W9-BXL-285

THE AUTHORITY SINCE 1868

THE WORLD ALMANAC®
AND BOOK OF FACTS
1996

WORLD ALMANAC BOOKS
AN IMPRINT OF FUNK & WAGNALLS CORPORATION
A K-III Communications Company

THE WORLD ALMANAC®
AND BOOK OF FACTS
1996

Editor: Robert Famighetti
Deputy Editor: Patricia Coleman
Associate Editors: Christina Cheddar, Matthew Friedlander, Judith Leale
Desktop Publishing Associate: Melissa Janssens
Chronology Editor: Donald Young
Index: AEIOU Inc.
Cover: Bill Smith Studio

Funk & Wagnalls
Vice President & Editorial Director: Leon L. Bram
Vice President–Manufacturing: Sally McCravey
Director of Editorial Production: Andrea J. Pitluk
Desktop Publishing Assistant: Hana Shaki

World Almanac Books
Vice President & Publisher: Richard W. Eiger
Sales Manager: James R. Keenley   **Director of Marketing:** Joyce H. Stein

The editors acknowledge with thanks the many letters of helpful comment and criticism from readers of THE WORLD ALMANAC. Because of the volume of mail directed to the editorial offices, it is not possible to reply to each letter writer. However, every communication is read by the editors and all comments and suggestions receive careful attention. THE WORLD ALMANAC's e-mail address is Walmanac@aol.com.

THE WORLD ALMANAC does not decide wagers.

The first edition of THE WORLD ALMANAC, a 120-page volume with 12 pages of advertising, was published by the New York World in 1868. Annual publication was suspended in 1876. Joseph Pulitzer, publisher of the New York World, revived THE WORLD ALMANAC in 1886 with the goal of making it a "compendium of universal knowledge." It has been published annually since then.

WORLD ALMANAC BOOKS
An Imprint of Funk & Wagnalls Corporation
One International Boulevard, Suite 444
Mahwah, New Jersey 07495-0017

CONTENTS

031
W92w
1996

GENERAL INDEX 4

THE TOP 10 NEWS STORIES 33

FEATURE ARTICLES 33

   CAMERAS IN THE COURTROOM 33
   BY JONATHAN ALTER

   TERRORISM: AT HOME 35
   BY JEFFREY D. SIMON

   THE YEAR OF THE CONGRESS 37
   BY NORMAN J. ORNSTEIN

NOTABLE SUPREME COURT DECISIONS,
   1994-95 40

THE 1995 NOBEL PRIZES 40

1996 PRESIDENTIAL PRIMARIES 41

CHRONOLOGY OF THE YEAR'S EVENTS 42

NOTABLE QUOTES IN 1995 72

HISTORICAL ANNIVERSARIES 73

OBITUARIES 76

UNITED STATES GOVERNMENT 78

CABINETS OF THE U.S. 104

ECONOMICS 110

AGRICULTURE 137

EMPLOYMENT 146

NATIONAL DEFENSE 158

COMPUTERS 167

SCIENCE AND TECHNOLOGY 174

METEOROLOGY 179

ENVIRONMENT 187

1995 IN PICTURES 193

ENERGY 201

TRADE AND TRANSPORTATION 206

EDUCATION 217

ARTS AND MEDIA 249

DISASTERS 264

ASTRONOMY AND CALENDAR 274

AEROSPACE 315

AWARDS, MEDALS, PRIZES 323

NOTED PERSONALITIES 340

UNITED STATES POPULATION 382

PRESIDENTIAL ELECTIONS 446

FLAGS AND MAPS 481

UNITED STATES HISTORY 497

BIOGRAPHIES OF U.S. PRESIDENTS 530

UNITED STATES FACTS 540

WORLD HISTORY 551

HISTORICAL FIGURES 577

WORLD EXPLORATION AND GEOGRAPHY 586

WEIGHTS AND MEASURES. 600

HEALTH 608

ASSOCIATIONS AND SOCIETIES 619

POSTAL INFORMATION 631

LANGUAGE 636

RELIGIOUS INFORMATION 644

STATES AND OTHER AREAS OF THE U.S. 655

CITIES OF THE U.S. 686

BUILDINGS, BRIDGES, TUNNELS, DAMS 696

SOCIAL SECURITY 708

CONSUMER INFORMATION 713

TAXES 730

NATIONS OF THE WORLD 737

1995 IN PICTURES (CONTINUED) 777

SPORTS 849

CRIME 956

VITAL STATISTICS 961

OFFBEAT NEWS STORIES 975

MISCELLANEOUS FACTS 975

QUICK REFERENCE INDEX 976

GENERAL INDEX

Note: Page numbers in *italics* indicate photos.

— A —

Abbreviations
- Canada, postal 633
- Common 638
- International organizations 842-43
- States, postal 633
- UN agencies 845

A-bomb. *See* Atomic bomb
Abortion
- Legalized (1973) 506, 524
- Number, by state 963-64

Academy Awards (Oscars) 336-38
Accidents and disasters 264-73
- Assassinations 272-73, 539
- Aviation 265-66, 320
- Blizzards 268
- Deaths (number, causes) 966
- Earthquakes (1989, 1994, 1995) 48, 271, 508, 510
- Explosions 269-70
  - Oklahoma City bombing (1995) 54, 55-56, 64, *196-97*
- Fires (1994) 269, 510
- Floods (1993) 268, 509
- Home 967
- Hurricanes 268
- Kidnappings 273
- Mining 267
- Motor vehicle 966
- Nuclear (1979) 270, 507, 574
- Occupational 150
- Oil spills (1989) 270, 508
- Railroad 266-67
  - Amtrak Arizona derailment (1995) 70
  - Tokyo nerve-gas attack (1995) 52, 57, *778*
- Ship (1915, 1989) 264-65, 502, 508
- Space exploration (1986) 315, 316, 317, 508
- Storms 268
- Tidal waves 268
- Tornadoes 267
- Typhoons 268
- Volcanic eruptions (1980) 507, 588-89

Acquired Immune Deficiency Syndrome
- Deaths, new cases (1985-94) 510, 973
- Epidemic (1986) 508
- Help organizations 616
- Louganis HIV-positive status (1995) 51
- Reported, estimated cases worldwide 840

Actors, actresses
- Birthplaces, birth dates 366-76
- Movies (1994-95) 249
- Movie, theater, TV awards 335-36, 336-38, 339
- New York theater (1994-95) 251, *780*
- Notable past 377-80
- Original names 380-81

Adams, John 479, 480, 539
- Biography 530
- Burial site 539
- Cabinet 104-6
- Electoral vote 478

Adams, John Quincy 479
- Biography 531
- Burial site 539
- Cabinet 104-6
- Popular, electoral votes 478

Address, forms of 641
Addresses
- Abbreviations, postal
  - Canada 633
  - States 633
- Armed forces, U.S. 164
- Associations and societies 619-30
- Businesses, major U.S. 714-19
- Colleges and universities 224-48
- Internet sites 169-70
- Labor unions 156-57
- Religious groups, U.S. 645-46
- Sports, pro organizations 901-02
- Television, cable networks 260
- U.S. government departments 78-81
- U.S. independent agencies 81-82
- U.S. judiciary 92-95
- ZIP codes 396-426, 445

Admirals, USN 158
- Address, forms of 641
- Personal salutes, honors 159

Adventist churches 644, 645
Advertising 263
Aerospace. *See* Aviation; Space developments
Afghanistan 481, 492, 575, 576, 737, 846
AFL. *See* American Football League
AFL-CIO. *See* American Federation of Labor and Congress of Industrial Organizations
Africa
- AIDs cases 840
- Area 838
- Commercial fishing 145
- Gold production 134
- Highest, lowest points 597
- History 554, 558, 560, 567, 572-73, 575, 576
- Lakes 598
- Languages 642-43
- Map 494-95
- Mountain peaks 590
- Population 838
  - Projections (2010, 2020) 838-39
  - Religious adherents 646
- Volcanoes 589
- Waterfalls 599
- *see also specific countries*

African Americans. *See* Blacks
Agencies
- United Nations 845
- U.S. government 81-82, 151

Agriculture 137-45
- Acreage, number of farms 137
- Employment 137, 147, 149
  - Minimum hourly rates 154
  - Social Security benefits 710
- Exports, imports 140, 144, 207
- Foreign production 144, 737-837
- Income 140
- Land grants (1862) 500
- Legislation (1916, 1929) 502, 503
- Occupational injuries 150
- Population 137
- Prices received 143
- Production
  - Crops 141-42, 144
  - Meat, eggs 138
- Real estate debt 141
- Subsidies 139
- U.S. programs 139
- *see also* Food; Grains

Agriculture, Department of 79
- Employees, payroll 151
- Expenditures 110
- Internet address 169
- Secretaries 78, 79, 107

AIDS. *See* Acquired Immune Deficiency Syndrome
Air
- Composition, temperature 292
- Density 292, 605
- Pollution 187

Air Commerce Act (1926) 503
Air conditioning 203
Aircraft. *See* Aviation
Air Force, Department of the
- Employees, payroll 151
- Secretary 79

Air Force, U.S.
- Academy 160, 234
- Address for information 164
- Flights, notable 322
- Generals, active duty 158
- Insignia 160
- Military units 159
- Personnel, active duty 161
- Secretary 79
- Training centers 159
- Women, active duty 162
- *see also* Armed forces, U.S.

Airlines, leading 319
- *see also* Aviation

Air mail 633, 634-35
Airplane pilots 320
Airports, busiest
- International 319
- U.S. 319

Airships 265, 322
Akron, OH 686
- Mayor 96
- Population 390, 417, 686

Alabama 655
- Admission, area, capital 542, 543, 655
- Agriculture 137-42
- Altitudes (high, low) 541
- Birth, death statistics 962
- Budget 116
- Coastline 541
- Congressional representation 82, 84, 384
- Courts, U.S. 93
- Crime, prisons, death penalty 959
- Energy consumption 203
- Federally owned land 545
- Governor, state officials 99, 100
- Immigrants' intended residence 393
- Indians, American 550
- Interest laws, rates 721, 722
- Marriage, divorce laws 728, 729
- Motor vehicle statistics 211
- Name origin, nickname 544, 655
- Population 384-85, 388
  - Cities, towns 396, 687, 691
  - Counties, county seats 427
- Port traffic 208
- Presidential elections 446, 447, 476
- Public libraries 223
- Schools 218, 219, 222
- Taxes 211, 735, 736
- Temperature, precipitation 181, 183
- Toxic chemical pollution 187
- Unemployment benefits 146
- Welfare assistance 395

Alaska 655-56
- Accession 545
- Admission, area, capital 542, 543, 655
- Agriculture 137-41
- Altitudes (high, low) 541
- Birth, death statistics 962
- Budget 116
- Coastline 541
- Commercial fishing 145
- Congressional representation 82, 84, 384
- Courts, U.S. 93
- Crime, prisons, death penalty 959
- Energy consumption 203
- Federally owned land 545
- Governor, state officials 99, 100
- Immigrants' intended residence 393
- Indians, American 550
- Interest laws, rates 721, 722
- Marriage, divorce laws 728, 729
- Motor vehicle statistics 211
- Name origin, nickname 544, 655
- Population 384-85, 388
  - Census divisions 427
  - Cities, towns 396, 686
- Port traffic 208
- Presidential elections 446, 447-48, 476
- Public libraries 223
- Schools 218, 219, 222
- Taxes 211, 735
- Temperature, precipitation 181, 183
- Time zones 313
- Unemployment benefits 146
- Welfare assistance 395

Albania 481, 737-38, 846
Albany, NY 96, 696
Albuquerque, NM 686
- Mayor 96
- Population 390, 415, 686

Alcohol boiling point 605
Alcoholic beverages. *See* Liquor
Alcohol, Tobacco, and Firearms, Bureau of 79, 82
- Waco (TX) standoff (1993, 1994, 1995) 61-62, 509

Aleutian Islands 592
Aleuts, U.S. 382, 386, 550
Alexander the Great 554
Algeria 47, 481, 738, 846
Aliens
- Admissions, exclusions, U.S. 840-41
- Illegal, amnesty (1988) 508
- Legislation (1952, 1990) 504, 840-41
- Naturalization 841
- Passports, visas 840-41

Allen, Ethan (1775) 348, 498
Allentown, PA 96, 420
Alps 590-91
Altitudes
- Cities (U.S, world) 593-95
- Highest, lowest
  - U.S. 541
  - World 597
- Mountains 590-91

Aluminum 132, 134
Alzheimer's disease 615, 617
Amazon River 596
Ambassadors and envoys 846-48
- Address, form of 641
- Salute to (artillery) 159

"America" ("My Country 'Tis of Thee") 528
American Federation of Labor and Congress of Industrial Organizations
- Address, affiliates 156-57
- AFL formed (1886) 501
- CIO formed (1935) 503
- Kirkland retirement (1995) 59
- Merger (1955) 504

American Football League
- Conference leaders (1960-69) 871
- Division champions 870
- Professional records 876-77
- *see also* Football, pro

American Kennel Club registrations 192

American League (baseball) 946-48
American Manual Alphabet 643
American Revolution (1775-83) 564
Articles of Confederation (1777) . 498, 514
Battlefields, monuments 546-47
Battles (1775, 1776, 1777, 1779, 1780,
1781) 498
Black troops 162
Casualties, numbers serving 166
Costs 163
Declaration of Independence
(1776) 498, 512-13
Liberty Bell 528-29
Military leaders 348-50
Americans, notable 340-81
Actors, actresses 336-38, 366-80
Architects 341-42
Artists 342-44
Athletes 924-26
Blacks 334, 345
Business leaders 346-47
Cartoonists 328-29, 334, 347
Composers 332-33, 360-62
Contemporary personalities 340-41
Country music artists 364
Dancers, choreographers 362-63
Economists 325, 347-48
Educators 355-56
Historians 330-31, 347-48
Industrialists 346-47
Jazz, blues artists 363-64
Lyricists 362
Military leaders 348-50
Obituaries (1994-95) 76-77
Opera singers 363
Philanthropists 346-47
Philosophers 350
Photographers 329, 342-44
Playwrights 330, 336, 356, 357-60
Poets 332
Political leaders 351-53
Religionists 350
Rock & Roll musicians 339, 364-65
Scientists 323-24, 353-55
Social reformers 355-56
Social scientists 347-48
Statesmen, stateswomen . . . 325, 351-53
Writers 324-25, 330-32, 333-34,
356, 357-60
American Samoa. See Samoa, American
American's Creed 525
American Stock Exchange
Address 629
Volume, transactions 130
America's Cup (yachting) 935, 784
"America, the Beautiful" 528
Ames, Aldrich (1994, 1995) . . . 42, 44, 510
Ames, Rosario (1994, 1995) 42, 510
Amnesty
Confederate citizens (1872) 501
Illegal aliens (1988) 508
Vietnam draft evaders (1977) 507
Anaheim, CA 686
Mayor 96
Population 390, 397, 686
Anchorage, AL 686
Mayor 96
Population 390, 396, 686
Ancient civilizations 551-56
Archaeological finds (1995) . . . 48, 199
Historical figures 577
Measures 605
Seven Wonders 555
Andaman Sea 593
Andorra 481, 738
Anesthesia (1842) 500
Anglicanism 829
Angola 206, 481, 575, 738-39, 846
Chronology (1994-95) 43, 50
Anguilla 830
Animals
American Kennel Club 192
Cat breeds 192
Classification 192
Collectives, names for 638
Endangered species 188, 189
Farm (see Livestock)
Gestation, incubation 189
Longevity 189
Speeds 189
Venomous 190
Westminster Kennel Club 918
Young, names for 639
Zoos, major 191
Annapolis (MD) (Naval Academy) . 160, 234
Anniversaries
Historical events (1896, 1946, 1971) 73-75
Holidays 314
Wedding 726
Antarctica
Area 838

Australian Territory 741
British Territory 831
Explorations 587-88
French 764
Highest, lowest points 597
Mountain peaks 591
Volcanoes 589
Antigua and Barbuda . . 481, 592, 739, 846
Antilles. See Netherlands Antilles
Antoinette Perry Awards (Tonys) . 336, 780
Apartheid 576, 818
APEC. See Asia-Pacific Economic Coopera-
tion Group
Aphelion, perihelion 282-83, 291
Apogee of moon 291
Apollo space missions (1969) . 315-16, 506
Appliances, home 203
Appomattox Court House (1865) . 500, 546
Apportionment, Congressional 384
Arabia. See Middle East; Saudi Arabia
Arab-Israeli conflict
East Jerusalem land seizure (1995) . . . 57
Lebanon 575, 576, 776, 791
October War (1973) 506, 575, 760,
776, 814
Palestinian self-rule (1994-95) . 43, 47, 49,
54-55, 62, 69, 71, 776, 778
Palestinian uprising 576, 776
Six-Day War (1967) . 574, 760, 776, 814
Arab League 573, 842
Arafat, Yasir 43, 49, 55, 62, 69, 778
Archaeological finds (1995) 48, 199
Archery 863
Architects, notable 335, 341-42
Archives, National 685
Arctic explorations 586-88
Arctic Ocean
Area, depth 593
Coast length, U.S. 541
Islands, areas 592
Area codes, telephone 396-426
Areas (geographical)
Continents 838
Earth 292
Islands 592
Lakes 598
Largest country (Russia) 838
National parks 546-47
National recreation 545, 549
Nations, world 737-837
Oceans, seas, gulfs 593
United States 387, 540
Counties, by state 427-45
States 542, 655-80
Territories 445, 545, 681-83
Areas (mathematical)
Formulas 607
Measures (units) 600-607
Arenas, stadiums
Baseball 951
Basketball 911
Football 877
Argentina 739-40
Ambassadors, envoys 846
Flag 481
History 573, 575
Motor vehicle production 212
Nuclear power 205
Arizona 656
Admission, area, capital . . 542, 543, 656
Agriculture 137-42
Altitudes (high, low) 541
Birth, death statistics 962
Budget 116
Congressional representation . 82, 84, 384
Courts, U.S. 93
Crime, prisons, death penalty 959
116
Energy consumption 203
Federally owned land 545
Governor, state officials 99, 100
Immigrants' intended residence 393
Indians, American 550
Interest laws, rates 721, 722
Marriage, divorce laws 728, 729
Mineral production 132
Motor vehicle statistics 211
Name origin, nickname 544, 656
Population 384-85, 388
Cities, towns . . 396-97, 691, 693, 695
Counties, county seats 427
Presidential elections . . . 446, 448, 476
Public libraries 223
Schools 218, 219, 222
Taxes 211, 735
Temperature, precipitation 181, 183
Unemployment benefits 146
Welfare assistance 395
Arkansas 656-57
Admission, area, capital . . 542, 543, 656
Agriculture 137-42

Altitudes (high, low) 541
Birth, death statistics 962
Budget 116
Congressional representation . 82, 84, 384
Courts, U.S. 93
Crime, prisons, death penalty 959
Energy consumption 203
Federally owned land 545
Governor, state officials 99, 100
Immigrants' intended residence 393
Indians, American 550
Interest laws, rates 722
Marriage, divorce laws 728, 729
Motor vehicle statistics 211
Name origin, nickname 544, 656
Population 384-85, 388
Cities, towns 397, 690
Counties, county seats 427-28
Presidential elections . . . 446, 448, 476
Public libraries 223
Schools 218, 219, 222
Taxes 211, 735, 736
Temperature, precipitation 181, 183
Unemployment benefits 146
Welfare assistance 395
Arkansas River 596
Arlington National Cemetery (VA) 685
Arlington, TX 96, 390, 422, 686
Armed forces (general)
Leaders, notable past 348-50
Military strength (by country) 164
Per 1,000 persons (by country) 164
see also specific countries
Armed forces, U.S. 158-66
Academies, service 160, 234
Address, forms of 641
Addresses for information 164
Base closings (1995) 61
Battlefields and parks, national . . 547-48
Black troops 162
Casualties, by wars 166
Commands 158
Defense contracts 162
Expenditures 110
Generals 158
Homosexual issues (1993, 1995) . 52, 509
Insignia 160
Joint Chiefs of Staff (1989) 508
Chairmen 79, 158, 165
Leaders, notable past 348-50
Medal of Honor 163
Military strength 163, 164
Pay scales 165
Personnel 158, 161, 162, 163, 164
Salutes 159
Secretaries 79, 105-6
Time, 24-hour 313
Training centers 158-59
Troop strength, by wars 166
Units 159
Veterans 162, 163
Women, active duty 162
First general (1970) 506
see also Weapons; specific branches
Armenia 481, 740, 846
Arms control 165
Limitations of Armaments Conference
(1921) 502
Mid-range missiles ban 165
Nuclear test-ban treaty (1963) . . . 165, 505
Pacifist pacts (1920s) 570
SALT (1972, 1979) 165
START (1991, 1993) 165
Army, Department of the
Employees, payroll 151
Secretary 79
Army, U.S.
Academy (West Point) 160, 234
Address for information 164
Generals 158
Address, form of 641
Salutes, honors 159
Women, first (1970) 506
Insignia 160
Leaders, notable past 348-50
Personnel, active duty 161
Secretary 79
Training centers 158
Units 159
Women, active duty 161, 162
Art
Abstract 570, 571
Artists, notable 342-44
Baroque 562
Beaux Arts 567
Gothic 560, 565
Impressionist 567
Neoclassical 564
Pop 574
Renaissance 561, 562
Rococo 564

Art *(continued)*
Romanesque 560
Romanticism 565
Artemis, Temple at Ephesus 555
Arthur, Chester A. 479, 480
Biography 533
Burial site 539
Cabinet 104-7
Articles of Confederation (1777) 498, 514
Artillery salutes 159
Artists, notable 342-44
Aruba 592, 802
Ascension Island 592, 831
ASEAN. *See* Association of Southeast Asian Nations
Ashmore and Cartier Islands 741
Ash Wednesday 647, 648
Asia
AIDS cases 840
Area 838
Commercial fishing 145
Highest, lowest points 597
Lakes 598
Languages 642-43
Maps 491, 492-93
Mountain peaks 590, 591
Population 838-39
Religious adherents 646
Trade 206
Volcanoes 589
Waterfalls 599
see also specific countries
Asians, U.S., Population 382, 386, 392
Asia-Pacific Economic Cooperation Group 842
Assassinations 272-73
Attempts 273
Clinton, Bill (1994) 42, 53, 273
Ford, Gerald R. (1975) 273
Gilgorov, Kiro (1995) 70
John Paul II, Pope (1981) 273
Mubarak, Hosni (1995) 60
Reagan, Ronald (1981) 273, 507
Shevardnadze, Eduard (1995) 66
Truman, Harry S. (1950) 273, 504
Wallace, George C. (1972) 273, 506
International
Gandhi, Indira (1984) 272, 576
Gandhi, Rajiv (1991) 272
Karami, Rashid (1987) 272, 576
Ngo Dinh Diem (1963) 272, 505
Palme, Olaf (1986) 272
Premadasa, Ranasinghe (1993) 272
Sadat, Anwar al- (1981) 272, 576
Presidents, U.S. 539
Garfield, James A. (1881) 272, 501, 533
Kennedy, John F. (1963) 272, 505, 536
Lincoln, Abraham (1865) 272, 500, 532
McKinley, William (1901) 272, 501, 534
United States
Kennedy, Robert F. (1968) 272, 506
King, Martin Luther (1968) 272, 506
Lennon, John (1980) 507
Long, Huey (1935) 272, 503
Assemblies of God 645
Association of Southeast Asian Nations 206, 842
Associations and societies 619-30
Health care 616-18
Sports 902
Astrological signs 291
Astronauts
First on moon (1969) 506
First orbit (1962) 505
First women (1983) 315, 316, 507
Hall of Fame 320-21
Missions 315-17
Numbers of 318
U.S.-Russian space linkup (1995) 59, *198*
Astronomy 274-308
Auroras 289
Calendar (1996) 297-308
Celestial highlights 274-77
Constants 287
Constellations 287-88
Earth 290, 292-94
Eclipses (1996) 289
Eclipses, total (1940-2000) 295-96
Moon 274-77, 289, 291-92, 296
Planets 277-85, 290
Configurations 274-77, 282-83
Rising, setting 284-85
Signs and symbols 282
Star tables 286-87
Morning, evening 286
Sun 277, 289, 290-91, 296
Time 286, 293
Twilight 294-95
Athletics. *See specific sports*; Sports
Atlanta, GA 686
Airport traffic 319
Buildings, tall 696
Mayor 96
Population 390, 403, 686
Atlantic cable, first (1858) 500
Atlantic Charter (1941) 503
Atlantic Ocean
Area, depth 593
Coasts, U.S.
Highest point 540
Length 541
Ports 208, 209
Commercial fishing 145
Crossings, notable (1819) 322, 499
Islands, areas 592
Atmosphere (air pressure) 607
Atmosphere (earth's) 292
Atolls 592, 683
Atomic bomb (1945)65-66, 74, *200*, 504, 572
see also Nuclear arms
Atomic clock 294
Atomic energy. *See* Nuclear energy
Atomic weights 177-78
Attila 557
Attorneys general, U.S. 78, 79, 106
Aunu'u Island 681
Aurora, CO 96, 390, 686
Auroras 289, 555
Austin, TX 686
Buildings, tall 696
Mayor 96
Population 390, 422, 686
Australia 568, 740-41
Ambassadors, envoys 846
Area 838
Flag 481
Gold production 134
Great Barrier Reef 555
Highest, lowest points 597
Lakes 598
Map 496
Merchant fleet 209
Motor vehicle production 212
Mountain peaks 590
Population 838
Projections (2010, 2020) 838, 839
Territories 741
Unemployment rates 147
Wages, hourly 152
Waterfalls 599
Australian Antarctic 741
Australian Open (tennis) 929
Austral Islands 764
Austria 741
Ambassadors, envoys 846
Flag 481
History 561, 565, 569
Motor vehicle production 212
Rulers 581
Wages, hourly 152
Authors, notable. *See* Writers, notable
Automobiles
Accidents, deaths 966
Colors, most popular 213
Drivers
Licensed (by age) 213
By state 211
Expenditures, driver 214
Exports, imports 207, 208
First cross-country trip (1903) 502
Fuel
Consumption 211, 214
Prices, retail 204
Tax 211
Inventions 174
Japanese luxury-car tariffs (1995) 57, 60
Production 210, 212
Registration 211
Safety belt laws
By country 214
By U.S. states 211
Sales 211, 212
Top-selling 213
Theft 956, 958, 960
Union merger (1995) 62
Auto racing 929-31
Autumn 293
Autumnal Equinox 276, 283, 293
Aviation
Accidents 265-66, 320
Air cargo 319
Air Commerce Act (1926) 503
Aircraft operation statistics 320
Airlines, leading 319
Air mail 633, 634-35
Airmen, airwomen 320
Air mileage, between world cities 216
Airships 265, 322
Balloon flights 321
Earhart lost (1937) 503
Fatalities 967
Federal agency 80, 82
Flights, notable 322
Gliders 321
Hall of Fame 320-21
Helicopters 321
Inventions 174
Wright brothers (1903) 502, 568
Jet, first U.S. passenger (1958) 505
Records, 1994 321
Safety 320
Traffic 319
Traffic controllers strike (1981) 507
Transatlantic, first flight (1919) 322, 502
Transatlantic, first nonstop flight (1927) 322, 503
Transcontinental, first flight (1911) 502
Union merger (1995) 62
Avoirdupois measures 601, 602, 603
Awards, prizes 323-39
Baseball 938, 941, 942
Broadcasting 334, 335-36, 339
Football 870, 874, 877
Hockey, ice 892-94
Journalism 325-29, 334
Literature 324-25, 330-32, 333-34
Medal of Honor 163
Miscellaneous 335
Miss America 335
Movies 336-38, 339
Music 332-33, 339
Nobel Prizes 40, 323-25
Pulitzer Prizes 325-33
Recording 258-59, 339, *780*
Spingarn Medal 334
Television 335-36
Theater 336, *780*
Video, music 259
Azerbaijan 481, 741-42, 846
Azores 592, 810
Aztecs 563, 586, 797

— B —

Badminton 863
Baha'i Faith 644, 645, 646
Bahamas 209, 481, 592, 742, 846
Bahrain 481, 592, 742, 846
Baker Islands 683
Bakersfield, CA 96, 391, 686
Balance of trade 135, 206, 207, 576
Balearic Islands 592, 819
Bali 592
Balkan War (1994-95) 43, 44-45, 46-47, 50, 52, 57, 59-60, 62-63, 65, 68, 70-71, *777*
Ballet
Companies, U.S. 253
Notable figures 362-63
Balloon flights (1994 records) 321
Baltic Sea 592, 593
Baltimore, MD 686-87
Buildings, tall 696
Mayor 96
Population 390, 408, 686
Port traffic 208
Bangladesh 206, 481, 742-43, 846
Bankruptcy 115
Banks
Charter, first (1781) 498
Chase-Chemical merger (1995) 67
Closed (1933) 503
Deposits, U.S. 118
Failures 119
Farm credit 141
Federal Reserve System (1913) 81, 502
Financial panics (1873, 1893, 1907) 501, 502
Gold reserves (world) 128, 132
International 43, 845
Largest
U.S. 118
World 118
Modern, beginning of 562
Mortgages 726, 727
Number, U.S. 118
Savings and loan crisis (1989) 508
Baptist churches
Addresses, U.S. headquarters 645
Beliefs, practices 652-53
Membership 644
Barbados 481, 743, 846
Barley production 141, 142, 143
Baseball
Addresses, team 901
All-Star games 949
Batting records 940-41
Cy Young Award 941
First black major league player (1947) 504
Gold Glove Awards (1994) 938
Hall of Fame, museum 949
Home run leaders 938-39
Leaders
All-time 951
League (1995) 950
Little League 954

Mantle death (1995) 77, *782*, 849, 953
Most Valuable Players 942
NCAA champions 955
Olympic champions (1992) 863
Pennant, division winners 936-37
American League (1995) 946-48
National League (1995) 943-45
Pitching records 941, 950
Players' strike (1994-95) 50, 53, 55, 510, 936
RBI leaders 939-40
Ripken record (1995) 69-70, *782*
Rookies of the Year 942
Stadiums 951
World Series 952-54
Basketball
Addresses, team 901
All-time leaders 910
Hall of Fame 911
Jordan return (1995) *783*
NBA
Arenas 911
Champions (1947-95) 905-06
Championship (1995) 60, *783*, 904
Coaching victories 911
Most Valuable Players 905
Player draft (1995) 910
Rookies of the Year (1954-95) 907
NCAA
Coaches, Division I 916
Tournament champions 55, 913-915
Women's champions 55, *783*, 917
Wooden Award 915
Olympic champions (1992) 863
Baton Rouge, LA 687
Mayor 96
Population 390, 407, 687
Port traffic 208
Battlefields, national 547
Beans. *See* Legumes
Beef
Livestock population 137
Nutritive value 610
Prices, farm 143
Production, consumption 138
Belarus 481, 743, 846
Belgian Congo. *See* Zaire
Belgium 743-44
Ambassadors, envoys 846
Flag 481
Gold reserves 128
Motor vehicle production 212
Nuclear power 204, 205
Rulers, royal family 381, 583, 744
Wages, hourly 152
Belize 481, 744, 846
Bell, Alexander Graham (1915) 502
Belmont Stakes 896
Benin 481, 744, 846
Bering, Vitus (1740-41) 497, 587
Bering Sea 593
Berlin, Germany
Blockade, airlift (1948) 504, 572
Wall built, opened (1961, 1989) 574, 576, 766
Bermuda 209, 592, 830-31
Beverages
Nutritive value 610, 611
see also specific kinds
Bhutan 481, 745, 846
Bhutto, Benazir (1995) 68
Biafra 804
Biathlon 850
Bible, books of the 649
Biblical measures 605
Bicycles. *See* Cycling
Bill of Rights (1791) 498, 519
Biology
Animal, plant classification 192
Discoveries 176-77
Birmingham, AL 687
Buildings, tall 696
Mayor 96
Population 390, 396, 687
Births
Certificates, records 726
Infant mortality rates 961, 962, 963
Life expectancy 974
Notable personalities, birth dates 340-81
Number, rate
By country (*see specific countries*)
By mothers receiving welfare 395
By states 962
Birthstones 726
Black Death 561
Black Friday (1869) 501
Blacks
Bus boycott (1955) 504
Civil Rights Act (1875) 501
Civil Rights Act (1964) 505, 574
Civil rights amendments 520-21
Civil rights bill (1957) 505
Civil rights workers (1964) 505
Companies, leading (1994) 124
Disabled people 392
Education 220, 221
Employment, unemployment 149, 153
First astronauts 316, 317
First governor since Reconstruction (1989) 508
First in colonies (1619) 497
First Joint Chiefs chairman (1989) 508
First major league baseball player (1947) 504
First senator since Reconstruction (1966) 505
First Supreme Court justice (1967) 506
First woman representative (1968) 506
Households 964
Income distribution 394
Ku Klux Klan (1866, 1921) 500, 502
March on Washington (1963) 505
Million Man March (1995) 33
Notable personalities 345
Population 386, 382, 387, 391, 392
Poverty rates 394
Race riots (1943, 1965, 1967, 1992) 503, 505-6, 509
Salaries and wages 149, 152
Sit-ins (1960) 505
Spingarn Medal 334
Voting rights (1957, 1965) 505
War service 162
see also Desegregation; Slavery
Black Sea 593
Blindness
Diabetes-caused 615
Help organizations 617
Income tax deduction 732
Blizzards 268
Characteristics 179
Great (1888) 268, 501
Blood pressure 616
Blues artists, notable 363-64
Boat racing
America's Cup *784*
Olympic champions (1992) 865
Power boat 935
Bobsledding 849-50
Body weight tables 612
Boer War (1899-1902) 567, 818
Boiling points 605
Bolivia 745
Ambassadors, envoys 846
Flag 481
History 573, 575
Bombings. *See* Terrorism
Bonaire 802
Bonaparte, Napoleon (1798, 1803) 499, 564, 565
Bonds
Defined 135, 136
Portraits on U.S. 120
Yields 129
Books
Awards 324-25, 330-32, 333-34
Best-selling (1994) 255-56
Copyright law, U.S. 724-25
Notable (1995) 254-55
Postal rates 632
Writers, notable 356, 357-60
Booth, John Wilkes (1865) 272, 500, 532
Borneo 592
Bosnia and Herzegovina 745-46
Ambassadors, envoys 846
Chronology (1994-95) 43, 44-45, 46-47, 50, 52, 57, 59-60, 62-63, 65, 68, 70-71, *777*
Flag 481
Map 490
Boston, MA 687
Buildings, tall 696
Education, compulsory (1636) 497
Historical sites 546
Massacre (1770) 498
Mayor 96
News Letter (1704) 497
Population 390, 409, 687
Port traffic 208
Tea Party (1773) 498
Botany, (plant classification) 192
Botswana 481, 746, 846
Boundary lines, U.S 543
Bourbon, House of 580
Bowl games (football)
College 879-81
Super Bowl 48, *782*, 870, 877
Bowling 898-99
Boxer Rebellion (1900) 501
Boxing
Champions (by class) 932-34
Foreman title (1995) 43
Heavyweight title bouts 934
Olympic champions 862-63
Tyson return (1995) 66-67, *784*
Boy Scouts
Address 620
Founded (1910) 502
Brady Bill (1993) 509
Branch Davidians (1993, 1994, 1995) 61-62, 509, 510
Brazil 746-47
Ambassadors, envoys 846
Cities (largest) 838
Flag 481
History 563, 565
Merchant fleet 209
Military strength 164
Motor vehicle production 212
Nuclear power 205
Rio de Janiero harbor 555
Bread, Nutritive value 610
Breeders' Cup 897
Brethren churches 644, 645
Brezhnev, Leonid 575, 585
Bridge (card game) 607
Bridges 702-5
Britain. *See* United Kingdom
British Antarctic Territory 831
British Honduras. *See* Belize
British Indian Ocean Territory 831
British Isles. *See* United Kingdom
British West Indies 830
Broadcasting. *See* Radio; Television
Broadway. *See* Theater
Bronx, NY 191, 437
Brooklyn, NY 388
Brooklyn Bridge (1883) 501, 702
Brunei 481, 747, 846
Bubonic plague 561
Buchanan, James 477, 479, 539
Biography 532
Burial site 539
Cabinet 104-7
Popular, electoral votes 478
Buddhism
Address, U.S. headquarters 645
Adherents, world, U.S. 644, 646
Beliefs, practices 654
History 554, 562, 575
Budget
Economic terms defined 135-36
Federal 110-11
Balanced-budget amendment (1995) 46, 51
Balanced-budget legislation (1995) 56-57, 59, *194*
Deficit 111-12, 135
Deficit reduction legislation (1993) 509
First trillion-dollar (1987) 508
Proposed, 1996 fiscal year 49
States 116-17
Buffalo, NY 687
Buildings, tall 696
Mayor 96
Population 390, 415, 687
Buildings, tall 696-702
Bulgaria 747
Ambassadors, envoys 846
Flag 481
Merchant fleet 209
Nuclear power 204, 205
Bull Run, Battle of (1861) 500
Bunker Hill, Battle of (1775) 498
Burglaries 956, 958, 960
Burkina Faso 481, 747-48, 846
Burma. *See* Myanmar
Burr, Aaron (1804) 479, 480, 499
Burundi 481, 748, 846
Buses, desegregation (1955) 504
Bush, George 477, 479, 480
Biography 537
Cabinet 104-8
Chronology (1995) 55
Notable quote (1995) 72
Popular, electoral votes 446-75, 475, 478
Presidential library 539
Business
Advertising expenditures 263
Air travel 319
Black-owned, largest (1994) 124
Capital gains tax 125
Charitable contributions 713
Consumer products, parent company 720
Corporate tax rates 125
Defense contracts 162
Directory 714-19
Empowerment zones 730
Franchises, fastest growing (1994) 124
International transactions, U.S. 126
Internet addresses 170
Leaders, notable past 346-47
Leading (1994) 122-23
Media business alliances *195*
Mergers/acquisitions
Banking (1995) 67

Entertainment, media (1995) 33, 62, 66, 70
Largest 123
Multinational companies 124
Occupational injuries 150
Patents granted 177
Profits (by industry) 115
Rotary club, first (1905) 502
Sherman Antitrust Act (1890) 501
Tax deductions 731, 733
Tobacco industry lawsuits (1995) 64-65
U.S. investments abroad 128
see also Banks; Economics; Industries, U.S.; Stocks
Butter, (nutritive value) 609, 610
Byzantine Empire 558

— C —

Cabinet, U.S. 104-8
Address, form of 641
Clinton administration 104-8
Personal salutes, honors 159
Salute (artillery) 159
Cable (measure) 601
Cable television
Advertising expenditures 263
Company mergers (1995) 70
Networks
Addresses, phone numbers 260
Internet addresses 170
Top 20 260
Subscribers 261
Systems, U.S. 260
Viewing shares 261
Cabot, John (1497) 497, 586
Cabrera Island 819
Caicos Island 830
Calcium (dietary) 609, 610-11, 612
Calendar
Celestial (1996) 274-77
Daily astronomical (1996) 297-308
Days between two dates 312
Episcopal Church 647
Eras, cycles (1996) 294
Greek Orthodox Church 647
Gregorian 309
Islamic 647
Jewish 648
Julian 309, 312
Leap years 309
Lenten 647, 648
Lunar 312
Perpetual 310-11
Twilight (1993) 295
Year 293
Caliber (measure) 604
California 657
Admission, area, capital 542, 657
Agriculture 137-42
Altitudes (high, low) 541
Birth, death statistics 962
Budget 116
Coastline 541
Congressional representation 82, 84-85, 384
Courts, U.S. 93
Crime, prisons, death penalty 959
Desert Protection Act (1994) 510
Earthquake (1994) 510
Energy consumption 203
Federally owned land 545
Governor, state officials 99, 100
Immigrants' intended residence 393
Indians, American 550
Interest laws, rates 721, 722
Marriage, divorce laws 728, 729
Mineral production 132
Motor vehicle statistics 211
Name origin, nickname 544, 657
Orange County bankruptcy (1994) 44
Population 384-85, 388
Cities, towns 397-400, 686, 689, 690, 692, 693, 694, 695
Counties, county seats 428
Port traffic 208
Presidential elections 446, 449, 476
Public libraries 223
Schools 218, 219, 222
Taxes 211, 735, 736
Temperature, precipitation 181, 183
Unemployment benefits 146
Welfare assistance 395
California, Gulf of 593
Calories 609, 610-11
Labels, nutrition 612
Calvin, John 350, 562
Cambodia 748-49
Ambassadors, envoys 846
Flag 481
History 573, 575
Mayaguez seized (1975) 507
U.S. invasion (1970) 506
Cameroon 481, 749, 846
Canada 749-50
Ambassadors, envoys 846
Buildings, tall 696, 697-98, 699, 701-2
Distances to ports 209
Energy production, consumption 202
Flag 481
Football 878
Grey Cup 878
French and Indian War (1754-63) 497
Gold production, reserves 128, 134
Islands 592
Lakes, largest 598
Latitudes, longitudes, altitudes 594-95
Libraries, public 223
Map 485
Mineral resources 132, 133
Motor vehicle production 212
Mountain peaks 590
Newspaper circulation 256
Nuclear power 204, 205
Postal codes, rates 633, 634
Prime ministers 750
Provinces, territories 750
Religions 651
Rivers 596-97
St. Lawrence Seaway (1959) 505
Trade 206, 749
Unemployment rates 147
U.S. immigrants from 393
Wages, hourly 152
Waterfalls 599
Zoos 191
Canadian Football League 878
Canals
Erie (1825) 499
Panama (1978) 507, 806
Suez 573, 760
Canary Islands 592, 819
Cancer
Deaths, new cases 972
Help organizations 617
Prevention 613, 614
Warning signals 614
Canoeing 863
Cape Verde 481, 750-51, 846
Capital gains 135
Capital punishment. *See* Death penalty
Capitals
States, U.S. 542
U.S. (*see* Washington, DC)
World (*see specific countries*)
Capitol, U.S. 684
Burned (1814) 499
Carat (measure) 604
Carbohydrates 609, 610-11
Cardinals, Roman Catholic 649
Cardiovascular disease 972
Cards, playing (odds) 607
Caribbean Community 842
Caribbean Sea
Area, depth 593
Islands, area 592, 682-83
Map 485
Volcanoes 589
CARICOM. *See* Caribbean Community
Carlsbad Caverns (NM) 546, 670
Caroline Islands 592, 683
Carolingian dynasty 581
Cars. *See* Automobiles
Carter, Jimmy 475, 477, 479, 480
Biography 537
Bosnia crisis (1994, 1995) 45, 57
Cabinet 104-8
Popular, electoral votes 478
Presidential library 539
Cartier and Ashmore Islands 741
Cartoonists
Awards 328-29, 334
Notable American 347
Castro, Fidel 573, 756
Casualties, U.S. wars 166
Catacombs (Egypt) 555
Cat breeds 192
Catholic Church. *See* Roman Catholicism
Cattle. *See* Beef; Livestock; Meats
Caucasus Mountains 591
Caves, U.S. 546
Cayman Islands 830
CD-ROM
Defined 172
Household computers with 170
School usage 217
Software, top selling 171
Celebes 592
Celebrities. *See* Notable personalities; *specific fields*
Celestial events (1996) 274-77
Celsius scale 605
Cemeteries
Arlington National (VA) 685
Presidential burial sites 539
Census. *See* Population, U.S.; Population, world
Census, Bureau of the 80, 82, 169, 383
Census Act (1790) 498
Census of U.S. Governments (1992) 100
Census Test (1995) 383
Central African Republic 481, 751, 846
Central America 576
Maps 485, 488
Trade 206
Volcanoes 589
see also specific countries
Central American Common Market 206
Central Intelligence Agency 81
Ames spy case (1994) 42, 44, 510
Directors 81, 109
Chronology (1994-95) 44, 49, 51, 56
Internet address 169
Century, defined 309
Cereals, Nutritive value 609, 610
Ceuta 819
Ceylon. *See* Sri Lanka
Chad 751
Ambassadors, envoys 846
Flag 481
History 560, 575
Challenger (space shuttle) (1983, 1984, 1986) 316, 317, 507, 508
Chambers of Commerce. *See* Cities, U.S.; States, U.S.
Champlain, Samuel de (1609) 497, 586
Channel Islands 592, 830
Charitable contributions 713, 714
Charlemagne 558, 579
Charlotte, NC 687
Buildings, tall 696
Mayor 96
Population 390, 417, 687
Chatham Islands 592, 803
Chechnya revolt (1994-95) 45, 47, 50, 52, 60, 63, *779*
Cheese, Nutritive value 609, 610
Chemicals
Exports, imports 207
Toxic 187
Chemistry
Discoveries 176-77
Elements (atomic weights, numbers) 177-78
Nobel Prizes 40, 323-24
Chess 71, 955
Chesterfield Islands 764
Chiang Kai-shek 570
Chicago, IL 687
Airport traffic 319
Buildings, tall 696-97
Fire (1871) 269, 501
Mayor 96
Population 390, 404, 687
Port traffic 208
Chicago Board of Trade 129
Chicken
Nutritive value 610
Prices, farm 143
Children
Average height, weight 974
Child care 382
Child support 382
Cost of raising 722
Immunization schedule 613
Income taxes, federal 730, 734
Internet addresses 170
Living arrangements 964
Population 386, 391
Single-parent families 382
Social Security benefits 709
Welfare assistance 395
Children's books
Awards 333-34
Notable (1995) 254-55
Chile 751-52
Ambassadors, envoys 846
Chronology (1995) 58
Commercial fishing 145
Flag 481
History 575
Rulers 584
China, dynastic 566, 567, 568
Boxer Rebellion (1900) 501
Chou 552, 554, 585
Great Wall 554, 555
Han 556, 585
Kuomintang 569, 570, 571, 572
Manchu 563, 569, 585
Ming 562, 585
Open Door Policy (1899) 501
Opium War (1839-1842) 565-66
Revolution (1911) 569
Seven Wonders, Middle Ages 555

Shang . . . 552, 585
Sung . . . 559, 585
Tang . . . 559, 585
Yuan . . . 560, 585
China, People's Republic of . . . 752-53
Ambassadors, envoys . . . 846
Chronology (1994-95) . . . 49-50, 66
UN women's conference (1995) . . . 68
Cities (largest) . . . 838
Commercial fishing . . . 145
Energy production, consumption . . . 202
Flag . . . 481
Gold production . . . 134
History . . . 572, 573, 574-75, 576, 752-53
Leaders . . . 585, 752-53
Maoism . . . 574-75, 752-53
Map . . . 492-93
Merchant fleet . . . 209
Military strength . . . 164
Motor vehicle production . . . 212
Nixon visit (1972) . . . 506
Nuclear power . . . 205
Population, world's greatest . . . 838
Tiananmen Square . . . 576
Trade, U.S. . . . 206
U.S. immigrants from . . . 393
China, Republic of. *See* Taiwan
China Sea . . . 593
Chinese lunar calendar . . . 312
Chirac, Jacques . . . 57, 62, *779*
Cholesterol
Heart disease . . . 616
Labels, nutrition . . . 612
Choreographers, notable . . . 362-63
Chou Dynasty . . . 552, 554, 585
Christ. *See* Jesus Christ
Christianity
Denominations . . . 644-47, 652-53
History . . . 556-57, 559-60, 562
Population, world . . . 646
Christmas Day . . . 314
Christmas Island . . . 592, 741
Chromium . . . 132, 133
Chronological eras, cycles (1996) . . . 294
Chronology of 1994-95 . . . 42-71
Churches
Addresses, U.S. headquarters . . . 645-46
Calendars . . . 647-48
Denominations . . . 652-53
Feast, fast, holy days . . . 647-48
Memberships . . . 644-45, 646, 651
Number, U.S. . . . 644-45
Churchill, Sir Winston . . . 351
Yalta Agreement (1945) . . . 504
Church of Christ, Scientist . . . 644, 645
Church of England . . . 829
Church of Jesus Christ of Latter-Day Saints. *See* Latter-Day Saints, Church of
CIA. *See* Central Intelligence Agency
Cigarettes. *See* Smoking
Cincinnati, OH . . . 687
Buildings, tall . . . 697
Mayor . . . 96
Population . . . 390, 418, 687
Cinema. *See* Movies
CIO. *See* American Federation of Labor and Congress of Industrial Organizations
Circle (mathematical formulas) . . . 607
Circulation (newspapers, magazines) 254, 256
Circumference (formula) . . . 607
Circumnavigation . . . 322
Cities, U.S. . . . 686-95
Area codes, telephone . . . 396-426
Buildings, tall . . . 696-702
Climatological data . . . 180-84, 185
Consumer price indexes . . . 113
Farthest east, north, south, west . . . 540
Housing prices . . . 727
Immigrants (1994) . . . 393
Latitudes, longitudes, altitudes . . . 594-95
Libraries, public . . . 223
Mayors . . . 96-99
Mileage tables
Air . . . 216
Road . . . 215
Newspaper circulation . . . 256
Orchestras, opera companies . . . 252-53
Population . . . 396-426, 686-95
Metropolitan areas (1990-92) . 382, 389
100 largest . . . 390-91
Ports . . . 208
Precipitation . . . 180, 182
Stadiums, arenas . . . 877
Temperatures . . . 180, 182
Theater companies . . . 251
Time differences . . . 314
Wind velocities . . . 182, 185
ZIP codes . . . 396-426
Cities, world
Air mileage . . . 216
Bridges, buildings . . . 702, 705
Latitudes, longitudes, altitudes . . . 593
Population (by country) . . . 737-837
Population of largest . . . 838
Port distances . . . 209
Temperatures, precipitation . . . 184
Time differences . . . 313
Citizenship, U.S.
American Indians (1924) . . . 502
14th Amendment . . . 520-21
Naturalization process . . . 841
Civil rights
Act (1875) . . . 501
Act (1964) . . . 505, 574
Bill signed (1957) . . . 505
Bill vetoed (1990) . . . 509
Commission, U.S. . . . 81
Congressional compliance (1995) . . . 46
Constitutional amendments . . 520-21, 522
Disabilities Act (1990) . . . 509
see also Desegregation; Elections, voting rights; Women
Civil War, U.S. (1861-65) . . . 500
Amnesty Act (1872) . . . 501
Appomattox Court House (1865) . 500, 546
Battlefields . . . 547
Black troops . . . 162
Bull Run (1861) . . . 500
Casualties, numbers serving . . . 166
Confederate States (1861) . . . 500, 523
Costs . . . 163
Draft riots (1863) . . . 500
Emancipation Proclamation (1863) . . 500
Ft. Sumter (1861) . . . 500
Gettysburg Address (1863) . . . 500, 523
Historical parks, sites . . . 546, 547-48
Lincoln assassination (1865) 272, 500, 533
Military leaders . . . 348, 349
Secession of states . . . 523
Sherman's March (1864) . . . 500
Classical music . . . 360-61
Classification, animal/plant . . . 192
Clergy, forms of address . . . 641
Cleveland, Grover . . . 477, 479, 539
Biography . . . 533
Burial site . . . 539
Cabinet . . . 104-7
Popular, electoral votes . . . 478
Cleveland, OH . . . 687
Buildings, tall . . . 697
Mayor . . . 96
Population . . . 390, 418, 687
Climate, U.S. . . . 180-84, 185
Clinton, Bill
Administration . . . 78-81, 479, 480
Assassination attempt (1994) . 42, 53, 273
Biography . . . 538
Cabinet . . . 78, 104-8
Chronology (1994-95) . 42, 43, 44, 46, 47, 48-49, 50, 51, 52, 54, 55, 56, 57, 58, 61, 62, 63, 64, 71
Foster suicide (1993, 1995) . . 61, 64, 509
Health-care reform (1993, 1994) . 509, 510
Inauguration (1993) . . . 509
Mideast peace process (1995) . . . 69, *778*
Presidential election (1992) . 446-75, 475, 477, 509
Popular, electoral votes . . . 446-75, 478
Salary . . . 78
Sexual harassment suit (1994) . . . 44, 510
State of the Union (1995) . . . 46
Vetoes (1995) . . . 58, 65, 91, *194*
Whitewater scandal (1994-95) . 44, 49, 51, 56, 58, 61, 64, 67, 509, 510
Clinton, Hillary Rodham . . . 538
Biography . . . 539
Gingrich White House tour (1995) . . . 46
Health-care reform (1993) . . . 509
UN women's conference (1995) . . . 68
Whitewater scandal (1993, 1994, 1995) 58, 61, 64, 509, 510
Clothing
Exports, imports . . . 207
Price index . . . 112, 113
Clubs, organizations . . . 619-30
Coal
Exports, imports . . . 201, 207
Mining strikes (1922, 1946) . . . 502, 504
Production, consumption . . . 201
Coast Guard, U.S. . . . 82
Academy . . . 160
Address for information . . . 164
Commandants . . . 80, 158
Insignia . . . 160
Personnel, active duty . . . 161
Women, active duty . . . 162
Coastlines, U.S. . . . 541
Cobalt . . . 132, 133
Cocoa (exports, imports) . . . 207
Cocos (Keeling) Island . . . 741
Coffee (exports, imports) . . . 207
Coinage . . . 120, 121
Cold War . . . 572, 575-76
Colleges and universities . 220-22, 224-48
ACT scores . . . 221
Addresses . . . 224-48
Affirmative action programs (1995) . . . 62
Coeducation, first (1833) . . . 499
Desegregation (1962) . . . 505
Enrollment . . . 220, 224-48
Faculty
Number . . . 224-48
Salaries . . . 222
Faulkner Citadel withdrawal (1995) . . . 65
Founding dates . . . 224-48
Four-year . . . 224-38
Freshman attitudes (1994) . . . 248
Governing officials . . . 224-48
Graduates . . . 383
Land Grant Act (1862) . . . 500
SAT scores . . . 221, 222
Sports
Baseball . . . 955
Basketball . . . 55, *783*, 912-17
Football . . . 879-886
Ice hockey . . . 894
Team nicknames, colors . . . 882-84
Wrestling . . . 902
State university, first (1795) . . . 498
Tuition and costs . . . 220, 221
Two-year . . . 238-48
Women's, first (1821) . . . 499
Colombia . . . 753-54
Ambassadors, envoys . . . 846
Drug lord arrests (1995) . . . 60, 66
Flag . . . 481
Gold production . . . 134
Rulers . . . 584
Colorado . . . 657-58
Admission, area, capital . . . 542, 543, 657
Agriculture . . . 137-42
Altitudes (high, low) . . . 541
Birth, death statistics . . . 962
Budget . . . 116
Congressional representation . 82, 85, 384
Courts, U.S. . . . 93
Crime, prisons, death penalty . . . 959
Energy consumption . . . 203
Federally owned land . . . 545
Governor, state officials . . . 99, 100
Immigrants' intended residence . . . 393
Indians, American . . . 550
Interest laws, rates . . . 721, 722
Marriage, divorce laws . . . 728, 729
Motor vehicle statistics . . . 211
Name origin, nickname . . . 544, 657
Population . . . 384-85, 388
Cities, towns . . . 400, 686, 687, 688
Counties, county seats . . . 428
Presidential elections . . . 446, 449-50, 476
Public libraries . . . 223
Schools . . . 218, 219, 222
Taxes . . . 211, 735
Temperature, precipitation . . . 181, 183
Unemployment benefits . . . 146
Welfare assistance . . . 395
Colorado River . . . 586, 596
Colorado Springs, CO . . . 687-88
Mayor . . . 96
Population . . . 390, 400, 687
Colors
Colleges, universities . . . 882-84
Of spectrum . . . 606
Colosseum (Rome) . . . 555
Colossus of Rhodes . . . 555
Columbia (space shuttle) (1981, 1982) 316, 317, 507
Columbia River . . . 596
Columbium . . . 132, 133
Columbus, Christopher (1492) . 497, 561, 586
Columbus, GA . . . 96, 391, 688
Columbus, OH . . . 688
Buildings, tall . . . 697
Mayor . . . 96
Population . . . 390, 418, 688
Columbus Day . . . 314
Comecon . . . 573
Commands, U.S. . . . 158
Commerce. *See* Commodities; Exports, imports; Shipping
Commerce, Department of . . . 79-80
Employees, payroll . . . 151
Expenditures . . . 110
Internet address . . . 169
Secretaries . . . 78, 79, 107-8
Brown investigation (1995) . . . 56
Commission on Civil Rights . . . 81
Committee for Industrial Organization. *See* American Federation of Labor and Congress of Industrial Organizations
Commodities
Exports, imports . . . 207

Commodities *(continued)*
Price indexes 112, 113
Production 138, 141, 142, 143
Common Market. *See* European Community
Common Sense (Paine), Excerpt 511
Commonwealth, The (British Common-
wealth) 842
Commonwealth of Independent States 842
Communications
Inventions 174-76
Media business alliances (1995) . . 62, 66,
70, *195*
Satellite, first (1962) 505
see also specific communications media
Communism
Post-World War II 572
Russian revolution (1917) 569
Soviet Bloc breakup (1989) 576
U.S.
Red scare (1920) 502
Trials, convictions (1949) 504
see also Cold War
Communist China. *See* China, People's
Republic of
Community colleges 238-48
Comoros 481, 754, 846
Composers, notable 360-62
Compound interest table 605
Computers 167-73
CD-ROM households 170
CD-ROM software 171
Glossary of terms 172-73
Media business alliances *195*
Sales, ownership 171
School usage 217
Software, top-selling 171
Usage rates 170, 383
see also Internet
Concentration camps 571, 572
Concerts, top-grossing (1985-94) . . . 257
Cone, Volume formula 607
Confederate States of America
Amnesty Act (1872) 501
Battlefield memorials 547
Civil War (1861-65) 500
Casualties, numbers serving 166
Costs 163
Flags 523
Government 523
Confucianism
Adherents 646
Confucius (551 BC) 554
Congo, Democratic Republic of. *See* Zaire
Congo, Republic of 481, 754, 846
Congo (Zaire) River 596
Congregational churches 644
Congress, U.S. 82-91
Address, forms of 641
Apportionment 384
Bill-into-law process 522
Chronology (1994-95) . . 42, 43, 45-46, 48,
49, 51, 53, 56, 59,
61-62, 63, 64, 65
Committees 90-91
Constitutional powers 516
Elections 82-90
Republican control (1994) . . 37-39, 42,
43-44, *193*, 510
Employees, payroll 151
Expenditures 110
House of Representatives 84-90, 91
Committees 90, 91
Constitutional powers 515, 516
First woman (1916) 502
Floor leaders 43, 84
Members 84-90
Party representation 91
Revenue bills origination 516
Salaries, term 84
Speakers 84, 109, *193*, *194*
Internet addresses 169, 170
Nonvoting members 90
Political division (1965-95) 91
Presidential vetoes (1789-95) 58, 91, *193*
Presidents, vice presidents 479-80
Qualifications 515
Salary amendment (1992) 509, 522
Senate 82-83
Committees 90
Election of senators 515, 521
Floor leaders 82, 109
Members 82-83
Packwood case (1995) . . . 56, 64, 67
Party representation 91
Salaries, term 82
Term limits, Supreme Court rulings . . 524
Visitors, admission of 684
Welfare reform efforts (1995) 51, 68
Women members (1916) 502
see also Continental Congress; Library of
Congress

Congress of Industrial Organizations. *See*
American Federation of Labor and
Congress of Industrial Organizations
Congress of Vienna (1814-15) 565
Connecticut 658
Admission, area, capital 542, 658
Agriculture 137-42
Altitudes (high, low) 541
Birth, death statistics 962
Budget 116
Coastline 541
Congressional representation . 82, 85, 384
Courts, U.S. 93
Crime, prisons, death penalty 959
Energy consumption 203
Federally owned land 545
Governor, state officials 99, 101
Immigrants' intended residence 393
Indians, American 550
Interest laws, rates 721, 722
Marriage, divorce laws 728, 729
Motor vehicle statistics 211
Name origin, nickname 544, 658
Population 384-85, 388
Cities, towns 400-401
Counties, county seats 428
Presidential elections 446, 450, 476
Public libraries 223
Schools 218, 219, 222
Taxes 211, 735, 736
Temperature, precipitation 181, 183
Unemployment benefits 146
Welfare assistance 395
Conservation. *See* Environment
Constantinople 558
Constants, astronomical 287
Constellations 287-88
Constitution, U.S. 515-22
Amendments 519-22
Balanced budget (1995) 46, 51
ERA proposed (1972, 1982) . 506, 507
Poll tax barred 522
Procedure for 518
Prohibition (1917, 1933) . 502, 503, 521
Reconstruction 520-21
Slavery abolished (1865) . . 500, 520
Term limits (1995) 51-52
27th ratified (1992) 509
Voting age (1971) 506, 522
Bill of Rights 519
Internet address 170
Origin 514
Preamble 515
Ratification (1787) 498, 514
Constitutional Convention (1787) 498, 514
Construction industry, (occupational
injuries) 150
Consumer electronics products 259
Consumer Price Indexes 112, 113
Chronology (1994-95) . . 42, 44, 46, 48,
51, 54, 56, 58, 61, 64, 67, 70
Consumer Product Safety Commission 81
Consumers and consumption
At-home shopping 713
Business directory 714-19
Charitable giving 713, 714
Consumer Information Catalog 713
Credit 721-22
Debt 121
Electronics products 259
Energy 201, 202, 203
Food
Labeling, nutrition 612
Meats 138
Nutritive values 609-11
Housing prices 727
Information 713-27
Loan rates 721
Mortgages 726, 727
Personal expenditures 131
Price indexes 112, 113
Products
Parent companies 720
Pure Food and Drug Act (1906) . . . 502
Safety Commission 81
Transportation 211, 212, 214
Continental Congress
Articles of Confederation (1777) . 498, 514
Declaration of Independence (1776) . 498,
512-13
First (1774) 498
Great Seal of the U.S. 525
Northwest Ordinance (1787) 498
Presidents, meetings 511
Stars and Stripes (1777) 498, 525-26
Continental Divide 542
Continents 586-91
Altitudes (highest, lowest) 597
Areas 838
Lakes 598
Maps 485-96

Mountain peaks 590-91
Population 838
Religious adherents 646
Rivers 596-97
Volcanoes 588-89
Waterfalls 599
see also specific continents
Contract With America (1995) . 46, 48, 49,
51-52, 53, 62
Convention sites, political 476
Cook Islands 803
Coolidge, Calvin 477, 479, 480
Biography 535
Burial site 539
Cabinet 104-7
Popular, electoral votes 478
Cooperstown (NY) (Baseball Hall
of Fame) 671, 949
Copper, Production, reserve . 132, 133, 134
Copyright law, U.S. 724-25
Chinese compliance (1995) 49-50
Corn
Exports, imports 144, 207
Nutritive value 611
Prices, farm 143
Production 141, 142, 144
Coronado, Francisco (1540) . . 497, 586
Corporation for Public Broadcasting
Corporations
Leading 122-23
Multinational 124
Profits (by industry) 115
Tax rates 125
see also Business
Corpus Christi, TX 688
Mayor 96
Population 390, 423, 688
Port traffic 208
Corsica 592, 764
Cortes, Hernando 563, 586
Cosmonauts 59, *198*, 315-17, 318
Costa Rica 481, 754-55, 846
Cost of living 135
Côte d'Ivoire (Ivory Coast) . . 481, 755, 846
Cotton
Exports, imports 207
Prices, farm 143
Production 141, 142
Cotton Bowl 880
Counterfeiting 960
Counties, U.S.
Areas and county seats 427-45
Elections (1988, 1992) 447-75
Largest, by population 388
Largest, smallest 540
Country music, notable artists 364
Courts. *See* Judiciary, U.S.; World Court
Courts of Appeal, U.S. 93
CPI. *See* Consumer Price Indexes
Credit
Consumer outstanding 121
Farm 141
Laws, rates 721, 722
Compound interest table 605
Mortgages 726, 727
Prime rate 136
Rating (how to check) 722
Credit cards 721, 722
Crime
Arrests 960
Assassinations 272-73, 539, 576
Chronology (1994-95)
Amtrak Arizona derailment 70
Colombian drug lord arrests 60, 66
Simpson case . . . 45, 48, 50-51, 53, 55,
58, 60-61, 63, 66, 69, 71, *195*, 510
Smith case 43, 63-64, *195*, 510
Unabomber investigation . . . 45, 54, 59,
67-68
Crime bills (1994, 1995) 49, 510
Death penalty (1890, 1977) . 501, 507, 960
Index, by crime, population, region . . . 956
Law enforcement officers 957
Prison population 959, 960
Rates, by type, region, state 958
Sentences versus time served 959
Terrorist incidents, U.S. (1990-94) . . . 960
see also War crimes
Crimean War (1853-56) 566
Croatia 481, 755-56, *777*, 846
Chronology (1994-95) . . 43, 44-45, 46-47,
50, 52, 57, 59-60, 62-63, 65, 68, 70-71
Crozet Archipelago 764
Crude oil. *See* Petroleum
Crusades 559
Cuba 756, 846
Area 592
Bay of Pigs (1961) 505, 573, 756
Castro, revolution (1959) 573, 756
Flag 481
Map 488

Missile crisis (1962) 505
Spanish-American War (1898) . . 501, 567
U.S. immigrants from 393
U.S. refugee policy (1995) 57
Vesco arrest (1995) 60
Cube, Volume formula 607
Curacao 592, 802
Currency, U.S.
Circulation, amount in 121
Denominations discontinued 120
Design, new 120
Dollar decline (1995) 52, 55, 64
Engraving, printing 684
Foreign exchange rates 125
Gold Standard dropped (1933) 503
Mint 120
Money supply 136
Portraits on 120
Silver coinage 120, 121
Customs, U.S. 79, 82
Exemptions, advice 722-23
U.S. receipts 110
Cycles, chronological (1996) 294
Cycling 863
Tour de France (1995) 926
Cyclones 179, 268
Cylinder (volume formula) 607
Cyprus 209, 481, 756-57, 846
Cy Young awards 941
Czechoslovakia 570, 571, 576, 757
Czech Republic . 205, 212, 481, 757-58, 846

— D —

Dahomey. *See* Benin
Dairy products
Exports, imports 207
Nutritive value 609, 610
Prices, farm 143
Dallas, TX 688
Airport traffic 319
Buildings, tall 697
Mayor 96
Population 388, 390, 423, 688
Dams, major 706-7
Dance
Companies, U.S. 253
Notable figures 362-63, 366-80
Dates
Days between two 312
Days of week, to find 310-11
Gregorian calendar 309
History, U.S. 497-510
History, world 551-76
International line 313, 484
Julian calendar 309
Julian period 312
Davis, Jefferson (1861) . . . 351, 500, 523
Davis Cup (tennis) 928
Daylight Saving Time 313
Days
Between two dates 312
Holidays 314
Length of 313
Names, non-English languages 640
Dayton, OH 688
Buildings, tall 697
Mayor 96
Population 391, 418, 688
Death penalty
Crime bill (1994) 49, 510
Electrocution, first (1890) 501
Gilmore execution (1977) 507
Rates, U.S. 959
States with 959
Death records, sources 726
Deaths
Accidental 966
AIDS 510
Aviation 265-66
Cancer 963
Cardiovascular disease 963
Critical illness, state laws 615
By execution 959
Firearms 966, 967
Fires 269
Infant rates 961, 962, 963
Leading causes 963
Motor vehicles 966
Obituaries (1994-95) 76-77
Occupational 150
Presidents, U.S. (dates) 479
Rates, U.S., by states, regions 962
Suicides 963, 964
Survivor benefits 709
United States 961
see also Accidents and disasters; Murders
Debt
Consumer 121
Farm, U.S. 141
National 136
State 116
Decathlon
Olympic champions 858
World record 865
Decibel (measure) 604
Decimals 606
Declaration of Independence
Adopted (1776) 498, 512
Signers 513-14
Text 512-13
Defense, Department of 79
Base closings (1995) 61
Employees, payroll 151
Expenditures 110
Internet address 169
Pentagon 685
Personal salutes, honors 159
Secretaries 78, 79, 105
Defense, national. *See* Armed forces, U.S.; Weapons
Defense contracts 162
Deficits, U.S. budget (1993) 509
Delaware 658
Admission, area, capital 542, 658
Agriculture 137-42
Altitudes (high, low) 541
Birth, death statistics 962
Budget 116
Coastline 541
Congressional representation . 82, 85, 384
Courts, U.S. 93
Crime, prisons, death penalty 959
Energy consumption 203
Federally owned land 545
Governor, state officials 99, 101
Immigrants' intended residence 393
Indians, American 550
Interest laws, rates 721, 722
Marriage, divorce laws 728, 729
Motor vehicle statistics 211
Name origin, nickname 544, 658
Population 384-85, 388
Cities, towns 401
Counties, county seats 428
Presidential elections 446, 450, 476
Public libraries 223
Schools 218, 219, 222
Taxes 211, 735, 736
Temperature, precipitation 181, 183
Unemployment benefits 146
Welfare assistance 395
Democratic Party
Chronology (1994-95) 42, 43, 46, 51, 59, 64, 70
Congressional members (1965-95) . . . 91
Convention sites 476
Elections (by county) 447-75
Presidential, vice presidential candidates 477
Denmark 758
Ambassadors, envoys 846
Flag 481
Merchant fleet 209
Rulers, royal family 381, 582
Trade 206
Wages, hourly 152
Denominations, religious . 644-47, 652-53
Density
Air 292, 605
Earth 290, 292
Gases 605
Planets 290
Sun 290
Denver, CO 688
Airport traffic 319
Buildings, tall 697
Mayor 96
Population 390, 400, 688
Departments, U.S.
Employees, payrolls 151
Executive personnel 78-81
Expenditures 110
Secretaries 78-81, 104-8
see also specific departments, name inverted
Depression, economic
Defined 135
Panic (1873) 501
Stock Market crash (1929) 503, 570
Worldwide (1929-39) 570-71
Desegregation
Baseball (1947) 504
Bus boycott (1955) 504
Mississippi, University of (1962) 505
Public schools (1954) 504, 524
Sit-ins (1960) 505
Supreme Court (1954, 1955, 1956) 504, 505
Deserts, world 599
Des Moines, IA 688
Buildings, tall 697
Mayor 96
Population 390, 406, 688
De Soto, Hernando (1539) 497, 586
Detroit, MI 688
Buildings, tall 697
Mayor 96
Population 390, 410, 688
Port traffic 208
Riots (1943, 1967) 503, 505-6
Diabetes 614-15, 617
Dice (odds) 607
Diet. *See* Nutrition
Dinosaurs *199*
Directories. *See* Addresses
Dirigibles
Hindenburg burned (1937) 265
Notable trips 322
Disability insurance 708-12
Disabled people
Anti-discrimination act (1990) 509
Ethnic, racial distribution 392
Help organizations 617
School programs 217
Disasters. *See* Accidents and disasters
Disciples of Christ Church
Address, headquarters 645
Beliefs, practices 652-53
Membership 644
Discoveries 176-78, 353-55
Chemical elements 177-78
Drugs 176-77
Explorers 586-88
Medicine 176-77
Discus throw
Olympic champions 857, 859
World records 865, 866
Diseases. *See* Health and medicine; *specific diseases*
District Courts, U.S. 93-95
District of Columbia. *See* Washington, DC
Diving
Louganis HIV-positive status (1995) . . . 51
Olympic champions 860-61, 862, 863
Divorce
Laws (by states) 729
Rates, patterns 961
Djibouti 481, 758, 846
Doctors
Age, sex, specialty 968
Patient visits 971
Documents. *See* Laws and documents
Dogs
American Kennel Club 192
Iditarod sled race 918
Westminster Kennel Club 918
Domain Name System (Internet) 167
Dominica 481, 592, 758-59, 846
Dominican Republic 759
Ambassadors, envoys 846
Flag 481
U.S. immigrants from 393
U.S. military government (1916) 502
U.S. troops (1965) 505
Dow Jones Industrial Average
Components 130
Defined 135
Milestones 130
Close above 4,000 (1995) 48
Record drop (1987) 508
Draft, U.S.
NYC riots (1863) 500
Peacetime, first (1940) 503
Selective Service System 81
Vietnam-era end (1973) 506
Vietnam evaders pardoned (1977) . . . 507
Drake, Sir Francis (1579) 497, 586
Dram (measure) 601, 602, 603, 604
Drama. *See* Theater
Dred Scott decision (1857) 500, 523
Drownings 966
Drug abuse
Colombian drug lord arrests (1995) 60, 66
Help organizations 616
Usage 965
Drugs, therapeutic
AIDS (1986) 508
Consumer protection (1906) 502
Discoveries 176-77
Most frequently prescribed 971
Duran, Francisco (1994, 1995) . 42, 53, 273
Dutch East Indies. *See* Indonesia
Duties. *See* Customs, U.S.
Duty-free imports 722-23

— E —

Earhart, Amelia
Lost (1937) 503
Notable flights 322
Earnings. *See* Salaries and wages
Earth 290, 292-94
Area 292
Atmosphere 292
Climate zones 293
Dimensions 292

Earth *(continued)*
Latitude, longitude 292
Poles 293-94
Rotation 294
Seasons 293
Sun, distance from 277, 290
Time 293
Earthquakes, major 271
Japan (1995) 48, 271
Los Angeles (1994) 271, 510
San Francisco (1906, 1989). 271, 502, 508
East China Sea 593
Eastern Atoll 683
Eastern Europe 571, 573, 574, 576
see also specific countries
Eastern Orthodox churches
Addresses, U.S. headquarters 645, 646
Beliefs, practices 652-53
Church calendar 647
Membership 644, 646
Russian church established 560
Easter Sunday 647, 648
East Germany. *See* Germany
Ebola virus (1995) 58
EC. *See* European Community
Eclipse Awards 897
Eclipses 289, 295-96
Ecology. *See* Environment
Economic indicators, leading
Chronology (1994-95) 42, 44, 46, 48, 51, 53-54, 56, 58, 61, 64, 67, 70
Defined 114, 136
Economics
Banking statistics 118-19
Bankruptcy 115
Budget, U.S. 110-11
Business leaders, notable past 346-47
Chronology (1994-95) 42, 44, 46, 48, 51, 52, 53-54, 55, 56, 58, 61, 64, 67, 70
Consumer credit 121
Consumer Price Indexes 112, 113
Depressions (1873, 1929). 501, 503, 570-71
Dow Jones Average 130, 135
Economists, notable 325, 347-48
GDP, GNP 114
Glossary of terms 135-36
Gold reserves 128, 132
Income, national 114, 127
Investments abroad 128
Nobel Prizes 40, 325
Reagan boom (1980s) 576
State finances 116-117
Stocks, bonds 129-31
U.S. net receipts 110-11
World Bank 845
see also Stocks
Ecuador 481, 759-60, 846
Edison, Thomas A. (1878, 1894) 354, 501
National historic site (NJ) 547
Education 217-48
Attainment
Annual earnings correlate 149, 383
By labor force status, occupation 149
Awards 335
Black enrollment 220, 221
Computer software, top-selling 171
Computers, technology in schools 217
Day schools, full-time 218
Desegregation, Supreme Court rulings (1954, 1955, 1956) 504, 505, 524
Disabled students 217
Educators, notable past 355-56
Enrollment
College 220
Elementary, secondary 217, 218
Food program costs 139
Graduates, high school 219, 220, 383
Historical summary (1939-93) 217
Revenues and expenditures, public schools 217, 218, 219
SAT, ACT scores 221-22
School prayer ban (1963) 505
see also Colleges and universities
Education, Department of 81
Employees, payroll 151
Expenditures 110
Internet address 169
Secretaries 78, 81, 108
EEC. *See* European Community
EEOC. *See* Equal Employment Opportunity Commission
EFTA. *See* European Free Trade Association
Eggs
Exports, imports 207
Nutritive value 609, 610
Prices
Farm 143
Per dozen, by state 138
Production, by state 138
Egypt 760
Ambassadors, envoys 846
Ancient 552, 554
Seven Wonders 555
Aswan Dam 707, 760
Distances to ports 209
Flag 481
Middle Ages 555
Military strength 164
Mubarak assassination attempt (1995) 60
Sadat assassination (1981) 272, 576, 760
Eisenhower, Dwight D. 475, 477, 479, 480
Biography 536
Burial site 539
Cabinet 104-8
Popular, electoral votes 478
Presidential library 539
Elba 565, 592, 785
Elderly (over 65)
Alzheimer's disease 615
Help organizations 616
Living arrangements 964
Medicare 710
Enacted (1966) 505
Population 382, 386, 391
Poverty levels 394
Social Security 708-12
Election Day 314
Elections
Congressional 42, 82-90
Presidential
Electoral College 476
Independent parties 477
1996 race 41, 49, 51, 54, 56, 58-59, 61, 65, 67, 70, *194*
Official results (1992) 475
Party nominees (1856-92) 477
Popular, electoral vote (1789-1992) 446-75, 478
Voter participation (1932-92) 475
Voting rights
Act signed, interpreted (1965, 1994) 505
Black males 521
18-year-olds (1971) 506, 522
Motor-voter bill (1993) 509
Turnout (1932-92) 475
Washington (DC) residents (1961) 522, 680
Women (1869, 1920) 501, 502, 521
Electoral College 476
Apportionment 384
Constitution on 516-17, 520
Map 476
Electrical appliance use 203
Electric power
Blackout, northeastern U.S. (1965) 505
Hydroelectric plants 706
Nuclear plants 205
Production, consumption 201, 203, 204
Unit measurements 604
Electronics products, consumer 259
Elements, chemical 177-78
Elevations, mountain 590-91
Elizabeth II, Queen (UK) 578, 829
Ellice Islands. *See* Tuvalu
Ellis Island (NYC) 529
El Paso, TX 688
Mayor 96
Population 390, 423, 688
El Salvador 393, 481, 760-61, 846
Em (measure) 604
E-mail (Internet) 167
Emancipation Proclamation (1863) 500
Emigration. *See* Immigration, emigration; *specific countries*
Emmy Awards 335-36
Empire State Building (NYC)
Height 699
Opened (1931) 503
Employment 146-57
Affirmative action programs (1995) 62
Agricultural 137, 147, 149
Benefit programs 148, 154
By cities (selected) 686-95
Earnings 153, 154, 155
By educational attainment 149
Employer costs 154
Full 135
Government 151
Immigration based on 840-41
Insurance 146, 148
Military 161, 162, 163
By nation (*see specific country*)
Occupational injuries, fatalities 150
Occupations 147, 149
Rates (1940-94) 146
Social Security benefits 708-12
Training services 148
Women 147, 149, 152, 153, 155, 382
see also Labor unions; Salaries and wages; Unemployment, U.S.
Endangered species 188, 189
Endeavour (space shuttle) (1993) 317, 509
Energy 201-5
Consumption 201, 202, 203
Exports, imports 201, 202, 207
Production 201, 202, 204
see also specific countries, sources, types
Energy, Department of 80
Employees, payroll 151
Expenditures 110
Internet address 169
Secretaries 78, 80, 108
England
History 561, 563, 564, 567, 829
Poets Laureate 357
Prime ministers 579
Rulers 577-78
see also United Kingdom
Engraving and Printing, Bureau of 79, 684
Enlightenment (18th century) 563
Entertainers
Awards 335-39
Birthplaces, birth dates 366-76
Notable past 377-80
Original names 380-81
see also Actors, actresses
Environment 187-92
Endangered species 188, 189
Hazardous waste sites 187
Legislation (1994) 510
Toxic releases 187
Water usage 192
Environmental Protection Agency 81
Employees, payroll 151
Expenditures 110
Internet address 169
Envoys. *See* Ambassadors and envoys
EPA. *See* Environmental Protection Agency
Ephemeris time 293
Epiphany (feast day) 647
Episcopal Church
Address, headquarters 645
Beliefs, practices 652-53
Calendar, fast days 647
Church of England 829
Membership 644
Eponyms 636
Equal Employment Opportunity Commission 81, 151
Equal Rights Amendment (1972, 1982) 506, 507
Equatorial Guinea 481, 761, 846
Equestrian sports 863
Equinoxes (1996) 275, 276, 282, 283, 293
ERA. *See* Equal Rights Amendment
Eras, chronological (1996) 294
Erie, Lake 598
Erie Canal (1825) 499
Eriksson, Leif 559
Eritrea 481, 761, 846
Eskimos 382, 386, 550
Estonia 481, 761-62, 846
Ethiopia 762
Ambassadors, envoys 846
Flag 482
History 558, 560, 571, 575
Ethnic, racial distribution (U.S.) 382, 387, 391, 392, 550
Etna, Mt. 589, 785
EU. *See* European Union
Europe
AIDS cases 840
Area 838
Commercial fishing 145
Highest, lowest points 597
Islands 592
Lakes 598
Languages 642-43
Map 490
Motor vehicle production 212
Mountain peaks 590-91
Population 838
Projections (2010, 2020) 838-39
Religious adherents 646
Rivers 596
Rulers, royal families 381, 577-84
Trade, U.S. 206
Volcanoes 588, 589
Waterfalls 599
see also specific countries
European Community 573, 575, 576, 842
European Free Trade Association 206, 573, 575, 842
European Union 206, 842
Evangelical churches 575, 644, 645
Evening stars (1996) 286
Events and anniversaries. *See* Anniversaries; Chronology of 1994-95
Everest, Mt. 555, 590, 591, 597
Evolution theory 566
Exchange rates, foreign 125
Executions, U.S. *See* Death penalty
Executive agencies, U.S. 78

Executive Office of the President 78
Exercise, (heart rate) 609
Expenditures, federal 110-11
Explorations, expeditions
  Antarctic. 587-88
  Arctic 586-87
  Space 315-19
  Western Hemisphere 559, 561, 563
  Major explorers 586
Explosions 269-70
  Oklahoma City bombing (1995) 54, 55-56,
    64, *196-97*
  Unabomber case (1994-95).45, 54, 59, 67-68
Exports, Imports 206-8
  Agricultural 140, 144, 207
  Automobiles 207, 208
  Balance of trade 135, 206, 207, 576
  Coal, coke 207
  Commodities. 207
  Energy. 201, 202, 207
  GATT 207, 573, 845
  International trade court, U.S. 95
  International transactions, U.S. 126
  Manufactures 207
  Merchant fleets 209-10
  NAFTA (1993). 509
  Petroleum. 201, 202, 207
Express Mail 631

— F —

FAA. *See* Federal Aviation Administration
Faeroe Islands 592, 758
Fahrenheit scale 605
Falkland Islands 592, 831
Families
  Child care. 382
  Child support 382
  Immigrant preference system. 840-41
  Living arrangements. 382
  One-parent. 382
  Poverty levels 394
  Welfare assistance. 395
  see also Households
FAO. *See* Food and Agriculture Organization
Farms. *See* Agriculture
Fastest trips, (air travel) 321-22
Fathom (measurement). 601
Fats and oils. 609, 610
  Labels, nutrition. 612
Faulkner, Shannon (1995) 65
FBI. *See* Federal Bureau of Investigation
FCC. *See* Federal Communications
  Commission
FDIC. *See* Federal Deposit Insurance
  Corporation
Federal agencies
  Budget receipts, outlays 110-11
  Civilian employment. 151
  Directory 81-82
  Internet addresses. 169
  see also specific agencies
Federal Aviation Administration ... 80, 82
Federal Bureau of Investigation
  Directors 79
  Expenditures. 110
  Headquarters 82, 684
  Ruby Ridge siege (1995). 65
Federal Claims Court, U.S. 95
Federal Communications Commission 81
Federal Deposit Insurance
  Corporation..... 81, 117, 135, 151
Federal government. *See* Government, U.S.
Federal Reserve System 81, 119
  Board actions (1994-95) 42, 48, 52, 55, 61
  Defined 135
  Discount rate 119
  Formed (1913) 502
Federal taxes. *See* Taxes, federal
Federal Trade Commission 81, 169
Fencing (sport) 863-64
Fertility rate 961
Fiber (labels, nutrition) 612
Field hockey 864
Figure skating. *See under* Skating
Fiji 482, 592, 762-63, 846
Fillmore, Millard 479, 480
  Biography. 532
  Burial site. 539
  Cabinet. 104-7
Films. *See* Movies
Finance. *See* Banks; Business; Economics;
  Stocks
Finland 763
  Ambassadors, envoys 846
  Flag 482
  Nuclear power. 204, 205
  Wages, hourly. 152
Firearms
  Crime bill (1994) 49, 510
  Deaths involving 967
  Gun control legislation (1993, 1994) 509, 510

  Gun gauge, caliber. 604
  Rifle, pistol champions (1994). 923
Fires
  Chicago, IL (1871) 269, 501
  Deaths 269
  Major (1994) 269, 510
  Property loss. 968
First aid 608
First ladies 169, 538
  Clinton, Hillary Rodham 538, 539
Fish and fishing
  Commercial
    U.S. 145
    World 145
  Endangered species 188, 189
  Exports, imports. 207
  Game fish records 919-20
  Nutritive food values. 609, 610
  Venomous species 190
  see also specific countries
Flags
  Confederacy 523
  United States. 525-27
    Display 526-27
    History 525-26
    Pledge to. 527
    21-gun-salute to 159
  World (color) 481-84
Flaxseed production 142
Fleets, merchant 209-10
Flights. *See* Aviation
Floods
  Characteristics. 179
  Johnstown (PA) (1889) 501
  Mississippi River (1993) 268, 509
  Worldwide. 268
Florida
  Accession (1819) 499, 545, 659
  Admission, area, capital. .. 542, 543, 659
  Agriculture 137-42
  Altitudes (high, low) 541
  Birth, death statistics. 962
  Budget 116
  Coastline 541
  Congressional representation . 82, 85, 384
  Courts, U.S. 94
  Crime, prisons, death penalty 959
  Energy consumption 203
  Federally owned land 545
  Governor, state officials. 99, 101
  Immigrants' intended residence. 393
  Indians, American. 550
  Interest laws, rates 721, 722
  Marriage, divorce laws 728, 729
  Mineral production 132
  Motor vehicle statistics 211
  Name origin, nickname 544, 659
  Population. 384-85, 388
    Cities, towns. 401-3, 689, 690,
      691, 694, 695
    Counties, county seats. 429
  Port traffic. 208
  Presidential elections .. 446, 450-51, 476
  Public libraries 223
  Schools 218, 219, 222
  Taxes 211, 735
  Temperature, precipitation. .. 181, 183
  Unemployment benefits. 146
  Welfare assistance 395
Fluid measures ... 600, 601, 602, 604, 605
Folger Shakespeare Library (DC). 684
Food 609-12
  Exports, imports. 207
  Federal assistance programs 139
  Internet addresses 170
  Labels, nutrition. 612
  Nutritive values. 609-11
    Dietary allowances 609, 612
  Price indexes. 112, 113
  Production (world) 144
  Pure Food and Drug Act (1906) 502
Food and Agriculture Organization
  (UN). 845
Food stamp program 139
  Reform efforts (1995) 51
Football, Canadian. 878
Football, college 879-86
  Bowl games 879-81
  Coaching 882-84, 885
  Conference champions 886
  Heisman Trophy. 884
  National champions 885
  Outland Award. 884
  Teams, Division I 882-84
  Winning percentage leaders. 885
  Winning streaks 886
Football, pro 867-77
  Addresses, teams. 902
  All-pro team (1994) 877
  All-time records 876-77
  Champions 867-69

  Expansion teams 867
  George Halas Trophy 874
  Hall of Fame 875
  Head coaches (1995) 869
  Jim Thorpe Trophy 874
  Player draft
    First round selections (1995) 875
    Number one choice (1936-95) 875
  Rookies of the Year (1964-1994) 874
  Stadiums 877
  Standings, final (1994). 867
  Statistical leaders (1994) 873-74
  Statistical leaders (by years). ... 871-72
  Super Bowl 48, *782*, 870, 877
Force, pressure measures. 607
Ford, Gerald R. .. 475, 477, 479, 480, 539
  Biography 537
  Cabinet. 104-8
  Popular, electoral votes 478
  Presidential library 539
Foreign idioms. 639
Foreign investment
  By U.S. abroad. 128
  In U.S. companies. 126
Foreign trade. *See* Exports, imports
Foreign words, phrases 637
Foreman, George (1995) 43
Forests (giant trees, U.S.) 190
Forgery 960
Formentera 819
Forms of address 641
Formulas, mathematical 607
Fortier, Michael (1995) 35, 56, 64
Fort Wayne, IN 688
  Mayor. 97
  Population. 391, 406, 688
Fort Worth, TX 688-89
  Buildings, tall 698
  Mayor. 97
  Population. 390, 423, 688
Foster, Vincent (1993, 1995) .. 61, 64, 509
Four Freedoms (1941). 503
Fractions-to-decimals reduction 606
France 763-64
  Ambassadors, envoys 846
  Chronology (1995) 48, 57, 62, 68-69, *199*
  Departments, territories 764
  Energy consumption 202
  Flag 482
  Gold reserves. 128
  History 561, 563, 564, 565,
      567, 571, 575, 576
    French and Indian War (1754-63) .. 497
    French Revolution (1789) 564
    New World settlements (1699) 497
  Merchant fleet 209
  Military strength 164
  Motor vehicle production 212
  Nuclear power 204, 205
  Rulers. 563, 564, 579-80, *779*
  Trade 206
  Unemployment rates 147
  Wages, hourly 152
Franchises. 124
Franconia, House of 581
Franklin, Benjamin (1732, 1752) . 351, 497
Freedom Statue (U.S. Capitol) 684
Freezing point, water 605
Freight statistics
  Air cargo. 319
  Merchant marine. 209-10
Fremont, CA 97, 391, 689
Fremont, John C. (1856) 500
French and Indian War (1754-63) 497
French Antarctica 764
French Guiana 764
French Open (tennis). 929
French Polynesia 764
French Revolution (1789) 564
Fresno, CA 689
  Mayor. 97
  Population. 390, 398, 689
Friends, Society of (Quakers). 644, 645
Fruits
  Exports, imports. 207
  Nutritive values. 609, 610
  Prices, farm 143
  Production 142
FTC. *See* Federal Trade Commission
Fuel. *See* Energy; *specific kinds*
Fulton, Robert (1807) 499
Futuna-Alofi Island 764
Futures (stock). 129, 136

— G —

Gabon 206, 482, 764-65, 846
Gadsden Purchase 545
Galapagos Islands 592, 760
Gambia 482, 765, 846
Gambier Islands 764
Gandhi, Indira 272, 576, 772

Gandhi, Mohandas 272, 571, 572, 772
GAO. *See* General Accounting Office
Garcia, Jerry (1995) 76, *781*
Garfield, James A. 477, 479
Assassinated (1881) 272, 501, 533, 539
Biography 533
Burial site 539
Cabinet 104-7
Popular, electoral votes 478
Garland, TX 97, 391, 689
Gas, natural. *See* Natural gas
Gas appliance use 203
Gases (densities) 605
Gasoline
Arab embargo (1973) 506
Automobile consumption 211, 214
Prices, retail 204
Taxes (by state) 211
GATT. *See* General Agreement on Tariffs and Trade
Gauge (measure) 604
Gays. *See* Homosexuality
Gaza. *See* Israel; Palestine
GDP. *See* Gross Domestic Product
General Accounting Office 82, 151
General Agreement on Tariffs and Trade (1994) 207, 510, 573, 845
see also World Trade Organization
Generals, U.S. 158
Address, form of 641
Insignia 160
Pay scale 165
Personal salutes, honors 159
Women, first (1970) 506
General Services Administration 81, 151
Geneva Conventions 845
Geodetic datum point 540
Geographic mobility, U.S. (1960-93) 391-92
Geography 540-45, 586-99
Geographic centers, U.S. 543
International boundary lines, U.S. 543
Superlative statistics, U.S. 540
George Halas Trophy 874
George Washington Bridge (NY-NJ) 702
Georgia 659-60
Admission, area, capital 542, 659
Agriculture 137-42
Altitudes (high, low) 541
Birth, death statistics 962
Budget 116
Coastline 541
Congressional representation 82, 85, 384
Courts, U.S. 94
Crime, prisons, death penalty 959
Energy consumption 203
Federally owned land 545
Governor, state officials 99, 101
Immigrants' intended residence 393
Indians, American 550
Interest laws, rates 721, 722
Marriage, divorce laws 728, 729
Mineral production 132
Motor vehicle statistics 211
Name origin, nickname 544, 659
Population 384-85, 388
Cities, towns 403-4, 686, 688
Counties, county seats 429-30
Port traffic 208
Presidential elections 446, 451-52, 476
Public libraries 223
Schools 218, 219, 222
Taxes 211, 735
Temperature, precipitation 181, 183
Unemployment benefits 146
Welfare assistance 395
Georgia, Republic of 66, 482, 491, 765-66, 846
Germany 766-67
Ambassadors, envoys 846
Chronology (1994-95) 43
Energy consumption 202
Flag 482
Gold reserves 128
History 559, 561, 564, 565, 566, 567, 571, 576
Munich Olympics (1972) 575
Reunification (1990) 766
Third Reich (1945) 504, 571, 572, 581, 766
Weimar Republic 570, 766
World War I (1917) 502, 569
Merchant flee 209
Military strength 164
Motor vehicle production 212
Nuclear power 204, 205
Rulers 559, 561, 581, 766
Trade 206
Unemployment rates 147
U.S. immigrants from 393
Wages, hourly 152
see also Berlin, Germany
Gestation, incubation (animal) 189
Gettysburg Address (1863) 500, 523
Ghana 767
Ambassadors, envoys 846
Flag 482
Gold production 134
History 558
GI Bill of Rights (1944) 503
Gibraltar 830
Gilgorov, Kiro (1995) 70
Gingrich, Newt 72, 84, 109, *193*, *194*
Chronology (1994-95) 42, 43, 44, 46, 58, 65
Girl Scouts
Address 623
Founded (1912) 502
Glendale, CA 97, 391, 689
Glenn, John H., Jr. (1962) 315, 320, 505
Gliders (1994 records) 321
GNP. *See* Gross National Product
Gold
Black Friday (1869) 501
Carats in pure 604
Discovered, U.S. (1835, 1848) 499, 500
Production 132, 133, 134
Reserves 128, 132
Golden Gate Bridge (CA) 702
Golf 921-23
Good Friday 314, 647
Gorbachev, Mikhail 575-76, 585, 812
Nobel Peace Prize 325
Summit talks (1985, 1987) 165, 508, 576
Gore, Albert, Jr. 78, 167, 480
Government, U.S. 78-95
Agencies 81-82, 151
Branches 78
Clinton administration 78-81
Internet addresses 169-79
Publications catalog 713
Revenue and expenditures 110-11
Governors, state 99-103
Address, form of 641
First women (1924) 503
Grains
Exports, imports 144, 207
Nutritive value 609, 610-11
Prices, farm 143
Production, U.S. 141, 142, 144
Production, world (by country) 144
Storage capacities 143
Grammy Awards 339, *780*
Grand Canyon (AZ) 546, 555, 656
Grand Coulee Dam 707
Grand Rapids, MI 97, 390, 689
Grant, Ulysses S. 477, 479
Biography 533
Burial site 539
Cabinet 104-7
Popular, electoral votes 478
Gravity
Atmosphere, effect on 292
Planets (relative) 290
Great Barrier Reef 555
Great Britain. *See* United Kingdom
Great Lakes 598
Commercial fishing 145
Great Seal of the U.S. 525
Great Wall 554, 555
Great White Fleet (1907) 502
Greece 767-68
Ambassadors, envoys 846
Chronology (1995) 70
Flag 482
History 565, 575
Merchant fleet 209
Wages, hourly 152
Greece, ancient
City-states 552
Hellenistic Era 554, 556
Leading figures 577
Measures 605
Minoan civilization 552
Philosophers 552
Seven Wonders 555
Greek Orthodox Church. *See* Eastern Orthodox churches
Greenland 559, 592, 758
Greensboro, NC 97, 391, 689
Greenwich meridian 313, 484
Greenwich sidereal time (1996) 286
Gregorian calendar 309
Grenada 768
Ambassadors, envoys 846
Flag 482
Invasion (1983) 508, 576, 768
Grenadines. *See* St. Vincent and the Grenadines
Grey Cup 878
Gross Domestic Product, U.S. 135
Gross National Product, U.S. 114
Group of Seven (G-7) 60, 842
Guadalcanal 592
Battle for (1942) 503, 572
Guadeloupe 592, 764
Guam 681-82
Accession (1898) 501, 545
Altitudes (high, low) 541
Area 445, 545, 592
Congressional delegate 90
Courts, U.S. 95
Immigrants' intended residence 393
Population 445
ZIP codes 445
Guangxi 753
Guatemala 482, 768-69, 846
Guernsey 830
Guiana, French 764
Guinea, Republic of 482, 769, 846
Guinea-Bissau 482, 769, 846
Gulf Coast, (length) 541
Gulfs 593
Gulf War. *See* Persian Gulf War
Guns. *See* Firearms
Guyana 482, 769-70, 846
Gymnastics
Olympic champions (1992) 864
Rhythmic 864
World championship (1995) 926)

— H —

Hagia Sophia Mosque 555
Haiti 770
Ambassadors, envoys 846
Chronology (1994-95) 47, 52-53
Flag 482
Map 488
U.S. occupation (1915, 1934) 502, 503
Halas Trophy 874
Hale, Nathan (1776) 498
Halicarnassus Mausoleum 555
Hall of Fame
Aviation 320-21
Baseball 949
Basketball 911
Bowling 898
Football, pro 875
Hambletonian (horse race) 898
Hammer throw
Olympic champions 857
World record 865
Hammurabi 551
Handball 864
Han dynasty 556, 585
Hanging Gardens of Babylon 555
Hanover, House of 578
Hapsburg dynasty 561, 566, 581
Harbors. *See* Ports
Harding, Warren G. 477, 479, 480, 539
Biography 535
Burial site 539
Cabinet 104-7
Popular, electoral votes 478
Harness racing 898
Harrison, Benjamin 477, 479
Biography 533-34
Burial site 539
Cabinet 104-7
Popular, electoral votes 478
Harrison, William Henry 479, 539
Biography 531
Burial site 539
Cabinet 104-6
Popular, electoral votes 478
Hartford, CT 97, 698
Hart Memorial Trophy 894
Harvest moon 291
Hawaii 660
Accession (1898) 501, 545
Admission, area, capital 542, 543, 660
Agriculture 137-42
Altitudes (high, low) 541
Area 592
Birth, death statistics 962
Budget 116
Coastline 541
Commercial fishing 145
Congressional representation 82, 85, 384
Courts, U.S. 94
Crime, prisons, death penalty 959
Energy consumption 203
Federally owned land 545
Governor, state officials 99, 101
Immigrants' intended residence 393
Indians, American 550
Interest laws, rates 721, 722
Marriage, divorce laws 728, 729
Motor vehicle statistics 211
Name origin, nickname 544, 660
Population 384-85, 388
Cities, towns 404, 689
Counties, county seats 430

Hawaii *(continued)*
Presidential elections 446, 452, 476
Public libraries 223
Schools 218, 219, 222
Taxes 211, 735, 736
Temperature, precipitation 181, 183
Unemployment benefits 146
Volcanoes 589
Welfare assistance 395
Wettest spot, U.S. 181
Hayes, Rutherford B. 477, 479
Biography 533
Burial site 539
Cabinet 104-7
Popular, electoral votes 478
Hay production 141, 142, 143
Hazardous waste sites 187
H-Bomb. *See* Hydrogen bomb
Health and Human Services, Department of 80
Employees, payroll 151
Expenditures 110
Internet address 169
Secretaries 78, 80, 108
Surgeon General 44, 80, 82
Foster nomination (1995) 48, 56, 59
see also Social Security Administration
Health and medicine
AIDS (1986, 1994) 508, 840
Alzheimer's disease 615
Anesthesia (1842) 500
Black Death 561
Cancer 613, 614
Critical illness, state laws 615
Diabetes 614-15
Disabled people 392
Doctor-office visits 971
Doctors 968
Drug usage 965, 971
Ebola virus outbreak (1995) 58
Emergency room visits 971
Expenditures 969
First aid 608
Heart, blood vessels 616
Artificial implant (1982) 507
Rate targets 609
Help organizations 616-18
High blood pressure 616
Hospice and home care 970
Immunization 613
Influenza epidemic (1918) 502
Internet addresses 170
Legionnaires' disease (1976) 507
Life expectancy 974
Medical discoveries 176-77
Nobel Prizes 40, 324
Occupational injuries, fatalities 150
Price Indexes 112, 113
Smoking regulations (1995) 64-65
Smoking risk reduction 613
see also Deaths
Health, Education, and Welfare, Department of 108
see also Education, Department of; Health and Human Services, Department of
Health insurance
Coverage 383, 970
Disability benefits 708-12
Medicare (1966) 505, 710, 731
Reform efforts (1993, 1994) 509, 510
Taxes, federal 730
Heart disease 615, 616, 617
Heart rate 609
Heat index 186
Hebrews. *See* Judaism
Hebrides 830
Height, weight (average adult, child) 612
Heimlich maneuver 608
Heisman Trophy 884
Helgoland 767
Helicopters (1994 records) 321
Henry, Patrick (1775) 498, 511
Heptathlon 858, 866
Herzegovina. *See* Bosnia and Herzegovina
Hialeah, FL 97, 390, 689
Hieroglyphic writing 552
High blood pressure 616
High jump
Olympic champions 856, 858-59
World records 865, 866
High schools
Computer, technology usage 217
Drug usage 965
Enrollment 217
Graduates 217, 219, 220, 383
SAT, ACT scores 221-22
Highways. *See* Roads
Hindenburg (dirigible) 265, 322
Hinduism
Adherents, U.S. 644
Beliefs, practices 654
Population, world 646
Hiroshima bombing (1945) 65-66, *200*, 504, 572
Hispanics
Disabled people 392
Education 220
Employment, unemployment 149
Households 964
Population 382, 386
Poverty rates 394
Salaries and wages 149, 152, 153
Hiss, Alger (1948) 504
Historic sites, national 547-48
History
Anniversaries 73-75
Historians, notable past 347-48
Leading figures 577-85
Parks, national 546-48
Pulitzer Prizes 330-31
U.S. 497-510
World 551-76
Hitler, Adolf 352, 571, 581, 766
Hockey, field 864
Hockey, ice 887-94
NCAA champions 894
NHL 887-94
Addresses, teams 901-2
All-time scorers 892
Individual leaders (1994-95) 888, 892
Individual scoring, by team (1994-95) 888-91
Most goals in a season 894
Players' strike (1994-95) 47-48, 510, 887
Stanley Cup 61, 887
Trophy winners 892-94
Olympic champions 853
Hog production 137, 138, 143
Holidays
International, selected 314
Legal, public (U.S.) 314
Flag display 526
Religious 647-48
Holland. *See* Netherlands
Holocaust Memorial Museum 684
Holy days 647-48
Holy Roman Empire 559
Home-accident deaths 967
Homes. *See* Housing
Homestead Act (1862) 500
Homosexuality (military conduct 1993, 1995) 52, 509
Honduras 482, 770-71, 846
Honduras, British. *See* Belize
Hong Kong 152, 209, 592, 831
Honolulu, HI 689
Buildings, tall 698
Mayor 97
Population 390, 404, 689
Hoover, Herbert 475, 477, 479, 480
Biography 535
Burial site 539
Cabinet 104-7
Popular, electoral votes 478
Presidential library 539
Hoover Dam 706, 707
Horsepower (measure) 604
Horse racing
American thoroughbred 895-98
Belmont Stakes 896
Breeders' Cup 897
Eclipse awards (1994) 897
Horses of Year 898
Jockey, annual leading 896
Kentucky Derby 895
Preakness 895-96
Triple Crown winners 895
Trotting, pacing 898
see also Equestrian sports
Household furnishings
Appliances in use 203
Consumer electronics products 259
Price index 112, 113
Households
Composition of 382
Housing units 382
Median income 383
Population (by type) 386
Poverty levels 394
Single-parent 382
Single-person 382
House of Representatives. *See* Congress, U.S.
Housing
Homeowners 382-83
Living conditions 383
Mortgages 383, 726, 727
Price Indexes 112, 113
Prices 383, 727
Rental 383
Units 382
Housing and Urban Development, Department of 80
Employees, payroll 151
Expenditures 110
Internet address 169
Secretaries 78, 80, 108
Houston, TX 689
Buildings, tall 698
Mayor 97
Population 390, 423, 689
Port traffic 208
Howland Island 683
Hubble Space Telescope (1993) *198*, 317, 509
HUD. *See* Housing and Urban Development, Department of
Hudson, Henry (1609) 497, 586
Hudson Bay 593
Hudson River 596
Hundred Years' War (1337-1453) 561
Hungary 771
Ambassadors, envoys 846
Flag 482
History 559, 561, 562, 569, 570, 571, 573, 576
Nuclear power 204, 205
Rulers 581
Hunter's moon 291
Huntington Beach, CA 689
Mayor 97
Population 391, 398, 689
Huon Islands 764
Huron, Lake 598
Hurricanes 268
Characteristics 179
Names of (1996) 185
Hussein, Saddam 63, 66, 774-75
Hussein I 49, 66, 69, *778*
Hydroelectric plants 201, 706
Hydrogen bomb (1950, 1952) 504, 573
see also Nuclear arms
Hypertension 616

—I—

IAEA. *See* International Atomic Energy Agency
Ibiza 819
ICAO. *See* International Civil Aviation Organization
ICC. *See* Interstate Commerce Commission
Ice hockey. *See* Hockey, ice
Iceland 482, 559, 771-72, 846
Ice skating. *See* Skating
IDA. *See* International Development Association
Idaho 660
Admission, area, capital 542, 543, 660
Agriculture 137-42
Altitudes (high, low) 541
Birth, death statistics 962
Budget 116
Congressional representation 82, 85, 384
Courts, U.S. 94
Crime, prisons, death penalty 959
Energy consumption 203
Federally owned land 545
Governor, state officials 99, 101
Immigrants' intended residence 393
Indians, American 550
Interest laws, rates 721, 722
Marriage, divorce laws 728, 729
Motor vehicle statistics 211
Name origin, nickname 544, 660
Population 384-85, 388
Cities, towns 404
Counties, county seats 430
Presidential elections 446, 452-53, 476
Public libraries 223
Schools 218, 219, 222
Taxes 211, 735, 736
Temperature, precipitation 181, 183
Unemployment benefits 146
Welfare assistance 395
Idioms
Foreign 639
Meanings, derivations 640
Iditarod sled race 918
IFC. *See* International Finance Corporation
Illinois 661
Admission, area, capital 542, 543, 661
Agriculture 137-42
Altitudes (high, low) 541
Birth, death statistics 962
Budget 116
Congressional representation 82, 85-86, 384
Courts, U.S. 94
Crime, prisons, death penalty 959
Energy consumption 203
Federally owned land 545
Governor, state officials 99, 101

Illinois *(continued)*
Immigrants' intended residence 393
Indians, American 550
Interest laws, rates. 721, 722
Marriage, divorce laws 728, 729
Motor vehicle statistics 211
Name origin, nickname. 544, 661
Population 384-85, 388
  Cities, towns 404-5, 687
  Counties, county seats 430-31
Port traffic 208
Presidential elections 446, 453, 476
Public libraries. 223
Schools 218, 219, 222
Taxes 211, 735, 736
Temperature, precipitation. 181, 183
Toxic chemical pollution 187
Unemployment benefits 146
Welfare assistance. 395
ILO. *See* International Labor Organization
IMF. *See* International Monetary Fund
Immigration and Naturalization Act
  (1952) 504
Immigration, emigration
Ellis Island (1892) 501, 529
Illegal aliens amnesty (1988) 508
Immigrants admitted
  Country of origin 382, 393
  Intended residence area 393
Naturalization 841
Quota system (1921, 1965) 502, 505
Rates of 382
Regulations, U.S.. 840-41
Immunization schedule 613
IMO. *See* International Maritime Organization
Impeachment
Articles of 515, 517
Johnson, Andrew (1868) 501, 532
Nixon hearings (1974) 506-7, 536
Imports. *See* Exports, imports
Incomes
Disposable 135
Distribution 394
Educational level correlate. 383
Farm 140
Median household 383
Minimum wage
  Enacted (1938). 503
  Hourly rates (1950-1991) 154
  Increased (1989) 508
National, U.S. 127
Pay differentials. 149
Per capita income
  Defined 136
  By foreign countries 737-837
  By U.S. states 655-80
Personal, U.S.
  Distribution of total 127
Poverty rate 383, 394
Wage, salary workers 153, 155
Welfare, by states 395
Income taxes 730-36
Federal 730-35
  Amendment authorizing 521
  Audits 735
  Children 730, 734
  Deductions 730-33
  Estimated 730
  Filing, forms. 734-35
  Health insurance 730
  Household employees 730
  Individual rates (1995) 731
  Paycheck withholding (1943) 503
  Recent changes, developments . . 730-31
  Reform Law (1986) 508
  Revenues 110
  Social Security 730, 733
  Tax cut proposals (1994-95) 44, 49, 53
  Taxpayers' rights 735
State 113, 735-36
Incubation, gestation (animal). 189
Independent political parties . 65, 67, 477
Index numbers
Consumer prices 112, 113
Economic indicators 114
Heat 186
Ultraviolet. 186
India 772
Ambassadors, envoys 846
Cities (largest). 838
Commercial fishing 145
Energy production, consumption. . . . 202
Flag 482
History 552, 556, 560,
  561, 565, 566, 567, 569, 571, 572, 575
Map 492
Merchant fleet 209
Military strength 164
Motor vehicle production 212
Nuclear power 205
Population 838

Trade 206
U.S. immigrants from 393
Indiana 661-62
Admission, area, capital. . . 542, 543, 661
Agriculture 137-42
Altitudes (high, low) 541
Birth, death statistics. 962
Budget 116
Congressional representation . 82, 86, 384
Courts, U.S. 94
Crime, prisons, death penalty 959
Energy consumption 203
Federally owned land 545
Governor, state officials. 99, 101
Immigrants' intended residence. 393
Indians, American. 550
Interest laws, rates 721, 722
Marriage, divorce laws 728, 729
Motor vehicle statistics 211
Name origin, nickname 544, 661
Population. 384-85, 388
  Cities, towns. 405-6, 688, 690
  Counties, county seats 431
Port traffic 208
Presidential elections . . 446, 453-54, 476
Public libraries 223
Schools 218, 219, 222
Taxes 211, 735, 736
Temperature, precipitation 181, 183
Toxic chemical pollution 187
Unemployment benefits 146
Welfare assistance 395
Indianapolis, IN 690
Buildings, tall 698
Mayor. 97
Population. 390, 406, 690
Indianapolis 500 (auto race). 929
Indian Ocean
Area, depth 593
Commercial fishing 145
Islands, areas 592
Indians, American 550
Custer's last stand (1876) 501
Geronimo surrender (1886) 501
Gold discovered (1835) 499
Population. 382, 392, 550
Reservations, trust lands 550
Sacagawea (1804) 499
Sand Creek Massacre (1864) 500
Seminole War (1835) 499
Tribes 550
U.S. citizenship (1924) 502
Wounded Knee, Battle of (1890) 501
Individual Retirement Accounts . 135, 732
Indochina. *See* Cambodia; Laos; Vietnam
Indochina War (1953) 504, 574
Indonesia 773
Ambassadors, envoys. 846
Commercial fishing 145
Flag 482
Maps 493, 496
Merchant fleet 209
Military strength 164
Motor vehicle production 212
Trade 206
Volcanoes 588, 589
Industrialists, notable 346-47
Industrial Revolution 564, 566
Industries, U.S.
Business directory 714-19
Corporate tax rates 125
Employees 147, 154
Mineral production 132-34
Multinational companies 124
National income by 127
Occupational injuries, fatalities 150
Profits 115
see also Business; *specific types*
Infant mortality 961, 962, 963
Inflation 135
Information superhighway. *See* Internet
Injuries
Accidental 966, 967
Cost of unintentional 967
Occupational
  Fatalities 150
  By industry, type 150
Inner Mongolia 753
Insects, venomous. 190
Insignia, military 160
Insurance
Life 969
Medical (1966). . . 383, 505, 710, 712, 970
  Reform efforts (1993, 1994) . . 509, 510
Social Security 708-12
Unemployment. 146, 148
Interest
Compound, table of 605
Defined. 135
Laws, rates 721, 722
Prime rate 136

Interior, Department of the 79
Employees, payroll 151
Expenditures 110
Internet address 169
Secretaries 78, 79, 107
Internal Revenue Service 79, 82
Audits 735
Expenditures 110
see also Income taxes
International Atomic Energy Agency . 845
International Bank for Reconstruction and
  Development 43, 845
International boundary lines, U.S. . 543
International Civil Aviation
  Organization 845
International Court of Justice 845
International Date Line 313, 484
International Development
  Association 845
International Finance Corporation . . . 845
International Fund for Agricultural
  Development 845
International Labor Organization 845
International Maritime Organization . . 845
International Monetary Fund 845
International organizations 842-45
International postage 634-35
International System (measurement). . 600
International Telecommunication
  Union. 845
Internet 167-70
Abbreviations, lingo 169
Accessing 167
Glossary of terms 168-69
Online services, commercial 167
Resources available 167-68
Security. 168
Site addresses 169-70
Interpol 842
Interstate Commerce Commission. . . . 81
Intolerable Acts (1774) 498
Inventions 174-76, 177
Investment
Foreign
  In U.S. companies 126
  By U.S companies 128
Glossary of terms 135-36
see also Business; Stocks
Iowa 662
Admission, area, capital . . . 542, 543, 662
Agriculture 137-42
Altitudes (high, low) 541
Birth, death statistics 962
Budget 116
Congressional representation . 82, 86, 384
Courts, U.S. 94
Crime, prisons, death penalty 959
Energy consumption 203
Federally owned land. 545
Governor, state officials 99, 101
Immigrants' intended residence 393
Indians, American 550
Interest laws, rates 721, 722
Marriage, divorce laws 728, 729
Motor vehicle statistics 211
Name origin, nickname 544, 662
Population 384-85, 388
  Cities, towns 406, 688
  Counties, county seats 431-32
Presidential elections . . 446, 454-55, 476
Public libraries 223
Schools 218, 219, 222
Taxes 211, 735, 736
Temperature, precipitation 181, 183
Unemployment benefits 146
Welfare assistance 395
IRA. *See* Individual Retirement Accounts
Iran 773-74, 846
Chronology (1994-95) 50, 55, 60
Energy production 202
Flag 482
Map 492
Merchant fleet 209
Military strength 164
Nuclear power 205
Persia 554, 557, 560,
  561, 570
Revolution (1979-80) 575, 774
Terrorism, international 576
U.S. embassy seizure (1979, 1980,
  1981) 507, 774
Iran-contra affair (1986, 1987, 1989, 1991,
  1993) 508, 509
Iran-Iraq War (1980-88) 576, 774
Iraq 774-75, 846
Arrested Americans freed (1995) 63
Flag 482
Gulf War (1991) 509, 776, 789, 814
Hussein family defections (1995) 66
Kuwait invasion (1990). 509, 775, 789, 814
Map 492

Military strength 164
U.S. helicopter tragedy (1995) 59
Ireland, Northern 830
Area 592
Chronology (1994-95) 44, 50, 52
History 575
Map 490
Ireland, Republic of 775
Ambassadors, envoys 846
Area 592
Chronology (1994-95) 44, 50, 52
Flag 482
History 558, 569
Map 490
Wages, hourly 152
Iron (dietary) 609, 610-11, 612
Iron (metal)
Exports, imports 207
Production 132, 133, 134
Reserve base, world 132
IRS. *See* Internal Revenue Service
Islam
Address, U.S. headquarters 645
Adherents, U.S. 644
Beliefs, practices 654
History 557, 558, 560, 575
Holy days 647
Population, world 646
Islands
Area, ownership 592
U.S. trusteeship 683
Isle of Man 209, 592, 830
Isle of Pines 764
Isle of Skye 830
Israel 775-76
Ambassadors, envoys 846
East Jerusalem land seizure (1995) 57
Flag 482
Formed (1948) 572
Jordanian peace treaty (1994) 776, 787
Map 492
Military strength 164
Palestinian militancy, uprisings 575, 576, 776
Palestinian self-rule (1994-95) 43, 47, 49, 54-55, 62, 69, 71, 776, *778*
Wages, hourly 152
Israeli-Arab wars. *See* Arab-Israeli conflict
Italy 776, 785
Ambassadors, envoys 846
Chronology (1994-95) 45, 47
Flag 482
Gold reserves 128
History 561, 566, 570, 571, 576
Merchant fleet 209
Military strength 164
Motor vehicle production 212
Rulers 583-84
Trade 206
Unemployment rates 147
Wages, hourly 152
ITU. *See* International Telecommunication Union
Ivory Coast. *See* Cote d'Ivoire
Iwo Jima
Area 592
Battle (1945) 504, 572
Memorial (statue) 685

— J —

Jackson, Andrew 479
Biography 531
Burial site 539
Cabinet 104-6
Popular, electoral votes 478
Jackson, MS 690
Mayor 97
Population 390, 412, 690
Jacksonville, FL 690
Buildings, tall 698
Mayor 97
Population 390, 402, 690
Jamaica 482, 785-86, 846
Japan 786
Ambassadors, envoys 846
Automobile production 210, 212
U.S. luxury-car tariffs (1995) 57, 60
Chronology (1994-95)
Atomic bombing anniversary 65-66
Earthquake 48, 271
Tokyo nerve-gas attack 52, 57, *778*
Cities (largest) 838
Commercial fishing 145
Energy consumption 202
Flag 482
Gold reserves 128
History 558-59, 562, 563, 566-67, 576, 579
Peace treaty, U.S. (1951) 504, 786
Perry treaty (1853) 500
World War II (1941-45) 503-4, 572
Islands, areas 592
Map 493
Merchant fleet 209
Military strength 164
Nuclear power 204, 205
Trade 206
Unemployment rates 147
Wages, hourly 152
Japan, Sea of 593
Jarvis Island 683
Java 592, 773
Javelin throw
Olympic champions 857-58, 859
World records 865, 866
Jazz artists, notable 363-64
Jefferson, Thomas 479, 480, 539
Biography 530
Burial site 539
Cabinet 104-6
Declaration of Independence 512-13
Electoral votes 478
Jefferson Memorial (DC) 684
Jehovah's Witnesses 644, 645, 652-53
Jersey, Isle of 592, 830
Jersey City, NJ 690
Mayor 97
Population 390, 414, 690
Jerusalem 554, 776
Jesuits 562
Jesus Christ 557
Jewelry
Birthstones 726
Carat weight, gold 604
Wedding anniversaries 726
Jewish people. *See* Judaism
Jim Thorpe Trophy 874
Jobs. *See* Employment
Jockeys, leading 896
John Paul II, Pope (1981, 1995) 53, 71, 72, 273, 650, *779*, 833
Johnson, Andrew 477, 479, 480
Biography 532
Burial site 539
Cabinet 104-7
Impeachment (1868) 501
Johnson, Lyndon B. 475, 477, 479, 480
Biography 536
Burial site 539
Cabinet 104-8
Popular, electoral votes 478
Presidential library 539
Johnston Atoll 683
Johnstown (PA) flood (1889) 501
Joint Chiefs of Staff 79
Chairmen 158, 165
Personal salutes, honors 159
Jordan 786-87
Ambassadors, envoys 846
Chronology (1995) 66
Flag 482
Israeli peace treaty (1994) 776, 787
Map 492
Jordan, Michael (1995) *783*
Joule (electrical unit) 604
Journalism awards 325-29, 334
see also Magazines; Newspapers
Judaism
Addresses, U.S. headquarters 646
Ancient Hebrews 552, 554, 605
Beliefs, practices 654
Holy days 648
Population, U.S., world 644, 646
Judiciary, U.S.
Address, forms of 641
Court addresses, judges 92-95
Employment, payroll 151
Expenditures 110
Supreme Court justices 92
Judo 864
Julian calendar 309
Julian Period 312
Junior colleges 238-48
Jupiter (planet) 279-80, 290
Morning, evening stars 286
Position by month 274-77, 282-83
Rises, sets 285
Sun, distance from 277, 290
Justice, Department of 79
Attorneys general 78, 79
First woman (1993) 509
Employees, payroll 151
Expenditures 110
Internet address 169
Ruby Ridge siege (1995) 65

— K —

Kampuchea. *See* Cambodia
Kansas 662-63
Admission, area, capital 542, 543, 662
Agriculture 137-42
Altitudes (high, low) 541
Birth, death statistics 962
Budget 116
Congressional representation 83, 86, 384
Courts, U.S 94
Crime, prisons, death penalty 959
Energy consumption 203
Federally owned land 545
Governor, state officials 99, 101
Immigrants' intended residence 393
Indians, American 550
Interest laws, rates 721, 722
Marriage, divorce laws 728, 729
Motor vehicle statistics 211
Name origin, nickname 544, 662
Population 384-85, 388
Cities, towns 406-7, 695
Counties, county seats 432
Presidential elections 446, 455-56, 476
Public libraries 223
Schools 218, 219, 222
Taxes 211, 735, 736
Temperatures, record 183
Unemployment benefits 146
Welfare assistance 395
Kansas City, MO 690
Buildings, tall 698
Mayor 97
Population 390, 412, 690
Kansas-Nebraska Act (1854) 500
Karami, Rashid 576
Kashmir 772
Kasparov, Gary (1995) 71
Kayaking 863
Kazakhstan 205, 482, 491, 787, 846
Kellogg-Briand Pact (1928) 570
Kennedy, John F. 475, 477, 479, 480
Assassination (1963) 272, 505, 536, 539
Warren Commission (1964) 505
Biography 536
Burial site 539, 685
Cabinet 104-8
Popular, electoral votes 478
Presidential library 539
Kennedy, John F., Center for the Performing Arts (DC) 684
Kennedy, Robert F.
Assassinated (1968) 272, 506
Burial site 685
Kentucky 663
Admission, area, capital 542, 663
Agriculture 137-42
Altitudes (high, low) 541
Birth, death statistics 962
Budget 116
Congressional representation 83, 86, 384
Courts, U.S. 94
Crime, prisons, death penalty 959
Energy consumption 203
Federally owned land 545
Governor, state officials 99, 101
Immigrants' intended residence 393
Indians, American 550
Interest laws, rates 721, 722
Marriage, divorce laws 728, 729
Motor vehicle statistics 211
Name origin, nickname 544, 663
Population 384-85, 388
Cities, towns 407, 690, 691
Counties, county seats 432-33
Presidential elections 446, 456, 476
Public libraries 223
Schools 218, 219, 222
Taxes 211, 735, 736
Temperature, precipitation 181, 183
Unemployment benefits 146
Welfare assistance 395
Kentucky Derby 895
First (1875) 501
Kenya 482, 787-88, 846
Kerguelen Archipelago 764
Key, Francis Scott 527
Khmer Empire 559
Khrushchev, Nikita S. (1959) 75, 505, 585, 811-12
Kidnappings, notable 273
Hearst, Patty (1975) 273, 507
Lindbergh baby (1932) 273, 503
Kilowatt-hour (electrical unit) 604
King, Martin Luther, Jr. 345
Assassinated (1968) 272, 506
Birthday (legal holiday) (1986) 314, 508
"I have a dream" speech (1963) 505
King George's War (1744) 497
Kingman Reef 683
Kiribati 482, 788, 846
Knot (measure) 604
Koran 557, 654
Korea, North (Democratic People's Republic of) 788, 846
Chronology (1994-95) 45, 47
Established 572

North Korea *(continued)*
- Flag . . . 482
- Invaded South Korea (1950) . . . 504, 573
- Map . . . 493
- Military strength . . . 164
- *Pueblo* incident (1968) . . . 506

Korea, South (Republic of) . . . 788-89
- Ambassadors, envoys . . . 847
- Commercial fishing . . . 145
- Established . . . 572
- Flag . . . 482
- Invaded by North Korea (1950) 504, 573
- Map . . . 493
- Merchant fleet . . . 209
- Military strength . . . 164
- Motor vehicle production . . . 212
- Nuclear power . . . 204, 205
- Trade . . . 206
- U.S. force (1945-1950) . . . 504, 573
- U.S. immigrants from . . . 393
- Wages, hourly . . . 152

Korean War (1950-53) . . . 573
- Beginning (1950) . . . 504, 573
- Casualties, U.S. forces . . . 166
- Costs . . . 163
- MacArthur removal (1951) . . . 504
- Medals of Honor . . . 163
- Veteran population . . . 162

Korean War Memorial (DC) . . . 684

Kosovo . . . 836

Krakatau volcano . . . 588, 589

Kublai Khan . . . 560

Ku Klux Klan (1866, 1921) . . . 500, 502

Kuomintang (China) . . . 569, 570, 571, 572, 752

Kuwait . . . 789
- Ambassadors, envoys . . . 847
- Flag . . . 482
- Gulf War (1991) . . . 509, 776, 789, 814
- Iraqi invasion (1990) . . 509, 775, 789, 814
- Map . . . 492
- Merchant fleet . . . 209

Kyrgyzstan . . . 482, 491, 789-90, 847

—L—

Labor. *See* Employment; Labor unions

Labor, Department of . . . 80
- Employees, payroll . . . 151
- Expenditures . . . 110
- Internet address . . . 169
- Secretaries . . . 78, 80, 107

Labor unions
- AFL-CIO merger (1955) . . . 504
- AFL formed (1886) . . . 501
- CIO formed (1935) . . . 503
- Contracts, first major (1937) . . . 503
- Directory . . . 156-57
- Haymarket riot (1886) . . . 501
- Industrial union merger (1995) . . . 62
- Kirkland resignation (1995) . . . 59
- Knights of Labor (1869) . . . 501
- Membership (1930-94) . . . 157
- Salary, wage correlate . . . 155
- Taft-Hartley act (1947) . . . 504
- *see also* Strikes

Lacrosse . . . 918, 933

LAFTA. *See* Latin American Free Trade Association

Lake Champlain, Battle of (1814) . . . 499

Lakes . . . 598

Lamb
- Nutritive value . . . 610
- Prices, farm . . . 143
- Production, consumption . . . 138

Land (public)
- California Desert Protection Bill (1994) 510
- Federally owned, by state . . . 545
- Homestead Act (1862) . . . 500
- Land Grant Act (1862) . . . 500
- National recreation areas . . . 545

Language . . . 636-43
- Abbreviations, common . . . 638
- Animal names . . . 638, 639
- Commonly confused words . . . 640
- Commonly misspelled words . . . 641
- Computer glossary . . . 172-73
- Days of week . . . 640
- Economic, financial glossary . . . 135-36
- Eponyms . . . 636
- Forms of address . . . 641
- Idioms . . . 639-40
- Internet terms . . . 168-69
- National Spelling Bee . . . 637
- New words, English . . . 636
- Non-English-speaking Americans . . . 382
- World languages . . . 637, 639, 642-43

Laos . . . 482, 573, 575, 790, 847

Lard . . . 138

La Salle, Sieur de (1682) . . . 497, 586

Las Vegas, NV . . . 690
- Buildings, tall . . . 698
- Mayor . . . 97
- Population . . . 390, 413, 690

Latin America. *See* Central America; South America

Latin American Free Trade Association . . . 206

Latinos. *See* Hispanics

Latitude
- Cities (U.S., world) . . . 593-95
- Position, reckoning . . . 292

Latter-Day Saints, Church of
- Address, headquarters . . . 645
- Beliefs, practices . . . 652-53
- Membership . . . 644
- Organized (1830) . . . 499
- Utah (1846) . . . 500

Latvia . . . 209, 482, 790, 847

Law enforcement
- Crime bills (1994, 1995) . . . 49, 510
- Officers . . . 957

Laws and documents
- Bill of Rights (1791) . . . 498, 519
- Civil rights (1875, 1964, 1990) . 501, 505, 509, 574
- Constitution . . . 515-22
- Consumer finance . . . 721
- Copyright . . . 724-25
- Crime bill (1994) . . . 49, 510
- Declaration of Independence (1776) . . . 498, 512-13
- Disabilities, anti-discrimination (1990) 509
- Divorce (by states) . . . 729
- Immigration (1952, 1990) . . . 504, 840-41
- Lend-Lease (1941) . . . 503
- Marriage (by states) . . . 728
- Mayflower Compact (1620) . . . 497, 511
- Personal records, obtaining . . . 726
- Safety belt . . . 211, 214
- Social Security (1935) . . . 503, 708-12
- Supreme Court, landmark decisions . . . 523-24
- Tax reform (1986) . . . 508, 730-31
- Voting rights (1957, 1965) . . . 505

Lazarus, Emma . . . 529

Lead (metal) . . . 132, 133, 134

League of Arab States . . . 573, 842

League of Nations (1920) . . 502, 569, 570

Leaning Tower of Pisa . . . 555

Leap years . . . 309

Lebanon . . . 791
- Ambassadors, envoys . . . 847
- Flag . . . 482
- Israeli-Palestinian conflicts . . . 575, 576, 776, 791
- Terrorism (1983) . . . 507, 791

Lee, Robert E. (1865) . . . 349, 500

Leeward Islands . . . 830

Legal holidays . . . 314

Legislation. *See* Laws and documents

Legislatures, state . . . 100-103

Legumes
- Nutritive value . . . 609, 611
- Production . . . 142

Lend-Lease Act (1941) . . . 503

Lent . . . 647, 648

Lesotho . . . 482, 791-92, 847

Lewis and Clark expedition (1804) . . . 499

Lexington, KY . . . 690
- Mayor . . . 97
- Population . . . 390, 407, 690

Liberia . . . 69, 209, 482, 792, 847

Liberty Bell . . . 528-29

Libraries
- Postal rates . . . 632
- Presidential . . . 539
- Public . . . 223

Library of Congress . . . 82, 684
- Employees, payroll . . . 151
- Internet address . . . 169
- Librarians . . . 109

Libya . . . 482, 792, 846

Liechtenstein . . . 381, 482, 793, 846

Life expectancy
- Animal longevity . . . 189
- Humans . . . 974

Life insurance . . . 969

Light, speed of . . . 287

Lincoln, Abraham . . . 477, 479
- Assassinated (1865) . . 272, 500, 532, 539
- Biography . . . 532
- Birthday (legal holiday) . . . 314
- Burial site . . . 539
- Cabinet . . . 104-7
- Emancipation Proclamation (1863) . . 500
- Gettysburg Address (1863) . . . 500, 523
- Popular, electoral votes . . . 478

Lincoln, NE . . . 690
- Mayor . . . 97
- Population . . . 390, 413, 690

Lincoln Memorial (DC) . . . 684

Lindbergh, Charles A.
- Flight (1927) . . . 322
- Son kidnapped (1932) . . . 273, 503

Linear measures . . . 600, 601, 603, 605

Lipari Islands . . . 785

Liquid measures . 600, 601, 602, 604, 605

Liquor
- Abuse, Help organizations . . . 616, 619
- Duty-free . . . 722-23
- Exports, imports . . . 207
- Measures . . . 606
- Prohibition (1917, 1933) . 502, 503, 521, 570

Liter (measure) . . . 600, 602, 604

Literature
- Awards . . . 324-25, 330-32, 333-34
- Best-selling books (1994) . . . 255-56
- Notable (1995) . . . 254-55
- Pen names . . . 642
- Writers, notable . . . 324-25, 330-32, 356, 357-60

Lithuania . . . 205, 482, 793, 847

Little Big Horn, Battle of (1876) . . . 501

Little Rock, AR . . . 690
- Buildings, tall . . . 698
- Mayor . . . 97
- Population . . . 391, 397, 690
- School desegregation (1957) . . . 505

Livestock . . . 137, 138, 140, 143
- *see also* Dairy products; Meats

Living wills . . . 615

Lizards, poisonous . . . 190

Loans. *See* Credit

Long Beach, CA . . . 690
- Mayor . . . 97
- Population . . . 390, 398, 690
- Port traffic . . . 208

Longevity, animal . . . 189

Long Island, NY (1776) . . . 498, 592

Longitude
- Cities (U.S., world) . . . 593-95
- Position, reckoning . . . 292

Long jump
- Olympic champions . . . 856, 859
- World records . . . 865, 866

Los Angeles, CA . . . 690-91
- Airport traffic . . . 319
- Buildings, tall . . . 698
- Earthquake (1994) . . . 271, 510
- Mayor . . . 97
- Population . . . 388, 390, 398, 690, 838
- Port traffic . . . 208
- Riots
  - Los Angeles (1992, 1993) . . . 509
  - Watts (1965) . . . 505

Louisiana . . . 663-64
- Admission, area, capital . . . 542, 543, 663
- Agriculture . . . 137-42
- Altitudes (high, low) . . . 541
- Birth, death statistics . . . 962
- Budget . . . 116
- Coastline . . . 541
- Congressional representation . . 83, 86, 384
- Courts, U.S. . . . 94
- Crime, prisons, death penalty . . . 959
- Energy consumption . . . 203
- Federally owned land . . . 545
- Governor, state officials . . . 99, 101
- Immigrants' intended residence . . . 393
- Indians, American . . . 550
- Interest laws, rates . . . 721, 722
- Marriage, divorce laws . . . 728, 729
- Motor vehicle statistics . . . 211
- Name origin, nickname . . . 544, 663
- Population . . . 384-85, 388
  - Cities, towns . . . 407-8, 687, 692, 694
  - Parishes, parish seats . . . 433
- Port traffic . . . 208
- Presidential elections . . . 446, 457, 476
- Public libraries . . . 223
- Schools . . . 218, 219, 222
- Taxes . . . 211, 735
- Temperature, precipitation . . . 181, 183
- Toxic chemical pollution . . . 187
- Unemployment benefits . . . 146
- Welfare assistance . . . 395

Louisiana Purchase (1803) . . . 499, 545

Louisville, KY . . . 691
- Buildings, tall . . . 699
- Mayor . . . 97
- Population . . . 390, 407, 691

Loyalty Islands . . . 764

Lubbock, TX . . . 691
- Mayor . . . 97
- Population . . . 391, 423, 691

Luge (sledding) . . . 850

Lunar calendar . . . 312

Luther, Martin . . . 350, 562, 652

Lutheran churches
- Addresses, headquarters . . . 645
- Beliefs, practices . . . 652-53
- Membership . . . 644

- **Luxembourg** 152, 210, 381, 482, 793, 847
- **Lyricists, notable** 362

— M —

- **Macao** 206, 810
- **MacArthur, Douglas** (1945, 1951) 349, 504
- **Macedonia** 70, 482, 554, 793-94
- **Madagascar** 482, 592, 794, 847
- **Madeira Islands** 592, 810
- **Madison, James** 479
  - Biography 530
  - Burial site 539
  - Cabinet 104-6
  - Electoral votes 478
- **Madison, WI** 97, 390, 691
- **Madura** 592
- **Magazines**
  - Advertising expenditures 263
  - Best-selling (1994) 254
  - Journalism awards 334
  - Postal rates 632
- **Magna Carta** (1215) 561
- **Magnetic poles** 293-94
- **Mailing information** 631-35
- **Maine** 664
  - Admission, area, capital 542, 664
  - Agriculture 137-42
  - Altitudes (high, low) 541
  - Birth, death statistics 962
  - Budget 116
  - Coastline 541
  - Congressional representation 83, 86, 384
  - Courts, U.S. 94
  - Crime, prisons, death penalty 959
  - Energy consumption 203
  - Federally owned land 545
  - Governor, state officials 99, 101
  - Immigrants' intended residence 393
  - Indians, American 550
  - Interest laws, rates 721, 722
  - Marriage, divorce laws 728, 729
  - Motor vehicle statistics 211
  - Name origin, nickname 544, 664
  - Population 384-85, 388
    - Cities, towns 408
    - Counties, county seats 433
  - Port traffic 208
  - Presidential elections 446, 457, 476
  - Public libraries 223
  - Schools 218, 219, 222
  - Taxes 211, 735
  - Temperature, precipitation 181, 183
  - Unemployment benefits 146
  - Welfare assistance 395
- **Majorca** 819
- **Malagasy Republic.** *See* Madagascar
- **Malawi** 482, 794-95, 847
- **Malaysia** 206, 210, 212, 482, 795, 847
- **Maldives** 482, 795, 847
- **Mali** 482, 795-96, 847
- **Malta** 210, 482, 796, 847
- **Man, Isle of** 592, 830
- **Management and Budget, Office of**
  - Director 78
  - Employees, payroll 151
  - Expenditures 110
- **Manchuria** 753
- **Mandela, Nelson** 818
- **Manganese** 132, 133
- **Manhattan, NY** (1626) 388, 497
- **Mantle, Mickey** (1995) 77, *782*
- **Manu'a Islands** 681
- **Manufactures**
  - Employees (by industry) 147
  - Exports, imports 207
  - Personal consumption expenditures 131
  - Workers' statistics 146-57
    - Occupational injuries 150
  - *see also specific industries*
- **Mao Zedong** (Mao Tse-tung) 574-75, 585, 752-53
- **Maps** (color) 485-96
  - World, time zones 484
- **Marathon**
  - Boston 955
  - New York 955
  - Olympic champions 856, 859
  - World records 865, 866
- **Mariana Islands.** *See* Northern Mariana Islands
- **Marine Corps, U.S.**
  - Address for information 164
  - Generals (active duty) 158
  - Insignia 160
  - Organization bases 159
  - Personnel, active duty 161
  - Training centers 159
  - War memorial 685
  - Women, active duty 162
- **Marine warnings, advisories** 179
- **Marquesas Islands** 592, 764
- **Marriage**
  - Age, lawful (by states) 728
  - Blood test requirements 728
  - Number, rate 382
  - Records, obtaining 726
  - Spousal Social Security benefits 709
  - Wedding anniversaries 726
- **Mars** (planet) 279, 290
  - Morning, evening stars 286
  - Position by month 274-77, 282-83
  - Rises, sets 284
  - Space exploration (1976) 279, 318, 507
  - Sun, distance from 277, 290
- **Marshall, Thurgood** (1967) 506
- **Marshall Islands** 683, 796
  - Ambassadors, envoys 847
  - Area 592
  - Flag 482
  - Immigrants' intended residence 393
  - Merchant fleet 210
- **Martinique** 592, 764
- **Maryland** 664-65
  - Admission, area, capital 542, 664
  - Agriculture 137-42
  - Altitudes (high, low) 541
  - Birth, death statistics 962
  - Budget 116
  - Coastline 541
  - Congressional representation 83, 86, 384
  - Courts, U.S. 94
  - Crime, prisons, death penalty 959
  - Energy consumption 203
  - Federally owned land 545
  - Governor, state officials 99, 101
  - Immigrants' intended residence 393
  - Indians, American 550
  - Interest laws, rates 721, 722
  - Marriage, divorce laws 728, 729
  - Motor vehicle statistics 211
  - Name origin, nickname 544, 664
  - Population 384-85, 388
    - Cities, towns 408-9, 686
    - Counties, county seats 433-34
  - Port traffic 208
  - Presidential elections 446, 457-58, 476
  - Public libraries 223
  - Schools 218, 219, 222
  - Taxes 211, 735, 736
  - Temperature, precipitation 181, 183
  - Unemployment benefits 146
  - Welfare assistance 395
- **Mass, units of** 600, 602, 603
- **Massachusetts** 665
  - Admission, area, capital 542, 665
  - Agriculture 137-42
  - Altitudes (high, low) 541
  - Birth, death statistics 962
  - Budget 116
  - Coastline 541
  - Congressional representation 83, 86, 384
  - Courts, U.S. 94
  - Crime, prisons, death penalty 959
  - Energy consumption 203
  - Federally owned land 545
  - Governor, state officials 99, 102
  - Immigrants' intended residence 393
  - Indians, American 550
  - Interest laws, rates 721, 722
  - Marriage, divorce laws 728, 729
  - Motor vehicle statistics 211
  - Name origin, nickname 544, 665
  - Population 384-85, 388
    - Cities, towns 409-10, 687
    - Counties, county seats 434
  - Port traffic 208
  - Presidential elections 446, 458, 476
  - Public libraries 223
  - Schools 218, 219, 222
  - Taxes 211, 735, 736
  - Temperature, precipitation 181, 183
  - Unemployment benefits 146
  - Welfare assistance 395
- **Mathematics**
  - Formulas 607
  - Fractions, decimals 606
- **Matsu** 823
- **Mauritania** 482, 796-97, 847
- **Mauritius** 482, 797, 847
- **Mayans** 554, 559
- **Mayflower Compact** (1620) 497, 511
- **Mayors** 96-99
  - Address, form of 641
  - First black (1967) 506
- **Mayotte** 764
- **McKinley, Mt.** 540, 541, 590, 597
- **McKinley, William** 477, 479
  - Assassinated (1901) 272, 501, 534, 539
  - Biography 534
  - Burial site 539
  - Cabinet 104-7
  - Popular, electoral votes 478
- **McVeigh, Timothy** (1995) 33, 35, 54, 55-56, 64, *197*
- **Mean time** 293
- **Measures** 600-7
- **Meats**
  - Consumption 138
  - Exports, imports 207
  - Inspection Act (1906) 502
  - Nutritive values 609, 610
  - Prices, farm 143
  - Production 137, 138
- **Medal of Honor** 163
- **Media.** *See* Cable television; Magazines; Newspapers; Radio; Television
- **Medicare**
  - Enacted (1966) 505
  - Federal tax 731
  - Program summary 710
- **Medicine.** *See* Health and medicine
- **Mediterranean Sea**
  - Area, depth 593
  - Islands, areas 592
- **Melilla** 819
- **Memorial Day** 314
- **Memorials, national** 547, 684-85
- **Memphis, TN** 691
  - Buildings, tall 699
  - Mayor 97
  - Population 390, 422, 691
- **Men**
  - Employment 147, 149
  - Height, weight 612
  - Life expectancy 974
  - Living alone 382
  - Marital status 382
  - One-parent families 82
  - Population (1790-1994) 386, 387, 391
  - Poverty rates 394
  - Salaries and wages
    - Annual earnings average 149
    - Hourly rates 153
    - Weekly earnings median 155
- **Mennonite churches** 644, 645
- **Mercantilism** 563
- **Merchant Marine**
  - Academy 160
  - Fleets, by country 209-10
- **Mercury** (planet) 277-78, 290
  - Morning, evening stars 286
  - Position by month 274-77, 282-83
  - Sun, distance from 277, 290
- **Mergers**
  - Banking (1995) 67
  - Corporate, largest 123
  - Entertainment, media (1995) 62, 66, 70
  - Labor unions (1955) 504
  - Sherman Antitrust Act (1890) 501
  - Takeovers, defined 136
- **Mesa, AZ** 691
  - Mayor 97
  - Population 390, 397, 691
- **Metals**
  - Exports, imports 207
  - Production 132, 133, 134
  - Reserve base, world 132
- **Meteorology** 179-86
- **Methodist churches**
  - Addresses, U.S. headquarters 646
  - Beliefs, practices 652-53
  - Membership 644
- **Metric measures** 600-604
- **Metropolitan areas, U.S.**
  - Average annual salaries 152
  - Immigrants' intended residence 393
  - Population (1990-92) 382, 389
- **Mexican War** (1846-48) 500
  - Casualties, U.S. forces 166
  - Costs 163
- **Mexico** 797-98
  - Ambassadors, envoys 847
  - Cession to U.S. (1846) 500, 545
  - Chronology (1994-95) 45, 47, 50, 52, 57-58
  - Energy production 202
  - Flag 483
  - Gold production 134
  - History 552, 559, 563, 586
  - Maps 485, 486-87
  - Military strength 164
  - Motor vehicle production 212
  - Mountain peaks 590
  - Nuclear power 205
  - Paricutin volcano 555
  - Revolution (1910) 569-70
  - U.S. immigrants from 382, 393
  - Wages, hourly 152
- **Mexico, Gulf of** 593
- **Mexico City, Mex.** 838
- **Miami, FL** 691
  - Buildings, tall 699
  - Mayor 97
  - Population 390, 402, 691

Michigan 665-66
Admission, area, capital 542, 543, 665
Agriculture 137-42
Altitudes (high, low) 541
Birth, death statistics 962
Budget 116
Congressional representation 83, 86-87, 384
Courts, U.S. 94
Crime, prisons, death penalty 959
Energy consumption 203
Federally owned land 545
Governor, state officials 99, 102
Immigrants' intended residence 393
Indians, American 550
Interest laws, rates 721, 722
Marriage, divorce laws 728, 729
Mineral production 132
Motor vehicle statistics 211
Name origin, nickname 544, 665
Population 384-85, 388
Cities, towns 410-11, 688, 689
Counties, county seats 434
Port traffic 208
Presidential elections 446, 458-59, 476
Public libraries 223
Schools 218, 219, 222
Taxes 211, 735, 736
Temperature, precipitation 181, 183
Unemployment benefits 146
Welfare assistance 395
Michigan, Lake 598
Micronesia 483, 683, 798, 847
Middle East
History 557, 558, 570, 574
see also Arab-Israeli conflict; Persian Gulf War; *specific countries*
Midway, Battle of (1942) 503, 572
Midway Atoll 683
MIGA. *See* Multilateral Investment Guarantee Agency
Mileage
Air 216
Road 215
Sea lanes 209
Miles (measurement) 600, 601, 603
Military. *See* Armed forces, U.S.; *specific branches*
Military Academy, U.S. (West Point, NY) 160, 234
Military leaders, notable 348-50
Military parks, national 547
Military strength
By country 164
U.S. 163, 164
Military time (24-hour) 313
Military training centers 158-59
Milk
Nutritive value 609, 610
Prices, farm 143
Million Man March 33
Milwaukee, WI 691
Buildings, tall 699
Mayor 97
Population 390, 426, 691
Minerals (dietary) 609, 610-11, 612
Minerals (industrial) 132-34, 207
Minimum wage, U.S.
Enacted (1938) 503
Hourly rates (1950-91) 154
Increased (1989) 508
Increase proposal (1995) 48-49
Mining
Coal 201
Disasters, U.S. 267
Gold, silver 132, 133, 134
Occupational injuries 150
Minneapolis, MN 691
Buildings, tall 699
Mayor 97
Population 390, 411, 691
Minnesota 666
Admission, area, capital 542, 543, 666
Agriculture 137-42
Altitudes (high, low) 541
Birth, death statistics 962
Budget 116
Congressional representation 83, 87, 384
Courts, U.S. 94
Crime, prisons, death penalty 959
Energy consumption 203
Federally owned land 545
Governor, state officials 99, 102
Immigrants' intended residence 393
Indians, American 550
Interest laws, rates 721, 722
Marriage, divorce laws 728, 729
Mineral production 132
Motor vehicle statistics 211
Name origin, nickname 544, 666
Population 384-85, 388
Cities, towns 411-12, 691, 694
Counties, county seats 434-35
Port traffic 208
Presidential elections 446, 459-60, 476
Public libraries 223
Schools 218, 219, 222
Taxes 211, 735
Temperature, precipitation 181, 183
Unemployment benefits 146
Welfare assistance 395
Minoans 552
Minorca 819
Mint, Bureau of the 79, 82
Minuit, Peter (1626) 497
Miquelon Island 764
Miscellaneous facts 975
Miss America 335
Missiles, rockets. *See* Nuclear arms; Space developments
Mississippi 666-67
Admission, area, capital 542, 543, 666, 667
Agriculture 137-42
Altitudes (high, low) 541
Birth, death statistics 962
Budget 116
Coastline 541
Congressional representation 83, 87, 384
Courts, U.S. 94
Crime, prisons, death penalty 959
Energy consumption 203
Federally owned land 545
Governor, state officials 99, 102
Immigrants' intended residence 393
Indians, American 550
Interest laws, rates 721, 722
Marriage, divorce laws 728, 729
Motor vehicle statistics 211
Name origin, nickname 544, 666
Population 384-85, 388
Cities, towns 412, 690
Counties, county seats 435
Port traffic 208
Presidential elections 446, 460, 476
Public libraries 223
Schools 218, 219, 222
Taxes 211, 735
Temperature, precipitation 181, 183
Toxic chemical pollution 187
Unemployment benefits 146
Welfare assistance 395
Mississippi River 596, 597
Bridges spanning 703, 704
First railroad crossing (1855) 500
Commerce 208
Discovered (1541) 497, 586
Floods (1993) 268, 509
Missouri 667
Admission, area, capital 542, 543, 667
Agriculture 137-42
Altitudes (high, low) 541
Birth, death statistics 962
Budget 116
Congressional representation 83, 87, 384
Courts, U.S. 94
Crime, prisons, death penalty 959
Energy consumption 203
Federally owned land 545
Governor, state officials 99, 102
Immigrants' intended residence 393
Indians, American 550
Interest laws, rates 721, 722
Marriage, divorce laws 728, 729
Mineral production 132
Motor vehicle statistics 211
Name origin, nickname 544, 667
Population 384-85, 388
Cities, towns 412-13, 690, 693
Counties, county seats 435-36
Port traffic 208
Presidential elections 446, 460-61, 476
Public libraries 223
Schools 218, 219, 222
Taxes 211, 735, 736
Temperature, precipitation 181, 183
Unemployment benefits 146
U.S. center of population 385
Welfare assistance 395
Missouri Compromise (1820) 499
Missouri River 596, 597
Bridges spanning 703, 704, 705
Mitterrand, François 57, *779*
Mobile, AL 691
Mayor 97
Population 390, 396, 691
Mobility, geographic, U.S. (1960-93) 391-92
Modems 170
Mohammed. *See* Muhammad
Moldova 483, 798, 847
Moluccas 592
Monaco 381, 483, 798
Money. *See* Currency, U.S.; Exchange rates, foreign
Mongolia 483, 799, 847
Mongolia, Inner 753
Mongols 560
Monroe, James 479, 539
Biography 530-31
Burial site 539
Cabinet 104-6
Electoral votes 478
Monroe Doctrine (1823) 499
Montana 667-68
Admission, area, capital 542, 543, 667, 668
Agriculture 137-42
Altitudes (high, low) 541
Birth, death statistics 962
Budget 116
Congressional representation 83, 87, 384
Courts, U.S. 94
Crime, prisons, death penalty 959
Energy consumption 203
Federally owned land 545
Governor, state officials 99, 102
Immigrants' intended residence 393
Indians, American 550
Interest laws, rates 721, 722
Marriage, divorce laws 728, 729
Motor vehicle statistics 211
Name origin, nickname 544, 667
Population 384-85, 388
Cities, towns 413
Counties, county seats 436
Presidential elections 446, 461, 476
Public libraries 223
Schools 218, 219, 222
Taxes 211, 735
Temperature, precipitation 181, 183
Unemployment benefits 146
Welfare assistance 395
Montgomery, AL 691-92
Mayor 97
Population 391, 396, 691
Montserrat 830
Monuments, national 548-49, 684-85
Largest, smallest U.S. 540
Moon 291-92
Apogee, perigee 291
Apollo missions (1969) 315-16, 506
Chinese lunar calendar 312
Conjunctions 274-77, 282-83
Eclipses (1996) 289
First man on (1969) 315, 506
Full 297-308
Harvest, Hunter's 291
Occultations 274-77
Phases of 292
Position by month 274-77
Rises, sets (1996) 296-308
Tides, effects on 185, 291
Moravian churches 645
Mormons. *See* Latter-Day Saints, Church of
Morning stars (1996) 286
Morocco 164, 483, 799, 847
Mortgages
Farm 141
Households, U.S. 383
Income needed 727
Tables 726
Motion pictures. *See* Movies
Motorcycle racing (1995) 931
Motor vehicles
Accidents and deaths 963, 966
Production 210, 212
see also Automobiles
Motto, U.S. 525
Mountains 590-91
Highest, Canada 590
Highest, U.S. 540, 541, 590, 591
Volcanoes 588-89
Mt. Etna 589, 785
Mt. Everest 555, 590, 591, 597
Mt. McKinley 540, 541, 590, 597
Mt. Rushmore 547, 675-76
Mt. St. Helens (1980) 507, 588, 589
Mt. Vesuvius 588, 589
Mount Vernon (VA) 685
Mouth-to-mouth resuscitation 608
Movies
Awards 336-38, 339
Jazz Singer (1927) 503
Kinetoscope (1894) 501
National Film Registry 250
Notable (1994-95) 249, *780*
Political criticism of (1995) 56
Sound-on-film, first (1923) 502
Stars, directors 249, 366-80
Talking (1927) 503
Top 50 films (1994) 249
Top grossing, all-time 250
Top videos (1994) 250

Mozambique 483, 799-800, 847
MSA. *See* Metropolitan Areas, U.S.
Mubarak, Hosni 43, 49, 60, 69, *778*
Muhammad 557, 647, 654
Multilateral Investment Guarantee Agency 845
Municipal bonds 129, 136
Murders
Arrests, sentences 959, 960
Assassinations 272-73, 539, 576
Incidence 956, 957, 958
Workplace 150
Muscat and Oman. *See* Oman
Museums
Natural History (NYC) *199*
Washington, DC 684-85
Music and musicians
Awards
Grammy 339
Pulitzer Prize 332-33, *780*
Classical 360-61
Composers, works 360-62
Concerts, top-grossing (1985-94) 257
Country music artists 364
Dance companies 253
Jazz, blues artists 363-64
Lyricists 362
Musicians, singers 363-80, *780*, *781*
Opera, operetta 252-53, 360-62, 363
Recordings 257, 258-59, 339
Rock & Roll notables 339, 364-65, *780*, *781*
Symphony orchestras 252
Theater 361-62, *780*
Videos 257, 258
Muslims. *See* Islam
Mutual funds 129, 136
Myanmar (Burma) 63, 164, 483, 572, 800, 847

— N —

NAACP. *See* National Association for the Advancement of Colored People
NAFTA. *See* North American Free Trade Agreement
Nagasaki bombing (1945) 66, 504, 572
Names
Animal collective 638
Animal young 639
Days, foreign languages 640
Original, entertainers 380-81
Pen names 642
States, origin and nicknames . . 544, 655-80
Namibia 483, 800-801, 847
Napoleon Bonaparte (1798, 1803) 499, 564, 565
NASA. *See* National Aeronautics and Space Administration
NASCAR (auto racing) 930, 931
NASDAQ Stock Exchange 130
Nashville, TN 692
Buildings, tall 699
Mayor 97
Population 390, 422, 692
National Aeronautics and Space Administration 81
Employees, payroll 151
Expenditures 110
Internet address 169
National Anthem
Composed (1814) 499, 527
Text 528
National Archives 685
National Association for the Advancement of Colored People
Director named (1995) 49
Founding (1909) 502
Spingarn Medal 334
National Basketball Association . . 60, *783*
Addresses, teams 901
National debt 136
National Film Registry 250
National Football League *782*, 867-77
Addresses, teams 902
National Foundation on the Arts and Humanities 81
National Gallery of Art (DC) 685
National historic sites 547-48
National Hockey League 61, 887-94
Addresses, teams 901-2
Players' strike (1994-95) . . 47-48, 510, 887
National income, U.S. 114, 127
National Labor Relations Board 81
National League (baseball) . . . 936-45, 950
National monuments 548-49, 684-85
Largest, smallest 540
National park system, U.S. 546-49
Visitors, number (1994) 549
National recreation areas 545, 549
National Science Foundation 81, 167
National seashores 549
National Spelling Bee 637
Nations of the World 737-848
Ambassadors and envoys 846-48
Cities (largest) 838
Direct dialing codes 848
Embassies 737-837
Energy production, consumption . . 202, 204
Exchange rates 125
Flags 481-84
Investment in U.S. 126
Maps 485-96
Merchant fleets 209-10
Military strength 164
Motor vehicle production 212
Population projections (2010, 2020) . 838-39
Refugees 840
Rulers 577-85
Safety belt laws 214
Stock exchanges 125
Trade 206
UN members 843-44
Native Americans. *See* Indians, American
NATO. *See* North Atlantic Treaty Organization
Natural gas
Exports, imports 201, 207
Production, consumption 201
Reserves 204
Naturalization 841
Barriers removed (1952) 504
see also Aliens
Nauru 483, 801, 847
Nautilus (nuclear submarine) (1954) . . 504
Naval Academy, U.S. (Annapolis, MD) 160, 234
Naval disasters 264-65
Lusitania, sinking of (1915) 264, 502
Naval leaders, notable 348-50
Navassa Island 683
Navigation Act (1660) 497
Navy, Department of the
Employees, payroll 151
Secretaries 79, 105-6
Navy, U.S.
Academy 160, 234
Address for information 164
Admirals (active duty) 158
Expansion Act (1938) 503
Insignia 160
Leaders, notable past 348, 349
Personnel, active duty 161
Secretary 79
Training centers 159
Women, active duty 162
Nazis 504, 571, 572, 581, 766
NBA. *See* National Basketball Association
Nebraska 668
Admission, area, capital . . . 542, 543, 668
Agriculture 137-42
Altitudes (high, low) 541
Birth, death statistics 962
Budget 116
Congressional representation . . 83, 87, 384
Courts, U.S. 94
Crime, prisons, death penalty 959
Energy consumption 203
Federally owned land 545
Governor, state officials 99, 102
Immigrants' intended residence 393
Indians, American 550
Interest laws, rates 721, 722
Marriage, divorce laws 728, 729
Motor vehicle statistics 211
Name origin, nickname 544, 668
Population 384-85, 388
Cities, towns 413, 690, 692
Counties, county seats 436-37
Presidential elections . . 446, 461-62, 476
Public libraries 223
Schools 218, 219, 222
Taxes 211, 735, 736
Temperature, precipitation 181, 183
Unemployment benefits 146
Welfare assistance 395
Necrology (1994-95) 76-77
Neolithic Revolution 551
Nepal 482, 801, 847
Neptune (planet) 281, 290
Morning, evening stars 286
Position by month 274-77, 282-83
Sun, distance from 277, 290
Netherlands 801-2
Ambassadors, envoys 847
Flag 483
Gold reserves 128
History 561, 563
New World settlements (1624, 1626, 1664) 497
Merchant fleet 210
Motor vehicle production 212
Nuclear power 205
Rulers, royal family 381, 583
Wages, hourly 152
Netherlands Antilles 802
Nevada 668-69
Admission, area, capital 542, 543, 668, 669
Agriculture 137-42
Altitudes (high, low) 541
Birth, death statistics 962
Budget 116
Congressional representation . . 83, 87, 384
Courts, U.S. 94
Crime, prisons, death penalty 959
Energy consumption 203
Federally owned land 545
Governor, state officials 99, 102
Immigrants' intended residence 393
Indians, American 550
Interest laws, rates 721, 722
Marriage, divorce laws 728, 729
Mineral production 132
Motor vehicle statistics 211
Name origin, nickname 544, 668
Population 384-85, 388
Cities, towns 413, 690
Counties, county seats 437
Presidential elections 446, 462, 476
Public libraries 223
Schools 218, 219, 222
Taxes 211, 735
Temperature, precipitation 181, 183
Unemployment benefits 146
Welfare assistance 395
Nevis. *See* St. Kitts and Nevis
New Amsterdam (1626, 1664) 497
Newark, NJ 692
Buildings, tall 699
Mayor 97
Population 390, 414, 692
Riots (1967) 505
Newbery Medal 333-34
New Britain 592
New Caledonia 592, 764
New Deal (1933) 503
Newfoundland 592
New Guinea. *See* Papua New Guinea
New Hampshire 669
Admission, area, capital 542, 669
Agriculture 137-42
Altitudes (high, low) 541
Birth, death statistics 962
Budget 116
Coastline 541
Congressional representation . . 83, 87, 384
Courts, U.S. 94
Crime, prisons, death penalty 959
Energy consumption 203
Federally owned land 545
Governor, state officials 99, 102
Immigrants' intended residence 393
Indians, American 550
Interest laws, rates 721, 722
Marriage, divorce laws 728, 729
Motor vehicle statistics 211
Name origin, nickname 544, 669
Population 384-85, 388
Cities, towns 413
Counties, county seats 437
Presidential elections . . 446, 462-63, 476
Public libraries 223
Schools 218, 219, 222
Taxes 211, 735, 736
Temperatures, record 183
Unemployment benefits 146
Welfare assistance 395
New Ireland 592
New Jersey 669-70
Admission, area, capital . . 542, 669, 670
Agriculture 137-42
Altitudes (high, low) 541
Birth, death statistics 962
Budget 116
Coastline 541
Congressional representation . . 83, 87, 384
Courts, U.S. 94
Crime, prisons, death penalty 959
Energy consumption 203
Federally owned land 545
Governor, state officials 99, 102
Immigrants' intended residence 393
Indians, American 550
Interest laws, rates 721, 722
Marriage, divorce laws 728, 729
Motor vehicle statistics 211
Name origin, nickname 544, 669
Population 384-85, 388
Cities, towns 413-15, 690, 692
Counties, county seats 437
Port traffic 208
Presidential elections 446, 463, 476
Public libraries 223
Schools 218, 219, 222
Taxes 211, 735, 736

New Jersey *(continued)*
Temperature, precipitation 181, 183
Unemployment benefits 146
Welfare assistance 395
see also specific cities
New Mexico 670
Admission, area, capital ... 542, 543, 670
Agriculture 137-42
Altitudes (high, low) 541
Birth, death statistics 962
Budget........................ 116
Congressional representation . 83, 87, 384
Courts, U.S.................. 94
Crime, prisons, death penalty....... 959
Energy consumption 203
Federally owned land 545
Governor, state officials 99, 102
Immigrants' intended residence 393
Indians, American 550
Interest laws, rates 721, 722
Marriage, divorce laws 728, 729
Motor vehicle statistics 211
Name origin, nickname 544, 670
Population 384-85, 388
Cities, towns 415, 686
Counties, county seats 437
Presidential elections ... 446, 463-64, 476
Public libraries 223
Schools 218, 219, 222
Taxes 211, 735, 736
Temperature, precipitation 181, 183
Unemployment benefits 146
Welfare assistance 395
New Orleans, LA 692
Buildings, tall 699
Mayor 98
Population 390, 407, 692
Port traffic 208
Newport News, VA 98, 391, 692
Newspapers
Advertising expenditures.......... 263
Boston News Letter (1704) 497
Dailies
First U.S. (1784) 498
Top U.S., Canadian............ 256
Journalism awards............ 334
Pulitzer Prize winners 325-29
Muckrakers................ 568
Offbeat stories (1995)........... 975
Unabomber case (1995) ... 54, 59, 67-68
News photos (1995)..... *193-200, 777-84*
New Testament................ 649
New words in English 636
New World
Central, South America........... 563
Explorers 559, 561, 563, 586
Jamestown (VA) colony (1607)....... 497
Mayflower Compact (1620) 497, 511
New Netherland colony (1664) 497
New Year, Chinese 312
New Year, Jewish 648
New Year's Day................ 314
New York (state) 670-71
Admission, area, capital ... 542, 670, 671
Agriculture 137-42
Altitudes (high, low) 541
Birth, death statistics 962
Budget...................... 116
Coastline 541
Congressional representation....... 83, 87-88, 384
Courts, U.S................ 94-95
Crime, prisons, death penalty....... 959
Energy consumption 203
Federally owned land 545
Governor, state officials 99, 102
Immigrants' intended residence 393
Indians, American 550
Interest laws, rates 721, 722
Marriage, divorce laws 728, 729
Motor vehicle statistics 211
Name origin, nickname 544, 670
Population 384-85, 388
Cities, towns 415-17, 687, 692, 693, 695
Counties, county seats 437-38
Port traffic 208
Presidential elections 446, 464, 476
Public libraries 223
Schools 218, 219, 222
Taxes 211, 735, 736
Temperature, precipitation 181, 183
Unemployment benefits 146
Welfare assistance 395
New York City 692
Airport traffic 319
Bridges, tunnels 702, 703, 704
Buildings, tall 699-700
Ellis Island 529
Mayor 98
Mileage to foreign ports 209
Population 388, 390, 416, 692, 838
Port traffic 208
Statue of Liberty (1886) 501, 529
Theater openings (1994-95) ... 251, *780*
United Nations 843
World Trade Center bombing (1993, 1994, 1995) 49, 509, 510
New York Stock Exchange
Address 629
Volume, transactions 130
see also Stocks
New Zealand 568, 802-3
Ambassadors, envoys........... 847
Flag 483
Islands, areas 592
Mountain peaks 590
Wages, hourly 152
Niagara Falls.................. 599
Nicaragua 483, 803, 847
Nichols, James (1995) 33, 54, 56, 64
Nichols, Terry (1995) 35, 54, 55-56, 64, *197*
Nickel (metal).............. 132, 133
Nicknames
College football teams......... 882-84
U.S. states 655-80
Niger 483, 803, 847
Nigeria 803-4
Ambassadors, envoys........... 847
Flag 483
History 554, 560, 573
Trade 206
Nile River 596
Niue Island 803
Nixon, Richard M. 475, 477, 479, 480
Biography 536
Burial site 539
Cabinet..................... 104-8
China visit (1972) 506
Impeachment hearings (1974) 506-7, 536
Moscow summit (1972) 506
Popular, electoral votes.......... 478
Presidential library 539
Resignation (1974).......... 507, 574
Watergate (1973, 1974)....... 506, 507
Nobel Prizes 40, 323-25
Nobility, forms of address 641
Norfolk, VA 692
Mayor 98
Population 390, 425, 692
Port traffic 208
Norfolk Island 741
Normandy, House of 577
Normandy invasion (1944) 503
North America
AIDS cases.................. 840
Area 838
Bridges 702-5
Buildings, tall.............. 696-702
Cities 390-91, 594-95, 686-95
Time differences............ 314
Commercial fishing............ 145
Explorations 586
Gold production 134
Highest, lowest points........... 597
Lakes 598
Map 485
Mountain peaks 590, 591
Population.................. 838
Projections (2010, 2020) 838-39
Religious adherents 646
Rivers 596-97
Trade 206
Tunnels 705
Volcanoes 588, 589
Waterfalls................... 599
see also Canada; Mexico; United States
North American Free Trade Agreement (1993) 509
North Atlantic Treaty Organization 842-43
Bosnia crisis (1994-95) 43, 44-45,57, 62-63, 65, 68, 70-71
Established (1949) 504, 572
International commands 158
North Carolina 671
Admission, area, capital 542, 671
Agriculture 137-42
Altitudes (high, low) 541
Birth, death statistics............ 962
Budget...................... 116
Coastline 541
Congressional representation.. 83, 88, 384
Courts, U.S.................. 95
Crime, prisons, death penalty...... 959
Energy consumption 203
Federally owned land 545
Governor, state officials........ 99, 102
Immigrants' intended residence..... 393
Indians, American.............. 550
Interest laws, rates 721, 722
Marriage, divorce laws 728, 729
Motor vehicle statistics........... 211
Name origin, nickname 544, 671
Population 384-85, 388
Cities, towns 417, 687, 689, 693
Counties, county seats 438
Presidential elections... 446, 464-65, 476
Public libraries 223
Schools.............. 218, 219, 222
Taxes.............. 211, 735, 736
Temperature, precipitation 181, 183
Toxic chemical pollution.......... 187
Unemployment benefits 146
Welfare assistance 395
North Dakota 671-72
Admission, area, capital .. 542, 543, 672
Agriculture 137-42
Altitudes (high, low)............. 541
Birth, death statistics............ 962
Budget 116
Congressional representation . 83, 88, 384
Courts, U.S. 95
Crime, prisons, death penalty 959
Energy consumption 203
Federally owned land 545
Governor, state officials 99, 102
Immigrants' intended residence 393
Indians, American 550
Interest laws, rates 721, 722
Marriage, divorce laws 728, 729
Motor vehicle statistics 211
Name origin, nickname 544, 672
Population 384-85, 388
Cities, towns 417
Counties, county seats 438
Presidential elections 446, 465, 476
Public libraries 223
Schools 218, 219, 222
Taxes 211, 735, 736
Temperature, precipitation 181, 183
Unemployment benefits 146
Welfare assistance 395
Northern Cyprus, Turkish Republic of 757
Northern Ireland. *See* Ireland, Northern
Northern Lights 289, 555
Northern Mariana Islands .. 545, 682, 683
Area 445
Courts, U.S. 95
Immigrants' intended residence 393
Population 445
ZIP codes 445
North Island............... 592, 803
North Korea. *See* Korea, North (Democratic People's Republic of)
North Pole
Discovery (1909) 502
Explorations 587
Magnetic force 293-94
North Sea 593
Northwest Ordinance (1787) 498
Northwest Territory, U.S. (1787)... 498, 543
Norway 804
Ambassadors, envoys 847
Flag 483
Merchant fleet 210
Rulers, royal family 381, 582
Trade 206
Wages, hourly 152
Notable personalities 340-81
Obituaries (1994-95) 76-77
Sports.................... 924-26
Novelists, notable. *See* Writers, notable
NRC. *See* Nuclear Regulatory Commission
Nubia 554
Nuclear arms
A-bomb
Dropped (1945) .. 65-66, *200*, 504, 572
Experiments (1939) 503
French underground testing (1995) . 68-69
H-bomb (1950, 1952) 504, 573
Nautilus submarine (1954) 504
Treaties, negotiations (1963-93) ... 165, 505, 506, 508
Nuclear energy
Accidents, major 270
Chernobyl (1986) 270
Three Mile Island (1979) .. 270, 507, 574
First chain reaction (1942) 503
Power production 201, 204, 205
By U.S. states 655-80
Nuclear Regulatory Commission . 81, 151
Numbers, large 607
Numerals, roman 607
Nutrition 609-12
Federal program costs 139
Help organizations 618
Internet addresses 170
Labels 612
Nuts
Nutritive value 609, 611
Prices, farm 143
Production 142

— O —

Oakland, CA 692
Buildings, tall 700
Mayor 98
Population 390, 399, 692
OAS. See Organization of American States
Oat production 141, 142, 143
OAU. See Organization of African Unity
Obesity 974
Obituaries (1994-95) 76-77
Occupations
Educational attainment 149
Injuries, fatalities 150
By sex 147
Oceans and seas
Areas, depths 593
Commercial fishing 145
Crossings, notable 322
Islands 592
Marine warnings, advisories 179
Territorial extent, U.S. 545
Odds (cards, dice) 607
OECD. See Organization for Economic
Cooperation and Development
Offbeat news stories (1995) 975
Ofu Island 681
O'Grady, Scott F. (1995) 59, 777
Ohio 672-73
Admission, area, capital ... 542, 543, 672
Agriculture 137-42
Altitudes (high, low) 541
Births, death statistics 962
Budget..................... 116
Congressional representation . 83, 88, 384
Courts 95
Crime, prisons, death penalty...... 959
Energy consumption 203
Federally owned land 545
Governor, state officials 99, 102
Immigrants' intended residence 393
Indians, American 550
Interest laws, rates 721, 722
Marriage, divorce laws 728, 729
Motor vehicle statistics 211
Name origin, nickname 544, 672
Population 384-85, 388
Cities, towns 417-19, 686, 687, 688, 695
Counties, county seats 439
Port traffic 208
Presidential elections ... 446, 465-66, 476
Public libraries 223
Schools 218, 219, 222
Taxes 211, 735, 736
Temperature, precipitation 181, 183
Toxic chemical pollution 187
Unemployment benefits 146
Welfare assistance 395
Ohio River 596, 597
Ohm (electrical unit) 604
Oil. See Petroleum
Oil spills (1989) 270, 508
Okhotsk, Sea of 593
Okinawa Island 572, 592, 786
Oklahoma.................... 673
Admission, area, capital ... 542, 543, 673
Agriculture 137-42
Altitudes (high, low) 541
Birth, death statistics 962
Budget..................... 116
Congressional representation . 83, 88, 384
Courts 95
Crime, prisons, death penalty...... 959
Energy consumption 203
Federally owned land 545
Governor, state officials 99, 103
Immigrants' intended residence 393
Indians, American 550
Interest laws, rates 721, 722
Marriage, divorce laws 728, 729
Motor vehicle statistics 211
Name origin, nickname 544, 673
Population 384-85, 388
Cities, towns 419, 692, 695
Counties, county seats 439
Presidential elections . 446, 466-67, 476
Public libraries 223
Schools 218, 219, 222
Taxes 211, 735, 736
Temperatures, record 183
Unemployment benefits 146
Welfare assistance 395
Oklahoma City, OK 692
Bombing (1995)........ 33, 35-37, 54,
55-56, 64, 196-97
Buildings, tall 700
Mayor 98
Population 390, 419, 692
Old-age insurance. See Social Security
Administration
Old Ironsides (1797) 498

Old Testament 649
Olosega Island 681
Olympic games
History, symbolism 854, 865
Summer 854-65
Games sites 854
Medal standings (1992) 854
Winter 850-53
Games sites 849
Medal standings (1994) 853
see also under specific sports
Olympics, Special 955
Omaha, NE 692
Buildings, tall 700
Mayor 98
Population 390, 413, 692
Oman 57, 483, 805, 847
Omnibus Violent Crime Control
and Prevention Act (1994) 510
Online services, commercial (Internet) . 167
Ontario, Lake................. 598
OPEC. See Organization of Petroleum
Exporting Countries
Open Door Policy (1899) 501
Opera
Companies, U.S. 252-53
Composers 360-62
Singers................... 363
Opium War 565-66
Options (stock) 129
Orange Bowl................. 879
Orbits, planetary 290
Orchestras, symphony (U.S.) 252
Oregon 673-74
Accession 545
Admission, area, capital . 542, 543, 673
Agriculture 137-42
Altitudes (high, low) 541
Birth, death statistics 962
Budget..................... 116
Coastline 541
Congressional representation 83,
88, 384
Courts 95
Crime, prisons, death penalty..... 959
Energy consumption 203
Federally owned land 545
Governor, state officials 99, 103
Immigrants' intended residence ... 393
Indians, American 550
Interest laws, rates 721, 722
Marriage, divorce laws 728, 729
Motor vehicle statistics 211
Name origin, nickname 544, 673
Population 384-85, 388
Cities, towns 419-20, 693
Counties, county seats 439-40
Port traffic 208
Presidential elections 446, 467, 476
Public libraries 223
Schools 218, 219, 222
Taxes 211, 735, 736
Temperature, precipitation 181, 183
Unemployment benefits 146
Welfare assistance 395
Organization for Economic Cooperation
and Development ... 202, 206, 843
Organization for Security and Cooperation
in Europe 63, 843
Organization of African Unity 843
Organization of American States
(1948) 504, 572, 843
Organization of Petroleum Exporting
Countries......... 201, 202, 206, 843
Organizations. See Associations and
societies; International organizations
Orinoco River 596
Orkney Islands 592, 830
Orlando, FL 98, 402, 700
Orleans, House of 580
Orthodox churches. See Eastern Orthodox
churches
Oscars. See Academy Awards
OSCE. See Organization for Security and
Cooperation in Europe
Ottoman Empire 560, 566, 568
Outland Award 884
Outlying areas, U.S. 681-83
Population.................. 445

— P —

Pacific Islanders, U.S.,
Population 382, 386, 392
Pacific Ocean
Area, depth 593
Coast, U.S.
Length 541
Ports, cargo, volume 208, 209
Commercial fishing 145
Crossings, notable 322
Discovery 586

Islands
Areas..................... 592
U.S. 592, 681-83
Map 496
Pacing, trotting 898
Packwood, Robert (1995) 56, 64, 67
Paine, Thomas 511
Painters, notable 342-44
Pakistan 805-6
Ambassadors, envoys 847
Flag 483
History 572, 575
Map 492
Military strength 164
Nuclear power 205
Palau 483, 806, 847
Paleontology 553
Palestine
East Jerusalem land seizure (1995) ... 57
History 570, 572
Militancy, uprisings 575, 576, 776
Self-rule (1994-95) 43, 47, 49, 54-55,
62, 69, 71, 776, 778
Palestine Liberation Organization 787
Gaza, West Bank self-rule ... 43, 47, 49,
54-55, 62, 69, 776, 778
Palm Sunday 647
Palmyra (atoll) 683
Panama 806
Ambassadors, envoys 847
Distances to ports 209
Flag 483
Merchant fleet 210
Treaties, U.S. (1903, 1978). 501-2, 507, 806
U.S. invasion (1989) 508, 806
Panama Canal 806
Employees, federal 151
Opened (1914)............... 502
Treaties (1903, 1978) ... 501-2, 507, 806
Pantelleria Island 785
Paper
Exports, imports 207
Invention 556
Measures 604
Papua New Guinea .. 483, 592, 806-7, 847
Parachuting (1994 records) 321
Paraguay 483, 807, 847
Parcel post rates 631-35
Parenthood 722
see also Households
Paricutin volcano 555
Parks, national (1994) 510, 546-49
Parliament
British 829
Oldest (Iceland) 771
Parthenon 552
Parthians................... 556
Passport regulations, U.S.......... 723
Patents, U.S. 177
Patrick, Saint 558
Pay. See Salaries and wages
Peace Prizes, Nobel 40, 325
Peale Atoll................... 683
Peanut production 142, 143
Pearl Harbor (1941) 503
Peary, Robert E. (1909) 502, 587
Peloponnesian Wars............. 552
Pemba 824
Penghu (Pescadores) 823
Pen names.................. 642
Pennsylvania................. 674
Admission, area, capital 542, 674
Agriculture 137-42
Altitudes (high, low)........... 541
Birth, death statistics 962
Budget..................... 116
Coastline 541
Congressional representation 83,
88-89, 384
Courts, U.S................. 95
Crime, prisons, death penalty 959
Energy consumption 203
Federally owned land........... 545
Governor, state officials 99, 103
Immigrants' intended residence 393
Indians, American 550
Interest laws, rates 721, 722
Marriage, divorce laws 728, 729
Motor vehicle statistics........... 211
Name origin, nickname 544, 674
Population 384-85, 388
Cities, towns 420-21, 692, 693
Counties, county seats 440
Port traffic 208
Presidential elections .. 446, 467-68, 476
Public libraries 223
Schools 218, 219, 222
Taxes 211, 735, 736
Temperature, precipitation 181, 183
Unemployment benefits 146
Welfare assistance 395

Pensions
Taxes, federal 731
Veterans 163
see also Social Security Administration
Pentagon (Defense Department) 685
Pentagon Papers (1971) 506
Pentathlon 864
Pentecostal churches
Addresses, U.S. headquarters 646
Beliefs, practices 652-53
Membership 645
Per capita income. *See under* Incomes
Per capita public debt (U.S.) 112
Perigee of moon 291
Perihelion. *See* Aphelion, perihelion
Peron, Juan 573, 740
Perot, H. Ross (1992, 1995) 65, 67, 446-75, 475, 477, 478, 509
Perpetual calendar 310-11
Perry, Matthew C. (1853) 500
Perry, Oliver H. (1813) 499
Pershing, John J. (1916) 502
Persia. *See under* Iran
Persian Gulf
Area, depth 593
Map 492
Persian Gulf War (1991) 509, 776, 789, 814
Black troops 162
Casualties, U.S. forces 166
Kuwait invaded (1990) . . 509, 775, 789, 814
Veteran population 162
Personal consumption, U.S. 112, 113
Personal income, U.S. 114, 127
Personalities, notable. *See* Notable personalities
Peru 807-8
Ambassadors, envoys 847
Ancient civilizations 554
Commercial fishing 145
Flag 483
Pescadores (Penghu) 823
Petroleum
Arab embargo (1973) 506
Exports, imports 201, 202, 207
First well (PA) (1859) 500
Oil spills (1989) 270, 508
OPEC 201, 202, 206, 843
Production, consumption, U.S. 201
Reserves, crude oil 204
U.S. dependence on 201, 202
see also Gasoline
Pharos of Alexandria 555
Phases of moon 292
Philadelphia, PA 692-93
Buildings, tall 700
Capital of U.S. (1790) 498
Liberty Bell 528-29
Mayor 98
Population 388, 390, 421, 692
Port traffic 208
Philanthropists, notable 346-47
Philippines, Republic of the 808-9
Accession, U.S. (1898) 501, 808
Ambassadors, envoys 847
Flag 483
Gold production 134
Independence (1946) 504, 572, 808
Insurrection (1899) 501
Islands, areas 592
Map 493
Merchant fleet 210
Trade 206
U.S. immigrants from 393
World War II (1944) 503, 572, 808
Philosophers, notable 350, 552
Phoenicians 551, 552
Phoenix, AZ 693
Buildings, tall 700
Mayor 98
Population 390, 397, 693
Photographers, notable 329, 342-44
Photographs of the year (1995) . . *193-200, 777-84*
Photography
Inventions, notable 174, 175
Pulitzer Prizes 329
Physicians. *See* Doctors
Physics
Discoveries 176-77
Nobel Prizes 40, 323
Physiology, Nobel Prizes 40, 324
Pierce, Franklin 479
Biography 532
Burial site 539
Cabinet 104-7
Popular, electoral votes 478
Pig iron production 134
Pilots, airplane 320
Ping-Pong 864
Pinochle (odds) 607
Pisa, Leaning Tower of 555
Pistol champions (1995) 923
Pitcairn Island 831
Pittsburgh, PA 693
Buildings, tall 700
Mayor 98
Population 390, 421, 693
Port traffic 208
Pizarro, Francisco 563, 586
Planets 274-85, 290
Configurations 274-77, 282-83
Earth 290, 292-94
Morning, evening stars 286
Rising, setting 284-85
Sun relationship 277, 290
see also Space developments
Plantagenet, House of 577
Plants
Classification 192
Endangered species 188, 189
Platinum 132, 133
Playing cards (odds) 607
Plays. *See* Theater
Playwrights, notable 336, 356, 357-60
Pulitzer Prizes 330
Pledge of allegiance 527
PLO. *See* Palestine Liberation Organization
Pluto (planet) 281-82, 290
Position by month 275-77, 282-83
Sun, distance from 277, 290
Plymouth colony (1620) 497, 563
Poets, notable 357-60
Awards 324-25, 332, 333
Laureates 357
Poisons
Animals, venomous 190
Chemical pollution 187
Death rates 964, 965
Poker odds 607
Poland 809
Ambassadors, envoys 847
Flag 483
History 559, 563, 564, 565, 576
Merchant fleet 210
Military strength 164
Motor vehicle production 212
Rulers 482
Solidarity (1982) 507, 576, 809
World War II 571-72, 809
Polar explorations 586-88
Poles of the earth 293-94
Pole vault
Olympic champions 857
World records 865, 866
Police 957
Political convention sites 476
Political leaders, notable 351-53
Political parties
Independent 65, 67, 477
see also Democratic Party; Republican Party
Polk, James K. 479
Biography 531-32
Burial site 539
Cabinet 104-6
Popular, electoral votes 478
Pollution. *See* Environment
Polynesia, French 764
Ponce de Leon (1513) 497, 586
Pony Express (1860) 500
Poor Richard's Almanac (1732) 497
Popes 649, 650
see also John Paul II, Pope
Population, U.S. 382-445, 838
Age, median (1790-1994) 382, 387
Asian-Pacific Islander 382, 386, 392
Birth, death statistics 961, 962, 963
Black 382, 386, 387, 391, 392
Census (1790-1990) 384-85
Census Act (1790) 498
Census Bureau 80, 82, 383
Census Test (1995) 383
Center of (1790-1990) 385
Children 386, 391
Cities 390-91, 396-426, 686-95
Colonies (1630-1780) 383
Congressional apportionment 384
Counties 427-45
Largest 388
Density (by state) 388
Disabled people 392
Drug use 965
Educational level 219, 383
Elderly (over 65) 382, 386, 391
Ethnic, racial distribution 386, 387, 391, 392, 550
Farm 137
Gender distribution 386, 387, 391
Geographic mobility (1960-93) 391-92
Hispanic 382, 386
Immigration
By intended residence 393
Rates of 382
Indian, American 382, 386, 392, 550
Languages spoken 382
Marital status 391
Metropolitan areas (1990-92) 382, 389
More than 5,000 (by state) 396-426
Poverty statistics 382, 383, 394
Projections, by race (1995-2050) 392
By region 391
Religious groups 644-45
Residence type 382, 386
States 382, 388, 427-45, 655-80
Census (1790-1990) 384-85
Veterans 162
Youth (under age 18) 382, 391
Population, world
Cities
By country 737-837
By largest 838
Continents 838
Growth (AD 1-1995) 553
Growth rate (by country) 737-837
Projections (2010, 2020) 838-39
Religious adherents 646
Porcelain Tower of Nanking 555
Pork
Nutritive value 610
Prices, farm 143
Production, consumption 138
Portland, OR 693
Buildings, tall 700
Mayor 98
Population 390, 419, 693
Ports 208, 209
Portugal 809-10
Ambassadors, envoys 847
Flag 483
History 569, 570, 575
Wages, hourly 152
Possessions, U.S. 681-83
Courts, U.S. 95
Governors 99
Populations 445
ZIP codes 445
Postage stamps (first adhesive, 1847) 500
Postal cards
First U.S. (1873) 501
International rates 634
Postal information 631-35
Abbreviations
Canadian 633
State 633
Domestic rates 631-32
International rates 634-35
Parcel post rates 631-35
Priority Mail 631
ZIP codes 396-426, 445
Postal Service, U.S. 81, 631-35
Abbreviations 633
Employees, payroll 151
Established (1970) 506, 631
Rates 631-35
Potatoes
Nutritive value 611
Prices, farm 143
Production 141, 142
Poultry products
Egg production 138
Nutritive value 609, 610
Prices
Egg (per dozen, by state) 138
Farm 143
Pound (measure) 601, 602, 603
Poverty
Rate, level 383, 394
Welfare assistance 395
Powell, Colin (1989, 1995) 67, 165, 508
Power-boat racing 935
Preakness Stakes 895-96
Precipitation
International 184
U.S.
Cities 180, 182
States 181
Wettest spot 181
see also Blizzards
Presbyterian churches
Addresses, U.S. headquarters 646
Beliefs, practices 652-53
Membership 645
Presidential elections 446-78
Clinton elected (1992) 509
Returns 446-75, 475, 478
Electoral College . . 384, 476, 516-17, 520
Independent parties 477
National convention sites 476
1996 aspirants 49, 51, 54, 56, 58-59, 61, 65, 67, 70, *194*
Party nominees 477

Popular, electoral votes 446, 478
Primaries (1996) 41
Returns (by states, counties) 447-75
Voter participation 475
Presidents, U.S.
  Address, form of 641
  Ages 479
  Aides 78
  Appointment powers 517
  Assassinations 272, 500, 501, 505,
                   532, 533, 534, 536, 539
  Biographies 530-38
  Birth, death dates 479
  Burial sites 539
  Cabinets 78, 104-8
  Children, number of 538
  Clinton administration 78-81
  Congresses 479-80
  Constitutional powers 517
  Disability 517, 525
  Elections. See Presidential elections
  Inauguration date........... 521
  Internet address 169
  Libraries.................... 539
  Notable facts................ 539
  Oath of office 517, 525
  Party 477
  Salary 78
  Salutes, honors 159
  Succession law 522, 525
  Term beginning, limit 78, 521-22
  Vetoes 91
  Vice presidents 479-80
  Voter turnout................ 475
  White House.............. 78, 685
  Wives 538, 539
  see also specific presidents
Press. See Magazines; Newspapers
Pressure and force measures...... 607
Price Index
  Consumer 112, 113, 114
  Producer 136
Priest, form of address 641
Primaries, presidential (1996)....... 41
Prime interest rate............. 136
Prime Meridian............ 313, 484
Príncipe. See Sao Tomé and Príncipe
Printer's measures............. 604
Priority Mail................. 631
Prism, rectangular, volume....... 607
Prisoners of war, Geneva Conventions. 845
Prison population 959
Prizes. See Awards, prizes
Probability (cards, dice) 607
Prohibition (1917, 1933) 502, 503,
                                521, 570
Protein 609, 610-11
Protestant churches
  Beliefs, practices............ 652-53
  Books of the Bible 649
  Membership 644-45, 646, 651
  Reformation 562
  see also specific denominations
Protestant Episcopal Church.
  See Episcopal Church
Providence, RI 98, 701
Prussia. See Germany
Public debt 136
Public holidays 314
Public libraries, U.S.......... 223
Public schools. See Education
Puerto Rico 682-83
  Accession (1898).......... 501, 545
  Altitudes (high, low) 541
  Area 445, 545, 592
  Cities (population) 445
  Congressional delegate 90
  Courts, U.S. 95
  Government 682
  Governor 99
  Immigrants' intended residence ... 393
  Interest laws, rates 721, 722
  Marriage, divorce laws 728, 729
  Name origin 544
  Port traffic 208
  Unemployment benefits 146
  ZIP codes................... 445
Pulitzer Prizes. 325-33
Pure Food and Drug Act (1906)...... 502
Pyramid (volume formula) 607
Pyramids (Egypt)............... 555
Pyrenees 591

— Q —

Qatar 483, 810, 847
Quakers (Society of Friends) 644, 645
Queen Anne's War (1701-13) 497
Queens, NY 388, 438
Quemoy 592, 823
Quire (measure)................. 604
Quotes, notable (1995) 72

— R —

Rabin, Yitzhak 43, 49, 57, 69, 776, *778*
Race
  Distribution 382, 386, 387, 550
  Disabled people 392
  Projections (1995-2050) 392
  By state.................... 655-80
  see also Aleuts, U.S.; Asians, U.S.; Blacks;
   Hispanics; Indians, American; Pacific
   Islanders, U.S.
Racing
  Airplane 321
  Automobile 929-31
  Bicycle 863
  Bobsled 849
  Harness 898
  Motorcycle 931
  NASCAR 930, 931
  Power boat 935
  Rowing..................... 864
  Skiing................. 851-52, 918
  Sled dog 918
  Speed skating 852-53
  Swimming 859-62, 903
  Thoroughbred horse 895-98
  Track and field........ 855-59, 865-66
  Yacht *784*, 865
Radio
  Advertising expenditures 263
  Awards 334
  Broadcast, first (1920) 502
  Commercial stations 257
  Inventions, notable 174
  Notable personalities 366-80
  Transatlantic, first (1901) 568
  War of the Worlds scare (1938) ... 503
Railroads, U.S.
  Accidents, deaths 266-67
  Amtrak Arizona derailment (1995) .. 70
  First Mississippi R. crossing (1855) .. 500
  First passenger (1828) 499
  Growth (19th century) 566
  Transcontinental (1869) 501
Railroads, world
  Accidents, deaths 266-67
  Growth (19th century) 566
  Tokyo nerve-gas attacks (1995) 52, 57, *778*
  Tunnels, longest............ 706
Rainfall. See Precipitation
Raleigh, NC 693
  Buildings, tall 701
  Mayor 98
  Population........... 390, 417, 693
Ramayana.................... 554
Rape 956, 957, 958, 959, 960
Reader's Digest (1922) 502
Reagan, Ronald ... 475, 477, 479, 480, 539
  Biography................... 537
  Cabinet.................... 104-8
  Chronology (1994-95) 43
  Popular, electoral votes 478
  Presidential library 539
Ream (measure)................. 604
Recession 136
  see also Depression, economic
Recommended Daily Dietary
  Allowances 609, 612
Reconstruction Era (1866) 500
  Constitutional amendments 520-21
Recordings
  Awards 258-59, 339, *780*
  Political criticism (1995)........ 56
  Sales 257, 258
Recreation areas, national 545, 549
Rectangle, Area 607
Red Sea 593
Reformation, Protestant 562
Reformed churches 645, 646
Refrigerators 203
Refugees, world 840
Religion 644-54
  Addresses, U.S. headquarters ... 645-46
  Adherents (U.S., world) ... 644-45, 646
  Beliefs, practices............ 652-54
  Bible 649
  Christian denominations 652-53
  Holy days 647-48
  Major world 652-54
  Membership
   Canada.................... 651
   U.S. 644-45
  Religionists, notable 335, 350
  School prayer banned (1963) ... 505
  see also specific faiths, denominations
Renaissance 561
Reno, Janet (1993, 1994, 1995) ... 62, 78,
                              79, 509, 510
Rents
  Consumer price index 112, 113, 114
  Housing units. 383

Reporters. See Journalism awards
Republican Party
  Congressional elections (1994) 42,
                              193, 510
  Congressional members (1965-95) ... 91
  Contract With America (1995) .. 46, 48,49,
                             51-52, 53, 62
  Convention sites............. 476
  Democratic defectors (1995).... 51, 53,
                              59, 64
  Elections (by county)....... 447-75
  First presidential nominee (1856).... 500
  Formed (1854) 500
  Presidential aspirants (1996).. 49, 51, 54,
               56, 58-59, 61, 65, 67, 70, 194
  Presidential, vice presidential
   candidates................ 477
Reservoirs, major 707
Réunion Island............ 592, 764
Revenue sharing 110-11
Revere, Paul (1775)............. 498
Revolutionary War. See American Revolution
Rheumatic heart disease
Rhode Island 674-75
  Admission, area, capital ... 542, 674
  Agriculture 137-42
  Altitudes (high, low) 541
  Birth, death statistics 962
  Budget 116
  Coastline 541
  Congressional representation .. 83, 89, 384
  Courts, U.S. 95
  Crime, prisons, death penalty 959
  Energy consumption 203
  Federally owned land 545
  Governor, state officials ... 99, 103
  Immigrants' intended residence ... 393
  Indians, American 550
  Interest laws, rates 721, 722
  Marriage, divorce laws 728, 729
  Motor vehicle statistics 211
  Name origin, nickname ... 544, 674
  Population 384-85, 388
   Cities, towns 421
   Counties, county seats 440
  Presidential elections 446, 468, 476
  Public libraries 223
  Schools 218, 219, 222
  Taxes 211, 735, 736
  Temperature, precipitation ... 181, 183
  Unemployment benefits 146
  Welfare assistance 395
Rhodesia. See Zimbabwe
Rice production 142, 143, 144
Richmond, VA 693
  Buildings, tall 701
  Confederate capital 523
  Mayor 98
  Population 390, 425, 693
Richmond County, NY (Staten Island). 438
Ride, Sally (1983)........... 316, 507
Rifle champions (1995) 923
Rig Veda 552
Ring of Fire volcanoes 588
Rio de Janiero, Brazil 555, 838
Rio Grande 596, 597
Riots
  Coal miner's strike (1922) 502
  Detroit (1943, 1967) 503, 505-6
  Haymarket (1886) 501
  Los Angeles
   King case (1992) 509
   Watts (1965) 505
  Newark (NJ) (1967) 505
  New York City
   Draft (1863) 500
   Harlem (1943) 503
   Slave revolt (1712) 497
Ripken, Cal, Jr. (1995).... 69-70, *782*, 937
Rivers
  North American 596-97
  World 596
  see also specific rivers
Riverside, CA 693
  Mayor 98
  Population 388, 390, 399, 693
Roads
  Interstate system (1956) 505
  Mileage................... 215
Robberies 956-60
Rochester, NY 693
  Buildings, tall 701
  Mayor 98
  Population 390, 416, 693
Rock & Roll
  Concerts, top-grossing (1985-94) ... 257
  Garcia death (1995) 76, *781*
  Notable personalities. 339, 364-65, *780*, *781*
Rockets. See Nuclear arms; Space
   developments
Rodeo champions 935

Roe v. Wade (1973) 506, 524
Rogers, Will (1935) 503
Roman Catholicism
  Address, U.S. headquarters. 646
  Beliefs, practices. 652-53
  Books of the Bible 649
  Clergy, forms of address 641
  Hierarchy 649
  Pope John Paul II (1981, 1995) . . 53, 71,
           72, 273, 650, *779*, 833
  Popes (chronological list) 650
  Population, U.S., world . . 645, 646, 651
  UN women's conference (1995) 68
  Vatican City 832-33, 847
Romania 810-11
  Ambassadors, envoys 847
  Flag 483
  History 570, 576
  Merchant fleet. 210
  Military strength. 164
  Nuclear power. 205
Roman numerals. 607
Romans, ancient
  Historical figures 577
  Measures 605
  Rulers, emperors 556, 583
Rome
  Founding 556
  Seven Wonders, Middle Ages 555
Roosevelt, Franklin D. 475, 477,
          479, 480, 539
  Biography 535
  Burial site 539
  Cabinet 104-8
  New Deal (1933) 503
  Popular, electoral votes 478
  Presidential library. 539
  World War II (1939, 1941, 1945). . 503, 504
Roosevelt, Theodore . . 477, 479, 480, 539
  Biography. 534
  Burial site 539
  Cabinet 104-7
  Popular, electoral votes 478
Rose Bowl 879
Rose Island 681
Ross, Betsy 526
Ross Dependency 803
Rowing 864
Royalty 577-85
  Address, forms of 641
  European families 381
Ruby Ridge siege (1995) 35-37, 65
Rural Credits Act (1916). 502
Rushmore, Mt. *See* Mt. Rushmore
Russia 811-12
  Ambassadors, envoys 847
  Area, world's largest country 838
  Bosnian war position 60, 68
  Chechen revolt (1994-95) . . 45, 47, 50,
         52, 60, 63, *779*
  Commercial fishing 145
  Energy production, consumption. . . . 202
  Flag. 483
  Iranian nuclear pact (1995) 50, 60
  Islands, areas 592
  Map 491
  Merchant fleet. 210
  Military strength. 164
  Mineral resources 132, 133
  Nuclear power. 204, 205
  Russian Federation 812
  Space exploration (1995) 59, *198*
  see also Soviet Union
Russian Empire (pre-1917) 560
  Alaska (1741, 1867) 497, 501
  Congress of Vienna 565
  Crimean War (1853-56) 566
  Japanese War (1904-5) 568
  Orthodox Church 560
  Tsars 560, 585
  see also Russia; Soviet Union (*for later*
     history)
Russian Federation. *See* Russia
Russian Orthodox churches. *See* Eastern
     Orthodox churches
Russian Revolution (1917) 569
Russo-Japanese War (1904-5) 568
Rwanda 812
  Ambassadors, envoys 847
  Civil unrest (1995) 55
  Flag 483
Rye production 142

— S —

Saba Island 802
SAC. *See* Strategic Air Command
Sacco-Vanzetti case (1920) 502
Sacramento, CA 693
  Buildings, tall 701
  Mayor 98
  Population 390, 399, 693

Sadat, Anwar al- (1981) . . . 272, 576, 760
Saints. *See name, inverted*
St. Croix Island 445, 683
St. Eustatius Island 802
St. Helena Island 592, 831
St. Helens volcano (1980) . 507, 588, 589
St. John Island 445, 683
St. Kitts and Nevis 483, 812-13, 847
St. Lawrence River
  Discovered 586
  Length, outflow 596, 597
St. Lawrence Seaway (1959) 505
St. Louis, MO 693
  Buildings, tall 701
  Mayor. 98
  Population. 390, 412, 693
  Port traffic 208
St. Lucia 483, 813, 847
St. Maarten 802
St. Paul, MN 694
  Buildings, tall 701
  Mayor. 98
  Population. 390, 412, 694
St. Petersburg, FL 694
  Mayor 98
  Population. 390, 402, 694
St. Pierre and Miquelon 764
St. Thomas Island 445, 683
St. Valentine's Day Massacre (1929) . 503
St. Vincent and the Grenadines . . . 210,
         483, 813, 847
Salaries and wages
  Armed Forces scale 165
  Average
    By education, sex, race 149
    By metropolitan area 152
  College professors 222
  Earnings 149, 153, 154, 155
  Employer costs 154
  Governors, state officials 99-103
  Hourly rate distribution 153
  Hourly rates, by country 152
  Judges, U.S. 93, 95
  Minimum wage
    Enacted (1938) 503
    Hourly rates 154
    Increased (1989) 508
    Increase proposal (1995) 48-49
  Pay, average 153, 155
  Paycheck withholding tax (1943) . . . 503
  Pay differentials 149
  President, U.S. 78
  Representatives, U.S. 84
  Senators, U.S. 82
  Supreme Court justices 92
  Teachers 218, 222
  Vice president, U.S. 78
  see also Income taxes
SALT I and II. *See* Strategic Arms Limitation
     Treaty, I and II
Salt Lake City, UT 98, 701
Salutations, persons of rank 641
Salutes and honors 159
Salvation Army 645, 646
Samoa, American 681
  Accession 545
  Altitudes (high, low) 541
  Area 445, 545, 592
  Congressional delegate 90
  Population 445
  ZIP code 445
Samoa, Western 484, 592, 834, 848
San Antonio, TX 694
  Buildings, tall 701
  Mayor 98
  Population 390, 423, 694
Sand Atoll 683
Sand Creek Massacre (1864) 500
San Diego, CA 694
  Buildings, tall 701
  Mayor 98
  Population 388, 390, 399, 694
San Francisco, CA 694
  Airport traffic 319
  Buildings, tall 701
  Earthquakes (1906, 1989) . 271, 502, 508
  Mayor 98
  Mileage to foreign ports 209
  Population 390, 399, 694
San Jose, CA 694
  Mayor 98
  Population 390, 399, 694
San Marino 483, 813
Santa Ana, CA 694
  Mayor 98
  Population 390, 399, 694
Sao Tomé and Príncipe 483,
         813-14, 847
Sardinia 592, 785
Sark Island 592, 830
Satellites, space. *See* Space developments

Saturn (planet) 280-81, 290
  Morning, evening stars 286
  Position by month 274-77, 282-83
  Rises, sets 285
  Sun, distance from 277, 290
Saudi Arabia 814
  Ambassadors, envoys 847
  Energy production 202
  Flag 483
  History 570, 574
  Map 492
  Persian Gulf War (1991) 509, 814
  Trade 206
Savings and loan crisis 117
Savings bonds, U.S. 120
Scandinavia 559
  see also Denmark; Norway; Sweden
School prayer ban (1963) 505
Schools. *See* Education
Science and technology 174-78
  Awards 323-24, 335
  Chemical elements 177-78
  Inventions, discoveries 174-78
  Scientific Revolution (1500-1700) . . . 562
  Scientists, notable . . . 323-24, 353-55
  see also Computers; Internet
Scorpions, poisonous 190
Scotland 578, 829-30
  see also United Kingdom
Sculptors, notable 342-44
Sea creatures, venomous 190
Seas. *See* Oceans and seas
Seashores, national 549
Seasons 282-83, 293
SEATO. *See* Southeast Asia Treaty
     Organization
Seattle, WA 694
  Buildings, tall 701
  Mayor 98
  Population 390, 425, 694
Secret Service, U.S. 79, 82
Securities and Exchange Commission 81, 151
Seeds, Nutritive value 611
Segregation. *See* Desegregation
Selective Service System. *See* Draft, U.S.
Self-employment
  Social Security benefits 709
  Taxes, federal 730, 731
Seminole War (1835) 499
Senate. *See* Congress, U.S.
Senegal 483, 814-15, 847
Sentences, prison 959
Serbia, Chronology (1994-95) . . 43, 44-45,
         46-47, 50, 52, 57, 59-60,
         62-63, 65, 68, 70-71, *777*
Seventh-Day Adventists 644
Seven Wonders of the World 555
Sexual harassment
  Clinton accuser (1994) 44
  Packwood case (1995) 56, 64, 67
  Reynolds conviction (1995) 64
  Thomas accuser (1991) 509
Seychelles 483, 815, 847
Shakespeare, William 359, 561
  Folger Library 684
Shaliskashvili, John 79
Shang Dynasty 552, 585
Shay's Rebellion (1787) 498
Sheep 137, 138, 143
Shepard, Alan B., Jr. (1961) . . 315, 505
Sherman Antitrust Act (1890) 501
Shetland Islands 592, 830
Shevardnadze, Eduard (1995) 66
Shi'ites. *See* Islam
Shintoism 558, 646
Shipping
  Distances between ports 209
  Merchant fleets 209-10
  Tonnage at ports 208, 209-10
Ships
  Disasters (1915, 1989) . . 264-65, 502, 508
  Frigates, famous U.S. (1797) 498
  Great White Fleet (1907) 502
  Steamboats
    First Atlantic crossing (1819) 499
    Fulton's (1807) 499
    Inventors 175
  see also Submarines
Shipwrecks 264-65
Shoko Asahara (1995) 52, 57, *778*
Shooting (sport)
  Olympic champions (1992) 864
  Rifle, pistol champions (1995) 923
Shot put
  Olympic champions 857, 859
  World records. 865, 866
Shreveport, LA 694
  Mayor 98
  Population 390, 408, 694
Siam. *See* Thailand
Sicily 592, 785

Sidereal day, year, time 286, 293
Sierra Leone 483, 815-16, 847
Sign language 643
Signs and symbols
Astronomical 282
Chemical elements 177-78
Zodiac 291
Sikhism 561, 565, 646
Sikkim 772
Silver
Production 132, 133, 134
Reserve base, world 132
Value in coins 120
Simpson, O. J. (1994-95) 33-35,45, 48, 50-51, 53, 55, 58, 60-61, 63, 66, 69, 71, *195*, 510
Singapore 816
Ambassadors, envoys 847
Distances to ports 209
Flag 483
Merchant fleet 210
Trade 206
Wages, hourly 152
Singers, notable 363-80
Single-parent households 382, 394
Sioux Indian War (1876) 501
Skating
Figure
Olympic champions (1908-94) 850
U.S., world champions 900
Speed, Olympic champions (1924-94) 852-53
Skiing
Olympic champions (1924-94) 851-52
World Cup Alpine Champions 918
Skye, Isle of 830
Skylab 316
Slavery
Abolished, 13th Amendment (1865) 500, 520
Abolitionist raids (1856, 1859) 500
Dred Scott decision (1857) 500, 523
Emancipation Proclamation (1863) 500
Importation outlawed (1808) 499
Introduced into America (1619) 497
Kansas-Nebraska Act (1854) 500
Missouri Compromise (1820) 499
Rebellions (1712, 1831) 497, 499
Slovakia 205, 483, 816, 847
Slovenia 205, 483, 816-17, 847
Small Business Administration 81, 151
Smith, Adam 348, 564
Smith, John (1607) 497
Smith, Susan (1994, 1995) 43, 63-64, *195*, 510
Smithsonian Institution 82, 108, 151, 685
Smoking
Benefits of quitting 613
Heart disease 616
High school students 965
Regulations, underage users (1995) 64-65
Smythe Trophy 894
Snakes, poisonous 190
Snowfall
Blizzards 268
Cities, U.S. 182
Mean annual 181
Soccer
Olympic champions (1992) 864
World Cup 935
Social reformers, notable 355-56
Social scientists, notable 347-48
Social Security Administration 81, 708-12
Act passed (1935) 503
Internet address 169
Medicare (1966) 505, 710
Tax revenues 110
Societies. *See* Associations and societies
Sodium (dietary)
Labels, nutrition 612
Nutritive value 610-11
Software, computer 171
Solar day 293
Solar system 274-94
Solidarity (Poland) (1982) 507, 576, 809
Solomon Islands 483, 817, 847
Solstices (1996) 275, 277, 283, 293
Somalia 817
Flag 483
Map 494-95
Peacekeeping troop withdrawal (1994, 1995) 42, 52
Somerset Island 592
Sorghum production 142, 143
Soto, Hernando de. *See* De Soto, Hernando
Sound
Measurements 604
Speed of 606
South Africa 817-18
Ambassadors, envoys 847
Apartheid 576, 818
Boer War (1899-1902) 567, 818
Distances to ports 209
Flag 483
Gold production 134
Mandela election 818
Map 495
Nuclear power 204, 205
Self-government (1910) 568
U.S. sanctions (1986) 508
South America
AIDS cases 840
Area 838
Commercial fishing 145
Explorations 586
Gold production 134
Highest, lowest points 597
Lakes 598
Languages 642-43
Largest country 746-47
Liberation wars, leaders 573, 584
Map 488-89
Mountain peaks 590
Population 838
Projections (2010, 2020) 838-39
Religious adherents 646
Trade 206
Volcanoes 589
Waterfalls 599
see also specific countries
South Carolina 675
Admission, area, capital 542, 675
Agriculture 137-42
Altitudes (high, low) 541
Birth, death statistics 962
Budget 116
Coastline 541
Congressional representation 83, 89, 384
Courts, U.S. 95
Crime, prisons, death penalty 959
Energy consumption 203
Federally owned land 545
Governor, state officials 99, 103
Immigrants' intended residence 393
Indians, American 550
Interest laws, rates 721, 722
Marriage, divorce laws 728, 729
Motor vehicle statistics 211
Name origin, nickname 544, 675
Population 384-85, 388
Cities, towns 421-22
Counties, county seats 440
Presidential elections 446, 468-69, 476
Public libraries 223
Schools 218, 219, 222
Taxes 211, 735, 736
Temperature, precipitation 181, 183
Unemployment benefits 146
Welfare assistance 395
South China Sea 593
South Dakota 675-76
Admission, area, capital 542, 543, 675
Agriculture 137-42
Altitudes (high, low) 541
Birth, death statistics 962
Budget 116
Congressional representation 83, 89, 384
Courts, U.S. 95
Crime, prisons, death penalty 959
Energy consumption 203
Federally owned land 545
Governor, state officials 99, 103
Immigrants' intended residence 393
Indians, American 550
Interest laws, rates 721, 722
Marriage, divorce laws 728, 729
Motor vehicle statistics 211
Name origin, nickname 544, 675
Population 384-85, 388
Cities, towns 422
Counties, county seats 440-41
Presidential elections 446, 469, 476
Public libraries 223
Schools 218, 219, 222
Taxes 211, 735
Temperature, precipitation 181, 183
Unemployment benefits 146
Welfare assistance 395
Southeast Asia
Map 493
see also Vietnam War; *specific countries*
Southeast Asia Treaty Organization (1954) 504, 572
South Island 592, 803
South Korea. *See* Korea, South (Republic of)
South Pole
Exploration 587-88
Magnetic force 293-94
South Yemen. *See* Yemen
Soviet Union 811-12
Berlin blockade (1948) 504
Chernobyl disaster (1986) 270
Cold War 572, 575-76
Cuban missle crisis (1962) 505
Eastern Bloc revolt (1989) 575-76
Glasnost 575-76, 812
Gold production 134
History 569, 570, 571
Hungarian revolt (1956) 573
Leaders 585
Nixon visit (1972) 506
Perestroika 575-76, 812
Space exploration 315-18, 573
Summit talks (1972, 1985, 1987) 506, 508
World War I 569
World War II 571-72
Yalta (1945) 504
see also Arms control; Russia; Russian Empire; *other former republics*
Soybean production 141, 142, 143
Space developments 315-18
Apollo missions (1969) 315-16, 506
Astronauts *198*, 315-17, 318
Cosmonauts 59, *198*, 315-17, 318
Explorer 1 (1958) 505
First men in space (1961) 315, 505
First women in space (1983) 315, 316, 507
Hall of Fame 320-21
Hubble telescope (1993) *198*, 317, 509
Mars *Viking* landings (1976) 279, 318, 507
Missions, proposed 319
Moonwalk, U.S. (1969) 315, 506
Outer Space Treaty (1967) 165
Payloads, worldwide 318
Planetary missions 318
Skylab 316
Space shuttles
Challenger (1983, 1984, 1986) 316, 317, 507, 508
Columbia (1981, 1982) 316, 317, 507
Discovery 316, 317
Endeavour (1993) 317, 509
Missions 316-17
Sputnik satellite 573
U.S.-Russian linkup (1995) 59, *198*
Spain 818-19
Ambassadors, envoys 847
Flag 483
History 558, 559, 561, 571, 575
Merchant fleet 210
Military strength 164
Motor vehicle production 212
Nuclear power 204, 205
Rulers, royal family 381, 584
Wages, hourly 152
Spanish-American War (1898) 501, 567
Casualties, U.S. forces 166
Costs 163
Spanish Civil War (1936-39) 571
Spanish Sahara 575
Spectrum, colors of 606
Speech, freedom of 519
Speed
Of animals 189
Of light 287
Of sound 606
Speedboat racing 935
Speed skating. *See under* Skating
Spelling
Commonly misspelled words 641
Spelling Bee, National 637
Sphere (formulas) 607
Spiders, poisonous 190
Spingarn Medal 334
Spirits. *See* Liquor
Spokane, WA 98, 391, 694
Sports
Directory 901-2
Dramatic events (1994-95) 849
Highlights (1995) *782-84*
Personalities, notable 924-926
see also specific sports
Spring (season) 293
Sputnik (1957) 573
Square, Area 607
Sri Lanka (Ceylon) 819
Ambassadors, envoys 847
Area 592
Flag 483
Trade 206
Wages, hourly 152
Stadiums, arenas
Baseball 951
Basketball 911
Football 877
Stalin, Joseph V. 572, 573, 811
Stamp Act (1765) 497
Stamps. *See* Postage stamps
Standard time 313, 314
Stanley Cup 61, 887
Stars
Constellations 287-88
Creation of *198*
Morning, evening 286
Tables 286-87

"Star-Spangled Banner" (1814) 499, 528
START I and II. *See* Strategic Arms Reduction Treaty, I and II
State, Department of 78
  Employees, payroll 151
  Expenditures 110
  Internet address 169
  Secretaries 78, 104
States, U.S. 655-80
  Abbreviations, postal 633
  Abortions 963-4
  Admission of new (law) 518
  Admitted to Union 542, 543, 655-80
  Agriculture 137-42
  Altitudes (high, low) 541
  Area, rank 540, 542
  Area codes, telephone 396-426
  Automobile data 211
  Births, deaths 961, 962, 963
  Bridges 702-5
  Budget 116, 117
  Capitals 542
  Census 384-85, 387-445, 388
  Census Test (1995) 383
  Chambers of Commerce 655-80
  Climate 181, 183-84
  Coastline, in miles 541
  Congressional representation 82-90
  Construction, value of 655-80
  Contiguous 48 540
  Counties, county seats 388, 427-45
  Courts, U.S. 93-95
  Crime, prisons, death penalty 956-60
  Critical illness, laws regarding 615
  Death penalty 959
  Deaths, births 961, 962, 963
  Education 218, 219, 222
  Electoral votes 446, 476
  Energy consumption 203
  Famous natives 655-80
  Federally owned land 545
  Finances 116
  Forested land 655-80
  Geographic centers 543
  Governors, state officials 99-103
  Immigrants' intended residence 393
  Income, per capita 655-80
  Indians, American
    Population 550
    Reservations, trust lands 550
  Inland water area 542
  Legislatures 100-103
  Marriage, divorce laws 728, 729
  Mineral production 132
  Motor vehicle registration 211
  Mountain peaks 590, 591
  Names, origin of 544
  Nicknames 655-80
  Original 13 383, 542
  Population, by states 382, 384-85, 388, 655-80
    Cities, more than 5,000 396-426
    Ethnic, racial distribution 550, 655-80
  Precipitation 181
  Presidential elections 446-75, 477
  Public lands
    Parks 546-49
    Recreation areas 545, 549
  Public libraries 223
  Revenues, expenditures 117
  Rivers 596-97
  Secession 523
  Settlement dates 542
  Taxes 211, 735-36
  Temperatures 181, 183-84
  Tourist attractions 655-80
  Toxic chemical pollution 187
  Unemployment benefits 146
  Union entry dates 542, 543
  Volcanoes 589
  Welfare assistance 395
  ZIP codes 396-426
Statesmen and stateswomen, notable 325, 351-53
Statistical Abstract of the United States 540
Statue of Liberty 529
  Dedicated (1886) 501
  Ellis Island 529
Steamships (1807, 1819) 175, 499
Steel
  Exports, imports 207
  Inventions 175
  Production 134
  Strikes (1892, 1952) 501, 504
  Union merger (1995) 62
Steeplechase (track and field)
  Olympic champions 855
  World record 865
Stewart Island 592, 803
Stocks 129-31
  Dow Jones Average 130
  Exchanges, global 125
  Exchanges, U.S. 129, 130, 629
  Foreign, U.S. holdings 131
  Glossary of terms 135-36
  Market crash (1929) 503, 570-71
  Market crash (1987) 508
  Most active (1994) 130
  Mutual funds 129, 136
Stockton, CA 98, 390, 695
Stonehenge 555
Storms
  Notable 268
  Watches, warnings, advisories 179
Strategic Air Command 158
Strategic Arms Limitation Treaty, I and II (1972, 1979) 165
Strategic Arms Reduction Treaty, I and II (1991, 1993) 165
Stratosphere 292
Strikes
  Air traffic controllers (1981) 507
  Baseball players (1994-95) 50, 53, 55, 510
  Coal miners (1922, 1946) 502, 504
  National Hockey League (1994-95) 47-48, 510, 887
  Number, days idle (1960-94) 155
  Steel mill seizure (1952) 504
  Steel workers (1892) 501
  Women weavers (1824) 499
Strokes
  Deaths 963, 972
  Diabetes 615
  Help organizations 618
  Warning signs 616
Students. *See* Colleges and universities; Education; High schools
Submarines
  Inventions 175
  Nautilus (1954) 504
  Sinkings 264
  Warfare (1917) 502, 569
Subway accidents 266-267
  Tokyo nerve-gas attack (1995) 52, 57, *778*
Succession, presidential 522, 525
Sudan 483, 820, 847
Suez Canal 573, 760
Suffrage, woman (amendment, 1920) 502, 521
Sugar
  Exports, imports 207
  Labels, nutrition 612
  Nutritive value 611
  Production 142
Sugar Bowl 879
Suicides
  By firearms 967
  Number 964
Sullivan Trophy 900
Sumatra 592
Sumeria 551
Summer (season) 293
Summer Olympics. *See under* Olympic games
Summer Solstice 275, 283, 293
Sun 290-91
  Eclipses 289, 295-96
  Planets' distance from 277, 290
  Rises, sets (1996) 296-308
  Twilight 294-95
  Ultraviolet index 186
Sung Dynasty 559, 585
Sunspots 290-91
Super Bowl 48, *782*, 870, 877
Superior, Lake 598
Superlative statistics, U.S. 540
Supplemental Security Income (SSI) 711
Supply-side economics 136
Supreme Court, U.S.
  Abortion legalization (1973) 506, 524
  Address, form of 641
  Appointments, salaries 92
  Created (1789) 498
  Decisions, notable 40, 523-24
    Dred Scott (1857) 500, 523
    Marbury v. *Madison* (1803) 499, 523
    Plessy v. *Ferguson* (1896) 501, 523
  Employees, payroll 151
  First black justice (1967) 506
  First woman justice (1981) 507
  Internet address 170
  Judicial powers (law) 517
  Justices 92
  Schools
    Desegregation (1954, 1955, 1956, 1995) 40, 504, 505, 524
    Prayer ban (1963) 505
Surgeon General, U.S. 44, 80, 82
  Foster nomination (1995) 48, 56, 59
Suriname 483, 820, 847
Surveyor's chain measure 601
Survivor insurance 709, 711
Svalbard Islands 804
Swahili 560
Swains Island 681
Swaziland 483, 820-21, 847
Sweden 821
  Ambassadors, envoys 847
  Flag 483
  History 559, 563, 575
  Merchant fleet 210
  Motor vehicle production 212
  Nuclear power 204, 205
  Rulers, royal family 381, 582
  Trade 206
  Unemployment rates 147
  Wages, hourly 152
Sweet-potato production 142
Swimming
  Olympic champions 859-62
  Synchronized 864
  World records 903
Switzerland 821-22
  Alps 590-91
  Ambassadors, envoys 847
  Flag 483
  Gold reserves 128
  Nuclear power 204, 205
  Wages, hourly 152
Symbols. *See* Signs and symbols
Symphony orchestras, U.S. 252
Syria 164, 483, 822, 847

— T —

Table tennis 864
Tacoma, WA 98, 391, 695
Taft, William H. 477, 479, 539
  Biography 534
  Burial site 539
  Cabinet 104-7
  Popular, electoral votes 478
Taft-Hartley Act (1947) 504
Tahiti 69, 592, 764
Taiwan 822-23, 846
  Area 592
  Flag 483
  Map 493
  Merchant fleet 210
  Military strength 164
  Motor vehicle production 212
  Nuclear power 204, 205
  Trade 206
  Wages, hourly 152
Tajikistan 484, 491, 823, 847
Taj Mahal 561
Tall buildings 696-702
Talmud 557
Tampa, FL 695
  Buildings, tall 701
  Mayor 98
  Population 390, 403, 695
  Port traffic 208
Tanganyika 824
Tang Dynasty 559, 585
Tantalum 132, 133
Tanzania 484, 823-24, 847
Taoism 554, 556
Tariff of Abominations (1828) 499
Tariffs. *See* Customs, U.S.
Ta'u Island 681
Taxes, federal 730-35
  Audits 735
  Capital gains 730, 731
  Corporate 125
  Court, U.S. 95
  Credits 730, 733
  Deductions 730-33
  Estimated 730
  Expenditures 110-11
  Filing, forms 734-35
  Income tax 730-35
    Amendment authorizing 521
  Pensions, annuities 731
  Receipts 110-11
  Recent changes, developments 730-31
  Social Security 708-12, 730, 731, 733
  Tax cut proposals (1994-95) 44, 49, 53
  Taxpayers' rights 735
Taxes, state
  Gasoline 211
  Income (by states) 735-36
  Per capita 116
Taylor, Zachary 479, 539
  Biography 532
  Burial site 539
  Cabinet 104-7
  Popular, electoral votes 478
Teachers
  Awards 335
  College, university 222, 224-48
  Pay, average 218, 222
  Public schools 217, 218

Technology. *See* Science and technology
Telegraph
Atlantic cable (1858) 500
First message (1844) 500
Inventions 175, 566
Transcontinental (1861) 500
Telephone
Area codes 396-426
AT&T breakup (1982) 507
First exchange (1878) 501
First transcontinental talk (1915) 502
International direct dial codes 848
Inventions 175
Transatlantic cable (1956) 505
Television *781*
Actors, actresses 366-80
Advertising expenditures 263
Awards 334, 335-36, 339
Company mergers (1995) 62, 66
Internet addresses 170
Inventions 175
Network addresses, phone numbers . . . 260
Programs, favorite 261-62
Sets, number of 259
Time spent viewing 260
Transcontinental, first (1951) 504
Viewing shares 261
see also Cable television
Temperature (weather)
Celsius-Fahrenheit conversion 605
Heat index 186
Heat wave deaths (1995) 61
Highest, lowest recorded 181
International 184
U.S. normal, highs, lows 180-84
Ten Commandments 649
Tennessee 676
Admission, area, capital . . . 542, 543, 676
Agriculture 137-42
Altitudes (high, low) 541
Birth, death statistics 962
Budget 116
Congressional representation 83, 89, 384
Courts, U.S. 95
Crime, prisons, death penalty 959
Energy consumption 203
Federally owned land 545
Governor, state officials 99, 103
Immigrants' intended residence 393
Indians, American 550
Interest laws, rates 721, 722
Marriage, divorce laws 728, 729
Motor vehicle statistics 211
Name origin, nickname 544, 676
Population 384-85, 388
Cities, towns 422, 691, 692
Counties, county seats 441
Port traffic 208
Presidential elections . . . 446, 469-70, 476
Public libraries 223
Schools 218, 219, 222
Taxes 211, 735, 736
Temperature, precipitation 181, 184
Toxic chemical pollution 187
Unemployment benefits 146
Welfare assistance 395
Tennessee Valley Authority 81, 151
Tennis 63, *784*, 927-29
Olympic champions (1992) 864
Territorial sea, U.S. 545
Territories, U.S.
Accession of 545
Altitudes (high, low) 541
Areas 445
Courts, U.S. 95
External 445, 681-83
Populations 445
Statehood 543
ZIP codes 445
Terrorism
International (1980-89) 36, 576
Lebanon (1983) 507, 791
Oklahoma City bombing (1995) . . 33, 35-37, 54, 55-56, 64, *196-97*
Unabomber (1994-95) 36, 45, 54, 59, 67-68
UN bombing plot trial (1995) 49, 70
World Trade Center bombing (1993, 1994, 1995) 35-37, 49, 509, 510
see also Assassinations
Texas 676-77
Accession 545, 677
Admission, area, capital . . . 542, 676, 677
Agriculture 137-42
Altitudes (high, low) 541
Birth, death statistics 962
Budget 116
Coastline 541
Congressional representation . 83, 89, 384
Courts, U.S. 95
Crime, prisons, death penalty 959
Energy consumption 203
Federally owned land 545
Governor, state officials 99, 103
Immigrants' intended residence 393
Indians, American 550
Interest laws, rates 721, 722
Marriage, divorce laws 728, 729
Mineral production 132
Motor vehicle statistics 211
Name origin, nickname 544, 676
Population 384-85, 388
Cities, towns 422-24, 686, 688, 689, 691, 694
Counties, county seats 441-43
Port traffic 208
Presidential elections . . 446, 470-71, 476
Public libraries 223
Schools 218, 219, 222
Taxes 211, 735
Temperature, precipitation 181, 184
Toxic chemical pollution 187
Unemployment benefits 146
Welfare assistance 395
Thailand (Siam) 824
Ambassadors, envoys 847
Commercial fishing 145
Flag 484
Military strength 164
Trade 206
World War II 572
Thames River 596
Thanksgiving Day 314
Theater 251
Actors, actresses 366-80
Awards 336, *780*
Composers 361-62
Dance companies 253
First in colonies (1716) 497
Long runs 251
Nonprofit professional 251
Notable openings (1994-95) . . . 251, *780*
Playwrights 336, 356, 357-60
Pulitzer Prizes 330
Theft 956, 957, 958, 959, 960
Third parties. *See* Independent political parties
Third Reich. *See under* Germany
Thirteen colonies 383, 542
Thirty Years War (1618-48) 562
Thorpe Trophy 874
Thunderstorm characteristics 179
Tibet 753
Ticonderoga, Ft. (1777) 498
Tidal waves 268
Tides 185, 291
Tierra del Fuego 592, 752
Tilden, Samuel J. (1876) 501
Timbuktu 560, 796
Time
Cities
North American 314
World 313
Computation 293
Daylight Saving 313
Differences, cities 313, 314
Earth's rotation 294
Greenwich 286, 313
International Date Line 313, 484
Mean, apparent 293
Military 313
Sidereal 286, 293
Solar 293
Standard 313, 314
24-hour 313
Zones (map) 484
Timor 592
Titanium 132
Tobacco
Exports, imports 207
Production 141, 142
see also Smoking
Tobago. *See* Trinidad and Tobago
Togo 484, 824-25, 847
Tokelau Island 803
Tokyo, Japan 838
Subway nerve-gas attack (1995) 52, 57, *778*
Toledo, OH 695
Buildings, tall 701
Mayor 98
Population 390, 419, 695
Ton (measure) 601, 602, 603
Tonga 484, 825, 847
Tonkin Resolution (1964) 505
Tonnage, gross, deadweight 209-10
Tony Awards 336, *780*
Top Ten News Stories, The (1995) 33
Tornadoes
Characteristics 179
Notable 267
Tour de France (1995) 926
Tourism
Expenditures (by states) 655-80
Foreign to U.S. 126
National parks, monuments 546-49
States, territories, cities 655-85
U.S. regulations 722-23
Washington (DC) sites 684-85
Townshend Acts (1767) 497
Toxic chemical pollution 187
Track and field
Olympic champions 855-59
World indoor, outdoor records . . . 865-66
see also Marathon
Trade 206-10
see also Exports, imports
Traffic
Airline 319
Motor vehicle 963, 966
Ports, major U.S. 208
Trails, national scenic 549
Training services, U.S. 148
Trains. *See* Railroads, U.S.; Railroads, world
Transportation 206-16
Expenditures, consumer 214
Occupational injuries 150
Price indexes 112, 113
see also specific types
Transportation, Department of 80
Employees, payroll 151
Expenditures 110
Internet address 169
Secretaries 78, 80, 108
Trapezoid, Area 607
Travel, foreign. *See* Tourism
Treasury, Department of 79
Bonds 129
Employees, payroll 151
Expenditures 110
Internet address 169
Secretaries 78, 79, 104-5
Bentsen resignation (1994) 44
Rubin confirmation (1995) 46
Waco (TX) standoff (1993, 1994, 1995) 61-62, 509, 510
see also Currency, U.S.; *specific bureaus*
Treaties. *See* Arms control; *specific treaties*
Trees
Giant (U.S.) 190
Official (by states) 655-80
Triangle, Area 607
Trieste 785
Trinidad and Tobago 484, 825, 847
Triple Crown winners 895
Triple jump
Olympic champions 857
World records 865, 866
Tripoli-U.S. War (1801) 499
Tristan da Cunha 592, 831
Tropical year 293
Trotsky, Leon 272, 353
Trotting, pacing 898
Troy weight (measure) 601, 602, 603
Trucks. *See* Motor vehicles
Truman, Harry S. 475, 477, 479, 480
Biography 535-36
Burial site 539
Cabinet 104-8
Popular, electoral votes 478
Presidential library 539
Trust funds, Social Security 711-12
Trust Territory, U.S. 683
Tsars, Russian 560, 585
Tucson, AZ 695
Mayor 98
Population 390, 397, 695
Tudor, House of 561, 578
Tuition, U.S. college 220, 221
Tulsa, OK 695
Buildings, tall 702
Mayor 99
Population 390, 419, 695
Tunisia 484, 825-26, 847
Tunnels 705-6
Turkey 826
Ambassadors, envoys 847
Flag 484
History 560, 566, 568, 569, 570, 575
Merchant fleet 210
Military strength 164
Turkey (meat), Prices, farm 143
Turkmenistan 484, 491, 826-27, 847
Turks and Caicos Islands 830
Turner, Nat (1831) 499
Tutuila Island 681
Tuvalu 484, 827, 847
TV. *See* Television
TVA. *See* Tennessee Valley Authority
21st century, start of 309
24-hour time 313
21-gun salute 159
Twilight 294-95

2-year colleges . . . 238-48
Tyler, John . . . 479
Biography . . . 531
Burial site . . . 539
Cabinet . . . 104-6
Typhoons . . . 268
Tyson, Mike (1995) . . . 66-67, *784*

—U—

Uganda . . . 484, 827, 847
Ukraine . . . 827-28
Ambassadors, envoys . . . 847
Chronology (1995) . . . 57
Energy consumption . . . 202
Flag . . . 484
Map . . . 491
Military strength . . . 164
Nuclear power . . . 204, 205
Ulster. *See* Northern Ireland
Ultraviolet index . . . 186
UN. *See* United Nations
Unabomber case (1994-95) . . . 36, 45, 54, 59, 67-68
Unemployment, U.S.
By educational attainment . . . 149
Rates, indicators . . . 146, 147, 149
Chronology (1994-95) . . 42, 44, 46, 48, 51, 53-54, 56, 58, 61, 64, 67, 70
Highest (1982) . . . 507
Training services . . . 148
Unemployment insurance . . . 146, 148
UNESCO. *See* United Nations Educational, Scientific, and Cultural Organization
UNICEF. *See* United Nations Children's Fund
Unified defense commands, U.S. . . . 158
Union of Soviet Socialist Republics. *See* Soviet Union
Unions. *See* Labor unions
Unitarian churches . . . 645, 646
United Arab Emirates . . . 484, 828, 847
United Arab Republic. *See* Egypt
United Church of Christ . 645, 646, 652-53
United Kingdom . . . 828-31
Ambassadors, envoys . . . 847
Chronology (1994-95) . . . 44, 50, 60, 62
Commonwealth . . . 842
Energy production, consumption . . . 202
Flag . . . 484
Gold reserves . . . 128
History . . . 568, 570, 576
World War I . . . 569
World War II (1945) . . . 504, 571-72
Islands, areas . . . 592
Merchant fleet . . . 210
Military strength . . . 164
Monarchs . . . 577-78, 829
Motor vehicle production . . . 212
Northern Ireland 44, 50, 52, 575, 592, 830
Nuclear power . . . 204, 205
Poets Laureate . . . 357
Prime ministers . . . 579
Royal family . . . 381
Scotland . . . 578, 829-30
Stonehenge . . . 555
Unemployment rates . . . 147
Wages, hourly . . . 152
Wales . . . 829
see also England
United Mine Workers
Membership . . . 156
Strikes (1922, 1946) . . . 502, 504
United Nations . . . 843-45
Agencies . . . 845
Bomb plot trial (1995) . . . 49, 70
Charter (1945) . . . 572, 843
50th anniversary (1995) . . . *200*
Headquarters . . . 843
Iraqi nuclear weapon disclosures (1995) 66
Members . . . 843-44
Peacekeeping efforts
Angola (1995) . . . 50
Bosnia (1994-95) . . . 43, 44-45, 46-47, 52, 57, 59-60, 62-63,65, 68, 70-71
Haiti (1995) . . . 47, 52-53
Somalia (1994, 1995) . . . 42, 52
Secretaries General . . . 844
U.S. Representatives . . . 844
Visitors' information . . . 843
Women's conference (1995) . . . 68
United Nations Children's Fund . . . 845
United Nations Educational, Scientific, and Cultural Organization . . . 845
United Nations High Commissioner for Refugees . . . 845
United States of America . . . 831
Accessions . . . 545
Agencies, government . . . 81-82
Altitudes (highest, lowest) . . . 541
Ambassadors, envoys . . . 846-48
Anthem, national . . . 527-28
Area codes . . . 396-426
Areas (square miles) . . . 387, 540, 542
Banks . . . 118
Bicentennial (1976) . . . 507
Births, deaths . . . 961, 962, 963
Boundaries . . . 543
Budget . . . 110-11
Cabinets . . . 78, 104-8
Capital . . . 680-81, 684-85, 695
Cities . . . 390-91, 686-95, 838
Latitudes, longitudes, altitudes . . 594-95
State capitals . . . 655-80
Clinton administration . . . 78-81
Coastline (by states) . . . 541
Congress . . . 82-91
Constitution . . . 515-22
Contiguous 48 . . . 540
Continental Divide . . . 542
Copyright law . . . 724-25
Courts . . . 92-95
Crime . . . 956-60
Currency . . . 121
Customs (traveler exemptions) . . 722-23
Dams . . . 706, 707
Debt, national . . . 112
Declaration of Independence . . . 512-13
Education . . . 217-48
Energy . . . 201, 202, 203, 204
Federal government employment, payroll . . . 151
Federally owned land . . . 545
Flag . . . 484, 525-27
Foreign investment in . . . 126
Foreign relations. *See* State, Department of; *specific countries*
Geographic centers . . . 543
Geographic superlatives . . . 540
Gold production, reserves . . . 134
Government . . . 78-95
Gross national/domestic products . . . 114
Historic parks, sites . . . 546-49
History . . . 497-510
Holidays . . . 314
Immigration . . . 382, 393, 840-41
Income, national . . . 114, 127
Income taxes . . . 730-36
Indians, American . . . 550
Investments abroad . . . 128
Island trusteeships . . . 683
Joint Chiefs of Staff . . . 79, 158, 165
Judiciary . . . 92-95
Labor force . . . 147
Lakes . . . 598
Land, federally owned . . . 545
Libraries, public . . . 223
Maps . . . 485, 486-87
Memorials, national . . . 547
Merchant fleet . . . 209
Military . . . 158-66
Mineral production . . . 132-34
Monuments, national . . . 548-49
Motto, national . . . 525
Mountains . . . 590, 591
Naturalization . . . 841
Nuclear arms treaties . . . 165
Nuclear power . . . 204, 205
Outlying areas . . . 445, 681-83
Parks, national . . . 546-47, 549
Passports . . . 723
Petroleum production, consumption . . 201
Poets Laureate . . . 357
Population . . . 382-445, 838
Postal information . . . 396-426, 631-35
Presidential elections . . . 446-78
Presidents . . . 479-80, 530-39
Recreation areas . . . 545, 549
Religions . . . 644-46
Reservoirs . . . 707
Social Security . . . 708-12
Space program . . . 315-18
Statehood dates . . . 542, 543, 655-80
States, individual . . . 655-80
Superlative statistics . . . 540
Trade . . . 206-8
Veterans . . . 162, 163
Vice presidents . . . 479-80
Vital statistics . . . 961-74
Wars
American Revolution . . . 498, 564
Casualties . . . 166
Civil War . . . 500
Costs in dollars . . . 163
Gulf War . . . 509, 776, 789, 814
Korean War . . . 504, 573
Mexican War . . . 500
Spanish-American War . . . 501, 567
Vietnam War . . . 574, 834
War of 1812 . . . 499
World War I . . . 502, 569
World War II . . . *200*, 503-4, 572
Water area . . . 387, 542
Waterfalls . . . 599
Weather . . . 180-84, 185
ZIP codes . . . 396-426, 445
Units
Electrical . . . 604
Of measurement . . . 600-607
Universal Postal Union . . . 845
Universities. *See* Colleges and universities
Unknown Soldier's Tomb . . . 685
Upanishads . . . 554
Upper Volta. *See* Burkina Faso
UPU. *See* Universal Postal Union
Uranus (planet) . . . 281, 290
Morning, evening stars . . . 286
Position by month . . . 274-77, 282-83
Sun, distance from . . . 277, 290
Urban areas. *See* Cities; Metropolitan areas, U.S.
Urban Development, Department of. *See* Housing and Urban Development, Department of
Uruguay . . . 484, 831-32, 847
U.S. Open (tennis) . . . 927
USSR. *See* Soviet Union
Utah . . . 677
Admission, area, capital . . . 542, 543, 677
Agriculture . . . 137-42
Altitudes (high, low) . . . 541
Birth, death statistics . . . 962
Budget . . . 116
Congressional representation . . 83, 89, 384
Courts, U.S. . . . 95
Crime, prisons, death penalty . . . 959
Energy consumption . . . 203
Federally owned land . . . 545
Governor, state officials . . . 99, 103
Immigrants' intended residence . . . 393
Indians, American . . . 550
Interest laws, rates . . . 721, 722
Marriage, divorce laws . . . 728, 729
Mineral production . . . 132
Motor vehicle statistics . . . 211
Name origin, nickname . . . 544, 677
Population . . . 384-85, 388
Cities, towns . . . 424
Counties, county seats . . . 443
Presidential elections . . 446, 471-72, 476
Public libraries . . . 223
Schools . . . 218, 219, 222
Taxes . . . 211, 735, 736
Temperature, precipitation . . . 181, 184
Toxic chemical pollution . . . 187
Unemployment benefits . . . 146
Welfare assistance . . . 395
UV index . . . 186
Uzbekistan . . . 484, 491, 832, 847

—V—

Valdez, AK . . . 208
Valois, House of . . . 580
Vanadium . . . 132
Van Buren, Martin . . . 479, 480
Biography . . . 531
Burial site . . . 539
Cabinet . . . 104-6
Popular, electoral votes . . . 478
Vanuatu . . . 210, 484, 832, 847
Varangians . . . 559
Vatican City . . . 832-33
Ambassadors, envoys . . . 847
Flag . . . 484
Popes . . . 649, 650
Veal
Nutritive value . . . 610
Prices, farm . . . 143
Production, consumption . . . 138
Vegetables
Nutritive value . . . 609, 611
Production . . . 142
Venezuela . . . 833
Ambassadors, envoys . . . 848
Energy production . . . 202
Flag . . . 484
Rulers . . . 584
Trade . . . 206
Venomous animals . . . 190
Venus (planet) . . . 278-79, 290
Morning, evening stars . . . 286
Position by month . . . 274-77, 282-83
Rises, sets . . . 284
Sun, distance from . . . 277, 290
Vermont . . . 677-78
Admission, area, capital . . . 542, 677
Agriculture . . . 137-42
Altitudes (high, low) . . . 541
Birth, death statistics . . . 962
Budget . . . 116
Congressional representation . 83, 89, 384
Courts, U.S. . . . 95
Crime, prisons, death penalty . . . 959
Energy consumption . . . 203
Federally owned land . . . 545

Governor, state officials 99, 103
Immigrants' intended residence 393
Indians, American 550
Interest laws, rates 721, 722
Marriage, divorce laws 728, 729
Motor vehicle statistics 211
Name origin, nickname 544, 677
Population 384-85, 388
Cities, towns 424
Counties, county seats 443
Presidential elections 446, 472, 476
Public libraries 223
Schools 218, 219, 222
Taxes 211, 735, 736
Temperature, precipitation 181, 184
Unemployment benefits 146
Welfare assistance 395
Vernal Equinox 275, 283, 293
Verrazano, Giovanni da (1524) 497, 586
Versailles conference (1919) 569
Vesuvius 588, 589
Veterans, U.S. 162, 163
Agent Orange suit (1984) 508
Court of Appeals 95
GI Bill (1944) 503
Veterans Affairs, Department of 81
Employees, payroll 151
Expenditures 110
Internet address 169
Secretaries 78, 81, 108
Veterans' Day 314
Vice presidents, U.S. 479-80
Internet address 169
Nominees 477
Presidential succession 522, 525
Salary 78
Salutes, honors 159
Victoria Falls 555
Videos
Games, top-selling (1994) 259
Movies, most popular (1994) 250
Music
Awards 259
Sales 257, 258
Vietnam 833-34
Ambassadors, envoys 848
Division (1954) 573
Flag 484
Indochina War (1953) 504, 573
Military strength 164
Nam-Viet Kingdom 559
Refugees (1975) 507, 575
Tet New Year 312
U.S. advisers, aid (1950) 504
U.S. diplomatic relations (1995) 47, 63
U.S. immigrants from 393
U.S. trade embargo (1994, 1995) 63, 510
Vietnam Veterans Memorial (DC) 685
Vietnam War 834
Agent Orange suit (1984) 508
Black troops 162
Bombings (1965, 1966, 1971, 1972) 505, 506
Casualties, U.S. forces 166
Costs 163
Demonstrations against (1969) 506
End (1975) 507, 575
McNamara perspective (1995) 54
Medals of Honor 163
Memorial (DC) 685
Mylai massacre (1969, 1971) 506
Participants 574
Peace talks, pacts (1969, 1973) 506
Pentagon Papers (1971) 506
Tet offensive (1968) 506
Tonkin Resolution (1964) 505
Troop withdrawal (1973 506
Veteran population 162
Women's memorial (DC) 685
Viking *I and II* (spacecraft) (1976) 279, 318, 507
Vikings 559, 586
Virginia 539, 678
Admission, area, capital 542, 678
Agriculture 137-42
Altitudes (high, low) 541
Birth, death statistics 962
Budget 116
Coastline 541
Congressional representation 83, 89, 384
Courts, U.S. 95
Crime, prisons, death penalty 959
Energy consumption 203
Federally owned land 545
Governor, state officials 99, 103
Immigrants' intended residence 393
Indians, American 550
Interest laws, rates 721, 722
Marriage, divorce laws 728, 729
Memorials, monuments 685
Motor vehicle statistics 211
Name origin, nickname 544, 678
Population 384-85, 388
Cities, towns 424-25, 692, 693, 695
Counties, county seats 443-44
Port traffic 208
Presidential elections 446, 472-73, 476
Public libraries 223
Schools 218, 219, 222
Taxes 211, 735, 736
Temperature, precipitation 181, 184
Unemployment benefits 146
Welfare assistance 395
Virginia Beach, VA 695
Mayor 99
Population 390, 425, 695
Virgin Islands, British 592, 830
Virgin Islands, U.S. 683
Accession (1916) 502, 545
Altitudes (high, low) 541
Area, capital, population 445, 545, 592, 683
Cities (population) 445
Citizenship 683
Congressional delegate 90
Courts, U.S. 95
Immigrants' intended residence 393
Unemployment benefits 146
ZIP codes 445
Vital statistics 961-74
Vitamins 609, 610-11, 612
Vojvodina 836
Volcanoes 588-89
Mt. St. Helens (1980) 507, 588, 589
Paricutin 555
Volleyball 864
Volume
Mathematical formulas 607
Measures, dry, fluid 600, 602, 604
Sun and planets 290
Voting rights. *See* Elections
Voting Rights Act (1965) 505

— W —

Waco (TX) standoff (1993, 1994, 1995) 61-62, 509, 510
Wages. *See* Salaries and wages
Wake Atoll 683
Wales 829
Walesa, Lech 576, 809
Freed (1982) 507
Nobel Peace Prize 325
Walking, Olympic champions 856
Wallis and Futuna Islands 764
Wall Street. *See* Stocks
War, Department of 105
see also Defense, Department of
War crimes
Bosnia (1995) 50, 63
Geneva Conventions 845
Nuremberg trials (1946) 572
Warehouse Act (1916) 502
War of 1812 (1812-15) 499
Casualties, numbers serving 166
Costs 163
War of the Worlds (broadcast) (1938) 503
Warren Commission (1964) 505
Wars
Battlefields, military parks 547
Casualties, U.S. 166
Costs, U.S. dollars 163
Geneva Conventions 845
Veterans, U.S. 162, 163
see also specific wars
Wars of the Roses (1455-85) 561
Washington (state) 678-79
Admission, area, capital 542, 543, 678
Agriculture 137-42
Altitudes (high, low) 541
Birth, death statistics 962
Budget 116
Coastline 541
Congressional representation 83, 89-90, 384
Courts, U.S. 95
Crime, prisons, death penalty 959
Energy consumption 203
Federally owned land 545
Governor, state officials 99, 103
Immigrants' intended residence 393
Indians, American 550
Interest laws, rates 721, 722
Marriage, divorce laws 728, 729
Motor vehicle statistics 211
Name origin, nickname 544, 678
Population 384-85, 388
Cities, towns 425-26, 694, 695
Counties, county seats 444
Port traffic 208
Presidential elections 446, 473, 476
Public libraries 223
Schools 218, 219, 222
Taxes 211, 735
Temperature, precipitation 181, 184
Unemployment benefits 146
Welfare assistance 395
Washington, Booker T. (1881) 345, 501
Washington, DC 680-81, 695
Altitudes (high, low) 541
Area, population 428, 542, 680
Birth, death, statistics 962
British burning of (1814) 499
Budget 111
Congressional delegate 90
Courts 94
Crime, prisons, death penalty 959
Energy consumption 203
Federally owned land 545
Federal workers 151
Immigrants' intended residence 393
Indians, American 550
Interest laws, rates 721, 722
Marches
Antiwar (1969) 506
Black civil rights (1963) 505
Million Man (1995) 33
Marriage, divorce laws 728, 729
Mayor 99
Memorials, monuments 684-85
Motor vehicle statistics 211
Museums, libraries 684-85
Name origin 544
Population 384-85, 388, 390, 401, 428, 695
Presidential elections 446, 450, 476
Public buildings 684-85
Public libraries 223
Schools 218, 219, 222
Taxes 211, 735
Temperature, precipitation 181, 183
Unemployment benefits 146
Voting rights 522, 680
Welfare assistance 395
White House 66, 685
Washington, George 479
Biography 530
Birthday (legal holiday) 314
Burial site 539
Cabinet 104-6
Commander-in-chief (1775) 498
Constitutional convention (1787) 498
Delaware crossing (1776) 498
Electoral votes 478
Farewell Address (1796) 498
Mount Vernon 685
Washington Monument (DC) 685
Water
Area (U.S.) 387, 542
Boiling, freezing points 605
Dams, reservoirs 706-7
Health, nutrition 609
Oceans, seas, gulfs 593
Pollution 187
Usag 192
Weights 605
Waterfalls 599
Watergate 536, 574
Break-in (1972) 506
Convictions (1973) 506
Cover-up (1973, 1975) 506, 507
Impeachment hearings (1974) 506-7
Nixon resignation (1974) 507, 574
"Plumbers" (1974) 506
Tapes (1973, 1974) 506, 507
Waterloo, Battle of (1815) 565
Water polo 864
Waterways. *See* Canals
Watt (electrical unit) 604
Weapons
Arrests, sentences 959, 960
Defense contracts 162
Firearms 604
see also Nuclear arms
Weather 179-86
Annual climatological data 182
Blizzards 179, 268
By cities, foreign 184
By cities and states, U.S. 180-84, 185
Floods (1993) 179, 268, 509
Hurricanes 179, 185, 268
Marine warnings, advisories 179
Precipitation 180-82, 184
Wettest spot 181
Storms 268
Watches, warnings 179
Temperatures 180-84
Heat index 186
Heat wave deaths (1995) 61
Highest, lowest recorded 181
Thunderstorms 179
Tornadoes 179, 267
Typhoons 268
Ultraviolet index 186
Wind chill 186
Winds, velocities 182, 185
Webster, Noah (1783, 1828) 498, 499

Wedding anniversaries 726
Weight, body
Children, average 974
Heart disease, impact on 616
Overweight adults 974
Recommended 612
Weight lifting 864
Weights, measures, numbers 600-607
Atomic 177-78
Electrical units 604
Energy measures 604
Equivalents, table of 601-2
Gases 605
Human 612, 616
Metric 600-604
Table of U.S. Customary 600-601
Temperature conversion 605
Water 605
Weimar Republic (1919) 570, 766
Welfare
Aid to Families with Dependent Children (by state) 395
Federal food programs 139
Mothers' fertility characteristics 395
Reform efforts (1995) 51, 68
Supplemental Security Income 711
West Bank. *See* Israel
Western Samoa. *See* Samoa, Western
West Germany. *See* Germany
West Indies, British 830
Westminster Kennel Club 918
West Point Military Academy 160, 234
West Virginia 679
Admission, area, capital 542, 679
Agriculture 137-42
Altitudes (high, low) 541
Birth, death statistics 962
Budget 116
Congressional representation 83, 90, 384
Courts, U.S. 95
Crime, prisons, death penalty 959
Energy consumption 203
Federally owned land 545
Governor, state officials 99, 103
Immigrants' intended residence 393
Indians, American 550
Interest laws, rates 721, 722
Marriage, divorce laws 728, 729
Motor vehicle statistics 211
Name origin, nickname 544, 679
Population 384-85, 388
Cities, towns 426
Counties, county seats 444
Port traffic 208
Presidential elections 446, 474, 476
Public libraries 223
Schools 218, 219, 222
Taxes 211, 735
Temperatures, record 184
Unemployment benefits 146
Welfare assistance 395
Wheat
Exports, imports 144, 207
Prices, farm 143
Production 141, 142, 144
Whiskey Rebellion (1794) 498
White House 685
Burning (1814) 499
Employees, payroll 151
Expenditures 110
Internet addresses 169
Security problems (1994, 1995) 44, 57
Staff 78
Whitewater scandal (1994-95) 44, 49, 51, 56, 58, 61, 64, 67, 509, 510
Whitney, Eli (1793) 498
WHO. *See* World Health Organization
Wichita, KS 695
Mayor 99
Population 390, 407, 695
Wilkes Atoll 683
Williams, Roger (1636) 497
William the Conqueror 559, 577
Wills, living 615
Wilson, Woodrow 477, 479
Biography 534-35
Burial site 539
Cabinet 104-7
Popular, electoral votes 478
Wimbledon (tennis tournament) 63, *784*
Wind chill factor 186
Windsor, House of 381, 578, 829
Wind speeds, U.S. 182, 185
Windward Islands. *See* Dominica; St. Lucia; St. Vincent and the Grenadines
Winston-Salem, NC 99, 702
Winter (season) 293
Winter Olympics. *See under* Olympic games
Winter Solstice 277, 283, 293
WIPO. *See* World Intellectual Property Organization
Wisconsin 679-80
Admission, area, capital 542, 543, 679, 680
Agriculture 137-42
Altitudes (high, low) 541
Birth, death statistics 962
Budget 116
Congressional representation 83, 90, 384
Courts, U.S. 95
Crime, prisons, death penalty 959
Energy consumption 203
Federally owned land 545
Governor, state officials 99, 103
Immigrants' intended residence 393
Indians, American 550
Interest laws, rates 721, 722
Marriage, divorce laws 728, 729
Motor vehicle statistics 211
Name origin, nickname 544, 679
Population 384-85, 388
Cities, towns 426, 691
Counties, county seats 444-45
Port traffic 208
Presidential elections 446, 474-75, 476
Public libraries 223
Schools 218, 219, 222
Taxes 211, 735, 736
Temperature, precipitation 181, 184
Unemployment benefits 146
Welfare assistance 395
WMO. *See* World Meteorological Organization
Women
Armed forces 161, 162
Generals, first U.S. (1970) 506
Vietnam memorial 685
Astronauts, first (1983) 315, 316, 507
Attorney general, first (1993) 382
Child support payments 382
College, first (1821) 499
Congresswoman, first (1916) 502
Employment, unemployment 147, 149, 152, 382
Equal Rights Amendment (1972, 1982) 506, 507
Equal rights convention (1848) 500
Faulkner withdrawal from Citadel (1995) 65
First ladies 538, 539
Governor, first U.S. (1924) 503
Health help organizations 618
Life expectancy 974
Living alone 382
Marital status 382, 391
Nobel Prize winners 323-25
Population (1790-1994) 386, 387, 391
Poverty rates 394
Salaries and wages
Annual earnings average 149
Hourly rates 153
Weekly earnings median 155
Single household heads 382
Strikers, first (1824) 499
Supreme Court justices (1981, 1993) 507, 509
UN world conference (1995) 68
Vice-presidential nominee (1984) 508
Voting rights (1869, 1920) 501, 502, 521
Weight, height 612
Wooden Award 915
Wool (farm prices) 143
Woolworth's Five and Dime (1879) 501
Workers. *See* Employment
World Almanac, *The*, First (1868) 501
World Bank 43, 845
World Court 845
World Cup
Skiing 918
Soccer 935
World Health Organization 58, 845
World history 551-76
World Intellectual Property Organization 845
World Meteorological Organization 845
World Series 952-53, 954
World Trade Center bombing (1993, 1994, 1995) 49, 509, 510
World Trade Organization 207, 845
World War I (1914-18) 569
Armistice (1918) 502
Black troops 162
Casualties, U.S. forces 166
Costs 163
Medals of Honor 163
Troop strength 166
U.S. neutrality (1914) 502
Versailles conference (1919) 569
Veteran population 162
World War II (1939-45) 503-4, 572
Atomic bombs (1945) 65-66, *200*, 504, 572
Black troops 162
Casualties, U.S. forces 166
Costs 163
50th anniversary remembrance *200*
Medals of Honor 163
Peace treaties, Japan (1951) 504
Pearl Harbor attack (1941) 503
Troop strength 166
Veteran population 162
World Wide Web 168, 169, 170
Wounded Knee, Battle of (1890) 501
Wrestling
NCAA champions 902
Olympic champions (1992) 864-65
Wright brothers 502, 547, 568
Writers, notable
Best-selling books (1994) 255-56
Children's books 254-55, 333-34
Contemporary 356
Deceased 357-60
Newbery Medal 333-34
Nobel Prizes 40, 324-25
Noteworthy literature (1995) 254
Pen names 642
Poets Laureate
England 357
U.S. 357
Pulitzer Prizes 325-32
Special awards 333
WTO. *See* World Trade Organization
Wyoming 680
Admission, area, capital 542, 543, 680
Agriculture 137-42
Altitudes (high, low) 541
Birth, death statistics 962
Budget 116
Congressional representation 83, 90, 384
Courts, U.S. 95
Crime, prisons, death penalty 959
Energy consumption 203
Federally owned land 545
Governor, state officials 99, 103
Immigrants' intended residence 393
Indians, American 550
Interest laws, rates 721, 722
Marriage, divorce laws 728, 729
Motor vehicle statistics 211
Name origin, nickname 544, 680
Population 384-85, 388
Cities, towns 426
Counties, county seats 445
Presidential elections 446, 475, 476
Public libraries 223
Schools 218, 219, 222
Taxes 211, 735
Temperature, precipitation 181, 184
Unemployment benefits 146
Welfare assistance 395

—X, Y, Z—

Xinjiang 753
Yacht racing
America's Cup 935, *784*
Olympic champions (1992) 865
Yalta Conference (1945) 504
Year
Calendar, perpetual 310-11
Chronological eras 294
Holidays 314
Sidereal, tropical 286, 293
Year in pictures (1995) *193-200, 777-84*
Yellow Sea 593
Yellowstone National Park 546, 680
Founded (1872) 501
Yeltsin, Boris 45, 47, 57, 60, 812
Yemen 484, 835, 848
Yonkers, NY 695
Mayor 99
Population 390, 417, 695
York, House of 578
Young, Brigham (1846) 500
Yugoslavia 212, 484, 570, 835-36, 848
Yukon River 596, 597
Zaire 836
Ambassadors, envoys 848
Ebola virus outbreak (1995) 58
Flag 484
Gold production 134
History 575
Zaire (Congo) River 596
Zambia 484, 837, 848
Zanzibar 592, 824
Zen Buddhism 562
Zeppelins 322
Zeus, Statue at Olympia 555
Zimbabwe 484, 575, 837, 848
Zinc 132, 133, 134
ZIP codes
Colleges and universities 224-48
U.S. outlying areas 445
U.S. states 396-426
Zodiac signs 291
Zones of earth 293
Zoological parks 191
Zoroaster 597

The World Almanac

and Book of Facts 1996

The Top 10 News Stories

In the worst terrorist act ever on U.S. soil, the Federal Building in Oklahoma City, OK, was the target of a car bomb on Apr. 19 that reduced the structure to rubble, killed 169 people, and left all of America stunned. Two Americans, Timothy McVeigh and Terry Nichols, were indicted in connection with the bombing.

The courtroom came to the living room via the television cameras during 1995 in what was called the "Trial of the Century," as O. J. Simpson was tried for the murders of his ex-wife Nicole Brown Simpson and her friend Ronald Goldman. On Oct. 3, after having been sequestered for 266 days and deliberating less than 4 hours, the jury found him not guilty.

The year of the Congress began at noon on Jan. 4, when the first Republican-controlled Congress in 40 years convened. Supplanting the executive branch as the dominant attention-getting force in the national government, the 104th Congress moved to curb federal spending and reduce or eliminate a number of major federal programs.

The continuing war in the Balkans seemed to take a new direction in Sept. when the Serbs, after suffering battlefield reverses, accepted a U.S.-brokered peace plan for Bosnia and Herzegovina that would divide the country into 2 autonomous entities—one controlled by a Croat-Muslim federation, the other by Bosnian Serbs.

Continuing the Middle East peace process, in a White House ceremony on Sept. 28 the Israelis and the Palestinians signed an agreement to expand Palestinian self-rule in the West Bank.

The release of sarin, a deadly nerve gas, in the Tokyo subway system on Mar. 20 killed 12 and injured more than 5,000 commuters. Shoko Asahara, founder and leader of the Aum Shinrikyo religious sect, and 40 of his followers were charged with organizing the attack.

Hundreds of thousands, mostly black men, gathered in Washington, DC, on Oct. 16 to participate in the Million Man March, inspired and organized by often-controversial Nation of Islam leader Louis Farrakhan, who challenged black men to assume personal responsibility for themselves and their families and to involve themselves in the renewal of their communities.

In a year marked by rapid change in the media industry, Time Warner and Turner Broadcasting announced, Sept. 22, their plan to merge and form the world's largest media company. This news came less than 2 months after Walt Disney announced its plans to acquire Capital Cities/ABC and Westinghouse Electric Corp. announced its plans to acquire CBS.

In the summer, it was the heat in the Midwest: During July, more than 500 people in Chicago alone died from it. And in the fall, it was the hurricanes, starting with Allison and abc'ing almost to Wendy. The 1995 Atlantic hurricane season was the most active since that of 1933.

Baltimore Oriole shortstop Cal Ripken, Jr., played his 2,131st consecutive game on Sept. 6 before a sold-out crowd at Oriole Park in Camden Yards, breaking the record set by baseball legend Lou Gehrig in 1939.

Cameras in the Courtroom: Justice, Education, or Entertainment?

by Jonathan Alter

Jonathan Alter is senior editor and columnist, Newsweek *magazine. Formerly, he was an editor of* The Washington Monthly.

The 1990s will long be remembered in the U.S. as the Era of Great Trials. William Kennedy Smith, Rodney King, Lyle and Erik Menendez, John Wayne Bobbitt, Susan Smith, and, most of all, O. J. Simpson are names that will linger in the minds of Americans. By 1995, with the nation at peace, the Cold War over (thereby decreasing the interest in foreign news), and highly publicized court cases thrust to the center of the nation's consciousness, a series of questions arose about the effects of these celebrated trials that will keep law professors and media critics busy for years: Does excessive pretrial publicity damage a defendant's right to a fair trial? Does the glare of attention generate social unrest? Has the presence of TV cameras changed the amount of coverage a trial receives? Do cameras create the media circus atmosphere so widely decried? Do they lengthen trials? Do they change behavior in the courtroom? Do they lessen respect for the legal process? Do they educate—or just titillate? There are plenty of theories and assumptions—and also some hard research on these questions.

We tend to think of the Simpson trial and the enormous fallout from his acquittal as somehow unprecedented, but celebrated cases predate television by hundreds of years. From the time of the ancient Greeks, legal proceedings—especially murder cases—have been inherently dramatic and a form of popular entertainment. Even in the U.S., most of the dozen or more cases labeled at various times the Trial of the Century predate cameras in the courtroom, for example, the Scopes "Monkey Trial," the Sacco and Vanzetti case, the espionage trial of Ethel and Julius Rosenberg, the Boston Strangler case, and the trial of the Chicago Seven. The Simpson trial would have received enormous coverage at any time because Simpson is the most famous person ever put on trial for murder in U.S. history, with the possible exception of the 1920s silent-screen comedian Fatty Arbuckle (who was eventually acquitted of rape and murder). Although scores of others have become enormously famous as a result of their trials, only Arbuckle and Simpson brought huge fame into their cases.

The Courtroom Comes to the Living Room

But the television age—especially the growth of cable and syndicated programs—has brought the coverage to new heights—or depths. The Simpson trial was not only carried live by Cable News Network (CNN), Court TV, and the E! Channel, it was fodder for tens of thousands of other hours of television, from *Nightline* to *The Tonight Show With Jay Leno* to hundreds of daytime talk shows and local news programs. Kathleen Hall Jamieson, dean of the Annenberg School of Communications, told the *Los Angeles Times*: "I guess we're going to have to revise all those theories about the 'MTV Generation' and the nation's short attention span. Anybody who says Americans don't have an extended attention span—and insatiable need for narrative—isn't watching O. J. Simpson."

The intensity of interest in the Simpson case and others in recent years has made an old-fashioned legal remedy to pretrial publicity—a change of venue—increasingly impractical. Because of the global reach of CNN (whose first televised trial was the New Bedford, MA, barroom rape trial), it's now often necessary to actually leave the country to find people who have not heard of the case. That's not legally possible, of course, not to mention that O. J. Simpson is a household name in many countries around the world.

So judges and attorneys have begun to accept as jurors people who have had considerable exposure to pretrial publicity. The fear has been that this prejudices the jury against the defendant, but in practice quite the opposite has taken place. In the Rodney King case, the original jury in Simi Valley, CA, had been exposed to repeated airings on TV of the videotape showing King being beaten by 4 Los Angeles police officers. That jury acquitted the officers. At the same time, had O. J. Simpson been an unknown black man accused of killing his wife, and blood evidence been found everywhere, he would likely have been quickly convicted, rather than becoming the subject of a months-long trial. All the pretrial publicity—from Simpson's football glory years to the famous Bronco ride down a Los Angeles freeway—enhanced the celebrity that became Simpson's greatest asset in court. If anything, all that publicity was unfair to the prosecution. With the discrediting of the testimony of racist police detective Mark Fuhrman, the Simpson case was often defined in racial terms. The tremendous racial issues unleashed after Simpson's acquittal have solidified it in the public mind as a race case. But it was above all a case about money and celebrity and the advantages (the "Dream Team" defense) they buy.

Often it seems that the greatest effect of the media on the criminal justice system comes long before the jury is selected. The daily diet of talk shows featuring abused spouses and dysfunctional families has fostered a psychological explanation for every type of aberrant social behavior. The result is a jury pool predisposed to believe many varieties of what has come to be known as the "abuse excuse." Verdicts in the Lorena Bobbitt case (she escaped serious punishment for dismembering her husband) and the first Menendez brothers murder case (a hung jury) seemed to indicate that the most powerful media in shaping the courtroom may be "Oprah" and "Geraldo."

Coverage Inside and Outside the Courtroom

With TV images so pervasive, trial verdicts can be social nitroglycerin, as the L.A. riots following the initial acquittals in the Rodney King case suggest. But in analyzing the effect of all the media attention, it's important to distinguish between coverage inside the courtroom and coverage outside the courtroom. Steven Brill, founder and president of Court TV, which televises many trials, argues in a paper called "Facts and Opinions About Cameras in the Courtroom" that the camera inside "acts as an antidote to the abuses of the 'circus' by allowing viewers to make their own judgments independent of the circus elements." Marvin Kitman, a well-respected TV critic for Newsday, agrees: "Everybody is saying the [Simpson] trial is out of control because of TV—let's pull the plug on TV coverage. That is not the answer. Court TV is doing a responsible, intelligent job. What's bad is the desperate media frenzy to annotate, comment on, go beyond the actual proceedings, notably the tabloid magazine shows." In fact, the worst distortions and inaccuracies growing out of the Simpson case were the result of leaks—not televised courtroom proceedings, which are by definition accurate.

Even the argument that cameras invariably turn the attorneys into Hollywood-style celebrities doesn't quite hold up. Moira Lasch, the prosecutor in the William Kennedy Smith rape trial, barely made an impression, despite appearing on television constantly. Conversely, flamboyant attorneys from William Jennings Bryan and Clarence Darrow to F. Lee Bailey and Gerry Spence have developed big reputations and followings largely without the help of courtroom cameras. Important, even sensational trials that aren't entertaining—such as New York's World Trade Center bombing case, in which public interest was hampered by a language barrier with the Arabs in the courtroom—would not be changed by the presence of cameras.

But the argument that the camera is so unobtrusive that it has no effect on the participants doesn't hold up either. Consider the money-hungry jurors, vexed judge, and TV-appropriate attire of the attorneys in the Simpson case. Visitors to the courtroom reported that the demeanor of the judge and the attorneys changed considerably once the camera came on.

The Judges Opine

Still, no correlation has been established between the length of a trial and the presence of cameras. The untelevised Charles Manson murder trial, for instance, took a full 9 months. The untelevised trial of Susan Smith, the Union, SC, woman accused of drowning her children, took only three weeks, which was instantly (and wrongly) related to the absence of cameras. The primary reason for the speed of the Smith trial was that Smith had confessed, which greatly reduced the witness list and simplified the trial.

Nonetheless, many judges in the 47 states that allow cameras in the courtroom are now choosing to bar them in the wake of the Simpson trial. In 24 of those states, strict rules severely limit TV coverage (only Indiana, Mississippi, South Dakota, and the District of Columbia prevent it entirely), and those rules are now being imposed more firmly. Progress toward televising federal trials has been stalled, and the television camera is not likely to be in the Supreme Court in the foreseeable future.

"I know for me, when there is a camera, there is an effect," said Judge William Howard, Jr., who presided over the Susan Smith trial. Old-fashioned sketch artists and journalists with notebooks covered that trial, in which a greater sense of courtroom decorum was reported. Although the lack of live coverage did not prevent tell-all books and magazine cover-story treatments, the "circus" was undoubtedly toned down by the absence of the play-by-play analysis that accompanies televised trials. And witnesses were not hounded in the grocery store, although the stigma of being associated with the case in a town the size of Union would exist without cameras.

In any event, the differences between the Simpson and Smith trials were not lost on other judges. Judge Lawrence Antolini, the California judge presiding over the trial of the accused murderer of Petaluma, CA, teenager Polly Klass, restricted TV coverage to the first five minutes of court each day. Antolini also issued a gag order on lawyers, vowing that "nothing like the O. J. Simpson case is going to happen in my courtroom."

As it happens, nothing like the Simpson case has taken place in other courtrooms. In the past 20 years, 41 states have studied the effect of cameras in the courtroom. Some criticism has surfaced, but the results have been positive overall, with judges in many states indicating that their experience with cameras overcame their initial reservations. While some of this approval can be chalked up to ego gratification, the surveys consistently show that judges found that the camera did not interfere. (In California, for example, 83 percent said they were "not at all distracted.") Many members of the bench have become believers in the educational potential of live coverage. New York's study, for instance, concluded that no witnesses had been lost because of camera coverage and that "the benefits of the program are substantial, with little or no adverse effect on anyone. Cameras in the courts serve a valuable educational function and promote public scrutiny of the judicial system. This in turn provides a deterrent against injustice and fosters a sense of confidence and respect for the judicial process."

The Media Reflect

But in 1995 the O. J. Simpson case threw all this favorable experience with cameras into a harsh light. As the Simpson trial wore on, opponents of cameras in the courtroom got a big boost from Don Hewitt, the legendary founder and executive producer of *60 Minutes*, the most successful program in the history of primetime network television. Writing in the *New York Times*, Hewitt acknowledged reversing a long-standing position in favor of cameras. "Letting cameras in can turn a courtroom into a movie set. In Los Angeles, we've got a movie in which the lead speaks no lines, a blonde bombshell turns out to be a man [the reference here appears to be to Kato Kaelin, a Simpson houseguest] and the $5-a-day extras in the jury box keep walking off the set," Hewitt wrote. "An occasional closed door in our face would be good for our souls and might even get some of us off our backsides and back to reporting instead of watching."

It's just such "reporting," of course, that often leads tothe tabloid excesses that so harm the reputation of the press. A strong case can be made that the way to avoid a circus is for the media to stick closely to the facts of the trial and the larger social commentary (about race, class, and so forth) and avoid the peripheral "scoops." This has been the approach of Court TV, and the effect has been to educate the public on the legal system. In the nearly 300 trials televised by Court TV in 28 states, not one appellate court has overturned a verdict because of the presence of the camera. "Cameras are an absolute godsend because the public has been educated to think that criminal trials are what they saw on Perry Mason and it ain't true," Professor John Langbein of Yale Law School told CBS News in the middle of the Simpson trial. "What it's showing people is the way the system really works."

The Decision

Unfortunately, the camera also showed the public arguments not directly meant for them. In his now famous summation, Johnnie Cochran directed his comments to the court—especially to the jury—but they were heard by the court of public opinion. The "race card," which might have been legitimate as part of a defense attorney's representation of a client, became inflammatory when conveyed to the outer world. Cochran and all attorneys must balance their obligations to their clients with their obligations to society at large.

Terrorism: At Home

By Jeffrey D. Simon

Jeffrey D. Simon is president of Political Risk Assessment Co. in Santa Monica, CA. He is the author of The Terrorist Trap: America's Experience With Terrorism *(Indiana University Press, 1994) and writes frequently on national and international affairs.*

Terrorism has not been a stranger to the American people. During the early days of the republic, hundreds of Americans were taken hostage off the high seas by the Barbary pirates of North Africa. Their sufferings evoked great sympathy in the country and led to the first arms-for-hostages deal and the first counterterrorist military operation in U.S. history. In more recent times, Americans have seen fellow citizens held hostage in Iran and Lebanon, planes with Americans onboard blown up in Europe, and U.S. symbols attacked by terrorists worldwide.

But although anti-U.S. terrorism has been a frequent event overseas, relatively few spectacular terrorist incidents have occurred on American soil. The majority of those happened during the anarchist and labor-management violence period of the late 19th and early 20th centuries. For most Americans, therefore, the threat of terrorism at home seemed quite remote. The public believed, or at least hoped, that the U.S. would be able to escape the terrorist violence that was sweeping the rest of the world.

The 1993 World Trade Center bombing in New York City shattered that illusion. Six people were killed and more than 1,000 others injured when a car bomb exploded in an underground parking garage of one of the twin towers. Yet as shocking as that incident was, it had all but faded from public attention by spring 1995. Most of the perpetrators of the bombing—a small group of Islamic extremists—had been sentenced to long prison terms, and there had not been any subsequent major terrorist incidents on U.S. soil. The American public believed that the worst was behind them.

The Oklahoma City Bombing

In the world of terrorism, however, it takes only one well-placed bomb to create new fears and reactions. That is what happened on the morning of Apr. 19, 1995, when a car bomb exploded in front of the federal building in Oklahoma City, killing 169 people (including one rescue worker). It was the worst terrorist act ever on U.S. soil, and it struck a special nerve throughout America. This was not a major, world-famous metropolis that had been attacked, but rather a small city in the heartland of the country. Every town and city across the U.S. could now be considered a potential target for terrorism. As millions of Americans watched on television the heart-wrenching scenes of dead babies being pulled from the wreckage, they could only wonder whether their country was now catching up with the rest of the world, where terrorism was a frequent event.

The psychological shock of the bombing was magnified with the disclosure that an American was being charged with causing the carnage. The public had become accustomed to equating anti-U.S. terrorism with Middle Eastern Islamic extremists. Now America faced the increased threat of home-grown terrorism. The prime suspect in the Oklahoma City bombing, Timothy McVeigh, had ties to a right-wing American militia group and reportedly set off the bomb in retaliation for the U.S. government's final assault on the Branch Davidian headquarters in Waco, TX. The bombing occurred on the second anniversary of that raid, in which some 80 members of the religious cult, which authorities said had large numbers of illegal weapons, died when their compound burst into flames. McVeigh and Terry Nichols, both of whom had served in the same army unit at Fort Riley, KS, were indicted on 11 counts related to the Oklahoma City bombing. Michael Fortier, another member of the army unit, pleaded guilty to lesser charges and was expected to testify against McVeigh and Nichols.

The Oklahoma City tragedy brought public and media attention to the rise of right-wing militias. These groups organized in several states following the Waco raid and a 1992 government siege at a white supremacist's cabin in Ruby Ridge, ID. In the latter incident, federal agents attempted to arrest the white supremacist, Randy Weaver, after he failed to appear in federal court on a weapons charge. An

11-day siege ensued in which Weaver's wife and son and a deputy marshal were killed before Weaver and an associate surrendered. The U.S. Justice Department agreed to pay $3.1 million to Weaver and his 3 surviving daughters in Aug. 1995 to settle a wrongful death suit. Five FBI agents were suspended for their actions during an internal investigation after the siege. The Ruby Ridge and Waco incidents, along with gun-control legislation, had been cited by the militias as evidence that the government intended to confiscate all weapons—thereby violating the constitutional right "to keep and bear arms"—and initiate a war against the citizenry. Some militia extremists believed that the U.S. government was being taken over by foreign powers under a "One World Government" or "New World Order" controlled by the United Nations. The militias saw themselves as the last hope to save the U.S. from tyrannical rule.

The national focus on the terrorist threat posed by militias and right-wing extremists following the Oklahoma City bombing was not surprising. It mirrored the national attention given to the threat of Islamic extremism following the World Trade Center bombing. Viewing the terrorist threat mainly in terms of the latest incident, however, ignores the diversity of terrorism and the potential for any number of groups to stage future attacks. Although right-wing, anti-government extremist groups advocating white supremacy, such as the Aryan Nations, the Order, and the American Front Skinheads, pose a terrorist threat within the U.S., the federal building in Oklahoma City could just as easily have been attacked by international radical terrorists, left-wing extremists, antiabortion militants, or others had they believed such an act would have furthered their interests. The threat of terrorism in the U.S. is not the domain of any single group or cause; it crosses all parts of the political, ideological, and ethnic-religious spectrum.

The Unabomber

The U.S. was still recovering from the shock of the Oklahoma City bombing when a new terrorist crisis erupted in June. This time a familiar name was behind the trouble: the elusive "Unabomber." Since 1978, an individual who claimed to be part of a larger group, but whom authorities believed worked alone, had terrorized people associated with universities and airlines—hence the code name Unabomber. In later years he targeted people associated with computers and other industries. His method was to send package bombs to his victims—occasionally he would leave a bomb at a university or computer store. Over a 17-year period, the Unabomber committed 16 attacks, killing 3 people and injuring 22 others. One bomb was mailed just a few days after the Oklahoma City bombing, killing a timber industry executive.

But it was a letter that he sent to the *San Francisco Chronicle* a week before the Fourth of July holiday that demonstrated how terrorism is unlike any other type of conflict. By simply threatening to place a bomb on an airliner flying out of Los Angeles International Airport, the Unabomber single-handedly increased public anxiety about terrorism; disrupted the U.S. Postal Service, as a temporary ban was placed on all air mail packages sent from California weighing more than 12 ounces; forced the authorities to increase security measures at California airports, which in turn led to major delays for travelers; and caused Secretary of Transportation Federico Peña to fly to Los Angeles to explain how the government intended to handle the crisis.

The ability of terrorists to elicit such reactions from government and the public is a key to the strategy of terrorism. Terrorists commit violent acts for a variety of reasons. The Unabomber's goal was to destroy what he called the "industrial-technological system" of modern society. In a letter to the *New York Times*, he stated that his original threat to place a bomb on a plane from Los Angeles was a hoax but

that he would resume sending package bombs to people unless the *New York Times* or the *Washington Post* published a 35,000-word manifesto calling for a revolution against the industrial-technological society. The *Washington Post*—with the *New York Times* sharing the printing costs—published the manifesto in September. Most terrorists, however, do not have such grandiose, global objectives in mind. Rather, their goals can range from overthrowing a particular government to winning the release of comrades from jail.

A common thread running through many acts of terrorism is the creation of fear in the general population. Terrorism is a psychological form of warfare, with terrorists often staging their violence to reach a wider audience than their immediate target. By hijacking a plane with a few hundred passengers onboard, terrorists deliver a message to all potential air travelers that they could be the next victims. By kidnapping people in a foreign country, terrorists state that living in, working in, or visiting that country is dangerous. By blowing up a building and killing scores of people, terrorists demonstrate that they can arbitrarily take the lives of innocent people.

Throughout the 1980s, Americans watched the dramas of terrorism unfold through extensive media coverage of major anti-U.S. incidents overseas. These included the bombing of the U.S. Marine headquarters in Beirut, Lebanon (1983), the hijacking of Trans World Airlines Flight 847 from Athens and its diversion to Beirut (1985), and the midair bombing of Pan American Flight 103 over Lockerbie, Scotland (1988). The public could thus vicariously live through the tragedies that terrorism brought to its victims and their loved ones. But terrorism on American soil has had a much deeper psychological impact on the country than anti-U.S. terrorism overseas. The terrorist threat could no longer be viewed as a distant phenomenon, but rather had to be seen as one that could surface in any city at any time. Following the Oklahoma City bombing, workers in federal buildings across the country worried about their safety. And the public, Congress, and others demanded to know what steps the government would take to protect America from future incidents.

The Federal Government Responds

President Bill Clinton responded by announcing a broad plan to combat domestic terrorism. The proposed measures included hiring 1,000 new federal officials to investigate, deter, and prosecute terrorist activity; establishing the Domestic Counterterrorism Center, headed by the FBI; requiring manufacturers to place microscopic particles, or taggants, in explosive substances to facilitate the tracing of bombing materials after an explosion; expanding court-authorized electronic surveillance of suspected terrorists; and allowing the military to assist in terrorism cases that involve chemical or biological weapons. These and other measures were added to a bill aimed at combating international terrorism that the Clinton administration had proposed to Congress following the World Trade Center bombing. The new package, which became known as the Comprehensive Terrorism Prevention Act of 1995, was under consideration in Congress in late 1995.

Clinton also ordered heightened security at federal buildings throughout the country, including restrictions on parking; greater use of metal detectors, security guards, and closed-circuit television; and the wearing of identification badges by employees and visitors. Many private businesses also began exploring ways to protect their facilities from terrorist attacks. Increased security will undoubtedly affect the way people live and work in America. Freedom of movement in certain places will be restricted, delays in travel will be encountered, and barriers and guards at buildings will be a constant reminder to people that they live in an age of terrorism. Just as most people have accepted the fact that before they can board a plane they must pass through a metal detector, so too are they likely to adapt to the new security measures that will be implemented in public and private buildings in the coming years. The reality is that even the most stringent security measures or new antiterrorist legislation cannot ensure that a terrorist group will not be successful in launching a spectacular attack. Too many opportunities and targets are available, and too many groups are willing to use terrorism for a variety of purposes. New tactics can always be introduced, as illustrated in October 1995 when several spikes were removed from rail tracks in Arizona, causing the derailment of an Amtrak passenger train. One person was killed and about 100 injured in the incident. A note found at the scene protested the government sieges at Waco and Ruby Ridge and was signed "Sons of the Gestapo," a previously unknown group.

Terrorism has actually been on the decline in terms of the number of incidents in recent years. The FBI reported that in 1994 there were no terrorist incidents in the U.S., whereas there had been 12 the previous year, the most significant being the World Trade Center bombing. (The FBI does not currently include the Unabomber's violence in its annual statistics on terrorism because, as noted above, the Unabomber is believed to be working alone. The FBI defines domestic terrorism as the "unlawful use of force or violence, committed by a group(s) of two or more individuals, against persons or property to intimidate or coerce a government, the civilian population, or any segment thereof, in furtherance of political or social objectives.") Similarly, the U.S. State Department reported that there were 431 incidents of international terrorism around the world in 1993, but only 321 incidents in 1994, the lowest annual total in 23 years. It is not, however, the total number of terrorist incidents that matters, but rather the effect that attacks can have on a government or society. In the U.S., the Oklahoma City bombing was indicative of a worldwide trend whereby terrorist incidents are becoming more deadly. Even though the number of incidents of international terrorism worldwide declined in 1994 from the previous year, the number of people killed actually increased from 109 in 1993 to 314 in 1994. The explosion of one car bomb near a Jewish cultural center in Buenos Aires in July 1994 killed some 100 persons.

Terrorism in America can be affected by global events. The U.S., by virtue of its status as the world's only super-power and its involvement in various conflicts, peace processes, and other issues, is a potential target for a variety of foreign extremists. Some of them may decide to strike within the U.S. to gain maximum publicity or revenge for their cause. The global village and telecommunications— faxes, cellular phones, computer networks—have also made it easier for foreign terrorists to establish a base of operations anywhere in the world, including the U.S.

The nature of international terrorism is changing as attacks by religious extremist groups are on the rise while attacks by secular terrorist organizations have been declining. Suicide terrorist incidents have also become more frequent. One of the most troublesome developments in terrorism is the potential for terrorists to acquire and use weapons of mass destruction. The release of the nerve agent sarin in the Tokyo subway system in March 1995 was a wake-up call that a new age of terrorism might be upon us. If chemical agents could be released in Tokyo's subway system, then any subway system in the world, including those in the U.S., could be vulnerable to similar attacks. Preventing terrorists from acquiring and using nuclear, chemical, and biological weapons will be an important challenge for the U.S. and other countries in the years ahead. This will require global cooperation in information, policy, and strategy.

Although terrorism can never be completely eliminated, the work of U.S. intelligence and law enforcement agencies can help reduce the risk of sustained campaigns of terrorism on American soil. For example, in 1993 the FBI uncovered a plot by Islamic extremists to bomb several targets in New York City, including the UN headquarters. The extremists and their spiritual leader, Sheik Omar Abdel Rahman, were arrested and eventually convicted by a federal jury in October 1995 of seditious conspiracy. Law enforcement and intelligence personnel have long been the front-line soldiers in the battle against terrorism, and their quiet efforts in tracking down suspected terrorists and identifying plots are crucial for protecting America from terrorism.

But it is the American people who have within themselves the most powerful weapon against terrorists. While Americans cannot prevent every single incident from occurring or take away every potential bomb from terrorists, they can take away the reaction that terrorists seek, which is panic, fear, and the general disruption of daily life.

The Year of the Congress

By Norman J. Ornstein

Norman J. Ornstein is a resident scholar at the American Enterprise Institute. He writes a regular column "Congress Inside Out" for Roll Call *and is an election analyst for CBS News. He was editor and cohost of* Congress: We the People, *an award-winning 26-part public television series.*

It was clear from the beginning that 1995 was destined to be the Year of the Congress. The House of Representatives convened at noon on Jan. 4 and elected Newt Gingrich of Georgia as the first Republican Speaker since Joe Martin of Massachusetts was elected in 1953. The House then debated, voted on, and passed a sweeping series of rules changes and reforms and, well after midnight, took up and passed its first piece of legislation, the Congressional Accountability Act, to require Congress to comply with the laws it applies to the private sector. When the Senate acted on the same bill several days later, it became the fastest a new Congress sent major legislation to the White House since the 1933 Emergency Banking Relief Act. The House's first day—normally a perfunctory hourlong session—finally concluded about 2:30 in the morning.

That first day was followed by another 90 remarkable ones. The 104th House started with an unprecedented pace and kept it up, overcoming the typical—and intrinsic—inertia of the institution. It managed to draft, mark up, debate, and pass a lengthy series of other bills and resolutions, fulfilling the majority Republicans' Contract With America and dominating the nation's policy agenda in an almost unprecedented version of congressional government.

Television networks, newspapers, and newsmagazines were filled with stories of the Congress's first 100 days. Near their conclusion, on April 7, Speaker of the House Newt Gingrich achieved another first, addressing the nation live in prime time on several television networks, including CBS, CNN, PBS, and C-SPAN. No Speaker had ever before unilaterally requested an opportunity to appear on national television to address the nation. That this Speaker asked—and that several prominent networks agreed—underscored the unusual dynamic of the 104th Congress, the first controlled wholly by the Republicans in 40 years.

Republicans Sweep 1994 Election

The Republican sweep in the Nov. 8, 1994, elections caught political experts and professionals on both sides of the political aisle off guard. In the *Washington Post*'s final election prediction survey, only 3 of the 14 analysts picked the Republicans to win both houses of Congress, and not one picked them to get the full 230 seats in the House that they actually received. (Democratic defections in 1995 brought GOP strength to 233 seats by midyear.)

The 1994 GOP victory was stunning and across the board. Republicans captured 53 seats in the House and 8 in the Senate, including a majority of Southern seats in both houses for the first time since Reconstruction. In the House, Republicans retained control of 17 out of 21 open GOP seats and captured 22 of the 31 open seats that had been held by Democrats. They gained 17 seats in the Midwest, 16 in the South, and 10 on the Pacific Coast. New England was the only region in which the Democrats held onto a solid majority. The only gains the Democrats made in the House at all were 4 open GOP seats—not a single GOP incumbent lost.

In the Senate, Republicans swept all 9 open-seat races, ousted 2 Democratic incumbents, equaled the House in not losing a single one of their own incumbents, and then achieved the bonus of 2 Democratic defections to their party, Alabama Sen. Richard Shelby (in Nov. 1994) and Colorado Sen. Ben Nighthorse Campbell (in Mar. 1995). The Senate freshman class consisted of 11 Republicans and zero Democrats—the first such shutout since 1914.

The 104th Congress Convenes

The first Republican majority in the House in 40 years convened with not one member among its 230 with experience in this role. The change wrought in 1994 continued a pattern of rapid change that has characterized the membership of Congress for several years. A full 52 percent of all House members in the 104th Congress arrived for the first time in the 1990s—including more than 60 percent of House Republicans. At the same time, the number of lawyers decreased slightly in the House in 1995, while the number of members with previous occupations in business or banking shot up 24 percent.

Freshmen Emerge as a Force

The 104th Congress freshman class entered as a major force in the institution. The Republican class came to Washington with substantial ballyhoo, making up nearly one-third of their party. As a group, they mostly ran on an agenda of term limits, balancing the budget, the line-item veto, reforming welfare, cutting government, and cutting taxes. They tended to be both young and inexperienced. Almost 55 percent of House freshmen were under 45 years of age, and only about 53 percent had previously held an elected office, versus 70 percent of returning lawmakers.

Although the freshman Republicans were grateful to Gingrich for his election help and strategy, and enthusiastic about his leadership, none got elected by pledging to march in lockstep with party leaders. A comment made in April by freshman Linda Smith of the state of Washington suggested that perfect party unity might not last: "We are here on a mission, and I will remain loyal to Gingrich only as long as he doesn't lose sight of what the people of Washington want us to accomplish. . . . My base is more populist than Republican."

If the early national spotlight focused on the House and its freshmen, the smaller Senate freshman class was equally populist and activist and proved anything but shy. Fresh-man Sen. Rick Santorum (R, PA) took the lead in challenging publicly a senior member from his own party, Sen. Mark Hatfield (R, OR), chairman of the Appropriations Committee, for his opposition to the balanced budget amendment, a major provision of the Contract With America. When some senior Republicans criticized Santorum for his brashness, his fellow freshman Senator Fred Thompson (R, TN) remarked emphatically, "Santorum's as much a senator as the most senior member, and he has a right to do and say anything he wants."

Leadership Develops Contrasting Approaches

Wielding an assertive, strategic vision of leadership, driven in part by the writings of management guru Peter Drucker, Speaker Gingrich began to implement his leadership vision long before the Republicans won the 1994 election. He was the driving force behind the Contract With America, making it easy for the party to follow his lead. Immediately after the election, Gingrich began to craft rules reforms and rules revisions to place more formal power in the speakership than at any time since the legendary Speakers Thomas Brackett Reed and Joseph Gurney Cannon held office in the 1890 to 1910 era.

Gingrich's vision turned on transforming the Speakership into a powerful public forum, with an eye toward supplanting President Bill Clinton as the primary source of ideas and vision about where the country should be heading. Most Speakers have had their primary focus inward, toward the House and its members. Gingrich turned at least as much focus outward, using his bully pulpit to shape the policy agenda and debate and to influence public opinion.

Gingrich's leadership approach contrasted significantly with that of Senate Majority Leader Bob Dole (R, KS). Dole, of course, was a prominent national figure for more than a decade before Gingrich even entered the House of Representatives. In his career, he served in the House as well as the Senate, as his party's 1976 vice presidential nominee, Senate Finance Committee Chairman, and Senate Minority and Majority Leader. And he ran unsuccessfully for the Republican presidential nomination twice, in 1980 and in 1988. Surprisingly, Dole found himself in the unusual position of spending the period from Nov. 1994 through Mar. 1995 as a secondary character, largely overshadowed by the new Speaker of the House. The lack of concentrated press coverage and attention, ironically, worked substantially to his personal advantage. Dole's approval in polls went from 39 percent to 51 percent by Apr. 1995, as he simultaneously became the overwhelming choice of Republicans for his party's 1996 presidential nomination.

In the meantime, the Senate's slow pace contrasted directly with the House's extraordinary level of activity. As the House churned out Contract provision after Contract provision, the Senate slowly, sometimes seriously, deliberated over a small number of items, only belatedly to discover—to Gingrich's and Dole's frustration—that they did not have the votes needed for passage.

House Fuels Legislative Action

The Gingrich team stampeded the House floor opening day and then maintained a frantic and mostly successful pace in order to fulfill the Contract. The Contract With America, a more ambitious plan for the first 100 days than that facing any Congress since the 73d under President Franklin Delano Roosevelt, served as the key organizing force for the newly minted majority. Instead of a chaotic transition filled with all-new GOP committee and subcommittee chairs, each declaring different priorities, the changeover was sharply focused, a result of the Contract, which became a powerful force for party unity in the new Congress.

The Senate, not tied to the Contract or its tight timetable, found itself in the unusual circumstance of being upstaged by the House. The intrinsic differences between the 2 bodies were underscored by their different treatment of the Congressional Accountability Act. The House took less than an hour on its first day to debate and pass the bill, unanimously. The Senate got around to the bill on its 3d day; 8 days later it passed the bill, 98 to 1.

The remarkable string of legislative successes that House Republicans achieved in the first 100 days—including a balanced budget constitutional amendment, a ban on unfunded mandates (or requirements that states take on certain tasks, without federal funds to pay for them), the line-item veto, crime legislation, a national security bill, product liability and tort reform, welfare reform, and tax cuts—overshadowed the few significant setbacks and disguised the difficulties that lay ahead for the new majority. With only 230 seats at the beginning of the session—the smallest majority in 40 years—the Republicans were left with a small cushion for a purely partisan success. And legislative successes in the House were no guarantee for comparable success in the Senate (and no guarantee that Clinton would sign the final legislation or that a presidential veto could be overridden).

To achieve their successes, the House Republicans showed a remarkable cohesion during their first 100 days, in equal parts a carryover from their discipline as a minority party, a tribute to the adroit performance of party leaders such as Gingrich, and a result of commitment to the Contract.

For most House Republicans, the solemn commitment to the Contract was reason enough to swallow philosophical or constituency differences and vote together. But the remaining 630 days of the 104th Congress would not have the superglue of the Contract to bind GOP lawmakers together.

As the 104th Congress moved from its first 100 days through its second and toward its third, the budget became a more dominant issue, supplanting much of the Contract agenda. At the same time, Medicare and Medicaid moved to the center of the congressional agenda. Republican House and Senate budgets each proposed removing about $1 trillion from the federal government's spending stream over 7 years, and more than 45 percent of all their cutbacks in spending growth came from the 2 health programs. Perhaps the greatest challenge facing Republican congressional leaders in the second part of their first year in the majority was finding ways to handle Medicare so artfully that real spending restraint could be achieved without hitting the elderly directly. And they needed to handle Medicaid without nicking nursing home care for the elderly or causing a revolution among the GOP's favorite politicians, the governors, who wanted block grants of federal aid to give them more flexibility in administering Medicaid but were fearful of formulas that would take away too much money from them. Success in that kind of agenda control would ensure a broader and comprehensive approach to budget balancing, one that could include zeroing out a number of programs as well as applying shorter leashes to all the others. Failure could mean that the Republican-controlled Congress would be discredited or at least significantly damaged in the eyes of voters, and the GOP agenda—to dismantle large parts of the federal government, shift other parts to the states, and also balance the federal budget—would be thwarted.

The Pace Slows

Could this Congress really deliver, meeting the expectations—often contradictory—of Americans to streamline government and reduce its role while simultaneously maintaining essential services, reducing tax burdens, and moving the country forward? The 104th Congress began in a fashion dramatically different from that of any other Congress in at least 30 years, perhaps in 60 years. New faces abounded, including familiar faces wielding gavels for the first time ever. Long-proposed reforms, ignored for years, were implemented swiftly in the House of Representatives. The normal inertia of the institution gave way to a frenetic pace through the first 100 days, with major legislation actually passing the House and even occasionally the Senate. The Congress acted more like a parliament than a traditional Congress.

But the second 3 months of the 104th Congress resembled a more typical Congress. The Senate checked the House, while the president, vetoing the first bill of his presidency in June of his 3d year, reminded the majority congressional Republicans that they could accomplish little without his support or acquiescence.

By the time of the August recess—a traditional stopping point and an opportunity for assessing the progress of the Congress—the bottom line showed the problems that had earlier been disguised by the promise of the new Congress's beginnings.

The 104th Congress had enacted only 20 public bills—compared with an average of 89 in the previous 7 Congresses. Even the much-maligned 103d Congress, summarily rejected by voters for its gridlock, had enacted 81 laws by its first August recess, including such consequential ones as the Clinton budget reconciliation package, the "motor voter" registration law, and the Family and Medical Leave Act. The most significant laws enacted through August 1995 by the 104th Congress were the Congressional Accountability Act, the unfunded mandates legislation, and a minor paperwork reduction act. The numerous top priorities expressed in the Contract With America—including term limits, a balanced budget constitutional amendment, a line-item veto, welfare reform, tort and product liability reform, elimination of a range of government programs and agencies, and dramatic changes in the role of the federal and state governments—all remained uncompleted.

Ample time, of course, remained in the Congress to enact all these items and more, but the path to action became trickier and more formidable as fall 1995 wore on.

The change from a parliamentary-type process was, of course, inevitable. The 1994 election was dramatic, but it did not repeal the constitutional system of checks and balances. But change to the norm did not mean inevitably a return to the same old patterns of partisan bickering, failure to enact major policies into law, and the dominance of scandals.

In the end, the performance of the 104th Congress and, in turn, the perceptions of American voters would be shaped by the skill of leaders in both parties, the behavior of rank-and-file lawmakers, especially the newer ones, and the role of the president, facing the Republican majority. These dynamics in turn would decide whether an enduring pattern of Republican majorities would emerge, whether the pattern of divided government—this time with a Democratic president—would endure at least for a time, and whether a pattern of stability or of continuing tumult would mark Congress as it—and America—approached the 21st century.

Notable Supreme Court Decisions, 1994-95

The Supreme Court's 1994-95 term began Oct. 3, 1994, and ended June 29, 1995, with the Court issuing signed decisions in only 82 cases, the fewest since the 1955-56 term. Of these decisions, 35, or 43% were unanimous, an increase from the 1993-94 Court term. Sixteen cases, including several that were among the term's most watched, were decided by 5-4 votes. Especially noteworthy was the Court's conservative shift, particularly in such areas as affirmative action, drug testing, and criminal law.

Justices Clarence Thomas and Antonin Scalia were most likely to vote together; they did so in 83% of the cases that were not unanimous. Justices Thomas and John Paul Stevens were least likely to agree; the pair voted the same way in only 11% of the divided opinions. Justice Anthony M. Kennedy most often cast the swing vote. He was in the majority in 13, or 81%, of the Court's 5-4 decisions. Justice Stevens was the most frequent dissenter. He voted with the majority in only 34% of the split decisions.

Some of the most notable decisions are described below.

Affirmative Action: The Court held (June 12), 5-4, that federal programs which classify people by race must meet the same strict constitutional standards as state and local programs in order to ensure all individuals the right to equal protection. The Constitution, Justice Sandra Day O'Connor wrote in the majority opinion, protected "persons, not groups."

Criminal Law: In a unanimous ruling, the Court declared (May 22) that when police execute a search warrant, they are ordinarily required to knock and announce their arrival prior to entering a house unless there are "reasonable" exceptions such as the imminent threat of violence or destruction of evidence.

Desegregation in the Schools: The Court overturned (June 12), 5-4, a lower federal court decision that had ordered the state of Missouri to fund teacher salary increases and to establish specialized "magnet" schools in the Kansas City school district to remedy past segregation. The Court's decision asserted that equal opportunity, not equal results, was the criterion by which a school district's policies should be judged.

Drug-Testing: In a 6-3 decision (June 26), the Court upheld an Oregon school district's random drug testing of student athletes; the Court cited the importance of student athletes as role models, the voluntary nature of sports programs, and the voluntary sacrifice of privacy inherent in such programs (for example, shared locker rooms) as outweighing the students' general right of privacy.

The Environment: In the only major environmental case heard by the Court in the 1994-95 term, the justices decided (June 29), 6-3, that the Dept. of the Interior has broad power to protect the habitats of endangered species, even on private property.

Federal Powers: In a case involving the boundaries between state and federal powers, for the first time in more than 60 years, the Court overturned (Apr. 26), 5-4, a federal law on the grounds that Congress had exceeded its constitutional powers to regulate interstate commerce. The statute in question was the Gun-Free School Zone Act of 1990, which made it a crime to carry a gun within 1,000 ft of a school.

Freedom of Speech: The Court, in a 6-3 ruling, reversed (Feb. 22) the ban that had prevented federal civil servants from receiving honoraria payments for speeches and published articles, even for those not connected with their jobs. In a case that could have implications for speech via computers, the rights of individuals to speak anonymously were upheld (Apr. 19), 7-2, by the Court when it struck down an Ohio law barring anonymous campaign leaflets. In a very high profile case, the Court unanimously ruled (June 19) that organizers of privately sponsored parades had a constitutional right to limit the messages conveyed in their events by excluding homosexual marchers from their parades. Although the Court had previously established the right of lawyers to advertise their services, in a 5-4 decision, the Court upheld (June 21) a Florida law that barred lawyers from soliciting accident victims until 30 days after the incident. Writing for the majority, Justice O'Connor stated that the law did not place an undue burden on the lawyers and was helpful in protecting the privacy of the victim.

Religion: Two cases eased the constitutional requirements for separation of church and state. In a case that marked the first time the Court had approved government funding for a religious organization, the Court ruled (June 29), 5-4, that the University of Virginia must fund a student-run religious publication in the same manner that it funded other student-run, secular publications. The Court also decided (June 29), 7-2, that the state could not forbid an Ohio chapter of the Ku Klux Klan from displaying a cross in a public park near the state capitol building because the park was a public forum, open to other private speakers.

Term Limits: The Court ruled (May 22), 5-4, that neither the states nor Congress may regulate the tenure of members of Congress. This case had the effect of invalidating term-limit measures in 23 states and making a constitutional amendment the only means to restrict the number of terms a member of Congress could serve.

Voting Rights: On the final day of the Court's session (June 29), the Court invalidated, 5-4, the 11th congressional district in Georgia, finding that the use of race as a "predominant factor" in drawing the majority black voting district was unconstitutional. Race, the Court said, should be only one of many factors considered when voting districts are drawn.

The 1995 Nobel Prizes

The 1995 Nobel Prizes were awarded in October. Each prize consisted of a large solid gold medal and a cash award worth more than $1 million. For prizes shared by more than one recipient, the names are in alphabetical order.

Chemistry: Paul Crutzen, a German, and two Americans—Mario Molina and F. Sherwood Rowland—shared the prize for their pioneering work in studying the chemical processes that deplete the earth's ozone shield.

Memorial Prize in Economic Science: Robert E. Lucas, an American, won the prize for his influence on macroeconomic research since 1970. Lucas's "rational expectation" hypothesis stated that people learn to anticipate the effects of government intervention on the economy, thereby lessening the intended efforts.

Literature: Seamus Heaney, an Irish poet whose works are deeply rooted in his Irish background, won the prize. His poetry collections include *Death of a Naturalist*,

Door Into the Dark, *North*, *Field Work*, and *Seeing Things*.

Peace: A Polish-born British physicist, Joseph Rotblat, won the prize. Rotblat helped to develop the atomic bomb, but he subsequently led a campaign to eliminate nuclear weapons.

Physics: Two Americans, Martin L. Perl and Frederick Reines, shared the prize for their discoveries of two subatomic particles. Working separately, Perl discovered the tau, a subatomic particle that belongs to a class of particles known as leptons, and Reines made the first detection of the neutrino, another lepton.

Physiology or Medicine: Two Americans—Edward B. Lewis and Eric F. Wieschaus—and Christiane Nüsslein-Volhard, a German, shared the prize for their work in exploring how genes work together to create from an embryo a complex organism.

U.S. Presidential Primary, Caucuses, and Convention Dates, 1996

Source: Democratic National Committee; Republican National Committee; as of Oct. 15, 1995

The table below indicates when and by what methods delegates to the 1996 Republican and Democratic national conventions will be chosen. Since 1992 many states have moved their presidential primaries or caucuses to dates earlier in the year. As a result, in 1996 about 70% of the delegates to the national conventions will be selected by the end of March. The Republicans planned to send a total of 1,984 delegates to the Republican National Convention in San Diego, Aug. 12-15, 1996. The Democrats planned to send 4,295 delegates, including 774 unpledged "super" delegates, to the Democratic National Convention in Chicago, Aug. 26-29, 1996. Super delegates are selected from among Democratic officeholders and party officials. Democrats abroad receive 25 delegates. Delegate allocation among the states is listed below for both parties and is subject to change. Delegates allocated to U.S. territories are not listed in the table. Democratic delegate totals include the super delegates. The general election will be held Nov. 5, 1996.

Republicans Delegates	Republicans Type	Date	State	Democrats Delegates	Democrats Type
14	Closed Caucuses	1/25-1/31[1]	HI		
19	Closed Caucuses	1/26-1/29[2]	AK		
25	Open Caucuses	2/12[3]	IA	56	Open Caucuses
16	Open Primary	2/20[3]	NH	26	Open Primary
12	Closed Primary	2/24	DE	22	Closed Primary
39	Closed Primary	2/27	AZ		
18	Open Primary	2/27[4]	ND		
18	Closed Primary	2/27[5]	SD	22	Closed Primary
37	Open Primary	3/2	SC		
27	Open Primary	3/5	CO	58	Open Primary
27	Closed Primary	3/5	CT	66	Closed Primary
42	Open Primary	3/5	GA	91	Open Primary
		3/5	ID	24	Open Caucuses
15	Open Primary	3/5	ME	32	Open Primary
32	Closed Primary	3/5	MD	86	Closed Primary
37	Open Primary	3/5	MA	115	Open Primary
33	Open Caucuses	3/5	MN	92	Open Caucuses
16	Open Primary	3/5	RI	31	Open Primary
		3/5	SC	52	Open Caucuses
12	Open Primary	3/5	VT	22	Open Primary
36	Open Caucuses	3/5[6]	WA	90	Open Caucuses
		3/7[7]	MO	93	Open Caucuses
102	Closed Primary	3/7	NY	289	Closed Primary
		3/9	AK	19	Open Caucuses
		3/9[8]	AZ	52	Open Caucuses
36	Open Caucuses	3/9[7]	MO		
		3/10[9]	NV	27	Closed Caucuses
98	Closed Primary	3/12	FL	177	Closed Primary
		3/12	HI	30	Closed Caucuses

Republicans Delegates	Republicans Type	Date	State	Democrats Delegates	Democrats Type
28	Closed Primary	3/12[10]	LA	75	Closed Primary
32	Open Primary	3/12	MS	48	Open Primary
38	Closed Primary	3/12	OK	52	Closed Primary
23	Closed Primary	3/12[11]	OR	56	Closed Primary
37	Open Primary	3/12	TN	83	Open Primary
123	Open Primary	3/12	TX	229	Open Caucuses
		3/16	MI	157	Open Caucuses
69	Open Primary	3/19	IL	194	Open Primary
57	Open Primary	3/19	MI		
67	Open Primary	3/19	OH	172	Open Primary
36	Open Primary	3/19	WI	90	Open Primary
20	Closed Caucuses	3/23[12]	WY	19	Closed Caucuses
28	Open Caucuses	3/25	UT	30	Open Caucuses
163	Closed Primary	3/26	CA	423	Closed Primary
14	Closed Primary	3/26[11]	NV		
36	Open Primary	3/26[6]	WA	90	Open Primary
		3/29[4]	ND	22	Open Caucuses
31	Open Primary	4/2	KS	41	Open Primary
53	Open Caucuses	4/13[13]	VA	96	Open Caucuses
73	Closed Primary	4/23	PA	195	Closed Primary
14	Closed Primary	5/7	DC	37	Closed Primary
52	Open Primary	5/7	IN	89	Open Primary
58	Open Primary	5/7	NC	98	Closed Primary
24	Open Primary	5/14	NE	33	Open Primary
18	Open Primary	5/14	WV	43	Closed Primary
20	Open Primary	5/21	AR	48	Open Primary
23	Open Primary	5/28	ID		
26	Closed Primary	5/28	KY	61	Closed Primary
40	Open Primary	6/4	AL	66	Open Primary
14	Open Primary	6/4	MT	25	Open Primary
48	Open Primary	6/4	NJ	120	Open Primary
18	Closed Primary	6/4	NM	34	Closed Primary

(1) Precinct caucuses are open to a limited number of party members who choose delegates to the state convention, held May 17-19. (2) Nonbinding straw polls begin a three-tiered selection process. The last step, the state convention, is scheduled for Apr. 27. (3) Tentative date, subject to change. (4) The Republican date varies by locale. The North Dakota Democratic Party holds nonbinding caucuses Feb. 29-Mar. 14. Delegates to the national convention are selected at the state convention on March 29. (5) Nonbinding statewide primary. Delegates to the national convention are selected at Mar. 9 caucuses. (6) The Washington selection process begins with Mar. 5 caucuses. All Democratic and half of the Republican delegates will be chosen on this date. The remaining Republican delegates will be chosen by a state primary on Mar. 26. Although the Democratic Party will participate in the primary, it will be a "beauty contest" vote. (7) A multi-tier caucus process begins. Process ends with the Democratic (May 4) and the Republican (May 17) state conventions. (8) The Arizona Democratic Party has requested permission from the Democratic National Committee to move its primary date to Feb. 27. (9) Due to a change in state election laws, the Democratic Party may consider holding a mail-in primary on Mar. 26. (10) Louisiana may change to a split method of delegate selection beginning on Feb. 6. The Louisiana Republican Party has set a state convention for that date, and several delegates may be chosen on that date. (11) Mail-in primary. (12) A two-step process begins. (Republican caucus dates may vary by locale.) Delegate selection ends with a state convention on May 4. (13) First round date. Second round will be held on Apr. 15.

Glossary of Election Terms

Beauty Contest. A term used to describe a primary or caucus vote that is nonbinding.

Caucus. (1) In some states, such as Iowa, a meeting of voters to choose a party's candidates or convention delegates. (2) A meeting, often closed, of officials, legislators, or party leaders to make decisions. Originally used to describe the closed meetings of party leaders where candidates were chosen.

Caucus, Open. A caucus in which a voter does not have to have previously stated a party affiliation to participate; the voter may attend a caucus of either party, but not both.

Caucus, Closed. A caucus in which a voter must have previously stated a party preference to participate in that party's caucus.

Precinct. The lowest level of political subdivision, usually an area in which all voters use a single polling place.

Primary. The election before an election, in which a party's candidates for the upcoming election or convention delegates are chosen.

Primary, Closed. A primary in states in which a voter must have previously stated a party preference to participate and then can vote only in that party's primary.

Primary, Open. A primary in states that have no party-registration requirements. In these states a voter does not have to have previously stated a party affiliation to participate and may vote in the primary of either party, but not both.

CHRONOLOGY OF THE YEAR'S EVENTS

Reported Month by Month in 3 Categories: National, International, and General
Nov. 1, 1994, to Oct. 15, 1995

NOVEMBER 1994

National

Senators Criticize CIA on Ames—The Central Intelligence Agency came under more criticism in Nov. for failing to discover, at an earlier date, that one of its counterintelligence officers, Aldrich Ames, was a spy for the Soviet Union and Russia. Ames and his wife, Rosario, had pleaded guilty to espionage and income-tax evasion in Apr. Aldrich Ames was sentenced to prison for life, his wife for a shorter period. In Aug, Aldrich Ames was interviewed by Sen. Dennis DeConcini (D, AZ), chairman of the Senate Select Committee on Intelligence. In a report issued **Nov. 1**, the committee said that Ames had admitted undermining more than 100 CIA operations, far more than he had previously acknowledged. Ames told DeConcini that he had originally planned to give only useless information to the Soviets, but that then "I sort of just threw myself at the KGB—lock, stock, and barrel." He received more than $2 million for his information. The committee report charged that the agency was "excessively tolerant" of employees' misconduct and that, because the CIA did not search employees, Ames was able to give 5 to 7 lb of classified documents to the KGB. The senators faulted CIA Dir. R. James Woolsey for being too lenient toward employees who had failed to discover Ames's treason more quickly.

Republicans Win Control of Congress—The Republican Party won a majority in both houses of Congress in the **Nov. 8** election. After the last votes had been counted and recounted—a process that took several weeks in some close races—the GOP held a 230-204 margin, with 1 independent, in the House of Representatives, and an advantage of 52-48 in the Senate, where only one-third of the seats had been up for election. The Republican advantage in the Senate widened to 53-47, **Nov. 9**, when Sen. Richard C. Shelby (AL), heretofore a Democrat with a conservative voting record, switched his allegiance to the Republicans. Shelby had not been up for reelection in 1994. The principal issues of the campaign were crime, on which the Republicans were perceived as being tougher, and Pres. Bill Clinton, whose personal popularity was not high and whose health-care proposals had failed to win wide public support. The economy was a concern in that many Americans apparently were not reassured by data showing that unemployment was low and that federal budget deficits were declining. Although many individual races were close, the overall results represented a dramatic change. Not since the 1952 election had the Republicans emerged with a majority in both houses. Their pickup in the House was 52 seats, and in the Senate, 8. The results meant that Rep. Newt Gingrich (R, GA) would become Speaker of the House and that Sen. Bob Dole (R, KS) would become Senate Majority Leader. Leading members of Congress—all Democrats—who were defeated included Rep. Tom Foley (WA), Speaker of the House; Rep. Dan Rostenkowski (IL), former chairman of the House Ways and Means Committee; and Sen. Jim Sasser (TN), who had been the leading candidate to become Democratic leader in the Senate. Both Sen. George Mitchell (D, ME), the Senate Majority Leader, and Rep. Robert Michel (IL), the House Republican leader, had retired. No Republican incumbent in either house was defeated for reelection, and the GOP won most races in which no incumbent was running. Democratic senators who survived the adverse tide included Daniel Patrick Moynihan (NY), Edward Kennedy (MA), and Charles Robb (VA). Robb edged out Republican Oliver North, the retired Marine officer who had figured prominently in the Iran-contra affair. In the year's nastiest and second most expensive campaign, the 2 savaged each other on the issues as well as on matters of personal character. The year's costliest race was in California, where Rep. Michael Huffington, a Republican, spent more than $25 million of his own money in an unsuccessful bid to unseat Sen. Dianne Feinstein. She was one of 8 women—an all-time high—who would serve in the next Senate. In the House, there would be 47 women and 38 blacks, both numbers the same as in the outgoing House. Among the nation's governorships, the Republicans emerged with a lopsided majority, 30-19, with 1 independent, Angus King, in Maine. Prominent Democrats defeated for reelection included Mario Cuomo of New York, who lost to George Pataki, and Ann Richards of Texas, who lost to George W. Bush, a son of former Pres. George Bush. Jeb Bush, another son of the former president, failed to unseat Gov. Lawton Chiles (D) of Florida. Republican Gov. Pete Wilson of California was reelected. Comeback-of-the-year honors went to Marion Barry (D), who recaptured his old job as mayor of Washington, DC, after serving a prison term for a drug conviction. In a ballot proposition, Californians voted to cut off access of illegal immigrants to state benefits in the areas of education, welfare, and nonemergency health care. Seven more states voted to impose term limits on elected officials; nearly half the states had backed limits since 1990. Clinton said, **Nov. 9**, that he accepted some responsibility for the outcome of the voting and added that he would do what he could to work with the Republican majority. Gingrich, **Nov. 9**, called Clinton and his staff "left-wing elitists" who would be "very, very dumb" to oppose the Republican agenda in the new Congress.

Interest Rates Climb Again—The Commerce Dept. reported, **Nov. 2**, that the index of leading economic indicators had remained unchanged in Sept. The Labor Dept. said, **Nov. 4**, that the unemployment rate had edged down 0.1 percentage points to 5.8% in Oct., its lowest level in 4 years. The department reported, **Nov. 10**, that an index of prices charged by producers for finished goods had declined by 0.5% in Oct.—a fall equal to the decline in Sept. The rather rapid growth in the economy prompted the Federal Reserve Board, **Nov. 15**, to jump 2 key short-term interest rates by 0.75 percentage points each. They were the federal funds rate, the rate banks charge one another on overnight loans (now 5.5%), and the discount rate, the rate the Federal Reserve Board charges on loans to commercial banks (now 4.75%). Both rates were at 3-year highs. Large banks responded by raising their prime rate to 8.5% from 7.75%. The Labor Dept. said, **Nov. 16**, that the consumer price index had risen only 0.1% in Oct. The U.S. trade deficit rose to $10.13 billion in Sept., the Commerce Dept. reported **Nov. 18**.

Gunman at White House Indicted—Francisco Duran, who had fired at least 27 rounds from a semiautomatic assault rifle at the White House in Oct., was indicted on **Nov. 17** for attempting to assassinate Pres. Bill Clinton. He was also charged with 10 other counts. Coworkers of Duran's in Colorado told investigators that he planned to "take out" the president. Duran, who was indicted on 4 more counts, **Dec. 8**, pleaded not guilty to all the charges.

International

UN Approves Somali Withdrawal—The UN Security Council voted unanimously, **Nov. 4**, to take its remaining peacekeeping troops out of Somalia by the end of Mar. 1995. The resolution stated that the UN forces had been unable to bring rival factions together and establish a government. Nineteen countries were represented in the UN force. The UN mission had saved hundreds of thousands of people from starvation, but Somali clans had repeatedly failed to uphold agreements brokered by the UN.

Bosnian Conflict Intensifies—In late Oct. and early Nov., Bosnian government forces, supported by Bosnian Croats, went on the offensive and gained considerable territory from the Bosnian Serbs. Before long, however, the Serbs had recovered much of the lost ground. On **Nov. 7**, the Yugoslav War Crimes Tribunal in The Hague, the Netherlands, indicted a Serb, the former commander of a detention camp in Bosnia, for crimes against humanity. The Bosnian capital of Sarajevo came under heavy shelling, **Nov. 8**, as Serbs retaliated for the recent government offensive. The Clinton administration, **Nov. 12**, pulled out unilaterally from enforcement of the UN arms embargo against the parties involved in the Bosnian conflict. Pres. Bill Clinton said, **Nov. 14**, that Congress, sympathetic to the Bosnian government side, appeared ready to support an end to U.S. commitment to the embargo. NATO said, **Nov. 15**, that its enforcement of the UN embargo would continue without U.S. participation. On **Nov. 21**, 39 NATO warplanes from 4 countries—Britain, France, the Netherlands, and the U.S.—bombed a Serb air base in Croatia in response to Serb air attacks near Bihac, Bosnia, an enclave and UN-declared "safe area." The Bosnian Serbs then seized an estimated 450 UN peacekeepers and 30 UN military observers and held them hostage. Serbs fired missiles at 2 British aircraft on NATO patrol, **Nov. 22**, and about 50 NATO aircraft responded with an attack on 3 Serb missile bases, **Nov. 23**. UN Undersecretary Gen. Kofi Annan declined, **Nov. 28**, to approve a NATO request to step up air attacks, saying that it "would be tantamount to going to war with the Serbs." By month's end, the Serbs had virtually surrounded Bihac.

Palestinian Police Fire on Militants—Violent acts by Islamic militants brought a lethal response from Palestinian police in Gaza City in Nov. Israel and the Palestine Liberation Organization approved, **Nov. 8**, measures that sought to buttress the position of PLO Chairman Yasir Arafat against the radicals. Arafat and Israeli Prime Minister Yitzhak Rabin, meeting at a border crossing, agreed to step up the timetable for transfer of administrative powers in Gaza to the Palestinian National Authority (PNA). Israel also agreed to issue 10,000 more permits for Palestinians to work in Israel and to move up the discussion of Israeli military pullbacks in the West Bank. On **Nov. 11**, a suicide-bomber on a bicycle killed 3 Israeli soldiers in the Gaza Strip. Egyptian Pres. Hosni Mubarak warned, **Nov. 17**, that foreign donors must move up their timetable for providing financial assistance to the Palestinians; he said, "In Gaza there are no jobs, no education, no infrastructure, no health care." Palestinian police fired, **Nov. 18**, on militants in Gaza City. Police claimed that the demonstrators fired first. Clashes across the city then occurred, leaving 14 militants and 1 policeman dead and as many as 200 demonstrators and 10 police officers wounded. The militant Hamas organization appealed, **Nov. 18**, for calm, and Arafat, warned, **Nov. 21**, against further violence. The World Bank and 22 donor nations met in Brussels, **Nov. 29** and **30**. Participants agreed to grant more than $200 million to the PNA quickly.

German Chancellor Reelected—Chancellor Helmut Kohl of Germany won a 4th term, **Nov. 15**, in the Bundestag, the lower house of parliament. The Oct. national election had given his ruling coalition a 10-seat majority in the 672-member body. The defection of 3 coalition members in the secret ballot left Kohl with only 338 votes, one more than the bare majority that he needed.

Angola Signs Treaty With Rebels—The government of Angola, **Nov. 20**, signed a peace treaty with the rebel group the National Union for the Total Independence of Angola (UNITA). The Angolan civil war had claimed more than 500,000 lives over 19 years. Treaties signed in 1989 and 1991 had not led to peace, but the latest effort was the first in which rebels were to be granted a share of power. UNITA members would hold some political offices, and military personnel would be absorbed into the national army. In an ominous note, Jonas Savimbi, UNITA's longtime leader, did not attend the signing in Lusaka, the capital of Zambia.

General

Mother Charged in Killing of 2 Young Sons—A widespread search for 2 young brothers that had attracted national media coverage came to a sad ending in Nov. A South Carolina woman, Susan Smith, told police, **Oct. 25**, that an armed black man had taken her car in Union, SC, and driven off with her two sons—Michael, age 3, and Alexander, 14 months. Susan Smith and her estranged husband, David, who accepted his wife's account, appeared on television several times to appeal for the return of the boys. Police, **Nov. 3**, charged Susan Smith with the children's murders. They said that, with the boys strapped to safety seats, she had driven to the edge of a lake near Union, left the car, and allowed it to roll into the lake, where her sons drowned. Police suggested, **Nov. 5**, that a failed romance may have prompted Susan Smith to act; reportedly, a boyfriend had told her he was ending their relationship because he wanted nothing to do with the children.

Reagan Stricken With Alzheimer's Disease—In a letter released **Nov. 5**, former Pres. Ronald Reagan disclosed that he was suffering from Alzheimer's disease, the symptoms of which include gradual memory loss and physical decline. He reported the diagnosis in a handwritten letter, saying that he had had symptoms of the disease for about a year. In his letter, Reagan, 83, wrote that he had begun "the journey that will lead me into the sunset of my life."

Foreman Regains Heavyweight Title at 45—George Foreman entered the record books in Nov. when, at age 45, he became the oldest man ever to win a boxing championship. He had won the heavyweight title in 1973, only to lose it the next year to Muhammad Ali. He retired from the ring in 1977 and then resumed fighting in 1987. His phenomenal comeback succeeded in Las Vegas, **Nov. 5**, when he knocked out Michael Moorer in the 10th round to take the International Boxing Federation and World Boxing Association heavyweight titles.

DECEMBER 1994

National

Congress Approves Free-Trade Treaty—Congress in Dec. completed its approval of the tariff-cutting provisions of the so-called Uruguay Round of the General Agreement on Tariffs and Trade (GATT). The House approved GATT, **Nov. 29**, 288-146, and the Senate gave its approval **Dec. 1**, 76-24.

Two Parties Choose Leaders for 1995—In late Nov. and early Dec., House and Senate Republicans and Democrats elected their leaders for the new 104th Congress, which would convene in Jan. 1995. On **Nov. 30**, House Democrats elected Rep. Richard Gephardt (MO) as their leader. Rep. David Bonior (MI) was elected Democratic whip. On **Dec. 2**, Sen. Tom Daschle (SD) edged out Sen. Christopher Dodd (CT), 24-23, in the vote to choose the Democratic leader in the Senate. Wendell Ford was renamed the Democratic whip. Bob Dole (KS) was approved without opposition, **Dec. 2**, to continue as Republican leader of the Senate, and, as a result of the Nov. voting, he would become majority leader. However, Sen. Alan Simpson (WY), the Republican whip and an ally of Dole, was upset, 27-26, by the more conservative Sen. Trent Lott (MS), who was supported by many of the newer Republican senators. On **Dec. 5**, as expected, House Republicans unanimously designated Rep. Newt Gingrich (GA) as their candidate for Speaker of the House—and the Republican majority meant that he would be the next Speaker. Republicans picked Rep. Richard Armey (TX) as their majority leader. The position of majority whip went to Rep. Tom DeLay (TX), the victor in a 3-way race.

Surgeon General Resigns—Dr. Joycelyn Elders, the U.S. surgeon general, resigned in Dec. Her strong advocacy of sex education and her support for legalizing some narcotics had long made her a controversial figure in the Clinton administration. On **Dec. 1**, at a UN-sponsored conference in New York, she said that masturbation was "something that perhaps should be taught" to school children as part of the effort to curb the spread of AIDS. This remark created a new furor, and Elders resigned, **Dec. 9**, at the request of Pres. Bill Clinton.

Decline in Jobless Rate Continues—The nation's unemployment rate continued to decline and stood at 5.6% in Nov., the Labor Dept. said, **Dec. 2**. Some 372,000 new jobs were created in Nov. Alan Greenspan, chairman of the Federal Reserve Board, warned Congress, **Dec. 7**, that continued economic expansion would bring on inflationary pressures, which the Fed would seek to suppress. The Labor Dept. reported, **Dec. 13**, that an index of prices charged by producers for finished goods had jumped 0.5% in Nov. The department reported, **Dec. 14**, that the consumer price index had risen 0.3% in Nov. The Commerce Dept., **Dec. 20**, put the Oct. trade deficit at $10.14 billion, the second highest monthly figure ever. In its final calculation of the gross domestic product for the 3d quarter, the Commerce Dept. said, **Dec. 22**, that the GDP had grown at an annual rate of 4%. On Wall Street on **Dec. 30**, the last trading day of the year, the Dow Jones industrial average closed at 3834.44, a modest increase of 80.35 points or 2.1% for all of 1994.

Two Linked to Whitewater Plead Guilty—Robert Palmer, a property appraiser, pleaded guilty, **Dec. 5**, in U.S. District Court in Little Rock to having conspired to falsify documents related to loans made by Madison Guaranty in the 1980s. Palmer agreed to cooperate with the investigation of the so-called Whitewater Affair being conducted by independent counsel Kenneth Starr. In a separate case before the same court, Webster Hubbell, a friend and adviser to Pres. Bill Clinton who had resigned from a top Justice Dept. post in Mar., pleaded guilty, **Dec. 6**, to effectively embezzling some $400,000 from the Rose Law Firm in Little Rock and from its clients through the submission of false bills and vouchers. In addition to pleading guilty to mail fraud, he also pleaded guilty to tax evasion and agreed to cooperate with the Whitewater investigation.

Bentsen Resigns As Treasury Secretary—Pres. Bill Clinton, **Dec. 6**, accepted the resignation of Treasury Sec. Lloyd Bentsen and announced that he would nominate Robert Rubin, chairman of the White House National Economic Council, to succeed him.

Orange County, CA, Declares Bankruptcy—Sending shock waves throughout the nation, Orange County, CA, officials announced, **Dec. 6**, that the county would file for bankruptcy under the Bankruptcy Code's Chapter 9 provisions. It was the biggest bankruptcy filing by a government unit and the first involving a large U.S. county. News had leaked, **Dec. 1**, that the county's so-called main fund—which supported the county's cities and towns, school districts, and public agencies—faced $1.5 billion in losses from a risky investment strategy that had been employed by county treasurer Robert Citron. The strategy, which relied on the purchasing of financial instruments known as derivatives, failed because the success of the investment was linked to the performance of fixed income securities and depended on interest rates falling. As interest rates rose, the risky strategy failed. Citron resigned, **Dec. 5**.

Skirmishing Over Tax Cut Begins—Pres. Bill Clinton and House Democratic Leader Richard Gephardt (MO) both put forward proposals in Dec. to cut taxes for the middle class, and Republicans were expected to unveil their own plan soon. Gephardt, saying that House Democrats would be working more as an equal partner with the White House in the formulation of policy, **Dec. 13** endorsed a tax cut for all families earning less than $75,000 a year. Clinton proposed, **Dec. 15**, a "middle-class bill of rights" that included $60 billion in tax

cuts over 5 years. Clinton said, **Dec. 19**, that he would pay for the reduction by overhauling federal agencies and backing cuts of $76 billion in federal spending over 5 years.

More Shots Fired at White House—Two months after a gunman had fired semiautomatic rounds at the White House, another shooting incident occurred early on **Dec. 17**. At least 4 small-caliber bullets were fired at the White House while Pres. Clinton and his family were asleep; no one was injured. One bullet went through the window of a state dining room.

Gingrich Yields on $4.5 Million Book Advance—Rep. Newt Gingrich (R, GA), who would become Speaker of the House when the new Congress convened in Jan., gave up a $4.5 million advance in Dec. for 2 books. Gingrich was to get the sum from HarperCollins Publishing Inc. for a book on conservative political philosophy and for providing a commentary for an anthology of writings on democracy. HarperCollins was owned by News Corp. Ltd., an Australian-based conglomerate headed by Rupert Murdoch, a naturalized U.S. citizen from Australia. News Corp. also owned Fox Broadcasting Co., and the U.S. Federal Communications Commission was examining whether that ownership violated U.S. laws limiting foreign control of television stations. David Bonior (D, MI), the House Democratic whip, said, **Dec. 22**, that the $4.5 million was a Christmas gift from Murdoch. Bob Dole (KS), the Senate Republican leader, said, **Dec. 29**, that the controversy over the book deal could distract attention from the GOP legislative agenda. Gingrich said, **Dec. 30**, that he would give up the $4.5 million advance but would go ahead with the books, for which he would receive royalties.

Suit Against Clinton Postponed—Federal District Court Judge Susan Webber Wright ruled, **Dec. 28**, that a sexual-harassment lawsuit filed against Pres. Clinton could not be tried until after Clinton left the White House. The plaintiff, Paula Jones, had waited nearly 3 years before filing the suit. The judge wrote that the president's responsibilities justified a temporary and limited immunity from trial. She also held, however, that Jones's attorneys could gather facts in the case; that could include interviewing the president.

CIA Director Resigns—R. James Woolsey, Jr., Director of Central Intelligence, resigned, **Dec. 28**. Woolsey had been criticized for his handling of the Aldrich Ames spy case and for not dealing sternly with officers who had failed to discover Ames's espionage more quickly. Woolsey had also been criticized for not revamping the CIA in light of the post-Soviet environment.

International

British, Sinn Fein Leaders Meet—British officials and representatives of Sinn Fein, the political wing of the Irish Republican Army, began talks in Dec. that sought to end 25 years of violence in Northern Ireland. British Prime Minister John Major, **Dec. 1**, said that the forthcoming talks would be "exploratory"; he wanted the IRA to disarm and make other concessions before more substantive talks began. On **Dec. 9**, the talks opened, the first time in 22 years that British officials and Sinn Fein members had met publicly. Ireland's parliament, **Dec. 15**, elected John Bruton of the Fine Gael party as the country's new prime minister; he said that achieving peace in Northern Ireland would be his top priority.

Truce Signed in Bosnian Conflict—The antagonists in the Bosnian civil war signed a truce in Dec. Earlier, on **Dec. 3**, UN Secretary Gen. Boutros Boutros-Ghali acknowledged that the UN and NATO were preparing for possible withdrawal of their forces from Bosnia and Herzegovina. Bosnian Serbs, **Dec. 8**, released 55 Canadian hostages, but still held 300 UN troops, as a means of discouraging NATO air strikes on Serb positions. The Serbs freed 187 French, Russian, and Ukrainian peacekeepers, **Dec. 10**, but on the same day Serb soldiers hijacked a UN fuel convoy near Sarajevo. Former U.S. Pres. Jimmy Carter, at the invitation of Bosnian Serb leader Radovan Karadzic, went to Bosnia to meet with leaders of the warring factions. Bosnian President Alija Izetbegovic, after meeting with Carter, **Dec. 18**, said that his government would agree only to a short-term cease-fire rather than to a long one that would tend to solidify territorial gains by the Serbs. Carter—who was in Bosnia as a private citizen, not as a representative of the U.S. government—announced, **Dec. 20**, that the parties had agreed to a cease-fire. In a settlement negotiated primarily by Lt. Gen. Sir Michael Rose, the UN commander in Bosnia, the adversaries signed, **Dec. 31**, an agreement—which was to last 4 months—providing for a cessation of hostilities.

Russian Troops Invade Rebel Republic—Chechnya, a republic in southern Russia, became a land of bloody strife in Dec. The Chechens, who were mostly Muslims, had been subdued by the Russians in the 19th century. Their current president, Dzhokhar Dudayev, had declared Chechen independence from Russia in 1991. Chechnya's oil reserves made the republic important to Russia. Russian army forces invaded Chechnya, **Dec. 11**, and began bombing raids on **Dec. 13**. After peace talks collapsed, Pres. Boris Yeltsin warned that the army would attack the capital of Grozny if the rebels did not surrender. The Russian parliament, **Dec. 14**, voted, 289-4, to oppose Yeltsin's use of force. Bombing of the capital began **Dec. 18**. Yeltsin, in a televised speech **Dec. 27**, ordered a cessation of bombing raids that could result in civilian fatalities, but within hours Russian planes bombed an orphanage and other civilian sites in the capital. This raised doubts among international observers that Yeltsin was fully in control of the situation. The U.S. State Dept., **Dec. 29**, criticized the attacks on civilians. On **Dec. 31**, Russian forces launched a full air and ground attack on Grozny. Although the presidential palace was in flames, Dudayev refused to surrender.

Italian Premier Resigns—Premier Silvio Berlusconi of Italy resigned in Dec. The nation's experiment in conservative government had begun to fray over a period of several months as a result of policy disputes within the ruling coalition. After one coalition partner, the Northern League, deserted Berlusconi's Forza Italia party on a key issue, **Dec. 14**, Berlusconi, **Dec. 15**, asked for a parliamentary vote of confidence. On **Dec. 21**, all 4 Northern League cabinet ministers resigned from the government, and Berlusconi, **Dec. 22**, choosing to avoid a probable defeat in parliament and take his chances in an election, submitted his resignation to Pres. Oscar Luigi Scalfaro. Berlusconi would head a caretaker government until new elections were held.

North Koreans Down U.S. Helicopter—North Korea shot down a U.S. Army reconnaissance helicopter that was flying over its territory, **Dec. 17**. Chief Warrant Officers David Hilemon and Bobby Hall were the only occupants of the copter. Hilemon died of his injuries, and Hall was taken prisoner. While conducting an investigation, North Korea declined to discuss the matter with the United States. U.S. and North Korean officials met at the village of Panmunjom, in the demilitarized zone on the border between North and South Korea, **Dec. 21**. The Koreans returned Hilemon's body, **Dec. 22**. On **Dec. 29**, North Korea released a statement that it said Hall had signed in which he admitted to a "criminal action." Hall was released, **Dec. 30**, after U.S. Deputy Assist. Sec. of State Thomas Hubbard met with Korean officials in the North Korean capital of Pyongyang. The U.S. agreed to express its "sincere regret" over the incident.

Mexican Peso Tumbles in Value—Mexico allowed the peso to fall sharply in value in Dec. as a means of making Mexican products more affordable on world markets. Mexico was experiencing large and growing international trade deficits. Effectively devaluing the peso, Mexico allowed the currency to fall nearly 15% against the U.S. dollar, **Dec. 20**. On **Dec. 21**, the government allowed the peso to float freely in currency markets, triggering an additional

15% decline in its value. The peso's decline, which continued after Dec. 21, caused sharp selloffs and drops in share prices on the Mexican stock exchange and of Mexican stocks listed on the New York Stock Exchange.

General

Jury Selection Completed in Simpson Case—The protracted and difficult process of selecting a jury in the trial of O. J. Simpson for 2 murders was completed, **Dec. 8**, with the seating of 12 alternate jurors. Those selected included 7 blacks, 4 whites, and 1 Hispanic person. The main jury, chosen in Nov., consisted of 8 blacks, 2 Hispanics, 1 white, and 1 person identified as half white and half Native American. Eight of the jurors were women, and 4 were men. The makeup of the jury and its likely sympathies were the subject of intense discussion in the media. Simpson was accused of fatally stabbing his former wife Nicole and a friend of hers, Ronald Goldman, in June 1994.

Mail Bomb Explodes, Kills Ad Executive—Early in the morning, **Dec. 11**, a mail bomb exploded in the kitchen of a North Caldwell, NJ, advertising executive. Federal Bureau of Investigation officials believed the bomb to be the work of the serial bomber they called *Unabomber*, an FBI condensation of "university and airline bomber." The Unabomber had been spotted only once in connection with the commitment of a crime, and authorities had only a rough sketch of a man wearing sunglasses and a cape. His attacks were a statement against modern technology, and the victims were chosen accordingly. He had been linked to 14 other bombings since 1978. The string of bombings had killed 2 men and wounded 22 others and had become more violent as the bombings progressed. In the past, targets of the bomber were members of the corporate and academic communities. This incident was unique because the victim, Thomas Mosser, was the first individual who worked in advertising to be targeted by the bomber. Mosser had recently gained public attention when he was promoted to general manager of leading firm Young and Rubicam Inc. Worldwide.

JANUARY 1995

National

Congress Convenes With GOP in Control—The curtain rose, **Jan. 4**, on the first day of business for the 104th Congress, whose members had been elected in Nov. 1994. Not since 1953 had a new Congress convened with Republicans in control of both houses. The GOP margin in the Senate was 53-47, and in the House, 230-204, with 1 independent. Sen. Bob Dole (R, KS) became Senate Majority Leader, and Rep. Newt Gingrich (R, GA) was formally elected Speaker of the House. Republicans became chairpersons of all Senate and House committees. The Senate had 11 new members, all Republicans. Almost all (73) of the 86 new members of the House were Republicans. Eight women, a record high, were members of the Senate. The House included 47 women, 38 blacks, 17 Hispanics, and 4 members of Asian descent, all figures unchanged from the previous Congress. **Jan. 4** and the early hours of **Jan. 5** proved to be productive for the House, as the Republican leadership kept the chamber in session for 14 hours. The purpose was to fulfill a pledge most Republicans had made to reform House rules. During the session the House voted to abolish 3 committees and 25 subcommittees and to eliminate about one-third (622) of all committee staff positions. The members also limited the service of a committee or subcommittee chairperson to 3 consecutive terms, and the tenure of a Speaker was limited to no more than 4 consecutive terms. All committee meetings and hearings, with rare exceptions, would be open to the public and to broadcast. Proxy voting in committees was forbidden, and publication of all votes in committee was required. Voting on the floor, permitted since 1993 under limited circumstances, by delegates from the District of Columbia and U.S. territories was banned. Many Democrats supported these and other rules changes. The minority did offer broad opposition to a proposal requiring a three-fifths majority to increase income taxes, but that rule change passed as well, 279-152.

Gingrich Finds Himself in the News—The new Speaker of the House, Newt Gingrich, was in the news often in Jan., sometimes in unwelcome ways. On **Jan. 4**, the day he was elected Speaker, CBS publicized that his mother, Kathleen Gingrich, had quoted him as saying that First Lady Hillary Rodham Clinton was a "bitch." During a taped interview with Connie Chung for the CBS news-magazine *Eye to Eye*, Mrs. Gingrich quoted her son after Chung assured her that the report of what he had said would be "just between you and me." On **Jan. 9**, Newt Gingrich asked for the resignation of Christina Jeffrey, a supporter whom he had appointed House historian, after it was revealed that she had once criticized a school program on the Holocaust for not including the "Nazi point of view" or that of the Ku Klux Klan. The dispute over a book contract that Gingrich had signed with HarperCollins flared anew in Jan. The *New York Daily News* reported, **Jan. 12**, that Gingrich had met with Rupert Murdoch, owner of the book company, in Nov., prior to agreeing to a contract under which Gingrich originally was to receive a $4.5 million advance. The two had discussed legal matters relating to Murdoch's broadcasting interests. On **Jan. 13**, Mrs. Clinton gave the Speaker and his mother a private tour of the White House as a gesture of friendship in the wake of the CBS incident. Gingrich said, **Jan. 17**, that he had promised no help to Murdoch during their Nov. meeting.

Congress to Comply With Its Own Laws—The first piece of legislation approved by the Republican-dominated Congress required that the Senate and House abide by a number of civil rights and labor statutes that it had applied to other Americans. Congress had been criticized for often exempting itself from such legislation, and the Contract With America, signed by many Republican candidates for the House in 1994, promised to rectify the situation. The law would extend various kinds of coverage to 30,000 congressional employees. For the first time they would be guaranteed a minimum wage, a maximum workday length, and time-and-a-half pay for overtime. Under the new law, they could bring labor-related claims against members of Congress, and could form unions. Employees were also given the protections of the 1964 Civil Rights Act, a 1967 age-discrimination act, the 1990 Americans With Disabilities Act, and the 1993 Family and Medical Leave Act. The House approved a bill, **Jan. 5**, 429-0, and the Senate approved its version, **Jan. 11**, 98-1. The House accepted the Senate bill, **Jan. 17**, and Pres. Bill Clinton signed it **Jan. 23**.

Jobless Rate Lowest Since 1990—The Labor Dept. reported, **Jan. 6**, that the unemployment rate in Dec. had stood at 5.4%, down 0.2 % from Nov., and at the lowest level since July 1990. Some 256,000 new jobs were created in Dec. In all of 1994, the economy added 3.5 million jobs, the highest annual total since 1984. The department said, **Jan. 10**, that in 1994 as a whole the prices charged by producers for finished goods had risen only 1.7%; the increase in Dec. had been 0.2%. The consumer price index was also up 0.2 % in Dec., the department announced, **Jan. 11**; for the entire year, consumer prices were up 2.7%. The Commerce Dept. said, **Jan. 19**, that the U.S. had posted a trade deficit of $10.53 billion in Nov. Commerce Dept. figures released **Jan. 27** showed that economic growth was accelerating at year's end. In the 4th quarter of 1994, the economy expanded at an annual rate of 4.5%, and the rate for the year was 4%, the highest level for an entire year since 1984.

New Treasury Secretary Confirmed—The Senate Finance Committee and the full Senate, **Jan. 10**, unanimously approved Pres. Clinton's nomination of Robert Rubin to serve as Secretary of the Treasury.

Democratic Party Names New Leaders—In the wake of a shocking defeat in the Nov. 1994 elections, delegates

to a meeting of the Democratic National Committee chose new party leaders in Jan. On **Jan. 21**, delegates chose Sen. Christopher Dodd (CT) as the committee's general chairman and named Donald Fowler, a former party leader in South Carolina, as national chairman and operating officer.

Clinton Gives State of Union Address—Pres. Clinton delivered his annual State of the Union address to the new Republican-led Congress, **Jan. 24**, and he showed both conciliation and defiance. He echoed GOP calls for a federal government that was smaller and more efficient and noted that he had eliminated hundreds of programs and cut 100,000 positions from the federal work force. He said that nearly 6 million jobs had been created in the past 2 years and that the combined rate of unemployment and inflation was at a 25-year low. He called for tax cuts to stimulate savings and for parents of college students, backed an increase in the minimum wage, and renewed his support for welfare and health-care reform. Noting that "a lot of people laid down their seats in Congress so that police officers and kids wouldn't have to lay down their lives under a hail of assault-weapon attack," he vowed to thwart any attempt to repeal the ban on assault weapons passed in 1994. In the Republican response to the president's address, Gov. Christine Todd Whitman (NJ), **Jan. 24**, said that the nationwide Republican revolution had been led by Republican governors who had cut taxes and spending and who had taken on the "tyranny of expanding welfare state policies." Whitman's address was noteworthy in that she was the first governor to be formally selected to reply to a president's State of the Union address; this was also the first time a woman gave such a reply.

House OKs Balanced-Budget Amendment—The U.S. House of Representatives, **Jan. 26**, approved, 300-132, an amendment to the U.S. Constitution that would require Congress, in each year beginning in fiscal year 2002, to approve a federal budget that was balanced. The language, however, contained a loophole allowing the approval of a budget with a deficit, providing that it received the support of three-fifths of the members of both houses. The so-called Contract With America, signed in 1994 by most Republican candidates for the House, had included a promise to pass a balanced-budget amendment. The contract had endorsed an amendment containing a provision that three-fifths of the full membership of Congress would have to approve any increase in taxes, but this approach failed in the House after Senate Majority Leader Bob Dole (R, KS) said, **Jan. 2**, that the Senate would not approve the requirement that only a super-majority could raise taxes. Even without this controversial provision, the proposed amendment received only 12 votes more than the two-thirds majority required for approving a constitutional amendment. Seventy-two Democrats supported the amendment; only 2 Republicans voted against it.

International

Shaky Truce Begins in Bosnia—A 4-month truce between the Muslim-led government and Bosnian Serbs went into effect in Bosnia, **Jan. 1**. On **Jan. 2**, Kresimir Zubak, the Bosnian Croat leader, also signed the truce. Under the agreement, the rival forces were to withdraw from the front line and allow UN peacekeepers to occupy the ground between them. Pres. Franjo Tudjman said, **Jan. 12**, that Croatia would not allow UN peacekeepers to remain in his country after their current mandate expired in Mar.; he said that the 12,000 troops did not "provide conditions necessary for establishing lasting peace and order." By mid-Jan, the truce in Bosnia began to fray. The Bosnian army seized 2 villages in NW Bosnia. Rebel Serbs in Croatia, **Jan. 30**, refused to accept a proposal, drafted by international mediators, that gave them limited autonomy.

Russians Advance Slowly in Chechnya—Russian forces attacking Grozny, the capital of the rebel Russian republic of Chechnya, advanced slowly against heavy resistance in Jan. The defenders, **Jan. 2**, turned back the first Russian attack on the capital, inflicting heavy casualties. They beat back a second assault, **Jan. 3**. Pres. Boris Yeltsin of Russia, **Jan. 4**, ordered an end to the bombing of Grozny, but reports of bombing continued. Chancellor Helmut Kohl of Germany warned, **Jan. 8**, that Russian brutality in Chechnya could jeopardize relations between Russia and the West. Russia declared a cease-fire, **Jan. 10**, but fighting resumed within hours. Pres. Dzhokhar Dudayev of Chechnya said, **Jan. 11**, that his forces could not defeat Russia and that a negotiated settlement would be necessary. The U.S. State Dept. said, **Jan. 11**, that Russia had broken an international agreement by making major troop movements without providing notification. The lower house of the Russian parliament recommended, **Jan. 13**, that Yeltsin seek a political solution in Chechnya. Public opinion in Russia had been influenced by gruesome photographs of casualties shown on television. Yeltsin said, **Jan. 18**, that he would not negotiate with Dudayev. The Russians, **Jan. 19**, captured the presidential palace in Grozny. Yeltsin, **Jan. 19**, removed 3 deputy defense ministers who had criticized the war. Russian forces renewed their attack on the rest of Grozny, **Jan. 24**, but the Chechens still held ground inside the city. The residents of the capital had no water or electricity and only limited heat and food.

Clinton Acts in Mexican Currency Crisis—Pres. Clinton sidestepped Congress in Jan. and took direct action to avert a financial collapse in Mexico, including a default on international debts. Earlier, on **Jan. 3**, in response to a sharp fall in the value of the peso, Pres. Ernesto Zedillo Ponce de Leon of Mexico proposed reductions in federal spending and a continuing 7% ceiling for wage increases. Mexico's trading partners, led by the U.S., supported the plan by extending an $18 billion line of credit. Clinton and leaders of the U.S. Congress agreed, **Jan. 12**, on a bailout package that would grant Mexico as much as $40 billion in loan guarantees, but the plan would require the approval of the Senate and House. On **Jan. 17**, in another attempt to bring stability and calm to their country, Zedillo and the leaders of Mexico's 4 largest political parties signed an agreement providing for a broad-based overhaul of election laws, including those relating to fundraising and spending. Government and opposition leaders also agreed to hold new elections in the states of Chiapas and Tabasco, where widespread fraud had been alleged in 1994. Meanwhile, the Mexican stock market and the value of the peso continued to slide. After the U.S. Congress failed to move quickly, Clinton, **Jan. 31**, invoked his emergency authority to provide a $20 billion loan to Mexico. The U.S. also obtained pledges of support from the International Monetary Fund and the Bank for International Settlements. Canada, Argentina, Brazil, and Colombia were other donors. The overall commitment to Mexico now stood at $49.5 billion. The $20 billion from the U.S. would consist of short-term loans and longer-term loan guarantees. As collateral, buyers of oil from the Mexican national oil company would deposit part of their payments into a U.S. Federal Reserve Bank fund.

Independent Becomes Premier of Italy—Lamberto Dini, who had served as treasury minister in the government of Silvio Berlusconi in 1994, became the new premier of Italy in Jan. Not identified with any party, Dini had previously served as director general of the Bank of Italy. In Berlusconi's cabinet, Dini had brought out an austerity budget that projected large spending cuts to reduce the country's huge deficit. Asked, **Jan. 13**, by Pres. Oscar Scalfaro, who chose not to call new elections, to form a new government, Dini announced his cabinet, also politically neutral, **Jan. 17**, and became premier **Jan. 18**.

U.S. Eases North Korea Trade Embargo—The Clinton administration announced, **Jan. 20**, that it would ease the trade embargo in effect against North Korea since the Korean War. The U.S. and North Korea had agreed in 1994 that North Korea would end its nuclear-development pro-

gram in return for U.S. oversight of construction of 2 light-water nuclear reactors, from which it was difficult to extract weapons-grade plutonium. The U.S. would also put together a $4 billion package of aid to pay for the reactors, to be used to generate electricity. In its Jan. gesture toward the North, the U.S. said American visitors could use credit cards. Phone calls between the countries would now be allowed. Each country could open news bureaus in the other, and the U.S. would accept imports from North Korea of magnesite, a mineral used in steel production.

Bombing in Israel Kills 21—Two Palestinians killed 18 Israeli soldiers, a civilian, and themselves, **Jan. 22**, when they detonated explosives outside a military camp in central Israel. About 65 people were injured. Islamic Jihad claimed responsibility for the bombing, which it said was in retaliation for the recent killing of several Palestinians. The Israeli government said negotiations with the Palestine Liberation Organization would continue, but Israel temporarily closed its border to Palestinians. Palestinian National Authority police said, **Jan. 25**, that they had arrested more than 20 Jihad militants. The Israeli cabinet, **Jan. 25**, approved construction of 2,200 housing units for Israeli settlers on the West Bank, near Jerusalem; the move appeared certain to increase tensions in the area.

U.S., Vietnam to Exchange Diplomats—The U.S. and Vietnam agreed, **Jan. 28**, to exchange low-level diplomats and open liaison offices in each other's capital city. The U.S. diplomats would live in a new embassy in Hanoi, and the Vietnamese, at the embassy building in Washington, DC, formerly occupied by South Vietnam. Vietnam agreed to pay $208.5 million to settle claims on U.S. property confiscated at the end of the Vietnam War. The U.S. would unfreeze $130 million in Vietnamese assets in the U.S.

UN Approves Peacekeepers in Haiti—U.S. Secretary of Defense William Perry said, **Jan. 29**, that Haiti was "safe and secure" and that U.S. troops had put an end to all but occasional incidents of violence. The UN Security Council, **Jan. 30**, authorized deployment of 6,000 peacekeepers to train Haiti's police and military and to help prepare for elections. They would take over from U.S. troops at the end of Mar. and remain in Haiti until Feb. 1996.

Bomb Kills 42 on Algiers Street—The conflict in Algeria between the military-run government and Muslim fundamentalists seeking to overthrow it reached a new high in bloodshed, **Jan. 30**, when a car bomb exploded in Algiers and claimed 42 lives. Nearly 300 people were wounded.

General

Labor Dispute Erases Half of Hockey Season—Almost one-half of the National Hockey League season was lost to a dispute between players and owners that was settled in Jan. The previous contract expired in 1993. In Oct. 1994, owners postponed the start of the 1994-95 season in the absence of a contract. On **Jan. 11**, the day by which owners said agreement would have to be reached if the season were to be salvaged, representatives of the NHL Players Association accepted the owners' final offer. With respect to one of the principal matters at issue, it was agreed that a player age 32 or older with 4 years of playing experience could become an unrestricted free agent, able to join a new team that would not be required to compensate the player's former team. The season began **Jan. 20**, with the teams playing a 48-game schedule instead of the usual 84.

Earthquake Kills 5,000 in Japan—An earthquake that measured 7.2 on the Richter scale devastated the city of Kobe and the surrounding area in W Japan, **Jan. 17**. More than 5,000 people were killed, and 26,500 were injured. Many buildings collapsed, and hundreds of fires were started. Some 300,000 people had to move to shelters, and 1 million were without water. More than 100,000 buildings were destroyed or damaged. The quake shut down one of the Far East's major ports and disrupted the flow of world trade.

Superb 30,000-Year-Old Art Found in France—Discovery of a magnificent display of Paleolithic cave art was announced in Paris in Jan. On **Dec. 18**, three explorers found a cave in the Ardèche region of S France, an area already known as a home for ancient cave art. A draft from the ground indicated that a larger space lay beyond the cave entrance, and on **Dec. 24** the explorers first saw the paintings. They soon found 4 large halls, as much as 70 yd long and 40 yd wide, joined by smaller galleries, all filled with paintings and engravings. Archaeologists soon came to the cave and proclaimed the art it contained one of the greatest finds ever of ancient art. The 300 images, ranging in size to as much as 12 ft long, had been done in yellow ochre, charcoal, and hematite. They included portraits of rhinos, bears, mammoths, oxen, and other animals. Skulls and bones of bears, knives, and remains of fireplaces were also found. In announcing the discovery, **Jan. 18**, the Minister of Culture, Jacques Toubon, said the cave was "of exceptional value because of its size and variety and because it was found undisturbed." There were no plans to open the cave to tourism. The French Culture Ministry announced, **June 7**, that testing done on charcoal pigments in the paintings dated them between 30,340 and 32,410 years old.

Opening Arguments Given in Simpson Case—The prosecution and defense presented their opening arguments to the jury in Jan. in the trial of O. J. Simpson for the murder of his ex-wife, Nicole Brown Simpson, and a friend of hers, Ronald Goldman. Earlier, on **Jan. 18**, Judge Lance Ito replaced 2 jurors with alternates, leaving a jury of 8 blacks, 2 whites, 1 Hispanic, and 1 person identified as half white and half Native American. Ito held, **Jan. 18**, that the jury could hear allegations that Simpson had sometimes attacked and beaten Nicole Brown Simpson during their marriage. Deputy District Attorneys Marcia Clark, the chief prosecutor, and Christopher Darden, in their opening statements, **Jan. 24**, said that a "trail of blood" would establish that Simpson had committed the murders. Darden said, "He killed her because he couldn't have her. And if he couldn't have her, he didn't want anyone else to have her." Johnnie Cochran, Jr., the lead defense attorney, addressed the jury, **Jan. 25**. Other members of the defense "dream team" included Robert Shapiro, F. Lee Bailey, and Alan Dershowitz. Cochran said there was no trail of blood because police work had been sloppy, and he suggested that some evidence may have been fabricated. He said testimony would be taken from 14 witnesses whom he had not previously identified. A book by Simpson, *I Want to Tell You*, published **Jan. 27**, asserted that he was innocent; Simpson wrote that the book was a response to the 300,000 letters he had received. After the prosecution charged that the defense had violated the law by not disclosing some of its witnesses earlier, Ito, **Jan. 30**, criticized the defense for seeking an "unfair tactical advantage."

49ers Win Super Bowl for Fifth Time—The San Francisco 49ers defeated the San Diego Chargers, 49-26, **Jan. 29**, in Super Bowl XXIX. Capturing their first title since 1990, the 49ers became the first team to win 5 Super Bowls. For the 11th consecutive time the champion of the National Football Conference prevailed over the representative of the American Football Conference, and many of those contests, including this one, were routs. The 49ers scored on their first 3 possessions, a record, and quarterback Steve Young threw 6 touchdown passes, breaking a Super Bowl record of 5 set by a former 49er, Joe Montana. Young, the league's most valuable player for the regular season, received the same honor for the title game, which was played in Joe Robbie Stadium in Miami.

FEBRUARY 1995

National

Congress Targets Unfunded Mandates—The Senate, **Jan. 27** (86-10), and the House, **Feb. 1** (360-74), approved bills making it difficult for Congress to pass laws that required action by the states and cities but that did not provide federal funds for implementation. Such laws and regulations, often related to pollution or workplace safety, had become common in the past few years. Action on these so-called unfunded mandates had been promised in the Contract With America signed by most Republican candidates for the House in 1994. Differences in the House and Senate bills would be reconciled by a conference committee.

Annual Trade Gap Tops $100 Billion—The U.S. deficit in trade in goods and services soared in 1994 to its highest level in 6 years, according to the Commerce Dept. in Feb. Earlier, on **Feb. 1**, the Federal Reserve Board increased the federal funds rate (the interest rate banks charged each other for overnight loans) by 0.5 percentage point to 6% and increased the discount rate (the interest rate charged by the Fed on loans to commercial banks) by 0.5 percentage point to 5.25%. Both rates were at their highest levels in 3 years. In response to these increases, most major banks raised their prime rate from 8.5% to 9.0%. The Commerce Dept. said, **Feb. 1**, that the index of leading economic indicators had edged upward 0.1% in Dec. The Labor Dept. reported, **Feb. 3**, that unemployment had advanced by 0.3 percentage point in Jan., to 5.7%. The department said, **Feb. 10**, that prices charged by producers for finished goods had risen 0.3% in Jan., and it reported, **Feb. 15**, that consumer prices had also risen 0.3% in the same month. The 1994 trade-deficit figure of $108.1 billion, announced **Feb. 17**, was 42% higher than the 1993 deficit and was the largest for a calendar year since 1988. On Wall Street, on **Feb. 23**, the Dow Jones industrial average closed above 4,000 for the first time, at 4003.33. Investors had responded favorably to the interest-rate increases by the Federal Reserve Board, which were aimed at checking inflation. Inflation had remained low and seemed unlikely to get out of control as the economy showed signs of slowing down.

Surgeon General Nominee Under Fire—On **Feb. 2**, Pres. Bill Clinton nominated Dr. Henry Foster to succeed Dr. Joycelyn Elders as U.S. Surgeon General. Foster was the former chairman of the Department of Obstetrics and Gynecology at Meharry Medical College, a predominantly black school in Nashville, TN. He had gained recognition for a program that encouraged teenagers to delay becoming sexually active. Within days of his nomination, Foster became ensnarled in a dispute with opponents of abortion over the number of abortions he had performed. On **Feb. 8**, he said that he had determined that he had performed 39 abortions and had participated in a clinical study of a vaginal suppository that had resulted in the termination of 55 pregnancies.

Clinton Backs $5.15 Minimum Wage—Pres. Clinton, who had previously endorsed an increase in the minimum wage, announced, **Feb. 3**, that he favored a minimum of $5.15, ninety cents higher than the current figure of $4.25. He said that if the minimum were not increased, in terms of real buying power it would stand at a 40-year low in 1996.

Clinton Budget Includes Middle-Class Tax Cuts—Pres. Clinton submitted to Congress his budget for the 1996 fiscal year, **Feb. 6**. As he had promised previously, the budget contained tax breaks for the middle class, including a tax credit for each child under 13 and a tax deduction for families or individuals who paid college tuition. Clinton's budget cut spending by $144 billion over 5 years, principally by continuing for 2 more years the cap on discretionary ("nonentitlement") spending. Administrative changes in entitlement programs would save $29 billion. The budget would eliminate 130 programs and consolidate 270, many of them in education and vocational training. The budget put spending at $1.61 trillion and projected continuing annual deficits of close to $200 billion through 2005.

House Approves Line-Item Veto—The House of Representatives, **Feb. 6**, approved, 294-134, a bill that dealt with a concept long advocated by conservatives—the line-item veto. The bill would give the president the authority to reject individual spending items in legislation before he signed the overall bill. Under the House line-item veto bill, the rejection by a president of a specific spending item would hold unless both houses of Congress overturned his veto within 20 days by two-thirds majorities. The line-item veto was already available to governors in 43 states. It had been endorsed in 1994 by most Republican candidates for the House in their Contract With America.

Defendant Pleads Guilty in UN Bomb Plot—The trial in U.S. federal court in New York of 12 men in a plot to bomb the UN building and kill political leaders took a surprise turn, **Feb. 6.** One of the accused men, Siddig Ibrahim Siddig Ali, changed his plea to guilty and said that Sheik Omar Abdel Rahman, one of his fellow defendants, had played a principal role in the conspiracy. Siddig Ali told the court that, in addition to the UN, the conspirators planned to bomb an FBI office, a bridge, and 2 tunnels. Siddig Ali said he had been Abdel Rahman's bodyguard and translator.

"Mastermind" in New York Bombing Arrested—The alleged mastermind in the 1993 bombing of the World Trade Center in New York was arrested in Islamabad, Pakistan, in Feb. The explosion killed 6 people and injured more than 1,000. Evidence heard during the trial of 4 other men in connection with the bombing had pointed toward Ramzi Ahmed Yousef as the leader of the plot. Authorities believed that Yousef had flown to New York in Sept. 1992 and then assembled the group of men who helped him plan the bombing. He flew from New York to Pakistan hours after the bomb went off. Yousef was arrested **Feb. 7** and flown to New York **Feb. 8.** In U.S. District Court in New York City, **Feb. 9,** Yousef pleaded not guilty to 11 counts.

Clinton Picks Ex-General to Head CIA—Pres. Clinton, **Feb. 8,** nominated Air Force General (ret.) Michael Carns as Director of Central Intelligence. If approved by the Senate, he would succeed R. James Woolsey, who had resigned in Jan. Carns, who had participated in 200 combat missions during the Vietnam War, had also served as vice chief of staff of the Air Force.

Republicans Decide on Presidential Race—The contest for the 1996 Republican presidential nomination began to take shape in Feb., although several prominent leaders would not be seeking the prize. Already, in Jan., former Defense Sec. Dick Cheney and Jack Kemp, a former congressman and secretary of housing aid urban development, took themselves out of consideration. Kemp said he was not willing to make the effort to raise the funds needed for a campaign. On **Feb. 9,** former Vice Pres. Dan Quayle, who had strong support among GOP conservatives, especially those concerned about family values, announced that he would not run. Within the past 3 months, Quayle had been hospitalized twice, for the treatment of blood clots in his lungs and for the removal of a benign tumor from his appendix. Ralph Reed, executive director of the Christian Coalition, said, **Feb. 10,** that evangelical Christians would not support the Republican ticket if either the presidential or the vice presidential nominee supported abortion rights. At a campaign dinner in Dallas, **Feb. 23,** Sen. Phil Gramm (TX) raised $4.1 million, believed to be a record for such an event, and on **Feb. 24** he announced his candidacy for president. Gramm, an outspoken conservative on fiscal and social issues, declared that he was committed to balancing the federal budget and pledged to overhaul the welfare system and end affirmative-action job programs. On **Feb. 27,** Gov. William Weld (MA), a rare liberal on social issues within GOP ranks, said he would not run for president. Lamar Alexander, a former governor of Tennessee and secretary of education, entered the contest **Feb. 28.** Positioning himself as an outsider, he was harshly critical of the Washington establishment and urged that many federal programs be eliminated and responsibility given to state governments.

House Takes New Approach on Crime—In Feb., the Republican-controlled House approved a bill that adopted a new approach to the nation's crime problem. In 1994, Pres.

Clinton had signed a $30 billion bill that provided $8.8 billion to hire 100,000 new police officers and over $6 billion for crime-prevention programs. On **Feb. 14,** in a 238-192 vote that closely followed party lines, the House voted to kill those outlays in favor of $10 billion in block grants to local authorities to use as they chose to fight crime. Republicans said that local officials were better able than the federal government to decide how to spend money against crime.

NAACP Replaces Its Chairman—Facing a $4 million debt and concerned about allegations of mismanagement against its chairman, the board of directors of the National Association for the Advancement of Colored People (NAACP) voted to replace him in Feb. William Gibson, a dentist, had served as chairman since 1985. The recent past had been difficult for the NAACP; in 1994 executive director Benjamin Chavis had been dismissed. On **Feb. 18,** the board, by a 30-29 margin, elected as chairwoman Myrlie Evers-Williams, widow of the assassinated civil rights leader Medgar Evers. She had been commissioner of the Los Angeles Board of Public Works and an executive at Atlantic Richfield and an advertising firm.

Whitewater Probe Leads to Indictment—An indictment, **Feb. 28,** by a federal grand jury in Little Rock, AR, grew out of the independent counsel Kenneth Starr's investigation of the Whitewater affair. The indictment of Neal Ainley, former president of the Perry County Bank in Perryville, AR, charged that he had attempted to conceal two 1990 transactions in which the bank transferred $52,500 in cash to a representative of the campaign of then-Gov. Bill Clinton. Federal law required that the Internal Revenue Service be notified of cash transactions greater than $10,000. On **Mar. 9,** Ainley pleaded not guilty.

International

Mideast Leaders Denounce Violence—Leaders playing a central role in the search for a permanent resolution of conflicts in the Middle East met at a summit in Cairo, **Feb. 2.** Those attending were Prime Minister Yitzhak Rabin of Israel; Yasir Arafat, chairman of the Palestine Liberation Organization; President Hosni Mubarak of Egypt; and King Hussein of Jordan. They condemned the recent instances of violence that had imperiled the peace process in the region. Also on **Feb. 2,** the Israeli municipal government in Jerusalem approved 6,500 housing units in a suburb for West Bank settlers, drawing swift protests from Palestinians and some pro-peace Israelis.

U.S., China Reach Copyright Agreement—An agreement signed in Feb. between the U.S. and China concerning copyright protection averted the application of U.S. sanctions on China. The U.S. had long been annoyed by China's apparent inability to prevent the domestic production of copies of U.S. motion pictures and music recordings that were, for the most part, then exported to other countries. Twenty-nine factories in S China, some of whose owners had ties to top Chinese officials, were believed to be sources of the copies of the pirated products. On **Feb. 4,** in response, U.S. Trade Representative Mickey Kantor announced the institution of tariffs of as much as 100% on a wide range of Chinese imports, including plastic articles, telephones, answering machines, bicycles, silk goods, and jewelry. China responded immediately, imposing tariffs on U.S. imports. Then, on **Feb. 15,** China announced that it had raided factories and seized illegal copies of recordings. On **Feb. 26,** before the tariff increases went into effect, China agreed to take a number of steps to enforce copyright laws and close down the illegal manufacturing.

President of Chechnya Flees Capital—After resisting Russian military power for 6 weeks, Pres. Dzhokhar Dudayev of the separatist republic of Chechnya announced **Feb. 8** that he and his commanders were pulling out of Grozny, the capital. Most civilians had already left the devastated city. Commanders on both sides agreed to a truce and prisoner exchange, **Feb. 13**, but that cease-fire and several others failed to last. A Russian commission estimated, **Feb. 21**, that as many as 24,400 civilians had died in Chechnya in 2 months as a result of the conflict.

UN to Send Peacekeepers to Angola—The UN Security Council voted unanimously, **Feb. 8**, to send 7,000 peacekeepers to Angola to maintain the peace there. In Nov. 1994, representatives of the government and the UNITA rebels had signed a peace treaty to end a civil war that had taken 500,000 lives. The UN force was expected to remain in Angola for as long as 2 years.

Mexico, U.S. Agree on Aid Package—In Feb., events of critical importance continued to test the mettle of Mexico's new president, Ernesto Zedillo Ponce de Leon. Zedillo, **Feb. 9**, ordered the army to take the offensive and capture Subcommandante Marcos and other leaders of the rebel Zapatista National Liberation Army (EZLN), which had launched an uprising in Chiapas state in 1994. Zedillo's ruling Institutional Revolutionary Party (PRI) suffered a stunning defeat, **Feb. 12**, in Jalisco state, losing the governorship, state legislative majority, and large-city mayoralties to candidates of the National Action Party. This was only the third time in 65 years that the PRI had lost a gubernatorial election. The vote came at a time of financial turmoil following the government's devaluation of the peso and its subsequent precipitous decline against the value of the U.S. dollar. Zedillo, **Feb. 14**, abruptly halted the army's offensive operations against the EZLN and said he would ask Congress to approve an amnesty for rebels who disarmed. On **Feb. 21**, the U.S. and Mexico reached an agreement on terms relating to a $20 billion U.S. loan package—which was intended to bolster the peso and prevent Mexico from defaulting on its debt—that Pres. Clinton had unveiled in Jan. The U.S. assistance, in turn, was part of an overall package of international support valued at about $50 billion. To receive the U.S. loan, Mexico agreed to reduce government spending and restrain growth of the money supply. As collateral, revenues due Mexico for oil and petrochemicals sold abroad would be deposited in the U.S. Federal Reserve Bank in New York. At the end of the month, Mexicans were stunned again by an announcement, **Feb. 28**, by the special prosecutor investigating the Sept. 1994 assassination of Jose Francisco Ruiz Massieu, the PRI's deputy leader. He said that Raul Salinas de Gortari, brother of Carlos Salinas de Gortari, whose term as president had ended in Dec., had been arrested in Ruiz Massieu's murder and that he was behind the killing.

Serb Leader Rejects Bosnian Peace Plan—Pres. Slobodan Milosevic of Serbia, the effective leader of what remained of Yugoslavia, rejected a 5-nation peace proposal for Bosnia and Herzegovina in Feb. Earlier, on **Feb. 13** in Geneva, a war crimes tribunal indicted 21 Serbs for crimes against humanity for actions they had taken in the war in Bosnia. Only one of those charged was in custody. One of the accused, Zeljko Meakic, former commander of a concentration camp, was also accused of genocide in connection with the mass killing of Muslims and Croats. This marked the first time that an international tribunal had charged an individual with genocide. On **Feb. 19**, Milosevic rejected a request by the 5 nations of the so-called Contact Group—France, Germany, Great Britain, Russia, and the U.S.—that he recognize the international borders of Bosnia and Croatia and accept a partition that would give 49% of Bosnia's territory to Bosnian Serbs. The Bosnian Serbs held 70% of the country's territory. The contact group had offered to lift international sanctions against Yugoslavia in return for Milosevic's support of the partition plan.

Plan for Northern Ireland Presented—The prime ministers of Great Britain and Ireland, John Major and John Bruton, presented a document in February that they hoped would lead to a resolution of the long conflict over North-ern Ireland. But on **Feb. 15**, even before the plan was formally made public, Unionists in Northern Ireland who favored continued ties with Britain denounced it. Major and Bruton presented their plan at a news conference in Belfast, **Feb. 22**. The plan contemplated creation of a cross-border assembly for Ulster (Northern Ireland) that would include representatives from Ulster and the parliament of Ireland. This "North-South" body would deal with economic and cultural development. Britain would continue to control taxation and security in Northern Ireland. Unionists denounced the cross-border assembly as a blueprint for uniting Ireland.

Russia Stands By Nuclear Pact With Iran—Georgi Mamedov, the deputy foreign minister of Russia, told U.S. officials in Washington, **Feb. 23** and 24, that Russia would go forward with an agreement with Iran to construct a nuclear-power reactor on the Persian Gulf. Although the project was purportedly for commercial usage, U.S. officials feared that Iran would gain expertise and materials that it could utilize to build nuclear weapons.

General

Clinton Whiffs in Baseball Dispute—Pres. Clinton failed in his Feb. attempt to resolve the baseball strike. In Jan., most of the owners had agreed to hire replacement players for the 1995 season. On **Feb. 1**, owners and representatives of the striking players met (in Washington, DC) for the first time in 1995, and on **Feb. 7**, Clinton, concerned about the thousands of jobs imperiled by the strike, invited the parties to come to the White House that day and make a final effort to reach an agreement. The principal issue was the owners' desire to impose a cap on players' salaries. After the meeting, Clinton said his efforts had not been successful, and, on **Feb. 8**, he sent a proposal for binding arbitration to Congress. Republican leaders, however, had already indicated that they did not favor congressional intervention.

Prosecution Opens Case Against Simpson—The prosecution in the double-murder trial of O. J. Simpson began presenting its case on **Jan. 31**. Denise Brown, sister of Nicole Brown Simpson, one of the slaying victims, testified, **Feb. 3**, that in the late 1980s O. J. Simpson had once thrown his wife against a wall and then out of the house. On **Feb. 7** and **8**, the prosecution sought to establish the approximate time of the murders as 10:15 PM, early enough to have allowed Simpson to dispose of evidence and catch a plane to Chicago before midnight. One neighbor said he heard Nicole Brown Simpson's dog barking plaintively at about that time. On **Feb. 24**, Judge Lance Ito agreed to let the defense question out of turn Rosa Maria Lopez, a former housekeeper for one of O. J. Simpson's neighbors, who said she was soon planning to return to El Salvador. With the jury absent, Lopez's testimony was videotaped **Feb. 27** for possible use later by the defense. Lopez said that she had seen O. J. Simpson's Ford Bronco outside his home at about 10:15 PM; prosecutors claimed that Simpson had driven the car to and from the scene of the crime. On **Mar. 2**, however, during cross-examination, Lopez modified her testimony, saying she had seen the car "shortly after 10."

Killer of 6 on Train Convicted—Colin Ferguson, an immigrant from Jamaica, was convicted, **Feb. 17**, by a Nassau County, NY, jury of killing 6 passengers on a commuter train in Dec. 1993. All had been shot to death with a handgun. Ferguson was also convicted of wounding 19 others. At his trial, Ferguson acted as his own lawyer. Investigators said they had found notes written by Ferguson, who was black, complaining that he was a victim of racism. During the trial, 12 survivors of the shooting identified the defendant as their assailant. Ferguson said the perpetrator was a man who had stolen his gun from his bag while he slept on the train. On **Mar. 22**, Ferguson was sentenced to 200 years to life in prison.

Olympic Champion Says He Has AIDS—Greg Louganis, who won 4 gold medals in the Olympic games of 1984 and 1988, and who was regarded as one of the greatest divers of all time, disclosed in a recorded television interview, **Feb. 24**, that he had AIDS. Louganis had said publicly in 1994 that he was a homosexual, one of the groups that was at high risk for contracting HIV, the virus that causes AIDS. At the 1988 Olympic competition in Seoul, South Korea, Louganis cut his head on the diving board, and blood spilled into the pool, but he did not then reveal that he knew he was HIV-positive. After his head was stitched up by a doctor who wore no protective gloves, Louganis returned to the competition and won a gold medal. Louganis was the author of a newly published autobiography.

MARCH 1995

National

Balanced-Budget Amendment Fails in Senate—An amendment to the U.S. Constitution requiring that the federal budget be balanced failed to receive the needed two-thirds approval of the Senate, **Mar. 2**. The House had approved the amendment in Jan. Senate Republican leaders supporting the amendment refused to agree to a provision that would have exempted Social Security funding from efforts to reduce the deficit; inclusion of the exemption could have brought several more Democrats to the support of the amendment. With 14 Democrats joining the Republican majority, the amendment was only one vote short of passage. One Republican, Mark Hatfield of Oregon, refused to support it, and some of his angry GOP colleagues sought to oust him as chairman of the Appropriations Committee. However, Senate Republican leaders rebuffed this effort at a party caucus, **Mar. 8**.

Another Democratic Senator Joins GOP—In Mar., for the second time since the Republicans swept the 1994 midterm elections, a Democratic senator switched parties. On **Mar. 3**, Sen. Ben Nighthorse Campbell of Colorado announced that he was joining the GOP ranks. A member of the Northern Cheyenne tribe, Campbell was the only Native American in Congress. Campbell had disagreed with some proposals from the Clinton administration, notably its support for higher grazing fees on federal lands.

Jobless Rate Drops Again to 5.4%—The Labor Dept. reported that the unemployment rate had fallen again, matching a recent low. On **Mar. 3**, the Commerce Dept. said that the index of leading economic indicators had remained unchanged in Jan. The Feb. unemployment rate of 5.4%, announced **Mar. 10**, equaled the 4-year low reported for Dec. The Labor Dept. reported, **Mar. 15**, that prices charged by producers for finished goods had risen 0.3% in Feb. The department said, **Mar. 16**, that consumer prices had also risen 0.3% in Feb. According to the Commerce Dept., **Mar. 22**, the U.S. trade deficit stood at an all-time monthly high, $12.23 billion, in Jan. On Wall Street, **Mar. 30**, the Dow Jones industrial average closed at an all-time high, 4172.56.

Nominee to Head CIA Withdraws—Air Force Gen. (ret.) Michael Carns withdrew, **Mar. 10**, as Pres. Bill Clinton's nominee to serve as Director of Central Intelligence. The FBI, in its background check on Carns, had turned up potential violations of labor and immigration law, involving a young family friend Carns had arranged to bring to the U.S. from the Philippines. Carns denounced allegations by the man, Elbino Runas, as outrageous. Clinton, **Mar. 10**, nominated John Deutch, the deputy secretary of defense, for the intelligence post.

Guilty Plea Entered in Whitewater Case—Charles Wade, a former financial manager of the Whitewater Development Corp., pleaded guilty in Federal District Court in Little Rock, AR, **Mar. 21**, to 2 counts of fraud. The cor-

poration had been owned in part by then-Gov. Bill Clinton and Hillary Rodham Clinton. Kenneth Starr, the independent counsel conducting the investigation of the Whitewater affair, said that Wade would cooperate with the investigation.

Clinton Signs "Unfunded Mandates" Bill—Congress in Mar. completed action on the bill intended to make difficult the approval of legislation that mandated action by the states without providing them with the funds needed to comply. A House-Senate conference committee, **Mar. 10**, approved a compromise bill that was weaker than what many Republican candidates had endorsed in their Contract With America in 1994. It required the Congressional Budget Office to calculate the costs that any bill would impose on state and local governments. When the cost was greater than $50 million, and if Congress did not intend to provide funding, consideration of a bill could proceed only under a special parliamentary motion. The Senate, **Mar. 15**, by a vote of 91-9, and the House, **Mar. 16**, 394-28, approved the conference report, and Pres. Clinton signed the bill **Mar. 22**.

Three More Republicans in Presidential Race—Three more Republicans announced their candidacies for the 1996 GOP presidential nomination in Mar. On **Mar. 20**, Patrick Buchanan, a journalist and television commentator who had served as an aide in the White House to 3 presidents, launched his second bid for the presidency. A conservative, Buchanan had challenged Pres. George Bush in the primaries in 1992. Alan Keyes, another journalist and commentator, and an assistant secretary of state in the Reagan administration, entered the contest **Mar. 26**. Keyes, an outspoken critic of abortion and declining moral values, was the first black to seek the Republican presidential nomination. Sen. Arlen Specter (PA) declared his intention **Mar. 30**. He supported abortion rights, and in his announcement he sharply criticized the conservative Christians now prominent in the party, saying that their social agenda would limit the civil rights of U.S. citizens.

House Approves Overhaul of Welfare—In a vote nearly along party lines, the House, **Mar. 24**, 234-199, approved a bill that would cut welfare spending by $69 billion over 5 years and replace more than 40 federal programs with block grants to the states. The bill would deny cash benefits to unwed mothers under 18 and set a 5-year limit on receiving benefits. Food stamps would be denied those able to work who did not find a job in 90 days. Welfare reform had been included in the Contract With America signed by most Republican candidates for the House in 1994.

Amendment Limiting Terms Fails in House—In Mar., for the first time one of the legislative initiatives endorsed in the Contract With America failed to win approval in the House. Four versions of a proposed constitutional amendment that would limit how long members of Congress could serve were rejected, **Mar. 29**, with none coming close to the two-thirds majority required for amendments. All versions limited members of the House and Senate to 12 years of service or less. One, offered by the Democrats and resoundingly defeated, would have counted time already served as part of a 12-year limit.

Judge Rebuffs Gays-in-Military Policy—The compromise 1994 policy allowing homosexuals to serve in the military under certain conditions was struck down in Mar. by a federal judge in New York City. The new "don't ask, don't tell, don't pursue" policy permitted gays to serve if they remained discreet about their sexual orientation. If they did not, they could be discharged. Six service members challenged the policy. On **Mar. 30**, U.S. District Court Judge Eugene Nickerson held that the policy violated the constitutional protection of free speech and equal rights for all. The Defense Dept. asked the Justice Dept. to appeal the ruling.

International

U.S. Dollar Tumbles Against Yen, Mark—The dollar, buffeted by concerns about the U.S. budget deficits and fears that the Mexican economic crisis could drag down the U.S. economy, fell to post–World War II lows against the Japanese yen and the German mark in Mar. The U.S. Federal Reserve Board tried to give a lift to the dollar by intervening in the currency markets. On **Mar. 2**, the Federal Reserve Bank of New York bought up to $300 million worth of dollars. On **Mar. 3**, the Fed and banks of a dozen other nations bought $1 billion in dollars. Nonetheless, on **Mar. 7**, the dollar hit a postwar low of 90.05 yen after a decline of 5% in just one week. Also on **Mar. 7**, the dollar fell to 1.3705 against the mark, a 12% decline in 3 months to another postwar low. On the bright side, U.S. officials saw the cheap dollar as an opportunity to increase exports and cut the trade deficit. By **Mar. 31**, the dollar had fallen to 86.55 yen and stood at 1.3715 marks.

UN Peacekeepers Leave Somalia—The UN pulled the last 2,400 members of its peacekeeping force out of Somalia in Mar. The UN Security Council, in Nov. 1994, had voted to end the effort after 2 years. The UN had saved millions of people from famine but had been unable to establish a stable government. Some 1,800 U.S. Marines and 400 Italian soldiers assisted in the withdrawal. While an international force waited offshore, U.S. Marines began coming ashore **Feb. 27**. Pakistani soldiers pulled out of the airport, **Mar. 1**, and were replaced by looters and an eruption of fighting between Somali clans. The Italians assisted in the evacuation from Mogadishu, the capital, **Mar. 2**. U.S. Marines killed and wounded several Somalis as the clans competed for areas vacated by the UN. The last UN peacekeepers and their escorts left Somali soil **Mar. 3**.

Mexican Drama Takes New Twists—More surprises were in store for citizens of Mexico in Mar. On **Mar. 3**, U.S. authorities arrested Mario Ruiz Massieu, a former deputy attorney general of Mexico, at Newark (NJ) International Airport. He was charged with not reporting that he was carrying $46,000 in cash. His brother, Jose Francisco Ruiz Massieu, deputy leader of the ruling party, had been murdered in 1994, and Raul Salinas de Gortari, brother of ex-Pres. Carlos Salinas, had already been charged in the murder. On **Mar. 3**, Carlos Salinas began a hunger strike and asked to meet with officials of the government of his successor, Pres. Ernesto Zedillo Ponce de Leon. Salinas ended the hunger strike, **Mar. 5**, after Zedillo said he would absolve Salinas of sole responsibility for the current economic crisis and of having obstructed the investigation into the murder of Luis Donaldo Colosio Murrieta, the ruling party's original nominee for president in 1994. Mexican officials, **Mar. 6**, charged Ruiz with obstructing the investigation into his brother's death. Zedillo, **Mar. 9**, announced new austerity measures in response to conditions tied to the $50 billion international aid package. To increase revenue, Zedillo hiked the price of state-produced gasoline and electricity and increased the value-added tax from 10% to 15%. The federal budget would be cut by 10%.

Russians Take Cities in Chechnya—Russian military headquarters claimed, **Mar. 6**, that Russian troops had pushed Chechen rebels from their last stronghold in Grozny, the capital of the rebellious republic of Chechnya. The last 2 cities held by the rebels, Gudermes and Shali, fell to the Russians—Gudermes on **Mar. 30** and Shali on **Mar. 31**. Fighting continued elsewhere.

Fighting Resumes in Bosnia—An offensive by the army of the government of Bosnia and Herzegovina abruptly ended the truce that had prevailed since the first of the year. Earlier, on **Mar. 9**, the *New York Times* reported that a classified CIA report had concluded that 90% of the barbaric "ethnic cleansing" in Bosnia could be attributed to the Serbs. Pres. Franjo Tudjman of Croatia, at a meeting with Vice Pres. Al Gore in Copenhagen, **Mar. 12**, agreed to let 5,000 UN peacekeepers (down from the current 15,000) remain in Croatia to patrol its borders with Serbia and Bosnia. On **Mar. 14**, in the most serious incident involving UN peacekeepers, 9 French soldiers were killed and 4 injured when their vehicle crashed south of Sarajevo. Although the truce in Bosnia had been broken sporadically, it had held fairly well until government forces launched an offensive, **Mar. 20**, against Serb positions. On one front, the government reportedly had taken 35 sq mi of territory. The Serbs, in turn, attacked Sarajevo, Gorazde, and Tuzla, all of which were UN-designated safe areas.

Clinton Meets Sinn Fein Leader—Gerry Adams, leader of Sinn Fein, the political wing of the Irish Republican Army (IRA), met with Pres. Clinton in Mar. The White House announced, **Mar. 9**, that Adams would be allowed an unlimited number of trips to the U.S. during the next 3 months and would be permitted to raise money. Prime Minister John Major of Great Britain, **Mar. 10**, urged Clinton to insist, when he met with Adams, that the IRA disarm as a step toward advancing negotiations with Britain over the future of Northern Ireland. Clinton greeted Adams briefly at a luncheon, **Mar. 16**, and then was host to Adams at the White House **Mar. 17**, St. Patrick's Day. Earlier that day, Clinton publicly called on the IRA to disarm. After the meeting, Adams was optimistic about upcoming talks with the British. In a phone conversation, **Mar. 19**, Clinton told Major that the U.S. would ensure that no money raised by the IRA in the U.S. would be used to buy weapons.

Nerve Gas Attack Kills 12 in Tokyo—The release of deadly nerve gas forced a partial closure of Tokyo's subway system during the morning rush hour, **Mar. 20**. Twelve people were killed in the attack, and more than 5,000 were made ill. The gas, sarin, can paralyze the central nervous system and cause death. Cannisters containing liquid sarin were placed on 5 subway cars, beginning at about 7 AM, and began to evaporate. Service was suspended on 3 subway lines and not resumed until **Mar. 21**. On **Mar. 22**, police raided 25 offices of the Aum Shinrikyo religious sect and seized 2 tons of chemicals, including compounds that could be used to make sarin. They also seized the equivalent of $7 million in cash and publications predicting mass death from gas in urban areas. Shoko Asahara, founder of the sect, and other sect leaders had fled their headquarters before the raid. More chemicals were seized at a warehouse, **Mar. 24**, and a newspaper reported that enough sarin could have been produced to kill 4.2 million people. In Russia, where the sect claimed 30,000 members, authorities, **Mar. 29**, seized its offices in Moscow.

UN Mission Replaces U.S. Force in Haiti—At the end of Mar., peacekeeping responsibilities in Haiti were transferred from U.S.-led forces to the UN Mission in Haiti (UNMH). Earlier, in a reminder that political unrest churned below the surface, a political opponent of Pres. Jean-Bertrand Aristide was shot to death, **Mar. 28**, in Port-au-Prince, the capital. The victim, Mireille Durocher Bertin, had been planning to run for president. **Mar. 31**, in ceremonies at Port-au-Prince attended by UN Secretary Gen. Boutros Boutros-Ghali and Pres. Clinton, the UNMH assumed its new role. Its force would consist of 6,000 military personnel and 900 police from 30 countries. The U.S. would provide 2,400 soldiers. The police would work with newly trained Haitian police. Clinton promised that the U.S. would continue to support Haiti's efforts to rebuild.

General

Labor Board, Judge Act in Baseball Strike—The major league baseball exhibition season opened, **Mar. 2**, with no solution in sight to the labor impasse that had halted play during the 1994 season. Twenty-seven of the 28 teams began exhibition play with replacement players. Only the Baltimore Orioles refused to hire replacements. The National Labor Relations Board (NLRB), **Mar. 15**, issued a complaint against the owners for "refusing to bargain collectively and in good faith." On **Mar. 26**, the NLRB voted, 3-2, to let its general counsel seek an injunction against baseball's management. In New York City, on **Mar. 27**, an NLRB regional director asked Federal District Court Judge Sonia Sotomayor to grant the injunction and reinstate the contract that had been in effect before the strike. The executive board of the Major League Baseball Players' Association voted unanimously, **Mar. 29**, to return to the playing field if the request was granted. Sotomayor issued the injunction, **Mar. 31**.

Policemen Testify Against Simpson—Police officers who had investigated the deaths of Nicole Brown Simpson and Ronald Goldman testified for the prosecution in Mar. at the trial of O. J. Simpson for the murders. Detective Tom Lange said, **Mar. 6** and **7**, that he believed both murders had been committed by the same killer using the same knife. Johnnie Cochran, the lead defense attorney, suggested during cross-examination of Lange, **Mar. 6-8**, that the crimes were drug related and that at least 2 killers had been involved. Detective Mark Fuhrman, who took the stand **Mar. 9**, testified that he had found a bloody glove— which matched another found at the crime scene—outside O. J. Simpson's home on the night of the murders. During cross-examination, **Mar. 13-16**, F. Lee Bailey, a defense attorney, suggested that Fuhrman could have planted the glove on O. J. Simpson's property. Fuhrman, **Mar. 14**, denied an allegation that he had made racist statements. Detective Philip Vannatter testified, **Mar. 17**, that a knuckle on Simpson's left middle finger had been cut and was swollen when examined the day after the murders. Vannatter said he believed that this wound was responsible for trails of blood found at the homes of Nicole Brown Simpson and O. J. Simpson. Simpson had told police that he had cut the finger on the day of the murders, though he didn't recall how, and again in Chicago the next morning, when he broke a glass after being told that his ex-wife had been killed. Brian "Kato" Kaelin, a houseguest at O. J. Simpson's estate, testified, **Mar. 22**, that Simpson had told him on the day of the murders that his relationship with his ex-wife was finally finished. He said that he and Simpson had returned from a restaurant at 9:40 PM and that he had not seen Simpson thereafter. Kaelin said that at 10:40 he heard 3 loud thumps on the wall of his room near where the glove was later found. In cross-examination, Kaelin said that Simpson had not seemed upset on the evening of the murders, contrary to what he had told the prosecution. Allan Park, a limousine driver who came to O. J. Simpson's estate to pick him up for a trip to Los Angeles International Airport for an 11:45 PM flight to Chicago for a long-scheduled business event, testified **Mar. 28**. He said that in driving around to look for Simpson's address, beginning at 10:22, he did not see Simpson's white Ford Bronco, which Simpson said was outside the estate all evening; the prosecution theorized that Simpson had driven it to the crime scene. Park said he repeatedly rang Simpson's doorbell, got no response, then at 10:56 observed a black person, 6 feet tall and 200 pounds, enter the house. Thirty seconds later, Park said, he buzzed again, and Simpson responded. Corroborating Kaelin's testimony, Park said that, although he assisted Simpson with other pieces of luggage, he heard Simpson insist that he (Simpson) pick up a small black bag himself. On **Mar. 29**, James Williams, an airport skycap, testified that Simpson boarded the flight with 3 pieces of luggage, 2 fewer than Park had observed. Park said he had seen a duffel bag on an airport trash can, with Simpson nearby. The prosecution theorized that the bag contained the small black bag, the murder weapon, and Simpson's blood-soaked clothes.

Pope Addresses Life and Death Issues—Pope John Paul II issued the 11th encyclical of his papacy, **Mar. 30**. In Evangelium Vitae, or Gospel of Life, he took strong stands on human birth and death issues. He opposed abortion, which he called "the deliberate killing of an innocent human being," as well as birth control and in vitro fertilization. Also rejecting euthanasia, he wrote that "true 'compassion' leads to sharing another's pain; it does not kill the person whose suffering we cannot bear." He said that public servants had no obligation to follow laws contrary to God's law. He rebuked economically advanced countries for promoting birth control in developing countries. He said that situations calling for the death penalty were "very rare, if not practically nonexistent."

APRIL 1995

National

Gunman Guilty of Trying to Kill Clinton—Francisco Duran, 26, a resident of Colorado Springs, CO, was convicted, **Apr. 4**, in federal court in Washington, DC, of attempting to assassinate Pres. Bill Clinton. In Oct. 1994, Duran had fired shots at the White House from an assault rifle. He had also been indicted for assault against Secret Service officers who had approached him, on weapons charges, and for damaging federal property. Defense lawyers contended that he had not intended to shoot anyone and that he was insane. Duran was convicted on all counts. On June 29, he was sentenced to 40 years in prison.

House Approves Cuts in Taxes—The House, **Apr. 5**, by a vote of 246-188, approved a bill that would cut taxes for individuals and corporations. A $500-per-child tax credit for families earning less than $200,000 would cut tax revenues by $105 billion over 5 years. Altogether, revenues would be reduced by $189 billion. The loss of revenue would be covered by reductions in social programs.

House GOP Celebrates Approval of Contract—House Republicans massed on the steps of the Capitol, **Apr. 7**, to celebrate their efforts to pass legislation promised in their 1994 Contract With America. Almost all the "contract" bills had sailed through the House, even though Republicans had only a small majority. A constitutional amendment limiting the number of terms a member of Congress could serve did fail to win approval. The Senate had failed to approve another amendment supported by the contract, requiring a balanced federal budget, and it had yet to act on most other bills sent it by the House. Pres. Clinton had signed contract legislation restricting unfunded mandates to the states and applying federal labor laws to Congress. The Republicans gained a House seat, **Apr. 10**, when Rep. Nathan Deal (GA) announced that he was switching parties.

Surge Continues on Wall Street—In Apr., while most economic statistics showed little change, investors in stocks continued to push equity prices higher. The Labor Dept. reported, **Apr. 7**, that the unemployment rate in Mar. had edged upward 0.1 percentage point to 5.5%. The department said, **Apr. 11**, that prices charged by producers for finished goods had been unchanged in Mar. It reported, **Apr. 12**, that consumer prices had risen 0.2% in Mar. The Commerce Dept. said, **Apr. 19**, that the trade gap declined sharply in Feb. to $9.01 billion. The department reported, **Apr. 28**, that the gross domestic product grew at an annual rate of 2.8% in the first quarter. On **Apr. 28**, the last day of trading for the month, the Dow Jones industrial average closed at an all-time high of 4321.27.

McNamara Calls Vietnam War a Mistake—Robert McNamara, who served as secretary of defense during much of the Vietnam War, wrote in a book published in Apr. that he and other American leaders had been "wrong, terribly wrong" about the war. His views in the book, *In Retrospect: The Tragedy and Lessons of Vietnam*, began to become public **Apr. 8** and **9**. In the 1960s, the conflict in Southeast Asia had been nicknamed McNamara's War because of his strong vocal support for U.S. intervention, but he now said that the U.S. should have withdrawn its troops by 1963 or soon thereafter. He wrote that the U.S. ally, South Vietnam, was incapable of defending its territory and that the U.S. had underestimated its North Vietnamese adversary and overestimated what high-technology weapons could accomplish. The book revived the public debate over Vietnam. Some complained that McNamara should have declared his opposition to U.S. policy in the 1960s when he could have influenced the course of the war.

Dole Makes Third Bid for White House—Sen. Bob Dole (KS) announced his candidacy, **Apr. 10**, for the Republican presidential nomination. Dole, who was seriously wounded during World War II and was now the Senate Majority Leader, had been the unsuccessful candidate for vice president on the GOP ticket in 1976, and he had also sought the nomination for the top spot without success in 1980 and 1988. Now, at age 71, he was leading public-opinion polls among Republican contenders for the nomination. A skilled legislator, he took less conservative positions on social and economic issues than did many other Republican leaders. Rep. Robert Dornan (CA) entered the Republican contest **Apr. 13**. An outspoken conservative, Dornan had often denounced abortion and homosexuality. Another foe of abortion, former Pennsylvania Gov. Robert Casey, said, **Apr. 18**, that health considerations prevented him from challenging Pres. Clinton for the Democratic nomination. Sen. Richard Lugar (IN) announced his candidacy for the Republican nomination, **Apr. 19**. Lugar had been mayor of Indianapolis for 8 years. A former chairman of the Senate Foreign Relations Committee and now head of the Agriculture Committee, Lugar emphasized his expertise in foreign policy in his declaration. He favored replacing the income tax with a national sales tax.

Bomb Explosion in Oklahoma City Kills 169—A bomb exploded outside a federal office building in Oklahoma City on the morning of Wednesday, **Apr. 19**, and caused the death of 169 people (including one rescue worker). The bomb had been left in a truck parked in front of the Alfred P. Murrah Federal Building. The explosion, which occurred at 9:02 AM, tore away the face of the 9-story building, damaged many other buildings in the vicinity, and left a crater 8 ft deep and 20 ft wide. Made of ammonium nitrate fertilizer and fuel oil, and estimated to weigh 5,000 lb, the bomb was similar to one used in 1993 at the World Trade Center in New York City, and international terrorists were initially viewed as likely perpetrators in the latest assault. Officials noted, however, that the federal building contained an office of the Bureau of Alcohol, Tobacco and Firearms, which had been denounced in some circles for its role in the 1993 assault on the Branch Davidian cult's complex near Waco, TX. That deadly confrontation had also occurred on **Apr. 19**. In addition to several other federal offices, the Oklahoma City building also contained a day-care center, and 19 young children were among those killed. More than 400 people were injured, including many outside the building who were struck by flying glass. From the moment of the explosion, rescue efforts were aimed at saving anyone still alive in the wreckage, but no living person was rescued after the evening of **Apr. 19**. Meanwhile, the death toll mounted as bodies were recovered. Investigators found a fragment of the destroyed truck that contained a vehicle identification number and traced the vehicle to a Ryder truck rental agency in Junction City, KS. The FBI, **Apr. 20**, released sketches of the 2 men identified as having rented the truck. The renter had used fake identification. A man already in custody was charged, **Apr. 21**, in connection with the bombing. The suspect, Timothy McVeigh, 27 years old, had been stopped by a policeman north of Oklahoma City about 90 minutes after the explosion because he was driving without license plates. The arresting officer had found that McVeigh had a pistol and so-called cop-killer bullets, and he was initially charged with carrying a concealed weapon. Two days later, on **Apr. 21**, when he was arraigned before a federal magistrate at Tinker Air Force Base, McVeigh entered no plea to a charge of malicious damage to federal property, and he reportedly refused to respond to questions about the

bombing. McVeigh was an Army infantry veteran who had participated in Operation Desert Storm, in Kuwait and Iraq, in 1991. Also on **Apr. 21**, 2 brothers, Terry and James Nichols, were taken into federal custody. McVeigh and Terry Nichols had, for a time, lived at the Decker, MI, farm of James Nichols. Terry had served with McVeigh in the Army. Investigators said, **Apr. 21**, that the Nicholses were involved with a paramilitary group called the Michigan Militia. The militia movement had been growing across the U.S., with many members sharing a concern about threats posed to private citizens by federal agents. On **Apr. 23**, Pres. Bill Clinton and Hillary Rodham Clinton attended a memorial service in Oklahoma City for the bombing victims. On **Apr. 24**, the president denounced those who "spread hate" and "leave the impression . . . that violence is acceptable," a presumed reference to the proliferation of radio talk shows that stressed distrust of, and hostility toward, the federal government. The Nichols brothers, **Apr. 25**, were charged with conspiring with McVeigh to build explosives. At a bail hearing for Terry Nichols, **Apr. 26**, in Wichita, KS, it was revealed that he had been providing information to the authorities. He said that McVeigh told him 3 days before the explosion that "something big is going to happen." At a bail hearing for McVeigh, **Apr. 27**, an FBI agent testified that residues of chemicals used in the bomb had been found on McVeigh's clothes. According to local officials, **Apr. 27**, 200 buildings had suffered structural damage; overall damage was estimated at $500 million.

Unabomber Kills Again Through Mail—A cunning killer who had become known as the Unabomber struck again in Apr. Since 1978 he had been linked to 16 mail-bomb incidents. Prior to Apr., 2 men had been killed and 22 persons wounded by well-crafted bombs sent through the mail. On **Apr. 24**, a bomb killed Gilbert Murray, president of the California Forestry Association, in Sacramento. It was learned, **Apr. 25 and 26**, that the Unabomber had sent 4 letters from the Oakland, CA, area. One was to the *New York Times*, to which the Unabomber had also written in 1993. In his new letter to the *Times*, the writer called himself an anarchist and said, "The people we are out to get are the scientists and engineers." He added that his goal was the destruction of the "worldwide industrial system."

International

Suicide Bombers Strike in Gaza—Violent events dominated the news from the Gaza Strip in Apr. An explosion in a building in the city of Gaza, **Apr. 2**, killed 8 people, including a leader of the military wing of Hamas, or the Islamic Resistance Movement, which opposed the ongoing peace process between Israel and the Palestine Liberation Organization (PLO). More than 30 persons were injured. The police chief for the Palestine National Authority (PNA) said that members of Hamas had been assembling a bomb, which went off accidentally. On **Apr. 9**, 2 suicide bombers killed themselves, 7 Israeli soldiers, and a Jewish student who was an American citizen when they detonated bombs in the Gaza Strip. At least 45 people, mostly Israeli soldiers, were injured. Hamas and Islamic Jihad, another radical organization, claimed responsibility. Yasir Arafat, chairman of the PLO and head of the PNA, ordered a crackdown on the radicals, 300 of whom, it was reported, were arrested within the next 3 days. PNA officials said, **Apr. 10**, that a member of Islamic Jihad had been sentenced to 15 years in prison for recruiting young men as suicide bombers. On **Apr. 11**, the PNA said a clergymen had received a life sentence for similar activities.

U.S. Dollar Continues to Slide—Again in Apr., the U.S. dollar slipped to postwar lows against the Japanese in international currency markets. The dollar fell to 85.85 against the yen during New York trading, **Apr. 3**, and rebounded only slightly at the close, after the Federal Reserve Bank of New York and Japan's central bank spent between $1 billion and $2 billion buying dollars and selling yen. The persistently large U.S. budget deficits and trade deficits with Japan contributed to the dollar's decline. Germany's central bank joined in the large-scale buying of dollars, with meager results, as the dollar stood at 1.3733 German marks in New York on **Apr. 5**, a near-record low. In intra-day trading in New York, **Apr. 19**, the dollar dipped briefly to less than 80 yen. By month's close, **Apr. 28**, the dollar rebounded in New York to 1.3874 marks and 84.26 yen.

2,000 Rwandans Die in Clash With Soldiers—Soldiers of the Rwandan government killed some 2,000 Hutu refugees in Apr. who attempted to resist them. The government, **Apr. 18**, began expelling refugees from camps in SW Rwanda, home to 250,000 people, contending that they were a destabilizing influence and hiding places for soldiers who had participated in massacres in 1994. Although most refugees abandoned the camps, 50,000 stayed at Kibeho. On **Apr. 22**, when some of them attempted to break through a military cordon, soldiers attacked with machine guns and grenades. This assault and the ensuing stampede took the heavy toll of life.

U.S. to Suspend All Trade With Iran—Pres. Bill Clinton announced, **Apr. 30**, that the U.S. would suspend all trade with Iran in protest against the latter's funding of terrorism and its plans to obtain nuclear weapons. U.S. oil companies and their foreign subsidiaries had been allowed to purchase oil from Iran for resale in other countries (but not the U.S.). The policy announced in Apr. would also virtually end all U.S. exports to Iran. Clinton restated his opposition to the sale by Russia to Iran of equipment that could be used to enrich uranium to make bombs. Clinton, **May 8**, signed the executive order establishing the embargo.

General

Baseball Strike Ends—Owners of major-league baseball teams, **Apr. 2**, accepted the offer by players to take the field. The players had acted after a judge ordered owners to reinstate the collective-bargaining agreement previously in effect. This agreement would now continue in effect while the opposing sides resumed efforts to reach a new accord. Owners released replacement players and reassigned them to the minor leagues or released them outright. Representatives of the owners and players, **Apr. 3**, approved an agreement that addressed the terms for what would be a shortened season, 144 games instead of the usual 162. An exhibition schedule began **Apr. 13**. Regular-season play got underway **Apr. 25** and was the first official action since the longest strike in sports history began in Aug. 1994. Major league teams had lost about $700 million because of the strike. A separate dispute was settled, **May 1**, when owners ended a lockout of umpires, agreeing to grant them raises ranging from 25% to 37.5%.

UCLA Wins NCAA Basketball Title—The University of California at Los Angeles (UCLA), once the dominant team in college basketball, reclaimed the championship in Apr. Earlier, on **Apr. 2**, the University of Connecticut women's team defeated Tennessee, 70-64, to win the National Collegiate Athletic Association's Division I women's title and complete a perfect 35-0 season. UConn forward Rebecca Lobo was named outstanding player in the women's tournament. On **Apr. 3**, UCLA defeated the defending champions, Arkansas, 89-78, to take the men's NCAA Division I title, its 11th overall and its first since 1975. UCLA forward Ed O'Bannon, who scored 30 points in the championship game, was named the men's tournament's outstanding player. UCLA finished the season with a 31-2 record.

Jury in Spotlight at Simpson Trial—Testimony at the double-murder trial of O. J. Simpson was almost overwhelmed in Apr. by difficulties within the jury. Dennis Fung, chief criminalist in the case, began his testimony, **Apr. 3**, and during the next 2 weeks defense lawyer Barry Scheck sought, with some apparent effect, to show, during cross-examination, that Fung's investigative work was sloppy and unreliable. Fung, on **Apr. 4**, acknowledged that it had not been true, as he had told the grand jury in 1994, that he had collected much of the blood evidence. In fact, he now said, most of the blood had been collected by a trainee. He later recanted other testimony that he had carried a vial of blood out of O. J. Simpson's home and put it in a police van. Meanwhile, on **Apr. 5**, Judge Lance Ito dismissed juror Jeanette Harris. She was the 6th juror to be excused, and only 6 alternates were now available. In interviews **Apr. 5** and **7**, Harris said that the jury had broken into factions supporting the defendant's guilt or innocence. She said that sheriff's deputies assigned to the jurors were fomenting racial discord. On **Apr. 20**, after another juror, Tracy Hampton, asked to be excused, Ito replaced the 3 deputies; in protest, **Apr. 21**, 13 jurors and alternates refused at first to go to court. Ito replaced Hampton, **May 1**.

MAY 1995

National

Second Man Charged in Oklahoma Bombing—A second suspect, Terry Nichols, was charged in May in the bombing of the federal building in Oklahoma City. The bombing killed 169 people. Federal authorities confirmed, **May 1**, that a receipt had been found showing that in Sept. 1994 Nichols had bought 2,000 lb of ammonium nitrate fertilizer, one of the components of the bomb. On **May 4**, more bodies were removed from the rubble of the Alfred P. Murrah Federal Building. Also, a nurse had been killed during the rescue effort. As of **May 4**, the search for survivors was considered over. The Oklahoma tragedy had sparked considerable nationwide discussion concerning the behavior of federal agents and of armed militias who perceived the agents as a menace to private citizens. It was reported, **May 10**, that former Pres. George Bush had resigned as a life member of the National Rifle Assn. after it sent out a fund-raising letter that referred to federal agents as "jackbooted Government thugs." Bush said the letter's language "deeply offends my own sense of decency and honor." Nichols, who had previously been charged with conspiring with his brother, James, and Timothy McVeigh to build bombs, was charged in the bombing itself, **May 10**. Specifically, he was accused of "malicious damage and destruction" of a federal building. He was also charged with aiding and abetting the bombing. An affidavit made public on **May 11** alleged that in Sept. 1994, Nichols had stored a ton of ammonium nitrate fertilizer in Herington, KS, and later stored another ton of the chemical in Council Grove, KS. It was further alleged that Nichols had bought diesel fuel for the bomb and that the yellow Ryder truck used in the bombing was parked behind Nichols's house in Herington 2 days before the explosion. Also on **May 11**, in Detroit, MI, a federal grand jury indicted James Nichols for allegedly conspiring with McVeigh and Terry Nichols to make and set off bombs on James's farm in Decker, MI. News reports, **May 20**, said that an Army friend of McVeigh, Michael Fortier, had implicated McVeigh. Fortier reportedly told investigators that about a week before the bombing, he and McVeigh had driven from Fortier's home in Kingman, AZ, to inspect the federal building in Oklahoma City. James Nichols, who had not been charged in the bombing itself, was released from custody, **May 23**. With the use of explosives, what was left of the federal building was razed, **May 23**. Three more victims of the bombing were found in the rubble, **May 29**.

Surgeon General Nominee Responds to Critics—Dr. Henry Foster, nominated by Pres. Bill Clinton to be U.S.

surgeon general, testified at his confirmation hearings in May before the Senate Labor and Human Resources Committee. Subsequent to his nomination, he and the White House had caused confusion concerning the number of abortions that he had performed. Foster, best known as founder of a program aimed at discouraging pregnancy and promiscuity among teenagers, told the senators that he believed, with the president, that abortions should be safe, legal, and rare, and he testified, **May 2**, "My life's work has been devoted to bringing healthy lives into this world, and trying to assure that every child born is a wanted child who has parents that can meet its needs." Foster, **May 3**, denied that he had known about a controversial program at Tuskegee University, prior to the time it was revealed publicly, that involved denying treatment to 400 poor black men who had syphilis, as part of a study of the disease. Foster had been a professor at Tuskegee at the time. The committee, **May 26**, recommended approval of Foster's nomination, 9-7, with 2 Republican senators joining all the committee's 7 Democrats in support.

Banker Pleads Guilty in Whitewater Case—The investigation by Kenneth Starr, the independent counsel, into the Whitewater Affair resulted in another conviction in May. Neal Ainley, ex-president of the Perry County Bank in Perryville, AR, pleaded guilty, **May 2**, in U.S. District Court in Little Rock, AR, to having "agreed with other persons" to divide a $30,000 withdrawal from his bank in 1990 into 4 smaller sums prior to its transfer to the reelection campaign of Gov. Bill Clinton. The purpose was to avoid compliance with a federal law requiring that cash transactions greater than $10,000 be reported to the Internal Revenue Service. Ainley also admitted preventing the filing of an IRS report on a $22,500 transaction in 1990. Ainley promised to cooperate with Starr's investigation.

Economic Growth May Be Slowing—The Commerce Dept. said, **May 3**, that the index of leading economic indicators had fallen 0.5% in Mar., the largest decline in 2 years. The Labor Dept. reported, **May 5**, that the unemployment rate had risen from 5.5% to 5.8% in Apr. The Federal Reserve Board said, **May 10**, that the pace of economic growth had slowed somewhat during 1995 and that the 7 interest-rate increases that it had imposed had kept inflationary pressures under control. The Labor Dept. said, **May 11**, that prices charged by manufacturers and farmers for finished goods had risen 0.5% in Apr. It reported, **May 12**, that consumer prices had gone up 0.4% in Apr. The U.S. trade deficit stood at $9.12 billion in Mar., the Commerce Dept. said, **May 18**. On **May 31**, on Wall Street, the Dow Jones industrial average closed at an all-time high of 4465.14.

New CIA Director Confirmed—The Senate, **May 9**, by a vote of 98-0, confirmed John Deutch as Director of Central Intelligence. Members of Congress had made it clear that they wanted Deutch, who had been nominated by Pres. Bill Clinton, to straighten out the covert operations section of the Central Intelligence Agency, which had been devastated in 1994 by the Aldrich Ames spy scandal.

Committee Cites Evidence Against Senator—The inquiry into the conduct of Sen. Bob Packwood (R, OR) moved forward, **May 17**, when the Senate Select Committee on Ethics released its preliminary report. The inquiry was an outgrowth of reports first made public in 1992 concerning unwanted sexual advances by Packwood toward a number of women. The committee said it had found "substantial credible evidence" of misconduct. Its next step would be to conduct hearings to determine if the Senate should censure or otherwise punish Packwood. The committee had interviewed 264 witnesses for a total of 11,000 hours. It identified incidents involving 17 women toward whom Packwood allegedly made harassing overtures. As well, the committee, in examining Packwood's diary, found evidence that the senator had asked lobbyists to find a job for his wife, from whom he was getting a divorce at the

time. Steady income for his wife would have reduced Sen. Packwood's alimony payments. The Ethics Committee saw this action, if true, as a violation of Senate rules against using one's official position for "personal financial gain." An employee of Packwood testified that the senator had altered passages in his diary after the investigation got underway, which could potentially constitute obstruction of justice. Packwood was chairman of the Senate Finance Committee, and the gathering storm about him came just as his committee was focusing on major legislation concerning taxation, welfare reform, and health care.

Movies Play a Role in GOP Contest—One way or another, the motion picture industry was featured in the contest for the Republican presidential nomination in May. Sen. Phil Gramm (R, TX), who was seeking conservative support for the nomination, acknowledged, **May 17**, that he had invested $7,500 in 1974 in a movie, *Beauty Queens*, which he said he was told "was to be an R-rated spoof of beauty contests." It was to have been produced by his then-brother-in-law, George Caton. Caton called it a "sexploitation" film. The film was never made. Caton said he redirected the money into another movie, *White House Madness*, a satire about Pres. Richard Nixon. On **May 31**, Sen. Bob Dole (KS), another candidate for the nomination, denounced the production of motion pictures and recordings that he called "nightmares of depravity." He said the entertainment industry was "bombarding our children with destructive messages" of casual sex and violence. He directed specific criticism at 2 recent movies, *Natural Born Killers* and *True Romance*. He rebuked Time Warner, Inc., a distributor of "gangsta rap" recordings that, according to Dole, extolled the "pleasures of raping, torturing, and mutilating women."

Clinton Threatens Veto of Spending Cuts—Pres. Bill Clinton said, **May 17**, that he would veto a bill moving through Congress that cut $16.4 billion in funding for domestic programs that the previous Congress had approved. This so-called rescissions bill deleted funding for some housing programs and for airport and highway construction and treatment of drinking water. Clinton especially objected to cuts in education and job-training programs. The House, **May 18** (235-189), and the Senate, **May 25** (61-38), approved the bill.

Commerce Secretary Faces Investigation—Sec. of Commerce Ron Brown, **May 16**, became the 3d member of the Clinton Cabinet to face investigation by an independent counsel. Attorney Gen. Janet Reno asked a panel of federal judges to appoint a counsel to investigate the personal finances of Brown. She said that a Justice Dept. inquiry had found reasonable grounds for further investigation.

Senate, House Aim for Balanced Budget—The House and the Senate approved budget resolutions in May that defined broad outlines of plans that sought to balance the budget by 2002. Differences in the House and Senate blueprints, essentially reflecting the wishes of the Republican majority in each chamber, would have to be resolved in conference committee. The House version, approved **May 18**, 238-193, provided a greater net reduction in the deficits, $1.04 trillion, and deeper tax cuts, $350 billion. In what was viewed as a challenge to Majority Leader Bob Dole (KS), his rival for the Republican presidential nomination, Sen. Phil Gramm (TX), sought to incorporate the House tax cuts into the Senate bill, but his amendment was defeated, **May 23**, by a 69-31 vote. The Senate bill, passed **May 25**, 57-42, provided for an unspecified future tax cut of $170 billion. It would cut the deficits by $961 billion.

White House Security Breached Again—New rules were adopted in May to increase security at the White House, but within days an armed intruder gained access to the mansion's lawn. On **May 19**, Treasury Sec. Robert Rubin, in response to several recent incidents at the White House as well as the bombing in Oklahoma City, approved new security provisions. On **May 20**, a 2-block stretch of

Pennsylvania Ave. in front of the White House was closed to all but pedestrian traffic. Rubin also recommended installing more bullet-proof glass in White House windows. On **May 23**, a man identified as Leland Modjeski, carrying an unloaded handgun, climbed over a fence and ran toward the White House. A Secret Service agent tackled him 60 ft from the building. A second agent fired a shot that wounded both the intruder and the first agent. Modjeski was charged, **May 24**, with assaulting federal officers and transporting a weapon across state lines.

International

Bosnian Serbs Seize UN Hostages—Another chaotic month in the Balkans began with an offensive, **May 1**, by Croat forces against a Serb-held area called the W Slavonian pocket, in Croatia. The attacks began on the day that a 4-month cease-fire, negotiated in part by former Pres. Jimmy Carter, expired. The Croats captured several towns. Croatian Serbs responded by shelling Zagreb, the capital of Croatia, **May 2** and **3**. The opposing forces, **May 3**, agreed to a cease-fire, which was broken the next day. By midmonth the Serbs were engaged in heavy fighting with the Croats and as well with government forces in Sarajevo, the capital of Bosnia and Herzegovina, and in other Bosnian towns. On **May 23**, Bosnian Serbs seized weapons from a UN-guarded weapons depot outside Sarajevo, and the Serbs also escalated their attacks on Sarajevo. NATO planes, **May 25** and **26**, bombed a weapons depot near Pale, the capital of the Bosnian Serbs. The Serbs, **May 25**, shelled 5 of the 6 UN-designated safe areas. The death toll in Tuzla, 71, was the highest of any single shelling incident in the war. The Serbs dramatically increased the level of tension in Bosnia, **May 25**, when they began taking UN peacekeepers hostage. Many were used as human shields, handcuffed and chained to potential targets of NATO planes. Two French peacekeepers were killed, **May 27**, in Sarajevo, when their unit clashed with Serbs over control of a bridge. By **May 28**, 325 UN soldiers were being held hostage. The Bosnian foreign minister, Irfan Ljubijankic, and 5 others were killed, **May 28**, when Serb forces downed their helicopter. By **May 30**, the U.S. had moved 7 ships and 12,000 Marines and sailors to the Adriatic Sea. Other Western nations sent reinforcements. UN peacekeepers were forced to abandon many of their positions.

U.S. Changes Cuban Refugee Policy—The U.S. announced, **May 2**, that Cuban boat people seeking asylum would henceforth be returned to Cuba. However, most of the 21,000 Cubans detained at the U.S. base at Guantanamo, Cuba, would be admitted into the U.S. These policies were pursuant to an agreement worked out with Cuba in Sept. 1994. The U.S. had agreed to accept at least 20,000 refugees a year. Attorney Gen. Janet Reno said, **May 2**, that Cubans could now apply for asylum at the U.S. Interests Section in Havana.

Chirac Elected President of France—Jacques Chirac, mayor of Paris, former premier of France, and leader of the neo-Gaullist Rally for the Republic, won the presidency of France in May, on his third try. Chirac defeated the Socialist Party candidate, Lionel Jospin, in a runoff, **May 7**, by a margin of 52.6% to 47.4%. François Mitterrand, a Socialist who had served two 7-year terms, had not sought reelection. Chirac's victory signaled a mild shift to the right in French politics. He had served as premier from 1974 to 1976 and again, under Mitterrand in a power-sharing agreement, from 1986 to 1988. He had cut taxes and privatized state-owned enterprises. Chirac had sought the presidency in 1981 and 1988. During the 1995 campaign, he had pledged to reduce France's 12.2% unemployment rate and had taken a restrained approach toward full French commitment to participation in the European Union. Chirac was inaugurated as president on **May 17**, and he named Alain Juppe, a former foreign minister, as premier.

Clinton-Yeltsin Summit Yields Little—Pres. Bill Clinton and Pres. Boris Yeltsin of Russia met in Moscow, **May 10**, but the summit produced few concrete results. Clinton's trip coincided with the 50th anniversary celebration of the end of World War II in Europe. Some U.S. political leaders had protested Clinton's visit while Russia was waging war against the secessionist republic of Chechnya. Clinton restated concerns about civilian casualties in Chechnya. **May 11** he met in Kiev, Ukraine, with Pres. Leonid Kuchma of Ukraine. On **May 12**, he attended a service at Babi Yar, where 100,000 persons were executed by Nazi soldiers during World War II.

U.S. Puts 100% Tariffs on Japanese Cars—U.S.-Japanese auto-trade talks having gotten nowhere, U.S. officials announced, **May 16**, that tariffs of 100% would be imposed on 13 Japanese-made luxury car models. The targeted cars included models manufactured by Honda, Mazda, Mitsubishi, Nissan, and Toyota. The cars accounted for about one-eighth of all Japanese cars sold in the U.S. The U.S. had been seeking without success to open Japanese markets for cars and car parts to foreign competition.

Japanese Cult Leader Held in Gas Attacks—The leader of a religious cult was arrested in Japan, **May 16**, and charged with murder and attempted murder in nerve-gas attacks in a Tokyo subway in Mar. The attacks had killed 12 and injured more than 5,000. The leader of the Aum Shinrikyo cult, Shoko Asahara, was captured in a raid on the cult's compound in Kamikuishiki. Forty other cult members, 26 of whom were in custody, were also charged in the gas attacks. The cultists were also suspects in a sarin-gas attack in Matsumoto in June 1994. That attack had killed 7 people and caused 200 injuries.

Israel Suspends Plan to Seize Arab Land—The Israeli Cabinet decided in May to suspend a plan to confiscate 134 acres of land in East Jerusalem. The land, mostly owned by Arabs, was to be the site of a police station and housing for Jews. Palestinians visualized East Jerusalem as a future capital. Oman, **May 17**, presented a UN Security Council resolution opposing the expropriation. Although it vetoed the resolution, **May 17**, the U.S. called the seizure of land "unhelpful" to the peace process. Facing 2 no-confidence votes in parliament, the government of Prime Minister Yitzhak Rabin, **May 22**, suspended the plan.

Mexico's Ruling Party Suffers Rare Defeat—On **May 28**, for only the 4th time in 66 years, Mexico's ruling Institutional Revolutionary Party (PRI) lost an election for a state governorship. In Guanajuato, the candidate of the right-wing National Action Party (PAN) prevailed by a 2-1 margin over the PRI candidate, and the result was interpreted as reflecting dissatisfaction over how Pres. Ernesto Zedillo Ponce de Leon was handling the country's economic crisis. In another gubernatorial election, in Yucatan state, the PRI candidate, Victor Cervera Pacheco, narrowly defeated Luis Correa Mena of PAN. Correa said, **May 30**, that he would challenge the result as fraudulent.

Chile Upholds Sentences in Washington, DC, Killings—The Supreme Court of Chile, **May 30**, unanimously upheld sentences imposed in the 1976 bombing deaths in Washington, DC, of a Chilean opposition leader, Orlando Letelier, and his secretary, Ronni Moffitt. In 1993, a Chilean court sentenced Gen. Manuel Contreras Sepulveda, former head of the secret police, to 7 years in prison, and Brig. Gen. Pedro Espinoza Bravo, his assistant, to 6 years, for roles in directing the murders. For the first time, top officials in the military regime of former Chilean leader Augusto Pinochet Ugarte faced prison terms for abuses of human rights.

General

Simpson Jury Hears Genetic Evidence—The prosecution in the double murder trial of O. J. Simpson presented genetic evidence in May. Testifying **May 1-5**, Gregory Matheson of the Los Angeles Police Dept. said that any mishandling of the evidence would not have resulted in the blood incorrectly matching that of the defendant or the victims. Robin Cotton of Cellmark Diagnostics, **May 10**, showed a match between Simpson's blood and blood found at the scene of the murders. On **May 11**, Cotton estimated that one in 170 million blacks and whites had a genetic pattern matching that of the defendant. A stain on a sock found at Simpson's home was almost certainly that of Nicole Brown Simpson, Cotton said: Only one of 6.8 billion people would have the same genetic type. Gary Sims of the California Dept. of Justice, testifying **May 16-22**, said he had found an apparent match between Ronald Goldman's blood and a stain on a glove found at O. J. Simpson's estate. In cross-examinations, the defense sought to suggest that the blood-stained evidence was planted or tainted beyond reliability because of mishandling.

Deadly Virus Reappears in Zaire—The deadly Ebola virus, which kills more than half its victims, was found to have returned to Zaire in May. The virus, which causes high fever and severe bleeding, was spread through bodily fluids and secretions. It had first been identified in Sudan and Zaire in 1976 and had killed 300 in Zaire that year. It had not been reported since 1979 in Sudan, but on **May 10** scientists from the U.S. Centers for Disease Control and Prevention and from the UN World Health Organization (WHO) found evidence that a mystery disease in Kikwit, Zaire, was caused by the Ebola virus. WHO said, **May 11**, that 27 of the 49 who had contracted the virus had died. Zairean officials said that the outbreak had been traced to a surgical patient who had infected medical workers. By **May 21**, according to WHO, 101 of 137 persons infected had died. WHO, **Aug. 24**, declared the outbreak over; 244 of the 315 known victims had died.

JUNE 1995

National

Economic Indicators Continue to Fall—In a signal that a recession might be on the way, the index of leading economic indicators had fallen for a third straight month, the Commerce Dept. reported, **June 2**. The index showed a decline of 0.6% in Apr., compared with Mar. The Labor Dept. said, **June 2**, that the unemployment rate had edged downward 0.1 percentage point in May, to 5.7%. Payroll jobs declined by 101,000 in May, the largest monthly drop in 4 years. The department reported, **June 9**, that prices charged by manufacturers and farmers for finished goods had not changed in May. It said, **June 13**, that consumer prices had risen 0.3% in May. The Commerce Dept. said, **June 21**, that the trade deficit had risen to $11.37 billion in Apr., highest since the new way of computing it began in Jan. 1992. On Wall Street, the Dow Jones industrial average closed, **June 22**, at an all-time high of 4589.64.

Clinton Casts First Veto—Pres. Bill Clinton, **June 7**, vetoed a bill passed by Congress, the first time he had done so. The disfavored piece of legislation was the so-called rescissions bill, which cut $16.4 billion from spending previously appropriated by Congress. Although he was willing to accept most of the rescissions, Clinton balked at $1.4 billion in cuts, principally in education programs. The bill had also included new expenditures for disaster relief and costs related to the bombing of the federal building in Oklahoma City. No attempt was made to override the veto, but Congress began to revise the bill.

Gov. Tucker of Arkansas Indicted—Gov. Jim Guy Tucker of Arkansas was indicted, **June 7**, for conspiring to defraud the Internal Revenue Service and the Small Business Administration. The governor and 2 codefendants pleaded not guilty, **June 22**, to the charges, which related to deals involving cable-television companies. The charges grew out of the investigation into the Whitewater affair, but were not directly related to the complex real-estate dealings that had cast a shadow over Pres. Bill Clinton and First

Lady Hillary Rodham Clinton. It was reported, **June 26**, that a confidential report prepared for the Resolution Trust Corp. had indicated that the Clintons, as they had claimed, had been only passive investors in the Whitewater Development Corp. The inquiry found no evidence that the Clintons knew about transactions involving Whitewater and Madison Guaranty Savings & Loan, which later went bankrupt. The study found that the Clintons had lost $42,000 in their Whitewater investment. On **June 28**, Webster Hubbell, a close friend of the Clintons and formerly associate attorney general in the Justice Dept., was sentenced to 21 months in prison for tax evasion and mail fraud. He was ordered to pay $135,000 in restitution. Documents submitted at the sentencing hearing showed that Hubbell, who had pleaded guilty in Dec., had defrauded the Rose Law Firm and 15 of its clients of $482,410 and had failed to pay $143,747 in taxes on the embezzled money.

Clinton, Gingrich Discuss Issues—Pres. Clinton and House Speaker Newt Gingrich (R, GA) discussed public issues in June before an audience in New Hampshire that consisted largely of senior citizens. Each was visiting the state that in every presidential-campaign cycle commanded great attention because it held the first primary election. Remarks by Clinton, **June 8**, opened the door to a possible joint meeting with Gingrich. After arriving in the state, Gingrich declined to rule out a bid for the Republican nomination, saying, **June 10**, that media speculation about his plans helped focus attention on his ideas. He surprised the Clinton entourage by saying he would be eager to meet with the president. A face-to-face discussion, which was televised nationally, was set up at a senior citizens' center in Claremont, **June 11**. The hour-long exchange was friendly, not confrontational, and both Clinton and Gingrich agreed that they and their parties needed to cooperate more often in a bipartisan way. Gingrich said that Medicare could be reformed without reducing benefits to beneficiaries, but Clinton said that he favored a smaller cutback combined with a smaller federal tax cut than that currently supported by Gingrich. After Clinton endorsed an increase in the federal minimum wage, Gingrich predicted that this would force employers to lay off some low-wage employees. Gingrich called the UN's management of military operations a nightmare, but Clinton responded that the UN was "better than nothing." Clinton and Gingrich shook hands as they agreed to establish a commission to recommend reforms in lobbying and campaign-financing laws.

California Gov. Wilson in Presidential Race—Gov. Pete Wilson of California, generally viewed as being in the moderate wing of the Republican Party, entered the GOP contest for the presidential nomination in June. He said, **June 8**, that he would continue to seek removal of the antiabortion plank in the Republican national platform. The 1992 plank had called for a constitutional amendment forbidding abortion. Wilson said, **June 15**, that there was "no doubt" he would seek the nomination, and he announced his intention formally, **June 22**, during a television interview on *Larry King Live*. Wilson had been mayor of San Diego and a U.S. senator before being elected governor in 1990 and again in 1994.

President of AFL-CIO to Step Down—The president of the 13.3-million-member AFL-CIO, Lane Kirkland, announced, **June 12**, that he would retire in Aug. Kirkland, 73, had been president for 16 years. Opponents within the confederation indicated that they would support for president a candidate who would be more vigorous than they said Kirkland had been in opposing Republican policies.

Congress Approves Plan to Balance Budget—The Republican-controlled Senate and House in June approved a budget resolution that endorsed slashing spending and reducing taxes for corporations and individuals and that sought to balance the budget by 2002. Earlier, on **June 13**, Pres. Clinton presented a plan to balance the budget by

2005, over a period of 10 years, not 7. His spending cuts totaled $1.1 trillion. The Senate and House plan, approved **June 29**, projected $894 billion in spending reductions and $245 billion in tax cuts over 7 years. The latter figure was a compromise, being much less than the $353 billion in tax cuts supported by the House. The "reductions" were from currently projected levels of spending, and actual spending, overall, would continue to grow, from $1.588 trillion in 1996 to $1.876 trillion in 2002. The Republican plan would cut Medicare and Medicaid spending, as well as programs to assist the poor. Spending for the arts, Amtrak, and Clinton's national-service program would be phased out. Congress would seek to implement the resolution's spending guidelines in a series of bills to be considered later in the year.

Officer Acquitted in Downing of 2 U.S. Helicopters— A military court, **June 20**, acquitted Air Force Capt. James Wang of dereliction of duty in connection with the downing of 2 U.S. Army helicopters over Iraq in Apr. 1994. He had been the senior director of an AWACS plane flying in the vicinity of the helicopters. The crew of the radar plane failed to warn 2 U.S. jets that the helicopters were friendly. Missiles fired from the jets downed both helicopters, which the crews of the jets believed to be Iraqi aircraft in a no-fly zone, killing all 26 aboard. Wang said he thought that the helicopters had landed. Wang, the only person to be prosecuted, said, after his acquittal, that the Air Force should investigate the incident further.

Surgeon General Nomination Fails—Pres. Clinton's nominee for surgeon general, Dr. Henry Foster, failed to win approval of the Senate in June. Opponents of abortion lobbied strongly against the nomination, and the debate in the Senate focused more on that issue than on any other aspect of Foster's record. Republicans filibustered, and 2 unsuccessful attempts were made, **June 21** and **22**, to shut off debate. The efforts to impose cloture both failed by a 3-vote margin, 57-43 (60 votes were required under Senate rules), with 11 Republicans joining all 46 Democrats to vote for cloture. Foster then abandoned the effort to win Senate approval.

Texas Congressman Joins GOP—Rep. Greg Laughlin (TX) switched from the Democratic Party to the Republican Party, **June 26**. A conservative, Laughlin said that his philosophy could not be found "in the agenda of the House Democratic leadership." Laughlin switched after Republican leaders promised to create a new seat on the Ways and Means Committee for him. Also in Texas, **June 26**, 18 state and local Democratic officeholders joined the GOP.

U.S. Shuttle, Russian Space Station Dock—History was made in space in June, when the U.S. shuttle *Atlantis* docked with the Russian space station *Mir*. Atlantis lifted off from Cape Canaveral, FL, **June 27**, on the 100th U.S. piloted space mission. *Mir* had been orbiting since 1986. On **June 29**, after *Atlantis* had closed to within 1,000 ft of *Mir*, Capt. Robert Gibson operated the U.S. spacecraft manually until its docking system made contact with the space station's docking port. Two hours later, Gibson opened the shuttle's hatch, and astronauts from both spacecraft greeted one another. The 10 persons on board were the greatest number ever to travel together, and the combined mass of 223 tons was the greatest of any space vehicle. *Atlantis* was 112 ft in length, and *Mir*, 122 ft. On **June 30**, the astronauts began conducting experiments on health problems related to long periods of time in space. Before the *Atlantis* and *Mir* decoupled, **July 4**, Norman E. Thagard, an American who had been traveling in *Mir* since flying to it in a Russian spacecraft in Mar., and 2 Russians joined the *Atlantis* crew, while 2 other Russians who had been launched with *Atlantis* went to *Mir*. *Atlantis* landed in Florida, **July 7**, and Thagard set a U.S. record of 115 consecutive days in space, 112 of which were spent in *Mir*.

Unabomber Asks Publication of Manuscript—The notorious Unabomber, who had killed 3 men and caused injuries to 22 other people with bombs sent through the mail, threatened in June to blow up an airliner flying out of Los Angeles. The threat was made in a letter received by the *San Francisco Chronicle*, **June 27**. On **June 28**, however, the *New York Times* received a letter in which the writer said his threat had been a prank and added, "We haven't tried to plant a bomb on an airline (recently)." The *Times*, **June 28**, and the *Washington Post*, **June 29**, received copies of the bomber's 35,000-word manuscript entitled "Industrial Society and Its Future." In it, he attacked technological advances and called the Industrial Revolution a disaster for humans. He wrote that he feared that in the future machines controlled by computer experts would rule the human race. The bomber threatened to continue his attacks unless his manuscript was published. The *Times* and the *Post* said, **June 29**, that they were considering publishing the manifesto. This prompted a debate over whether a newspaper should give in to demands from a terrorist.

International

Downed U.S. Pilot Rescued in Bosnia—A U.S. F-16 fighter jet was shot down by a Russian-made surface-to-air missile over Bosnia and Herzegovina in June, and the pilot was rescued by U.S. Marines 6 days later. The pilot, Air Force Capt. Scott O'Grady, was on patrol over Serb-occupied territory, **June 2**, when his plane was hit by the Serb-launched missile and broke apart. O'Grady ejected safely and landed behind Serb lines. The Serbs and the U.S. military both made intense efforts to find O'Grady. On **June 8**, a U.S. plane picked up a message from O'Grady's voice radio, "I'm alive. Help." While 40 U.S. aircraft flew overhead, 2 helicopters with 40 Marines landed near the woods where O'Grady was hiding, and the pilot ran toward his rescuers. O'Grady said he had eaten plants and insects and drunk rainwater. He said, **June 10**, "All I was, was a scared little bunny rabbit trying to hide." He received a hero's welcome in the U.S. and had lunch with Pres. Bill Clinton at the White House, **June 12**.

Bosnian Serbs Release UN Hostages—As June began, the Bosnian Serbs were holding 370 UN peacekeepers hostage, and fighting between the Serbs and Bosnian government troops erupted in Gorazde, one of the UN-designated safe areas. On **June 2**, the Serbs released 121 hostages—even while seizing others elsewhere—and on **June 7** they freed 111 more. On **June 7**, talks in Belgrade between Pres. Slobodan Milosevic of Serbia and U.S. Deputy Asst. Secretary of State Robert Frasure ended without an agreement. The U.S. had been urging Serbia to pressure the Bosnian Serbs to reach a peace agreement with the Bosnian government, in exchange for which UN-imposed sanctions on Yugoslavia (Serbia and Montenegro) would be lifted. The UN acknowledged, **June 10**, that the Serbs had seized 285 heavy weapons near Sarajevo, the Bosnian capital, when they took the hostages. The Bosnian government said, **June 13**, that troops were being deployed near Sarajevo to protect it from the weapons. On **June 13**, the Serbs released most of their remaining hostages. Bosnian government forces, **June 15**, began an offensive aimed at lifting the 38-month Serb siege of Sarajevo. The Serbs freed their last 26 hostages, **June 18**.

Drug Cartel Leader Seized in Colombia—Colombian police, **June 9**, in Cali, arrested Gilberto Rodriguez Orejuela, believed to be a leader of the Cali drug cartel. Rodriguez had been indicted on drug charges in the U.S. U.S. officials had estimated that the Cali cartel, which preferred nonviolent means such as bribery rather than the terrorism preferred by the Medellin cartel, controlled nearly 80% of the cocaine smuggled into the U.S.

Cuban Government Arrests U.S. Fugitive—Robert Vesco, a one-time financier who had fled the U.S. in 1972, was arrested in Havana, Cuba, in June. He had been indicted in the U.S. in 1973 on charges of embezzling $224 million from a mutual fund, Investment Overseas Services Ltd. In another indictment, in 1989, he was charged with helping the Medellin drug cartel smuggle cocaine into the U.S. Vesco had lived in several Caribbean and Central American countries until being granted asylum in Cuba in the early 1980s. In announcing, **June 10**, the arrest of the fugitive, the Cuban government said that Vesco was suspected of being an agent for "foreign special services." Cuba said, **June 19**, that it did not plan to extradite Vesco.

Chechen Rebels Attack Russian Town—Russian officials claimed, **June 13**, that they had captured the last stronghold of the Chechen rebels. On **June 14**, however, Chechens led by Shamil Basayev attacked Budyonnovsk, a town in the Russian Caucasus about 70 mi north of the Chechen border. At a hospital, Chechens took about 2,000 patients and medical staff hostage and threatened to kill them if the Russians did not stop their offensive in Chechnya. Russian troops, **June 17**, stormed the hospital twice, but were able to free only about 50 hostages; the Chechens released 150 more. Premier Viktor Chernomyrdin then agreed to negotiate with Basayev, and their conversations, by telephone, **June 18** and **19**, were broadcast live on television. Basayev, **June 19**, agreed to free the hostages, and Chernomyrdin said he would agree to a cease-fire in Chechnya and begin peace talks with Chechen leader Dzhokhar Dudayev. About 140 soldiers, rebels, hostages, and others had died during the week. The talks began, **June 19**, in Grozny, the Chechen capital, and on **June 20** negotiators agreed to a 3-day cease-fire. Many Russian leaders asserted that Russia had been humiliated by the hostage crisis and the agreement to negotiate with the rebels, and on **June 21** the Duma, the lower house of parliament, approved, 241-72, a motion declaring no confidence in the government. Pres. Boris Yeltsin, **June 30**, dismissed 3 of his ministers for their alleged failures in connection with the hostage crisis.

"Group of 7" Leaders Hold 21st Summit—The leaders of the world's 7 wealthiest industrial nations (the U.S., Canada, Great Britain, France, Germany, Italy, and Japan) convened their 21st annual summit in Halifax, Nova Scotia, **June 15**. Pres. Jacques Chirac of France, **June 15**, called on his colleagues to support deployment of a rapid reaction force to help the UN carry out its mission in Bosnia. Pres. Boris Yeltsin of Russia, a guest of the "Group of 7" leaders, said, **June 17**, that Russia would attempt to use its influence with Serbia to bring an end to the conflict in Bosnia. In an implied criticism of Russia, the leaders voted to urge all nations to "avoid any collaboration with Iran which might contribute to the acquisition of a nuclear-weapons capability." When Chechen rebels seized a hospital in Russia, **June 17**, the leaders urged that a solution be found without resort to force, but Yeltsin objected, and Chechnya was not mentioned in the final communiqué.

Prime Minister Major Confronts Critics—British Prime Minister John Major sought to force the hand of his critics within the Conservative Party in June, by resigning as party leader. For some time, Tory members of Parliament had been blaming Major for the party's decline in popularity. As well, the party's so-called Euroskeptics opposed Major on the European Union, and they wanted assurances that Britain would not participate in a unified European currency. Saying he wanted to put an end to "phony threats" to his leadership, Major announced his resignation, **June 22**, and set July 4 as the date for the election of a new leader. Secretary of State for Wales John Redwood resigned from his cabinet position, **June 26**, and said he would challenge Major for leader. Pending the election, Major continued as prime minister.

Attempt to Assassinate Mubarak Fails—Gunmen attempted to kill Pres. Hosni Mubarak of Egypt during his visit to Addis Ababa, the capital of Ethiopia, **June 26**. Militants seeking to overthrow Mubarak and establish an Islamic state in Egypt were suspected in the attack. The assassination attempt occurred while Mubarak was on his way to a summit meeting of the Organization of African Unity. Gunmen in a jeep, joined by comrades on rooftops and on the street, fired at his limousine with automatic weapons, but Mubarak was not injured. Two Ethiopian police officers and 2 of the assailants were killed, and other people were wounded.

U.S. Drops Tariff Hikes on Japanese Cars—The U.S., **June 28**, dropped its plan for 100% tariff increases, announced in May, on 13 makes of Japanese luxury cars. The sanctions had been a response to the failure of the U.S. and Japan to reach an agreement on opening the latter's automobile and auto-parts markets to competition from other countries. On **June 28**, hours before the tariffs were to take effect, an agreement was reached. The major Japanese auto companies announced that they would buy more parts from the U.S. and other countries and increase production at their U.S. plants. The manufacturers agreed to import $6 billion in parts within 2 years. The Japanese government said it would make it easier for U.S. manufacturers of auto parts to sell replacement parts in Japanese repair shops, and it endorsed an increase in the number of Japanese dealerships that would sell American cars.

General

Houston Retains NBA Title—The defending champion Houston Rockets retained their National Basketball Assn. title in June. During the 1994-95 season, the Rockets had posted a modest regular-season record and were seeded 6th in the Western Conference. But they then won 3 series to take the conference title. They had rallied after being down, 3 games to 1 in the second round, to overcome the Phoenix Suns in the 7th and deciding game, 115-114. The Orlando Magic, meanwhile, won the Eastern Conference title. In the second round, the Magic had eliminated the Chicago Bulls, who had been bolstered by the return from retirement of Michael Jordan. In the Eastern Conference final, Orlando outlasted the Indiana Pacers in 7 games. The championship series featured a confrontation between 2 of the game's most acclaimed players, centers Hakeem Olajuwon of the Rockets and Shaquille O'Neal of the Magic. In the first game, **June 7**, Houston won in overtime at Orlando, 120-118. The Rockets won the second game in Orlando and the third in Houston and then completed a 4-game sweep by defeating the Magic in Houston, 113-101, on **June 14**. Olajuwon (for the second straight year) was named most valuable player in the final series.

"The Gloves Don't Fit!" O. J. Simpson—One of the most dramatic moments at the double-murder trial of O. J. Simpson occurred in June when he put on the blood-stained gloves allegedly worn by the killer. Earlier, on **June 5**, Judge Lance Ito dismissed 2 more jurors, leaving only 2 alternates. During the first 2 weeks of June, the Los Angeles County chief medical examiner, Dr. Lakshmanan Sathyavagiswaran, testified that the murders of Nicole Brown Simpson and her friend, Ronald Goldman, could have taken place within a few minutes and that just one knife could have been used. The murder weapon had never been found. He showed graphic photos of the victims that unsettled the jury and others present. He said, **June 6**, that Dr. Irwin Golden, the forensic pathologist who had performed autopsies on the victims, had made as many as 30 mistakes, but that they were mainly of little significance. The prosecution, **June 15**, asked Simpson to try on the bloody gloves; one had been found at the crime scene, and Detective Mark Fuhrman had testified that he had found the other at the defendant's estate. In 1990, Nicole Brown Simpson had purchased, at Bloomingdale's Dept. Store in New York City, a pair of gloves of the same brand and size. Simpson seemed to have difficulty pulling on the gloves and remarked, "Too tight, too tight." Later, outside the courtroom, Defense Attorney Johnnie Cochran exclaimed to the press, "The gloves don't fit!"

New Jersey Devils Win Hockey Title—The New Jersey Devils won their first Stanley Cup championship in June. The hockey season, off to a late start because of a labor dispute, came to a surprise climax in Brendan Byrne Arena, in East Rutherford, NJ, **June 24**, when the Devils completed a 4-game sweep of the championship series against the Detroit Red Wings. The score of the final game was 5-2. Claude Lemieux, a right wing for the Devils who had scored 13 goals during the playoffs, was named the most valuable player in the playoffs.

JULY 1995

National

In Policy Shift, Key Interest Rate Is Cut—The Federal Reserve Board, **July 6**, cut the federal funds rate, the interest rate charged by banks on overnight loans to each other, from 6% to 5.75%. Throughout 1994 and until Feb. 1995, the Fed had been nudging rates upward as a means of slowing economic growth and controlling inflation. Now, in the face of some predictions that a recession was in sight, a key interest rate was cut for the first time since 1992. The Commerce Dept. reported, **July 6**, that the index of leading economic indicators had declined for the 4th consecutive month in May, by 0.2%, the longest slide since a 6-month fall during the 1989 recession. The Labor Dept. said, **July 7**, that unemployment had edged downward in June, from 5.7% to 5.6%, and that employers had added 215,000 payroll jobs. The department said, **July 13**, that prices charged by manufacturers and farmers for finished goods had declined 0.1% in June. Conversely, it reported, **July 14**, that consumer prices had edged upward 0.1%. The long, sustained run-up in stock prices continued on Wall Street; on **July 17**, the Dow Jones industrial average closed at another all-time high, 4736.29. The Commerce Dept. said, **July 18**, that the May trade deficit stood at $11.43 billion. The department reported, **July 28**, that the gross domestic product had grown at an annual rate of 0.5% in the 2d quarter, the lowest quarterly increase since 1991.

Fletcher Seeks GOP Nomination—Arthur Fletcher, who was chairman of the U.S. Civil Rights Commission under Pres. George Bush, announced, **July 7**, that he would seek the Republican presidential nomination. Serving in the Labor Dept. during the Nixon administration, Fletcher developed affirmative-action programs to help minorities who had experienced discrimination. Fletcher, an African-American, said he opposed Republicans "trying to destroy" civil rights for minorities.

Senate Holds Whitewater Hearings—A Senate committee opened hearings in July into some aspects of the Whitewater affair. The Senate's special Whitewater committee, consisting largely of members of the Banking Committee, concentrated initially on the apparent suicide in July 1993 of Deputy White House Counsel Vincent Foster, who had handled matters for Bill and Hillary Rodham Clinton relating to their investment in the Whitewater Development Corp. Robert Fiske, the special counsel who had investigated Whitewater in 1994, had found no wrongdoing in the handling of Foster's papers after his death and had found that his suicide had nothing to do with Whitewater. However, his successor as special counsel, Kenneth Starr, was continuing to investigate Foster's death. The Senate planned to investigate why then-White House Counsel Bernard Nussbaum had prevented police officers and federal agents from examining Foster's papers and why papers taken from Foster's office had been transferred to the Clintons. Webster Hubbell, associate attorney general in the Justice Dept. when Foster died, testified before the Senate panel, **July 19**, that he and others had urged Nussbaum, without success, to avoid any official role in the Foster inquiry because of his close personal friendship with Foster. Patsy Thomasson, a White House staff member,

testified, **July 25**, that on the night Foster died she had looked for a suicide note in his office and had found none, even in the briefcase where, 6 days later, White House aides said they found a torn-up note. Henry O'Neill, a Secret Service officer, testified, **July 26**, that he had seen Margaret Williams, chief of staff for First Lady Hillary Rodham Clinton, leave Foster's office on the night of his death carrying an armful of folders. Williams, testifying **July 26**, denied that she had taken files from the office. She did acknowledge that 2 days after his death she had removed files designated by Nussbaum and taken them to the Clintons. Michael Spafford, a lawyer for Foster's family, testified, **July 27**, that 2 days after Foster's death he had heard a White House lawyer call Nussbaum's attention to the suicide note.

Heat Wave Fatal to 800—At least 800 people died in the Middle West and Northeast as a result of a heat wave that smothered the region between **July 12** and 17. In Chicago, where the temperature reached an all-time high of 106 degrees on **July 13**, 536 deaths were blamed on the heat. Many of the victims were elderly people who lived alone and who could not afford air conditioning. Large numbers of cattle and chickens died. Pres. Bill Clinton announced, **July 21**, that $100 million in federal emergency aid would be distributed to 19 states.

Clinton Accepts Base-Closing Proposal—On **July 13**, Pres. Bill Clinton accepted the latest recommendations of the Defense Base Closure and Realignment Commission. The commission proposed to close 79 military bases and consolidate 26 others. The Defense Dept. estimated that these steps would save $1.6 billion a year. Directly or indirectly, the closings and consolidations would cause the loss of more than 90,000 jobs held by military personnel and civilians. Clinton deplored that most job losses were in only 2 states, California and Texas. Congress was now required to vote on the issue, and under a previous agreement the House and Senate could only vote the entire list of recommendations up or down, with no additions or deletions.

House Holds Hearings on Waco Cult Siege—Two House subcommittees began hearings, **July 19**, on the siege by federal agents in 1993 of a compound occupied by the Branch Davidian religious cult. Six cultists and 4 agents of the Bureau of Alcohol, Tobacco and Firearms (ATF) had died, Feb. 28, 1993, during an initial attempt to raid the compound and arrest cult leader David Koresh on weapons charges. On Apr. 19, after a 51-day standoff, agents attacked with tear gas and tanks, and a fire consumed the compound and killed about 80 cultists. The hearing opened with Democrats generally defending the actions of government agencies and Republicans contending that ineptitude of the Clinton administration was partly responsible for the large loss of life. Kiri Jewell, who was 14 years old, told the committee, **July 19**, that while she lived at the Waco compound she had been sexually molested by Koresh at age 10. She said that cultists had discussed ways of committing suicide. Robert Rodriguez, an ATF agent who had infiltrated the cult, testified, **July 24**, that his superiors had ignored his warning that Koresh had become aware of the impending February raid, and went ahead with it. Two of his superiors testified, **July 24**, that his warning had been too vague to prompt cancellation of the raid. Two Davidian lawyers testified, **July 25**, that Koresh would have surrendered if the FBI had honored his request that he be allowed to finish a paper on the Seven Seals described in the Bible. James Quintiere of the University of Maryland told the committee, **July 28**, that evidence indicated that cultists had started the fire in the compound. Clive Doyle, a Davidian, denied that the cultists planned a mass suicide and testified, **July 28**, that he had not heard anyone in the compound say anything on the day of the fire about spreading fuel for a fire. Then-Associate Attorney Gen. Webster Hubbell told the panel, **July 28**, that Pres. Bill Clinton had not pressured him to bring the standoff to a forceful end. Attorney Gen. Janet Reno testified, **Aug. 1**, that she had ordered the FBI to launch the gas attack, that Clinton had not tried to influence her decision, and that Koresh was responsible for the tragic ending.

Affirmative Action Programs Debated—Pres. Bill Clinton, **July 19**, strongly defended affirmative action programs, which were designed to ensure that minorities and women would not be victims of discrimination in the workplace, in college admissions, and in other areas. Republicans argued that such programs constituted reverse discrimination, causing better-qualified candidates for employment, promotion, and college admission to be passed over in favor of less-deserving applicants so that racial and gender "quotas" could be met. Contending that the best approach was "Mend it, but don't end it," Clinton, **July 19**, issued an executive order directing federal agencies to reform or eliminate programs if they created quota-based preference systems, gave preference to unqualified candidates, created reverse discrimination, or continued after the goal of attaining equal opportunity had been met. With the strong support of Gov. Pete Wilson (R), the California Board of Regents, **July 20**, voted, 14-10, to end consideration of race, sex, religion, color, ethnicity, or national origin in the admission of students. The board voted, 15-10, to end affirmative action in the hiring of faculty and awarding of contracts.

Curb on Regulations Fails in Senate—A Democratic filibuster in July killed a Republican-supported Senate bill that would have reduced the scope and force of federal regulations on business in such areas as health, safety, and the environment. A promise to reduce the burden of regulation had been included in the GOP Contract With America in 1994, and the House had passed a tough antiregulation bill earlier in 1995. The Senate bill would have required a cost-benefit analysis for any regulation costing the economy more than $100 million. It would have allowed Congress to kill new regulations seen as burdensome to industry and would have broadened rights of business owners to challenge federal agencies in court. On **July 20**, after a 58-40 vote on their 3d attempt to cut off debate fell 2 votes short of the required 60, Republicans gave up on the bill.

Clinton Signs Revision of Bill He Vetoed—Pres. Bill Clinton, **July 27**, signed a revised version of the rescissions bill that he had rejected in June when he cast his first veto. The new version, in many ways, did not differ greatly from its predecessor. It cut $16.3 billion from spending previously approved by Congress for fiscal 1995, but it restored $770 billion that Clinton wanted for education, training, and environmental programs. Environmentalists were angered by a provision in the new bill that allowed removal of dead and dying trees from federal lands in so-called salvage operations.

Three Large Industrial Unions Vote to Merge—On **July 27**, the leaders of the 3 largest industrial labor unions in the U.S.—the United Automobile Workers, the United Steel Workers of America, and the International Assn. of Machinists and Aerospace Workers—voted to merge by the year 2000. Together, the 3 unions had about 2 million members, but their ranks had been thinning and their bargaining power declining.

Senators Restrict Gifts to Themselves—Caught up in the reform fervor in Washington, the Senate, **July 28**, voted, 98-0, to bar senators and members of their staffs from accepting vacation trips and other expensive gifts, other than from close friends and relatives. Under these new rules, a senator could accept no more than $100 in gifts from a single source in a year, excepting only any gifts valued at under $10. Any gift from a close friend or family member valued at more than $250 was subject to approval by the Senate Ethics Committee. Lobbyists would now be unable to treat a senator to an expenses-paid golfing or skiing trip, and they would be unable to contribute to a senator's legal-defense fund.

Disney to Buy ABC in $19 Billion Deal—The Walt Disney Co. would buy Capital Cities/ABC Inc. for some $19 billion in stock and cash, the 2 companies announced, **July 31**. Disney was largely a creator of entertainment programs, and ABC was a major presenter of entertainment. Under new rule changes adopted by the Federal Communications Commission, networks would soon have greater flexibility in producing their own programming. Disney would borrow $10 billion to finance the purchase.

International

Tories Keep John Major as Party Leader—Prime Minister John Major of Great Britain won his big political gamble in July, as his colleagues reconfirmed him as leader of the Conservative Party. Having endured much criticism from Tory members of Parliament, Major resigned his party leadership in June to force party members to either endorse his leadership or replace him. Appealing to right-wing critics, Major declared, **July 3**, that he supported lower taxes, more privatization, and a smaller government, but, in a disappointment for the so-called Euroskeptics, he did not rule out participation in the economic and monetary union of the European Union. In the leadership vote among Conservative members of Parliament, **July 4**, 218 MPs backed Major, and 89 supported his challenger, former Secretary of State for Wales John Redwood.

Israel, PLO Reach New Agreement—Meeting in the Gaza Strip, **July 4**, Israeli Foreign Minister Shimon Peres and Yasir Arafat, leader of the Palestine National Authority, agreed in principle to the next phase of their agreement. Israeli soldiers would be redeployed away from centers of Palestinian population in the West Bank. Palestinian elections would follow. A Palestinian suicide bomber killed himself and 5 others in a bus in a Tel Aviv suburb, **July 24**.

Serbs Seize 2 Bosnian "Safe Areas"—The Bosnian Serbs in July seized 2 towns designated as safe areas. The UN had promised to protect civilians in the 6 towns so designated—Bihac, Gorazde, Sarajevo, Srebrenica, Tuzla, and Zepa. The Serbs began their advance on Srebrenica, **July 6**, overran 3 UN observation posts, and seized 30 Dutch peacekeepers, **July 8** and **9**. NATO planes—Dutch and American—attacked Serb positions twice, **July 11**, but suspended a third attack when the Serbs threatened to kill their hostages. Srebrenica fell, **July 11**, and Pres. Jacques Chirac of France said his country would be willing to use force to take it back, but other European nations did not support him. The Serbs, **July 12**, began transporting refugees from Srebrenica to Bosnian government territory. On **July 12** and **13**, tens of thousands of refugees from Srebrenica made their own way to Tuzla. Serbs in Srebrenica committed many atrocities, raping women and killing men and boys. By **July 16**, Serbs were closing in on Zepa. Government soldiers surrounded 79 Ukrainian peacekeepers, **July 18**, and threatened to use them as shields against the Serbs unless NATO attacked the advancing Serbs from the air. The Serbs, **July 20**, opened another offensive in the vicinity of Bihac. In Gorazde, government forces confiscated the weapons of about 400 UN peacekeepers in order to use them against an anticipated Serb attack. The U.S., **July 20**, got Britain's support for an air campaign against the Serbs to prevent further assaults on the safe areas. The Serbs, **July 21**, released 308 Dutch peacekeepers they had held hostage. France, **July 24**, backed air strikes. Zepa fell to the Serbs, **July 25**. In The Hague, the Netherlands, **July 25**, the International Criminal Tribunal for the Former Yugoslavia indicted Radovan Karadzic, leader of the Bosnian Serbs, and Gen. Ratko Mladac, the Bosnian Serb military commander, for crimes against humanity, including the killings and mass deportations of civilians and the seizing of hostages for use as human shields. Twenty-two other Serbs were also indicted. The U.S. Senate, **July 26**, passed, 69-29, a bill that would end U.S. participation in the arms embargo against the Bosnian government. Pres. Bill Clinton opposed the unilateral lifting of the embargo, because Britain and France had threatened to pull their peacekeepers out of Bosnia in that event, and the U.S. had promised to send troops into Bosnia to help evacuate the peacekeepers. In a reversal of fortune, **July 28**, Croatian and Bosnian Croat troops seized 2 Serb-held towns and cut off Serb access to the Serb-occupied Krajina region of Croatia. On **July 30**, after Pres. Franjo Tudjman of Croatia threatened to invade the Krajina, the Croatian Serbs agreed to fall back from Bihac.

Myanmar Junta Frees Winner of Nobel Prize—Daw Aung San Suu Kyi, a leading pro-democracy dissident in Myanmar (formerly Burma), was freed from house arrest, **July 10**. In 1988, she had helped found the National League for Democracy party, which had won the national election in 1990. The ruling junta nullified the results. Aung San Suu Kyi, meanwhile, had been placed under house arrest in 1989 for "endangering the state." In 1991, she received the Nobel Peace Prize. On **July 11**, she told supporters that she would continue to work for democracy.

U.S., Vietnam Open Diplomatic Relations—Twenty years after the U.S. military departed in haste from Saigon and after Communist-run North Vietnam absorbed South Vietnam, the U.S. and Vietnam formally established diplomatic relations in July. The effective bar to normalizing relations had been the belief by many Americans that Vietnam was not telling all it knew about 1,618 U.S. military personnel officially listed as missing in action in Vietnam. Vietnam had dribbled out information over the years. In Feb. 1994, Pres. Bill Clinton had lifted the U.S. trade embargo on Vietnam, to the delight of American business. Liaison offices were opened in the capitals of both countries in Jan. 1995. In May, Vietnam released more historical documentation on the MIAs. In announcing the opening of diplomatic ties, **July 11**, Clinton predicted that more information on missing U.S. combatants would be forthcoming. Reflecting views of those who opposed normalization, Senate Majority Leader Bob Dole (R, KS) said, **July 11**, that Vietnam was "willfully withholding information" on MIAs.

Iraq Frees 2 Americans—Two Americans arrested in Iraq in Mar. were freed in July. The two, William Barloon and David Daliberti, were employed by U.S. defense contractors in Kuwait. Relatives and friends of the 2 said that they had crossed the Iraq boundary in error while traveling to visit a friend at a border post. An Iraqi court sentenced them in Mar. to 8 years in prison. Rep. Bill Richardson (D, NM) initiated secret negotiations with Iraq to free the Americans, and he went to Iraq to meet with Pres. Saddam Hussein, **July 16**. After the meeting, Hussein announced he had pardoned and ordered the release of the Americans.

Truce Ends Fighting in Chechnya—Six weeks of peace talks in Grozny, the capital of the breakaway republic of Chechnya, ended in success, **July 30**, when Russian and Chechen negotiators signed an agreement to end the fighting. The talks, overseen by the Organization for Security and Cooperation in Europe, had begun after Chechens led by Shamil Basayev had seized 2,000 Russian hostages and demanded that the Russians negotiate seriously with the Chechens. Interior Minister Anatoly Kulikov, the chief Russian negotiator, said, **July 31**, that 1,800 Russian soldiers had been killed in the fighting and 6,500 had been wounded. Some 20,000 Russian and Chechen civilians had been killed. Although the agreement provided for the exchange of prisoners, the disarming of the Chechen forces, and the withdrawal of most Russian soldiers from the area, the future status of Chechnya was not resolved and was to be the subject of further talks.

General

O. J. Simpson's Defense Opens Its Case—The prosecution in the double-murder trial of O. J. Simpson rested its case, **July 6**, after presenting 58 witnesses and 488 exhibits during 92 days of testimony. The defense opened its case, **July 10**, with testimony from the defendant's mother, a sister, and his daughter from his first marriage. They said that Simpson was grief-stricken and distraught in the hours after he learned of his wife's death. A neighbor, Robert Heidstra, testified, **July 11**, that, while walking his dog at

about 10:40 PM, he had heard 2 men quarreling. Had the murders been committed that late, the defendant would have had little time to dispose of evidence, return home, change clothes, and meet the limousine driver at 11 PM. In cross-examination, **July 12**, Heidstra acknowledged that he had seen a white car similar to Simpson's Ford Bronco leaving the crime scene in haste at about 10:40. Dr. Robert Huizenga, who examined the defendant after the murders, testified, **July 14**, that he was in poor physical condition as a result of football injuries and arthritis, casting doubt that he could have committed 2 murders and acted with apparent necessary speed thereafter. The prosecution, **July 17** and **18**, played an exercise video Simpson had made 2 weeks before the murders in which he ran in place and did pushups and bodybends. Dr. Fredric Rieders, a forensic pathologist, testified, **July 24**, that blood matching that of Nicole Brown Simpson, found on a sock in O. J. Simpson's bedroom, and blood matching that of the defendant, found on a gate at the crime scene, contained a preservative indicating that the blood came from a test tube. This buttressed a defense theory that evidence in the case had been planted to frame the defendant. An FBI agent, Roger Martz, testified, **July 25**, that what Rieders had concluded was a preservative could just as well have been contamination from the testing instrument or any of a number of similar chemical compounds. On **July 27**, Herbert MacDonell, a member of the International Assn. of Blood Stain Pattern Analysts, testified that blood on the sock at the foot of Simpson's bed had gotten there by touch, not by splatter, and some had seeped through to the other side, which could not have happened if Simpson had been wearing it.

Sampras, Graf Win at Wimbledon—Steffi Graf of Germany won the All-England (Wimbledon) women's singles tennis title for the 6th time, **July 8**. The top-seeded Graf defeated the second seed, Arantxa Sanchez Vicario of Spain, 4-6, 6-1, 7-5, in the final. Pete Sampras of the U.S. won his third consecutive men's singles title, **July 9**, defeating Germany's Boris Becker, 6-7, 6-2, 6-4, 6-2. Sampras was the first American to win the men's title at Wimbledon 3 times in a row.

Mother Gets Life for Drowning 2 Sons—Susan Smith, the Union, SC, mother who had confessed in Nov. to drowning her two young sons by allowing a car to roll into a lake with the boys locked inside, was found guilty of 2 counts of first-degree murder, **July 22**. The prosecution sought the death penalty. The defense contended that her behavior was the outgrowth of a deeply troubled personal life. Her father had committed suicide, and she had been molested by her stepfather, Beverly Russell, at age 15 and had had an affair with him in 1993 and 1994. As a teenager, she had attempted suicide. Russell read a letter in court, **July 27**, that he had written to his daughter, acknowledging his heartbreak "for what I have done to you" and adding, "You don't have all the guilt in this tragedy." The apparent immediate cause of the 2 murders was a letter from Smith's boyfriend, Tom Findlay, saying he was breaking off with her because he didn't want a relationship with a mother with 2 children. The circuit court jury in Union, **July 28**, sentenced Smith to life in prison. She would be eligible for parole in 30 years. Smith's husband, David, said he was disappointed that she had not received the death penalty.

AUGUST 1995

National

Two Committees End Whitewater Hearings—A Senate special committee concluded its inquiry in Aug. into events that followed the apparent 1993 suicide of Deputy White House Counsel Vince Foster, who had handled matters relating to the Whitewater investment by Pres. Bill Clinton and First Lady Hillary Rodham Clinton. Philip

Heymann, who had been deputy attorney general in 1993, told the committee, **Aug. 2,** that on the day after Foster's death then-White House Counsel Bernard Nussbaum had agreed to let 2 Justice Dept. prosecutors examine Foster's files. Heymann said, however, that Nussbaum did not let them look at the files as he alone went through them. Two witnesses testified, **Aug. 3,** that Margaret Williams, the chief of staff for First Lady Hillary Rodham Clinton, had indicated that files Williams was removing from Foster's office would be going to Mrs. Clinton at her request and would be reviewed by her. Williams had testified in July that the files were not removed at Mrs. Clinton's request and she did not review them. At the onset, **Aug. 7,** of 4 days of hearings by the House Banking Committee, Chairman Jim Leach (R, IA) released hundreds of documents relating to ties between the Clintons and James McDougal involving Madison Guaranty Savings and Loan and the Whitewater Development Corp. McDougal was owner of Madison, which subsequently failed, and he and his then-wife Susan were partners with the Clintons in Whitewater. The documents seemed to suggest that the Clintons had taken more of an interest in Whitewater's finances than they had claimed. L. Jean Lewis, an investigator for the Resolution Trust Corp., a federal agency, testified at the House hearings, **Aug. 8** and **9,** that Treasury and Justice Dept. officials had obstructed her efforts to look into the relationship between Whitewater and Madison. At the Senate hearings, **Aug. 9** and **10,** Nussbaum asserted that as White House counsel he had had an ethical duty to protect the confidentiality of files related to the Clintons. He said there was no connection between Whitewater and how files were handled after Foster died. The Senate and House hearings concluded, **Aug. 10.** McDougal and his ex-wife were indicted **Aug. 17** by a federal grand jury for arranging fraudulent loans through Madison and an investment firm, Capital Management Services, to fund business ventures. The McDougals and Gov. Jim Guy Tucker (D), who had been indicted on other charges in June, were charged with laundering loans and other transactions through phony companies to conceal income.

Senate Rejects Public Hearings on Packwood—By a 52-48 margin the Senate voted, **Aug. 2,** not to hold public hearings into charges against Sen. Robert Packwood (R, OR). As reports of further allegations against him emerged, Packwood, **Aug. 25,** reversed his position and called for public hearings.

Slide in Economic Indicators Ends—After falling for 4 consecutive months, the index of leading economic indicators edged upward 0.2% in June, the Commerce Dept. said, **Aug. 2.** The Labor Dept. reported, **Aug. 4,** that the unemployment rate had increased slightly in July, from 5.6% to 5.7%. The Federal Reserve Board said, **Aug. 9,** that the economy was expanding, but at a slow rate. The Fed said that inflationary pressures were still present. Prices charged by manufacturers and farmers for finished goods remained unchanged in July, the Labor Dept. said, **Aug. 10.** The department reported, **Aug. 11,** that consumer prices had risen 0.2% in July. By mid-August the U.S. dollar had recovered most of the losses it had suffered in world currency markets during the first 4 months of 1995. On **Aug. 15,** after coordinated buying of dollars by the central banks of the U.S., Germany, Japan, and Switzerland, the dollar jumped to 96.99 yen and 1.4778 marks. The Commerce Dept. said, **Aug. 17,** that the trade deficit in June had been $11.31 billion.

Another House Democrat Joins GOP—Rep. W. J. "Billy" Tauzin (LA) announced, **Aug. 6,** he was switching from the Democratic Party to the Republican Party. He had supported all the provisions of the GOP Contract With America and had been a consistent defender of private property rights and an opponent of environmental regulations. The Republicans now had 233 House seats and the Democrats 201, and there was one independent.

Congressman Guilty on Sex Charges—Rep. Mel Reynolds (D, IL) was convicted in August on charges relating to his relationship with a teenage campaign worker. Beverly Heard had made allegations against Reynolds, later recanted them, and then testified in a Cook County courtroom, **Aug. 7** and **8,** that she had often had sex with Reynolds when she was 16. It was illegal in Illinois for an adult to have sex with a 16-year-old or for a person in a position of authority to have sex with a 17-year-old. Reynolds, **Aug. 22,** was convicted of sexual assault, sexual abuse, soliciting child pornography, and obstructing justice. He announced, **Sept. 1,** that he would resign from the House on Oct. 1. On **Sept. 28,** Reynolds was sentenced to 5 years in prison.

Guilty Plea Entered in Oklahoma Bombing—Michael Fortier, who had been implicated in the bombing of a federal building in Oklahoma City in April, pleaded guilty to 4 charges, **Aug. 10,** after reaching a plea-bargain agreement with prosecutors and agreeing to testify about the bombing. Fortier admitted conspiring to transport stolen firearms and then transporting them, making false statements to the FBI, and failing to report a crime. He was an Army friend of Timothy McVeigh, a prime suspect in the bombing. Both McVeigh and Terry Nichols were indicted on new charges, **Aug. 10,** including conspiracy to blow up the federal building and robbing a gun dealer, which, according to prosecutors, helped finance the plot. U.S. Attorney Patrick Ryan said, **Aug. 10,** that he would ask the death penalty for McVeigh and Nichols. On **Aug. 10,** in Detroit, charges against James Nichols, Terry's brother, related to the detonation of bombs on the former's property, were dropped. McVeigh and Terry Nichols pleaded not guilty, **Aug. 15,** to the new charges. The Oklahoma state medical examiner said, **Aug. 30,** that a severed leg, clad in a combat boot and found in the building rubble, was that of a black woman and that it did not belong to any known victim. The death count thus became 169, including a nurse killed during the rescue effort.

Clinton Seeks to Stop Under-18 Smoking—Pres. Bill Clinton, **Aug. 10,** endorsed proposed Food and Drug Administration regulations aimed at curbing the use of tobacco by young people. Clinton noted that 3,000 teenagers began to smoke each day, and one-third of them would eventually die of smoking-related causes. The FDA rules would allow tobacco to be sold only to persons 18 or older, prohibit the sale of cigarettes by mail or from vending machines, ban brand-name tobacco advertising at athletic events, keep outdoor tobacco advertising 1,000 yards from schools and playgrounds, and require the tobacco industry to spend $150 million a year on ads to discourage smoking by young people. In North Carolina, **Aug. 10,** 5 tobacco companies and an ad agency filed suit against the regulations, claiming that the FDA was exceeding its authority. In a suit in New York, **Aug. 10,** advertising groups and a publishing group asserted that the rules violated the First Amendment to the Constitution. The Philip Morris and R. J. Reynolds tobacco companies agreed, **Aug. 21,** to drop libel suits against ABC News after ABC apologized for reporting in 1994 that tobacco companies had added nicotine from outside sources to cigarettes in order to addict smokers.

Candidates Flock to Perot Conference—Ross Perot, the Texas billionaire who had captured 19% of the vote for president in 1992, was host to a conference in Dallas, **Aug. 11-13,** sponsored by his grassroots political organization, United We Stand America. The possible formation of a third party was a prime topic of discussion. Ten declared candidates for the 1996 Republican presidential nomination attended, and Patrick Buchanan got the most enthusiastic reception with a forceful speech attacking foreign aid, illegal immigration, affirmative action, and U.S. international trade policy. House Speaker Newt Gingrich (R, GA) headed a large congressional contingent at the conference. Addressing the conference on **Aug. 13,** Perot called for campaign-finance and lobbying reforms, term limits for members of Congress, and adoption of a balanced-budget amendment to the U.S. Constitution. Perot made no commitment concerning a run for president in 1996, and no consensus among grassroots activists on forming a third party emerged. Third-party talk flourished anew, **Aug. 16**, when Sen. Bill Bradley (D, NJ) announced that he would not seek reelection in 1996. He left the door open, **Aug. 17**, to an independent candidacy for president. He said that both political parties had "settled into familiar ruts" and had lost touch with average Americans. Gov. Pete Wilson of California, whose presidential efforts had been delayed by throat surgery and a conflict over the California state budget, restarted his campaign, **Aug. 28**, with a speech in New York using the Statue of Liberty as a backdrop. He emphasized his opposition to affirmative-action programs and government benefits for illegal aliens, and his record of cutting welfare spending and getting tough with criminals.

Admitted to Citadel, Woman Then Resigns—Shannon Faulkner won her long legal fight in Aug. to gain admission to the cadet corps of the Citadel, but she resigned 4 days later. Applying by mail in 1993, she had been accepted, but her admission was barred when the all-male school discovered she was a female. A federal appeals court held in Apr. 1995 that the Citadel must admit women until South Carolina established a comparable program open to women. An appeal by the academy to the U.S. Supreme Court was turned down by Chief Justice William Rehnquist and Justice Antonin Scalia, **Aug. 11**. Faulkner attended an orientation, **Aug. 12**, and was admitted to the cadet corps, **Aug. 14**. The Citadel was widely known for the harshness of its training and hazing of freshmen, but in a concession, Faulkner was not required to have her head shaved. During the first day of training she, as well as some other cadets, became ill in the 100-degree weather. On **Aug. 18**, Faulkner announced that she was leaving the Citadel and said she saw no point in "killing myself just for the political point." In all, 35 of 592 new cadets dropped out during the first week. Faulkner's lawyer said, **Aug. 22**, that another woman would become a plaintiff in the suit against the Citadel.

1992 Idaho Siege Still Rankles Government—A deadly standoff between white separatists and federal agents in Idaho in 1992 continued to trouble the U.S. government in Aug. During the siege at the cabin of the family of Randall Weaver in the Ruby Ridge area, 3 people were killed: a deputy U.S. marshal, William Degan, and Weaver's wife, Vicki, and son, Samuel. The Justice Dept. had found in 1994 that the FBI had withheld from prosecutors or destroyed documents relating to the siege. On **Aug. 11**, FBI Director Louis Freeh suspended 4 FBI officials indefinitely with pay as a result of that investigation, whose results had not been released. Those suspended included Larry Potts, who had been demoted from deputy FBI director in July. The Justice Dept. agreed, **Aug. 15**, to pay Weaver and his 3 daughters $3.1 million. The Weavers had filed wrongful death claims totaling $200 million. Hearings on the Ruby Ridge shootout, conducted in Sept. by a subcommittee of the Senate Judiciary Committee, did not produce significant new information.

International

Serbs Pounded on Ground and From Air—The Bosnian Serbs took a pounding in Aug., from their adversaries on the ground and from NATO aircraft. NATO, **Aug. 1**, warned the Serbs of air attacks if they attacked any of the UN's 4 remaining safe areas in Bosnia and Herzegovina. The U.S. House, **Aug. 1**, voted, 298-128, to require Pres. Bill Clinton to end U.S. participation in the arms embargo imposed on Bosnia. On **Aug. 4**, Croatian government forces attacked the Krajina region of Croatia, nearly 3,500 sq mi in size, which had been populated largely by Serbs for 500 years. A conflict in 1991-92 had left Serb military forces in control of the Krajina and Slavonia, also in Croa-

tia. Croatian forces had captured Western Slavonia in May, and in their newest offensive more than 100,000 Croatian troops advanced along a broad front and recaptured the entire Krajina by **Aug. 7**. The Croatian offensive raised the siege of Bihac, one of the safe areas in Bosnia, and the Bosnian army soon held sway in that region. Croatia acknowledged, **Aug. 7**, that it had been responsible for the deaths of 3 UN peacekeepers. Some 120,000 Serb civilians fled the Krajina for Serb-controlled areas. There were many reports of Croatian soldiers shooting Serb civilians. Pres. Slobodan Milosevic of Serbia, the principal component of what was left of Yugoslavia, said that the Bosnian Serbs were at fault for the continuing war and that Yugoslavia would not be dragged into the war. The U.S., **Aug. 10**, released spy-satellite photographs that may have shown mass graves near Srebrinica, which Bosnian Serb forces had seized in July. Thousands of Muslim men and boys from the area were missing. Clinton, **Aug. 11**, vetoed the bill passed by Congress that would have unilaterally ended U.S. participation in the arms embargo against the Bosnian government. Three U.S. negotiators, including U.S. Deputy Asst. Secretary of State Robert Frasure, were killed, **Aug. 19**, when their armored vehicle plunged from a mountain road near Sarajevo. Two mortar shells struck a market in Sarajevo, one of the safe areas, **Aug. 28**, and killed 38 persons. Later in the day, a hospital was struck. Pres. Alija Izetbegovic of Bosnia declared, **Aug. 29**, that his government would not participate in more peace talks until Serb artillery was withdrawn from around Sarajevo. The Bosnian Serb parliament said, **Aug. 29**, that an international peace plan reducing the amount of land controlled by the Serbs was acceptable as a basis of negotiations. This message was not enough to avert the punishing wrath of NATO air attacks in response to the shelling of Sarajevo. On **Aug. 30** and **31**, 60 NATO aircraft, which included 48 U.S. planes, attacked Serb missiles, artillery, ammunition depots, and barracks near Sarajevo. One French jet was downed by a surface-to-air missile, and the 2 pilots parachuted into Serb territory. On the ground, British, French, and Dutch soldiers lobbed artillery shells at Serb gun emplacements.

Anniversaries of Atomic Bombings Observed—The 50th anniversaries of the dropping of 2 atomic bombs over Japan in 1945, during World War II, were observed in Aug. The U.S. bombings, approved by Pres. Harry Truman, were carried out with the objective of shortening the war and averting the large number of casualties that could be expected if allied forces had invaded Japan on the ground. The morality and military justification for the attacks had been debated ever since. Some 100,000 people attended a service, **Aug. 6**, in Hiroshima, at the site of the first bombing. Mayor Takashi Hiraoka of Hiroshima apologized for atrocities committed by Japanese troops during the war. Premier Tomiichi Murayama rebuked China and France for continuing to test nuclear weapons. Japanese officials put the total deaths in the Hiroshima bombing at 192,020, including those who died later from radiation poisoning. The anniversary of the bombing of Nagasaki, where perhaps 100,000 died, then or later, was observed, **Aug. 9**. The bombings had brought World War II to a quick close. On **Aug. 15**, marking the 50th anniversary of the Japanese surrender, Murayama became the first Japanese premier to use the word *apology* in reference to Japan's "colonial rule and aggression" against other countries. Japan's hesitation to voice apologies over the decades had been a source of complaint from South Korea, China, the Philippines, and other countries. Murayama noted that Japan, as the first and still only country to suffer atomic devastation, had also been a victim in the war. In a speech in Honolulu, **Sept. 2**, the 50th anniversary of the formal Japanese surrender that ended World War II, Pres. Bill Clinton paid tribute to American veterans of what he called the most destructive conflict in all human history.

Roundup of Drug Cartel Leaders Continues—Police in Colombia, **Aug. 6**, captured Miguel Rodriguez Orejuela, reputed co-leader of the Cali drug cartel. He was specifically charged with shipping cocaine to Costa Rica. The cartel, believed to control most of the world's cocaine market, had seen 6 of its leaders arrested by police since June, and only one senior cartel leader was still at large.

Relatives of Iraqi President Defect—The regime of Pres. Saddam Hussein of Iraq was shaken, **Aug. 8**, when his 2 eldest daughters and their husbands and other senior army officers defected. The 2 sons-in-law, who were also brothers, had been important officials. Lt. Gen. Hussein Kamel Hassan al-Majid had headed the chemical, biological, and nuclear weapons program, and Lt. Col. Saddam Kamel Hassan al-Majid had been head of presidential security. It was announced, **Aug. 10**, that Jordan, a neighbor of Iraq, had granted asylum to all the defectors, and Jordan's King Hussein rejected an appeal from Pres. Hussein to extradite the defectors. Hussein Kamel said, **Aug. 12**, that he thought he could do more to bring down Pres. Hussein from outside the government, and he urged Iraq's army to overthrow the president. Anticipating that Hussein Kamel would disclose information on Iraqi nuclear weapons, Iraqi Deputy Premier Tariq Aziz, **Aug. 13**, said Iraq would provide data it had withheld from the UN. King Hussein said, **Aug. 14**, that it was time for a change in Iraq. Between **Aug. 17** and **20**, Rolf Ekeus, chairman of the UN Special Commission on Iraq, met in Baghdad with Iraqi officials who gave him information on biological and nuclear weapons. Iraq acknowledged that it had begun to work on a nuclear-weapons program in 1990, but that Allied bombing during the Gulf War in 1991 had set it back. UN officials said, **Aug. 22**, that Iraqis had also admitted manufacturing botulin and anthrax, 2 lethal bacteria. Ekeus met with Hussein Kamel in Amman, Jordan, **Aug. 22**. On **Aug. 25**, Ekeus said that in 1990 Iraq had launched a crash program to build a nuclear weapon.

China Convicts, Expels U.S. Citizen—Harry Wu, an American citizen and human rights activist, was expelled from China in Aug. after being convicted of spying. Originally a citizen of China, Wu had spent 19 years in Chinese labor camps for criticizing the Communist Party. He came to the U.S. in 1985 and became a naturalized citizen in 1994. Meanwhile, he had returned undercover to China several times, videotaping prison conditions. Wu wrote 2 books, including *The Chinese Gulag*. He was arrested in June when he attempted to enter China from Kazakhstan. He was tried despite U.S. protests. On **Aug. 24**, his conviction was announced, and he was expelled the same day.

Shevardnadze Survives Attempt on Life—Eduard Shevardnadze, the head of state in Georgia, survived an assassination attempt in Aug. while on his way to sign the country's new constitution. Parliament, **Aug. 24**, approved Georgia's first constitution since it became independent of the Soviet Union in 1991. It created the office of president, who would be both head of state and head of government. Shevardnadze was slightly wounded, **Aug. 29**, when a bomb went off near his motorcade in Tbilisi, the capital.

nounced African-Americans. Earlier, testimony appeared to undercut the DNA evidence that the prosecution had presented. John Gerdes, a molecular biologist, testified, **Aug. 2**, that the Los Angeles Police Dept. (LAPD) laboratory was "definitely" the worst he had ever seen and that there was a "tremendous risk of cross-contamination" of blood samples. Gerdes acknowledged, **Aug. 3**, that there was too much blood on a glove found at Simpson's estate, on a sock in his bedroom, and on a gate behind Nicole Brown's condominium for it to have been compromised; the defense was asserting that this blood was planted. Dr. Michael Baden, a forensic pathologist, testified, **Aug. 10**, that both victims had put up an extended struggle. The defense contended that Simpson did not have enough time to commit such crimes and still meet his limousine driver at 11 PM and that he did not have any injuries of the type that one would suffer while in such violent fights. With the jury out of the room, over a period of several days, Judge Lance Ito sought to resolve the question of how much evidence should be introduced to impeach the testimony of Detective Mark Fuhrman. From 1985 to 1994, Fuhrman had been interviewed for a total of 14 hours by Laura Hart McKinney, who planned to write a screenplay about police officers. Her tapes established that Fuhrman was extremely hostile toward African-Americans, and, contrary to his previous testimony, he had frequently used a slur offensive to blacks. On the tapes, he boasted of planting evidence in other cases. Dr. Henry Lee, head of the crime laboratory of the Connecticut State Police and a legendary expert on crime scenes, testified, **Aug. 22**, that he had found possible evidence of a shoe print near the victims that could not have been made by shoes the prosecution said Simpson wore on the night of the murders. He said, **Aug. 23**, that the fight between the killer and Goldman was "not a short struggle." The Fuhrman tapes, played in court, **Aug. 29**, with the jury still absent, stunned all present. Ito, however, ruled, **Aug. 31**, that only 2 short excerpts from the tapes could be heard by the jury.

Out of Prison, Tyson Wins First Fight—Mike Tyson, once the world heavyweight boxing champion, began his comeback, **Aug. 19**, in Las Vegas, after being freed from prison. Convicted of rape, Tyson had been in prison in Indiana from 1992 until his release in March. Interest in his first fight, against Peter McNeeley, ran high, and the fight grossed about $70 million in gate receipts and cable and worldwide television fees. Tyson decked McNeeley when the first round was only 8 seconds old, and after a second knockdown McNeeley's manager stopped the fight, which lasted only 89 seconds altogether.

Merger Creates $300 Billion Bank—Chase Manhattan Corp. and Chemical Banking Corp., 2 banks based in New York City, announced, **Aug. 28**, that they would merge. The new corporation, retaining the Chase name, would have assets of $297 billion, $40 billion more than Citicorp, then the largest U.S. bank.

SEPTEMBER 1995

General

Westinghouse to Buy CBS for $5 Billion—Westinghouse Electric Corp. announced, **Aug. 1**, that it would buy CBS Inc.—just one day after the Walt Disney Co. announced its purchase of Capital Cities/ABC Inc. Westinghouse would pay some $5 billion. The combined company would have 39 radio stations and 15 television stations.

Simpson Trial in Turmoil Over Racial Slurs—The double-murder trial of O. J. Simpson, which had approached chaos several times, almost fell apart in Aug. during a dispute over taped interviews in which Mark Fuhrman, a major prosecution witness, repeatedly de-

National

Fed Sees Continuing Economic Upswing—The Labor Dept. reported, **Sept. 1**, that 249,000 jobs had been added to business payrolls in Aug. The unemployment rate edged downward from 5.7% to 5.6% in Aug. The Commerce Dept. reported, **Sept. 1**, that the index of leading economic indicators had resumed its downward trend in July, declining 0.2% after a slight jump in June. The Labor Dept. said, **Sept. 12**, that prices charged by manufacturers and farmers for finished goods had declined 0.1% in Aug. The Federal Reserve Board said, **Sept. 13**, that it saw indications of an ongoing economic upswing across the country. It noted, for example, an apparent strengthening of construction activity in many areas. Business activity, however, was found to be declining in New York and Dallas. The Fed reported that inflationary pressures were weak. The Labor Dept. said, **Sept. 13**, that consumer prices had risen 0.1% in Aug. The Commerce Dept. reported, **Sept. 20**, that the trade deficit had risen to $11.5 billion in July.

Gen. Powell Considers Run for President— Presidential politics in Sept. was dominated by speculation on whether Gen. Colin Powell (ret.) would seek the big prize. Earlier, Sen. Bob Dole (R, KS), a candidate for the Republican presidential nomination, urged, **Sept. 4**, that English be made the official language of the U.S. He said that multilingual education undermined the nation's political and cultural cohesion and led to "ethnic separatism." The Christian Coalition held a 2-day conference in Washington, DC, **Sept 8** and **9**, that attracted GOP presidential candidates eager to embrace the organization's political agenda. Powell, former chairman of the Joint Chiefs of Staff, had retired in 1993 and had remained largely out of sight until Sept., when his autobiography, *My American Journey*, became available in bookstores. In excerpts, available **Sept. 9**, Powell wrote that "the time may be at hand for a third major party to emerge to represent the sensible center of the American political spectrum." He described himself as "a fiscal conservative with a social conscience" and said he didn't feel comfortable as either a Republican or a Democrat. A veteran of Vietnam who had headed the joint chiefs during the Gulf War, Powell was widely popular and was regarded as the first black American with a serious chance of being elected president. On **Sept. 15**, Powell said in a television interview that he supported abortion rights, affirmative action, and gun control and opposed organized prayer in the schools. In a book tour that began **Sept. 16**, Powell drew huge and admiring crowds. The GOP presidential field grew, **Sept. 22**, when magazine publisher Malcolm S. Forbes, Jr., declared that he would seek the Republican nomination. Steve Forbes, as he was generally known, had succeeded his father as publisher of *Forbes* magazine. An advocate of a flat income tax, he said he was optimistic that the economy could expand with lower taxes and less government regulation. He planned to finance his campaign out of his personal fortune. Ross Perot, the Texas billionaire who ran for president as an independent in 1992 and received 19% of the vote, announced, **Sept. 25**, that he was forming a new Independence Party, and he invited "outstanding" but unaligned public figures to seek his party's nomination. Gov. Pete Wilson (CA) announced, **Sept. 29**, that he was giving up his pursuit of the GOP presidential nomination. He had been unable either to raise much money or to raise his low numbers in public-opinion polls. He had angered Californians by going back on a promise made during his reelection campaign in 1994 to serve out a full 4-year term. As well, he had confused voters by shifting his positions on several issues, in an apparent attempt to catch the current political winds.

Judge Rejects Indictment of Governor—Federal District Judge Henry Woods, **Sept. 5**, quashed an indictment handed up in June against Gov. Jim Guy Tucker of Arkansas and 2 other men. The indictment had been sought by Kenneth Starr, the independent counsel investigating the Whitewater affair. Tucker was charged with obtaining a bank loan under false pretenses and participating in a scheme to avoid capital-gains taxes. Woods held that the charges "were not related at all" to Starr's mandate on Whitewater. Tucker had also been indicted in Aug. on charges that appeared more directly related to Whitewater.

Packwood Resigns From Senate—Sen. Robert Packwood (R, OR) announced in Sept. that he would resign from the Senate. The Senate Ethics Committee, **Sept. 6**, voted, 6-0, to recommend that he be expelled. It cited findings of sexual misconduct, influence peddling, and obstruction of justice on Packwood's part. An angry Packwood responded, "I am accused of kissing women . . . And when rebuffed, never approaching them again." Expulsion was the most severe penalty that the committee could recommend. After initially indicating that he would resist the expulsion move, Packwood addressed the Senate, **Sept. 7**, saying he had a duty to resign. He had served since first being elected in 1968. The committee, **Sept. 7**, released 10,145 pages of evidence relating to its investigation of Packwood. The committee found that Packwood had altered a 1989 entry in his diary to conceal an effort to get a job from a lobbyist for his wife, Georgie, who was divorcing him, in order to reduce his alimony payments. Packwood also had altered a 1992 passage in which he wrote, originally, that at a meeting with Sen. Phil Gramm (R, TX) and others, "what was said in that room would be enough to convict us all of something." According to the original entry, Gramm told Packwood that $100,000 being given to the Oregon GOP by the National Republican Senatorial Committee, which Gramm headed, would actually go to Packwood's reelection effort, although the legal limit was $17,500. Both Packwood and Gramm declared, in Sept., that no such agreement had been reached in their 1992 conversation. After Sen. Bob Dole (R, KS), the Senate majority leader, suggested, **Sept. 7**, that Packwood would remain in office for 3 months, a backlash from Packwood's critics forced Dole, **Sept. 8**, to ask him to leave on Oct. 1.

Paper Prints Bomber's 35,000-Word Text—On **Sept. 19** the *Washington Post* published the 35,000-word manifesto written by the notorious Unabomber. The author, a severe critic of modern technology, had been responsible for mailing letter bombs that had killed 3 men and injured 22 other people. In June, he had mailed his manuscript, "Industrial Society and Its Future," to the *Post* and the *New York Times*, informing the papers that he would not attempt to kill again if one of them published it and 3 annual follow-up messages. The publishers of the *Post* and the *Times* said, **Sept. 19**, that Attorney Gen. Janet Reno and FBI Director Louis Freeh had recommended publication, the cost of which the papers shared. The FBI hoped that editorial style or usage in the text would be recognized by someone who had seen previous writings by the bomber. Its investigation had already taken agents to universities at which the bomber may have studied in the 1970s and 1980s. The *Post* was criticized by some who objected to any concession to a terrorist. In his text, as published, the author claimed that the Industrial Revolution and its consequences had destabilized society, made life unfulfilling, subjected human beings to indignities, led to widespread psychological suffering, and inflicted severe damage on the natural world. He asserted, "You can't make rapid, drastic changes in the technology and the economy of a society without causing rapid changes in all other aspects of the society as well, and [these] inevitably break down traditional values."

Senate Bill Shifts Welfare to States—Reform of the nation's welfare system, a major subject of debate for years, moved closer to reality in Sept. when the Senate voted for an approach that would effectively make states responsible for welfare. Republicans had long complained of the system's expense and ineffectiveness, and during the 1992 presidential campaign Bill Clinton had pledged to "end welfare as we know it." The House, in Mar. 1995, and the Senate on **Sept. 19**, 87-12, approved bills with significant differences, which would be resolved in conference committee. Pres. Clinton backed the Senate version, which would save an estimated $65 billion over 7 years. The principal welfare program, Aid to Families With Dependent Children, would be replaced by block grants to the states.

International

Controversies Swirl at Women's Forums—The UN's Fourth World Conference on Women met in Beijing in Sept., and the UN-sanctioned Nongovernmental Organizations (NGOs) Forum on Women met nearby. The gatherings were productive, but the delegates had to surmount disputes among themselves and with their Chinese hosts. As the NGO forum, attended by 25,000 delegates, opened in Beijing's Olympic Stadium, **Aug. 30**, leaders urged the Chinese government to cease harassment of participants. The NGO forum then moved to the town of Huairou, an hour's drive from Beijing. Chinese security officials, **Aug. 31**, tried to seize a video on Tibet, a formerly independent country now under Chinese control, that had been shown at the forum. NGO leaders said, **Sept. 2**, that they would close the forum unless the Chinese stopped monitoring participants. The opening ceremony for the conference, which drew more than 4,000 delegates from 185 countries, took place, **Sept. 4**, at the Great Hall of the People in Beijing. The main issues were the ending of violence against women, political and economic empowerment of women, and the granting of sexual equality to women. In an address, **Sept. 4**, Prime Minister Benazir Bhutto of Pakistan deplored the preference among Asian men for sons, which, she said, led to the aborting of female fetuses. First Lady Hillary Rodham Clinton spoke, **Sept. 5**. Many persons in the U.S. had opposed her attending because of China's poor record on human rights. China's release of U.S. citizen Harry Wu in Aug. appeared sufficient to justify Clinton's trip to China. Without mentioning China by name, Clinton, in her address, lashed out at abuse of women by governments, and some of her reproaches applied to China. She said, "It is a violation of human rights when women are denied the right to plan their own families, and that includes being forced to have abortions or being sterilized against their will." She also condemned female genital mutilation, domestic violence against women, and the rape of women during war. Madeleine Albright, U.S. ambassador to the UN and head of the U.S. delegation to the conference, also made forceful remarks in an address, **Sept. 6**. During debate on the conference platform, **Sept. 6**, Mary Ann Glendon, the chief Vatican delegate, who was from the U.S., said that although the Vatican opposed abortion, it would accept language on reproductive rights based on the 1994 UN population conference. Clinton, **Sept. 7**, met with Mongolian leaders in Ulan Bator, the capital, and spoke at the Mongolia National University. China's news agency asserted, **Sept. 8**, that the constitution gave equal rights to women and that China's policy of one child per family freed women to pursue more opportunities. The NGO forum closed **Sept. 8**. The Vatican said, **Sept. 8**, that it would not contest language supporting the use of condoms to thwart the spread of AIDS. The majority compromised with conservative Muslim delegates opposing equal inheritance rights for women. An attempt to endorse equality based on sexual orientation failed. The conference closed, **Sept. 15**, after the approval of the platform. The Vatican and some 35 other countries announced formal reservations to parts of the text.

Combatants in Bosnia Agree to Peace Plan—In Sept., the warring parties in Bosnia and Herzegovina accepted a peace plan brokered by the U.S. Bombings by NATO planes on Serb positions in late Aug. and the rout of Serbs in the Krajina region of Croatia had been factors in getting the Serbs to accept the plan, in principle. On **Sept. 1**, Lt. Gen. Bernard Janvier of France, commander of UN forces in the former Yugoslavia, told Gen. Ratko Mladic, chief of the Bosnian Serb military, that the Serbs must stop attacking the remaining UN safe areas and withdraw from the exclusion zone within 12.5 mi of Sarajevo, the Bosnian capital. Janvier, **Sept. 2**, refused to meet counterdemands by Mladic, and NATO, **Sept. 3**, embodied its terms in an ultimatum that the Serbs comply by **Sept. 4** or face new attacks. As the deadline passed, some of the 300 Serb artillery pieces and tanks had been moved back from around Sarajevo. NATO air strikes resumed, **Sept. 5**, with artillery, missile bases, ammunition depots, and communications

posts around Sarajevo and near the self-proclaimed Bosnian Serb capital of Pale being the principal targets. German aircraft were now assuming a limited role, taking reconnaissance photographs, thus playing a part in combat missions for the first time since World War II. Russia, a traditional ally of Serbia, deplored the renewal of the raids, **Sept. 5**. Against the backdrop of military confrontation, U.S. Asst. Secretary of State Richard Holbrooke, chief U.S. negotiator in Bosnia, had been engaged in shuttle diplomacy with the parties, and on **Sept. 8** they agreed to the creation of 2 self-governing entities within Bosnia's current boundaries: the Federation of Bosnia and Herzegovina and the Republic of Serbia. The former would encompass the current Muslim-Croat federation, and the latter would be the home of the Bosnian Serbs. The Muslim-dominated Bosnian government, Croatia, and Yugoslavia, representing the Bosnian Serbs, were parties to the agreement. The federation would get 51% of the land and the Serbs 49%, which meant that the Serbs would have to give up much of the 70% of Bosnia that they then controlled. No agreement had been reached on which areas would be assigned to each entity. The lower house of the Russian parliament, **Sept. 10**, condemned the NATO attacks and urged Russia to lift unilaterally UN sanctions against Yugoslavia. NATO attacks continued, meanwhile, and on **Sept. 10** the U.S. warship *Normandy* fired 13 Tomahawk cruise missiles at about 10 communications sites. On **Sept. 11**, Bosnian Croats and the Croatian army attacked Serb towns in W Bosnia and sent 40,000 civilians fleeing. By **Sept. 13**, NATO had carried out 850 bombing raids. Gen. Mladic, **Sept. 14**, agreed to the NATO ultimatum, and the bombing campaign was stopped to allow the Serbs to withdraw. The Bosnian government and the Bosnian Croats agreed, **Sept. 19**, to NATO's insistence that the ground offensive be halted. As a result of the latest offensive, Serb-controlled land in Bosnia had declined to about 50%. UN and NATO officials said, **Sept. 21**, that Serb weapons had been withdrawn from around Sarajevo. Regular delivery of relief supplies began to reach the capital on **Sept. 21**. The Muslim-Croat federation and the Bosnian Serbs, **Sept. 26**, agreed on the structure for the new government of Bosnia. It would include a group Presidency, a Parliament, and a Constitutional Court. "Free and democratic elections" would be conducted under international supervision.

French Nuclear Test Met With Protests—France conducted an underground nuclear test—the first in a new series—in Sept., against vociferous protests from many quarters. French navy commandos boarded and seized 2 Greenpeace protest ships, **Sept. 1**, to prevent them from entering the test area; commandos had also raided one of the ships in July. Commandos boarded a sailboat, **Sept. 3**. France detonated the bomb, having an explosive power of less than 20,000 tons of TNT, on **Sept. 5**, at the Mururoa Atoll in the South Pacific. Nuclear opponents set afire the main terminal of Tahiti's international airport, **Sept. 6**, forcing cancellation of outbound flights. By **Sept. 6**, the U.S., Japan, Australia, Russia, and other nations had made known their opposition to the test.

Peace Plan Implemented in Liberia—Implementation of a peace agreement worked out in Aug. among Liberia's warring militias moved forward, **Sept. 1**, with the swearing in of a 6-member interim ruling council. It included 3 civilians and the leaders of 3 factions. Since 1989, many factions had become involved in a civil war that had claimed 150,000 lives.

Israel, Palestinians Sign New Accord—Israel and the Palestinians signed their "Phase 2" agreement in Sept. Negotiators for both sides said, **Sept. 8**, that the question of protecting Israeli settlers in Hebron had stalled the peace process. The parties were now working on the second phase of the peace settlement, in which the Israelis would grant the Palestinians administrative control over West Bank areas Israel had occupied for almost 30 years. Several hundred Israelis had chosen to settle in Hebron, a Palestinian city of 100,000. The government had pledged to protect the settlers, and Prime Minister Yitzhak Rabin therefore sought, temporarily at least, to retain responsibility for security in Hebron. A breakthrough occurred 2 weeks later, **Sept. 24**, with an agreement on a plan to divide Hebron into 3 zones: Israel would patrol one zone, Palestinians another, and the third would be jointly patrolled. Palestinians would have overall control of security in Hebron. The Israeli pullback was worked out in detail, town by town. A 12,000-member Palestinian security force would take over. Elections to a Palestinian Council would take place 22 days after Israel withdrew from populated areas. Prime Minister Yitzhak Rabin of Israel and PLO Chairman Yasir Arafat signed the agreement in Washington, **Sept. 28.** Pres. Bill Clinton, Pres. Hosni Mubarak of Egypt, and King Hussein of Jordan were among those present. Jewish settlers in Hebron vowed to respect no authority there except the Israeli army. The third and final phase of the negotiating process, scheduled for 1996, would focus on the future of Jerusalem, Arab refugees, and the West Bank settlements.

General

Simpson Murder Case Goes to the Jury—The marathon trial of O. J. Simpson for 2 murders went to the jury at the end of Sept. after both sides completed the presentation of their cases. The defense, **Sept. 5**, presented 3 witnesses who disputed the previous testimony of prosecution witness Mark Fuhrman, a retired police detective, who had claimed to have found a bloody glove at Simpson's estate matching one found at the crime scene. Fuhrman had denied using the so-called "N word," offensive to blacks, in the past 10 years, but Laura Hart McKinny, a screenwriter, testified that he had used the word "approximately 42 times" during her taped interviews with him. Kathleen Bell and Natalie Singer described a number of distasteful and racist remarks made by Fuhrman. Bell said he had told her that if he had his way, all black people "in the world would be gathered together and burned." Fuhrman returned to the courtroom, **Sept. 6**, with the jury absent, and asserted his 5th Amendment privilege against self-incrimination in response to several questions, including: "Did you plant or manufacture any evidence in this case?" A California state appeals court, **Sept. 8**, rejected instructions that Judge Lance Ito proposed to read to the jury, to the effect that Fuhrman was not available for further testimony and that the jury could make inferences from that. Ito, **Sept. 11**, denied a defense request to call Fuhrman back to the stand with the jury present. On **Sept. 11**, even though the defense had not yet rested its case, Ito directed the prosecution to begin its rebuttal. Richard Rubin, a former executive at Aris Isotoner, testified, **Sept. 12**, that he was certain that gloves Simpson wore at a football game in 1991—as shown in photographs—were identical to gloves found at the crime scene and at Simpson's estate. No more than 240 pairs of the gloves had been sold. Nicole Brown Simpson had purchased one such pair in New York. FBI agent William Bodziak, disputing the testimony of Dr. Henry Lee, asserted, **Sept. 15**, that evidence of a shoe print that Lee had found at the scene might in fact have been only traces of trowels rubbing on wet concrete when the walkway was put down. The defense, **Sept. 19**, called Larry and Craig Fiato, 2 brothers and former organized-crime figures now cooperating with the FBI. They testified that Detective Philip Vannatter, chief detective in the Simpson case, had told them that police entered O. J. Simpson's estate on the night of the murders (without a warrant) because he was a suspect, not because they wanted to notify him of his wife's death. Judge Lance Ito, **Sept. 20**, denied a defense motion to throw out evidence seized during the warrantless entry. Ito held, **Sept. 21**, that the jury, if it chose to convict Simp-

son, could find him guilty of either first- or second-degree murder. On **Sept. 22**, the defense answered the question in millions of minds: Would O. J. take the stand? With the jury absent, Ito permitted the defendant a brief statement. Simpson said, "As much as I would like to address some of the misrepresentations about myself . . . I am mindful of the mood and stamina of this jury. . . . I have confidence . . . that they will find as the record stands now, that I did not, could not and would not have committed this crime." Simpson then waived his right to testify, and the defense rested. In her final arguments, **Sept. 26**, Deputy District Attorney Marcia Clark stressed that the defendant's whereabouts were unknown for 78 minutes on the night of the murders. She argued that the ferocity and brutality of the killings were not the hallmarks of a professional killer, but of someone in a state of rage: "A knife is up close and personal, and that's the type of murders these are, ladies and gentlemen." Deputy District Attorney Christopher Darden contended, **Sept. 26** and **27**, that Simpson was hot-tempered and had an emotional fuse that burned shorter and shorter on the day of the murders as the defendant realized that his ex-wife would not return to him. In his closing arguments, **Sept. 27** and **28**, defense attorney Johnnie Cochran pushed the theme, in reference to the bloody glove and other prosecution evidence, "If it doesn't fit, you must acquit." Cochran charged that the police had taken the socks from a hamper and "spiked" one with blood. He urged the jury to send the police a message by acquitting Simpson. As a rapt nation saw the year-long trial accelerate as it approached a climax, the drama outside the courtroom reached a new intensity. In separate statements, **Sept. 28**, Fred Goldman, father of Ron Goldman, and the family of O. J. Simpson argued the guilt or innocence of the defendant with deep emotion. Barry Scheck, the defense team's specialist on physical evidence, told the jury, **Sept. 28**, "There is something terribly wrong about this evidence." He asserted, offering painstaking detail, that the physical evidence had been "contaminated, corrupted, and compromised." In her rebuttal argument, **Sept. 29**, an unusually emotional Marcia Clark played a 911 tape of Nicole Brown Simpson expressing fear of O. J. Simpson. Ito then gave instructions to the jury, and deliberations began after a weekend recess.

Ripken Breaks Gehrig's "Iron Man" Record—On **Sept. 6**, shortstop Cal Ripken, Jr., of the Baltimore Orioles played in his 2,131st consecutive game, breaking the record of 2,130 set in 1939 by Lou Gehrig, first baseman for the New York Yankees. The legendary Yankee star died 2 years later from amyotrophic lateral sclerosis, commonly known thereafter as Lou Gehrig's disease. Ripken, like Gehrig, was widely admired as a person, and he received 20 minutes of applause from the crowd, which included Pres. Bill Clinton, when he set the record. He had been named rookie of the year (1982) and most valuable player (1983, 1991) in the American League and had played in 13 All-Star games, a record.

Graf, Sampras Win U.S. Open—On **Sept. 9**, Steffi Graf of Germany defeated Monica Seles, 7-6, 0-6, 6-3, to gain her 4th U.S. Open women's singles title. Seles's appearance in the tournament was her first in a Grand Slam event since being stabbed by a tennis fan during a match in 1993. On **Sept. 10**, Pete Sampras won his 3d U.S. Open men's singles title by defeating Andre Agassi, 6-4, 6-3, 4-6, 7-5.

Time Warner, Turner Broadcasting to Merge—Time Warner Inc. and the Turner Broadcasting System announced, **Sept. 22**, that they would merge. With revenues projected at $19.8 billion, the new company would be bigger even than the Walt Disney Company after its merger with Capital Cities/ABC Inc. Holdings would include *Time* magazine, Warner Brothers, Cable News Network, Home Box Office, and the Cartoon Network. Time Warner would buy the 82% of Turner stock it didn't already own, an outlay of about $7 billion. Ted Turner, the innovative founder of CNN and chairman of Turner Broadcasting, would become vice chairman of Time Warner.

OCTOBER 1995

National

Ten Convicted in New York Terrorist Plot—Ten Muslims were convicted in New York, **Oct. 1**, of conspiring to conduct a terrorist campaign, including bombings and assassinations, in the New York City area. The acts of violence, which were not carried out, were to include a "day of terror"—bombings at the UN, a bridge and 2 tunnels, and the principal U.S. government building in Manhattan. An objective was to force the U.S. to drop its support for Israel and Egypt. The 10 men were convicted on 48 of 50 counts. Leader of the group, and one of those convicted, was Sheik Omar Abdel Rahman, a blind Egyptian cleric who had attracted a following among Islamic fundamentalists in the New York metropolitan area with fiery rhetoric denouncing U.S. policy in the Middle East. Abdel Rahman was convicted of directing the conspiracy and of plotting to kill Pres. Hosni Mubarak of Egypt. El Sayyid Nosair was convicted of the 1990 Manhattan killing of Rabbi Meir Kahane. Nosair, in 1991, had been acquitted of the murder in a state court, and in this case the federal government had charged him under a conspiracy law; indeed, the killing of Kahane, an extreme opponent of Palestinian aspirations, was now seen as the first step in the agenda of the terrorists. In the current trial, the government had relied on secret tapes made by Emad Salem, an FBI informant, which, for example, showed 4 defendants mixing diesel oil and fertilizer, to make bombs, in a garage in Queens.

Most Economic Data Encouraging—The Commerce Dept. said, **Oct. 4**, that the index of leading economic indicators had risen 0.2% in Aug. The Labor Dept. reported, **Oct. 6**, that, although the unemployment rate had held steady at 5.6% in Sept., 121,000 payroll jobs had been added to the economy. The department said, **Oct. 12**, that prices received by producers of finished goods had risen 0.3% in Sept., the largest advance in 8 months. Inflation at the retail level remained in check; the department reported, **Oct. 13**, that consumer prices had edged upward 0.1% in Sept.

Buchanan Asks Campaign, Lobbying Reform—Patrick Buchanan, a candidate for the Republican presidential nomination, proposed sweeping changes, **Oct. 5**, in campaign financing, lobby laws, and congressional perquisites. He urged that political action committees be eliminated and that congressional candidates be allowed to raise money only in their own districts or states. He urged tighter restrictions on foreign lobbyists and called for elimination of congressional pensions and free-mailing privileges for members of Congress. Buchanan's proposals closely tracked reforms advocated by Ross Perot, the independent candidate for president in 1992. Ten GOP presidential candidates met at a forum in Manchester, NH, **Oct. 11**. The format permitted little opportunity for the aspirants to challenge one another's views directly. Participants included Morry Taylor, owner of a tire and wheel manufacturing company, who had entered the contest and was spending mostly his own money.

Sabatoge Derails Amtrak Train in Arizona—An Amtrak train carrying 248 passengers and a crew of 20 went off the tracks on a remote stretch of land SW of Phoenix, during the predawn hours of **Oct. 9**. The train had been traveling around a slight curve at about 50 mi an hour. At the point of derailment, 4 cars plunged completely or partly into a ravine 30 ft deep. One member of the crew was killed and about 100 people injured. Rescuers needed more than an hour to reach the site. Amtrak reported, **Oct. 9**, that the derailment had been caused by the removal of bolts that held a connecting bar, or joint, to 2 pieces of rail. According to Amtrak, the perpetrator knew enough about trains to attach a wire to each end of the rails on either side of the joint so that electric current would continue and the train's engineer would see green lights in the trackside signals. The track was owned by the Southern Pacific Railroad. Several copies of a note, whose text was not immediately made public, were found near the crash. Responsibility was claimed by Sons of the Gestapo, a name that investigators said they did not recognize. On **Oct. 13**, law enforcement officials made public the contents of the typewritten note. It contained an account of the attack by federal agents on the Branch Davidian compound near Waco, TX, that resulted in the death of about 80 people. The note raised these questions: "Who is policing the ATF, FBI, state troopers, county sheriffs and local police? What . . . agency investigates each and every choke hold killing committed by a police officer? Each and every beating of a drunk wether (sic) or not a passerby videotapes it? . . . Each and every killing at Ruby Ridge?"

Sen. Nunn to Retire—The Senate's leading authority on military matters, Sam Nunn, announced, **Oct. 9**, that he would not seek reelection in 1996. Nunn had served as chairman of the Senate Armed Services Committee for 8 years while the Democrats held a majority, and he had been the leading advocate among Democratic senators for a strong military. Nunn was the 8th Democratic senator (out of 15 up for reelection) who had announced that he would not run again. With his departure, the Democrats' electoral prospects continued to fade, especially in the South.

International

Macedonian President Wounded Seriously—In Macedonia, a comparatively peaceful part of the former Yugoslavia, a bomb explosion in Oct. nearly claimed the life of Pres. Kiro Gilgorov. Macedonia had split from Yugoslavia in 1991. Its relations had grown tense with its S neighbor, Greece, because of the latter's concerns that the new state might want to unite with Greece's northern area, also called Macedonia. In Sept., Gilgorov had signed an agreement with Greece ending a dispute over the name "Macedonia" and the design of its flag. U.S. troops were currently assigned to Macedonia as part of a UN peacekeeping force seeking to ensure that the war in Bosnia and Herzegovina would not spread to Macedonia. A bomb exploded near the president's car, **Oct. 3**, as he was being driven to the National Parliament building in Skopje, the capital. Gilgorov suffered a serious head injury. His driver was killed, and 3 bystanders were wounded. No one claimed responsibility for the attack. Parliament, **Oct. 4**, named an interim president after it became apparent that Gilgorov, 78, would be unable to fulfill his duties. He was replaced by the Speaker of Parliament, Stojan Andov.

Cease-Fire Takes Effect in Bosnia—Bosnia and Herzegovina, which had seen many temporary cease-fires, welcomed another one in Oct. that many observers thought might hold. Earlier, NATO confronted the Bosnian Serbs again in Oct. Bosnian Serb planes had been bombing Bosnian government positions in an area designated by NATO as a no-flight zone. As NATO planes flew in routine patrol over the zone, **Oct. 4**, Serb missile batteries locked their radar systems on the planes in apparent preparation to fire. The NATO planes struck at the batteries with anti-radiation missiles, with unknown results. On **Oct. 5**, Pres. Bill Clinton announced that the warring parties had agreed to a cease-fire, to take effect 5 days later providing that gas and electrical service had been restored to Sarajevo. Asst. Secretary of State Richard Holbrooke had worked out the agreement in Sarajevo. The UN said, **Oct. 5**, that during Oct. it would reduce the number of troops assigned to Bosnia from 30,000 to 21,000. On **Oct. 8**, 2 days before the cease-fire was to begin, Bosnian Serbs attacked a Muslim refugee camp, killing 10 and wounding 34. Government and Croatian sources said that the Serbs had bombed several villages. Serbs shelled UN "safe areas," and NATO planes responded by bombing and destroying a Bosnian Serb command and control bunker. When the date for the cease-fire arrived, **Oct. 10**, gas and electricity had not been restored to Sarajevo. Later on **Oct. 10**, Serbs reportedly were engaged in a new "ethnic cleansing" operation, forcing 10,000 Muslims and Croats from their homes in and near the Serb stronghold of Banja Luka. With the restoration of utility service to Sarajevo, the cease-fire was finally declared to be in effect, **Oct. 12**. During the 2-day delay, the Bosnian army had made further territorial gains. As the government army and the Croats continued to advance in NW Bosnia, the Serbs demanded that NATO bomb their positions. Bosnian officers said, **Oct. 14**, that they had been ordered to halt their advance. It was believed, **Oct. 15**, that Serbs had killed or taken prisoner some 500 civilian men in Sanski, most in the days before it fell to the Bosnian army. The mayor said that the bodies of 86 men had been found.

Israel Frees 900 Palestinians—Some 900 Palestinian men were freed from Israeli detention, **Oct. 10**. As implementation of the second phase of the peace process began on the West Bank, the Israelis also pulled out of 4 towns, as Palestinians celebrated. Guerrillas with the Iranian-backed Party of God killed 3 Israeli soldiers in S Lebanon, **Oct. 12**, and 6 more soldiers were killed in a similar attack, **Oct. 15**. After pulling out of Lebanon in 1985, Israel had established a security zone inside Lebanon along the border with Israel.

General

O. J. Simpson Found Not Guilty of 2 Murders—Orenthal James Simpson, one of football's finest running backs who went on to a successful career as a sports broadcaster, actor, and endorser of products, was found not guilty in Oct. of the murders of his former wife Nicole Brown Simpson and a friend of hers, Ronald Goldman. The defendant smiled, members of his family cheered, and members of the families of the victims were subdued or shaken. Judge Lance Ito told Simpson he was free to leave after checking out of his cell. He had been in custody for 474 days. Across the country, blacks generally hailed the verdict, while a majority of whites disapproved of the result. Simpson quickly returned to his estate in Brentwood. At a press conference, Johnnie Cochran, the lead defense attorney, said he had been confident that "if we could shatter the prosecution's timeline so that O. J. Simpson couldn't have committed this crime . . . there would be a reasonable doubt." He said that the prosecution, not the defense, had injected race into the trial by relying heavily on the testimony of former detective Mark Fuhrman, who had frequently used racial slurs. In a separate interview, however, Robert Shapiro, another defense attorney, criticized Cochran's closing argument, saying Cochran had not only played the race card but "dealt it from the bottom of the deck." Jason Simpson, O. J. Simpson's son from his first marriage, read a statement from his father saying that his first obligation would be to his 2 youngest children, Sidney, 9, and Justin, 7, "who will be raised in the way that Nicole and I had always planned." The children lived with their maternal grandparents, who had obtained legal custody after their father was arrested. District Attorney Gil Garcetti said, "This was not, in our opinion, a close case." He said of the jury, "Apparently their decision was based on emotion that overcame reason." Jesse Jackson, the civil rights leader, said, **Oct. 4**, "It is not a time for wild celebration. This is a legal victory, not a moral victory for social change. O. J. is free, but we have all been diminished during this tragedy." Simpson was reunited with his children, **Oct. 4**, for the first time in 15 months. While Cochran was being interviewed by Larry King on television, **Oct. 4**, Simpson phoned in to say, "Fortunately for me, the jury listened to what the witnesses said and not Marcia Clark or Chris Darden's rendition or anything else." Simpson, **Oct. 9**, agreed to a live one-hour interview with NBC News. On **Oct. 11**, prior to the interview, he pulled out. Instead, he called the *New York Times* and spoke with a reporter for 45 minutes. He said he had dropped the NBC interview because his lawyers believed "I was being set up." They were concerned that what he said might be used against him in upcoming civil trials. Simpson proclaimed his innocence, said it was wrong to have beaten his wife, and said he was willing to meet with battered women to discuss his relationship with his wife. Simpson said he had not been left broke by the payment of lawyer fees. He said there was no conflict between him and the Brown family over his and Nicole's children.

Pope John Paul II Visits U.S. 4th Time—John Paul II, leader of the Roman Catholic Church and by far the most traveled pontiff ever, visited the U.S. in Oct. for the 4th time since he became pope in 1978. Although his personal popularity remained high, many in his American flock disagreed with his strict opposition to birth control and abortion. Landing in Newark, NJ, **Oct. 4**, the Pope was welcomed by Pres. Bill Clinton, other political leaders, and almost all the Roman Catholic hierarchy in the U.S. After a message of greeting at the airport, the pope conducted a prayer service at Sacred Heart Cathedral in Newark. In an address, **Oct. 5**, at the UN, the pope expressed regret that the fear of other people, even within the same nation, can lead to the denial of the humanity of others and to a cycle of violence in which not even children are spared. In a homily delivered to 83,000 of the faithful at Giants Stadium in East Rutherford, NJ, **Oct. 5**, the pope called on the U.S. to keep its doors open to immigrants. He asked, "If America were to turn in on itself, would this not be the beginning of the end of what constitutes the very essence of the American experience?" The pope conducted a morning mass for 75,000 people at Aqueduct Race Track in New York City, **Oct. 6**. In a sumptuous outdoor setting, the Great Lawn in Central Park in Manhattan, the Pope conducted mass for 120,000 persons, **Oct. 7**. He called on young people, in particular, to care for the poor, the homeless, the hungry, and those ill with AIDS. On **Oct. 8**, the Pope went to Baltimore, in Maryland, the first Roman Catholic settlement established in the English colonies of the New World. Speaking to 50,000 people at the city's baseball stadium, he called on Catholics to carry their religious values into the political arena. The Pope then flew back to Rome.

Kasparov Retains Chess Title—Gary Kasparov, the world's top chess player for the past decade, won a world championship match in Oct. He ensured victory, **Oct. 10**, over Viswanathan Anand by obtaining a draw and an insurmountable lead of 10½ to 7½. The match was sponsored by the Professional Chess Assn., which Kasparov had launched in 1993. The International Chess Federation, which had stripped Kasparov of its title and did not recognize the match with Anand, was expected to hold its own championship match soon. Interest in the Kasparov-Anand match, which was held on the 107th floor of the World Trade Center in New York City, was great. As many as 1,200 spectators attended daily, 250 foreign journalists sent reports around the world, and in India alone (Anand's country) 300 million people followed the match live on television. Kasparov received a purse of $900,000, and Anand, in his first championship match at age 25, got $450,000.

Notable Quotes in 1995

"Not guilty"
Deirdre Robertson, law clerk to Judge Lance Ito, announcing the verdict in the O. J. Simpson murder trial

"A very short one."
Oldest known living person, *Jeanne Calment*, 120, of France, commenting on what sort of future she anticipated

"If combat means living in a ditch, females have biological problems staying in a ditch for 20 days because they get infections . . . males are biologically driven to go out and hunt giraffes. "
Newt Gingrich, speaking to students about why most women are not suited to traditional military combat

"Pray for me. Don't brag. And don't talk to Connie Chung."
Barbara Bush, on what son and Texas Gov. George W. Bush asks of her

"God! I sound like a breath mint!"
Robin Williams, wowed by the description of his talents at a black-tie affair in his honor

"This is the hottest issue we will take up this session."
Texas state Sen. *Eddie Lucio*, after his colleagues adopted a resolution declaring the jalapeño the official state pepper

"How's the wound?"
Former Pres. *George Bush*, to the second of two spectators he accidentally struck with a golf ball during a charity game. The first needed stitches.

"I just don't think they could make it another four months."
Editor *Jim Witt* of the *Arlington* (Texas) *Star-Telegram*, on the disbanding of a mock jury that had nearly come to blows watching the O. J. Simpson trial on TV

"It's always a privilege to introduce someone who also speaks with an accent."
Henry Kissinger, introducing a foreign policy speech by Pres. Bill Clinton

"This would be the biggest thing to happen to this town since, well, since he retired."
Matt Hein, a Chicago basketball fan, on the expected return of Michael Jordan to the Chicago Bulls

"I'm delighted to be in Cobb County, the locale in our country that builds the wide-bodies that dominate the world, and for you Republicans in the audience, I'm not talking about Newt."
Sen. *Sam Nunn*, speaking in Marietta, GA, where large Lockheed jets are built

"Marty, Jean's out of control. Shred her!"
Oliver North, instructing an assistant to hang up on an angry caller on the first day of his radio talk show

"We want to combine the Bureau of Alcohol, Tobacco, and Firearms with both the Bureau of Fisheries and the Interstate Trucking Commission. We're going to call it the Department of Guys."
Pres. *Bill Clinton*, jokingly suggesting a way to improve his standing among male voters

"I can see myself saying, 'Who's up next? Who cares? Who's up now? Who cares?'"
Play-by-play announcer *Jon Miller*, on the prospect of "replacement player" baseball games had the strike not been settled

"With the exception of Bob Dole, to borrow a baseball analogy, these are replacement players."
Democratic strategist *Bob Beckel*, on the field of GOP presidential candidates

"I am encouraged by the example of Kato Kaelin, who was relatively unknown until two weeks ago."
Former Tennessee governor *Lamar Alexander*, on his chances in the '96 GOP presidential race

"Our sensors are detecting absolutely no sounds of survivors. Our cameras show only death."
Rescue worker *Dan Schroder*, on searching for survivors in the collapsed Oklahoma City federal building days after a car-bomb exploded, in April, killing and injuring hundreds

"Let that baby cry. It sounds like music today."
Rev. *Mark Estep*, commenting on a baby's cry during a funeral service for Dana Cooper, the woman who ran the day-care center at the Oklahoma City federal building, and her 2-year-old son, Anthony

"I've never met a cigarette that didn't make me do that anyway. I thought that's what they were for."
Albany, NY, smoker *Chris Edwards*, on the recall of defective Philip Morris cigarettes that could cause dizziness, coughing, and wheezing and eye, nose, and throat irritation

"Four words I thought I'd never say: Good news from Bosnia."
An *unknown Pentagon briefer* announcing the rescue of F-16 pilot Capt. Scott O'Grady, whose plane had been shot down over Bosnia and Herzegovina in June

"I had four ladies from Verona last month, and none of them was a Juliet."
One of Moscow's busiest and best-known plastic surgeons, *Dr. Igor Volf*, on the number of European clients who come to him to avoid the high costs of cosmetic surgery in the West

"I think most of us learned some time ago that if you don't like the president's position on a particular issue, you simply need to wait a few weeks."
Democrat Rep. *David Obey*, on Clinton's budget proposal

"That's absurd. Actually, it was a passenger pigeon."
Actor *Sylvester Stallone*, on the rumor that he broke up with a former girlfriend via Federal Express

"Houston, we have capture."
Commander *Robert "Hoot" Gibson*, on the successful docking of the space shuttle *Atlantis* with the Russian space station *Mir*

"I'd like to stay here for a few more days."
Teenager *Yoo Ji Hwan*, joking with rescuers who pulled her from a collapsed South Korean department store where she had been trapped for 12 days

"I can't believe that we are going to let a majority of the people decide what's best for this state."
Louisiana state Rep. *John Travis,* on an apparently popular measure

"Certainly, there's irony. But we're bound by the law, the same law he violated."
Larry Field, director of Oklahoma's Corrections Department, justifying a doctor's revival of convicted killer Robert Brecheen, who had overdosed on sedatives just hours before his scheduled execution

"In lieu of flowers, a 'Yes' vote on the new baseball stadium would be appreciated."
Death notice for *Thomas Fallihee*, 80, an ardent Seattle Mariners fan who favored a referendum that would finance a replacement for the deteriorating Kingdome

"[The poor] too have a role to play in building a society truly worthy of the human person—a society in which none are so poor that they have nothing to give and none are so rich that they have nothing to receive."
Pope John Paul II, in an address delivered at Newark International Airport during his Oct. 1995 visit to the U.S.

"Death, taxes, and Cal."
The three things one can count on as seen on a T-shirt at Camden Yards the night Baltimore Oriole shortstop Cal Ripken, Jr., surpassed Lou Gehrig's record of 2,130 consecutive games played

Historical Anniversaries
1896 — 100 Years Ago

Immigrants pour into U.S. cities, providing cheap labor for rapidly growing industry, as the country recovers from the depression of the late 1800s and begins to come into its own as a world industrial power.

Utah is admitted to the union, **Jan. 4**, as the 45th state; woman suffrage is part of Utah's constitution.

The first motion picture, which includes scenes of a comic boxing match and two girls dancing with umbrellas, is shown to the public, **Apr. 23**, at Koster and Bial's Music Hall in New York City.

The U.S. Supreme Court, in *Plessy* v. *Ferguson*, approves racial segregation, **May 18**, under the "separate but equal" doctrine.

A tornado strikes St. Louis, MO, **May 27**, damaging some 5,000 homes and killing an estimated 400 people.

Henry Ford completes work on the first Ford automobile, a 4-horsepower "Quadricycle," **June 4**, in Detroit, MI.

An earthquake, followed by destructive tidal waves, strikes the island of Honshu, Japan, **June 15**, killing some 27,000 and leaving an estimated 60,000 homeless.

Gold is discovered in Canada's Yukon Territory along the Klondike River, **Aug. 12**, setting off the "Klondike Stampede" of 1897-98.

Rural free postal delivery in the U.S. is established, **Oct. 1**.

Republican presidential candidate William McKinley, who favored the gold standard's tight controls on money, defeats Democratic candidate William Jennings Bryan in the general election, **Nov. 3**. Bryan had won his party's nomination, **July 8**, at the Democratic National Convention in Chicago, after delivering his "Cross of Gold" speech, which urged unlimited coinage of silver and gold.

Duryea Motor Wagon Co. of Springfield, MA, produces the Haynes-Duryea motorcar, the first U.S. motorcar to be offered for public sale.

Journalism. Using $75,000 of borrowed funds, Adolf Ochs gains control of the *New York Times*, **Aug. 18**; he adds a book review section and a Sunday magazine and on **Oct. 25** adopts the slogan, "All the News That's Fit to Print."

A one-panel yellow-colored cartoon by Richard F. Outcault called "Down Hogan's Alley," the first comic panel to be printed in color in a newspaper, appears in Joseph Pulitzer's *New York World* in **Feb.** Words are soon added to the weekly drawing, which depicts the adventures of a boy in a long, yellow outfit. Noting the popularity of the cartoon and wanting to build readership for his *New York Journal*, William Randolf Hearst lures Outcault to his newspaper where "The Yellow Kid" debuts in **Oct.**, establishing color comics as a regular newspaper feature.

The first "advice to the lovelorn" column, written by Elizabeth Gilmer under the pen name Dorothy Dix, appears in the *New Orleans Picayune*.

Literature. *Joan of Arc* by Mark Twain, *The Country of the Pointed Firs* by Sarah Orne Jewett, *A Shropshire Lad* by A. E. Housman.

Art. Winslow Homer's *All's Well*, Paul Cézanne's *The Clock Maker*, Henri de Toulouse-Lautrec's *The Toilette*.

Theater. *The Sea Gull* by Anton Chekhov in St. Petersburg, Russia; *Salomé* by Oscar Wilde, in Paris; *Rosemary* by Louis Napoleon.

Musicals. *El Capitán* with music by John Philip Sousa; *The Geisha*, in London, with music by Sidney Jones, lyrics by Harry Greenbank.

Opera. Gilbert & Sullivan's last operetta, *The Grand Duke*, at London's Savoy Theatre; *Andrea Chénier*, at Milan's Teatro alla Scala, with music by Umberto Giordano.

Popular Songs. "Sweet Rosie O'Grady" by Maude Nugent Jerome; "When the Saints Go Marching In" by James M. Black, lyrics by Katherine E. Purvis.

Sports. The first modern Olympics opens in Athens, Greece, with 311 athletes from 13 nations competing in 9 sports. Winners receive a silver medal and a crown of olive branches. The first women's intercollegiate basketball game is played between Stanford Univ. and the Univ. of California.

Miscellaneous. Cracker Jack, the candy coated popcorn mixed with peanuts, and Tootsie Rolls, the first paper-wrapped candies, are introduced. Henry M. Flagler opens Miami's Royal Palm Hotel, which begins the city's fame as a winter resort. The St. Louis brewery Anheuser-Busch introduces Michelob beer. The first trading stamps, S&H green stamps, are introduced in the U.S.

1946 — 50 Years Ago

Postwar America is a paradox of plenty and need as record-breaking crops (the greatest in history to date, 26% above the 1922-32 average and 2% above the 1942 record) and expanding business are juxtaposed with food shortages, price controls, and crippling labor conflicts.

The first session of the UN General Assembly convenes in London, **Jan. 10**, with 51 nations represented; the International Atomic Energy Commission is established **Jan. 20**.

The U.S. Army Signal Corps makes the first radar contact with the moon, **Jan. 10**; the signal covers the 477,714 mi round-trip distance in 2.4 sec.

Pres. Harry Truman establishes the Central Intelligence Group, the forerunner of the Central Intelligence Agency, by executive order, **Jan. 20**.

The United Steel Workers of America shut down the steel industry, **Jan. 21**, when an estimated 750,000 workers strike. The strike is settled, **Feb. 17**, when U.S. Steel Corp. agrees to increase the hourly wage by 18½¢.

Tensions between the West and the USSR are evident as Winston Churchill declares "from Stettin in the Baltic to Trieste in the Adriatic, an iron curtain has descended across the Continent" in a speech in Fulton, MO, **Mar. 5**, and urges a U.S.-British military alliance to strengthen the UN and work for peace.

As part of the "Eat Less" drive, the U.S. National Famine Emergency Committee, **Mar. 11**, lists 39 ways to save food, including open sandwiches, thinner bread slices, and coverless pies. U.S. bakers are ordered, **Mar. 15**, to cut the weight of bread and rolls by 10%, without a reduction in price.

Juan Peron is elected, **Mar. 28**, to a 6-year term as president of Argentina.

Japanese women vote for the first time ever, **Apr. 10**, as voters approve a new constitution and expand the powers of parliament in Japan's first postwar national election. Having declared, **Jan. 1**, that his divinity was a matter of "legends and myths," Emperor Hirohito officially promulgates the new constitution before the Japanese Diet, **Nov. 3**. It reduces the throne to a national symbol, establishes a democratic form of government, declares the emperor to be only the symbolic head of state, and renounces Japan's right to declare war.

Strikes continue in the U.S. as 400,000 soft coal miners strike, **Apr. 1**; the federal government seizes the mines,

May 22, and miners settle, **May 29**, with an 18½¢ per hour wage increase and the establishment of welfare and retirement funds. They strike again, **Nov. 21**, but return to work by federal court order, **Dec. 7**.

Gen. Zhou Enlai, second in command in the Chinese Communist Party, declares all-out war, **Apr. 14**, with the Chinese Nationalists.

The League of Nations officially expires, **Apr. 18**, and turns over its physical assets to the UN.

Pres. Truman seizes the nation's railroads, **May 17**, in an effort to avert a strike. However, the strike is called, although it ends after 48 hr, **May 25**, when workers agree to an 18½¢ per hour wage increase. Pres. Truman had appeared to a joint session of Congress that same day asking for emergency power to break strikes; the House immediately passed such legislation, but it was blocked in the Senate.

In *Morgan* v. *the Commonwealth*, the U.S. Supreme Court, **June 3**, rules 6-1 that racial segregation of passengers on interstate vehicles is unconstitutional.

In a continuing response to the world food crisis, Pres. Truman reports, **June 27**, that 5,500,000 tons of bread grain had been exported to Europe since **Jan. 1**. For the first time in history, **July 21**, the British government rations bread, flour, and cake.

As part of a U.S. government test, an atomic bomb is dropped, **July 1**, from 30,000 ft over an obsolete fleet of 73 vessels anchored off Bikini Atoll in the Pacific Ocean; a second test, the first underwater atomic explosion in history, is conducted at the same site, **July 25**.

A new, scanty two-piece bathing suit, dubbed the "bikini" by designer Louis Réard, who considered his creation as explosive as the atomic bomb, is introduced **July 5** at a Paris fashion show. It is made of a cotton fabric printed with press clippings, symbolizing the union of fashion and current events.

The Philippines becomes an independent republic, **July 4**, with Manuel Roxas as its first elected president.

Mother Frances Xavier Cabrini is named a saint of the Roman Catholic Church, **July 7**; she is the first American citizen to be canonized.

The Paris Peace Conference convenes, **July 29-Oct. 15**; foreign ministers of Great Britain, France, the USSR, and the U.S. (the Big 4) are joined by ministers of 17 other nations to draft World War II treaties with Italy, Finland, Bulgaria, Hungary, and Romania. The Big 4 Council of Foreign Ministers meets again in New York City, **Nov. 4**, to write the final treaties, which are completed **Dec. 6** and signed Feb. 10, 1947.

The McMahon Act, which allows the U.S. Army and Navy to manufacture atomic weapons and prohibits distribution of information on atomic energy, is passed, **Aug. 1**, by Congress. It establishes the civilian U.S. Atomic Energy Commission.

The Fulbright Act is passed, **Aug. 1**, establishing grants for international academic exchange.

The International Military Tribunal at Nuremberg, Germany, finds 19 Nazi defendants, including Herman Göring and Rudolf Hess, guilty, **Sept. 30**, of crimes against humanity; 12 are sentenced, **Oct. 1**, to death.

The first session of the UN General Assembly reconvenes, **Oct. 23**, in Flushing, NY, and votes, **Dec. 14**, to accept a site in New York City, offered as a gift by John D. Rockefeller, for its headquarters.

Republicans win a landslide victory in the **Nov. 5th** election, gaining control of both houses of Congress and a majority of state governorships.

After a 4-year stabilization program, Pres. Truman lifts price, wage, and salary controls (excluding rents, sugar, and rice), **Nov. 9**.

Pres. Truman issues a proclamation, **Dec. 31**, formally ending World War II hostilities.

John W. Mauchly and J. Presper Eckert complete work on the first electronic computer, ENIAC (Electronic Numerical Integrator and Calculator).

Pediatrician and psychiatrist Benjamin Spock presents his theories on raising children in *The Common Sense Book of Baby and Child Care*, which influences a generation of postwar American parents and becomes an all-time bestseller.

Literature. *Hiroshima* by John Hersey, *All the King's Men* by Robert Penn Warren, *Paterson* by William Carlos Williams, *Delta Wedding* by Eudora Welty, *This Side of Innocence* by Taylor Caldwell.

Art. Grandma Moses' *Out for Christmas Trees*, Pablo Picasso's *Françoise With a Yellow Necklace*, Jackson Pollock's *Eyes in the Heat*, Marc Chagall's *The Cow With a Parasol*.

Theater. *The Iceman Cometh* by Eugene O'Neill; *Another Part of the Forest* by Lillian Hellman; *Born Yesterday* by Garson Kanin; *The Respectful Prostitute* by Jean-Paul Sartre, in Paris.

Musicals. Ethel Merman stars in *Annie Get Your Gun*, with music and lyrics by Irving Berlin; songs include "There's No Business Like Show Business," "They Say It's Wonderful," "I Got the Sun in the Morning."

Movies. William Wyler's *The Best Years of Our Lives* with Fredric March and Myrna Loy; Frank Capra's *It's a Wonderful Life* with James Stewart, Lionel Barrymore, and Donna Reed; Edmund Goulding's *The Razor's Edge* with Tyrone Power and Gene Tierney; John Ford's *My Darling Clementine* with Henry Fonda, Victor Mature, and Linda Darnell; Vincente Minnelli's *Ziegfeld Follies* with William Powell, Judy Garland, Fred Astaire, and Gene Kelly. The first international Cannes Film Festival opens in Cannes, France, **Sept. 20**.

Popular Songs. "Let It Snow" by Sammy Cahn and Jule Styne; "(Get Your Kicks on) Route 66" by Bob Troup; "Seems Like Old Times" by Carmen Lombardo and John Jacob Loeb; "The Christmas Song (Chestnuts Roasting on an Open Fire)" by Mel Tormé and Robert Wells.

Sports. The Basketball Association of America (forerunner of the NBA) is organized. The invention of the automatic pinspotter revolutionizes bowling. The first U.S. Women's Open golf tournament is played in Spokane, WA.

Television. *Hour Glass*, the first hour-long entertainment series, debuts. WNBT in association with NBC begins feeding its programs to Philadelphia and Schenectady, creating the first east-coast regional television network.

Miscellaneous. *Tide* detergent is introduced by Procter & Gamble. Joakim Lehmkuhl introduces the mass-produced Timex watch, which, at $6.95 and up, will soon account for 40% of U.S. wristwatch sales.

1971 — 25 Years Ago

As the U.S. begins its second decade of involvement in Vietnam, **Jan. 21** marks the 100th meeting of the U.S., South Vietnam, North Vietnam, and the Provisional Revolutionary Government at the Paris peace talks. Public outcry in the U.S. against the war continues as Vietnam veterans demonstrate for 5 days, **Apr. 19-23**, and some 200,000 people march, **Apr. 24**, in Washington, DC. Demonstrations persist, **May 3-5**, and police arrest some 12,600.

The pullout of U.S. forces from Vietnam continues throughout the year, but late in **Dec.**, U.S. Air Force and

Navy planes carry out massive attacks on military installations in North Vietnam, the heaviest since a bombing halt had been declared in Nov. 1968.

A federal ban on cigarette advertising on U.S. radio and television networks begins, **Jan. 2**.

Charles Manson and 3 of his followers are found guilty, **Jan. 26**, of first degree murder in the brutal 1969 slayings of actress Sharon Tate and 6 others.

A major earthquake, registering 6.6 on the Richter scale, hits the San Fernando Valley, in southern California, **Feb. 9**, killing 65 and injuring hundreds more.

A treaty prohibiting installation of nuclear weapons on the seabed beyond any nation's 12-mi coastal zone is signed, **Feb. 11**, by 63 nations, including the U.S. and the USSR.

The Twenty-sixth Amendment to the U.S. Constitution, which lowers the voting age to 18 in all elections, is ratified, **June 30**, when Ohio becomes the 38th state to approve it.

A court-martial jury of 6 officers, **Mar. 29**, convicts Lt. William L. Calley, Jr., of the premeditated murder of 22 South Vietnamese men, women, and children at Mylai on Mar. 16, 1968. He is sentenced to life imprisonment, **Mar. 31**; the sentence is reduced to 20 yr, **Aug. 20**, and the verdict is overturned, Sept. 24, 1974, by a federal court.

In a move to raise revenues, New York City opens betting windows, **Apr. 7**, enabling horseplayers to participate in the first legalized off-track-betting (OTB) operated by any U.S. city.

The new nation of Bangladesh is proclaimed, **Apr. 17**, by East Pakistani rebels.

The USSR launches *Salyut 1*, an unpiloted, scientific space station, **Apr. 19**; 3 cosmonauts dock their spacecraft with the orbiting lab, **Apr. 24**, but fail to enter. Another team of cosmonauts docks with and later enters the spacelab, **June 7**, but after nearly 24 days in space, they die, **June 30**, during their return to earth.

The U.S. Supreme Court unanimously upholds the legality of busing of schoolchildren to achieve racial balance, **Apr. 20**, in the case of *Swann v. Charlotte-Mecklenburg Board of Education*.

Pres. Richard Nixon lifts the 21-year trade embargo with China, **June 10**, and in a surprise announcement, **July 15**, says that he will visit that country before May 1972, becoming the first U.S. president to be received by a Chinese government.

Publication of classified Pentagon papers on the U.S. involvement in Vietnam begins, **June 13**, by the *New York Times*. The Justice Dept. secures a restraining order, **June 15**, against publication of the "Pentagon Papers," pending a ruling on a permanent injunction. In a 6-3 vote, the U.S. Supreme Court, **June 30**, upholds the right of the *New York Times* and the *Washington Post* to publish the documents under First Amendment protection. Daniel Ellsberg, admitted leaker of the 47-volume Pentagon analysis, is indicted, **June 28**, on charges of unauthorized possession of secret documents. Conspiracy and other charges are added, **Dec. 30**; all charges are dismissed May 13, 1973.

Special ceremonies in Washington, DC, **July 1**, mark the inauguration of the semi-independent U.S. Postal Service, which replaces the 182-year-old Post Office Dept.

Rock musician/poet Jim Morrison dies in Paris, **July 3**, of an apparent drug overdose.

As part of the *Apollo 15* mission, Col. Randolf Scott and Lt. Col. James Irwin take the first car-ride on the moon when they explore the lunar surface in the electric, four-wheeled Lunar Rover 1, **Jul. 31-Aug. 2**.

Pres. Nixon begins a sweeping new economic program, **Aug. 15**, calling for a 90-day wage, price, and rent freeze,

to be effective immediately. He also frees the dollar to fluctuate in value against other currencies by cutting its tie with gold, and he halts the conversion of foreign-held dollars into gold.

The flamboyant former USSR Communist Party chief and premier Nikita Khrushchev dies, **Sept. 11**, in Moscow.

More than 1,000 NY state troopers and police storm the Attica State Correctional Facility in Attica, NY, **Sept. 13**, ending a 4-day takeover of the facility by inmates, leaving 10 hostages and 33 convicts dead.

Emperor Hirohito stops over in Anchorage, Alaska, **Sept. 26**, to meet briefly with Pres. Nixon. The occasion marks the first time that a U.S. president and an emperor of Japan meet, as well as the first visit to American soil in the Japanese imperial dynasty's history.

China is granted UN membership, **Oct. 25**, when the General Assembly adopts a resolution to seat the mainland Communists and oust the Taiwan Nationalists.

The House of Commons, **Oct. 28**, approves British entry into the European Economic Community.

The interplanetary probe *Mariner 9* becomes the first artificial satellite to orbit another planet when it begins to circle Mars, **Nov. 13**.

Det. Frank Serpico testifies, **Dec. 14**, about New York City police corruption before the Knapp Commission in New York City.

The U.S. experiences its first trade deficit since 1888 when imports top exports by $2.05 bil.

Journalism. *Look* magazine ceases publication with its **Oct. 19** issue.

Literature. *Rabbit Redux* by John Updike, *Winds of War* by Herman Wouk, *The Drifters* by James Michener, *Our Gang* by Philip Roth, *The Book of Daniel* by E. L. Doctorow.

Art. David Hockney's *Portrait of an Artist (Pool With Two People)*.

Theater. *The Prisoner of Second Avenue* by Neil Simon. The John F. Kennedy Center for the Performing Arts opens in Washington, DC, **Sept. 8**, with the first performance of Leonard Bernstein's Mass.

Musicals. *Follies*, with music and lyrics by Stephen Sondheim; *Jesus Christ Superstar*, with music by Andrew Lloyd Webber and lyrics by Tim Rice.

Movies. William Friedkin's *The French Connection* with Gene Hackman; Peter Bogdanovich's *The Last Picture Show* with Timothy Bottoms, Jeff Bridges, and Cybill Shepherd; Alan J. Pakula's *Klute* with Jane Fonda and Donald Sutherland; Stanley Kubrick's *A Clockwork Orange* with Malcom McDowell and Michael Bates.

Television. Norman Lear's *All in the Family* on CBS, with Carroll O'Connor, Jean Stapleton, Sally Struthers, and Rob Reiner.

Popular Songs. "It's Too Late" by Carol King, "Stairway to Heaven" by Robert Plant and Jimmy Page (Led Zeppelin), "Maggie May" by Rod Stewart, "Theme From Shaft" by Isaac Hayes, "Take Me Home, Country Roads" by John Denver.

Sports. Members of the U.S. Ping-Pong team visit China, **Apr. 10**, on invitation from the Chinese government. The National Hockey Assn. adds 2 franchise sites—Long Island, NY, and Atlanta, GA. The U.S. Supreme Court, **June 28**, reverses the draft-evasion conviction of heavyweight boxer Muhammad Ali, in an 8-0 decision.

Miscellaneous. Amtrak, the nation's new rail-passenger system, goes into operation, **May 1**. Walt Disney World opens, **Oct. 1**, near Orlando, FL. Women's all-occasion short-shorts called "hot pants" hit the fashion scene.

Obituaries

Deaths, Nov. 1, 1994–Oct. 15, 1995

A

Abbot, George, 107; playwright, director, actor, and producer in more than 120 productions, including *Damn Yankees*; Miami Beach, FL, Jan 31, 1995.

Alfven Hannes, 86; Nobel-prize-winning physicist who founded the field of magnetohydrodynamics; Djursholm, Sweden, Apr. 2, 1995.

Aspin, Les, 56; Democratic representative from Wisconsin and former secretary of defense; Washington, DC, May 21, 1995.

Atanasoff, John Vincent, 91; inventor of the first electronic computer in 1939; Monrovia, MD, June 15, 1995.

B

Ballantine, Ian, 79; founder of Penguin USA, Bantam Books, and Ballantine Books; Bearsville, NY, Mar. 9, 1995.

Baskerville, Charles, 98; portrait painter and muralist whose subjects included heads of state; New York, NY, Nov. 20, 1994.

Bazargan, Mehdi, late 80s; Iran's first prime minister after the Islamic revolution of 1979; Zurich, Switzerland, Jan. 20, 1995.

Belladonna, Giorgio, 72; one of the greatest bridge players of all time; Rome, May 12, 1995.

Bernays, Edward, 103; father of public relations and leader in opinion making; Cambridge, MA, Mar. 9, 1995.

Bill, Max, 85; painter, sculptor, and architect, among the last surviving students of the Bauhaus; Berlin, Dec. 9, 1994.

Bingham, Mary, 90; matriarch of the Bingham newspaper empire; Louisville, KY, Apr. 18, 1995.

Blair, Frank, 79; anchor of the *Today* show for 22 years; Hilton Head Island, SC, Mar. 14, 1995.

Bolt, Robert, 70; Oscar-winning screenwriter, whose credits included *Lawrence of Arabia* and *Dr. Zhivago*; Hampshire, England, Feb. 20, 1995.

Botvinnik, Mikhail, 83; world chess champion of the 1950s; Moscow, May 5, 1995.

Brazzi, Rossano, 78; starred in the movie *South Pacific* and played other romantic film roles; Rome, Dec. 24, 1994.

Burger, Warren E., 87; 15th chief justice of the U.S.; Washington, DC, June 25, 1995.

C

Calloway, Cab, 86; "Hi-de-ho" man of jazz, model for Sportin' Life; Hockessin, DE, Nov. 18, 1994.

Chandrasekhar, Subrahmanyan, 84; Nobel laureate in physics whose discovery about the evolution of stars pointed toward the existence of "black holes"; Chicago, IL, Aug. 21, 1995.

Christiansen, Godtfred K., 75; Danish executive of the company that created Lego plastic bulding-brick sets; Billund, Denmark, July 13, 1995.

Cohen, Stanley, 66; creator of Moppets; Mount Kisco, NY, Apr. 28, 1995.

Coleman, Earl, 69; jazz-ballad singer; New York, NY, July 12, 1995.

Cook, Peter, 57; British writer and performer; London, Jan. 9, 1995.

Cosell, Howard, 77; outspoken and controversial sportscaster on television and radio; New York, NY, Apr. 23, 1995.

Critchfield, Richard Patrick, 63; author and journalist who lived among and wrote about people of the third world; Washington, DC, Dec. 10, 1994.

Crosby, Gary, 62; singer, actor, eldest son of Bing Crosby; Burbank, CA, Aug. 25, 1995.

Cyr, Frank W., 95; an authority on rural education who was called the Father of the Yellow School Bus; Stamford, NY, Aug. 1, 1995.

D

Dahmer, Jeffrey, 34; multiple killer, notorious for exploits of necrophilia and dismemberment; murdered in a Wisconsin prison, Nov. 28, 1994.

Day, Leon, 78; former Negro League baseball star, only recently selected to the Baseball Hall of Fame; Baltimore, MD, Mar. 13, 1995.

Delany, Bessie, 104; author of *Having Our Say* and one of the first black women to become a dentist; Mt. Vernon, NY, Sept. 25, 1995.

Desai, Morarji, 99; prime minister of India's first non-Congress Party government in 1977; Bombay, Apr. 10, 1995.

Djilas, Milovan, 83; Yugoslav critic of communism; Belgrade, Apr. 20, 1995.

Douglas-Home, Sir Alec, 92; former prime minister of Great Britain; Berwickshire, Scotland, Oct. 9, 1995.

Duke, Angier Biddle, 79; ambassador and tobacco family heir; Southampton, NY, Apr. 30, 1995.

Dzubas, Friedel, 79; abstract painter of the New York School; Newton, MA, Dec. 11, 1994.

E

Easy-E, 31; founder and performer of gangster rap; Los Angeles, CA, Mar. 26, 1995.

Eckert, J. Presper, 76; coinventor of the Eniac computer in 1945; Bryn Mawr, PA, June 3, 1995.

Eisenstaedt, Alfred, 96; pioneering photographer whose *Life* magazine images helped define photojournalism; Martha's Vineyard, MA, Aug. 23, 1995.

Elgart, Les, 77; trumpet player and leader of a big band; Dallas, TX, July 29, 1995.

Elkin, Stanley, 65; writer of fiction, whose works included The Magic Kingdom; St. Louis, MO, May 31, 1995.

F

Fangio, Juan Manuel, 84; 5-time world champion race driver; Buenos Aires, July 17, 1995.

Faubus, Orval, 84; governor of Arkansas (1955-67), champion of segregation in the South; Conway, AR, Dec. 14, 1994.

Flanders, Ed, 60; actor known for his work in "St. Elsewhere"; Denny, CA, Feb. 22, 1995.

Fleet, Preston, 60; founder of the Fotomat company and inventor of Omnimax; Santa Barbara, CA, Jan. 31, 1995.

Fleming, Art, 70; original host of TV's *Jeopardy*; Crystal River, FL, Apr. 25, 1995.

Franklin, Melvin, 52; original member of the Temptations; Los Angeles, CA, Feb. 23, 1995.

Fulbright, J. William, 89; U.S. senator (1945-74) and creator of the Fulbright fellowships; Washington, DC, Feb. 9, 1995.

G

Gabor, Eva, 74; actress best known for her TV role in *Green Acres* and as one of 3 celebrated sisters; Los Angeles, CA, July 4, 1995.

Garcia, Jerry, 53; lead guitarist of the Grateful Dead and counterculture icon of the 1960s and '70s; Forest Knolls, CA, Aug. 9, 1995.

Glaser, Elizabeth, 47; crusader for pediatric AIDS; Santa Monica, CA, Dec. 3, 1994.

Godunov, Alexander, 45; Russian ballet dancer and film actor; West Hollywood, CA, May 18, 1995.

Gonzalez, Pancho, 67; U.S. tennis champion; Las Vegas, NV, July 3, 1995.

Gonzalez, Pedro, 99; folk hero, advocate for social justice, and infamous member of Pancho Villa's rebel forces; Lodi, CA, Mar. 17, 1995.

Gordon, Gale, 89; TV actor who played opposite Lucille Ball; Escondido, CA, June 30, 1995.

Gorman, Margaret, 90; the first Miss America; Washington, DC, Oct. 1, 1995.

Grace, J. Peter, 81; head of W. R. Grace & Co. for 47 years; New York, NY, Apr. 19, 1995.

Griswold, Erwin, 90; U.S. solicitor general and dean of Harvard Law School; Boston, MA, Nov. 19, 1994.

Guardino, Harry, 69; stage, television, and movie actor; Palm Springs, CA, July 17, 1995.

Gucci, Paolo, 64; former design chief and central player in the leather goods company; London, Oct. 10, 1995.

H

Harris, Phil, 91; band leader, radio comedian, and voice of Baloo the Bear in Disney's *Jungle Book*; Rancho Mirage, CA, Aug. 11, 1995.

Harris, Thomas, 85; psychiatrist and author of *I'm OK—You're OK*; Sacramento, CA, May 4, 1995.

Hawkins, Erick, 85; pioneering choreographer of American dance; New York, NY, Nov. 23, 1994.

Hayward, Thomas, 77; leading tenor at the Metropolitan Opera in the 1940s and '50s; Las Vegas, NV, Feb. 2, 1995.

Herriot, James, 78; veterinarian author of *All Creatures Great and Small*; Yorkshire, England, Feb. 23, 1995.

Highsmith, Patricia, 74; crime writer who created Tom Ripley; Locarno, Switzerland, Feb. 5, 1995.

Hobby, Oveta Culp, 90; creator of the Women's Army Corps, first secretary of Health, Education, and Welfare, and former owner of the *Houston Post*; Houston, TX, Aug. 16, 1995.

Holman, Nat, 98; basketball great of the 1920s and coach, known as "Mr. Basketball"; Riverdale, NY, Feb. 12, 1995.

Horn, Milton, 88; sculptor known for public artworks; Chicago, IL, Mar. 29, 1995.

Hunter, Howard William, 87; 14th leader of the Mormon Church; Salt Lake City, UT, Mar. 3, 1995.

I

Ives, Burl, 85; folk singer and Academy

Award-winning actor; Anacortes, WA, Apr. 14, 1995.

J

Johnson, Helene, 89; Harlem Renaissance poet; New York, NY, July 7, 1995.

K

Kelsey, Hugh, 69; famed bridge writer and expert player; Edinburgh, Scotland, Mar. 18, 1995.

Kennedy, Rose Fitzgerald, 104; matriarch of a political dynasty that included Pres. John F. Kennedy and 2 U.S. senators; Hyannis Port, MA, Jan. 22, 1995.

Kenyon, Jane, 47; poet laureate of New Hampshire; Wilmot, NH, Apr. 22, 1995.

Kirby, George, 71; comedian and singer; Las Vegas, NV, Sept. 30, 1995.

Koch, Howard, 93; screenwriter for Casablanca and author of Orson Welles's radio adaptation of *The War of the Worlds*; Kingston, NY, Aug. 17, 1995.

Kuhn, Maggie, 89; founder of the Gray Panthers; Philadelphia, PA, Apr. 22, 1995.

Kunstler, William, 76; lawyer for social outcasts and civil rights champion; New York, NY, Sept. 4, 1995.

L

Lester, Jerry, 85; comedian and host of early TV talk show; Miami, FL, Mar. 23. 1995.

Levitz, Ralph, 82; co-founder of Levitz Furniture Corp.; La Costa, CA, Mar. 25, 1995.

Levin, Morton L., 91; one of the first epidemiologists to link cigarette smoking to lung cancer; Riverhead, NY, July 7, 1995.

Listyev, Vladislav, 38; television journalist; Moscow, Mar. 1, 1995.

Lowe, Edward, 75; discoverer of Kitty Litter and creator of a multimillion dollar Kitty Litter industry; Sarasota, FL, Oct. 4, 1995.

Luciano, Ron, 57; former major league umpire; Endicott, NY, Jan. 18, 1995.

Lupino, Ida, 77; film actress and director; Burbank, CA, Aug. 3, 1995.

M

Mantle, Mickey, 63; the most powerful switch-hitter in baseball history and New York Yankee folk hero; Dallas, TX, Aug. 13, 1995.

Martell, René M., 68: leader of cognac company; Nice, France, June 6, 1995.

Martin, Charles Elmer, 85; artist known for his cartoons and covers for the *New Yorker*; Portland, ME, June 16, 1995.

Maxwell, Vera, 93; pioneering women's sportswear designer; Rincon, Puerto Rico, Jan. 15, 1995.

McClure, Doug, 59; actor who starred in such TV westerns as *The Virginian*; Sherman Oaks, CA, Feb. 5, 1995.

McRae, Carmen, 74; jazz singer known for her lyrical interpretations; Beverly Hills, CA, Nov. 10, 1994.

Meister, Alton, 72; biochemist active in AIDS research; Stamford, CT, Apr. 6, 1995.

Merrill, James, 68; prize-winning poet, one of the most admired in America; Tucson, AZ, Feb. 6, 1995.

Moncion, Francisco, 76; leading dancer and charter member of the New York City Ballet; Woodstock, NY, Apr. 1, 1995.

Montgomery, Elizabeth, 57; star of the TV comedy *Bewitched*; Los Angeles, CA, May 18, 1995.

Moses, Gilbert, 52; award-winning stage director; New York, NY, Apr. 14, 1995.

Muir, Jean, 66; British designer of classic fashions; London, May 28, 1995.

N

Nelson, Lindsey, 76; sports broadcaster; Atlanta, GA, June 10, 1995.

Nizer, Louis, 92; shrewd and voluble trial lawyer whose clients were a roster of celebrities; New York, NY, Nov. 10, 1994.

Nu, U, 87; first prime minister of Burma (now called Myanmar); Yangon, Myanmar, Feb. 14, 1995.

O

Onganía, Juan Carlos, 81; fromer president of Argentina; Buenos Aires, June 8, 1995.

Osborn, Robert, 90; caricaturist, cartoonist, and satiric commentator; Salisbury, CT, Dec. 20, 1994.

Osborne, John, 65; British playwright; Shropshire, England, Dec. 24, 1994.

P

Penick, Harvey, 90; golf instructor and author of best-selling sports book in history; Austin, TX, Apr. 2, 1995.

Perry, Frank, 65; director whose films included *David and Lisa*; New York, NY, Aug. 29, 1995.

Perry, Frederick John, 85; British tennis star of the 1930s; Melbourne, Australia, Feb. 2, 1995.

Potamkin, Victor, 83; controller of an automotive empire that included 50 Cadillac franchises; Miami, FL, June 5, 1995.

Q

Quintanilla, Selena, 23; Grammy award-winning Tejano singer; Corpus Christi, TX, Mar. 31, 1995.

R

Redenbacher, Orville, 88; agricultural scientist who became famous for his popcorn; Coronado, CA, Sept. 19, 1995.

Rich, Charlie, 62; country singer known as the Silver Fox; Hammond, LA, July 25, 1995.

Rogers, Ginger, 83; Academy Award-winning actress and dancer; Rancho Mirage, CA, Apr. 25, 1995.

Rome, Esther, 49; author of *Our Bodies, Ourselves*; Somerville, MA, June 24, 1995.

Romney, George, 88; president of American Motors, 3-term governor of Michigan, Republican presidential candidate, and member of the Nixon cabinet; Bloomfield Hills, MI, July 26, 1995.

Roosa, Stuart A., 61; astronaut who made 3d moon landing; Falls Church, VA, Dec. 12, 1994.

Ross, Bob, 52; host of public television's *Joy of Painting*; July 4, 1995.

Rubin, Jerry, 56; '60s radical and standard bearer of the counterculture and opposition to the Vietnam War; Los Angeles, CA, Nov. 28, 1994.

Rudolph, Wilma, 54; first woman to win 3 gold medals in track and field in one Olympics; Brentwood, TN, Nov. 12, 1994.

Rusk, Dean, 85; secretary of state for presidents Kennedy and Johnson; Athens, GA, Dec. 20, 1994.

S

Salk, Jonas, 80; renowned scientist who developed the first successful vaccine against poliomyelitis; San Diego, CA, June 23, 1995.

Sarton, May, 83; poet, novelist, and individualist, a heroine to feminists; York, ME, July 16, 1995.

Scali, John A., 77; former ABC News correspondent and U.S. ambassador to the UN; Washington, DC, Oct. 9, 1995.

Shulman, Irving, 81; novelist and screenwriter, who wrote the screenplay for the movie *Rebel Without a Cause*; Los Angeles, CA, Mar. 23, 1995.

Siad Barre, Mohamed, 70s; former president of Somalia; Nigeria, Jan 2, 1995.

Simpson, Adele, 91; designer of women's fashions; Greenwich, CT, Aug. 23, 1995.

Singh, Brajendra, 76; the last maharajah of Bharatpur; Rajasthan State, India, July 8, 1995.

Skala, Lilia, 90s; actress, known for work in *Lilies of the Field*; Bay Shore, NY, Dec. 18, 1994.

Smith, Margaret Chase, 97; Maine Republican who was the first woman to win election to both houses of Congress and the first whose name was advanced for the presidency at a national convention; Skowhegan, ME, May 29, 1995.

Smith, Ralph H., 80; the town crier of Mariemont, OH, believed to be the only elected town crier in the U.S.; Cincinnati, OH, July 31, 1995.

Spender, Stephen, 86; British poet, critic, and novelist; London, July 16, 1995.

Stennis, John, 93; Democratic senator from Mississippi for more than 41 years; Jackson, MS, Apr. 23, 1995.

Swayze, John Cameron, 89; early TV newscaster and announcer and pitchman for Timex watches; Sarasota, FL, Aug. 15, 1995.

T

Taylor, Art, 65; leading jazz drummer and bandleader; New York, NY, Feb. 6, 1995.

Timsley, Marion, 68; checkers champion who was considered the best player in the history of the game; Humble, TX, Apr. 3, 1995.

Townsend, Dallas, Jr., 76; CBS radio broadcaster; Montclair, NJ, June 1, 1995.

Townsend, Peter, 80; Princess Margaret's love; Paris, June 19, 1995.

Trueblood, Elton, 94; Quaker scholar, teacher, and author; Lansdale, PA, Dec. 20, 1994.

Turner, Lana, 75; movie star who first appeared on screen as a teenage "sweater girl"; Los Angeles, CA, June 29, 1995.

W

Waterman, Willard, 80; radio, TV, film, and theater actor, known for his role as "The Great Gildersleeve"; Burlingame, CA, Feb. 1, 1995.

Wayne, David, 81; actor who played on Broadway, in films, and in television; Santa Monica, CA, Feb. 9, 1995.

Wigner, Eugene, 92; Nobel Prize-winning physicist; Princeton, NJ, Jan. 1, 1995.

Wilson, Harold, 79; former British prime minister and Labor Party leader; London, May 24, 1995.

Wolfman Jack, 57; rock-and-roll disc jockey and raspy-voiced radio show host; Belvidere, NC, July 1, 1995.

Wood, Evelyn, 86; promoter and developer of speed-reading techniques; Tucson, AZ, Aug. 26, 1995.

Z

Zelazny, Roger, 58; science fiction writer; Santa Fe, NM, June 14, 1995.

UNITED STATES GOVERNMENT

EXECUTIVE BRANCH	LEGISLATIVE BRANCH	JUDICIAL BRANCH
PRESIDENT **Vice President Cabinet** **Executive Office of the President** White House Office Office of Management and Budget Council of Economic Advisers National Security Council Office of the U.S. Trade Representative Council on Environmental Quality Office of Science and Technology Policy Office of National Drug Control Policy Office of Administration	**CONGRESS** **Senate House** Architect of the Capitol U.S. Botanic Garden General Accounting Office Government Printing Office Library of Congress Congressional Budget Office	**Supreme Court of the United States** Courts of Appeals District Courts Territorial Courts Court of International Trade Court of Federal Claims Court of Military Appeals Tax Court Court of Veterans Appeals Administrative Office of the Courts Federal Judicial Center Sentencing Commission

The Clinton Administration

As of Oct. 15, 1995; all mailing addresses listed are for Washington, DC

Terms of office of the president and vice president: Jan. 20, 1993, to Jan. 20, 1997. No person may be elected president of the United States for more than two 4-year terms.

President — Bill Clinton of Arkansas receives salary of $200,000 a year taxable; in addition an expense allowance of $50,000 to assist in defraying expenses resulting from his official duties. Also there may be expended not exceeding $100,000, nontaxable, a year for travel expenses and $20,000 for official entertainment available for allocation within the Executive Office of the President.

Vice President — Albert Gore, Jr., of Tennessee receives salary of $171,500 a year and $10,000 for expenses, all of which is taxable.

The Cabinet Department Heads

(Salary: $148,400 per annum)

Secretary of State — Warren M. Christopher
Secretary of the Treasury — Robert E. Rubin
Secretary of Defense — William J. Perry
Attorney General — Janet Reno
Secretary of the Interior — Bruce Babbitt
Secretary of Agriculture — Dan Glickman
Secretary of Commerce — Ronald H. Brown
Secretary of Labor — Robert B. Reich
Secretary of Health and Human Services — Donna E. Shalala
Secretary of Housing and Urban Development — Henry G. Cisneros
Secretary of Transportation — Federico F. Peña
Secretary of Energy — Hazel R. O'Leary
Secretary of Education — Richard W. Riley
Secretary of Veterans Affairs — Jesse Brown

The White House Staff

1600 Pennsylvania Ave. NW 20500

Chief of Staff — Leon Panetta
Asst. to the President & Deputy Chief of Staff for Policy and Political Affairs — Harold Ickes
Asst. to the President & Deputy Chief of Staff for Operations — Erskine Bowles
Counselor to the President — Thomas F. McLarty 3d
Senior Adviser on Policy and Strategy — George Stephanopoulos
Assistants to the President:
  Counsel to the President — Jack Quinn
  Domestic Policy Council — Carol Rasco
  Presidential Personnel — Bob Nash
  Press Secretary — Michael McCurry
  Legislative Affairs — Patrick Griffin
  Strategic Planning — Don Baer
  National Economic Policy — Laura D'Andrea Tyson
  Intergovernmental Affairs — Marcia Hale
  National Security — W. Anthony Lake
  Staff Secretary — Todd Stern
  Political Affairs — Doug Sosnik

  Public Liaison — Alexis Herman
  Management & Administration — Jodie R. Torkelson

Executive Agencies

Council of Economic Advisers — Joseph Stiglitz, chmn.
Office of Administration — Franklin S. Reeder, dir.
Office of Science & Technology Policy — John H. Gibbons
Office of National AIDS Policy — Patricia Fleming
Office of National Drug Control Policy — Lee P. Brown
Office of Management and Budget — Alice Rivlin, dir.
U.S. Trade Representative — Michael Kantor, amb.
Council on Environmental Policy — Kathleen McGinty, chmn.

Department of State

2201 C St. NW 20520

Secretary of State — Warren M. Christopher
Deputy Secretary — Strobe Talbott
Chief of Staff & Asst. Sec. for Public Affairs — Thomas E. Donilon
U.S. Ambassador to the United Nations — Madeleine K. Albright
Under Sec. for Political Affairs — Peter Tarnoff
Under Sec. for Management — Richard M. Moose
Under Sec. for Global Affairs — Timothy E. Wirth
Under Sec. for Economic, Business, & Agricultural Affairs — Joan E. Spero
Under Sec. for Arms Control & International Security Affairs — Lynn E. Davis
Policy Planning Director — James B. Steinberg
Chief of Protocol — Molly M. Raiser
Inspector General — Jacqueline L. Williams-Bridgers
Legal Adviser — Conrad K. Harper
Director Gen. of the Foreign Service & Dir. of Personnel — Genta Hawkins Holmes
Assistant Secretaries for:
  Administration — Patrick F. Kennedy
  African Affairs — George E. Moose
  Consular Affairs — Mary A. Ryan
  Democracy, Human Rights, & Labor — John Shattuck
  Diplomatic Security — Tony Quainton
  East Asian & Pacific Affairs — Winston Lord
  Economic & Business Affairs — Daniel K. Tarullo
  European & Canadian Affairs — Richard Holbrooke
  Intelligence & Research — Toby T. Gati
  Inter-American Affairs — Alexander F. Watson
  International Narcotics and Law — Robert S. Gelbard
  International Organization Affairs — Douglas J. Bennett
  Legislative Affairs — Wendy R. Sherman
  Near Eastern Affairs — Robert H. Pelletreau
  Oceans, International Environmental, & Scientific Affairs — Elinor G. Constable
  Politico-Military Affairs — Thomas E. McNamara
  Population, Refugees, and Migration — Phyllis E. Oakley

Department of the Treasury
1500 Pennsylvania Ave. NW 20220
Secretary of the Treasury — Robert E. Rubin
Deputy Sec. of the Treasury — Lawrence Summers
Under Sec. for Domestic Finance — John Hawke
Under Sec. for International Affairs — vacant
Under Sec. for Enforcement — Ronald K. Noble
General Counsel — Edward Knight
Inspector General — Valerie Lau
Assistant Secretaries for:
  Economic Policy — Alicia Hancock Munnell
  Enforcement — vacant
  Fiscal Affairs — Gerald Murphy
  International Affairs — vacant
  Legislative Affairs — Linda Robertson
  Public Affairs — Howard Schloss
  Tax Policy — Leslie B. Samuels
  Management — George Muñoz
  Financial Institutions — Richard Carnell
Treasurer of the U.S. — Mary Ellen Withrow
Bureaus:
  Alcohol, Tobacco & Firearms — John W. Magaw, dir.
  Comptroller of the Currency — Eugene A. Ludwig, comm.
  Customs — George J. Weise, comm.
  Engraving & Printing — Larry Rolufs, dir.
  Federal Law Enforcement Training Center — Charles F. Rinkevich, dir.
  Financial Management Service — Russell Morris, comm.
  Internal Revenue Service — Margaret Milner Richardson, comm.
  Mint — Philip Diehl, dir.
  Public Debt — Richard L. Gregg, comm.
  U.S. Secret Service — Eljay B. Bowron, dir.
  Office Thrift Supervision — Jonathan Fiechter

Department of Defense
The Pentagon 20301
Secretary of Defense — William J. Perry
Deputy Secretary — John P. White
Under Sec. for Acquisition and Technology — Paul Kaminski
Under Sec. for Policy — Walter B. Slocombe
Asst. Secretaries for:
  Command, Control, Communications & Intelligence — Emmett Paige Jr.
  Personnel and Readiness — Edwin Dorn
  Health Affairs — Stephen C. Joseph
  International Security Policy — Ashton B. Carter
  Legislative Affairs — Sandra Stuart
  Program Analysis & Evaluation — William J. Lynn III
  Public Affairs — Kenneth Bacon
  Reserve Affairs — Deborah Lee
  Special Operations & Low Intensity Conflict— H. Allen Holmes
Comptroller— John Hamre
General Counsel — Judith Miller
Administration — Ann Reese, dir.
Operational Test & Evaluation — Phillip E. Coyle III
Chairman, Joint Chiefs of Staff — Gen. John Shalikashvili
Secretary of the Army — Togo West
Secretary of the Navy — John Dalton
Secretary of the Air Force — Sheila Widnall

Department of Justice
Constitution Ave. & 10th St. NW 20530
Attorney General — Janet Reno
Deputy Attorney General — Jamie S. Gorelick
Associate Attorney General — John R. Schmidt
Solicitor General — Drew S. Days 3d
Office of Inspector General — Michael R. Bromwich
Assistants:
  Antitrust Division — Anne K. Bingaman
  Civil Division — Frank W. Hunger
  Civil Rights Division — Deval L. Patrick
  Criminal Division — Jo Ann Harris
  Environment & Natural Resources Division — Lois J. Schiffer
  Justice Programs — Laurie Robinson

Legal Counsel — Walter Dellinger
Policy Development — Eleanor D. Acheson
Legislative Affairs — Kent Marcus, act.
Administration — Steve R. Colgate
Tax Division — Loretta C. Argrett
Executive Secretariat — Anna Gatons
Office of Public Affairs — Carl Stern
Office of Information and Privacy — Richard L. Huff/Daniel J. Metcalf
Community Oriented Policing Services — Joseph Brann, dir.
Fed. Bureau of Investigation — Louis J. Freeh, dir.
Exec. Off. for Immigration Review — Tony Moscato, dir.
Bureau of Prisons — Kathleen M. Hawk, dir.
Comm. Relations Service — Jeffrey Weiss, dir.
Drug Enforcement Adm. — Tom Constantine
Office of Intelligence Policy and Review — Richard Scruggs, counsel
Exec. Off. for National Security — Mark Steinberg, dir.
Office of Professional Responsibility — Michael E. Shaheen Jr.
Exec. Off. for U.S. Trustees — Joseph Patchan, act. dir.
Foreign Claims Comm. — Delissa Ridgeway, comm.
Exec. Off. for U.S. Attorneys — Carol DiBattiste, dir.
Immigration and Naturalization Service — Doris Meissner, comm.
Pardon Attorney — Margaret C. Love
U.S. Parole Commission — Edward F. Reilly Jr., chmn.
U.S. Marshals Service — Eduardo Gonzalez, dir.
U.S. Natl. Central Bureau of INTERPOL — Shelley G. Altenstadtero, chief

Department of the Interior
1849 C St. NW 20240
Secretary of the Interior — Bruce Babbitt
Deputy Secretary — John Garamenol
Assistant Secretaries for:
  Fish, Wildlife, and Parks — George T. Framton Jr.
  Indian Affairs — Ada E. Deer
  Land & Minerals — Robert Armstrong
  Policy, Budget, and Management — Bonnie R. Cohen
  Intergovernmental Affairs — Leslie Turner
  Water & Science — Elizabeth A. Reike
Bureau of Land Management — Michael Dombeck, act. dir.
Bureau of Mines — Rhea Graham, dir.
Bureau of Reclamation — Daniel T. Beard, comm.
Fish & Wildlife Service — Mollie Beattie, dir.
Geological Survey — Gordon P. Eaton, dir.
National Park Service — Roger Kennedy, dir.
Communications — Michael Gauldin, dir.
Office of Congressional and Legislative Affairs — Melanie Beller
Solicitor — John D. Leshy
External Affairs — Ken Smith
Executive Secretariat & Regulatory Affairs — Julie Faulkner

Department of Agriculture
14th St. and Independence Ave. SW 20250
Secretary of Agriculture — Dan Glickman
Deputy Secretary — Richard Rominger
Assistant Secretaries for:
  Administration — Wardell Townsend Jr.
  Congressional Relations — Scott Shearer, act.
  Research, Education & Economics — Karl Stauber
  Food, Nutrition & Consumer Services — Ellen Haas
  Food Safety — Mike Taylor, act.
  Farm & Foreign Agriculture Services — Eugene Moos
  Marketing & Regulatory Program— Patricia Jensen, act.
  Natural Resources & Environment — James Lyons
  Rural Economic & Community Development — Mike Dunn, act.
General Counsel — James Gilliland
Inspector General — Roger Vladero
Communications — Ali Webb
Press Secretary — Tom Amontree

Department of Commerce
14th St. between Constitution & Pennsylvania Ave. NW 20230
Secretary of Commerce — Ronald H. Brown
Deputy Secretary — David Barram

(continued)

Department of Commerce (continued)

Chief of Staff — William W. Ginsberg
General Counsel — Ginger Lew
Assistant Secretaries for:
  Chief Financial Officer & Asst. for Administration — Thomas Bloom
  Economic Development Adm. — vacant
  Export Enforcement — John Despres
  Import Administration — Susan Esserman
  Intl. Economic Policy — Charles Meissner
  Legislative Affairs — vacant
  Natl. Telecommunications Information Adm. — Clarence Irving Jr.
  Oceans & Atmosphere — Douglas K. Hall
  Patent & Trademark Office & Act. Asst. Comm. — Bruce Lehman
  Trade Development — Raymond Vickery Jr.
Bureau of the Census — Martha Farnsworth Riche
Bureau of Economic Analysis — J. Steven Landerfeld, act. dir.
Under Sec. for International Trade — vacant
Under Sec. for Econ. Affairs — Everett Ehrlich
Under Sec. for Technology — Mary Lowe Good
Natl. Technical Info. Service — Donald Johnson
Natl. Institute for Standards & Technology — Arati Prabhakar, dir.
Minority Business Development Agency — Joan Parrott-Fonseca
Public Affairs — Jill Schuker

Department of Labor

200 Constitution Ave. NW 20210

Secretary of Labor — Robert B. Reich
Deputy Secretary — Thomas P. Glynn
Chief of Staff — Leslie Loble
Assistant Secretaries for:
  Administration and Management — Cynthia A. Metzler
  Congressional & Intergovernmental Affairs — Geri Palast
  Employment & Training — Timothy Barnicle
  Employment Standards — Bernard E. Anderson
  Occupational Safety & Health — Joseph A. Dear
  Mine Safety & Health—Davitt McAteer
  Office of American Workplace—Charles L. Smith, act.
  Pension & Welfare Benefits — E. Olena Berg
  Policy — Anne H. Lewis
  Public Affairs — Susan R. King, act.
  Veterans Employment & Training — Preston M. Taylor Jr.
Solicitor of Labor — Thomas S. Williamson Jr.
Bureau of International Affairs — Joaquin F. Otero
Women's Bureau — Karen Nussbaum
Inspector General — Charles C. Masten
Bureau of Labor Statistics — Katharine G. Abraham

Department of Health and Human Services

200 Independence Ave. SW 20201

Secretary of HHS — Donna E. Shalala, Ph.D.
Deputy Secretary — Walter D. Broadnax, Ph.D.
Chief of Staff — Kevin L. Thurm
Assistant Secretaries for:
  Health — Philip Lee, M.D.
  Legislation — Jerry D. Klepner
  Management & Budget — John Callahan
  Planning & Evaluation — Peter Edelman, act.
  Public Affairs — Melissa Skolfield, act.
General Counsel — Harriet Rabb
Inspector General — June Gibbs Brown
Surgeon General — Audrey Manley, act.
Office of Consumer Affairs — Bernice Friedlander, act.
Administration on Aging—Fernando Torres–Gil
Health Care Financing Adm. — Bruce C. Vladeck
Administration for Children & Families — Mary Jo Bane

Department of Housing and Urban Development

451 7th St. SW 20410

Secretary of Housing & Urban Development — Henry G. Cisneros

Deputy Secretary — Dwight P. Robinson, act.
Asst. to Dep. Sec. for Field Mgt.—John Wilson
Assistant Secretaries for:
  Administration — Marilynn A. Davis
  Community Planning & Development — Andrew Cuomo
  Fair Housing & Equal Opportunity — vacant
  Housing & Federal Housing Commissioner — Nicolas P. Retsinas
  Labor Relations — vacant
  Congressional & Intergovernmental Relations — vacant
  Policy Development & Research — Michael Stegman
  Public Affairs — Jean Nolan
  Public & Indian Housing — Joseph Shuldiner
General Counsel — Nelson Diaz
Inspector General — Susan Gaffney

Department of Transportation

400 7th St. SW 20590

Secretary of Transportation — Federico F. Peña
Deputy Secretary — Mortimer L. Downey
Assistant Secretaries for:
  Administration — Melissa Spillenkothen
  Budget & Programs — Louise F. Stoll
  Governmental Affairs — Steven O. Palmer
  Aviation & International Affairs — Mark Gerchick, act.
  Transportation—Frank E. Kreusi
  Public Affairs — Steve Akey
U.S. Coast Guard Commandant — Adm. Robert E. Kramek
Federal Aviation Admin. — David R. Hinson
Federal Highway Admin. — Rodney E. Slater
Federal Railroad Admin. — Jolene Molitoris
Maritime Admin. — Albert Herberger
National Highway Traffic Safety Adm. — Ricardo Martinez
Federal Transit Admin. — Gordon J. Linton
Research & Special Programs Admin. — Dharmendra K. Sahama
Saint Lawrence Seaway Development Corp. — David Sanders, act.

Department of Energy

1000 Independence Ave. SW 20585

Secretary of Energy — Hazel R. O'Leary
Deputy Secretary — Charles B. Curtis
Under Secretary — vacant
Chief of Staff — Richard Rosenzweig
Deputy Chief of Staff —Dan Reicher
General Counsel — Robert Nordhaus
Inspector General — John C. Layton
Assistant Secretaries for:
  Congressional & Intergovernmental Affairs — Carolyn Herr Watts, act.
  Energy Efficiency & Renewable Energy — Christine Ervin
  Defense Programs — Victor Reis
  Policy, Planning, & Program Evaluation — Jack Riggs, act.
  Environmental Restoration & Waste Management — Thomas Grumbly
  Administration and Human Resource Management — Archer L. Durham
  Environment, Safety & Health — Tara Jeanne O'Toole
  Fossil Energy — Patricia Godley
Nuclear Energy — Terry Lash, dir.
Energy Information Adm. — Jay E. Hakes, adm.
Economic Impact and Diversity — Corlis Moody, dir.
Hearings & Appeals — George Breznay, dir.
Energy Research — Martha Krebs, dir.
Civilian Radioactive Waste Management — Daniel A. Dreyfuss, dir.
Nonproliferation & National Security — Kenneth E. Baker, act. dir.
Science, Education & Technical Information — Terry Cornwell Rumsey, dir.
Public and Consumer Affairs — Carmen MacDougall, act. dir.
Chief Financial Officer — Joseph F. Vivona
Field Management —Don Pearman
Quality Management — Nancy K. Weidenfeller, dir.
Energy Advisory Board — Peter F. Didisheim, act. dir.

Department of Education
600 Independence Ave. SW 20202

Secretary of Education — Richard W. Riley
Deputy Secretary — Madeleine Kunin
Under Secretary — Marshall S. Smith
Chief of Staff — Frank Holleman
Inspector General — vacant
General Counsel — Judith Winston
Assistant Secretaries for:
　Adult & Vocational Education — Patricia McNeal, act.
　Civil Rights — Norma V. Cantu
　Educational Research and Improvement — Sharon Porter Robinson
　Elementary and Secondary Education — Thomas W. Payzant
　Intergovernmental & Interagency Affairs — Mario Moreno
　Legislation & Congressional Affairs — Kay Casstevens
　Management — Rod McCowan
　Postsecondary Education — David Longanecker
　Special Education and Rehabilitative Services — Judith Heumann
Bilingual & Minority Language Affairs — Eugene Garcia, dir.

Rehabilitation Services Admin. — Frederic K. Schroeder, comm.

Department of Veterans Affairs
810 Vermont Ave. NW 20420

Secretary of Veterans Affairs — Jesse Brown
Deputy — Hershel W. Gober
Assistant Secretaries for:
　Congressional Affairs — Edward P. Scott
　Finance & Information Resources Mgmt. — D. Mark Catlett
　Human Resources & Adm. — Eugene Brickhouse
　Policy & Planning — Dennis Duffy
　Public & Intergovernmental Affairs — Kathy E. Jurado
Inspector General — Stephen Trodden
Under Sec. for Benefits — R. John Vogel
Under Sec. for Health — Kenneth W. Kizer, M.D.
National Cemetery System — Jerry W. Bowen, dir.
General Counsel — Mary Lou Keener
Board of Veterans Appeals — Charles L. Cragin, chmn.
Board of Contract Appeals — Guy H. McMichael III, chmn.
Small & Disadvantaged Business Equalization — Scott S. Denniston, dir.
Veterans Service Organization Liason — Robert L. Jones

Notable U.S. Government Independent Agencies
Source: *The U.S. Government Manual*, National Archives and Records Administration; World Almanac research

All addresses are Washington, DC, unless otherwise noted; as of mid-1995

Central Intelligence Agency — John M. Deutch, dir. (Wash., DC 20505).
Commission on Civil Rights — Mary Frances Berry, chmn. (624 9th St. NW, 20425).
Commodity Futures Trading Commission — Mary L. Shapiro, chmn. (3 Lafayette Center, 1155 21st St. NW, 20581).
Consumer Product Safety Commission — Ann Brown, chmn. (East West Towers, 4330 East West Hwy., Bethesda, MD 20814).
Environmental Protection Agency — Carol M. Browner, adm. (401 M St. SW, 20460).
Equal Employment Opportunity Commission — Gilbert Casellas, chmn. (1801 L St. NW, 20507).
Export-Import Bank of the United States — Kenneth D. Brody, pres. and chmn. (811 Vermont Ave. NW, 20571).
Farm Credit Administration — Marsha P. Martin, chmn., Farm Credit Administration Board (1501 Farm Credit Drive, McLean, VA 22102).
Federal Communications Commission — Reed E. Hundt, chmn. (1919 M St. NW, 20554).
Federal Deposit Insurance Corporation — Ricki R. Halfer-Tigert, chmn. (550 17th St. NW, 20429).
Federal Election Commission — Danny McDonald, chmn. (999 E St. NW, 20463).
Federal Emergency Management Agency — James Lee Witt, dir. (500 C St. SW, 20472).
Federal Housing Finance Board — Bruce A. Morrison, chmn. (1777 F St. NW, 20006).
Federal Labor Relations Authority — Phyllis Segal, chmn. (607 14th St. NW, 20424).
Federal Maritime Commission — William D. Hathaway, chmn. (800 N. Capitol St. NW, 20573).
Federal Mediation and Conciliation Service — John Calhoun Wells, dir. (2100 K St. NW, 20427).
Federal Mine Safety & Health Review Commission — Mary Lu Jordan, chmn. (1730 K St. NW, 20006).
Federal Reserve System — Alan Greenspan, chairman, Board of Governors (20th St. & C St. NW, 20551).
Federal Retirement Thrift Investment Board — James H. Atkins, chmn. (1250 H St. NW, Suite 400, 20005).
Federal Trade Commission — Robert Pitofsky, chmn. (Pennsylvania Ave. at 6th St. NW, 20580).
General Services Administration — Roger W. Johnson, adm. (18th St. & F St. NW, 20405).
Inter-American Foundation — Maria Otero, chmn. (901 N. Stuart St., Arlington, VA 22203).
Interstate Commerce Commission — Linda J. Morgan, chmn. (1201 Constitution Ave. NW, 20423).
Merit Systems Protection Board — Benjamin L. Erdreich, chmn. (1120 Vermont Ave. NW, 20419).
National Aeronautics and Space Administration — Daniel S. Goldin, adm. (300 E St. SW, 20546).
National Archives & Records Administration — John W. Carlin, archivist (7th St. & Pennsylvania Ave. NW, 20408).
National Credit Union Administration — Norman E. D'Amours, chmn. (1775 Duke St., Alexandria, VA 22314).

National Foundation on the Arts and the Humanities — Jane Alexander, chmn. (arts) 1100 Pennsylvania Ave. NW, 20506; Sheldon Hackney, chmn. (humanities) same address; Jennifer Dowley, dir. (museum services) same address.
National Labor Relations Board — William B. Gould IV, chmn. (1099 14th St. NW, 20570).
National Mediation Board — Magdalena G. Jacobsen, chmn. (Suite 250 East, 1301 K St. NW, 20572).
National Railroad Passenger Corporation (Amtrak) — Thomas M. Downs, chmn. (60 Massachusetts Ave. NE, 20002).
National Science Foundation — Frank H. T. Rhodes, chmn., National Science Board (4201 Wilson Blvd., Arlington, VA 22230).
National Transportation Safety Board — Jim Hall, chmn. (490 L'Enfant Plaza SW, 20594).
Nuclear Regulatory Commission — Shirley A. Jackson, chmn. (20555).
Occupational Safety and Health Review Commission — Stuart E. Weisberg, chmn. (1120 20th St. NW, 20036).
Office of Government Ethics — Stephen D. Potts, dir. (1201 New York Ave. NW, Suite 500, 20005).
Office of Personnel Management — James B. King, dir. (1900 E St. NW, 20415-0001).
Office of Special Counsel — Kathleen Day Koch, sp. counsel (1730 M St. NW, Suite 216, 20036).
Peace Corps — Mark Gearan, dir. (1990 K St. NW, 20526).
Pension Benefit Guaranty Corporation — Robert B. Reich, chmn., Board of Directors (1200 K St. NW, 20005).
Postal Rate Commission — Edward J. Gleiman, chmn. (1333 H St. NW, 20268).
Railroad Retirement Board — Glen L. Bower, chmn. (Main Office: 844 N. Rush St., Chicago, IL 60611).
Resolution Trust Corporation — John E. Ryan, chmn. (801 17th St. NW, 20434).
Securities and Exchange Commission — Arthur Levitt, chmn. (450 5th St. NW, 20549).
Selective Service System — Gil Coronado, dir. (National Headquarters, 1515 Wilson Blvd., Arlington, VA 22209-2425).
Small Business Administration — Philip Lader, adm. (409 Third St. SW, 20416).
Social Security Administration — Shirley S. Chater, act. comm. (6401 Security Blvd., Baltimore, MD 20235).
Tennessee Valley Authority — Craven Crowell, chmn., Board of Directors (400 W. Summit Hill Dr., Knoxville, TN 37902, and One Mass. Ave. NW, Suite 300, 20444).
Thrift Depositor Protection Oversight Board — Robert E. Rubin, chmn., Board of Directors (808 17th St. NW, 20232).[1]
Trade and Development Agency — J. Joseph Grand Maison, dir. (State Annex 16, Room 309, 20523).
United States Arms Control & Disarmament Agency — John D. Holum, dir. (320 21st St. NW, 20451).
United States Information Agency — Joseph D. Duffey, dir. (301 4th St. SW, 20547).
United States International Trade Commission — Peter S. Watson, chmn. (500 E St. SW, 20436).
United States Postal Service — Marvin Runyon, Postmaster General (475 L'Enfant Plaza SW, 20260).

(1) Scheduled for closure in early 1996.

Other Notable U.S. Government Agencies

Source: *The U.S. Government Manual*, National Archives and Records Administration; unless otherwise noted, all addresses are Washington, DC

Bureau of Alcohol, Tobacco, and Firearms — John W. Magaw, dir. (Dept. of Treasury, 650 Mass. Ave NW, 20226).

Bureau of the Census — Martha Farnsworth Riche, dir. (Dept. of Commerce, 20233).

Bureau of Economic Analysis — J. Steven Landerfeld, act. dir. (Dept. of Commerce, 20230).

Bureau of Indian Affairs — Ada E. Deer, asst. sec. (Dept. of the Interior, 20240).

Bureau of Prisons — Kathleen M. Hawk, dir. (Dept. of Justice, 320 First St. NW, 20534).

Centers for Disease Control & Prevention — David Satcher, dir. (Dept. of HHS, 1600 Clifton Rd. NE, Atlanta, GA 30333).

Federal Aviation Administration — David R. Hinson, adm. (Dept. of Transportation, 800 Independence Ave. SW, 20591).

Federal Bureau of Investigation — Louis J. Freeh, dir. (Dept. of Justice, 9th St. and Pennsylvania Ave. NW, 20535).

Federal Energy Regulatory Commission — Elizabeth A. Moler, chair (825 N Capitol St. NW 20426).

Federal Highway Administration — Rodney E. Slater, adm. (Dept. of Trans., 400 7th St. SW, 20590).

Fish & Wildlife Service — Mollie Beattie, dir. (Dept. of the Interior, 20240).

Food and Drug Administration — David A. Kessler, comm. (Dept. of HHS, 5600 Fishers Ln., Rockville, MD 20857).

Forest Service — Jack W. Thomas, chief (Dept. of Agriculture, PO Box 96090, 20090).

General Accounting Office — (congressional agency) Charles A. Bowsher, comptroller gen. (441 G St. NW, 20548).

Government Printing Office — (congressional agency) Michael F. DiMario, public printer (N. Capitol and H. Sts. NW, 20401).

Immigration & Naturalization Service — Doris Meissner, comm. (Dept. of Justice, 425 I St. NW, 20536).

Internal Revenue Service — Margaret Milner Richardson, comm. (Dept. of Treas., 1111 Constitution Ave. NW, 20224).

Library of Congress — (congressional agency) James H. Billington, Librarian of Congress (101 Independence Av. SE, 20540).

National Institutes of Health — Harold E. Varmus, dir. (Dept. of HHS, 9000 Rockville Pike, Bethesda, MD 20892).

National Oceanic and Atmospheric Administration — D. James Baker, undersec. (Dept. of Commerce, 20230).

National Park Service — Roger G. Kennedy, dir. (Dept. of the Interior, 20240).

Smithsonian Institution — (quasi-official agency) Ira M. Hayman, sec. (1000 Jefferson Dr. SW, 20560).

Surgeon General — Audrey Manley, act. (Public Health Service, Dept. of HHS, 200 Independence Ave. SW, 20201 & 5600 Fishers Ln., Rockville, MD 20857).

U.S. Customs Service — George J. Weise, comm. (Dept. of the Treasury, 1301 Constitutional Ave. NW, 20229).

U.S. Coast Guard — Adm. Robert E. Kramek, commandant, (Dept. of Trans., 2100 2d St. SW, 20593).

U.S. Mint — Philip N. Diehl, dir. (Dept. of Treas., 633 3d St. NW, 20220).

U.S. Secret Service — Eljay B. Bowron, dir. (Dept. of Treas., 1800 G St. NW, 20223).

The One Hundred and Fourth Congress

With Official 1994 Election Results

Source: Voter News Service; World Almanac research

The 104th Congress convened on Jan. 4, 1995. Membership shown here as of Oct. 15, 1995.

The Senate

Rep., 53; Dem., 46; Vacant, 1; Total, 100. *Incumbent. Boldface denotes the 1994 election winner.

Terms are for 6 years and end Jan. 3 of the year preceding the senator's name in the following table. Annual salary, $133,600; President Pro Tempore, Majority Leader, and Minority Leader, $148,400. To be eligible for the U.S. Senate, a person must be at least 30 years of age, a citizen of the United States for at least 9 years, and a resident of the state from which he or she is chosen. The Congress must meet annually on Jan. 3, unless it has, by law, appointed a different day.

The ZIP code of the Senate is 20510; the telephone number is 202-224-3121.

Senate officials in 1995-97 (104th Congress) were: President Pro Tempore, Strom Thurmond; Majority Leader, Bob Dole; Majority Whip, Trent Lott; Minority Leader, Tom Daschle; Minority Whip, Wendell Ford.

D-Democrat; R-Republican; ACP-A Connecticut Party; I-Independent; L-Liberal; C-Conservative

Term ends	Senator (Party)/Service from[1]	1994 Election	Term ends	Senator (Party)/Service from[1]	1994 Election
	Alabama			**Delaware**	
1997	Howell Heflin (D)/1979		1997	Joseph R. Biden, Jr. (D)/1973	
1999	Richard C. Shelby (R)[2]/1/6/87		2001	**William V. Roth, Jr.*** (R)/1/1/71	111,088
	Alaska			Charles M. Oberly (D)	84,554
1997	Ted Stevens (R)/12/24/68			**Florida**	
1999	Frank H. Murkowski (R)/1981		1999	Bob Graham (D)/1/6/87	
	Arizona		2001	**Connie Mack*** (R)/1989	2,894,726
1999	John McCain (R)/1/6/87			Hugh E. Rodham (D)	1,210,412
2001	**Jon Kyl** (R)/1/4/95	606,999		**Georgia**	
	Sam Coppersmith (D)	442,510	1997	Sam Nunn (D)/11/8/72	
	Arkansas		1999	Paul Coverdell (R)/1993	
1997	David H. Pryor (D)/1979			**Hawaii**	
1999	Dale Bumpers (D)/1975		1999	Daniel K. Inouye (D)/1963	
	California		2001	**Daniel K. Akaka*** (D)/4/28/90	256,189
1999	Barbara Boxer (D)/1993			Maria M. Hustace (R)	86,320
2001	**Dianne Feinstein*** (D)/11/10/92	3,977,063		**Idaho**	
	Michael Huffington (R)	3,811,501	1997	Larry E. Craig (R)/1991	
	Colorado		1999	Dirk Kempthorne (R)/1993	
1997	Hank Brown (R)/1991			**Illinois**	
1999	Ben Nighthorse Campbell (R)[3]/1993		1997	Paul Simon (D)/1985	
	Connecticut		1999	Carol Moseley-Braun (D)/1993	
1999	Christopher J. Dodd (D)/1981			**Indiana**	
2001	**Joe Lieberman*** (D,ACP)/1989	723,842	1999	Daniel R. Coats (R)/1989	
	Jerry Labriola (R)	334,833	2001	**Richard G. Lugar*** (R)/1977	1,039,625
				James Jontz (D)	470,799
				Iowa	
			1997	Tom Harkin (D)/1985	
			1999	Charles E. Grassley (R)/1981	

Term ends	Senator (Party)/Service from[1]	1994 Election
Kansas		
1997	Nancy Landon Kassebaum (R)/12/23/78	
1999	Bob Dole (R)/1969	
Kentucky		
1997	Mitch McConnell (R)/1985	
1999	Wendell H. Ford (D)/12/28/74	
Louisiana		
1997	J. Bennett Johnston (D)/11/14/72	
1999	John B. Breaux (D)/1/6/87	
Maine		
1997	William S. Cohen (R)/1979	
2001	**Olympia J. Snowe** (R)/1/4/95	308,244
	Thomas H. Andrews (D)	186,042
Maryland		
1999	Barbara A. Mikulski (D)/1/6/87	
2001	**Paul S. Sarbanes*** (D)/1977	809,125
	William Brock (R)	559,908
Massachusetts		
1997	John F. Kerry (D)/1/2/85	
2001	**Edward M. Kennedy*** (D)/11/7/62	1,256,997
	W. Mitt Romney (R)	894,000
Michigan		
1997	Carl Levin (D)/1979	
2001	**Spencer Abraham** (R)/1/4/95	1,578,770
	Bob Carr (D)	1,300,960
Minnesota		
1997	Paul David Wellstone (D)/1991	
2001	**Rod Grams** (R)/1/4/95	869,653
	Ann Wynia (D)	781,860
Mississippi		
1997	Thad Cochran (R)/12/27/78	
2001	**Trent Lott*** (R)/1989	418,333
	Ken Harper (D)	189,752
Missouri		
1999	Christopher "Kit" Bond (R)/1/6/87	
2001	**John Ashcroft** (R)/1/4/95	1,060,149
	Alan Wheat (D)	633,697
Montana		
1997	Max Baucus (D)/12/15/78	
2001	**Conrad Burns*** (R)/1989	218,542
	Jack Mudd (D)	131,845
Nebraska		
1997	J. James Exon (D)/1979	
2001	**Bob Kerrey*** (D)/1989	317,297
	Jan Stoney (R)	260,668
Nevada		
1999	Harry M. Reid (D)/1/6/87	
2001	**Richard H. Bryan*** (D)/1989	193,804
	Hal Furman (R)	156,020
New Hampshire		
1997	Robert Smith (R)/12/7/90	
1999	Judd Gregg (R)/1993	
New Jersey		
1997	Bill Bradley (D)/1979	
2001	**Frank R. Lautenberg*** (D)/12/27/82	1,033,487
	Garabed "Chuck" Haytaian (R)	966,244
New Mexico		
1997	Pete V. Domenici (R)/1973	
2001	**Jeff Bingaman*** (D)/1983	249,989
	Colin R. McMillan (R)	213,025
New York		
1999	Alfonse M. D'Amato (R)/1981	
2001	**Daniel Patrick Moynihan*** (D,L)/1977	2,646,541
	Bernadette Castro (R,C)	1,988,308
North Carolina		
1997	Jesse Helms (R)/1973	
1999	Lauch Faircloth (R)/1993	

Term ends	Senator (Party)/Service from[1]	1994 Election
North Dakota		
1999	Byron L. Dorgan (D)/12/14/92	
2001	**Kent Conrad*** (D)/1/6/87	137,157
	Ben Clayburgh (R)	99,390
Ohio		
1999	John Glenn (D)/12/24/74	
2001	**Mike Dewine** (R)/1/4/95	1,836,556
	Joel Hyatt (D)	1,348,213
Oklahoma		
1997	**James M. Inhofe** (R)[4]/11/21/94	542,390
	Dave McCurdy (D)	392,488
1999	Don Nickles (R)/1981	
Oregon		
1997	Mark O. Hatfield (R)/1/10/67	
1999	Bob Packwood (R)[5]/1969	
Pennsylvania		
1999	Arlen Specter (R)/1981	
2001	**Rick Santorum** (R)/1/4/95	1,735,691
	Harris Wofford* (D)/5/8/91	1,648,481
Rhode Island		
1997	Claiborne Pell (D)/1961	
2001	**John H. Chafee*** (R)/12/29/76	222,856
	Linda J. Kushner (D)	122,532
South Carolina		
1997	Strom Thurmond (R)/11/7/56	
1999	Ernest F. "Fritz" Hollings (D)/11/9/66	
South Dakota		
1997	Larry Pressler (R)/1979	
1999	Thomas A. Daschle (D)/1/6/87	
Tennessee		
1997	**Fred Thompson** (R)[6]/12/9/94	885,998
	Jim Cooper (D)	565,930
2001	**Bill Frist** (R)/1/4/95	834,226
	Jim Sasser* (D)/1977	623,164
Texas		
1997	Phil Gramm (R)/1985	
2001	**Kay Bailey Hutchison*** (R)/6/5/93	2,604,218
	Richard Fisher (D)	1,639,615
Utah		
1999	Robert F. Bennett (R)/1993	
2001	**Orrin G. Hatch*** (R)/1977	357,297
	Patrick A. Shea (D)	146,938
Vermont		
1999	Patrick J. Leahy (D)/1975	
2001	**Jim Jeffords*** (R)/1989	106,505
	Jan Backus (D)	85,868
Virginia		
1997	John W. Warner (R)/1/2/79	
2001	**Charles S. Robb*** (D)/1989	938,376
	Oliver L. "Ollie" North (R)	882,213
	J. Marshall Coleman (I)	235,324
Washington		
1999	Patty Murray (D)/1993	
2001	**Slade Gorton*** (R)/1989	947,821
	Ron Sims (D)	752,352
West Virginia		
1997	John D. Rockefeller IV (D)/1/15/85	
2001	**Robert C. Byrd*** (D)/1959	290,495
	Stan Klos (R)	130,441
Wisconsin		
1999	Russell D. Feingold (D)/1993	
2001	**Herbert H. Kohl*** (D)/1989	912,662
	Robert T. Welch (R)	636,989
Wyoming		
1997	Alan K. Simpson (R)/1/1/79	
2001	**Craig Thomas** (R)/1/4/95	118,754
	Mike Sullivan (D)	79,287

(1)Jan. 3, unless otherwise noted. (2)Democratic Sen. Richard C. Shelby announced Nov. 9, 1994, that he changed his party designation to Republican. (3)Democratic Sen. Ben Nighthorse Campbell announced Mar. 3, 1995, that he changed his party designation to Republican. (4)A special election was held, Nov. 8, 1994, to fill the seat left vacant by the resignation of Sen. David Boren (D) to become president of the Univ. of Oklahoma. The winner will serve the remainder of Boren's term. (5)A special election (by mail) was scheduled for Jan. 30, 1996, to fill the seat left vacant when Republican Senator Bob Packwood resigned, Oct. 1, 1995, after the Senate Ethics Committee had concluded that Packwood had engaged in sexual and official misconduct while a senator. This would be the first time a U.S. senator would be elected by a mail-in vote. (6)A special election was held Nov. 8, 1994, to fill the seat left vacant by the resignation of Al Gore, Jr., to become vice president in 1993. The winner will serve the remainder of Gore's term.

The House of Representatives

Rep. 233; Dem. 199; Ind., 1; Vacant, 2; Total, 435. *Incumbent. Boldface denotes the 1994 election winner.

Members' terms to Jan. 3, 1997. Annual salary, $133,600; Speaker of the House, $171,500; Majority Leader and Minority Leader, $148,400. To be eligible for membership, a person must be at least 25 years of age, a U.S. citizen for at least 7 years, and a resident of the state from which he or she is chosen. The ZIP code of the House is 20515; the telephone number is 202-225-3121.

House officials in 1995-97 (104th Congress) were: Speaker, Newt Gingrich; Majority Leader, Dick Armey; Majority Whip, Tom DeLay; Minority Leader, Richard A. Gephardt; Minority Whip, David E. Bonior.

D-Democrat; R-Republican; ACP-A Connecticut Party; B-Libertarian; C-Conservative; CC-Change Congress; GR-Green; I-Independent; IF-Independent Fusion; IN-Independent Neighbors; L-Liberal; LI-Long Island First; PF-Peace & Freedom; T-Right to Life; TX-Taxpayers; WE-We the People.

Dist.	Representative (Party)	1994 Election	Dist.	Representative (Party)	1994 Election
	Alabama			Ellen Schwartz (D)	90,523
1.	**H. L. "Sonny" Callahan*** (R)	**103,431**	11.	**Richard Pombo*** (R)	**99,302**
	Don Womack (D)	50,227		Randy A. Perry (D)	55,794
2.	**Terry Everett*** (R)	**124,465**	12.	**Tom Lantos*** (D)	**118,408**
	Brian Dowling (D)	44,694		Deborah Wilder (R)	57,228
3.	**Glen Browder*** (D)	**93,924**	13.	**Fortney "Pete" Stark*** (D)	**97,344**
	Ben Hand (R)	53,757		Larry Molton (D)	45,555
4.	**Tom Bevill*** (D) . . . . Unopposed		14.	**Anna G. Eshoo*** (D)	**120,713**
5.	**Bud Cramer*** (D)	**88,693**		Ben Brink (R)	78,475
	Wayne Parker (R)	86,923	15.	**Norm Mineta*** (D)[1]	**119,921**
6.	**Spencer Bachus*** (R)	**155,047**		Robert Wick (R)	80,266
	Larry Fortenberry (D)	41,030	16.	**Zoe Lofgren** (D)	**74,935**
7.	**Earl F. Hilliard*** (D)	**116,150**		Lyle J. Smith (R)	40,409
	Alfred J. Middleton, Sr. (R)	34,814	17.	**Sam Farr*** (D)	**87,222**
	Alaska			Bill McCampbell (R)	74,380
	Don Young* (R), ...	**118,537**	18.	**Gary A. Condit*** (D)	**91,105**
	Tony Smith (D)	68,172		Tom Carter (R)	44,046
	Joni Whitmore (GR)	21,277	19.	**George P. Radanovich** (R)	**104,435**
	Arizona			Rick Lehman* (D)	72,912
1.	**Matt Salmon** (R)	**101,350**	20.	**Cal Dooley*** (D)	**57,394**
	Chuck Blanchard (D)	70,627		Paul Young (R)	43,836
2.	**Ed Pastor*** (D)	**62,589**	21.	**Bill Thomas*** (R)	**116,874**
	Robert MacDonald (R)	32,797		John L. Evans (D)	47,517
3.	**Bob Stump*** (R)	**145,396**	22.	**Andrea Seastrand** (R)	**102,987**
	Howard Lee Sprague (D)	61,939		Walter Holden Capps (D)	101,424
4.	**John Shadegg** (R)	**116,714**	23.	**Elton Gallegly*** (R)	**114,043**
	Carol Cure (D)	69,760		Kevin Ready (D)	47,345
5.	**Jim Kolbe*** (R)	**149,514**	24.	**Anthony C. Beilenson*** (D)	**95,342**
	Gary Auerbach (D)	63,436		Rich Sybert (R)	91,806
6.	**J. D. Hayworth** (R)	**107,060**	25.	**Howard "Buck" McKeon*** (R)	**110,301**
	Karan English* (D)	81,321		James H. Gilmartin (D)	53,445
	Arkansas		26.	**Howard L. Berman*** (D)	**55,145**
1.	**Blanche M. Lambert*** (D)	**95,290**		Gary E. Forsch (R)	28,423
	Warren Dupwe (R)	83,147	27.	**Carlos J. Moorhead*** (R)	**88,341**
2.	**Ray Thornton*** (D)	**97,580**		Doug Kahn (D)	70,267
	Bill Powell (R)	72,473	28.	**David Dreier*** (R)	**110,179**
3.	**Tim Hutchinson*** (R)	**129,800**		Tommy Randle (D)	50,022
	Berta L. Seitz (D)	61,883	29.	**Henry A. Waxman*** (D)	**129,413**
4.	**Jay Dickey*** (R)	**87,469**		Paul Stepanek (R)	53,801
	Jay Bradford (D)	81,370	30.	**Xavier Becerra*** (D)	**43,943**
	California			David A. Ramirez (R)	18,741
1.	**Frank Riggs** (R)	**106,870**	31.	**Matthew G. Martinez*** (D)	**50,541**
	Dan Hamburg* (D)	93,717		John V. Flores (R)	34,926
2.	**Wally Herger*** (R)	**137,863**	32.	**Julian C. Dixon*** (D)	**98,017**
	Mary Jacobs (D)	55,958		Ernie A. Farhat (R)	22,190
3.	**Vic Fazio*** (D)	**97,093**	33.	**Lucille Roybal-Allard*** (D)	**33,814**
	Tim Lefever (R)	89,964		Kermit Booker (PF)	7,694
4.	**John T. Doolittle*** (R)	**144,936**	34.	**Esteban E. Torres*** (D)	**72,439**
	Katie Hirning (D)	82,505		Albert J. Nunez (R)	40,068
5.	**Robert T. Matsui*** (D)	**125,042**	35.	**Maxine Waters*** (D)	**65,688**
	Robert S. Dinsmore (R)	52,905		Nate Truman (R)	18,390
6.	**Lynn C. Woolsey*** (D)	**137,642**	36.	**Jane Harman*** (D)	**93,939**
	Michael J. Nugent (R)	88,940		Susan Brooks (R)	93,127
7.	**George Miller*** (D)	**116,105**	37.	**Walter R. Tucker III*** (D)	**64,166**
	Charles V. Hughes (R)	45,698		Guy Wilson (B)	18,502
8.	**Nancy Pelosi*** (D)	**137,642**	38.	**Steve Horn*** (R)	**85,225**
	Elsa C. Cheung (R)	30,528		Peter Mathews (D)	53,681
9.	**Ronald V. Dellums*** (D)	**129,233**	39.	**Ed Royce*** (R)	**113,037**
	Deborah Wright (R)	40,448		R. O. "Bob" Davis (D)	49,459
10.	**Bill Baker*** (R)	**138,916**	40.	**Jerry Lewis*** (R)	**115,728**
				Donald M. "Don" Rusk (D)	48,003
			41.	**Jay Kim*** (R)	**81,854**
				Ed Tessier (D)	49,924

Dist.	Representative (Party)	1994 Election
42.	**George E. Brown, Jr.*** (D)	**58,888**
	Rob Guzman (R).	56,259
43.	**Ken Calvert*** (R)	**84,500**
	Mark A. Takano (D)	59,342
44.	**Sonny Bono** (R).	**95,521**
	Steve Clute (D).	65,370
45.	**Dana Rohrabacher*** (R)	**124,006**
	Brett Williamson (D)	55,489
46.	**Robert K. "Bob" Dornan*** (R)	**50,126**
	Michael P. "Mike" Farber (D).	32,577
47.	**Christopher Cox*** (R)	**152,413**
	Gary Kingsbury (D)	53,035
48.	**Ron Packard*** (R)	**143,275**
	Andrei Leschick (D)	43,446
49.	**Brian P. Bilbray** (R)	**90,283**
	Lynn Schenk* (D)	85,597
50.	**Bob Filner*** (D).	**59,214**
	Mary Alice Acevedo (R)	36,955
51.	**Randy "Duke" Cunningham*** (R) . . .	**138,547**
	Rita K. Tamerius (D)	57,374
52.	**Duncan Hunter*** (R).	**109,201**
	Janet M. Gastil (D)	53,024

Colorado

Dist.	Representative (Party)	1994 Election
1.	**Patricia Schroeder*** (D)	**93,123**
	William F. Eggert (R).	61,978
2.	**David Skaggs*** (D).	**105,938**
	Patricia "Pat" Miller (R)	80,723
3.	**Scott McInnis*** (R)	**145,365**
	Linda Powers (D)	63,427
4.	**Wayne Allard*** (R)	**136,251**
	Cathy Kipp (D)	52,202
5.	**Joel Hefley*** (R)	**Unopposed**
6.	**Dan Schaefer*** (R)	**124,079**
	John Hallen (D).	49,701

Connecticut

Dist.	Representative (Party)	1994 Election
1.	**Barbara Bailey Kennelly*** (D,ACP) . .	**138,637**
	Douglas T. Putnam (R)	46,865
2.	**Sam Gejdenson*** (D)	**79,188**
	Edward W. Munster (R)	79,167
	David Bingham (ACP).	27,716
3.	**Rosa L. DeLauro*** (D)	**111,261**
	Susan Johnson (R,ACP)	64,094
4.	**Christopher Shays*** (R)	**109,436**
	Jonathan D. Kantrowitz (D)	34,962
5.	**Gary A. Franks*** (R)	**93,471**
	James H. Maloney (D,ACP)	81,523
6.	**Nancy L. Johnson*** (R)	**123,101**
	Charlotte Koskoff (D,ACP)	60,701

Delaware

	Michael N. Castle* (R)	**137,960**
	Carol Ann DeSantis (D)	51,803

Florida

Dist.	Representative (Party)	1994 Election
1.	**Joe Scarborough** (R)	**112,901**
	Vince Whibbs, Jr. (D)	70,389
2.	**Pete Peterson*** (D).	**117,404**
	Carole Griffin (R).	74,011
3.	**Corrine Brown*** (D)	**63,845**
	Marc Little (R).	46,895
4.	**Tillie K. Fowler*** (R)	**Unopposed**
5.	**Karen L. Thurman*** (D)	**125,780**
	Don "Big Daddy" Garlits (R)	94,093
6.	**Clifford B. "Cliff" Stearns*** (R) . . .	**Unopposed**
7.	**John L. Mica*** (R)	**131,711**
	Edward D. Goddard (D)	47,747
8.	**Bill McCollum*** (R).	**Unopposed**
9.	**Michael Bilirakis*** (R)	**Unopposed**
10.	**C. W. Bill Young*** (R)	**Unopposed**
11.	**Sam M. Gibbons*** (D)	**76,814**
	Mark Sharpe (R).	72,119
12.	**Charles T. Canady*** (R)	**106,123**
	Robert Connors (D)	57,203
13.	**Dan Miller*** (R).	**Unopposed**
14.	**Porter J. Goss*** (R)	**Unopposed**
15.	**Dave Weldon** (R)	**117,027**
	Sue Munsey (D)	100,513

Dist.	Representative (Party)	1994 Election
16.	**Mark Foley** (R).	**122,734**
	John Comerford (D)	88,646
17.	**Carrie P. Meek*** (D)	**Unopposed**
18.	**Ileana Ros-Lehtinen*** (R)	**Unopposed**
19.	**Harry Johnston*** (D)	**147,591**
	Peter J. Tsakanikas (R)	75,779
20.	**Peter Deutsch*** (D)	**114,615**
	Beverly "Bev" Kennedy (R)	72,516
21.	**Lincoln Diaz-Balart*** (R)	**Unopposed**
22.	**Clay Shaw*** (R)	**119,690**
	Hermine L. Wiener (D)	69,215
23.	**Alcee L. Hastings*** (D)	**Unopposed**

Georgia

Dist.	Representative (Party)	1994 Election
1.	**Jack Kingston*** (R)	**88,788**
	Raymond Beckworth (D).	27,197
2.	**Sanford Bishop*** (D)	**65,383**
	John Clayton (R)	33,429
3.	**Mac Collins*** (R)	**94,717**
	Fred Overby (D)	49,828
4.	**John Linder*** (R)	**90,063**
	Comer Yates (D)	65,566
5.	**John Lewis*** (D)	**85,094**
	Dale Dixon (R)	37,999
6.	**Newt Gingrich*** (R)	**119,432**
	Ben Jones (D)	66,700
7.	**Bob Barr** (R)	**71,265**
	George "Buddy" Darden* (D)	65,978
8.	**Saxby Chambliss** (R)	**89,591**
	Craig Mathis (D)	53,408
9.	**Nathan Deal*** (R)[2]	**79,145**
	Robert L. Castello (D)	57,568
10.	**Charlie Norwood** (R)	**96,099**
	Don Johnson* (D).	51,192
11.	**Cynthia McKinney*** (D)	**71,560**
	Woodrow Lovett (R)	37,533

Hawaii

Dist.	Representative (Party)	1994 Election
1.	**Neil Abercrombie*** (D).	**94,754**
	Orson Swindle (R)	76,623
2.	**Patsy Takemoto Mink*** (D)	**124,431**
	Robert H. (Lopaka) Garner (R)	42,891

Idaho

Dist.	Representative (Party)	1994 Election
1.	**Helen Chenoweth** (R)	**111,728**
	Larry LaRocco* (D).	89,826
2.	**Mike Crapo*** (R).	**143,593**
	Penny Fletcher (D)	47,936

Illinois

Dist.	Representative (Party)	1994 Election
1.	**Bobby L. Rush*** (D)	**112,474**
	William J. Kelly (R)	36,038
2.	**Mel Reynolds*** (D)[3]	**Unopposed**
3.	**William O. Lipinski*** (D)	**92,353**
	Jim Nalepa (R)	78,163
4.	**Luis V. Gutierrez*** (D)	**46,695**
	Steven Valtierra (R)	15,384
5.	**Michael Patrick Flanagan** (R)	**75,328**
	Dan Rostenkowski* (D).	63,065
6.	**Henry J. Hyde*** (R)	**115,664**
	Tom Berry (D)	37,163
7.	**Cardiss Collins*** (D)	**93,457**
	Charles "Chuck" Mobley (R)	24,011
8.	**Philip M. Crane*** (R)	**88,225**
	Robert C. Walberg (R)	47,654
9.	**Sidney R. Yates*** (D)	**94,404**
	George Edward Larney (R).	48,419
10.	**John E. Porter*** (R)	**114,884**
	Andrew M. Krupp (D)	38,191
11.	**Gerald C. "Jerry" Weller** (R)	**97,241**
	Frank Giglio (D)	63,150
12.	**Jerry F. Costello*** (D)	**101,391**
	Jan Morris (R)	52,419
13.	**Harris W. Fawell*** (R)	**124,312**
	William A. Riley (D)	45,709
14.	**J. Dennis Hastert*** (R)	**110,204**
	Steve Denari (D).	33,891
15.	**Thomas W. Ewing*** (R)	**108,857**
	Paul Alexander (D)	50,874

Dist.	Representative (Party)	1994 Election
16.	**Donald Manzullo*** (R)	117,238
	Pete Sullivan (D)	48,736
17.	**Lane Evans*** (D)	95,312
	Jim Anderson (R)	79,471
18.	**Ray LaHood*** (R)	119,838
	G. Douglas Stephens (D)	78,332
19.	**Glenn Poshard*** (D)	115,045
	Brent Winters (R)	81,995
20.	**Richard J. Durbin*** (D).	108,034
	Bill Owens (R).	88,964

Indiana

Dist.	Representative (Party)	1994 Election
1.	**Peter J. Visclosky*** (D)	68,612
	John Larson (R)	52,920
2.	**David M. McIntosh** (R).	93,592
	Joseph H. Hogsett (D)	78,241
3.	**Tim Roemer*** (D)	72,497
	Richard Burkett (R)	58,878
4.	**Mark Edward Souder** (R).	88,584
	Jill L. Long* (D)	71,235
5.	**Steve Buyer*** (R)	111,031
	J. D. Beatty (D).	45,224
6.	**Dan Burton*** (R).	136,876
	Natalie M. Bruner (D)	40,815
7.	**John T. Myers*** (R)	104,359
	Michael M. Harmless (D).	55,941
8.	**John Hostettler** (R)	93,529
	Frank McCloskey* (D)	84,857
9.	**Lee H. Hamilton*** (D)	91,459
	Jean Leising (R)	84,315
10.	**Andrew Jacobs, Jr.*** (D)	58,573
	Marvin Bailey Scott (R)	50,998

Iowa

Dist.	Representative (Party)	1994 Election
1.	**Jim Leach*** (R).	110,448
	Glen Winekauf (D)	69,461
2.	**Jim Nussle*** (R)	111,076
	Dave Nagle (D).	86,087
3.	**Jim Ross Lightfoot*** (R)	111,862
	Elaine Baxter (D)	79,310
4.	**Greg Ganske** (R)	111,935
	Neal Smith* (D).	98,824
5.	**Tom Latham** (R)	114,796
	Sheila McGuire (D)	73,627

Kansas

Dist.	Representative (Party)	1994 Election
1.	**Pat Roberts*** (R)	169,531
	Terry L. Nichols (D).	49,477
2.	**Sam Brownback** (R)	135,725
	John Carlin (D)	71,025
3.	**Jan Meyers*** (R).	102,218
	Judy Hancock (D)	78,401
4.	**Todd Tiahrt** (R)	111,653
	Dan Glickman* (D)	99,366

Kentucky

Dist.	Representative (Party)	1994 Election
1.	**Edward Whitfield** (R).	64,849
	Tom Barlow* (D)	62,387
2.	**Ron Lewis*** (R)	90,535
	David Adkisson (D)	60,867
3.	**Mike Ward** (D)	67,663
	Susan B. Stokes (R)	67,238
	Richard Lewis (TX)	17,591
4.	**Jim Bunning*** (R).	96,695
	Sally Harris Skaggs (D).	33,717
5.	**Harold "Hal" Rogers*** (R)	82,291
	Walter "Doc" Blevins (D)	21,318
6.	**Scotty Baesler*** (D)	70,085
	Matthew Eric Wills (R).	49,032

Louisiana

Dist.	Representative (Party)	1994 Election
1.	**Robert L. "Bob" Livingston*** (R). . . .	
2.	**William J. Jefferson*** (D)	
3.	**W. J. "Billy" Tauzin*** (R)[4].	
4.	**Cleo Fields*** (D)	

Dist.	Representative (Party)	1994 Election
5.	**Jim McCrery*** (R).	
6.	**Richard Baker*** (R)	
7.	**James A. "Jimmy" Hayes*** (D)	

In Louisiana, all candidates of all parties run against each other in an open primary, unless they are unopposed incumbents, in which case they are declared elected. All candidates who receive more than 50 percent of the primary vote are also declared elected and do not appear on the general election ballot. In 1994 all congressional candidates were declared elected.

Maine

Dist.	Representative (Party)	1994 Election
1.	**James B. Longley, Jr.** (R)	136,316
	Dennis L. Dutremble (D).	126,373
2.	**John Baldacci** (D).	109,615
	Richard A. Bennett (R)	97,754

Maryland

Dist.	Representative (Party)	1994 Election
1.	**Wayne T. Gilchrest*** (R)	120,975
	Ralph T. Gies (D)	57,712
2.	**Robert L. Ehrlich, Jr.** (R)	125,162
	Gerry L. Brewster (D)	74,275
3.	**Benjamin L. Cardin*** (D)	117,269
	Robert Ryan Tousey (R)	47,966
4.	**Albert R. Wynn*** (D)	93,148
	Michele Dyson (R)	30,999
5.	**Steny H. Hoyer*** (D).	98,821
	Donald Devine (R)	69,211
6.	**Roscoe Bartlett*** (R)	122,809
	Paul Muldowney (D)	63,411
7.	**Kweisi Mfume*** (D)	97,016
	Kenneth Kondner (R)	22,007
8.	**Constance A. Morella*** (R)	143,449
	Steven Van Grack (D)	60,660

Massachusetts

Dist.	Representative (Party)	1994 Election
1.	**John W. Olver*** (D) . . . . Unopposed	
2.	**Richard E. Neal*** (D)	117,178
	John M. Briare (R)	72,732
3.	**Peter I. Blute*** (R)	115,810
	Kevin O'Sullivan (D)	93,689
4.	**Barney Frank*** (D). . . . . Unopposed	
5.	**Martin T. Meehan*** (D).	140,725
	David E. Coleman (R).	60,734
6.	**Peter G. Torkildsen*** (R)	120,952
	John F. Tierney (D)	113,481
7.	**Edward J. Markey*** (D)	146,246
	Brad Bailey (R)	80,674
8.	**Joseph P. Kennedy II*** (D) . . . . Unopposed	
9.	**John Joseph Moakley*** (D)	146,287
	Michael M. Murphy (R)	63,369
10.	**Gerry E. Studds*** (D)	172,753
	Keith Jason Hemeon (R)	78,487

Michigan

Dist.	Representative (Party)	1994 Election
1.	**Bart Stupak*** (D)	121,433
	Gil Ziegler (R).	89,660
2.	**Peter Hoekstra*** (R).	146,164
	Marcus Hoover (D)	46,097
3.	**Vernon J. Ehlers*** (R)	136,711
	Betsy J. Flory (D)	43,580
4.	**Dave Camp*** (R)	145,176
	Damion Frasier (D).	50,544
5.	**James A. Barcia*** (D)	126,456
	William T. Anderson (R)	61,342
6.	**Fred Upton*** (R).	121,923
	David Taylor (R)	42,348
7.	**Nick Smith*** (R)	115,621
	Kim McCaughtry (D)	57,326
8.	**Dick Chrysler** (R)	109,663
	Bob Mitchell (D)	95,383
9.	**Dale E. Kildee*** (D)	97,096
	Megan O'Neill (R)	89,148
10.	**David E. Bonior*** (D)	121,876
	Donald J. Lobsinger (R)	73,862
11.	**Joe Knollenberg*** (R)	154,696
	Mike Breshgold (D)	69,168
12.	**Sander Levin*** (D)	103,508
	John Pappageorge (R)	92,762

Dist.	Representative (Party)	1994 Election
13.	Lynn Nancy Rivers (D)	89,573
	John A. Schall (R)	77,908
14.	John Conyers, Jr.* (D)	128,463
	Richard Charles Fournier (R)	26,215
15.	Barbara-Rose Collins* (D)	119,442
	John W. Savage II (R)	20,074
16.	John D. Dingell* (D)	105,849
	Ken Larkin (R)	71,159

Minnesota

Dist.	Representative (Party)	1994 Election
1.	Gil Gutknecht (R)	117,613
	John C. Hottinger (D)	95,328
2.	David Minge* (D)	114,289
	Gary B. Revier (R)	98,881
3.	Jim Ramstad* (R)	173,223
	Bob Olson (D)	62,211
4.	Bruce F. Vento* (D)	115,638
	Dennis Newinski (R)	88,344
5.	Martin Olav Sabo* (D)	121,515
	Dorothy LeGrand (R)	73,258
6.	William P. "Bill" Luther (D)	113,740
	Tad Jude (R)	113,190
7.	Collin C. Peterson* (D)	108,023
	Bernie Omann (R)	102,623
8.	James L. Oberstar* (D)	153,161
	Phil Herwig (R)	79,818

Mississippi

Dist.	Representative (Party)	1994 Election
1.	Roger Wicker (R)	80,553
	Bill Wheeler (D)	47,192
2.	Bennie G. Thompson* (D)	68,014
	Bill Jordan (R)	49,270
3.	G. V. "Sonny" Montgomery* (D)	83,163
	Dutch Dabbs (R)	39,826
4.	Mike Parker* (D)	82,939
	Mike Wood (R)	38,200
5.	Gene Taylor* (D)	73,179
	George Barlos (R)	48,575

Missouri

Dist.	Representative (Party)	1994 Election
1.	William "Bill" Clay, Sr.* (D)	97,061
	Donald R. Counts (R)	50,303
2.	James M. Talent* (R)	154,882
	Pat Kelly (D)	70,480
3.	Richard A. Gephardt* (D)	117,601
	Gary Gill (R)	80,977
4.	Ike Skelton* (D)	137,876
	James A. Noland, Jr. (R)	65,616
5.	Karen McCarthy (D)	100,391
	Ron Freeman (R)	77,120
6.	Pat "Patsy Ann" Danner* (D)	140,108
	Tina Tucker (R)	71,709
7.	Melton D. "Mel" Hancock* (R)	112,228
	James R. Fossard (D)	77,836
8.	Bill Emerson* (R)	129,320
	James L. "Jay" Thompson (D)	48,987
9.	Harold L. Volkmer* (D)	103,443
	Kenny Hulshof (R)	92,301

Montana

Dist.	Representative (Party)	1994 Election
	Pat Williams* (D)	171,372
	Cy Jamison (R)	148,715

Nebraska

Dist.	Representative (Party)	1994 Election
1.	Doug Bereuter* (R)	117,967
	Patrick Combs (D)	70,369
2.	Jon Christensen (R)	92,516
	Peter Hoagland* (D)	90,750
3.	Bill Barrett* (R)	154,919
	Gil Chapin (D)	41,943

Nevada

Dist.	Representative (Party)	1994 Election
1.	John Ensign (R)	73,769
	James H. Bilbray* (D)	72,333
2.	Barbara F. Vucanovich* (R)	142,202
	Janet Greeson (D)	65,390

New Hampshire

Dist.	Representative (Party)	1994 Election
1.	Bill Zeliff* (R)	97,017
	Bill Verge (D)	42,481
2.	Charles Bass (R)	83,121
	Dick Swett* (D)	74,243

New Jersey

Dist.	Representative (Party)	1994 Election
1.	Robert E. Andrews* (D)	108,155
	James N. Hogan (R)	41,505
2.	Frank A. LoBiondo (R)	102,566
	Louis N. Magazzu (D)	56,151
3.	Jim Saxton* (R)	115,750
	James B. Smith (D)	54,441
4.	Christopher H. Smith* (R)	109,818
	Ralph Walsh (D)	49,537
5.	Marge Roukema* (R)	139,964
	Bill Auer (D)	41,275
6.	Frank Pallone, Jr.* (D)	88,922
	Mike Herson (R)	55,287
7.	Bob Franks* (R)	98,814
	Karen Carroll (D)	64,231
8.	Bill Martini (R)	70,494
	Herb Klein* (D)	68,661
9.	Robert G. Torricelli* (D)	99,984
	Peter J. Russo (R)	57,651
10.	Donald M. Payne* (D)	74,622
	Jim Ford (R)	21,524
11.	Rodney Frelinghuysen (R)	127,868
	Frank Herbert (D)	50,211
12.	Dick Zimmer* (R)	125,939
	Joseph D. Youssouf (D)	55,977
13.	Robert Menendez* (D)	67,688
	Fernando A. Alonso (R)	24,071

New Mexico

Dist.	Representative (Party)	1994 Election
1.	Steven H. Schiff* (R)	119,996
	Peter L. Zollinger (D)	42,316
2.	Joseph R. Skeen* (R)	89,966
	Benjamin Anthony Chavez (D)	45,316
3.	Bill Richardson* (D)	99,900
	F. Gregg Bemis, Jr. (R)	53,515

New York

Dist.	Representative (Party)	1994 Election
1.	Michael P. Forbes (R/WE,C,T)	90,491
	George J. Hochbrueckner* (D,LI)	80,146
2.	Rick A. Lazio* (R/WE,C)	100,107
	James L. Manfre (D, LI)	41,102
3.	Peter T. King* (R,C)	115,236
	Norma Grill (D)	77,774
4.	Daniel Frisa (R)	87,815
	Philip M. Schiliro (D)	65,286
5.	Gary L. Ackerman* (D,L)	93,896
	Grant M. Lally (R,C)	73,884
6.	Floyd H. Flake* (D)	68,596
	Denny D. Bhagwandin (R,C)	16,675
7.	Thomas J. Manton* (D)	58,935
	Robert E. Hurley (C)	8,698
8.	Jerrold L. Nadler* (D,L)	110,066
	David L. Askren (R)	21,169
9.	Charles E. Schumer* (D,L)	95,139
	James P. McCall (R,C)	35,880
10.	Edolphus Towns* (D,L)	77,026
	Amelia Smith Parker (R)	7,995
11.	Major R. Owens* (D,L)	61,945
	Gary S. Popkin (R,B)	6,605
12.	Nydia M. Velázquez* (D,L)	39,929
	Genevieve R. Brennan (R)	2,747
13.	Susan Molinari* (R,C)	96,491
	Tyrone G. Butler (D,L)	33,937
14.	Carolyn B. Maloney* (D,IN)	98,479
	Charles Millard (R,L)	54,277
15.	Charles B. Rangel* (D,L)	77,830
	Jose Suero (T,IF)	2,812
16.	José E. Serrano* (D,L)	59,414
	Michael Walters (R)	1,415
17.	Eliot L. Engel* (D,L)	73,321
	Edward T. Marshall (R)	16,896
18.	Nita M. Lowey* (D)	91,663
	Andrew C. Hartzell, Jr. (R,C)	65,517

Dist.	Representative (Party)	1994 Election
19.	**Sue W. Kelly** (R)	**100,173**
	Hamilton Fish, Jr. (D)	70,696
	Joseph J. DioGuardi (C,T)	19,761
20.	**Benjamin A. Gilman*** (R)	**120,334**
	Gregory B. Julian (D)	52,345
21.	**Michael R. McNulty*** (D,C)	**147,804**
	Joseph Gomez (R)	68,745
22.	**Gerald B. H. Solomon*** (R,C,T)	**157,717**
	L. Robert Lawrence, Jr. (D)	57,064
23.	**Sherwood L. Boehlert*** (R)	**124,486**
	Charles W. Skeele, Jr. (D)	40,786
24.	**John M. McHugh*** (R,C)	**124,645**
	Danny M. Francis (D)	34,032
25.	**James T. Walsh*** (R,C)	**113,949**
	Rhea Jezer (D,CC)	83,853
26.	**Maurice D. Hinchey*** (D,L)	**94,610**
	Bob Moppert (R,C)	94,244
27.	**Bill Paxon*** (R,C,T)	**152,610**
	William A. Long, Jr. (D)	52,160
28.	**Louise M. Slaughter*** (D)	**110,987**
	Renee Forgensi Davison (R,C)	78,516
29.	**John J. LaFalce*** (D,L)	**103,053**
	William E. Miller, Jr. (R,C)	80,355
30.	**Jack Quinn*** (R,C)	**124,738**
	David A. Franczyk (D,L)	61,392
31.	**Amo Houghton*** (R,C)	**121,178**
	Gretchen S. McManus (T)	21,747

North Carolina

Dist.	Representative (Party)	1994 Election
1.	**Eva M. Clayton*** (D)	**66,827**
	Ted Tyler (R)	42,602
2.	**David Funderburk** (R)	**79,207**
	Richard Moore (D)	62,122
3.	**Walter B. Jones, Jr.** (R)	**72,464**
	H. Martin Lancaster* (D)	65,013
4.	**Frederick Kenneth Heineman** (R)	**77,773**
	David E. Price* (D)	76,558
5.	**Richard Burr** (R)	**84,741**
	A. P. "Sandy" Sands (D)	63,194
6.	**Howard Coble*** (R)	**Unopposed**
7.	**Charles G. Rose III*** (D)	**62,670**
	Robert C. Anderson (R)	58,849
8.	**W. G. "Bill" Hefner*** (D)	**62,845**
	Sherrill Morgan (R)	57,140
9.	**Sue Myrick** (R)	**82,374**
	Rory Blake (D)	44,379
10.	**T. Cass Ballenger*** (R)	**107,829**
	Robert Wayne Avery (D)	42,939
11.	**Charles H. Taylor*** (R)	**115,826**
	Maggie Palmer Lauterer (D)	76,862
12.	**Mel Watt*** (D)	**57,655**
	Joseph A. "Joe" Martino (R)	29,933

North Dakota

	Representative (Party)	1994 Election
	Earl Pomeroy* (D)	**123,134**
	Gary Porter (R)	105,988

Ohio

Dist.	Representative (Party)	1994 Election
1.	**Steve Chabot** (R)	**92,997**
	David Mann* (D)	72,822
2.	**Rob Portman*** (R)	**150,128**
	Les Mann (D)	43,730
3.	**Tony P. Hall*** (D)	**105,342**
	David A. Westbrock (R)	72,314
4.	**Michael G. Oxley*** (R)	**Unopposed**
5.	**Paul E. Gillmor*** (R)	**135,879**
	Jarrod Tudor (D)	49,335
6.	**Frank A. Cremeans** (R)	**91,263**
	Ted Strickland* (D)	87,861
7.	**David L. Hobson*** (R)	**Unopposed**
8.	**John A. Boehner*** (R)	**Unopposed**
9.	**Marcy Kaptur*** (D)	**118,120**
	R. Randy Whitman (R)	38,665
10.	**Martin R. Hoke*** (R)	**95,226**
	Francis E. Gaul (D)	70,918
	Joseph J. Jacobs, Jr. (I)	17,495
11.	**Louis Stokes*** (D)	**114,220**
	James J. Sykora (R)	33,705

Dist.	Representative (Party)	1994 Election
12.	**John R. Kasich*** (R)	**114,608**
	Cynthia L. Ruccia (D)	57,294
13.	**Sherrod Brown*** (D)	**93,147**
	Gregory A. White (R)	86,422
14.	**Thomas C. Sawyer*** (D)	**96,274**
	Lynn Slaby (R)	89,106
15.	**Deborah Pryce*** (R)	**112,912**
	Bill Buckel (D)	46,480
16.	**Ralph Regula*** (R)	**137,322**
	J. Michael Finn (D)	45,781
17.	**James A. Traficant, Jr.*** (D)	**149,004**
	Mike G. Meister (R)	43,490
18.	**Bob Ney** (R)	**103,115**
	Greg L. DiDonato (D)	87,926
19.	**Steven C. LaTourette** (R)	**99,997**
	Eric D. Fingerhut* (D)	89,701

Oklahoma

Dist.	Representative (Party)	1994 Election
1.	**Steve Largent** (R)	**107,085**
	Stuart Price (D)	63,753
2.	**Tom Coburn** (R)	**82,476**
	Virgil R. Cooper (D)	75,943
3.	**Bill K. Brewster*** (D)	**115,731**
	Darrel Dewayne Tallant (R)	41,147
4.	**J. C. Watts** (R)	**80,251**
	David Perryman (D)	67,237
5.	**Ernest Istook*** (R)	**136,877**
	Tom Keith (I)	38,270
6.	**Frank Lucas*** (R)	**106,961**
	Jeffrey S. Tollett (D)	45,399

Oregon

Dist.	Representative (Party)	1994 Election
1.	**Elizabeth Furse*** (D)	**121,147**
	Bill Witt (R)	120,846
2.	**Wes Cooley** (R)	**134,255**
	Sue C. Kupillas (D)	90,822
3.	**Ron Wyden*** (D)	**161,624**
	Everett Hall (R)	43,211
4.	**Peter DeFazio*** (D)	**158,981**
	John D. Newkirk (R)	78,947
5.	**Jim Bunn** (R)	**121,369**
	Catherine Webber (D)	114,015

Pennsylvania

Dist.	Representative (Party)	1994 Election
1.	**Thomas M. Foglietta*** (D)	**99,669**
	Roger F. Gordon (R)	22,595
2.	**Chaka Fattah** (D)	**120,553**
	Lawrence R. Watson (R)	19,824
3.	**Robert A. Borski*** (D)	**92,702**
	James C. Hasher (R)	55,209
4.	**Ron Klink*** (D)	**119,115**
	Ed Peglow (R)	66,509
5.	**William F. "Bill" Clinger, Jr.*** (R)	**Unopposed**
6.	**Tim Holden*** (D)	**90,023**
	Fred Levering (R)	68,610
7.	**Curt Weldon*** (R)	**137,480**
	Sara Nichols (D)	59,845
8.	**Jim Greenwood*** (R)	**110,499**
	John P. Murray (D)	44,559
9.	**Bud Shuster*** (R)	**Unopposed**
10.	**Joseph M. McDade*** (R)	**106,992**
	Daniel J. Schreffler (D)	50,635
11.	**Paul E. Kanjorski*** (D)	**101,966**
	J. Andrew Podolak (R)	51,295
12.	**John P. Murtha*** (D)	**117,825**
	Bill Choby (R)	53,147
13.	**Jon D. Fox** (R)	**96,254**
	Marjorie Margolies-Mezvinsky* (D)	88,073
14.	**William J. Coyne*** (D)	**105,310**
	John Robert Clark (R)	53,221
15.	**Paul McHale*** (D)	**72,073**
	Jim Yeager (R)	71,602
16.	**Robert S. Walker*** (R)	**109,759**
	Bill Chertok (D)	47,680
17.	**George W. Gekas*** (R)	**Unopposed**
18.	**Mike Doyle** (D)	**101,784**
	John McCarty (R)	83,881

Dist.	Representative (Party)	1994 Election
19.	**Bill Goodling*** (R)	Unopposed
20.	**Frank R. Mascara** (D)	95,251
	Mike McCormick (R)	84,156
21.	**Phil English** (R)	89,439
	Bill Leavens (D)	84,796

Rhode Island

Dist.	Representative (Party)	1994 Election
1.	**Patrick J. Kennedy** (D)	89,832
	Kevin Vigilante (R)	76,069
2.	**John F. Reed*** (D)	119,659
	A. John Elliot (R)	56,348

South Carolina

Dist.	Representative (Party)	1994 Election
1.	**Mark Sanford** (R)	97,803
	Robert Barber (D)	47,769
2.	**Floyd D. Spence*** (R)	Unopposed
3.	**Lindsey Graham** (R)	90,123
	James E. Bryan, Jr. (D)	59,932
4.	**Bob Inglis*** (R)	109,626
	Jerry L. Fowler (D)	39,396
5.	**John Spratt*** (D)	77,311
	Larry Bigham (R)	70,967
6.	**James E. Clyburn*** (D)	88,635
	Gary McLeod (R)	50,259

South Dakota

Dist.	Representative (Party)	1994 Election
	Tim Johnson* (D)	183,036
	Jan Berkhout (R)	112,054

Tennessee

Dist.	Representative (Party)	1994 Election
1.	**James H. "Jimmy" Quillen*** (R)	102,947
	J. Carr "Jack" Christian (D)	34,691
2.	**John J. Duncan, Jr.*** (R)	128,937
	Randon J. Krieg (I)	6,854
	Greg Samples (I)	6,682
3.	**Zach Wamp** (R)	84,583
	Randy Button (D)	73,839
4.	**Van Hilleary** (R)	81,539
	Jeff Whorley (D)	60,489
5.	**Bob Clement*** (D)	95,953
	John Osborne (R)	61,692
6.	**Bart Gordon*** (D)	90,933
	Steve Gill (R)	88,759
7.	**Ed Bryant** (R)	102,587
	Harold Byrd (D)	65,851
8.	**John Tanner*** (D)	97,951
	Neal R. Morris (R)	55,573
9.	**Harold E. Ford*** (D)	94,805
	Rod DeBerry (R)	69,226

Texas

Dist.	Representative (Party)	1994 Election
1.	**Jim Chapman*** (D)	86,480
	Mike Blankenship (R)	63,911
2.	**Charles Wilson*** (D)	87,709
	Donna Peterson (R)	66,071
3.	**Sam Johnson*** (R)	157,011
	Tom Donahue (B)	15,611
4.	**Ralph M. Hall*** (D)	99,303
	David L. Bridges (R)	67,267
5.	**John Bryant*** (D)	61,877
	Pete Sessions (R)	58,521
6.	**Joe Barton*** (R)	152,038
	Terry Jesmore (D)	44,286
7.	**Bill Archer*** (R)	Unopposed
8.	**Jack Fields*** (R)	148,473
	Russ Klecka (I)	12,831
9.	**Steve Stockman** (R)	81,353
	Jack Brooks* (D)	71,643
10.	**Lloyd Doggett** (D)	113,738
	A. Jo Baylor (R)	80,382
11.	**Chet Edwards*** (D)	76,667
	Jim Broyles (R)	52,876
12.	**Pete Geren*** (D)	96,372
	Ernest J. Anderson, Jr. (R)	43,959
13.	**William M. "Mac" Thornberry** (R)	79,466
	Bill Sarpalius* (D)	63,923
14.	**Greg Laughlin*** (R)[5]	86,175
	Jim Deats (R)	68,793
15.	**E. "Kika" de la Garza*** (D)	61,527
	Tom Haughey (R)	41,119
16.	**Ronald Coleman*** (D)	49,815
	Bobby Ortiz (R)	37,409
17.	**Charles W. Stenholm*** (D)	83,497
	Phil Boone (R)	72,108
18.	**Sheila Jackson-Lee** (D)	84,790
	Jerry Burley (R)	28,153
19.	**Larry Combest*** (R)	Unopposed
20.	**Henry B. Gonzalez*** (D)	60,114
	Carl Bill Colyer (R)	36,035
21.	**Lamar Smith*** (R)	165,595
	Kerry L. Lowry (I)	18,480
22.	**Tom DeLay*** (R)	120,302
	Scott Douglas Cunningham (D)	38,826
23.	**Henry Bonilla*** (R)	73,815
	Rolando L. Rios (D)	44,101
24.	**Martin Frost*** (D)	65,019
	Ed Harrison (R)	58,062
25.	**Ken Bentsen** (D)	61,959
	Gene Fontenot (R)	53,321
26.	**Dick Armey*** (R)	135,398
	LeEarl Ann Bryant (D)	39,763
27.	**Solomon P. Ortiz*** (D)	65,325
	Erol A. Stone (R)	44,693
28.	**Frank Tejeda*** (D)	73,986
	David C. Slatter (R)	28,777
29.	**Gene Green*** (D)	44,102
	Harold "Oilman" Eide (R)	15,952
30.	**Eddie Bernice Johnson*** (D)	73,166
	Lucy Cain (R)	25,848

Utah

Dist.	Representative (Party)	1994 Election
1.	**James V. Hansen*** (R)	104,954
	Bobbie Coray (D)	57,664
2.	**Enid Greene Waldholtz** (R)	85,507
	Karen Shepherd* (D)	66,911
	Merrill Cook (I)	34,167
3.	**Bill Orton*** (D)	91,505
	Dixie Thompson (R)	61,839

Vermont

Dist.	Representative (Party)	1994 Election
	Bernard Sanders* (I)	105,502
	John Carroll (R)	98,523

Virginia

Dist.	Representative (Party)	1994 Election
1.	**Herbert H. "Herb" Bateman*** (R)	142,930
	Mary F. Sinclair (D)	45,173
2.	**Owen B. Pickett*** (D)	81,372
	J. L. "Jim" Chapman IV (R)	56,375
3.	**Robert C. "Bobby" Scott*** (D)	108,532
	Thomas E. "Tom" Ward (R)	28,080
4.	**Norman Sisisky*** (D)	115,055
	A. George Sweet III (R)	71,678
5.	**L. F. Payne, Jr.*** (D)	95,308
	George C. Landrith III (R)	83,555
6.	**Robert W. "Bob" Goodlatte*** (R)	Unopposed
7.	**Thomas J. "Tom" Bliley, Jr.*** (R)	176,941
	Gerald E. "Jerry" Berg (I)	33,220
8.	**James P. Moran, Jr.*** (D)	120,281
	Kyle E. McSlarrow (R)	79,568
9.	**Frederick C. "Rick" Boucher*** (D)	102,876
	S. H. "Steve" Fast (R)	72,133
10.	**Frank R. Wolf*** (R)	153,311
	Alan R. Ogden (I)	13,687
	Robert L. "Bob" Rilee (I)	8,267
11.	**Thomas M. Davis III** (R)	98,216
	Leslie L. Byrne* (D)	84,104

Washington

Dist.	Representative (Party)	1994 Election
1.	**Rick White** (R)	100,554
	Maria Cantwell* (D)	94,110
2.	**Jack Metcalf** (R)	107,430
	Harriet A. Spanel (D)	89,096
3.	**Linda Smith** (R)	100,188
	Jolene Unsoeld* (D)	85,826
4.	**Doc Hastings** (R)	92,828
	Jay Inslee* (D)	81,198
5.	**George Nethercutt** (R)	110,057
	Thomas S. Foley* (D)	106,074

Dist.	Representative (Party)	1994 Election
6.	Norm Dicks* (D)	105,480
	Benjamin Gregg (R)	75,322
7.	Jim McDermott* (D)	148,353
	Keith Harris (R)	49,091
8.	Jennifer Dunn* (R)	140,409
	Jim Wyrick (D)	44,165
9.	Randy Tate (R)	77,833
	Mike Kreidler* (D)	72,451
West Virginia		
1.	Alan B. Mollohan* (D)	103,177
	Sally Rossy Riley (R)	43,590
2.	Bob Wise* (D)	90,757
	Sam Cravotta (R)	51,691
3.	Nick Joe Rahall II* (D)	74,967
	Ben Waldman (R)	42,382
Wisconsin		
1.	Mark W. Neumann (R)	83,937
	Peter W. Barca* (D)	82,817

Dist.	Representative (Party)	1994 Election
2.	Scott L. Klug* (R)	133,734
	Thomas C. Hecht (D)	55,406
3.	Steve Gunderson* (R)	89,338
	Harvey Stower (D)	65,758
4.	Gerald D. Kleczka* (D)	93,789
	Tom Reynolds (R)	78,225
5.	Tom Barrett* (D)	87,806
	Stephen B. Hollingshead (R)	51,145
6.	Thomas E. Petri* (R)	Unopposed
7.	David R. Obey* (D)	97,184
	Scott West (R)	81,706
8.	Toby Roth* (R)	114,319
	Stan Gruszynski (D)	65,065
9.	F. James Sensenbrenner, Jr.* (R)	Unopposed
Wyoming		
	Barbara Cubin (R)	104,426
	Bob Schuster (D)	81,022

The following members of Congress are nonvoting: Carlos A. Romero Barceló (D), resident commissioner, Puerto Rico; Eleanor Holmes Norton (D), District of Columbia; Robert Underwood (D), Guam; Eni F. H. Faleomavaega (D), American Samoa; Victor O. Frazer (I), Virgin Islands.

(1) Democratic Rep. Norm Mineta resigned, Oct. 10, 1995, to become a vice president at Lockheed Martin Corp. A special election to fill the vacant seat was scheduled for Feb. 6, 1996. (2) Democratic Rep. Nathan Deal announced, Apr. 10, 1995, that he changed his party designation to Republican. (3) Democratic Rep. Mel Reynolds resigned, Oct. 1, 1995, after his criminal conviction relating to his allegedly having had sex with a minor. Reynolds appealed his conviction. A special election to fill the vacant seat was scheduled for Dec. 12, 1995. (4) Democratic Rep. W. J. "Billy" Tauzin announced, Aug. 6, 1995, that he changed his party designation to Republican. (5) Democratic Rep. Greg Laughlin announced, June 26, 1995, that he changed his party designation to Republican.

Congressional Committees

Senate Standing Committees
(as of Oct. 15, 1995)

Agriculture, Nutrition, and Forestry
Chairman: Richard G. Lugar, IN
Ranking Dem.: Patrick J. Leahy, VT
Appropriations
Chairman: Mark O. Hatfield, OR
Ranking Dem.: Robert C. Byrd, WV
Armed Services
Chairman: Strom Thurmond, SC
Ranking Dem.: Sam Nunn, GA
Banking, Housing, and Urban Affairs
Chairman: Alfonse M. D'Amato, NY
Ranking Dem.: Paul S. Sarbanes, MD
Budget
Chairman: Pete V. Domenici, NM
Ranking Dem.: J. James Exon, NE
Commerce, Science, and Transportation
Chairman: Larry Pressler, SD
Ranking Dem.: Ernest F. "Fritz" Hollings, SC

Energy and Natural Resources
Chairman: Frank H. Murkowski, AK
Ranking Dem.: J. Bennett Johnston, LA
Environment and Public Works
Chairman: John H. Chafee, RI
Ranking Dem.: Max Baucus, MT
Finance
Chairman: William V. Roth, Jr., DE
Ranking Dem.: Daniel Patrick Moynihan, NY
Foreign Relations
Chairman: Jesse Helms, NC
Ranking Dem.: Claiborne Pell, RI
Governmental Affairs
Chairman: Ted Stevens, AK
Ranking Dem.: John Glenn, OH
Indian Affairs
Chairman John McCain, AZ
Ranking Dem.: Daniel K. Inouye, HI

Judiciary
Chairman: Orrin G. Hatch, UT
Ranking Dem.: Joseph R. Biden, Jr., DE
Labor and Human Resources
Chairman: Nancy Landon Kassebaum, KS
Ranking Dem.: Edward M. Kennedy, MA
Rules and Administration
Chairman: John W. Warner, VA
Ranking Dem.: Wendell H. Ford, KY
Small Business
Chairman: Christopher "Kit" Bond, MO
Ranking Dem.: Dale Bumpers, AR
Veterans' Affairs
Chairman: Alan K. Simpson, WY
Ranking Dem.: John D. Rockefeller IV, WV

Senate Select Committees
(as of Oct. 15, 1995)

Aging
Chairman: William S. Cohen, ME
Ranking Dem.: David H. Pryor, AR
Ethics
Chairman: Mitch McConnell, KY
V. Chairman: Richard H. Bryan, NV
Intelligence
Chairman: Arlen Specter, PA
V. Chairman: Bob Kerrey, NE

House Select Committees
(as of Oct. 15, 1995)

Intelligence
Chairman: Larry Combest, TX
Ranking Dem.: Norman Dicks, WA

Joint Committees of Congress
(as of Oct. 15, 1995)

Economic
Chairman: Sen. Connie Mack, FL
V. Chairman: Rep. Jim Saxton, NJ

Library
Chairman: Sen. Mark O. Hatfield, OR
V. Chairman: Rep. Bill Thomas, CA

Printing
Chairman: Rep. Bill Thomas, CA
V. Chairman: Sen. John W. Warner, VA

Taxation
Chairman: Rep. Bill Archer, TX
V. Chairman: Sen. William V. Roth, Jr., DE

House Standing Committees
(as of Oct. 15, 1995)

Agriculture
Chairman: Pat Roberts, KS
Ranking Dem.: E. "Kika" de la Garza, TX

Appropriations
Chairman: Robert L. "Bob" Livingston, LA
Ranking Dem.: David R. Obey, WI

Banking and Financial Services
Chairman: Jim Leach, IA
Ranking Dem.: Henry B. Gonzalez, TX

Budget
Chairman: John R. Kasich, OH
Ranking Dem.: Martin Olav Sabo, MN

Commerce
Chairman: Thomas J. "Tom" Bliley, Jr., VA
Ranking Dem.: John D. Dingell, MI

Economic and Educational Opportunities
Chairman: Bill Goodling, PA
Ranking Dem.: William "Bill" Clay, Sr., MO

Government Reform and Oversight
Chairman: William F. "Bill" Clinger, Jr., PA
Ranking Dem.: Cardiss Collins, IL

House Oversight
Chairman: Bill Thomas, CA
Ranking Dem.: Vic Fazio, CA

International Relations
Chairman: Benjamin A. Gilman, NY
Ranking Dem.: Lee H. Hamilton, IN

Judiciary
Chairman: Henry J. Hyde, IL
Ranking Dem.: John Conyers, Jr., MI

National Security
Chairman: Floyd D. Spence, SC
Ranking Dem.: Ronald V. Dellums, CA

Resources
Chairman: Don Young, AK
Ranking Dem.: George Miller, CA

Rules
Chairman: Gerald B. H. Solomon, NY
Ranking Dem.: John Joseph Moakley, MA

Science
Chairman: Robert S. Walker, PA
Ranking Dem.: George E. Brown, Jr., CA

Small Business
Chairman: Jan Meyers, KS
Ranking Dem.: John J. LaFalce, NY

Standards of Official Conduct
Chairman: Nancy L. Johnson, CT
Ranking Dem.: Jim McDermott, WA

Transportation and Infrastructure
Chairman: Bud Shuster, PA
Ranking Dem.: James L. Oberstar, MN

Veterans' Affairs
Chairman: Bob Stump, AZ
Ranking Dem.: G. V. "Sonny" Montgomery, MS

Ways and Means
Chairman: Bill Archer, TX
Ranking Dem.: Sam M. Gibbons, FL

Political Divisions of the U.S. Senate and House of Representatives, 1965-95
Source: Clerk of the House of Representatives; Secretary of the Senate; Voter News Service
(All figures reflect immediate post-election party breakdown.)

Congress	Years	Senate					House of Representatives				
		Number of Senators	Democrats	Republicans	Other parties	Vacant	Number of Representatives	Democrats	Republicans	Other parties	Vacant
89th . . .	1965-67	100	68	32			435	295	140		
90th . . .	1967-69	100	64	36			435	248	187		
91st . . .	1969-71	100	58	42			435	243	192		
92d . . .	1971-73	100	54	44	2		435	255	180		
93d	1973-75	100	56	42	2		435	242	192	1	
94th . . .	1975-77	100	61	37	2		435	291	144		
95th . . .	1977-79	100	61	38	1		435	292	143		
96th . . .	1979-81	100	58	41	1		435	277	158		
97th . . .	1981-83	100	46	53	1		435	242	192	1	
98th . . .	1983-85	100	46	54			435	269	166		
99th . . .	1985-87	100	47	53			435	253	182		
100th . . .	1987-89	100	55	45			435	258	177		
101st . . .	1989-91	100	55	45			435	260	175		
102d . . .	1991-93	100	56	44			435	267	167	1	
103d . . .	1993-95	100	57	43			435	258	176	1	
104th . . .	1995-97	100	48[1]	52[1]			435	204[1]	230[1]	1[1]	

(1)As of Oct. 15, 1995, there were 53 Republicans, 46 Democrats, and 1 vacant seat in the Senate, and 233 Republicans, 199 Democrats, 1 Independent, and 2 vacant seats in the House of Representatives.

Congressional Bills Vetoed, 1789-1995
Source: Senate Library

	Regular vetoes	Pocket vetoes	Total vetoes	Vetoes over-ridden		Regular vetoes	Pocket vetoes	Total vetoes	Vetoes over-ridden
Washington	2	—	2	—	Benjamin Harrison	19	25	44	1
John Adams	—	—	—	—	Cleveland	42	128	170	5
Jefferson	—	—	—	—	McKinley	6	36	42	—
Madison	5	2	7	—	Theodore Roosevelt	42	40	82	1
Monroe	1	—	1	—	Taft	30	9	39	1
John Q. Adams	—	—	—	—	Wilson	33	11	44	6
Jackson	5	7	12	—	Harding	5	1	6	—
Van Buren	—	1	1	—	Coolidge	20	30	50	4
William Harrison	—	—	—	—	Hoover	21	16	37	3
Tyler	6	4	10	1	Franklin Roosevelt	372	263	635	9
Polk	2	1	3	—	Truman	180	70	250	12
Taylor	—	—	—	—	Eisenhower	73	108	181	2
Fillmore	—	—	—	—	Kennedy	12	9	21	—
Pierce	9	—	9	5	Lyndon Johnson	16	14	30	—
Buchanan	4	3	7	—	Nixon	26	17	43	7
Lincoln	2	5	7	—	Ford	48	18	66	12
Andrew Johnson	21	8	29	15	Carter	13	18	31	2
Grant	45	48	93	4	Reagan	39	39	78	9
Hayes	12	1	13	1	Bush[1]	29	15	44	1
Garfield	—	—	—	—	Clinton[2]	3	—	3	—
Arthur	4	8	12	1					
Cleveland	304	110	414	2	Total[1]	1,451	1,065	2,516	104

(1)Excluded from the figures are 2 additional bills, which Pres. Bush claimed to be vetoed but Congress considered enacted into law because the president failed to return them to Congress during a recess period. (2) As of Oct. 15, 1995.

Judiciary of the U.S.

(data as of mid-1995)

Justices of the United States Supreme Court

The Supreme Court comprises the chief justice of the U.S. and 8 associate justices, all appointed by the president with advice and consent of the Senate. Salaries: chief justice $171,500 annually, associate justice $164,100. The Supreme Court is at the U.S. Supreme Court Bldg., 1 First St. NE, Washington, DC 20543.

Members of the Supreme Court at the start of the 1995–96 term (Oct. 2, 1995): Chief justice: William H. Rehnquist; associate justices: Stephen Breyer, Ruth Bader Ginsburg, Anthony M. Kennedy, Sandra Day O'Connor, Antonin Scalia, David H. Souter, John Paul Stevens, Clarence Thomas.

Name,[1] apptd from	Service Term	Yrs	Born	Died	Name,[1] apptd from	Service Term	Yrs	Born	Died
John Jay, NY	1789-1795	5	1745	1829	William H. Moody, MA	1906-1910	3	1853	1917
John Rutledge, SC	1789-1791	1	1739	1800	Horace H. Lurton, TN	1909-1914	4	1844	1914
William Cushing, MA	1789-1810	20	1732	1810	Charles E. Hughes, NY	1910-1916	5	1862	1948
James Wilson, PA	1789-1798	8	1742	1798	Willis Van Devanter, WY	1910-1937	26	1859	1941
John Blair, VA	1789-1796	6	1732	1800	Joseph R. Lamar, GA	1910-1916	5	1857	1916
James Iredell, NC	1790-1799	9	1751	1799	*Edward D. White,* LA	1910-1921	10	1845	1921
Thomas Johnson, MD	1791-1793	1	1732	1819	Mahlon Pitney, NJ	1912-1922	10	1858	1924
William Paterson, NJ	1793-1806	13	1745	1806	James C. McReynolds,				
John Rutledge,[2] SC	1795	—	1739	1800	TN	1914-1941	26	1862	1946
Samuel Chase, MD	1796-1811	15	1741	1811	Louis D. Brandeis, MA	1916-1939	22	1856	1941
Oliver Ellsworth, CT	1796-1800	4	1745	1807	John H. Clarke, OH	1916-1922	5	1857	1945
Bushrod Washington, VA	1798-1829	31	1762	1829	*William H. Taft,* CT	1921-1930	8	1857	1930
Alfred Moore, NC	1799-1804	4	1755	1810	George Sutherland, UT	1922-1938	15	1862	1942
John Marshall, VA	1801-1835	34	1755	1835	Pierce Butler, MN	1922-1939	16	1866	1939
William Johnson, SC	1804-1834	30	1771	1834	Edward T. Sanford, TN	1923-1930	7	1865	1930
Henry B. Livingston, NY	1806-1823	16	1757	1823	Harlan F. Stone, NY	1925-1941	16	1872	1946
Thomas Todd, KY	1807-1826	18	1765	1826	*Charles E. Hughes,* NY	1930-1941	11	1862	1948
Joseph Story, MA	1811-1845	33	1779	1845	Owen J. Roberts, PA	1930-1945	15	1875	1955
Gabriel Duval, MD	1811-1835	22	1752	1844	Benjamin N. Cardozo,				
Smith Thompson, NY	1823-1843	20	1768	1843	NY	1932-1938	6	1870	1938
Robert Trimble, KY	1826-1828	2	1777	1828	Hugo L. Black, AL	1937-1971	34	1886	1971
John McLean, OH	1829-1861	32	1785	1861	Stanley F. Reed, KY	1938-1957	19	1884	1980
Henry Baldwin, PA	1830-1844	14	1780	1844	Felix Frankfurter, MA	1939-1962	23	1882	1965
James M. Wayne, GA	1835-1867	32	1790	1867	William O. Douglas, CT	1939-1975	36	1898	1980
Roger B. Taney, MD	1836-1864	28	1777	1864	Frank Murphy, MI	1940-1949	9	1890	1949
Philip P. Barbour, VA	1836-1841	4	1783	1841	*Harlan F. Stone,* NY	1941-1946	5	1872	1946
John Catron, TN	1837-1865	28	1786	1865	James F. Byrnes, SC	1941-1942	1	1879	1972
John McKinley, AL	1837-1852	15	1780	1852	Robert H. Jackson, NY	1941-1954	12	1892	1954
Peter V. Daniel, VA	1841-1860	19	1784	1860	Wiley B. Rutledge, IA	1943-1949	6	1894	1949
Samuel Nelson, NY	1845-1872	27	1792	1873	Harold H. Burton, OH	1945-1958	13	1888	1964
Levi Woodbury, NH	1845-1851	5	1789	1851	*Fred M. Vinson,* KY	1946-1953	7	1890	1953
Robert C. Grier, PA	1846-1870	23	1794	1870	Tom C. Clark, TX	1949-1967	18	1899	1977
Benjamin R. Curtis, MA	1851-1857	6	1809	1874	Sherman Minton, IN	1949-1956	7	1890	1965
John A. Campbell, AL	1853-1861	8	1811	1889	*Earl Warren,* CA	1953-1969	16	1891	1974
Nathan Clifford, ME	1858-1881	23	1803	1881	John Marshall Harlan,				
Noah H. Swayne, OH	1862-1881	18	1804	1884	NY	1955-1971	16	1899	1971
Samuel F. Miller, IA	1862-1890	28	1816	1890	William J. Brennan Jr.,				
David Davis, IL	1862-1877	14	1815	1886	NJ	1956-1990	33	1906	—
Stephen J. Field, CA	1863-1897	34	1816	1899	Charles E. Whittaker,				
Salmon P. Chase, OH	1864-1873	8	1808	1873	MO	1957-1962	5	1901	1973
William Strong, PA	1870-1880	10	1808	1895	Potter Stewart, OH	1958-1981	23	1915	1985
Joseph P. Bradley, NJ	1870-1892	21	1813	1892	Byron R. White, CO	1962-1993	31	1917	—
Ward Hunt, NY	1872-1882	9	1810	1886	Arthur J. Goldberg, IL	1962-1965	3	1908	1990
Morrison R. Waite, OH	1874-1888	14	1816	1888	Abe Fortas, TN	1965-1969	4	1910	1982
John M. Harlan, KY	1877-1911	34	1833	1911	Thurgood Marshall, NY	1967-1991	24	1908	1993
William B. Woods, GA	1880-1887	6	1824	1887	*Warren E. Burger,* VA	1969-1986	17	1907	1995
Stanley Matthews, OH	1881-1889	7	1824	1889	Harry A. Blackmun, MN	1970-1994	24	1908	—
Horace Gray, MA	1881-1902	20	1828	1902	Lewis F. Powell Jr., VA	1972-1987	15	1907	—
Samuel Blatchford, NY	1882-1893	11	1820	1893	William H. Rehnquist, AZ	1972-1986	14	1924	—
Lucius Q.C. Lamar, MS	1888-1893	5	1825	1893	John Paul Stevens, IL	1975-	—	1920	—
Melville W. Fuller, IL	1888-1910	21	1833	1910	Sandra Day O'Connor,				
David J. Brewer, KS	1889-1910	20	1837	1910	AZ	1981-	—	1930	—
Henry B. Brown, MI	1890-1906	15	1836	1913	*William H. Rehnquist,* AZ	1986-		1924	—
George Shiras Jr., PA	1892-1903	10	1832	1924	Antonin Scalia, VA	1986-		1936	—
Howell E. Jackson, TN	1893-1895	2	1832	1895	Anthony M. Kennedy, CA	1988-		1936	—
Edward D. White, LA	1894-1910	16	1845	1921	David H. Souter, NH	1990-		1939	—
Rufus W. Peckham, NY	1895-1909	13	1838	1909	Clarence Thomas, VA.	1991-		1948	—
Joseph McKenna, CA	1898-1925	26	1843	1926	Ruth Bader Ginsburg,				
Oliver W. Holmes, MA	1902-1932	29	1841	1935	DC	1993-		1933	—
William R. Day, OH	1903-1922	19	1849	1923	Stephen Breyer, MA	1994-		1938	—

(1) Chief justices in italics. (2) Rejected Dec. 15, 1795.

U.S. Courts of Appeals

(Salaries, $141,700. CJ means Chief Judge)

Federal Circuit — Glenn L. Archer Jr., CJ; Helen W. Nies, Giles S. Rich, Pauline Newman, H. Robert Mayer, Paul R. Michel, S. Jay Plager, Alan D. Lourie, Raymond C. Clevenger III, Randall R. Rader, Alvin A. Schall, William C. Bryson; Clerk's Office, Washington, DC 20439.

District of Columbia —Harry T. Edwards, CJ; Patricia M. Wald, Laurence H. Silberman, James L. Buckley, Stephen F. Williams, Douglas Ginsburg, David B. Sentelle, Karen Le-Craft Henderson, A. Raymond Randolph, Judith W. Rogers, David S. Tatel; Clerk's Office, Washington, DC 20001.

First Circuit (ME, MA, NH, RI, Puerto Rico) — Juan R. Torruella, CJ; Bruce M. Selya, Conrad K. Cyr, Michael Boudin, Norman H. Stahl, Sandra Lynch; Clerk's Office, Boston, MA 02109.

Second Circuit (CT, NY, VT) — Jon O. Newman, CJ; Amalya Lyle Kearse, Ralph K. Winter, Roger J. Miner, Frank X. Altimari, J. Daniel Mahoney, John M. Walker Jr., Joseph M. McLaughlin, Dennis G. Jacobs, Pierre N. Leval, Guido Calabresi, José A. Cabranes, Fred I. Parker; Clerk's Office, New York, NY 10007.

Third Circuit (DE, NJ, PA, Virgin Islands) — Dolores K. Sloviter, CJ; Edward R. Becker, Walter K. Stapleton, Carol Los Mansmann, Morton I. Greenberg, William D. Hutchinson, Anthony J. Scirica, Robert E. Cowen, Richard L. Nygaard, Samuel A. Alito Jr., Jane R. Roth, Timothy K. Lewis, Theodore A. McKee, H. Lee Sarokin; Clerk's Office, Philadelphia, PA 19106.

Fourth Circuit (MD, NC, SC, VA, WV) — Sam J. Ervin III, CJ; Donald Stuart Russell, H. Emory Widener Jr., Kenneth K. Hall, Francis D. Murnaghan Jr., J. Harvie Wilkinson III, William W. Wilkins Jr., Paul V. Niemeyer, Clyde H. Hamilton, J. Michael Luttig, Karen J. Williams, M. Blane Michael, Diana G. Motz; Clerk's Office, Richmond, VA 23219.

Fifth Circuit (LA, MS, TX) — Henry A. Politz, CJ; Carolyn Dineen King, Will Garwood, E. Grady Jolly, Patrick E. Higginbotham, W. Eugene Davis, Jerry E. Smith, Edith Hollan Jones, John M. Duhé Jr., Rhesa A. Barksdale, Jacques L. Wiener Jr., Emilio M. Garza, Harold R. DeMoss Jr., Fortunato P. Benavides, Carl E. Stewart, Robert M. Parker; Clerk's Office, New Orleans, LA 70130.

Sixth Circuit (KY, MI, OH, TN) — Gilbert S. Merritt, CJ; Boyce F. Martin Jr., Cornelia G. Kennedy, H. Ted Milburn, David A. Nelson, James L. Ryan, Danny J. Boggs, Alan E. Norris, Richard H. Suhrheinrich, Eugene E. Siler Jr., Alice M. Batchelder, Martha Craig Daughtrey, Karen Nelson Moore; Clerk's Office, Cincinnati, OH 45202.

Seventh Circuit (IL, IN, WI) — Richard A. Posner, CJ; William J. Bauer, Walter J. Cummings, Richard D. Cudahy, John L. Coffey, Joel M. Flaum, Frank H. Easterbrook, Kenneth F. Ripple, Daniel A. Manion, Michael S. Kanne, Ilana D. Rovner, Wilbur F. Pell Jr., Thomas E. Fairchild, Harlington Wood, Jesse E. Eschbach, Diane P. Wood; Clerk's Office, Chicago, IL 60604.

Eighth Circuit (AR, IA, MN, MO, NE, ND, SD) — Richard S. Arnold, CJ; Theodore McMillian, George G. Fagg, Pasco M. Bowman, Roger L. Wollman, Frank J. Magill, C. Arlen Beam, James B. Loken, David R. Hansen, Morris S. Arnold, Diana E. Murphy; Clerk's Office, St. Louis, MO 63101.

Ninth Circuit (AK, AZ, CA, HI, ID, MT, NV, OR, WA, Guam, N. Mariana Islands) — J. Clifford Wallace, CJ; James R. Browning, Procter Hug Jr., Mary M. Schroeder, Betty B. Fletcher, Jerome Farris, Harry Pregerson, Cecil F. Poole, William C. Canby Jr., Stephen Reinhardt, Robert R. Beezer, Cynthia Holcomb Hall, Charles E. Wiggins, Melvin Brunetti, Alex Kozinski, John T. Noonan, David R. Thompson, Diarmuid F. O'Scannlain, Edward Leavy, Stephen S. Trott, Ferdinand F. Fernandez, Pamela Ann Rymer, Thomas G. Nelson, Andrew J. Kleinfeld, Michael D. Hawkins; Clerk's Office, San Francisco, CA 94119.

Tenth Circuit (CO, KS, NM, OK, UT, WY) — Stephanie K. Seymour, CJ; John P. Moore, Stephen H. Anderson, Deanell R. Tacha, Bobby R. Baldock, Wade Brorby, David M. Ebel, Paul J. Kelly Jr., Robert H. Henry, Mary Beck Briscoe, Carlos Lucero; Clerk's Office, Denver, CO 80294.

Eleventh Circuit (AL, FL, GA)— Gerald B. Tjoflat, CJ; Peter T. Fay, Phyllis A. Kravitch, Joseph W. Hatchett, R. Lanier Anderson III, J. L. Edmondson, Emmett R. Cox, Stanley F. Birch Jr., Joel F. Dubina, Susan H. Black, Edward E. Carnes, Rosemary Barkett; Clerk's Office, Atlanta GA 30303.

U.S. District Courts

(Salaries, $133,600. CJ means Chief Judge)

Alabama — **Northern:** Sam C. Pointer Jr., CJ; James Hughes Hancock, Robert B. Propst, U. W. Clemon, William M. Acker Jr., Edwin L. Nelson, Sharon Lovelace Blackburn; Clerk's Office, Birmingham 35203. **Middle:** Myron H. Thompson, CJ; W. Harold Albritton, Ira Dement; Clerk's Office, Montgomery 36101. **Southern:** Charles R. Butler Jr., CJ; Alex T. Howard Jr., Richard W. Vollmer Jr.; Clerk's Office, Mobile 36602.

Alaska — John K. Singleton, CJ; H. Russel Holland, John W. Sedwick; Clerk's Office, Anchorage 99513.

Arizona — Robert C. Bloomfield, CJ; William D. Browning, Richard M. Bilby, Paul G. Rosenblat, Roger G. Strand, Stephen M. McNamee, John M. Roll, Roslyn Silver; Clerk's Office, Phoenix 85025.

Arkansas — **Eastern:** Stephen M. Reasoner, CJ; Henry Woods, George Howard Jr., Susan Weber Wright, G. Thomas Eisele, Elsiejane Trimble Roy, William R. Wilson Jr., James M. Moody; Clerk's Office, Little Rock 72203. **Western:** H. Franklin Waters, CJ; Jimm Larry Hendren, Harry F. Barnes; Clerk's Office, Fort Smith 72902.

California — **Northern:** Thelton E. Henderson, CJ; Stanley A. Weigel, Samuel Conti, Spencer Williams, William H. Orrick Jr., William A. Ingram, William W. Schwarzer, Robert P. Aguilar, Marilyn H. Patel, Eugene F. Lynch, Charles A. Legge, D. Lowell Jensen, Fern M. Smith, Vaughn R. Walker, James Ware, Saundra Brown Armstrong, Ronald M. Whyte, Claudia Wilken, Maxine M. Chesney, Susan Illston; Clerk's Office, San Francisco 94102. **Eastern:** Robert E. Coyle, CJ; Lawrence K. Karlton, CJ Emeritus; Edward J. Garcia, William B. Shubb, David F. Levi, Oliver W. Wanger, Garland E. Burrell Jr.; Clerk's Office, Sacramento 95814. **Central:** William Matthew Byrne Jr., CJ; Manuel L. Real, Robert M. Takasugi, Mariana R. Pfaelzer, Terry J. Hatter Jr., A. Wallace Tashima, Consuelo Bland Marshall, David V. Kenyon, Richard A. Gadbois, Edward Rafeedie, Harry L. Hupp, Alicemarie H. Stotler, James M. Ideman, William J. Rea, William D. Keller, Stephen V. Wilson, J. Spencer Letts, Dickran M. Tevrizian Jr., John G. Davies, Ronald S. W. Lew, Gary L. Taylor, Linda Hodge McLaughlin, Lourdes G. Baird, Audrey B. Collins, Richard A. Paez, Robert J. Timlin, Stephen V. Wilson, George H. King; Clerk's Office, Los Angeles 90012. **Southern:** Judith N. Keep, CJ; Rudi M. Brewster, John S. Rhoades, Marilyn L. Huff, Irma E. Gonzalez, Napoleon A. Jones Jr.; Clerk's Office, San Diego 92101.

Colorado — Richard P. Matsch, CJ; John L. Kane Jr., Jim R. Carrigan, Zita L. Weinshienk, Lewis T. Babcock, Edward W. Nottingham, Daniel B. Sparr, Wiley Y. Daniel; Clerk's Office, Denver 80294.

Connecticut — Peter C. Dorsey, CJ; T. F. Gilroy Daly, Alan H. Nevas, Alfred V. Covello, Robert N. Chatigny, Dominic J. Squatrito, Alvin W. Thompson, Janet Bond Arterton; Clerk's Office, New Haven 06510.

Delaware — Joseph J. Longobardi, CJ; Joseph J. Farnan Jr., Sue L. Robinson, Roderick R. McKelvie; Clerk's Office, Wilmington 19801.

(continued)

U.S. District Courts (*continued*)

District of Columbia — John Garrett Penn, CJ; Charles R. Richey, Norma Holloway Johnson, Thomas P. Jackson, Thomas F. Hogan, Stanley S. Harris, Stanley Sporkin, Royce C. Lamberth, Gladys Kessler, Paul L. Friedman, Ricardo M. Urbina, Emmet G. Sullivan, James Robertson; Clerk's Office, Washington DC 20001.

Florida — **Northern:** Maurice M. Paul, CJ; C. Roger Vinson, Lacey A. Collier, William H. Stafford; Clerk's Office, Tallahassee 32301. **Middle:** John H. Moore II, CJ; William Terrell Hodges, Elizabeth A. Kovachevich, George Kendall Sharp, Patricia C. Fawsett, Harvey E. Schlesinger, Ralph W. Nimmons Jr., Anne C. Conway, Steven D. Merryday, Susan C. Bucklew, Henry L. Adams Jr.; Clerk's Office, Jacksonville 32201. **Southern:** Norman C. Roettger, CJ; Jose A. Gonzalez Jr., Edward B. Davis, Lenore C. Nesbitt, Stanley Marcus, William J. Zloch, Kenneth L. Ryskamp, Federico A. Moreno, Shelby Highsmith, Donald L. Graham, K. Michael Moore, Ursula Ungaro-Benages, Wilkie D. Ferguson Jr., Daniel T. K. Hurley; Clerk's Office, Miami 33128.

Georgia — **Northern:** Robert L. Vining Jr., CJ; William C. O'Kelley, Harold L. Murphy, G. Ernest Tidwell, Orinda D. Evans, J. Owen Forrester, Jack T. Camp, Julie E. Carnes, Clarence Cooper, Frank M. Hull, Willis B. Hunt Jr.; Clerk's Office, Atlanta 30303. **Middle:** Wilbur D. Owens Jr., CJ; J. Robert Elliott, Duross Fitzpatrick, W. Louis Sands; Clerk's Office, Macon 31202. **Southern:** B. Avant Edenfield, CJ; Dudley H. Bowen Jr., William T. Moore Jr.; Clerk's Office, Savannah 31412.

Hawaii — Alan C. Kay, CJ; David A. Ezra, Helen Gillmor; Clerk's Office, Honolulu 96850.

Idaho — Edward J. Lodge, CJ; B. Lynn Winmill; Clerk's Office, Boise 83724.

Illinois — **Northern:** Marvin E. Aspen, CJ; Charles P. Kocoras, William T. Hart, Paul E. Plunkett, Charles R. Norgle Sr., James F. Holderman, Ann C. Williams, Brian Barnett Duff, Harry D. Leinenweber, James B. Zagel, James H. Alesia, Suzanne B. Conlon, George M. Marovich, George W. Lindberg, Wayne R. Andersen, Philip G. Reinhard, Ruben Castillo, Blanche M. Manning, David H. Coar, Robert W. Gettleman, Elaine E. Buciclo; Clerk's Office, Chicago 60604. **Central:** Michael M. Mihm, CJ; Richard Mills, Joe Billy McDade; Clerk's Office, Springfield 62705. **Southern:** J. Phil Gilbert, CJ; William D. Stiehl, Paul E. Riley, James L. Foreman, William L. Beatty; Clerk's Office, East St. Louis 62201.

Indiana — **Northern:** Allen Sharp, CJ; William C. Lee, James T. Moody, Robert L. Miller Jr., Rudy Lozano; Clerk's Office, South Bend 46601. **Southern:** Sarah E. Barker, CJ; Gene E. Brooks, S. Hugh Dillin, Larry J. McKinney, John D. Tinder, David F. Hamilton; Clerk's Office, Indianapolis 46204.

Iowa — **Northern:** Michael J. Melloy, CJ; Mark W. Bennett; Clerk's Office, Cedar Rapids 52401. **Southern:** Charles R. Wolle, CJ; Harold D. Vietor, R. E. Longstaff; Clerk's Office, Des Moines 50309.

Kansas — G. Thomas Van Bebber, CJ; Sam A. Crow, John W. Lungstrum, Monti L. Belot, Kathryn H. Vratil; Clerk's Office, Wichita 67202.

Kentucky — **Eastern:** William Bertelsman, CJ; Henry R. Wilhoit Jr., Karl S. Forester, Joseph M. Hood, Jennifer B. Coffman; Clerk's Office, Lexington 40596-3074. **Western:** Charles R. Simpson III, CJ; John G. Heyburn II, Jennifer B. Coffman, Thomas B. Russell, Joseph H. McKinley Jr.; Clerk's Office, Louisville 40202.

Louisiana — **Eastern:** Morley L. Sear, CJ; A. J. McNamara, Martin L. C. Feldman, Marcel Livaudais Jr., Edith Brown Clement, Ginger Berrigan, Stanwood R. Duval Jr., Eldon E. Fallon, Sarah S. Vance, Okla Jones II, G. Thomas Porteous Jr.; Clerk's Office, New Orleans 70130. **Middle:** John V. Parker, CJ; Frank J. Polozola; Clerk's Office, Baton Rouge 70801. **Western:** John M. Shaw, CJ; F. A. Little Jr., Donald E. Walter, Richard Haiks, James T. Trimble, Rebecca F. Doherty, Tucker L. Melancon; Clerk's Office, Shreveport 71101.

Maine — Gene Carter, CJ; D. Brock Hornby, Morton A. Brody; Clerk's Office, Portland 04101.

Maryland — J. Frederick Motz, CJ; Frederic N. Smalkin, William M. Nickerson, Marvin J. Garbis, Benson Everett Legg, Catherine C. Blake, Andre M. Davis, Deborah K. Chasanow, Peter J. Messitte, Alexander Williams Jr.; Clerk's Office, Baltimore 21201.

Massachusetts — Joseph L. Tauro, CJ; Robert E. Keeton, Rya W. Zobel, William G. Young, Mark L. Wolf, Douglas P. Woodlock, Edward F. Harrington, Nathaniel M. Gorton, Richard G. Stearns, Reginald C. Lindsay, Patti B. Saris, Nancy Gertner, George A. O'Toole, Nathaniel M. Gorton, Michael A. Ponsor; Clerk's Office, Boston 02109.

Michigan — **Eastern:** Julian A. Cook Jr., CJ; Avern Cohn, Anna Diggs Taylor, George La Plata, Barbara K. Hackett, Lawrence P. Zatkoff, Patrick J. Duggan, Bernard A. Friedman, Paul V. Gadola, Gerald E. Rosen, Robert H. Cleland, Nancy G. Edmunds, Denise Page-Hood, Paul D. Borman, John Corbett O'Meara; Clerk's Office, Detroit 48226. **Western:** Richard A. Enslen, CJ; Benjamin F. Gibson, Robert H. Bell, David W. McKeague, Gordon J. Quist; Clerk's Office, Grand Rapids 49503.

Minnesota — Paul A. Magnuson, CJ; James M. Rosenbaum, David S. Doty, Richard H. Kyle, Michael J. Davis; Clerk's Office, St. Paul 55101.

Mississippi — **Northern:** L. T. Senter Jr., CJ; Neal Biggers, Glen H. Davidson; Clerk's Office, Oxford 38655. **Southern:** William H. Barbour Jr., CJ; Henry T. Wingate, Tom S. Lee, Walter J. Gex III, Charles W. Pickering Sr., David Bramlette; Clerk's Office, Jackson 39201.

Missouri — **Eastern:** Jean Hamilton, CJ; Stephen N. Limbaugh, George F. Gunn Jr., Donald J. Stohr, Carol E. Jackson, Charles A. Shaw, Catherine D. Perry; Clerk's Office, St. Louis 63101. **Western:** D. Brook Bartlett, CJ; Joseph E. Stevens Jr., Dean Whipple, Fernando J. Gaitan Jr., Ortrie D. Smith; Clerk's Office, Kansas City 64106.

Montana — Paul G. Hatfield, CJ; Charles C. Lovell, Jack D. Shanstrom; Clerk's Office, Billings 59101.

Nebraska — William G. Cambridge, CJ; Lyle E. Strom, Richard G. Kopf, Thomas M. Shanahan; Clerk's Office, Omaha 68101.

Nevada — Lloyd D. George, CJ; Howard D. McKibben, Philip M. Pro, David W. Hagen; Clerk's Office, Las Vegas 89101, Reno 89509.

New Hampshire — Joseph A. DiClerico, CJ; Paul J. Barbadoro, Steven J. McAuliffe; Clerk's Office, Concord 03301.

New Jersey — Anne E. Thompson, CJ; John W. Bissell, Maryanne Trump Barry, Joseph H. Rodriguez, Garrett E. Brown Jr., A. J. Lechner Jr., Nicholas H. Politan, Alfred M. Wolin, John C. Lifland, William G. Bassler, Mary Little Parell, Joseph E. Irenas, Jerome E. Simandle, William H. Walls; Clerk's Office, Newark 07101.

New Mexico — John E. Conway, CJ; James A. Parker, C. Leroy Hansen, Martha Vazquez; Clerk's Office, Albuquerque 87103.

New York — **Northern:** Thomas J. McAvoy, CJ; Con G. Cholakis, Frederick J. Scullin Jr., Rosemary S. Pooler; Clerk's Office, Syracuse 13261-7367. **Eastern:** Charles P. Sifton, CJ; Thomas C. Platt Jr., Raymond J. Dearie, Edward R. Korman, Reena Raggi, Arthur D. Spatt, Carol Bagley Amon, Sterling Johnson Jr., Denis R. Hurley, David G. Trager, Joanna Seybert, Allyne Ross, John Gleeson, Fredric Block; Clerk's Office, Brooklyn 11201. **Southern:** Thomas P. Griesa, CJ; David N. Edelstein, Charles L. Brieant, Kevin Thomas Duffy, Leonard B. Sand, Charles S. Haight Jr., John E. Sprizzo, Shirley Wohl Kram, John F. Keenan, Peter K. Leisure, Louis L. Stanton, Miriam G. Cedarbaum, Lewis A. Kaplan, Michael B. Mukasey, Kimba Wood, Robert P. Patterson Jr., Lawrence McKenna, John S. Martin Jr., Loretta A. Preska, Sonia Sotomayer, Harold Baer Jr., Deborah A. Batts, Denny Chin, Denise L. Cote, John Koeltl, Allen G. Schwartz, Barrington D. Parker Jr., Shira A. Scheindlin, Sidney H. Stein; Clerk's Office New York City 10007. **Western:** Michael A. Telesca, CJ; Richard J.

Arcara, David G. Larimer, William M. Skretny, John T. Curtin, John T. Elfvin; Clerk's Office, Buffalo 14202.

North Carolina — Eastern: James C. Fox, CJ; W. Earl Britt, Terrence W. Boyle, Malcolm J. Howard; Clerk's Office, Raleigh 27611. **Middle:** Frank W. Bullock, CJ; N. Carlton Tilley Jr., William L. Osteen Sr., James A. Beaty Jr.; Clerk's Office, Greensboro 27402. **Western:** Richard L. Voorhees, CJ; Graham C. Mullen, Lacy H. Thornburg; Clerk's Office, Asheville 28801.

North Dakota — Rodney S. Webb, CJ; Patrick A. Conmy; Clerk's Office, Bismarck 58502.

Ohio — Northern: George W. White, CJ; David D. Dowd Jr., Sam H. Bell, Paul R. Matia, Lesley Brooks Wells, James G. Carr, Solomon Oliver Jr., David A. Katz, Kathleen O'Malley, Peter C. Economus, Donald C. Nugent, Ann Aldrich; Clerk's Office, Cleveland 44114. **Southern:** John D. Holschuh, CJ; Walter Herbert Rice, Herman J. Weber, James L. Graham, George C. Smith, Sandra S. Beckwith; Clerk's Office, Columbus 43215.

Oklahoma — Northern: Thomas R. Brett, CJ; Terry C. Kern, Sven Erik Holmes, Michael Burrage; Clerk's Office, Tulsa 74103. **Eastern:** Frank H. Seay, CJ; Michael Burrage; Clerk's Office, Muskogee 74401. **Western:** David L. Russell, CJ; Ralph G. Thompson, Wayne Alley, Robin Cauthron, Tim Leonard, Michael Burrage, Vicki Miles-LaGrange; Clerk's Office, Oklahoma City 73102.

Oregon — Michael R. Hogan, CJ; Helen J. Frye, Malcolm F. Marsh, Robert E. Jones, Ancer L. Haggerty; Clerk's Office, Portland 97205.

Pennsylvania — Eastern: Edward N. Cahn, CJ; Norma L. Shapiro, James T. Giles, James McGirr Kelly, Thomas N. O'Neill Jr., Marvin Katz, Edmund V. Ludwig, Robert F. Kelly, Franklin S. Van Antwerpen, Robert S. Gawthrop III, Lowell A. Reed Jr., Jan E. Dubois Herbert J. Hutton, Jay C. Waldman, Ronald L. Buckwalter, Stewart Dalzell, William H. Yohn Jr., Harvey Bartle III, John R. Padova, J. Curtis Joyner, Eduardo C. Robreno, Anita B. Brody, Marjorie O. Rendell; Clerk's Office, Philadelphia 19106. **Middle:** Sylvia H. Rambo, CJ; Edward M. Kosik, James F. McClure Jr., Thomas I. Vanaskie; Clerk's Office, Scranton 18501. **Western:** Donald E. Ziegler, CJ; Alan N. Bloch, William L. Standish, D. Brooks Smith, Donald J. Lee, Donetta W. Ambrose, Gary L. Lancaster, Robert J. Cindrich, Sean J. McLaughlin; Clerk's Office, Pittsburgh 15230.

Rhode Island — Ronald R. Lagueux, CJ; Ernest C. Torres, Mary M. Lisi; Clerk's Office, Providence 02903.

South Carolina — C. Weston Houck, CJ; Matthew J. Perry Jr., G. Ross Anderson Jr., Joseph F. Anderson Jr., David C. Norton, Dennis W. Shedd, Henry M. Herlong Jr., William B. Traxler, Cameron M. Currie; Clerk's Office, Columbia 29201.

South Dakota — Richard H. Battey, CJ; Lawrence L. Piersol, Charles B. Kornmann; Clerk's Office, Sioux Falls 57102.

Tennessee — Eastern: James H. Jarvis, CJ; Thomas G. Hull, R. Allan Edgar, Leon Jordan, Curtis Collier; Clerk's Office, Knoxville 37901. **Middle:** John T. Nixon, CJ; Thomas A. Wiseman Jr., Thomas A. Higgins, Robert L. Echols; Clerk's Office, Nashville 37203. **Western:** Julia S. Gibbons, CJ; James D. Todd, Jerome Turner, John Phipps McCalla; Clerk's Office, Memphis 38103.

Texas — Northern: Jerry Buchmeyer, CJ; Barefoot Sanders, Mary Lou Robinson, A. Joe Fish, Robert B. Maloney, Sidney A. Fitzwater, Samuel R. Cummings, John H. McBryde, Jorge A. Solis, Terry Means, Joe Kendall; Clerk's Office, Dallas 75242. **Southern:** Norman W. Black, CJ; George P. Kazen, Filemon B. Vela, Hayden W. Head Jr., Ricardo H. Hinojosa, Lynn N. Hughes, David Hittner, Kenneth M. Hoyt, Simeon T. Lake III, Melinda Harmon, John D. Rainey, Samuel B. Kent, Ewing Werlein Jr., Lee H. Rosenthal, Janis Graham Jack, Vanessa Gilmore, Nancy F. Atlas; Clerk's Office, Houston 77208. **Eastern:** Richard A. Schell, CJ; William Wayne Justice, Howell Cobb, Paul N. Brown, John Hannah Jr., David Folsom, Thad Heartfield; Clerk's Office, Tyler 75702. **Western:** Harry Lee Hudspeth, CJ; David Briones, Hipolito F. Garcia, Edward C. Prado, Fred Biery, Orlando L. Garcia,

James R. Nowlin, Sam Sparks, Walter S. Smith Jr., W. Royal Furgeson; Clerk's Office, San Antonio 78206.

Utah — David K. Winder, CJ; J. Thomas Greene, David Sam, Dee Benson, Tena Campbell; Clerk's Office, Salt Lake City 84101.

Vermont — J. Garvan Murtha, CJ; William K. Sessions III; Clerk's Office, Burlington 05402.

Virginia — Eastern: James C. Cacheris, CJ; Robert G. Doumar, Claude M. Hilton, James R. Spencer, Thomas S. Ellis III, Rebecca Beach Smith, Henry Coke Morgan Jr., Robert E. Payne, Raymond A. Jackson, Leonie M. Brinkema; Clerk's Office, Alexandria 22320. **Western:** Jackson L. Kiser, CJ; James C. Turk, James H. Michael Jr., Samuel G. Wilson; Clerk's Office, Roanoke 24006.

Washington — Eastern: W. Fremming Nielsen, CJ; Alan A. McDonald, Fred Van Sickle, Robert H. Whaley; Clerk's Office, Spokane 99210. **Western:** Carolyn R. Dimmick, CJ; Barbara J. Rothstein, John C. Coughenour, Robert J. Bryan, William L. Dwyer, Thomas Zilly, Franklin D. Burgess; Clerk's Office, Seattle 98104.

West Virginia — Northern: Frederick P. Stamp Jr., CJ; Irene M. Keeley; Clerk's Office, Wheeling 26003. **Southern:** Charles H. Haden II, CJ; John T. Copenhaver Jr., Elizabeth V. Hallanan, David A. Faber, Joseph R. Goodwin; Clerk's Office, Charleston 25329.

Wisconsin — Eastern: Terence T. Evans, CJ; Thomas J. Curran, J. P. Stadtmueller, Rudolph T. Randa, Aaron E. Goodstein, Patricia J. Gorence; Clerk's Office, Milwaukee 53202. **Western:** Barbara B. Crabb, CJ; John C. Shabaz; Clerk's Office, Madison 53701.

Wyoming — Alan B. Johnson, CJ; Clarence A. Brimmer, William F. Downes; Clerk's Office, Cheyenne 82001.

U.S. Territorial District Courts

Guam — John S. Unpingco, CJ; Clerk's Office, Agana 96910.

Northern Mariana Islands — Alex R. Munson, CJ; Clerk's Office, Saipan MP 96950.

Puerto Rico — Carmen Consuelo Cerezo, CJ; Juan M. Perez-Gimenez, Hector M. Laffitte, Jose Antonio Fuste, Salvador Casellas, Daniel Dominguez; Clerk's Office, Hato Rex 00918.

Virgin Islands — Thomas K. Moore, CJ; Raymond L. Finch; Clerk's Office, St. Croix 00820.

U.S. Court of International Trade
New York, NY 10007 (Salaries, $133,600)

Chief Judge — Dominick L. DeCarlo.

Judges — Gregory W. Carmen, Jane A. Restani, Thomas J. Aquilino Jr., Nicholas Tsoucalas, R. Kenton Musgrave, Richard W. Goldberg, Donald C. Pogue, Evan J. Wallach.

U.S. Court of Federal Claims
Washington, DC 20005 (Salaries, $133,600)

Chief Judge — Loren A. Smith.

Judges — James F. Merow, John P. Wiese, Robert J. Yock, Lawrence S. Margolis, Christine Odell Cook Miller, Moody R. Tidwell 3d, Marian Blank Horn, Eric G. Bruggink, Bohdan A. Futey, Wilkes C. Robinson, Roger B. Andewelt, James T. Turner, Robert H. Hodges Jr., Diane Gilbert Weinstein.

U.S. Tax Court
Washington, DC 20217 (Salaries, $133,600)

Chief Judge — Lapsley W. Hamblen Jr.

Judges — Renato Beghe, Herbert L. Chabot, Mary Ann Cohen, John O. Colvin, Joel Gerber, Julien I. Jacobs, Carolyn Miller Parr, Robert P. Ruwe, James S. Halpern, Carolyn P. Chiechi, David Laro, Stephen Swift, Thomas Wells, Laurence J. Whalen, Lawrence A. Wright, Maurice B. Foley, Juan F. Vasquez.

U.S. Court of Veterans Appeals
Washington, D.C. 20004 (Salaries, $133,600)

Chief Judge — Frank Q. Nebeker.

Judges — Kenneth B. Kramer, John J. Farley 3d, Hart T. Mankin, Ronald M. Holdaway, Donald L. Ivers, Jonathan R. Steinberg.

Mayors of Selected U.S. Cities

The expiration date for the mayor's term of office appears next to each name.

D, Democrat; R, Republican; N-P, Non-Partisan; I, Independent

(data as of mid-1995)

City	Name	Term	City	Name	Term
Abilene, TX	Gary McCaleb, N-P	1996, May	Casper, WY	Ed Opella, N-P.	1996, Jan.
Akron, OH	D. L. Plusquellic, D	1996, Jan.	Cedar Rapids, IA	Larry Serbousek, N-P	1995, Dec.
Alameda, CA	Ralph J. Appezato, N-P	1996, Apr.	Champaign, IL	Dan McCollum, N-P	1999, May
Albany, GA	Paul Keenan, D	1996, Jan.	Chandler, AZ	Jay Tibshraeny, N-P	1996, Mar.
Albany, NY	Gerald D. Jennings, D	1997, Dec.	Charleston, SC	Joseph P. Riley Jr., D	1996, Jan.
Albuquerque, NM	Martin Chavez, D	1997, Nov.	Charleston, WV	G. Kemp Melton, D	1996, Apr.
Alexandria, LA	Edward Randolph Jr., D	1998, Nov.	Charlotte, NC	Richard Vinroot, R	1995, Dec.
Alexandria, VA	Patricia S. Ticer, D	1997, June	Charlottesville, VA	David Toscano, D	1996, June
Alhambra, CA	Talmage Burke, N-P	1996, Aug.	Chattanooga, TN	Gene Roberts, R	1997, Apr.
Allentown, PA	William Heydt, R	1997, Dec.	Chesapeake, VA	William Ward, N-P	1996, June
Amarillo, TX	Kel Seliger, N-P	1997, May	Chester, PA	Barbara Bohannan-Shepperd, D	1996, Dec.
Ames, IA	Larry R. Curtis, N-P	1997, Dec.	Cheyenne, WY	Leo Pando, N-P	1997, Jan.
Anaheim, CA	Tom Daly, N-P	1998, Nov.	Chicago, IL	Richard M. Daley, D	1999, Apr.
Anchorage, AK	Rick Mystrom, R	1997, July	Chicopee, MA	Joseph Chessey, D	1995, Dec.
Anderson, IN	J. Mark Lawler, D	1995, Dec.	Chino, CA	Eunice M. Ulloa, R	1996, Nov.
Anderson, SC	Darwin Wright, D	1998, June	Chula Vista, CA	Shirley Horton, I	1998, Nov.
Ann Arbor, MI	Ingrid B. Sheldon, R	1996, Nov.	Cicero, IL	Betty Loren-Maltese, R	1997, Apr.
Appleton, WI	Richard De Broux, N-P	1996, Apr.	Cincinnati, OH	Roxanne Qualls, D	1995, Nov.
Arcadia, CA	Dennis A. Lojeski, N-P	1996, Apr.	Clarksville, TN	Don Trotter, N-P	1999, Jan.
Arlington, MA	Donald R. Marquis, N-P	1995, Nov.	Clearwater, FL	Rita Garvey, N-P	1996, Apr.
Arlington, TX	Richard Greene, N-P	1997, May	Cleveland, OH	Michael White, D	1997, Dec.
Arlington Hts., IL	Arlene J. Mulder, N-P	1997, Apr.	Cleveland Hts., OH	Carol Edwards, N-P	1996, Jan.
Arvada, CO	Robert G. Frie, N-P	1995, Nov.	Clifton, NJ	James Anzaldi, R	1998, July
Asheville, NC	Russel Martin, N-P	1995, Dec.	Colorado Spgs., CO	Robert M. Isaac, N-P	1997, Apr.
Athens, GA	Gwenn O'Looney, D	1998, Dec.	Columbia, MO	Darwin Hindman, N-P	1998, Apr.
Atlanta, GA	Bill Campbell, D	1997, Dec.	Columbia, SC	Robert Coble, N-P	1998, June
Atlantic City, NJ	Jim Whelan, N-P	1998, July	Columbus, GA	Bobby Peters, D	1999, Jan.
Augusta, GA	Charles DeVaney, N-P.	1998, Jan.	Columbus, OH	Gregory Lashutka, R	1995, Dec.
Aurora, CO	Paul E. Tauer, N-P	1995, Nov.	Compton, CA	Omar Bradley, N-P.	1997, June
Aurora, IL	David L. Pierce, N-P	1997, Apr.	Concord, CA	Helen M. Allen, N-P	1995, Nov.
Austin, TX	Bruce Todd, N-P	1997, June	Coon Rapids, MN	William Thompson, N-P	1995, Dec.
Bakersfield, CA	Bob Price, N-P	1996, Dec.	Coral Gables, FL	Raul Valdes-Sauli, N-P.	1996, Mar.
Baldwin Park, CA	Fidel A. Vargas, N-P	1996, Apr.	Coral Springs, FL	John Sommerer, N-P	1996, Mar.
Baltimore, MD	Kurt Schmoke, D	1995, Dec.	Corona, CA	Jeff Bennett, N-P	1995, Nov.
Baton Rouge, LA	Tom E. McHugh, D	1996, Dec.	Corpus Christi, TX.	Mary Rhodes, N-P	1997, Apr.
Battle Creek, MI	John Gallagher, N-P	1995, Nov.	Costa Mesa, CA	Joe Erickson, N-P.	1996, Dec.
Bayonne, NJ	Leonard P. Kiczek, N-P	1998, June	Council Bluffs, IA	Tom Hanafan, N-P	1997, Dec.
Baytown, TX	Pete C. Alfaro, N-P	1996, May	Covington, KY	Denny Bowman, D	1996, Jan.
Beaumont, TX	David W. Moore, N-P	1996, May	Cranston, RI	Michael Traficante, R	1998, Dec.
Belleville, IL	Roger C. Cook, I	1997, May	Cuyahoga Falls, OH	Donald L. Robart, R	1997, Dec.
Belleville, NJ	Jim Messina, D	1998, May	Dallas, TX	Ronald Kirk, N-P	1999, May
Bellevue, WA	Don Davidson, N-P	1995, Dec.	Daly City, CA	Madolyn Agrimonti, N-P	1995, Nov.
Bellingham, WA	Tim Douglas, N-P	1995, Nov.	Danbury, CT	Gene Eriquez, D	1995, Nov.
Bellflower, CA	Randy Boomgaars, N-P	1996, Apr.	Danville, VA	F. S. Anderson Jr., N-P.	1996, July
Berkeley, CA	Shirley Dean, N-P	1998, Nov.	Davenport, IA	Patrick J. Gibbs, R	1995, Dec.
Bethlehem, PA	Kenneth Smith, R	1997, Dec.	Davis, CA	Dave Rosenberg, N-P.	1996, July
Beverly Hills, CA	Allan Alexander, N-P	1996, Apr.	Dayton, OH	Michael R. Turner, N-P.	1998, Jan.
Billings, MT	Richard L. Larsen, N-P	1995, Dec.	Daytona Beach, FL.	Paul A. Carpenella, N-P	1995, Nov.
Biloxi, MS	A. J. Holloway, R	1997, July	Dearborn , MI	Michael Guido, N-P	1998, Jan.
Binghamton, NY	Richard Bucci, R	1997, Dec.	Dearborn Hts., MI	Ruth A. Canfield, N-P	1997, Dec.
Birmingham, AL	Richard Arrington Jr., D	1995, Oct.	Decatur, IL	Terry M. Howley, N-P	1999, May
Bismarck, ND	Bill Sorensen, R	1998, June	Delray Beach, FL	Thomas E. Lynch, N-P	1996, Mar.
Bloomfield, NJ	James P. Norton, R	1995, Dec.	Denton, TX	Bob Castleberry, N-P	1996, May
Bloomington, IL	Jesse Smart, R	1997, May	Denver, CO	Wellington Webb, N-P	1997, May
Bloomington, IN	Tomilea Allison, D	1996, Jan.	Des Moines, IA	John Dorrian, D	1995, Dec.
Bloomington, MN	Neil Peterson, N-P	1995, Dec.	Des Plaines, IL	Ted Sherwood, N-P	1997, Apr.
Boca Raton, FL	Carol G. Hanson, N-P	1997, Apr.	Detroit, MI	Dennis W. Archer, D	1997, Dec.
Boise, ID	H. Brent Coles, N-P	1997, Dec.	Dothan, AL	Alfred Saliba, N-P.	1997, July
Bossier City, LA	George Dement, N-P	1997, May	Downey, CA	Barbara Riley, N-P	1998, July
Boston, MA	Thomas M. Menino, D	1998, Jan.	Dubuque, IA	Terrance M. Duggan, N-P	1997, Dec.
Boulder, CO	Leslie L. Durgin, N-P	1995, Nov.	Duluth, MN	Gary L. Doty, N-P.	1996, Jan.
Bridgeport, CT	Joseph Ganim, D	1995, Dec.	Durham, NC	Sylvia S. Kerckhoff, N-P.	1995, Dec.
Bristol, CT	Frank N. Nicastro, D	1995, Nov.	East Hartford, CT	Robert DeCrescenzo, D	1995, Nov.
Brockton, MA	Winthrop Farwell Jr., D	1996, Jan.	East Lansing, MI	Robert J. Phipps, N-P	1995, Nov.
Broken Arrow, OK	Jim Reynolds, N-P	1999, Apr.	East Orange, NJ	Cardell Cooper, D	1996, Dec.
Brooklyn Park, MN	Grace Arborgast	1998, Dec.	Edison, NJ	George Spadoro, D	1997, Dec.
Brownsville, TX	Henry Gonzalez, N-P	1995, Nov.	Edmond, OK.	Robert Rudkin, N-P	1997, Apr.
Bryan, TX	Lonnie Stabler, N-P	1998, May	El Cajon, CA	Joan Shoemaker, N-P	1998, July
Buena Park, CA	Don Griffin, N-P.	1996, Nov.	Elgin, IL	Kevin Kelly, N-P	1999, Apr.
Buffalo, NY	Anthony Masiello, D	1997, Nov.	Elizabeth, NJ	J. C. Bollwage, D	1996, Dec.
Burbank, CA	Dave Golonski, N-P	1996, May	Elkhart, IN	James Perron, D	1996, Jan.
Burlington, VT	Peter Clavelle, Prog. Coalition	1997, Apr.	El Monte, CA	Patricia Wallach, D	1996, Apr.
Calumet City, IL	Gerome P. Genova, I	1997, Apr.	El Paso, TX	Larry Francis, N-P	1995, June
Camarillo, CA	Michael D. Morgan, N-P.	1998, Dec.	Elyria, OH	Michael Keys, D	1995, Dec.
Cambridge, MA	Kenneth Reeves, N-P	1995, Dec.	Enfield, CT	Ann M. Petronella, N-P.	1995, Nov.
Camden, NJ	Arnold Webster, D	1996, Dec.	Enid, OK	Mike Cooper, N-P	1997, May
Canton, OH	Richard Watkins, R	1995, Nov.	Erie, PA	Joyce Savocchio, D	1997, Dec.
Cape Coral, FL	Roger G. Butler, N-P	1996, Nov.	Escondido, CA	Sid Hollins, N-P	1996, June
Carlsbad, CA	Claude Lewis, N-P.	1998, Dec.	Euclid, OH	David Lynch, R.	1996, Jan.
Carson, CA	Michael Mitoma, N-P	1997, Mar.	Eugene, OR	Ruth Bascom, N-P	1997, Jan.

City	Name	Term	City	Name	Term
Evanston, IL	Lorraine Morton, N-P	1997, Apr.	Kokomo, IN	Robert Sargent, D	1995, Dec.
Evansville, IN.	Frank McDonald, D	1995, Dec.	LaCrosse, WI	Patrick Zielke, N-P	1997, Apr.
Everett, WA.	Edward D. Hansen, N-P.	1997, Dec.	Lafayette, IN.	James Riehle, D.	1995, Dec.
Fairbanks, AK	James C. Hayes	1998, Oct.	Lafayette, LA	Kenneth Bowen, D.	1996, June
Fairfield, CA	Chuck Hamond, N-P	1997, Jan.	La Habra, CA	Juan Garcia, N-P	1994, Dec.
Fairfield, CT.	Paul A. Audley, R	1995, Nov.	Lake Charles, LA	Willie L. Mount, D	1997, June
Fall River, MA	John Mitchell, D	1996, Jan.	Lakeland, FL	Ralph L. Fletcher	1996, Dec.
Fargo, ND	Bruce Furness, N-P	1998, May	Lakewood, CA	Wayne Piercy, N-P	1997, Mar.
Farmington Hills, MI	Joanne Smith, N-P	1995, Nov.	Lakewood, CO	Linda Morton, N-P	1995, Nov.
Fayetteville, NC	J. L. Dawkins, N-P.	1995, Nov.	Lakewood, OH	David Harbarger, R.	1995, Dec.
Fitchburg, MA	Jeffrey Bean, D	1997, Jan.	La Mesa, CA	Arthur Madrid, N-P	1998, Nov.
Flagstaff, AZ	Christopher Bavasi, N-P.	1996, Apr.	La Mirada, CA	C. David Peters, N-P	1996, Apr.
Flint, MI.	Woodrow Stanley, D	1995, Nov.	Lancaster, CA.	George Runner, N-P	1996, Apr.
Florissant, MO.	James J. Eagan, N-P.	1999, Apr.	Lancaster, PA.	Janice Stork, D.	1997, Dec.
Fontano, CA	David Eshleman, D	1998, Nov.	Lansing, MI	David Hollister, N-P	1997, Dec.
Ft. Collins, CO.	Ann Azari, N-P.	1997, Apr.	Laredo, TX.	Saul N. Ramirez Jr., N-P.	1998, May
Ft. Lauderdale, FL.	Jim Naugle, N-P	1997, Mar.	Largo, FL.	Thomas Feaster, N-P	1997, Apr.
Ft. Smith, AR.	Ray Baker, N-P	1998, Dec.	Las Cruces, NM	Ruben A. Smith, D	1995, Nov.
Ft. Wayne, IN	Paul Helmke, R	1996, Jan.	Las Vegas, NV	Jan Laverty Jones, D	1995, June
Ft. Worth, TX.	Kay Granger, N-P	1997, May	Lauderhill, FL	Ilene Lieberman, D.	1996, Mar.
Fountain Valley, CA	George Scott, N-P.	1996, Dec.	Lawrence, KS.	Bob Moody, N-P.	1996, Apr.
Fremont, CA	Gus Morrison, N-P.	1996, Nov.	Lawrence, MA	Mary Claire Kennedy,	
Fresno, CA	Jim Patterson, N-P	1997, Mar.		N-P	1997, Dec.
Fullerton, CA.	Julie Sa, N-P.	1995, Dec.	Lawton, OK	John T. Marley, N-P	1996, Apr.
Gadsden, AL.	Steve Means, N-P.	1998, Oct.	Lexington, KY.	Pam Miller, N-P	1998, Dec.
Gainesville, FL.	James Painter, N-P.	1996, May	Lima, OH	David Berger, N-P	1997, Dec.
Galveston, TX	Barbara K. Crews, N-P	1996, May	Lincoln, NE.	Mike Johanns, R	1999, May
Gardena, CA.	Donald L. Dear, N-P	1996, Apr.	Little Rock, AR	Jim Dailey, N-P	1999, Jan.
Garden Grove, CA.	Bruce Broadwater, N-P	1996, Dec.	Livermore, CA	Cathie Brown, N-P	1995, Nov.
Garland, TX.	James B. Ratliff, N-P	1996, May	Livonia, MI	Robert Bennett, N-P	1996, Jan.
Gary, IN	Thomas Barnes, D	1996, Jan.	Lodi, CA.	Stephen J. Mann, N-P	1996, Dec.
Gastonia, NC.	James B. Garland, N-P	1997, Nov.	Long Beach, CA	Beverly O'Neill, N-P	1998, July
Glendale, AZ	Elaine Scruggs, N-P	1996, Apr.	Longmont,CO	Leona Stoecker, N-P	1995, Nov.
Glendale, CA.	Richard M. Reyes, N-P	1997, Apr.	Longview, TX	I. J. Patterson Jr., N-P.	1996, May
Grand Forks, ND	Michael Polovitz, D	1996, June	Lorain, OH	Alex Olejko, D	1995, Dec.
Grand Prairie, TX.	Charles V. England, N-P	1996, May	Los Angeles, CA.	Richard Riordan, N-P	1997, June
Grand Rapids, MI.	John Logie, N-P	1996, Jan.	Louisville, KY	Jerry Abramson, D	1997, Dec.
Greeley, CO	William Morton, N-P.	1995, Nov.	Lowell, MA	Richard Howe, N-P	1996, Jan.
Green Bay, WI.	Paul F. Jadin, N-P	1999, Apr.	Lubbock, TX.	David Langston, N-P	1996, May
Greenville, SC	William Workman III, R.	1995, Nov.	Lynchburg, VA	James Whitaker, N-P	1996, July
Greensboro, NC	Carolyn Allen, N-P.	1995, Dec.	Lynn, MA	Patrick McManus, D	1995, Dec.
Greenwich, CT.	John Margenot, R	1995, Dec.	Lynwood, CA	Paul Richards, III, N-P	1995, Dec.
Groton, CT	Dolores Hauber, N-P	1995, Nov.	Macon, GA	David L. Carter, R.	1995, Nov.
Gulfport, MS	Ken Combs, R	1997, June	Madison, WI	Paul Soglin, D	1999, Apr.
Hamden, CT	Lillian Clayman, D	1995, Nov.	Malden, MA	Edwin C. Lucey, D	1995, Dec.
Hamilton, OH.	Charles R. Furmon, N-P.	1995, Dec.	Manchester, CT	Stephen Cassano, N-P	1995, Nov.
Hammond, IN	Duane W. Dadelow, R	1996, Jan.	Manchester, NH.	Ray Wieczorek, R.	1996, Jan.
Hampton, VA.	James L. Eason, N-P.	1996, June	Mansfield, OH.	Lydia J. Reid, D	1995, Nov.
Harrisburg, PA.	Stephen Reed, D.	1997, Dec.	Marietta, GA	Ansley L. Meaders, D	1997, Dec.
Hartford, CT	Mike Peters, N-P.	1995, Dec.	McAllen, TX	Othal Brand, R	1997, May
Haverhill, MA.	James Rurak, D	1995, Dec.	Medford, MA.	Michael McGlynn, D	1996, Jan.
Hawthorne, CA	Larry Guidi, N-P	1995, Nov.	Medford, OR.	Jerry Lausman, N-P	1996, Dec.
Hayward, CA.	Roberta Cooper, N-P.	1998, Apr.	Melbourne, FL	Joseph F. Mullins, N-P.	1996, Nov.
Henderson, NV	Robert Groesbeck, N-P	1997, June	Memphis, TN	W. W. Herenton, D	1995, Dec.
Hesperia, CA.	Diana J. Nourse	1998, Dec.	Mentor, OH	James F. Struna, N-P.	1995, Dec.
Hialeah, FL	Raul Martinez, R	1997, Nov.	Merced, CA	Richard Bernasconi, N-P.	1995, Nov.
High Point, NC.	Rebecca Smothers, N-P	1995, Dec.	Meriden, CT.	Joseph Marinan Jr., N-P.	1995, Dec.
Hollywood, FL.	Mara Giulianti, N-P.	1996, Mar.	Meridian, MS	John Robert Smith, R	1997, June
Holyoke, MA	William Hamilton, R.	1995, Dec.	Mesa, AZ	Willie Wong, N-P	1996, June
Honolulu, HI	Jeremy Harris, N-P	1996, Dec.	Mesquite, TX	Cathye Ray, N-P	1997, May
Houston, TX	Bob Lanier, N-P	1995, Dec.	Miami, FL.	Steve Clark, N-P	1997, Nov.
Huntington, WV	Jean Dean, R	1997, June	Miami Beach, FL.	Seymour Gelber, D.	1995, Nov.
Huntington Beach,			Midland, TX	Robert E. Burns, N-P	1996, June
CA	Victor Leipzig	1996, Dec.	Midwest City, OK	Eddie O. Reed, N-P	1998, Apr.
Huntington Park, CA	Tom Jackson, N-P.	1996, Feb.	Milford, CT	Frederick Lisman, R	1995, Nov.
Huntsville, AL	Steve Hettinger, N-P	1996, Oct.	Milpitas, CA	Peter McHugh, N-P	1996, Nov.
Idaho Falls, ID	Linda Milam, N-P.	1998, Jan.	Milwaukee, WI	John Norquist, D	1996, Apr.
Independence, MO	Ron Stewart, N-P	1998, Apr.	Minneapolis, MN	Sharon Sayles Belton, D.	1997, Dec.
Indianapolis, IN1994	Steve Goldsmith, R	1995, Dec.	Minnetonka, MN	Karen J. Anderson, N-P	1995, Dec.
Inglewood, CA.	Edward Vincent, D.	1999, Jan.	Mobile, AL	Michael Dow, R, I.	1997, Oct.
Iowa City, IA	Susan M. Horowitz, N-P.	1996, Jan.	Modesto, CA	Richard Lang, N-P	1995, Nov.
Irvine, CA	Mike Ward, N-P.	1996, Dec.	Monroe, LA	Robert Powell, D	1996, July
Irving, TX	Morris Parrish, N-P	1997, May	Montclair, NJ	James Bishop, R	1996, July
Irvington, NJ	Sara A. Bost, D	1998, July	Montebello, CA.	Art Payan, D	1995, Nov.
Jackson, MS	Kane Ditto, D	1997, July	Monterey Park, CA.	Rita Valenzula, N-P	1996, Mar.
Jacksonville, FL.	Ed Austin, D	1995, July	Montgomery, AL	Emory Folmar, R	1995, Nov.
Janesville, WI	Steven Sheiffer, N-P	1996, Apr.	Moreno Valley, CA	Greg G. Lefler, N-P	1996, Dec.
Jersey City, NJ	Bret Schundler, R	1997, May	Mt. Prospect, IL	Gerald "Skip" Farley, N-P	1997, May
Johnson City, TN	Mickii Carter, N-P	1996, May	Mt. Vernon, NY.	Ronald Blackwood, D	1995, Nov.
Joliet, IL	Arthur Schultz, N-P	1999, May	Mountain View, CA	Patricia Figueroa, N-P	1996, Jan.
Kalamazoo, MI	Edward Annen, N-P	1995, Nov.	Muncie, IN	David M. Dominick, R	1995, Dec.
Kansas City, KS.	Carol Marinovich, N-P	1999, Apr.	Muskogee, OK	Kathy Hewitt, N-P.	1996, May
Kansas City, MO	Emanuel Cleaver II, D	1999, Apr.	Napa, CA.	Ed Solomon, R.	1996, July
Kenner, LA	Aaron F. Broussard, D.	1998, July	Naperville, IL	George Pradel, N-P	1999, Apr.
Kenosha, WI	John Antaramian, D.	1996, Apr.	Nashua, NH	Rob Wagner, D.	1996, Jan.
Kettering, OH	Richard Hartmann, R	1997, Dec.	Nashville, TN	Philip Bredesen, D	1995,Sept.
Killeen, TX.	Raul Villaronga, N-P	1996, May	National City, CA	George H. Waters, R	1998, Nov.
Knoxville, TN	Victor Ashe, R.	1995, Dec.	Newark, NJ	Sharpe James, D.	1998, July

City	Name	Term	City	Name	Term
New Bedford, MA..	Rosemary Tierney, D..	1996, Jan.	Rockville, MD.....	James F. Coyle, N-P.....	1995, Nov.
New Britain, CT...	Linda Blogoslawski, R	1995, Nov.	Rome, NY.....	Joseph Griffo, R.....	1995, Dec.
New Haven, CT...	John DeStafano, D.....	1995, Dec.	Rosemead, CA...	Joe Vasquez, N-P.....	1997, Mar.
New Orleans, LA..	Marc Morial, D.....	1998, May	Roseville, MI.....	Gerald K. Alsip, N-P.....	1997, Nov.
Newport, RI.....	David S. Roderick, N-P.....	1996, Jan.	Roswell, NM.....	Thomas Jennings, N-P.....	1998, Mar.
Newport Beach, CA	John Hedges, N-P.....	1995, Nov.	Royal Oak, MI.....	Dennis G. Cowan, N-P.....	1995, Dec.
Newport News, VA.	Barry E. Duval, N-P.....	1996, Nov.	Sacramento, CA...	Joseph Serna Jr., N-P.....	1996, June
New Rochelle, NY..	Timothy Idoni, D.....	1996, Jan.	Saginaw, MI.....	Gary L. Loster, N-P.....	1995, Nov.
Newton, MA.....	Thomas Concannon, N-P..	1997, Dec.	St. Charles, MO...	Robert L. Moeller, N-P.....	1999, Apr.
New York, NY...	Rudolph Giuliani, R.....	1997, Dec.	St. Clair Shores, MI.	William Callahan, N-P.....	1995, Nov.
Niagara Falls, NY..	Jacob A. Palillo, R.....	1996, Jan.	St. Cloud, MN.....	Charles Winkleman, N-P..	1997, Nov.
Norfolk, VA.....	Paul D. Fraim, N-P.....	1996, July	St. Joseph, MO....	Larry Stobbs, N-P.....	1998, Mar.
Norman, OK.....	William Nation, N-P.....	1998, Mar.	St. Louis, MO....	Freeman R. Bosley Jr., D	1997, Apr.
North Charleston, SC	R. Keith Summey, R.....	1999, July	St. Louis Park, MN	Lyle Hanks, N-P.....	1995, Dec.
N. Little Rock, AR.	Patrick Hayes, D.....	1996, Dec.	St. Paul, MN.....	Norm Coleman, N-P.....	1997, Dec.
Norwalk, CA....	Judith Brennan, N-P.....	1996, Apr.	St. Petersburg, FL..	David Fischer, N-P.....	1997, Mar.
Norwalk, CT.....	Frank Esposito, R.....	1995, Nov.	Salem, OR.....	Roger Gertenrich, N-P.....	1996, Dec.
Novato, CA.....	Bernard H. Meyers, N-P	1995, Nov.	Salinas, CA.....	Alan Styles, N-P.....	1997, June
Oakland, CA....	Elihu Mason Harris, N-P..	1999, Jan.	Salt Lake City, UT..	Deedee Corradini, D.....	1995, Dec.
Oak Park, IL.....	Lawrence Christmas, N-P	1997, Apr.	San Angelo, TX...	Dick Funk, N-P.....	1997, May
Oceanside, CA...	Dick Lyon, N-P.....	1996, Dec.	San Antonio, TX...	William Thornton, N-P.....	1997, May
Odessa, TX.....	Lorraine Perryman, N-P...	1996, Apr.	San Bernardino, CA	Tom Minor, R.....	1997, June
Ogden, UT.....	Glenn Mecham, N-P.....	1995, Dec.	San Diego, CA...	Susan Golding, R.....	1996, Dec.
Oklahoma City, OK	Ronald Norick, N-P.....	1998, Apr.	Sandy, UT.....	Thomas M. Dolan, N-P...	1998, Jan.
Omaha, NE.....	Hal Daub, R.....	1997, June	San Francisco, CA.	Frank Jordan, D	1996, Jan.
Ontario, CA.....	Gus James Skropos, N-P..	1998, Nov.	San Jose, CA....	Susan Hammer.....	1999, Jan.
Orange, CA.....	Joanne Coontz, N-P.....	1996, Nov.	San Leandro, CA..	Ellen M. Corbett, N-P.....	1998, May
Orlando, FL.....	Glenda E. Hood, N-P..	1996, Oct.	San Mateo, CA....	Claire Mack, N-P.....	1995, Dec.
Oshkosh, WI....	Richard A. Wollangk, N-P..	1996, Apr.	San Rafael, CA....	Albert J. Boro, N-P.....	1995, Nov.
Overland Park, KS.	Ed Eilert, R.....	1997, Apr.	Santa Ana, CA....	Miguel Pulido, N-P.....	1996, Nov.
Owensboro, KY...	David C. Adkisson, N-P..	1995, Dec.	Santa Barbara, CA	Harriet Miller, N-P.....	1995, Dec.
Oxnard, CA.....	Manuel M. Lopez, N-P....	1996, Nov.	Santa Clara, CA..	Judy Nadler, N-P.....	1998, Nov.
Palm Springs, CA.	Lloyd Maryanov, N-P.....	1996, Apr.	Santa Clarita, CA..	JoAnne Darcy, N-P.....	1995 Dec.
Palo Alto, CA.....	Joe Simitian, N-P.....	1995, Dec.	Santa Cruz, CA...	Katherine Beiers, N-P.....	1995, Nov.
Parma, OH.....	Gerald M. Boldt, D.....	1996, Jan.	Santa Fe, NM.....	Debbie Jaramillo, N-P.....	1998, Mar.
Pasadena, CA...	William M. Paparian, N-P.	1997, May	Santa Maria, CA...	Roger Bunch, N-P.....	1996, Nov.
Pasadena, TX...	Johnny Isbell, N-P.....	1997, June	Santa Monica, CA.	Paul Rosenstein, N-P.....	1996, Nov.
Passaic, NJ.....	Margie Semler, N-P.....	1997, June	Santa Rosa, CA...	James Pedgrift, N-P.....	1996, Nov.
Paterson, NJ.....	William Pascrell, D.....	1998, July	Sarasota, FL.....	David Merrill, N-P.....	1996, Mar.
Pawtucket, RI....	Robert Metivier, D.....	1995, Dec.	Savannah, GA.....	Susan Weiner, N-P.....	1995, Dec.
Peabody, MA.....	Peter Torigian, D.....	1997, Jan.	Schaumburg, IL...	Al Larson, N-P.....	1999, Apr.
Pembroke Pines, FL	Alex G. Fekete, N-P.....	1996, Mar.	Schenectady, NY..	Frank Duci, R.....	1995, Dec.
Pensacola, FL....	John Fogg, N-P.....	1997, June	Scottsdale, AZ....	Herbert Drinkwater, R.....	1996, Apr.
Peoria, IL.....	James A. Maloof, N-P.....	1997, May	Scranton, PA.....	James Connors, R.....	1997, Dec.
Philadelphia, PA..	Edward Rendell, D.....	1996, Jan.	Seattle, WA.....	Norman Rice, D.....	1997, Dec.
Phoenix, AZ.....	Skip Rimza, N-P.....	1996, Jan.	Sheboygan, WI....	Richard Schneider, N-P..	1997, Apr.
Pico Rivera, CA...	Garth Gardner, N-P.....	1996, Apr.	Shreveport, LA...	Robert W. Williams, R.....	1998, Nov.
Pine Bluff, AR....	Jerry Taylor, I.....	1996, Dec.	Simi Valley, CA....	Greg Stratton, N-P.....	1996, Nov.
Pittsburgh, PA....	Tom Murphy, D.....	1997, Dec.	Sioux City, IA.....	Robert Scott, N-P.....	1997, Dec.
Pittsfield, MA.....	Edward Reilly, N-P	1995, Dec.	Sioux Falls, SD...	Gary Hanson, N-P.....	1999, Fall
Plainfield, NJ....	Mark Fury, N-P.....	1997, Dec.	Skokie, IL.....	Jacqueline B. Gorell, N-P.	1997, Apr.
Plano, TX.....	James N. Muns, N-P.....	1996, May	Somerville, MA....	Michael Capuano, D.....	1996, Jan.
Plantation, FL....	Frank Veltri, D.....	1999, Mar.	South Bend, IN....	Joseph Kernan, D.....	1995, Dec.
Pocatello, ID.....	Peter Angstadt, N-P.....	1997, Dec.	South Gate, CA...	Albert Robles, N-P.....	1996, Apr.
Pomona, CA.....	Eddie Cortez, N-P.....	1996, Apr.	Southfield, MI....	Donald F. Fracassi, R....	1997, Dec.
Pompano Beach, FL	Emma Lou Olson, N-P..	1996, Mar.	Sparks, NV.....	Bruce Breslow, N-P.....	1999, June
Pontiac, MI.....	Charles Harrison Jr., N-P.	1997, Dec.	Spartanburg, SC..	James E. Talley, N-P.....	1998, Jan.
Port Arthur, TX...	Robert T. Morgan, D.....	1998, May	Spokane, WA.....	Jack Geraghty, N-P.....	1997, Dec.
Portland, ME.....	Philip John Dawson, N-P.	1996, June	Springfield, IL.....	Karen Hasara, N-P.....	1999, Apr.
Portland, OR.....	Vera Katz, D.....	1996, Dec.	Springfield, MA...	Robert Markel, D.....	1996, Jan.
Portsmouth, VA...	Gloria O. Webb, N-P.....	1996, June	Springfield, MO...	Leland L. Gannaway, N-P.	1997, Apr.
Poughkeepsie, NY.	Sheila Newman, N-P.....	1995, Dec.	Springfield, OH...	Dale A. Henry, N-P.....	1995, Dec.
Providence, RI....	Vincent Cianci Jr., R, I....	1998, Dec.	Stamford, CT.....	Stanley Esposito, R.....	1995, Nov.
Provo, UT.....	George O. Stewart, N-P...	1997, Dec.	Sterling Hts., MI...	Richard J. Notte, N-P.....	1995, Nov.
Quincy, IL.....	Charles W. Scholz, D.....	1997, Apr.	Stockton, CA.....	Joan Darrah, N-P.....	1996, Dec.
Quincy, MA.....	James Sheets, D.....	1996, Jan.	Stratford, CT.....	Rudolf Weiss, N-P.....	1995, Nov.
Racine, WI.....	James M. Smith, N-P.....	1999, Apr.	Sunnyvale, CA...	Barbara Waldman, N-P...	1995, Nov.
Raleigh, NC.....	Tom Fetzer, N-P.....	1995, Dec.	Suffolk, VA.....	S. Chris Jones, N-P.....	1998, July
Rancho Cucamanga,			Sunrise, FL.....	Steve Effman, N-P.....	1997, Mar.
CA.....	William Alexander.....	1996, Dec.	Syracuse, NY....	Roy A. Bernardi, R.....	1997, Dec.
Rapid City, SD....	Edward McLaughlin, N-P.	1997, May	Tacoma, WA.....	Harold G. Moss, N-P.....	1995, Dec.
Reading, PA.....	Warren Haggerty Jr., D...	1995, Dec.	Tallahassee, FL...	Scott Maddox, N-P.....	1996, Mar.
Redding, CA.....	Robert Anderson, N-P....	1996, Apr.	Tampa, FL.....	Dick Greco, D.....	1999, Mar.
Redondo Beach, CA	Brad Parton, N-P.....	1997, May	Taunton, MA.....	Robert Nunes, D.....	1995, Dec.
Redwood City, CA.	Danaiela Gastarini, N-P..	1995, Nov.	Taylor, MI.....	Cameron Priebe, D.....	1997, Nov.
Reno, NV.....	Jeff Griffin, N-P.....	1999, June	Tempe, AZ.....	Neil Giuliano, N-P.....	1996, July
Rialto, CA.....	John Longville, N-P.....	1996, Nov.	Temple, TX.....	J. W. Perry, N-P.....	1996, May
Richardson, TX...	Gary Slagel, N-P.....	1997, May	Terre Haute, IN....	Pete Chalos, D.....	1995, Dec.
Richmond, CA....	Rosemary Corbin, D.....	1997, Nov.	Thornton, CO.....	Margaret Carpenter, N-P..	1995, Nov.
Richmond, VA....	Leonidas B. Young, N-P.	1998, July	Thousand Oaks, CA	Jaime Zukowski, N-P.....	1996, Nov.
Riverside, CA....	Ronald O. Loveridge, N-P.	1997, Dec.	Titusville, FL.....	Tom Mariani, N-P.....	1996, Nov.
Roanoke, VA.....	David Bowers, D.....	1996, June	Toledo, OH.....	Carty Finkbeiner, N-P.....	1998, Jan.
Rochester, MN....	Chuck Hazama, N-P.....	1995, Dec.	Topeka, KS.....	Harry Felker, R.....	1997, Apr.
Rochester, NY....	Bill Johnson, D.....	1997, Dec.	Torrance, CA.....	Dee Hardison, N-P.....	1998, Mar.
Rochester Hills, MI.	Billie Ireland, R.....	1995, Nov.	Trenton, NJ.....	Douglas Palmer, N-P.....	1998, July
Rock Hill, SC.....	Elizabeth D. Rhea, N-P..	1997, Dec.	Troy, MI.....	Jeanne M. Stine, N-P.....	1988, Nov.
Rock Island, IL....	Mark W. Schwiebert, N-P..	1997, Apr.	Troy, NY.....	Eugene Eaton, R.....	1996, Jan.
Rockford, IL.....	Charles Box, D.....	1997, Apr.	Tucson, AZ.....	George Miller, D.....	1995, Dec.

City	Name	Term	City	Name	Term
Tulsa, OK	M. Susan Savage, D	1998, Mar.	W. Covina, CA	Steve Herfert, N-P	1996, Apr.
Tuscaloosa, AL . . .	Alvin DuPont, D.	1997, Oct.	W. Hartford, CT . . .	Sandy Klebanoff, D	1995, Nov.
Tyler, TX.	Smith Reynolds Jr., N-P. .	1996, May	W. Haven, CT.	H. Richard Borer Jr., D . . .	1995, Dec.
Union City, NJ	Bruce D. Walter, D	1996, May	Westland, MI	Robert Thomas, D	1997, Dec.
Upland, CA	Robert R. Nolan, N-P. . . .	1996, Nov.	Westminster, CA. .	Charles V. Smith, N-P. . . .	1996, Nov.
Utica, NY.	Louis Lapolla, R	1995, Dec.	Westminster, CO . .	Nancy Heil, N-P	1995, Nov.
Vacaville, CA.	David A. Fleming, N-P . . .	1998, Nov.	W. Palm Beach, FL.	Nancy M. Graham, N-P. . .	1998, Mar.
Vallejo, CA	Anthony Intintoli Jr., N-P .	1995, Dec.	Wheaton, IL	James C. Carr, N-P	1995, Nov.
Vancouver, WA . . .	Bruce E. Hagensen, N-P .	1995, Dec.	White Plains, NY. . .	S. J. Schulman, D	1997, Dec.
Vineland, NJ	Joseph Romano, I	1996, June	Whittier, CA	Michael Sullens, N-P	1996, Apr.
Virginia Beach, VA.	Meyera E. Oberndorf, I . .	1996, June	Wichita, KS	Bob Knight, N-P	1999, Apr.
Visalia, CA	Basil A. Perch, N-P	1995, Nov.	Wichita Falls, TX. . .	Michael Lam, N-P.	1996, May
Vista, CA	Gloria McClellan, R	1998, Dec.	Wilkes-Barre, PA . .	Lee Namey, D	1996, Jan.
Waco, TX	Robert Sheehy Jr., N-P . .	1996, May	Wilmington, DE. . . .	Jim Sills, D.	1996, Dec.
Walnut Creek, CA .	Ed Dimmick, N-P.	1995, Nov.	Wilmington, NC. . . .	Don Betz, N-P	1995, Dec.
Waltham, MA.	William Stanley, D	1996, Jan.	Winston-Salem, NC.	Martha S. Wood, N-P	1997, Dec.
Warren, MI	Ronald Bonkowski, N-P . .	1995, Nov.	Woodbridge, NJ . . .	James McGreevey, D	1996, Jan.
Warren, OH.	Daniel Sferra, D	1996, Jan.	Woonsocket, RI . . .	Francis Lanctot, N-P.	1995, Dec.
Warwick, RI.	Lincoln D. Chafee, R	1996, Dec.	Worcester, MA	Raymond Mariano, N-P . . .	1996, Jan.
Washington, DC . .	Marion Barry, D	1999, Jan.	Wyandotte, MI	James R. DeSana, D	1997, Apr.
Waterbury, CT. . . .	Edward D. Bergin, D	1995, Nov.	Wyoming, MI	Jack Magnuson, N-P	1995, Nov.
Waterloo, IA	John Rooff III, R	1995, Dec.	Yakima, WA	Pat Berndt, N-P	1996, Jan.
Waukegan, IL	William F. Durkin, D.	1997, Apr.	Yonkers, NY.	Terence Zaleski, D	1995, Dec.
Waukesha, WI	Carol Opel, N-P.	1998, Apr.	York, PA	C. Robertson D	1997, Dec.
Wauwatosa, WI . . .	Maricolette Walsh, N-P . .	1996, Apr.	Youngstown, OH. . .	Patrick Ungaro, D.	1997, Dec.
W. Allis, WI	John Turck, N-P	1996, Apr.	Yuma, AZ.	Marilyn R. Young, N-P . . .	1997, Dec.

Governors of States and Puerto Rico

(as of mid-1995)

State	Capital, Zip Code	Governor	Party	Term years	Term expires	Annual salary[1]
Alabama	Montgomery 36103	Fob James Jr.	Rep.	4	Jan. 1999	$87,643
Alaska.	Juneau 99811.	Tony Knowles	Dem.	4	Dec. 1998	81,648
Arizona	Phoenix 85007	Fife Symington	Rep.	4	Jan. 1999	75,000
Arkansas.	Little Rock 72201	Jim Guy Tucker	Dem.	4	Jan. 1999	60,000
California.	Sacramento 95814	Pete Wilson	Rep.	4	Jan. 1999	120,000
Colorado.	Denver 80203.	Roy Romer	Dem.	4	Jan. 1999	70,000
Connecticut. . . .	Hartford 06106	John G. Rowland	Rep.	4	Jan. 1999	78,000
Delaware.	Dover 19901.	Thomas R. Carper.	Dem.	4	Jan. 1997	95,000
Florida	Tallahassee 32399	Lawton Chiles	Dem.	4	Jan. 1999	104,817[2]
Georgia.	Atlanta 30334	Zell Miller	Dem.	4	Jan. 1999	91,092
Hawaii.	Honolulu 96813.	Ben Cayetano	Dem.	4	Dec. 1998	94,780
Idaho	Boise 83720	Phil Batt	Rep.	4	Jan. 1999	85,000
Illinois	Springfield 62706	Jim Edgar	Rep.	4	Jan. 1999	119,439
Indiana	Indianapolis 46204	Evan Bayh	Dem.	4	Jan. 1997	77,200
Iowa	Des Moines 50319	Terry E. Branstad	Rep.	4	Jan. 1999	76,700
Kansas	Topeka 66612.	Bill Graves	Rep.	4	Jan. 1999	80,340
Kentucky.	Frankfort 40601	Brereton C. Jones	Dem.	4	Dec. 1995	86,352
Louisiana	Baton Rouge 70804	Edwin W. Edwards	Dem.	4	May 1996	95,000[3]
Maine	Augusta 04333	Angus King Jr.	Ind.	4	Jan. 1999	69,992
Maryland.	Annapolis 21401	Parris N. Glendening	Dem.	4	Jan. 1999	120,000
Massachusetts .	Boston 02113	William F. Weld	Rep.	4	Jan. 1999	75,000
Michigan	Lansing 48909	John Engler	Rep.	4	Jan. 1999	112,025
Minnesota.	St. Paul 55155	Arne H. Carlson.	Rep.	4	Jan. 1999	114,506
Mississippi.	Jackson 39205	Kirk Fordice	Rep.	4	Jan. 1996	83,160[2]
Missouri	Jefferson City 65102	Mel Carnahan	Dem.	4	Jan. 1997	94,563
Montana	Helena 59620	Marc Racicot.	Rep.	4	Jan. 1997	59,310
Nebraska	Lincoln 68509.	Ben Nelson	Dem.	4	Jan. 1999	65,000
Nevada	Carson City 89710	Bob Miller	Dem.	4	Jan. 1999	90,000
New Hampshire. .	Concord 03301	Steve Merrill	Rep.	2	Jan. 1997	86,235
New Jersey. . . .	Trenton 08625	Christine Todd Whitman. . . .	Rep.	4	Jan. 1998	85,000
New Mexico. . . .	Santa Fe 87503	Gary Johnson	Rep.	4	Jan. 1999	90,000
New York	Albany 12224	George E. Pataki.	Rep.	4	Jan. 1999	130,000
North Carolina . .	Raleigh 27603	James B. Hunt Jr.	Dem.	4	Jan. 1997	110,076
North Dakota. . .	Bismarck 58505	Edward T. Schafer.	Rep.	4	Jan. 1997	69,650
Ohio	Columbus 43215.	George V. Voinovich	Rep.	4	Jan. 1999	115,762
Oklahoma	Oklahoma City 73105	Frank Keating	Rep.	4	Jan. 1999	70,000
Oregon	Salem 97310	John Kitzhaber	Dem.	4	Jan. 1999	80,000
Pennsylvania. . .	Harrisburg 17120	Tom Ridge	Rep.	4	Jan. 1999	105,000
Rhode Island. . .	Providence 02903	Lincoln C. Almond	Rep.	4	Jan. 1999	69,900
South Carolina. .	Columbia 29211	David Beasley.	Rep.	4	Jan. 1999	101,959
South Dakota. . .	Pierre 57501.	William J. Janklow	Rep.	4	Jan. 1999	79,875
Tennessee	Nashville 37243	Don Sundquist	Rep.	4	Jan. 1999	85,000
Texas	Austin 78711	George W. Bush	Rep.	4	Jan. 1999	99,122
Utah	Salt Lake City 84114	Michael O. Leavitt	Rep.	4	Jan. 1997	77,250
Vermont	Montpelier 05609	Howard Dean	Dem.	2	Jan. 1997	80,724
Virginia	Richmond 23219.	George F. Allen.	Rep.	4	Jan. 1998	110,000
Washington. . . .	Olympia 98504	Mike Lowry	Dem.	4	Jan. 1997	121,000
West Virginia . . .	Charleston 25305	Gaston Caperton.	Dem.	4	Jan. 1997	72,500
Wisconsin	Madison 53707	Tommy G. Thompson	Rep.	4	Jan. 1999	101,861
Wyoming.	Cheyenne 82002.	Jim Geringer	Rep.	4	Jan. 1999	95,000
Puerto Rico	San Juan 00936	Pedro J. Rosselló	—	4	Jan. 1996	—

(1)Salary as of mid-1995 unless otherwise noted. (2)Salary effective 1/1/96. (3)Salary effective 1/8/96.

1992 Census of U.S. Governments—Popularly Elected Officials

Source: U.S. Dept. of Commerce, Economics and Statistics Administration; Bureau of the Census

A census of U.S. governments is taken at 5-year intervals (beginning in 1957). One of the major subject areas includes popularly elected officials. The term *elected officials* refers to officials who are directly elected by the voters, plus the president and the vice president of the U.S., who are elected by presidential electors rather than direct election by the people. Officials who are selected by the governing body of one or more governments are not classified as elected officials.

There were 85,006 governments in the U.S. as of Jan. 1992. In addition to the federal government and the 50 state governments, there were 84,955 units of local government. Of these, 38,978 are general-purpose local governments—3,043 county governments, and 35,935 subcounty general-purpose governments (including 19,279 municipal governments and 16,656 town or township governments). The remainder, more than half the total number, are special-purpose local governments, including 14,422 school district governments and 31,555 special district governments.

The 85,006 governments in the U.S. in 1992 had 513,200 elected officials—approximately one elected official for every 485 inhabitants. There were 542 federal and 18,828 state elected officials, which accounted for only 3.8% of the total. The majority were officials of the various local governments.

Elected Officials of State and Local Governments by State, 1992

Source: U.S. Dept. of Commerce, Economics and Statistics Administration; Bureau of the Census

	Total	State	Local	%change 1987-92		Total	State	Local	%change 1987-92
AL ...	4,385	436	3,949	1.6	MT ...	5,106	201	4,905	−9.6
AK ...	1,929	255	1,674	8.9	NE ...	13,899	201	13,698	−7.7
AZ ...	3,289	239	3,050	3.3	NV ...	1,218	141	1,077	3.7
AR ...	8,408	349	8,059	.9	NH ...	7,347	430	6,917	9.3
CA ...	18,925	226	18,699	−1.6	NJ ...	9,042	121	8,921	−3.3
CO ...	8,605	280	8,325	7.1	NM ...	2,201	220	1,981	5.0
CT ...	9,147	333	8,814	7.8	NY ...	25,932	950	24,982	−.3
DE ...	1,171	80	1,091	−4.5	NC ...	5,820	593	5,227	5.2
DC ...	348	—	348	7.1	ND ...	15,482	205	15,277	2.2
FL ...	5,588	934	4,654	6.3	OH ...	19,366	231	19,135	−1.9
GA ...	6,529	465	6,064	−.4	OK ...	8,989	362	8,627	−3.2
HI ...	183	91	92	14.3	OR ...	7,833	290	7,543	−6.3
ID ...	4,775	171	4,604	2.1	PA ...	30,476	1,200	29,276	3.0
IL ...	42,336	623	41,713	8.7	RI ...	1,138	155	983	1.6
IN ...	11,624	506	11,118	2.4	SC ...	3,943	195	3,748	6.8
IA ...	16,479	319	16,160	−3.3	SD ...	9,684	155	9,529	4.7
KS ...	18,895	343	18,552	15.1	TN ...	6,950	321	6,629	1.6
KY ...	7,060	565	6,495	−4.4	TX ...	27,628	815	26,813	2.6
LA ...	5,051	629	4,422	1.7	UT ...	2,711	200	2,511	4.8
ME ...	6,556	210	6,346	−6.0	VT ...	8,534	186	8,348	6.4
MD ...	2,123	356	1,767	9.3	VA ...	3,104	143	2,961	−.3
MA ...	22,173	225	21,948	62.6	WA ...	7,724	537	7,187	−3.8
MI ...	18,704	652	18,052	−3.0	WV ...	2,772	205	2,567	−2.3
MN ...	18,870	623	18,247	−.3	WI ...	17,829	450	17,379	−2.2
MS ...	4,754	296	4,458	−3.8	WY ...	2,742	121	2,621	17.2
MO ...	17,281	994	16,287	1.0	U.S. ...	512,658	18,828	493,830	3.1

State Officials, Salaries, Party Membership

As of mid-1995; † ind. or other party.

Alabama

Governor — Fob James, Jr., R, $87,643
Lt. Gov. — Don Siegelman, D, $12 per day, plus $50 per day expenses, plus $3,780 per mo expenses
Sec. of State — Jim Bennett, D, $61,779
Atty. Gen. — Jeff Sessions, R, $115,695
Treasurer — Lucy Baxley, D, $61,779
Legislature: meets annually at Montgomery the 3d Tues. in Apr., 1st year of term of office; 1st Tues. in Feb., 2d and 3d yr; 2d Tues. in Jan., 4th yr. Members receive $10 per day salary, plus $50 per day expenses, plus $2,280 per mo expenses.
Senate — Dem., 23; Rep., 12. Total, 35
House — Dem., 83; Rep., 22. Total, 105

Alaska

Governor — Tony Knowles, D, $81,648
Lt. Gov. — Fran Ulmer, D, $76,188
Atty. General — Bruce Botelho, D, $84,000
Legislature: meets annually in Jan. at Juneau for 120 days with a 10-day extension possible upon 2/3 vote. First session in odd years. Members receive $24,120 annually, plus per diem as follows: beginning of session to Apr. 29, $148 per day; Apr. 30 to end of session, $160 per day.
Senate — Dem., 8; Rep., 12. Total, 20
House — Dem., 17; Rep., 22; 1 other. Total, 40

Arizona

Governor — Fife Symington, R, $75,000
Sec. of State — Jane Dee Hull, R, $54,600
Atty. Gen. — Grant Woods, R, $76,440
Treasurer — Tony West, R, $54,600
Legislature: meets annually in Jan. at Phoenix. Each member receives an annual salary of $15,000.
Senate — Dem., 11; Rep., 19. Total, 30
House — Dem., 22; Rep., 38. Total, 60

Arkansas

Governor — Jim Guy Tucker, D, $60,000
Lt. Gov. — Mike Huckabee, R, $29,000
Sec. of State — Sharon Priest, D, $37,500
Atty. Gen. — Winston Bryant, D, $50,000
Treasurer — Jimmie Lou Fisher, D, $37,500
Auditor — Gus Wingfield, D, $37,500
General Assembly: meets odd years in Jan. at Little Rock. Members receive $12,500 annually.
Senate — Dem., 28; Rep., 7. Total, 35
House — Dem., 89; Rep., 11; Total, 100

California

Governor — Pete Wilson, R, $120,000
Lt. Gov. — Gray Davis, D, $90,000
Sec. of State — Bill Jones, R, $90.000
Controller — Kathleen Connell, D, $90,000
Atty. Gen. — Dan Lungren, R, $102,000
Legislature: meets at Sacramento on the 1st Mon. in Dec. of even-numbered years; each session lasts 2 years. Members receive $52,500 annually, plus $101 per diem.
Senate — Dem., 21; Rep., 17; 2 ind. Total, 40
Assembly — Dem., 39; Rep., 41. Total, 80

Colorado

Governor — Roy Romer, D, $70,000
Lt. Gov. — Gail Schoettler, D, $48,500
Sec. of State — Victoria (Vikki) Buckley, R, $48,500
Atty. Gen. — Gale Norton, R, $60,000
Treasurer — Bill Owens, $48,500
General Assembly: meets annually in Jan. at Denver. Members receive $17,500 annually.
Senate — Dem., 16; Rep., 19. Total, 35
House — Dem., 24; Rep., 41. Total, 65

Connecticut

Governor — John G. Rowland, R, $78,000
Lt. Gov. — M. Jodi Rell, R, $55,000
Sec. of State — Miles S. Rapoport, D, $50,000
Treasurer — Christopher B. Burnham, R, $50,000
Comptroller — Nancy S. Wyman, D, $50,000
Atty. Gen. — Richard Blumenthal, D, $60,000
General Assembly: meets annually odd years in Jan. and even years in Feb., at Hartford. Members receive $15,200 annually, plus $4,500 (senator), $3,500 (representative) per yr for expenses.
Senate — Dem., 17; Rep., 19. Total, 36
House — Dem., 91; Rep., 60. Total, 151

Delaware

Governor — Thomas R. Carper, D, $95,000
Lt. Gov. — Ruth Ann Minner, D, $40,700
Sec. of State — Edward J. Freel, D, $85,600
Atty. Gen. — M. Jane Brady, R, $94,300
Treasurer — Janet C. Rzewnicki, R, $75,900
General Assembly: meets annually the 2d Tues. in Jan. and continues until June 30. Members receive $27,000 annually, plus $5,500 expense allowance.
Senate — Dem., 12; Rep., 9. Total, 21
House — Dem., 14; Rep., 27. Total, 41

Florida

Governor — Lawton Chiles, D, $104,817[1]
Lt. Gov. — Kenneth "Buddy" McKay, D, $100,403[1]
Sec. of State — Sandra Mortham, R, $103,757[1]
Comptroller — Robert R. Milligan, R, $103,757[1]
Atty. Gen. — Robert Butterworth, D, $103,757[1]
Treasurer — Bill Nelson, D, $103,757[1]
Legislature: meets annually at Tallahassee. Members receive $24,180 annually, plus expense allowance for official business.
Senate — Dem., 18; Rep., 22. Total, 40
House — Dem., 63; Rep., 57. Total, 120

Georgia

Governor — Zell Miller, D, $91,092
Lt. Gov. — Pierre Howard, D, $59,145
Sec. of State — Max Cleland, D, $72,966
Insurance Comm. — Tim Ryles, D, $72,954
Atty. Gen. — Michael J. Bowers, R, $74,645
General Assembly: meets annually at Atlanta. Members receive $10,641 annually ($59 per diem, and $4,800 expense reimbursement).
Senate — Dem., 35; Rep., 21. Total, 56
House — Dem., 114; Rep., 66. Total, 180

Hawaii

Governor — Benjamin Cayetano, D, $94,780
Lt. Gov. — Mazie Hirono, D, $90,041
Atty. Gen. — Margery Bronster, $85,302
Comptroller — Sam Callejo, $85,302
Dir. of Budget & Finance — Earl Anzai, $85,302
Legislature: meets annually on 3d Wed. in Jan. at Honolulu. Members receive $32,000 annually, plus expenses.
Senate — Dem., 23; Rep., 2. Total, 25
House — Dem., 45; Rep., 6. Total, 51

Idaho

Governor — Philip E. Batt, R, $85,000
Lt. Gov. — C. L. "Butch" Otter, R, $22,500
Sec. of State — Pete T. Cenarrusa, R, $67,500
Treasurer — Lydia Justice Edwards, R, $67,500
Atty. Gen. — Alan Lance, R, $75,000
Legislature: meets annually the Mon. on or nearest Jan. 9 at Boise. Members receive $12,000 annually, plus $70 per day during session if required to maintain a 2d residence; $40 if no 2d residence, plus $50 per day when engaged in legislative business when legislature is not in session.
Senate — Dem., 8; Rep., 27. Total, 35
House — Dem., 13; Rep., 57. Total, 70

Illinois

Governor — Jim Edgar, R, $119,439
Lt. Gov. — Bob Kustra, R, $84,310
Sec. of State — George H. Ryan, R, $105,387
Comptroller — Loleta C. Didrickson, R, $91,336
Atty. Gen. — Jim Ryan, R, $105, 387
Treasurer — Judy Baar Topinka, R, $91,336
General Assembly: meets annually in Jan. at Springfield. Members receive $42,265 annually.
Senate — Dem., 26; Rep., 33. Total, 59
House — Dem., 54; Rep., 64. Total, 118

Indiana

Governor — Evan Bayh, D, $77,200
Lt. Gov. — Frank O'Bannon, D, $64,000
Sec. of State — Sue Anne Gilroy, R, $46,000
Atty. Gen. — Pamela Carter, D, $59,200
Treasurer — Joyce Brinkman, R, $46,000
Auditor — Morris Wooden, R, $46,000
General Assembly: meets annually in Jan. Members receive $11,600 annually, plus $105 per day while in session, $25 per day while not in session.
Senate — Dem., 19; Rep., 31. Total, 50
House — Dem., 55; Rep., 45. Total, 100

Iowa

Governor — Terry E. Branstad, R, $76,700
Lt. Gov. — Joy Corning, R, $60,000
Sec. of State — Paul D. Pate, R, $60,000
Atty. Gen. — Tom Miller, D, $73,600
Treasurer — Michael L. Fitzgerald, D, $60,000
Auditor — Richard D. Johnson, R, $60,000
Sec. of Agriculture — Dale M. Cochran, D, $60,000
General Assembly: meets annually in Jan. at Des Moines. Members receive $18,100 annually, plus expense allowance.
Senate — Dem., 27; Rep., 23. Total, 50
House — Dem., 36; Rep., 64. Total, 100

Kansas

Governor — Bill Graves, R, $80,340
Lt. Gov. — Sheila Frahm, R, $81,600
Sec. of State — Ron Thornburgh, R, $62, 412
Atty. Gen. — Carla Stovall, R, $71,772
Treasurer — Sally Thompson, D, $62,412
Legislature: meets annually in Jan. at Topeka. Members receive $63 per day salary, plus $73 per day expenses while in session, and $600 per month while not in session.
Senate — Dem., 13; Rep., 27. Total, 40
House — Dem., 44; Rep., 81. Total, 125

Kentucky

Governor — Brereton C. Jones, D, $86,352
Lt. Gov. — Paul Patton, D, $73,411
Sec. of State — Bob Babbage, D, $73,411
Atty. Gen. — Chris Gorman, D, $73,411
Treasurer — Francis J. Mills, D, $73,411
Auditor — A. B. Chandler III, D, $73,411
General Assembly: meets even years in Jan. at Frankfort. Members receive $100 per day, plus $75 per day expenses during session and $950 per month for expenses for interim.
Senate — Dem., 21; Rep., 17. Total, 38
House — Dem., 62; Rep., 37; 1 vacancy. Total, 100

Louisiana

Governor — Edwin W. Edwards, D, $95,000[2]
Lt. Gov. — Melinda Schwegmann, D, $85,000[2]
Sec. of State — Fox McKeithen, R, $85,000[2]
Atty. Gen. — Richard Ieyoub, D, $85,000[2]
Treasurer — Mary Landrieu, D, $85,000[2]
Legislature: meets in odd-numbered years on last Mon. in Mar. for 60 legislative days of 85 calendar days; meets in even-numbered years on last Mon. in Apr. for 30 legislative days of 45 calendar days. Members receive $16,800 annually, plus $75 per day expenses while in session.
Senate — Dem., 33; Rep., 6. Total, 39.
House — Dem., 88; Rep., 16; 1 ind. Total, 105.

Maine

Governor — Angus King, Jr., †, $69,992
Sec. of State — G. William Diamond, D, $49,587
Atty. Gen. — Andrew Ketterer, $66,123
Treasurer — Samuel Shapiro, D, $60,008
Legislature: meets annually at Augusta the first Wed. in Dec. and the Wed. after the first Tues. in Jan., in even numbered years. Members receive $10,500 for first regular session, $7,500 for second regular session, plus expenses; presiding officers receive 50% more.
Senate — Dem., 16; Rep., 18; 1 ind. Total, 35
House — Dem., 75; Rep., 75; 1 vacancy. Total, 151

Maryland

Governor — Parris Glendening, D, $120,000
Lt. Gov. — Kathleen Kennedy Townsend, D, $100,000
Comptroller — Louis L. Goldstein, D, $100,000
Atty. Gen. — J. Joseph Curran, Jr., D, $100,000
Sec. of State — John Willis, D, $70,000
Treasurer — Lucille Maurer, D, $100,000
General Assembly: meets 90 consecutive days annually beginning on the 2d Wed. in Jan. at Annapolis. Members receive $27,000 annually, plus expenses.
Senate — Dem., 32; Rep., 15. Total, 47
House — Dem., 100; Rep., 41. Total, 141

(continued)

State Officials, Salaries, Party Membership (*continued*)

Massachusetts
Governor — William F. Weld, R, $75,000
Lt. Gov. — A. Paul Cellucci, R, $60,000
Sec. of State — William Francis Galvin, D, $60,000
Atty. Gen. — L. Scott Harshbarger, D, $65,000
Treasurer — Joseph Malone, R, $60,000
Auditor — A. Joseph DeNucci, D, $60,000
General Court (legislature): meets each Jan. in Boston. Members receive $30,000 annually.
Senate — Dem., 31; Rep., 9. Total, 40
House — Dem., 121; Rep., 33; 1 ind.; 5 vacancies. Total, 160

Michigan
Governor — John Engler, R, $112,025
Lt. Gov. — Connie Binsfeld, R, $84,315
Sec. of State — Candice Miller, R, $111,200
Atty. Gen. — Frank J. Kelley, D, $111,200
Treasurer — Douglas B. Roberts, (appointed), $87,300
Legislature: meets annually in Jan. at Lansing. Members receive $47,723 annually.
Senate — Dem., 16; Rep., 22. Total, 38
House — Dem., 54; Rep., 56. Total, 110

Minnesota
(DFL means Democratic-Farmer-Labor. IR means Independent Republican.)
Governor — Arne H. Carlson, R, $114,506
Lt. Gov. — Joanell Dyrstad, IR, $62,980
Sec. of State — Joan Anderson Growe, DFL, $62,980
Atty. Gen. — Hubert H. Humphrey 3d, DFL, $89,454
Treasurer — Michael McGrath, DFL, $62,980
Auditor — Mark Dayton, IR, $68,709
Legislature: meets for a total of 120 days within every 2 years at St. Paul. Members receive $29,657 annually, plus expense allowance during session.
Senate — DFL, 43; IR, 24. Total, 67
House — DFL, 69; IR, 65. Total, 134

Mississippi
Governor — Kirk Fordice, R, $83,160[1]
Lt. Gov. — Eddie Briggs, R, $40,800
Sec. of State — Dick Molpus, D, $59,400
Atty. Gen. — Mike Moore, D, $68,400
Treasurer — Marshall Bennett, D, $59,400
Legislature: meets annually in Jan. at Jackson. Members receive $10,000 per regular session, plus travel allowance, and $800 per month while not in session.
Senate — Dem., 37; Rep., 15. Total, 52
House — Dem., 90; Rep., 30; 2 ind. Total, 122

Missouri
Governor — Mel Carnahan, D, $94,563
Lt. Gov. — Roger Wilson, D, $57,145
Sec. of State — Rebecca McDowell Cook, D, $75,854
Atty. Gen. — Jeremiah W. Nixon, D, $82,090
Treasurer — Bob Holden, D, $75,854
State Auditor — Margaret Kelly, R, $75,854
General Assembly: meets annually in Jefferson City on the first Wed. after first Mon. in Jan. Members receive $24,313 annually.
Senate — Dem., 19; Rep., 15. Total, 34
House — Dem., 87; Rep., 76. Total, 163

Montana
Governor — Marc Racicot, R, $59,310
Lt. Gov. — Dennis Rehberg, R, $43,242
Sec. of State — Mike Cooney, D, $40,101
Atty. Gen. — Joe Mazurek, D, $54,329
Legislative Assembly: meets odd years in Jan. at Helena. Members receive $55.50 per legislative day, plus $50 per day for expenses while in session.
Senate — Dem., 19; Rep., 31. Total, 50
House — Dem., 33; Rep., 67. Total, 100

Nebraska
Governor — Ben Nelson, D, $65,000
Lt. Gov. — Kim Robak, D, $47,000
Sec. of State — Scott Moore, R, $52,000
Atty. Gen. — Don Stenberg, R, $64,500
Treasurer — David Heineman, R, $49,500
Legislature: meets annually in Jan. at Lincoln. Members receive $12,000 annually, plus expenses.
Unicameral body composed of 49 members who are elected on a nonpartisan ballot and are called senators.

Nevada
Governor — Bob Miller, D, $90,000
Lt. Gov. — Lonnie Hammargren, R, $20,000
Sec. of State — Dean Heller, R, $62,500
Comptroller — Darrel Daines, R, $62,500

Atty. Gen. — Frankie Sue Del Papa, D, $85,000
Treasurer — Bob Seale, R, $62,500
Legislature: meets at Carson City odd years third Mon. in Jan. for 60 days. Members receive $130 per day salary plus $66 per day expenses, while in session
Senate — Dem., 8; Rep., 13. Total, 21
Assembly — Dem., 21; Rep., 21. Total, 42

New Hampshire
Governor — Steve Merrill, R, $86,235
Sec. of State — William M. Gardner, D, $68,768
Atty. Gen. — Jeffrey Howard, R, $76,983
Treasurer — Georgie A. Thomas, R, $68,768.
General Court (Legislature): meets every year in Jan. at Concord. Members receive $200, presiding officers $250, annually.
Senate — Dem., 6; Rep., 18. Total, 24
House — Rep., 282; Dem., 110; 1 ind.; 7 vac. Total, 400

New Jersey
Governor — Christine Todd Whitman, R, $85,000
Sec. of State — Lonna R. Hooks, R, $100,225
Atty. Gen. — Deborah T. Poritz, R, $100,225
Treasurer — Bryan W. Clymer, R, $100,225
Legislature: meets throughout the year at Trenton. Members receive $35,000 annually, except president of Senate and speaker of Assembly who receive 1/3 more.
Senate — Dem., 16; Rep., 24. Total, 40
Assembly — Dem., 27; Rep., 53. Total, 80

New Mexico
Governor — Gary Johnson, R, $90,000
Lt. Gov. — Walter Bradley, R, $65,000
Sec. of State — Stephanie Gonzales, D, $65,000
Atty. Gen. — Tom Udall, D, $72,500
Treasurer — Michael A. Montoya, D, $65,000
Legislature: meets on the 3d Tues. in Jan. at Santa Fe; odd years for 60 days, even years for 30 days. Members receive $75 per day while in session.
Senate — Dem., 27; Rep., 15. Total, 42
House — Dem., 46; Rep., 24. Total, 70

New York
Governor — George E. Pataki, R, $130,000
Lt. Gov. — Elizabeth McCaughey, R, $110,000
Sec. of State — Alexander F. Treadwell, $90,832
Comptroller — H. Carl McCall, D, $110,000
Atty. Gen. — Dennis Vacco, R, $110,000
Legislature: meets annually in Jan. at Albany. Members receive $57,500 annually, plus $89 per day expenses.
Senate — Dem., 25; Rep., 36. Total, 61
Assembly — Dem., 94; Rep., 56; Total, 150

North Carolina
Governor — James B. Hunt Jr., D, $98,576, plus $11,500 per yr expenses
Lt. Gov. — Dennis Wicker, D, $87,000, plus expenses
Sec. of State — Rufus L. Edmisten, D, $87,000
Atty. Gen. — Michael Easley, D, $87,000
Treasurer — Harlan E. Boyles, D, $87,000
General Assembly: meets odd years in Jan. at Raleigh. Members receive $13,951 annually and an expense allowance of $559 per month, plus subsistence and travel allowance while in session.
Senate — Dem., 26; Rep., 24. Total, 50
House — Dem., 52; Rep., 68. Total, 120

North Dakota
Governor — Edward T. Schafer, R, $69,650
Lt. Gov. — Rosemarie Myrdal, R, $57,238
Sec. of State — Alvin A. Jaeger, R, $52,787
Atty. Gen. — Heidi Heitkamp, D, $59,576
Treasurer — Kathi Gilmore, D, $52,787
Legislative Assembly: meets odd years in Jan. at Bismarck. Members receive $480 per month salary, plus $90 per day salary and $35 per day expenses during session.
Senate — Dem., 20; Rep., 29. Total, 49
House — Dem., 23; Rep., 75. Total, 98

Ohio
Governor — George V. Voinovich, R, $115,762
Lt. Gov. — Nancy Hollister, R, $59,861
Sec. of State — Bob Taft, R, $85,516
Atty. Gen. — Betty Montgomery, R, $85,516
Treasurer — J. Kenneth Blackwell, R, $85,516
Auditor — Jim Petro, $85,516
General Assembly: meets odd years at Columbus on 1st Mon. in Jan.; no limit on session. Members receive $42,426 annually.
Senate — Dem., 13; Rep., 20. Total, 33
House — Dem., 43; Rep., 56. Total, 99

Oklahoma
Governor — Frank Keating, R, $70,000
Lt. Gov. — Mary Fallin, R, $62,500
Sec. of State — Tom Cole, R, $42,500
Atty. Gen. — Drew Edmondson, D, $75,000
Treasurer — Robert Butkin, D, $70,000
Auditor— Clifton Scott, D, $70,000
Legislature: meets annually the first Mon. in Feb. at Oklahoma City. Members receive $32,000 annually.
Senate — Dem., 35; Rep., 13. Total, 48
House — Dem., 65; Rep., 36. Total, 101

Oregon
Governor — John Kitzhaber, D, $80,000
Sec. of State — Phil Keisling, D, $61,500
Atty. Gen. — Ted Kulongoski, D, $66,000
Treasurer — Jim Hill, D, $61,500
Legislative Assembly: meets odd years in Jan. at Salem. Members receive $1,092 monthly, plus $77 expenses per day both during and out of session.
Senate — Dem., 11; Rep., 19. Total, 30
House — Dem., 26; Rep., 34. Total, 60

Pennsylvania
Governor — Tom Ridge, R, $105,000
Lt. Gov. — Mark Schweiker, R, $83,000
Sec. of the Commonwealth — Yvette Kane, $72,000
Atty. Gen. — Thomas W. Corbett, Jr., R, $84,000
Treasurer — Catherine Baker Knoll, D, $84,000
General Assembly — convenes annually in Jan. at Harrisburg. Members receive $47,000 annually, plus expenses.
Senate — Dem., 21; Rep., 27; 2 vacancies. Total, 50.
House — Dem., 100 Rep., 102; 1 vacancy. Total, 203

Rhode Island
Governor — Lincoln C. Almond, R, $69,900
Lt. Gov. — Robert A. Weygand, D, $52,000
Sec. of State — James R. Langevin, D, $52,000
Atty. Gen. — Jeffrey B. Pine, R, $55,000
Treasurer — Nancy J. Mayer, R, $52,000
General Assembly: meets annually in Jan. at Providence. Members receive $10,000 annually.
Senate — Dem., 40; Rep., 10. Total, 50
House — Dem., 84; Rep., 16. Total, 100

South Carolina
Governor — David M. Beasley, R, $101,959
Lt. Gov. — Robert L. Peeler, R, $44,737
Sec. of State — Jim Miles, R, $92,007.
Comptroller Gen. — Earle E. Morris Jr., D, $92,007
Atty. Gen. — Charles M. Condon, R, $92,007
Treasurer — Richard Eckstrom, R, $85,000
General Assembly: meets annually in Jan. at Columbia. Members receive $10,400 annually, plus $79 per day for expenses.
Senate — Dem., 26; Rep., 19; 1 ind. Total, 46
House — Dem., 54; Rep., 65; 4 ind.; 1 vacancy. Total, 124

South Dakota
Governor — William Janklow, R, $79,875
Lt. Gov. — Carole Hillard, R, $10,581
Sec. of State — Joyce Hazeltine, R, $54,272
Treasurer — Dick Butler, D, $54,272
Atty. Gen. — Mark Barnett, R, $67,841
Auditor — Vernon Larson, R, $54,272
Legislature: meets annually in Jan. at Pierre. Members receive $4,267 for 40-day session in odd-numbered years, and $3,733 for 35-day session in even-numbered years, plus $75 per legislative day.
Senate — Dem., 16; Rep., 19. Total, 35
House — Dem., 24; Rep., 46. Total, 70

Tennessee
Governor — Don Sundquist, R, $85,000
Lt. Gov. — John S. Wilder, D, $49,500
Sec. of State — Riley C. Darnell, D, $80,700
Comptroller — William Snodgrass, D, $80,700
Atty. Gen. — Charles W. Burson, D, $101,820
General Assembly: meets annually in Jan. at Nashville. Members receive $16,500 annual salary, plus $78 per day expenses while in session.
Senate — Dem., 18; Rep., 15. Total, 33
House — Dem., 59; Rep., 40. Total, 99

Texas
Governor — George W. Bush, R, $99,122
Lt. Gov. — Bob Bullock, D, $7,200
Sec. of State — Antonio Garza, Jr., R, $76,966
Comptroller — John Sharp, D, $79,247
Atty. Gen. — Dan Morales, D, $79,247

Treasurer — Martha Whitehead, D, $79,247
Railroad Commissioners — Barry Williamson, R, Chairman; Carole Keeton Rylander, R; Charles R. Matthews, R; $79,247
Legislature: meets odd years in Jan. at Austin. Members receive $7,200 annually, plus $95 per day expenses while in session.
Senate — Dem., 17; Rep., 14. Total, 31
House — Dem., 89; Rep., 61. Total, 150

Utah
Governor — Michael O. Leavitt, R, $77,250
Lt. Gov. — Olene S. Walker, R, $60,000
Atty. Gen. — Jan Graham, D, $65,000
Treasurer — Edward T. Alter, R, $60,000
Legislature: convenes for 45 days on 2d Mon. in Jan. each year; Members receive $85 per day, plus $35 a day expenses.
Senate — Dem., 10; Rep., 19. Total, 29
House — Dem., 20; Rep., 55. Total, 75

Vermont
Governor — Howard Dean, D, $80,724
Lt. Gov. — Barbara W. Snelling, R, $33,654
Sec. of State — Jim Milne, R, $50,794
Atty. Gen. — Jeffrey Amestoy, R, $61,027
Treasurer — James Douglas, R, $50,794
General Assembly: meets in Jan. at Montpelier (annual and biennial session). Members receive $510 per week while in session plus $100 per day for special session, plus expenses.
Senate — Dem., 12; Rep., 18. Total, 30
House — Dem., 86; Rep., 61; Prog. Coalition, 1; 2 ind. Total, 150

Virginia
Governor — George F. Allen, R, $110,000
Lt. Gov. — Donald S. Beyer, Jr., D, $32,000
Atty. Gen. — James S. Gilmore III, R, $97,500
Sec. of the Commonwealth — Elizabeth Beamer, R, $73,023
Treasurer — Ronald L. Tillett, $89,500
General Assembly: meets annually in Jan. at Richmond. Members receive $18,000 (senate), $17,640 (assembly) annually, plus expense and mileage allowances.
Senate — Dem., 22; Rep., 18. Total, 40
House — Dem., 52; Rep., 47; 1 ind. Total, 100

Washington
Governor — Mike Lowry, D, $121,000
Lt. Gov. — Joel Pritchard, R, $62,700
Sec. of State — Ralph Munro, R, $64,300
Atty. Gen. — Christine Gregoire, D, $92,000
Treasurer — Daniel K. Grimm, D, $79,500
Legislature: meets annually in Jan. at Olympia. Members receive $25,900 annually, plus $66 per diem while in session, and $66 per diem for attending meetings during interim.
Senate — Dem., 24; Rep., 24; 1 vacancy. Total, 49
House — Dem., 37; Rep., 61. Total, 98

West Virginia
Governor — Gaston Caperton, D, $72,500
Sec. of State — Ken Hechler, D, $43,200
Atty. Gen. — Darrell McGraw, D, $50,400
Treasurer — Larrie Bailey, D, $50,400
Comm. of Agric. — Gus Douglass, D, $46,800
Auditor — Glen B. Gainer 3d, D, $46,800
Legislature: meets annually in Jan. at Charleston. Members receive $15,000 annually.
Senate — Dem., 26; Rep., 8. Total, 34
House — Dem., 69; Rep., 31. Total, 100

Wisconsin
Governor — Tommy G. Thompson, R, $101,861
Lt. Gov. — Scott McCallum, R, $54,795
Sec. of State — Douglas La Follette, D, $49,719
Treasurer — Jack Voight, R, $49,719
Atty. Gen. — James E. Doyle, D, $97,756
Legislature: meets in Jan. at Madison. Members receive $35,070 annually, plus $64 per day expenses.
Senate — Dem., 16; Rep., 17. Total, 33
Assembly — Dem., 47; Rep., 52. Total, 99

Wyoming
Governor — Jim Geringer, R, $95,000
Sec. of State — Diana J. Ohman, R, $77,000
Atty. Gen. — William U. Hill, $77,000
Treasurer — Stan Smith, R, $77,000
Auditor — Dave Ferrari, R, $77,000
Legislature: meets odd years in Jan., even years in Feb., at Cheyenne. Members receive $125 per day while in session, plus $80 per day for expenses.
Senate — Dem., 10; Rep., 20. Total, 30.
House — Dem., 13; Rep., 47. Total, 60.

(1) Salary effective 1/1/96. (2) Salaries effective 1/8/96.

CABINETS OF THE U.S.

Role of the Cabinet

The Cabinet as a governmental institution is not provided for in the U.S. Constitution. It developed as an advisory body out of the desire of presidents to consult the heads of the executive departments on policy issues and problems. Aside from its role as a consultative and advisory body, the Cabinet has no function and wields no executive authority. The president may or may not consult the Cabinet and is not bound by its advice. Most presidents also consult numerous advisers outside the Cabinet. A group of regular informal advisers to the president has been known in American history as a "kitchen cabinet." The formal Cabinet (which may include other officials designated by the president, as well as the department heads) meets at times set by the president, often once a week. Members of Pres. Bill Clinton's Cabinet listed here are as of Oct. 15, 1995.

Secretaries of State

The Department of Foreign Affairs was created by act of Congress on July 27, 1789, and the name changed to Department of State on Sept. 15.

President	Secretary	Home	Apptd.	President	Secretary	Home	Apptd.
Washington	Thomas Jefferson	VA	1789	Harrison, B.	James G. Blaine	ME	1889
"	Edmund Randolph	VA	1794	"	John W. Foster	IN	1892
"	Timothy Pickering	PA	1795	Cleveland	Walter Q. Gresham	IN	1893
Adams, J.	Timothy Pickering	PA	1797	"	Richard Olney	MA	1895
"	John Marshall	VA	1800	McKinley	Richard Olney	MA	1897
Jefferson	James Madison	VA	1801	"	John Sherman	OH	1897
Madison	Robert Smith	MD	1809	"	William R. Day	OH	1898
"	James Monroe	VA	1811	"	John Hay	DC	1898
Monroe	John Quincy Adams	MA	1817	Roosevelt, T.	John Hay	DC	1901
Adams, J.Q.	Henry Clay	KY	1825	"	Elihu Root	NY	1905
Jackson	Martin Van Buren	NY	1829	"	Robert Bacon	NY	1909
"	Edward Livingston	LA	1831	Taft	Robert Bacon	NY	1909
"	Louis McLane	DE	1833	"	Philander C. Knox	PA	1909
"	John Forsyth	GA	1834	Wilson	Philander C. Knox	PA	1913
Van Buren	John Forsyth	GA	1837	"	William J. Bryan	NE	1913
Harrison, W.H.	Daniel Webster	MA	1841	"	Robert Lansing	NY	1915
Tyler	Daniel Webster	MA	1841	"	Bainbridge Colby	NY	1920
"	Abel P. Upshur	VA	1843	Harding	Charles E. Hughes	NY	1921
"	John C. Calhoun	SC	1844	Coolidge	Charles E. Hughes	NY	1923
Polk	John C. Calhoun	SC	1845	"	Frank B. Kellogg	MN	1925
"	James Buchanan	PA	1845	Hoover	Frank B. Kellogg	MN	1929
Taylor	James Buchanan	PA	1849	"	Henry L. Stimson	NY	1929
"	John M. Clayton	DE	1849	Roosevelt, F.D.	Cordell Hull	TN	1933
Fillmore	John M. Clayton	DE	1850	"	E.R. Stettinius Jr.	VA	1944
"	Daniel Webster	MA	1850	Truman	E.R. Stettinius Jr.	VA	1945
"	Edward Everett	MA	1852	"	James F. Byrnes	SC	1945
Pierce	William L. Marcy	NY	1853	"	George C. Marshall	PA	1947
Buchanan	William L. Marcy	NY	1857	"	Dean G. Acheson	CT	1949
"	Lewis Cass	MI	1857	Eisenhower	John Foster Dulles	NY	1953
"	Jeremiah S. Black	PA	1860	"	Christian A. Herter	MA	1959
Lincoln	Jeremiah S. Black	PA	1861	Kennedy	Dean Rusk	NY	1961
"	William H. Seward	NY	1861	Johnson, L.B.	Dean Rusk	NY	1963
Johnson, A.	William H. Seward	NY	1865	Nixon	William P. Rogers	NY	1969
Grant	Elihu B. Washburne	IL	1869	"	Henry A. Kissinger	DC	1973
"	Hamilton Fish	NY	1869	Ford	Henry A. Kissinger	DC	1974
Hayes	Hamilton Fish	NY	1877	Carter	Cyrus R. Vance	NY	1977
"	William M. Evarts	NY	1877	"	Edmund S. Muskie	ME	1980
Garfield	William M. Evarts	NY	1881	Reagan	Alexander M. Haig Jr.	CT	1981
"	James G. Blaine	ME	1881	"	George P. Shultz	CA	1982
Arthur	James G. Blaine	ME	1881	Bush	James A. Baker 3d.	TX	1989
"	F.T. Frelinghuysen	NJ	1881	"	Lawrence S. Eagleburger	MI	1992
Cleveland	F.T. Frelinghuysen	NJ	1885	Clinton	Warren M. Christopher	CA	1993
"	Thomas F. Bayard	DE	1885				
Harrison, B.	Thomas F. Bayard	DE	1889				

Secretaries of the Treasury

The Treasury Department was organized by act of Congress on Sept. 2, 1789.

President	Secretary	Home	Apptd.	President	Secretary	Home	Apptd.
Washington	Alexander Hamilton	NY	1789	Tyler	George M. Bibb	KY	1844
"	Oliver Wolcott	CT	1795	Polk	Robert J. Walker	MS	1845
Adams, J.	Oliver Wolcott	CT	1797	Taylor	William M. Meredith	PA	1849
"	Samuel Dexter	MA	1801	Fillmore	Thomas Corwin	OH	1850
Jefferson	Samuel Dexter	MA	1801	Pierce	James Guthrie	KY	1853
"	Albert Gallatin	PA	1801	Buchanan	Howell Cobb	GA	1857
Madison	Albert Gallatin	PA	1809	"	Phillip F. Thomas	MD	1860
"	George W. Campbell	TN	1814	"	John A. Dix	NY	1861
"	Alexander J. Dallas	PA	1814	Lincoln	Salmon P. Chase	OH	1861
"	William H. Crawford	GA	1816	"	William P. Fessenden	ME	1864
Monroe	William H. Crawford	GA	1817	"	Hugh McCulloch	IN	1865
Adams, J.Q.	Richard Rush	PA	1825	Johnson, A.	Hugh McCulloch	IN	1865
Jackson	Samuel D. Ingham	PA	1829	Grant	George S. Boutwell	MA	1869
"	Louis McLane	DE	1831	"	William A. Richardson	MA	1873
"	William J. Duane	PA	1833	"	Benjamin H. Bristow	KY	1874
"	Roger B. Taney	MD	1833	"	Lot M. Morrill	ME	1876
"	Levi Woodbury	NH	1834	Hayes	John Sherman	OH	1877
Van Buren	Levi Woodbury	NH	1837	Garfield	William Windom	MN	1881
Harrison, W.H.	Thomas Ewing	OH	1841	Arthur	Charles J. Folger	NY	1881
Tyler	Thomas Ewing	OH	1841	"	Walter Q. Gresham	IN	1884
"	Walter Forward	PA	1841	"	Hugh McCulloch	IN	1884
"	John C. Spencer	NY	1843				

President	Secretary	Home	Apptd.	President	Secretary	Home	Apptd.
Cleveland	Daniel Manning	NY	1885	Truman	John W. Snyder	MO	1946
"	Charles S. Fairchild	NY	1887	Eisenhower	George M. Humphrey	OH	1953
Harrison, B.	William Windom	MN	1889	"	Robert B. Anderson	CT	1957
"	Charles Foster	OH	1891	Kennedy	C. Douglas Dillon	NJ	1961
Cleveland	John G. Carlisle	KY	1893	Johnson, L.B.	C. Douglas Dillon	NJ	1963
McKinley	Lyman J. Gage	IL	1897	"	Henry H. Fowler	VA	1965
Roosevelt, T.	Lyman J. Gage	IL	1901	"	Joseph W. Barr	IN	1968
"	Leslie M. Shaw	IA	1902	Nixon	David M. Kennedy	IL	1969
"	George B. Cortelyou	NY	1907	"	John B. Connally	TX	1971
Taft	Franklin MacVeagh	IL	1909	"	George P. Shultz	IL	1972
Wilson	William G. McAdoo	NY	1913	"	William E. Simon	NJ	1974
"	Carter Glass	VA	1918	Ford	William E. Simon	NJ	1974
"	David F. Houston	MO	1920	Carter	W. Michael Blumenthal	MI	1977
Harding	Andrew W. Mellon	PA	1921	"	G. William Miller	RI	1979
Coolidge	Andrew W. Mellon	PA	1923	Reagan	Donald T. Regan	NY	1981
Hoover	Andrew W. Mellon	PA	1929	"	James A. Baker 3d	TX	1985
"	Ogden L. Mills	NY	1932	"	Nicholas F. Brady	NJ	1988
Roosevelt, F.D.	William H. Woodin	NY	1933	Bush	Nicholas F. Brady	NJ	1989
"	Henry Morgenthau, Jr.	NY	1934	Clinton	Lloyd Bentsen	TX	1993
Truman	Fred M. Vinson	KY	1945	"	Robert E. Rubin	NY	1995

Secretaries of Defense

The Department of Defense, originally designated the National Military Establishment, was created Sept. 18, 1947. It is headed by the secretary of defense, who is a member of the president's cabinet.

The departments of the army, of the navy, and of the air force function within the Department of Defense, and since 1947 their respective secretaries are not members of the president's cabinet.

President	Secretary	Home	Apptd.	President	Secretary	Home	Apptd.
Truman	James V. Forrestal	NY	1947	Nixon	Melvin R. Laird	WI	1969
"	Louis A. Johnson	WV	1949	"	Elliot L. Richardson	MA	1973
"	George C. Marshall	PA	1950	"	James R. Schlesinger	VA	1973
"	Robert A. Lovett	NY	1951	Ford	James R. Schlesinger	VA	1974
Eisenhower	Charles E. Wilson	MI	1953	"	Donald H. Rumsfeld	IL	1975
"	Neil H. McElroy	OH	1957	Carter	Harold Brown	CA	1977
"	Thomas S. Gates Jr.	PA	1959	Reagan	Caspar W. Weinberger	CA	1981
Kennedy	Robert S. McNamara	MI	1961	"	Frank C. Carlucci	PA	1987
Johnson, L.B.	Robert S. McNamara	MI	1963	Bush	Richard B. Cheney	WY	1989
"	Clark M. Clifford	MD	1968	Clinton	Les Aspin	WI	1993
				"	William J. Perry	CA	1994

Secretaries of War

The War Department (which included jurisdiction over the navy until 1798) was created by act of Congress on Aug. 7, 1789, and Gen. Henry Knox was commissioned secretary of war under that act on Sept. 12, 1789.

President	Secretary	Home	Apptd.	President	Secretary	Home	Apptd.
Washington	Henry Knox	MA	1789	Grant	John A. Rawlins	IL	1869
"	Timothy Pickering	PA	1795	"	William T. Sherman	OH	1869
"	James McHenry	MD	1796	"	William W. Belknap	IA	1869
Adams, J.	James McHenry	MD	1797	"	Alphonso Taft	OH	1876
"	Samuel Dexter	MA	1800	"	James D. Cameron	PA	1876
Jefferson	Henry Dearborn	MA	1801	Hayes	George W. McCrary	IA	1877
Madison	William Eustis	MA	1809	"	Alexander Ramsey	MN	1879
"	John Armstrong	NY	1813	Garfield	Robert T. Lincoln	IL	1881
"	James Monroe	VA	1814	Arthur	Robert T. Lincoln	IL	1881
"	William H. Crawford	GA	1815	Cleveland	William C. Endicott	MA	1885
Monroe	John C. Calhoun	SC	1817	Harrison, B.	Redfield Proctor	VT	1889
Adams, J.Q.	James Barbour	VA	1825	"	Stephen B. Elkins	WV	1891
"	Peter B. Porter	NY	1828	Cleveland	Daniel S. Lamont	NY	1893
Jackson	John H. Eaton	TN	1829	McKinley	Russel A. Alger	MI	1897
"	Lewis Cass	MI	1831	"	Elihu Root	NY	1899
"	Benjamin F. Butler	NY	1837	Roosevelt, T.	Elihu Root	NY	1901
Van Buren	Joel R. Poinsett	SC	1837	"	William H. Taft	OH	1904
Harrison, W.H.	John Bell	TN	1841	"	Luke E. Wright	TN	1908
Tyler	John Bell	TN	1841	Taft	Jacob M. Dickinson	TN	1909
"	John C. Spencer	NY	1841	"	Henry L. Stimson	NY	1911
"	James M. Porter	PA	1843	Wilson	Lindley M. Garrison	NJ	1913
"	William Wilkins	PA	1844	"	Newton D. Baker	OH	1916
Polk	William L. Marcy	NY	1845	Harding	John W. Weeks	MA	1921
Taylor	George W. Crawford	GA	1849	Coolidge	John W. Weeks	MA	1923
Fillmore	Charles M. Conrad	LA	1850	"	Dwight F. Davis	MO	1925
Pierce	Jefferson Davis	MS	1853	Hoover	James W. Good	IL	1929
Buchanan	John B. Floyd	VA	1857	"	Patrick J. Hurley	OK	1929
"	Joseph Holt	KY	1861	Roosevelt, F.D.	George H. Dern	UT	1933
Lincoln	Simon Cameron	PA	1861	"	Harry H. Woodring	KS	1937
"	Edwin M. Stanton	PA	1862	"	Henry L. Stimson	NY	1940
Johnson, A.	Edwin M. Stanton	PA	1865	Truman	Robert P. Patterson	NY	1945
"	John M. Schofield	IL	1868	"	*Kenneth C. Royall	NC	1947

* Last member of the Cabinet. The War Department became the Department of the Army and became a branch of the Department of Defense, created Sept. 18, 1947.

Secretaries of the Navy

The Navy Department was created by act of Congress on Apr. 30, 1798.

President	Secretary	Home	Apptd.	President	Secretary	Home	Apptd.
Adams, J.	Benjamin Stoddert	MD	1798	"	Robert Smith	MD	1801
Jefferson	Benjamin Stoddert	MD	1801	Madison	Paul Hamilton	SC	1809

(continued)

Secretaries of the Navy *(continued)*

President	Secretary	Home	Apptd.	President	Secretary	Home	Apptd.
"	William Jones......	PA....	1813	"	George M. Robeson..	NJ.....	1869
"	Benjamin W. Crowninshield	MA ...	1814	Hayes........	Richard W. Thompson	IN	1877
Monroe.......	Benjamin W. Crowninshield	MA ...	1817	"	Nathan Goff Jr.	WV	1881
"	Smith Thompson	NY ...	1818	Garfield.......	William H. Hunt ..	LA....	1881
"	Samuel L. Southard ..	NJ ...	1823	Arthur........	William E. Chandler ..	NH ...	1882
Adams, J.Q. ...	Samuel L. Southard ..	NJ ...	1825	Cleveland	William C. Whitney...	NY ...	1885
Jackson	John Branch	NC ...	1829	Harrison, B....	Benjamin F. Tracy ...	NY ...	1889
"	Levi Woodbury......	NH ...	1831	Cleveland	Hilary A. Herbert	AL....	1893
"	Mahlon Dickerson....	NJ....	1834	McKinley.......	John D. Long	MA ...	1897
Van Buren.....	Mahlon Dickerson....	NJ....	1837	Roosevelt, T....	John D. Long	MA ...	1901
"	James K. Paulding ...	NY ...	1838	"	William H. Moody....	MA ...	1902
Harrison, W.H.	George E. Badger ...	NC ...	1841	"	Paul Morton......	IL	1904
Tyler.........	George E. Badger ...	NC ...	1841	"	Charles J. Bonaparte .	MD	1905
"	Abel P. Upshur......	VA....	1841	"	Victor H. Metcalf.....	CA	1906
"	David Henshaw	MA ...	1843	"	Truman H. Newberry .	MI.....	1908
"	Thomas W. Gilmer ...	VA....	1844	Taft	George von L. Meyer .	MA ...	1909
"	John Y. Mason......	VA....	1844	Wilson	Josephus Daniels....	NC ...	1913
Polk	George Bancroft.....	MA ...	1845	Harding.......	Edwin Denby	MI.....	1921
"	John Y. Mason......	VA....	1846	Coolidge......	Edwin Denby	MI.....	1923
Taylor........	William B. Preston ...	VA....	1849	"	Curtis D. Wilbur	CA	1924
Fillmore.......	William A. Graham ...	NC ...	1850	Hoover	Charles Francis Adams	MA ...	1929
"	John P. Kennedy	MD ...	1852	Roosevelt, F.D.	Claude A. Swanson ..	VA ...	1933
Pierce........	James C. Dobbin	NC ...	1853	"	Charles Edison	NJ....	1940
Buchanan	Isaac Toucey	CT....	1857	"	Frank Knox	IL	1940
Lincoln	Gideon Welles	CT....	1861	"	James V. Forrestal...	NY	1944
Johnson, A....	Gideon Welles	CT....	1865	Truman.......	*James V. Forrestal ..	NY	1945
Grant	Adolph E. Borie	PA....	1869				

* Last member of Cabinet. The Navy Department became a branch of the Department of Defense, created Sept. 18, 1947.

Attorneys General

The office of attorney general was organized by act of Congress on Sept. 24, 1789. The Department of Justice was created June 22, 1870.

President	Attorney General	Home	Apptd.	President	Attorney General	Home	Apptd.
Washington....	Edmund Randolph ..	VA....	1789	Cleveland	Richard Olney	MA ...	1893
"	William Bradford...	PA....	1794	"	Judson Harmon	OH ...	1895
"	Charles Lee.......	VA....	1795	McKinley.......	Joseph McKenna ...	CA....	1897
Adams, J.	Charles Lee.......	VA....	1797	"	John W. Griggs	NJ ...	1898
Jefferson......	Levi Lincoln	MA....	1801	"	Philander C. Knox ...	PA....	1901
"	John Breckenridge ..	KY....	1805	Roosevelt, T....	Philander C. Knox ...	PA....	1901
"	Caesar A. Rodney ..	DE....	1807	"	William H. Moody ...	MA ...	1904
Madison	Caesar A. Rodney ..	DE....	1807	"	Charles J. Bonaparte	MD ...	1906
"	William Pinkney....	MD....	1811	Taft	George W. Wicker-		
"	Richard Rush......	PA....	1814		sham.	NY....	1909
Monroe.......	Richard Rush......	PA....	1817	Wilson	J.C. McReynolds ...	TN	1913
"	William Wirt	VA....	1817	"	Thomas W. Gregory .	TX....	1914
Adams, J.Q. ...	William Wirt	VA....	1825	"	A. Mitchell Palmer ..	PA....	1919
Jackson	John M. Berrien	GA....	1829	Harding.......	Harry M. Daugherty .	OH ...	1921
"	Roger B. Taney	MD....	1831	Coolidge......	Harry M. Daugherty .	OH ...	1923
"	Benjamin F. Butler ..	NY....	1833	"	Harlan F. Stone	NY....	1924
Van Buren.....	Benjamin F. Butler ..	NY....	1837	"	John G. Sargent.....	VT....	1925
"	Felix Grundy	TN....	1838	Hoover	William D. Mitchell ..	MN	1929
"	Henry D. Gilpin....	PA....	1840	Roosevelt, F.D.	Homer S. Cummings .	CT....	1933
Harrison, W.H.	John J. Crittenden ..	KY....	1841	"	Frank Murphy	MI	1939
Tyler.........	John J. Crittenden ..	KY....	1841	"	Robert H. Jackson ..	NY....	1940
"	Hugh S. Legare	SC....	1841	"	Francis Biddle	PA....	1941
"	John Nelson.......	MD....	1843	Truman.......	Thomas C. Clark	TX....	1945
Polk	John Y. Mason.....	VA....	1845	"	J. Howard McGrath ..	RI	1949
"	Nathan Clifford.....	ME....	1846	"	J.P. McGranery	PA....	1952
"	Isaac Toucey	CT....	1848	Eisenhower....	Herbert Brownell Jr. .	NY....	1953
Taylor........	Reverdy Johnson....	MD....	1849	"	William P. Rogers...	MD ...	1957
Fillmore.......	John J. Crittenden ..	KY....	1850	Kennedy......	Robert F. Kennedy..	MA ...	1961
Pierce........	Caleb Cushing	MA....	1853	Johnson, L.B. ..	Robert F. Kennedy..	MA ...	1963
Buchanan	Jeremiah S. Black ...	PA....	1857	"	N. de B. Katzenbach .	IL....	1964
"	Edwin M. Stanton...	PA....	1860	"	Ramsey Clark	TX....	1967
Lincoln	Edward Bates	MO ...	1861	Nixon	John N. Mitchell	NY....	1969
"	James Speed......	KY....	1864	"	Richard G. Kleindi-		
Johnson, A....	James Speed......	KY....	1865		enst	AZ....	1972
"	Henry Stanbery	OH....	1866	"	Elliot L. Richardson .	MA ...	1973
"	William M. Evarts ...	NY....	1868	"	William B. Saxbe ...	OH ...	1974
Grant	Ebenezer R. Hoar...	MA....	1869	Ford	William B. Saxbe ...	OH ...	1974
"	Amos T. Akerman...	GA....	1870	"	Edward H. Levi	IL....	1975
"	George H. Williams..	OR....	1871	Carter........	Griffin B. Bell	GA....	1977
"	Edwards Pierrepont .	NY....	1875	"	Benjamin R. Civiletti .	MD ...	1979
"	Alphonso Taft......	OH....	1876	Reagan.......	William French Smith	CA....	1981
Hayes........	Charles Devens	MA....	1877	"	Edwin Meese 3d	CA....	1985
Garfield.......	Wayne MacVeagh ..	PA....	1881	"	Richard Thornburgh .	PA....	1988
Arthur........	Benjamin H. Brewster	PA....	1882	Bush.........	Richard Thornburgh .	PA....	1989
Cleveland	Augustus Garland...	AR....	1885	"	William P. Barr.....	NY....	1991
Harrison, B....	William H. H. Miller ..	IN	1889	Clinton	Janet Reno	FL....	1993

Secretaries of the Interior

The Department of the Interior was created by act of Congress on Mar. 3, 1849.

President	Secretary	Home	Apptd.	President	Secretary	Home	Apptd.
Taylor	Thomas Ewing	OH	1849	Taft	Walter L. Fisher	IL	1911
Fillmore	Thomas M. T. McKennan	PA	1850	Wilson	Franklin K. Lane	CA	1913
"	Alex H. H. Stuart	VA	1850	"	John B. Payne	IL	1920
Pierce	Robert McClelland	MI	1853	Harding	Albert B. Fall	NM	1921
Buchanan	Jacob Thompson	MS	1857	"	Hubert Work	CO	1923
Lincoln	Caleb B. Smith	IN	1861	Coolidge	Hubert Work	CO	1923
"	John P. Usher	IN	1863	"	Roy O. West	IL	1929
Johnson, A.	John P. Usher	IN	1865	Hoover	Ray Lyman Wilbur	CA	1929
"	James Harlan	IA	1865	Roosevelt, F.D.	Harold L. Ickes	IL	1933
"	Orville H. Browning	IL	1866	Truman	Harold L. Ickes	IL	1945
Grant	Jacob D. Cox	OH	1869	"	Julius A. Krug	WI	1946
"	Columbus Delano	OH	1870	"	Oscar L. Chapman	CO	1949
"	Zachariah Chandler	MI	1875	Eisenhower	Douglas McKay	OR	1953
Hayes	Carl Schurz	MO	1877	"	Fred A Seaton	NE	1956
Garfield	Samuel J. Kirkwood	IA	1881	Kennedy	Stewart L. Udall	AZ	1961
Arthur	Henry M. Teller	CO	1882	Johnson, L.B.	Stewart L. Udall	AZ	1963
Cleveland	Lucius Q.C. Lamar	MS	1885	Nixon	Walter J. Hickel	AK	1969
"	William F. Vilas	WI	1888	"	Rogers C.B. Morton	MD	1971
Harrison, B.	John W. Noble	MO	1889	Ford	Rogers C.B. Morton	MD	1971
Cleveland	Hoke Smith	GA	1893	"	Stanley K. Hathaway	WY	1975
"	David R. Francis	MO	1896	"	Thomas S. Kleppe	ND	1975
McKinley	Cornelius N. Bliss	NY	1897	Carter	Cecil D. Andrus	ID	1977
"	Ethan A. Hitchcock	MO	1898	Reagan	James G. Watt	CO	1981
Roosevelt, T.	Ethan A. Hitchcock	MO	1901	"	William P. Clark	CA	1983
"	James R. Garfield	OH	1907	"	Donald P. Hodel	OR	1985
Taft	Richard A. Ballinger	WA	1909	Bush	Manuel Lujan	NM	1989
				Clinton	Bruce Babbitt	AZ	1993

Secretaries of Agriculture

The Department of Agriculture was created by act of Congress on May 15, 1862. On Feb. 8, 1889, its commissioner was renamed secretary of agriculture and became a member of the Cabinet.

President	Secretary	Home	Apptd.	President	Secretary	Home	Apptd.
Cleveland	Norman J. Colman	MO	1889	Truman	Charles F. Brannan	CO	1948
Harrison, B.	Jeremiah M. Rusk	WI	1889	Eisenhower	Ezra Taft Benson	UT	1953
Cleveland	J. Sterling Morton	NE	1893	Kennedy	Orville L. Freeman	MN	1961
McKinley	James Wilson	IA	1897	Johnson, L.B.	Orville L. Freeman	MN	1963
Roosevelt, T.	James Wilson	IA	1901	Nixon	Clifford M. Hardin	IN	1969
Taft	James Wilson	IA	1909	"	Earl L. Butz	IN	1971
Wilson	David F. Houston	MO	1913	Ford	Earl L. Butz	IN	1974
"	Edwin T. Meredith	IA	1920	"	John A. Knebel	VA	1976
Harding	Henry C. Wallace	IA	1921	Carter	Bob Bergland	MN	1977
Coolidge	Henry C. Wallace	IA	1923	Reagan	John R. Block	IL	1981
"	Howard M. Gore	WV	1924	"	Richard E. Lyng	CA	1986
"	William M. Jardine	KS	1925	Bush	Clayton K. Yeutter	NE	1989
Hoover	Arthur M. Hyde	MO	1929	"	Edward Madigan	IL	1991
Roosevelt, F.D.	Henry A. Wallace	IA	1933	Clinton	Mike Espy	MS	1993
"	Claude R. Wickard	IN	1940	"	Dan Glickman	KS	1995
Truman	Clinton P. Anderson	NM	1945				

Secretaries of Commerce and Labor

The Department of Commerce and Labor, created by Congress on Feb. 14, 1903, was divided by Congress Mar. 4, 1913, into separate departments of Commerce and Labor. The secretary of each was made a Cabinet member.

President	Secretary	Home	Apptd.
Nixon	George P. Shultz	IL	1969

Secretaries of Commerce and Labor

President	Secretary	Home	Apptd.				
Roosevelt, T.	George B. Cortelyou	NY	1903	"	James D. Hodgson	CA	1970
"	Victor H. Metcalf	CA	1904	"	Peter J. Brennan	NY	1973
"	Oscar S. Straus	NY	1906	Ford	Peter J. Brennan	NY	1974
Taft	Charles Nagel	MO	1909	"	John T. Dunlop	CA	1975
				"	W.J. Usery Jr.	GA	1976
				Carter	F. Ray Marshall	TX	1977
				Reagan	Raymond J. Donovan	NJ	1981

Secretaries of Labor

President	Secretary	Home	Apptd.
Wilson	William B. Wilson	PA	1913
Harding	James J. Davis	PA	1921
Coolidge	James J. Davis	PA	1923
Hoover	James J. Davis	PA	1929
"	William N. Doak	VA	1930
Roosevelt, F.D.	Frances Perkins	NY	1933
Truman	L.B. Schwellenbach	WA	1945
"	Maurice J. Tobin	MA	1949
Eisenhower	Martin P. Durkin	IL	1953
"	James P. Mitchell	NJ	1953
Kennedy	Arthur J. Goldberg	IL	1961
"	W. Willard Wirtz	IL	1962
Johnson, L.B.	W. Willard Wirtz	IL	1963

Continuing the right column:

President	Secretary	Home	Apptd.
"	William E. Brock	TN	1985
"	Ann D. McLaughlin	DC	1987
Bush	Elizabeth Hanford Dole	NC	1989
"	Lynn Martin	IL	1991
Clinton	Robert B. Reich	MA	1993

Secretaries of Commerce

President	Secretary	Home	Apptd.
Wilson	William C. Redfield	NY	1913
"	Joshua W. Alexander	MO	1919
Harding	Herbert C. Hoover	CA	1921
Coolidge	Herbert C. Hoover	CA	1923
"	William F. Whiting	MA	1928
Hoover	Robert P. Lamont	IL	1929
"	Roy D. Chapin	MI	1932

(continued)

Secretaries of Commerce *(continued)*

Roosevelt, F.D.	Daniel C. Roper	SC	1933
"	Harry L. Hopkins	NY	1939
"	Jesse Jones	TX	1940
"	Henry A. Wallace	IA	1945
Truman	Henry A. Wallace	IA	1945
"	W. Averell Harriman	NY	1947
"	Charles Sawyer	OH	1948
Eisenhower	Sinclair Weeks	MA	1953
"	Lewis L. Strauss	NY	1958
"	Frederick H. Mueller	MI	1959
Kennedy	Luther H. Hodges	NC	1961
Johnson, L.B.	Luther H. Hodges	NC	1963
"	John T. Connor	NJ	1965
"	Alex B. Trowbridge	NJ	1967
Johnson, L.B.	Cyrus R. Smith	NY	1968
Nixon	Maurice H. Stans	MN	1969
"	Peter G. Peterson	IL	1972
"	Frederick B. Dent	SC	1973
Ford	Frederick B. Dent	SC	1974
"	Rogers C.B. Morton	MD	1975
"	Elliot L. Richardson	MA	1975
Carter	Juanita M. Kreps	NC	1977
"	Philip M. Klutznick	IL	1979
Reagan	Malcolm Baldrige	CT	1981
"	C. William Verity Jr.	OH	1987
Bush	Robert A. Mosbacher	TX	1989
"	Barbara H. Franklin	PA	1992
Clinton	Ronald H. Brown	DC	1993

Secretaries of Housing and Urban Development

The Department of Housing and Urban Development was created by act of Congress on Sept. 9, 1965.

President	Secretary	Home	Apptd.	President	Secretary	Home	Apptd.
Johnson, L.B.	Robert C. Weaver	WA	1966	Carter	Patricia Roberts Harris	DC	1977
"	Robert C. Wood	MA	1969	"	Moon Landrieu	LA	1979
Nixon	George W. Romney	MI	1969	Reagan	Samuel R. Pierce Jr.	NY	1981
"	James T. Lynn	OH	1973	Bush	Jack F. Kemp	NY	1989
Ford	James T. Lynn	OH	1974	Clinton	Henry G. Cisneros	TX	1993
"	Carla Anderson Hills	CA	1975				

Secretaries of Transportation

The Department of Transportation was created by act of Congress on Oct. 15, 1966.

President	Secretary	Home	Apptd.	President	Secretary	Home	Apptd.
Johnson, L.B.	Alan S. Boyd	FL	1966	Reagan	Andrew L. Lewis Jr.	PA	1981
Nixon	John A. Volpe	MA	1969	"	Elizabeth Hanford Dole	NC	1983
"	Claude S. Brinegar	CA	1973	"	James H. Burnley	NC	1987
Ford	Claude S. Brinegar	CA	1974	Bush	Samuel K. Skinner	IL	1989
"	William T. Coleman Jr.	PA	1975	"	Andrew H. Card Jr.	MA	1992
Carter	Brock Adams	WA	1977	Clinton	Federico F. Peña	CO	1993
Carter	Neil E. Goldschmidt	OR	1979				

Secretaries of Energy

The Department of Energy was created by federal law on Aug. 4, 1977.

President	Secretary	Home	Apptd.	President	Secretary	Home	Apptd.
Carter	James R. Schlesinger	VA	1977	Reagan	Donald P. Hodel	OR	1982
"	Charles Duncan Jr.	WY	1979	"	John S. Herrington	CA	1985
Reagan	James B. Edwards	SC	1981	Bush	James D. Watkins	CA	1989
				Clinton	Hazel R. O'Leary	MN	1993

Secretaries of Health, Education, and Welfare

The Department of Health, Education, and Welfare, created by Congress on Apr. 11, 1953, was divided by Congress on Sept. 27, 1979, into separate departments of Education and of Health and Human Services. The secretary of each is a Cabinet member.

President	Secretary	Home	Apptd.	President	Secretary	Home	Apptd.
Eisenhower	Oveta Culp Hobby	TX	1953	Nixon	Robert H. Finch	CA	1969
"	Marion B. Folsom	NY	1955	"	Elliot L. Richardson	MA	1970
"	Arthur S. Flemming	OH	1958	"	Caspar W. Weinberger	CA	1973
Kennedy	Abraham A. Ribicoff	CT	1961	Ford	Caspar W. Weinberger	CA	1974
"	Anthony J. Celebrezze	OH	1962	"	Forrest D. Mathews	AL	1975
Johnson, L.B.	Anthony J. Celebrezze	OH	1963	Carter	Joseph A. Califano Jr.	DC	1977
"	John W. Gardner	NY	1965	"	Patricia Roberts Harris	DC	1979
"	Wilbur J. Cohen	MI	1968				

Secretaries of Health and Human Services

President	Secretary	Home	Apptd.	President	Secretary	Home	Apptd.
Carter	Patricia Roberts Harris	DC	1979	Reagan	Otis R. Bowen	IN	1985
Reagan	Richard S. Schweiker	PA	1981	Bush	Louis W. Sullivan	GA	1989
"	Margaret M. Heckler	MA	1983	Clinton	Donna E. Shalala	WI	1993

Secretaries of Education

President	Secretary	Home	Apptd.	President	Secretary	Home	Apptd.
Carter	Shirley Hufstedler	CA	1979	Bush	Lauro F. Cavazos	TX	1989
Reagan	Terrel Bell	UT	1981	"	Lamar Alexander	TN	1991
"	William J. Bennett	NY	1985	Clinton	Richard W. Riley	SC	1993
"	Lauro F. Cavazos	TX	1988				

Secretaries of Veterans Affairs

The Department of Veterans Affairs was created on Oct. 25, 1988, when Pres. Reagan signed a bill that made the Veterans Administration into a Cabinet department as of Mar. 15, 1989.

President	Secretary	Home	Apptd.	President	Secretary	Home	Apptd.
Bush	Edward J. Derwinski	IL	1989	Clinton	Jesse Brown	IL	1993

Directors of the Central Intelligence Agency

On June 13, 1942, Pres. Franklin D. Roosevelt established the Office of Strategic Services (OSS) and named William J. Donovan as its director. The OSS was disbanded Oct. 1, 1945, and its functions absorbed by the State and War departments. Pres. Truman, Jan. 22, 1946, established the Central Intelligence Agency Group (CIG) to operate under the direction of the National Intelligence Authority (NIA). The National Security Act of 1947 replaced the NIA with the National Security Council and the CIG with the Central Intelligence Agency.

Director	Served	Appointed by President	Director	Served	Appointed by President
Adm. Sidney W. Souers	1946	Truman	William E. Colby	1973-1976	Nixon
Gen. Hoyt S. Vandenberg	1946-1947	Truman	George Bush	1976-1977	Ford
Adm. Roscoe H. Hillenkoetter	1947-1950	Truman	Adm. Stansfield Turner	1977-1981	Carter
Gen. Walter Bedell Smith	1950-1953	Truman	William J. Casey	1981-1987	Reagan
Allen W. Dulles	1953-1961	Eisenhower	William H. Webster	1987-1991	Reagan
John A. McCone	1961-1965	Kennedy	Robert M. Gates	1991-1993	Bush
Adm. William F. Raborn Jr.	1965-1966	Johnson	R. James Woolsey	1993-1995	Clinton
Richard Helms	1966-1973	Johnson	John M. Deutch	1995-	Clinton
James R. Schlesinger	1973	Nixon			

Speakers of the House of Representatives

Party designations: A, American; D, Democratic; DR, Democratic-Republican; F, Federalist; R, Republican; W, Whig

Name	Party	State	Tenure	Name	Party	State	Tenure
Frederick Muhlenberg	F	PA	1789-1791	Theodore M. Pomeroy	R	NY	1869
Jonathan Trumbull	F	CT	1791-1793	James G. Blaine	R	ME	1869-1875
Frederick Muhlenberg	F	PA	1793-1795	Michael C. Kerr	D	IN	1875-1876
Jonathan Dayton	F	NJ	1795-1799	Samuel J. Randall	D	PA	1876-1881
Theodore Sedgwick	F	MA	1799-1801	Joseph W. Keifer	R	OH	1881-1883
Nathaniel Macon	DR	NC	1801-1807	John G. Carlisle	D	KY	1883-1889
Joseph B. Varnum	DR	MA	1807-1811	Thomas B. Reed	R	ME	1889-1891
Henry Clay	DR	KY	1811-1814	Charles F. Crisp	D	GA	1891-1895
Langdon Cheves	DR	SC	1814-1815	Thomas B. Reed	R	ME	1895-1899
Henry Clay	DR	KY	1815-1820	David B. Henderson	R	IA	1899-1903
John W. Taylor	DR	NY	1820-1821	Joseph G. Cannon	R	IL	1903-1911
Philip P. Barbour	DR	VA	1821-1823	Champ Clark	D	MO	1911-1919
Henry Clay	DR	KY	1823-1825	Frederick H. Gillett	R	MA	1919-1925
John W. Taylor	D	NY	1825-1827	Nicholas Longworth	R	OH	1925-1931
Andrew Stevenson	D	VA	1827-1834	John N. Garner	D	TX	1931-1933
John Bell	D	TN	1834-1835	Henry T. Rainey	D	IL	1933-1935
James K. Polk	D	TN	1835-1839	Joseph W. Byrns	D	TN	1935-1936
Robert M. T. Hunter	D	VA	1839-1841	William B. Bankhead	D	AL	1936-1940
John White	W	KY	1841-1843	Sam Rayburn	D	TX	1940-1947
John W. Jones	D	VA	1843-1845	Joseph W. Martin Jr.	R	MA	1947-1949
John W. Davis	D	IN	1845-1847	Sam Rayburn	D	TX	1949-1953
Robert C. Winthrop	W	MA	1847-1849	Joseph W. Martin Jr.	R	MA	1953-1955
Howell Cobb	D	GA	1849-1851	Sam Rayburn	D	TX	1955-1961
Linn Boyd	D	KY	1851-1855	John W. McCormack	D	MA	1962-1971
Nathaniel P. Banks	A	MA	1856-1857	Carl Albert	D	OK	1971-1977
James L. Orr	D	SC	1857-1859	Thomas P. O'Neill Jr.	D	MA	1977-1987
William Pennington	R	NJ	1860-1861	James Wright	D	TX	1987-1989
Galusha A. Grow	R	PA	1861-1863	Thomas S. Foley	D	WA	1989-1995
Schuyler Colfax	R	IN	1863-1869	Newt Gingrich	R	GA	1995-

Floor Leaders in the U.S. Senate Since the 1920s

Majority Leaders				Minority Leaders			
Name	Party	State	Tenure	Name	Party	State	Tenure
Charles Curtis[1]	R	KS	1925-1929	Oscar W. Underwood[2]	D	AL	1920-1923
James E. Watson	R	IN	1929-1933	Joseph T. Robinson	D	AR	1923-1933
Joseph T. Robinson	D	AR	1933-1937	Charles L. McNary	R	OR	1933-1944
Alben W. Barkley	D	KY	1937-1947	Wallace H. White	R	ME	1944-1947
Wallace H. White	R	ME	1947-1949	Alben W. Barkley	D	KY	1947-1949
Scott W. Lucas	D	IL	1949-1951	Kenneth S. Wherry	R	NE	1949-1951
Ernest W. McFarland	D	AZ	1951-1953	Henry Styles Bridges	R	NH	1951-1953
Robert A. Taft	R	OH	1953	Lyndon B. Johnson	D	TX	1953-1955
William F. Knowland	R	CA	1953-1955	William F. Knowland	R	CA	1955-1959
Lyndon B. Johnson	D	TX	1955-1961	Everett M. Dirksen	R	IL	1959-1969
Mike Mansfield	D	MT	1961-1977	Hugh D. Scott	R	PA	1969-1977
Robert C. Byrd	D	WV	1977-1981	Howard H. Baker Jr.	R	TN	1977-1981
Howard H. Baker Jr.	R	TN	1981-1985	Robert C. Byrd	D	WV	1981-1987
Robert J. Dole	R	KS	1985-1987	Robert J. Dole	R	KS	1987-1995
Robert C. Byrd	D	WV	1987-1989	Thomas A. Daschle	D	SD	1995-
George J. Mitchell	D	ME	1989-1995				
Robert J. Dole	R	KS	1995-				

(1) First Republican to be designated floor leader. (2) First Democrat to be designated floor leader.

Librarians of Congress

Librarian	Served	Appointed by President	Librarian	Served	Appointed by President
John J. Beckley	1802-1807	Jefferson	Herbert Putnam	1899-1939	McKinley
Patrick Magruder	1807-1815	Jefferson	Archibald MacLeish	1939-1944	F. Roosevelt
George Watterston	1815-1829	Madison	Luther H. Evans	1945-1953	Truman
John Silva Meehan	1829-1861	Jackson	L. Quincy Mumford	1954-1974	Eisenhower
John G. Stephenson	1861-1864	Lincoln	Daniel J. Boorstin	1975-1987	Ford
Ainsworth Rand Spofford	1864-1897	Lincoln	James H. Billington	1987-	Reagan
John Russell Young	1897-1899	McKinley			

ECONOMICS

U.S. Budget Receipts and Outlays—1991-94

Source: Financial Management Service, U.S. Dept. of the Treasury

(Fiscal year ends Sept. 30)
(millions of dollars; some figures may not add due to independent rounding)
(outlays incl. selected departments and agencies)

Classification	Fiscal 1991	Fiscal 1992	Fiscal 1993	Fiscal 1994
Net Receipts				
Individual income taxes	$467,827	$476,465	$509,680	$542,738
Corporation income taxes	98,086	100,270	117,520	140,385
Social insurance taxes and contributions:				
Federal old-age and survivors insurance	265,503	273,137	281,735	302,607
Federal disability insurance	28,382	29,289	30,199	32,419
Federal hospital insurance	72,842	79,109	81,224	90,062
Railroad retirement fund	3,799	3,957	3,781	3,723
Total employment taxes and contributions	**370,526**	**385,491**	**396,939**	**428,810**
Other insurance and retirement:				
Unemployment	20,922	23,410	26,556	28,004
Federal employees retirement	4,459	4,683	4,709	4,563
Non-federal employees	108	105	96	98
Total social insurance taxes and contributions	**396,016**	**413,689**	**428,300**	**461,475**
Excise taxes	42,402	45,570	48,057	55,225
Estate and gift taxes	11,138	11,143	12,577	15,225
Customs duties	15,949	17,359	18,802	20,099
Deposits of earnings-Federal Reserve Banks	19,158	22,920	14,908	18,023
All other miscellaneous receipts	3,688	4,275	3,382	4,018
Net Budget Receipts	**$1,054,265**	**$1,091,692**	**$1,153,175**	**$1,257,187**
Net Outlays				
Legislative Branch	$2,296	$2,677	$2,406	$2,561
The Judiciary	1,989	2,295	2,628	2,659
Executive Office of the President:				
The White House Office	32	36	40	40
Office of Management and Budget	53	54	55	57
Total Executive Office	**193**	**190**	**194**	**229**
Funds appropriated to the President:				
International security assistance	9,531	7,203	7,322	6,306
Multilateral assistance	1,520	1,717	1,547	1,670
Agency for International Development	1,835	2,142	2,099	2,544
International Development Assistance	3,444	4,029	3,855	4,444
Total funds appropriated to the President	**11,724**	**11,108**	**11,526**	**10,511**
Agriculture Department:				
Food stamp program	19,649	22,800	24,602	25,549
Farmers Home Admin.	6,629	4,455	2,061	1,880
Forest Service	3,001	3,293	3,292	3,353
Total Agriculture Department	**54,119**	**56,436**	**63,143**	**60,812**
Commerce Department:				
Bureau of the Census	451	302	346	250
Total Commerce Department	**2,585**	**2,567**	**2,798**	**2,915**
Defense Department (military):				
Military personnel	83,439	81,171	75,904	73,137
Operation and maintenance	101,769	92,042	94,121	87,895
Procurement	82,028	74,881	69,936	61,758
Research, development, test, evaluation	34,589	34,632	36,968	34,786
Military construction	3,497	4,262	4,831	4,979
Total Defense Department (military)	**261,925**	**286,632**	**278,586**	**268,635**
Defense Department (civil)	26,543	28,265	29,266	30,402
Education Department	25,339	26,047	30,290	24,699
Energy Department	12,459	15,439	16,801	17,840
Health and Human Services Department:				
Food and Drug Administration	648	752	733	801
National Institutes of Health	7,677	8,376	9,543	10,165
Public Health Service	15,348	17,447	18,872	19,760
Health Care Financing Adm.	205,776	239,366	266,452	285,117
Total Health and Human Services Dept.	**217,969**	**257,961**	**282,781**	**310,837**
Social Security (Off Budget)	266,395	281,418	298,349	313,881
Housing and Urban Development Department	22,751	24,470	25,181	25,774
Interior Department	6,096	6,555	6,720	6,910
Justice Department:				
Federal Bureau of Investigation	1,695	1,832	1,975	2,106
Total Justice Department	**8,244**	**9,826**	**10,170**	**10,005**
Labor Department:				
Unemployment Trust Fund	28,434	41,294	39,869	30,458
Total Labor Department	**34,040**	**47,193**	**44,738**	**36,918**
State Department	4,252	5,007	5,385	5,718
Transportation Department:				
Federal Aviation Administration	7,241	8,155	8,800	8,784
Total Transportation Department	**30,503**	**32,560**	**34,457**	**37,279**
Treasury Department:				
Internal Revenue Service	13,689	17,904	18,437	21,488
Interest on the public debt	285,472	292,330	292,502	296,278
Total Treasury Department	**276,352**	**293,428**	**298,802**	**307,258**
Veterans Affairs Department	31,214	33,737	35,487	37,401
Environmental Protection Agency	5,770	5,932	5,930	5,855
General Services Administration	487	469	743	334
National Aeronautics and Space Administration	13,878	13,961	14,305	13,694

Classification	Fiscal 1991	Fiscal 1992	Fiscal 1993	Fiscal 1994
Office of Personnel Management	$34,808	$35,596	$36,794	$38,596
Small Business Administration	613	394	785	779
Other independent agencies:				
Action	192	194	208	182
Board for International Broadcasting	228	210	246	213
Corporation for Public Broadcasting.	299	327	319	275
District of Columbia	671	691	698	698
Equal Employment Opportunity Commission . . .	192	209	218	229
Export-Import Bank of the United States	−88	−119	−747	−832
Federal Communications Commission.	66	78	94	49
Federal Deposit Insurance Corporation	7,363	3,666	−8,412	−11,048
Federal Trade Commission.	60	71	64	69
Interstate Commerce Commission.	45	40	41	43
Legal Services Corporation.	344	329	389	375
National Archives & Records Adm.	172	226	269	261
National Foundation on the Arts and Humanities	325	331	343	354
National Labor Relations Board.	143	155	171	173
National Science Foundation	2,081	2,249	2,452	2,642
Nuclear Regulatory Commission	−1	50	−19	46
Railroad Retirement Board	4,358	4,843	4,782	4,780
Securities and Exchange Commission.	143	117	99	68
Smithsonian Institution	340	378	395	400
Tennessee Valley Authority	740	1,469	1,629	1,210
U.S. Information Agency.	1,001	1,050	1,088	1,165
Total other independent agencies	81,217	18,876	−9,992	11,525
Undistributed offsetting receipts	−110,005	−117,118	−119,711	−123,470
Net Budget Outlays	**$1,323,757**	**$1,381,895**	**$1,408,532**	**$1,460,557**
Less net receipts	1,054,265	1,091,692	1,153,175	1,257,187
Deficit	**$−269,492**	**$−290,204**	**$−255,306**	**$−203,370**

Summary of Receipts, Outlays, and Surpluses or Deficits, 1936-90

Source: Financial Management Service, U.S. Dept. of the Treasury

(millions of dollars)

Year[1]	Receipts	Outlays	Surplus or Deficit (−)	Year[1]	Receipts	Outlays	Surplus or Deficit (−)
1936	$3,923	$8,228	$−4,304	1964	$112,613	$118,528	$−5,915
1937	5,387	7,580	−2,193	1965	116,817	118,228	−1,411
1938	6,751	6,840	−89	1966	130,835	134,532	−3,698
1939	6,295	9,141	−2,846	1967	148,822	157,464	−8,643
1940	6,548	9,468	−2,920	1968	152,973	178,134	−25,161
1941	8,712	13,653	−4,941	1969	186,882	183,640	3,242
1942	14,634	35,137	−20,503	1970	192,807	195,649	−2,842
1943	24,001	78,555	−54,554	1971	187,139	210,172	−23,033
1944	43,747	91,304	−47,557	1972	207,309	230,681	−23,373
1945	45,159	92,712	−47,553	1973	230,799	245,707	−14,908
1946	39,296	55,232	−15,936	1974	263,224	269,359	−6,135
1947	38,514	34,496	4,018	1975	279,090	332,332	−53,242
1948	41,560	29,764	11,796	1976	298,060	371,779	−73,719
1949	39,415	38,835	580	Transition quarter[2] . . .	81,232	95,973	−14,741
1950	39,443	42,562	−3,119	1977	355,559	409,203	−53,644
1951	51,616	45,514	6,102	1978	399,561	458,729	−59,168
1952	66,167	67,686	−1,519	1979	463,302	503,464	−40,162
1953	69,608	76,101	−6,493	1980	517,112	590,920	−73,808
1954	69,701	70,855	−1,154	1981	599,272	678,209	−78,936
1955	65,451	68,444	−2,993	1982	617,766	745,706	−127,940
1956	74,587	70,640	3,947	1983	600,562	808,327	−207,764
1957	79,990	76,578	3,412	1984	666,457	851,781	−185,324
1958	79,636	82,405	−2,769	1985	734,057	946,316	−212,260
1959	79,249	92,098	−12,849	1986	769,091	990,231	−221,140
1960	92,492	92,191	301	1987	854,143	1,003,804	−149,661
1961	94,388	97,723	−3,335	1988	908,166	1,063,318	−155,151
1962	99,676	106,821	−7,146	1989	990,701	1,144,020	−153,319
1963	106,560	111,316	−4,756	1990	1,031,308	1,251,776	−220,469

(1) Fiscal years: 1936 to 1976, July 1-June 30; starting with 1977, Oct. 1-Sept. 30. (2) Transition quarter covers July 1, 1976-Sept. 30, 1976.

Net Receipts and Outlays, 1789-1935

Source: U.S. Dept. of the Treasury; annual statements for year ending June 30

(thousands of dollars)

Yearly Average	Receipts	Outlays	Yearly Average	Receipts	Outlays	Yearly Average	Receipts	Outlays
1789-1800[1]. . .	$5,717	$5,776	1866-1870	447,301	377,642	1901-1905. . . .	559,481	535,559
1801-1810[2]. . .	13,056	9,086	1871-1875	336,830	287,460	1906-1910. . . .	628,507	639,178
1811-1820[2]. . .	21,032	23,943	1876-1880	288,124	255,598	1911-1915. . . .	710,227	720,252
1821-1830[2]. . .	21,928	16,162	1881-1885	366,961	257,691	1916-1920. . . .	3,483,652	8,065,333
1831-1840[2]. . .	30,461	24,495	1886-1890	375,448	279,134	1921-1925. . . .	4,306,673	3,578,989
1841-1850[2]. . .	28,545	34,097	1891-1895	352,891	363,599	1926-1930. . . .	4,069,138	3,182,807
1851-1860 . . .	60,237	60,163	1896-1900	434,877	457,451	1931-1935. . . .	2,770,973	5,214,874
1861-1865 . . .	160,907	683,785						

(1) Average for period March 4, 1789, to Dec. 31, 1800. (2) Years ended Dec. 31, 1801 to 1842; average for 1841-1850 is for the period Jan. 1, 1841, to June 30, 1850.

Public Debt of the U.S.

Source: Bureau of Public Debt, U.S. Dept. of the Treasury

Fiscal year	Debt (billions)	Per. cap. (dollars)	Interest paid (billions)	% of federal outlays	Fiscal year	Debt (billions)	Per. cap. (dollars)	Interest paid (billions)	% of federal outlays
1870	$2.4	$61.06	—	—	1978	$771.5	$3,463	$48.7	10.6
1880	2.0	41.60	—	—	1979	826.5	3,669	59.8	11.9
1890	1.1	17.80	—	—	1980	907.7	3,985	74.9	12.7
1900	1.2	16.60	—	—	1981	997.9	4,338	95.6	14.1
1910	1.1	12.41	—	—	1982	1,142.0	4,913	117.4	15.7
1920	24.2	228	—	—	1983	1,377.2	5,870	128.8	15.9
1930	16.1	131	—	—	1984	1,572.3	6,640	153.8	18.1
1940	43.0	325	$1.0	10.5	1985	1,823.1	7,598	178.9	18.9
1945	258.7	1,849	3.8	4.1	1986	2,125.3	8,774	190.2	19.2
1950	256.1	1,688	5.7	13.4	1987	2,350.3	9,615	195.4	19.5
1955	272.8	1,651	6.4	9.4	1988	2,602.3	10,534	214.1	20.1
1960	284.1	1,572	9.2	10.0	1989	2,857.4	11,545	240.9	21.0
1965	313.8	1,613	11.3	9.6	1990	3,233.3	13,000	264.8	21.1
1970	370.1	1,814	19.3	9.9	1991	3,665.3	14,436	285.4	21.5
1975	533.2	2,475	32.7	9.8	1992	4,064.6	15,846	292.3	21.1
1976	620.4	2,852	37.1	10.0	1993	4,351.2	16,871	292.5	20.8
1977	698.8	3,170	41.9	10.2	1994	4,692.8	18,026	296.3	20.3

Note: Through 1976 the fiscal year ended June 30. From 1977 on, the fiscal year ends Sept. 30.

Consumer Price Index

The Consumer Price Index (CPI) is a measure of the average change in prices over time of basic consumer goods and services. From Jan. 1978, the Bureau of Labor Statistics began publishing CPI's for 2 population groups: (1) a CPI for all urban consumers (CPI-U), which covers about 80% of the total population; and (2) a CPI for urban wage earners and clerical workers (CPI-W), which covers about 32% of the total population. The CPI-U includes, in addition to wage earners and clerical workers, groups such as professional, managerial, and technical workers, the self-employed, short-term workers, the unemployed, retirees, and others not in the labor force.

The CPI is based on prices of food, clothing, shelter, fuels, transportation fares, charges for doctors' and dentists' services, drugs, and prices of the other goods and services bought for day-to-day living. The index measures price changes from a designated reference period, 1982-84, which equals 100.0.

Use of this reference period began in Jan. 1988.

Consumer Price Indexes, 1994-95

Source: Bureau of Labor Statistics, U.S. Dept. of Labor

		CPI-U				CPI-W		
	Unadjusted indexes Aug. 1995	Unadjusted percent change to Aug. 1995 from		Seasonally adjusted percent change from July to Aug.	Unadjusted indexes Aug. 1995	Unadjusted percent change to Aug. 1994 from		Seasonally adjusted percent change from July to Aug.
(1982-84=100)		Aug. 1994	July 1995			Aug. 1994	July 1995	
Food, beverages.......	148.9	2.5	0.2	0.2	148.3	2.3	0.2	0.3
Housing	149.6	2.5	0.3	0.3	146.5	2.4	0.3	0.3
Apparel, upkeep	130.1	–0.8	1.4	0.3	129.1	–0.8	1.3	0.3
Transportation	139.2	2.4	–0.6	–0.6	138.9	2.7	–0.6	–0.6
Medical care..........	221.6	4.4	0.4	0.4	221.1	4.5	0.4	0.5
Entertainment.........	154.1	2.6	0.3	0.4	152.0	2.5	0.3	0.4
Other goods, services	207.7	4.2	1.0	0.5	205.0	3.8	0.8	0.5
Services.............	169.8	3.4	0.4	0.2	167.0	3.3	0.3	0.2
Special indexes								
All items less food......	153.7	2.6	0.2	0.1	150.6	2.6	0.2	0.1
Commodities less food ..	129.7	1.0	0.2	0.1	129.9	1.2	0.0	–0.2
Nondurables..........	139.3	1.4	0.2	–0.1	138.9	1.2	0.1	–0.1
Energy..............	107.4	–1.0	–0.6	–0.8	106.8	–1.3	–0.7	–0.9
All items less energy	159.0	2.8	0.3	0.2	156.3	2.9	0.3	0.2

Consumer Price Indexes[1] Annual Percent Change, 1983-94

Source: Bureau of Labor Statistics, U.S. Dept. of Labor

	1983[2]	1984	1985	1986	1987	1988	1989	1990	1991	1992	1993	1994
All items	3.2	4.3	3.6	1.9	3.6	4.1	4.8	5.4	4.2	3.0	3.0	2.6
Food	2.1	3.8	2.3	3.2	4.1	4.1	5.8	5.8	2.9	1.2	2.2	2.4
Shelter..............	2.3	4.9	5.6	5.5	4.7	4.8	4.5	5.4	4.5	3.3	3.0	3.1
Rent, residential	5.8	5.2	6.2	5.8	4.1	3.8	3.9	5.6	6.1	2.5	2.3	2.5
Fuel & other utilities.......	5.6	4.6	1.6	–2.3	–1.1	–1.4	3.3	3.5	3.3	2.2	3.0	1.0
Apparel and upkeep	2.5	1.9	2.8	0.9	4.4	4.3	2.8	4.6	3.7	2.5	1.4	–0.2
Private transportation	2.3	4.3	2.5	–4.7	–3.0	3.3	4.9	5.2	2.6	2.2	2.3	3.1
New cars	2.6	2.9	3.2	4.2	3.6	2.0	2.0	1.8	3.8	2.5	2.4	3.4
Gasoline.............	–3.3	–1.6	0.8	–21.9	–4.0	0.9	9.5	14.1	–1.8	–0.2	–1.3	0.5
Public transportation	4.8	6.2	4.5	5.9	3.5	1.8	5.0	10.1	4.4	1.7	10.3	3.0
Medical care...........	8.8	6.2	6.3	7.5	6.6	6.5	7.7	9.0	8.7	7.4	5.9	4.8
Entertainment...........	4.3	3.7	3.9	3.4	3.3	4.3	5.2	4.7	4.5	2.8	2.5	2.9
Commodities	2.9	3.4	2.1	–0.9	3.2	3.5	4.7	5.2	4.2	2.0	1.9	1.7

(1) The Consumer Price Index (CPI-U) measures the average change in prices of goods and services purchased by all urban consumers. (2) Change from 1982.

Consumer Price Indexes for Selected Items and Groups, 1970-94

Source: Bureau of Labor Statistics, U.S. Dept. of Labor

(1982-84 = 100. Annual averages of monthly figures. All urban consumers = CPI-U.)

	1970	1975	1980	1985	1990	1992	1993	1994
All Items	**38.8**	**53.8**	**82.4**	**107.6**	**130.7**	**140.3**	**144.5**	**148.2**
Food and beverages	**40.1**	**60.2**	**86.7**	**105.6**	**132.1**	**138.7**	**141.6**	**144.9**
Food	39.2	59.8	86.8	105.6	132.4	137.9	140.9	144.3
Food at home	39.9	61.8	88.4	104.3	132.3	136.8	140.1	144.1
Cereals, bakery prods.	37.1	62.9	83.9	107.9	140.0	151.5	156.6	163.0
Meats, poultry, fish, eggs	44.6	67.0	92.0	100.1	130.0	130.9	135.5	137.2
Dairy prods.	44.7	62.6	90.9	103.2	126.5	128.5	129.4	131.7
Fruits, vegetables	37.8	56.9	82.1	106.4	149.0	155.4	159.0	165.0
Sugar, sweets	30.5	65.3	90.5	105.8	124.7	133.1	133.4	135.2
Fats, oils	39.2	73.5	89.3	106.9	126.3	129.8	130.0	133.5
Nonalcoholic beverages	27.1	41.3	91.4	104.3	113.5	114.3	114.6	123.2
Other prepared foods	39.6	58.9	83.6	106.4	131.2	140.1	143.7	147.5
Food away from home	37.5	54.5	83.4	108.3	133.4	140.7	143.2	147.7
Alcoholic beverages	52.1	65.9	86.4	106.4	129.3	147.3	149.6	151.5
Housing	**36.4**	**50.7**	**81.1**	**107.7**	**128.5**	**137.5**	**141.2**	**144.8**
Shelter	35.5	48.8	81.0	109.8	140.0	151.2	155.7	160.5
Rent	46.5	58.0	80.9	111.8	146.7	160.9	165.0	169.4
Maintenance, repairs	35.8	54.1	82.4	106.5	122.2	128.6	130.6	130.8
Fuel, other utilities	29.1	45.4	75.4	106.5	111.6	117.8	121.3	122.8
Energy services	31.8	50.0	75.8	106.9	117.4	114.8	118.5	119.2
Household furnishings & operation	46.8	63.4	86.3	103.8	113.3	118.0	119.3	121.0
House furnishings	55.5	69.8	88.5	101.7	106.7	109.0	109.5	111.0
Apparel & upkeep	**59.2**	**72.5**	**90.9**	**105.0**	**124.1**	**131.9**	**133.7**	**133.4**
Apparel commodities	63.3	76.7	92.9	104.0	122.0	129.4	131.0	130.4
Men's & boys'	62.2	75.5	89.4	105.0	120.4	126.5	127.5	126.4
Women's & girls'	71.8	85.5	96.0	104.9	122.6	130.4	132.6	130.9
Footwear	56.8	69.6	91.8	102.3	117.4	125.0	125.9	126.0
Transportation	**37.5**	**50.1**	**83.1**	**106.4**	**120.5**	**126.5**	**130.4**	**134.3**
Private	37.5	50.6	84.2	106.2	118.8	124.6	127.5	131.4
New cars	53.0	62.9	88.4	106.1	121.4	128.4	131.5	136.0
Used cars	31.2	43.8	62.3	113.7	117.6	123.2	133.9	141.7
Gasoline	27.9	45.1	97.5	98.6	101.0	99.0	97.7	98.2
Public	35.2	43.5	69.0	110.5	142.6	151.4	167.0	172.0
Medical care	**34.0**	**47.5**	**74.9**	**113.5**	**162.8**	**190.1**	**201.4**	**211.0**
Entertainment	**47.5**	**62.0**	**83.6**	**107.9**	**132.4**	**142.3**	**145.8**	**150.1**
Other goods & services	**40.9**	**53.9**	**75.2**	**114.5**	**159.0**	**183.3**	**192.9**	**198.5**
Tobacco products	43.1	54.7	72.0	116.7	181.5	219.8	228.4	220.0
Personal care	43.5	57.9	81.9	106.3	130.4	138.3	141.5	144.6
Toilet goods	42.7	58.0	79.6	107.6	128.2	136.5	139.0	141.5
Personal care services	44.2	57.7	83.7	108.9	132.8	140.0	144.0	147.9
Personal, educational expenses	35.5	48.7	70.9	119.1	170.2	197.4	210.7	223.2

Consumer Price Index by Region and Selected Cities, 1994-95

Source: Bureau of Labor Statistics, U.S. Dept. of Labor

Area (1982-84 = 100)	CPI-U Indexes June 1995	CPI-U Indexes July 1995	CPI-U Indexes Aug. 1995	Percentage change Aug. 1994- Aug. 1995	CPI-W Indexes June 1995	CPI-W Indexes July 1995	CPI-W Indexes Aug. 1995	Percentage change Aug. 1994- Aug. 1995
U.S. city average	**152.5**	**152.5**	**152.9**	**2.6**	**149.9**	**149.9**	**150.2**	**2.5**
Northeast urban	**158.9**	**159.2**	**159.7**	**2.4**	**156.4**	**156.6**	**157.1**	**2.4**
More than 1,200,000	159.6	159.8	160.3	2.4	156.1	156.1	156.7	2.4
500,000 to 1,200,000	156.5	157.5	157.9	2.0	154.5	155.3	155.7	1.9
50,000 to 500,000	157.2	157.8	158.5	3.1	158.9	159.2	159.8	3.0
North Central urban	**148.7**	**148.8**	**148.9**	**2.5**	**145.6**	**145.5**	**145.6**	**2.4**
More than 1,200,000	149.5	149.5	149.8	2.4	145.7	145.6	145.8	2.2
360,000 to 1,200,000	147.7	148.0	147.8	2.4	144.2	144.1	144.0	2.1
50,000 to 360,000	149.9	149.6	149.9	2.7	147.4	147.1	147.3	2.6
Less than 50,000	145.4	146.0	145.7	3.5	143.7	144.2	144.0	3.2
South urban	**149.1**	**149.2**	**149.7**	**2.9**	**147.8**	**147.8**	**148.3**	**2.9**
More than 1,200,000	148.8	148.8	149.4	2.5	147.2	147.2	147.6	2.4
450,000 to 1,200,000	151.3	151.5	152.0	2.8	147.8	147.9	148.3	2.6
50,000 to 450,000	148.5	148.4	149.4	3.5	148.6	148.5	149.4	3.6
Less than 50,000	147.8	148.1	147.8	3.4	148.1	148.3	148.3	3.6
West urban	**153.6**	**153.5**	**153.7**	**2.4**	**150.7**	**150.5**	**150.7**	**2.4**
More than 1,250,000	154.1	154.0	154.1	1.9	149.8	149.5	149.6	1.8
50,000 to 330,000	156.6	156.7	157.0	3.9	153.8	153.7	153.9	3.6
Selected areas								
Chicago, IL–Gary–Lake County, IL–IN–WI	153.5	153.6	153.8	2.7	148.5	148.7	148.8	2.5
L.A.–Anaheim–Riverside, CA	154.8	154.5	154.4	1.6	149.7	149.3	149.2	1.6
New York, NY–Northern NJ–Long Island, NY–NJ–CT	162.2	162.3	162.8	2.3	158.4	158.3	158.9	2.3
Philadelphia–Wilmington–Trenton, PA– NJ–DE–MD	158.4	158.9	159.6	2.5	158.1	158.5	159.2	2.5
San Francisco–Oakland–San Jose, CA	151.7	151.5	151.5	1.4	149.6	149.3	149.3	1.5
Baltimore, MD.	—	151.5	—	—	—	150.5	—	—
Boston–Lawrence–Salem, MA–NH	—	157.8	—	—	—	156.6	—	—
Cleveland–Akron–Lorain, OH	—	148.1	—	—	—	140.3	—	—
Miami–Ft. Lauderdale, FL	—	148.3	—	—	—	146.5	—	—
St. Louis–East St. Louis, MO–IL	—	145.6	—	—	—	145.2	—	—
Washington, DC–MD–VA	—	156.1	—	—	—	153.5	—	—
Dallas–Fort Worth, TX	144.4	—	145.1	2.0	144.4	—	144.8	2.3
Detroit–Ann Arbor, MI	148.3	—	148.8	2.4	143.7	—	144.0	2.1
Houston–Galveston–Brazoria, TX	139.9	—	140.1	0.6	139.5	—	139.8	0.7
Pittsburgh–Beaver Valley, PA	149.2	—	150.1	3.0	143.0	—	143.7	3.1

Percentage Change in Consumer Prices in Selected Countries

Source: International Monetary Fund

Country	1975-1980, avg.	1980-1985, avg.	1989-1990, avg.	1990-1991, avg.	1991-1992, avg.	1992-1993, avg.	1993-1994, avg.
Canada	8.7	7.4	4.8	5.6	1.5	1.8	0.2
France	10.5	9.6	3.4	3.1	2.4	2.1	1.7
Germany	4.1	3.9	2.7	3.5	4.0	4.1	3.0
Italy	16.3	13.7	6.4	6.3	5.2	4.5	4.0
Japan	6.5	2.7	3.1	3.3	1.7	1.3	0.7
Spain	18.6	12.2	6.7	5.9	5.9	4.6	4.7
Sweden	10.5	9.0	10.5	9.3	2.3	4.6	2.2
Switzerland	2.3	4.3	5.4	5.8	4.0	3.3	0.8
United Kingdom	14.4	7.2	9.5	5.9	3.7	1.6	2.5
United States	8.9	5.5	5.4	4.2	3.0	3.0	2.6

Index of Leading Economic Indicators

Source: Bureau of Economic Analysis, U.S. Dept. of Commerce

The index of leading economic indicators is used to project the U.S. economy's performance 6 months or a year ahead. The index is made up of 11 measurements of economic activity that tend to change direction long before the overall economy does.

Components

Average work week of production workers in manufacturing

Average weekly claims for state unemployment insurance

New orders for consumer goods and materials, adjusted for inflation

Vendor performance (companies receiving slower deliveries from suppliers)

Contracts and orders for plant and equipment, adjusted for inflation

Index of new private housing units authorized by local building permits

Change in manufacturers' unfilled orders, durable goods

Change in sensitive materials prices

Index of stock prices

Money supply: M-2, adjusted for inflation

Index of consumer expectations

Gross Domestic Product, Gross National Product, Net National Product, National Income, and Personal Income

Source: Bureau of Economic Analysis, U.S. Dept. of Commerce

(billions of dollars)

	1960	1970	1980	1990	1993	1994
Gross domestic product	—	—	—	$5,546.1	$6,343.3	$6,738.4
Gross national product	$515.3	$1,015.5	$2,732.0	5,567.8	6,347.8	6,726.9
Less: Capital consumption allowances	46.4	88.8	303.8	602.7	669.1	715.3
Equals: Net national product	468.9	926.6	2,428.1	4,965.1	5,678.7	6,011.5
Less: Indirect business tax and nontax liability	45.3	94.0	213.3	444.0	525.3	554.0
Business transfer payments	2.0	4.1	12.1	26.8	28.7	30.7
Statistical discrepancy	−2.8	−1.1	4.9	7.8	2.3	−30.9
Plus: Subsidies less current surplus of government enterprises	0.4	2.9	5.7	4.5	9.0	0.7
Equals: National income	424.9	832.6	2,203.5	4,491.0	5,131.4	5,458.4
Less: Corporate profits with inventory valuation and capital consumption adjustments	49.5	74.7	177.2	380.6	485.8	542.7
Net interest	11.3	41.2	200.9	463.7	399.5	409.7
Contributions for social insurance	21.9	62.2	216.5	503.1	585.6	626.0
Wage accruals less disbursements	0.0	0.0	0.0	0.1	20.0	0.0
Plus: Government transfer payments to persons	27.5	81.8	312.6	666.3	892.6	939.9
Personal interest income	24.9	69.3	271.9	698.2	637.9	664.0
Personal dividend income	12.9	22.2	52.9	144.4	181.3	194.3
Business transfer payments	2.0	4.1	12.1	21.3	22.8	23.5
Equals: Personal income	409.4	831.8	2,258.5	4,673.8	5,375.1	5,701.7

Gross Domestic Product

Source: Bureau of Economic Analysis, U.S. Dept. of Commerce

(billions of dollars)

	1993	1994	First Quarter 1995[1]		1993	1994	First Quarter 1995[1]
Gross domestic product	$6,343.3	$6,738.4	$6,977.4	Change in business inventories	15.4	52.2	54.5
Personal consumption expenditures	4,378.2	4,628.4	4,782.1	Nonfarm	20.1	45.9	54.1
Durable goods	538.0	591.5	615.2	Farm	−4.7	6.4	0.4
Nondurable goods	1,339.2	1,394.3	1,432.2	Net exports of goods and services	−65.3	−98.2	−111.1
Services	2,501.0	2,642.7	2,734.8	Exports	659.1	718.7	778.8
Gross private domestic investment	882.0	1,032.9	1,107.8	Imports	724.3	816.9	889.9
Fixed investment	866.7	980.7	1,053.3	Government purchases	1,148.4	1,175.3	1,198.7
Nonresidential	616.1	697.6	766.4	Federal	443.6	437.3	434.4
Structures	173.4	182.8	198.6	National defense	302.7	292.3	283.7
Producers' durable equipment	442.7	514.8	567.8	Nondefense	140.9	145.0	150.6
Residential	250.6	283.0	286.8	State and local	704.7	738.0	764.3

(1) Seasonally adjusted at annual rates.

U.S. Corporate Profits by Industry

Source: Bureau of Economic Analysis, U.S. Dept. of Commerce

(billions of dollars)

	1993	1994	First quarter 1995[1]		1993	1994	First quarter 1995[1]
Corporate profits with inventory valuation and capital consumption adjustments	485.8	542.7	569.7	Durable goods	49.4	72.1	76.5
Domestic industries	420.5	482.3	501.0	Primary metal industries . . .	0.2	0.5	2.6
Financial.	89.5	88.3	98.0	Fabricated metal prods.	6.8	9.3	10.4
Nonfinancial	330.9	394.0	403.0	Industrial machinery and equip.	7.4	9.1	13.4
Rest of the world.	65.3	60.5	68.7	Electronic and other electric equip.	11.9	19.8	21.0
Receipts from the rest of the world	74.2	84.2	99.4	Motor vehicles and equip. . .	4.1	10.5	6.8
Less: Payments to the rest of the world	8.9	23.7	30.7	Other	19.0	23.0	22.3
Corporate profits with inventory valuation adjustment	456.2	505.0	531.6	Nondurable goods	64.9	73.5	67.5
Domestic industries	391.0	444.6	462.9	Food and kindred prods. . . .	16.9	20.2	16.5
Financial.	103.7	104.0	115.2	Chemicals and allied prods.	17.5	19.2	19.3
Federal Reserve banks	16.0	17.3	19.8	Petroleum and coal prods. .	4.7	6.1	5.4
Other	87.7	86.7	95.5	Other	25.8	28.1	26.2
Nonfinancial	287.3	340.6	347.7	Transportation and public utilities	65.0	72.3	77.6
Manufacturing	114.2	145.6	143.9	Wholesale and retail trade.	61.2	67.6	66.7
				Other.	46.9	55.1	59.5
				Rest of the world	65.3	60.5	68.7

(1) Seasonally adjusted at annual rates.

Chapter 11

Chapter 11 refers to the provisions in the Federal Bankruptcy Code for court-supervised reorganization of debtor companies. A company files for Chapter 11 protection when it can no longer pay its creditors or when it expects future liabilities it cannot hope to pay, like product liability damage awards. In 1991, the U.S. Supreme Court ruled that the provision of federal bankruptcy law that permits corporations to reorganize while continuing to operate was also available for use by individuals. The Bankruptcy Reform Act of 1994 further amended Chapter 11.

Process

1. Bankruptcy filing imposes an automatic stay.
• Creditors generally cannot file or continue suits for repayment.
• Debts are frozen and creditors generally must stop collection actions. This is called the "automatic stay."
• Debtor's day-to-day operations continue.
• Spending, borrowing, and asset sales that are outside of the debtor's normal course of business must be approved by the court.
• Secured creditors can ask the court for exemption from the automatic stay to undertake or continue to recover the collateral that secures their claim.

2. Unsecured creditors form a committee.
• The U.S. trustee appoints the committee, which ordinarily consists of the 7 largest unsecured creditors who are willing to serve on the panel.
• The U.S. trustee can appoint additional committees to represent other creditors and shareholders.
• The committee chooses representatives to deal with the debtor company.
• The committee and U.S. trustee oversee the debtor's business operations.
• Creditors and the U.S. trustee can ask the court to appoint an examiner to investigate possible fraud or mismanagement.
• Creditors and the U.S. trustee can ask the court to order the appointment of a case trustee to run the debtor company.
• If the court orders the appointment, the U.S. trustee selects the case trustee unless a party asks that creditors be allowed to elect the case trustee.

3. The committee, other creditors, and the debtor company negotiate a reorganization plan.
• Parties negotiate a plan for the reorganization of the debtor's business and repayment of frozen debts. This step can take months or years.
• Only the debtor can file a reorganization plan with the court for the first 120 days of the bankruptcy case. The court can extend the so-called "exclusivity" period and often does so.
• If the debtor does not file a plan during the exclusivity period, if the debtor's plan is not approved by the court, or if a trustee is appointed, any party can file a plan.
• The proponent of the plan prepares a disclosure statement, which must be approved by the court at a separate hearing.

4. Creditors and shareholders vote on the plan.
• Only creditors and shareholders whose claims and interests are impaired or affected by the plan vote on it.
• A class of creditors accepts the plan if the plan is approved by creditors who hold more than half of the claims in the class by number and at least two-thirds of the claims by amount.
• A class of shareholders accepts the plan if the plan is approved by shareholders who hold at least two-thirds of the equity interest in the class by amount.

5. Judge considers the plan.
• The bankruptcy judge approves the plan if it complies with the Bankruptcy Code and all impaired classes approve.
• If at least one of the impaired classes approves the plan and it meets certain statutory tests, the judge can confirm the plan in a so-called "cramdown" even if all impaired classes do not approve.

6. Reorganized company emerges.
• Generally, the debtor's debts are discharged.
• The debtor and creditors must comply with the confirmed plan.
• The automatic stay ends and a permanent injunction goes into effect against any effort to collect prepetition debts other than as provided in the plan.
• The reorganized debtor operates like a normal company.
• Only 17% of the debtors who file Chapter 11 cases get their plans confirmed.

Expedited Procedure for Small Businesses

• The Bankruptcy Reform Act of 1994 included an expedited confirmation process to be used in Chapter 11 cases filed by small businesses.
• The debtor can elect to use the new process if it has less than $2 million in debts and its primary business is not owning or operating real estate.
• The court can order that a creditors' committee not be appointed.
• Unless the court orders otherwise, the debtor's exclusivity period for filing a plan is shortened to 100 days and all plans must be filed within 160 days.
• The court may conditionally approve the disclosure statement. This saves time by combining the court hearing on the disclosure statement with the hearing on confirmation of the plan.

State Finances

Revenue, Expenditures, Debt, and Taxes

Source: Census Bureau, U.S. Dept. of Commerce

(fiscal year 1993)

State	Revenue (millions)	Expenditures (millions)	Debt (millions)	Per cap.[1] debt	Per cap.[1] taxes	Per cap.[1] expenditures
Alabama	$11,389	$10,242	$4,163	$994	$1,108	$2,446
Alaska	7,358	5,423	4,427	7,391	3,718	9,053
Arizona	10,843	9,783	3,053	776	1,342	2,485
Arkansas	6,446	5,915	1,884	777	1,214	2,440
California	108,222	104,567	41,295	1,323	1,562	3,350
Colorado	10,028	8,673	3,117	874	1,062	2,432
Connecticut	12,744	12,507	12,848	3,921	2,037	3,817
Delaware	2,876	2,557	3,490	4,986	1,914	3,653
Florida	33,216	30,103	13,635	997	1,199	2,201
Georgia	16,565	15,308	4,519	653	1,178	2,213
Hawaii	5,543	5,605	5,023	4,286	2,345	4,783
Idaho	3,408	2,776	1,290	1,174	1,419	2,526
Illinois	30,351	28,133	19,893	1,701	1,240	2,405
Indiana	14,653	14,136	5,458	955	1,210	2,474
Iowa	8,224	7,766	1,837	653	1,387	2,760
Kansas	6,730	5,742	935	370	1,294	2,269
Kentucky	11,011	10,543	6,820	1,800	1,393	2,783
Louisiana	13,348	12,893	9,585	2,232	1,017	3,002
Maine	3,926	3,889	2,999	2,421	1,424	3,138
Maryland	14,842	13,537	8,731	1,759	1,445	2,727
Massachusetts	21,493	21,557	25,415	4,227	1,727	3,586
Michigan	28,760	27,051	8,849	934	1,390	2,854
Minnesota	16,245	14,295	4,145	918	1,801	3,165
Mississippi	7,205	6,235	1,659	628	1,129	2,359
Missouri	12,559	10,809	6,516	1,245	1,047	2,065
Montana	3,023	2,663	1,749	2,085	1,347	3,174
Nebraska	3,890	3,823	1,587	988	1,233	2,379
Nevada	4,500	4,051	1,653	1,190	1,589	2,916
New Hampshire	3,011	2,970	5,242	4,660	883	2,640
New Jersey	29,614	28,923	21,779	2,764	1,653	3,671
New Mexico	6,303	5,599	1,597	989	1,718	3,465
New York	78,209	74,280	59,219	3,254	1,720	4,082
North Carolina	19,377	16,916	4,002	576	1,405	2,436
North Dakota	2,288	2,129	830	1,307	1,380	3,353
Ohio	38,341	31,665	12,486	1,126	1,153	2,855
Oklahoma	8,679	8,272	3,919	1,213	1,290	2,560
Oregon	10,826	9,013	5,821	1,920	1,207	2,973
Pennsylvania	37,779	34,359	12,989	1,078	1,378	2,852
Rhode Island	3,765	4,176	5,147	5,147	1,433	4,176
South Carolina	10,637	10,388	4,901	1,345	1,177	2,852
South Dakota	1,942	1,686	1,818	2,543	824	2,359
Tennessee	11,864	11,028	2,632	516	1,004	2,162
Texas	42,019	39,091	8,684	482	1,012	2,168
Utah	5,348	4,834	2,193	1,179	1,189	2,599
Vermont	1,953	1,849	1,419	2,463	1,376	3,211
Virginia	16,307	14,721	7,438	1,146	1,167	2,268
Washington	19,930	18,003	7,848	1,493	1,694	3,426
West Virginia	6,047	5,943	2,684	1,475	1,360	3,265
Wisconsin	18,677	14,621	7,674	1,523	1,579	2,902
Wyoming	2,181	1,887	781	1,661	1,408	4,014
United States	**$804,495**	**$742,936**	**$387,680**	**$1,507**	**$1,373**	**$2,887**

(1) Per capita amounts are based on population figures of the resident U.S. population (excluding the District of Columbia) as of July 1, 1993.

State and Local Government Receipts and Expenditures

Source: Bureau of Economic Analysis, U.S. Dept. of Commerce

(billions of dollars)

	1993	1994	First Quarter 1995[1]		1993	1994	First Quarter 1995[1]
Receipts	891.0	943.2	981.2	Transfer payments to persons	250.4	273.3	285.6
Personal tax and nontax receipts	166.1	176.5	182.8	Net interest paid	−53.4	−54.8	−55.6
Income taxes	123.3	131.5	136.4	Interest paid	65.1	65.5	65.9
Nontaxes	22.7	23.8	24.3	Less: Interest received by			
Other	20.1	21.2	22.0	government	118.4	120.4	121.5
Corporate profits tax accruals	30.3	35.4	38.0	Less: Dividends received by			
Indirect business tax and nontax				government	10.4	10.9	11.6
accruals	440.7	462.9	476.5	Subsidies less current surplus of			
Sales taxes	212.4	226.2	233.5	government enterprises	−26.7	−28.6	−29.6
Property taxes	184.0	190.8	196.4	Subsidies	0.4	0.4	0.4
Other	44.3	46.0	46.5	Less: Current surplus of			
Contributions for social insurance	67.8	70.9	73.0	government enterprises	27.1	28.9	30.0
Federal grants-in-aid	186.1	197.6	211.0	Less: Wage accruals less			
Expenditures	864.7	917.0	953.1	disbursements	0.0	0.0	0.0
Purchases	704.7	738.0	764.3	**Surplus or deficit (−), national**			
Compensation of employees	483.0	506.4	521.9	**income and product accounts**	**26.3**	**26.2**	**28.2**
Other	221.7	231.6	242.4				

(1) Seasonally adjusted at annual rates.

State and Local Government Expenditures by Type and Function

Source: Bureau of Economic Analysis, U.S. Dept. Of Commerce

(millions of dollars)

	1992 Expenditures	1992 Purchases	1992 (1)	1993 Expenditures	1993 Purchases	1993 (1)
Total	818,115	676,331	165,831	864,696	704,749	186,689
Central executive, legislative, and judicial activities	50,522	49,831	691	52,755	52,033	722
Administrative, legislative, and judicial activities...	27,672	27,672	...	28,996	28,996	...
Tax collection and financial management	22,850	22,159	691	23,759	23,037	722
Civilian safety	80,708	80,639	69	84,492	84,418	74
Police	35,927	35,927	...	37,529	37,529	...
Fire	14,814	14,814	...	15,538	15,538	...
Correction	29,967	29,898	69	31,425	31,351	74
Education	307,996	301,707	6,289	321,073	314,282	6,791
Elementary and secondary	236,026	236,026	...	247,414	247,414	...
Higher	54,315	54,315	...	55,070	55,070	...
Libraries	4,120	4,120	...	4,276	4,276	...
Other	13,535	7,246	6,289	14,313	7,522	6,791
Health and hospitals	27,937	27,629	308	25,621	25,296	325
Health	20,617	20,617	...	21,505	21,505	...
Hospitals	7,320	7,012	308	4,116	3,791	325
Income support, social security, and welfare ...	187,009	34,894	152,115	206,257	37,342	168,915
Government employees retirement and disability ..	−11,495	3,407	−14,902	−8,621	3,971	−12,592
Workers' Compensation and temporary disability insurance	9,839	1,593	8,246	10,339	1,792	8,547
Medical care	122,520	...	122,520	135,817	...	135,817
Welfare and social services	66,145	29,894	36,251	68,722	31,579	37,143
Veterans benefits and services	182	168	14	190	174	16
Housing and community services	14,986	24,649	...	15,733	26,723	...
Housing, community development, and urban renewal	3,052	3,196	...	2,475	3,280	...
Water	1,843	7,520	...	2,633	8,682	...
Sewerage	4,571	8,413	...	4,544	8,680	...
Sanitation	5,520	5,520	...	6,081	6,081	...
Recreational and cultural activities	12,192	12,192	...	12,467	12,467	...
Energy	−5,393	3,608	...	−5,377	4,171	...
Gas utilities	−58	459	...	−47	518	...
Electric utilities	−5,335	3,149	...	−5,330	3,653	...
Agriculture	3,793	3,793	...	3,884	3,884	...
Natural resources	7,666	7,666	...	8,336	8,336	...
Transportation	76,402	72,487	...	79,909	76,042	...
Highways	60,911	63,304	...	64,499	67,035	...
Water	143	686	...	137	727	...
Air	1,359	3,815	...	1,053	3,750	...
Transit and railroad	13,989	4,682	...	14,220	4,530	...
Economic development, regulation, and services	6,299	6,299	...	6,387	6,387	...
Labor training and services	5,646	4,528	1,118	5,904	4,802	1,102
Commercial activities	−8,981	317	...	−9,764	307	...
Publicly owned liquor store systems	−545	9	...	−550	8	...
Government-administered lotteries and pari-mutuels	−8,539	...	...	−9,257	...	...
Other	103	308	...	43	299	...
Net interest paid[2]	5,227	...	5,227	8,744	...	8,744
Other and unallocable	45,924	45,924	...	48,085	48,085	...

(1) Transfer payments and net interest paid less dividends. (2) Excludes interest received by social insurance funds, which is netted against expenditures for the appropriate functions.

Federal Deposit Insurance Corporation (FDIC)

The Federal Deposit Insurance Corporation (FDIC) is the independent deposit insurance agency created by Congress to maintain stability and public confidence in the nation's banking system. In its unique role as deposit insurer of banks and savings associations, and in cooperation with other federal and state regulatory agencies, the FDIC promotes the safety and soundness of insured depository institutions in the U.S. financial system by identifying, monitoring, and addressing risks to the deposit insurance funds. The FDIC promotes public understanding and sound public policies by providing financial and economic information and analyses. It minimizes disruptive effects from the failure of banks and savings associations. It assures fairness in the sale of financial products and the provision of financial services. The FDIC's income consists of assessments on insured banks and income from investments; it receives no appropriations from Congress. The Corporation may borrow from the U.S. Treasury not to exceed $30 billion outstanding, but has made no such borrowings since it was organized in 1933. The FDIC's Bank Insurance Fund was $24.7 billion (unaudited) and the Savings Association Insurance Fund stood at $2.6 billion (unaudited), as of June 30, 1995.

The Savings and Loan Crisis

Congress authorized the Resolution Trust Corporation (RTC) $105 billion for resolving insolvent savings institutions that failed between 1989 and June 30, 1995. The sunset date for the RTC is Dec. 31, 1995. The RTC has estimated that the S&L cleanup will cost no more than $105 billion and based on current economic conditions could total approximately $90 billion. This does not include $60 billion spent before 1989.

All Banks in U.S.—Number, Deposits

Source: Federal Reserve System, 1925-1960; Federal Deposit Insurance Corp., 1965-95

Comprises all national banks in the U.S. and all state commercial banks, trust companies, mutual stock savings banks, private and industrial banks, and special types of institutions that are treated as banks by the federal bank supervisory agencies. Data as of June 30 prior to 1975, and for 1995.

| | Number of banks | | | | | Total deposits (millions of dollars) | | | | |
| | | F.R.S. members | | Nonmembers | | | F.R.S. members | | Nonmembers | |
Year	Total all banks	Total	Natl.	State	Mutual savings	Other	Total all banks	Total	Natl.	State	Mutual savings	Other
1925	28,479	9,538	8,066	1,472	621	18,320	$51,641	$32,457	$19,912	$12,546	$7,089	$12,095
1930	23,855	8,315	7,247	1,068	604	14,936	59,828	38,069	23,235	14,834	9,117	12,642
1935	16,047	6,410	5,425	985	569	9,068	51,149	34,938	22,477	12,461	9,830	6,381
1940	14,955	6,398	5,164	1,234	551	8,008	70,770	51,729	33,014	18,715	10,631	8,410
1945	14,542	6,840	5,015	1,825	539	7,163	151,033	118,378	76,534	41,844	14,413	18,242
1950	14,674	6,885	4,971	1,914	527	7,262	163,770	122,707	82,430	40,277	19,927	21,137
1955	14,309	6,611	4,744	1,867	525	7,173	208,850	154,670	98,636	56,034	27,310	26,870
1960	14,006	6,217	4,542	1,675	513	7,276	249,163	179,519	116,178	63,341	35,316	34,328
1965	13,876	6,220	4,815	1,405	329	7,327	377,399	275,994	194,337	81,657	45,887	55,518
1970	13,829	5,767	4,620	1,147	327	7,735	541,858	385,176	283,664	101,512	62,684	93,998
1975	14,699	5,787	4,741	1,046	327	8,585	873,335	590,999	447,590	143,409	98,126	184,210
1980	14,758	5,422	4,425	997	323	9,013	1,327,155	847,935	656,752	191,183	134,909	344,311
1985	14,799	6,029	4,959	1,070	392	8,378	2,296,874	1,596,460	1,241,875	354,585	178,786	521,628
1990	12,817	4,988	3,979	1,009	474	7,355	2,864,222	1,956,712	1,558,915	397,797	214,091	693,419
1993	11,567	4,273	3,304	969	609	6,685	2,996,040	2,052,817	1,576,724	476,093	241,705	701,518
1994	11,077	4,050	3,075	975	627	6,400	3,115,829	2,163,277	1,629,997	533,280	241,508	711,044
1995	10,793	3,940	2,946	994	625	6,228	3,162,550	2,187,325	1,617,200	570,125	255,507	719,718

Largest U.S. Commercial Banks

Source: *American Banker* (as of Dec. 31, 1994)

Bank	Assets (millions)	Bank	Assets (millions)
Citibank, New York	$210,487.0	State Street Bank & Trust Co., Boston	$21,610.6
Bank of America, San Francisco	147,670.0	Texas Commerce Bank, Houston	19,804.7
Chemical Bank, New York	135,742.0	Marine Midland Bank, Buffalo, New York	18,336.3
Morgan Guaranty Trust Co., New York	124,384.4	Bank One, Texas, Dallas	18,242.3
Chase Manhattan Bank, New York	94,193.1	NationsBank, Bethesda, Maryland	18,018.3
Bankers Trust Co., New York	71,000.0	Bank of America, Illinois, Chicago	17,551.0
Wells Fargo Bank, San Francisco	52,215.8	Shawmut Bank Connecticut, Hartford	17,116.7
PNC Bank, Pittsburgh	44,624.8	NationsBank of Georgia, Atlanta	16,784.1
First National Bank, Chicago	42,542.9	Union Bank, San Francisco	16,761.1
NationsBank of Texas, Dallas	39,329.0	National Westminster Bank USA, New York	16,661.6
Bank of New York	39,287.4	Seattle Fleet National Bank	15,458.0
First National Bank, Boston	36,886.5	Norwest Bank Minnesota, Minneapolis	15,453.9
First Fidelity Bank, Elkton, Maryland	33,411.4	Key Bank of New York, Albany	14,945.1
Mellon Bank, Pittsburgh	32,489.5	Northern Trust Co., Chicago	14,735.5
Republic National Bank of New York	32,395.5	First Bank, Minneapolis	14,567.0
NBD Bank, Detroit	31,493.5	Wachovia Bank of Georgia, Atlanta	14,550.4
First Union National Bank of Florida, Jacksonville	31,338.6	Shawmut Bank, Boston	14,431.9
NationsBank (Carolinas), Charlotte	31,280.0	Fleet Bank of New York, Albany	14,176.5
Comerica Bank, Detroit	27,044.1	Midlantic Bank, Newark, New Jersey	12,950.9
First Interstate Bank of California, Los Angeles	25,250.8	Meridian Bank, Reading, Pennsylvania	12,845.4
Society National Bank, Cleveland	24,571.4	First of America Bank-Michigan, Kalamazoo	12,383.0
First Union National Bank of North Carolina, Charlotte	23,082.2	United Jersey Bank, Hackensack, New Jersey	12,273.2
NationsBank of Florida, Tampa	22,918.0	Huntington National Bank, Columbus, Ohio	11,968.6
Wachovia Bank of North Carolina, Winston-Salem	22,225.4	Harris Trust & Savings Bank, Chicago	11,944.3
CoreStates Bank, Philadelphia	21,889.0	Bank One, Arizona, Phoenix	11,936.2

World's Largest Banking Companies[1]

Source: *American Banker* (as of Dec. 31, 1994; Japan data as of Mar. 31, 1995)

Banks	Assets (millions)	Banks	Assets (millions)
Sanwa Bank Ltd., Osaka, Japan	$588,349	Barclays Bank Plc, London	$244,753
Dai-Ichi Kangyo Bank Ltd., Tokyo, Japan	587,773	National Westminster Bank Plc, London	244,753
Fuji Bank, Ltd., Tokyo	577,107	Compagnie Financiere de Paribas, Paris	242,146
Sumitomo Bank Ltd., Osaka	571,942	Westdeutsche Landesbank Girozentrale,	
Sakura Bank, Ltd., Tokyo	565,381	Dusseldorf, Germany	237,292
Mitsubishi Bank Ltd., Tokyo	553,515	Toyo Trust & Banking Co. Ltd., Tokyo	236,612
Norinchukin Bank, Tokyo	500,434	Union Bank of Switzerland, Zurich, Switzerland	226,966
Industrial Bank of Japan, Ltd., Tokyo	437,853	Commerzbank, Frankfurt	220,478
Mitsubishi Trust & Banking Corp., Tokyo	394,001	BankAmerica Corp., San Francisco, United States	214,406
Long-Term Credit Bank of Japan Ltd., Tokyo	375,515	Bayerische Vereinsbank, Munich, Germany	204,214
Deutsche Bank, AG, Frankfurt, Germany	367,883	Shoko Chukin Bank, Tokyo	186,800
Sumitomo Trust & Banking Co., Ltd., Osaka	355,984	Nippon Credit Bank, Ltd., Tokyo	183,862
Tokai Bank Ltd., Nagoya, Japan	351,637	Bayerische Hypotheken und Wechsel Bank,	
Mitsui Trust & Banking Co., Ltd., Tokyo	331,209	Munich	177,354
Credit Agricole Mutuel, Paris, France	328,054	Credit Suisse, Zurich	176,910
Credit Lyonnais, Paris	327,806	Zenshinren Bank, Tokyo	175,190
Asahi Bank, Ltd., Tokyo	317,472	Bayerische Landesbank Girozentrale, Munich	171,640
HSBC Holdings, Plc, London, United Kingdom	314,368	Chemical Banking Corp., New York	170,319
Daiwa Bank, Ltd., Osaka	304,716	NationsBank Corp., Charlotte, NC, United States	168,920
ABN-AMRO Bank, N.V., Amsterdam, Netherlands	290,666	Swiss Bank Corp., Basel, Switzerland	162,128
Societe Generale, Paris	277,923	Bankgesellschaft Berlin, AG, Berlin, Germany	158,769
Bank of Tokyo, Ltd.	274,075	Deutsche Genossenschaftsbank, Frankfurt	158,065
Yasuda Trust & Banking Co. Ltd., Tokyo	271,580	Rabobank Nederland, Utrecht, Netherlands	154,992
Banque Nationale de Paris	271,561	J.P. Morgan & Co., Inc., New York	154,331
Dresdner Bank, Frankfurt	258,079	Istituto Bancario San Paolo di Torino, Turin, Italy	153,711
Citicorp, New York, United States	249,049	Abbey National, Plc, London	147,138

(1) Includes bank holding companies and commercial and savings banks. **Note:** Data for U.S. companies in this table include assets not included in "Largest U.S. Commercial Banks" table.

Bank Failures

Source: Federal Deposit Insurance Corp.

Year	Closed or assisted	Year	Closed or assisted	Year	Closed or assisted	Year	Closed or assisted	Year	Closed or assisted
1934	61	1959	3	1969	9	1979	10	1987	203
1935	32	1960	2	1970	8	1980	11	1988	221
1936	72	1961	9	1971	6	1981	10	1989	207
1937	84	1963	2	1972	3	1982	42	1990	169
1938	81	1964	8	1973	6	1983	48	1991	127
1939	72	1965	9	1975	14	1984	80	1992	122
1940	48	1966	8	1976	17	1985	120	1993	41
1955	5	1967	4	1978	7	1986	145	1994	13

Federal Reserve Board Discount Rate

The discount rate is the rate of interest set by the Federal Reserve that member banks are charged when borrowing money through the Federal Reserve System. Data are as of Oct. 1995.

Effective date	Rate	Effective date	Rate	Effective date	Rate	Effective date	Rate	Effective date	Rate	Effective date	Rate
1980:		**1981:**		Oct. 12	9½	**1986:**		**1989:**		**1992:**	
Feb. 15	13	May 5	14	Nov. 22	9	March 7	7	Feb. 24	7	July 3	3
May 30	12	Nov. 2	13	Dec. 15	8½	April 21	6½	**1990:**		**1994:**	
June 13	11	Dec. 4	12	**1984:**		July 11	6	Dec. 18	6½	May 17	3½
July 28	10	**1982:**		April 9	9	Aug. 21	5½	**1991:**		Aug. 16	4
Sept. 26	11	July 20	11½	Nov. 21	8½	**1987:**		Apr. 30	5½	Nov. 15	4¾
Nov. 17	12	Aug. 2	11	Dec. 24	8	Sept. 4	6	Sept. 13	5	**1995:**	
Dec. 5	13	Aug. 16	10½	**1985:**		**1988:**		Nov. 6	4½	Feb. 1	5¼
		Aug. 27	10	May 20	7½	Aug. 9	6½	Dec. 20	3½		

Federal Reserve System

(as of Oct. 1995)

The Federal Reserve System is the central bank for the U.S. The system was established on Dec. 23, 1913, originally to give the country an elastic currency, to provide facilities for discounting commercial paper, and to improve the supervision of banking. Since then, the system's responsibilities have been broadened. Over the years, stability and growth of the economy, a high level of employment, stability in the purchasing power of the dollar, and reasonable balance in transactions with other countries have come to be recognized as primary objectives of governmental economic policy.

The Federal Reserve System consists of the Board of Governors, the 12 District Reserve Banks and their branch offices, and the Federal Open Market Committee. Several advisory councils help the board meet its varied responsibilities.

The hub of the system is the 7-member Board of Governors in Washington. The members of the board are appointed by the president and confirmed by the Senate, to serve 14-year terms. The president also appoints the chairman and vice chairman of the board from among the board members for 4-year terms that may be renewed. Currently, the board members are: Alan Greenspan, Chairman; Alan S. Blinder, Vice Chairman; Edward W. Kelley, Jr.; Lawrence B. Lindsey; Susan M. Phillips; Janet Yellen; and 1 vacancy.

The board is the policy-making body. In addition to its policy-making responsibilities, it supervises the budget and operations of the Reserve Banks, approves the appointments of their presidents, and appoints 3 of each District Bank's directors, including the chairman and vice chairman of each Reserve Bank's board.

The 12 Reserve Banks and their branch offices serve as the decentralized portion of the system, carrying out day-to-day operations such as circulating currency and coin and providing fiscal agency functions and payments mechanism services. The District Banks are in Boston, New York, Philadelphia, Cleveland, Richmond, Atlanta, Chicago, St. Louis, Minneapolis, Kansas City, Dallas, and San Francisco.

The system's principal function is monetary policy, which it controls using 3 tools: reserve requirements, the discount rate, and open market operations. Uniform reserve requirements, set by the board, are applied to the transaction accounts and nonpersonal time deposits of all depository institutions. Responsibility for setting the discount rate (the interest rate at which depository institutions can borrow money from the Reserve Banks) is shared by the Board of Governors and the Reserve Banks. Changes in the discount rate are recommended by the individual boards of directors of the Reserve Banks and are subject to approval by the Board of Governors. The most important tool of monetary policy is open market operations (the purchase and sale of government securities). Responsibility for influencing the cost and availability of money and credit through the purchase and sale of government securities lies with the Federal Open Market Committee (FOMC). This committee is composed of the 7 members of the Board of Governors, the president of the Federal Reserve Bank of New York, and 4 other Federal Reserve Bank presidents, who serve one-year terms on a rotating basis. The committee bases its decisions on current economic and financial developments and outlook, setting yearly growth objectives for key measures of money supply and credit. The decisions of the committee are carried out by the Domestic Trading Desk of the Federal Reserve Bank of New York.

The Federal Reserve Act prescribes a Federal Advisory Council, consisting of one member from each Federal Reserve District, elected annually by the Board of Directors of each of the 12 Federal Reserve Banks. They meet with the Federal Reserve Board 4 times a year to discuss business and financial conditions and to make advisory recommendations.

The Consumer Advisory Council is a statutory body, including both consumer and creditor representatives, which advises the Board of Governors on its implementation of consumer regulations and other consumer-related matters.

Following the passage of the Monetary Control Act of 1980, the Board of Governors established the Thrift Institutions Advisory Council to provide information and views on the special needs and problems of thrift institutions. The group is composed of representatives of mutual savings banks, savings and loan associations, and credit unions.

United States Mint

Source: United States Mint, U.S. Dept. of the Treasury

The United States Mint was created by an act of Congress on April 2, 1792, which established the U.S. national coinage system. Supervision of the mint was a function of the secretary of state, but in 1799 the mint became an independent agency reporting directly to the president. The mint was made a statutory bureau of the Treasury Department in 1873, with a director appointed by the President to oversee its operations.

The mint manufactures and ships all U.S. coins for circulation to the Federal Reserve banks and branches, which issue coins to the public and the business community through depository institutions. The mint also safeguards the Treasury Department's stored gold and silver and other monetary assets.

The composition of dimes, quarters, and half dollars, traditionally produced from silver, was changed by the Coinage Act of 1965, which mandated that these coins be minted from a cupronickel-clad alloy and reduced the silver content of the half dollar to 40%. In 1970, legislative action mandated that the half dollar and a dollar coin be minted from the same cupronickel-clad alloy.

The Eisenhower dollar was minted from 1971 through 1978, when legislation called for the minting of the smaller Susan B. Anthony dollar coin. The Anthony dollar, which was minted from 1979 through 1981, marked the first time that a woman, other than a mythical figure, appeared on a U.S. coin produced for general circulation.

Mint headquarters is in Washington, DC. Mint production facilities are in Philadelphia, Denver, San Francisco, and West Point, NY. In addition, the mint is responsible for the U.S. Bullion Depository at Fort Knox, KY.

Proof coin sets, silver proof coin sets, and uncirculated coin sets are available annually from the mint. The mint also produces ongoing series of national and historic medals in honor of outstanding persons or events and sites of special meaning to the American people.

Since 1982, the mint has produced the following congressionally authorized commemorative coins: the 1982 George Washington commemorative half dollar; 1984 U.S. Olympic coins; 1986 U.S. Statue of Liberty coins; 1987 Bicentennial of the U.S. Constitution coins; 1989 U.S. Congressional coins; the 1990 Eisenhower Centennial coin; the 1991 United Services Organization 59th Anniversary coin; the 1991 Korean War Memorial coin; 1991 Mount Rushmore Anniversary coins; 1992 U.S. Olympic coins; the 1992 White House 200th Anniversary coin; 1992 Christopher Columbus Quincentenary coins; 1993 Bill of Rights coins; 1993 World War II 50th Anniversary coins; 1994 World Cup USA coins; the Thomas Jefferson 250th Anniversary coin; the U.S. Veterans Commemorative coins (featuring the Prisoner of War coin, the Vietnam Veterans Memorial coin, and the Women in Military Service for America coin); the Bicentennial of the U.S. Capitol Commemorative Silver Dollar; and 1995 Civil War Battlefield coins.

Sales of the 1995 and 1996 Atlanta Centennial Olympic coins will help support staging of the 1996 Olympic Games in Atlanta. Sales of the 1996 National Community Service Silver Dollar will benefit innovative community service programs at U.S. universities.

The congressionally authorized American eagle gold and silver bullion coins produced by the mint are available through dealers worldwide. The gold eagles are sold in one-ounce, half-ounce, quarter-ounce, and one-tenth-ounce sizes; the price of the coins fluctuates with the daily market value of gold. The American eagle silver bullion coin contains one troy ounce of .999 fine silver and is priced according to the daily market value of silver. These coins also are available in proof condition, separately priced.

The mint offers free public tours and operates sales centers at the U.S. mints in Denver and Philadelphia, and also operates a sales center at Union Station in Washington, DC.

Information about mint programs and products is available from the United States Mint, Customer Service Center, 10001 Aerospace Rd., Lanham, MD 20706. Telephone: (202) 283-COIN.

Portraits on U.S. Treasury Bills, Bonds, Notes, and Savings Bonds

Denomination	Savings bonds	Treasury bills*	Treasury bonds*	Treasury notes*
50	Washington		Jefferson	
75	Adams			
100	Jefferson		Jackson	
200	Madison			
500	Hamilton		Washington	
1,000	Franklin	H. McCulloch	Lincoln	Lincoln
5,000	Revere	J. G. Carlisle	Monroe	Monroe
10,000	J. Wilson	J. Sherman	Cleveland	Cleveland
50,000		C. Glass		
100,000		A. Gallatin	Grant	Grant
1,000,000		O. Wolcott	T. Roosevelt	T. Roosevelt
100,000,000				Madison
500,000,000				McKinley

*The U.S. Treasury discontinued issuing treasury bill, bond, and note certificates in 1986. Since then, all issues of marketable treasury securities have only been available in book-entry form, although some certificates remain in circulation.

Denominations of U.S. Currency

The largest denomination of U.S. currency now being issued is the $100 bill. Issuance of currency in denominations larger than $100 was discontinued in 1969. As large-denomination bills reach the Federal Reserve Bank, they are removed from circulation. Because some discontinued currency is expected to be in the hands of holders for many years, the description of the various denominations below is continued.

Amt.	Portrait	Embellishment on back	Amt.	Portrait	Embellishment on back
$ 1	Washington	Great Seal of U.S.	$ 100	Franklin	Independence Hall
2	Jefferson	Signers of Declaration	500	McKinley	Ornate denominational marking
5	Lincoln	Lincoln Memorial	1,000	Cleveland	Ornate denominational marking
10	Hamilton	U.S. Treasury	5,000	Madison	Ornate denominational marking
20	Jackson	White House	10,000	Chase	Ornate denominational marking
50	Grant	U.S. Capitol	100,000*	W. Wilson	Ornate denominational marking

* For use only in transactions between Federal Reserve System and Treasury Department.

New U.S. Currency Design

U.S. Treasury Secretary Robert E. Rubin and Federal Reserve Board Chairman Alan Greenspan announced, Sept. 27, 1995, that the U.S. will issue a new $100 note that has been redesigned to incorporate many new and modified anticounterfeiting features. The new note, scheduled for release in early 1996, is the first of the U.S. currency series to be redesigned. New currency will be issued at a rate of one denomination per year. Old notes will be removed from circulation as they are returned to the Federal Reserve but all U.S. currency will continue to be honored at full face value. The new $100 bill will have the following features: a larger portrait, moved off-center to create space to incorporate a watermark; a watermark (seen only when held up to the light) to the right of the portrait, depicting the same historical figure; a security thread (to be located in a unique position on each denomination) that will glow red when exposed to ultraviolet light in a dark environment; color-shifting ink that changes from green to black when viewed at different angles, to appear in the numeral on the lower, front right-hand corner of the bill; microprinting in the numeral in the note's lower, front left-hand corner and on the portrait (on Benjamin Franklin's lapel); and other features for security, machine authentication, and processing of the currency. Many or all of these features are expected to appear in all subsequent denominations. More information on the new currency is available on the Treasury's interactive fax system: (202) 622-2040.

U.S. Currency and Coin

Source: Financial Management Service, U.S. Dept. of the Treasury (Mar. 31, 1995)

Amounts Outstanding and in Circulation

Currency	Total currency and coin	Total currency	Federal Reserve notes[1]	U.S. notes	Currency no longer issued
Amounts outstanding	$476,206,751,539	$453,562,839,641	$452,980,333,318	$322,539,016	$259,967,307
Less amounts held by:					
Treasury	373,714,472	46,753,867	6,351,929	40,201,239	200,699
Federal Reserve banks . .	74,223,427,618	73,789,758,962	73,789,755,362	—	3,600
Amounts in circulation . . .	$401,609,609,449	$379,726,326,812	$379,184,226,027	$282,337,777	$259,763,008

Coins[2]	Total	Dollars[3]	Fractional coins
Amounts outstanding	$22,643,911,898	$2,024,703,898	$20,619,208,000
Less amounts held by:			
Treasury	326,960,605	247,063,163	79,897,442
Federal Reserve banks . .	433,668,656	44,515,498	389,153,158
Amounts in circulation . . .	$21,883,282,637	$1,733,125,237	$20,150,157,400

Currency in Circulation by Denominations

Denomination		Total currency in circulation	Federal Reserve notes[1]	U.S. notes	Currency no longer issued
1	Dollar	$5,845,268,648	$5,696,261,845	$143,481	$148,863,322
2	Dollars	1,003,940,584	871,251,242	132,676,766	12,576
5	Dollars	6,948,740,110	6,804,255,990	110,912,910	33,571,210
10	Dollars	13,013,456,290	12,990,258,310	5,950	23,192,030
20	Dollars	76,265,781,080	76,245,675,540	3,380	20,102,160
50	Dollars	42,906,224,700	42,894,728,700	—	11,496,000
100	Dollars	233,423,525,300	233,362,953,900	38,595,200	21,976,000
500	Dollars	145,442,500	145,254,500	—	188,000
1,000	Dollars	168,722,000	168,516,000	—	206,000
5,000	Dollars	1,775,000	1,720,000	—	55,000
10,000	Dollars	3,450,000	3,350,000	—	100,000
Fractional parts		485	—	—	485
Partial notes[4]		115	—	90	25
Total currency		**$379,726,326,812**	**$379,184,226,027**	**$282,337,777**	**$259,763,008**

Comparative Totals of Money in Circulation — Selected Dates

Date	Dollars (in millions)	Per capita[5]	Date	Dollars (in millions)	Per capita[5]	Date	Dollars (in millions)	Per capita[5]
Mar. 31, 1995	401,610.0	1,531.39	June 30, 1975	81,196.4	380.08	June 30, 1940	7,847.5	59.40
Mar. 31, 1994	371,466.0	1,428.37	June 30, 1970	54,351.0	265.39	June 30, 1935	5,567.1	43.75
Mar. 31, 1993	332,822.7	1,293.58	June 30, 1965	39,719.8	204.14	June 30, 1930	4,522.0	36.74
Mar. 31, 1992	303,215.0	1,219.15	June 30, 1960	32,064.6	177.47	June 30, 1925	4,815.2	41.56
Mar. 31, 1990	257,664.4	1,028.71	June 30, 1955	30,229.3	182.90	June 30, 1920	5,467.6	51.36
June 30, 1985	185,890.7	778.58	June 30, 1950	27,156.3	179.03	June 30, 1915	3,319.6	33.01
June 30, 1980	127,097.2	558.28	June 30, 1945	26,746.4	191.14	June 30, 1910	3,148.7	34.07

(1) Issued on and after July 1, 1929. (2) Excludes coin sold to collectors at premium prices. (3) Includes $481,781,898 in standard silver dollars. (4) Represents value of certain partial denominations not presented for redemption. (5) Based on Bureau of the Census estimates of population.

The requirement for a gold reserve against U.S. notes was repealed by Public Law 90-269 approved Mar. 18, 1968. Silver certificates issued on and after July 1, 1929, became redeemable from the general fund on June 24, 1968. The amount of security after those dates has been reduced accordingly.

Consumer Credit Outstanding, 1992-94

Source: Federal Reserve System

(billions of dollars)

Estimated amounts of credit outstanding as of end of year. Not seasonally adjusted.

	1992[R]	1993[R]	1994[R]		1992[R]	1993[R]	1994[R]
Credit outstanding	804.6	863.5	984.7	Commercial banks	109.6	122.0	141.9
Ratio to disposable personal				Finance companies	57.3	56.1	61.6
income[1] (percent)	18.2	18.4	19.9	Pools of securitized assets[3]	33.9	39.5	34.9
Installment[2]	748.1	809.4	925.0	Revolving	271.9	301.8	352.3
By major holder				Commercial banks	133.0	149.9	180.2
Commercial banks	330.1	367.6	427.9	Finance companies	44.5	50.1	55.3
Finance companies	118.3	116.5	134.8	Pools of securitized assets[3]	74.9	79.9	94.4
Credit unions	91.7	101.6	119.6	Other	218.0	226.1	254.5
Savings institutions	37.0	37.9	38.5	Commercial banks	87.5	95.6	105.8
Nonfinancial business	49.6	55.3	61.0	Finance companies	61.0	60.4	73.2
Pools of securitized assets[3]	121.4	130.6	143.3	Nonfinancial business	5.1	5.2	5.6
By major type of credit[4]				Pools of securitized assets[3]	12.6	11.3	14.0
Automobile	258.2	281.5	318.2	**Noninstallment**	**56.5**	**54.1**	**59.7**

(1) Based on fourth quarter seasonally adjusted disposable personal income at annual rates as published by the U.S. Bureau of Economic Analysis. (2) The Board's series on amounts of credit covers most short- and intermediate-term credit extended to individuals that is scheduled to be repaid in two or more installments. (3) Outstanding balances of pools upon which securities have been issued; these balances are no longer carried on the balance sheets of the loan originator. (4) Totals include estimates for certain holders for which only consumer credit totals are available. (R) Revised.

Leading U.S. Businesses in 1994

Source: *FORTUNE* Magazine

(millions of dollars in revenues)

Aerospace

Boeing	$21,924
United Technologies	21,197
McDonnell Douglas	13,176
Lockheed	13,130
AlliedSignal	12,817
Martin Marietta	9,874
Textron	9,683
Northrop Grumman	6,711
General Dynamics	3,702
Gencorp	1,740

Airlines

AMR	$16,137
UAL	13,950
Delta Air Lines	12,359
Northwest Airlines	9,143
USAir Group	6,997
Continental Airlines	5,670
Trans World Airlines	3,408
Southwest Airlines	2,592
America West	1,409
Alaska Air Group	1,316

Apparel

Levi Strauss Associates	$6,074
VF	4,972
Fruit of the Loom	2,298
Liz Claiborne	2,163
Kellwood	1,203
Russell	1,098
Warnaco Group	789

Beverages

Coca-Cola	$16,172
Anheuser-Busch	12,054
Coca-Cola Enterprises	6,011
Whitman	2,659
Adolph Coors	1,663
Brown-Forman	1,401

Brokerage

Merrill Lynch	$18,233
Lehman Brothers	9,190
Salomon	6,278
Paine Webber Group	3,964
Bear Stearns	3,441
Charles Schwab	1,263

Building Materials, Glass

Corning	$4,799
Owens-Illinois	3,653
Owens-Corning Fiberglas	3,351
Armstrong World Ind.	2,753
USG	2,290

Chemicals

E. I. Du Pont De Nemours	$34,968
Dow Chemical	20,015
Occidental Petroleum	9,416
Monsanto	8,272
W. R. Grace	6,381
PPG Industries	6,331
Union Carbide	4,865
Eastman Chemical	4,329
FMC	4,051
Lyondell Petrochemical	3,857

Commercial Banks

Citicorp	$31,650
Bankamerica Corp.	16,531
Nationsbank Corp.	13,126
Chemical Banking Corp.	12,685
J. P. Morgan & Co.	11,915
Chase Manhattan Corp.	11,187
Banc One Corp.	7,857
Bankers Trust N.Y. Corp.	7,503
First Union Corp.	6,254
Norwest Corp.	6,032

Computers, Office Equipment

IBM	$64,052
Hewlett-Packard	24,991
Digital Equipment	13,451
Compaq Computer	10,866
Apple Computer	9,189
Unisys	7,400
Sun Microsystems	4,690
Pitney Bowes	3,823
Seagate Technology	3,500
Dell Computer	3,475

Diversified Financials

ITT	$23,767
Fed. Natl. Mortgage Assn.	18,572
American Express	15,593
Loews	13,515
Morgan Stanley Group	9,376
Federal Home Loan Mtg.	6,923
Dean Witter Discover	6,603
American General	4,841
Household International	4,603
Berkshire Hathaway	3,847

Electric and Gas Utilities

Pacific Gas and Electric	$10,447
SCECorp	8,345
Southern	8,297
UNICOM	6,278
Consol. Edison of N.Y.	6,240
Entergy	5,963
Public Service Ent. Group	5,916
Texas Utilities	5,664
American Electric Power	5,505
FPL Group	5,423

Electronics, Electrical Equip.

General Electric	$64,687
Motorola	22,245
Intel	11,521
Rockwell International	11,205
Texas Instruments	10,315
Raytheon	10,013
Westinghouse Electric	9,208
Emerson Electric	8,607
Whirlpool	8,104
Cooper Industries	6,258

Entertainment

Walt Disney	$10,055
Viacom	7,637
Time Warner	7,396
Capital Cities/ABC	6,379
CBS	3,712
Turner Broadcasting	2,809

Food

Philip Morris	$53,776
Conagra	23,512
Sara Lee	15,536
IBP	12,075
Archer Daniels Midland	11,374
General Mills	8,517
Ralston Purina	7,705
CPC International	7,425
H. J. Heinz	7,047
Campbell Soup	6,691

Food and Drug Stores

Kroger	$22,959
American Stores	18,355
Safeway	15,627
Albertson's	11,895
Winn-Dixie Stores	11,082
Great Atl. & Pacific Tea	10,384
Walgreen	9,235
Publix Super Markets	8,742
Supermarkets Genl. Hldgs.	7,226
Vons	4,997

Food Services

Pepsico	$28,472
McDonald's	8,321
Aramark	5,162
Flagstar	3,526
Wendy's International	1,398
Morrison Restaurants	1,213
Shoney's	1,166
Family Restaurants	1,113
Foodmaker	1,053
Brinker International	878

Forest and Paper Products

International Paper	$14,966
Georgia-Pacific	12,738
Weyerhaeuser	10,398
Kimberly-Clark	7,364
Stone Container	5,749
James River Corp. of VA	5,417
Champion International	5,318
Mead	5,123
Scott Paper	4,726
Boise Cascade	4,142

Furniture

Leggett & Platt	$1,858
Interco	1,736
Herman Miller	953
Hon Industries	846
Kimball International	822
La-Z-Boy Chair	805

General Merchandisers

Wal-Mart Stores	$83,412
Sears Roebuck	54,559
Kmart	34,313
Dayton Hudson	21,311
J. C. Penney	21,082
May Department Stores	12,223
Federated Dept. Stores	8,316
Dillard Dept. Stores	5,729
Nordstrom	3,894
Harcourt General	3,640

Industrial and Farm Equip.

Caterpillar	$14,328
Tenneco	13,222
Deere	9,030
Dresser Industries	5,331
Black & Decker	5,248
Cummins Engine	4,737
Ingersoll-Rand	4,507
American Standard	4,457
Dover	3,085
Parker Hannifin	2,576

Insurance (Stock)

American Intl. Group	$22,386
Travelers Inc.	18,465
Cigna	18,392
Aetna Life & Casualty	17,525
Lincoln National	6,984

Insurance (Mutual)

State Farm Group	$38,850
Prudential Ins. of America	36,946
Metropolitan Life Insurance	22,258
New York Life Insurance	12,067
Nationwide Insurance Ent.	11,183

Metal Products

Gillette	$6,070
Masco	4,468
Crown Cork & Seal	4,452
Illinois Tool Works	3,461
Tyco International	3,263
Ball	2,595
Stanley Works	2,511
Newell	2,075
Mascotech	1,702
Hillenbrand Industries	1,577

Metals

Alcoa	$10,392
Reynolds Metals	6,013
Bethlehem Steel	4,819
LTV	4,529
Inland Steel Industries	4,497
Phelps Dodge	3,289
Nucor	2,976
Alumax	2,755
Maxxam	2,116
AK Steel Holding	2,017

Motor Vehicles and Parts

General Motors	$154,951
Ford Motor	128,439
Chrysler	52,224
TRW	9,087
Johnson Controls	6,871
Dana	6,741
Eaton	6,052
Navistar International	5,337
Paccar	4,499
Lear Seating	3,147

Petroleum Refining

Exxon	$101,459
Mobil	59,621
Texaco	33,768
Chevron	31,064
Amoco	26,953
USX	16,799
Atlantic Richfield	15,682
Phillips Petroleum	12,367
Coastal	10,013
Ashland	9,505

Pharmaceuticals

Johnson & Johnson	$15,734
Merck	14,970
Bristol-Myers Squibb	11,984
Abbott Laboratories	9,156
American Home Products	8,966
Pfizer	8,281
Eli Lilly	7,001
Warner-Lambert	6,417
Schering-Plough	4,657
Upjohn	3,566

Publishing & Printing

R.R. Donnelley & Sons	$4,889
Times Mirror	3,856
Gannett	3,825
Reader's Digest Assn.	2,806
McGraw-Hill	2,761
Knight-Ridder	2,649
New York Times	2,358
Tribune	2,155
Dow Jones	2,091
American Greetings	1,781

Rubber and Plastic Prods.

Goodyear Tire & Rubber	$12,288
Premark International	3,451
Rubbermaid	2,169
M. A. Hanna	1,839
Raychem	1,462
Cooper Tire & Rubber	1,406
Mark IV Industries	1,313
Foamex	1,088
Standard Products	872

Scientific, Photographic, and Control Equip.

Xerox	$17,837
Eastman Kodak	16,862
Minnesota Mining & Mfg.	15,079
Baxter International	9,324
Honeywell	6,057
EG&G	2,633
Becton Dickinson	2,559
Polaroid	2,313
Bausch & Lomb	1,851
Thermo Electron	1,585

Soaps, Cosmetics

Procter & Gamble	$30,296
Colgate-Palmolive	7,588
Avon Products	4,325
Dial	3,547
Clorox	1,856
Intl. Flavors & Fragr.	1,315
Alberto-Culver	1,216
Helene Curtis Industries	1,187
Safety-Kleen	791

Specialist Retailers

Price/Costco	$16,481
Home Depot	12,477
Melville	11,286
Toys "R" Us	8,746
Woolworth	8,293
Limited	7,321
Lowe's	6,111
Tandy	4,944
Office Depot	4,266
Circuit City Stores	4,130

Telecommunications

AT&T	$75,094
GTE	19,944
BellSouth	16,845
Bell Atlantic	13,791
MCI Communications	13,338
NYNEX	13,307
Sprint	12,662
Ameritech	12,570
SBC Communications	11,619
US West	11,506

Textiles

Shaw Industries	$2,789
Burlington Industries	2,127
Springs Industries	2,069
Westpoint Stevens	1,597
Collins & Aikman	1,536
Mohawk Industries	1,437
UNIFI	1,385
TRIARC	1,074
Fieldcrest Cannon	1,064
JPS Textile Group	828

Tobacco

RJR Nabisco Holdings	$15,366
American Brands	8,442
Universal	2,975
UST	1,198
Standard Commercial	1,047
Dibrell Brothers	919

Toys, Sporting Goods

Mattel	$3,205
Hasbro	2,670

Transportation Equipment

Brunswick	$2,836
Trinity Industries	1,785
Harley-Davidson	1,542
Polaris Industries	826

U.S. Corporations With Largest Revenues in 1994

Source: *FORTUNE* Magazine

(millions of dollars)

Company, headquarters	Revenues	Company, headquarters	Revenues
General Motors, Detroit, MI	$154,951	Chrysler, Highland Park, MI	$52,224
Ford Motor, Dearborn, MI	128,439	State Farm Group, Bloomington, IL	38,850
Exxon, Irving, TX	101,459	Prudential Ins. Co. of America, Newark, NJ	36,946
Wal-Mart Stores, Bentonville, AR	83,412	E. I. Du Pont de Nemours, Wilmington, DE	34,968
AT&T, New York, NY	75,094	Kmart, Troy, MI	34,313
General Electric, Fairfield, CT	64,687	Texaco, White Plains, NY	33,768
IBM, Armonk, NY	64,052	Citicorp, New York, NY	31,650
Mobil, Fairfax, VA	59,621	Chevron, San Francisco, CA	31,064
Sears Roebuck, Chicago, IL	54,559	Procter & Gamble, Cincinnati, OH	30,296
Philip Morris, New York, NY	53,776	Pepsico, Purchase, NY	28,472

Largest Corporate Mergers or Acquisitions in U.S.

Source: Securities Data Co.

(as of Oct. 1995; most recent mergers and acquisitions may not be complete)

Company	Acquirer	Dollars	Year	Company	Acquirer	Dollars	Year
RJR Nabisco	Kohlberg Kravis Roberts	30.6 bil	1989	Marathon Oil	U.S. Steel	6.4 bil	1982
McCaw Cellular Communications	AT&T	18.9 bil	1994	Upjohn	Pharmacia AB	6.3 bil	1995
Capital Cities/ABC	Walt Disney	18.8 bil	1995	Contel	GTE	6.2 bil	1991
Warner Communications	Time	14.1 bil	1989	Medco	Merck	6.2 bil	1993
				Marion Laboratories	Dow Chemical	6.2 bil	1989
US West-Domestic Cellular	AirTouch Communications	13.5 bil	1994	Beatrice	BCI Holdings	6.1 bil	1986
Kraft	Philip Morris	13.4 bil	1988	Pillsbury	Grand Metropolitan	5.8 bil	1989
Gulf Oil	Standard Oil of Calif.	13.4 bil	1984	First Financial Management	First Data	5.8 bil	1995
NYNEX-Cellular Phone Bus.	Bell Atlantic	13.0 bil	1995	MCA	Seagram	5.7 bil	1995
Squibb	Bristol-Myers	12.1 bil	1989	Superior Oil	investor group	5.7 bil	1983
Allstate	shareholders	12.0 bil	1995	Superior Oil	Mobil Oil	5.7 bil	1984
Getty Oil	Texaco	10.1 bil	1984	General Foods	Philip Morris	5.7 bil	1985
Chase Manhattan	Chemical Banking	9.9 bil	1995	Shell Oil	Royal Dutch/Shell	5.7 bil	1985
Paramount	Viacom	9.6 bil	1994	Hospital Corp. of America	Columbia Healthcare	5.6 bil	1994
American Cyanamid	American Home Products	9.6 bil	1994	Safeway Stores	SSI Holdings	5.3 bil	1986
PacTel	shareholders	8.6 bil	1994	Syntex	Roche Holding	5.3 bil	1994
Blockbuster	Viacom	8.0 bil	1994	First Chicago	NBD Bancorp	5.3 bil	1995
SmithKline Beckman	Beecham Group	7.9 bil	1989	Healthtrust-The Hospital	Columbia/HCA Healthcare	5.2 bil	1995
NCR	AT&T	7.9 bil	1991	Lockheed	Martin Marietta	5.2 bil	1995
Standard Oil	British Petroleum	7.9 bil[1]	1987	Farmers Group	B.A.T. Industries	5.2 bil	1988
Conoco	Du Pont	7.6 bil	1981	Texasgulf	Elf Aquitaine	5.1 bil	1981
MCA	Matsushita Electrical	7.4 bil	1991	Sterling Drug	Eastman Kodak	5.1 bil	1988
Marion Merrell Dow	Hoechst AG	7.1 bil	1995	Signal	Allied	5.1 bil	1985
Turner Broadcasting System	Time Warner	6.9 bil	1995	First Fidelity	First Union	5.1 bil	1995
Scott Paper	Kimberly-Clark	6.8 bil	1995	Dean Witter Discover	shareholders	5.0 bil	1993
RCA	General Electric	6.6 bil	1986	Hughes Aircraft	General Motors	5.0 bil	1985
Federated Dept. Stores	Campeau	6.5 bil	1988	CBS	Westinghouse Electric	5.0 bil	1995

(1) For the 45% of Standard Oil that British Petroleum did not already own.

U.S Multinational Companies[1], 1982-93

Source: Bureau of Economic Analysis, U.S. Dept. of Commerce

	MNCs worldwide[2]	U.S. Parent Companies	Foreign Affiliates		MNCs worldwide[2]	U.S. Parent Companies	Foreign Affiliates
Total assets				1990	4,737,147	3,243,721	1,493,426
Millions of dollars:				1991	4,794,100	3,252,534	1,541,566
1982	3,493,105	2,741,619	751,486	1992	4,904,955	3,330,886	1,574,069
1983	3,653,616	2,902,793	750,823	1993	5,068,946	3,495,055	1,573,891
1984	3,820,025	3,060,031	759,994	Percentage change at annual rates:			
1985	4,297,034	3,462,398	834,636	1982-89	4.3	4.2	4.6
1986	4,723,294	3,792,001	931,293	1989-90	7.1	3.4	16.2
1987	5,285,962	4,175,308	1,110,654	1990-91	1.2	0.3	3.2
1988	5,569,767	4,363,441	1,206,326	1991-92	2.3	2.4	2.1
1989	6,182,401	4,852,373	1,330,028	1992-93	3.3	4.9	(*)
1990	6,510,086	4,951,048	1,559,038	**Number of employees**			
1991	6,861,631	5,183,286	1,678,345	Thousands:			
1992	7,341,796	5,579,798	1,761,998	1982	25,344.8	18,704.6	6,640.2
1993	8,138,040	6,084,571	2,053,469	1983	24,782.6	18,399.5	6,383.1
Percentage change at annual rates:				1984	24,548.4	18,130.9	6,417.5
1982-89	8.5	8.5	8.5	1985	24,531.9	18,112.6	6,419.3
1989-90	5.3	2.0	17.2	1986	24,082.0	17,831.8	6,250.2
1990-91	5.4	4.7	7.7	1987	24,255.4	17,985.8	6,269.6
1991-92	7.0	7.6	5.0	1988	24,141.1	17,737.6	6,403.5
1992-93	10.8	9.0	16.5	1989	25,387.5	18,765.4	6,622.1
Sales				1990	25,263.6	18,429.7	6,833.9
Millions of dollars:				1991	24,837.1	17,958.9	6,878.2
1982	3,284,168	2,348,388	935,780	1992	24,189.7	17,529.6	6,660.1
1983	3,263,802	2,377,488	886,314	1993	24,413.4	17,682.3	6,731.1
1984	3,407,337	2,508,779	898,558	Percentage change at annual rates:			
1985	3,482,155	2,586,695	895,460	1982-89	(*)	(*)	(*)
1986	3,473,354	2,544,439	928,915	1989-90	−0.5	−1.8	3.2
1987	3,742,022	2,689,227	1,052,795	1990-91	−1.7	−2.6	0.6
1988	4,022,942	2,828,209	1,194,733	1991-92	−2.6	−2.4	−3.2
1989	4,421,731	3,136,837	1,284,894	1992-93	0.9	0.9	1.1

(1) Banks not included. (2) The MNC totals for assets and sales contain duplication because they do not exclude positions and transactions between parent companies and foreign affiliates. (*) Less than 0.05 percent.

Fastest Growing Franchises in 1994[1]

Source: Reprinted with permission from *Entrepreneur* Magazine, January 1995

Company	Business	Minimum start-up cost[2]	Company	Business	Minimum start-up cost[2]
Subway	submarine sandwiches	$43,000	Furniture Medic	cabinet refacing	$5,600
Choice Hotels Intl.	hotels and motels	1,500,000	Chem-Dry Carpet Drapery & Upholstery Cleaning	carpet, upholstery, and drapery services	3,550
McDonald's	hamburgers	400,000	Century 21 Real Estate		
7-Eleven Convenience Stores	convenience stores	12,500+	Corp.	real estate services	varies
Burger King Corp.	hamburgers	73,000	Holiday Inn Worlwide	hotels and motels	varies
Dunkin' Donuts	donuts	181,600	Baskin-Robbins USA Co.	ice cream	80,200
The Historical Research Center	misc. retail products	20,000	Play It Again Sports	sports equipment and apparel	94,000
Hardee's	hamburgers	497,200	Super 8 Motels Inc.	hotels and motels	300,000
Tower Cleaning Systems	commercial cleaning	1,190	Futurekids	children's computer learning centers	45,000
Coverall North America Inc.	commercial cleaning	350			
Mail Boxes Etc.	postal and business services	68,500	Merry Maids	residential cleaning	6,950
Re/Max Intl. Inc.	real estate services	60,000	Arby's Inc.	misc. fast foods	525,000
Jackson Hewitt Tax Service	income tax services	13,000	Applebee's Neighborhood Grill & Bar	misc. full-service restaurants	1,130,000
Coldwell Banker Residential Affiliates Inc.	real estate services	4,000 or 25,000	Super Coups	direct-mail advertising	3,470
GNC Franchising Inc.	health food stores	73,700	Great Clips Inc.	hair care	55,600
Jani-King	commercial cleaning	2,400+	Pretzel Time	pretzels	112,700

(1) Based on the number of new franchise units added. (2) Not including franchise fee, which varies.

Largest U.S. Black-Owned Companies in 1994

Source: *Black Enterprise* Magazine

Company, Location (Business)	Sales (millions)	Company, Location (Business)	Sales (millions)
TLC Beatrice International Holdings Inc., New York (international food processor & distributor)	$1,800.0	RMS Technologies Inc., New Castle, DE (computer & tech. services)	$137.0
Johnson Publishing Co. Inc., Chicago (publishing, broadcasting, TV prod., cosmetics, hair care)	306.6	The Anderson-Dubose Co., Solon, OH (food distributor)	118.0
Philadelphia Coca-Cola Bottling Co. Inc., Philadelphia	305.0	Gold Line Refining Ltd., Houston (oil refinery)	108.6
H. J. Russell & Co., Atlanta (construction, communications, airport concessions)	154.7	Uniworld Group Inc., New York (advertising, public relations, event marketing, TV programming)	104.1
Pulsar Data Systems Inc., Marlton, NJ (systems integration, office automation, computer reseller)	115.2	BET Holdings, Washington, DC (cable TV network, magazine pub.)	97.5

Capital Gains Tax

Source: U.S. Chamber of Commerce; as of Oct. 15, 1995

The following shows how the maximum tax rate on net long-term capital gains for individuals has changed since 1960.

Year	Maximum rate (percentage)	Year	Maximum rate (percentage)	Year	Maximum rate (percentage)	Year	Maximum rate (percentage)	Year	Maximum rate (percentage)
1960	25.0	1971	32.5	1978	28.0	1987	28.0	1990	28.0[3]
1970	29.5	1972	35.0[1]	1981	20.0	1988	33.0[2]		

(1) From 1972 to 1976, the interplay of minimum tax and maximum tax resulted in a marginal rate of 49.125%. (2) Statutory maximum of 28%, but "phase-out" notch increased marginal rate to 33%; interplay of all "phase outs" could have increased marginal rate to 49.5%. (3) The Budget Act of 1990 increased the statutory rate to 31%, and capped the marginal rate at 28%; however, some taxpayers will face effective marginal rates of more than 34% due to the phase out of personal exemptions and itemized deductions.

1995 Federal Corporate Tax Rates

Taxable Income Amount	Tax Rate	Taxable Income Amount	Tax Rate
Not more than $50,000	15%	$335,001 to $10,000,000	34%
$50,001 to $75,000	25%	$10,000,001 to $15,000,000	35%
$75,001 to $100,000	34%	$15,000,001 to $18,333,333	38%
$100,001 to $335,000	39%	More than $18,333,333	35%

Personal service corporations (used by professional individuals such as attorneys and doctors) pay a flat rate of 35%.

Global Stock Markets

Source: Bureau of Economic Analysis, U.S. Dept. Of Commerce; not seasonally adjusted

Stock price indexes (1967=100):	1994	1995 Jan.	Feb.	Mar.	Apr.	May	June	July	Aug.
United States ...	500.8	506.1	524.2	536.4	552.5	569.8	586.7	606.3	608.2
Japan.........	1,449.6	1,344.3	1,277.1	1,190.1	1,182.2	1,180.2	1,109.1	(p)1,193.9	(p)1,279.5
Germany	376.8	361.7	366.0	343.6	338.9	349.6	354.6	(p)364.1	(p)373.8
France	1,034.4	(p)925.2	(p)921.2	(p)902.1	(p)954.6	(p)988.9	(p)961.1	(p)969.1	(p)978.6
United Kingdom .	1,478.3	1,420.4	1,420.4	1,421.4	1,472.6	1,514.4	(p)1,528.7	(p)1,556.3	(p)1,587.9
Italy	717.2	691.6	697.8	643.6	644.1	682.7	(p)657.4	(p)668.0	(p)692.0
Canada	484.0	454.0	466.1	487.4	483.6	502.7	511.5	521.5	(p)518.8

(p) = preliminary.

Foreign Exchange Rates: 1970 to 1994

Source: International Monetary Fund

(National currency units per dollar except as indicated; data are annual averages)

Year	Australia[1] (dollar)	Austria (schilling)	Belgium (franc)	Canada (dollar)	Denmark (krone)	France (franc)	Germany[2] (deutsche mark)	Greece (drachma)
1970	1.1136	25.880	49.680	1.0103	7.489	5.5200	3.6480	30.00
1975	1.3077	17.443	36.799	1.0175	5.748	4.2876	2.4613	32.29
1980	1.1400	12.945	29.237	1.1693	5.634	4.2250	1.8175	42.62
1985	.7003	20.690	59.378	1.3655	10.596	8.9852	2.9440	138.12
1988	.7842	12.348	36.768	1.2307	6.732	5.9569	1.7562	141.86
1989	.7925	13.231	39.404	1.1840	7.310	6.3801	1.8800	162.42
1990	.7813	11.370	33.418	1.1668	6.189	5.4453	1.6157	158.51
1991	.7791	11.676	34.148	1.1457	6.396	5.6421	1.6595	182.27
1992	.7353	10.989	32.150	1.2087	6.036	5.2938	1.5617	190.62
1993	.6801	11.632	34.597	1.2901	6.484	5.6632	1.6533	229.25
1994	.7317	11.422	33.456	1.3656	6.361	5.5520	1.6228	242.60

Year	India (rupee)	Ireland[1] (pound)	Italy (lira)	Japan (yen)	Malaysia (ringgit)	Mexico (new peso)	Netherlands (guilder)	Norway (kroner)
1970	7.576	2.3959	623	357.60	3.0900	—	3.5970	7.1400
1975	8.409	2.2216	653	296.78	2.4030	—	2.5293	5.2282
1980	7.887	2.0577	856	226.63	2.1767	—	1.9875	4.9381
1985	12.369	1.0656	1,909	238.54	2.4830	—	3.3214	8.5972
1988	13.917	1.5261	1,302	128.15	2.6188	2.2731	1.9766	6.5170
1989	16.226	1.4190	1,372	137.96	2.7088	2.4615	2.1207	6.9045
1990	17.504	1.6585	1,198	144.79	2.7049	2.8126	1.8209	6.2597
1991	22.742	1.6155	1,241	134.71	2.7501	3.0184	1.8697	6.4829
1992	25.918	1.7053	1,232	126.65	2.5474	3.0949	1.7585	6.2145
1993	30.493	1.4671	1,574	111.20	2.5741	3.1156	1.8573	7.0941
1994	31.374	1.4978	1,612	102.21	2.6243	3.3751	1.8200	7.0576

Year	Portugal (escudo)	Singapore (dollar)	South Korea (won)	Spain (peseta)	Sweden (krona)	Switzerland (franc)	Thailand (baht)	United Kingdom[1] (pound)
1970	28.75	3.0800	310.57	69.72	5.1700	4.3160	21.000	2.3959
1975	25.51	2.3713	484.00	57.43	4.1530	2.5839	20.379	2.2216
1980	50.08	2.1412	607.43	71.76	4.2309	1.6772	20.476	2.3243
1985	170.39	2.2002	870.02	170.04	8.6039	2.4571	27.159	1.2963
1988	143.95	2.0124	731.47	116.49	6.1272	1.4633	25.294	1.7814
1989	157.46	1.9503	671.46	118.38	6.4469	1.6359	25.702	1.6397
1990	142.55	1.8125	707.76	101.93	5.9188	1.3892	25.585	1.7847
1991	144.48	1.7276	733.35	103.91	6.0475	1.4340	25.517	1.7694
1992	135.00	1.6290	780.65	102.38	5.8238	1.4062	25.400	1.7655
1993	160.80	1.6158	802.67	127.26	7.7834	1.4776	25.319	1.5020
1994	165.99	1.5274	803.45	133.96	7.7160	1.3677	25.150	1.5316

(1) Value of one unit of foreign currency in dollars. (2) W. Germany prior to 1991.

Tourism: International Visitors to the U.S., 1994

Source: U.S. Travel & Tourism Administration; Bureau of Economic Analysis

Country of origin	Visitors (millions)	Expenditures (billions)	Expenditures per visitor	Country of origin	Visitors (millions)	Expenditures (billions)	Expenditures per visitor
Canada	15.0	$7.4	$494	Brazil	0.7	(*)	—
Mexico	11.3	5.5	485	Italy	0.6	1.8	3,267
Japan	4.1	16.7	4,103	South Korea	0.5	(*)	—
United Kingdom	2.9	8.5	2,911	Venezuela	0.4	1.3	3,066
Germany	1.7	5.1	2,931	All countries	45.4	$77.9	$1,712
France	0.9	$2.9	$3,360				

Note: Excludes international passenger fare payments and cruise travel. (*) Not provided by the Bureau of Economic Analysis.

Foreign Direct Investment[1] in the U.S. by Selected Countries

Source: Bureau of Economic Analysis; U.S. Dept. of Commerce

(millions of dollars)

	1993	1994		1993	1994
All countries[2]	$464,110	$504,401	Brazil	760	785
Canada	40,143	43,223	Mexico	1,214	2,187
Europe[2]	287,084	312,876	Panama	3,985	3,603
Austria	602	886	Other Western Hemisphere[2]	14,042	17,273
Belgium	3,852	3,606	Bahamas	1,272	1,120
Denmark	1,066	1,908	Bermuda	775	1,156
Finland	1,649	1,806	Africa[2]	902	866
France	29,420	33,496	Middle East[2]	5,221	5,579
Germany	34,849	39,550	Israel	1,854	2,159
Ireland	4,894	4,641	Kuwait	1,551	1,581
Italy	2,014	2,437	Saudi Arabia	1,622	1,704
Luxembourg	1,136	2,067	Asia and Pacific[2]	110,612	117,835
Netherlands	72,172	70,645	Australia	6,296	7,884
Norway	1,039	1,686	Hong Kong	1,629	1,723
Spain	1,217	1,781	Japan	99,208	103,120
Sweden	8,244	9,112	Malaysia	291	451
Switzerland	22,161	25,330	Singapore	267	1,135
United Kingdom	102,351	113,504	South Korea	849	1,158
South and Central America[2]	6,106	6,749	Taiwan	1,329	1,438

(1) The book value of foreign direct investors' equity in, and net outstanding loans to, their U.S. affiliates. A U.S. affiliate is a U.S. business enterprise in which a single foreign direct investor owns at least 10% of the voting securities or the equivalent. (2) Totals include countries not shown.

U.S. International Transactions

Source: Bureau of Economic Analysis, U.S. Dept. of Commerce

(millions of dollars)

	1965	1970	1975	1980	1985	1990	1993	1994
Exports of goods, services, and income[1]	$42,722	$68,387	$157,936	$344,440	$382,747	$697,426	$763,826	$838,820
Merchandise, adjusted, excluding military[2]	26,461	42,469	107,088	224,250	215,915	389,307	456,823	502,485
Services	8,824	14,171	25,497	47,584	73,155	147,819	187,755	198,716
Income receipts on U.S. assets abroad	7,437	11,748	25,351	72,606	93,677	160,300	119,248	137,619
Imports of goods, services, and income	−32,708	−59,901	−132,745	−333,774	−484,037	−756,694	−829,668	−954,304
Merchandise, adjusted, excluding military[2]	−21,510	−39,866	−98,185	−249,750	−338,088	−498,337	−589,441	−668,584
Services	−9,111	−14,520	−21,996	−41,491	−72,862	−118,783	−129,979	−138,829
Income payments on foreign assets in the U.S.	−2,088	−5,515	−12,564	−42,532	−73,087	−139,574	−110,248	−146,891
Unilateral transfers, net	−4,583	−6,156	−7,075	−8,349	−22,954	−33,393	−34,084	−35,761
U.S. assets abroad, net (increase/capital outflow [−])	−5,716	−9,337	−39,703	−86,967	−39,889	−74,011	−184,589	−125,851
U.S. official reserve assets, net	1,225	2,481	−849	−8,155	−3,858	−2,158	−1,379	5,346
U.S. Government assets, other than official reserve assets, net	−1,605	−1,589	−3,474	−5,162	−2,821	2,307	−330	−322
U.S. private assets, net	−5,336	−10,229	−35,380	−73,651	−33,211	−74,160	−182,880	−130,875
Foreign assets in the U.S., net (increase/capital inflow [+])	742	6,359	15,670	58,112	141,183	122,192	248,529	291,365
Statistical discrepancy (sum of above items with sign reversed)	−457	−219	5,917	25,386	22,950	44,480	35,985	−14,269
Memorandum:								
Balance on current account	5,431	2,331	18,116	2,317	−124,243	−92,661	−99,925	−151,245

(1) Excludes transfers of goods and services under U.S. military grant programs. (2) Excludes exports of goods under U.S. military agency sales contracts identified in Census export documents, excludes imports of goods under direct defense expenditures identified in Census import documents, and reflects various other adjustments.

National Income by Industry

Source: Bureau of Economic Analysis, U.S. Dept. of Commerce

(billions of dollars)

	1960	1970	1975	1980	1990	1993	1994
National income without capital consumption adjustment	$428.6	$835.1	$1,315.0	$2,263.9	$4,497.5	$5,156.4	$5,483.9
Domestic industries	425.1	827.8	1,297.4	2,216.3	4,486.7	5,151.9	5,495.5
Private industries	371.6	695.4	1,088.3	1,894.5	3,828.9	4,386.7	4,702.0
Agriculture, forestry, fisheries	17.8	25.9	46.5	61.4	97.1	95.1	101.9
Mining	5.6	8.4	21.2	43.8	38.1	40.4	40.2
Construction	22.5	47.4	69.9	126.6	234.4	215.4	238.3
Manufacturing	125.3	215.6	317.5	532.1	846.9	911.9	979.7
Durable goods	73.4	127.7	185.0	313.7	484.3	514.3	562.4
Nondurable goods	52.0	87.9	132.5	218.4	362.6	397.6	417.4
Transportation, public utilities	35.8	64.4	101.1	177.3	328.7	384.8	407.5
Transportation	18.5	31.5	48.0	85.8	139.4	166.1	177.5
Communications	8.2	17.6	26.8	48.1	96.4	107.6	113.4
Electric, gas, sanitary services . . .	9.1	86.8	90.2	43.4	92.9	111.1	116.5
Wholesale trade	25.0	47.5	83.0	143.3	263.6	288.6	310.2
Retail trade	41.3	79.9	123.1	189.4	392.1	444.9	475.6
Finance, insurance, real estate	51.3	96.4	143.9	279.5	679.8	846.0	894.2
Services	46.9	109.8	182.1	341.0	948.3	1,159.6	1,254.4
Government	53.5	132.4	209.1	321.8	657.9	765.2	793.4

National Income by Type of Income

Source: Bureau of Economic Analysis, U.S. Dept. of Commerce

(billions of dollars)

	1960	1970	1980	1990	1992	1993	1994
National income[1]	$424.9	$832.6	$2,203.5	$4,459.6	$4,743.4	$5,131.4	$5,458.4
Compensation of employees	296.7	618.3	1,638.2	3,290.3	3,525.2	3,780.4	4,004.6
Wages and salaries	272.8	551.5	1,372.0	2,738.9	2,916.6	3,100.8	3,279.0
Government	49.2	117.1	260.1	514.0	562.5	583.8	602.8
Other	223.7	434.3	1,111.8	2,224.9	2,354.1	2,517.0	2,676.2
Supplements to wages, salaries	23.8	66.8	266.3	551.4	608.6	679.6	725.6
Employer contrib. for social ins. . . .	12.6	34.3	127.9	277.3	302.9	324.3	344.6
Other labor income	11.2	32.5	138.4	274.0	305.7	355.3	381.0
Propietors' income	52.1	80.2	180.7	373.2	404.5	441.6	473.7
Farm	11.6	14.7	20.5	42.5	39.5	37.3	39.5
Nonfarm	40.5	65.4	160.1	330.7	364.9	404.3	434.2
Rental income of persons with capital consumption adjustment	15.3	18.2	6.6	−12.9	4.7	24.1	27.7
Corp. profits with inventory adjustment	49.8	69.5	194.0	319.0	393.8	456.2	505.0
Corp. profits before tax	49.9	76.0	237.1	332.3	371.6	462.4	524.5
Corp. profits tax liability	22.7	34.4	84.8	135.3	140.2	173.2	202.5
Corp. profits after tax	27.2	41.7	152.3	197.0	231.4	289.2	322.0
Dividends	12.9	22.5	54.7	133.7	149.3	191.7	205.2
Undistributed profits	14.3	19.2	97.6	63.3	82.1	97.5	116.9
Inventory valuation adjustment	−0.2	−6.6	−43.1	−14.2	−7.4	−6.2	−19.5
Net interest	11.3	41.2	200.9	490.1	415.2	399.5	409.7

(1) National income is the aggregate of labor and property earnings that arises in the current production of goods and services. It is the sum of employee compensation, proprietors' income, rental income, corporate profits, and net interest. It measures the total factor costs of the goods and services produced by the economy. Income is measured before deduction of taxes on income.

Distribution of Total Personal Income[1]

Source: Bureau of Economic Analysis, U.S. Dept. of Commerce

(billions of dollars)

Year	Personal income	Personal taxes	Disposable personal income	Personal outlays	Personal Savings Amount	Personal Savings As pct. of disposable income
1960	$ 402.3	$50.4	$ 352.0	$332.3	$19.7	5.6%
1965	540.7	64.9	475.8	442.1	33.7	7.1
1970	811.1	115.8	695.3	639.5	55.8	8.0
1975	1,265.0	168.9	1,096.1	1,001.8	94.3	8.6
1980	2,165.3	336.5	1,828.9	1,718.7	110.2	6.0
1981	2,429.5	387.7	2,041.7	1,904.3	137.4	6.7
1982	2,584.6	404.1	2,180.5	2,044.5	136.0	6.2
1983	2,838.6	410.5	2,428.1	2,297.4	130.6	5.4
1984	3,108.7	440.2	2,668.6	2,504.5	164.1	6.1
1985	3,325.3	486.6	2,838.7	2,713.3	125.4	4.4
1986	3,526.2	512.9	3,013.3	2,888.5	124.9	4.1
1987	3,776.6	571.7	3,205.9	3,104.1	101.8	3.2
1988	4,070.8	591.6	3,479.2	3,333.6	145.6	4.2
1989	4,384.3	658.8	3,725.5	3,553.7	171.8	4.6
1990	4,679.8	621.0	4,058.8	3,853.1	205.8	5.1
1991	4,828.4	618.7	4,209.6	4,009.9	199.6	4.7
1992	5,058.1	627.3	4,430.6	4,218.1	212.6	4.8
1993	5,375.1	686.4	4,688.7	4,496.2	192.6	4.1
1994	5,701.7	742.1	4,959.6	4,756.5	203.1	4.1

(1) Figures may not add because of rounding.

U.S. Direct Investment[1] Abroad in Selected Countries

Source: Bureau of Economic Analysis, U.S. Dept. of Commerce

(millions of dollars)

	1990	1993	1994		1990	1993	1994
All countries[2]	$424,096	$559,733	$612,109	Luxembourg	1,390	5,376	5,730
Africa[2]	NA	5,473	5,472	Netherlands	22,658	20,945	24,150
Egypt	1,465	1,463	1,360	Portugal............	598	1,260	1,458
Nigeria	161	544	402	Spain	7,704	6,734	8,048
S. Africa............	956	903	1,044	United Kingdom	68,224	104,313	102,244
Asia and Pacific (excl. Japan)[2]	NA	61,377	71,375	Other Europe[2]	33,552	45,104	49,028
Australia	14,846	19,054	20,054	Austria[3]	889	1,333	1,611
China	—	933	1,699	Finland[3]	551	419	602
Hong Kong..........	6,187	10,177	11,986	Norway	3,815	3,768	4,286
India.............	513	611	818	Sweden[3]	1,600	2,428	2,719
Indonesia..........	3,226	4,770	5,015	Switzerland..........	25,199	32,782	34,485
Malaysia	1,384	1,988	2,382	Turkey.............	494	997	1,084
New Zealand........	NA	3,090	3,577	Japan	20,997	31,184	37,027
Philippines	1,629	1,945	2,374	South America[2]......	23,760	31,457	37,972
Singapore	3,385	8,867	10,972	Argentina	2,956	4,331	5,666
South Korea	2,178	3,124	3,612	Brazil	14,918	16,822	18,977
Taiwan	2,014	3,128	3,882	Chile	1,368	2,847	4,457
Thailand	1,585	2,947	3,762	Colombia	1,728	3,075	3,442
Bermuda...........	21,737	28,696	29,232	Ecuador...........	387	549	728
Canada	67,033	69,612	72,808	Peru	410	628	836
Europe[2]	211,194	280,506	300,177	Venezuela	1,490	2,419	2,978
European Union	177,642	235,402	251,149	Central America[2]......	17,719	28,317	31,321
Belgium...........	9,050	11,488	13,966	Mexico	9,398	15,229	16,375
Denmark	1,597	1,740	1,993	Panama...........	7,409	12,190	13,775
France	18,874	24,281	27,894	Middle East[2]	3,973	6,573	6,727
Germany	27,259	36,879	39,886	Israel	756	1,604	1,350
Greece	288	410	446	Saudi Arabia	1,981	2,618	2,717
Ireland............	6,880	9,224	10,337	United Arab Emirates. ...	519	524	589
Italy	13,117	12,750	14,998				

(1) The book value of U.S. direct investors' equity in, and net outstanding loans to, their foreign affiliates. A foreign affiliate is a foreign business enterprise in which a single U.S. investor owns at least 10% of the voting securities or the equivalent. (2) Total includes countries not shown. (3) Joined the European Union at the beginning of 1995. NA = not available.

Gold Reserves of Central Banks and Governments

Source: *International Financial Statistics,* IMF; million fine troy ounces

Year end	All countries[1]	United States	Canada	Japan	Belgium	France	Germany	Italy	Nether-lands	Switzer-land	United Kingdom
1975	1,018.71	274.71	21.95	21.11	42.17	100.93	117.61	82.48	54.33	83.20	21.03
1976	1,014.23	274.68	21.62	21.11	42.17	101.02	117.61	82.48	54.33	83.28	21.03
1977	1,029.19	277.55	22.01	21.62	42.45	101.67	118.30	82.91	54.63	83.28	22.23
1978	1,036.82	276.41	22.13	23.97	42.59	101.99	118.64	83.12	54.78	83.28	22.83
1979	944.44	264.60	22.18	24.23	34.21	81.92	95.25	66.71	43.97	83.28	18.25
1980	952.99	264.32	20.98	24.23	34.18	81.85	95.18	66.67	43.94	83.28	18.84
1981	953.72	264.11	20.46	24.23	34.18	81.85	95.18	66.67	43.94	83.28	19.03
1982	949.16	264.03	20.26	24.23	34.18	81.85	95.18	66.67	43.94	83.28	19.01
1983	947.84	263.39	20.17	24.23	34.18	81.85	95.18	66.67	43.94	83.28	19.01
1984	946.79	262.79	20.14	24.23	34.18	81.85	95.18	66.67	43.94	83.28	19.03
1985	949.39	262.65	20.11	24.33	34.18	81.85	95.18	66.67	43.94	83.28	19.03
1986	949.11	262.04	19.72	24.23	34.18	81.85	95.18	66.67	43.94	83.28	19.01
1987	944.49	262.38	18.52	24.23	33.63	81.85	95.18	66.67	43.94	83.28	19.01
1988	946.65	261.87	17.14	24.23	33.67	81.85	95.18	66.67	43.94	83.28	19.00
1989	940.93	261.93	16.10	24.23	30.23	81.85	95.18	66.67	43.94	83.28	18.99
1990	938.90	261.91	14.76	24.23	30.23	81.85	95.18	66.67	43.94	83.28	18.94
1991	937.80	261.91	12.96	24.23	30.23	81.85	95.18	66.67	43.94	83.28	18.89
1992	929.29	261.84	9.94	24.23	25.04	81.85	95.18	66.67	43.94	83.28	18.61
1993	912.60	261.79	6.05	24.23	25.04	81.85	95.18	66.67	35.05	83.28	18.45
1994	909.79	261.73	3.89	24.23	25.04	81.85	95.18	66.67	34.77	83.28	18.44

(1) Covers IMF members with reported gold holdings. For countries not listed above, see *International Financial Statistics,* a monthly publication of the International Monetary Fund.

Trade-Weighted Index of Foreign Currency Value of the Dollar

Source: Office of Foreign Exchange Operations, U.S. Dept. of the Treasury

These indexes are presented to provide measures of the general foreign exchange value of the dollar that are broader than those provided by single exchange rate levels. They do not purport to represent a guide to measuring the impact of exchange rate levels on U.S. international transactions. The indexes are computed as geometric averages of individual currency levels with weights derived from the share of each country's trade with the U.S. during 1982-83.

End of period (Dec. 1980 = 100)	Index of industrial country currencies[1]	End of period (Dec. 1980 = 100)	Index of industrial country currencies[1]	End of period (Dec. 1980 = 100)	Index of industrial country currencies[1]
1985	127.8	1991	93.7	Feb.	(r)97.3
1986	114.4	1992	101.1	Mar.	(r)94.4
1987	97.8	1993	103.3	Apr.	(r)92.1
1988	98.4	1994	(r)99.0	May	92.0
1989	100.0	1995		June	92.7
1990	94.4	Jan.	(r)98.2	July	93.2

(r)=revised. (1) Each index covers (a) 22 currencies of countries represented in the Organization for Economic Cooperation and Development (OECD): Australia, Austria, Belgium-Luxembourg, Canada, Denmark, Finland, France, Germany, Greece, Iceland, Ireland, Italy, Japan, the Netherlands, New Zealand, Norway, Portugal, Spain, Sweden, Switzerland, Turkey, and the United Kingdom; and (b) currencies of four major trading economies outside the OECD: Hong Kong, South Korea, Singapore, and Taiwan. Exchange rates are drawn from the International Monetary Fund's *International Financial Statistics* when available.

Average Yields of Long-Term Treasury, Corporate, and Municipal Bonds

Source: Office of Market Finance, U.S. Dept. of the Treasury

Period	Treasury 30-year bonds	New Aa corporate bonds[1]	New Aa municipal bonds[2]	Period	Treasury 30-year bonds	New Aa corporate bonds[1]	New Aa municipal bonds[2]
1984				**1992**			
June	13.44	14.49	10.44	June	7.84	8.45	6.32
Dec.	11.52	12.47	9.65	Dec.	7.44	8.12	6.02
1985				**1993**			
June	10.45	11.33	8.46	June	6.81	7.48	5.54
Dec.	9.54	10.42	8.44	Dec.	6.25	7.22	5.27
1986				**1994**			
June	7.57	9.39	7.75	Jan.	6.29	7.16	5.19
Dec.	7.37	8.87	6.70	Feb.	6.49	7.27	5.16
1987				Mar.	6.91	7.64	5.47
June	8.57	9.64	7.69	Apr.	7.27	7.95	5.59
Dec.	9.12	10.22	7.83	May	7.41	8.17	5.79
1988				June	7.40	8.16	5.96
June	9.00	10.08	7.67	July	7.58	8.30	6.11
Dec.	9.01	10.05	7.40	Aug.	7.49	8.25	6.07
1989				Sept.	7.71	8.48	6.10
June	8.27	9.24	6.94	Oct.	7.94	8.76	6.31
Dec.	7.90	9.23	6.76	Nov.	8.08	8.89	6.79
1990				Dec.	7.87	8.66	6.63
June	8.46	9.69	6.98	**1995**			
Dec.	8.24	9.55	6.85	Jan.	7.85	8.59	6.48
1991				Feb.	7.61	8.39	6.09
June	8.47	9.37	6.90	Mar.	7.45	8.23	5.91
Dec.	7.70	8.55	6.43				

(1) Treasury series based on 3-week moving average of reoffering yields of new corporate bonds rated Aa by Moody's Investors Service with an original maturity of at least 20 years. (2) Index of new reoffering yields on 20-year general obligations rated Aa by Moody's Investors Service. Source: U.S. Treasury, 1984-90; Moody's, 1991-95.

Performance of Mutual Funds by Type

Source: CDA/Wiesenberger, Rockville, MD, 800-232-2285

(data for period ending Aug. 31, 1995)

Fund type	Fund objective	1-Yr Total return No.	1-Yr Total return Avg.	5-Yr Annual return No.	5-Yr Annual return Avg.	Fund type	Fund objective	1-Yr Total return No.	1-Yr Total return Avg.	5-Yr Annual return No.	5-Yr Annual return Avg.
Stock	Natural resources	30	7.68	19	5.94	**International**					
	Equity income	113	13.99	54	13.24	**stock**	Pacific area	76	−9.34	17	7.13
	Financial services	14	17.68	9	27.12		Other foreign	188	−1.19	53	7.47
	Precious metals	39	−2.17	30	3.56	**Hybrid**	Asset allocation	81	14.07	33	11.56
	Growth and current						Balanced	210	14.19	68	12.38
	income	412	16.52	175	13.91		Flexible income	66	12.24	39	13.32
	Health care	15	24.69	10	16.81	**Bond**	Corporate bond	487	9.42	161	8.85
	Long-term growth	656	19.68	297	15.36		Corporate high yield	121	10.43	70	13.23
	Max. capital gain	119	22.78	69	16.86		Govt. mortgage-				
	Other specialized	39	10.87	28	15.17		backed	178	5.86	49	7.85
	Small company	292	24.90	94	19.02		Govt. securities	421	8.91	165	8.31
	Technology	28	54.58	14	27.14		International	165	7.61	39	7.09
	Utilities	79	10.53	21	12.48	**Municipal**					
International						**bond**	National	428	7.07	189	7.88
stock	Emerging markets	44	−20.49	2	10.89		California	144	6.90	58	8.03
	Global	126	5.27	41	10.73		New York	114	6.73	48	8.19
	European	33	8.51	16	5.38		Other state	777	7.19	188	8.04

Chicago Board of Trade, Contracts Traded 1985-94

	1985	1994	Percent change 1985-94		1985	1994	Percent change 1985-94
Futures group				Metals	10,819	5,952	−45
Agricultural	22,998,602	36,091,553	157	Insurance	—	9,420	—
Financial	43,727,876	139,483,486	319	**Total options**	13,293,562	43,806,394	330
Stock index	2,624,062	0	—	**Combined futures**			
Metals	1,203,357	122,637	−90	**and options**			
Insurance	—	4	—	Agricultural	24,202,937	42,348,484	175
Total futures	70,553,897	175,697,680	249	Financial	55,806,284	177,017,577	317
Options group				Stock index	2,624,062	0	—
Agricultural	1,204,335	6,256,931	520	Metals	1,214,176	128,589	−89
Financial	12,078,408	37,534,091	311	Insurance	—	9,424	—
Stock index	—	0	—	**Grand total**	83,847,459	219,504,074	262

Dow Jones Industrial Average Since 1961

	High		Year		Low			High		Year		Low	
Dec.	13	734.91	**1961**	Jan.	3	610.25	Oct.	5	897.61	**1979**	Nov.	7	796.67
Jan.	3	726.01	**1962**	June	26	535.76	Nov.	20	1000.17	**1980**	Apr.	21	759.13
Dec.	18	767.21	**1963**	Jan.	2	646.79	Apr.	27	1024.05	**1981**	Sept.	25	824.01
Nov.	18	891.71	**1964**	Jan.	2	766.08	Dec.	27	1070.55	**1982**	Aug.	12	776.92
Dec.	31	969.26	**1965**	June	28	840.59	Nov.	29	1287.20	**1983**	Jan.	3	1027.04
Feb.	9	995.15	**1966**	Oct.	7	744.32	Jan.	6	1286.64	**1984**	July	24	1086.57
Sept.	25	943.08	**1967**	Jan.	3	786.41	Dec.	16	1553.10	**1985**	Jan.	4	1184.96
Dec.	3	985.21	**1968**	Mar.	21	825.13	Dec.	2	1955.57	**1986**	Jan.	22	1502.29
May	14	968.85	**1969**	Dec.	17	769.93	Aug.	25	2722.42	**1987**	Oct.	19	1738.74
Dec.	29	842.00	**1970**	May	6	631.16	Oct.	21	2183.50	**1988**	Jan.	20	1879.14
Apr.	28	950.82	**1971**	Nov.	23	797.97	Oct.	9	2791.41	**1989**	Jan.	3	2144.64
Dec.	11	1036.27	**1972**	Jan.	26	889.15	July	16	2999.75	**1990**	Oct.	11	2365.10
Jan.	11	1051.70	**1973**	Dec.	5	788.31	Dec.	31	3168.83	**1991**	Jan.	9	2470.30
Mar.	13	891.66	**1974**	Dec.	6	577.60	June	1	3413.21	**1992**	Oct.	9	3136.58
July	15	881.81	**1975**	Jan.	2	632.04	Dec.	29	3794.33	**1993**	Jan.	20	3241.95
Sept.	21	1014.79	**1976**	Jan.	2	858.71	Jan.	31	3978.36	**1994**	Apr.	4	3593.35
Jan.	3	999.75	**1977**	Nov.	2	800.85	Sept.	14	4801.80	**1995***	Jan.	30	3832.08
Sept.	8	907.74	**1978**	Feb.	28	742.12							

*As of Oct. 1

Components of Dow Jones Industrial Average

Allied-Signal	DuPont	Minn. Mining & Manuf.
Aluminum Co. of Amer. (Alcoa)	Eastman Kodak	Morgan (J.P.)
American Express	Exxon	Philip Morris
AT&T	General Electric	Procter & Gamble
Bethlehem Steel	General Motors	Sears
Boeing	Goodyear	Texaco
Caterpillar	IBM	Union Carbide
Chevron	International Paper	United Technologies
Coca-Cola	McDonald's	Westinghouse
Disney	Merck	Woolworth

Components of Dow Jones Transportation Average

AMR Corp.	Consolidated Rail	Southwest Air Lines
Airborne Freight	Delta Air Lines	UAL
Alaska Air	Federal Express	Union Pacific
American President	Norfolk Southern	USAir Group
Burlington Northern	Roadway Services	XTRA Corp.
CSX	Ryder System	Yellow Corp.
Consolidated Freightways	Santa Fe Pacific	

Components of Dow Jones Utility Average

American Electric Power	Houston Industries	Peco Energy
Centerior Energy	Niagara Mohawk Power	Peoples Energy
Consolidated Edison	NorAm Energy	Public Service Enterprises
Consolidated Natural Gas	Pacific Gas & Electric	SCE
Detroit Edison	Panhandle Eastern	Unicom

Milestones of the Dow Jones Industrial Average

First close over...		First close over...		First close over...	
100	Jan. 12, 1906	2,000	Jan. 8, 1987	4,500	June 16, 1995
500	March 12, 1956	2,500	July 17, 1987	4,600	July 5, 1995
1,000	Nov. 14, 1972	3,000	April 17, 1991	4,700	July 7, 1995
1,500	Dec. 11, 1985	3,500	May 19, 1993	4,800	Sept. 14, 1995
		4,000	Feb. 23, 1995		

Most Active Common Stocks in 1994

New York Exchange	Volume (millions of shares)	American Exchange	Volume (millions of shares)	NASDAQ	Volume (millions of shares)
Teléfonos de Mexico	1,048.7	XCL Limited	236.7	Intel	1,184.1
RJR Nabisco	780.7	Cheyenne Software	173.2	Cisco Systems	1,007.5
General Motors	702.2	Echo Bay Mines	166.5	Microsoft	841.6
Merck	679.1	Viacom B	164.6	Novell	836.0
Wal-Mart Stores	661.2	Royal Oak Mines	115.7	MCI Communications	773.0
I.B.M	600.8	Ivax	107.6	Tele-Communications "A"	663.0
Ford Motor	593.3	Ensco (Energy Services)	93.0	Oracle Systems	565.5
Philip Morris	576.4	Amdahl	80.4	Apple Computer	510.2
Chrysler	571.4	Hasbro	69.2	Lotus Development	434.9
Compaq	528.4	Interdigital Communications	61.4	DSC Communications	424.9
Hanson	519.3	U.S. Bioscience	54.9	3Com	413.6
A.T.&T.	514.1	Top Source Technologies	52.2	Dell Computer	395.6
Motorola	472.0	New York Times "A"	51.9	Bay Networks	382.9
General Electric	463.2	Atari	50.5	U.S. Healthcare	376.3
Citicorp	458.2	Pegasus Gold	49.4	Sun Microsystems	366.4

U.S. Holdings of Foreign Stocks

Source: Bureau of Economic Analysis, U.S. Dept. Of Commerce

(billions of dollars)

	1993	1994		1993	1994
Total holdings	297.7	313.9	Canada	23.1	24.6
Western Europe	123.2	137.3	Japan	42.7	66.2
Of which: United Kingdom	41.9	42.7	Latin America	35.8	22.0
Germany	23.0	25.5	Of which: Mexico	25.7	15.9
Netherlands	18.0	20.0	Other countries	72.9	63.8
France	16.3	17.3			

Selected Personal Consumption Expenditures in the U.S.

Source: Bureau of Economic Analysis, U.S. Dept. of Commerce

(billions of dollars)

	1987	1988	1989	1990	1991	1992	1993
Personal consumption expenditures	$3,009.4	$3,296.1	$3,523.1	$3,761.2	$3,906.4	$4,139.9	$4,378.2
Food & Tobacco	566.4	569.8	605.6	648.2	666.8	684.5	700.3
Food purchased for off-premise consumption	353.7	351.7	373.7	400.2	411.1	418.0	422.2
Purchased meals and beverages	165.5	171.7	180.6	193.1	198.5	203.5	215.2
Tobacco products	35.6	36.2	40.5	43.4	45.4	50.9	50.5
Clothing, accessories, jewelry	222.3	231.8	248.7	259.3	264.3	282.4	293.9
Shoes	25.9	27.4	30.1	31.4	31.3	32.3	33.0
Clothing and accessories less shoes	152.5	158.9	170.1	175.7	181.6	195.7	202.1
Jewelry and watches	24.7	28.8	29.7	31.3	31.6	34.0	36.2
Personal care	44.4	51.4	55.8	59.2	60.9	63.2	65.8
Toilet articles, preparations	26.3	31.8	34.1	36.8	38.2	39.3	41.1
Barbershops, beauty parlors, health clubs	18.2	19.6	21.6	22.4	22.6	23.9	24.6
Housing	468.9	484.2	514.4	547.5	574.4	600.0	629.0
Owner-occupied nonfarm dwellings space rent	316.9	334.1	355.8	379.5	399.1	417.8	438.3
Tenant-occupied nonfarm dwellings rent	123.6	125.3	132.6	141.1	147.7	153.8	160.2
Rental value of farm dwellings	10.3	4.9	5.0	5.2	5.3	5.3	5.6
Household operation	363.3	398.9	422.6	437.3	452.7	475.2	508.2
Furniture, incl. bedding	31.8	34.0	36.9	36.7	36.8	40.0	42.5
Kitchen, other household appliances	26.7	24.1	25.7	26.4	27.1	29.2	31.3
China, glassware, tableware, utensils	15.3	16.4	17.9	18.7	19.4	21.0	22.1
Other durable house furnishings	33.5	37.7	40.2	42.0	41.9	45.2	47.2
Semidurable house furnishings	16.0	19.4	20.4	21.2	21.9	23.6	25.2
Household utilities	125.8	127.3	134.1	136.7	145.3	149.9	159.3
Telephone, telegraph	44.1	50.2	51.7	53.8	56.2	58.7	68.2
Medical care	399.0	487.7	536.4	597.8	651.7	704.6	760.5
Drug preparations, sundries	32.3	50.8	55.0	60.6	64.4	65.9	69.0
Physicians	94.0	110.6	121.6	133.8	144.0	153.1	165.6
Dentists	25.0	27.9	30.0	31.6	32.9	36.4	38.6
Hospitals and nursing homes	166.3	190.9	209.5	231.3	255.3	279.6	346.8
Health insurance	25.3	26.4	31.2	36.6	40.0	45.9	46.2
Personal business	215.4	255.0	272.2	296.0	323.4	356.0	373.3
Brokerage charges, investment counseling	20.5	19.3	21.6	22.0	24.3	28.5	34.8
Bank service charges, trust services, safe deposit box	14.6	19.8	22.0	23.7	25.2	27.6	31.2
Legal services	35.0	41.7	45.5	49.2	49.9	54.0	56.1
Funeral, burial expenses	7.0	7.8	7.9	8.5	9.0	9.6	10.4
Transportation	379.7	413.2	437.3	453.9	434.6	463.1	504.2
User-operated transportation	346.3	376.9	399.6	414.0	395.5	423.9	461.9
New autos	93.5	101.0	99.9	96.6	79.5	87.3	93.4
Used autos	38.5	30.5	32.5	33.1	36.7	39.5	45.9
Repair, greasing, washing, parking, storage, rental, leasing	55.9	73.5	79.1	82.6	82.4	89.5	98.4
Gasoline and oil	75.3	86.9	96.2	108.4	102.9	103.4	105.6
Tolls	1.9	1.8	2.1	2.0	2.0	2.1	2.5
Insurance premiums less claims paid	15.4	16.8	16.8	18.1	22.7	24.6	27.5
Purchased local transportation	8.2	8.3	8.1	8.9	9.1	9.2	9.3
Mass transit systems	4.0	5.4	5.3	5.7	5.7	5.9	5.9
Taxicab	3.5	2.9	2.8	3.2	3.4	3.3	3.4
Purchased intercity transportation	25.5	28.0	29.5	30.9	30.0	30.0	33.0
Railway (excl. commutation)	0.7	0.6	0.7	0.7	0.7	0.7	0.7
Bus	1.4	2.2	1.7	1.4	1.5	1.5	1.3
Airline	20.8	23.0	24.7	26.4	25.6	25.7	28.5
Recreation	223.2	246.8	266.0	285.7	299.4	318.8	339.9
Books, maps	9.5	14.6	15.8	17.5	18.3	20.2	20.8
Magazines, newspapers, sheet music	15.4	20.8	22.0	23.8	24.7	25.4	26.8
Nondurable toys and sport supplies	26.2	27.5	30.0	32.1	33.5	35.2	37.4
Wheel goods, durable toys, sports equipment, boats, pleasure aircraft	33.2	30.0	31.0	31.3	31.4	34.0	33.0
Video & audio prods., computers, musical instruments	—	44.5	47.3	50.4	55.4	59.1	65.7
Flowers, seeds, potted plants	7.0	9.3	10.1	10.3	10.4	11.0	12.4
Admissions to specified spectator amusements	11.3	11.1	12.1	14.0	14.9	16.1	16.8
Motion picture theaters	4.2	3.6	3.9	4.7	5.0	5.5	5.6
Legitimate theater, opera	4.0	3.6	3.9	4.5	4.7	5.1	5.5
Spectator sports	3.0	3.9	4.3	4.9	5.2	5.5	5.7
Clubs, fraternal organizations	5.5	7.6	8.0	8.4	8.6	9.0	9.5
Commercial participant amusements	17.1	19.1	20.5	23.1	23.8	25.7	28.0
Education & Research	50.9	71.6	79.4	86.2	91.8	98.2	105.5
Higher education	17.7	36.7	40.3	44.0	47.3	50.8	56.1
Nursery, elementary and secondary schools	15.5	17.1	19.2	19.8	20.6	21.6	22.1
Religious and welfare activities	68.1	86.0	92.7	101.6	105.7	116.2	123.0

Minerals

Source: Bureau of Mines, U.S. Dept. of the Interior; as of mid-1995

Aluminum: the second most abundant metallic element in the earth's crust. Bauxite is the main source of aluminum; convert to aluminum equivalent by multiplying by 0.232. Guinea and Australia have 49% of the world's reserves. Aluminum is used in the U.S. principally in transportation (28%), packaging (28%), and building (17%).

Chromium: some two-thirds of the world's production of chromite, the chief source of chromium, is in Kazakhstan and South Africa. The chemical and metallurgical industries use about 90% of the chromite consumed in the world.

Cobalt: used in superalloys for jet engines, chemicals (paint driers, catalysts, magnetic coatings), permanent magnets, and cemented carbides for cutting tools. More than 90% of the world's cobalt is produced in Canada, Finland, Norway, Russia, Zaire, and Zambia. The U.S. uses about one-third of total world consumption. Although its resources are relatively large, the U.S. has not produced cobalt since 1971; most cobalt resources are low grade, and production from these deposits is not economically feasible.

Columbium: used mostly as an additive in steelmaking and in superalloys. Brazil and Canada are the world's leading columbium raw materials (feedstock) producers. There is no U.S. columbium mining industry.

Copper: main uses of copper in the U.S. are in building construction (42%), electrical and electronic products (24%), industrial machinery and equipment (13%), transportation (11%), and consumer and general products (10%). The leading producer is Chile, followed by the U.S., Canada, Russia, Australia, Zambia, Poland, and China. Principal mining states are Arizona, New Mexico, and Utah.

Gold: used in the U.S. in jewelry and the arts (70%), the electronics and other industries (23%), and dentistry (7%). South Africa has about half the world's resources; significant quantities are also present in the U.S., Canada, the former USSR, and Brazil. Gold is mined in nearly all the western states and in Alaska.

Iron ore: the source of primary iron for the world's iron and steel industries. Major iron ore producers include Australia, Brazil, China, and the former USSR.

Lead: the U.S., Australia, China, Peru, and Canada are the world's largest producers of lead. Transportation accounts for the major end use in the U.S., with 83% used in batteries, bearings, casting metals, and solders. Other uses include emergency power supply batteries, construction sheeting, sporting ammunition, and power cable coverings. The U.S. produces and consumes more than 20% of the world's lead metal.

Manganese: essential to iron and steel production. The U.S., Japan, and Western Europe have all nearly exhausted their economically minable manganese. South Africa and the former USSR have about 80% of the world's reserves.

Nickel: vital to the stainless steel industry and played a key role in the development of the chemical and aerospace industries. Leading producers include Russia, Canada, Australia, New Caledonia, and Indonesia.

Platinum-Group Metals: the platinum group consists of 6 closely related metals: platinum, palladium, rhodium, ruthenium, iridium, and osmium. They commonly occur together in nature and are among the scarcest of the metallic elements. They are consumed in the U.S. by the following industries: automotive, electrical and electronic, chemical, and dental and medical. The automotive, chemical, and petroleum-refining industries use platinum-group metals mainly as catalysts. The former USSR and South Africa have nearly all the world's reserves.

Silver: used in the following U.S. industries: photography; electrical and electronic products; sterlingware, electroplated ware, and jewelry. Silver is mined in more than 60 countries. Nevada produces more than 46% of U.S. silver, Idaho 11%.

Tantalum: a refractory metal with unique electrical, chemical, and physical properties; it is used in the U.S. mostly to produce electronic components, mainly tantalum capacitors. Australia, Brazil, Canada, and Thailand are the leading tantalum raw material (feedstock) producers. There is no U.S. tantalum mining industry.

Titanium: as a metal, titanium is used mostly in commercial and military aerospace applications. Titanium metal is produced in Russia, Kazakhstan, Japan, the U.S., and China.

Vanadium: used as an alloying element in steel and aerospace aluminum-titanium alloys, as a catalyst in the production of maleic and phthalic anhydride, and in the production of sulfuric acid. China, South Africa, and Russia are the world's largest producers of vanadium-bearing ores and concentrates.

Zinc: used as a protective coating on steel, as diecastings, as an alloying metal with copper to make brass, and as a component of chemical compounds in rubber and paints. It is mined in more than 50 countries. Canada is the leading producer, followed by Australia, China, the former USSR, Peru, and the U.S. In the U.S., mine production comes mostly from Alaska, Tennessee, New York, and Missouri.

World Mineral Reserve Base

Source: Bureau of Mines, U.S. Dept. of the Interior; as of mid-1995

Mineral	Reserve Base[1]	Mineral	Reserve Base[1]
Aluminum.	28,000 mil metric tons[2]	Manganese.	4,8900 mil metric tons
Chromium	6,700 mil metric tons	Nickel.	110 mil metric tons
Cobalt	8.8 mil metric tons	Platinum-Group Metals	66,000 metric tons
Columbium.	4,200 mil kilograms	Silver	420,000 metric tons
Copper.	590 mil metric tons	Tantalum	35 mil kilograms
Gold	60,000 metric tons	Titanium	595 mil metric tons[4]
Iron ore	230,000 mil metric tons[3]	Vanadium.	27 mil metric tons
Lead	130 mil metric tons	Zinc	330 mil metric tons

(1) Includes demonstrated resources that are currently economic (reserves) or marginally economic (marginal reserves) and some of those that are currently subeconomic. (2) Bauxite. (3) Crude ore. (4) Titanium dioxide (TiO_2) content.

U.S. Nonfuel Mineral Production—10 Leading States in 1994

Source: Bureau of Mines, U.S. Dept. of the Interior

Rank/State	Value (millions)	Percent of U.S. total	Principal minerals
1. Arizona	$3,323	9.71	Copper, sand & gravel (construction), cement, molybdenum
2. Nevada	2,761	8.07	Gold, sand & gravel (construction), diatomite, cement
3. California	2,497	7.30	Cement, sand & gravel (construction), gold, boron minerals
4. Michigan	1,621	4.74	Iron ore, cement, sand & gravel (construction), magnesium compounds
5. Georgia	1,535	4.49	Clay, stone (crushed), cement, stone (dimension)
6. Florida	1,468	4.29	Phosphate rock, stone (crushed), cement, sand & gravel (construction)
7. Utah	1,428	4.17	Copper, gold, magnesium metal, sand & gravel (construction)
8. Texas	1,409	4.12	Cement, stone (crushed), magnesium metal, sand & gravel (construction)
9. Minnesota	1,352	3.95	Iron ore, sand & gravel (construction), stone (crushed), sand & gravel (industrial)
10. Missouri	1,003	2.93	Stone (crushed), cement, lead, lime

U.S. Nonfuel Mineral Production
Source: Bureau of Mines, U.S. Dept. of the Interior

Production as measured by mine shipments, sales, or marketable production (including consumption by producers)

		1989	1990	1991	1992	1993	1994
Antimony (ore and concentrate)		W	W	W	W	W	W
Bauxite		W	W	W	W	W	W
Beryllium (metal equivalent)	metric tons	184	182	174	193	198	173
Copper (recoverable content of ores, etc.)	thousand metric tons	1,498	1,588	1,630	1,760	1,800	1,810
Gold (recoverable content of ores, etc.)	metric tons	265.7	294.2	294.1	330.2	331.0	326.2
Iron ore, usable (includes byproduct material)	million metric tons	59.0	56.4	56.8	55.6	55.7	58.4
Lead (in concentrate)	thousand metric tons	420	495	477	407	362	370
Magnesium metal (primary)	thousand metric tons	152	139		137	132	128
Molybdenum (content of ore and concentrate)	metric tons	63,105	61,611	53,364	49,725	36,803	46,810
Nickel (content of ore and concentrate)	metric tons	—	330	5,523	6,671	2,464	—
Silver (recoverable content of ores, etc.)	metric tons	2,008	2,120	1,860	1,800	1,640	1,480
Tungsten (content of ore and concentrate)	metric tons	W	W	W	W	W	W
Zinc (recoverable content of ores, etc.)	thousand metric tons	276	515	518	523	488	570
Asbestos	thousand metric tons	17	W	20	16	14	10
Barite	thousand metric tons	290	430	448	326	315	583
Boron minerals	thousand metric tons	562	608	626	554	574	550
Bromine	million kilograms	175	177	170	171	177	195
Cement (portland, masonry, etc.)	thousand short tons	77,189	77,111	74,068	76,704	81,358	86,436
Clays	thousand metric tons	42,254	42,904	41,017	40,237	40,700	41,700
Diatomite	thousand metric tons	617	631	610	595	599	613
Feldspar	thousand metric tons	655	630	580	725	770	765
Fluorspar	thousand metric tons	66	64	58	51	56	49
Garnet (industrial)	metric tons	42,605	47,009	50,860	54,139	48,502	56,218
Gem stones	million dollars	42.9	52.9	84.4	66.2	57.7	50.5
Gypsum	thousand short tons	17,624	16,406	15,456	16,269	17,429	18,960
Helium (extracted from natural gas)	million cubic meters	66.3	64.6	86.4	92.0	99.3	106.0E
Helium (Grade A)	million cubic meters	79.9	84.8	88.1	94.4	95.6	96.0E
Iodine	thousand kilograms	1,508	1,973	1,999	1,995	1,935	1,630
Lime	thousand metric tons	15,560	15,832	15,667	16,199	16,932	17,095
Mica (scrap & flake)	thousand metric tons	119	109	103	85	88	110
Peat	thousand metric tons	690	692	632	599	616	574
Perlite (sold and used by producers)	thousand metric tons	545	576	514	541	569	644
Phosphate rock (marketable product)	thousand metric tons	49,817	46,343	48,096	46,965	35,494	41,115
Pumice and pumicite	thousand metric tons	424	443	401	481	469	490
Salt	thousand metric tons	35,250	36,916	35,902	34,784	38,770	39,483
Sand and gravel (construction)	thousand short tons	897,300E	913,500	780,300E	919,300	957,600	985,000E
Sand and gravel (industrial)	thousand short tons	26,494	25,769	23,224	25,195	26,220	27,900
Soda ash (sodium carbonate)	thousand metric tons	8,995	9,156	9,005	9,379	8,959	9,321
Sodium sulfate (natural)	thousand metric tons	340	349	354	337	322	298
Stone (crushed)	million metric tons	1,213	1,222E	1,103	1,162	1,230	1,350
Stone (dimension)[1]	thousand short tons	1,238	1,232	1,275	1,169	1,362	1,465
Sulfur	thousand metric tons	11,592	11,560	10,820	10,663	10,959	11,500
Talc and pyrophyllite	thousand metric tons	1,253	1,267	1,037*	997*	968*	935*
Vermiculite	thousand metric tons	249	209E	180	190	190	180

(E) Estimated. (W) Withheld to avoid disclosing company proprietary data. (—) No production. *Talc only. (1) After 1990 production includes Puerto Rico.

U.S. Reliance on Foreign Supplies of Minerals
Source: Bureau of Mines, U.S. Dept. of the Interior

Mineral	Percent imported in 1994	Major sources (1990-1994)	Major uses
Columbium	100%	Brazil, Canada, Germany	Steelmaking, superalloys
Graphite (natural)	100	Mexico, Canada, China, Madagascar	Refractories, brake linings, packings
Manganese	100	South Africa, France, Brazil, Australia	Steelmaking
Mica (sheet)	100	India, Belgium, China, Argentina	Electronic and electrical equipment
Strontium (celestite)	100	Mexico	Television picture tubes, pyrotechnics, ferrite magnets
Bauxite and alumina	99	Australia, Jamaica, Guinea, Brazil, Guyana	Aluminum production, abrasives, refractories
Asbestos	95	Canada, South Africa	Roofing products, friction products
Diamonds (industrial)	95	Ireland, Britain, Zaire	Machinery for grinding and cutting
Tungsten	94	China, Bolivia, Peru, Germany	Machinery, lamps and
Platinum group	91	South Africa, Russia, Britain	Catalysts, electrical and electronic equipment
Fluorspar	88	China, Mexico, South Africa	Hydrofluoric acid production, steelmaking
Tantalum	86	Germany, Australia, Canada, Brazil	Electronic components
Tin	84	Brazil, Bolivia, China, Indonesia	Cans, electrical, construction
Barite	82	China, India, Mexico	Oil and gas well drilling fluids
Cobalt	79	Zambia, Zaire, Canada, Norway, Finland	Aerospace alloys, catalysts, paint driers, magnetic alloys
Chromium	75	South Africa, Turkey, Zimbabwe, Yugoslavia	Ferroalloys, chemicals, refractories
Potash	74	Canada, Israel, former USSR, Germany	Fertilizer
Nickel	66	Canada, Norway, Australia, Dominican Rep.	Stainless steel, other alloys
Stone (dimension)	65	Italy, Spain, Canada	Construction
Antimony	62	China, Mexico, South Africa, Hong Kong	Flame retardants, batteries
Iodine	58	Japan, Chile	Animal feed supplements, catalysts, inks, disinfectants
Cadmium	50	Canada, Mexico, Australia, Belgium	Batteries, pigments, plating and coating of metals

U.S. Copper, Lead, and Zinc Production, 1950-94

Source: Bureau of Mines, U.S. Dept. of the Interior; E=estimated

Year	Copper Quantity (metric tons)	Copper Value ($1,000)	Lead Quantity (metric tons)	Lead Value ($1,000)	Zinc Quantity (metric tons)	Zinc Value ($1,000)	Year	Copper Quantity (metric tons)	Copper Value ($1,000)	Lead Quantity (metric tons)	Lead Value ($1,000)	Zinc Quantity (metric tons)	Zinc Value ($1,000)
1950	827	379,122	390,839	113,078	565,516	167,000	1988	1,417	3,764,000	384,983	315,222	244,314	324,249
1960	1,037	733,706	223,774	57,722	395,013	112,365	1989	1,497	4,323,000	410,915	356,476	275,883	499,103
1965	1,226	957,028	273,196	93,959	554,429	178,284	1990	1,586	4,310,000	483,704	490,750	515,355	847,485
1970	1,560	1,984,484	518,698	178,609	484,560	163,650	1991	1,630	3,931,000	465,931	343,907	517,804	602,426
1975	1,282	1,814,763	563,783	267,230	425,792	366,097	1992	1,760	4,167,000	397,076	307,337	523,430	673,800
1980	1,181	2,666,931	550,366	515,189	317,103	261,671	1993	1,800	3,635,000	355,185	248,540	488,283	496,795
1985	1,105	1,631,000	413,955	174,008	226,545	201,607	1994	1,810	4,430,000	363,000	298,000	570,162	600,000ᴱ

U.S. Pig Iron and Raw Steel Output, 1940-94

Source: American Iron and Steel Institute

(net tons)

Year	Total pig iron	Raw steel	Year	Total pig iron	Raw steel
1940	46,071,666	66,982,686	1986	43,952,000	81,606,000
1945	53,223,169	79,701,648	1987	48,410,000	89,151,000
1950	64,586,907	96,836,075	1988	55,745,000	99,924,000
1960	66,480,648	99,281,601	1989	55,873,000	97,943,000
1965	88,184,901	131,461,601	1990	54,750,000	98,906,000
1970	91,435,000	131,514,000	1991	48,637,000	87,896,000
1975	79,923,000	116,642,000	1992	52,224,000	92,949,000
1980	68,721,000	111,835,000	1993	53,082,000	97,877,000
1985	50,446,000	88,259,000	1994	54,426,000	100,579,000

Steel figures include only that portion of the capacity and production of steel for castings used by foundries that were operated by companies producing steel ingots.

World Gold Production, 1972-94

Source: Bureau of Mines, U.S. Dept. of the Interior

(troy ounces)

Year	World prod.	South Africa	Africa Ghana	Africa Zaireʳ	North and South America United States	North and South America Canada	North and South America Mexico	North and South America Colombia	Other Australia	Other China	Other Philippines	Other USSR
1972	44,843,374	29,245,273	724,051	80,377	1,449,943	2,078,567	146,061	188,137	754,866	NA	606,730	NA
1975	38,476,371	22,937,820	523,889	115,743	1,052,252	1,653,611	144,710	308,864	526,821	NA	502,577	NA
1978	38,983,019	22,648,558	402,034	32,151	998,832	1,735,077	202,003	246,446	647,579	NA	586,531	NA
1980	39,197,315	21,669,468	353,000	96,452	969,782	1,627,477	195,991	510,439	547,591	NA	753,452	8,425,000
1982	43,082,814	21,355,111	331,000	135,033	1,465,686	2,081,230	214,349	472,674	866,815	1,800,000	834,439	8,550,000
1984	46,929,444	21,860,933	287,000	321,507	2,084,615	2,682,786	270,998	730,670	1,295,963	1,900,000	827,149	8,650,000
1985	49,283,691	21,565,230	299,363	257,206	2,427,232	2,815,118	265,693	1,142,385	1,881,491	1,950,000	1,062,997	8,700,000
1986	51,534,056	20,513,665	287,127	257,206	3,739,015	3,364,700	250,615	1,285,878	2,413,842	2,100,000	1,296,400	8,850,000
1987	53,033,614	19,176,500	327,598	385,809	4,947,040	3,724,000	256,822	853,600	3,558,954	2,300,000	1,048,081	8,850,000
1988	60,308,973	19,965,611	355,620	401,884	6,459,534	4,334,338	292,508	932,822	5,046,059	2,507,758	980,019	8,925,046
1989	65,335,998	19,530,290	429,470	340,798	8,543,449	5,127,850	276,914	948,640	6,544,702	2,893,567	964,265	9,773,826
1990	70,206,932	19,454,414	541,419	299,002	9,458,395	5,446,722	311,283	943,689	7,849,186	3,215,074	790,619	9,709,524
1991	70,422,599	19,326,133	845,918	282,927	9,454,311	5,676,278	326,073	1,120,260	7,530,283	3,858,089	833,219	8,359,193
1992	73,529,583	19,742,838	997,702	225,055	10,616,561	5,189,194	318,003	1,032,618	7,825,491	4,501,104	729,886	8,231,554*
1993	74,210,568	19,907,772	1,261,434	192,904	10,642,314	4,916,781	356,873	883,149	7,947,535	5,144,119	508,818	8,228,179*
1994ᴱ	73,618,833	18,637,078	1,430,869	34,562	10,488,247	4,694,008	446,895	883,149	8,236,634	5,144,119	469,754	8,172,719*

NA=not available. r=revised to reflect improved data. *USSR as constituted prior to Dec. 1991. E=estimated, except for U.S. data.

U.S. and World Silver Production, 1930-94

Source: Bureau of Mines, U.S. Dept. of the Interior; E=estimated

(metric tons)

Largest production of silver in the United States in 1915—2,332 metric tons.

Year	United States	World	Year	United States	World	Year	United States	World
1930	1,578	7,736	1965	1,238	8,007	1988	1,661	15,484
1935	1,428	6,865	1970	1,400	9,670	1989	2,008	16,041
1940	2,164	8,565	1975	1,087	9,428	1990	2,120	16,600
1945	904	5,039	1980	1,006	10,556	1991	1,860	15,600
1950	1,347	6,323	1985	1,227	13,051	1992	1,800	14,600
1955	1,134	6,967	1986	1,074	12,970	1993	1,640	14,300
1960	1,120	7,505	1987	1,241	14,019	1994	1,480	13,900ᴱ

Aluminum Summary, 1980-94

Source: Bureau of Mines, U.S. Dept. of the Interior

Item	Unit	1980	1985	1989	1990	1991	1992	1993	1994
U.S. production	1,000 metric tons	5,914	5,262	6,084	6,441	6,407	6,798	6,635	6,379
Primary aluminum	1,000 metric tons	4,654	3,500	4,030	4,048	4,121	4,042	3,695	3,299
Secondary aluminum[1]	1,000 metric tons	1,260	1,762	2,054	2,393	2,286	2,756	2,940	3,080
Primary aluminum value	Bil. dol	7.3	6.3	7.8	6.6	5.4	5.1	4.3	5.2
Price (Primary alum.)[2]	Cents/lb	71.6	81.0	87.8	74.0	59.5	57.5	53.3	71.2
Imports for consumption[3]	1,000 metric tons	647	1,420	1,470	1,514	1,490	1,725	2,540	3,380
Exports[3]	1,000 metric tons	1,346	908	1,613	1,659	1,762	1,453	1,210	1,370
World production	1,000 metric tons	15,383	15,398	19,104	19,299	19,575	19,462	19,700	19,100ᴱ

(1) Recoverable metal content from purchased scrap, old and new. (2) Average prices for primary aluminum, quoted by *Metals Week*. (3) Crude and semicrude (including metal and alloys, plates, bars, etc., and scrap). (E) Estimated.

Economic and Financial Glossary

Acquisition: The purchase of one company by another.

Arbitrage: A form of hedged investment meant to capture slight differences in the prices of two related securities—for example, buying gold in London and selling it at a higher price in New York.

Balanced budget: A budget is balanced when receipts equal current expenditure.

Balance of payments: The difference between all payments made to and from foreign countries over a set period of time. A *favorable* balance exists when more payments are coming in than going out; an *unfavorable* balance, when the reverse is true. Payments include gold, the cost of merchandise and services, interest and dividend payments, money spent by travelers, and repayment of principal on loans.

Balance of trade (trade gap):   The difference between exports and imports, in both actual funds and credit. A nation's balance of trade is *favorable* when exports exceed imports and *unfavorable* when the reverse is true.

Bear market: A market in which prices are falling.

Bearer bond: A bond issued in bearer form rather than being registered in the owner's name. Ownership is determined by possession.

Bond: A written promise or IOU by the issuer to repay a fixed amount of borrowed money on a specified date and to pay a set annual rate of interest in the meantime, usually at semi-annual intervals. Bonds are generally considered safe because the borrower (whether a company or the government) usually must make interest payments before the money is spent on anything else.

Bull market: A market in which prices are on the rise.

Capital gain (loss):   An increase (decrease) in the market value of an asset above (below) the price originally paid, at the time the asset is sold.

Commercial paper: An extremely short-term corporate IOU, generally due in 270 days or less. Available in face amounts of $100,000, $250,000, $500,000, $1,000,000 and combinations thereof.

Convertible bond: A corporate bond (see below) that may be converted into a stated number of shares of common stock. Its price tends to fluctuate along with fluctuations in the price of the stock and with changes in interest rates.

Corporate bond: Evidence of debt by a corporation. The bond normally has a stated life and pays a fixed rate of interest. Considered safer than the common or preferred stock of the same company.

Cost of living: The cost of maintaining a standard of living measured in terms of purchased goods and services. A rise in the cost of living mirrors the rate of inflation.

Cost-of-living benefits: Benefits that go to those persons whose money receipts increase automatically as prices rise.

Credit crunch (liquidity crisis):   The period when cash for lending to business and consumers is in short supply.

Debenture: An unsecured long-term debt obligation backed only by the general credit of the issuing corporation.

Deficit spending: The practice whereby a government goes into debt to finance some of its expenditures.

Depression: A long period of economic decline when prices are low, unemployment is high, and there are many business failures.

Derivatives: Custom-designed financial contracts whose values are based on, or *derived* from, a financial market like stocks, interest rates, or currencies.

Devaluation: The official lowering of a nation's currency, decreasing its value in relation to foreign currencies.

Discount rate: The rate of interest set by the Federal Reserve that member banks are charged when borrowing money through the Federal Reserve System.

Disposable income: Income after taxes which is available to persons for spending and saving.

Dividend: Payment by a corporation to its shareholders, usually in the form of cash, stock shares, or other property.

Dow-Jones Industrial Average: A measure of stock market prices, based on 30 leading companies on the New York Stock Exchange.

Econometrics: The application of mathematical and statistical methods to the study of economic and financial data.

Economic growth: The steady process of increasing productive capacity of the economy, and hence of increasing national income.

Federal Deposit Insurance Corporation (FDIC):   A government-sponsored corporation that insures accounts in national banks and other qualified institutions.

Federal Reserve System: The entire banking system of the U.S., incorporating 12 Federal Reserve banks (one in each of 12 Federal Reserve districts), 24 Federal Reserve branch banks all national banks and state-chartered commercial banks and trust companies that have been admitted to its membership. The system greatly influences the nation's monetary and credit policies.

Full employment: The economy is said to be at full employment when only fractional unemployment exists. That is, everyone who wishes to work at the going wage-rate for his type of labor is employed. Since it takes time to switch from one job to another, there will be at any given time a small amount of unemployment.

Golden parachute: Provisions in the employment contracts of executives guaranteeing substantial severance benefits if they lose their position in a corporate takeover.

Government bond: An IOU of the U.S. Treasury, considered the safest security in the investment world. They are divided into two categories, those that are not marketable and those that are. *Savings Bonds* cannot be bought and sold once the original purchase is made. These include the familiar Series EE bonds. You buy them at 50 percent of their face value and when they mature, 12 years later, they will pay you back 100 percent of face value if you cash them in. Another type, Series H, are not discounted, but issued in amounts of $500, $1,000, $5,000, and $10,000 and pay their interest in semiannual checks. Marketable bonds fall into 12 categories. *Treasury Bills* are short-term U.S. obligations, maturing in 3, 6, or 12 months. They are sold at a discount of the face value, and the minimum denomination is $10,000. *Treasury Notes* mature in up to 10 years. Denominations range from $500, $1,000 to $5,000, $10,000 and up. *Treasury Bonds* mature in 10 to 30 years. The minimum investment is $1,000.

Greenmail: A company buys back its own shares from a suitor for more than the going market price to avoid a hostile takeover.

Gross domestic product (GDP):   The market value of all goods and services that have been bought for final use during a year. It became the official measure of the U.S. economy in 1991, and replaced the *Gross National Product (GNP),* which had been in use since 1941. The GDP covers workers and capital employed within the nation's borders. The GNP covers production by American residents, regardless of location. The switch aligned the U.S. with most other industrialized countries, making comparisons easier.

Hedge fund: A flexible investment fund for a limited number of large investors (the minimum investment is typically $1 million). Hedge funds can use almost any investment technique, including those not allowed for mutual funds, such as short-selling and heavy leveraging.

Hedging: Taking two positions that will offset each other if prices change, in order to limit financial risk.

Individual retirement account (IRA):   A self-funded retirement plan that allows employed individuals to contribute a maximum yearly sum toward their retirement. Interest earned in the account is tax deferred.

Inflation: An increase in the average level of prices.

Insider information: Important facts about the condition or plans of a corporation that have not been released to the general public.

Interest: Money paid for the use of money. There are two kinds of interest. Simple interest is interest that is earned and paid. Compound interest is the accumulated interest that is added to the principal amount.

Junk bonds: Debt securities that sell at relatively low prices, because of the low credit rating of their issuers.

Leading indicators: A series of eleven indicators from different segments of the economy used by the Commerce Department to foretell what will happen in the economy in the near future.

Leverage: A way to amplify the potential gain or loss of an investment, usually by investing with borrowed money.

Leveraged buy-out: An acquisition of a publicly traded company by a small group, often including the company's management, which takes the company private. Much of the purchase price is borrowed, with the debt repaid from company profits or by selling company assets.

Liquid assets: Assets that include cash or those items that are easily converted into cash.

Margin account: A brokerage account that allows a person to trade securities on credit. A **margin call** is a demand for more collateral on the account.

Money supply: The currency held by the public plus checking accounts in commercial banks and savings institutions.

Mortgage-backed securities: Created when a bank, builder, or government agency gathers together a group of mortgages and then sells bonds to other institutions and the public. The investors receive their proportionate share of the interest payments on the loans as well as the principal payments. Usually, these mortgages are guaranteed by the government.

Municipal bond: Issued by governmental units such as states, cities, local taxing authorities, and other agencies. Interest is exempt from U.S. — and sometimes state and local — income tax. *Municipal Bond Unit Investment Trusts* allow you to invest in a portfolio of many different municipal bonds chosen by professionals. The income is exempt from federal income taxes.

Mutual fund: A portfolio, or selection, of professionally bought and managed stocks in which you pool your money along with thousands of other people. A share price is based on net asset value, or the value of all the investments owned by the funds, less any debt, and divided by the total number of shares. The major advantage is less risk — it is spread out over many stocks and, if one or two do badly, the remainder may shield you from the losses. *Bond Funds* are mutual funds that deal in the bond market exclusively. *Money Market Mutual Funds* buy in the so-called "Money Market" — institutions that need to borrow large sums of money for short terms. Usually the individual investor cannot afford the denominations required in the "Money Market" (i.e. treasury bills, commercial paper, certificates of deposit), but through a money market mutual fund he can take advantage of these instruments when interest rates are high. These funds offer special checking account advantages.

National debt: The debt of the national government as distinguished from the debts of the political subdivisions of the nation and private business and individuals.

National debt ceiling: Limit set by Congress beyond which the national debt cannot rise. This limit is periodically raised by congressional vote.

Option: A contractual agreement between a buyer and a seller to buy or sell shares of a security. A **Call** option contract gives the right to purchase shares of a specific stock at a stated price within a given period of time. A **Put** option contract gives the buyer the right to sell shares of a specific stock at a stated price within a given period of time.

Per capita income: The nation's total income divided by the number of people in the nation.

Prime interest rate: The rate charged by banks on short-term loans to large commercial customers with the highest credit rating.

Producer price index: A statistical measure of the change in the price of wholesale goods. It is reported for 3 different stages of the production chain: crude, intermediate, and finished goods.

Program trading: A term used for trading techniques involving large numbers and large blocks of stocks, usually used in conjunction with computer programs. Techniques include *Index Arbitrage,* in which traders profit from price differences between stocks and futures contracts on stock indexes, and *Portfolio Insurance,* which is the use of stock-index futures to protect stock investors from large losses when the market drops.

Public debt: The total of the nation's debts owed by state, local, and national government. This is considered a good measure of how much of the nation's spending is financed by borrowing rather than taxation.

Recession: A mild decrease in economic activity marked by a decline in real GDP, employment, and trade, usually lasting 6 months to a year, and marked by widespread decline in many sectors of the economy.

Savings Association Insurance Fund (SAIF): Created in 1989 to insure accounts in savings and loan associations up to $100,000.

Seasonal adjustment: Statistical changes made to compensate for regular fluctuations in data that are so great they tend to distort the statistics and make comparisons meaningless. For instance, seasonal adjustments are made in mid-winter for a slowdown in housing construction and for the rise in farm income in the fall after the summer crops are harvested.

Short-selling: Borrowing shares of stock from a brokerage firm and selling them, hoping to buy the shares back at a lower price, return them, and realize a profit from the decline in prices.

Stagnation: A period of economic slowdown in which there is little growth in GDP, capital investment, and real income.

Stock: *Common Stocks* are shares of ownership in a corporation; they are the most direct way to participate in the fortunes of a company. There can be wide swings in the prices of this kind of stock. *Preferred Stock* is a type of stock on which a fixed dividend must be paid before holders of common stock are issued their share of the issuing corporation's earnings. Prices are higher and yields lower than comparable bonds. However, they are attractive to corporate investors because 85% of preferred dividends are tax exempt to corporations. *Convertible Preferred Stock* can be converted into the common stock of the company that issued the preferred. This stock has the advantage of producing a higher yield than common stock and it also has appreciation potential. *Over-the-Counter Stock* is not traded on the major or regional exchanges, but rather through dealers from whom you buy directly. *Blue Chip* stocks are so called because they have been leading stocks for a long time. *Growth* stocks are stocks whose earnings have grown over several years.

Stock-index futures: A futures contract is an agreement to buy or sell a specific amount of a commodity or financial instrument at a particular price at a set date. Futures on a stock index (such as the Standard & Poor's 500) are bets on the future price of that group of stocks.

Supply-side economics: The school of economic thinking that stresses the importance of the costs of production as a means of revitalizing the economy. Advocates policies that raise capital and labor output by increasing the incentives to produce.

Takeover: The passing of control of one company by another company or group by sale or merger. A friendly takeover occurs when the acquired company's management is agreeable to the merger; when management is opposed to the merger it is an unfriendly takeover. Takeover **arbitrage** is the purchase and/or selling of the securities of companies involved in takeover situations in order to realize a profit.

Tender offer: A public offer to buy a company's stock; usually priced at a premium above the market.

Unit investment trust: A portfolio of many different corporate bonds, preferred stocks, government-backed securities, or utility common stocks in which you can invest with as little as $1,000. Professional managers choose the securities, arrange for safekeeping, and collect the income. You receive your pro rata share of income every month.

Zero coupon bond: A corporate or government bond that is issued at a deep discount from the maturity value and pays no interest during the life of the bond. It is redeemable at face value.

AGRICULTURE

The U.S. Farm Population

Source: U.S. Dept. of Agriculture, Economic Research Service, *The Farm Entrepreneurial Population, 1988-90*, by Margaret Butler

When first separately counted in the 1920 census, the farm population was defined as people living on farms, regardless of occupation or source of income. Many people who live on farms today have no one in the household employed primarily in agriculture, and those employed in agriculture often do not live on farms. Thirty-five percent of persons in farm operator or manager households did not live on a farm in 1992, and 38% of farm residents were members of households in which no one operated or managed a farm or received farm self-employment income. Thus, the conventional farm residence definition has lost some of its former validity and has been discontinued.

In 1993, about 4.9 million people lived in households associated with the operation of farms, as indicated by a household member's occupation or source of income. This farm population definition is now identified as the farm entrepreneurial population. The Midwest was home to a larger proportion of that population—47%—than any other region of the country.

Persons in Farm Occupations, 1850-1993

Source: U.S. Dept. of Agriculture, Economic Research Service

(in thousands)

Year	Total workers*	Farm occupations Number	Farm occupations % of total	Year	Total workers*	Farm occupations Number	Farm occupations % of total
1850	7,697	4,902	63.7	1970	79,802	2,881	3.6
1870	12,925	6,850	53.0	1980	104,058	2,818	2.7
1900	29,030	10,888	37.5	1985 (March)	106,214	2,949	2.8
1920	42,206	11,390	27.0	1990 (March)	117,491	2,864	2.4
1930	48,686	10,321	21.2	1991 (March)	116,000	2,848	2.5
1940	51,742	8,995	17.4	1992 (March)	116,442	2,936	2.5
1950	59,230	6,858	11.6	1993 (March)	117,238	2,988	2.5
1960	67,990	4,132	6.1				

* Total workers for 1985 to 1993 are employed workers ages 15 years and older; total workers for 1970 and 1980 are members of the experienced civilian labor force ages 16 years and older; total workers for 1900 to 1960 are members of the experienced civilian labor force ages 14 years and older; and total workers for 1850 to 1890 are gainfully employed workers ages 10 years and older.

Farms–Number and Acreage by State, 1984 and 1994

Source: National Agricultural Statistics Service, U.S. Dept. of Agriculture

State	Farms (1,000) 1984	Farms (1,000) 1994	Acreage (mil) 1984	Acreage (mil) 1993	Acreage per farm 1984	Acreage per farm 1994	State	Farms (1,000) 1984	Farms (1,000) 1994	Acreage (mil) 1984	Acreage (mil) 1993	Acreage per farm 1984	Acreage per farm 1994
U.S.	2,334	2,065	1,018	973	436	471	Montana	24	23	61	60	2,525	2,653
Alabama	53	46	11	10	215	222	Nebraska	61	55	47	47	774	856
Alaska	1	1	2	1	2,031	1,788	Nevada	3	2	9	9	3,179	3,667
Arizona	8	7	38	35	4,518	4,784	New Hampshire	3	2	1	(Z)	159	183
Arkansas	55	44	16	15	291	343	New Jersey	9	9	1	1	105	97
California	82	79	33	30	400	378	New Mexico	14	14	46	44	3,271	3,274
Colorado	27	25	35	33	1,281	1,292	New York	47	36	9	8	200	219
Connecticut	4	4	(Z)	(Z)	114	103	N. Carolina	79	58	11	9	139	160
Delaware	4	3	1	1	183	228	N. Dakota	36	32	41	40	1,155	1,263
Florida	40	39	12	10	310	264	Ohio	90	75	16	15	176	203
Georgia	51	45	14	62	265	269	Oklahoma	73	70	33	34	452	486
Hawaii	5	5	2	2	402	331	Oregon	37	38	18	18	486	461
Idaho	25	21	15	14	598	659	Pennsylvania	58	51	9	8	150	153
Illinois	96	77	29	28	299	365	Rhode Island	1	1	(Z)	(Z)	95	90
Indiana	82	63	16	16	200	254	S. Carolina	28	23	6	5	200	222
Iowa	113	101	34	33	297	329	S. Dakota	37	34	45	44	1,203	1,300
Kansas	74	65	48	48	649	735	Tennessee	95	83	13	12	141	145
Kentucky	101	89	15	14	144	158	Texas	194	200	137	129	705	645
Louisiana	35	28	10	8	287	300	Utah	14	13	12	11	843	854
Maine	8	8	2	1	199	179	Vermont	7	6	2	1	233	226
Maryland	18	15	3	2	152	152	Virginia	56	46	10	9	173	187
Massachusetts	7	6	1	1	106	100	Washington	38	36	16	16	424	439
Michigan	63	52	11	11	179	206	W. Virginia	22	20	4	4	173	185
Minnesota	97	85	30	30	313	349	Wisconsin	86	79	18	17	209	214
Mississippi	50	39	14	13	284	328	Wyoming	9	9	35	35	3,824	3,761
Missouri	116	105	31	30	267	287							

(Z) Fewer than 500 farms or 500,000 acres

Livestock on Farms in the U.S., 1900-95

Source: National Agricultural Statistics Service, U.S. Dept. of Agriculture

(in thousands)

Year (On Jan. 1)	All cattle	Milk cows	Sheep	Hogs[1]	Year (On Jan. 1)	All cattle	Milk cows	Sheep	Hogs[1]
1900	59,739	16,544	48,105	51,055	1965[2]	109,000	16,981	25,127	56,106
1910	58,993	19,450	50,239	48,072	1970	112,369	12,091	20,423	57,046
1920	70,400	21,455	40,743	60,159	1980	111,242	10,758	12,699	67,318
1925	63,373	22,575	38,543	55,770	1985	109,582	10,777	10,716	54,073
1930	61,003	23,032	51,565	55,705	1990*	95,816	10,015	11,358	53,788
1935	68,846	26,082	51,808	39,066	1991*	96,393	9,966	11,174	54,416
1940	68,309	24,940	52,107	61,165	1992*	97,556	9,728	10,797	57,649
1945	85,573	27,770	46,520	59,373	1993*	99,176	9,658	10,201	58,202
1950	77,963	23,853	29,826	58,937	1994*	100,988	9,528	9,742	57,904
1955	96,592	23,462	31,582	50,474	1995[3]	103,265	9,532	8,895	59,992
1960	96,236	19,527	33,170	59,026					

* Figures revised by USDA NASS, Jan. 1995. (1)As of Dec. 1 of preceding year. (2)From 1965, milk cows and heifers that have calved. (3)Total estimated value on farms as of Jan. 1, 1995, was (avg. value per head in parentheses): cattle $63,583,416,000 ($616.00); sheep $664,065,000 ($74.70); hogs $3,191,574,000 ($53.20).

U.S. Farms, 1940-94

Source: U.S. Dept. of Agriculture

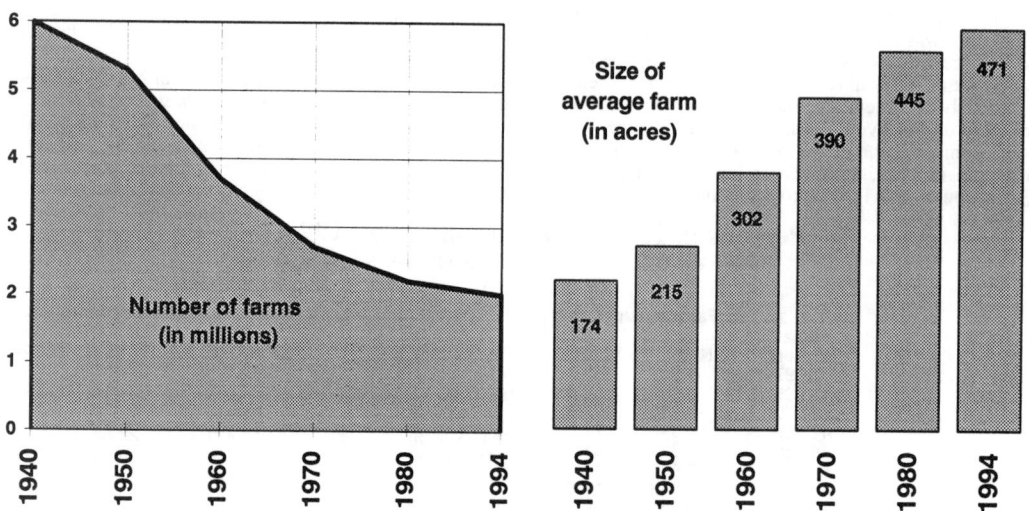

Eggs: U.S. Production, Price, and Value, 1993-94[1]

Source: Economic Research Service, U.S. Dept. of Agriculture

State	Eggs produced[2] 1993	Eggs produced[2] 1994	Price per dozen[2] 1993	Price per dozen[2] 1994	Value of production 1993	Value of production 1994	State	Eggs produced[2] 1993	Eggs produced[2] 1994	Price per dozen[2] 1993	Price per dozen[2] 1994	Value of production 1993	Value of production 1994
	(mil)		(cents)		(1,000 dollars)			(mil)		(cents)		(1,000 dollars)	
AL ..	2,538	2,732	103.0	90.2	217,845	205,355	NE. ..	2,027	2,027	43.0	36.0	72,634	60,810
AK ..	0.5	0.5	179.0	171.0	75	71	NV. ..	1.1	1.4	41.3	43.8	38	51
AZ ..	88	81	50.6	49.1	3,711	3,314	NH. ..	45	39	105.0	97.0	3,938	3,153
AR ..	3,645	3,803	94.1	104.0	285,829	329,593	NJ ..	526	451	76.0	71.0	33,313	26,684
CA ..	7,029	6,602	49.1	46.4	287,603	255,277	NM ..	313	300	64.0	59.8	16,693	14,950
CO ..	837	778	68.8	66.0	47,988	42,790	NY. ..	1,028	1,049	60.7	57.2	52,000	50,002
CT ..	988	972	103.0	99.7	84,803	80,757	NC. ..	3,082	3,214	76.0	73.5	195,193	196,858
DE ..	162	152	106.0	108.0	14,310	13,680	ND. ..	60	51	43.0	36.0	2,150	1,530
FL. ..	2,475	2,538	51.8	46.5	106,838	98,348	OH. ..	5,075	5,644	48.1	48.7	203,423	229,052
GA ..	4,449	4,543	74.6	74.5	276,580	282,045	OK. ..	880	765	100.0	89.9	73,333	57,311
HI. ..	210.6	187	85.5	85.9	15,005	13,386	OR. ..	673	708	79.0	78.3	44,306	46,197
ID. ..	232	253	66.4	64.8	12,837	13,662	PA. ..	5,642	5,597	51.0	51.1	239,785	238,339
IL. ..	807	768	59.0	64.0	39,678	40,960	RI ..	53	55	98.1	94.9	4,333	4,350
IN. ..	5,281	5,452	55.9	50.8	246,007	230,801	SC. ..	1,282	1,326	65.0	63.7	69,442	70,389
IA. ..	3,328	3,808	45.1	39.8	125,077	126,299	SD. ..	627	535	37.5	32.5	19,594	14,490
KS ..	334	352	44.1	38.8	12,275	11,381	TN. ..	258	255	79.0	72.0	16,985	15,300
KY ..	629	679	68.0	63.7	35,643	36,044	TX. ..	3,569	3,860	68.1	61.6	202,541	198,147
LA ..	450	441	92.3	111.0	34,613	40,793	UT. ..	498	489	57.0	45.1	23,655	18,378
ME. ..	1,204	1,403	96.1	92.2	96,420	107,797	VT. ..	30	20	104.0	99.3	2,600	1,655
MD. ..	831	852	57.6	63.7	39,888	45,227	VA. ..	926	943	84.8	88.5	65,437	69,546
MA ..	202	205	103.0	98.7	17,338	16,861	WA ..	1,283	1,371	69.8	73.0	74,628	83,403
MI. ..	1,401	1,435	46.0	42.5	53,705	50,823	WV ..	213	248	110.0	115.0	19,525	23,767
MN. ..	2,692	2,669	46.0	40.0	103,193	88,967	WI ..	820	883	47.0	41.0	32,117	30,169
MS ..	1,435	1,515	88.5	96.4	105,831	121,705	WY ..	2.8	2.9	74.0	67.6	173	163
MO ..	1,644	1,713	45.8	43.3	62,746	61,811	U.S.[3]	71,936	73,866	63.4	61.4	3,800,237	3,776,795
MT ..	125	95	63.0	55.0	6,563	4,354							

(1)Estimates cover the 12-month period from Dec. 1 of the previous year through Nov. 30. (2) Average of all eggs sold by producers, including hatching eggs. (3) Total states may not equal U.S. total due to rounding.

U.S. Meat Production and Consumption, 1940-94

Source: Economic Research Service, U.S. Dept. of Agriculture

(in millions of pounds)

Year	Beef Production	Beef Consumption[2]	Veal Production	Veal Consumption[2]	Lamb and mutton Production	Lamb and mutton Consumption[2]	Pork (exclud. lard) Production	Pork (exclud. lard) Consumption[2]	All meats[1] Production	All meats[1] Consumption[2]	Lard Production	Lard Consumption[3]
1940	7,175	7,257	981	981	876	873	10,044	9,701	19,076	18,812	2,288	1,901
1950	9,534	9,529	1,230	1,206	597	596	10,714	10,390	22,075	21,721	2,631	1,891
1960	14,728	15,465	1,109	1,118	769	857	13,905	14,057	30,511	31,497	2,562	1,358
1970	21,684	23,451	588	613	551	669	14,699	14,957	37,522	39,689	1,913	939
1980	21,643	23,560	400	420	318	351	16,617	16,838	38,978	41,701	1,207	588
1990	22,743	24,031	327	325	363	397	15,354	16,031	38,787	40,784	4	4
1991	22,917	24,113	306	305	363	396	15,999	16,399	39,585	41,214	4	4
1992	23,086	24,261	310	312	348	388	17,233	17,474	40,977	42,435	4	4
1993	23,049	24,006	285	286	337	381	17,088	18,213	40,759	42,092	4	4
1994	24,386	25,127	293	291	308	345	17,696	17,829	42,683	43,592	4	4

(1)Meats may not add to total. (2) Includes shipments. (3) Direct use. Excludes lard used in such products as table spreads and shortenings. (4) Data collection discontinued.

Government Agricultural Payments by State, 1994[1]

Source: Economic Research Service, U.S. Dept. of Agriculture

(in thousands of dollars)

State	Feed Grains	Wheat	Rice	Cotton	Wool Act	Conservation[2]	Miscellaneous[3]	Total
Alabama	2,534	2,861	0	31,757	130	30,213	21,891	89,386
Alaska.	107	0	0	0	9	1,098	134	1,348
Arizona	1,817	4,893	0	54,491	1,701	2,982	6,189	72,073
Arkansas.	3,715	19,721	132,487	56,247	541	17,016	73,025	302,752
California.	8,042	22,747	67,688	92,978	9,952	14,642	56,732	272,781
Colorado	22,046	44,813	0	0	8,064	85,020	17,166	177,109
Connecticut	340	0	0	0	42	372	1,614	2,368
Delaware.	1,228	468	0	0	5	554	3,335	5,590
Florida	1,407	485	83	3,607	34	15,674	37,347	58,637
Georgia.	7,653	9,552	0	31,112	37	32,504	58,967	139,825
Hawaii.	0	0	0	0	11	714	2,186	2,911
Idaho	18,626	44,217	0	0	5,195	42,134	17,117	127,289
Illinois	178,702	16,903	0	0	768	70,044	36,742	303,159
Indiana	79,347	9,003	0	0	330	37,247	11,093	137,020
Iowa	238,875	214	0	0	3,013	195,251	295,214	732,567
Kansas	73,921	199,236	0	31	2,141	163,653	29,376	467,710
Kentucky.	16,073	5,175	10	0	190	29,653	3,793	54,894
Louisiana	3,078	3,392	52,7800	71,842	38	10,036	40,409	181,575
Maine	317	2	0	0	134	4,556	9,092	14,101
Maryland	4,558	1,510	0	0	136	2,479	6,951	15,634
Massachusetts . .	154	0	0	0	80	645	3,815	4,694
Michigan	39,406	10,516	0	0	999	24,400	26,771	102,092
Minnesota	127,841	53,596	25,045	0	2,054	108,551	330,283	622,325
Mississippi.	2,254	4,906	10,098	112,018	19	41,666	39,575	225,483
Missouri	36,842	24,143	0	18,036	1,622	124,561	52,095	267,397
Montana	35,731	89,417	0	0	11,772	109,925	9,306	256,151
Nebraska	160,832	42,787	0	0	1,959	85,384	57,371	348,333
Nevada.	156	515	0	0	1,583	822	1,709	4,785
New Hampshire . .	129	0	0	0	79	726	541	1,475
New Jersey	1,089	267	0	0	42	650	5,548	7,596
New Mexico.	4,897	6,050	0	5,409	9,223	21,722	13,791	61,092
New York	13,250	2,574	0	0	521	8,094	18,004	42,443
North Carolina . . .	12,796	5,135	0	18,509	120	10,403	30,683	77,646
North Dakota. . . .	70,409	167,520	0	0	3,403	114,754	101,260	457,346
Ohio	51,119	17,592	113	0	1,699	31,263	15,424	117,097
Oklahoma	4,996	105,634	0	17,322	2,764	55,121	21,086	207,036
Oregon	3,911	25,511	0	0	3,534	29,685	11,785	74,426
Pennsylvania. . . .	7,997	913	0	0	700	9,992	13,084	32,686
Rhode Island. . . .	1	0	0	0	10	89	351	451
South Carolina. . .	6,828	5,681	0	12,951	8	14,141	20,589	60,198
South Dakota . . .	53,556	51,285	0	0	11,174	74,697	98,502	289,214
Tennessee	7,043	5,504	63	34,343	92	26,996	21,5699	95,610
Texas	66,636	73,464	48,334	265,472	89,820	182,416	137,071	863,213
Utah	2,162	3,536	0	0	8,496	11,043	6,814	32,051
Vermont	335	1	0	0	216	1,913	1,769	4,234
Virginia	5,801	2,750	0	618	811	6,995	17,279	34,254
Washington	16,196	66,698	0	0	872	56,992	12,096	152,854
West Virginia	725	60	0	0	425	2,346	1,957	5,513
Wisconsin	50,901	1,518	0	0	610	54,146	129,309	236,484
Wyoming.	2,309	3,477	0	0	14,753	12,329	5,260	38,128
United States . . .	**1,448,688**	**1,156,242**	**336,701**	**826,743**	**201,931**	**1,977,661**	**1,933,070**	**7,881,036**

(1)Includes both cash payments and payment-in-kind (PIK). (2)Includes amount paid under agriculture and conservation programs (Conservation Reserve, Agriculture Conservation, Emergency Conservation, and Great Plains Program). (3) The programs included Rural Clean Water, Forestry Incentive Long Term, Water Bank Practice Cost Share, Dairy Indemnity, Dairy Termination, Extended Warehouse Storage, Extended Farm Storage, Colorado River Salinity, Livestock Emergency Assistance, Interest Payments, Disaster, Loan Deficiency, Market Gains, Naval Stores Conservation, Milk Marketing Fee, Options Pilot, Milk Diversion, Emergency Feed, Rice Marketing, 90 Day Rule, Payment Limitation Refund, Additional Intervest, Arkansas Beaver Lake, and Wetlands Reserve.

Federal Food Assistance Programs, 1985-94[1]

Source: Food and Nutrition Service, U.S. Dept. of Agriculture

(in millions of dollars)

Program	1985	1986	1987	1988	1989	1990	1991	1992	1993	1994
Food stamps[2]	$11,703	$11,638	$11,605	$12,317	$12,932	$15,491	$18,769	$22,462	$23,653	$24,492
Puerto Rico nutrition asst.[3] . .	825	820	853	879	908	937	963	1,002	1,040	1,079
Natl. school lunch[4]	3,380	3,537	3,685	3,730	3,769	3,834	4,224	4,564	4,751	4,964
School breakfast[5]	379	406	447	482	513	596	685	787	869	959
WIC[6]	1,489	1,583	1,680	1,798	1,911	2,122	2,301	2,597	2,829	3,169
Summer food service[4]	112	115	129	133	146	164	182	204	220	231
Child/adult care[4]	452	496	548	628	697	813	945	1,104	1,223	1,358
Special milk	16	16	15	19	18	19	20	20	19	18
Nutrition for the elderly[4]	134	137	139	146	146	142	144	151	150	153
Food distrib. to Indian reserv..	60	60	63	62	65	66	65	62	62	65
Commodity supp. food prog.[4,7]	48	48	56	62	73	85	93	105	112	107
Food dist.—charitable inst.[8] . .	170	240	158	159	136	104	93	116	92	101
Emergency food assistance..	1,026	895	895	645	276	257	256	236	238	201
Soup kitchens/food banks . . .	0	0	0	0	34	77	45	36	35	40
Other costs[9]	56	60	62	58	68	71	78	92	107	116
Total[10]	**$19,851**	**$20,051**	**$20,335**	**$21,118**	**$21,692**	**$24,776**	**$28,863**	**$33,538**	**$35,400**	**$37,052**

(1) Data are for fiscal (not calendar) years. (2) Includes the federal share of state administrative expenses and other federal costs. (3) Puerto Rico participated in the Food Stamp Program from FY 1975 until July 1982, when it initiated a separate grant program. (4) Includes the value of commodities (entitlement, bonus, and cash in lieu). (5) Excludes startup costs. (6) Includes program studies and the WIC Farmers Market Nutrition Program. (7) Includes elderly feeding projects. (8) Includes summer camps. (9)Includes child nutrition state administration expenses, nutrition studies, nutrition education and training, Northern Marianas nutrition assistance grant, and commodity disaster relief. (10) Excludes food program administration costs.

Farm Marketings by State, 1993-94

Source: Economic Research Service, U.S. Dept. of Agriculture

(in thousands of dollars)

State/Rank	1994 Farm marketings			1993 Farm marketings		
	Total	Crops	Livestock and products	Total	Crops	Livestock and products
Alabama (26).........	2,904,463	745,060	2,159,403	2,857,094	728,031	2,129,063
Alaska (50)..........	27,716	21,685	6,031	26,763	20,834	5,929
Arizona (32).........	1,868,642	1,044,621	824,021	1,945,902	1,027,581	918,321
Arkansas (11)........	5,275,623	2,161,534	3,114,089	4,354,224	1,453,568	2,900,656
California (1)........	20,238,064	14,840,518	5,397,546	19,954,273	14,642,815	5,311,458
Colorado (17)........	4,028,834	1,250,177	2,778,657	4,197,400	1,204,991	2,992,409
Connecticut (44)......	472,741	221,848	250,893	474,510	214,495	260,015
Delaware (40)........	660,191	154,807	505,384	611,054	144,060	466,994
Florida (9)..........	5,977,970	4,786,346	1,191,624	6,069,496	4,858,365	1,211,331
Georgia (14).........	4,715,685	2,046,757	2,668,928	4,232,365	1,663,837	2,548,528
Hawaii (41)..........	498,099	421,576	76,523	507,204	421,835	85,369
Idaho (23)...........	2,954,516	1,755,529	1,198,987	2,890,394	1,723,322	1,167,072
Illinois (5)..........	8,222,796	6,158,108	2,064,688	8,150,527	5,916,210	2,234,317
Indiana (12).........	4,837,594	3,072,192	1,765,402	5,340,897	3,427,646	1,913,251
Iowa (3)............	10,084,316	4,964,427	5,119,889	10,389,722	4,605,688	5,784,034
Kansas (6)..........	7,687,299	2,878,598	4,808,701	7,335,486	2,478,065	4,857,421
Kentucky (22)........	3,230,277	1,584,844	1,645,433	3,414,258	1,689,532	1,724,726
Louisiana (31)........	2,012,687	1,308,964	703,723	1,795,135	1,090,195	704,940
Maine (42)...........	482,729	206,701	276,028	453,287	184,759	268,528
Maryland (36)........	1,344,680	551,193	793,487	1,345,320	524,559	820,761
Massachusetts (45)....	458,731	341,421	117,310	490,598	369,501	121,097
Michigan (20)........	3,418,874	2,009,236	1,409,638	3,327,519	1,959,479	1,368,040
Minnesota (7)........	6,522,323	3,075,068	3,447,255	6,334,387	2,579,833	3,754,554
Mississippi (25).......	2,916,359	1,210,043	1,706,316	2,632,254	1,064,193	1,568,061
Missouri (15)........	4,524,209	2,072,076	2,452,133	4,111,941	1,836,384	2,275,557
Montana (33).........	1,857,217	990,433	866,784	1,801,742	853,576	948,166
Nebraska (4).........	8,561,321	3,157,866	5,403,455	8,870,838	3,024,941	5,845,897
Nevada (47).........	299,121	109,696	189,425	295,700	102,586	193,114
New Hampshire (48)...	151,911	87,885	64,026	152,431	86,275	66,156
New Jersey (39).......	768,405	585,841	182,564	699,685	502,376	197,309
New Mexico (34)......	1,523,959	425,073	1,098,886	1,536,797	413,468	1,123,329
New York (27)........	2,857,581	970,556	1,887,025	2,859,586	978,076	1,881,510
North Carolina (8)....	6,369,139	3,036,625	3,332,514	6,019,322	2,829,349	3,189,973
North Dakota (24)....	2,934,691	2,307,377	627,314	2,948,826	2,348,419	600,407
Ohio (16)...........	4,475,151	2,897,802	1,577,349	4,490,584	2,834,933	1,655,651
Oklahoma (18).......	3,864,455	1,164,650	2,699,805	3,949,327	1,141,304	2,808,023
Oregon (28)..........	2,651,530	1,925,560	725,970	2,557,447	1,809,465	747,982
Pennsylvania (19).....	3,755,276	1,143,263	2,612,013	3,806,940	1,186,935	2,620,005
Rhode Island (49).....	80,748	68,461	12,287	80,461	66,657	13,804
South Carolina (35)...	1,361,759	746,869	614,890	1,249,116	648,891	600,225
South Dakota (21).....	3,342,603	1,698,537	1,644,066	3,200,009	1,236,183	1,963,826
Tennessee (30).......	2,151,724	1,169,745	981,979	2,025,569	1,063,968	961,601
Texas (2)...........	12,552,238	4,324,186	8,228,052	12,662,294	4,492,070	8,170,224
Utah (37)............	818,862	221,289	597,573	831,399	217,691	613,708
Vermont (43).........	480,548	90,770	389,778	489,196	87,330	401,866
Virginia (29).........	2,159,252	773,057	1,386,195	2,094,682	697,008	1,397,674
Washington (13)......	4,720,482	3,111,831	1,608,651	4,632,786	3,074,675	1,558,111
West Virginia (46)....	402,749	74,201	328,548	404,574	81,117	323,457
Wisconsin (10).......	5,384,188	1,439,320	3,944,868	5,395,090	1,294,250	4,100,840
Wyoming (38)........	778,364	157,348	621,016	840,955	180,505	660,450
United States........	**179,668,692**	**91,561,570**	**88,107,122**	**177,137,366**	**87,101,826**	**90,035,540**

Value of U.S. Agricultural Exports and Imports, 1974-94

Source: Economic Research Service, U.S. Dept. of Agriculture

(in billions of dollars, except percent)

Year	Trade balance	Exports, domestic products	Percentage of all exports	Imports for consumption	Percentage of all imports	Year	Trade balance	Exports, domestic products	Percentage of all exports	Imports for consumption	Percentage of all imports
1974 ..	$11.8	$22.0	23	$10.2	10	1985...	$9.1	$29.0	13	$20.0	6
1975 ..	12.6	21.9	21	9.3	10	1986...	4.8	26.2	13	21.5	6
1976 ..	12.0	23.0	20	11.0	9	1987...	8.3	28.7	12	20.4	5
1977 ..	10.2	23.6	20	13.4	9	1988...	16.1	37.1	12	21.0	5
1978 ..	14.6	29.4	21	14.8	9	1989...	18.2	39.9	11	21.7	5
1979 ..	18.0	34.7	19	16.7	8	1990...	16.6	39.4	10	22.8	5
1980 ..	23.9	41.2	19	17.4	7	1991...	16.5	39.2	10	22.7	5
1981 ..	26.6	43.3	18	16.8	6	1992...	18.3	42.9	10	24.6	5
1982 ..	21.2	36.6	17	15.4	6	1993...	17.6	42.6	10	25.0	4
1983 ..	19.5	36.1	18	16.6	6	1994...	18.9	45.7	10	26.8	4
1984 ..	18.5	37.8	17	19.3	6						

Farm Real Estate Debt Outstanding by Lender Groups,[1] 1960-94

Source: Economic Research Service, U.S.Dept. of Agriculture

(in thousands of dollars)

Dec. 31	Total farm real estate debt[2]	Federal land banks[2]	Amounts held by principal lender groups — Farmers Home Adminis-tration[3]	Life in-surance com-panies[4]	All commer-cial banks	Other[5]
1960	$12,867,524	$2,539,000	$723,000	$2,975,000	$1,592,000	$5,039,000
1970	30,492,357	7,145,363	2,440,043	5,610,300	3,772,377	11,524,000
1980	97,486,996	36,196,103	8,163,270	12,927,800	8,563,457	31,636,000
1985	105,739,201	44,583,842	10,426,971	11,830,400	11,384,920	27,507,000
1986	95,879,799	37,757,626	10,348,597	10,940,200	12,710,650	24,123,000
1987	87,717,601	32,637,687	10,083,239	9,895,800	14,455,162	20,646,000
1988	82,952,518	30,326,707	9,606,796	9,581,700	15,416,700	18,020,000
1989	80,482,189	28,506,713	8,719,822	9,597,900	16,646,179	17,011,577
1990	78,903,115	27,390,156	8,092,982	10,186,300	17,227,171	16,006,500
1991	78,304,937	26,760,206	7,462,411	10,029,300	18,436,918	16,616,072
1992	80,419,686	26,886,261	6,779,546	9,208,000	19,862,622	17,683,259
1993	80,738,586	26,460,450	6,216,178	9,469,174	20,847,783	17,745,000
1994	82,971,224	26,300,421	5,852,920	9,562,841	22,555,042	18,700,000

(1) Includes operator households. (2) Includes data for joint stock land banks and real estate loans by Agricultural Credit Assn. (3) Includes loans made directly by FmHA for farm ownership, soil and water loans to individuals, Native American tribe land acquisition, grazing associations, and half of economic emergency loans. Also includes loans for rural housing on farm tracts and labor housing. (4) American Council of Life Insurance. (5) Estimated by ERS, USDA. Includes Commodity Credit Corporation storage and drying facility loans.

Grain, Hay, Potato, Cotton, Soybean, Tobacco Production, by State, 1994

Source: Economic Research Service, U.S. Dept. of Agriculture

1994 State	Barley (1,000 bu)	Corn, grain (1,000 bu)	Cotton lint (1,000 b)	All hay (1,000 t)	Oats (1,000 bu)	Potatoes (1,000 cwt)	Soybeans (1,000 bu)	Tobacco (1,000 lb)	All wheat (1,000 bu)
Alabama.	—	24,960	740.0	2,025	1,815	1,628	9,145	—	4,560
Alaska	—	—	—	—	—	—	—	—	—
Arizona	3,135	2,550	870.0	1,326	—	1,670	—	—	11,186
Arkansas	—	10,800	1,760.0	2,505	1,540	—	115,600	—	40,480
California	14,300	28,050	2,910.0	8,210	2,800	—	—	—	44,365
Colorado	7,470	133,500	—	4,060	1,440	15,267	—	—	79,734
Connecticut. . . .	—	—	—	191	—	28,720	—	2,625	—
Delaware	1,890	18,750	—	61	—	—	8,140	—	3,780
Florida	—	6,800	100.0	744	—	816	1,302	16,575	630
Georgia	—	57,240	1,550.0	1,950	3,350	9,992	15,500	80,660	20,400
Hawaii	—	—	—	—	—	—	—	—	—
Idaho.	54,000	4,900	—	4,438	1,300	134,340	—	—	100,280
Illinois	—	1,786,200	—	3,175	5,490	1,450	438,380	—	50,400
Indiana	—	858,240	—	2,110	1,855	1,148	219,960	15,265	38,430
Iowa	—	1,930,400	—	5,775	26,660	328	447,270	—	2,115
Kansas	532	304,590	1.7	5,925	5,520	—	75,600	—	433,200
Kentucky	1,106	156,160	—	5,400	—	—	42,940	458,075	25,200
Louisiana	—	35,190	1,500.0	812	—	—	32,480	—	2,590
Maine	—	—	—	406	1,820	17,250	—	—	—
Maryland	4,200	46,020	—	668	270	250	19,800	12,750	12,100
Massachusetts . .	—	—	—	217	—	775	—	803	—
Michigan.	1,632	260,910	—	4,865	6,270	14,910	58,520	—	30,740
Minnesota.	30,000	915,900	—	7,530	24,750	20,035	229,600	—	71,948
Mississippi	—	30,500	2,150.0	1,875	—	—	59,520	—	6,400
Missouri	—	273,700	595.0	6,770	1,768	1,734	173,280	8,190	49,500
Montana.	52,800	2,700	—	4,540	3,600	3,200	—	—	170,590
Nebraska	304	1,153,700	—	7,415	7,500	5,296	137,280	—	71,400
Nevada	340	—	—	1,400	—	2,760	—	—	670
New Hampshire .	—	—	—	163	—	—	—	—	—
New Jersey	265	9,639	—	273	—	—	5,145	—	1,344
New Mexico. . . .	—	12,750	90.0	1,499	—	588	—	—	5,520
New York	—	68,440	—	3,961	7,040	4,238	—	—	6,095
North Carolina . .	1,750	81,900	820.0	1,187	2,600	7,805	41,850	597,525	30,380
North Dakota . . .	132,000	54,000	—	4,510	33,550	3,186	18,910	—	356,404
Ohio	—	486,500	—	4,384	6,720	28,200	175,560	19,295	68,440
Oklahoma.	222	16,500	240.0	4,128	1,110	1,348	9,280	—	143,100
Oregon	9,490	3,400	—	2,840	4,500	25,784	—	—	58,580
Pennsylvania. . .	4,875	123,600	—	4,528	8,480	3,780	13,545	18,360	7,920
Rhode Island . . .	—	—	—	18	—	253	—	—	—
South Carolina . .	504	29,325	380.0	650	2,840	—	15,660	110,450	18,000
South Dakota . . .	13,020	367,200	—	7,330	31,360	1,540	94,380	—	95,278
Tennessee	—	66,120	890.0	3,795	—	—	38,850	134,672	15,000
Texas	264	238,680	5,052.0	8,455	5,200	2,900	7,140	—	75,400
Utah	8,025	2,860	—	2,525	600	1,590	—	—	7,012
Vermont	—	—	—	649	—	—	—	—	—
Virginia	6,351	34,300	79.2	2,342	—	1,425	17,160	108,752	14,000
Washington. . . .	14,335	19,425	—	2,785	1,160	88,920	—	—	134,000
West Virginia . . .	—	3,675	—	1,110	225	—	—	3,600	550
Wisconsin	4,452	437,100	—	6,550	25,380	25,740	36,520	5,800	7,940
Wyoming	7,600	5,856	—	2,049	1,344	476	—	—	4,949
United States . .	**374,862**	**10,103,030**	**19,727.9**	**150,124**	**229,857**	**459,342**	**2,558,317**	**1,593,397**	**2,320,610**

Production of Principal U.S. Crops, 1985-94

Source: National Agricultural Statistics Service, U.S. Dept. of Agriculture

Year	Corn for grain (1,000 bu)	Oats (1,000 bu)	Barley (1,000 bu)	Sorghum for grain (1,000 bu)	All wheat (1,000 bu)	Rye (1,000 bu)	Flax-seed (1,000 bu)	Cotton lint (1,000 b)	Cotton-seed (1,000 t)
1985	8,875,453	518,490	590,213	1,120,271	2,424,115	20,373	8,293	13,432	5,279
1986	8,225,764	384,996	608,532	938,869	2,090,570	19,067	11,538	9,731	3,801
1987	7,131,300	373,713	521,499	730,809	2,107,685	19,526	7,444	14,760	5,769
1988	4,928,681	217,600	289,994	576,686	1,812,201	14,689	1,615	15,412	6,062
1989	7,525,493	373,587	404,203	615,420	2,036,618	13,647	1,215	12,196	4,677
1990	7,934,028	357,524	422,196	573,303	2,736,428	10,176	3,812	15,505	5,969
1991	7,475,480	243,451	464,326	584,860	1,981,139	9,761	6,200	17,614	6,926
1992	9,476,698	294,229	455,090	875,022	2,466,798	11,440	3,288	16,219	6,230
1993	6,336,470	206,770	398,041	534,172	2,396,440	10,340	3,480	16,134	6,343
1994	10,103,030	229,857	374,862	655,021	2,320,610	11,138	2,922	19,728	7,669

Year	Tobacco (1,000 lb)	All hay (1,000 t)	Beans, dry edible (1,000 cwt)	Peas, dry edible (1,000 cwt)	Peanuts (1,000 lb)	Soy-beans (1,000 bu)	Potatoes (1,000 cwt)	Sweet potatoes (1,000 cwt)
1985	1,511,638	148,719	22,298	NA	4,122,787	2,099,056	407,109	14,573
1986	1,161,940	155,385	22,960	3,196	3,697,085	1,942,558	361,511	12,368
1987	1,188,868	147,319	26,031	3,385	3,616,010	1,938,087	385,774	11,611
1988	1,369,500	126,010	19,253	3,868	3,980,917	1,548,841	356,438	10,945
1989	1,367,188	145,512	23,729	3,883	3,989,995	1,923,666	370,444	11,358
1990	1,626,380	146,820	32,379	2,372	3,602,770	1,925,947	402,110	12,594
1991	1,664,372	153,325	33,765	3,715	4,926,570	1,986,539	417,622	11,203
1992	1,721,671	146,903	22,615	2,535	4,284,416	2,190,354	425,367	12,005
1993	1,614,364	146,799	21,913	3,292	3,392,415	1,870,958	428,693	11,053
1994	1,593,397	150,124	29,187	2,255	4,264,550	2,558,317	459,342	13,081

Year	Rice (1,000 cwt)	Sugar-cane (1,000 t)	Sugar beets (1,000 t)	Pecans (1,000 t)	Almonds (1,000 t)	Wal-nuts (1,000 t)	Hazel-nuts[1] (1,000 t)	Oranges[2] (1,000 bx)	Grape-fruit[2] (1,000 bx)
1985	134,913	28,213	22,529	122.2	375.6	219.0	24.6	158,350	56,150
1986	133,356	30,311	25,150	136.4	201.3	180.0	15.1	175,440	57,870
1987	129,603	29,218	28,072	131.1	519.0	247.0	21.8	181,175	63,775
1988	159,897	29,904	24,810	154.1	451.9	209.0	16.5	200,250	68,700
1989	154,487	29,426	25,131	125.3	394.7	229.0	13.0	209,050	69,500
1990	156,088	28,136	27,513	102.5	519.7	227.0	21.7	186,075	48,600
1991	157,457	30,252	28,203	149.5	385.8	259.0	25.5	178,950	55,500
1992	179,658	30,363	29,143	83.0	454.4	203.0	27.7	209,610	55,265
1993	156,110	31,101	26,249	182.5	401.0	260.0	38.2	257,660	68,675
1994	197,779	31,816	32,008	99.5	365.0	232.0	20.1	239,250	64,900

NA=Not available. (1) Formerly called filberts. (2) Crop year ending in year cited.

Principal U.S. Crops: Area Planted and Harvested, 1992-94

Source: Natl. Agricultural Statistics Service, U.S. Dept. of Agriculture

(in thousand acres)

State	Area planted[1] 1992	1993	1994	Area harvested[1] 1992	1993	1994	State	Area planted[1] 1992	1993	1994	Area harvested[1] 1992	1993	1994
AL	2,216	2,256	2,289	2,105	2,116	2,170	NE	19,021	18,532	19,043	18,104	17,718	18,619
AZ	744	710	750	736	695	744	NV	407	530	497	403	527	491
AR	8,310	8,755	8,360	8,110	8,305	8,160	NH	105	109	98	103	107	96
CA	4,901	4,791	5,119	4,444	4,402	4,674	NJ	446	456	458	391	413	410
CO	5,968	6,052	6,103	5,544	5,661	5,632	NM	1,301	1,276	1,252	1,051	986	985
CT	131	117	130	125	111	123	NY	3,325	3,187	3,119	3,085	3,101	3,071
DE	531	512	510	515	499	494	NC	4,757	4,482	4,731	4,519	4,168	4,489
FL	1,147	1,133	1,090	1,088	1,077	1,048	ND	21,782	21,982	21,714	21,091	19,832	20,719
GA	4,039	4,068	4,276	3,693	3,551	3,874	OH	10,379	10,231	10,408	10,037	10,009	10,277
HI	68	70	67	68	70	67	OK	11,012	10,690	10,826	9,372	8,780	8,788
ID	4,177	4,506	4,402	4,006	4,322	4,244	OR	2,236	2,317	2,318	2,147	2,240	2,240
IL	23,940	23,533	23,801	23,237	21,241	23,393	PA	4,161	4,111	4,154	4,048	4,035	4,063
IN	12,219	12,038	12,237	11,759	11,768	12,071	RI	13	13	12	13	13	12
IA	24,272	23,662	24,207	23,716	22,001	23,967	SC	1,988	1,837	2,042	1,885	1,602	1,926
KS	21,886	21,899	22,540	20,237	20,485	21,724	SD	16,847	15,231	16,391	15,658	14,073	15,714
KY	5,553	5,600	5,558	5,335	5,375	5,353	TN	4,512	4,690	4,658	4,316	4,458	4,396
LA	4,190	3,947	3,896	4,069	3,811	3,810	TX	23,820	22,012	21,817	18,769	18,108	17,529
ME	385	379	349	377	364	339	UT	1,050	1,083	1,114	995	1,032	1,050
MD	1,679	1,627	1,569	1,619	1,569	1,506	VT	443	413	418	433	404	409
MA	141	138	141	135	133	135	VA	2,898	2,854	2,906	2,745	2,682	2,749
MI	6,956	6,726	7,013	6,714	6,554	6,815	WA	4,233	4,378	4,057	3,957	4,227	3,922
MN	19,905	19,277	20,077	19,301	16,940	19,534	WV	652	630	646	639	621	636
MS	4,990	4,841	4,881	4,855	4,709	4,813	WI	8,668	8,020	8,438	8,096	7,511	8,074
MO	13,121	12,749	12,674	12,826	11,483	12,466	WY	1,729	1,890	1,713	1,668	1,806	1,637
MT	9,240	9,378	9,357	8,459	8,816	8,988	U.S.[2]	326,453	319,553	324,256	306,652	295,529	308,474

(1) Crops included in area planted are corn, sorghum, oats, barley, winter wheat, rye, durum wheat, other spring wheat, rice, soybeans, peanuts, sunflower, cotton, dry edible beans, potatoes, and sugar beets. Harvested acreage is used for all hay, tobacco, and sugarcane in computing total area planted. Includes double-cropped acres and unharvested small grains planted as cover crops. (2) State figures do not add to U.S. totals due to sunflower and sugar-beet unallocated acreage.

Average Prices Received by U.S. Farmers, 1940-94

Source: Natl. Agricultural Statistics Service, U.S. Dept. of Agriculture

The figures represent dollars per 100 lb for hogs, beef cattle, veal calves, sheep, lamb, and milk (wholesale); dollars per head for milk cows; cents per lb for chickens, broilers, turkeys, and wool; cents per dozen for eggs; weighted calendar year prices for livestock and livestock products other than wool. For 1943-63, wool prices are weighted on marketing year basis. The marketing year was changed in 1964 from a calendar year to a Dec.-Nov. basis for hogs, chickens, broilers, and eggs.

Year	Hogs	Cattle (beef)	Calves (veal)	Sheep	Lambs	Milk cows	Milk	Chickens (excl. broilers)	Broilers	Turkeys	Eggs	Wool
1940	5.39	7.56	8.83	3.95	8.10	61	1.82	13.0	17.3	15.2	18.0	28.4
1950	18.00	23.30	26.30	11.60	25.10	198	3.89	22.2	27.4	32.8	36.3	62.1
1960	15.30	20.40	22.90	5.61	17.90	223	4.21	12.2	16.9	25.4	36.1	42.0
1970	22.70	27.10	34.50	7.51	26.40	332	5.71	9.1	13.6	22.6	39.1	35.4
1975	46.10	32.20	27.20	11.30	42.10	412	8.75	9.9	26.3	34.8	54.5	44.8
1979	41.80	66.10	88.80	26.30	66.70	1,040	12.00	14.4	25.9	41.3	58.3	86.3
1980	38.00	62.40	76.80	21.30	63.60	1,190	13.05	11.0	27.7	41.3	56.3	88.1
1984	47.10	57.30	59.90	16.40	60.10	895	13.46	15.9	33.7	48.9	72.3	79.5
1985	44.00	53.70	62.10	23.90	67.70	860	12.76	14.8	30.1	49.1	57.1	63.3
1986	49.30	52.60	61.10	25.60	69.00	820	12.51	12.5	34.5	47.1	61.6	66.8
1987	51.20	61.10	78.50	29.50	77.60	920	12.54	11.0	28.7	34.8	54.9	91.7
1988	42.30	66.60	89.20	25.60	69.10	990	12.26	9.2	33.1	38.6	52.8	138.0
1989	42.50	69.50	90.80	24.40	66.10	1,030	13.56	14.9	36.6	40.9	68.9	124.0
1990	53.70	74.60	95.60	23.20	55.50	1,160	13.74	9.3	32.6	39.4	70.9	80.0
1991	49.10	72.70	98.00	19.70	52.20	1,100	12.27	7.1	30.8	38.4	67.8	55.0
1992	41.60	71.30	89.00	25.80	59.50	1,130	13.15	8.6	31.8	37.7	57.6	74.0
1993	45.20	72.60	91.20	28.60	64.40	1,160	12.84	10.0	34.0	39.0	63.4	51.0
1994	39.90	66.70	87.20	30.90	65.60	1,170	13.01	7.6	35.0	40.4	61.4	78.0

The figures represent cents per lb for cotton, apples, and peanuts; dollars per bushel for oats, wheat, corn, barley, and soybeans; dollars per 100 lb for rice, sorghum, and potatoes; dollars per ton for cottonseed and baled hay; weighted crop year prices.

Crop years are as follows: apples, June-May; wheat, oats, barley, hay, and potatoes, July-June; cotton, rice, peanuts, and cottonseed, Aug.-July; soybeans, Sept.-Aug.; and corn and sorghum grain, Oct.-Sept.

	Corn	Wheat	Upland cotton*	Oats	Barley	Rice	Soybeans	Sorghum	Peanuts	Cottonseed	Hay	Potatoes	Apples
1940	0.62	0.67	9.8	0.30	0.39	1.80	0.89	0.87	3.7	21.70	9.78	0.85	...
1950	1.52	2.00	39.9	0.79	1.19	5.09	2.47	1.88	10.9	86.60	21.10	1.50	...
1960	1.00	1.74	30.1	0.60	0.84	4.55	2.13	1.49	10.0	42.50	21.70	2.00	2.7
1970	1.33	1.33	21.9	0.62	0.97	5.17	2.85	2.04	12.8	56.40	26.10	2.21	6.5
1975	2.54	3.55	51.1	1.45	2.42	8.35	4.92	4.21	19.0	97.00	52.10	4.48	8.8
1979	2.52	3.78	62.3	1.36	2.29	10.50	6.28	4.18	20.6	121.00	59.50	3.43	15.4
1980	3.11	3.91	74.4	1.79	2.86	12.80	7.57	5.25	25.1	129.00	71.00	6.55	12.1
1984	2.63	3.39	58.7	1.67	2.29	8.04	5.84	4.15	27.9	99.50	72.70	5.69	15.5
1985	2.23	3.08	56.8	1.23	1.98	6.53	5.05	3.45	24.4	66.00	67.60	3.92	17.3
1986	1.50	2.42	51.5	1.21	1.61	3.75	4.78	2.45	29.2	80.00	59.70	5.03	19.1
1987	1.94	2.57	63.7	1.56	1.81	7.27	5.88	3.04	28.0	82.50	65.00	4.38	12.7
1988	2.54	3.72	55.6	2.61	2.80	6.83	7.42	4.05	28.0	118.00	85.20	6.02	17.4
1989	2.36	3.72	63.6	1.49	2.42	7.35	5.69	3.75	28.0	105.00	85.40	7.36	13.9
1990	2.28	2.61	67.1	1.14	2.14	6.68	5.74	3.79	34.7	121.00	80.60	6.08	20.9
1991	2.37	3.00	56.8	1.21	2.10	7.58	5.58	4.01	28.3	71.00	71.20	4.96	25.1
1992	2.07	3.24	53.7	1.32	2.04	5.89	5.56	3.38	30.0	97.50	74.30	5.52	19.5
1993	2.50	3.26	58.1	1.36	1.99	7.98	6.40	4.13	30.4	113.00	84.70	6.18	18.4
1994	2.25	3.45	72.1	1.22	2.03	6.70	5.45	3.75	29.0	101.00	86.00	5.36	18.2

*Beginning in 1964, 480 lb net weight bales.

Grain Storage Capacity at Principal U.S. Grain Centers, Aug. 1995

Source: Chicago Board of Trade Market Information Department

(in bushels)

	Capacity			Capacity
Atlantic Coast	12,800,000		**Southwest**	
Great Lakes			Texas High Plains	72,900,000
Toledo, OH	63,100,000		Fort Worth, TX	68,000,000
Duluth, MN	57,600,000		Enid, OK.	NA
Chicago, IL	52,400,000		**Gulf Points**	
Buffalo, NY	15,200,000		South Mississippi Region	46,600,000
Milwaukee, WI	NA		Texas Gulf	45,800,000
River Points			**Plains**	
Kansas City, MO	95,200,000		Topeka, KS.	53,300,000
Minneapolis, MN	78,900,000		Salina, KS	50,600,000
St. Joseph, MO	22,300,000		Wichita, KS	37,400,000
Atchison, KS	20,100,000		Lincoln, NE.	33,700,000
St. Louis, MO.	10,300,000		Hutchinson, KS.	29,600,000
Omaha-Council Bluffs, NE	8,200,000		Hastings-Grand Island, NE.	25,600,000
Sioux City, IA.	3,800,000		**Pacific NW**	
			Puget Sound (incl. Portland).	32,100,000
			California Ports	NA

NA= Not available.

Atlantic Coast — Albany, NY, Philadelphia, PA, Baltimore, MD, Norfolk, VA. **Gulf Points, South Mississippi Region** — New Orleans, Baton Rouge, Ama, Belle Chasse, LA; Mobile, AL. **Texas Gulf** — Houston, Galveston, Beaumont, Port Arthur, Corpus Christi, Brownsville, TX. **Pacific NW** — Seattle, Tacoma, WA; Portland, OR; Columbia River. **Texas High Plains** — Amarillo, Lubbock, Hereford, Plainview, TX. NA = not available.

World Wheat, Rice, and Corn Production, 1991

Source: UN Food and Agriculture Organization

(in thousands of metric tons)

Country	Wheat	Rice	Corn	Country	Wheat	Rice	Corn
Afghanistan........	1,750F	350F	360F	Laos	—	1,653	77
Argentina.........	10,680	606	10,246	Madagascar........	1F	2,360	155
Australia.........	8,803*	1,017	258*	Malaysia	—	2,040	40*
Austria...........	1,265	—	1,476*	Mexico...........	3,589	375	19,193
Bangladesh.......	1,131	27,537	3	Morocco..........	5,523	70	350
Belgium-Lux.......	1,490	—	228	Myanmar.........	109	19,057	271
Brazil	2,276	10,582	32,305	Nepal............	899	3,496	1,254
Bulgaria	3,788	2	1,362	Netherlands	961	—	83
Cambodia.........	—	1,800F	64F	New Zealand	181F	—	173F
Canada..........	23,350	—	7,043	Nigeria.:	30*	3,857	2,000F
Chile............	1,271	133	937	Pakistan..........	15,114	5,269	1,288*
China	101,205*	178,251*	103,550*	Panama..........	—	200*	103F
Colombia.........	99	1,679	1,185	Peru	130	1,381	726
Croatia	750	—	1,685	Philippines	—	10,150*	5,400*
Cuba............	—	166F	90F	Poland...........	7,658	—	189
Czech Rep........	3,713	—	91	Portugal..........	454	115	661
Denmark.........	3,709	—	—	Romania.........	5,991	622*	9,300
Ecuador	26	1,366	495	Russian Fed.	32,094	390	879
Egypt	4,437	4,582	4,883	Slovakia..........	2,145	—	521
Ethiopia..........	1,180F	—	1,711	South Africa	1,850	3F	11,811
Finland	337	—	—	Spain............	4,312	79	2,268
France	30,652	124	13,040	Sri Lanka	—	2,582	31F
Germany	16,429	—	2,357	Sweden	1,360	—	—
Greece	2,387	120F	1,818	Switzerland	550	—	180
Hungary	4,900	14	4,920	Syria	3,814	—	260F
India............	59,131	118,400	10,500*	Thailand..........	1*	18,447	3,800*
Indonesia	—	46,245	6,617	Turkey	17,500	200	1,850
Iran.............	11,500*	2,700*	210F	Turkmenistan	1,063	149	252
Iraq.............	1,008*	220F	285F	Ukraine	13,657	—	1,539
Ireland	540	—	—	United Kingdom	13,100	—	—
Israel	145*	—	4F	United States	63,141	8,972	256,629
Italy	7,805	1,324	7,661	Uruguay..........	300F	680	128F
Japan	565	14,978	—	Uzbekistan	1,200*	544*	200F
Kazakhstan.......	9,052	283	233	Venezuela	—	738	884
Kenya...........	230*	50F	2,970	Vietnam	—	22,500*	950F
Korea, North	1008	2,104F	2,140*	Yugoslavia	3,535	—	4,860*
Korea, South......	2F	7,056*	75*	**World, total ....**	**527,982**	**534,701**	**569,557**

Note: * Unofficial figure. F=Food and Agriculture Organization (FAO) estimate. Where production is small or nonexistent, — is indicated. Because not all countries are reported on this table, country totals do not add to world totals.

Wheat, Rice, and Corn—Exports and Imports of 10 Leading Countries

Source: UN Food and Agriculture Organization

(in thousands of metric tons)

Leading exporters	Exports[1] Wheat			Leading importers	Imports[1] Wheat		
	1991	1992	1993		1991	1992	1993
U.S.	34,482	35,205	37,141	China	13,442	11,622	7,369
France	19,732	19,762	20,990	Japan	5,693	5,979	5,814
Canada...........	23,510	23,878	18,414	Russian Fed.	NA	18,904	5,773
Australia	12,020	8,204	9,582	Brazil...........	4,677	4,433	5,654
Argentina	5,784	6,268	6,019	Italy...........	6,526	6,332	5,066
Germany	3,465	5,755	4,514	Egypt	6,188	5,683	5,038
United Kingdom......	4,128	4,088	4,014	South Korea.	4,790	3,546	4,939
Saudi Arabia	952	2,001	2,001	Algeria.........	3,637	4,037	4,116
Italy	2,466	2,604	1,902	Uzbekistan......	NA	3,734	4,100*
Bel-Lux...........	1,596	1,749	1,797	Pakistan	972	2,018	2,890
	Rice				**Rice**		
	1991	1992	1993		1991	1992	1993
Thailand	4,333	5,151	4,989	Iran............	629	873	1,050*
U.S.	2,243	2,164	2,680	Saudi Arabia	253	489	650*
Vietnam	1,033	1,946	1,765	Brazil..........	960	583	650*
China	818	1,034	1,507	Iraq...........	300	450*	600*
Pakistan	1,205	1,512	1,032	South Africa.....	374	362	450F
India............	678	580	628*	Malaysia	399	443	389
Italy	644	739	574	Hong Kong	391	400	372
Uruguay	270	328	505	Côte d'Ivoire	317	330	372*
Australia	425	519	482	United Arab Em...	281	362	370*
Indonesia	1	42	350	Cuba..........	262	300F	370*
	Corn				**Corn**		
	1991	1992	1993		1991	1992	1993
U.S.	44,558	43,236	40,365	Japan	16,646	16,382	16,863
China	7,783	10,340	11,098	South Korea.	5,477	6,612	6,207
Argentina	3,898	6,093	4,871	Russian Fed. ...	NA	5,490	4,391
France	4,777	7,042	4,632	Spain	1,678	1,790	2,401
Bel-Lux...........	101	98	414	Egypt	1,300	1,444	2,148*
Canada...........	735	399	357	Malaysia	1,464	1,817	1,797
Germany..........	272	254	216	United Kingdom ..	1,518	1,690	1,450
Italy	15	114	213	Brazil...........	815	528	1,370*
Thailand	123	145	213	Bel-Lux	1,299	947	1,284
Netherlands........	12	13	212	Venezuela	321	822	1,189

Note: * Unofficial figure. NA=Not available. F=Food and Agriculture Organization (FAO) estimate. (1) Marketing years.

World Commercial Catch of Fish, Crustaceans, and Mollusks,[1] by Major Fishing Areas, 1988-93

Source: U.S. Dept. of Commerce, Natl. Oceanic and Atmospheric Admin., Natl. Marine Fisheries Service

(in thousands of metric tons; live weight)

Area	1988	1989	1990	1991	1992	1993
Marine						
Pacific Ocean . . .	53,446	54,678	52,939	52,011	51,782	53.569
Atlantic Ocean. . .	26,550	25,314	23,552	23,760	24,204	23,391
Indian Ocean . . .	5,680	6,198	6,199	6,689	7,089	7,289
Total	85,676	86,190	82,690	82,460	83,075	84,249
Inland Waters						
N. America	540	546	552	548	600	584
S. America	356	340	335	331	363	387
Europe	476	520	511	484	494	487
Former USSR . . .	1,002	1,030	988	824	700	595
Asia	9,222	9,658	10,402	10,920	11,756	13,301
Africa	1,787	1,807	1,930	1,812	1,772	1,792
Oceania	26	24	24	23	25	23
Total	13,409	13,925	14,742	14,942	15,710	17,169
Grand total	99,085	100,115	97,432	97,402	98,785	101,418

(1) Does not include marine mammals and aquatic plants.

World Commercial Catch of Fish, Crustaceans, and Mollusks,[1] by Country, 1988-93

Source: U.S. Dept. of Commerce, Natl. Oceanic and Atmospheric Admin., Natl. Marine Fisheries Service

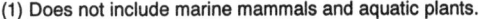

(in thousands of metric tons; live weight)

Country	1988	1989	1990	1991	1992	1993
China	10,358	11,220	12,095	13,135	15,007	17,568
Peru.	6,641	6,854	6,875	6,949	6,871	8,451
Japan.	11,966	11,173	10,354	9,301	8,502	8,128
Chile	5,209	6,454	5,195	6,003	6,502	6,038
United States[2,3] . .	5,956	5,775	5,868	5,486	5,588	5,939
Russia	—	—	—	7,047	5,611	4,461
India.	3,125	3,640	3,794	4,044	4,232	4,324
Indonesia	2,795	2,948	3,044	3,252	3,442	3,638
Thailand	2,642	2,700	2,786	2,968	3,240	3,348
South Korea	2,731	2,841	2,843	2,521	2,696	2,649

(1) Does not include marine mammals and aquatic plants. (2) Includes weight of clam, oyster, scallop, and other mollusk shells.
(3) Statistics on quantities caught by recreational anglers in the U.S. are excluded.

U.S. Commercial Landings of Fish and Shellfish, 1984-94[1]

Source: U.S. Dept. of Commerce, Natl. Oceanic and Atmospheric Admin., Natl. Marine Fisheries Service

Year	Landings for human food		Landings for industrial purposes[2]		Total	
	mil lb	mil dollars	mil lb	mil dollars	mil lb	mil dollars
1984	3,320	$2,206	3,118	$144	6,438	$2,350
1985	3,294	2,198	2,964	128	6,258	2,326
1986	3,393	2,641	2,638	122	6,031	2,763
1987	3,946	2,979	2,950	136	6,896	3,115
1988	4,588	3,362	2,604	158	7,192	3,520
1989	6,204	3,111	2,259	127	8,463	3,238
1990	7,041	3,366	2,363	156	9,404	3,522
1991	7,031	3,169	2,453	139	9,484	3,308
1992	7,618	3,531	2,019	147	9,637	3,678
1993	8,214	3,317	2,253	154	10,467	3,471
1994	7,936	3,751	2,525	95	10,461	3,846

Note: Data do not include landings outside the 50 states or products of aquaculture, except oysters and clams.

(1) Statistics on landings are shown in round weight for all items except univalve and bivalve mollusks such as clams, oysters, and scallops, which are shown in weight of meats (excluding the shell). All data are preliminary. (2) Processed into meal, oil, solubles, and shell products or used as bait or animal food.

U.S. Domestic Landings, by Regions, 1993-94[1]

Source: U.S. Dept. of Commerce, Natl. Oceanic and Atmospheric Admin., Natl. Marine Fisheries Service

Region	1993		1994	
	1,000 lb	1,000 dollars	1,000 lb	1,000 dollars
New England	604,697	$552,280	558,046	$583,228
Middle Atlantic	257,537	154,989	253,237	148,741
Chesapeake	813,283	161,516	648,442	161,748
South Atlantic	250,346	161,314	286,674	214,997
Gulf	1,714,772	630,738	2,152,719	806,270
Pacific Coast and Alaska . .	6,759,704	1,722,396	6,505,716	1,849,695
Great Lakes	31,974	19,145	29,464	19,268
Hawaii	34,582	69,082	27,090	62,451
Total	10,466,895	$3,471,460	10,461,388	3,846,398

(1) Landings are reported in round (live) weight for all items except univalve and bivalve mollusks such as clams, oysters, and scallops, which are reported in weight of meats (excluding shell). Landings for Mississippi River Drainage Area states are not available.

EMPLOYMENT

Employment and Unemployment in the U.S., 1940-94

Source: Bureau of Labor Statistics, U.S. Dept. of Labor

(civilian labor force, persons 16 years of age and older; in thousands)

Year[1]	Employed	Unemployed	Unemployment rate	Year[1]	Employed	Unemployed	Unemployment rate
1940[2]	47,520	8,120	14.6%	1986[3]	109,597	8,237	7.0%
1950	58,918	3,288	5.0	1987	112,440	7,425	6.2
1960	65,778	3,852	5.5	1988	114,988	6,701	5.5
1970	78,678	4,093	4.9	1989	117,342	6,528	5.3
1980	99,303	7,637	7.1	1990	117,914	6,874	5.5
1982	99,526	10,678	9.7	1991	116,877	8,426	6.7
1983	100,834	10,717	9.6	1992	117,598	9,384	7.4
1984	105,005	8,539	7.5	1993	119,306	8,734	6.8
1985	107,150	8,312	7.2	1994[3]	123,060	7,996	6.1

(1) **Early unemployment rates:** 1915, 9.7; 1916, 4.8; 1917, 4.8; 1918, 1.4; 1919, 2.3; 1920, 4.0; 1921, 11.9; 1922, 7.6; 1923, 3.2; 1924, 5.5; 1925, 4.0; 1926, 1.9; 1927, 4.1; 1928, 4.4; 1929, 3.2; 1930, 8.7; 1931, 15.9; 1932, 23.6; 1933, 24.9; 1934, 21.7; 1935, 20.1; 1936, 16.9; 1937, 14.3; 1938, 19.0; 1939, 17.2. (2) Persons 14 years of age and older. (3) Not strictly comparable with prior years.

Selected Unemployment Insurance Data, by State, 1994

Source: Employment and Training Admin., U.S. Dept. of Labor; state programs only

State	Monetarily eligible claimants	First payments	Final payments	Initial claims	Benefits paid	Average weekly benefit amount	Employers subject to state law
AL	160,325	136,651	30,922	305,469	$178,541,366	$131.21	81,518
AK	51,022	46,804	21,336	100,329	114,709,866	169.99	14,680
AZ	101,706	76,469	28,685	164,508	164,908,730	147.93	87,069
AR	85,765	81,360	27,738	204,057	155,351,823	161.37	53,651
CA	1,743,165	1,310,730	586,615	3,368,185	3,416,374,759	153.92	772,574
CO	108,487	73,001	29,951	143,460	178,424,906	194.72	102,128
CT	147,149	143,341	52,612	258,915	512,094,848	221.96	92,677
DE	27,785	23,485	6,308	40,644	58,680,841	182.72	21,013
DC	25,049	24,194	13,828	35,056	101,196,476	219.82	22,500
FL	356,674	285,055	138,150	512,134	707,080,528	168.65	334,547
GA	265,109	188,392	57,793	392,270	267,171,329	152.60	153,408
HI	62,727	41,023	15,372	101,871	184,936,107	265.72	27,111
ID	52,780	44,924	13,984	105,939	81,086,895	167.24	31,145
IL	411,391	321,373	124,595	682,652	1,108,295,318	198.60	258,973
IN	167,514	106,316	34,064	230,174	196,567,600	158.02	116,130
IA	87,851	71,184	18,229	126,453	153,128,523	182.93	65,032
KS	74,890	60,323	21,629	121,341	165,705,740	191.74	61,415
KY	180,009	164,165	24,158	344,011	226,141,761	159.41	74,969
LA	103,708	82,224	25,529	187,785	145,100,370	117.85	85,522
ME	56,401	50,972	17,846	109,827	109,025,154	160.79	36,323
MD	166,549	118,776	46,913	235,927	346,395,764	179.93	117,754
MA	252,805	211,611	84,818	384,057	844,323,921	237.07	149,102
MI	458,034	323,674	104,524	672,202	880,180,282	212.77	196,266
MN	128,221	115,216	37,896	202,875	373,637,885	217.44	109,197
MS	86,640	58,172	16,520	161,496	94,405,498	128.56	47,977
MO	205,154	144,792	51,669	375,397	299,668,768	150.07	132,854
MT	33,543	27,409	9,838	57,059	54,259,262	155.54	26,362
NE	36,109	26,912	7,151	54,324	40,899,390	140.00	41,676
NV	71,884	51,851	15,561	108,040	128,574,571	184.82	32,730
NH	32,123	24,901	3,145	47,874	40,271,990	145.87	32,825
NJ	343,735	297,723	148,434	562,421	1,257,293,353	245.61	202,335
NM	36,411	27,834	9,769	61,133	66,665,909	140.00	38,103
NY	637,348	581,477	262,085	1,100,775	2,200,827,492	203.35	432,621
NC	304,258	190,384	36,863	625,115	296,614,689	175.02	142,910
ND	16,792	13,984	5,243	28,585	27,015,439	159.56	18,255
OH	322,293	254,573	76,709	539,497	722,562,288	190.87	218,532
OK	62,753	48,059	19,809	109,799	113,689,076	168.16	69,231
OR	159,763	138,286	47,874	343,104	361,960,309	178.57	87,434
PA	567,641	470,271	154,824	1,091,799	1,579,184,001	211.95	233,717
PR	133,657	133,631	69,619	253,417	227,513,117	89.37	48,932
RI	66,174	56,920	25,369	125,052	181,682,502	219.78	32,578
SC	155,489	99,770	29,548	304,061	180,831,134	153.75	75,363
SD	10,433	7,678	854	18,407	10,888,968	137.68	20,232
TN	220,235	154,068	49,090	398,844	251,372,759	141.73	100,230
TX	501,641	374,993	176,735	740,481	1,046,955,310	184.94	351,584
UT	40,755	30,656	9,065	56,014	65,924,354	186.66	39,500
VT	26,332	22,515	5,288	42,637	54,588,025	163.95	19,347
VA	183,501	114,426	32,242	323,990	215,240,582	169.31	140,470
VI	5,724	4,039	3,111	4,505	18,127,886	191.11	2,115
WA	284,741	241,606	90,891	549,233	876,870,002	206.41	161,033
WV	66,656	57,366	13,594	96,092	130,652,822	166.51	37,036
WI	221,362	191,952	39,805	430,452	405,625,564	187.53	110,454
WY	16,743	11,770	3,268	25,251	26,663,702	172.54	16,762
US	**10,125,006**	**7,959,281**	**2,977,468**	**17,664,995**	**21,645,889,554**	**182.17**	**5,977,894**

Unemployment Rates, by Selected Country, 1975-95

Source: Bureau of Labor Statistics, U.S. Dept. of Labor; civilian labor force, seasonally adjusted; Aug. 1995

Time period	U.S.	Canada	Australia	Japan	France	Germany[1]	Italy[2]	Sweden	United Kingdom
1975	8.5	6.9	4.9	1.9	4.2	3.4	3.4	1.6	4.6
1980	7.1	7.5	6.1	2.0	6.5	2.8	4.4	2.0	7.0
1981	7.6	7.6	5.8	2.2	7.6	4.0	4.9	2.5	10.5
1982	9.7	11.0	7.2	2.4	8.3	5.6	5.4	3.1	11.3
1983	9.6	11.9	10.0	2.7	8.6	6.9[3]	5.9	3.5	11.8
1984	7.5	11.3	9.0	2.8	10.0	7.1	5.9	3.1	11.8
1985	7.2	10.5	8.3	2.6	10.5	7.2	6.0	2.8	11.2
1986	7.0	9.6	8.1	2.8	10.6	6.6	7.5[3]	2.6	11.2
1987	6.2	8.9	8.1	2.9	10.8	6.3	7.9	2.2[3]	10.3
1988	5.5	7.8	7.2	2.5	10.3	6.3	7.9	1.9	8.6
1989	5.3	7.5	6.2	2.3	9.6	5.7	7.8	1.6	7.3
1990	5.5	8.1	6.9	2.1	9.1	5.0	7.0	1.8	6.9
1991	6.7	10.4	9.6	2.1	9.6	4.3P	6.9[3]	3.1	8.8
1992	7.4	11.3	10.8	2.2	10.5R	4.6P	7.3P	5.6	10.0
1993	6.8	11.2	10.9	2.5	11.9R	5.8P	10.3P[3]	9.3	10.4P
1994	6.1[3]	10.4	9.7	2.9	12.7R	6.5P	11.4P	9.6	9.5P
1st quarter ...	6.6	11.0	10.4	2.8	12.7R	6.4P	11.0P	9.8	9.9P
2d quarter....	6.2	10.6	10.0	2.9	12.7R	6.5P	11.6P	9.7	9.7P
3d quarter....	6.0	10.2	9.5	3.0	12.7R	6.5P	11.1P	9.7	9.5P
4th quarter ...	5.6	9.8	9.1	2.9R	12.6R	6.5P	11.8P	9.3	9.0P
1995									
1st quarter ...	5.5	9.7	8.9	3.0	12.5R	6.5R,P	12.2P	9.3	8.7P
2d quarter....	5.7	9.5	8.4	3.2	NA	NA	12.2P	9.4	NA

NA=Not available. R=Revised. P=Preliminary. **Note:** For the sake of making comparisions, U.S. unemployment rate concepts were applied to unemployment data collected from Canada, Australia, Japan, France, Germany, Italy, Sweden, and the United Kingdom. Quarterly and monthly figures for France and Germany were calculated by applying annual adjustment factors to current published data and therefore should be viewed as less precise indicators of unemployment under U.S. concepts than the annual figures. (1) Former West Germany. (2) Quarterly rates are for the first month of the quarter. (3) Due to various revisions in survey methodology, there are breaks in the data series for the U.S. (1994), Germany (1983), Italy (1986, 1991, 1993), and Sweden (1987); as a result, data prior to a survey change are not fully comparable to data released after a survey change.

Employed Persons, by Occupation, Sex, and Age, 1993-94

Source: Bureau of Labor Statistics, U.S. Dept. of Labor

(in thousands)

Occupation	Total 16 years and older		Men 16 years and older		Women 16 years and older	
	1993	1994	1993	1994	1993	1994
Total	119,306	123,060	64,700	66,450	54,606	56,610
Managerial and professional specialty	32,280	33,847	16,839	17,583	15,441	16,264
Executive, administrative, and managerial	15,376	16,312	8,923	9,298	6,452	7,014
Officials and administrators, public administration ..	659	673	380	375	278	298
Other executive, administrative, and managerial ...	10,561	11,364	6,578	6,941	3,984	4,422
Management-related occupations	4,155	4,269	1,965	1,977	2,190	2,291
Professional specialty	16,904	17,536	7,916	8,285	8,988	9,250
Engineers................................	1,716	1,866	1,568	1,711	148	155
Mathematical and computer scientists..........	1,051	1,186	711	787	340	399
Natural scientists	531	535	371	369	160	166
Health diagnosing occupations	909	932	723	731	186	200
Health assessment and treating occupations......	2,602	2,708	353	375	2,249	2,333
Teachers, college and university..............	772	838	444	482	328	356
Teachers, except college and university	4,397	4,330	1,093	1,087	3,304	3,244
Lawyers and judges	814	861	629	648	185	213
Other professional specialty occupations.........	4,111	4,279	2,024	2,095	2,087	2,184
Technical, sales, and administrative support	36,814	37,306	13,311	13,322	23,503	23,984
Technicians and related support	4,014	3,869	1,985	1,856	2,028	2,013
Sales occupations.........................	14,245	14,817	7,389	7,543	6,857	7,273
Administrative support, including clerical	18,555	18,620	3,937	3,923	14,618	14,697
Service occupations	16,522	16,912	6,688	6,840	9,833	10,072
Precision production, craft, and repair	13,326	13,489	12,185	12,241	1,141	1,248
Mechanics and repairers.....................	4,416	4,419	4,261	4,219	156	201
Construction trades........................	5,004	5,008	4,909	4,900	95	108
Other precision production, craft, and repair........	3,906	4,062	3,015	3,123	890	939
Operators, fabricators, and laborers..............	17,038	17,876	12,862	13,535	4,176	4,341
Machine operators, assemblers, and inspectors.....	7,415	7,754	4,548	4,800	2,868	2,954
Transportation and material moving occupations	5,004	5,136	4,539	4,654	465	483
Motor vehicle operators	3,825	3,882	3,412	3,454	413	428
Other transportation and material moving occupations	1,179	1,254	1,127	1,200	52	54
Handlers, equipment cleaners, helpers, and laborers .	4,619	4,986	3,776	4,081	843	904
Constuction laborers	658	740	635	714	23	27
Other handlers, equipment cleaners, etc.	3,962	4,245	3,141	3,368	821	878
Farming, forestry, and fishing	3,326	3,629	2,814	2,928	512	701

Note: Data for 1994 are not fully comparable to data for 1993 and earlier years because of the introduction of the occupational classification system used in the 1990 census and new surveying methodology.

Employment and Training Services and Unemployment Insurance

Source: Employment and Training Administration, U.S. Dept. of Labor; September 1995

Employment Service

The Federal-State Employment Service consists of the United States Employment Service and affiliated state employment services that make up the nation's public employment service system. From July 1, 1994, to June 30, 1995, the public employment service listed 6.6 million job openings and placed more than 2.7 million people in jobs.

The employment service refers employable applicants to job openings that use their highest skills and helps the unemployed obtain services or training to make them employable. It also provides special attention to handicapped workers, migrants and seasonal farmworkers, workers who lose their jobs because of foreign trade competition, and other worker groups. Veterans receive priority services, including referral to jobs and training. During program year 1994, 2.5 million registered for the program; 559,000 veterans were placed in jobs.

Job Training

The Job Training Partnership Act (JTPA), which became fully operational on Oct. 1, 1983, provides job training and employment services for economically disadvantaged youths and adults, dislocated workers, and others who face significant employment barriers. The goal of the act is to move as many jobless workers as possible into permanent, unsubsidized, self-sustaining employment.

As of the end of program year 1993, JTPA had provided approximately 10 million Americans with training and employment services since its inception. Its placement rate is almost 69%, making it one of the most successful job and training efforts ever undertaken.

Title I establishes an administrative structure for the delivery of job and training services. Generally, state governors receive block grants from the Labor Department, and the funds are then distributed to Service Delivery Areas— areas of 200,000 population or more where local elected officials work with Private Industry Councils to plan and conduct local training projects.

Title II has 3 parts. During program year 1993, more than 1.4 million people were served under Titles II-A, II-B, and II-C. Title II-A spells out the act's provision of employment and training projects for the economically disadvantaged. In program year 1993 (July 1, 1993, to June 30, 1994), these projects served nearly 638,000 adults.

Title II-B outlines a summer youth program offering basic and remedial education, institutional and on-the-job training, work experience, and supportive services. This program had nearly 568,000 participants in calendar year 1994. Beginning July 1, 1993, a new Title II-C provided for a year-round youth training program that provided basic skills training, occupational skills training, preemployment skills training, work experience, and supportive services to economically disadvantaged youths. In program year 1993, 280,000 youths participated in this program.

Title III, Economic Dislocation and Worker Adjustment Assistance, provides for job and training help for dislocated workers—workers who lose jobs and are unlikely to return to their previous industries or occupations. This includes workers who lose their jobs because of plant closings or mass layoffs; long-term unemployed persons with limited local opportunities for jobs in their fields; farmers, ranchers, and other self-employed persons who become jobless due to general economic conditions or natural disasters; and, under certain circumstances, displaced homemakers. In program year 1993, 306,340 workers participated in these programs.

Title IV authorizes programs to address the employment and training needs of specific groups facing significant barriers to productive employment, including Native Americans, migrant and seasonal farmworkers, and the disabled. In program year 1993, these programs served 24,924 Native Americans; 37,320 migrant and seasonal farmworkers; 97,357 older workers; and more than 6,950 persons with disabilities.

In addition, Title IV includes the Job Corps, which each year enrolls approximately 60,000 young people ages 16 to 21 in 110 residential and nonresidential job training centers throughout the U.S.; the National Commission for Employment Policy; and nationally administered programs for technical assistance, labor market information, research and evaluation, and pilots and demonstrations.

Title VII authorized the establishment of state human resource investment councils, which would oversee all federal human resource programs. Currently, 20 states have established these state councils.

Trade Adjustment Assistance for Workers

Trade Adjustment Assistance (TAA) is available to workers who lose their jobs or whose hours of work and wages are reduced as a result of increased imports. TAA includes a variety of benefits and reemployment services to help unemployed workers prepare for and obtain suitable employment. Workers may be eligible for training, job search, relocation, and other reemployment services. Additionally, weekly trade readjustment allowances (TRA) may be payable to eligible workers following their exhaustion of unemployment insurance benefits. In fiscal year 1994, about 30,803 workers received $130 million in TRA payments; 26,318 workers entered training; 60 workers were involved in job search visits; and 2,288 workers relocated in order to obtain long term jobs.

The TAA program is administered by the Employment and Training Administration's Office of Trade Adjustment Assistance. State employment security agencies serve as agents of the U.S., under an agreement with the Secretary of Labor, for administering the TAA benefit provisions in the Trade Act of 1974, as amended.

Unemployment Insurance

Unlike old-age and survivors insurance, which is entirely a federal program, the unemployment insurance program is a federal-state system that provides insured wage earners partial replacement for lost wages during a period of involuntary unemployment. The program protects most workers. During fiscal year 1994, an estimated 111 million workers in commerce, industry, agriculture, and government, including the armed forces, were covered under the federal-state system.

Each state, as well as the District of Columbia, Puerto Rico, and the Virgin Islands, has its own law and operates its own program. The amount and duration of the weekly benefits are determined by state laws, based on prior wages and length of employment. States are required to extend the duration of benefits when unemployment rises to and remains above specified state levels; costs of extended benefits are shared by the state and federal governments.

Under the Federal Unemployment Tax Act, the federal tax rate is 6.2% on the first $7,000 paid to each employee of employers with one or more employees in 20 weeks of the year or a quarterly payroll of $1,500. A credit of up to 5.4% is allowed for taxes paid under state unemployment insurance laws that meet certain criteria, leaving the net federal rate at 0.8% of taxable wages. Subject employers also pay a state unemployment tax.

The secretary of labor certified states for administrative grants to operate the program (under the Social Security Act) and for employer tax credit (under the Federal Unemployment Tax Act).

Benefits are financed solely by employer contributions, except in Alaska, Pennsylvania, and New Jersey, where employees also contribute. Benefits are paid through the states' public employment offices, at which unemployed workers must register for work and to which they must report regularly for referral to a possible job during the time when they are drawing weekly benefit payments. During the fiscal year 1994, $21.8 billion in benefits was paid under state unemployment insurance programs (including the state share of extended benefit programs) to 8.2 million beneficiaries. Beneficiaries received an average weekly payment of $181.53 for total unemployment for an average of 15.4 weeks.

U.S. Unemployment, by Selected Characteristics, 1992-95

Source: Bureau of Labor Statistics, U.S. Dept. of Labor; seasonally adjusted, quarterly averages

Category Characteristic	1992			1993				1994				1995	
	II	III	IV	I	II	III	IV	I	II	III	IV	I	II
Total (all civilian workers)	7.5	7.5	7.3	7.0	7.0	6.7	6.5	6.6	6.2	6.0	5.6	5.5	5.7
Men, 20 years and older	7.2	7.1	6.9	6.6	6.5	6.4	6.0	5.9	5.5	5.3	4.9	4.8	4.9
Women, 20 years and older. . . .	6.2	6.4	6.2	6.0	5.9	5.8	5.7	5.9	5.5	5.3	4.9	4.9	5.0
Both sexes, 16 to 19 years	20.6	20.6	19.4	19.6	19.8	18.2	18.3	18.2	18.1	17.5	16.7	16.8	17.2
White.	6.6	6.6	6.4	6.2	6.1	5.9	5.8	5.7	5.4	5.2	4.9	4.8	5.0
Black and other.	12.8	12.7	12.7	12.3	12.1	11.5	11.0	11.4	10.6	10.4	9.8	9.3	9.5
Black	14.3	14.1	14.1	13.6	13.3	12.6	12.0	12.7	11.7	11.1	10.4	10.0	10.4
Hispanic origin	11.3	11.7	11.6	11.3	10.3	10.2	10.7	10.3	10.3	10.0	9.1	9.4	9.3
Married men, spouse present. . .	5.0	5.2	4.9	4.6	4.5	4.4	4.1	4.2	3.8	3.5	3.2	3.2	3.4
Married women, spouse present	5.1	5.1	5.0	4.6	4.7	4.6	4.5	4.4	4.2	4.1	3.8	3.7	4.0
Women who maintain families . .	10.0	10.1	10.0	9.8	9.7	9.2	9.5	9.4	8.9	8.6	8.8	8.2	8.5
Occupation[1]													
Managerial and professional specialty.	3.1	3.3	3.2	3.3	3.0	2.7	2.9	2.8	2.7	2.6	2.4	2.3	2.4
Technical, sales, and adminis-trative support.	5.8	5.9	5.8	5.4	5.5	5.3	5.2	5.5	5.2	4.8	4.5	4.4	4.7
Precision production, craft, and repair.	8.7	8.6	8.6	8.1	8.3	7.9	7.3	6.9	6.4	6.0	5.7	5.5	6.0
Operators, fabricators, and laborers	11.2	11.1	10.6	10.1	9.9	10.2	9.4	9.5	9.1	8.9	8.3	7.8	8.4
Farming, forestry, and fishing. . .	8.0	8.6	8.4	8.5	8.0	7.8	8.2	9.1	7.7	8.7	7.9	7.7	8.8
Industry													
Nonagricultural private wage and salary workers.	7.7	7.8	7.6	7.3	7.2	7.0	6.8	6.8	6.4	6.2	5.8	5.6	5.9
Goods-producing industries. . .	9.8	9.8	9.5	8.9	9.0	9.0	8.1	7.6	7.0	6.6	6.3	6.0	6.7
Mining	8.1	8.8	6.9	6.8	8.5	6.9	6.9	5.5	6.2	5.4	4.3	5.4	4.5
Construction.	16.8	16.5	15.5	14.8	15.0	14.9	12.9	13.3	11.9	10.8	10.7	11.0	11.7
Manufacturing	7.8	7.9	7.9	7.3	7.2	7.3	6.7	6.1	5.6	5.4	5.0	4.5	5.2
Durable goods	7.8	8.2	8.3	7.2	7.2	7.2	6.6	5.5	5.3	5.3	4.6	4.1	4.6
Nondurable goods.	7.8	7.6	7.3	7.5	7.2	7.5	6.9	6.9	6.0	5.5	5.7	5.1	6.0
Service-producing industries	6.9	7.0	6.8	6.6	6.5	6.2	6.2	6.5	6.2	6.0	5.6	5.4	5.6
Transportation and public utilities	5.2	5.5	5.7	4.9	5.0	5.2	5.3	5.1	5.0	4.8	4.4	4.6	4.4
Wholesale and retail trade. .	8.4	8.7	8.0	7.9	8.0	7.5	7.7	8.0	7.4	7.3	7.0	6.4	6.5
Finance, insurance, and real estate	4.5	4.6	4.7	4.3	4.3	4.0	3.7	3.5	3.6	3.9	3.3	3.2	3.5
Services.	6.6	6.4	6.7	6.4	6.0	5.9	5.9	6.4	6.0	5.7	5.3	5.2	5.6
Government workers.	3.5	3.4	3.5	3.6	3.3	3.2	3.1	3.6	3.6	3.4	3.0	2.9	3.0
Agricultural wage/salary workers	12.7	13.2	12.7	12.2	11.5	11.3	11.1	13.1	9.4	11.4	10.6	10.1	11.9

Note: Data, beginning with 1994, are not directly comparable with data for 1993 and earlier years due to a major redesign of the survey used. (1) Seasonally adjusted data for service occupations are not available because the seasonal components are small relative to the trend-cycle and/or irregular components and consequently cannot be separated with sufficient precision.

Annual Earnings, by Education Attainment, Sex, Race, and Hispanic Origin, 1992

Source: Bureau of the Census, U.S. Dept. of Commerce; averages per person

Characteristic	Total	Not a high school graduate	High school graduate	Some college or an associate degree	Bachelor's degree	Advanced degree
Total	$23,227	$12,809	$18,737	$20,866	$32,629	$48,653
Male	28,448	14,934	22,978	25,660	40,039	58,324
Female.	17,145	9,311	14,128	16,023	23,991	33,814
White	23,932	13,193	19,265	21,357	33,092	49,346
Black	17,416	11,077	15,260	17,768	27,457	39,088
Hispanic origin[1]	16,824	11,836	16,714	19,215	28,260	41,296

(1) May be of any race.

Educational Attainment by Labor Force Status and Occupation, March 1994

Source: Bureau of the Census, Dept. of Commerce

Characteristics	Number of persons (1,000)	Percentage with		
		High school degree or more	Some college or more	Bachelor's degree or more
Civilian labor force, 25 years and older	108,593	88.6	54.6	27.1
Employed.	102,325	89.3	55.6	28.0
Not employed	6,268	75.9	37.2	13.5
Not in the labor force.	55,151	65.5	30.4	12.4
Total, employed persons, 25-64 years old	98,743	89.7	56.1	28.2
Executive, admin., and managerial	14,370	97.5	76.9	47.0
Professional specialty occupations	15,759	99.2	93.1	75.4
Technicians and related support occupations.	3,441	98.6	78.7	29.3
Sales occupations	10,681	94.1	61.1	30.0
Administrative support occupations, includ. clerical.	15,031	96.6	54.0	15.3
Private household occupations	548	58.0	21.4	6.4
Other service occupations	11,523	80.5	36.1	9.0
Farming, forestry, and fishing	2,377	68.4	30.4	10.0
Precision products, craft, and repair	11,398	83.5	35.7	6.8
Machine operators, assemblers, and inspectors. . .	6,222	75.0	22.6	3.7
Transportation and material moving	4,344	79.5	24.7	4.9
Handlers, equipment cleaners, helpers, and laborers	3,050	71.0	24.3	4.6

Occupational Illnesses, by Industry and Type of Illness, 1993

Source: Bureau of Labor Statistics, U.S. Dept. of Labor

(Incidence rate per total injuries and illnesses)

| Occupational illness | Goods producing | | | | | Service producing | | | | |
	Private sector[1]	Agriculture[2]	Mining[3]	Construction	Manufacturing	Trans. and pub. utilities	Wholesale	Retail	Finance[4]	Service
Total [2,252,600 cases] ..	100.0	100.0	100.0	100.0	100.0	100.0	100.0	100.0	100.0	100.0
Nature of injury, illness:										
Sprains, strains.........	42.6	35.6	42.3	37.6	38.1	49.8	45.7	39.9	36.8	48.5
Bruises, contusions......	9.4	9.5	10.8	7.4	9.1	9.9	9.6	10.3	7.5	9.6
Cuts, lacerations........	7.5	10.0	5.8	8.9	8.2	4.0	6.5	11.7	5.5	5.1
Fractures	6.1	6.4	11.2	10.0	6.1	5.9	6.6	5.2	8.1	4.6
Carpal tunnel syndrome...	1.8	0.6	0.3	0.6	3.2	1.1	1.1	1.2	4.5	1.6
Heat burns	1.7	0.7	1.5	1.3	1.5	0.5	0.8	3.8	0.5	1.4
Tendonitis.............	1.1	0.6	—	0.6	2.3	0.5	0.8	0.7	1.5	0.8
Chemical burns........	0.7	0.8	0.8	0.7	0.9	0.5	0.8	0.6	0.5	0.6
Amputations	0.5	0.6	0.9	0.6	1.1	0.2	0.6	0.3	0.4	0.2
Multiple injuries	3.2	4.3	5.8	3.5	2.9	3.3	3.4	3.1	4.5	3.2
Event or exposure:										
Contact with object/equip. ...	27.3	33.4	39.1	34.0	32.8	22.3	28.2	29.1	19.1	19.2
Struck by object	13.1	16.5	21.0	17.2	13.5	10.5	13.7	16.0	9.3	9.5
Struck against object....	7.2	8.7	8.5	8.2	7.7	6.2	6.9	8.4	6.3	5.8
Caught in object	4.4	4.7	8.4	3.7	8.0	2.9	5.0	2.8	2.3	2.3
Fall to lower level	4.9	8.1	8.3	11.6	3.0	6.0	5.0	3.9	8.9	3.9
Fall to same level	10.8	8.9	8.9	7.6	7.3	9.3	8.0	14.9	15.2	14.1
Slips, trips.............	3.7	4.3	1.8	3.4	3.0	4.6	3.8	4.2	3.5	3.8
Overexertion...........	28.2	19.2	28.7	22.7	26.9	29.0	31.9	26.6	20.5	33.3
Overexertion in lifting....	16.9	11.5	11.3	13.3	15.2	16.5	20.4	18.3	12.5	19.3
Repetitive motion	4.2	1.8	0.8	1.5	8.5	2.2	2.4	2.3	8.6	3.2
Exposed to harmful substance...........	5.0	5.3	4.7	4.3	5.4	3.5	3.2	5.9	4.3	5.2
Transportation accidents ..	3.2	4.1	1.8	2.7	1.6	7.5	5.0	2.0	4.8	3.3
Fires, explosions........	0.2	0.2	0.3	0.4	0.2	0.1	0.4	0.2	0.2	0.1
Assault, by person.......	0.9	0.2	—	0.1	0.1	0.4	0.2	1.0	1.2	2.7
Source of injury, illness:										
Chemicals/chem. products.	1.9	1.9	5.7	1.4	2.5	1.3	1.5	1.7	1.9	1.9
Containers	14.7	10.4	5.6	5.4	14.6	19.9	22.8	21.9	9.6	9.3
Furniture, fixtures	3.9	0.8	0.6	1.7	2.9	2.1	2.9	5.8	5.8	5.8
Machinery.............	6.8	7.3	11.7	6.3	11.0	2.7	7.9	6.5	5.5	4.2
Parts and materials	11.1	8.5	17.8	24.6	16.6	8.9	12.2	7.1	4.4	4.1
Worker motion or position...	14.7	13.4	5.4	12.2	18.9	15.1	13.5	11.6	18.6	13.9
Floor, ground surface	15.1	16.2	15.4	17.8	9.8	14.8	12.9	18.0	23.0	17.4
Tools, instruments, equip. ...	6.3	8.6	8.5	10.5	6.5	4.0	4.2	7.4	5.5	5.1
Vehicles	7.0	8.0	8.2	4.7	4.6	16.3	11.4	5.7	7.3	6.0
Health care patient	4.4	—	—	—	—	0.8	—	—	0.6	18.1

Note: Dashes (—) indicate data that are not available or data that do not meet publication guidelines. Because of rounding and classifications not shown, percentages may not add to 100. All injuries and illnesses reported involved days away from work. (1) Private sector includes all industries except government, but excludes farms with fewer than 11 employees. (2) Agriculture includes forestry and fishing, but excludes farms with fewer than 11 employees. (3) Data conforming to OSHA definition for mining operators in coal, metal, and nonmetal mining and for employers in railroad transportation are provided to the Bureau of Labor Statistics by the Mine Safety and Health Administration, U.S. Dept. of Labor; and by the Federal Railroad Administration, U.S. Dept. of Transportation. Independent mining contractors are excluded from the coal, metal, and nonmental industries. (4) Finance includes insurance and real estate.

Fatal Occupational Injuries, 1994

Source: Bureau of Labor Statistics, U.S. Dept. of Labor

| Event or exposure | Fatalities | | Event or exposure | Fatalities | |
	Number	Percentage		Number	Percentage
Total	**6,588**	**100**	Struck by object	589	9
Transportation incidents	**2,740**	**42**	Struck by falling object	371	6
Highway	1,336	20	Struck by flying object	67	1
Collision between vechicles	650	10	Caught in or compressed by equipment or objects	280	4
Vehicle struck stationary object	255	4			
Noncollision	370	6	Caught in or crushed by collapsing materials	132	2
Nonhighway (farm, industrial premises)	407	6	**Falls**	**661**	**10**
Aircraft	424	6	Fall to lower level	577	9
Worker struck by a vehicle	383	6	Fall on same level	62	1
Water vehicle	92	1	**Exposure to harmful substances or environments**	**638**	**10**
Railway	81	1	Contact with electric current	346	5
Assaults and violent acts	**1,308**	**20**	Contact with temperature extremes	50	1
Homicide	1,071	16	Exposure to caustic, noxious, or allergenic substances	131	1
Shooting	925	14	Oxygen deficiency	110	2
Stabbing	60	1	**Fires and explosions**	**202**	**3**
Self-inflicted injury	210	3	Other events or exposures[1]	24	—
Contact with objects and equipment	**1,015**	**15**			

Note: Totals for major categories may include subcategories not shown separately. Percentage, based on incidence rate per total fatalities, may not add to totals because of rounding. (1) Includes the category "Bodily reaction and exertion."

Civilian Employment of the Federal Government, May 1995

Source: Workforce Analysis and Statistics Division, U.S. Office of Personnel Management

(payroll in thousands of dollars, for the month of May 1995)

Agency	All Areas Employment	Payroll	United States Employment	Payroll	Wash., DC MSA Employment	Payroll	Overseas Employment	Payroll
Total, all agencies[1]	2,939,422	$9,233,548	2,831,215	$8,907,468	358,870	$1,390,788	108,207	$326,080
Legislative Branch	34,279	122,986	34,230	122,763	32,418	115,481	49	223
Congress	18,020	62,207	18,020	62,207	18,020	62,207	—	—
U.S. Senate	7,194	23,943	7,194	23,943	7,194	23,943	—	—
House of Rep. Summary	10,812	38,207	10,812	38,207	10,812	38,207	—	—
Comm. on Scty & Coop in Eur	14	57	14	57	14	57	—	—
Architect of the Capitol	2,127	6,070	2,127	6,070	2,127	6,070	—	—
Botanic Garden	51	146	51	146	51	146	—	—
Comm. on Legal Immi. Reform	18	89	18	89	18	89	—	—
Competit Policy Council	7	52	7	52	7	52	—	—
Congressional Budget Ofc	218	1,114	218	1,114	218	1,114	—	—
General Accounting Ofc	4,408	20,763	4,365	20,579	3,006	14,483	43	184
Government Printing Ofc	4,158	13,857	4,158	13,857	3,738	12,780	—	—
John C. Stennis Ctr Pub Dev	5	17	5	17	—	—	—	—
Library of Congress	4,677	16,015	4,671	15,976	4,651	15,923	6	39
Ofc Technology Assessment	191	841	191	841	191	841	—	—
Physician Payment Rev. Comm.	3	16	3	16	—	—	—	—
Prosptv Paymt. Assessmt. Comm.	11	24	11	24	11	24	—	—
U.S. Court of Vets Appeals	81	324	81	324	81	324	—	—
U.S. Tax Court	304	1,451	304	1,451	299	1,428	—	—
Judicial Branch	28,325	104,576	28,018	103,460	1,892	8,075	307	1,116
Supreme Court	373	1,176	373	1,176	373	1,176	—	—
U.S. Courts	27,952	103,400	27,645	102,284	1,519	6,899	307	1,116
Executive Branch	2,876,818	9,005,986	2,768,967	8,681,245	324,560	1,267,232	107,851	324,741
Exec Ofc of the President	1,575	7,378	1,568	7,338	1,568	7,338	7	40
White House Office	378	1,595	378	1,595	378	1,595	—	—
Ofc of Vice President	18	97	18	97	18	97	—	—
Ofc of Mgt & Budget	538	2,686	538	2,686	538	2,686	—	—
Office of Administration	187	696	187	696	187	696	—	—
Council Economic Advisors	27	110	27	110	27	110	—	—
Council on Environ Qual	18	100	18	100	18	100	—	—
Ofc of Policy Development	28	158	28	158	28	158	—	—
Exec Residence at WH	88	413	88	413	88	413	—	—
National Security Council	47	244	47	244	47	244	—	—
Ofc of Natl Drug Control	38	233	38	233	38	233	—	—
Ofc of Sci and Tech Policy	34	201	34	201	34	201	—	—
Ofc of U.S. Trade Rep.	174	845	167	805	167	805	7	40
Executive Departments	1,804,806	5,837,153	1,717,100	5,569,332	241,181	941,352	87,706	267,821
State	25,092	105,329	8,890	37,874	7,842	32,319	16,202	67,455
Treasury	168,051	533,698	166,930	528,785	23,451	98,091	1,121	4,913
Defense, Total	848,385	2,586,775	786,533	2,419,540	82,760	280,255	61,852	167,235
Dept of the Army	276,425	658,184	250,449	592,031	23,795	44,240	25,976	66,153
Army, Mil Func Total	246,777	581,694	220,884	515,822	22,634	40,718	25,893	65,872
Army, Civil Func Total	29,648	76,490	29,565	76,209	1,161	3,522	83	281
Corps of Engineers	29,535	76,170	29,452	75,889	1,048	3,202	83	281
Cemeterial Expenses	113	320	113	320	113	320	—	—
Dept of the Navy	246,748	894,000	235,335	859,938	33,137	123,908	11,413	34,062
Dept of the Air Force	181,793	606,531	173,651	587,878	5,771	23,872	8,142	18,653
Defense Log Agcy	52,079	126,178	51,310	125,362	2,977	11,532	769	816
Other Defense Activities	91,340	301,882	75,788	254,331	17,080	76,703	15,552	47,551
Justice	100,999	392,035	99,005	384,346	21,780	89,314	1,994	7,689
Interior	76,921	224,936	76,580	223,897	9,039	33,016	341	1,039
Agriculture	108,410	303,717	107,036	300,389	12,322	46,526	1,374	3,328
Commerce	37,832	128,570	36,892	124,679	19,995	77,861	940	3,891
Labor	16,340	59,009	16,301	58,847	5,645	22,065	39	162
Health and Human Services	60,118	223,281	59,910	222,394	27,409	110,043	208	887
Housing & Urban Dev	11,960	43,988	11,861	43,639	3,349	14,751	99	349
Transportation	63,522	307,013	63,011	304,566	9,737	48,100	511	2,447
Energy	19,986	96,309	19,978	96,255	7,179	44,106	8	54
Education	4,989	19,599	4,984	19,581	3,369	13,970	5	18
Veterans Affairs	262,201	812,894	259,189	804,540	7,304	30,935	3,012	8,354
Independent Agencies[1]	1,070,437	3,161,455	1,050,299	3,104,575	81,811	318,542	20,138	56,880
Environmtl Protect Agcy	18,297	72,553	18,273	72,460	6,067	26,876	24	93
Equal Employ Opp Comm	2,838	10,246	2,838	10,246	722	3,007	—	—
Federal Deposit Ins Corp	15,712	70,426	15,705	70,389	3,817	19,562	7	37
Fed Emergency Mgmt Agcy	5,287	16,258	5,238	16,096	1,870	6,503	49	162
General Svcs Admin	16,698	58,105	16,608	57,825	5,510	22,210	90	280
Natl Archives & Recds Admin.	2,867	6,293	2,867	6,293	1,156	3,423	—	—
Natl Aero Space Admin	21,996	95,085	21,976	94,966	4,987	23,174	20	119
Nuclear Regulatory Comm	3,264	19,048	3,264	19,048	2,203	13,231	—	—
Office of Personnel Mgmt	4,875	13,488	4,853	13,448	2,109	7,745	22	40
Panama Canal Commission	8,940	21,438	17	82	7	45	8,923	21,356
Securities & Exchnge Comm	2,803	12,142	2,803	12,142	1,779	7,658	—	—
Small Business Admin	5,524	18,322	5,459	18,143	833	3,530	65	189
Smithsonian, Summary	5,401	16,132	5,218	15,657	4,803	14,260	183	475
Tennessee Valley Auth	16,587	76,967	16,587	76,967	11	56	—	—
U.S. Information Agency	7,554	27,241	3,727	15,609	3,536	14,458	3,827	11,632
U.S. Intnatl Dev Coop Agcy	3,867	17,516	2,288	10,154	2,287	10,150	1,579	7,362
U.S. Postal Service	839,381	2,314,916	835,444	2,302,458	24,073	71,891	3,937	12,458

(1) Included in total are other independent agencies with fewer than 2,500 employees.

10 Facts About Women Workers

Source: Women's Bureau, U.S. Dept. of Labor

1. Of the 102 million women 16 and older in the U.S., 60 million were labor force participants (working or looking for work) during 1994. Women accounted for 60% of labor force growth between 1984 and 1994.
2. Women represented 46% of all persons in the civilian labor force in 1994. Women are projected to constitute 48% of the labor force by the year 2005.
3. Teenage women (16-19 years old) are not as active in the labor force as adult women (20 years of age and older). Only 51% of teenage women were in the labor force, compared with 59% of adult women. In addition, teenage women's unemployment rate was 3 times as high as that of adult women—16.2% and 5.4%, respectively.
4. The unemployment rate for all women in the labor force was 6.0% in 1994. Teenage black and Hispanic women continued to experience very high unemployment rates— 32.6% and 22.2%, respectively.
5. Of the 57 million employed women in the U.S. in 1994, 41 million worked full time (35 or more hours per week); nearly 16 million, or 28% of all women workers, held part-time jobs. Two-thirds (67%) of all part-time workers were women.
6. Women have made substantial progress in obtaining jobs in virtually all managerial and professional specialty occupations. In 1984 they held 42% (10.3 million) of these high-paying jobs; in 1994 they held 48% (16.3 million). Women employed in managerial and professional specialty occupations had 1994 median weekly earnings between $285 and $917.
7. Women are still overrepresented in low-paying jobs. Two-fifths (42%) of employed women work in technical, sales, and administrative support jobs—24 million women. Even though the earnings gap between men and women is slowly closing, women earn only 76 cents for every dollar earned by men when comparing 1994 median weekly earnings of full-time workers ($399 for women and $522 for men). The most lucrative occupations for women are lawyer, physician, engineer, computer systems analyst, scientist, and university and college teachers. (This list excludes any occupation at which fewer than 50,000 females are employed.)
8. Median income for female high school graduates age 25 and older (with no college) working year-round, full time in 1993 were less than those of fully employed men who were high school dropouts—$19,963 and $21,752, respectively. During the 10-year period 1983-93, the income gap between the 2 groups has slowly declined from $4,374 to $1,789. Female high school graduates (with no college) continue to earn substantially less than their male counterparts—$19,963 versus $27,370. In addition, men with an associate's degree working year-round, full time had incomes comparable to similarly employed women with a bachelor's degree— $33,690 and $34,307, respectively.
9. Of the approximately 67 million families in the U.S. in 1993, 12 million (18%) were maintained by women. In black families, women maintained 48%; in Hispanic families, 24%; and in white families, 14%. The median weekly earnings of families maintained by women in 1993 was $393, compared with $804 for married-couple families and $523 for families maintained by men.
10. In 1993 women represented 62% of all persons 18 years and older who were living below the poverty level. The poverty rate for families maintained by women with no husband present was 5.5 times as high as for married-couple families—35.6% and 6.5%, respectively. Women maintained 53% of all poor families in 1993. Women maintained 76% of poor black families, about 48% of poor Hispanic families, and 44% of poor white families.

Hourly Compensation Costs, by Selected Country, 1975-93

Source: Bureau of Labor Statistics, U.S. Dept. of Labor

(in U.S. dollars, compensation for production workers in manufacturing)

Country	1975	1985	1990	1993	Country	1975	1985	1990	1993
United States	$6.36	$13.01	$14.91	$16.73	Finland	$4.61	$8.16	$21.03	$16.56
Canada	5.96	10.94	15.83	16.33	France	4.52	7.52	15.23	16.23
Mexico	1.47	1.59	1.64	2.59	Germany[1]	6.35	9.60	21.96	25.71
Australia	5.62	8.20	13.07	12.49	Greece	1.69	3.66	6.71	NA
Hong Kong	0.76	1.73	3.20	4.29	Ireland	3.03	5.92	11.76	12.18
Israel	2.25	4.06	8.55	8.82	Italy	4.67	7.63	17.74	15.99
Japan	3.00	6.34	12.80	19.01	Luxembourg	6.35	7.72	16.37	NA
Korea, South	0.32	1.23	3.71	5.53	Netherlands	6.58	8.75	18.29	19.95
New Zealand	3.21	4.47	8.33	8.01	Norway	6.77	10.37	21.47	20.21
Singapore	0.84	2.47	3.78	5.25	Portugal	1.58	1.53	3.77	4.60
Sri Lanka	0.28	0.28	0.35	0.42	Spain	2.53	4.66	11.33	11.50
Taiwan	0.40	1.50	3.95	5.22	Sweden	7.18	9.66	20.93	17.70
Austria	4.51	7.58	17.75	20.27	Switzerland	6.09	9.66	20.83	22.63
Belguim	6.41	8.97	19.22	21.21	United Kingdom	3.37	6.27	12.71	12.76
Denmark	6.28	8.13	17.96	19.12					

NA=Not available. (1) Former West Germany.

Top 15 Metropolitan Areas, by Average Annual Salary, 1993

Source: Bureau of Labor Statistics, U.S. Dept. of Labor

Rank	Metropolitan area	Average annual salary[1]	Rank	Metropolitan area	Average annual salary[1]
1.	New York, NY	$39,381	8.	Bergen-Passaic, NJ	$34,126
2.	San Jose, CA	38,040	9.	Anchorage, AK	33,782
3.	Middlesex–Somerset–Hunterdon, NJ.	35,573	10.	Washington, DC–MD–VA	33,170
4.	San Francisco, CA	35,278	11.	Jersey City, NJ	32,815
5.	Newark, NJ	35,129	12.	Hartford, CT	32,555
6.	New Haven–Bridgeport–Stamford–		13.	Los Angeles-Long Beach, CA	31,760
	Danbury–Waterbury, CT	35,058	14.	Oakland, CA	31,701
7.	Trenton, NJ	34,365	15.	Detroit, MI	31,622

Note: Jacksonville, NC, recorded the lowest annual pay level among the metropolitan statistical areas in 1993—$15,919—followed by Myrtle Beach, SC ($17,012), McAllen–Edinburg–Mission, TX ($17,173), Brownsville–Harlingen–San Benito, TX ($17,757), and Yuma, AZ ($17,759). The average annual salary in the 5 bottom-ranked metropolitan areas averaged 36-42% below the nationwide metropolitan average of $27,051. A total of 28 metropolitan areas reported average pay levels below $20,000 annually. (1) Data are preliminary and include workers covered by Unemployment Insurance and Unemployment Compensation for Federal Employees programs.

Distribution of Wage and Salary Workers Paid Hourly Rates, 1994

Source: Bureau of Labor Statistics, U.S. Dept. of Labor; unpublished tabulations from Current Population Survey

(in thousands)

	Total paid hourly rates	$4.25[1] or less	Less than $10.00	$10.00 or more
Sex and age				
Total, 16 years and older.....................	66,549	4,127	41,892	24,657
16 to 24 years	15,258	2,217	14,001	1,257
20 to 24 years	9,765	922	8,610	1,155
25 years and older	51,291	1,911	27,892	23,399
25 to 54 years	44,797	1,572	23,973	20,824
25 to 34 years	18,179	814	11,148	7,031
35 to 44 years	16,260	491	7,904	8,356
45 to 54 years	10,357	266	4,920	5,437
55 years and older..................	6,495	339	3,919	2,576
55 to 64 years	5,028	181	2,776	2,252
65 years and older	1,467	158	1,143	324
Men, 16 years and older	33,528	1,565	18,335	15,193
16 to 24 years	7,939	955	7,118	821
20 to 24 years	5,165	372	4,412	753
25 years and older	25,589	610	11,248	14,341
Women, 16 years and older....................	33,021	2,563	23,557	9,464
16 to 24 years	7,319	1,262	6,883	436
20 to 24 years	4,599	550	4,157	402
25 years and older	25,702	1,301	16,674	9,028
Race and Hispanic origin				
White				
Total, 16 years and older	55,151	3,384	34,078	21,073
Men.......................................	27,956	1,273	14,826	13,130
Women	27,196	2,111	19,253	7,943
Black				
Total, 16 years and older	8,586	561	5,993	2,593
Men.......................................	4,116	214	2,630	1,486
Women	4,471	347	3,364	1,107
Hispanic origin				
Total, 16 years and older	7,130	612	5,296	1,834
Men.......................................	4,308	315	3,023	1,285
Women	2,822	297	2,273	549
Full- and part-time status and sex				
Full-time workers				
Total, 16 years and older	49,682	1,519	27,766	21,916
Men.......................................	28,224	674	13,692	14,532
Women	21,458	845	14,074	7,384
Part-time workers				
Total, 16 years and older	16,773	2,602	14,068	2,705
Men.......................................	5,251	889	4,614	637
Women	11,522	1,713	9,453	2,069

Note: Data exclude the incorporated self-employed. (1) $4.25 = minimum wage from April 1, 1991.

Average Hours and Earnings of Production Workers, 1966-94

Source: Bureau of Labor Statistics, U.S. Dept. of Labor

(annual averages)

	Weekly hours	Total private[1] Hourly earnings	Weekly earnings		Weekly hours	Total private[1] Hourly earnings	Weekly earnings
1966	38.6	$2.56	$98.82	1981	35.2	$7.25	$255.20
1967	38.0	2.68	101.84	1982	34.8	7.68	267.26
1968	37.8	2.85	107.73	1983	35.0	8.02	280.70
1969	37.7	3.04	114.61	1984	35.2	8.32	292.86
1970	37.1	3.23	119.83	1985	34.9	8.57	299.09
1971	36.9	3.45	127.31	1986	34.8	8.76	304.85
1972	37.0	3.70	136.90	1987	34.8	8.98	312.50
1973	36.9	3.94	145.39	1988	34.7	9.28	322.02
1974	36.5	4.24	154.76	1989	34.6	9.66	334.24
1975	36.1	4.53	163.53	1990	34.5	10.01	345.35
1976	36.1	4.86	175.45	1991	34.3	10.32	353.98
1977	36.0	5.25	189.00	1992	34.4	10.57	363.61
1978	35.8	5.69	203.70	1993	34.5	10.83	373.64
1979	35.7	6.16	219.91	1994	34.7	11.13	386.21
1980	35.3	6.66	235.10				

(1) Data relate to production workers in mining and manufacturing; construction workers in construction; and nonsupervisory workers in transportation and public utilities; wholesale and retail trade; finance, insurance, and real estate; and services.

Employer Costs for Employee Compensation, March 1995

Source: Bureau of Labor Statistics, U.S. Dept. of Labor; dollar figures are costs per hour worked

The following table discusses average employee compensation costs for all civilian employees (private industry and state and local governments).

In private industry, March 1995 employer compensation costs averaged $17.10 per hour worked. This figure was composed of $12.25 per hour in straight-time wages and $4.85 per hour in benefits costs, including legally required benefits. Compensation costs averaged more for workers in goods-producing industries ($20.75 per hour worked) than for those in service-producing industries ($15.88 per hour worked).

During the same period, employer compensation costs for state and local government employees averaged $24.86 per hour worked. Of this amount, costs for straight-time wages and salaries averaged $17.31 per hour, and benefit costs, including legally required benefits, averaged $7.56 per hour. Among work activities, average compensation costs were higher per hour worked in services (that is, health and educational services) than in public administration ($25.92 per hour and $22.82 per hour, respectively). These 2 categories account for most state and local government employment.

	Total compensation	Wages and salaries	Benefit Costs					
			Total[1]	Paid leave	Supplemental pay	Insurance	Retirement and savings	Legally required benefits
Civilian workers	$18.38	$13.12	$5.26	$1.22	$0.42	$1.29	$0.71	$1.59
Occupational group:								
White-collar occupations	21.87	15.94	5.93	1.54	0.42	1.46	0.86	1.63
Professional specialty and technical	29.07	21.42	7.65	1.95	0.39	1.87	1.36	2.04
Executive, administrative, and managerial	32.34	23.14	9.20	2.77	0.94	1.83	1.32	2.30
Administrative support including clerical	14.86	10.51	4.36	1.10	0.26	1.31	0.50	1.17
Blue-collar occupations	16.92	11.39	5.53	1.00	0.59	1.38	0.65	1.87
Service occupations	9.96	7.21	2.77	.57	0.16	0.66	0.36	1.01
Industry group:								
Services	19.53	14.38	5.15	1.28	0.25	1.32	0.79	1.51
Health services	19.59	13.90	5.69	1.59	0.56	1.42	0.56	1.55
Hospitals	21.14	14.83	6.31	1.81	0.64	1.62	0.62	1.60
Educational services	24.99	18.51	6.48	1.49	0.07	1.81	1.46	1.63
Elementary and secondary education	24.57	18.27	6.30	1.34	0.05	1.88	1.43	1.57
Higher education	28.11	20.43	7.68	2.05	0.12	1.85	1.83	1.82
	Percent of Total Compensation							
Civilian workers	100.0%	71.4%	28.6%	6.6%	2.3%	7.0%	3.9%	8.7%
Occupational group:								
White-collar occupations	100.0	72.9	27.1	7.0	1.9	6.7	3.9	7.5
Professional specialty and technical	100.0	73.7	26.3	6.7	1.4	6.4	4.7	7.0
Executive, administrative, and managerial	100.0	71.5	28.5	8.6	2.9	5.6	4.1	7.1
Administrative support including clerical	100.0	70.7	29.3	7.4	1.7	8.8	3.4	7.9
Blue-collar occupations	100.0	67.3	32.7	5.9	3.5	8.1	3.8	11.1
Service occupations	100.0	72.2	27.8	5.7	1.6	6.6	3.6	10.1
Industry group:								
Services	100.0	73.6	26.4	6.5	1.3	6.7	4.1	7.7
Health services	100.0	71.0	29.0	8.1	2.8	7.2	2.9	7.9
Hospitals	100.0	70.2	29.8	8.6	3.0	7.7	2.9	7.6
Educational services	100.0	74.1	25.9	6.0	0.3	7.2	5.8	6.5
Elementary and secondary education	100.0	74.4	25.6	5.5	0.2	7.7	5.8	6.4
Higher education	100.0	72.7	27.3	7.3	0.4	6.6	6.5	6.5

(1) Includes severance pay and supplemental unemployment benefits, not listed separately.

Federal Minimum Hourly Wage Rates Since 1950

Source: Bureau of Labor Statistics, U.S. Dept. of Labor

The Fair Labor Standards Act of 1938 and subsequent amendments provide for minimum wage coverage applicable to specified nonsupervisory employment categories. Exempt from coverage are executives and administrators or professionals.

Minimum Rates for Nonfarm Workers

Effective date	Laws prior to 1966[1]	Percent, avg earnings[2]	1966 and later[3]	Minimum rates for farm workers[4]
Jan. 25, 1950	$.75	54	NA	NA
Mar. 1, 1956	1.00	52	NA	NA
Sept. 3, 1961	1.15	50	NA	NA
Sept. 3, 1963	1.25	51	NA	NA
Feb. 1, 1967	1.40	50	$1.00	$1.00
Feb. 1, 1968	1.60	54	1.15	1.15
Feb. 1, 1969	(5)	(5)	1.30	1.30
Feb. 1, 1970	(5)	(5)	1.45	(5)
Feb. 1, 1971	(5)	(5)	1.60	(5)
May 1, 1974	2.00	46	1.90	1.60

Minimum Rates for Nonfarm Workers

Effective date	Laws prior to 1966[1]	Percent, avg earnings[2]	1966 and later[3]	Minimum rates for farm workers[4]
Jan. 1, 1975	$2.10	45	$2.00	$1.80
Jan. 1, 1976	2.30	46	2.20	2.00
Jan. 1, 1977	(5)	(5)	2.30	2.20
Jan. 1, 1978	2.65	44	2.65	2.65
Jan. 1, 1979	2.90	45	2.90	2.90
Jan. 1, 1980	3.10	43	3.10	3.10
Jan. 1, 1981	3.35	42	3.35	3.35
Apr. 1, 1990	3.80[6]	35	3.80[6]	3.80[6]
Apr. 1, 1991	4.25[6]	38	4.25[6]	4.25[6]

NA = not applicable. (1) Applies to workers covered prior to 1961 Amendments and, after Sept. 1965, to workers covered by 1961 Amendments. Rates set by 1961 Amendments were: Sept. 1961, $1.00; Sept. 1964, $1.15; and Sept. 1965, $1.25. (2) Percent of gross average hourly earnings of production workers in manufacturing. (3) Applies to workers newly covered by Amendments of 1966, 1974, and 1977, and Title IX of Education Amendments of 1972. (4) Included in coverage as of 1966, 1974, and 1977 Amendments. (5) No change in rate. (6) Training wage for workers age 16-19 in first six months of first job: 1990, $3.35; 1991, $3.62 and from Apr. 1, 1991, additional requirements refer to subsequent employment by a different employer for an additional 90 days. The training wage expired Mar. 31, 1993.

Median Weekly Earnings of Full-Time Wage and Salary Workers by Age, Sex, and Union Affiliation, 1993-94

Source: Bureau of Labor Statistics, U.S. Dept. of Labor

Sex and age	1993				1994			
	Total	Members of unions[1]	Represented by unions[2]	Non-union	Total	Members of unions[1]	Represented by unions[2]	Non-union
Total, 16 years and older	$463	$575	$569	$426	$467	$592	$587	$432
16 to 24 years	283	377	366	277	286	366	364	281
25 years and older	493	585	581	468	500	603	599	474
25 to 34 years	439	520	514	420	439	532	522	421
35 to 44 years	519	595	593	499	537	623	618	508
45 to 54 years	543	622	620	507	566	639	636	520
55 to 64 years	492	576	573	462	501	588	589	472
65 years and older	394	467	462	381	384	549	549	361
Men, 16 years and older	514	608	606	490	522	621	620	495
16 to 24 years	289	393	383	283	294	374	371	288
25 years and older	559	617	616	524	576	635	635	544
25 to 34 years	478	555	549	459	479	572	566	460
35 to 44 years	598	623	623	586	617	657	656	603
45 to 54 years	656	670	671	641	671	685	684	661
55 to 64 years	586	610	612	564	603	617	624	591
65 years and older	453	529	524	434	441	608	604	405
Women, 16 years and older ...	395	504	500	374	399	522	517	377
16 to 24 years	274	344	340	270	276	350	348	271
25 years and older	416	511	508	396	421	535	527	401
25 to 34 years	396	481	474	383	397	483	478	385
35 to 44 years	437	526	524	412	448	570	560	419
45 to 54 years	441	540	537	407	450	573	572	415
55 to 64 years	396	482	480	372	398	506	504	374
65 years and older	335	400	399	316	336	458	450	323

Note: Data refer to the sole or principal job of full-time workers. Excluded are self-employed workers whose businesses are incorporated although they technically qualify as wage and salary workers. (1) Data refer to members of a labor union or an employee association similar to a union. (2) Data refer to members of a labor union or an employee association similar to a union as well as workers who report no union affiliation but whose jobs are covered by a union or an employee association contract.

Work Stoppages (Strikes) in the U.S., 1960-94

Source: Bureau of Labor Statistics, U.S. Dept. of Labor ; involving 1,000 workers or more

	Number stoppages[1]	Workers involved[1] (thousands)	Work days idle[1] (thousands)		Number stoppages[1]	Workers involved[1] (thousands)	Work days idle[1] (thousands)
1960........	222	896	13,260	1982........	96	656	9,061
1965........	268	999	15,140	1983........	81	909	17,461
1970........	381	2,468	52,761	1984........	62	376	8,499
1971........	298	2,516	35,538	1985........	54	324	7,079
1972........	250	975	16,764	1986........	69	533	11,861
1973........	317	1,400	16,260	1987........	46	174	4,481
1974........	424	1,796	31,809	1988........	40	118	4,364
1975........	235	965	17,563	1989........	51	452	16,996
1976........	231	1,519	23,962	1990........	44	185	5,926
1977........	298	1,212	21,258	1991........	40	392	4,584
1978........	219	1,006	23,774	1992........	35	364	3,989
1979........	235	1,021	20,409	1993........	35	182	3,981
1980........	187	795	20,844	1994........	45	322	5,020
1981........	145	729	16,908				

(1) The number of stoppages and workers relate to stoppages that began in the year. Days of idleness include all stoppages in effect. Workers are counted more than once if they were involved in more than one stoppage during the year.

Work Stoppages Involving 5,000 Workers or More Beginning in 1994

Source: Bureau of Labor Statistics, U.S. Dept. of Labor

Employer, location, and union	Began	Ended	Workers involved[1]	Estimated days idle in 1994[1]
United Parcel Service, interstate; Teamsters (IBT)	2/7	2/7	40,000	40,000
General Motors Corp., Dayton, OH; Automobile Workers (UAW)	3/14	3/16	10,900	16,900
Trucking Management, Inc., interstate; Teamsters (IBT)	4/6	4/29	71,000	1,180,500
Hawaii State and County governments, Hawaii; State County, and Municipal Employees (AFSCME)	4/18	4/29	15,800	136,500
Caterpillar, Inc., IL; Automobile Workers (UAW)	5/16	5/20	7,500	37,500
Connecticut Construction Contractors (heavy/highway) Connecticut and vicinity; Teamsters (IBT)	6/6	6/18	6,000	60,000
Long Island Rail Road, Long Island, NY; Transportation (UTU)	6/17	6/18	5,400	5,400
Caterpillar, Inc., IL, MI, PA, and CO; Automobile Workers (UAW)	6/20	(2)	14,000	1,489,000
Los Angeles Metropolitan Transit Authority, Los Angeles, CA; Transit (ATU)	7/25	8/2	7,200	50,400
Food Employers, Inc., Portland, OR, and Vancouver, WA; Food and Commercial Workers (UFCW)	8/18	11/12	7,000	413,000
General Motors Corp., Inland Fisher Guide Plant, Anderson, IN; Automobile Workers (UAW)	8/23	8/25	46,400	63,300
General Motors Corp., Buick City facility, Flint, MI; Automobile Workers (UAW)	9/27	9/30	22,300	74,000

(1) Workers and days idle are rounded to the nearest 100. (2) Strike continued into 1995.

Labor Union Directory

Source: Bureau of Labor Statistics, U.S. Dept. of Labor; AFL-CIO; World Almanac questionnaire

(*) Independent union; all others affiliated with AFL-CIO

American Federation of Labor & Congress of Industrial Organizations (AFL-CIO), 815 16th St. NW, Washington, DC 20006; founded 1955; Thomas R. Donahue, Interim Pres. (since 1995); 13.3 mil. members.

Actors and Artistes of America, Associated (AAAA), 165 W 46th St., New York, NY 10036; founded 1919; Theodore Bikel, Pres.; no individual members, 7 National Performing Arts Unions are affiliates; approx. 100,000 combined membership.

Actors' Equity Association, 165 W 46th St., New York, NY 10036; founded 1913; Ron Silver, Pres. (since 1991); 32,000 active members.

Air Line Pilots Association, 1625 Massachusetts Ave. NW, Washington, DC 20036; founded 1933; J. Randolph Babbitt, Pres. (since 1990); 41,000 members.

Aluminum, Brick & Glass Workers International Union (ABGWIU), 3362 Hollenberg Drive, Bridgeton, MO 63044; founded 1953; Ernie J. Labaff, Pres. (since 1985); 44,000 members, 375 locals.

Automobile, Aerospace & Agricultural Implement Workers of America, International Union, United (UAW), 8000 E Jefferson Ave., Detroit, MI 48214; founded 1935; Stephen P. Yokich, Pres. (since 1995); 1.3 mil. members, 1,100 locals.

Bakery, Confectionery & Tobacco Workers International Union (BC&T), 10401 Connecticut Ave., Kensington, MD 20895; founded 1886; Frank Hurt, Pres. (since 1992); 125,000 members.

Boilermakers, Iron Ship Builders, Blacksmiths, Forgers and Helpers, International Brotherhood of (IBBISB/BF&H), 753 State Ave., Suite 570, Kansas City, KS 66101; founded 1880; Charles W. Jones, Pres. (since 1983); 80,000 members, 357 locals.

Bricklayers and Allied Craftsmen, International Union of, 815 15th St. NW, Washington, DC 20005; founded 1865; John T. Joyce, Pres.; 100,000 members, 400 locals.

Carpenters and Joiners of America, United Brotherhood of, 101 Constitution Ave. NW, Washington, DC 20001; founded 1881; Sigurd Lucassen, Gen. Pres. (since 1988); 500,000 members, 1,000 locals.

Chemical Workers Union, International (ICWU), 1655 West Market St., Akron, OH 44313; founded 1944; Frank D. Martino, Pres. (since 1975); 50,000 members, 350 locals.

Clothing and Textile Workers Union, Amalgamated (ACTWU), 15 Union Square, New York, NY 10003; founded 1976 (by merger of 2 unions); Jack Sheinkman, Pres. (since 1987); 26,500 members.

Communications Workers of America (CWA), 501 3d St. NW, Washington, DC 20001-2797; founded 1938; Morton Bahr, Pres. (since 1985); 600,000 members, 1,200 locals.

Distillery, Wine & Allied Workers International Union (DWU), 66 Grand Ave., Englewood, NJ 07631; founded 1940; George J. Orlando, Pres. (since 1984).

***Education Association, National,** 1201 16th St. NW, Washington, DC 20036; founded 1857; Keith Geiger, Pres. (since 1989); 2 mil. members, 13,250 affiliates.

Electrical Workers, International Brotherhood of (IBEW), 1125 15th St. NW, Washington, DC 20005; founded 1891; John J. Barry, Int'l Pres. (since 1986); 800,000 members, 1,134 locals.

Electronic, Electrical, Salaried, Machine and Furniture Workers, International Union of (IUE), 1126 16th St. NW, Washington, DC 20036; founded 1949; William H. Bywater, Pres. (since 1982); 140,000 members, 450 locals.

Farm Workers of America, United (UFW), 29700 Woodfoel Tehachapi Rd., PO Box 62, Keene, CA 93531; founded 1962; Arturo S. Rodríguez, Pres. (since 1993); 50,000 members.

***Federal Employees, National Federation of (NFFE),** 1016 16th St. NW, Washington, DC 20036; founded 1917; Sheila K. Velazco, Pres.; 148,000 members, 392 locals.

Fire Fighters, International Association of, 1750 New York Ave. NW, Washington, DC 20006; founded 1918; Alfred K. Whitehead, Pres. (since 1988); 200,000 members, 2,280 locals.

Firemen and Oilers, International Brotherhood of, 1100 Circle 75 Parkway, Suite 350, Atlanta, GA 30339; founded 1899; Jimmy L. Walker, Pres.; 25,000 members, 210 locals.

Food and Commercial Workers International Union, United (UFCW), 1775 K St. NW, Washington, DC 20006-1598;

founded 1979 following merger; Douglas H. Dority, Int'l Pres. (since 1994); 1.4 mil. members, 660 locals.

Garment Workers of America, United (UGWA), 4207 Lebanon Rd., Hermitage, TN 37076; founded 1891; Dave Johnson, Gen. Pres. (since 1991); 20,000 members, 120 locals.

Glass, Molders, Pottery, Plastics & Allied Workers Intl. Union (GMP), 608 E Baltimore Pike, PO Box 607, Media, PA 19063; founded 1842; James E. Hatfield, Int'l Pres. (since 1977); 72,000 members, 450 locals.

Government Employees, American Federation of (AFGE), 80 F St. NW, Washington, DC 20001; founded 1932; John N. Sturdivant, Natl. Pres. (since 1988); 200,000 members, 1,200 locals.

Grain Millers, American Federation of (AFGM), 4949 Olson Memorial Hwy., Minneapolis, MN 55422; founded 1936; Larry R. Jackson, Gen. Pres. (since 1991); 27,000 members, 180 locals.

Graphic Communications International Union (GCIU), 1900 L St. NW, Washington, DC 20036; founded 1983; James J. Norton, Pres. (since 1985); 165,000 members, 450 locals.

Hotel Employees and Restaurant Employees International Union, 1219 28th St. NW, Washington, DC 20007; Edward T. Henley, Gen. Pres.(since 1973); 400,000 members, 190 locals.

Iron Workers, International Association of Bridge, Structural and Ornamental, 1750 New York Ave. NW, Suite 400, Washington, DC 20006; founded 1896; Jake West, Gen. Pres. (since 1989); 130,000 members, 245 locals.

Laborers' International Union of North America (LIUNA), 905 16th St. NW, Washington, DC 20006; founded 1903; Arthur A. Coia, Gen. Pres. (since 1993); 700,000 members, 622 locals.

Ladies' Garment Workers' Union, International (ILGWU), 1710 Broadway, New York, NY 10019; founded 1900; Jay Mazur, Pres. (since 1986); 150,000 members, 245 locals.

Leather Goods, Plastic and Novelty Workers' Union, International, 265 W 14th St., New York, NY 10011; Andrew McKenzie, Gen. Pres. (since 1992); 6,000 members, 85 locals.

Letter Carriers, National Association of (NALC), 100 Indiana Ave. NW, Washington, DC 20001; founded 1889; Vincent R. Sombrotto, Pres. (since 1978); 310,000 members, 3,190 locals.

***Locomotive Engineers, Brotherhood of (BLE),** The Standard Bldg., 1370 Ontario Ave., Cleveland, OH 44113-1702; founded 1863; Ronald P. McLaughlin, Pres. (since 1991); 50,500 members, 610 divisions.

Longshoremen's Association, International, 17 Battery Pl., New York, NY 10004; John Bowers, Pres., (since 1987); 65,000 members, 331 locals.

***Longshoremen's & Warehousemen's Union, International (ILWU),** 1188 Franklin St., San Francisco, CA 94109-6800; founded 1937; Brian McWilliams, Pres. (since 1994); 45,000 members, 60 locals.

Machinists and Aerospace Workers, International Association of (IAM), 9000 Machinists Pl., Upper Marlboro, MD 20772-2687; founded 1888; George J. Kourpias, Int'l Pres. (since 1989); 731,780 members, 1,370 locals.

Maintenance of Way Employees, Brotherhood of (BMWE), 26555 Evergreen Rd., Suite 200, Southfield, MI 48076; founded 1887; Mac A. Fleming, Pres. (since 1990); 50,000 members, 801 locals.

Marine Engineer Beneficial Assn. (MEBA), 444 N Capitol St. NW, Suite 800, Washington, DC 20001; founded 1875; Joel E. Bem, Pres. (since 1994); 4,242 members, 25 locals.

Maritime, National, Union (NMU), 1125 15th St. NW, Suite 501, Washington, DC 20005; Louis Parise, Pres.; 50,000 members.

***Mine Workers of America, United (UMWA),** 900 15th St. NW, Washington, DC 20005; founded 1890; Richard L. Trumka, Int'l Pres. (since 1982); 240,000 members, 900 locals.

Musicians of the United States and Canada, American Federation of (AF of M), 1501 Broadway, Suite 600, New York, NY 10036; founded 1896; Mark Tully Massagli, Pres. (since 1991); 150,000 members, 340 locals.

Newspaper Guild, The (TNG), 8611 Second Ave., Silver Spring, MD 20910; founded 1933; Charles B. Dale, Pres. (since 1987); 32,000 members, 76 locals.

***Nurses Association, American (ANA),** 600 Maryland Ave. SW, Suite 100W, Washington, DC 20024-2571; founded 1896; Virginia Trotter-Betts, JD, RN, Pres. (since 1992); 205,000 members, 53 constituent state assns.

Office and Professional Employees International Union (OPEIU), 265 W 14th St., New York, NY 10011; founded 1945 (AFL Charter); Michael Goodwin, Int'l Pres. (since 1994); 130,000 members, 250 locals.

Oil, Chemical and Atomic Workers International Union (OCAW), 255 Union Blvd., PO Box 281200, Lakewood, CO 80228; Robert E. Wages, Pres. (since 1991); 87,000 members, 350 locals.

Operating Engineers, International Union of (IUOE), 1125 17th St. NW, Washington, DC 20036; founded 1896; Frank Hanley, Gen. Pres.; 400,000 members, 200 locals.

Painters and Allied Trades, International Brotherhood of (IBPAT), 1750 New York Ave. NW, Washington, DC 20006; founded 1887; A. L. "Mike" Monroe, Gen. Pres.; 128,243 members, 550 locals.

Paperworkers International Union, United (UPIU), 3340 Perimeter Hill Dr., Nashville, TN 37211; founded 1884; Wayne E. Glenn, Pres. (since 1978); 275,000 members, 1,300 locals.

*Plant Guard Workers of America, International Union, United (UPGWA), 25510 Kelly Rd., Roseville, MI 48066; founded 1948; Gene McConville, Pres.; 28,000 members, 176 locals.

Plasterers' and Cement Masons' International Association of the United States & Canada, Operative, 1125 17th St. NW, 6th Fl., Washington, DC 20036; founded 1864; Dominic A. Martell, Gen. Pres.; 40,000 members, 250 locals.

Plumbing and Pipefitting Industry of the United States and Canada, United Association of Journeymen and Apprentices of the, 901 Massachusetts Ave. NW, Washington, DC 20001; founded 1889; Marvin J. Boede, Pres. (since 1982); 292,000 members, 424 locals.

*Police, Fraternal Order of, 1410 Donelson Pike, Nashville, TN 37217; Dewey R. Stokes, Natl. Pres., and Jerry Atnip, Natl. Secy.; 253,000 members, 1,860 affiliates.

*Postal Supervisors, National Association of, 1727 King St., Suite 400, Alexandria, VA 22314-2753; Vincent Palladino, Pres. (since 1992); 37,464 members, 407 locals.

Postal Workers Union, American (APWU), 1300 L St. NW, Washington, DC 20005; founded 1971; Moe Biller, Pres. (since 1980); 350,000 members, 1,850 locals.

Railway Carmen Division of Transportation Communications Int'l. Union (BRC Division/TCU), 3 Research Pl., Rockville, MD 20850; founded 1888; R. P. Wojtowicz, Gen. Pres. (since 1992); 50,000 members, 265 locals.

Retail, Wholesale and Department Store Union, 30 E 29th St., New York, NY 10016; Lenore Miller, Pres.; 100,000 members, 157 locals.

Roofers, Waterproofers & Allied Workers, United Union of, 1125 17th St. NW, Washington, DC 20036; founded 1903; Earl J. Kruse, Pres. (since 1985); 25,000 members, 110 locals.

Rubber, Cork, Linoleum and Plastic Workers of America, United (URW), 570 White Pond Dr., Akron, OH 44320-1156; founded 1935; Kenneth L. Coss, Int'l Pres. (since 1990); 90,000 members, 360 locals.

*Rural Letter Carriers' Association, National, 1630 Duke St., 4th floor, Alexandria, VA 22314; founded 1903; Scottie B. Hicks, Pres. (since 1994); 48,000 members; 50 state organizations.

Seafarers International Union of North America (SIUNA), 5201 Auth Way, Camp Springs, MD 20746; founded 1938; Michael Sacco, Pres. (since 1988); 85,000 members, 18 locals.

Service Employees International Union (SEIU), 1313 L St. NW, Washington, DC 20005; founded 1921; John J. Sweeney, Pres. (since 1980); 1 mil. members, 290 locals.

Sheet Metal Workers' International Association (SMWIA), 1750 New York Ave. NW, Washington, DC 20006; founded 1888; Arthur Moore, Gen. Pres. (since 1993); 135,000 members, 213 locals.

State, County and Municipal Employees, American Federation of, 1625 L St. NW, Washington, DC 20036; Gerald McEntee, Pres. (since 1981); 1.3 mil. members, 3,515 locals.

Steelworkers of America, United (USWA), 5 Gateway Center, Pittsburgh, PA 15222; founded 1936; George Becker, Int'l Pres. (since 1994); 550,000 members, 2,300 locals.

Teachers, American Federation of (AFT), 555 New Jersey Ave. NW, Washington, DC 20001; founded 1916; Albert Shanker, Pres. (since 1964); 875,000 members, 2,100 locals.

Teamsters, Chauffeurs, Warehousemen and Helpers of America, International Brotherhood of (IBT), 25 Louisiana Ave. NW, Washington, DC 20001; founded 1903; Ronald R. Carey, Pres. (since 1992); 1.4 mil. members, 615 locals.

Television and Radio Artists, American Federation of, 260 Madison Ave., 7th Floor, New York, NY 10016; founded 1937; Shelby Scott, Pres.; 75,000 members, 30 locals.

Textile Workers of America, United (UTWA), 2 Echelon Plaza, Suite 200, Laurel Rd., Voorhees, NJ 08043; founded 1901; Ron Myslowka, Intl. Pres. (since 1992); 30,000 members, 125 locals.

Theatrical Stage Employees and Moving Picture Machine Operators of the United States and Canada, International Alliance of (IATSE), 1515 Broadway, Suite 601, New York, NY 10036; founded 1893; Thomas C. Short, Pres. (since 1994); 75,000 members, 552 locals.

Transit Union, Amalgamated (ATU), 5025 Wisconsin Ave. NW, Washington, DC 20016; founded 1892; James LaSala, Intl. Pres. (since 1986); 160,000 members, 275 locals.

Transportation Communications International Union (TCU), 3 Research Place, Rockville, MD 20850; founded 1899; Robert A. Scardelletti, Int'l Pres. (since 1991); 123,081 members, 920 locals.

*Transportation Union, United (UTU), 14600 Detroit Ave., Cleveland, OH 44107; founded 1969; G. Thomas DuBose, Pres. (since 1991); 134,000 members, 712 locals.

Transport Workers Union of America, 80 West End Ave., New York, NY 10023; founded 1934; Sonny Hall, Int'l Pres. (since 1993); 125,000 members, 92 locals.

*Treasury Employees Union, National (NTEU), 901 E St. NW, Suite 600, Washington, DC 20004; founded 1938; Robert M. Tobias, Natl. Pres. (since 1983); 150,000 represented, 250 chapters.

*University Professors, American Association of (AAUP), 1012 14th St. NW, Washington, DC 20005; founded 1915; James Perley, Pres.; 41,000 members, 1,000 chapters.

Utility Workers Union of America (UWUA), 815 16th St. NW, Suite 605, Washington, DC 20006; founded 1945; Marshall M. Hicks, Natl. Pres. (since 1991); 50,000 members, 210 locals.

U.S. Union Membership, 1930-94

Source: Bureau of Labor Statistics, U.S. Dept. of Labor

Year	Labor force[1] (thousands)	Union members[2] (thousands)	Percentage	Year	Labor force[1] (thousands)	Union members[2] (thousands)	Percentage
1930	29,424	3,401	11.6	1985	94,521	16,996	18.0
1935	27,053	3,584	13.2	1986	96,903	16,975	17.5
1940	32,376	8,717	26.9	1987	99,303	16,913	17.0
1945	40,394	14,322	35.5	1988	101,407	17,002	16.8
1950	45,222	14,267	31.5	1989	103,480	16,960	16.4
1955	50,675	16,802	33.2	1990	103,905	16,740	16.1
1960	54,234	17,049	31.4	1991	102,786	16,568	16.1
1965	60,815	17,299	28.4	1992	103,688	16,390	15.8
1970	70,920	19,381	27.3	1993	105,067	16,598	15.8
1975	76,945	19,611	25.5	1994	107,989	16,748	15.5
1980	90,564	19,843	21.9				

(1) Does not include agricultural employment; from 1985, data do not include self-employed or unemployed persons. (2) From 1930 to 1980 data are the number of dues-paying members of traditional trade unions with members counted regardless of employment status; from 1985, members include employee associations that engage in collective bargaining with employers.

NATIONAL DEFENSE

Data as of mid-1995

Chairman, Joint Chiefs of Staff
Gen. John M. Shalikashvili

Vice Chairman
Adm. David E. Jeremiah

The Joint Chiefs of Staff consists of the Chairman and Vice Chairman of the Joint Chiefs of Staff; the Chief of Staff, U.S. Army; the Chief of Naval Operations; the Chief of Staff, U.S. Air Force; and the Commandant of the Marine Corps.

Army

Chief of Staff—Gen. Dennis J. Reimer

Generals	Date of Rank
Downing, Wayne A.	May 20, 1993
Franks, Frederick M., Jr.	Aug. 23, 1991
Joulwan, George A.	Nov. 21, 1990
Luck, Gary E.	July 1, 1993
Maddox, David M.	July 9, 1992
McCaffrey, Barry R.	Feb. 17, 1994
Peay, J.H. Binford III.	Mar. 26, 1993
Salomon, Leon E.	Feb. 11, 1994
Shalikashvili, John M.	Jun. 24, 1992

Air Force

Chief of Staff—Gen. Ronald R. Fogleman

Generals	Date of Rank
Ashy, Joseph W.	July 15, 1994
Boles, Billy J.	June 20, 1995
Boyd, Charles G.	Dec. 1, 1992
Jamerson, James L.	July 15, 1994
Loh, John M.	June 1, 1990
Lorber, John G.	Oct. 12, 1994
Moorman, Thomas S.	July 15, 1994
Ralston, Joseph W.	July 1, 1995
Rutherford, Robert L.	Feb. 1, 1993
Viccellio, Henry, Jr.	Dec. 10, 1992
Yates, Ronald W.	Apr. 1, 1990

Navy

Chief of Naval Operations
Adm. Jeremy M. Boorda (surface warfare)

Admirals	Date of Rank
Chiles, Henry G., Jr. (submariner)	Feb. 14, 1994
Demars, Bruce (submariner)	Nov. 1, 1988
Flanagan, William (surface warfare)	Nov. 1, 1994
Larson, Charles R. (submariner)	Mar. 1, 1990
Macke, Richard C. (aviator)	Oct. 1, 1994
Prueher, Joseph W. (aviator)	June 1, 1995
Reason, J. Paul (surface warfare)	Feb. 1, 1991
Smith, Leighton W., Jr. (aviator)	May 1, 1994
Zlatoper, Ronald J. (aviator)	Oct. 5, 1994

Marine Corps

Corps Commandant (CMC), with rank of General

Charles C. Krulak	July 1, 1995

Assistant Commandant (ACMC)

Richard D. Hearny	July 15, 1994

Coast Guard

Commandant, with rank of Admiral

Robert E. Kramek	June 1, 1994

Vice Commandant, with rank of Vice Admiral

Arthur E. Henn	June 17, 1994

Unified Defense Commands Commanders in Chief

(as of mid-1995)

U.S. European Command, Brussels, Belgium — Gen. George A. Joulwan (USA) (concurrently NATO Supreme Allied Commander, Europe)

U.S. Southern Command, Quarry Heights, Panama Canal Zone — Gen. Barry R. McCaffrey (USA)

U.S. Atlantic Command, Norfolk, Virginia — Gen. John J. Sheehan (USMC) (concurrently NATO Supreme Allied Commander, Atlantic)

U.S. Pacific Command, Honolulu, Hawaii — Adm. Richard C. Macke (USN)

U.S. Space Command, Peterson AFB, Colo. — Gen. Joseph W. Ashy (USAF)

U.S. Strategic Command, Omaha, Neb. — Adm. Henry G. Chiles, Jr. (USN)

U.S. Forces Command, Fort McPherson, Ga. — Gen. John H. Tilelli Jr. (USA)

U.S. Transportation Command, Scott AFB, Ill. — Gen. Robert L. Rutherford (USAF)

U.S. Special Operations Command, Fort Walton Beach, Fla. — Gen. Wayne A. Downing (USA)

U.S. Central Command, MacDill AFB, Fla. — Gen. J.H. Binford Peay, III (USA)

North Atlantic Treaty Organization International Commands

(as of mid-1995)

Supreme Allied Commander, Europe (SACEUR) — Gen. George A. Joulwan (USA)

Deputy Supreme Allied Commander, Europe (DSACEUR) — Gen. Sir Jeremy MacKenzie (UKA)

Commander in Chief Allied Forces Northern Europe — Adm. B. Kibsgaard (NoN)

Commander in Chief Allied Forces Central Europe — Gen. Helge Hansen (GEA)

Commander in Chief Allied Forces Southern Europe — Adm. Leighton W. Smith, Jr. (USN)

Chairman, NATO Military Committee — Field Marshall Sir Richard Vincent (UKA)

Principal U.S. Military Training Centers

Army

Name, P.O. address	Zip	Nearest city	Name, P.O. address	Zip	Nearest city
Aberdeen Proving Ground, MD	21005	Aberdeen	Fort Leavenworth, KS	66027	Leavenworth
Carlisle Barracks, PA	17013	Carlisle	Fort Lee, VA	23801	Petersburg
Fort Benning, GA	31905	Columbus	Fort McClellan, AL	36205	Anniston
Fort Bliss, TX	79916	El Paso	Fort Monmouth, NJ	07703	Red Bank
Fort Bragg, NC	28307	Fayetteville	Fort Rucker, AL	36362	Dothan
Fort Devens, MA	01433	Ayer	Fort Sill, OK	73503	Lawton
Fort Dix, NJ	08640	Trenton	Fort Leonard Wood, MO	65473	Rolla
Fort Eustis, VA	23604	Newport News	Joint Readiness, Ft. Chaffee, AR	72905	Fort Smith
Fort Gordon, GA	30905	Augusta	National Training Center	92311	Barstow, CA
Fort Sam Houston, TX	78234	San Antonio	The Judge Advocate General		
Fort Huachuca, AZ	85613	Sierra Vista	School, VA	22901	Charlottesville
Fort Jackson, SC	29207	Columbia	U.S. Military Acad., NY	10996	West Point
Fort Knox, KY	40121	Louisville			

Navy

Name	Zip	Nearest city	Name	Zip	Nearest city
Atlantic Fleet	02841	Norfolk, VA	Naval Education & Training Ctr.	02841	Newport, RI
Pacific Fleet	92143	San Diego, CA	Naval Submarine School	06349	Groton, CT
Great Lakes, IL	60088	North Chicago	Naval Training Center	92133	San Diego, CA
Naval Air Training	78419	Corpus Christi,TX	Naval Training Center	32813	Orlando, FL

Marine Corps

Name, P.O. address	Zip	Nearest city	Name, P.O. address	Zip	Nearest city
MCB Camp Lejeune, NC	28542	Jacksonville	MCAS Cherry Point, NC	28533	Havelock
MCB Camp Pendleton, CA.	92055	Oceanside	MCAS El Toro, CA	92709	Santa Ana
MCAGCC Twentynine Palms, CA	92278	Palm Springs	MCAS New River, NC	28545	Jacksonville
			MCAS Kaneohe Bay, HI	96863	Kailua
MCCDC Quantico, VA.	22134	Quantico			
MCRD Parris Island, SC	29905	Beaufort	MCAS Beaufort, SC	29904	Beaufort
MCRD San Diego, CA.	92140	San Diego	MCAS Yuma, AZ	85369	Yuma
			MCMWTC Bridgeport, CA.	93517	Bridgeport

MCB = Marine Corps Base. MCCDC = Marine Corps Combat Development Command. MCAS = Marine Corps Air Station. MCRD = Marine Corps Recruit Depot. MCAGCC = Marine Corps Air-Ground Combat Center. MCMWTC = Marine Corps Mountain Warfare Training Center.

Air Force

Name, P.O. address	Zip	Nearest city	Name, P.O. address	Zip	Nearest city
Goodfellow AFB, TX	76908	San Angelo	Lackland AFB, TX	78236	San Antonio
Gunter AFB, AL	36114	Montgomery	Maxwell AFB, AL	36112	Montgomery
Keesler AFB, MS	39534	Biloxi	Sheppard AFB, TX	76311	Wichita Falls

All are Air Education and Training Command Bases.

Personal Salutes and Honors

The United States national salute, 21 guns, is also the salute to a national flag. The independence of the U.S. is commemorated by the salute to the Union — one gun for each state — fired at noon on July 4, at all military posts provided with suitable artillery.

A 21-gun salute on arrival and departure, with 4 ruffles and flourishes, is rendered to the president of the United States, to an ex-president, and to a president-elect. The national anthem or "Hail to the Chief," as appropriate, is played for the president, and the national anthem for the others. A 21-gun salute on arrival and departure, with 4 ruffles and flourishes, also is rendered to the sovereign or chief of state of a foreign country or a member of a reigning royal family; the national anthem of his or her country is played. The music is considered an inseparable part of the salute and immediately follows the ruffles and flourishes without pause. Regarding the Honors March, generals receive the "General's March," admirals receive the "Admiral's March," and all others receive the 32-bar medley of "The Stars and Stripes Forever."

Grade, title, or office	Salute — guns Arrive — Leave		Ruffles and flourishes	Music
Vice President of United States.	19		4	Hail, Columbia
Speaker of the House.	19		4	Honors March
American or foreign ambassador.	19		4	Nat. anthem of official
Premier or prime minister.	19		4	Nat. anthem of official
Secretary of Defense, Army, Navy, or Air Force	19	19	4	Honors March
Other Cabinet members, Senate President pro tempore, Governor, or Chief Justice of U.S.	19		4	Honors March
Chairman, Joint Chiefs of Staff.	19	19	4	
Army Chief of Staff, Chief of Naval Operations, Air Force Chief of Staff, Marine Commandant	19	19	4	Honors March
General of the Army, General of the Air Force, Fleet Admiral.	19	19	4	
Generals, Admirals	17	17	4	
Assistant secretaries of Defense, Army, Navy, or Air Force	17	17	4	Honors March
Chairman of a committee of Congress.	17		4	Honors March

Other salutes (on arrival only) include 15 guns, along with 3 ruffles and flourishes, for U.S. envoys or ministers and foreign envoys or ministers accredited to the U.S.; 15 guns, for a lieutenant general or vice admiral; 13 guns, along with 2 ruffles and flourishes, for a major general or rear admiral (upper half) and for U.S. ministers resident and ministers resident accredited to the U.S.; 11 guns, along with 1 ruffle and flourish, for a brigadier general or rear admiral (lower half) and for U.S. charges d'affaires and like officials accredited to the U.S.; and 11 guns, and no ruffles and flourishes, for consuls general accredited to the U.S.

Military Units, U.S. Army and Air Force

Army Units. Squad: In infantry usually 10 enlisted personnel under a staff sergeant. **Platoon:** In infantry 4 squads under a lieutenant. **Company:** Headquarters section and 4 platoons under a captain. (Company-size unit in the artillery is a battery; in the cavalry, a troop.) **Battalion:** Hdqts. and 4 or more companies under a lieutenant colonel. (Battalion-size unit in the cavalry is a squadron.) **Brigade:** Hdqts. and 3 or more battalions under a colonel. **Division:** Hdqts. and 3 brigades with artillery, combat support, and combat service support units under a major general. **Army Corps:** Two or more divisions with corps troops under a lieutenant general. **Field Army:** Hdqts. and two or more corps with field Army troops under a general.

Air Force Units. Flight: Numerically designated flights are the lowest level unit in the Air Force. They are used primarily where there is a need for small mission elements to be incorporated into an organized unit. **Squadron:** A squadron is the basic unit in the Air Force. It is used to designate the mission units in operational commands. **Group:** The group is a flexible unit composed of two or more squadrons whose functions may be operational, support, or administrative in nature. **Wing:** An operational wing normally has two or more assigned mission squadrons in an area such as combat, flying training, or airlift. **Numbered Air Forces:** Normally an operationally oriented agency, the numbered air force is designed for the control of two or more air divisions or units of comparable strength. It is a flexible organization and may be of any size. Its wings may be assigned to air divisions or directly under the numbered air force. **Major Command:** A major subdivision of the Air Force that is assigned a major segment of the USAF mission.

The Federal Service Academies

U.S. Military Academy, West Point, NY. Founded 1802. Awards BS degree and Army commission for a 5-year service obligation. For admissions information, write Admissions Office, USMA, West Point, NY 10996.

U.S. Naval Academy, Annapolis, MD. Founded 1845. Awards BS degree and Navy or Marine Corps commission for a 6-year service obligation. For admissions information, write Dean of Admissions, Naval Academy, Annapolis, MD 21402.

U.S. Air Force Academy, Colorado Springs, CO. Founded 1954. Awards BS degree and Air Force commission for a 6-year service obligation. For admissions information, write Registrar, U.S. Air Force Academy, CO 80840.

U.S. Coast Guard Academy, New London, CT. Founded 1876. Awards BS degree and Coast Guard commission for a 5-year service obligation. For admissions information, write Director of Admissions, Coast Guard Academy, New London, CT 06320.

U.S. Merchant Marine Academy, Kings Point, NY. Founded 1943. Awards BS degree, a license as a deck, engineer, or dual officer, and a U.S. Naval Reserve commission. Service obligations vary according to options taken by the graduate. For admissions information, write Admission Office, U.S. Merchant Marine Academy, Kings Point, NY 11024.

U.S. Army and Air Force Insignia and Chevrons

Source: Dept. of the Army, Dept. of the Air Force, U.S. Dept. of Defense

Army

General of the Armies

General John J. Pershing, the only person to have held this rank, was authorized to prescribe his own insignia, but never wore in excess of four stars. The rank originally was established by Congress for George Washington in 1799, and he was promoted to the rank by joint resolution of Congress, approved by Pres. Gerald Ford, Oct. 19, 1976.

General of the Army. . . Five silver stars fastened together in a circle and the coat of arms of the United States in gold color metal with shield and crest enameled.

General	Four silver stars
Lieutenant General.	Three silver stars
Major General	Two silver stars
Brigadier General.	One silver star
Colonel	Silver eagle
Lieutenant Colonel	Silver oak leaf
Major	Gold oak leaf
Captain	Two silver bars
First Lieutenant	One silver bar
Second Lieutenant.	One gold bar

Warrant Officers

Grade Four—Silver bar with 4 enamel black squares
Grade Three—Silver bar with 3 enamel black squares
Grade Two—Silver bar with 2 enamel black squares
Grade One—Silver bar with 1 enamel black square

Noncommissioned Officers

Sergeant Major of the Army (E-9). Same as Command Sergeant Major (below) but with 2 stars. Also wears distinctive red and white shield on lapel.

Command Sergeant Major (E-9). Three chevrons above 3 arcs with a 5-pointed star with a wreath around the star between the chevrons and arcs.

Sergeant Major (E-9). Three chevrons above 3 arcs with a 5-pointed star between the chevrons and arcs.

First Sergeant (E-8). Three chevrons above 3 arcs with a lozenge between the chevrons and arcs.

Master Sergeant (E-8). Three chevrons above 3 arcs.

Sergeant First Class (E-7). Three chevrons above 2 arcs.

Staff Sergeant (E-6). Three chevrons above 1 arc.

Sergeant (E-5). Three chevrons.

Corporal (E-4). Two chevrons.

Specialists

Specialist (E-4). Eagle device only.

Other enlisted

Private First Class (E-3). One chevron above one arc.

Private (E-2). One chevron.

Private (E-1). None.

Air Force

Insignia for Air Force officers are identical to those of the Army. Insignia for enlisted personnel are worn on both sleeves and consist of a star and an appropriate number of rockers. Chevrons appear above 5 rockers for the top 3 noncommissioned officer ranks, as follows (in ascending order): Master Sergeant, 1 chevron; Senior Master Sergeant, 2 chevrons; and Chief Master Sergeant, 3 chevrons. The insignia of the Chief Master Sergeant of the Air Force has 3 chevrons and a wreath around the star design.

U.S. Navy, Marine Corps, and Coast Guard Insignia

Source: Dept. of the Navy, U.S. Dept. of Defense

Navy

Stripes and corps device are of gold embroidery.

Stripes

Fleet Admiral.	1 two inch with 4 one-half inch
Admiral.	1 two inch with 3 one-half inch
Vice Admiral	1 two inch with 2 one-half inch
Rear Admiral (upper half)	1 two inch with 1 one-half inch
Rear Admiral (lower half).	1 two inch
Captain.	4 one-half inch
Commander	3 one-half inch
Lieut. Commander.	2 one-half inch with 1 one-quarter inch between
Lieutenant.	2 one-half inch
Lieutenant (j.g.).	1 one-half inch with one-quarter inch above
Ensign	1 one-half inch

Warrant Officers—One ½" broken with ½" intervals of blue as follows:

Warrant Officer W-4 — 1 break
Warrant Officer W-3 — 2 breaks, 2" apart
Warrant Officer W-2 — 3 breaks, 2" apart

The breaks are symmetrically centered on outer face of the sleeve.

Enlisted personnel (noncommissioned petty officers)—A rating badge worn on the upper left arm, consisting of a spread eagle, appropriate number of chevrons, and centered specialty mark.

Marine Corps

Marine Corps and Army officer insignia are similar. Marine Corps and Army enlisted insignia, although basically similar, differ in color and design, and there are fewer Marine Corps subdivisions. The Marine Corps' distinctive cap and collar ornament is a combination of the American eagle, a globe, and an anchor.

Coast Guard

Coast Guard insignia follow Navy custom, with certain minor changes such as the officer cap insignia. The Coast Guard shield is worn on both sleeves of officers and on the right sleeve of all enlisted personnel.

U.S. Army Personnel on Active Duty[1]

Source: Department of the Army, U.S. Dept. of Defense

Date[2]	Total strength	Commissioned officers				Warrant officers		Enlisted personnel		
		Total	Male	Female[3]	Male[4]	Female	Total	Male	Female
1940	267,767	17,563	16,624	939	763	—	249,441	249,441	—
1942	3,074,184	203,137	190,662	12,475	3,285	—	2,867,762	2,867,762	—
1943	6,993,102	557,657	521,435	36,222	21,919	0	6,413,526	6,358,200	55,325
1944	7,992,868	740,077	692,351	47,726	36,893	10	7,215,888	7,144,601	71,287
1945	8,266,373	835,403	772,511	62,892	56,216	44	7,374,710	7,283,930	90,780
1946	1,889,690	257,300	240,643	16,657	9,826	18	1,622,546	1,605,847	16,699
1950	591,487	67,784	63,375	4,409	4,760	22	518,921	512,370	6,551
1955	1,107,606	111,347	106,173	5,174	10,552	48	985,659	977,943	7,716
1960	871,348	91,056	86,832	4,224	10,141	39	770,112	761,833	8,279
1965	967,049	101,812	98,029	3,783	10,285	23	854,929	846,409	8,520
1970	1,319,735	143,704	138,469	5,235	23,005	13	1,153,013	1,141,537	11,476
1975	781,316	89,756	85,184	4,572	13,214	22	678,324	640,621	37,703
1980 (Sept. 30)	772,661	85,339	77,843	7,496	13,265	113	673,944	612,593	61,351
1985 (Sept. 30)	776,244	94,103	83,563	10,540	15,296	288	666,557	598,639	67,918
1990 (Mar. 31)	746,220	91,330	79,520	11,810	15,177	470	639,713	567,015	72,698
1992 (Mar. 31)	661,391	85,953	74,326	11,627	13,840	494	561,104	496,335	64,769
1993 (Mar. 31)	590,324	76,714	66,336	10,378	12,359	441	500,810	443,942	56,868
1994	553,627	74,956	64,281	10,675	12,448	535	465,688	405,664	60,024
1995	521,036	72,646	62,250	10,396	12,053	599	435,807	377,832	57,975

(1) Represents strength of the active Army, including Philippine Scouts, retired Regular Army personnel on extended active duty, and National Guard and Reserve personnel on extended active duty; excludes U.S. Military Academy cadets, contract surgeons, and National Guard and Reserve personnel not on extended active duty.
(2) June 30, unless otherwise noted; data for 1940 to 1946 include personnel in the Army Air Forces and its predecessors (Air Service and Air Corps).
(3) Includes women doctors, dentists, and Medical Service Corps officers for 1946 and subsequent years, women in the Army Nurse Corps for all years, and the Women's Army Corps and Women's Medical Specialists Corps (dietitians, physical therapists, and occupational specialists) for 1943 and subsequent years.
(4) Act of Congress approved Apr. 27, 1926, directed the appointment as warrant officers of field clerks still in active service. Includes flight officers as follows: 1943, 5,700; 1944, 13,615; 1945, 31,117; 1946, 2,580.

U.S. Navy Personnel on Active Duty

Date	Officers	Nurses	Enlisted	Officer Candidates	Total
1940 (June)	13,162	442	144,824	2,569	160,997
1945 (June)	320,293	11,086	2,988,207	61,231	3,380,817
1950 (June)	42,687	1,964	331,860	5,037	381,538
1960 (June)	67,456	2,103	544,040	4,385	617,984
1970 (June)	78,488	2,273	605,899	6,000	692,660
1980 (June)[1]	63,100	—	464,100	—	527,200
1990 (Sept.)	74,429	—	530,133	—	604,562
1992 (Mar.)	71,826	—	500,459	—	572,285
1993 (Mar.)	66,787	—	445,409	—	512,196
1994 (Apr.)	64,430	—	418,378	—	482,808
1995 (May)	61,075	—	402,626	—	463,701

(1) Starting in 1980, "Nurses" are included with "Officers," and "Officer Candidates" are included with "Enlisted."

U.S. Marine Corps Personnel on Active Duty

(midyear personnel figures)

Year	Officers	Enlisted	Total	Year	Officers	Enlisted	Total	Year	Officers	Enlisted	Total
1940	1,800	26,545	28,345	1970	24,941	234,796	259,737	1993	18,878	161,205	180,083
1945	37,067	437,613	474,680	1980	18,198	170,271	188,469	1994	18,430	159,949	178,379
1950	7,254	67,025	74,279	1990	19,958	176,694	196,652	1995	18,017	153,929	171,946
1960	16,203	154,418	170,621								

U.S. Air Force Personnel on Active Duty

Year[1]	Strength	Year[1]	Strength	Year[1]	Strength	Year[1]	Strength
1907	3	1941	152,125	1950	411,277	1990	535,233
1918	195,023	1942	764,415	1960	814,213	1991	510,432
1920	9,050	1943	2,197,114	1970	791,078	1992	470,315
1930	13,531	1944	2,372,292	1980	557,969	1993	444,351
1940	51,165	1945	2,282,259	1986	608,200	1994	426,327
						1995	400,051

(1) Prior to 1947, data are for U.S. Army Air Corps and Air Service of the Signal Corps.

U.S. Coast Guard Personnel on Active Duty

Year	Total	Officers	Cadets	Enlisted	Year	Total	Officers	Cadets	Enlisted
1970	37,689	5,512	653	31,524	1986 . . .	37,284	6,577	754	29,953
1975	36,788	5,630	1,177	29,981	1987 . . .	38,576	6,644	859	31,073
1980	39,381	6,463	877	32,041	1988 . . .	37,723	6,530	887	30,306
1981	39,760	6,519	981	32,260	1990 . . .	37,308	6,475	820	29,860
1982	38,248	6,431	902	30,915	1991 . . .	38,280	7,095	900	30,285
1983	39,708	6,535	811	32,362	1992 . . .	39,185	7,348	919	30,918
1984	38,705	6,790	759	31,156	1993 . . .	38,832	7,724	691	30,417
1985	38,595	6,775	733	31,087	1994 . . .	37,284	7,401	881	29,002

Defense Contracts
Source: U.S. Dept. of Defense
(in thousands of dollars)

The 50 companies (including their subsidiaries) receiving the largest dollar volume of prime contract awards from the Department of Defense during fiscal 1994.

Company	Amount	Company	Amount	Company	Amount
McDonnell Douglas	$9,266,462	TRW	848,045	Allied Signal	453,338
Lockheed	6,518,209	Fulcrum II Ltd. Prtnrshp.	797,525	Johns Hopkins University	442,341
Northrop-Grumman	5,202,162	GTE	788,301	Olin	436,358
Martin Marietta	3,133,682	E-Systems	769,395	Mitre	425,274
General Motors	3,040,540	Texas Instruments	690,486	Alliant Techsystems	421,849
General Dynamics	2,800,828	Unisys	639,587	Oshkosh Truck	409,359
Raytheon	2,737,562	ITT	608,651	NV Kon Nederlandse Pet.	351,104
General Electric	2,704,796	Computer Sciences	589,159	Foundation Health	350,586
United Technologies	2,677,444	FMC	582,256	Johnson Controls	340,120
Loral	1,681,127	IBM	562,414	Gencorp	331,339
Litton Industries	1,575,547	AT&T	537,587	CAE	330,025
Westinghouse Electric	1,357,125	Exxon	530,368	Boeing Sikorsky LHX Program Office	327,548
Textron	1,235,577	Carlyle Prtnrs. Lev. Cap.	528,049		
Boeing	1,194,641	Tenneco	495,366	Federal Express	327,175
Rockwell International	1,061,583	Dyncorp	488,781	Harris	323,665
Avondale Industries	902,098	Tracor	465,146	MIT	318,409
Science Application Intl.	867,683	Black & Decker	453,653	Renco Group	290,521

Women in the Armed Forces
Source: U.S. Dept. of Defense

Women in the Army, Navy, Air Force, Marines, and Coast Guard are fully integrated with male personnel. Expansion of military women's programs began in the Department of Defense in fiscal year 1973.

Admission of women to the service academies began in the fall of 1976.

Under rules instituted in 1993, women are allowed to fly combat aircraft and to serve aboard warships. Women are still restricted from service in ground combat units.

Between Apr. 1993 and July 1994, almost 260,000 positions in the armed forces had been opened to women. In July 1994, 80.2% of all jobs and 92% of all career fields in the military had been opened to women. As of June 30, 1995, women made up 12.6% of the armed forces.

Women Active Duty Troops in 1995

Service	% Women
Army	13.2
Navy	12.0
Marines	4.7
Air Force	15.8
Coast Guard (1994)	8.7

Women on Active Duty, All Services*: 1973-95

Year	% Women	Year	% Women
1973	2.5	1987	10.2
1975	4.6	1993	11.6
1981	8.9	1995	12.6

*Not including the Coast Guard, which is a part of the Dept. of Transportation.

African American Service in U.S. Wars

American Revolution. About 5,000 blacks served in the Continental Army, mostly in integrated units, some in all-black combat units.

Civil War. Some 200,000 blacks served in the Union Army; 38,000 were killed, 22 won the Medal of Honor (the nation's highest award).

Word War I. About 367,000 blacks served in the armed forces, 100,000 in France.

World War II. More than 1 million blacks served in the armed forces; all-black fighter and bomber AAF units and infantry divisions gave distinguished service. (By 1954, the armed forces were completely desegregated.)

Vietnam War. 274,937 blacks served in the armed forces (1965-74); 5,681 were killed in combat.

Persian Gulf War. About 104,000 blacks served in the Kuwaiti theater—20% of U.S. soldiers, compared with 8.7% for World War II and 9.8% for Vietnam.

Veteran Population
Source: U.S. Dept. of Veterans Affairs; as of July 1994
(in thousands)

Total veterans in civilian life[a,b]	**26,487**
Total wartime veterans	**20,425**
Total Persian Gulf War	1,236
Persian Gulf War with service in Vietnam era	204
Persian Gulf War with no prior wartime service	1,032
Total Vietnam era	8,281
Vietnam era with service in Korean conflict	533
Vietnam era with no prior wartime service	7,748
Total Korean conflict	4,597
Korean conflict with service in WWII	765
Korean conflict with no prior wartime service	3,832
World War II	7,795
World War I	19
Total peacetime veterans	**6,072**
Total post-Vietnam era	3,048
Service between Korean conflict and Vietnam era only	2,859
Other peacetime	166

Note: Detail may not add to total shown due to rounding. (a) The category "wartime veterans" equals the sum of Persian Gulf War (no service in Vietnam era), Vietnam era (no service in Korean conflict), Korean conflict (no service in World War II), World War II, and World War I. The data refer only to veterans living in the U.S. and Puerto Rico since data on veterans living elsewhere are not available. (b) There are an indeterminate number of Mexican Border period veterans, 34 of whom were receiving benefits in July 1995.

Veterans Compensation and Pension Case Payments

Fiscal year	Living veteran cases	Deceased veteran cases	Total cases	Total disbursement (dollars)	Fiscal year	Living veteran cases	Deceased veteran cases	Total cases	Total disbursement (dollars)
1900	752,510	241,019	993,529	$138,462,130	1970	3,127,338	1,487,176	4,614,514	$5,113,649,490
1910	602,622	318,461	921,083	159,974,056	1980	3,195,395	1,450,785	4,646,180	11,045,412,000
1920	419,627	349,916	769,543	316,418,029	1990	2,746,329	837,596	3,583,925	15,535,069,000
1930	542,610	298,223	840,833	418,432,808	1991 ...	2,709,500	799,677	3,509,177	15,975,440,000
1940	610,122	239,176	849,298	429,138,465	1992 ...	2,673,833	753,981	3,427,814	16,145,203,000
1950	2,368,238	658,123	3,026,361	2,009,462,298	1993 ...	2,660,030	713,758	3,373,788	16,881,938,000
1960	3,008,935	950,802	3,959,737	3,314,761,383	1994 ...	2,658,704	683,200	3,341,904	18,256,764,000

Active Duty U.S. Military Personnel Strengths, Worldwide

Source: U.S. Dept. of Defense

(as of Sept. 30, 1994)

U.S. Territories & Special Locations
U.S., 48 contiguous states	1,073,309
Alaska	19,049
Hawaii	42,161
Guam	6,319
Johnston Atoll	289
Puerto Rico	2,782
Transients	35,449
Afloat	144,483
Total[1]	**1,323,896**

Western & Southern Europe
Belgium	1,670
Germany	87,955
Greece	492
Greenland	122
Iceland	2,474
Italy	12,743
Macedonia	535
Netherlands	826
Norway	196
Portugal	1,173
Spain	2,790
Turkey	4,077
United Kingdom	13,781
Afloat	8,528
Total[1]	**137,575**

East Asia & Pacific
Australia	330
Japan	45,398
Korea, South	36,796
Philippines	232
Singapore	165
Thailand	102
Afloat	15,011
Total[1]	**98,269**

North Africa, Middle East & South Asia
Bahrain	444
Diego Garcia	888
Egypt	1,146
Kuwait	269
Saudi Arabia	710
Afloat	4,595
Total[1]	**8,322**

Sub-Saharan Africa
Somalia	933
Afloat	3,473
Total[1]	**4,752**

Other Western Hemisphere
Bermuda	466
Canada	282
Cuba (Guantánamo)	3,760
Haiti	17,495
Honduras	248
Panama	9,479
Suriname	168
Afloat	3,865
Total[1]	**36,288**
Total Worldwide	**1,610,490**

(1) Area totals include countries with fewer than 100 assigned U.S. military members.

Estimates of Total Dollar Costs of American Wars

Source: *The Military Budget and National Economic Priorities,* revised and updated by James L. Clayton

(millions of dollars, except percent)

Item	World War II	Vietnam Conflict	Korean Conflict	World War I	Civil War: Union	Civil War: Confederacy	Spanish American War	American Revolution	War of 1812	Mexican War
Original increment, direct costs:[1]										
Current dollars	360,000	140,600	50,000	32,700	2,300	1,000	270	100-140	89	82
Constant (1967) dollars .	816,300	148,800	69,300	100,000	8,500	3,700	1,100	400-680	170	300
Percent 1 year's GNP ..	188	14	15	43	74	123	2	10	14	4
Service-connected veterans' benefits[2]	96,666	32,288	19,512	19,580	3,290	—	2,111	28	20	26
Interest, pmts. on war loans[3]	(5)	(5)	(5)	11,000	1,200	(5)	60	20	14	10
Current cost to 1990[4]	466,000	179,000	72,000	63,500	6,790	(5)	2,441	170	120	120

Note: The U.S. Department of Defense reported that, as of 1991, the total cost of the **Persian Gulf War** was $61.1 billion; this figure includes $7.4 billion from the U.S. and $53.7 billion in contributions from other countries.
(1) Figures are rounded and taken from Claudia D. Goldin, *Encyclopedia of American Economic History.* (2) Total cost to Oct. 1, 1990. For World War I and later wars, benefits are actual service-connected figures from *Annual Report* of Veterans Administration. For earlier wars, service-connected veterans' benefits are estimated at 40% of total, the approximate ratio of service-connected to total benefits since World War I. (3) Total cost to 1990. Interest payments are a very rough approximation based on the percentage of the original costs of each war financed by money creation and debt, the difference between the level of public debt at the beginning of the war and at its end, and the approximate time required to pay off the war debts. (4) Figures are rounded estimates. (5) Unknown.

The Medal of Honor

The Medal of Honor is the highest military award for bravery that can be given to any individual in the United States. The first Army Medals were awarded on Mar. 25, 1863, and the first Navy Medals went to sailors and Marines on Apr. 3, 1863.

The Medal of Honor, established by Joint Resolution of Congress, July 12, 1862 (amended by Acts of Congress, July 9, 1918, and July 25, 1963), is awarded in the name of Congress to a person who, while a member of the Armed Forces, distinguishes himself or herself conspicuously by gallantry and intrepidity at the risk of life above and beyond the call of duty while engaged in an action against any enemy of the United States; while engaged in military operations involving conflict with an opposing foreign force; or while serving with friendly foreign forces engaged in an armed conflict against an opposing armed force in which the United States is not a belligerent party. The deed performed must have been one of personal bravery or self-sacrifice so conspicuous

as to clearly distinguish the individual above his or her comrades and must have involved risk of life. Incontestable proof of the performance of service is required, and each recommendation for award of this decoration is considered on the standard of extraordinary merit.

Prior to World War I, the 2,625 Army Medal of Honor awards up to that time were reviewed to determine which past awards met new stringent criteria. The Army removed 911 names from the list, most of them former members of a volunteer infantry group during the Civil War who had been induced to extend their enlistments when they were promised the medal.

Since that review, Medals of Honor have been awarded in the following numbers:

World War I.	 96	Korean War	 131
World War II	... 432	Vietnam War	... 238
		Somalia	 2

For Further Information on the U.S. Armed Forces

Army — Office of the Chief of Public Affairs, 1500 Army Pentagon, Wash., DC 20310-1500.

Navy — Chief of Information, Dept. of the Navy, Wash., DC 20350-2000.

Air Force — Office of Public Affairs, Air Force, 1690 Pentagon, Wash., DC 20330-1690.

Marine Corps — Commandant of the Marine Corps (Code PA), Headquarters, Marine Corps, Wash., DC 20380-0001.

Coast Guard — Commandant (G-CP), U.S. Coast Guard, 2100 Second St. SW, Wash., DC 20593-0001.

Armed Forces per 1,000 Persons, 1993[1]

Source: U.S. Arms Control and Disarmament Agency

Argentina	1.9	India	1.4	Pakistan	4.6
Australia	3.8	Indonesia	1.4	Philippines	1.5
Austria	NA	Iran	8.5	Poland	4.7
Belgium	7.0	Iraq	21.2	Portugal	6.5
Bolivia	4.2	Israel	36.8	Romania	7.2
Brazil	1.9	Italy	7.8	Russia	15.1
Bulgaria	5.9	Japan	1.9	Singapore	19.8
Canada	2.7	Jordan	26.2	South Africa	1.7
Chile	6.7	Korea, North	53.0	Spain	5.2
China	2.6	Korea, South	16.8	Sweden	5.0
Colombia	4.0	Kuwait	7.1	Switzerland	4.4
Cuba	16.0	Lebanon	10.4	Syria	28.5
Denmark	5.2	Libya	17.4	Taiwan	21.0
Egypt	7.1	Mexico	1.9	Thailand	5.0
El Salvador	8.7	Mongolia	7.6	Turkey	11.3
Finland	6.1	Morocco	7.0	United Kingdom	4.7
France	8.8	Netherlands	5.6	Venezuela	3.7
Germany	4.9	Nicaragua	3.8	Vietnam	11.9
Greece	20.3	Norway	9.8		
Hungary	NA	Oman	21.3		

(1) Includes active-duty personnel performing national security functions. Does not include reserves or paramilitary forces. NA=not available.

Nations With Largest Armed Forces, by Active-Duty Troop Strength, 1994

Source: *The Military Balance, 1994-95* (Internatl. Institute for Strategic Studies, published by Brassey's U.K.)

	Troop strength				Navy			
	Active troops	Reserve troops	Defense expend.	Tanks (MBT)	Cruisers/ Frigates/	Sub-	Combat aircraft	
	(thousands)		($bil)[1]	(army only)	Destroyers	marines	FGA (air force only)	fighters
1 **China**	2,930.0	1,200+	2.7[2]	7,500-8,000	37F/18D	50	500	4000 est.
2 **Russia**	1,714.0	20,000	NA	19,500	25C/112F/22D*	185	775	625
3 **U.S.**	1,650.5	2,048.0	280.6[3]	14,524	34C/51F/41D*	104	53 tactical ftr. sqn	
4 India	1,265.0	300.0	7.0[2]	3,400	18F/5D*	15	407	364
5 N. Korea	1,128.0	540.0	5.3[2]	3,700	3F	25	294	360
6 S. Korea	633.0	4,500.0	11.4[2]	1,900	32F/8D	2	238	96
7 Pakistan	587.0	313.0	3.3[2]	1,950+	6F/3D	6	126	244
8 Vietnam	572.0	3-4,000	0.7	1,300	7F	-	65	125
9 **Ukraine**	517.0	1,000.0	5.3	5,380	-	-	185	522
10 Iran	513.0	350.0	2.3	1,245	3F/2D	2	150	115
11 Turkey	503.8	952.3	6.3	4,919	16F/5D	15	14 sqn	6 sqn
12 Egypt	440.0	254.0	2.1	3,234	4F/1D	3	121	340
13 Taiwan	425.0	1,657.5	10.0	309	11F/22D	4	393 total FGA/ftr.	
14 **France**	409.6	339.8	34.4[2]	998	1C/36F/4D*	18	9 sqn	9 sqn
15 Syria	408.0	400.0	2.2	4,500	2F	1	154	280
16 Iraq	382.0	650.0	2.6[2]	2,200	1F	-	130 est.	180 est.
17 Germany	367.3	442.7	35.2	2,855	8F/4D	20	8 sqn	7 sqn
18 Brazil	336.8	1,115.0	4.3	†	14F/6D*	4	74	16
19 Italy	322.3	584.0	NA	1,210	1C/23F/4D*	9	8 sqn	7 sqn
20 Myanmar	286.0	NA	1.0[4]	56	-	-	24	36
21 Poland	283.6	465.5	2.2[2]	2,110	1F/1D	3	118	256
22 Indonesia	276.0	400.0	1.8	†	6F	2	39	14
23 Thailand	256.0	200.0	2.9	253+	9F	-	22	37
24 **U.K.**	254.3	376.2	41.7	921	23F/12D*	17	11 sqn	6 sqn
25 Japan	237.7	47.9	5.9	1,160	55F/7D	17	50	280
26 Romania	230.5	427.0	1.7	2,395	5F/1D	1	189	181
27 Spain	206.5	498.0	7.7[2]	1,012	16F*	8	4 sqn	8 sqn
28 Morocco	195.5	150.0	NA	524	1F	-	30	15
29 Mexico	175.0	300.0	NA	-	2F/3D	-	-	-
30 Israel	172.0	430.0	6.9	3,895	-	3	442 total FGA/ftr.	

Bold face denotes nations with known strategic nuclear capability; MBT=main battle tank; FGA=fighter, ground attack; sqn= squadron (18-24 aircraft); †= light tanks only; * denotes navies with aircraft carriers, as follows: Russia 2, USA 11, India 2, France 2, Brazil 1, Italy 1, U.K. 3, Spain 1. (1) 1992 figures unless otherwise noted. (2) 1993. (3) 1994. (4) 1991. NA = not available.

Nuclear Arms Treaties and Negotiations: An Historical Overview

Aug. 5, 1963—Limited Test Ban Treaty signed in Moscow by the U.S., USSR, and Great Britain; prohibited testing of nuclear weapons in space, above ground, and under water.

Jan. 27, 1967—Outer Space Treaty banned the introduction of nuclear weapons and other weapons of mass destruction into space.

July 1, 1968—Nuclear Nonproliferation Treaty, with U.S., USSR, and Great Britain as major signers, limited the spread of military nuclear technology by agreement not to assist nonnuclear nations in getting or making nuclear weapons. Extended indefinitely, May 11, 1995.

May 26, 1972—Strategic Arms Limitation Treaty (SALT I) signed in Moscow by U.S. and USSR. An interim short-term agreement putting a ceiling on numbers of offensive nuclear weapons. The treaty imposed a 5-year freeze on testing and deployment of intercontinental ballistic missiles (ICBMs) and submarine-launched ballistic missiles (SLBMs). SALT I was in effect until Oct. 3, 1977. In the area of defensive nuclear weapons, the separate **ABM Treaty** limited antiballistic missiles to 2 sites of 100 antiballistic missile launchers in each country (amended in 1974 to one site in each country).

July 3, 1974—ABM Treaty Revision (protocol on antiballistic missile systems) and **Threshold Test Ban Treaty** on limiting underground testing of nuclear weapons to 150 kilotons were signed by U.S. and USSR in Moscow.

Sept. 1977—U.S. and USSR agreed to continue to abide by SALT I, despite its expiration date.

June 18, 1979—SALT II, signed in Vienna by the U.S. and USSR, constrained offensive nuclear weapons, limiting each side to 2,400 missile launchers and heavy bombers with that ceiling to apply until Jan. 1, 1985. The treaty also set a subceiling of 1,320 ICBMs and SLBMs with multiple warheads on each side. Although approved by the U.S. Senate Foreign Relations Committee, the treaty never reached the Senate floor for ratification because Pres. Jimmy Carter withdrew his support for the treaty following the Dec. 1979 invasion of Afghanistan by Soviet troops.

Dec. 8, 1987—Intermediate-Range Nuclear Forces (INF) Treaty signed in Washington, D.C., by USSR leader Mikhail Gorbachev and U.S. Pres. Ronald Reagan, eliminating all U.S. and Soviet intermediate- and shorter-range nuclear missiles from Europe and Asia; ratified with conditions by U.S. Senate on May 27, 1988.

July 31, 1991—Strategic Arms Reduction Treaty (START I) signed in Moscow by Soviet Pres. Mikhail Gorbachev and U.S. Pres. George Bush to reduce strategic offensive arms by approximately 30% in 3 phases over 7 years. START I was the first treaty to mandate reductions by the superpowers. The treaty was approved by the U.S. Senate Oct. 1, 1992. With the breakup of the Soviet Union in Dec. 1991, 4 former Soviet republics became independent nations with strategic nuclear weapons on their territory—Russia, Ukraine, Kazakhstan, and Belarus. The last 3 agreed in principle in 1992 to transfer their nuclear weapons to Russia and ratify START I. The Russian Supreme Soviet voted to ratify Nov. 4, 1992, but Russia decided not to provide the instruments of ratification until Ukraine, Kazakhstan, and Belarus each ratified START I and acceded to the Nuclear Nonproliferation Treaty (NPT) as nonnuclear nations. By late 1993, Belarus and Kazakhstan had ratified START I and acceded to the nonproliferation treaty. In Feb. 1994, Ukraine ratified START I and subsequently acceded to the NPT. The treaty entered into force on Dec. 5, 1994.

Jan. 3, 1993—START II signed in Moscow by U.S. Pres. George Bush and Russian Pres. Boris Yeltsin. Potentially the broadest disarmament pact in history, it called for both sides to reduce their long-range nuclear arsenals to about one-third of their then-current levels within a decade and would entirely eliminate land-based multiple-warhead missiles. START II required ratification only by the U.S. Senate and the legislature of Russia (under the guidelines for START I finalization, the only remaining nuclear republic of the former Soviet Union).

Monthly Military Pay Scale

Source: U.S. Dept. of Defense; effective Jan. 1, 1995

Rank/Grade	Years of Service						
	2	4	8	12	16	20	26
General—0-10	$7,223.70	$7,223.70	$7,223.70	$7,916.70	$8,482.80	$9,016.80	$9,018.80
Lt. General—0-9	6,346.50	6,481.80	6,646.50	6,923.10	7,501.20	7,916.70	8,482.80
Major General—0-8	5,769.60	5,906.40	6,346.50	6,646.50	6,923.10	7,501.20	7,686.00
Brig. General—0-7	4,971.00	4,971.00	5,193.90	5,494.80	6,346.50	6,783.00	6,783.00
Colonel—0-6	3,790.20	4,038.60	4,038.60	4,038.60	4,838.30	5,193.90	5,959.50
Lt. Colonel—0-5	3,239.70	3,463.80	3,463.80	3,760.80	4,313.10	4,698.60	4,862.70
Major—0-4	2,832.00	3,021.00	3,212.70	3,624.90	3,956.70	4,065.60	4,065.60
Captain—0-3	2,416.50	2,858.10	3,102.30	3,432.00	3,516.30	3,516.30	3,516.30
1st Lt.—0-2	2,058.00	2,556.00	2,608.80	2,608.80	2,608.80	2,608.80	2,608.80
2d Lt.—0-1	1,703.10	2,058.00	2,058.00	2,058.00	2,058.00	2,058.00	2,058.00
Chief Warrant—W-4	2,362.50	2,416.50	2,637.60	2,940.60	3,185.10	3,375.90	3,760.80
Warrant Officer—W-1	1,674.30	1,814.10	1,977.60	2,143.20	2,307.30	2,472.90	2,472.90
Sgt. Major—E-9	0.00	0.00	0.00	2,619.00	2,739.90	2,855.70	3,297.90
Master Sgt.—E-8	0.00	0.00	2,148.00	2,268.00	2,388.30	2,502.90	2,945.10
Sgt. 1st class—E-7	1,619.10	1,737.90	1,854.30	1,973.40	2,121.00	2,208.30	2,649.90
Staff Sgt.—E-6	1,406.40	1,527.30	1,641.60	1,789.50	1,905.30	1,934.10	1,934.10
Sergeant—E-5	1,232.40	1,348.50	1,495.80	1,612.20	1,641.60	1,641.60	1,641.60
Corporal—E-4	1,115.40	1,272.00	1,322.40	1,322.40	1,322.40	1,322.40	1,322.40
Pvt. 1st class—E-3	1,049.70	1,134.60	1,134.60	1,134.60	1,134.60	1,134.60	1,134.60
Private—E-2	957.60	957.60	957.60	957.60	957.60	957.60	957.60
Recruit—E-1	854.40	854.40	854.40	854.40	854.40	854.40	854.40

Chairmen of the Joint Chiefs of Staff

Gen. of the Army Omar N. Bradley, USA 8/16/49–8/14/ 53
Adm. Arthur W. Radford, USN 8/15/53– 8/14/ 57
Gen. Nathan F. Twining, USAF ... 8/15/57 – 9/30/ 60
Gen. Lyman L. Lemnitzer, USA .. 10/1/60 – 10/30/62
Gen. Maxwell D. Taylor, USA .... 10/1/62 – 7/3/64
Gen. Earle G. Wheeler, USA ..... 7/3/64 – 7/2/70

Adm. Thomas H. Moorer, USN ... 7/3/70 – 6/30/74
Gen. George S. Brown, USAF .... 7/1/74 – 6/20/78
Gen. David C. Jones, USAF ..... 6/21/78 – 6/18/82
Gen. John W. Vessey Jr., USA ... 6/18/82 – 9/30/85
Adm. William J. Crowe, Jr., USN . 10/1/85 – 9/30/89
Gen. Colin L. Powell, USA ...... 10/1/89 – 9/30/93
Gen. John M. Shalikashvili, USA . 10/1/93 –

Casualties in Principal Wars of the U.S.

Source: U.S. Dept. of Defense

Data prior to World War I are based on incomplete records in many cases. Casualty data are confined to dead and wounded personnel and therefore exclude personnel captured or missing in action who were subsequently returned to military control. Dash (—) indicates information is not available.

War	Branch of service	Number serving	Casualties Battle deaths	Other deaths	Wounds not mortal[7]	Total
Revolutionary War	**Total**	—	**4,435**	—	**6,188**	—
1775-83	Army	184,000	4,044	—	6,004	—
	Navy	to	342	—	114	—
	Marines	250,000	49	—	70	—
War of 1812	**Total**	**286,730[8]**	**2,260**	—	**4,505**	**6,765**
1812-15	Army	—	1,950	—	4,000	5,950
	Navy	—	265	—	439	704
	Marines	—	45	—	66	111
Mexican War	**Total**	**78,718[8]**	**1,733**	**11,550**	**4,152**	**17,435**
1846-48	Army	—	1,721	11,500	4,102	17,373
	Navy	—	1	—	3	4
	Marines	—	11	—	47	58
Civil War	**Total**	**2,213,363[8]**	**140,414**	**224,097**	**281,881**	**646,392**
Union forces	Army	2,128,948	138,154	221,374	280,040	639,568
1861-65	Navy	—	2,112	2,411	1,710	6,233
	Marines	84,415	148	312	131	591
Confederate forces	**Total**	—	**74,524**	**59,297**	—	**133,821**
(estimate)[1]	Army	600,000	—	—	—	—
1863-66	Navy	to	—	—	—	—
	Marines	1,500,000	—	—	—	—
Spanish-American	**Total**	**306,760**	**385**	**2,061**	**1,662**	**4,108**
War	Army[3]	280,564	369	2,061	1,594	4,024
1898	Navy	22,875	10	0	47	57
	Marines	3,321	6	0	21	27
World War I	**Total**	**4,743,826**	**53,513**	**63,195**	**204,002**	**320,710**
April 6, 1917-	Army[4]	4,057,101	50,510	55,868	193,663	300,041
Nov. 11, 1918	Navy	599,051	431	6,856	819	8,106
	Marines	78,839	2,461	390	9,520	12,371
	Coast Guard	8,835	111	81	—	192
World War II	**Total**	**16,353,659**	**292,131**	**115,185**	**670,846**	**1,078,162**
Dec. 7, 1941-	Army[5]	11,260,000	234,874	83,400	565,861	884,135
Dec. 31, 1946[2]	Navy[6]	4,183,466	36,950	25,664	37,778	100,392
	Marines	669,100	19,733	4,778	67,207	91,718
	Coast Guard	241,093	574	1,343	—	1,917
Korean War[9]	**Total**	**5,764,143**	**33,651**	—	**103,284**	—
June 25, 1950-	Army	2,834,000	27,709	—	77,596	—
July 27, 1953	Navy	1,177,000	474	176	1,576	2,226
	Marines	424,000	4,270	339	23,744	28,353
	Air Force	1,285,000	1,198	298	368	1,864
	Coast Guard	44,143	—	—	—	—
Vietnam War[10]	**Total**	**8,744,000**	**47,369**	**10,799**	**153,303**	**211,471**
Aug. 4, 1964-	Army	4,368,000	30,911	7,274	96,802	134,987
Jan. 27, 1973	Navy	1,842,000	1,631	927	4,178	6,736
	Marines	794,000	13,083	1,754	51,392	66,229
	Air Force	1,740,000	1,739	842	931	3,512
	Coast Guard	—	5	2	—	7
Persian Gulf War	**Total**	**467,539[11]**	**148**	**145**	**467**	**760**
1991	Army	246,682	98	105	—	—
	Navy	98,852	6	8	—	—
	Marines	71,254	24	26	—	—
	Air Force	50,751	20	6	—	—

(1) Authoritative statistics for the Confederate forces are not available. An estimated 26,000-31,000 Confederate personnel died in Union prisons.

(2) Data are for the period Dec. 1, 1941 through Dec. 31, 1946, when hostilities were officially terminated by Presidential Proclamation, but few battle deaths or wounds not mortal were incurred after the Japanese acceptance of Allied peace terms on Aug. 14, 1945. Numbers serving Dec. 1, 1941-Aug. 31, 1945 were: Total—14,903,213; Army—10,420,000; Navy—3,883,520; and Marine Corps—599,693.

(3) Number serving covers the period April 21-Aug. 13, 1898, while dead and wounded data are for the period May 1-Aug. 31, 1898. Active hostilities ceased on Aug. 13, 1898, but ratifications of the treaty of peace were not exchanged between the United States and Spain until April 11, 1899.

(4) Includes Army Air Forces battle deaths and wounds not mortal, as well as casualties suffered by American forces in Northern Russia to Aug. 25, 1919, and in Siberia to April 1, 1920. Other deaths covered the period April 1, 1917-Dec. 31, 1918.

(5) Includes Army Air Forces.

(6) Battle deaths and wounds not mortal include casualties incurred in Oct. 1941 due to hostile action.

(7) Marine Corps data for World War II, the Spanish-American War, and prior wars represent the number of individuals wounded, whereas all other data in this column represent the total number (incidence) of wounds.

(8) As reported by the Commissioner of Pensions in his Annual Report for Fiscal Year 1903.

(9) Battle deaths and other deaths associated with the conflict differ from previously reported figures due to a reexamination of individual files by the U.S. Dept. of Defense.

(10) Number serving covers the period Aug. 4, 1964-Jan. 27, 1973 (date of ceasefire). Number of casualties incurred in connection with the conflict in Vietnam covers the period Jan. 1, 1961-Sept. 30, 1977. Includes casualties incurred in Mayaguez Incident. Wounds not mortal exclude 150,375 persons not requiring hospital care.

(11) Estimated, because deployment figures changed continually.

COMPUTERS

The Internet

For more details about terms used here, see the Glossary of Internet Terms that follows.

What Is the Internet?

The Internet is a vast computer network of computer networks. Estimates are that some 20-30 million computer users populated this electronic global village by mid-1995.

Some other facts about the Internet:

- Annual rate of growth for World Wide Web traffic: 341,000%
- Number of countries reachable by electronic mail: 159 (approx.)
- Date after which more than half the registered networks were commercial: August 1991
- Amount of time it takes for U.S. Supreme Court decisions to become available on the Internet: less than one day
- Number of financial service firms with Internet sites in early 1995: 398

The Internet is *not* owned or funded by any one institution, organization, or government. It doesn't have a CEO, and it is not a commercial service. The Internet is, however, directed by the Internet Society (ISOC), which is composed of volunteers. The ISOC appoints a subcouncil, the Internet Architecture Board (IAB), and members of this board work out issues of standards, network resources, network addresses, and so on. Another volunteer group, the Internet Engineering Task Force (IETF), takes care of the day-to-day issues of Internet operation.

Practically speaking, the Internet, also referred to as the Information Superhighway, is composed of people, hardware, and software. With the proper equipment, you can sit at your computer and communicate with someone any place in the world as long as that person also has the proper equipment. You can also use the Internet to access vast amounts of information, including text, graphics, sound, and video. From your computer, you can view masterpieces from the Louvre, take an aerial tour of Hawaii, or dissect a virtual frog. You can search databases at the Library of Congress, send e-mail, receive electronic newsletters, and "chat" with others online.

How Did It Originate?

In the late 1960s, a group of scientists at the U.S. Department of Defense's Advanced Research Projects Agency (ARPA) wanted to share information with others working on similar research projects, many of whom were government contractors working at large universities. Thus, ARPAnet was spawned. When people at these institutions discovered the enormous utility of a network that linked them with colleagues around the world, the project mushroomed.

As the network expanded throughout the 1970s, members of the computer industry began to participate, and the Internet became an online haven for computer jocks, researchers, and academics. The first commercial online service, CompuServe, started up in 1969 and for several years was itself primarily an online hangout for computer jocks.

In 1986, the National Science Foundation (NSF) created NSFNET to connect supercomputer sites around the U.S. It also connected computers at research sites and schools that were near the supercomputers. Within 2 years, NSFNET had totally replaced ARPAnet.

In 1991, Vice President Al Gore, then a U.S. senator, proposed widening the architecture of NSFNET to include more K-12 schools, community colleges, and 2-year colleges. The resulting legislation expanded NSFNET and renamed it NREN (National Research and Educational Network). This bill also allowed businesses to purchase part of the network for commercial uses. The mass commercialization of today's Internet is the direct result of this legislation.

How Can You Get There?

First, you need the equipment. You can get basic Internet access with any computer that has a modem that is connected to a phone line. However, to take full advantage of all the Internet has to offer, you need either a Macintosh that has a 68040 or higher CPU or a PC that has an 80486 or higher CPU. With either system, you also need the following:

- At least 4 megabytes of RAM (8 is recommended)
- A 250 megabyte hard drive
- A 14.4 bps modem (28.8 is even better)

You can access the Internet in 4 ways: directly; with a SLIP/PPP account; with a shell, or dial-up, account; and via a commercial online service. *Direct access* is primarily the province of large institutions and businesses that have computers that are part of a network that is part of the Internet. *SLIP* (Serial Line Interface Protocol) and *PPP* (Point-to-Point Protocol) accounts attach your computer to a network of computers that is directly attached to the Internet. You use software that you purchase or download off the Net. A *shell account* gives you text-only access through a Unix system.

Commercial online services—collections of networked computers that provide content to subscribers—constitute the fastest-growing segment of the Internet, and almost all now provide access to the Internet. Free installation software is available for most of these services and is often bundled with modems and new computers. It can also often be found in computer publications. Some of the most well-known commercial online services are America Online, CompuServe, and Prodigy. None of these charge a startup fee. All charge a monthly subscription rate and charge additionally for connect time beyond that included in the monthly rate.

Internet Resources

What you can do on the Internet depends on which resource you access. The basic resources are e-mail, FAQs, FTP, Gopher, newsgroups, and the World Wide Web.

E-mail. Electronic mail is probably the most popular and widely used resource on the Internet. To use it, however, you must know the address of the person or organization. An e-mail address consists of a *username*, a *service*, and a *domain*. For example, The World Almanac's e-mail address is `Walmanac@aol.com`. `Walmanac` is the username, `aol` is the service (in this case, America Online), and `com` is the domain (in this case, a commercial organization). The domains are identified in the Domain Name System. Here are the most familiar:

Domain name	What it is
com	a commercial organization, business, or company
edu	an educational institution
int	an international organization
gov	a nonmilitary government entity
mil	a military organization
net	a network administration
org	other organizations: nonprofit, nonacademic, or nongovernmental

FAQs. Frequently Asked Questions documents contain the answers to common Internet questions. Reading some of these documents, which can be found in many areas of the Internet, is a first step for anyone new to the Internet.

FTP. File Transfer Protocol is a method of transferring files on the Internet and a type of Internet site. Using FTP, you log on to a remote site, usually a server, view the available files, and copy them to your computer. The address for an FPT site begins with ftp.

Gopher. Developed at the University of Minnesota, home of the Golden Gophers, Gopher is a hierarchy of menus you can use to browse the Internet or search for a specific file. These menus are available on numerous Gopher servers on the Internet. Any Internet address that begins with gopher points to a location on a Gopher server.

Newsgroups. Newsgroups, a classic institution of the Internet, are found on the part of the Internet called Usenet. In a newsgroup, messages concerning a particular topic are posted in a public forum. You can simply read the postings, or you can post an article yourself.

The World Wide Web. The Web may be the most complete realization of the Internet to date. It was developed in the early 1990s at the European Center for Nuclear Research as an environment in which scientists in Geneva, Switzerland, could share information. It has evolved into a medium that consists of text, graphics, audio, animation, and video. The address of a site on the Web begins with http://www. The World Wide Web is a graphical environment that can be navigated through hyperlinks. From one site you click on hyperlinks to go to any number of related sites.

Safety and Security on the Internet

The Internet has no governing body through which laws and policies are enforced, and its original inhabitants were known for their opposition to censorship and their strongly-held beliefs about free speech.

That said, common sense dictates some basic codes of conduct.

- If you encounter an area that you find offensive, for example, a newsgroup or a chat room, remove that area from your list of places to visit. In fact, any time you feel uncomfortable, remember: The computer is under your control. You can always turn it off.
- If you feel that someone is being threatening or dangerous, you can inform your Internet service provider, which can issue a warning or can even withdraw entirely the person's online privileges.
- Be as conscious of your privacy on the Internet as you would in any other situation in which you interact with strangers. Children, especially, should never give out their home phone number or address or any other personal information.
- Be extremely careful about giving out credit card numbers. The Internet is not 100% secure.

Glossary of Internet Terms

For general computer terms, see the Computer Glossary later in this section.

Archie   A system of servers that searches for publicly available files in FTP archives. *See* **FTP.**

browser   A tool that you can use to look around at sites on the Internet.

chat room   An area of an online service where people can communicate from their computers in real time.

cyberspace   The online culture that the Internet creates.

dial-up account   A basic access to a text-only Unix system.

directory service   a provider of online directories of Web sites and search engines. *See* **search engine.**

domain   The portion of a URL that designates its type. *See* **URL.**

emoticon   A combination of keyboard characters that depicts an emotional response (also called smiley). For example, :-) is a smiley face, indicating happiness. If you don't get it, turn this page sideways and look.

FAQ   An abbreviation for Frequently Asked Questions, a document that assembles answers to common questions about sites or areas of the Internet.

Fetch   A program for finding and accessing FTP files.

flame   A derisive, possibly insulting message posted on a newsgroup.

forum   An online gathering place for groups of people with a similar interest.

FTP   An abbreviation for File Transfer Protocol. As a noun, FTP is a protocol for the transfer of data on the Internet. As a verb, it is a method for transferring data. As an adjective, it is a type of site on the Internet.

Gopher   A menu-based tool for find, accessing, and organizing Internet resources.

Gopher hole   A Gopher site.

Gopherspace   The worldwide Gopher system.

home page   The first screen you see when you go to a site on the World Wide Web; also the site itself.

HTML   An abbreviation for Hypertext Markup Language, the language used to create World Wide Web documents.

hyperlink   A highlighted (and sometimes underlined) word, phrase, or image in a Web document that connects to another part of the document, another document, or even a document on a different server.

Internet service provider   A network, commercial or otherwise, to which you can connect in order to get access to the Internet.

Jughead   A Gopher search program that searches a specific set of Gopher menus.

link   *See* **hyperlink.**

logon   The process of identifying oneself to a computer after connecting to it.

lurk   To read articles in a newsgroup or e-mail discussion list without joining in. A perfectly acceptable practice for a newbie. *See* **newbie.**

Lynx   A nongraphical Web browser. With it, you can see text on the World Wide Web and iconic representations of the graphics.

mailing list   An electronic version of the printed kind. If your name is on a mailing list, you receive, via e-mail, anything that is sent to those on the list.

moderated   A description of a newsgroup or mailing list whose contents are monitored by a human being.

Mosaic   Any of several programs that you can use to browse the Web. *See* **browser.**

Net   Short for the Internet.

netiquette   The Internet code of conduct

Netizen   An Internet user.

newbie   A new or an inexperienced user of the Internet.

newsgroup   Usenet message areas, each of which focuses on a particular topic.

password   A unique string of characters that a user types to identify himself or herself when logging on to a protected computer system.

posting   Submitting an article to a newsgroup; also the article itself. *See* **thread.**

PPP   An abbreviation for Point-to-Point protocol, a set of rules or standards for direct Internet access over the phone lines.

protocol   A set of rules or standards that enables computers to communicate with as little error as possible.

search engine   software that finds and retrieves data.

shell account   A Unix-based Internet access account.

site   A location on the Internet.

SLIP   An abbreviation for Serial Line Internet Protocol, a set of rules or standards for direct Internet access over the phone lines.

smiley   *See* **emoticon.**

snail mail   Items that travel via the postal service, which in the Information Age is viewed as terribly slow.

spamming   Sending junk e-mail.

system administrator   The person who organizes, maintains, troubleshoots, and generally oversees a network.

TCP/IP   An abbreviation for Transmission Control Protocol/Internet Protocol, the underlying standards that define the Internet.

Telnet   A protocol to log in to remote computers on the Internet. It can be used to access databases or one's own accounts from a remote location.

thread   A series of newsgroup postings on the same subject. *See* **posting**.

TIA   An abbreviation for The Internet Adapter, a shareware program that enables you to use a less expensive shell account to access the World Wide Web.

Unix   A text-based, as opposed to a graphical, operating system in which you must type commands rather than pointing and clicking with a mouse.

URL   An abbreviation for Uniform Resource Locator, an address or location of a document on the World Wide Web.

Usenet   An informal, anarchistic worldwide newsgroup network that exchanges public messages on specific topics.

username   The name that is used in an e-mail address.

Veronica   A search program for Gophers.

Web   *See* World Wide Web

Web browser   *See* **browser**.

World Wide Web (WWW)   A loose network of documents that are connected through hyperlinks.

Yahoo   A search and reference tool, specific to the World Wide Web.

Internet Lingo

The following abbreviations are commonly used in Internet documents and in e-mail.

BTW	By the way	**HHOS**	Ha, ha—only serious
F2F	Face to face, a personal meeting	**IMHO**	In my humble opinion
FCOL	For crying out loud	**IMO**	In my opinion
FWIW	For what it's worth	**LOL**	Laughing out loud
FYI	For your information	**OTOH**	On the other hand
GOK	God only knows	**ROFL** or **ROTFL**	Rolling on the floor laughing
HHOK	Ha, ha—only kidding	**TAFN**	That's all for now

Emoticons, or smileys, are a series of typed characters that, when turned sideways, resemble a face and express an emotion. Here are some smileys that are often encountered on the Internet.

:-)	Smile	:-(	Unhappy	=:o	Argh!
;-)	Wink	:-o	Shouting	{*}	A hug and a kiss
:-*	Kiss	:-b...	Drooling	:p	Raz

Internet Directory to Selected Sites

The e-mail and site addresses listed below are but a small sampling of what is available on the Internet. When you enter an address, you must type it exactly as written, including capital and lowercase letters, any nonalphanumeric characters, and spaces. You may be unable to connect to a site for the following reasons: (1) You have mistyped the address; (2) the site is busy; (3) the site has moved; (4) the site no longer exists.

U.S. Government

To send e-mail to the president, the vice president, or the first lady, use the following addresses:

```
president@whithouse.gov
vice.president@whitehouse.gov
first.lady@whitehouse.gov
```

To take a virtual tour of the White House, connect to the following site:

```
http://www.whitehouse.gov
```

The White House FAQ is at the following address:

```
faq@whitehouse.gov
```

To receive White House documents and publications by e-mail, send the message `Send  Info` to `publications@whitehouse gov.`

To get a complete listing of the e-mail addresses and Web sites of the members of Congress, connect to:

```
www.yahoo.com/Government/
Legislative_Branch/Congressional_E_Mail_
Addresses/
```

Census Bureau
```
http://www.census.gov
```
Central Intelligence Agency
```
http://www.odci.gov/cia
```
Department of Agriculture
```
http://www.usda.gov/
```
Department of Commerce
```
http://www.doc.gov/
```
Department of Defense
```
http://www.dtic.dla.mil/defenselink/
```

Department of Education
```
http://gopher.ed.gov/
```
Department of Energy
```
http://www.doe.gov
```
Department of Health and Human Services
```
http://www.os.dhhs.gov/
```
Department of Housing and Urban Development
```
http://www.hud.gov/
```
Department of the Interior
```
http://info.er.usgs.gov/doi/doi.html
```
Department of Justice
```
http://www.usdoj.gov/
```
Department of Labor
```
http://www.dol.gov
```
Department of State
```
http://dosfan.lib.uic.edu/dosfan.html
```
Department of Transportation
```
http://www.dot.gov/
```
Department of the Treasury
```
http://www.ustreas.gov/
```
Department of Veterans Affairs
```
http://www.va.gov
```
Environmental Protection Agency
```
http://www.epa.gov/
```
Federal Trade Commisssion
```
http://www.ftc.gov/Welcome.html
```
Library of Congress
```
http://www.loc.gov/
```
NASA
```
http://www.nasa.gov/
```
Social Security On Line
```
http://www.ssa.gov/SSA_Home.html
```
THOMAS: Legislative Information
```
http://thomas.loc.gov/
```

Internet Sites *(continued)*

United States Constitution
(At this site, you can access the complete text of the U.S. Constitution.)
`http://www.house.gov/Constitution/`
  `Constitution.html`
U.S. House of Representatives
`http://www.house.gov/`
U.S. Supreme Court Decisions
`http://www.law.cornell.edu/supct/supct.`
  `table.html`
U.S. Supreme Court Justices
(biographical data on and decisions of each justice)
`http://www.law.cornell.edu/supct/`
  `justices/fullcourt.html`

Television

CBS—Columbia Broadcasting System, Inc.
`http://www.cbs.com/`
CNBC—Consumer News and Business Channel
`http://www.cnbc.com`
CNN—Cable News Network
`http://www.cnn.com`
NBC—National Broadcasting Company
`http://www.nbc.com`
NICK—Nickelodeon/Nick at Nite
`http://nick-at-nite.viacom.com`
PBS—Public Broadcasting Service
`http://www.pbs.org/`

Kids' Places

Blue Dog Can Count
`http://fedida.ini.cmu.edu:5550/bdf.html`
Buena Vista MoviePlex
`http:/www.disney.com`
CRAYON (CReAte Your Own Newspaper)
`http://sun.bucknell.edu/~boulter/crayon/`
Interactive Frog Dissection
`http://curry.edschool.virginia.edu/`
  `~insttech/frog/`
International Kids' Space
`http://www.interport./kids-space`
Lite Brite Images
`http://www.galcit.caltech.edu/~ta/lb/`
  `lb.html`
Uncle Bob's Kids' Page
`http://gagme.wwa.com/~boba/kids.html`
VolcanoWorld
`http://volcano.und.nodak.edu/`

Health and Fitness

Multimedia Medical Reference Library
`http://www.tiac.net/users/jtward/`
  `index.html`
The On-line Allergy Center
`http://www.sig.net:80/~allergy/`
  `welcome.html`
The Running Page
`http://sunsite.unc.edu:80/drears/running`
  `/running.html`
Tennis Server
`http://arganet.tenagra.com:80/`
  `Racquet_Workshop/Tennis.html`

Food and Drink

CheeseNet95
`http://www.efn.org:80/~kpw/cheesenet95/`
The Chile-Heads Home Page
`http://chile.ucdmc.ucdavis.edu:8000/www/`
  `chile.html`
Cooking and Recipes
`http://www.yatcom.com/neworl/food/`
  `cooktop.html`
the electronic Gourmet Guide (eGG)
`http://www.deltanet.com/food/egg/`
  `index.html`
The Gumbo Pages
`http://www.Webcom.com/~gumbo/`
  `welcome.html`
Hawaii's Best Espresso Company
`http://hoohana.aloha.net/~bec`
Mimi's Cyber Kitchen
`http://www.smartlink.net:80/~hiller/`
  `food/`
Virtual Vineyards
`http://www.virtualvin.com`

Corporations

AT&T
`http://www.att.com/`
Coca-Cola
`http://www.cocacola.com/`
Federal Express Page
(track your shipment's progress)
`http://www.fedex.com/`
General Electric
`http://www.ge.com/`
IBM
`http://www.ibm.com/`
Microsoft
`http://www.microsoft.com/`
Wal-Mart Stores
`http://www.wal-mart.com/`

World Wide Web Directory Services

Excite
`http://www.excite.com`
Info Seek Net Search
`http://www.infoseek.com`
Lycos
`http://lycos.cs.cmu.edu`
Open Text
`http://www.opentext.com`
Webcrawler
`http://www.webcrawler.com`
Yahoo
`http://www.yahoo.com`

Miscellaneous

Impact Online
(seeks volunteers and donations for nonprofit organizations)
`http://www.webcom.com/~iol`
Shoppers Advantage
(online superstore)
`http://www.cuc.com`
Virtual Tourist II
`http://wings.buffalo.edu/world/vt2`

Households With Computers, CD-ROM Drives, and Modems in Use, 1995

Source: Inteco, Norwalk, CT

(estimates, as of June 1995)

An estimated 35% of U.S. households had computers in June 1995. Of those computers,

  11.5% had CD-ROM drives   15.8% had modems

Of the personal computer households with modems,

  10.8% had the modem connected to a phone line   6.4% used online services

Top-Selling Software, 1995

Source: PC Data, Reston, VA

(based on average U.S. sales, Jan.-June 1995)

CD-ROM, All Categories

1. Myst, Brøderbund
2. Dark Forces, LucasArts
3. Print Shop Deluxe CD Ensemble, Brøderbund
4. Doom II, GT Interactive
5. D!Zone Collector's Edition, Wizard Works
6. The Lion King Storybook, Disney
7. Quicken CD-ROM Deluxe, Intuit
8. NASCAR Racing, Papyrus
9. Descent, Interplay
10. Aladdin Activity Center, Disney
11. Microsoft Encarta, Microsoft
12. 7th Guest, Virgin
13. Corel Gallery, Corel
14. X-Wing Collector's CD, LucasArts
15. Wing Commander III, Electronic Arts

Games (MS-DOS/Windows)

1. Myst, Brøderbund
2. Doom II, GT Interactive
3. Dark Forces, LucasArts
4. D!Zone Collector's Edition, Wizard Works
5. Microsoft Flight Simulator, Microsoft
6. NASCAR Racing, Papyrus
7. Descent, Interplay
8. Sim City 2000, Maxis
9. X-Wing Collector's CD, LucasArts
10. The Best of Microsoft Entertainment Pack, Microsoft
11. Wing Commander III, Electronic Arts/Origin
12. 7th Guest, Virgin
13. Tie Fighter, LucasArts
14. Sim City 2000 Collection, Maxis
15. 5 Ft. 10 Pak Vol. II, Sirius

Games (Macintosh)

1. Myst, Brøderbund
2. Marathon, Bungee
3. Sim City 2000, Maxis
4. Star Wars Rebel Assault, LucasArts
5. Links Pro, Access
6. Chessmaster 3000, Mindscape
7. Wolfenstein 3D, Interplay
8. Sim Tower, Maxis
9. FA-18 Hornet, Graphic Simulations
10. Mindscape CD Mac Pack, Mindscape

Home Education (MS-DOS/Windows)

1. The Lion King Story Book, Disney
2. Aladdin Activity Center, Disney
3. Where in the World Is Carmen Sandiego? Brøderbund
4. Mavis Beacon Teaches Typing, Mindscape
5. Oregon Trail Deluxe, MECC
6. Math Blaster: In Search of Spot, Davidson
7. 3 Ft. 6 Pak, Sirius
8. Reader Rabbit 1, Learning Company
9. Interactive Reading Journey, Learning Company
10. Where in the USA Is Carmen Sandiego? Brøderbund

Home Education (Macintosh)

1. Aladdin Activity Center, Disney
2. Mavis Beacon Teaches Typing, Mindscape
3. Kid Pix Studio, Brøderbund
4. Where in the World Is Carmen Sandiego? Brøderbund
5. Mario Teaches Typing, Interplay
6. Sim Town, Maxis
7. Oregon Trail Deluxe, MECC
8. Where in the USA Is Carmen Sandiego? Brøderbund
9. A.D.A.M. Inside Story, A.D.A.M. Software
10. Kid's Pix 2, Brøderbund

Reference Software

1. Microsoft Encarta, Microsoft
2. Compton's Interactive Encyclopedia, Compton's New Media
3. Microsoft Bookshelf, Microsoft
4. Grolier Encyclopedia, Grolier
5. 70 Million Households Phone Book, American Business Info

Personal Productivity (MS-DOS/Windows)

1. TurboTax Final, Intuit
2. Quicken, Intuit
3. Quicken Deluxe, Intuit
4. Print Shop Deluxe, Brøderbund
5. TaxCut Final, Block
6. Street Atlas USA, DeLorme
7. TurboTax Deluxe, Intuit
8. Family Treemaker Deluxe, Brøderbund
9. 3-D Home Architect, Brøderbund
10. Print Shop Deluxe for Windows, Brøderbund
11. One Stop CD Shop Vol. I, Softkey
12. State TurboTax CA, Intuit
13. Expert Clipart, Expert
14. Expert Home Design 3-D, Expert
15. Printmaster Gold, Micrologic

Personal Productivity (Macintosh)

1. Macintax Final, Intuit
2. Quicken, Intuit
3. Print Shop Deluxe CD Ensemble, Brøderbund
4. Print Ship Deluxe, Brøderbund
5. Family Doctor, Creative Multimedia

U.S. Computer Sales and Ownership, 1982-96

Source: Electronic Industries Association, Arlington, VA, August 1995

(U.S. sales through retail consumer channels)

Year	Unit sales to dealers (thousands)	Dollar sales to dealers (millions)	Percentage of households with owners	Year	Unit sales to dealers (thousands)	Dollar sales to dealers (millions)	Percentage of households with owners
1982	1,550	1,375	NA	1989	3,900	3,711	21
1983	3,750	2,070	7	1990	4,000	4,187	22
1984	3,975	2,385	13	1991	3,900	4,287	25
1985	3,200	2,175	15	1992	4,875	5,573	27
1986	2,950	3,060	16	1993	5,850	6,921	30
1987	3,125	3,100	18	1994[1]	6,725	8,070	33
1988	3,500	3,340	20	1995[1]	8,225	10,281	37
				1996[1]	9,525	11,906	NA

NA = not available. (1) Estimated figures. Sales and households with owners estimated through the end of the calendar year.

Glossary of Computer Terms

For terms specific to the Internet, see the Internet Glossary earlier in this section.

application   A computer program designed to help people perform a certain type of work. An application can manipulate text, numbers, graphics, or a combination of those elements.

artificial intelligence (AI)   The branch of computer science that deals with enabling computers to emulate such aspects of intelligence as speech recognition, deduction, inference, creative response, the ability to learn from past experience, and the ability to make reasonable inferences from incomplete information.

ASCII   (pronounced "askee"); acronym for American Standard Code for Information Interchange, a coding scheme that assigns numeric values to letters, numbers, punctuation marks, and certain other characters.

back up (noun); backup (verb)   As a noun, a duplicate copy of a program, a disk, or data. As a verb, to make a backup copy.

bandwidth   In communications, the difference between the highest and lowest frequencies in a given range. In computer networks, greater bandwidth indicates faster data-transfer capability.

baud rate   Commonly, a reference to the speed at which a modem can transmit data.

BBS   An abbreviation for bulletin board system, a computer system equipped with one or more modems that serves as an information and message-passing center for dial-up users.

bit   Short for binary digit; either 1 or 0 in the binary number system. In processing and storage, a bit is the smallest unit of information handled by a computer.

boot   As a verb, to start up a computer. As a noun, the process of starting or resetting a computer.

broadband network   A type of local area network on which transmissions travel as radio-frequency signals over separate inbound and outbound channels. Stations on a broadband network are connected by coaxial or fiber-optic cable. The cable itself can be made to carry data, voice, and video simultaneously.

bug   An error in software or hardware. In software, a bug is an error in coding or logic that causes a program to malfunction or to produce incorrect results.

bulletin board system   *See* **BBS.**

byte   Abbreviation for binary term. A unit of information consisting of 8 bits; in computer processing and storage, the equivalent of a single character.

CD-ROM   Acronym for compact disc read-only memory, a form of storage characterized by high capacity (roughly 600 megabytes) and the use of laser optics rather than magnetic means for reading data.

central processing unit (CPU)   The computational and control unit of a computer; the device that interprets and executes instructions.

chip   *See* **integrated circuit.**

client   On a local area network, a computer that accesses shared network resources provided by another computer (called a server). *See also* **server.**

computer   Any machine that does three things: accepts structured input, processes it according to prescribed rules, and produces the results as output.

copy protection   A software "lock" placed on a computer program by its developer to prevent the product from being copied and distributed without approval or authorization.

CPU   *See* **central processing unit.**

cursor   A special on-screen indicator that marks the place at which keystrokes will occur when typed.

database   Loosely any aggregation of data; a file consisting of a number of records (or tables), each of which is constructed of fields (columns) of a particular type, together with a collection of operations that facilitate searching, sorting, recombination, and similar activities.

debug   With software, to detect, locate, and correct logical or syntactical errors in a computer program.

desktop publishing   The use of a computer and specialized software to combine text and graphics to create a document that can be printed on either a laser printer or a typesetting machine.

disk   A round, flat piece of flexible plastic (floppy disk) or inflexible metal (hard disk) coated with a magnetic material that can be electrically influenced to hold information recorded in digital (binary) format.

disk drive   An electromechanical device that reads from and writes to disks.

disk operating system   Abbreviated DOS. A generic term describing any operating system that is loaded from disk devices when the system is started or rebooted.

document   As a noun, any self-contained piece of work created with an application program and, if saved on disk, given a unique filename by which it can be retrieved.

DOS   *See* **disk operating system.**

download   In communications, the process of transferring a copy of a file from a remote computer to the requesting computer by means of a modem or network.

electronic mail   The transmission of messages over a communications network.

e-mail   *See* **electronic mail.**

Ethernet   A local area network developed by Xerox in 1976, originally for linking minicomputers at the Palo Alto Research Center.

file   A complete, named collection of information, such as a program, a set of data used by a program, or a user-created document.

filename   The set of letters, numbers, and allowable symbols assigned to a file that distinguishes it from all other files in a particular directory on a disk.

file server   A file-storage device on a local area network that is accessible to all users on the network. On local area networks, a file server is often a computer with a large hard disk that is dedicated only to the task of managing shared files.

floppy disk   *See* **disk.**

format   As a noun, the structure or appearance of a unit of data, such as a file, fields in a database record, a cell in a spreadsheet, or the text in a word-processed document. As a verb, to format text or the contents of a cell in a spreadsheet means to change the appearance of the selected material.

graphical user interface   Abbreviated GUI (pronounced "gooey"). A type of display format that enables the user to choose commands, start programs, and see lists of files and other options by pointing to pictorial representations (icons) and lists of menu items on the screen. *See also* **icon.**

hacker   Originally, a computerphile—a person totally engrossed in computer programming and computer technology. In the 1980s, with the advent of personal computers and dial-up computer networks, *hacker* acquired a pejorative connotation, often referring to someone who secretively invades others' computers.

hard copy   Printed output on paper, film, or other permanent media. *See* **soft copy.**

hard disk   *See* **disk.**

host   The main computer in a system of computers or terminals connected by communications links.

icon   In graphical environments, a small graphics image displayed on the screen to represent an object that can be manipulated by the user.

integrated circuit Also called a chip. In electronics, the packing of circuit elements, such as transistors and resistors, onto a single chip of silicon crystal or other material.

interactive Operating in a back-and-forth, often conversational, manner, as when a user enters a question or command and the system immediately responds.

KB *See* **kilobyte.**

kilobyte Abbreviated KB, K, or Kbyte. One thousand twenty-four (1024) bytes.

kludge Pronounced "klooj." With computers, a term used to describe a piece of hardware or software that basically operates properly but whose construction or design is severely lacking in elegance or logical efficiency.

LAN Rhymes with "can." Acronym for local area network, a group of computers and other devices dispersed over a relatively limited area and connected by a communications link that enables any device to interact with any other on the network.

laptop computer *See* **portable computer.**

mainframe computer A high-level computer designed for the most intensive computational tasks.

MB *See* **megabyte.**

megabyte Abbreviated MB. Either 1 million bytes or 1,048,576 bytes (2^{20}).

memory Circuitry that allows information to be stored and retrieved. In common usage, it refers only to the fast semiconductor storage (RAM) directly connected to the processor. *See* **RAM.**

menu A list of options from which a program user can select in order to perform a desired action, such as choosing a command or applying a particular format to part of a document.

microcomputer A computer built around a single-chip microprocessor. *See* **chip; microprocessor.**

microprocessor A central processing unit (CPU) on a single chip. *See also* **integrated circuit.**

minicomputer A mid-level computer built to perform complex computations while dealing efficiently with a high level of input and output from users connected via terminals.

CPU *See* **central processing unit.**

monitor The device on which images generated by the computer's video adapter are displayed.

motherboard The main circuit board containing the primary components of a computer system.

mouse A common pointing device, popularized by its inclusion as standard equipment with the Apple Macintosh. By moving the mouse on a surface (such as a desk), the user typically controls an on-screen cursor. *See* **cursor.**

multimedia The combination of sound, graphics, animation, and video.

multitasking A mode of operation offered by an operating system in which a computer works on more than one task at a time.

network A group of computers and associated devices that are connected by communications facilities.

online Activated and ready for operation; capable of communicating with or being controlled by a computer.

operating system The software responsible for controlling the allocation and usage of hardware resources such as memory, central processing unit (CPU) time, disk space, and peripheral devices.

optical fiber A thin strand of transparent material used to carry optical signals.

packet In general usage, a unit of information transmitted as a whole from one device to another on a network.

PC Abbreviation for personal computer.

Pentium A microprocessor introduced by Intel Corporation in 1993.

peripheral Devices, such as disk drives, printers, modems, and joysticks, that are connected to a computer and are controlled by its microprocessor.

pixel Short for picture element; sometimes called a pel.

portable computer Any computer designed to be moved easily.

port In computer hardware, a location for passing data in and out of a computing device.

printer A computer peripheral that puts text or a computer-generated image on paper or on another medium, such as a transparency.

program Synonymous with *software;* a sequence of instructions that can be executed by a computer.

RAM Pronounced "ram." Acronym for random access memory. Semiconductor-based memory that can be read and written by the microprocessor or other hardware devices.

server On a local area network, a computer running administrative software that controls access to all or part of the network and its resources (such as disk drives or printers). *See* **LAN.**

soft copy The temporary images presented on a computer display screen. *See* **hard copy**.

software Computer programs; instructions that cause the hardware—the machines—to do work.

spreadsheet program An application program commonly used for budgets, forecasting, and other finance-related tasks.

supercomputer A large, extremely fast, and expensive computer used for complex or sophisticated calculations.

telecommuting The practice of working in one location (often, at home) and communicating with a main office in a different location through a personal computer equipped with a modem and communications software.

teleconferencing The use of audio, video, or computer equipment linked through a communications system to enable geographically separated individuals to participate in a meeting or discussion.

Unix Pronounced "ewe-niks." A multiuser, multitasking operating system originally developed by Ken Thompson and Dennis Ritchie at AT&T Bell Laboratories in 1969 for use on minicomputers.

upload In communications, the process of transferring a copy of a file from a local computer to a remote computer by means of a modem or network.

user-friendly An adjective meaning easy to learn and easy to use.

user interface The portion of a program with which a user interacts.

virtual memory Also called disk memory. A technique that allows an application to see the system as providing a large uniform primary memory, which in reality is smaller, more fragmented, and/or partially simulated by secondary storage, such as a hard disk.

virus A program that "infects" computer files (usually other executable programs) by inserting in those files copies of itself.

WAN *See* **wide area network.**

wide area network A communications network that connects geographically separated areas.

window In applications and graphical interfaces, a portion of the screen that can contain its own document or message.

word processor An application program for manipulating text-based documents; the electronic equivalent of paper, pen, typewriter, eraser, and, most likely, dictionary and thesaurus.

workstation In general, a combination of input, output, and computing hardware that can be used for work by an individual.

WYSIWYG Pronounced "wizzywig." Acronym for "What you see is what you get." A display method that shows documents and graphics characters on the screen as they will appear when printed, WYSIWYG attempts to duplicate print output as closely as possible but is not always exact.

SCIENCE AND TECHNOLOGY
Inventions

Inventions	Date	Inventor	Nation
Adding machine	1642	Pascal	French
Adding machine	1885	Burroughs	U.S.
Aerosol spray	1926	Rotheim	Norwegian
Air brake	1868	Westinghouse	U.S.
Air conditioning	1911	Carrier	U.S.
Air pump	1654	Guericke	German
Airplane, automatic pilot	1912	Sperry	U.S.
Airplane, experimental	1896	Langley	U.S.
Airplane jet engine	1939	Ohain	German
Airplane with motor	1903	Wright bros.	U.S.
Airplane, hydro	1911	Curtiss	U.S.
Airship	1852	Giffard	French
Airship, rigid dirigible	1900	Zeppelin	German
Arc welder	1919	Thomson	U.S.
Aspartame	1965	Schlatter	U.S.
Autogyro	1920	de la Cierva	Spanish
Automobile, differential gear	1885	Benz	German
Automobile, electric	1892	Morrison	U.S.
Automobile, exp'mtl.	1864	Marcus	Austrian
Automobile, gasoline	1889	Daimler	German
Automobile, gasoline	1892	Duryea	U.S.
Automobile magneto	1897	Bosch	German
Automobile muffler	...	Maxim, H.P.	U.S.
Automobile self-starter	1911	Kettering	U.S.
Babbitt metal	1839	Babbitt	U.S.
Bakelite	1907	Baekeland	Belg., U.S.
Balloon	1783	Montgolfier	French
Barometer	1643	Torricelli	Italian
Bicycle, modern	1885	Starley	English
Bifocal lens	1780	Franklin	U.S.
Block signals, railway	1867	Hall	U.S.
Bomb, depth	1916	Tait	U.S.
Bottle machine	1895	Owens	U.S.
Braille printing	1829	Braille	French
Burner, gas	1855	Bunsen	German
Calculating machine	1833	Babbage	English
Calculator, electronic pocket	1972	Merryman, Van Tassel	U.S.
Camera, Kodak	1888	Eastman, Walker	U.S.
Camera, Polaroid Land	1948	Land	U.S.
Car coupler	1873	Janney	U.S.
Carburetor, gasoline	1893	Maybach	German
Card time recorder	1894	Cooper	U.S.
Carding machine	1797	Whittemore	U.S.
Carpet sweeper	1876	Bissell	U.S.
Cash register	1879	Ritty	U.S.
Cassette, audio	1963	Philips Co.	Dutch
Cassette, videotape	1969	Sony	Japanese
Cathode ray oscilloscope	1897	Braun	German
Cathode ray tube	1878	Crookes	English
CAT, or CT, scan (computerized tomography)	1973	Hounsfield	English
Cellophane	1908	Brandenberger	Swiss
Celluloid	1870	Hyatt	U.S.
Cement, Portland	1824	Aspdin	English
Chronometer	1761	Harrison	English
Circuit breaker	1925	Hilliard	U.S.
Circuit, integrated	1959	Kilby, Noyce, Texas Instr.	U.S.
Clock, pendulum	1657	Huygens	Dutch
Coaxial cable system	1929	Affel, Espensched	U.S.
Coke oven	1893	Hoffman	Austrian
Compressed air rock drill	1871	Ingersoll	U.S.
Comptometer	1887	Felt	U.S.
Computer, automatic sequence	1944	Aiken, et al.	U.S.
Computer, mini	1960	Digital Corp	U.S.
Condenser microphone (telephone)	1916	Wente	U.S.
Contraceptive, oral	1954	Pincus, Rock	U.S.
Corn, hybrid	1917	Jones	U.S.
Cotton gin	1793	Whitney	U.S.
Cream separator	1878	DeLaval	Swedish
Cultivator, disc	1878	Mallon	U.S.
Cystoscope	1878	Nitze	German
Diesel engine	1895	Diesel	German
Disc, compact	1972	RCA	U.S.
Disk, floppy	1970	IBM	U.S.
Disc player, compact	1979	Sony, Philips Co.	Japan, Dutch
Disk, video	1972	Philips Co.	Dutch
Dynamite	1866	Nobel	Swedish
Dynamo, continuous current	1871	Gramme	Belgian
Dynamo, hydrogen cooled	1915	Schuler	U.S.
Electric battery	1800	Volta	Italian
Electric fan	1882	Wheeler	U.S.
Electrocardiograph	1903	Einthoven	Dutch
Electroencephalograph	1929	Berger	German
Electromagnet	1824	Sturgeon	English
Electron spectrometer	1944	Deutsch, Elliott, Evans	U.S.
Electron tube multigrid	1913	Langmuir	U.S.
Electroplating	1805	Brugnatelli	Italian
Electrostatic generator	1929	Van de Graaff	U.S.
Elevator brake	1852	Otis	U.S.
Elevator, push button	1922	Larson	U.S.
Engine, automatic transmission	1910	Fottinger	German
Engine, coal-gas 4-cycle	1876	Otto	German
Engine, compression ignition	1883	Daimler	German
Engine, electric ignition	1883	Benz	German
Engine, gas, compound	1926	Eickemeyer	U.S.
Engine, gasoline	1872	Brayton, Geo.	U.S.
Engine, gasoline	1889	Daimler	German
Engine, jet	1930	Whittle	English
Engine, steam, piston	1705	Newcomen	English
Engine, steam, piston	1769	Watt	Scottish
Engraving, half-tone	1852	Talbot	U.S.
Fiberglass	1938	Owens-Corning	U.S.
Fiber optics	1955	Kapany	English
Filament, tungsten	1913	Coolidge	U.S.
Flanged rail	1831	Stevens	U.S.
Flatiron, electric	1882	Seely	U.S.
Food, frozen	1924	Birdseye	U.S.
Freon (low-boiling fluorine compounds)	1930	Midgley, et al.	U.S.
Furnace (for steel)	1858	Siemens	German
Galvanometer	1820	Sweigger	German
Gas discharge tube	1922	Hull	U.S.
Gas lighting	1792	Murdoch	Scottish
Gas mantle	1885	Welsbach	Austrian
Gasoline (lead ethyl)	1922	Midgley	U.S.
Gasoline, cracked	1913	Burton	U.S.
Gasoline, high octane	1930	Ipatieff	Russian
Geiger counter	1913	Geiger	German
Glass, laminated safety	1909	Benedictus	French
Glider	1853	Cayley	English
Gun, breechloader	1811	Thornton	U.S.
Gun, Browning	1897	Browning	U.S.
Gun, magazine	1875	Hotchkiss	U.S.
Gun, silencer	1908	Maxim, H.P.	U.S.
Guncotton	1847	Schoenbein	German
Gyrocompass	1911	Sperry	U.S.
Gyroscope	1852	Foucault	French
Harvester-thresher	1818	Lane	U.S.
Heart, artificial	1982	Jarvik	U.S.
Helicopter	1939	Sikorsky	U.S.
Hydrometer	1768	Baume	French
Hydrogen bomb	1952	U.S. government scientists	U.S
Ice-making machine	1851	Gorrie	U.S.
Iron lung	1928	Drinker, Slaw	U.S.
Kaleidoscope	1817	Brewster	Scottish
Kinetoscope	1889	Edison	U.S.
Lacquer, nitrocellulose	1921	Flaherty	U.S.
Lamp, arc	1847	Staite	English
Lamp, flourescent	1938	General Electric, Westinghouse	U.S.
Lamp, incandescent	1879	Edison	U.S.
Lamp, incand., frosted	1924	Pipkin	U.S.
Lamp, incand., gas	1913	Langmuir	U.S.
Lamp, klieg	1911	Kliegl, A. & J.	U.S.
Lamp, mercury vapor	1912	Hewitt	U.S.
Lamp, miner's safety	1816	Davy	English
Lamp, neon	1909	Claude	French
Lathe, turret	1845	Fitch	U.S.
Launderette	1934	Cantrell	U.S.
Lens, achromatic	1758	Dollond	English
Lens, fused bifocal	1908	Borsch	U.S.
Leyden jar (condenser)	1745	von Kleist	German
Lightning rod	1752	Franklin	U.S.
Linoleum	1860	Walton	English
Linotype	1884	Mergenthaler	U.S.
Lock, cylinder	1851	Yale	U.S.
Locomotive, electric	1851	Vail	U.S.
Locomotive, exp'mtl.	1802	Trevithick	English
Locomotive, exp'mtl.	1812	Fenton, et al.	English
Locomotive, exp'mtl.	1813	Hedley	English
Locomotive, exp'mtl.	1814	Stephenson	English
Locomotive, practical	1829	Stephenson	English
Locomotive, 1st U.S.	1830	Cooper, P.	U.S.
Loom, power	1785	Cartwright	English
Loudspeaker, dynamic	1924	Rice, Kellogg	U.S.

Inventions

Inventions	Date	Inventor	Nation
Machine gun	1861	Gatling	U.S.
Machine gun, improved	1872	Hotchkiss	U.S.
Machine gun (Maxim)	1883	Maxim, H.S.	U.S., Eng.
Magnet, electro	1828	Henry	U.S.
Mantle, gas	1885	Welsbach	Austrian
Mason jar	1858	Mason, J.	U.S.
Match, friction	1827	John Walker	English
Mercerized textiles	1843	Mercer, J.	English
Meter, induction	1888	Shallenberg	U.S.
Metronome	1816	Malezel	German
Microcomputer	1973	Truong, et al.	French
Micrometer	1636	Gascoigne	English
Microphone	1877	Berliner	U.S.
Microprocessor	1971	Intel Corp.	U.S.
Microscope, compound	1590	Janssen	Dutch
Microscope, electronic	1931	Knoll, Ruska	German
Microscope, field ion	1951	Mueller	German
Monitor, warship	1861	Ericsson	U.S.
Monotype	1887	Lanston	U.S.
Motor, AC	1892	Tesla	U.S.
Motor, DC	1837	Davenport	U.S.
Motor, induction	1887	Tesla	U.S.
Motorcycle	1885	Daimler	German
Movie machine	1894	Jenkins	U.S.
Movie, panoramic	1952	Waller	U.S.
Movie, talking	1927	Warner Bros.	U.S.
Mower, lawn	1831	Budding, Ferrabee	English
Mowing machine	1822	Bailey	U.S.
Neoprene	1930	Carothers	U.S.
Nylon synthetic	1930	Carothers	U.S.
Nylon	1937	Du Pont lab	U.S.
Oil cracking furnace	1891	Gavrilov	Russian
Oil filled power cable	1921	Emanueli	Italian
Oleomargarine	1869	Mege-Mouries	French
Ophthalmoscope	1851	Helmholtz	German
Paper	105	Lun	Chinese
Paper machine	1809	Dickinson	U.S.
Parachute	1785	Blanchard	French
Pen, ballpoint	1938	Biro	Hungarian
Pen, fountain	1884	Waterman	U.S.
Pen, steel	1780	Harrison	English
Pendulum	1583	Galileo	Italian
Percussion cap	1807	Forsythe	Scottish
Phonograph	1877	Edison	U.S.
Photo, color	1892	Ives	U.S.
Photo film, celluloid	1893	Reichenbach	U.S.
Photo film, transparent	1884	Eastman, Goodwin	U.S.
Photoelectric cell	1895	Elster	German
Photographic paper	1835	Talbot	English
Photography	1835	Talbot	English
Photography	1835	Daguerre	French
Photography	1816	Niepce	French
Photophone	1880	Bell	U.S.-Scot.
Phototelegraphy	1925	Bell Labs	U.S.
Piano	1709	Cristofori	Italian
Piano, player	1863	Fourneaux	French
Pin, safety	1849	Hunt	U.S.
Pistol (revolver)	1836	Colt	U.S.
Plow, cast iron	1785	Ransome	English
Plow, disc	1896	Hardy	U.S.
Pneumatic hammer	1890	King	U.S.
Powder, smokeless	1884	Vieille	French
Printing press, rotary	1845	Hoe	U.S.
Printing press, web	1865	Bullock	U.S.
Propeller, screw	1804	Stevens	U.S.
Propeller, screw	1837	Ericsson	Swedish
Pulsars	1967	Bell	English
Punch card accounting	1889	Hollerith	U.S.
Quasars	1963	Schmidt	U.S.
Radar	1940	Watson-Watt	Scottish
Radio amplifier	1906	De Forest	U.S.
Radio beacon	1928	Donovan	U.S.
Radio crystal oscillator	1918	Nicolson	U.S.
Radio receiver, cascade tuning	1913	Alexanderson	U.S.
Radio receiver, heterodyne	1913	Fessenden	U.S.
Radio transmitter triode modulation	1914	Alexanderson	U.S.
Radio tube diode	1905	Fleming	English
Radio tube oscillator	1915	De Forest	U.S.
Radio tube triode	1906	De Forest	U.S.
Radio, signals	1895	Marconi	Italian
Radio, magnetic detector	1902	Marconi	Italian
Radio FM, 2-path	1933	Armstrong	U.S.
Rayon (acetate)	1895	Cross	English
Rayon (cuprammonium)	1890	Despeissis	French
Rayon (nitrocellulose)	1884	Chardonnet	French
Razor, electric	1917	Schick	U.S.
Razor, safety	1895	Gillette	U.S.
Reaper	1834	McCormick	U.S.
Record, cylinder	1887	Bell, Tainter	U.S.
Record, disc	1887	Berliner	U.S.
Record, long playing	1947	Goldmark	U.S.
Record, wax cylinder	1888	Edison	U.S.
Refrigerator car	1868	David	U.S.
Resin, synthetic	1931	Hill	English
Richter scale	1935	Richter	U.S.
Rifle, repeating	1860	Spencer	U.S.
Rocket engine	1926	Goddard	U.S.
Rubber, vulcanized	1839	Goodyear	U.S.
Saccharin	1879	Remsen, Fahlberg	U.S.
Saw, band	1808	Newberry	English
Saw, circular	1777	Miller	English
Sewing machine	1846	Howe	U.S.
Shoe-sewing machine	1860	McKay	U.S.
Shrapnel shell	1784	Shrapnel	English
Shuttle, flying	1733	Kay	English
Sleeping-car	1865	Pullman	U.S.
Slide rule	1620	Oughtred	English
Soap, hardwater	1928	Bertsch	German
Spectroscope	1859	Kirchoff, Bunsen	German
Spectroscope (mass)	1918	Dempster	U.S.
Spinning jenny	c. 1764	Hargreaves	English
Spinning mule	1779	Crompton	English
Steamboat, exp'mtl	1778	Jouffroy	French
Steamboat, exp'mtl	1785	Fitch	U.S.
Steamboat, exp'mtl	1787	Rumsey	U.S.
Steamboat, exp'mtl	1788	Miller	Scottish
Steamboat, exp'mtl	1803	Fulton	U.S.
Steamboat, exp'mtl	1804	Stevens	U.S.
Steamboat, practical	1802	Symington	Scottish
Steamboat, practical	1807	Fulton	U.S.
Steam car	1770	Cugnot	French
Steam turbine	1884	Parsons	English
Steel (converter)	1856	Bessemer	English
Steel alloy	1891	Harvey	U.S.
Steel alloy, high-speed	1901	Taylor, White	U.S.
Steel, electric	1900	Heroult	French
Steel, manganese	1884	Hadfield	English
Steel, stainless	1916	Brearley	English
Stereoscope	1838	Wheatstone	English
Stethoscope	1819	Laennec	French
Stethoscope, binaural	1840	Cammann	U.S.
Stock ticker	1870	Edison	U.S.
Storage battery, rechargeable	1859	Plante	French
Stove, electric	1896	Hadaway	U.S.
Submarine	1891	Holland	U.S.
Submarine, even keel	1894	Lake	U.S.
Submarine, torpedo	1776	Bushnell	U.S.
Superconductivity (BCS theory)	1957	Bardeen, Cooper, Schreiffer	U.S.
Tank, military	1914	Swinton	English
Tape recorder, magnetic	1899	Poulsen	Danish
Teflon	1938	Du Pont	U.S.
Telegraph, magnetic	1837	Morse	U.S.
Telegraph, quadruplex	1864	Edison	U.S.
Telegraph, railroad	1887	Woods	U.S.
Telegraph, wireless high frequency	1895	Marconi	Italian
Telephone	1876	Bell	U.S.-Scot.
Telephone amplifier	1912	De Forest	U.S.
Telephone, automatic	1891	Stowger	U.S.
Telephone, radio	1900	Poulsen, Fessenden	Danish
Telephone, radio	1906	De Forest	U.S.
Telephone, radio, l. d.	1915	AT&T	U.S.
Telephone, recording	1898	Poulsen	Danish
Telephone, wireless	1899	Collins	U.S.
Telescope	1608	Lippershey	Neth.
Telescope	1609	Galileo	Italian
Telescope, astronomical	1611	Kepler	German
Teletype	1928	Morkrum, Kleinschmidt	U.S.
Television, iconoscope	1923	Zworykin	U.S.
Television, electronic	1927	Farnsworth	U.S.
Television, mech. scanner	1923	Baird	Scottish
Thermometer	1593	Galileo	Italian
Thermometer	1730	Reaumur	French
Thermometer, mercury	1714	Fahrenheit	German
Time recorder	1890	Bundy	U.S.
Time, self-regulator	1918	Bryce	U.S.
Tire, double-tube	1845	Thomson	Scottish
Tire, pneumatic	1888	Dunlop	Scottish
Toaster, automatic	1918	Strite	U.S.
Tool, pneumatic	1865	Law	English
Torpedo, marine	1804	Fulton	U.S.
Tractor, crawler	1904	Holt	U.S.
Transformer, AC	1885	Stanley	U.S.
Transistor	1947	Shockley, Brattain, Bardeen	U.S.

(continued)

Inventions (*continued*)

Inventions	Date	Inventor	Nation
Trolley car, electric	1884-87	Van DePoele, Sprague	U.S.
Tungsten, ductile	1912	Coolidge	U.S.
Tupperware	1945	Tupper	U.S.
Turbine, gas	1849	Bourdin	French
Turbine, hydraulic	1849	Francis	U.S.
Turbine, steam	1884	Parsons	English
Type, movable	1447	Gutenberg	German
Typewriter	1867	Sholes, Soule, Glidden	U.S.
Vacuum cleaner, electric	1907	Spangler	U.S.
Velcro	1948	de Mestral	Swiss
Video game ("Pong")	1972	Buschnel	U.S.
Video home system (VHS)	1975	Matsushita, JVC	Japanese
Washer, electric	1901	Fisher	U.S.
Welding, atomic hydrogen	1924	Langmuir, Palmer	U.S.
Welding, electric	1877	Thomson	U.S.
Wind tunnel	1912	Eiffel	French
Wire, barbed	1874	Glidden	U.S.
Wire, barbed	1875	Haisn	U.S.
Wrench, double-acting	1913	Owen	U.S.
X-ray tube	1913	Coolidge	U.S.
Zipper	1891	Judson	U.S.

Discoveries and Innovations: Chemistry, Physics, Biology, Medicine

	Date	Discoverer	Nation
Acetylene gas	1862	Berthelot	French
ACTH	1927	Evans, Long	U.S.
Adrenalin	1901	Takamine	Japanese
Aluminum, electrolytic process	1886	Hall	U.S.
Aluminum, isolated	1825	Oersted	Danish
Anesthesia, ether	1842	Long	U.S.
Anesthesia, local	1885	Koller	Austrian
Anesthesia, spinal	1898	Bier	German
Aniline dye	1856	Perkin	English
Anti-rabies	1885	Pasteur	French
Antiseptic surgery	1867	Lister	English
Antitoxin, diphtheria	1891	Von Behring	German
Argyrol	1897	Bayer	German
Arsphenamine	1910	Ehrlich	German
Aspirin	1889	Dresser	German
Atabrine	...	Mietzsch, et al.	German
Atomic numbers	1913	Moseley	English
Atomic theory	1803	Dalton	English
Atomic time clock	1948	Lyons	U.S.
Atomic time clock, cesium beam	1948	Essen	English
Atom-smashing theory	1919	Rutherford	English
Bacitracin	1945	Johnson, et al.	U.S.
Bacteria (described)	1676	Leeuwenhoek	Dutch
Barbital	1903	Fischer	German
Bleaching powder	1798	Tennant	English
Blood, circulation	1628	Harvey	English
Bordeaux mixture	1885	Millardet	French
Bromine from sea	1924	Edgar Kramer	U.S.
Calcium carbide	1888	Wilson	U.S.
Calculus	1670	Newton	English
Camphor synthetic	1896	Haller	French
Canning (food)	1804	Appert	French
Carbomycin	1952	Tanner	U.S.
Carbon oxides	1925	Fisher	German
Chloamphenicol	1947	Burkholder	U.S.
Chlorine	1774	Scheele	Swedish
Chloroform	1831	Guthrie, S.	U.S.
Chlortetracycline	1948	Duggen	U.S.
Classification of plants and animals	1735	Linnaeus	Swedish
Cocaine	1860	Niermann	German
Combustion explained	1777	Lavoisier	French
Conditioned reflex	1914	Pavlov	Russian
Cortisone	1936	Kendall	U.S.
Cortisone, synthesis	1946	Sarett	U.S.
Cosmic rays	1910	Gockel	Swiss
Cyanamide	1905	Frank, Caro	German
Cyclotron	1930	Lawrence	U.S.
DDT	1874	Zeidler	German
(not applied as insecticide until 1939)			
Deuterium	1932	Urey, Brickwedde, Murphy	U.S.
DNA (structure)	1951	Crick	English
		Watson	U.S.
		Wilkins	English
Electric resistance (law)	1827	Ohm	German
Electric waves	1888	Hertz	German
Electrolysis	1852	Faraday	English
Electromagnetism	1819	Oersted	Danish
Electron	1897	Thomson, J.	English
Electron diffraction	1936	Thomson, G.	English
		Davisson	U.S.
Electroshock treatment	1938	Cerletti, Bini	Italian
Erythromycin	1952	McGuire	U.S.
Evolution, natural selection	1858	Darwin	English
Falling bodies, law	1590	Galileo	Italian
Gases, law of combining volumes	1808	Gay-Lussac	French
Geometry, analytic	1619	Descartes	French
Gold (cyanide process for extraction)	1887	MacArthur, Forest	British
Gravitation, law	1687	Newton	English
Holograph	1948	Gabor	British
Human heart transplant	1967	Barnard	S. African
Human immunodeficiency virus identified	1984	Montagnier, Gallo	French, U.S.
Indigo, synthesis of	1880	Baeyer	German
Induction, electric	1830	Henry	U.S.
Insulin	1922	Banting, Best, Macleod	Canadian, Scottish
Intelligence testing	1905	Binet, Simon	French
In vitro fertilization	1978	Steptoe, Edwards	English
Isoniazid	1952	Hoffman-La-Roche	U.S.
		Domagk	German
Isotopes, theory	1912	Soddy	English
Laser (light amplification by stimulated emission of radiation)	1958	Townes, Schawlow	U.S.
Lasting machine	1883	Jan Matzelieger	U.S.
Light, velocity	1675	Roemer	Danish
Light, wave theory	1690	Huygens	Dutch
Lithography	1796	Senefelder	Bohemian
Lobotomy	1935	Egas Moniz	Portuguese
LSD-25	1943	Hoffman	Swiss
Mendelian laws	1866	Mendel	Austrian
Mercator projection (map)	1568	Mercator(Kremer)	Flemish
Methanol	1661	Boyle	Irish
Milk condensation	1853	Borden	U.S.
Molecular hypothesis	1811	Avogadro	Italian
Motion, laws of	1687	Newton	English
Neomycin	1949	Waksman, Lechevalier	U.S.
Neutron	1932	Chadwick	English
Nitric acid	1648	Glauber	German
Nitric oxide	1772	Priestley	English
Nitroglycerin	1846	Sobrero	Italian
Oil cracking process	1891	Dewar	U.S.
Oxygen	1774	Priestley	English
Oxytetracycline	1950	Finlay, et al.	U.S.
Ozone	1840	Schonbein	German
Paper, sulfite process	1867	Tilghman	U.S.
Paper, wood pulp, sulfate process	1884	Dahl	German
Penicillin	1929	Fleming	Scottish
practical use	1941	Florey, Chain	English
Periodic law and table of elements	1869	Mendeleyev	Russian
Planetary motion, laws	1609	Kepler	German
Plutonium fission	1940	Kennedy, Wahl, Seaborg, Segre	U.S.
Polymyxin	1947	Ainsworth	English
Positron	1932	Anderson	U.S.
Proton	1919	Rutherford	N. Zealand
Psychoanalysis	1900	Freud	Austrian
Quantum theory	1900	Planck	German
Quasars	1963	Matthews, Sandage	U.S.
Quinine synthetic	1946	Woodward, Doering	U.S.
Radioactivity	1896	Becquerel	French

	Date	Discoverer	Nation		Date	Discoverer	Nation
Radiocarbon dating	1947	Libby	U.S.			Einstein,	
Radium	1898	Curie, Pierre . . .	French			Pegram,	
		Curie, Marie . .	Pol.-Fr.			Wheeler	U.S.
Relativity theory	1905	Einstein	German	Uranium fission,		Fermi,	
Reserpine	1949	Jal Vaikl	Indian	atomic reactor	1942	Szilard	U.S.
Schick test	1913	Schick	U.S.	Vaccine, measles	1954	Enders, Peebles	U.S.
Silicon	1823	Berzelius	Swedish	Vaccine, meningitis			
Smallpox eradication . . .	1979	World Health		(first conjugate)	1987	Gordon, et. al.,	
		Organization .	United			Connaught	
			Nations			Lab.,	
Streptomycin	1945	Schatz,				Inc.	U.S.
		Waksman . . .	U.S.	Vaccine, polio	1955	Salk	U.S.
Sulfanilamide	1935	Bovet, Trefouel .	French	Vaccine, polio, oral	1955	Sabin	U.S.
Sulfanilamide theory . . .	1908	Gelmo	German	Vaccine, rabies	1885	Pasteur	French
Sulfapyridine	1938	Ewins, Phelps . .	English	Vaccine, smallpox	1796	Jenner	English
Sulfathiazole	...	Fosbinder,		Vaccine, typhus	1909	Nicolle	French
		Walter.	U.S.	Vaccine, varicella	1974	Takahashi	Japan
Sulfuric acid	1831	Phillips.	English	Van Allen belts,			
Sulfuric acid, lead	1746	Roebuck	English	radiation	1958	Van Allen	U.S.
				Vitamin A	1913	McCollum, Davis	U.S.
Thiacetazone	1950	Belmisch,		Vitamin B	1916	McCollum.	U.S.
		Mietzsch,		Vitamin C	1928	Szent-Gyorgyi,	
		Domagk	German			King	U.S.
Tuberculin	1890	Koch	German	Vitamin D	1922	McCollum.	U.S.
Uranium fission		Hahn, Meitner,		Wassermann test	1906	Wassermann . .	German
(theory).	1939	Strassmann . .	German	Xerography	1938	Carlson	U.S.
		Bohr.	Danish	X ray.	1895	Roentgen	German
		Fermi	Italian				

Top 20 Corporations Receiving U.S. Patents in 1994

Source: *Technology Assessment and Forecast Report*, Patent and Trademark Office, U.S. Department of Commerce

Rank	Company	Number of patents	Rank	Company	Number of patents
1.	International Business Machines Corp.	1,298	11.	Sony Corp.	656
2.	Canon K. K.	1,096	12.	Xerox Corp.	611
3.	Hitachi, Ltd.	976	13.	AT&T Corp.	595
4.	Mitsubishi Denki K. K.	972	14.	Fujitsu, Ltd.	592
5.	General Electric Company	970	15.	Fuji Photo Film Co., Ltd.	545
6.	Toshiba Corporation	968	16.	Minnesota Mining & Manufacturing Co.	519
7.	NEC Corp.	897	17.	E. I. du Pont de Nemours & Co.	486
8.	Eastman Kodak Company	888	18.	Texas Instruments, Inc.	479
9.	Motorola, Inc.	837	19.	Sharp K. K.	454
10.	Matsushita Electric Industrial Co., Ltd.	771	20.	Hewlett-Packard Corp.	428

Chemical Elements, Atomic Weights, Discoverers

Source: Glenn T. Seaborg, Ph.D., Ernest Orlando Lawrence Berkeley National Laboratory, Berkeley, CA

Atomic weights, based on the exact number 12 as the assigned atomic mass of the principal isotope of carbon, carbon 12, are provided through the courtesy of the International Union of Pure and Applied Chemistry and Butterworth Scientific Publications. For the radioactive elements, with the exception of uranium and thorium, the mass number of either the isotope of longest half-life (*) or the better known isotope (**) is given.

Chemical element	Symbol	Atomic number	Atomic weight	Year discov.	Discoverer
Actinium	Ac	89	227*	1899	Debierne
Aluminum	Al	13	26.9815	1825	Oersted
Americium	Am	95	243*	1944	Seaborg, et al.
Antimony.	Sb	51	121.75	1450	Valentine
Argon	Ar	18	39.948	1894	Rayleigh, Ramsay
Arsenic	As	33	74.9216	13th c.	Albertus Magnus
Astatine.	At	85	210*	1940	Corson, et al.
Barium	Ba	56	137.34	1808	Davy
Berkelium	Bk	97	249**	1949	Thompson, Ghiorso, Seaborg
Beryllium	Be	4	9.0122	1798	Vauquelin
Bismuth.	Bi	83	208.980	15th c.	Valentine
Boron	B	5	10.811[a]	1808	Gay-Lussac, Thenard
Bromine	Br	35	79.904[b]	1826	Balard
Cadmium	Cd	48	112.40	1817	Stromeyer
Calcium.	Ca	20	40.08	1808	Davy
Californium	Cf	98	251*	1950	Thompson, et al.
Carbon	C	6	12.01115[a]	BC	unknown
Cerium	Ce	58	140.12	1803	Klaproth
Cesium	Cs	55	132.905	1860	Bunsen, Kirchhoff
Chlorine	Cl	17	35.453[b]	1774	Scheele
Chromium	Cr	24	51.996[b]	1797	Vauquelin
Cobalt	Co	27	58.9332	1735	Brandt
Copper	Cu	29	63.546[b]	BC	unknown
Curium	Cm	96	247*	1944	Seaborg, James, Ghiorso
Dysprosium	Dy	66	162.50*	1886	Boisbaudran
Einsteinium	Es	99	254*	1952	Ghiorso, et al.
Erbium	Er	68	167.26	1843	Mosander
Europium	Eu	63	151.96	1901	Demarcay
Fermium	Fm	100	257*	1953	Ghiorso, et al.
Fluorine.	F	9	18.9984	1771	Scheele

(continued)

Chemical Elements (continued)

Chemical element	Symbol	Atomic number	Atomic weight	Year discov.	Discoverer
Francium	Fr	87	223*	1939	Perey
Gadolinium	Gd	64	157.25	1886	Marignac
Gallium	Ga	31	69.72	1875	Boisbaudran
Germanium	Ge	32	72.59	1886	Winkler
Gold	Au	79	196.967	BC	unknown
Hafnium	Hf	72	178.49	1923	Coster, Hevesy
Hahnium	Ha	105	262*	1970	Ghiorso, et al.
Hassium	Hs	108	265*	1984	Münzenberg, et al.
Helium	He	2	4.0026	1868	Janssen, Lockyer
Holmium	Ho	67	164.930	1878	Soret, Delafontaine
Hydrogen	H	1	1.00797[a]	1766	Cavendish
Indium	In	49	114.82	1863	Reich, Richter
Iodine	I	53	126.9044	1811	Courtois
Iridium	Ir	77	192.2	1804	Tennant
Iron	Fe	26	55.847[b]	BC	unknown
Krypton	Kr	36	83.80	1898	Ramsay, Travers
Lanthanum	La	57	138.91	1839	Mosander
Lawrencium	Lr	103	262*	1961	Ghiorso, T. Sikkeland, A.E. Larsh, and R.M. Latimer
Lead	Pb	82	207.19	BC	unknown
Lithium	Li	3	6.939	1817	Arfvedson
Lutetium	Lu	71	174.97	1907	Welsbach, Urbain
Magnesium	Mg	12	24.312	1829	Bussy
Manganese	Mn	25	54.9380	1774	Gahn
Meitnerium	Mt	109	266*	1982	Münzenberg, et al.
Mendelevium	Md	101	258*	1955	Ghiorso, et al.
Mercury	Hg	80	200.59	BC	unknown
Molybdenum	Mo	42	95.94	1782	Hjelm
Neodymium	Nd	60	144.24	1885	Welsbach
Neon	Ne	10	20.183	1898	Ramsay, Travers
Neptunium	Np	93	237*	1940	McMillan, Abelson
Nickel	Ni	28	58.71	1751	Cronstedt
Nielsbohrium	Ns	107	262*	1981	Münzenberg, et al.
Niobium[1]	Nb	41	92.906	1801	Hatchett
Nitrogen	N	7	14.0067	1772	Rutherford
Nobelium	No	102	259*	1958	Ghiorso, et al.
Osmium	Os	76	190.2	1804	Tennant
Oxygen	O	8	15.9994[a]	1774	Priestley, Scheele
Palladium	Pd	46	106.4	1803	Wollaston
Phosphorus	P	15	30.9738	1669	Brand
Platinum	Pt	78	195.09	1735	Ulloa
Plutonium	Pu	94	242**	1940	Seaborg, et al.
Polonium	Po	84	210**	1898	P. and M. Curie
Potassium	K	19	39.102	1807	Davy
Praseodymium	Pr	59	140.907	1885	Welsbach
Promethium	Pm	61	147**	1945	Glendenin, Marinsky, Coryell
Protactinium	Pa	91	231*	1917	Hahn, Meitner
Radium	Ra	88	226*	1898	P. and M. Curie, Bemont
Radon	Rn	86	222*	1900	Dorn
Rhenium	Re	75	186.2	1925	Noddack, Tacke, Berg
Rhodium	Rh	45	102.905	1803	Wollaston
Rubidium	Rb	37	85.47	1861	Bunsen, Kirchhoff
Ruthenium	Ru	44	101.07	1845	Klaus
Rutherfordium	Rf	104	261*	1969	Ghiorso, et al.
Samarium	Sm	62	150.35	1879	Boisbaudran
Scandium	Sc	21	44.956	1879	Nilson
Seaborgium	Sg	106	266*	1974	Ghiorso, et al.
Selenium	Se	34	78.96	1817	Berzelius
Silicon	Si	14	28.086[a]	1823	Berzelius
Silver	Ag	47	107.868[b]	BC	unknown
Sodium	Na	11	22.9898	1807	Davy
Strontium	Sr	38	87.62	1790	Crawford
Sulfur	S	16	32.064[a]	BC	unknown
Tantalum	Ta	73	180.948	1802	Ekeberg
Technetium	Tc	43	99**	1937	Perrier and Segre
Tellurium	Te	52	127.60	1782	Von Reichenstein
Terbium	Tb	65	158.924	1843	Mosander
Thallium	Tl	81	204.37	1861	Crookes
Thorium	Th	90	232.038	1828	Berzelius
Thulium	Tm	69	168.934	1879	Cleve
Tin	Sn	50	118.69	BC	unknown
Titanium	Ti	22	47.90	1791	Gregor
Tungsten (Wolfram)	W	74	183.85	1783	d'Elhujar
Uranium	U	92	238.03	1789	Klaproth
Vanadium	V	23	50.942	1830	Sefstrom
Xenon	Xe	54	131.30	1898	Ramsay, Travers
Ytterbium	Yb	70	173.04	1878	Marignac
Yttrium	Y	39	88.905	1794	Gadolin
Zinc	Zn	30	65.37	BC	unknown
Zirconium	Zr	40	91.22	1789	Klaproth

(1) Formerly Columbium. (a) Atomic weights so designated are known to be variable because of natural variations in isotopic composition. The observed ranges are: hydrogen±0.0001; boron±0.003; carbon±0.005; oxygen±0.0001; silicon±0.001; sulfur±0.003. (b) Atomic weights so designated are believed to have the following experimental uncertainties: chlorine±0.001; chromium±0.001; iron±0.003; copper±0.001; bromine±0.001; silver±0.001.

Note: Due to different nomenclature systems, the names of elements 101 through 109 may vary.

METEOROLOGY

National Weather Service Watches and Warnings

Source: National Weather Service, NOAA, U.S. Dept. of Commerce; *Glossary of Meteorology,* American Meteorological Society

National Weather Service forecasters issue a Severe Thunderstorm or Tornado Watch for a specific area where a severe convective storm that usually covers a relatively small geographic area or moves in a narrow path is sufficiently intense to threaten life and/or property. Examples include thunderstorms with large hail, damaging winds, and/or tornadoes. Additionally, excessive localized convective rains are classified as severe storms but are often the product of severe local storms. Such rainfall may result in related phenomena that threaten life and property, such as flash floods. Although cloud-to-ground lightning is not a criterion for severe local storms, it is acknowledged to be highly dangerous and a leading cause of deaths, injuries, and damage from thunderstorms.

A *Watch* alerts people that threatening weather is likely. Under a Watch, persons should remain alert for approaching storms, activate a plan for action, and monitor ongoing events closely. A *Warning* means that severe weather is occurring or has been indicated by radar; **immediate** action should be taken.

Severe Thunderstorm—A thunderstorm that produces a tornado, winds of at least 50 knots (58 mph), and/or hail at least 3/4 inch in diameter. A thunderstorm with winds of at least 35 knots (40 mph) and/or hail at least 1/2 inch in diameter is defined as approaching severe. A Severe Thunderstorm Watch is issued for a specific area where such storms are most likely to develop. A Severe Thunderstorm Warning indicates that a severe thunderstorm has been sighted or indicated by radar.

Tornado—A violent rotating column of air (winds up to 300 mph), usually pendant to a cumulonimbus cloud, with circulation reaching the ground. A tornado nearly always starts as a funnel cloud and may be accompanied by a loud roaring noise. On a local scale, it is the most destructive of all atmospheric phenomena. Tornado paths have varied in length from a few feet to nearly 300 miles (avg. 5 mi); in diameter from a few feet to more than a mile (avg. 220 yd); average forward speed, 30 mph.

Cyclone—An atmospheric circulation of winds rotating counterclockwise in the northern hemisphere and clockwise in the southern hemisphere. Tornadoes, hurricanes, and the lows shown on weather maps are all examples of cyclones of various size and intensity. Cyclones are usually accompanied by precipitation or stormy weather.

Subtropical Storm—An atmospheric circulation of one-minute sustained surface winds, 34 knots (39 mph) or more. Depending on its characteristics and intensity, it can develop into a tropical storm or a hurricane.

Tropical Storm—An atmospheric circulation of one-minute sustained surface winds within a range of 34 to 63 knots (39 to 73 mph). A *Tropical Storm Watch* is an announcement that a tropical storm or tropical storm conditions may pose a threat to coastal areas generally within 36 hours. A *Tropical Storm Warning* is an announcement that tropical storm conditions pose a threat along a specified segment of coastline within 24 hours.

Hurricane—A severe cyclone originating over tropical ocean waters and having one-minute sustained surface winds, 64 knots (73 mph) or higher. (West of the international date line, in the western Pacific, such storms are known as *typhoons*.) The area of hurricane-force winds takes the form of a circle or an oval, sometimes as wide as 300 mi in diameter. In the lower latitudes, hurricanes usually move west or northwest at 10 to 15 mph. When the center approaches 25° to 30° North Latitude, direction of motion often changes to northeast, with increased forward speed.

Blizzard—A severe weather condition characterized by strong winds bearing a great amount of snow. The National Weather Service specifies winds of 35 mph or higher and sufficient falling and/or blowing snow to frequently reduce visibility to less than 1/4 mile for a duration of at least 3 hours.

Flood—Flooding takes many forms. *River Flood:* A natural process that occurs seasonally when winter or spring rains are coupled with melting snow, filling river basins with too much water, too quickly; torrential rains from decaying hurricanes or tropical systems can also produce river flooding. *Coastal Flooding:* Winds generated from tropical storms and hurricanes or intense offshore low pressure systems can drive ocean water inland and cause significant flooding. Coastal floods can also be produced by sea waves called *Tsunamis,* sometimes referred to as tidal waves; these waves are produced by earthquakes or volcanic activity. *Urban Flooding:* Urbanization increases runoff 2-6 times over what would occur on natural terrain. During periods of urban flooding, streets can become swift-moving rivers, and basements can become death traps as they fill with water. *Flash Flooding:* The result of copious amounts of rain in a short period of time; flash flooding occurs within 6 hours of the rain event. *Ice Jam Flooding:* Ice can accumulate at natural or artificial obstructions and stop the flow of water. As the water flow is stopped, water builds up and flooding occurs.

Flash Flood or Flood Watch: Persons should be alert that flash flooding or flooding is possible within a designated area.

Flash Flood or Flood Warning: Flash flooding or flooding has been reported, and all necessary precautions should be taken immediately.

Urban and Small Stream Advisory: Small streams, streets, and low-lying areas such as railroad underpasses and urban storm drains are flooding.

National Weather Service Marine Warnings and Advisories

Small Craft Advisory: A Small Craft Advisory alerts mariners to sustained (exceeding 2 hours) weather and/or sea conditions, either present or forecast, potentially hazardous to small boats. Although there is no definition of a small craft, hazardous conditions generally include winds of 18 to 33 knots and/or dangerous wave conditions. It is the responsibility of the mariner, based on experience and on the location and size or type of boat, to determine if the conditions are hazardous. When a mariner becomes aware of a Small Craft Advisory, he or she should immediately obtain the latest marine forecast to determine the reason for the advisory.

Gale Warning indicates that winds within the range 34 to 47 knots, not directly associated with a tropical storm, are forecast for the area.

Tropical Storm Warning indicates that winds of 34 to 63 knots are forecast in a specified coastal area within 24 hours or less. Only issued for winds of tropical weather systems.

Storm Warning indicates that winds 48 knots or above, not directly associated with a tropical storm, are forecast for the area.

Hurricane Warning indicates that winds 64 knots or greater are forecast for the area. Only issued for winds produced by tropical weather systems.

Special Marine Warning: A warning for potentially hazardous weather conditions, usually of short duration (2 hours or less) and producing wind speeds of 34 knots or more, not adequately covered by existing marine warnings.

Primary sources of dissemination are commercial radio, TV, U.S. Coast Guard radio stations, and NOAA VHF-FM broadcasts. These broadcasts on 162.40 to 162.55 MHz can usually be received 20-40 mi from the transmitting antenna site, depending on terrain and quality of the receiver used. Where transmitting antennas are on high ground, the range may be somewhat greater, reaching 60 mi or more.

Monthly Normal Temperatures, Precipitation

Source: National Climatic Data Center, NESDIS, NOAA, U.S. Dept. of Commerce

The normal temperatures below are based on records for the 30-year period 1961-90 inclusive. For stations that did not have continuous records from the same instrument site for the entire 30 years, the means have been adjusted to the record at the present site.

Airport station; *city stations. T, temperature in Fahrenheit; P, precipitation in inches; L, less than 0.05 inch.

Station	Jan.		Feb.		Mar.		Apr.		May		June		July		Aug.		Sept.		Oct.		Nov.		Dec.	
	T	P	T	P	T	P	T	P	T	P	T	P	T	P	T	P	T	P	T	P	T	P	T	P
Albany, NY	21	2.4	24	2.3	34	2.9	46	3.0	58	3.4	67	3.6	72	3.2	70	3.5	61	3.0	50	2.8	40	3.2	27	2.9
Albuquerque, NM	34	0.4	40	0.5	47	0.5	55	0.5	64	0.5	74	0.6	79	1.4	76	1.6	69	1.0	57	0.9	44	0.4	35	0.5
Anchorage, AK	15	0.8	19	0.8	26	0.7	36	0.7	47	0.7	54	1.1	58	1.7	56	2.4	48	2.7	35	2.0	21	1.1	16	1.1
Asheville, NC	36	3.3	39	3.9	47	4.6	55	3.4	63	4.4	69	4.2	73	4.5	72	4.7	66	3.9	56	3.6	48	3.6	40	3.5
Atlanta, GA	41	4.8	45	4.8	54	5.8	62	4.3	69	4.3	76	3.6	79	5.0	78	3.7	73	3.4	62	3.1	53	3.9	45	4.3
Atlantic City, NJ	31	3.5	33	3.1	42	3.6	50	3.6	60	3.3	69	2.6	75	3.8	73	4.1	66	2.9	55	2.8	46	3.6	36	3.3
Baltimore, MD	32	3.1	35	3.1	44	3.4	53	3.1	63	3.7	73	3.7	77	3.7	76	3.9	69	3.4	57	3.0	47	3.3	37	3.4
Barrow, AK	–13	0.2	–18	0.2	–15	0.2	–2	0.2	19	0.2	34	0.3	39	0.9	38	1.0	31	0.6	14	0.5	–2	0.3	–11	0.2
Birmingham, AL	42	5.1	46	4.7	54	6.2	62	5.0	69	4.9	76	3.7	80	5.3	79	3.6	73	3.9	63	2.8	53	4.3	45	5.1
Bismarck, ND	9	0.5	16	0.4	28	0.8	43	1.7	55	2.2	64	2.7	71	2.1	68	1.7	57	1.5	46	0.9	29	0.5	14	0.5
Boise, ID	29	1.5	36	1.2	43	1.3	49	1.2	58	1.1	67	1.8	74	0.4	73	0.4	63	0.8	52	0.8	40	1.5	30	1.4
Boston, MA	29	3.6	30	3.6	39	3.7	48	3.6	58	3.3	68	3.1	74	2.8	72	3.2	65	3.1	55	3.3	45	4.2	34	4.0
Buffalo, NY	24	2.7	25	2.3	34	2.7	45	2.9	57	3.1	66	3.6	71	3.1	69	4.2	62	3.5	51	3.1	41	3.8	29	3.7
Burlington, VT	16	1.8	18	1.6	31	2.2	44	2.8	56	3.1	65	3.5	71	3.7	68	4.1	59	3.3	48	2.9	37	3.1	23	2.4
Caribou, ME	9	2.4	12	1.9	25	2.4	38	2.5	51	3.1	61	2.9	66	4.0	63	4.1	54	3.5	43	3.1	31	3.6	15	3.2
Charleston, SC	48	3.5	51	3.3	58	4.3	65	2.7	73	4.0	78	6.4	82	6.8	81	7.2	76	4.7	67	2.9	58	2.5	51	3.2
Chicago, IL	21	1.5	25	1.4	37	2.7	49	3.6	59	3.3	69	3.8	73	3.7	72	4.2	64	3.8	53	2.4	40	2.9	27	2.5
Cleveland, OH	25	2.0	27	2.2	37	2.9	48	3.1	58	3.5	68	3.7	72	3.5	70	3.4	64	3.4	53	2.5	43	3.2	31	3.1
Columbus, OH	26	2.2	30	2.2	41	3.3	51	3.2	61	3.9	69	4.0	73	4.3	72	3.7	66	3.0	54	2.2	43	3.2	32	2.9
Dallas-Ft. Worth, TX	43	1.8	48	2.2	57	2.8	66	3.5	73	4.9	81	3.0	85	2.3	85	2.2	77	3.4	67	3.5	56	2.3	47	1.8
Denver, CO	30	0.5	33	0.6	39	1.3	48	1.7	57	2.4	67	1.8	74	1.9	71	1.5	62	1.2	51	1.0	39	0.9	31	0.6
Des Moines, IA	19	1.0	25	1.1	37	2.3	51	3.4	62	3.7	72	4.5	77	3.8	74	4.2	65	3.5	54	2.6	39	1.8	24	1.3
Detroit, MI	23	1.8	25	1.7	36	2.6	47	3.0	58	2.9	68	3.6	72	3.2	71	3.4	63	2.9	51	2.1	40	2.7	28	2.8
Dodge City, KS	30	0.5	35	0.6	43	1.6	55	2.0	64	3.0	74	3.1	80	3.2	78	2.7	69	1.9	57	1.3	43	0.8	32	0.6
Duluth, MN	7	1.2	12	0.8	24	1.9	39	2.3	51	3.0	60	3.8	66	3.6	64	4.0	54	3.8	44	2.5	28	1.8	13	1.2
Fairbanks, AK	–10	0.5	–4	0.4	11	0.4	31	0.3	49	0.6	60	1.4	63	1.9	57	2.0	46	1.0	25	0.9	3	0.8	–7	0.9
Fresno, CA	46	2.0	51	1.8	55	1.9	61	1.0	69	0.3	77	0.1	82	L	80	L	75	0.2	65	0.5	54	1.4	45	1.4
Galveston, TX*	53	3.3	55	2.3	62	2.2	69	2.4	76	3.6	81	4.4	83	4.0	84	4.5	80	5.9	73	2.8	64	3.4	56	3.5
Grand Junction, CO	25	0.6	34	0.5	43	0.9	52	0.7	62	0.9	72	0.5	79	0.6	76	0.8	67	0.8	55	1.0	40	0.7	29	0.6
Grand Rapids, MI	22	1.8	24	1.4	34	2.6	46	3.4	58	3.1	67	3.7	72	3.2	70	3.6	61	4.2	50	2.8	38	3.3	27	2.9
Hartford, CT	25	3.4	28	3.2	38	3.6	49	3.9	60	4.1	69	3.8	74	3.2	72	3.7	63	3.8	52	3.6	42	4.0	30	3.9
Helena, MT	20	0.6	26	0.4	34	0.7	43	1.0	53	1.8	62	1.9	69	1.1	67	1.3	55	1.2	45	0.6	32	0.5	21	0.6
Honolulu, HI	73	3.6	73	2.2	74	2.2	76	1.5	78	1.1	79	0.5	81	0.6	81	0.4	81	0.8	80	2.3	77	3.0	74	3.8
Houston, TX	50	3.2	54	3.3	61	2.7	68	4.2	75	4.7	80	4.0	83	3.3	82	3.7	78	4.9	70	3.7	61	3.4	54	3.7
Huron, SD	13	0.4	19	0.8	32	1.2	46	2.0	58	2.7	68	3.3	74	2.3	72	2.0	61	1.4	49	1.4	32	0.7	18	0.5
Indianapolis, IN	26	2.3	30	2.5	41	3.8	52	3.7	63	4.0	72	3.5	75	4.5	73	3.6	67	2.9	55	2.6	43	3.2	31	3.3
Jackson, MS	44	5.2	48	4.7	57	5.8	65	5.6	72	5.1	79	3.2	82	4.5	81	3.8	76	3.6	65	3.3	56	4.8	48	5.9
Jacksonville, FL	52	3.3	55	3.9	61	3.7	67	2.8	73	3.6	79	5.7	82	5.6	81	7.9	78	7.0	70	2.9	62	2.1	55	2.7
Juneau, AK	24	4.5	28	3.7	33	3.3	40	2.8	47	3.4	53	3.1	56	4.2	55	5.3	49	6.7	42	7.8	32	4.9	27	4.4
Kansas City, MO	26	1.1	31	1.1	43	2.5	55	3.1	64	5.0	73	4.7	79	4.4	76	4.0	68	4.9	57	3.3	43	1.9	30	1.6
Knoxville, TN	36	4.2	40	4.1	49	5.1	58	3.7	65	4.1	73	4.0	77	4.7	76	3.1	70	3.1	58	2.8	49	3.8	40	4.5
Lander, WY	20	0.5	25	0.6	34	1.2	43	2.1	53	2.3	63	1.5	71	0.8	69	0.5	58	1.1	47	1.1	31	0.8	21	0.6
Lexington, KY	31	2.9	35	3.2	45	4.4	55	3.9	64	4.5	72	3.7	76	5.0	75	3.9	68	3.2	57	2.6	46	3.4	36	4.0
Little Rock, AR	39	3.9	44	4.4	53	5.3	62	6.2	70	7.0	78	7.8	82	8.2	81	8.1	74	7.4	63	6.3	52	5.2	43	4.3
Los Angeles, CA*	58	2.9	60	3.1	61	2.6	63	1.0	66	0.2	70	L	74	L	75	0.1	74	0.5	70	0.3	63	2.0	58	2.0
Louisville, KY	32	2.9	36	3.3	46	4.7	56	4.2	65	4.6	73	3.5	77	4.5	76	3.5	70	3.2	58	2.7	47	3.7	37	3.6
Marquette, MI*	12	2.2	14	1.7	24	2.8	37	2.6	50	3.0	59	3.5	65	2.9	63	3.4	54	4.1	44	3.6	30	2.9	17	2.6
Memphis, TN	40	3.7	44	4.4	53	5.4	63	5.5	71	5.0	79	3.6	83	3.8	81	3.4	74	3.5	63	3.0	53	5.1	44	5.7
Miami, FL	67	2.0	69	2.1	72	2.4	75	2.9	79	6.2	81	9.3	83	5.7	83	7.6	82	7.6	78	5.6	74	2.7	69	1.8
Milwaukee, WI	19	1.6	23	1.5	33	2.7	44	3.5	55	2.8	65	3.2	71	3.5	69	3.5	62	3.4	50	2.4	38	2.5	24	2.3
Minneapolis, MN	12	1.0	18	0.9	31	1.9	46	2.4	59	3.4	68	4.1	74	3.5	71	3.6	61	2.7	49	2.2	33	1.6	18	1.1
Mobile, AL	50	4.8	53	5.5	61	6.4	68	4.5	75	5.7	80	5.0	82	6.9	82	7.0	78	5.9	68	2.9	60	4.1	53	5.3
Moline, IL	20	1.5	25	1.2	37	3.0	50	3.9	61	4.3	71	4.3	75	5.0	73	4.2	65	4.0	53	2.9	40	2.5	25	2.2
Nashville, TN	36	3.6	40	3.8	50	4.9	59	4.4	68	4.9	76	3.6	79	4.0	78	3.5	72	3.5	60	2.6	50	4.1	41	4.6
Newark, NJ	31	3.4	33	3.0	42	3.9	52	3.8	63	4.1	73	3.2	78	4.5	76	3.9	69	3.7	58	3.1	47	3.9	36	3.5
New Orleans, LA	51	5.1	54	6.0	62	4.9	69	4.5	75	4.6	80	5.8	82	6.1	82	6.2	78	5.5	69	3.1	61	4.4	55	5.8
New York, NY*	32	3.4	34	3.3	42	4.1	53	4.2	63	4.4	72	3.7	77	4.4	76	4.0	68	3.9	58	3.6	48	4.5	37	3.9
Norfolk, VA	39	3.8	41	3.5	49	3.7	57	3.1	66	3.8	74	3.8	78	5.1	77	4.8	72	3.9	61	3.2	53	2.9	44	3.2
Oklahoma City, OK	36	1.1	41	1.6	50	2.7	60	2.8	68	5.2	77	4.3	82	2.6	81	2.6	73	3.8	62	3.2	50	2.0	39	1.4
Omaha, NE	21	0.7	27	0.8	39	2.0	52	2.7	62	4.5	72	3.9	77	3.5	74	3.2	65	3.7	53	2.3	39	1.5	25	1.0
Philadelphia, PA	30	3.2	33	2.8	42	3.5	52	3.6	63	3.8	72	3.7	77	4.3	76	3.8	68	3.4	56	2.6	46	3.3	36	3.4
Phoenix, AZ	54	0.7	58	0.7	62	0.9	70	0.2	79	0.1	88	0.1	94	0.8	92	1.0	86	0.9	75	0.7	62	0.7	54	1.0
Pittsburgh, PA	26	2.5	29	2.4	39	3.4	50	3.2	60	3.6	68	3.7	72	3.8	71	3.2	64	3.0	52	2.4	42	2.9	32	2.9
Portland, ME	21	3.5	23	3.3	33	3.7	43	4.1	53	3.6	62	3.4	69	3.1	67	2.9	59	3.1	49	3.9	39	5.2	27	4.6
Portland, OR	40	5.4	44	3.9	47	3.6	51	2.4	57	2.1	64	1.5	68	0.6	69	1.1	63	1.8	55	2.7	46	5.3	40	6.1
Providence, RI	28	4.1	30	3.7	37	4.3	47	4.0	57	3.5	67	2.8	73	3.0	71	4.0	64	3.5	54	3.8	44	4.2	33	4.5
Raleigh, NC	39	3.6	42	3.4	50	3.7	59	2.9	67	3.7	74	3.7	78	4.4	77	4.4	71	3.3	60	2.7	51	2.9	43	3.1
Rapid City, SD	22	0.4	27	0.5	34	1.0	45	1.9	55	2.7	65	3.1	72	2.0	71	1.7	60	1.2	49	1.1	35	0.6	24	0.5
Reno, NV	33	1.1	38	1.0	43	0.7	49	0.4	57	0.7	65	0.5	72	0.3	70	0.3	60	0.4	51	0.4	40	0.9	33	1.0
Richmond, VA	37	3.2	39	3.2	48	3.6	57	3.0	66	3.8	74	3.6	78	5.0	77	4.4	70	3.3	59	3.5	50	3.2	40	3.3
St. Louis, MO	29	1.8	34	2.1	45	3.6	57	3.5	66	4.0	75	3.7	80	3.9	78	2.9	70	3.1	58	2.7	46	3.3	34	3.0
Salt Lake City, UT	28	1.1	34	1.2	42	1.9	50	2.1	59	1.8	69	0.9	78	0.8	76	0.9	65	1.3	53	1.4	41	1.3	30	1.4
San Antonio, TX	49	1.7	54	1.8	62	1.5	69	2.5	76	4.2	82	3.8	85	2.2	85	2.5	79	3.4	70	3.2	60	2.6	52	1.5
San Diego, CA	57	1.8	59	1.5	60	1.8	62	0.8	64	0.2	67	0.1	71	L	73	0.1	71	0.2	68	0.4	62	1.5	57	1.6
San Francisco, CA	49	4.4	52	3.2	53	3.1	56	1.4	58	0.2	62	0.1	63	L	64	0.1	65	0.2	61	1.2	55	2.9	49	3.1
San Juan, PR	77	2.8	77	2.1	78	2.3	79	3.8	81	5.9	82	4.0	83	4.4	83	5.3	82	5.3	82	5.7	80	5.9	78	4.7
Sault Ste. Marie, MI*	13	2.4	14	1.7	24	2.3	38	2.4	51	2.7	58	3.1	64	2.7	63	3.6	55	3.7	45	3.2	33	3.5	19	2.9
Savannah, GA	49	3.6	52	3.2	59	3.8	66	3.0	74	4.1	79	5.7	82	6.4	81	7.4	77	4.5	67	2.4	59	2.2	52	3.0
Scottsbluff, NE	25	0.5	30	0.5	36	1.1	47	1.6	56	2.8	67	2.6	74	2.1	72	1.1	61	1.1	50	0.8	36	0.6	26	0.6
Seattle, WA	41	5.4	44	4.0	47	3.8	50	2.5	56	1.8	61	1.6	65	0.9	66	1.2	61	1.9	54	3.3	46	5.7	42	6.0
Spokane, WA	27	2.0	33	1.5	39	1.5	46	1.2	54	1.4	62	1.3	69	0.7	68	0.7	59	0.7	47	1.0	35	2.2	28	2.4
Springfield, MO	31	1.8	36	2.2	46	3.9	56	4.2	65	4.4	73	5.1	78	2.9	77	3.5	69	4.6	58	3.6	46	3.8	35	3.2
Syracuse, NY	22	2.3	24	2.2	34	2.8	46	3.3	57	3.3	65	3.8	70	3.8	68	3.5	62	3.8	51	3.2	41	3.7	28	3.2
Tampa, FL	60	2.0	62	3.1	67	3.0	71	1.2	77	3.1	81	5.5	82	6.6	82	7.6	81	6.0	75	2.0	68	1.8	62	2.2
Washington, DC	31	2.7	34	2.8	43	3.2	53	3.1	62	4.0	71	3.9	76	3.5	74	3.9	67	3.4	55	3.2	45	3.3	35	3.2
Wilmington, DE	31	3.0	33	2.9	43	3.4	52	3.4	63	3.8	72	3.6	76	4.2	75	3.4	68	3.4	56	2.9	46	3.3	36	3.5

Normal High and Low Temperatures, Precipitation

Source: National Climatic Data Center, NESDIS, NOAA, U.S. Dept. of Commerce

The normal temperatures below are based on records for the 30-year period 1961-90. The extreme temperatures (through 1990) are listed for the stations shown and may not agree with the state records shown on p. 183.

Airport stations; * designates city stations. The minus (–) sign indicates temperatures below zero. Fahrenheit thermometer registration.

| State | Station | Normal temperature | | | | Extreme temperature | | Normal annual precipitation (inches) |
| | | January | | July | | | | |
		Max.	Min.	Max.	Min.	Highest	Lowest	
Alabama	Mobile	60	40	91	73	104	3	63.96
Alaska	Anchorage	21	8	65	52	85	–34	15.91
Alaska	Barrow	–7	–19	45	34	79	–56	4.49
Arizona	Phoenix	66	41	106	81	122	17	7.66
Arkansas	Little Rock	49	29	92	72	112	–5	72.10
California	Los Angeles*	68	49	84	65	112	28	14.77
California	San Diego	66	49	76	66	111	29	9.9
California	San Francisco	56	42	72	54	106	20	19.70
Colorado	Denver	43	16	88	59	104	–30	15.40
Connecticut	Hartford	33	16	85	62	102	–26	44.14
Delaware	Wilmington	39	22	86	67	102	–14	40.84
District of Columbia	Washington–National	42	27	89	71	104	–5	38.63
Florida	Jacksonville	64	41	91	72	105	7	51.32
Florida	Miami	75	59	89	76	98	30	55.91
Georgia	Atlanta	50	32	88	70	105	–8	50.77
Georgia	Savannah	60	38	91	72	105	3	49.22
Hawaii	Honolulu	80	66	88	74	94	53	22.02
Idaho	Boise	36	22	90	58	111	–25	12.11
Illinois	Chicago	29	13	84	63	104	–27	35.82
Illinois	Moline	28	11	86	65	106	–27	39.08
Indiana	Indianapolis	34	17	86	65	104	–23	39.94
Iowa	Des Moines	28	11	87	67	108	–24	33.12
Lexington	Kentucky	39	22	86	66	103	–21	44.55
Kentucky	Louisville	40	23	87	67	105	–20	44.39
Louisiana	New Orleans	61	42	91	73	102	11	61.88
Maine	Caribou	19	–2	77	55	96	–41	36.60
Maine	Portland	30	11	79	58	103	–39	44.34
Maryland	Baltimore	40	23	87	67	105	–7	40.76
Massachusetts	Boston	36	22	82	65	102	–12	41.51
Michigan	Detroit	30	16	83	61	104	–21	32.62
Michigan	Sault Ste. Marie*	21	5	76	51	98	–36	34.23
Minnesota	Duluth	16	–2	77	55	97	–39	30.00
Minnesota	Minneapolis-St. Paul	21	3	84	63	105	–34	28.32
Mississippi	Jackson	56	33	92	71	106	2	55.37
Missouri	Kansas City	35	17	89	68	109	–23	37.62
Missouri	St. Louis	38	21	89	70	107	–18	37.51
Montana	Helena	30	10	85	53	105	–42	11.60
Nebraska	Omaha	31	11	88	66	114	–23	29.86
Nebraska	Scottsbluff	38	12	90	59	109	–42	15.27
Nevada	Reno	45	21	92	51	105	–16	7.53
New Jersey	Atlantic City	40	21	85	65	106	–11	40.29
New Mexico	Albuquerque	47	22	93	64	105	–17	8.88
New York	Albany	30	11	84	60	100	–28	36.17
New York	Buffalo	30	17	80	62	99	–20	38.58
New York	New York–La Guardia	37	26	84	69	107	–3	42.12
North Carolina	Asheville	47	25	83	62	100	–16	47.59
North Carolina	Raleigh	49	29	88	68	105	–9	41.43
North Dakota	Bismarck	20	–2	84	56	109	–44	15.47
Ohio	Cleveland	32	18	82	61	104	–19	36.63
Ohio	Columbus	34	19	84	63	102	–19	38.09
Oregon	Portland	45	34	80	57	107	–3	36.30
Pennsylvania	Philadelphia	38	23	86	67	104	–7	41.41
Pennsylvania	Pittsburgh	34	19	83	62	103	–18	36.85
Rhode Island	Providence	37	19	82	63	104	–13	45.53
South Carolina	Charleston	58	38	90	73	104	6	51.53
South Dakota	Huron	24	2	87	62	112	–39	20.08
South Dakota	Rapid City	34	11	86	58	110	–30	16.64
Tennessee	Memphis	49	31	92	73	108	–13	52.10
Tennessee	Nashville	46	27	90	69	107	–17	47.30
Texas	Galveston*	58	47	87	79	101	8	42.28
Texas	Houston	61	40	93	72	107	7	46.07
Utah	Salt Lake City	36	19	92	64	107	–30	16.18
Vermont	Burlington	25	8	81	60	101	–30	34.47
Virginia	Norfolk	47	31	86	70	104	–3	44.64
Virginia	Richmond	46	26	88	68	105	–12	43.16
Washington	Seattle-Tacoma	45	35	75	55	99	0	37.19
Washington	Spokane	33	21	83	54	108	–25	16.49
Wisconsin	Milwaukee	26	12	80	62	103	–26	32.93
Wyoming	Lander	31	8	86	56	101	–37	13.01

Mean Annual Snowfall (inches) based on record through 1990: Boston, MA, 42; Sault Ste. Marie, MI, 113; Albany, NY, 65.2; Burlington, VT, 78.6; Lander, WY, 66; Juneau, AK, 105.8.

Wettest Spot: Mount Waialeale, HI, on the island of Kauai, is the rainiest place in the world, according to the National Geographic Society, with an average annual rainfall of 460 inches.

Highest Temperature: A temperature of 136° F observed at Azizia, Tripolitania, in northern Africa on Sept. 13, 1922, is generally accepted as the world's highest temperature recorded under standard conditions.

The record high in the United States was 134° F in Death Valley, CA, July 10, 1913.

Lowest Temperature: A record low temperature of –128.6° F was recorded at the Soviet Antarctica station Vostok on July 21, 1983.

The record low in the United States was –80° F at Prospect Creek, AK, Jan. 23, 1971.

The lowest official temperature on the North American continent was recorded at –81° F in February 1947, at a lonely airport in the Yukon called Snag.

These are the meteorological champions—the official temperature extremes—but there are plenty of other claimants to thermometer fame. However, sun readings are unofficial records, since meteorological data to qualify officially must be taken on instruments in a sheltered and ventilated location.

Annual Climatological Data

Source: National Climatic Data Center, NESDIS, NOAA, U.S. Dept. of Commerce

1994

Station	Elev. ft	Temperature °F Highest	Date	Lowest	Date	Precipitation Total (in.)	Greatest in 24 hours	Date	Sleet or snow Total (in.)	Greatest in 24 hours	Date	Fastest wind MPH	Date	No. of days Clear*	Cloudy*	Prec. .01 in. or more	Snow, sleet 1 in. or more
Albany, NY	275	95	6/18	−23	1/27	34.72	1.85	8/17	88.3	11.3	1/17	30	11/2	72	181	146	22
Albuquerque, NM	5,311	107	6/26	12	2/2	11.15	2.13	8/14	1.7	1.1	3/27	44	1/25	143	98	63	0
Anchorage, AK	114	76	8/3	−15	11/25	13.12	0.90	6/24	122.0	14.1	11/20	44	2/20	52	259	106	34
Asheville, NC	2,140	88	6/22	−5	1/19	57.46	3.98	3/27	3.0	2.3	1/3	35	12/25	84	177	147	1
Atlanta, GA	1,010	95	8/30	6	1/19	60.02	6.47	7/4	T	T	1/15	35	10/2	100	158	124	0
Atlantic City, NJ	64	96	7/9	−3	1/19	42.49	2.80	3/2	5.1	2.4	2/8	41	3/2	98	150	116	2
Baltimore, MD	148	101	6/15	−5	1/19	43.42	2.72	9/22	14.6	4.1	2/10	46	7/25	101	168	130	4
Barrow, AK	31	68	8/10	−49	12/24	4.28	0.67	8/17	35.0	3.6	10/6	41	11/3	120	197	76	9
Birmingham, AL	620	94	6/15	9	1/19	60.25	3.59	9/22	T	T	7/27	—	—	120	0	
Bismarck, ND	1,647	99	7/18	−43	2/9	18.94	4.34	9/14	71.0	8.3	4/25	41	10/6	99	158	107	20
Boise, ID	2,838	106	7/22	7	11/21	9.40	0.65	12/1	23.9	3.7	11/17	35	6/11	121	165	81	11
Boston, MA	15	97	7/21	−4	1/16	47.62	2.88	9/22	86.3	14.5	2/8	48	12/24	86	175	135	22
Buffalo, NY	705	95	6/18	−10	1/19	36.72	2.80	6/23	85.8	7.1	1/17	41	4/16	60	199	157	27
Burlington, VT	332	97	6/18	−29	1/27	34.86	1.47	11/1	98.3	17.4	3/3	37	7/2	59	207	153	22
Caribou, ME	624	90	7/21	−32	1/19	38.40	1.42	7/1	138.8	19.0	1/17	39	12/29	—	160	31	
Charleston, SC	40	95	8/31	17	1/19	70.54	4.75	10/2	0.0	0.0	—	35	6/26	82	171	131	0
Chicago, IL	658	95	7/5	−21	1/19	29.59	3.79	6/23	47.4	8.8	2/22	39	11/28	84	171	115	18
Cleveland, OH	777	94	6/16	−20	1/19	29.56	3.65	8/13	51.3	6.5	1/3	37	6/20	71	186	133	18
Columbus, OH	813	98	6/19	−22	1/19	31.62	1.95	7/2	28.4	7.8	1/16	28	3/18	59	185	123	8
Dallas-Ft. Worth, TX	551	103	8/19	18	1/18	44.10	4.17	9/1	0.1	0.1	2/10	44	5/14	125	159	91	0
Denver, CO	5,282	104	6/26	−3	12/31	11.00	0.88	11/13	57.4	12.1	11/13	37	3/17	130	115	80	23
Des Moines, IA	938	95	7/19	−18	1/15	28.20	1.98	9/4	37.8	8.6	2/22	35	2/25	104	143	106	10
Detroit, MI	633	99	6/18	−20	1/19	31.01	2.18	8/13	52.5	10.1	1/6	37	11/28	74	171	121	13
Duluth, MN	1,428	85	7/11	−35	1/30	30.53	1.85	4/25	88.1	16.3	1/6	38	11/27	83	174	136	25
Fairbanks, AK	436	93	8/5	−45	12/7	9.73	1.02	8/24	88.3	6.9	11/14	31	8/18	55	223	119	29
Fresno, CA	328	106	8/15	29	12/10	10.12	0.84	12/24	T	T	2/18	28	3/5	169	104	51	0
Galveston, TX[3]	7	95	8/15	35	2/2	22.76	1.57	5/15	T	T	2/1	30	3/9	—	83	0	
Grand Rapids, MI	784	96	6/18	−22	1/19	46.58	4.03	6/23	66.4	7.0	12/6	38	11/28	72	183	137	20
Hartford, CT	169	97	7/7	−10	1/27	52.98	3.52	9/22	83.2	10.5	3/2	30	11/2	76	182	144	20
Helena, MT	3,828	98	8/15	−27	2/8	7.47	0.54	6/15	32.4	5.0	11/26	47	4/21	—	85	10	
Honolulu, HI	7	95	9/19	56	1/19	15.59	4.14	2/13	0.0	0.0	—	31	12/9	97	92	80	0
Houston, TX	96	101	8/15	27	2/2	43.15	4.87	10/17	0.1	0.1	2/1	32	11/5	61	183	103	0
Huron, SD	1,281	93	8/25	−41	2/9	20.78	1.89	6/4	52.0	9.2	1/26	41	6/4	114	151	94	13
Indianapolis, IN	792	96	6/18	−27	1/19	31.61	3.09	6/26	24.9	7.9	1/16	39	4/27	92	165	120	7
Jackson, MS	291	95	8/30	14	1/19	56.21	4.72	1/26	0.0	0.0	—	41	12/16	91	95	102	0
Jacksonville, FL	26	96	7/17	26	2/3	67.26	4.68	9/20	T	T	2/2	39	6/25	53	180	140	0
Kansas City, MO	973	97	8/12	−1	1/18	28.34	3.23	4/27	17.3	5.1	3/1	35	8/19	122	148	94	4
Knoxville, TN	979	92	7/6	−4	1/18	63.27	5.77	3/27	3.9	2.5	1/17	26	6/15	96	151	138	1
Lander, WY	5,557	94	8/26	−13	2/9	11.92	1.87	10/16	89.6	9.6	10/3	37	12/3	135	123	64	26
Lexington, Ky.	966	97	6/19	−20	1/19	45.70	2.37	3/9	24.2	10.2	1/16	31	3/18	86	159	119	6
Little Rock, AR	257	99	6/29	14	1/18	53.40	2.92	11/4	0.8	0.7	2/9	—	—	116	0	
Los Angeles, CA	270	104	8/12	40	11/19	8.66	1.05	12/24	0.0	0.0	—	—	—	35	0	
Louisville, KY	477	98	7/5	−22	1/19	35.98	1.94	1/16	23.9	15.9	1/16	37	11/21	—	113	2	
Marquette, MI	1,415	91	6/15	−27	2/10	24.15	1.93	8/27	112.3	12.9	3/23	—	—	149	32	
Memphis, TN	258	97	7/5	9	1/19	49.49	2.75	12/9	3.1	2.1	2/9	51	6/9	113	170	115	2
Miami, FL	7	96	6/10	50	1/6	79.56	6.86	8/11	0.0	0.0	—	38	3/2	46	131	147	0
Milwaukee, WI	676	100	6/16	−21	1/19	27.36	1.61	6/23	83.3	9.7	2/25	35	11/18	75	182	126	24
Minn.-St. Paul, MN	834	95	6/14	−27	1/19	29.67	2.61	9/13	56.2	8.4	1/16	40	11/18	79	180	115	16
Mobile, AL	211	94	7/25	21	1/19	54.92	4.36	10/1	T	T	2/1	29	12/29	83	170	111	0
Moline, IL	582	98	6/18	−23	1/19	32.15	2.58	7/13	36.1	9.6	2/22	35	4/15	103	163	105	12
Nashville, TN	590	95	6/21	−1	1/19	59.77	3.23	6/26	3.3	2.2	1/17	31	6/2	86	166	118	1
Newark, NJ	7	102	6/19	−2	1/27	47.32	2.32	8/21	60.6	18.0	2/11	38	6/29	87	181	129	14
New Orleans, LA	4	95	8/15	26	2/2	51.91	3.18	9/15	T	T	2/1	25	12/10	67	180	109	0
New York, NY	132	98	6/19	−2	1/19	47.39	2.53	8/21	46.5	12.8	2/11	29	3/3	—	124	12	
Norfolk, VA	24	99	7/9	5	1/19	52.40	4.02	3/1	8.9	3.1	1/30	36	9/22	116	151	126	3
Oklahoma City, OK	1,285	103	6/27	8	2/9	29.10	2.89	11/19	6.5	4.0	3/9	46	11/20	—	75	2	
Omaha, NE[4]	997	96	8/24	−13	2/9	26.50	4.27	6/22	29.0	6.3	2/22	44	4/25	—	92	10	
Philadelphia, PA	5	100	6/19	−5	1/19	44.92	3.45	7/18	22.2	5.3	2/8	46	8/14	93	161	116	5
Phoenix, AZ	1,110	117	6/29	35	11/28	8.78	1.36	9/2	T	T	2/4	43	7/28	—	33	0	
Pittsburgh, PA	1,137	97	6/19	−22	1/19	41.34	2.14	8/2	55.5	13.4	1/3	36	11/28	63	187	155	15
Portland, ME[5]	43	94	7/22	−18	1/27	44.05	4.10	9/23	63.7	9.7	1/17	38	11/7	—	129	16	
Portland, OR	21	103	7/20	22	1/19	34.96	4.44	10/26	4.0	2.0	2/24	35	12/31	78	215	143	1
Providence, RI	51	94	7/13	−3	1/16	44.69	2.78	11/18	54.4	9.8	2/11	46	12/24	89	171	123	16
Raleigh, NC	416	96	6/16	2	1/19	36.41	3.79	10/13	1.3	0.6	2/2	33	1/4	106	154	125	0
Rapid City, SD	3,162	103	8/26	−25	2/9	10.50	0.83	10/15	48.4	7.7	4/25	55	10/6	112	129	91	17
Reno, NV	4,404	101	7/28	3	11/19	5.20	0.63	5/6	21.5	6.5	11/25	48	11/9	142	137	41	7
Richmond, VA	164	99	7/9	−1	1/19	43.81	2.69	9/21	4.6	1.6	2/10	30	6/29	105	154	122	2
St. Louis, MO	535	97	8/13	−8	1/18	34.70	3.15	4/27	7.7	2.4	1/16	35	11/27	89	171	107	2
Salt Lake City, UT.	4,221	106	8/4	10	11/22	15.28	0.99	11/12	71.3	9.9	2/22	45	7/5	134	145	92	17
San Antonio, TX.	788	104	7/25	20	2/2	40.43	4.82	10/7	T	T	3/27	46	3/27	69	167	90	0
San Diego, CA	13	99	10/9	39	11/19	9.43	1.14	3/24	0.0	0.0	—	34	2/7	129	111	42	0
San Francisco, CA	8	94	6/10	35	12/30	19.32	2.43	11/5	T	T	2/18	40	4/21	166	102	66	0
San Juan, PR	13	95	10/15	68	12/30	40.98	1.62	9/19	0.0	0.0	—	28	6/30	135	56	197	0
Sault Ste. Marie, MI	718	91	6/17	−29	1/15	27.99	1.65	7/21	81.8	7.3	1/17	35	11/21	70	200	149	25
Savannah, GA	46	97	8/30	21	1/19	69.44	8.86	10/12	T	T	2/2	32	6/25	86	166	116	0
Scottsbluff, NE	3,957	102	8/26	−18	2/9	15.97	1.85	6/20	40.0	4.6	12/30	44	2/1	96	148	77	12
Seattle, WA	22	94	7/20	23	12/4	34.85	1.84	12/19	2.5	1.5	12/5	—	—	142	2	
Spokane, WA.	2,356	102	7/22	3	2/8	13.81	1.23	10/26	30.4	5.2	11/4	35	2/23	102	175	95	9
Springfield, MO	1,268	97	7/4	3	1/19	49.02	3.28	4/9	11.3	6.7	3/8	29	11/27	104	173	112	1
Syracuse, NY	410	93	6/18	−21	1/16	37.34	1.43	8/13	126.2	18.0	1/4	43	1/29	—	172	34	
Tampa, FL	19	94	8/27	35	2/3	47.23	3.20	7/29	0.0	0.0	—	39	7/18	85	131	114	0
Washington, DC.	290	99	6/15	−7	1/21	44.26	4.05	7/27	15.9	4.9	3/1	40	6/19	91	167	120	6
Wilmington, DE	74	100	6/19	−5	1/19	45.40	2.57	7/14	15.3	4.7	2/11	36	11/28	—	116	5	

*To get partly cloudy days, deduct the total of clear and cloudy days from 365 (1 yr). T—trace. (1) Date shown is the starting date of the storm (in some cases it lasted more than one day). (2) Sustained for at least 1 minute, not peak gust. (3) Data compiled through Oct. 1994. (4) Wind data compiled through Aug. 1994. (5) Snow/sleet data compiled through Aug. 1994.

Record Temperatures by State Through 1994

Source: National Climatic Data Center, NESDIS, NOAA, U.S. Dept. of Commerce

State	Lowest °F	Highest	Latest date	Station	Approximate elevation in feet
Alabama.	-27		Jan. 30, 1966	New Market	760
		112	Sept. 5, 1925	Centerville	345
Alaska	-80		Jan. 23, 1971	Prospect Creek Camp	1,100
		100	June 27, 1915	Fort Yukon	420
Arizona	-40		Jan. 7, 1971	Hawley Lake.	8,180
		128	June 29, 1994 [1]	Lake Havasu City	505
Arkansas	-29		Feb. 13, 1905	Pond	1,250
		120	Aug. 10, 1936	Ozark.	396
California	-45		Jan. 20, 1937	Boca	5,532
		134	July 10, 1913	Greenland Ranch	-178
Colorado	-61		Feb. 1, 1985	Maybell.	5,920
		118	July 11, 1888	Bennett	5,484
Connecticut	-32		Feb. 16, 1943	Falls Village	585
		105	July 21, 1991 [1]	Danbury	450
Delaware	-17		Jan. 17, 1893	Millsboro.	20
		110	July 21, 1930	Millsboro.	20
Dist. of Col..	-15		Feb. 11, 1899	Washington	112
		106	July 20, 1930	Washington	112
Florida	-2		Feb. 13, 1899	Tallahassee	193
		109	June 29, 1931	Monticello.	207
Georgia	-17		Jan. 27, 1940	CCC Camp F-16	1,000
		112	Jul. 24, 1952	Louisville	132
Hawaii	12		May 17, 1979	Mauna Kea.	13,770
		100	Apr. 27, 1931	Pahala.	850
Idaho	-60		Jan. 18, 1943	Island Park Dam	6,285
		118	July 28, 1934	Orofino.	1,027
Illinois	-35		Jan. 22, 1930	Mount Carroll	817
		117	July 14, 1954	E. St. Louis.	410
Indiana.	-36		Jan. 19, 1994	New Whiteland	785
		116	July 14, 1936	Collegeville.	672
Iowa.	-47		Jan. 12, 1912	Washta.	1,157
		118	July 20, 1934	Keokuk.	614
Kansas.	-40		Feb. 13, 1905	Lebanon.	1,812
		121	July 24, 1936 [1]	Alton (near).	1,651
Kentucky	-34		Jan. 28, 1963	Cynthiana.	684
		114	July 28, 1930	Greensburg	581
Louisiana	-16		Feb. 13, 1899	Minden.	194
		114	Aug. 10, 1936	Plain Dealing	268
Maine.	-48		Jan. 19, 1925	Van Buren	510
		105	July 10, 1911 [1]	North Bridgton.	450
Maryland	-40		Jan. 13, 1912	Oakland	2,461
		109	July 10, 1936 [1]	Cumberland and Frederick	623; 325
Massachusetts	-35		Jan. 12, 1981	Chester	640
		107	Aug. 2, 1975	Chester and New Bedford	120; 640
Michigan	-51		Feb. 9, 1934	Vanderbilt.	785
		112	July 13, 1936	Mio.	963
Minnesota	-59		Feb. 16, 1903 [1]	Pokegama Dam	1,280
		114	July 6, 1936 [1]	Moorhead.	904
Mississippi	-19		Jan. 30, 1966	Corinth	420
		115	July 29, 1930	Holly Springs.	600
Missouri	-40		Feb. 13, 1905	Warsaw	700
		118	July 14, 1954 [1]	Warsaw and Union	687; 560
Montana.	-70		Jan. 20, 1954	Rogers Pass.	5,470
		117	July 5, 1937	Medicine Lake.	1,950
Nebraska	-47		Feb. 12, 1899	Camp Clarke.	3,700
		118	July 24, 1936 [1]	Minden.	2,169
Nevada	-50		Jan. 8, 1937	San Jacinto.	5,200
		125	June 29, 1994	Laughlin	605
New Hampshire	-46		Jan. 28 1925	Pittsburgh.	1,575
		106	July 4, 1911	Nashua.	125
New Jersey	-34		Jan. 5, 1904	River Vale.	70
		110	July 10, 1936	Runyon.	18
New Mexico	-50		Feb. 1, 1951	Gavilan.	7,350
		122	June 27, 1994	Waste Isolat. Pilot Plt.	3,418
New York	-52		Feb. 18, 1979	Old Forge	1,720
		108	July 22, 1926	Troy	35
North Carolina	-34		Jan. 21, 1985	Mt. Mitchell	6,525
		110	Aug. 21, 1983	Fayetteville.	213
North Dakota	-60		Feb. 15, 1936	Parshall	1,929
		121	July 6, 1936	Steele.	1,857
Ohio.	-39		Feb. 10, 1899	Milligan.	800
		113	July 21, 1934 [1]	Gallipolis (near).	673
Oklahoma.	-27		Jan. 18, 1930	Watts	958
		120	June 27, 1994 [1]	Tipton.	1,350
Oregon.	-54		Feb. 10, 1933 [1]	Seneca.	4,700
		119	Aug. 10, 1898	Pendleton.	1,074
Pennsylvania	-42		Jan. 5, 1904	Smethport.	1,500
		111	July 10, 1936 [1]	Phoenixville	100
Rhode Island	-23		Jan. 11, 1942	Kingston	100
		104	Aug. 2, 1975	Providence	51
South Carolina	-19		Jan. 21, 1985	Caesar's Head	3,100
		111	June 28, 1954 [1]	Camden.	170
South Dakota	-58		Feb. 17, 1936	McIntosh.	2,277
		120	July 5, 1936	Gannvalley.	1,750

State	Lowest °F	Highest	Latest date	Station	Approximate elevation in feet
Tennessee	-32		Dec. 30, 1917	Mountain City	2,471
		113	*Aug. 9, 1930*[1]	*Perryville*	*377*
Texas	-23		Feb. 8, 1933	Seminole	3,275
		120	*Aug. 12, 1936*	*Seymour*	*1,291*
Utah	-69		Feb. 1, 1985	Peter's Sink	8,092
		117	*Jul. 5, 1985*	*Saint George*	*2,880*
Vermont	-50		Dec. 30, 1933	Bloomfield	915
		105	*July 4, 1911*	*Vernon*	*310*
Virginia	-30		Jan. 22, 1985	Mountain Lake Bio. Station	3,870
		110	*July 15, 1954*	*Balcony Falls*	*725*
Washington	-48		Dec. 30, 1968	Mazama and Winthrop	2,120; 1,765
		118	*Aug. 5, 1961*[1]	*Ice Harbor Dam*	*475*
West Virginia	-37		Dec. 30, 1917	Lewisburg	2,200
		112	*July 10, 1936*[1]	*Martinsburg*	*435*
Wisconsin	-54		Jan. 24, 1922	Danbury	908
		114	*July 13, 1936*	*Wisconsin Dells*	*900*
Wyoming	-66		Feb. 9, 1933	Riverside R.S.	6,650
		114	*July 12, 1900*	*Basin*	*3,500*

(1) Also on earlier dates at the same or other places.

International Temperature and Precipitation

Source: Environmental Data Service, U.S. Dept. of Commerce

A standard period of 30 years has been used to obtain the average daily maximum and minimum temperatures and precipitation. The length of record of extreme maximum and minimum temperatures includes all available years of data for a given location and is usually for a longer period.

Station	Elev. Feet	Temperature °F — Average Daily January Max.	January Min.	July Max.	July Min.	Extreme Max.	Extreme Min.	Average annual precipitation (inches)
Addis Ababa, Ethiopia	8,038	75	43	69	50	94	32	48.7
Algiers, Algeria	194	59	49	83	70	107	32	30.0
Amsterdam, Netherlands	5	40	34	69	59	95	3	25.6
Athens, Greece	351	54	42	90	72	109	20	15.8
Auckland, New Zealand	23	73	60	56	46	90	33	49.1
Bangkok, Thailand	53	89	67	90	76	104	50	57.8
Beirut, Lebanon	111	62	51	87	73	107	30	35.1
Berlin, Germany	187	35	26	74	55	96	-15	23.1
Bogotá, Colombia	8,355	67	48	64	50	75	30	41.8
Bombay, India	27	88	62	88	75	110	46	71.2
Bucharest, Romania	269	33	20	86	61	105	-18	22.8
Budapest, Hungary	394	35	26	82	61	103	-10	24.2
Buenos Aires, Argentina	89	85	63	57	42	104	22	37.4
Cairo, Egypt	381	65	47	96	70	117	34	1.1
Capetown, South Africa	56	78	60	63	45	103	28	20.0
Caracas, Venezuela	3,418	75	56	78	61	91	45	32.9
Casablanca, Morocco	164	63	45	79	65	110	31	15.9
Copenhagen, Denmark	43	36	29	72	55	91	-3	23.3
Damascus, Syria	2,362	53	36	96	64	113	21	8.6
Dublin, Ireland	155	47		67	51	86	8	29.7
Geneva, Switzerland	1,329	39	29	77	58	101	-1	33.9
Havana, Cuba	80	79	65	89	75	104	43	48.2
Hong Kong	109	64	56	87	78	97	32	85.1
Istanbul, Turkey	59	45	36	81	65	100	17	31.5
Jerusalem, Israel	2,654	55	41	87	63	107	26	19.7
Lagos, Nigeria	10	88	74	83	74	104	60	72.3
La Paz, Bolivia	12,001	63	43	62	33	80	26	22.6
Lima, Peru	394	82	66	67	57	93	49	1.6
London, England	149	44	35	73	55	99	9	22.9
Madrid, Spain	2,188	47	33	87	62	102	14	16.5
Manila, Philippines	49	86	69	88	75	101	58	82.0
Mexico City, Mexico	7,340	66	42	74	54	92	24	23.0
Montreal, Canada	187	21	6	78	61	97	-35	40.8
Moscow, Russia	505	21	9	76	55	96	-27	24.8
Nairobi, Kenya	5,971	77	54	69	51	87	41	37.7
Oslo, Norway	308	30	20	73	56	93	-21	26.9
Paris, France	164	42	32	76	55	105	1	22.3
Prague, Czech Republic	662	34	25	74	58	98	-16	19.3
Reykjavik, Iceland	92	36	28	58	48	74	4	33.9
Rome, Italy	377	54	39	88	64	104	20	29.5
San Salvador, El Salvador	2,238	90	60	89	65	105	45	70.0
Santiago, Chile	1,706	85	53	59	37	99	24	14.2
Sao Paolo, Brazil	2,628	77	63	66	53	100	32	57.3
Shanghai, China	16	47	32	91	75	104	10	45.0
Singapore	33	86	73	88	75	97	66	95.0
Stockholm, Sweden	146	31	23	70	55	97	-26	22.4
Sydney, Australia	62	78	65	60	46	114	35	46.5
Tehran, Iran	3,937	45	27	99	72	109	-5	9.7
Tokyo, Japan	19	47	29	83	70	101	17	61.6
Toronto, Canada	379	30	16	79	59	105	-26	32.2
Tripoli, Libya	72	61	47	85	71	114	33	15.1
Vienna, Austria	664	34	26	75	59	98	-14	25.6
Warsaw, Poland	294	30	21	75	56	98	-22	22.0

Tides and Their Causes

Source: U.S. Dept. of Commerce, Natl. Oceanic & Atmospheric Admin. (NOAA), Natl. Ocean Service (NOS)

The tides are a natural phenomenon involving the alternating rise and fall in the large fluid bodies of the earth caused by the combined gravitational attraction of the sun and moon. The combination of these two variable force influences produces the complex recurrent cycle of the tides. Tides may occur in both oceans and seas, to a limited extent in large lakes, the atmosphere, and, to a very minute degree, in the earth itself. The period between succeeding tides varies as the result of many factors and force influences.

The tide-generating force represents the difference between (1) the centrifugal force produced by the revolution of the earth around the common center-of-gravity of the earth-moon system and (2) the gravitational attraction of the moon acting upon the earth's overlying waters. Since, on the average, the moon is only 238,852 miles from the earth compared with the sun's much greater distance of 92,956,000 miles, this closer distance outranks the much smaller mass of the moon compared with that of the sun, and the moon's tide-raising force is, accordingly, 2.5 times that of the sun.

The effect of the tide-generating forces of the moon and sun acting tangentially to the earth's surface (the so-called "tractive force") tends to cause a maximum accumulation of the waters of the oceans at two diametrically opposite positions on the surface of the earth and to withdraw compensating amounts of water from all points 90° removed from the positions of these tidal bulges. As the earth rotates beneath the maxima and minima of these tide-generating forces, a sequence of two high tides, separated by two low tides, ideally is produced each day (semidiurnal tide).

Twice in each lunar month, when the sun, moon, and earth are directly aligned, with the moon between the earth and the sun (at new moon) or on the opposite side of the earth from the sun (at full moon), the sun and the moon exert their gravitational force in a mutual or additive fashion. The highest high tides and lowest low tides are produced at these times. These are called *spring* tides. At two positions 90° in between, the gravitational forces of the moon and sun — imposed at right angles— tend to counteract each other to the greatest extent,

and the range between high and low tides is reduced. These are called *neap* tides. This semi-monthly variation between the spring and neap tides is called the *phase inequality*.

The inclination of the moon's monthly orbit to the equator and the inclination of the sun during the earth's yearly orbit to the equator produce a difference in the height of succeeding high tides and in the extent of depression of succeeding low tides that is known as the diurnal inequality. In most cases, this produces a type of tide called a mixed tide. In extreme cases, these phenomena can result in only one high tide and one low tide each (diurnal tide). There are also other monthly and yearly variations in the tide due to the elliptical shape of the orbits themselves.

The datum for Charting and Predictions is Mean Lower Low Water (MLLW). This became effective January 1989 according to the convention of 1980, which prescribed that data on all United States coastlines would be the same; namely, Mean Higher High Water (MHHW), Mean High Water (MHW), Mean Tide Level (MTL), Mean Sea Level (MSL), Mean Low Water (MLW), Mean Lower Low Water (MLLW). Diurnal range of tide is the difference in height between MHHW and MLLW. Mean range of tide is the difference in height between MHW and MLW.

The actual range of tide in the waters of the open oceans may amount to only one to three feet. However, as the ocean tide approaches shoal waters and its effects are augmented the tidal range may be greatly increased. In Nova Scotia along the narrow channel of the Bay of Fundy, the range of tides, or difference between high and low waters, may reach 43-1/2 feet or more (under spring tide conditions) due to resonant amplification.

At New Orleans, the periodic rise and fall of the diurnal tide is affected by the seasonal stages of the Mississippi River, being about 10 inches at low stage and zero at high. The Canadian Tide Tables for 1972 gave a maximum range of nearly 50 feet at Leaf Basin, Ungava Bay, Quebec.

In every case, actual high or low tide can vary considerably from the average, due to weather conditions such as strong winds, abrupt barometric pressure changes, or prolonged periods of extreme high or low pressure.

The Average Rise and Fall of Tides[1]

Places	Ft.	In.	Places	Ft.	In.	Places	Ft.	In.
Baltimore, MD.	1	8	Hampton Roads, VA . . .	2	10	St. John's, Nfld.	2	7[2]
Boston, MA	10	4	Key West, FL	1	10	St. Petersburg, FL.	2	3
Charleston, SC	5	10	Mobile, AL	1	6	San Diego, CA	5	9
Cristobal, Panama	1	1	New London, CT.	3	1	Sandy Hook, NJ	5	2
Eastport, ME	19	4	Newport, RI	3	11	San Francisco, CA	5	10
Ft. Pulaski, GA	7	6	New York, NY.	5	1	Seattle, WA	11	4
Galveston, TX.	1	5	Philadelphia, PA	6	9	Vancouver, B.C.	10	6
Halifax, N.S.	4	5[2]	Portland, ME	9	11	Washington, DC	3	2

(1) Diurnal range. (2) Mean range.

Hurricane Names in 1996

Source: National Weather Service, NOAA, U.S. Dept. of Commerce

Names assigned to Atlantic hurricanes, 1996 —Arthur, Bertha, Cesar, Dolly, Edouard, Fran, Gustav, Hortense, Isadore, Josephine, Kyle, Lili, Marco, Nana, Omar, Paloma, Rene, Sally, Teddy, Vicky, Wilfred.

Names assigned to Eastern Pacific hurricanes, 1996 —Alma, Boris, Cristina, Douglas, Elida, Fausto, Genevieve, Hernan, Iselle, Julio, Kenna, Lowell, Marie, Norbert, Odile, Polo, Rachel, Simon, Trudy, Vance, Winnie, Xavier, Yolanda, Zeke.

Speed of Winds in the U.S.

Source: National Climatic Data Center, NESDIS, NOAA, U.S. Dept. of Commerce

Miles per hour — average through 1993. High through 1993. Wind velocities in true values.

Station	Avg.	High	Station	Avg.	High	Station	Avg.	High
Albuquerque, NM. . . .	9.0	(b)90	Helena, MT.	7.7	73	Mt. Washington, NH . .	35.3	231
Anchorage, AK.	7.0	75	Honolulu, HI	11.3	(b)67	New Orleans, LA. . . .	8.2	(b)98
Atlanta, GA.	9.1	60	Houston, TX.	7.9	51	New York, NY(c).	9.4	(b)70
Baltimore, MD.	9.2	80	Indianapolis, IN.	9.6	46	Omaha, NE	10.5	(b)109
Bismarck, ND	10.2	(b)72	Jacksonville, FL	8.0	(b)82	Philadelphia, PA	9.6	73
Boston, MA	12.5	(b)61	Kansas City, MO.	10.8	(b)70	Phoenix, AZ	6.2	(b)86
Buffalo, NY.	11.9	91	Lexington, KY.	9.2	46	Pittsburgh, PA	9.1	58
Cape Hatteras, NC . . .	11.1	(b)110	Little Rock, AR	7.8	65	Portland, OR	7.9	88
Casper, WY	12.9	81	Los Angeles, CA.	6.2	49	St. Louis, MO	9.6	(b)60
Chicago, IL.	10.4	84	Louisville, KY	8.3	(b)61	Salt Lake City, UT. . . .	8.8	71
Cleveland, OH	10.6	(b)74	Memphis, TN	8.8	46	San Diego, CA	7.0	56
Dallas-Ft. Worth, TX . .	10.7	73	Miami, FL.	9.3	(a)86	San Francisco, CA . . .	8.7	47
Denver, CO	8.7	60	Milwaukee, WI	11.5	54	Seattle, WA	9.0	66
Detroit, MI	10.4	48	Minn.-St. Paul, MN . . .	10.5	(b)92	Spokane, WA	8.9	59
Galveston, TX.	11.0	(d)100	Mobile, AL	9.0	63	Washington, DC	9.4	(b)78

(a) Highest velocity ever recorded in Miami area was 132 mph, at former station in Miami Beach in September 1926. (b) Previous location. (c) Data for Central Park; Battery Place data through 1960, avg. 14.5, high 113. (d) Recorded before anemometer blew away. Estimated high 120.

Wind Chill Table
Source: National Weather Service, NOAA, U.S. Dept. of Commerce

Both temperature and wind cause heat loss from body surfaces. A combination of cold and wind makes a body feel colder than the actual temperature. The table shows, for example, that a temperature of 20 degrees Fahrenheit, plus a wind of 20 miles per hour, causes a body heat loss equal to that in minus 10 degrees with no wind. In other words, the wind makes 20 degrees feel like minus 10.

Top line of figures shows actual temperatures in degrees Fahrenheit. Column at left shows wind speeds. (Wind speeds greater than 45 mph have little additional chilling effect.)

MPH	35	30	25	20	15	10	5	0	-5	-10	-15	-20	-25	-30	-35	-40	-45
5	33	27	21	16	12	7	0	-5	-10	-15	-21	-26	-31	-36	-42	-47	-52
10	22	16	10	3	-3	-9	-15	-22	-27	-34	-40	-46	-52	-58	-64	-71	-77
15	16	9	2	-5	-11	-18	-25	-31	-38	-45	-51	-58	-65	-72	-78	-85	-92
20	12	4	-3	-10	-17	-24	-31	-39	-46	-53	-60	-67	-74	-81	-88	-95	-103
25	8	1	-7	-15	-22	-29	-36	-44	-51	-59	-66	-74	-81	-88	-96	-103	-110
30	6	-2	-10	-18	-25	-33	-41	-49	-56	-64	-71	-79	-86	-93	-101	-109	-116
35	4	-4	-12	-20	-27	-35	-43	-52	-58	-67	-74	-82	-89	-97	-105	-113	-120
40	3	-5	-13	-21	-29	-37	-45	-53	-60	-69	-76	-84	-92	-100	-107	-115	-123
45	2	-6	-14	-22	-30	-38	-46	-54	-62	-70	-78	-85	-93	-102	-109	-117	-125

Heat Index

The heat index is a measure of the contribution that high humidity makes with abnormally high temperatures in reducing the body's ability to cool itself. For example, the index shows that for an actual air temperature of 100 degrees Fahrenheit and a relative humidity of 50%, the effect on the human body would be same as 120 degrees. Sunstroke and heat exhaustion are likely when the heat index reaches 105. This index is a measure of what hot weather "feels like" to the average person for various temperatures and relative humidities.

Relative Humidity	Air Temperature* 70	75	80	85	90	95	100	105	110	115	120
	Apparent Temperature*										
0%	64	69	73	78	83	87	91	95	99	103	107
10%	65	70	75	80	85	90	95	100	105	111	116
20%	66	72	77	82	87	93	99	105	112	120	130
30%	67	73	78	84	90	96	104	113	123	135	148
40%	68	74	79	86	93	101	110	123	137	151	
50%	69	75	81	88	96	107	120	135	150		
60%	70	76	82	90	100	114	132	149			
70%	70	77	85	93	106	124	144				
80%	71	78	86	97	113	136					
90%	71	79	88	102	122						
100%	72	80	91	108							

*Degrees Fahrenheit.

Ultraviolet (UV) Index Forecast
Source: National Weather Service, NOAA, U.S. Dept. of Commerce

The National Weather Service (NWS), the Environmental Protection Agency (EPA), and the Centers for Disease Control and Prevention (CDC) developed the UV Index in an effort to raise the visibility of the risks associated with prolonged exposure to ultraviolet radiation. The NWS, EPA, and CDC began offering an experimental UV index on a limited basis on June 28, 1994, in response to increasing incidence of skin cancer, cataracts, and other effects from exposure to the sun's harmful rays. The NWS UV Index is now a regular element of atmospheric forecasts.

UV Index number and forecast. The UV Index number, ranging between 0 and 10+, is an indication of the amount of UV radiation reaching the earth's surface over the one-hour period around noon. The lower the number, the lesser the amount of UV radiation. The UV Index forecast is produced by the NWS Climate Analysis Center, Camp Springs, MD, about a day in advance of the time for which the forecast is effective. The forecast is based on several factors: latitude, day of year, time of day, total ozone in the atmosphere, elevation, and the predicted cloud conditions at solar noon time. A forecast is given for 58 listed cities. The index is valid for a radius of about 30 miles around a listed city; however, adjustments should be made for a number of factors.

Ozone. Total ozone is measured by a NOAA polar orbiting satellite. This measurement is combined with the aforementioned factors to help determine how much atmosphere the UV rays must pass through to reach the surface; the greater the distance and more ozone, the lower the UV radiation at the surface.

Cloudiness. Rapid changes in cloud amount can alter the predicted UV Index. Increased cloudiness will lower the index number.

Reflectivity. Reflective surfaces will intensify UV exposure to varying degrees. For example, grass reflects 2.5% to 3% of the UV radiation reaching the surface; sand, 20% to 30%; snow and ice, 80% to 90%; water, up to 100% (depending on the angle of reflection).

Elevation. Trips to the mountains and to the beach will increase exposure to UV radiation. At higher elevations, the distance by which UV radiation has to travel to reach the surface is shortened, so there is less atmosphere to absorb the rays. For every 4,000 ft. one travels above sea level, the UV Index increases by 1 unit. The presence of snow and the lack of pollutants in the atmosphere also intensify UV exposure at higher altitudes. At the beach, several factors increase UV exposure: light-colored sand and water reflect UV rays, and people usually wear less clothing and often lie in a horizontal position.

Latitude. The closer someone is to the equator, the higher the UV radiation level. It makes good sense to cover exposed areas and wear sunglasses when traveling in tropical regions. (A person can suffer a bad sunburn in the Tropics even during winter.)

Accuracy. By gathering data from 20 UV sensors (June-Oct. 1994), the NWS determined 32% of UV Index forecasts were correct, 76% were within plus or minus 1 UV Index unit, and about 90% were within plus or minus 2 units. Unpredictable cloudiness, haze, and pollution contribute to forecast error.

SPF number. The UV Index is not linked in any way to the SPF number found on suntan lotions and sunscreens. For an explanation of the SPF factor for a particular product, contact the manufacturer or the Food and Drug Administration.

Further information. For questions about health aspects or what precautions to take after learning the UV Index number, call the U.S. EPA hot line (800-296-1996) or a doctor/optometrist. For questions about scientific aspects, call the NWS at 301-713-0622.

ENVIRONMENT

Hazardous Waste Sites in the U.S., 1995

Source: Environmental Protection Agency, *Natl. Priorities List*, April 1995

State	Final Gen	Final Fed	Proposed Gen	Proposed Fed	Total	State	Final Gen	Final Fed	Proposed Gen	Proposed Fed	Total
Alabama	9	3	1	0	13	Montana	8	0	1	0	9
Alaska	2	6	0	0	8	Nebraska	8	1	1	0	10
Arizona	7	3	0	0	10	Nevada	1	0	0	0	1
Arkansas	12	0	0	0	12	New Hampshire	16	1	0	0	17
California	69	23	4	0	96	New Jersey	100	6	1	0	107
Colorado	13	3	2	0	18	New Mexico	8	2	1	0	11
Connecticut	14	1	0	0	15	New York	77	4	0	0	81
Delaware	18	1	0	0	19	North Carolina	21	2	0	0	23
District of Columbia	0	0	0	0	0	North Dakota	2	0	0	0	2
Florida	49	5	4	0	58	Ohio	31	3	2	2	38
Georgia	11	2	0	0	13	Oklahoma	9	1	1	0	11
Hawaii	1	3	0	0	4	Oregon	9	2	1	0	12
Idaho	6	2	2	0	10	Pennsylvania	95	5	1	1	102
Illinois	33	4	0	0	37	Rhode Island	10	2	0	0	12
Indiana	32	0	1	0	33	South Carolina	23	2	0	0	25
Iowa	17	1	1	0	19	South Dakota	2	1	1	0	4
Kansas	9	1	1	1	12	Tennessee	13	3	1	1	18
Kentucky	19	1	0	0	20	Texas	24	4	1	0	29
Louisiana	12	1	4	0	17	Utah	8	4	4	0	16
Maine	7	3	1	0	11	Vermont	8	0	0	0	8
Maryland	8	4	1	1	14	Virginia	18	6	0	0	24
Massachusetts	22	8	0	0	30	Washington	35	20	0	0	55
Michigan	75	0	1	1	77	West Virginia	4	2	0	0	6
Minnesota	36	3	0	0	39	Wisconsin	40	0	0	0	40
Mississippi	2	0	3	0	5	Wyoming	2	1	0	0	3
Missouri	19	3	0	0	22	Total	1,074	153	42	7	1,276

Note: Gen=general superfund sites.

Toxics Release Inventory, 1992-93

Source: Environmental Protection Agency

Reported industrial releases of toxic chemicals into the nation's environment by major manufacturing facilities (excluding power plants and mining facilities) continued to decrease in 1993, according to the EPA's *Toxics Release Inventory (TRI)*. The pollutants reported released in 1993 decreased 12.6% from the 1992 figure and decreased 42.7% from the 1988 figure, the baseline year.

Pollutant releases	1992 mil lb	1993 mil lb	Top industries, total releases	1992 mil lb	1993 mil lb
Air releases	1,845	1,672	Chemicals	1,536	1,316
Underground injection	726	576	Primary metals	345	329
Land releases	338	289	Paper	233	216
Water releases	273	271	Transportation equipment	137	136
Total	**3,182**	**2,808**	Plastics	138	127
Pollutant transfers			**Carcinogens, air/water/land releases**		
To recycling	2,840	3,252	Dichloromethane	74	64
To energy recovery	478	487	Styrene	33	33
To treatment	393	328	Chloroform	18	14
To disposal/other	276	325	Formaldehyde	12	12
To publicly owned treatment works	381	314	Tetrachloroethylene	12	12
Total	**4,368**	**4,706**	Benzene	13	11

Top 10 States, Total Releases 1992-93

Source: Environmental Protection Agency

(air, water, land, and underground injection)

State	1992 mil lb	1993 mil lb	State	1992 mil lb	1993 mil lb
Louisiana	465	451	Alabama	112	106
Texas	420	352	Illinois	118	101
Tennessee	194	188	Indiana	124	98
Ohio	144	138	Utah (#13 in 1992)	79	92
Mississippi	120	118	North Carolina	104	91

Release of Toxic Substances, 1988-93

Source: Environmental Protection Agency

Releases	% change 1992-93	% change 1988-93	Transfers[1]	% change 1992-93	% change 1988-93
Water releases	−1.8	−13.0	Disposal	23.3	—[2]
Air releases	−10.7	−38.8	Recycling	10.8	—[2]
			Energy recovery	3.1	—[2]
Land releases	−15.1	−43.7	Treatment	−17.4	—[2]
Underground injection	−20.6	−57.1	Publicly owned treatment works	−28.0	—[2]
Total	**−12.6**	**−42.7**	**Total**	**4.1**	**—[2]**

(1)Reported transfers increased by 4.1% in 1993, primarily because of increased transfers for recycling. (2)1993 transfers cannot be directly compared with 1988 transfers because of a change in reporting requirements.

Some Endangered Species

Source: Fish and Wildlife Service, U.S. Dept. of Interior; as of Aug. 20, 1994.

For a complete list of threatened and endangered species, write to Publications Unit, U.S. Fish and Wildlife Service, 113 WEBB, Washington, DC 20240.

Mammals

Common name	Scientific name	Range
Armadillo, giant	Pridontes maximus (giganteus)	Venezuela, Guyana to Argentina
Bat, gray	Myotis grisescens	central, southeastern U.S.
Bear, American black	Ursus americanus	N. America
Bear, brown or grizzly	Ursus arctos horribilis	U.S. (48 conterminous states)
Beaver, Point Arena mountain	Aplodontia rufa nigra	U.S. (CA)
Bobcat	Felis rufus escuinapae	Central Mexico
Caribou, woodland	Rangifer tarandus caribou	U.S., Canada
Cheetah	Acinonyx jubatus	Africa to India
Cougar, eastern	Felis concolor couguar	eastern N. America
Dolphin, Chinese river	Lipotes vexillifer	China
Elephant, Asian	Elephas maximus	south central & southeast Asia
Fox, northern swift	Vulpes velox hebes	U.S., Canada
Gorilla	Gorilla gorilla	central & western Africa
Leopard	Panthera pardus	Africa and Asia
Lion, Asiatic	Panthera leo persica	Turkey to India
Lion, mountain	Felis concolor	Canada to S. America
Manatee, West Indian (Florida)	Trichechus manatus	U.S. (SE), Caribbean Sea, S. America
Ocelot	Felis pardalis	U.S. (TX, AZ) to Central & S. America
Otter, marine	Lutra felina	Peru south to Straits of Magellan
Panda, giant	Ailuropoda melanoleuca	China
Panther, Florida	Felis concolor coryi	U.S. (LA, AR east to SC, FL)
Rabbit, lower keys	Sylvilagus palustris hefneri	U.S. (FL)
Rhinoceros, black	Diceros bicornis	Sub-Saharan Africa
Rhinoceros, northern white	Ceratotherium simum cottoni	Zaire, Sudan, Uganda, C. African Rep.
Sea lion, stellar (northern)	Eumetopias jubatus	U.S. (AK, CA, OR, WA), N. Pacific Ocean
Squirrel, Carolina northern flying	Glaucomys sabrinus coloratus	U.S. (NC, TN)
Tiger	Panthera tigris	Asia
Whale, gray	Eschrichtius robustus	North Pacific Ocean
Whale, humpback	Megaptera novaeangliae	Oceanic
Wolf, red	Canis rufus	southeastern U.S. to central TX
Yak, wild	Bos grunniens mutus	China (Tibet), India
Zebra, mountain	Equus zebra zebra	South Africa

Birds

Common name	Scientific name	Range
Bobwhite, masked (quail)	Colinus virginianus ridgwayi	U.S. (AZ), Mexico (Sonora)
Condor, California	Gymnogyps californianus	U.S. (OR, CA), Mexico (Baja)
Crane, hooded	Grus monacha	Japan, Russia
Crane, whooping	Grus americana	Canada, Mexico, U.S. (Rocky Mts. to Carolinas)
Curlew, Eskimo	Numenius borealis	Alaska, northern Canada to Argentina
Falcon, American peregrine	Falco peregrinus anatum	Canada to Mexico
Hawk, Hawaiian	Buteo solitarius	U.S. (HI)
Ibis, Japanese crested	Nipponia nippon	China, Japan, Russia, Korea
Kite, Everglade snail	Rostrhamus sociabilis plumbeus	U.S. (FL), Cuba
Macaw, indigo	Anodorhynchus leari	Brazil
Ostrich, West African	Struthio camelus spatzi	western Sahara
Owl, northern spotted	Strix occidentalis caurina	U.S. (CA, OR, WA), Canada, (BC)
Parakeet, golden	Aratinga guarouba	Brazil
Parrot, imperial	Amazona imperialis	West Indies (Dominica)
Tern, roseate	Sterna dougallii dougallii	tropical and temperate coasts of Atlantic basin and E. Africa
Warbler, Bachman's (wood)	Vermivora bachmanii	southeastern U.S., Cuba
Woodpecker, ivory-billed	Campephilus principalis	south central and southeastern U.S., Cuba

Reptiles

Common name	Scientific name	Range
Alligator, American	Alligator mississippiensis	southeastern U.S
Crocodile, American	Crocodylus acutus	U.S. (FL), Mexico, C. and S. America
Sea turtle, leatherback	Dermochelys coriacea	tropical, temperate, and subpolar seas
Tortoise, Galapagos	Geochelone elephantopus	Ecuador (Galapagos Islands)
Turtle, Plymouth red-bellied	Pseudemys rubiventris bangsi	U.S. (MA)

Fishes

Common name	Scientific name	Range
Salmon, chinook	Oncorhynchus tshawytscha	North Pacific basin from U.S. to Japan
Salmon, sockeye (red)	Oncorhynchus nerka	North Pacific basin from U.S. to Russia
Sturgeon, shortnose	Acipenser brevirostrum	U.S. & Canada

Flowering Plants

Common name	Scientific name	Range
Buttercup, autumn	Ranunculus acriformis var. aestivalis	U.S. (UT)
Cactus, Bakersfield	Opuntia treleasei	U.S. (CA)
Cinquefoil, Robbins'	Potentilla robbinsiana	U.S. (NH, VT)
Daisy, Maguire	Erigeron maguirei var. maguirei	U.S. (UT)
Heather, mountain golden	Hudsonia montana	U.S. (NC)
Meadowrue, Cooley's	Thalictrum cooleyi	U.S. (NC, FL)
Peperomia, Wheeler's	Peperomia wheeleri	U.S. (PR)
Rhododendron, chapman	Rhododendron chapmanii	U.S. (FL)

U.S. List of Endangered and Threatened Species

Source: Fish and Wildlife Service, U.S. Dept. of Interior; as of Aug. 4, 1994

Group	Endangered U.S. only	Endangered Foreign only	Threatened U.S. only	Threatened Foreign only	Total listed species	Species with recovery plans
Mammals	55	252	9	19	335	40
Birds	76	177	16	6	275	69
Reptiles	14	65	19	14	112	30
Amphibians	7	8	5	0	20	11
Fishes	68	11	37	0	116	68
Snails	15	1	7	0	23	11
Clams	51	2	6	0	59	42
Crustaceans	14	0	3	0	17	4
Insects	20	4	9	0	33	20
Arachnids	5	0	0	0	5	4
Animals, subtotal	325	520	111	39	995	300
Flowering plants	406	1	90	0	497	200
Conifers	2	0	0	2	4	1
Ferns and others	26	0	2	0	28	12
Plant, subtotal	434	1	92	2	529	213
Grand total	759	521	203	41	1,524[1]	513[2]

(1)When separate populations of a species are listed as endangered and as threatened, those species are tallied twice. Those species are the chimpanzee, leopard, gray wolf, bald eagle, piping plover, roseate tern, green sea turtle, and olive ridley sea turtle. (2)There are 411 approved recovery plans. Some recovery plans cover more than one species, and a few species have separate plans covering different parts of their ranges. Recovery plans are drawn up only for listed species that occur in the U.S.

Gestation, Longevity, and Incubation of Animals

Information reviewed and updated as of mid-1994 by Ronald M. Nowak, ed. *Walker's Mammals of the World* (5th ed., Johns Hopkins University Press, 1991). Average longevity figures were supplied by Ronald T. Reuther. They refer to animals in captivity; the potential life span of animals is rarely attained in nature. Figures on gestation and incubation are averages based on estimates by leading authorities.

Animal	Gestation (days)	Average longevity (years)	Maximum longevity (yr-mo)
Ass	365	12	47
Baboon	187	20	45
Bear: Black	219	18	36-10
Grizzly	225	25	50
Polar	240	20	38
Beaver	105	5	50
Bison	285	15	40
Camel (Bactrian)	406	12	50
Cat (domestic)	63	12	28
Chimpanzee	230	20	53
Chipmunk	31	6	8
Cow	284	15	30
Deer (white-tailed)	201	8	20
Dog (domestic)	61	12	20
Elephant (African)	660	35	70
Elephant (Asian)	645	40	77
Elk	250	15	26-8
Fox (red)	52	7	14
Giraffe	425	10	33-7
Goat (domestic)	151	8	18
Gorilla	258	20	54
Guinea pig	68	4	8
Hippopotamus	238	41	54-4
Horse	330	20	50
Kangaroo (gray)	36	7	24

Animal	Gestation (days)	Average longevity (years)	Maximum longevity (yr-mo)
Leopard	98	12	23
Lion	100	15	30
Monkey (rhesus)	166	15	37
Moose	240	12	27
Mouse (meadow)	21	3	4
Mouse (dom. white)	19	3	6
Opossum (American) . .	13	1	5
Pig (domestic)	112	10	27
Puma	90	12	20
Rabbit (domestic)	31	5	13
Rhinoceros (black)	450	15	45
Rhinoceros (white)	480	20	50
Sea lion (California) . . .	350	12	30
Sheep (domestic)	154	12	20
Squirrel (gray)	44	10	23-6
Tiger	105	16	26-3
Wolf (maned)	63	5	13
Zebra (Grant's)	365	15	50

Incubation time	days
Chicken	21
Duck	30
Goose	30
Pigeon	18
Turkey	26

Speeds of Animals

Source: *Natural History* magazine, March 1974. Copyright © The American Museum of Natural History, 1974

Animal	mph	Animal	mph	Animal	mph
Cheetah	70	Mongolian wild ass	40	Human	27.89
Pronghorn antelope	61	Greyhound	39.35	Elephant	25
Wildebeest	50	Whippet	35.50	Black mamba snake	20
Lion	50	Rabbit (domestic)	35	Six-lined race runner	18
Thomson's gazelle	50	Mule deer	35	Wild turkey	15
Quarterhorse	47.5	Jackal	35	Squirrel	12
Elk	45	Reindeer	32	Pig (domestic)	11
Cape hunting dog	45	Giraffe	32	Chicken	9
Coyote	43	White-tailed deer	30	Spider (Tegenaria atrica)	1.17
Gray fox	42	Wart hog	30	Giant tortoise	0.17
Hyena	40	Grizzly bear	30	Three-toed sloth	0.15
Zebra	40	Cat (domestic)	30	Garden snail	0.03

Most of these measurements are for maximum speeds over approximate quarter-mile distances. Exceptions are the lion and elephant, whose speeds were clocked in the act of charging; the whippet, which was timed over a 200-yd course; the cheetah, timed over a 100-yd distance; the human, timed for a 15-yd segment of a 100-yd run (of 13.6 sec); and the black mamba, six-lined race runner, spider, giant tortoise, three-toed sloth, and garden snail, which were measured over various small distances.

Major Venomous Animals

Snakes

Asian pit viper - from 2 ft to 5 ft long, throughout Asia; reactions and mortality vary, but most bites cause tissue damage, and mortality is generally low.

Australian brown snake - 4 ft to 7 ft long; very slow onset of cardiac or respiratory distress; moderate mortality, but because death can be sudden and unexpected, it is the most dangerous of the Australian snakes; antivenom.

Barba Amarilla or **Fer-de-lance** - as much as 7 ft long, from tropical Mexico to Brazil; severe tissue damage common; moderate mortality; antivenom.

Black mamba - as much as 14 ft long, fast-moving; S and C Africa; rapid onset of dizziness, difficulty breathing, erratic heart-beat; mortality high, nears 100% without antivenom.

Boomslang - less than 6 ft long, in African savannahs; rapid onset of nausea and dizziness, often followed by slight recovery and then sudden death from internal hemorrhaging; bites rare, mortality high; antivenom.

Bushmaster - as much as 12 ft long, wet tropical forests of C and S America; few bites occur, but mortality rate is high.

Common or Asian cobra - 4 ft to 8 ft long, throughout southern Asia; considerable tissue damage, sometimes paralysis; mortality probably not more than 10%; antivenom.

Copperhead - less than 4 ft long, from New England to Texas; pain and swelling; very seldom fatal; antivenom seldom needed.

Coral snake - 2 ft to 5 ft long, in Americas south of Canada; bite may be painless; slow onset of paralysis, impaired breathing; mortalities rare, but high without antivenom and mechnical respiration.

Cottonmouth water moccasin - as much as 5 ft long, wetlands of southern U.S. from Virginia to Texas. Rapid onset of severe pain, swelling; mortality low, but tissue destruction can be extensive; antivenom.

Death adder - less than 3 ft long, Australia; rapid onset of faintness, cardiac and respiratory distress; at least 50% mortality without antivenom.

Desert horned viper - in dry areas of Africa and western Asia; swelling and tissue damage; low mortality; antivenom.

European viper - from 1 ft to 3 ft long; bleeding and tissue damage; mortality low; antivenom.

Gaboon viper - more than 6 ft long, fat; 2-in. fangs; south of the Sahara; massive tissue damage, internal bleeding; few recorded bites.

King cobra - as much as 16 ft long, throughout southern Asia; rapid swelling, dizziness, loss of consciousness, difficulty breathing, erratic heartbeat; mortality varies sharply with amount of venom involved, most bites involve nonfatal amounts; antivenom.

Krait - as much as 5 ft long, in SE Asia; rapid onset of sleepiness; numbness; as much as 50% mortality even with antivenom.

Puff adder - as much as 5 ft long, fat; south of the Sahara and throughout the Middle East; rapid large swelling, great pain, dizziness; moderate mortality often from internal bleeding; antivenom.

Rattlesnake - 2 ft to 6 ft long, throughout W Hemisphere. Rapid onset of severe pain, swelling; mortality low, but amputation of affected digits is sometimes necessary; antivenom. Mojave rattler may produce temporary paralysis.

Ringhals, or spitting, cobra - 5 ft to 7 ft long; southern Africa; squirts venom through holes in front of fangs as a defense; venom is severely irritating, can cause blindness.

Russell's viper or **tic-polonga** - more than 5 ft long, throughout Asia; internal bleeding; moderate mortality rate; bite reports common.

Saw-scaled or carpet viper - as much as 2 ft long, in dry areas from India to Africa; severe bleeding, fever; high mortality, causes more human fatalities than any other snake; antivenom.

Sea snakes - throughout Pacific, Indian oceans except NE Pacific; almost painless bite, variety of muscle pain, paralysis; mortality rate low, many bites are not envenomed; some antivenoms.

Sharp-nosed pit viper or One Hundred Pace Snake - as much as 5 ft long, in S Vietnam, Taiwan, and China; the most toxic of Asian pit vipers; very rapid onset of swelling and tissue damage, internal bleeding; moderate mortality; antivenom.

Taipan - as much as 11 ft long, in Australia and New Guinea; rapid paralysis with severe breathing difficulty; mortality nears 100% without antivenom.

Yellow or Cape cobra - 7 ft long, in S Africa; most toxic venom of any cobra; rapid onset of swelling, breathing and cardiac difficulties; mortality high without treatment; antivenom.

Tiger snake - 2 ft to 6 ft long, S Australia; pain, numbness, mental disturbances with rapid onset of paralysis; may be the most deadly of all land snakes although antivenom is quite effective.

Notes: Not all bites by venomous snakes are actually envenomed. Any animal bite, however, carries the danger of tetanus, and anyone suffering a venomous snake bite should seek medical attention. Antivenoms do not cure; they are only an aid in the treatment of bites. Mortality rates above are for envenomed bites; low mortality, as much as 2% result in death; moderate, 2%–5%; high, 5%–15%.

Lizards

Gila monster - as much as 24 in. long with heavy body and tail, in high desert in SW U.S. and N Mexico; immediate severe pain and transient low blood pressure; no recent mortality.

Mexican beaded lizard - similar to Gila monster, Mexican west coast; reaction and mortality rate similar to Gila monster.

Insects

Ants, bees, wasps, hornets, etc. Global distribution. Usual reaction is piercing pain in area of sting. Not directly fatal, except in cases of massive multiple stings. Many people suffer allergic reactions — swelling and rashes — and a few may die within minutes from severe sensitivity to the venom (anaphylactic shock).

Spiders, Scorpions

Atrax spider - also known as funnel whip spider; several varieties, often large, in Australia; slow onset of breathing, circulation difficulties; low mortality; antivenom.

Black widow - small, round-bodied with red hour-glass marking; the widow and its relatives are found in tropical and temperate zones; severe musculoskeletal pain, weakness, breathing difficulty, convulsions; may be more serious in small children; low mortality; antivenom. The **redback** spider of Australia has the hour-glass marking on its back, rather than on its front, but is otherwise identical to the black widow.

Recluse or fiddleback and brown spider - small, oblong body; throughout U.S.; pain with later ulceration at place of bite; in severe cases fever, nausea, and stomach cramps; ulceration may last months; very low mortality.

Scorpion - crablike body with stinger in tail, various sizes, many varieties throughout tropical and subtropical areas; various symptoms may include severe pain spreading from the wound, numbness, severe agitation, cramps; severe reaction may include respiratory failure; low mortality, usually in children; antivenoms.

Tarantula - large, hairy spider found around the world; the American tarantula, and probably all others, are **harmless**, though their bite may cause some pain and swelling.

Sea Life

Cone-shell - mollusk in small, beautiful shell in the S Pacific and Indian oceans; shoots barbs into victims; paralysis; low mortality.

Octopus - global distribution, usually in warm waters; all varieties produce venom, but only a few can cause death; rapid onset of paralysis with breathing difficulty.

Portuguese man-of-war - jellyfishlike, with tentacles as much as 70 ft long, in most warm water areas; immediate severe pain; not fatal, though shock may cause death in rare cases.

Sea wasp - jellyfish, with tentacles as much as 30 ft, in the S Pacific; very rapid onset of circulatory problems; high mortality because of speed of toxic reaction; antivenom.

Stingray - several varieties of differing sizes, found in tropical and temperate seas and some fresh water; severe pain, rapid onset of nausea, vomiting, breathing difficulties; wound area may ulcerate, gangrene may appear; seldom fatal.

Stonefish - brownish fish that lies motionless as a rock on bottom in shallow water; throughout S Pacific and Indian oceans; extraordinary pain, rapid paralysis; low mortality; antivenom available, amount determined by number of puncture wounds; warm water relieves pain.

Giant Trees of the U.S.

Source: American Forests, Washington, DC

Approximately 850 native and naturalized species of trees are grown in the U.S. The oldest living tree is believed to be a bristlecone pine tree in California named Methusalah, estimated to be 4,700 years old. The world's largest living tree, the General Sherman giant sequoia in California, weighs more than 6,167 tons—as much as 41 blue whales or 740 elephants.

American Forests recognizes and lists the National Champion (largest by total mass) of each U.S. tree species. Anyone can nominate candidates for this National Register of Big Trees. For information, write to American Forests, PO Box 2000, Washington, DC 20013.

Major U.S. Public Zoological Parks

Source: *World Almanac* questionnaire, 1995; budget and attendance in millions

Zoo	Budget	Atten-dance	Acres	Species	Major attractions
Atlanta	$9.1	0.9	39	231	Gorilla exhibit, Ford African rainforest *for further information: (404) 624-5600*
Arizona-Sonora Desert Museum (Tucson)	4.7	0.6	30	1,703	"Living" museum, 90% outdoors, hummingbird aviary *for further information: (602) 883-2702.*
Audubon (New Orleans)	7.6	0.9	58	383	White alligators, Louisiana Swamp, Reptile Encounter *for further information: (504) 861-2537.*
Baltimore	6.9	0.6	180	1,200	Children's zoo, Chimpanzee Forest, Leopard Lair Exhibit *for further information: (410)-366-LION*
Bronx (NYC)	29.0	2.0	265	674	Himalayan Highlands, Jungle World, baboon reserve *for further information: (718) 367-1010.*
Buffalo	3.0	0.5	24	183	Gorilla Habitat, World of Wildlife Building *for further information: (716) 837-3900.*
Chicago (Brookfield)	35.0	2.0	215	400	7 Seas Panorama, Tropic World, Habitat Africa! *for further information: (708) 485-0263.*
Cincinnati	13.0	1.3	70	731	Gorilla World, white Bengal tigers, Jungle Trails *for further information: (513) 281-4701.*
Cleveland	8.2	1.2	165	400	Rhino/Cheetah Exhibit, RainForest, Nothern Trek *for further information: (216) 661-6500.*
Columbus (Powell, OH)	NA	1.25	404	607	Discovery Reef, koalas, reptiles, gorillas *for further information: (614)-645-3400*
Dallas	1.7	0.4	70	393	25-acre Wilds of Africa with monorail, forest aviary *for further information: (214) 946-5145.*
Denver	9.0	1.7	80	600	Tropical Discovery, Primate Panorama, Northern Shores *for further information: (303) 331-4100.*
Detroit	9.0	1.0	125	280	Penguinarium, Chimps of Harambee *for further information: (810) 398-0900.*
Houston	6.3	2.5	55	650	McGovern Mammal Marina, rainforest birds in free flight *for further information: (713) 525-5888.*
Lincoln Park (Chicago)	12.0	3.0+	35	250	Great Ape house, polar bear pool, Farm-in-the-Zoo *for further information: (312) 742-2000.*
Los Angeles	17.0	1.4	80	440	Koala House, World of Birds, Tiger Falls *for further information: (213) 666-4090.*
Miami Metrozoo	7.0	0.6	290	260	Koalas, aviary, cageless exhibits, Asian River Life *for further information: (305) 251-0400.*
Milwaukee	15.1	1.4	200	300	Aquatic and Reptile Center, wolf woods, bear dens *for further information: (414) 256-5412.*
Minnesota	13.7	1.2	500	450	Dolphin shows, World of Birds *for further information: (612) 431-9200.*
National (Washington, DC)	18.0	3.0 est.	163	491	Giant pandas, Komodo dragon lizards, gorillas *for further information: (202) 673-4800.*
Oklahoma City	12.0	0.6	110	605	Aquaticus, Great EscApe *for further information: (405) 424-3344.*
Omaha/Henry Doorly Zoo	7.0	1.4	120	543	Indoor rainforest, free-flight aviary, aquarium *for further information: (402) 733-8401.*
Point Defiance (Tacoma, WA)	4.6	.5	27	295	Marine mammal complex, polar bear exhibit *for futher information: (206)-591-5335.*
Philadelphia	15.5	1.3	42	437	Carnivore Kingdom, white lions, red pandas *for further information: (215) 243-1100.*
Phoenix	8.0	1.0	125	374	Tropical rainforest, Arizona Trail, 200 endangered animals *for further information: (602) 273-1341.*
Rio Grande (Albuquerque)	5.8	0.6	63	271	Sea lion pool, white Bengal tigers *for further information: (505) 764-6200.*
Riverbanks (Columbia, SC)	5.0	1.0	100	489	Aquarium Reptile Complex, Riverbanks Farm *for further information: (803) 779-8717.*
St. Louis	19.0	2.7	83	699	Living World, Bear Pits, Jungle of the Apes, herpetarium *for further information: (314) 781-0900.*
San Diego	50.0	3.0	125	800	Tiger River, Gorilla Tropics, Hippo Beach *for further information: (619) 234-1515.*
San Diego (Wild Animal Park)	24.0	1.3	1,850	460	Mixed-species enclosures, exotic species, monorail tour *for further information: (619) 747-8702.*
San Francisco	13.0	.8	125	265	Primate Discovery Center, Koala Crossing, Gorilla World *for further information: (415) 753-7080.*
Toledo	9.9	0.9	30	524	Hippoquarium, aquarium, Kingdom of the Apes *for further information: (419) 385-5721.*
Washington Park (Portland, OR)	18.3	1.1	64	188	Asian elephants, Penguinarium, African rainforest *for further information: (503) 226-1561.*
Woodland Park (Seattle)	9.0	1.0	92	260	Tropical rainforest, Tropical Asia & Elephant Forest *for further information: (206) 684-4800.*

Note: NA=Not Available.

Major Canadian Public Zoological Parks

Source: *World Almanac* questionnaire, 1995; budget in millions of dollars (Canadian), attendance in millions

Zoo	Budget	Atten-dance	Acres	Species	Major attractions
Calgary	10.0	0.8	80	336	Canadian Wilds, Prehistoric Park *for further information: (403) 232-9300.*
Granby (Quebec)	5.0	0.4	60	225	Reptile House, Bear Mountain, Big Cats Pavilion *for further information: (514) 372-9113.*
Toronto	22.0	1.2	710	440	Indoor Zoo, South American Waterfall, Underground Zoo *for further information: (416) 392-5938.*
Vancouver Aquarium	8.6	0.8	2	627	Stellar sea lions, beluga whale, Amazon rainforest *for further information: (604) 268-9900.*
Winnipeg (Assiniboine Park)	2.5	0.4	90	242	Kinsmen Discovery Center, rare colder climate animals *for further information: (204) 986-6920.*

Top 50 American Kennel Club Registrations

Source: American Kennel Club, New York, NY; dogs registered Jan. 1, 1994, to Dec. 31, 1994

Breed	Rank	Number registered 1994	Rank	Number registered 1993	Breed	Rank	Number registered 1994	Rank	Number registered 1993
Labrador Retriever	1	126,393	1	124,899	Pug	26	15,464	28	15,722
Rottweiler	2	102,596	2	104,160	Pekingese	27	15,306	26	16,869
German Shepherd Dog	3	78,999	3	79,936	Lhasa Apso	28	14,504	24	17,124
Golden Retriever	4	64,322	5	68,125	German Shorthaired Pointer	29	14,154	30	13,931
Poodle	5	61,775	6	67,850	Collie	30	14,073	27	15,952
Cocker Spaniel	6	60,888	4	75,882	Brittany	31	12,741	31	13,635
Beagle	7	59,215	7	61,051	Bichon Frise	32	11,363	32	12,120
Dachshund	8	46,129	8	48,573	Bulldog	33	11,357	33	12,105
Dalmatian	9	42,621	9	42,816	Great Dane	34	11,155	35	10,929
Pomeranian	10	39,947	11	40,805	Akita	35	11,014	34	11,574
Yorkshire Terrier	11	38,626	12	39,827	West Highland White Terrier	36	8,441	36	9,459
Shih Tzu	12	37,017	13	39,773	Pembroke Welsh Corgi	37	6,554	38	6,707
Shetland Sheepdog	13	36,853	10	41,113	Scottish Terrier	38	6,091	37	6,724
Miniature Schnauzer	14	33,344	14	37,267	St. Bernard	39	6,063	40	5,595
Chihuahua	15	32,705	16	32,435	Australian Shepherd	40	5,906	44	5,364
Boxer	16	30,629	17	30,757	Weimaraner	41	5,678	41	5,590
Chow Chow	17	25,415	15	33,824	Chesapeake Bay Retriever	42	5,198	45	5,361
Siberian Husky	18	24,804	18	25,565	Samoyed	43	5,017	39	6,172
Doberman Pinscher	19	19,822	19	21,469	Alaskan Malamute	44	4,855	42	5,451
Basset Hound	20	18,043	21	19,982	Cairn Terrier	45	4,653	43	5,386
English Springer Spaniel	21	17,404	20	19,989	Great Pyrenees	46	4,273	47	4,005
Maltese	22	17,030	23	17,491	Keeshond	47	4,002	46	5,125
Miniature Pinscher	23	16,538	29	14,987	Mastiff	48	3,884	49	3,567
Boston Terrier	24	16,453	25	17,091	Airedale Terrier	49	3,798	48	3,889
Chinese Shar-Pei	25	15,834	22	19,465	Schipperke	50	3,562	50	3,519

Cat Breeds

Source: Cat Fanciers' Assn., Manasquan, NJ

Only a small percentage of house cats in the U.S. are pedigreed or registered with one of the official registering bodies, the largest of which is the Cat Fanciers' Assn., sponsor of more than 600 clubs. The Cat Fanciers' Assn. recognized 36 breeds as of mid-1995 (in order of registration totals): Persian, Maine Coon, Siamese, Abyssinian, Exotic, Scottish Fold, Oriental, American Shorthair, Birman, Burmese, Ocicat, Cornish Rex, Tonkinese, Devon Rex, Manx, Somali, Russian Blue, Colorpoint Shorthair, British Shorthair, Ragdoll, Norwegian Forest Cat, Japanese Bobtail, Balinese, Egyptian Mau, Chartreux, American Curl, Turkish Angora, Javanese, Korat, Bombay, Singapura, American Wirehair, Havana Brown, Turkish Van, Selkirk Rex, and European Burmese.

Classification

Source: Funk & Wagnalls New Encyclopedia.

In biology, classification is the identification, naming, and grouping of organisms into a formal system. The 2 fields that are most directly concerned with classification are taxonomy and systematics. Although the 2 disciplines overlap considerably, taxonomy is more concerned with nomenclature (naming) and with constructing hierarchical systems, and systematics with uncovering evolutionary relationships. Two kingdoms of living forms, Plantae and Animalia, have been recognized since Aristotle established the first taxonomy in the 4th century BC. In addition, there are the following 3 kingdoms: Protista (one-celled organisms), Monera (bacteria and blue-green algae), also known as the kingdom Procaryotae, and Fungi. The 7 basic categories of classification (from most general to most specific) are: kingdom, phylum (division), class, order, family, genus, and species. Below are 2 examples:

Zoological hierarchy

Kingdom	Phylum	Class	Order	Family	Genus	Species Name	Common name
Animalia	Chordata	Mammalia	Primates	Hominidae	Homo	Homo sapiens	Human

Botanical hierarchy

Kingdom	Division*	Class	Order	Family	Genus	Species Name	Common name
Plantae	Magnoliophyta	Magnoliopsida	Magnoliales	Magnoliaceae	Magnolia	M. virginiana	Sweet Bay

* In botany, the division is generally used in place of phylum.

How Much Water Is Used...?

Source: American Water Works Association; U.S. Geological Survey

Total freshwater withdrawals for all offstream uses in the U.S. were estimated to be 339 bil gal per day during 1990, about the same as during 1985. Offstream use is defined as water withdrawn or diverted from a ground- or surface-water source for public water supply; domestic, commercial, or industrial use; irrigation; livestock; mining; and thermoelectric power.

Total water withdrawals in 1990 from lakes, reservoirs, streams, wells, and springs were estimated at 408 bil gal per day, including 69 bil gal per day of salt water.

The following are some answers to the question "How much water is used...?"

1. In the average residence during a year? 110,000 gal
2. By an average person daily? 100 gal
3. To flush a non low-flow toilet? 5-7 gal
4. To take a shower? 15-30 gal or 5-10 gal per min
5. To brush your teeth (water running)? 1-2 gal
6. To shave (water running)? 10-15 gal
7. To wash dishes by hand? 20 gal
8. To run a dishwasher? 10-25 gal
9. By a dripping faucet? 1,000 gal or more per year
10. To manufacture a new car? 39,090 gal

1995 IN
PICTURES

New era: On Jan. 4, 1995, Representative Newt Gingrich of Georgia was sworn in as Speaker of the House, the first Republican Speaker in more than 40 years.

NATIONAL SCENE

Pres. Bill Clinton and House Speaker Newt Gingrich exchanged views in an unusual town-meeting style discussion on June 11, 1995, at a senior citizens' center in New Hampshire.

BROOKS KRAFT/SYGMA

MARTIN SIMON/SABA

In a year of sharp conflicts over the budget, Pres. Clinton, on June 7, 1995, signed the first veto of his presidency, rejecting a 1995 budget bill.

Republican hopefuls in the race for the 1996 presidential nomination, shown here posing at a Manchester, NH, fundraiser, included (left to right) commentator Pat Buchanan, U.S. senators Phil Gramm and Arlen Specter, Senate Majority Leader Bob Dole, former Tennessee governor Lamar Alexander, Representative Bob Dornan, former ambassador Alan Keyes, and Senator Richard Lugar.

REUTERS/BETTMANN

Susan Smith, who confessed to drowning her 2 small sons, was sentenced to life in prison by a jury in her hometown of Union, SC, on July 28, 1995.

The trial of the most famous person ever to be accused of murder in the U.S. ended on Oct. 3, 1995, when O. J. Simpson was found not guilty of the murders of Nicole Brown Simpson and Ronald Goldman.

Media giants: Microsoft and DreamWorks SKG formed an alliance to create entertainment products. Shown here in March 1995 are (left to right) DreamWorks' Jeffrey Katzenberg and David Geffen, Microsoft's Bill Gates, and Steven Spielberg of DreamWorks.

THE OKLAHOMA CITY BOMBING

On Apr. 19, 1995, a bomb ripped through the Federal Building in Oklahoma City, OK, causing massive destruction (below) and horrendous loss of human life. Right, firefighter Chris Fields holds one-year-old Baylee Almon, whom he pulled from the wreckage; she died soon after this photograph was taken. Facing page, top: Rescue workers hunt for survivors in the rubble.

AP/WIDE WORLD PHOTOS

AP/WIDE WORLD PHOTOS

STEVE SISNEY/DAILY OKLAHOMAN/SABA

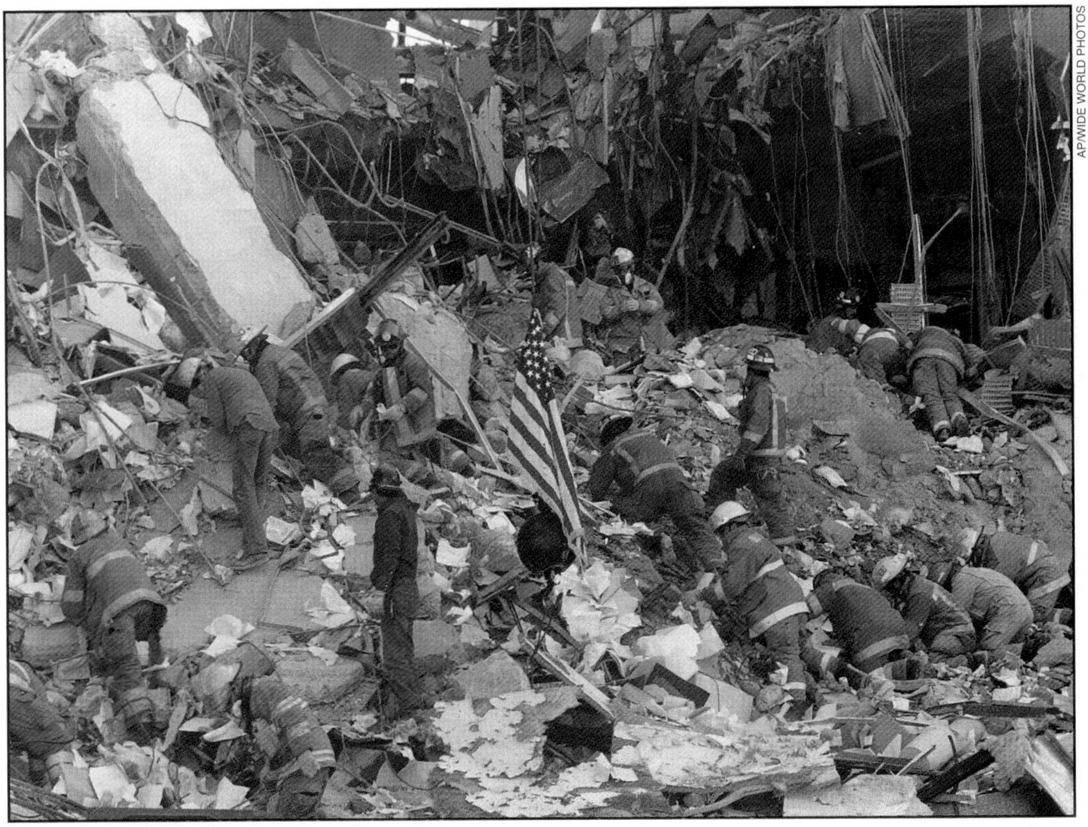

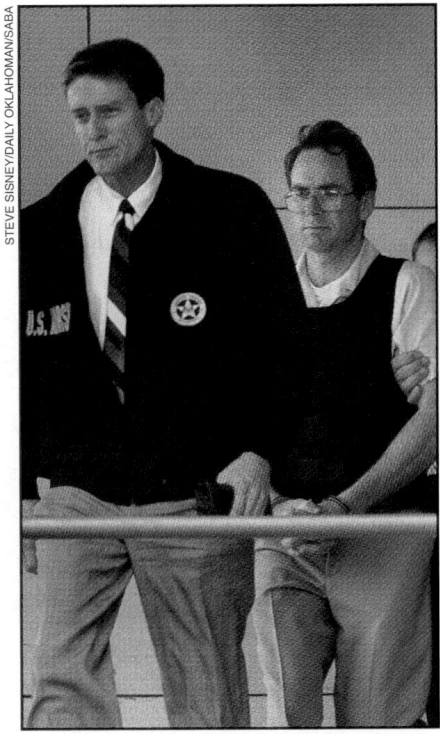

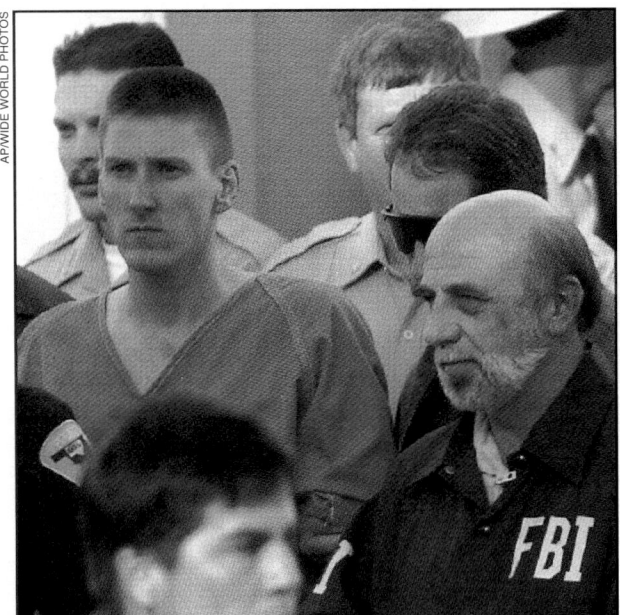

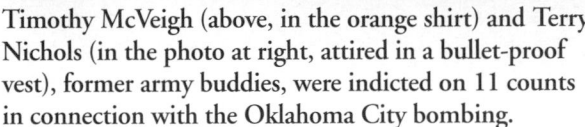

Timothy McVeigh (above, in the orange shirt) and Terry Nichols (in the photo at right, attired in a bullet-proof vest), former army buddies, were indicted on 11 counts in connection with the Oklahoma City bombing.

SCIENCE AND TECHNOLOGY

Below: U.S. astronaut Norman E. Thagard (left) and Russian cosmonaut Gennady M. Strekalov at work in the Russian space station *Mir.* On Mar. 16, 1995, Thagard, who had traveled on a Russian spacecraft, became the first American to board *Mir,* which had been in orbit since 1986. On June 29, *Mir* docked with the U.S. space shuttle *Atlantis.*

Above: *Atlantis* commander Robert Gibson (right) shakes hands with *Mir* commander Vladimir Dezhurov after the linkup. By the time Thagard returned to earth on *Atlantis,* he had set the record for American duration in space (112 days).

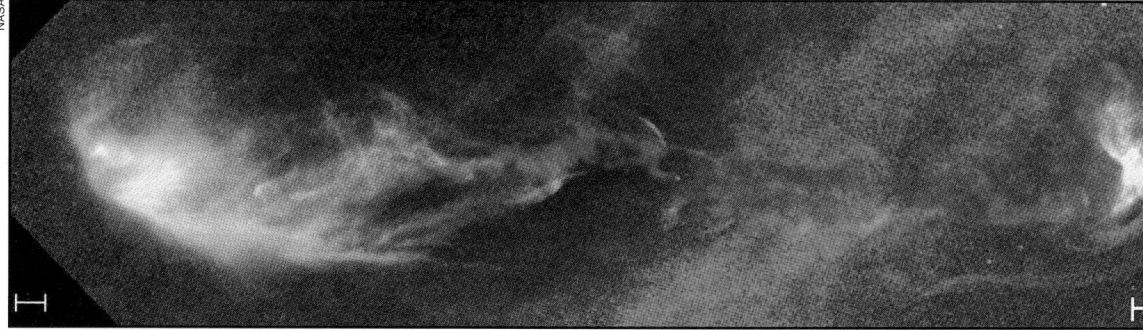

A star is born: The Hubble Space Telescope has provided the most detailed images ever taken of this cataclysmically violent process. This photo shows a 3 trillion mile long jet of gas blasting out of the star.

Ancient Art and Animals

This cave painting, some 30,000 years old, is one of 300 recently discovered in southern France—one of the most important archeological finds of the century.

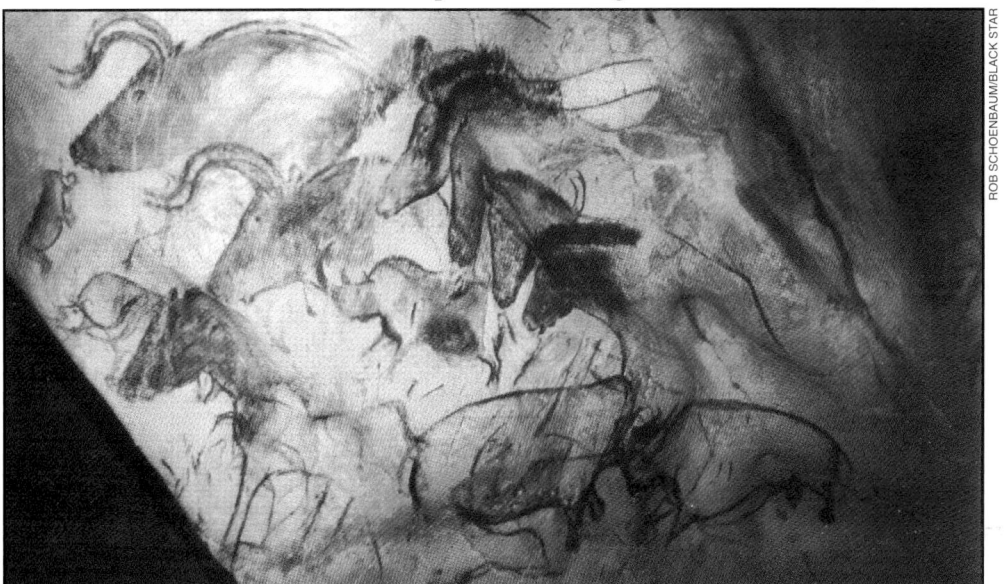

ROB SCHOENBAUM/BLACK STAR

In June 1995, the American Museum of Natural History in New York City debuted the largest, most scientifically ambitious dinosaur exhibit in the world.

REUTERS/BETTMANN

REMEMBERING 1945

This nighttime explosion of light in Moscow on May 9, 1995, celebrated the 50th anniversary of the end of World War II in Europe.

BILL SWERSEY/GAMMA LIAISON

Japanese umbrellas, part of an artwork, float on the Motoyasu River in Hiroshima, marking the 50th anniversary of the atomic bombing (Aug. 6).

DENNIS BRACK/BLACK STAR

SCHNEIDER/GAMMA LIAISON

To celebrate its 50th birthday, the United Nations turned on the lights during the summer of 1995. Delegates from 50 nations, meeting in San Francisco, approved the charter establishing the UN in June 1945.

Photos continue on page 777   200

ENERGY

U.S. Energy Summary

Source: Energy Information Administration, U.S. Dept. of Energy, *Annual Energy Review 1994*

A reviving domestic economy, low energy prices, and cold weather in the first quarter of 1994 contributed to the third consecutive year of growth in U.S. total energy consumption, which rose to a record 88 quadrillion Btu. The increase came as a result of a rise in the consumption of petroleum, natural gas, coal, nuclear electric power, and renewable energy. The growing economy and continued low prices for crude oil led to a modest increase in petroleum consumption, which rose 0.4 million barrels per day from the 1993 level to 18 million barrels per day. This increase was primarily due to a greater demand in the transportation and industrial sectors, which rely so heavily on petroleum that even relatively small increases in consumption affect the total. Consumption of petroleum by electric utilities decreased slightly in 1994, while consumption by the residential and commercial sectors rose 4.4%.

Energy consumption per dollar of gross domestic product (GDP) declined for the third consecutive year. About 17,000 Btu of energy were consumed for each 1987 dollar in 1994, compared with 23,000 Btu in the early 1970s.

U.S. total energy production rose 3.1% to 70 quadrillion Btu in 1994, after three years of decline. Most of the increase was attributed to higher coal production (which had been depressed in 1993 due to the strike by the United Mine Workers of America), higher natural gas production, and higher production of nuclear electric power. Production of crude oil (including lease condensate) dropped 0.5 quadrillion Btu to 14 quadrillion Btu, the lowest level in 40 years. Total renewable energy production also declined, due to a lower level of conventional hydroelectric power production.

U.S. net imports of energy rose to 18 quadrillion Btu in 1994, an increase of 6.6% from the 1993 level and the highest net import volume since 1977. Petroleum net imports rose 4.4% to 17 quadrillion Btu, natural gas net imports rose 8.0% to 2.4 quadrillion Btu, and coal net exports declined 5.1% to 1.7 quadrillion Btu. U.S. net imports of petroleum totaled 8.0 million barrels per day in 1994. Members of OPEC supplied 4.2 million barrels per day, more than half the total. Despite a sharp decline from the 1992 level, coal remained the primary U.S. energy export. Coal exports totaled 71 million short tons in 1994.

U.S. Energy Overview, 1960-94

Source: Energy Information Administration, U.S. Dept. of Energy, *Annual Energy Review 1994*

(in quadrillion Btu)

Activity and energy source	1960	1970	1975	1980	1985	1990[1]	1991	1992	1993	1994[P]
Production	41.49	62.07	59.86	64.76	64.87	70.68[R]	70.33[R]	69.87[R]	68.32[R]	70.43
Fossil fuels	39.87	59.19	54.73	59.01	57.54	58.56	57.83	57.55	55.86[R]	57.79
Coal	10.82	14.61	14.99	18.60	19.33	22.46	21.59	21.59	20.22[R]	22.00
Natural gas (dry)	12.66	21.67	19.64	19.91	16.98	18.36	18.23	18.38	18.74[R]	19.36
Crude oil[2]	14.93	20.40	17.73	18.25	18.99	15.57	15.70	15.22	14.49[R]	14.03
Natural gas plant liquids	1.46	2.51	2.37	2.25	2.24	2.17	2.31	2.36	2.41[R]	2.39
Nuclear electric power	0.01	0.24	1.90	2.74	4.15	6.16	6.58	6.61	6.52	6.83
Hydroelectric pumped storage[3]	(4)	(4)	(4)	(4)	(4)	-0.04	-0.05	-0.04	-0.04	-0.04
Renewable energy	1.61	2.65	3.23	3.01	3.18	5.99	5.97	5.75	5.98	5.85
Conventional hydroelectric power[5]	1.61	2.63	3.15	2.90	2.97	3.01	2.98	2.61	2.88	2.67
Geothermal energy	(*)	0.01	0.07	0.11	0.20	0.25	0.25	0.26	0.26	0.27
Biofuels[6]	(*)	(*)	(*)	(*)	0.01	2.63	2.64	2.78	2.74	2.80
Solar energy	0	0	0	0	0	0.07	0.07	0.07	0.07	0.07
Wind energy	0	0	0	0	(*)	0.02	0.03	0.03	0.03	0.04
Imports	4.23	8.39	14.11	15.97	12.10	18.99	18.58	19.65	21.53[R]	22.41
Natural gas	0.16	0.85	0.98	1.01	0.95	1.55	1.80	2.16	2.40[R]	2.58
Crude oil[7]	2.20	2.81	8.72	11.19	6.81	12.77	12.55	13.25	14.75[R]	15.26
Petroleum products[8]	1.80	4.66	4.23	3.46	3.80	4.35	3.79	3.71	3.76[R]	3.84
Other[9]	0.07	0.07	0.19	0.31	0.54	0.32	0.43	0.52	0.62[R]	0.72
Exports	1.48	2.66	2.36	3.72	4.23	4.91	5.22	5.02	4.35[R]	4.09
Coal	1.02	1.94	1.76	2.42	2.44	2.77	2.85	2.68	1.96[R]	1.88
Crude oil	0.43	0.55	0.44	1.16	1.66	1.82	2.13	2.01	2.12[R]	1.99
Other[10]	0.03	0.18	0.16	0.14	0.14	0.31	0.24	0.33	0.27[R]	0.22
Adjustments[11]	-0.43	-1.37	-1.07	-1.05	1.24	-0.67	0.28	0.66	1.38[R]	-0.30
Consumption	43.80	66.43	70.55	75.96	73.98	84.09[R]	83.96[R]	85.16[R]	86.88[R]	88.45
Fossil fuels	42.14	63.52	65.35	69.98	66.22	71.96	71.23	72.55	74.13	75.37
Coal	9.84	12.26	12.66	15.42	17.48	19.10	18.77	18.87	19.43[R]	19.54
Coal coke net imports	-0.01	-0.06	0.01	-0.04	-0.01	(*)	0.01	0.03	0.02	0.02
Natural gas[12]	12.39	21.79	19.95	20.39	17.83	19.30	19.61	20.13	20.84[R]	21.16
Petroleum[13]	19.92	29.52	32.73	34.20	30.92	33.55	32.85	33.53	33.84[R]	34.65
Nuclear electric power	0.01	0.24	1.90	2.74	4.15	6.16	6.58	6.61	6.52	6.83
Hydroelectric pumped storage[3]	(4)	(4)	(4)	(4)	(4)	-0.04	-0.05	-0.04	-0.04	-0.04
Renewable energy	1.66	2.67	3.29	3.23	3.61	6.01	6.20	6.04	6.28	6.28
Conventional hydroelectric power[5,14]	1.66	2.65	3.22	3.12	3.40	3.03	3.21	2.90	3.18	3.11
Geothermal energy	(*)	0.01	0.07	0.11	0.20	0.25	0.25	0.26	0.26	0.27
Biofuels[6]	(*)	(*)	(*)	(*)	0.01	2.63	2.64	2.78	2.74	2.80
Solar energy	0	0	0	0	0	0.07	0.07	0.07	0.07	0.07
Wind energy	0	0	0	0	(*)	0.02	0.03	0.03	0.03	0.04

(1) Starting in 1990, expanded coverage of nonelectric utility use of renewable energy caused an increase in total energy production and consumption figures. (2) Includes lease condensate. (3) Total pumped storage facility production minus energy used for pumping. (4) Before 1990, pumped storage is included in conventional hydroelectric power. (5) Starting in 1990, pumped storage is removed and expanded coverage of industrial use of hydroelectric power is included. (6) Includes wood, wood waste, peat, wood liquors, railroad ties, pitch, wood sludge, municipal solid waste, agricultural waste, straw, tires, landfill gases, fish oils, and/or other waste. (7) Includes imports of crude oil for the Strategic Petroleum Reserve, which began in 1977. (8) Includes imports of unfinished oils and natural gas plant liquids. (9) "Other" imports are coal, electricity, and coal coke. (10) "Other" exports are natural gas, petroleum products, electricity, and coal coke. (11) A balancing item. Includes stock changes, losses, gains, miscellaneous blending components, and unaccounted for supply. (12) Includes supplemental gaseous fuels. (13) Petroleum products supplied, including natural gas plant liquids and crude oil burned as fuel. (14) Includes net imports of electricity. R= Revised data. P= Preliminary data. (*)=Less than 0.005 quadrillion Btu. **Note:** Totals may not equal sum of components due to independent rounding.

World Energy Consumption and Production Trends

Source: Energy Information Administration, U.S. Dept. of Energy, *International Energy Annual 1993* and International Energy Database, May 1995

The world's consumption of primary energy—petroleum, natural gas, coal, and net hydroelectric, nuclear, geothermal, solar, and wind electric power—remained unchanged between 1990 and 1993, compared with increases of 1.7% from 1980 to 1985 and 2.8% from 1986 to 1989. The 24 countries of the Organization for Economic Cooperation and Development (OECD), which includes some of the world's largest economies (the U.S., Japan, Germany), continued to dominate global energy use. OECD nations consumed about 53% of the world's primary energy supply in 1993. Consumption by non-OECD nations in recent years has been affected both by a surge of economic growth and expansion in Asia and other developing countries and by significant downturns in most of Eastern Europe and the former USSR. World production increased from 343 quadrillion Btu in 1992 to 346 quadrillion Btu in 1993. In 1993 world production of petroleum was about 67.7 million barrels per day, or 137 quadrillion Btu; petroleum remained the most heavily used source of energy.

In 1993 three countries—the U.S., Russia, and China—were the world's leading producers (41%) and consumers (42%) of energy. Russia and the U.S. alone supplied 31% of the world total. The U.S. accounted for 24% of the world's total energy consumption. The U.S. consumed 28% more than it produced—an imbalance of 18.6 quadrillion Btu.

World's Major Producers of Primary Energy, 1993

Source: Energy Information Administration, International Energy Database, May 1995; quadrillion Btu

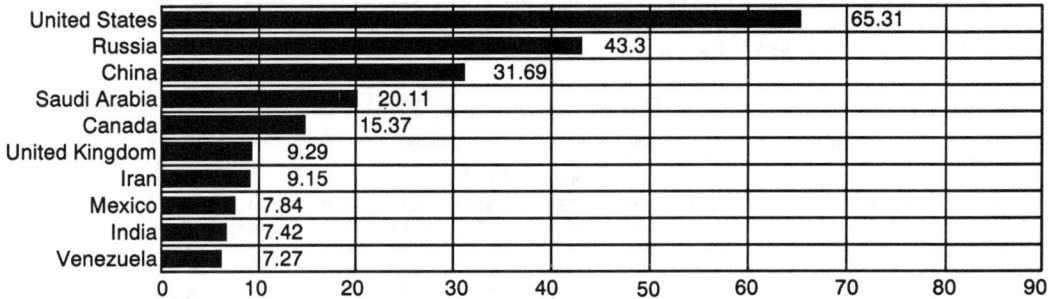

World's Major Consumers of Primary Energy, 1993

Source: Energy Information Administration, International Energy Database, May 1995; quadrillion Btu

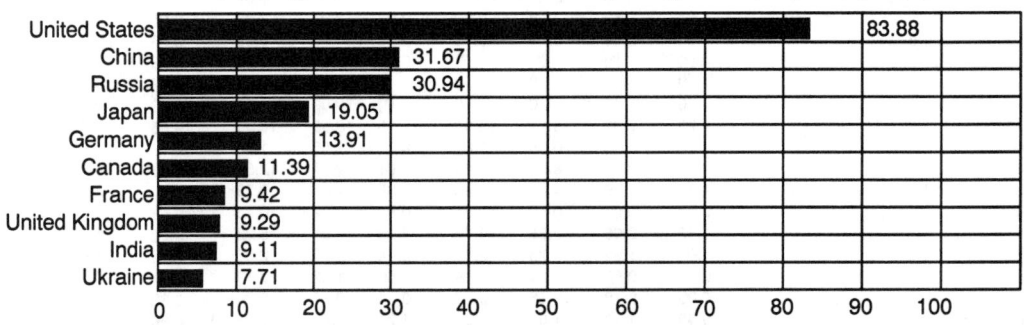

U.S. Net Imports of Petroleum, 1973-94

Source: Energy Information Administration, U.S. Dept. of Energy, *Monthly Energy Review*, May 1995

(in thousands of barrels per day)

Average annual rate	From Arab OPEC[2]	From OPEC[3]	From all countries	Petroleum products supplied	Average annual rate	From Arab OPEC[2]	From OPEC[3]	From all countries	Petroleum products supplied
	Net Imports[1]					Net Imports[1]			
1973	914	2,991	6,025	17,308	1984	817	2,037	4,715	15,726
1974	752	3,277	5,892	16,653	1985	470	1,821	4,286	15,726
1975	1,382	3,599	5,846	16,322	1986	1,160	2,828	5,439	16,281
1976	2,423	5,063	7,090	17,461	1987	1,272	3,053	5,914	16,665
1977	3,184	6,190	8,565	18,431	1988	1,837	3,513	6,587	17,283
1978	2,962	5,747	8,002	18,847	1989	2,128	4,124	7,202	17,325
1979	3,054	5,633	7,985	18,513	1990	2,243	4,285	7,161	16,988
1980	2,549	4,293	6,365	17,056	1991	2,057	4,064	6,626	16,714
1981	1,844	3,315	5,401	16,058	1992	1,972	4,071	6,938	17,033
1982	852	2,136	4,298	15,296	1993	1,995	4,253	7,618	17,237
1983	630	1,843	4,312	15,231	1994......	1,968	4,215	7,986	17,679

(1) Net Imports are imports minus exports. Imports from members of the Organization of Petroleum Exporting Countries (OPEC) exclude indirect imports, which are petroleum products primarily from Caribbean and West European areas and refined from crude oil produced by OPEC. (2) The Arab members of OPEC are Algeria, Iraq, Kuwait, Libya, Qatar, Saudi Arabia, and the United Arab Emirates. Net imports from the Neutral Zone between Kuwait and Saudi Arabia are included in net imports from Arab OPEC. (3) OPEC currently consists of Gabon, Indonesia, Iran, Nigeria, and Venezuela, as well as the Arab members; prior to 1993, it also included Ecuador. **Notes:** Beginning in October 1977, Strategic Petroleum Reserves are included. U.S. geographic coverage includes the 50 states and the District of Columbia.

Appliance Use in U.S. Households, 1978-93

Source: Energy Information Administration, U.S. Dept. of Energy, *Annual Energy Review 1994*

(percentage of households)

Appliance	1978	1980	1982	1984	1987	1990	1993	Change 1980-93
Total households	100	100	100	100	100	100	100	—
Type of appliances								
Electric appliances								
Television set (color)	NA	82	85	88	93	96	98	16
Television set (B/W)	NA	51	47	43	36	31	20	-31
Clothes washer	75	75	72	74	76	76	77	2
Range (stove-top burner)	53	54	53	54	57	58	61	7
Oven, regular or microwave . .	54	59	59	63	79	88	91	32
Oven, microwave	8	14	21	34	61	79	84	70
Clothes dryer	45	47	45	46	51	53	57	10
Separate freezer	35	38	37	37	34	35	35	-3
Dishwasher	35	37	36	38	43	45	45	8
Dehumidifier	NA	9	9	9	10	12	9	(1)
Waterbed heaters	NA	NA	NA	10	14	15	12	NA
Window or ceiling fan	NA	NA	28	35	46	51	60	NA
Whole house fan	NA	NA	8	8	9	10	4	NA
Evaporative cooler	NA	4	4	4	3	4	3	-1
Personal computer	NA	NA	NA	NA	NA	16	23	NA
Pump for well water	NA	NA	NA	NA	NA	15	13	NA
Swimming-pool pump[2]	NA	4	3	NA	NA	5	5	1
Gas appliances[3]								
Range (stove-top burner)	48	46	47	45	43	42	38	-8
Oven	47	42	42	42	41	41	36	-6
Clothes dryer	14	14	15	16	15	16	15	1
Outdoor gas grill	NA	9	11	13	20	26	29	20
Outdoor gas light	2	2	2	1	1	1	1	-1
Swimming pool heater[4]	NA	NA	NA	1	1	2	1	NA
Refrigerators[5]								
One	86	86	86	88	86	84	85	-1
Two or more	14	14	13	12	14	15	15	1
Air Conditioning								
Central[6]	23	27	28	30	36	39	44	17
Individual room units[6]	33	30	30	30	30	29	25	-5
None	44	43	42	40	36	32	32	-11
Portable Kerosene Heaters . . .	(1)	(1)	3	6	6	5	2	2

(1) Less than 0.5%. (2) All reported swimming pools were assumed to have an electric pump for filtering and circulating the water, except for 1993 when a filtering system was made explicit. (3) Includes natural gas or liquefied petroleum gases. (4) In 1984 and 1987, also includes heaters for jacuzzis and hot tubs. (5) Fewer than 0.5% of the households do not have a refrigerator. (6) Households with both central and individual room units are counted only under "Central." NA= not available.

Energy Consumption and Consumption per Capita by State, 1993

Source: Energy Information Administration, U.S. Dept. of Energy, *Annual Energy Review 1994*

	Consumption Trillion			Consumption Trillion			Consumption per Capita Million			Million
Rank	State	Btu	Rank	State	Btu	Rank	State	Btu	Rank State	Btu
1.	Texas	10,081.1	27.	Colorado	1,023.1	1.	Alaska	1,001.6	27. Oregon	315.3
2.	California.	6,988.4	28.	Iowa	965.8	2.	Wyoming . . .	864.6	28. Utah	311.4
3.	Ohio	3,790.6	29.	Mississippi	963.1	3.	Louisiana . . .	840.3	29. District of	
4.	New York	3,701.7	30.	Arizona	958.0				Columbia	308.3
5.	Pennsylvania . .	3,665.9	31.	Oregon	957.0	4.	Texas.	559.4	30. New Jersey	308.2
6.	Louisiana. . . .	3,604.7	32.	Arkansas	853.2	5.	North Dakota.	519.5	31. Maine	306.7
7.	Illinois	3,582.1	33.	West Virginia	825.5	6.	West Virginia.	454.1	32. Illinois	306.5
8.	Florida	3,128.2	34.	Connecticut	761.6	7.	Indiana	440.6	33. Michigan	306.4
9.	Michigan	2,898.7	35.	Alaska	599.0	8.	Montana	425.6	34. South Dakota	305.8
10.	Indiana	2,513.8	36.	New Mexico	594.9	9.	Oklahoma. . .	419.1	35. Missouri	305.1
11.	New Jersey . . .	2,421.9	37.	Utah	579.1	10.	Kansas.	417.1	36. Pennsylvania	304.7
12.	Georgia.	2,236.7	38.	Nebraska	532.6	11.	Kentucky	415.7	37. North Carolina	302.6
13.	North Carolina .	2,103.6	39.	Nevada	446.1	12.	Alabama. . . .	399.3	38. Virginia	295.3
14.	Washington . . .	1,943.6	40.	Wyoming	406.4	13.	Washington. .	369.6	39. Wisconsin	290.4
15.	Virginia	1,911.4	41.	Idaho	399.2	14.	Delaware . . .	368.5	40. Colorado	287.1
16.	Tennessee . . .	1,832.4	42.	Maine	380.3	15.	New Mexico .	368.2	41. Maryland	251.3
17.	Alabama	1,669.4	43.	Montana	357.9	16.	Mississippi . .	364.8	42. Vermont	246.2
18.	Missouri	1,597.4	44.	North Dakota	330.9	17.	Idaho	362.9	43. Rhode Island	244.9
19.	Kentucky	1,577.0	45.	Delaware	257.2	18.	Tennessee . .	359.7	44. Arizona	242.8
20.	Wisconsin	1,464.7	46.	New Hamp-shire	245.7	19.	South Carolina	353.3	45. Massachusetts	233.9
21.	Minnesota	1,432.2	47.	Rhode Island	244.9	20.	Arkansas . . .	351.7	46. Connecticut	232.3
22.	Massachusetts	1,407.9	48.	Hawaii	229.3	21.	Ohio.	342.7	47. Florida	227.9
23.	Oklahoma . . .	1,354.9	49.	South Dakota	219.0	22.	Iowa.	342.4	48. California	223.9
24.	South Carolina	1,278.8	50.	District of Columbia	178.5	23.	Nebraska . . .	330.2	49. New Hamp-shire	218.6
25.	Maryland	1,245.8	51.	Vermont	141.8	24.	Georgia	324.1	50. New York	203.9
26.	Kansas	1,057.3	**Total United States**	**83,957.8**		25.	Nevada.	322.8	51. Hawaii	196.6
						26.	Minnesota. . .	316.6	**Total United States**	**325.7**

World Crude Oil and Natural Gas Reserves, Jan. 1, 1994

Sources: Energy Information Administration, U.S. Dept. of Energy, *Annual Energy Review 1994; Oil and Gas Journal,* Penn Well Publishing Company, Dec. 1993; *World Oil,* Gulf Publishing Company, Aug. 1994

Region and country	Crude oil (billion barrels) Oil and Gas Journal	World Oil	Natural gas (trillion cubic feet) Oil and Gas Journal	World Oil	Region and country	Crude oil (billion barrels) Oil and Gas Journal	World Oil	Natural gas (trillion cubic feet) Oil and Gas Journal	World Oil
North America......	79.0	72.1	328.2	325.7	Iran............	92.9	60.0	730.0	612.0
Canada.........	5.1	4.7	94.8	93.2	Iraq............	100.0	99.6	109.5	109.2
Mexico	50.9	44.4	71.0	70.0	Kuwait..........	96.5	94.2	52.9	51.4
United States	23.0	23.0	162.4	162.4	Oman	4.7	5.0	20.0	20.0
Central and South					Qatar...........	3.7	4.2	250.0	165.0
America........	74.1	77.7	197.5	204.1	Saudi Arabia	261.2	262.4	185.9	186.1
Argentina........	1.6	1.9	26.5	26.5	United Arab Emirates	98.1	64.5	204.6	198.4
Bolivia..........	0.1	0.1	3.9	4.5	Other...........	5.7	5.4	22.2	23.2
Brazil..........	3.6	3.8	4.8	4.9	**Africa............**	62.0	73.9	343.5	347.8
Colombia........	1.9	3.0	10.0	7.2	Algeria.........	9.2	10.1	128.0	130.7
Ecuador........	2.0	2.3	3.8	3.9	Cameroon	0.4	0.3	3.9	3.9
Trinidad and Tobago	0.5	0.5	8.5	8.5	Egypt	6.3	3.4	15.4	20.5
Venezuela	63.3	64.4	128.9	138.0	Libya...........	22.8	37.9	45.8	45.5
Other...........	1.0	1.5	11.1	10.8	Nigeria.........	17.9	17.5	120.0	121.9
Western Europe	16.9	38.5	194.0	261.6	Tunisia.........	1.7	0.4	3.2	0.9
Denmark	0.8	0.7	4.3	4.6	Other...........	3.7	4.3	27.2	24.5
Germany	0.4	0.2	12.1	7.9	**Far East and Oceania**	44.6	53.3	354.5	309.7
Italy...........	0.6	0.6	10.7	10.3	Australia	1.6	3.1	19.6	18.2
Netherlands	0.1	0.1	68.2	66.2	Brunei	1.4	1.3	14.0	13.3
Norway	9.3	18.9	70.5	113.2	China	24.0	29.5	59.0	45.0
United Kingdom ...	4.6	16.9	21.5	54.7	India	5.9	5.9	25.4	22.8
Other...........	1.1	1.1	6.7	4.7	Indonesia........	5.8	6.2	64.4	67.5
Eastern Europe and					Malaysia	4.3	5.1	76.7	80.8
Former USSR ...	58.9	183.0	2,014.9	1,891.4	New Zealand	0.2	0.1	3.2	3.0
Former USSR.....	57.0	181.7	1,997.0	1,877.0	Pakistan	0.2	0.2	22.9	23.0
Other[1]	1.9	1.3	17.9	14.4	Thailand	0.2	0.2	5.7	6.2
Middle East.........	662.9	595.4	1,581.0	1,370.8	Other...........	1.1	1.6	63.6	29.8
Bahrain..........	0.1	0.1	5.9	5.6	**World ....**	998.3	1,093.8	5,013.6	4,711.2

(1) Albania, Bulgaria, former Czechoslovakia, Hungary, Poland, and Romania. **Notes:** Data for Kuwait and Saudi Arabia include one-half of the reserves in the Neutral Zone between Kuwait and Saudi Arabia. All reserve figures except those for the former USSR and natural gas reserves in Canada are proved reserves recoverable with present technology and prices. Former USSR figures are "explored reserves," which include proved, probable, and some partially possible. The Canadian natural gas figure includes proved and some probable. The latest Energy Information Administration data for the U.S. are for Dec. 31, 1993. Totals may not equal sum of components due to independent rounding.

Gasoline Retail Prices, U.S. City Average, 1973-94

Source: Energy Information Administration, U.S. Dept. of Energy, *Monthly Energy Review,* May 1995

(cents per gallon, including taxes)

Average	Leaded regular	Unleaded regular	Unleaded premium	All types[1]	Average	Leaded regular	Unleaded regular	Unleaded premium	All types[1]
1973 ...	38.8	NA	NA	NA	1984 ...	112.9	121.2	136.6	119.8
1974 ...	53.2	NA	NA	NA	1985 ...	111.5	120.2	134.0	119.6
1975 ...	56.7	NA	NA	NA	1986 ...	85.7	92.7	108.5	93.1
1976 ...	59.0	61.4	NA	NA	1987 ...	89.7	94.8	109.3	95.7
1977 ...	62.2	65.6	NA	NA	1988 ...	89.9	94.6	110.7	96.3
1978 ...	62.6	67.0	NA	65.2	1989 ...	99.8	102.1	119.7	106.0
1979 ...	85.7	90.3	NA	88.2	1990 ...	114.9	116.4	134.9	121.7
1980 ...	119.1	124.5	NA	122.1	1991 ...	NA	114.0	132.1	119.6
1981[2] ...	131.1	137.8	147.0[3]	135.3	1992 ...	NA	112.7	131.6	119.0
1982 ...	122.2	129.6	141.5	128.1	1993 ...	NA	110.8	130.2	117.3
1983 ...	115.7	124.1	138.3	122.5	1994 ...	NA	111.2	130.5	117.4

(1) Also includes types of motor gasoline not shown separately. (2) In Sept. 1981, the Bureau of Labor Statistics changed the weights used in the calculation of average motor gasoline prices. From Sept. 1981 forward, gasohol is included in the average for all types, and unleaded premium is weighted more heavily. (3) Based on Sept. through Dec. data only. **Notes:** Geographic coverage for 1973-77 is 56 urban areas; for 1978 forward, 85 urban areas. NA = not available.

Nuclear Electricity Gross Generation by Selected Country, February 1995

Source: Energy Information Administration, U.S. Dept. of Energy; *Monthly Energy Review,* May 1995

(billion kilowatt-hours)

Belgium.............	3.7	Hungary.............	1.1	Sweden.............	6.3
Bulgaria.............	2.1	Japan	21.5	Switzerland	2.2
Canada	8.4	Russia..............	8.9	Taiwan	2.3
Finland	1.5	South Africa.........	0.7	Ukraine	7.5
France.............	31.7	South Korea	4.9	United Kingdom.......	6.8
Germany............	13.1	Spain...............	4.6	United States........	54.3

World Nuclear Power

Source: International Atomic Energy Agency, Dec. 31, 1994

Country	Reactors in operation No. of units	Reactors in operation Total MW(e)	Reactors under construction No. of units	Reactors under construction Total MW(e)	Nuclear electricity supplied in 1994 TW(e) .h[1]	Nuclear electricity supplied in 1994 % of total	Total operating experience to Dec. 31, 1994 Years	Total operating experience to Dec. 31, 1994 Months
Argentina	2	935	1	692	7.68	13.77	32	7
Belgium	7	5,527	—	—	38.20	55.77	128	7
Brazil	1	626	1	1,245	0.04	0.01	12	9
Bulgaria	6	3,538	—	—	15.33	45.63	77	1
Canada	22	15,755	—	—	101.73	19.07	326	11
China	3	2,100	—	—	13.50*	1.49*	5	4
Czech Republic. . . .	4	1,648	2	1,824	12.13*	28.22*	34	8
Finland	4	2,310	—	—	18.33	29.51	63	4
France	56	58,493	4	5,810	341.80	75.29	822	10
Germany	21	22,657	—	—	143.00	29.33	490	1
Hungary	4	1,729	—	—	13.23	43.73	38	2
India.	9	1,493	5	1,010	4.32	1.37	119	3
Iran	—	—	2	2,146	—	—	—	—
Japan.	49	38,875	5	4,799	258.30	30.70	652	2
Kazakhstan.	1	70	—	—	0.38	0.58	21	6
Korea, South	10	8,170	6	4,820	55.92	35.48	90	4
Lithuania	2	2,370	—	—	6.63	76.37	18	6
Mexico	2	1,308	—	—	4.28	3.22	5	11
Netherlands	2	504	—	—	3.70	4.86	47	9
Pakistan	1	125	1	300	0.52	1.01	23	3
Romania.	—	—	5	3,250	—	—	—	—
Russia	29	19,843	4	3,375	97.83	11.39	497	6
South Africa	2	1,842	—	—	9.69	5.69	20	3
Slovakia	4	1,632	4	1,552	12.13	49.05	57	5
Slovenia	1	632	—	—	4.39	38.01	13	3
Spain	9	7,105	—	—	52.80	34.97	138	2
Sweden	12	10,002	—	—	70.20	51.13	207	2
Switzerland.	5	2,985	—	—	22.98	36.84	98	10
Taiwan	6	4,890	—	—	33.48	31.72	80	1
Ukraine	15	12,679	6	5,700	68.85	34.20	158	11
United Kingdom . . .	34	11,720	1	1,188	79.40	25.79	1,028	5
United States	109	98,784	1	1,165	639.36	21.98	1,919	8
Total	**432**	**340,347**	**48**	**44,369**	**2,130.13**	**—**	**7,230**	**8**

(1) 1 terawatt-hour [TW(e).h] = 10^6 megawatt-hour [MW(e).h]. For an average power plant, 1 TW(e).h = 0.39 megatonnes of coal equivalent (input) and 0.23 megatonnes of oil equivalent (input). *Not officially confirmed. **Notes:** In 1994, construction was suspended at 3 reactors—2 in Cuba, 1 in the U.S. Also, 2 reactors were shut down—1 in France, 1 in the U.K.

U.S. Nuclear Power Plant Operations

Source: Energy Information Administration, U.S. Dept. of Energy, *Monthly Energy Review,* May 1995

	Operable reactors (number)	Nuclear-based electricity generation (million net kilowatt-hours)	Nuclear portion of domestic electricity generation (percent)		Operable reactors (number)	Nuclear-based electricity generation (million net kilowatt-hours)	Nuclear portion of domestic electricity generation (percent)
1976.	61	191,104	9.4	1986.	100	414,038	16.6
1977.	65	250,883	11.8	1987.	107	455,270	17.7
1978.	70	276,403	12.5	1988.	108	526,973	19.5
1979.	68	255,155	11.4	1989.	110	529,355	19.0
1980.	70	251,116	11.0	1990.	111	576,862	20.5
1981.	74	272,674	11.9	1991	111	612,565	21.7
1982.	77	282,773	12.6	1992	109	618,776	22.1
1983.	80	293,677	12.7	1993.	109	610,291	21.2
1984.	86	327,634	13.6	1994.	109	640,440	22.0
1985.	95	383,691	15.5				

Status of U.S. Nuclear Reactor Units

Source: Energy Information Administration, U.S. Dept. of Energy, *Monthly Energy Review,* May 1995

(number of reactor units)

	Licensed for operation Operable	Licensed for operation In startup	Construction permits Granted	Construction permits Pending	On order	Announced	Total	Total design capacity (million net kilowatts)
1980	70	2	82	12	3	0	169	163
1981	74	0	75	11	3	0	163	157
1982	77	2	60	3	2	0	144	135
1983	80	3	53	0	2	0	138	129
1984	86	6	38	0	2	0	132	123
1985	95	3	30	0	2	0	130	121
1986	100	7	19	0	2	0	128	119
1987	107	4	14	0	2	0	127	119
1988	108	3	12	0	0	0	123	115
1989	110	1	10	0	0	0	121	113
1990	111	0	8	0	0	0	119	111
1991	111	0	8	0	0	0	119	111
1992	109	0	8	0	0	0	117	111
1993	109	0	7	0	0	0	116	110
1994	109	0	7	0	0	0	116	110

TRADE AND TRANSPORTATION

U.S. Trade With Leading Countries and Areas, 1994

Source: Office of Trade and Economic Analysis, U.S. Dept. of Commerce

(millions of dollars, not seasonally adjusted)

Country/Area	Trade balance	Rank	Exports	Rank	Imports	Rank
Total	$–150,629.2	(X)	$512,626.5	(X)	$663,255.7	(X)
Japan	–65,888.0	1	53,487.7	2	119,155.7	2
China	–29,504.9	2	9,281.8	14	38,786.7	4
Canada	–13,967.4	3	114,438.5	1	128,405.9	1
Germany	–12,515.3	4	19,229.0	5	31,744.3	5
Taiwan	–9,597.0	5	17,106.8	7	26,705.8	6
Italy	–7,619.4	6	7,182.7	16	14,802.2	11
Malaysia	–7,012.6	7	6,969.0	17	13,981.7	12
Thailand	5,440.7	8	4,865.1	21	10,305.8	13
Venezuela	–4,332.0	9	4,039.3	25	8,371.3	16
Nigeria	–3,920.9	10	508.1	61	4,429.9	26
Indonesia	–3,738.2	11	2,808.8	29	6,546.9	18
France	–3,080.2	12	13,618.7	8	16,690.0	9
India	–3,015.5	13	2,294.0	35	5,309.5	23
Sweden	–2,522.5	14	2,516.4	34	5,040.9	25
Singapore	–2,337.8	15	13,019.9	10	15,357.7	10
Angola	–1,884.0	16	197.3	83	2,061.3	35
Philippines	–1,683.0	17	3,888.0	26	5,719.1	22
Saudi Arabia	–1,674.6	18	6,013.4	18	7,688.0	17
Korea, South	–1,603.9	19	18,025.4	6	19,629.3	8
Gabon	–1,094.1	20	40.2	129	1,134.3	48
Norway	–1,088.1	21	1,267.3	44	2,353.4	33
Denmark	–906.8	22	1,214.8	45	2,121.6	34
Sri Lanka	–895.2	23	197.7	82	1,093.0	51
Bangladesh	–848.0	24	232.1	75	1,080.1	52
Macao	–770.1	25	21.2	135	791.3	56
North America	–12,617.6	(X)	165,282.0	(X)	177,899.6	(X)
Western Europe	–12,552.3	(X)	118,177.4	(X)	130,730.2	(X)
European Union (EU)	–8,056.9	(X)	102,818.2	(X)	110,875.2	(X)
European Free Trade Association	–5,689.4	(X)	11,975.4	(X)	17,664.8	(X)
Eastern Europe	–530.9	(X)	5,301.0	(X)	5,831.9	(X)
Former Soviet Republics	–286.0	(X)	3,561.6	(X)	3,847.6	(X)
Organization for Economic Cooperation & Development (OECD) in Europe	–12,577.5	(X)	117,556.0	(X)	130,133.5	(X)
Pacific Rim Countries	–113,573.8	(X)	147,779.4	(X)	261,153.2	(X)
Asia—Near East	232.5	(X)	16,044.9	(X)	15,812.4	(X)
Asia—NICS	–11,793.3	(X)	59,595.0	(X)	71,388.4	(X)
Asia—South	–5,162.0	(X)	3,454.9	(X)	8,616.9	(X)
Assn. of Southeast Asian Nations (ASEAN)	–20,032.1	(X)	31,924.7	(X)	51,956.8	(X)
South/Central America	3,247.5	(X)	41,706.4	(X)	38,461.0	(X)
Twenty Latin American Republics	3,159.8	(X)	87,804.9	(X)	84,615.1	(X)
Central American Common Market	547.1	(X)	5,350.8	(X)	4,803.8	(X)
Latin American Free Trade Association (LAFTA)	1,829.5	(X)	78,169.2	(X)	76,339.7	(X)
Organization of Petroleum Exporting Countries (OPEC)	–13,516.6	(X)	17,868.4	(X)	31,665.0	(X)
Unidentified[1]	252.7	(X)	252.7	(X)	(X)	(X)

(1) The export totals reflect shipments of certain grains, oilseeds, and satellites that are not included in the country/area totals. (X) Not applicable. **Note:** Details may not equal totals due to rounding.

Definitions of areas:

North America—Canada, Mexico.

Western Europe—Andorra, Austria, Belgium, Bosnia and Herzegovina, Croatia, Cyprus, Denmark, Faroe Islands, Finland, France, Germany, Gibraltar, Greece, Iceland, Ireland, Italy, Liechtenstein, Luxembourg, Macedonia, Monaco, Netherlands, Norway, Portugal, San Marino, Slovenia, Spain, Svalbard/Jan Mayen Island, Sweden, Switzerland, Turkey, United Kingdom, Vatican City, Yugoslavia.

European Union—Belgium, Denmark, France, Germany, Greece, Ireland, Italy, Luxembourg, Netherlands, Portugal, Spain, United Kingdom.

European Free Trade Association —Austria, Finland, Iceland, Liechtenstein, Norway, Sweden, Switzerland.

Eastern Europe—Albania, Armenia, Azerbaijan, Belarus, Bulgaria, Czech Republic, Estonia, Georgia, Hungary, Kazakhstan, Kyrgyzstan, Latvia, Lithuania, Moldova, Poland, Romania, Russia, Slovakia, Tajikistan, Turkmenistan, Ukraine, Uzbekistan.

Former Soviet Republics—Armenia, Azerbaijan, Belarus, Estonia, Georgia, Kazakhstan, Kyrgyzstan, Latvia, Lithuania, Moldova, Russia, Tajikistan, Turkmenistan, Ukraine, Uzbekistan.

OECD—Austria, Belgium, Denmark, Finland, France, Germany, Greece, Iceland, Ireland, Italy, Liechtenstein, Luxembourg, Monaco, Netherlands, Norway, Portugal, San Marino, Spain, Svalbard/Jan Mayen Island, Sweden, Switzerland, Turkey, United Kingdom.

Pacific Rim Countries—Australia, Brunei, China, Hong Kong, Indonesia, Japan, South Korea, Macao, Malaysia, New Zealand, Papua New Guinea, Philippines, Singapore, Taiwan.

Asia Near East—Bahrain, Iran, Iraq, Israel, Jordan, Kuwait, Lebanon, Oman, Qatar, Saudi Arabia, Syria, United Arab Emirates, Yemen.

Asia NICS—Hong Kong, South Korea, Singapore, Taiwan.

Asia South—Afghanistan, Bangladesh, India, Nepal, Pakistan, Sri Lanka.

ASEAN—Brunei, Indonesia, Malaysia, Philippines, Singapore, Thailand.

South/Central America—Anguilla, Antigua and Barbuda, Argentina, Aruba, Bahamas, Barbados, Belize, Bermuda, Bolivia, Brazil, British Virgin Islands, Cayman Islands, Chile, Colombia, Costa Rica, Cuba, Dominica, Dominican Republic, Ecuador, El Salvador, Falkland Islands, French Guiana, Grenada, Guadeloupe, Guatemala, Guyana, Haiti, Honduras, Jamaica, Martinique, Montserrat, Netherland Antilles, Nicaragua, Panama, Paraguay, Peru, St. Kitts and Nevis, St. Lucia, St. Vincent and the Grenadines, Suriname, Trinidad and Tobago, Turks and Caicos Islands, Uruguay, Venezuela.

Twenty Latin American Republics—Argentina, Bolivia, Brazil, Chile, Colombia, Costa Rica, Cuba, Dominican Republic, Ecuador, El Salvador, Guatemala, Haiti, Honduras, Mexico, Nicaragua, Panama, Paraguay, Peru, Uruguay, Venezuela.

Central American Common Market—Costa Rica, El Salvador, Guatemala, Honduras, Nicaragua.

LAFTA—Argentina, Bolivia, Brazil, Chile, Colombia, Ecuador, Mexico, Paraguay, Peru, Uruguay, Venezuela.

OPEC—Algeria, Gabon, Indonesia, Iran, Iraq, Kuwait, Libya, Nigeria, Qatar, Saudi Arabia, United Arab Emirates, Venezuela.

U.S. Exports and Imports by Principal Commodity Groupings, 1994

Source: Office of Trade and Economic Analysis, U.S. Dept. of Commerce

(millions of dollars, not seasonally adjusted, current dollar basis)

Item	Exports	Imports	Item	Exports	Imports
Total	**$512,627**	**$663,256**	Lighting, plumbing	$1,249	$2,024
Agricultural commodities	**44,936**	**25,955**	Metal manufactures	7,034	8,847
Animal feeds	3,353	433	Metalworking machinery	3,897	4,596
Bulbs	112	238	Motorcycles, bicycles	1,515	2,322
Cereal flour	1,159	970	Nickel	210	736
Cocoa.	34	696	Optical goods.	965	1,817
Coffee.	53	2,270	Paper and paperboard	7,448	9,066
Corn.	4,197	65	Photographic equipment	3,016	4,576
Cotton, raw and linters	2,641	21	Plastic articles	3,574	4,517
Dairy products; eggs	717	583	Platinum	306	1,325
Fur skins, raw	131	78	Pottery.	104	1,555
Grains, unmilled.	696	181	Power generating mach.	20,345	19,543
Hides and skins.	1,391	126	Printed materials.	3,971	2,234
Live animals	587	1,392	Records/magnetic media.	5,864	3,612
Meat and preparations	5,195	2,627	Rubber articles.	795	1,253
Oils/fats, animal.	586	21	Rubber tires and tubes	1,614	3,034
Oils/fats, vegetable	963	1,051	Scientific instruments	16,475	9,963
Plants.	117	106	Ships, boats.	1,165	808
Rice	1,009	130	Silver and bullion	256	488
Seeds	315	152	Spacecraft	444	219
Soybeans	4,355	46	Specialized ind. mach.	19,677	16,733
Sugar	5	552	Telecommunications equip.	15,872	32,418
Tobacco, unmanufactured	1,304	697	Textile yarn, fabric	6,445	9,207
Vegetables and fruit.	6,757	6,075	Toys/games/sporting goods. . . .	3,079	11,824
Wheat	4,055	291	Travel goods	233	3,085
Other agricultural.	5,225	7,134	Vehicles/new cars - Canada . . .	7,465	21,687
Manufactured goods	**402,674**	**557,310**	Vehicles/new cars - Japan.	1,787	24,020
ADP equipment; office mach. . . .	30,867	52,058	Vehicles/new cars - other	5,824	13,470
Airplanes.	18,803	3,719	Vehicles/trucks.	5,128	10,355
Airplane parts	9,824	2,727	Vehicles/chassis/bodies	427	429
Aluminum	2,787	4,943	Vehicles/parts.	21,314	19,609
Artwork/antiques	1,184	2,432	Watches/clocks/parts	276	2,641
Basketware, etc.	1,816	2,588	Wood manufactures	1,543	3,390
Chemicals - cosmetics	3,537	1,998	Zinc.	47	787
Chemicals - dyeing	2,330	1,869	Other manufactured goods	28,102	42,156
Chemicals - fertilizers.	2,703	1,298	**Mineral fuel**	**8,911**	**56,391**
Chemicals - inorganic.	4,067	4,087	Coal	2,966	646
Chemicals - medicinal	6,096	4,674	Crude oil	49	38,479
Chemicals - organic.	12,789	10,805	Petroleum preparations.	3,157	10,270
Chemicals - plastics	12,485	5,941	Liquefied propane/butane	195	873
Chemicals - other	7,657	3,235	Natural gas	254	3,937
Clothing	5,461	36,748	Electricity	31	973
Copper	1,266	2,295	Other mineral fuels	2,248	1,213
Electrical machinery.	44,454	57,750	**Selected commodities:**		
Footwear.	646	11,712	Fish and preparations	3,036	6,590
Furniture and parts	3,131	7,565	Cork, wood, lumber.	5,572	6,680
Gem diamonds	184	5,756	Pulp and waste paper	3,794	2,315
General industrial mach..	21,816	21,330	Metal ores; scrap	3,713	3,262
Glass	1,503	1,350	Crude fertilizers	1,446	1,026
Glassware.	560	1,158	Cigarettes	4,965	70
Gold, nonmonetary	5,689	1,933	Alcoholic bev., distilled	355	1,828
Iron and steel mill products. . . .	3,554	12,896	**All other.**	**3,243**	**1,831**

Note: Details may not equal totals due to rounding.

U.S. Exports and Imports, 1950-94

Source: Office of Trade and Economic Analysis, U.S. Dept. of Commerce

(millions of dollars)

Year	Exports	Imports	Year	Exports	Imports	Year	Exports	Imports
1950	$ 9,997	$ 8,954	1970	$ 42,681	40,356	1991	$421,730	485,453
1955	14,298	11,566	1975	107,652	98,503	1992	448,164	532,665
1960	19,659	15,073	1980	220,626	244,871	1993	465,091	580,659
1965	26,742	21,520	1985	213,133	345,276	1994	512,627	663,256
			1990	394,030	495,042			

General Agreement on Tariffs and Trade

Following World War II, the major economic powers of the world, recognizing that obstacles to trade hindered economic development and growth, negotiated a set of rules for reducing and limiting barriers to trade and for settling trade disputes. These rules were called the General Agreement on Tariffs and Trade (GATT). Headquarters to oversee the administration of the GATT were established in Geneva, Switzerland.

Periodically, rounds of multilateral trade negotiations under the GATT have been carried out since the late 1940s. The 8th round began in 1986 in Punta del Este, Uruguay, and is usually referred to as the Uruguay Round. The Uruguay Round concluded on Dec. 15, 1993, when 117 countries completed a new trade-liberalization agreement. One of the provisions of the agreement changed the name of the GATT to the World Trade Organization (WTO).

The agreement required ratification by the legislatures of many countries, including the U.S. The U.S. House of Representatives approved legislation to implement the Uruguay Round on Nov. 29, 1994, by a vote of 288-146, and the Senate voted 76-24 to approve it on Dec. 1, 1994. Pres. Bill Clinton signed the legislation Dec. 8, 1994. The WTO formally took effect on Jan. 1, 1995. The trade pact had a formal deadline for ratification of July 1, 1995. By that time, 100 nations had approved it.

New Passenger Cars Imported Into the U.S., by Country of Origin,[1] 1968-94

Source: Bureau of the Census, U.S. Dept. of Commerce

	Japan	Germany[2]	Italy	United Kingdom	Sweden	France	South Korea	Mexico	Canada	Total[3]
1968 ..	169,849	707,972	33,843	96,787	52,515	39,551	N.A.	N.A.	500,881	1,620,452
1969 ..	260,005	642,157	41,569	104,050	41,008	24,457	N.A.	N.A.	691,146	1,846,717
1970 ..	381,338	674,945	42,520	76,257	57,844	37,114	N.A.	N.A.	692,783	2,013,420
1971 ..	703,672	770,807	51,469	106,710	61,925	23,316	N.A.	0	802,281	2,587,484
1972 ..	697,788	676,967	64,614	72,038	64,541	14,713	N.A.	9	842,300	2,485,901
1973 ..	624,805	677,465	56,102	64,140	58,626	8,219	N.A.	4,469	871,557	2,437,345
1974 ..	791,791	619,757	107,071	72,512	60,817	21,331	N.A.	3,914	817,559	2,572,557
1975 ..	695,573	370,012	102,344	67,106	51,993	15,647	N.A.	0	733,766	2,074,653
1976 ..	1,128,936	349,804	82,500	77,190	37,466	21,916	N.A.	0	825,590	2,536,792
1977 ..	1,341,530	423,492	55,437	56,889	39,370	19,215	N.A.	N.A.	849,814	2,790,144
1978 ..	1,563,047	416,231	69,689	54,478	56,140	28,502	N.A.	6	833,061	3,024,982
1979 ..	1,617,328	495,565	72,456	46,911	65,907	27,887	N.A.	4	677,008	3,005,523
1980 ..	1,991,502	338,711	46,899	32,517	61,496	47,386	N.A.	1	594,770	3,116,448
1981 ..	1,911,525	234,052	21,635	12,728	68,042	42,477	N.A.	1	563,943	2,856,286
1982 ..	1,801,185	259,385	9,402	13,023	89,231	50,032	N.A.	27	702,495	2,926,407
1983 ..	1,871,192	239,807	5,442	17,261	114,726	40,823	N.A.	2	835,665	3,133,836
1984 ..	1,948,714	335,032	8,582	19,833	114,854	37,788	N.A.	N.A.	1,073,425	3,559,427
1985 ..	2,527,467	473,110	8,689	24,474	142,640	42,882	N.A.	13,647	1,144,805	4,397,653
1986 ..	2,618,711	451,699	11,829	27,506	148,700	10,869	169,309	41,983	1,162,226	4,691,297
1987 ..	2,417,509	377,542	8,648	50,059	138,565	26,707	399,856	126,266	926,927	4,589,010
1988 ..	2,123,051	264,249	6,053	31,636	108,006	15,990	455,741	148,065	1,191,357	4,450,213
1989 ..	2,051,525	216,881	9,319	29,378	101,571	4,885	270,609	133,049	1,151,122	4,042,728
1990 ..	1,867,794	245,286	11,045	27,271	93,084	1,976	201,475	215,986	1,220,221	3,944,602
1991 ..	1,762,347	171,097	2,886	14,862	62,905	1,727	186,740	249,498	1,109,248	3,612,665
1992 ..	1,598,919	205,248	1,791	10,997	76,832	65	130,110	266,111	1,119,223	3,447,200
1993 ..	1,501,953	180,383	1,178	20,029	58,742	23	122,943	299,634	1,371,856	3,604,361
1994 ..	1,488,159	178,774	1,010	28,217	63,867	58	213,962	360,367	1,525,746	3,909,079

(1) Excludes passenger cars assembled in U.S. foreign trade zones. (2) Figures prior to 1991 are for West Germany. (3) Includes countries not shown separately.

50 Busiest U.S. Ports, 1993

Source: Corps of Engineers, Dept. of the Army, U.S. Dept. of Defense

(ports ranked by tonnage handled, all figures in tons)

Rank	Port	Total	Domestic	Foreign	Imports	Exports
1	South Louisiana, LA, Port of	193,796,104	100,062,787	93,733,317	32,417,949	61,315,368
2	Houston, TX.	141,476,979	64,329,185	77,147,794	51,446,146	25,701,648
3	New York, NY and NJ.	116,735,760	74,021,708	42,714,052	35,504,203	7,209,849
4	Valdez, AK.	85,722,337	85,711,858	10,479	9,738	741
5	Baton Rouge, LA	85,078,863	44,623,571	40,455,292	27,503,859	12,951,433
6	New Orleans, LA	67,037,285	38,028,470	29,008,815	13,850,243	15,158,572
7	Corpus Christi, TX	59,649,751	23,589,020	36,060,731	29,070,847	6,989,884
8	Long Beach, CA.	54,320,932	24,202,970	30,117,962	13,605,504	16,512,458
9	Texas City, TX.	53,652,781	17,437,367	36,215,414	33,908,578	2,306,836
10	Plaquemine, LA, Port of	53,110,120	36,213,860	16,896,260	5,125,492	11,770,768
11	Norfolk Harbor, VA.	45,543,792	8,350,108	37,193,684	4,590,832	32,602,852
12	Lake Charles, LA	45,436,380	18,692,954	26,743,426	21,350,976	5,392,450
13	Tampa, FL.	44,992,777	27,672,005	17,320,772	5,847,493	11,473,279
14	Pittsburgh, PA	44,490,094	44,490,094	0	0	0
15	Mobile, AL.	43,959,704	22,774,048	21,185,656	9,320,986	11,864,670
16	Los Angeles, CA	43,622,807	19,089,706	24,533,101	13,696,983	10,836,118
17	Philadelphia, PA.	42,707,684	15,112,279	27,595,405	27,070,418	524,987
18	Port Arthur, TX.	38,326,902	5,866,533	32,460,369	28,044,238	4,416,131
19	Duluth-Superior, MN & WI.	37,679,398	28,729,550	8,949,848	951,218	7,998,630
20	Baltimore, MD	37,170,223	12,392,908	24,777,315	12,028,320	12,748,995
21	Marcus Hook, PA.	30,907,303	14,325,567	16,581,736	16,493,408	88,328
22	Portland, OR	29,804,208	12,381,837	17,422,371	3,344,986	14,077,385
23	St. Louis, MO & IL.	27,551,350	27,551,350	0	0	0
24	Pascagoula, MS.	27,020,433	10,048,072	16,972,361	13,584,266	3,388,095
25	Beaumont, TX.	25,409,757	13,523,388	11,886,369	8,207,459	3,678,910
26	Chicago, IL.	25,048,025	21,206,362	3,841,663	3,038,706	802,957
27	Richmond, CA.	24,570,112	18,842,297	5,727,815	1,768,878	3,958,937
28	Huntington, WV	22,833,285	22,833,285	0	0	0
29	Paulsboro, NJ	22,614,762	10,293,290	12,321,472	12,223,023	98,449
30	Seattle, WA.	21,693,410	7,608,714	14,084,696	7,123,683	6,961,013
31	Boston, MA	19,447,857	9,445,237	10,002,620	9,319,378	683,242
32	Jacksonville, FL.	18,849,849	10,780,031	8,069,818	6,708,859	1,360,959
33	Tacoma, WA	18,651,709	6,337,559	12,314,150	4,364,682	7,949,468
34	Detroit, MI	17,421,533	13,991,379	3,430,154	2,928,032	502,122
35	Newport News, VA.	16,734,878	3,928,574	12,806,304	1,713,160	11,093,144
36	Port Everglades, FL.	16,297,269	10,605,185	5,692,084	4,698,001	994,083
37	Indiana Harbor, IN	15,546,403	15,375,637	170,766	138,666	32,100
38	Savannah, GA.	14,962,844	3,280,116	11,682,728	5,404,795	6,277,933
39	New Castle, DE	14,242,529	6,620,221	7,622,308	7,542,827	79,481
40	San Juan, PR	14,153,403	8,888,806	5,264,597	4,629,285	635,312
41	Cleveland, OH	14,083,014	11,847,085	2,235,929	2,065,308	170,621
42	Freeport, TX	14,024,604	5,377,333	8,647,271	7,404,082	1,243,189
43	Lorain, OH.	13,676,686	13,649,902	26,784	19,184	7,600
44	Cincinnati, OH	13,648,255	13,648,255	0	0	0
45	Memphis, TN.	13,332,165	13,332,165	0	0	0
46	Anacortes, WA.	13,123,794	11,416,492	1,707,302	539,693	1,167,609
47	Oakland, CA.	12,733,691	3,892,826	8,840,865	4,051,681	4,789,184
48	Toledo, OH	12,149,760	7,225,259	4,924,501	1,194,365	3,730,136
49	Portland, ME	11,171,097	2,144,768	9,026,329	8,834,786	191,543
50	Two Harbors, MN.	10,711,059	10,711,059	0	0	0

Shortest Navigable Distances[1] Between Ports

Source: Defense Mapping Agency, Hydrographic/Topographic Center, July 1995

Distances shown are in nautical mi (1,852 m or about 6,076.115 ft). For statute mi, multiply by 1.15.

From	To	Distance	From	To	Distance
New York, New York	Barcelona, Spain	3,714	Colón,[3] Panama	Copenhagen, Denmark	5,433
”	Cape Town, South Africa	6,786	”	Galveston, Texas	1,508
”	Cherbourg, France	3,134	”	Gibraltar[2]	4,332
”	Copenhagen, Denmark	3,720	”	Hamburg, Germany	5,061
”	Galveston, Texas	1,935	”	Helsinki, Finland	5,970
”	Glasgow, Scotland	3,210	”	Lagos, Nigeria	5,050
”	Hamburg, Germany	3,654	”	Lisbon, Portugal	4,152
”	Havana, Cuba	1,186	”	Oslo, Norway	5,053
”	Helsinki, Finland	4,257	”	Piraeus, Greece	5,759
”	Oslo, Norway	3,644	”	Port Said, Egypt	6,251
”	Piraeus, Greece	4,688	”	St. John's, Nfld.	2,695
”	Southampton, England	3,169	”	Southampton, England	4,576
Montreal, Canada	Algiers, Algeria	3,842	San Francisco, Calif.	Bombay, India	9,794
”	Barcelona, Spain	3,939	”	Calcutta, India	9,384
”	Cape Town, South Africa	7,118	”	Colón, Panama	3,285
”	Gibraltar[2]	3,429	Vancouver, Canada	Calcutta, India	8,727
”	Halifax, Nova Scotia	895	”	Melbourne, Australia	7,365
”	Havana, Cuba	3,326	Panama, Panama	Jakarta, Indonesia	10,603
”	Istanbul, Turkey	5,226	Port Said, Egypt	Ho Chi Minh City, Vietnam	5,684
”	Kingston, Jamaica	3,269	”	Hong Kong	6,489
”	Lagos, Nigeria	6,505	”	Manila, Philippines	6,365
”	Marseille, France	4,116	”	Melbourne, Australia	7,886
”	Naples, Italy	4,406	”	Singapore	5,035
”	Oslo, Norway	3,957	”	Yokohama, Japan	7,924
”	Piraeus, Greece	4,856	Cape Town,[4] S. Africa	Jakarta, Indonesia	5,276
”	Port Said, Egypt	5,348	”	Melbourne, Australia	6,600
”	Southampton, England	3,397	”	Singapore	5,614
Colón,[3] Panama	Buenos Aires, Argentina	5,385	Singapore	Jakarta, Indonesia	525

(1) Traveling through station points. (2) Gibraltar (port) is 24 nautical mi E of the Strait of Gibraltar. (3) Colón on the Atlantic is 44 nautical mi from Panamá (port) on the Pacific. (4) Cape Town is 35 nautical mi NW of the Cape of Good Hope.

Major Merchant Fleets of the World

Source: Maritime Administration, U.S. Dept of Commerce

Fleets of oceangoing steam and motor ships totaling 1,000 gross tons or more as of Jan. 1995. Excludes ships operating exclusively on the Great Lakes and inland waterways and special types such as channel ships, icebreakers, cable ships, and merchant ships owned by any military force. Gross tonnage is a volume measurement; each cargo gross ton represents 100 cubic ft of enclosed space. Deadweight tonnage is the carrying capacity of a ship in long tons (2,240lb). Tonnage figures may not add, due to rounding.

(tonnage in thousands)

	Total			Freighters			Type of vessel Bulk carriers			Tankers		
	No. of ships	Gross tons	Dwt tons	No. of ships	Gross tons	Dwt tons	No. of ships	Gross tons	Dwt tons	No. of ships	Gross tons	Dwt tons
All countries[1]	25,092	433,840	685,885	13,386	117,449	135,716	5,316	142,809	250,947	6,007	167,469	297,603
United States	543	14,126	19,968	308	6,578	6,866	22	592	1,042	200	6,763	11,945
Privately owned	354	11,462	16,477	158	4,558	4,362	22	592	1,042	172	6,272	11,059
Government owned	189	2,664	3,491	150	2,020	2,504	0	0	0	28	491	886
Australia	72	2,467	3,513	18	247	268	29	1,035	1,718	25	1,185	1,527
Bahamas	910	22,121	35,065	484	5,513	6,724	132	4,264	7,488	240	11,075	20,582
Bermuda	57	2,826	4,497	17	271	250	8	151	245	31	2,393	3,998
Brazil	211	5,065	8,650	58	558	701	65	2,216	3,912	87	2,290	4,036
Bulgaria	115	1,235	1,795	60	390	457	36	579	912	17	264	426
China	1,387	14,590	22,257	837	6,098	8,349	318	5,992	10,071	203	2,308	3,745
Cyprus	1,436	23,222	39,706	707	5,573	7,741	561	12,474	22,341	155	5,040	9,572
Denmark	345	4,871	6,763	246	2,713	2,956	15	562	1,032	84	1,596	2,775
France	67	1,604	2,616	23	335	421	3	103	182	34	1,079	1,987
Germany	440	5,068	6,371	385	4,357	5,355	10	281	469	40	320	511
Greece	981	29,386	53,633	215	2,014	2,734	470	13,123	23,452	272	14,000	27,362
Hong Kong	215	7,834	13,486	72	1,284	1,424	120	5,788	10,721	23	762	1,341
India	284	5,994	10,066	83	691	971	118	2,738	4,640	81	2,554	4,450
Indonesia	413	1,836	2,741	286	1,036	1,467	16	173	259	104	611	1,001
Iran	124	3,656	6,708	42	427	580	50	1,057	1,757	32	2,172	4,371
Isle of Man	70	1,845	3,159	36	415	422	6	224	417	28	1,206	2,320
Italy	395	5,568	8,398	120	1,231	1,160	39	1,548	2,833	224	2,662	4,350
Japan	812	17,839	26,950	275	3,198	2,581	206	6,532	12,125	316	7,906	12,188
Korea, South	407	6,123	9,819	203	1,927	2,188	119	3,550	6,462	85	646	1,169
Kuwait	45	2,134	3,553	16	323	442	0	0	0	29	1,811	3,111
Latvia	96	813	1,022	62	342	322	0	0	0	34	471	700
Liberia	1,534	57,703	95,392	397	7,441	7,446	450	16,129	28,229	651	33,093	59,527

(continued)

Major Merchant Fleets of the World (*continued*)

	Total			Freighters			Type of vessel Bulk carriers			Tankers		
	No. of ships	Gross tons	Dwt tons	No. of ships	Gross tons	Dwt tons	No. of ships	Gross tons	Dwt tons	No. of ships	Gross tons	Dwt tons
Luxembourg	43	1,135	1,791	12	136	153	12	558	1,003	19	441	635
Malaysia	219	2,451	3,737	113	675	954	30	721	1,299	76	1,055	1,484
Malta	925	15,225	26,082	404	2,985	4,041	290	6,183	10,894	225	5,988	11,122
Marshall Islands.......	36	2,128	4,094	2	27	43	23	539	910	11	1,562	3,141
Netherlands..........	394	3,592	4,401	315	2,425	2,748	14	255	430	59	764	1,192
Norway	678	19,662	31,528	230	3,395	3,265	147	4,783	8,452	287	11,095	19,741
Panama	3,488	62,185	95,616	1,856	18,082	19,226	806	22,100	38,296	789	21,444	37,956
Philippines..........	536	8,836	14,319	236	1,875	2,115	238	6,506	11,393	57	420	794
Poland	161	2,316	3,401	81	675	729	73	1,509	2,479	5	109	185
Romania	231	2,412	3,713	175	1,042	1,415	45	986	1,626	11	384	672
Russia	1,579	10,183	13,216	1,287	6,218	6,915	85	1,767	2,853	196	2,152	3,439
Saint Vincent........	589	5,133	8,134	404	2,189	3,033	101	1,873	3,218	82	1,060	1,878
Singapore	575	11,494	18,098	236	3,175	3,325	98	3,149	5,557	241	5,170	9,216
Spain	143	808	1,362	88	226	356	11	59	104	43	521	899
Sweden.............	174	2,217	2,127	99	1,463	989	9	42	61	63	620	1,063
Taiwan	194	5,793	8,967	122	2,329	2,712	54	2,499	4,621	18	965	1,634
Turkey	416	5,126	8,725	213	880	1,268	135	3,235	5,698	64	992	1,753
United Kingdom	152	3,050	3,380	65	1,237	1,237	7	69	109	61	1,241	1,914
Vanuatu	106	1,861	2,377	46	702	476	46	1,028	1,715	14	131	186

(1) Includes combination passenger & cargo ships.

Passenger Car Production, U.S. Plants

Source: American Automobile Manufacturers Assn.

	1993	1994		1993	1994
Chrysler Corp.			Aurora.	0	27,558
Neon	1,522	119,955	Delta 88	70,132	86,937
Acclaim	52,460	28,210	Oldsmobile 98	24,351	27,542
Sundance................	101,326	21,472	Achieva.	51,665	69,591
Total Plymouth	**155,308**	**169,637**	Cutlass Supreme	101,037	124,420
Cirrus.	0	29,558	Ciera.	151,566	145,404
LeBaron Sedan.	27,359	7,932	**Total Oldsmobile.**	**398,717**	**481,452**
LeBaron J Coupe	32,601	40,465	LeSabre	157,125	165,063
Fifth Avenue (Y)	11,185	0	Roadmaster.	33,092	43,483
Imperial	3,286	0	Park Avenue	65,875	64,395
New Yorker (C)	10,388	0	Riviera	0	24,235
Total Chrysler-Plymouth	**240,127**	**247,630**	Century.................	93,379	124,373
Neon	2,754	122,757	Skylark	52,918	61,480
Shadow	126,153	30,908	**Total Buick**	**402,389**	**483,029**
Daytona	2,055	0	DeVille (C).	71,883	0
Spirit	64,724	27,577	DeVille (K).	42,066	138,108
Stratus.................	0	2,912	Fleetwood	29,744	20,551
Dynasty	27,466	0	Eldorado	23,621	25,942
Intrepid................	29,341	116,709	Seville.	45,231	41,528
Viper	1,953	2,815	Allante	2,262	7
Total Dodge	**254,446**	**303,678**	**Total Cadillac**	**214,807**	**226,136**
Total Chrysler Corp..	**494,573**	**551,308**	Saturn..................	281,479	280,363
Ford Motor Co.			**Total General Motors Corp...**	**2,542,455**	**2,719,764**
Contour	0	57,108	**Diamond Star**		
Thunderbird	125,659	146,848	Mitsubishi Eclipse	54,694	57,019
Taurus.................	428,718	431,755	Mitsubishi Galant	42,896	64,958
Tempo..................	157,460	73,562	Dodge Avenger	0	13,849
Escort	208,263	312,191	Plymouth Laser	11,571	1,031
Mustang................	106,238	199,048	Chrysler Sebring	0	1,103
Total Ford	**1,026,338**	**1,220,512**	Eagle Talon.	26,874	31,869
Cougar.................	76,901	81,936	**Total Diamond Star**	**136,035**	**169,829**
Mystique	0	25,930	**Honda**		
Sable...................	137,262	121,237	Accord	283,038	360,591
Topaz..................	64,795	31,148	Civic	120,737	138,119
Lincoln Town Car	114,491	121,078	**Total Honda**	**403,775**	**498,710**
Mark	35,688	26,666	**Auto Alliance**		
Continental..............	34,224	32,843	Probe	103,323	113,849
Total Lincoln-Mercury	**463,361**	**440,838**	Mazda MX-6/626	115,773	133,142
Total Ford Motor Co.	**1,489,699**	**1,661,350**	**Total Auto Alliance**	**219,096**	**246,991**
General Motors Corp.			**Nissan**		
Caprice	93,941	110,534	Altima	155,563	173,416
Corvette.	22,578	25,390	Sentra..................	136,619	137,968
Beretta-Corsica.	202,819	230,761	200 SX	0	1,291
Cavalier	287,750	170,135	**Total Nissan**	**292,182**	**312,675**
Geo Prizm	84,988	114,827	**Subaru Legacy**.............	**47,117**	**54,002**
Total Chevrolet	**692,116**	**651,647**	**Toyota**		
Grand Prix	119,847	138,115	Avalon	0	11,768
Grand Am.	230,070	288,740	Corolla	122,054	114,576
Bonneville H.............	91,285	107,982	Camry..................	234,060	272,997
Sunbird	111,745	57,677	**Total Toyota**	**356,114**	**399,341**
Sunfire	0	4,623			
Total Pontiac	**552,947**	**597,137**	**Total Passenger Cars.**	**5,981,046**	**6,613,970**

Selected Motor Vehicle Statistics

Source: Federal Highway Administration; U.S. Dept. of Transportation; Insurance Institute for Highway Safety; 1993 figures unless otherwise specified.

State	Driving age Jan. 1, 1995 (1) Regular	(2) Juvenile	State gas tax cents/gal. (Jan. 1, 1995)	Safety belt use law[3] (Sept. 1, 1995)	Licensed drivers per 1,000 resident population	Registered motor ve-hicles per 1,000 resident population	Licensed drivers per registered motor vehicle	Gallons of fuel used per vehicle	Miles per gallon	Annual miles driven per vehicle	Vehicle miles per licensed driver
Alabama.....	16	—	18	S	719	810	0.89	812	17.19	13,962	15,734
Alaska......	16	—	8	S	731	816	0.90	734	10.92	8,012	8,951
Arizona.....	16	—	18	S	667	735	0.91	786	17.22	13,539	14,922
Arkansas....	16	—	18.7	S	722	630	1.15	1,111	14.14	15,707	13,705
California....	16/18	14	18	P	645	731	0.88	649	17.98	11,672	13,239
Colorado....	18	16	22	S	727	850	0.85	610	17.68	10,791	12,628
Connecticut ..	16/18	—	33	P	665	792	0.84	586	17.77	10,408	12,384
Delaware....	16/18	—	23	S	723	792	0.91	721	17.24	12,434	13,619
Dist. of Col. ..	18	16	20	S	624	456	1.37	743	17.79	13,219	9,652
Florida......	16	—	12.3	S	787	743	1.06	707	16.76	11,846	11,194
Georgia.....	16	—	7.5	S*	667	814	0.82	872	15.96	13,924	17,000
Hawaii......	15	—	16	P	627	652	0.96	522	20.25	10,575	10,994
Idaho......	17	15	21	S	701	931	0.75	672	16.71	11,221	14,903
Illinois......	16/18	—	19	S	638	690	0.92	692	16.06	11,114	12,020
Indiana.....	16/18	—	15	S	664	818	0.81	769	16.82	12,946	15,949
Iowa.......	16/18	—	20	P	675	973	0.69	611	15.02	9,173	13,224
Kansas.....	16	14	18	S	701	760	0.92	775	16.18	12,545	13,593
Kentucky....	16	—	16.4	S	652	694	0.94	957	15.74	15,061	16,038
Louisiana....	15/17	15	20	P	600	737	0.81	731	15.71	11,481	14,108
Maine......	16/17	16	19	No	731	829	0.88	696	17.04	11,851	13,453
Maryland....	16/18	16	23.5	S	660	717	0.92	681	17.86	12,168	13,227
Massachusetts	17/18	16½	21	S	692	638	1.08	686	17.75	12,165	11,219
Michigan....	16/18	14	15	S	689	781	0.88	695	16.67	11,581	13,127
Minnesota ...	16/18	15	20	S	584	823	0.71	667	17.04	11,360	16,006
Mississippi ...	15	—	18.4	S	621	757	0.82	838	16.03	13,434	16,377
Missouri.....	16	—	15	S	663	777	0.85	841	16.04	13,484	15,789
Montana	15/16	13	27	S	632	1,119	0.57	619	14.99	9,270	16,405
Nebraska....	16	14	26.3	S	710	895	0.79	691	14.86	10,269	12,949
Nevada.....	16	14	24	S	703	675	1.04	914	13.56	12,403	11,907
New Hampshire .	16/18	16	18.7	No	772	852	0.91	599	18.00	10,787	11,907
New Jersey ..	17	16	10.5	S	693	716	0.97	604	17.54	10,588	10,941
New Mexico ..	15/16	—	18	P	710	879	0.81	762	17.50	13,335	16,499
New York	17/18	16	21.92	P	567	558	1.02	627	17.61	11,045	10,869
North Carolina	16/18	—	21.6	P	680	772	0.88	759	17.07	12,954	14,709
North Dakota .	16	14	18	S	690	1,042	0.66	667	13.95	9,304	14,061
Ohio	16/18	14	22	S	688	837	0.82	624	16.74	10,453	12,704
Oklahoma ...	16	—	17	S	723	858	0.84	763	16.81	12,820	15,207
Oregon	16	14	24	P	783	866	0.90	665	16.25	10,804	11,947
Pennsylvania .	17/18	16	22.35	S	669	687	0.97	690	15.88	10,952	11,261
Rhode Island .	16/18	—	29	S	675	695	0.97	592	17.56	10,394	10,708
South Carolina	16	15	16	S	667	737	0.91	855	15.74	13,461	14,863
South Dakota .	16	14	18	S	708	1,129	0.63	614	14.94	9,178	14,634
Tennessee ..	16	14	20	S	695	974	0.71	644	16.30	10,498	14,710
Texas	16/18	15	20	P	659	728	0.91	789	16.20	12,777	14,113
Utah	16	—	19	S	640	718	0.89	731	17.47	12,778	14,338
Vermont	18	16	16	S	748	839	0.89	760	16.27	12,367	13,880
Virginia	16/19	—	17.5	S	706	833	0.85	688	17.24	11,867	14,012
Washington ..	16/18	—	23	S	704	840	0.84	624	16.76	10,454	12,473
West Virginia .	16/18	16	25.35	S	715	739	0.97	771	16.17	12,471	12,886
Wisconsin ...	16/18	14	23.4	S	695	757	0.92	698	18.47	12,889	14,038
Wyoming	16	14	9	S	744	1,186	0.63	918	13.23	12,141	19,339
Average.....					671	752	0.89	707	16.74	11,834	13,264

(1) Unrestricted operation of private passenger car. When 2 ages are shown, license is issued at lower age upon completion of approved driver education course. (2) Juvenile license issued with consent of parent or guardian. (3) P = an officer may stop a vehicle for a violation (primary); S = an officer may issue a seat belt citation only when the vehicle is stopped for another moving violation (secondary); *Although the Georgia law is secondary, for persons 4-18 years of age it is enforced primarily.

U.S. Car Sales by Vehicle Size and Type, 1984-94

Source: American Automobile Manufacturers Assn.

Year	Small (%)	Midsize (%)	Large (%)	Luxury (%)	Total (%)
1994	29.2	45.6	11.7	13.5	100.0
1993	32.8	43.3	11.1	12.8	100.0
1992	32.9	44.5	9.2	13.4	100.0
1991	33.0	44.9	8.3	13.9	100.0
1990	32.8	44.8	9.4	13.0	100.0
1989	36.6	41.9	11.9	11.6	100.0
1988	37.6	42.5	10.0	9.9	100.0
1987	38.4	42.3	9.1	10.2	100.0
1986	37.6	42.5	9.8	10.1	100.0
1985	37.9	42.1	9.8	10.2	100.0
1984	39.1	39.6	11.6	9.7	100.0

U.S. Car Sales by Type of Buyer, 1980-94

Source: American Automobile Manufacturers Assn.

Year	Consumer	Sales in thousands Business	Government	Total	% of total sales Consumer	Business
1994	4,624	4,496	115	9,235	50.1	48.7
1993	4,669	3,941	108	8,718	53.6	45.2
1992	4,558	3,683	113	8,354	54.6	44.1
1991	4,538	3,752	97	8,387	54.1	44.8
1990	5,768	3,567	149	9,484	60.8	37.6
1989	6,375	3,402	136	9,913	64.3	34.3
1988	6,802	3,699	138	10,639	63.9	34.8
1987	6,748	3,395	135	10,278	65.7	33.0
1986	7,658	3,666	127	11,450	66.9	32.0
1985	7,083	3,822	134	11,039	64.2	34.6
1984	6,590	3,669	135	10,394	63.4	35.3
1983	6,054	3,006	119	9,179	66.0	32.7
1982	5,285	2,593	102	7,980	66.2	32.5
1981	5,623	2,787	116	8,535	66.0	32.7
1980	6,062	2,791	126	8,979	67.5	31.1

Domestic and Imported Retail Car Sales in the U.S., 1980-94

Source: American Automobile Manufacturers Assn.

Calendar year	Domestic	Imports From Japan	From Germany	From other countries	Total imports	Total U.S. sales	Import % Total	Japan	U.S.-sponsored imports
1980	6,581,307	1,905,968	305,219	186,700	2,397,887	8,979,194	26.7	21.2	223,310
1981	6,208,760	1,858,896	282,881	185,502	2,327,279	8,536,039	27.3	21.8	174,665
1982	5,758,586	1,801,969	247,080	174,508	2,223,557	7,982,143	27.9	22.6	139,767
1983	6,795,295	1,915,621	279,748	191,403	2,386,772	9,182,067	26.0	20.9	136,798
1984	7,951,523	1,906,206	344,416	188,220	2,438,842	10,390,365	23.5	18.3	116,965
1985	8,204,542	2,217,837	423,983	195,925	2,837,745	11,042,287	25.7	20.1	206,252
1986	8,214,897	2,382,614	443,721	418,286	3,244,621	11,459,518	28.3	20.8	314,358
1987	7,080,858	2,190,405	347,881	657,465	3,195,751	10,276,609	31.1	21.3	348,154
1988	7,526,038	2,022,602	280,099	700,991	3,003,692	10,529,730	28.5	19.2	393,412
1989	7,072,902	1,897,143	248,561	553,660	2,699,364	9,772,266	27.6	19.4	340,425
1990	6,896,888	1,719,384	265,116	418,823	2,403,323	9,300,211	25.8	18.5	296,778
1991	6,136,757	1,500,309	192,776	344,814	2,037,899	8,174,656	24.9	18.4	280,673
1992	6,276,557	1,451,766	200,851	283,938	1,936,555	8,213,112	23.6	17.7	228,927
1993	6,741,667	1,328,445	186,177	261,570	1,776,192	8,517,859	20.9	15.6	185,284
1994	7,255,303	1,239,450	192,241	303,489	1,735,180	8,990,483	19.3	13.8	95,399

World Motor Vehicle Production, 1950-94

Source: American Automobile Manufacturers Assn.

(in thousands)

Year	United States	Canada	Europe	Japan	Other	World total	U.S. % of world total
1994	12,263	2,322	16,028	10,554	8,526	49,693	24.7
1993	10,898	2,246	14,825	11,228	7,205	46,402	23.5
1992	9,729	1,961	17,307	12,499	6,269	47,765	24.5
1991	8,811	1,888	17,563	13,245	5,180	46,687	18.9
1990	9,783	1,928	18,651	13,487	4,496	48,345	20.2
1985	11,653	1,933	16,015	12,271	2,939	44,811	26.0
1980	8,010	1,324	15,445	11,043	2,692	38,514	20.8
1970	8,284	1,160	13,033	5,289	1,637	29,403	28.2
1960	7,905	398	6,837	482	866	16,488	47.9
1950	8,006	388	1,991	32	160	10,577	75.7

Note: As far as can be determined, production refers to vehicles locally manufactured.

Motor Vehicle Production by Selected Countries, 1994

Source: American Automobile Manufacturers Assn.

Country	Passenger cars	Commercial vehicles	Total	Country	Passenger cars	Commercial vehicles	Total
Argentina	338,355	70,422	408,777	Japan	7,801,317	2,752,802	10,554,119
Australia.	328,909	9,159	338,068	Korea, South	1,805,895	505,768	2,311,663
Austria	44,533	3,396	47,929	Malaysia	171,411	7,752	179,163
Belgium	408,541	71,241	479,782	Mexico	855,973	266,143	1,122,116
Brazil	1,248,773	332,616	1,581,389	Netherlands.	92,044	22,513	114,557
Canada	1,215,830	1,105,981	2,321,811	Poland	326,150	25,076	351,226
China.	250,000	1,100,000	1,350,000	Spain	1,821,696	320,566	2,142,262
Commonwealth of Independent States	869,797	254,358	1,124,155	Sweden	352,951	82,044	434,995
Czech Republic	152,402	27,691	180,093	Taiwan	291,347	131,971	423,318
France	3,175,213	383,225	3,558,438	United Kingdom . . .	1,466,823	227,815	1,694,638
Germany	4,093,685	262,453	4,356,138	United States.	6,613,970	5,648,767	12,262,737
India	249,280	237,583	486,863	Yugoslavia	7,648	1,557	9,205
Indonesia	41,807	283,214	325,021				
Italy	1,340,878	193,591	1,534,469	Total.	35,365,228	14,327,704	49,692,932

Top-Selling Passenger Cars in the U.S. by Calendar Year, 1991-94
(Domestic and Import)

Source: American Automobile Manufacturers Assn.

1994

1. Ford Taurus	397,031	8. Chevrolet Corsica/Beretta	222,129	15. Oldsmobile Ciera 141,100
2. Honda Accord	367,615	9. Toyota Corolla	210,926	16. Buick Century 138,948
3. Ford Escort	336,967	10. Chevrolet Cavalier	187,263	17. Dodge Intrepid 133,475
4. Toyota Camry	321,979	11. Nissan Sentra	172,148	18. Ford Thunderbird 130,713
5. Saturn	286,003	12. Nissan Altima	163,138	19. Cadillac DeVille 124,804
6. Honda Civic	267,023	13. Buick LeSabre	159,500	20. Chevrolet Lumina...... 122,314
7. Pontiac Grand Am	262,310	14. Ford Mustang	158,421	

1993

1. Ford Taurus	360,448
2. Honda Accord	330,030
3. Toyota Camry	299,737
4. Chevrolet Cavalier	273,617
5. Ford Escort	269,034
6. Honda Civic	255,579
7. Saturn	229,356
8. Chevrolet Lumina	219,683
9. Ford Tempo	217,644
10. Pontiac Grand Am	214,761

1992

1. Ford Taurus	409,751
2. Honda Accord	393,477
3. Toyota Camry	286,602
4. Ford Escort	236,622
5. Honda Civic/CRX	219,228
6. Chevrolet Lumina	218,114
7. Chevrolet Cavalier	212,374
8. Pontiac Grand Am	210,332
9. Ford Tempo	207,173
10. Saturn	196,126

1991

1. Honda Accord	399,297
2. Ford Taurus	299,659
3. Toyota Camry	263,818
4. Chevrolet Cavalier	259,385
5. Ford Escort	247,864
6. Chevrolet Corsica/Beretta	231,227
7. Chevrolet Lumina	217,555
8. Honda Civic	205,715
9. Toyota Corolla	199,083
10. Ford Tempo	189,457

The Most Popular Colors, by Type of Vehicle, 1994 Model Year

Source: American Automobile Manufacturers. Assn.

Luxury cars		Full size/ intermediate cars		Compact/sports cars		Light trucks and vans	
Color	Percentage	Color	Percentage	Color	Percentage	Color	Percentage
Green	18.3	Green	19.4	White	15.3	White	21.7
White	15.6	White	18.1	Green	12.8	Green	17.3
Light brown	10.6	Light brown	11.8	Bright red	11.2	Medium/dark red	12.2
Black	9.2	Medium red	10.0	Medium red	10.5	Teal/aqua	9.8
White metallic	8.7	Black	5.7	Black	10.1	Black	9.0
Medium red	7.4	Teal/aqua	5.5	Teal/aqua	9.8	Bright red	8.3
Silver	7.1	Silver	4.6	Purple	6.2	Medium/dark blue	6.5
Medium gray	5.1	Bright red	4.2	Bright blue	5.4	Light brown	4.7
Dark blue	4.9	Medium blue	4.0	Light brown	5.0	Bright blue	3.9
Dark red	4.5	Dark red	3.3	Light blue	2.9	Silver	2.1
Medium blue	3.7	Light blue	3.0	Silver	2.4	Medium/dark gray	1.7
Light blue	2.2	Purple	2.7	Dark blue	2.4	Purple	1.0
Other	2.7	Other	7.7	Other	6.0	Other	1.8

Licensed Drivers, by Age

Source: Federal Highway Administration, U.S. Dept. of Transportation

	1993				Estimated 1994			Percent change
Age	Male	Female	Total	Percent male	Male	Female	Total	total drivers 1983-93
Under 16	19,256	17,878	37,134	51.86	19,000	18,000	38,000	−70.53
16	772,758	707,576	1,480,334	52.20	782,000	716,000	1,497,000	−12.30
17	1,095,074	990,634	2,085,708	52.50	1,108,000	1,002,000	2,110,000	−19.90
18	1,298,035	1,165,513	2,463,548	52.69	1,313,000	1,179,000	2,492,000	−23.75
19	1,432,245	1,282,111	2,714,356	52.77	1,449,000	1,297,000	2,745,000	−25.51
(19 and under)	4,617,368	4,163,712	8,781,080	52.58	4,670,000	4,211,000	8,881,000	−22.24
20	1,474,501	1,348,009	2,822,510	52.24	1,491,000	1,363,000	2,855,000	−24.17
21	1,551,672	1,468,621	3,020,293	51.37	1,569,000	1,485,000	3,055,000	−23.61
22	1,755,654	1,643,466	3,399,120	51.65	1,776,000	1,662,000	3,438,000	−16.34
23	1,848,555	1,727,899	3,576,454	51.69	1,870,000	1,748,000	3,617,000	−12.98
24	1,917,746	1,801,785	3,719,531	51.56	1,940,000	1,822,000	3,762,000	−9.26
(20-24)	8,548,128	7,989,780	16,537,908	51.69	8,646,000	8,081,000	16,727,000	−17.09
25-29	9,506,409	9,017,911	18,524,320	51.32	9,615,000	9,121,000	18,736,000	−8.29
30-34	10,498,138	10,212,801	20,710,939	50.69	10,618,000	10,329,000	20,948,000	12.61
35-39	10,197,325	10,048,144	20,245,469	50.37	10,314,000	10,163,000	20,477,000	31.05
40-44	9,084,430	8,970,619	18,055,049	50.32	9,188,000	9,073,000	18,261,000	48.52
45-49	7,714,567	7,557,639	15,272,206	50.51	7,803,000	7,644,000	15,447,000	47.44
50-54	6,060,765	5,904,745	11,965,510	50.65	6,130,000	5,972,000	12,102,000	17.23
55-59	5,006,385	4,839,817	9,846,202	50.85	5,064,000	4,895,000	9,959,000	−2.76
60-64	4,615,506	4,461,330	9,076,836	50.85	4,668,000	4,512,000	9,181,000	0.73
65-69	4,312,138	4,263,443	8,575,581	50.28	4,361,000	4,312,000	8,674,000	20.04
70 and over	7,832,290	7,725,923	15,558,213	50.34	7,922,000	7,814,000	15,736,000	53.94
Total	87,993,449	85,155,864	173,149,313	50.82	89,000,000	86,128,000	175,128,000	12.15

Some Countries With Safety Belt Use Laws

Source: American Automobile Manufacturers Assn.

Country	Effective Date	Country	Effective Date
Australia	1/72	Iceland	10/81
Austria	7/76	Ireland	2/79
Belgium	6/75	Israel	7/75
Brazil	6/72	Japan	12/71
Bulgaria	1976	Jordan	12/83
Canadian Provinces		Luxembourg	6/75
Alberta	7/87	Malaysia	4/79
British Columbia	10/77	Netherlands	6/75
Manitoba	4/84	New Zealand	6/72
Newfoundland	7/82	Norway	9/75
New Brunswick	11/83	Poland	1/84
Nova Scotia	1/85	Portugal	1/78
Ontario	1/76	Singapore	7/81
Prince Edward Island	1/88	South Africa	12/77
Quebec	7/76	Spain	10/74
Saskatchewan	7/77	Sweden	1/75
Côte d'Ivoire	1970	Switzerland	1/76
Denmark	1/76	Turkey	10/84
Finland	7/75	United Kingdom	1/83
France	10/79	USSR	1/76
Greece	12/79	West Germany	1/76
Hong Kong	10/83	Yugoslavia	1/85
Hungary	7/77	Zimbabwe	7/80

Personal Consumption Expenditures for Transportation

Source: American Automobile Manufacturers Assn.; Bureau of Economic Analysis, U.S. Dept. of Commerce

(in millions of dollars)

	1982	1984	1986	1988	1990	1992	1993	1994
User-operated transportation								
New autos	$53,336	$77,560	$100,328	$101,041	$96,692	$87,265	$91,319	$98,698
Net purchases of used autos	13,551	21,152	25,356	30,532	33,663	39,453	43,008	54,403
Other motor vehicles*	15,605	28,589	40,818	45,577	49,586	53,879	62,443	69,222
Tires, tubes, accessories and parts	15,230	17,302	18,353	20,685	22,483	23,687	25,540	28,834
Repair, greasing, washing, parking, storage, and rental	37,903	49,723	60,695	73,531	82,538	89,468	97,344	105,455
Gasoline and oil	94,125	94,532	79,699	86,899	108,471	103,444	103,727	107,221
Bridge, tunnel, ferry, and road tolls	1,306	1,387	1,794	1,774	2,024	2,116	2,260	2,571
Insurance premiums, less claims paid	9,150	10,099	12,724	16,842	18,066	24,572	29,706	28,558
Total user-operated transportation	**$240,206**	**$300,344**	**$339,767**	**$376,881**	**$413,523**	**$423,885**	**$455,347**	**$494,961**
Purchased local transportation								
Transit systems	$3,839	$4,244	$4,913	$5,377	$5,707	$5,940	$5,762	$6,077
Taxicabs	1,513	2,498	2,998	2,935	3,209	,285	3,372	3,468
Total purchased local transportation	**$5,352**	**$6,742**	**$7,911**	**$8,312**	**$8,916**	**$9,225**	**$9,134**	**$9,545**
Purchased intercity transportation								
Railway, excluding commutation	$317	$415	$472	$588	$708	$698	$692	$654
Bus	1,665	1,632	1,469	2,181	1,396	1,451	1,412	1,141
Airline	14,706	17,721	18,993	22,993	26,467	25,684	27,062	29,042
Other	1,173	1,360	1,737	2,229	2,644	2,185	2,428	2,649
Total purchased intercity transportation	**$17,861**	**$21,128**	**$22,671**	**$27,991**	**$31,215**	**$30,018**	**$31,594**	**$33,484**
Total transportation expenditures	**$263,419**	**$328,214**	**$370,349**	**$413,184**	**$453,654**	**$463,128**	**$496,075**	**$537,991**
Total personal consumption expenditures	**$2,059,179**	**$2,460,288**	**$2,850,553**	**$3,296,126**	**$3,748,417**	**$4,139,901**	**$4,391,790**	**$4,628,434**

* New and used trucks, recreation vehicles, etc.

Road Mileage Between Selected U.S. Cities

	Atlanta	Boston	Chicago	Cincinnati	Cleveland	Dallas	Denver	Des Moines	Detroit	Houston
Atlanta, Ga.	...	1,037	674	440	672	795	1,398	870	699	789
Boston, Mass..	1,037	...	963	840	628	1,748	1,949	1,280	695	1,804
Chicago, Ill.	674	963	...	287	335	917	996	327	266	1,067
Cincinnati, Oh. . . .	440	840	287	...	244	920	1,164	571	259	1,029
Cleveland, Oh.	672	628	335	244	...	1,159	1,321	652	170	1,273
Dallas Tex.	795	1,748	917	920	1,159	...	781	684	1,143	243
Denver, Col.	1,398	1,949	996	1,164	1,321	781	...	669	1,253	1,019
Detroit, Mich.	699	695	266	259	170	1,143	1,253	584	...	1,265
Houston, Tex.	789	1,804	1,067	1,029	1,273	243	1,019	905	1,265	...
Indianapolis, Ind.. . .	493	906	181	106	294	865	1,058	465	278	987
Kansas City, Mo.. . .	798	1,391	499	591	779	489	600	195	743	710
Los Angeles, Cal. . .	2,182	2,979	2,054	2,179	2,367	1,387	1,059	1,727	2,311	1,538
Memphis, Tenn. . . .	371	1,296	530	468	712	452	1,040	599	713	561
Milwaukee, Wis. . . .	761	1,050	87	374	422	991	1,029	361	353	1,142
Minneapolis, Minn. .	1,068	1,368	405	692	740	936	841	252	671	1,157
New Orleans, La. . .	479	1,507	912	786	1,030	496	1,273	978	1,045	356
New York, N.Y.. . . .	841	206	802	647	473	1,552	1,771	1,119	637	1,608
Omaha, Neb.	986	1,412	459	693	784	644	537	132	716	865
Philadelphia, Pa.. . .	741	296	738	567	413	1,452	1,691	1,051	573	1,508
Pittsburgh, Pa.	687	561	452	287	129	1,204	1,411	763	287	1,313
Portland Ore.	2,601	3,046	2,083	2,333	2,418	2,009	1,238	1,786	2,349	2,205
St. Louis, Mo.	541	1,141	289	340	529	630	857	333	513	779
San Francisco	2,496	3,095	2,142	2,362	2,467	1,753	1,235	1,815	2,399	1,912
Seattle, Wash.	2,618	2,976	2,013	2,300	2,348	2,078	1,307	1,749	2,279	2,274
Tulsa, Okla.	772	1,537	683	736	925	257	681	443	909	478
Washington, D.C. . .	608	429	671	481	346	1,319	1,616	984	506	1,375

	Indianapolis	Kansas City	Los Angeles	Louisville	Memphis	Milwaukee	Minneapolis	New Orleans	New York	Omaha
Atlanta, Ga.	493	798	2,182	382	371	761	1,068	479	841	986
Boston, Mass..	906	1,391	2,979	941	1,296	1,050	1,368	1,507	206	1,412
Chicago, Ill.	181	499	2,054	292	530	87	405	912	802	459
Cincinnati, Oh.	106	591	2,179	101	468	374	692	786	647	693
Cleveland Oh..	294	779	2,367	345	712	422	740	1,030	473	784
Dallas, Tex.	865	489	1,387	819	452	991	936	496	1,552	644
Denver, Col.	1,058	600	1,059	1,120	1,040	1,029	841	1,273	1,771	537
Detroit, Mich.	278	743	2,311	360	713	353	671	1,045	637	716
Houston, Tex.	987	710	1,538	928	561	1,142	1,157	356	1,608	865
Indianapolis, Ind.. . .	...	485	2,073	111	435	268	586	796	713	587
Kansas City, Mo.. . .	485	...	1,589	520	451	537	447	806	1,198	201
Los Angeles, Cal. . .	2,073	1,589	...	2,108	1,817	2,087	1,889	1,883	2,786	1,595
Memphis, Tenn. . . .	435	451	1,817	367	...	612	826	390	1,100	652
Milwaukee, Wis. . . .	268	537	2,087	379	612	...	332	994	889	493
Minneapolis, Minn. .	586	447	1,889	697	826	332	...	1,214	1,207	357
New Orleans, La. . .	796	806	1,883	685	390	994	1,214	...	1,311	1,007
New York, N.Y.. . . .	713	1,198	2,786	748	1,100	889	1,207	1,311	...	1,251
Omaha, Neb.	587	201	1,595	687	652	493	357	1,007	1,251	...
Philadelphia, Pa.. . .	633	1,118	2,706	668	1,000	825	1,143	1,211	100	1,183
Pittsburgh, Pa.	353	838	2,426	388	752	539	857	1,070	368	895
Portland, Ore.	1,227	1,809	959	2,320	2,259	2,010	1,678	2,505	2,885	1,654
St. Louis, Mo.	235	257	1,845	263	285	363	552	673	948	449
San Francisco	2,256	1,835	379	2,349	2,125	2,175	1,940	2,249	2,934	1,683
Seattle, Wash.	2,194	1,839	1,131	2,305	2,290	1,940	1,608	2,574	2,815	1,638
Tulsa, Okla.	631	248	1,452	659	401	757	695	647	1,344	387
Washington, D.C. . .	558	1,043	2,631	582	867	758	1,076	1,078	233	1,116

	Philadelphia	Pittsburgh	Portland	St. Louis	Salt Lake City	San Francisco	Seattle	Toledo	Tulsa	Wash., D.C.
Atlanta, Ga.	741	687	2,601	541	1,878	2,496	2,618	640	772	608
Boston, Mass..	296	561	3,046	1,141	2,343	3,095	2,976	739	1,537	429
Chicago, Ill.	738	452	2,083	289	1,390	2,142	2,013	232	683	671
Cincinnati, Oh.	567	287	2,333	340	1,610	2,362	2,300	200	736	481
Cleveland Oh..	413	129	2,418	529	1,715	2,467	2,348	111	925	346
Dallas, Tex.	1,452	1,204	2,009	630	1,242	1,753	2,078	1,084	257	1,319
Denver, Col.	1,691	1,411	1,238	857	504	1,235	1,307	1,218	681	1,616
Detroit, Mich.	576	287	2,349	513	1,647	2,399	2,279	59	909	506
Houston, Tex.	1,508	1,313	2,205	779	1,438	1,912	2,274	1,206	478	1,375
Indianapolis, Ind.. . .	633	353	2,227	235	1,504	2,256	2,194	219	631	558
Kansas City, Mo.. . .	1,118	838	1,809	257	1,086	1,835	1,839	687	248	1,043
Los Angeles, Cal. . .	2,706	2,426	959	1,845	715	379	1,131	2,276	1,452	2,631
Memphis, Tenn. . . .	1,000	752	2,259	285	1,535	2,125	2,290	654	401	867
Milwaukee, Wis. . . .	825	539	2,010	363	1,423	2,175	1,940	319	757	758
Minneapolis, Minn. .	1,143	857	1,678	552	1,186	1,940	1,608	637	695	1,076
New Orleans, La. . .	1,211	1,070	2,505	673	1,738	2,249	2,574	986	647	1,078
New York, N.Y.. . . .	100	368	2,885	948	2,182	2,934	2,815	578	1,344	233
Omaha, Neb.	1,183	895	1,654	449	931	1,683	1,638	681	387	1,116
Philadelphia, Pa.. . .	...	288	2,821	868	2,114	2,866	2,751	514	1,264	133
Pittsburgh, Pa.	288	...	2,535	588	1,826	2,578	2,465	228	984	221
Portland, Ore.	2,821	2,535	...	2,060	767	636	172	2,315	1,913	2,754
St. Louis, Mo.	868	588	2,060	...	1,337	2,089	2,081	454	396	793
San Francisco	2,866	2,578	636	2,089	752	...	808	2,364	1,760	2,799
Seattle, Wash.	2,751	2,465	172	2,081	836	808	...	2,245	1,982	2,684
Tulsa, Okla.	1,264	984	1,913	396	1,172	1,760	1,982	850	...	1,189
Washington, D.C. . .	133	221	2,754	793	2,047	2,799	2,684	447	1,189	...

Air Distances Between Selected World Cities in Statute Miles

Point-to-point measurements are usually from City Hall.

	Bangkok	Beijing	Berlin	Cairo	Cape Town	Caracas	Chicago	Hong Kong	Hono-lulu	Lima
Bangkok.........	...	2,046	5,352	4,523	6,300	10,555	8,570	1,077	6,609	12,244
Beijing..........	2,046	...	4,584	4,698	8,044	8,950	6,604	1,217	5,077	10,349
Berlin...........	5,352	4,584	...	1,797	5,961	5,238	4,414	5,443	7,320	6,896
Cairo...........	4,523	4,698	1,797	...	4,480	6,342	6,141	5,066	8,848	7,726
Cape Town.......	6,300	8,044	5,961	4,480	...	6,366	8,491	7,376	11,535	6,072
Caracas.........	10,555	8,950	5,238	6,342	6,366	...	2,495	10,165	6,021	1,707
Chicago.........	8,570	6,604	4,414	6,141	8,491	2,495	...	7,797	4,256	3,775
Hong Kong.......	1,077	1,217	5,443	5,066	7,376	10,165	7,797	...	5,556	11,418
Honolulu.........	6,609	5,077	7,320	8,848	11,535	6,021	4,256	5,556	...	5,947
London..........	5,944	5,074	583	2,185	5,989	4,655	3,958	5,990	7,240	6,316
Los Angeles......	7,637	6,250	5,782	7,520	9,969	3,632	1,745	7,240	2,557	4,171
Madrid..........	6,337	5,745	1,165	2,087	5,308	4,346	4,189	6,558	7,872	5,907
Melbourne.......	4,568	5,643	9,918	8,675	6,425	9,717	9,673	4,595	5,505	8,059
Mexico City.......	9,793	7,753	6,056	7,700	8,519	2,234	1,690	8,788	3,789	2,639
Montreal.........	8,338	6,519	3,740	5,427	7,922	2,438	745	7,736	4,918	3,970
Moscow.........	4,389	3,607	1,006	1,803	6,279	6,177	4,987	4,437	7,047	7,862
New York.......	8,669	6,844	3,979	5,619	7,803	2,120	714	8,060	4,969	3,639
Paris...........	5,877	5,120	548	1,998	5,786	4,732	4,143	5,990	7,449	6,370
Rio de Janeiro	9,994	10,768	6,209	6,143	3,781	2,804	5,282	11,009	8,288	2,342
Rome...........	5,494	5,063	737	1,326	5,231	5,195	4,824	5,774	8,040	6,750
San Francisco	7,931	5,918	5,672	7,466	10,248	3,902	1,859	6,905	2,398	4,518
Singapore	883	2,771	6,164	5,137	6,008	11,402	9,372	1,605	6,726	11,689
Stockholm	5,089	4,133	528	2,096	6,423	5,471	4,331	5,063	6,875	7,166
Tokyo...........	2,865	1,307	5,557	5,958	9,154	8,808	6,314	1,791	3,859	9,631
Warsaw.........	5,033	4,325	322	1,619	5,935	5,559	4,679	5,147	7,366	7,215
Washington, D.C. ..	8,807	6,942	4,181	5,822	7,895	2,047	596	8,155	4,838	3,509

	London	Los Angeles	Madrid	Mel-bourne	Mexico City	Mon-treal	Mos-cow	New Delhi	New York	Paris
Bangkok.........	5,944	7,637	6,337	4,568	9,793	8,338	4,389	1,813	8,669	5,877
Beijing..........	5,074	6,250	5,745	5,643	7,753	6,519	3,607	2,353	6,844	5,120
Berlin...........	583	5,782	1,165	9,918	6,056	3,740	1,006	3,598	3,979	548
Cairo...........	2,185	7,520	2,087	8,675	7,700	5,427	1,803	2,758	5,619	1,998
Cape Town.......	5,989	9,969	5,308	6,425	8,519	7,922	6,279	5,769	7,803	5,786
Caracas.........	4,655	3,632	4,346	9,717	2,234	2,438	6,177	8,833	2,120	4,732
Chicago.........	3,958	1,745	4,189	9,673	1,690	745	4,987	7,486	714	4,143
Hong Kong.......	5,990	7,240	6,558	4,595	8,788	7,736	4,437	2,339	8,060	5,990
Honolulu.........	7,240	2,557	7,872	5,505	3,789	4,918	7,047	7,412	4,969	7,449
London..........	...	5,439	785	10,500	5,558	3,254	1,564	4,181	3,469	214
Los Angeles......	5,439	...	5,848	7,931	1,542	2,427	6,068	7,011	2,451	5,601
Madrid..........	785	5,848	...	10,758	5,643	3,448	2,147	4,530	3,593	655
Melbourne.......	10,500	7,931	10,758	...	8,426	10,395	8,950	6,329	10,359	10,430
Mexico City.......	5,558	1,542	5,643	8,426	...	2,317	6,676	9,120	2,090	5,725
Montreal.........	3,254	2,427	3,448	10,395	2,317	...	4,401	7,012	331	3,432
Moscow.........	1,564	6,068	2,147	8,950	6,676	4,401	...	2,698	4,683	1,554
New York.......	3,469	2,451	3,593	10,359	2,090	331	4,683	7,318	...	3,636
Paris...........	214	5,601	655	10,430	5,725	3,432	1,554	4,102	3,636	...
Rio de Janeiro	5,750	6,330	5,045	8,226	4,764	5,078	7,170	8,753	4,801	5,684
Rome...........	895	6,326	851	9,929	6,377	4,104	1,483	3,684	4,293	690
San Francisco	5,367	347	5,803	7,856	1,887	2,543	5,885	7,691	2,572	5,577
Singapore	6,747	8,767	7,080	3,759	10,327	9,203	5,228	2,571	9,534	6,673
Stockholm	942	5,454	1,653	9,630	6,012	3,714	716	3,414	3,986	1,003
Tokyo...........	5,959	5,470	6,706	5,062	7,035	6,471	4,660	3,638	6,757	6,053
Warsaw.........	905	5,922	1,427	9,598	6,337	4,022	721	3,277	4,270	852
Washington, D.C. ..	3,674	2,300	3,792	10,180	1,885	489	4,876	7,500	205	3,840

	Rio de Janeiro	Rome	San Francisco	Singa-pore	Stock-holm	Tehran	Tokyo	Vienna	Warsaw	Wash., D.C.
Bangkok.........	9,994	5,494	7,931	883	5,089	3,391	2,865	5,252	5,033	8,807
Beijing..........	10,768	5,063	5,918	2,771	4,133	3,490	1,307	4,648	4,325	6,942
Berlin...........	6,209	737	5,672	6,164	528	2,185	5,557	326	322	4,181
Cairo...........	6,143	1,326	7,466	5,137	2,096	1,234	5,958	1,481	1,619	5,822
Cape Town.......	3,781	5,231	10,248	6,008	6,423	5,241	9,154	5,656	5,935	7,895
Caracas.........	2,804	5,195	3,902	11,402	5,471	7,320	8,808	5,372	5,559	2,047
Chicago.........	5,282	4,824	1,859	9,372	4,331	6,502	6,314	4,698	4,679	596
Hong Kong.......	11,009	5,774	6,905	1,605	5,063	3,843	1,791	5,431	5,147	8,155
Honolulu.........	8,288	8,040	2,398	6,726	6,875	8,070	3,859	7,632	7,366	4,838
London..........	5,750	895	5,367	6,747	942	2,743	5,959	771	905	3,674
Los Angeles......	6,330	6,326	347	8,767	5,454	7,682	5,470	6,108	5,922	2,300
Madrid..........	5,045	851	5,803	7,080	1,653	2,978	6,706	1,128	1,427	3,792
Melbourne.......	8,226	9,929	7,856	3,759	9,630	7,826	5,062	9,790	9,598	10,180
Mexico City.......	4,764	6,377	1,887	10,327	6,012	8,184	7,035	6,320	6,337	1,885
Montreal.........	5,078	4,104	2,543	9,203	3,714	5,880	6,471	4,009	4,022	489
Moscow.........	7,170	1,483	5,885	5,228	716	1,532	4,660	1,043	721	4,876
New York.......	4,801	4,293	2,572	9,534	3,986	6,141	6,757	4,234	4,270	205
Paris...........	5,684	690	5,577	6,673	1,003	2,625	6,053	645	852	3,840
Rio de Janeiro	...	5,707	6,613	9,785	6,683	7,374	11,532	6,127	6,455	4,779
Rome...........	5,707	...	6,259	6,229	1,245	2,127	6,142	477	820	4,497
San Francisco	6,613	6,259	...	8,448	5,399	7,362	5,150	5,994	5,854	2,441
Singapore	9,785	6,229	8,448	...	5,936	4,103	3,300	6,035	5,843	9,662
Stockholm	6,683	1,245	5,399	5,936	...	2,173	5,053	780	494	4,183
Tokyo...........	11,532	6,142	5,150	3,300	5,053	4,775	...	5,689	5,347	6,791
Warsaw.........	6,455	820	5,854	5,843	494	1,879	5,689	347	...	4,472
Washington, D.C. ..	4,779	4,497	2,441	9,662	4,183	6,341	6,791	4,438	4,472	...

EDUCATION

Historical Summary of Public Elementary and Secondary Schools

Source: National Center for Education Statistics, U.S. Dept. of Education

Pupils and teachers (thousands)	1939-40	1949-50	1959-60[1]	1969-70[1]	1979-80[1]	1989-90[1]	1990-91[1]	1991-92[1]	1992-93[1]
Total U.S. population	130,880	149,199	179,323	203,212	224,567	246,819	249,399	252,137	255,078
Population 5-17 years of age	30,150	30,223	43,881	52,490	48,041	44,947	45,307	45,918	46,668
Percentage 5-17 years of age	23.0	20.3	24.5	25.8	21.4	18.2	18.2	18.2	18.3
Enrollment (thousands)									
Elementary and secondary	25,434	25,112	36,087	45,619	41,651	40,543	41,217	42,047	42,816
Kindergarten and grades 1-8	18,833	19,387	27,602	32,513	28,034	29,152	29,878	30,506	31,081
Grades 9-12	6,601	5,725	8,485	13,037	13,616	11,390	11,338	11,541	11,735
Percentage pop. 5-17 enrolled	84.4	83.1	82.2	86.9	86.7	90.2	91.0	91.6	91.7
Percentage in high schools	26.0	22.8	23.5	28.5	32.7	28.1	27.5	27.4	27.4
High school graduates (thousands)	1,143	1,063	1,627	2,589	2,748	2,320	2,2375	2,212	2,233
Average school term (in days)	175.0	177.9	178.0	178.9	178.5	—	179.8	—	—
Total instructional staff (thousands)	912	963	1,464	2,253	2,406	—	—	3,104	3,140
Teachers, librarians, and other non-supervisory instructional staff (thousands)	875	920	1,393	2,195	2,300	2,860	2,924	2,975	3,017
Revenue & expenditures (millions)									
Total revenue	$2,261	$5,437	$14,747	$40,267	$96,881	$207,573	$223,341	$234,486	$248,496
Total expenditures	2,344	5,838	15,613	40,683	95,962	212,100	229,430	241,567	253,859
Current elem. and secondary	1,942	4,687	12,239	34,218	86,984	187,558	202,038	211,216	221,353
Capital outlay	258	1,014	2,662	4,659	6,506	17,788	19,771	20,797	22,669
Interest on school debt	131	101	490	1,171	1,874	3,770	4,325	5,162	5,439
Other	13	36	133	636	598	2,985	3,296	4,392	4,399
Salaries and pupil cost				(data in unadjusted dollars)					
Annual salary of instructional staff[2]	$1,441	$3,010	$5,174	$8,840	$16,715	$32,638	$34,412	$35,550	$36,454
Expenditure per capita total pop.	17.91	39	87	200	427	859	920	958	995
Current expenditure per pupil ADA[3]	88.09	210	375	816	2,272	4,962	5,258	5,421	5,594

(1) Because of a modification in scope, "current expenditures for elementary and secondary schools" data for 1959-60 and later years are not entirely comparable with data for prior years. (2) Includes supervisors, principals, teachers, and nonsupervisory instructional staff. (3) ADA means average daily attendance in elementary and secondary day schools.

Programs for the Disabled[1], 1984-93

Source: Office of Special Education and Rehabilitative Services, U.S. Dept. of Education

(Number of children 0 to 21 years old served annually in educational programs for the disabled; in thousands.)

Type of Disability	1984-85	1985-86	1986-87	1987-88	1988-89	1989-90	1990-91	1991-92	1992-93
All disabilities	4,315	4,317	4,374	4,446	4,544	4,641	4,771	4,949	5,125
Learning disabilities	1,832	1,862	1,914	1,928	1,987	2,050	2,130	2,234	2,354
Speech impairments	1,126	1,125	1,136	953	967	973	987	997	996
Mental retardation	694	660	643	582	564	548	536	538	519
Serious emotional disturbance	372	375	383	373	376	381	391	399	401
Hearing impairments	69	66	65	56	56	57	58	60	60
Orthopedic impairments	56	57	57	47	47	48	49	51	52
Visual impairments	28	27	26	22	23	22	23	24	23
Other health impairments	68	57	52	45	43	52	55	58	65
Multiple disabilities	69	86	97	77	85	86	96	97	102
Deaf-blindness	2	2	2	12	2	2	1	1	1
Autism and other	—	—	—					5	19
Preschool disables[2]	3	3	3	361	394	422	441	484	531

Note: Counts are based on reports from the 50 states, the District of Columbia, and Puerto Rico (i.e., figures from U.S. territories are not included). Increases since 1987-88 are due in part to new legislation enacted fall 1986, which mandates public school special education services for all disabled children ages 3 -5. Details may not add to totals because of rounding.

(1)Includes students served under Chapter I and Individuals with Disabilities Education Act (IDEA). (2)Includes preschool children 3-5 years and 0-5 years served under Chapter I and IDEA respectively. (3)Prior to 1987-88, these students were included in the counts by disabling condition. Beginning in 1987-88, states are no longer required to report disabled preschool students (0-5 years) by disabling condition.

Technology in Public Schools, 1992-95

Source: Quality Education Data, Inc., Denver, CO

Technology	Number of schools				Percentage of schools			
	1992	1993	1994	1995	1992	1993	1994	1995
Schools with interactive videodisc players[1]	6,502	11,729	17,489	24,534	8.0	14.0	21.0	29.1
Elementary[2]	2,921	5,986	9,247	13,292	6.0	12.0	18.0	26.0
Junior high[3]	1,258	2,386	3,580	4,924	10.0	18.0	26.0	36.0
Senior high[4]	2,106	3,129	4,548	5,990	14.0	19.0	27.0	35.4
Schools with modems[1]	13,597	18,471	22,611	30,768	16.0	22.0	27.0	37.0
Elementary[2]	5,831	8,492	10,878	16,010	11.0	17.0	21.0	31.0
Junior high[3]	2,608	3,431	4,246	5,652	20.0	26.0	31.0	41.1
Senior high[4]	5,001	6,371	7,402	8,790	30.0	38.0	44.0	52.0
Schools with networks[1]	4,184	11,657	17,522	24,604	5.0	14.0	21.0	29.2
Elementary[2]	1,583	4,683	7,545	11,693	3.0	9.0	15.0	23.0
Junior high[3]	776	2,030	3,220	4,599	6.0	15.0	24.0	33.4
Senior high[4]	1,736	4,895	6,576	8,159	10.0	29.0	39.0	48.3
Schools with CD-ROMs[1]	5,706	11,021	20,943	34,480	7.0	13.0	25.0	41.0
Elementary[2]	1,897	4,457	9,791	18,343	4.0	9.0	19.0	36.0
Junior high[3]	1,231	2,326	4,261	6,510	9.0	17.0	31.0	47.4
Senior high[4]	2,543	4,168	6,713	9,327	15.0	25.0	40.0	55.2

(1)Includes schools for special and adult education, not shown separately. (2)Includes K-12, preschool, preschool through 3, K-6, and K-8. (3)Includes schools with grade spans of 4-8 and 7-9. (4)Includes 7-12, 9-12,10-12, vocational technical, and alternative high schools.

Enrollment and Teachers in Full-Time Elementary and Secondary Day Schools, Fall 1993

Source: National Center for Education Statistics, U.S. Dept. of Education; National Education Association

	Local school districts	Classroom teachers	Total enrollment	Pupils per teacher	Teacher's average pay (1993-94)[1]	Instructional aides	Expenditure per pupil
U.S.	**14,881**	**2,505,075**	**43,476,267**	**17.4**	**$35,819**	**450,598**	**$5,594**
Alabama	127	43,002	734,469	17.1	28,705	3,897	3,761
Alaska	56	7,193	125,948	17.5	47,512	2,146	8,735
Arizona	228	37,493	709,453	18.9	31,800	9,519	4,510
Arkansas	315	26,014	444,271	17.1	28,098	2,501	4,124
California	1,002	221,779	5,328,558	24.0	40,264	55,984	4,780
Colorado	176	33,661	625,062	18.6	33,826	4,995	5,139
Connecticut	166	34,526	496,298	14.4	49,769	6,178	7,970
Delaware	19	6,380	105,547	16.5	37,469	846	6,271
District of Columbia	1	6,056	80,678	13.3	42,543	366	9,419
Florida	67	110,653	2,040,763	18.4	31,944	22,238	5,314
Georgia	181	75,602	1,265,304	16.3	30,712	20,058	4,686
Hawaii	1	10,111	180,430	17.8	36,564	2,203	5,704
Idaho	113	12,007	236,774	19.7	27,756	1,709	3,690
Illinois	922	110,874	1,893,078	17.1	39,387	17,609	5,898
Indiana	294	55,107	965,599	17.5	35,712	13,633	5,344
Iowa	397	31,616	498,519	15.8	30,760	4,945	5,257
Kansas	304	30,283	457,614	15.1	33,919	4,178	5,442
Kentucky	176	37,324	655,265	17.6	31,625	9,322	4,874
Louisiana	66	46,913	800,560	16.6	26,285	9,431	4,428
Maine	282	15,344	216,995	14.1	30,996	3,452	6,073
Maryland	24	44,171	772,638	17.5	39,453	7,277	6,813
Massachusetts	351	58,766	877,726	14.9	40,852	10,611	6,627
Michigan	558	80,267	1,599,377	19.9	45,186[1]	12,629	6,494
Minnesota	405	46,956	810,233	17.3	36,146	6,089	5,554
Mississippi	149	28,376	505,907	17.8	25,153	8,886	3,382
Missouri	541	54,543	875,639	16.1	30,310	6,047	4,885
Montana	495	9,950	163,009	16.4	28,200	1,725	5,425
Nebraska	695	19,553	285,097	14.6	29,564	3,325	5,336
Nevada	17	12,579	235,800	18.7	33,955	1,257	5,066
New Hampshire	178	11,972	185,360	15.5	34,121	2,902	5,644
New Jersey	608	84,564	1,151,307	13.6	44,693	12,808	9,415
New Mexico	88	18,404	322,292	17.5	27,922	4,066	4,071
New York	714	179,413	2,733,813	15.2	45,772	26,272	8,902
North Carolina	121	69,421	1,133,231	16.3	29,728	20,721	4,763
North Dakota	260	7,755	119,127	15.4	25,506	1,290	4,575
Ohio	661	107,444	1,807,319	16.8	35,678	9,804	6,005
Oklahoma	554	39,031	604,076	15.5	27,009	6,172	4,355
Oregon	280	26,488	516,611	19.5	37,590	5,236	6,296
Pennsylvania	501	101,301	1,744,082	17.2	42,411	12,676	6,890
Rhode Island	36	9,823	145,676	14.8	39,261	1,320	6,938
South Carolina	95	38,620	643,859	16.7	29,566	7,121	4,624
South Dakota	178	9,557	142,825	14.9	25,259	1,801	4,357
Tennessee	140	46,066	866,991	18.8	30,514	8,981	3,993
Texas	1,046	224,830	3,608,262	16.0	30,519	38,816	4,670
Utah	40	19,053	471,365	24.7	27,706	4,309	3,180
Vermont	285	8,102	102,755	12.7	34,517	2,378	6,675
Virginia	141	70,220	1,045,471	14.9	33,009	11,209	4,980
Washington	296	45,524	915,952	20.1	35,863	7,940	5,614
West Virginia	55	21,029	314,383	14.9	30,549	2,858	5,527
Wisconsin	427	52,822	844,001	16.0	35,990	7,565	6,475
Wyoming	49	6,537	100,899	15.4	30,952	1,301	5,822

(1) National Education Association estimate.

Revenues for Public Schools by Source, 1990-95

Source: National Education Association

(in thousands)

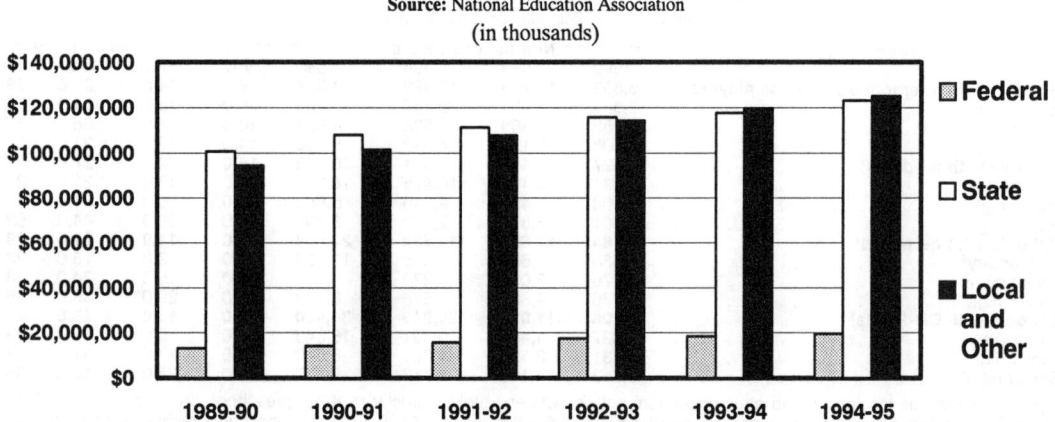

Estimated Revenues[1] for Public Elementary and Secondary Schools, by State, 1994-95

Source: National Education Association

(in thousands)

State	Total	Federal Amount	%	State Amount	%	Local and intermediate Amount	%
U.S.	$267,749,793	$19,587,397	7.3	$123,086,439	46.0	$125,075,957	46.7
Alabama	3,145,583	355,798	11.3	2,181,272	69.3	608,513	19.3
Alaska	1,059,103*	133,199*	12.6*	673,368*	63.6*	252,536*	23.8*
Arizona	3,713,546*	325,635*	8.8*	1,565,990*	42.2*	1,821,921*	49.1*
Arkansas	1,943,643	184,515	9.5	1,236,100	63.6	523,028	26.9
California	28,856,813	2,607,952	9.0	15,679,005	54.3	10,569,856	36.6
Colorado	3,273,796	194,064	5.9	1,552,290	47.4	1,527,290	46.7
Connecticut	4,443,893	197,710	4.4	1,763,841	39.7	2,482,342	55.9
Delaware	757,512	64,604	8.5	494,707	65.3	198,201	26.2
District of Columbia	622,000	80,000	12.9	—		542,000	87.1
Florida	12,626,925	921,137	7.3	6,344,224	50.2	5,361,564	42.5
Georgia	6,864,526	583,401	8.5	3,465.639	50.5	6,864,526	41.0
Hawaii	1,212,242	98,408	8.1	1,088,388	89.8	25,446	2.1
Idaho	999,575*	83,886*	8.4*	606,197*	60.6*	309,492*	31.0*
Illinois	11,793,500	1,080,600	9.2	3,792,200	32.2	6,920,700	58.7
Indiana	5,898,233*	325,450*	5.5*	3,061,111*	51.9*	2,511,672*	42.6*
Iowa	2,823,736	162,191	5.7	1,366,696	48.4	1,294,849	45.9
Kansas	2,591,395	141,857	5.5	1,287,014	49.7	1,162,524	44.9
Kentucky	3,475,343	345,565	9.9	2,344,532	67.5	785,246	22.6
Louisiana	3,768,960	468,917	12.4	2,078,290	55.1	1,221,753	32.4
Maine	1,334,550	88,760	6.7	649,879	48.7	595,911	44.7
Maryland	5,236,173	271,000	5.2	2,044,424	39.0	2,920,749	55.8
Massachusetts	6,123,672*	362,611*	5.9*	2,115,193*	34.5*	3,645,868*	59.5*
Michigan	11,507,509*	679,343*	5.9*	3,690,562*	32.1	7,137,604*	62.0
Minnesota	5,229,256*	265,524*	5.1*	2,261,158*	43.2	2,702,574*	51.7
Mississippi	1,997,808*	335,956*	16.8	1,070,556*	53.6	591,296*	29.6
Missouri	4,647,724	320,293	6.9	1,725,650	37.1	2,601,781	56.0
Montana	882,800	81,000	9.2	471,800	53.4	330,000	37.4
Nebraska	1,455,554*	61,514*	4.2*	587,799*	40.4*	806,241*	55.4*
Nevada	1,317,067	64,805	4.9	443,919	33.7	808,343	61.4
New Hampshire	1,278,071	35,663	2.8	108,065	8.5	1,134,343	88.8
New Jersey	11,539,724	485,172	4.2	4,784,097	41.5	6,270,455	54.3
New Mexico	1,887,799	189,971	10.1	1,274,000	66.1	450,828	23.9
New York	24,769,000	1,375,000	5.6	9,889,000	39.9	13,505,000	54.5
North Carolina	5,777,128	648,000	11.2	3,591,076	62.2	1,538,052	26.6
North Dakota	578,273*	71,640*	12.4*	254,037*	43.9*	252,596*	43.7*
Ohio	11,215,000	706,000	6.3	4,867,000	43.4	5,642,000	50.3
Oklahoma	2,799,949*	203,568*	7.3*	1,780,088*	63.6	816,293*	29.2*
Oregon	2,970,100	213,700	7.2	1,478,400	49.8	1,278,000	43.0
Pennsylvania	13,674,911	891,285	6.5	5,483,202	40.1	7,300,424	53.4
Rhode Island	1,036,981	46,281	4.5	416,546	40.2	574,154	55.4
South Carolina	3,211,357	309,936	9.7	1,503,152	46.8	1,398,269	43.5
South Dakota	674,994*	81,255*	12.0	184,429*	27.3*	409,310*	60.6*
Tennessee	3,734,744	316,701	8.5	1,873,128	50.2	1,544,915	41.4
Texas	19,930,447	1,794,597	9.0	8,582,167	43.1	9,553,683	47.9
Utah	1,891,899	126,612	6.7	1,054,373	55.7	710,914	37.6
Vermont	730,378*	37,756*	5.2*	235,377*	32.2*	457,245*	62.6*
Virginia	6,038,983	325,912	5.4	2,148,425	35.6	3,564,646*	59.0*
Washington	5,850,453	380,565	6.5	4,129,992	70.6	1,339,966	22.9
West Virginia	1,894,117	154,653	8.2	1,223,779	64.6	515,685	27.2
Wisconsin	6,019,048	268,435	4.5	2,291,372	38.1	6,019,048	57.5
Wyoming	644,000	39,000	6.1	320,000	49.7	285,000	44.3

* Indicates NEA estimate. (1)Included as revenue receipts are all appropriations from general funds of federal, state, county, and local governments; receipts from taxes levied for school purposes; income from permanent school funds and endowments; and income from leases of school lands and miscellaneous sources (interest on bank deposits, tuition, gifts, school lunch charges, etc.).

Public High School Graduation Rates, 1992-93

Source: National Center for Education Statistics, U.S. Dept. of Education

	Graduation rate (%)[1]	Rank		Graduation rate (%)[1]	Rank		Graduation rate (%)[1]	Rank
U.S.	71.1		Kentucky	72.7	33	Ohio	75.0	27
Alabama	61.7	46	Louisiana	56.3	51	Oklahoma	75.9	21
Alaska	73.4	31	Maine	74.3	29	Oregon	72.6	34
Arizona	72.0	35	Maryland	75.6	22T	Pennsylvania	80.6	14
Arkansas	78.4	16T	Massachusetts . .	78.1	18	Rhode Island	75.5	24
California	67.9	40	Michigan	69.9	37	South Carolina . . .	59.2	50
Colorado	75.3	25	Minnesota	89.1	1T	South Dakota . . .	89.1	1T
Connecticut	80.8	12	Mississippi	63.5	45	Tennessee	67.4	42
Delaware	70.2	36	Missouri	72.8	32	Texas	59.4	49
D.C.	64.6	44	Montana	86.7	6	Utah	80.7	13
Florida	61.4	48	Nebraska	86.9	4T	Vermont	82.0	11
Georgia	61.6	47	Nevada	69.6	38	Virginia	74.2	30
Hawaii	74.9	28	New Hampshire . .	78.4	16T	Washington	75.6	22T
Idaho	82.3	10	New Jersey	85.8	7T	West Virginia	77.9	20
Illinois	78.0	19	New Mexico	68.2	39	Wisconsin	83.5	9
Indiana	75.1	26	New York	65.4	43	Wyoming	86.9	4T
Iowa	87.5	3	North Carolina . . .	67.6	41			
Kansas	80.3	15	North Dakota	85.8	7T			

Note: T=Tied in rank with one or more states. (1) Graduates as percentage of Fall 1989 9th grade enrollment.

College Enrollment Rates of High School Graduates, by Race/Ethnicity and Sex, 1960-94

Source: American College Testing Program; Bureau of the Census, U.S. Department of Commerce; U.S. Department of Labor

(in thousands)

	High school graduates[1]					Enrolled in college[2]					
Year	Total	Male	Female	White[3]	Black[3,4]	Hispanic[4]	Total	Male	Female	White[3]	Black[3,4]	Hispanic[4]
1960..	1,679	756	923	1,565	—	—	758	408	350	717	—	—
1961..	1,763	756	923	1,612	—	—	847	445	402	840	—	—
1962..	1,838	872	966	1,660	—	—	900	488	420	840	—	—
1963..	1,741	794	947	1,615	—	—	784	415	420	736	—	—
1964..	2,145	997	1,148	1,964	—	—	1,037	570	467	967	—	—
1965..	2,659	1,254	1,405	2,417	—	—	1,354	718	636	1,249	—	—
1966..	2,612	1,207	1,405	2,403	—	—	1,309	709	600	1,243	—	—
1967..	2,525	1,142	1,383	2,267	—	—	1,311	658	653	1,202	—	—
1968..	2,606	1,184	1,422	2,303	—	—	1,444	748	696	1,304	—	—
1969..	2,842	1,352	1,490	2,538	—	—	1,516	812	704	2,538	—	—
1970..	2,757	1,343	1,414	2,461	—	—	1,427	741	686	1,280	—	—
1971..	2,872	1,369	1,503	2,461	—	—	1,535	788	747	1,402	—	—
1972..	2,961	1,420	1,541	2,614	—	—	1,457	749	708	1,292	—	—
1973..	3,101	1,491	1,610	2,707	—	—	1,425	730	695	1,302	—	—
1974..	3,101	1,491	1,610	2,736	—	—	1,474	736	738	1,288	—	—
1975..	3,186	1,513	1,673	2,825	—	—	1,615	796	819	1,446	—	—
1976..	2,987	1,450	1,537	2,640	320	152	1,458	685	773	1,291	134	80
1977..	3,140	1,482	1,658	2,768	335	156	1,590	773	817	1,403	166	80
1978..	3,161	1,485	1,676	2,750	352	133	1,584	758	826	1,378	161	57
1979..	3,160	1,474	1,686	2,776	324	154	1,559	743	816	1,376	147	69
1980..	3,089	1,500	1,589	2,682	361	129	1,524	701	823	1,339	151	68
1981..	3,053	1,490	1,563	2,626	359	146	1,646	816	830	1,434	154	76
1982..	3,100	1,508	1,592	2,644	384	174	1,568	739	829	1,376	140	75
1983..	2,964	1,390	1,574	2,496	392	138	1,562	721	841	1,372	151	75
1984..	3,012	1,429	1,583	2,514	438	185	1,662	800	862	1,455	176	82
1985..	2,666	1,286	1,380	2,241	333	141	1,539	754	785	1,332	141	72
1986..	2,786	1,331	1,455	2,307	386	169	1,499	744	755	1,292	141	75
1987..	2,647	1,278	1,369	2,207	337	176	1,503	746	757	1,249	175	59
1988..	2,673	1,334	1,339	2,187	382	179	1,575	761	814	1,328	172	102
1989..	2,454	1,208	1,245	2,051	337	168	1,463	696	767	1,238	178	93
1990..	2,355	1,169	1,185	1,921	341	112	1,410	676	735	1,182	158	53
1991..	2,276	1,139	1,137	1,867	320	154	1,420	656	763	1,207	146	88
1992..	2,398	1,216	1,182	1,900	353	199	1,479	725	754	1,204	169	109
1993..	2,338	1,118	1,219	1,910	302	200	1,464	668	797	1,200	168	125
1994..	2,517	1,244	1,273	2,065	318	178	1,559	754	805	1,313	162	87

— Data not available. (1)Individuals age 16 to 24 who graduated from high school during the preceding 12 months. (2)Enrollment in college as of October of each year for individuals age 16 to 24 who graduated from high school during the preceding 12 months. (3)Includes persons of Hispanic origin. (4)Due to the small sample size, data are subject to relatively large sampling errors.

Institutions of Higher Education–Charges, 1969-70 to 1993-94

Source: National Center for Education Statistics, U.S. Dept. of Education

Data are for the entire academic year ending in year shown. Figures for 1969-70 are average charges for full-time resident degree-credit students; figures for later years are average charges per full-time equivalent student. Room and board are based on full-time students.

Academic control and year	Tuition and required fees			Board rates (7-day basis)[1]			Dormitory charges		
	All institutions	2-yr	4-yr	All institutions	2-yr	4-yr	All institutions	2-yr	4-yr
Public (in-state)									
1969-70	$323	$178	$427	$511	$465	$540	$369	$308	$395
1979-80	583	355	840	867	894	898	715	572	749
1989-90	1,356	756	2,035	1,635	1,581	1,728	1,513	962	1,561
1990-91	1,454	824	2,159	1,691	1,594	1,767	1,612	1,050	1,658
1991-92	1,624	937	2,410	1,780	1,612	1,852	1,731	1,074	1,789
1992-93	1,782	1,025	2,349	1,841	1,668	1,854	1,756	1,106	1,816
1993-94[2].......	1,939	1,114	2,543	1,880	1,688	1,894	1,877	1,204	1,937
Private									
1969-70	1,533	1,034	1,809	561	546	608	436	413	503
1979-80	3,130	2,062	3,811	955	924	1,078	827	769	999
1989-90	8,147	5,196	10,348	1,948	1,811	2,339	1,923	1,663	2,411
1990-91	8,772	5,570	11,379	2,074	1,989	2,470	2,063	1,744	2,654
1991-92	9,434	5,752	12,192	2,252	2,090	2,727	2,221	1,789	2,860
1992-93	9,942	6,059	10,294	2,344	1,875	2,354	2,348	1,970	2,362
1993-94[2].......	10,594	6,343	10,994	2,440	1,981	2,451	2,498	2,113	2,513

(1) Data for 1989-90 through 1993-94 reflect 20 meals per week rather than 7 days per week. (2) Preliminary data based on fall 1992 enrollment weights.

Tuition and College Costs, 1995-96

Based on the Peterson's Guides Annual Survey of Undergraduate Institutions, the average cost of tuition, mandatory fees, and college room and board at 4-year private colleges is $15,648. The average cost at 4-year public colleges is $6,585 for state residents and $11,009 for nonresidents. Two-year public colleges are the least expensive group of institutions; tuition and fees average $1,767 for state residents and $4,178 for nonresidents. Tuition and fees at 2-year private colleges average $6,334.

The most expensive 4-year institutions, including tuition, mandatory fees, and college room and board, are Sarah Lawrence College ($28,448); Barnard College ($28,012); Brandeis University ($27,885); Yale University ($27,630); Brown University ($27,489); Hampshire College ($27,385); Tufts University ($27,336); New York University ($27,298); Stanford University ($27,237); and the Massachusetts Institute of Technology ($27,150). The least expensive 4-year undergraduate institutions are the U.S. service academies, which are all free.

American College Testing (ACT) Program Mean Scores and Characteristics of College-Bound Students, 1985-94

Source: The American College Testing Program

(for school year ending in year shown)

Type of test and mean test scores[1]	Unit	1985	1986[2]	1987[2]	1988[2]	1989[2]	1990[2]	1991[2]	1992[2]	1993[2]	1994[2]
Composite	**Points ...**	**18.6**	**20.8**	**20.8**	**20.8**	**20.6**	**20.6**	**20.6**	**20.6**	**20.7**	**20.8**
Male	Points ...	19.4	19.6	19.5	19.6	19.3	21.0	20.9	20.9	21.0	20.9
Female	Points ...	17.9	18.1	18.1	18.1	18.0	20.3	20.4	20.5	20.5	20.7
English	**Points ...**	**18.1**	**18.5**	**18.4**	**18.5**	**18.4**	**20.5**	**20.3**	**20.2**	**20.3**	**20.3**
Male	Points ...	17.6	17.9	17.9	18.0	17.8	20.1	19.8	19.8	19.8	19.8
Female	Points ...	18.6	18.9	18.9	19.0	18.9	20.9	20.7	20.6	20.6	20.7
Math	**Points ...**	**17.2**	**17.3**	**17.2**	**17.2**	**17.1**	**19.9**	**20.0**	**20.0**	**20.1**	**20.2**
Male	Points ...	18.6	18.8	18.6	18.4	18.3	20.7	20.6	20.7	20.8	20.8
Female	Points ...	16.0	16.0	16.1	16.1	16.1	19.3	19.4	19.5	19.6	19.6
Participants											
Total	**1,000 ....**	**739**	**730**	**777**	**842**	**855**	**817**	**796**	**832**	**875**	**892**
Male	Percent ..	46	46	46	46	46	46	45	45	45	45
White	Percent ..	82	82	81	81	80	79	79	79	79	79
Black	Percent ..	8	8	8	9	9	9	9	9	9	9
Obtaining composite scores of											
27 or above	Percent ..	14	14	14	14	14	12	11	12	12	13
18 or below	Percent ..	32	31	31	31	32	35	35	35	35	34

(1)Minimum score, 1; maximum score, 36. Test scores and characteristics of college-bound students are based on the performance of all ACT-tested students who graduated in the spring of a given school year and who took the ACT Assessment during junior or senior year of high school. (2)Beginning with the Oct. 1989 test (1990 scores), an entirely new ACT Assessment was introduced. The Enhanced ACT Assessment increases the emphasis on rhetorical skills in the measurement of writing proficiency, increases the number of advanced math items, and includes a new reading test that features inferential and reasoning skills and a test designed to measure science reasoning. The Enhanced ACT also provides subscores in English, mathematics, and reading. The composite scores for 1986-89 have been converted to provide a basis of comparison; all 1990-94 scores are for the Enhanced ACT. It is not possible to compare directly these data and data from earlier years.

SAT Mean Scores and Characteristics of College-Bound Seniors, 1980-95

Source: College Entrance Examination Board

(for school year ending in year shown)

Type of test and characteristic	Unit	1980	1985	1987	1988	1989	1990	1991	1992	1993	1994	1995
Test scores[1]												
Verbal, total[1]	**Points**	**424**	**431**	**430**	**428**	**427**	**424**	**422**	**423**	**424**	**423**	**428**
Male	Points	428	437	435	435	434	429	426	428	428	425	429
Female	Points	420	425	425	422	421	419	418	419	420	421	426
Math, total[1]	**Points**	**466**	**475**	**476**	**476**	**476**	**476**	**474**	**476**	**478**	**479**	**482**
Male	Points	491	499	500	498	500	499	497	499	502	501	503
Female	Points	443	452	453	455	454	455	453	456	457	460	463
Participants												
Total	**(thousands)**	**989**	**1,080**	**1,134**	**1,088**	**1,025**	**1,033**	**1,032**	**1,034**	**1,109**	**1,050**	**1,067**
Male	Percent	48.2	48.3	48.0	48.0	48.0	48.0	48.0	48.0	47.0	47.0	46.0
White	Percent	82.1	80.0	78.0	77.0	75.0	73.0	72.0	71.0	70.0	69.0	69.0
Black	Percent	9.1	8.9	9.0	9.0	10.0	10.0	10.0	10.0	11.0	11.0	11.0
Obtaining scores of												
600 or above												
Verbal	Percent	7.2	7.0	8.0	7.0	7.8	7.0	7.0	7.0	7.0	7.0	8.0
Math	Percent	15.1	17.0	18.0	17.0	18.0	18.0	17.0	18.0	19.0	18.0	21.0
Below 400												
Verbal	Percent	41.8	40.0	40.0	42.0	40.5	41.0	43.0	42.0	42.0	42.0	40.0
Math	Percent	30.2	28.0	29.0	27.0	28.0	28.0	29.0	27.0	28.0	26.0	28.0

(1) Minimum score, 200; maximum score, 800. (2)The College Board reports that SAT scores for the class of 1995 have not been recentered. Aggregated recentered scores will be reported for the first time in 1996.

SAT Mean Scores by State, 1991-95

Source: College Entrance Examination Board

	1991 Verbal	1991 Math	1992 Verbal	1992 Math	1993 Verbal	1993 Math	1994 Verbal	1994 Math	1995[1] Verbal	1995[1] Math	% Graduates Taking SAT[2]
Alabama	476	515	476	520	480	526	482	529	491	538	8
Alaska.	439	481	433	475	438	477	434	477	445	489	47
Arizona	442	490	440	493	444	497	443	496	448	496	27
Arkansas.	482	523	474	516	478	519	417	518	482	523	6
California.	415	482	416	484	415	484	413	482	417	485	45
Colorado.	453	506	453	507	454	509	456	513	462	518	29
Connecticut	429	468	430	470	430	474	426	472	431	477	81
Delaware.	428	464	432	463	429	465	428	464	429	468	68
Dist. of Columbia	405	435	405	437	405	441	406	443	412	445	53
Florida	416	466	416	468	416	466	413	466	420	469	48
Georgia.	400	444	398	444	399	445	398	446	406	448	65
Hawaii.	405	478	401	477	401	478	401	480	407	482	57
Idaho	463	505	460	503	465	507	461	508	468	511	15
Illinois	471	535	473	537	475	541	478	546	488	560	13
Indiana	408	457	409	459	409	460	410	466	415	467	58
Iowa	515	578	512	584	520	583	506	574	516	583	5
Kansas	493	546	487	546	494	548	494	550	503	557	9
Kentucky.	473	520	470	518	476	522	474	523	477	522	11
Louisiana	476	518	471	520	481	527	481	530	486	535	9
Maine	421	458	422	460	422	463	420	463	427	469	68
Maryland.	429	475	431	476	431	478	429	479	430	479	64
Massachusetts	426	470	428	474	427	476	426	475	430	477	80
Michigan	461	519	464	523	469	528	472	537	484	549	11
Minnesota	480	543	492	561	489	556	495	562	506	579	9
Mississippi.	477	520	478	526	481	521	485	528	498	540	4
Missouri	476	526	475	529	481	532	485	532	495	550	9
Montana	464	518	465	523	459	516	463	523	473	536	21
Nebraska	481	543	478	540	479	544	482	543	494	556	9
Nevada	435	484	434	488	432	488	429	484	434	483	30
New Hampshire.	440	481	440	483	442	487	438	486	444	491	70
New Jersey	417	469	420	471	419	473	418	475	420	478	70
New Mexico.	474	522	475	521	478	525	475	528	485	530	11
New York	413	468	416	466	416	471	416	472	419	473	74
North Carolina	400	444	405	450	406	453	405	455	411	454	60
North Dakota.	502	571	501	567	518	583	497	559	515	592	5
Ohio	450	496	450	501	454	505	456	510	460	515	23
Oklahoma	476	521	480	527	482	530	482	537	491	536	9
Oregon	439	483	439	486	441	492	436	491	448	499	51
Pennsylvania.	417	459	418	459	418	460	417	462	419	461	70
Rhode Island.	421	459	421	460	419	464	420	462	425	463	70
South Carolina.	395	437	394	437	396	442	395	443	401	443	58
South Dakota	496	551	490	550	502	558	483	548	505	563	5
Tennessee	487	528	484	529	486	531	488	535	497	543	12
Texas	411	463	410	466	413	472	412	474	419	474	47
Utah	494	537	496	545	500	549	509	558	513	563	4
Vermont	424	466	429	468	426	467	427	472	429	472	68
Virginia	424	466	425	468	425	469	424	469	428	468	65
Washington.	433	480	432	484	435	486	434	488	443	494	48
West Virginia.	441	485	440	484	439	485	439	482	448	484	17
Wisconsin	481	542	481	548	485	551	487	557	501	572	9
Wyoming.	466	514	462	516	463	507	459	521	476	525	10
National Average	**422**	**474**	**423**	**476**	**424**	**478**	**423**	**479**	**428**	**482**	**41**

(1)The College Board reports that SAT scores for the class of 1995 have not been recentered. Aggregated recentered scores will be reported for the first time in 1996. (2)Based on number of high school graduates in 1995, as projected by the Western Interstate Commission for Higher Education, and number of students in the class of 1995 who took the SAT. **Note:** Comparing states or ranking them on the basis of SAT scores alone is invalid, and the College Entrance Examination Board strongly discourages doing so.

Salaries of College Professors, 1994-95

Source: American Association of University Professors

	Women	Women Type of institution Private/ Independent	Women Church-related	Men	Men Type of institution Private/ Independent	Men Church-related
Academic rank	Public	Independent	Church-related	Public	Independent	Church-related
Doctoral level						
Professor	$61,710	$76,690	$68,190	$68,350	$85,940	$73,890
Associate	48,880	53,680	50,460	49,890	57,320	53,360
Assistant	39,470	44,990	41,890	42,630	48,830	44,740
Master's level						
Professor	53,650	57,490	55,470	57,590	61,610	61,220
Associate	44,060	45,810	44,850	46,760	48,410	48,430
Assistant	37,080	38,130	37,730	39,280	39,990	39,930
General 4-year						
Professor	49,770	55,040	44,510	51,870	58,800	47,290
Associate	41,800	43,050	37,370	42,990	44,790	39,090
Assistant	35,040	35,960	32,120	36,290	36,880	32,950
2-year						
Professor	49,070	37,930	33,380	52,690	43,410	33,700
Associate	40,860	32,980	30,420	43,430	39,920	30,310
Assistant	35,010	29,600	25,760	36,920	31,980	25,910

Top 50[1] Public Libraries in the U.S. and Canada, 1994-95

Source: World Almanac questionnaire; Public Library Association

Population served	Library name and location	No. of branches	No. of bound volumes	Circulation	Annual acquisition expenditures
3,620,500	Los Angeles Public Library (CA)	63	6,064,978	18,312,251	$4,762,642
3,280,020	Los Angeles County Public Library (Downey, CA)	84	5,855,534	11,875,807	9,365,813[2]
3,070,302	New York Public Library, The Branch Libraries (NY)	78	4,616,033	10,215,045	7,822,000[3]
2,783,726	Chicago Public Library (IL)	82	11,463,011	7,156,442	9,100,000[2]
2,300,664	Brooklyn Public Library (NY)	59	5,947,870	9,219,814	7,000,000
2,122,101	Maricopa County Library District (Phoenix, AZ)	11	543,908	1,693,070	801,700
1,951,598	Queens Borough Public Library (NY)	63	9,681,898	13,636,119	6,857,913[2]
1,690,180	Houston Public Library (TX)	34	4,113,095	6,482,882	2,823,900
1,627,866	Miami-Dade Public Library System (FL)	31	3,300,000	8,000,000	5,000,000
1,585,577	Free Library of Philadelphia (PA)	53	5,129,439	6,178,951	5,488,460[2]
1,438,505	Orange County Public Library (Santa Ana, CA)	27	2,212,956	NA	5,726,975[2]
1,371,946	Broward County Library System (Fort Lauderdale, FL)	28	2,070,939	6,465,591	4,244,981[2]
1,336,449	Carnegie Library of Pittsburgh (PA)	17	1,963,557	2,999,206	1,400,000
1,185,394	San Antonio Public Library (TX)	17	1,811,207	3,610,878	2,237,000[2]
1,184,800	San Diego Public Library (CA)	32	2,335,881	6,051,510	1,882,079[2]
1,100,000	Sacramento Public Library (CA)	24	1,364,207	3,900,000	1,000,000
1,081,200	Riverside City and County Public Library (CA)	23	1,503,545	3,866,757	1,122,603
1,052,000	Phoenix Public Library (AZ)	11	1,680,000	6,267,000	2,375,000[2]
1,030,678	Montréal, Bibliothèque Municipale De (Quebec)	25	2,051,419	4,485,653	3,092,900[4]
1,027,954	Detroit Public Library (MI)	25	1,680,000	1,267,000	2,375,000
1,022,497	Dallas Public Library (TX)	20	2,644,788	4,276,354	1,784,339
1,003,464	Providence Public Library (RI)	9	1,127,366	643,734	251,645[2]
969,600	San Bernardino County Library (CA)	27	1,049,230	2,999,087	763,410
968,584	Buffalo & Erie County Public Library (NY)	52	4,000,000	8,500,000	2,700,000
950,000	King County Library System (Seattle, WA)	39	2,710,611	12,287,434	5,461,900
904,997	San Diego County Library (CA)	32	982,547	2,845,685	843,394
878,000	Fairfax County Public Library (VA)	23	2,103,937	8,500,000	5,900,000
866,228	Cincinnati & Hamilton County, Public Library of (OH)	41	4,655,058	11,724,356	7,124,320
866,134	Tampa-Hillsborough County Public Library (FL)	18	1,208,404	3,007,915	1,768,757[3]
844,000	Memphis Shelby County Public Library (TN)	21	1,726,329	3,689,112	1,168,868[2]
842,936	St. Louis County Library (MO)	17	2,013,472	9,456,114	3,095,022[3]
834,000	San Jose Public Library System (CA)	17	1,300,000	4,700,000	1,400,000
799,900	Montgomery County Dept. of Public Libraries (Rockville, MD)	23	2,042,035	8,386,220	3,800,000
776,000	Contra Costa County Library (Pleasant Hill, CA)	21	1,080,300	3,943,975	711,506
770,684	Indianapolis-Marion County Public Library (IN)	21	1,145,941	7,720,766	4,150,420
752,830	Prince George's County Memorial Library System (Hyattsville, MD)	20	2,321,931	5,149,286	2,494,358[2]
739,092	Jacksonville Public Libraries (FL)	18	2,561,664	3,296,906	3,144,096
738,235	Fresno County Library (CA)	32	657,543	1,731,470	460,000
738,184	Calgary Public Library (Alberta)	0	1,524,245	9,603,295	3,410,500[3,4]
736,014	Enoch Pratt Free Library (Baltimore, MD)	28	2,293,980	1,460,421	2,094,052
734,247	Tucson-Pima Library (AZ)	18	1,138,300	5,200,000	1,836,730
729,030	Las Vegas Clark County Library District (NV)	24	1,467,314	4,065,065	3,744,274[2]
726,700	San Francisco Public Library (CA)	26	2,008,619	3,363,144	1,015,855[2]
714,418	Atlanta-Fulton Public Library (GA)	31	1,950,552	2,104,745	2,446,408[2]
713,968	Rochester Public Library (NY)	10	932,813	1,525,083	923,570[3]
708,582	Columbus Metropolitan Library (OH)	20	2,212,476	10,918,703	6,414,308
699,506	Baltimore County Public Library (Towson, MD)	15	1,742,778	10,989,985	3,810,156[2]
694,487	Orange County Library System (Orlando, FL)	11	1,498,102	4,681,881	2,000,000
683,502	Hennepin County Library (Minnetonka, MN)	25	1,257,362	8,909,315	3,578,013[2]
664,937	Louisville Free Public Library (KY)	15	888,988	2,540,810	2,225,000

(1)By population served. (2)1993-94 fiscal year (3)1992-93 fiscal year (4)Canadian dollars.

Number of Public Libraries and Operating Income, by State, 1993

Source: U.S. Dept. of Education; National Center for Education Statistics

(operating income in thousands)

State	No. of libraries	Operating income[1]	State	No. of libraries	Operating income[1]	State	No. of libraries	Operating income[1]
Alabama	208	$42,165	Kentucky	116	43,483	Ohio	250	381,506
Alaska	85	17,913	Louisiana	65	62,048	Oklahoma	110	33,928
Arizona	39	63,127	Maine	225	17,382[2]	Oregon	124	59,467
Arkansas	36	19,848	Maryland	24	116,358	Pennsylvania	448	163,127[2]
California	169	602,394	Massachusetts	374	128,241	Rhode Island	51	18,631
Colorado	120	82,415	Michigan	377	171,733[2]	S. Carolina	40	42,528
Connecticut	194	88,195	Minnesota	132	104,545	S. Dakota	113	9,910
Deleware	29	7,842	Mississippi	47	22,565	Tennessee	137	51,631
District of Columbia	1	20,819	Missouri	148	90,533	Texas	498	175,821[2]
Florida	100	225,779	Montana	83	10,541	Utah	69	32,651
Georgia	54	85,846	Nebraska	269	24,632[2]	Vermont	201	7,894[2]
Hawaii	1	24,918	Nevada	26	41,520	Virginia	90	122,487
Idaho	107	13,967	New Hampshire	229	21,123	Washington	70	136,838
Illinois	606	351,151	New Jersey	310	233,541	W. Virginia	97	16,970
Indiana	238	151,990	New Mexico	69	18,355	Wisconsin	380	108,125
Iowa	517	47,364	New York	758	600,407	Wyoming	23	10,168
Kansas	320	46,850	N. Carolina	74	91,593	**U.S. Total**	**8,929**	**$5,068,999**
			N. Dakota	78	6,132			

(1)Total income represents data for libraries that reported total operating income and/or all sources of income. Totals may be underestimated due to nonresponse. (2)Data reported are for fiscal year 1992.

American Colleges and Universities
General Information for the 1994–95 Academic Year
Source: Peterson's Guides, Copyright 1995

These listings include all accredited undergraduate degree-granting institutions in the United States and U.S. territories that have a total institutional enrollment of 1,000 or more. Four-year colleges (those that award a bachelor's as their highest undergraduate degree) are listed first, followed by two-year colleges (those that award an associate as their highest or primary undergraduate degree).

All institutions are coeducational except those where the zip code is directly followed by: (1)–men only, (2)–primarily men, (3)–women only, (4)–primarily women.

Year is that of founding.

Governing official is the chief executive officer.

Institutional control: 1–independent (nonprofit), 2–independent-religious, 3–proprietary (profit making), 4–federal, 5–state, 6–commonwealth (Puerto Rico), 7–territory (U.S. territories), 8–county, 9–district, 10–city, 11–state and local, 12–state related.

Highest degree offered: B–bachelor's, M–master's, F–first professional, D–doctorate.

Enrollment is the total number of matriculated undergraduate and (if applicable) graduate students.

Faculty is the total number of faculty members teaching undergraduate courses and (if available) graduate courses.

Any data not reported are indicated as NR.

Data reported for institutions that provided updated information on Peterson's Annual Survey of Undergraduate Institutions for the 1994–95 academic year.

Four-Year Colleges

Name, address	Year	Governing official, control, and highest degree offered		Enroll-ment	Faculty
Abilene Christian U, Abilene, TX 79699	1906	Dr. Royce Money	2-F	4,207	255
Acad of Art Coll, San Francisco, CA 94105-3410	1929	Ms. Elisa Stephens	3-M	3,621	303
Adams State Coll, Alamosa, CO 81102	1921	Dr. J. Thomas Gilmore	5-M	2,494	149
Adelphi U, Garden City, NY 11530	1896	Dr. Peter Diamandopoulos	1-D	8,012	688
Adrian Coll, Adrian, MI 49221-2575	1859	Dr. Stanley P. Caine	2-B	1,059	112
Alabama A&M U, Normal, AL 35762-1357	1875	Dr. David B. Henson	5-D	5,543	378
Alabama State U, Montgomery, AL 36101-0271	1874	Dr. William H. Harris	5-M	5,800	270
Albany State Coll, Albany, GA 31705-2717	1903	Dr. Billy C. Black	5-M	3,062	150
Albion Coll, Albion, MI 49224-1831	1835	Dr. Melvin L. Vulgamore	2-B	1,641	125
Albright Coll, Reading, PA 19612-5234	1856	Dr. Ellen S. Hurwitz	2-B	1,072	88
Alcorn State U, Lorman, MS 39096-9402	1871	Dr. Rudolph E. Waters	5-M	2,742	194
Alfred U, Alfred, NY 14802-1232	1836	Dr. Edward G. Coll, Jr.	1-D	2,326	197
Allegheny Coll, Meadville, PA 16335	1815	Dr. Daniel F. Sullivan	2-B	1,809	198
Allentown Coll of St Francis de Sales, Center Valley, PA 18034-9568	1962	Rev. Daniel Gambet, OSFS	2-M	2,166	96
Alma Coll, Alma, MI 48801-1599	1886	Dr. Alan J. Stone	2-B	1,404	133
Alvernia Coll, Reading, PA 19607-1799	1958	Dr. Daniel N. DeLucca	2-B	1,300	109
Alverno Coll, Milwaukee, WI 53234-3922 (3)	1887	Sr. Joel Read	2-B	1,876	210
Ambassador U, Big Sandy, TX 75755	1947	NR	2-B	1,111	79
Amber U, Garland, TX 75041-5595	1971	Dr. Douglas W. Warner	2-M	1,610	65
American International Coll, Springfield, MA 01109-3189	1885	Dr. Harry J. Courniotes	1-M	1,839	122
American U, Washington, DC 20016-8001	1893	Dr. Benjamin Ladner	2-D	11,708	1,335
Amherst Coll, Amherst, MA 01002	1821	Dr. Tom Gerety	1-B	1,608	165
Anderson U, Anderson, IN 46012-3462	1917	Dr. James L. Edwards	2-M	2,245	202
Andrews U, Berrien Springs, MI 49104	1874	Dr. Niels-Erik Andreasen	2-D	2,952	312
Angelo State U, San Angelo, TX 76909	1928	Dr. E. James Hindman	5-M	6,276	246
Anna Maria Coll, Paxton, MA 01612	1946	Dr. William R. Dill	2-M	1,797	158
Appalachian State U, Boone, NC 28608	1899	Dr. Francis T. Borkowski	5-M	11,866	730
Aquinas Coll, Grand Rapids, MI 49506-1799	1886	Mr. R. Paul Nelson	2-M	2,443	191
Arizona State U, Tempe, AZ 85287	1885	Dr. Lattie F. Coor	5-D	42,189	1,798
Arizona State U West, Phoenix, AZ 85069-7100	1984	NR	5-M	2,026	249
Arkansas State U, State University, AR 72467	1909	Dr. Leslie Wyatt	5-D	9,631	446
Arkansas Tech U, Russellville, AR 72801-2222	1909	Dr. Robert C. Brown	5-M	4,700	254
Armstrong State Coll, Savannah, GA 31419-1997	1935	Dr. Robert A. Burnett	5-B	5,040	373
Art Ctr Coll of Design, Pasadena, CA 91103-1999	1930	Mr. David R. Brown	1-M	1,164	427
Asbury Coll, Wilmore, KY 40390-1198	1890	Dr. David J. Gyertson	2-B	1,143	135
Ashland U, Ashland, OH 44805-3702	1878	Dr. G. William Benz	2-M	5,826	202
Assumption Coll, Worcester, MA 01615-0005	1904	Dr. Joseph H. Hagan	2-M	2,588	214
Athens State Coll, Athens, AL 35611-1902	1822	Dr. Jerry F. Bartlett	5-B	3,200	182
Auburn U, Auburn University, AL 36849-0001	1856	Dr. William V. Muse	5-D	21,226	1,288
Auburn U at Montgomery, Montgomery, AL 36117-3596	1967	Dr. Roy H. Saigo	5-M	6,341	356
Audrey Cohen Coll, New York, NY 10014-4502	1964	Dr. Audrey C. Cohen	1-M	1,087	73
Augsburg Coll, Minneapolis, MN 55454-1351	1869	Dr. Charles S. Anderson	2-M	2,958	256
Augusta Coll, Augusta, GA 30904-2200	1925	Dr. William A. Bloodworth, Jr.	5-M	5,673	264
Augustana Coll, Rock Island, IL 61201-2296	1860	Dr. Thomas Tredway	2-B	2,054	169
Augustana Coll, Sioux Falls, SD 57197	1860	Dr. Ralph H. Wagoner	2-M	1,667	157
Aurora U, Aurora, IL 60506-4892	1893	Dr. Thomas H. Zarle	1-M	2,025	240
Austin Coll, Sherman, TX 75090-4440	1849	Dr. Oscar C. Page	2-M	1,152	100
Austin Peay State U, Clarksville, TN 37044-0001	1927	Dr. Sal D. Rinella	5-M	8,207	477
Averett Coll, Danville, VA 24541-3692	1859	Dr. Frank R. Campbell	2-M	2,423	57
Avila Coll, Kansas City, MO 64145-1698	1916	Dr. Larry Kramer	2-M	1,429	151
Azusa Pacific U, Azusa, CA 91702-2701	1899	Dr. Richard E. Felix	2-D	4,386	374
Babson Coll, Babson Park, MA 02157-0310	1919	Mr. William F. Glavin	1-M	3,263	178
Baker Coll of Flint, Flint, MI 48507-5508	1911	Dr. Julianne T. Princinsky	1-M	4,043	179
Baker Coll of Muskegon, Muskegon, MI 49442-3497	1888	Dr. Rick Amidon	1-M	1,597	93
Baker Coll of Owosso, Owosso, MI 48867-4400	1984	NR	1-M	1,605	89
Baker U, Baldwin City, KS 66006-0065	1858	Dr. Daniel M. Lambert	2-M	1,997	83
Baldwin-Wallace Coll, Berea, OH 44017-2088	1845	Dr. Neal Malicky	2-M	4,716	314
Ball State U, Muncie, IN 47306-1099	1918	Dr. John E. Worthen	5-D	19,515	1,110
Bard Coll, Annandale-on-Hudson, NY 12504	1860	Dr. Leon Botstein	1-M	1,148	135
Barnard Coll, New York, NY 10027-6598 (3)	1889	Prof. Judith R. Shapiro	1-B	2,274	283
Barry U, Miami Shores, FL 33161-6695	1940	Sr. Jeanne O'Laughlin, OP	2-D	7,000	500
Barton Coll, Wilson, NC 27893	1902	Dr. James B. Hemby	2-B	1,465	90

Name, address	Year	Governing official, control, and highest degree offered		Enroll-ment	Faculty
Baruch Coll of the City U of New York, New York, NY 10010-5585	1919	Dr. Matthew Goldstein	11-D	14,750	820
Bates Coll, Lewiston, ME 04240-6028	1855	Dr. Donald W. Harward	1-B	1,562	166
Bayamón Central U, Bayamón, PR 00960-1725	1970	Rev. Vincent A. M. Van Rooij, OP	2-M	3,269	117
Bayamón Tech U Coll, Bayamón, PR 00959-1919	1971	Prof. Carmen A. Rivera	6-B	4,263	181
Baylor U, Waco, TX 76798	1845	Dr. Robert B. Sloan, Jr.	2-D	12,240	655
Beaver Coll, Glenside, PA 19038-3295	1853	Dr. Bette E. Landman	2-M	2,387	214
Belhaven Coll, Jackson, MS 39202-1789	1883	Dr. Dan Fredericks	2-B	1,109	80
Bellarmine Coll, Louisville, KY 40205-0671	1950	Dr. Joseph J. McGowan, Jr.	2-M	2,411	237
Bellevue U, Bellevue, NE 68005-3098	1965	Dr. John B. Muller	1-M	2,159	83
Belmont U, Nashville, TN 37212-3757	1951	Dr. William E. Troutt	2-M	2,961	330
Beloit Coll, Beloit, WI 53511-5596	1846	Mr. Victor E. Ferrall, Jr.	1-M	1,256	137
Bemidji State U, Bemidji, MN 56601-2699	1919	Dr. M. James Bensen	5-M	4,174	222
Benedict Coll, Columbia, SC 29204	1870	Dr. David H. Swinton	2-B	1,501	109
Bentley Coll, Waltham, MA 02154-4705	1917	Dr. Joseph M. Cronin	1-M	6,599	350
Berea Coll, Berea, KY 40404	1855	Dr. Larry D. Shinn	1-B	1,550	125
Berklee Coll of Music, Boston, MA 02215-3693	1945	Dr. Lee Eliot Berk	1-B	2,686	280
Berry Coll, Mount Berry, GA 30149-0159	1902	Dr. Gloria M. Shatto	1-M	1,876	105
Bethel Coll, Mishawaka, IN 46545-5591	1947	Dr. Norman Bridges	2-M	1,200	111
Bethel Coll, St Paul, MN 55112-6999	1871	Dr. George K. Brushaber	2-M	2,208	190
Bethune-Cookman Coll, Daytona Beach, FL 32114-3099	1904	Dr. Oswald P. Bronson, Sr.	2-B	2,345	184
Biola U, La Mirada, CA 90639-0001	1908	Dr. Clyde Cook	2-D	2,961	219
Birmingham-Southern Coll, Birmingham, AL 35254	1856	Dr. Neal R. Berte	2-M	1,583	146
Black Hills State U, Spearfish, SD 57799-9501	1883	Dr. Thomas O. Flickema	5-M	2,964	110
Bloomfield Coll, Bloomfield, NJ 07003-9981	1868	Dr. John F. Noonan	2-B	2,174	200
Bloomsburg U of Pennsylvania, Bloomsburg, PA 17815-1905	1839	Dr. Jessica Kozloff	5-M	7,277	398
Bluefield State Coll, Bluefield, WV 24701-2198	1895	Dr. Robert E. Moore	5-B	2,604	154
Boise State U, Boise, ID 83725-0399	1932	Dr. Charles Ruch	5-D	14,647	892
Boricua Coll, New York, NY 10032-1560	1974	Dr. Victor G. Alicea	1-B	1,228	128
Boston Coll, Chestnut Hill, MA 02167-9991	1863	Rev. J. Donald Monan, SJ	2-D	14,698	985
Boston U, Boston, MA 02215	1839	Dr. John Silber	1-D	28,664	2,544
Bowdoin Coll, Brunswick, ME 04011-2546	1794	Mr. Robert H. Edwards	1-B	1,489	172
Bowie State U, Bowie, MD 20715-3318	1865	Dr. Nathanael Pollard, Jr.	5-M	4,946	193
Bowling Green State U, Bowling Green, OH 43403	1910	Dr. Sidney A. Ribeau	5-D	17,564	866
Bradley U, Peoria, IL 61625-0002	1897	Dr. John R. Brazil	1-M	5,882	444
Brandeis U, Waltham, MA 02254-9110	1948	Dr. Jehuda Reinharz	1-D	4,008	490
Brenau U, Gainesville, GA 30501-3697 (4)	1878	Dr. John S. Burd	1-M	2,241	182
Brewton-Parker Coll, Mt Vernon, GA 30445	1904	Dr. Y. Lynn Holmes	2-B	2,250	231
Briar Cliff Coll, Sioux City, IA 51104-2100	1930	Sr. Margaret Wick	2-B	1,157	73
Bridgewater State Coll, Bridgewater, MA 02325-0001	1840	Dr. Adrian Tinsley	5-M	8,166	558
Brigham Young U, Provo, UT 84602-1001	1875	Dr. Rex E. Lee	2-D	30,413	1,697
Brigham Young U–Hawaii Cmps, Laie, Oahu, HI 96762-1294	1955	Dr. Eric B. Shumway	2-B	2,096	120
Brooklyn Coll of the City U of New York, Brooklyn, NY 11210-2889	1930	Dr. Vernon E. Lattin	11-M	13,045	925
Brown U, Providence, RI 02912	1764	Dr. Vartan Gregorian	1-D	7,801	676
Bryant Coll, Smithfield, RI 02917-1287	1863	Dr. William E. Trueheart	1-M	3,739	188
Bryn Mawr Coll, Bryn Mawr, PA 19010-2899 (3)	1885	Dr. Mary Patterson McPherson	1-D	1,778	221
Bucknell U, Lewisburg, PA 17837	1846	Dr. Wiliam D. Adams	1-M	3,528	264
Buena Vista U, Storm Lake, IA 50588	1891	Dr. Frederick V. Moore	2-B	1,085	92
Butler U, Indianapolis, IN 46208-3485	1855	Dr. Geoffrey Bannister	1-M	3,758	383
Cabrini Coll, Radnor, PA 19087-3698	1957	Dr. Antoinette Iadarola	2-M	1,932	149
Caldwell Coll, Caldwell, NJ 07006-6195	1939	Sr. Patrice Werner	2-M	1,688	118
California Coll for Health Sciences, National City, CA 91950-6605	1977	NR	3-M	4,671	23
California Coll of Arts and Crafts, Oakland, CA 94618	1907	Mr. Lorne Buchman	1-M	1,135	251
California Inst of Tech, Pasadena, CA 91125-0001	1891	Dr. Thomas E. Everhart	1-D	1,929	295
California Inst of the Arts, Valencia, CA 91355-2340	1961	Dr. Steven D. Lavine	1-M	1,051	212
California Lutheran U, Thousand Oaks, CA 91360-2787	1959	Dr. Luther S. Luedtke	2-M	2,824	241
California Polytechnic State U, San Luis Obispo, San Luis Obispo, CA 93407	1901	Dr. Warren J. Baker	5-M	15,440	839
California State Polytechnic U, Pomona, Pomona, CA 91768-2557	1938	Dr. Bob Suzuki	5-M	16,304	920
California State U, Bakersfield, Bakersfield, CA 93311-1022	1970	Dr. Tomas A. Arciniega	5-M	5,081	289
California State U, Chico, Chico, CA 95929-0150	1887	Dr. Manuel A. Esteban	5-M	14,232	823
California State U, Dominguez Hills, Carson, CA 90747-0001	1960	Dr. Robert Detweiler	5-M	9,744	401
California State U, Fresno, Fresno, CA 93740	1911	Dr. John D. Welty	5-D	17,277	918
California State U, Fullerton, Fullerton, CA 92634-9480	1957	Dr. Milton A. Gordon	5-M	22,097	1,013
California State U, Hayward, Hayward, CA 94542-3000	1957	Dr. Norma Rees	5-M	12,567	636
California State U, Long Beach, Long Beach, CA 90840-0119	1949	Dr. Robert C. Maxson	5-M	26,227	1,292
California State U, Los Angeles, Los Angeles, CA 90032-4221	1947	Dr. James M. Rosser	5-M	18,224	946
California State U, Northridge, Northridge, CA 91330	1958	Dr. Blenda J. Wilson	5-M	24,310	1,306
California State U, Sacramento, Sacramento, CA 95819-6048	1947	Dr. Donald R. Gerth	5-M	22,726	1,171
California State U, San Bernardino, San Bernardino, CA 92407-2397	1965	Dr. Anthony H. Evans	5-M	11,864	571
California State U, San Marcos, San Marcos, CA 92096	1990	NR	5-M	2,753	105
California State U, Stanislaus, Turlock, CA 95382	1957	Dr. Marvalene Hughes	5-M	5,877	335
California U of Pennsylvania, California, PA 15419-1394	1852	Dr. Angelo Armenti, Jr.	5-M	6,215	345
Calumet Coll of Saint Joseph, Whiting, IN 46394-2195	1951	Dr. Dennis C. Rittenmeyer	2-B	1,132	110
Calvin Coll, Grand Rapids, MI 49546-4388	1876	Dr. Gaylen J. Byker	2-M	3,793	294
Cameron U, Lawton, OK 73505-6377	1908	Dr. Don Davis	5-M	5,927	227
Campbellsville Coll, Campbellsville, KY 42718-2799	1906	Dr. Kenneth W. Winters	2-M	1,260	97
Campbell U, Buies Creek, NC 27506	1887	Dr. Norman A. Wiggins	2-F	6,646	349
Canisius Coll, Buffalo, NY 14208-1098	1870	Rev. Vincent M. Cooke, S.J.	2-M	4,789	375
Capital U, Columbus, OH 43209-2394	1830	NR	2-F	3,924	180
Cardinal Stritch Coll, Milwaukee, WI 53217-3985	1937	Sr. Mary Lea Schneider	2-M	5,654	564
Carleton Coll, Northfield, MN 55057-4001	1866	Dr. Stephen R. Lewis, Jr.	1-B	1,754	161
Carlow Coll, Pittsburgh, PA 15213-3165 (4)	1929	Dr. Grace Ann Geibel, RSM	2-M	1,670	189
Carnegie Mellon U, Pittsburgh, PA 15213-3891	1900	Dr. Robert Mehrabian	1-D	7,141	749
Carroll Coll, Helena, MT 59625-0002	1909	Dr. Matthew J. Quinn	2-B	1,438	110
Carroll Coll, Waukesha, WI 53186-5593	1846	Dr. Frank Falcone	2-M	2,279	129
Carson-Newman Coll, Jefferson City, TN 37760	1851	Dr. J. Cordell Maddox	2-M	2,163	176
Carthage Coll, Kenosha, WI 53140-1994	1847	Dr. F. Gregory Campbell	2-M	2,147	123
Case Western Reserve U, Cleveland, OH 44106	1826	Dr. Agnar Pytte	1-D	9,569	1,875
Castleton State Coll, Castleton, VT 05735	1787	Dr. Martha K. Farmer	5-M	1,800	179
Catawba Coll, Salisbury, NC 28144-2488	1851	Mr. J. Fred Corriher, Jr.	2-M	1,056	85
The Catholic U of America, Washington, DC 20064	1887	Br. Patrick Ellis, FSC, PhD	2-D	6,128	669

Name, address	Year	Governing official, control, and highest degree offered		Enrollment	Faculty
Cedar Crest Coll, Allentown, PA 18104-6132 (4)	1867	Dr. Dorothy Gulbenkian Blaney	2-B	1,545	140
Cedarville Coll, Cedarville, OH 45314-0601	1887	Dr. Paul H. Dixon	2-B	2,378	170
Centenary Coll of Louisiana, Shreveport, LA 71134-1188	1825	Dr. Kenneth L. Schwab	2-M	1,014	109
Central Coll, Pella, IA 50219-1999	1853	Dr. William M. Wiebenga	2-B	1,452	128
Central Connecticut State U, New Britain, CT 06050-4010	1849	Dr. Merle W. Harris	5-M	9,703	734
Central Methodist Coll, Fayette, MO 65248-1198	1854	Dr. Marianne Inman	2-B	1,134	82
Central Michigan U, Mount Pleasant, MI 48859	1892	Dr. Leonard E. Plachta	5-D	16,126	817
Central Missouri State U, Warrensburg, MO 64093	1871	Dr. Ed Elliott	5-M	10,805	514
Central Washington U, Ellensburg, WA 98926	1891	Dr. Ivory V. Nelson	5-M	8,468	322
Chadron State Coll, Chadron, NE 69337	1911	Dr. Samuel H. Rankin	5-M	3,296	147
Chaminade U of Honolulu, Honolulu, HI 96816-1578	1955	Dr. Mary Wesselkamper	2-M	2,700	195
Chapman U, Orange, CA 92666-1011	1861	Dr. James Doti	2-M	3,285	310
Charleston Southern U, Charleston, SC 29423-8087	1964	Dr. Jairy C. Hunter, Jr.	2-M	2,519	129
Charter Oak State Coll, Newington, CT 06111-2646	1973	Dr. Merle W. Harris	5-B	1,186	NR
Chestnut Hill Coll, Philadelphia, PA 19118-2695 (3)	1924	Dr. Carol J. Vale, SSJ	2-M	1,196	149
Cheyney U of Pennsylvania, Cheyney, PA 19319	1837	Dr. Douglas Covington	5-M	1,357	114
Chicago State U, Chicago, IL 60628	1867	Dr. Dolores Cross	5-M	10,001	482
Christian Brothers U, Memphis, TN 38104-5581	1871	Dr. Michael J. McGinniss, FSC	2-M	1,710	149
Christopher Newport U, Newport News, VA 23606-2998	1961	Dr. Anthony R. Santoro	5-M	4,705	340
The Citadel, The Military Coll of South Carolina, Charleston, SC 29409 (1)	1842	Lt. Gen. Claudius E. Watts, III	5-M	3,600	166
City Coll of the City U of New York, New York, NY 10031	1847	Dr. Yolanda T. Moses	11-D	14,885	1,244
City U, Bellevue, WA 98004-6442	1973	Dr. Michael A. Pastore	1-M	8,192	1,130
Clarion U of Pennsylvania, Clarion, PA 16214	1867	Dr. Diane L. Reinhard	5-M	5,637	375
Clark Atlanta U, Atlanta, GA 30314	1869	NR	2-D	5,193	316
Clarke Coll, Dubuque, IA 52001-3198	1843	Dr. Catherine Dunn, BVM	2-M	1,002	64
Clarkson U, Potsdam, NY 13699	1896	Dr. Dennis G. Brown	1-D	2,601	176
Clark U, Worcester, MA 01610-1477	1887	Dr. Richard P. Traina	1-D	2,670	NR
Clayton State Coll, Morrow, GA 30260-0285	1969	NR	5-B	4,760	191
Clemson U, Clemson, SC 29634	1889	Dr. Constantine W. Curris	5-D	16,296	1,389
Cleveland State U, Cleveland, OH 44115	1964	Dr. Claire A. Van Ummersen	5-D	16,504	800
Clinch Valley Coll of the U of Virginia, Wise, VA 24293	1954	Dr. L. Jay Lemons	5-B	1,387	90
Coastal Carolina U, Myrtle Beach, SC 29578-1954	1954	Dr. Ronald R. Ingle	5-M	4,461	249
Coe Coll, Cedar Rapids, IA 52402-5070	1851	Dr. John E. Brown	2-M	1,343	124
Colby Coll, Waterville, ME 04901	1813	William R. Cotter	1-B	1,650	150
Colgate U, Hamilton, NY 13346-1386	1819	Dr. Neil R. Grabois	1-M	2,759	254
Coll for Lifelong Learning of the U System of NH, Concord, NH 03301	1972	Dr. Victor Montana	11-B	1,228	300
Coll Misericordia, Dallas, PA 18612-1098	1924	Dr. Carol A. Jobe	2-M	1,822	142
Coll of Aeronautics, Flushing, NY 11371 (2)	1932	Dr. Richard B. Goetze, Jr.	1-B	1,092	80
Coll of Charleston, Charleston, SC 29424-0002	1770	Dr. Alexander M. Sanders, Jr.	5-M	9,943	584
Coll of Insurance, New York, NY 10007-2165	1962	Dr. Ellen Thrower	1-M	2,388	93
Coll of Mount St Joseph, Cincinnati, OH 45233-1670	1920	Sr. Francis Marie Thrailkill, OSU	2-M	2,508	194
Coll of Mount Saint Vincent, Riverdale, NY 10471-1093	1911	Dr. Mary C. Stuart	1-M	1,235	117
Coll of New Rochelle, New Rochelle, NY 10805-2308 (4)	1904	Sr. Dorothy Ann Kelly, OSU	1-M	2,383	212
Coll of Notre Dame, Belmont, CA 94002-1997	1851	Dr. Margaret Huber	2-M	1,707	179
Coll of Notre Dame of Maryland, Baltimore, MD 21210-2476 (3)	1873	Sr. Rosemarie Nassif	2-M	2,085	85
Coll of Saint Benedict, Saint Joseph, MN 56374 (3)	1887	Sr. Colman O'Connell, OSB	2-B	1,796	188
Coll of St Catherine, St Paul, MN 55105-1789 (3)	1905	Dr. Anita Pampusch	2-M	2,763	252
Coll of Saint Elizabeth, Morristown, NJ 07960-6989 (4)	1899	Sr. Jacqueline Burns	2-M	1,484	116
Coll of St Francis, Joliet, IL 60435-6188	1920	Dr. James A. Doppke	2-M	1,200	124
Coll of Saint Mary, Omaha, NE 68124-2377 (3)	1923	Dr. Kenneth Nielsen	2-B	1,172	131
Coll of Saint Rose, Albany, NY 12203-1419	1920	Dr. Louis C. Vaccaro	1-M	3,879	241
Coll of St Scholastica, Duluth, MN 55811-4199	1912	Dr. Daniel H. Pilon	2-M	1,849	167
Coll of Santa Fe, Santa Fe, NM 87505	1947	Dr. James A. Fries	1-M	1,365	60
Coll of Staten Island of the City U of New York, Staten Island, NY 10314-6600	1955	Dr. Marlene Springer	11-M	12,512	751
Coll of the Holy Cross, Worcester, MA 01610	1843	Rev. Gerard C. Reedy, SJ	2-B	2,720	265
Coll of the Ozarks, Point Lookout, MO 65726	1906	Dr. Jerry C. Davis	2-B	1,527	123
The Coll of West Virginia, Beckley, WV 25802-2830	1933	Dr. Charles H. Polk	1-B	1,736	110
Coll of William and Mary, Williamsburg, VA 23187-8795	1693	Mr. Timothy J. Sullivan	5-D	7,547	653
The Coll of Wooster, Wooster, OH 44691	1866	Dr. Susanne Woods	2-B	1,644	144
Colorado Christian U, Lakewood, CO 80226-1053	1914	Dr. Ronald Schmidt	2-M	2,568	72
The Colorado Coll, Colorado Springs, CO 80903-3294	1874	Dr. Kathryn Mohrman	1-M	1,933	203
Colorado Sch of Mines, Golden, CO 80401-1887	1874	Dr. George S. Ansell	5-D	3,146	235
Colorado State U, Fort Collins, CO 80523	1870	Dr. Albert C. Yates	5-D	21,461	1,001
Colorado Tech Coll, Colorado Springs, CO 80907-3896	1965	Mr. David D. O'Donnell	3-D	1,413	93
Columbia Coll, Chicago, IL 60605-1997	1890	Mr. John B. Duff	1-M	7,620	885
Columbia Coll, New York, NY 10027	1754	Dr. Austin E. Quigley	1-B	3,518	NR
Columbia Coll, Columbia, SC 29203-5998 (3)	1854	Dr. Peter T. Mitchell	2-M	1,229	104
Columbia U, Sch of Engineering & Applied Sci, New York, NY 10027	1864	Dr. Donald Goldfarb	1-D	996	NR
Columbia U, Sch of General Studies, New York, NY 10027	1754	Dr. Gillian Lindt	1-M	2,600	450
Columbia U, Sch of Nursing, New York, NY 10032-3702 (4)	1892	NR	1-D	612	40
Columbus Coll, Columbus, GA 31907-5645	1958	Dr. Frank D. Brown	5-M	5,534	228
Columbus Coll of Art and Design, Columbus, OH 43215-1758	1879	Mr. Joseph V. Canzani	1-B	1,726	130
Concord Coll, Athens, WV 24712-1000	1872	Dr. Jerry L. Beasley	5-B	2,623	150
Concordia Coll, Moorhead, MN 56562	1891	Dr. Paul J. Dovre	2-B	2,970	282
Concordia Coll, St Paul, MN 55104-5494	1893	Dr. Robert Holst	2-M	1,275	109
Concordia U, River Forest, IL 60305-1499	1864	Dr. George C. Heider	2-M	2,497	216
Concordia U, Portland, OR 97211-6099	1905	Dr. Charles E. Schlimpert	2-B	1,095	89
Concordia U Wisconsin, Mequon, WI 53097-2402	1881	Dr. R. John Buuck	2-M	3,209	135
Connecticut Coll, New London, CT 06320-4196	1911	Dr. Claire L. Gaudiani	1-M	1,919	169
Converse Coll, Spartanburg, SC 29302-0006 (3)	1889	Dr. Sandra C. Thomas	1-M	1,160	83
Cooper Union for the Advancement of Science & Art, New York, NY 10003-7120	1859	Dr. John Jay Iselin	1-M	1,064	235
Coppin State Coll, Baltimore, MD 21216-3698	1900	Dr. Calvin W. Burnett	5-M	3,380	232
Cornell Coll, Mount Vernon, IA 52314-1098	1853	Dr. Leslie H. Garner, Jr.	2-B	1,133	126
Cornell U, Ithaca, NY 14853-0001	1865	Dr. Hunter R. Rawlings	1-D	18,811	1,581
Creighton U, Omaha, NE 68178-0001	1878	Rev. Michael G. Morrison, SJ	2-D	6,341	1,180
Culver-Stockton Coll, Canton, MO 63435-1299	1853	Dr. Edwin B. Strong, Jr.	2-B	1,057	73
Cumberland Coll, Williamsburg, KY 40769-1372	1889	Dr. James Taylor	2-M	1,550	104
Cumberland U, Lebanon, TN 37087-3554	1842	Dr. Clair Eugene Martin	1-M	1,013	60
Curry Coll, Milton, MA 02186-9984	1879	Dr. Catherine W. Ingold	1-M	1,179	148
Daemen Coll, Amherst, NY 14226-3592	1947	Dr. Robert S. Marshall	1-M	1,884	150
Dakota State U, Madison, SD 57042-1799	1881	Dr. Jerald Tunheim	5-B	1,438	68
Dallas Baptist U, Dallas, TX 75211-9299	1965	Dr. Gary R. Cook	2-M	2,989	179

Name, address	Year	Governing official, control, and highest degree offered		Enroll-ment	Faculty
Dartmouth Coll, Hanover, NH 03755	1769	Mr. James O. Freedman	1-D	5,300	488
Davenport Coll of Business, Grand Rapids, MI 49503	1866	Mr. Donald W. Maine	1-B	3,455	162
Davenport Coll of Business, Kalamazoo Cmps, Kalamazoo, MI 49006-2791 (4)	1866	Ms. Patricia Dolly	1-B	1,315	78
Davenport Coll of Business, Lansing Cmps, Lansing, MI 48933-2197	1979	Mr. Don Colizzi	1-B	1,518	102
David Lipscomb U, Nashville, TN 37204-3951	1891	Dr. Harold Hazelip	2-M	2,432	181
Davidson Coll, Davidson, NC 28036-1719	1837	Dr. John W. Kuykendall	2-B	1,614	147
Delaware State U, Dover, DE 19901-2277	1891	Dr. William B. DeLauder	5-M	3,381	174
Delaware Valley Coll, Doylestown, PA 18901-2697	1896	Dr. William L. George	1-B	1,340	106
Delta State U, Cleveland, MS 38733-0001	1925	Dr. F. Kent Wyatt	5-D	3,775	278
Denison U, Granville, OH 43023	1831	Dr. Michele Tolela Myers	1-B	1,834	162
Denver Tech Coll, Denver, CO 80224-1658	1945	NR	3-B	1,400	67
DePaul U, Chicago, IL 60604-2287	1898	Rev. John P. Minogue, CM	2-D	16,747	1,149
DePauw U, Greencastle, IN 46135-1772	1837	Dr. Robert G. Bottoms	2-B	2,042	198
Detroit Coll of Business, Dearborn, MI 48126-3799	1962	Dr. James Mendola	1-B	3,076	192
Detroit Coll of Business, Warren Cmps, Warren, MI 48092-5209	1975	Ms. Janet Guggenheim	1-B	1,683	83
DeVry Inst of Tech, Phoenix, AZ 85021-2995	1967	Mr. James A. Dugan	3-B	2,637	80
DeVry Inst of Tech, Pomona, CA 91768-2642	1983	Dr. Rose Marie Dishman	3-B	2,845	140
DeVry Inst of Tech, Decatur, GA 30030-2198	1969	Dr. Ronald Bush	3-B	2,710	101
DeVry Inst of Tech, Addison, IL 60101-6106	1982	Mr. Jerry R. Dill	3-B	2,871	102
DeVry Inst of Tech, Chicago, IL 60618-5994	1931	Dr. E. Arthur Stunnard	3-B	2,858	120
DeVry Inst of Tech, Kansas City, MO 64131-3698	1931	Mr. Charles R. Levalley	3-B	1,927	71
DeVry Inst of Tech, Columbus, OH 43209-2764	1952	Mr. Richard A. Czerniak	3-B	2,667	78
DeVry Inst of Tech, Irving, TX 75063-2440	1969	Dr. Francis V. Cannon	3-B	2,019	111
Dickinson Coll, Carlisle, PA 17013-2896	1773	Dr. A. Lee Fritschler	1-B	1,875	184
Dickinson State U, Dickinson, ND 58601-4896	1918	Dr. Philip W. Conn	5-B	1,591	98
Dillard U, New Orleans, LA 70122-3097	1869	Dr. Samuel DuBois Cook	2-B	1,675	124
Doane Coll, Crete, NE 68333-2430	1872	Dr. Frederic D. Brown	2-M	1,294	96
Dominican Coll of Blauvelt, Orangeburg, NY 10962-1210	1952	Sr. Kathleen Sullivan	1-M	1,743	145
Dominican Coll of San Rafael, San Rafael, CA 94901-8008	1890	Dr. Joseph R. Fink	2-M	1,249	151
Dordt Coll, Sioux Center, IA 51250-1697	1955	Dr. John B. Hulst	2-M	1,156	90
Dowling Coll, Oakdale, NY 11769-1999	1955	Dr. Victor P. Meskill	1-M	5,683	383
Drake U, Des Moines, IA 50311-4516	1881	Dr. Michael R. Ferrari	1-D	5,954	278
Drew U, Madison, NJ 07940-1493	1867	Mr. Thomas H. Kean	2-D	2,047	183
Drexel U, Philadelphia, PA 19104-2875	1891	C. R. Pennoni	1-D	9,782	710
Drury Coll, Springfield, MO 65802-3791	1873	Dr. John E. Moore, Jr.	1-M	1,377	107
Duke U, Durham, NC 27708-0586	1838	Dr. Nannerl O. Keohane	2-D	11,352	2,105
Duquesne U, Pittsburgh, PA 15282-0001	1878	Dr. John E. Murray, Jr.	2-D	9,001	712
Dyke Coll, Cleveland, OH 44115-1096	1848	Dr. John C. Corfias	1-B	1,362	92
D'Youville Coll, Buffalo, NY 14201-1084	1908	Dr. Denise A. Roche, GNSH	1-M	1,825	148
East Carolina U, Greenville, NC 27858-4353	1907	Dr. Richard Eakin	5-D	16,373	1,160
East Central U, Ada, OK 74820-6899	1909	Dr. Bill S. Cole	5-M	4,538	225
Eastern Coll, St Davids, PA 19087-3696	1932	Dr. Roberta Hestenes	2-M	1,939	206
Eastern Connecticut State U, Willimantic, CT 06226-2295	1889	Dr. David G. Carter	5-M	4,522	192
Eastern Illinois U, Charleston, IL 61920-3099	1895	Dr. David L. Jorns	5-M	11,301	657
Eastern Kentucky U, Richmond, KY 40475-3102	1906	Dr. Hanly Funderburk	5-M	16,060	855
Eastern Mennonite U, Harrisonburg, VA 22801-2462	1917	Dr. Joseph L. Lapp	2-F	1,106	103
Eastern Michigan U, Ypsilanti, MI 48197	1849	Dr. William E. Shelton	5-D	23,321	1,138
Eastern Nazarene Coll, Quincy, MA 02170-2999	1918	Dr. Kent R. Hill	2-M	1,287	66
Eastern New Mexico U, Portales, NM 88130	1934	Dr. Everett L. Frost	5-M	3,853	224
Eastern Oregon State Coll, La Grande, OR 97850-2899	1929	Dr. David E. Gilbert	5-M	1,956	147
Eastern Washington U, Cheney, WA 99004-2431	1882	Dr. Marshall Drummond	5-M	8,360	423
East Stroudsburg U of Pennsylvania, East Stroudsburg, PA 18301-2999	1893	Dr. James Gilbert	5-M	5,247	277
East Tennessee State U, Johnson City, TN 37614-0734	1911	Dr. Roy S. Nicks	5-D	11,512	659
East Texas Baptist U, Marshall, TX 75670-1498	1912	Dr. Bob E. Riley	2-M	1,333	103
East Texas State U, Commerce, TX 75429-3011	1889	Dr. Jerry D. Morris	5-D	7,952	383
East Texas State U at Texarkana, Texarkana, TX 75505-5518	1971	Dr. Stephen R. Hensley	5-M	1,210	59
Eckerd Coll, St Petersburg, FL 33711	1958	Dr. Peter H. Armacost	2-B	1,387	124
Edgewood Coll, Madison, WI 53711-1998	1927	Dr. James A. Ebben	2-M	1,893	140
Edinboro U of Pennsylvania, Edinboro, PA 16444	1857	Mr. Foster F. Diebold	5-M	7,484	423
Elizabeth City State U, Elizabeth City, NC 27909-7806	1891	Dr. Jimmy R. Jenkins	5-B	2,099	136
Elizabethtown Coll, Elizabethtown, PA 17022-2298	1899	Dr. Gerhard E. Spiegler	2-B	1,818	151
Elmhurst Coll, Elmhurst, IL 60126-3296	1871	Dr. Bryant L. Cureton	2-B	2,775	135
Elmira Coll, Elmira, NY 14901	1855	Dr. Thomas K. Meier	1-M	1,121	76
Elms Coll, Chicopee, MA 01013-2839 (3)	1928	Sr. Kathleen Keating	2-M	1,182	105
Elon Coll, Elon College, NC 27244	1889	Dr. J. Fred Young	2-M	3,496	218
Embry-Riddle Aeronautical U, Prescott, AZ 86301-3720	1978	Dr. Stephen Kahbe	1-B	1,400	84
Embry-Riddle Aeronautical U, Daytona Beach, FL 32114-3900	1926	Dr. Steven M. Sliwa	1-M	4,210	238
Embry-Riddle Aeronautical U, Extended Cmps, Daytona Beach, FL 32114-3900	1970	Dr. Leon E. Flancher	1-M	6,935	2,211
Emerson Coll, Boston, MA 02116-1511	1880	Dr. Jacqueline W. Liebergott	1-D	3,409	259
Emmanuel Coll, Boston, MA 02115 (4)	1919	Sr. Janet Eisner, SND	2-M	1,528	94
Emory U, Atlanta, GA 30322-1100	1836	Dr. William M. Chace	2-D	10,800	2,085
Emporia State U, Emporia, KS 66801-5087	1863	Dr. Robert E. Glennen	5-D	6,075	290
Eugene Lang Coll, New Sch for Social Research, New York, NY 10011-8601	1978	Dr. Beatrice Banu	1-B	363	59
Evangel Coll, Springfield, MO 65802-2191	1955	Dr. Robert H. Spence	2-B	1,541	122
The Evergreen State Coll, Olympia, WA 98505	1967	Dr. Jane L. Jervis	5-M	3,672	169
Fairfield U, Fairfield, CT 06430-5195	1942	Rev. Aloysius P. Kelley, SJ	2-M	4,969	367
Fairleigh Dickinson U, Teaneck-Hackensack Cmps, Teaneck, NJ 07666-1914	1942	Dr. Francis J. Mertz	1-D	7,321	580
Fairmont State Coll, Fairmont, WV 26554	1865	Dr. Robert J. Dillman	5-B	6,355	435
Fashion Inst of Tech, New York, NY 10001-5992	1944	Dr. Allan F. Hershfield	11-M	8,422	931
Faulkner U, Montgomery, AL 36109-3398	1942	Dr. Billy D. Hilyer	2-F	2,363	125
Fayetteville State U, Fayetteville, NC 28301	1867	Dr. Donna J. Benson	5-M	4,109	240
Felician Coll, Lodi, NJ 07644-2198	1942	Sr. Theresa Martin	2-B	1,068	97
Ferris State U, Big Rapids, MI 49307	1884	Dr. William Sederburg	5-F	10,258	608
Ferrum Coll, Ferrum, VA 24088-9001	1913	Dr. Jerry M. Boone	2-B	1,124	98
Finch U of Health Sciences/Chicago Medical Sch, North Chicago, IL 60064-3037	1912	Mr. Herman M. Finch	1-D	1,285	23
Fitchburg State Coll, Fitchburg, MA 01420-2697	1894	Dr. Vincent J. Mara	5-M	6,149	431
Flagler Coll, St Augustine, FL 32085-1027	1968	Dr. William L. Proctor	1-B	1,350	123
Florida A&M U, Tallahassee, FL 32307	1887	Dr. Frederick Humphries	5-D	10,101	678

Name, address	Year	Governing official, control, and highest degree offered		Enrollment	Faculty
Florida Atlantic U, Boca Raton, FL 33431-0991	1961	Dr. Anthony James Catanese	5-D	17,484	684
Florida Inst of Tech, Melbourne, FL 32901-6988	1958	Dr. Lynn E. Weaver	1-D	4,564	446
Florida International U, Miami, FL 33199	1965	Dr. Modesto A. Maidique	5-D	22,052	1,171
Florida Memorial Coll, Miami, FL 33054	1879	Dr. Albert E. Smith	2-B	1,800	NR
Florida Southern Coll, Lakeland, FL 33801-5698	1885	Dr. Thomas L. Reuschling	2-M	1,820	126
Florida State U, Tallahassee, FL 32306	1857	Dr. Talbot D'Alemberte	5-D	29,630	1,568
Fontbonne Coll, St Louis, MO 63105-3098	1917	Dr. Dennis C. Golden	2-M	1,681	124
Fordham U, New York, NY 10458	1841	Rev. Joseph A. O'Hare, SJ	2-D	14,423	765
Fort Hays State U, Hays, KS 67601-4099	1902	Dr. Edward H. Hammond	5-M	5,496	272
Fort Lewis Coll, Durango, CO 81301-3999	1911	Mr. Joel M. Jones	5-B	4,109	249
Fort Valley State Coll, Fort Valley, GA 31030-3262	1895	Dr. Oscar L. Prater	5-F	2,820	151
Framingham State Coll, Framingham, MA 01701-9101	1839	Dr. Paul F. Weller	5-M	5,151	219
Franciscan U of Steubenville, Steubenville, OH 43952-6701	1946	Rev. Michael Scanlan, TOR	2-M	1,908	133
Francis Marion U, Florence, SC 29501-0547	1970	Dr. Lee A. Vickers	5-M	3,892	219
Franklin and Marshall Coll, Lancaster, PA 17604-3003	1787	Dr. Richard Kneedler	1-B	1,834	169
Franklin Pierce Coll, Rindge, NH 03461-0060	1962	Dr. Walter Peterson	1-B	1,164	105
Franklin U, Columbus, OH 43215-5399	1902	Dr. Paul J. Otte	1-M	3,915	212
Freed-Hardeman U, Henderson, TN 38340-2399	1869	Dr. Milton R. Sewell	2-M	1,467	91
Fresno Pacific Coll, Fresno, CA 93702-4709	1944	Dr. Richard Kriegbaum	2-M	1,548	160
Friends U, Wichita, KS 67213	1898	Dr. Biff Green	1-M	2,326	119
Frostburg State U, Frostburg, MD 21532-2302	1898	Dr. Catherine R. Gira	5-M	5,443	305
Furman U, Greenville, SC 29613	1826	Dr. David E. Shi	1-M	2,663	198
Gallaudet U, Washington, DC 20002-3625	1864	Dr. I. King Jordan	1-D	2,175	330
Gannon U, Erie, PA 16541	1925	Msgr. David A. Rubino, PhD	2-M	3,669	303
Gardner-Webb U, Boiling Springs, NC 28017	1905	Dr. M. Christopher White	2-M	2,259	174
Geneva Coll, Beaver Falls, PA 15010-3599	1848	Dr. John H. White	2-M	1,679	103
George Fox Coll, Newberg, OR 97132-2697	1891	Dr. Edward F. Stevens	2-D	1,658	115
George Mason U, Fairfax, VA 22030-4445	1957	Dr. George W. Johnson	5-D	21,774	1,246
Georgetown Coll, Georgetown, KY 40324-1696	1829	Dr. William H. Crouch, Jr.	2-M	1,405	109
Georgetown U, Washington, DC 20057	1789	Rev. Leo J. O'Donovan, SJ	2-D	12,617	1,843
The George Washington U, Washington, DC 20052	1821	Mr. Stephen J. Trachtenberg	1-D	19,298	2,171
Georgia Coll, Milledgeville, GA 31061	1889	Dr. Edwin G. Speir	5-M	5,655	290
Georgia Inst of Tech, Atlanta, GA 30332-0001	1885	Dr. Gerald W. Clough	5-D	12,901	634
Georgian Court Coll, Lakewood, NJ 08701-2697 (4)	1908	Sr. Barbara Williams	2-M	2,539	189
Georgia Southern U, Statesboro, GA 30460-8033	1906	Dr. Nicholas Henry	5-D	14,138	678
Georgia Southwestern Coll, Americus, GA 31709-4693	1906	Dr. William H. Capitan	5-M	2,533	155
Georgia State U, Atlanta, GA 30303-3083	1913	Dr. Carl V. Patton	5-D	23,776	1,335
Gettysburg Coll, Gettysburg, PA 17325-1411	1832	Dr. Gordon A. Haaland	1-B	1,950	174
Glenville State Coll, Glenville, WV 26351-1200	1872	Dr. William K. Simmons	5-B	2,269	160
GMI Engineering & Management Inst, Flint, MI 48504-4898	1919	Dr. James E. A. John	1-M	3,258	150
Golden Gate U, San Francisco, CA 94105-2968	1853	Dr. Thomas M. Stauffer	1-D	5,881	537
Goldey-Beacom Coll, Wilmington, DE 19808-1999	1886	Mr. William R. Baldt	1-M	1,795	73
Gonzaga U, Spokane, WA 99258	1887	Rev. Bernard J. Coughlin, SJ	2-D	5,000	276
Gordon Coll, Wenham, MA 01984-1899	1889	Dr. R. Judson Carlberg	2-B	1,178	103
Goshen Coll, Goshen, IN 46526-4794	1894	Dr. Victor Stoltzfus	2-B	1,011	125
Goucher Coll, Baltimore, MD 21204-2794	1885	Dr. Judy Jolley Mohraz	1-M	1,130	138
Governors State U, University Park, IL 60466	1969	Dr. Paula Wolff	5-M	5,708	294
Graceland Coll, Lamoni, IA 50140	1895	Dr. William T. Higdon	2-B	1,116	90
Grambling State U, Grambling, LA 71245	1901	Dr. Raymond A. Hicks	5-D	8,000	224
Grand Canyon U, Phoenix, AZ 85017-3030	1949	Dr. Bill Williams	2-M	2,083	182
Grand Valley State U, Allendale, MI 49401-9403	1960	Mr. Arend D. Lubbers	5-M	13,553	719
Grand View Coll, Des Moines, IA 50316-1599	1896	Dr. Arthur E. Puotinen	2-B	1,418	121
Grinnell Coll, Grinnell, IA 50112-0805	1846	Dr. Pamela A. Ferguson	1-B	1,295	153
Grove City Coll, Grove City, PA 16127-2104	1876	Dr. Jerry H. Combee	2-B	2,280	145
Guilford Coll, Greensboro, NC 27410-4173	1837	Dr. William R. Rogers	2-B	1,187	124
Gustavus Adolphus Coll, St Peter, MN 56082-1498	1862	Dr. Axel D. Steuer	2-B	2,334	221
Gwynedd-Mercy Coll, Gwynedd Valley, PA 19437	1948	Dr. Linda M. Bevilacqua, OP	2-M	1,860	204
Hamilton Coll, Clinton, NY 13323-1218	1812	Dr. Eugene M. Tobin	1-B	1,664	199
Hamline U, St Paul, MN 55104-1284	1854	Dr. Larry G. Osnes	2-F	2,698	245
Hampshire Coll, Amherst, MA 01002	1965	Dr. Gregory S. Prince, Jr.	1-B	1,086	100
Hampton U, Hampton, VA 23668	1868	Dr. William R. Harvey	1-D	5,769	351
Hanover Coll, Hanover, IN 47243	1827	Dr. Russell L. Nichols	2-B	1,092	108
Harding U, Searcy, AR 72149-0001	1924	Dr. David B. Burks, Jr.	2-M	3,817	216
Hardin-Simmons U, Abilene, TX 79698-0001	1891	Dr. Lanny Hall	2-F	2,133	154
Harris-Stowe State Coll, St Louis, MO 63103-2136	1857	Dr. Henry Givens, Jr.	5-B	1,757	99
Hartwick Coll, Oneonta, NY 13820-4020	1797	Dr. Richard A. Detweiler	1-B	1,502	159
Harvard U, Cambridge, MA 02138	1636	Dr. Neil Rudenstine	1-D	18,694	1,990
Hastings Coll, Hastings, NE 68902-0269	1882	Dr. Thomas J. Reeves	2-M	1,064	96
Haverford Coll, Haverford, PA 19041-1392	1833	Dr. Tom G. Kessinger	1-B	1,109	111
Hawaii Pacific U, Honolulu, HI 96813-2785	1965	Mr. Chatt Wright	1-M	7,910	492
Heidelberg Coll, Tiffin, OH 44883-2462	1850	Dr. William C. Cassell	2-M	1,372	108
Henderson State U, Arkadelphia, AR 71999-0001	1890	Dr. Charles D. Dunn	5-M	3,796	187
High Point U, High Point, NC 27262-3598	1924	Dr. Jacob C. Martinson, Jr.	2-M	2,452	199
Hillsdale Coll, Hillsdale, MI 49242-1298	1844	Dr. George C. Roche, III	1-B	1,160	112
Hofstra U, Hempstead, NY 11550-1090	1935	Dr. James M. Shuart	1-D	11,545	929
Hollins Coll, Roanoke, VA 24020-1657 (3)	1842	Dr. Jane Margaret O'Brien	1-M	1,070	91
Holy Family Coll, Philadelphia, PA 19114-2094	1954	Sr. Francesca Onley	2-M	2,569	241
Hood Coll, Frederick, MD 21701-8575 (4)	1893	Mrs. Shirley D. Peterson	2-M	2,022	129
Hope Coll, Holland, MI 49422-9000	1862	Dr. John H. Jacobson, Jr.	2-B	2,825	255
Houghton Coll, Houghton, NY 14744	1883	Dr. Daniel R. Chamberlain	2-B	1,332	100
Houston Baptist U, Houston, TX 77074-3298	1960	Dr. E. Douglas Hodo	2-M	2,131	140
Howard Payne U, Brownwood, TX 76801-2715	1889	Dr. Don Newbury	2-B	1,488	116
Howard U, Washington, DC 20059-0002	1867	H. Patrick Swygert, Esq.	1-D	10,961	2,021
Humboldt State U, Arcata, CA 95521-8299	1913	Dr. Alistair W. McCrone	5-M	7,049	411
Hunter Coll of the City U of New York, New York, NY 10021-5085	1870	Dr. Blanche D. Blank	11-M	18,390	696
Husson Coll, Bangor, ME 04401-2999	1898	Dr. William H. Beardsley	1-M	2,077	78
ICI U, Irving, TX 75063-2631	1967	NR	2-M	8,998	NR
Idaho State U, Pocatello, ID 83209	1901	Dr. Richard Bowen	5-D	11,877	659
Illinois Benedictine Coll, Lisle, IL 60532-0900	1887	Dr. William J. Carroll	2-M	2,860	245
Illinois Inst of Tech, Chicago, IL 60616	1890	Mr. Lewis Collens	1-D	7,157	474
Illinois State U, Normal, IL 61790-2200	1857	Dr. Thomas P. Wallace	5-D	19,166	949
Illinois Wesleyan U, Bloomington, IL 61702-2900	1850	Dr. Minor Myers, Jr.	1-B	1,855	181
Immaculata Coll, Immaculata, PA 19345-0900 (4)	1920	Sr. Marie Roseanne Bonfini	2-D	2,088	160
Incarnate Word Coll, San Antonio, TX 78209-6397	1881	Dr. Louis J. Agnese, Jr.	2-M	2,801	214

Name, address	Year	Governing official, control, and highest degree offered		Enroll-ment	Faculty
Indiana Inst of Tech, Fort Wayne, IN 46803-1297	1930	Mr. Donald J. Andorfer	1-B	1,050	42
Indiana State U, Terre Haute, IN 47809-1401	1865	Dr. John W. Moore	5-D	11,641	641
Indiana U Bloomington, Bloomington, IN 47405	1820	Dr. Kenneth R. R. Gros Louis	5-D	35,594	1,557
Indiana U East, Richmond, IN 47374-1289	1971	Dr. David J. Fulton	5-B	2,387	185
Indiana U Kokomo, Kokomo, IN 46904-9003	1945	Dr. Emita B. Hill	5-M	3,257	195
Indiana U Northwest, Gary, IN 46408-1197	1959	Dr. Hilda Richards	5-M	5,639	382
Indiana U of Pennsylvania, Indiana, PA 15705	1875	Dr. Lawrence K. Pettit	5-D	13,814	835
Indiana U–Purdue U Fort Wayne, Fort Wayne, IN 46805-1499	1917	Dr. Michael A. Wartell	5-M	11,513	674
Indiana U–Purdue U Indianapolis, Indianapolis, IN 46202-2896	1969	Mr. Gerald L. Bepko	5-D	26,766	1,997
Indiana U South Bend, South Bend, IN 46634-7111	1922	Dr. Lester C. Lamon	5-M	7,936	599
Indiana U Southeast, New Albany, IN 47150-6405	1941	Dr. Leon Rand	5-M	5,464	403
Indiana Wesleyan U, Marion, IN 46953-4999	1920	Dr. James Barnes	2-M	4,738	150
Inter American U of PR, Arecibo Cmps, Arecibo, PR 00614-4050	1957	Dr. Zaida Vega	1-B	4,633	244
Inter Amer U of PR, Barranquitas Regional Coll, Barranquitas, PR 00618	1957	Mr. Vidal Rivera Garcia	1-B	1,618	85
Inter American U of PR, San Germán Cmps, San Germán, PR 00683-5008	1912	Prof. Agnes Mojica	1-M	6,392	324
Iona Coll, New Rochelle, NY 10801-1890	1940	NR	1-M	6,197	431
Iowa State U of Science and Tech, Ames, IA 50011	1858	Dr. Martin C. Jischke	5-D	24,728	1,759
Ithaca Coll, Ithaca, NY 14850	1892	Dr. James J. Whalen	1-M	5,556	550
Jackson State U, Jackson, MS 39217	1877	Dr. James E. Lyons, Sr.	5-D	6,224	388
Jacksonville State U, Jacksonville, AL 36265-9982	1883	Dr. Harold J. McGee	5-M	7,553	342
Jacksonville U, Jacksonville, FL 32211-3394	1934	Dr. James J. Brady	1-M	2,480	227
James Madison U, Harrisonburg, VA 22807	1908	Dr. Ronald E. Carrier	5-M	11,539	729
Jamestown Coll, Jamestown, ND 58405	1883	Dr. James Walker	2-B	1,083	72
Jersey City State Coll, Jersey City, NJ 07305-1957	1927	Dr. Carlos Hernandez	5-M	7,199	245
John Brown U, Siloam Springs, AR 72761-2121	1919	Dr. A. LeVon Balzer	2-B	1,114	88
John Carroll U, University Heights, OH 44118-4581	1886	Dr. Frederick Travis, SJ	2-M	4,342	338
John F Kennedy U, Orinda, CA 94563-2689	1964	Mr. Charles E. Glasser	1-F	1,796	88
John Jay Coll of Criminal Justice of City U of NY, New York, NY 10019-1093	1964	Dr. Gerald Lynch	11-M	9,599	496
Johns Hopkins U, Baltimore, MD 21218-2699	1876	Dr. William C. Richardson	1-D	4,812	470
Johnson & Wales U, Providence, RI 02903-2807	1914	Dr. John A. Yena	1-M	7,892	435
Johnson & Wales U, Charleston, SC 29403	1984	NR	1-B	1,150	66
Johnson C Smith U, Charlotte, NC 28216	1867	Dr. Dorothy Cowser Yancy	1-B	1,391	91
Johnson State Coll, Johnson, VT 05656-9405	1828	Dr. Robert Hahn	5-M	1,648	119
Juniata Coll, Huntingdon, PA 16652-2119	1876	Dr. Robert W. Neff	1-B	1,068	104
Kalamazoo Coll, Kalamazoo, MI 49006-3295	1833	Dr. Lawrence Bryan	1-B	1,241	108
Kansas Newman Coll, Wichita, KS 67213-2084	1933	Sr. Tarcisia Roths	2-M	1,954	305
Kansas State U, Manhattan, KS 66506	1863	Dr. Jon Wefald	5-D	20,664	1,132
Kean Coll of New Jersey, Union, NJ 07083	1855	Dr. Henry J. Ross	5-M	11,386	824
Keene State Coll, Keene, NH 03435-1701	1909	Dr. Stanley J. Yarosewick	5-M	3,931	343
Kennesaw State Coll, Marietta, GA 30061-0444	1963	Dr. Betty L. Siegel	5-M	11,915	484
Kent State U, Kent, OH 44242-0001	1910	Dr. Carol A. Cartwright	5-D	21,413	1,299
Kentucky State U, Frankfort, KY 40601	1886	Dr. Mary L. Smith	12-M	2,564	149
Kenyon Coll, Gambier, OH 43022-9623	1824	Dr. Robert A. Oden, Jr.	1-B	1,510	145
King's Coll, Wilkes-Barre, PA 18711-0801	1946	Rev. James Lackenmier, CSC	2-M	2,271	175
Knox Coll, Galesburg, IL 61401	1837	Mr. Frederick C. Nahm	1-B	1,056	91
Kutztown U of Pennsylvania, Kutztown, PA 19530	1866	Dr. David E. McFarland	5-M	7,916	449
Lafayette Coll, Easton, PA 18042-1798	1826	Mr. Arthur J. Rothkopf	2-B	2,219	232
Lake Forest Coll, Lake Forest, IL 60045-2399	1857	Dr. David Spadafora	1-M	1,013	119
Lake Superior State U, Sault Sainte Marie, MI 49783-1699	1946	Dr. Robert D. Arbuckle	5-M	3,301	106
Lamar U–Beaumont, Beaumont, TX 77710	1923	Dr. Rex Cottle	5-D	8,356	725
Lambuth U, Jackson, TN 38301	1843	Dr. Thomas F. Boyd	2-B	1,209	90
Lander U, Greenwood, SC 29649-2099	1872	Dr. William C. Moran	5-M	2,779	166
Langston U, Langston, OK 73050-0907	1897	Dr. Ernest L. Holloway	5-M	4,200	128
La Roche Coll, Pittsburgh, PA 15237-5898	1963	Msgr. William Kerr	2-M	1,700	131
La Salle U, Philadelphia, PA 19141-1199	1863	Br. Joseph Burke	2-M	5,376	324
La Sierra U, Riverside, CA 92515	1922	Dr. Lawrence T. Geraty	2-D	1,456	108
Lawrence Tech U, Southfield, MI 48075-1058	1932	Dr. Charles M. Chambers	1-M	4,503	307
Lawrence U, Appleton, WI 54912-0599	1847	Dr. Richard Warch	1-B	1,161	137
Lebanon Valley Coll, Annville, PA 17003-0501	1866	Mr. John A. Synodinos	2-M	1,754	104
Lee Coll, Cleveland, TN 37311-4475	1918	Dr. Paul Conn	2-B	2,197	144
Lehigh U, Bethlehem, PA 18015-3094	1865	Dr. Peter Likins	1-D	6,447	504
Lehman Coll of the City U of New York, Bronx, NY 10468-1589	1931	Dr. Ricardo R. Fernandez	11-M	8,921	NR
Le Moyne Coll, Syracuse, NY 13214	1946	Rev. Robert A. Mitchell, SJ	2-M	2,756	216
LeMoyne-Owen Coll, Memphis, TN 38126-6595	1862	Dr. Burnett Joiner	2-M	1,440	100
Lenoir-Rhyne Coll, Hickory, NC 28603	1891	Dr. Ryan A. LaHurd	2-M	1,418	111
Lesley Coll, Cambridge, MA 02138-2790 (3)	1909	Ms. Margaret A. McKenna	1-D	6,024	885
LeTourneau U, Longview, TX 75607-7001	1946	Dr. Alvin O. Austin	2-M	2,047	205
Lewis & Clark Coll, Portland, OR 97219-7879	1867	Dr. Michael J. Mooney	1-F	3,234	286
Lewis-Clark State Coll, Lewiston, ID 83501-2698	1893	Dr. James Hottois	5-B	3,347	302
Lewis U, Romeoville, IL 60441	1932	Br. James Gaffney, FSC	2-M	4,399	330
Liberty U, Lynchburg, VA 24506-8001	1971	Dr. A. Pierre Guillermin	2-D	4,879	191
Lincoln Memorial U, Harrogate, TN 37752	1897	Dr. Scott D. Miller	1-M	1,914	116
Lincoln U, Jefferson City, MO 65102	1866	Dr. Wendell G. Rayburn, Sr.	5-M	3,512	218
Lincoln U, Lincoln University, PA 19352	1854	Dr. Niara Sudarkasa	12-M	1,400	138
Lindenwood Coll, St Charles, MO 63301-1695	1827	Dr. Dennis Spellmann	2-M	3,375	162
Lindsey Wilson Coll, Columbia, KY 42728-1298	1903	Dr. John B. Begley	2-B	1,277	55
Linfield Coll, McMinnville, OR 97128-6894	1849	Dr. Vivian A. Bull	2-B	1,570	134
Lock Haven U of Pennsylvania, Lock Haven, PA 17745-2390	1870	Dr. Craig Dean Willis	5-M	3,687	226
Long Island U, Brooklyn Cmps, Brooklyn, NY 11201-8423	1926	Dr. David J. Steinberg	1-D	8,006	507
Long Island U, C W Post Cmps, Brookville, NY 11548-1300	1954	NR	1-D	7,919	1,008
Long Island U, Southampton Cmps, Southampton, NY 11968-9822	1963	Dr. David J. Steinberg	1-M	1,441	120
Longwood Coll, Farmville, VA 23909-1800	1839	Dr. William F. Dorrill	5-M	3,277	205
Loras Coll, Dubuque, IA 52004-0178	1839	Dr. Joachim W. Froehlich	2-M	1,933	134
Louisiana Coll, Pineville, LA 71359-0001	1906	Dr. Robert L. Lynn	2-B	1,013	92
Louisiana State U and A&M Coll, Baton Rouge, LA 70803-3103	1860	Dr. William E. Davis	5-D	25,317	1,287
Louisiana State U in Shreveport, Shreveport, LA 71115-2399	1965	Dr. John R. Darling, Jr.	5-M	4,237	208
Louisiana State U Medical Ctr, New Orleans, LA 70112-2223	1931	Dr. Mervin L. Trail	5-D	3,217	NR
Louisiana Tech U, Ruston, LA 71272	1894	Dr. Daniel D. Reneau	5-D	10,023	464
Lourdes Coll, Sylvania, OH 43560-2898	1958	Sr. Ann Francis Klimkowski, OSF	2-B	1,666	131
Loyola Coll, Baltimore, MD 21210-2699	1852	Rev. Harold Ridley, S.J.	2-D	6,169	436
Loyola Marymount U, Los Angeles, CA 90045-2699	1911	Rev. Thomas P. O'Malley, SJ	2-F	6,546	591

Name, address	Year	Governing official, control, and highest degree offered		Enrollment	Faculty
Loyola U Chicago, Chicago, IL 60611-2196	1870	Rev. John J. Piderit, SJ	2-D	13,806	1,107
Loyola U, New Orleans, New Orleans, LA 70118-6195	1912	Rev. Bernard Patrick Knoth, SJ	2-F	5,634	435
Lubbock Christian U, Lubbock, TX 79407-2099	1957	Dr. Ken Jones	2-M	1,117	97
Luther Coll, Decorah, IA 52101-1045	1861	Dr. H. George Anderson	2-B	2,383	201
Lycoming Coll, Williamsport, PA 17701-5192	1812	Dr. James E. Douthat	2-B	1,507	139
Lynchburg Coll, Lynchburg, VA 24501-3199	1903	Dr. Charles O. Warren, Jr.	2-M	2,067	169
Lyndon State Coll, Lyndonville, VT 05851	1911	Dr. Margaret R. Williams	5-M	1,178	105
Lynn U, Boca Raton, FL 33431-5598	1962	Dr. Donald E. Ross	1-M	1,444	119
Macalester Coll, St Paul, MN 55105-1899	1874	Dr. Robert M. Gavin, Jr.	2-B	1,796	192
Madonna U, Livonia, MI 48150-1173	1947	Sr. Mary Francilene	2-M	4,155	241
Malone Coll, Canton, OH 44709-3897	1892	Dr. Ronald G. Johnson	2-M	2,004	149
Manchester Coll, North Manchester, IN 46962-1225	1889	Dr. Parker G. Marden	2-M	1,004	98
Manhattan Coll, Riverdale, NY 10471	1853	Br. Thomas J. Scanlan	2-M	3,250	266
Mankato State U, Mankato, MN 56002-8400	1868	Dr. Richard R. Rush	5-M	12,624	715
Mannes Coll of Music, New Sch for Social Research, New York, NY 10024-4402	1916	Dr. Charles Kaufman	1-M	267	216
Mansfield U of Pennsylvania, Mansfield, PA 16933	1857	Mr. Rod C. Kelchner	5-M	2,992	216
Marian Coll, Indianapolis, IN 46222-1997	1851	Dr. Daniel A. Felicetti	2-B	1,352	135
Marian Coll of Fond du Lac, Fond du Lac, WI 54935-4699	1936	Mr. Matthew G. Flanigan	2-M	2,510	113
Marietta Coll, Marietta, OH 45750-4000	1835	Dr. Lauren R. Wilson	1-M	1,319	125
Marist Coll, Poughkeepsie, NY 12601-1387	1929	Dr. Dennis J. Murray	1-M	4,276	377
Marquette U, Milwaukee, WI 53201-1881	1881	Rev. Albert J. DiUlio, SJ	2-D	10,749	1,048
Marshall U, Huntington, WV 25755-2020	1837	Dr. J. Wade Gilley	5-D	12,659	801
Mars Hill Coll, Mars Hill, NC 28754	1856	Dr. Fred B. Bentley	2-B	1,056	123
Mary Baldwin Coll, Staunton, VA 24401 (4)	1842	Dr. Cynthia H. Tyson	2-M	1,300	113
Marygrove Coll, Detroit, MI 48221-2599	1910	Dr. John E. Shay, Jr.	2-M	1,218	72
Marylhurst Coll, Marylhurst, OR 97036-0261	1893	Dr. Nancy A. Wilgenbusch	2-M	1,183	276
Marymount Coll, Tarrytown, NY 10591-3796 (4)	1907	Dr. Brigid Driscoll, RSHM	1-B	1,031	126
Marymount Manhattan Coll, New York, NY 10021-4597	1936	Dr. Regina Peruggi	1-B	1,973	207
Marymount U, Arlington, VA 22207-4299	1950	Sr. Eymard Gallagher, RSHM	2-M	3,456	375
Maryville U of Saint Louis, St Louis, MO 63141-7299	1872	Dr. Keith Lovin	1-M	3,425	276
Mary Washington Coll, Fredericksburg, VA 22401-5358	1908	Dr. William M. Anderson, Jr.	5-M	3,489	235
Marywood Coll, Scranton, PA 18509-1598	1915	Sr. Mary Reap, IHM	2-M	3,068	266
Massachusetts Coll of Art, Boston, MA 02115-5882	1873	Dr. William F. O'Neil	5-M	1,367	86
Mass Coll of Pharmacy and Allied Health Sciences, Boston, MA 02115-5896	1823	Dr. Sumner M. Robinson	1-D	1,436	122
Massachusetts Inst of Tech, Cambridge, MA 02139-4307	1861	Dr. Charles M. Vest	1-D	9,774	962
McKendree Coll, Lebanon, IL 62254-1299	1828	Dr. James M. Dennis	2-B	1,632	163
McMurry U, Abilene, TX 79697	1923	Dr. Robert E. Shimp	2-B	1,384	131
McNeese State U, Lake Charles, LA 70609-2495	1939	Dr. Robert D. Hebert	5-M	8,729	300
Medaille Coll, Buffalo, NY 14214-2695	1875	Mr. Kevin I. Sullivan	1-B	1,144	94
Medical Coll of Georgia, Augusta, GA 30912-1003	1828	Dr. Francis J. Tedesco	5-D	2,098	791
Medical Coll of Pennsylvania & Hahnemann U, Philadelphia, PA 19102	1848	Mr. Sherif Abdelhak	1-D	1,736	752
Medical U of South Carolina, Charleston, SC 29425-0002	1824	Dr. James B. Edwards	5-D	2,278	2,276
Mercer U, Macon, GA 31207-0003	1833	Dr. R. Kirby Godsey	2-F	6,823	670
Mercer U, Cecil B Day Cmps, Atlanta, GA 30341-4155	1968	Dr. R. Kirby Godsey	2-D	1,663	38
Mercy Coll, Dobbs Ferry, NY 10522-1189	1951	Dr. Jay Sexter	1-M	6,242	670
Mercyhurst Coll, Erie, PA 16546	1926	Dr. William P. Garvey	2-M	2,487	156
Meredith Coll, Raleigh, NC 27607-5298 (3)	1891	Dr. John E. Weems	2-M	2,336	213
Merrimack Coll, North Andover, MA 01845-5800	1947	Mr. Richard J. Santagati	2-B	3,021	178
Mesa State Coll, Grand Junction, CO 81502-2647	1925	Dr. Ray N. Kieft	5-B	4,638	244
Messiah Coll, Grantham, PA 17027	1909	Dr. Rodney J. Sawatsky	2-B	2,320	197
Methodist Coll, Fayetteville, NC 28311-1420	1956	Dr. M. Elton Hendricks	2-M	1,612	85
Metropolitan State Coll of Denver, Denver, CO 80217-3362	1963	Dr. Sheila Kaplan	5-B	16,296	918
Metropolitan State U, St Paul, MN 55106-5000	1971	Dr. Susan A. Cole	5-M	5,510	611
Miami U, Oxford, OH 45056	1809	Dr. Paul G. Risser	12-D	15,882	982
Michigan State U, East Lansing, MI 48824-1020	1855	Mr. M. Peter McPherson	5-D	40,254	2,496
Michigan Tech U, Houghton, MI 49931-1295	1885	Dr. Curtis J. Tompkins	5-D	6,460	387
MidAmerica Nazarene Coll, Olathe, KS 66062-1899	1966	Dr. Richard Spindle	2-M	1,445	117
Middlebury Coll, Middlebury, VT 05753-6000	1800	Dr. John McCardell	1-D	1,940	234
Middle Tennessee State U, Murfreesboro, TN 37132	1911	Dr. James E. Walker	5-D	17,120	877
Midland Lutheran Coll, Fremont, NE 68025-4200	1883	Dr. Carl L. Hansen	2-B	1,119	70
Midwestern State U, Wichita Falls, TX 76308-2096	1922	Dr. Louis J. Rodriguez	5-M	5,819	262
Millersville U of Pennsylvania, Millersville, PA 17551-0302	1855	Dr. Joseph A. Caputo	5-M	7,400	406
Millikin U, Decatur, IL 62522-2084	1901	Dr. Curtis L. McCray	2-B	1,863	213
Millsaps Coll, Jackson, MS 39210-0001	1890	Dr. George M. Harmon	2-M	1,437	114
Mills Coll, Oakland, CA 94613-1000 (3)	1852	Dr. Janet L. Holmgren	1-M	1,169	140
Milwaukee Sch of Engineering, Milwaukee, WI 53202-3109	1903	Dr. Hermann Viets	1-M	3,031	253
Minot State U, Minot, ND 58707-0002	1913	Dr. H. Erik Shaar	5-M	3,793	233
Mississippi Coll, Clinton, MS 39058	1826	Dr. Howell Todd	2-F	3,781	234
Mississippi State U, Mississippi State, MS 39762	1878	Dr. Donald W. Zacharias	5-D	13,371	860
Mississippi U for Women, Columbus, MS 39701-9998 (4)	1884	Dr. Clyda S. Rent	5-M	3,020	180
Mississippi Valley State U, Itta Bena, MS 38941-1400	1946	Dr. William W. Sutton	5-M	2,182	138
Missouri Baptist Coll, St Louis, MO 63141-8698	1968	Dr. Alton Lacey	2-B	1,935	80
Missouri Southern State Coll, Joplin, MO 64801-1595	1937	Dr. Julio Leon	5-B	5,334	299
Missouri Valley Coll, Marshall, MO 65340-3197	1889	Dr. J. Kenneth Bryant	2-B	1,206	68
Missouri Western State Coll, St Joseph, MO 64507-2294	1915	Dr. Janet Gorman Murphy	5-B	5,124	317
Molloy Coll, Rockville Centre, NY 11571-5002	1955	Dr. Janet A. Fitzgerald, OP	1-M	2,139	188
Monmouth U, West Long Branch, NJ 07764-1898	1933	Dr. Rebecca Stafford	1-M	4,118	314
Montana State U–Billings, Billings, MT 59101-0298	1927	Dr. Ronald P. Sexton	5-M	3,843	211
Montana State U–Bozeman, Bozeman, MT 59717	1893	Dr. Michael P. Malone	5-D	10,962	647
Montana State U–Northern, Havre, MT 59501-7751	1929	Dr. William Daehling	5-M	1,710	113
Montana Tech of The U of Montana, Butte, MT 59701-8997	1895	Dr. Lindsay D. Norman, Jr.	5-M	1,900	115
Montclair State U, Upper Montclair, NJ 07043-1624	1908	Dr. Irvin D. Reid	5-M	12,675	769
Moody Bible Inst, Chicago, IL 60610-3284	1886	Dr. Joseph M. Stowell, III	2-M	1,532	140
Moorhead State U, Moorhead, MN 56563-0002	1885	Dr. Roland Barden	5-M	7,037	399
Moravian Coll, Bethlehem, PA 18018-6650	1742	Dr. Roger Harry Martin	2-M	1,353	123
Morehead State U, Morehead, KY 40351	1922	Dr. Ronald Eaglin	5-M	8,697	433
Morehouse Coll, Atlanta, GA 30314 (1)	1867	Dr. Walter Massey	1-B	2,992	178
Morgan State U, Baltimore, MD 21239	1867	Dr. Earl Richardson	5-D	5,858	340
Morningside Coll, Sioux City, IA 51106-1751	1894	Dr. Jerry Israel	2-M	1,214	120
Morris Brown Coll, Atlanta, GA 30314-4195	1881	Dr. Samuel D. Jolley, Jr.	2-B	1,897	125
Mount Aloysius Coll, Cresson, PA 16630-1900	1939	Dr. Edward F. Pierce	2-B	1,046	120
Mount Holyoke Coll, South Hadley, MA 01075-1414 (3)	1837	Dr. Joanne V. Creighton	1-M	1,925	213
Mount Marty Coll, Yankton, SD 57078-3724	1936	Sr. Jacquelyn Ernster	2-M	1,024	81
Mount Mary Coll, Milwaukee, WI 53222-4597 (3)	1913	Ms. Sally Mahoney	2-M	1,533	167

Name, address	Year	Governing official, control, and highest degree offered		Enroll-ment	Faculty
Mount Mercy Coll, Cedar Rapids, IA 52402-4797	1928	Dr. Thomas R. Feld	2-B	1,235	98
Mount Saint Mary Coll, Newburgh, NY 12550-3494.	1960	Sr. Ann Sakac	1-M	2,260	177
Mount St Mary's Coll, Los Angeles, CA 90049-1597 (4)	1925	Sr. Karen Kennelly	2-M	1,621	199
Mount Saint Mary's Coll, Emmitsburg, MD 21727-7799	1808	Mr. George R. Houston, Jr.	2-M	1,818	156
Mount Union Coll, Alliance, OH 44601-3993	1846	Dr. Harold M. Kolenbrander	2-B	1,481	96
Mount Vernon Nazarene Coll, Mount Vernon, OH 43050-9509	1964	Dr. E. LeBron Fairbanks	2-M	1,344	70
Muhlenberg Coll, Allentown, PA 18104-5586.	1848	Mr. Arthur R. Taylor	2-B	1,704	164
Murray State U, Murray, KY 42071-0009.	1922	Dr. Kern Alexander	5-M	7,960	376
Muskingum Coll, New Concord, OH 43762	1837	Dr. Samuel W. Speck, Jr.	2-M	1,251	108
National–Louis U, Evanston, IL 60201-1730	1886	NR	1-D	7,307	283
National U, San Diego, CA 92108-4107.	1971	Dr. Jerry C. Lee	1-M	9,063	1,500
Nazareth Coll of Rochester, Rochester, NY 14618-3790.	1924	Dr. Rose Marie Beston	1-M	2,723	172
Nebraska Wesleyan U, Lincoln, NE 68504-2796	1887	Dr. John W. White, Jr.	2-B	1,610	157
Neumann Coll, Aston, PA 19014	1965	Dr. Nan B. Hechenberger	2-M	1,335	122
New Hampshire Coll, Manchester, NH 03106-1045.	1932	Dr. Richard A. Gustafson	1-M	1,181	174
New Jersey Inst of Tech, Newark, NJ 07102-1982.	1881	Dr. Saul K. Fenster	12-D	7,504	514
New Mexico Highlands U, Las Vegas, NM 87701	1893	Mr. Selimo Rael	5-M	2,797	163
New Mexico Inst of Mining and Tech, Socorro, NM 87801	1889	Dr. Daniel H. Lopez	5-D	1,657	106
New Mexico State U, Las Cruces, NM 88003-8001.	1888	Dr. J. Michael Orenduff.	5-D	15,645	795
New Orleans Baptist Theological Sem, New Orleans, LA 70126-4858	1917	Dr. Landrum P. Leavell, II.	2-D	1,854	18
New Sch Bach of Arts, New Sch for Social Research, New York, NY 10011-8603.	1919	NR	1-D	266	545
New York Inst of Tech, Old Westbury, NY 11568-8000	1955	Dr. Matthew Schure.	1-F	10,221	934
New York U, New York, NY 10012-1019	1831	Dr. L. Jay Oliva.	1-D	33,428	3,911
Niagara U, Niagara University, NY 14109	1856	Rev. Paul L. Golden, CM	1-M	2,862	245
Nicholls State U, Thibodaux, LA 70301	1948	Dr. Donald J. Ayo.	5-M	7,205	265
Nichols Coll, Dudley, MA 01571.	1815	Dr. Lowell C. Smith	1-M	1,768	47
Norfolk State U, Norfolk, VA 23504-3907.	1935	Dr. Harrison B. Wilson	5-M	8,667	604
North Adams State Coll, North Adams, MA 01247-4100.	1894	Dr. Thomas D. Aceto	5-M	1,510	111
North Carolina Ag and Tech State U, Greensboro, NC 27411	1891	Dr. Edward B. Fort.	5-D	8,050	507
North Carolina Central U, Durham, NC 27707-3129	1910	Mr. Julius L. Chambers.	5-F	5,634	381
North Carolina State U, Raleigh, NC 27695	1887	Dr. Larry K. Monteith.	5-D	27,577	1,568
North Central Bible Coll, Minneapolis, MN 55404-1322.	1930	Dr. Gordon L. Anderson.	2-B	1,054	64
North Central Coll, Naperville, IL 60566-7063.	1861	Dr. Harold R. Wilde.	2-M	2,446	171
North Dakota State U, Fargo, ND 58105.	1890	NR	5-D	9,734	497
Northeastern Illinois U, Chicago, IL 60625-4699.	1961	Dr. Salme H. Steinberg.	5-M	10,228	376
Northeastern State U, Tahlequah, OK 74464-2399	1846	Dr. W. Roger Webb	5-D	9,023	329
Northeastern U, Boston, MA 02115-5096.	1898	Dr. John A. Curry	1-D	28,154	2,164
Northeast Louisiana U, Monroe, LA 71209-0001	1931	Mr. Lawson L. Swearingen, Jr., JD .	5-D	11,379	533
Northeast Missouri State U, Kirksville, MO 63501-4221	1867	Dr. Jack Magruder	5-M	6,317	390
Northern Arizona U, Flagstaff, AZ 86011	1899	Dr. Clara M. Lovett	5-D	19,242	754
Northern Illinois U, De Kalb, IL 60115-2864.	1895	Dr. John E. LaTourette	5-D	22,881	1,233
Northern Kentucky U, Highland Heights, KY 41099	1968	Dr. Leon E. Boothe	5-F	11,978	750
Northern Michigan U, Marquette, MI 49855-5301.	1899	Dr. William E. Vandament	5-M	7,898	366
Northern State U, Aberdeen, SD 57401-7198.	1901	Dr. John Hutchinson	5-M	3,078	143
North Georgia Coll, Dahlonega, GA 30597-1001	1873	Dr. Delmas J. Allen	5-M	2,877	197
North Park Coll, Chicago, IL 60625-4895.	1891	Dr. David G. Horner.	2-D	1,647	80
Northwestern Coll, Orange City, IA 51041-1996	1882	Dr. James E. Bultman.	2-B	1,150	93
Northwestern Coll, St Paul, MN 55113-1598.	1902	Dr. Donald Ericksen.	2-B	1,269	116
Northwestern Oklahoma State U, Alva, OK 73717-2799.	1897	Dr. Joe J. Struckle.	5-M	1,861	113
Northwestern State U of Louisiana, Natchitoches, LA 71497	1884	Dr. Robert A. Alost.	5-M	8,762	324
Northwestern U, Evanston, IL 60208	1851	Dr. Henry S. Bienen.	1-D	12,179	962
Northwest Missouri State U, Maryville, MO 64468-6001	1905	Dr. Dean L. Hubbard.	5-M	6,025	274
Northwest Nazarene Coll, Nampa, ID 83686-5897	1913	Dr. Richard Hagood.	2-M	1,236	101
Northwood U, Midland, MI 48640-2398	1959	Dr. David E. Fry.	1-M	1,435	56
Norwich U, Northfield, VT 05663	1819	Dr. Richard Schneider.	1-M	2,650	179
Notre Dame Coll, Manchester, NH 03104-2299	1950	Dr. Carol J. Descoteaux, CSC	2-M	1,300	90
Nova Southeastern U, Fort Lauderdale, FL 33314-7721.	1964	Dr. Ovid C. Lewis.	1-D	11,918	580
Oakland U, Rochester, MI 48309-4401	1957	Dr. Gary D. Russi.	5-D	13,165	623
Oakwood Coll, Huntsville, AL 35896.	1896	Dr. Benjamin F. Reaves	2-B	1,534	120
Oberlin Coll, Oberlin, OH 44074-1090	1833	Dr. Nancy Schrom Dye.	1-B	2,744	217
Occidental Coll, Los Angeles, CA 90041-3392	1887	Dr. John B. Slaughter	1-M	1,604	187
Oglethorpe U, Atlanta, GA 30319-2797	1835	Dr. Donald S. Stanton.	1-M	1,280	114
Ohio Dominican Coll, Columbus, OH 43219-2099	1911	Sr. Mary Andrew Matesich.	2-B	1,713	107
Ohio Northern U, Ada, OH 45810.	1871	Dr. DeBow Freed.	2-F	2,872	243
The Ohio State U, Columbus, OH 43210.	1870	Dr. E. Gordon Gee.	5-D	49,542	3,835
Ohio State U at Marion, Marion, OH 43302-5695	1957	Dr. F. Dominic Dottavio.	5-B	1,209	90
Ohio State U–Lima Cmps, Lima, OH 45804-3576	1960	Dr. Violet I. Meek.	5-B	1,232	89
Ohio State U–Mansfield Cmps, Mansfield, OH 44906-1547.	1958	Dr. John O. Riedl, Jr.	5-B	1,504	69
Ohio State U–Newark Cmps, Newark, OH 43055-1797	1957	Dr. Rafael L. Cortado.	5-B	1,560	102
Ohio U, Athens, OH 45701-2979.	1804	Dr. Robert Glidden.	5-D	18,855	976
Ohio U–Chillicothe, Chillicothe, OH 45601-0629	1946	Dr. Delbert Meyer.	5-B	1,917	115
Ohio U–Eastern, St Clairsville, OH 43950-9724.	1957	Dr. James W. Newton.	5-B	1,050	110
Ohio U–Lancaster, Lancaster, OH 43130-1097.	1968	Dr. Charles P. Bird.	5-M	1,554	127
Ohio U–Zanesville, Zanesville, OH 43701-2695	1946	Dr. Craig D. Laubenthal.	5-M	1,270	49
Ohio Wesleyan U, Delaware, OH 43015.	1842	Dr. Thomas B. Courtice.	2-B	1,732	187
Oklahoma Baptist U, Shawnee, OK 74801-2558	1910	Dr. Bob R. Agee.	2-M	2,440	158
Oklahoma Christian U of Science and Arts, Oklahoma City, OK 73136-1100	1950	Dr. J. Terry Johnson	2-M	1,508	125
Oklahoma City U, Oklahoma City, OK 73106-1402	1904	Dr. Jerald C. Walker	2-F	4,571	332
Oklahoma Panhandle State U, Goodwell, OK 73939-0430	1909	Dr. Carl O. Westbrook.	5-B	1,259	78
Oklahoma State U, Stillwater, OK 74078.	1890	Dr. James E. Halligan.	5-D	18,561	868
Old Dominion U, Norfolk, VA 23529	1930	Dr. James V. Koch.	5-D	16,500	1,037
Olivet Nazarene U, Kankakee, IL 60901-0592	1907	Dr. John C. Bowling.	2-M	2,269	120
Oral Roberts U, Tulsa, OK 74171-0001	1963	Mr. Richard Roberts	2-D	3,318	261
Oregon Health Sciences U, Portland, OR 97201-3098	1974	Dr. Peter O. Kohler	5-D	1,757	76
Oregon Inst of Tech, Klamath Falls, OR 97601-8801	1947	Dr. Lawrence J. Wolf.	5-B	2,478	171
Oregon State U, Corvallis, OR 97331.	1868	Dr. John V. Byrne.	5-D	14,336	2,285
Orlando Coll, Orlando, FL 32810-5674.	1918	Mrs. Ouida B. Kirby.	3-M	2,240	106
Otterbein Coll, Westerville, OH 43081	1847	Dr. C. Brent DeVore.	2-M	2,599	161
Ouachita Baptist U, Arkadelphia, AR 71998-0001	1886	Dr. Ben M. Elrod.	2-B	1,440	123
Our Lady of Holy Cross Coll, New Orleans, LA 70131-7399	1916	Rev. Thomas E. Chambers, CSC	2-M	1,276	99
Our Lady of the Lake U of San Antonio, San Antonio, TX 78207-4689	1895	Sr. Elizabeth Anne Sueltenfuss	2-D	3,338	205

Name, address	Year	Governing official, control, and highest degree offered	Enroll-ment	Faculty
Pace U, New York, NY 10038	1906	Dr. Patricia Ewers 1-D	12,312	1,012
Pacific Lutheran U, Tacoma, WA 98447	1890	Dr. Loren J. Anderson............. 2-M	3,257	322
Pacific Union Coll, Angwin, CA 94508	1882	Dr. D. Malcolm Maxwell 2-M	1,597	125
Pacific U, Forest Grove, OR 97116-1797	1849	Dr. Faith Gabelnick 1-F	1,837	176
Palm Beach Atlantic Coll, West Palm Beach, FL 33416-4708	1968	Dr. Paul R. Corts 2-M	1,894	131
Palmer Coll of Chiropractic, Davenport, IA 52803-5287	1895	Dr. Virgil V. Strang 1-F	1,974	122
Park Coll, Parkville, MO 64152-4358	1875	Dr. Donald J. Breckon............. 2-M	1,160	111
Parsons Sch of Design, New Sch for Social Research, New York, NY 10011-8878	1896	Mr. Charles S. Olton 1-M	1,912	413
Pembroke State U, Pembroke, NC 28372-1510	1887	Dr. Joseph B. Oxendine 5-M	3,017	210
Penn State U at Erie, The Behrend Coll, Erie, PA 16563	1948	Dr. John M. Lilley 12-M	3,090	211
Penn State U at Harrisburg—The Capital Coll, Middletown, PA 17057-4898	1966	Dr. John G. Bruhn 12-D	3,628	198
Penn State U Univ Park Cmps, University Park, PA 16802-1503 .	1855	Dr. Joab L. Thomas............... 12-D	38,294	2,201
Pepperdine U, Malibu, CA 90263-0001	1937	Dr. David Davenport 2-D	7,264	297
Peru State Coll, Peru, NE 68421	1867	Dr. Robert L. Burns 5-M	1,682	79
Pfeiffer Coll, Misenheimer, NC 28109-0960	1885	Dr. Zane E. Eargle................ 2-M	1,057	91
Philadelphia Coll of Bible, Langhorne, PA 19047-2990	1913	Dr. W. Sherrill Babb.............. 2-M	1,050	113
Philadelphia Coll of Pharmacy and Science, Philadelphia, PA 19104-4495	1821	Dr. Philip R. Gerbino 1-D	1,933	205
Philadelphia Coll of Textiles and Science, Philadelphia, PA 19144-5497	1884	Dr. James P. Gallagher........... 1-M	3,308	165
Pittsburg State U, Pittsburg, KS 66762-5880	1903	Dr. Tom W. Bryant................ 5-M	6,377	304
Plymouth State Coll of the U System of NH, Plymouth, NH 03264-1600	1871	Dr. Donald P. Wharton 5-M	4,000	200
Point Loma Nazarene Coll, San Diego, CA 92106-2899	1902	Dr. Jim L. Bond.................. 2-M	2,440	170
Point Park Coll, Pittsburgh, PA 15222-1984	1960	Dr. J. Matthew Simon 1-M	2,397	219
Polytechnic U, Brooklyn Cmps, Brooklyn, NY 11201-2990	1854	Dr. David C. Chang 1-D	2,187	325
Pomona Coll, Claremont, CA 91711	1887	Dr. Peter W. Stanley 1-B	1,382	188
Pontifical Catholic U of Puerto Rico, Ponce, PR 00731-6382.....	1948	Rev. F. Tosello Giangiacomo....... 2-M	12,250	581
Portland State U, Portland, OR 97207-0751	1946	Dr. Judith Ramaley 5-D	14,426	629
Prairie View A&M U, Prairie View, TX 77446-0188	1878	Dr. Charles A. Hines 5-M	5,849	303
Pratt Inst, Brooklyn, NY 11205-3899	1887	Dr. Thomas F. Schutte 1-M	2,979	590
Presbyterian Coll, Clinton, SC 29325	1880	Dr. Kenneth B. Orr................ 2-B	1,122	112
Princeton U, Princeton, NJ 08544-1019	1746	Mr. Harold T. Shapiro 1-D	6,444	869
Providence Coll, Providence, RI 02918	1917	Rev. Philip A. Smith, OP 2-D	5,842	372
Purchase Coll, State U of NY, Purchase, NY 10577-1400	1967	Mr. Bill Lacy.................... 5-M	2,498	314
Purdue U, West Lafayette, IN 47907-1968	1869	Dr. Steven C. Beering............. 5-D	34,484	2,199
Purdue U Calumet, Hammond, IN 46323-2094	1951	Dr. James Yackel 5-M	9,100	457
Purdue U North Central, Westville, IN 46391-9543	1967	Dr. Dale W. Alspaugh 5-M	3,588	218
Queens Coll, Charlotte, NC 28274-0002	1857	Dr. Billy O. Wireman 2-M	1,572	115
Queens Coll of the City U of New York, Flushing, NY 11367-1597	1937	Dr. Allen Lee Sessoms 11-M	17,958	1,124
Quincy U, Quincy, IL 62301-2699	1860	Rev. James Toal, OFM............ 2-M	1,164	100
Quinnipiac Coll, Hamden, CT 06518-1904	1929	Dr. John L. Lahey................ 1-F	5,000	333
Radford U, Radford, VA 24142	1910	Dr. Douglas Covington 5-M	9,105	545
Ramapo Coll of New Jersey, Mahwah, NJ 07430-1681	1969	Dr. Robert A. Scott 5-M	4,706	274
Randolph-Macon Coll, Ashland, VA 23005-5505	1830	Dr. Ladell Payne................. 2-B	1,093	157
Reed Coll, Portland, OR 97202-8199	1909	Dr. Steven Koblik 1-M	1,279	126
Regis Coll, Weston, MA 02193-1571 (3)	1927	Dr. Sheila Megley, RSM 2-M	1,162	118
Regis U, Denver, CO 80221-1099	1877	Rev. Michael J. Sheeran, SJ....... 2-M	6,471	87
Rensselaer Polytechnic Inst, Troy, NY 12180-3590	1824	Dr. R. Byron Pipes 1-D	6,331	418
Rhode Island Coll, Providence, RI 02908-1924	1854	Dr. John Nazarian 5-M	9,900	502
Rhode Island Sch of Design, Providence, RI 02903-2784	1877	Mr. Roger Mandle 1-M	2,011	302
Rhodes Coll, Memphis, TN 38112-1690	1848	Dr. James H. Daughdrill, Jr. 2-M	1,469	149
Rice U, Houston, TX 77005	1912	Dr. Malcolm Gillis 1-D	4,073	554
The Richard Stockton Coll of New Jersey, Pomona, NJ 08240-9988	1971	Dr. Vera King Farris............... 5-B	5,145	305
Rider U, Lawrenceville, NJ 08648-3001	1865	Dr. J. Barton Luedeke............. 1-M	5,026	378
Rivier Coll, Nashua, NH 03060-5086	1933	Sr. Jeanne Perreault 2-M	2,759	190
Roanoke Coll, Salem, VA 24153-3794	1842	Dr. David M. Gring............... 2-B	1,694	160
Robert Morris Coll, Coraopolis, PA 15108-1189	1921	Dr. Edward A. Nicholson 1-M	5,346	292
Roberts Wesleyan Coll, Rochester, NY 14624-1997	1866	Dr. William C. Crothers........... 2-M	1,181	107
Rochester Inst of Tech, Rochester, NY 14623-5604	1829	Dr. Albert J. Simone 1-D	12,250	1,085
Rockford Coll, Rockford, IL 61108-2393	1847	Dr. William A. Shields 1-M	1,610	137
Rockhurst Coll, Kansas City, MO 64110-2561	1910	Rev. Thomas J. Savage, SJ 2-M	2,658	217
Roger Williams U, Bristol, RI 02809	1948	Mr. Anthony J. Santoro............ 1-F	2,111	229
Rollins Coll, Winter Park, FL 32789-4499	1885	Dr. Rita Bornstein................ 1-M	3,284	251
Roosevelt U, Chicago, IL 60605-1394	1945	Dr. Theodore L. Gross 1-M	6,709	508
Rosary Coll, River Forest, IL 60305-1099	1901	Ms. Donna M. Carroll 2-M	1,851	116
Rose-Hulman Inst of Tech, Terre Haute, IN 47803-3920.........	1874	Dr. Samuel F. Hulbert 1-M	1,420	105
Rowan Coll of New Jersey, Glassboro, NJ 08028-1702	1923	Dr. Herman D. James 5-M	8,936	340
Rush U, Chicago, IL 60612-3832	1969	Dr. Leo M. Henikoff 1-D	1,321	170
Russell Sage Coll, Troy, NY 12180-4115 (3)	1916	Dr. Jeanne K. Neff 1-M	2,378	180
Rust Coll, Holly Springs, MS 38635-2328	1866	Dr. David L. Beckley 2-B	1,180	65
Rutgers, State U of NJ, Camden Coll of Arts & Scis, Camden, NJ 08102-1401	1927	NR 5-B	2,420	NR
Rutgers, State U of NJ, Coll of Engineering, Piscataway, NJ 08855-0909	1864	Dr. Ellis H. Dill.................. 5-B	2,260	NR
Rutgers, State U of NJ, Coll of Nursing, Newark, NJ 07102-1803	1956	Dr. Dorothy J. DeMaio 5-D	372	NR
Rutgers, State U of NJ, Coll of Pharmacy, Piscataway, NJ 08855-0789	1927	Dr. John Louis Colaizzi............ 5-D	938	NR
Rutgers, State U of NJ, Cook Coll, New Brunswick, NJ 08903-2101	1921	Dr. Daryl B. Lund 5-B	3,010	NR
Rutgers, State U of NJ, Douglass Coll, New Brunswick, NJ 08903-0270 (3)	1918	Dr. Martha A. Cotter 5-B	2,986	NR
Rutgers, State U of NJ, Livingston Coll, New Brunswick, NJ 08903	1969	NR 5-B	3,273	NR
Rutgers, State U of NJ, Mason Gross Sch of Arts, New Brunswick, NJ 08903-0270	1976	Dr. Marilyn F. Somville 5-D	647	NR
Rutgers, State U of NJ, Newark Coll of Arts & Scis, Newark, NJ 07102-1896	1946	Dr. David Hosford................ 5-B	3,724	NR
Rutgers, State U of NJ, Rutgers Coll, New Brunswick, NJ 08903-2101	1766	Dr. Carl Kirschner................ 5-B	8,908	NR

Name, address	Year	Governing official, control, and highest degree offered		Enroll-ment	Faculty
Rutgers, State U of NJ, U Coll–Camden, Camden, NJ 08102-1401	1950	Dr. Robert A. Catlin	5-B	764	NR
Rutgers, State U of NJ, U Coll–Newark, Newark, NJ 07102-1896	1934	NR	5-B	1,865	NR
Rutgers, State U of NJ, U Coll–New Brunswick, New Brunswick, NJ 08903	1934	NR	5-B	5,132	NR
Sacred Heart U, Fairfield, CT 06432-1000	1963	Dr. Anthony J. Cernera	2-M	5,453	358
Saginaw Valley State U, University Center, MI 48710	1963	Dr. Eric R. Gilbertson	5-M	7,066	397
St Ambrose U, Davenport, IA 52803-2898	1882	Dr. Edward J. Rogalski	2-B	2,584	197
Saint Anselm Coll, Manchester, NH 03102-1310	1889	Rev. Jonathan DeFelice, OSB	2-B	1,858	161
Saint Augustine's Coll, Raleigh, NC 27610-2298	1867	Dr. Bernard W. Franklin	2-B	1,918	92
St Bonaventure U, St Bonaventure, NY 14778-2284	1858	Dr. Robert J. Wickenheiser	2-M	2,509	138
St Cloud State U, St Cloud, MN 56301-4498	1869	Dr. Bruce Grube	5-D	14,673	694
St Edward's U, Austin, TX 78704-6489	1885	Dr. Patricia Hayes	2-M	3,129	234
Saint Francis Coll, Fort Wayne, IN 46808-3994	1890	Sr. M. Elise Kriss	2-M	1,005	80
St Francis Coll, Brooklyn Heights, NY 11201-4398	1884	Br. Donald Sullivan, OSF	1-B	2,166	153
Saint Francis Coll, Loretto, PA 15940-0600	1847	Rev. Christian R. Oravec	2-M	1,886	182
St John Fisher Coll, Rochester, NY 14618-3597	1948	Dr. William L. Pickett	2-M	2,164	186
Saint John's U, Collegeville, MN 56321 (1)	1857	Br. Dietrich Reinhart, OSB	2-M	1,820	174
St John's U, Jamaica, NY 11439	1870	Rev. Donald J. Harrington, CM	2-D	17,820	1,012
Saint Joseph Coll, West Hartford, CT 06117-2700 (3)	1932	Dr. Winifred E. Coleman	2-M	1,987	150
Saint Joseph's Coll, Rensselaer, IN 47978-0850	1889	Dr. Albert J. Shannon	2-M	1,037	88
St Joseph's Coll, New York, Brooklyn, NY 11205-3688	1916	Sr. George Aquin O'Connor	1-B	1,189	119
St Joseph's Coll, Suffolk Cmps, Patchogue, NY 11772-2399	1916	Sr. George Aquin O'Connor	1-B	2,303	184
Saint Joseph's U, Philadelphia, PA 19131-1376	1851	Rev. Nicholas S. Rashford, SJ	2-M	6,771	366
St Lawrence U, Canton, NY 13617-1455	1856	Dr. Patti McGill Peterson	1-M	2,045	174
Saint Louis U, St Louis, MO 63103-2097	1818	Rev. Lawrence Biondi, SJ	2-D	10,768	2,927
Saint Mary-of-the-Woods Coll, Saint Mary-of-the-Woods, IN 47876 (3)	1840	Dr. Barbara Doherty, SP	2-M	1,215	55
Saint Mary's Coll, Notre Dame, IN 46556 (3)	1844	Dr. William A. Hickey	2-B	1,545	188
Saint Mary's Coll of California, Moraga, CA 94575	1863	Br. Mel Anderson, FSC	2-M	4,247	231
St Mary's Coll of Maryland, St Mary's City, MD 20686	1840	Dr. Edward T. Lewis	5-B	1,376	164
Saint Mary's Coll of Minnesota, Winona, MN 55987-1399	1912	Br. Louis DeThomasis, FSC	2-M	7,620	285
St Mary's U of San Antonio, San Antonio, TX 78228-8507	1852	Rev. John Moder, SM	2-D	4,166	312
Saint Michael's Coll, Colchester, VT 05439	1904	Dr. Paul J. Reiss	2-M	2,565	167
St Norbert Coll, De Pere, WI 54115-2099	1898	Dr. Thomas A. Manion	2-M	2,092	156
St Olaf Coll, Northfield, MN 55057-1098	1874	Dr. Mark U. Edwards, Jr.	2-B	2,958	431
Saint Peter's Coll, Jersey City, NJ 07306	1872	NR	2-M	3,561	420
St Thomas Aquinas Coll, Sparkill, NY 10976	1952	Dr. Margaret M. Fitzpatrick, SC	1-M	1,454	115
St Thomas U, Miami, FL 33054-6459	1961	Rev. Msgr. Franklyn M. Casale	2-F	2,388	133
Saint Vincent Coll, Latrobe, PA 15650	1846	Rev. John F. Murtha, OSB	2-M	1,077	106
Saint Xavier U, Chicago, IL 60655-3105	1847	Dr. Richard Yanikoski	2-M	4,060	249
Salem State Coll, Salem, MA 01970-5353	1854	Dr. Nancy D. Harrington	5-M	10,132	409
Salisbury State U, Salisbury, MD 21801-6837	1925	Dr. Thomas E. Bellavance	5-M	6,048	349
Salve Regina U, Newport, RI 02840-4192	1934	Dr. Therese Antone, RSM	2-D	2,071	208
Samford U, Birmingham, AL 35229-0002	1841	Dr. Thomas E. Corts	2-F	4,571	382
Sam Houston State U, Huntsville, TX 77341-2448	1879	Dr. Martin J. Anisman	5-D	12,906	508
San Diego State U, San Diego, CA 92182	1897	Dr. Thomas B. Day	5-D	27,787	2,126
San Francisco State U, San Francisco, CA 94132-1722	1899	Dr. Robert A. Corrigan	5-D	26,552	1,384
San Jose State U, San Jose, CA 95192-0001	1857	Dr. Robert L. Chret	5-M	26,299	1,735
Santa Clara U, Santa Clara, CA 95053-0001	1851	Rev. Paul L. Locatelli, SJ	2-D	7,513	575
Sarah Lawrence Coll, Bronxville, NY 10708	1926	Dr. Alice Stone Ilchman	1-M	1,306	227
Savannah Coll of Art and Design, Savannah, GA 31401-3146	1978	Mr. Richard G. Rowan	1-M	2,488	143
Savannah State Coll, Savannah, GA 31404	1890	NR	5-B	3,100	149
Sch of the Art Inst of Chicago, Chicago, IL 60603-3103	1866	Dr. Carol Becker	1-M	2,891	304
Sch of Visual Arts, New York, NY 10010-3994	1947	Mr. David Rhodes	3-M	3,049	621
Seattle Pacific U, Seattle, WA 98119-1997	1891	NR	2-D	3,406	211
Seattle U, Seattle, WA 98122	1891	Rev. William J. Sullivan, SJ	2-D	6,091	463
Seton Hall U, South Orange, NJ 07079-2697	1856	Rev. Thomas R. Peterson, OP	2-D	8,400	752
Shawnee State U, Portsmouth, OH 45662-4344	1986	NR	5-B	3,185	239
Shaw U, Raleigh, NC 27601-2399	1865	Dr. Talbert O. Shaw	2-B	2,432	269
Shenandoah U, Winchester, VA 22601-5195	1875	Dr. James A. Davis	2-M	1,652	217
Shepherd Coll, Shepherdstown, WV 25443	1871	Dr. Michael P. Riccards	5-B	3,648	256
Shippensburg U of Pennsylvania, Shippensburg, PA 17257	1871	Dr. Anthony F. Ceddia	5-M	6,603	363
Shorter Coll, Rome, GA 30165-4298	1873	Dr. Larry Lee McSwain	2-B	1,455	141
Siena Coll, Loudonville, NY 12211-1462	1937	Fr. William McConville, OFM	2-B	3,232	257
Siena Heights Coll, Adrian, MI 49221-1796	1919	Dr. Richard Artman	2-M	1,141	110
Simmons Coll, Boston, MA 02115 (3)	1899	Dr. Barbara Graham	1-D	3,456	354
Simpson Coll, Indianola, IA 50125-1297	1860	Dr. Stephen G. Jennings	2-B	1,613	158
Skidmore Coll, Saratoga Springs, NY 12866-1632	1903	Dr. David H. Porter	1-M	2,198	220
Slippery Rock U of Pennsylvania, Slippery Rock, PA 16057	1889	Dr. Robert Aebersold	5-M	7,563	412
Smith Coll, Northampton, MA 01063 (3)	1871	Ms. Ruth Simmons	1-D	3,036	292
Sonoma State U, Rohnert Park, CA 94928-3609	1960	Dr. Ruben Arminana	5-M	6,610	403
South Carolina State U, Orangeburg, SC 29117-0001	1896	Dr. Barbara R. Hatton	5-D	4,873	246
South Dakota Sch of Mines and Tech, Rapid City, SD 57701-3995	1885	Dr. Richard J. Gowen	5-D	2,463	145
South Dakota State U, Brookings, SD 57007	1881	Dr. Robert T. Wagner	5-D	9,140	511
Southeastern Coll of the Assemblies of God, Lakeland, FL 33801-6099	1935	Dr. James Hennesy	2-B	1,137	89
Southeastern Louisiana U, Hammond, LA 70402	1925	Dr. G. Warren Smith	5-M	13,912	599
Southeastern Oklahoma State U, Durant, OK 74701-0609	1909	Dr. Larry Williams	5-M	4,104	205
Southeast Missouri State U, Cape Girardeau, MO 63701-4799	1873	Dr. Kala M. Stroup	5-M	7,921	436
Southern Arkansas U–Magnolia, Magnolia, AR 71753	1909	Dr. Steven G. Gamble	5-M	2,957	221
Southern California Coll, Costa Mesa, CA 92626-6597	1920	Mr. Wayne E. Kraiss	2-M	1,083	51
Southern Coll of Seventh-day Adventists, Collegedale, TN 37315-0370	1892	Dr. Donald R. Sahly	2-B	1,652	125
Southern Coll of Tech, Marietta, GA 30060-2896	1948	Dr. Stephen R. Cheshier	5-M	3,904	203
Southern Connecticut State U, New Haven, CT 06515-1355	1893	Mr. Michael J. Adanti	5-M	11,652	726
Southern Illinois U at Carbondale, Carbondale, IL 62901-6806	1869	Dr. John C. Guyon	5-D	23,162	1,543
Southern Illinois U at Edwardsville, Edwardsville, IL 62026-0001	1957	Dr. Nancy G. Belck	5-F	10,938	743
Southern Methodist U, Dallas, TX 75275	1911	Dr. R. Gerald Turner	2-D	9,014	648
Southern Nazarene U, Bethany, OK 73008-2694	1899	Dr. Loren P. Gresham	2-M	1,737	101
Southern Oregon State Coll, Ashland, OR 97520	1926	Dr. Stephen Reno	5-M	4,554	279
Southern U and A&M Coll, Baton Rouge, LA 70813	1880	Dr. Marvin L. Yates	5-D	9,800	603
Southern U at New Orleans, New Orleans, LA 70126-1009	1959	Dr. Robert B. Gex	5-M	4,500	235
Southern Utah U, Cedar City, UT 84720-2498	1897	Dr. Gerald R. Sherratt	5-M	5,026	206
Southern Wesleyan U, Central, SC 29630-1020	1906	Dr. David J. Spittal	2-M	1,381	173

Name, address	Year	Governing official, control, and highest degree offered		Enroll- ment	Faculty
Southwest Baptist U, Bolivar, MO 65613-2597	1878	Dr. Roy Blunt	2-M	3,202	208
Southwestern Assemblies of God U, Waxahachie, TX 75165-2342	1927	Dr. Delmer Guynes	2-B	1,007	28
Southwestern Oklahoma State U, Weatherford, OK 73096-3098	1901	Dr. Joe Anna Hibler	5-M	4,737	237
Southwestern U, Georgetown, TX 78626	1840	Dr. Roy B. Shilling, Jr.	2-B	1,238	143
Southwest Missouri State U, Springfield, MO 65804-0094	1905	Dr. John H. Keiser	5-M	17,310	824
Southwest State U, Marshall, MN 56258-3306	1963	Dr. Doug Sweetland	5-B	2,362	136
Southwest Texas State U, San Marcos, TX 78666	1899	Dr. Jerome Supple	5-M	20,899	915
Spalding U, Louisville, KY 40203-2188	1814	Dr. Thomas R. Oates	2-D	1,221	115
Spelman Coll, Atlanta, GA 30314-4399 (3)	1881	Dr. Johnnetta B. Cole	1-B	1,976	209
Springfield Coll, Springfield, MA 01109-3797	1885	Dr. Randolph W. Bromery	1-D	2,961	232
Spring Hill Coll, Mobile, AL 36608-1791	1830	Rev. William J. Rewak, SJ	2-M	1,362	106
Stanford U, Stanford, CA 94305-9991	1891	Mr. Gerhard Casper	1-D	14,031	1,428
State U of NY at Binghamton, Binghamton, NY 13902-6000	1946	Dr. Lois B. DeFleur	5-D	12,088	710
State U of NY at Buffalo, Buffalo, NY 14260	1846	Mr. William R. Greiner	5-D	24,943	2,070
State U of NY at New Paltz, New Paltz, NY 12561-2449	1828	Dr. Alice Chandler	5-M	7,897	600
State U of NY at Oswego, Oswego, NY 13126	1861	Dr. Stephen Weber	5-M	8,819	391
State U of NY at Stony Brook, Stony Brook, NY 11794	1957	Dr. Shirley Strum Kenny	5-D	17,621	1,600
State U of NY Coll at Brockport, Brockport, NY 14420-2997	1867	Dr. John E. Van de Wetering	5-M	7,910	513
State U of NY Coll at Buffalo, Buffalo, NY 14222-1095	1867	Dr. F. C. Richardson	5-M	11,528	605
State U of NY Coll at Cortland, Cortland, NY 13045	1868	Dr. Judson H. Taylor	5-M	6,060	459
State U of NY Coll at Fredonia, Fredonia, NY 14063	1826	Dr. Donald A. MacPhee	5-M	4,892	332
State U of NY Coll at Geneseo, Geneseo, NY 14454-1401	1871	Dr. Christopher Dahl	5-M	5,754	325
State U of NY Coll at Old Westbury, Old Westbury, NY 11568-0210	1965	Dr. L. Eudora Pettigrew	5-B	3,988	263
State U of NY Coll at Oneonta, Oneonta, NY 13820	1889	Dr. Alan B. Donovan	5-M	5,829	306
State U of NY Coll at Plattsburgh, Plattsburgh, NY 12901	1889	Dr. Horace A. Judson	5-M	5,772	376
State U of NY Coll at Potsdam, Potsdam, NY 13676	1816	Dr. William Merwin	5-M	4,293	275
State U of NY Coll of Environ Sci and Forestry, Syracuse, NY 13210-2779	1911	Dr. Ross S. Whaley	5-D	1,787	134
State U of NY Empire State Coll, Saratoga Springs, NY 12866-4391	1971	Dr. James W. Hall	5-M	7,199	329
State U of NY Health Science Ctr at Brooklyn, Brooklyn, NY 11203-2098	1858	Dr. Russell L. Miller	5-D	1,641	156
State U of NY Health Science Ctr at Syracuse, Syracuse, NY 13210-2334	1950	Dr. Gregory L. Eastwood	5-D	1,100	45
State U of NY Inst of Tech at Utica/Rome, Utica, NY 13504-3050	1966	Dr. Peter J. Cayan	5-M	2,544	138
Stephen F Austin State U, Nacogdoches, TX 75962	1923	Dr. Daniel D. Angel	5-D	12,206	677
Stetson U, DeLand, FL 32720-3781	1883	Dr. H. Douglas Lee	1-F	2,883	197
Stevens Inst of Tech, Hoboken, NJ 07030	1870	Dr. Harold J. Raveche	1-D	2,872	223
Stonehill Coll, North Easton, MA 02357-0001	1948	Rev. Bartley MacPhaidin, CSC	2-B	1,932	184
Strayer Coll, Washington, DC 20005-2603	1892	Mr. Ron K. Bailey	3-M	6,726	283
Suffolk U, Boston, MA 02108-2770	1906	Mr. David J. Sargent	1-D	5,920	443
Sullivan Coll, Louisville, KY 40232	1864	NR	3-B	2,002	83
Sul Ross State U, Alpine, TX 79832	1920	Dr. R. Vic Morgan	5-M	3,145	138
Susquehanna U, Selinsgrove, PA 17870-1001	1858	Dr. Joel L. Cunningham	2-B	1,512	151
Swarthmore Coll, Swarthmore, PA 19081-1397	1864	Dr. Alfred H. Bloom	1-B	1,320	174
Syracuse U, Syracuse, NY 13244-0003	1870	Dr. Kenneth A. Shaw	1-D	14,550	1,682
Tampa Coll, Tampa, FL 33614-5899	1890	Mr. David Zorn	3-M	1,150	50
Tarleton State U, Stephenville, TX 76402	1899	Dr. Dennis P. McCabe	5-M	6,460	329
Taylor U, Upland, IN 46989-1001	1846	Dr. Jay L. Kesler	1-B	1,831	138
Teikyo Marycrest U, Davenport, IA 52804-4096	1939	Dr. Laurence M. Conner	1-M	1,323	88
Teikyo Post U, Waterbury, CT 06723-2540	1890	Dr. Phyllis C. DeLeo	1-B	1,794	166
Temple U, Philadelphia, PA 19122	1884	Mr. Peter J. Liacouras	12-D	26,952	2,646
Tennessee State U, Nashville, TN 37209-1561	1912	Dr. James A. Hefner	5-D	8,180	430
Tennessee Tech U, Cookeville, TN 38505	1915	Dr. Angelo A. Volpe	5-D	8,250	509
Texas A&M International U, Laredo, TX 78041	1969	Dr. Leo Sayavedra	5-M	1,964	84
Texas A&M U, College Station, TX 77843-1244	1876	Dr. Ray M. Bowen	5-D	42,018	2,331
Texas A&M U at Galveston, Galveston, TX 77553-1675	1962	Dr. David J. Schmidly	5-B	1,238	86
Texas A&M U–Corpus Christi, Corpus Christi, TX 78412-5503	1947	Dr. Robert R. Furgason	5-D	5,152	313
Texas A&M U–Kingsville, Kingsville, TX 78363	1925	Dr. Manuel L. Ibanez	5-D	6,548	337
Texas Christian U, Fort Worth, TX 76129-0002	1873	Dr. William E. Tucker	2-D	6,706	496
Texas Lutheran Coll, Seguin, TX 78155-5999	1891	Dr. Jon Moline	2-B	1,268	92
Texas Southern U, Houston, TX 77004-4584	1947	Dr. Joann Horton	5-D	10,872	516
Texas Tech U, Lubbock, TX 79409	1923	Dr. Robert W. Lawless	5-D	24,083	947
Texas Wesleyan U, Fort Worth, TX 76105-1536	1890	Dr. Jake B. Schrum	2-F	2,593	198
Texas Woman's U, Denton, TX 76204 (4)	1901	Dr. Carol Surles	5-D	10,090	762
Thomas Edison State Coll, Trenton, NJ 08608-1176	1972	Dr. George A. Pruitt	5-B	8,619	346
Thomas Jefferson U, Philadelphia, PA 19107	1824	Dr. Paul C. Brucker	1-M	1,533	83
Thomas More Coll, Crestview Hills, KY 41017-3495	1921	Rev. William F. Cleves	2-B	1,161	130
Tiffin U, Tiffin, OH 44883-2161	1888	Dr. George Kidd, Jr.	1-M	1,099	81
Tougaloo Coll, Tougaloo, MS 39174	1869	NR	2-B	1,105	91
Touro Coll, New York, NY 10010	1971	NR	1-F	8,876	810
Towson State U, Towson, MD 21204-7097	1866	Dr. Hoke L. Smith	5-M	14,551	1,070
Trenton State Coll, Trenton, NJ 08650-4700	1855	Dr. Harold Eickhoff	5-M	6,981	589
Trevecca Nazarene Coll, Nashville, TN 37210-2834	1901	Dr. Millard Reed	2-M	1,358	81
Trinity Coll, Hartford, CT 06106-3100	1823	Dr. Evan S. Dobelle	1-M	2,146	237
Trinity Coll, Washington, DC 20017-1094 (3)	1897	NR	2-M	1,362	121
Trinity U, San Antonio, TX 78212-7200	1869	Dr. Ronald K. Calgaard	2-M	2,479	286
Tri-State U, Angola, IN 46703-0307	1884	Dr. R. John Reynolds	1-B	1,097	86
Troy State U, Troy, AL 36082	1887	Dr. Jack Hawkins, Jr.	5-M	5,480	349
Troy State U at Dothan, Dothan, AL 36304-0368	1961	Dr. Thomas Harrison	5-M	2,500	144
Troy State U in Montgomery, Montgomery, AL 36103-4419	1957	Dr. Glenda S. McGaha	5-M	3,408	189
Tufts U, Medford, MA 02155	1852	Dr. John A. DiBiaggio	1-D	8,042	1,059
Tulane U, New Orleans, LA 70118-5669	1834	Dr. Eamon M. Kelly	1-D	11,362	1,201
Tusculum Coll, Greeneville, TN 37743-9997	1794	Dr. Robert E. Knott	2-M	1,217	104
Tuskegee U, Tuskegee, AL 36088	1881	Dr. Benjamin F. Payton	1-F	3,322	298
Union Coll, Barbourville, KY 40906-1499	1879	Dr. Jack C. Phillips	2-M	1,003	65
Union Coll, Schenectady, NY 12308-2311	1795	Dr. Roger H. Hull	1-D	2,374	197
The Union Inst, Cincinnati, OH 45206-1947	1964	Dr. Robert T. Conley	1-D	1,639	113
Union U, Jackson, TN 38305	1823	Dr. Hyran E. Barefoot	2-M	2,036	146
United States Air Force Acad, USAF Academy, CO 80840-5025	1954	Lt. Gen. Paul E. Stein	4-B	4,000	517
United States International U, San Diego, CA 92131-1799	1952	Dr. Garry D. Hays	1-D	1,281	112
United States Military Acad, West Point, NY 10996	1802	Lt. Gen. Howard D. Graves	4-B	4,095	491
United States Naval Acad, Annapolis, MD 21402-5000	1845	Adm. Charles Larson	4-B	4,216	650

Name, address	Year	Governing official, control, and highest degree offered		Enroll-ment	Faculty
Universidad Politécnica de Puerto Rico, Hato Rey, PR 00919	1966	Mr. Ernesto Vazquez-Barquet	1-M	4,996	227
U at Albany, State U of NY, Albany, NY 12222-0001	1844	Dr. Karen R. Hitchcock	5-D	14,798	938
U of Akron, Akron, OH 44325-0001	1870	Dr. Peggy Gordon Elliott	5-D	26,009	1,692
U of Alabama, Tuscaloosa, AL 35487	1831	Dr. E. Roger Sayers	5-D	19,366	1,065
U of Alabama at Birmingham, Birmingham, AL 35294	1969	Dr. J. Claude Bennett	5-D	16,252	1,863
The U of Alabama in Huntsville, Huntsville, AL 35899	1950	Dr. Frank Franz	5-D	7,531	457
U of Alaska Anchorage, Anchorage, AK 99508-8060	1954	Mr. Edward Lee Gorcuch	5-M	15,113	1,203
U of Alaska Fairbanks, Fairbanks, AK 99775-7480	1917	Dr. Joan K. Wadlow	5-D	7,807	717
U of Arizona, Tucson, AZ 85721	1885	Dr. Manuel T. Pacheco	5-D	35,306	1,587
U of Arkansas, Fayetteville, AR 72701-1201	1871	Dr. Daniel E. Ferritor	5-D	14,655	803
U of Arkansas at Little Rock, Little Rock, AR 72204-1000	1927	Dr. Charles E. Hathaway	5-D	11,509	740
U of Arkansas at Monticello, Monticello, AR 71656	1909	Dr. Fred J. Taylor	5-M	2,398	126
U of Arkansas at Pine Bluff, Pine Bluff, AR 71601-2799	1873	Dr. Lawrence A. Davis, Jr.	5-M	4,075	193
U of Arkansas for Medical Sciences, Little Rock, AR 72205-7199	1879	Dr. Harry P. Ward	5-D	1,864	NR
U of Baltimore, Baltimore, MD 21201-5779	1925	Dr. H. Mebane Turner	5-F	5,204	330
U of Bridgeport, Bridgeport, CT 06601	1927	Dr. Richard L. Robenstein	1-D	1,939	255
U of California, Berkeley, Berkeley, CA 94720	1868	Dr. Chang-Lin Tien	5-D	29,634	1,787
U of California, Davis, Davis, CA 95616	1905	Larry N. Vanderhoef	5-D	22,442	1,565
U of California, Irvine, Irvine, CA 92717	1965	Ms. Laurel L. Wilkening	5-D	17,092	811
U of California, Los Angeles, Los Angeles, CA 90024-1301	1919	Dr. Charles E. Young	5-D	35,110	3,210
U of California, Riverside, Riverside, CA 92521-0102	1954	Dr. Raymond L. Orbach	5-D	8,591	692
U of California, San Diego, La Jolla, CA 92093-5003	1959	Dr. Richard C. Atkinson	5-D	17,776	1,359
U of California, Santa Barbara, Santa Barbara, CA 93106	1909	Dr. Henry T. Yang	5-D	17,834	829
U of California, Santa Cruz, Santa Cruz, CA 95064	1965	Dr. Karl S. Pister	5-D	10,117	530
U of Central Arkansas, Conway, AR 72035-0001	1907	Dr. Winfred L. Thompson	5-M	9,192	566
U of Central Florida, Orlando, FL 32816	1963	Dr. John C. Hitt	5-D	25,363	1,112
U of Central Oklahoma, Edmond, OK 73034-5209	1890	Mr. George Nigh	5-M	16,039	704
The U of Charleston, Charleston, WV 25304-1099	1888	Dr. Edwin H. Welch	1-M	1,363	111
U of Chicago, Chicago, IL 60637-1513	1891	Mr. Hugo F. Sonneschein	1-D	11,427	1,232
U of Cincinnati, Cincinnati, OH 45221	1819	Dr. Joseph A. Steger	5-D	18,473	986
U of Colorado at Boulder, Boulder, CO 80309	1876	NR	5-D	24,548	1,124
U of Colorado at Colorado Springs, Colorado Springs, CO 80933-7150	1965	Dr. Linda Bunnell Shade	5-D	5,801	369
U of Colorado at Denver, Denver, CO 80217-3364	1912	Mr. John Buechner	5-D	9,537	569
U of Colorado Health Sciences Ctr, Denver, CO 80262	1883	Dr. Vincent A. Fulginiti	5-D	2,188	1,104
U of Connecticut, Storrs, CT 06269	1881	Dr. Harry J. Hartley	5-D	15,626	1,165
U of Connecticut at Hartford, West Hartford, CT 06117-2620	1946	Dr. Russell F. Farnen	5-B	1,065	91
U of Connecticut at Stamford, Stamford, CT 06903-2899	1951	NR	5-M	1,600	93
U of Dallas, Irving, TX 75062-4799	1956	Dr. Robert F. Sasseen	2-D	2,737	117
U of Dayton, Dayton, OH 45469-1611	1850	Br. Raymond L. Fitz, SM	2-D	10,204	813
U of Delaware, Newark, DE 19716	1743	Dr. David P. Roselle	12-D	18,080	1,013
U of Denver, Denver, CO 80208	1864	Mr. Daniel Ritchie	1-D	8,522	399
U of Detroit Mercy, Detroit, MI 48219-0900	1877	Sr. Maureen A. Fay, OP	2-D	7,461	566
U of Dubuque, Dubuque, IA 52001-5050	1852	Dr. John J. Agria	2-M	1,042	64
U of Evansville, Evansville, IN 47722-0002	1854	Dr. James S. Vinson	2-M	3,162	179
The U of Findlay, Findlay, OH 45840-3653	1882	Dr. Kenneth E. Zirkle	2-M	3,663	250
U of Florida, Gainesville, FL 32611-8140	1853	Dr. John V. Lombardi	5-D	38,277	NR
U of Georgia, Athens, GA 30602	1785	Dr. Charles B. Knapp	5-D	29,469	1,924
U of Great Falls, Great Falls, MT 59405	1932	Dr. Frederick W. Gilliard	2-M	1,168	88
U of Guam, Mangilao, GU 96923	1952	Dr. John C. Salas	7-M	3,979	230
U of Hartford, West Hartford, CT 06117-1500	1877	Dr. Humphrey Tonkin	1-D	7,253	705
U of Hawaii at Hilo, Hilo, HI 96720-4091	1970	Dr. Kenneth Perrin	5-B	2,870	281
U of Hawaii at Manoa, Honolulu, HI 96822	1907	Dr. Kenneth P. Mortimer	5-D	19,983	1,484
U of Houston, Houston, TX 77204	1927	Dr. Glenn Goerke	5-D	31,298	1,892
U of Houston–Clear Lake, Houston, TX 77058-1098	1974	Dr. Glenn A. Goerke	5-M	7,136	359
U of Houston–Downtown, Houston, TX 77002-1001	1974	Dr. Max Castillo	5-B	7,715	361
U of Houston–Victoria, Victoria, TX 77901-4450	1973	Dr. Karen S. Haynes	5-M	1,616	74
U of Idaho, Moscow, ID 83844	1889	Dr. Thomas O. Bell	5-D	11,730	570
U of Illinois at Chicago, Chicago, IL 60680	1946	Dr. David C. Broski	5-D	24,865	2,629
U of Illinois at Springfield, Springfield, IL 62794-9243	1969	Dr. Naomi B. Lynn	5-M	4,384	256
U of Illinois at Urbana-Champaign, Champaign, IL 61820-5711	1867	Dr. Michael Aiken	5-D	36,191	1,995
U of Indianapolis, Indianapolis, IN 46227-3697	1902	Dr. G. Benjamin Lantz, Jr.	2-M	3,878	276
The U of Iowa, Iowa City, IA 52242	1847	Dr. Peter E. Nathan	5-D	26,932	1,803
U of Kansas, Lawrence, KS 66045	1866	Dr. Robert E. Hemenway	5-D	28,046	2,049
U of Kentucky, Lexington, KY 40506-0032	1865	Dr. Charles T. Wethington, Jr.	5-D	23,622	2,075
U of La Verne, La Verne, CA 91750-4443	1891	Dr. Stephen Morgan	1-D	2,285	165
U of Louisville, Louisville, KY 40292-0001	1798	Dr. John W. Shumaker	5-D	21,377	1,763
U of Maine, Orono, ME 04469-5703	1865	Dr. Frederick E. Hutchinson	5-D	11,001	735
U of Maine at Farmington, Farmington, ME 04938-1911	1863	Dr. Theodora J. Kalikow	5-B	1,972	148
U of Maine at Presque Isle, Presque Isle, ME 04769-2888	1903	Dr. W. Michael Easton	5-B	1,308	106
U of Mary, Bismarck, ND 58504-9652	1959	Sr. Thomas Welder	2-M	1,776	118
U of Mary Hardin-Baylor, Belton, TX 76513	1845	Dr. Jerry G. Bawcom	2-M	2,244	156
U of Maryland Baltimore County, Baltimore, MD 21228-5398	1963	Dr. Freeman A. Hrabowski	5-D	10,315	696
U of Maryland Coll Park, College Park, MD 20742	1856	Dr. William E. Kirwan	5-D	32,493	1,638
U of Maryland Eastern Shore, Princess Anne, MD 21853	1886	Dr. William P. Hytche	5-D	2,925	250
U of Maryland U Coll, College Park, MD 20742-1600	1947	Dr. T. Benjamin Massey	5-M	36,302	1,538
U of Massachusetts Amherst, Amherst, MA 01003-0001	1863	Dr. David K. Scott	5-D	22,332	1,290
U of Massachusetts Boston, Boston, MA 02125-3393	1964	Dr. Jean F. MacCormack	5-D	10,436	842
U of Massachusetts Dartmouth, North Dartmouth, MA 02747-2300	1895	Dr. Peter H. Cressy	5-M	5,245	414
U of Massachusetts Lowell, Lowell, MA 01854-2881	1894	Dr. William T. Hogan	5-D	12,731	615
The U of Memphis, Memphis, TN 38152	1912	Dr. V. Lane Rawlins	5-D	19,848	1,181
U of Miami, Coral Gables, FL 33124	1925	Mr. Edward T. Foote, II	1-D	13,410	1,454
U of Michigan, Ann Arbor, MI 48109	1817	Dr. James J. Duderstadt	5-D	36,543	3,380
U of Michigan–Dearborn, Dearborn, MI 48128-1491	1959	Dr. James C. Renick	5-M	7,453	385
U of Michigan–Flint, Flint, MI 48502-2186	1956	Dr. Charlie Nelms	5-M	6,236	242
U of Minnesota, Duluth, Duluth, MN 55812-2496	1947	Dr. Kathryn A. Martin	5-M	7,497	430
U of Minnesota, Morris, Morris, MN 56267	1959	Dr. David C. Johnson	5-B	1,933	142
U of Minnesota, Twin Cities Cmps, Minneapolis, MN 55455-0213	1851	Dr. Nils Hasselmo	5-D	36,699	2,953
U of Mississippi, University, MS 38677	1844	NR	5-D	10,075	507
U of Mississippi Medical Ctr, Jackson, MS 39216-4505	1955	Dr. A. Wallace Conerly	5-D	1,817	545
U of Missouri–Columbia, Columbia, MO 65211	1839	Dr. Charles A. Kiesler	5-D	22,136	1,559
U of Missouri–Kansas City, Kansas City, MO 64110-2499	1929	Dr. Eleanor B. Schwartz	5-D	9,962	820
U of Missouri–Rolla, Rolla, MO 65401-0249	1870	Dr. John T. Park	5-D	5,472	354
U of Missouri–St Louis, St Louis, MO 63121-4499	1963	Dr. Blanche M. Touhill	5-D	12,045	951
U of Mobile, Mobile, AL 36663-0220	1961	Dr. Michael A. Magnoli	2-M	1,994	191
The U of Montana–Missoula, Missoula, MT 59812-0002	1893	Dr. George M. Dennison	5-D	11,067	640
U of Montevallo, Montevallo, AL 35115	1896	Dr. Robert M. McChesney	5-M	3,282	190

Name, address	Year	Governing official, control, and highest degree offered		Enroll-ment	Faculty
U of Nebraska at Kearney, Kearney, NE 68849-0001	1903	Dr. Gladys Styles Johnston	5-M	7,584	423
U of Nebraska at Omaha, Omaha, NE 68182	1908	Dr. Del D. Weber	5-D	15,570	782
U of Nebraska–Lincoln, Lincoln, NE 68588	1869	Dr. Joan Leitzel	5-D	23,854	1,521
U of Nebraska Medical Ctr, Omaha, NE 68198-0001	1869	Dr. Carol A. Aschenbrenner	5-D	2,778	912
U of Nevada, Las Vegas, Las Vegas, NV 89154-9900	1957	Dr. Carol Harter	5-D	20,239	1,138
U of Nevada, Reno, Reno, NV 89557	1874	Dr. Joseph N. Crowley	5-D	11,746	584
U of New England, Biddeford, ME 04005-9526	1939	Dr. Sandra Featherman	1-F	1,510	153
U of New Hampshire, Durham, NH 03824	1866	Mr. Walter R. Peterson	5-D	12,518	856
U of New Haven, West Haven, CT 06516-1916	1920	Dr. Lawrence J. DeNardis	1-D	5,497	546
U of New Mexico, Albuquerque, NM 87131-2039	1889	Dr. Richard E. Peck	5-D	24,344	2,454
U of New Orleans, New Orleans, LA 70148	1958	Dr. Gregory M. St.L. O'Brien	5-D	15,239	698
U of North Alabama, Florence, AL 35632-0001	1872	Mr. Robert L. Potts	5-M	5,221	270
U of North Carolina at Asheville, Asheville, NC 28804-3299	1927	Dr. Patsy Reed	5-M	3,195	248
U of North Carolina at Chapel Hill, Chapel Hill, NC 27599	1795	Dr. Michael K. Hooker, III	5-D	24,463	2,297
U of North Carolina at Charlotte, Charlotte, NC 28223	1946	Dr. James H. Woodward, Jr.	5-D	15,513	901
U of North Carolina at Greensboro, Greensboro, NC 27412-0001	1891	Dr. Patricia A. Sullivan	5-D	12,094	716
U of North Carolina at Wilmington, Wilmington, NC 28403-3201	1947	Dr. James R. Leutze	5-M	8,435	457
U of North Dakota, Grand Forks, ND 58202	1883	Dr. Kendall Baker	5-D	11,521	715
U of Northern Colorado, Greeley, CO 80639	1890	Dr. Herman D. Lujan	5-D	10,426	535
U of Northern Iowa, Cedar Falls, IA 50614	1876	Dr. Constantine W. Curris	5-D	12,572	855
U of North Florida, Jacksonville, FL 32224-2645	1965	Dr. Adam W. Herbert	5-D	10,064	574
U of North Texas, Denton, TX 76203-6737	1890	Dr. Alfred F. Hurley	5-D	25,605	1,009
U of Notre Dame, Notre Dame, IN 46556	1842	Rev. Edward A. Malloy, CSC.	2-D	10,000	912
U of Oklahoma, Norman, OK 73019	1890	Mr. David L. Boren	5-D	19,683	989
U of Oklahoma Health Sciences Ctr, Oklahoma City, OK 73190	1890	Dr. Jay H. Stein	5-D	3,044	961
U of Oregon, Eugene, OR 97403	1872	Mr. David Frohnmayer	5-D	16,681	803
U of Osteopathic Medicine and Health Sciences, Des Moines, IA 50312-4104	1898	Dr. David Marker	1-F	1,350	108
U of Pennsylvania, Philadelphia, PA 19104	1740	Dr. Judith Rodin	1-D	22,720	3,680
U of Phoenix, Phoenix, AZ 85072-2069	1976	Mr. William Gibbs	3-M	19,719	1,500
U of Pittsburgh, Pittsburgh, PA 15260-0001	1787	Dr. Mark A. Nordenberg	12-D	26,328	3,386
U of Pittsburgh at Bradford, Bradford, PA 16701-2812	1963	Dr. Richard E. McDowell	12-B	1,334	107
U of Pittsburgh at Greensburg, Greensburg, PA 15601-5860	1963	Dr. George F. Chambers	12-B	1,387	90
U of Pittsburgh at Johnstown, Johnstown, PA 15904-2990	1927	Dr. Albert L. Etheridge.	12-B	3,138	191
U of Portland, Portland, OR 97203-5798	1901	Rev. David T. Tyson, CSC	2-M	2,600	209
U of Puerto Rico at Arecibo, Arecibo, PR 00613	1967	Prof. Juan Ramirez Silva	6-B	3,837	218
U of Puerto Rico at Ponce, Ponce, PR 00732-7186	1970	Ms. Antonia Lopez	6-B	2,918	140
U of Puerto Rico, Cayey U Coll, Cayey, PR 00737	1967	Jose Luis Monserrate	6-B	3,149	194
U of Puerto Rico, Humacao U Coll, Humacao, PR 00791	1962	Dr. Roberto Marrero	6-B	3,925	260
U of Puerto Rico, Mayagüez Cmps, Mayagüez, PR 00681-5000	1911	Dr. Stuart J. Ramos	6-D	11,123	640
U of Puget Sound, Tacoma, WA 98416-0005	1888	Dr. Susan Resneck Pierce	1-M	3,163	235
U of Redlands, Redlands, CA 92373-0999	1907	Dr. James R. Appleton	1-M	3,950	156
U of Rhode Island, Kingston, RI 02881	1892	Dr. Robert L. Carothers	5-D	12,110	696
U of Richmond, Richmond, VA 23173	1830	Dr. Richard L. Morrill	2-F	4,315	400
U of Rio Grande, Rio Grande, OH 45674	1876	Dr. Barry M. Dorsey	1-M	2,042	135
U of Rochester, Rochester, NY 14627-0001	1850	Mr. Thomas H. Jackson	1-D	8,336	1,376
U of St Thomas, St Paul, MN 55105-1089	1885	Rev. Dennis Dease	2-D	10,161	678
U of St Thomas, Houston, TX 77006-4694	1947	Dr. Joseph M. McFadden	2-D	2,298	181
U of San Diego, San Diego, CA 92110-2492	1949	Dr. Alice B. Hayes	2-D	6,381	510
U of San Francisco, San Francisco, CA 94117-1080	1855	Rev. John P. Schlegel, SJ	2-D	7,921	887
U of Science and Arts of Oklahoma, Chickasha, OK 73018-0001	1908	Dr. Roy Troutt	5-B	1,687	74
U of Scranton, Scranton, PA 18510-4622	1888	Rev. J. A. Panuska, SJ	2-M	4,946	401
U of South Alabama, Mobile, AL 36688-0002	1963	Dr. Frederick P. Whiddon	5-D	12,386	841
U of South Carolina, Columbia, SC 29208	1801	Dr. John M. Palms	5-D	26,754	1,416
U of South Carolina–Aiken, Aiken, SC 29801-6309	1961	Dr. Robert E. Alexander	5-M	3,245	218
U of South Carolina–Spartanburg, Spartanburg, SC 29303-4932	1967	Dr. John C. Stockwell	5-M	3,422	218
U of South Dakota, Vermillion, SD 57069-2390	1862	Dr. Betty Turner Asher	5-D	7,739	471
U of Southern California, Los Angeles, CA 90089	1880	Dr. Steven B. Sample	1-D	27,864	2,621
U of Southern Colorado, Pueblo, CO 81001-4901	1933	Dr. Robert Shirley	5-M	5,300	278
U of Southern Indiana, Evansville, IN 47712-3590	1965	Dr. H. Ray Hoops	5-M	7,443	374
U of Southern Maine, Portland, ME 04103	1878	Dr. Richard L. Pattenaude	5-F	9,628	536
U of Southern Mississippi, Hattiesburg, MS 39406-5001	1910	Dr. Aubrey K. Lucas	5-D	11,587	655
U of South Florida, Tampa, FL 33620-9951	1956	Mrs. Betty Castor	5-D	36,058	1,504
U of Southwestern Louisiana, Lafayette, LA 70504	1898	Dr. Ray P. Authement	5-D	16,789	672
The U of Tampa, Tampa, FL 33606-1490	1931	Dr. Ronald L. Vaughn	1-M	2,388	167
U of Tennessee at Chattanooga, Chattanooga, TN 37403-2504	1886	Dr. Frederick W. Obear	5-M	8,281	528
The U of Tennessee at Martin, Martin, TN 38238-1000	1927	Dr. Margaret N. Perry	5-M	5,627	285
U of Tennessee, Knoxville, Knoxville, TN 37996	1794	Dr. William T. Snyder	5-D	25,890	1,191
U of Tennessee, Memphis, Memphis, TN 38163-0002	1911	NR	5-D	2,095	914
U of Texas at Arlington, Arlington, TX 76019	1895	Dr. Robert E. Witt	5-D	23,280	935
U of Texas at Austin, Austin, TX 78712	1883	Dr. Robert M. Berdahl	5-D	47,957	2,367
The U of Texas at Brownsville, Brownsville, TX 78520-4991	1973	NR	5-M	1,675	390
U of Texas at Dallas, Richardson, TX 75083-0688	1969	Dr. Franklyn G. Jenifer	5-D	8,487	NR
U of Texas at El Paso, El Paso, TX 79968-0001	1913	Dr. Diana Natalicio	5-D	17,188	808
U of Texas at San Antonio, San Antonio, TX 78249	1969	Dr. Samuel A. Kirkpatrick	5-D	17,579	765
U of Texas at Tyler, Tyler, TX 75799-0001	1971	Dr. George F. Hamm	5-M	3,988	219
U of Texas Health Science Ctr at San Antonio, San Antonio, TX 78284-6200	1976	Dr. John P. Howe, III	5-D	2,800	1,213
U of Texas-Houston Health Science Ctr, Houston, TX 77225-0036	1943	Dr. M. David Low	5-D	3,183	1,076
U of Texas Medical Branch at Galveston, Galveston, TX 77555	1891	Dr. Thomas N. James	5-D	2,327	145
U of Texas of the Permian Basin, Odessa, TX 79762-0001	1969	Dr. Charles A. Sorber	5-M	2,315	120
U of Texas–Pan American, Edinburg, TX 78539-2999	1927	Dr. Miguel A. Nevarez	5-D	13,298	478
U of Texas Southwestern Medical Ctr at Dallas, Dallas, TX 75235-9002	1943	Dr. C. Kern Wildenthal	5-D	1,700	344
U of the Arts, Philadelphia, PA 19102-4944	1870	NR	1-M	1,298	362
U of the District of Columbia, Washington, DC 20008-1175	1976	Dr. Tilden J. LeMelle	9-M	10,599	583
U of the Pacific, Stockton, CA 95211-0197	1851	Donald DeRosa	1-D	4,140	322
U of the Sacred Heart, Santurce, PR 00914	1935	Dr. Jose Jaime Rivera	2-M	5,199	366
U of the South, Sewanee, TN 37383-1000	1857	Dr. Samuel R. Williamson	2-D	1,298	133
U of the State of NY, Regents Coll, Albany, NY 12203-5159	1970	Mr. C. Wayne Williams	1-B	17,269	NR
U of the Virgin Islands, Charlotte Amalie, St Thomas, VI 00802-9999	1962	Dr. Orville Kean	7-M	3,127	266
U of Toledo, Toledo, OH 43606-3398	1872	Dr. Frank E. Horton	5-D	23,107	1,377
U of Tulsa, Tulsa, OK 74104-3126	1894	Dr. Robert H. Donaldson	2-D	4,573	445
U of Utah, Salt Lake City, UT 84112	1850	Dr. Arthur K. Smith	5-D	25,226	1,430
U of Vermont, Burlington, VT 05405-0160	1791	Mr. Thomas P. Salmon	5-D	9,072	1,000
U of Virginia, Charlottesville, VA 22903	1819	Mr. John T. Casteen, III	5-D	17,704	2,029

Name, address	Year	Governing official, control, and highest degree offered		Enroll-ment	Faculty
U of Washington, Seattle, WA 98195	1861	Dr. Richard McCormick	5-D	33,719	3,604
U of West Alabama, Livingston, AL 35470	1835	Dr. Donald C. Hines	5-M	2,320	120
U of West Florida, Pensacola, FL 32514-5750	1963	Dr. Morris L. Marx	5-M	7,816	255
U of Wisconsin–Eau Claire, Eau Claire, WI 54702-4004	1916	Dr. Larry Schnack	5-M	10,331	508
U of Wisconsin–Green Bay, Green Bay, WI 54311-7001	1968	Dr. Mark L. Perkins	5-M	5,630	256
U of Wisconsin–La Crosse, La Crosse, WI 54601-3742	1909	Dr. Judith L. Kuipers	5-M	8,589	448
U of Wisconsin–Madison, Madison, WI 53706-1380	1848	Dr. David Ward	5-D	38,139	2,325
U of Wisconsin–Milwaukee, Milwaukee, WI 53201-0413	1956	Dr. John H. Schroeder, Jr.	5-D	22,984	1,358
U of Wisconsin–Oshkosh, Oshkosh, WI 54901-3551	1871	Dr. John E. Kerrigan	5-M	10,567	534
U of Wisconsin–Parkside, Kenosha, WI 53141-2000	1968	Dr. Eleanor J. Smith	5-M	4,993	293
U of Wisconsin–Platteville, Platteville, WI 53818-3099	1866	Dr. Robert G. Culbertson	5-M	4,943	280
U of Wisconsin–River Falls, River Falls, WI 54022-5013	1874	Dr. Gary A. Thibodeau	5-M	6,432	295
U of Wisconsin–Stevens Point, Stevens Point, WI 54481-3897	1894	Dr. Keith R. Sanders	5-M	8,424	NR
U of Wisconsin–Stout, Menomonie, WI 54751	1891	Dr. Charles Sorensen	5-M	7,413	370
U of Wisconsin–Superior, Superior, WI 54880-2873	1893	Dr. Betty J. Youngblood	5-M	2,420	146
U of Wisconsin–Whitewater, Whitewater, WI 53190-1790	1868	Dr. H. Gaylon Greenhill	5-M	10,438	471
U of Wyoming, Laramie, WY 82071	1886	Dr. Terry P. Roark	5-D	12,020	738
Upper Iowa U, Fayette, IA 52142-1857	1857	Dr. Ralph L. McKay	1-B	3,140	230
Urbana U, Urbana, OH 43078-2091	1850	Dr. Francis E. Hazard	2-B	1,000	75
Ursinus Coll, Collegeville, PA 19426-1000	1869	Dr. John Strassburger	2-B	1,163	135
Ursuline Coll, Pepper Pike, OH 44124-4398 (4)	1871	Anne Marie Diederich, OSU, PhD	2-M	1,563	141
Utah State U, Logan, UT 84322	1888	Dr. George H. Emert	5-D	20,371	802
Utica Coll of Syracuse U, Utica, NY 13502-4892	1946	Dr. Michael K. Simpson	1-B	1,841	141
Valdosta State U, Valdosta, GA 31698	1906	Dr. Hugh C. Bailey	5-D	9,160	472
Valparaiso U, Valparaiso, IN 46383-6493	1859	Dr. Alan F. Harre	2-F	3,480	366
Vanderbilt U, Nashville, TN 37240-1001	1873	Mr. Joe B. Wyatt	1-D	10,088	1,899
Vassar Coll, Poughkeepsie, NY 12601	1861	Dr. Frances D. Fergusson	1-M	2,312	227
Villa Julie Coll, Stevenson, MD 21153	1952	Dr. Carolyn Manuszak	1-B	1,827	139
Villanova U, Villanova, PA 19085-1699	1842	Rev. Edmund J. Dobbin, OSA	2-D	10,760	783
Virginia Commonwealth U, Richmond, VA 23284-9005	1838	Dr. Eugene P. Trani	5-D	21,523	2,606
Virginia Military Inst, Lexington, VA 24450 (1)	1839	Maj. Gen. John W. Knapp	5-B	1,179	115
Virginia Polytechnic Inst and State U, Blacksburg, VA 24061-0202	1872	Dr. Paul E. Torgersen	5-D	25,842	1,974
Virginia State U, Petersburg, VA 23806-0001	1882	Mr. Eddie N. Moore, Jr.	5-M	4,007	239
Virginia Union U, Richmond, VA 23220-1170	1865	Dr. S. Dallas Simmons	2-D	1,500	139
Virginia Wesleyan Coll, Norfolk, VA 23502-5599	1961	Dr. William T. Greer, Jr.	2-B	1,568	94
Viterbo Coll, La Crosse, WI 54601-4797	1890	Dr. William J. Medland	2-M	1,701	153
Wagner Coll, Staten Island, NY 10301	1883	Dr. Norman R. Smith	1-M	1,856	177
Wake Forest U, Winston-Salem, NC 27109	1834	Dr. Thomas K. Hearn, Jr.	1-D	5,748	1,510
Walla Walla Coll, College Place, WA 99324-3000	1892	Dr. W. G. Nelson	2-M	1,725	190
Walsh Coll of Accountancy and Business Admin, Troy, MI 48007-7006	1922	Dr. David A. Spencer	1-M	3,619	107
Walsh U, North Canton, OH 44720-3396	1958	Rev. Richard Mucowski	2-M	1,483	113
Wartburg Coll, Waverly, IA 50677-1033	1852	Dr. Robert Vogel	2-B	1,405	136
Washburn U of Topeka, Topeka, KS 66621	1865	Dr. Hugh Thompson	10-F	6,439	430
Washington and Jefferson Coll, Washington, PA 15301-4801	1781	Dr. Howard J. Burnett	1-B	1,104	104
Washington and Lee U, Lexington, VA 24450	1749	Dr. John W. Elrod	1-F	1,990	167
Washington State U, Pullman, WA 99164	1890	Dr. Samuel H. Smith	5-D	19,314	1,151
Washington U, St Louis, MO 63130-4899	1853	Dr. Mark S. Wrighton	1-D	11,655	3,462
Waynesburg Coll, Waynesburg, PA 15370-1222	1849	Mr. Timothy R. Thyreen	2-M	1,319	113
Wayne State Coll, Wayne, NE 68787	1910	Dr. Donald J. Mash	5-M	3,886	228
Wayne State U, Detroit, MI 48202	1868	Mr. David Adamany	5-D	32,906	2,695
Weber State U, Ogden, UT 84408-0002	1889	Dr. Paul H. Thompson	5-M	14,230	453
Webster U, St Louis, MO 63119-3194	1915	Dr. Richard S. Meyers	1-D	10,834	1,372
Wellesley Coll, Wellesley, MA 02181 (3)	1870	Ms. Diana Chapman Walsh	1-B	2,288	313
Wentworth Inst of Tech, Boston, MA 02115-5998	1904	Dr. John F. Van Domelen	1-B	2,377	225
Wesleyan U, Middletown, CT 06459-0260	1831	Douglas J. Bennett, Jr.	1-D	3,424	337
Wesley Coll, Dover, DE 19901	1873	Dr. Reed M. Stewart	2-B	1,355	106
West Chester U of Pennsylvania, West Chester, PA 19383	1871	Dr. Madeleine Wing Adler	5-M	11,168	678
West Coast U, Los Angeles, CA 90020-1765	1909	Dr. Robert M. L. Baker, Jr.	1-M	1,600	250
Western Carolina U, Cullowhee, NC 28723	1889	Dr. John W. Bardo	5-M	6,619	499
Western Connecticut State U, Danbury, CT 06810-6885	1903	Dr. James R. Roach	5-M	5,462	326
Western Illinois U, Macomb, IL 61455-1390	1899	Dr. Donald S. Spencer	5-M	12,599	645
Western International U, Phoenix, AZ 85021-2718	1978	Mr. James Haynes	1-M	1,469	86
Western Kentucky U, Bowling Green, KY 42101-3576	1906	Dr. Thomas C. Meredith	5-M	14,765	879
Western Maryland Coll, Westminster, MD 21157-4390	1867	Dr. Robert H. Chambers	1-M	2,357	198
Western Michigan U, Kalamazoo, MI 49008	1903	Dr. Diether H. Haenicke	5-D	25,673	1,081
Western Montana Coll of The U of Montana, Dillon, MT 59725-3598	1893	Dr. Sheila M. Stearns	5-B	1,150	42
Western New England Coll, Springfield, MA 01119-2654	1919	Dr. Beverly W. Miller	1-F	4,795	269
Western New Mexico U, Silver City, NM 88062-0680	1893	Dr. John E. Counts	5-M	2,240	126
Western Oregon State Coll, Monmouth, OR 97361	1856	Dr. Bill Cowart	5-M	3,871	282
Western State Coll of Colorado, Gunnison, CO 81231	1911	Dr. Kaye Howe	5-B	2,443	138
Western Washington U, Bellingham, WA 98225-5996	1893	Dr. Karen Morse	5-M	10,598	534
Westfield State Coll, Westfield, MA 01086	1838	Dr. Ronald L. Applbaum	5-M	5,026	330
West Georgia Coll, Carrollton, GA 30118	1933	Dr. Beheruz N. Sethna	5-M	8,310	376
West Liberty State Coll, West Liberty, WV 26074	1837	Dr. Clyde D. Campbell	5-B	2,381	143
Westminster Coll, New Wilmington, PA 16172-0001	1852	Dr. Oscar E. Remick	2-M	1,620	120
Westminster Coll of Salt Lake City, Salt Lake City, UT 84105-3697	1875	Dr. Peggy Stock	1-M	2,113	208
Westmont Coll, Santa Barbara, CA 93108-1099	1940	Dr. David K. Winter	2-B	1,280	116
West Texas A&M U, Canyon, TX 79016-0001	1909	Dr. Russell C. Long	5-M	6,738	332
West Virginia Inst of Tech, Montgomery, WV 25136	1895	Dr. John P. Carrier	5-M	2,695	227
West Virginia State Coll, Institute, WV 25112-1000	1891	NR	5-B	4,756	239
West Virginia U, Morgantown, WV 26506	1867	Mr. David C. Hardesty, Jr.	5-D	22,500	1,617
West Virginia Wesleyan Coll, Buckhannon, WV 26201	1890	Mr. William R. Haden	2-M	1,680	136
Wheaton Coll, Wheaton, IL 60187-5571	1860	Dr. A. Duane Litfin	2-D	2,642	268
Wheaton Coll, Norton, MA 02766	1834	Dr. Dale Rogers Marshall	1-B	1,331	120
Wheeling Jesuit Coll, Wheeling, WV 26003-6295	1954	Fr. Thomas S. Acker, SJ	2-M	1,482	90
Wheelock Coll, Boston, MA 02215 (4)	1888	Dr. Marjorie Bakken	1-M	1,288	182
Whitman Coll, Walla Walla, WA 99362-2083	1859	Dr. Thomas Cronin	1-B	1,295	166
Whittier Coll, Whittier, CA 90608-0634	1887	Dr. James L. Ash, Jr.	1-F	2,182	122
Whitworth Coll, Spokane, WA 99251-0001	1890	Dr. William P. Robinson	2-M	2,003	95
Wichita State U, Wichita, KS 67260	1895	Dr. Eugene Morgan Hughes	5-D	14,558	514
Widener U, Chester, PA 19013-5792	1821	Dr. Robert J. Bruce	1-D	8,628	310
Wilkes U, Wilkes-Barre, PA 18766-0002	1933	Dr. Christopher N. Breiseth	1-M	3,065	225

Name, address	Year	Governing official, control, and highest degree offered		Enroll-ment	Faculty
Willamette U, Salem, OR 97301-3931	1842	Dr. Jerry E. Hudson	2-F	2,519	243
William Carey Coll, Hattiesburg, MS 39401-5499	1906	Dr. James W. Edwards	2-M	2,139	115
William Jewell Coll, Liberty, MO 64068-1843	1849	Dr. W. Christian Sizemore	2-B	1,322	157
William Paterson Coll of New Jersey, Wayne, NJ 07470-8420	1855	Dr. Arnold Speert	5-M	9,669	328
Williams Coll, Williamstown, MA 01267	1793	Dr. Harry C. Payne	1-M	2,126	258
William Woods U, Fulton, MO 65251-1098 (4)	1870	Dr. Jahnae Barnett	2-M	1,000	73
Wilmington Coll, New Castle, DE 19720-6491	1967	Dr. Audrey K. Doberstein	1-D	3,500	394
Wilmington Coll, Wilmington, OH 45177	1870	Dr. Daniel DiBiasio	2-B	1,006	65
Wingate U, Wingate, NC 28174	1896	Dr. Jerry E. McGee	2-M	1,383	107
Winona State U, Winona, MN 55987-5838	1858	Dr. Darrell Krueger	5-M	7,500	350
Winston-Salem State U, Winston-Salem, NC 27110-0003	1892	Dr. Cleon F. Thompson, Jr.	5-B	2,846	172
Winthrop U, Rock Hill, SC 29733	1886	Dr. Anthony DiGiorgio	5-M	5,164	413
Wittenberg U, Springfield, OH 45501-0720	1845	Dr. Baird Tipson	2-B	2,160	166
Wofford Coll, Spartanburg, SC 29303-3663	1854	Dr. Joab M. Lesesne	2-B	1,106	96
Woodbury U, Burbank, CA 91510	1884	Dr. Paul E. Sago	1-M	1,062	195
Worcester Polytechnic Inst, Worcester, MA 01609-2247	1865	Dr. Edward A. Parrish, Jr.	1-D	3,794	259
Worcester State Coll, Worcester, MA 01602-2597	1874	Dr. Kalyan K. Ghosh	5-M	5,772	250
Wright State U, Dayton, OH 45435	1964	Dr. Harley E. Flack	5-D	16,823	950
Xavier U, Cincinnati, OH 45207-5311	1831	Rev. James E. Hoff, SJ	2-M	6,180	411
Xavier U of Louisiana, New Orleans, LA 70125-1098	1925	Dr. Norman C. Francis	2-F	3,486	252
Yale U, New Haven, CT 06520	1701	Mr. Richard C. Levin	1-D	10,964	2,782
Yeshiva U, New York, NY 10033-3201	1886	Dr. Norman Lamm	1-D	5,205	1,092
York Coll of Pennsylvania, York, PA 17405-7199	1787	Dr. George W. Waldner	1-M	4,868	310
York Coll of the City U of New York, Jamaica, NY 11451-0001	1967	Dr. Thomas K. Minter	11-B	6,889	466
Youngstown State U, Youngstown, OH 44555-0002	1908	Dr. Leslie H. Cochran	5-D	13,979	852

Two-Year Colleges

The highest undergraduate degree offered for all two-year colleges is the associate degree.

Name, address	Year	Governing official, control		Enroll-ment	Faculty
Abraham Baldwin Ag Coll, Tifton, GA 31794-2601	1933	Dr. Harold J. Loyd	5	2,751	113
Adirondack Comm Coll, Queensbury, NY 12804	1960	Dr. Roger Andersen	11	3,475	226
Aiken Tech Coll, Aiken, SC 29802-0600	1972	Dr. Kathleen A. Noble	11	2,308	123
Aims Comm Coll, Greeley, CO 80632-0069	1967	Dr. George R. Conger	9	6,970	431
Alabama Southern Comm Coll, Monroeville, AL 36460	1965	Dr. John A. Johnson	5	1,800	107
Alabama Southern Comm Coll, Thomasville, AL 36784-0489	1965	Dr. John A. Johnson	5	1,225	119
Alamance Comm Coll, Graham, NC 27253-8000	1959	Dr. W. Ronald McCarter	5	3,340	145
Albuquerque Tech Vocational Inst, Albuquerque, NM 87106-4096	1965	NR	5	14,841	603
Allan Hancock Coll, Santa Maria, CA 93454-6399	1920	Dr. Ann F. Stephenson	11	7,570	417
Allegany Comm Coll, Cumberland, MD 21502	1961	Dr. Donald L. Alexander	11	2,877	217
Allen County Comm Coll, Iola, KS 66749-1607	1923	Mr. John Masterson	11	1,646	135
Alpena Comm Coll, Alpena, MI 49707-1495	1952	Dr. Donald L. Newport	11	1,942	89
Alvin Comm Coll, Alvin, TX 77511-4898	1949	Dr. A. Rodney Allbright	11	3,864	141
Amarillo Coll, Amarillo, TX 79178-0001	1929	Dr. Luther Bud Joyner	11	6,767	384
American River Coll, Sacramento, CA 95841-4286	1955	Dr. Marie Smith	9	19,695	700
Angelina Coll, Lufkin, TX 75902-1768	1968	Dr. Larry M. Phillips	11	3,478	151
Anne Arundel Comm Coll, Arnold, MD 21012-1895	1961	Dr. Martha A. Smith	11	12,387	577
Anoka-Ramsey Comm Coll, Coon Rapids, MN 55433-3499	1965	Dr. Patrick M. Johns	5	4,706	218
Antelope Valley Coll, Lancaster, CA 93536-5426	1929	Dr. Allan W. Kurki	11	10,751	400
Arapahoe Comm Coll, Littleton, CO 80160-9002	1965	Dr. James F. Weber	5	7,346	298
Arizona Western Coll, Yuma, AZ 85366-0929	1962	Dr. James R. Carruthers	11	5,653	287
Arkansas State U–Beebe Branch, Beebe, AR 72012-1008	1927	Dr. Eugene McKay, Jr.	5	1,962	71
Art Inst of Atlanta, Atlanta, GA 30326-1018	1949	Mr. Hal R. Griffith	3	1,329	104
Art Inst of Dallas, Dallas, TX 75231-5993	1978	Thomas M. Hauser	3	1,100	84
Art Inst of Fort Lauderdale, Fort Lauderdale, FL 33316-3000	1968	Mr. David Pauldine	3	1,850	150
The Art Inst of Houston, Houston, TX 77056-4115	1978	NR	3	1,189	91
The Art Inst of Philadelphia, Philadelphia, PA 19103-5198	1966	Mr. Robert P. Gioella	3	1,400	90
Art Inst of Pittsburgh, Pittsburgh, PA 15222-3269	1921	Ms. Saundra M. Van Dyke	3	1,959	107
Art Inst of Seattle, Seattle, WA 98121-1642	1982	Leslie E. Pritchard	3	1,605	101
Asheville-Buncombe Tech Comm Coll, Asheville, NC 28801-4897	1959	Mr. K. Ray Bailey	5	4,104	216
Asnuntuck Comm-Tech Coll, Enfield, CT 06082-3800	1972	Dr. Harvey S. Irlen	5	2,104	112
Athens Area Tech Inst, Athens, GA 30601-1500	1958	NR	5	1,658	100
Atlanta Metropolitan Coll, Atlanta, GA 30310-4498	1974	Dr. Harold E. Wade	5	1,882	77
Atlantic Comm Coll, Mays Landing, NJ 08330-2699	1966	Dr. John May	8	6,400	390
Austin Comm Coll, Austin, MN 55912-1407	1940	Dr. Vicky R. Smith	5	1,373	73
Austin Comm Coll, Austin, TX 78752-4342	1972	Dr. Bill Segura	9	25,275	1,388
Bainbridge Coll, Bainbridge, GA 31717	1972	Dr. Edward D. Mobley	5	1,049	39
Bakersfield Coll, Bakersfield, CA 93305-1299	1913	Dr. Richard Wright	11	12,267	496
Barstow Coll, Barstow, CA 92311-6699	1959	Dr. Judith Strattan	11	3,569	128
Barton County Comm Coll, Great Bend, KS 67530-9283	1969	Dr. Jimmie L. Downing	11	7,000	289
Bay de Noc Comm Coll, Escanaba, MI 49829-2511	1963	Dr. Dwight E. Link	8	2,248	143
Beaufort County Comm Coll, Washington, NC 27889-1069	1967	Dr. Ron Champion	5	1,233	110
Bee County Coll, Beeville, TX 78102-2197	1965	Dr. Norman Wallace	8	2,417	134
Belleville Area Coll, Belleville, IL 62221-5899	1946	Dr. Joseph Cipfl	9	15,707	893
Bellevue Comm Coll, Bellevue, WA 98007-6484	1966	Mrs. B. Jean Floten	5	10,249	640
Belmont Tech Coll, St Clairsville, OH 43950-9766	1971	Dr. Wesley R. Channell	5	1,689	101
Bergen Comm Coll, Paramus, NJ 07652-1595	1965	Dr. Judith K. Winn	8	9,233	679
Berkeley Coll of Business, West Paterson, NJ 07424-3353	1931	Mr. Kevin L. Luing	3	1,458	104
Berkshire Comm Coll, Pittsfield, MA 01201-5786	1960	Dr. Barbara A. Viniar	5	2,445	149
Bessemer State Tech Coll, Bessemer, AL 35021-0308	1966	Dr. W. Michael Bailey	5	1,840	91
Bevill State Comm Coll, Sumiton, AL 35148	1969	Dr. Harold Wade	5	1,145	63
Big Bend Comm Coll, Moses Lake, WA 98837-3299	1962	Dr. William C. Bonaudi	5	1,868	146
Bishop State Comm Coll, Mobile, AL 36603-5898	1965	NR	5	4,478	229
Bismarck State Coll, Bismarck, ND 58501-1299	1939	Dr. Donna Thigpen	5	2,349	117
Black Hawk Coll, Moline, IL 61265-5899	1946	Dr. Judith A. Redwine	11	5,881	305
Blackhawk Tech Coll, Janesville, WI 53547-5009	1968	Dr. James C. Catania	9	3,915	293
Blinn Coll, Brenham, TX 77833-4049	1883	Dr. Donald E. Voelter	11	9,020	361
Blue Mountain Comm Coll, Pendleton, OR 97801-1000	1962	Mr. Ronald L. Daniels	11	4,175	245
Blue Ridge Comm Coll, Flat Rock, NC 28731	1969	Dr. David W. Sink	11	1,514	98
Blue Ridge Comm Coll, Weyers Cave, VA 24486-0080	1965	Dr. James R. Perkins	5	3,996	154
Borough of Manhattan Comm Coll of City U of NY, New York, NY 10007-1079	1963	Dr. Marcia V. Keizs	11	16,968	1,080
Bossier Parish Comm Coll, Bossier City, LA 71111-5801	1967	Mr. Thomas N. Carleton	11	4,687	134

Name, address	Year	Governing official, control		Enrollment	Faculty
Bowling Green State U–Firelands Coll, Huron, OH 44839-9791	1968	Dr. R. Darby Williams	5	1,404	85
Bramson ORT Tech Inst, Forest Hills, NY 11375-4239	1977	Mr. Barry M. Glotzer	1	1,200	57
Brazosport Coll, Lake Jackson, TX 77566-3199	1948	Dr. John R. Grable	11	3,094	163
Brevard Comm Coll, Cocoa, FL 32922-6597	1960	Dr. Maxwell C. King	5	14,529	976
Briarcliffe–The Coll for Business & Tech, Woodbury, NY 11797-2015	1966	Mr. Richard Turan	3	1,252	112
Bristol Comm Coll, Fall River, MA 02720-7395	1965	Ms. Eileen Farley	5	3,906	183
Bronx Comm Coll of City U of NY, Bronx, NY 10453	1959	NR	11	8,357	390
Brookdale Comm Coll, Lincroft, NJ 07738	1967	Dr. Peter F. Burnham	8	9,988	443
Brookhaven Coll, Farmers Branch, TX 75244-4997	1978	Dr. Walter G. Bumphus	8	9,060	525
Broome Comm Coll, Binghamton, NY 13902-1017	1946	Dr. Donald A. Dellow	11	6,011	377
Broward Comm Coll, Fort Lauderdale, FL 33301-2298	1960	Dr. Willis N. Holcombe	5	28,433	775
Brown Inst, Minneapolis, MN 55407-1932	1946	Dr. Jim Otten	3	1,180	79
Brunswick Coll, Brunswick, GA 31520-3644	1961	Dr. Dorothy L. Lord	5	2,029	74
Bucks County Comm Coll, Newtown, PA 18940-1525	1964	Dr. James J. Linksz	8	10,300	375
Bunker Hill Comm Coll, Boston, MA 02129	1973	NR	5	6,002	145
Burlington County Comm Coll, Pemberton, NJ 08068-1599	1966	Dr. Robert Messina	8	6,798	322
Butler County Comm Coll, El Dorado, KS 67042-3280	1927	Dr. James Stringer	11	7,500	473
Butler County Comm Coll, Butler, PA 16003-1203	1965	Dr. Frederick F. Bartok	8	3,094	220
Butte Coll, Oroville, CA 95965-8399	1966	Dr. Betty M. Dean	9	12,838	575
Cabrillo Coll, Aptos, CA 95003-3194	1959	Mr. John D. Hurd	9	13,500	552
Caldwell Comm Coll and Tech Inst, Hudson, NC 28638-2397	1964	Dr. Kenneth A. Boham	5	2,938	203
Camden County Coll, Blackwood, NJ 08012-0200	1967	Dr. Phyllis Della Vecchia	11	14,543	701
Cañada Coll, Redwood City, CA 94061-1099	1968	Dr. Marie E. Rosenwasser	9	5,714	263
Cape Cod Comm Coll, West Barnstable, MA 02668	1961	NR	5	3,758	263
Cape Fear Comm Coll, Wilmington, NC 28401-3993	1959	Mr. Eric B. McKeithan	5	3,615	205
Capital Comm Tech Coll, Hartford, CT 06105-2354	1946	NR	5	3,260	174
Carl Albert State Coll, Poteau, OK 74953-5208	1934	NR	5	1,887	160
Carl Sandburg Coll, Galesburg, IL 61401-9576	1967	NR	11	2,800	208
Carteret Comm Coll, Morehead City, NC 28557-2989	1963	Dr. Donald W. Bryant	5	1,602	93
Casper Coll, Casper, WY 82601-4699	1945	Dr. LeRoy Strausner	9	3,874	185
Catawba Valley Comm Coll, Hickory, NC 28602-9699	1960	Dr. Cuyler A. Dunbar	11	3,499	235
Catonsville Comm Coll, Catonsville, MD 21228-5381	1957	Dr. Frederick J. Walsh	8	10,288	534
Cayuga County Comm Coll, Auburn, NY 13021-3099	1953	Dr. Lawrence H. Poole	11	2,081	183
Cecil Comm Coll, North East, MD 21901-1999	1968	Dr. Robert L. Gell	8	1,064	96
Cedar Valley Coll, Lancaster, TX 75134-3799	1977	Dr. Carol J. Spencer	5	3,136	130
Central Alabama Comm Coll, Alexander City, AL 35010-0699	1965	Dr. James H. Cornell	5	2,421	139
Central Arizona Coll, Coolidge, AZ 85228-9779	1961	Dr. John J. Klein	8	14,724	440
Central Carolina Comm Coll, Sanford, NC 27330-9000	1962	Dr. Marvin R. Joyner	11	3,122	189
Central Carolina Tech Coll, Sumter, SC 29150-2499	1963	Dr. Herbert C. Robbins	5	2,400	144
Central Comm Coll–Grand Island Cmps, Grand Island, NE 68802-4903	1976	Dr. William Giddings	11	1,265	165
Central Comm Coll–Hastings Cmps, Hastings, NE 68902-1024	1966	Dr. Judy Dresser	11	1,522	111
Central Comm Coll–Platte Cmps, Columbus, NE 68602-1027	1968	Dr. M. Richard Shaink	11	1,019	100
Central Florida Comm Coll, Ocala, FL 34478-1388	1957	NR	11	5,972	178
Centralia Coll, Centralia, WA 98531-4099	1925	Dr. Henry P. Kirk	5	1,800	112
Central Lakes Coll, Brainerd, MN 56401-3904	1938	Ms. Sally Jane Ihne	5	2,042	97
Central Ohio Tech Coll, Newark, OH 43055-1767	1971	Dr. Rafael L. Cortada	5	1,712	99
Central Oregon Comm Coll, Bend, OR 97701-5998	1949	Dr. Robert L. Barber	9	3,137	184
Central Piedmont Comm Coll, Charlotte, NC 28235-5009	1963	Dr. Paul A. Zeiss	11	15,336	1,220
Central Texas Coll, Killeen, TX 76542-4199	1967	Dr. James R. Anderson	11	8,600	328
Central Virginia Comm Coll, Lynchburg, VA 24502-4907	1966	Dr. Belle S. Wheelan	5	4,145	200
Central Wyoming Coll, Riverton, WY 82501-2273	1966	Dr. JoAnne McFarland	11	1,550	110
Cerritos Coll, Norwalk, CA 90650-6298	1956	Dr. Fred Gaskin	11	22,068	642
Cerro Coso Comm Coll, Ridgecrest, CA 93555-9571	1973	Dr. Raymond A. McCue	5	4,118	262
Chabot Coll, Hayward, CA 94545-5001	1961	Dr. Raul J. Cardoza	5	15,290	957
Chaffey Coll, Rancho Cucamonga, CA 91737-3002	1883	Dr. Jerry W. Young	9	12,651	540
Champlain Coll, Burlington, VT 05402-0670	1878	Dr. Roger H. Perry	1	1,846	128
Charles County Comm Coll, La Plata, MD 20646-0910	1958	Dr. John Sine	11	5,910	355
Charles Stewart Mott Comm Coll, Flint, MI 48503-2089	1923	Dr. Allen Arnold	9	10,434	414
Chattahoochee Tech Inst, Marietta, GA 30060	1961	NR	5	1,959	76
Chattahoochee Valley State Comm Coll, Phenix City, AL 36869-7928	1974	Dr. Richard Federinko	5	2,126	123
Chattanooga State Tech Comm Coll, Chattanooga, TN 37406-1018	1965	Dr. James L. Catanzaro	5	8,728	599
Chemeketa Comm Coll, Salem, OR 97309-7070	1955	Dr. Gerard Berger	11	9,812	881
Chesapeake Coll, Wye Mills, MD 21679-0008	1965	Dr. John R. Kotula	11	2,107	106
Chesterfield-Marlboro Tech Coll, Cheraw, SC 29520-1007	1967	Dr. Ronald W. Hampton	11	1,028	70
Chipola Jr Coll, Marianna, FL 32446-3065	1947	Dr. H. Dale O'Daniel	5	2,689	142
Chippewa Valley Tech Coll, Eau Claire, WI 54701-6120	1912	William A. Ihlenfeldt	9	3,800	400
Cincinnati State Tech and Comm Coll, Cincinnati, OH 45223-2690	1966	Dr. James P. Long	5	5,496	351
Cisco Jr Coll, Cisco, TX 76437-9321	1940	Dr. Roger C. Schustereit	11	2,690	98
Citrus Coll, Glendora, CA 91741-1899	1915	NR	11	10,489	389
City Colls of Chicago, Harold Washington Coll, Chicago, IL 60601-2420	1962	Ms. Nancy DeSombre	11	8,117	197
City Colls of Chicago, Harry S Truman Coll, Chicago, IL 60640-5616	1956	Dr. Donald B. Smith	11	5,175	160
City Colls of Chicago, Kennedy-King Coll, Chicago, IL 60621-3733	1935	Dr. Wayne Watson	11	2,421	106
City Colls of Chicago, Malcolm X Coll, Chicago, IL 60612-3145	1911	Ms. Zerrie D. Campbell	11	3,484	93
City Colls of Chicago, Olive-Harvey Coll, Chicago, IL 60628-1645	1970	Mr. Homer D. Franklin	11	3,306	97
City Colls of Chicago, Richard J Daley Coll, Chicago, IL 60652-1242	1960	Dr. Ted Martinez, Jr.	11	5,557	155
City Colls of Chicago, Wilbur Wright Coll, Chicago, IL 60634-1591	1934	Mr. Raymond F. LeFevour	11	6,949	161
Clackamas Comm Coll, Oregon City, OR 97045-7998	1966	Dr. John S. Keyser	8	6,354	459
Clark Coll, Vancouver, WA 98663-3598	1933	Dr. Earl P. Johnson	5	10,300	320
Clark State Comm Coll, Springfield, OH 45501-0570	1962	Mr. Albert A. Salerno	5	2,826	189
Clatsop Comm Coll, Astoria, OR 97103	1958	Dr. John W. Wubben	8	2,474	165
Cleveland Comm Coll, Shelby, NC 28150	1965	Dr. L. Steve Thornburg	5	1,642	92
Cleveland Inst of Electronics, Cleveland, OH 44114-3636 (2)	1934	Mr. John R. Drinko	3	2,300	5
Cleveland State Comm Coll, Cleveland, TN 37320-3570	1967	Dr. Owen Cargol	5	3,182	182
Clinton Comm Coll, Clinton, IA 52732-6299	1946	Ms. Karen Vickers	5	1,274	75
Clinton Comm Coll, Plattsburgh, NY 12901-9573	1969	Dr. Jay L. Fennell	11	2,117	179

Name, address	Year	Governing official, control		Enroll-ment	Faculty
Cloud County Comm Coll, Concordia, KS 66901-1002	1965	Dr. James P. Ihrig	11	3,112	218
Clovis Comm Coll, Clovis, NM 88101-8381	1971	Dr. Jay Gurley	5	3,328	NR
Coastal Carolina Comm Coll, Jacksonville, NC 28546-6877	1964	Dr. Ronald K. Lingle, Jr.	11	3,285	195
Coastline Comm Coll, Fountain Valley, CA 92708-2597	1976	Dr. Leslie N. Purdy	11	13,760	437
Cochise Coll, Douglas, AZ 85607-9724	1962	Dr. Walter S. Patton	11	1,341	88
Cochise Coll, Douglas, AZ 85607-9724	1977	NR	11	2,955	253
Coffeyville Comm Coll, Coffeyville, KS 67337-5063	1923	Dr. Ronald E. Thomas	11	2,300	86
Colby Comm Coll, Colby, KS 67701-4099	1964	Dr. Mikel Ary	11	1,095	63
Coll of Alameda, Alameda, CA 94501-2109	1970	Dr. Edward J. Veleau	11	5,597	NR
Coll of DuPage, Glen Ellyn, IL 60137	1967	Dr. Michael T. Murphy	11	31,132	1,842
Coll of Eastern Utah, Price, UT 84501-2699	1937	Dr. Michael A. Petersen	5	3,123	122
Coll of Lake County, Grayslake, IL 60030-1198	1967	Dr. Gretchen J. Naff	9	14,994	822
Coll of Marin, Kentfield, CA 94904	1926	Dr. James E. Middleton	11	8,845	464
Coll of St Catherine–Minneapolis, Minneapolis, MN 55454-1494	1964	Dr. Anita M. Pampusch	2	1,232	156
Coll of San Mateo, San Mateo, CA 94402-3784	1922	Mr. Peter Landsberger	11	12,000	476
Coll of Southern Idaho, Twin Falls, ID 83303-1238	1964	Mr. Gerald R. Meyerhoeffer	11	3,804	248
Coll of The Albemarle, Elizabeth City, NC 27906-2327	1960	Dr. Larry R. Donnithorne	5	2,033	118
Coll of the Canyons, Santa Clarita, CA 91355-1899	1969	Dr. Dianne G. Van Hook	11	6,250	258
Coll of the Desert, Palm Desert, CA 92260-9305	1959	Dr. David A. George	11	9,753	320
Coll of the Mainland, Texas City, TX 77591-2499	1967	Mr. Larry L. Stanley	11	4,013	180
Coll of the Redwoods, Eureka, CA 95501-9300	1964	Dr. Cedric A. Sampson	11	6,968	376
Coll of the Sequoias, Visalia, CA 93277-2234	1925	Dr. M. Douglas Kechter	11	8,771	443
Coll of the Siskiyous, Weed, CA 96094-2899	1957	Dr. Martha Romero	11	2,835	146
Collin County Comm Coll, McKinney, TX 75070-2906	1985	NR	11	9,865	540
Colorado Inst of Art, Denver, CO 80203-2903	1952	Mr. Elliott B. Jones, Sr.	3	1,368	112
Columbia Basin Coll, Pasco, WA 99301-3397	1955	Dr. Lee R. Thornton	5	7,382	350
Columbia Coll, Sonora, CA 95370	1968	Dr. Kenneth White	11	3,618	121
Columbia-Greene Comm Coll, Hudson, NY 12534-0327	1969	Dr. Terry A. Cline	11	1,711	115
Columbia State Comm Coll, Columbia, TN 38402-1315	1966	Dr. Paul Sands	5	2,541	178
Columbus State Comm Coll, Columbus, OH 43216-1609	1963	Dr. Harold M. Nestor	5	17,042	842
Comm Coll of Allegheny County Allegheny Cmps, Pittsburgh, PA 15212-6003	1966	Dr. J. David Griffin	8	6,163	564
Comm Coll of Allegheny County Boyce Cmps, Monroeville, PA 15146-1348	1966	Dr. Jacqueline D. Taylor	8	3,971	358
Comm Coll of Allegheny County North Cmps, Pittsburgh, PA 15237-5353	1972	Dr. Patricia A. McDonald	8	4,494	563
Comm Coll of Allegheny County South Cmps, West Mifflin, PA 15122-3029	1967	Dr. Thomas A. Juravich	8	4,890	394
Comm Coll of Aurora, Aurora, CO 80011-9036	1983	Dr. Larry Carter	5	4,670	197
Comm Coll of Beaver County, Monaca, PA 15061-2588	1966	Dr. Margaret Williams-Betlyn	5	2,635	150
Comm Coll of Denver, Denver, CO 80217-3363	1970	Dr. Byron McClenney	5	11,897	271
Comm Coll of Philadelphia, Philadelphia, PA 19130-3991	1964	Dr. Frederick W. Capshaw	11	18,713	1,182
Comm Coll of Rhode Island, Warwick, RI 02886-1807	1964	Mr. Edward Liston	5	12,265	697
Comm Coll of Southern Nevada, North Las Vegas, NV 89030-4296	1971	Dr. Richard Moore	5	16,718	925
Comm Coll of the Air Force, Maxwell Air Force Base, AL 36112-6655	1972	Col. Paul A. Reid	4	121,495	6,028
Comm Coll of Vermont, Waterbury, VT 05676-0120	1970	Barbara Murphy	5	2,922	496
Compton Comm Coll, Compton, CA 90221-5393	1927	Dr. Byron R. Skinner	11	5,700	347
Connors State Coll, Warner, OK 74469-9700	1908	Dr. Ronald D. Garner	5	2,416	113
Contra Costa Coll, San Pablo, CA 94806-3195	1948	Dr. D. Candy Rose	11	7,052	222
Copiah-Lincoln Comm Coll, Wesson, MS 39191-0457	1928	Dr. Billy B. Thames	11	1,705	116
Corning Comm Coll, Corning, NY 14830-3297	1956	Dr. Eduardo J. Marti	11	3,957	179
Cosumnes River Coll, Sacramento, CA 95823-5799	1970	Dr. Merilee R. Lewis	9	11,245	425
County Coll of Morris, Randolph, NJ 07869-2086	1966	Dr. Edward J. Yaw	8	9,627	481
Cowley County Comm Coll and Voc-Tech Sch, Arkansas City, KS 67005-2662	1922	Dr. Patrick J. McAtee	11	2,856	184
Crafton Hills Coll, Yucaipa, CA 92399-1799	1972	Dr. Luis S. Gomez	11	5,041	183
Craven Comm Coll, New Bern, NC 28562-4984	1965	Dr. Lewis S. Redd	5	2,391	211
Crowder Coll, Neosho, MO 64850-9160	1963	Dr. Kent A. Farnsworth	11	1,702	147
Cuesta Coll, San Luis Obispo, CA 93403-8106	1964	Dr. Grace N. Mitchell	9	7,917	292
Culinary Inst of America, Hyde Park, NY 12538-1499	1946	Mr. Ferdinand E. Metz	1	2,874	124
Cumberland County Coll, Vineland, NJ 08360-0517	1963	Dr. Roland J. Chapdelaine	11	2,783	118
Cuyahoga Comm Coll, Eastern Cmps, Highland Hills, OH 44122-6104	1971	Dr. Lawrence Simpson	11	5,602	234
Cuyahoga Comm Coll, Metropolitan Cmps, Cleveland, OH 44115-3123	1963	Dr. Alex Johnson	11	6,594	474
Cuyahoga Comm Coll, Western Cmps, Parma, OH 44130-5199	1966	Mr. Ronald M. Sobel	11	13,078	536
Cuyamaca Coll, El Cajon, CA 92019-4304	1978	Dr. Sherrill L. Amador	5	4,377	NR
Cypress Coll, Cypress, CA 90630-5897	1966	Dr. Christine Johnson	11	14,142	434
Dabney S Lancaster Comm Coll, Clifton Forge, VA 24422	1964	Dr. Richard R. Teaff	5	1,622	160
Dalton Coll, Dalton, GA 30720-3797	1963	Dr. James A. Burran	5	3,005	109
Danville Area Comm Coll, Danville, IL 61832-5199	1946	Dr. Harry J. Braun	11	3,429	143
Danville Comm Coll, Danville, VA 24541-4088	1967	Dr. B. Carlyle Ramsey	5	3,785	144
Darton Coll, Albany, GA 31707-3098	1965	Dr. Peter J. Sireno	5	2,657	150
Davidson County Comm Coll, Lexington, NC 27293-1287	1958	Dr. J. Bryan Brooks	11	2,277	136
Daytona Beach Comm Coll, Daytona Beach, FL 32120-2811	1958	NR	5	12,274	785
Dean Coll, Franklin, MA 02038-1941	1865	Dr. Paula M. Rooney	1	2,172	126
De Anza Coll, Cupertino, CA 95014-5793	1967	Dr. Martha J. Kanter	11	22,915	1,179
DeKalb Coll, Decatur, GA 30034-3897	1964	Dr. Jacquelyn Belcher	5	16,349	1,038
Delaware County Comm Coll, Media, PA 19063-1094	1967	Dr. Richard D. De Cosmo	11	10,127	486
Delaware Tech & Comm Coll, Stanton/Wilmington Cmps, Newark, DE 19702	1968	Dr. Orlando J. George, Jr.	5	6,424	348
Delaware Tech & Comm Coll, Terry Cmps, Dover, DE 19904	1972	Dr. Marguerite M. Johnson	5	1,847	105
Delaware Tech & Comm Coll, Jack F Owens Cmps, Georgetown, DE 19947	1967	Dr. G. Timothy Kavel	5	3,110	159
Delgado Comm Coll, New Orleans, LA 70119-4399	1921	Dr. Ione Elioff	5	14,845	1,015
Del Mar Coll, Corpus Christi, TX 78404-3897	1935	Dr. Terry L. Dicianna	11	10,757	514
Delta Coll, University Center, MI 48710	1961	Dr. Peter D. Boyse	9	10,446	515
Des Moines Area Comm Coll, Ankeny, IA 50021-8995	1966	Dr. Joseph Borgen	11	11,034	NR
DeVry Tech Inst, Woodbridge, NJ 07095-1407	1969	NR	3	2,180	81
Diablo Valley Coll, Pleasant Hill, CA 94523-1544	1949	Dr. Phyllis L. Peterson	11	20,000	800
Dixie Coll, St George, UT 84770-3876	1911	Dr. Robert Huddleston	5	3,016	109
Dodge City Comm Coll, Dodge City, KS 67801-2399	1935	Dr. Thomas E. Gamble	11	2,260	163
Doña Ana Branch Comm Coll, Las Cruces, NM 88003-8001	1973	NR	11	3,768	158
Dundalk Comm Coll, Baltimore, MD 21222-4694	1970	Dr. Harold D. McAninch	8	3,444	224

Name, address	Year	Governing official, control		Enroll-ment	Faculty
Durham Tech Comm Coll, Durham, NC 27703-5023............	1961	Dr. Phail Wynn, Jr..................	5	4,859	410
Dutchess Comm Coll, Poughkeepsie, NY 12601-1595..........	1957	Dr. D. David Conklin...............	11	6,643	432
Dyersburg State Comm Coll, Dyersburg, TN 38024	1969	Dr. Karen A. Bowyer	5	2,155	153
East Arkansas Comm Coll, Forrest City, AR 72335-9598........	1974	Dr. George McCormick.............	5	1,303	89
East Central Coll, Union, MO 63084-0529...................	1968	Dr. Dale Gibson	9	2,971	155
East Central Comm Coll, Decatur, MS 39327-0129...........	1928	Dr. Eddie M. Smith	11	1,482	85
Eastern Arizona Coll, Thatcher, AZ 85552-0769.............	1888	Mr. Gherald L. Hoopes, Jr.	11	1,817	248
Eastern New Mexico U–Roswell, Roswell, NM 88202-6000......	1958	Dr. Loyd R. Hughes...............	5	2,825	150
Eastern Oklahoma State Coll, Wilburton, OK 74578-4999	1908	NR	5	2,474	52
Eastern Wyoming Coll, Torrington, WY 82240-1699	1948	Dr. Jack L. Bottenfield............	11	1,641	136
Eastfield Coll, Mesquite, TX 75150-2099..................	1970	Dr. Robert Aguero	11	8,716	NR
East Los Angeles Coll, Monterey Park, CA 91754-6001	1945	Mr. Ernest H. Moreno	11	13,423	450
East Mississippi Comm Coll, Scooba, MS 39358-0158.........	1927	Dr. Thomas L. Davis	11	1,363	70
Edgecombe Comm Coll, Tarboro, NC 27886-9399	1968	Dr. Hartwell H. Fuller, Jr.	11	1,922	135
Edison Comm Coll, Fort Myers, FL 33906-6210..............	1962	Dr. Kenneth Walker...............	11	9,836	724
Edison State Comm Coll, Piqua, OH 45356-9253	1973	Dr. Kenneth A. Yowell	5	3,297	183
Edmonds Comm Coll, Lynnwood, WA 98036-5999	1967	Dr. Carl Opgaard.................	11	8,525	381
Elaine P Nunez Comm Coll, Chalmette, LA 70043-1249	1992	Dr. Carol S. Hopson	5	1,467	112
El Camino Coll, Torrance, CA 90506-0001	1947	Dr. Sam Schauerman	9	25,260	533
El Centro Coll, Dallas, TX 75202-3604....................	1966	Dr. Wright L. Lassiter, Jr.	8	6,328	331
Elgin Comm Coll, Elgin, IL 60123-7193	1949	Dr. Roy Flores...................	11	9,085	460
El Paso Comm Coll, El Paso, TX 79998-0500	1969	Dr. Adriana Barrera	8	22,264	1,098
Enterprise State Jr Coll, Enterprise, AL 36331-1300	1965	Dr. Stafford L. Thompson..........	5	1,943	125
Erie Comm Coll, City Cmps, Buffalo, NY 14203-2601.........	1971	Dr. Louis M. Ricci................	11	3,594	241
Erie Comm Coll, North Cmps, Williamsville, NY 14221-7095.....	1946	Dr. Louis M. Ricci................	11	6,868	392
Erie Comm Coll, South Cmps, Orchard Park, NY 14127-2199 ...	1974	Dr. Louis M. Ricci................	11	3,427	316
Essex Comm Coll, Baltimore, MD 21237-3899...............	1957	Dr. Donald J. Slowinski............	11	9,653	536
Eugenio María de Hostos Comm Coll of City U of NY, Bronx, NY 10451................	1968	Dr. Isaura Santiago	11	5,291	315
Everett Comm Coll, Everett, WA 98201-1327	1941	Dr. Susan C. Carroll	5	6,922	268
Evergreen Valley Coll, San Jose, CA 95135-1598	1975	NR	11	9,799	275
Fayetteville Tech Comm Coll, Fayetteville, NC 28303-0236	1961	Dr. Craig Allen...................	5	7,407	401
Fergus Falls Comm Coll, Fergus Falls, MN 56537-1009	1960	Mr. Dan F. True...................	5	1,420	63
Finger Lakes Comm Coll, Canandaigua, NY 14424-8395	1965	Dr. Daniel T. Hayes	11	4,075	234
Fiorello H LaGuardia Comm Coll of City U of NY, Long Island City, NY 11101-3071	1970	Dr. Raymond C. Bowen	11	10,923	914
Flathead Valley Comm Coll, Kalispell, MT 59901-2622.........	1967	Dr. David Beyer	11	1,658	112
Florence-Darlington Tech Coll, Florence, SC 29501-0548	1963	Dr. Charles W. Gould	5	3,025	201
Florida Comm Coll at Jacksonville, Jacksonville, FL 32202-4030 .	1963	Dr. Charles C. Spence	5	19,630	1,533
Florida Keys Comm Coll, Key West, FL 33040-4397...........	1965	Dr. William A. Seeker	5	2,200	94
Florida National Coll, Hialeah, FL 33012		NR	3	1,000	70
Floyd Coll, Rome, GA 30162-1864	1970	Dr. H. Lynn Cundiff	5	2,981	66
Foothill Coll, Los Altos Hills, CA 94022-4599	1958	Dr. Bernadine Chuck Fong	11	16,147	578
Forsyth Tech Comm Coll, Winston-Salem, NC 27103-5197......	1964	Dr. Desna L. Wallin	5	4,947	535
Fort Scott Comm Coll, Fort Scott, KS 66701................	1919	Dr. Laura Meeks..................	11	1,694	59
Fox Valley Tech Coll, Appleton, WI 54913-2277	1967	Dr. H. Victor Baldi	11	6,370	1,241
Frank Phillips Coll, Borger, TX 79008-5118................	1948	Dr. William A. Griffin	11	1,146	93
Frederick Comm Coll, Frederick, MD 21702-2097	1957	Dr. Lee J. Betts..................	11	4,336	267
Fresno City Coll, Fresno, CA 93741-0002.................	1910	Dr. Brice W. Harris...............	9	18,598	832
Front Range Comm Coll, Westminster, CO 80030-2105.........	1968	Dr. Thomas Gonzales	5	10,742	517
Fullerton Coll, Fullerton, CA 92632-2095.................	1913	Dr. Vera M. Martinez	11	18,708	678
Fulton-Montgomery Comm Coll, Johnstown, NY 12095-3790	1964	Dr. Priscilla J. Bell	11	1,787	94
Gadsden State Comm Coll, Gadsden, AL 35902-0227..........	1985	NR	5	5,754	NR
Gainesville Coll, Gainesville, GA 30503-1358	1964	Dr. J. Foster Watkins.............	5	2,642	102
Galveston Coll, Galveston, TX 77550-7496................	1967	NR	11	2,461	121
Garden City Comm Coll, Garden City, KS 67846-6399.........	1919	Dr. James H. Tangeman	9	2,219	147
Garland County Comm Coll, Hot Springs, AR 71914-3470.......	1973	NR	11	2,020	100
Gaston Coll, Dallas, NC 28034-1499....................	1963	Dr. Patricia Skinner	11	4,037	363
Gateway Comm Coll, Phoenix, AZ 85034-1795..............	1968	Dr. Phil Randolph.................	11	6,046	253
Gateway Comm-Tech Coll, New Haven, CT 06511-5918	1968	Dr. Antonio Perez	5	5,005	299
Gateway Tech Coll, Kenosha, WI 53144-1690	1911	Dr. Carole Johnson	11	10,568	850
Gavilan Coll, Gilroy, CA 95020-9599.....................	1919	Dr. Glenn E. Mayle	11	4,029	164
Genesee Comm Coll, Batavia, NY 14020-9704	1966	Dr. Stuart Steiner	11	4,435	291
George Corley Wallace State Comm Coll, Selma, AL 36702-1049.................	1966	Dr. Julius Ray Brown..............	5	1,847	78
George C Wallace State Comm Coll, Dothan, AL 36303	1949	Dr. Larry Beaty	5	4,000	180
Georgia Military Coll, Milledgeville, GA 31061..............	1879	Maj Gen. Peter J. Boylam, Jr........	11	3,949	179
Germanna Comm Coll, Locust Grove, VA 22508-0339	1970	Dr. Francis S. Turnage	5	2,596	135
Glendale Comm Coll, Glendale, AZ 85302-3090.............	1965	Dr. John R. Waltrip	11	18,033	687
Glendale Comm Coll, Glendale, CA 91208-2894.............	1927	Dr. John A. Davitt.................	11	15,337	345
Glen Oaks Comm Coll, Centreville, MI 49032-9719............	1965	Dr. Philip G. Ward	11	1,211	114
Gloucester County Coll, Sewell, NJ 08080	1967	Dr. Richard H. Jones..............	8	5,292	215
Gogebic Comm Coll, Ironwood, MI 49938.................	1932	Mr. Thomas J. Cuengros	11	1,300	91
Golden West Coll, Huntington Beach, CA 92647-2748	1966	Dr. Philip Westin.................	11	13,094	421
Gordon Coll, Barnesville, GA 30204-1762	1852	Dr. Jerry M. Williamson	5	2,241	121
Grand Rapids Comm Coll, Grand Rapids, MI 49503-3201.......	1914	Mr. Richard Calkins...............	9	13,726	554
Grays Harbor Coll, Aberdeen, WA 98520-7599	1930	Dr. Jewell Manspeaker	5	2,815	87
Grayson County Coll, Denison, TX 75020-8299	1964	Dr. Jim M. Williams	11	3,286	176
Great Lakes Jr Coll of Business, Saginaw, MI 48607-1158	1907	NR	1	1,778	130
Greenfield Comm Coll, Greenfield, MA 01301-9739	1962	Mr. Lawrence A. Dean	5	1,863	131
Green River Comm Coll, Auburn, WA 98092-3699	1965	Mr. Richard A. Rutkowski..........	5	9,200	342
Greenville Tech Coll, Greenville, SC 29606-5616............	1962	Dr. Thomas E. Barton, Jr.	5	8,734	539
Grossmont Coll, El Cajon, CA 92020-1799	1961	Dr. Richard M. Sanchez	11	14,500	600
Guilford Tech Comm Coll, Jamestown, NC 27282-0309	1958	Dr. Don Cameron.................	11	7,550	539
Gulf Coast Comm Coll, Panama City, FL 32401-1058..........	1957	Dr. Robert L. McSpadden	5	6,991	355
Gwinnett Tech Inst, Lawrenceville, GA 30246-1505	1984	NR	5	3,096	84
Hagerstown Jr Coll, Hagerstown, MD 21742-6590	1946	Dr. Norman P. Shea	8	3,035	177
Halifax Comm Coll, Weldon, NC 27890-0809................	1967	Dr. Elton L. Newbern, Jr.	11	1,360	68
Harford Comm Coll, Bel Air, MD 21015-1698...............	1957	Dr. Claudia E. Chiesi..............	11	5,304	382
Harrisburg Area Comm Coll, Harrisburg, PA 17110-2999	1964	Dr. Mary L. Fifield................	11	10,904	560
Hartnell Coll, Salinas, CA 93901-1697	1920	Dr. Edward J. Valeau..............	9	6,754	363
Hawkeye Comm Coll, Waterloo, IA 50704-8015..............	1967	Dr. Phillip O. Barry...............	11	3,426	283
Haywood Comm Coll, Clyde, NC 28721-9453	1964	Dr. Dan W. Moore	11	1,281	120
Heartland Comm Coll, Bloomington, IL 61701	1990	NR	9	2,769	191

Name, address	Year	Governing official, control		Enrollment	Faculty
Henry Ford Comm Coll, Dearborn, MI 48128-1495	1938	Dr. Andrew A. Mazzara	9	14,235	994
Herkimer County Comm Coll, Herkimer, NY 13350	1966	Dr. Ronald F. Williams	11	2,542	143
Hesser Coll, Manchester, NH 03103-7245	1900	Mr. Linwood W. Galeucia	3	3,000	60
Hibbing Comm Coll, Hibbing, MN 55746-3300	1916	Dr. Anthony Kuznik	5	1,060	65
Highland Comm Coll, Freeport, IL 61032-9341	1962	Dr. Ruth Mercedes Smith	11	2,679	159
Highland Comm Coll, Highland, KS 66035-0068	1858	Dr. Betty Stevens	11	2,600	182
Highline Comm Coll, Des Moines, WA 98198-9800	1961	Dr. Edward M. Command	5	10,300	432
Hill Coll of the Hill Jr Coll District, Hillsboro, TX 76645-0619	1923	Dr. W. R. Auvenshine	9	2,000	80
Hillsborough Comm Coll, Tampa, FL 33631-3127	1968	Dr. Andreas A. Paloumpis	5	19,094	691
Hinds Comm Coll, Raymond, MS 39154	1917	NR	11	9,191	695
Hocking Tech Coll, Nelsonville, OH 45764-9588	1968	Dr. John J. Light	5	5,995	253
Holmes Comm Coll, Goodman, MS 39079-0369	1928	NR	11	2,386	125
Holyoke Comm Coll, Holyoke, MA 01040-1099	1946	Dr. David M. Bartley	5	3,558	235
Horry-Georgetown Tech Coll, Conway, SC 29526	1965	Dr. D. Kent Sharples	11	2,814	215
Housatonic Comm-Tech Coll, Bridgeport, CT 06608-2453	1966	Dr. Vincent S. Darnowski	5	2,855	135
Houston Comm Coll System, Houston, TX 77270-7849	1971	Dr. Charles Green	11	45,893	2,352
Howard Coll, Big Spring, TX 79720-3702	1945	Dr. Cheryl T. Sparks	11	2,600	147
Howard Comm Coll, Columbia, MD 21044-3197	1966	Dr. Dwight A. Burrill	11	5,000	320
Hudson County Comm Coll, Jersey City, NJ 07306-4301	1974	NR	11	3,959	237
Hudson Valley Comm Coll, Troy, NY 12180-6096	1953	Dr. Joseph J. Bulmer	11	10,086	511
ICS Ctr for Degree Studies, Scranton, PA 18515	1975	Mr. Gary Keisling	3	20,363	5
Illinois Central Coll, East Peoria, IL 61635-0001	1967	Dr. Thomas K. Thomas	11	12,208	626
Illinois Eastern Comm Colls, Frontier Comm Coll, Fairfield, IL 62837-2601	1976	Mr. Richard Mason	11	2,093	158
Illinois Eastern Comm Colls, Lincoln Trail Coll, Robinson, IL 62454-9524	1969	Dr. John Arabatgis	11	1,115	77
Illinois Eastern Comm Colls, Olney Central Coll, Olney, IL 62450-1043	1962	Mr. Ed Covey	11	1,535	72
Illinois Eastern Comm Colls, Wabash Valley Coll, Mount Carmel, IL 62863-2657	1960	Dr. Harry K. Benson	11	2,075	78
Imperial Valley Coll, Imperial, CA 92251-0158	1922	Mr. William Sechrist	11	5,226	290
Independence Comm Coll, Independence, KS 67301-0708	1925	Dr. Don Schoening	5	1,848	153
Indiana Business Coll, Indianapolis, IN 46204-1108	1902	Mr. Kenneth J. Konesco	3	1,700	70
Indian Hills Comm Coll, Ottumwa, IA 52501-1398	1966	Dr. Lyle A. Hellyer	11	3,257	137
Indian River Comm Coll, Fort Pierce, FL 34981-5599	1960	Dr. Edwin R. Massey	5	6,697	577
Interboro Inst, New York, NY 10019-3602	1888	Mr. Bruce R. Kalish	3	1,101	53
Inver Hills Comm Coll, Inver Grove Heights, MN 55076-3209	1969	Dr. Steve Wallace	5	5,451	210
Iowa Central Comm Coll, Fort Dodge, IA 50501-5798	1966	Dr. Robert A. Paxton	11	2,200	105
Iowa Lakes Comm Coll, Estherville, IA 51334-2295	1967	Mr. James E. Billings	11	1,574	40
Iowa Western Comm Coll, Council Bluffs, IA 51502	1966	Dr. Dan Kinney	9	3,581	162
Irvine Valley Coll, Irvine, CA 92720-4399	1979	Dr. Daniel R. Larios	11	10,287	223
Isothermal Comm Coll, Spindale, NC 28160-0804	1965	Dr. Willard L. Lewis	5	1,579	92
Itasca Comm Coll, Grand Rapids, MN 55744	1922	Dr. James Clark	5	1,163	73
Itawamba Comm Coll, Fulton, MS 38843-1099	1947	Dr. David Cole	11	3,500	102
Ivy Tech State Coll–Central Indiana, Indianapolis, IN 46206-1763	1963	Dr. Meredith L. Carter	5	5,069	367
Ivy Tech State Coll–Columbus, Columbus, IN 47203-1868	1963	NR	5	2,926	179
Ivy Tech State Coll–Eastcentral, Muncie, IN 47302-9448	1968	Dr. Thomas C. Henry	5	2,152	251
Ivy Tech State Coll–Kokomo, Kokomo, IN 46901-2548	1968	Dr. Shanon Christiansen	5	1,554	159
Ivy Tech State Coll–Lafayette, Lafayette, IN 47903-6299	1968	Dr. Elizabeth J. Doversberger	5	2,067	137
Ivy Tech State Coll–Northcentral, South Bend, IN 46619-3837	1968	Dr. Carl F. Lutz	5	2,428	239
Ivy Tech State Coll–Northeast, Fort Wayne, IN 46805-1430	1969	Mr. Jon L. Rupright	5	3,479	292
Ivy Tech State Coll–Northwest, Gary, IN 46409-1499	1963	NR	5	2,335	210
Ivy Tech State Coll–Southcentral, Sellersburg, IN 47172-1829	1968	Mr. James R. Wells	5	1,918	144
Ivy Tech State Coll–Southwest, Evansville, IN 47710-3398	1963	NR	5	2,680	245
Ivy Tech State Coll–Wabash Valley, Terre Haute, IN 47802	1966	Dr. Sam E. Borden	5	2,312	167
Ivy Tech State Coll–Whitewater, Richmond, IN 47374-1220	1963	Mr. James Steck	5	1,122	115
Jackson Comm Coll, Jackson, MI 49201-8399	1928	Dr. Lee Howser	8	8,100	435
Jackson State Comm Coll, Jackson, TN 38301-3797	1967	Dr. Walter L. Nelms	5	3,315	182
James H Faulkner State Comm Coll, Bay Minette, AL 36507-2619	1965	Dr. Gary L. Branch	5	3,496	173
James Sprunt Comm Coll, Kenansville, NC 28349-0398	1964	Dr. Donald L. Reichard	5	1,000	99
Jamestown Comm Coll, Jamestown, NY 14701-1999	1950	Dr. Gregory T. DeCinque	11	4,110	NR
Jefferson Coll, Hillsboro, MO 63050-2441	1963	Dr. Gregory D. Adkins	11	4,220	190
Jefferson Comm Coll, Watertown, NY 13601	1961	Dr. John W. Deans	11	2,593	217
Jefferson Comm Coll, Steubenville, OH 43952-3598	1966	Dr. Edward L. Florak	11	1,528	114
Jefferson State Comm Coll, Birmingham, AL 35215-3098	1965	Dr. Judy M. Merritt	5	6,749	317
John A Logan Coll, Carterville, IL 62918	1967	Dr. Ray Hancock	11	4,889	246
John C Calhoun State Comm Coll, Decatur, AL 35609-2216	1965	Dr. Richard Carpenter	5	7,899	422
John M Patterson State Tech Coll, Montgomery, AL 36116-2699	1962	Mr. J. L. Taunton	5	1,073	41
Johnson County Comm Coll, Overland Park, KS 66210-1299	1967	Dr. Charles J. Carlsen	11	15,035	694
Johnston Comm Coll, Smithfield, NC 27577-2350	1969	Dr. John L. Tart	5	2,848	254
John Tyler Comm Coll, Chester, VA 23831	1967	Dr. Marshall W. Smith	5	5,882	237
John Wood Comm Coll, Quincy, IL 62301-9147	1974	Dr. Robert C. Keys	9	2,500	143
Joliet Jr Coll, Joliet, IL 60436-9352	1901	Dr. Raymond A. Pietak	11	10,369	496
Jones County Jr Coll, Ellisville, MS 39437-3901	1928	Dr. T. Terrell Tisdale	11	4,351	168
J Sargeant Reynolds Comm Coll, Richmond, VA 23285-5622	1972	Dr. S. A. Burnette	5	9,642	599
Kalamazoo Valley Comm Coll, Kalamazoo, MI 49003-4070	1966	Dr. Marilyn J. Schlack	11	9,202	387
Kankakee Comm Coll, Kankakee, IL 60901-0888	1966	Dr. Larry D. Huffman	11	3,629	222
Kansas City Kansas Comm Coll, Kansas City, KS 66112-3003	1923	Dr. Thomas R. Burke	11	6,142	388
Kaskaskia Coll, Centralia, IL 62801-7878	1966	Dr. Alice Marie Mumaw	11	3,247	227
Kellogg Comm Coll, Battle Creek, MI 49017-3306	1956	Dr. Paul R. Ohm	11	9,108	253
Kent State U, Ashtabula Cmps, Ashtabula, OH 44004-2299	1958	Dr. John K. Mahan	5	1,100	74
Kent State U, Stark Cmps, Canton, OH 44720-7599	1967	Dr. William G. Bittle	5	2,461	107
Kent State U, Trumbull Cmps, Warren, OH 44483-1998	1954	Dr. David A. Allen, Jr.	5	2,010	100
Kent State U, Tuscarawas Cmps, New Philadelphia, OH 44663-9447	1962	NR	5	1,167	83
Kilgore Coll, Kilgore, TX 75662-3299	1935	NR	11	4,351	260
Kingsborough Comm Coll of City U of NY, Brooklyn, NY 11235	1963	Dr. Leon M. Goldstein	11	15,518	648
Kings River Comm Coll, Reedley, CA 93654-2099	1926	Dr. Richard J. Giese	11	6,500	221
Kirkwood Comm Coll, Cedar Rapids, IA 52406-2068	1966	Dr. Norm Nielsen	11	9,752	456
Kirtland Comm Coll, Roscommon, MI 48653-9699	1966	Dr. Dorothy N. Franke	9	1,352	95
Kishwaukee Coll, Malta, IL 60150	1967	Dr. Norman L. Jenkins	11	3,407	70
Labette Comm Coll, Parsons, KS 67357-4299	1923	Mr. Joseph C. Birmingham	11	2,598	261

Name, address	Year	Governing official, control		Enroll-ment	Faculty
Lake Area Vocational-Tech Inst, Watertown, SD 57201	1964	NR	5	1,030	65
Lake City Comm Coll, Lake City, FL 32025	1962	Dr. Muriel Kay Heimer	5	3,038	225
Lake Land Coll, Mattoon, IL 61938-9366	1966	Dr. Robert K. Luther	11	4,831	271
Lakeland Comm Coll, Kirtland, OH 44094-5198	1967	Dr. Ralph R. Doty	11	8,698	544
Lakeshore Tech Coll, Cleveland, WI 53015-1414	1967	Dr. Dennis Ladwig	11	2,500	336
Lake-Sumter Comm Coll, Leesburg, FL 34788-8751	1962	Dr. Robert Westrick	11	2,394	117
Lake Tahoe Comm Coll, South Lake Tahoe, CA 96150-4524	1975	Dr. Guy F. Lease	11	2,500	121
Lakewood Comm Coll, White Bear Lake, MN 55110-5697	1967	Dr. James M. Meznek	5	6,251	189
Lamar U–Orange, Orange, TX 77630-5899	1969	Dr. J. Michael Shahan	5	1,473	63
Lamar U–Port Arthur, Port Arthur, TX 77641-0310	1909	Dr. Sam Monroe	5	2,470	111
Lane Comm Coll, Eugene, OR 97405-0640	1964	Dr. Jerry Moskus	11	9,600	542
Laney Coll, Oakland, CA 94607-4893	1953	Mr. Odell Johnson	11	10,433	379
Lansing Comm Coll, Lansing, MI 48901-7210	1957	Dr. Abel B. Sykes, Jr.	11	16,816	1,085
Laramie County Comm Coll, Cheyenne, WY 82007-3299	1968	Dr. Charles Bohlen	8	4,272	255
Laredo Comm Coll, Laredo, TX 78040-4395	1946	Dr. Roger L. Worsley	11	7,019	297
Las Positas Coll, Livermore, CA 94550-7650	1988	NR	5	5,100	NR
Lassen Coll, Susanville, CA 96130	1925	Dr. Dennis P. Adams	11	2,825	204
Lawson State Comm Coll, Birmingham, AL 35221-1798	1965	Dr. Perry W. Ward	5	1,942	111
Lee Coll, Baytown, TX 77522-0818	1934	Dr. Jackson N. Sasser	9	5,628	326
Lehigh Carbon Comm Coll, Schnecksville, PA 18078-2598	1967	Dr. James R. Davis	11	4,384	155
Lenoir Comm Coll, Kinston, NC 28501	1960	Dr. Lonnie H. Blizzard	5	2,069	163
Lewis and Clark Comm Coll, Godfrey, IL 62035-2466	1970	NR	9	5,534	305
Lima Tech Coll, Lima, OH 45804-3597	1971	Dr. James J. Countryman	5	2,583	167
Lincoln Land Comm Coll, Springfield, IL 62794-9256	1967	Dr. Norman Stephens, Jr.	9	9,486	245
Linn-Benton Comm Coll, Albany, OR 97321	1966	Mr. Jon Carnahan	11	5,649	617
Long Beach City Coll, Long Beach, CA 90808-1780	1927	Ms. Barbara A. Adams	5	27,000	763
Longview Comm Coll, Lee's Summit, MO 64081-2105	1969	Mr. Aldo W. Leker	11	8,353	409
Lorain County Comm Coll, Elyria, OH 44035	1963	Dr. Roy Church	11	7,753	339
Lord Fairfax Comm Coll, Middletown, VA 22645-0047	1969	Dr. Marilyn C. Beck	5	3,072	148
Los Angeles City Coll, Los Angeles, CA 90029-3590	1929	Mr. Jose Robledo	9	15,217	625
Los Angeles Harbor Coll, Wilmington, CA 90744-2311	1949	Mr. James L. Heinselman	11	7,837	350
Los Angeles Mission Coll, Sylmar, CA 91342-3200	1974	Dr. William Norcund, EdD	11	6,027	115
Los Angeles Pierce Coll, Woodland Hills, CA 91371-0001	1947	Dr. Mary E. Lee	11	16,987	519
Los Angeles Southwest Coll, Los Angeles, CA 90047-4810	1967	Dr. Carolyn G. Williams	11	5,802	223
Los Angeles Trade-Tech Coll, Los Angeles, CA 90015-4108	1925	Mr. Thomas L. Stevens, Jr.	11	13,076	600
Los Angeles Valley Coll, Van Nuys, CA 91401-4096	1949	Ms. Tyree Wieder	11	17,768	482
Los Medanos Coll, Pittsburg, CA 94565-5197	1974	Dr. Helen Spencer	9	7,191	236
Louisiana State U at Alexandria, Alexandria, LA 71302-9121	1960	Dr. Robert Cavanaugh	5	2,481	87
Louisiana State U at Eunice, Eunice, LA 70535-1129	1967	Dr. Michael Smith	5	2,861	120
Lower Columbia Coll, Longview, WA 98632-0310	1934	Dr. Vernon R. Pickett	5	4,091	160
Lurleen B Wallace State Jr Coll, Andalusia, AL 36420-1418	1969	Dr. Seth Hammett	5	1,159	60
Luzerne County Comm Coll, Nanticoke, PA 18634-9804	1966	Mr. Thomas J. Moran	8	7,001	584
Macomb Comm Coll, Warren, MI 48093-3896	1954	Dr. Albert L. Lorenzo	9	28,165	841
Macon Coll, Macon, GA 31297	1968	Dr. S. Aaron Hyatt	5	4,907	141
Madison Area Tech Coll, Madison, WI 53704-2599	1911	Dr. Beverly S. Simone	9	18,201	2,006
Manatee Comm Coll, Bradenton, FL 34206-7046	1957	Dr. Stephen J. Korcheck	5	7,911	311
Manchester Comm-Tech Coll, Manchester, CT 06045-1046	1963	Dr. Jonathan M. Daube	5	6,686	205
Maple Woods Comm Coll, Kansas City, MO 64156-1299	1969	Dr. Stephen R. Brainard	11	4,755	197
Marion Tech Coll, Marion, OH 43302-5694	1971	Dr. John Richard Bryson	12	1,800	105
Marshalltown Comm Coll, Marshalltown, IA 50158-4760	1927	Dr. William Simpson	9	1,266	107
Marymount Coll, Palos Verdes, California, Rancho Palos Verdes, CA 90275-6299	1932	Dr. Thomas M. McFadden	2	1,021	80
Massachusetts Bay Comm Coll, Wellesley Hills, MA 02181-5359	1961	Mr. Roger A. Van Winkle	5	5,033	291
Massasoit Comm Coll, Brockton, MA 02402-3996	1966	Dr. Gerard F. Burke	5	7,500	427
McCook Comm Coll, McCook, NE 69001-2631	1926	Dr. Robert G. Smallfoot	11	1,100	64
McHenry County Coll, Crystal Lake, IL 60012-2761	1967	Mr. Robert C. Bartlett	11	4,368	161
McIntosh Coll, Dover, NH 03820-3990	1896	NR	3	1,050	27
McLennan Comm Coll, Waco, TX 76708-1499	1965	Dr. Dennis F. Michaelis	8	5,540	284
Mendocino Coll, Ukiah, CA 95482-0300	1973	Dr. Carl J. Ehmann	11	3,400	169
Merced Coll, Merced, CA 95348-2898	1962	Dr. E. Jan Moser	11	6,616	421
Mercer County Comm Coll, Trenton, NJ 08690-1004	1966	Dr. Thomas Sepe	11	7,001	361
Meridian Comm Coll, Meridian, MS 39307	1937	Dr. William F. Scaggs	11	2,872	236
Merritt Coll, Oakland, CA 94619-3196	1953	Mr. Wise Allen	11	5,769	NR
Mesa Comm Coll, Mesa, AZ 85202-4866	1965	Dr. Larry K. Christiansen	11	20,622	852
Metropolitan Comm Coll, Omaha, NE 68103-0777	1974	Dr. J. Richard Gilliland	11	10,686	549
Miami-Dade Comm Coll, Miami, FL 33132-2296	1960	Dr. Robert H. McCabe	11	52,940	2,013
Miami U–Hamilton Cmps, Hamilton, OH 45011-3399	1968	Dr. Jack Rhodes	5	2,229	140
Miami U–Middletown Cmps, Middletown, OH 45042-3497	1966	Dr. Michael P. Governanti	5	2,251	165
Middle Georgia Coll, Cochran, GA 31014-1599	1884	Dr. Joe Ben Welch	5	2,167	82
Middlesex Comm Coll, Bedford, MA 01730-1655	1970	Dr. Carole A. Cowan	5	6,554	470
Middlesex Comm– Tech Coll, Middletown, CT 06457-4889	1966	Dr. Leila Gonzalez Sullivan	5	3,230	130
Middlesex County Coll, Edison, NJ 08818-3050	1964	Dr. Flora M. Edwards	8	12,500	287
Midland Coll, Midland, TX 79705-6399	1969	Dr. David E. Daniel	11	3,885	192
Midlands Tech Coll, Columbia, SC 29202-2408	1974	Dr. James L. Hudgins	11	9,356	673
Mid Michigan Comm Coll, Harrison, MI 48625-9447	1965	Dr. Charles J. Corrigan	11	3,304	227
Mid-Plains Comm Coll, North Platte, NE 69101-9420	1965	Dr. William A. Griffin, Jr.	9	2,024	91
Mid-State Tech Coll, Wisconsin Rapids, WI 54494-5599	1917	Mr. Brian Oehler	11	2,808	86
Milwaukee Area Tech Coll, Milwaukee, WI 53233-1443	1912	Dr. John R. Birkholz	9	23,099	1,759
Mineral Area Coll, Park Hills, MO 63601	1922	Dr. Dixie A. Kohn	9	2,588	154
Minneapolis Comm Coll, Minneapolis, MN 55403-1779	1965	Dr. Mary Retterer	5	4,498	225
MiraCosta Coll, Oceanside, CA 92056-3899	1934	Dr. Tim T. L. Dong	5	8,038	374
Mission Coll, Santa Clara, CA 95054-1897	1977	Dr. Michael Rao	11	9,540	376
Mississippi County Comm Coll, Blytheville, AR 72316-1109	1975	Dr. John P. Sullins	5	1,603	99
Mississippi Delta Comm Coll, Moorhead, MS 38761-0668	1926	Dr. Bobby Garvin	9	2,403	128
Mississippi Gulf Coast Comm Coll, Perkinston, MS 39573-0067	1911	Dr. Richard Miller	9	8,790	753
Mitchell Comm Coll, Statesville, NC 28677-5293	1852	Dr. Douglas O. Eason	5	1,526	90
Moberly Area Comm Coll, Moberly, MO 65270-1392	1927	Dr. Andrew Komar, Jr.	11	1,846	95
Modesto Jr Coll, Modesto, CA 95350-5800	1921	Dr. Maria Sheehan	11	8,510	477
Mohave Comm Coll, Kingman, AZ 86401-1299	1971	Dr. Charles W. Hall	5	5,216	349
Mohawk Valley Comm Coll, Utica, NY 13501-5394	1946	Dr. Michael I. Schafer	11	6,500	353
Monroe Coll, Bronx, NY 10468-5407	1933	Mr. Stephen J. Jerome	3	2,303	100
Monroe Comm Coll, Rochester, NY 14623-5780	1961	Dr. Peter A. Spina	11	13,731	660
Monroe County Comm Coll, Monroe, MI 48161-9047	1964	Mr. Gerald D. Welch	8	3,923	201
Montcalm Comm Coll, Sidney, MI 48885-0300	1965	Dr. Donald C. Burns	11	1,890	134
Monterey Peninsula Coll, Monterey, CA 93940-4799	1947	Dr. Edward Orest Gould	5	8,500	390
Montgomery Coll–Germantown Cmps, Germantown, MD 20876	1975	Dr. Robert E. Parilla	11	3,732	185
Montgomery Coll–Rockville Cmps, Rockville, MD 20850-1196	1965	Dr. Robert E. Parilla	11	13,623	705

Name, address	Year	Governing official, control		Enroll-ment	Faculty
Montgomery Coll–Takoma Park Cmps, Takoma Park, MD 20912.	1946	Dr. Robert E. Parilla	11	4,950	219
Montgomery County Comm Coll, Blue Bell, PA 19422-0796	1964	Dr. Edward M. Sweitzer	8	9,206	465
Moorpark Coll, Moorpark, CA 93021-1695.	1967	Dr. Darlene Pacheco	8	10,226	450
Moraine Park Tech Coll, Fond du Lac, WI 54936-1940	1967	Dr. John J. Shanahan	11	6,100	291
Moraine Valley Comm Coll, Palos Hills, IL 60465-0937	1967	Dr. Vernon O. Crawley	11	13,273	632
Morton Coll, Cicero, IL 60650-4398	1924	Dr. John A. Neuhaus	11	4,356	252
Motlow State Comm Coll, Tullahoma, TN 37388-8100	1969	Dr. A. Frank Glass	5	3,263	245
Mountain Empire Comm Coll, Big Stone Gap, VA 24219-0700	1972	Dr. Robert H. Sandel	5	2,800	133
Mountain View Coll, Dallas, TX 75211-6599	1970	Dr. Monique Amerman	8	6,093	268
Mt Hood Comm Coll, Gresham, OR 97030-3300	1966	Dr. Paul Kreider	11	7,742	549
Mount Ida Coll, Newton Centre, MA 02159-3310	1899	Dr. Bryan E. Carlson	1	1,848	206
Mt San Antonio Coll, Walnut, CA 91789-1399	1946	Dr. William H. Feddersen	9	22,571	799
Mt San Jacinto Coll, San Jacinto, CA 92583-2399	1963	Dr. Roy B. Mason, II	11	5,610	181
Mount Wachusett Comm Coll, Gardner, MA 01440-1000	1963	Dr. Daniel M. Asquino	5	1,900	112
Murray State Coll, Tishomingo, OK 73460-3130	1908	Dr. Glen Pedersen	5	1,532	69
Muscatine Comm Coll, Muscatine, IA 52761-5396	1929	Dr. Victor G. McAvoy	5	1,114	68
Muskingum Area Tech Coll, Zanesville, OH 43701-2694	1969	Dr. Lynn H. Willett	11	2,135	104
Napa Valley Coll, Napa, CA 94558-6236	1942	Dr. Diane E. Carey	11	6,094	297
Nash Comm Coll, Rocky Mount, NC 27804-0488	1967	Dr. J. Reid Parrott, Jr.	5	1,880	106
Nashville State Tech Inst, Nashville, TN 37209-4515.	1970	Dr. George H. Van Allen	5	6,302	294
Nassau Comm Coll, Garden City, NY 11530-6793	1959	Dr. Sean A. Fanelli	11	21,955	1,573
Naugatuck Valley Comm–Tech Coll, Waterbury, CT 06708-3000	1967	Dr. Richard L. Sanders	5	5,667	165
Navajo Comm Coll, Tsaile, AZ 86556	1968	Dr. Tommy Lewis, Jr.	4	2,019	156
Navarro Coll, Corsicana, TX 75110-4899	1946	Dr. Gerald Burson	11	3,246	175
Neosho County Comm Coll, Chanute, KS 66720-2699	1936	Dr. Theodore W. Wischropp	11	1,750	125
Newbury Coll, Brookline, MA 02146-5750	1962	Mr. Edward J. Tassinari	1	1,137	84
New England Inst of Tech, Warwick, RI 02886-2244	1940	Dr. Richard I. Gouse	1	2,131	168
New England Inst of Tech & Florida Culinary Inst, West Palm Beach, FL 33407-2384	1983	Mr. William Bennett	3	1,000	68
New Hampshire Tech Inst, Concord, NH 03301-7412	1964	Dr. David E. Larrabee, Sr.	5	1,551	145
New Mexico Jr Coll, Hobbs, NM 88240-9123	1965	Dr. Charles D. Hays	11	2,829	114
New Mexico State U–Alamogordo, Alamogordo, NM 88310	1958	Dr. Charles R. Reidlinger	5	2,113	109
New Mexico State U–Carlsbad, Carlsbad, NM 88220-3509	1950	Dr. Douglas E. Burghan	5	1,203	69
New River Comm Coll, Dublin, VA 24084-1127	1969	Dr. Edwin L. Barnes	5	1,641	169
Niagara County Comm Coll, Sanborn, NY 14132-9460	1962	Mr. Gerald L. Miller	11	5,702	453
Nicolet Area Tech Coll, Rhinelander, WI 54501-0518	1968	Dr. Adrian Lorbetske	11	1,700	84
Normandale Comm Coll, Bloomington, MN 55431-4399	1968	Dr. Thomas J. Horak	5	8,171	300
Northampton County Area Comm Coll, Bethlehem, PA 18017-7599	1967	Dr. Robert J. Kopecek	11	6,135	374
North Arkansas Comm/Tech Coll, Harrison, AR 72601	1974	Dr. Bill Baker	11	1,584	116
North Central Michigan Coll, Petoskey, MI 49770-8717	1958	Mr. Robert B. Graham	8	2,141	102
North Central Missouri Coll, Trenton, MO 64683-1824	1925	Dr. James Selby	9	1,142	70
North Central Tech Coll, Mansfield, OH 44901-0698	1961	Dr. Byron E. Kee	5	2,862	182
Northcentral Tech Coll, Wausau, WI 54401-1880	1912	Dr. Robert Ernst	9	4,881	211
North Central Texas Coll, Gainesville, TX 76240-4699	1924	Dr. Ronnie Glasscock	8	4,031	175
North Country Comm Coll, Saranac Lake, NY 12983-2046	1967	Dr. Gail Rogers Rice	11	1,823	140
North Dakota State Coll of Science, Wahpeton, ND 58076	1903	Dr. Jerry Olson	5	2,429	150
Northeast Alabama State Comm Coll, Rainsville, AL 35986-0159.	1963	Dr. Charles M. Pendley	5	1,686	51
Northeast Comm Coll, Norfolk, NE 68702-0469	1973	Dr. James C. Underwood	11	3,564	122
Northeastern Jr Coll, Sterling, CO 80751-2344	1941	NR	11	2,734	79
Northeastern Oklahoma A&M Coll, Miami, OK 74354-6434	1919	Dr. Jerry D. Carroll	5	2,600	133
Northeast Iowa Comm Coll, Peosta Cmps, Peosta, IA 52068-9776	1970	Ms. Karla Berns	11	1,450	66
Northeast Metro Tech Coll, White Bear Lake, MN 55110	1970	NR	5	1,800	95
Northeast State Tech Comm Coll, Blountville, TN 37617-0246	1966	Dr. R. Wade Powers	5	4,995	166
Northeast Texas Comm Coll, Mount Pleasant, TX 75456-1307	1985	NR	11	2,105	93
Northeast Wisconsin Tech Coll, Green Bay, WI 54307-9042	1913	Dr. Gerald D. Prindiville	11	8,594	310
Northern Essex Comm Coll, Haverhill, MA 01830	1960	Dr. John R. Dimitry	5	6,359	457
Northern Maine Tech Coll, Presque Isle, ME 04769-2016	1963	Dr. Durward Huffman	12	1,043	100
Northern New Mexico Comm Coll, Española, NM 87532	1909	Ms. Connie A. Valdez	5	1,601	154
Northern Oklahoma Coll, Tonkawa, OK 74653-0310	1901	Dr. Joe Kinzer	5	2,250	80
Northern Virginia Comm Coll, Annandale, VA 22003-3796	1965	Dr. Richard J. Ernst	5	38,531	1,452
North Florida Comm Coll, Madison, FL 32340-1602	1958	Mr. William O. Brazil	5	1,038	30
North Hennepin Comm Coll, Minneapolis, MN 55445-2231	1966	Dr. Katherine H. Sloan	5	5,750	220
North Idaho Coll, Coeur d'Alene, ID 83814-2199	1933	Dr. C. Robert Bennett	11	3,324	192
North Iowa Area Comm Coll, Mason City, IA 50401-7299	1918	Dr. David Buettner	11	2,878	107
North Lake Coll, Irving, TX 75038-3899	1977	Dr. James F. Horton, Jr.	8	6,800	280
Northland Pioneer Coll, Holbrook, AZ 86025-0610	1974	Dr. John H. Anderson	11	4,779	400
North Seattle Comm Coll, Seattle, WA 98103-3599	1970	Dr. Constance Rice	5	9,200	290
North Shore Comm Coll, Danvers, MA 01923-4093	1965	Dr. George Traicoff	5	4,600	NR
NorthWest Arkansas Comm Coll, Bentonville, AR 72712-1408	1989	NR	11	2,035	147
Northwest Coll, Powell, WY 82435-1898	1946	Dr. John P. Hanna	11	1,991	181
Northwestern Coll, Lima, OH 45805-1498	1920	Mr. Loren R. Jarvis	1	1,800	59
Northwestern Connecticut Comm-Tech Coll, Winsted, CT 06098	1965	Dr. R. Eileen Baccus	5	2,103	94
Northwestern Michigan Coll, Traverse City, MI 49686-3061	1951	Dr. Timothy G. Quinn	11	3,928	96
Northwest Indian Coll, Bellingham, WA 98226	1978	NR	4	1,200	73
Northwest Mississippi Comm Coll, Senatobia, MS 38668-1701	1927	Dr. David M. Haraway	11	4,200	180
Northwest-Shoals Comm Coll, Phil Campbell, AL 35581-9399	1961	Dr. Larry McCoy	5	2,049	83
Northwest State Comm Coll, Archbold, OH 43502-9542	1968	Dr. Larry G. McDougle	5	1,832	118
Norwalk Comm-Tech Coll, Norwalk, CT 06854-1655	1961	Dr. William H. Schwab	5	5,244	241
Oakland Comm Coll, Bloomfield Hills, MI 48304-2266	1964	Dr. Patsy J. Calkins	11	27,129	788
Oakton Comm Coll, Des Plaines, IL 60016-1268	1969	Dr. Thomas TenHoeve	9	11,254	495
Ocean County Coll, Toms River, NJ 08754-2001	1964	Dr. Milton Shaw	8	8,162	367
Odessa Coll, Odessa, TX 79764-7127	1946	Dr. Vance W. Gipson	11	4,500	238
Ohlone Coll, Fremont, CA 94539-5884	1967	Dr. Floyd M. Hogue	11	9,827	434
Okaloosa-Walton Comm Coll, Niceville, FL 32578-1295	1963	Dr. James R. Richburg	11	5,820	297
Oklahoma City Comm Coll, Oklahoma City, OK 73159-4419	1969	Dr. Bobby Gaines	5	11,185	342
Oklahoma State U, Oklahoma City, Oklahoma City, OK 73107-6120	1961	Dr. James Hooper	5	4,357	205
Oklahoma State U, Okmulgee, Okmulgee, OK 74447-3901	1946	Dr. Robert Klabenes	5	2,188	138
Olympic Coll, Bremerton, WA 98337-1699	1946	Dr. Wallace A. Simpson	5	6,536	323
Onondaga Comm Coll, Syracuse, NY 13215	1962	Dr. Bruce H. Leslie	5	7,400	536
Orangeburg-Calhoun Tech Coll, Orangeburg, SC 29115-8299	1968	Dr. Jeffery R. Olson	11	1,768	120
Orange Coast Coll, Costa Mesa, CA 92628-5005	1947	Mr. David A. Grant	11	25,208	878
Orange County Comm Coll, Middletown, NY 10940-6437	1950	Dr. William F. Messner	11	4,965	311
Otero Jr Coll, La Junta, CO 81050-3415	1941	Dr. Joe M. Treece	5	1,064	53

Name, address	Year	Governing official, control		Enrollment	Faculty
Owensboro Comm Coll, Owensboro, KY 42303-1899	1986	NR	5	2,614	124
Owens Comm Coll, Findlay, OH 45840	1983	NR	5	1,572	91
Owens Comm Coll, Toledo, OH 43699-1947	1966	NR	5	8,683	514
Oxnard Coll, Oxnard, CA 93033-6699	1975	Dr. Elise D. Schneider	8	6,500	288
Palm Beach Comm Coll, Lake Worth, FL 33461-4796	1933	Dr. Edward M. Eissey	5	16,679	656
Palo Alto Coll, San Antonio, TX 78224-2499	1987	NR	11	7,110	317
Palomar Coll, San Marcos, CA 92069-1487	1946	Dr. George R. Boggs	11	22,845	1,097
Palo Verde Coll, Blythe, CA 92225-1118	1947	Dr. Wilford J. Beumel	11	1,200	69
Panola Coll, Carthage, TX 75633	1947	Dr. W. F. Edmonson	11	1,600	80
Paradise Valley Comm Coll, Phoenix, AZ 85032-1200	1985	NR	11	5,235	224
Paris Jr Coll, Paris, TX 75460-6298	1924	Mr. Bobby R. Walters	11	2,450	117
Parkland Coll, Champaign, IL 61821-1899	1967	Dr. Zelema M. Harris	9	8,463	673
Pasadena City Coll, Pasadena, CA 91106-2041	1924	Dr. Jack A. Scott	9	21,756	824
Pasco-Hernando Comm Coll, Dade City, FL 33525-7599	1972	Dr. Robert W. Judson, Jr.	5	7,318	255
Passaic County Comm Coll, Paterson, NJ 07505-1179	1968	Mr. Elliott Collins	8	3,597	253
Patrick Henry Comm Coll, Martinsville, VA 24115-5311	1962	NR	5	2,449	88
Paul D Camp Comm Coll, Franklin, VA 23851-0737	1971	Dr. Jerome J. Friga	5	1,629	59
Pearl River Comm Coll, Poplarville, MS 39470	1909	Dr. Ted J. Alexander	11	2,727	167
Peirce Coll, Philadelphia, PA 19102-4603	1865	Dr. Arthur J. Lendo	1	1,200	57
Pellissippi State Tech Comm Coll, Knoxville, TN 37933-0990	1974	Dr. Allen G. Edwards	5	7,686	447
Peninsula Coll, Port Angeles, WA 98362-2779	1961	Dr. Wallace Sigmar	5	3,550	149
Pennsylvania Coll of Tech, Williamsport, PA 17701-5778	1965	Dr. Robert Breuder	12	4,781	330
Penn State U Abington-Ogontz Cmps, Abington, PA 19001-3918	1950	Dr. Karen Wiley Sandler	12	2,958	152
Penn State U Altoona Cmps, Altoona, PA 16601-3760	1929	Dr. Allen C. Meadors	12	2,468	132
Penn State U Berks Cmps, Reading, PA 19610-6009	1924	Dr. Frederick H. Gaige	12	1,723	103
Penn State U Delaware County Cmps, Media, PA 19063-5596	1966	Dr. Edward S. J. Tomezsko	12	1,416	81
Penn State U Hazleton Cmps, Hazleton, PA 18201-1291	1934	Dr. James J. Staudenmeier	12	1,211	78
Penn State U Mont Alto Cmps, Mont Alto, PA 17237-9703	1929	Dr. Corrinne A. Caldwell	12	1,111	60
Penn State U New Kensington Cmps, New Kensington, PA 15068-1798	1958	Dr. Katherine Gannon	12	1,040	68
Penn State U Schuylkill Cmps, Schuylkill Haven, PA 17972-2208	1934	Dr. Wayne Lammie	12	1,018	63
Penn State U Shenango Cmps, Sharon, PA 16146-1537	1965	Dr. Albert N. Skomra	12	1,103	76
Penn State U Worthington Scranton Cmps, Dunmore, PA 18512-1699	1923	Dr. James D. Gallagher	12	1,268	80
Penn State U York Cmps, York, PA 17403-3298	1926	Dr. Donald A. Gogniat	12	1,868	114
Penn Valley Comm Coll, Kansas City, MO 64111	1969	Dr. E. Paul Williams	11	5,023	424
Pensacola Jr Coll, Pensacola, FL 32504-8998	1948	Dr. Horace E. Hartsell	5	12,000	950
Phillips County Comm Coll, Helena, AR 72342-0785	1965	Dr. Steven Jones	11	1,494	107
Phoenix Coll, Phoenix, AZ 85013-4234	1920	Dr. Marie Pepicello	11	11,266	540
Piedmont Virginia Comm Coll, Charlottesville, VA 22902-8714	1972	Dr. Deborah M. DiCroce	5	4,316	262
Pierce Coll, Tacoma, WA 98498-1999	1967	Dr. George Delaney	5	8,159	542
Pikes Peak Comm Coll, Colorado Springs, CO 80906-5498	1968	Dr. Marijane Axtell Paulsen	5	6,747	417
Pima Comm Coll, Tucson, AZ 85709-1010	1966	Dr. Robert Jensen	5	27,960	1,567
Pitt Comm Coll, Greenville, NC 27835-7007	1961	Dr. Charles E. Russell	11	4,673	248
Polk Comm Coll, Winter Haven, FL 33881-4299	1964	Dr. Maryly VanLeer Peck	5	6,026	260
Porterville Coll, Porterville, CA 93257-6058	1927	Dr. Bonnie L. Rogers	5	2,778	128
Portland Comm Coll, Portland, OR 97280-0990	1961	Dr. Daniel F. Moriarty	11	34,028	1,215
Potomac State Coll of West Virginia U, Keyser, WV 26726	1901	Dr. Kathryn A. Brailer	5	1,056	83
Prairie State Coll, Chicago Heights, IL 60411-1275	1958	Dr. T. Lightfield	11	5,000	289
Pratt Comm Coll and Area Vocational Sch, Pratt, KS 67124-8317	1938	Dr. William Wojciechowski	9	1,291	54
Prince George's Comm Coll, Largo, MD 20772-2199	1958	Dr. Robert I. Bickford	8	12,201	554
Pueblo Comm Coll, Pueblo, CO 81004-1499	1979	Dr. Joe May	5	3,910	327
Queensborough Comm Coll of City U of NY, Bayside, NY 11364	1958	Dr. Kurt R. Schmeller	11	12,000	553
Quincy Coll, Quincy, MA 02169-4522	1958	Dr. Linda B. Wilson	10	2,331	69
Quinebaug Valley Comm-Tech Coll, Danielson, CT 06239-1440	1971	Ms. Dianne E. Williams	5	1,166	55
Quinsigamond Comm Coll, Worcester, MA 01606-2092	1963	Dr. Sandra Kurtinitis	5	4,558	238
Rancho Santiago Coll, Santa Ana, CA 92706-3398	1915	Dr. Vivian B. Blevins	5	26,379	2,210
Randolph Comm Coll, Asheboro, NC 27204-1009	1962	Dr. Larry K. Linker	5	1,477	73
Rappahannock Comm Coll, Glenns, VA 23149-0287	1970	Dr. John H. Upton	11	2,129	131
Raritan Valley Comm Coll, Somerville, NJ 08876-1265	1965	Dr. Cary A. Israel	8	4,445	276
Reading Area Comm Coll, Reading, PA 19603-1706	1971	Dr. Gust Zogas	8	3,233	249
Redlands Comm Coll, El Reno, OK 73036	1938	Dr. Larry F. Devane	5	2,041	159
Red Rocks Comm Coll, Lakewood, CO 80401	1969	Dr. Dorothy A. Horrell	5	6,952	276
Rend Lake Coll, Ina, IL 62846-9801	1967	Mr. Mark S. Kern	5	3,759	201
Richard Bland Coll of the Coll of William and Mary, Petersburg, VA 23805-7100	1961	Dr. Clarence Maze, Jr.	5	1,024	48
Richland Coll, Dallas, TX 75243-2199	1972	Dr. Stephen Mittelstet	11	13,391	665
Richland Comm Coll, Decatur, IL 62521-8513	1971	Dr. Charles R. Novak	9	3,801	213
Richmond Comm Coll, Hamlet, NC 28345-1189	1964	Mr. Joseph W. Grimsley	5	1,144	100
Ricks Coll, Rexburg, ID 83460-4107	1888	Dr. Steven D. Bennion	2	7,989	387
Rio Hondo Coll, Whittier, CA 90601-1699	1960	Mr. Tim Wood	11	14,500	710
Rio Salado Comm Coll, Phoenix, AZ 85003-1558	1978	Dr. Linda Thor	11	9,442	511
Riverside Comm Coll, Riverside, CA 92506-1293	1916	Dr. Salvatore Rotella	11	20,000	550
Roane State Comm Coll, Harriman, TN 37748-5011	1971	Dr. Sherry L. Hoppe	5	5,641	333
Robert Morris Coll of Chicago, Chicago, IL 60601-2501	1913	Mr. Michael Viollt	1	3,100	180
Robeson Comm Coll, Lumberton, NC 28359-1420	1965	Mr. Fred W. Williams, Jr.	5	1,322	114
Rochester Comm Coll, Rochester, MN 55904-4999	1915	Dr. Karen E. Nagle	5	3,926	225
Rockingham Comm Coll, Wentworth, NC 27375-0038	1964	Dr. N. J. Owens, Jr.	5	2,033	114
Rock Valley Coll, Rockford, IL 61114-5699	1964	Dr. Karl J. Jacobs	9	8,682	222
Rogers State Coll, Claremore, OK 74017-2099	1909	Dr. Richard H. Mosier	5	3,875	270
Rogue Comm Coll, Grants Pass, OR 97527-9298	1970	Dr. Harvey Bennett	11	2,839	279
Rose State Coll, Midwest City, OK 73110-2799	1968	Dr. Larry Nutter	11	9,083	471
Rowan-Cabarrus Comm Coll, Salisbury, NC 28145-1595	1963	Dr. Richard L. Brownell	5	3,500	130
Sacramento City Coll, Sacramento, CA 95822-1386	1916	Dr. Robert M. Harris	11	16,103	420
Saddleback Coll, Mission Viejo, CA 92692-3697	1967	NR	11	23,303	638
Saint Augustine Coll, Chicago, IL 60640-3501	1980	Fr. Carlos A. Plazas	1	1,346	150
Saint Charles County Comm Coll, St Peters, MO 63376-0975	1986	NR	5	4,567	227
St Clair County Comm Coll, Port Huron, MI 48061-5015	1923	Dr. R. Ernest Dear	8	4,629	263
St Cloud Tech Coll, St Cloud, MN 56303-1240	1948	NR	5	3,600	102
St Johns River Comm Coll, Palatka, FL 32177-3807	1958	Dr. R. L. McLendon, Jr.	5	3,500	157
St Louis Comm Coll at Florissant Valley, St Louis, MO 63135-1499	1963	Mr. Michael Maguire	9	8,804	405
St Louis Comm Coll at Forest Park, St Louis, MO 63110-1316	1962	Dr. Henry D. Shannon	9	8,365	373

Name, address	Year	Governing official, control		Enrollment	Faculty
St Louis Comm Coll at Meramec, Kirkwood, MO 63122-5720	1963	Mr. Richard A. Black	9	13,716	839
St Paul Tech Coll, St Paul, MN 55102-1800	1922	Dr. Donovan Schwichtenberg	11	3,401	565
St Petersburg Jr Coll, St Petersburg, FL 33733-3489	1927	Dr. Carl M. Kuttler, Jr.	11	23,488	861
St Philip's Coll, San Antonio, TX 78203-2098	1898	Dr. Charles A. Taylor	9	5,844	334
Salem Comm Coll, Carneys Point, NJ 08069-2799	1971	Dr. Linda C. Jolly	8	1,428	74
Salt Lake Comm Coll, Salt Lake City, UT 84130-0808	1948	Dr. Frank W. Budd	5	18,534	1,042
Sampson Comm Coll, Clinton, NC 28328-0318	1965	Dr. Clifton W. Paderick	11	1,086	102
San Antonio Coll, San Antonio, TX 78212-4299	1925	Dr. Ruth Burgos-Sasscer	11	19,908	847
San Bernardino Valley Coll, San Bernardino, CA 92410-2748	1926	Dr. Donald L. Singer	11	11,750	375
Sandhills Comm Coll, Pinehurst, NC 28374-8299	1963	Dr. John Dempsey	11	2,371	150
San Diego Mesa Coll, San Diego, CA 92111-4998	1964	Dr. Constance Carroll	9	22,586	676
San Diego Miramar Coll, San Diego, CA 92126-2999	1969	Dr. Louis C. Murillo	9	9,820	174
San Jacinto Coll–North Cmps, Houston, TX 77049-4599	1974	Dr. Edwin E. Lehr	11	3,913	188
San Jacinto Coll–South Cmps, Houston, TX 77089-6099	1979	Dr. Parker Williams	11	5,157	204
San Joaquin Delta Coll, Stockton, CA 95207-6370	1935	Dr. L. H. Horton, Jr.	9	15,777	579
San Jose City Coll, San Jose, CA 95128-2797	1921	Dr. Raul Rodriguez	9	10,044	390
San Juan Coll, Farmington, NM 87402-4699	1958	Dr. James C. Henderson	8	4,390	195
Santa Barbara City Coll, Santa Barbara, CA 93109-2394	1908	Dr. Peter R. MacDougall	9	11,254	476
Santa Fe Comm Coll, Gainesville, FL 32606-6200	1966	Dr. Larry W. Tyree	9	11,813	539
Santa Monica Coll, Santa Monica, CA 90405-1644	1929	Dr. Piedad F. Robertson	11	22,127	664
Santa Rosa Jr Coll, Santa Rosa, CA 95401-4395	1918	Dr. Robert F. Agrella	11	21,815	972
Sauk Valley Comm Coll, Dixon, IL 61021	1965	Dr. Richard L. Behrendt	9	2,633	152
Schenectady County Comm Coll, Schenectady, NY 12305-2294	1968	Dr. Gabriel J. Basil	11	3,834	225
Schoolcraft Coll, Livonia, MI 48152-2696	1961	Dr. Richard W. McDowell	9	9,536	406
Scott Comm Coll, Bettendorf, IA 52722-6804	1966	Dr. Lenny E. Stone	11	4,000	235
Scottsdale Comm Coll, Scottsdale, AZ 85250-2699	1969	NR	11	10,322	380
Seattle Central Comm Coll, Seattle, WA 98122-2400	1966	Dr. Charles H. Mitchell	5	9,673	388
Seminole Comm Coll, Sanford, FL 32773-6199	1966	Dr. Earl S. Weldon	11	7,371	502
Seminole Jr Coll, Seminole, OK 74818-0351	1931	Dr. James J. Cook	5	1,533	85
Seward County Comm Coll, Liberal, KS 67905-1137	1969	Dr. James Grote	11	1,694	147
Shasta Coll, Redding, CA 96049-6006	1948	Dr. Douglas Treadway	11	12,820	424
Shawnee Comm Coll, Ullin, IL 62992-9725	1967	NR	11	2,500	194
Shelby State Comm Coll, Memphis, TN 38174-0568	1970	Mr. Mark L. Stansbury	5	6,579	342
Shelton State Comm Coll, Tuscaloosa, AL 35405-4093	1979	Dr. Thomas E. Umphrey	5	7,000	NR
Sheridan Coll, Sheridan, WY 82801-1500	1948	Dr. Stephen Maier	11	2,508	177
Shoreline Comm Coll, Seattle, WA 98133-5696	1964	Mr. Gary L. Oertli	5	8,575	333
Sierra Coll, Rocklin, CA 95677-3397	1936	Dr. Kevin M. Ramirez	5	13,735	510
Sinclair Comm Coll, Dayton, OH 45402-1453	1887	Dr. David H. Ponitz	11	20,075	974
Skagit Valley Coll, Mount Vernon, WA 98273-5899	1926	Dr. Lydia Ledesma	5	6,893	325
Skyline Coll, San Bruno, CA 94066-1698	1969	Ms. Linda Graef Salter	8	8,172	268
Snead State Comm Coll, Boaz, AL 35957	1935	Dr. William H. Osborn	5	1,607	76
Snow Coll, Ephraim, UT 84627-1203	1888	Dr. Gerald Day	5	2,471	127
Solano Comm Coll, Suisun City, CA 94585-3197	1945	Stan R. Arterberry	11	10,347	374
South Arkansas Comm Coll, El Dorado, AR 71731-7010	1975	Dr. Ben Whitfield	5	1,000	81
Southeast Comm Coll, Beatrice Cmps, Beatrice, NE 68310-9683	1976	NR	9	1,050	50
Southeast Comm Coll, Lincoln Cmps, Lincoln, NE 68520-1299	1973	NR	9	4,704	535
Southeastern Comm Coll, Whiteville, NC 28472-0151	1964	Dr. Stephen C. Scott	5	1,750	145
Southeastern Comm Coll, North Cmps, West Burlington, IA 52655-0605	1968	Dr. R. Gene Gardner	11	1,998	94
Southeastern Illinois Coll, Harrisburg, IL 62946-9804	1960	Dr. Ben Cullers	5	3,382	184
Southern Arkansas U Tech, Camden, AR 71701	1968	Dr. George J. Brown	5	1,197	114
Southern Maine Tech Coll, South Portland, ME 04106	1946	Dr. Wayne H. Ross	5	2,524	148
Southern State Comm Coll, Hillsboro, OH 45133-9487	1975	Dr. Lawrence N. Dukes	5	1,560	123
Southern Union State Comm Coll, Wadley, AL 36276	1922	Dr. Roy W. Johnson	5	3,274	168
Southern West Virginia Comm and Tech Coll, Mount Gay, WV 25637	1971	Dr. Michael Allkins	5	3,251	198
South Florida Comm Coll, Avon Park, FL 33825-9356	1965	Dr. Catherine P. Cornelius	5	1,620	232
South Georgia Coll, Douglas, GA 31533-5098	1906	Dr. Edward D. Jackson, Jr.	5	1,267	59
South Mountain Comm Coll, Phoenix, AZ 85040	1979	Dr. John A. Cordova	11	2,491	178
South Plains Coll, Levelland, TX 79336-6595	1958	Dr. Gary D. McDaniel	11	5,866	356
South Puget Sound Comm Coll, Olympia, WA 98512-6292	1970	Dr. Kenneth J. Minnaert	5	5,350	215
South Seattle Comm Coll, Seattle, WA 98106-1499	1970	Dr. Peter Ku	5	3,568	375
Southside Virginia Comm Coll, Alberta, VA 23821-9719	1970	Dr. John J. Cavan	5	2,256	214
South Suburban Coll, South Holland, IL 60473-1270	1927	Dr. Richard Fonte	11	7,783	332
Southwestern Coll, Chula Vista, CA 91910-7299	1961	Mr. Joseph M. Conte	11	15,427	604
Southwestern Comm Coll, Creston, IA 50801	1966	NR	5	1,191	65
Southwestern Comm Coll, Sylva, NC 28779-9578	1964	Dr. Barry W. Russell	5	1,674	199
Southwestern Michigan Coll, Dowagiac, MI 49047-9793	1964	Mr. David C. Briegel	11	2,665	180
Southwestern Oregon Comm Coll, Coos Bay, OR 97420-2911	1961	Dr. Stephen J. Kridelbaugh	11	1,434	393
Southwest Mississippi Comm Coll, Summit, MS 39666	1918	NR	9	1,520	89
Southwest Texas Jr Coll, Uvalde, TX 78801-6296	1946	Mr. Billy Word	11	3,162	166
Southwest Virginia Comm Coll, Richlands, VA 24641	1968	Dr. Charles R. King	5	4,762	235
Southwest Wisconsin Comm Coll, Fennimore, WI 53809-9778	1967	Dr. Richard A. Rogers	11	3,178	101
Spartanburg Tech Coll, Spartanburg, SC 29305-4386	1961	Dr. Jack A. Powers	5	2,500	NR
Spokane Comm Coll, Spokane, WA 99207-5399	1963	Dr. James Williams	5	6,776	481
Spoon River Coll, Canton, IL 61520-9801	1959	Dr. Felix T. Haynes	5	2,101	133
Springfield Tech Comm Coll, Springfield, MA 01105-1296	1967	Dr. Andrew M. Scibelli	5	6,193	331
Stanly Comm Coll, Albemarle, NC 28001-7458	1971	Dr. Jan J. Crawford	5	1,651	76
Stark Tech Coll, Canton, OH 44720-7299	1970	Dr. John J. McGrath	11	4,207	210
State Comm Coll of East St Louis, East St Louis, IL 62201-1100	1969	NR	5	1,268	83
State Fair Comm Coll, Sedalia, MO 65301-2199	1966	Dr. Marvin Fielding	9	2,369	98
State Tech Inst at Memphis, Memphis, TN 38134-7693	1967	Dr. Charles Temple	5	11,117	527
State U of NY Coll of A&T at Cobleskill, Cobleskill, NY 12043	1916	Dr. Kenneth E. Wing	5	2,650	152
State U of NY Coll of A&T at Morrisville, Morrisville, NY 13408	1908	Dr. Frederick W. Woodward	5	3,151	171
State U of NY Coll of Tech at Alfred, Alfred, NY 14802	1908	Dr. William Rezak	5	3,493	176
State U of NY Coll of Tech at Canton, Canton, NY 13617	1906	Dr. Joseph L. Kennedy	5	2,278	107
State U of NY Coll of Tech at Delhi, Delhi, NY 13753	1913	Dr. Mary Ellen Duncan	5	2,184	144
State U of NY Coll of Tech at Farmingdale, Farmingdale, NY 11735	1912	Dr. Frank A. Cipriani	5	6,717	417
Suffolk County Comm Coll–Ammerman Cmps, Selden, NY 11784-2851	1962	Dr. John F. Cooper	11	13,154	782
Suffolk County Comm Coll–Eastern Cmps, Riverhead, NY 11901	1977	Dr. Elizabeth Blake	11	2,680	216
Suffolk County Comm Coll–Western Cmps, Brentwood, NY 11717	1974	Mr. Salvatore J. LaLima	11	6,097	349
Sullivan County Comm Coll, Loch Sheldrake, NY 12759-4002	1962	Dr. Jeffrey B. Willens	11	2,085	98
Surry Comm Coll, Dobson, NC 27017-0304	1965	Dr. James Reeves	5	3,036	98
Sussex County Comm Coll, Newton, NJ 07860	1981	NR	11	2,213	170

Name, address	Year	Governing official, control		Enrollment	Faculty
Tacoma Comm Coll, Tacoma, WA 98465-1997	1965	Dr. Raymond Needham	5	5,461	308
Tallahassee Comm Coll, Tallahassee, FL 32304-2895	1966	Dr. T. K. Wetherall	11	10,163	384
Tarrant County Jr Coll, Fort Worth, TX 76102-6599	1967	Mr. C. A. Roberson	8	26,842	971
Tech Career Institutes, New York, NY 10001-2705	1974	Mr. Eric Biederman	3	3,300	136
Tech Coll of the Lowcountry, Beaufort, SC 29901-1288	1972	Dr. Anne S. McNutt	5	1,600	69
Temple Jr Coll, Temple, TX 76504-7435	1926	Dr. Marvin R. Felder	9	2,363	113
Terra State Comm Coll, Fremont, OH 43420-9670	1968	Dr. Charlotte J. Lee	5	2,591	148
Texarkana Coll, Texarkana, TX 75599-0001	1927	Dr. Carl M. Nelson	11	3,990	196
Texas Southmost Coll, Brownsville, TX 78520-4991	1926	Dr. Juliet V. Garcia	9	6,429	390
Texas State Tech Coll–Harlingen Cmps, Harlingen, TX 78550-3697	1967	Dr. J. Gilbert Leal	5	2,888	141
Texas State Tech Coll–Waco/Marshall Cmps, Waco, TX 76705-1695	1965	Dr. Fred L. Williams	5	3,116	341
Thomas Nelson Comm Coll, Hampton, VA 23670-0407	1968	Dr. Shirley R. Pippins	5	7,496	321
Three Rivers Comm Coll, Poplar Bluff, MO 63901-2393	1966	Dr. Stephen M. Poort	5	3,061	67
Three Rivers Comm-Tech Coll, Norwich, CT 06360	1963	Dr. Booker T. DeVaughn	5	4,138	180
Tidewater Comm Coll, Portsmouth, VA 23703	1968	Dr. Larry Whitworth	5	17,747	817
Tomball Coll, Tomball, TX 77375-4036	1988	NR	11	3,950	187
Tompkins Cortland Comm Coll, Dryden, NY 13053-9533	1968	Dr. Carl Haynes	11	2,899	196
Treasure Valley Comm Coll, Ontario, OR 97914-3423	1962	Dr. Berton L. Glandon	11	2,925	110
Tri-County Tech Coll, Pendleton, SC 29670-0587	1962	Dr. Don C. Garrison	5	3,162	250
Trident Tech Coll, Charleston, SC 29423-8067	1964	Dr. Mary Thornley	11	9,627	497
Trinidad State Jr Coll, Trinidad, CO 81082-2396	1925	Dr. Harold Deselms	5	1,676	111
Trinity Valley Comm Coll, Athens, TX 75751-2765	1946	Mr. Ron Baugh	11	4,786	224
Triton Coll, River Grove, IL 60171-1995	1964	Dr. George Jorndt	5	11,898	793
Trocaire Coll, Buffalo, NY 14220-2094	1958	Barbara Ciarico, RSM	1	1,105	103
Truckee Meadows Comm Coll, Reno, NV 89512-3901	1971	Dr. Rita Gubanich	5	8,826	495
Truett-McConnell Coll, Cleveland, GA 30528-9799	1946	Dr. T. Clark Bryan	2	1,957	39
Tunxis Comm Tech Coll, Farmington, CT 06032-3026	1969	Dr. Cathryn Addy	5	2,465	175
Tyler Jr Coll, Tyler, TX 75711-9020	1926	Dr. William R. Crowe	11	7,984	364
Ulster County Comm Coll, Stone Ridge, NY 12484	1961	Mr. Robert T. Brown	11	2,750	194
Umpqua Comm Coll, Roseburg, OR 97470-0226	1964	Dr. James M. Kraby	11	2,300	145
Union County Coll, Cranford, NJ 07016-1528	1933	Dr. Thomas H. Brown	11	10,457	422
The U of Akron–Wayne Coll, Orrville, OH 44667-9192	1972	Dr. Peggy Gordon Elliott	5	1,461	109
U of Alaska Anchorage, Kenai Peninsula Coll, Soldotna, AK 99669-9798	1964	NR	5	1,795	87
U of Alaska Anchorage, Matanuska-Susitna Coll, Palmer, AK 99645-2889	1958	Mr. Glenn Massay	5	1,654	114
U of Alaska Southeast, Sitka Cmps, Sitka, AK 99835-9418	1962	Ms. Elaine Sunde	5	1,470	69
U of Cincinnati Clermont Coll, Batavia, OH 45103-1785	1972	Dr. Roger J. Barry	5	1,918	135
U of Cincinnati Raymond Walters Coll, Cincinnati, OH 45236-1007	1967	Dr. Barbara A. Bardes	5	2,857	233
U of Hawaii–Hawaii Comm Coll, Hilo, HI 96720-4091	1954	NR	5	2,729	98
U of Hawaii–Honolulu Comm Coll, Honolulu, HI 96817-4598	1920	NR	5	5,148	285
U of Hawaii–Kapiolani Comm Coll, Honolulu, HI 96816-4421	1957	Mr. John F. Morton	5	7,639	317
U of Hawaii–Maui Comm Coll, Kahului, HI 96732	1967	Dr. Clyde Sakamoto	5	2,553	147
U of Kentucky, Ashland Comm Coll, Ashland, KY 41101-3683	1937	Dr. Charles Dassance	5	2,760	142
U of Kentucky, Elizabethtown Comm Coll, Elizabethtown, KY 42701-3081	1964	Dr. Charles E. Stebbins	5	4,042	136
U of Kentucky, Hazard Comm Coll, Hazard, KY 41701-2403	1968	Dr. G. Edward Hughes	5	1,870	121
U of Kentucky, Henderson Comm Coll, Henderson, KY 42420-4623	1963	Dr. Patrick R. Lake	5	1,396	96
U of Kentucky, Hopkinsville Comm Coll, Hopkinsville, KY 42241-2100	1965	Dr. Jim Kerley	5	2,612	158
U of Kentucky, Jefferson Comm Coll, Louisville, KY 40202-2005	1968	Dr. Ronald J. Horvath	5	10,236	490
U of Kentucky, Lexington Comm Coll, Lexington, KY 40506-0235	1965	Dr. Janice N. Friedel	5	5,001	302
U of Kentucky, Madisonville Comm Coll, Madisonville, KY 42431-9185	1968	Dr. Arthur D. Stumpf	5	2,545	167
U of Kentucky, Maysville Comm Coll, Maysville, KY 41056	1967	Dr. James C. Shires	5	1,409	111
U of Kentucky, Paducah Comm Coll, Paducah, KY 42002-7380	1932	Dr. Leonard O'Hara	5	2,918	102
U of Kentucky, Prestonsburg Comm Coll, Prestonsburg, KY 41653-1815	1964	Dr. Deborah Lee Floyd	5	2,866	124
U of Kentucky, Somerset Comm Coll, Somerset, KY 42501-2973	1965	Dr. Rollin J. Watson	5	2,700	153
U of Kentucky, Southeast Comm Coll, Cumberland, KY 40823-1099	1960	Dr. W. Bruce Ayers	5	2,634	107
U of Maine at Augusta, Augusta, ME 04330-9410	1965	Charles R. MacRoy	5	5,334	180
U of New Mexico–Gallup Branch, Gallup, NM 87301-5603	1968	Dr. Robert Carlson	5	2,836	117
U of New Mexico–Los Alamos Branch, Los Alamos, NM 87544-2233	1980	Dr. Carlos B. Ramirez	5	1,023	96
U of New Mexico–Valencia Cmps, Los Lunas, NM 87031-7633	1981	Dr. Alice V. Lietteney	5	1,440	93
U of South Carolina at Beaufort, Beaufort, SC 29902-4601	1959	Dr. Chris P. Plyler	5	1,159	64
U of South Carolina at Lancaster, Lancaster, SC 29721-0889	1959	Dr. Joseph Pappin, III	5	1,039	52
U of South Carolina at Sumter, Sumter, SC 29150-2498	1966	Dr. C. Leslie Carpenter	5	1,566	97
U of Wisconsin Ctr–Fox Valley, Menasha, WI 54952-8002	1933	Dr. James W. Perry	5	1,315	58
U of Wisconsin Ctr–Marathon County, Wausau, WI 54401-5396	1933	Dr. G. Dennis Massey	5	1,047	71
U of Wisconsin Ctr–Waukesha County, Waukesha, WI 53188-2720	1966	Dr. Mary S. Knudten	5	1,858	86
Utah Valley State Coll, Orem, UT 84058-0001	1941	Dr. Kerry D. Romesburg	5	11,332	568
Valencia Comm Coll, Orlando, FL 32802-3028	1967	Dr. Paul C. Gianini, Jr.	5	23,564	999
Vance-Granville Comm Coll, Henderson, NC 27536-0917	1969	Dr. Ben F. Currin	5	2,547	191
Ventura Coll, Ventura, CA 93003-3899	1925	Dr. Larry Calderon	11	12,158	541
Vernon Regional Jr Coll, Vernon, TX 76384-4092	1972	Dr. Wade Kirk	11	1,803	98
Victoria Coll, Victoria, TX 77901-4494	1925	Dr. Jimmy Goodson	8	3,667	120
Victor Valley Coll, Victorville, CA 92392-5849	1961	Dr. Edward O. Gould	5	8,000	325
Vincennes U, Vincennes, IN 47591-5202	1801	Dr. Phillip M. Summers	5	7,211	400
Vincennes U–Jasper Ctr, Jasper, IN 47546-9393	1970	NR	5	1,188	62
Virginia Highlands Comm Coll, Abingdon, VA 24212-0828	1967	Dr. F. David Wilkin, Jr.	5	1,938	131
Virginia Western Comm Coll, Roanoke, VA 24038-4065	1966	Dr. Charles L. Downs	5	6,590	202
Vista Comm Coll, Berkeley, CA 94704-5102	1974	Dr. Barbara Beno	11	3,227	138
Volunteer State Comm Coll, Gallatin, TN 37066-3146	1970	Dr. Hal R. Ramer	5	6,257	348
Wake Tech Comm Coll, Raleigh, NC 27603-5696	1958	Dr. Bruce I. Howell	11	7,340	405
Wallace State Comm Coll, Hanceville, AL 35077-2000	1966	Dr. James C. Bailey	5	5,454	301
Walla Walla Comm Coll, Walla Walla, WA 99362-9267	1967	Dr. Steven L. VanAusdle	5	4,858	267
Walters State Comm Coll, Morristown, TN 37813-6899	1970	Dr. Jack E. Campbell	5	5,683	253

Name, address	Year	Governing official, control		Enroll-ment	Faculty
Warren County Comm Coll, Washington, NJ 07882-9605	1981	NR	11	1,418	41
Washington State Comm Coll, Marietta, OH 45750-9225	1971	Dr. Carson K. Miller	5	2,152	132
Washtenaw Comm Coll, Ann Arbor, MI 48106	1965	Dr. Gunder A. Myran	11	10,541	757
Waubonsee Comm Coll, Sugar Grove, IL 60554-9799	1966	Dr. John J. Swalec	9	7,761	494
Waukesha County Tech Coll, Pewaukee, WI 53072-4601	1923	Dr. Richard T. Anderson	11	4,700	520
Wayne Comm Coll, Goldsboro, NC 27533-8002	1957	Dr. Edward H. Wilson, Jr.	11	2,379	153
Wayne County Comm Coll, Detroit, MI 48226-3010	1967	Dr. Richard M. Turner, III	11	10,024	400
Weatherford Coll, Weatherford, TX 76086-5699	1869	Dr. Jim Boyd	11	2,277	94
Wenatchee Valley Coll, Wenatchee, WA 98801-1799	1939	Dr. Woody Ahn	11	3,419	168
Westark Comm Coll, Fort Smith, AR 72913-3649	1928	Mr. Joel R. Stubblefield	11	5,323	236
Westchester Comm Coll, Valhalla, NY 10595-1698	1946	Dr. Joseph N. Hankin	11	17,118	722
Western Iowa Tech Comm Coll, Sioux City, IA 51102-0265	1966	Dr. Robert E. Dunker	5	2,750	157
Western Nebraska Comm Coll–Scottsbluff Cmps, Scottsbluff, NE 69361-1899	1926	Dr. John N. Harms	11	1,910	56
Western Nevada Comm Coll, Carson City, NV 89703-7316	1971	Dr. James Randolph	5	4,668	358
Western Oklahoma State Coll, Altus, OK 73521-1397	1926	Dr. Ray Brown	5	1,639	78
Western Piedmont Comm Coll, Morganton, NC 28655-9978	1964	Dr. Jim A. Richardson	5	2,592	132
Western Texas Coll, Snyder, TX 79549-9502	1969	Dr. Harry L. Krenek	11	1,200	55
Western Wisconsin Tech Coll, La Crosse, WI 54602-0908	1911	Dr. James Lee Rasch	9	4,230	187
Western Wyoming Comm Coll, Rock Springs, WY 82902-0428	1959	Dr. T. L. Boggs	11	3,094	232
West Hills Comm Coll, Coalinga, CA 93210-1399	1932	Dr. Frank P. Gornick	5	2,810	160
West Los Angeles Coll, Culver City, CA 90230-3500	1969	Dr. Evelyn C. Wong	11	8,958	320
Westmoreland County Comm Coll, Youngwood, PA 15697	1970	Dr. Daniel C. Krezenski	8	6,321	390
West Shore Comm Coll, Scottville, MI 49454-9716	1967	Dr. William M. Anderson	9	1,487	71
West Valley Coll, Saratoga, CA 95070-5697	1963	Dr. Sam Schauerman	11	14,224	560
West Virginia Northern Comm Coll, Wheeling, WV 26003	1972	Dr. Linda S Dunn	5	2,921	158
West Virginia U at Parkersburg, Parkersburg, WV 26101-9577	1971	Dr. Eldon L. Miller	5	3,600	161
Wharton County Jr Coll, Wharton, TX 77488-3298	1946	Dr. Frank R. Vivelo	11	3,395	161
Whatcom Comm Coll, Bellingham, WA 98226-8003	1970	Dr. Harold G. Heiner	5	2,424	166
Wilkes Comm Coll, Wilkesboro, NC 28697	1965	Dr. Swanson Richards	5	1,957	225
William Rainey Harper Coll, Palatine, IL 60067-7398	1965	Dr. Paul N. Thompson	11	14,834	1,018
Willmar Comm Coll, Willmar, MN 56201-0797	1961	Mr. Harold G. Conradi	5	1,341	81
Willmar Tech Coll, Willmar, MN 56201-1097	1961	NR	5	1,175	90
Wilson Tech Comm Coll, Wilson, NC 27893-3310	1958	Dr. Frank L. Eagles	5	1,301	74
Wisconsin Indianhead Tech Coll, New Richmond Cmps, New Richmond, WI 54017-1738	1972	Mr. Tim Schreiner	9	1,300	65
Wisconsin Indianhead Tech Coll, Rice Lake Cmps, Rice Lake, WI 54868-2435	1941	Ms. Thomas B. Lemler	9	1,136	79
Wood Coll, Mathiston, MS 39752-0289	1886	Dr. Doyce W. Gunter	2	1,500	35
Wor-Wic Comm Coll, Salisbury, MD 21801	1976	NR	11	1,506	103
Wytheville Comm Coll, Wytheville, VA 24382-3308	1967	Dr. William F. Snyder	5	2,748	137
Yakima Valley Comm Coll, Yakima, WA 98907-1647	1928	Dr. Donald Hughes	5	4,109	374
Yavapai Coll, Prescott, AZ 86301-3297	1966	Dr. Doreen Dailey	11	6,274	384
York Tech Coll, Rock Hill, SC 29730-3395	1961	Mr. Dennis F. Merrell	5	3,480	236
Yuba Coll, Marysville, CA 95901-7699	1927	Dr. Stephen Epler	11	9,390	267

College Freshman Attitudes, 1994

According to the 29th annual survey of college freshmen conducted by the American Council on Education and UCLA, college freshmen are less interested and less involved in politics than ever before. Only 31.9% of freshmen—the lowest percentage in 29 years—report that "keeping up with political affairs" is an important goal (compared with 42.4% in 1990 and 57.8% in 1966). There was also less discussion of politics reported in 1994 (16.0% compared with 18.8% in 1993, the highest point being 29.9% in 1968). In line with these trends, the report reveals a considerable decline in the number of students who claim that a very important goal in life is to "participate in community action programs" (24.4% in 1994, a decrease from 26.1% in 1992), "participate in programs to help clean up the environment" (24.4% in 1994, a decrease from 26.1% in 1992), and "help promote racial understanding" (35.8% in 1994, a decrease from 42.0% in 1992).

Politically, 52.6% of freshmen identify themselves as "middle of the road" (an increase from 49.9% in 1993). Consistent with this move to the political center, students exhibit a variety of liberal and conservative trends. For the 5th straight year, support for legalization of marijuana grew (32.1% in 1994, compared with 28.2% in 1993 and 16.7% in 1989), while support for legislation to outlaw homosexuality fell to an all-time low (33.9% in 1994, compared with 36.2% in 1993 and 53.2% in 1987). On the conservative side, support for abolishing capital punishment dropped to 20.1%—the lowest point in the history of the survey—(compared with 22.1% in 1993 and a high point of 57.6% in 1971). An all-time high 73.0% of students (compared with 67.6% in 1993 and 50.1% in 1973) agrees that "there is too much concern in the courts for the rights of criminals." Support for increased government efforts to protect the environment (84.0%), control hand-gun sales (79.9%), promote energy conservation (71.9%), develop a national health-care plan (70.5%), and raise taxes on the wealthy (67.3%) declined between 1993 and 1994.

In 1994, interest in medical careers reached an all-time high of 8.9% (compared with 8.4% in 1993, and 4.1% in 1969). More women than men plan to seek medical degrees (9.9% compared with 7.7%). Interest in engineering careers fell to 7.1%—the lowest point in 19 years—(compared with 7.7% in 1993, and 12.0% in 1982). In 1994, 53.6% of entering freshmen were women (compared with 49.3% in 1977 and 44.4% in 1967).

Finances concern more students than ever before. In 1994, students who are "not sure I will have enough funds to complete college" climbed to an all-time high of 18.9% (compared with 17.4% in 1992, and 8.4% in 1968). Reliance on Perkins loans, Stafford loans, and loans from other sources reached an all-time high, as students have to borrow more to finance their college education.

Students are feeling increasingly stressed. Of freshmen, 24.1%—a record high number—report that they have frequently "felt overwhelmed by all I have to do." The number of students who frequently "felt depressed" increased for the 4th straight year, while students' self-ratings on "emotional and physical health" reached all-time lows.

For the 6th time in the past 7 years, the percentage of college freshmen who smoke cigarettes rose (12.5%, compared with 11.6% in 1993 and 9.1% in 1985). The 1994 figure was the highest level since 1979, when 13.3% said they smoked cigarettes. In contrast, the percentage who report drinking beer fell to an all-time low of 53.2% (compared with 54.4% in 1993 and 75.2% in 1981).

ARTS AND MEDIA

Notable Movies of the Year, Sept. 1994-Aug. 1995

Movie	Stars	Director
Apollo 13	Tom Hanks, Kevin Bacon, Bill Paxton, Gary Sinise, Ed Harris	Ron Howard
Basketball Diaries	Leonardo DiCaprio, Mark Wahlberg, Patrick McGaw, James Maddio	Scott Kalvert
Batman Forever	Val Kilmer, Chris O'Donnell, Jim Carrey, Tommy Lee Jones	Joel Schumacher
Before Sunrise	Ethan Hawke, Julie Delpy	Richard Linklater
Billy Madison	Adam Sandler, Ben Stiller, Shaun Weiss	Arne Glimcher
Boys on the Side	Whoopi Goldberg, Drew Barrymore, Mary-Louise Parker	Herbert Ross
The Brady Bunch Movie	Shelly Long, Gary Cole, Michael McKean	Betty Thomas
Braveheart	Mel Gibson, Sophie Marceau, Patrick McGoohan	Mel Gibson
Bridges of Madison County	Meryl Streep, Clint Eastwood	Clint Eastwood
Bullets Over Broadway	John Cusak, Dianne Wiest	Woody Allen
Casper	Christina Ricci, Bill Pullman, Cathy Moriarty, Eric Idle	Brad Silberling
Circle of Friends	Minnie Driver, Geraldine O'Rawe, Saffron Burrows	Pat O'Connor
Clueless	Alicia Silverstone, Stacey Dash, Wallace Shawn	Amy Heckerling
Congo	Dylan Walsh, Laura Linney, Ernie Hudson, Tim Curry	Frank Marshall
Crimson Tide	Denzel Washington, Gene Hackman	Tony Scott
Dangerous Minds	Michelle Pfeiffer, George Dzunda, Courtney B. Vance	John N. Smith
Disclosure	Demi Moore, Michael Douglas	Barry Levinson
Dolores Claiborne	Kathy Bates, Jennifer Jason Leigh	Taylor Hackford
Drop Zone	Wesley Snipes, Gary Busey, Yancy Butler, Michael Jeter	John Badham
Dumb and Dumber	Jim Carrey, Jeff Daniels	Peter Farrelly
Ed Wood	Johnny Depp, Martin Landau, Sarah Jessica Paker	Tim Burton
Exit to Eden	Dana Delany, Paul Mercurio, Dan Aykroyd, Rosie O'Donnell	Garry Marshall
French Kiss	Meg Ryan, Kevin Kline	Lawrence Kasdan
Higher Learning	Jennifer Connelly, Ice Cube, Omar Epps, Michael Rapaport	John Singleton
I.Q.	Walter Matthau, Meg Ryan, Tim Robbins	Fred Schepisi
Interview With the Vampire	Tom Cruise, Brad Pitt, Antonio Banderas, Christian Slater	Neil Jordan
Junior	Arnold Schwarzenegger, Danny De Vito	Ivan Reitman
Just Cause	Sean Connery, Blair Underwood, Laurence Fishburne	Arne Glimcher
Kids	Leo Fitzpatrick, Justin Pierce, Cathy Konrad, Christine Vachon	Larry Clark
Legends of the Fall	Brad Pitt, Anthony Hopkins, Aidan Quinn, Henry Thomas	Edward Zwick
Little Women	Susan Sarandon, Winona Ryder, Trini Alvarado, Kirsten Dunst, Claire Danes, Gabriel Byrne, Eric Stoltz, Christian Bale	Gillian Armstrong
Major Payne	Damon Wayans, Karyn Parsons, William Hickey, Michael Ironside	Nick Castle
Mary Shelley's Frankenstein	Kenneth Branagh, Robert De Niro, Helena Bonham Carter	Kenneth Branagh
Murder in the First	Kevin Bacon, Christian Slater, Gary Oldman	Marc Rocco
Nell	Jodie Foster, Liam Neeson, Natasha Richardson	Michael Apted
The Net	Sandra Bullock, Jeremy Northam	Irwin Winkler
Nine Months	Hugh Grant, Julianne Moore	Chris Columbus
Nobody's Fool	Paul Newman, Jessica Tandy, Bruce Willis, Melanie Griffith	Robert Benton
Only You	Marisa Tomei, Robert Downey Jr., Bonnie Hunt, Fisher Stevens	Norman Jewison
Outbreak	Dustin Hoffman, Morgan Freeman, Rene Russo, Donald Sutherland	Wolfgang Petersen
Pocahontas	Mel Gibson, Irene Bedard, Judy Kuhn, Russell Means, David Ogden Stiers, Linda Hunt	Mike Gabriel, Eric Goldberg
Pulp Fiction	Samuel L. Jackson, Harvey Keitel, Amanda Plummer, Tim Roth, Bruce Willis, Uma Thurman, Eric Stoltz, John Travolta	Quentin Tarantino
Quiz Show	Ralph Fiennes, John Turturro, Rob Morrow, Mira Sorvino, David Paymer, Barry Levinson	Robert Redford
Richie Rich	Macaulay Culkin, John Larroquette, Edward Herrmann	Donald Petrie
The River Wild	Meryl Streep, David Strathairn, Kevin Bacon	Curtis Hanson
Rob Roy	Liam Neeson, Jessica Lange, John Hurt, Tim Roth, Eric Stoltz	Michael Caton-Jones
The Santa Clause	Tim Allen, Eric Lloyd, David Krumholz	John Pasquin
The Shawshank Redemption	Morgan Freeman, Tim Robbins, Bob Gunton, William Sadler	Frank Darabont
The Specialist	Sharon Stone, Stylveste Stallone	Luis Llosa
Star Trek: Generations	William Shatner, Patrick Stewart	David Carson
Tales From the Crypt: Demon Knight	Billy Zane, William Sadler, Jada Pinkett, Brenda Bakke	Ernest Dickerson
Terminal Velocity	Charlie Sheen, Natassja Kinski	Deran Serafian
Waterworld	Kevin Costner, Jeanne Tripplehorn, Tina Majorino, Dennis Hopper	Kevin Reynolds
While You Were Sleeping	Sandra Bullock, Bill Pullman, Peter Gallagher, Peter Boyle	Jon Turteltaub

Top 50 Movies, 1994

Source: *Variety*, Jan. 30-Feb. 5, 1995; box office grosses in the U.S. during calendar year 1994

Rank/Title	Gross (millions)	Rank/Title	Gross (millions)	Rank/Title	Gross (millions)
1. The Lion King**	$298.9	19. Pulp Fiction**	$62.4	34. Timecop	$44.5
2. Forrest Gump**	298.1	20. Dumb and Dumber**	59.1	35. City Slickers II: The Legend	
3. True Lies	146.3	21. Grumpy Old Men*	58.0	of Curly's Gold	43.6
4. The Santa Clause**	134.6	22. The Specialist**	55.8	36. Beverly Hills Cop III	42.6
5. The Flintstones	130.5	23. Four Weddings and a		37. Tombstone*	39.6
6. Clear and Present Danger**	121.7	Funeral	52.7	38. The Paper	38.8
7. Speed	121.2	24. The Little Rascals	51.9	39. On Deadly Ground	38.6
8. The Mask**	118.6	25. Naked Gun 33-1/3: The Final		40. It Could Happen to You	37.9
9. Mrs. Doubtfire*	107.4	Insult	51.1	41. The Shadow	32.1
10. Maverick	101.6	26. The Crow	50.7	42. I Love Trouble	30.8
11. Interview With the Vampire	100.0	27. Angels in the Outfield	50.2	43. Major League II	30.6
12. The Client	92.1	28. Natural Born Killers**	50.2	44. Blank Check	30.6
13. Schindler's List*	91.1	29. When a Man Loves a		45. Blown Away	30.2
14. Philadelphia	76.9	Woman	50.0	46. Junior**	30.2
15. Ace Ventura: Pet Detective	72.2	30. The Pelican Brief*	48.8	47. In the Army Now**	28.9
16. Star Trek Generations**	70.4	31. Disclosure**	46.3	48. Guarding Tess	27.1
17. Stargate**	68.2	32. D2: The Mighty Ducks	45.6	49. A Low Down Dirty Shame**	26.5
18. Wolf	65.0	33. The River Wild**	45.2	50. Beethoven's 2nd*	26.4

*1993 releases; 1994 gross only. **Box office receipts through Dec. 31, 1994. In release at the start of 1995.

All-Time Top 50 American Movies

Source: *Variety*, Feb. 20-26, 1995

Rank/Title/Date	Gross[1] (millions)	Rank/Title/Date	Gross[1] (millions)	Rank/Title/Date	Gross[1] (millions)
1. E.T. The Extra-Terrestrial (1982)	$399.8	19. Indiana Jones and the Last Crusade (1989)	197.2	34. Batman Returns (1992)	162.8
2. Jurassic Park (1993)	356.8	20. Gone With the Wind (1939)	191.7	35. The Sound of Music (1965)	160.5
3. Star Wars (1977)	322.0	21. Dances With Wolves (1990)	184.2	36. The Firm (1993)	158.3
4. The Lion King (1993)	310.1	22. The Fugitive (1993)	183.9	37. Fatal Attraction (1987)	156.6
5. Forrest Gump (1993)	300.6	23. Indiana Jones and the Temple of Doom (1984)	179.9	38. The Sting (1973)	156.0
6. Home Alone (1990)	285.8	24. Pretty Woman (1990)	178.4	39. Who Framed Roger Rabbit? (1988)	154.1
7. Return of the Jedi (1983)	263.0	25. Tootsie (1982)	177.2	40. Beverly Hills Cop II (1987)	153.7
8. Jaws (1975)	260.0	26. Top Gun (1986)	176.8	41. Grease (1978)	153.1
9. Batman (1989)	251.2	27. Snow White and the Seven Dwarfs (1937)	175.3	42. Rambo: First Blood Part II (1985)	150.4
10. Raiders of the Lost Ark (1981)	242.4	28. Crocodile Dundee (1986)	174.6	43. Gremlins (1984)	148.2
11. Beverly Hills Cop (1984)	234.8	29. Home Alone 2 (1992)	173.6	44. Lethal Weapon 2 (1989)	147.2
12. The Empire Strikes Back (1980)	222.7	30. Rain Man (1989)	172.8	45. True Lies (1994)	146.3
13. Ghostbusters (1984)	220.9	31. Three Men and a Baby (1987)	167.8	46. Beauty and the Beast	145.8
14. Mrs. Doubtfire (1993)	219.2	32. Robin Hood: Prince of Thieves (1991)	165.5	47. Lethal Weapon 3 (1992)	144.7
15. Ghost (1990)	217.6	33. The Exorcist (1973)	165.0	48. 101 Dalmations (1961)	144.0
16. Aladdin (1992)	217.4			49. The Santa Clause (1994)	142.7
17. Back to the Future (1985)	208.2			50. National Lampoon's Animal House (1978)	141.6
18. Terminator 2 (1991)	204.8				

(1) Gross is in absolute dollars. Ticket prices favor recent films, but older films have the advantage of reissues.

Most Popular Movie Videos, 1994

Source: Alexander & Associates/Video Flash, New York, NY

Top 10 Rentals
1. Mrs. Doubtfire
2. The Fugitive
3. The Firm
4. Ace Ventura: Pet Detective
5. Jurassic Park
6. Tombstone
7. Sleepless in Seattle
8. Aladdin
9. Barney (various)
10. Cliffhanger

Top 10 Sales
1. Snow White and the Seven Dwarfs
2. Jurassic Park
3. The Fox and the Hound
4. Mrs. Doubtfire
5. The Return of Jafar
6. Aladdin
7. Barney (various)
8. Once Upon a Forest
9. Free Willy
10. The Fugitive

National Film Registry, 1989-94

Source: National Film Registry, Library of Congress

"Culturally, historically, or esthetically significant" films placed on the National Film Registry, Library of Congress. Films selected in 1994 are in **boldface**. Titles are in alphabetic order.

Adam's Rib (1949)
The African Queen (1951)
All About Eve (1950)
All Quiet on the Western Front (1930)
An American in Paris (1951)
Annie Hall (1977)
The Apartment (1960)
Badlands (1973)
The Bank Dick (1940)
The Battle of San Pietro (1945)
The Best Years of Our Lives (1946)
Big Business (1929)
The Big Parade (1925)
The Birth of a Nation (1915)
The Black Pirate (1926)
Blade Runner (1982)
The Blood of Jesus (1941)
Bonnie and Clyde (1967)
Bringing Up Baby (1938)
Carmen Jones (1954)
Casablanca (1942)
Castro Street (1966)
Cat People (1942)
The Cheat (1915)
Chinatown (1974)
Chulas Fronteras (1976)
Citizen Kane (1941)
City Lights (1931)
The Cool World (1963)
A Corner in Wheat (1909)
The Crowd (1928)
David Holzman's Diary (1968)
Detour (1946)
Dodsworth (1936)
Dog Star Man (1964)
Double Indemnity (1944)
Dr. Strangelove (or, How I Learned to Stop Worrying and Love the Bomb) (1964)
Duck Soup (1933)
Eaux D'Artifice (1953)

E.T. the Extra-Terrestrial (1982)
The Exploits of Elaine (1914)
Fantasia (1940)
Footlight Parade (1933)
Force of Evil (1948)
Frankenstein (1931)
Freaks (1932)
The Freshman (1925)
The General (1927)
Gertie the Dinosaur (1914)
Gigi (1958)
The Godfather (1972)
The Godfather, Part II (1974)
The Gold Rush (1925)
Gone with the Wind (1939)
The Grapes of Wrath (1940)
The Great Train Robbery (1903)
Greed (1924)
Harlan County, U.S.A. (1976)
Hell's Hinges (1916)
High Noon (1952)
High School (1968)
His Girl Friday (1940)
Hospital (1970)
How Green Was My Valley (1941)
I Am a Fugitive From a Chain Gang (1932)
Intolerance (1916)
Invasion of the Body Snatchers (1956)
It Happened One Night (1934)
It's a Wonderful Life (1946)
The Italian (1915)
Killer of Sheep (1977)
King Kong (1933)
The Lady Eve (1941)
Lassie Come Home (1943)
Lawrence of Arabia (1962)
The Learning Tree (1969)

Letter From an Unknown Woman (1948)
Louisiana Story (1948)
Love Me Tonight (1932)
The Manchurian Candidate (1962)
Magical Maestro (1952)
The Magnificent Ambersons (1942)
The Maltese Falcon (1941)
March of Time: Inside Nazi Germany—1938 (1938)
Marty (1955)
Meet Me in St. Louis (1944)
Meshes of the Afternoon (1943)
Midnight Cowboy (1969)
Modern Times (1936)
Morocco (1930)
A Movie (1958)
Mr. Smith Goes to Washington (1939)
My Darling Clementine (1946)
Nanook of the North (1922)
Nashville (1975)
A Night at the Opera (1935)
The Night of the Hunter (1955)
Ninotchka (1939)
Nothing But a Man (1964)
On the Waterfront (1954)
One Flew Over the Cuckoo's Nest (1975)
Out of the Past (1947)
Paths of Glory (1957)
Pinocchio (1940)
A Place in the Sun (1951)
Point Of Order (1964)
The Poor Little Rich Girl (1917)
Primary (1960)
The Prisoner of Zenda (1937)
Psycho (1960)
Raging Bull (1980)
Rebel Without a Cause (1955)

Red River (1948)
Ride the High Country (1962)
The River (1937)
Safety Last (1923)
Salesman (1969)
Salt of the Earth (1954)
Scarface (1932)
The Searchers (1956)
Shadow of a Doubt (1943)
Shadows (1959)
Shane (1953)
Sherlock, Jr. (1924)
Singin' in the Rain (1952)
Snow White (1933)
Snow White and the Seven Dwarfs (1937)
Some Like It Hot (1959)
Star Wars (1977)
Sullivan's Travels (1941)
Sunrise (1927)
Sunset Boulevard (1950)
Sweet Smell of Success (1957)
Tabu (1933)
Taxi Driver (1976)
Tevye (1939)
Top Hat (1935)
Touch of Evil (1958)
The Treasure of the Sierra Madre (1948)
Trouble in Paradise (1932)
2001: A Space Odyssey (1968)
Vertigo (1958)
What's Opera, Doc? (1957)
Where Are My Children? (1916)
The Wind (1928)
Within Our Gates (1920)
The Wizard of Oz (1939)
A Woman Under the Influence (1974)
Yankee Doodle Dandy (1942)
Zapruder Film (1963)

Record Long-Run Broadway Plays[1]
Source: *Variety*, July 31-Aug. 6, 1995

Title	Performances	Title	Performances	Title	Performances
Chorus Line	6,137	Dancin'	1,774	The Music Man	1,375
*Cats	5,341	La Cage aux Folles	1,761	Funny Girl	1,348
Oh, Calcutta (revival)	5,959	Hair	1,750	Mumenschanz	1,326
42nd Street	3,486	The Wiz	1,672	Oh! Calcutta! (original)	1,314
*Les Misérables	3,429	Born Yesterday	1,642	Brighton Beach Memoirs	1,299
Grease	3,388	Ain't Misbehavin'	1,604	Angel Street	1,295
Fiddler on the Roof	3,242	Best Little Whorehouse in Texas	1,584	Lightnin'	1,291
Life With Father	3,224	Mary, Mary	1,572	Promises, Promises	1,281
Tobacco Road	3,182	Evita	1,567	The King and I	1,246
*Phantom of the Opera	3,127	Voice of the Turtle	1,557	Cactus Flower	1,234
Hello Dolly	2,844	Barefoot in the Park	1,530	Sleuth	1,222
My Fair Lady	2,717	Dreamgirls	1,521	Torch Song Trilogy	1,222
Annie	2,377	Mame	1,508	"1776"	1,217
Man of La Mancha	2,328	Same Time, Next Year	1,453	Equus	1,209
Abie's Irish Rose	2,327	Arsenic and Old Lace	1,444	Sugar Babies	1,208
Oklahoma!	2,212	The Sound of Music	1,443	Guys and Dolls	1,200
Pippin	1,944	*Crazy for You	1,428	Amadeus	1,181
South Pacific	1,925	How to Succeed in Business		Cabaret	1,165
Magic Show	1,920	Without Really Trying (original)	1,417	Mister Roberts	1,157
Deathtrap	1,792	Me and My Girl	1,412	Annie Get Your Gun	1,147
Gemini	1,788	Hellzapoppin	1,404		
*Miss Saigon	1,781				
Harvey	1,775				

(1) Number of performances through July 23, 1995. * Still running July 23, 1995.

Notable New York Theater Openings, 1994-95 Season

After-Play. A comedy about a reunion between 2 couples, one from New York and the other from Los Angeles, who contemplate their lives over dinner after seeing a thought-provoking play. By Anne Meara. Directed by David Saint. With Rue McClanahan, Barbara Barrie, Merwin Goldsmith, and Larry Keith.

Hamlet. The William Shakespeare tradegy. Directed by Jonthan Kent. With Ralph Fiennes, Francesca Annis, Terence Rigby, Tara FitzGerald, James Laurenson, Peter Eyre, and Damian Lewis.

Having Our Say. Adaptation of the best-selling autobiography of the same title by Sarah and A. Elizabeth Delany. Retells the stories of black centenarian sisters. Written and directed by Emily Mann. With Gloria Foster and Mary Alice.

The Heiress. Revival of a 1947 adaptation of the Henry James novel *Washington Square*. By Ruth and Augustus Goetz. Directed by Geral Guiterrez. With Philip Bosco, Cherry Jones, Jon Tenney, and Frances Sternhagen.

How to Succeed in Business Without Really Trying. Revival of the 1961 musical. Words and lyrics by Frank Loesser. Book by Abe Burrows, Jack Weinstock, and Willie Gilbert. Directed by Des McAnuff. Choreography by Wayne Cilento. With Matthew Broderick, Jonathan Freeman, Ronn Carroll, Megan Mullally, Victoria Clark, Jeff Blumenkrantz, Lillias White.

Indiscretions. Adaptation of the 1938 Jean Cocteau play *Les Parents Terribles*. The story of a mother obsessed with her son's life. Translated by Jeremy Sams. Directed by Sean Mathia. With Kathleen Turner, Eileen Atkins, Roger Rees, Jude Law, and Cynthia Nixon.

London Suite. Collection of four one-act comedies by Neil Simon, all set in a fashinonable London hotel suite. Directed by Daniel Sullivan. With Carole Shelley, Paxton Whitehead, Kate Burton, Jeffrey Jones, and Brooks Ashmanskas.

Love! Valour! Compassion! Drama about a group of gay men who spend 3 summer weekends in a rural New York farmhouse. By Terrace McNally. Directed by Joe Mantello. With Stephen Bogardus, John Benjamin Hickey, Stephen Spinella, John Glover, Nathan Lane, Justin Kirk, and Randy Becker.

Smokey Joe's Cafe: The Songs of Leiber and Stoller. Musical revue featuring the music of the pop songwriting duo Jerry Leiber and Mike Stoller ("Hound Dog," "Love Potion No.9," and "Stand By Me"). Directed by Jerry Zaks. Musical staging by Joey McKneely. With Victor Cook, B. J. Crosby, and Brenda Braxton.

Travels With My Aunt. Adaptation of a Graham Greene novel. A repressed banker, beginning retirement, learns from his eccentric aunt. Adapted and directed by Giles Havergal. With Jim Dale, Brian Murray, Tom Beckett, and Martin Rayner.

Some Notable Nonprofit Professional Theater Companies in the U.S.
Source: Theatre Communications Group, Inc., July 1995

Theater Company	City	State	Theater Company	City	State
Actors Theatre of Louisville	Louisville	KY	Lincoln Center Theater	New York	NY
Alabama Shakespeare Festival	Montgomery	AL	Long Wharf Theatre	New Haven	CT
Alley Theater	Houston	TX	Manhattan Theatre Club	New York	NY
Alliance Theatre Company	Atlanta	GA	Mark Taper Forum	Los Angeles	CA
American Conservatory Theatre	San Francisco	CA	McCarter Theatre Center for the		
American Repertory Theatre	Cambridge	MA	Performing Arts	Princeton	NJ
Arena Stage	Washington	DC	Milwaukee Repertory Theater	Milwaukee	WI
Arizona Theatre Company	Tucson	AZ	Missouri Repertory Theatre	Kansas City	MO
Asolo Theatre Company	Sarasota	FL	Oregon Shakespeare Festival	Ashland	OR
Berkeley Repertory Theatre	Berkeley	CA	Pittsburgh Public Theater	Pittsburgh	PA
Center Stage	Baltimore	MD	Public Theater, The	New York	NY
Children's Theatre Company, The	Minneapolis	MN	Repertory Theatre of St. Louis	St. Louis	MO
Cincinnati Playhouse in the Park	Cincinnati	OH	Roundabout Theatre	New York	NY
Cleveland Play House, The	Cleveland	OH	Seattle Repertory Theatre	Seattle	WA
Dallas Theater Center	Dallas	TX	Shakespeare Theatre, The	Washington	DC
Denver Center Theater Company	Denver	CO	South Coast Repertory	Costa Mesa	CA
Goodman Theatre	Chicago	IL	Studio Arena Theatre	Buffalo	NY
Guthrie Theater, The	Minneapolis	MN	Syracuse Stage	Syracuse	NY
Hartford Stage Company	Hartford	CT	Trinity Repertory Theatre	Providence	RI
Huntington Theatre Company	Boston	MA	Walnut Street Theatre Company,		
Indiana Repertory Theatre	Indianapolis	IN	The	Philadelphia	PA

Some Notable Symphony Orchestras in the U.S.

Source: American Symphony Orchestra League, 1156 Fifteenth St. NW, Suite 800, Washington, DC 20005; July 1995

Symphony Orchestra[1]	Music Director[2]	Symphony Orchestra[1]	Music Director[2]
American Composers (NY)	Dennis Russell Davies	Naples Philharmonic (FL)	Christopher Seaman
American (NY)	Leon Botstein	The Nashville Symphony (TN)	Kenneth S. Schermerhorn
Atlanta (GA)	Yoel Levi	National (Washington, DC)	Leonard Slatkin
Austin (TX)	Sung Kwak	New Haven (CT)	Michael Palmer
Baltimore (MD)	David Zinman	New Jersey (Newark)	Zdenek Macal
Baton Rouge (LA)	James Paul	New Mexico (Albuquerque)	Neal H. Stulberg
Boston (MA)	Seiji Ozawa	New World Symphony (Miami	
Brooklyn Philharmonic (NY)	Dennis Russell Davies	Beach, FL)	Michael Tilson Thomas
Buffalo Philharmonic (NY)	Maximiano Valdez	New York Chamber Sym. of	
Cedar Rapids (IA)	Christian Tiemeyer	the 92nd St. Y (NYC)	Gerard Schwarz
Charleston (SC)	David Stahl	New York Philharmonic (NYC)	Kurt Masur
Charlotte (NC)	Peter McCoppin	New York Pops, Inc. (NY)	Skitch Henderson
Chattanooga, & Opera Assn.		North Carolina (Raleigh)	Gerhardt Zimmermann
(TN)	Robert Bernhardt	Oklahoma City Philharmonic (OK)	Joel A. Levine
Chicago (IL)	Daniel Barenboim	Omaha (NE)	Victor Yampolsky
Cincinnati (OH)	Jesus Lopez-Cobos	Oregon (Portland)	James DePreist
Cleveland (OH)	Christoph von Dohnanyi	Pacific Symphony (Irvine, CA)	Carl St. Clair
Colorado (Denver)	Marin Alsop	The Philadelphia Orchestra (PA)	Wolfgang Sawallisch
Colorado Springs (CO)	Christopher P. Wilkins	Phoenix (AZ)	James L. Sedares
Columbus (OH)	Alessandro Siciliani	Philharmonia Baroque (CA)	Nicholas McGegan
Dallas (TX)	Andrew Litton	Pittsburgh (PA)	Lorin Maazel
Dayton Philharmonic (OH)	Isaiah Jackson	Portland (ME)	Toshiyuki Shimada
Delaware (Wilmington)	Stephen Gunzenhauser	Puerto Rico (Santurce)	Eugene Kohn
Detroit (MI)	Neeme Jarvi	Rhode Island Philharmonic Or.	
The Florida Orchestra (Tampa)	Jahja Ling	(Providence)	Zuohuang Chen
Florida Philharmonic (Ft. Lauderdale)	James Judd	The Richmond Symphony (VA)	George Manahan
Florida Symphonic Pops (Boca Raton)	Derek Stannard	Rochester Philharmonic Or. (NY)	Peter Bay
Florida West Coast (FL)	Paul C. Wolfe	Sacramento (CA)	Geoffrey Simon
Fort Wayne Philharmonic (IN)	Edward Chivzel	St. Louis (MO)	Hans Vonk
Fort Worth (TX)	John Giordano	St. Paul Chamber Or. (MN)	Hugh Wolff
Grand Rapids (MI)	Catherine Comet	San Antonio (TX)	Christopher P. Wilkins
Grant Park (Chicago, IL)	Hugh Wolff	San Diego (CA)	Yoav Talmi
Greenville (SC)	Davis Pollitt	San Francisco (CA)	Herbert Blomstedt
Hartford (CT)	Michael Lankester	San Jose (CA)	Leonid Grin
Houston (TX)	Christoph Eschenbach	Santa Barbara (CA)	Gisele Ben-Dor
Hudson Valley Philharmonic		Savannah (GA)	Philip B. Greenberg
(Poughkeepsie, NY)	Randall Craig Fleischer	Seattle (WA)	Gerard Schwarz
Indianapolis (IN)	Raymond Leppard	Shreveport (LA)	Peter Leonard
Jacksonville (FL)	Roger Nierenberg	Spokane (WA)	Fabio Mechetti
Kansas City (MO)	William McGlaughlin	Springfield (MA)	Raymond C. Harvey
Knoxville (TN)	Kirk Trevor	Syracuse (NY)	Fabio Mechetti
Long Beach (CA)	JoAnn Falletta	Toldeo (OH)	Andrew Massey
Long Island Philharmonic (NY)	Marin Alsop	Tucson (AZ)	Robert E. Bernhardt
Los Angeles Chamber Or. (CA)	Christof Perick	Tulsa Philharmonic Or. (OK)	Bernard Rubenstein
Los Angeles Philharmonic (CA)	Esa-Pekka Salonen	Utah (Salt Lake City)	Joseph Silverstein
The Louisville Orchestra (KY)	Joseph Silverstein	The Virginia Symphony (Norfolk)	JoAnn Falletta
Memphis (TN)	Alan Balter	West Virginia (Charleston)	Thomas B. Conlin
Milwaukee (WI)	Zdenek Macal	Wichita (KS)	Zuohuang Chen
The Minnesota Orchestra (Minneapolis)	Edo de Waart	Winston-Salem Piedmont	
Mississippi (Jackson)	Colman Pearce	Triad Symphony (NC)	Peter J. Perret
Music of the Baroque (IL)	Thomas S. Wikman		

(1) Orchestra name = place name + Symphony Orchestra, unless otherwise noted. (2) General title; listed is highest-ranking member of conducting personnel.

U.S. Opera Companies With Budgets of $500,000 or More

Source: OPERA America, 1156 15th Street NW, Washington, DC 20005-1704; July 1995

Albuquerque Civic Light Opera (NM); Linda E. McVey, exec. dir.
American Music Theater Festival (Phila.); Marjorie Samoff, prod. dir.
Anchorage Opera (AK); Peter Brown, gen. dir.
Arizona Opera Co. (Tucson); Glynn Ross, gen. dir.
Aspen Opera Theatre Center (CO); Thomas Eirman, gen. mgr.
The Atlanta Opera (GA); Alfred Kennedy, gen. dir.
Augusta Opera (GA); Edward Bradberry, gen. dir.
The Austin Lyric Opera (TX); Joseph McClain, gen. dir.
Baltimore Opera Co. (MD); Michael Harrison, gen. dir.
Birmingham Opera Theatre (AL); Gregory Thomas, exec. dir.
Boston Lyric Opera Company (MA); Janice Mancini Del Sesto, gen. dir.
Boston Opera Theatre; Robert Canon, exec. dir.
Brooklyn Academy of Music; Harvey Lichtenstein, pres. & exec. prod.
Central City Opera (Denver, CO); Daniel Rule, gen. mgr.
Chautauqua Opera (NY); Jay Lesenger, art. dir.
Chicago Opera Theater; Alan Stone, art. dir.
The Cincinnati Opera; Paul A. Stuhlreyer III, mng. dir.
Cleveland Opera; David Bamberger, gen. dir.
Connecticut Grand Opera & Stamford State Opera, Laurence Gilgore, art. dir.

Connecticut Opera (Hartford); George Osborne, gen. dir.
The Dallas Opera; Plato Karayanis, gen. dir.
Dayton Opera Assn. (OH); Jane Nelson, gen. dir.
Des Moines Metro Opera (Indianola, IA); Robert Larsen, art. dir.
Florentine Opera of Milwaukee; Dennis Hanthorn, gen. mgr.
Florida Grand Opera; Robert Heuer, gen. mgr.
Fort Lauderdale Opera (FL); Marvin David Levy, art. dir.
Fort Worth Opera; William Walker, gen. dir.
Fullerton Civic Light Opera (CA); Griff Duncan, gen. mgr.
Glimmerglass Opera (Cooperstown, NY); Paul Kellogg, gen. mgr.
Goodspeed Opera House (E. Haddam, CT); Michael Price, exec. dir.
Greater Buffalo Opera (NY); Gary Burgess, gen. dir.
Hawaii Opera Theatre; J. Mario Ramos, gen. dir.
Houston Grand Opera Assn.; David Gockley, gen. dir
Indianapolis Opera; Nando Scheller, gen. dir.
Kentucky Opera Assn. (Louisville); Thomson Smillie, gen. dir.
Knoxville Opera (TN); Robert Lyall, gen. dir.
L.A. Music Center Opera Assn.; Peter Hemmings, gen. dir.
Long Beach Civic Light Opera (CA); Clare Faulkner, gen. mgr.
Long Beach Opera (CA); Michael Milenski, gen. dir.
Lyric Opera Cleveland (OH); Jane Keegan Evans, mng. dir.
Lyric Opera of Chicago; Ardis Krainik, gen. dir.

Lyric Opera of Kansas City (MO); Russell Patterson, gen. dir. & art. dir.
Magic Circle Opera Repertory Ensemble (NY); Ray Evans Harrell, art. dir.
Metro Lyric Opera (NJ); Era M. Tognoli, gen. & art. dir.
Metropolitan Opera Assn. (NYC); Joseph Volpe, gen. mgr.
Michigan Opera Theatre (Detroit); David DiChiera, gen. dir.
The Minnesota Opera Co. (St. Paul); Kevin Smith, gen. dir.
Music-Theatre Group (NY & Stockbridge, MA); Lyn Austin, prod. dir.
National Grand Opera, Inc. (NY); Linda Holgers, gen. dir.
Nevada Opera (Reno); Esther Nelson, gen. dir.
Nevada Opera Theatre; Eileen Hayes, gen. & art. dir.
New Jersey State Opera (Newark); Alfredo Silipigni, art. dir.
New Orleans Opera Assn.; Arthur Cosenza, gen. dir.
New York City Opera Natl. Co.; Clifford Kellas, tour coordinator
New York City Opera; Christopher Keene, gen. dir.
Ohio Light Opera; James Stuart, art. dir.
Opera Carolina (Charlotte, NC); James Wright, gen. dir.
Opera Colorado (Denver); Nathaniel Merrill, art. dir.
Opera Company of Boston; Sarah Caldwell, art. dir.
Opera Company of Philadelphia; Robert B. Driver, gen. dir.
Opera Festival of NJ (Princeton Junction); Deborah S. Sandler, gen. dir.
Opera Grand Rapids (MI); Robert Lyall, gen. dir.
Opera Memphis (TN); Michael Ching, gen./art. dir
Opera Northeast (NY); Donald Westwood, art. dir.
Opera Omaha (NE); Hal France, interim gen. dir.
Opera Orchestra of NY (NYC); Eve Queler, art. dir.
Opera Pacific (Costa Mesa, CA); David DiChiera, gen. dir.
Opera San José (CA); Irene Dalis, gen. dir.
Opera Theatre at Wildwood (AZ); Ann Chotard, art. dir.
Opera Theatre of St. Louis (MO); Charles MacKay, gen. dir.
Opera/Columbus (OH); William F. Russell, gen. dir.

OperaDelaware (Wilmington); Leland Kimball, gen. dir.
Orlando Opera Co. (FL); Robert Swedberg, gen. dir.
Palm Beach Opera (FL); Herbert P. Benn, gen. dir.
The Pennsylvania Opera Theater; Barbara Silverstein, art. dir.
Pittsburgh Civic Light Opera; Charles Gray, exec. dir.
Pittsburgh Opera; Tito Capobianco, gen. dir.
Playwrights Horizons (NYC); Leslie Marcus, mng. dir.
Portland Opera Assn. (OR); Robert Bailey, exec. dir.
Sacramento Opera Assn. (CA); Marianne H. Oaks, gen. dir.
The St. Ann Center for Restoration and the Arts (Brooklyn, NY); Susan Feldman, art. dir.
San Diego Civic Light Opera Assn.; Leon Drew, gen. mgr.
San Diego Opera Assn.; Ian Campbell, gen. dir.
San Francisco Opera Center (Western Opera Theater); Christopher Hahn, dir.
San Francisco Opera; Lotfi Mansouri, gen. dir.
San José Civic Light Opera (CA); Dianna Shuster, dir.
The Santa Fe Opera (NM); John Crosby, gen. dir.
Sarasota Opera Assn. (FL); Deane Allyn, exec. dir.
Seattle Opera Assn.; Speight Jenkins, gen. dir.
Skylight Opera Theatre (Milwaukee); Joan Lounsbery, mng. dir.
Southeastern Regional Opera (SC); Einar Anderson, art. dir.
Syracuse Opera (NY); Julie Richard, mng. dir.
Teatro de la Opera, Inc. (PR); Alberto Esteves, art. dir.
Texas Opera Theater (Houston); James Ireland, gen. mgr.
Toledo Opera (OH); James Meena, art. dir.
Tri-Cities Opera (Binghamton, NY); Marilyn Cotter, exec. dir.
Tulsa Opera (OK); Myrna S. Ruffner, gen. mgr.
Utah Opera (Salt Lake City); Anne Ewers, gen. dir.
Virginia Opera (Norfolk); Peter Mark, gen. dir.
The Washington Opera (DC); Patricia Mossel, exec. dir.
Wolf Trap Opera (Vienna, VA); Peter Russell, gen. dir.

Some Notable U.S. Dance Companies

Source: Dance/USA, 1156 15th Street NW, Washington, DC 20005-1704; July 1995

African-American Dance Ensemble, Durham, NC
Alvin Ailey American Dance Theater, New York, NY
Aman Folk Ensemble, Los Angeles, CA
American Ballet Theatre, New York, NY
American Repertory Ballet Company, Princeton, NJ
Atlanta Ballet, GA
Avaz International Dance Theatre, Los Angeles, CA
Ballet Arizona, Phoenix, AZ
Ballet Concierto de Puerto Rico, Santurce, PR
Ballet Florida, West Palm Beach, FL
Ballet Hispanico of New York, New York, NY
BalletMet Columbus, Columbus, OH
Ballet Omaha, NE
Ballet West, Salt Lake City, UT
Karen Bamonte Dance Works, Philadelphia, PA
Tandy Beal and Company, Santa Cruz, CA
Maria Benitez Teatro Flamenco, Santa Fe, NM
Boston Ballet, Boston, MA
Trisha Brown Company, New York, NY
Donald Byrd/The Group, New York, NY
Caribbean Dance Company of the Virgin Isl., St. Croix, VI
Chen & Dancers, New York, NY
Lucinda Childs Dance Company, New York, NY
Cincinnati Ballet, Cincinnati, OH
Cleveland San Jose Ballet, Cleveland, OH
Cunningham Dance Foundation, New York, NY
Dallas Black Dance Theatre, Dallas, TX
Dance Alloy, Pittsburgh, PA
Dance Exchange, Washington, DC
Dance Theatre of Harlem, New York, NY
DanceBrazil, New York, NY
Dayton Ballet, Dayton, OH
Dayton Contemporary Dance Company, Dayton, OH
Laura Dean Musicians and Dancers, New York, NY
Eiko & Koma, New York, NY
Eugene Ballet Company, Eugene, OR
Garth Fagan Dance, Rochester, NY
Feld Ballets/NY, New York, NY
Fort Worth Dallas Ballet, Fort Worth, TX
Joe Goode Performance Group, San Francisco, CA
David Gordon/Pick Up Co., New York, NY
Martha Graham Dance Co., New York, NY
Hartford Ballet, Hartford, CT
Erick Hawkins Dance Co., New York, NY
Joseph Holmes Dance Theater, Chicago, IL
Houston Ballet, Houston, TX
Hubbard Street Dance Chicago, Chicago, IL
Indianapolis Ballet Theatre, Indianapolis, IN
Isaacs, McCaleb & Dancers, San Diego, CA
Jazz Tap Ensemble, Los Angeles, CA
Margaret Jenkins Dance Company, San Francisco, CA
The Joffrey Ballet, New York, NY

Bill T. Jones/Arnie Zane Company, New York, NY
Ko-Thi Dance Company, Bronx, NY
Ralph Lemon Company, New York, NY
Lewitzky Dance Company, Los Angeles, CA
Limón Dance Company, New York, NY
LINES Contemporary Ballet, San Francisco, CA
Louisville Ballet, Louisville, KY
Lar Lubovitch Dance Company, New York, NY
Miami City Ballet, Miami Beach, FL
Bebe Miller and Company, New York, NY
Elisa Monte Dance Company, New York, NY
Montgomery Ballet, Montgomery, AL
Mordine & Company, Chicago, IL
Mark Morris Dance Group, New York, NY
Muntu Dance Theatre, Chicago, IL
Nashville Ballet, Nashville, TN
Nevada Dance Theatre, Las Vegas, NV
New York City Ballet, New York, NY
Nikolais and Murray Louis Dance, New York, NY
North Carolina Dance Theatre, Charlotte, NC
Oakland Ballet, Oakland, CA
ODC/San Francisco, San Francisco, CA
Ohio Ballet, Akron, OH
Oregon Ballet Theatre, Portland, OR
Pacific Northwest Ballet, Seattle, WA
The Parsons Dance Company, New York, NY
Pennsylvania Ballet, Philadelphia, PA
Pepatián, Bronx, NY
Philadanco, Philadelphia, PA
Pilobolus Dance Theater, Washington, CT
Stuart Pimsler Dance & Theater, Columbus, OH
Pittsburgh Ballet Theatre, Pittsburgh, PA
Rhythm in Shoes, Spring Valley, OH
Richmond Ballet, Richmond, VA
Ririe-Woodbury Dance Company, Salt Lake City, UT
Cleo Parker Robinson Dance Ensemble, Denver, CO
Betty Salamun's DANCECIRCUS, Milwaukee, WI
San Francisco Ballet, San Francisco, CA
Carlota Santana Spanish Dance Arts Co., New York, NY
James Sewell Dance, Minneapolis, MN
Solomons Company/Dance, New York, NY
State Ballet of Missouri, Kansas City, MO
Elizabeth Streb Ringside, New York, NY
Paul Taylor Dance Company, New York, NY
Tulsa Ballet Theatre, Tulsa, OK
Urban Bush Women, New York, NY
Washington Ballet, Washington, DC
Lula Washington's L.A. Contemporary Dance Theatre, Los Angeles, CA
June Watanabe in Company, San Rafael, CA
Zivili Kolo Ensemble, Granville, OH

100 Best-Selling U.S. Magazines, 1994

Source: Audit Bureau of Circulations, Schaumburg, IL

General magazines, exclusive of groups and comics; also exclusive of magazines that failed to file reports to ABC by press time. Based on total average paid circulation during the 6 months prior to Dec. 31, 1994.

Magazine	Circulation	Magazine	Circulation	Magazine	Circulation
1. NRTA/AARP Bulletin	21,875,436	33. Field & Stream	2,004,087	67. Entertainment Weekly	1,115,024
2. Modern Maturity . . .	21,716,727	34. Money	1,982,123	68. Kiplinger's	1,095,652
3. Reader's Digest . . .	15,126,664	35. Seventeen	1,978,155	69. PC Magazine	1,051,381
4. TV Guide	14,037,062	36. Ebony	1,937,095	70. Family Handyman. .	1,041,098
5. The Conde Nast Select	12,850,436	37. YM.	1,933,775	71. Scouting	1,037,291
6. National Geographic	9,203,079	38. Country Living.	1,932,840	72. Weight Watchers. . .	1,031,177
7. Better Homes & Gar-		39. Parents	1,852,517	73. House Beautiful . . .	1,023,697
dens.	7,613,661	40. Popular Science . . .	1,808,140	74. Globe.	1,021,929
8. Good Housekeeping	5,223,935	41. Popular Mechanics .	1,636,210	75. Country Home	1,018,362
9. Ladies' Home Journal	5,048,081	42. Life	1,596,862	76. Home Mechanix . . .	1,009,347
10. Family Circle.	5,005,301	43. Outdoor Life	1,503,257	77. Discover.	1,008,916
11. Woman's Day	4,724,500	44. Sunset	1,498,417	78. Home.	1,005,751
12. McCall's	4,611,848	45. Golf Digest	1,465,494	79. Country America. . .	1,001,089
13. Time	4,036,146	46. Soap Opera Digest .	1,422,958	80. Endless Vacation . .	975,869
14. Prevention	3,427,803	47. Penthouse	1,304,719	81. Disney Adventures .	961,992
15. AAA World	3,425,655	48. Mademoiselle	1,304,059	82. AAA Going Places .	953,194
16. People	3,424,858	49. New Woman.	1,301,859	83. PC World	951,849
17. Redbook	3,401,775	50. 'Teen	1,280,148	84. Motor Trend	951,650
18. Playboy	3,401,264	51. Golf	1,269,642	85. Essence.	950,634
19. Sports Illustrated . . .	3,252,641	52. Men's Health	1,258,493	86. Martha Stewart Living	948,838
20. Newsweek	3,158,617	53. Cooking Light	1,248,939	87. Jet	948,254
21. National Enquirer . .	3,066,032	54. Boys' Life	1,242,594	88. Travel & Leisure . . .	927,790
22. American Legion. . .	2,945,123	55. First for Women . . .	1,236,019	89. Health	916,952
23. Star	2,752,280	56. Rolling Stone	1,221,417	90. Gourmet.	912,342
24. Cosmopolitan	2,527,928	57. Consumer's Digest .	1,208,643	91. Conde Nast Traveler	909,092
25. Southern Living. . . .	2,472,649	58. Self	1,201,395	92. Victoria.	907,034
26. U.S. News & World		59. Bon Appetit.	1,187,437	93. Elle	905,498
Report	2,240,710	60. Vogue	1,181,313	94. PC/Computing	900,165
27. Smithsonian	2,214,509	61. Us	1,177,395	95. Fortune	887,205
28. Motorland.	2,194,221	62. Woman's World . . .	1,167,314	96. Architectural Digest.	881,232
29. Glamour.	2,181,316	63. True Story Plus	1,143,479	97. Business Week. . . .	880,357
30. Home & Away.	2,146,295	64. Vanity Fair	1,130,993	98. Nation's Business . .	861,620
31. NEA Today.	2,115,968	65. Car and Driver	1,125,119	99. Parenting	856,019
32. VFW	2,038,216	66. Sesame Street	1,116,756	100. Midwest Life	852,704

Notable Books, 1995

Source: American Library Association, Chicago, IL; as of Jan. 1995

Fiction

In the Time of the Butterflies, Julia Alvarez
The Birthday Boys, Beryl Bainbridge
Souls Raised From the Dead, Doris Betts
The End of Vandalism, Tom Drury
Scar Tissue, Michael Ignatieff
Ancestral Truths, Sara Maitland
Open Secrets, Alice Munro
The Bird Artist, Howard Norman
In the Lake of the Woods, Tim O'Brien

The Collected Stories, Grace Paley
The Grass Dancer, Susan Power
The Cage, Audrey Schulman

Poetry

The Ghost Trio: Poems, Linda Bierds
A Silence Opens, Amy Clampitt

Nonfiction

Warriors Don't Cry, Melba Bealbs
A Man on the Moon, Andrew Chaikin

Train Go Sorry, Leah Hager Cohen
Colored People, Henry Gates
Shot in the Heart, Mikal Gilmore
No Ordinary Time, Doris Goodwin
Out of Silenced, Russell Martin
How We Die, Sherwin Nuland
A Whole New Life, Reynolds Price
The Beak of the Finch, Jonathan Weiner
9 Highland Rd., Michael Winerip
In Pharaoh's Army, Tobias Wolff

Notable Books for Children and Young Adults, 1995

Source: American Library Association, Chicago, IL; as of Jan. 1995

All Ages

Smoky Night, Eve Bunting
The Passover Journey, Barbara Diamond Goldin
Swamp Angel, Anne Isaacs
The Creation, James Weldon Johnson
De Colores and Other Latin-American Folk Songs, Jose Luis Orozco
Winter Poems, Barbara Rogasky
Time Flies, Eric Rohmann
The Christmas Alphabet, Robert Sabuda

Younger Readers

The Golly Sisters Ride Again, Betsy Byars
Barnyard Banter, Denise Fleming
Tough Boris, Mem Fox
The Rattlebang Picnic, Margaret Mahy
Harvey Potter's Balloon Farm, Jerdine Nolen

How To Make Apple Pie and See The World, Marjorie Priceman
Good Night, Gorilla, Peggy Rathmann
The Surprise Family, Lynn Reiser
How Now, Brown Cow, Alice Schertle
Hi!, Ann Herbert Scott
Don't Fidget a Feather, Erica Silverman
A Hat for Minerva Louise, Janet Morgan Stoeke
Too Tired, Ann Turnbull
Going Home, Margaret Wild
Out Granny, Maragaret Wild

Middle Grade Readers

Misoso, Verna Aardema
Coming Home, Floyd Cooper
Sister Shako and Kolo the Goat, Vedat Dalakoy
The Big Bug Book, Margery Facklam
Beast Feast, Douglas Florian

Meet Danitra Brown, Nikki Grimes
Sweet and Sour Animal Book, Langston Hughes
Russian Girl, Russ Kendall
The Three Princes, Eric Kimmel
Three Terrible Trins, Dick King-Smith
The Librarian Who Measured the Earth, Kathryn Lasky
John Henry, Julius Lester
Seven Spiders Spinning, Gregory Maguire
Outside and Inside Birds, Sandra Markle
Hob and the Goblins, William Mayne
Coyote, Gerald McDermott
My Rotten Redheaded Older Brother, Patricia Polacco
Pink and Say, Patricia Polacco
Cleopatra, Diane Stanley and Peter Vennema

Junior High School Age Readers

The Barn, Avi
Tell Them We Remember, Susan Bachrach
The Amazing Paper Cuttings of Hans Christian Andersen, Beth Wagner Brust
I See the Moon, C.B. Christiansen
Walk Two Moons, Sharon Creech
Catherine, Called Birdy, Karen Cushman
Guests, Michael Dorris
The Ear, the Eye, and the Arm, Nancy Farmer
Flour Babies, Anne Fine
War Game, Michael Foreman
Kids at Work, Russell Freedman
It's Perfectly Normal, Robie Harris
Phoenix Rising, Karen Hesse
Adam and Eve and Pinch-Me, Julie Johnson
Tiger, Tiger, Burning Bright, Ron Koertge
Jazz, Morgan Monceaux
Earthshine, Theresa Nelson
Iblis, Shulamith Oppenheim
Celebrate America, Nora Panzer
Flip-Flop Girl, Katherine Paterson
The Boys of St. Petri, Bjarne Reuter
Under the Blood Red Sun, Graham Salisbury
I Am an American, Jerry Stanley
Focus, Sylvia Wolf
I Hadn't Meant to Tell You This, Jacqueline Woodson

Young Adult (Teenage)—Fiction

In the Time of the Butterflies, Julia Alvarez
Tell Them We Remember, Susan Bachrach
Am I Blue?, Marion Dane Bauer
Song of Be, Lesley Beake
Dakota Dream, James Bennett
Heartbreak and Roses, Janet Bode and Stan Mack
Looking After Lily, Cindy Bonner
The Examination, Malcolm Bosse

Traveling on Into the Light: And Other Stories, Martha Brooks
Pigs Don't Fly, Mary Brown
Finder: A Novel of the Borderlands, Emma Bull
Parable of the Sower, Octavia E. Butler
Cool Salsa, Lori M. Carlson
Driver's Ed., B. Caroline Cooney
Oddly Enough, Bruce Coville
Catherine, Called Birdy, Karen Cushman
The Ear, the Eye, and the Arm, Nancy Farmer
Flight of the Dragon Kyn, Susan Fletcher
Kids at Work, Russell Freedman
Billy, Albert French
Stranger at the Wedding, Barbara Hambly
No Effect, Daniel Hayes
Phoenix Rising, Karen Hesse
It's Nothing to a Mountain, Sid Hite
Say it Loud! The Story of Rap Music, Maurice K. Jones
Wolf-Woman, Sherryl Jordan
Deliver Us From Evie, M.E. Kerr
Owl in Love, Patrice Kindl
The Beekeeper's Apprentice, R. Laurie King
Zoo Book: The Evolution of Wildlife Conservation Centers, Linda Koebner
Tiger, Tiger, Burning Bright, Ron Koertge
Spite Fences, Trudy Krisher
After a Suicide: Young People Speak Up, Susan Kuklin
Beyound the Burning Time, Kathryn Laksy
Shadow Catcher: The Life & Work of Edwards S. Curtis, Laurie Lawlor
Escape From Egypt, Sonia Levitin
Gypsy Davey, Chris Lynch
Iceman, Chris Lynch
Unconditional Surrender: U.S. Grant & the Civil War, Albert Marrin
Letters From the Inside, John Marsden
Makes Me Wanna Holler, Nathan McCall
The Glory Field, Walter Dean Myers

Sarajevo: A Portrait of the Seige, Matthew Naythons
Earthshine, Theresa Nelson
The Great Apes: Between Two Worlds, Michael Nichols
The Magic and the Healing, Nick O'Donohoe
Celebrate America, Nora Panzer
Winterdance: The Fine Madness of Running the Iditarod, Gary Paulsen
Something Terrible Happened, Barbara Ann Porte
The Grass Dancer, Susan Power
Come in From the Cold, Marsha Qualey
Missing the Piano, Adam Rapp
The Boys From St. Petri, Bjarne Reuter
Too Soon for Jeff, Marilyn Reynolds
Those Who Love the Game: Glenn "Doc" Rivers on Life in the NBA and Elsewhere, Glenn Rivers and Bruce Brooks
Hannah In Between, Colby Rodowsky
Shakespeare & MacBeth: The Story Behind the Play, Stewart Ross
Billy, Laura Roybal
Something Permanent, Cynthia Rylant and Walker Evans
Under the Blood-Red Sun, Graham Salisbury
The Cage, Audrey Schulman
Wish You Were Here, Barbara Shoup
Coffee Will Make You Black, April Sinclair
Toughing It, Nancy Springer
Cezanne Pinto, Mary Stolz
Hearing Us Out: Voices from the Gay & Lesbian Community, Roger Sutton
Shadow, Joyce Sweeney
The Ramsay Scallop, Frances Temple
When She Hollers, Cynthia Voigt
My Brother, My Sister, and I, Yoko Kawashima Watkins
Mysterium, Robert Charles Wilson
Focus: Five Women Photographers, Syliva Wolf
I Hadn't Meant to Tell You This, Jacqueline Woodson

Best-Selling Books, 1994

Source: *Publishers Weekly*, Mar. 20, 1995.

Rankings are determined by sales figures provided by publishers; the numbers used in ranking titles generally reflect reports of copies "shipped and billed" in 1994, not final net sales.

Hardcover Fiction

1. *The Chamber*, John Grisham
2. *Debt of Honor*, Tom Clancy
3. *The Celestine Prophecy*, James Redfield
4. *The Gift*, Danielle Steel
5. *Insomnia*, Stephen King
6. *Politically Correct Bedtime Stories*, James Finn Garner
7. *Wings*, Danielle Steel
8. *Accident*, Danielle Steel
9. *The Bridges of Madison County*, Robert James Waller
10. *Disclosure*, Michael Crichton
11. *Nothing Lasts Forever*, Sidney Sheldon
12. *Taltos*, Anne Rice
13. *Dark Rivers of the Heart*, Dean Koontz
14. *The Lottery Winner*, Mary Higgins Clark
15. *Remember Me*, Mary Higgins Clark

Hardcover Nonfiction

1. *In the Kitchen with Rosie*, Rosie Daley
2. *Men Are From Mars, Women Are From Venus*, John Gray
3. *Crossing the Threshold of Hope*, by John Paul II
4. *Magic Eye I*, N.E. Thing Enterprises
5. *The Book of Virtues*, William J. Bennett
6. *Magic Eye II*, N.E. Thing Enterprises
7. *Embraced by the Light*, Betty J. Eadie with Curtis Taylor
8. *Don't Stand Too Close to a Naked Man*, Tim Allen

9. *Couplehood*, Paul Reiser
10. *Magic Eye III*, N.E. Thing Enterprises
11. *Dolly*, Dolly Parton
12. *James Herriott's Cat Stories*, James Herriott
13. *Barbara Bush*, Barbara Bush
14. *Nicole Brown Simpson*, Faye D. Resnick
15. *The Bubba Gump Shrimp Co. Cookbook*, Oxmoor House/Leisure Arts

Trade Paperback

1. *Schindler's List*, Thomas Keneally
2. *Homicidal Psycho Jungle Cat*, Bill Waterson
3. *Chicken Soup for the Soul*, Jack Canfield and Mark Victor Hansen
4. *The T-Factor Fat Gram Counter*, Jamie Pope-Cordle and Martin Katahn
5. *Care of the Soul*, Thomas Moore
6. *The Curse of Madame "C"*, Gary Larson
7. *The Shipping News*, E. Annie Proulx
8. *Butter Busters: The Cookbook*, Pam Mycoskie
9. *Gumpisms*, Winston Groom
10. *Magic Eye Poster Book*, N.E. Thing Enterprises
11. *Magic Eye Book of Postcards*, N.E. Thing Enterprises
12. *Lasher*, Anne Rice
13. *Beavis & Butthead's Ensucklopedia*, Mike Judge
14. *The Pocket Powter*, Susan Powter
15. *Pigs in Heaven*, Barbara Kingsolver

(continued)

Best-Selling Books, 1994 *(continued)*

Mass-Market Paperback

1. *The Client*, John Grisham
2. *Disclosure*, Michael Crichton
3. *Without Remorse*, Tom Clancy
4. *Vanished*, Danielle Steel
5. *I'll Be Seeing You*, Mary Higgins Clark
6. *Interview With the Vampire*, Anne Rice
7. *Nightmares & Dreamscapes*, Stephen King
8. *A Case of Need*, Michael Crichton
9. *Winter Moon*, Dean Koontz
10. *Pleading Guilty*, Scott Turow
11. *The Door to December*, Dean Koontz
12. *Mr. Murder*, Dean Koontz
13. *Ruby*, V.C. Andrews
14. *Pearl in the Mist*, V.C. Andrews
15. *Slow Waltz in Cedar Bend*, Robert James Waller

Almanacs, Atlases, and Annuals

1. *The World Almanac and Book of Facts 1995*, ed. Robert Famighetti
2. *The World Almanac and Book of Facts 1994*, ed. Robert Famighetti
3. *J. K. Lasser's Your Income Tax, 1995*, The J. Lasser Institute
4. *The 1994 Information Please Almanac*
5. *The Ernst & Young Tax Guide 1994*, Ernst & Young

Leading U.S. and Canadian Daily Newspapers, 1994

Source: 1995 Editor & Publisher International Yearbook

(Circulation as of Sept. 30, 1994; m = morning, e = evening)

As of Feb. 1, 1995, U.S. daily newspapers had declined to 1,548, a net loss of 8 when compared with the same date in 1994. When comparing the average daily circulation for the 6-month period ending Sept. 30, 1994, with the average for the same period in 1993, circulation dropped 506,158, from 59,811,594 to 59,305,436. Although both the number of Saturday editions and Sunday editions increased during 1994—by 3 and 2 respectively—the average Sunday circulation decreased for the 6-month period ending Sept. 30, 1994, falling 270,775, from 62,565,574 to 62,294,799.

As of Feb. 1, 1995, there were 2 fewer Canadian dailies, bringing the total number of daily newspapers in Canada to 107. Six fewer evening and 4 additional morning editions account for the changes. Canadian circulation fell by 128,682 in the 6-month period prior to Sept. 30, 1994. During the same period, Sunday circulation decreased by 47,423. Loss of Sunday circulation was accompanied by a drop of 2 in the number of Sunday papers.

Newspaper		Circulation
1. *Wall Street Journal* (New York, NY)	(m)	1,780,442
2. *USA Today* (Arlington, VA)	(m)	1,465,926
3. *Times* (New York, NY)	(m)	1,114,905
4. *Times* (Los Angeles, CA).	(m)	1,062,202
5. *Post* (Washington, DC)	(m)	810,675
6. *Daily News* (New York, NY)	(m)	753,024
7. *Newsday* (Long Isl./New York, NY)	(all day)	693,556
8. *Tribune* (Chicago, IL)	(m)	678,081
9. *Free Press* (Detroit, MI).	(m)	554,606
10. *Sun-Times* (Chicago, IL)	(m)	518,094
11. *Chronicle* (San Francisco,CA) . . .	(m)	509,548
12. *Globe* (Boston, MA)	(m)	506,545
13. *Star* (Toronto, Ont.)	(m)	494,719
14. *Morning News* (Dallas, TX)	(m)	491,480
15. *Inquirer* (Philadelphia, PA).	(m)	478,999
16. *Star-Ledger* (Newark, NJ)	(m)	455,919
17. *Chronicle* (Houston, TX)	(m)	409,340
18. *Star Tribune* (Minneapolis, MN) . .	(m)	407,504
19. *Post* (New York, NY).	(m)	405,318
20. *Plain Dealer* (Cleveland, OH). . . .	(m)	394,692
21. *Herald* (Miami, FL)	(m)	393,791
22. *Union-Tribune* (San Diego, CA) . .	(all day)	372,466
23. *Arizona Republic* (Phoenix, AZ) . .	(m)	362,199
24. *News* (Detroit, MI).	(e)	355,970
25. *Times* (St. Petersburg, FL)	(m)	354,164
26. *Register* (Orange County, CA) . . .	(m)	350,887
27. *Rocky Mountain News* (Denver, CO)	(m)	344,585
28. *Oregonian* (Portland, OR)	(all day)	334,744
29. *Post-Dispatch* (St. Louis, MO) . . .	(m)	333,968
30. *Herald* (Boston, MA)	(m)	309,935
31. *Constitution* (Atlanta, GA)	(m)	309,906
32. *Globe and Mail* (Toronto, Ont.). . .	(m)	306,260
33. *News* (Buffalo, NY)	(all day)	296,820
34. *Star* (Kansas City, MO)	(m)	290,650
35. *Post* (Denver, CO)	(m)	287,213
36. *Mercury News* (San Jose, CA). . .	(all day)	283,590
37. *Post* (Houston, TX)	(m)	281,628
38. *Bee* (Sacramento, CA)	(m)	275,696
39. *Le Journal* (Montreal, Que.)	(m)	273,588
40. *Sentinel* (Orlando, FL).	(all day)	270,970
41. *Times-Picayune* (New Orleans, LA)	(all day)	267,938
42. *Sun-Sentinel* (Ft. Lauderdale, FL)	(m)	263,256
43. *Tribune* (Tampa, FL)	(m)	264,400
44. *Dispatch* (Columbus, OH)	(m)	260,355
45. *Sun* (Baltimore, MD)	(m)	248,520
46. *Post-Gazette* (Pittsburgh, PA) . . .	(m)	248,183
47. *Sun* (Toronto, Ont.).	(m)	243,336
48. *Courier-Journal* (Louisville, KY) . .	(m)	239,595
49. *Star-Telegram* (Ft. Worth, TX) . . .	(all day)	237,031
50. *Observer* (Charlotte, NC).	(m)	236,579
51. *World-Herald* (Omaha, NE)	(all day)	233,035
52. *Express-News* (San Antonio, TX)	(all day)	232,037
53. *Star* (Indianapolis, IN)	(m)	231,423
54. *Times* (Seattle, WA).	(e)	230,286
55. *Courant* (Hartford, CT)	(m)	226,533
56. *Journal* (Milwaukee, WI)	(e)	214,243
57. *Times-Dispatch* (Richmond, VA) . .	(m)	211,227
58. *Pioneer Press* (St. Paul, MN)	(m)	207,802
59. *Daily Oklahoman* (Oklahoma City, OK)	(m)	207,759
60. *Daily News* (Los Angeles, CA) . . .	(m)	207,011
61. *Post-Intelligencer* (Seattle, WA) . .	(m)	203,679
62. *Enquirer* (Cincinnati, OH)	(m)	203,118
63. *Daily News* (Philadelphia, PA). . . .	(m)	196,239
64. *Journal* (Providence, RI)	(all day)	190,876
65. *Sun* (Vancouver, B.C.)	(m)	187,984
66. *La Presse* (Montreal, Que)	(m)	186,546
67. *Commercial Appeal* (Memphis, TN)	(m)	185,834
68. *Register* (Des Moines, IA).	(m)	184,591
69. *Times-Union* (Jacksonville, FL) . . .	(m)	181,841
70. *Investor's Business Daily* (Los Angeles, CA).	(m)	176,740
71. *American-Statesman* (Austin, TX) .	(m)	176,696
72. *Sentinel* (Milwaukee, WI)	(m)	175,330
73. *Democrat-Gazette* (Little Rock, AR)	(m)	174,883
74. *Palm Beach Post* (West Palm Beach, FL)	(m)	172,744
75. *World* (Tulsa, OK)	(m)	170,208
76. *Viginian-Pilot* (Norfolk, VA)	(m)	165,940
77. *Press* (Asbury Park, NJ).	(e)	163,282
78. *Daily News* (Dayton, OH)	(m)	162,039
79. *Press-Enterprise* (Riverside, CA). .	(m)	161,659
80. *Citizen* (Ottawa, Ont.).	(all day)	161,394
81. *Province* (Vancouver, B.C.)	(m)	161,032
82. *News* (Birmingham, AL)	(e)	159,823
83. *Record* (Hackensack, NJ).	(m)	159,545
84. *Beacon Journal* (Akron, OH)	(m)	155,812
85. *Journal* (Edmonton, Alb.)	(m)	155,590
86. *Gazette* (Montreal, Ont.)	(m)	154,171
87. *Bee* (Fresno, CA).	(m)	150,438
88. *Blade* (Toledo, OH)	(m)	149,760
89. *News & Observer* (Raleigh, NC) . .	(m)	148,618
90. *Press* (Grand Rapids, MI)	(e)	147,530
91. *Tennessean* (Nashville, TN)	(m)	144,331
92. *Democrat and Chronicle* (Rochester, NY).	(m)	143,392
93. *Journal* (Atlanta, GA)	(e)	140,473
94. *Review-Journal* (Las Vegas, NV) .	(m)	137,153
95. *Morning Call* (Allentown, PA)	(m)	136,645
96. *State* (Columbia, SC)	(m)	130,649
97. *Morning News Tribune* (Tacoma, WA)	(m)	128,932
98. *News Journal* (Wilmington, DE). . .	(all day)	125,742
99. *Tribune* (Salt Lake City, UT)	(m)	125,037
100. *Daily Herald* (Chicago, IL).	(m)	124,595

U.S. Commercial Radio Stations, by Format, 1989-95

Source: M Street Coporation, New York, NY © 1995; counts are for Aug. of each year

Stations, by primary format	1989	1990	1991	1992	1993	1994	1995
Country	2,448	2,452	2,457	2,552	2,612	2,642	2,608
Adult Comtemporary (AC)	2,058	2,135	2,088	1,963	1,895	1,784	1,661
News, Talk, Business, Sports . . .	308	405	527	648	841	1,028	1,165
Religion (Teaching and Music) . .	696	745	799	837	915	926	970
Rock (Album, Modern, Classic) .	365	419	529	592	643	721	808
Oldies	545	659	704	731	734	714	718
Spanish and Ethnic	313	342	370	385	421	470	492
Adult Standards	332	383	408	412	421	435	469
Urban, Black, Urban AC.	284	294	311	313	321	328	342
Top-40	951	824	675	578	441	358	324
Easy Listening	328	240	210	171	116	106	85
Variety	134	97	81	72	68	63	63
Jazz and New Age	64	68	53	52	45	43	58
Classical, Fine Arts	49	52	51	48	45	44	39
Pre-Teen	0	3	4	3	13	19	26
Comedy	1	1	0	0	0	1	0
Off Air	112	210	308	352	345	369	323
Changing formats/not available .	266	115	19	15	14	6	9
Total stations	9,254	9,444	9,594	9,724	9,890	10,057	10,160

Top-Grossing North American Concert Appearances, 1994

Source: Pollstar, Fresno, CA

Rank	Artist	Venue	Location	Total performances	Total gross (in millions)
1.	Barbara Streisand	Madison Square Garden	New York, NY	7	$16.5
2.	Elton John/Billy Joel	Giants Stadium	East Rutherford, NJ	5	14.9
3.	Barbara Streisand	MGM Grand Garden	Las Vegas, NV	2	13.6
4.	Barbara Streisand	Arrowhead Pond of Anaheim	Anaheim, CA	6	12.4
5.	The Rolling Stones	Giants Stadium	East Rutherford, NJ	4	9.5
6.	The Rolling Stones	Oakland Stadium	Oakland, CA	4	9.4
7.	Barbara Streisand	Palace of Auburn Hills	Auburn Hills, MI	3	7.8
8.	Elton John/Billy Joel	Veterans Stadium	Philadelphia, PA	3	7.3
9.	The Rolling Stones	Rose Bowl	Pasadena, CA	2	6.2
10.	Luis Miguel	Auditorio Nacional	Mexico City, Mex.	15	(1)
11.	Pink Floyd	Olympic Stadium	Montreal, Que.	3	(2)
12.	Pink Floyd	Oakland Stadium	Oakland, CA	3	5.2
13.	Pink Floyd	Autodromo	Mexico City, Mex.	2	(3)
14.	The Eagles	Great Woods	Mansfield, MA	6	5.1
15.	The Eagles	Giants Stadium	East Rutherford, NJ	2	5.1
16.	Pink Floyd	Veterans Stadium	Philadelphia, PA	3	5.1
17.	The Eagles	Irvine Meadows Amphitheater	Irvine, CA	4	5.1
18.	Pink Floyd	Foxboro Stadium	Foxboro, MA	3	5.0
19.	The Eagles	Shoreline Amphitheatre	Mountain View, CA	5	4.8
20.	Pink Floyd	Rose Bowl	Pasadena, CA	2	4.7

(1) 1,800 million pesos. (2) 7.3 million Canadian dollars. (3) 1,700 million pesos.

Top-Grossing North American Concert Tours, 1985-94

Source: Pollstar, Fresno, CA

	Artist (Year)	Total gross[1]	Cities/ Shows		Artist (Year)	Total gross[1]	Cities/ Shows
1.	The Rolling Stones (1994)	$121.2	43/60	11.	Billy Joel (1990)	$43.0	53/95
2.	Pink Floyd (1994)	103.5	39/59	12.	The Who (1989)	41.7	27/39
3.	The Rolling Stones (1989)	98.0	33/60	13.	Bruce Springsteen & the E St.		
4.	The Eagles (1994)	79.4	32/54		Band (1985)	39.1	21/40
5.	The New Kids on the Block			14.	Paul McCartney (1990)	37.9	21/32
	(1990)	74.1	122/152	15.	Bon Jovi (1989)	36.7	129/143
6.	U2 (1992)	67.0	61/73	16.	U2 (1987)	35.1	50/79
7.	Barbara Streisand (1994)	58.9	6/22	17.	The Grateful Dead (1991)	34.7	27/76
8.	The Grateful Dead (1994)	52.4	29/84	18.	The Grateful Dead (1992)	31.2	23/55
9.	Elton John/Billy Joel (1994)	47.7	14/21	19.	Guns N' Roses/Metallica (1992)	31.1	25/25
10.	The Grateful Dead (1993)	45.6	29/81	20.	Rod Stewart (1993)	30.5	54/68

(1) In millions. Not adjusted for inflation.

Sales of Recorded Music and Music Videos, by Format and Genre, 1990-94

Source: Recording Industry Assn. of America, New York, NY

Characteristic	1990	1991	1992	1993	1994	Characteristic	1990	1991	1992	1993	1994
Genre											
Rock	36.1	34.8	31.6	30.2	35.1	Format					
Country	9.6	12.8	17.4	18.7	16.3	Compact disc	31.1	38.9	46.5	51.2	58.4
Pop	13.7	12.1	11.5	11.9	10.3	CD single	0.2	0.9	1.2	0.9	1.9
Urban Contemp.	11.6	9.9	9.8	10.6	9.6						
Rap	8.5	10.0	8.6	9.2	7.9	Cassette	54.7	49.8	43.6	38.0	32.1
Classical	3.1	3.2	3.7	3.3	3.7	Cassette single	6.6	6.5	5.4	7.8	4.9
Jazz	4.8	4.0	3.8	3.1	3.0	LP	4.7	1.7	1.3	0.3	0.8
Gospel	2.5	3.8	2.8	3.2	3.3	7" single	0.8	0.4	0.3	0.2	0.4
Soundtracks	0.8	0.7	0.7	0.7	1.0	12" single	1.1	1.0	0.6	0.3	0.2
Children's	0.5	0.3	0.5	0.4	0.4	Music video	NA	NA	1.0	1.3	0.8
Other	7.5	6.5	7.4	6.6	7.1						

NA = Not available. **Note:** Percentage of recorded music sold for calendar year. Totals may not equal 100% due to "Don't know/no answer" responses to survey.

Sales of Recorded Music and Music Videos, by Units Shipped and Value, 1985-94

Source: Recording Industry Assn. of America, New York, NY

(in millions, net after returns)

Format	1985	1987	1988	1989	1990	1991	1992	1993	1994	Percentage change 1993-94
Compact disc (CD)										
Units shipped	22.6	102.1	149.7	207.2	286.5	333.3	407.5	495.4	662.1	33.6
Dollar value	389.5	1,593.6	2,089.9	2,587.5	3,451.6	4,337.7	5,326.5	6,511.4	8,464.5	30.0
CD single										
Units shipped	NA	NA	1.6	−0.1	1.1	5.7	7.3	7.8	9.3	19.0
Dollar value	NA	NA	9.8	−0.7	6.0	35.1	45.1	45.8	56.1	22.5
Cassette										
Units shipped	339.1	410.0	450.1	446.2	442.2	360.1	366.4	339.5	345.4	1.7
Dollar value	2,411.5	2,959.7	3,385.1	3,345.8	3,472.4	3,019.6	3,116.3	2,915.8	2,976.4	2.1
Cassette single										
Units shipped	NA	5.1[2]	22.5	76.2	87.4	69.0	84.6	85.6	81.1	−5.1
Dollar value	NA	14.3[2]	57.3	194.6	257.9	230.4	298.8	298.5	274.9	−7.9
LP/EP										
Units shipped	167.0	107.0	72.4	34.6	11.7	4.8	2.3	1.2	1.9	58.3
Dollar value	1,280.5	793.1	532.2	220.3	86.5	29.4	13.5	10.6	17.8	67.9
Vinyl single										
Units shipped	120.7	82.0	65.6	36.6	27.6	22.0	19.8	15.1	11.7	−22.5
Dollar value	281.0	203.3	180.4	116.4	94.4	63.9	66.4	51.2	47.2	−7.8
Music video										
Units shipped	NA	NA	NA	6.1	9.2	6.1	7.6	11.0	11.2	1.8
Dollar value	NA	NA	NA	115.4	172.3	118.1	157.4	213.3	231.1	8.3
Total units	653.0[1]	706.8[1]	761.9	806.7	865.7	801.0	895.5	955.6	1,122.7	17.5
Total value	4,378.8[1]	5,567.5[1]	6,254.8	6,579.4	7,541.1	7,834.2	9,024.0	10,046.6	12,068.0	20.1

NA = Not applicable. (1) Total includes discontinued configurations not itemized in the table. (2) Cassette singles were introduced in the second half of the year. The figure here represents six month sales for cassette singles.

Multi-Platinum and Platinum Awards for Recorded Music and Music Videos, 1994

Source: Recording Industry Assn. of America, New York, NY

To achieve platinum status, an album must reach a minimum sale of 1 million units in LPs, tapes, and CDs, with a manufacturer's dollar volume of at least $2 million based on one-third of the suggested retail list price for each record, tape, or CD sold. To achieve multi-platinum status, an album must reach a minimum sale of at least 2 million units in LPs, tapes, and CDs, with a manufacturer's dollar volume of at least $4 million based on one-third of the list price. Singles must sell 1 million units to achieve a platinum award and must sell at least 2 million to achieve a multi-platinum award. EP singles count as two units. Music videos (long form) must sell 100,000 units to qualify for a platinum award and must sell more than 200,000 units to qualify for a multi-platinum award. Video singles, which must have a maximum running time of 15 minutes and no more than two songs per title, must sell 50,000 units to qualify for a platinum award and must sell at least 100,000 units to qualify for a multi-platinum award. Awards in 1994 were for albums and singles released in 1994 and for music videos released at any time. No multi-platinum singles were awarded for singles released in 1994. No multi-platinum music video singles were awarded in 1994.

Albums, Multi-Platinum

(number in parentheses = millions sold)

Alice in Chains, *Jar of Flies* (2)
All 4 One, *All 4 One* (2)
Benedictine Monks of Santo Domingo de Silos, *Chant* (2)
Boyz II Men, *II* (5)
Mariah Carey, *Merry Christmas* (3)
Eric Clapton, *From the Cradle* (2)
Green Day, *Dookie* (3)
Reba McEntire, *Read My Mind* (2)
Tim McGraw, *Not a Moment Too Soon* (3)
John Michael Montgomery, *Kickin' It Up* (2)
Offspring, *Smash* (3)
Pink Floyd, *The Division Bell* (2)
R.E.M., *Monster* (2)
Bonnie Raitt, *Longing in Their Hearts* (2)
The Rolling Stones, *Voodoo Lounge* (2)
Soundgarden, *Superunknown* (3)
Soundtrack, *Above the Rim* (2)
Soundtrack, *Forrest Gump* (3)
Soundtrack, *Reality Bites* (2)
Soundtrack, *The Lion King* (7)
Stone Temple Pilots, *Purple* (3)
Warren G, *Regulate. . .G Funk Era* (2)
Yanni, *Live at the Acropolis* (2)

Albums, Platinum

Aaliyah, *Age Ain't Nothing But a Number*
Tori Amos, *Under the Pink*
Anita Baker, *Rhythm of Love*
Beastie Boys, *Ill Communicaton*
Bon Jovi, *Crossroad*

Bone Thugs-n-Harmony, *Creepin on Ah Come Up*
Boston, *Walk On*
Brooks & Dunn, *Waitin' on Sundown*
Jimmy Buffett, *Fruitcakes*
Mary Chapin Carpenter, *Stones in the Road*
Carreras, Domingo, Pavarotti, *The Three Tenors in Concert 1994*
Collective Soul, *Hints*
Coolio, *It Takes a Thief*
The Cranberries, *No Need to Argue*
Enigma, *The Cross of Changes*
Gloria Estefan, *Hold Me, Thrill Me, Kiss Me*
Vince Gill, *When Love Finds You*
Amy Grant, *House of Love*
Hammer, *The Funky Headhunter*
Alan Jackson, *Who I Am*
Richard Marx, *Paid Vacation*
John Mellencamp, *Dance Naked*
Willie Nelson, *City of New Orleans*
Nine Inch Nails, *The Downward Spiral*
Jimmy Paige and Robert Plant, *No Quarter*
Queensryche, *Promise Land*
Scarface, *The Diary*
Bob Seger and the Silver Bullet Band, *Greatest Hits*
Smashing Pumpkins, *Pices Iscariot*
Soundtrack, *Jason's Lyric*
Soundtrack, *Murder Was the Case*
Soundtrack, *Pulp Fiction*
Soundtrack, *The Crow*
Barbara Streisand, *The Concert*
Keith Sweat, *Get Up on It*
The Tractors, *The Tractors*
Travis Tritt, *Ten Feet Tall and Bulletproof*
Luther Vandross, *Songs*

Various, *The Lion King Sing-Along*
Various, *Rhythm, Country & Blues*
Barry White, *The Icon is Love*
ZZ Top, *Antenna*

Singles, Platinum

69 Boyz, "Tootsee Roll"
All 4 One, "I Swear"
Boyz II Men, "I'll Make Love to You"
Changing Faces, "Stroke You Up"
Coolio, "Fantastic Voyage"
Da Brat, "Funkdafied"
Ini Kamoze, "Here Comes the Hotstepper"
Craig Mack, "Flava in Ya Ear"
R. Kelly, "Bump and Grind"
Various, "The Lion King Read-Along"
Warren G & Nate Dogg, "Regulate"

Music Videos, Multi-Platinum

(number in parenthesis = units sold)

Pamela Conn Beall and Susan Hagen Nipp, *Wee Sing Presents Grandpa's Magical Toys* (300,000)

Pamela Conn Beall and Susan Hagen Nipp, *Wee Sing Presents King Cole's Party* (200,000)
Pamela Conn Beall and Susan Hagen Nipp, *Wee Sing in Sillyville* (300,000)
Pamela Conn Beall and Susan Hagen Nipp, *Wee Sing Together* (500,000)
Pamela Conn Beall and Susan Hagen Nipp, *Wee Sing in the Big Rock Candy Mountains* (200,000)
Pamela Conn Beall and Susan Hagen Nipp, *Wee Sing the Best Christmas Ever* (200,000)
Carreras, Domingo, Pavarotti, *In Concert* (500,000)
Carreras, Domingo, Pavarotti with Mehta, *The Three Tenors In Concert 1994* (500,000)
Billy Ray Cyrus, *Billy Ray Cyrus* (400,000)
Jan Hammer, *Beyond the Mind's Eye* (300,000)
Madonna, *The Immaculate Collection* (300,000)
Mary Kate and Ashley Olsen, *Our First Video* (400,000)
Mary Kate and Ashley Olsen, *The Case of Thorn Mansion* (300,000)
Mary Kate and Ashley Olsen, *The Case of the Logical I Ranch* (300,000)
Barbara Streisand, *The Concert* (300,000)
Various, Simply *Mad About the Mouse* (200,000)
Yanni, *Live at the Acropolis* (300,000)

Top-Selling Video Games, 1994

Source: The NPD TRSTS report, The NPD Group, Inc., Port Washington, NY; ranked by units sold

Title
1. Super Nintendo Donkey Kong Country
2. Genesis NBA Jam
3. Genesis Mortal Kombat II
4. Super Nintendo NBA Jam
5. Super Nintendo Mortal Kombat II
6. Genesis Sonic 3
7. Genesis Sonic and Knuckles
8. Genesis Madden NFL'95

Title
9. Super Nintendo Aladdin
10. Genesis Mortal Kombat
11. Genesis NHL '95
12. Genesis Street Fighter II
13. Super Nintendo Ken Griffey Jr. Presents: Major League Baseball
14. Genesis World Series Baseball
15. Genesis Mighty Morphin Power Rangers

Household Penetration of Some Consumer Electronics Products, 1995

Source: Electronic Industries Association Market Research Department; as of January 1995

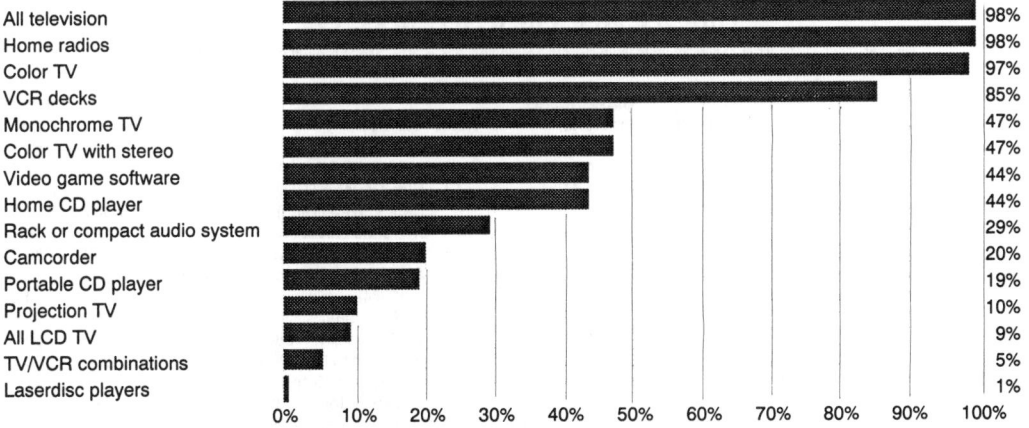

All television	98%
Home radios	98%
Color TV	97%
VCR decks	85%
Monochrome TV	47%
Color TV with stereo	47%
Video game software	44%
Home CD player	44%
Rack or compact audio system	29%
Camcorder	20%
Portable CD player	19%
Projection TV	10%
All LCD TV	9%
TV/VCR combinations	5%
Laserdisc players	1%

U.S. Television Set Ownership, 1995

Source: Neilsen Media Research; May 1995

Of the 95.4 million homes (98% of U.S. households) that own at least one TV set:

99% have color televisions
38% have 2 TV sets

28% have 3 or more TV sets
81% have a VCR

65% receive basic cable
31% receive pay cable

Some Television Addresses and Phone Numbers

BROADCAST

ABC–American Broadcasting Company
77 W 66th St.
New York, NY 10023   (212) 456-7777

CBS–Columbia Broadcasting System, Inc.
51 W 52nd St.
New York, NY 10019   (212) 975-4321

NBC–National Broadcasting Company
30 Rockefeller Plaza
New York, NY 10112   (212) 664-4444

Westinghouse Broadcasting and Cable Inc.
200 Park Ave.
New York, NY 10106   (212) 885-2600

Fox Television
205 E 67th St.
New York, NY 10021   (212) 452-5555

PBS–Public Broadcasting Service
1320 Braddock Place
Alexandria, VA 22314   (703) 739-5000

CABLE

A&E–Arts & Enterntainment Network
235 E 45th St.
New York, NY 10017   (212) 661-4500

AMC, BRV–American Movie Classics, Bravo
Rainbow Programming Holdings, Inc.
150 Crossways Pk. W
Woodbury, NY 11797   (516) 364-2222

BET–Black Entertainment Television
1232 31st St. NW
Washington, DC 20007 (202) 608-2000

CNBC–Consumer News and Business Channel
2200 Fletcher Ave.
Fort Lee, NJ 07024   (201) 585-2622

CNN–Cable News Network
One CNN Center, Box 105366
Atlanta, GA 30348-5366 (404) 827-1500

C-SPAN–Cable-Satellite Public Affairs Network
400 N Capitol St. NW, Suite 650
Washington, DC 20001   (202) 737-3220

DIS–The Disney Channel
3800 W Alameda Ave.
Burbank, CA 91505   (818) 569-7500

ESPN–ESPN, Inc.
ESPN Plaza
Bristol, CT 06010-9454 (860) 585-2000

LIF–Lifetime
309 W 49th St.
New York, NY 10019   (212) 424-7000

MTV–Music Television
MTV Networks, Inc.
1515 Broadway
New York, NY 10036   (212) 258-8000

NICK–Nickelodeon/Nick at Nite
MTV Networks, Inc.
1515 Broadway
New York, NY 10036   (212) 258-8000

TBS–Turner Broadcasting System
One CNN Center, Box 105366
Atlanta, GA 30348-5366
(404) 827-1700

TDC–The Discovery Channel
Discovery Communications
7700 Wisconsin Ave., Suite 700
Bethesda, MD 20814-3522
(301) 986-0444

USA–USA Network
USA Networks
1230 Ave. of the Americas
New York, NY 10020   (212) 408-9100

Average Television Viewing Time, 1995

Source: Nielsen Media Research, May 1995 (Hours:Minutes per week)

		Mon.-Fri. 10 AM- 4:30 PM	Mon.-Fri. 4:30 PM- 7:30 PM	Mon.-Sun. 8-11 PM	Sat. 7 AM-1 PM	Mon.-Fri. 11:30 PM- 1 AM
Total		4:10	3:23	7:59	0:42	1:13
Women	18+	5:34	3:55	9:14	0:37	1:28
	18-24	4:45	2:47	6:25	0:26	1:17
	25-54	4:29	3:05	8:31	0:35	1:28
	55+	8:04	5:59	11:47	0:46	1:34
Men	18+	3:25	2:59	8:27	0:37	1:26
	18-24	3:31	2:25	5:54	0:31	1:25
	25-54	2:42	2:25	7:56	0:37	1:25
	55+	5:08	4:40	11:02	0:38	1:28
Teens	12-17	2:11	3:07	6:14	0:42	0:46
Children	2-5	5:22	2:59	4:08	1:02	0:23
	6-11	1:49	3:07	5:13	1:04	0:22

Top 20 Cable Video Networks, 1995

Source: *Cable Television Developments*, Natl. Cable Television Assn., Apr. 1995; ranked by number of subscribers

Rank	Network[1]	Systems	Subscribers (millions)	Rank	Network[1]	Systems	Subscribers (millions)
1.	ESPN (1979)	26,700	64.9	11.	MTV: Music Television (1981)	8,750	59.4
2.	CNN (1980)	11,593	64.7	12.	LIFETIME Television (1984)	5,800	59.0
3.	TBS (1976)	11,668	64.4	13.	Nickelodeon (1979)	9,171	59.0
4.	TNN (The Nashville Network) (1983)	13,639	63.6		Nick at Nite (1985)	4,381	
5.	USA Network (1980)	12,500	63.0	14.	Headline News (1982)	6,147	56.8
6.	The Discovery Channel (1985)	10,036	63.0	15.	The Weather Channel (1982)	5,550	55.7
7.	TNT (Turner Network Television) (1988)	9,840	63.0	16.	AMC (American Movie Classics) (1984)	NA	54.0
8.	C-SPAN (1979)	5,162	61.7	17.	CNBC (1989)	4,000	52.0
9.	The Family Channel (1977)	10,555	61.4	18.	QVC Network (1986)	5,199	50.5
10.	Arts & Entertainment Network (1984)	9,500	60.0	19.	VH-1 (Video Hits One) (1985)	5,304	50.2
				20.	BET (Black Entertainment Television) (1980)	2,622	40.1

NA = Not available. **Note:** Data include noncable affiliates. (1) Date in parentheses is year service began.

Number of Cable TV Systems: 1972-95

Source: *Television and Cable Factbook*, Warren Publishing, Inc., Washington, DC; estimates as of Jan. 1

Year	Systems	Year	Systems	Year	Systems	Year	Systems
1972	2,841	1978	3,875	1984	6,200	1990	9,575
1973	2,991	1979	4,150	1985	6,600	1991	10,704
1974	3,158	1980	4,225	1986	7,500	1992	11,073
1975	3,506	1981	4,375	1987	7,900	1993	11,108
1976	3,681	1982	4,825	1988	8,500	1994	11,214
1977	3,832	1983	5,600	1989	9,050	1995	11,215

U.S. Households With Cable Television, 1977-94

Source: Nielsen Media Research, New York, NY

Year	Basic cable subscribers	Percentage of households with TVs	Year	Basic cable subscribers	Percentage of households with TVs
1977	12,168,450	16.6	1986	42,237,140	48.1
1978	13,391,910	17.9	1987	44,970,880	50.5
1979	14,814,380	19.4	1988	48,636,520	53.8
1980	17,671,490	22.6	1989	52,564,470	57.1
1981	23,219,200	28.3	1990	54,871,330	59.0
1982	29,340,570	35.0	1991	55,786,390	60.6
1983	34,113,790	40.5	1992	57,211,600	61.5
1984	37,290,870	43.7	1993	58,834,440	62.5
1985	39,872,520	46.2	1994	60,483,600	63.4

TV Viewing Shares: Broadcast Years 1985/86-1993/94[1]

Source: *Cable TV Facts*, Cable Advertising Bureau, New York, NY

	Total Television Households '85/'86 '87 '88 '89 '90 '91 '92 '93 '94									All Cable Households '85/'86/'87/'88/'89/'90/'91/'92/'93/ '86 '87 '88 '89 '90 '91 '92 '93 '94									Pay Cable Households '85/'86/'87/'88/'89/'90/'91/'92/'93/ '86 '87 '88 '89 '90 '91 '92 '93 '94								
Broadcast Network Affiliates	66	64	61	58	55	53	54	53	52	56	53	52	49	46	46	47	46	44	51	48	48	45	43	41	43	42	42
Independent TV Stations[2]	18	20	20	20	20	21	20	21	21	17	17	17	16	16	17	16	17	17	17	16	17	16	16	16	16	16	17
Public TV Stations	3	4	4	3	3	3	3	4	4	3	3	3	3	3	2	3	3	3	3	3	3	2	2	2	2	2	3
Basic Cable Networks[2]	11	13	15	17	21	24	24	25	26	19	23	25	28	32	35	35	36	37	19	23	24	27	30	34	33	35	36
Pay Cable Services	5	4	7	7	6	6	6	5	5	10	10	11	11	10	9	8	8	8	17	17	18	18	18	17	17	16	15

(1) For all television viewing Monday-Sunday, 24 hours/day. Due to multiset use and rounding off of numbers, totals are more than 100. (2) For broadcast year 1985/1986, superstation shares are divided between independent stations and basic cable networks categories; for broadcast years 1986/1987-1993/1994, TBS has been counted in the basic cable networks category. Independent shares include those for Fox.

America's Favorite Prime-Time Television Programs, 1994-95

Source: Nielsen Media Research

Data are for regularly scheduled network programs (Sept. 19, 1994-Apr. 16, 1995). Average audience percentages, or ratings, are estimates based on the percentage of TV households and persons in TV households watching a program. Audience share percentages are estimates based on the total number of televisions that are turned on in TV households.

Rank	Program	Average audience (%)	Audience share (%)	Rank	Program	Average audience (%)	Audience share (%)
1.	Seinfeld	20.5	31	26.	America's Funniest Home Videos	12.4	20
2.	E.R.	20.0	33	27.	Law and Order	12.2	21
3.	Home Improvement	19.9	29	28.	Chicago Hope	12.0	19
4.	Grace Under Fire	18.8	29	28.	NBC Sunday Movie	12.0	19
5.	NFL Monday Night Football	17.8	30	30.	Wings	11.9	19
6.	60 Minutes	17.1	28	31.	Primetime Live	11.7	20
7.	NYPD Blue	16.5	27	31.	ABC Monday Night Movie	11.7	18
8.	Friends	16.1	25	31.	Martin Short Show	11.7	18
9.	Roseanne	15.6	24	34.	Family Matters	11.6	21
9.	Murder, She Wrote	15.6	24	34.	Dateline NBC, Tues.	11.6	19
11.	Mad About You	15.2	25	36.	Thunder Alley	11.5	19
12.	Madman of the People	14.9	23	36.	Turning Point	11.5	20
13.	Ellen	14.7	23	36.	Boy Meets World	11.5	20
14.	Hope and Gloria	14.6	24	38.	Step by Step	11.4	20
15.	Frasier	14.3	21	38.	Newsradio	11.4	18
16.	Murphy Brown	14.1	21	40.	Hangin' with Mr. Cooper	11.2	19
17.	20/20	14.0	25	40.	Walker, Texas Ranger	11.2	20
18.	CBS Sunday Movie	13.7	22	40.	Northern Exposure	11.2	19
19.	NBC Monday Night Movies	13.6	21	43.	John Larroquette Show	11.1	17
20.	Dave's World	13.4	20	43.	In the House	11.1	18
21.	Me and the Boys	13.1	20	45.	Beverly Hills 90210	11.0	18
22.	Cybill	12.8	19	46.	Love and War	10.9	16
23.	ABC Sunday Night Movie	12.7	20	47.	Rescue: 911	10.8	17
24.	The Nanny	12.5	19	49.	Dr. Quinn Medicine Woman	10.7	20
24.	Full House	12.5	20	49.	Dateline NBC, Wed.	10.7	17

Favorite Syndicated Programs, 1994-95

Source: Nielsen Media Research, Aug. 30, 1994-Apr. 16, 1995

Average audience percentages, or ratings, are estimates based on the percentage of TV households and persons in TV households watching a program.

Rank	Program	Avg. audience (%)	Rank	Program	Avg. audience (%)
1.	Wheel of Fortune (syndicated)	13.7	11.	Wheel of Fortune (weekend)	6.7
2.	Jeopardy	11.4	12.	Baywatch	6.4
3.	Oprah Winfrey Show	8.6	12.	Hard Copy	6.4
4.	Buena Vista I	8.1	12.	Inside Edition	6.4
5.	Entertainment Tonight	7.9	15.	Turner Pictures II	6.2
5.	Star Trek	7.9	16.	Imagination I	6.1
7.	National Geographic on Assignment	7.6	17.	Family Matters	5.9
8.	Star Trek: Deep Space Nine	7.4	17.	Married With Children	5.9
9.	Magic II	7.3	19.	Journeys of Hercules	5.8
10.	Roseanne	7.0	20.	Simpsons	5.7

All-Time Top Television Programs

Source: Nielsen Media Research; Jan. 1961-May 28, 1995

Estimates exclude unsponsored or joint network telecasts or programs under 30 minutes long. Ranked by rating (percentage of average TV audience).

Rank	Program	Telecast date	Network	Rating (%)	Avg. audience (000)
1.	M*A*S*H (last episode)	2/28/83	CBS	60.2	50,150
2.	Dallas (Who Shot J.R.?)	11/21/80	CBS	53.3	41,470
3.	Roots-Pt. 8	1/30/77	ABC	51.1	36,380
4.	Super Bowl XVI	1/24/82	CBS	49.1	40,020
5.	Super Bowl XVII	1/30/83	NBC	48.6	40,480
6.	XVII Winter Olympics - 2d Wed.	2/23/94	CBS	48.5	45,690
7.	Super Bowl XX	1/26/86	NBC	48.3	41,490
8.	Gone With the Wind-Pt. 1	11/7/76	NBC	47.7	33,960
9.	Gone With the Wind-Pt. 2	11/8/76	NBC	47.4	33,750
10.	Super Bowl XII	1/15/78	CBS	47.2	34,410
11.	Super Bowl XIII	1/21/79	NBC	47.1	35,090
12.	Bob Hope Christmas Show	1/15/70	NBC	46.6	27,260
13.	Super Bowl XVIII	1/22/84	CBS	46.4	38,800
13.	Super Bowl XIX	1/20/85	ABC	46.4	39,390
15.	Super Bowl XIV	1/20/80	CBS	46.3	35,330
16.	ABC Theater (The Day After)	11/20/83	ABC	46.0	38,550
17.	Roots-Pt. 6	1/28/77	ABC	45.9	32,680
17.	The Fugitive	8/29/67	ABC	45.9	25,700
19.	Super Bowl XXI	1/25/87	CBS	45.8	40,030
20.	Roots-Pt. 5	1/27/77	ABC	45.7	32,540
21.	Super Bowl XXVIII	1/29/94	NBC	45.5	42,860
21.	Cheers (last episode)	5/20/93	NBC	45.5	42,360
23.	Ed Sullivan	2/9/64	CBS	45.3	23,240
24.	Super Bowl XXVII	1/31/93	NBC	45.1	41,990
25.	Bob Hope Christmas Show	1/14/71	NBC	45.0	27,050
26.	Roots-Pt. 3	1/25/77	ABC	44.8	31,900
27.	Super Bowl XI	1/9/77	NBC	44.4	31,610
27.	Super Bowl XV	1/25/81	NBC	44.4	34,540
29.	Super Bowl VI	1/16/72	CBS	44.2	27,450
30.	XVII Winter Olympics - 2d Fri.	2/25/94	CBS	44.1	41,540
30.	Roots-Pt. 2	1/24/77	ABC	44.1	31,400
32.	Beverly Hillbillies	1/8/64	CBS	44.0	22,570
33.	Roots-Pt. 4	1/26/77	ABC	43.8	31,190
33.	Ed Sullivan	2/16/64	CBS	43.8	22,445
35.	Super Bowl XXIII	1/22/89	NBC	43.5	39,320
36.	Academy Awards	4/7/70	ABC	43.4	25,390
37.	Thorn Birds-Pt. 3	3/29/83	ABC	43.2	35,990
38.	Thorn Birds-Pt. 4	3/30/83	ABC	43.1	35,900
39.	CBS NFC Championship	1/10/82	CBS	42.9	34,960
40.	Beverly Hillbillies	1/15/64	CBS	42.8	21,960
41.	Super Bowl VII	1/14/73	NBC	42.7	27,670
42.	Thorn Birds-Pt. 2	3/28/83	ABC	42.5	35,400

Top-Rated TV Shows of Each Season, 1950-51 to 1994-95

Source: Nielsen Media Research; regular series programs, Sept.-Apr. season

Season	Program	Rating	TV households (in thousands)	Season	Program	Rating	TV households (in thousands)
1950-51	Texaco Star Theatre	61.6	10,320	1973-74	All in the Family	31.2	66,200
1951-52	Godfrey's Talent Scouts	53.8	15,300	1974-75	All in the Family	30.2	68,500
1952-53	I Love Lucy	67.3	20,400	1975-76	All in the Family	30.1	69,600
1953-54	I Love Lucy	58.8	26,000	1976-77	Happy Days	31.5	71,200
1954-55	I Love Lucy	49.3	30,700	1977-78	Laverne & Shirley	31.6	72,900
1955-56	$64,000 Question	47.5	34,900	1978-79	Laverne & Shirley	30.5	74,500
1956-57	I Love Lucy	43.7	38,900	1979-80	60 Minutes	28.2	76,300
1957-58	Gunsmoke	43.1	41,920	1980-81	Dallas	31.2	79,900
1958-59	Gunsmoke	39.6	43,950	1981-82	Dallas	28.4	81,500
1959-60	Gunsmoke	40.3	45,750	1982-83	60 Minutes	25.5	83,300
1960-61	Gunsmoke	37.3	47,200	1983-84	Dallas	25.7	83,800
1961-62	Wagon Train	32.1	48,555	1984-85	Dynasty	25.0	84,900
1962-63	Beverly Hillbillies	36.0	50,300	1985-86	Bill Cosby Show	33.8	85,900
1963-64	Beverly Hillbillies	39.1	51,600	1986-87	Bill Cosby Show	34.9	87,400
1964-65	Bonanza	36.3	52,700	1987-88	Bill Cosby Show	27.8	88,600
1965-66	Bonanza	31.8	53,850	1988-89	Roseanne	25.5	90,400
1966-67	Bonanza	29.1	55,130	1989-90	Roseanne	23.4	92,100
1967-68	Andy Griffith	27.6	56,670	1990-91	Cheers	21.6	93,100
1968-69	Rowan & Martin Laugh-In	31.8	58,250	1991-92	60 Minutes	21.7	92,100
1969-70	Rowan & Martin Laugh-In	26.3	58,500	1992-93	60 Minutes	21.6	93,100
1970-71	Marcus Welby, MD	29.6	60,100	1993-94	Home Improvement	21.9	94,200
1971-72	All in the Family	34.0	62,100	1994-95	Seinfeld	20.5	95,400
1972-73	All in the Family	33.3	64,800				

(1) Data prior to 1988-89 exclude Alaska and Hawaii.

100 Leading U.S. Advertisers, 1994

Source: Competitive Media Reporting and Publishers Information Bureau, New York, © Copyright 1995

(in thousands)

Rank	Advertiser	Ad spending 1994	Rank	Advertiser	Ad spending 1994	Rank	Advertiser	Ad spending 1994
1.	Procter & Gamble	$1,464,994.6	32.	National Amusements	$294,376.4	66.	Gillette	$129,349.2
2.	General Motors	1,398,806.2	33.	Warner-Lambert	284,308.0	67.	Wal-Mart Stores	128,743.4
3.	Philip Morris	1,307,661.6	34.	J. C. Penney	283,109.3	68.	SmithKline Beecham	124,600.5
4.	Ford Motor	920,264.6	35.	Seagram	279,427.5	69.	Chrysler (dealers)	124,415.5
5.	Chrysler	758,684.2	36.	RJR Nabisco	275,832.5	70.	Nissan Motor (local)	123,896.0
6.	AT&T	700,429.2	37.	Coca-Cola	269,852.7	71.	Benckiser	121,639.4
7.	Pepsico	669,686.6	38.	Ford Motor (dealers)	253,134.1	72.	Turner Broadcasting	121,143.2
8.	Toyota Motor	536,123.0	39.	KMart	243,800.9	73.	Cadbury Schwepps	116,826.8
9.	Sears Roebuck	507,622.2	40.	Dayton Hudson Corp.	243,140.8	74.	BAT Industries	115,247.3
10.	Walt Disney	503,621.2	41.	Mazda Motor	225,817.6	75.	Schering-Plough	112,785.1
11.	General Mills	492,064.6	42.	Hasbro Inc.	220,276.7	76.	Visa	111,749.7
12.	Kellogg	483,742.4	43.	Toyota (local)	219,881.4	77.	Montgomery Ward	110,825.3
13.	Time Warner	476,383.5	44.	American Express	203,057.8	78.	SC Johnson & Sons	108,882.2
14.	Johnson & Johnson	472,691.8	45.	Mars	200,700.6	79.	Kimberly-Clark	107,347.8
15.	Nestlé	458,072.4	46.	Sprint	188,989.1	80.	General Electric	105,615.8
16.	McDonalds	425,823.1	47.	Valassis Com-		81.	Broadway Stores	103,920.0
17.	General Motors			munications	180,523.0	82.	Dean Witter/Discover	103,690.9
	(dealers)	418,231.7	48.	Quaker Oats	177,295.4	83.	Citicorp	102,781.9
18.	Unilever	408,319.0	49.	Mattel	175,067.8	84.	Hershey Foods	101,005.4
19.	News Corp.	377,895.3	50.	U.S. Government	172,509.2	85.	Reckitt & Colman	100,936.4
20.	Ford Motor (local)	377,450.5	51.	Bristol-Myers Squibb	165,044.8	86.	Toyota (dealers)	99,247.1
21.	Honda Motor	359,644.5	52.	Sara Lee	163,645.9	87.	Volkswagen	98,630.4
22.	Federated Dept.		53.	Mitsubishi	163,003.2	88.	Dillard Dept. Stores	98,556.6
	Stores	354,090.2	54.	Chrysler (local)	158,840.8	89.	Upjohn	95,279.9
23.	Grand Metropolitan	352,726.2	55.	Roll International	156,920.1	90.	Ciba-Geigy	95,195.9
24.	Sony	349,743.7	56.	Wendy's	156,492.4	91.	Delta Air Lines	94,772.0
25.	Nissan Motor	345,027.3	57.	Clorox	156,091.7	92.	Bertelsmann	94,265.5
26.	May Dept. Stores	338,309.5	58.	Campbell Soup	152,376.3	93.	United Dairy Assn.	94,031.9
27.	MCI Communications	325,651.9	59.	Ralston Purina	149,859.6	94.	Helene Curtis	93,083.6
28.	American Home		60.	Tandy	140,883.0	95.	Conagra	93,079.0
	Products	321,028.0	61.	Nike	137,442.9	96.	BMW	91,937.0
29.	General Motors		62.	IBM	134,454.8	97.	American Stores	90,635.7
	(local)	314,514.0	63.	Wrigley	134,300.3	98.	Honda (local)	90,553.0
30.	Anheuser-Busch	306,328.5	64.	Bayer	133,379.1	99.	Goodyear Tire & Rubber	90,264.7
31.	Circuit City Stores	304,820.3	65.	Coors	129,861.8	100.	Prudential	90,005.2

Total U.S. Ad Spending by Category and Medium, 1994

Source: Competitive Media Reporting and Publishers Information Bureau, New York, © Copyright 1995

(in millions, fiscal year 1994)

Category	Total ad spending	Magazine	Sunday magazines	Local newspaper	Network TV	Spot TV	Syndicated TV	Cable TV	Network radio
Total.	$55,022.0	$8,463.0	$1,000.0	$11,744.6	$11,893.2	$12,718.8	$2,358.1	$2,970.2	$599.8
Automotive	8,988.1	1,210.8	39.5	2,521.4	1,692.8	2,758.1	72.7	325.6	42.3
Retail	8,522.5	210.1	109.1	4,550.5	605.7	2,253.4	71.8	170.3	126.6
Business, consumer svcs.	6,518.6	661.4	45.2	1,562.2	1,101.6	1,794.4	128.7	360.6	77.1
Entertainment	4,388.1	76.1	3.6	691.1	1,308.5	1,723.9	133.5	206.9	3.2
Food	3,914.7	510.9	49.6	22.1	1,480.5	987.9	435.6	286.0	44.4
Toiletries & cosmetics . .	2,822.5	854.0	27.5	11.5	1,187.3	303.7	215.7	191.9	15.1
Drugs & remedies	2,561.2	432.8	72.4	104.0	972.3	398.0	231.9	202.0	89.4
Travel & hotels	2,290.0	436.7	45.4	891.3	224.3	285.9	5.0	107.4	18.5
Direct response cos. . . .	1,676.6	823.3	404.2	66.2	36.0	64.8	150.9	41.6	21.8
Candy, snacks & soft drinks . . .	1,435.8	80.1	4.9	5.9	638.2	302.2	176.4	145.0	27.0
Sporting goods, toys . . .	1,134.3	173.5	0.9	6.8	309.6	271.7	198.9	164.2	0.4
Apparel, footwear	1,106.6	539.0	46.6	19.1	283.5	70.1	19.9	99.0	2.9
Publishing & media . . .	1,068.4	257.0	9.0	195.5	42.8	249.9	48.7	81.5	43.4
Computers, office equip.	928.1	414.6	5.1	58.6	193.0	30.0	17.3	44.8	4.6
Beer & wine	798.0	38.9	4.1	5.9	360.3	185.2	33.6	72.5	7.8
Household equipment . .	773.0	141.8	12.2	7.5	317.7	127.2	62.8	77.6	18.0
Electronic equipment. . .	692.4	102.8	9.1	11.4	164.9	116.3	197.2	61.5	15.3
Soaps & cleansers	591.0	66.6	4.4	0.8	279.1	83.3	77.1	74.7	3.6
Cigarettes.	455.8	285.0	21.6	21.7	0.7	0.2	0.0	0.3	0.0
Building materials	393.5	108.2	7.6	33.2	67.1	90.6	12.6	57.1	5.0
Jewelry, optical	385.5	178.8	9.6	3.4	108.7	22.3	7.0	35.7	2.8
Miscellaneous.	363.9	140.4	3.4	85.5	0.0	14.9	0.9	0.4	0.2
Gasoline & lubricants. . .	343.0	26.4	0.3	8.4	77.1	143.3	4.4	24.9	1.6
Household furnishings . .	342.5	164.5	18.8	30.3	50.4	42.9	20.2	9.4	0.3
Horticulture & farming . .	255.7	26.7	12.2	49.7	40.3	63.2	9.6	23.9	4.6
Pets & pet foods	241.2	51.9	3.1	11.4	75.2	41.9	17.3	36.2	0.0
Liquor.	207.0	158.9	12.1	4.6	0.0	155.2	0.0	0.0	0.0
Freight, industrial.	156.3	44.2	0.0	2.9	49.0	28.9	0.3	10.0	1.1
Insurance & real estate .	144.6	160.3	18.2	648.6	174.8	250.9	6.8	44.6	15.7
Industrial materials	138.9	43.4	0.0	2.8	50.5	8.2	0.1	13.2	7.2
Business propositions . .	60.0	34.8	0.3	7.6	0.7	2.9	1.4	0.4	0.2
Airplanes (not travel) . . .	22.5	9.1	0.0	3.0	0.5	2.3	0.0	0.8	0.0

DISASTERS

Disasters are reported as of Sept. 1995.

Some Notable Shipwrecks Since 1850

(Figures indicate estimated lives lost.)

1854, Mar.—City of Glasgow; Brit. steamer missing in N Atlantic; 480.

1854, Sept. 27—Arctic; U.S. (Collins Line) steamer sunk in collision with French steamer Vesta near Cape Race; 285-351.

1856, Jan. 23—Pacific; U.S. (Collins Line) steamer missing in N Atlantic; 186-286.

1858, Sept. 23—Austria; German steamer destroyed by fire in N Atlantic; 471.

1863, Apr. 27—Anglo-Saxon; Brit. steamer wrecked at Cape Race; 238.

1865, Apr. 27—Sultana; a Mississippi River steamer blew up near Memphis, TN; 1,450.

1869, Oct. 27—Stonewall; steamer burned on Mississippi River below Cairo, IL; 200.

1870, Jan. 25—City of Boston; Brit. (Inman Line) steamer vanished between New York and Liverpool; 177.

1870, Oct. 19—Cambria; Brit. steamer wrecked off N Ireland; 196.

1872, Nov. 7—Mary Celeste; U.S. half-brig sailed from New York for Genoa; found abandoned in Atlantic 4 weeks later in mystery of sea; crew never heard from; loss of life unknown.

1873, Jan. 22—Northfleet; Brit. steamer foundered off Dungeness, England; 300.

1873, Apr. 1—Atlantic; Brit. (White Star) steamer wrecked off Nova Scotia; 585.

1873, Nov. 23—Ville du Havre; French steamer, sunk after collision with Brit. sailing ship Loch Earn; 226.

1875, May 7—Schiller; German steamer wrecked off Scilly Isles; 312.

1875, Nov. 4—Pacific; U.S. steamer sunk after collision off Cape Flattery; 236.

1878, Sept. 3—Princess Alice; Brit. steamer sank after collision in Thames River; 700.

1878, Dec. 18—Byzantin; French steamer sank after Dardanelles collision; 210.

1881, May 24—Victoria; steamer capsized in Thames River, Canada; 200.

1883, Jan. 19—Cimbria; German steamer sunk in collision with Brit. steamer Sultan in North Sea; 389.

1887, Nov. 15—Wah Yeung; Brit. steamer burned at sea; 400.

1890, Feb. 17—Duburg; Brit. steamer wrecked, China Sea; 400.

1890, Sept. 19—Ertogrul; Turkish frigate foundered off Japan; 540.

1891, Mar. 17—Utopia; Brit. steamer sank in collision with Brit. ironclad Anson off Gibraltar; 562.

1895, Jan. 30—Elbe; German steamer sank in collision with Brit. steamer Craithie in North Sea; 332.

1895, Mar. 11—Reina Regenta; Spanish cruiser foundered near Gibraltar; 400.

1898, Feb. 15—Maine; U.S. battleship blown up in Havana Harbor; 260.

1898, July 4—La Bourgogne; French steamer sunk in collision with Brit. sailing ship Cromartyshire off Nova Scotia; 549.

1898, Nov. 26—Portland; U.S. steamer wrecked off Cape Cod; 157.

1904, June 15—General Slocum; excursion steamer burned in East River, New York City; 1,030.

1904, June 28—Norge; Danish steamer wrecked on Rockall Island, Scotland; 620.

1906, Aug. 4—Sirio; Italian steamer wrecked off Cape Palos, Spain; 350.

1908, Mar. 23—Matsu Maru; Japanese steamer sank in collision near Hakodate, Japan; 300.

1909, Aug. 1—Waratah; Brit. steamer, Sydney to London, vanished; 300.

1910, Feb. 9—General Chanzy; French steamer wrecked off Minorca, Spain; 200.

1911, Sept. 25—Liberté; French battleship exploded at Toulon; 285.

1912, Mar. 5—Principe de Asturias; Spanish steamer wrecked off Spain; 500.

1912, Apr. 14-15—Titanic; Brit. (White Star) steamer hit iceberg in N Atlantic; 1,503.

1912, Sept. 28—Kichemaru; Japanese steamer sank off Japanese coast; 1,000.

1914, May 29—Empress of Ireland; Brit. (Canadian Pacific) steamer sunk in collision with Norwegian collier in St. Lawrence River; 1,014.

1915, May 7—Lusitania; Brit. (Cunard Line) steamer torpedoed and sunk by German submarine off Ireland; 1,198.

1915, July 24—Eastland; excursion steamer capsized in Chicago River; 812.

1916, Feb. 26—Provence; French cruiser sank in Mediterranean; 3,100.

1916, Mar. 3—Principe de Asturias; Spanish steamer wrecked near Santos, Brazil; 558.

1916, Aug. 29—Hsin Yu; Chinese steamer sank off Chinese coast; 1,000.

1917, Dec. 6—Mont Blanc, Imo; French ammunition ship and Belgian steamer collided in Halifax Harbor; 1,600.

1918, Apr. 25—Kiang-Kwan; Chinese steamer sank in collision off Hankow; 500.

1918, July 12—Kawachi; Japanese battleship blew up in Tokayama Bay; 500.

1918, Oct. 25—Princess Sophia; Canadian steamer sank off Alaskan coast; 398.

1919, Jan. 17—Chaonia; French steamer lost in Straits of Messina, Italy; 460.

1919, Sept. 9—Valbanera; Spanish steamer lost off Florida coast; 500.

1921, Mar. 18—Hong Kong; steamer wrecked in South China Sea; 1,000.

1922, Aug. 26—Niitaka; Japanese cruiser sank in storm off Kamchatka, USSR; 300.

1927, Oct. 25—Principessa Mafalda; Italian steamer blew up, sank off Porto Seguro, Brazil; 314.

1928, Nov. 12—Vestris; Brit. steamer sank in gale off Virginia; 113.

1934, Sept. 8—Morro Castle; U.S. steamer, Havana to New York, burned off Asbury Park, NJ; 134.

1939, May 23—Squalus; U.S. submarine sank off Portsmouth, NH; 26.

1939, June 1—Thetis; Brit. submarine, sank in Liverpool Bay; 99.

1942, Feb. 18—Truxtun and Pollux; U.S. destroyer and cargo ship ran aground, sank off Newfoundland; 204.

1942, Oct. 2—Curacao; Brit. cruiser sank after collision with liner Queen Mary; 338.

1944, Dec. 17-18—3 U.S. Third Fleet destroyers sank during typhoon in Philippine Sea; 790.

1947, Jan. 19—Himera; Greek steamer hit a mine off Athens; 392.

1947, Apr. 16—Grandcamp; French freighter exploded in Texas City, TX, Harbor, starting fires; 510.

1948, Nov.—Chinese army evacuation ship exploded and sunk off S Manchuria; 6,000.

1948, Dec. 3—Kiangya; Chinese refugee ship wrecked in explosion S of Shanghai; 1,100+.

1949, Sept. 17—Noronic; Canadian Great Lakes Cruiser burned at Toronto dock; 130.

1952, Apr. 26—Hobson and Wasp; U.S. destroyer and aircraft carrier collided in Atlantic; 176.

1954, May 26—Pennington sunk off RI coast; 103.

1954, Sept. 26—Toya Maru; Japanese ferry sank in Tsugaru Strait, Japan; 1,172.

1956, July 26—Andrea Doria and Stockholm; Italian liner and Swedish liner collided off Nantucket; 51.

1957, July 14—Eshghabad; Soviet ship ran aground in Caspian Sea; 270.

1960, Dec. 19—Constitution, U.S. aircraft carrier, caught fire in Brooklyn Navy Yard, NY; 49.

1961, July 8—Save; Portuguese ship ran aground off Mozambique; 259.

1962, Apr. 8—Dara; Brit. liner exploded and sunk in Persian Gulf; 236.

1963, Apr. 10—Thresher; U.S. Navy atomic submarine sank in N Atlantic; 129.

1964, Feb. 10—Voyager, Melbourne; Australian destroyer sank after collision with Australian aircraft carrier Melbourne off New South Wales; 82.

1965, Nov. 13—Yarmouth Castle; Panamanian registered cruise ship burned and sank off Nassau; 90.

1967, July 29—Forrestal; U.S. aircraft carrier caught fire off N Vietnam; 134.

1968, Jan. 25—Dakar; Israeli submarine vanished in Mediterranean Sea; 69.

1968, late May—Scorpion; U.S. nuclear submarine sank in Atlantic near Azores; 99 (located Oct. 31).

1969, June 2—Evans; U.S. destroyer cut in half by Australian carrier Melbourne, S China Sea; 74.

1970, Mar. 4—Eurydice; French submarine sank in Mediterranean near Toulon; 57.

1970, Dec. 15—Namyong-Ho; South Korean ferry sank in Korea Strait; 308.

1974, May 1—Motor launch capsized off Bangladesh; 250.

1974, Sept. 26— Soviet destroyer burned and sank in Black Sea; 200+.

1976, Oct. 20—George Prince and Frosta; ferryboat and Norwegian tanker collided on Mississippi R. at Luling, LA; 77.

1976, Dec. 25—Patria; Egyptian liner caught fire and sank in the Red Sea; c. 100.

1979, Aug. 14—23 yachts competing in Fastnet yacht race sunk or abandoned during storm in S Irish Sea; 18.

1981, Jan. 27—Tamponas II; Indonesian passenger ship caught fire and sank in Java Sea; 580.

1981, May 26—Nimitz; U.S. Marine combat jet crashed on deck of U.S. aircraft carrier; 14.

1983, Feb. 12—Marine Electric; coal freighter sank during storm off Chincoteague, VA; 33.

1983, May 25—10th of Ramadan; Nile steamer caught fire and sank in L. Nassar; 357.

1986, Apr. 20—overcrowded ferry sinks near Barisal, Bangladesh; 262.

1986, Aug. 31—Soviet passenger ship **Admiral Nakhimov** and Soviet freighter **Pyotr Vasev** collided in Black Sea; 398.

1987, Mar. 6—Brit. ferry capsized off Zeebrugge, Belg.; 189.

1987, Dec. 20—Philippine ferry **Dona Paz** and oil tanker **Victor** collided in Tablas Strait; 3,000+.

1988, Aug. 6—Indian ferry capsized on Ganges R.; 400+.

1989, Apr. 19—USS Iowa; U.S. battleship; explosion in gun turret; 47.

1989, Aug. 20—Brit. barge **Bowbelle** struck Brit. pleasure cruiser **Marchioness** on Thames R. in central London; 56.

1989, Sept. 10—Romanian pleasure boat and Bulgarian barge collided on Danube R.; 161.

1991, Apr. 10—Auto ferry and oil tanker collided outside Livorno Harbor, Italy; 140.

1991, Dec. 14—Salem Express; ferry rammed coral reef nr. Safaga, Egypt; 462.

1993, Feb. 17—Neptune; ferry capsized off Port-au-Prince, Haiti; 500+.

1993, Oct. 10—West Sea Ferry; capsized in Yellow Sea near W South Korea during storm; 285.

1994, Sept. 28—Estonia; ferry sank in Baltic Sea when water entered through bow door; 1,049.

Some Notable Aircraft Disasters Since 1937

Date	Aircraft	Site of accident	Deaths
1937, May 6	German zeppelin Hindenburg	Burned at mooring, Lakehurst, NJ	36
1944, Aug. 23	U.S. Air Force B-24	Hit school, Freckelton, England	76[1]
1945, July 28	U.S. Army B-25	Hit Empire State Building, New York, NY	14[1]
1952, Dec. 20	U.S. Air Force C-124	Fell, burned, Moses Lake, WA	87
1953, Mar. 3	Canadian Pacific Comet Jet	Karachi, Pakistan	11[2]
1953, June 18	U.S. Air Force C-124	Crashed, burned near Tokyo	129
1955, Nov. 1	United Air Lines DC-6B	Exploded, crashed near Longmont, CO	44[3]
1956, June 20	Venezuelan Super-Constellation	Crashed in Atlantic off Asbury Park, NJ	74
1956, June 30	TWA Super-Const., United DC-7	Collided over Grand Canyon, AZ	128
1960, Dec. 16	United DC-8 jet, TWA Super-Const.	Collided over New York City	134[4]
1962, Mar. 16	Flying Tiger Super-Const.	Vanished in W Pacific	107
1962, June 3	Air France Boeing 707 jet	Crashed on takeoff from Paris	130
1962, June 22	Air France Boeing 707 jet	Crashed in storm, Guadeloupe, W.I.	113
1963, June 3	Chartered Northw. Airlines DC-7	Crashed in Pacific off British Columbia	101
1963, Nov. 29	Trans-Canada Airlines DC-8F	Crashed after takeoff from Montreal	118
1965, May 20	Pakistani Boeing 720-B	Crashed at Cairo, Egypt, airport	121
1966, Jan. 24	Air India Boeing 707 jetliner	Crashed on Mont Blanc, France-Italy	117
1966, Feb. 4	All-Nippon Boeing 727	Plunged into Tokyo Bay	133
1966, Mar. 5	BOAC Boeing 707 jetliner	Crashed on Mount Fuji, Japan	124
1966, Dec. 24	U.S. military-chartered CL-44	Crashed into village in South Vietnam	129[1]
1967, Apr. 20	Swiss Britannia turboprop	Crashed at Nicosia, Cyprus	126
1967, July 19	Piedmont Boeing 727, Cessna 310	Collided in air, Hendersonville, NC	82
1968, Apr. 20	S. African Airways Boeing 707	Crashed on takeoff, Windhoek, SW Africa	122
1968, May 3	Braniff International Electra	Crashed in storm near Dawson, TX	85
1969, Mar. 16	Venezuelan DC-9	Crashed after takeoff from Maracaibo, Venezuela	155[5]
1969, Dec. 8	Olympia Airways DC-6B	Crashed near Athens in storm	93
1970, Feb. 15	Dominican DC-9	Crashed into sea on takeoff from Santo Domingo	102
1970, July 3	British chartered jetliner	Crashed near Barcelona, Spain	112
1970, July 5	Air Canada DC-8	Crashed near Toronto International Airport	108
1970, Aug. 9	Peruvian turbojet	Crashed after takeoff from Cuzco, Peru	101[1]
1970, Nov. 14	Southern Airways DC-9	Crashed in mountains near Huntington, WV	75[6]
1971, July 30	All-Nippon Boeing 727 and Japanese Air Force F-86	Collided over Morioka, Japan	162[7]
1971, Sept. 4	Alaska Airlines Boeing 727	Crashed into mountain near Juneau, AK	111
1972, Aug. 14	E German Ilyushin-62	Crashed on take-off East Berlin	156
1972, Oct. 13	Aeroflot Ilyushin-62	E German airline crashed near Moscow	176
1972, Dec. 3	Chartered Spanish airliner	Crashed on take-off, Canary Islands	155
1972, Dec. 29	Eastern Airlines Lockheed Tristar	Crashed on approach to Miami Intl. Airport	101
1973, Jan. 22	Chartered Boeing 707	Burst into flames during landing, Kano Airport, Nigeria	176
1973, Feb. 21	Libyan jetliner	Shot down by Israeli fighter planes over Sinai	108
1973, Apr. 10	British Vanguard turboprop	Crashed during snowstorm at Basel, Switzerland	104
1973, June 3	Soviet Supersonic TU-144	Crashed near Goussainville, France	14[8]
1973, July 11	Brazilian Boeing 707	Crashed on approach to Orly Airport, Paris	122
1973, July 31	Delta Airlines jetliner	Crashed, landing in fog at Logan Airport, Boston	89
1973, Dec. 23	French Caravelle jet	Crashed in Morocco	106
1974, Mar. 3	Turkish DC-10 jet	Crashed at Ermenonville near Paris	346
1974, Apr. 23	Pan American 707 jet	Crashed in Bali, Indonesia	107
1974, Dec. 1	TWA-727	Crashed in storm, Upperville, VA	92
1974, Dec. 4	Dutch-chartered DC-8	Crashed in storm near Colombo, Sri Lanka	191
1975, Apr. 4	Air Force Galaxy C-5B	Crashed near Saigon, South Vietnam, after takeoff with load of orphans	172
1975, June 24	Eastern Airlines 727 jet	Crashed in storm, JFK Airport, NY	113
1975, Aug. 3	Chartered 707	Hit mountainside, Agadir, Morocco	188
1976, Sept. 10	British Airways Trident, Yugoslav DC-9	Collided near Zagreb, Yugoslavia	176
1976, Sept. 19	Turkish 727	Hit mountain, S Turkey	155
1976, Oct. 13	Bolivian 707 cargo jet	Crashed in Santa Cruz, Bolivia	100[9]
1977, Mar. 27	KLM 747, Pan American 747	Collided on runway, Tenerife, Canary Islands	582
1977, Nov. 19	TAP Boeing 727	Crashed on Madeira	130
1977, Dec. 4	Malaysian Boeing 737	Hijacked, then exploded in mid-air over Straits of Johore	100
1977, Dec. 13	U.S. DC-3	Crashed after takeoff at Evansville, IN	29[10]
1978, Jan. 1	Air India 747	Exploded, crashed into sea off Bombay	213
1978, Sept. 25	Boeing 727, Cessna 172	Collided in air, San Diego, CA	150
1978, Nov. 15	Chartered DC-8	Crashed near Colombo, Sri Lanka	183

(continued)

Some Notable Aircraft Disasters Since 1937 (*continued*)

Date	Aircraft	Site of accident	Deaths
1979, May 25	American Airlines DC-10	Crashed after takeoff at O'Hare Intl. Airport, Chicago	275[11]
1979, Aug. 17	Two Soviet Aeroflot jetliners	Collided over Ukraine	173
1979, Nov. 26	Pakistani Boeing 707	Crashed near Jidda, Saudi Arabia	156
1979, Nov. 28	New Zealand DC-10	Crashed into mountain in Antarctica	257
1980, Mar. 14	Polish Ilyushin 62	Crashed making emergency landing, Warsaw	87[2]
1980, Aug. 19	Saudi Arabian Tristar	Burned after emergency landing, Riyadh	301
1981, Dec. 1	Yugoslavian DC-9	Crashed into mountain in Corsica	174
1982, Jan. 13	Air Florida Boeing 737	Crashed into Potomac R. after takeoff	78
1982, July 9	Pan Am Boeing 727	Crashed after takeoff in Kenner, LA.	153[13]
1983, Sept. 1	S. Korean Boeing 747	Shot down after violating Soviet airspace	269
1983, Nov. 27	Colombian Boeing 747	Crashed near Barajas Airport, Madrid	183
1985, Feb. 19	Spanish Boeing 727	Crashed into Mt. Oiz, Spain	148
1985, June 23	Air-India Boeing 747	Crashed into Atlantic Ocean S of Ireland	329
1985, Aug. 2	Delta Air Lines jumbo jet	Crashed at Dallas-Ft. Worth Intl. Airport	137
1985, Aug. 12	Japan Air Lines Boeing 747	Crashed into Mt. Ogura, Japan	520[14]
1985, Dec. 12	Arrow Air DC-8	Crashed after takeoff in Gander, Newfoundland	256[15]
1986, Mar. 31	Mexican Boeing 727	Crashed NW of Mexico City	166
1986, Aug. 31	Aeromexico DC-9	Collided with Piper PA-28 over Cerritos, CA	82[16]
1987, May 9	Ilyushin 62M	Crashed after takeoff in Warsaw, Poland	183
1987, Aug. 16	Northwest Airlines MD-82	Crashed after takeoff in Romulus, MI.	156
1988, July 3	Iranian A300 Airbus	Shot down by U.S. Navy warship *Vincennes* over Persian Gulf	290
1988, Dec. 21	Pan Am Boeing 747	Exploded and crashed in Lockerbie, Scotland	270[17]
1989, Feb. 8	Boeing 707	Crashed into mountain in Azores Islands off Portugual	144
1989, June 7	Suriname DC-8	Crashed near Paramaribo Airport, Suriname	168
1989, July 19	United Airlines DC-10	Crashed while landing with a disabled hydraulic system, Sioux City, IA	111
1989, Sept. 19	French DC-10	Exploded in air over Niger	171
1991, May 26	Lauda-Air Boeing 767-300	Exploded over rural Thailand	223
1991, July 11	Nigerian DC-8	Crashed while landing at Jidda, Saudi Arabia	261
1994, Jan. 3	Aeroflot TU-154	Crashed and exploded after takeoff in Irkhutsk, Russia	125[18]
1994, Apr. 26	China Airlines Airbus A-300-600R	Crashed at Japan's Nagoya Airport	264
1994, June 16	China Northwest Airlines TU-154	Crashed 10 min. after takeoff	160
1994, Sept. 8	USAir Boeing 737-300	Crashed in Aliquippa, PA, near Pittsburgh Intl. Airport	132
1994, Oct. 31	American Eagle ATR-72-210	Crashed in field near Roselawn, IN	68
1995, Aug. 11	Aviateca Boeing 737	Crashed into Chichontepec volcano, El Salvador	65

(1) Including those on the ground and in buildings. (2) First fatal crash of commercial jet plane. (3) Caused by bomb planted by John G. Graham in insurance plot to kill his mother, a passenger. (4) Including all 128 aboard the planes and 6 on ground. (5) Killed 84 on plane and 71 on ground. (6) Including 43 Marshall U. football players and coaches. (7) Airliner-fighter crash, pilot of fighter parachuted to safety, was arrested for negligence. (8) First supersonic plane crash killed 6 crewmen and 8 on the ground; there were no passengers. (9) Crew of 3 killed; 97, mostly children, killed on ground. (10) Including U. of Evansville basketball team. (11) Highest death toll in U.S. aviation history. (12) Including 22 members of U.S. boxing team. (13) Including 8 on ground. (14) Worst single-plane disaster. (15) Incl. 248 members of U.S. 101st Airborne Division. (16) Incl. 15 on the ground. (17) Incl. 11 on the ground. (18) Incl. 1 on the ground.

Some Notable Railroad Disasters

Date	Location	Deaths	Date	Location	Deaths
1876, Dec. 29	Ashtabula, OH	92	1926, Sept. 5	Waco, CO	30
1880, Aug. 11	Mays Landing, NJ	40	1928, Aug. 24	I.R.T. subway, Times Sq., NY	18
1887, Aug. 10	Chatsworth, IL	81	1937, July 16	Nr. Patna, India	107
1888, Oct. 10	Mud Run, PA	55	1938, June 19	Saugus, MT	47
1891, June 14	Nr. Basel, Switzerland	100	1939, Aug. 12	Harney, NV	24
1896, July 30	Atlantic City, NJ	60	1939, Dec. 22	Nr. Magdeburg, Germany	132
1903, Dec. 23	Laurel Run, PA	53	1939, Dec. 22	Nr. Friedrichshafen, Germany	99
1904, Aug. 7	Eden, CO	96	1940, Apr. 19	Little Falls, NY	31
1904, Sept. 24	New Market, TN	56	1940, July 31	Cuyahoga Falls, OH	43
1906, Mar. 16	Florence, CO	35	1943, Aug. 29	Wayland, NY	27
1906, Oct. 28	Atlantic City, NJ	40	1943, Sept. 6	Frankford Junction, Philadelphia, PA	79
1906, Dec. 30	Washington, DC	53	1943, Dec. 16	Between Rennert and Buie, NC.	72
1907, Jan. 2	Volland, KS	33	1944, Jan. 16	Leon Province, Spain	500
1907, Jan. 19	Fowler, IN	29	1944, Mar. 2	Salerno, Italy	521
1907, Feb. 16	New York, NY	22	1944, July 6	High Bluff, TN	35
1907, Feb. 23	Colton, CA	26	1944, Aug. 4	Near Stockton, GA	47
1907, May 11	Lompoc, CA	36	1944, Sept. 14	Dewey, IN.	29
1907, July 20	Salem, MI	33	1944, Dec. 31	Bagley, UT	50
1910, Mar. 1	Wellington, WA	96	1945, Aug. 9	Michigan, ND	34
1910, Mar. 21	Green Mountain, IA	55	1946, Mar. 20	Aracaju, Mexico	185
1911, Aug. 25	Manchester, NY	29	1946, Apr. 25	Naperville, IL.	45
1912, July 4	East Corning, NY	39	1947, Feb. 18	Gallitzin, PA	24
1912, July 5	Ligonier, PA	23	1949, Oct. 22	Nr. Dwor, Poland	200+
1914, Aug. 5	Tipton Ford, MO	43	1950, Feb. 17	Rockville Centre, NY	31
1914, Sept. 15	Lebanon, MO	28	1950, Sept. 11	Coshocton, OH	33
1915, May 22	Nr. Gretna, Scotland	227	1950, Nov. 22	Richmond Hill, NY	79
1916, Mar. 29	Amherst, OH	27	1951, Feb. 6	Woodbridge, NJ.	84
1917, Sept. 28	Kellyville, OK.	23	1951, Nov. 1	Wyuta, WY	17
1917, Dec. 12	Modane, France	543[1]	1951, Nov. 25	Woodstock, AL	17
1917, Dec. 20	Shepherdsville, KY.	46	1952, Mar. 4	Nr. Rio de Janeiro, Brazil	119
1918, June 22	Ivanhoe, IN	68	1952, July 9	Rzepin, Poland	160
1918, July 9	Nashville, TN.	101	1952, Oct. 8	Harrow, England	112
1918, Nov. 1	Brooklyn, NY.	97	1953, Mar. 27	Conneaut, OH.	21
1919, Jan. 12	South Byron, NY	22	1955, Apr. 3	Guadalajara, Mexico	300
1919, Dec. 20	Onawa, ME.	23	1956, Jan. 22	Los Angeles, CA	30
1921, Feb. 27	Porter, IN	37	1956, Feb. 28	Swampscott, MA	13
1921, Dec. 5	Woodmont, PA	27	1956, Sept. 5	Springer, NM.	20
1922, Aug. 5	Sulphur Spring, MO	34	1957, June 11	Vroman, CO	12
1922, Dec. 13	Humble, TX.	22	1957, Sept. 1	Kendal, Jamaica	178
1923, Sept. 27	Lockett, WY	31	1957, Sept. 29	Montgomery, W Pakistan	250
1925, June 16	Hackettstown, NJ.	50	1957, Dec. 4	London, England	90
1925, Oct. 27	Victoria, MS	21	1958, May 8	Rio de Janeiro, Brazil	128

Date	Location	Deaths	Date	Location	Deaths
1958, Sept. 15	Elizabethport, NJ	48	1977, Jan. 18	Granville, Australia	82
1960, Mar. 14	Bakersfield, CA	14	1977, Feb. 4	Chicago, IL, elevated train	11
1960, Nov. 14	Pardubice, Czech.	110	1981, June 6	Bihar, India	500+
1962, Jan. 8	Woerden, Netherlands	91	1982, Jan. 27	El Asnam, Algeria	130
1962, May 3	Tokyo, Japan.	163	1982, July 11	Tepic, Mexico	120
1962, July 28	Steelton, PA	19	1983, Feb. 19	Empalme, Mexico	100
1964, July 26	Oporto, Portugal	94	1987, Jan. 4	Essex, MD	16
1966, Dec. 28	Everett, MA.	13	1988, Dec. 12	London, England	115
1970, Feb. 1	Buenos Aires, Argentina	236	1989, Jan. 15	Maizdi Khan, Bangladesh	110+
1971, June 10	Salem, IL	11	1990, Jan. 4	Sindh Province, Pakistan	210+
1972, June 16	Vierzy, France	107	1991, May 14	Shigaraki, Japan	42
1972, July 21	Seville, Spain	76	1993, Sept. 22	Big Bayou Conot, AL	47
1972, Oct. 6	Saltillo, Mexico	208	1994, Mar. 8	Nr. Durban, South Africa	63
1972, Oct. 30	Chicago, IL	45	1994, Sept. 22	Tolunda, Angola	300
1974, Aug. 30	Zagreb, Yugoslavia	153	1995, Mar. 20	Tokyo subway	12[2]

(1) World's worst train wreck; passenger train derailed. (2) Sarin nerve gas released in subway.

Principal U.S. Mine Disasters Since 1900

Source: Bureau of Mines, U.S. Dept. of the Interior; Mine Safety and Health Admin., U.S. Dept. of Labor

Note: Prior to 1968, only disasters with losses of 65 or more lives are listed; since 1968, all disasters in which 5 or more people were killed are listed. Only fatalities to mining company employees are included. All bituminous-coal mines unless otherwise noted.

Date	Location	Deaths	Date	Location	Deaths
1900, May 1	Scofield, UT	200	1923, Aug. 14	Kemmerer, WY.	99
1902, May 19	Coal Creek, TN	184	1924, Mar. 8	Castle Gate, UT	171
1902, July 10	Johnstown, PA.	112	1924, Apr. 28	Benwood, WV	119
1903, June 30	Hanna, WY.	169	1926, Jan. 13	Wilburton, OK	91
1904, Jan. 25	Cheswick, PA.	179	1927, Apr. 30	Everettville, WV.	97
1905, Feb. 20	Virginia City, AL	112	1928, May 19	Mather, PA	195
1907, Jan. 29	Stuart WV	84	1930, Nov. 5	Millfield, OH	79
1907, Dec. 6	Monongah, WV	361	1940, Jan. 10	Bartley, WV.	91
1907, Dec. 19	Jacobs Creek, PA.	239	1940, Mar. 16	St. Clairsville, OH	72
1908, Nov. 28	Marianna, PA.	154	1943, Feb. 27	Washoe, MT	74
1909, Jan. 12	Switchback, WV	67	1944, July 5	Belmont, OH	66
1909, Nov. 13	Cherry, IL.	259	1947, Mar. 25	Centralia, IL	111
1910, Jan. 31	Primero, CO.	75	1951, Dec. 21	West Frankfort, IL	119
1910, May 5	Palos, AL.	90	1968, Mar. 6	Calumet, LA[3].	21
1910, Nov.8	Delagua, CO	79	1968, Nov. 20	Farmington, WV	78
1911, Apr. 7	Throop, PA[1].	72	1970, Dec. 30	Hyden, KY	38
1911, Apr. 8	Littleton, AL	128	1972, May 2	Kellogg, ID[2].	91
1911, Dec.9	Briceville, TN	84	1976, Mar. 9, 11	Oven Fork, KY	23
1912, Mar. 20	McCurtain, OK	73	1977, Mar. 1	Tower City, PA	9
1912, Mar. 26	Jed, WV.	83	1979, June 8	Franklin, LA[3].	5
1913, Apr. 23	Finleyville, PA	96	1980, Nov. 7	Clothier, WV	5
1913, Oct. 22	Dawson, NM	263	1981, Apr. 15	Redstone, CO	15
1914, Apr. 28	Eccles, WV	181	1981, Dec. 7	Topmost, KY	8
1915, Mar. 2	Layland, WV	112	1981, Dec. 8	Whitwell, TN	13
1917, Apr. 27	Hastings, CO	121	1982, Jan. 20	Floyd County, KY	7
1917, June 8	Butte, MT[2].	163	1983, June 21	Dante, VA.	7
1919, June 5	Wilkes-Barre, PA[3].	92	1984, Dec. 19	Huntington, UT	27
1922, Nov. 6	Spangler, PA	77	1986, Feb. 6	Fairmont, WV	5
1922, Nov. 22	Dolomite, AL	90	1989, Sept. 13	Sturgis, KY	10
1923, Feb. 8	Dawson, NM	120	1992, Dec. 7	Norton, VA	8

Note: World's worst mine disaster killed 1,549 workers in Honkeiko Colliery in Manchuria Apr. 25, 1942. (1) Anthracite mine. (2) Metal mine. (3) Nonmetal mine.

Some Notable U.S. Tornadoes Since 1925

Date	Location	Deaths	Date	Location	Deaths
1925, Mar. 18	MO, IL, IN	689	1966, Mar. 3	Mississippi, Alabama	61
1927, Apr. 12	Rock Springs, TX	74	1967, Apr. 21	IL, MI	33
1927, May 9	Arkansas, Poplar Bluff, MO	92	1968, May 15	Midwest	71
1927, Sept. 29	St. Louis, MO.	90	1969, Jan. 23	Mississippi	32
1930, May 6	Hill, Navarro, Ellis Co., TX.	41	1971, Feb. 21	Mississippi delta.	110
1932, Mar. 21	AL (series of tornadoes)	268	1973, May 26-27	South, Midwest (series)	47
1936, Apr. 5	MS, GA.	455	1974, Apr. 3-4	AL, GA, TN, KY, OH.	315
1936, Apr. 6	Gainesville, GA	203	1977, Apr. 4	AL, MS, GA.	22
1938, Sept. 29	Charleston, SC	32	1979, Apr. 10	TX, OK.	60
1942, Mar. 16	Central to NE Mississippi.	75	1980, June 3	Grand Island, NE (series)	4
1942, Apr. 27	Rogers and Mayes Co., OK.	52	1982, Mar. 2-4	South, Midwest (series)	17
1944, June 23	OH, PA, WV, MD	150	1982, May 29	southern IL	10
1945, Apr. 12	OK-AR	102	1983, May 18-22	TX	12
1947, Apr. 9	TX, OK and KS	169	1984, Mar. 28	NC, SC.	57
1948, Mar. 19	Bunker Hill & Gillespie, IL	33	1984, Apr. 21-22	Mississippi	15
1949, Jan. 3	LA and AR.	58	1984, Apr. 26	OK to MN (series)	17
1952, Mar. 21	AR, MO, TN (series)	208	1985, May 31	NY, PA, OH, Ont. (series)	75
1953, May 11	Waco, TX	114	1987, May 22	Saragosa, TX	29
1953, June 8	MI, OH	142	1989, Nov. 15	Huntsville, AL	18
1953, June 9	Worcester and vicinity, MA	90	1989, Nov. 16	Newburgh, NY.	9
1953, Dec. 5	Vicksburg, MS	38	1990, June 2-3	Midwest, Great Lakes.	13
1955, May 25	KS, MO, OK, TX.	115	1990, Aug. 28	northern IL	25
1957, May 20	KS, MO.	48	1991, Apr. 26	KS, OK.	23
1958, June, 4	NW Wisconsin	30	1992, Nov. 21-23	South, Midwest	26
1959, Feb. 10	St. Louis, MO.	21	1994, Mar. 27-28	AL, TN, GA, NC, SC (series)	52
1960, May 5, 6	SE Oklahoma, Arkansas	30	1994, Apr. 26	cen. TX.	4
1965, Apr. 11	IN, IL, OH, MI, WI.	271	1995, May 6-7	southern OK, northern TX	23
1966, Mar. 3	Jackson, MS	57	1995, May 19-20	TX to MD (series).	4

Some Notable Hurricanes, Typhoons, Blizzards, Other Storms

Names of hurricanes and typhoons in italics: H.—hurricane; T.—typhoon

Date	Location	Deaths	Date	Location	Deaths
1888, Mar. 11-14	Blizzard, eastern U.S.	400	1967, Sept. 5-23	H. *Beulah,* Carib., Mex., TX	54
1900, Aug.-Sept.	H., Galveston, TX	6,000	1967, Dec. 12-20	Blizzard, SW, U.S.	51
1906, Sept. 19-24	H., LA, MS	350	1968, Nov. 18-28	T. *Nina,* Philippines	63
1906, Sept. 18	Typhoon, Hong Kong	10,000	1969, Aug. 17-18	H. *Camille,* MS, LA	256
1915, Sept. 29	H., LA	500	1970, July 30-		
1926, Sept. 11-22	H., FL, AL	243	Aug. 5	H. *Celia,* Cuba, FL, TX.	31
1926, Oct. 20	H., Cuba	600	1970, Aug. 20-21	H. *Dorothy,* Martinique	42
1928, Sept. 6-20	H., southern FL	1,836	1970, Sept. 15	T. *Georgia,* Philippines	300
1930, Sept. 3	H., Dominican Rep.	2,000	1970, Oct. 14	T. *Sening,* Philippines	583
1938, Sept. 21	H., Long Island, NY, New England	600	1970, Oct. 15	T. *Titang,* Philippines	526
1940, Nov. 11-12	Blizzard, U.S. NE, Midwest	144	1970, Nov. 13	Cyclone, Bangladesh	300,000
1942, Oct. 15-16	H., Bengal, India	40,000	1971, Aug. 1	T. *Rose,* Hong Kong	130
1944, Sept. 9-16	H., NC to New England	46	1972, June 19-29	H. *Agnes,* FL to NY	118
1947, Dec. 26	Blizzard, New York, NY, N Atlantic	55	1972, Dec. 3	T. *Theresa,* Philippines	169
	states		1973, June-Aug.	Monsoon rains in India	1,217
1952, Oct. 22	Typhoon, Philippines	440	1974, June 11	Storm Dinah, Luzon Is., Phil.	71
1954, Aug. 30	H. *Carol,* northeastern U.S.	68	1974, July 11	T. *Gilda,* Japan, S. Korea	108
1954, Oct. 5-18	H. *Hazel,* eastern U.S., Haiti	347	1974, Sept. 19-20	H. *Fifi,* Honduras	2,000
1955, Aug. 12-13	H. *Connie,* NC, SC, VA, MD	43	1974, Dec. 25	Cyclone leveled Darwin, Aus.	50
1955, Aug. 7-21	H. *Diane,* eastern U.S.	400	1975, Sept. 13-27	H. *Eloise,* Caribbean, NE U.S.	71
1955, Sept. 19	H. *Hilda,* Mexico	200	1976, May 20	T. *Olga,* floods, Philippines	215
1955, Sept. 22-28	H. *Janet,* Caribbean	500	1977, July 25, 31	T. *Thelma,* T. *Vera,* Taiwan	39
1956, Feb. 1-29	Blizzard, W Europe	1,000	1978, Oct. 27	T. *Rita,* Philippines	c. 400
1957, June 25-30	H. *Audrey,* TX to AL	390	1979, Aug. 30-		
1958, Feb. 15-16	Blizzard, northeastern U.S.	171	Sept. 7	H. *David,* Caribbean, E U.S.	1,100
1959, Sept. 17-19	T. *Sarah,* Japan, S. Korea	2,000	1980, Aug. 4-11	H. *Allen,* Caribbean, TX	272
1959, Sept. 26-27	T. *Vera,* Honshu, Japan	4,466	1981, Nov. 25	T. *Irma,* Luzon Is., Phil.	176
1960, Sept. 4-12	H. *Donna,* Caribbean, E U.S.	148	1983, June	Monsoon, India	900
1961, Sept. 11-14	H. *Carla,* TX	46	1983, Aug. 18	H. *Alicia,* southern TX	17
1961, Oct. 31	H. *Hattie,* Br. Honduras	400	1984, Sept. 2	T. *Ike,* S Philippines	1,363
1963, May 28-29	Windstorm, Bangladesh	22,000	1985, May 25	Cyclone, Bangladesh	10,000
1963, Oct. 4-8	H. *Flora,* Caribbean	6,000	1985, Oct. 26-		
1964, Oct. 4-7	H. *Hilda,* LA, MS, GA	38	Nov. 6	H. *Juan,* SE U.S.	97
1964, June 30	T. *Winnie,* N Philippines	107	1987, Nov. 25	T. *Nina,* Philippines	650
1964, Sept. 5	T. *Ruby,* Hong Kong and China	735	1988, Sept. 10-17	H. *Gilbert,* Caribbean, G. of Mexico	260
1965, May 11-12	Windstorm, Bangladesh	17,000	1989, Sept. 16-22	H. *Hugo,* Caribbean, SE U.S.	504
1965, June 1-2	Windstorm, Bangladesh	30,000	1990, May 6-11	Cyclones, SE India	450
1965, Sept. 7-12	H. *Betsy,* FL, MS, LA	74	1991, Apr. 30	Cyclone, Bangladesh	139,000
1965, Dec. 15	Windstorm, Bangladesh	10,000	1992, Aug. 24-26	H. *Andrew,* southern FL, LA	14
1966, June 4-10	H. *Alma,* Honduras, SE U.S.	51	1993, Mar. 13-14	Blizzard, eastern U.S.	200
1966, Sept. 24-30	H. *Inez,* Carib., FL, Mex.	293	1993, June	Monsoon, Bangladesh	2,000
1967, July 9	T. *Billie,* SW Japan	347	1994, Nov. 8-18	Storm Gordon, Caribbean, FL	830

Some Notable Floods, Tidal Waves

Date	Location	Deaths	Date	Location	Deaths
1228	Holland	100,000	1969, Oct. 1-8	Tunisia	500
1642	China	300,000	1970, May 20	cen. Romania	160
1883, Aug. 27	Indonesia	36,000	1970, July 22	Himalayas, India	500
1887	Huang He River, China	900,000	1971, Feb. 26	Rio de Janeiro, Brazil	130
1889, May 31	Johnstown, PA	2,209	1972, Feb. 26	Buffalo Creek, WV	118
1900, Sept. 8	Galveston, TX	5,000	1972, June 9	Rapid City, SD	236
1903, June 15	Heppner, OR	325	1972, Aug. 7	Luzon Is., Philippines	454
1911	Chang Jiang River, China	100,000	1972, Aug. 19-31	Pakistan	1,500
1913, Mar. 25-27	Ohio, Indiana	732	1974, Mar. 29	Tubaro, Brazil	1,000
1915, Aug. 17	Galveston, TX	275	1974, Aug. 12	Monty-Long, Bangladesh	2,500
1928, Mar. 13	Collapse of St. Francis, Dam,		1976, June 5	Teton Dam collapse, ID	11
	Saugus, CA	450	1976, July 31	Big Thompson Canyon, CO	139
1928, Sept. 13	Lake Okeechobee, FL	2,000	1976, Nov. 17	East Java, Indonesia	136
1931, Aug.	Huang He River, China	3,700,000	1977, July 19-20	Johnstown, PA	68
1937, Jan. 22	Ohio, MS Valleys	250	1978, June-Sept.	N India	1,200
1939	N China	200,000	1979, Jan.-Feb.	Brazil	204
1946, Apr. 1	Hawaii, Alaska	159	1979, July 17	Lomblem Is., Indonesia	539
1947, Sept. 20	Honshu Island, Japan	1,900	1979, Aug. 11	Morvi, India	15,000
1951, Aug.	Manchuria	1,800	1980, Feb. 13-22	southern CA, AZ	26
1953, Jan. 31	W Europe	2,000	1981, Apr.	N China	550
1954, Aug. 17	Farahzad, Iran	2,000	1981, July	Sichuan, Hubei Prov., China	1,300
1955, Oct. 7-12	India, Pakistan	1,700	1982, Jan. 23	Nr. Lima, Peru	600
1959, Nov. 1	W Mexico	2,000	1982, May 12	Guangdong, China	430
1959, Dec. 2	Frejus, France	412	1982, Sept. 17-21	El Salvador, Guatemala	1,300+
1960, Oct. 10	Bangladesh	6,000	1983, Feb.-Mar.	CA coast	13
1960, Oct. 31	Bangladesh	4,000	1983, Apr. 6-12	AL, LA, MS, TN.	15
1962, Feb. 17	German North Sea coast	343	1984, May 27	Tulsa, OK	13
1962, Sept. 27	Barcelona, Spain	445	1984, Aug.-Sept.	S. Korea	200+
1963, Oct. 9	Dam collapse, Vaiont, Italy	1,800	1985, July 19	N Italy, dam burst	361
1966, Nov. 3-4	Florence, Venice, Italy	113	1987, Aug.-Sept.	N Bangladesh	1,000+
1967, Jan. 18-24	E Brazil	894	1988, Sept.	N India	1,000+
1967, Mar. 19	Rio de Janeiro, Brazil	436	1990, June 14	Shadyside, OH	23
1967, Nov. 26	Lisbon, Portugal	464	1991, Dec. 18-26	Texas	18
1968, Aug. 7-14	Gujarat State, India	1,000	1992, Feb. 9-15	southern CA	13
1968, Oct. 7	NE India	780	1993, July-Aug.	Midwest	48
1969, Jan. 18-26	S CA	100	1994, July	Georgia, Alabama	32
1969, Mar. 17	Mundau Valley, Alagoas, Brazil	218	1995, Jan. 30-Feb. 9	NW Europe	40
1969, Aug. 20-22	W Virginia	189	1995, March 8-15	California	15
1969, Sept. 15	South Korea	250	1995, July	Hunan Province, China	1,200
			1995, Aug. 19	SW Morocco	136

Some Notable Fires Since 1835

Date	Location	Deaths	Date	Location	Deaths
1835, Dec. 16	New York, NY, 500 bldgs. destroyed	—	1966, Oct. 17	New York, NY, bldg. (firefighters)	12
1845, May	Canton, China, theater	1,670	1966, Dec. 7	Erzurum, Turkey, barracks	68
1871, Oct. 8	Chicago, $196 million loss	250	1967, Feb. 7	Montgomery, AL, restaurant	25
1871, Oct. 8	Peshtigo, WI, forest fire	1,182	1967, May 22	Brussels, Belgium, store	322
1872, Nov. 9	Boston, 800 bldgs. destroyed	—	1967, July 16	Jay, FL, state prison	37
1876, Dec. 5	Brooklyn, NY, theater	295	1968, Feb. 26	Shrewsbury, England, hospital	22
1877, June 20	St. John, N. B., Canada	100	1968, May 11	Vijayawada, India, wedding hall	58
1881, Dec. 8	Ring Theater, Vienna	850	1968, Nov. 18	Glasgow, Scotland, factory	24
1887, May 25	Opera Comique, Paris	200	1969, Dec. 2	Notre Dame, Can., nursing home	54
1887, Sept. 4	Exeter, England, theater	200	1970, Jan. 9	Marietta, OH, nursing home	27
1894, Sept. 1	MN, forest fire	413	1970, Mar. 20	Seattle, WA, hotel	19
1897, May 4	Paris, charity bazaar	150	1970, Nov. 1	Grenoble, France, dance hall	145
1900, June 30	Hoboken, NJ, docks	326	1970, Dec. 20	Tucson, AZ, hotel	28
1902, Sept. 20	Birmingham, AL, church	115	1971, Mar. 6	Burghoezli, Switzerland, psychiatric clinic	28
1903, Dec. 30	Iroquois Theater, Chicago	602	1971, Apr., 20	Bangkok, Thailand, hotel	24
1908, Jan. 13	Rhoads Theater, Boyertown, PA	170	1971, Dec., 25	Seoul, South Korea, hotel	162
1908, Mar. 4	Collinwood, OH, school	176	1972, May 13	Osaka, Japan, nightclub	116
1911, Mar. 25	Triangle Shirtwaist factory, NY, NY	146	1972, July 5	Sherborne, England, hospital	30
1913, Oct. 14	Mid Glamorgan, Wales, colliery	439	1973, Feb. 6	Paris, France, school	21
1918, Apr. 13	Norman OK, state hospital	38	1973, Nov. 6	Fukui, Japan, train	28
1918, Oct. 12	Cloquet, MN, forest fire	400	1973, Nov. 29	Kumamoto, Japan, department store	107
1919, June 20	Mayagüez Theater, San Juan	150	1973, Dec. 2	Seoul, South Korea, theater	50
1923, May 17	Camden, SC, school	76	1974, Feb. 1	Sao Paulo, Brazil, bank building	189
1924, Dec. 24	Babb's Switch, OK, school	35	1974, June 30	Port Chester, NY, discotheque	24
1929, May 15	Cleveland, OH, clinic	125	1974, Nov. 3	Seoul, South Korea, hotel, discotheque	88
1930, Apr. 21	Columbus, OH, penitentiary	320	1975, Dec. 12	Mina, Saudi Arabia, tent city	138
1931, July 24	Pittsburgh, PA, home for aged	48	1976, Oct. 24	Bronx, NY, social club	25
1934, Dec. 11	Hotel Kerns, Lansing, MI	34	1977, Feb. 25	Moscow, Rossiya hotel	45
1938, May 16	Atlanta, GA, Terminal Hotel	35	1977, May 28	Southgate, KY, nightclub	164
1940, Apr. 23	Natchez, MS, dance hall	198	1977, June 9	Abidjan, Ivory Coast, nightclub	41
1942, Nov. 28	Cocoanut Grove, Boston	491	1977, June 26	Columbia, TN, jail	42
1942, Dec. 12	St. John's,Nfld., hostel	100	1977, Nov. 14	Manila, Philippines, hotel	47
1943, Sept. 7	Gulf Hotel, Houston	55	1978, Jan. 28	Kansas City, Coates House Hotel	16
1944, July 6	Ringling Circus, Hartford, CT	168	1979, July 14	Saragossa, Spain, hotel	80
1946, June 5	LaSalle Hotel, Chicago	61	1979, Dec. 31	Chapais, Quebec, social club	42
1946, Dec. 7	Winecoff Hotel, Atlanta	119	1980, May 20	Kingston, Jamaica, nursing home	157
1946, Dec. 12	New York, NY, ice plant, tenement	37	1980, Nov. 21	MGM Grand Hotel, Las Vegas	84
1949, Apr. 5	Effingham, IL, hospital	77	1980, Dec. 4	Stouffer Inn, Harrison, NY	26
1950, Jan. 7	Davenport, IA, Mercy Hospital	41	1981, Jan. 9	Keansburg, NJ, boarding home	30
1953, Mar. 29	Largo, FL, nursing home	35	1981, Feb. 10	Las Vegas Hilton	8
1953, Apr. 16	Chicago, metalworking plant	35	1981, Feb. 14	Dublin, Ireland, discotheque	44
1957, Feb. 17	Warrenton, MO, home for aged	72	1982, Sept. 4	Los Angeles, apartment house	24
1958, Mar. 19	New York, NY, loft building	24	1982, Nov. 8	Biloxi, MS, county jail	29
1958, Dec. 1	Chicago, parochial school	95	1983, Feb. 13	Turin, Italy, movie theater	64
1958, Dec. 16	Bogota, Colombia, store	83	1983, Dec. 17	Madrid, Spain, discotheque	83
1959, June 23	Stalheim, Norway, resort hotel	34	1984, May 11	Great Adventure Amusement Pk., NJ	8
1960, Mar. 12	Pusan, Korea, chemical plant	68	1985, Apr. 21	Tabaco, Phil., movie theater	44
1960, July 14	Guatemala City, mental hospital	225	1985, Apr. 26	Buenos Aires, Arg. hospital	79
1960, Nov. 13	Amude, Syria, movie theater	152	1985, May 11	Bradford, England, soccer stadium	53
1961, Jan. 6	Thomas Hotel, San Francisco	20	1986, Dec. 31	Puerto Rico, Dupont Plaza Hotel	96
1961, Dec. 8	Hartford, CT, hospital	16	1987, May 6-June 2	N China, forest fire	193
1961, Dec. 17	Niteroi, Brazil, circus	323	1987, Nov. 17	London, England subway	30
1963, May 4	Diourbel, Senegal, theater	64	1990, Mar. 25	NY City, social club	87
1963, Nov. 18	Surfside Hotel, Atlantic City, NJ	25	1991, Sept. 3	Hamlet, NC, chicken-processing plant	25
1963, Nov. 23	Fitchville, OH, rest home	63	1991, Oct. 20-21	Oakland, Berkeley, CA, wildfire	24
1963, Dec. 29	Roosevelt Hotel, Jacksonville, FL	22	1993, Apr. 19	Waco, TX, cult compound	72
1964, May 8	Manila, apartment bldg.	30	1994, May 10	Bangkok, Thailand, toy factory	213
1964, Dec. 18	Fountaintown, IN, nursing home	20	1994, July 4-10	Glenwood Springs, CO (firefighters)	14
1965, Mar. 1	LaSalle, Canada, apartment	28	1994, Dec. 10	Karamay, China, theater	300
1965, Aug. 11-16	Watts riot fires, CA	30+	1994, Nov. 2	Durunka, Egypt, burning fuel flood	500
1966, Mar. 11	Numata, Japan, 2 ski resorts	31			
1966, Aug. 13	Melbourne, Australia, hotel	29			
1966, Sept. 12	Anchorage, AK, hotel	14			

Some Notable Explosions Since 1910

Date	Location	Deaths	Date	Location	Deaths
1910, Oct. 1	Los Angeles Times Bldg.	21	1942, June 5	Ordnance plant, Elwood, IL	49
1913, Mar. 7	Dynamite, Baltimore harbor	55	1944, Apr. 14	Bombay, India, harbor	700
1915, Sept. 27	Gasoline tank car, Ardmore, OK	47	1944, July 17	Port Chicago, CA, pier	322
1917, Apr. 10	Munitions plant, Eddystone, PA	133	1944, Oct. 21	Liquid gas tank, Cleveland	135
1917, Dec. 6	Halifax Harbor, Canada	1,654	1947, Apr. 16	Texas City, TX, pier	576
1918, May 18	Chemical plant, Oakdale, PA	193	1948, July 28	Farben works, Ludwigshafen, Germ.	184
1918, July 2	Explosives, Split Rock, NY	50	1950, May 19	Munitions barges, S. Amboy, NJ	30
1918, Oct. 4	Shell plant, Morgan Station, NJ	64	1956, Aug. 7	Dynamite trucks, Cali, Colombia	1,100
1919, May 22	Food plant, Cedar Rapids, IA	44	1958, Apr. 18	Sunken munitions ship, Okinawa	40
1920, Sept. 16	Wall Street, New York, bomb	30	1958, May 22	Nike missiles, Leonardo, NJ	10
1921, Sept. 21	Chem. storage facility, Oppau, Germ.	561	1959, Apr. 10	World War II bomb, Philippines	38
1924, Jan. 3	Food plant, Pekin, IL.	42	1959, June 28	Rail tank cars, Meldrin, GA	25
1927, May 18	Bath school, Lansing, MI	38	1959, Aug. 7	Dynamite truck, Roseburg, OR	13
1928, April 13	Dance hall, West Plains, MO	40	1959, Nov. 2	Jamuri Bazar, India, explosives	46
1937, Mar. 18	New London, TX, school	413	1959, Dec. 13	Dortmund, Germ., 2 apt. bldgs.	26
1940, Sept. 12	Hercules Powder, Kenvil, NJ	55	1960, Mar. 4	Belgian munitions ship, Havana	100

(continued)

Some Notable Explosions Since 1910 (continued)

Date	Location	Deaths	Date	Location	Deaths
1960, Oct. 25	Gas, Windsor, Ont., store	11	1977, Dec. 22	Grain elevator, Westwego, LA	35
1962, Jan. 16	Gas pipeline, Edson, Alberta	8	1978, Feb. 24	Derailed tank car, Waverly, TN	12
1962, Oct. 3	Telephone Co. office, NY City	23	1978, July 11	Propylene tank truck, Spanish	
1963, Jan. 2	Packing plant, Terre Haute, IN	16		coastal campsite	150
1963, Mar. 9	Dynamite plant, S. Africa.	45	1980, Oct. 23	School, Ortuella, Spain.	64
1963, Aug. 13	Explosives dump, Gauhiti, India	32	1982, Apr. 25	Antiques exhibition, Todi, Italy	33
1963, Oct. 31	State Fair Coliseum, Indianapolis	73	1982, Nov. 2	Salang Tunnel, Afghanistan	1,000-
1964, July 23	Bone, Algeria, harbor munitions	100			3,000
1965, Mar. 4	Gas pipeline, Natchitoches, LA	17	1984, Feb. 25	Oil pipeline, Cubatao, Brazil	508
1965, Aug. 9	Missile silo, Searcy, AR	53	1984, June 21	Naval supply depot, Severomorsk,	
1965, Oct. 21	Bridge, Tila Bund, Pakistan	80		USSR	200+
1965, Oct. 30	Cartagena, Colombia	48	1984, Nov. 19	Gas storage area, NE Mexico City . . .	334
1965, Nov. 24	Armory, Keokuk, IA	20	1984, Dec. 3	Chemical plant, Bhopal, cen. India . . .	3,849
1966, Oct. 13	Chemical plant, La Salle, Que..	11	1984, Dec. 5	Coal mine, Taipei, Taiwan.	94
1967, Feb. 17	Chemical plant, Hawthorne, NJ	11	1985, June 25	Fireworks factory, Hallett, OK	21
1967, Dec. 25	Apartment bldg., Moscow	20	1988, July 6	Oil rig, North Sea.	167
1968, Apr. 6	Sports store, Richmond, IN	43	1989, June 3	Gas pipeline, between Ufa, Asha, USSR	650+
1970, Apr. 8	Subway construction, Osaka, Jap. . . .	73	1992, Mar. 3	Coal mine, Kozlu, Turkey	270+
1971, June 24	Tunnel, Sylmar, CA	17	1992, Apr. 22	Sewer, Guadalajara, Mexico	190
1971, June 28	School, fireworks, Puebla, Mex.	13	1992, May 9	Coal mine, Plymouth, Nova Scotia . . .	26
1971, Oct. 21	Shopping center, Glasgow, Scot.	20	1993, Feb. 26	World Trade Center, NY City.	6
1973, Feb., 10	Liquefied gas tank, Staten Is., NY. . . .	40	1994, Jul. 18	Jewish community center, Buenos	
1975, Dec. 27	Chasnala, India, mine.	431		Aires	100
1976, Apr. 13	Lapua, Finland, munitions works	40	1995, Apr. 19	Federal office bldg., Oklahoma City . .	169[1]
1977, Nov. 11	Freight train, Iri, South Korea.	57	1995, Apr. 29	Subway construction, South Korea. . .	110

(1) Includes a rescue worker who died during the rescue effort.

Notable Nuclear Accidents

Oct. 7, 1957 — A fire in the Windscale plutonium production reactor N of Liverpool, England, spread radioactive material throughout the countryside. In 1983, the British government said that 39 people probably died of cancer as a result.

1957 — A chemical explosion in Kasli, USSR (now in Russia), in tanks containing nuclear waste, spread radioactive material and forced a major evacuation.

Jan. 3, 1961 — An experimental reactor at a federal installation near Idaho Falls, ID, killed three workers—the only deaths in U.S. reactor operations. The plant had high radiation levels, but damage was contained.

Oct. 5, 1966 — A sodium cooling system malfunction caused a partial core meltdown at the Enrico Fermi demonstration breeder reactor near Detroit, MI. Radiation was contained.

Jan. 21, 1969 — A coolant malfunction from an experimental underground reactor at Lucens Vad, Switzerland, resulted in the release of a large amount of radiation into a cavern, which was then sealed.

Mar. 22, 1975 — A technician checking for air leaks with a lighted candle caused a $100 million fire at the Brown's Ferry reactor in Decatur, AL. The fire burned out electrical controls, lowering the cooling water to dangerous levels.

Mar. 28, 1979 — The worst commercial nuclear accident in the U.S. occurred as equipment failures and human mistakes led to a loss of coolant and partial core meltdown at the Three Mile Island reactor in Middletown, PA.

Feb. 11, 1981 — Eight workers were contaminated when more than 100,000 gallons of radioactive coolant leaked into the containment building of the TVA's Sequoyah 1 plant in Tennessee.

Apr. 25, 1981 — Some 100 workers were exposed to radioactive material during repairs of a nuclear plant at Tsuruga, Japan.

Jan. 6, 1986 — A cylinder of nuclear material burst after being improperly heated at a Kerr-McGee plant at Gore, OK. One worker died, and 100 were hospitalized.

Apr. 26, 1986 — In the worst accident in the history of the nuclear power industry, fires and explosions resulting from an unauthorized experiment at the Chernobyl nuclear power plant near Kiev, USSR (now in Ukraine), left at least 31 people dead in the immediate aftermath of the disaster and spread significant quantities of radioactive material over much of Europe. An estimated 135,000 people were evacuated from areas around Chernobyl, some of which were rendered uninhabitable for years. As a result of the radiation released into the atmosphere, tens of thousands of excess cancer deaths (as well as increased rates of birth defects) were expected in succeeding decades.

Record Oil Spills

As a rule, the number of tons can be multiplied by 7 to estimate the number of barrels spilled; the exact number of barrels in a ton varies with the type of oil. Each barrel contains 42 gallons.

Name, place	Date	Cause	Tons
Ixtoc I oil well, S Gulf of Mexico	June 3, 1979.	Blowout	600,000
Nowruz oil field, Persian Gulf	Feb. 1983.	Blowout	600,000 (est.)
Atlantic Empress & Aegean Captain, off Trinidad and Tobago. . . .	July 19, 1979	Collision	300,000
Castillo de Bellver, off Cape Town, South Africa	Aug. 6, 1983	Fire	250,000
Amoco Cadiz, near Portsall, France.	Mar. 16, 1978	Grounding.	223,000
Torrey Canyon, off Land's End, England	Mar. 18, 1967	Grounding.	119,000
Sea Star, Gulf of Oman	Dec. 19, 1972	Collision	115,000
Urquiola, La Coruna, Spain.	May 12, 1976	Grounding.	100,000
Hawaiian Patriot, N Pacific	Feb. 25, 1977	Fire	99,000
Othello, Tralhavet Bay, Sweden	Mar. 20, 1970	Collision	60,000-100,000

Other Notable Oil Spills

Name, place	Date	Cause	Gallons
Persian Gulf	Jan. 23, 1991 (began)	Spillage by Iraq	130,000,000[1]
Braer, off Shetland Islands	Jan. 5, 1993	Grounding	26,000,000
Aegean Sea, off N Spain	Dec. 3, 1992	Unknown	21,500,000
World Glory, off South Africa.	June 13, 1968.	Hull failure	13,524,000
Burmah Agate, Galveston Bay, TX	Nov. 1, 1979.	Collision	10,700,000
Exxon Valdez, Prince William Sound, AK	Mar. 24, 1989	Grounding	10,080,000
Keo, off MA	Nov. 5, 1969.	Hull failure	8,820,000
Storage tank, Sewaren, NJ.	Nov. 4, 1969.	Tank rupture	8,400,000
Ekofisk oil field, North Sea	Apr. 22, 1977	Well blowout	8,200,000
Argo Merchant, Nantucket, MA	Dec. 15, 1976	Grounding	7,700,000
Pipeline, West Delta, LA.	Oct. 15, 1967	Dragging anchor	6,720,000
Tanker off Japan.	Nov. 30, 1971	Ship broke in half	6,258,000
Usinsk, Russian Arctic.	Aug. 12, 1994	Pipeline rupture	4,300,000
Storage tank, Monongahela River	Jan. 2, 1988	Tank rupture	3,800,000[2]

(1) Estimated by Saudi Arabia. Some estimates are as low as 25 mln. gallons. (2) Some estimates are as high as 84.6 mln. gallons.

Major Earthquakes

Source: Global Volcanism Network, Smithsonian Institution; U.S. Geological Survey, Dept. of the Interior; World Almanac research

Magnitude of earthquakes (Mag.), distinct from deaths or damage caused, is measured on the Richter scale, on which each higher number represents a tenfold increase in energy measured in ground motion. Adopted in 1935, the scale has been applied in the following table to earthquakes as far back as reliable seismograms are available.

Date	Location	Deaths	Mag.	Date	Location	Deaths	Mag.
526, May 20	Antioch, Syria	250,000	NA	1966, Aug. 19	E Turkey	2,520	6.9
856	Corinth, Greece	45,000	"	1968, Aug. 31	NE Iran	12,000	7.4
1057	Chihli, China	25,000	"	1970, Jan. 5	Yunnan Province,		
1169, Feb. 11	nr. Mt. Etna, Sicily	15,000[1]	"		China	10,000	7.7
1268	Cilicia, Asia Minor	60,000	"	1970, Mar. 28	W Turkey	1,086	7.4
1290, Sept. 27	Chihli, China	100,000	"	1970, May 31	N Peru	66,794	7.7
1293, May 20	Kamakura, Japan	30,000	"	1971, Feb. 9	San Fernando Valley,		
1531, Jan. 26	Lisbon, Portugal	30,000	"		CA	65	6.6
1556, Jan. 24	Shaanxi, China	830,000	"	1972, Apr. 10	S Iran	5,057	6.9
1667, Nov.	Shemaka, Caucasia	80,000	"	1972, Dec. 23	Nicaragua	5,000	6.2
1693, Jan. 11	Catania, Italy	60,000	"	1974, Dec. 28	Pakistan (9 towns)	5,200	6.3
1730, Dec. 30	Hokkaido, Japan	137,000	"	1975, Sept. 6	Turkey (Lice, etc.)	2,312	6.8
1737, Oct. 11	India, Calcutta	300,000	"	1976, Feb. 4	Guatemala	22,778	7.5
1755, June 7	N Persia	40,000	"	1976, May 6	NE Italy	946	6.5
1755, Nov. 1	Lisbon, Portugal	60,000	8.75*	1976, June 26	Irian Jaya, New Guinea	443	7.1
1783, Feb. 4	Calabria, Italy	30,000	NA	1976, July 28	Tangshan, China	242,000	8.2
1797, Feb. 4	Quito, Ecuador	41,000	"	1976, Aug. 17	Mindanao, Phil.	8,000	7.8
1811-12	New Madrid, MO			1976, Nov. 24	E Turkey	4,000	7.9
	(series)	NA	8.7*	1977, Mar. 4	Romania	1,541	7.5
1822, Sept. 5	Asia Minor, Aleppo	22,000	NA	1977, Aug. 19	Indonesia	200	8.0
1828, Dec. 28	Echigo, Japan	30,000	"	1977, Nov. 23	NW Argentina	100	8.2
1868, Aug. 13-15	Peru, Ecuador	40,000	"	1978, Sept. 16	NE Iran	25,000	7.7
1875, May 16	Venezuela, Colombia	16,000	"	1979, Sept. 12	Indonesia	100	8.1
1886, Aug. 31	Charleston, SC	60	6.6	1979, Dec. 12	Colombia, Ecuador	800	7.9
1896, June 15	Japan, sea wave	27,120	NA	1980, Oct. 10	NW Algeria	4,500	7.3
1906, Apr. 18-19	San Francisco, CA	503[2]	8.3	1980, Nov. 23	S Italy	4,800	7.2
1906, Aug. 16	Valparaiso, Chile	20,000	8.6	1982, Dec. 13	N Yemen	2,800	6.0
1908, Dec. 28	Messina, Italy	83,000	7.5	1983, May 26	N Honshu, Japan	81	7.7
1915, Jan. 13	Avezzano, Italy	29,980	7.5	1983, Oct. 30	E Turkey	1,300	7.1
1918, Oct. 11	Mona Passage, P.R.	116	7.5	1985, Mar. 3	Chile	146	7.8
1920, Dec. 16	Gansu, China	100,000	8.6	1985, Sept. 19, 21	Mexico City	4,200+	8.1
1923, Sept. 1	Yokohama, Japan	200,000	8.3	1987, Mar. 5-6	NE Ecuador	4,000+	7.3
1927, May 22	Nan-Shan, China	200,000	8.3	1988, Aug. 20	India/Nepal border	1,000+	6.5
1932, Dec. 26	Gansu, China	70,000	7.6	1988, Nov. 6	China/Burma border	1,000	7.3
1933, Mar. 2	Japan	2,990	8.9	1988, Dec. 7	NW Armenia	55,000+	6.8
1933, Mar. 10	Long Beach, CA	115	6.2	1989, Oct. 17	San Francisco Bay		
1934, Jan. 15	India, Bihar-Nepal	10,700	8.4		area	62	6.9
1935, May 31	Quetta, India	50,000	7.5	1990, May 30	N Peru	115	6.3
1939, Jan. 24	Chillan, Chile	28,000	8.3	1990, June 21	NW Iran	40,000+	7.7
1939, Dec. 26	Erzincan, Turkey	30,000	7.9	1990, July 16	Luzon, Philippines	1,621	7.7
1946, Dec. 21	Honshu, Japan	2,000	8.4	1991, Feb. 1	Pakistan, Afghanistan		
1948, June 28	Fukui, Japan	5,131	7.3		border	1,200	6.8
1949, Aug. 5	Pelileo, Ecuador	6,000	6.8	1992, Mar. 13, 15	E Turkey	4,000	6.2/6.0
1950, Aug. 15	Assam, India	1,530	8.7	1992, June 28	S CA	1	7.5/6.6
1953, Mar. 18	NW Turkey	1,200	7.2	1992, Dec. 12	Flores Isl., Indonesia	2,500	7.5
1956, June 10-17	N Afghanistan	2,000	7.7	1993, July 12	off Hokkaido, Japan	200+	7.7
1957, July 2	N Iran	2,500	7.4	1993, Sept. 29	Maharashtra, S India	9,748[3]	6.4
1957, Dec. 13	W Iran	2,000	7.1	1994, Jan. 17	Northridge, CA	61	6.8
1960, Feb. 29	Agadir, Morocco	12,000	5.8	1994, Feb. 15	S Sumatra, Indon.	215	7.0
1960, May 21-30	S Chile	5,000	8.3	1994, June 6	Cauca, SW Col.	1,000	6.8
1962, Sept. 1	NW Iran	12,230	7.1	1994, Aug. 19	N Algeria	164	6.0
1963, July 26	Skopje, Yugoslavia	1,100	6.0	1995, Jan. 16	Kobe, Japan	5,477[4]	7.2
1964, Mar. 27	Alaska	131	8.4	1995, May 27	Sakhalin Isl., Russia	2,000	7.6

(*) estimated from earthquake intensity. NA=not available. (1) Once thought to be a volcanic eruption; evidence indicates a destructive earthquake and tsunami occurred on this date. (2) With subsequent fires, death toll rose to 700. (3) Official death toll released by Indian government. Other sources reported 30,000 deaths. (4) Official Japanese death toll as of Sept. 1995.

Some Recent Earthquakes

Source: Global Volcanism Network, Smithsonian Institution; dates are Greenwich Mean Time

Date	Location	Magnitude	Date	Location	Magnitude
1995, April 28	Kuril Isl.	6.9	Jan. 16	Kobe, Japan	7.2
April 21	Philippine Isl.	7.3	1994, Nov. 14	Mindoro, Philippines	7.2
April 7	Tonga Isl.	7.5	Oct. 4	Kuril Isl., nr. Japan	8.2
May 27	Sakhalin Isl., Russia	7.6	Sept. 1	off N California coast	7.0
May 16	Loyalty Isl.	7.7	July 13	N Vanuatu Isl.	7.3
May 14	Timor Isl. region, Indon.	6.9	June 18	South Isl., New Zealand	7.1
May 5	Samar Isl., Philippines	7.0	June 9	La Paz, Bolivia	8.2
Mar. 19	S coast Iran Jaya, Indon.	7.2	June 6	Cauca, SW Colombia	6.8
Feb. 5	New Zealand	7.5	June 2	S of Java, Indon.	7.7
Jan. 27	Irian Jaya, Idon.	6.9			

Historic Assassinations Since 1865

1865—Apr. 14. U.S. Pres. Abraham Lincoln, shot by John Wilkes Booth in Washington, DC; died Apr. 15.

1881—Mar. 13. Alexander II, of Russia.—July 2. U.S. Pres. James A. Garfield, shot by Charles J. Guiteau, Washington DC; died Sept. 19.

1900—July 29. Umberto I, king of Italy.

1901—Sept. 6. U.S. Pres. William McKinley in Buffalo, NY, died Sept. 14. Leon Czolgosz executed for the crime Oct. 29.

1913—Feb. 23. Mexican Pres. Francisco I. Madero and Vice Pres. Jose Pino Suarez.—Mar. 18. George, king of Greece.

1914—June 28. Archduke Francis Ferdinand of Austria-Hungary and his wife in Sarajevo, Bosnia (later part of Bosnia and Herzegovina), by Gavrilo Princip.

1916—Dec. 30. Grigori Rasputin, politically powerful Russian monk.

1918—July 12. Grand Duke Michael of Russia, at Perm.—July 16. Nicholas II, abdicated as czar of Russia; his wife, the Czarina Alexandra; their son, Czarevitch Alexis; their daughters, Grand Duchesses Olga, Tatiana, Marie, Anastasia; and 4 members of their household were executed by Bolsheviks at Ekaterinburg.

1920—May 20. Mexican Pres. Gen. Venustiano Carranza in Tlaxcalantongo.

1922—Aug. 22. Michael Collins, Irish revolutionary.— Dec. 16. Polish President Gabriel Narutowicz in Warsaw by an anarchist.

1923—July 20. Gen. Francisco "Pancho" Villa, ex-rebel leader, in Parral, Mexico.

1928—July 17. Gen. Alvaro Obregon, president-elect of Mexico, in San Angel, Mexico.

1934—July 25. In Vienna, Austrian Chancellor Engelbert Dollfuss by Nazis.

1935—Sept. 8. U.S. Sen. Huey P. Long, shot in Baton Rouge, LA, by Dr. Carl Austin Weiss, who was slain by Long's bodyguards; Long died Sept. 10.

1940—Aug. 20. Leon Trotsky (Lev Bronstein), 63, exiled Russian war minister, near Mexico City. Killer identified as Ramon Mercador del Rio, a Spaniard, served 20 years in Mexican prison.

1948—Jan. 30. Mohandas K. Gandhi, 78, shot in New Delhi, India, by Nathuram Vinayak Godse.— Sept. 17. Count Folke Bernadotte, UN mediator for Palestine, ambushed in Jerusalem.

1951—July 20. King Abdullah ibn Hussein of Jordan. — Oct. 16. Prime Min. Liaquat Ali Khan of Pakistan shot in Rawalpindi.

1956—Sept. 21. Pres. Anastasio Somoza of Nicaragua, in Leon; died Sept. 29.

1957—July 26. Pres. Carlos Castillo Armas of Guatemala, in Guatemala City by one of his own guards.

1958—July 14. King Faisal of Iraq; his uncle, Crown Prince Abdullah; and July 15, Premier Nuri as-Said, by rebels in Baghdad.

1959—Sept. 25. Prime Minister Solomon Bandaranaike of Ceylon, by Buddhist monk in Colombo.

1961—Jan. 17. Ex-Premier Patrice Lumumba of the Congo, in Katanga Province—May 30. Dominican dictator Rafael Leonidas Trujillo Molina shot to death by assassins near Ciudad Trujillo.

1963—June 12. Medgar W. Evers, NAACP's Mississippi field secretary, in Jackson, MS.—Nov. 2. Pres. Ngo Dinh Diem of South Vietnam and his brother, Ngo Dinh Nhu, in a military coup.—Nov. 22. U.S. Pres. John F. Kennedy fatally shot in Dallas, TX; accused Lee Harvey Oswald murdered by Jack Ruby while awaiting trial.

1965—Jan. 21. Iranian premier Hassan Ali Mansour fatally wounded by assassin in Teheran; 4 executed.—Feb. 21. Malcolm X, black nationalist, fatally shot in NY City.

1966—Sept. 6. Prime Minister Hendrik F. Verwoerd of South Africa stabbed to death in parliament at Cape Town.

1968—Apr. 4. Rev. Dr. Martin Luther King Jr. fatally shot in Memphis, TN by James Earl Ray.—June 5. Sen. Robert F. Kennedy (D-NY) fatally shot in Los Angeles; Sirhan Sirhan, resident alien, convicted of murder.

1971—Nov. 28. Prime Minister Wasfi Tal of Jordan, in Cairo, by Palestinian guerrillas.

1973—Mar. 2. U.S. Ambassador Cleo A. Noel Jr., U.S. Charge d'Affaires George C. Moore and Belgian Charge d'Affaires Guy Eid killed by Palestinian guerrillas in Khartoum, Sudan.

1974—Aug. 19. U.S. Ambassador to Cyprus, Rodger P. Davies, killed by sniper's bullet in Nicosia.

1975—Feb. 11. Pres. Richard Ratsimandrava, of Madagascar, shot in Tananarive.—Mar. 25. King Faisal of Saudi Arabia shot by nephew Prince Musad Abdel Aziz, in royal palace, Riyadh.— Aug. 15. Bangladesh Pres. Sheik Mujibur Rahman killed in coup.

1976—Feb. 13. Nigerian head of state, Gen. Murtala Ramat Mohammed, slain by self-styled "young revolutionaries."

1977—Mar. 16. Kamal Jumblat, Lebanese Druse chieftain, was shot near Beirut.— Mar. 18. Congo Pres. Marien Ngouabi shot in Brazzaville.

1978—July 9. Former Iraqi Premier Abdul Razak Al-Naif shot in London.

1979—Feb. 14. U.S. Ambassador Adolph Dubs shot and killed by Afghan Muslim extremists in Kabul.— Aug. 27. Lord Mountbatten, World War II hero, and 2 others were killed when a bomb exploded on his fishing boat off the coast of Co. Sligo, Ire. The IRA claimed responsibility. — Oct. 26. South Korean President Park Chung Hee and 6 bodyguards fatally shot by Kim Jae Kyu, head of South Korean CIA, and 5 aides in Seoul.

1980—Apr. 12. Liberian President William R. Tolbert slain in military coup.—Sept. 17. Former Nicaraguan President Anastasio Somoza Debayle shot in Paraguay.

1981— Oct. 6. Egyptian President Anwar al-Sadat fatally shot by a band of commandos while reviewing a military parade in Cairo.

1982—Sept. 14. Lebanese President-elect Bashir Gemayel killed by bomb in east Beirut.

1983— Aug. 21. Philippine opposition political leader Benigno Aquino Jr. fatally shot by a gunman at Manila International Airport.

1984—Oct. 31. Indian Prime Minister Indira Gandhi shot and killed by 2 of her bodyguards, who were members of the minority Sikh sect, in New Delhi.

1986—Feb. 28. Swedish Premier Olaf Palme shot and killed by a gunman in Stockholm.

1987—June 1. Lebanese Premier Rashid Karami killed when a bomb exploded aboard a helicopter in which he was traveling.

1988—Apr. 16. PLO military chief Khalil Wazir (Abu Jihad) was gunned down by Israeli commandos in Tunisia.

1989—Aug. 18. Colombian Liberal Party presidential candidate Luis Carlos Galan was killed by Medellín cartel drug traffickers at a campaign rally in Bogotá.—Nov. 22. Lebanese President Rene Moawad was killed when a bomb exploded next to his motorcade.

1990—Mar. 22. Colombian Patriotic Union presidential candidate Bernando Jamamillo Ossa was shot by a gunman at an airport in Bogotá.

1991—May 21. Rajiv Gandhi, former prime minister of India, was killed when a bomb exploded during an election rally in Madras.

1992—June 29. Mohammed Boudiaf, president of Algeria, was shot by a gunman in Annaba.

1993—May 1. Ranasinghe Premadasa, president of Sri Lanka, killed by bomb in Colombo.

1994—Mar. 23. Luis Donaldo Colosio, Mexican presidential candidate, was shot by a gunman.—Apr. 6. Burundian President Cyprien Ntaryamira and Rwandan President Juvenal Habyarimana were killed, with 8 others, when their plane was apparently shot down.

Assassination Attempts

1912—Oct. 14. Former U.S. President Theodore Roosevelt shot and seriously wounded by demented man in Milwaukee, WI

1933—Feb. 15. In Miami, FL, Joseph Zangara, anarchist, shot at Pres.-elect Franklin D. Roosevelt, but a woman seized his arm, and the bullet fatally wounded Mayor Anton J. Cermak, of Chicago, who died Mar. 6. Zangara was electrocuted on Mar. 20, 1933.

1950—Nov. 1. In an attempt to assassinate President Truman, 2 members of a Puerto Rican nationalist movement—Griselio Torresola and Oscar Collazo—tried to shoot their way into Blair House. Torresola was killed, and a guard, Pvt. Leslie Coffelt, was fatally shot. Collazo was convicted, Mar. 7, 1951, for the murder of Coffelt.

1970—Nov. 27. Pope Paul VI unharmed by knife-wielding assailant who attempted to attack him in Manila airport.

1972—May 15. Alabama Gov. George Wallace shot in Laurel, MD, by Arthur Bremer; seriously crippled.

1975—Sept. 5. Pres. Gerald R. Ford was unharmed when a Secret Service agent grabbed a pistol aimed at him by Lynette (Squeaky) Fromme, a Charles Manson follower, in Sacramento.

1975—Sept. 22. Pres. Ford escaped unharmed when Sara Jane Moore, a political activist, fired a revolver at him.

1980—May 29. Civil rights leader Vernon E. Jordan Jr. shot and wounded in Ft. Wayne, IN.

1981—Jan. 16. Irish political activist Bernadette Devlin McAliskey and her husband were shot and seriously wounded by 3 members of a Protestant paramilitary group in Co. Tyrone, Ire.

1981—Mar. 30. Pres. Ronald Reagan, Press Sec. James Brady, Secret Service agent Timothy J. McCarthy, and Washington, DC, policeman Thomas Delahanty were shot and seriously wounded by John W. Hinckley Jr. in Washington, DC

1981—May 13. Pope John Paul II and 2 bystanders were shot and wounded by Mehmet Ali Agca, an escaped Turkish murderer, in St. Peter's Square, Rome.

1982—May 12. Pope John Paul II was unharmed when a man with a knife was overpowered by guards, in Fatima, Portugal.

1984—Oct. 12. British Prime Minister Margaret Thatcher narrowly escaped injury when a bomb, said to be planted by the Irish Republican Army, exploded at the Grand Hotel in Brighton, England, during the annual Conservative Party conference. Four died, including a Conservative member of Parliament.

1986—Sept. 7. Chilean President Gen. Augusto Pinochet Ugarte escaped unharmed when his motorcade was attacked by rebels using rockets, bazookas, grenades, and rifles.

1994—Oct. 29. President Bill Clinton was unharmed when Francisco Duran, later convicted of attempted assassination, shot at a tourist resembling Clinton outside the White House.

Notable U.S. Kidnappings Since 1924

Robert Franks, 13, in Chicago, **May 22, 1924,** by 2 youths, Richard Loeb and Nathan Leopold, who killed boy. Demand for $10,000 ignored. Loeb died in prison, Leopold paroled 1958.

Charles A. Lindbergh Jr., 20 mos. old, in Hopewell, NJ, **Mar. 1, 1932;** found dead May 12. Ransom of $50,000 was paid to man identified as Bruno Richard Hauptmann, 35, paroled German convict who entered U.S. illegally. Hauptmann was convicted after spectacular trial at Flemington, and electrocuted in Trenton, NJ, prison, Apr. 3, 1936.

William A. Hamm Jr., 39, in St. Paul, **June 15, 1933.** $100,000 paid. Alvin Karpis given life, paroled in 1969.

Charles F. Urschel, in Oklahoma City, **July 22, 1933.** Released July 31 after $200,000 paid. George (Machine Gun) Kelly and 5 others given life.

Brooke L. Hart, 22, in San Jose, CA, Thomas Thurmond and John Holmes arrested after demanding $40,000 ransom. When Hart's body was found in San Francisco Bay, **Nov. 26, 1933,** a mob attacked the jail at San Jose and lynched the 2 kidnappers.

George Weyerhaeuser, 9, in Tacoma, WA, **May 24, 1935.** Returned home June 1 after $200,000 paid. Kidnappers given 20 to 60 years.

Charles Mattson, 10, in Tacoma, WA, **Dec. 27, 1936.** Found dead Jan. 11, 1937. Kidnapper asked $28,000, failed to contact.

Arthur Fried, in White Plains, NY, **Dec. 4, 1937.** Body not found. Two kidnappers executed.

Robert C. Greenlease, 6, taken from Kansas City, MO, school **Sept. 28, 1953,** and held for $600,000. Body found Oct. 7. Bonnie Brown Heady and Carl A. Hall pleaded guilty and were executed.

Peter Weinberger, 32 days old, Westbury, NY, **July 4, 1956,** for $2,000 ransom, not paid. Child found dead. Angelo John LaMarca, 31, convicted, executed.

Lee Crary, 8, in Everett, WA, **Sept. 22, 1957;** $10,000 ransom, not paid. He escaped after 3 days, led police to George E. Collins, who was convicted.

Frank Sinatra Jr., 19, from hotel room in Lake Tahoe, CA, **Dec. 8, 1963.** Released **Dec. 11** after his father paid $240,000 ransom. Three men sentenced to prison.

Barbara Jane Mackle, 20, abducted **Dec. 17, 1968,** from Atlanta, GA, motel, was found unharmed 3 days later, buried in a coffin-like wooden box 18 inches underground,

after her father had paid $500,000 ransom; Gary Steven Krist sentenced to life, Ruth Eisenmann-Schier to 7 years.

Mrs. Roy Fuchs, 35, and 3 children held hostage 2 hours, **May 14, 1969,** in Long Island, NY, released after her husband, a bank manager, paid kidnappers $129,000 in bank funds; 4 men arrested, ransom recovered.

Virginia Piper, 49, abducted **July 27, 1972,** from her home in suburban Minneapolis; found unharmed near Duluth 2 days later after her husband paid $1 million ransom.

Patricia "Patty" Hearst, 19, taken from her Berkeley, CA, apartment **Feb. 4, 1974.** Symbionese Liberation Army demanded her father, Randolph A. Hearst, publisher, give millions to poor. She was identified by FBI as taking part in a San Francisco bank holdup, **Apr. 15.** FBI, **Sept. 18, 1975,** captured her and others in San Francisco; they were indicted on various charges. Patricia Hearst convicted of bank robbery, **Mar. 20, 1976.** She was released from prison under executive clemency, **Feb. 1, 1979.** In 1978, William and Emily Harris were sentenced to 10 years to life for the Hearst kidnapping. Both were paroled in 1983.

J. Reginald Murphy, 40, an editor of *Atlanta* (GA) *Constitution,* kidnapped **Feb. 20, 1974;** freed **Feb. 22** after payment of $700,000 ransom by the newspaper. Police arrested William A. H. Williams, a contractor; most of the money was recovered.

E. B. Reville, Hepzibah, GA, banker, and wife, Jean, kidnapped **Sept. 30, 1974.** Ransom of $30,000 paid. He was found alive; Jean Reville was found dead **Oct. 2.**

Jack Teich, Kings Point, NY, steel executive, seized **Nov. 12, 1974;** released **Nov. 19** after payment of $750,000.

Adam Walsh, 6, was abducted from a Hollywood, FL, department store, **July 27,** 1981. Although his severed head was found 2 weeks later at Vero Beach, FL, his body was never recovered. John Walsh, Adam's father, became active in raising awareness about missing children.

Sidney J. Reso, oil co. executive, seized **Apr. 29, 1992;** died May 3; Arthur D. Seale and wife, Irene, arrested **June 19.** Arthur Seale pleaded guilty and was sentenced to life in prison; Irene Seale was sentenced to a 20-year prison term.

Polly Klaas, 12, Petaluma, CA, abducted at knife-point, **Oct. 1, 1993,** during a slumber party at her home; found dead **Dec. 4** in wooded area of Cloverdale, CA. Police arrested Richard Allen Davis on **Nov. 30.** Davis pleaded not guilty, **Dec. 21.**

ASTRONOMY AND CALENDAR

Edited by Dr. Kenneth L. Franklin, Astronomer Emeritus
American Museum of Natural History-Hayden Planetarium

Celestial Events Summary, 1996

(Greenwich Mean Time, or GMT)

Early this year, Venus and Saturn have the evening stage to themselves, but the show depends on Venus, because Saturn will be fainter than usual all year. Saturn is such a reluctant performer because its rings are still very narrow from our point of view. We will see them edge-on for the last time in mid-Feb., but they will slowly be seen more widely for the next 7 years. This will then give Saturn a larger screen from which to return sunlight to us, so the ringed planet will gradually grow brighter. By the end of Feb., Saturn dives into the afternoon sun's glare, to return to visibility in the morning sky in Apr. By the end of May, dazzling Venus will also leave the evening sky to enliven the morning twilight by July. As Venus leaves the western sky, the eastern evening sky will be taken over by Jupiter, which will rise in mid-evening. In the summer, by the time we have gotten used to Jupiter, now in the west, Saturn will appear in the east, but much fainter than Jupiter. However, Saturn will be in a part of the sky devoid of the bright stars Aquarius and Pisces, and thus will appear prominent. In late Dec., Jupiter and Mercury will be close in the evening twilight, Jupiter perhaps leading the gaze to Mercury.

The morning sky provides more drama, but much of it is in the wings, as it were. In the listing of events, below, note is made of a gathering of planets for Mar. 22 and 23. A good telescope will be needed for this accumulation, because it takes place too close to the sun in the bright twilight for easy viewing. From May 31 to the end of June, Mercury, Mars, and Venus play tag, but they are usually several degrees apart at their closest. A distant approach is also true of Venus and Mars in early Sept.

There are, however, some interesting appulses with the fainter planets Uranus and Neptune. Mercury is only 0°.07 north of Neptune, Feb. 11, at 9 AM EST, an event visible from any place before dawn at that time. Mercury is 0°.2 from Uranus, Feb. 16, but in the afternoon in the U.S. Look at the close approach of these planets in the mornings before and after this event, and do the same for the occultation of Mercury, June 14. The Feb. 22 occultation of Venus may be seen as a fine close approach by observers on the west coast. Another fine close approach between Venus and the moon occurs on July 12. If you have kept track of Regulus as it descends into the evening twilight, a telescope may let you see Mercury just one moon-diameter from the star on Aug. 1. Look a day on either side of this date also. Use this technique for Venus and Regulus on Oct. 4.

A series of occultations of Aldebaran begins Aug. 8. Even if the time is propitious at your location, such as on the evening of Dec. 22 and 23, the shadow of the moon may not pass near you. That shadow is only 2,000 mi across and can pass a world away from where you are. But each of these events can be interesting to see how the moon moves in the sky against the background of stars. Try watching occultations and near misses with a telescope to see this dramatic motion.

Jupiter is observable for almost the entire year. Followers of the giant planet will be seeing how the scars of the great comet crash of 1994 are healing. After about a year, the signs of the impacts were fading and coalescing along the band into which the comet fragments dropped. The energy and foreign material injected into this region of the planet are expected to have results observable, at least by professional equipment, for several more years.

Discovered on July 23, 1995, by amateur astronomers Alan Hale and Thomas Bopp, comet Hale-Bopp may become the brightest comet to be seen in several decades. Future comet brightness is notoriously difficult to predict, but comet Hale-Bopp should be at its brightest and well placed for northern hemisphere observers in the early evenings of late Mar. to early Apr. of 1997.

Celestial Events Highlights, 1996

(GMT, or as indicated)

January

Mercury begins the year as an evening object in the bright twilight to the right of the just-set sun, stationary on the 9th, starting its retrograde motion prior to its passage through inferior conjunction on the 18th, resuming its direct motion on the 30th.

Venus, much brighter than Mercury, is farther to the right than Mercury in the evening twilight.

Mars, fainter than a first magnitude star, is lost in the bright western twilight.

Jupiter begins the year as a bright object in the morning twilight, quickly emerging from the about-to-rise sun's glare in the first weeks of January.

Saturn appears as a first magnitude star among the fainter stars of eastern Aquarius.

Moon passes Jupiter on the 18th, Venus on the 23d, and Saturn on the 24th.

Jan. 1—Mercury 0°.9 south of Uranus; Mars is 1°.6 south of Neptune.

Jan. 2—Mercury is at greatest elongation, 19° east of the sun.

Jan. 4—Earth is at perihelion, 91.4 million miles from the sun; Quadrantid meteor shower.

Jan. 8—Mars is 0°.6 south of Uranus.

Jan. 9—Mercury is stationary, beginning its retrograde motion.

Jan. 13—Mercury is 3° north of Mars.

Jan. 16—Neptune is in conjunction with the sun.

Jan. 18—Jupiter is 5° south of the moon; Mercury is in inferior conjunction, between the earth and the sun.

Jan. 19—Sun enters Capricornus.

Jan. 21—Uranus is in conjunction.

Jan. 23—Venus is 5° south of the three day old crescent moon.

Jan. 24—Saturn is 5° south of the moon.

Jan. 30—Mercury is stationary, resuming its direct motion.

February

Mercury is at greatest western elongation on the 11th, 26° from the morning sun, looking like a zero magnitude star to the right of the sunrise point.

Venus, over a hundred times brighter than Saturn, passes the ringed planet on the 3d, and is occulted by the moon on the 22d.

Mars is lost in the sun's glare all month.

Jupiter is much easier to see as a minus 2d magnitude star in Sagittarius in the morning sky.

Saturn, in Aquarius, is hard to find in the evening twilight as it approaches the sun.

Moon passes Jupiter on the 15th, Neptune on the 16th, Uranus and Mercury on the 17th, Saturn on the 20th, and occults Venus on the 22d.

Feb. 3—Venus is 1°.3 north of Saturn.

Feb. 11—Mercury is 0°.07 north of Neptune; Mercury at greatest elongation, 26° west of the sun.

Feb. 12—Earth passes from north to south through the ring plane of Saturn, the last such passage until 2010.

Feb. 15—Jupiter is 5° south of the moon.

Feb. 16—Neptune is 5° south of the moon; Mercury is 0°.2 north of Uranus; Sun enters Aquarius.

Feb. 17—Uranus is 6° south of the moon; Mercury is 5° south of the moon.

Feb. 20—Saturn is 4° south of the moon.

Feb. 22—Venus is 0°06 north of the thin crescent moon which occults it.

March

Mercury remains in the morning sky until the 28th of this month.

Venus remains the dazzling evening star, so beautiful in the evening twilight.

Mars is in conjunction early this month, so is lost to view.

Jupiter is prominent in Sagittarius, as it will be all year.

Saturn passes through conjunction in mid-month and is lost to view.

Moon passes Jupiter on the 14th, Neptune and Uranus on the 15th, and Venus on the 23d.

Mar. 4—Mars is in conjunction.

Mar. 7—Pluto is stationary, beginning its retrograde motion in Ophiuchus.

Mar. 11—Sun enters Pisces.

Mar. 14—Jupiter is 5° south of the moon.

Mar. 15—Neptune is 5° south and Uranus 6° south of the moon.

Mar. 17—Saturn is in conjunction with the sun.

Mar. 20—Vernal equinox at 8:03 GMT (3:03 AM, EST); spring begins in the northern hemisphere, fall in the southern hemisphere.

Mar. 22—Mars is 1°3 north of Saturn.

Mar. 23—Venus is 5° north of the moon; Mercury is 0°3 north of Saturn and 0°9 south of Mars.

Mar. 28—Mercury is in superior conjunction with the sun, on the far side of its orbit from us.

April

Mercury is in the evening sky all month, reaching its greatest elongation on the 23d.

Venus is at its greatest elongation on the 1st, and passes Aldebaran on the 15th.

Mars, in Pisces all month, is a difficult object to observe in the bright morning twilight.

Jupiter, in Sagittarius, dominates the morning sky.

Saturn moves into western Pisces as a first magnitude star.

Moon is totally eclipsed on the 4th, passes Jupiter on the 10th, Neptune on the 11th, Uranus on the 12th, Saturn on the 16th, partially eclipses the sun on the 17th, passes Mercury on the 19th, and Venus on the 21st.

Apr. 1—Venus at greatest elongation, 46° east of the sun.

Apr. 4—Total eclipse of the moon.

Apr. 10—Jupiter 5° south of the moon.

Apr. 11—Neptune 5° south of the moon.

Apr. 12—Uranus 6° south of the moon.

Apr. 15—Venus 10° north of Aldebaran.

Apr. 16—Saturn 4° south of the moon.

Apr. 17—Partial eclipse of the sun.

Apr. 18—Sun enters Aries.

Apr. 19—Mercury 5° north of the moon.

Apr. 21—Venus 9° north of the moon.

Apr. 23—Mercury at greatest elongation, 20° east of the sun.

Apr. 29—Neptune stationary, beginning its retrograde motion.

May

Mercury is stationary on the 4th, beginning retrograde motion before its inferior conjunction on the 15th, to resume direct motion on the 27th.

Venus is at its greatest brilliance, minus 4.5 magnitude, on the 4th, its spectacular final performance in the evening sky before diving into the bright evening twilight by the beginning of June.

Mars is fainter than a 1st magnitude star all month in Aries.

Jupiter asserts its dominance by becoming still brighter all month in the morning sky, and begins its retrograde motion when it is stationary on the 4th.

Saturn is a 1st magnitude star in western Pisces.

Moon passes Jupiter and Neptune on the 8th, Uranus on the 9th, Saturn on the 13th, and Mars on the 16th, and Venus on the 20th.

May 4—Mercury stationary beginning retrograde motion; Venus at greatest brilliancy; Jupiter stationary beginning retrograde motion.

May 8—Jupiter 5° south of the moon; Neptune 5° south of the moon.

May 9—Uranus stationary beginning retrograde motion; Uranus 6° south of the moon.

May 13—Saturn 3° south of the moon; sun enters Taurus.

May 15—Mercury in inferior conjunction with the sun.

May 16—Mars 1°7 north of the moon.

May 20—Venus 8° north of the moon; Venus stationary, beginning its retrograde motion.

May 22—Pluto at opposition to the sun in Ophiuchus.

May 27—Mercury stationary, resuming its direct motion in the morning sky.

May 31—Mercury is 4° south of Mars.

June

Mercury is at greatest western elongation on the 10th, is occulted by the moon and passes Mars on the 14th, passes Aldebaran on the 21st, and Venus on the 23d.

Venus is in inferior conjunction on the 10th, leaving the evening sky to be in the morning sky for the remainder of the year.

Mars is now in Taurus, passing Aldebaran on the 27th.

Jupiter attains a magnitude of minus 2.7 by mid-month, brighter than all but the moon in the night sky, justifying it name as the ruler of the gods.

Saturn does nothing spectacular this month other than brightening almost imperceptibly.

Moon passes Jupiter on the 4th, Neptune and Uranus on the 5th, Saturn on the 9th, and occults Mercury on the 14th.

June 4—Jupiter is 5° south of the moon.

June 5—Neptune is 5° and Uranus is 6° south of the moon.

June 9—Saturn is 3° south of the moon.

June 10—Mercury is at greatest elongation, 24° west of the sun; Venus is in inferior conjunction.

June 14—Mercury is 0°4 north of the moon which occults it; Mars is 4° north of the moon; Mercury is 3° south of Mars.

June 20—Sun enters Gemini.

June 21—Summer solstice at 2:24 GMT (10:24 PM EDT, June 20th); summer begins in the northern hemisphere, winter in the southern; Mercury is 4° north of Aldebaran.

June 23—Mercury is 1°6 north of Venus.

June 27—Mars is 6° north of Aldebaran.

June 30—Venus is 4° south of Mars.

July

Mercury is in superior conjunction with the sun on the 11th, thus difficult to find in mid-month.

Venus is stationary on the 2d, resuming its direct motion, and passes its greatest morning brilliancy, minus 4.5 magnitude, on the 17th.

Mars, while emerging from the morning twilight and passing from Taurus into Gemini, fades to magnitude 1.5.

Jupiter is opposite to the sun on the 4th, thus rising at sunset and setting at sunrise.

Saturn is stationary on the 20th, beginning its retrograde motion, moving westward in western Pisces.

Moon, in its Full phase, passes Jupiter on the 1st, Neptune and Uranus on the 2d, Saturn on the 7th, occults Venus and passes Mars on the 12th, Jupiter on the 28th, Neptune on the 29th, and Uranus on the 30th, again at Full phase.

July 1—Jupiter 5° south of the moon.

July 2—Venus stationary, resuming direct motion; Neptune 4° south of the moon; Uranus 5° south of the moon.

July 4—Jupiter at opposition.

July 5—Earth at aphelion, 94.4 million miles from the sun.

July 7—Saturn 3° south of the moon.

July 11—Mercury in superior conjunction with the sun.

July 12—Venus 0°4 south of the moon which occults it; Mars is 5° north of the moon.

July 17—Venus at greatest brilliancy, minus 4.5 magnitude.

July 18—Neptune at opposition.

July 20—Saturn stationary, beginning its retrograde motion; sun enters Cancer.

July 25—Uranus at opposition.

July 28—Jupiter 5° south of the moon.

July 29—Neptune 4° south of the moon.

July 30—Uranus 5° south of the moon.

August

Mercury appearing as a 1st magnitude star passes the real 1st magnitude star, Regulus, 0°5 north on the 1st, is occulted by the 2 day old moon on the 16th, and reaches greatest elongation in the evening sky on the 21st.

Venus passes 1°2 north of the thick crescent moon in the morning sky of the 10th, and is at its greatest western elongation on the 20th.

Mars, in Gemini, is at its faintest for the year looking like a star of magnitude 1.5.

Jupiter is the prominent object in the southeastern sky after sunset.

Saturn, rising about 8:30 PM in mid-month, at about magnitude 0.6 is the brightest star-like object in western Pisces.

Moon passes Saturn on the 3d, begins a series of occultions of Aldebaran on the 8th, passes Venus and Mars on the 10th, occults Mercury on the 16th, passes Jupiter on the 24th, Neptune and Uranus on the 26th, and Saturn, again, on the 30th.

Aug. 1—Mercury is 0°5 north of Regulus.

Aug. 3—Saturn is 3° south of the moon.

Aug. 8—Moon passes 1°0 north of Aldebaran, occulting it.

Aug. 10—Venus is 1°2 north of the moon; Mars is 6° north of the moon; sun enters Leo.

Aug. 11—Look for the Perseid meteor shower tonight and tomorrow night.

Aug. 13—Pluto is stationary, resuming its direct motion.

Aug. 16—Moon is 0°3 south Mercury, occulting it.

Aug. 20—Venus at greatest elongation, 46° west of the sun.

Aug. 21—Mercury is at greatest elongation, 27° east of the sun.

Aug. 24—Jupiter is 5° south of the moon.

Aug. 26—Neptune and Uranus are each 5° south of the moon.

Aug. 30—Saturn is 3° south of the moon.

Aug. 31—Mars is 6° south of Pollux.

September

Mercury, stationary on the 3d, begins its retrograde motion prior to its inferior conjunction on the 17th, and resumes its direct motion on the 25th when it is again stationary.

Venus, the brilliant morning star, remains in Cancer for nearly the whole month.

Mars, still a faint 1.5 magnitude, may be found 3° north of Venus on the 4th.

Jupiter is stationary on the 3d, resuming its direct motion, beginning its move toward Capricorn.

Saturn attains its greatest brilliance of the year, 0.5 magnitude, when it is at opposition to the sun on the 26th.

Moon occults Aldebaran on the 4th, 0°9 north of the star, passes Mars and Venus on the 8th, Jupiter on the 21st, Neptune and Uranus on the 22d, and Saturn on the 27th, when it is also totally eclipsed.

Sept. 2—Venus is 9° south of Pollux.

Sept. 3—Jupiter and Mercury are stationary.

Sept. 4—Moon is 0°9 north of Aldebaran, occulting it; Venus is 3° south of Mars.

Sept. 8—Mars is 6° north of the moon; Venus is 3° north of the moon.

Sept. 16—Sun enters Virgo.

Sept. 17—Mercury is in inferior conjunction.

Sept. 21—Jupiter is 6° south of the moon.

Sept. 22—Neptune is 5° south of the moon; the autumnal equinox occurs at 18:00 GMT (2:00 PM EDT), fall beginning in the northern hemisphere, spring in the southern; Uranus is 6° south of the moon.

Sept. 25—Mercury is stationary, resuming its direct motion.

Sept. 26—Saturn is at opposition, rising at sunset and setting at dawn.

Sept. 27—Total lunar eclipse; Saturn 3° south of the moon.

October

Mercury, in the morning twilight, reaches greatest elongation on the 3d.

Venus passes very close to Regulus the morning of the 4th.

Mars passes close to Regulus on the 29th.

Jupiter is the prominent bright object in the southwest after sunset.

Saturn is the brightest star in Pisces.

Moon occults Aldebaran on the 1st, passes Mars on the 7th, Venus on the 9th, partially eclipses the sun on the 12th, passes Jupiter on the 18th, Neptune on the 19th, Uranus on the 20th, Saturn on the 24th, and occults Aldebaran again on the 29th.

Oct. 1—Moon passes 0°8 north of Aldebaran, occulting it.

Oct. 3—Mercury at greatest elongation, 18° west of the sun.

Oct. 4—Venus passes 0°2 south of Regulus.

Oct. 6—Neptune stationary, resuming its direct motion.

Oct. 7—Mars is 6° north of the moon.

Oct. 9—Venus is 4° north of the moon.

Oct. 10—Uranus stationary, resuming its direct motion.

Oct. 12—Partial solar eclipse.

Oct. 18—Jupiter 6° south of the moon.

Oct. 19—Neptune 5° south of the moon.

Oct. 20—Uranus 6° south of the moon.

Oct. 21—Orionid meteor shower.

Oct. 24—Saturn 3° south of the moon.

Oct. 29—Mars 1°2 north of Regulus; moon 0°9 north of Aldebaran, occulting it; sun enters Libra.

November

Mercury moves from the morning sky to the evening sky when it passes through superior conjunction on the 2d.

Venus passes close to the thin crescent moon in the dawn twilight the morning of the 8th.

Mars begins to brighten in eastern Leo.

Jupiter is the dazzler low in the southwest evening twilight.

Saturn, higher than Jupiter, somewhat between faint Aquarius and faint Pisces, sets an hour or two after midnight nearly due west.

Moon passes Mars on the 5th, Venus on the 8th, Jupiter and Neptune on the 15th, Uranus on the 16th, Saturn on the 20th, and occults Aldebaran on the 25th.

Nov. 2—Mercury at superior conjunction.

Nov. 5—Mars 5° north of the moon.

Nov. 8—Venus 1°4 north of the moon.

Nov. 15—Jupiter 5° south of the moon; Neptune 4° south of the moon.

Nov. 16—Uranus 5° south of the moon; Venus 4° north of Spica.

Nov. 17—Leonid meteor shower.

Nov. 20—Saturn 3° south of the moon; Mercury 3° north of Antares.

Nov. 22—Sun enters Scorpio.

Nov. 25—Pluto in conjunction with the sun; moon is 0°9 north of Aldebaran, occulting it.

Nov. 29—Sun enters Ophiuchus.

December

Mercury is at greatest elongation on the 15th, passing close to Jupiter about the 20th, and is stationary on the 23d, beginning its retrograde motion.

Venus and the crescent moon make a pretty picture in the dawn twilight of the 8th.

Mars noticeably brightens this month while it slows its approach to Virgo.

Jupiter and Mercury are close in the evening twilight about the 20th, Mercury to the left.

Saturn resumes its direct motion when it is stationary on the 4th.

Moon passes Mars on the 3d, Venus on the 8th, Mercury and Jupiter on the 12th, Neptune and Uranus on the 13th, Saturn on the 17th, and occults Aldebaran on the 23d.

Dec. 3—Mars is 4° north of the moon.

Dec. 4—Saturn is stationary, resuming its direct motion.

Dec. 8—Venus is 2° south of the moon.

Dec. 12—Mercury is 7° south of the moon; Jupiter is 5° south of the moon.

Dec. 13—Neptune is 4° south of the moon; Uranus is 5° south of the moon; Geminid meteor shower.

Dec. 15—Mercury is at greatest elongation, 20° east of the sun.

Dec. 16—Sun enters Sagittarius.

Dec. 17—Saturn is 3° south of the moon.

Dec. 21—Winter solstice at 14:06 GMT (9:06 AM, EST); winter begins in the northern hemisphere, spring in the southern.

Dec. 23—Moon is 0°9 north of Aldebaran, occulting it; Mercury is stationary, beginning its retrograde motion.

Dec. 24—Venus is 6° north of Antares.

Planets and the Sun

The planets of the solar system, in order of their mean distance from the sun, are Mercury, Venus, the earth, Mars, Jupiter, Saturn, Uranus, Neptune, and Pluto. Both Uranus and Neptune are visible through good field glasses, but Pluto is so distant and so small that only large telescopes or long-exposure photographs can make it visible.

Because Mercury and Venus are nearer to the sun than is the earth, their motions about the sun are seen from the earth as wide swings first to one side of the sun and then to the other, although they are both passing continuously around the sun in orbits that are almost circular. When their passage takes them either between the earth and the sun or beyond the sun as seen from the earth, they are invisible to us. Because of the laws that govern the motions of planets about the sun, both Mercury and Venus require much less time to pass between the earth and the sun than around the far side of the sun; so their periods of visibility and invisibility are unequal.

The planets that lie farther from the sun than does the earth may be seen for longer periods of time and are invisible only when they are so located in our sky that they rise and set at about the same time as the sun, when, of course, they are overwhelmed by the sun's great brilliance. None of the planets has any light of its own; each shines only by reflecting sunlight from its surface. Mercury and Venus, because they are between the earth and the sun, show phases very much as the moon does. The planets farther from the sun are always seen as full, although Mars does occasionally present a slightly gibbous phase — like the moon when not quite full.

The planets move rapidly among the stars because they are very much nearer to us. The stars are also in motion, some of them at tremendous speeds, but they are so far away that their motion does not change their apparent positions in the heavens sufficiently for anyone to perceive that change in a single lifetime. The very nearest star is about 7,000 times as far away as the most distant planet.

Planets of the Solar System

Mercury

Mercury, the nearest planet to the sun, is the second smallest of the 9 planets known to be orbiting the sun. Its diameter is 3,100 miles, and its mean distance from the sun is 36,000,000 miles.

Mercury moves with great speed in its journey about the sun, averaging about 30 miles a second to complete its circuit in 88 of our days. Mercury rotates upon its axis over a period of nearly 59 days, thus exposing all its surface periodically to the sun. It is believed that the surface passing before the sun may have a temperature of about 800° F and that the temperature on the side turned temporarily away from the sun does not fall as low as might be expected. This night temperature has been described by Russian astronomers as "room temperature" — possibly about 70° F. This would contradict the former belief that Mercury did not possess an atmosphere, for some sort of atmosphere would be needed to retain the fierce solar radiation that strikes Mercury. A shallow but dense layer of carbon dioxide would produce the "greenhouse" effect, in which heat accumulated during exposure to the sun would not completely escape at night. The actual presence of a carbon dioxide atmosphere is in dispute. Other research, however, has indicated a nighttime temperature approaching −300° F.

This uncertainty about conditions on Mercury and its motion arise from its shorter angular distance from the sun as seen from the earth. Mercury is always too much in line with the sun to be observed against a dark sky, but is always seen during either morning or evening twilight.

Mariner 10 passed Mercury 3 times in 1974 and 1975. A large fraction of the surface was photographed from varying distances, revealing a degree of cratering similar to that of the moon. An atmosphere of hydrogen and helium may be made up of gases of the solar wind temporarily concentrated by the presence of Mercury. The discovery of a weak but permanent magnetic field was a surprise. It has been held that both a fluid core and rapid rotation were necessary for the generation of a planetary magnetic field. Mercury may demonstrate these conditions to be unnecessary, or the field may reveal something about the history of Mercury.

Venus

Venus, slightly smaller than the earth, moves about the sun at a mean distance of 67,000,000 miles in 225 of our days. Its synodical revolution — its return to the same relationship with the earth and the sun, which is a result of the combination of its own motion with that of the earth — is 584 days. Every 19 months, then, Venus will be nearer to the earth than any other planet in the solar system. The planet is covered with a dense, white, cloudy atmosphere that conceals whatever is below it. This same cloud reflects sunlight efficiently so that when Venus is favorably situated it is the third brightest object in the sky, exceeded only by the sun and the moon.

Spectral analysis of sunlight reflected from Venus's cloud tops has shown features that can best be explained by identifying material of the clouds as sulfuric acid (oil of vitriol). Infrared spectroscopy from a balloon-borne telescope nearly 20 miles above the earth's surface gave indications of a small amount of water vapor present in the same region of the atmosphere of Venus. In 1956, radio astronomers at the Naval Research Laboratories in Washington, DC, found a temperature for Venus of about 600° F, in marked contrast to –125° F previously found at the cloud tops. Subsequent radio work confirmed a high temperature and produced evidence for this temperature to be associated with the solid body of Venus. With this peculiarity in mind, space scientists devised experiments for the U.S. space probe *Mariner 2* to perform when it flew by in 1962. *Mariner 2* confirmed the high temperature and the fact that it pertained to the ground rather than to some special activity of the atmosphere. In addition, *Mariner 2* was unable to detect the existence of a magnetic field even as weak as 1/100,000 of that of the earth.

In 1967, a Russian space probe, *Venera 4*, and the American *Mariner 5* arrived at Venus within a few hours of each other. *Venera 4* was designed to allow an instrument package to land gently on the surface via parachute. It ceased to transmit information in about 75 minutes when its temperature reading went above 500° F. After considerable controversy, it was agreed that the instrument package still had 20 miles to go to reach the surface. *Mariner 5* went around the dark side of Venus at a distance of about 6,000 miles. Again, it detected no significant field, but its radio signals passed to earth through Venus's atmosphere twice —once on the night side and once on the day side. The results were startling. Venus's atmosphere is nearly all carbon dioxide and must exert a pressure at the planet's surface of as much as 100 times the earth's normal sea-level pressure of one atmosphere. Because the earth and Venus are about the same size and were presumably formed at the same time, by the same general process and from the same mixture of chemical elements, one is faced with the question: Which is the planet with the unusual history—the earth or Venus?

Radar astronomers using powerful transmitters as well as sensitive receivers and computers succeeded in determining the rotation period of Venus. It turns out to be 243 days clockwise—in other words, contrary to the spin of the other planets and to its own motion around the sun. If it were exactly 243.16 days, Venus would present the same face toward the earth at every inferior conjunction. This rate and sense of rotation allows a "day" on Venus of 117.4 earth days. Any part of Venus will receive sunlight on its clouds for more than 58 days and will be in darkness for 58 days. Earth-based radar observations have shown surface features below the clouds. Large craters, continent-sized highlands, and extensive, dry "ocean" basins were identified.

Mariner 10 passed Venus before traveling on to Mercury in 1974. The carbon dioxide molecule found in such abundance in the atmosphere is rather opaque to certain ultraviolet wavelengths, enabling sensitive television cameras to photograph the Venusian cloud cover. Photos radioed to earth showed a spiral pattern in the clouds from the equator to the poles.

In Dec. 1978, two U.S. *Pioneer* probes arrived at Venus. One went into orbit around Venus; the other split into 5 separate probes targeted for widely spaced entry points to sample different conditions. The instrument ensemble was selected on the basis of previous missions that had shown the range of conditions to be studied. The probes confirmed expected high surface temperatures and high winds aloft. Winds of about 200 miles per hour there may account for the transfer of heat into the night side despite the low rotation speed of the planet. However, surface winds were light at the time. Atmosphere and cloud chemistries were examined in detail, providing much data for continued analysis. The probes detected 4 layers of clouds and more light on the surface than expected solely from sunlight. This light allowed Russian scientists to obtain at least 2 photos of rocks on the surface. Sulfur seems to play a large role in the chemistry of Venus, and reactions involving sulfur may be responsible for the glow. To learn more about the weather and atmospheric circulation on Venus, the orbiter took daily photos of the daylight-side cloud cover. It confirmed the cloud pattern and its circulation shown by *Mariner 10*. The ionosphere showed large variability. The orbiter's radar operated in 2 modes: one for ground elevation variability, and the second for ground reflectivity in 2 dimensions, thus "imaging" the surface. Radar maps of the entire planet showing the large features mentioned above were produced.

The Venus orbiter *Magellan* was launched May 4, 1989. It was equipped to observe Venus by a side-scanning radar system, together with one to gather data on the variations in elevations directly beneath the craft. *Magellan* mapped all but a small fraction of the planet. The side-looking radar illuminates the surface and its features with radio waves and records the strength and distance of the returning echoes. Computer processing produces what seems to be a view of the landscape as if seen through a clear atmosphere from above, near sunset, with a resolution better than about 500 feet on Venus. Information on vertical relief has a resolution of about 30 feet.

Craters more than 20 miles wide are believed to have been caused by impacting bodies. One 150-mile-wide crater has been named for Margaret Mead. Smaller craters are probably the result of volcanic action. One such caldera has been named Sakajawea. Many lava flows have been seen, and some old craters and plains seem to be filled with lava.

Most of the surface is believed to be younger than 1 billion to 500 million years old. Modifications of previously existing surface features have been caused by tectonic actions such as faulting and by weathering. Tectonic actions on Venus in general are distinctly different from such actions on earth. The intense heat at the surface of Venus can prevent the surface materials from cooling to the same brittle condition as on earth. The same actions may produce somewhat different results on earth than they would on Venus. No activity on Venus seems to be similar to the earth's moving tectonic plates, but local stretching and compressing may produce rift valleys and higher plains and mountains. Although no weathering is due to water on Venus, the action of the winds is in evidence. Extensive sand dunes have been seen, and windblown deposits indicate stable wind patterns for very long periods of time. Although there are deep regions, somewhat similar to earth's ocean basins, there is no water to fill them.

The tremendous amount of information about the topography of Venus's surface obtained by *Magellan* will keep teams of analysts and theoreticians busy for years. The orbit of *Magellan* has been adjusted to a nearly circular shape about 300 miles from the planet's surface. In this mode, variation in its orbital speed reveals information on irregularities in the gravitational field presumably due to details in the internal structure of the planet.

Mars

Mars is the first planet beyond the earth, away from the sun. Mars's diameter is about 4,200 miles, although a determination of the radius and mass of Mars by the space probe *Mariner 4*, which flew by Mars at a distance of less than 6,000 miles on July 14, 1965, indicated that these dimensions were slightly larger than had been previously estimated. Although Mars's orbit is nearly circular, it is somewhat more eccentric than the orbits of many of the other planets, and Mars is more than 30 million miles farther from the sun in some parts of its year than it is at others. Mars takes 687 of our days to make one circuit of the sun, traveling at about 15 miles a second. Mars rotates upon its axis in almost the same period of time that the earth does — 24 hours and 37 minutes. Mars's mean distance from the sun is 141 million miles; so the temperature on Mars would be lower than that on the earth even if Mars's atmosphere were about the same as ours. The atmosphere is not, however, for *Mariner 4* reported that atmospheric pressure on Mars is between 1% and 2% of the earth's atmospheric pressure. This thin atmosphere appears to be largely carbon dioxide. No evidence of free water was found.

There appears to be no magnetic field about Mars. This would eliminate the previous conception of a dangerous radiation belt around Mars. The same lack of a magnetic field would expose the surface of Mars to an influx of cosmic radiation about 100 times as intense as that on earth.

Deductions from years of telescopic observation indicate that ⅝ of the surface of Mars is a desert of reddish rock, sand, and soil. The rest of Mars is covered by irregular patches that appear generally green in hues that change through the Martian year. These were formerly held to be some sort of primitive vegetation, but with the findings of *Mariner 4* of a complete lack of water and oxygen, such growth does not appear possible. The nature of the green areas is now unknown. They may be regions covered with volcanic salts whose color changes with changing temperatures and atmospheric conditions, or they may be gray rather than green. When large gray areas are placed beside large red areas, the gray areas appear green to the eye.

Mars's axis of rotation is inclined from a vertical to the plane of its orbit about the sun by about 25°, and therefore Mars has seasons as does the earth, except that the Martian seasons are longer because Mars's year is longer. White caps form about the winter pole of Mars, growing in the winter and shrinking in the summer. These polar caps are now believed to be both water ice and carbon dioxide ice. It is the carbon dioxide that is seen to come and go with the seasons. The water ice is apparently in many layers with dust between them, indicating climatic cycles.

The canals of Mars have become more of a mystery than they were before the voyage of *Mariner 4*. Markings forming a network of fine lines crossing much of the surface of Mars have been seen there by those who have devoted much time to the study of the planet, but no canals have shown clearly enough in previous photographs to be universally accepted. A few of the 21 photographs sent back to earth by *Mariner 4* covered areas crossed by canals. The pictures show faint, ill-defined, broad, dark markings, but no positive identification of the nature of the markings.

Mariners 6 and *7* in 1969 sent back many more photographs of higher quality than those of the pioneering *Mariner 4*. These pictures showed cratering similar to the earlier views, but in addition showed 2 other types of terrain. Some regions seemed featureless for many square miles, but others were chaotic, showing high relief without apparent organization into mountain chains or craters.

Mariner 9, the first artificial body to be placed in an orbit about Mars, has transmitted more than 10,000 photographs covering 100% of the planet's surface. Preliminary study of these photos and other data shows that Mars resembles no other planet we know. Using terrestrial terms, however, scientists describe features that seem to be clearly of volcanic origin. One of these features is Nix Olympica (now called Olympus Mons), apparently a shield volcano whose caldera is more than 50 miles wide, whose outer slopes are more than 300 miles in diameter, and which stands about 90,000 feet above the surrounding plain. Some features may have been produced by cracking (faulting) of the surface and the sliding of one region over or past another. Many craters seem to have been produced by impacting bodies that may have come from the nearby asteroid belt. Features near the south pole may have been produced by glaciers that are no longer present. Flowing water, non-existent on Mars at the present time, probably carved canyons, one 10 times longer and 3 times deeper than the Grand Canyon.

Although the Russians landed a probe on the Martian surface, it transmitted for only 20 seconds. In 1976, the U.S. landed 2 *Viking* spacecraft on the Martian surface. The landers had devices aboard to perform chemical analyses of the soil in search of evidence of life. The results have been inconclusive. The 2 *Viking* orbiters have returned the best pictures yet of Martian topographic features. Many features can be explained only if Mars once had large quantities of flowing water.

Mars's position in its orbit and its speed around that orbit in relation to the earth's position and speed bring Mars fairly close to the earth on occasions about 2 years apart and then move Mars and the earth too far apart for accurate observation and photography. Every 15-17 years, the close approaches are especially favorable to close observation.

Mars has 2 satellites, discovered in 1877 by Asaph Hall. The outer satellite, Deimos, revolves around Mars in about 31 hours. The inner satellite, Phobos, whips around Mars in a little more than 7 hours, making 3 trips around the planet each Martian day. *Mariner* and *Viking* photos show these bodies to be irregularly shaped and pitted with numerous craters. Phobos also shows a system of linear grooves, each about ⅓ mile across and roughly parallel. Phobos measures about 8 by 12 miles and Deimos about 5 by 7.5 miles.

Jupiter

Jupiter is the largest of the planets. Its equatorial diameter is 88,000 miles, 11 times the diameter of the earth. Its polar diameter is about 6,000 miles shorter. This is an equilibrium condition resulting from the liquidity of the planet and its extremely rapid rate of rotation: a Jupiter day is only 10 earth hours long. For a planet this size, this rotational speed is amazing, and it moves a point on Jupiter's equator at a speed of 22,000 miles an hour, as compared with 1,000 miles an hour for a point on the earth's equator. Jupiter is at an average distance of 480 million miles from the sun and takes almost 12 of our years to make one complete circuit of the sun.

The major observable chemical constituents of Jupiter's atmosphere are methane (CH_4) and ammonia (NH_3), but it is reasonable to assume the same mixture of elements available to make Jupiter as to make the sun. This would mean a large fraction of hydrogen and helium must be present also, as well as water (H_2O). The temperature at the tops of the clouds may be about –260° F. The clouds are probably ammonia ice crystals, becoming ammonia droplets lower down. There may be a space before water ice crystals show up as clouds: in turn, these become water droplets near the bottom of the entire cloud layer. The total atmosphere may be only a few hundred miles in depth, pulled down by the surface gravity (= 2.64 times earth's) to a relatively thin layer. Of course, the gases become denser with depth until they may turn into a slush or a slurry. Perhaps there is no surface — no real interface between the gaseous atmosphere and the body of Jupiter. *Pioneers 10* and *11* provided evidence for considering Jupiter almost entirely liquid hydrogen. Long before a rocky core about the size of the earth is reached, hydrogen mixed with helium becomes a liquid metal at very high temperature and pressure. Jupiter's cloudy atmosphere is a fairly good reflector of sunlight and makes it appear far brighter than any of the stars.

Fourteen of Jupiter's 17 or more satellites have been found through earth-based observations. Four of the moons are large and bright, rivaling the earth's moon and the planet Mercury in diameter, and may be seen through a field glass. They move rapidly around Jupiter, and their change of position from night to night is extremely interesting to watch. The other satellites are much smaller and in all but one instance much farther from Jupiter and cannot be seen except through powerful telescopes. The 4 outermost satellites are revolving around Jupiter clockwise as seen from the north, contrary to the motions of the great majority of the satellites in the solar system and to the direction of revolution of the planets around the sun. The reason for this retrograde motion is not known, but one theory is that Jupiter's tremendous gravitational power may have captured 4 of the minor planets or asteroids that move about the sun between Mars and Jupiter and that these would necessarily revolve backward. At the great distance of these bodies from Jupiter — some 14 million miles — direct motion would result in decay of the orbits, while retrograde orbits would be stable. Jupiter's mass is more than twice the mass of all the other planets put together, which accounts for Jupiter's tremendous gravitational field and so, probably, for its numerous satellites and its dense atmosphere.

In Dec. 1973, *Pioneer 10* passed about 80,000 miles from the equator of Jupiter and was whipped into a path that would take it beyond the system of planets on June 13, 1983, and out of the earth's solar system in about 50 years. In Dec. 1974, *Pioneer 11* passed within 30,000 miles of Jupiter, moving roughly from south to north, over the poles.

Photographs from both encounters were useful at the time but were far surpassed by those of *Voyagers I* and *II*, both of which were launched in 1977 and rendezvoused with Jupiter in 1979. Thousands of high-resolution multicolor pictures show rapid variations of features both large and small. The Great Red Spot exhibits internal counterclockwise rotation. Much turbulence is seen in adjacent material passing north or south of it. The satellites Amalthea, Io, Europa, Ganymede, and Callisto were photographed, some in great detail. Each is individual and unique, with no similarities to other known planets or satellites. Io has active volcanoes that probably have ejected material into a doughnut-shaped ring enveloping its orbit about Jupiter. This is not to be confused with the thin flat disklike ring closer to Jupiter's surface.

Beginning July 16, 1994, the 21 large fragments of the comet Shoemaker-Levy 9 collided with Jupiter in a dramatic 6-day barrage. Moving at 134,000 mph, stretched out like a 21-car freight train, the fragments impacted one after another against the side of Jupiter facing away from the earth. The high speed of the planet's rotation, allowing the impact sites to rotate quickly into view, along with the sheer scope of the reactions, provided a show unprecedented in astronomy. Massive plumes of gas erupted from the impact sites, forming brilliant fireballs and leaving dark blotches and smears behind. For example, one of the largest chunks, labeled the G fragment, impacted with the force of 6 million megatons of TNT, 100,000 times the power of the largest nuclear bomb ever detonated. It produced a plume 1,200-1,600 miles high and 5,000 miles wide and left a dark discoloration larger than the earth. These impacts, predicted a year in advance, were closely observed and produced a massive amount of data for scientists and astronomers to analyze, even as they continue to observe Jupiter for the event's aftermath.

Saturn

Saturn, last of the planets visible to the unaided eye, is almost twice as far from the sun as Jupiter, almost 900 million miles. It is second in size to Jupiter, but its mass is much smaller. Saturn's specific gravity is less than that of water. Its diameter is about 71,000 miles at the equator; its rotational speed spins it completely around in a little more than 10 hours, and its atmosphere is much like that of Jupiter, except that its temperature at the top of its cloud layer is at least 100° F lower. At about 300° F below zero, the ammonia would be frozen out of Saturn's clouds. The theoretical construction of Saturn resembles that of Jupiter; it is either all gas, or it has a small dense center surrounded by a layer of liquid and a deep atmosphere.

Detecting the precise number of satellites surrounding Saturn is complicated by the fact that the clearest observations can be made only at those times when the planet's rings are edge-on and virtually invisible. Until *Pioneer 11* passed Saturn in Sept. 1979, only 10 satellites of the planet were known from ground-based observation. Since that time, the *Voyager I* and *II* fly-bys and improved scientific equipment have yielded more information about Saturn's icy satellites. In 1995, astronomers using the Hubble Space Telescope detected at least 2 previously unknown moons of Saturn, bringing the total to at least 24, some sharing orbits.

Saturn's ring system begins about 7,000 miles above the visible disk of Saturn, lying above its equator and extending about 35,000 miles into space. The diameter of the ring system visible from earth is about 170,000 miles; the rings are estimated to be no thicker than 10 miles. In 1973, radar observation showed the ring particles to be large chunks of material averaging a meter on a side.

Voyager I and *II* observations showed the rings to be considerably more complex than had been believed, so much so that interpretation will take much time. To the untrained eye, the *Voyager* photographs could be mistaken for pictures of a colorful phonograph record.

Uranus

Voyager II, after passing Saturn in Aug. 1981, headed for a rendezvous with Uranus, culminating in a fly-by Jan. 24, 1986. This encounter answered many questions and raised others.

Uranus, discovered by Sir William Herschel on Mar. 13, 1781, lies at a distance of 1.8 billion miles from the sun, taking 84 years to make its circuit around our star. Uranus has a diameter of about 32,000 miles and spins once in some 16.8 hours, according to fly-by data. One of the most fascinating features of Uranus is how far over it is tipped. Its north pole lies 98° from being directly up and down to its orbit plane. Thus, its seasons are extreme. When the sun rises at the north pole, it stays up for 42 years; then it sets, and the north pole is in darkness (and winter) for 42 years.

The satellite system of Uranus consists of at least 15 moons (the 5 largest having been known before the fly-by), which have orbits lying in the plane of the planet's equator. In that plane there is also a complex of rings, 9 of which were discovered in 1978. Invisible from earth, the 9 original rings were found by observers watching Uranus pass before a star. As they waited, they saw their photoelectric equipment register several short eclipses of the star; then the planet occulted the star as expected. After the star came out from behind Uranus, the star winked out several more times. Subsequent observations and analyses indicated the 9 narrow, nearly opaque rings circling Uranus. Evidence from the *Voyager II* fly-by has shown the ring particles to be predominantly a yard or so in diameter.

In addition to photos of the 10 new, very small satellites, *Voyager II* returned detailed photos of the 5 large satellites. As in the case of other satellites newly observed in the *Voyager* program, these bodies proved to be entirely different from one another and from any others. Miranda has grooved markings, reminiscent of Jupiter's Ganymede, but often arranged in a chevron pattern. Ariel shows rifts and channels. Umbriel is extremely dark, prompting some observers to regard its surface as among the oldest in the system. Titania has rifts and fractures, but not the evidence of flow found on Ariel. Oberon's main feature is its surface saturated with craters, unrelieved by other formations.

The structure of Uranus is subject to some debate. Basically, however, it may have a rocky core surrounded by a thick icy mantle on top of which is a crust of hydrogen and helium that gradually becomes an atmosphere. Perhaps continued analysis of the wealth of data returned by *Voyager II* will shed some light on this problem.

Neptune

Neptune, currently the most distant planet from the sun (until 1999), lies at an average distance of 2.8 billion miles. It was the last planet visited in *Voyager II*'s epic 12-year trek (1977-89) from earth. Although much new information was immediately perceived, much more must await analysis of the tremendous amount of data returned from the spacecraft.

As with the other giant planets, Neptune may have no solid surface to give real meaning to a measure of a diameter. However, a mean value of 30,600 miles may be assigned to a diameter between atmosphere levels where the pressure is about the same as sea level on earth, as determined by radio experimenters. A different radio observational technique gave evidence of a rotation period for the bulk of Neptune of 16.1 hours, a shorter value than the 18.2 hours given by the clouds seen in the blue atmosphere. Neptune orbits the sun in 164 years in nearly a circular orbit.

Voyager II, which passed 3,000 miles from Neptune's north pole, found a magnetic field that is considerably asymmetric to the planet's structure, similar to, but not so extreme as, that found at Uranus.

Neptune's atmosphere was seen to be quite blue, with quickly changing white clouds often suspended high above an apparent surface. In that apparent surface were found features, one of which was reminiscent of the Great Red Spot of Jupiter, even to the counterclockwise rotation expected in a high-pressure system in the southern hemisphere. Atmospheric constituents are mostly hydrocarbon compounds. Although lightning and auroras have been found on other giant planets, only the aurora phenomenon has been seen on Neptune.

Six new satellites were discerned around Neptune, one confirming a 1981 sighting that was then difficult to recover for proper identification. Five of these satellites orbit Neptune in a half day or less. Of the 8 satellites of Neptune, the largest, Triton, is in a retrograde orbit suggesting that it was captured rather than being coeval with Neptune. Triton's large size, sufficient to raise significant tides on Neptune, will one day, say 100 million years from now, cause Triton to come close enough to Neptune for it to be torn apart. Nereid was found in 1949 and is in a long looping orbit suggesting that it too was captured. Each of the satellites that has been photographed by the 2 *Voyagers* in the planetary encounters has been different from any of the other satellites, and certainly different from any of the planets. Only about half of Triton has been observed, but its terrain shows cratering and a strange regional feature described as resembling the skin of a cantaloupe. Triton has a tenuous atmosphere of nitrogen with a trace of hydrocarbons and has evidence of active geysers injecting material into it. At –238 degrees Celsius, Triton is one of the coldest objects in the solar system observed by *Voyager II*.

In addition to the satellite system, *Voyager II* confirmed the existence of at least 3 rings composed of very fine particles. There may be some clumpiness in the rings' structure. It is not known if Neptune's satellites influence the formation or maintenance of the rings, as they have in other systems.

As with the other giant planets, Neptune is emitting more energy than it receives from the sun, *Voyager* finding the excess to be 2.7 times the solar contribution. These excesses are thought to be cooling from internal heat sources and from the heat of formation of the planets.

Pluto

Although Pluto on the average stays about 3.6 billion miles from the sun, its orbit is so eccentric that its minimum distance of 2.7 billion miles is less than the current distance of Neptune. Thus, Pluto, until 1999, is temporarily planet number 8 from the sun. At its mean distance, Pluto takes 247.7 years to circumnavigate the sun, a ³/₂ resonance with Neptune. Until recently, this was about all that was known of Pluto.

About a century ago, a hypothetical planet was believed to lie beyond Neptune and Uranus because neither planet followed the paths predicted by astronomers even when all known gravitational influences were considered. Little more than a guess, a mass of one earth was assigned to the mysterious body, and mathematical searches were begun. Amid some controversy about the validity of the predictive process, Pluto was found nearly where it was predicted to be. It was found by Clyde Tombaugh at the Lowell Observatory in Flagstaff, AZ, in 1930.

At the U.S. Naval Observatory, also in Flagstaff, on July 2, 1978, James Christy obtained a photograph of Pluto that was distinctly elongated. Repeated observations of this shape and its variation were convincing evidence of the discovery of a satellite of Pluto, now named Charon. Subsequent observations show it to be 750 miles across, at adistance of more than 12,000 miles from Pluto, and taking 6.4 days to move around Pluto. In this same length of time Pluto and Charon each rotate once around their individual axes. The Pluto-Charon system thus appears to rotate as virtually a ridged body. Gravitational laws allow these interactions to give the mass of Pluto as 0.0020 of the earth. This mass, together with a new diameter for Pluto of 1,430 miles, make the density about twice that of water. Theorists predict a rocky core for Pluto surrounded by a thick mantle of ice.

It is now clear that Pluto, the body found by Tombaugh, could not have influenced Neptune and Uranus to go astray. Theorists are again at work looking for a new planet X.

Because the rotational axis of the system is tipped from the reference plane of the solar system by about 98°.3, similar to that of Uranus, there is only a short interval every half solar period when Pluto and Charon alternately eclipse each other. Analysis of the variations in light in and out of the recent eclipses has led to the diameters quoted above and to interesting knowledge of other aspects of the system. Both components are approximately spherical, but they are otherwise different. Pluto is red, Charon gray. Charon's surface is identified as water ice; Pluto's surface is frozen methane. Large regions on Pluto are dark, others light; Pluto has spots and, perhaps, polar caps. Although extremely cold, Pluto's methane surface produces a tenuous atmosphere that may be slowly escaping into space, perhaps going to Charon. When Pluto occulted a star, the star's light faded in such a way as to have passed through a haze layer lying above the planet's surface, indicating an inversion of temperatures — 110°K above and 50°K below — suggesting Pluto has primitive weather.

There are tentative plans for a spacecraft reconnaissance of the Pluto system, thus completing direct, close-up observation of each planet of the solar system.

Astronomical Signs and Symbols

☉	The Sun	⊕	The Earth	♅	Uranus	□	Quadrature
☽	The Moon	♂	Mars	♆	Neptune	☍	Opposition
☿	Mercury	♃	Jupiter	♇	Pluto	☊	Ascending Node
♀	Venus	♄	Saturn	☌	Conjunction	☋	Descending Node

Two heavenly bodies are in *conjunction* (☌) when they are due north and south of each other, either in Right Ascension (with respect to the north celestial pole) or in Celestial Longitude (with respect to the north ecliptic pole). If the bodies are seen near each other, they will rise and set at nearly the same time. They are in *opposition* (☍) when their Right Ascensions differ by exactly 12 hours, or when their Celestial Longitudes differ by 180°. One of the two objects in opposition will rise while the other is setting. *Quadrature* (□) refers to the arrangement when the coordinates of 2 bodies differ by exactly 90°. These terms may refer to the relative positions of any 2 bodies as seen from the earth, but one of the bodies is so frequently the sun that mention of the sun is omitted; otherwise, both bodies are named. The geocentric angular separation between sun and object is termed *elongation*. Elongation is limited only for Mercury and Venus; the *greatest elongation* for each of these bodies is noted in the appropriate tables and is approximately the time for longest observation. When a planet is in its *ascending* (☊) or *descending* (☋) node, it is passing northward or southward, respectively, through the plane of the earth's orbit, across the celestial circle called the ecliptic. The term *perihelion* means nearest to the sun, and *aphelion*, farthest from the sun. An *occultation* of a planet or a star is an eclipse of it by some other body, usually the moon.

Planetary Configurations, 1996

Greenwich Mean Time (0 designates midnight; 12 designates noon; ✳ = star; ☽ = moon)

Month	d	h	m				
Jan.	1	01	-	☿	☌	♅	☿ 0°.9 S
	1	07	-	♂	☌	♆	♂ 1°.6 S
	2	16	-				☿ Gr. Elong. 19° E of ☉
	4	07	-				⊕ Perihelion
	8	00	-	♂	☌	♅	♂ 0°.6 S
	9	12	-				☿ Stationary; begins retrograde motion
	13	00	-	☿	☌	♂	☿ 3° N
	16	03	-	♆	☌	☉	
	18	20	-	♃	☌	☽	♃ 5° S
	18	22	-	☿	☌	☉	Inferior Conj.
	21	07	-	♅	☌	☉	
	23	08	-	♀	☌	☽	♀ 5° S
	24	04	-	♄	☌	☽	♄ 5° S
	30	06	-				☿ Stationary; resumes direct motion
Feb.	3	02	-	♀	☌	♄	♀ 1°.3 N
	11	14	-	☿	☌	♆	☿ 0°.07 N
	11	21	-				☿ Gr. Elong. 26° W of ☉
	12	02	-				⊕ passes through ♄ ring plane, N to S
	15	15	-	♃	☌	☽	♃ 5° S
	16	20	-	♆	☌	☽	♆ 5° S
	16	22	-	☿	☌	♅	☿ 0°.2 N
	17	05	-	♅	☌	☽	♅ 6° S
	17	06	-	☿	☌	☽	☿ 5° S
	20	19	-	♄	☌	☽	♄ 4° S
	22	05	-	♀	☌	☽	♀ 0°.06 N; Occultation
Mar.	4	14	-	♂	☌	☉	
	7	20	-				♇ Stationary; begins retrograde motion
	14	06	-	♃	☌	☽	♃ 5° S
	15	05	-	♆	☌	☽	♆ 5° S
	15	16	-	♅	☌	☽	♅ 6° S
	17	19	-	♄	☌	☉	
	20	08	03				Vernal Equinox; Spring begins in Northern Hemi-

Month	d	h	m	Configuration	Remarks
					sphere
	22	20	-	♂ ☌ ♄	♂ 1°.3 N
	23	00	-	♀ ☌ ☽	♀ 5° N
	23	11	-	☿ ☌ ♄	☿ 0°.3 N
	23	20	-	☿ ☌ ♂	☿ 0°.9 S
	28	08	-	☿ ☌ ☉	Superior conj.
Apr.	1	01			♀ Gr. Elong. 46° E of ☉
	4	00	-	☽ ☍ ☉	Total lunar eclipse
	10	17	-	♃ ☌ ☽	♃ 5° S
	11	12	-	♆ ☌ ☽	♆ 5° S
	12	00	-	♅ ☌ ☽	♅ 6° S
	15	22	-	♀ ☌ ✱	♀ 10° N of Aldebaran
	16	01	-	♄ ☌ ☽	♄ 4° S
	17	23	-	☽ ☌ ☉	Partial solar eclipse
	19	10	-	☿ ☌ ☽	☿ 5° N
	21	14	-	♀ ☌ ☽	♀ 9° N
	23	08	-		☿ Gr. Elong. 20° E of ☉
	29	09	-		♆ Stationary; begins retrograde motion
May	4	10	-		☿ Stationary; begins retrograde motion
	4	14	-		♀ Gr. Brilliancy
	4	17	-		♃ Stationary; begins retrograde motion
	8	00	-	♃ ☌ ☽	♃ 5° S
	8	17	-	♆ ☌ ☽	♆ 5° S
	9	00	-		♅ Stationary; begins retrograde motion
	9	06	-	♆ ☌ ☽	♆ 6° S
	13	13	-	♄ ☌ ☽	♄ 3° S
	15	01	-	☿ ☌ ☉	Inferior Conj.
	16	03	-	♂ ☌ ☽	♂ 1°.7 N
	20	01		♀ ☌ ☽	♀ 8° N
	20	07			♀ Stationary; begins retrograde motion
	22	14	-	♇ ☍ ☉	
	27	07	-		☿ Stationary; resumes direct motion
	31			☿ ☌ ♂	☿ 4° S
June	4	06	-	♃ ☌ ☽	♃ 5° S
	5	00	-	♆ ☌ ☽	♆ 5° S
	5	12	-	♅ ☌ ☽	♅ 6° S
	9	22	-	♄ ☌ ☽	♄ 3° S
	10	09	-		☿ Gr. Elong. 24° W of ☉
	10	16	-	♀ ☌ ☉	Inferior Conj.
	14	00	-	☿ ☌ ☽	☿ 0°.4 N; Occultation
	14	01	-	♂ ☌ ☽	♂ 4° N
	14	13	-	☿ ☌ ♂	☿ 3° S
	21	02	24		Summer Solstice; Summer begins in Northern Hemisphere
	21	11	-	☿ ☌ ✱	☿ 4° N of Aldebaran
	23	12	-	☿ ☌ ♀	☿ 1°.6 N
	27	12	-	♂ ☌ ✱	♂ 6° N of Aldebaran
	30	04	-	♀ ☌ ♂	♀ 4° S
July	1	10	-	♃ ☌ ☽	♃ 5° S
	2	00	-		♀ Stationary; resumes direct motion
	2	08	-	♆ ☌ ☽	♆ 4° S
	2	20	-	♅ ☌ ☽	♅ 5° S
	4	12	-	♃ ☍ ☉	
	5	18	-		⊕ at aphelion
	7	06	-	♄ ☌ ☽	♄ 3° S
	11	09	-	☿ ☌ ☉	Superior Conj.
	12	09	-	♀ ☌ ☽	♀ 0°.4 S; Occultation
	12	23	-	♂ ☌ ☽	♂ 5° N
	17	09	-		♀ Gr. Brilliancy
	18	18	-	♆ ☍ ☉	
	20	00	-		♄ Stationary; begins retrograde motion
	25	07	-	♅ ☍ ☉	
	28	16	-	♃ ☌ ☽	♃ 5° S
	29	18	-	♆ ☌ ☽	♆ 4° S
	30	04	-	♅ ☌ ☽	♅ 5° S
Aug.	1	10	-	☿ ☌ ✱	☿ 0°.5 N of Regulus
	3	13	-	♄ ☌ ☽	♄ 3° S
	8	07	-	☽ ☌ ✱	☽ 1° N of Aldebaran: Occultation
	10	04	-	♀ ☌ ☽	♀ 1°.2 N
	10	21	-	♂ ☌ ☽	♂ 6° N
	13	14	-		♇ Stationary; resumes direct motion
	16	18	-	☿ ☌ ☽	☿ 0°.3 N; Occultation
	20	04	-		♀ Gr. Elong. 46° W of ☉
	21	16	-		☿ Gr. Elong. 27° E of ☉
	24	22	-	♃ ☌ ☽	♃ 5° S
	26	03	-	♆ ☌ ☽	♆ 5° S
	26	13	-	♅ ☌ ☽	♅ 5° S
	30	21	-	♄ ☌ ☽	♄ 3° S
	31	17	-	♂ ☌ ✱	♂ 6°S of Pollux
Sept.	2	05	-	♀ ☌ ✱	♀ 9° S of Pollux
	3	14	-		♃ Stationary; resumes direct motion
	3	20	-		☿ Stationary, begins retrograde motion
	4	14	-	☽ ☌ ✱	☽ 0°.9 N of Aldebaran; Occultation
	4	15	-	♀ ☌ ♂	♀ 3° S
	8	19	-	♂ ☌ ☽	♂ 6° N
	8	23	-	♀ ☌ ☽	♀ 3° N
	17	13	-	☿ ☌ ☉	Inferior Conj.
	21	06	-	♃ ☌ ☽	♃ 6° S
	22	11	-	♆ ☌ ☽	♆ 5° S
	22	18	00		Autumnal Equinox; Fall begins in Northern Hemisphere
	22	21	-	♅ ☌ ☽	♅ 6° S
	25	22	-		☿ Stationary; resumes direct motion
	26	16	-	♄ ☍ ☉	
	27	03	-	☽ ☍ ☉	Total lunar eclipse
	27	04	-	♄ ☌ ☽	♄ 3° S
Oct.	1	22	-	☽ ☌ ✱	☽ 0°.8 N of Aldebaran; Occultation
	3	06	-		☿ Gr. Elong. 18° W of ☉
	4	00	-	♀ ☌ ✱	♀ 0°.2 S of Regulus
	6	12	-		♆ Stationary; resumes direct motion
	7	15	-	♂ ☌ ☽	♂ 6° N
	9	04	-	♀ ☌ ☽	♀ 4° N
	10	03	-		♅ Stationary, resumes direct motion
	12	14	-	☽ ☌ ☉	Partial Solar Eclipse
	18	16	-	♃ ☌ ☽	♃ 6° S
	19	17	-	♆ ☌ ☽	♆ 5° S
	20	03	-	♅ ☌ ☽	♅ 6° S
	24	10	-	♄ ☌ ☽	♄ 3° S
	29	04	-	♂ ☌ ✱	♂ 1°.2 N of Regulus
	29	08	-	☽ ☌ ✱	☽ 0°.9 N of Aldebaran; Occultation
Nov.	2	00	-	☿ ☌ ☉	Superior Conj.
	5	08	-	♂ ☌ ☽	♂ 5° N
	8	10	-	♀ ☌ ☽	♀ 1°.4 N
	15	05	-	♃ ☌ ☽	♃ 5° S
	15	23	-	♆ ☌ ☽	♆ 4° S
	16	09	-	♅ ☌ ☽	♅ 5° S
	16	18	-	♀ ☌ ✱	♀ 4° N of Spica
	20	15	-	♄ ☌ ☽	♄ 3° S
	20	17	-	☿ ☌ ✱	☿ 3° N of Antares
	25	00	-	♇ ☌ ☉	
	25	17	-	☽ ☌ ✱	☽ 0°.9 N of Aldebaran
Dec.	3	21	-	♂ ☌ ☽	♂ 4° N
	4	11	-		♄ Stationary; resumes direct motion
	8	13	-	♀ ☌ ☽	♀ 2° S
	12	05	-	☿ ☌ ☽	☿ 7° S
	12	23	-	♃ ☌ ☽	♃ 5° S
	13	07	-	♆ ☌ ☽	♆ 4° S
	13	18	-	♅ ☌ ☽	♅ 5° S
	15	19	-		☿ Gr. Elong. 20° E of ☉
	17	20	-	♄ ☌ ☽	♄ 3° S
	21	14	06		Winter Solstice; Winter begins in Northern Hemisphere
	23	00	-	☽ ☌ ✱	☽ 0°.9 N of Aldebaran; Occultation
	23	14	-		☿ Stationary; begins retrograde motion
	24	07	-	♀ ☌ ✱	♀ 6° N of Antares

Rising and Setting of Planets, 1996

Greenwich Mean Time (0 designates midnight)

Venus, 1996

Date		20° N Latitude Rise	Set	30° N Latitude Rise	Set	40° N Latitude Rise	Set	50° N Latitude Rise	Set	60° N Latitude Rise	Set
Jan.	1	8:49	19:58	9:05	19:42	9:26	19:22	9:54	18:54	10:40	18:08
	11	8:52	20:13	9:04	20:01	9:20	19:46	9:41	19:25	10:15	18:51
	21	8:51	20:27	9:00	20:19	9:10	20:09	9:24	19:55	9:46	19:34
	31	8:49	20:39	8:53	20:36	8:58	20:31	9:04	20:25	9:14	20:15
Feb.	10	8:45	20:51	8:44	20:51	8:44	20:52	8:43	20:03	8:42	20:55
	20	8:40	21:01	8:35	21:06	8:29	21:12	8:21	21:21	8:08	21:34
Mar.	2	8:35	21:11	8:25	21:20	8:14	21:32	7:58	21:48	7:34	22:14
	12	8:30	21:20	8:16	21:34	7:59	21:51	7:36	22:15	6:59	22:53
	22	8:25	21:29	8:08	21:47	7:46	22:09	7:15	22:40	6:23	23:33
Apr.	1	8:21	21:37	8:00	21:58	7:34	22:25	6:56	23:03	5:48	0:12
	11	8:17	21:41	7:53	22:05	7:23	22:36	6:39	23:21	5:14	0:47
	21	8:11	21:42	7:46	22:07	7:13	22:41	6:24	23:30	4:42	1:13
May	1	8:02	21:34	7:35	22:01	7:00	22:36	6:09	23:27	4:15	1:22
	11	7:44	21:16	7:17	21:43	6:42	22:17	5:51	23:09	3:56	1:03
	21	7:14	20:43	6:48	21:08	6:15	21:42	5:25	22:31	3:41	0:14
	31	6:29	19:51	6:05	20:14	5:34	20:45	4:49	21:30	3:21	22:56
June	10	5:31	18:43	5:10	19:05	4:43	19:31	4:04	20:10	2:53	21:19
	20	4:32	17:36	4:14	17:54	3:51	18:17	3:18	18:50	2:21	19:45
	30	3:44	16:42	3:27	16:58	3:06	17:19	2:37	17:48	1:49	18:36
July	10	3:09	16:06	2:53	16:22	2:33	16:42	2:05	17:09	1:19	17:56
	20	2:45	15:44	2:29	16:00	2:09	16:21	1:40	16:49	0:53	17:37
	30	2:31	15:32	2:14	15:49	1:52	16:11	1:22	16:41	0:32	17:31
Aug.	9	2:23	15:27	2:06	15:45	1:43	16:08	1:12	16:39	0:19	17:32
	19	2:22	15:27	2:03	15:45	1:41	16:08	1:09	16:40	0:14	17:35
	29	2:24	15:29	2:06	15:47	1:44	16:09	1:12	16:41	0:19	17:34
Sep.	8	2:30	15:32	2:14	15:48	1:52	16:09	1:23	16:39	0:33	17:28
	18	2:39	15:34	2:24	15:49	2:05	16:08	1:39	16:34	0:56	17:16
	28	2:49	15:36	2:36	15:48	2:21	16:04	1:59	16:25	1:24	16:59
Oct.	8	3:00	15:36	2:50	15:46	2:39	15:57	2:22	16:13	1:57	16:38
	18	3:11	15:36	3:05	15:42	2:58	15:49	2:47	15:59	2:31	16:14
	28	3:23	15:35	3:20	15:37	3:18	15:39	3:14	15:43	3:07	15:49
Nov.	7	3:35	15:33	3:36	15:32	3:38	15:30	3:41	15:27	3:44	15:23
	17	3:48	15:33	3:53	15:27	4:00	15:20	4:09	15:11	4:23	14:57
	27	4:01	15:33	4:11	15:24	4:22	15:12	4:38	14:56	5:02	14:32
Dec.	7	4:16	15:36	4:29	15:23	4:45	15:07	5:08	14:44	5:43	14:09
	17	4:32	15:42	4:49	15:25	5:09	15:05	5:37	14:36	6:23	13:50
	27	4:49	15:50	5:08	15:31	5:32	15:07	6:05	14:34	7:01	13:37

Mars, 1996

Date		20° N Latitude Rise	Set	30° N Latitude Rise	Set	40° N Latitude Rise	Set	50° N Latitude Rise	Set	60° N Latitude Rise	Set
Jan.	1	7:37	18:33	7:57	18:13	8:22	17:48	8:58	17:13	9:59	16:11
	11	7:28	18:29	7:46	18:11	8:09	17:48	8:42	17:16	9:36	16:22
	21	7:17	18:26	7:34	18:09	7:55	17:49	8:23	17:20	9:10	16:34
	31	7:06	18:21	7:20	18:07	7:38	17:50	8:02	17:25	8:41	16:47
Feb.	10	6:54	18:17	7:06	18:05	7:20	17:51	7:40	17:31	8:12	17:00
	20	6:40	18:12	6:50	18:03	7:01	17:52	7:17	17:36	7:41	17:12
Mar.	2	6:26	18:07	6:33	18:00	6:41	17:52	6:52	17:41	7:09	17:25
	12	6:11	18:01	6:15	17:57	6:20	17:52	6:27	17:46	6:37	17:36
	22	5:56	17:55	5:57	17:54	5:59	17:52	6:01	17:50	6:04	17:48
Apr.	01	5:40	17:49	5:39	17:50	5:37	17:52	5:35	17:55	5:31	17:59
	11	5:25	17:42	5:21	17:46	5:16	17:51	5:09	17:58	4:58	18:09
	21	5:09	17:35	5:03	17:42	4:54	17:50	4:43	18:02	4:26	18:20
May	01	4:54	17:29	4:45	17:38	4:33	17:49	4:18	18:05	3:53	18:30
	11	4:39	17:22	4:27	17:34	4:13	17:48	3:53	18:08	3:22	18:40
	21	4:25	17:15	4:11	17:29	3:54	17:47	3:30	18:11	2:51	18:50
	31	4:11	17:09	3:55	17:25	3:35	17:45	3:07	18:13	2:21	18:59
June	10	3:58	17:02	3:40	17:20	3:18	17:42	2:46	18:14	1:53	19:08
	20	3:45	16:55	3:26	17:14	3:02	17:39	2:27	18:14	1:27	19:14
	30	3:34	16:47	3:13	17:08	2:47	17:34	2:09	18:12	1:03	19:19
Jul.	10	3:23	16:39	3:01	17:01	2:34	17:28	1:54	18:08	0:43	19:20
	20	3:12	16:30	2:50	16:53	2:22	17:21	1:41	18:02	0:26	19:17
	30	3:02	16:21	2:40	16:43	2:11	17:12	1:30	17:53	0:14	19:09
Aug.	09	2:52	16:10	2:30	16:32	2:01	17:01	1:21	17:41	0:06	18:56
	19	2:42	15:58	2:20	16:20	1:53	16:47	1:13	17:27	0:01	18:39
	29	2:32	15:45	2:11	16:06	1:44	16:33	1:07	17:10	23:59	18:17
Sep.	08	2:21	15:31	2:01	15:51	1:36	16:16	1:01	16:51	23:59	17:53
	18	2:10	15:16	1:52	15:34	1:28	15:57	0:56	16:30	23:59	17:26
	28	1:58	14:59	1:41	15:16	1:20	15:37	0:50	16:07	0:00	16:57
Oct.	08	1:46	14:41	1:30	14:57	1:11	15:16	0:44	15:42	0:00	16:26
	18	1:32	14:22	1:19	14:36	1:02	14:53	0:38	15:17	23:59	15:55
	28	1:18	14:02	1:06	14:14	0:51	14:29	0:30	14:50	23:57	15:23
Nov.	07	1:03	13:41	0:53	13:52	0:40	14:05	0:22	14:22	23:53	14:50
	17	0:47	13:20	0:38	13:28	0:27	13:39	0:12	13:54	23:48	14:17
	27	0:29	12:57	0:22	13:04	0:13	13:12	0:01	13:25	23:41	13:43
Dec.	7	0:10	12:32	0:04	12:38	23:56	12:45	23:48	12:55	23:31	13:10
	17	23:50	12:07	23:43	12:11	23:38	12:17	23:32	12:24	23:19	12:36
	27	23:27	11:41	23:22	11:44	23:18	11:47	23:14	11:53	23:04	12:01

Jupiter, 1996

Date		20° N Latitude Rise	Set	30° N Latitude Rise	Set	40° N Latitude Rise	Set	50° N Latitude Rise	Set	60° N Latitude Rise	Set
Jan.	1	5:50	16:43	6:12	16:22	6:38	15:55	7:15	15:18	8:21	14:12
	11	5:21	16:13	5:42	15:52	6:08	15:26	6:46	14:48	7:52	13:42
	21	4:51	15:43	5:12	15:22	5:38	14:56	6:16	14:19	7:22	13:13
	31	4:21	15:13	4:42	14:52	5:08	14:26	5:45	13:49	6:51	12:44
Feb.	10	3:50	14:43	4:11	14:22	4:37	13:56	5:14	13:19	6:19	12:14
	20	3:19	14:12	3:39	13:51	4:05	13:25	4:42	12:49	5:46	11:44
Mar.	2	2:47	13:40	3:07	13:20	3:33	12:54	4:10	12:18	5:13	11:14
	12	2:14	13:08	2:34	12:48	3:00	12:22	3:36	11:46	4:39	10:43
	22	1:40	12:35	2:01	12:14	2:26	11:49	3:02	11:13	4:04	10:11
Apr.	1	1:06	12:01	1:26	11:40	1:51	11:15	2:27	10:39	3:28	9:38
	11	0:30	11:25	0:50	11:05	1:15	10:40	1:51	10:04	2:52	9:03
	21	23:49	10:48	0:13	10:28	0:38	10:03	1:14	9:28	2:15	8:27
May	1	23:11	10:10	23:31	9:50	23:56	9:25	0:35	8:50	1:36	7:49
	11	22:32	9:31	22:52	9:11	23:17	8:46	23:52	8:10	0:57	7:10
	21	21:51	8:50	22:11	8:30	22:36	8:05	23:12	7:29	0:17	6:28
	31	21:09	8:08	21:29	7:48	21:55	7:22	22:30	6:47	23:32	5:45
June	10	20:26	7:25	20:47	7:04	21:12	6:39	21:48	6:03	22:50	5:01
	20	19:42	6:40	20:03	6:20	20:29	5:54	21:05	5:18	22:08	4:15
	30	18:58	5:55	19:19	5:35	19:45	5:09	20:21	4:32	21:25	3:29
Jul.	10	18:14	5:10	18:34	4:50	19:00	4:24	19:37	3:47	20:42	2:42
	20	17:29	4:26	17:50	4:05	18:16	3:38	18:54	3:01	19:59	1:56
	30	16:45	3:41	17:06	3:20	17:33	2:54	18:10	2:16	19:16	1:11
Aug.	9	16:02	2:58	16:23	2:37	16:50	2:10	17:28	1:33	18:34	0:26
	19	15:20	2:16	15:41	1:54	16:08	1:28	16:46	0:50	17:52	23:39
	29	14:39	1:35	15:01	1:13	15:27	0:47	16:05	0:09	17:12	22:58
Sep.	8	14:00	0:55	14:21	0:34	14:48	0:07	15:26	23:25	16:33	22:18
	18	13:22	0:17	13:43	23:52	14:10	23:25	14:48	22:47	15:55	21:40
	28	12:45	23:37	13:06	23:15	13:33	22:49	14:11	22:11	15:18	21:04
Oct.	8	12:10	23:01	12:31	22:40	12:57	22:13	13:35	21:36	14:42	20:29
	18	11:35	22:27	11:56	22:06	12:23	21:39	13:00	21:02	14:06	19:56
	28	11:02	21:54	11:23	21:33	11:49	21:06	12:26	20:29	13:32	19:24
Nov.	7	10:29	21:22	10:50	21:01	11:16	20:35	11:53	19:58	12:58	18:53
	17	9:57	20:50	10:18	20:30	10:43	20:04	11:20	19:27	12:24	18:23
	27	9:25	20:20	9:46	19:59	10:11	19:34	10:48	18:58	11:50	17:55
Dec.	7	8:54	19:50	9:15	19:30	9:43	19:07	10:15	18:29	11:17	17:27
	17	8:24	19:20	8:44	19:00	9:12	18:38	9:43	18:01	10:43	17:01
	27	7:53	18:51	8:13	18:31	8:40	18:10	9:11	17:33	10:10	16:35

Saturn, 1996

Date		20° N Latitude Rise	Set	30° N Latitude Rise	Set	40° N Latitude Rise	Set	50° N Latitude Rise	Set	60° N Latitude Rise	Set
Jan.	1	10:49	22:35	10:54	22:30	11:01	22:24	11:09	22:15	11:21	22:03
	11	10:12	21:59	10:17	21:54	10:23	21:48	10:31	21:40	10:42	21:29
	21	9:36	21:23	9:40	21:18	9:46	21:13	9:53	21:06	10:04	20:55
	31	8:59	20:48	9:03	20:44	9:08	20:39	9:15	20:32	9:25	20:22
Feb.	10	8:23	20:13	8:27	20:09	8:32	20:05	8:37	19:59	8:46	19:50
	20	7:48	19:39	7:51	19:35	7:55	19:31	8:00	19:26	8:08	19:18
Mar.	2	7:12	19:04	7:15	19:01	7:18	18:58	7:23	18:53	7:30	18:47
	12	6:36	18:30	6:39	18:28	6:42	18:25	6:46	18:21	6:52	18:15
	22	6:01	17:56	6:03	17:54	6:05	17:52	6:09	17:48	6:13	17:44
Apr.	1	5:25	17:22	5:27	17:20	5:29	17:18	5:32	17:16	5:35	17:12
	11	4:50	16:48	4:51	16:47	4:53	16:45	4:54	16:43	4:57	16:41
	21	4:14	16:13	4:15	16:13	4:16	16:12	4:17	16:10	4:19	16:09
May	1	3:38	15:39	3:39	15:38	3:39	15:38	3:40	15:37	3:41	15:36
	11	3:02	15:04	3:02	15:04	3:03	15:03	3:03	15:03	3:03	15:03
	21	2:26	14:28	2:26	14:29	2:26	14:29	2:25	14:29	2:25	14:30
	31	1:49	13:53	1:49	13:53	1:48	13:53	1:48	13:54	1:46	13:56
June	10	1:12	13:16	1:12	13:17	1:11	13:18	1:10	13:19	1:08	13:21
	20	0:35	12:39	0:34	12:40	0:33	12:41	0:32	12:42	0:30	12:45
	30	23:53	12:02	23:52	12:02	23:51	12:04	23:50	12:05	23:47	12:08
Jul.	10	23:14	11:23	23:14	11:24	23:13	11:25	23:11	11:27	23:08	11:30
	20	22:36	10:44	22:35	10:45	22:34	10:46	22:32	10:48	22:29	10:51
	30	21:56	10:05	21:55	10:05	21:54	10:07	21:53	10:08	21:50	10:10
Aug.	9	21:16	9:24	21:15	9:25	21:15	9:26	21:13	9:27	21:11	9:29
	19	20:36	8:43	20:35	8:44	20:34	8:44	20:33	8:45	20:32	8:47
	29	19:55	8:02	19:54	8:02	19:54	8:02	19:53	8:03	19:52	8:04
Sep.	8	19:13	7:20	19:13	7:20	19:13	7:20	19:13	7:20	19:12	7:20
	18	18:32	6:37	18:32	6:37	18:32	6:37	18:32	6:37	18:33	6:36
	28	17:50	5:55	17:51	5:54	17:51	5:54	17:52	5:53	17:53	5:52
Oct.	8	17:08	5:12	17:09	5:11	17:10	5:10	17:11	5:09	17:13	5:08
	18	16:27	4:30	16:28	4:29	16:29	4:27	16:30	4:26	16:33	4:24
	28	15:45	3:48	15:47	3:46	15:48	3:45	15:50	3:43	15:52	3:41
Nov.	7	15:04	3:06	15:06	3:05	15:07	3:03	15:09	3:01	15:12	2:58
	17	14:24	2:25	14:25	2:24	14:27	2:22	14:29	2:20	14:33	2:16
	27	13:44	1:45	13:45	1:43	13:47	1:41	13:49	1:39	13:53	1:36
Dec.	7	13:04	1:05	13:06	1:04	13:08	1:02	13:10	1:00	13:13	0:56
	17	12:25	0:27	12:27	0:25	12:28	0:23	12:31	0:21	12:34	0:18
	27	11:47	23:45	11:48	23:43	11:50	23:42	11:52	23:40	11:54	23:37

Morning and Evening Stars, 1996

(Greenwich Mean Time)

	Morning	Evening		Morning	Evening
Jan.	Mercury, from Jan. 18	Mercury, from Jan. 1 to Jan. 18		Saturn Uranus Neptune	
	Jupiter, from Jan. 1	Venus, from Jan. 1	**July**	Mercury, to Jul. 11	Mercury, from Jul. 11
	Uranus, from Jan. 21	Mars, from Jan. 1		Venus	Jupiter, from July 4
	Neptune, from Jan. 16	Saturn, from Jan. 1		Mars	Uranus
		Uranus, to Jan. 17		Jupiter, to Jul. 4	Uranus, from Jul. 25
		Neptune, to Jan. 13		Saturn	Neptune, from Jul. 18
Feb.	Mercury	Venus		Uranus, to Jul. 25	
	Jupiter	Mars		Neptune, to Jul. 18	
	Uranus	Saturn	**Aug.**	Venus	Mercury
	Neptune			Mars	Jupiter
Mar.	Mercury, to Mar. 28	Mercury, from Mar. 28		Saturn	Uranus
	Mars, from Mar. 4	Venus			Neptune
	Jupiter	Mars, to Mar. 4	**Sept.**	Mercury, from Sept. 17	Mercury, to Sept. 17
	Saturn, from Mar. 17	Saturn, to Mar. 6		Venus	Jupiter
	Uranus			Mars	Saturn, from Sept. 26
	Neptune			Saturn, to Sep. 26	Uranus
Apr.	Mars	Mercury			Neptune
	Jupiter	Venus	**Oct.**	Mercury	Jupiter
	Saturn			Venus	Saturn
	Uranus			Mars	Uranus
	Neptune				Neptune
			Nov.	Mercury, to Nov. 2	Mercury, from Nov. 2
May	Mars	Mercury, to May 15		Venus	Jupiter
	Jupiter	Venus		Mars	Saturn
	Saturn				Uranus
	Uranus				Neptune
	Neptune		**Dec.**	Venus	Mercury
June	Mercury	Venus, to June 10		Mars	Jupiter
	Venus, from June 10				Saturn
	Mars				Uranus
	Jupiter				Neptune

Greenwich Sidereal Time for 0ʰ GMT, 1996

(Add 12 hours to obtain Right Ascension of Mean Sun)

Date	d	h	m	Date	d	h	m	Date	d	h	m
Jan.	1	6	39.7	May	10	15	12.3	Sept.	7	23	5.40
	11	7	19.2		20	15	51.7		17	23	44.8
	21	7	58.6		30	16	31.1		27	0	24.2
	31	8	38.0	June	9	17	10.6	Oct.	7	1	03.7
Feb.	10	9	17.5		19	17	50.0		17	1	43.1
	20	9	56.9		29	18	29.4		27	2	22.5
Mar.	1	10	36.3	July	9	19	08.8	Nov.	6	3	02.0
	11	11	15.7		19	19	48.3		16	3	41.4
	21	11	55.2		29	20	27.7		26	4	20.8
	31	12	34.6	Aug.	8	21	07.1	Dec.	6	5	00.2
Apr.	12	13	14.0		18	21	46.5		16	5	39.7
	22	13	53.4		28	22	26.0		26	6	19.1
	30	14	32.9								

Star Tables

These tables include stars of visual magnitude 2.5 and brighter. Coordinates are for mid-1996. If no parallax figures are given, the trigonometric parallax figure is smaller than the margin for error, and the distance given is obtained by indirect methods. Stars of variable magnitude are designated by v.

To find the time when the star is on meridian, subtract Right Ascension of Mean Sun, from the sidereal time table above, from the star's right ascension, first adding 24h to the latter, if necessary. Mark this result PM, if less than 12h; but if greater than 12, subtract 12h and mark the remainder AM.

	Star	Magni-tude	Paral-lax ʺ	Light yrs.	Right ascen. h m	Decli-nation ° ′		Star	Magni-tude	Paral-lax ʺ	Light yrs.	Right ascen. h m	Decli-nation ° ′
α	Andromedae (Alpheratz)	2.06	0.02	90	0 08.2	29 04	β	Andromedae	2.06	0.04	76	1 09.5	35 36
β	Cassiopeiae	2.27 v	0.07	45	0 09.0	59 08	α	Eridani (Achernar)	0.46	0.02	118	1 37.6	−57 15
α	Phoenicis	2.39	0.04	93	0 26.1	−42 20	γ	Andromedae	2.26		260	2 03.7	42 19
α	Cassiopeiae (Schedir)	2.23	0.01	150	0 40.3	56 31	α	Arietis	2.00	0.04	76	2 07.0	23 27
β	Ceti	2.04	0.06	57	0 43.4	−18 00	o	Ceti	2.00	0.01	103	2 19.2	−3 00
γ	Cassiopeiae	2.47 v	0.03	96	0 56.5	60 42	α	Ursae Min. (Pole Star)	2.02 v		680	2 28.0	89 15
							β	Persei (Algol)	2.12 v	0.03	105	3 07.9	40 57

Star	Magnitude	Parallax "	Light yrs.	Right ascen. h m	Declination ° '	Star	Magnitude	Parallax "	Light yrs.	Right ascen. h m	Declination ° '
α Persei	1.80	0.03	570	3 24.1	49 51	γ Crucis	1.63		220	12 31.0	-57 06
α Tauri						γ Centauri	2.17		160	12 41.3	-48 56
(Aldebaran)	0.85 v	0.05	68	4 35.7	16 30	β Crucis	1.25 v		490	12 47.5	-59 40
β Orionis (Rigel)	0.12 v		900	5 14.3	-8 12	ε Ursae Majoris					
α Aurigae						(Alioth)	1.77 v	0.01	68	12 53.9	55 59
(Capella)	0.08	0.07	45	5 16.3	46 00	ζ Ursae Majoris					
γ Orionis (Bellatrix)	1.64	0.03	470	5 24.9	6 21	(Mizar)	2.05	0.04	88	13 23.8	54 57
β Tauri (El Nath)	1.65	0.02	300	5 26.1	28 36	α Virginis (Spica)	0.97 v	0.02	220	13 25.0	-11 09
δ Orionis	2.23 v		1500	5 31.8	-0 18	ε Centauri	2.30 v		570	13 39.7	-53 27
ε Orionis	1.70		1600	5 36.0	-1 12	η Ursae Majoris					
ζ Orionis	2.05	0.02	1600	5 40.6	-1 57	(Alkaid)	1.86		210	13 47.4	49 20
κ Orionis	2.06	0.01	2100	5 47.6	-9 40	β Centauri	0.61 v	0.02	490	14 03.6	-60 21
α Orionis						θ Centauri	2.06	0.06	55	14 06.5	-36 21
(Betelgeuse)	0.50 v		520	5 55.0	7 24	α Bootis					
β Aurigae	1.90	0.04	88	5 59.3	44 57	(Arcturus)	-0.04	0.09	36	14 15.5	19 12
β Canis Majoris	1.98	0.01	750	6 22.5	-17 57	η Centauri	2.31 v		390	14 35.3	-42 09
α Carinae						α Centauri	-0.01	0.75	4.3	14 39.4	-60 49
(Canopus)	-0.72	0.02	98	6 23.9	-52 42	α Lupi	2.30 v		430	14 41.7	-47 22
γ Geminorum	1.93	0.03	105	6 37.5	16 24	ε Bootis	2.40	0.01	103	14 44.8	27 05
α Canis Majoris						β Ursae Minoris	2.08	0.03	105	14 50.7	74 10
(Sirius)	-1.46	0.38	8.7	6 45.0	-16 43	α Coronae Bo-					
ε Canis Majoris	1.50		680	6 58.5	-28 58	realis	2.23 v	0.04	76	15 34.5	26 44
δ Canis Majoris	1.86		2100	7 08.2	-26 23	δ Scorpii	2.32		590	16 00.1	-22 37
η Canis Majoris	2.44		2700	7 24.0	-29 18	α Scorpii					
α Geminorum						(Antares)	0.96 v	0.02	520	16 29.2	-26 25
(Castor)	1.99	0.07	45	7 34.3	31 54	α Trianguli Aus-					
α Canis Minoris						tralis	1.92	0.02	82	16 48.3	-69 01
(Procyon)	0.38	0.29	11.3	7 39.1	5 14	ε Scorpii	2.29	0.05	66	16 49.9	-34 17
β Geminorum						η Ophiuchi	2.43	0.05	69	17 10.2	-15 43
(Pollux)	1.14	0.09	35	7 45.1	28 02	λ Scorpii	1.63 v		310	17 33.4	-37 06
ζ Puppis	2.25		2400	8 03.5	-40 00	α Ophiuchi	2.08	0.06	58	17 34.8	12 34
γ Velorum	1.82		520	8 09.4	-47 20	θ Scorpii	1.87	0.02	650	17 37.1	-43 00
ε Carinae	1.86		340	8 22.4	-59 30	κ Scorpii	2.41 v		470	17 42.2	-39 02
δ Velorum	1.96	0.04	76	8 44.6	-54 42	γ Draconis	2.23	0.02	108	17 56.5	51 29
λ Velorum	2.21	0.02	750	9 07.9	-43 25	ε Sagittarii	1.85	0.02	124	18 23.9	-34 23
β Carinae	1.68	0.04	86	9 13.2	-69 42	α Lyrae (Vega)	0.03	0.12	26.5	18 36.8	38 47
ι Carinae	2.25		750	9 17.0	-59 16	σ Sagittarii	2.02		300	18 55.0	-26 18
κ Velorum	2.50	0.01	470	9 22.0	-55 00	α Aquilae					
α Hydrae	1.98	0.02	94	9 27.4	-8 39	(Altair)	0.77	0.20	16.5	19 50.6	8 52
α Leonis (Regulus)	1.35	0.04	84	10 08.2	11 59	γ Cygni	2.20		750	20 22.1	40 15
γ Leonis	1.90	0.02	90	10 19.8	19 54	α Pavonis	1.94		310	20 25.4	-56 45
β Ursae Majoris						α Cygni (Deneb)	1.25		1600	20 41.3	45 16
(Merak)	2.37	0.04	78	11 01.6	56 24	ε Cygni	2.46	0.04	74	20 46.1	33 57
α Ursae Majoris						α Cephei	2.44	0.06	52	21 18.5	62 34
(Dubhe)	1.79	0.03	105	11 03.5	61 47	ε Pegasi	2.39		780	21 44.0	9 52
β Leonis						α Gruis	1.74	0.05	64	22 08.0	-46 59
(Denebola)	2.14	0.08	43	11 48.9	14 35	β Gruis	2.11 v		280	22 42.5	-46 54
γ Ursae Majoris						α Piscis Austrinis					
(Phecda)	2.44	0.02	90	11 53.6	53 43	(Fomalhaut)	1.16	0.14	22.6	22 57.5	-29 39
α Crucis	1.58		370	12 26.4	-63 05	β Pegasi	2.42 v	0.02	210	23 03.6	28 04
						α Pegasi	2.49	0.03	109	23 04.6	15 11

Astronomical Constants; Speed of Light

The following were adopted in 1968, in accordance with the resolutions and recommendations of the International Astronomical Union (Hamburg 1964): **Speed of light**, 299,792.5 kilometers per second, or about 186,282.3976 statute miles per second; **solar parallax**, 8".794; **constant of nutation**, 9".210; and **constant of aberration**, 20".496.

Constellations

Culturally, constellations are imagined patterns among the stars that, in some cases, have been recognized through millenia of tradition. In the early days of astronomy, knowledge of the constellations was necessary in order to function as an astronomer. For today's astronomers, constellations are simply areas on the entire sky in which interesting objects await observation and interpretation.

Because western culture has prevailed in establishing modern science, equally viable and interesting constellations and celestial traditions of other cultures (of Asia or Africa, for example) are not well known outside their regions of origin. Even the patterns with which we are most familiar today have undergone considerable change over the centuries, because the western heritage em-braces teachings of cultures disparate in time as well as place.

Today, students of the sky the world over recognize 88 constellations that cover the entire celestial sphere. Many of these have their origins in ancient days; many are "modern," contrived out of unformed stars by astronomers a few centuries ago. Unformed stars were those usually too faint or inconveniently placed to be included in depicting the more prominent constellations.

When astronomers began to travel to South Africa in the 16th and 17th centuries, they found a sky that itself was unformed and showing numerous brilliant stars. Thus, we find constellations in the southern hemisphere like the "air pump," the "microscope," the "furnace," and other technological marvels of the time, as well as some arguably traditional forms, such as the "fly."

Many of the commonly recognized constellations had their origins in ancient Asia Minor—Syria, Babylon, etc. These were adopted by the Greeks and Romans, who translated their names and stories into their own languages, modifying some details in the process. After the declines of these cultures, most such knowledge entered oral tradition or remained hidden in monastic libraries. Beginning in the 8th century, the Muslim explosion spread through the Mediterranean world. Wherever possible, everything was translated into Arabic to be taught in the universities the Muslims established all over their new-found world.

In the 13th century, Alphonsus XX of Spain, an avid student of astronomy, succeeded in having Claudius Ptolemy's *Almagest,* as its Arabian title was known, translated into Latin. It thus became widely available to European scholars. In the process, the constellation names were translated, but the star names were retained in their Arabic forms. Transliterating Arabic into the Roman alphabet has never been an exact art, so many of the star names we use today only "seem" Arabic to all but scholars.

Names of stars often indicated what parts of the traditional figures they represented: Deneb, the tail of the swan; Betelgeuse, the armpit of the giant. Thus, the names were an indication of the position in the sky of a particular star, provided one recognized the traditional form of the mythic figure.

In English, usage of the Latin names for the constellations couples often inconceivable creatures, represented in unimaginable configurations, with names that often seem unintelligible. Avoiding traditional names, astronomers may designate the brighter stars in a constellation with Greek letters, usually in order of brightness. Thus, the "alpha star" is often the brightest star of that constellation. The "of" implies possession, so the genitive (possessive) form of the constellation name is used, as in Alpha Orionis, the first star of Orion (Betelgeuse). Astronomers usually use a 3-letter form for the constellation name, understanding it to be read as either the nominative or genitive case of the name.

Until the 1920s, astronomers used curved boundaries for the constellation areas. As these were rather arbitrary at best, the International Astronomical Union adopted boundaries that ran due north-south and east-west, filling the sky much as the contiguous states fill up the area of the "lower 48" United States.

Within these boundaries, and occasionally crossing them, popular "asterisms" are recognized: the Big Dipper is a small part of Ursa Major, the big bear; the Sickle is the traditional head and mane of Leo, the lion; one of the horntips of Taurus, the bull, properly belongs to Auriga, the charioteer; the northeast star of the Great Square of Pegasus is Alpha Andromedae.

It is unlikely that further change will occur in the realm of the celestial constellations.

Name	Genitive	Abbre-viation	Meaning
Andromeda	Andromedae	And	Chained Maiden
Antlia	Antliae	Ant	Air Pump
Apus	Apodis	Aps	Bird of Paradise
Aquarius	Aquarii	Aqr	Water Bearer
Aquila	Aquilae	Aql	Eagle
Ara	Arae	Ara	Altar
Aries	Arietis	Ari	Ram
Auriga	Aurigae	Aur	Charioteer
Bootes	Bootis	Boo	Herdsmen
Caelum	Caeli	Cae	Chisel
Camelopardalis	Camelopardalis	Cam	Giraffe

Name	Genitive	Abbre-viation	Meaning
Cancer	Cancri	Cnc	Crab
Canes Venatici	Canum Venaticorum	CVn	Hunting Dogs
Canis Major	Canis Majoris	CMa	Great Dog
Canis Minor	Canis Minoris	CMi	Little Dog
Capricornus	Capricorni	Cap	Sea-goat
Carina	Carinae	Car	Keel
Cassiopeia	Cassiopeiae	Cas	Queen
Centaurus	Centauri	Cen	Centaur
Cepheus	Cephei	Cep	King
Cetus	Ceti	Cet	Whale
Chamaeleon	Chamaeleontis	Cha	Chameleon
Circinus	Circini	Cir	Compasses (art)
Columba	Columbae	Col	Dove
Coma Berenices	Comae Berenices	Com	Berenice's Hair
Corona Australis	Coronae Australis	CrA	Southern Crown
Corona Borealis	Coronae Borealis	CrB	Northern Crown
Corvus	Corvi	Crv	Crow
Crater	Crateris	Crt	Cup
Crux	Crucis	Cru	Cross (southern)
Cygnus	Cygni	Cyg	Swan
Delphinus	Delphini	Del	Dolphin
Dorado	Doradus	Dor	Goldfish
Draco	Draconis	Dra	Dragon
Equuleus	Equulei	Equ	Little Horse
Eridanus	Eridani	Eri	River
Fornax	Fornacis	For	Furnace
Gemini	Geminorum	Gem	Twins
Grus	Gruis	Gru	Crane (bird)
Hercules	Herculis	Her	Hercules
Horologium	Horologii	Hor	Clock
Hydra	Hydrae	Hya	Water Snake (female)
Hydrus	Hydri	Hyi	Water Snake (male)
Indus	Indi	Ind	Indian
Lacerta	Lacertae	Lac	Lizard
Leo	Leonis	Leo	Lion
Leo Minor	Leonis Minoris	LMi	Little Lion
Lepus	Leporis	Lep	Hare
Libra	Librae	Lib	Balance
Lupus	Lupi	Lup	Wolf
Lynx	Lyncis	Lyn	Lynx
Lyra	Lyrae	Lyr	Lyre
Mensa	Mensae	Men	Table Mountain
Microscopium	Microscopii	Mic	Microscope
Monoceros	Monocerotis	Mon	Unicorn
Musca	Muscae	Mus	Fly
Norma	Normae	Nor	Square (rule)
Octans	Octantis	Oct	Octant
Ophiuchus	Ophiuchi	Oph	Serpent Bearer
Orion	Orionis	Ori	Hunter
Pavo	Pavonis	Pav	Peacock
Pegasus	Pegasi	Peg	Flying Horse
Perseus	Persei	Per	Hero
Phoenix	Phoenicis	Phe	Phoenix
Pictor	Pictoris	Pic	Painter
Pisces	Piscium	Psc	Fishes
Piscis Austrinius	Piscis Austrini	PsA	Southern Fish
Puppis	Puppis	Pup	Stern (deck)
Pyxis	Pyxidis	Pyx	Compass (sea)
Reticulum	Reticuli	Ret	Reticle
Sagitta	Sagittae	Sge	Arrow
Sagittarius	Sagittarii	Sgr	Archer
Scorpius	Scorpii	Sco	Scorpion
Sculptor	Sculptoris	Scl	Sculptor
Scutum	Scuti	Sct	Shield
Serpens	Serpentis	Ser	Serpent
Sextans	Sextantis	Sex	Sextant
Taurus	Tauri	Tau	Bull
Telescopium	Telescopii	Tel	Telescope
Triangulum	Trianguli	Tri	Triangle
Triangulum Australe	Trianguli Australis	TrA	Southern Triangle
Tucana	Tucanae	Tuc	Toucan
Ursa Major	Ursae Majoris	UMa	Great Bear
Ursa Minor	Ursae Minoris	UMi	Little Bear
Vela	Velorum	Vel	Sail
Virgo	Virginis	Vir	Maiden
Volans	Volantis	Vol	Flying Fish
Vulpecula	Vulpeculae	Vul	Fox

Aurora Borealis and Aurora Australis

The Aurora Borealis, also called the Northern Lights, is a broad display of rather faint light in the northern skies at night. The Aurora Australis, a similar phenomenon, appears at the same time in southern skies. The aurora appears in a wide variety of forms. Sometimes it is seen as a quiet glow, almost foglike in character; sometimes as vertical streamers in which there may be considerable motion; sometimes as a series of luminous expanding arcs. There are many colors, with white, yellow, and red predominating.

The auroras are most vivid and most frequently seen at about 20 degrees from the magnetic poles, along the northern coast of the North American continent and the eastern part of the northern coast of Europe. The Aurora Borealis has been seen as far south as Key West, and the Aurora Australis has been seen as far north as Australia and New Zealand. Such occurences are rare, however.

Although the cause of the auroras is not known beyond question, there does seem to be a definite correlation between auroral displays and sunspot activity. It is thought that atomic particles expelled from the sun by the forces that cause solar flares speed through space at velocities of 400 to 600 miles per second. These particles are entrapped by the earth's magnetic field, forming what are termed the Van Allen belts. The encounter of these clouds of the solar wind with the earth's magnetic field weakens the field so that previously trapped particles are allowed to impact the upper atmosphere. The collisions between solar and terrestrial atoms result in the glow in the upper atmosphere called the aurora. The glow may be vivid where the lines of magnetic force converge near the magnetic poles.

The auroral displays appear at heights ranging from 50 to about 600 miles and have given us a means of estimating the extent of the earth's atmosphere.

The auroras are often accompanied by magnetic storms whose forces, also guided by the lines of force of the earth's magnetic field, disrupt electrical communication.

Eclipses, 1996

(Greenwich Mean Time)

There are four eclipses, two of the Sun and two of the Moon.

I. Total eclipse of the Moon, April 3-4.

The beginning of the umbral phase is visible in extreme eastern North America, South America, (except for the northwest and west coast), southern and eastern Greenland, Europe, Africa, western and central Asia, the extreme western coast of Australia, parts of Antarctica, most of the North Atlantic Ocean, the South Atlantic Ocean, and the Indian Ocean. The end of the umbral phase is visible in eastern and central regions of the United States and Canada, most of Mexico, Central America, South America, Greenland, Europe, Africa, western Asia, parts of Antarctica, the eastern South Pacific Ocean, the Atlantic Ocean, and the western Indian Ocean.

Circumstances of the Eclipse

Event	Date		h	m
Moon enters penumbra	April	3	21	15.7
Moon enters umbra		3	22	20.9
Moon enters totality		3	23	26.5
Middle of eclipse		4	0	9.7
Moon leaves totality		4	0	53.0
Moon leaves umbra		4	1	58.7
Moon leaves penumbra		4	3	3.7

Magnitude of the eclipse: 1.38

II. Partial eclipse of the Sun, April 17-18.

This partial solar eclipse is visible in most of New Zealand, parts of Antarctica, and some of the southern South Pacific Ocean.

Circumstances of the Eclipse

Event	Date		h	m
Eclipse begins	April	17	20	31.4
Greatest eclipse		17	22	37.2
Eclipse ends		18	0	43.3

Magnitude of greatest eclipse: 0.88.

III. Total eclipse of the Moon, September 27.

The beginning of the umbral phase of this eclipse is visible in eastern and central regions of the United States and Canada, most of Mexico, Central America, South America, Greenland, Europe, Africa, western Asia, parts of Antarctica, the eastern South Pacific Ocean, the Atlantic Ocean, and the western half of the Indian Ocean. The end is visible in North America (except the extreme western part of Alaska), Hawaii, Central America, South America, the western half of Africa, Europe (except for the extreme east), Greenland, parts of Antarctica, the eastern Pacific Ocean, and the Atlantic Ocean.

Circumstances of the Eclipse

Event	Date		h	m
Moon enters penumbra	Sept.	27	0	12.4
Moon enters umbra		27	1	12.3
Moon enters totality		27	2	19.3
Middle of eclipse		27	2	54.4
Moon leaves totality		27	3	29.4
Moon leaves umbra		27	4	36.3
Moon leaves penumbra		27	5	36.4

Magnitude of the eclipse: 1.24.

IV. Partial eclipse of the Sun, October 12.

This partial solar eclipse is visible from Europe, northern Arabian peninsula, North Africa, most of the North Atlantic Ocean, most of Greenland, and northeast Canada.

Circumstances of the Eclipse

Event	Date		h	m
Eclipse begins	Oct.	12	11	59.5
Greatest eclipse		12	14	2.0
Eclipse ends		12	16	4.8

Magnitude of greatest eclipse: 0.76.

The Planets: Motion, Distance, and Brightness

Planet	Mean daily motion "	Orbital velocity miles per sec.	Sidereal revolution days	Synodical revolution days	Distance from sun in millions of mi Max.	Min.	Dist. from Earth in millions of mi Max.	Min.	Light at[1] peri-helion	aphe-helion
Mercury....	14732	29.75	88.0	115.9	43.4	28.6	136	50	10.58	4.59
Venus....	5768	21.76	224.7	583.9	67.7	66.8	161	25	1.94	1.89
Earth......	3548	18.51	365.3	—	94.6	91.4	—	—	1.03	0.97
Mars......	1886	14.99	687.0	779.9	155.0	128.5	248	35	0.524	0.360
Jupiter....	299	8.12	4331.8	398.9	507.0	460.6	600	368	0.0408	0.0333
Saturn.....	120	5.99	10760.0	378.1	937.5	838.4	1031	745	0.01230	0.00984
Uranus	42	4.23	30684.0	369.7	1859.7	1669.3	1953	1606	0.00300	0.00250
Neptune ...	21	3.38	60188.3	367.5	2821.7	2760.4	2915	2667	0.00114	0.00109
Pluto......	14	2.95	90466.8	366.7	4551.4	2756.4	4644	2663	0.00114	0.00042

(1) Light at perihelion and aphelion is solar illumination in units of mean illumination at earth.

Orbital Elements of the Planets, 1996

Planet	Mean longitude of:[1] ascending node ° ' "	perihelion ° ' "	Inclination[1] of orbit to ecliptic ° ' "	Mean[1] distance[2]	Eccentricity[1] of orbit	Mean longitude at the epoch[1] ° ' "
Mercury ...	48 17 37	77 24 26	7 0 18	0.387098	0.205631	248 31 31
Venus	76 39 6	131 31 11	3 23 41	0.723330	0.006773	148 17 52
Earth.....	0 0 0	102 53 0	0 0 0	1.000001	0.016710	52 23 35
Mars.....	49 32 2	336 0 9	1 50 59	1.523679	0.093398	115 38 2
Jupiter....	100 25 57	14 16 51	1 18 12	5.202603	0.048490	299 12 35
Saturn	113 38 17	92 59 43	2 29 20	9.554910	0.055519	371 44 21
Uranus ...	73 59 23	172 57 31	0 46 23	19.218446	0.046297	300 35 7
Neptune ...	131 44 58	48 4 44	1 46 13	30.110387	0.008988	297 27 31
Pluto[3]	110 05 49	223 35 53	17 09 44	39.469800	0.248646	244 33 30

(1) Consistent for the standard epoch: 1996 November 13, Ephemeris Time. (2) Astronomical units. (3) Consistent for the standard epoch: 1990 April 19 Ephemeris Time.

Planets and the Sun, by Selected Characteristics

Sun and planets	Semi-diameter at unit dis-tance ' "	at mean least dist. ' "	in miles mean s.d.	Volume ⊕=1	Mass ⊕=1	Den -sity ⊕=1	Sidereal period of rotation d h m s	Gravity at sur-face ⊕=1	Re-flect-ing power Pct.	Prob-able tem perature °F
Sun..........	959.62	——	432449	1299370	332946	0.26	24 16 48	27.90	——	+10,000
Mercury.......	3.37	5.5	1515	0.0559	0.0553	1.00	58 15 30	0.37	0.11	+620
Venus........	8.34	30.1	3760	0.8541	0.8150	0.97	243 R	0.88	0.65	+900
Earth.........	—	—	3963	1.000	1.000	1.00	23 56 6.7	1.00	0.37	+72
Moon.........	2.40	932.4	1080	0.020	0.0123	0.62	27 7 43	0.17	0.12	−10
Mars.........	4.69	8.95	2108.5	0.1506	0.1074	0.73	24 37 26	0.38	0.15	−10
Jupiter........	98.35	23.4	44419	1403	317.89	0.25	9 3 30	2.64	0.52	−240
Saturn........	82.83	9.7	37448	832	95.18	0.13	10 39 22	1.15	0.47	−300
Uranus	35.4	1.9	15881	63	14.54	0.23	17 14 R	1.15	0.40	−340
Neptune	33.4	1.2	15387	55	17.15	0.30	16 6	1.12	0.35	−370
Pluto.........	1.9	0.05	714	0.006	0.0020	0.37	6 9 17	0.04	0.5	?

R = Retrograde of Venus and Uranus.

The Sun

The sun, the controlling body of the earth's solar system, is a star whose dimensions cause it to be classified among stars as average in size, temperature, and brightness. Its proximity to the earth makes it appear tremendously large and bright. A series of thermonuclear reactions involving the atoms of the elements of which it is composed produces the heat and light that make life possible on earth.

The sun has a diameter of 864,000 miles and is distant, on the average, 92,900,000 miles from the earth. It is 1.41 times as dense as water. The light of the sun reaches the earth in 499.012 seconds, or in slightly more than 8 minutes. The average solar surface temperature has been measured by several indirect methods that agree closely on a value of 6,000 Kelvin, or about 10,000° F. The interior temperature of the sun is about 35,000,000° F.

When sunlight is analyzed with a spectroscope, it is found to consist of a continuous spectrum composed of all the colors of the rainbow in order, crossed by many dark lines. The "absorption lines" are produced by gaseous materials in the atmosphere of the sun. More than 60 of the natural terrestrial elements have been identified in the sun, all in gaseous form because of the intense heat of the sun.

Spheres and Corona

The radiating surface of the sun is called the **photosphere,** and just above it is the **chromosphere**. The chromosphere is visible to the naked eye only at times of total solar eclipses, appearing then to be a pinkish-violet layer with occasional great prominences projecting above its general level. With proper instruments the chromosphere can be seen or photographed whenever the sun is visible without waiting for a total eclipse. Above the chromosphere is the corona, also visible to the naked eye only at times of total eclipse. Instruments also permit the brighter portions of the **corona** to be studied whenever conditions are favorable. The pearly light of the corona surges millions of miles from the sun. Iron, nickel, and calcium are believed to be principal contributors to the composition of the corona, all in a state of extreme attenuation and high ionization that indicates temperatures on the order of a million degrees Fahrenheit.

Sunspots

There is an intimate connection between sunspots and the corona. At times of low sunspot activity, the fine streamers of the corona are longer above the sun's equator than over the polar regions of the sun; during high sunspot activity, the corona extends fairly evenly outward from all regions of the sun, but to a much greater distance in space. Sunspots are dark, irregularly shaped regions whose diameters may reach tens of thousands of miles. The average life of a sunspot group is from 2 to 3 weeks, but some sunspot groups have lasted for more than a year by being carried repeatedly around as the sun rotated upon its axis.

The record for the duration of a sunspot is 18 months. Sunspots reach a low point every 11.3 years, with a peak of activity occurring irregularly between 2 successive minima.

The sun is 400,000 times as bright as the full moon and gives the earth 6 million times as much light as do all the other stars put together. Actually, most of the stars that can be easily seen on any clear night are brighter than the sun.

The Zodiac

The sun's apparent yearly path among the stars is known as the **ecliptic.** The zone, 16° wide, 8° on each side of the ecliptic, is known as the **zodiac.** Inside this zone are the apparent paths of the sun, moon, earth, and major planets. Beginning at the point on the ecliptic that marks the position of the sun at the vernal equinox and proceeding eastward, the zodiac is divided into 12 signs of 30° each, as shown here.

These signs are named from the 12 constellations of the zodiac with which the signs coincided in the time of the astronomer Hipparchus, about 2,000 years ago. Owing to the precession of the equinoxes, that is to say, to the retrograde motion of the equinoxes along the ecliptic, each sign in the zodiac has, in the course of 2,000 years, moved backward 30° into the constellation west of it; the sign Aries is now in the constellation Pisces, for example, and so on.

The vernal equinox will move from Pisces into Aquarius about the middle of the 26th century. The signs of the zodiac with their Latin and English names are as follows:

Spring	1.	♈	Aries	The Ram
	2.	♉	Taurus	The Bull
	3.	♊	Gemini	The Twins
Summer	4.	♋	Cancer	The Crab
	5.	♌	Leo	The Lion
	6.	♍	Virgo	The Virgin
Autumn	7.	♎	Libra	The Balance
	8.	♏	Scorpius	The Scorpion
	9.	♐	Sagittarius	The Archer
Winter	10.	♑	Capricorn	The Goat
	11.	♒	Aquarius	The Water Bearer
	12.	♓	Pisces	The Fishes

The Moon

The moon completes a circuit around the earth in a period whose mean or average duration is 27 days, 7 hours, 43.2 minutes. This is the moon's **sidereal period.** Because of the motion of the moon in common with the earth around the sun, the mean duration of the lunar month — the period from one new moon to the next new moon — is 29 days, 12 hours, 44.05 minutes. This is the moon's **synodical period.**

The mean distance of the moon from the earth according to the American Ephemeris is 238,857 miles. Because the orbit of the moon about the earth is not circular but elliptical, however, the maximum distance from the earth that the moon may reach is 252,710 miles and the least distance is 221,463 miles. All distances are from the center of one object to the center of the other.

The moon's diameter is 2,160 miles. If we deduct the radius of the moon, 1,080 miles, and the radius of the earth, 3,963 miles, from the minimum distance, or **perigee,** we shall have for the nearest approach of the bodies' surfaces 216,420 miles.

The moon rotates on its axis in a period of time that is exactly equal to its sidereal revolution about the earth — 27.321666 days. The moon's revolution about the earth is irregular because of its elliptical orbit. The moon's rotation, however, is regular, and this, together with the irregular revolution, produces what is called "libration in longitude," which permits us to see first farther around the east side

and then farther around the west side of the moon. The moon's variation north or south of the ecliptic permits us to see farther over first one pole and then the other of the moon; this is called "libration in latitude." These two libration effects permit us to see a total of about 60% of the moon's surface over a period of time. The hidden side of the moon was photographed in 1959 by the Soviet space vehicle *Lunik III.* Since then, many excellent pictures of nearly all of the moon's surface have been transmitted to earth by Lunar Orbiters launched by the U.S.

The tides are caused mainly by the moon, because of its proximity to the earth. The ratio of the tide-raising power of the moon to that of the sun is 11 to 5.

Harvest Moon and Hunter's Moon

The Harvest Moon, the full moon nearest the autumnal equinox, ushers in a period of several successive days when the moon rises soon after sunset. This phenomenon gives farmers in temperate latitudes extra hours of light in which to harvest their crops before frost and winter come. The 1996 Harvest Moon falls on Sept. 27 GMT. Harvest Moon in the south temperate latitudes falls on Apr. 4.

The next full moon after Harvest Moon is called the Hunter's Moon, accompanied by a similar phenomenon but less marked. In 1996, the Hunter's Moon occurs on Oct. 26, northern hemisphere; May 3, southern hemisphere.

Moon's Perigee and Apogee, 1996

	Perigee						Apogee				
Month	**Day**	**h**	**Month**	**Day**	**h**	**Month**	**Day**	**h**	**Month**	**Day**	**h**
Jan.	19	18	July	30	3	Jan.	5	7	July	16	9
Feb.	17	4	Aug.	27	12	Feb.	1	11	Aug.	12	11
Mar.	16	1	Sept.	24	17	Feb.	29	2	Sept.	8	21
Apr.	10	22	Oct.	22	4	Mar.	27	22	Oct.	6	13
May	6	17	Nov.	16	0	Apr.	24	17	Nov.	3	9
June	3	11	Dec.	12	23	May	22	11	Dec.	1	6
July	1	17				June	19	1	Dec.	29	0

Moon Phases, 1996

(Eastern Standard Time)

Month	New Moon d	h	m	Month	First Quarter d	h	m	Month	Full Moon d	h	m	Month	Last Quarter d	h	m
Jan.	20	7	50	Jan.	27	6	14	Jan.	5	15	51	Jan.	13	15	45
Feb.	18	18	30	Feb.	26	0	52	Feb.	4	10	58	Feb.	12	3	37
Mar.	19	5	45	Mar.	26	20	31	Mar.	5	4	23	Mar.	12	12	15
Apr.	17	17	49	Apr.	25	15	40	Apr.	3	19	7	Apr.	10	18	36
May	17	6	46	May	25	9	13	May	3	6	48	May	10	0	4
June	15	20	36	June	24	0	23	June	1	15	47	June	8	6	5
July	15	11	15	July	23	12	49	June	30	22	58	July	7	13	55
Aug.	14	2	34	Aug.	21	22	36	July	30	5	35	Aug.	6	0	25
Sept.	12	18	7	Sept.	20	6	23	Aug.	28	12	52	Sept.	4	14	6
Oct.	12	9	14	Oct.	19	13	9	Sept.	26	21	51	Oct.	4	7	4
Nov.	10	23	16	Nov.	17	20	9	Oct.	26	9	11	Nov.	3	2	50
Dec.	10	11	56	Dec.	17	4	31	Nov.	24	23	10	Dec.	3	0	6
								Dec.	24	15	41				

The Earth: Size, Computation of Time, Seasons

Size and Dimensions

The earth is the 5th largest planet and the 3d from the sun. Its mass is 6 sextillion, 588 quintillion short tons. Using the parameters of an ellipsoid adopted by the International Astronomical Union in 1964 and recognized by the International Union of Geodesy and Geophysics in 1967, the length of the equator is 24,901.55 miles, the length of a meridian is 24,859.82 miles, the equatorial diameter is 7,926.41 miles, and the area of this reference ellipsoid is approximately 196,938,800 square miles.

The earth is considered a solid, rigid mass with a dense core of magnetic, probably metallic material. The outer part of the core is probably liquid. Around the core is a thick shell or mantle of heavy crystalline rock that in turn is covered by a thin crust forming the solid granite and basalt base of the continents and ocean basins. Over broad areas of the earth's surface the crust has a thin cover of sedimentary rock such as sandstone, shale, and limestone formed by weathering of the earth's surface and deposition of sands, clays, and plant and animal remains.

The temperature in the earth increases about 1° F with every 100 to 200 feet in depth, in the upper 100 kilometers of the earth, and the temperature near the core is believed to be near the melting point of the core materials under the conditions at that depth. The heat of the earth is believed to be derived from radioactivity in the rocks, pressures developed within the earth, and the original heat of formation.

Atmosphere of the Earth

The earth's atmosphere is a blanket composed of nitrogen, oxygen, and argon, in amounts of about 78%, 21%, and 1% by volume. Also present in minute quantities are carbon dioxide, hydrogen, neon, helium, krypton, and xenon.

Water vapor displaces other gases and varies from nearly zero to about 4% by volume. The height of the ozone layer varies from approximately 12 to 21 miles above the earth. Traces exist as low as 6 miles and as high as 35 miles. Traces of methane have been found.

The atmosphere rests on the earth's surface with the weight equivalent to a layer of water 34 ft deep. For about 300,000 ft upward the gases remain in the proportions stated. Gravity holds the gases to the earth.

The weight of the air compresses it at the bottom so that the greatest density is at the earth's surface. Pressure, as well as density, decreases as height increases because the weight pressing upon any layer is always less than that pressing upon the layers below.

The temperature of the air drops with increased height until the **tropopause** is reached. This may vary from 25,000 to 60,000 ft. The atmosphere below the tropopause is the **troposphere;** the atmosphere for about 20 miles above the tropopause is the **stratosphere,** where the temperature generally increases with height except at high latitudes in winter. A temperature maximum near the 30-mile level is called the **stratopause.** Above this boundary is the **mesosphere,** where the temperature decreases with height to a minimum, the **mesopause,** at a height of 50 miles. Extending above the mesosphere to the outer fringes of the atmosphere is the **thermosphere,** a region where temperature increases with height to a value measured in thousands of degrees Fahrenheit. The lower portion of this region, extending from 50 to about 400 miles in altitude, is characterized by a high ion density and is thus called the **ionosphere.** The outer region is called the **exosphere;** this is the region where gas molecules traveling at high speed may escape into outer space, above 600 miles.

Latitude, Longitude

Position on the globe is measured by means of meridians and parallels. Meridians, which are imaginary lines drawn around the earth through the poles, determine **longitude.** The meridian running through Greenwich, England, is the **prime meridian of longitude,** and all others are either east or west. Parallels, which are imaginary circles parallel with the equator, determine **latitude.** The length of a degree of longitude varies as the cosine of the latitude. At the equator a degree is 69.171 statute miles; this is gradually reduced toward the poles. Value of a longitude degree at the poles is zero.

Latitude is reckoned by the number of degrees north or south of the equator, an imaginary circle on the earth's surface everywhere equidistant between the two poles. According to the International Astronomical Union ellipsoid of 1964, the length of a degree of latitude is 68.708 statute miles at the equator and varies slightly north and south because of the oblate form of the globe; at the poles it is 69.403 statute miles.

Definitions of Time

The earth rotates on its axis and follows an elliptical orbit around the sun. The rotation makes the sun appear to move across the sky from East to West. It determines day and night, and the complete rotation, in relation to the sun, is called the **apparent** or **true solar day.** This varies, but an average determines the **mean solar day** of 24 hours.

The mean solar day is in universal use for civil purposes. It may be obtained from apparent solar time by correcting observations of the sun for the equation of time, but when high precision is required, the mean solar time is calculated from its relation to sidereal time. These relations are extremely complicated, but for most practical uses, they may be considered as follows:

Sidereal time is the measure of time defined by the diurnal motion of the vernal equinox and is determined from observation of the meridian transits of stars. One complete rotation of the earth relative to the equinox is called the **sidereal day.** The **mean sidereal day** is 23 hours, 56 minutes, 4.091 seconds of mean solar time.

The **Calendar Year** begins at 12 o'clock midnight precisely local clock time, on the night of Dec. 31-Jan. 1. The day and the calendar month also begin at midnight by the clock. The interval required for the earth to make one absolute revolution around the sun is a **sidereal year;** it consisted of 365 days, 6 hours, 9 minutes, and 9.5 seconds of mean solar time (approximately 24 hours per day) in 1900 and is increasing at the rate of 0.0001 second annually.

The **Tropical Year,** on which the return of the seasons depends, is the interval between 2 consecutive returns of the sun to the vernal equinox. The tropical year consisted of 365 days, 5 hours, 48 minutes, and 46 seconds in 1900. It is decreasing at the rate of 0.530 second per century.

In 1956 the unit of time interval was defined to be identical with the second of **Ephemeris Time,** 1/31,556,925.9747 of the tropical year for 1900 January 0d 12th hour E.T. A physical definition of the second based on a quantum transition of cesium (atomic second) was adopted in 1964. The atomic second is equal to 9,192,631,770 cycles of the emitted radiation. In 1967 this atomic second was adopted as the unit of time interval for the International System of Units.

The Zones and Seasons

The 5 zones of the earth's surface are Torrid, lying between the Tropics of Cancer and Capricorn; North Temperate, between Cancer and the Arctic Circle; South Temperate, between Capricorn and the Antarctic Circle; the Frigid Zones, between the polar Circles and the Poles.

The inclination or tilt of the earth's axis with respect to the sun determines the seasons. These are commonly marked in the North Temperate Zone, where spring begins at the vernal equinox, summer at the summer solstice, autumn at the autumnal equinox, and winter at the winter solstice.

In the South Temperate Zone, the seasons are reversed. Spring begins at the autumnal equinox, summer at the winter solstice, etc.

If the earth's axis were perpendicular to the plane of the earth's orbit around the sun, there would be no change of seasons. Day and night would be of nearly constant length, and there would be equable conditions of temperature. But the axis is tilted 23° 27′ away from a perpendicular to the orbit, and only in March and September is the axis at right angles to the sun.

The points at which the sun crosses the equator are the equinoxes, when day and night are most nearly equal. The points at which the sun is at a maximum distance from the equator are the solstices. Days and nights are then most unequal.

In June the North Pole is tilted 23° 27′ toward the sun, and the days in the northern hemisphere are longer than the nights, while the days in the southern hemisphere are shorter than the nights. In December the North Pole is tilted 23° 27′ away from the sun, and the situation is reversed.

The Seasons in 1996

In 1996 the 4 seasons will begin as follows: add one hour to Eastern Standard Time for Atlantic Time; subtract one hour for Central, 2 hours for Mountain, 3 hours for Pacific, 4 hours for Alaska, 5 hours for Hawaii-Aleutian. Also shown is Greenwich Mean Time.

Seasons	Date	GMT	EST
Vernal Equinox.	Mar. 20	8:03	3:03
Summer Solstice	June 21	2:24	21:24*
Autumnal Equinox	Sept. 22	17:58	12:58
Winter Solstice	Dec. 21	14:07	9:06

*Previous day.

Poles of the Earth

The geographic (rotation) poles, or points where the earth's axis of rotation cuts the surface, are not absolutely fixed in the body of the earth. The pole of rotation describes an irregular curve about its mean position.

Two periods have been detected in this motion: (1) an annual period due to seasonal changes in barometric pressure, to load of ice and snow on the surface, and to other phenomena of seasonal character; (2) a period of about 14 months due to the shape and constitution of the earth.

In addition there are small but as yet unpredictable irregularities. The whole motion is so small that the actual pole at any time remains within a circle of 30 or 40 feet in radius centered at the mean position of the pole.

The pole of rotation for the time being is of course the pole having a latitude of 90° and an indeterminate longitude.

Magnetic Poles

The **north magnetic pole** of the earth is that region where the magnetic force is vertically downward, and the **south magnetic pole** is that region where the magnetic force is vertically upward. A compass placed at the magnetic poles experiences no directive force in azimuth.

There are slow changes in the distribution of the earth's magnetic field. These changes were at one time attributed in part to a periodic movement of the magnetic poles around the geographical poles, but later evidence refutes this theory and points, rather, to a slow migration of "disturbance" foci over the earth.

There appear shifts in position of the magnetic poles due to the changes in the earth's magnetic field. The center of the area designated as the north magnetic pole was estimated to be in about latitude 70.5° N and longitude 96° W in 1905; from recent nearby measurements and studies of the secular changes, the position in 1970 was estimated as latitude 76.2° N and longitude 101° W. Improved data rather than actual motion account for at least part of the change.

The position of the south magnetic pole in 1912 was near 71° S and longitude 150° E. In 1970 it was estimated at latitude 66° S and longitude 139.1° E.

The direction of the horizontal components of the magnetic field at any point is known as magnetic north at that point, and the angle by which it deviates east or west of true north is known as the magnetic declination or, in the mariner's terminology, the **variation of the compass.**

A compass without error points in the direction of magnetic north. (In general, this is not the direction of the magnetic north pole.) If one follows the direction indicated by the north end of the compass, he or she will travel along a rather irregular curve that eventually reaches the north magnetic pole (though not usually by a great-circle route). However, the action of the compass should not be thought of as due to any influence of the distant pole, but simply as an indication of the distribution of the earth's magnetism at the place of observation.

Rotation of the Earth

The speed of rotation of the earth about its axis has been found to be slightly variable. The variations may be classified as:

(A) **Secular.** Tidal friction acts as a brake on the rotation and causes a slow secular increase in the length of the day, about 1 millisecond per century.

(B) **Irregular.** The speed of rotation may increase for a number of years, about 5 to 10, and then start decreasing. The maximum difference from the mean in the length of the day during a century is about 5 milliseconds. The accumulated difference in time has amounted to approximately 44 seconds since 1900. The cause is probably motion in the interior of the earth.

(C) **Periodic.** Seasonal variations exist with periods of 1 year and 6 months. The cumulative effect is such that each year the earth is late about 30 milliseconds near June 1 and is ahead about 30 milliseconds near Oct. 1. The maximum seasonal variation in the length of the day is about 0.5 millisecond. It is believed that the principal cause of the annual variation is the seasonal change in the wind patterns of the northern and southern hemispheres. The semiannual variation is due chiefly to tidal action of the sun, which distorts the shape of the earth slightly.

The secular and irregular variations were discovered by comparing time based on the rotation of the earth with time based on the orbital motion of the moon about the earth and of the planets about the sun. The periodic variation was determined largely with the aid of quartz-crystal clocks. The introduction of the cesium-beam atomic clock in 1955 made it possible to determine in greater detail than before the nature of the irregular and periodic variations.

Chronological Eras, 1996

The year 1996 of the Christian Era comprises the latter part of the 220th and the beginning of the 221st year of the independence of the U.S.

Era	Year	Begins in 1996	Era	Year	Begins in 1996
Byzantine	7505....	Sept. 14	Grecian (Seleucidae).........	2308	Sept. 14 or
Jewish[1]	5757....	Sept. 14			Oct. 14
Roman (Ab Urbe Condita)	2749....	Jan. 14	Diocletian.................	1713	Sept. 11
Nabonassar (Babylonian)	2745....	Apr. 24	Indian (Saka)	1918	Mar. 21
Japanese	2656....	Jan. 1	Islamic/Muslim (Hegira)[1]	1417	May 18

(1) Year begins at sunset.

Chronological Cycles, 1996

Dominical Letter..........	GF	Golden Number (Lunar Cycle)	II	Roman Indiction..........	4
Epact.................	10	Solar Cycle.............	17	Julian Period (year of)	6709

Twilight

Twilight is that evening period of waning light from the time of sunset to dark, often termed dusk. Morning twilight, a time of increasing light, is called dawn. The source of this light is the sun shining on the atmosphere above the observer. Twilight is a time of very slowly changing sky illumination with no abrupt variations. Nevertheless, there are 3 commonly accepted divisions in this smooth continuum defined by the distance the sun lies below the astronomical horizon: civil twilight, nautical twilight, and astronomical twilight. The astronomical horizon is that great circle lying 90° from the zenith, the point directly over the observer's head. Twilight ends in the evening or begins in the morning at a particular time. Nominally, evening events are repeated in reverse order in the morning.

Civil twilight is the time between the moment of sunset, when the sun's apparent upper edge is just at the horizon,

until the center of the sun is 6° directly below the horizon. In many states, this is the time in the evening when automobile headlights must be turned on, not to see better, but to be seen by other drivers. After this time, a newspaper becomes increasingly difficult to read in the absence of artificial light.

Nautical twilight ends when the sun's center is 12° below the horizon. By this time in the evening, the bright stars used by navigators have appeared, and the horizon may still be seen. After this time, the horizon is more difficult to perceive, preventing navigators from sighting stars.

Astronomical twilight ends in the evening when the sun is 18° below the horizon and when the sky is dark enough, at least away from the sun's location, to allow astronomical work to proceed. Sunlight, however, is still shining on the higher levels of the atmosphere from the observer's zenith to the horizon toward the sun. Although not named as a period of twilight, when the sun is 24° below the horizon, no part of the observer's atmosphere, even toward the sun, receives any sunlight.

In the tropics, the sun moves nearly vertically, accomplishing its 6°, 12°, or 18° depression very quickly. In the polar regions, the sun's diurnal motion may actually be nearly along the horizon, prolonging the twilight period or even not permitting darkness to fall at all. In mid-latitudes,

civil twilight may last about a half hour; nautical, an hour; and astronomers can go to work in about 90 minutes.

The twilight tables given in *The World Almanac* are for astronomical twilight and are presented for reference only. Although the instant of the sun's horizontal depression may be calculated precisely, the phenomena associated with the event are sufficiently imprecise that the table is not recalculated each year.

Astronomical Twilight—Meridian of Greenwich

Date 1993[1]	20° Begin h	m	20° End h	m	30° Begin h	m	30° End h	m	40° Begin h	m	40° End h	m	50° Begin h	m	50° End h	m	60° Begin h	m	60° End h	m
Jan. 1	5	16	6	50	5	30	6	35	5	45	6	21	6	00	6	07	6	18	5	49
11	5	19	6	56	5	33	6	43	5	46	6	30	6	00	6	17	6	15	6	01
21	5	21	7	01	5	32	6	51	5	43	6	40	5	55	6	30	6	06	6	18
Feb. 1	5	21	7	07	5	29	6	58	5	38	6	51	5	45	6	44	5	51	6	38
11	5	18	7	11	5	24	7	05	5	29	7	01	5	32	6	59	5	32	7	01
21	5	13	7	15	5	17	7	12	5	17	7	12	5	16	7	14	5	09	7	23
Mar. 1	5	08	7	18	5	08	7	19	5	06	7	21	4	59	7	29	4	44	7	45
11	5	00	7	21	4	58	7	24	4	50	7	32	4	38	7	46	4	12	8	12
21	4	52	7	24	4	45	7	32	4	33	7	44	4	14	8	04	3	37	8	43
Apr. 1	4	42	7	28	4	31	7	39	4	14	7	57	3	47	8	25	2	53	9	21
11	4	32	7	32	4	18	7	47	3	56	8	09	3	20	8	47	2	03	10	10
21	4	23	7	36	4	04	7	54	3	37	8	23	2	52	9	11	0	37	11	47
May 1	4	14	7	41	3	52	8	04	3	19	8	37	2	22	9	39				
11	4	08	7	46	3	41	8	13	3	03	8	53	1	49	10	09				
21	4	02	7	52	3	32	8	22	2	48	9	07	1	13	10	46				
June 1	3	58	7	58	3	26	8	30	2	36	9	20	0	21	11	52				
11	3	56	8	03	3	22	8	36	2	29	9	30								
21	3	57	8	06	3	22	8	40	2	28	9	35								
July 1	3	59	8	07	3	25	8	41	2	30	9	35								
11	4	03	8	06	3	30	8	39	2	40	9	30								
21	4	08	8	03	3	39	8	33	2	52	9	18	1	12	11	23				
Aug. 1	4	15	7	56	3	48	8	23	3	09	9	01	1	49	10	20				
11	4	20	7	50	3	56	8	13	3	22	8	46	2	21	9	46				
21	4	24	7	41	4	05	8	01	3	34	8	27	2	47	9	15				
Sept. 1	4	29	7	31	4	14	7	46	3	51	8	08	3	13	8	43	1	40	10	02
11	4	32	7	20	4	20	7	33	4	02	7	50	3	33	8	16	2	36	9	12
21	4	35	7	11	4	26	7	19	4	14	7	31	3	52	7	52	3	11	8	31
Oct. 1	4	38	7	02	4	33	7	05	4	25	7	13	4	10	7	28	3	41	7	54
11	4	40	6	53	4	40	6	53	4	35	6	58	4	26	7	05	4	07	7	23
21	4	43	6	47	4	45	6	44	4	45	6	43	4	41	6	46	4	32	6	55
Nov. 1	4	46	6	41	4	52	6	34	4	56	6	30	4	58	6	27	4	56	6	27
11	4	50	6	38	4	59	6	28	5	06	6	21	5	13	6	14	5	17	6	08
21	4	55	6	36	5	06	6	25	5	16	6	15	5	26	6	04	5	37	5	52
Dec. 1	5	00	6	37	5	13	6	24	5	25	6	11	5	38	5	58	5	53	5	42
11	5	06	6	40	5	20	6	26	5	34	6	12	5	48	5	57	6	06	5	38
21	5	11	6	45	5	25	6	30	5	39	6	16	5	55	6	00	6	15	5	40
31	5	15	6	50	5	30	6	35	5	44	6	21	6	00	6	06	6	18	5	48

(1)Although the instant of the sun's horizontal depression may be calculated precisely, the phenomena associated with astronomical twilight are sufficiently imprecise that the table is not recalculated each year.

Total Eclipses, 1940-2000

Date	Duration m	s	Width miles	Path of Totality
1940 Oct. 1	5	35	135	Colombia, Brazil, Atlantic Ocean, S Africa
1941 Sept. 21	3	21	88	Soviet Union, China, Pacific Ocean
1943 Feb. 4	2	39	142	Japan, Pacific Ocean, Alaska
1944 Jan. 25	4	08	90	Peru, Brazil, W Africa
1945 July 9	1	15	57	U.S., Canada, Greenland, Scandinavia, Soviet Union
1947 May 20	5	13	121	South America, Atlantic Ocean, Africa
1948 Nov. 1	1	55	52	Africa, Indian Ocean
1950 Sept. 12	1	13	83	Arctic Ocean, Siberia, Pacific Ocean
1952 Feb. 25	3	09	85	Africa, Middle East, Soviet Union
1954 June 30	2	35	95	U.S., Canada, Iceland, Europe, Middle East
1955 June 20	7	07	157	SE Asia, Philippines, Pacific Ocean
1956 June 8	4	44	266	South Pacific Ocean
1958 Oct. 12	5	10	129	Pacific Ocean, Chile, Argentina
1959 Oct. 2	3	01	75	New England, Atlantic Ocean, Africa
1961 Feb. 15	2	45	160	Europe, Soviet Union
1962 Feb. 5	4	08	91	Borneo, New Guinea, Pacific Ocean
1963 July 20	1	39	63	Pacific Ocean, Alaska, Canada, Maine
1965 May 30	5	15	123	New Zealand, Pacific Ocean
1966 Nov. 12	1	57	52	Pacific Ocean, South America, Atlantic Ocean
1968 Sept. 22	0	39	64	Soviet Union, China
1970 Mar. 7	3	27	95	Pacific Ocean, Mexico, Eastern U.S., Canada
1972 July 10	2	35	109	Siberia, Alaska, Canada
1973 June 30	7	03	159	Atlantic Ocean, Central Africa, Indian Ocean
1974 June 20	5	08	214	Indian Ocean, Australia
1976 Oct. 23	4	46	123	Africa, Indian Ocean, Australia

Date	Duration		Width	Path of Totality
	m	s	miles	
1977 Oct. 12	2	37	61	Pacific Ocean, Colombia, Venezuela
1979 Feb. 26	2	49	185	NW U.S., Canada, Greenland
1980 Feb. 16	4	08	92	Africa, Indian Ocean, India, Burma, China
1981 July 31	2	02	67	Soviet Union, Pacific Ocean
1983 June 11	5	10	123	Indian Ocean, Indonesia, New Guinea
1984 Nov. 22	1	59	53	New Guinea, Pacific Ocean
1985 Nov. 12	1	58	430	Antarctica
1986 Oct. 3h	0	01	1	North Atlantic Ocean
1987 Mar. 29h	0	07	3	South Atlantic Ocean, Africa
1988 Mar. 18	3	46	104	Sumatra, Borneo, Philippines, Pacific Ocean
1990 July 22	2	32	125	Finland, Soviet Union, Aleutian Islands
1991 July 11	6	53	160	Hawaii, Mexico, Central America, Colombia, Brazil
1992 June 30	5	20	182	South Atlantic Ocean
1994 Nov. 3	4	23	117	Peru, Bolivia, Paraguay, Brazil
1995 Oct. 24	2	09	48	Iran, India, SE Asia
1997 Mar. 9	2	50	221	Mongolia, Siberia
1998 Feb. 26	4	08	94	Galapagos Islands, Panama, Colombia, Venezuela
1999 Aug. 11	2	22	69	Europe, Middle East, India

h = indicates annular-total hybrid eclipse.

Calculation of Rise Times

The *Daily Calendar* pages contain rise and set times for the sun and moon for the Greenwich Meridian at north latitudes 20°, 30°, 40°, 50°, and 60°. You probably live somewhere west of the Greenwich Meridian, 0° longitude, and within the range of latitudes in the table. Notice that from day to day, the values for the sun at any particular latitude do not change very much. This slow variation for the sun means that no important correction needs to be made from one day to the next, once a proper correction for your latitude has been made. Thus, whenever the sun rises or sets at the 0° meridian, that will also be the time of that phenomenon at your Standard Time meridian. Any correction necessary for you to be able to observe that phenomenon from your location will be to account for your distance from the Standard Time meridian and for your latitude.

The moon, however, moves its own diameter, about one-half degree, in an hour, or about 12°.5 in one complete turn of the earth—one day. Most of this is eastward against the background stars of the sky, but some is also north or south of the equator. If there is little change on the same day of the times over the range of latitudes, the moon is near the celestial equator. All this motion considerably affects the times of rise or set, as you can see from the adjacent entries in the table. Thus, it is necessary to take your longitude into account in addition to your latitude. If you have no need for total accuracy, simply note that the time will be between the 4 values you find surrounding your location and the dates of interest.

The process of finding more accurate corrections is called interpolation. In the example, linear interpolation involving simple differences is used. In extreme cases, higher order interpolation should be used. If such cases are important to you, it is suggested that you plot the times, draw smooth curves through the plots, and interpolate by eye between the relevant curves. Some people find this exercise fun.

Let's find the time of the first July Full Moon at Rapid City, SD.

First, where is Rapid City, SD? Find Rapid City's latitude and longitude in the "Latitude, Longitude, and Altitude of U.S. and Canadian Cities" table found in the World Exploration and Geography section of *The World Almanac*.

I. Rapid City, SD: 44° 04′ 52″ N
103° 13′ 11″ W

IA. Convert these values to decimals:
52/60 = 0.87
4 + 0.87 = 4.87
4.87/60 = 0.08
44 + 0.08 = 44.08 N
11/60 = 0.18
13 + 0.18 = 13.18
13.18/60 = 0.22
103 + 0.22 = 103.22 W

IB. Fraction Rapid City lies between 40° and 50°:
44.08 − 40 = 4.08; 4.08/10 = 0.408

IC. Fraction world must turn between Greenwich and Rapid City:
103.22/360 = 0.287

ID. The MST meridian is 105°, thus 103.22 is 105 − 103.22 = 1.78 degrees east of the Mountain Standard Meridian. In 24 hours, there are 24 × 60 = 1,440 minutes; 1,440/360 = 4 minutes for every degree around the earth. So events happen 4 × 1.78 = 7.2 minutes earlier in Rapid City than at the 105° meridian.

IE. The values IB and IC are interpolates for Rapid City; ID is the time correction from local to Standard time for Rapid City. These values need never be calculated again for Rapid City.

IIA. We need the Greenwich times for moonrise at latitudes 40° and 50°, and for July 1 and 2 the day of the Full Moon and the next day.

	40°	Diff.	50°
July 1	19:42	0:27	20:09
July 2	20:32	0:23	20:55

IIB. We want IB and the July 1 time difference:
0.408 × 27 = 11.0
Add this to the July 1, 40° time;
19:42 + 11.0 = 19:53.0
And for July 13:
0.408 × 23 = 9.4
Add this to the July 2 rise time:
20:32 + 9.4 = 20:41.4
These two times are for the latitude of Rapid City, but for the Greenwich meridian.

IIC. To get the time for Rapid City, take the difference between these two times just determined,
20:41.4 − 19:53.0 = 48.4 minutes,
and find what fraction of this 24-hour change took place while the earth turned between Greenwich and Rapid City, 0.287 (See IC).
49.4 × 0.287 = 14.2 minutes after 19:52.
Thus 19:53 + 14.2 = 20:07 is the time the Full Moon will rise in the local time of Rapid City.

IID. But this happens 7.1 minutes (See ID) earlier than MST clock time at Rapid City, thus
20:07 − 7.1 = 19:59 MST.
But this is summer, and daylight time is in effect;
19:59 + 1:00 = 20:59 MDT is the rise time for the Full Moon at Rapid City the evening of July 1, 1996. Can you confirm that sunset will be at 20:49?

1st Month   **January 1996**   **31 days**

Greenwich Mean Time

NOTE: For each day, numbers on first line indicate Sun. *Italic* numbers on second line indicate *Moon*.
Degrees are North Latitude.

FM = full moon; LQ = last quarter; NM = new moon; FQ = first quarter.

CAUTION: Must be converted to local time. For instructions see page 296.

Day of month week year	Sun on Meridian Moon Phase h m s	Sun's Declina- tion ° ´	20° Rise Sun / Moon h m	20° Set Sun / Moon h m	30° Rise Sun / Moon h m	30° Set Sun / Moon h m	40° Rise Sun / Moon h m	40° Set Sun / Moon h m	50° Rise Sun / Moon h m	50° Set Sun / Moon h m	60° Rise Sun / Moon h m	60° Set Sun / Moon h m
1 MO 1	12 3 18	-23 4	6: 35 *14: 23*	17: 32 *2: 47*	6: 56 *14: 8*	17: 11 *3: 1*	7: 22 *13: 50*	16: 45 *3: 18*	7: 59 *13: 25*	16: 8 *3: 42*	9: 3 *12: 44*	15: 4 *4: 20*
2 TU 2	12 3 46	-22 19	6: 7 *15: 7*	17: 18 *3: 38*	6: 7 *14: 51*	17: 18 *3: 53*	7: 8 *14: 30*	16: 18 *4: 13*	7: 8 *14: 2*	16: 17 *4: 41*	9: 8 *13: 15*	15: 6 *5: 26*
3 WE 3	12 4 14	-22 19	6: 8 *15: 53*	17: 19 *4: 27*	6: 8 *15: 36*	17: 19 *4: 44*	7: 8 *15: 14*	16: 19 *5: 6*	7: 8 *14: 44*	16: 18 *5: 36*	9: 9 *13: 54*	15: 7 *6: 25*
4 TH 4	12 4 42	-22 20	6: 8 *16: 41*	17: 20 *5: 16*	6: 8 *16: 24*	17: 20 *5: 33*	7: 9 *16: 2*	16: 20 *5: 55*	7: 9 *15: 32*	16: 20 *6: 25*	9: 9 *14: 42*	15: 9 *7: 16*
5 FR 5	12 5 9 20 51 FM	-22 21	6: 9 *17: 30*	17: 21 *6: 2*	6: 9 *17: 14*	17: 21 *6: 19*	7: 9 *16: 53*	16: 21 *6: 40*	7: 9 *16: 24*	16: 21 *7: 10*	9: 9 *15: 37*	15: 10 *7: 58*
6 SA 6	12 5 36	-22 22	6: 10 *18: 20*	17: 22 *6: 47*	6: 10 *18: 5*	17: 22 *7: 3*	7: 10 *17: 46*	16: 22 *7: 22*	7: 10 *17: 21*	16: 22 *7: 48*	8: 10 *16: 40*	15: 12 *8: 31*
7 SU 7	12 6 2	-22 23	6: 10 *19: 9*	17: 23 *7: 30*	6: 10 *18: 57*	17: 23 *7: 43*	7: 10 *18: 41*	16: 23 *8: 0*	7: 10 *18: 20*	16: 23 *8: 22*	8: 10 *17: 47*	15: 14 *8: 58*
8 MO 8	12 6 28	-22no	6: 11 *19: 59*	17: no *8: 10*	6: 11 *19: 49*	17: no *8: 21*	7: 11 *19: 38*	16: no *8: 34*	7: 11 *19: 22*	16: no *8: 52*	8: 10 *18: 57*	15: 16 *9: 20*
9 TU 9	12 6 53	-22 0	6: 12 *20: 49*	17: 0 *8: 49*	6: 11 *20: 42*	17: 0 *8: 57*	7: 11 *20: 35*	16: 0 *9: 7*	7: 11 *20: 25*	16: 1 *9: 19*	8: 11 *20: 8*	15: 18 *9: 39*
10 WE 10	12 7 18	-22 1	6: 12 *21: 39*	17: 1 *9: 28*	6: 12 *21: 36*	17: 1 *9: 32*	7: 12 *21: 33*	16: 2 *9: 37*	7: 12 *21: 28*	16: 2 *9: 44*	8: 11 *21: 22*	15: 20 *9: 55*
11 TH 11	12 7 42	-21 2	6: 13 *22: 29*	17: 2 *10: 6*	6: 13 *22: 30*	17: 2 *10: 7*	7: 13 *22: 32*	16: 3 *10: 8*	7: 12 *22: 34*	16: 3 *10: 9*	8: 12 *22: 36*	15: 22 *10: 11*
12 FR 12	12 8 6	-21 3	6: 14 *23: 22*	17: 3 *10: 45*	6: 14 *23: 26*	17: 3 *10: 42*	7: 14 *23: 32*	16: 4 *10: 38*	7: 13 *23: 40*	16: 5 *10: 34*	8: 12 *23: 53*	15: 24 *10: 26*
13 SA 13	12 8 29 20 45 LQ	-21 4	6: 15 *no: ne*	17: 4 *11: 25*	6: 15 *no: ne*	17: 4 *11: 19*	7: 15 *no: ne*	16: 5 *11: 11*	7: 14 *no: ne*	16: 6 *11: 0*	8: 13 *no: ne*	15: 26 *10: 43*
14 SU 14	12 8 51	-21 5	6: 16 *0: 16*	17: 5 *12: 8*	6: 16 *0: 24*	17: 5 *11: 58*	7: 16 *0: 35*	16: 6 *11: 46*	7: 15 *0: 49*	16: 7 *11: 29*	8: 14 *1: 12*	15: 28 *11: 3*
15 MO 15	12 9 13	-21 6	6: 17 *1: 13*	17: 6 *12: 56*	6: 17 *1: 25*	17: 6 *12: 42*	7: 17 *1: 39*	16: 7 *12: 26*	7: 17 *2: 0*	16: 7 *12: 3*	8: 16 *2: 33*	15: 30 *11: 28*
16 TU 16	12 9 34	-21 7	6: 19 *2: 12*	17: 7 *13: 47*	6: 18 *2: 27*	17: 7 *13: 31*	7: 18 *2: 45*	16: 7 *13: 12*	7: 18 *3: 11*	16: 8 *12: 45*	8: 17 *3: 54*	15: 32 *12: 0*
17 WE 17	12 9 55	-20 8	6: 20 *3: 13*	17: 8 *14: 44*	6: 19 *3: 30*	17: 8 *14: 27*	7: 19 *3: 52*	16: 8 *14: 5*	7: 19 *4: 21*	16: 8 *13: 35*	8: 19 *5: 10*	15: 35 *12: 45*
18 TH 18	12 10 15	-20 8	6: 21 *4: 16*	17: 8 *15: 46*	6: 21 *4: 33*	17: 8 *15: 28*	7: 20 *4: 56*	16: 9 *15: 6*	7: 20 *5: 27*	16: 9 *14: 35*	8: 20 *6: 18*	15: 37 *13: 44*
19 FR 19	12 10 34	-20 9	6: 22 *5: 17*	17: 9 *16: 50*	6: 22 *5: 34*	17: 9 *16: 34*	7: 22 *5: 55*	17: 9 *16: 14*	7: 22 *6: 25*	16: 9 *15: 45*	8: 22 *7: 13*	15: 39 *14: 58*
20 SA 20	12 10 52 NM 12 50	-20 10	6: 22 *6: 15*	17: 10 *17: 56*	6: 23 *6: 30*	17: 10 *17: 42*	7: 23 *6: 49*	17: 9 *17: 25*	7: 23 *7: 14*	16: 9 *17: 2*	8: 23 *7: 55*	15: 42 *16: 23*
21 SU 21	12 11 10	-20 10	6: 23 *7: 10*	17: 10 *19: 1*	6: 23 *7: 22*	17: 10 *18: 51*	7: no *7: 36*	17: 10 *18: 38*	7: no *7: 56*	16: 10 *18: 21*	8: no *8: 26*	15: 44 *17: 54*
22 MO 22	12 11 27	-19 11	6: no *8: 1*	17: 11 *20: 3*	6: no *8: 8*	17: 11 *19: 57*	7: 0 *8: 18*	17: 10 *19: 50*	7: 0 *8: 31*	16: 10 *19: 40*	8: 0 *8: 51*	15: 47 *19: 24*
23 TU 23	12 11 43	-19 12	6: 0 *8: 48*	17: 12 *21: 3*	6: 0 *8: 51*	17: 11 *21: 1*	7: 1 *8: 56*	17: 11 *20: 59*	7: 1 *9: 2*	16: 10 *20: 56*	8: 2 *9: 12*	15: 49 *20: 51*
24 WE 24	12 11 58	-19 13	6: 1 *9: 32*	17: 12 *22: 0*	6: 1 *9: 31*	17: 12 *22: 3*	7: 2 *9: 31*	17: 12 *22: 6*	7: 2 *9: 31*	16: 11 *22: 10*	8: 3 *9: 30*	15: 52 *22: 16*
25 TH 25	12 12 13	-19 13	6: 2 *10: 14*	17: 13 *22: 56*	6: 2 *10: 10*	17: 13 *23: 2*	7: 3 *10: 5*	17: 12 *23: 10*	7: 3 *9: 58*	16: 11 *23: 20*	8: 4 *9: 48*	15: 54 *23: 37*
26 FR 26	12 12 27	-18 14	6: 3 *10: 56*	17: 14 *23: 49*	6: 3 *10: 48*	17: 13 *23: 59*	7: 3 *10: 39*	17: 13 *no: ne*	7: 4 *10: 26*	16: 12 *no: ne*	8: 5 *10: 6*	15: 57 *no: ne*
27 SA 27	12 12 40 11 14 FQ	-18 41	6: 37 *11: 38*	17: 48 *no: ne*	6: 53 *11: 27*	17: 32 *no: ne*	7: 14 *11: 14*	17: 12 *0: 11*	7: 41 *10: 55*	16: 45 *0: 28*	8: 27 *10: 26*	15: 59 *0: 54*
28 SU 28	12 12 52	-18 26	6: 37 *12: 21*	17: 49 *0: 42*	6: 53 *12: 7*	17: 33 *0: 55*	7: 13 *11: 50*	17: 13 *1: 10*	7: 40 *11: 27*	16: 46 *1: 32*	8: 25 *10: 50*	16: 2 *2: 7*
29 MO 29	12 13 3	-18 10	6: 37 *13: 5*	17: 50 *1: 33*	6: 52 *12: 50*	17: 34 *1: 48*	7: 12 *12: 30*	17: 15 *2: 7*	7: 39 *12: 3*	16: 48 *2: 33*	8: 22 *11: 19*	16: 5 *3: 15*
30 TU 30	12 13 14	-17 54	6: 36 *13: 51*	17: 50 *2: 23*	6: 52 *13: 34*	17: 35 *2: 40*	7: 11 *13: 13*	17: 16 *3: 1*	7: 37 *12: 43*	16: 50 *3: 29*	8: 20 *11: 55*	16: 7 *4: 17*
31 WE 31	12 13 23	-17 38	6: 36 *14: 38*	17: 51 *3: 12*	6: 51 *14: 21*	17: 36 *3: 29*	7: 10 *13: 59*	17: 17 *3: 51*	7: 36 *13: 29*	16: 51 *4: 21*	8: 18 *12: 39*	16: 10 *5: 11*

2nd Month   **February 1996**   **29 days**

Greenwich Mean Time

NOTE: For each day, numbers on first line indicate Sun. *Italic* numbers on second line indicate *Moon*. Degrees are North Latitude.

FM = full moon; LQ = last quarter; NM = new moon; FQ = first quarter.

CAUTION: Must be converted to local time. For instructions see page 296.

Day of month / week / year	Sun on Meridian / Moon Phase (h m s)	Sun's Declina-tion (° ')	20° Rise Sun/Moon	20° Set Sun/Moon	30° Rise Sun/Moon	30° Set Sun/Moon	40° Rise Sun/Moon	40° Set Sun/Moon	50° Rise Sun/Moon	50° Set Sun/Moon	60° Rise Sun/Moon	60° Set Sun/Moon
1 TH 32	12 13 32	-17 22	6: 36	17: 52	6: 51	17: 37	7: 9	17: 18	7: 35	16: 53	8: 16	16: 12
32			*15: 26*	*3: 59*	*15: 9*	*4: 16*	*14: 48*	*4: 38*	*14: 19*	*5: 7*	*13: 31*	*5: 56*
2 FR 33	12 13 40	-17 5	6: 35	17: 52	6: 50	17: 37	7: 8	17: 19	7: 33	16: 55	8: 13	16: 15
33			*16: 15*	*4: 45*	*16: 0*	*5: 1*	*15: 41*	*5: 21*	*15: 14*	*5: 48*	*14: 31*	*6: 33*
3 SA 34	12 13 47	-16 47	6: 35	17: 53	6: 50	17: 38	7: 7	17: 21	7: 32	16: 56	8: 11	16: 18
34			*17: 5*	*5: 28*	*16: 52*	*5: 42*	*16: 35*	*6: 0*	*16: 13*	*6: 24*	*15: 36*	*7: 2*
4 SU 35	12 13 53 / *15 58 FM*	-16 30	6: 35	17: 53	6: 49	17: 39	7: 6	17: 22	7: 30	16: 58	8: 8	16: 20
35			*17: 55*	*6: 10*	*17: 45*	*6: 21*	*17: 32*	*6: 36*	*17: 14*	*6: 55*	*16: 46*	*7: 26*
5 MO 36	12 13 59	-16 12	6: 34	17: 54	6: 48	17: 40	7: 5	17: 23	7: 29	17: 0	8: 6	16: 23
36			*18: 45*	*6: 50*	*18: 38*	*6: 59*	*18: 29*	*7: 9*	*18: 16*	*7: 24*	*17: 57*	*7: 46*
6 TU 37	12 14 3	-15 54	6: 34	17: 54	6: 48	17: 41	7: 4	17: 24	7: 27	17: 2	8: 4	16: 25
37			*19: 36*	*7: 29*	*19: 32*	*7: 34*	*19: 27*	*7: 41*	*19: 20*	*7: 50*	*19: 10*	*8: 4*
7 WE 38	12 14 7	-15 36	6: 34	17: 55	6: 47	17: 42	7: 3	17: 25	7: 26	17: 3	8: 1	16: 28
38			*20: 26*	*8: 7*	*20: 26*	*8: 9*	*20: 26*	*8: 12*	*20: 25*	*8: 15*	*20: 25*	*8: 20*
8 TH 39	12 14 10	-15 17	6: 33	17: 55	6: 46	17: 42	7: 2	17: 27	7: 24	17: 5	7: 58	16: 31
39			*21: 18*	*8: 46*	*21: 21*	*8: 44*	*21: 26*	*8: 42*	*21: 32*	*8: 40*	*21: 41*	*8: 36*
9 FR 40	12 14 13	-14 58	6: 33	17: 56	6: 45	17: 43	7: 1	17: 28	7: 22	17: 7	7: 56	16: 33
40			*22: 11*	*9: 26*	*22: 18*	*9: 21*	*22: 27*	*9: 14*	*22: 39*	*9: 6*	*22: 58*	*8: 53*
10 SA 41	12 14 14	-14 39	6: 32	17: 56	6: 45	17: 44	7: 0	17: 29	7: 21	17: 8	7: 53	16: 36
41			*23: 6*	*10: 7*	*23: 16*	*9: 59*	*23: 30*	*9: 48*	*23: 48*	*9: 34*	*no: ne*	*9: 11*
11 SU 42	12 14 15	-14 19	6: 32	17: 57	6: 44	17: 45	6: 59	17: 30	7: 19	17: 10	7: 51	16: 39
42			*no: ne*	*10: 52*	*no: ne*	*10: 40*	*no: ne*	*10: 25*	*no: ne*	*10: 5*	*0: 16*	*9: 34*
12 MO 43	12 14 15 / *8 37 LQ*	-13 60	6: 31	17: 57	6: 43	17: 46	6: 58	17: 31	7: 17	17: 12	7: 48	16: 41
43			*0: 3*	*11: 40*	*0: 16*	*11: 26*	*0: 33*	*11: 7*	*0: 57*	*10: 42*	*1: 35*	*10: 2*
13 TU 44	12 14 14	-13 40	6: 31	17: 58	6: 42	17: 47	6: 56	17: 33	7: 16	17: 14	7: 45	16: 44
44			*1: 1*	*12: 33*	*1: 17*	*12: 16*	*1: 37*	*11: 56*	*2: 5*	*11: 27*	*2: 51*	*10: 40*
14 WE 45	12 14 13	-13 20	6: 30	17: 58	6: 41	17: 47	6: 55	17: 34	7: 14	17: 15	7: 43	16: 47
45			*2: 1*	*13: 30*	*2: 18*	*13: 13*	*2: 40*	*12: 51*	*3: 10*	*12: 20*	*4: 0*	*11: 30*
15 TH 46	12 14 11	-12 60	6: 30	17: 59	6: 41	17: 48	6: 54	17: 35	7: 12	17: 17	7: 40	16: 49
46			*3: 0*	*14: 31*	*3: 17*	*14: 14*	*3: 39*	*13: 53*	*4: 9*	*13: 23*	*4: 59*	*12: 34*
16 FR 47	12 14 8	-12 39	6: 29	17: 59	6: 40	17: 49	6: 53	17: 36	7: 10	17: 19	7: 37	16: 52
47			*3: 58*	*15: 34*	*4: 14*	*15: 19*	*4: 34*	*15: 0*	*5: 1*	*14: 34*	*5: 46*	*13: 51*
17 SA 48	12 14 4	-12 18	6: 29	18: 0	6: 39	17: 50	6: 51	17: 37	7: 8	17: 21	7: 35	16: 54
48			*4: 53*	*16: 38*	*5: 7*	*16: 26*	*5: 23*	*16: 11*	*5: 46*	*15: 50*	*6: 22*	*15: 17*
18 SU 49	12 14 0 / *23 30 NM*	-11 57	6: 28	18: 0	6: 38	17: 50	6: 50	17: 38	7: 6	17: 22	7: 32	16: 57
49			*5: 46*	*17: 42*	*5: 56*	*17: 33*	*6: 8*	*17: 23*	*6: 25*	*17: 9*	*6: 50*	*16: 47*
19 MO 50	12 13 55	-11 36	6: 27	18: 1	6: 37	17: 51	6: 49	17: 40	7: 5	17: 24	7: 29	17: 0
50			*6: 35*	*18: 43*	*6: 41*	*18: 39*	*6: 48*	*18: 34*	*6: 58*	*18: 27*	*7: 13*	*18: 16*
20 TU 51	12 13 50	-11 15	6: 27	18: 1	6: 36	17: 52	6: 47	17: 41	7: 3	17: 26	7: 26	17: 2
51			*7: 21*	*19: 43*	*7: 23*	*19: 43*	*7: 25*	*19: 43*	*7: 28*	*19: 44*	*7: 33*	*19: 44*
21 WE 52	12 13 43	-10 53	6: 26	18: 2	6: 35	17: 53	6: 46	17: 42	7: 1	17: 27	7: 24	17: 5
52			*8: 6*	*20: 41*	*8: 4*	*20: 45*	*8: 1*	*20: 50*	*7: 57*	*20: 58*	*7: 52*	*21: 9*
22 TH 53	12 13 36	-10 32	6: 25	18: 2	6: 34	17: 54	6: 45	17: 43	6: 59	17: 29	7: 21	17: 8
53			*8: 49*	*21: 37*	*8: 43*	*21: 45*	*8: 36*	*21: 55*	*8: 26*	*22: 9*	*8: 11*	*22: 30*
23 FR 54	12 13 29	-10 10	6: 25	18: 2	6: 33	17: 54	6: 43	17: 44	6: 57	17: 31	7: 18	17: 10
54			*9: 33*	*22: 32*	*9: 23*	*22: 43*	*9: 11*	*22: 57*	*8: 56*	*23: 16*	*8: 31*	*23: 47*
24 SA 55	12 13 20	-9 48	6: 24	18: 3	6: 32	17: 55	6: 42	17: 45	6: 55	17: 32	7: 15	17: 13
55			*10: 16*	*23: 25*	*10: 4*	*23: 39*	*9: 48*	*23: 56*	*9: 27*	*no: ne*	*8: 54*	*no: ne*
25 SU 56	12 13 12	-9 26	6: 23	18: 3	6: 31	17: 56	6: 40	17: 46	6: 53	17: 34	7: 12	17: 15
56			*11: 1*	*no: ne*	*10: 46*	*no: ne*	*10: 28*	*no: ne*	*10: 2*	*0: 20*	*9: 22*	*0: 59*
26 MO 57	12 13 2 / *5 52 FQ*	-9 4	6: 23	18: 4	6: 30	17: 56	6: 39	17: 48	6: 51	17: 36	7: 9	17: 18
57			*11: 46*	*0: 16*	*11: 30*	*0: 32*	*11: 10*	*0: 52*	*10: 41*	*1: 19*	*9: 55*	*2: 5*
27 TU 58	12 12 52	-8 41	6: 22	18: 4	6: 29	17: 57	6: 38	17: 49	6: 49	17: 38	7: 7	17: 20
58			*12: 33*	*1: 6*	*12: 16*	*1: 23*	*11: 55*	*1: 44*	*11: 25*	*2: 14*	*10: 36*	*3: 2*
28 WE 59	12 12 41	-8 19	6: 21	18: 4	6: 28	17: 58	6: 36	17: 50	6: 47	17: 39	7: 4	17: 23
59			*13: 21*	*1: 54*	*13: 4*	*2: 11*	*12: 43*	*2: 33*	*12: 14*	*3: 2*	*11: 25*	*3: 51*
29 TH 60	12 12 30	-7 56	6: 20	18: 5	6: 27	17: 59	6: 35	17: 51	6: 45	17: 41	7: 1	17: 25
60			*14: 10*	*2: 40*	*13: 54*	*2: 57*	*13: 34*	*3: 17*	*13: 7*	*3: 45*	*12: 22*	*4: 31*

3rd Month   March 1996   31 days

Greenwich Mean Time

NOTE: For each day, numbers on first line indicate Sun. *Italic* numbers on second line indicate *Moon*. Degrees are North Latitude.

FM = full moon; LQ = last quarter; NM = new moon; FQ = first quarter.

CAUTION: Must be converted to local time. For instructions see page 296.

Day of month week year	Sun on Meridian Moon Phase h m s	Sun's Declina-tion ° '	20° Rise Sun/Moon	20° Set Sun/Moon	30° Rise Sun/Moon	30° Set Sun/Moon	40° Rise Sun/Moon	40° Set Sun/Moon	50° Rise Sun/Moon	50° Set Sun/Moon	60° Rise Sun/Moon	60° Set Sun/Moon
1 FR	12 12 18	-7 33	6: 20	18: 5	6: 26	17: 59	6: 33	17: 52	6: 43	17: 43	6: 58	17: 28
61			*14: 59*	*3: 24*	*14: 45*	*3: 39*	*14: 28*	*3: 58*	*14: 4*	*4: 23*	*13: 25*	*5: 3*
2 SA	12 12 6	7 11	6: 19	18: 6	6: 25	18: 0	6: 32	17: 53	6: 41	17: 44	6: 55	17: 31
62			*15: 49*	*4: 7*	*15: 38*	*4: 19*	*15: 23*	*4: 35*	*15: 4*	*4: 56*	*14: 33*	*5: 30*
3 SU	12 11 54	-6 48	6: 18	18: 6	6: 24	18: 1	6: 30	17: 54	6: 39	17: 46	6: 52	17: 33
63			*16: 39*	*4: 47*	*16: 31*	*4: 57*	*16: 20*	*5: 10*	*16: 6*	*5: 26*	*15: 44*	*5: 51*
4 MO	12 11 40	-6 25	6: 17	18: 6	6: 22	18: 1	6: 29	17: 55	6: 37	17: 47	6: 49	17: 36
64			*17: 30*	*5: 27*	*17: 25*	*5: 34*	*17: 19*	*5: 42*	*17: 10*	*5: 53*	*16: 57*	*6: 10*
5 TU	12 11 27	-6 1	6: 17	18: 7	6: 21	18: 2	6: 27	17: 56	6: 35	17: 49	6: 46	17: 38
65	*9 23 FM*		*18: 21*	*6: 6*	*18: 20*	*6: 10*	*18: 18*	*6: 14*	*18: 15*	*6: 19*	*18: 11*	*6: 27*
6 WE	12 11 13	-5 38	6: 16	18: 7	6: 20	18: 3	6: 26	17: 58	6: 33	17: 51	6: 43	17: 41
66			*19: 14*	*6: 46*	*19: 16*	*6: 45*	*19: 18*	*6: 45*	*19: 22*	*6: 44*	*19: 28*	*6: 44*
7 TH	12 10 58	-5 15	6: 15	18: 7	6: 19	18: 3	6: 24	17: 59	6: 30	17: 52	6: 40	17: 43
67			*20: 7*	*7: 26*	*20: 13*	*7: 22*	*20: 20*	*7: 17*	*20: 30*	*7: 10*	*20: 45*	*7: 0*
8 FR	12 10 43	-4 52	6: 14	18: 8	6: 18	18: 4	6: 22	18: 0	6: 28	17: 54	6: 37	17: 46
68			*21: 2*	*8: 7*	*21: 11*	*8: 0*	*21: 23*	*7: 51*	*21: 39*	*7: 38*	*22: 4*	*7: 19*
9 SA	12 10 28	-4 28	6: 13	18: 8	6: 17	18: 5	6: 21	18: 1	6: 26	17: 56	6: 34	17: 48
69			*21: 58*	*8: 51*	*22: 11*	*8: 40*	*22: 26*	*8: 27*	*22: 48*	*8: 9*	*23: 23*	*7: 40*
10 SU	12 10 13	-4 5	6: 13	18: 8	6: 16	18: 5	6: 19	18: 2	6: 24	17: 57	6: 31	17: 51
70			*22: 55*	*9: 38*	*23: 11*	*9: 25*	*23: 30*	*9: 8*	*23: 56*	*8: 44*	*no: ne*	*8: 7*
11 MO	12 9 57	-3 41	6: 12	18: 8	6: 14	18: 6	6: 18	18: 3	6: 22	17: 59	6: 28	17: 53
71			*23: 54*	*10: 29*	*no: ne*	*10: 13*	*no: ne*	*9: 53*	*no: ne*	*9: 26*	*0: 39*	*8: 41*
12 TU	12 9 41	-3 18	6: 11	18: 9	6: 13	18: 7	6: 16	18: 4	6: 20	18: 0	6: 25	17: 55
72	*17 15 LQ*		*no: ne*	*11: 24*	*0: 11*	*11: 6*	*0: 32*	*10: 45*	*1: 1*	*10: 15*	*1: 50*	*9: 26*
13 WE	12 9 25	-2 54	6: 10	18: 9	6: 12	18: 7	6: 15	18: 5	6: 18	18: 2	6: 22	17: 58
73			*0: 52*	*12: 21*	*1: 9*	*12: 4*	*1: 31*	*11: 43*	*2: 1*	*11: 13*	*2: 51*	*10: 23*
14 TH	12 9 8	-2 30	6: 9	18: 9	6: 11	18: 8	6: 13	18: 6	6: 15	18: 4	6: 19	18: 0
74			*1: 48*	*13: 22*	*2: 5*	*13: 6*	*2: 25*	*12: 46*	*2: 54*	*12: 19*	*3: 40*	*11: 33*
15 FR	12 8 51	-2 7	6: 8	18: 10	6: 10	18: 8	6: 11	18: 7	6: 13	18: 5	6: 16	18: 3
75			*2: 43*	*14: 23*	*2: 57*	*14: 10*	*3: 15*	*13: 53*	*3: 40*	*13: 30*	*4: 19*	*12: 53*
16 SA	12 8 34	-1 43	6: 7	18: 10	6: 9	18: 9	6: 10	18: 8	6: 11	18: 7	6: 13	18: 5
76			*3: 35*	*15: 25*	*3: 46*	*15: 15*	*4: 0*	*15: 2*	*4: 20*	*14: 45*	*4: 50*	*14: 18*
17 SU	12 8 17	-1 19	6: 7	18: 10	6: 7	18: 10	6: 8	18: 9	6: 9	18: 9	6: 10	18: 8
77			*4: 24*	*16: 26*	*4: 32*	*16: 19*	*4: 41*	*16: 12*	*4: 54*	*16: 2*	*5: 14*	*15: 45*
18 MO	12 7 60	0 55	6: 6	18: 11	6: 6	18: 10	6: 6	18: 10	6: 7	18: 10	6: 7	18: 10
78			*5: 10*	*17: 25*	*5: 14*	*17: 23*	*5: 19*	*17: 21*	*5: 26*	*17: 18*	*5: 36*	*17: 12*
19 TU	12 7 42	0 32	6: 5	18: 11	6: 5	18: 11	6: 5	18: 11	6: 5	18: 12	6: 4	18: 13
79	*10 45 NM*		*5: 55*	*18: 24*	*5: 55*	*18: 26*	*5: 55*	*18: 29*	*5: 55*	*18: 32*	*5: 55*	*18: 38*
20 WE	12 7 24	0 8	6: 4	18: 11	6: 4	18: 12	6: 3	18: 12	6: 2	18: 13	6: 1	18: 15
80			*6: 40*	*19: 21*	*6: 35*	*19: 27*	*6: 30*	*19: 35*	*6: 24*	*19: 45*	*6: 14*	*20: 1*
21 TH	12 7 7	0 16	6: 3	18: 11	6: 3	18: 12	6: 2	18: 13	6: 0	18: 15	5: 58	18: 18
81			*7: 24*	*20: 17*	*7: 16*	*20: 27*	*7: 6*	*20: 39*	*6: 53*	*20: 56*	*6: 34*	*21: 22*
22 FR	12 6 49	0 39	6: 2	18: 12	6: 1	18: 13	6: 0	18: 14	5: 58	18: 16	5: 55	18: 20
82			*8: 8*	*21: 12*	*7: 57*	*21: 25*	*7: 43*	*21: 41*	*7: 25*	*22: 3*	*6: 56*	*22: 38*
23 SA	12 6 31	1 3	6: 1	18: 12	6: 0	18: 13	5: 58	18: 15	5: 56	18: 18	5: 52	18: 22
83			*8: 53*	*22: 6*	*8: 39*	*22: 21*	*8: 22*	*22: 39*	*7: 59*	*23: 5*	*7: 22*	*23: 48*
24 SU	12 6 13	1 27	6: 0	18: 12	5: 59	18: 14	5: 57	18: 16	5: 54	18: 20	5: 49	18: 25
84			*9: 39*	*22: 57*	*9: 23*	*23: 14*	*9: 4*	*23: 34*	*8: 37*	*no: ne*	*7: 53*	*no: ne*
25 MO	12 5 55	1 50	6: 0	18: 12	5: 58	18: 15	5: 55	18: 17	5: 52	18: 21	5: 46	18: 27
85			*10: 26*	*23: 47*	*10: 9*	*no: ne*	*9: 48*	*no: ne*	*9: 19*	*0: 3*	*8: 31*	*0: 50*
26 TU	12 5 36	2 14	5: 59	18: 13	5: 56	18: 15	5: 54	18: 18	5: 49	18: 23	5: 43	18: 30
86			*11: 14*	*no: ne*	*10: 57*	*0: 4*	*10: 36*	*0: 25*	*10: 6*	*0: 55*	*9: 18*	*1: 43*
27 WE	12 5 18	2 37	5: 58	18: 13	5: 55	18: 16	5: 52	18: 19	5: 47	18: 24	5: 40	18: 32
87	*1 31 FQ*		*12: 3*	*0: 34*	*11: 46*	*0: 51*	*11: 26*	*1: 11*	*10: 58*	*1: 40*	*10: 12*	*2: 27*
28 TH	12 5 0	3 1	5: 57	18: 13	5: 54	18: 16	5: 50	18: 20	5: 45	18: 26	5: 37	18: 35
88			*12: 52*	*1: 19*	*12: 37*	*1: 34*	*12: 19*	*1: 54*	*11: 53*	*2: 20*	*11: 12*	*3: 3*
29 FR	12 4 42	3 24	5: 56	18: 14	5: 53	18: 17	5: 49	18: 21	5: 43	18: 28	5: 34	18: 37
89			*13: 41*	*2: 2*	*13: 29*	*2: 15*	*13: 13*	*2: 32*	*12: 52*	*2: 55*	*12: 18*	*3: 31*
30 SA	12 4 24	3 48	5: 55	18: 14	5: 52	18: 18	5: 47	18: 22	5: 41	18: 29	5: 31	18: 40
90			*14: 31*	*2: 43*	*14: 21*	*2: 54*	*14: 9*	*3: 8*	*13: 53*	*3: 26*	*13: 27*	*3: 55*
31 SU	12 4 6	4 11	5: 54	18: 14	5: 51	18: 19	5: 45	18: 23	5: 39	18: 31	5: 28	18: 42
91			*15: 22*	*3: 23*	*15: 15*	*3: 31*	*15: 7*	*3: 41*	*14: 56*	*3: 54*	*14: 39*	*4: 14*

4th Month   **April 1996**   **30 days**

Greenwich Mean Time

NOTE: For each day, numbers on first line indicate Sun. *Italic* numbers on second line indicate *Moon*.
Degrees are North Latitude.

FM = full moon; LQ = last quarter; NM = new moon; FQ = first quarter.

CAUTION: Must be converted to local time. For instructions see page 296.

Day of month / week / year	Sun on Meridian / Moon Phase (h m s)	Sun's Declination (° ′)	20° Rise Sun / Moon	20° Set Sun / Moon	30° Rise Sun / Moon	30° Set Sun / Moon	40° Rise Sun / Moon	40° Set Sun / Moon	50° Rise Sun / Moon	50° Set Sun / Moon	60° Rise Sun / Moon	60° Set Sun / Moon
1 MO	12 3 48	4 34	5: 54	18: 14	5: 49	18: 19	5: 44	18: 24	5: 36	18: 32	5: 25	18: 44
92			*6: 13*	*4: 2*	*16: 10*	*4: 7*	*16: 6*	*4: 13*	*16: 1*	*4: 21*	*15: 53*	*4: 32*
2 TU	12 3 30	4 57	5: 53	18: 15	5: 48	18: 19	5: 42	18: 25	5: 34	18: 34	5: 22	18: 47
93			*17: 5*	*4: 42*	*17: 5*	*4: 43*	*17: 6*	*4: 44*	*17: 7*	*4: 46*	*17: 9*	*4: 49*
3 WE	12 3 12	5 20	5: 52	18: 15	5: 47	18: 20	5: 41	18: 26	5: 32	18: 35	5: 19	18: 49
94			*17: 58*	*5: 22*	*18: 3*	*5: 19*	*18: 8*	*5: 16*	*18: 16*	*5: 12*	*18: 28*	*5: 6*
4 TH	12 2 55	5 43	5: 51	18: 15	5: 46	18: 21	5: 39	18: 27	5: 30	18: 37	5: 16	18: 52
95	0 7 FM		*18: 54*	*6: 4*	*19: 2*	*5: 57*	*19: 12*	*5: 50*	*19: 26*	*5: 40*	*19: 48*	*5: 24*
5 FR	12 2 37	6 6	5: 50	18: 15	5: 44	18: 21	5: 37	18: 28	5: 28	18: 38	5: 13	18: 54
96			*19: 51*	*6: 48*	*20: 2*	*6: 38*	*20: 17*	*6: 26*	*20: 36*	*6: 10*	*21: 8*	*5: 45*
6 SA	12 2 20	6 29	5: 49	18: 16	5: 43	18: 22	5: 36	18: 30	5: 26	18: 40	5: 10	18: 57
97			*20: 49*	*7: 35*	*21: 4*	*7: 22*	*21: 22*	*7: 6*	*21: 46*	*6: 44*	*22: 27*	*6: 10*
7 SU	12 2 3	6 51	5: 48	18: 16	5: 42	18: 22	5: 34	18: 31	5: 24	18: 42	5: 7	18: 59
98			*21: 48*	*8: 25*	*22: 5*	*8: 10*	*22: 25*	*7: 51*	*22: 54*	*7: 25*	*23: 41*	*6: 42*
8 MO	12 1 47	7 14	5: 48	18: 16	5: 41	18: 23	5: 33	18: 32	5: 21	18: 43	5: 4	19: 1
99			*22: 47*	*9: 20*	*23: 4*	*9: 3*	*23: 26*	*8: 42*	*23: 56*	*8: 12*	*no: ne*	*7: 24*
9 TU	12 1 30	7 36	5: 47	18: 17	5: 40	18: 24	5: 31	18: 33	5: 19	18: 45	5: 1	19: 4
100			*23: 44*	*10: 17*	*no: ne*	*9: 59*	*no: ne*	*9: 38*	*no: ne*	*9: 8*	*0: 46*	*8: 18*
10 WE	12 1 14	7 58	5: 46	18: 17	5: 39	18: 24	5: 30	18: 34	5: 17	18: 46	4: 58	19: 6
101	23 36 LQ		*no: ne*	*11: 16*	*0: 1*	*11: 0*	*0: 22*	*10: 39*	*0: 51*	*10: 11*	*1: 39*	*9: 24*
11 TH	12 0 58	8 20	5: 45	18: 17	5: 38	18: 25	5: 28	18: 35	5: 15	18: 48	4: 55	19: 9
102			*0: 39*	*12: 16*	*0: 54*	*12: 2*	*1: 13*	*11: 44*	*1: 39*	*11: 20*	*2: 20*	*10: 40*
12 FR	12 0 43	8 42	5: 44	18: 17	5: 36	18: 25	5: 27	18: 36	5: 13	18: 49	4: 52	19: 11
103			*1: 30*	*13: 16*	*1: 43*	*13: 5*	*1: 58*	*12: 51*	*2: 19*	*12: 32*	*2: 53*	*12: 2*
13 SA	12 0 27	9 4	5: 43	18: 18	5: 35	18: 26	5: 25	18: 37	5: 11	18: 51	4: 49	19: 14
104			*2: 19*	*14: 16*	*2: 28*	*14: 8*	*2: 39*	*13: 59*	*2: 55*	*13: 46*	*3: 18*	*13: 26*
14 SU	12 0 12	9 26	5: 43	18: 18	5: 34	18: 27	5: 24	18: 38	5: 9	18: 53	4: 46	19: 16
105			*3: 5*	*15: 14*	*3: 10*	*15: 10*	*3: 17*	*15: 6*	*3: 26*	*15: 0*	*3: 40*	*14: 50*
15 MO	11 59 58	9 47	5: 42	18: 18	5: 33	18: 27	5: 22	18: 39	5: 7	18: 54	4: 43	19: 19
106			*3: 49*	*16: 12*	*3: 51*	*16: 12*	*3: 53*	*16: 13*	*3: 55*	*16: 13*	*3: 59*	*16: 14*
16 TU	11 59 44	10 9	5: 41	18: 19	5: 32	18: 28	5: 21	18: 40	5: 5	18: 56	4: 40	19: 21
107			*4: 33*	*17: 8*	*4: 30*	*17: 13*	*4: 27*	*17: 18*	*4: 23*	*17: 26*	*4: 17*	*17: 37*
17 WE	11 59 30	10 30	5: 40	18: 19	5: 31	18: 29	5: 19	18: 41	5: 3	18: 57	4: 37	19: 24
108	22 49 NM		*5: 16*	*18: 4*	*5: 10*	*18: 12*	*5: 2*	*18: 22*	*4: 52*	*18: 36*	*4: 36*	*18: 58*
18 TH	11 59 17	10 51	5: 40	18: 19	5: 30	18: 29	5: 18	18: 42	5: 1	18: 59	4: 34	19: 26
109			*6: 0*	*19: 0*	*5: 50*	*19: 11*	*5: 38*	*19: 25*	*5: 22*	*19: 45*	*4: 57*	*20: 16*
19 FR	11 59 4	11 12	5: 39	18: 20	5: 29	18: 30	5: 16	18: 43	4: 59	19: 0	4: 31	19: 29
110			*6: 44*	*19: 54*	*6: 32*	*20: 8*	*6: 16*	*20: 26*	*5: 55*	*20: 50*	*5: 21*	*21: 29*
20 SA	11 58 51	11 32	5: 38	18: 20	5: 28	18: 30	5: 15	18: 44	4: 57	19: 2	4: 28	19: 31
111			*7: 30*	*20: 47*	*7: 15*	*21: 3*	*6: 57*	*21: 23*	*6: 31*	*21: 50*	*5: 50*	*22: 36*
21 SU	11 58 39	11 53	5: 37	18: 20	5: 27	18: 31	5: 13	18: 45	4: 55	19: 4	4: 25	19: 34
112			*8: 18*	*21: 38*	*8: 1*	*21: 55*	*7: 41*	*22: 16*	*7: 12*	*22: 45*	*6: 26*	*23: 34*
22 MO	11 58 27	12 13	5: 37	18: 21	5: 26	18: 32	5: 12	18: 46	4: 53	19: 5	4: 23	19: 36
113			*9: 6*	*22: 27*	*8: 49*	*22: 44*	*8: 27*	*23: 5*	*7: 58*	*23: 34*	*7: 9*	*no: ne*
23 TU	11 58 16	12 33	5: 36	18: 21	5: 25	18: 32	5: 10	18: 47	4: 51	19: 7	4: 20	19: 39
114			*9: 55*	*23: 13*	*9: 38*	*23: 29*	*9: 17*	*23: 49*	*8: 48*	*no: ne*	*8: 0*	*0: 22*
24 WE	11 58 5	12 53	5: 35	18: 21	5: 24	18: 33	5: 9	18: 48	4: 49	19: 8	4: 17	19: 41
115			*10: 44*	*23: 57*	*10: 28*	*no: ne*	*10: 9*	*no: ne*	*9: 42*	*0: 16*	*8: 59*	*1: 1*
25 TH	11 57 55	13 13	5: 35	18: 22	5: 23	18: 34	5: 8	18: 49	4: 47	19: 10	4: 14	19: 44
116	20 40 FQ		*11: 33*	*no: ne*	*11: 19*	*0: 11*	*11: 3*	*0: 29*	*10: 40*	*0: 53*	*10: 2*	*1: 33*
26 FR	11 57 45	13 32	5: 34	18: 22	5: 22	18: 34	5: 6	18: 50	4: 45	19: 11	4: 11	19: 46
117			*12: 22*	*0: 38*	*12: 11*	*0: 51*	*11: 58*	*1: 6*	*11: 39*	*1: 26*	*11: 10*	*1: 58*
27 SA	11 57 36	13 51	5: 33	18: 22	5: 21	18: 35	5: 5	18: 51	4: 43	19: 13	4: 8	19: 48
118			*13: 12*	*1: 19*	*13: 4*	*1: 28*	*12: 54*	*1: 39*	*12: 41*	*1: 55*	*12: 20*	*2: 19*
28 SU	11 57 27	14 10	5: 33	18: 23	5: 20	18: 36	5: 4	18: 52	4: 42	19: 14	4: 6	19: 51
119			*14: 2*	*1: 58*	*13: 58*	*2: 4*	*13: 52*	*2: 11*	*13: 44*	*2: 22*	*13: 32*	*2: 37*
29 MO	11 57 18	14 29	5: 32	18: 23	5: 19	18: 36	5: 2	18: 53	4: 40	19: 16	4: 3	19: 53
120			*14: 53*	*2: 39*	*14: 52*	*2: 39*	*14: 51*	*2: 43*	*14: 49*	*2: 47*	*14: 47*	*2: 54*
30 TU	11 57 11	14 48	5: 31	18: 23	5: 18	18: 37	5: 1	18: 54	4: 38	19: 17	4: 0	19: 56
121			*15: 46*	*3: 16*	*15: 49*	*3: 15*	*15: 52*	*3: 14*	*15: 57*	*3: 13*	*16: 4*	*3: 10*

5th Month   **May 1996**   **31 days**

Greenwich Mean Time

NOTE: For each day, numbers on first line indicate Sun. *Italic* numbers on second line indicate *Moon*.
Degrees are North Latitude.

FM = full moon; LQ = last quarter; NM = new moon; FQ = first quarter.

CAUTION: Must be converted to local time. For instructions see page 296.

Day of month week year	Sun on Meridian Moon Phase h m s	Sun's Declina- tion ° '	20° Rise Sun h m	20° Set Sun h m	30° Rise Sun h m	30° Set Sun h m	40° Rise Sun h m	40° Set Sun h m	50° Rise Sun h m	50° Set Sun h m	60° Rise Sun h m	60° Set Sun h m
1 WE	11 57 3	15 6	5: 31	18: 24	5: 17	18: 37	5: 0	18: 55	4: 36	19: 19	3: 57	19: 58
122			*16: 41*	*3: 57*	*16: 47*	*3: 52*	*16: 55*	*3: 47*	*17: 6*	*3: 39*	*17: 24*	*3: 28*
2 TH	11 56 56	15 24	5: 30	18: 24	5: 16	18: 38	4: 59	18: 56	4: 34	19: 21	3: 55	20: 1
123			*17: 38*	*4: 40*	*17: 48*	*4: 32*	*18: 0*	*4: 22*	*18: 18*	*4: 8*	*18: 45*	*3: 47*
3 FR	11 56 50	15 42	5: 30	18: 24	5: 15	18: 39	4: 57	18: 57	4: 33	19: 22	3: 52	20: 3
124	*11 48 FM*		*18: 37*	*5: 26*	*18: 50*	*5: 15*	*19: 7*	*5: 0*	*19: 30*	*4: 41*	*20: 7*	*4: 11*
4 SA	11 56 44	15 59	5: 29	18: 25	5: 14	18: 39	4: 56	18: 58	4: 31	19: 24	3: 49	20: 6
125			*19: 37*	*6: 17*	*19: 53*	*6: 2*	*20: 13*	*5: 44*	*20: 40*	*5: 20*	*21: 26*	*4: 40*
5 SU	11 56 39	16 16	5: 28	18: 25	5: 14	18: 40	4: 55	18: 59	4: 29	19: 25	3: 47	20: 8
126			*20: 38*	*7: 11*	*20: 55*	*6: 54*	*21: 17*	*6: 34*	*21: 47*	*6: 5*	*22: 37*	*5: 19*
6 MO	11 56 35	16 33	5: 28	18: 25	5: 13	18: 41	4: 54	19: 0	4: 28	19: 27	3: 44	20: 11
127			*21: 38*	*8: 9*	*21: 55*	*7: 51*	*22: 17*	*7: 30*	*22: 46*	*6: 59*	*23: 36*	*6: 9*
7 TU	11 56 31	16 50	5: 27	18: 26	5: 12	18: 41	4: 53	19: 1	4: 26	19: 28	3: 42	20: 13
128			*22: 35*	*9: 9*	*22: 51*	*8: 52*	*23: 10*	*8: 31*	*23: 38*	*8: 2*	*no: ne*	*7: 13*
8 WE	11 56 27	17 6	5: 27	18: 26	5: 11	18: 42	4: 52	19: 2	4: 24	19: 30	3: 39	20: 16
129			*23: 28*	*10: 10*	*23: 41*	*9: 55*	*23: 58*	*9: 36*	*no: ne*	*9: 10*	*0: 22*	*8: 28*
9 TH	11 56 24	17 22	5: 26	18: 27	5: 11	18: 43	4: 51	19: 3	4: 23	19: 31	3: 36	20: 18
130			*no: ne*	*11: 11*	*no: ne*	*10: 59*	*no: ne*	*10: 43*	*0: 21*	*10: 22*	*0: 57*	*9: 49*
10 FR	11 56 22	17 38	5: 26	18: 27	5: 10	18: 43	4: 50	19: 4	4: 21	19: 33	3: 34	20: 21
131	*5 4 LQ*		*0: 17*	*12: 11*	*0: 28*	*12: 2*	*0: 41*	*11: 51*	*0: 58*	*11: 36*	*1: 25*	*11: 13*
11 SA	11 56 20	17 54	5: 26	18: 27	5: 9	18: 44	4: 49	19: 5	4: 20	19: 34	3: 31	20: 23
132			*1: 4*	*13: 9*	*1: 11*	*13: 4*	*1: 19*	*12: 58*	*1: 30*	*12: 49*	*1: 47*	*12: 36*
12 SU	11 56 19	18 9	5: 25	18: 28	5: 8	18: 45	4: 48	19: 6	4: 18	19: 35	3: 29	20: 25
133			*1: 48*	*14: 5*	*1: 51*	*14: 5*	*1: 54*	*14: 3*	*1: 59*	*14: 2*	*2: 6*	*13: 59*
13 MO	11 56 19	18 24	5: 25	18: 28	5: 8	18: 45	4: 47	19: 7	4: 17	19: 37	3: 27	20: 28
134			*2: 31*	*15: 1*	*2: 30*	*15: 4*	*2: 28*	*15: 8*	*2: 27*	*15: 13*	*2: 24*	*15: 21*
14 TU	11 56 19	18 38	5: 24	18: 29	5: 7	18: 46	4: 46	19: 8	4: 15	19: 38	3: 24	20: 30
135			*3: 13*	*15: 56*	*3: 8*	*16: 3*	*3: 2*	*16: 11*	*2: 54*	*16: 23*	*2: 42*	*16: 41*
15 WE	11 56 20	18 53	5: 24	18: 29	5: 7	18: 46	4: 45	19: 9	4: 14	19: 40	3: 22	20: 32
136			*3: 55*	*16: 51*	*3: 47*	*17: 1*	*3: 37*	*17: 14*	*3: 23*	*17: 31*	*3: 2*	*17: 58*
16 TH	11 56 21	19 7	5: 24	18: 29	5: 6	18: 47	4: 44	19: 9	4: 12	19: 41	3: 20	20: 35
137			*4: 39*	*17: 45*	*4: 27*	*17: 58*	*4: 13*	*18: 14*	*3: 54*	*18: 37*	*3: 24*	*19: 13*
17 FR	11 56 23	19 20	5: 23	18: 30	5: 5	18: 48	4: 43	19: 10	4: 11	19: 42	3: 17	20: 37
138	*11 46 NM*		*5: 24*	*18: 38*	*5: 10*	*18: 53*	*4: 52*	*19: 12*	*4: 28*	*19: 39*	*3: 50*	*20: 22*
18 SA	11 56 25	19 34	5: 23	18: 30	5: 5	18: 48	4: 42	19: 11	4: 10	19: 44	3: 15	20: 39
139			*6: 10*	*19: 30*	*5: 54*	*19: 46*	*5: 34*	*20: 7*	*5: 7*	*20: 36*	*4: 22*	*21: 24*
19 SU	11 56 28	19 47	5: 23	18: 31	5: 4	18: 49	4: 41	19: 12	4: 9	19: 45	3: 13	20: 42
140			*6: 58*	*20: 20*	*6: 41*	*20: 37*	*6: 20*	*20: 58*	*5: 51*	*21: 28*	*5: 2*	*22: 17*
20 MO	11 56 31	19 59	5: 22	18: 31	5: 4	18: 50	4: 40	19: 13	4: 7	19: 46	3: 11	20: 44
141			*7: 47*	*21: 7*	*7: 30*	*21: 24*	*7: 9*	*21: 44*	*6: 39*	*22: 13*	*5: 50*	*23: 0*
21 TU	11 56 35	20 12	5: 22	18: 31	5: 3	18: 50	4: 40	19: 14	4: 6	19: 48	3: 9	20: 46
142			*8: 36*	*21: 52*	*8: 20*	*22: 7*	*8: 0*	*22: 26*	*7: 32*	*22: 52*	*6: 46*	*23: 34*
22 WE	11 56 40	20 24	5: 22	18: 32	5: 3	18: 51	4: 39	19: 15	4: 5	19: 49	3: 7	20: 48
143			*9: 26*	*22: 35*	*9: 11*	*22: 48*	*8: 53*	*23: 4*	*8: 28*	*23: 27*	*7: 48*	*no: ne*
23 TH	11 56 45	20 35	5: 21	18: 32	5: 2	18: 51	4: 38	19: 16	4: 4	19: 50	3: 5	20: 50
144			*10: 15*	*23: 15*	*10: 3*	*23: 26*	*9: 48*	*23: 39*	*9: 27*	*23: 57*	*8: 54*	*0: 2*
24 FR	11 56 50	20 47	5: 21	18: 33	5: 2	18: 52	4: 38	19: 17	4: 3	19: 52	3: 3	20: 53
145			*11: 4*	*23: 54*	*10: 55*	*no: ne*	*10: 43*	*no: ne*	*10: 27*	*no: ne*	*10: 2*	*0: 24*
25 SA	11 56 56	20 58	5: 21	18: 33	5: 1	18: 53	4: 37	19: 17	4: 2	19: 53	3: 1	20: 55
146	*14 13 FQ*		*11: 53*	*no: ne*	*11: 47*	*0: 2*	*11: 39*	*0: 11*	*11: 29*	*0: 24*	*11: 13*	*0: 43*
26 SU	11 57 3	21 8	5: 21	18: 33	5: 1	18: 53	4: 36	19: 18	4: 1	19: 54	2: 59	20: 57
147			*12: 43*	*0: 32*	*12: 40*	*0: 37*	*12: 37*	*0: 42*	*12: 33*	*0: 49*	*12: 26*	*1: 0*
27 MO	11 57 10	21 18	5: 21	18: 34	5: 1	18: 54	4: 36	19: 19	4: 0	19: 55	2: 57	20: 59
148			*13: 34*	*1: 11*	*13: 35*	*1: 12*	*13: 36*	*1: 13*	*13: 38*	*1: 14*	*13: 40*	*1: 16*
28 TU	11 57 17	21 28	5: 20	18: 34	5: 0	18: 54	4: 35	19: 20	3: 59	19: 56	2: 55	21: 1
149			*14: 27*	*1: 50*	*14: 31*	*1: 47*	*14: 37*	*1: 44*	*14: 45*	*1: 40*	*14: 57*	*1: 33*
29 WE	11 57 25	21 38	5: 20	18: 35	5: 0	18: 55	4: 35	19: 21	3: 58	19: 57	2: 54	21: 2
150			*15: 22*	*2: 31*	*15: 30*	*2: 25*	*15: 41*	*2: 17*	*15: 55*	*2: 7*	*16: 17*	*1: 50*
30 TH	11 57 33	21 47	5: 20	18: 35	5: 0	18: 55	4: 34	19: 21	3: 57	19: 58	2: 52	21: 4
151			*16: 20*	*3: 15*	*16: 32*	*3: 6*	*16: 46*	*2: 53*	*17: 7*	*2: 37*	*17: 39*	*2: 11*
31 FR	11 57 42	21 55	5: 20	18: 35	5: 0	18: 56	4: 34	19: 22	3: 56	20: 0	2: 51	21: 6
152			*17: 20*	*4: 4*	*17: 35*	*3: 51*	*17: 53*	*3: 34*	*18: 19*	*3: 12*	*19: 1*	*2: 37*

6th Month   **June 1996**   **30 days**

Greenwich Mean Time

NOTE: For each day, numbers on first line indicate Sun. *Italic* numbers on second line indicate *Moon*.
Degrees are North Latitude.

FM = full moon; LQ = last quarter; NM = new moon; FQ = first quarter.

CAUTION: Must be converted to local time. For instructions see page 296.

Day of month week year	Sun on Meridian Moon Phase h m s	Sun's Declination ° ′	20° Rise Sun Moon h m	20° Set Sun Moon h m	30° Rise Sun Moon h m	30° Set Sun Moon h m	40° Rise Sun Moon h m	40° Set Sun Moon h m	50° Rise Sun Moon h m	50° Set Sun Moon h m	60° Rise Sun Moon h m	60° Set Sun Moon h m
1 SA 153	11 57 51 *20 47 FM*	22 4	5: 20 *18: 22*	18: 36 *4: 56*	4: 59 *18: 39*	18: 57 *4: 41*	4: 33 *19: 0*	19: 23 *4: 21*	3: 56 *19: 29*	20: 1 *3: 54*	2: 49 *20: 17*	21: 8 *3: 11*
2 SU 154	11 58 0	22 12	5: 20 *19: 24*	18: 36 *5: 54*	4: 59 *19: 42*	18: 57 *5: 37*	4: 33 *20: 3*	19: 24 *5: 15*	3: 55 *20: 34*	20: 2 *4: 45*	2: 48 *21: 24*	21: 10 *3: 56*
3 MO 155	11 58 10	22 19	5: 20 *20: 24*	18: 37 *6: 55*	4: 59 *20: 41*	18: 58 *6: 38*	4: 32 *21: 2*	19: 24 *6: 16*	3: 54 *21: 31*	20: 2 *5: 46*	2: 46 *22: 18*	21: 11 *4: 55*
4 TU 156	11 58 20	22 26	5: 20 *21: 21*	18: 37 *7: 58*	4: 59 *21: 36*	18: 58 *7: 42*	4: 32 *21: 54*	19: 25 *7: 22*	3: 54 *22: 19*	20: 3 *6: 54*	2: 45 *22: 59*	21: 13 *6: 8*
5 WE 157	11 58 30	22 33	5: 20 *22: 14*	18: 37 *9: 1*	4: 59 *22: 25*	18: 59 *8: 48*	4: 32 *22: 40*	19: 26 *8: 31*	3: 53 *22: 59*	20: 4 *8: 8*	2: 44 *23: 30*	21: 14 *7: 30*
6 TH 158	11 58 41	22 39	5: 20 *23: 2*	18: 38 *10: 3*	4: 59 *23: 10*	18: 59 *9: 53*	4: 32 *23: 20*	19: 26 *9: 41*	3: 53 *23: 34*	20: 5 *9: 23*	2: 43 *23: 54*	21: 16 *8: 56*
7 FR 159	11 58 52	22 45	5: 20 *23: 48*	18: 38 *11: 3*	4: 58 *23: 52*	18: 59 *10: 57*	4: 31 *23: 57*	19: 27 *10: 49*	3: 52 *no: ne*	20: 6 *10: 38*	2: 42 *no: ne*	21: 17 *10: 22*
8 SA 160	11 59 4 *11 5 LQ*	22 51	5: 20 *no: ne*	18: 38 *12: 1*	4: 58 *no: ne*	19: 0 *11: 59*	4: 31 *no: ne*	19: 27 *11: 56*	3: 52 *0: 4*	20: 7 *11: 52*	2: 41 *0: 15*	21: 18 *11: 46*
9 SU 161	11 59 16	22 56	5: 20 *0: 31*	18: 39 *12: 57*	4: 58 *0: 31*	19: 0 *12: 59*	4: 31 *0: 32*	19: 28 *13: 1*	3: 51 *0: 32*	20: 7 *13: 4*	2: 40 *0: 33*	21: 20 *13: 8*
10 MO 162	11 59 28	23 1	5: 20 *1: 13*	18: 39 *13: 52*	4: 58 *1: 10*	19: 1 *13: 58*	4: 31 *1: 5*	19: 28 *14: 5*	3: 51 *1: 0*	20: 8 *14: 14*	2: 39 *0: 51*	21: 21 *14: 28*
11 TU 163	11 59 40	23 5	5: 20 *1: 55*	18: 39 *14: 46*	4: 58 *1: 48*	19: 1 *14: 55*	4: 31 *1: 39*	19: 29 *15: 7*	3: 51 *1: 27*	20: 9 *15: 22*	2: 38 *1: 9*	21: 22 *15: 46*
12 WE 164	11 59 52	23 9	5: 20 *2: 38*	18: 40 *15: 40*	4: 58 *2: 27*	19: 2 *15: 52*	4: 31 *2: 14*	19: 29 *16: 7*	3: 51 *1: 57*	20: 9 *16: 28*	2: 38 *1: 30*	21: 23 *17: 1*
13 TH 165	12 0 5	23 13	5: 20 *3: 21*	18: 40 *16: 32*	4: 58 *3: 8*	19: 2 *16: 47*	4: 31 *2: 52*	19: 30 *17: 5*	3: 50 *2: 29*	20: 10 *17: 31*	2: 37 *1: 54*	21: 24 *18: 12*
14 FR 166	12 0 17	23 16	5: 20 *4: 7*	18: 40 *17: 24*	4: 58 *3: 51*	19: 2 *17: 41*	4: 31 *3: 32*	19: 30 *18: 1*	3: 50 *3: 6*	20: 10 *18: 29*	2: 37 *2: 23*	21: 25 *19: 16*
15 SA 167	12 0 30	23 19	5: 20 *4: 53*	18: 41 *18: 14*	4: 58 *4: 37*	19: 3 *18: 32*	4: 31 *4: 16*	19: 31 *18: 53*	3: 47 *3: 50*	20: 11 *19: 23*	2: 36 *2: 59*	21: 25 *20: 12*
16 SU 168	12 0 43 *1 36 NM*	23 21	5: 21 *5: 42*	18: 41 *19: 3*	4: 59 *5: 24*	19: 3 *19: 20*	4: 31 *5: 3*	19: 31 *19: 41*	3: 50 *4: 33*	20: 11 *20: 10*	2: 36 *3: 44*	21: 26 *20: 59*
17 MO 169	12 0 56	23 23	5: 21 *6: 31*	18: 41 *19: 49*	4: 59 *6: 14*	19: 3 *20: 5*	4: 31 *5: 53*	19: 31 *20: 25*	3: 50 *5: 24*	20: 12 *20: 52*	2: 36 *4: 36*	21: 26 *21: 37*
18 TU 170	12 1 10	23 24	5: 21 *7: 20*	18: 41 *20: 32*	4: 59 *7: 5*	19: 3 *20: 47*	4: 31 *6: 46*	19: 32 *21: 4*	3: 50 *6: 19*	20: 12 *21: 28*	2: 36 *5: 36*	21: 27 *22: 7*
19 WE 171	12 1 23	23 25	5: 21 *8: 9*	18: 42 *21: 14*	4: 59 *7: 56*	19: 4 *21: 25*	4: 31 *7: 40*	19: 32 *21: 40*	3: 50 *7: 17*	20: 12 *22: 0*	2: 36 *6: 40*	21: 27 *22: 31*
20 TH 172	12 1 36	23 26	5: 21 *8: 58*	18: 42 *21: 53*	4: 59 *8: 48*	19: 4 *22: 2*	4: 31 *8: 35*	19: 32 *22: 13*	3: 50 *8: 17*	20: 13 *22: 28*	2: 36 *7: 48*	21: 28 *22: 51*
21 FR 173	12 1 49	23 26	5: 22 *9: 47*	18: 42 *22: 31*	5: 0 *9: 40*	19: 4 *22: 37*	4: 31 *9: 30*	19: 32 *22: 44*	3: 51 *9: 18*	20: 13 *22: 54*	2: 36 *8: 58*	21: 28 *23: 8*
22 SA 174	12 2 2	23 26	5: 22 *10: 36*	18: 42 *23: 9*	5: 0 *10: 32*	19: 4 *23: 11*	4: 32 *10: 27*	19: 32 *23: 14*	3: 51 *10: 20*	20: 13 *23: 18*	2: 36 *10: 9*	21: 28 *23: 24*
23 SU 175	12 2 15	23 25	5: 22 *11: 26*	18: 42 *23: 47*	5: 0 *11: 25*	19: 5 *23: 46*	4: 32 *11: 24*	19: 33 *23: 44*	3: 51 *11: 23*	20: 13 *23: 43*	2: 36 *11: 21*	21: 28 *23: 40*
24 MO 176	12 2 28 *5 23 FQ*	23 24	5: 22 *12: 16*	18: 43 *no: ne*	5: 0 *12: 19*	19: 5 *no: ne*	4: 32 *12: 23*	19: 33 *no: ne*	3: 52 *12: 28*	20: 13 *no: ne*	2: 37 *12: 35*	21: 28 *23: 56*
25 TU 177	12 2 40	23 23	5: 23 *13: 9*	18: 43 *0: 26*	5: 0 *13: 16*	19: 5 *0: 21*	4: 32 *13: 24*	19: 33 *0: 16*	3: 52 *13: 35*	20: 13 *0: 8*	2: 37 *13: 52*	21: 28 *no: ne*
26 WE 178	12 2 53	23 21	5: 23 *14: 4*	18: 43 *1: 7*	5: 1 *14: 14*	19: 5 *0: 59*	4: 33 *14: 27*	19: 33 *0: 49*	3: 53 *14: 44*	20: 13 *0: 36*	2: 38 *15: 11*	21: 27 *0: 15*
27 TH 179	12 3 5	23 19	5: 23 *15: 2*	18: 43 *1: 52*	5: 1 *15: 15*	19: 5 *1: 41*	4: 33 *15: 32*	19: 33 *1: 27*	3: 53 *15: 55*	20: 13 *1: 7*	2: 39 *16: 31*	21: 27 *0: 37*
28 FR 180	12 3 17	23 16	5: 23 *16: 2*	18: 43 *2: 42*	5: 1 *16: 18*	19: 5 *2: 27*	4: 34 *16: 38*	19: 33 *2: 9*	3: 53 *17: 5*	20: 13 *1: 45*	2: 40 *17: 51*	21: 27 *1: 6*
29 SA 181	12 3 29	23 13	5: 24 *17: 4*	18: 43 *3: 36*	5: 2 *17: 22*	19: 5 *3: 20*	4: 34 *17: 43*	19: 33 *2: 59*	3: 54 *18: 13*	20: 13 *2: 31*	2: 40 *19: 3*	21: 26 *1: 44*
30 SU 182	12 3 41	23 10	5: 24 *18: 6*	18: 43 *4: 35*	5: 2 *18: 24*	19: 5 *4: 18*	4: 34 *18: 45*	19: 33 *3: 56*	3: 54 *19: 15*	20: 13 *3: 26*	2: 41 *20: 5*	21: 25 *2: 35*

7th Month   **July 1996**   **31 days**

Greenwich Mean Time

NOTE: For each day, numbers on first line indicate Sun. *Italic* numbers on second line indicate *Moon*. Degrees are North Latitude.

FM = full moon; LQ = last quarter; NM = new moon; FQ = first quarter.

CAUTION: Must be converted to local time. For instructions see page 296.

Day of month / week / year	Sun on Meridian Moon Phase (h m s)	Sun's Declination (° ′)	20° Rise Sun / Moon	20° Set Sun / Moon	30° Rise Sun / Moon	30° Set Sun / Moon	40° Rise Sun / Moon	40° Set Sun / Moon	50° Rise Sun / Moon	50° Set Sun / Moon	60° Rise Sun / Moon	60° Set Sun / Moon
1 MO	12 3 53	23 6	5: 24	18: 43	5: 3	19: 5	4: 35	19: 33	3: 55	20: 12	2: 42	21: 25
183	*3 58 FM*		*19: 6*	*5: 38*	*19: 22*	*5: 22*	*19: 42*	*5: 0*	*20: 9*	*4: 31*	*20: 54*	*3: 42*
2 TU	12 4 4	23 2	5: 25	18: 43	5: 3	19: 5	4: 35	19: 32	3: 56	20: 12	2: 44	21: 24
184			*20: 3*	*6: 43*	*20: 16*	*6: 28*	*20: 32*	*6: 10*	*20: 55*	*5: 44*	*21: 30*	*5: 1*
3 WE	12 4 15	22 57	5: 25	18: 44	5: 3	19: 5	4: 36	19: 32	3: 56	20: 12	2: 45	21: 23
185			*20: 55*	*7: 48*	*21: 5*	*7: 36*	*21: 17*	*7: 22*	*21: 33*	*7: 1*	*21: 59*	*6: 28*
4 TH	12 4 25	22 52	5: 25	18: 44	5: 4	19: 5	4: 37	19: 32	3: 57	20: 11	2: 46	21: 22
186			*21: 44*	*8: 51*	*21: 50*	*8: 43*	*21: 57*	*8: 33*	*22: 7*	*8: 20*	*22: 21*	*7: 58*
5 FR	12 4 36	22 47	5: 26	18: 44	5: 4	19: 5	4: 37	19: 32	3: 58	20: 11	2: 47	21: 21
187			*22: 29*	*9: 52*	*22: 31*	*9: 48*	*22: 33*	*9: 43*	*22: 36*	*9: 37*	*22: 41*	*9: 26*
6 SA	12 4 46	22 41	5: 26	18: 44	5: 5	19: 5	4: 38	19: 32	3: 59	20: 10	2: 49	21: 20
188			*23: 13*	*10: 51*	*23: 11*	*10: 51*	*23: 8*	*10: 51*	*23: 5*	*10: 51*	*22: 59*	*10: 52*
7 SU	12 4 55	22 35	5: 26	18: 43	5: 5	19: 5	4: 38	19: 31	4: 0	20: 10	2: 50	21: 19
189	*18 55 LQ*		*23: 55*	*11: 47*	*23: 50*	*11: 51*	*23: 42*	*11: 57*	*23: 33*	*12: 4*	*23: 18*	*12: 14*
8 MO	12 5 5	22 28	5: 27	18: 43	5: 6	19: 4	4: 39	19: 31	4: 1	20: 9	2: 52	21: 17
190			*no: ne*	*12: 42*	*no: ne*	*12: 50*	*no: ne*	*13: 0*	*no: ne*	*13: 13*	*23: 38*	*13: 34*
9 TU	12 5 14	22 21	5: 27	18: 43	5: 6	19: 4	4: 40	19: 31	4: 2	20: 8	2: 53	21: 16
191			*0: 38*	*13: 36*	*0: 29*	*13: 47*	*0: 17*	*14: 1*	*0: 2*	*14: 20*	*no: ne*	*14: 50*
10 WE	12 5 22	22 13	5: 27	18: 43	5: 7	19: 4	4: 40	19: 30	4: 2	20: 8	2: 55	21: 15
192			*1: 21*	*14: 29*	*1: 9*	*14: 43*	*0: 54*	*15: 0*	*0: 33*	*15: 24*	*0: 0*	*16: 2*
11 TH	12 5 30	22 6	5: 28	18: 43	5: 7	19: 4	4: 41	19: 30	4: 3	20: 7	2: 57	21: 13
193			*2: 6*	*15: 21*	*1: 51*	*15: 37*	*1: 33*	*15: 56*	*1: 8*	*16: 23*	*0: 28*	*17: 8*
12 FR	12 5 38	21 57	5: 28	18: 43	5: 8	19: 3	4: 42	19: 29	4: 4	20: 6	2: 58	21: 12
194			*2: 51*	*16: 11*	*2: 35*	*16: 28*	*2: 15*	*16: 49*	*1: 47*	*17: 18*	*1: 1*	*18: 7*
13 SA	12 5 45	21 49	5: 28	18: 43	5: 8	19: 3	4: 42	19: 29	4: 6	20: 5	3: 0	21: 10
195			*3: 39*	*17: 0*	*3: 22*	*17: 17*	*3: 0*	*17: 38*	*2: 31*	*18: 8*	*1: 42*	*18: 57*
14 SU	12 5 52	21 40	5: 29	18: 43	5: 9	19: 3	4: 43	19: 28	4: 7	20: 4	3: 2	21: 8
196			*4: 27*	*17: 47*	*4: 10*	*18: 3*	*3: 49*	*18: 23*	*3: 20*	*18: 52*	*2: 31*	*19: 38*
15 MO	12 5 58	21 31	5: 29	18: 43	5: 9	19: 2	4: 44	19: 28	4: 8	20: 4	3: 4	21: 7
197	*16 15 NM*		*5: 16*	*18: 31*	*5: 0*	*18: 46*	*4: 40*	*19: 4*	*4: 13*	*19: 30*	*3: 28*	*20: 10*
16 TU	12 6 3	21 21	5: 30	18: 42	5: 10	19: 2	4: 45	19: 27	4: 9	20: 3	3: 6	21: 5
198			*6: 6*	*19: 13*	*5: 51*	*19: 26*	*5: 34*	*19: 42*	*5: 10*	*20: 3*	*4: 31*	*20: 37*
17 WE	12 6 9	21 11	5: 30	18: 42	5: 10	19: 2	4: 45	19: 26	4: 10	20: 2	3: 8	21: 3
199			*6: 55*	*19: 53*	*6: 43*	*20: 3*	*6: 29*	*20: 16*	*6: 9*	*20: 32*	*5: 37*	*20: 58*
18 TH	12 6 13	21 1	5: 30	18: 42	5: 11	19: 1	4: 46	19: 26	4: 11	20: 1	3: 10	21: 1
200			*7: 44*	*20: 32*	*7: 35*	*20: 39*	*7: 24*	*20: 47*	*7: 9*	*20: 59*	*6: 46*	*21: 17*
19 FR	12 6 17	20 50	5: 31	18: 42	5: 11	19: 1	4: 47	19: 25	4: 12	19: 59	3: 12	20: 59
201			*8: 32*	*21: 9*	*8: 27*	*21: 13*	*8: 20*	*21: 18*	*8: 11*	*21: 24*	*7: 56*	*21: 33*
20 SA	12 6 21	20 39	5: 31	18: 41	5: 12	19: 0	4: 48	19: 24	4: 14	19: 58	3: 14	20: 57
202			*9: 21*	*21: 47*	*9: 19*	*21: 47*	*9: 17*	*21: 48*	*9: 13*	*21: 48*	*9: 8*	*21: 49*
21 SU	12 6 24	20 27	5: 31	18: 41	5: 13	19: 0	4: 49	19: 24	4: 15	19: 57	3: 16	20: 55
203			*10: 11*	*22: 25*	*10: 12*	*22: 22*	*10: 14*	*22: 18*	*10: 16*	*22: 13*	*10: 20*	*22: 5*
22 MO	12 6 26	20 16	5: 32	18: 41	5: 13	18: 59	4: 50	19: 23	4: 16	19: 56	3: 18	20: 53
204			*11: 2*	*23: 4*	*11: 7*	*22: 58*	*11: 13*	*22: 50*	*11: 21*	*22: 39*	*11: 34*	*22: 22*
23 TU	12 6 28	20 3	5: 32	18: 41	5: 14	18: 59	4: 50	19: 22	4: 17	19: 55	3: 21	20: 51
205	*17 49 FQ*		*11: 54*	*23: 46*	*12: 3*	*23: 36*	*12: 13*	*23: 24*	*12: 27*	*23: 8*	*12: 50*	*22: 42*
24 WE	12 6 29	19 51	5: 33	18: 40	5: 14	18: 58	4: 51	19: 21	4: 19	19: 53	3: 23	20: 49
206			*12: 49*	*no: ne*	*13: 1*	*no: ne*	*13: 15*	*no: ne*	*13: 35*	*23: 41*	*14: 8*	*23: 7*
25 TH	12 6 29	19 38	5: 33	18: 40	5: 15	18: 58	4: 52	19: 20	4: 20	19: 52	3: 25	20: 46
207			*13: 46*	*0: 32*	*14: 1*	*0: 19*	*14: 19*	*0: 3*	*14: 44*	*no: ne*	*15: 25*	*23: 39*
26 FR	12 6 29	19 25	5: 33	18: 39	5: 16	18: 57	4: 53	19: 19	4: 21	19: 51	3: 27	20: 44
208			*14: 46*	*1: 22*	*15: 2*	*1: 7*	*15: 23*	*0: 48*	*15: 52*	*0: 21*	*16: 39*	*no: ne*
27 SA	12 6 29	19 12	5: 34	18: 39	5: 16	18: 57	4: 54	19: 18	4: 23	19: 49	3: 30	20: 42
209			*15: 47*	*2: 18*	*16: 4*	*2: 1*	*16: 26*	*1: 39*	*16: 56*	*1: 10*	*17: 46*	*0: 21*
28 SU	12 6 27	18 58	5: 34	18: 39	5: 17	18: 56	4: 55	19: 18	4: 24	19: 48	3: 32	20: 39
210			*16: 47*	*3: 18*	*17: 4*	*3: 0*	*17: 25*	*2: 39*	*17: 54*	*2: 9*	*18: 41*	*1: 18*
29 MO	12 6 25	18 44	5: 34	18: 38	5: 17	18: 55	4: 56	19: 17	4: 25	19: 47	3: 34	20: 37
211			*17: 46*	*4: 21*	*18: 0*	*4: 5*	*18: 19*	*3: 45*	*18: 44*	*3: 17*	*19: 25*	*2: 30*
30 TU	12 6 23	18 30	5: 35	18: 38	5: 18	18: 55	4: 57	19: 16	4: 27	19: 45	3: 36	20: 35
212	*10 35 FM*		*18: 41*	*5: 26*	*18: 53*	*5: 13*	*19: 7*	*4: 56*	*19: 27*	*4: 32*	*19: 58*	*3: 54*
31 WE	12 6 20	18 15	5: 35	18: 37	5: 18	18: 54	4: 58	19: 15	4: 28	19: 44	3: 39	20: 32
213			*19: 33*	*6: 32*	*19: 41*	*6: 22*	*19: 50*	*6: 9*	*20: 4*	*5: 52*	*20: 24*	*5: 24*

8th Month   **August 1996**   **31 days**

Greenwich Mean Time

NOTE: For each day, numbers on first line indicate Sun. *Italic* numbers on second line indicate *Moon*. Degrees are North Latitude.

FM = full moon; LQ = last quarter; NM = new moon; FQ = first quarter.

CAUTION: Must be converted to local time. For instructions see page 296.

Day of month / week / year	Sun on Meridian / Moon Phase (h m s)	Sun's Declination (° ')	20° Rise Sun/Moon	20° Set Sun/Moon	30° Rise Sun/Moon	30° Set Sun/Moon	40° Rise Sun/Moon	40° Set Sun/Moon	50° Rise Sun/Moon	50° Set Sun/Moon	60° Rise Sun/Moon	60° Set Sun/Moon
1 TH 214	12 6 16	17 60	5: 35	18: 37	5: 19	18: 53	4: 58	19: 13	4: 30	19: 42	3: 41	20: 30
214			*20: 21*	*7: 36*	*20: 25*	*7: 29*	*20: 30*	*7: 22*	*20: 36*	*7: 12*	*20: 46*	*6: 55*
2 FR 215	12 6 12	17 45	5: 36	18: 36	5: 20	18: 52	4: 59	19: 12	4: 31	19: 40	3: 44	20: 27
215			*21: 7*	*8: 37*	*21: 7*	*8: 35*	*21: 7*	*8: 33*	*21: 6*	*8: 30*	*21: 6*	*8: 25*
3 SA 216	12 6 7	17 29	5: 36	18: 36	5: 20	18: 52	5: 0	19: 11	4: 32	19: 39	3: 46	20: 25
216			*21: 52*	*9: 37*	*21: 47*	*9: 39*	*21: 42*	*9: 42*	*21: 35*	*9: 46*	*21: 25*	*9: 52*
4 SU 217	12 6 1	17 13	5: 37	18: 35	5: 21	18: 51	5: 1	19: 10	4: 34	19: 37	3: 48	20: 22
217			*22: 36*	*10: 34*	*22: 28*	*10: 40*	*22: 18*	*10: 48*	*22: 5*	*10: 59*	*21: 45*	*11: 15*
5 MO 218	12 5 55	16 57	5: 37	18: 35	5: 21	18: 50	5: 2	19: 9	4: 35	19: 36	3: 51	20: 19
218			*23: 20*	*11: 30*	*23: 8*	*11: 40*	*22: 55*	*11: 52*	*22: 36*	*12: 8*	*22: 7*	*12: 34*
6 TU 219	12 5 48	16 41	5: 37	18: 34	5: 22	18: 49	5: 3	19: 8	4: 37	19: 34	3: 53	20: 17
219 5 25 LQ			*no: ne*	*12: 24*	*23: 50*	*12: 37*	*23: 33*	*12: 53*	*23: 10*	*13: 14*	*22: 33*	*13: 49*
7 WE 220	12 5 41	16 24	5: 38	18: 34	5: 23	18: 48	5: 4	19: 7	4: 38	19: 32	3: 55	20: 14
220			*0: 4*	*13: 17*	*no: ne*	*13: 32*	*no: ne*	*13: 50*	*23: 48*	*14: 16*	*23: 4*	*14: 58*
8 TH 221	12 5 33	16 7	5: 38	18: 33	5: 23	18: 47	5: 5	19: 5	4: 40	19: 31	3: 58	20: 12
221			*0: 50*	*14: 8*	*0: 34*	*14: 24*	*0: 15*	*14: 45*	*no: ne*	*15: 13*	*23: 42*	*16: 0*
9 FR 222	12 5 25	15 50	5: 38	18: 32	5: 24	18: 47	5: 6	19: 4	4: 41	19: 29	4: 0	20: 9
222			*1: 37*	*14: 57*	*1: 20*	*15: 14*	*0: 59*	*15: 35*	*0: 30*	*16: 5*	*no: ne*	*16: 53*
10 SA 223	12 5 16	15 33	5: 38	18: 32	5: 24	18: 46	5: 7	19: 3	4: 43	19: 27	4: 3	20: 6
223			*2: 24*	*15: 44*	*2: 7*	*16: 1*	*1: 46*	*16: 22*	*1: 17*	*16: 50*	*0: 28*	*17: 37*
11 SU 224	12 5 6	15 15	5: 39	18: 31	5: 25	18: 45	5: 8	19: 2	4: 44	19: 25	4: 5	20: 3
224			*3: 13*	*16: 29*	*2: 57*	*16: 45*	*2: 37*	*17: 4*	*2: 9*	*17: 30*	*1: 22*	*18: 13*
12 MO 225	12 4 56	14 57	5: 39	18: 30	5: 26	18: 44	5: 9	19: 0	4: 45	19: 23	4: 7	20: 1
225			*4: 2*	*17: 12*	*3: 48*	*17: 26*	*3: 29*	*17: 42*	*3: 4*	*18: 5*	*2: 23*	*18: 41*
13 TU 226	12 4 46	14 39	5: 39	18: 30	5: 26	18: 43	5: 10	18: 59	4: 47	19: 22	4: 10	19: 58
226			*4: 51*	*17: 53*	*4: 39*	*18: 4*	*4: 23*	*18: 18*	*4: 2*	*18: 36*	*3: 28*	*19: 5*
14 WE 227	12 4 35	14 20	5: 40	18: 29	5: 27	18: 42	5: 11	18: 58	4: 48	19: 20	4: 12	19: 55
227 7 34 NM			*5: 41*	*18: 32*	*5: 31*	*18: 40*	*5: 19*	*18: 50*	*5: 2*	*19: 4*	*4: 36*	*19: 24*
15 TH 228	12 4 23	14 2	5: 40	18: 28	5: 27	18: 41	5: 12	18: 56	4: 50	19: 18	4: 15	19: 52
228			*6: 30*	*19: 10*	*6: 23*	*19: 15*	*6: 15*	*19: 21*	*6: 3*	*19: 29*	*5: 46*	*19: 42*
16 FR 229	12 4 11	13 43	5: 40	18: 28	5: 28	18: 40	5: 13	18: 55	4: 51	19: 16	4: 17	19: 50
229			*7: 19*	*19: 48*	*7: 15*	*19: 50*	*7: 11*	*19: 52*	*7: 6*	*19: 54*	*6: 57*	*19: 58*
17 SA 230	12 3 58	13 24	5: 41	18: 27	5: 29	18: 39	5: 14	18: 54	4: 53	19: 14	4: 20	19: 47
230			*8: 8*	*20: 26*	*8: 8*	*20: 24*	*8: 8*	*20: 22*	*8: 9*	*20: 19*	*8: 9*	*20: 14*
18 SU 231	12 3 45	13 5	5: 41	18: 26	5: 29	18: 38	5: 15	18: 52	4: 54	19: 12	4: 22	19: 44
231			*8: 58*	*21: 5*	*9: 2*	*20: 59*	*9: 6*	*20: 53*	*9: 13*	*20: 44*	*9: 22*	*20: 31*
19 MO 232	12 3 31	12 45	5: 41	18: 26	5: 30	18: 37	5: 16	18: 51	4: 56	19: 10	4: 24	19: 41
232			*9: 50*	*21: 45*	*9: 57*	*21: 37*	*10: 6*	*21: 26*	*10: 18*	*21: 12*	*10: 37*	*20: 49*
20 TU 233	12 3 17	12 25	5: 41	18: 25	5: 30	18: 36	5: 16	18: 49	4: 57	19: 8	4: 27	19: 38
233			*10: 43*	*22: 29*	*10: 53*	*22: 17*	*11: 6*	*22: 3*	*11: 24*	*21: 43*	*11: 52*	*21: 12*
21 WE 234	12 3 2	12 6	5: 42	18: 24	5: 31	18: 35	5: 17	18: 48	4: 59	19: 6	4: 29	19: 35
234			*11: 38*	*23: 16*	*11: 51*	*23: 1*	*12: 8*	*22: 44*	*12: 31*	*22: 19*	*13: 8*	*21: 40*
22 TH 235	12 2 47	11 45 3 36 FQ		5: 42	18: 23	5: 31	18: 34	5: 18	18: 46	5: 0	19: 4	4: 32	19: 32
235			*12: 34*	*no: ne*	*12: 50*	*23: 51*	*13: 10*	*23: 31*	*13: 37*	*23: 3*	*14: 21*	*22: 17*
23 FR 236	12 2 31	11 25	5: 42	18: 23	5: 32	18: 33	5: 19	18: 45	5: 2	19: 2	4: 34	19: 29
236			*13: 33*	*0: 7*	*13: 50*	*no: ne*	*14: 11*	*no: ne*	*14: 40*	*23: 55*	*15: 29*	*23: 5*
24 SA 237	12 2 15	11 5	5: 42	18: 22	5: 33	18: 31	5: 20	18: 44	5: 3	19: 0	4: 36	19: 27
237			*14: 31*	*1: 3*	*14: 48*	*0: 46*	*15: 9*	*0: 24*	*15: 39*	*no: ne*	*16: 28*	*no: ne*
25 SU 238	12 1 58	10 44	5: 43	18: 21	5: 33	18: 30	5: 21	18: 42	5: 5	18: 58	4: 39	19: 24
238			*15: 29*	*2: 3*	*15: 45*	*1: 46*	*16: 4*	*1: 25*	*16: 31*	*0: 56*	*17: 16*	*0: 8*
26 MO 239	12 1 41	10 23	5: 43	18: 20	5: 34	18: 29	5: 22	18: 41	5: 6	18: 56	4: 41	19: 21
239			*16: 25*	*3: 6*	*16: 38*	*2: 51*	*16: 55*	*2: 32*	*17: 17*	*2: 6*	*17: 53*	*1: 24*
27 TU 240	12 1 24	10 2	5: 43	18: 19	5: 34	18: 28	5: 23	18: 39	5: 8	18: 54	4: 43	19: 18
240			*17: 18*	*4: 10*	*17: 28*	*3: 58*	*17: 40*	*3: 43*	*17: 57*	*3: 22*	*18: 23*	*2: 49*
28 WE 241	12 1 6	9 41 17 52 FM		5: 43	18: 18	5: 35	18: 27	5: 24	18: 37	5: 9	18: 52	4: 46	19: 15
241			*18: 8*	*5: 14*	*18: 14*	*5: 6*	*18: 22*	*4: 55*	*18: 32*	*4: 41*	*18: 47*	*4: 19*
29 TH 242	12 0 48	9 20	5: 44	18: 18	5: 35	18: 26	5: 25	18: 36	5: 11	18: 50	4: 48	19: 12
242			*18: 56*	*6: 17*	*18: 58*	*6: 13*	*19: 0*	*6: 8*	*19: 4*	*6: 1*	*19: 8*	*5: 50*
30 FR 243	12 0 30	8 59	5: 44	18: 17	5: 36	18: 25	5: 26	18: 34	5: 12	18: 48	4: 51	19: 9
243			*19: 43*	*7: 19*	*19: 40*	*7: 19*	*19: 38*	*7: 19*	*19: 34*	*7: 20*	*19: 28*	*7: 20*
31 SA 244	12 0 11	8 37	5: 44	18: 16	5: 36	18: 23	5: 27	18: 33	5: 14	18: 46	4: 53	19: 6
244			*20: 28*	*8: 19*	*20: 22*	*8: 23*	*20: 14*	*8: 29*	*20: 4*	*8: 36*	*19: 49*	*8: 47*

9th Month   September 1996   30 days

Greenwich Mean Time

NOTE: For each day, numbers on first line indicate Sun. *Italic* numbers on second line indicate *Moon*.
Degrees are North Latitude.

FM = full moon; LQ = last quarter; NM = new moon; FQ = first quarter.

CAUTION: Must be converted to local time. For instructions see page 296.

Day of month week year	Sun on Meridian Moon Phase h m s	Sun's Declina- tion ° ′	20° Rise Sun Moon h m	20° Set Sun Moon h m	30° Rise Sun Moon h m	30° Set Sun Moon h m	40° Rise Sun Moon h m	40° Set Sun Moon h m	50° Rise Sun Moon h m	50° Set Sun Moon h m	60° Rise Sun Moon h m	60° Set Sun Moon h m
1 SU 245	11 59 52	8 15	5: 44 *21: 13*	18: 15 *9: 17*	5: 37 *21: 4*	18: 22 *9: 25*	5: 28 *20: 52*	18: 31 *9: 36*	5: 15 *20: 36*	18: 44 *9: 49*	4: 55 *20: 11*	19: 3 *10: 11*
2 MO 246	11 59 33	7 54	5: 45 *21: 59*	18: 14 *10: 14*	5: 38 *21: 46*	18: 21 *10: 25*	5: 29 *21: 31*	18: 30 *10: 39*	5: 17 *21: 9*	18: 41 *10: 59*	4: 58 *20: 36*	19: 0 *11: 30*
3 TU 247	11 59 13	7 32	5: 45 *22: 45*	18: 13 *11: 9*	5: 38 *22: 30*	18: 20 *11: 23*	5: 30 *22: 12*	18: 28 *11: 40*	5: 18 *21: 46*	18: 39 *12: 4*	5: 0 *21: 6*	18: 57 *12: 43*
4 WE 248	11 58 53 *19 6 LQ*	7 10	5: 45 *23: 32*	18: 12 *12: 1*	5: 39 *23: 16*	18: 19 *12: 17*	5: 31 *22: 56*	18: 26 *12: 37*	5: 20 *22: 28*	18: 37 *13: 4*	5: 2 *21: 42*	18: 54 *13: 49*
5 TH 249	11 58 33	6 47	5: 45 *no: ne*	18: 12 *12: 52*	5: 39 *no: ne*	18: 17 *13: 9*	5: 32 *23: 43*	18: 25 *13: 30*	5: 21 *223: 13*	18: 35 *13: 59*	5: 5 *22: 25*	18: 51 *14: 47*
6 FR 250	11 58 13	6 25	5: 45 *0: 20*	18: 11 *13: 40*	5: 40 *0: 4*	18: 16 *13: 57*	5: 33 *no: ne*	18: 23 *14: 18*	5: 23 *no: ne*	18: 33 *14: 47*	5: 7 *23: 17*	18: 48 *15: 34*
7 SA 251	11 57 53	6 3	5: 46 *1: 9*	18: 10 *14: 26*	5: 40 *0: 53*	18: 15 *14: 42*	5: 33 *0: 32*	18: 22 *15: 2*	5: 24 *0: 4*	18: 31 *15: 29*	5: 9 *no: ne*	18: 45 *16: 13*
8 SU 252	11 57 32	5 40	5: 46 *1: 58*	18: 9 *15: 10*	5: 41 *1: 43*	18: 14 *15: 24*	5: 34 *1: 24*	18: 20 *15: 42*	5: 26 *0: 58*	18: 28 *16: 6*	5: 12 *0: 15*	18: 42 *16: 44*
9 MO 253	11 57 11	5 18	5: 46 *2: 47*	18: 8 *15: 52*	5: 41 *2: 34*	18: 13 *16: 3*	5: 35 *2: 17*	18: 18 *16: 18*	5: 27 *1: 55*	18: 26 *16: 38*	5: 14 *1: 18*	18: 39 *17: 9*
10 TU 254	11 56 50	4 55	5: 46 *3: 36*	18: 7 *16: 31*	5: 42 *3: 26*	18: 11 *16: 41*	5: 36 *3: 12*	18: 17 *16: 52*	5: 29 *2: 54*	18: 24 *17: 7*	5: 17 *2: 25*	18: 36 *17: 30*
11 WE 255	11 56 29	4 32	5: 47 *4: 25*	18: 6 *17: 10*	5: 42 *4: 18*	18: 10 *17: 16*	5: 37 *4: 8*	18: 15 *17: 24*	5: 30 *3: 55*	18: 22 *17: 33*	5: 19 *3: 35*	18: 33 *17: 48*
12 TH 256	11 56 8 *23 7 NM*	4 9	5: 47 *5: 15*	18: 5 *17: 48*	5: 43 *5: 10*	18: 9 *17: 51*	5: 5 *5: 5*	18: 13 *17: 54*	5: 32 *4: 57*	18: 20 *17: 59*	5: 21 *4: 46*	18: 30 *18: 5*
13 FR 257	11 55 47	3 46	5: 47 *6: 4*	18: 4 *18: 26*	5: 44 *6: 3*	18: 8 *18: 26*	5: 39 *6: 2*	18: 12 *18: 25*	5: 33 *6: 0*	18: 17 *18: 23*	5: 24 *5: 58*	18: 27 *18: 22*
14 SA 258	11 55 26	3 23	5: 47 *6: 55*	18: 3 *19: 5*	5: 44 *6: 57*	18: 6 *19: 1*	5: 40 *7: 0*	18: 10 *18: 56*	5: 35 *7: 5*	18: 15 *18: 49*	5: 26 *7: 11*	18: 24 *18: 38*
15 SU 259	11 55 5	3 0	5: 47 *7: 46*	18: 2 *19: 46*	5: 45 *7: 52*	18: 4 *19: 38*	5: 41 *8: 0*	18: 8 *19: 29*	5: 36 *8: 10*	18: 13 *19: 16*	5: 28 *8: 26*	18: 57 *18: 57*
16 MO 260	11 54 43	2 37	5: 48 *8: 39*	18: 2 *20: 28*	5: 45 *8: 48*	18: 4 *20: 17*	5: 42 *9: 0*	18: 7 *20: 4*	5: 38 *9: 16*	18: 11 *19: 46*	5: 31 *9: 41*	18: 17 *19: 18*
17 TU 261	11 54 22	2 14	5: 48 *9: 33*	18: 1 *21: 14*	5: 46 *9: 46*	18: 3 *21: 0*	5: 43 *10: 1*	18: 5 *20: 44*	5: 39 *10: 22*	18: 9 *20: 21*	5: 33 *10: 57*	18: 14 *19: 44*
18 WE 262	11 54 1	1 51	5: 48 *10: 29*	18: 0 *22: 3*	5: 46 *10: 44*	18: 1 *21: 47*	5: 44 *11: 2*	18: 3 *21: 28*	5: 41 *11: 28*	18: 6 *21: 1*	5: 35 *12: 10*	18: 11 *20: 18*
19 TH 263	11 53 39	1 27	5: 48 *11: 26*	17: 59 *22: 56*	5: 47 *11: 42*	18: 0 *22: 39*	5: 45 *12: 3*	18: 2 *22: 18*	5: 42 *12: 31*	18: 4 *21: 49*	5: 38 *13: 19*	18: 8 *21: 1*
20 FR 264	11 53 18 *11 23 FQ*	1 4	5: 48 *12: 23*	17: 58 *23: 53*	5: 47 *12: 40*	17: 59 *23: 36*	5: 46 *13: 1*	18: 0 *23: 15*	5: 44 *13: 30*	18: 2 *22: 45*	5: 40 *14: 19*	18: 5 *21: 57*
21 SA 265	11 52 57	0 41	5: 49 *13: 19*	17: 57 *no: ne*	5: 48 *13: 35*	17: 58 *no: ne*	5: 47 *13: 55*	17: 58 *no: ne*	5: 45 *14: 23*	18: 0 *23: 50*	5: 42 *15: 9*	18: 2 *23: 5*
22 SU 266	11 52 36	0 18	5: 49 *14: 13*	17: 56 *0: 52*	5: 48 *14: 28*	17: 56 *0: 37*	5: 48 *14: 46*	17: 57 *0: 17*	5: 47 *15: 10*	17: 58 *no: ne*	5: 45 *15: 50*	17: 59 *no: ne*
23 MO 267	11 52 15	0 6	5: 49 *15: 6*	17: 55 *1: 54*	5: 49 *15: 17*	17: 55 *1: 40*	5: 49 *15: 31*	17: 55 *1: 24*	5: 48 *15: 51*	17: 55 *1: 1*	5: 47 *16: 21*	17: 56 *0: 23*
24 TU 268	11 51 54	0 29	5: 49 *15: 56*	17: 54 *2: 56*	5: 49 *16: 4*	17: 54 *2: 46*	5: 50 *16: 14*	17: 54 *2: 33*	5: 50 *16: 27*	17: 53 *2: 16*	5: 49 *16: 47*	17: 53 *1: 49*
25 WE 269	11 51 33	0 53	5: 50 *16: 44*	17: 53 *3: 58*	5: 50 *16: 48*	17: 53 *3: 52*	5: 51 *16: 53*	17: 52 *3: 44*	5: 51 *16: 59*	17: 51 *3: 34*	5: 52 *17: 10*	17: 50 *3: 17*
26 TH 270	11 51 12	-1 16	5: 50 *17: 31*	17: 52 *5: 0*	5: 51 *17: 31*	17: 51 *4: 58*	5: 52 *17: 30*	17: 50 *4: 55*	5: 53 *17: 30*	17: 49 *4: 52*	5: 54 *17: 30*	17: 47 *4: 46*
27 FR 271	11 50 52 *2 51 FM*	-1 39	5: 50 *18: 17*	17: 51 *6: 0*	5: 51 *18: 13*	17: 50 *6: 3*	5: 52 *18: 7*	17: 49 *6: 5*	5: 54 *18: 1*	17: 47 *6: 9*	5: 56 *17: 50*	17: 44 *6: 15*
28 SA 272	11 50 32	-2 3	5: 50 *19: 3*	17: 51 *7: 0*	5: 52 *18: 55*	17: 49 *7: 6*	5: 53 *18: 45*	17: 47 *7: 14*	5: 56 *18: 32*	17: 44 *7: 24*	5: 59 *18: 12*	17: 41 *7: 41*
29 SU 273	11 50 12	-2 26	5: 50 *19: 49*	17: 50 *7: 58*	5: 52 *19: 38*	17: 48 *8: 8*	5: 54 *19: 24*	17: 45 *8: 21*	5: 57 *19: 5*	17: 42 *8: 37*	6: 1 *18: 36*	17: 38 *9: 4*
30 MO 274	11 49 52	-2 49	5: 51 *20: 36*	17: 49 *8: 55*	5: 53 *20: 22*	17: 46 *9: 8*	5: 55 *20: 5*	17: 44 *9: 24*	5: 59 *19: 42*	17: 40 *9: 46*	6: 4 *19: 4*	17: 35 *10: 22*

10th Month   **October 1996**   **31 days**

Greenwich Mean Time

NOTE: For each day, numbers on first line indicate Sun. *Italic* numbers on second line indicate *Moon*. Degrees are North Latitude.

FM = full moon; LQ = last quarter; NM = new moon; FQ = first quarter.

CAUTION: Must be converted to local time. For instructions see page 296.

Day of month week year	Sun on Meridian Moon Phase h m s	Sun's Declina- tion ° '	20° Rise Sun Moon h m	20° Set Sun Moon h m	30° Rise Sun Moon h m	30° Set Sun Moon h m	40° Rise Sun Moon h m	40° Set Sun Moon h m	50° Rise Sun Moon h m	50° Set Sun Moon h m	60° Rise Sun Moon h m	60° Set Sun Moon h m
1 TU 275	11 49 33	-3 13	5: 51 *21: 24*	17: 48 *9: 50*	5: 53 *21: 9*	17: 45 *10: 6*	5: 56 *20: 49*	17: 42 *10: 24*	6: 0 *20: 22*	17: 38 *10: 51*	6: 6 *19: 38*	17: 32 *11: 33*
2 WE 276	11 49 13	-3 36	5: 51 *22: 13*	17: 47 *10: 43*	5: 54 *21: 56*	17: 44 *11: 0*	5: 57 *21: 36*	17: 40 *11: 20*	6: 2 *21: 7*	17: 36 *11: 49*	6: 8 *20: 19*	17: 29 *12: 36*
3 TH 277	11 48 55	-3 59	5: 51 *23: 2*	17: 46 *11: 34*	5: 55 *22: 46*	17: 43 *11: 50*	5: 58 *22: 25*	17: 39 *12: 11*	6: 3 *21: 56*	17: 34 *12: 40*	6: 11 *21: 8*	17: 26 *13: 28*
4 FR 278	11 48 36 *12 4 LQ*	-4 22	5: 52 *23: 52*	17: 45 *12: 21*	5: 55 *23: 36*	17: 42 *12: 37*	5: 59 *23: 16*	17: 37 *12: 57*	6: 5 *22: 49*	17: 31 *13: 25*	6: 13 *22: 5*	17: 23 *14: 11*
5 SA 279	11 48 18	-4 45	5: 52 *no: ne*	17: 44 *13: 6*	5: 56 *no: ne*	17: 40 *13: 21*	6: 0 *no: ne*	17: 36 *13: 39*	6: 6 *23: 45*	17: 29 *14: 4*	6: 15 *23: 6*	17: 20 *14: 45*
6 SU 280	11 48 1	-5 8	5: 52 *0: 41*	17: 44 *13: 48*	5: 56 *0: 27*	17: 39 *14: 1*	6: 1 *0: 9*	17: 34 *14: 17*	6: 8 *no: ne*	17: 27 *14: 38*	6: 18 *no: ne*	17: 17 *15: 12*
7 MO 281	11 47 43	-5 31	5: 52 *1: 30*	17: 43 *14: 29*	5: 57 *1: 18*	17: 38 *14: 39*	6: 2 *1: 4*	17: 32 *14: 51*	6: 10 *0: 44*	17: 25 *15: 8*	6: 20 *0: 12*	17: 14 *15: 35*
8 TU 282	11 47 27	-5 54	5: 53 *2: 19*	17: 42 *15: 8*	5: 58 *2: 10*	17: 37 *15: 15*	6: 3 *1: 59*	17: 31 *15: 24*	6: 11 *1: 44*	17: 23 *15: 36*	6: 23 *1: 21*	17: 11 *15: 54*
9 WE 283	11 47 10	-6 17	5: 53 *3: 8*	17: 41 *15: 46*	5: 58 *3: 3*	17: 36 *15: 50*	6: 4 *2: 56*	17: 29 *15: 55*	6: 13 *2: 46*	17: 21 *16: 1*	6: 25 *2: 31*	17: 8 *16: 11*
10 TH 284	11 46 54	-6 40	5: 53 *3: 58*	17: 40 *16: 24*	5: 59 *3: 56*	17: 35 *16: 25*	6: 5 *3: 53*	17: 28 *16: 26*	6: 14 *3: 49*	17: 19 *16: 26*	6: 28 *3: 43*	17: 5 *16: 28*
11 FR 285	11 46 39	-7 3	5: 54 *4: 48*	17: 39 *17: 3*	5: 59 *4: 50*	17: 33 *17: 0*	6: 6 *4: 51*	17: 26 *16: 57*	6: 16 *4: 53*	17: 17 *16: 52*	6: 30 *4: 56*	17: 2 *16: 44*
12 SA 286	11 46 24 *14 14 NM*	-7 25	5: 54 *5: 40*	17: 39 *17: 44*	6: 0 *5: 45*	17: 32 *17: 37*	6: 7 *5: 51*	17: 25 *17: 29*	6: 17 *5: 59*	17: 15 *17: 19*	6: 32 *6: 11*	16: 59 *17: 2*
13 SU 287	11 46 10	-7 48	5: 54 *6: 33*	17: 38 *18: 26*	6: 1 *6: 41*	17: 31 *18: 16*	6: 9 *6: 52*	17: 23 *18: 4*	6: 19 *7: 6*	17: 13 *17: 48*	6: 35 *7: 28*	16: 56 *17: 23*
14 MO 288	11 45 56	-8 10	5: 55 *7: 28*	17: 37 *19: 11*	6: 1 *7: 39*	17: 30 *18: 59*	6: 10 *7: 54*	17: 22 *18: 43*	6: 21 *8: 13*	17: 10 *18: 22*	6: 37 *8: 45*	16: 53 *17: 48*
15 TU 289	11 45 43	-8 32	5: 55 *8: 24*	17: 36 *20: 0*	6: 2 *8: 38*	17: 28 *19: 45*	6: 11 *8: 56*	17: 20 *19: 26*	6: 22 *9: 21*	17: 8 *19: 1*	6: 40 *10: 0*	16: 50 *18: 19*
16 WE 290	11 45 30	-8 54	5: 55 *9: 21*	17: 36 *20: 52*	6: 3 *9: 37*	17: 28 *20: 36*	6: 12 *9: 57*	17: 19 *20: 15*	6: 24 *10: 25*	17: 6 *19: 46*	6: 42 *11: 12*	16: 48 *18: 59*
17 TH 291	11 45 18	-9 16	5: 56 *10: 18*	17: 35 *21: 48*	6: 3 *10: 35*	17: 27 *21: 31*	6: 13 *10: 56*	17: 17 *21: 10*	6: 25 *11: 26*	17: 4 *20: 40*	6: 45 *12: 15*	16: 45 *19: 51*
18 FR 292	11 45 6	-9 38	5: 56 *11: 14*	17: 34 *22: 46*	6: 4 *11: 31*	17: 26 *22: 30*	6: 14 *11: 52*	17: 16 *22: 10*	6: 27 *12: 21*	17: 2 *21: 41*	6: 47 *13: 8*	16: 42 *20: 55*
19 SA 293	11 44 55 *18 9 FQ*	-9 60	5: 56 *12: 9*	17: 33 *23: 46*	6: 5 *12: 24*	17: 25 *23: 31*	6: 15 *12: 42*	17: 14 *23: 14*	6: 29 *13: 8*	17: 0 *22: 49*	6: 50 *13: 50*	16: 39 *22: 9*
20 SU 294	11 44 45	-10 22	5: 57 *13: 0*	17: 33 *no: ne*	6: 5 *13: 13*	17: 24 *no: ne*	6: 16 *13: 29*	17: 13 *no: ne*	6: 30 *13: 50*	16: 58 *no: ne*	6: 52 *14: 24*	16: 36 *23: 30*
21 MO 295	11 44 35	-10 43	5: 57 *13: 49*	17: 32 *0: 46*	6: 6 *13: 59*	17: 23 *0: 35*	6: 17 *14: 10*	17: 12 *0: 20*	6: 32 *14: 26*	16: 57 *0: 1*	6: 55 *14: 50*	16: 33 *no: ne*
22 TU 296	11 44 26	-11 4	5: 57 *14: 37*	17: 31 *1: 46*	6: 7 *14: 42*	17: 22 *1: 38*	6: 18 *14: 49*	17: 10 *1: 29*	6: 33 *14: 59*	16: 55 *1: 15*	6: 57 *15: 13*	16: 31 *0: 55*
23 WE 297	11 44 18	-11 25	5: 58 *15: 22*	17: 31 *2: 46*	6: 7 *15: 24*	17: 21 *2: 42*	6: 19 *15: 26*	17: 9 *2: 37*	6: 35 *15: 29*	16: 53 *2: 31*	7: 0 *15: 33*	16: 28 *2: 21*
24 TH 298	11 44 10	-11 46	5: 58 *16: 8*	17: 30 *3: 45*	6: 8 *16: 5*	17: 20 *3: 45*	6: 20 *16: 2*	17: 7 *3: 46*	6: 37 *15: 59*	16: 51 *3: 46*	7: 2 *15: 53*	16: 25 *3: 47*
25 FR 299	11 44 3	-12 7	5: 58 *16: 53*	17: 29 *4: 44*	6: 9 *16: 46*	17: 19 *4: 48*	6: 21 *16: 39*	17: 6 *4: 54*	6: 38 *16: 29*	16: 49 *5: 1*	7: 5 *16: 13*	16: 22 *5: 12*
26 SA 300	11 43 57 *14 11 FM*	-12 28	5: 59 *17: 39*	17: 29 *5: 42*	6: 10 *17: 29*	17: 18 *5: 50*	6: 23 *17: 17*	17: 5 *6: 1*	6: 40 *17: 1*	16: 47 *6: 15*	7: 7 *16: 36*	16: 19 *6: 36*
27 SU 301	11 43 51	-12 48	5: 59 *18: 26*	17: 28 *6: 40*	6: 10 *18: 13*	17: 17 *6: 52*	6: 24 *17: 57*	17: 4 *7: 6*	6: 42 *17: 35*	16: 45 *7: 26*	7: 10 *17: 2*	16: 17 *7: 57*
28 MO 302	11 43 46	-13 8	6: 0 *19: 14*	17: 27 *7: 36*	6: 11 *18: 59*	17: 16 *7: 51*	6: 25 *18: 40*	17: 2 *8: 8*	6: 43 *18: 14*	16: 43 *8: 33*	7: 13 *17: 33*	16: 14 *9: 13*
29 TU 303	11 43 42	-13 28	6: 0 *20: 3*	17: 27 *8: 31*	6: 12 *19: 46*	17: 15 *8: 47*	6: 26 *19: 26*	17: 1 *9: 7*	6: 45 *18: 58*	16: 42 *9: 35*	7: 15 *18: 11*	16: 11 *10: 21*
30 WE 304	11 43 39	-13 48	6: 1 *20: 53*	17: 26 *9: 24*	6: 12 *20: 36*	17: 14 *9: 41*	6: 27 *20: 15*	17: 0 *10: 2*	6: 47 *19: 46*	16: 40 *10: 31*	7: 18 *18: 57*	16: 9 *11: 19*
31 TH 305	11 43 36	-14 7	6: 1 *21: 43*	17: 26 *10: 13*	6: 13 *21: 26*	17: 14 *10: 30*	6: 28 *21: 6*	16: 59 *10: 51*	6: 48 *20: 38*	16: 38 *11: 19*	7: 20 *19: 51*	16: 6 *12: 6*

11th Month   **November 1996**   **30 days**

Greenwich Mean Time

NOTE: For each day, numbers on first line indicate Sun. *Italic* numbers on second line indicate *Moon*. Degrees are North Latitude.

FM = full moon; LQ = last quarter; NM = new moon; FQ = first quarter.

CAUTION: Must be converted to local time. For instructions see page 296.

Day of month / week / year	Sun on Meridian Moon Phase (h m s)	Sun's Declination (° ')	20° Rise Sun / Rise Moon	20° Set Sun / Set Moon	30° Rise Sun / Rise Moon	30° Set Sun / Set Moon	40° Rise Sun / Rise Moon	40° Set Sun / Set Moon	50° Rise Sun / Rise Moon	50° Set Sun / Set Moon	60° Rise Sun / Rise Moon	60° Set Sun / Set Moon
1 FR	11 43 35	-14 27	6: 2	17: 25	6: 14	17: 13	6: 29	16: 57	6: 50	16: 36	7: 23	16: 3
306			*22: 33*	*11: 0*	*22: 18*	*11: 15*	*21: 59*	*11: 35*	*21: 34*	*12: 1*	*20: 52*	*12: 44*
2 SA	11 43 34	-14 46	6: 2	17: 25	6: 15	17: 12	6: 30	16: 56	6: 52	16: 35	7: 25	16: 1
307			*23: 22*	*11: 44*	*23: 9*	*11: 57*	*22: 53*	*12: 14*	*22: 32*	*12: 38*	*21: 57*	*13: 15*
3 SU	11 43 34	-15 5	6: 3	17: 24	6: 16	17: 11	6: 32	16: 55	6: 53	16: 33	7: 28	15: 58
308	*7 50 LQ*		*no: ne*	*12: 25*	*no: ne*	*12: 36*	*23: 48*	*12: 50*	*23: 31*	*13: 9*	*23: 4*	*13: 39*
4 MO	11 43 35	-15 23	6: 3	17: 24	6: 16	17: 11	6: 33	16: 54	6: 55	16: 32	7: 30	15: 56
309			*0: 11*	*13: 4*	*0: 1*	*13: 13*	*no: ne*	*13: 23*	*no: ne*	*13: 37*	*no: ne*	*13: 59*
5 TU	11 43 36	-15 42	6: 3	17: 23	6: 17	17: 10	6: 34	16: 53	6: 57	16: 30	7: 33	15: 53
310			*1: 0*	*13: 43*	*0: 53*	*13: 48*	*0: 44*	*13: 55*	*0: 32*	*14: 3*	*0: 13*	*14: 17*
6 WE	11 43 39	-15 60	6: 4	17: 23	6: 18	17: 9	6: 35	16: 52	6: 58	16: 28	7: 36	15: 51
311			*1: 49*	*14: 20*	*1: 45*	*14: 22*	*1: 41*	*14: 25*	*1: 34*	*14: 28*	*1: 24*	*14: 33*
7 TH	11 43 42	-16 18	6: 5	17: 23	6: 19	17: 8	6: 36	16: 51	7: 0	16: 27	7: 38	15: 48
312			*2: 39*	*14: 59*	*2: 39*	*14: 57*	*2: 38*	*14: 56*	*2: 38*	*14: 53*	*2: 37*	*14: 50*
8 FR	11 43 47	-16 35	6: 5	17: 22	6: 19	17: 8	6: 37	16: 50	7: 2	16: 25	7: 41	15: 46
313			*3: 30*	*15: 38*	*3: 33*	*15: 33*	*3: 37*	*15: 27*	*3: 43*	*15: 19*	*3: 51*	*15: 7*
9 SA	11 43 52	-16 52	6: 6	17: 22	6: 20	17: 7	6: 38	16: 49	7: 3	16: 24	7: 43	15: 44
314			*4: 23*	*16: 20*	*4: 29*	*16: 12*	*4: 38*	*16: 1*	*4: 49*	*15: 48*	*5: 7*	*15: 26*
10 SU	11 43 58	-17 9	6: 6	17: 22	6: 21	17: 6	6: 40	16: 48	7: 5	16: 22	7: 46	15: 41
315			*5: 17*	*17: 5*	*5: 28*	*16: 53*	*5: 40*	*16: 39*	*5: 58*	*16: 19*	*6: 25*	*15: 49*
11 MO	11 44 4	-17 26	6: 7	17: 21	6: 22	17: 6	6: 41	16: 47	7: 7	16: 21	7: 48	15: 39
316	*4 16 NM*		*6: 14*	*17: 53*	*6: 27*	*17: 39*	*6: 44*	*17: 21*	*7: 7*	*16: 57*	*7: 44*	*16: 18*
12 TU	11 44 12	-17 42	6: 7	17: 21	6: 23	17: 5	6: 42	16: 46	7: 8	16: 20	7: 51	15: 37
317			*7: 12*	*18: 45*	*7: 28*	*18: 29*	*7: 47*	*18: 9*	*8: 15*	*17: 41*	*8: 59*	*16: 55*
13 WE	11 44 20	-17 59	6: 8	17: 21	6: 24	17: 5	6: 43	16: 45	7: 10	16: 18	7: 53	15: 34
318			*8: 11*	*19: 41*	*8: 28*	*19: 24*	*8: 49*	*19: 3*	*9: 19*	*18: 33*	*10: 8*	*17: 44*
14 TH	11 44 30	-18 14	6: 8	17: 20	6: 24	17: 4	6: 44	16: 44	7: 11	16: 17	7: 56	15: 32
319			*9: 9*	*20: 40*	*9: 26*	*20: 23*	*9: 48*	*20: 2*	*10: 17*	*19: 33*	*11: 6*	*18: 45*
15 FR	11 44 40	-18 30	6: 9	17: 20	6: 25	17: 4	6: 45	16: 44	7: 13	16: 16	7: 59	15: 30
320			*10: 5*	*21: 40*	*10: 21*	*21: 25*	*10: 41*	*21: 6*	*11: 8*	*20: 40*	*11: 52*	*19: 57*
16 SA	11 44 51	-18 45	6: 10	17: 20	6: 26	17: 3	6: 46	16: 43	7: 15	16: 14	8: 1	15: 28
321			*10: 58*	*22: 41*	*11: 12*	*22: 28*	*11: 29*	*22: 13*	*11: 52*	*21: 51*	*12: 29*	*21: 17*
17 SU	11 45 3	-18 60	6: 10	17: 20	6: 27	17: 3	6: 48	16: 42	7: 16	16: 13	8: 4	15: 26
322			*11: 48*	*23: 40*	*11: 59*	*23: 31*	*12: 12*	*23: 20*	*12: 29*	*23: 5*	*12: 57*	*22: 40*
18 MO	11 45 15	-19 14	6: 11	17: 20	6: 28	17: 3	6: 49	16: 41	7: 18	16: 12	8: 6	15: 24
323	*1 9 FQ*		*12: 35*	*no: ne*	*12: 42*	*no: ne*	*12: 51*	*no: ne*	*13: 2*	*no: ne*	*13: 20*	*no: ne*
19 TU	11 45 29	-19 28	6: 11	17: 19	6: 29	17: 2	6: 50	16: 41	7: 19	16: 11	8: 8	15: 22
324			*13: 20*	*0: 39*	*13: 23*	*0: 34*	*13: 27*	*0: 28*	*13: 32*	*0: 19*	*13: 40*	*0: 5*
20 WE	11 45 43	-19 42	6: 12	17: 19	6: 29	17: 2	6: 51	16: 40	7: 21	16: 10	8: 11	15: 20
325			*14: 4*	*1: 37*	*14: 3*	*1: 36*	*14: 2*	*1: 35*	*14: 1*	*1: 33*	*13: 59*	*1: 29*
21 TH	11 45 58	-19 55	6: 13	17: 19	6: 30	17: 1	6: 52	16: 39	7: 23	16: 9	8: 13	15: 18
326			*14: 48*	*2: 35*	*14: 43*	*2: 37*	*14: 37*	*2: 41*	*14: 30*	*2: 46*	*14: 18*	*2: 53*
22 FR	11 46 14	-20 8	6: 13	17: 19	6: 31	17: 1	6: 53	16: 39	7: 24	16: 8	8: 16	15: 16
327			*15: 32*	*3: 31*	*15: 24*	*3: 38*	*15: 13*	*3: 46*	*15: 0*	*3: 58*	*14: 39*	*4: 15*
23 SA	11 46 30	-20 21	6: 14	17: 19	6: 32	17: 1	6: 54	16: 38	7: 26	16: 7	8: 18	15: 14
328			*16: 17*	*4: 28*	*16: 6*	*4: 38*	*15: 52*	*4: 51*	*15: 32*	*5: 8*	*15: 2*	*5: 36*
24 SU	11 46 48	-20 33	6: 14	17: 19	6: 33	17: 1	6: 55	16: 38	7: 27	16: 6	8: 20	15: 13
329			*17: 4*	*5: 24*	*16: 50*	*5: 37*	*16: 33*	*5: 54*	*16: 9*	*6: 16*	*15: 30*	*6: 53*
25 MO	11 47 6	-20 45	6: 15	17: 19	6: 34	17: 0	6: 57	16: 37	7: 29	16: 5	8: 23	15: 11
330	*4 10 FM*		*17: 53*	*6: 20*	*17: 37*	*6: 35*	*17: 17*	*6: 54*	*16: 49*	*7: 21*	*16: 5*	*8: 4*
26 TU	11 47 24	-20 57	6: 16	17: 19	6: 34	17: 0	6: 58	16: 37	7: 30	16: 4	8: 25	15: 9
331			*18: 43*	*7: 13*	*18: 26*	*7: 30*	*18: 5*	*7: 51*	*17: 35*	*8: 20*	*16: 47*	*9: 7*
27 WE	11 47 44	-21 8	6: 16	17: 19	6: 35	17: 0	6: 59	16: 37	7: 32	16: 4	8: 27	15: 8
332			*19: 33*	*8: 4*	*19: 16*	*8: 21*	*18: 55*	*8: 43*	*18: 26*	*9: 12*	*17: 38*	*10: 0*
28 TH	11 48 4	-21 19	6: 17	17: 19	6: 36	17: 0	7: 0	16: 36	7: 33	16: 3	8: 29	15: 6
333			*20: 24*	*8: 53*	*20: 8*	*9: 9*	*19: 48*	*9: 29*	*19: 21*	*9: 57*	*18: 36*	*10: 43*
29 FR	11 48 25	-21 29	6: 18	17: 19	6: 37	17: 0	7: 1	16: 36	7: 34	16: 2	8: 31	15: 5
334			*21: 14*	*9: 38*	*21: 0*	*9: 53*	*20: 42*	*10: 11*	*20: 18*	*10: 36*	*19: 40*	*11: 17*
30 SA	11 48 47	-21 39	6: 18	17: 19	6: 38	17: 0	7: 2	16: 36	7: 36	16: 2	8: 33	15: 4
335			*22: 3*	*10: 21*	*21: 52*	*10: 33*	*21: 37*	*10: 49*	*21: 18*	*11: 10*	*20: 47*	*11: 43*

12th Month December 1996 **31 days**

Greenwich Mean Time

NOTE: For each day, numbers on first line indicate Sun. *Italic* numbers on second line indicate *Moon*. Degrees are North Latitude.

FM = full moon; LQ = last quarter; NM = new moon; FQ = first quarter.

CAUTION: Must be converted to local time. For instructions see page 296.

Day of month / week / year	Sun on Meridian Moon Phase (h m s)	Sun's Declination (° ')	20° Rise Sun/Moon	20° Set Sun/Moon	30° Rise Sun/Moon	30° Set Sun/Moon	40° Rise Sun/Moon	40° Set Sun/Moon	50° Rise Sun/Moon	50° Set Sun/Moon	60° Rise Sun/Moon	60° Set Sun/Moon
1 SU	11 49 9	-21 48	6: 19	17: 19	6: 38	17: 0	7: 3	16: 35	7: 37	16: 1	8: 35	15: 2
336			*22: 52*	*11: 1*	*22: 43*	*11: 11*	*22: 33*	*11: 23*	*22: 18*	*11: 40*	*21: 55*	*12: 5*
2 MO	11 49 32	-21 58	6: 19	17: 20	6: 39	17: 0	7: 4	16: 35	7: 38	16: 0	8: 37	15: 1
337			*23: 41*	*11: 39*	*23: 35*	*11: 46*	*23: 28*	*11: 55*	*23: 19*	*12: 6*	*23: 5*	*12: 24*
3 TU	11 49 56 / *5 6 LQ*	-22 6	6: 20	17: 20	6: 40	17: 0	7: 5	16: 35	7: 40	16: 0	8: 39	15: 0
338			*no: ne*	*12: 17*	*no: ne*	*12: 21*	*no: ne*	*12: 25*	*no: ne*	*12: 31*	*no: ne*	*12: 40*
4 WE	11 50 20	-22 15	6: 21	17: 20	6: 41	17: 0	7: 6	16: 35	7: 41	16: 0	8: 41	14: 59
339			*0: 29*	*12: 54*	*0: 27*	*12: 55*	*0: 25*	*12: 55*	*0: 21*	*12: 56*	*0: 16*	*12: 56*
5 TH	11 50 45	-22 22	6: 21	17: 20	6: 41	17: 0	7: 7	16: 35	7: 42	15: 59	8: 43	14: 58
340			*1: 19*	*13: 33*	*1: 20*	*13: 29*	*1: 22*	*13: 26*	*1: 25*	*13: 20*	*1: 28*	*13: 12*
6 FR	11 51 10	-22 30	6: 22	17: 20	6: 42	17: 0	7: 8	16: 35	7: 43	15: 59	8: 45	14: 57
341			*2: 10*	*14: 12*	*2: 15*	*14: 6*	*2: 21*	*13: 58*	*2: 30*	*13: 47*	*2: 43*	*13: 30*
7 SA	11 51 36	-22 37	6: 23	17: 21	6: 43	17: 0	7: 8	16: 35	7: 44	15: 59	8: 46	14: 56
342			*3: 3*	*14: 55*	*3: 12*	*14: 45*	*3: 22*	*14: 33*	*3: 37*	*14: 16*	*3: 59*	*13: 50*
8 SU	11 52 3	-22 43	6: 23	17: 21	6: 44	17: 0	7: 9	16: 35	7: 45	15: 58	8: 48	14: 56
343			*3: 59*	*15: 42*	*4: 10*	*15: 29*	*4: 25*	*15: 13*	*4: 45*	*14: 50*	*5: 18*	*14: 16*
9 MO	11 52 30	-22 49	6: 24	17: 21	6: 44	17: 0	7: 10	16: 35	7: 47	15: 58	8: 50	14: 55
344			*4: 57*	*16: 32*	*5: 11*	*16: 17*	*5: 29*	*15: 58*	*5: 55*	*15: 31*	*6: 36*	*14: 48*
10 TU	11 52 57 / *16 56 NM*	-22 55	6: 24	17: 21	6: 45	17: 1	7: 11	16: 35	7: 48	15: 58	8: 51	14: 55
345			*5: 56*	*17: 28*	*6: 13*	*17: 11*	*6: 33*	*16: 50*	*7: 2*	*16: 20*	*7: 50*	*15: 32*
11 WE	11 53 25	-22 60	6: 25	17: 22	6: 46	17: 1	7: 12	16: 35	7: 49	15: 58	8: 53	14: 54
346			*6: 56*	*18: 27*	*7: 14*	*18: 10*	*7: 35*	*17: 48*	*8: 5*	*17: 18*	*8: 55*	*16: 28*
12 TH	11 53 53	-23 5	6: 26	17: 22	6: 46	17: 1	7: 13	16: 35	7: 50	15: 58	8: 54	14: 54
347			*7: 55*	*19: 29*	*8: 12*	*19: 13*	*8: 33*	*18: 53*	*9: 2*	*18: 25*	*9: 49*	*17: 39*
13 FR	11 54 21	-23 9	6: 26	17: 22	6: 47	17: 1	7: 13	16: 35	7: 50	15: 58	8: 55	14: 53
348			*8: 52*	*20: 31*	*9: 7*	*20: 18*	*9: 25*	*20: 1*	*9: 50*	*19: 37*	*10: 31*	*18: 59*
14 SA	11 54 50	-23 13	6: 27	17: 23	6: 48	17: 2	7: 14	16: 35	7: 51	15: 58	8: 56	14: 53
349			*9: 45*	*21: 33*	*9: 56*	*21: 23*	*10: 11*	*21: 10*	*10: 31*	*20: 52*	*11: 3*	*20: 24*
15 SU	11 55 19	-23 16	6: 27	17: 23	6: 48	17: 2	7: 15	16: 36	7: 52	15: 58	8: 57	14: 53
350			*10: 34*	*22: 34*	*10: 42*	*22: 27*	*10: 53*	*22: 19*	*11: 6*	*22: 8*	*11: 28*	*21: 50*
16 MO	11 55 48	-23 19	6: 28	17: 24	6: 49	17: 3	7: 15	16: 36	7: 53	15: 59	8: 58	14: 53
351			*11: 20*	*23: 33*	*11: 25*	*23: 30*	*11: 30*	*23: 27*	*11: 38*	*23: 22*	*11: 49*	*23: 16*
17 TU	11 56 18 / *9 31 FQ*	-23 21	6: 28	17: 24	6: 50	17: 3	7: 16	16: 36	7: 54	15: 59	8: 59	14: 53
352			*12: 5*	*no: ne*	*12: 5*	*no: ne*	*12: 6*	*no: ne*	*12: 7*	*no: ne*	*12: 8*	*no: ne*
18 WE	11 56 47	-23 23	6: 29	17: 25	6: 50	17: 3	7: 17	16: 37	7: 54	15: 59	9: 0	14: 53
353			*12: 48*	*0: 30*	*12: 44*	*0: 32*	*12: 40*	*0: 33*	*12: 35*	*0: 36*	*12: 27*	*0: 39*
19 TH	11 57 17	-23 25	6: 30	17: 25	6: 51	17: 4	7: 17	16: 37	7: 55	16: 0	9: 1	14: 54
354			*13: 31*	*1: 27*	*13: 24*	*1: 32*	*13: 15*	*1: 39*	*13: 4*	*1: 47*	*12: 46*	*2: 1*
20 FR	11 57 46	-23 26	6: 30	17: 25	6: 51	17: 4	7: 18	16: 38	7: 56	16: 0	9: 2	14: 54
355			*14: 15*	*2: 22*	*14: 5*	*2: 31*	*13: 52*	*2: 42*	*13: 34*	*2: 57*	*13: 8*	*3: 21*
21 SA	11 58 16	-23 26	6: 31	17: 26	6: 52	17: 5	7: 18	16: 38	7: 56	16: 0	9: 2	14: 54
356			*15: 0*	*3: 17*	*14: 47*	*3: 30*	*14: 31*	*3: 45*	*14: 8*	*4: 5*	*13: 33*	*4: 38*
22 SU	11 58 46	-23 26	6: 31	17: 26	6: 52	17: 5	7: 19	16: 39	7: 57	16: 1	9: 3	14: 55
357			*15: 47*	*4: 12*	*15: 32*	*4: 27*	*15: 13*	*4: 45*	*14: 46*	*5: 10*	*14: 4*	*5: 51*
23 MO	11 59 16	-23 26	6: 32	17: 27	6: 53	17: 6	7: 19	16: 39	7: 57	16: 2	9: 3	14: 56
358			*16: 36*	*5: 5*	*16: 19*	*5: 22*	*15: 58*	*5: 42*	*15: 29*	*6: 10*	*14: 42*	*6: 57*
24 TU	11 59 46 / *20 41 FM*	-23 25	6: 32	17: 28	6: 53	17: 6	7: 20	16: 40	7: 57	16: 2	9: 3	14: 56
359			*17: 25*	*5: 57*	*17: 8*	*6: 14*	*16: 47*	*6: 35*	*16: 18*	*7: 5*	*15: 29*	*7: 54*
25 WE	12 0 15	-23 23	6: 32	17: 28	6: 54	17: 7	7: 20	16: 40	7: 58	16: 3	9: 3	14: 57
360			*18: 16*	*6: 47*	*17: 59*	*7: 3*	*17: 39*	*7: 24*	*17: 11*	*7: 53*	*16: 24*	*8: 41*
26 TH	12 0 45	-23 22	6: 33	17: 29	6: 54	17: 7	7: 21	16: 41	7: 58	16: 4	9: 4	14: 58
361			*19: 6*	*7: 33*	*18: 51*	*7: 49*	*18: 33*	*8: 8*	*18: 7*	*8: 35*	*17: 25*	*9: 18*
27 FR	12 1 14	-23 19	6: 33	17: 29	6: 54	17: 8	7: 21	16: 42	7: 58	16: 4	9: 4	14: 59
362			*19: 56*	*8: 17*	*19: 43*	*8: 31*	*19: 28*	*8: 48*	*19: 6*	*9: 11*	*18: 31*	*9: 48*
28 SA	12 1 44	-23 17	6: 34	17: 30	6: 55	17: 9	7: 21	16: 42	7: 58	16: 4	9: 5	15: 0
363			*20: 45*	*8: 58*	*20: 35*	*9: 10*	*20: 23*	*9: 24*	*20: 6*	*9: 42*	*19: 39*	*10: 11*
29 SU	12 2 13	-23 13	6: 34	17: 30	6: 55	17: 9	7: 21	16: 43	7: 58	16: 6	9: 3	15: 1
364			*21: 34*	*9: 38*	*21: 27*	*9: 46*	*21: 18*	*9: 56*	*21: 7*	*10: 10*	*20: 48*	*10: 31*
30 MO	12 2 42	-23 10	6: 34	17: 31	6: 55	17: 10	7: 22	16: 44	7: 59	16: 7	9: 3	15: 3
365			*22: 22*	*10: 15*	*22: 18*	*10: 21*	*22: 14*	*10: 27*	*22: 8*	*10: 35*	*21: 58*	*10: 48*
31 TU	12 3 10	-23 5	6: 35	17: 32	6: 56	17: 11	7: 22	16: 45	7: 59	16: 8	9: 3	15: 4
366			*23: 11*	*10: 52*	*23: 10*	*10: 54*	*23: 10*	*10: 57*	*23: 10*	*11: 0*	*23: 9*	*11: 4*

Julian and Gregorian Calendars; Leap Year; Century

Calendars based on the movements of the sun and moon have been used since ancient times, but none has been perfect. The **Julian calendar**, under which Western nations measured time until AD 1582, was authorized by Julius Caesar in 46 BC, the year 709 of Rome. His expert was a Greek, Sosigenes. The Julian calendar, on the assumption that the true year was 365 1/4 days, gave every fourth year 366 days. St. Bede the Venerable, an Anglo-Saxon monk, announced in AD 730 that the 365 1/4-day Julian year was 11 min, 14 sec too long, a cumulative error of about a day every 128 years, but nothing was done about it for more than 800 years.

By 1582 the accumulated error was estimated to amount to 10 days. In that year Pope Gregory XIII decreed that the day following Oct. 4, 1582, should be called Oct. 15, thus dropping 10 days and initiating what became known as the **Gregorian calendar.**

However, with common years 365 days and a 366-day leap year every fourth year, the error in the length of the year would have recurred at the rate of a little more than 3 days every 400 years. Therefore, 3 of every 4 centesimal years (years ending in 00) were made common years, not leap years. Thus, 1600 was a leap year; 1700, 1800, and 1900 were not, but 2000 will be. **Leap years** are those years divisible by 4, except centesimal years, which are common unless divisible by 400.

The Gregorian calendar was adopted at once by France, Italy, Spain, Portugal, and Luxembourg. Within 2 years most German Catholic states, Belgium, and parts of Switzerland and the Netherlands were brought under the new calendar, and Hungary followed in 1587. The rest of the Netherlands, along with Denmark and the German Protestant states, made the change in 1699-1700 (German Protestants retained the old reckoning of Easter until 1776).

The British government imposed the Gregorian calendar on all its possessions, including the American colonies, in 1752. The British decreed that the day following Sept. 2, 1752, should be called Sept. 14, a loss of 11 days. All dates preceding were marked OS, for Old Style. In addition, New Year's Day was moved to Jan. 1 from Mar. 25 (e.g., under the old reckoning, Mar. 24, 1700, had been followed by Mar. 25, 1701). George Washington's birthdate, which was Feb. 11, 1731, OS, became Feb. 22, 1732, New Style (NS). In 1753 Sweden too went Gregorian, retaining the old Easter rules until 1844.

In 1793 the French revolutionary government adopted a calendar of 12 months of 30 days each with 5 extra days in September of each common year and a 6th extra day every 4th year. Napoleon reinstated the Gregorian calendar in 1806.

The Gregorian system later spread to non-European regions, first in the European colonies and then in the independent countries, replacing traditional calendars at least for official purposes. Japan in 1873, Egypt in 1875, China in 1912, and Turkey in 1925 made the change, usually in conjunction with political upheavals. In China, the republican government began reckoning years from its 1911 founding — e.g., 1948 was designated the year 37. After 1949, the Communists adopted the Common, or Christian Era, year count, even for the traditional lunar calendar.

In 1918 the revolutionary government in the Soviet Union decreed that the day after Jan. 31, 1918, OS, would become Feb. 14, 1918, NS. Greece followed in 1923. (The Russian Orthodox Church has retained the Julian calendar, as have various Middle Eastern Christian sects.) For the first time in history, all major cultures have one calendar.

To convert from the Julian to the Gregorian calendar, add 10 days to dates Oct. 5, 1582, through Feb. 28, 1700; after that date add 11 days through Feb. 28, 1800; 12 days through Feb. 28, 1900; and 13 days through Feb. 28, 2100.

A **century** consists of 100 consecutive calendar years. The 1st century AD consisted of the years 1 through 100. The 20th century consists of the years 1901 through 2000 and will end Dec. 31, 2000. The 21st century will begin Jan. 1, 2001.

Julian Calendar

To find which of the 14 calendars printed on pages 310-11 applies to any year, starting Jan. 1, under the Julian system, find the century for the desired year in the 3 leftmost columns below; read across. Then find the year in the 4 top rows; read down. The number in the intersection is the calendar designation for that year.

Year (last 2 figures of desired year)

			01 02 03 04	05 06 07 08	09 10 11 12	13 14 15 16	17 18 19 20	21 22 23 24	25 26 27 28
			29 30 31 32	33 34 35 36	37 38 39 40	41 42 43 44	45 46 47 48	49 50 51 52	53 54 55 56
			57 58 59 60	61 62 63 64	65 66 67 68	69 70 71 72	73 74 75 76	77 78 79 80	81 82 83 84
Century		00	85 86 87 88	89 90 91 92	93 94 95 96	97 98 99			
0	700	1400	12 7 1 2	10 5 6 7	8 3 4 5	13 1 2 3	11 6 7 1	9 4 5 6	14 2 3 4 12
100	800	1500	11 6 7 1	9 4 5 6	14 2 3 4	12 7 1 2	10 5 6 7	8 3 4 5	13 1 2 3 11
200	900	1600	10 5 6 7	8 3 4 5	13 1 2 3	11 6 7 1	9 4 5 6	14 2 3 4	12 7 1 2 10
300	1000	1700	9 4 5 6	14 2 3 4	12 7 1 2	10 5 6 7	8 3 4 5	13 1 2 3	11 6 7 1 9
400	1100	1800	8 3 4 5	13 1 2 3	11 6 7 1	9 4 5 6	14 2 3 4	12 7 1 2	10 5 6 7 8
500	1200	1900	14 2 3 4	12 7 1 2	10 5 6 7	8 3 4 5	13 1 2 3	11 6 7 1	9 4 5 6 14
600	1300	2000	13 1 2 3	11 6 7 1	9 4 5 6	14 2 3 4	12 7 1 2	10 5 6 7	8 3 4 5 13

Gregorian Calendar

Choose the desired year from the table below or from page 310 (for years 1803 to 2080). The number shown with each year designates which calendar to use for that year, as shown on pages 310-11. (The Gregorian calendar was inaugurated Oct. 15, 1582. From that date to Dec. 31, 1582, use calendar 6.)

1583-1802

Year	#	Year	#	Year	#	Year	#	Year	#	Year	#	Year	#	Year	#	Year	#	Year	#	Year	#
1583	7	1603	4	1623	1	1643	5	1663	2	1683	6	1703	2	1723	6	1743	3	1763	7	1783	4
1584	8	1604	12	1624	9	1644	13	1664	10	1684	14	1704	10	1724	14	1744	11	1764	8	1784	12
1585	3	1605	7	1625	4	1645	1	1665	5	1685	2	1705	5	1725	2	1745	6	1765	3	1785	7
1586	4	1606	1	1626	5	1646	2	1666	6	1686	3	1706	6	1726	3	1746	7	1766	4	1786	1
1587	5	1607	2	1627	6	1647	3	1667	7	1687	4	1707	7	1727	4	1747	1	1767	5	1787	2
1588	13	1608	10	1628	14	1648	11	1668	8	1688	12	1708	8	1728	12	1748	9	1768	13	1788	10
1589	1	1609	5	1629	2	1649	6	1669	3	1689	7	1709	3	1729	7	1749	4	1769	1	1789	5
1590	2	1610	6	1630	3	1650	7	1670	4	1690	1	1710	4	1730	1	1750	5	1770	2	1790	6
1591	3	1611	7	1631	4	1651	1	1671	5	1691	2	1711	5	1731	2	1751	6	1771	3	1791	7
1592	11	1612	8	1632	12	1652	9	1672	13	1692	10	1712	13	1732	10	1752	14	1772	11	1792	8
1593	6	1613	3	1633	7	1653	4	1673	1	1693	5	1713	1	1733	5	1753	2	1773	6	1793	3
1594	7	1614	4	1634	1	1654	5	1674	2	1694	6	1714	2	1734	6	1754	3	1774	7	1794	4
1595	1	1615	5	1635	2	1655	6	1675	3	1695	7	1715	3	1735	7	1755	4	1775	1	1795	5
1596	9	1616	13	1636	10	1656	14	1676	11	1696	8	1716	11	1736	8	1756	12	1776	9	1796	13
1597	4	1617	1	1637	5	1657	2	1677	6	1697	3	1717	6	1737	3	1757	7	1777	4	1797	1
1598	5	1618	2	1638	6	1658	3	1678	7	1698	4	1718	7	1738	4	1758	1	1778	5	1798	2
1599	6	1619	3	1639	7	1659	4	1679	1	1699	5	1719	1	1739	5	1759	2	1779	6	1799	3
1600	14	1620	11	1640	8	1660	12	1680	9	1700	6	1720	9	1740	13	1760	10	1780	14	1800	4
1601	2	1621	6	1641	3	1661	7	1681	4	1701	7	1721	4	1741	1	1761	5	1781	2	1801	5
1602	3	1622	7	1642	4	1662	1	1682	5	1702	1	1722	5	1742	2	1762	6	1782	3	1802	6

Perpetual Calendar

The number shown for each year indicates which Gregorian calendar to use. For 1583-1802, see "Gregorian Calendar" on page 309. For 1803-20, use numbers for 1983-2000, respectively. For Julian Calendar, see "Julian Calendar" on page 309.

1821	2	1847	6	1873	4	1899	1	1925	5	1951	2	1977	7	2003	4	2029	2	2055	6
1822	3	1848	14	1874	5	1900	2	1926	6	1952	10	1978	1	2004	12	2030	3	2056	14
1823	4	1849	2	1875	6	1901	3	1927	7	1953	5	1979	2	2005	7	2031	4	2057	2
1824	12	1850	3	1876	14	1902	4	1928	8	1954	6	1980	10	2006	1	2032	12	2058	3
1825	7	1851	4	1877	2	1903	5	1929	3	1955	7	1981	5	2007	2	2033	7	2059	4
1826	1	1852	12	1878	3	1904	13	1930	4	1956	8	1982	6	2008	10	2034	1	2060	12
1827	2	1853	7	1879	4	1905	1	1931	5	1957	3	1983	7	2009	5	2035	2	2061	7
1828	10	1854	1	1880	12	1906	2	1932	13	1958	4	1984	8	2010	6	2036	10	2062	1
1829	5	1855	2	1881	7	1907	3	1933	1	1959	5	1985	3	2011	7	2037	5	2063	2
1830	6	1856	10	1882	1	1908	11	1934	2	1960	13	1986	4	2012	8	2038	6	2064	10
1831	7	1857	5	1883	2	1909	6	1935	3	1961	1	1987	5	2013	3	2039	7	2065	5
1832	8	1858	6	1884	10	1910	7	1936	11	1962	2	1988	13	2014	4	2040	8	2066	6
1833	3	1859	7	1885	5	1911	1	1937	6	1963	3	1989	1	2015	5	2041	3	2067	7
1834	4	1860	8	1886	6	1912	9	1938	7	1964	11	1990	2	2016	13	2042	4	2068	8
1835	5	1861	3	1887	7	1913	4	1939	1	1965	6	1991	3	2017	1	2043	5	2069	3
1836	13	1862	4	1888	8	1914	5	1940	9	1966	7	1992	11	2018	2	2044	13	2070	4
1837	1	1863	5	1889	3	1915	6	1941	4	1967	1	1993	6	2019	3	2045	1	2071	5
1838	2	1864	13	1890	4	1916	14	1942	5	1968	9	1994	7	2020	11	2046	2	2072	13
1839	3	1865	1	1891	5	1917	2	1943	6	1969	4	1995	1	2021	6	2047	3	2073	1
1840	11	1866	2	1892	13	1918	3	1944	14	1970	5	1996	9	2022	7	2048	11	2074	2
1841	6	1867	3	1893	1	1919	4	1945	2	1971	6	1997	4	2023	1	2049	6	2075	3
1842	7	1868	11	1894	2	1920	12	1946	3	1972	14	1998	5	2024	9	2050	7	2076	11
1843	1	1869	6	1895	3	1921	7	1947	4	1973	2	1999	6	2025	4	2051	1	2077	6
1844	9	1870	7	1896	11	1922	1	1948	12	1974	3	2000	14	2026	5	2052	9	2078	7
1845	4	1871	1	1897	6	1923	2	1949	7	1975	4	2001	2	2027	6	2053	4	2079	1
1846	5	1872	9	1898	7	1924	10	1950	1	1976	12	2002	3	2028	14	2054	5	2080	9

1 1995

JANUARY

S	M	T	W	T	F	S
1	2	3	4	5	6	7
8	9	10	11	12	13	14
15	16	17	18	19	20	21
22	23	24	25	26	27	28
29	30	31				

FEBRUARY

S	M	T	W	T	F	S
			1	2	3	4
5	6	7	8	9	10	11
12	13	14	15	16	17	18
19	20	21	22	23	24	25
26	27	28				

MARCH

S	M	T	W	T	F	S
			1	2	3	4
5	6	7	8	9	10	11
12	13	14	15	16	17	18
19	20	21	22	23	24	25
26	27	28	29	30	31	

APRIL

S	M	T	W	T	F	S
						1
2	3	4	5	6	7	8
9	10	11	12	13	14	15
16	17	18	19	20	21	22
23	24	25	26	27	28	29
30						

MAY

S	M	T	W	T	F	S
	1	2	3	4	5	6
7	8	9	10	11	12	13
14	15	16	17	18	19	20
21	22	23	24	25	26	27
28	29	30	31			

JUNE

S	M	T	W	T	F	S
				1	2	3
4	5	6	7	8	9	10
11	12	13	14	15	16	17
18	19	20	21	22	23	24
25	26	27	28	29	30	

JULY

S	M	T	W	T	F	S
						1
2	3	4	5	6	7	8
9	10	11	12	13	14	15
16	17	18	19	20	21	22
23	24	25	26	27	28	29
30	31					

AUGUST

S	M	T	W	T	F	S
		1	2	3	4	5
6	7	8	9	10	11	12
13	14	15	16	17	18	19
20	21	22	23	24	25	26
27	28	29	30	31		

SEPTEMBER

S	M	T	W	T	F	S
					1	2
3	4	5	6	7	8	9
10	11	12	13	14	15	16
17	18	19	20	21	22	23
24	25	26	27	28	29	30

OCTOBER

S	M	T	W	T	F	S
1	2	3	4	5	6	7
8	9	10	11	12	13	14
15	16	17	18	19	20	21
22	23	24	25	26	27	28
29	30	31				

NOVEMBER

S	M	T	W	T	F	S
			1	2	3	4
5	6	7	8	9	10	11
12	13	14	15	16	17	18
19	20	21	22	23	24	25
26	27	28	29	30		

DECEMBER

S	M	T	W	T	F	S
					1	2
3	4	5	6	7	8	9
10	11	12	13	14	15	16
17	18	19	20	21	22	23
24	25	26	27	28	29	30
31						

2

JANUARY

S	M	T	W	T	F	S
	1	2	3	4	5	6
7	8	9	10	11	12	13
14	15	16	17	18	19	20
21	22	23	24	25	26	27
28	29	30	31			

FEBRUARY

S	M	T	W	T	F	S
				1	2	3
4	5	6	7	8	9	10
11	12	13	14	15	16	17
18	19	20	21	22	23	24
25	26	27	28			

MARCH

S	M	T	W	T	F	S
				1	2	3
4	5	6	7	8	9	10
11	12	13	14	15	16	17
18	19	20	21	22	23	24
25	26	27	28	29	30	31

APRIL

S	M	T	W	T	F	S
1	2	3	4	5	6	7
8	9	10	11	12	13	14
15	16	17	18	19	20	21
22	23	24	25	26	27	28
29	30					

MAY

S	M	T	W	T	F	S
		1	2	3	4	5
6	7	8	9	10	11	12
13	14	15	16	17	18	19
20	21	22	23	24	25	26
27	28	29	30	31		

JUNE

S	M	T	W	T	F	S
					1	2
3	4	5	6	7	8	9
10	11	12	13	14	15	16
17	18	19	20	21	22	23
24	25	26	27	28	29	30

JULY

S	M	T	W	T	F	S
1	2	3	4	5	6	7
8	9	10	11	12	13	14
15	16	17	18	19	20	21
22	23	24	25	26	27	28
29	30	31				

AUGUST

S	M	T	W	T	F	S
			1	2	3	4
5	6	7	8	9	10	11
12	13	14	15	16	17	18
19	20	21	22	23	24	25
26	27	28	29	30	31	

SEPTEMBER

S	M	T	W	T	F	S
						1
2	3	4	5	6	7	8
9	10	11	12	13	14	15
16	17	18	19	20	21	22
23	24	25	26	27	28	29
30						

OCTOBER

S	M	T	W	T	F	S
	1	2	3	4	5	6
7	8	9	10	11	12	13
14	15	16	17	18	19	20
21	22	23	24	25	26	27
28	29	30	31			

NOVEMBER

S	M	T	W	T	F	S
				1	2	3
4	5	6	7	8	9	10
11	12	13	14	15	16	17
18	19	20	21	22	23	24
25	26	27	28	29	30	

DECEMBER

S	M	T	W	T	F	S
						1
2	3	4	5	6	7	8
9	10	11	12	13	14	15
16	17	18	19	20	21	22
23	24	25	26	27	28	29
30	31					

3

JANUARY

S	M	T	W	T	F	S
		1	2	3	4	5
6	7	8	9	10	11	12
13	14	15	16	17	18	19
20	21	22	23	24	25	26
27	28	29	30	31		

FEBRUARY

S	M	T	W	T	F	S
					1	2
3	4	5	6	7	8	9
10	11	12	13	14	15	16
17	18	19	20	21	22	23
24	25	26	27	28		

MARCH

S	M	T	W	T	F	S
					1	2
3	4	5	6	7	8	9
10	11	12	13	14	15	16
17	18	19	20	21	22	23
24	25	26	27	28	29	30
31						

APRIL

S	M	T	W	T	F	S
	1	2	3	4	5	6
7	8	9	10	11	12	13
14	15	16	17	18	19	20
21	22	23	24	25	26	27
28	29	30				

MAY

S	M	T	W	T	F	S
			1	2	3	4
5	6	7	8	9	10	11
12	13	14	15	16	17	18
19	20	21	22	23	24	25
26	27	28	29	30	31	

JUNE

S	M	T	W	T	F	S
						1
2	3	4	5	6	7	8
9	10	11	12	13	14	15
16	17	18	19	20	21	22
23	24	25	26	27	28	29
30						

JULY

S	M	T	W	T	F	S
	1	2	3	4	5	6
7	8	9	10	11	12	13
14	15	16	17	18	19	20
21	22	23	24	25	26	27
28	29	30	31			

AUGUST

S	M	T	W	T	F	S
				1	2	3
4	5	6	7	8	9	10
11	12	13	14	15	16	17
18	19	20	21	22	23	24
25	26	27	28	29	30	31

SEPTEMBER

S	M	T	W	T	F	S
1	2	3	4	5	6	7
8	9	10	11	12	13	14
15	16	17	18	19	20	21
22	23	24	25	26	27	28
29	30					

OCTOBER

S	M	T	W	T	F	S
		1	2	3	4	5
6	7	8	9	10	11	12
13	14	15	16	17	18	19
20	21	22	23	24	25	26
27	28	29	30	31		

NOVEMBER

S	M	T	W	T	F	S
					1	2
3	4	5	6	7	8	9
10	11	12	13	14	15	16
17	18	19	20	21	22	23
24	25	26	27	28	29	30

DECEMBER

S	M	T	W	T	F	S
1	2	3	4	5	6	7
8	9	10	11	12	13	14
15	16	17	18	19	20	21
22	23	24	25	26	27	28
29	30	31				

4 1997

JANUARY

S	M	T	W	T	F	S
			1	2	3	4
5	6	7	8	9	10	11
12	13	14	15	16	17	18
19	20	21	22	23	24	25
26	27	28	29	30	31	

FEBRUARY

S	M	T	W	T	F	S
						1
2	3	4	5	6	7	8
9	10	11	12	13	14	15
16	17	18	19	20	21	22
23	24	25	26	27	28	

MARCH

S	M	T	W	T	F	S
						1
2	3	4	5	6	7	8
9	10	11	12	13	14	15
16	17	18	19	20	21	22
23	24	25	26	27	28	29
30	31					

APRIL

S	M	T	W	T	F	S
		1	2	3	4	5
6	7	8	9	10	11	12
13	14	15	16	17	18	19
20	21	22	23	24	25	26
27	28	29	30			

MAY

S	M	T	W	T	F	S
				1	2	3
4	5	6	7	8	9	10
11	12	13	14	15	16	17
18	19	20	21	22	23	24
25	26	27	28	29	30	31

JUNE

S	M	T	W	T	F	S
1	2	3	4	5	6	7
8	9	10	11	12	13	14
15	16	17	18	19	20	21
22	23	24	25	26	27	28
29	30					

JULY

S	M	T	W	T	F	S
		1	2	3	4	5
6	7	8	9	10	11	12
13	14	15	16	17	18	19
20	21	22	23	24	25	26
27	28	29	30	31		

AUGUST

S	M	T	W	T	F	S
					1	2
3	4	5	6	7	8	9
10	11	12	13	14	15	16
17	18	19	20	21	22	23
24	25	26	27	28	29	30
31						

SEPTEMBER

S	M	T	W	T	F	S
	1	2	3	4	5	6
7	8	9	10	11	12	13
14	15	16	17	18	19	20
21	22	23	24	25	26	27
28	29	30				

OCTOBER

S	M	T	W	T	F	S
			1	2	3	4
5	6	7	8	9	10	11
12	13	14	15	16	17	18
19	20	21	22	23	24	25
26	27	28	29	30	31	

NOVEMBER

S	M	T	W	T	F	S
						1
2	3	4	5	6	7	8
9	10	11	12	13	14	15
16	17	18	19	20	21	22
23	24	25	26	27	28	29
30						

DECEMBER

S	M	T	W	T	F	S
	1	2	3	4	5	6
7	8	9	10	11	12	13
14	15	16	17	18	19	20
21	22	23	24	25	26	27
28	29	30	31			

5

JANUARY

S	M	T	W	T	F	S
				1	2	3
4	5	6	7	8	9	10
11	12	13	14	15	16	17
18	19	20	21	22	23	24
25	26	27	28	29	30	31

FEBRUARY

S	M	T	W	T	F	S
1	2	3	4	5	6	7
8	9	10	11	12	13	14
15	16	17	18	19	20	21
22	23	24	25	26	27	28

MARCH

S	M	T	W	T	F	S
1	2	3	4	5	6	7
8	9	10	11	12	13	14
15	16	17	18	19	20	21
22	23	24	25	26	27	28
29	30	31				

APRIL

S	M	T	W	T	F	S
			1	2	3	4
5	6	7	8	9	10	11
12	13	14	15	16	17	18
19	20	21	22	23	24	25
26	27	28	29	30		

MAY

S	M	T	W	T	F	S
					1	2
3	4	5	6	7	8	9
10	11	12	13	14	15	16
17	18	19	20	21	22	23
24	25	26	27	28	29	30
31						

JUNE

S	M	T	W	T	F	S
	1	2	3	4	5	6
7	8	9	10	11	12	13
14	15	16	17	18	19	20
21	22	23	24	25	26	27
28	29	30				

JULY

S	M	T	W	T	F	S
			1	2	3	4
5	6	7	8	9	10	11
12	13	14	15	16	17	18
19	20	21	22	23	24	25
26	27	28	29	30	31	

AUGUST

S	M	T	W	T	F	S
						1
2	3	4	5	6	7	8
9	10	11	12	13	14	15
16	17	18	19	20	21	22
23	24	25	26	27	28	29
30	31					

SEPTEMBER

S	M	T	W	T	F	S
		1	2	3	4	5
6	7	8	9	10	11	12
13	14	15	16	17	18	19
20	21	22	23	24	25	26
27	28	29	30			

OCTOBER

S	M	T	W	T	F	S
				1	2	3
4	5	6	7	8	9	10
11	12	13	14	15	16	17
18	19	20	21	22	23	24
25	26	27	28	29	30	31

NOVEMBER

S	M	T	W	T	F	S
1	2	3	4	5	6	7
8	9	10	11	12	13	14
15	16	17	18	19	20	21
22	23	24	25	26	27	28
29	30					

DECEMBER

S	M	T	W	T	F	S
		1	2	3	4	5
6	7	8	9	10	11	12
13	14	15	16	17	18	19
20	21	22	23	24	25	26
27	28	29	30	31		

6

JANUARY

S	M	T	W	T	F	S
					1	2
3	4	5	6	7	8	9
10	11	12	13	14	15	16
17	18	19	20	21	22	23
24	25	26	27	28	29	30
31						

FEBRUARY

S	M	T	W	T	F	S
	1	2	3	4	5	6
7	8	9	10	11	12	13
14	15	16	17	18	19	20
21	22	23	24	25	26	27
28						

MARCH

S	M	T	W	T	F	S
	1	2	3	4	5	6
7	8	9	10	11	12	13
14	15	16	17	18	19	20
21	22	23	24	25	26	27
28	29	30	31			

APRIL

S	M	T	W	T	F	S
				1	2	3
4	5	6	7	8	9	10
11	12	13	14	15	16	17
18	19	20	21	22	23	24
25	26	27	28	29	30	

MAY

S	M	T	W	T	F	S
						1
2	3	4	5	6	7	8
9	10	11	12	13	14	15
16	17	18	19	20	21	22
23	24	25	26	27	28	29
30	31					

JUNE

S	M	T	W	T	F	S
		1	2	3	4	5
6	7	8	9	10	11	12
13	14	15	16	17	18	19
20	21	22	23	24	25	26
27	28	29	30			

JULY

S	M	T	W	T	F	S
				1	2	3
4	5	6	7	8	9	10
11	12	13	14	15	16	17
18	19	20	21	22	23	24
25	26	27	28	29	30	31

AUGUST

S	M	T	W	T	F	S
1	2	3	4	5	6	7
8	9	10	11	12	13	14
15	16	17	18	19	20	21
22	23	24	25	26	27	28
29	30	31				

SEPTEMBER

S	M	T	W	T	F	S
			1	2	3	4
5	6	7	8	9	10	11
12	13	14	15	16	17	18
19	20	21	22	23	24	25
26	27	28	29	30		

OCTOBER

S	M	T	W	T	F	S
					1	2
3	4	5	6	7	8	9
10	11	12	13	14	15	16
17	18	19	20	21	22	23
24	25	26	27	28	29	30
31						

NOVEMBER

S	M	T	W	T	F	S
	1	2	3	4	5	6
7	8	9	10	11	12	13
14	15	16	17	18	19	20
21	22	23	24	25	26	27
28	29	30				

DECEMBER

S	M	T	W	T	F	S
			1	2	3	4
5	6	7	8	9	10	11
12	13	14	15	16	17	18
19	20	21	22	23	24	25
26	27	28	29	30	31	

The Julian Period

How many days have you lived? To determine this, multiply your age by 365, add the number of days since your last birthday until today, and account for all leap years. Chances are your answer would be wrong. Astronomers, however, find it convenient to express dates and time intervals in days rather than in years, months, and days. This is done by placing events within the Julian period.

The Julian period was devised in 1582 by the French classical scholar Joseph Scaliger (1540-1609) and named after his father Julius Caesar Scaliger (1484-1558), not after the Julian calendar. Joseph Scaliger began Julian Day (JD) #1 at noon, Jan. 1, 4713 BC, the most recent time that 3 major chronological cycles began on the same day—(1)

the 28-year solar cycle, after which dates in the Julian calendar (e.g., Feb. 11) return to the same days of the week (e.g., Monday); (2) the 19-year lunar cycle, after which the phases of the moon return to the same dates of the year; and (3) the 15-year indiction cycle, used in ancient Rome to regulate taxes. It will take 7,980 years to complete the period, the product of 28, 19, and 15.

Noon of Dec. 31, 1995, marks the beginning of JD 2,450,084; that many days will have passed since the start of the Julian period. The JD at noon of any date in 1996 may be found by adding to this figure the day of the year for that date, which can be obtained from the left half of the "Days Between Two Dates" chart.

Days Between Two Dates

Table covers period of 2 ordinary years. Example—Days between Feb. 10, 1994, and Dec. 15, 1995; subtract 41 from 714; answer is 673 days. For leap year, such as 1996, one day must be added: answer for days between Feb. 10, 1995, and Dec. 15, 1996, would be 674.

Date	Jan.	Feb.	Mar.	April	May	June	July	Aug.	Sept.	Oct.	Nov.	Dec.	Date	Jan.	Feb.	Mar.	April	May	June	July	Aug.	Sept.	Oct.	Nov.	Dec.
1	1	32	60	91	121	152	182	213	244	274	305	335	1	366	397	425	456	486	517	547	578	609	639	670	700
2	2	33	61	92	122	153	183	214	245	275	306	336	2	367	398	426	457	487	518	548	579	610	640	671	701
3	3	34	62	93	123	154	184	215	246	276	307	337	3	368	399	427	458	488	519	549	580	611	641	672	702
4	4	35	63	94	124	155	185	216	247	277	308	338	4	369	400	428	459	489	520	550	581	612	642	673	703
5	5	36	64	95	125	156	186	217	248	278	309	339	5	370	401	429	460	490	521	551	582	613	643	674	704
6	6	37	65	96	126	157	187	218	249	279	310	340	6	371	402	430	461	491	522	552	583	614	644	675	705
7	7	38	66	97	127	158	188	219	250	280	311	341	7	372	403	431	462	492	523	553	584	615	645	676	706
8	8	39	67	98	128	159	189	220	251	281	312	342	8	373	404	432	463	493	524	554	585	616	646	677	707
9	9	40	68	99	129	160	190	221	252	282	313	343	9	374	405	433	464	494	525	555	586	617	647	678	708
10	10	41	69	100	130	161	191	222	253	283	314	344	10	375	406	434	465	495	526	556	587	618	648	679	709
11	11	42	70	101	131	162	192	223	254	284	315	345	11	376	407	435	466	496	527	557	588	619	649	680	710
12	12	43	71	102	132	163	193	224	255	285	316	346	12	377	408	436	467	497	528	558	589	620	650	681	711
13	13	44	72	103	133	164	194	225	256	286	317	347	13	378	409	437	468	498	529	559	590	621	651	682	712
14	14	45	73	104	134	165	195	226	257	287	318	348	14	379	410	438	469	499	530	560	591	622	652	683	713
15	15	46	74	105	135	166	196	227	258	288	319	349	15	380	411	439	470	500	531	561	592	623	653	684	714
16	16	47	75	106	136	167	197	228	259	289	320	350	16	381	412	440	471	501	532	562	593	624	654	685	715
17	17	48	76	107	137	168	198	229	260	290	321	351	17	382	413	441	472	502	533	563	594	625	655	686	716
18	18	49	77	108	138	169	199	230	261	291	322	352	18	383	414	442	473	503	534	564	595	626	656	687	717
19	19	50	78	109	139	170	200	231	262	292	323	353	19	384	415	443	474	504	535	565	596	627	657	688	718
20	20	51	79	110	140	171	201	232	263	293	324	354	20	385	416	444	475	505	536	566	597	628	658	689	719
21	21	52	80	111	141	172	202	233	264	294	325	355	21	386	417	445	476	506	537	567	598	629	659	690	720
22	22	53	81	112	142	173	203	234	265	295	326	356	22	387	418	446	477	507	538	568	599	630	660	691	721
23	23	54	82	113	143	174	204	235	266	296	327	357	23	388	419	447	478	508	539	569	600	631	661	692	722
24	24	55	83	114	144	175	205	236	267	297	328	358	24	389	420	448	479	509	540	570	601	632	662	693	723
25	25	56	84	115	145	176	206	237	268	298	329	359	25	390	421	449	480	510	541	571	602	633	663	694	724
26	26	57	85	116	146	177	207	238	269	299	330	360	26	391	422	450	481	511	542	572	603	634	664	695	725
27	27	58	86	117	147	178	208	239	270	300	331	361	27	392	423	451	482	512	543	573	604	635	665	696	726
28	28	59	87	118	148	179	209	240	271	301	332	362	28	393	424	452	483	513	544	574	605	636	666	697	727
29	29	—	88	119	149	180	210	241	272	302	333	363	29	394	—	453	484	514	545	575	606	637	667	698	728
30	30	—	89	120	150	181	211	242	273	303	334	364	30	395	—	454	485	515	546	576	607	638	668	699	729
31	31	—	90	—	151	—	212	243	—	304	—	365	31	396	—	455	—	516	—	577	608	—	669	—	730

Lunar Calendar, Chinese New Year, Vietnamese Tet
Source: Chinese Information and Culture Center, New York, NY

The Chinese lunar calendar is divided into 12 months of either 29 or 30 days (compensating for the lunar month's mean duration of 29 days, 12 hr, 44.05 min). The calendar is synchronized with the solar year by the addition of extra months at fixed intervals.

The Chinese calendar runs on a sexagenary cycle, i.e., a 60-year cycle. The cycles 1876-1935 and 1936-95, with the years grouped under their 12 animal designations, are printed below. A new cycle will begin in 1996 and last until 2055. The year 1996 (Lunar Year 4694) is found in the 1st column, under Rat, and is known as a Year of the Rat. Readers can find the animal name for the year of their birth, marriage, etc., in the same chart. (Note: The first 3-7 weeks of each Western year belong to the previous Chinese year and animal designation.)

Both the Western (Gregorian) and traditional lunar calendars are used publicly in China and in North and South Korea, and 2 New Year's celebrations are held. In Taiwan, in overseas Chinese communities, and in Vietnam, the lunar calendar is used only to set the dates for traditional festivals, with the Gregorian system in general use.

The 4-day Chinese New Year, Hsin Nien, the 3-day Vietnamese New Year festival, Tet, and the 3-to-4-day Korean festival, Suhl, begin at the second new moon after the winter solstice. Because the date is fixed according to the date of the new moon in the Far East, which is west of the International Date Line, the date may be one day later than that of the new moon in the U.S. The day may fall, therefore, between Jan. 21 and Feb. 19 of the Gregorian calendar. Feb. 19, 1996, marks the start of the new Chinese year.

Rat	Ox	Tiger	Hare (Rabbit)	Dragon	Snake	Horse	Sheep (Goat)	Monkey	Rooster	Dog	Pig
1876	1877	1878	1879	1880	1881	1882	1883	1884	1885	1886	1887
1888	1889	1890	1891	1892	1893	1894	1895	1896	1897	1898	1899
1900	1901	1902	1903	1904	1905	1906	1907	1908	1909	1910	1911
1912	1913	1914	1915	1916	1917	1918	1919	1920	1921	1922	1923
1924	1925	1926	1927	1928	1929	1930	1931	1932	1933	1934	1935
1936	1937	1938	1939	1940	1941	1942	1943	1944	1945	1946	1947
1948	1949	1950	1951	1952	1953	1954	1955	1956	1957	1958	1959
1960	1961	1962	1963	1964	1965	1966	1967	1968	1969	1970	1971
1972	1973	1974	1975	1976	1977	1978	1979	1980	1981	1982	1983
1984	1985	1986	1987	1988	1989	1990	1991	1992	1993	1994	1995
1996	1997	1998	1999	2000	2001	2002	2003	2004	2005	2006	2007
2008	2009	2010	2011	2012	2013	2014	2015	2016	2017	2018	2019

Standard Time, Daylight Saving Time, and Others

Source: Defense Mapping Agency Hydrographic/Topographic Center; U.S. Dept. of Transportation

Standard Time

Standard Time is reckoned from Greenwich, England, recognized as the Prime Meridian of Longitude. The world is divided into 24 zones, each 15° of arc, or one hour in time apart. The Greenwich meridian (0°) extends through the center of the initial zone, and the zones to the east are numbered from 1 to 12 with the prefix "minus" indicating the number of hours to be subtracted to obtain Greenwich Time. Each zone extends 7½° on either side of its central meridian.

Westward zones are similarly numbered, but prefixed "plus" showing the number of hours that must be added to get Greenwich Time. Although these zones apply generally to sea areas, the Standard Time maintained in many countries does not coincide with zone time. A graphical representation of the zones is shown on the Standard Time Zone Chart of the World published by the U.S. Geological Survey Distribution Center, PO Box 25286, Denver, CO 80225.

The U.S. and possessions are divided into 10 Standard Time zones. Each zone is approximately 15° of longitude in width. All places in each zone use, instead of their own local time, the time counted from the transit of the "mean sun" across the Standard Time meridian that passes near the middle of that zone. These time zones are designated as Atlantic, Eastern, Central, Mountain, Pacific, Alaska, Hawaii-Aleutian, Samoa, Wake Island, and Guam, and the time in these zones is basically reckoned from the 60th, 75th, 90th, 105th, 120th, 135th, 150th, and 165th meridians west of Greenwich and the 165th and 150th meridians east of Greenwich. The time zone line wanders to conform to local geographical regions. The time in the various zones in the U.S. and U.S. territories is earlier than Greenwich Time by 4, 5, 6, 7, 8, 9, 10, and 11 hours respectively. However, Wake Island and Guam cross the International Date Line and are 12 and 10 hours ahead of Greenwich Time respectively.

24-Hour Time

Twenty-four-hour time is widely used in scientific work throughout the world. In the U.S. it is used also in operations of the armed forces. In Europe it is frequently used by the transportation networks in preference to the 12-hour AM and PM system. With the 24-hour system, the day begins at midnight and is designated 0000 through 2359.

International Date Line

The Date Line is a zig-zag line that approximately coincides with the 180th meridian, and it separates the calendar dates. The date must be advanced one day when crossing in a westerly direction and set back one day when crossing in an easterly direction. The line is deflected eastward through the Bering Strait and westward of the Aleutians to prevent separating these areas by date. The line is again deflected eastward of the Tonga and New Zealand Islands in the South Pacific for the same reason.

Daylight Saving Time

Daylight Saving Time is achieved by advancing the clock one hour. Since 1987, Daylight Saving Time has begun at 2 AM on the first Sunday in Apr. and ends at 2 AM on the last Sunday in Oct.

Daylight Saving Time was first observed in the U.S. during World War I, and then again during World War II. In the intervening years, some states and communities observed Daylight Saving Time using whatever beginning and ending dates they chose. In 1966, Congress passed the Uniform Time Act, which provided that any state or territory that chooses to observe Daylight Saving Time must begin and end on the federal dates. Any state could, by law, exempt itself; a 1972 amendment to the act authorized states split by time zones to observe Daylight Saving Time in one time zone and standard time in the other time zone. Currently, Arizona, Hawaii, the eastern time zone portion of Indiana, Puerto Rico, the U.S. Virgin Islands, and American Samoa do not observe Daylight Saving Time.

Congress and the Secretary of Transportation both have authority to change time zone boundaries. Since 1966 there have been a number of changes to U.S. time zone boundaries. Efforts to conserve energy have also prompted various changes to the times that Daylight Saving Time was observed in the past.

International Usage

Adjusting clock time to be able to use the added daylight on summer evenings is common throughout the world.

Canada, which lies over 6 time zones, observes Daylight Saving Time from the last Sunday of Apr. until the last Sunday of Oct. Saskatchewan remains on standard time throughout the year. Communities elsewhere in Canada also may choose to exempt themselves from Daylight Saving Time.

Beginning in 1996, member nations of the European Union (EU) will begin observance of the "summer-time period," the EU's version of Daylight Saving Time, from the last Sunday of March until the last Sunday in Oct.

Russia, which lies over 11 time zones, maintains its Standard Time 1 hour fast of the zone designation. Additionally, it proclaims Daylight Saving Time from the fourth Sunday in March until the fourth Sunday in Sept.

China, which lies across 5 time zones, has decreed that the entire country be placed on Greenwich Time plus 8 hours. Daylight Saving Time is not observed. Japan, which lies in one time zone, and Mexico, which occupies 3 times zones, also do not modify their legal time during the summer months.

Many countries in the Southern Hemisphere maintain Daylight Saving Time, generally from Oct. to March; however, most countries near the equator do not deviate from Standard Time.

Standard Time Differences—World Cities

The time indicated in the table is fixed by law and is called the legal time or, more generally, Standard Time. Use of Daylight Saving Time varies widely. * Indicates morning of the following day. At 12:00 noon, Eastern Standard Time, the Standard Time (in 24-hour time) in selected cities is as follows:

City	Time	City	Time	City	Time	City	Time
Addis Ababa	20 00	Cape Town	19 00	Lima	12 00	Santiago (Chile)	13 00
Alexandria	19 00	Caracas	13 00	Lisbon	17 00	Seoul	2 00*
Amsterdam	18 00	Casablanca	17 00	Liverpool	17 00	Shanghai	1 00*
Athens	19 00	Copenhagen	18 00	London	17 00	Singapore	1 00*
Auckland	5 00*	Delhi	22 30	Madrid	18 00	Stockholm	18 00
Baghdad	20 00	Dhaka	23 00	Manila	1 00*	Sydney (Australia)	3 00*
Bangkok	0 00	Dublin	17 00	Mecca (Saudi Arabia)	20 00	Tashkent	23 00
Beijing	1 00*	Gdánsk	18 00	Melbourne	3 00*	Tehran	20 30
Belfast	17 00	Geneva	18 00	Mexico City	11 00	Tel Aviv	19 00
Berlin	18 00	Havana	12 00	Montevideo	14 00	Tokyo	2 00*
Bogotá	12 00	Helsinki	19 00	Moscow	20 00	Valparaíso	13 00
Bombay	22 30	Ho Chi Minh City	0 00	Nagasaki	2 00*	Vienna	18 00
Bremen	18 00	Hong Kong	1 00*	Oslo	18 00	Vladivostok	3 00*
Brussels	18 00	Istanbul	19 00	Paris	18 00	Vienna	18 00
Bucharest	19 00	Jakarta	0 00	Prague	18 00	Warsaw	18 00
Budapest	18 00	Jerusalem	19 00	Rio de Janeiro	14 00	Wellington (NZ)	5 00*
Buenos Aires	14 00	Johannesburg	19 00	Rome	18 00	Yangon (Rangoon)	23 30
Cairo	19 00	Karachi	22 00	St. Petersburg	20 00	Yokohama	2 00*
Calcutta	22 30	Le Havre	18 00			Zürich	18 00

Standard Time Differences — North American Cities

At 12:00 noon, Eastern Standard Time, the Standard Time in North American cities is as follows:

City	Time		City	Time		City	Time	
Akron, OH	12 00	Noon	Frankfort, KY	12 00	Noon	*Phoenix, AZ	10 00	AM
Albuquerque, NM	10 00	AM	Galveston, TX	11 00	AM	Pierre, SD	11 00	AM
Atlanta, GA	12 00	Noon	Grand Rapids, MI	12 00	Noon	Pittsburgh, PA	12 00	Noon
Austin, TX	11 00	AM	Halifax, NS	1 00	PM	Portland, ME	12 00	Noon
Baltimore, MD	12 00	Noon	Hartford, CT	12 00	Noon	Portland, OR	9 00	AM
Birmingham, AL	11 00	AM	Helena, MT	10 00	AM	Providence, RI	12 00	Noon
Bismarck, ND	11 00	AM	*Honolulu, HI	7 00	AM	*Regina, Sask.	11 00	AM
Boise, ID	10 00	AM	Houston, TX	11 00	AM	Reno, NV	9 00	AM
Boston, MA	12 00	Noon	*Indianapolis, IN	12 00	Noon	Richmond, VA	12 00	Noon
Buffalo, NY	12 00	Noon	Jacksonville, FL	12 00	Noon	Rochester, NY	12 00	Noon
Butte, MT	10 00	AM	Juneau, AK	8 00	AM	Sacramento, CA	9 00	AM
Calgary, Alta.	10 00	AM	Kansas City, MO	11 00	AM	St. John's, Nfld.	1 30	PM
Charleston, SC	12 00	Noon	Knoxville, TN	12 00	Noon	St. Louis, MO	11 00	AM
Charleston, WV	12 00	Noon	Lexington, KY	12 00	Noon	St. Paul, MN	11 00	AM
Charlotte, NC.	12 00	Noon	Lincoln, NE	11 00	AM	Salt Lake City, UT	10 00	AM
Charlottetown, PEI.	1 00	PM	Little Rock, AR	11 00	AM	San Antonio, TX	11 00	AM
Chattanooga, TN	12 00	Noon	Los Angeles, CA	9 00	AM	San Diego, CA	9 00	AM
Cheyenne, WY	10 00	AM	Louisville, KY	12 00	Noon	San Francisco, CA	9 00	AM
Chicago, IL	11 00	AM	*Mexico City	11 00	AM	Santa Fe, NM	10 00	AM
Cleveland, OH	12 00	Noon	Memphis, TN	11 00	AM	Savannah, GA	12 00	Noon
Colorado Spr., CO	10 00	AM	Miami, FL	12 00	Noon	Seattle, WA	9 00	AM
Columbus, OH	12 00	Noon	Milwaukee, WI	11 00	AM	Shreveport, LA	11 00	AM
Dallas, TX	11 00	AM	Minneapolis, MN	11 00	AM	Sioux Falls, SD	11 00	AM
*Dawson, Yuk.	9 00	AM	Mobile, AL.	11 00	AM	Spokane, WA	9 00	AM
Dayton, OH	12 00	Noon	Montreal, Que	12 00	Noon	Tampa, FL	12 00	Noon
Denver, CO	10 00	AM	Nashville, TN	11 00	AM	Toledo, OH	12 00	Noon
Des Moines, IA	11 00	AM	New Haven, CT	12 00	Noon	Topeka, KS	11 00	AM
Detroit, MI	12 00	Noon	New Orleans, LA	11 00	AM	Toronto, Ont.	12 00	Noon
Duluth, MN	11 00	AM	New York, NY	12 00	Noon	*Tucson, AZ	10 00	AM
El Paso, TX	10 00	AM	Nome, AK	8 00	AM	Tulsa, OK	11 00	AM
Erie, PA	12 00	Noon	Norfolk, VA	12 00	Noon	Vancouver, BC	9 00	AM
Evansville, IN.	11 00	AM	Oklahoma City, OK	11 00	AM	Washington, DC	12 00	Noon
Fairbanks, AK	8 00	AM	Omaha, NE	11 00	AM	Wichita, KS	11 00	AM
Flint, MI.	12 00	Noon	Peoria, IL	11 00	AM	Wilmington, DE	12 00	Noon
*Fort Wayne, IN	12 00	Noon	Philadelphia, PA	12 00	Noon	Winnipeg, Man	11 00	AM
Fort Worth, TX	11 00	AM						

* Cities with an asterisk do not observe Daylight Saving Time. During much of the year, it is necessary to add one hour to the time in cities that do observe Daylight Saving Time to get the proper time relation.

U.S. Legal or Public Holidays, 1996

Technically, the U.S. observes no national holidays; each state has jurisdiction over its holidays, which are designated by legislative enactment or executive proclamation. In practice, however, most states observe the federal legal public holidays, even though the president and the U.S. Congress can legally designate holidays only for the District of Columbia and for federal employees. Federal legal public holidays are New Year's Day, Martin Luther King Jr. Day, Washington's Birthday, Memorial Day, Independence Day, Labor Day, Columbus Day, Veterans Day, Thanksgiving, and Christmas.

Chief Legal or Public Holidays

When a holiday falls on a Sunday or a Saturday, it is usually observed on the following Monday or the preceding Friday. For some holidays, government and business closing practices vary. In most cases, the office of the secretary of state can provide details for holiday closings. The following will be legal or public holidays in most states in 1996:

Jan. 1 (Mon.) — New Year's Day
Jan. 15 (3d Mon. in Jan.) — Martin Luther King Jr. Day
Feb. 12 (Mon.) — Lincoln's Birthday
Feb. 19 (3d Mon. in Feb.) — Washington's Birthday, or Presidents' Day, or Washington-Lincoln Day
May 27 (last Mon. in May) — Memorial Day, or Decoration Day

July 4 (Thur.) — Independence Day
Sept. 2 (1st Mon. in Sept.) — Labor Day
Nov. 11 (Mon.) — Veterans Day
Nov. 28 (4th Thurs. in Nov.) — Thanksgiving
Dec. 25 (Wed.) — Christmas Day

In some states, the following will be legal or public holidays in 1996:

Apr. 5 (Fri.) — Good Friday. (In some states, observed for half or part of day.)
Oct. 14 (2d Mon. in Oct.) — Columbus Day, or Discoverers' Day, or Pioneers' Day
Nov. 5 (1st Tues. after 1st Mon. in Nov.) — Election Day

Selected International Holidays, 1996

Jan 20-21 — Ati-Atihan Festival, Philippines
Jan. 29 — Australia Day obsvd., Australia
Feb. 5 — Constitution Day, Mexico
Feb. 11 — National Foundation Day, Japan
Feb. 17-20 — Carnival, Brazil
Mar. 11 — Commonwealth Day, Canada, Great Britain
Mar. 17 — St. Patrick's Day, Ireland
Mar. 21 — Benito Juarez's Birthday, Mexico
Apr. 8 — Buddha's Birthday, Korea, Japan
May 5 — Cinco de Mayo (Battle of Puebla Day), Mexico
May 17 — Constitution Day, Norway
May 20 — Victoria Day, Canada
July 1 — Canada Day, Canada

July 14 — Bastille Day, France
Sept. 2 — Labor Day, Canada
Sept. 15 — Respect for the Aged Day, Japan
Sept. 16 — Independence Day, Mexico
Sept. 19 — St. Gennaro, Italy
Sept. 28 — Confucius' Birthday/Teachers' Day, Taiwan
Oct. 14 — Thanksgiving Day, Canada
Nov. 1-2 — Day of the Dead, Mexico
Nov. 5 — Guy Fawkes Day, Great Britain
Nov. 11 — Remembrance Day, Canada
Dec. 12 — Jamhuri Day, Kenya; Guadalupe Day, Mexico
Dec. 26 — Boxing Day, Australia, Canada, Great Britain

AEROSPACE

Memorable Moments in Human Spaceflight

Sources: National Aeronautics and Space Administration; Congressional Research Service; World Almanac research

Note: U.S. space missions are in boldface. Other missions were sponsored by the former Soviet Union or the Commonwealth of Independent States. All dates are Eastern standard time. EVA = extravehicular activity. ASTP = Apollo-Saturn Test Project.

DATES	VEHICLE NAME	CREW (no. of flights)	CREW DURATION (HR:MIN)	REMARKS
4/12/61	Vostok 1	Yuri A. Gagarin	1:48	1st human orbital flight
5/5/61	**Mercury-Redstone 3**	**Alan B. Shepard Jr.**	**0:15**	**1st American in space**
7/21/61	**Mercury-Redstone 4**	**Virgil I. Grissom**	**0:15**	**Spacecraft sank, Grissom rescued**
8/6/61-8/7/61	Vostok 2	Gherman S. Titov	25:18	1st spaceflight of more than 24 hrs
2/20/62	**Mercury-Atlas 6**	**John H. Glenn Jr.**	**4:55**	**1st American in orbit; 3 orbits**
5/24/62	**Mercury-Atlas 7**	**M. Scott Carpenter**	**4:56**	**Manual retrofire error caused 250-mi landing overshoot**
8/11/62-8/15/62	Vostok 3	Andrian G. Nikolayev	94:22	Vostok 3 and 4 made 1st group flight
8/12/62-8/15/62	Vostok 4	Pavel R. Popovich	70:57	On 1st orbit it came within 3 mi of Vostok 3
5/15/63-5/16/63	**Mercury-Atlas 9**	**L. Gordon Cooper**	**34:19**	**1st U.S. evaluation of effects of one day in space on a person; 22 orbits**
6/14/63-6/19/63	Vostok 5	Valery F. Bykovsky	119:06	Vostok 5 and 6 made 2d group flight
6/16/63-6/19/63	Vostok 6	Valentina V. Tereshkova	70:50	1st woman in space; passes within 3 mi of Vostok 5
10/12/64-10/13/64	Voskhod 1	Vladimir M. Komarov, Konstantin P. Feoktistov, Boris B. Yegorov	24:17	1st 3-man orbital flight; 1st without space suits
3/18/65-3/19/65	Voskhod 2	Pavel I. Belyayev, Aleksei A. Leonov	26:02	Leonov made 1st "space walk" (10 min)
3/23/65	**Gemini-Titan 3**	**Grissom (2), John W. Young**	**4:53**	**1st piloted spacecraft to change its orbital path**
6/3/65-6/7/65	**Gemini-Titan 4**	**James A. McDivitt, Edward H. White 2d**	**97:56**	**White was 1st American to "walk in space" (36 min)**
12/4/65-12/18/65	**Gemini-Titan 6**	**Frank Borman, James A. Lovell**	**330:35**	**Longest duration Gemini flight**
12/15/65-12/16/65	**Gemini-Titan 7**	**Schirra (2), Thomas P. Stafford**	**25:51**	**Completed 1st U.S. space rendezvous, with Gemini 6**
3/16/66-3/17/66	**Gemini-Titan 8**	**Neil A. Armstrong, David R. Scott**	**10:41**	**1st docking of one space vehicle with another; mission aborted, control malfunction; 1st Pacific landing**
7/18/66-7/21/66	**Gemini-Titan 10**	**Young (2), Michael Collins**	**70:47**	**1st use of Agena target vehicle's propulsion systems; 1st orbital docking**
11/11/66-11/15/66	**Gemini-Titan 12**	**Lovell (2), Edwin W. "Buzz" Aldrin Jr.**	**94:34**	**Final Gemini mission; record 5½ hr of EVA**
4/23/67-4/24/67	Soyuz 1	Komarov (2)	26:40	Crashed on reentry killing Komarov
10/11/68-10/22/68	**Apollo-Saturn 7**	**Schirra (3), Donn F. Eisele, R. Walter Cunningham**	**260:09**	**1st piloted flight of Apollo spacecraft command-service module only; live TV footage of crew**
12/21/68-12/27/68	**Apollo-Saturn 8**	**Borman (2), Lovell (3), William A. Anders**	**147:00**	**1st lunar orbit and piloted lunar return reentry (command-service module only); views of lunar surface televised to earth**
1/14/69-1/17/69	Soyuz 4	Vladimir A. Shatalov	71:21	Docked with Soyuz 5
1/15/69-1/18/69	Soyuz 5	Boris V. Volyanov, Aleksei S. Yeliseyev, Yevgeny V. Khrunov	72:54	Docked with 4; Yeliseyev and Khrunov transferred to Soyuz 4 via a spacewalk
3/3/69-3/13/69	**Apollo-Saturn 9**	**McDivitt (2), Scott (2), Russell L. Schweickart**	**241:00**	**1st piloted flight of lunar module**
5/18/69-5/26/69	**Apollo-Saturn 10**	**Stafford (3), Young (3), Cernan(2)**	**192:03**	**1st lunar module orbit of moon, 50,000 ft from moon surface**
7/16/69-7/24/69	**Apollo-Saturn 11**	**Armstrong (2), Collins (2), Aldrin (2)**	**195:18**	**1st lunar landing made by Armstrong and Aldrin (7/20/69); collected 48.5 lb of soil, rock samples; lunar stay time 21:36:21**
10/11/69-10/16/69	Soyuz 6	Georgi S. Shonin, Valery N. Kubasov	118:43	1st welding of metals in space
10/12/69-10/17/69	Soyuz 7	Anatoly V. Flipchenko, Vladislav N. Volkov, Viktor V. Gorbatko	118:40	Space lab construction test made; Soyuz 6, 7, and 8: 1st time 3 spacecraft, 7 crew members orbited the earth at once
10/13/69[1]	Soyuz 8	Shatalov (2), Yeliseyev (2)	118:51	Part of space lab construction team
11/14/69-11/24/69	**Apollo-Saturn 12**	**Conrad (3), Richard F. Gordon Jr. (2), Alan L. Bean**	**244:36**	**Conrad and Bean made 2d moon landing; collected 74.7 lb of samples, lunar stay time 31:31**
4/11/70-4/17/70	**Apollo-Saturn 13**	**Lovell (4), Fred W. Haise Jr., John L. Swigart Jr.**	**142:54**	**Aborted after service module oxygen tank ruptured; crew returned safely using lunar module**

DATES	VEHICLE NAME	CREW (no. of flights)	CREW DURATION (HR:MIN)	REMARKS
1/31/71-2/9/71	Apollo-Saturn 14	A. Shepard (2), Stuart A. Roosa, Edgar D. Mitchell	216:01	Shepard and Mitchell made 3d moon landing, collected 96 lb of lunar samples; lunar stay 33:31
4/19/71[1]	Salyut 1[2]	(Occupied by Soyuz 11 crew)		1st space station
4/22/71[1]	Soyuz 10	Shatalov (3), Yeliseyev (3), Nikolay N. Rukavishnikov	47:46	1st successful docking with a space station; failed to enter space station
6/6/71-6/30/71	Soyuz 11	Georgi T. Dobrovolskiy, V. Volkov (2), Viktor I. Patsayev	570:22	Docked and entered Salyut 1 space station; orbited in Salyut 1 for 23 days, crew died during reentry from loss of pressurization
7/26/71-8/7/71	Apollo-Saturn 15	Scott (3), James B. Irwin, Alfred M. Worden	295:12	Scott and Irwin made 4th moon landing; 1st lunar rover use; 1st deep space walk; 170 lb of samples; 66:55 stay
4/16/72-4/27/72	Apollo-Saturn 16	Young (4), Charles M. Duke Jr., Thomas K. Mattingly	265:51	Young and Duke made 5th moon landing; colleced 213 lb of lunar samples; lunar stay 71:2
12/7/72-12/19/72	Apollo-Saturn 17	Cernan (3), Ronald E. Evans, Harrison H. Schmitt	301:51	Cernan and Schmitt made 6th piloted lunar landing; collected 243 lb of samples; record lunar stay of more than 75 hr
5/14/73[1]	Skylab 1[3]	(Occupied by Skylab 2, 3, and 4 crews)		1st U.S. space station
5/25/73-6/22/73	Skylab 2	Conrad (4), Joseph P. Kerwin, Paul J. Weitz	672:49	1st Amer. piloted orbiting space station; crew repaired damage caused during boost
7/28/73-9/25/73	Skylab 3	Bean (2), Owen K. Garriott, Jack R. Lousma	1,427:09	Crew systems and operational tests, exceeded pre-mission plans for scientific activities; EVA total 13:44
11/16/73-2/8/74	Skylab 4	Gerald P. Carr, Edward G. Gibson, William Pogue	2,017:15	Final Skylab mission
7/15/75-7/21/75	Soyuz 19 (ASTP)	Leonov (2), Kubasov (2)	143:31	U.S.-USSR joint flight; crews linked up in space (7/17), conducted experiments, shared meals, and held a joint news conference
7/15/75-7/24/75	Apollo (ASTP)	Vance Brand, Stafford (4), Donald K. Slayton	217:28	Joint flight with Soyuz 19
12/10/77[1]	Soyuz 26	Yuri V. Romanenko, Georgiy M. Grechko (2)	2,314:00	1st multiple docking to a space station (Soyuz 26 and 27 docked at Salyut 6)
1/10/78[1]	Soyuz 27	Vladimir A. Dzhanibekov	142:59	See Soyuz 26
3/2/78[1]	Soyuz 28	Aleksei A. Gubarev (2), Vladimir Remek	190:16	1st international crew launch; Remek was 1st Czech in space
4/12/81-4/14/81	Columbia	Young (5), Robert L. Crippen	54:21	1st space shuttle flight[4]
11/11/82-11/16/82	Columbia	Brand (2), Robert Overmyer, William Lenoir, Joseph Allen	122:14	1st reuse of space shuttle; 1st 4-person crew
6/18/83-6/24/83	Challenger	Crippen (2), Frederick Hauck, Sally K. Ride, John W. Fabian, Norman Thagard	146:24	Ride was 1st U.S. woman in space; 1st 5-person crew
6/27/83[1]	Soyuz T-9	Vladimir A. Lyakhov (2), A. P. Aleksandrov	3,585:46	Docked at Salyut 7; 1st construction in space
8/30/83-9/5/83	Challenger	Truly (2), Daniel Brandenstein, William Thornton, Guion Bluford, Dale Gardner	3,585:46	Bluford was 1st U.S. black in space
11/28/83-12/8/83	Columbia	Young (6), Brewster Shaw Jr., Robert Parker, Garriott (2), Byron Lichtenberg, Ulf Merbold	247:47	1st 6-person crew
2/3/84-2/11/84	Challenger	Brand (3), Robert Gibson, Ronald McNair, Bruce McCandless, Robert Stewart	191:16	1st untethered EVA
4/6/84-4/13/84	Challenger	Crippen (3), Francis R. Scobee, George D. Nelson, Terry J. Har, James D. Van Hoften	167:40	1st in-orbit satellite repair
7/17/84[1]	Soyuz T-12	Dzhanibekov (4), Svetlana Y. Savitskaya (2), Igor P. Volk,	283:14	Docked at Salyut 7; Savitskaya was 1st woman to perform EVA
10/5/84-10/13/84	Challenger	Crippen (4), Jon A. McBride, Kathryn D. Sullivan, Ride (2), Marc Garneau, David C. Leestma, Paul D. Scully-Power	197:24	1st 7-person crew
11/8/84-11/16/84	Discovery	Hauck (2); David M. Walker, Dr. Anna L. Fisher, J. Allen (2), D. Gardner (2)	191:45	1st satellite retrieval/repair
4/12/85-4/19/85	Discovery	Karol J. Bobko, Donald E. Williams, Jake Garn, Charles D. Walker, Jeffrey A. Hoffman, S. David Griggs, M. Rhea Seddon	167:55	Garn was 1st senator in space
6/17/85-6/24/85	Discovery	Brandenstein (2), John O. Creighton, Shannon W. Lucid, Steven R. Nagel, Fabian (2), Prince Sultan Salman al-Saud, Patrick Baudry	169:39	Launched 4 satellites; Salman al-Saud was 1st Arab in space; Baudry was 1st French person on U.S. mission

DATES	VEHICLE NAME	CREW (no. of flights)	CREW DURATION (HR:MIN)	REMARKS
10/3/85-10/7/85	Atlantis	Bobko (3), Ronald J. Grabe, David C. Hilmers, Stewart (2), William A. Pailes	97:47	1st Atlantis flight
10/30/85-11/6/85	Challenger	Hartsfield (3), Steven R. Nagel, Buchli (2), Bluford (2), Bonnie J. Dunbar, Wubbo J. Ockels, Richard Furrer, Ernst Messerschmid	168:44	1st 8-person crew
11/26/85-12/3/85	Atlantis	Shaw (2), Bryan D. O'Connor, Sherwood C. Spring, Mary L. Cleave, Jerry L. Ross, C. Walker (3), Rodolfo Neri	165:05	Neri was 1st Mexican in space
1/12/86-1/18/86	Columbia	R. Gibson (2), Charles F. Bolden Jr., Hawley (2), G. Nelson (2), Franklin R. Chang-Diaz, Robert J. Cenker, Bill Nelson	146:04	B. Nelson was 1st congressman in space
1/28/86	Challenger	Scobee (2), Michael J. Smith, Judith A. Resnik (2), Ellison S. Onizuka (2), Ronald E. McNair, Gregory B. Jarvis, Christa McAuliffe		Exploded 73 sec after liftoff; all were killed
2/20/86[1]	Mir[2]	Space station with 6 docking ports		
3/13/86[1]	Soyuz T-15	Leonid Kizim (3), Vladmir Solovyov (2)	3,000:01	Ferry between stations; docked at Mir
2/5/87-12/29/87	Soyuz TM-2	Romanenko (3), Aleksandr I. Laveikin	7,835:38	Romanenko set endurance record, since broken
12/21/87-12/21/88	Soyuz TM-4	V. Titov (2), Muso Manarov, Anatoly Levchenko	8,782:39	Docked at Mir
9/29/88-10/3/88	Discovery	Hauck (3), Richard O. Covey (2), Hilmers (2), G. Nelson (2), John M. Lounge (2)	97:00	Redesigned shuttle makes 1st flight
4/24/90-4/29/90	Discovery	McCandless (2), Sullivan (2), Loren J. Shriver (2), Bolden (2), Steven A. Hawley (3)	121:15	Launched Hubble telescope
5/7/92-5/16/92	Endeavour	Brandenstein (4), Kevin C. Chilton, Bruce E. Melnick (2), Pierre J. Thuot (2), Richard J. Hieb (2), Karen Thornton (2), Akers (2)	213:18	1st 3-person EVA
9/12/92-9/21/92	Endeavour	R. Gibson (4), Curtis L. Brown Jr., Mark Lee (2), Jay Apt (2), N. Jan Davis, Mae Carol Jemison, Mamoru Mohri	190:30	Jemison was 1st black woman in space; Lee and Davis were 1st married couple to travel together in space
4/8/93-4/17/93	Discovery	Kenneth D. Cameron, Stephen S. Oswald (2), C. Michael Foale (2), Ellen Ochoa, Kenneth D. Cockrell	222:08	Ochoa was 1st Hispanic woman in space
12/2/93-12/13/93	Endeavour	Covey (3), Kenneth D. Bowersox (2), Claude Nicollier (2), Story Musgrave (5), Akers (3), K. Thornton (3), Hoffman (4)	259:58	Hubble space telescope repaired; Akers set new U.S. EVA duration record (29 hr, 40 min)
2/3/94-2/11/94	Discovery	Bolden (3), Kenneth S. Reightler Jr. (2), Davis, (2), Chang-Diaz (3), Ronald M. Sega, Sergei K. Krikalev	199:10	Krikalev was 1st Russian on U.S. shuttle
7/8/94-7/23/94	Columbia	Robert D. Cabana (3), James D. Halsell Jr., Hieb (3), Carl E. Walz (2), Leroy Chiao, Donald A. Thomas; Chiaki Naito-Mukai	353:56	Studied effects of weightlessness on aquatic animals; 2d longest space shuttle flight
2/3/95-2/11/95	Discovery	James D. Wetherbee (3), Eileen M. Collins, Bernard A. Harris (2), Foale (3), Janice Voss (2), V. Titov (4)	198:29	*Discovery* and Russian space station rendezvous
3/16/95-3/22/95	Soyuz/Mir-18	Thagard (2), Vladimir Dezhurov, Gennadi Strekalov	2,688[4]	Docked with Mir 3/16/95; Thagard was the 1st American aboard the Russian spacecraft; Valery Polyakov returned to earth, 3/22/95, after a record stay in space (439 days)
3/2/95-3/18/95	Endeavour	Oswald (3), William G. Gregory, Samuel T. Durrance (2), Ronald Parise (2), Wendy B. Lawrence, Tamara Jenigan (3), John M. Grunsfeld	399:09	Set record for longest U.S. space shuttle flight; shuttle data available on the Internet; astronomy research conducted
6/27/95-7/7/95	Atlantis	Charles J. Precourt (2), Ellen S. Baker (3), Gregory J. Harbaugh (3), Dunbar (4), Anatoly Y. Solovyev (4) (to *Mir*), Nikolai M. Budarin (to *Mir*), Thagard (from *Mir*), Strekalov (from *Mir*), Dezhurov (from *Mir*)	269:47	Docked with Mir; exchanged crew members, including Thagard, who set U.S. individual duration in space record (115 days)
7/13/95-7/22/95[5]	Discovery	Terence T. Henricks (3), Kevin R. Kregel, Thomas (2), Nancy J. Currie (2), Mary Ellen Weber	214:20	New mission control system inaugurated; NASA satellite launched

Note: Four Soviets died in spaceflights: Komarov on Soyuz 1 (1967) when the parachute lines tangled during descent; the 3-man Soyuz 11 crew (1971) asphyxiated. Seven Americans died in the 1986 Challenger explosion; 3 astronauts—Virgil I. Grissom, Edward H. White, and Roger B. Chaffee—died in the Jan. 27, 1967, Apollo 204 fire on the ground at Cape Kennedy, FL. (1) Launch date. (2) Space stations, such as the Salyuts and Mir, have been used to house crews since 1971. (3) Spacelab 1 deteriorated and fell from orbit without burning up upon entering the atmosphere. Pieces fell on Australia and the Indian Ocean; however, no one was injured. (4) Approximate crew duration for Thagard's stay. Crew did not return together. (5) As of July 1995, there have been 70 space shuttle flights; 45 since the Challenger explosion. Active shuttles include the *Columbia* (17 flights), the *Discovery* (21), the *Atlantis* (14), and the *Endeavour* (8).

Individuals Who Have Flown in Space, 1961-94

Source: Congressional Research Service; as of Dec. 31, 1994

Country	Number of individuals	Country	Number of individuals	Country	Number of individuals
United States	204	France[1,2]	5	Poland[1]	1
Russia/CIS	80	Germany[1,2]	7	Romania[1]	1
Afghanistan[1]	1	Hungary[1]	1	Saudi Arabia[2]	1
Austria[1]	1	India[1]	1	Switzerland[2]	1
Belguim[2]	1	Italy[2]	1	Syria[1]	1
Bulgaria[1]	2	Japan[1,2]	3	United Kingdom[1]	1
Canada[2]	3	Mexico[2]	1	Vietnam[1]	1
Cuba[1]	1	Mongolia[1]	1	**Total**	**322**
Czechoslovokia[1]	1	Netherlands[2]	1		

Note: All cosmonauts who were citizens of the Soviet Union at the time of launch are included here under "Russia/CIS." "Germany" incorporates the former East and West Germany. (1) Aboard Russian/CIS-sponsored mission. (2) Aboard U.S.-sponsored mission.

Summary of Worldwide Successful Announced Payloads, 1957-94

Source: National Aeronautics and Space Administration

(A payload is something carried into space by a rocket.)

Year	Total[1]	CIS/ USSR[2]	United States	Japan	China	European Space Agency	France	United Kingdom	India	Germany	Canada
1957-59	24	6	18	—	—	—	—	—	—	—	—
1960-69	1,035	399	614	—	—	2	4	1	—	—	—
1970-79	1,366	1,028	247	18	8	5	14	6	1	3	4
1980-89	1,431	1,132	191	26	16	14	5	4	9	7	5
1990	159	96	31	7	5	1	2	5	1	1	0
1991	157	101	30	2	1	4	6	2	1	1	2
1992	128	77	27	3	2	1	3	0	2	1	1
1993	104	59	29	1	1	2	2	0	1	0	0
1994	109	64	27	4	5	1	0	0	2	2	0
Total	**4,513**	**2,961**	**1,214**	**61**	**38**	**34**	**32**	**18**	**17**	**15**	**12**

(1) Includes launches sponsored by countries not shown. (2) Figures for 1986-91 are for the Soviet Union; 1992-94 figures are for the Commonwealth of Independent States.

Notable U.S. Planetary Science Missions

Source: National Aeronautics and Space Administration

Spacecraft	Launch date (GMT)	Mission	Remarks
Mariner 2	Aug. 27, 1962	Venus	Passed within 22,000 mi from Venus 12/14/62; contact lost 1/3/63 at 54 million mi
Ranger 7	July 28, 1964	Moon	Yielded over 4,000 photos of lunar surface
Mariner 4	Nov. 28, 1964	Mars	Passed behind Mars 7/14/65; took 22 photos from 6,000 mi
Ranger 8	Feb. 17, 1965	Moon	Yielded over 7,000 photos of lunar surface
Surveyor 3	Apr. 17, 1967	Moon	Scooped and tested lunar soil
Mariner 5	June 14, 1967	Venus	In solar orbit; closest Venus fly-by 10/19/67
Mariner 6	Feb. 24, 1969	Mars	Came within 2,000 mi of Mars 7/31/69; sent back data, photos
Mariner 7	Mar. 27, 1969	Mars	Came within 2,000 mi of Mars 8/5/69
Mariner 9	May 30, 1971	Mars	First craft to orbit Mars 11/13/71; sent back more than 7,000 photos
Pioneer 10	Mar. 2, 1972	Jupiter	Passed Jupiter 12/3/73; exited the planetary system 6/13/83; still operating in outer solar system
Mariner 10	Nov. 3, 1973	Venus, Mercury	Passed Venus 2/5/74; arrived Mercury 3/29/74. First time gravity of one planet (Venus) used to whip spacecraft toward another (Mercury)
Viking 1	Aug. 20, 1975	Mars	Landed on Mars 7/20/76; did scientific research, sent photos; functioned 6½ years
Viking 2	Sept. 9, 1975	Mars	Landed on Mars 9/3/76; functioned 3½ years
Voyager 1	Sept. 5, 1977	Jupiter, Saturn	Encountered Jupiter 3/5/79, provided evidence of Jupiter ring; passed near Saturn 11/12/80
Voyager 2	Aug. 20, 1977	Jupiter, Saturn, Uranus, Neptune	Encountered Jupiter 7/9/79; Saturn 8/25/81; Uranus 1/24/86; Neptune 8/25/8
Pioneer Venus 1	May 20, 1978	Venus	Entered Venus orbit 12/4/78; spent 14 years studying planet; ceased operating 10/19/92
Pioneer Venus 2	Aug. 8, 1978	Venus	Encountered Venus 12/9/78; probes impacted on surface
Magellan	May 4, 1989	Venus	Orbit and map Venus; monitoring geological activity on surface; first planetary spacecraft to lower its orbit by using planet's atmosphere (aerobraking) 5/25/93-8/3/93; ceased operating 10/12/94
Titan IV	June 14, 1989	Orbit earth	First of 41 such rockets whose primary purpose is defense
Galileo	Oct. 18, 1989	Jupiter	Used earth's gravity to propel it toward Jupiter; encountered Venus Feb. 1991; launched robot to Jupiter 7/13/95
Mars Observer	Sept. 25, 1992	Mars	Communication was lost 8/21/93

Notable Proposed U.S. Space Missions

Source: National Aeronautics and Space Administration

Year	Mission	Purpose
1996	Mars Environmental Survey Pathfinder	Technical demonstration of Mars Environmental Survey
1997	Cassini	Study of Saturn's atmosphere, rings, magnetosphere, and moons
1998	Earth Observing System	Provide long-term data sets of interactions between earth's land, atmosphere, water, and life
1998, 1999	Advanced X-ray Astrophysics Facility (2 spacecraft)	Study of dark matter, stellar evolution, galactic clusters
TBD	Pluto Fast Fly-by	First fly-by of Pluto for photographic survey and other studies
2001	Space Infrared Telescope Facility	High sensitivity observations of celestial sources

Note: All spacecraft to be launched by expendable rockets. TBD=To Be Determined.

Traffic at World Airports, 1994

Source: Airport Council International-North America

Airport	Total Passengers	Airport	Total Passengers
London, UK (Heathrow)	51,717,918	Osaka, Japan (Osaka Intl.)	20,366,293
Tokyo/Haneda, Japan (Tokyo Intl.)	42,245,667	Rome, Italy (Fiumicino)	20,316,058
Frankfurt, Germany (Rheim/Main)	35,122,528	Mexico City, Mexico (Mexico City)	18,889,256
Paris, France (Charles De Gaulle)	29,630,222	Madrid, Spain (Barajas)	18,427,086
Seoul, South Korea (Kimpo Intl.)	27,333,241	Sydney, Australia (Kingsford Smith)	17,483,193
Paris, France (Orly)	26,617,556	Sapporo, Japan (Chitose)	15,093,583
Hong Kong (Hong Kong Intl.)	25,948,789	Manchester, UK (Manchester)	14,814,299
Tokyo, Japan (New Tokyo Intl.)	23,745,240	Zurich, Switzerland (Zurich)	14,506,865
Amsterdam, Netherlands (Schiphol)	23,559,456	Fukuoka, Japan (Fukuoka Intl.)	14,475,617
Singapore (Changi)	21,644,677	Palma De Mallorca, Spain (Palma De Mallorca)	14,142,035
London, UK (Gatwick)	21,212,117	Dusseldorf, Germany (Dusseldorf)	14,003,365
Bangkok, Thailand (Bangkok Intl.)	21,009,259	Copenhagen, Denmark (Copenhagen)	13,955,178
Toronto, Ontario (Lester B. Pearson Intl.)	20,863,922		

Traffic at U.S. Airports, 1994

Source: Air Transport Association of America

Airport	Passenger Arrivals and Departures	Airport	Passenger Arrivals and Departures
Chicago (O'Hare–ORD)	66,435,252	Detroit (DTW)	26,797,876
Atlanta (Hartsfield Intl.–ATL)	54,090,579	Pheonix (Sky Harbor Intl.–PHX)	25,619,704
Dallas/Ft. Worth (DFW)	52,601,125	Boston (Logan Intl.–BOS)	25,360,104
Los Angeles (LAX)	51,050,275	Minneapolis/St. Paul (MSP)	24,513,419
San Francisco (SFO)	34,550,652	St. Louis (Lambert St. Louis Intl.–STL)	23,362,671
Denver (Stapleton Intl.–DEN)	33,129,126	Houston (IAH)	22,521,655
Miami (MIA)	30,203,269	Honolulu (HNL)	22,473,611
New York (J. F. Kennedy Intl.–JFK)	28,799,275	Orlando (MCO)	22,347,412
Newark (EWR)	27,995,721	Seattle-Tacoma (SEA)	20,972,819
Las Vegas (McCarran Intl.–LAS)	26,810,020	New York (LaGuardia Intl.–LGA)	20,808,242

U.S. Scheduled Airline Traffic, 1992-94

Source: Air Transport Association of America; in thousands

	1992	1993	1994
Passenger traffic			
Revenue passengers enplaned	475,108	488,520	528,376
Revenue passenger miles	478,553,708	489,684,421	519,161,222
Available seat miles	752,772,435	771,640,648	783,839,740
Revenue passenger load factor (%)	63.6	63.5	66.2
Cargo traffic (ton miles)	13,198,674	14,119,818	15,989,691
Revenue freight and express (ton miles)	11,129,962	11,943,595	13,720,625
Revenue U.S. Mail (ton miles)	2,068,962	2,176,223	2,269,066
Financial			
Passenger revenue	$59,828,487	$63,945,223	$64,849,849
Net profit	−$4,791,284	−$2,135,626[1]	−$276,407
Employees	540,413	537,111	543,325

(1) Excludes 1993 debt forgiven during bankruptcy proceedings for Continental and Trans World.

Leading U.S. Passenger Airlines, 1994

Source: Air Transport Association of America

(in thousands)

Airline	Passengers	Airline	Passengers	Airline	Passengers
Delta	88,922	Trans World	20,880	Morris	3,393
American	81,082	America West	15,629	Reno	3,370
United	74,070	Alaska	8,885	Atlantic Southeast	3,120
USAir	59,494	Aloha	5,032	Continental Micronesia	2,281
Northwest	45,496	Hawaiian	4,576	Markair	2,094
Southwest	44,238	Simmons	4,517	ValuJet	1,968
Continental	39,947	Horizon Air	3,481		

U.S. Airline Safety, Scheduled Commercial Carriers, 1979-94

Source: National Transportation Safety Board

	Departures (millions)	Fatal accidents	Fatalities	Fatal accidents per 100,000 departures		Departures (millions)	Fatal accidents	Fatalities	Fatal accidents per 100,000 departures
1979....	5.4	4	351	0.074	1987	6.6	4[1]	231	0.046[1]
1980....	5.4	0	0	0.000	1988	6.7	3[1]	285	0.030[1]
1981....	5.2	4	4	0.077	1989	6.6	11	278	0.166
1982....	5.0	4	233	0.060	1990	6.9	6	39	0.087
1983....	5.0	4	15	0.079	1991	6.8	4	62	0.059
1984....	5.4	1	4	0.018	1992	7.1	4	33	0.057
1985....	5.8	4	197	0.069	1993	7.2	1	1	0.014
1986....	6.4	2	5	0.016	1994	7.5	4	237	0.053

(1) Sabotage-caused accidents are included in the number of fatal accidents, but not in the calculation of accident rates.

Aircraft Operating Statistics, 1993

Source: Air Transport Association of America; figures are averages for most commonly used models

	Number of seats	Speed airborne (mph)	Flight length (miles)	Fuel (gallons per hour)	Aircraft operating cost per hour
B747-400	367	507	4,639	3,393	$6,592
B747-100	393	478	3,131	3,590	5,571
B747-200/300	355	494	3,879	3,701	7,257
DC-10-40	288	444	1,901	2,596	3,904
L-1011-100/200............	283	429	1,422	2,376	3,783
DC-10-10	280	439	1,577	2,254	4,504
DC-10-30	266	479	2,788	2,551	4,349
A300-600	262	393	1,162	1,752	3,648
MD-11....................	260	484	3,436	2,302	5,024
L-1011-500	222	486	3,162	2,534	3,958
B767-300ER	219	452	2,252	1,583	3,100
B757-200	186	397	1,118	1,028	2,362
B767-200ER	179	443	2,160	1,407	2,973
A310-300	172	465	2,864	1,513	3,597
B727-200	148	357	707	1,260	2,241

Active Airmen and Airwomen, 1993-94

Source: Federal Aviation Administration, U.S. Dept. of Transportation; as of Dec. 31, 1994

	1993		1994	
Category	Total	Percentage women	Total	Percentage women
Total pilots	665,069	5.9	654,088	6.0
Student......................	103,583	12.3	96,254	12.5
Private......................	283,700	6.0	284,236	6.0
Commercial	143,014	4.2	138,728	4.3
Airline Transport	117,070	2.3	117,434	2.5
Other[1]	17,702	5.4	17,436	5.6
Total nonpilots	559,726	2.2	571,358	2.3
Mechanic	401,060	1.2	411,071	1.3
Ground Instructor	76,050	6.1	77,789	6.2
Flight Engineer	60,277	2.3	59,467	2.4
Other[2]	22,339	6.7	23,031	5.0
Flight instructors...................	72,148	5.5	76,171	5.9

Note: Excludes military personnel. (1) Includes helicopter (only), glider (only), and recreational pilot certificates. (2) Includes flight navigators, parachute riggers, and dispatchers.

National Aviation Hall of Fame

The National Aviation Hall of Fame at Dayton, OH, is dedicated to honoring the outstanding pioneers of air and space.

Allen, William M.
Andrews, Frank M.
Armstrong, Neil A.
Arnold, Henry H. "Hap"
Atwood, John Leland

Balchen, Bernt
Baldwin, Thomas S.
Beachey, Lincoln
Beech, Olive A.
Beech, Walter H.
Bell, Alexander Graham
Bell, Lawrence D.
Bellanca, Giuseppe Mario
Bendix, Vincent T.
Boeing, William E.
Bong, Richard I.
Borman, Frank
Boyd, Albert
Bradley, Mark E.

Brown, George "Scratchley"
Byrd, Richard E.

Cessna, Clyde V.
Chamberlin, Clarence D.
Chanute, Octave
Chennault, Claire L.
Cochran (Odlum), Jacqueline
Collins, Michael
Conrad Jr., Charles
Crawford, Frederick C.
Crossfield, A. Scott
Cunningham, Alfred A.
Curtiss, Glenn H.

Davis Jr., Benjamin O.
DeSeversky, Alexander P.
Doolittle, James H.

Douglas, Donald W.
Draper, Charles S.

Eaker, Ira C.
Earhart (Putnam), Amelia
Eielson, C. Benjamin
Ellyson, Theodore G.
Ely, Eugene B.
Everest, Frank K.

Fairchild, Sherman M.
Fleet, Reuben H.
Fokker, Anthony H.G.
Ford, Henry
Foss, Joseph
Foulois, Benjamin D.
Frye, Jack

Gabreski, Francis S.
Gilruth, Robert R.

Gentile, Dominic "Don"
Glenn Jr., John H.
Goddard, George W.
Goddard, Robert H.
Godfrey, Arthur
Goldwater, Barry M.
Grissom, Virgil I.
Gross, Robert E.
Grumman, Leroy R.
Guggenheim, Harry F.

Haughton, Daniel J.
Hegenberger, Albert F.
Heinemann, Edward H.
Hoover, Robert A.
Hughes, Howard R.

Ingalls, David S.

James Jr., Daniel "Chappie"	Macready, Carl B.	Rentschler, Frederick B.	Taylor, Charles E.
Jeppesen, Elrey B.	Macready, John A.	Richardson, Holden C.	Thomas, Lowell
Johnson, Clarence L.	Martin, Glenn L.	Rickenbacker, Edward V.	Towers, John H.
Johnston, Alvin M. "Tex"	McDonnell, James S.	Rodgers, Calbraith P.	Trippe, Juan T.
Jones, Thomas V.	Mitscher, Marc A.	Rogers, Will	Turner, Roscoe
	Meyer, John C.	Rushworth, Robert A.	Twining, Nathan F.
	Mitchell, William "Billy"		
Kenney, George C.	Montgomery, John J.		Vandenberg, Hoyt
Kettering, Charles F.	Moorer, Thomas H.	Rutan, Elbert "Burt" L.	von Braun, Wernher
Kindelberger, James H.	Moss, Sanford A.	Ryan, T. Claude	von Karman, Theodore
Knabenshue, A. Roy			von Ohain, Hans P.
Knight, William J.	Neumann, Gerhard	Schirra, Walter M.	Vought, Chance M.
	Nichols, Ruth R.	Schriever, Bernard A.	
Lahm, Frank P.	Norden, Carl L.	Selfridge, Thomas E.	Wade, Leigh
Langley, Samuel P.	Northrop, John K.	Shepard Jr., Alan B.	Walden, Henry W.
Lear Sr., William P.		Sikorsky, Igor I.	Wells, Edward
LeMay, Curtis E.	Pangborn, Clyde Edward	Six, Robert F.	Wilson, Thornton A.
LeVier, Anthony W.	Patterson, William A.	Smith, C.R.	Woolman, Collett Everman
Lindbergh, Anne M.	Piper Sr., William T.	Spaatz, Carl A.	"C.E."
Lindbergh, Charles A.	Pitcairn, Harold Frederick	Sperry Sr., Elmer A.	Wright, Orville
Link, Edwin A.	Post, Wiley H.	Sperry Sr., Lawrence B.	Wright, Wilbur
Lockheed, Allan H.		Stanley, Robert M.	
Loening, Grover	Read, Albert C.	Stapp, John P.	Yeager, Charles E.
Luke Jr., Frank	Reeve, Robert C.	Stearman, Lloyd C.	Young, John W.

Memorable Flight Records, 1994

Source: National Aeronautic Association of the USA, 1815 North Fort Myer Dr., Arlington, VA 22209

The National Aeronautic Association of the USA is the U.S. representative of the Fédération Aéronautique Internationale, the certifying agency for world aviation and space records. The International Aeronautical Federation was formed in 1905 by representatives from Belgium, France, Germany, Great Britain, Spain, Italy, Switzerland, and the U.S., with headquarters in Paris. Regulations for the control of official records were signed Oct. 14, 1905.

World abosolute records are defined as maximum performance, regardless of class or type of aircraft used. Absolute records for space flight are kept separately. All other records, also international in scope, are termed "World Class" records and are divided into 17 classes, including: Class A, free balloons; Class B, airships; Class C-1, airplanes; Class C-2, seaplanes; Class C-3, amphibians; Class D, gliders; and Class E, rotorcrafts, such as helicopters. Classes are subdivided into 4 groups based on their power source: Group I—piston engine, Group II—turboprop, Group III—jet engine, Group IV—rocket engine. Sometimes there are also further divisions for weight subclasses, such as Class C-1d, which is a light airplane weighing 3,858 to 6,614 lb.

In 1994, the NAA certified more than 160 aviation records. Of those records the NAA's Contest and Records Board selected the following memorable record flights of 1994.

Orbital Space Missions

Duration — 14 days, 17 hr, 54 min, 50 sec — Robert D. Cabana, Cmdr.; James D. Halsell Jr., Pilot; Leroy Chiao, Mission Specialist; Richard J. Hieb, Mission Specialist; Donald A. Thomas, Mission Specialist; Carl E. Walz, Mission Specialist; Chiaki Naito-Mukai, Payload Specialist; Space Shuttle Orbiter *Columbia*; John F. Kennedy Space Center, FL, 7/8-7/23/94.

Balloons, Subclass AX-9 (3,000-4,000 m³)

Altitude — 32,657 ft — Jetta Miller Schantz; Aerostar Rally, China Lake, CA, 8/19/94.

Gliders, Single Place

Free Distance — 891.66 mi — Karl H. Striedieck; Schleicher ASW 20B, Julian, PA, 5/12/94.

Light Airplanes, Piston Engine (661-1,102 lb)

Time to climb to 6,000 meters — 12 min, 50 sec — Bruce Bohannon; Miller Special, M-105, Oshkosh, WI, 7/30/94.

Light Airplanes, Piston Engine (2,204-3,858 lb)

Speed over a closed circuit (2,000 km speed without payload) — 257.11 mph — Michael W. Melvill; Rutan Catbird, Lake Hughes, CA–Boise, ID, 3/2/94.

Heavy Airplanes, Jet Engine (330,690-440,920 lb)

Speed over a closed circuit (10,000 km speed without payload) — 594.61 mph — Capt. R. F. Lewandowski, Cmdr.; Capt. Kevin T. Kalen, Pilot; Lt. Col. Timothy W. Van Splunder, OSO; Capt. Jerrold A. Wangberg, DSO; Rockwell International B-1B, Grand Forks, ND–Monroeville, AL–Mullan, ID, 4/7-4/8/94.

Heavy Airplanes, Jet Engine (440,920-551,150 lb)

Speed over a closed circuit (10,000 km speed without payload) — 599.59 mph — Capt. Michael S. Menser, Cmdr.; Capt. Brain P. Gallagher, Pilot; Capt. Robert P. Bornan, OSO; Capt. Matthew E. Grant, WSO; Rockwell International B-1B, Grand Forks, ND–Monroeville, AL–Mullan, ID, 4/7-4/8/94.

STOL (Short Take-Off and Landing) Aircraft, Jet Engine

Greatest mass carried to a height of 2,000 meters — 44,088 lb — Maj. Andre A. Gerner, Pilot; John D. Burns, Aircraft Cmdr.; Craig S. Johnson, Loadmaster; McDonnell Douglas C-17A, Edwards Airforce Base, CA, 6/3/94.

Helicopters, Turbine Engine

Speed around the world, eastbound — 40.99 mph — Joe Ronald Bower, Bell JetRanger III, Hurst, TX, 6/28–7/22/94.

Parachutes

Largest canopy formation — 46 persons — Luke Aikins, Lon Baillargeon, David Bassinger, Nasser Basir, Schantz Basir, Francis Bender, Teresa Bizzell, Ian Bobo, Alex Borsutzky, Chas Buncn, John Carlisle, Ted Cheung, John Coldren, Scott Fiore, Scott Franklin, Andy Gamache, Chris Gay, Lillian Goodin, Al Gutshall, Rich Hall, Jackson Hoffman, Kevin Ingley, Tommy Lentz, Pat Linder, R.G. Long, Frank Matrone, Terrina McMichael, Bill Mershon, Joe O'Leary, Red Payne, Pasi Pirttikoski, Mark Puckett, Kevin Reiseck, David Richardson, Bruce Robertson, Peter Schaller, Ray Sermet, Jon Sikorksy, Scott Smith, Ken Smith, Terry Sparrow, Bill Thomasson, Kirk Van Zandt, Kevin Vetter, Shaun Vineyard, Robert Williamson; Davis, CA, 10/12/94.

Notable Around-the-World and Intercontinental Trips

	From/To	Miles	Time	Date
Nellie Bly.	New York/New York		72d 06h 11m	1889
George Francis Train	New York/New York		67d 12h 03m	1890
Charles Fitzmorris	Chicago/Chicago		60d 13h 29m	1901
J. W. Willis Sayre.	Seattle/Seattle		54d 09h 42m	1903
J. Alcock-A.W. Brown [1]	Newfoundland/Ireland	1,960	16h 12m	June 14-15, 1919
Two U.S. Army airplanes	Seattle/Seattle	26,103	35d 01h 11m	1924
Richard E. Byrd [2]	Spitsbergen/N. Pole	1,545	15h 30m	May 9, 1926
Amundsen-Ellsworth-Nobile Expedition . . .	Spitsbergen/Teller, Alaska.		80h	May 11-14,1926
E.S. Evans and L. Wells (N.Y.World) [3]	New York/New York	18,410	28d 14h 36m 05s	June 16-July 14, 1926
Charles Lindbergh [4]	New York/Paris.	3,610	33h 29m 30s	May 20-21, 1927
Amelia Earhart, W. Stultz, L. Gordon	Newfoundland/Wales		20h 40m	June 17-18, 1928
Graf Zeppelin	Friedrichshafen, Ger./Lakehurst, NJ	6,630	4d 15h 46m	Oct. 11-15, 1928
Graf Zeppelin	Friedrichshafen, Ger./Lakehurst, NJ	21,700	20d 04h	Aug. 14-Sept. 4, 1929
Wiley Post and Harold Gatty (Monoplane Winnie Mae) . .	New York/New York	15,474	8d 15h 51m	July 1, 1931
C. Pangborn-H. Herndon Jr. [5]	Misawa, Japan/Wenatchee, Wash. .	4,458	41h 34m	Oct. 3-5, 1931
Amelia Earhart [6]	Newfoundland/Ireland	2,026	14h 56m	May 20-21, 1932
Wiley Post (Monoplane Winnie Mae)[7]	New York/New York	15,596	115h 36m 30s	July 15-22, 1933
Hindenburg Zeppelin	Lakehurst, NJ/Frankfort, Ger..		42h 53m	Aug. 9-11, 1936
H. R. Ekins (Scripps-Howard Newspapers in race) (Zeppelin Hindenburg to Germany, airplanes from Frankfurt)	Lakehurst, NJ/Lakehurst, NJ	25,654	18d 11h 14m 33s	Sept, 30-Oct. 19, 1936
Howard Hughes and 4 assistants	New York/New York.	14,824	3d 19h 08m 10s	July 10-13, 1938
Douglas Corrigan.	New York/Dublin.		28h 13m	July 17-18, 1938
Mrs. Clara Adams (Pan American Clipper)	Port Washington, NY/Newark, NJ		16d 19h 04m	June 28-July 15, 1939
Globester, U.S. Air Transport Command	Washington, DC/Washington, DC .	23,279	149h 44m	Oct. 4, 1945
Capt. William P. Odom (A-26 Reynolds Bombshell)	New York/New York	20,000	78h 55m 12s	Apr. 12-16, 1947
America, Pan American 4-engine Lockheed Constellation [8] . .	New York/New York	22,219	101h 32m	June 17-30, 1947
Col. Edward Eagan	New York/New York	20,559	147h 15m	Dec. 13, 1948
USAF B-50 Lucky Lady II (Capt. James Gallagher) [9] . .	Ft. Worth, TX/Ft. Worth, TX	23,452	94h 01m	Feb. 26-Mar. 2, 1949
Col. D. Schilling, USAF [10] . . .	England/Limestone, ME	3,300	10h 01m	Sept. 22, 1950
C.F. Blair Jr.	Norway/Alaska	3,300	10h 29m	May 29, 1951
Two U.S. S-55.	Massachusetts/Scotland	3,410	42h 30m	July 15-31, 1952
Canberra Bomber [11]	N. Ireland/Newfoundland.	2073	04h 34m	Aug. 26, 1952
	Newfoundland/N. Ireland	2073	03h 25m	Aug. 26, 1952
Three USAF B-52 Stratofortresses [12]	Merced, CA/CA	24,325	45h 19m	Jan. 15-18, 1957
Max Conrad.	Chicago/Rome	5,000	34h 03m	Mar. 5-6, 1959
USSR TU-114 [13]	Moscow/New York	5,092	11h 06m	June 28, 1959
Boeing 707-320	New York/Moscow	c.5090	08h 54m	July 23, 1959
Peter Gluckmann (solo)	San Francisco/San Francisco	22,800	29d	Aug. 22-Sept. 20, 1959
Sue Snyder.	Chicago/Chicago	21,219	62h 59m	June 22-24, 1960
Max Conrad (solo)	Miami/Miami.	25,946	8d 18h 35m 57s	Feb. 28-Mar. 8, 1961
Sam Miller & Louis Fodor	New York/New York		46h 28m	Aug. 3-4, 1963
Robert & Joan Wallick	Manila/Manila.	23,129	5d 06h 17m 10s	June 2-7, 1966
Arthur Godfrey, Richard Merrill Fred Austin, Karl Keller	New York/New York	23,333	86h 9m 01s	June 4-7, 1966
Trevor K. Brougham.	Darwin, Australia/Darwin	24,800	5d 05h 57m	Aug. 5-10, 1972
Walter H. Mullikin, Albert Frink, Lyman Watt, Frank Cassaniti, Edward Shields	New York/New York	23,137	1d 22h 50s	May 1-3, 1976
David Kunst [14]	Waseca, MN/Waseca, MN.	14,500	4yr 3mos 16d	June 10, 1970-Oct. 5, 1974
Arnold Palmer	Denver/Denver.	22,985	57h 7m 12s	May 17-19, 1976
Boeing 747 [15]	San Francisco/San Francisco	26,382	57h 25m 42s	Oct. 28-31, 1977
Concorde.	Paris/New York	1,037.50 mph	03h 30m 11s	Aug. 22, 1978
Richard Rutan & Jeana Yeager[16]	Edwards AFB, CA.	24,986	09d 03m 44s	Dec. 14-23, 1986
Concorde.	New York/New York	1,114 mph	31h 27m 49s	Aug. 15-16, 1995

(1) Nonstop transatlantic flight. (2) Polar flight. (3) Mileage by train and auto, 4,110; by plane, 6,300; by steamship, 8,000. (4) Solo transatlantic flight in the Ryan monoplane the "Spirit of St. Louis". (5) Nonstop Pacific flight. (6) Women's transoceanic solo flight. (7) First to fly solo around northern circumference of the world, also first to fly twice around the world. (8) Inception of regular commercial global air service. (9) First nonstop round-the-world flight, refueled 4 times in flight. (10) Nonstop jet transatlantic flight. (11) Transatlantic round trip on same day. (12) First nonstop global flight by jet planes; refueled in flight by KC-97 aerial tankers; average speed approx. 525 mph. (13) Nonstop between Moscow and New York. (14) First to circle the earth on foot. (15) Speed record around the world over both the earth's poles. (16) Circled the earth nonstop without refueling.

AWARDS — MEDALS — PRIZES
The Alfred B. Nobel Prize Winners

Alfred B. Nobel (1833-96), inventor of dynamite, bequeathed $9,000,000, the interest to be distributed yearly to those who had most benefited humankind in physics, chemistry, medicine-physiology, literature, and peace. Prizes in these 5 areas were first awarded in 1901. The first Nobel Memorial Prize in Economic Science was awarded in 1969, funded by the central bank of Sweden. If the year is omitted, no awards were given that year. In 1994, each prize was worth approximately $900,000.

Physics

1994 Bertram N. Brockhouse, Can.; Clifford G. Shull, U.S.
1993 Joseph H. Taylor, Russell A. Hulse, both U.S.
1992 Georges Charpak, Pol.-Fr.
1991 Pierre-Giles de Gennes, Fr.
1990 Richard E. Taylor, Can.; Jerome I. Friedman, Henry W. Kendall, both U.S.
1989 Norman F. Ramsey, U.S.; Hans G. Dehmelt, Ger.-U.S.; Wolfgang Paul, Ger.
1988 Leon M. Lederman, Melvin Schwartz, Jack Steinberger, all U.S.
1987 K. Alex Müller, Swiss; J. Georg Bednorz, W. Ger.
1986 Ernest Ruska, Ger.; Gerd Binnig, W. Ger.; Heinrich Rohrer, Swiss
1985 Klaus von Klitzing, W. Ger.
1984 Carlo Rubbia, It.; Simon van der Meer, Dutch
1983 Subrahmanyan Chandrasekhar, William A. Fowler, both U.S.
1982 Kenneth G. Wilson, U.S.
1981 Nicolaas Bloembergen, Arthur Schaalow, both U.S.; Kai M. Siegbahn, Swed.
1980 James W. Cronin, Val L. Fitch, both U.S.
1979 Steven Weinberg, Sheldon L. Glashow, both U.S.; Abdus Salam, Pakistani
1978 Pyotr Kapitsa, USSR; Arno Penzias, Robert Wilson, both U.S.
1977 John H. Van Vleck, Philip W. Anderson, both U.S.; Nevill F. Mott, Br.
1976 Burton Richter, Samuel C.C. Ting, both U.S.
1975 James Rainwater, U.S.; Ben Mottelson, U.S.-Danish; Aage Bohr, Danish
1974 Martin Ryle, Antony Hewish, both Br.
1973 Ivar Giaever, U.S.; Leo Esaki, Jpn.; Brian D. Josephson, Br.
1972 John Bardeen, Leon N. Cooper, John R. Schrieffer, all U.S.
1971 Dennis Gabor, Br.
1970 Louis Neel, Fr.; Hannes Alfven, Swed.
1969 Murray Gell-Mann, U.S.
1968 Luis W. Alvarez, U.S.
1967 Hans A. Bethe, U.S.
1966 Alfred Kastler, Fr.
1965 Richard P. Feynman, Julian S. Schwinger, both U.S.; Shinichiro Tomonaga, Jpn.
1964 Nikolai G. Basov, Aleksander M. Prochorov, both USSR; Charles H. Townes, U.S.
1963 Maria Goeppert-Mayer, Eugene P. Wigner, both U.S.; J. Hans D. Jensen, Ger.
1962 Lev. D. Landau, USSR
1961 Robert Hofstadter, U.S.; Rudolf L. Mossbauer, Ger.
1960 Donald A. Glaser, U.S.
1959 Owen Chamberlain, Emilio G. Segre, both U.S.
1958 Pavel Cherenkov, Ilya Frank, Igor Y. Tamm, all USSR
1957 Tsung-dao Lee, Chen Ning Yang, both U.S.
1956 John Bardeen, Walter H. Brattain, William Shockley, all U.S.
1955 Polykarp Kusch, Willis E. Lamb, both U.S.
1954 Max Born, Br.; Walter Bothe, Ger.
1953 Frits Zernike, Dutch
1952 Felix Bloch, Edward M. Purcell, both U.S.
1951 Sir John D. Cockroft, Br.; Ernest T. S. Walton, Ir.
1950 Cecil F. Powell, Br.
1949 Hideki Yukawa, Jpn.
1948 Patrick M. S. Blackett, Br.
1947 Sir Edward V. Appleton, Br.
1946 Percy Williams Bridgman, U.S.
1945 Wolfgang Pauli, U.S.
1944 Isidor Isaac Rabi, U.S.
1943 Otto Stern, U.S.
1939 Ernest O. Lawrence, U.S.
1938 Enrico Fermi, It.-U.S.
1937 Clinton J. Davisson, U.S.; Sir George P. Thomson, Br.
1936 Carl D. Anderson, U.S.; Victor F. Hess, Aus.
1935 Sir James Chadwick, Br.
1933 Paul A. M. Dirac, Br.; Erwin Schrodinger, Aus.
1932 Werner Heisenberg, Ger.
1930 Sir Chandrasekhara V. Raman, Indian
1929 Prince Louis-Victor de Broglie, Fr.
1928 Owen W. Richardson, Br.
1927 Arthur H. Compton, U.S.; Charles T. R. Wilson, Br.
1926 Jean B. Perrin, Fr.
1925 James Franck, Gustav Hertz, both Ger.
1924 Karl M. G. Siegbahn, Swed.
1923 Robert A. Millikan, U.S.
1922 Niels Bohr, Danish
1921 Albert Einstein, Ger.-U.S.
1920 Charles E. Guillaume, Fr.
1919 Johannes Stark, Ger.
1918 Max K. E. L. Planck, Ger.
1917 Charles G. Barkla, Br.
1915 Sir William H. Bragg, Sir William L. Bragg, both Br.
1914 Max von Laue, Ger.
1913 Heike Kamerlingh-Onnes, Dutch
1912 Nils G. Dalen, Swed.
1911 Wilhelm Wien, Ger.
1910 Johannes D. van der Waals, Dutch
1909 Carl F. Braun, Ger.; Guglielmo Marconi, It.
1908 Gabriel Lippmann, Fr.
1907 Albert A. Michelson, U.S.
1906 Sir Joseph J. Thomson, Br.
1905 Philipp E. A. von Lenard, Ger.
1904 John W. Strutt, Lord Rayleigh, Br.
1903 Antoine Henri Becquerel, Pierre Curie, both Fr.; Marie Curie, Pol.-Fr.
1902 Hendrik A. Lorentz, Pieter Zeeman, both Dutch
1901 Wilhelm C. Roentgen, Ger.

Chemistry

1994 George A. Olah, U.S.
1993 Kary B. Mullis, U.S.; Michael Smith, Br.-Canadian
1992 Rudolph A. Marcus, Can.-U.S.
1991 Richard R. Ernst, Swiss
1990 Elias James Corey, U.S.
1989 Thomas R. Cech, Sidney Altman, both U.S.
1988 Johann Deisenhofer, Robert Huber, Hartmut Michel, all W. Ger.
1987 Donald J. Cram, Charles J. Pedersen, both U.S.; Jean-Marie Lehn, Fr.
1986 Dudley Herschbach, Yuan T. Lee, both U.S.; John C. Polanyi, Can.
1985 Herbert A. Hauptman, Jerome Karle, both U.S.
1984 Bruce Merrifield, U.S.
1983 Henry Taube, Canadian
1982 Aaron Klug, S. African
1981 Kenichi Fukui, Jpn.; Roald Hoffmann, U.S.
1980 Paul Berg, Walter Gilbert, both U.S.; Frederick Sanger, U.K.
1979 Herbert C. Brown, U.S.; George Wittig, Ger.
1978 Peter Mitchell, Br.
1977 Ilya Prigogine, Belg.
1976 William N. Lipscomb, U.S.
1975 John Cornforth, Austral.-Br.; Vladimir Prelog, Yugo.-Swiss
1974 Paul J. Flory, U.S.
1973 Ernst Otto Fischer, W. Ger.; Geoffrey Wilkinson, Br.
1972 Christian B. Anfinsen, Stanford Moore, William H. Stein, all U.S.
1971 Gerhard Herzberg, Canadian
1970 Luis F. Leloir, Arg.
1969 Derek H. R. Barton, Br.; Odd Hassel, Nor.
1968 Lars Onsager, U.S.
1967 Manfred Eigen, Ger.; Ronald G. W. Norrish, George Porter, both Br.
1966 Robert S. Mulliken, U.S.
1965 Robert B. Woodward, U.S.
1964 Dorothy C. Hodgkin, Br.
1963 Giulio Natta, It.; Karl Ziegler, Ger.
1962 John C. Kendrew, Max F. Perutz, both Br.
1961 Melvin Calvin, U.S.
1960 Willard F. Libby, U.S.
1959 Jaroslav Heyrovsky, Czech.
1958 Frederick Sanger, Br.
1957 Sir Alexander R. Todd, Br.
1956 Sir Cyril N. Hinshelwood, Br.; Nikolai N. Semenov, USSR
1955 Vincent du Vigneaud, U.S.
1954 Linus C. Pauling, U.S.
1953 Hermann Staudinger, Ger.
1952 Archer J. P. Martin, Richard L. M. Synge, both Br.
1951 Edwin M. McMillan, Glenn T. Seaborg, both U.S.
1950 Kurt Alder, Otto P. H. Diels, both Ger.
1949 William F. Giauque, U.S.
1948 Arne W. K. Tiselius, Swed.
1947 Sir Robert Robinson, Br.
1946 James B. Sumner, John H. Northrop, Wendell M. Stanley, all U.S.
1945 Artturi I. Virtanen, Finnish
1944 Otto Hahn, Ger.
1943 Georg de Hevesy, Hung.
1939 Adolf F. J. Butenandt, Ger.; Leopold Ruzicka, Swiss
1938 Richard Kuhn, Ger.
1937 Walter N. Haworth, Br.; Paul Karrer, Swiss
1936 Peter J. W. Debye, Dutch
1935 Frederic Joliot-Curie, Irene Joliot-Curie, both Fr.
1934 Harold C. Urey, U.S.
1932 Irving Langmuir, U.S.
1931 Friedrich Bergius, Karl Bosch, both Ger.
1930 Hans Fischer, Ger.
1929 Sir Arthur Harden, Br.; Hans von Euler-Chelpin, Swed.
1928 Adolf O. R. Windaus, Ger.
1927 Heinrich O. Wieland, Ger.
1926 Theodor Svedberg, Swed.
1925 Richard A. Zsigmondy, Ger.
1923 Fritz Pregl, Aus.
1922 Francis W. Aston, Br.
1921 Frederick Soddy, Br.
1920 Walther H. Nernst, Ger.
1918 Fritz Haber, Ger.

(continued)

Chemistry *(continued)*

1915	Richard M. Willstatter, Ger.
1914	Theodore W. Richards, U.S.
1913	Alfred Werner, Swiss
1912	Victor Grignard, Paul Sabatier, both Fr.
1911	Marie Curie, Pol.-Fr.
1910	Otto Wallach, Ger.
1909	Wilhelm Ostwald, Ger.
1908	Ernest Rutherford, Br.
1907	Eduard Buchner, Ger.
1906	Henri Moissan, Fr.
1905	Adolf von Baeyer, Ger.
1904	Sir William Ramsay, Br.
1903	Svante A. Arrhenius, Swed.
1902	Emil Fischer, Ger.
1901	Jacobus H. van't Hoff, Dutch

Physiology or Medicine

1994 Alfred G. Gilman, Martin Rodbell, both U.S.
1993 Phillip A. Sharp, U.S.; Richard J. Roberts, Br.
1992 Edmond H. Fisher, Edwin G. Krebs, both U.S.
1991 Edwin Neher, Bert Sakmann, both Ger.
1990 Joseph E. Murray, E. Donnall Thomas, both U.S.
1989 J. Michael Bishop, Harold E. Varmus, both U.S.
1988 Gertrude B. Elion, George H. Hitchings, both U.S; Sir James Black, Br.
1987 Susumu Tonegawa, Jpn.
1986 Rita Levi-Montalcini, It.-U.S., Stanley Cohen, U.S.
1985 Michael S. Brown, Joseph L. Goldstein, both U.S.
1984 Cesar Milstein, Brit.-Arg.; Georges J. F. Koehler, Ger.; Niels K. Jerne, Brit.-Dan.
1983 Barbara McClintock, U.S.
1982 Sune Bergstrom, Bengt Samuelsson, both Swed.; John R. Vane, Br.
1981 Roger W. Sperry, David H. Hubel, Tosten N. Wiesel, all U.S.
1980 Baruj Benacerraf, George Snell, both U.S.; Jean Dausset, Fr.
1979 Alian M. Cormack, U.S.; Geoffrey N. Hounsfield, Br.
1978 Daniel Nathans, Hamilton O. Smith, both U.S.; Werner Arber, Swiss
1977 Rosalyn S. Yalow, Roger C.L. Guillemin, Andrew V. Schally, all U.S.
1976 Baruch S. Blumberg, Daniel Carleton Gajdusek, both U.S.
1975 David Baltimore, Howard Temin, both U.S.; Renato Dulbecco, It.-U.S.
1974 Albert Claude, Lux.-U.S.; George Emil Palade, Rom.-U.S.; Christian Rene de Duve, Belg.
1973 Karl von Frisch, Ger.; Konrad Lorenz, Ger.-Aus.; Nikolaas Tinbergen, Br.

1972 Gerald M. Edelman, U.S.; Rodney R. Porter, Br.
1971 Earl W. Sutherland Jr., U.S.
1970 Julius Axelrod, U.S.; Sir Bernard Katz, Br.; Ulf von Euler, Swed.
1969 Max Delbrück, Alfred D. Hershey, Salvador Luria, all U.S.
1968 Robert W. Holley, H. Gobind Khorana, Marshall W. Nirenberg, all U.S.
1967 Ragnar Granit, Swed.; Haldan Keffer Hartline, George Wald, both U.S.
1966 Charles B. Huggins, Francis Peyton Rous, both U.S.
1965 François Jacob, Andre Lwoff, Jacques Monod, all Fr.
1964 Konrad E. Bloch, U.S.; Feodor Lynen, Ger.
1963 Sir John C. Eccles, Australian; Alan L. Hodgkin, Andrew F. Huxley, both Br.
1962 Francis H. C. Crick, Maurice H. F. Wilkins, both Br.; James D. Watson, U.S.
1961 Georg von Bekesy, U.S.
1960 Sir F. MacFarlane Burnet, Australian; Peter B. Medawar, Br.
1959 Arthur Kornberg, Severo Ochoa, both U.S.
1958 George W. Beadle, Edward L. Tatum, Joshua Lederberg, all U.S.
1957 Daniel Bovet, It.
1956 Andre F. Cournand, Dickinson W. Richards Jr., both U.S.; Werner Forssmann, Ger.
1955 Alex H. T. Theorell, Swed.
1954 John F. Enders, Frederick C. Robbins, Thomas H. Weller, all U.S.
1953 Hans A. Krebs, Br.; Fritz A. Lipmann, U.S.
1952 Selman A. Waksman, U.S.
1951 Max Theiler, U.S.
1950 Philip S. Hench, Edward C. Kendall, both U.S.; Tadeus Reichstein, Swiss
1949 Walter R. Hess, Swiss; Antonio Moniz, Port.
1948 Paul H. Müller, Swiss
1947 Carl F. Cori, Gerty T. Cori, both U.S.; Bernardo A. Houssay, Arg.

1946 Hermann J. Muller, U.S.
1945 Ernst B. Chain, Sir Alexander Fleming, Sir Howard W. Florey, all Br.
1944 Joseph Erlanger, Herbert S. Gasser, both U.S.
1943 Henrik C. P. Dam, Dan.; Edward A. Doisy, U.S.
1939 Gerhard Domagk, Ger.
1938 Corneille J. F. Heymans, Belg.
1937 Albert Szent-Gyorgyi, Hung.-U.S.
1936 Sir Henry H. Dale, Br.; Otto Loewi, U.
1935 Hans Spemann, Ger.
1934 George R. Minot, William P. Murphy, G. H. Whipple, all U.S.
1933 Thomas H. Morgan, U.S.
1932 Edgar D. Adrian, Sir Charles S. Sherrington, both Br.
1931 Otto H. Warburg, Ger.
1930 Karl Landsteiner, U.S.
1929 Christiaan Eijkman, Dutch; Sir Frederick G. Hopkins, Br.
1928 Charles J. H. Nicolle, Fr.
1927 Julius Wagner-Jauregg, Aus.
1926 Johannes A. G. Fibiger, Dan.
1924 Willem Einthoven, Dutch
1923 Frederick G. Banting, Can.; John J. R. Macleod, Scottish
1922 Archibald V. Hill, Br.; Otto F. Meyerhof, Ger.
1920 Schack A. S. Krogh, Dan.
1919 Jules Bordet, Belg.
1914 Robert Barany, Aus.
1913 Charles R. Richet, Fr.
1912 Alexis Carrel, Fr.
1911 Allvar Gullstrand, Swed.
1910 Albrecht Kossel, Ger.
1909 Emil T. Kocher, Swiss
1908 Paul Ehrlich, Ger.; Elie Metchnikoff, Fr.
1907 Charles L. A. Laveran, Fr.
1906 Camillo Golgi, It.; Santiago Ramon y Cajal, Span.
1905 Robert Koch, Ger.
1904 Ivan P. Pavlov, Russ.
1903 Niels R. Finsen, Dan.
1902 Sir Ronald Ross, Br.
1901 Emil A. von Behring, Ger.

Literature

1994 Kenzaburo Oe, Jpn.
1993 Toni Morrison, U.S.
1992 Derek Walcott, West Indian
1991 Nadine Gordimer, S. African
1990 Octavio Paz, Mex.
1989 Camilo José Cela, Span.
1988 Naguib Mahfouz, Eg.
1987 Joseph Brodsky, USSR-U.S.
1986 Wole Soyinka, Nigerian
1985 Claude Simon, Fr.
1984 Jaroslav Siefert, Czech.
1983 William Golding, Br.
1982 Gabriel Garcia Marquez, Colombian-Mex.
1981 Elias Canetti, Bulg.-Br.
1980 Czeslaw Milosz, Pol.-U.S.
1979 Odysseus Elytis, Gk.
1978 Isaac Bashevis Singer, U.S.
1977 Vicente Aleixandre, Span.
1976 Saul Bellow, U.S.
1975 Eugenio Montale, It.
1974 Eyvind Johnson, Harry Edmund Martinson, both Swed.
1973 Patrick White, Austral.
1972 Heinrich Böll, W. Ger.

1971 Pablo Neruda, Chilean
1970 Aleksandr I. Solzhenitsyn, USSR
1969 Samuel Beckett, Ir.
1968 Yasunari Kawabata, Jpn.
1967 Miguel Angel Asturias, Guate.
1966 Samuel Joseph Agnon, Isr.; Nelly Sachs, Swed.
1965 Mikhail Sholokhov, USSR
1964 Jean Paul Sartre, Fr. (Prize declined)
1963 Giorgos Seferis, Gk.
1962 John Steinbeck, U.S.
1961 Ivo Andric, Yugo.
1960 Saint-John Perse, Fr.
1959 Salvatore Quasimodo, It.
1958 Boris L. Pasternak, USSR (Prize declined)
1957 Albert Camus, Fr.
1956 Juan Ramon Jimenez, Span.
1955 Halldor K. Laxness, Icelandic
1954 Ernest Hemingway, U.S.
1953 Sir Winston Churchill, Br.
1952 Francois Mauriac, Fr.
1951 Par F. Lagerkvist, Swed.
1950 Bertrand Russell, Br.

1949 William Faulkner, U.S.
1948 T.S. Eliot, Br.
1947 Andre Gide, Fr.
1946 Hermann Hesse, Swiss
1945 Gabriela Mistral, Chilean
1944 Johannes V. Jensen, Dan.
1939 Frans E. Sillanpaa, Finnish
1938 Pearl S. Buck, U.S.
1937 Roger Martin du Gard, Fr.
1936 Eugene O'Neill, U.S.
1934 Luigi Pirandello, It.
1933 Ivan A. Bunin, USSR
1932 John Galsworthy, Br.
1931 Erik A. Karlfeldt, Swed.
1930 Sinclair Lewis, U.S.
1929 Thomas Mann, Ger.
1928 Sigrid Undset, Nor.
1927 Henri Bergson, Fr.
1926 Grazia Deledda, Italian
1925 George Bernard Shaw, Ir.-Br.
1924 Wladyslaw S. Reymont, Pol.
1923 William Butler Yeats, Ir.
1922 Jacinto Benavente, Spanish
1921 Anatole France, Fr.

1920	Knut Hamsun, Nor.	1912	Gerhart Hauptmann, Ger.	1905	Henryk Sienkiewicz, Pol.
1919	Carl F. G. Spitteler, Swiss	1911	Maurice Maeterlinck, Belg.	1904	Frederic Mistral, Fr.; Jose
1917	Karl A. Gjellerup, Henrik Pon-	1910	Paul J. L. Heyse, Ger.		Echegaray, Span.
	toppidan, both Dan.	1909	Selma Lagerlof, Swed.	1903	Bjornsterne Bjornson, Nor.
1916	Verner von Heidenstam, Swed.	1908	Rudolf C. Eucken, Ger.	1902	Theodor Mommsen, Ger.
1915	Romain Rolland, Fr.	1907	Rudyard Kipling, Br.	1901	Rene F. A. Sully Prudhomme,
1913	Rabindranath Tagore, Indian	1906	Giosue Carducci, It.		Fr.

Peace

1994	Yasir Arafat, Palestine; Shimon Peres, Yitzhak Rabin, both Isr.	1971	Willy Brandt, W. Ger.	1931	Jane Addams, Nicholas Murray Butler, both U.S.
1993	Frederik W. de Klerk, Nelson Mandela, both South African	1970	Norman E. Borlaug, U.S.	1930	Nathan Soderblom, Swed.
		1969	Intl. Labor Organization	1929	Frank B. Kellogg, U.S.
1992	Rigoberta Menchú, Guatemalan	1968	Rene Cassin, Fr.	1927	Ferdinand E. Buisson, Fr.; Lud-
1991	Aung San Suu Kyi, Myanmarese	1965	U.N. Children's Fund (UNICEF)		wig Quidde, Ger.
1990	Mikhail S. Gorbachev, USSR	1964	Martin Luther King Jr., U.S.	1926	Aristide Briand, Fr.; Gustav Stre-
1989	Dalai Lama, Tibetan	1963	International Red Cross,		semann, Ger.
1988	United Nations Peacekeeping Forces		League of Red Cross Societies	1925	Sir J. Austen Chamberlain, Brit.; Charles G. Dawes, U.S.
1987	Oscar Arias Sanchez, Costa Ri- can	1962	Linus C. Pauling, U.S.	1922	Fridtjof Nansen, Nor.
		1961	Dag Hammarskjold, Swed.	1921	Karl H. Branting, Swed.;
1986	Elie Wiesel, Romanian-U.S.	1960	Albert J. Luthuli, S. African		Christian L. Lange, Nor.
1985	Intl. Physicians for the Preven- tion of Nuclear War, U.S.	1959	Philip J. Noel-Baker, Br.	1920	Leon V.A. Bourgeois, Fr.
		1958	Georges Pire, Belg.	1919	Woodrow Wilson, U.S.
1984	Bishop Desmond Tutu, S. African	1957	Lester B. Pearson, Can.	1917	International Red Cross
1983	Lech Walesa, Pol.	1954	Office of the UN High Commissioner for Refugees	1913	Henri La Fontaine, Belg.
1982	Alva Myrdal, Swedish; Alfonso Garcia Robles, Mex.			1912	Elihu Root, U.S.
		1953	George C. Marshall, U.S.	1911	Tobias M.C. Asser, Dutch; Alfred H. Fried, Aus.
1981	Office of UN High Commissioner for Refugees	1952	Albert Schweitzer, Fr.		
		1951	Leon Jouhaux, Fr.	1910	Permanent Intl. Peace Bureau
1980	Adolfo Perez Esquivel, Arg.	1950	Ralph J. Bunche, U.S.	1909	Auguste M. F. Beernaert, Belg.; Paul H. B. B. d'Estournelles de Constant, Fr.
1979	Mother Teresa of Calcutta, Al- banian-Indian	1949	Lord John Boyd Orr of Brechin Mearns, Br.		
1978	Anwar Sadat, Eg.; Menachem Begin, Isr.	1947	Friends Service Council, Br.; American Friends Service Committee, U.S.	1908	Klas P. Arnoldson, Swed.; Fredrik Bajer, Dan.
1977	Amnesty International	1946	Emily G. Balch, John R. Mott, both U.S.	1907	Ernesto T. Moneta, It.; Louis Renault, Fr.
1976	Mairead Corrigan, Betty Wil- liams, both N. Ir.	1945	Cordell Hull, U.S.	1906	Theodore Roosevelt, U.S.
1975	Andrei Sakharov, USSR	1944	International Red Cross	1905	Baroness Bertha von Suttner, Aus.
1974	Eisaku Sato, Jpn.; Sean MacBride, Ir.	1938	Nansen International Office for Refugees	1904	Institute of International Law
1973	Henry Kissinger, U.S.; Le Duc Tho, N. Vietnamese (Tho declined)	1937	Viscount Cecil of Chelwood, Br.	1903	Sir William R. Cremer, Br.
		1936	Carlos de Saavedra Lamas, Arg.	1902	Elie Ducommun, Charles A. Gobat, both Swiss
		1935	Carl von Ossietzky, Ger.		
		1934	Arthur Henderson, Br.	1901	Jean H. Dunant, Swiss; Frederic Passy, Fr.
		1933	Sir Norman Angell, Br.		

Nobel Memorial Prize in Economic Science

1994	John C. Harsanyi, John F. Nash, both U.S.	1985	Franco Modigliani, It.-U.S.	1975	Tjalling Koopmans, Dutch-U.S.; Leonid Kantorovich, USSR
		1984	Richard Stone, Br.		
1993	Robert W. Fogel, Douglass C. North, both U.S.	1983	Gerard Debreu, Fr.-U.S.	1974	Gunnar Myrdal, Swed.; Friedrich A. von Hayek, Aus.
		1982	George J. Stigler, U.S.		
1992	Gary S. Becker, U.S.	1981	James Tobin, U.S.	1973	Wassily Leontief, U.S.
1991	Ronald H. Coase, Br.-U.S.	1980	Lawrence R. Klein, U.S.	1972	Kenneth J. Arrow, U.S.; John R. Hicks, Br.
1990	Harry M. Markowitz, William F. Sharpe, Merton H. Miller, all U.S.	1979	Theodore W. Schultz, U.S.; Sir Arthur Lewis, Br.		
		1978	Herbert A. Simon, U.S.	1971	Simon Kuznets, U.S.
1989	Trygve Haavelmo, Nor.	1977	Bertil Ohlin, Swedish; James E. Meade, Br.	1970	Paul A. Samuelson, U.S.
1988	Maurice Allais, Fr.			1969	Ragnar Frisch, Norwegian; Jan Tinbergen, Dutch
1987	Robert M. Solow, U.S.				
1986	James M. Buchanan, U.S.	1976	Milton Friedman, U.S.		

Pulitzer Prizes in Journalism, Letters, and Music

The Pulitzer Prizes were endowed by Joseph Pulitzer (1847-1911), publisher of the *New York World*, in a bequest to Co-lumbia University and are awarded annually by the president of the university on recommendation of the Pulitzer Prize Board for work done during the preceding year. The administrator is Seymour Topping of Columbia University. All prizes are $3,000 (originally $500) in each category, except Meritorious Public Service, for which a gold medal is given. If a year is omitted, no award was given that year.

Journalism

Meritorious Public Service

For distinguished and meritorious public service by a United States newspaper.
1918—New York Times. Also special award to Minna Lewinson and Henry Beetle Hough
1919—Milwaukee Journal
1921—Boston Post
1922—New York World
1923—Memphis Commercial Appeal
1924—New York World
1926—Enquirer-Sun, Columbus, GA
1927—Canton (OH) Daily News
1928—Indianapolis Times
1929—New York Evening World
1931—Atlanta (GA) Constitution
1932—Indianapolis (IN) News
1933—New York World-Telegram

1934—Medford (OR) Mail-Tribune
1935—Sacramento (CA) Bee
1936—Cedar Rapids (IA) Gazette
1937—St.Louis Post-Dispatch
1938—Bismarck (ND) Tribune
1939—Miami (FL) Daily News
1940—Waterbury (CT) Republican and American
1941—St.Louis Post-Dispatch
1942—Los Angeles Times
1943—Omaha World Herald
1944—New York Times
1945—Detroit Free Press
1946—Scranton (PA) Times.
1947—Baltimore Sun
1948—St. Louis Post-Dispatch
1949—Nebraska State Journal
1950—Chicago Daily News; St. Louis Post-Dispatch

(continued)

Meritorious Public Service (continued)

1951—Miami (FL) Herald and Brooklyn Eagle
1952—St. Louis Post-Dispatch
1953—Whiteville (NC) News Reporter; Tabor City (NC) Tribune
1954—Newsday (Long Island, NY)
1955—Columbus (GA) Ledger and Sunday Ledger-Enquirer
1956—Watsonville (CA) Register-Pajaronian
1957—Chicago Daily News
1958—Arkansas Gazette, Little Rock
1959—Utica (NY) Observer-Dispatch and Utica Daily Press
1960—Los Angeles Times
1961—Amarillo (TX) Globe-Times
1962—Panama City (FL) News-Herald
1963—Chicago Daily News
1964—St.Petersburg (FL) Times
1965—Hutchinson (KS) News
1966—Boston Globe
1967—Louisville Courier-Journal; Milwaukee Journal
1968—Riverside (CA) Press-Enterprise
1969—Los Angeles Times
1970—Newsday (Long Island, NY)
1971—Winston Salem (NC) Journal & Sentinel
1972—New York Times
1973—Washington Post
1974—Newsday (Long Island, NY)
1975—Boston Globe
1976—Anchorage Daily News
1977—Lufkin (TX) News
1978—Philadelphia Inquirer
1979—Point Reyes (CA) Light
1980—Gannett News Service
1981—Charlotte (NC) Observer
1982—Detroit News
1983—Jackson (MS) Clarion-Ledger
1984—Los Angeles Times
1985—Ft. Worth (TX) Star-Telegram
1986—Denver Post
1987—Pittsburgh Press
1988—Charlotte Observer
1989—Anchorage Daily News
1990—Philadelphia Inquirer, Gilbert M. Gaul; Washington (NC) Daily News
1991—Des Moines Register, Jane Schorer
1992—Sacramento Bee, Tom Knudson
1993—Miami Herald
1994—Akron Beacon Journal
1995—The Virgin Islands Daily News, St. Thomas

Reporting

This category originally embraced all fields—local, national, and international. Later, separate categories were created for national and international reporting.

1917—Herbert Bayard Swope, New York World
1918—Harold A. Littledale, New York Evening Post
1920—John J. Leary Jr., New York World
1921—Louis Seibold, New York World
1922—Kirke L. Simpson, Associated Press
1923—Alva Johnston, New York Times
1924—Magner White, San Diego Sun
1925—James W. Mulroy and Alvin H. Goldstein, Chicago Daily News
1926—William Burke Miller, Louisville Courier-Journal
1927—John T. Rogers, St. Louis Post-Dispatch
1929—Paul Y. Anderson, St. Louis Post-Dispatch
1930—Russell D. Owens, New York Times. Also $500 to W.O. Dapping, Auburn (NY) Citizen
1931—A.B. MacDonald, Kansas City (MO) Star
1932—W.C. Richards, D.D. Martin, J.S. Pooler, F.D. Webb, J.N.W. Sloan, Detroit Free Press
1933—Francis A. Jamieson, Associated Press
1934—Royce Brier, San Francisco Chronicle
1935—William H. Taylor, New York Herald Tribune
1936—Lauren D. Lyman, New York Times
1937—John J. O'Neill, NY Herald Tribune; William L. Laurence, NY Times; Howard W. Blakeslee, AP; Gobind Behari Lal, Universal Service; and David Dietz, Scripps-Howard Newspapers
1938—Raymond Sprigle, Pittsburgh Post-Gazette
1939—Thomas L. Stokes, Scripps-Howard Newspaper Alliance
1940—S. Burton Heath, New York World-Telegram
1941—Westbrook Pegler, New York World-Telegram
1942—Stanton Delaplane, San Francisco Chronicle
1943—George Weller, Chicago Daily News
1944—Paul Schoenstein, New York Journal-American
1945—Jack S. McDowell, San Francisco Call-Bulletin
1946—William L. Laurence, New York Times
1947—Frederick Woltman, New York World-Telegram
1948—George E. Goodwin, Atlanta Journal
1949—Malcolm Johnson, New York Sun

1950—Meyer Berger, New York Times
1951—Edward S. Montgomery, San Francisco Examiner
1952—George de Carvalho, San Francisco Chronicle

(1) General or Spot; (2) Special or Investigative

1953—(1) Providence (RI) Journal and Evening Bulletin; (2) Edward J. Mowery, New York World-Telegram & Sun
1954—(1) Vicksburg (MS) Sunday Post-Herald; (2) Alvin Scott McCoy, Kansas City (MO) Star
1955—(1) Mrs. Caro Brown, Alice (TX) Daily Echo; (2) Roland K. Towery, Cuero (TX) Record
1956—(1) Lee Hills, Detroit Free Press; (2) Arthur Daley, New York Times
1957—(1) Salt Lake Tribune, Salt Lake City, UT; (2) Wallace Turner and William Lambert, Portland Oregonian
1958—(1) Fargo, (ND) Forum; (2) George Beveridge, Evening Star, Washington, DC
1959—(1) Mary Lou Werner, Washington Evening Star; (2) John Harold Brislin, Scranton (PA) Tribune, and The Scrantonian
1960—(1) Jack Nelson, Atlanta Constitution; (2) Miriam Ottenberg, Washington Evening Star
1961—(1) Sanche de Gramont, New York Herald Tribune; (2) Edgar May, Buffalo Evening News
1962—(1) Robert D. Mullins, Deseret News, Salt Lake City; (2) George Bliss, Chicago Tribune
1963—(1) Shared by Sylvan Fox, William Longgood, and Anthony Shannon, New York World-Telegram & Sun; (2) Oscar Griffin Jr., Pecos (TX) Independent and Enterprise
1964—(1) Norman C. Miller, Wall Street Journal; (2) Shared by James V. Magee, Albert V. Gaudiosi, and Frederick A. Meyer, Philadelphia Bulletin
1965—(1) Melvin H. Ruder, Hungry Horse News (Columbia Falls, MT); (2) Gene Goltz, Houston Post
1966—(1) Los Angeles Times Staff; (2) John A. Frasca, Tampa (FL) Tribune
1967—(1) Robert V. Cox, Chambersburg (PA) Public Opinion; (2) Gene Miller, Miami Herald
1968—(1) Detroit Free Press Staff; (2) J. Anthony Lukas, New York Times
1969—(1) John Fetterman, Louisville Courier-Journal and Times; (2) Albert L. Delugach, St. Louis Globe Democrat, and Denny Walsh, Life
1970—(1) Thomas Fitzpatrick, Chicago Sun-Times; (2) Harold Eugene Martin, Montgomery Advertiser & Alabama Journal
1971—(1) Akron Beacon Journal Staff; (2) William Hugh Jones, Chicago Tribune
1972—(1) Richard Cooper and John Machacek, Rochester Times-Union; (2) Timothy Leland, Gerard M. O'Neill, Stephen A. Kurkjian and Anne De Santis, Boston Globe
1973—(1) Chicago Tribune; (2) Sun Newspapers of Omaha
1974—(1) Hugh F. Hough, Arthur M. Petacque, Chicago Sun-Times; (2) William Sherman, New York Daily News
1975—(1) Xenia (OH) Daily Gazette; (2) Indianapolis Star
1976—(1) Gene Miller, Miami Herald; (2) Chicago Tribune
1977—(1) Margo Huston, Milwaukee Journal; (2) Acel Moore, Wendell Rawls Jr., Philadelphia Inquirer
1978—(1) Richard Whitt, Louisville Courier-Journal; (2) Anthony R. Dolan, Stamford (CT) Advocate
1979—(1) San Diego (CA) Evening Tribune; (2) Gilbert M. Gaul, Elliot G. Jaspin, Pottsville (PA) Republican
1980—(1) Philadelphia Inquirer; (2) Stephen A. Kurkjian, Alexander B. Hawes Jr., Nils Bruzelius, Joan Vennochi, Robert M. Porterfield, Boston Globe
1981—(1) Longview (WA) Daily News staff; (2) Clark Hallas and Robert B. Lowe, Arizona Daily Star
1982—(1) Kansas City Star, Kansas City Times; (2) Paul Henderson, Seattle Times
1983—(1) Fort Wayne (IN) News-Sentinel; (2) Loretta Tofani, Washington Post
1984—(1) Newsday (NY); (2) Boston Globe
1985—(1) Thomas Turcol, Virginian-Pilot and Ledger-Star, Norfolk, VA; (2) William K. Marimow, Philadelphia Inquirer; Lucy Morgan & Jack Reed, St. Petersburg (FL) Times
1986—(1) Edna Buchanan, Miami Herald; (2) Jeffrey A. Marx & Michael M. York, Lexington (KY) Herald-Leader
1987—(1) Akron Beacon Journal; (2) Daniel R. Biddle, H.G. Bissinger, Fredric N. Tulsky, Philadelphia Inquirer; John Woestendiek, Philadelphia Inquirer
1988—(1) Alabama Journal; Lawrence (MA) Eagle-Tribune; (2) Walt Bogdanich, Wall Street Journal
1989—(1) Louisville Courier-Journal; (2) Bill Dedman, Atlanta Journal and Constitution
1990—(1) San Jose Mercury News; (2) Lon Kilzer, Chris Ison, Star Tribune, Minneapolis-St. Paul
1991—(1) Miami Herald; (2) Joseph T. Hallinan, Susan M. Headden, Indianapolis Star
1992—(1) New York Newsday; (2) Lorraine Adams, Dan Malone, Dallas Morning News
1993—(1) Los Angeles Times; Jeff Brazil, Steve Berry, Orlando Sentinel

1994—(1) New York Times staff; (2) Providence Journal-Bulletin staff
1995—(1) Los Angeles Times staff; (2) Brian Donovan, Stephanie Saul, Newsday

Criticism or Commentary

(1) Criticism; (2) Commentary
1970—(1) Ada Louise Huxtable, New York Times; (2) Marquis W. Childs, St. Louis Post-Dispatch
1971—(1) Harold C. Schonberg, New York Times; (2) William A. Caldwell, The Record, Hackensack, NJ
1972—(1) Frank Peters Jr., St. Louis Post-Dispatch; (2) Mike Royko, Chicago Daily News
1973—(1) Ronald Powers, Chicago Sun-Times; (2) David S. Broder, Washington Post
1974—(1) Emily Genauer, Newsday (NY); (2) Edwin A. Roberts Jr., National Observer
1975—(1) Roger Ebert, Chicago Sun Times; (2) Mary McGrory, Washington Star
1976—(1) Alan M. Kriegsman, Washington Post; (2) Walter W. (Red) Smith, New York Times
1977—(1) William McPherson, Washington Post; (2) George F. Will, Washington Post Writers Group
1978—(1) Walter Kerr, New York Times; (2) William Safire, New York Times
1979—(1) Paul Gapp, Chicago Tribune; (2) Russell Baker, New York Times
1980—(1) William A. Henry III, Boston Globe; (2) Ellen Goodman, Boston Globe
1981—(1) Jonathan Yardley, Washington Star; (2) Dave Anderson, New York Times
1982—(1) Martin Bernheimer, Los Angeles Times; (2) Art Buchwald, Los Angeles Times Syndicate
1983—(1) Manuela Hoelterhoff, Wall St. Journal; (2) Claude Sitton, Raleigh (NC) News & Observer
1984—(1) Paul Goldberger, New York Times; (2) Vermont Royster, Wall St. Journal
1985—(1) Howard Rosenberg, Los Angeles Times; (2) Murray Kempton, Newsday (NY)
1986—(1) Donal J. Henahan, New York Times; (2) Jimmy Breslin, New York Daily News
1987—(1) Richard Eder, Los Angeles Times; (2) Charles Krauthammer, Washington Post
1988—(1) Tom Shales, Washington Post; (2) Dave Barry, Miami Herald
1989—(1) Michael Skube, News and Observer, Raleigh, NC; (2) Clarence Page, Chicago Tribune
1990—(1) Allan Temko, San Francisco Chronicle; (2) Jim Murray, Los Angeles Times
1991—(1) David Shaw, Los Angeles Times; (2) Jim Hoagland, Washington Post
1992—(1) No award; (2) Anna Quindlen, New York Times
1993—(1) Michael Dirda, Washington Post; (2) Liz Balmaseda, Miami Herald
1994—(1) Lloyd Schwartz, Boston Phoenix; (2) William Raspberry, Washington Post
1995—(1) Margo Jefferson, New York Times; (2) Jim Dwyer, Newsday

National Reporting

1942—Louis Stark, New York Times
1944—Dewey L. Fleming, Baltimore Sun
1945—James B. Reston, New York Times
1946—Edward A. Harris, St. Louis Post-Dispatch
1947—Edward T. Folliard, Washington Post
1948—Bert Andrews, New York Herald Tribune; Nat S. Finney, Minneapolis Tribune
1949—Charles P. Trussell, New York Times
1950—Edwin O. Guthman, Seattle Times
1952—Anthony Leviero, New York Times
1953—Don Whitehead, Associated Press
1954—Richard Wilson, Des Moines Register
1955—Anthony Lewis, Washington Daily News
1956—Charles L. Bartlett, Chattanooga Times
1957—James Reston, New York Times
1958—Relman Morin, AP; Clark Mollenhoff, Des Moines Register & Tribune
1959—Howard Van Smith, Miami (FL) News
1960—Vance Trimble, Scripps-Howard, Washington, DC
1961—Edward R. Cony, Wall Street Journal
1962—Nathan G. Caldwell and Gene S. Graham, Nashville Tennessean
1963—Anthony Lewis, New York Times
1964—Merriman Smith, UPI
1965—Louis M. Kohlmeier, Wall Street Journal
1966—Haynes Johnson, Washington Evening Star
1967—Monroe Karmin and Stanley Penn, Wall Street Journal

1968—Howard James, Christian Science Monitor; Nathan K. Kotz, Des Moines Register
1969—Robert Cahn, Christian Science Monitor
1970—William J. Eaton, Chicago Daily News
1971—Lucinda Franks & Thomas Powers, UPI
1972—Jack Anderson, United Feature Syndicate
1973—Robert Boyd and Clark Hoyt, Knight Newspapers
1974—James R. Polk, Washington Star-News; Jack White, Providence Journal-Bulletin
1975—Donald L. Barlett and James B. Steele, Philadelphia Inquirer
1976—James Risser, Des Moines Register
1977—Walter Mears, Associated Press
1978—Gaylord D. Shaw, Los Angeles Times
1979—James Risser, Des Moines Register
1980—Charles Stafford, Bette Swenson Orsini, St. Petersburg (FL) Times
1981—John M. Crewdson, New York Times
1982—Rick Atkinson, Kansas City Times
1983—Boston Globe
1984—John Noble Wilford, New York Times
1985—Thomas J. Knudson, Des Moines (IA) Register
1986—Craig Flournoy & George Rodrigue, Dallas Morning News; Arthur Howe, Philadelphia Inquirer
1987—Miami Herald; New York Times
1988—Tim Weiner, Philadelphia Inquirer
1989—Donald L. Barlett & James B. Steele, Philadelphia Inquirer
1990—Ross Anderson, Bill Dietrich, Mary Ann Gwinn, Eric Nalder, Seattle Times
1991—Marjie Lundstrom, Rochelle Sharpe, Gannett News Service
1992—Jeff Taylor, Mike McGraw, Kansas City Star
1993—David Maraniss, Washington Post
1994—Eileen Welsome, Albuquerque Tribune
1995—Tony Horwitz, Wall Street Journal

International Reporting

1942—Laurence Edmund Allen, Associated Press
1943—Ira Wolfert, North American Newspaper Alliance
1944—Daniel DeLuce, Associated Press
1945—Mark S. Watson, Baltimore Sun
1946—Homer W. Bigart, New York Herald Tribune
1947—Eddy Gilmore, Associated Press
1948—Paul W. Ward, Baltimore Sun
1949—Price Day, Baltimore Sun
1950—Edmund Stevens, Christian Science Monitor
1951—Keyes Beech and Fred Sparks, Chicago Daily News; Homer Bigart and Marguerite Higgins, New York Herald Tribune; Relman Morin and Don Whitehead, AP
1952—John M. Hightower, Associated Press
1953—Austin C. Wehrwein, Milwaukee Journal
1954—Jim G. Lucas, Scripps-Howard Newspapers
1955—Harrison Salisbury, New York Times
1956—William Randolph Hearst Jr., Frank Conniff, Hearst Newspapers; Kingsbury Smith, INS
1957—Russell Jones, United Press
1958—New York Times
1959—Joseph Martin and Philip Santora, New York Daily News
1960—A.M. Rosenthal, New York Times
1961—Lynn Heinzerling, Associated Press
1962—Walter Lippmann, New York Herald Tribune Syndicate
1963—Hal Hendrix, Miami (FL) News
1964—Malcolm W. Browne, AP; David Halberstam, New York Times
1965—J.A. Livingston, Philadelphia Bulletin
1966—Peter Arnett, AP
1967—R. John Hughes, Christian Science Monitor
1968—Alfred Friendly, Washington Post
1969—William Tuohy, Los Angeles Times
1970—Seymour M. Hersh, Dispatch News Service
1971—Jimmie Lee Hoagland, Washington Post
1972—Peter R. Kann, Wall Street Journal
1973—Max Frankel, New York Times
1974—Hedrick Smith, New York Times
1975—William Mullen and Ovie Carter, Chicago Tribune
1976—Sydney H. Schanberg, New York Times
1978—Henry Kamm, New York Times
1979—Richard Ben Cramer, Philadelphia Inquirer
1980—Joel Brinkley, Jay Mather, Louisville (KY) Courier-Journal
1981—Shirley Christian, Miami Herald
1982—John Darnton, New York Times
1983—Thomas L. Friedman, New York Times; Loren Jenkins, Washington Post
1984—Karen Elliot House, Wall St. Journal
1985—Josh Friedman, Dennis Bell, Ozler Muhammad, Newsday (NY)
1986—Lewis M. Simons, Pete Carey, Katherine Ellison, San Jose (CA) Mercury News
1987—Michael Parks, Los Angeles Times
1988—Thomas L. Friedman, New York Times

(continued)

International Reporting *(continued)*

1989—Glenn Frankel, Washington Post; Bill Keller, New York Times
1990—Nicholas D. Kirstof, Sheryl WuDunn, New York Times
1991—Caryle Murphy, Washington Post; Serge Schmemann, New York Times
1992—Patrick J. Sloyan, Newsday (NY)
1993—John F. Burns, New York Times; Roy Gutman, Newsday (NY)
1994—Dallas Morning News team
1995—Mark Fritz, Associated Press

Correspondence

For Washington or foreign correspondence. Category was merged with those in national and international reporting in 1948.
1929—Paul Scott Mowrer, Chicago Daily News
1930—Leland Stowe, New York Herald Tribune
1931—H.R. Knickerbocker, Philadelphia Public Ledger and New York Evening Post
1932—Walter Duranty, New York Times, and Charles G. Ross, St. Louis Post-Dispatch
1933—Edgar Ansel Mowrer, Chicago Daily News
1934—Frederick T. Birchall, New York Times
1935—Arthur Krock, New York Times
1936—Wilfred C. Barber, Chicago Tribune
1937—Anne O'Hare McCormick, New York Times
1938—Arthur Krock, New York Times
1939—Louis P. Lochner, Associated Press
1940—Otto D. Tolischus, New York Times
1941—Bronze plaque to commemorate work of American correspondents on war fronts
1942—Carlos P. Romulo, Philippines Herald
1943—Hanson W. Baldwin, New York Times
1944—Ernest Taylor Pyle, Scripps-Howard Newspaper Alliance
1945—Harold V. (Hal) Boyle, Associated Press
1946—Arnaldo Cortesi, New York Times
1947—Brooks Atkinson, New York Times

Editorial Writing

1917—New York Tribune
1918—Louisville (KY) Courier-Journal
1920—Harvey E. Newbranch, Omaha Evening World-Herald
1922—Frank M. O'Brien, New York Herald
1923—William Allen White, Emporia Gazette
1924—Frank Buxton, Boston Herald, Special Prize; Frank I. Cobb, New York World
1925—Robert Lathan, Charleston (SC) News and Courier
1926—Edward M. Kingsbury, New York Times
1927—F. Lauriston Bullard, Boston Herald
1928—Grover C. Hall, Montgomery Advertiser
1929—Louis Isaac Jaffe, Norfolk Virginian-Pilot
1931—Chas. Ryckman, Fremont (NE) Tribune
1933—Kansas City (MO) Star
1934—E. P. Chase, Atlantic (IA) News Telegraph
1936—Felix Morley, Washington Post; George B. Parker, Scripps-Howard Newspapers
1937—John W. Owens, Baltimore Sun
1938—W.W. Waymack, Des Moines (IA) Register and Tribune
1939—Ronald G. Callvert, Portland Oregonian
1940—Bart Howard, St. Louis Post-Dispatch
1941—Reuben Maury, Daily News, NY
1942—Geoffrey Parsons, New York Herald Tribune
1943—Forrest W. Seymour, Des Moines (IA) Register and Tribune
1944—Henry J. Haskell, Kansas City (MO) Star
1945—George W. Potter, Providence (RI) Journal-Bulletin
1946—Hodding Carter, Greenville (MS) Delta Democrat-Times
1947—William H. Grimes, Wall Street Journal
1948—Virginius Dabney, Richmond (VA) Times-Dispatch
1949—John H. Crider, Boston (MA) Herald; Herbert Elliston, Washington Post
1950—Carl M. Saunders, Jackson (MI) Citizen-Patriot
1951—William H. Fitzpatrick, New Orleans States
1952—Louis LaCoss, St. Louis Globe Democrat
1953—Vermont C. Royster, Wall Street Journal
1954—Don Murray, Boston Herald
1955—Royce Howes, Detroit Free Press
1956—Lauren K. Soth, Des Moines (IA) Register and Tribune
1957—Buford Boone, Tuscaloosa (AL) News
1958—Harry S. Ashmore, Arkansas Gazette
1959—Ralph McGill, Atlanta Constitution
1960—Lenoir Chambers, Norfolk Virginian-Pilot
1961—William J. Dorvillier, San Juan (Puerto Rico) Star
1962—Thomas M. Storke, Santa Barbara (CA) News-Press
1963—Ira B. Harkey Jr., Pascagoula (MS) Chronicle
1964—Hazel Brannon Smith, Lexington (MS) Advertiser
1965—John R. Harrison, Gainesville (FL) Sun
1966—Robert Lasch, St. Louis Post-Dispatch

1967—Eugene C. Patterson, Atlanta Constitution
1968—John S. Knight, Knight Newspapers
1969—Paul Greenberg, Pine Bluff (AR) Commercial
1970—Philip L. Geyelin, Washington Post
1971—Horance G. Davis Jr., Gainesville (FL) Sun
1972—John Strohmeyer, Bethlehem (PA) Globe-Times
1973—Roger B. Linscott, Berkshire Eagle, Pittsfield, MA
1974—F. Gilman Spencer, Trenton (NJ) Trentonian
1975—John D. Maurice, Charleston (WV) Daily Mail
1976—Philip Kerby, Los Angeles Times
1977—Warren L. Lerude, Foster Church, and Norman F. Cardoza, Reno (NV) Evening Gazette and Nevada State Journal
1978—Meg Greenfield, Washington Post
1979—Edwin M. Yoder, Washington Star
1980—Robert L. Bartley, Wall Street Journal
1982—Jack Rosenthal, New York Times
1983—Editorial board, Miami Herald
1984—Albert Scardino, Georgia Gazette
1985—Richard Aregood, Philadelphia Daily News
1986—Jack Fuller, Chicago Tribune
1987—Jonathan Freedman, Tribune (San Diego)
1988—Jane Healy, Orlando Sentinel
1989—Lois Wille, Chicago Tribune
1990—Thomas J. Hylton, Pottstown (PA) Mercury
1991—Ron Casey, Harold Jackson, Joey Kennedy, Birmingham (AL) News
1992—Maria Henson, Lexington (KY) Herald-Leader
1993—No award
1994—R. Bruce Dold, Chicago Tribune
1995—Jeffrey Good, St. Petersburg (FL) Times

Editorial Cartooning

1922—Rollin Kirby, New York World
1924—Jay N. Darling, Des Moines Register
1925—Rollin Kirby, New York World
1926—D. R. Fitzpatrick, St. Louis Post-Dispatch
1927—Nelson Harding, Brooklyn Eagle
1928—Nelson Harding, Brooklyn Eagle
1929—Rollin Kirby, New York World
1930—Charles Macauley, Brooklyn Eagle
1931—Edmund Duffy, Baltimore Sun
1932—John T. McCutcheon, Chicago Tribune
1933—H. M. Talburt, Washington Daily News
1934—Edmund Duffy, Baltimore Sun
1935—Ross A. Lewis, Milwaukee Journal
1937—C. D. Batchelor, New York Daily News
1938—Vaughn Shoemaker, Chicago Daily News
1939—Charles G. Werner, Daily Oklahoman
1940—Edmund Duffy, Baltimore Sun
1941—Jacob Burck, Chicago Times
1942—Herbert L. Block, Newspaper Enterprise Assn.
1943—Jay N. Darling, Des Moines Register
1944—Clifford K. Berryman, Washington Star
1945—Bill Mauldin, United Feature Syndicate
1946—Bruce Alexander Russell, Los Angeles Times
1947—Vaughn Shoemaker, Chicago Daily News
1948—Reuben L. (Rube) Goldberg, New York Sun
1949—Lute Pease, Newark (NJ) Evening News
1950—James T. Berryman, Washington Star
1951—Reginald W. Manning, Arizona Republic
1952—Fred L. Packer, New York Mirror
1953—Edward D. Kuekes, Cleveland Plain Dealer
1954—Herbert L. Block, Washington Post & Times-Herald
1955—Daniel R. Fitzpatrick, St. Louis Post-Dispatch
1956—Robert York, Louisville (KY) Times
1957—Tom Little, Nashville Tennessean
1958—Bruce M. Shanks, Buffalo Evening News
1959—Bill Mauldin, St. Louis Post-Dispatch
1961—Carey Orr, Chicago Tribune
1962—Edmund S. Valtman, Hartford Times
1963—Frank Miller, Des Moines Register
1964—Paul Conrad, Denver Post
1966—Don Wright, Miami News
1967—Patrick B. Oliphant, Denver Post
1968—Eugene Gray Payne, Charlotte Observer
1969—John Fischetti, Chicago Daily News
1970—Thomas F. Darcy, Newsday
1971—Paul Conrad, Los Angeles Times
1972—Jeffrey K. MacNelly, Richmond News-Leader
1974—Paul Szep, Boston Globe
1975—Garry Trudeau, Universal Press Syndicate
1976—Tony Auth, Philadelphia Inquirer
1977—Paul Szep, Boston Globe
1978—Jeffrey K. MacNelly, Richmond News Leader
1979—Herbert L. Block, Washington Post
1980—Don Wright, Miami (FL) News
1981—Mike Peters, Dayton (OH) Daily News
1982—Ben Sargent, Austin American-Statesman
1983—Richard Lochner, Chicago Tribune

1984—Paul Conrad, Los Angeles Times
1985—Jeffrey K. MacNelly, Chicago Tribune
1986—Jules Feiffer, Village Voice (NY)
1987—Berke Breathed, Washington Post
1988—Doug Marlette, Atlanta Constitution, Charlotte Observer
1989—Jack Higgins, Chicago Sun-Times
1990—Tom Toles, Buffalo News
1991—Jim Borgman, Cincinnati Enquirer
1992—Signe Wilkinson, Philadelphia Daily News
1993—Stephen R. Benson, Arizona Republic
1994—Michael P. Ramirez, Commercial Appeal, Memphis, TN
1995—Mike Luckovich, Atlanta Constitution

Spot News Photography

1942—Milton Brooks, Detroit News
1943—Frank Noel, Associated Press
1944—Frank Filan, AP; Earl L. Bunker, Omaha World-Herald
1945—Joe Rosenthal, Associated Press, for photograph of planting American flag on Iwo Jima
1947—Arnold Hardy, amateur, Atlanta, GA
1948—Frank Cushing, Boston Traveler
1949—Nathaniel Fein, New York Herald Tribune
1950—Bill Crouch, Oakland (CA) Tribune
1951—Max Desfor, Associated Press
1952—John Robinson and Don Ultang, Des Moines Register and Tribune
1953—William M. Gallagher, Flint (MI) Journal
1954—Mrs. Walter M. Schau, amateur
1955—John L. Gaunt Jr., Los Angeles Times
1956—New York Daily News
1957—Harry A. Trask, Boston Traveler
1958—William C. Beall, Washington Daily News
1959—William Seaman, Minneapolis Star
1960—Andrew Lopez, UPI
1961—Yasushi Nagao, Mainichi Newspapers, Tokyo
1962—Paul Vathis, Associated Press
1963—Hector Rondon, La Republica, Caracas, Venezuela
1964—Robert H. Jackson, Dallas Times-Herald
1965—Horst Faas, Associated Press
1966—Kyoichi Sawada, UPI
1967—Jack R. Thornell, Associated Press
1968—Rocco Morabito, Jacksonville Journal
1969—Edward Adams, AP
1970—Steve Starr, AP
1971—John Paul Filo, Valley Daily News & Daily Dispatch of Tarentum & New Kensington, PA
1972—Horst Faas and Michel Laurent, AP
1973—Huynh Cong Ut, AP
1974—Anthony K. Roberts, AP
1975—Gerald H. Gay, Seattle Times
1976—Stanley Forman, Boston Herald American
1977—Neal Ulevich, Associated Press; Stanley Forman, Boston Herald American
1978—John H. Blair, UPI
1979—Thomas J. Kelly III, Pottstown (PA) Mercury
1980—UPI
1981—Larry C. Price, Ft. Worth (TX) Star-Telegram
1982—Ron Edmonds, Associated Press
1983—Bill Foley, AP
1984—Stan Grossfeld, Boston Globe
1985—The Register, Santa Ana, CA
1986—Carol Guzy & Michel duCille, Miami Herald
1987—Kim Komenich, San Francisco Examiner
1988—Scott Shaw, Odessa (TX) American
1989—Ron Olshwanger, St. Louis Post-Dispatch
1990—Oakland (CA) Tribune photo staff
1991—Greg Marinovich, Associated Press
1992—Associated Press staff
1993—Ken Geiger, William Snyder, Dallas Morning News
1994—Paul Watson, Toronto Star
1995—Carol Guzy, Washington Post

Feature Photography

1968—Toshio Sakai, UPI
1969—Moneta Sleet Jr., Ebony
1970—Dallas Kinney, Palm Beach Post
1971—Jack Dykinga, Chicago Sun-Times
1972—Dave Kennerly, UPI
1973—Brian Lanker, Topeka Capitol-Journal
1974—Slava Veder, AP
1975—Matthew Lewis, Washington Post
1976—Louisville Courier-Journal and Louisville Times
1977—Robin Hood, Chattanooga News-Free Press
1978—J. Ross Baughman, AP
1979—Staff photographers, Boston Herald American
1980—Erwin H. Hagler, Dallas Times-Herald
1981—Taro M. Yamasaki, Detroit Free Press
1982—John H. White, Chicago Sun-Times
1983—James B. Dickman, Dallas Times-Herald
1984—Anthony Suad, Denver Post

1985—Stan Grossfeld, Boston Globe; Larry C. Price, Philadelphia Inquirer
1986—Tom Gralish, Philadelphia Inquirer
1987—David Peterson, Des Moines Register
1988—Michel duCille, Miami Herald
1989—Manny Crisostomo, Detroit Free Press
1990—David C. Turnley, Detroit Free Press
1991—William Snyder, Dallas Morning News
1992—John Kaplan, Block Newspapers (Toledo, OH)
1993—Associated Press staff
1994—Kevin Carter, New York Times
1995—Associated Press staff

Special Citation

1938—Edmonton (Alberta) Journal, bronze plaque
1941—New York Times
1944—Byron Price and Mrs. William Allen White. Also to Richard Rodgers and Oscar Hammerstein 2d, for musical, Oklahoma!
1945—Press cartographers for war maps
1947—(Pulitzer centennial year.) Columbia Univ. and the Graduate School of Journalism, and St. Louis Post-Dispatch
1948—Dr. Frank Diehl Fackenthal
1951—Cyrus L. Sulzberger, New York Times
1952—Max Kase, New York Journal-American, Kansas City Star
1953—New York Times; Lester Markel
1957—Kenneth Roberts, for his historical novels
1958—Walter Lippmann, New York Herald Tribune
1960—Garrett Mattingly, for The Armada
1961—American Heritage Picture History of the Civil War
1964—Gannett Newspapers
1973—James T. Flexner, for biography of George Washington
1976—John Hohenberg, for services to American journalism
1977—Alex Haley, for Roots
1978—Richard Lee Strout, Christian Science Monitor and New Republic
    —E.B. White
1984—Theodore Geisel ("Dr. Seuss")
1985—William Schuman, composer, educational leader
1987—Joseph Pulitzer Jr.
1992—Art Spiegelman, for Maus

Feature Writing

1979—Jon D. Franklin, Baltimore Evening Sun
1980—Madeleine Blais, Miami Herald Tropic Magazine; Janet Cooke, Washington Post
1981—Teresa Carpenter, Village Voice, New York City
1982—Saul Pett, Associated Press
1984—Peter M. Rinearson, Seattle Times
1985—Alice Steinbach, Baltimore Sun
1986—John Camp, St. Paul Pioneer Press & Dispatch
1987—Steve Twomey, Philadelphia Inquirer
1988—Jacqui Banaszynski, St. Paul Pioneer Press Dispatch
1989—David Zucchino, Philadelphia Inquirer
1990—Dave Curtin, Colorado Springs Gazette Telegraph
1991—Sheryl James, St. Petersburg Times
1992—Howell Raines, New York Times
1993—George Lardner Jr., Washington Post
1994—Isabel Wilkerson, New York Times
1995—Ron Suskind, Wall Street Journal

Explanatory Journalism

1985—Jon Franklin, Baltimore Evening Sun
1986—New York Times staff
1987—Jeff Lyon & Peter Gorner, Chicago Tribune
1988—Daniel Hertzberg, James B. Stewart, Wall Street Journal
1989—David Hanners, William Snyder, Karen Blessen, Dallas Morning News
1990—David A. Vise, Steve Coll, Washington Post
1991—Susan C. Faludi, Wall Street Journal
1992—Robert S. Capers, Eric Lipton, Hartford (CT) Courant
1993—Mike Toner, Atlanta Journal-Constitution
1994—Ronald Kotulak, Chicago Tribune
1995—Leon Dash, Lucian Perkins, Washington Post

Specialized Reporting (1985-90)
(discontinued category)

1985—Randall Savage, Jackie Crosby, Macon (GA) Telegraph and News
1986—Andrew Schneider & Mary Pat Flaherty, Pittsburgh Press
1987—Alex S. Jones, New York Times
1988—Dean Baquet, William Gaines, Ann Marie Lipinski, Chicago Tribune
1989—Edward Humes, Orange County (CA) Register
1990—Tamar Stieber, Albuquerque Journal

Beat Reporting

1991—Natalie Angier, New York Times
1992—Deborah Blum, Sacramento Bee
1993—Paul Ingrassia, Joseph B. White, Wall Street Journal
1994—Eric Freedman, Jim Mitzelfeld, Detroit News
1995—David Shribman, Boston Globe

Letters

Fiction

For fiction in book form by an American author, preferably dealing with American life.
1918—Ernest Poole, His Family
1919—Booth Tarkington, The Magnificent Ambersons
1921—Edith Wharton, The Age of Innocence
1922—Booth Tarkington, Alice Adams
1923—Willa Cather, One of Ours
1924—Margaret Wilson, The Able McLaughlins
1925—Edna Ferber, So Big
1926—Sinclair Lewis, Arrowsmith (Refused prize)
1927—Louis Bromfield, Early Autumn
1928—Thornton Wilder, Bridge of San Luis Rey
1929—Julia M. Peterkin, Scarlet Sister Mary
1930—Oliver LaFarge, Laughing Boy
1931—Margaret Ayer Barnes, Years of Grace
1932—Pearl S. Buck, The Good Earth
1933—T. S. Stribling, The Store
1934—Caroline Miller, Lamb in His Bosom
1935—Josephine W. Johnson, Now in November
1936—Harold L. Davis, Honey in the Horn
1937—Margaret Mitchell, Gone With the Wind
1938—John P. Marquand, The Late George Apley
1939—Marjorie Kinnan Rawlings, The Yearling
1940—John Steinbeck, The Grapes of Wrath
1942—Ellen Glasgow, In This Our Life
1943—Upton Sinclair, Dragon's Teeth
1944—Martin Flavin, Journey in the Dark
1945—John Hersey, A Bell for Adano
1947—Robert Penn Warren, All the King's Men
1948—James A. Michener, Tales of the South Pacific
1949—James Gould Cozzens, Guard of Honor
1950—A. B. Guthrie Jr., The Way West
1951—Conrad Richter, The Town
1952—Herman Wouk, The Caine Mutiny
1953—Ernest Hemingway, The Old Man and the Sea
1955—William Faulkner, A Fable
1956—MacKinlay Kantor, Andersonville
1958—James Agee, A Death in the Family
1959—Robert Lewis Taylor, The Travels of Jaimie McPheeters
1960—Allen Drury, Advise and Consent
1961—Harper Lee, To Kill a Mockingbird
1962—Edwin O'Connor, The Edge of Sadness
1963—William Faulkner, The Reivers
1965—Shirley Ann Grau, The Keepers of the House
1966—Katherine Anne Porter, Collected Stories of Katherine Anne Porter
1967—Bernard Malamud, The Fixer
1968—William Styron, The Confessions of Nat Turner
1969—N. Scott Momaday, House Made of Dawn
1970—Jean Stafford, Collected Stories
1972—Wallace Stegner, Angle of Repose
1973—Eudora Welty, The Optimist's Daughter
1975—Michael Shaara, The Killer Angels
1976—Saul Bellow, Humboldt's Gift
1978—James Alan McPherson, Elbow Room
1979—John Cheever, The Stories of John Cheever
1980—Norman Mailer, The Executioner's Song
1981—John Kennedy Toole, A Confederacy of Dunces
1982—John Updike, Rabbit Is Rich
1983—Alice Walker, The Color Purple
1984—William Kennedy, Ironweed
1985—Alison Lurie, Foreign Affairs
1986—Larry McMurtry, Lonesome Dove
1987—Peter Taylor, A Summons to Memphis
1988—Toni Morrison, Beloved
1989—Anne Tyler, Breathing Lessons
1990—Oscar Hijuelos, The Mambo Kings Play Songs of Love
1991—John Updike, Rabbit at Rest
1992—Jane Smiley, A Thousand Acres
1993—Robert Olen Butler, A Good Scent From a Strange Mountain
1994—E. Annie Proulx, The Shipping News
1995—Carol Shields, The Stone Diaries

Drama

For an American play, preferably original and dealing with American life.
1918—Jesse Lynch Williams, Why Marry?
1920—Eugene O'Neill, Beyond the Horizon
1921—Zona Gale, Miss Lulu Bett
1922—Eugene O'Neill, Anna Christie
1923—Owen Davis, Icebound
1924—Hatcher Hughes, Hell-Bent for Heaven
1925—Sidney Howard, They Knew What They Wanted

1926—George Kelly, Craig's Wife
1927—Paul Green, In Abraham's Bosom
1928—Eugene O'Neill, Strange Interlude
1929—Elmer Rice, Street Scene
1930—Marc Connelly, The Green Pastures
1931—Susan Glaspell, Alison's House
1932—George S. Kaufman, Morrie Ryskind, and Ira Gershwin, Of Thee I Sing
1933—Maxwell Anderson, Both Your Houses
1934—Sidney Kingsley, Men in White
1935—Zoe Akins, The Old Maid
1936—Robert E. Sherwood, Idiot's Delight
1937—George S. Kaufman and Moss Hart, You Can't Take It With You
1938—Thornton Wilder, Our Town
1939—Robert E. Sherwood, Abe Lincoln in Illinois
1940—William Saroyan, The Time of Your Life
1941—Robert E. Sherwood, There Shall Be No Night
1943—Thornton Wilder, The Skin of Our Teeth
1945—Mary Chase, Harvey
1946—Russel Crouse and Howard Lindsay, State of the Union
1948—Tennessee Williams, A Streetcar Named Desire
1949—Arthur Miller, Death of a Salesman
1950—Richard Rodgers, Oscar Hammerstein 2d, and Joshua Logan, South Pacific
1952—Joseph Kramm, The Shrike
1953—William Inge, Picnic
1954—John Patrick, Teahouse of the August Moon
1955—Tennessee Williams, Cat on a Hot Tin Roof
1956—Frances Goodrich and Albert Hackett, The Diary of Anne Frank
1957—Eugene O'Neill, Long Day's Journey Into Night
1958—Ketti Frings, Look Homeward, Angel
1959—Archibald MacLeish, J. B.
1960—George Abbott, Jerome Weidman, Sheldon Harnick, and Jerry Bock, Fiorello
1961—Tad Mosel, All the Way Home
1962—Frank Loesser and Abe Burrows, How to Succeed in Business Without Really Trying
1965—Frank D. Gilroy, The Subject Was Roses
1967—Edward Albee, A Delicate Balance
1969—Howard Sackler, The Great White Hope
1970—Charles Gordone, No Place to Be Somebody
1971—Paul Zindel, The Effect of Gamma Rays on Man-in-the-Moon Marigolds
1973—Jason Miller, That Championship Season
1975—Edward Albee, Seascape
1976—Michael Bennett, James Kirkwood, Nicholas Dante, Marvin Hamlisch, and Edward Kleban, A Chorus Line
1977—Michael Cristofer, The Shadow Box
1978—Donald L. Coburn, The Gin Game
1979—Sam Shepard, Buried Child
1980—Lanford Wilson, Talley's Folly
1981—Beth Henley, Crimes of the Heart
1982—Charles Fuller, A Soldier's Play
1983—Marsha Norman, 'night, Mother
1984—David Mamet, Glengarry Glen Ross
1985—Stephen Sondheim and James Lapine, Sunday in the Park With George
1987—August Wilson, Fences
1988—Alfred Uhry, Driving Miss Daisy
1989—Wendy Wasserstein, The Heidi Chronicles
1990—August Wilson, The Piano Lesson
1991—Neil Simon, Lost in Yonkers
1992—Robert Schenkkan, The Kentucky Cycle
1993—Tony Kushner, Angels in America: Millennium Approaches
1994—Edward Albee, Three Tall Women
1995—Horton Foote, The Young Man From Atlanta

History

For a book on the history of the United States.
1917—J. J. Jusserand, With Americans of Past and Present Days
1918—James Ford Rhodes, History of the Civil War
1920—Justin H. Smith, The War With Mexico
1921—William Sowden Sims, The Victory at Sea
1922—James Truslow Adams, The Founding of New England
1923—Charles Warren, The Supreme Court in United States History
1924—Charles Howard McIlwain, The American Revolution: A Constitutional Interpretation
1925—Frederick L. Paxton, A History of the American Frontier
1926—Edward Channing, A History of the U.S.
1927—Samuel Flagg Bemis, Pinckney's Treaty
1928—Vernon Louis Parrington, Main Currents in American Thought

1929—Fred A. Shannon, The Organization and Administration of the Union Army, 1861-65
1930—Claude H. Van Tyne, The War of Independence
1931—Bernadotte E. Schmitt, The Coming of the War, 1914
1932—Gen. John J. Pershing, My Experiences in the World War
1933—Frederick J. Turner, The Significance of Sections in American History
1934—Herbert Agar, The People's Choice
1935—Charles McLean Andrews, The Colonial Period of American History
1936—Andrew C. McLaughlin, The Constitutional History of the United States
1937—Van Wyck Brooks, The Flowering of New England
1938—Paul Herman Buck, The Road to Reunion, 1865-1900
1939—Frank Luther Mott, A History of American Magazines
1940—Carl Sandburg, Abraham Lincoln: The War Years
1941—Marcus Lee Hansen, The Atlantic Migration, 1607-1860
1942—Margaret Leech, Reveille in Washington
1943—Esther Forbes, Paul Revere and the World He Lived In
1944—Merle Curti, The Growth of American Thought
1945—Stephen Bonsal, Unfinished Business
1946—Arthur M. Schlesinger Jr., The Age of Jackson
1947—James Phinney Baxter 3d, Scientists Against Time
1948—Bernard De Voto, Across the Wide Missouri
1949—Roy F. Nichols, The Disruption of American Democracy
1950—O. W. Larkin, Art and Life in America
1951—R. Carlyle Buley, The Old Northwest: Pioneer Period 1815-1840
1952—Oscar Handlin, The Uprooted
1953—George Dangerfield, The Era of Good Feelings
1954—Bruce Catton, A Stillness at Appomattox
1955—Paul Horgan, Great River: The Rio Grande in North American History
1956—Richard Hofstadter, The Age of Reform
1957—George F. Kennan, Russia Leaves the War
1958—Bray Hammond, Banks and Politics in America—From the Revolution to the Civil War
1959—Leonard D. White and Jean Schneider, The Republican Era; 1869-1901
1960—Margaret Leech, In the Days of McKinley
1961—Herbert Feis, Between War and Peace: The Potsdam Conference
1962—Lawrence H. Gibson, The Triumphant Empire: Thunderclouds Gather in the West
1963—Constance McLaughlin Green, Washington: Village and Capital, 1800-1878
1964—Sumner Chilton Powell, Puritan Village: The Formation of a New England Town
1965—Irwin Unger, The Greenback Era
1966—Perry Miller, Life of the Mind in America
1967—William H. Goetzmann, Exploration and Empire: The Explorer and Scientist in the Winning of the American West
1968—Bernard Bailyn, The Ideological Origins of the American Revolution
1969—Leonard W. Levy, Origin of the Fifth Amendment
1970—Dean Acheson, Present at the Creation: My Years in the State Department
1971—James McGregor Burns, Roosevelt: The Soldier of Freedom
1972—Carl N. Degler, Neither Black nor White
1973—Michael Kammen, People of Paradox: An Inquiry Concerning the Origins of American Civilization
1974—Daniel J. Boorstin, The Americans: The Democratic Experience
1975—Dumas Malone, Jefferson and His Time
1976—Paul Horgan, Lamy of Santa Fe
1977—David M. Potter, The Impending Crisis
1978—Alfred D. Chandler Jr., The Visible Hand: The Managerial Revolution in American Business
1979—Don E. Fehrenbacher, The Dred Scott Case: Its Significance in American Law and Politics
1980—Leon F. Litwack, Been in the Storm So Long
1981—Lawrence A. Cremin, American Education: The National Experience, 1783-1876
1982—C. Vann Woodward, ed., Mary Chesnut's Civil War
1983—Rhys L. Issac, The Transformation of Virginia, 1740-1790
1985—Thomas K. McCraw, Prophets of Regulation
1986—Walter A. McDougall, … The Heavens and the Earth
1987—Bernard Bailyn, Voyagers to the West
1988—Robert V. Bruce, The Launching of Modern American Science 1846-1876
1989—Taylor Branch, Parting the Waters: America in the King Years, 1954-63; and James M. McPherson, Battle Cry of Freedom: The Civil War Era
1990—Stanley Karnow, In Our Image: America's Empire in the Philippines
1991—Laurel Thatcher Ulrich, A Midwife's Tale: The Life of Martha Ballard, based on her diary, 1785-1812
1992—Mark E. Neely Jr., The Fate of Liberty: Abraham Lincoln and Civil Liberties

1993—Gordon S. Wood, The Radicalism of the American Revolution
1995—Doris Kearns Goodwin, No Ordinary Time: Franklin and Eleanor Roosevelt: The Home Front in World War II

Biography or Autobiography

For a distinguished biography or autobiography by an American author.

1917—Laura E. Richards and Maude Howe Elliott, assisted by Florence Howe Hall, Julia Ward Howe
1918—William Cabell Bruce, Benjamin Franklin, Self-Revealed
1919—Henry Adams, The Education of Henry Adams
1920—Albert J. Beveridge, The Life of John Marshall
1921—Edward Bok, The Americanization of Edward Bok
1922—Hamlin Garland, A Daughter of the Middle Border
1923—Burton J. Hendrick, The Life and Letters of Walter H. Page
1924—Michael Pupin, From Immigrant to Inventor
1925—M. A. DeWolfe Howe, Barrett Wendell and His Letters
1926—Harvey Cushing, Life of Sir William Osler
1927—Emory Holloway, Whitman: An Interpretation in Narrative
1928—Charles Edward Russell, The American Orchestra and Theodore Thomas
1929—Burton J. Hendrick, The Training of an American: The Earlier Life and Letters of Walter H. Page
1930—Marquis James, The Raven (Sam Houston)
1931—Henry James, Charles W. Eliot
1932—Henry F. Pringle, Theodore Roosevelt
1933—Allan Nevins, Grover Cleveland
1934—Tyler Dennett, John Hay
1935—Douglas Southall Freeman, R. E. Lee
1936—Ralph Barton Perry, The Thought and Character of William James
1937—Allan Nevins, Hamilton Fish: The Inner History of the Grant Administration
1938—Divided between Odell Shepard, Pedlar's Progress; Marquis James, Andrew Jackson
1939—Carl Van Doren, Benjamin Franklin
1940—Ray Stannard Baker, Woodrow Wilson, Life and Letters
1941—Ola Elizabeth Winslow, Jonathan Edwards
1942—Forrest Wilson, Crusader in Crinoline
1943—Samuel Eliot Morison, Admiral of the Ocean Sea (Columbus)
1944—Carleton Mabee, The American Leonardo: The Life of Samuel F. B. Morse
1945—Russell Blaine Nye, George Bancroft; Brahmin Rebel.
1946—Linny Marsh Wolfe, Son of the Wilderness
1947—William Allen White, The Autobiography of William Allen White
1948—Margaret Clapp, Forgotten First Citizen: John Bigelow
1949—Robert E. Sherwood, Roosevelt and Hopkins
1950—Samuel Flag Bemis, John Quincy Adams and the Foundations of American Foreign Policy
1951—Margaret Louise Colt, John C. Calhoun: American Portrait
1952—Merlo J. Pusey, Charles Evans Hughes
1953—David J. Mays, Edmund Pendleton, 1721-1803
1954—Charles A. Lindbergh, The Spirit of St. Louis
1955—William S. White, The Taft Story
1956—Talbot F. Hamlin, Benjamin Henry Latrobe
1957—John F. Kennedy, Profiles in Courage
1958—Douglas Southall Freeman (decd. 1953), George Washington, Vols. I-VI; John Alexander Carroll and Mary Wells Ashworth, Vol. VII
1959—Arthur Walworth, Woodrow Wilson: American Prophet
1960—Samuel Eliot Morison, John Paul Jones
1961—David Donald, Charles Sumner and the Coming of the Civil War
1963—Leon Edel, Henry James: Vol. II, The Conquest of London, 1870-1881; Vol. III, The Middle Years, 1881-1895
1964—Walter Jackson Bate, John Keats
1965—Ernest Samuels, Henry Adams
1966—Arthur M. Schlesinger Jr., A Thousand Days
1967—Justin Kaplan, Mr. Clemens and Mark Twain
1968—George F. Kennan, Memoirs (1925-1950)
1969—B. L. Reid, The Man From New York: John Quinn and His Friends
1970—T. Harry Williams, Huey Long
1971—Lawrence Thompson, Robert Frost: The Years of Triumph, 1915-1938
1972—Joseph P. Lash, Eleanor and Franklin
1973—W. A. Swanberg, Luce and His Empire
1974—Louis Sheaffer, O'Neill, Son and Artist
1975—Robert A. Caro, The Power Broker: Robert Moses and the Fall of New York
1976—R.W.B. Lewis, Edith Wharton: A Biography
1977—John E. Mack, A Prince of Our Disorder: The Life of T.E. Lawrence
1978—Walter Jackson Bate, Samuel Johnson

(continued)

Biography or Autobiography *(continued)*

1979—Leonard Baker, Days of Sorrow and Pain: Leo Baeck and the Berlin Jews
1980—Edmund Morris, The Rise of Theodore Roosevelt
1981—Robert K. Massie, Peter the Great: His Life and World
1982—William S. McFeely, Grant: A Biography
1983—Russell Baker, Growing Up
1984—Louis R. Harlan, Booker T. Washington
1985—Kenneth Silverman, The Life and Times of Cotton Mather
1986—Elizabeth Frank, Louise Bogan: A Portrait
1987—David J. Garrow, Bearing the Cross: Martin Luther King Jr. and the Southern Christian Leadership Conference
1988—David Herbert Donald, Look Homeward: A Life of Thomas Wolfe
1989—Richard Ellmann, Oscar Wilde
1990—Sebastian de Grazia, Machiavelli in Hell
1991—Steven Naifeh and Gregory White Smith, Jackson Pollock: An American Saga
1992—Lewis B. Puller Jr., Fortunate Son: The Healing of a Vietnam Vet
1993—David McCullough, Truman
1994—David Levering Lewis, W.E.B. DuBois: Biography of a Race, 1868-1919
1995—Joan D. Hedrick, Harriet Beecher Stowe: A Life

American Poetry

Before this prize was established in 1922, awards were made from gifts provided by the Poetry Society: 1918—Love Songs, by Sara Teasdale. 1919—Old Road to Paradise, by Margaret Widemer; Corn Huskers, by Carl Sandburg.
1922—Edwin Arlington Robinson, Collected Poems
1923—Edna St. Vincent Millay, The Ballad of the Harp-Weaver; A Few Figs From Thistles; Eight Sonnets in American Poetry, 1922; A Miscellany
1924—Robert Frost, New Hampshire: A Poem With Notes and Grace Notes
1925—Edwin Arlington Robinson, The Man Who Died Twice
1926—Amy Lowell, What's O'Clock
1927—Leonora Speyer, Fiddler's Farewell
1928—Edwin Arlington Robinson, Tristram
1929—Stephen Vincent Benet, John Brown's Body
1930—Conrad Aiken, Selected Poems
1931—Robert Frost, Collected Poems
1932—George Dillon, The Flowering Stone
1933—Archibald MacLeish, Conquistador
1934—Robert Hillyer, Collected Verse
1935—Audrey Wurdemann, Bright Ambush
1936—Robert P. Tristram Coffin, Strange Holiness
1937—Robert Frost, A Further Range
1938—Marya Zaturenska, Cold Morning Sky
1939—John Gould Fletcher, Selected Poems
1940—Mark Van Doren, Collected Poems
1941—Leonard Bacon, Sunderland Capture
1942—William Rose Benet, The Dust Which Is God
1943—Robert Frost, A Witness Tree
1944—Stephen Vincent Benet, Western Star
1945—Karl Shapiro, V-Letter and Other Poems
1947—Robert Lowell, Lord Weary's Castle
1948—W. H. Auden, The Age of Anxiety
1949—Peter Viereck, Terror and Decorum
1950—Gwendolyn Brooks, Annie Allen
1951—Carl Sandburg, Complete Poems
1952—Marianne Moore, Collected Poems
1953—Archibald MacLeish, Collected Poems
1954—Theodore Roethke, The Waking
1955—Wallace Stevens, Collected Poems
1956—Elizabeth Bishop, Poems, North and South
1957—Richard Wilbur, Things of This World
1958—Robert Penn Warren, Promises: Poems 1954-1956
1959—Stanley Kunitz, Selected Poems 1928-1958
1960—W. D. Snodgrass, Heart's Needle
1961—Phyllis McGinley, Times Three: Selected Verse from Three Decades
1962—Alan Dugan, Poems
1963—William Carlos Williams, Pictures From Breughel
1964—Louis Simpson, At the End of the Open Road
1965—John Berryman, 77 Dream Songs

1966—Richard Eberhart, Selected Poems
1967—Anne Sexton, Live or Die
1968—Anthony Hecht, The Hard Hours
1969—George Oppen, Of Being Numerous
1970—Richard Howard, Untitled Subjects
1971—William S. Merwin, The Carrier of Ladders
1972—James Wright, Collected Poems
1973—Maxine Winokur Kumin, Up Country
1975—Gary Snyder, Turtle Island
1976—John Ashbery, Self-Portrait in a Convex Mirror
1977—James Merrill, Divine Comedies
1978—Howard Nemerov, Collected Poems
1979—Robert Penn Warren, Now and Then: Poems 1976-1978
1980—Donald Justice, Selected Poems
1981—James Schuyler, The Morning of the Poem
1982—Sylvia Plath, The Collected Poems
1983—Galway Kinnell, Selected Poems
1984—Mary Oliver, American Primitive
1985—Carolyn Kizer, Yin
1986—Henry Taylor, The Flying Change
1987—Rita Dove, Thomas and Beulah
1988—William Meredith, Partial Accounts: New and Selected Poems
1989—Richard Wilbur, New and Collected Poems
1990—Charles Simic, The World Doesn't End
1991—Mona Van Duyn, Near Changes
1992—James Tate, Selected Poems
1993—Louise Glück, The Wild Iris
1994—Yusef Komunyakaa, Neon Vernacular
1995—Philip Levine, The Simple Truth

General Nonfiction

1962—Theodore H. White, The Making of the President 1960
1963—Barbara W. Tuchman, The Guns of August
1964—Richard Hofstadter, Anti-Intellectualism in American Life
1965—Howard Mumford Jones, O Strange New World
1966—Edwin Way Teale, Wandering Through Winter
1967—David Brion Davis, The Problem of Slavery in Western Culture
1968—Will and Ariel Durant, Rousseau and Revolution
1969—Norman Mailer, The Armies of the Night; Rene Jules Dubos, So Human an Animal: How We Are Shaped by Surroundings and Events
1970—Eric H. Erikson, Gandhi's Truth
1971—John Toland, The Rising Sun
1972—Barbara W. Tuchman, Stilwell and the American Experience in China, 1911-1945
1973—Frances FitzGerald, Fire in the Lake: The Vietnamese and the Americans in Vietnam; Robert Coles, Children of Crisis, Volumes II & III
1974—Ernest Becker, The Denial of Death
1975—Annie Dillard, Pilgrim at Tinker Creek
1976—Robert N. Butler, Why Survive? Being Old in America
1977—William W. Warner, Beautiful Swimmers
1978—Carl Sagan, The Dragons of Eden
1979—Edward O. Wilson, On Human Nature
1980—Douglas R. Hofstadter, Gödel, Escher, Bach: An Eternal Golden Braid
1981—Carl E. Schorske, Fin-de-Siecle Vienna: Politics and Culture
1982—Tracy Kidder, The Soul of a New Machine
1983—Susan Sheehan, Is There No Place on Earth for Me?
1984—Paul Starr, Social Transformation of American Medicine
1985—Studs Terkel, The Good War
1986—Joseph Lelyveld, Move Your Shadow; J. Anthony Lukas, Common Ground
1987—David K. Shipler, Arab and Jew
1988—Richard Rhodes, The Making of the Atomic Bomb
1989—Neil Sheehan, A Bright Shining Lie: John Paul Vann and America in Vietnam
1990—Dale Maharidge and Michael Williamson, And Their Children After Them
1991—Bert Holldobler and Edward O. Wilson, The Ants
1992—Daniel Yergin, The Prize: The Epic Quest for Oil
1993—Garry Wills, Lincoln at Gettysburg
1994—David Remnick, Lenin's Tomb: The Last Days of the Soviet Empire
1995—Jonathan Weiner, The Beak of the Finch: A Story of Evolution in Our Time

Music

For composition by an American (before 1977, by a composer resident in the U.S.), in the larger forms of chamber, orchestra, or choral music or for an operatic work including ballet. A special posthumous award was granted in 1976 to Scott Joplin.

1943—William Schuman, Secular Cantata No. 2, A Free Song
1944—Howard Hanson, Symphony No. 4, Op. 34
1945—Aaron Copland, Appalachian Spring

1946—Leo Sowerby, The Canticle of the Sun
1947—Charles E. Ives, Symphony No. 3
1948—Walter Piston, Symphony No. 3
1949—Virgil Thomson, Louisiana Story
1950—Gian-Carlo Menotti, The Consul
1951—Douglas Moore, Giants in the Earth
1952—Gail Kubik, Symphony Concertante

1954—Quincy Porter, Concerto for Two Pianos and Orchestra
1955—Gian-Carlo Menotti, The Saint of Bleecker Street
1956—Ernest Toch, Symphony No. 3
1957—Norman Dello Joio, Meditations on Ecclesiastes
1958—Samuel Barber, Vanessa
1959—John La Montaine, Concerto for Piano and Orchestra
1960—Elliott Carter, Second String Quartet
1961—Walter Piston, Symphony No. 7
1962—Robert Ward, The Crucible
1963—Samuel Barber, Piano Concerto No. 1
1966—Leslie Bassett, Variations for Orchestra
1967—Leon Kirchner, Quartet No. 3
1968—George Crumb, Echoes of Time and The River
1969—Karel Husa, String Quartet No. 3
1970—Charles W. Wuorinen, Time's Encomium
1971—Mario Davidovsky, Synchronisms No. 6
1972—Jacob Druckman, Windows
1973—Elliott Carter, String Quartet No. 3
1974—Donald Martino, Notturno. (Special Citation) Roger Sessions
1975—Dominick Argento, From the Diary of Virginia Woolf
1976—Ned Rorem, Air Music

1977—Richard Wernick, Visions of Terror and Wonder
1978—Michael Colgrass, Deja Vu for Percussion and Orchestra
1979—Joseph Schwantner, Aftertones of Infinity
1980—David Del Tredici, In Memory of a Summer Day
1982—Roger Sessions, Concerto for Orchestra (Special Citation) Milton Babbitt
1983—Ellen T. Zwilich, Three Movements for Orchestra
1984—Bernard Rands, Canti del Sole
1985—Stephen Albert, Symphony, RiverRun
1986—George Perle, Wind Quintet IV
1987—John Harbison, The Flight Into Egypt
1988—William Bolcom, 12 New Etudes for Piano
1989—Roger Reynolds, Whispers Out of Time
1990—Mel Powell, Duplicates: A Concerto for Two Pianos and Orchestra
1991—Shulamit Ran, Symphony
1992—Wayne Peterson, The Face of the Night, The Heart of the Dark
1993—Christopher Rouse, Trombone Concerto
1994—Gunther Schuller, Of Reminiscences and Reflections
1995—Morton Gould, String Music

Miscellaneous Book Awards
Awarded in 1994 or 1995

Academy of American Poets Awards, Fellowship for Distinguished Poetic Achievement, $20,000: (1994) David Ferry, (1995) Denise Levertov; Lamont Poetry Selection, $1,000 and purchase of 2,000 copies of book: (1994) Brigit Pegeen Kelly, *Song;* Lavan Younger Poet Awards, $1,000 each: (1994) Peter Gizzi, Li-Young Lee, Cythina Zarin; Walt Whitman Award, $1,000 and the purchase of 3,000 copies of the book: (1995) Nicole Cooley, *Resurrection;* Landon Translation Award, $1,000: (1995) Robert Pinsky, *The Inferno of Dante: A New Verse Translation;* Lenore Marshall Poetry Prize, $10,000: (1994) W. S. Merwin; Tanning Prize: $100,000: (1994) W. S. Merwin, (1995) James Tate
American Academy of Arts and Letters, 1995 gold medal for fiction: William Maxwell; Howells medal, best novel 1990-95: John Updike, *Rabbit at Rest;* award of merit, $5,000: Larry Woiwode; academy awards in literature, $7,500: poets, Jane Cooper, Stephen Dunn, John Haines, Miller Williams; fiction, Louis Begley, R. V. Cassill, Josephine Humphreys; playwright, Horton Foote; Rosenthal Award, $5,000: Laura Hendrie, *Stygo;* Kaufman Prize, $2,500: Jim Grimsley, *Winter Birds;* E. M. Forster Award, $12,500: Colm Toibin
Bollingen Prize in American Poetry, awarded every two years, $25,000: Kenneth Koch
Booker Prize, British award for fiction, $32,000: James Kelman, *How Late It Was, How Late*
Curtis Benjamin Award, for creative publishing: James Laughlin, president and publisher of New Directions
Caldecott Medal, by American Library Assn., for most distinguished American picture book: David Diaz, illustrator, *Smoky Night* by Eve Bunting
Christopher Awards, by The Christophers, for expression of highest values of human spirit, bronze medallion each: Eva Fogelman, *Conscience & Courage: Rescuers of Jews During the Holocaust;* Joan D. Hedrick, *Harriet Beecher Stowe: A Life;* Paul F. Morrissey, *Let Someone Hold You: The Journey of a Hospice Priest;* Nelson Mandela, *Long Walk to Freedom, The Autobiography of Nelson Mandela;* David Hilfiker, M.D., *Not All of Us Are Saints: A Doctor's Journey With the Poor*
Golden Kite Awards, by Society of Children's Book Writiers and Illustrators: fiction: Karen Cushman, *Catherine, Called Birdy;* nonfiction: Russell Freedman, *Kids at Work: Lewis Hine and the Crusade Against Child Labor;* picture-illustration: Keith Baker, *Big Fat Hen*
Society of American Historians, Francis Parkman Prize: John Demos, *The Unredeemed Captive*
Ruth Lilly Poetry Prize, by *Poetry* magazine, $75,000: A. R. Ammons
Lincoln Prize, by Lincoln Soldiers Institute at Gettysburg College, for lifetime contribution to Civil War studies, $35,000 and a bronze bust of Lincoln: *The Presidency of Abraham Lincoln,* Phillip Shaw Paludan
National Book Awards, by National Book Foundation, $10,000 each: nonfiction: Sherwin B. Nuland, *How We Die: Reflections on Life's Final Chapter;* poetry: James Tate, *Worshipful Company of Fletchers;* fiction: William Gaddis, *A Frolic of His Own;* Medal for Distinguished Contribution to American Letters: Gwendolyn Brooks
National Book Critics Circle Awards, fiction: Carol Shields, *The Stone Diaries;* nonfiction: Lynn H. Nicholas, *The Rape of Europa: The Fate of Europe's Treasures in the Third Reich and the Second World War;* criticism: Gerald Early, *The Culture of Bruising: Essays on Prizefighting, Literature and Modern American Culture;* biography: Mikal Gilmore, *Shot in the Heart;* poetry: Mark Rudman, *Rider;* reviewing: JoAnn C. Gutin; lifetime *achievement:* William Maxwell
Newbery Award, by American Library Assn., for most distinguished contribution to American literature for children: Sharon Creech, *Walk Two Moons*
PEN/Faulkner Award, for fiction, $15,000: David Guterson, *Snow Falling on Cedars*
Edgar Allan Poe Awards, by the Mystery Writers of America: Grand Master award: Mickey Spillane; best mystery 1994: Mary Willis Walker, *The Red Scream*

Newbery Medal Books

The Newbery Medal is awarded annually by the Association for Library Service to Children, a division of the American Library Association, to the author of the most distinguished contribution to American literature for children.

Year Awarded	Book, Author	Year Awarded	Book, Author
1922	*The Story of Mankind,* Hendrik Willem van Loon	1939	*Thimble Summer,* Elizabeth Enright
1923	*The Voyages of Dr. Dolittle,* Hugh Lofting	1940	*Daniel Boone,* James Daugherty
1924	*The Dark Frigate,* Charles Boardman Hawes	1941	*Call It Courage,* Armstrong Sperry
1925	*Tales From Silver Lands,* Charles Joseph Finger	1942	*The Matchlock Gun,* Walter D. Edmonds
1926	*Shen of the Sea,* Arthur Bowie Chrisman	1943	*Adam of the Road,* Elizabeth Janet Gray
1927	*Smoky, the Cowhorse,* Will James	1944	*Johnny Tremain,* Esther Forbes
1928	*Gay-Neck,* Dhan Gopal Mukerji	1945	*Rabbit Hill,* Robert Lawson
1929	*The Trumpeter of Krakow,* Eric P. Kelly	1946	*Strawberry Girl,* Lois Lenski
1930	*Hitty, Her First Hundred Years,* Rachel Field	1947	*Miss Hickory,* Carolyn S. Bailey
1931	*The Cat Who Went to Heaven,* Elizabeth Coatsworth	1948	*Twenty-One Balloons,* William Pène Du Bois
1932	*Waterless Mountain,* Laura Adams Armer	1949	*King of the Wind,* Marguerite Henry
1933	*Young Fu of the Upper Yangtze,* Elizabeth Foreman Lewis	1950	*The Door in the Wall,* Marguerite de Angeli
		1951	*Amos Fortune, Free Man,* Elizabeth Yates
1934	*Invincible Louisa,* Cornelia Lynde Meigs	1952	*Ginger Pye,* Eleanor Estes
1935	*Dobry,* Monica Shannon	1953	*Secret of the Andes,* Ann Nolan Clark
1936	*Caddie Woodlawn,* Carol Ryrie Brink	1954	*. . . And Now Miguel,* Joseph Krumgold
1937	*Roller Skates,* Ruth Sawyer	1955	*The Wheel on the School,* Meindert DeJong
1938	*The White Stag,* Kate Seredy	1956	*Carry On, Mr. Bowditch,* Jean Lee Latham

(continued)

Newbery Medal Books *(continued)*

1957 *Miracles on Maple Hill,* Virginia Sorensen	1977 *Roll of Thunder, Hear My Cry,* Mildred D. Taylor
1958 *Rifles for Watie,* Harold Keith	1978 *Bridge to Terabithia,* Katherine Paterson
1959 *The Witch of Blackbird Pond,* Elizabeth George Speare	1979 *The Westing Game,* Ellen Raskin
1960 *Onion John,* Joseph Krumgold	1980 *A Gathering of Days,* Joan Blos
1961 *Island of the Blue Dolphins,* Scott O'Dell	1981 *Jacob Have I Loved,* Katherine Paterson
1962 *The Bronze Bow,* Elizabeth George Speare	1982 *A Visit to William Blake's Inn: Poems for Innocent and Experienced Travelers,* Nancy Willard
1963 *A Wrinkle in Time,* Madeleine L'Engle	
1964 *It's Like This, Cat,* Emily Cheney Neville	1983 *Dicey's Song,* Cynthia Voigt
1965 *Shadow of a Bull,* Maja Wojciechowska	1984 *Dear Mr. Henshaw,* Beverly Cleary
1966 *I, Juan de Pareja,* Elizabeth Borton de Trevino	1985 *The Hero and the Crown,* Robin McKinley
1967 *Up a Road Slowly,* Irene Hunt	1986 *Sarah, Plain and Tall,* Patricia MacLachlan
1968 *From the Mixed-Up Files of Mrs. Basil E. Frankweiler,* E. L. Konigsburg	1987 *The Whipping Boy,* Sid Fleischman
	1988 *Lincoln: A Photobiography,* Russell Freedman
1969 *The High King,* Lloyd Alexander	1989 *Joyful Noise: Poems for Two Voices,* Paul Fleischman
1970 *Sounder,* William H. Armstrong	1990 *Number the Stars,* Lois Lowry
1971 *The Summer of the Swans,* Betsy Byars	1991 *Maniac Magee,* Jerry Spinelli
1972 *Mrs. Frisby and the Rats of NIMH,* Robert C. O'Brien	1992 *Shiloh,* Phyllis Reynolds Naylor
1973 *Julie of the Wolves,* Jean George	1993 *Missing May,* Cynthia Rylant
1974 *The Slave Dancer,* Paula Fox	1994 *The Giver,* Lois Lowry
1975 *M. C. Higgins the Great,* Virginia Hamilton	1995 *Walk Two Moons,* Sharon Creech
1976 *Grey King,* Susan Cooper	

Journalism

National Journalism Awards, by Scripps Howard Foundation, for print journalism: service to literacy, $2,500 each: *Naples* (FL) *Daily News,* WDEF-TV, Chattanooga, TN; human interest writing, $2,500: Lisa Pollak, *The* (Raleigh, NC) *News & Observer;* editorial writing, $2,000: Jay Bookman, *The Atlanta Journal-Constitution;* environmental reporting, $2,000 each: Marla Cone, *Los Angeles Times,* Ken Ward, Jr., *The Charleston (WV) Gazette;* public service reporting, $2,500 each: *New York Newsday, The Virgin Island Daily News;* service to First Amendment, $2,500: *The State,* Columbia, SC; cartoonist, $2,000: Duk "Frank" Cho, Univ. of Maryland; excellence in broadcast journalism, $2,000 each: KTRK-TV, Houston, TX, WBRC-TV, Birmingham, AL, KGO-AM, San Francisco, CA, KGLT-FM, Bozeman, MT

National Magazine Awards, by American Society of Magazine Editors and Columbia Univ. Graduate School of Journalism: general excellence, circulation over 1 million: *Entertainment Weekly;* 400,000 to 1 million: *The New Yorker,* 100,000 to 400,000: *Men's Journal;* under 100,000: *I.D.;* single topic issue: *Discover* magazine; special interests: Alan Richman, *GQ;* feature writing: Tom Junod, *GQ;* fiction: *Story magazine;* design: *Martha Stewart Living;* photography: *Rolling Stone;* reporting: *The Atlantic Monthly;* personal service: *Smart Money;* public interest: *The New Republic;* essays and criticism: Lewis Lapham, *Harper's Magazine*

George Foster Peabody Awards, by the Univ. of Georgia, *Tobacco Stories,* National Public Radio, Washington, DC; *Schizophrenia: Voices of an Illness,* Litchtenstein Creative Media, N.Y., NY; *Wade in the Water: African American Sacred Music Traditions,* National Public Radio and the Smithsonian Inst., Washington, DC; *D-Day and 50 Years,* Cincinnati, OH; *The Rise and Fall of Vee-Jay,* WRKS-FM, N.Y., NY; *Fascinatn' Rhythm,* WXXI-FM, N.Y., NY; *Rush to Read,* ABC News PrimeTime Live, N.Y., NY; *CBS Reports: D-Day,* CBS News, N.Y., NY; *Rwanda,* KGO-TV, San Francisco, CA; *The Atomic Bombshell,* KSEE-TV, Fresno, CA; *Fat Chance,* National Film Board of Canada; *Sewer Solvent Scandal,*

KGAN-TV, Cedar Rapids, IA; *The Battle of the Bulge,* WGBH-TV, Boston, MA; *Just Because: Tales of Violence, Dreams of Peace,* KSBW-TV, Salinas, CA; *The Hunger Inside,* ABC News 20/20, N.Y., NY; *FDR,* WGBH-TV, Boston, MA; *Normandy: The Great Crusade,* Discovery Communications, Bethesda, MD; *China: Beyond the Clouds,* WETA-TV, Washington, DC; *Malcolm X: Make It Plain,* WGBH-TV, Boston, MA; *Buddy Check 12,* WTLV-TV, Jacksonville, FL; *Reflections on Elephants,* National Geographic Television, Washington, DC; *Fourways Farm,* Case TV, London, England; *Break the Silence: Kids Against Child Abuse,* CBS-TV, N.Y., NY; *Nick News,* Nickelodeon and Lucky Duck Productions, N.Y., NY; *ER,* NBC-TV; *Armistead Maupin's Tales of the City,* American Playhouse, KQED, San Francisco, CA; *Frasier,* NBC-TV; *MTV Unplugged,* MTV Network, N.Y., NY, *Mad About You,* NBC-TV; *Barbra Streisand The Concert,* J.E.G. Prod., HBO; *Moon Shot,* Turner Original Prod., Atlanta, GA

George Polk Awards, by Long Island Univ., for excellence in journalism: national: Joel Brinkley, Deborah Sontag, Stephen Engelberg, *New York Times;* metropolitan: David Armstrong, Shelley Murphy, Stephen Kurkjian, *Boston Globe;* local: Sonia Nazario, *Los Angeles Times;* foreign: Barbara Demick, *Philadelphia Inquirer;* political: Joe Stephens, *Kansas City Star;* education: Olive Talley, *Dallas Morning News;* medical: Joan Mazzolini, Dave Davis, *Cleveland Plain Dealer;* environmental: Jim Lynch, Karen Dorn Steele, *Spokesman Review;* magazine reporting: Allan Naim, *The Nation;* TV reporting: *Day One,* ABC; TV documentary: *Jihad in America,* PBS; career: Philip Hamburger, *The New Yorker*

Reuben Awards, by National Cartoonists Society: best cartoonist of 1994: Gary Larson; editorial cartoon: Jim Borgman; advertising illustration: Jerry Buckley; greeting cards: Roy Doty; comic books: Dan Jurgens; newspaper panels: Dave Coverly; gag cartoons: John Reiner; newspaper illustration: Jerry Dowling; animation: David Silverman; newspaper comic strip: Garry Trudeau; magazine and book illustration: Rick Geary

The Spingarn Medal

The Spingarn Medal has been awarded annually since 1914 by the National Association for the Advancement of Colored People for the highest achievement by a black American. The award is presented for accomplishments in the previous year.

1915	Ernest E. Just	1936	John Hope	1957	Martin Luther King Jr.	1976	Alvin Ailey
1916	Charles Young	1937	Walter White	1958	Mrs. Daisy Bates and the Little Rock Nine	1977	Alex Haley
1917	Harry T. Burleigh	1938	no award			1978	Andrew Young
1918	William S. Braithwaite	1939	Marian Anderson	1959	Edward Kennedy (Duke) Ellington	1979	Mrs. Rosa L. Parks
1919	Archibald H. Grimké	1940	Louis T. Wright			1980	Dr. Rayford W. Logan
1920	W. E. B. Du Bois	1941	Richard Wright	1960	Langston Hughes	1981	Coleman Young
1921	Charles S. Gilpin	1942	A. Philip Randolph	1961	Kenneth B. Clark	1982	Dr. Benjamin E. Mays
1922	Mary B. Talbert	1943	William H. Hastie	1962	Robert C. Weaver	1983	Lena Horne
1923	George W.Carver	1944	Charles Drew	1963	Medgar W. Evers	1984	Thomas Bradley
1924	Roland Hayes	1945	Paul Robeson	1964	Roy Wilkins	1985	Bill Cosby
1925	James W. Johnson	1946	Thurgood Marshall	1965	Leontyne Price	1986	Dr. Benjamin L. Hooks
1926	Carter G. Woodson	1947	Dr. Percy L. Julian	1966	John H. Johnson	1987	Percy E. Sutton
1927	Anthony Overton	1948	Channing H. Tobias	1967	Edward W. Brooke	1988	Frederick D. Patterson
1928	Charles W. Chesnutt	1949	Ralph J. Bunche	1968	Sammy Davis Jr.	1989	Jesse Jackson
1929	Mordecai W. Johnson	1950	Charles H. Houston	1969	Clarence M. Mitchell Jr.	1990	L. Douglas Wilder
1930	Henry A. Hunt	1951	Mabel K. Staupers	1970	Jacob Lawrence	1991	Gen. Colin L. Powell
1931	Richard B. Harrison	1952	Harry T. Moore	1971	Leon H. Sullivan	1992	Barbara Jordan
1932	Robert R. Moton	1953	Paul R. Williams	1972	Gordon Parks	1993	Dorothy I. Height
1933	Max Yergan	1954	Theodore K. Lawless	1973	Wilson C. Riles	1994	Maya Angelou
1934	William T. B. Williams	1955	Carl Murphy	1974	Damon Keith	1995	John Hope Franklin
1935	Mary McLeod Bethune	1956	Jack R. Robinson	1975	Henry (Hank) Aaron		

Miscellaneous Awards

American Institute of Architects Gold Medal, Cesar Pelli

Charles Frankel Prizes, by National Endowment for the Humanities, for those who have increased public awareness of the humanities, $5,000 each: Ernest L. Boyer, William Kittredge, Peggy Whitman Prenshaw, Sharon Percy Rockefeller, Dorothy Porter Wesley

National Inventor of the Year Awards, by Intellectual Property Owners, recognizing most outstanding inventors: Harold E. Aller, Adam C. Hsu

John F. Kennedy Center for the Performing Arts Awards, for contribution to U.S. cultural life: Pete Seeger, Aretha Franklin, Kirk Douglas, Harold Prince, Morton Gould.

Library of the Year Award, by Gale Research, Inc., and *Library Journal,* $10,000 grant: Public Library of Charlotte & Mecklenburg County, Charlotte, NC

National Medal of Arts, by White House, for outstanding contributions to cultural life in the U.S.: Harry Belafonte; Dave Brubeck; Celia Cruz; Dorothy DeLay; Julie Harris; Erick Hawkin;, Gen; Kelly; Pete Seeger; Catherine Filene Shouse; Wayne Thiebaud; Richard Wilbur; N.Y.C. nonprofit organization, Young Audiences

Pritzker Architecture Prize, by the Hyatt Foundation, $100,000: Tadeo Ando

1995 Teacher of the Year, by the Council of Chief State School Officers and Scholastic Inc.: Elaine Griffin

Templeton Prize for Progress in Religion, by Templeton Foundation, about $1 million: Paul Davies

Westinghouse Talent Search, 1st prize, $40,000 scholarship: Irene Ann Chen, La Jolla High School, San Diego, CA.

Miss America Winners

1921	Margaret Gorman, Washington, D.C.	1964	Donna Axum, El Dorado, Arkansas
1922-23	Mary Campbell, Columbus, Ohio	1965	Vonda Kay Van Dyke, Phoenix, Arizona
1924	Ruth Malcolmson, Philadelphia, Pennsylvania	1966	Deborah Irene Bryant, Overland Park, Kansas
1925	Fay Lamphier, Oakland, California	1967	Jane Anne Jayroe, Laverne, Oklahoma
1926	Norma Smallwood, Tulsa, Oklahoma	1968	Debra Dene Barnes, Moran, Kansas
1927	Lois Delander, Joliet, Illinois	1969	Judith Anne Ford, Belvidere, Illinois
1933	Marion Bergeron, West Haven, Connecticut	1970	Pamela Anne Eldred, Birmingham, Michigan
1935	Henrietta Leaver, Pittsburgh, Pennsylvania	1971	Phyllis Ann George, Denton, Texas
1936	Rose Coyle, Philadelphia, Pennsylvania	1972	Laurie Lea Schaefer, Columbus, Ohio
1937	Bette Cooper, Bertrand Island, New Jersey	1973	Terry Anne Meeuwsen, DePere, Wisconsin
1938	Marilyn Meseke, Marion, Ohio	1974	Rebecca Ann King, Denver, Colorado
1939	Patricia Donnelly, Detroit, Michigan	1975	Shirley Cothran, Fort Worth, Texas
1940	Frances Marie Burke, Philadelphia, Pennsylvania	1976	Tawney Elaine Godin, Yonkers, New York
1941	Rosemary LaPlanche, Los Angeles, California	1977	Dorothy Kathleen Benham, Edina, Minnesota
1942	Jo-Caroll Dennison, Tyler, Texas	1978	Susan Perkins, Columbus, Ohio
1943	Jean Bartel, Los Angeles, California	1979	Kylene Barker, Galax, Virginia
1944	Venus Ramey, Washington, D.C.	1980	Cheryl Prewitt, Ackerman, Mississippi
1945	Bess Myerson, New York City, New York	1981	Susan Powell, Elk City, Oklahoma
1946	Marilyn Buferd, Los Angeles, California	1982	Elizabeth Ward, Russellville, Arkansas
1947	Barbara Walker, Memphis, Tennessee	1983	Debra Maffett, Anaheim, California
1948	BeBe Shopp, Hopkins, Minnesota	1984	Vanessa Williams, Milwood, New York*
1949	Jacque Mercer, Litchfield, Arizona		Suzette Charles, Mays Landing, New Jersey
1951	Yolande Betbeze, Mobile, Alabama	1985	Sharlene Wells, Salt Lake City, Utah
1952	Coleen Kay Hutchins, Salt Lake City, Utah	1986	Susan Akin, Meridian, Mississippi
1953	Neva Jane Langley, Macon, Georgia	1987	Kellye Cash, Memphis, Tennessee
1954	Evelyn Margaret Ay, Ephrata, Pennsylvania	1988	Kaye Lani Rae Rafko, Monroe, Michigan
1955	Lee Meriwether, San Francisco, California	1989	Gretchen Carlson, Anoka, Minnesota
1956	Sharon Ritchie, Denver, Colorado	1990	Debbye Turner, Columbia, Missouri
1957	Marian McKnight, Manning, South Carolina	1991	Marjorie Vincent, Oak Park, Illinois
1958	Marilyn Van Derbur, Denver, Colorado	1992	Carolyn Suzanne Sapp, Honolulu, Hawaii
1959	Mary Ann Mobley, Brandon, Mississippi	1993	Leanza Cornett, Jacksonville, Florida
1960	Lynda Lee Mead, Natchez, Mississippi	1994	Kimberly Aiken, Columbia, South Carolina
1961	Nancy Fleming, Montague, Michigan	1995	Heather Whitestone, Birmingham, Alabama
1962	Maria Fletcher, Asheville, North Carolina	1996	Shawntel Smith, Muldrow, Oklahoma
1963	Jacquelyn Mayer, Sandusky, Ohio		

* Resigned July 23, 1984.

Entertainment Awards

1994-95 Emmy Awards

Prime-Time Emmy Awards

Drama series: *NYPD Blue,* ABC

Comedy series: *Frasier,* NBC

Miniseries: *Joseph,* TNT

Television movie: *Indictment: The McMartin Trial,* HBO

Variety, music, comedy special: *Barbra Streisand: The Concert,* HBO

Variety, music, comedy series: *The Tonight Show With Jay Leno,* NBC

Lead actor, drama series: Mandy Patinkin, *Chicago Hope,* CBS

Lead actress, drama series: Kathy Baker, *Picket Fences,* CBS

Lead actor, comedy series: Kelsey Grammer, *Frasier,* NBC

Lead actress, comedy series: Candice Bergen, *Murphy Brown,* CBS

Lead actor, miniseries/special: Raul Julia, *The Burning Season,* HBO

Lead actress, miniseries/special: Glenn Close, *Serving in Silence: The Margarethe Cammermeyer Story,* NBC

Supporting actor, drama series: Ray Walston, *Picket Fences,* CBS

Supporting actress, drama series: Julianna Margulies, *ER,* NBC

Supporting actor, comedy series: David Hyde Pierce, *Frasier,* NBC

Supporting actress, comedy series: Christine Baranski, *Cybill,* CBS

Supporting actor, miniseries/special: Donald Sutherland, *Citizen X,* HBO

Supporting actress, miniseries/special: (TIE) Judy Davis, *Serving in Silence: The Margarethe Cammermeyer Story,* NBC; Shirley Knight, *Indictment: The McMartin Trial,* HBO

Individual performance, variety/music program: Barbra Streisand, *Barbra Streisand: The Concert,* HBO

Directing, drama series: Mimi Leder, *ER: Love's Labor Lost,* NBC

Directing, comedy series: David Lee, *Frasier: The Matchmaker,* NBC

Directing, miniseries/special: John Frankenheimer, *The Burning Season,* HBO

Directing, variety/music program: Jeff Margolis, *The 67th Annual Academy Awards,* ABC

Writing, drama series: Lance Gentile, *ER: The Pilot,* NBC

Writing, comedy series: *Frasier: An Affair to Forget,* NBC

Writing, miniseries/special: Alison Cross, *Serving in Silence: The Margarethe Cammermeyer Story,* NBC

Writing, variety/music program: *Dennis Miller Live,* HBO

Daytime Emmy Awards

Drama series: *General Hospital*, ABC
Actress: Erika Slezak, *One Life to Live*, ABC
Actor: Justin Deas, *Guiding Light*, CBS
Supporting actress: Rena Sofer, *General Hospital*, ABC
Supporting actor: Jerry ver Dorn, *Guiding Light*, CBS
Directing team: *All My Children*, ABC
Writing team: *General Hospital*, ABC

Game/Audience participation show: *Jeopardy!*
Game show host: Bob Barker
Children's series: *Nick News*, Nickelodeon
Animated children's program: *Where on Earth Is Carmen San Diego?* FOX
Outstanding talk show: *The Oprah Winfrey Show*
Talk show host: Oprah Winfrey

1994-95 Tony (Antoinette Perry) Awards

Play: *Love! Valour! Compassion!*, by Terrence McNally
Musical: *Sunset Boulevard*
Actor, play: Ralph Fiennes, *Hamlet*
Actress, play: Cherry Jones, *The Heiress*
Actor, musical: Matthew Broderick, *How to Succeed in Business Without Really Trying*
Actress, musical: Glenn Close, *Sunset Boulevard*
Musical score: Andrew Lloyd Webber (music), Christopher Hampton, Don Black (lyrics), *Sunset Boulevard*
Director, play: Gerald Gutierrez, *The Heiress*
Director, musical: Harold Prince, *Show Boat*

Play revival: *The Heiress*
Musical revival: *Show Boat*
Featured actor, play: John Glover, *Love! Valour! Compassion!*
Featured actress, play: Frances Sternhagen, *The Heiress*
Featured actor, musical: George Hearn, *Sunset Boulevard*
Featured actress, musical: Gretha Boston, *Show Boat*
Choreography: Susan Stroman, *Show Boat*
Costume design: Florence Klotz, *Show Boat*
Scenic design: John Napier, *Sunset Boulevard*
Lighting design: Andrew Bridge, *Sunset Boulevard*
Lifetime achievement: Carol Channing, Harvey Sabinson

Academy Awards (Oscars)

1927-28
Picture: *Wings*, Paramount
Actor: Emil Jannings, *The Way of All Flesh*
Actress: Janet Gaynor, *Seventh Heaven*
Director: Frank Borzage, *Seventh Heaven*; Lewis Milestone, *Two Arabian Knights*
1928-29
Picture: *Broadway Melody*, MGM
Actor: Warner Baxter, *In Old Arizona*
Actress: Mary Pickford, *Coquette*
Director: Frank Lloyd, *The Divine Lady*
1929-30
Picture: *All Quiet on the Western Front*, University
Actor: George Arliss, *Disraeli*
Actress: Norma Shearer, *The Divorcee*
Director: Lewis Milestone, *All Quiet on the Western Front*
1930-31
Picture: *Cimarron*, RKO
Actor: Lionel Barrymore, *Free Soul*
Actress: Marie Dressler, *Min and Bill*
Director: Norman Taurog, *Skippy*
1931-32
Picture: *Grand Hotel*, MGM
Actor: Fredric March, *Dr. Jekyll and Mr. Hyde*; Wallace Beery, *The Champ* (tie)
Actress: Helen Hayes, *The Sin of Madelon Claudet*
Director: Frank Borzage, *Bad Girl*
Special: Walt Disney, *Mickey Mouse*
1932-33
Picture: *Cavalcade*, Fox
Actor: Charles Laughton, *The Private Life of Henry VIII*
Actress: Katharine Hepburn, *Morning Glory*
Director: Frank Lloyd, *Cavalcade*
1934
Picture: *It Happened One Night*, Columbia
Actor: Clark Gable, *It Happened One Night*
Actress: Claudette Colbert, *It Happened One Night*
Director: Frank Capra, *It Happened One Night*
1935
Picture: *Mutiny on the Bounty*, MGM
Actor: Victor McLaglen, *The Informer*
Actress: Bette Davis, *Dangerous*
Director: John Ford, *The Informer*
1936
Picture: *The Great Ziegfeld*, MGM
Actor: Paul Muni, *Story of Louis Pasteur*
Actress: Luise Rainer, *The Great Ziegfeld*
Sup. Actor: Walter Brennan, *Come and Get It*

Sup. Actress: Gale Sondergaard, *Anthony Adverse*
Director: Frank Capra, *Mr. Deeds Goes to Town*
1937
Picture: *Life of Emile Zola*, Warner
Actor: Spencer Tracy, *Captains Courageous*
Actress: Luise Rainer, *The Good Earth*
Sup. Actor: Joseph Schildkraut, *Life of Emile Zola*
Sup. Actress: Alice Brady, *In Old Chicago*
Director: Leo McCarey, *The Awful Truth*
1938
Picture: *You Can't Take It With You*, Columbia
Actor: Spencer Tracy, *Boys Town*
Actress: Bette Davis, *Jezebel*
Sup. Actor: Walter Brennan, *Kentucky*
Sup. Actress: Fay Bainter, *Jezebel*
Director: Frank Capra, *You Can't Take It With You*
1939
Picture: *Gone With the Wind*, Selznick International
Actor: Robert Donat, *Goodbye, Mr. Chips*
Actress: Vivien Leigh, *Gone With the Wind*
Sup. Actor: Thomas Mitchell, *Stage Coach*
Sup. Actress: Hattie McDaniel, *Gone With the Wind*
Director: Victor Fleming, *Gone With the Wind*
1940
Picture: *Rebecca*, Selznick International
Actor: James Stewart, *The Philadelphia Story*
Actress: Ginger Rogers, *Kitty Foyle*
Sup. Actor: Walter Brennan, *The Westerner*
Sup. Actress: Jane Darwell, *The Grapes of Wrath*
Director: John Ford, *The Grapes of Wrath*
1941
Picture: *How Green Was My Valley*, 20th Cent.-Fox
Actor: Gary Cooper, *Sergeant York*
Actress: Joan Fontaine, *Suspicion*
Sup. Actor: Donald Crisp, *How Green Was My Valley*
Sup. Actress: Mary Astor, *The Great Lie*
Director: John Ford, *How Green Was My Valley*
1942
Picture: *Mrs. Miniver*, MGM
Actor: James Cagney, *Yankee Doodle Dandy*
Actress: Greer Garson, *Mrs. Miniver*

Sup. Actor: Van Heflin, *Johnny Eager*
Sup. Actress: Teresa Wright, *Mrs. Miniver*
Director: William Wyler, *Mrs. Miniver*
1943
Picture: *Casablanca*, Warner
Actor: Paul Lukas, *Watch on the Rhine*
Actress: Jennifer Jones, *The Song of Bernadette*
Sup. Actor: Charles Coburn, *The More the Merrier*
Sup. Actress: Katina Paxinou, *For Whom the Bell Tolls*
Director: Michael Curtiz, *Casablanca*
1944
Picture: *Going My Way*, Paramount
Actor: Bing Crosby, *Going My Way*
Actress: Ingrid Bergman, *Gaslight*
Sup. Actor: Barry Fitzgerald, *Going My Way*
Sup. Actress: Ethel Barrymore, *None But the Lonely Heart*
Director: Leo McCarey, *Going My Way*
1945
Picture: *The Lost Weekend*, Paramount
Actor: Ray Milland, *The Lost Weekend*
Actress: Joan Crawford, *Mildred Pierce*
Sup. Actor: James Dunn, *A Tree Grows in Brooklyn*
Sup. Actress: Anne Revere, *National Velvet*
Director: Billy Wilder, *The Lost Weekend*
1946
Picture: *The Best Years of Our Lives*, Goldwyn, RKO
Actor: Fredric March, *The Best Years of Our Lives*
Actress: Olivia de Havilland, *To Each His Own*
Sup. Actor: Harold Russell, *The Best Years of Our Lives*
Sup. Actress: Anne Baxter, *The Razor's Edge*
Director: William Wyler, *The Best Years of Our Lives*
1947
Picture: *Gentleman's Agreement*, 20th Cent.-Fox
Actor: Ronald Colman, *A Double Life*
Actress: Loretta Young, *The Farmer's Daughter*
Sup. Actor: Edmund Gwenn, *Miracle on 34th Street*
Sup. Actress: Celeste Holm, *Gentleman's Agreement*
Director: Elia Kazan, *Gentleman's Agreement*
1948
Picture: *Hamlet*, Two Cities Film, Universal International
Actor: Laurence Olivier, *Hamlet*

Actress: Jane Wyman, *Johnny Belinda*
Sup. Actor: Walter Huston, *Treasure of Sierra Madre*
Sup. Actress: Claire Trevor, *Key Largo*
Director: John Huston, *Treasure of Sierra Madre*

1949
Picture: *All the King's Men,* Columbia
Actor: Broderick Crawford, *All the King's Men*
Actress: Olivia de Havilland, *The Heiress*
Sup. Actor: Dean Jagger, *Twelve O'Clock High*
Sup. Actress: Mercedes McCambridge, *All the King's Men*
Director: Joseph L. Mankiewicz, *Letter to Three Wives*

1950
Picture: *All About Eve,* 20th Century-Fox
Actor: Jose Ferrer, *Cyrano de Bergerac*
Actress: Judy Holliday, *Born Yesterday*
Sup. Actor: George Sanders, *All About Eve*
Sup. Actress: Josephine Hull, *Harvey*
Director: Joseph L. Mankiewicz, *All About Eve*

1951
Picture: *An American in Paris,* MGM
Actor: Humphrey Bogart, *The African Queen*
Actress: Vivien Leigh, *A Streetcar Named Desire*
Sup. Actor: Karl Malden, *A Streetcar Named Desire*
Sup. Actress: Kim Hunter, *A Streetcar Named Desire*
Director: George Stevens, *A Place in the Sun*

1952
Picture: *The Greatest Show on Earth,* C.B. DeMille, Paramount
Actor: Gary Cooper, *High Noon*
Actress: Shirley Booth, *Come Back, Little Sheba*
Sup. Actor: Anthony Quinn, *Viva Zapata!*
Sup. Actress: Gloria Grahame, *The Bad and the Beautiful*
Director: John Ford, *The Quiet Man*

1953
Picture: *From Here to Eternity,* Columbia
Actor: William Holden, *Stalag 17*
Actress: Audrey Hepburn, *Roman Holiday*
Sup. Actor: Frank Sinatra, *From Here to Eternity*
Sup. Actress: Donna Reed, *From Here to Eternity*
Director: Fred Zinnemann, *From Here to Eternity*

1954
Picture: *On the Waterfront,* Horizon-American, Columbia
Actor: Marlon Brando, *On the Waterfront*
Actress: Grace Kelly, *The Country Girl*
Sup. Actor: Edmond O'Brien, *The Barefoot Contessa*
Sup. Actress: Eva Marie Saint, *On the Waterfront*
Director: Elia Kazan, *On the Waterfront*

1955
Picture: *Marty,* Hecht and Lancaster's Steven Prods., U.A.
Actor: Ernest Borgnine, *Marty*
Actress: Anna Magnani, *The Rose Tattoo*
Sup. Actor: Jack Lemmon, *Mister Roberts*
Sup. Actress: Jo Van Fleet, *East of Eden*
Director: Delbert Mann, *Marty*

1956
Picture: *Around the World in 80 Days,* Michael Todd, U.A.
Actor: Yul Brynner, *The King and I*
Actress: Ingrid Bergman, *Anastasia*
Sup. Actor: Anthony Quinn, *Lust for Life*
Sup. Actress: Dorothy Malone, *Written on the Wind*
Director: George Stevens, *Giant*

1957
Picture: *The Bridge on the River Kwai,* Columbia
Actor: Alec Guinness, *The Bridge on the River Kwai*
Actress: Joanne Woodward, *The Three Faces of Eve*
Sup. Actor: Red Buttons, *Sayonara*
Sup. Actress: Miyoshi Umeki, *Sayonara*
Director: David Lean, *The Bridge on the River Kwai*

1958
Picture: *Gigi,* Arthur Freed Production, MGM
Actor: David Niven, *Separate Tables*
Actress: Susan Hayward, *I Want to Live*
Sup. Actor: Burl Ives, *The Big Country*
Sup. Actress: Wendy Hiller, *Separate Tables*
Director: Vincente Minnelli, *Gigi*

1959
Picture: *Ben-Hur,* MGM
Actor: Charlton Heston, *Ben-Hur*
Actress: Simone Signoret, *Room at the Top*
Sup. Actor: Hugh Griffith, *Ben-Hur*
Sup. Actress: Shelley Winters, *Diary of Anne Frank*
Director: William Wyler, *Ben-Hur*

1960
Picture: *The Apartment,* Mirisch Co., U.A.
Actor: Burt Lancaster, *Elmer Gantry*
Actress: Elizabeth Taylor, *Butterfield 8*
Sup. Actor: Peter Ustinov, *Spartacus*
Sup. Actress: Shirley Jones, *Elmer Gantry*
Director: Billy Wilder, *The Apartment*

1961
Picture: *West Side Story,* United Artists
Actor: Maximilian Schell, *Judgment at Nuremberg*
Actress: Sophia Loren, *Two Women*
Sup. Actor: George Chakiris, *West Side Story*
Sup. Actress: Rita Moreno, *West Side Story*
Director: Jerome Robbins, Robert Wise, *West Side Story*

1962
Picture: *Lawrence of Arabia,* Columbia
Actor: Gregory Peck, *To Kill a Mockingbird*
Actress: Anne Bancroft, *The Miracle Worker*
Sup. Actor: Ed Begley, *Sweet Bird of Youth*
Sup. Actress: Patty Duke, *The Miracle Worker*
Director: David Lean, *Lawrence of Arabia*

1963
Picture: *Tom Jones,* Woodfall Prod., U.A.-Lopert Pictures
Actor: Sidney Poitier, *Lilies of the Field*
Actress: Patricia Neal, *Hud*
Sup. Actor: Melvyn Douglas, *Hud*
Sup. Actress: Margaret Rutherford, *The V.I.P.s*
Director: Tony Richardson, *Tom Jones*

1964
Picture: *My Fair Lady,* Warner Bros.
Actor: Rex Harrison, *My Fair Lady*
Actress: Julie Andrews, *Mary Poppins*
Sup. Actor: Peter Ustinov, *Topkapi*
Sup. Actress: Lila Kedrova, *Zorba the Greek*
Director: George Cukor, *My Fair Lady*

1965
Picture: *The Sound of Music,* 20th Century-Fox
Actor: Lee Marvin, *Cat Ballou*
Actress: Julie Christie, *Darling*
Sup. Actor: Martin Balsam, *A Thousand Clowns*
Sup. Actress: Shelley Winters, *A Patch of Blue*
Director: Robert Wise, *The Sound of Music*

1966
Picture: *A Man for All Seasons,* Columbia
Actor: Paul Scofield, *A Man for All Seasons*
Actress: Elizabeth Taylor, *Who's Afraid of Virginia Woolf?*
Sup. Actor: Walter Matthau, *The Fortune Cookie*
Sup. Actress: Sandy Dennis, *Who's Afraid of Virginia Woolf?*
Director: Fred Zinnemann, *A Man for All Seasons*

1967
Picture: *In the Heat of the Night*
Actor: Rod Steiger, *In the Heat of the Night*
Actress: Katharine Hepburn, *Guess Who's Coming to Dinner*
Sup. Actor: George Kennedy, *Cool Hand Luke*
Sup. Actress: Estelle Parsons, *Bonnie and Clyde*
Director: Mike Nichols, *The Graduate*

1968
Picture: *Oliver!*
Actor: Cliff Robertson, *Charly*
Actress: Katharine Hepburn, *The Lion in Winter;* Barbra Streisand, *Funny Girl* (tie)
Sup. Actor: Jack Albertson, *The Subject Was Roses*
Sup. Actress: Ruth Gordon, *Rosemary's Baby*
Director: Sir Carol Reed, *Oliver!*

1969
Picture: *Midnight Cowboy*
Actor: John Wayne, *True Grit*
Actress: Maggie Smith, *The Prime of Miss Jean Brodie*
Sup. Actor: Gig Young, *They Shoot Horses, Don't They?*
Sup. Actress: Goldie Hawn, *Cactus Flower*
Director: John Schlesinger, *Midnight Cowboy*

1970
Picture: *Patton*
Actor: George C. Scott, *Patton* (refused)
Actress: Glenda Jackson, *Women in Love*
Sup. Actor: John Mills, *Ryan's Daughter*
Sup. Actress: Helen Hayes, *Airport*
Director: Franklin Schaffner, *Patton*

1971
Picture: *The French Connection*
Actor: Gene Hackman, *The French Connection*
Actress: Jane Fonda, *Klute*
Sup. Actor: Ben Johnson, *The Last Picture Show*
Sup. Actress: Cloris Leachman, *The Last Picture Show*
Director: William Friedkin, *The French Connection*

1972
Picture: *The Godfather*
Actor: Marlon Brando, *The Godfather* (refused)
Actress: Liza Minnelli, *Cabaret*
Sup. Actor: Joel Grey, *Cabaret*
Sup. Actress: Eileen Heckart, *Butterflies Are Free*
Director: Bob Fosse, *Cabaret*

1973
Picture: *The Sting*
Actor: Jack Lemmon, *Save the Tiger*
Actress: Glenda Jackson, *A Touch of Class*
Sup. Actor: John Houseman, *The Paper Chase*
Sup. Actress: Tatum O'Neal, *Paper Moon*
Director: George Roy Hill, *The Sting*

1974
Picture: *The Godfather, Part II*
Actor: Art Carney, *Harry and Tonto*
Actress: Ellen Burstyn, *Alice Doesn't Live Here Anymore*

(continued)

Academy Awards *(continued)*

Sup. Actor: Robert DeNiro, *The Godfather, Part II*
Sup. Actress: Ingrid Bergman, *Murder on the Orient Express*
Director: Francis Ford Coppola, *The Godfather, Part II*

1975
Picture: *One Flew Over the Cuckoo's Nest*
Actor: Jack Nicholson, *One Flew Over the Cuckoo's Nest*
Actress: Louise Fletcher, *One Flew Over the Cuckoo's Nest*
Sup. Actor: George Burns, *The Sunshine Boys*
Sup. Actress: Lee Grant, *Shampoo*
Director: Milos Forman, *One Flew Over the Cuckoo's Nest*

1976
Picture: *Rocky*
Actor: Peter Finch, *Network*
Actress: Faye Dunaway, *Network*
Sup. Actor: Jason Robards, *All the President's Men*
Sup. Actress: Beatrice Straight, *Network*
Director: John G. Avildsen, *Rocky*

1977
Picture: *Annie Hall*
Actor: Richard Dreyfuss, *The Goodbye Girl*
Actress: Diane Keaton, *Annie Hall*
Sup. Actor: Jason Robards, *Julia*
Sup. Actress: Vanessa Redgrave, *Julia*
Director: Woody Allen, *Annie Hall*

1978
Picture: *The Deer Hunter*
Actor: Jon Voight, *Coming Home*
Actress: Jane Fonda, *Coming Home*
Sup. Actor: Christopher Walken, *The Deer Hunter*
Sup. Actress: Maggie Smith, *California Suite*
Director: Michael Cimino, *The Deer Hunter*

1979
Picture: *Kramer vs. Kramer*
Actor: Dustin Hoffman, *Kramer vs. Kramer*
Actress: Sally Field, *Norma Rae*
Sup. Actor: Melvyn Douglas, *Being There*
Sup. Actress: Meryl Streep, *Kramer vs. Kramer*
Director: Robert Benton, *Kramer vs. Kramer*

1980
Picture: *Ordinary People*
Actor: Robert DeNiro, *Raging Bull*
Actress: Sissy Spacek, *Coal Miner's Daughter*
Sup. Actor: Timothy Hutton, *Ordinary People*
Sup. Actress: Mary Steenburgen, *Melvin & Howard*
Director: Robert Redford, *Ordinary People*

1981
Picture: *Chariots of Fire*
Actor: Henry Fonda, *On Golden Pond*
Actress: Katharine Hepburn, *On Golden Pond*
Sup. Actor: John Gielgud, *Arthur*
Sup. Actress: Maureen Stapleton, *R*

1982
Picture: *Gandhi*
Actor: Ben Kingsley, *Gandhi*
Actress: Meryl Streep, *Sophie's Choice*
Sup. Actor: Louis Gossett, Jr., *An Officer and a Gentleman*
Sup. Actress: Jessica Lange, *Tootsie*
Director: Richard Attenborough, *Gandhi*

1983
Picture: *Terms of Endearment*
Actor: Robert Duvall, *Tender Mercies*
Actress: Shirley MacLaine, *Terms of Endearment*
Sup. Actor: Jack Nicholson, *Terms of Endearment*
Sup. Actress: Linda Hunt, *The Year of Living Dangerously*
Director: James L. Brooks, *Terms of Endearment*

1984
Picture: *Amadeus*
Actor: F. Murray Abraham, *Amadeus*
Actress: Sally Field, *Places in the Heart*
Sup. Actor: Haing S. Ngor, *The Killing Fields*
Sup. Actress: Peggy Ashcroft, *A Passage to India*
Director: Milos Forman, *Amadeus*

1985
Picture: *Out of Africa*
Actor: William Hurt, *Kiss of the Spider Woman*
Actress: Geraldine Page, *The Trip to Bountiful*
Sup. Actor: Don Ameche, *Cocoon*
Sup. Actress: Anjelica Huston, *Prizzi's Honor*
Director: Sydney Pollack, *Out of Africaeds*
Director: Warren Beatty, *Reds*

1986
Picture: *Platoon*
Actor: Paul Newman, *The Color of Money*
Actress: Marlee Matlin, *Children of a Lesser God*
Sup. Actor: Michael Caine, *Hannah and Her Sisters*
Sup. Actress: Dianne Wiest, *Hannah and Her Sisters*
Director: Oliver Stone, *Platoon*

1987
Picture: *The Last Emperor*
Actor: Michael Douglas, *Wall Street*
Actress: Cher, *Moonstruck*
Sup. Actor: Sean Connery, *The Untouchables*
Sup. Actress: Olympia Dukakis, *Moonstruck*
Director: Bernardo Bertolucci, *The Last Emperor*

1988
Picture: *Rain Man*
Actor: Dustin Hoffman, *Rain Man*
Actress: Jodie Foster, *The Accused*
Sup. Actor: Kevin Kline, *A Fish Called Wanda*
Sup. Actress: Geena Davis, *The Accidental Tourist*
Director: Barry Levinson, *Rain Man*

1989
Picture: *Driving Miss Daisy*
Actor: Daniel Day-Lewis, *My Left Foot*
Actress: Jessica Tandy, *Driving Miss Daisy*
Sup. Actor: Denzel Washington, *Glory*
Sup. Actress: Brenda Fricker, *My Left Foot*
Director: Oliver Stone, *Born on the Fourth of July*

1990
Picture: *Dances With Wolves*
Actor: Jeremy Irons, *Reversal of Fortune*
Actress: Kathy Bates, *Misery*
Sup. Actor: Joe Pesci, *Goodfellas*
Sup. Actress: Whoopi Goldberg, *Ghost*
Director: Kevin Costner, *Dances With Wolves*

1991
Picture: *The Silence of the Lambs*
Actor: Anthony Hopkins, *The Silence of the Lambs*
Actress: Jodie Foster, *The Silence of the Lambs*
Sup. Actor: Jack Palance, *City Slickers*
Sup. Actress: Mercedes Ruehl, *The Fisher King*
Director: Jonathan Demme, *The Silence of the Lambs*

1992
Picture: *Unforgiven*
Actor: Al Pacino, *Scent of a Woman*
Actress: Emma Thompson, *Howards End*
Sup. Actor: Gene Hackman, *Unforgiven*
Sup. Actress: Marisa Tomei, *My Cousin Vinny*
Director: Clint Eastwood, *Unforgiven*

1993
Picture: *Schindler's List*
Actor: Tom Hanks, *Philadelphia*
Actress: Holly Hunter, *The Piano*
Sup. Actor: Tommy Lee Jones, *The Fugitive*
Sup. Actress: Anna Paquin, *The Piano*
Director: Steven Spielberg, *Schindler's List*

1994
Picture: *Forrest Gump*
Actor: Tom Hanks, *Forrest Gump*
Actress: Jessica Lange, *Blue Sky*
Sup. Actor: Martin Landau, *Ed Wood*
Sup. Actress: Dianne Weist, *Bullets Over Broadway*
Director: Robert Zemeckis, *Forrest Gump*
Foreign Film: *Burnt by the Sun*, Russia
Original Screenplay: Quentin Tarantino, Roger Avery, *Pulp Fiction*
Adapted Screenplay: Eric Roth, *Forrest Gump*
Cinematography: John Toll, *Legends of the Fall*
Art Direction: Ken Adams, Carolyn Scott, *The Madness of King George*
Editing: Arthur Schmidt, *Forrest Gump*
Original Song: "Can You Feel the Love Tonight," from *The Lion King*, Elton John and Tim Rice
Costume: Lizzy Gardiner, Tim Chappel, *The Adventures of Priscilla, Queen of the Desert*
Makeup: Rick Baker, Ve Neill, Yolanda Toussieng, *Ed Wood*
Documentary Short Subject: Charles Guggenheim, *A Time for Justice*
Visual Effects: Ken Ralson, George Murphy, Stephen Rosenbaum, Allen Hall, *Forrest Gump*
Sound: Gregg Landaker, Steve Maslow, Bob Beemer, David R. B. MacMillan, *Speed*.
Documentary Feature: Freida Lee Mock, Terrry Sanders, *Maya Lin: A Strong Clear Vision*
Short Film, Live: (Tie) Peter Capaldi, Ruth Kenley-Letts, *Franz Kafka's It's a Wonderful Life*; Peggy Rajski, Randy Stone, *Trevor*
Short Film, Animated: Alison Snowden, David Fine, *Bob's Birthday*
Honorary Award: Michelangelo Antonioni
Jean Hersholt Humanitarian Award: Quincy Jones
Irving G. Thalberg Memorial Award: Clint Eastwood
Technical Award of Merit: Eastman Kodak Co.; Petro and Paul Vlahos

Grammy Awards, 1958-93

Source: National Academy of Recording Arts & Sciences

(The first Grammys were awarded for records released in 1958.)

Record	Year	Album
Domenico Modugno, Nel Blu Dipinto Di Blu (Volare)	1958	Henry Mancini, The Music From Peter Gunn
Bobby Darin, Mack the Knife	1959	Frank Sinatra, Come Dance With Me
Percy Faith, Theme From a Summer Place	1960	Bob Newhart, Button Down Mind
Henry Mancini, Moon River	1961	Judy Garland, Judy at Carnegie Hall
Tony Bennett, I Left My Heart in San Francisco	1962	Vaughn Meader, The First Family
Henry Mancini, The Days of Wine and Roses	1963	The Barbra Streisand Album
Stan Getz, Astrud Gilberto, The Girl From Ipanema	1964	Stan Getz, Astrud Gilberto, Getz/Gilberto
Herb Alpert, A Taste of Honey	1965	Frank Sinatra, September of My Years
Frank Sinatra, Strangers in the Night	1966	Frank Sinatra, A Man and His Music
5th Dimension, Up, Up and Away	1967	The Beatles, Sgt. Pepper's Lonely Hearts Club Band
Simon & Garfunkel, Mrs. Robinson	1968	Glen Campbell, By the Time I Get to Phoenix
5th Dimension, Aquarius/Let the Sunshine In	1969	Blood, Sweat and Tears
Simon & Garfunkel, Bridge Over Troubled Water	1970	Simon & Garfunkel, Bridge Over Troubled Water
Carole King, It's Too Late	1971	Carole King, Tapestry
Roberta Flack, The First Time Ever I Saw Your Face	1972	The Concert for Bangla Desh
Roberta Flack, Killing Me Softly With His Song	1973	Stevie Wonder, Innervisions
Olivia Newton-John, I Honestly Love You	1974	Stevie Wonder, Fulfillingness' First Finale
Captain & Tennille, Love Will Keep Us Together	1975	Paul Simon, Still Crazy After All These Years
George Benson, This Masquerade	1976	Stevie Wonder, Songs in the Key of Life
Eagles, Hotel California	1977	Fleetwood Mac, Rumours
Billy Joel, Just the Way You Are	1978	Bee Gees, Saturday Night Fever
The Doobie Brothers, What a Fool Believes	1979	Billy Joel, 52nd Street
Christopher Cross, Sailing	1980	Christopher Cross, Christopher Cross
Kim Carnes, Bette Davis Eyes	1981	John Lennon, Yoko Ono, Double Fantasy
Toto, Rosanna	1982	Toto, Toto IV
Michael Jackson, Beat It	1983	Michael Jackson, Thriller
Tina Turner, What's Love Got to Do With It	1984	Lionel Richie, Can't Slow Down
USA for Africa, We Are the World	1985	Phil Collins, No Jacket Required
Steve Winwood, Higher Love	1986	Paul Simon, Graceland
Paul Simon, Graceland	1987	U2, The Joshua Tree
Bobby McFerrin, Don't Worry, Be Happy	1988	George Michael, Faith
Bette Midler, Wind Beneath My Wings	1989	Bonnie Raitt, Nick of Time
Phil Collins, Another Day in Paradise	1990	Quincy Jones, Back on the Block
Natalie Cole, with Nat "King" Cole, Unforgettable	1991	Natalie Cole, with Nat "King" Cole, Unforgettable
Eric Clapton, Tears in Heaven	1992	Eric Clapton, Unplugged
Whitney Houston, I Will Always Love You	1993	Whitney Houston, The Bodyguard

Selected 1994 Grammy Awards

(awarded in March 1995 for 1994 releases)

Record: "All I Wanna Do," Sheryl Crow
Album: *MTV Unplugged*, Tony Bennett
Song: "Streets of Philadelphia," Bruce Springsteen
New artist: Sheryl Crow
Female pop vocalist: Sheryl Crow, "All I Wanna Do"
Male pop vocalist: Elton John, "Can You Feel the Love Tonight"
Traditional pop vocalist: Tony Bennett, *MTV Unplugged*
Pop album: *Longing in Their Hearts*, Bonnie Raitt
Rock vocalist, female: Melissa Etheridge, "Come to My Window"
Rock vocalist, male: Bruce Springsteen, "Streets of Philadelphia"
Rock song: "Streets of Philadelphia," Bruce Springsteen
Rock album: *Voodoo Lounge*, Rolling Stones

R & B song: "I'll Make Love to You," Babyface
R & B album: *II*, Boyz II Men
Rap solo: Queen Latifah, "U.N.I.T.Y."
Rap duo or group: Salt-N-Pepa, "None of Your Business"
Jazz vocalist: Etta James, "Mystery Lady"
Traditional blues album: *From the Cradle*, Eric Clapton
Country vocalist, female: Mary Chapin Carpenter, "Shut up and Kiss Me"
Country vocalist, male: Vince Gill, "When Love Finds You"
Country song: "I Swear," Gary Baker, Frank J. Myers
Classical album: *Bartok: Concerto for Orchestra*, Pierre Boulez and the Chicago Symphony Orchestra

Other Entertainment Awards

Christopher Awards, by The Christophers: movies: *Forrest Gump, Little Women*; television: *Break the Silence: Kids Against Child Abuse; CBS Schoolbreak Special: The Writing on the Wall; Christy; One More Mountain; Place For Annie; The Vernon Johns Story*

Directors Guild of America Awards, movie director: Robert Zemeckis, *Forrest Gump*; documentary: Steve James, *Hoop Dreams*

Golden Globe Awards, movies: drama: *Forrest Gump*; musical/comedy: *The Lion King*; actress, drama: Jessica Lange, *Blue Sky*; actor, drama: Tom Hanks, *Forrest Gump*; actress, musical/comedy: Jamie Lee Curtis, *True Lies*; actor, musical/comedy: Hugh Grant, *Four Weddings and a Funeral*; supporting actress, drama: Dianne Wiest, *Bullets Over Broadway*; supporting actor, drama: Martin Landau, *Ed Wood*; director: Robert Zemeckis, *Forrest Gump*; screenplay: Quentin Tarantino, Roger Avary, *Pulp Fiction*; television: series: *X-Files*; actress, drama: Claire Danes, *My So-Called Life*; actor, drama: Dennis Franz, *NYPD Blue*; series, musical/comedy: *Frasier, Mad About You* (tie); actress, musical/comedy: Helen Hunt,

Mad About You; actor, musical/comedy: Tim Allen, *Home Improvement*; miniseries, movie made for TV: *The Burning Season*

Los Angeles Film Critics Awards, film: *Pulp Fiction*; director: Quentin Tarantino, *Pulp Fiction*; actor: John Travolta, *Pulp Fiction*; actress: Jessica Lange, *Blue Sky*

National Society of Film Critics Awards, film: *Pulp Fiction*; actor: Paul Newman, *Nobody's Fool*; actress: Jennifer Jason Leigh, *Mrs. Parker and the Vicious Circle*; director: Quentin Tarantino, *Pulp Fiction*; supporting actor: Martin Landau, *Ed Wood*; supporting actress: Dianne Weist, *Bullets Over Broadway*; cinematography: Stefan Czapsky, *Ed Wood*; screen writer: Quentin Tarantino, Roger Avary, *Pulp Fiction*; foreign language film: *Red*; documentary: *Hoop Dreams*

New York Film Critics Awards, film: *Quiz Show*; director: Quentin Tarantino, *Pulp Fiction*; actor: Paul Newman, *Nobody's Fool*; actress: Linda Florentino, *The Last Seduction*

Rock-and-Roll Hall of Fame, 1995 inductees: the Allman Brothers Band, Al Green, Janis Joplin, Led Zeppelin, Martha and the Vandellas, Neil Young, Frank Zappa

NOTED PERSONALITIES

Widely Known Americans of the Present

Government and political leaders, journalists, authors of nonfiction, and other widely
known persons who may not be listed in other categories.

(as of mid-1995)

Name (Birthplace)	Birthdate	Name (Birthplace)	Birthdate
Adler, Mortimer (New York, NY)	12/2/02	Dukakis, Michael S. (Boston, MA)	11/3/33
Ailes, Roger (Knoxville, TN)	7/3/40	Edelman, Marian Wright (Bennettsville, SC)	6/6/39
Albright, Madeleine (Prague, Czech.)	5/15/37	Eisner, Michael (New York, NY)	3/7/42
Alexander, Lamar (Knoxville, TN)	7/3/40	Ephron, Nora (New York, NY)	5/19/41
Ambrose, Stephen E. (Decatur, IL)	1/10/36	Evers-Williams, Myrlie (Vicksburg, MS)	3/17/33
Anderson, Jack (Long Beach, CA)	10/19/22	Falwell, Jerry (Lynchburg, VA)	8/11/33
Annenberg, Walter H. (Milwaukee, WI)	3/13/08	Feinstein, Dianne (San Francisco, CA)	6/22/33
Arledge, Roone (Forest Hills, NY)	7/8/31	Foote, Shelby (Greenville, MS)	11/17/16
Armey, Richard K. (Cando, ND)	7/7/40	Ford, Betty (Chicago, IL)	4/8/18
Armstrong, Neil (Wapakoneta, OH)	8/5/30	Ford, Gerald R. (Omaha, NE)	7/14/13
Babbitt, Bruce (Los Angeles, CA)	6/27/38	Friedan, Betty (Peoria, IL)	2/4/21
Bailey, F. Lee (Waltham, MA)	6/10/33	Friedman, Milton (Brooklyn, NY)	7/31/12
Baker, Russell (Loudoun Co., VA)	8/14/25	Galbraith, John Kenneth (Iona Station, Ontario)	10/15/08
Barry, Dave (Armonk, NY)	7/3/47	Gates, Bill (Seattle, WA)	10/28/55
Barry, Marion (Itta Bena, MS)	3/6/36	Gates, Henry Louis, Jr. (Keyser, WV)	9/16/50
Barthelmy, Sidney K. (New Orleans, LA)	3/17/42	Geffen, David (Brooklyn, NY)	2/21/43
Bennett, William J. (Brooklyn, NY)	7/31/43	Gephardt, Richard (St. Louis, MO)	1/31/41
Bentsen, Lloyd (Mission, TX)	2/11/21	Gergen, David R. (Durham, NC)	5/9/42
Biden, Joseph R., Jr. (Scranton, PA)	11/20/42	Gibson, Charles (Evanston, IL)	3/9/43
Blackmun, Harry (Nashville, IL)	11/12/08	Gingrich, Newt (Harrisburg, PA)	6/17/43
Bombeck, Erma (Dayton, OH)	2/21/27	Ginsberg, Allen (Paterson, NJ)	6/3/21
Bonior, David (Detroit, MI)	6/6/45	Ginsburg, Ruth Bader (Brooklyn, NY)	3/15/33
Boorstin, Daniel (Atlanta, GA)	10/1/14	Giuliani, Rudolph (New York, NY)	5/28/44
Boxer, Barbara (Brooklyn, NY)	11/11/40	Glenn, John (Cambridge, OH)	7/18/21
Bradlee, Ben (Boston, MA)	8/26/21	Goldwater, Barry M. (Phoenix, AZ)	1/1/09
Bradley, Bill (Crystal City, MO)	7/28/43	Goodman, Ellen (Newton, MA)	4/11/41
Bradley, Ed (Philadelphia, PA)	6/22/41	Gore, Al (Washington, DC)	3/31/48
Brennan, William J., Jr. (Newark, NJ)	4/25/06	Gore, Tipper (Washington, DC)	8/19/48
Breslin, Jimmy (Jamaica, NY)	10/17/30	Gottlieb, Robert A. (New York, NY)	4/29/31
Breyer, Stephen (San Francisco, CA)	8/15/38	Gould, Stephen Jay (New York, NY)	9/10/41
Brinkley, David (Wilmington, NC)	7/10/20	Graham, Billy (Charlotte, NC)	11/7/18
Brody, Jane (Brooklyn, NY)	5/19/41	Graham, Katharine (New York, NY)	6/16/17
Broder, David (Chicago Heights, IL)	9/11/29	Gramm, Phil (Ft. Benning, GA)	7/8/42
Brokaw, Tom (Webster, SD)	2/6/40	Greenfield, Meg (Seattle, WA)	12/27/30
Brothers, Joyce (New York, NY)	9/20/28	Greenspan, Alan (New York, NY)	3/6/26
Brown, Helen Gurley (Green Forest, AR)	2/18/22	Gumbel, Bryant (New Orleans, LA)	9/29/48
Brown, Jerry (San Francisco, CA)	4/7/38	Halberstam, David (New York, NY)	4/10/34
Brown, Ron (Washington, DC)	8/1/41	Harvey, Paul (Tulsa, OK)	9/4/18
Buchanan, Pat (Washington, DC)	11/2/38	Hatch, Orrin (Homestead Park, PA)	3/22/34
Buchwald, Art (Mt. Vernon, NY)	10/20/25	Heflin, Howell (Poulan, GA)	6/19/21
Buckley, William F. (New York, NY)	11/24/25	Helms, Jesse (Monroe, NC)	10/18/21
Buffett, Warren (Omaha, NE)	8/30/30	Helmsley, Leona (New York, NY)	c1920
Buscaglia, Leo (Los Angeles, CA)	3/31/24	Heloise (Waco, TX)	4/15/51
Bush, Barbara (Rye, NY)	6/8/25	Huizenga, H. Wayne (Evergreen Park, IL)	12/29/39
Bush, George Herbert Walker (Milton, MA)	6/12/24	Hutchison, Kay Bailey (Galveston, TX)	7/22/43
Byrd, Robert (N. Wilkesboro, NC)	11/20/17	Iacocca, Lee A. (Allentown, PA)	10/15/24
Carter, Jimmy (Plains, GA)	10/1/24	Ireland, Patricia (Oak Park, IL)	10/19/45
Carter, Rosalynn (Plains, GA)	8/18/27	Ito, Lance (Los Angeles, CA)	8/2/50
Chancellor, John (Chicago, IL)	7/14/27	Ivins, Molly (Monterey, CA)	8/30/44
Child, Julia (Pasadena, CA)	8/15/12	Jackson, Jesse (Greenville, SC)	10/8/41
Christopher, Warren (Scranton, PA)	10/27/25	Jennings, Peter (Toronto, Ontario)	8/29/38
Chung, Connie (Washington, DC)	8/20/46	Johnson, Lady Bird (Karnack, TX)	12/22/12
Cisneros, Henry (San Antonio, TX)	6/11/47	Jordan, Barbara (Houston, TX)	2/21/36
Claiborne, Liz (Brussels, Belg.)	3/31/29	Kasich, John R. (McKees Rocks, PA)	5/13/52
Clark, Marcia (Berkeley, CA)	8/31/53	Kantor, Mickey (Nashville, TN)	8/7/39
Clinton, Bill (Hope, AR)	8/19/46	Karan, Donna (Forest Hills, NY)	10/2/48
Clinton, Chelsea (Little Rock, AR)	2/27/80	Kassebaum, Nancy (Topeka, KS)	7/29/32
Clinton, Hillary Rodham (Chicago, IL)	10/26/47	Katzenberg, Jefferey (New York, NY)	1950
Cochran, Johnnie L., Jr.(Shreveport, LA)	10/2/37	Kemp, Jack (Los Angeles, CA)	7/13/35
Commager, Henry Steele (Pittsburgh, PA)	10/25/02	Kennedy, Anthony (Sacramento, CA)	7/23/36
Cooney, Joan Ganz (Phoenix, AZ)	10/30/29	Kennedy, Caroline (Boston, MA)	11/27/57
Costas, Bob (New York, NY)	3/22/52	Kennedy, Edward M. (Brookline, MA)	2/22/32
Couric, Katie (Washington, DC)	1/7/57	Kennedy, John F., Jr. (Washington, DC)	11/25/60
Cronkite, Walter (St. Joseph, MO)	11/4/16	Keyes, Alan (New York, NY)	8/7/50
Cuomo, Mario (Queens, NY)	6/15/32	King, Coretta Scott (Marion, AL)	4/27/27
Daley, Richard M. (Chicago, IL)	4/24/42	King, Larry (Brooklyn, NY)	11/19/34
D'Amato, Alfonse M. (Brooklyn, NY)	8/1/37	Kinsley, Michael (Detroit, MI)	3/9/51
Daschle, Thomas (Aberdeen, SD)	12/9/47	Kirkland, Lane (Camden, SC)	3/12/22
DeLay, Tom D. (Laredo, TX)	4/8/47	Kirkpatrick, Jeane (Duncan, OK)	11/19/26
Dellums, Ronald (Oakland, CA)	11/24/35	Kissinger, Henry (Fuerth, Germany)	5/27/23
Dershowitz, Alan (Brooklyn, NY)	9/1/38	Klein, Calvin (New York, NY)	11/19/42
Diller, Barry (San Francisco, CA)	2/2/42	Koch, Edward I. (New York, NY)	12/12/24
Dodd, Christopher (Willimantic, CT)	5/27/44	Koop, C. Everett (Brooklyn, NY)	10/14/16
Dole, Elizabeth (Salisbury, NC)	7/29/36	Koppel, Ted (Lancashire, England)	2/8/40
Dole, Robert (Russell, KS)	7/22/23	Kristol, William (New York, NY)	12/23/52
Domenici, Pete (Albuquerque, NM)	5/7/32	Kuralt, Charles (Wilmington, NC)	9/10/34
Donaldson, Sam (El Paso, TX)	3/11/34	Landers, Ann (Sioux City, IA)	7/4/18
Dove, Rita (Akron, OH)	8/28/52	Lauder, Estee (New York, NY)	9/1/08
Drew, Elizabeth (Cincinnati, OH)	11/16/35	Lauren, Ralph (Bronx, NY)	10/14/39

Name (Birthplace)	Birthdate
Lear, Norman (New Haven, CT)	7/27/22
Lehrer, Jim (Wichita, KS)	5/19/34
Lewis, Anthony (New York, NY)	3/27/27
Limbaugh, Rush (Cape Girardeau, MO)	1/12/51
Lindbergh, Anne Morrow (Englewood, NJ)	1906
Lorenzo, Frank (New York, NY)	5/19/40
Lott, Trent (Grenada, MS)	10/9/41
Lugar, Richard G. (Indianapolis, IN)	4/4/32
Lunden, Joan (Sacramento, CA)	9/19/50
MacNeil, Robert (Montreal, Quebec)	1/19/31
Manchester, William (Attleboro, MA)	4/1/22
Maslin, Janet (New York, NY)	8/12/49
McGovern, George (Avon, SD)	7/19/22
McNamara, Robert (San Francisco, CA)	6/9/16
Metzenbaum, Howard (Cleveland, OH)	6/4/17
Mikulski, Barbara (Baltimore, MD)	7/20/36
Millet, Kate (St. Paul, MN)	9/14/34
Mondale, Walter (Ceylon, MN)	1/5/28
Moseley-Braun, Carol (Chicago, IL)	8/16/47
Moyers, Bill (Hugo, OK)	6/5/34
Moynihan, Daniel P. (Tulsa, OK)	3/16/27
Mudd, Roger (Washington, DC)	2/9/28
Murdoch, Rupert (Melbourne, Australia)	3/11/31
Nader, Ralph (Winsted, CT)	2/27/34
North, Oliver (San Antonio, TX)	10/7/43
Norton, Eleanor Holmes (Washington, DC)	6/13/37
Novak, Robert (Joliet, IL)	2/26/31
Nunn, Sam (Perry, GA)	9/8/38
O'Connor, Sandra Day (nr. Duncan, AZ)	3/26/30
Osgood, Charles (New York, NY)	1/8/33
O'Rouke, P. J. (Toledo, OH)	11/14/47
Ovitz, Michael (Encino, CA)	12/14/46
Packwood, Bob (Portland, OR)	9/11/32
Paglia, Camille (Endicott, NY)	—
Panetta, Leon F. (Monterey, CA)	6/28/38
Parks, Rosa (Tuskegee, AL)	2/4/13
Pauley, Jane (Indianapolis, IN)	10/31/50
Perot, H. Ross (Texarkana, TX)	6/27/30
Perry, William (Vandergrift, PA)	10/11/27
Plimpton, George (New York, NY)	3/18/27
Podhoretz, Norman (New York, NY)	1/16/30
Poussaint, Alvin F. (New York, NY)	5/15/34
Powell, Colin (New York, NY)	4/5/37
Powell, Lewis, Jr. (Suffolk, VA)	9/19/07
Quayle, Dan (Indianapolis, IN)	2/4/47
Quindlen, Anna (Phildelphia, PA)	7/8/53
Quinn, Jane Bryant (Niagara Falls, NY)	2/5/39
Rather, Dan (Wharton, TX)	10/31/31
Redstone, Sumner M. (Boston, MA)	5/27/23
Reagan, Nancy (New York, NY)	7/6/23
Reagan, Ronald (Tampico, IL)	2/6/11
Reed, Ralph (Portsmouth, VA)	6/24/61
Rehnquist, William (Milwaukee, WI)	10/1/24
Reich, Robert B. (Scranton, PA)	6/24/46
Reno, Janet (Miami, FL)	7/21/38
Rich, Frank (Washington, DC)	6/2/49
Richards, Ann (Waco, TX)	9/3/33
Ride, Sally K. (Encino, CA)	5/26/51
Riley, Richard (Greenville, SC)	1/2/33
Riordan, Richard (Flushing, NY)	1930
Roberts, Oral (nr. Ada, OK)	1/24/18
Robertson, Pat (Lexington, VA)	3/22/30
Rockefeller, David (New York, NY)	6/12/15
Rockefeller, John D., 4th, "Jay" (New York, NY)	6/18/37
Rockefeller, Laurance S. (New York, NY)	5/26/10
Rooney, Andy (Albany, NY)	1/14/19
Rukeyser, Louis (New York, NY)	1/30/33
Royko, Mike (Chicago, IL)	9/19/32
Safer, Morley (Toronto, Ontario)	11/8/31
Safire, William (New York, NY)	12/17/29
Sagan, Carl (New York, NY)	11/9/34

Name (Birthplace)	Birthdate
Sawyer, Diane (Glasgow, KY)	12/22/45
Scalia, Antonin (Trenton, NJ)	3/11/36
Schlesinger, Arthur, Jr. (Columbus, OH)	10/15/17
Schroeder, Patricia (Portland, OR)	7/30/40
Schuller, Robert (Alton, IA)	9/16/26
Schwarzkopf, H. Norman (Trenton, NJ)	8/22/34
Scott, Willard (Alexandria, VA)	3/7/34
Scowcroft, Brent (Ogden, UT)	3/19/25
Seaborg, Glenn T. (Ishpeming, MI)	4/19/12
Shalala, Donna E. (Cleveland, OH)	2/14/41
Shalikashvili, John (Warsaw, Poland)	6/27/36
Shanker, Albert (New York, NY)	9/14/28
Shapiro, Robert (Plainfield, NJ)	9/2/42
Shaw, Bernard (Chicago, IL)	1940
Shriver, Maria (Chicago, IL)	11/6/55
Shultz, George P. (New York, NY)	12/13/20
Simpson, Alan K. (Cody, WY)	9/2/31
Simpson, O. J. (San Francisco, CA)	7/9/47
Smith, Harry (Lansing, IL)	8/21/51
Smith, Hedrick (Kilmacolm, Scotland)	7/9/33
Smith, Liz (Ft. Worth, TX)	2/2/23
Souter, David H. (Melrose, MA)	9/17/39
Specter, J. Arlen (Wichita, KS)	2/12/30
Spock, Benjamin (New Haven, CT)	5/2/03
Stahl, Lesley (Lynn, MA)	12/16/41
Steinbrenner, George (Rocky River, OH)	7/4/30
Steinem, Gloria (Toledo, OH)	3/25/34
Stephanopolous, George (Fall River, MA)	2/10/61
Stern, David J. (New York, NY)	9/22/42
Stevens, John Paul (Chicago, IL)	4/20/20
Sulzberger, Arthur Ochs, Sr. (New York, NY)	2/5/26
Sulzberger, Arthur Ochs, Jr. (Mt. Kisco, NY)	9/22/51
Sununu, John H. (Havana, Cuba)	7/2/39
Tagliabue, Paul (Jersey City, NJ)	11/24/40
Tartikoff, Brandon (Long Island, NY)	1/13/49
Taylor, Susan (New York, NY)	1/23/46
Terkel, Studs (New York, NY)	5/16/12
Thomas, Clarence (Savannah, GA)	6/23/48
Thomas, R. David (Altantic City, NJ)	7/2/32
Thompson, Hunter (Louisville, KY)	7/18/37
Thurmond, J. Strom (Edgefield, SC)	12/5/02
Tisch, Laurence (New York, NY)	3/15/23
Toffler, Alvin (New York, NY)	10/4/28
Toland, John (LaCrosse, WI)	6/29/12
Trillin, Calvin (Kansas City, MO)	12/5/35
Truman, Margaret (Independence, MO)	2/17/24
Trump, Donald (New York, NY)	1946
Turner, Ted (Cincinnati, OH)	11/19/38
Udall, Morris K. (St. Johns, AZ)	6/15/22
Ueberroth, Peter (Chicago, IL)	9/2/37
Valenti, Jack (Houston, TX)	9/5/21
Van Buren, Abigail (Sioux City, IA)	7/4/18
Wallace, George (Clio, AL)	8/25/19
Wallace, Mike (Brookline, MA)	5/9/18
Walters, Barbara (Boston, MA)	9/25/31
Wattleton, Faye (St. Louis, MO)	7/8/43
Wenner, Jann (New York, NY)	1/7/46
Westheimer, Ruth (Frankfurt, Germany)	1928
White, Bill (Lakewood, FL)	1/28/34
White, Byron (Ft. Collins, CO)	6/8/17
Whitman, Christine Todd (New York)	9/26/46
Wicker, Tom (Hamlet, NC)	6/18/26
Wiesel, Elie (Sighet, Romania)	9/30/28
Wilder, L. Douglas (Richmond, VA)	1/17/31
Will, George (Champaign, IL)	5/4/41
Wilson, Pete (Lake Forest, IL)	8/23/33
Yard, Molly (Shanghai, China)	c1910
Young, Coleman (Tuscaloosa, AL)	5/24/18
Zahn, Paula (Omaha, NE)	2/24/56
Zuckerman, Mortimer (Montreal, Quebec)	6/4/37

American Architects and Some of Their Achievements

Max Abramovitz, b 1908, Avery Fisher Hall, NYC; U.S. Steel Building (now USX Towers), Pittsburgh, PA.

Henry Bacon, 1866-1924, Lincoln Memorial, Washington, DC.

Pietro Belluschi, 1899-1994, Juilliard School of Music, Lincoln Center, Pan Am Bldg. (now MetLife Bldg.) (with Walter Gropius), all NYC.

Marcel Breuer, 1902-81, Whitney Museum of American Art, (with Hamilton Smith), NYC.

Charles Bulfinch, 1763-1844, State House, Boston; Capitol (part), Washington, DC.

Gordon Bunshaft, 1909-90, Lever House, Park Ave, NYC; Hirshhorn Museum, Washington, DC.

Daniel H. Burnham, 1846-1912, Union Station, Washington DC; Flatiron Bldg., NYC.

Irwin Chanin, 1892-1988, theaters, skyscrapers, NYC.

Ralph Adams Cram, 1863-1942, Cathedral of St. John the Divine, NYC; U.S. Military Academy (part), West Point, NY.

R. Buckminster Fuller, 1895-1983, U.S. Pavilion (geodesic domes), Expo 67, Montreal.

Cass Gilbert, 1859-1934, Custom House, Woolworth Bldg., NYC; Supreme Court Bldg., Washington, DC.

Bertram G. Goodhue, 1869-1924, Capitol, Lincoln, Nebraska; St. Thomas's Church, St. Bartholomew's Church, NYC.

Walter Gropius, 1883-1969, Pan Am Building (now MetLife Bldg.) (with Pietro Belluschi), NYC.

Peter Harrison, 1716-75, Touro Synagogue, Redwood Library, Newport, RI.

Wallace K. Harrison, 1895-1981, Metropolitan Opera House, Lincoln Center, NYC.

Thomas Hastings, 1860-1929, NY Public Library (with John Carrère), Frick Mansion, NYC.

James Hoban, 1762-1831, The White House, Washington, DC.

Raymond Hood, 1881-1934, Rockefeller Center (part), Daily News, NYC; Tribune, Chicago, IL.

Richard M. Hunt, 1827-95, Metropolitan Museum (part), NYC; National Observatory, Washington, DC.

William Le Baron Jenney, 1832-1907, Home Insurance (demolished 1931), Chicago, IL.

Philip C. Johnson, b 1906, AT&T headquarters (now 550 Madison Ave.), NYC; Transco Tower, Houston, TX.

Albert Kahn, 1869-1942, General Motors Bldg., Detroit, MI.

Louis Kahn, 1901-74, Salk Laboratory, La Jolla, CA; Yale Art Gallery, New Haven, CT.

Christopher Grant LaFarge, 1862-1938, Roman Catholic Chapel, West Point, NY.

Benjamin H. Latrobe, 1764-1820, Capitol (part), Washington, DC; State Capitol Building, Richmond, VA.

William Lescaze, 1896-1969, Philadelphia Savings Fund Society; Borg-Warner Bldg., Chicago.

Maya Lin, b 1959, Vietnam Veterans Memorial, Washington, DC.

Bernard R. Maybeck, 1862-1957, Hearst Hall, Univ. of CA, Berkeley; First Church of Christ Scientist, Berkeley, CA.

Charles F. McKim, 1847-1909, Public Library, Boston; Columbia Univ. (part), NYC.

Charles M. McKim, b 1920, KUHT-TV Transmitter Building, Lutheran Church of the Redeemer, Houston, TX.

Ludwig Mies van der Rohe, 1886-1969, Seagram Building, (with Philip C. Johnson), NYC; National Gallery, Berlin.

Robert Mills, 1781-1855, Washington Monument, Washington, DC.

Charles Moore, 1925-93, Sea Ranch, near San Francisco; Faculty Club, Santa Barbara, CA; Piazza d'Italia, New Orleans, LA.

Richard J. Neutra, 1892-1970, Mathematics Park, Princeton, NJ; Orange Co. Courthouse, Santa Ana, CA.

Gyo Obata, b 1923, Natl. Air & Space Museum, Smithsonian Inst., Washington, DC; Dallas-Ft. Worth Airport.

Frederick L. Olmsted, 1822-1903, Central Park, NYC; Fairmount Park, Philadelphia, PA.

I(eoh) M(ing) Pei, b 1917, East Wing, Natl. Gallery of Art, Washington, DC; Pyramid, The Louvre, Paris.

Cesar Pelli, b 1926, World Financial Center, Carnegie Hall Tower, NYC.

William Pereira, 1909-85, Cape Canaveral; Transamerica Bldg., San Francisco, CA.

John Russell Pope, 1874-1937, National Gallery, Washington, DC.

John Portman, b 1924, Peachtree Center, Atlanta, GA.

George Browne Post, 1837-1913, New York Stock Exchange, NYC; Capitol, Madison, WI.

James Renwick, Jr., 1818-95, Grace Church, St. Patrick's Cathedral, NYC.; Corcoran Gallery (now Renwick Gallery for arts and crafts), Washington, DC.

Henry H. Richardson, 1838-86, Trinity Church, Boston, MA.

Kevin Roche, b 1922, Oakland Museum, Oakland, CA; Fine Arts Center, University of Massachusetts, Amherst.

James Gamble Rogers, 1867-1947, Columbia-Presbyterian Medical Center, NYC; Northwestern Univ., Evanston, IL.

John Wellborn Root, 1887-1963, Palmolive Building, Chicago; Hotel Statler, Washington, DC.

Paul Rudolph, b 1918, Jewitt Art Center, Wellesley Colllege, in MA; Art & Architecture Bldg., Yale, New Haven, CT.

Eero Saarinen, 1910-61, Gateway to the West Arch, St. Louis, MO; Trans World Flight Center, NYC.

Louis Skidmore, 1897-1962, Atomic Energy Commission town site, Oak Ridge, TN; Terrace Plaza Hotel, Cincinnati, OH.

Clarence S. Stein, 1882-1975, Temple Emanu-El, NYC.

Edward Durell Stone, 1902-78, U.S. Embassy, New Delhi, India; (H. Hartford) Gallery of Modern Art, NYC.

Louis H. Sullivan, 1856-1924, Auditorium Building, Chicago, IL.

Richard Upjohn, 1802-78, Trinity Church, NYC.

Max O. Urbahn, 1912-95, (Ger.-U.S.) Vehicle Assembly Bldg., Cape Canaveral, FL.

Ralph T. Walker, 1889-1973, N.Y. Telephone Bldg. (now NYNEX), NYC; IBM Research Lab, Poughkeepsie, NY.

Roland A. Wank, 1898-1970, Cincinnati Union Terminal, Cincinnati, OH; head architect (1933-44), Tennessee Valley Authority.

Stanford White, 1853-1906, Washington Arch in Washington Square Park, first Madison Square Garden, NYC.

Frank Lloyd Wright, 1867 (or 1869)-1959, Imperial Hotel, Tokyo; Guggenheim Museum, NYC; Unity Church, Oak Park, IL; Robie House, Chicago, IL; Taliesin, Spring Green, WI.

William Wurster, 1895-1973, Ghirardelli Sq., San Francisco; Cowell College, UC, Berkeley, CA.

Minoru Yamasaki, 1912-86, World Trade Center, NYC.

Noted Artists, Photographers, and Sculptors of the Past

Artists are painters unless otherwise indicated.

Berenice Abbot, 1898-1991, (U.S.) photographer. Documentary of New York City, *Changing New York* (1939).

Ansel Easton Adams, 1902-84, (U.S.) photographer. Landscapes of the American Southwest.

Washington Allston, 1779-1843, (U.S.) landscapist. *Belshazzar's Feast.*

Albrecht Altdorfer, 1480-1538, (Ger.) landscapist. Battle of Alexander.

Andrea del Sarto, 1486-1530, (It.) frescoes. *Madonna of the Harpies.*

Fra Angelico, c1400-55, (It.) Renaissance muralist. *Madonna of the Linen Drapers' Guild.*

Diane Arbus, 1923-71, (U.S.) photographer. Photographs of disturbing images on bizarre individuals.

Alexsandr Archipenko, 1887-1964, (U.S.) sculptor. *Boxing Match, Medranos.*

Eugène Atget, 1856-1927, (Fr.) photographer. Parisian life.

John James Audubon, 1785-1851, (U.S.) *Birds of America.*

Hans Baldung-Grien, 1484-1545, (Ger.) *Todentanz.*

Ernst Barlach, 1870-1938, (Ger.) Expressionist sculptor. *Man Drawing a Sword.*

Frederic-Auguste Bartholdi, 1834-1904, (Fr.) *Liberty Enlightening the World, Lion of Belfort.*

Fra Bartolommeo, 1472-1517, (It.) *Vision of St. Bernard.*

Aubrey Beardsley, 1872-98, (Br.) illustrator. *Salome, Lysistrata, Morte d'Arthur, Volpone.*

Max Beckmann, 1884-1950, (Ger.) Expressionist. *The Descent from the Cross.*

Gentile Bellini, 1426-1507, (It.) Renaissance. *Procession in St. Mark's Square.*

Giovanni Bellini, 1428-1516, (It.) *St. Francis in Ecstasy.*

Jacopo Bellini, 1400-70, (It.) *Crucifixion.*

George Wesley Bellows, 1882-1925, (U.S.) sports artist, portraitist, landscapist. *Stag at Sharkey's, Edith Clavell.*

Thomas Hart Benton, 1889-1975, (U.S.) American regionalist. *Threshing Wheat, Arts of the West.*

Gianlorenzo Bernini, 1598-1680, (It.) Baroque sculpture. *The Assumption.*

Albert Bierstadt, 1830-1902, (U.S.) landscapist. *The Rocky Mountains, Mount Corcoran.*

George Caleb Bingham, 1811-79, (U.S.) *Fur Traders Descending the Missouri.*

William Blake, 1752-1827, (Br.) engraver. *Book of Job, Songs of Innocence, Songs of Experience.*

Rosa Bonheur, 1822-99, (Fr.) *The Horse Fair.*

Pierre Bonnard, 1867-1947, (Fr.) Intimist. *The Breakfast Room, Girl in a Straw Hat.*

Gutzon Borglum, 1871-1941, (U.S.) sculptor. Mt. Rushmore Memorial.

Hieronymus Bosch, 1450-1516, (Flem.) religious allegories. *The Crowning with Thorns.*

Sandro Botticelli, 1444-1510, (It.) Renaissance. *Birth of Venus, Adoration of the Magi, Guiliano de'Medici.*

Margaret Bourke-White, 1906-71, (U.S.) photographer, photojournalist. WW2, USSR, rural South during the Depression.

Mathew Brady, c1823-96, (U.S.) photographer. Official photographer of the Civil War.

Constantin Brancusi, 1876-1957, (Rom.) Nonobjective sculptor. *Flying Turtle, The Kiss.*

Georges Braque, 1882-1963, (Fr.) Cubist. *Violin and Palette.*

Pieter Bruegel the Elder, c1525-69, (Flem.) *The Peasant Dance, Hunters in the Snow, Magpie on the Gallows.*

Pieter Bruegel the Younger, 1564-1638, (Flem.) *Village Fair, The Crucifixion.*

Edward Burne-Jones, 1833-98, (Br.) Pre-Raphaelite artist-craftsman. *The Mirror of Venus.*

Alexander Calder, 1898-1976, (U.S.) sculptor. *Lobster Trap and Fish Tail.*

Julia Cameron, 1815-79, (Br.) photographer. Considered one of the most important portraitists of the 19th cent.

Robert Capa (Andrei Friedmann), 1913-54, (Hung.-U.S.) photographer. War photojournalist; invasion of Normandy.

Michelangelo Merisi da Caravaggio, 1573-1610, (It.) Baroque. *The Supper at Emmaus.*

Emily Carr, 1871-1945, (Can.) landscapist. *Blunden Harbour, Big Raven, Rushing Sea of Undergrowth.*

Carlo Carrà, 1881-1966, (It.) Metaphysical school. *Lot's Daughters, The Enchanted Room.*

Mary Cassatt, 1844-1926, (U.S.) Impressionist. *The Cup of Tea, Woman Bathing, The Boating Party.*

George Catlin, 1796-1872, (U.S.) American Indian life. *Gallery of Indians, Buffalo Dance.*

Benvenuto Cellini, 1500-71, (It.) Mannerist sculptor, goldsmith. *Perseus and Medusa, Salt Cellar of Francis I.*

Paul Cézanne, 1839-1906, (Fr.) *Card Players, Mont-Sainte-Victoire with Large Pine Trees.*

Marc Chagall, 1887-1985, (Russ.) Jewish life and folklore. *I and the Village, The Praying Jew.*

Jean Simeon Chardin, 1699-1779, (Fr.) still lifes. *The Kiss, The Grace.*

Frederick Church, 1826-1900, (U.S.) Hudson River school. *Niagara, Andes of Ecuador.*

Giovanni Cimabue, 1240-1302, (It.) Byzantine mosaicist. *Madonna Enthroned with St. Francis.*

Claude Lorrain, 1600-82, (Fr.) ideal-landscapist. *The Enchanted Castle.*

Thomas Cole, 1801-48, (U.S.) Hudson River school. *The Ox-Bow, In the Catskills.*

John Constable, 1776-1837, (Br.) landscapist. *Salisbury Cathedral from the Bishop's Grounds.*

John Singleton Copley, 1738-1815, (U.S.) portraitist. *Samuel Adams, Watson and the Shark.*

Lovis Corinth, 1858-1925, (Ger.) Expressionist. *Apocalypse.*

Jean-Baptiste-Camille Corot, 1796-1875, (Fr.) landscapist. *Souvenir de Mortefontaine, Pastorale.*

Correggio, 1494-1534, (It.) Renaissance muralist. *Mystic Marriages of St. Catherine.*

Gustave Courbet, 1819-77, (Fr.) Realist. *The Artist's Studio.*

Lucas Cranach the Elder, 1472-1553, (Ger.) Protestant Reformation portraitist. *Luther.*

Imogen Cunningham, 1883-1976, (U.S.) photographer, portraitist. Plant photography.

Nathaniel Currier, 1813-88, and **James M. Ives,** 1824-95, (both U.S.) lithographers. *A Midnight Race on the Mississippi, American Forest Scene—Maple Sugaring.*

John Steuart Curry, 1897-1946, (U.S.) Americana, murals. *Baptism in Kansas.*

Salvador Dalí, 1904-89, (Sp.) Surrealist. *Persistence of Memory, The Crucifixion.*

Honoré Daumier, 1808-79, (Fr.) caricaturist. *The Third-Class Carriage.*

Jacques-Louis David, 1748-1825, (Fr.) Neoclassicist. *The Oath of the Horatii.*

Arthur Davies, 1862-1928, (U.S.) Romantic landscapist. *Unicorns, Leda and the Dioscuri.*

Edgar Degas, 1834-1917, (Fr.) *The Ballet Class.*

Eugène Delacroix, 1798-1863, (Fr.) Romantic. *Massacre at Chios, Liberty Leading the People.*

Paul Delaroche, 1797-1856, (Fr.) historical themes. *Children of Edward IV.*

Luca Della Robbia, 1400-82, (It.) Renaissance terracotta artist. *Cantoria* (singing gallery), Florence cathedral.

Donatello, 1386-1466, (It.) Renaissance sculptor. *David, Gattamelata.*

Jean Dubuffet, 1902-85, (Fr.) painter, sculptor, printmaker. *Group of Four Trees.*

Marcel Duchamp, 1887-1968, (Fr.) Dada artist. *Nude Descending a Staircase, No. 2.*

Raoul Dufy, 1877-1953, (Fr.) Fauvist. *Chateau and Horses.*

Asher Brown Durand, 1796-1886, (U.S.) Hudson River school. *Kindred Spirits.*

Albrecht Dürer, 1471-1528, (Ger.) Renaissance painter, engraver, woodcuts. *St. Jerome in His Study, Melencolia I.*

Anthony van Dyck, 1599-1641, (Flem.) Baroque portraitist. *Portrait of Charles I Hunting.*

Thomas Eakins, 1844-1916, (U.S.) Realist. *The Gross Clinic.*

Alfred Eisenstaedt, 1898-1995, (Ger.-U.S.) photographer, photojournalist. Famous for V-J Day, Aug. 14, 1945, photograph of sailor and nurse in Times Square, NYC.

Peter Henry Emerson, 1856-1936, (Br.) photographer. Promoted photography as an independent art form.

Jacob Epstein, 1880-1959, (Br.) religious and allegorical sculptor. *Genesis, Ecce Homo.*

Jan van Eyck, c1390-1441, (Flem.) naturalistic panels. *Adoration of the Lamb.*

Roger Fenton, 1819-68, (Br.) photographer. Crimean War photographer.

Anselm Feuerbach, 1829-80, (Ger.) Romantic Classicist. *Judgment of Paris, Iphigenia.*

John Bernard Flannagan, 1895-1942, (U.S.) animal sculptor. *Triumph of the Egg.*

Jean-Honore Fragonard, 1732-1806, (Fr.) Rococo. *The Swing.*

Daniel Chester French, 1850-1931, (U.S.) *The Minute Man of Concord;* seated *Lincoln,* Lincoln Memorial, Washington, D.C.

Caspar David Friedrich, 1774-1840, (Ger.) Romantic landscapes. *Man and Woman Gazing at the Moon.*

Thomas Gainsborough, 1727-88, (Br.) portraitist. *The Blue Boy, The Watering Place, Orpin the Parish Clerk.*

Alexander Gardner, 1821-82, (U.S.) photographer. Civil War; railroad construction; Great Plains Indians.

Paul Gauguin, 1848-1903, (Fr.) Post-impressionist. *The Tahitians, Spirit of the Deadwatching.*

Lorenzo Ghiberti, 1378-1455, (It.) Renaissance sculptor. Gates of Paradise baptistery doors, Florence.

Alberto Giacometti, 1901-66, (Swiss) attenuated sculptures of solitary figures. *Man Pointing.*

Giorgione, c1477-1510, (It.) Renaissance. *The Tempest.*

Giotto di Bondone, 1267-1337, (It.) Renaissance. *Presentation of Christ in the Temple.*

François Girardon, 1628-1715, (Fr.) Baroque sculptor of classical themes. *Apollo Tended by the Nymphs.*

Vincent van Gogh, 1853-90, (Dutch) *The Starry Night, L'Arlesienne, Bedroom at Arles, Self-Portrait.*

Arshile Gorky, 1905-48, (U.S.) Surrealist. *The Liver Is the Cock's Comb.*

Francisco de Goya y Lucientes, 1746-1828, (Sp.) *The Naked Maja, The Disasters of War* (etchings).

El Greco, 1541-1614, (Sp.) *View of Toledo, Assumption of the Virgin.*

Horatio Greenough, 1805-52, (U.S.) Neo-classical sculptor. *George Washington.*

Matthias Grünewald, 1480-1528, (Ger.) mystical religious themes. *The Resurrection.*

Frans Hals, c1580-1666, (Dutch) portraitist. *Laughing Cavalier, Gypsy Girl.*

Childe Hassam, 1859-1935, (U.S.) Impressionist. *Southwest Wind, July 14 Rue Daunon.*

Edward Hicks, 1780-1849, (U.S.) folk painter. *The Peaceable Kingdom.*

Lewis Wickes Hine, 1874-1940, (U.S.) photographer. Studies of immigrants, children in industry.

Hans Hofmann, 1880-1966, (U.S.) early abstract Expressionist. *Spring, The Gate.*

William Hogarth, 1697-1764, (Br.) caricaturist. *The Rake's Progress.*

Katsushika Hokusai, 1760-1849, (Jpn.) printmaker. *Crabs.*

Hans Holbein the Elder, 1460-1524, (Ger.) late Gothic. *Presentation of Christ in the Temple.*

Hans Holbein the Younger, 1497-1543, (Ger.) portraitist. *Henry VIII, The Frence Ambassadors.*

Winslow Homer, 1836-1910, (U.S.) marine themes. *Marine Coast, High Cliff.*

Edward Hopper, 1882-1967, (U.S.) realistic urban scenes. *Sunlight in a Cafeteria.*

Jean-Auguste-Dominique Ingres, 1780-1867, (Fr.) Classicist. *Valpincon Bather.*

George Inness, 1825-94, (U.S.) luminous landscapist. *Delaware Water Gap.*

William Henry Jackson, 1843-1942, (U.S.) photographer. American West, building of Union Pacific Railroad.

Donald Judd, 1928-94, (U.S.) sculptor, major figure in Minimalist art.

Vasily Kandinsky, 1866-1944, (Russ.) abstractionist. *Capricious Forms, Improvisation 38 (second version).*

Paul Klee, 1879-1940, (Swiss) Abstractionist. *Twittering Machine, Pastoral, Death and Fire.*

Oscar Kokoschka, 1886-1980, (Aus.) Expressionist. *View of Prague, Harbor of Marseilles.*

Kathe Kollwitz, 1867-1945, (Ger.) printmaker, social justice themes. *The Peasant War.*

Gaston Lachaise, 1882-1935, (U.S.) figurative sculptor. *Standing Woman.*

John La Farge, 1835-1910, (U.S.) muralist. *Red and White Peonies, The Ascension.*

Dorothea Lange, 1895-1965, (U.S.), photographer. Depression photographs, migrant farm workers.

Fernand Léger, 1881-1955, (Fr.) machine art. *The Cyclists.*

Leonardo da Vinci, 1452-1519, (It.) *Mona Lisa, Last Supper, The Annunciation.*

Emanuel Leutze, 1816-68, (U.S.) historical themes. *Washington Crossing the Delaware.*

Jacques Lipchitz, 1891-1973, (Fr.) Cubist sculptor. *Harpist.*

Filippino Lippi, 1457-1504, (It.) Renaissance. *The Vision of St. Bernard.*

Fra Filippo Lippi, 1406-69, (It.) Renaissance. *Coronation of the Virgin, Madonna and Child with Angels.*

Morris Louis, 1912-62, (U.S.) abstract Expressionist. *Signa, Stripes, Alpha-Phi.*

Aristide Maillol, 1861-1944, (Fr.) sculptor. *L'Harmonie.*

Édouard Manet, 1832-83, (Fr.) forerunner of Impressionism. *Luncheon on the Grass, Olympia.*

Andrea Mantegna, 1431-1506, (It.) Renaissance frescoes. *Triumph of Caesar.*

Franz Marc, 1880-1916, (Ger.) Expressionist. *Blue Horses.*

John Marin, 1870-1953, (U.S.) Expressionist seascapes. *Maine Island.*

Reginald Marsh, 1898-1954, (U.S.) satirical artist. *Tattoo and Haircut.*

Masaccio, 1401-28, (It.) Renaissance. *The Tribute Money.*

Henri Matisse, 1869-1954, (Fr.) Fauvist. *Woman with the Hat.*

Michelangelo Buonarroti, 1475-1564, (It.) *Pieta, David, Moses, The Last Judgment,* Sistine Chapel ceiling.

Jean-Francois Millet, 1814-75, (Fr.) painter of peasant subjects. *The Gleaners, The Man with a Hoe.*

Joan Miró, 1893-1983, (Sp.) Exuberant colors, playful images. Catalan landscape, *Dutch Interior.*

Amedeo Modigliani, 1884-1920, (It.) *Reclining Nude.*

Piet Mondrian, 1872-1944, (Dutch) Abstractionist. *Composition with Red, Yellow and Blue.*

Claude Monet, 1840-1926, (Fr.) Impressionist. *The Bridge at Argenteuil, Haystacks.*

Henry Moore, 1898-1986, (Br.) sculptor of large-scale, abstract works. *Reclining Figure* (several).

Gustave Moreau, 1826-98, (Fr.) Symbolist. *The Apparition, Dance of Salome.*

James Wilson Morrice, 1865-1924, (Can.) landscapist. *The Ferry, Quebec, Venice, Looking Over the Lagoon.*

Grandma Moses, 1860-1961, (U.S.) folk painter. *Out for the Christmas Trees, Thanksgiving Turkey.*

Edvard Munch, 1863-1944, (Nor.) Expressionist. *The Cry.*

Bartolome Murillo, 1618-82, (Sp.) Baroque religious artist. *Vision of St. Anthony, The Two Trinities.*

Eadweard Muybridge, 1830-1904, (Br.-U.S.) photographer. Studies of motion, *Animal Locomotion.*

Nadar (Gaspar-Félix Tournachon) 1820-1910, (F.) photographer, charicaturist, portraitist. Invented photo-essay.

Barnett Newman, 1905-70, (U.S.) abstract Expressionist. *Stations of the Cross.*

Isamu Noguchi, 1904-88, (U.S.) abstract sculptor, designer. *Kouros, BirdC(MU),* sculptural gardens.

Georgia O'Keeffe, 1887-1986, (U.S.) Southwest motifs. *Cow's Skull: Red, White, and Blue, The Shelton with Sunspots.*

José Clemente Orozco, 1883-1949, (Mex.) frescoes. *House of Tears, Pre-Columbian Golden Age.*

Timothy H. O'Sullivan, 1840-82, (U.S.) Civil War photographer.

Charles Willson Peale, 1741-1827, (U.S.) American Revolutionary portraitist. *The Staircase Group,* U.S. presidents.

Rembrandt Peale, 1778-1860, (U.S.) portraitist. Thomas Jefferson.

Pietro Perugino, 1446-1523, (It.) Renaissance. *Delivery of the Keys to St. Peter.*

Pablo Picasso, 1881-1973, (Sp.) painter, sculptor. *Guernica; Dove; Head of a Woman; Head of a Bull, Metamorphosis.*

Piero della Francesca, c1415-92, (It.) Renaissance. *Duke of Urbino, Flagellation of Christ.*

Camille Pissarro, 1830-1903, (Fr.) Impressionist. *Morning Sunlight, Bather in the Woods.*

Jackson Pollock, 1912-56, (U.S.) abstract Expressionist. *Autumn Rhythm.*

Nicolas Poussin, 1594-1665, (Fr.) Baroque pictorial classicism. *St. John on Patmos.*

Maurice B. Prendergast, c1860-1924, (U.S.) Post-impressionist water colorist. *Umbrellas in the Rain.*

Pierre-Paul Prud'hon, 1758-1823, (Fr.) Romanticist. *Crime Pursued by Vengeance and Justice.*

Pierre Cecile Puvis de Chavannes, 1824-98, (Fr.) muralist. *The Poor Fisherman.*

Raphael Sanzio, 1483-1520, (It.) Renaissance. *Disputa, School of Athens, Sistine Madonna.*

Man Ray, 1890-1976, (U.S.) Dadaist. *Observing Time, The Lovers, Marquis de Sade.*

Odilon Redon, 1840-1916, (Fr.) Symbolist painter, lithographer. *In the Dream, Vase of Flowers.*

Rembrandt van Rijn, 1606-69, (Dutch) *The Bridal Couple, The Night Watch.*

Frederic Remington, 1861-1909, (U.S.) painter, sculptor. Portrayer of the American West. *Bronco Buster.*

Pierre-Auguste Renoir, 1841-1919, (Fr.) Impressionist. *The Luncheon of the Boating Party, Dance in the Country.*

Joshua Reynolds, 1723-92, (Br.) portraitist. *Mrs. Siddons As the Tragic Muse.*

Diego Rivera, 1886-1957, (Mex.) frescoes. *The Fecund Earth.*

Henry Peach Robinson, 1830-1901 (Br.) photographer. A leader of "high art" photography.

Norman Rockwell, 1894-1978, (U.S.) painter, illustrator. *Saturday Evening Post* covers.

Auguste Rodin, 1840-1917, (Fr.) sculptor. *The Thinker, The Burghers of Calais.*

Mark Rothko, 1903-70, (U.S.) abstract Expressionist. *Light, Earth and Blue.*

Georges Rouault, 1871-1958, (Fr.) Expressionist. *Three Judges.*

Henri Rousseau, 1844-1910, (Fr.) primitive exotic themes. *The Snake Charmer.*

Theodore Rousseau, 1812-67, (Swiss-Fr.) landscapist. *Under the Birches, Evening.*

Peter Paul Rubens, 1577-1640, (Flem.) Baroque. *Mystic Marriage of St. Catherine.*

Jacob van Ruisdael, c1628-82, (Dutch) landscapist. *Jewish Cemetery.*

Charles M. Russell, 1866-1926, (U.S.) Western life.

Salomon van Ruysdael, c1600-70, (Dutch) landscapist. *River with Ferry-Boat.*

Albert Pinkham Ryder, 1847-1917, (U.S.) seascapes and allegories. *Toilers of the Sea.*

Augustus Saint-Gaudens, 1848-1907, (U.S.) memorial statues. *Farragut, Mrs. Henry Adams (Grief).*

Andrea Sansovino, 1460-1529, (It.) Renaissance sculptor. *Baptism of Christ.*

Jacopo Sansovino, 1486-1570, (It.) Renaissance sculptor. *St. John the Baptist.*

John Singer Sargent, 1856-1925, (U.S.) Edwardian society portraitist. The Wyndham Sisters, Madam X.

Georges Seurat, 1859-91, (Fr.) Pointillist. *Sunday Afternoon on the Island of Grande Jatte.*

Gino Severini, 1883-1966, (It.) Futurist and Cubist. *Dynamic Hieroglyph of the Bal Tabarin.*

Ben Shahn, 1898-1969, (U.S.) social and political themes. Sacco and Vanzetti series, *Seurat's Lunch, Handball.*

Charles Sheeler, 1883-1965, (U.S.) abstractionist.

David Alfaro Siqueiros, 1896-1974, (Mex.) political muralist. *March of Humanity.*

John F. Sloan, 1871-1951, (U.S.) depictions of New York City. *Wake of the Ferry.*

David Smith, 1906-65, (U.S.) welded metal sculpture. *Hudson River Landscape, Zig, Cubi* series.

Edward Steichen, 1879-1973, (U.S.) photographer. Credited with the transformation of photography into an art form.

Alfred Stieglitz, 1864-1946, (U.S.) photographer.

Paul Strand, 1890-1976, (U.S.) photographer. People, nature, landscapes.

Gilbert Stuart, 1755-1828, (U.S.) portraitist. George Washington, Thomas Jefferson, James Madison.

Thomas Sully, 1783-1872, (U.S.) portraitist. *Col. Thomas Handasyd Perkins, The Passage of the Delaware.*

William Henry Fox Talbot, 1800-77, (Br.) photographer. *Pencil of Nature,* one of the first photographically illustrated books.

George Tames, 1919-94, (U.S.) photographer. Chronicled presidents, political leaders.

Yves Tanguy, 1900-55, (Fr.) Surrealist. *Rose of the Four Winds, Mama, Papa is Wounded!*

Giovanni Battista Tiepolo, 1696-1770, (It.) Rococo frescoes. *The Crucifixion.*

Jacopo Tintoretto, 1518-94, (It.) Mannerist. *The Last Supper.*

Titian, c1485-1576, (It.) Renaissance. *Venus and the Lute Player, The Bacchanal.*

Jose Rey Toledo, 1916-94, (U.S.) Native American artist. Captured the essence of tribal dances on canvas.

Henri de Toulouse-Lautrec, 1864-1901, (Fr.) *At the Moulin Rouge.*

John Trumbull, 1756-1843, (U.S.) historical themes. *The Declaration of Independence.*

J(oseph) M(allord) W(illiam) Turner, 1775-1851, (Br.) Romantic landscapist. *Snow Storm.*

Paolo Uccello, 1397-1475, (It.) Gothic-Renaissance. *The Rout of San Romano.*

Maurice Utrillo, 1883-1955, (Fr.) Impressionist. *Sacre-Coeur de Montmartre.*

John Vanderlyn, 1775-1852, (U.S.) Neo-classicist. *Ariadne Asleep on the Island of Naxos.*

Diego Velázquez, 1599-1660, (Sp.) Baroque. *Las Meninas, Portrait of Juan de Pareja.*

Jan Vermeer, 1632-75, (Dutch) interior genre subjects. *Young Woman with a Water Jug.*

Paolo Veronese, 1528-88, (It.) devotional themes, vastly peopled canvases. *The Temptation of St. Anthony.*

Andrea del Verrocchio, 1435-88, (It.) Florentine sculptor. *Colleoni.*

Maurice de Vlaminck, 1876-1958, (Fr.) Fauvist landscapist.

Andy Warhol, 1928-87, (U.S.) Pop Art. *Campbell's Soup Cans, Marilyn Diptych.*

Antoine Watteau, 1684-1721, (Fr.) Rococo painter of "scenes of gallantry." *The Embarkation for Cythera.*

George Frederic Watts, 1817-1904, (Br.) painter and sculptor of grandiose allegorical themes. *Hope.*

Benjamin West, 1738-1820, (U.S.) realistic historical themes. *Death of General Wolfe.*

Edward Weston, 1886-1958, (U.S.) photographer. Landscapes of American West.

James Abbott McNeill Whistler, 1834-1903, (U.S.) *Arrangement in Grey and Black, No. 1: The Artist's Mother.*

Archibald M. Willard, 1836-1918, (U.S.) *The Spirit of '76.*

Grant Wood, 1891-1942, (U.S.) Midwestern regionalist. *American Gothic, Daughters of Revolution.*

Ossip Zadkine, 1890-1967, (Russ.) School of Paris sculptor. *The Destroyed City, Musicians, Christ.*

Noted Black Americans of the Past

Ralph David Abernathy, 1926-90, organizer, 1957, president, 1968, Southern Christian Leadership Conference.

Crispus Attucks, c1723-70, agitator who led group that precipitated the "Boston Massacre," Mar. 5, 1770.

James Baldwin, 1924-87, author, playwright; *The Fire Next Time, Blues for Mister Charlie, Just Above My Head.*

Benjamin Banneker, 1731-1806, inventor, astronomer, mathematician, and gazetteer; served on commission that surveyed and planned Washington, DC.

James P. Beckwourth, 1798-c 1867, western fur trader, scout; Beckwourth Pass in northern California named for him.

Mary McCleod Bethune, 1875-1955, adviser to presidents Franklin Roosevelt and Harry Truman; founder, president, Bethune-Cookman College.

Henry Blair, 19th century, obtained patents (believed among first issued to a black) for a corn-planter, 1834, and for a cotton-planter, 1836.

Edward Bouchet, 1852-1918, first black to earn a PhD at a U.S. university (Yale, 1876); first black elected to Phi Beta Kappa.

Sterling A. Brown, 1901-89, poet, literature professor; helped establish African-American literary criticism.

William Wells Brown, 1815-84, novelist, dramatist; first American black to publish a novel.

Ralph Bunche, 1904-71, first black to win the Nobel Peace Prize, 1950; undersecretary of the UN, 1950.

George Washington Carver, 1864-1943, botanist, chemist, and educator; his extensive experiments in soil building and plant diseases revolutionized the economy of the South.

Charles Waddell Chesnutt, 1858-1932, author known primarily for his short stories, including *The Conjure Woman.*

James Cleveland, 1931-91, composer, musician, singer; first black gospel artist to appear in Carnegie Hall.

Countee Cullen, 1903-46, poet, played a prominent role in the Harlem Renaissance of the 1920s; *The Black Christ.*

Benjamin O. Davis, Sr., 1877-1970, first black general, 1940, in U. S. Army.

William L. Dawson, 1886-1970, Illinois congressman, first black chairman of a major U.S. House of Representatives committee.

Aaron Douglas, 1900-79, painter; called father of black American art.

Frederick Douglass, 1817-95, author, editor, orator, diplomat; edited the abolitionist weekly, *The North Star,* in Rochester, NY; U.S. minister and consul general to Haiti.

St. Clair Drake, 1911-90, black studies pioneer, *Black Metropolis* (1945, with Horace R. Cayton); first permanent director, African and African American Studies, Stanford Univ.

Charles Richard Drew, MD, 1904-50, pioneer in development of blood banks; director of American Red Cross blood donor project in WW2.

William Edward Burghardt (W.E.B.) Du Bois, 1868-1963, historian, sociologist; a founder of the National Association for the Advancement of Colored People (NAACP), 1909, and founder of its magazine *The Crisis.*

Paul Laurence Dunbar, 1872-1906, poet, novelist; won fame with *Lyrics of Lowly Life,* 1896.

Jean Baptiste Point du Sable, c1750-1818, pioneer trader and first settler of Chicago, 1779.

Henry O. Flipper, 1856-1940, first black to graduate, 1877, from West Point.

Marcus Garvey, 1887-1940, founded Universal Negro Improvement Assn., 1911.

Ewart Guinier, 1911-90, trade unionist; first chairman of Harvard Univ.'s Department of African American Studies.

Jupiter Hammon, c1720-1800, poet; the first black American to have his works published, 1761.

Lorraine Hansberry, 1930-65, playwright; won New York Drama Critics Circle Award, 1959; *A Raisin in the Sun.*

William H. Hastie, 1904-76, first black federal judge, appointed 1937; governor of Virgin Islands, 1946-49.

Matthew A. Henson, 1866-1955, member of Peary's 1909 expedition to the North Pole; placed U.S. flag at the pole.

Chester Himes, 1909-84, novelist. *Cotton Comes to Harlem.*

William A. Hinton, MD, 1883-1959, developed the Hinton and Davies-Hinton tests for detection of syphilis; first black professor, 1949, at Harvard Medical School.

Charles Hamilton Houston, 1895-1950, lawyer, Howard University instructor, and champion of minority rights.

Langston Hughes, 1902-67, poet, lyric writer, author; a major influence in the Harlem Renaissance of the 1920s.

Daniel James, Jr., 1920-78, first black 4-star general, 1975; Commander, North American Air Defense Command.

Henry Johnson, 1897-1929, the first American decorated by France in WW1 with the Croix de Guerre.

James Weldon Johnson, 1871-1938, poet, novelist, diplomat; lyricist for *Lift Every Voice and Sing.*

Ernest Everett Just, 1883-1941, marine biologist, studied egg development; author, *Biology of Cell Surfaces,* 1941.

Martin Luther King, Jr., 1929-68, led 382-day Montgomery, AL, boycott that brought 1956 U.S. Supreme Court decision holding segregation on buses unconstitutional; founder, president, Southern Christian Leadership Conference, 1957.

Lewis H. Latimer, 1848-1928, associate of Edison; supervised installation of first electric street lighting in NYC.

Mickey Leland, 1944-89, U.S. representative from Texas, 1978 until death; chairman of Congressional Black Caucus.

Malcolm X (Little), 1925-65, Black Muslim leader, black nationalist; leader in black pride movements in the 1960s.

Thurgood Marshall, 1908-93, first black U.S. solicitor general, 1965; first black justice of the U.S. Supreme Court, 1967-91; as a lawyer led the legal battery that won the Supreme Court decision *Brown* v. *Board of Education of Topeka,* 1954.

Jan Matzeliger, 1852-89, invented lasting machine, patented 1883, which revolutionized the shoe industry.

Benjamin Mays, 1895-1984, educator, civil rights leader; headed Morehouse College, 1940-67.

Ronald McNair, 1950-86, physicist, astronaut; killed in *Challenger* explosion.

Dorie Miller, 1919-43, Navy hero of Pearl Harbor attack; awarded the Navy Cross.

Willard Motley, 1912-65, novelist; *Knock on Any Door.*

Elijah Muhammad, 1897-1975, founded Black Muslims, 1931.

Pedro Alonzo Niño, navigator of the Niña, one of Columbus's 3 ships on his first voyage to the New World, 1492.

Frederick D. Patterson, 1901-88, founder of United Negro College Fund, 1944.

Harold R. Perry, 1916-91, first black American Roman Catholic bishop in the 20th century, 1966; first black clergyman to deliver the opening prayer in the U.S. Congress, 1964.

Adam Clayton Powell, 1908-72, early civil rights leader, congressman, 1945-69.

Joseph H. Rainey, 1832-87, first black elected to U.S. House of Representatives, 1869, from South Carolina.

A. Philip Randolph, 1889-1979, organized the Brotherhood of Sleeping Car Porters, 1925; an organizer of 1941 and 1963 March on Washington movements.

Hiram R. Revels, 1822-1901, first black U.S. senator, elected in Mississippi, served 1870-71.

Norbert Rillieux, 1806-94; invented a vacuum pan evaporator, 1846, revolutionizing the sugar-refining industry.

Paul Robeson, 1898-1976, actor, singer, civil rights activist; graduated first in class at Rutgers, 1918, Phi Beta Kappa.

Max Robinson, 1939-88, TV journalist, first black to anchor network news, 1978.

John B. Russwurm, 1799-1851, with **Samuel E. Cornish,** 1793-1858, founded, 1827, the nation's first black newspaper, *Freedom's Journal,* in NYC.

Bayard Rustin, 1910-87, an organizer of the 1963 March on Washington; executive director, A. Philip Randolph Institute.

Peter Salem, at the Battle of Bunker Hill, June 17, 1775, shot and killed British commander Maj. John Pitcairn.

Stephen Spottswood, 1897-1974, board chairman of NAACP, 1961-74.

Willard Townsend, 1895-1957, organized the United Transport Service Employees (redcaps), 1935.

Sojourner Truth, 1797-1883, born Isabella Baumfree; preacher, abolitionist; worked for black educational opportunities.

Harriet Tubman, 1823-1913, Underground Railroad conductor, served as nurse and spy for Union Army in the Civil War.

Nat Turner, 1800-31, led the most significant of more than 200 slave revolts in U.S., in Southampton, VA; hanged.

Booker T. Washington, 1856-1915, founder, 1881, and first president of Tuskegee Institute; author, *Up From Slavery.*

Harold Washington, 1922-87, first black mayor of Chicago, from 1983 until death.

Ida B. Wells (Barnett), 1862-1931, journalist who waged anti-lynching crusade.

Phillis Wheatley, c1753-84, poet; second American woman and first black woman to have her works published, 1770.

Walter White, 1893-1955, exec. secretary, NAACP, 1931-55.

Roy Wilkins, 1901-81, exec. director, NAACP, 1955-77.

Daniel Hale Williams, MD, 1858-1931, performed one of first two open-heart operations, 1893; first black elected a fellow of the American College of Surgeons.

Granville T. Woods, 1856-1910, invented the third-rail system now used in subways, and automatic air brake.

Carter G. Woodson, 1875-1950, historian; founded Assn. for the Study of Negro Life and History.

Frank Yerby, 1916-91, 1st best-selling American black novelist.

Noted Business Leaders, Industrialists, and Philanthropists of the Past

Elizabeth Arden (F. N. Graham), 1884-1966, (U.S.) Canadian-born founder of cosmetics empire.

Philip D. Armour, 1832-1901, (U.S.) industrialist; streamlined meatpacking.

John Jacob Astor, 1763-1848, (U.S.) German-born fur trader, banker, real estate magnate; at death, richest in U.S.

Francis W. Ayer, 1848-1923, (U.S.) ad industry pioneer.

August Belmont, 1816-90, (U.S.) German-born financier.

James B. (Diamond Jim) Brady, 1856-1917, (U.S.) financier, philanthropist, legendary bon vivant.

Adolphus Busch, 1839-1913, (U.S.) German-born businessman; established brewery empire.

Asa Candler, 1851-1929, (U.S.) founded Coca-Cola Co.

Andrew Carnegie, 1835-1919, (U.S.) Scottish-born industrialist; founded U.S. Steel; financed more than 2,800 libraries.

Tom Carvel, 1908-89, (Gr.-U.S.) founded ice cream chain.

William Colgate, 1783-1857, (Br.-U.S.) Br.-born businessman, philanthropist; founded soap-making empire.

Jay Cooke, 1821-1905, (U.S.) financier; sold $1 billion in Union bonds during Civil War.

Peter Cooper, 1791-1883, (U.S.) industrialist, inventor, philanthropist; founder Cooper Union (1859).

Ezra Cornell, 1807-74, (U.S.) businessman, philanthropist; headed Western Union, established university.

Erastus Corning, 1794-1872, (U.S.) financier; headed N.Y. Central.

Charles Crocker, 1822-88, (U.S.) railroad builder, financier.

.Samuel Cunard, 1787-1865, (Can.) pioneered trans-Atlantic steam navigation.

Marcus Daly, 1841-1900, (U.S.) Irish-born copper magnate.

George T. Delacorte, 1893-1991, (U.S.) publisher; Central Park donations included Alice in Wonderland statue.

W. Edwards Deming, 1900-93, (U.S.) quality-control expert who revolutionized Japanese manufacturing.

Walt Disney, 1901-66, (U.S.) pioneer in cinema animation; built entertainment empire.

Herbert H. Dow, 1866-1930, (U.S.) founder of chemical co.

James Duke, 1856-1925, (U.S.) founded American Tobacco, Duke Univ.

Eleuthere I. du Pont, 1771-1834, (Fr.-U.S.) gunpowder manufacturer; founded one of the largest business empires.

Thomas C. Durant, 1820-85, (U.S.) railroad official, financier.

William C. Durant, 1861-1947, (U.S.) industrialist; formed General Motors.

George Eastman, 1854-1932, (U.S.) inventor; manufacturer of photographic equipment.

Marshall Field, 1834-1906, (U.S.) merchant; founded Chicago's largest department store.

Harvey Firestone, 1868-1938, (U.S.) founded tire company.

Avery Fisher, 1906-94, (U.S.) industrialist, philanthropist, founded Fisher electronics.

Henry M. Flagler, 1830-1913, (U.S.) financier; helped form Standard Oil; developed Florida as resort state.

Malcolm Forbes, 1919-90, (U.S.) magazine publisher.

Henry Ford, 1863-1947, (U.S.) auto maker; developed first popular low-priced car.

Henry Ford 2d, 1917-87, (U.S.) headed auto company founded by grandfather.

Henry C. Frick, 1849-1919, (U.S.) industrialist; helped organize U.S. Steel.

Jakob Fugger (Jakob the Rich), 1459-1525, (Ger.) headed leading banking, trading house, in 16th-century Europe.

Alfred C. Fuller, 1885-1973, (U.S.) Canadian-born businessman; founded brush co.

Elbert H. Gary, 1846-1927, (U.S.) one of the organizers of U.S. Steel; chariman of the board of directors, 1903-27.

Jean Paul Getty, 1892-1976, (U.S.) founded oil empire.

Amadeo P. Giannini, 1870-1949, (U.S.) founded Bank of America.

Stephen Girard, 1750-1831, (U.S.) French-born financier, philanthropist; richest man in U.S. at his death.

Jay Gould, 1836-92, (U.S.) railroad magnate, financier, speculator.

Hetty Green, 1834-1916, (U.S.) financier, the "witch of Wall St."; richest woman in U.S. in her day.

William Gregg, 1800-67, (U.S.) launched textile industry in the South.

Meyer Guggenheim, 1828-1905, (U.S.) Swiss-born merchant, philanthropist; built merchandising, mining empires.

Armand Hammer, 1898-1990, (U.S.) headed Occidental Petroleum; promoted U.S.-Soviet ties.

Edward H. Harriman, 1848-1909, (U.S.) railroad financier, administrator; headed Union Pacific.

William Randolph Hearst, 1863-1951, (U.S.) a dominant figure in American journalism; built vast publishing empire.

Henry J. Heinz, 1844-1919, (U.S.) founded food empire.

James J. Hill, 1838-1916, (U.S.) Canadian-born railroad magnate, financier; founded Great Northern Railway.

Conrad N. Hilton, 1888-1979, (U.S.) hotel chain founder.

Howard Hughes, 1905-76, (U.S.) industrialist, movie maker.

H. L. Hunt, 1889-1974, (U.S.) oil magnate.

Collis P. Huntington, 1821-1900, (U.S.) railroad magnate.

Henry E. Huntington, 1850-1927, (U.S.) railroad builder, philanthropist.

Walter L. Jacobs, 1898-1985, (U.S.) founder of the first rental car agency, which later became Hertz.

Howard Johnson, 1896-1972, (U.S.) founded restaurants.

Henry J. Kaiser, 1882-1967, (U.S.) industrialist; built empire in steel, aluminum.

Minor C. Keith, 1848-1929, (U.S.) railroad magnate; founded United Fruit Co.

Will K. Kellogg, 1860-1951, (U.S.) businessman, philanthropist; founded breakfast food co.

Richard King, 1825-85, (U.S.) cattleman; founded half-million acre King Ranch in Texas.

William S. Knudsen, 1879-1948, (U.S.) Danish-born auto industry executive.

Samuel H. Kress, 1863-1955, (U.S.) businessman, art collector, philanthropist; founded "dime store" chain.

Ray A. Kroc, 1902-84, (U.S.) founded McDonald's fast food.

Alfred Krupp, 1812-87, (Ger.) armaments magnate.

William Levitt, 1907-94, (U.S.) industrialist, "suburb maker".

Thomas Lipton, 1850-1931, (Scot.) merchant, tea empire.

James McGill, 1744-1813, (Scot.-Can.) founded university.

Andrew W. Mellon, 1855-1937, (U.S.) financier, industrialist; benefactor of National Gallery of Art.

Charles E. Merrill, 1885-1956, (U.S.) financier; developed firm of Merrill Lynch.

John Pierpont Morgan, 1837-1913, (U.S.) most powerful figure in finance and industry at the turn of the century.

Malcolm Muir, 1885-1979, (U.S.) created *Business Week* magazine; headed *Newsweek,* 1937-61.

Samuel Newhouse, 1895-1979, (U.S.) publishing and broadcasting magnate; built communications empire.

Aristotle Onassis, 1906-75, (Gr.) shipping magnate.

William S. Paley, 1901-90, (U.S.) built CBS communications empire.

George Peabody, 1795-1869, (U.S.) merchant, financier, philanthropist.

James C. Penney, 1875-1971, (U.S.) businessman; developed department store chain.

William C. Procter, 1862-1934, (U.S.) headed soap company.

John D. Rockefeller, 1839-1937, (U.S.) industrialist; established Standard Oil.

John D. Rockefeller, Jr., 1874-1960, (U.S.) philanthropist; established foundation; provided land for United Nations.

Meyer A. Rothschild, 1743-1812, (Ger.) founded international banking house.

Thomas Fortune Ryan, 1851-1928, (U.S.) financier; a founder of American Tobacco.

Russell Sage, 1816-1906, (U.S.) financier.

David Sarnoff, 1891-1971, (U.S.) broadcasting pioneer; established first radio network, NBC.

Richard Sears, 1863-1914, (U.S.) founded mail-order co.

(Ernst) Werner von Siemens, 1816-92, (Ger.) industrialist; inventor.

Alfred P. Sloan, 1875-1966, (U.S.) industrialist, philanthropist; headed General Motors.

A. Leland Stanford, 1824-93, (U.S.) railroad official, philanthropist; founded university.

Nathan Straus, 1848-1931, (U.S.) German-born merchant, philanthropist; headed Macy's.

Levi Strauss, c1829-1902, (U.S.) pants manufacturer.

Clement Studebaker, 1831-1901, (U.S.) wagon, carriage manufacturer.

Gustavus Swift, 1839-1903, (U.S.) pioneer meatpacker; promoted refrigerated railroad cars.

Gerard Swope, 1872-1957, (U.S.) industrialist, economist; headed General Electric.

James Walter Thompson, 1847-1928, (U.S.) ad executive.

Alice Tully, 1902-93, (U.S.) philanthropist, arts patron.

Theodore N. Vail, 1845-1920, (U.S.) organized Bell Telephone system; headed AT&T.

Cornelius Vanderbilt, 1794-1877, (U.S.) financier; established steamship, railroad empires.

Henry Villard, 1835-1900, (U.S.) German-born railroad executive, financier.

George Westinghouse, 1846-1914, (U.S) inventor, manufacturer; organized Westinghouse Electric Co., 1886.

Charles R. Walgreen, 1873-1939, (U.S.) founded drugstore chain.

DeWitt Wallace, 1890-1981, (U.S.) and **Lila Wallace,** 1890-1984, (U.S.) co-founders of *Reader's Digest* magazine.

Sam Walton, 1918-92, (U.S.) founder of Wal-Mart stores.
John Wanamaker, 1838-1922, (U.S.) pioneered department-store merchandising.
Aaron Montgomery Ward, 1843-1913, (U.S.) established first mail-order firm.
Thomas J. Watson, 1874-1956, (U.S.) IBM head, 1924-49.

John Hay Whitney, 1905-82, (U.S.) publisher, sportsman, philanthropist.
Charles E. Wilson, 1890-1961, (U.S.) auto industry executive; public official.
Frank W. Woolworth, 1852-1919, (U.S.) created 5 & 10 chain.
William Wrigley, Jr., 1861-1932, (U.S.) founded chewing gum company.

Noted American Cartoonists

Charles Addams, 1912-88, macabre cartoons.
Brad Anderson, b 1924, Marmaduke.
Peter Arno, 1904-68, *New Yorker* urban characterizations.
Tex Avery, 1908-80, animator of Bugs Bunny, Porky Pig, and Daffy Duck.
Arthur Babbitt, 1907-92, Disney cartoonist.
George Baker, 1915-75, The Sad Sack.
C. C. Beck, 1910-89, Captain Marvel.
Jim Berry, b 1932, Berry's World.
Herb Block (Herblock), b 1909, political cartoonist.
George Booth, b 1926, *New Yorker* cartoonist.
Berke Breathed, b 1957, Bloom County.
Clare Briggs, 1875-1930, Mr. & Mrs.
Dik Browne, 1917-89, Hi & Lois, Hagar the Horrible.
Marjorie Buell, 1904-93, Little Lulu.
Ernie Bushmiller, 1905-82, Nancy.
Milton Caniff, 1907-88, Terry & the Pirates, Steve Canyon.
Al Capp, 1909-79, Li'l Abner.
Roz Chast, b 1954, *New Yorker* "bonfire of the banalities."
Paul Conrad, 1924, political cartoonist.
Roy Crane, 1901-77, Captain Easy, Buz Sawyer.
Robert Crumb, b 1943, "Underground" cartoonist.
Jay N. Darling (Ding), 1876-1962, political cartoonist.
Jack Davis, b 1926, *Mad* magazine.
Jim Davis, b 1945, Garfield.
Billy DeBeck, 1890-1942, Barney Google.
Rudolph Dirks, 1877-1968, The Katzenjammer Kids.
Walt Disney, 1901-66, producer of animated cartoons, created Mickey Mouse and Donald Duck.
Steve Ditko, b 1927, Spider-Man.
Mort Drucker, b 1929, *Mad* magazine.
Jules Feiffer, b 1929, satirical *Village Voice* cartoonist.
Bud Fisher, 1884-1954, Mutt & Jeff.
Ham Fisher, 1900-55, Joe Palooka.
James Montgomery Flagg, 1877-1960, illustrator, created the famous Uncle Sam recruiting poster during WWI.
Max Fleischer, 1883-1972, creator of Betty Boop, Popeye.
Hal Foster, 1892-1982, Tarzan, Prince Valiant.
Fontaine Fox, 1884-1964, Toonerville Folks.
Isadore "Friz" Freleng, 1905-95, animator, Yosemite Sam, Porky Pig, Sylvestor and Tweety.
Al Frueh, 1880-1968, *The New Yorker* cartoonist.
Rube Goldberg, 1883-1970, Boob McNutt.
Chester Gould, 1900-85, Dick Tracy.
Harold Gray, 1894-1968, Little Orphan Annie.
Matt Groening, b 1954, Life Is Hell, The Simpsons.
Cathy Guisewite, b 1950, Cathy.
Bill Hanna, b 1910, **& Joe Barbera,** b 1911, animators of Tom & Jerry, Huckleberry Hound, Yogi Bear, Flintstones.
Johnny Hart, b 1931, BC, Wizard of Id.
Alfred Harvey, 1913-94, created Casper the Friendly Ghost
Jimmy Hatlo, 1898-1963, Little Iodine.
John Held, Jr., 1889-1958, "Jazz Age" cartoonist.
George Herriman, 1881-1944, Krazy Kat.
Harry Hershfield, 1885-1974, Abie the Agent.
Al Hirschfeld, b 1903, *N.Y. Times* theater caricaturist.
Burne Hogarth, b 1911, Tarzan.
Helen Hokinson, 1900-49, satirized clubwomen.
Nicole Hollander, b 1939, Sylvia.
Lynn Johnston, b 1947, For Better or For Worse.
Chuck Jones, b 1912, animator, Bugs Bunny, Porky Pig, Daffy Duck

Bob Kane, b 1916, Batman.
Bil Keane, b 1922, The Family Circus.
Walt Kelly, 1913-73, Pogo.
Hank Ketcham, b 1920, Dennis the Menace.
Ted Key, b 1912, Hazel.
Frank King, 1883-1969, Gasoline Alley.
Jack Kirby, 1917-94, Fantastic Four, The Incredible Hulk.
Rollin Kirby, 1875-1952, political cartoonist.
B(ernard) Kliban, 1935-91, cat books.
Edward Koren, b 1935, *New Yorker* woolly characters.
Harvey Kurtzman, 1921-93, *Mad* magazine.
Walter Lantz, 1900-94, Woody Woodpecker.
Gary Larson, b 1950, The Far Side.
Mell Lazarus, b 1929, Momma, Miss Peach.
Stan Lee, b 1922, Marvel Comics.
David Levine, b 1926, *N.Y. Review of Books* caricatures.
Doug Marlette, b 1949, editorial cartoonist, Kudzu.
Don Martin, b 1931, *Mad* magazine.
Bill Mauldin, b 1921, depicted squalid life of the G.I. in WW2.
Jeff MacNelly, b 1947, political cartoonist, Shoe.
Winsor McCay, 1872-1934, Little Nemo.
John T. McCutcheon, 1870-1949, midwestern rural life.
George McManus, 1884-1954, Bringing Up Father.
Dale Messick, b 1906, Brenda Starr.
Norman Mingo, 1896-1980, Alfred E. Neuman.
Bob Montana, 1920-75, Archie.
Dick Moores, 1909-86, Gasoline Alley.
Willard Mullin, 1902-78, sports cartoonist, created Dodgers "Bum" and Mets "Kid."
Russell Myers, b 1938, Broom Hilda.
Thomas Nast, 1840-1902, political cartoonist, created the Democratic donkey and Republican elephant.
Pat Oliphant, b 1935, political cartoonist.
Frederick Burr Opper, 1857-1937, Happy Hooligan.
Richard Outcault, 1863-1928, Yellow Kid, Buster Brown.
Mike Peters, b 1943, editorial cartoons. Mother Goose & Grimm.
George Price, 1901-95, *New Yorker* lower-class life.
Alex Raymond, 1909-56, Flash Gordon, Jungle Jim.
Forrest (Bud) Sagendorf, 1915-94, Popeye
Art Sansom, 1920-91, The Born Loser.
Charles Schulz, b 1922, Peanuts.
Elzie C. Segar, 1894-1938, Popeye.
Jerry Siegel, b 1914, **& Joe Shuster,** 1914-92, Superman.
Sydney Smith, 1887-1935, The Gumps.
Otto Soglow, 1900-75, Little King, Canyon Kiddies.
Art Spiegelman, b 1948, Raw, Maus.
William Steig, b 1907, *New Yorker* cartoonist.
James Swinnerton, 1875-1974, Little Jimmy.
Paul Terry, 1887-1971, animator of Mighty Mouse.
Bob Thaves, b 1924, Frank and Ernest.
James Thurber, 1894-61, *New Yorker* cartoonist.
Garry Trudeau, b 1948, Doonesbury.
Mort Walker, b 1923, Beetle Bailey.
Bill Watterson, b 1958, Calvin and Hobbes.
Russ Westover, 1887-1966, Tillie the Toiler.
Frank Willard, 1893-1958, Moon Mullins.
J. R. Williams, 1888-1957, The Willets Family, Out Our Way.
Gahan Wilson, b 1930, cartoonist of the macabre.
Tom Wilson, b 1931, Ziggy.
Art Young, 1866-1943, political radical and satirist.
Chic Young, 1901-73, Blondie.

Noted Historians, Economists, and Social Scientists of the Past

Brooks Adams, 1848-1927, (U.S.) historian, political theoretician; *The Law of Civilization and Decay.*
Henry Adams, 1838-1918, (U.S.) historian; *History of the United States of America, The Education of Henry Adams.*
Francis Bacon, 1561-1626, (Eng.) philosopher, essayist, and statesman; applied scientific induction to philosophy.
George Bancroft, 1800-91, (U.S.) historian; wrote 10-volume *History of the United States.*
Jack Barbash, 1911-94, (U.S.) labor economist who helped create the AFL-CIO.
Charles A. Beard, 1874-1948, (U.S.) historian; *The Economic Basis of Politics;* helped found New School for Social Research.
Bede (the Venerable), c673-735, (Eng.) scholar historian whose writings virtually constitute the learning of his time.

Ruth Benedict, 1887-1948, (U.S.) anthropologist; studied Indian tribes of the Southwest.
Bruno Bettleheim, 1903-90, (Aus.-U.S.) psychoanalyst specializing in autistic children; *The Uses of Enchantment.*
Louis Blanc, 1811-82, (Fr.) Socialist leader and historian whose ideas were a link between utopian and Marxist socialism.
Leonard Bloomfield, 1887-1949, (U.S.) linguist; *Language.*
Franz Boas, 1858-1942, (U.S.) German-born anthropologist; studied American Indians.
Van Wyck Brooks, 1886-1963, (U.S.) historian; critic of New England culture, especially literature.
Edmund Burke, 1729-97, (Ir.) British parliamentarian and political philosopher; influenced many Federalists.
Joseph Campbell, 1904-87, (U.S.) author, editor, teacher; wrote books on mythology, folklore.

Thomas Carlyle, 1795-1881, (Sc.) historian, critic; *Sartor Resartus, Past and Present, The French Revolution.*

Edward Channing, 1856-1931, (U.S.) historian; wrote 6-volume *History of the United States.*

John R. Commons, 1862-1945, (U.S.) economist, labor historian; *Legal Foundations of Capitalism.*

Benedetto Croce, 1866-1952, (It.) philosopher, statesman, and historian; *Philosophy of the Spirit.*

Bernard A. De Voto, 1897-1955, (U.S.) historian; wrote trilogy on American West; edited Mark Twain manuscripts.

Ariel Durant, 1898-1981, (U.S.) historian; collaborated with husband on 11-volume *Story of Civilization.*

Will Durant, 1885-1981, (U.S.) historian; *The Story of Civilization, The Story of Philosophy.*

Emile Durkheim, 1858-1917, (Fr.) a founder of modern sociology; *The Rules of Sociological Method.*

Friedrich Engels, 1820-95, (Ger.) political writer; with Marx wrote the *Communist Manifesto.*

Erik Erikson, 1902-94, (U.S.) psychoanalyst, author; theory of developmental stages of life, *Childhood and Society.*

Irving Fisher, 1867-1947, (U.S.) economist; contributed to the development of modern monetary theory.

John Fiske, 1842-1901, (U.S.) historian and lecturer; popularized Darwinian theory of evolution.

Charles Fourier, 1772-1837, (Fr.) utopian socialist.

Henry George, 1839-97, (U.S.) economist, reformer; led single-tax movement.

Edward Gibbon, 1737-94, (Br.) historian; wrote *The History of the Decline and Fall of the Roman Empire.*

Francesco Guicciardini, 1483-1540, (It.) historian; wrote *Storia d'Italia,* principal historical work of the 16th cent.

Thomas Hobbes, 1588-1679, (Eng.) political philosopher; *Leviathan.*

Richard Hofstadter, 1916-70, (U.S.) historian; *The Age of Reform.*

John Maynard Keynes, 1883-1946, (Br.) economist; principal advocate of deficit spending.

Alfred L. Kroeber, 1876-1960, (U.S.) cultural anthropologist; studied Indians of North and South America.

Christopher Lasch, 1932-94, (U.S.) social critic, historian; *The Culture of Narcissism.*

James L. Laughlin, 1850-1933, (U.S.) economist; helped establish Federal Reserve System.

Lucien Lévy-Bruhl, 1857-1939, (Fr.) philosopher; studied the psychology of primitive societies; *Primitive Mentality.*

Kurt Lewin, 1890-1947, (U.S.) German-born psychologist, studied human motivation and group dynamics.

John Locke, 1632-1704, (Eng.) philosopher; *Essay Concerning Human Understanding.*

Konrad Lorenz, 1904-89, (Aus.) ethologist; pioneer in study of animal behavior.

Thomas B. Macauley, 1800-59, (Br.) historian, statesman.

Bronislaw Malinowski, 1884-1942, (Pol.) considered the father of social anthropology.

Thomas R. Malthus, 1766-1834, (Br.) economist; famed for *Essay on the Principle of Population.*

Karl Mannheim, 1893-1947, (Hung.) sociologist, historian; *Ideology and Utopia.*

Karl Marx, 1818-83, (Ger.) political philosopher, proponent of modern communism; *Communist Manifesto, Das Kapital.*

Giuseppe Mazzini, 1805-72, (It.) political philosopher.

George H. Mead, 1863-1931, (U.S.) philosopher, social psychologist.

Margaret Mead, 1901-78, (U.S.) cultural anthropologist; popularized field, *Coming of Age in Samoa.*

James Mill, 1773-1836, (Sc.) philosopher, historian, economist; a proponent of Utilitarianism.

Perry G. Miller, 1905-63, (U.S.) historian; interpreted 17th-century New England.

Theodor Mommsen, 1817-1903, (Ger.) historian; *The History of Rome.*

Charles-Louis Montesquieu, 1689-1755, (Fr.) social philosopher; *The Spirit of Laws.*

Samuel Eliot Morison, 1887-1976, (U.S.) historian; chronicled voyages of early explorers.

Lewis Mumford, 1895-1990, (U.S.) sociologist, critic; *The Culture of Cities.*

Gunnar Myrdal, 1898-1987, (Swed.) economist, social scientist; *Asian Drama: An Inquiry into the Poverty of Nations.*

Joseph Needham, 1900-95, (Br.) scientific historian; *Science and Civilization in China.*

Allan Nevins, 1890-1971, (U.S.) historian, biographer; *The Ordeal of the Union.*

José Ortega y Gasset, 1883-1955, (Sp.) philosopher; advocated control by elite, *The Revolt of the Masses.*

Robert Owen, 1771-1858, (Br.) political philosopher, reformer; pioneer in cooperative movement.

Vilfredo Pareto, 1848-1923, (It.) economist, sociologist.

Francis Parkman, 1823-93, (U.S.) historian; *France and England in North America, 1851-92.*

Marco Polo, c1254-1324, (It.) narrated an account of his travels to China.

William Prescott, 1796-1859, (U.S.) early American historian; *The Conquest of Peru.*

Pierre Joseph Proudhon, 1809-65, (Fr.) social theorist; the father of anarchism, *The Philosophy of Property.*

François Quesnay, 1694-1774, (Fr.) economic theorist; demonstrated circular flow of economic activity through society.

David Ricardo, 1772-1823, (Br.) economic theorist; advocated free international trade.

James H. Robinson, 1863-1936, (U.S.) historian, educator.

Carl Rogers, 1902-87, (U.S.) psychotherapist, author.

Jean-Jacques Rousseau, 1712-78, (Fr.) social philosopher; the father of romantic sensibility; *Confessions.*

Lee Salk, 1926-92, (U.S.) child psycologist, author.

Edward Sapir, 1884-1939, (Ger.-U.S.) anthropologist; studied ethnology and linguistics of some U.S. Indian groups.

Ferdinand de Saussure, 1857-1913, (Swiss) a founder of modern linguistics.

Hjalmar Schacht, 1877-1970, (Ger.) economist.

Joseph Schumpeter, 1883-1950, (Czech.-U.S.) economist; championed big business, capitalism.

Albert Schweitzer, 1875-1965, (Alsatian) organist, social philosopher, theologian, medical missionary.

George Simmel, 1858-1918, (Ger.) sociologist, philosopher; helped establish German sociology.

B. F. Skinner, 1904-89, (U.S.) psychologist; behaviorism.

Adam Smith, 1723-90, (Br.) economist; advocated laissez-faire economy and free trade.

Jared Sparks, 1789-1866, (U.S.) historian, educator, editor; *The Library of American Biography.*

Oswald Spengler, 1880-1936, (Ger.) philosopher and historian; *The Decline of the West.*

William G. Sumner, 1840-1910, (U.S.) social scientist, economist; laissez-faire economy, Social Darwinism.

Hippolyte Taine, 1828-93, (Fr.) historian; basis of naturalistic school; *The Origins of Contemporary France.*

Frank W. Taussig, 1859-1940, (U.S.) economist, educator.

A(lan) J(ohn) P(ercivale) Taylor, 1906-89, (Br.) historian; *The Origins of the Second World War.*

Nikolaas Tinbergen, 1907-88, (Dutch-Br.) ethologist; pioneer in study of animal behavior.

Alexis de Tocqueville, 1805-59, (Fr.) political scientist, historian; *Democracy in America.*

Francis E. Townsend, 1867-1960, (U.S.) led old-age pension movement, 1933.

Arnold Toynbee, 1889-1975, (Br.) historian.

Heinrich von Treitschke, 1834-96, (Ger.) historian, political writer; *A History of Germany in the 19th Century.*

George Trevelyan, 1838-1928, (Br.) historian, statesman; favored "literary" over "scientific" history; *History of England.*

Barbara Tuchman, 1912-89, (U.S.) author of popular history books, *The Guns of August, The March of Folly.*

Frederick J. Turner, 1861-1932, (U.S.) historian, educator; *The Frontier in American History.*

Thorstein B. Veblen, 1857-1929, (U.S.) economist, social philosopher; *The Theory of the Leisure Class.*

Giovanni Vico, 1668-1744, (It.) historian, philosopher; regarded by many as first modern historian; *New Science.*

Voltaire (F.M. Arouet), 1694-1778, (Fr.) philosopher, historian; writer of "philosophical romances"; *Candide.*

Izaak Walton, 1593-1683, (Eng.) wrote biographies; political-philosophical study of fishing, *The Compleat Angler.*

Sidney J., 1859-1947, and wife **Beatrice,** 1858-1943, **Webb,** (Br.) leading figures in Fabian Society and Br. Labour Party.

Walter P. Webb, 1888-1963, (U.S.) historian of the West.

Max Weber, 1864-1920, (Ger.) sociologist; *The Protestant Ethic and the Spirit of Capitalism.*

Notable Military and Naval Leaders of the Past

Creighton Abrams, 1914-74, (U.S.) commanded forces in Vietnam, 1968-72.

Harold Alexander, 1891-1969, (Br.) led Allied invasion of Italy, 1943, WW2.

Ethan Allen, 1738-89, (U.S.) headed Green Mountain Boys; captured Ft. Ticonderoga, 1775, American Revolution.

Edmund Allenby, 1861-1936, (Br.) in Boer War, WW1; led Egyptian expeditionary force, 1917-18.

Benedict Arnold, 1741-1801, (U.S.) victorious at Saratoga; tried to betray West Point to British, American Revolution.

Henry "Hap" Arnold, 1886-1950, (U.S.) commanded Army Air Force in WW2.

John Barry, 1745-1803, (U.S.) won numerous sea battles during American Revolution.

Pierre Beauregard, 1818-93, (U.S.) Confederate general, ordered bombardment of Ft. Sumter that began the Civil War.

Gebhard von Blücher, 1742-1819, (Ger.) helped defeat Napoleon at Waterloo.

Napoleon Bonaparte, 1769-1821, (Fr.) defeated Russia and Austria at Austerlitz, 1805; invaded Russia, 1812; defeated at Waterloo, 1815.

Edward Braddock, 1695-1755, (Br.) commanded forces in French and Indian War.

Omar N. Bradley, 1893-1981, (U.S.) headed U.S. ground troops in Normandy invasion, 1944, WW2.

John Burgoyne, 1722-92, (Br.) defeated at Saratoga, American Revolution.

Claire Chennault, 1890-1958, (U.S.) headed Flying Tigers in WW2.

Mark Clark, 1896-1984, (U.S.) led forces in WW2 and Korean War.

Karl von Clausewitz, 1780-1831, (Prussian) wrote books on military theory.

Lucius D. Clay, 1897-1978, (U.S.) led Berlin airlift, 1948-49.

Henry Clinton, 1738-95, (Br.) commander of forces in American Revolution, 1778-81.

Cochise, c1815-74, (Native American) chief of Chiricahua band of Apache Indians in Southwest.

Charles Cornwallis, 1738-1805, (Br.) victorious at Brandywine, 1777; surrendered at Yorktown, American Revolution.

Crazy Horse, 1849-77, (Native American) Sioux war chief victorious at Little Big Horn.

George A. Custer, 1839-76, (U.S.) defeated and killed at Little Big Horn.

Moshe Dayan, 1915-81, (Isr.) directed campaigns in the 1967, 1973 Arab-Israeli wars.

Stephen Decatur, 1779-1820, (U.S.) naval hero of Barbary wars, War of 1812.

Anton Denikin, 1872-1947, (Russ.) led White forces in Russian civil war.

George Dewey, 1837-1917, (U.S.) destroyed Spanish fleet at Manila, 1898, Spanish-American War.

Hugh C. Dowding, 1883-1970, (Br.) headed RAF, 1936-40, WW2.

Jubal Early, 1816-94, (U.S.) Confederate general led raid on Washington, 1864, Civil War.

Dwight D. Eisenhower, 1890-1969, (U.S.) commanded Allied forces in Europe, WW2.

David Farragut, 1801-70, (U.S.) Union admiral, captured New Orleans, Mobile Bay, Civil War.

Ferdinand Foch, 1851-1929, (Fr.) headed victorious Allied armies, 1918, WW1.

Nathan Bedford Forrest, 1821-77, (U.S.) Confederate general, led cavalry raids against Union supply lines, Civil War.

Frederick the Great, 1712-86, (Prussian) led Prussia in The Seven Years War.

Horatio Gates, 1728-1806, (U.S.) commanded army at Saratoga, American Revolution.

Geronimo, 1829-1909 (Native American) leader of Chiricahua band of Apache Indians.

Charles G. Gordon, 1833-85, (Br.) led forces in China, Crimean War; killed at Khartoum.

Ulysses S. Grant, 1822-85, (U.S.) headed Union army, Civil War, 1864-65; forced Lee's surrender, 1865.

Nathanael Greene, 1742-86, (U.S.) defeated British in Southern campaign, 1780-81.

Heinz Guderian, 1888-1953, (Ger.) tank theorist, led panzer forces in Poland, France, Russia, WW2.

Douglas Haig, 1861-1928, (Br.) led British armies in France, 1915-18, WW1.

William F. Halsey, 1882-1959, (U.S.) defeated Japanese fleet at Leyte Gulf, 1944, WW2.

Sir Arthur Travers Harris, 1895-1984, (Br.) led Britain's WW2 bomber command.

Richard Howe, 1726-99, (Br.) commanded navy in American Revolution, 1776-78; June 1 victory against French, 1794.

William Howe, 1729-1814, (Br.) commanded forces in American Revolution, 1776-78.

Isaac Hull, 1773-1843, (U.S.) sunk British frigate *Guerriere*, War of 1812.

Thomas (Stonewall) Jackson, 1824-63, (U.S.) Confederate general led Shenandoah Valley campaign, Civil War.

Joseph Joffre, 1852-1931, (Fr.) headed Allied armies, won Battle of the Marne, 1914, WW1.

John Paul Jones, 1747-92, (U.S.) commanded *Bonhomme Richard* in victory over Serapis, American Revolution, 1779.

Stephen Kearny, 1794-1848, (U.S.) headed Army of the West in Mexican War.

Ernest J. King, 1878-1956, (U.S.) chief naval strategist in WW2.

Horatio H. Kitchener, 1850-1916, (Br.) led forces in Boer War; victorious at Khartoum; organized army in WW1.

Lavrenti Kornilov, 1870-1918, (Russ.) commander-in-chief, 1917; led counter-revolutionary march on Petrograd.

Thaddeus Kosciusko, 1746-1817, (Pol.) aided American cause in American Revolution.

Mikhail Kutuzov, 1745-1813, (Russ.) fought French at Borodino, Napoleonic Wars, 1812; abandoned Moscow; forced French retreat.

Marquis de Lafayette, 1757-1834, (Fr.) aided American cause in American Revolution.

T(homas) E. Lawrence (of Arabia), 1888-1935, (Br.) organized revolt of Arabs against Turks in WW1.

Henry (Light-Horse Harry) Lee, 1756-1818, (U.S.) cavalry officer in American Revolution.

Robert E. Lee, 1807-70, (U.S.) Confederate general defeated at Gettysburg, Civil War; surrendered to Grant, 1865.

Lyman Lemnitzer, 1899-1988, (U.S.) WW2 hero, later general, chairman of Joint Chiefs of Staff.

James Longstreet, 1821-1904, (U.S.) aided Lee at Gettysburg, Civil War.

Douglas MacArthur, 1880-1964, (U.S.) commanded forces in SW Pacific in WW2; headed occupation forces in Japan, 1945-51; UN commander in Korean War.

Francis Marion, 1733-95, (U.S.) led guerrilla actions in South Carolina during American Revolution.

Duke of Marlborough, 1650-1722, (Br.) led forces against Louis XIV in War of the Spanish Succession.

George C. Marshall, 1880-1959, (U.S.) chief of staff in WW2; authored Marshall Plan.

George B. McClellan, 1826-85, (U.S.) Union general, commanded Army of the Potomac, 1861-62, Civil War.

George Meade, 1815-72; (U.S.) commanded Union forces at Gettysburg, Civil War.

Billy Mitchell, 1879-1936, (U.S.) WW1 air-power advocate; court-martialed for insubordination, later vindicated.

Helmuth von Moltke, 1800-91, (Ger.) victorious in Austro-Prussian, Franco-Prussian wars.

Louis de Montcalm, 1712-59, (Fr.) headed troops in Canada, French and Indian War; defeated at Quebec, 1759.

Bernard Law Montgomery, 1887-1976, (Br.) stopped German offensive at Alamein, 1942, WW2; helped plan Normandy invasion.

Daniel Morgan, 1736-1802, (U.S.) victorious at Cowpens, 1781, American Revolution.

Louis Mountbatten, 1900-79, (Br.) Supreme Allied Commander of SE Asia, 1943-46, WW2.

Joachim Murat, 1767-1815, (Fr.) leader of cavalry at Marengo, 1800; Austerlitz, 1805; and Jena, 1806, Napoleonic Wars.

Horatio Nelson, 1758-1805, (Br.) naval commander destroyed French fleet at Trafalgar.

Michel Ney, 1769-1815, (Fr.) commanded forces in Switz., Aus., Russ., Napoleonic Wars; defeated at Waterloo.

Chester Nimitz, 1885-1966, (U.S.) commander of naval forces in Pacific in WW2.

George S. Patton, 1885-1945, (U.S.) led assault on Sicily, 1943, Third Army invasion of Europe, WW2.

Oliver Perry, 1785-1819, (U.S.) won Battle of Lake Erie in War of 1812.

John Pershing, 1860-1948, (U.S.) commanded Mexican border campaign, 1916, American Expeditionary Force, WW1.

Henri Philippe Pétain, 1856-1951, (Fr.) defended Verdun, 1916; headed Vichy government in WW2.

George E. Pickett, 1825-75, (U.S.) Confederate general famed for "charge" at Gettysburg, Civil War.

Hyman Rickover, 1900-86, (U.S.) father of nuclear navy.

Erwin Rommel, 1891-1944, (Ger.) headed Afrika Korps, WW2.

Gerd von Rundstedt, 1875-1953, (Ger.) supreme commander in West, 1942-45, WW2.

Aleksandr Samsonov, 1859-1914, (Russ.) led invasion of E. Prussia, WW1, defeated at Tannenberg, 1914.

Winfield Scott, 1786-1866, (U.S.) hero of War of 1812; headed forces in Mexican war, took Mexico City.

Philip Sheridan, 1831-88, (U.S.) Union cavalry officer, headed Army of the Shenandoah, 1864-65, Civil War.

William T. Sherman, 1820-91, (U.S.) Union general, sacked Atlanta during "march to the sea," 1864, Civil War.

Carl Spaatz, 1891-1974, (U.S.) directed strategic bombing against Germany, later Japan, in WW2.

Raymond Spruance, 1886-1969, (U.S.) victorious at Midway Island, 1942, WW2.

Joseph W. Stilwell, 1883-1946, (U.S.) headed forces in the China, Burma, India theater in WW2.

J.E.B. Stuart, 1833-64, (U.S.) Confederate cavalry commander, Civil War.

George H. Thomas, 1816-70, (U.S.) saved Union army at Chattanooga, 1863; victorious at Nashville, 1864, Civil War.

Semyon Timoshenko, 1895-1970, (USSR) defended Moscow, Stalingrad, WW2; led winter offensive, 1942-43.

Alfred von Tirpitz, 1849-1930, (Ger.) responsible for submarine blockade in WW1.

Jonathan M. Wainwright, 1883-1953, (U.S.) forced to surrender on Corregidor, 1942, WW2.

George Washington, 1732-99, (U.S.) led Continental army, 1775-83, American Revolution.
Archibald Wavell, 1883-1950, (Br.) commanded forces in N. and E. Africa, and SE Asia in WW2.
Anthony Wayne, 1745-96, (U.S.) captured Stony Point, 1779, American Revolution.

Duke of Wellington, 1769-1852, (Br.) defeated Napoleon at Waterloo.
James Wolfe, 1727-59, (Br.) captured Quebec from French, 1759, French and Indian War.
Georgi Zhukov, 1895-1974, (Russ.) defended Moscow, 1941, led assault on Berlin, 1945, WW2.

Noted Philosophers and Religionists of the Past

Lyman Abbott, 1835-1922, (U.S.) clergyman, reformer; advocate of Christian Socialism.
Pierre Abelard, 1079-1142, (Fr.) philosopher, theologian, teacher; used dialectic method to support Christian dogma.
Felix Adler, 1851-1933, (U.S.) German-born founder of the Ethical Culture Society.
Aristotle, 384-322 BC, (Gr.) philosopher; emphasized direct observation of nature.
St. Augustine, 354-430, Latin bishop considered the founder of formalized Christian theology.
Averroes, 1126-98, (Sp.) Islamic philosopher.
Roger Bacon, c1214-94, (Eng.) philosopher and scientist.
Bahaullah (Mirza Husayn Ali), 1817-92, (Pers.) founder of Bahá'í faith.
Karl Barth, 1886-1968, (Sw.) theologian; a leading force in 20th-century Protestantism.
St. Benedict, c480-547, (It.) founded the Benedictines.
Jeremy Bentham, 1748-1832, (Br.) philosopher, reformer; founder of Utilitarianism.
Henri Bergson, 1859-1941, (Fr.) philosopher of evolution.
George Berkeley, 1685-1753, (Ir.) philosopher, churchman.
John Biddle, 1615-62, (Eng.) founder of English Unitarianism.
Jakob Boehme, 1575-1624, (Ger.) theosophist and mystic.
William Brewster, 1567-1644, (Eng.) headed Pilgrims.
Emil Brunner, 1889-1966, (Sw.) Protestant theologian.
Giordano Bruno, 1548-1600, (It.) philosopher; first to state the cosmic theory.
Martin Buber, 1878-1965, (Ger.) Jewish philosopher, theologian; wrote *I and Thou.*
Buddha (Siddhartha Gautama), c563-c 483 BC, (Ind.) philosopher, founded Buddhism.
Kenneth Burke, 1897-1993 (U.S.), one of the founders of New Criticism literary philosophy, *A Grammar of Motives.*
John Calvin, 1509-64, (Fr.) theologian; a key figure in the Protestant Reformation.
Rudolph Carnap, 1891-1970, (U.S.) German-born philosopher; a founder of logical positivism.
William Ellery Channing, 1780-1842, (U.S.) clergyman; early spokesman for Unitarianism.
Auguste Comte, 1798-1857, (Fr.) philosopher; the founder of positivism.
Confucius, 551-479 BC, (Chin.) founder of Confucianism.
John Cotton, 1584-1652, (Eng.) Puritan theologian.
Thomas Cranmer, 1489-1556, (Eng.) churchman; wrote much of *Book of Common Prayer.*
René Descartes, 1596-1650, (Fr.) philosopher, mathematician; "father of modern philosophy."
John Dewey, 1859-1952, (U.S.) philosopher, educator; helped inaugurate the progressive education movement.
Denis Diderot, 1713-84, (Fr.) philosopher, encyclopedist.
Mary Baker Eddy, 1821-1910, (U.S.) founder of Christian Science, wrote *Science and Health.*
Jonathan Edwards, 1703-58, (U.S.) preacher, theologian.
(Desiderius) Erasmus, c1466-1536, (Du.) Renaissance humanist; wrote *On the Freedom of the Will.*
Johann Fichte, 1762-1814, (Ger.) philosopher; the first of the Transcendental Idealists.
George Fox, 1624-91, (Br.) founder of Society of Friends.
St. Francis of Assisi, 1182-1226, (It.) founded Franciscans.
al-Ghazali, 1058-1111, Islamic philosopher.
Georg W. Hegel, 1770-1831, (Ger.) Idealist philosopher.
Martin Heidegger, 1889-1976, (Ger.) existentialist philosopher; affected fields ranging from physics to literary criticism.
Johann G. Herder, 1744-1803, (Ger.) philosopher, cultural historian; a founder of German Romanticism.
David Hume, 1711-76, (Sc.) philosopher, historian.
Jan Hus, 1369-1415, (Czech.) religious reformer.
Edmund Husserl, 1859-1938, (Ger.) philosopher; founded the Phenomenological movement.
Thomas Huxley, 1825-95, (Br.) philosopher, educator.
Ignatius of Loyola, 1491-1556, (Sp.) founder of the Jesuits.
William Inge, 1860-1954, (Br.) theologian; explored the mystic aspects of Christianity.
William James, 1842-1910, (U.S.) philosopher, psychologist; advanced theory of the pragmatic nature of truth.
Karl Jaspers, 1883-1969, (Ger.) existentialist philosopher.
Immanuel Kant, 1724-1804, (Ger.) metaphysician; preeminent founder of modern critical philosophy; *Critique of Pure Reason.*
Soren Kierkegaard, 1813-55, (Dan.) philosopher; considered the father of Existentialism.

Russell Kirk, 1918-94, (U.S.), social philosopher; *The Conservative Mind.*
John Knox, 1505-72, (Sc.) leader of the Protestant Reformation in Scotland.
Lao-Tzu, 604-531 BC, (Chin.) philosopher; considered the founder of the Taoist religion.
Gottfried von Leibniz, 1646-1716, (Ger.) philosopher, mathematician; influenced German Enlightenment.
Martin Luther, 1483-1546, (Ger.) leader of the Protestant Reformation, founded Lutheran church.
Maimonides, 1135-1204, (Sp.) Jewish philosopher.
Jacques Maritain, 1882-1973, (Fr.) Neo-Thomist philosopher.
Cotton Mather, 1663-1728, (U.S.) defender of orthodox Puritanism; founded Yale, 1701.
Philipp Melanchthon, 1497-1560, (Ger.) theologian, humanist; an important voice in the Reformation.
Thomas Merton, 1915-68, (U.S.) Trappist monk, spiritual writer; *The Seven Storey Mountain.*
John Stuart Mill, 1806-73, (Br.) philosopher, economist.
Muhammad, c570-632, (Arab) the prophet of Islam.
Dwight Moody, 1837-99, (U.S.) evangelist.
George E. Moore, 1873-1958, (Br.) ethical theorist.
Elijah Muhammad, 1897-1975, (U.S.) leader of the Black Muslim sect.
Heinrich Muhlenberg, 1711-87, (Ger.) organized the Lutheran Church in America.
John H. Newman, 1801-90, (Br.) Roman Catholic cardinal; led Oxford Movement; *Apologia pro Vita Sua.*
Reinhold Niebuhr, 1892-1971, (U.S.) Protestant theologian.
Friedrich Nietzsche, 1844-1900, (Ger.) moral philosopher; *The Birth of Tragedy, Thus Spake Zarathustra.*
Blaise Pascal, 1623-62, (Fr.) philosopher, mathematician.
St. Patrick, c389-c 461, brought Christianity to Ireland.
St. Paul, ?-c67, a proponent of Christianity; his epistles are first Christian theological writing.
Norman Vincent Peale, 1898-1993, (U.S.) religious leader, author; *The Power of Positive Thinking.*
Charles S. Peirce, 1839-1914, (U.S.) philosopher, logician; originated concept of Pragmatism, 1878.
Plato, c428-347 BC, (Gr.) philosopher; argued for inde-pendent reality of ideas; *Republic.*
Josiah Royce, 1855-1916, (U.S.) Idealist philosopher.
Charles T. Russell, 1852-1916, (U.S.) founder of Jehovah's Witnesses.
Fredrich von Schelling, 1775-1854, (Ger.) philosopher of romantic movement.
Friedrich Schleiermacher, 1768-1834, (Ger.) theologian; a founder of modern Protestant theology.
Arthur Schopenhauer, 1788-1860, (Ger.) philosopher.
Joseph Smith, 1805-44, (U.S.) founded Latter Day Saints (Mormon) movement, 1830.
Socrates, 469-399 BC, (Gr.) philosopher.
Herbert Spencer, 1820-1903, (Br.) philosopher of evolution.
Baruch Spinoza, 1632-77, (Dutch) rationalist philosopher.
Billy Sunday, 1862-1935, (U.S.) evangelist.
Daisetz Teitaro Suzuki, 1870-1966, (Jpn.) Buddhist scholar.
Emanuel Swedenborg, 1688-1772, (Swed.) philosopher, mystic.
Thomas à Becket, 1118-70, (Eng.) archbishop of Canterbury; opposed Henry II.
Thomas à Kempis, c1380-1471, (Ger.) theologian; probably wrote *Imitation of Christ.*
Thomas Aquinas, 1225-74, (It.) Roman Catholic scholar, saint; wrote *Summa Theologica.*
Paul Tillich, 1886-1965, (U.S.) German-born philosopher and theologian; brought depth psychology to Protestantism.
John Wesley, 1703-91, (Br.) theologian, evangelist; founded Methodism.
Alfred North Whitehead, 1861-1947, (Br.) philosopher, mathematician; *Principia Mathematica* (with Bertrand Russell).
William of Occam, c1285-c1349 (Eng.) medieval scholastic philosopher.
Roger Williams, c1603-83, (U.S.) clergyman; championed religious freedom and separation of church and state.
Ludwig Wittgenstein, 1889-1951, (Aus.) philosopher; influenced language philosophy.
John Wycliffe, 1320-84, (Eng.) theologian, reformer.
Brigham Young, 1801-77, (U.S.) Mormon leader after Smith's assassination, colonized Utah.
Huldrych Zwingli, 1484-1531, (Swed.) theologian; led Swiss Protestant Reformation.

Noted Political Leaders of the Past

(U.S. presidents and vice presidents, Supreme Court justices, signers of Declaration of Independence listed elsewhere.)

Abu Bakr, 573-634, Muslim leader, first caliph, chosen successor to Muhammad.

Dean Acheson, 1893-1971, (U.S.) secretary of state; chief architect of cold war foreign policy.

Samuel Adams, 1722-1803, (U.S.) patriot, Boston Tea Party firebrand.

Konrad Adenauer, 1876-1967, (Ger.) W. German chancellor.

Emilio Aguinaldo, 1869-1964, (Philip.) revolutionary; fought against Spain and the U.S.

Akbar, 1542-1605, greatest Mogul emperor of India.

Salvador Allende Gossens, 1908-1973, (Chilean) president; advocate of democratic socialism.

Herbert H. Asquith, 1852-1928, (Br.) liberal prime minister; instituted an advanced program of social reform.

Atahualpa, ?-1533, Inca (ruling chief) of Peru.

Kemal Atatürk, 1881-1938, (Turk.) founded modern Turkey.

Clement Attlee, 1883-1967, (Br.) Labour party leader, prime minister; enacted natl. health, nationalized many industries.

Stephen F. Austin, 1793-1836, (U.S.) led Texas colonization.

Mikhail Bakunin, 1814-76, (Russ.) revolutionary; leading exponent of anarchism.

Arthur J. Balfour, 1848-1930, (Br.) foreign secretary under Lloyd George; issued Balfour Declaration expressing official British approval of Zionism.

Bernard M. Baruch, 1870-1965, (U.S.) financier, govt. adviser.

Fulgencio Batista y Zaldívar, 1901-73, (Cuban) ruler overthrown by Castro.

Lord Beaverbrook, 1879-1964, (Br.) financier, statesman, newspaper owner.

Menachem Begin, 1913-92, (Isr.) Israeli prime minister, won 1978 Nobel Peace Prize.

Eduard Benes, 1884-1948, (Czech.) president during interwar and post-WW2 eras.

David Ben-Gurion, 1886-1973, (Isr.) first prime minister of Israel, 1948-53, 1955-63.

Thomas Hart Benton, 1782-1858, (U.S.) Missouri senator; championed agrarian interests and westward expansion.

Lavrenti Beria, 1899-1953, (USSR) Communist leader prominent in political purges under Stalin.

Aneurin Bevan, 1897-1960, (Br.) Labour party leader.

Ernest Bevin, 1881-1951, (Br.) Labour party leader, foreign minister; helped lay foundation for NATO.

Otto von Bismarck, 1815-98, (Ger.) statesman known as the Iron Chancellor, uniter of Germany, 1870.

James G. Blaine, 1830-93, (U.S.) Republican politician, diplomat; influential in launching Pan-American movement.

Léon Blum, 1872-1950, (Fr.) socialist leader, writer; headed first Popular Front government.

Simón Bolívar, 1783-1830, (Venez.) S. American revolutionary who liberated much of the continent from Spanish rule.

William E. Borah, 1865-1940, (U.S.) isolationist senator; instrumental in blocking U.S. membership in League of Nations and the World Court.

Cesare Borgia, 1476-1507, (It.) soldier, politician; an outstanding figure of the Italian Renaissance.

Willy Brandt, 1913-92, (Ger.) statesman, chancellor of West Germany, 1969-74; promoted East/West peace, *Ostpolitik.*

Leonid Brezhnev, 1906-82, (USSR) leader of the Soviet Union, 1964-82.

Aristide Briand, 1862-1932, (Fr.) foreign minister; chief architect of Locarno Pact and anti-war Kellogg-Briand Pact.

William Jennings Bryan, 1860-1925, (U.S.) Democratic, populist leader, orator; 3 times lost race for presidency.

Nikolai Bukharin, 1888-1938, (USSR) communist leader.

William C. Bullitt, 1891-1967, (U.S.) diplomat; first ambassador to USSR, ambassador to France.

Ralph Bunche, 1904-71, (U.S.) a founder and key diplomat of United Nations for more than 20 years.

John C. Calhoun, 1782-1850, (U.S.) political leader; champion of states' rights and a symbol of the Old South.

Robert Castlereagh, 1769-1822, (Br.) foreign secretary; guided Grand Alliance against Napoleon.

Camillo Benso Cavour, 1810-61, (It.) statesman; largely responsible for uniting Italy under the House of Savoy.

Nicolae Ceausescu, 1918-89, (Rom.) Communist leader, head of state 1967-89.

Austen Chamberlain, 1863-1937, (Br.) Conservative party leader; largely responsible for Locarno Pact of 1925.

Neville Chamberlain, 1869-1940, (Br.) Conservative prime minister whose appeasement of Hitler led to Munich Pact.

Salmon P. Chase, 1808-73, (U.S.) public official, abolitionist, jurist; 6th chief justice of the U.S.

Chiang Kai-shek, 1887-1975, (Chin.) Nationalist Chinese president whose government was driven from mainland to Taiwan.

Winston Churchill, 1874-1965, (Br.) prime minister, soldier, author; guided Britain through WW2.

Galeazzo Ciano, 1903-44, (It.) fascist foreign minister; helped create Rome-Berlin Axis, executed by Mussolini.

Henry Clay, 1777-1852, (U.S.) "The Great Compromiser," one of the most influential pre-Civil War political leaders.

Georges Clemenceau, 1841-1929, (Fr.) twice premier, Wilson's antagonist at Paris Peace Conference after WW1.

DeWitt Clinton, 1769-1828, (U.S.) political leader; responsible for promoting idea of the Erie Canal.

Robert Clive, 1725-74, (Br.) first administrator of Bengal; laid foundation for British Empire in India.

Jean Baptiste Colbert, 1619-83, (Fr.) statesman; influential under Louis XIV, created the French navy.

Oliver Cromwell, 1599-1658, (Br.) Lord Protector of England, led parliamentary forces during Civil War.

Curzon of Kedleston, 1859-1925, (Br.) viceroy of India, foreign secretary; major force in dealing with post-WW1 problems in Europe and Far East.

Édouard Daladier, 1884-1970, (Fr.) radical socialist politician, arrested by Vichy, interned by Germans until 1945.

Georges Danton, 1759-94, (Fr.) a leading figure in the French Revolution.

Jefferson Davis, 1808-89, (U.S.) president of the Confederate States of America.

Charles G. Dawes, 1865-1951, (U.S.) statesman, banker; advanced Dawes Plan, 1924, to stabilize post-WW1 German finances.

Alcide De Gasperi, 1881-1954, (It.) prime minister; founder of the Christian Democratic party.

Charles DeGaulle, 1890-1970, (Fr.) general, statesman; first president of the Fifth Republic.

Eamon De Valera, 1882-1975, (Ir.-U.S.) statesman; led fight for Irish independence.

Thomas E. Dewey, 1902-71, (U.S.) New York governor; twice loser in try for presidency.

Ngo Dinh Diem, 1901-63, (Viet.) South Vietnamese president; assassinated in government take-over.

Everett M. Dirksen, 1896-1969, (U.S.) Senate Republican minority leader, orator.

Benjamin Disraeli, 1804-81, (Br.) prime minister; considered founder of modern Conservative party.

Engelbert Dollfuss, 1892-1934, (Aus.) chancellor; assassinated by Austrian Nazis.

Andrea Doria, 1466-1560, (It.) Genoese admiral, statesman; called "Father of Peace" and "Liberator of Genoa."

Stephen A. Douglas, 1813-61, (U.S.) Democratic leader, orator; opposed Lincoln for the presidency.

Alexander Dubcek, 1921-92, (Czech.) statesman whose attempted liberalization was crushed, 1968.

John Foster Dulles, 1888-1959, (U.S.) secretary of state under Eisenhower, cold war policy maker.

Friedrich Ebert, 1871-1925, (Ger.) Social Democratic movement leader; 1st president of Weimar Republic, 1919-25.

Sir Anthony Eden, 1897-1977, (Br.) foreign secretary, prime minister during Suez invasion of 1956.

Ludwig Erhard, 1897-1977, (Ger.) economist, West German chancellor; led nation's economic rise after WW2.

Hamilton Fish, 1808-93, (U.S.) secretary of state, successfully mediated disputes with Great Britain, Latin America.

James V. Forrestal, 1892-1949, (U.S.) secretary of navy, first secretary of defense.

Francisco Franco, 1892-1975, (Sp.) leader of rebel forces during Spanish Civil War and dictator of Spain.

Benjamin Franklin, 1706-90, (U.S.) printer, publisher, author, inventor, scientist, diplomat.

Louis de Frontenac, 1620-98, (Fr.) governor of New France (Canada); encouraged explorations, fought Iroquois.

J. William Fulbright, 1905-95, (U.S.) U.S. senator; leading figure in U.S. foreign policy during cold war years.

Hugh Gaitskell, 1906-63, (Br.) Labour party leader; major force in reversing its stand for unilateral disarmament.

Albert Gallatin, 1761-1849, (U.S.) secretary of treasury who was instrumental in negotiating end of War of 1812.

Léon Gambetta, 1838-82, (Fr.) statesman, politician; one of the founders of the Third Republic.

Indira Gandhi, 1917-84, (In.) daughter of Jawaharlal Nehru, prime minister of India, 1966-77, 1980-84; assassinated.

Mohandas K. Gandhi, 1869-1948, (In.) political leader, ascetic; led nationalist movement against British rule.

Giuseppe Garibaldi, 1807-82, (It.) patriot, soldier; a leading figure in the Risorgimento, the Italian unification movement.

Genghis Khan, c1167-1227, Mongol conqueror, ruler of vast Asian empire.

William E. Gladstone, 1809-98, (Br.) prime minister 4 times; dominant force of Liberal party from 1868 to 1894.

Paul Joseph Goebbels, 1897-1945, (Ger.) Nazi propagandist, master of mass psychology.

Klement Gottwald, 1896-1953, (Czech.) communist leader; ushered communism into his country.

Che (Ernesto) Guevara, 1928-67, (Arg.) guerrilla leader; prominent in Cuban revolution, killed in Bolivia.

Haile Selassie, 1891-1975, (Eth.) emperor; maintained monarchy through invasion, occupation, internal resistance.

Alexander Hamilton, 1755-1804, (U.S.) first treasury secretary; champion of strong central government.

Dag Hammarskjold, 1905-61, (Swed.) statesman; UN secretary-general.

John Hancock, 1737-93, (U.S.) revolutionary leader; first signer of Declaration of Independence.

John Hay, 1838-1905, (U.S.) secretary of state; primarily associated with Open Door Policy toward China.

Patrick Henry, 1736-99, (U.S.) major revolutionary figure, remarkable orator.

Édouard Herriot, 1872-1957, (Fr.) Radical Socialist leader; twice premier, president of National Assembly.

Theodor Herzl, 1860-1904, (Aus.) founder of modern Zionism.

Heinrich Himmler, 1900-45, (Ger.) notorious head of Nazi SS and Gestapo.

Paul von Hindenburg, 1847-1934, (Ger.) field marshal,WW1; 2d president of Weimar Republic, 1925-34.

Hirohito, 1902-89 (Jpn.); emperor of Japan,1926-89.

Adolf Hitler, 1889-1945, (Ger.) dictator; founder of National Socialism; wrote *Mein Kampf,* strategy for world domination.

Ho Chi Minh, 1890-1969, (Viet.) North Vietnamese president, Vietnamese Communist leader.

Harry L. Hopkins, 1890-1946, (U.S.) New Deal administrator; closest adviser to FDR during WW2.

Edward M. House, 1858-1938, (U.S.) diplomat; confidential adviser to Woodrow Wilson.

Samuel Houston, 1793-1863, (U.S.) leader of struggle to win control of Texas from Mexico.

Cordell Hull, 1871-1955, (U.S.) secretary of state, 1933-44; initiated reciprocal trade to lower tariffs, helped organize UN.

Hubert H. Humphrey, 1911-78, (U.S.) Minnesota Democrat, senator, vice president; spent 32 years in public service.

Ibn Saud, c1888-1953, (Saudi Arabian) founder of Saudi Arabia and its first king.

Jacob Javits, 1904-86 (U.S.) U.S. senator from NY for 24 yrs.

Jinnah, Muhammed Ali, 1876-1948, (Pak.) founder, first governor-general of Pakistan.

Benito Juarez, 1806-72, (Mex.) rallied his country against foreign threats, sought to create democratic, federal republic.

Kamehameha I, c1758-1819, (Hawaiian) founder, first monarch of unified Hawaii.

Frank B. Kellogg, 1856-1937, (U.S.) secretary of state; negotiated Kellogg-Briand Pact to outlaw war.

Robert F. Kennedy, 1925-68, (U.S.) attorney general, senator; assassinated while seeking presidential nomination.

Aleksandr Kerensky, 1881-1970, (Russ.) revolutionary; served as prime minister after Feb. 1917 revolution until Bolshevik overthrow.

Ruhollah Khomeini, 1900-89, (Iranian), religious leader with Islamic title "ayatollah," directed overthrow of shah, 1979.

Nikita Khrushchev, 1894-1971, (USSR) premier, first secretary of Communist party; initiated de-Stalinization.

Kim Il Sung, 1912-94, (Korean) leader of North Korea from 1948 until his death.

Lajos Kossuth, 1802-94, (Hung.) principal figure in 1848 Hungarian revolution.

Pyotr Kropotkin, 1842-1921, (Russ.) anarchist; championed the peasants but opposed Bolshevism.

Kublai Khan, c1215-94, Mongol emperor; founder of Yüan dynasty in China.

Béla Kun, 1886-c1939, (Hung.) communist; member of 3d Communist Intl., tried to foment worldwide revolution.

Robert M. LaFollette, 1855-1925, (U.S.) Wisconsin public official; leader of progressive movement.

Pierre Laval, 1883-1945, (Fr.) politician, Vichy foreign minister; executed for treason.

Andrew Bonar Law, 1858-1923, (Br.) Conservative party politician; led opposition to Irish home rule.

Vladimir Ilyich Lenin (Ulyanov), 1870-1924, (Russ.) revolutionary; founder of Bolshevism, Soviet leader 1917-24.

Ferdinand de Lesseps, 1805-94, (Fr.) diplomat, engineer; conceived idea of Suez Canal.

Rene Levesque, 1922-87, (Can.) premier of Quebec, 1976-85; led unsuccessful fight to separate from Canada.

Maxim Litvinov, 1876-1951, (Pol.-Russ.) revolutionary, commissar of foreign affairs; favored cooperation with West.

Liu Shaoqi, c1898-1974, (Chin.) communist leader; fell from grace during "cultural revolution."

David Lloyd George, 1863-1945, (Br.) Liberal party prime minister; laid foundations for modern welfare state.

Henry Cabot Lodge, 1850-1924, (U.S.) Republican senator; led opposition to participation in League of Nations.

Huey P. Long, 1893-1935, (U.S.) Louisiana political demagogue, governor; assassinated.

Rosa Luxemburg, 1871-1919, (Ger.) revolutionary; leader of the German Social Democratic party and Spartacus party.

J. Ramsay MacDonald, 1866-1937, (Br.) first Labour party prime minister of Great Britain.

Harold Macmillan, 1895-1987, (Br.) prime minister of Great Britain, 1957-63.

Joseph R. McCarthy, 1908-57, (U.S.) senator notorious for his witch hunt for communists in the government.

Makarios III, 1913-77, (Cypriot) Greek Orthodox archbishop; first president of Cyprus.

Mao Zedong, 1893-1976, (Chin.) chief Chinese Marxist theorist, soldier; led Chinese revolution establishing his nation as an important communist state.

Jean Paul Marat, 1743-93, (Fr.) revolutionary, politician; identified with radical Jacobins, assassinated.

José Martí, 1853-95, (Cub.) patriot, poet; leader of Cuban struggle for independence.

Jan Masaryk, 1886-1948, (Czech.) foreign minister; died by mysterious suicide following communist coup.

Thomas G. Masaryk, 1850-1937, (Czech.) statesman, philosopher; first president of Czechoslovak Republic.

Jules Mazarin, 1602-61, (Fr.) cardinal, statesman; prime minister under Louis XIII and queen regent Anne of Austria.

Giuseppe Mazzini, 1805-72, (It.), reformer dedicated to Risorgimento, 19th-century movement for renewal of Italy.

Tom Mboya, 1930-69, (Kenyan) political leader; instrumental in securing independence for Kenya.

Cosimo I de' Medici, 1519-74, (It.) Duke of Florence, grand duke of Tuscany.

Lorenzo de' Medici, the Magnificent, 1449-92, (It.) merchant prince; a towering figure in Italian Renaissance.

Catherine de Medicis, 1519-89, (Fr.) queen consort of Henry II, regent of France; influential in Catholic-Huguenot wars.

Golda Meir, 1898-1979, (Isr.) a founder of the state of Israel and prime minister, 1969-74.

Klemens W. N. L. Metternich, 1773-1859, (Aus.) statesman; arbiter of post-Napoleonic Europe.

Anastas Mikoyan, 1895-1978, (USSR) president of the Presidium of the Supreme Soviet of the USSR, 1964-65.

Guy Mollet, 1905-75, (Fr.) social politician, resistance leader.

Henry Morgenthau, Jr., 1891-1967, (U.S.) secy. of treasury; raised funds to finance New Deal and U.S. WW2 activities.

Gouverneur Morris, 1752-1816, (U.S.) statesman, diplomat; financial expert who helped plan decimal coinage system.

Muhammad Ali, 1769?-1849, (Egypt) pasha; founder of dynasty that inspired emergence of modern Egyptian state.

Benito Mussolini, 1883-1945, (It.) dictator and leader of the Italian fascist state.

Imre Nagy, c1896-1958, (Hung.) communist premier; assassinated after Soviets crushed 1956 uprising.

Gamal Abdel Nasser, 1918-70, (Egypt.) leader of Arab unification, second Egyptian president.

Jawaharlal Nehru, 1889-1964, (Indian) prime minister; guided India through its early years of independence.

Kwame Nkrumah, 1909-72, (Ghan.) 1st prime minister, 1957-60, and president, 1960-66, of Ghana.

Frederick North, 1732-92, (Br.) prime minister; his inept policies led to loss of American colonies.

Daniel O'Connell, 1775-1847, (Ir.) political leader; known as The Liberator.

Omar, c581-644, Muslim leader; 2d caliph, led Islam to become an imperial power.

Thomas P. (Tip) O'Neill, Jr., 1912-94, (U.S.) U.S. congressman, Speaker of the House, 1977-86.

Ignace Paderewski, 1860-1941, (Pol.) statesman, pianist; composer, briefly prime minister, an ardent patriot.

Viscount Palmerston, 1784-1865, (Br.) Whig-Liberal prime minister, foreign minister; embodied British nationalism.

Georgios Papandreou, 1888-1968, (Gk.) Republican politician; served 3 times as prime minister.

Franz von Papen, 1879-1969, (Ger.) politician; played major role in overthrow of Weimar Republic and rise of Hitler.

Charles Stewart Parnell, 1846-1891, (Ir.) nationalist leader; "uncrowned king of Ireland."

Lester Pearson, 1897-1972, (Can.) diplomat, Liberal party leader, prime minister.

Robert Peel, 1788-1850, (Br.) reformist prime minister, founder of Conservative party.

Juan Perón, 1895-1974, (Arg.) president of Argentina (1946-55 and 1973-74).

Joseph Pilsudski, 1867-1935, (Pol.) statesman; instrumental in reestablishing Polish state in the 20th century.

Charles Pinckney, 1757-1824, (U.S.) founding father; his Pinckney plan was largely incorporated into constitution.

Christian Pineau, 1905-95, (Fr.) leader of French Resistance during WW2; French foreign minister, 1956-58.

William Pitt, the Elder, 1708-78, (Br.) statesman; called the "Great Commoner," transformed Britain into imperial power.

William Pitt, the Younger, 1759-1806, (Br.) prime minister during French Revolutionary wars.

Georgi Plekhanov, 1857-1918, (Russ.) revolutionary, social philosopher; called "father of Russian Marxism."

Raymond Poincaré, 1860-1934, (Fr.) 9th president of the Republic; advocated harsh punishment of Germany after WW1.

Georges Pompidou, 1911-74, (Fr.) Gaullist political leader; president from 1969-74.

Grigori Potemkin, 1739-91, (Russ.) field marshal; favorite of Catherine II.

Edmund Randolph, 1753-1813, (U.S.) attorney; prominent in drafting, ratification of constitution.

John Randolph, 1773-1833, (U.S.) southern planter; strong advocate of states' rights.

Jeannette Rankin, 1880-1973, (U.S.) pacifist; first woman member of U.S. Congress.

Walter Rathenau, 1867-1922, (Ger.) industrialist, statesman.

Sam Rayburn, 1882-1961, (U.S.) Democratic leader; representative for 47 years, House Speaker for 17.

Paul Reynaud, 1878-1966, (Fr.) statesman; premier in 1940 at the time of France's defeat by Germany.

Syngman Rhee, 1875-1965, (Korean) first president of the Republic of Korea.

Cecil Rhodes, 1853-1902, (Br.) imperialist, industrial magnate; established Rhodes scholarships in his will.

Cardinal de Richelieu, 1585-1642, (Fr.) statesman; known as "red eminence," chief minister to Louis XIII.

Maximilien Robespierre, 1758-94, (Fr.) leading figure of French Revolution, responsible for much of Reign of Terror.

Nelson Rockefeller, 1908-79, (U.S.) Republican governor of NY, 1959-73; U.S. vice president, 1974-77.

George W. Romney, 1907-95, (U.S.) president of American Motors; 3-term Republican governor of Michigan.

Eleanor Roosevelt, 1884-1962, (U.S.) humanitarian, United Nations diplomat.

Elihu Root, 1845-1937, (U.S.) lawyer, statesman, diplomat; leading Republican supporter of the League of Nations.

Dean Rusk, 1909-95, (U.S.) statesman; Secretary of State, 1961-69, during Vietnam War.

John Russell, 1792-1878, (Br.) Liberal prime minister during the Irish potato famine.

Anwar al-Sadat, 1918-81, (Egypt.) president, 1970-1981, promoted peace with Israel; assassinated.

António de O. Salazar, 1889-1970, (Port.) statesman; longtime dictator.

José de San Martin, 1778-1850, South American revolutionary; protector of Peru.

Eisaku Sato, 1901-75, (Jpn.) prime minister; presided over Japan's post-WW2 emergence as major world power.

Philipp Scheidemann, 1865-1939, (Ger.) Social Democratic leader; first chancellor of the German republic.

Robert Schuman, 1886-1963, (Fr.) statesman; founded European Coal and Steel Community.

Carl Schurz, 1829-1906, (U.S.) German-American political leader, journalist, orator, dedicated reformer.

Kurt Schuschnigg, 1897-1977, (Aus.) chancellor; unsuccessful in stopping his country's annexation by Germany.

William H. Seward, 1801-72, (U.S.) anti-slavery activist; as U.S. secretary of state purchased Alaska.

Carlo Sforza, 1872-1952, (It.) foreign minister, anti-fascist.

Sitting Bull, c1831-90, (Native American) Sioux leader in Battle of Little Bighorn over George A. Custer, 1876.

Alfred E. Smith, 1873-1944, (U.S.) New York Democratic governor; first Roman Catholic to run for presidency.

Margaret Chase Smith, 1897-1995, (U.S.) congresswoman, senator; 1st woman elected to both houses of Congress.

Jan C. Smuts, 1870-1950, (S. African) statesman, philosopher, soldier, prime minister.

Paul Henri Spaak, 1899-1972, (Belg.) statesman, socialist leader.

Joseph Stalin, 1879-1953, (USSR) Soviet dictator, 1924-53.

Edwin M. Stanton, 1814-69, (U.S.) secretary of war, 1862-68, during the Civil War.

Edward R. Stettinius, Jr., 1900-49, (U.S.) industrialist, secretary of state who coordinated aid to WW2 allies.

Adlai E. Stevenson, 1900-65, (U.S.) Democratic leader, diplomat, Illinois governor, presidential candidate.

Henry L. Stimson, 1867-1950, (U.S.) statesman; served in 5 administrations, foreign policy adviser in 1930s and 1940s.

Gustav Stresemann, 1878-1929, (Ger.) chancellor, foreign minister; strove to regain friendship for post-WW1 Germany.

Sukarno, 1901-70, (Indon.) dictatorial first president of the Indonesian republic.

Sun Yat-sen, 1866-1925, (Chin.) revolutionary; leader of Kuomintang, regarded as the father of modern China.

Robert A. Taft, 1889-1953, (U.S.) conservative Senate leader, called "Mr. Republican."

Charles de Talleyrand, 1754-1838, (Fr.) statesman, diplomat; the major force of the Congress of Vienna of 1814-15.

U Thant, 1909-74 (Bur.) statesman, UN secretary-general.

Norman M. Thomas, 1884-1968, (U.S.) social reformer; 6 times unsuccessful Socialist party presidential candidate.

Josip Broz Tito, 1892-1980, (Yug.) president of Yugoslavia from 1953, WW2 guerrilla chief, postwar rival of Stalin.

Palmiro Togliatti, 1893-1964, (It.) major leader of Italian Communist party.

Hideki Tojo, 1885-1948, (Jpn.) statesman, soldier; prime minister during most of WW2.

François Toussaint L'Ouverture, c1744-1803, (Haitian) patriot, martyr; thwarted French colonial aims.

Leon Trotsky, 1879-1940, (Russ.) revolutionary, founded Red Army, expelled from party in conflict with Stalin.

Rafael L. Trujillo Molina, 1891-1961, (Dom.) absolute dictator of Dominican Republic, 1930-61; assassinated.

Moise K. Tshombe, 1919-69, (Cong.) politician; president of secessionist Katanga, premier of Republic of Congo (Zaire).

William M. Tweed, 1823-78, (U.S.) politician; absolute leader of Tammany Hall, NYC's Democratic political machine.

Walter Ulbricht, 1893-1973, (Ger.) communist leader of German Democratic Republic.

Arthur H. Vandenberg, 1884-1951, (U.S.) senator; proponent of anti-communist bipartisan foreign policy after WW2.

Eleutherios Venizelos, 1864-1936, (Gk.) most prominent Greek statesman in early 20th century; expanded territory.

Hendrik F. Verwoerd, 1901-66, (S. African) prime minister; rigorously applied apartheid policy despite protest.

Robert Walpole, 1676-1745, (Br.) statesman; generally considered Britain's first prime minister.

Daniel Webster, 1782-1852, (U.S.) orator, politician; advocate of business interests during Jacksonian agrarianism.

Chaim Weizmann, 1874-1952, (Russ.-Isr.) Zionist leader, scientist; first Israeli president.

Wendell L. Willkie, 1892-1944, (U.S.) Republican who tried to unseat FDR when he ran for his 3d term.

Harold Wilson, 1916-95, (Br.) Labour party leader; prime minister, 1964-70, 1974-76.

Emiliano Zapata, c1879-1919, (Mex.) revolutionary; major influence on modern Mexico.

Zhou Enlai, 1898-1976, (Chin.) diplomat, prime minister; a leading figure of the Chinese Communist party.

Noted Scientists of the Past

Howard H. Aiken, 1900-73, (U.S.) mathematician; credited with designing forerunner of digital computer.

Albertus Magnus, 1193-1280, (Ger.) theologian, philosopher; established medieval Christian study of natural science.

Andre-Marie Ampère, 1775-1836, (Fr.) scientist known for contributions to electrodynamics.

Amedeo Avogadro, 1776-1856, (It.) chemist, physicist; advanced important theories on properties of gases.

John Bardeen, 1908-91, (U.S.) co-inventor of the transistor that led to modern electronics.

A. C. Becquerel, 1788-1878, (Fr.) physicist; pioneer in electrochemical science.

A. H. Becquerel, 1852-1908, (Fr.) physicist; discovered radioactivity in uranium.

Alexander Graham Bell, 1847-1922, (U.S.) inventor; first to patent and commercially exploit the telephone, 1876.

Daniel Bernoulli, 1700-82, (Swiss) mathematician; advanced kinetic theory of gases and fluids.

Jöns Jakob Berzelius, 1779-1848, (Swed.) chemist; developed modern chemical symbols and formulas.

Henry Bessemer, 1813-98, (Br.) engineer; invented Bessemer steel-making process.

Louis Blériot, 1872-1936, (Fr.) engineer; pioneer aviator, invented and constructed monoplanes.

Niels Bohr, 1885-1962, (Dan.) physicist; leading figure in the development of quantum theory.

Max Born, 1882-1970, (Ger.) physicist known for research in quantum mechanics.

Satyendranath Bose, 1894-1974, (In.) physicist, chemist, mathematician; forerunner of modern quantum theory.

Walter Brattain, 1902-87, (U.S.) inventor; worked on invention of transistor.

Louis de Broglie, 1893-1987, (Fr.) physicist; best known for wave theory.

Robert Bunsen, 1811-99, (Ger.) chemist; invented Bunsen burner.

Luther Burbank, 1849-1926, (U.S.) plant breeder whose work developed plant breeding into a modern science.

Vannevar Bush, 1890-1974, (U.S.) electrical engineer; developed differential analyzer, 1st electronic analogue computer.

Marvin Camras, 1916-95, (U.S.) inventor, electrical engineer; invented magnetic tape recording.

Alexis Carrel, 1873-1944, (Fr.) surgeon, biologist; developed methods of suturing blood vessels and transplanting organs.

George Washington Carver, 1864-1943, (U.S.) botanist, chemist, and educator.

Henry Cavendish, 1731-1810, (Br.) chemist, physicist; discovered hydrogen.

James Chadwick, 1891-1974, (Br.) physicist; discovered the neutron.

Darly Chapin, 1906-95, (U.S.) physicist; co-developer of the solar energy cell.

Jean M. Charcot, 1825-93, (Fr.) neurologist known for work on hysteria, hypnotism, sclerosis.

Albert Claude, 1899-1983, (Belg.) a founder of modern cell biology.

John D. Cockcroft, 1897-1967, (Br.) nuclear physicist; constructed first atomic particle accelerator with E. T. S. Walton.

Nicholas Copernicus, 1473-1543, (Pol.) astronomer who first described solar system, with Earth as one of planets revolving around sun.

William Crookes, 1832-1919, (Br.) physicist, chemist; discovered thallium, invented a cathode-ray tube, radiometer.

Marie Curie, 1867-1934, (Pol.-Fr.) physical chemist known for work on radium and its compounds.

Pierre Curie, 1859-1906, (Fr.) physical chemist known for work, with his wife Marie, on radioactivity.

Gottlieb Daimler, 1834-1900, (Ger.) engineer, inventor; pioneer automobile manufacturer.

John Dalton, 1766-1844, (Br.) chemist, physicist; formulated atomic theory, made first table of atomic weights.

Charles Darwin, 1809-82, (Br.) naturalist; established theory of organic evolution; *Origin of Species.*

Humphry Davy, 1778-1829, (Br.) chemist; research in electrochemistry led to isolation of potassium, sodium, calcium, barium, boron, magnesium, and strontium.

Lee De Forest, 1873-1961, (U.S.) inventor; pioneer in development of wireless telegraphy, sound pictures, television.

Max Delbruck, 1907-81, (U.S.) pioneer in modern molecular genetics.

Rudolf Diesel, 1858-1913, (Ger.) mechanical engineer; patented Diesel engine.

Thomas Dooley, 1927-61, (U.S.) "jungle doctor," noted for efforts to supply medical aid to developing countries.

Christian Doppler, 1803-53, (Aus.) physicist; showed change in energy wavelengths caused by motion, Doppler effect.

J. Presper Eckert, Jr., 1919-95, (U.S.) co-inventor with John W. Mauchly of the first electronic digital computer, the Eniac.

Thomas A. Edison, 1847-1931, (U.S.) inventor; held more than 1,000 patents, including incandescent electric lamp.

Paul Ehrlich, 1854-1915, (Ger.) bacteriologist; pioneer in modern immunology and bacteriology.

Albert Einstein, 1879-1955, (Ger.-U.S.) theoretical physicist; known for formulation of relativity theory.

John F. Enders, 1897-1985, (U.S.) virologist who helped discover vaccines against polio, measles, and mumps.

Leonhard Euler, 1707-83, (Swiss) mathematician, physicist; authored first calculus book.

Gabriel Fahrenheit, 1686-1736, (Ger.) physicist; introduced Fahrenheit scale for thermometers.

Michael Faraday, 1791-1867, (Br.) chemist, physicist; known for work in field of electricity.

Pierre de Fermat, 1601-65, (Fr.) mathematician; founded modern theory of numbers and calculus of probabilities.

Enrico Fermi, 1901-54, (It.-U.S.) physicist; one of primary architects of the nuclear age.

Galileo Ferraris, 1847-97, (It.) physicist; electrical engineer, discovered principle of rotary magnetic field.

Richard Feynman, 1918-88, (U.S.) a leading theoretical physicist of the postwar generation.

Camille Flammarion, 1842-1925, (Fr.) astronomer; popularized study of astronomy.

Alexander Fleming, 1881-1955, (Br.) bacteriologist; discovered penicillin.

Jean B. J. Fourier, 1768-1830, (Fr.) mathematician; discovered theorem governing periodic oscillation.

James Franck, 1882-1964, (Ger.) physicist; proved value of quantum theory.

Sigmund Freud, 1856-1939, (Aus.) psychiatrist; founder of psychoanalysis.

Galileo Galilei, 1564-1642, (It.) astronomer, physicist; a founder of the experimental method.

Luigi Galvani, 1737-98, (It.) physician, physicist; known as founder of galvanism.

Carl Friedrich Gauss, 1777-1855, (Ger.) mathematician, astronomer, physicist.

Joseph Gay-Lussac, 1778-1850, (Fr.) chemist, physicist; investigated behavior of gases, discovered law of combining volumes.

Josiah W. Gibbs, 1839-1903, (U.S.) theoretical physicist, chemist; founded chemical thermodynamics.

Robert H. Goddard, 1882-1945, (U.S.) physicist; father of modern rocketry.

George W. Goethals, 1858-1928, (U.S.) army engineer; built the Panama Canal.

William C. Gorgas, 1854-1920, (U.S.) sanitarian, U.S. army surgeon-general; his work to prevent yellow fever, malaria helped ensure construction of Panama Canal.

Ernest Haeckel, 1834-1919, (Ger.) zoologist, evolutionist; a strong proponent of Darwin.

Otto Hahn, 1879-1968, (Ger.) chemist; worked on atomic fission.

J. B. S. Haldane, 1892-1964, (Br.) scientist; known for work as geneticist and application of mathematics to science.

James Hall, 1761-1832, (Br.) geologist, chemist; founded experimental geology, geochemistry.

Edmund Halley, 1656-1742, (Br.) astronomer; calculated the orbits of many planets.

William Harvey, 1578-1657, (Eng.) physician, anatomist; discovered circulation of the blood.

Hermann von Helmholtz, 1821-94, (Ger.) physicist, anatomist, physiologist.

William Herschel, 1738-1822, (Br.) astronomer; discovered Uranus.

Heinrich Hertz, 1857-94, (Ger.) physicist; his discoveries led to wireless telegraphy.

David Hilbert, 1862-1943, (Ger.) mathematician; formulated 1st satisfactory set of axioms for modern Euclidean geometry.

Edwin P. Hubble, 1889-1953, (U.S.) astronomer; produced first observational evidence of expanding universe.

Alexander von Humboldt, 1769-1859, (Ger.) explorer, naturalist; earth scientist; originated ecology, geophysics.

Julian Huxley, 1887-1975, (Br.) biologist; a gifted exponent and philosopher of science.

Edward Jenner, 1749-1823, (Br.) physician; discovered vaccination.

William Jenner, 1815-98, (Br.) physician, pathological anatomist.

Frederic Joliot-Curie, 1900-58, (Fr.) physicist; with his wife continued work of Curies on radioactivity.

Irene Joliot-Curie, 1897-1956, (Fr.) physicist; continued work of Curies in radioactivity.

James P. Joule, 1818-89, (Br.) physicist; determined relationship between heat and mechanical energy (conservation of energy).

Carl Jung, 1875-1961, (Swiss) psychiatrist; founder of analytical psychology.

Wm. Thomson Kelvin, 1824-1907, (Br.) mathematician, physicist; known for work on heat and electricity.

Sister Elizabeth Kenny, 1886-1952, (Austral.) nurse; developed method of treatment for polio.

Johannes Kepler, 1571-1630, (Ger.) astronomer; discovered important laws of planetary motion.

Georges Köhler, 1946-95, (Ger.) immunologist; co-inventor of monoclonal antibody technique.

Joseph Lagrange, 1736-1813, (Fr.) geometer, astronomer; number theorist, analytical and celestial mechanics.

Jean B. Lamarck, 1744-1829, (Fr.) naturalist; forerunner of Darwin in evolutionary theory.

Edwin Land, 1910-91, (U.S.) invented Polaroid camera.

Irving Langmuir, 1881-1957, (U.S.) physical chemist; colloid research and biochemistry.

Pierre S. Laplace, 1749-1827, (Fr.) astronomer, physicist; put forth nebular hypothesis of origin of solar system.

Antoine Lavoisier, 1743-94, (Fr.) chemist; founder of modern chemistry.

Ernest O. Lawrence, 1901-58, (U.S.) physicist; invented the cyclotron.

Jerome Lejeune, 1927-94, (Fr.) geneticist; discovered the cause of Down's syndrome.

Louis Leakey, 1903-72, (Br.) anthropologist; discovered important fossils, remains of early hominids.

Anton van Leeuwenhoek, 1632-1723, (Dutch) microscopist; father of microbiology.

Gottfried Wilhelm Leibniz, 1646-1716, (Ger.) mathematician; developed theories of differential and integral calculus.

Justus von Liebig, 1803-73, (Ger.) chemist; established quantitative organic chemical analysis.

Joseph Lister, 1827-1912, (Br.) pioneered antiseptic surgery.

Percival Lowell, 1855-1916, (U.S.) astronomer; predicted the existence of Pluto.

Louis, 1864-1984, and **Auguste Lumière,** 1862-1954, (Fr.) invented cinematograph.

Guglielmo Marconi, 1874-1937, (It.) physicist; known for his development of wireless telegraphy.

John W. Mauchly, 1908-80, (U.S.) co-inventor with J. Presper Eckert of the first electronic digital computer, the Eniac.

James Clerk Maxwell, 1831-79, (Br.) physicist; known especially for his work in electricity and magnetism.

Maria Goeppert Mayer, 1906-72, (Ger.-U.S.) physicist; independently developed theory of structure of atomic nuclei.

Barbara McClintock, 1902-92, (U.S.) geneticist; significant studies in the nature of mobile genetic elements.

Lise Meitner, 1878-1968, (Aus.) physicist whose work contributed to the development of the atomic bomb.

Gregor J. Mendel, 1822-84, (Aus.) botanist; known for his experimental work on heredity.

Franz Mesmer, 1734-1815, (Ger.) physician; developed theory of animal magnetism.

Albert A. Michelson, 1852-1931, (U.S.) physicist; established speed of light as a fundamental constant.

Robert A. Millikan, 1868-1953, (U.S.) physicist; studied elementary electronic charge and photoelectric effect.

Thomas Hunt Morgan, 1866-1945, (U.S.) geneticist, embryologist; established chromosome theory of heredity.

Isaac Newton, 1642-1727, (Eng.) natural philosopher, mathematician; discovered law of gravitation, laws of motion.

Robert N. Noyce, 1927-89, (U.S.) inventor of the microchip, which revolutionized the electronics industry.

J. Robert Oppenheimer, 1904-67, (U.S.) physicist; director of Los Alamos during development of the atomic bomb.

Wilhelm Ostwald, 1853-1932, (Ger.) physical chemist, philosopher; primary founder of physical chemistry.

Robert Morris Page, 1903-92, (U.S.) physicist; a leading figure in development of radar technology.

Louis Pasteur, 1822-95, (Fr.) chemist; originated process of pasteurization.

Linus C. Pauling, 1901-94, (U.S.) chemist; specializing in chemical bonds; political activist.

Max Planck, 1858-1947, (Ger.) physicist; originated and developed quantum theory.

Roy J. Plunkett, 1922-94, (U.S.) chemist; created Teflon ™.

Henri Poincaré, 1854-1912, (Fr.) mathematician, physicist; influenced cosmology, relativity, and topology.

Joseph Priestley, 1733-1804, (Br.) chemist; one of the discoverers of oxygen.

Isidor Isaac Rabi, 1899-1988, (U.S.) physicist; pioneered atom exploration.

Walter S. Reed, 1851-1902, (U.S.) army pathologist, bacteriologist; proved mosquitoes transmit yellow fever.

Bernhard Riemann, 1826-66, (Ger.) mathematician; contributed to development of calculus and mathematical physics.

Wilhelm Roentgen, 1845-1923, (Ger.) physicist; discovered the X ray.

Bertrand Russell, 1872-1970, (Br.) logician, philosopher; one of the founders of modern logic.

Ernest Rutherford, 1871-1937, (Br.) physicist; discovered the atomic nucleus.

Albert B. Sabin, 1906-93, (Russ.-U.S.) In 1954, developed oral polio live-virus vaccine, which was licensed in 1961.

Jonas Salk, 1914-95, (U.S.) developed the first successful polio vaccine, which came into widespread use in 1955 when it was found to be safe and effective.

Giovanni Schiaparelli, 1835-1910, (It.) astronomer; hypothesized canals on the surface of Mars.

Angelo Secchi, 1818-78, (It.) astronomer; pioneer in classifying stars by their spectra.

Harlow Shapley, 1885-1972, (U.S.) astronomer; noted for his studies of the galaxy.

Roger Sperry, 1913-94, (U.S.) brain expert; studied relationship between the right and left sides of the brain.

Charles P. Steinmetz, 1865-1923, (Ger.-U.S.) electrical engineer; developed basic ideas on alternating current systems.

Frederick Stewart, 1904-93, (Br.) botanist; cell biologist; studies considered foundations of molecular biology.

George Stibitz, 1904-95. (U.S.), invented first digital computer.

Leo Szilard, 1898-1964, (Hung.-U.S.) physicist; helped create first sustained nuclear reaction.

Nikola Tesla, 1856-1943, (Croatia-U.S.) electrical engineer; contributed to most developments in electronics.

Rudolf Virchow, 1821-1902, (Ger.) pathologist; a founder of cellular pathology.

Alessandro Volta, 1745-1827, (It.) physicist; pioneer in electricity.

Werner von Braun, 1912-77, (Ger.-U.S.) pioneered development of rockets for warfare and space exploration.

Alfred Russell Wallace, 1823-1913, (Br.) naturalist; proposed concept of evolution similar to Darwin's.

August von Wasserman, 1866-1925, (Ger.) bacteriologist; discovered reaction used as test for syphilis.

James E. Watt, 1736-1819, (Br.) mechanical engineer, inventor; invented modern steam-condensing engine.

Alfred L. Wegener, 1880-1930, (Ger.) meteorologist, geophysicist; postulated theory of continental drift.

Norbert Wiener, 1894-1964, (U.S.) mathematician; founder of the science of cybernetics.

Eugene Wigner, 1902-95, (U.S.) quantum theorist, nuclear physicist; helped perfect world's first nuclear reactor.

Sewall Wright, 1889-1988, (U.S.) evolutionary theorist.

Ferdinand von Zeppelin, 1838-1917, (Ger.) soldier, aeronaut, airship designer.

Noted Social Reformers and Educators of the Past

Jane Addams, 1860-1935, (U.S.) co-founder of Hull House; won Nobel Peace Prize, 1931.

Susan B. Anthony, 1820-1906, (U.S.) a leader in temperance, anti-slavery, and woman suffrage movements.

Henry Barnard, 1811-1900, (U.S.) public school reformer.

Thomas Barnardo, 1845-1905, (Br.) social reformer; pioneered in the care of destitute children.

Clara Barton, 1821-1912, (U.S.) organizer of the American Red Cross.

Henry Ward Beecher, 1813-87, (U.S.) clergyman, abolitionist.

Sarah G. Blanding, 1899-1985, (U.S.) head of Vassar College, 1946-64.

Amelia Bloomer, 1818-94, (U.S.) social reformer.

William Booth, 1829-1912, (Br.) founded the Salvation Army.

John Brown, 1800-59, (U.S.) abolitionist who led murder of 5 pro-slavery men, was hanged.

Nicholas Murray Butler, 1862-1947, (U.S.) educator; headed Columbia Univ., 1902-45; Nobel Peace Prize, 1931.

Frances X. (Mother) Cabrini, 1850-1917, (It.-U.S.) Italian-born nun; founded charitable institutions; first American canonized as a saint of the Roman Catholic church, 1946.

Carrie Chapman Catt, 1859-1947, (U.S.) suffragette; helped win passage of the 19th amendment.

Cesar Chavez, 1927-93, (U.S.) labor leader; helped establish United Farm Workers of America.

Clarence Darrow, 1857-1938, (U.S.) lawyer; defender of "underdog," opponent of capital punishment.

Dorothy Day, 1897-1980, (U.S.) founder of Catholic Worker Movement.

Eugene V. Debs, 1855-1926, (U.S.) labor leader; led Pullman strike, 1894; 4-time Socialist presidential candidate.

Melvil Dewey, 1851-1931, (U.S.) devised decimal system of library-book classification.

Dorothea Dix, 1802-87, (U.S.) crusader for the mentally ill.

William Lloyd Garrison, 1805-79, (U.S.) abolitionist.

Giovanni Gentile, 1875-1944, (It.) philosopher, educator; reformed Italian educational system.

Emma Goldman, 1869-1940, (Russ.-U.S.) published anarchist *Mother Earth,* birth-control advocate.

Samuel Gompers, 1850-1924, (U.S.) labor leader; a founder and president of AFL.

William Green, 1873-1952, (U.S.) president of AFL, 1924-52.

Michael Harrington, 1928-89, (U.S.) revealed poverty in affluent U.S. in *The Other America,* 1963.

Sidney Hillman, 1887-1946, (U.S.) labor leader; helped organize CIO.

John Holt, 1924-85, (U.S.) educator and author.

Samuel G. Howe, 1801-76, (U.S.) social reformer; changed public attitudes toward the handicapped.

Helen Keller, 1880-1968, (U.S.) crusader for better treatment for the handicapped.

Maggie Kuhn, 1905-95, (U.S.) founded Gray Panthers, 1970.

William Kunstler, 1919-95, (U.S.) civil liberties attorney.

John L. Lewis, 1880-1969, (U.S.) labor leader; headed United Mine Workers, 1920-60.

Horace Mann, 1796-1859, (U.S.) pioneered modern public school system.

William H. McGuffey, 1800-73, (U.S.) author of *Reader,* the mainstay of 19th-century U.S. public education.

Alexander Meiklejohn, 1872-1964, (U.S.) Br.-born educator; championed academic freedom and experimental curricula.

Karl Menninger, 1893-1991, (U.S.) with brother William found Menninger Clinic, and Menninger Foundation in Topeka, KS.

Maria Montessori, 1870-1952, (It.) educator, physician; originated Montessori method of student self-motivation.

Lucretia Mott, 1793-1880, (U.S.) reformer, pioneer feminist.

Philip Murray, 1886-1952, (Br.-U.S.) Scotch-born labor leader.

Florence Nightingale, 1820-1910, (Br.) founder of modern nursing.

Emmeline Pankhurst, 1858-1928, (Br.) woman suffragist.

Elizabeth P. Peabody, 1804-94, (U.S.) education pioneer and; founded 1st kindergarten in U.S., 1860.

Walter Reuther, 1907-70, (U.S.) labor leader; headed UAW.

Jacob Riis, 1849-1914, (U.S.) crusader for urban reforms.

Margaret Sanger, 1883-1966, (U.S.) social reformer; pioneered the birth-control movement.

Elizabeth Seton, 1774-1821, (U.S.) established parochial school education in U.S.

Earl of Shaftesbury (A. A. Cooper), 1801-85, (Br.) social reformer.

Elizabeth Cady Stanton, 1815-1902, (U.S.) woman suffrage pioneer.

Lucy Stone, 1818-93, (U.S.) feminist, abolitionist.

Philip Vera Cruz, 1905-94, (Filipino-U.S.) helped to found the United Farm Workers Union.

Walter F. White, 1893-1955, (U.S.) headed NAACP, 1931-55.

William Wilberforce, 1759-1833, (Br.) social reformer; prominent in struggle to abolish the slave trade.

Emma Hart Willard, 1787-1870, (U.S.) pioneered higher education for women.

Frances E. Willard, 1839-98, (U.S.) temperance, women's rights leader.

Mary Wollstonecraft, 1759-97, (Br.) wrote *Vindication of the Rights of Women.*

Notable Writers of the Present

Name (Birthplace)	Birthdate
Chinua Achebe (Ogidi, Nigeria)	11/16/30
Alice Adams (Fredericksburg, VA)	8/14/26
Edward Albee (Washington, DC)	3/12/28
Jorge Amado (Bahia, Brazil)	8/1/12
Martin Amis (Oxford, England)	8/25/49
Oscar Arias Sanchez (Heredia, Costa Rica)	9/13/41
Margaret Atwood (Ottawa, Ontario)	11/18/39
Louis Auchincloss (Lawrence, NY)	9/27/17
John Barth (Cambridge, MD)	5/27/30
Ann Beattie (Washington, DC)	9/7/47
Saul Bellow (Lachine, Quebec)	7/10/15
Peter Benchley (New York, NY)	5/8/40
Thomas Berger (Cincinnati, OH)	7/20/24
Judy Blume (Elizabeth, NJ)	2/12/38
Ray Bradbury (Waukegan, IL)	8/22/20
Gwendolyn Brooks (Topeka, KS)	6/7/17
Hortense Calisher (New York, NY)	12/20/11
Tom Clancy (Baltimore, MD)	1947
Mary Higgins Clark (New York, NY)	12/24/31
Beverly Cleary (McMinnville, OR)	1916
Evan S. Connell (Kansas City, MO)	8/17/24
Pat Conroy (Atlanta, GA)	10/26/45
Harry Crews (Alma, GA)	6/6/35
Michael Crichton (Chicago, IL)	10/23/42
Janet Dailey (Storm Lake, IA)	5/21/44
Robertson Davies (Thamesville, Ontario)	8/28/13
Peter De Vries (Chicago, IL)	2/27/10
Joan Didion (Sacramento, CA)	12/5/34
E. L. Doctorow (New York, NY)	1/6/31
Takako Doi (Hyogo, Japan)	11/30/28
Rita Dove (Akron, OH)	8/28/52
John Gregory Dunne (Hartford, CT)	5/25/32
Stanley Elkin (New York, NY)	5/11/30
Howard Fast (New York, NY)	11/11/14
Paula Fox (New York, NY)	4/22/23
Marilyn French (New York, NY)	11/21/29
Charles Fuller (Philadelphia, PA)	3/5/39
William Gaddis (New York, NY)	1922
Frank Gilroy (New York, NY)	10/13/25
Gail Godwin (Birmingham, AL)	6/18/37
William Goldman (Chicago, IL)	8/12/31
Mary Gordon (Long Island, NY)	12/8/49
Shirley Ann Grau (New Orleans, LA)	7/8/29
John Grisham (Jonesboro, AR)	2/8/55
John Guare (New York, NY)	2/5/38
Arthur Hailey (Luton, England)	4/5/20
John Hawkes (Stamford, CT)	8/17/25
Joseph Heller (Brooklyn, NY)	5/1/23
Mark Helprin (New York, NY)	6/28/47
S. E. Hinton (Tulsa, OK)	1948
John Irving (Exeter, NH)	3/2/42
John Jakes (Chicago, IL)	3/31/32
P. D. James (Oxford, England)	8/3/20
Erica Jong (New York, NY)	3/26/42
Garrison Keillor (Anoka, MN)	8/7/42
William Kennedy (Albany, NY)	1/16/28
Jean Kerr (Scranton, PA)	7/10/23
Stephen King (Portland, ME)	9/21/47
Maxine Hong Kingston (Stockton, CA)	10/27/40
John Knowles (Fairmont, WV)	9/16/26
Judith Krantz (New York, NY)	1/9/28
Maxine Kumin (Philadelphia, PA)	6/6/25
Tony Kushner	—
John le Carré (Poole, England)	10/19/31
Ursula LeGuin (Berkeley, CA)	10/21/29

Name (Birthplace)	Birthdate
Madeleine L'Engle (New York, NY)	11/29/18
Elmore Leonard (New Orleans, LA)	10/11/25
Doris Lessing (Kermanshah, Persia)	10/22/19
Ira Levin (New York, NY)	8/27/29
Robert Ludlum (New York, NY)	5/25/27
Alison Lurie (Chicago, IL)	9/3/26
Norman Mailer (Long Branch, NJ)	1/31/23
David Mamet (Chicago, IL)	11/30/47
Gabriel Garcia Marquez (Aracata, Colombia)	3/6/28
Cormac McCarthy (Providence, RI)	7/20/33
Thomas McGuane (Wyandotte, MI)	12/11/39
Larry McMurtry (Wichita Falls, TX)	6/3/36
James A. Michener (New York, NY)	2/3/07
Arthur Miller (New York, NY)	10/17/15
Wright Morris (Central City, NE)	1/6/10
Toni Morrison (Lorain, OH)	2/18/31
Alice Munro (Wingham, Ontario)	7/10/31
Joyce Carol Oates (Lockport, NY)	6/16/38
Cynthia Ozick (New York, NY)	4/17/28
Grace Paley (New York, NY)	12/11/22
Marge Piercy (Detroit, MI)	3/31/36
Chaim Potok (New York, NY)	2/17/29
Reynolds Price (Macon, NC)	2/1/33
E. Annie Proulx (Norwich, CT)	8/22/35
Mario Puzo (New York, NY)	10/15/20
Thomas Pynchon (Glen Cove, NY)	5/8/37
David Rabe (Dubuque, IA)	3/10/40
Ishmael Reed (Chattanooga, TN)	2/22/38
Anne Rice (New Orleans, LA)	10/14/41
Henry Roth (Austria-Hungary)	2/8/06
Philip Roth (Newark, NJ)	3/19/33
Salman Rushdie (Bombay, India)	6/19/47
J. D. Salinger (New York, NY)	1/1/19
Lawrence Sanders (New York, NY)	1920
Maurice Sendak (New York, NY)	6/10/28
Sam Shepard (Ft. Sheridan, IL)	11/5/43
Carol Shields (Oak Park, IL)	6/2/35
Shel Silverstein (Chicago, IL)	1932
Neil Simon (New York, NY)	7/4/27
Mickey Spillane (Brooklyn, NY)	3/9/18
Danielle Steel (New York, NY)	8/14/47
Richard Stern, (New York, NY)	2/25/28
Robert Stone (Brooklyn, NY)	8/21/37
William Styron (Newport News, VA)	6/11/25
Amy Tan (Oakland, CA)	2/19/52
Peter Taylor (Trenton, TN)	1/8/17
Paul Theroux (Medford, MA)	4/10/41
Scott F. Turow (Chicago, IL)	4/12/49
Anne Tyler (Minneapolis, MN)	10/25/41
John Updike (Shillington, PA)	3/18/32
Leon Uris (Baltimore, MD)	8/3/24
Gore Vidal (West Point, NY)	10/3/25
Kurt Vonnegut Jr. (Indianapolis, IN)	11/11/22
Alice Walker (Eatonton, GA)	2/9/44
Robert James Waller (Rockford, IA)	8/1/39
Joseph Wambaugh (East Pittsburgh, PA)	1/22/37
Wendy Wasserstein (New York, NY)	—
Eudora Welty (Jackson, MS)	4/13/09
John Edgar Wideman (Pittsburgh, PA)	6/14/41
August Wilson (Pittsburgh, PA)	4/27/45
Lanford Wilson (Lebanon, MO)	4/13/37
Tom Wolfe (Richmond, VA)	3/2/31
Tobias Wolff (Birmingham, AL)	6/19/45
Herman Wouk (New York, NY)	5/27/15

Poets Laureate of England

There is no authentic record of the origin of the office of Poet Laureate of England. According to Warton, there was a Versificator Regis, or King's Poet, in the reign of Henry III (1216-72), and he was paid 100 shillings a year. Geoffrey Chaucer (1340-1400) assumed the title of Poet Laureate and in 1389 got a royal grant of a yearly allowance of wine. In the reign of Edward IV (1461-83), John Kay held the post. Under Henry VII (1485-1509), Andrew Bernard was the Poet Laureate and was succeeded under Henry VIII (1509-47) by John Skelton. Next came Edmund Spenser, who died in 1599; then Samuel Daniel, appointed 1599, and then Ben Jonson, 1619. Sir William D'Avenant was appointed in 1637. He was a godson of William Shakespeare.

Others were: John Dryden, 1670; Thomas Shadwell, 1688; Nahum Tate, 1692; Nicholas Rowe, 1715; the Rev. Laurence Eusden, 1718; Colley Cibber, 1730; William Whitehead, 1757, on the refusal of Thomas Gray; Rev. Thomas Warton, 1785, on the refusal of William Mason; Henry J. Pye, 1790; Robert Southey, 1813, on the refusal of Sir Walter Scott; William Wordsworth, 1843; Alfred, Lord Tennyson, 1850; Alfred Austin, 1896; Robert Bridges, 1913; John Masefield, 1930; Cecil Day Lewis, 1967; Sir John Betjeman, 1972; Ted Hughes, 1984.

U.S. Poets Laureate

Robert Penn Warren—the poet, novelist, and essayist—was named the country's first official Poet Laureate on Feb. 26, 1986. The only writer to have won the Pulitzer Prize for fiction and poetry (twice), Warren was chosen by Daniel J. Boorstin, the Librarian of Congress. The appointment began in Sept. 1986. Other appointments, all beginning in Sept., are: 1987, Richard Wilbur; 1988, Howard Nemerov; 1990, Mark Strand; 1991, Joseph Brodsky; 1992, Mona Van Duyn, the first female poet laureate; 1993, Rita Dove, the first black poet laureate; 1995, Robert Hass.

Noted Writers of the Past

George Ade, 1866-1944, (U.S.) humorist. *Fables in Slang.*
Conrad Aiken, 1889-1973, (U.S.) poet, critic. *Ushant.*
Louisa May Alcott, 1832-88, (U.S.) novelist. *Little Women.*
Sholom Aleichem, 1859-1916, (Russ.) Yiddish writer. *Tevye's Daughter, Adventures of Mottel, The Old Country.*
Vicente Aleixandre, 1898-1984, (Sp.) poet. *La destrucción o el amor, Dialogolos del conocimiento.*
Horatio Alger, 1832-1899, (U.S.) "rags-to-riches" books.
Hans Christian Andersen, 1805-75, (Dan.) author of fairy tales. *The Princess and the Pea, The Ugly Duckling.*
Maxwell Anderson, 1888-1959, (U.S.) playwright. *What Price Glory?, High Tor, Winterset, Key Largo.*
Sherwood Anderson, 1876-1941, (U.S.) short-story writer. "Death in the Woods"; *Winesburg, Ohio* (collection).
Matthew Arnold, 1822-88, (Br.) poet, critic. "Thrysis," "Dover Beach," "The Gypsy Scholar"; "Culture and Anarchy."
Isaac Asimov, 1920-92, (U.S.) science fiction writer. *I Robot.*
Jane Austen, 1775-1817, (Br.) novelist. *Pride and Prejudice, Sense and Sensibility, Emma, Mansfield Park.*
Isaac Babel, 1894-1941, (Russ.) short-story writer, playwright. *Odessa Tales, Red Cavalry.*
Honoré de Balzac, 1799-1850, (Fr.) novelist. *Le Père Goriot, Cousine Bette, Eugénie Grandet, The Human Comedy.*
James M. Barrie, 1860-1937, (Br.) playwright, novelist. *Peter Pan, Dear Brutus, What Every Woman Knows.*
Charles Baudelaire, 1821-67, (Fr.) symbolist poet. *Les Fleurs du Mal.*
L. Frank Baum, 1856-1919, (U.S.) writer. Wizard of Oz series of children's books.
Simone de Beauvoir, 1908-86, (Fr.) novelist, essayist. *The Second Sex, Memoirs of a Dutiful Daughter.*
Samuel Beckett, 1906-89, (Ir.) novelist, playwright. *Waiting for Godot, Endgame* (plays); *Murphy, Watt, Molloy* (novels).
Brendan Behan, 1923-64, (Ir.) playwright. *The Quare Fellow, The Hostage, Borstal Boy.*
Robert Benchley, 1889-1945, (U.S.) humorist. *From Bed to Worse, My Ten Years in a Quandary.*
Stephen Vincent Benét, 1898-1943, (U.S.) poet, novelist. *John Brown's Body.*
John Berryman, 1914-72, (U.S.) poet. *Homage to Mistress Bradstreet.*
Ambrose Bierce, 1842-1914, (U.S.) short-story writer, journalist. *In the Midst of Life, The Devil's Dictionary.*
William Blake, 1757-1827, (Br.) poet, artist. *Songs of Innocence, Songs of Experience, The Marriage of Heaven and Hell.*
Giovanni Boccaccio, 1313-75, (It.) poet, storyteller. *Decameron, Filostrato.*
Jorge Luis Borges, 1900-86, (Arg.) short-story writer, poet, essayist. *Labyrinths.*
James Boswell, 1740-95, (Sc.) biographer. *The Life of Samuel Johnson, A Journal of a Tour of the Hebrides.*
Pierre Boulle, (1913-94) (Fr.) author. *The Bridge Over the River Kwai, Planet of the Apes.*
Anne Bradstreet, c1612-72, (U.S.) poet. *The Tenth Muse Lately Sprung Up in America.*
Bertolt Brecht, 1898-1956, (Ger.) dramatist, poet. *The Threepenny Opera, Mother Courage and Her Children.*

Charlotte Brontë, 1816-55, (Br.) novelist. *Jane Eyre.*
Emily Brontë, 1818-48, (Br.) novelist. *Wuthering Heights.*
Elizabeth Barrett Browning, 1806-61, (Br.) poet. *Sonnets From the Portuguese, Aurora Leigh.*
Robert Browning, 1812-89, (Br.) poet. "My Last Duchess," "Fra Lippo Lippi," *The Ring and The Book.*
Pearl Buck, 1892-1973, (U.S.) novelist. *The Good Earth.*
Mikhail Bulgakov, 1891-1940, (Russ.) novelist, playwright. *The Heart of a Dog, The Master and Margarita.*
John Bunyan, 1628-88, (Br.) writer. *Pilgrim's Progress.*
Anthony Burgess, 1917-93, (Br.) author. *A Clockwork Orange.*
Robert Burns, 1759-96, (Sc.) poet. "Flow Gently, Sweet Afton," "My Heart's in the Highlands," "Auld Lang Syne."
Virginia Lee Burton, 1909-68, (U.S.), children's author. *Mike Mulligan and His Steam Shovel, The Little House.*
Edgar Rice Burroughs, 1875-1950, (U.S.) novelist. *Tarzan of the Apes.*
George Gordon Byron, Lord Byron, 1788-1824, (Br.) poet. *Don Juan, Childe Harold, Manfred, Cain.*
Italo Calvino, 1923-85, (It.) novelist, short-story writer. *If on a Winter's Night a Traveler.*
Albert Camus, 1913-60, (Fr.) writer. *The Stranger.*
Karel Capek, 1890-1938, (Czech.) playwright, novelist, essayist. *R.U.R. (Rossum's Universal Robots).*
Lewis Carroll, 1832-98, (Br.) writer, mathematician. *Alice's Adventures in Wonderland, Through the Looking Glass.*
Giacomo Casanova, 1725-98, (It.) adventurer, memoirist.
Willa Cather, 1873-1947, (U.S.) novelist, essayist. *O Pioneers! My Ántonia, Death Comes for the Archbishop.*
Miguel de Cervantes Saavedra, 1547-1616, (Sp.) novelist, dramatist, poet. *Don Quixote de la Mancha.*
Raymond Chandler, 1888-1959, (U.S.) writer of detective fiction. Philip Marlowe series.
Geoffrey Chaucer, c1340-1400, (Br.) poet. *The Canterbury Tales, Troilus and Criseyde.*
John Cheever, 1912-82, (U.S.) short-story writer, novelist. *The Wapshot Scandal,* "The Country Husband."
Anton Chekhov, 1860-1904, (Russ.) short-story writer, dramatist. *Uncle Vanya, The Cherry Orchard, The Three Sisters.*
G. K. Chesterton, 1874-1936, (Br.) critic, novelist. Father Brown series of mysteries.
Kate Chopin, 1851-1904, (U.S.) writer. *The Awakening.*
Agatha Christie, 1890-1976, (Br.) mystery writer. *And Then There Were None, Murder on the Orient Express.*
James Clavell, 1925-94, (Br.-U.S.) novelist. *Noble House, Shogun, King Rat.*
Jean Cocteau, 1889-1963, (Fr.) writer, visual artist, filmmaker. *The Beauty and the Beast, Les Enfants Terribles.*
Samuel Taylor Coleridge, 1772-1834, (Br.) poet, critic. "Kubla Khan," "The Rime of the Ancient Mariner."
(Sidonie) Colette, 1873-1954, (Fr.) novelist. *Claudine, Gigi.*
Joseph Conrad, 1857-1924, (Br.) novelist. *Lord Jim, Heart of Darkness, The Nigger of the Narcissus, Nostromo.*
James Fenimore Cooper, 1789-1851, (U.S.) novelist. Leatherstocking Tales.
Pierre Corneille, 1606-84, (Fr.) dramatist. *Medeé, Le Cid, Horace, Cinna, Polyeucte.*

Hart Crane, 1899-1932, (U.S.) poet. "The Bridge."

Stephen Crane, 1871-1900, (U.S.) novelist, short-story writer. *The Red Badge of Courage,* "The Open Boat."

E. E. Cummings, 1894-1962, (U.S.) poet. *Tulips and Chimneys.*

Roald Dahl, 1916-90, (Br.-U.S.) writer. *Charlie and the Chocolate Factory.*

Gabriele D'Annunzio, 1863-1938, (It.) poet, novelist, dramatist. *The Child of Pleasure, The Intruder, The Victim.*

Dante Alighieri, 1265-1321, (It.) poet. The Divine Comedy.

Daniel Defoe, 1660-1731, (Br.) writer. *Robinson Crusoe, Moll Flanders, Journal of the Plague Year.*

Charles Dickens, 1812-70, (Br.) novelist. *David Copperfield, Oliver Twist, Great Expectations, The Pickwick Papers.*

Emily Dickinson, 1830-86, (U.S.) poet.

Isak Dinesen (Karen Blixen), 1885-1962, (Dan.) author. *Out of Africa, Seven Gothic Tales, Winter's Tales.*

John Donne, 1573-1631, (Br.) poet. *Songs and Sonnets.*

John Dos Passos, 1896-1970, (U.S.) novelist. *U.S.A.*

Fyodor Dostoyevsky, 1821-81, (Russ.) novelist. *Crime and Punishment, The Brothers Karamazov, The Possessed.*

Arthur Conan Doyle, 1859-1930, (Br.) novelist. Sherlock Holmes mystery series.

Theodore Dreiser, 1871-1945, (U.S.) novelist. *An American Tragedy, Sister Carrie.*

John Dryden, 1631-1700, (Br.) poet, dramatist, critic. *All for Love, Mac Flecknoe, Absalom and Achitopel.*

Alexandre Dumas, 1802-70, (Fr.) novelist, dramatist. *The Three Musketeers, The Count of Monte Cristo.*

Alexandre Dumas (fils), 1824-95, (Fr.) dramatist, novelist. *La Dame aux Camélias, Le Demi-Monde.*

Ilya G. Ehrenburg, 1891-1967, (Russ.) writer. *The Thaw.*

George Eliot (Mary Ann Evans or Marian Evans), 1819-80, (Br.) novelist. *Middlemarch, The Mill on the Floss.*

T. S. Eliot, 1888-1965, (Br.) poet, critic. *The Waste Land,* "The Love Song of J. Alfred Prufrock," *Four Quartets.*

Ralph Ellison, 1914-94, (U.S.), writer. *Invisible Man.*

Ralph Waldo Emerson, 1803-82, (U.S.) poet, essayist. "Brahma," "Nature," "The Over-Soul," "Self-Reliance."

James T. Farrell, 1904-79, (U.S.) novelist. *Studs Lonigan.*

William Faulkner, 1897-1962, (U.S.) novelist. *Sanctuary, Light in August, The Sound and the Fury, Absalom, Absalom!*

Edna Ferber, 1887-1968, (U.S.) novelist, short-story writer, playwright. *The Girls, Ice Palace, Dinner at Eight.*

Henry Fielding, 1707-54, (Br.) novelist. *Tom Jones.*

F. Scott Fitzgerald, 1896-1940, (U.S.) short-story writer, novelist. *The Great Gatsby, Tender Is the Night.*

Gustave Flaubert, 1821-80, (Fr.) novelist. *Madame Bovary.*

C. S. Forester, 1899-1966, (Br.) writer. Horatio Hornblower.

E. M. Forster, 1879-1970, (Br.) novelist. *A Passage to India.*

Anatole France, 1844-1924, (Fr.) writer. *Penguin Island, My Friend's Book, The Crime of Sylvestre Bonnard.*

Robert Frost, 1874-1963, (U.S.) poet. "Birches," "Fire and Ice," "Stopping by Woods on a Snowy Evening."

John Galsworthy, 1867-1933, (Br.) novelist, dramatist. *The Forsyte Saga, A Modern Comedy.*

Erle Stanley Gardner, 1889-1970, (U.S.) novelist. Perry Mason series of mysteries.

Jean Genet, 1911-86, (Fr.) playwright, novelist. *The Blacks, The Maids, The Balcony.*

Kahlil Gibran, 1883-1931, (Lebanese-U.S.) mystical novelist, essayist, poet. *The Prophet.*

André Gide, 1869-1951, (Fr.) writer. *The Immoralist, The Pastoral Symphony, Strait Is the Gate.*

Jean Giraudoux, 1882-1944, (Fr.) novelist, dramatist. *Electra, The Madwoman of Chaillot, Ondine, Tiger at the Gate.*

Johann Wolfgang von Goethe, 1749-1832, (Ger.) poet, dramatist, novelist. *Faust, The Sorrows of Young Werther.*

Nikolai Gogol, 1809-52, (Russ.) short-story writer, dramatist, novelist. *Dead Souls, The Inspector General.*

William Golding, 1911-93, (Br.) writer. *Lord of the Flies.*

Oliver Goldsmith, 1730?-74, (Br.-Ir.) writer. *The Vicar of Wakefield, She Stoops to Conquer.*

Maxim Gorky, 1868-1936, (Russ.) writer. *The Lower Depths.*

Robert Graves, 1895-1985, (Br.) poet, classical scholar, novelist. *I, Claudius; The White Goddess.*

Thomas Gray, 1716-71, (Br.) poet. "Elegy Written in a Country Churchyard," "The Progress of Poesy."

Graham Greene, 1904-91, (Br.) novelist. *The Power and the Glory, The Heart of the Matter, The Ministry of Fear.*

Zane Grey, 1872-1939, (U.S.) writer of western stories.

Jakob Grimm, 1785-1863, (Ger.) philologist, folklorist. *German Methodology, Grimm's Fairy Tales.*

Wilhelm Grimm, 1786-1859, (Ger.) philologist, folklorist. *Grimm's Fairy Tales.*

Alex Haley, 1921-92, (U.S.) author. *Roots, The Autobiography of Malcolm X.*

Dashiell Hammett, 1894-1961, (U.S.) writer of detective fiction, created Sam Spade.

Knute Hamsun, 1859-1952 (Nor.) novelist. *Hunger.*

Thomas Hardy, 1840-1928, (Br.) novelist, poet. *The Return of the Native, Tess of the D'Urbervilles, Jude the Obscure.*

Joel Chandler Harris, 1848-1908, (U.S.) short-story writer. Uncle Remus series.

Moss Hart, 1904-61, (U.S.) playwright. *Once in a Lifetime, You Can't Take It With You, The Man Who Came to Dinner.*

Bret Harte, 1836-1902, (U.S.) short-story writer, poet. *The Luck of Roaring Camp.*

Jaroslav Hasek, 1883-1923, (Czech.) writer. *The Good Soldier Schweik.*

Nathaniel Hawthorne, 1804-64, (U.S.) novelist, short-story writer. *The Scarlet Letter,* "The Artist of the Beautiful."

Heinrich Heine, 1797-1856, (Ger.) poet. *Book of Songs.*

Lillian Hellman, 1905-84, (U.S.) playwright, author of memoirs. "The Little Foxes," *An Unfinished Woman, Pentimento.*

Ernest Hemingway, 1899-1961, (U.S.) novelist, short-story writer. *A Farewell to Arms, For Whom the Bell Tolls.*

O. Henry (W. S. Porter), 1862-1910, (U.S.) short-story writer. "The Gift of the Magi."

James Herriot (James Alfred Wight), 1916-95, (Br.) novelist, veterinarian. *All Creatures Great and Small.*

John Hersey, 1914-93, (U.S.) novelist, journalist. *Hiroshima, A Bell for Adano.*

Hermann Hesse, 1877-1962, (Ger.) novelist, poet. *Death and the Lover, Steppenwolf, Siddhartha.*

Oliver Wendell Holmes, 1809-94, (U.S.) poet, novelist. *The Autocrat of the Breakfast-Table.*

Alfred E. Housman, 1859-1936, (Br.) poet. *A Shropshire Lad.*

William Dean Howells, 1837-1920, (U.S.) novelist, critic. *The Rise of Silas Lapham.*

Langston Hughes, 1902-67, (U.S.) poet, playwright. *The Weary Blues, One-Way Ticket, Shakespeare in Harlem.*

Victor Hugo, 1802-85, (Fr.) poet, dramatist, novelist. *Notre Dame de Paris, Les Misérables.*

Nora Zeale Hurston, 1903-60, (U.S.) novelist, folklorist. *Their Eyes Were Watching God, Mules and Men.*

Aldous Huxley, 1894-1963, (Br.) writer. *Brave New World.*

Henrik Ibsen, 1828-1906, (Nor.) dramatist, poet. *A Doll's House, Ghosts, The Wild Duck, Hedda Gabler.*

Eugene Ionesco, 1910-94, (Fr.) surrealist writer. *The Bald Soprano, The Chairs.*

Washington Irving, 1783-1859, (U.S.) writer. "Rip Van Winkle," "The Legend of Sleepy Hollow."

Shirley Jackson, 1919-65, (U.S.) writer. "The Lottery."

Henry James, 1843-1916, (U.S.) novelist, short-story writer, critic. *The Portrait of a Lady, The American, Daisy Miller.*

Robinson Jeffers, 1887-1962, (U.S.) poet, dramatist. *Tamar and Other Poems, Medea.*

Samuel Johnson, 1709-84, (Br.) author, scholar, critic. *Dictionary of the English Language.*

Ben Jonson, 1572-1637, (Br.) dramatist, poet. *Volpone.*

James Joyce, 1882-1941, (Ir.) writer. *Ulysses, Dubliners, A Portrait of the Artist As a Young Man, Finnegans Wake.*

Franz Kafka, 1883-1924, (Ger.) novelist, short-story writer. *The Trial, Amerika, The Castle, The Metamorphosis.*

George S. Kaufman, 1889-1961, (U.S.) playwright. *The Man Who Came to Dinner, You Can't Take It With You, Stage Door.*

Nikos Kazantzakis, 1883?-1957, (Gk.) novelist. *Zorba the Greek, A Greek Passion.*

John Keats, 1795-1821, (Br.) poet. "Ode on a Grecian Urn," "Ode to a Nightingale," "La Belle Dame Sans Merci."

Joyce Kilmer, 1886-1918, (U.S.) poet, "Trees."

Rudyard Kipling, 1865-1936, (Br.) author, poet. "The White Man's Burden," "Gunga Din," *The Jungle Book.*

Jean de la Fontaine, 1621-95, (Fr.) poet. *Fables choisies.*

Pär Lagerkvist, 1891-1974, (Swed.) poet, dramatist, novelist. *Barabbas, The Sybil.*

Selma Lagerlöf, 1858-1940, (Swed.) novelist. *Jerusalem, The Ring of the Lowenskolds.*

Alphonse de Lamartine, 1790-1869, (Fr.) poet, novelist, statesman. *Méditations poétiques.*

Charles Lamb, 1775-1834, (Br.) essayist. *Specimens of English Dramatic Poets, Essays of Elia.*

Giuseppe di Lampedusa, 1896-1957, (It.) novelist. *The Leopard.*

Ring Lardner, 1885-1933, (U.S.) short-story writer, humorist. *You Know Me, Al.*

D. H. Lawrence, 1885-1930, (Br.) novelist. *Sons and Lovers, Women in Love, Lady Chatterley's Lover.*

Mikhail Lermontov, 1814-41, (Russ.) novelist, poet. "Demon," *Hero of Our Time.*

Alain-René Lesage, 1668-1747, (Fr.) novelist. *Gil Blas de Santillane.*

Gotthold Lessing, 1729-81, (Ger.) dramatist, philosopher, critic. *Miss Sara Sampson, Minna von Barnhelm.*

Sinclair Lewis, 1885-1951, (U.S.) novelist. *Babbitt, Main Street, Arrowsmith, Dodsworth.*

Vachel Lindsay, 1879-1931, (U.S.) poet. *General William Booth Enters into Heaven, The Congo.*

Hugh Lofting, 1886-1947, (Br.) writer. Dr. Doolittle series.

Jack London, 1876-1916, (U.S.) novelist, journalist. *Call of the Wild, The Sea-Wolf.*

Henry Wadsworth Longfellow, 1807-82, (U.S.) poet. *Evangeline, The Song of Hiawatha.*

Amy Lowell, 1874-1925, (U.S.) poet, critic. "Lilacs."

James Russell Lowell, 1819-91, (U.S.) poet, editor. *Poems, The Biglow Papers.*

Robert Lowell, 1917-77, (U.S.) poet. "Lord Weary's Castle".

Niccolò Machiavelli, 1469-1527, (It.) writer, statesman. *The Prince, Discourses on Livy.*

Bernard Malamud, 1914-86, (U.S.) short-story writer, novelist. "The Magic Barrel," *The Assistant, The Fixer.*

Stéphane Mallarmé, 1842-98, (Fr.) poet. *Poésies.*

Thomas Malory, ?-1471, (Br.) writer. *Morte d'Arthur.*

Andre Malraux, 1901-76, (Fr.) novelist. *Man's Fate.*

Osip Mandelstam, 1891-1938, (Russ.) poet. *Stone, Tristia.*

Thomas Mann, 1875-1955, (Ger.) novelist, essayist. *Buddenbrooks, Death in Venice, The Magic Mountain.*

Katherine Mansfield, 1888-1923, (Br.) writer. "Bliss."

Christopher Marlowe, 1564-93, (Br.) dramatist, poet. *Tamburlaine the Great, Dr. Faustus, The Jew of Malta.*

John Masefield, 1878-1967, (Br.) poet. "Sea Fever," "Cargoes," *Salt Water Ballads.*

Edgar Lee Masters, 1869-1950, (U.S.) poet, biographer. *Spoon River Anthology.*

W. Somerset Maugham, 1874-1965, (Br.) author. *Of Human Bondage, The Razor's Edge, The Moon and Sixpence.*

Guy de Maupassant, 1850-93, (Fr.) novelist, short-story writer. "A Life," "Bel-Ami," "The Necklace."

François Mauriac, 1885-1970, (Fr.) novelist, dramatist. *Viper's Tangle, The Kiss to the Leper.*

Vladimir Mayakovsky, 1893-1930, (Russ.) poet, dramatist. *The Cloud in Trousers.*

Mary McCarthy, 1912-89, (U.S.) critic, novelist. *Memories of a Catholic Girlhood.*

Carson McCullers, 1917-67, (U.S.) novelist. *The Heart Is a Lonely Hunter, Member of the Wedding.*

Herman Melville, 1819-91, (U.S.) novelist, poet. *Moby Dick, Typee, Billy Budd, Omoo.*

H. L. Mencken, 1880-1956, (U.S.) author, critic, editor. *Prejudices, The American Language.*

George Meredith, 1828-1909, (Br.) novelist, poet. *The Ordeal of Richard Feverel, The Egoist.*

Prosper Mérimée, 1803-70, (Fr.) author. *Carmen.*

James Merrill, 1926-95, (U.S.)poet. *Divine Comedies.*

Edna St. Vincent Millay, 1892-1950, (U.S.) poet. *The Harp Weaver and Other Poems, A Few Figs from Thistles.*

Henry Miller, 1891-1980, (U.S.) writer. *Tropic of Cancer.*

A. A. Milne, 1882-1956, (Br.) author. *Winnie-the-Pooh.*

John Milton, 1608-74, (Br.) poet. *Paradise Lost.*

Mishima Yukio (Hiraoka Kimitake), 1925-70, (Jpn.) writer. *Confessions of a Mask.*

Gabriela Mistral, 1889-1957, (Chil.) poet. *Sonnets of Death.*

Margaret Mitchell, 1900-49, (U.S.) author. *Gone With the Wind.*

Jean Baptiste Molière, 1622-73, (Fr.) dramatist. *Le Tartuffe, Le Misanthrope, Le Bourgeois Gentilhomme.*

Ferenc Molnár, 1878-1952, (Hung.) dramatist, novelist. *Liliom, The Guardsman, The Swan.*

Michel de Montaigne, 1533-92, (Fr.) essayist. *Essais.*

Eugenio Montale, 1896-1981, (It.) poet.

Clement C. Moore, 1779-1863, (U.S.) poet, educator. "A Visit From Saint Nicholas."

Marianne Moore, 1887-1972, (U.S.) poet. *Collected Poems.*

Thomas More, 1478-1535, (Br.) writer. *Utopia.*

H. H. Munro (Saki), 1870-1916, (Br.) writer. *Reginald, The Chronicles of Clovis, Beasts and Super-Beasts.*

Murasaki Shikibu, c978-1031?, (Jpn.) novelist. *The Tale of Genji.*

Alfred de Musset, 1810-57, (Fr.) poet, dramatist. *La Confession d'un Enfant du Siècle.*

Vladimir Nabokov, 1899-1977, (Russ.-U.S.) novelist. *Lolita.*

Ogden Nash, 1902-71, (U.S.) poet. *Hard Lines, I'm a Stranger Here Myself, The Private Dining Room.*

Pablo Neruda, 1904-73, (Chil.) poet. *Twenty Love Poems and One Song of Despair, Toward the Splendid City.*

Sean O'Casey, 1884-1964, (Ir.) dramatist. *Juno and the Paycock, The Plough and the Stars.*

Flannery O'Connor, 1925-64, (U.S.) novelist, short-story writer. *Wise Blood,* "A Good Man Is Hard to Find."

Clifford Odets, 1906-63, (U.S.) playwright. *Waiting for Lefty, Awake and Sing, Golden Boy, The Country Girl.*

John O'Hara, 1905-70, (U.S.) novelist, short-story writer. *From the Terrace, Appointment in Samarra, Pal Joey.*

Omar Khayyam, c1028-1122, (Per.) poet. *Rubaiyat.*

Eugene O'Neill, 1888-1953, (U.S.) playwright. *Emperor Jones, Anna Christie, Long Day's Journey into Night.*

George Orwell, 1903-50, (Br.) novelist, essayist. *Animal Farm, Nineteen Eighty-Four.*

John Osborne, 1929-95, (Br.) dramatist, novelist. *Look Back in Anger, The Entertainer.*

Thomas (Tom) Paine, 1737-1809, (U.S.) writer, political theorist. *Common Sense.*

Dorothy Parker, 1893-1967, (U.S.) poet, short-story writer. *Enough Rope, Laments for the Living.*

Boris Pasternak, 1890-1960, (Russ.) poet, novelist. *Doctor Zhivago, My Sister, Life.*

Samuel Pepys, 1633-1703, (Br.) public official, diarist.

S. J. Perelman, 1904-79, (U.S.) humorist. *The Road to Miltown, Under the Spreading Atrophy.*

Francesco Petrarca, 1304-74, (It.) poet. *Africa, Trionfi, Canzoniere, On Solitude.*

Luigi Pirandello, 1867-1936, (It.) novelist, dramatist. *Six Characters in Search of an Author.*

Sylvia Plath, 1932-63, (U.S.) author, poet. *The Bell Jar.*

Edgar Allan Poe, 1809-49, (U.S.) poet, short-story writer, critic. "Annabel Lee," "The Raven," "The Purloined Letter."

Alexander Pope, 1688-1744, (Br.) poet. *The Rape of the Lock, An Essay on Man.*

Katherine Anne Porter, 1890-1980, (U.S.) novelist, short-story writer. *Ship of Fools.*

Ezra Pound, 1885-1972, (U.S.) poet. *Cantos.*

Marcel Proust, 1871-1922, (Fr.) novelist. *Remembrance of Things Past.*

Aleksandr Pushkin, 1799-1837, (Russ.) poet, prose writer. *Boris Godunov, Eugene Onegin, The Bronze Horseman.*

François Rabelais, 1495-1553, (Fr.) writer. *Gargantua.*

Jean Racine, 1639-99, (Fr.) dramatist. *Andromaque, Phèdre, Bérénice, Britannicus.*

Ayn Rand, 1905-82, (Russ.-U.S.) novelist, philosopher. *The Fountainhead, Atlas Shrugged.*

Erich Maria Remarque, 1898-1970, (Ger.-U.S.) novelist. *All Quiet on the Western Front.*

Samuel Richardson, 1689-1761, (Br.) novelist. *Clarissa Harlowe, Pamela; or Virtue Rewarded.*

Rainer Maria Rilke, 1875-1926, (Ger.) poet. *Life and Songs, Duino Elegies, Poems from the Book of Hours.*

Arthur Rimbaud, 1854-91, (Fr.) poet. *A Season in Hell.*

Edwin Arlington Robinson, 1869-1935, (U.S.) poet. "Richard Cory," "Miniver Cheevy."

Theodore Roethke, 1908-63, (U.S.) poet. *Open House, The Waking, The Far Field.*

Romain Rolland, 1866-1944, (Fr.) novelist, biographer. *Jean-Christophe.*

Pierre de Ronsard, 1524-85, (Fr.) poet. *Sonnets pour Hélène, La Franciade.*

Edmond Rostand, 1868-1918, (Fr.) poet, dramatist. *Cyrano de Bergerac.*

Damon Runyon, 1880-1946, (U.S.) short-story writer, journalist. *Guys and Dolls, Blue Plate Special.*

John Ruskin, 1819-1900, (Br.) critic, social theorist. *Modern Painters, The Seven Lamps of Architecture.*

Antoine de Saint-Exupéry, 1900-44, (Fr.) writer. *Wind, Sand and Stars, The Little Prince.*

George Sand (Amandine Lucie Aurore Dupin), 1804-76, (Fr.) novelist. *Consuelo, The Haunted Pool, The Master Bell-Ringer.*

Carl Sandburg, 1878-1967, (U.S.) poet. *The People, Yes; Chicago Poems, Smoke and Steel, Harvest Poems.*

George Santayana, 1863-1952, (U.S.) poet, essayist, philosopher. *The Sense of Beauty, The Realms of Being.*

William Saroyan, 1908-81, (U.S.) playwright, novelist. *The Time of Your Life, The Human Comedy.*

May Sarton, 1914-95, (Belg.-U.S.) poet, novelist. *Encounter in April, Anger.*

Jean-Paul Sartre, 1905-80, (Fr.) philosopher, novelist, playwright. *Nausea, No Exit, Being and Nothingness.*

Richard Scarry, 1920-94, (U.S.) author of children's books. *Richard Scarry's Best Story Book Ever.*

Friedrich von Schiller, 1759-1805, (Ger.) dramatist, poet, historian. *Don Carlos, Maria Stuart, Wilhelm Tell.*

Sir Walter Scott, 1771-1832, (Sc.) novelist, poet. *Ivanhoe.*

Jaroslav Seifert, 1902-86, (Czech.) poet.

Dr. Seuss (Theodor Seuss Geisel), 1904-91, (U.S.) children's book author and illustrator. *The Cat in the Hat.*

William Shakespeare, 1564-1616, (Br.) dramatist, poet. *Romeo and Juliet, Hamlet, King Lear, Julius Caesar,* sonnets.

George Bernard Shaw, 1856-1950, (Ir.-Br.) playwright, critic. *St. Joan, Pygmalion, Major Barbara, Man and Superman.*

Mary Wollstonecraft Shelley, 1797-1851, (Br.) novelist, feminist. *Frankenstein, The Last Man.*

Percy Bysshe Shelley, 1792-1822, (Br.) poet. *Prometheus Unbound, Adonais,* "Ode to the West Wind," "To a Skylark."

Richard B. Sheridan, 1751-1816, (Br.) dramatist. *The Rivals, School for Scandal.*

William I. Shirer, 1904-93, (U.S.) author. *The Rise and Fall of the Third Reich.*
Mikhail Sholokhov, 1906-84, (Russ.) writer. *The Silent Don.*
Upton Sinclair, 1878-1968, (U.S.) novelist. *The Jungle.*
Isaac Bashevis Singer, 1904-91, (Pol.-U.S.) novelist, short story writer, in Yiddish. *The Magician of Lubin.*
Stephen Spender, 1909-95, (Br.) poet, critic, novelist. *Twenty Poems,* "Elegy for Margaret."
Edmund Spenser, 1552-99, (Br.) poet. *The Faerie Queen.*
Christina Stead, 1903-83, (Austral.) novelist, short-story writer. *The Man Who Loved Children.*
Richard Steele, 1672-1729, (Br.) essayist, playwright, began the *Tatler* and *Spectator. The Conscious Lovers.*
Lincoln Steffens, 1866-1936, (U.S.) editor, writer. *The Shame of the Cities.*
Gertrude Stein, 1874-1946, (U.S.) writer. *Three Lives.*
John Steinbeck, 1902-68, (U.S.) novelist. *The Grapes of Wrath, Of Mice and Men, The Winter of Our Discontent.*
Stendhal (Marie Henri Beyle), 1783-1842, (Fr.) novelist. *The Red and the Black, The Charterhouse of Parma.*
Laurence Sterne, 1713-68, (Br.) novelist. *Tristram Shandy.*
Wallace Stevens, 1879-1955, (U.S.) poet. *Harmonium, The Man With the Blue Guitar, Notes Toward a Supreme Fiction.*
Robert Louis Stevenson, 1850-94, (Br.) novelist, poet, essayist. *Treasure Island, A Child's Garden of Verses.*
Rex Stout, 1886-1975, (U.S.) novelist, created Nero Wolfe.
Harriet Beecher Stowe, 1811-96, (U.S.) novelist. *Uncle Tom's Cabin.*
Lytton Strachey, 1880-1932, (Br.) biographer, critic. *Eminent Victorians, Queen Victoria, Elizabeth and Essex.*
August Strindberg, 1849-1912, (Swed.) dramatist, novelist. *The Father, Miss Julie, The Creditors.*
Jonathan Swift, 1667-1745, (Br.) writer. *Gulliver's Travels.*
Algernon C. Swinburne, 1837-1909, (Br.) writer. *Atalanta in Calydon.*
John M. Synge, 1871-1909, (Ir.) poet, dramatist. *Riders to the Sea, The Playboy of the Western World.*
Rabindranath Tagore, 1861-1941, (Ind.) author, poet. *Sadhana, The Realization of Life, Gitanjali.*
Booth Tarkington, 1869-1946, (U.S.) novelist. *Seventeen, Alice Adams, Penrod.*
Peter Taylor, 1917-94, (U.S.) novelist. *A Summons to Memphis.*
Sara Teasdale, 1884-1933, (U.S.) poet. *Helen of Troy and Other Poems, Rivers to the Sea, Flame and Shadow.*
Tennyson, Alfred, Lord, 1809-92, (Br.) poet. *Idylls of the King, In Memoriam,* "The Charge of the Light Brigade."
William Makepeace Thackeray, 1811-63, (Br.) novelist. *Vanity Fair, Henry Esmond, Pendennis.*
Dylan Thomas, 1914-53, (Welsh) poet. *Under Milk Wood, A Child's Christmas in Wales.*
Henry David Thoreau, 1817-62, (U.S.) author. *Walden.*
James Thurber, 1894-1961, (U.S.) humorist, cartoonist. "The Secret Life of Walter Mitty," *My Life and Hard Times.*
J. R. R. Tolkien, 1892-1973, (Br.) writer. *Lord of the Rings.*

Leo Tolstoy, 1828-1910, (Russ.) novelist, short-story writer. *War and Peace, Anna Karenina,* "The Death of Ivan Ilyich."
Anthony Trollope, 1815-82, (Br.) novelist. *The Warden, Barchester Towers,* The Palliser novels.
Ivan Turgenev, 1818-83, (Russ.) novelist, short-story writer. *Fathers and Sons, First Love, A Month in the Country.*
Mark Twain (Samuel Clemens), 1835-1910, (U.S.) novelist, humorist. *The Adventures of Huckleberry Finn, Tom Sawyer.*
Sigrid Undset, 1881-1949, (Nor.) novelist, poet. *Kristin Lavransdatter.*
Paul Valéry, 1871-1945, (Fr.) poet, critic. *La Jeune Parque, The Graveyard by the Sea.*
Jules Verne, 1828-1905, (Fr.) novelist. *Twenty Thousand Leagues Under the Sea.*
François Villon, 1431-63?, (Fr.) poet. *The Lays, The Grand Testament.*
Evelyn Waugh, 1903-66, (Br.) novelist. *The Loved One.*
H. G. Wells, 1866-1946, (Br.) novelist. *The Time Machine, The Invisible Man, The War of the Worlds.*
Rebecca West, 1893-1983, (Br.) critic. *Black Lamb and Grey Falcon.*
Edith Wharton, 1862-1937, (U.S.) novelist. *The Age of Innocence, The House of Mirth, Ethan Frome.*
E. B. White, 1899-1985, (U.S.) essayist, novelist. *Here Is New York, Charlotte's Web, Stuart Little.*
T. H. White, 1906-64, (Br.) author. *The Once and Future King, A Book of Beasts.*
Walt Whitman, 1819-92, (U.S.) poet. *Leaves of Grass.*
John Greenleaf Whittier, 1807-92, (U.S.) poet, journalist. *Snow-Bound.*
Oscar Wilde, 1854-1900, (Ir.) playwright, story-writer. *The Picture of Dorian Gray, The Importance of Being Earnest.*
Laura Ingalls Wilder, 1867-1957, (U.S.) novelist. Little House on the Prairie series of children's books.
Thornton Wilder, 1897-1975, (U.S.) playwright. *Our Town, The Skin of Our Teeth, The Matchmaker.*
Tennessee Williams, 1911-83, (U.S.) playwright. *A Streetcar Named Desire, Cat on a Hot Tin Roof, The Glass Menagerie.*
William Carlos Williams, 1883-1963, (U.S.) poet. *Tempers, Al Que Quiere! Paterson.*
Edmund Wilson, 1895-1972, (U.S.) critic, novelist. *Axel's Castle, To the Finland Station.*
P. G. Wodehouse, 1881-1975, (Br.-U.S.) humorist. The "Jeeves" novels, *Anything Goes.*
Thomas Wolfe, 1900-38, (U.S.) novelist. *Look Homeward, Angel, You Can't Go Home Again, Of Time and the River.*
Virginia Woolf, 1882-1941, (Br.) novelist, essayist. *Mrs. Dalloway, To the Lighthouse, The Waves, A Room of One's Own.*
William Wordsworth, 1770-1850, (Br.) poet. "Tintern Abbey," "Ode: Intimations of Immortality," *The Prelude.*
Richard Wright, 1908-60, novelist; *Native Son, Black Boy.*
William Butler Yeats, 1865-1939, (Ir.) poet, playwright. *The Wild Swans at Coole, The Tower, Last Poems.*
Émile Zola, 1840-1902, (Fr.) novelist. *Nana, The Dram Shop.*

Composers of Classical Music

Carl Philipp Emanuel Bach, 1714-88, (Ger.) Cantatas, passions, numerous keyboard and instrumental works.
Johann Christian Bach, 1735-82, (Ger.) Concertos, operas, sonatas.
Johann Sebastian Bach, 1685-1750, (Ger.) St. Matthew Passion, The Well-Tempered Clavier.
Samuel Barber, 1910-81, (U.S.) Adagio for Strings, Vanessa.
Béla Bartók, 1881-1945, (Hung.) Concerto for Orchestra, The Miraculous Mandarin.
Ludwig van Beethoven, 1770-1827, (Ger.) Concertos (Emperor), sonatas (Moonlight, Pathetique), 9 symphonies.
Vincenzo Bellini, 1801-35, (It.) I Puritani, La Sonnambula, Norma.
Alban Berg, 1885-1935, (Aus.) Wozzeck, Lulu.
Hector Berlioz, 1803-69, (Fr.) Damnation of Faust, Symphonie Fantastique, Requiem.
Leonard Bernstein, 1918-90, (U.S.) Chichester Psalms, Jeremiah Symphony, Mass.
Georges Bizet, 1838-75, (Fr.) Carmen, Pearl Fishers.
Ernest Bloch, 1880-1959, (Swiss-U.S.) Macbeth (opera), Schelomo, Voice in the Wilderness.
Luigi Boccherini, 1743-1805, (It.) Chamber music, and guitar pieces.
Alexander Borodin, 1833-87, (Russ.) Prince Igor, In the Steppes of Central Asia, Polovtzian Dances.
Johannes Brahms, 1833-97, (Ger.) Liebeslieder Waltzes, Academic Festival Overture, chamber music, 4 symphonies.
Benjamin Britten, 1913-76, (Br.) Peter Grimes, Turn of the Screw, A Ceremony of Carols, War Requiem.
Anton Bruckner, 1824-96, (Aus.) 9 symphonies.
Dietrich Buxtehude, 1637-1707, (Dan.) Organ works, vocal music.
William Byrd, 1543-1623, (Br.) Masses, motets.
Emmanuel Chabrier, 1841-94, (Fr.) Le Roi Malgré Lui, Espana.

Gustave Charpentier, 1860-1956, (Fr.) Louise.
Frédéric Chopin, 1810-49, (Pol.) Mazurkas, waltzes, etudes, nocturnes, polonaises (Polonaise No. 6 in A flat major [Heroic]), sonatas.
Aaron Copland, 1900-90, (U.S.) Appalachian Spring, Fanfare for the Common Man, Lincoln Portrait.
Claude Debussy, 1862-1918, (Fr.) Pelleas et Melisande, La Mer, Prelude to the Afternoon of a Faun.
Gaetano Donizetti, 1797-1848, (It.) Elixir of Love, Lucia di Lammermoor, Daughter of the Regiment.
Paul Dukas, 1865-1935, (Fr.) Sorcerer's Apprentice.
Antonin Dvorak, 1841-1904, (Czech.) Songs My Mother Taught Me, Symphony in E Minor (From the New World).
Edward Elgar, 1857-1934, (Br.) Enigma Variations, Pomp and Circumstance.
Manuel de Falla, 1876-1946, (Sp.) El Amor Brujo, La Vida Breve, The Three-Cornered Hat.
Gabriel Fauré, 1845-1924, (Fr.) Requiem, Elègie for Cello and Piano.
Cesar Franck, 1822-90, (Belg.) Symphony in D minor , Violin Sonata.
George Gershwin, 1898-1937, (U.S.) Rhapsody in Blue, An American in Paris, Porgy and Bess.
Mikhail Glinka, 1804-57, (Russ.) A Life for the Tsar, Ruslan and Ludmilla.
Christoph W. Gluck, 1714-87, (Ger.) Alceste, Iphigènie en Tauride.
Charles Gounod, 1818-93, (Fr.) Faust, Romeo and Juliet.
Edvard Grieg, 1843-1907, (Nor.) Peer Gynt Suite, Concerto in A minor for piano.
George Frideric Handel, 1685-1759, (Ger.-Br.) Messiah, Water Music.

Howard Hanson, 1896-1981, (U.S.) Symphonies No. 1 (Nordic) and No. 2 (Romantic).
Roy Harris, 1898-1979, (U.S.) Symphonies.
Joseph Haydn, 1732-1809, (Aus.) Symphonies (Clock, London Toy), chamber music, oratorios.
Paul Hindemith, 1895-1963, (U.S.) Mathis der Maler.
Gustav Holst, 1874-1934, (Br.) The Planets.
Arthur Honegger, 1892-1955, (Fr.) Judith, Le Roi David, Pacific 231.
Alan Hovhaness, b 1911, (U.S.) Symphonies, Magnificat.
Engelbert Humperdinck, 1854-1921, (Ger.) Hansel and Gretel.
Charles Ives, 1874-1954, (U.S.) Concord Sonata, symphonies.
Aram Khachaturian, 1903-78, (Russ.) Ballets, piano pieces, Sabre Dance.
Zoltán Kodaly, 1882-1967, (Hung.) Háry János, Psalmus Hungaricus.
Fritz Kreisler, 1875-1962, (Aus.) Caprice Viennois, Tambourin Chinois.
Edouard Lalo, 1823-92, (Fr.) Symphonie Espagnole.
Ruggero Leoncavallo, 1857-1919, (It.) Pagliacci.
Franz Liszt, 1811-86, (Hung.) 20 Hungarian rhapsodies, symphonic poems.
Edward MacDowell, 1861-1908, (U.S.) To a Wild Rose.
Gustav Mahler, 1860-1911, (Aus.) Das Lied von der Erde.
Pietro Mascagni, 1863-1945, (It.) Cavalleria Rusticana.
Jules Massenet, 1842-1912, (Fr.) Manon, Le Cid, Thaïs.
Felix Mendelssohn, 1809-47, (Ger.) A Midsummer Night's Dream, Songs Without Words, violin concerto.
Gian-Carlo Menotti, b 1911, (It.-U.S.) The Medium, The Consul, Amahl and the Night Visitors.
Claudio Monteverdi, 1567-1643, (It.) Opera, masses, madrigals.
Modest Moussorgsky, 1839-81, (Russ.) Boris Godunov, Pictures at an Exhibition.
Wolfgang Amadeus Mozart, 1756-91, (Aus.) Chamber music, concertos, operas (Magic Flute, Marriage of Figaro), 41 symphonies.
Jacques Offenbach, 1819-80, (Fr.) Tales of Hoffmann.
Carl Orff, 1895-1982, (Ger.) Carmina Burana.
Johann Pachelbel, 1653-1706, (Ger.) Canon and Gigue in D major.
Ignacy Paderewski, 1860-1941, (Pol.) Minuet in G.
Niccolò Paganini, 1782-1840, (It.) Caprices for violin solo.
Palestrina, c1525-94, (It.) Masses, madrigals.
Francis Poulenc, 1899-1963, (Fr.) Dialogues des Carmèlites.
Sergei Prokofiev, 1891-1953, (Russ.) Classical Symphony, Love for Three Oranges, Peter and the Wolf.

Giacomo Puccini, 1858-1924, (It.) La Boheme, Manon Lescaut, Tosca, Madama Butterfly.
Henry Purcell, 1659-95, (Eng.) Dido and Aeneas.
Sergei Rachmaninov, 1873-1943, (Russ.) Concertos, preludes (Prelude in csharp minor), symphonies.
Maurice Ravel, 1875-1937, (Fr.) Bolèro, Daphnis et Chloè, Piano Concerto in D for Left Hand Alone.
Nikolai Rimsky-Korsakov, 1844-1908, (Russ.) Golden Cockerel, Capriccio Espagnol, Scheherazade, Russian Easter Overture, Flight of the Bumblebee.
Gioacchino Rossini, 1792-1868, (It.) Barber of Seville, Othello, William Tell.
Camille Saint-Saëns, 1835-1921, (Fr.) Carnival of Animals (The Swan), Samson and Delilah, Danse Macabre.
Alessandro Scarlatti, 1660-1725, (It.) Cantatas, oratorios, operas.
Domenico Scarlatti, 1685-1757, (It.) Harpsichord works.
Arnold Schoenberg, 1874-1951, (Aus.) Pelleas and Melisande, Pierrot Lunaire, Verklärte Nacht.
Franz Schubert, 1797-1828, (Aus.) Chamber music (Trout Quintet), lieder, symphonies (Unfinished).
Robert Schumann, 1810-56, (Ger.) Die Frauenliebe und Leben, Traümeri.
Dimitri Shostakovich, 1906-75, (Russ.) Symphonies, Lady Macbeth of the District Mzensk.
Jean Sibelius, 1865-1957, (Finn.) Finlandia.
Bedrich Smetana, 1824-84, (Czech.) The Bartered Bride.
Karlheinz Stockhausen, b 1928, (Ger.) KontraPunkte, Kontakte for Electronic Instruments.
Richard Strauss, 1864-1949, (Ger.) Salome, Elektra, Der Rosenkavalier, Thus Spake Zarathustra.
Igor Stravinsky, 1882-1971, (Russ.) Noah and the Flood, The Rake's Progress, The Rite of Spring.
Peter I. Tchaikovsky, 1840-93, (Russ.) Nutcracker, Swan Lake, The Sleeping Beauty.
Virgil Thomson, 1896-1989, (U.S.) Opera, film music, Four Saints in Three Acts.
Ralph Vaughan Williams, 1872-1958, (Eng.) Fantasiz on a Theme by Thomas Tallis, symphonies, vocal music.
Giuseppe Verdi, 1813-1901, (It.) Aida, Rigoletto, Don Carlo, Il Trovatore, La Traviata, Falstaff, Macbeth.
Heitor Villa-Lobos, 1887-1959, (Brazil) Bachianas Brasileiras.
Antonio Vivaldi, 1678-1741, (It.) Concerto grossos (The Four Seasons).
Richard Wagner, 1813-83, (Ger.) Rienzi, Tannhäuser, Lohengrin, Tristan und Isolde.
Carl Maria von Weber, 1786-1826, (Ger.) Der Freischutz.

Composers of Operettas, Musicals, and Popular Music

Richard Adler, b 1921, (U.S.) *Pajama Game; Damn Yankees.*
Milton Ager, 1893-1979, (U.S.) I Wonder What's Become of Sally; Hard Hearted Hannah; Ain't She Sweet?
Arthur Altman, 1910-94, (U.S.) All or Nothing at All.
Leroy Anderson, 1908-75, (U.S.) Syncopated Clock.
Paul Anka, b 1941, (Can.) My Way; Tonight Show theme.
Harold Arlen, 1905-86, (U.S.) Stormy Weather; Over the Rainbow; Blues in the Night; That Old Black Magic.
Burt Bacharach, b 1928, (U.S.) Raindrops Keep Fallin' on My Head; Walk on By; What the World Needs Now Is Love.
Ernest Ball, 1878-1927, (U.S.) Mother Machree; When Irish Eyes Are Smiling.
Irving Berlin, 1888-1989, (U.S.) *Annie Get Your Gun; Call Me Madam;* God Bless America; White Christmas.
Leonard Bernstein, 1918-90, (U.S.) *On the Town; Wonderful Town; Candide; West Side Story.*
Eubie Blake, 1883-1983, (U.S.) *Shuffle Along;* I'm Just Wild about Harry.
Jerry Bock, b 1928, (U.S.) *Mr. Wonderful; Fiorello; Fiddler on the Roof; The Rothschilds.*
Carrie Jacobs Bond, 1862-1946, (U.S.) I Love You Truly.
Nacio Herb Brown, 1896-1964, (U.S.) Singing in the Rain; You Were Meant for Me; All I Do Is Dream of You.
Hoagy Carmichael, 1899-1981, (U.S.) Stardust; Georgia on My Mind; Old Buttermilk Sky.
George M. Cohan, 1878-1942, (U.S.) Give My Regards to Broadway; You're A Grand Old Flag; Over There.
Cy Coleman, b 1929, (U.S.) *Sweet Charity;* Witchcraft.
Noel Coward, 1899-1973, (Br.) *Bitter Sweet;* Mad Dogs and Englishmen; Mad About the Boy.
Neil Diamond, b 1941, (U.S.) I'm a Believer; Sweet Caroline.
Walter Donaldson, 1893-1947, (U.S.) My Buddy; Carolina in the Morning; You're Driving Me Crazy; Makin' Whoopee.
Vernon Duke, 1903-69, (U.S.) April in Paris.
Bob Dylan, b 1941, (U.S.) Blowin' in the Wind.
Gus Edwards, 1879-1945, (U.S.) School Days; By the Light of the Silvery Moon; In My Merry Oldsmobile.
Sherman Edwards, 1919-81, (U.S.) See You in September; Wonderful! Wonderful!

Duke Ellington, 1899-1974, (U.S.) Sophisticated Lady; Satin Doll; It Don't Mean a Thing; Solitude.
Sammy Fain, 1902-89, (U.S.) I'll Be Seeing You; Love Is a Many-Splendored Thing.
Fred Fisher, 1875-1942, (U.S.) Peg O' My Heart; Chicago.
Stephen Collins Foster, 1826-64, (U.S.) My Old Kentucky Home; Old Folks at Home.
Rudolf Friml, 1879-1972, (Czech-U.S.) *The Firefly; Rose Marie; Vagabond King; Bird of Paradise.*
John Gay, 1685-1732, (Br.) *The Beggar's Opera.*
George Gershwin, 1898-1937, (U.S.) Someone to Watch Over Me; I've Got a Crush on You; Embraceable You.
Ferde Grofe, 1892-1972, (U.S.) Grand Canyon Suite.
Marvin Hamlisch, b 1944, (U.S.) The Way We Were, Nobody Does It Better, *A Chorus Line.*
Ray Henderson, 1896-1970, (U.S.) *George White's Scandals;* That Old Gang of Mine; Five Foot Two, Eyes of Blue.
Victor Herbert, 1859-1924, (Ir.-U.S.) *Mlle. Modiste; Babes in Toyland; The Red Mill; Naughty Marietta; Sweethearts.*
Jerry Herman, b 1932, (U.S.) *Hello Dolly; Mame.*
Brian Holland, b 1941, **Lamont Dozier,** b 1941, **Eddie Holland,** b 1939, (all U.S.) Heat Wave; Stop! In the Name of Love; Baby, I Need Your Loving.
Antonio Carlos Jobim, 1927-94, (Brazilian) *The Girl From Ipanema, Desafinado, One Note Samba.*
Billy (William Martin) Joel, b 1949, (U.S.) *Just the Way You Are,* Honesty, Piano Man.
Scott Joplin, 1868-1917, (U.S.) *Treemonisha.*
John Kander, b 1927, (U.S.) *Cabaret; Chicago; Funny Lady.*
Jerome Kern, 1885-1945, (U.S.) *Sally; Sunny; Show Boat.*
Carole King, b 1942, (U.S.) Will You Love Me Tomorrow?; Natural Woman; One Fine Day; Up on the Roof.
Burton Lane, b 1912, (U.S.) *Finian's Rainbow.*
Franz Lehar, 1870-1948, (Hung.) *Merry Widow.*
Jerry Leiber, & Mike Stoller, both b 1933, (both U.S.) Hound Dog; Searchin'; Yakety Yak; Love Me Tender.
Mitch Leigh, b 1928, (U.S.) *Man of La Mancha.*
John Lennon, 1940-80, & **Paul McCartney,** b 1942, (both Br.) I Want to Hold Your Hand; She Loves You.

Frank Loesser, 1910-69, (U.S.) *Guys and Dolls; Where's Charley?; The Most Happy Fella; How to Succeed ....*

Frederick Loewe, 1901-88, (Aus.-U.S.) *Brigadoon; Paint Your Wagon; My Fair Lady; Camelot.*

Henry Mancini, 1924-94, (U.S.) *Moon River; Days of Wine and Roses; Pink Panther Theme.*

Barry Mann, b 1939, & **Cynthia Weil,** b 1937, (both U.S.) *You've Lost That Loving Feeling.*

Jimmy McHugh, 1894-1969, (U.S.) *Don't Blame Me; I'm in the Mood for Love; I Feel a Song Coming On.*

Alan Menken, b 1950, (U.S.) *Little Shop of Horrors.*

Joseph Meyer, 1894-1987, (U.S.) *If You Knew Susie; California, Here I Come; Crazy Rhythm.*

Chauncey Olcott, 1858-1932, (U.S.) *Mother Machree.*

Jerome "Doc" Pomus, 1925-91, (U.S.) *Save the Last Dance for Me, A Teenager in Love.*

Cole Porter, 1893-1964, (U.S.) *Anything Goes; Kiss Me Kate; Can Can; Silk Stockings.*

Smokey Robinson, b 1940, (U.S.) *Shop Around; My Guy; My Girl; Get Ready.*

Richard Rodgers, 1902-79, (U.S.) *Oklahoma!; Carousel; South Pacific; The King and I; The Sound of Music.*

Sigmund Romberg, 1887-1951, (Hung.) *Maytime; The Student Prince; Desert Song; Blossom Time.*

Harold Rome, 1908-93, (U.S.) *Pins and Needles; Call Me Mister; Wish You Were Here; Fanny; Destry Rides Again.*

Vincent Rose, b 1880-1944, (U.S.) *Avalon; Whispering; Blueberry Hill.*

Harry Ruby, 1895-1974, (U.S.) *Three Little Words; Who's Sorry Now?*

Arthur Schwartz, 1900-84, (U.S.) *The Band Wagon; Dancing in the Dark; By Myself; That's Entertainment.*

Neil Sedaka, b 1939, (U.S.) *Breaking Up Is Hard to Do.*

Paul Simon, b 1942, (U.S.) *Sounds of Silence; I Am a Rock; Mrs. Robinson; Bridge Over Troubled Waters.*

Stephen Sondheim, b 1930, (U.S.) *A Little Night Music; Company; Sweeney Todd; Sunday in the Park with George.*

John Philip Sousa, 1854-1932, (U.S.) *El Capitan;* Stars and Stripes Forever.

Oskar Straus, 1870-1954, (Aus.) *Chocolate Soldier.*

Johann Strauss, 1825-99, (Aus.) *Gypsy Baron; Die Fledermaus;* waltzes: Blue Danube, Artist's Life.

Charles Strouse, b 1928, (U.S.) *Bye Bye, Birdie; Annie.*

Jule Styne, 1905-94, (Br.-U.S.) *Gentlemen Prefer Blondes; Bells Are Ringing; Gypsy; Funny Girl.*

Arthur S. Sullivan, 1842-1900, (Br.) *H.M.S. Pinafore, Pirates of Penzance; The Mikado.*

Deems Taylor, 1885-1966, (U.S.) *Peter Ibbetson.*

Harry Tobias, 1905-94, (U.S.) *I'll Keep the Lovelight Burning.*

Egbert van Alstyne, 1882-1951, (U.S.) *In the Shade of the Old Apple Tree; Memories; Pretty Baby.*

Jimmy Van Heusen, 1913-90, (U.S.) *Moonlight Becomes You; Swinging on a Star; All the Way; Love and Marriage.*

Albert von Tilzer, 1878-1956, (U.S.) *I'll Be With You in Apple Blossom Time; Take Me Out to the Ball Game.*

Harry von Tilzer, 1872-1946, (U.S.) *Only a Bird in a Gilded Cage; On a Sunday Afternoon.*

Fats Waller, 1904-43, (U.S.) *Honeysuckle Rose; Ain't Misbehavin'.*

Harry Warren, 1893-1981, (U.S.) *You're My Everything; We're in the Money; I Only Have Eyes for You.*

Jimmy Webb, b 1946, (U.S.) *Up, Up and Away; By the Time I Get to Phoenix; Didn't We?; Wichita Lineman.*

Andrew Lloyd Webber, b 1948, (Br.) *Jesus Christ Superstar, Evita, Cats, The Phantom of the Opera.*

Kurt Weill, 1900-50, (Ger.-U.S.) *Threepenny Opera; Lady in the Dark; Knickerbocker Holiday; One Touch of Venus.*

Percy Wenrich, 1887-1952, (U.S.) *When You Wore a Tulip; Moonlight Bay; Put On Your Old Gray Bonnet.*

Richard A. Whiting, 1891-1938, (U.S.) *Till We Meet Again; Sleepytime Gal; Beyond the Blue Horizon; My Ideal.*

John Williams, b 1932, (U.S.) *Jaws, E.T., Star Wars* series, *Raiders of the Lost Ark* series.

Meredith Willson, 1902-84, (U.S.) *The Music Man.*

Stevie Wonder, b 1950, (U.S.) *You Are the Sunshine of My Life; Signed, Sealed, Delivered, I'm Yours.*

Vincent Youmans, 1898-1946, (U.S.) *Two Little Girls in Blue; Wildflower; No, No, Nanette; Hit the Deck; Rainbow; Smiles.*

Lyricists

Howard Ashman, 1950-91, (U.S.) Little Shop of Horrors, The Little Mermaid.

Johnny Burke, 1908-84, (U.S.) What's New?; Misty; Imagination; Polka Dots and Moonbeams.

Sammy Cahn, 1913-93, (U.S.) High Hopes; Love and Marriage; The Second Time Around; It's Magic.

Betty Comden, b 1919, (U.S.) and **Adolph Green,** b 1915, (U.S.) The Party's Over; Just in Time; New York, New York.

Hal David, b 1921, (U.S.) What the World Needs Now Is Love.

Buddy De Sylva, 1895-1950, (U.S.) When Day Is Done; Look for the Silver Lining; April Showers.

Howard Dietz, 1896-1983, (U.S.) Dancing in the Dark; You and the Night and the Music; That's Entertainment.

Al Dubin, 1891-1945, (U.S.) Tiptoe Through the Tulips; Anniversary Waltz; Lullaby of Broadway.

Fred Ebb, b 1936, (U.S.) Cabaret, Zorba, Woman of the Year.

Dorothy Fields, 1905-74, (U.S.) On the Sunny Side of the Street; Don't Blame Me; The Way You Look Tonight.

Ira Gershwin, 1896-1983, (U.S.) The Man I Love; Fascinating Rhythm; S'Wonderful; Embraceable You.

William S. Gilbert, 1836-1911, (Br.) The Mikado; H.M.S. Pinafore, Pirates of Penzance.

Gerry Goffin, b 1939, (U.S.) Will You Love Me Tomorrow, Take Good Care of My Baby, Up on the Roof.

Mack Gordon, 1905-59, (Pol.-U.S.) You'll Never Know; The More I See You; Chattanooga Choo-Choo.

Oscar Hammerstein II, 1895-1960, (U.S.) Ol' Man River; Oklahoma; Carousel.

E. Y. (Yip) Harburg, 1898-1981, (U.S.) Brother, Can You Spare a Dime; April in Paris; Over the Rainbow.

Lorenz Hart, 1895-1943, (U.S.) Isn't It Romantic; Blue Moon; Lover; Manhattan; My Funny Valentine.

DuBose Heyward, 1885-1940, (U.S.) Summertime; A Woman Is a Sometime Thing.

Gus Kahn, 1886-1941, (U.S.) Memories; Ain't We Got Fun.

Alan J. Lerner, 1918-86, (U.S.) Brigadoon; My Fair Lady; Camelot; Gigi; On a Clear Day You Can See Forever.

Johnny Mercer, 1909-76, (U.S.) Blues in the Night; Come Rain or Come Shine; Laura; That Old Black Magic.

Bob Merrill, b 1921, (U.S.) People; Don't Rain on My Parade.

Jack Norworth, 1879-1959, (U.S.) Take Me Out to the Ball Game; Shine On Harvest Moon.

Mitchell Parish, 1901-93, (U.S.) Stairway to the Stars; Stardust.

Andy Razaf, 1895-1973, (U.S.) Honeysuckle Rose, Ain't Misbehavin', S'posin'.

Leo Robin, 1900-84, (U.S.) Thanks for the Memory; Hooray for Love; Diamonds Are a Girl's Best Friend.

Paul Francis Webster, 1907-84, (U.S.) Secret Love, The Shadow of Your Smile, Love Is a Many-Splendored Thing.

Jack Yellen, 1892-1991, (U.S.) Down by the O-Hi-O; Ain't She Sweet; Happy Days Are Here Again.

Some Notable Figures of the Past in Dance

Source: Reviewed by Gary Parks, Reviews editor, *Dance* magazine

Alvin Ailey, 1931-89, (U.S.) modern dancer, choreographer; melded modern dance and Afro-Caribbean techniques.

Frederick Ashton, 1904-88, (Br.) ballet choreographer; director of Great Britain's Royal Ballet, 1963-70.

Fred Astaire, 1899-1987, (U.S.) dancer, actor; teamed with dancer/actress **Ginger Rogers** (1911-95) in movie musicals.

George Balanchine, 1904-83, (Russ.-U.S.) ballet choreographer, teacher; most influential exponent of the neoclassical style, co-founded with **Lincoln Kirstein,** b 1907 (U.S.), School of American Ballet and New York City Ballet.

Carlo Blasis, 1803-78, (It.) ballet dancer, choreographer, writer; his teaching methods are standards of classical dance.

August Bournonville, 1805-79, (Dan.) ballet dancer, choreographer, teacher; developed a distinctly Danish style known for its exuberance and lightness.

Enrico Cecchetti, 1850-1928, (It.) ballet dancer, teacher of many leading dancers of Russia's Imperial Ballet; his technique is basis for Great Britain's Imperial Society of Teachers of Dancing.

Gower Champion, 1921-80, (U.S.) dancer, choreographer, director; with his wife **Marge,** b 1923, (U.S.), choreographed and danced in Broadway musicals and films.

John Cranko, 1927-73, (S. African) choreographer; created narrative ballets based on literary works.

Agnes de Mille, 1909-93, (U.S.) ballet dancer, choreographer; known for using American themes, she choreographed the ballet *Rodeo* and the musical *Oklahoma.*

Sergei Diaghilev, 1872-1929, (Russ.) impresario; founded Les Ballet Russes; saw ballet as an art unifying dance, drama, music, and decor.

Isadora Duncan, 1877-1927, (U.S.) expressive dancer who united free movement with serious music; one of the founders of modern dance.

Fanny Elssler, 1810-84, (Aus.) ballerina of the Romantic period; known for dramatic skill and sensual style.

Michel Fokine, 1880-1942, (Russ.) ballet dancer, choreographer, teacher; rejected strict classicism in favor of dramatically expressive style.

Margot Fonteyn, 1919-91, (Br.) prima ballerina, Royal Ballet of Great Britain; famed performance partner of Rudolf Nureyev.

Bob Fosse, 1927-87, (U.S.) jazz dancer, choreographer, director; Broadway musicals and film.

Martha Graham, 1893-1991, (U.S.) modern dancer, choreographer, created and codified her own dramatic technique.

Doris Humphrey, 1895-1958, (U.S.) modern dancer, choreographer, writer, teacher; known for her intellect and choreographic range.

Robert Joffrey, 1930-88, (U.S.) ballet dancer, choreographer; co-founded with **Gerald Arpino,** b 1928, (U.S.), the Joffrey Ballet.

Kurt Jooss, 1901-79, (Ger.) choreographer, teacher; created expressionist works utilizing modern and classical techniques.

Tamara Karsavina, 1885-1978, (Russ.) prima ballerina of Russia's Imperial Ballet and Diaghilev's Ballets Russes; partner of Nijinsky.

Serge Lifar, 1905-86, (Russ.-F.) premier danseur, choreographer; director of dance at Paris Opera, 1930-45, 1947-58.

José Limón, 1908-72, (Mex.-U.S.) modern dancer, choreographer, teacher; developed technique based on that of mentor Doris Humphrey.

Catherine Littlefield, 1908-51, (U.S.) ballet dancer, choreographer, teacher; pioneer of American ballet.

Léonide Massine, 1896-1979, (Russ.-U.S.) ballet dancer, choreographer; created "symphonic ballet" using concert music previously thought unsuitable for dance.

Kenneth MacMillan, 1929-92, (Br.) ballet dancer, choreographer; director of Royal Ballet of Great Britain 1970-77.

Vaslav Nijinsky, 1890-50, (Russ.) premier danseur, choreographer; leading member of Diaghilev's Ballets Russes; his ballets were revolutionary for their time.

Alwin Nikolais, 1910-93, (U.S.) modern choreographer; created dance theater utilizing mixed media effects.

Jean-George Noverre, 1727-1810, (Fr.) ballet choreographer, teacher, writer; his theories on dramatic ballet remain influential; called the "Shakespeare of the dance."

Rudolf Nureyev, 1938-93, (Russ.) premier danseur, choreographer; leading male dancer of his generation; director of dance at Paris Opera, 1983-89.

Ruth Page, 1903-91, (U.S.) ballet dancer, choreographer; danced and directed ballet at Chicago Lyric Opera.

Anna Pavlova, 1881-1931, (Russ.) prima ballerina; toured all over the world with her own company to great acclaim.

Marius Petipa, 1818-1910, (Fr.) ballet dancer, choreographer; as ballet master of the Imperial Ballet, he established Russian classicism as leading style of late 19th century.

Pearl Primus, 1919-95, (Trinidad-U.S.) modern dancer, choreographer, scholar; combined African, Caribbean, and African-American styles.

Bill (Bojangles) Robinson, 1878-1949, (U.S.) tap dancer; called the King of Tapology, he attained fame on stage and screen rare for an African-American of his era.

Ruth St. Denis, 1877-1968, (U.S.) interpretive dancer, choreographer, teacher; touring widely, she influenced many early modern dancers.

Ted Shawn, 1891-1972, (U.S.) modern dancer, choreographer; teamed with Ruth St. Denis to form Denishawn dance company and school.

Marie Taglioni, 1804-84, (It.) ballerina, teacher; in the title role of *La Sylphide* she established the image of the ethereal ballerina.

Mary Wigman, 1886-1973, (Ger.) modern dancer, choreographer, teacher; influential in European expressionist dance.

Agrippina Vaganova, 1879-1951, (Russ.) ballet teacher, director; codified Soviet ballet technique that developed virtuosity.

Antony Tudor, 1908-87, (Br.) choreographer, teacher; exponent of the "psychological ballet."

Selected Notable Opera Singers of the Past

Frances Alda, 1883-1952, (NZ.) soprano
Paul Althouse, 1889-1954, (U.S.) tenor
Pasquale Amato, 1878-1942, (It.) baritone
Marion Anderson, 1902-93, (U.S.) contralto
Jussi Björling, 1911-60, (Swed.) tenor
Lucrezia Bori, 1887-1960, (It.) soprano
Maria Callas, 1923-77, (U.S.) soprano
Emma Calvé, 1858-1942, (Fr.) soprano
Enrico Caruso, 1873-1921, (It.) tenor
Feodor Chaliapin, 1873-1938, (Russ.) bass
Richard Crooks, 1900-72, (U.S.) tenor
Giuseppe De Luca, 1876-1950, (It.) baritone
Edouard De Reszke, 1853-1917, (Pol.) bass
Jean De Reszke, 1850-1925, (Pol.) tenor
Emmy Destinn, 1878-1930, (Czech.) soprano
Emma Eames, 1865-1952, (U.S.) soprano
Geraldine Farrar, 1882-1967, (U.S.) soprano
Kirsten Flagstad, 1895-1962, (Nor.) soprano.
Olive Fremstad, 1871-1951, (Swed.-U.S.) soprano
Amelita Galli-Curci, 1882-1963, (It.) soprano
Mary Garden, 1874-1967, (Br.) soprano
Beniamino Gigli, 1890-1957, (It.) tenor
Tito Gobbi, 1913-84, (It.) baritone
Frieda Hempel, 1885-1955, (Ger.) soprano

Maria Jeritza, 1887-1982, (Czech.) soprano
Alexander Kipnis, 1891-1978, (Russ.-U.S.) bass
Lilli Lehmann, 1848-1929, (Ger.) soprano
Lotte Lehmann, 1888-1976, (Ger.-U.S.) soprano
Jenny Lind, 1820-87, (Swed.) soprano
John McCormack, 1884-1945, (Ir.) tenor
Blanche Marchesi, 1863-1940, (Fr.) soprano
Nellie Melba, 1861-1931, (Aus.) soprano.
Lauritz Melchior, 1890-1973, (Dan.) tenor
Zinka Milanov, 1906-89, (Yugo.) soprano
Lillian Nordica, 1857-1914, (U.S.) soprano
Adelina Patti, 1843-1919, (It.) soprano
Peter Pears, 1910-86, (Eng.) tenor
Jan Peerce, 1904-84, (U.S.) tenor
Ezio Pinza, 1892-1957, (It.) bass
Lily Pons, 1898-1976, (Fr.) soprano
Rosa Ponselle, 1897-1981, (U.S.) soprano
Marcella Sembrich, 1858-1935, (Pol.) soprano
Eleanor Steber, 1916-90, (U.S.) soprano
Luisa Tetrazzini, 1871-1940, (It.) soprano
Lawrence Tibbett, 1896-1960, (U.S.) baritone
Richard Tucker, 1913-75, (U.S.) tenor
Pauline Viardot, 1821-1910, (Fr.) mezzo-soprano
Leonard Warren, 1911-60, (U.S.) baritone

Some Notable Blues and Jazz Artists of the Past

Blues originated from the songs of the black American slave. Traditionally, soloists accompanied themselves with a harmonica or guitar. Blues developed as its own genre, but it is linked in many ways to jazz. Jazz has been called America's only completely unique contribution to Western culture. It is traditionally complex in rhythm and is noted for improvisation.

Julian "Cannonball" Adderley, 1928-75, alto sax
Louis "Satchmo" Armstrong, 1900-71, trumpet, singer; originated the "scat" vocal
Mildred Bailey, 1907-51, blues singer
Chet Baker, 1929-88, trumpet
Count Basie, 1904-84, orchestra leader, piano
Sidney Bechet, 1897-1959, early innovator, soprano sax
Bix Beiderbecke, 1903-31, cornet, piano, composer
Tommy Benford, 1906-94, drummer
Bunny Berigan, 1909-42, trumpet, singer
Barney Bigard, 1906-80, clarinet
Ed Blackwell, 1929-92, drummer
Jimmy Blanton, 1921-42, bass
Charles "Buddy" Bolden, 1868-1931, cornet; formed the first jazz band in the 1890s
Big Bill Broonzy, 1893-1958, blues singer, guitar
Don Byas, 1912-72, tenor sax
Cab Calloway, 1907-94, band leader

Harry Carney, 1910-74, baritone sax
Sidney Catlett, 1910-51, drums
Charlie Christian, 1919-42, guitar
Kenny Clarke, 1914-85, pioneer of modern drums
Buck Clayton, 1911-91, trumpet, arranger
James Cleveland, 1931-91, gospel singer
Al Cohn, 1925-88, tenor sax, composer
Cozy Cole, 1909-81, drums
John Coltrane, 1926-67, tenor sax innovator
Eddie Condon, 1904-73, guitar, band leader; Dixieland
Tadd Dameron, 1917-65, piano, composer
Eddie "Lockjaw" Davis, 1921-86, tenor sax
Miles Davis, 1926-91, trumpet; pioneer of cool jazz
Wild Bill Davison, 1906-89, cornet, early Chicago jazz
Paul Desmond, 1924-77, alto sax
Vic Dickenson, 1906-84, trombone, composer
Willy Dixon, 1915-92, songwriter, blues, "You Shook Me"
Warren "Baby" Dodds, 1898-1959, Dixieland drummer

Johnny Dodds, 1892-1940, clarinet
Jimmy Dorsey, 1904-57, clarinet, alto sax; band leader
Tommy Dorsey, 1905-56, trombone; band leader
Roy Eldridge, 1911-89, trumpet, drums, singer
Duke Ellington, 1899-1974, piano, band leader, composer
Bill Evans, 1929-80, piano
Gil Evans, 1912-88, composer, arranger, piano
"Red" Garland, 1923-84; piano
Erroll Garner, 1921-77, piano, composer, "Misty"
Stan Getz, 1927-91, tenor sax
Dizzy Gillespie, 1917-93, trumpet, composer; bop developer
Benny Goodman, 1909-86, clarinet, band and combo leader
Dexter Gordon, 1923-90, tenor sax; bop-derived style
Bobby Hackett, 1915-76, trumpet, cornet
Herbie Hancock, b 1940, piano, composer
W. C. Handy, 1873-1958, composer, "St Louis Blues"
Coleman Hawkins, 1904-69, tenor sax; "Body and Soul," 1939
Fletcher Henderson, 1898-1952, orchestra leader, arranger
Woody Herman, 1913-87, clarinet, alto sax, band leader
Jay C. Higginbotham, 1906-73, trombone
Earl "Fatha" Hines, 1905-83, piano, songwriter
Johnny Hodges, 1906-70, alto sax
Billie Holiday, 1915-59, blues singer, "Strange Fruit"
Sam "Lightnin'" Hopkins, 1912-82, blues singer, guitar
Mahalia Jackson, 1911-72, gospel singer
Blind Lemon Jefferson, 1897-1930, blues singer, guitar
Bunk Johnson, 1879-1949, cornet, trumpet
James P. Johnson, 1891-1955, piano, composer
Robert Johnson, 1911-32, blues songwriter, singer
Jo Jones, 1911-85, drums
Philly Joe Jones, 1923-85, drums
Thad Jones, 1923-86, trumpet, cornet
Scott Joplin, 1868-1917, composer, "Maple Leaf Rag"
Louis Jordan, 1908-75, singer, alto sax
Stan Kenton, 1912-79, orchestra leader, composer, piano
Albert King, 1923-92, blues guitarist
Gene Krupa, 1909-73, drums, band and combo leader
Scott LaFaro, 1936-61, bass
Huddie Ledbetter (Leadbelly), 1888-1949, blues singer, guitar
Mel Lewis, 1929-90, drummer, orchestra leader
Jimmie Lunceford, 1902-47, band leader, sax
Jimmy McPartland, 1907-91, trumpet
Carmen McRae, 1920-94, jazz singer
Glenn Miller, 1904-44, trombone, dance band leader
Charles Mingus, 1922-79, bass, composer, combo leader
Thelonious Monk, 1920-82, piano, composer, combo leader; a developer of bop
Wes Montgomery, 1925-68, guitar
"Jelly Roll" Morton, 1885-1941, composer, piano, singer
Bennie Moten, 1894-1935, piano
Turk Murphy, 1915-87, trombone, band leader
Theodore "Fats" Navarro, 1923-50, trumpet
Red Nichols, 1905-65, cornet, combo leader

King Oliver, 1885-1938, cornet, band leader; teacher of Louis Armstrong
Sy Oliver, 1910-88, Swing Era arranger, composer, conductor
Kid Ory, 1886-1973, trombone, "Muskrat Ramble"
Charlie "Bird" Parker, 1920-55, alto sax, composer; rated by many as the greatest jazz improviser
Joe Pass, 1929-94, guitarist
Art Pepper, 1925-82, alto sax
Oscar Pettiford, 1922-60, a leading bassist in the bop era
Bud Powell, 1924-66, piano; modern jazz pioneer
Don Pullen, 1942?095, piano; percussive pianist
Sun Ra, 1915?-93, big band leader, pianist, composer
Gertrude "Ma" Rainey, 1886-1939, blues singer
Don Redman, 1900-64, composer, arranger
Django Reinhardt, 1910-53, guitar; Belgian gypsy, first European to influence American jazz
Buddy Rich, 1917-87, drums, band leader
Red Rodney, 1928-94, trumpeter
Frank Rosolino, 1926-78, trombone
Jimmy Rushing, 1903-72, blues singer
Pee Wee Russell, 1906-69, clarinet
Zoot Sims, 1925-85, tenor, alto sax; clarinet
Zutty Singleton, 1898-1975, Dixieland drummer
Bessie Smith, 1894-1937, blues singer
Clarence "Pinetop" Smith, 1904-29, piano, singer; pioneer of boogie woogie
Willie "The Lion" Smith, 1897-1973, stride style pianist
Muggsy Spanier, 1906-67, cornet, band leader
Billy Strayhorn, 1915-67, composer, piano
Sonny Stitt, 1924-82, alto, tenor sax
Art Tatum, 1910-56, piano; technical virtuoso
Art Taylor, 1929-95, jazz drummer, bandleader
Jack Teagarden, 1905-64, trombone, singer
Dave Tough, 1908-48, drums
Lennie Tristano, 1919-78, piano, composer
Joe Turner, 1911-85, blues singer
Sarah Vaughan, 1924-90, singer
Stevie Ray Vaughn, 1954-90, virtuoso guitarist, singer
Joe Venuti, 1904-78, first great jazz violinist
T-Bone Walker, 1910-75, guitarist; pioneered electric blues guitar sound
Thomas "Fats" Waller, 1904-43, piano, singer, composer
Dinah Washington, 1924-63, singer
Ethel Waters, 1896-1977, jazz and blues singer
Muddy Waters, 1915-83, blues singer, songwriter
Chick Webb, 1902-39, band leader, drums
Ben Webster, 1909-73, tenor sax
Paul Whiteman, 1890-1967, jazz orchestra leader.
Charles "Cootie" Williams, 1908-85, trumpet, band leader
Mary Lou Williams, 1914-81, piano, composer
Teddy Wilson, 1912-86, piano, composer
Kai Winding, 1922-83, trombone, composer
Jimmy Yancey, 1894-1951, piano
Lester "Pres" Young, 1909-59, tenor sax, composer.

Noted Country Music Artists of the Past

Country music is a style of U.S. popular music rooted in southern traditional music, portraying the life experience of poor rural whites. It was popularized by the *Grand Ole Opry* radio show, which began broadcasting nationally from Memphis, TN, in 1939. Still broadcasting today, the *Grand Ole Opry* is the oldest continuous radio show in the U.S.

Roy Acuff, 1903-92, guitarist, singer, songwriter, "Precious Jewel"
Boudleaux Bryant, 1920-87, songwriter, singer, "Hey Joe"
"Mother" Maybelle Carter, 1909-78, singer
Patsy Cline, 1932-63, singer
Vernon Dalhart, 1883-1948, singer
Lester Flatt, 1914-79, singer
Red Foley, 1910-68, singer
Tennessee Ernie Ford, 1919-91, singer
Lefty Frizzell, 1928-75, singer, guitarist
Kendall L. Hayes, 1936-95, song writer, "Walk On By"
Uncle Dave Macon, 1870-1952, singer, banjo player
Jim Reeves, 1924-64, singer
Charlie Rich (Silver Fox), 1932-95, singer, songwriter, "The Most Beautiful Girl"
Tex Ritter, 1907-74, singer

Marty Robbins, 1925-82, singer, songwriter, "A White Sport Coat and a Pink Carnation"
Jimmie Rodgers, 1897-1933, singer
Fred Rose, 1898-1954, songwriter, singer, musician, "Blue Eyes Cryin' in the Rain"
Original Sons of the Pioneers, Len Slye (Roy Rogers), b 1912, Bob Nolan, 1908-80, singers, songwriters, "Tumbling Tumbleweed"; Tim Spencer, 1905-74, singer, songwriter, "Careless Kisses"; Hugh Farr, 1903-80, Karl Farr, 1909-61, Lloyd Perryman, 1917-77, singers
Merle Travis, 1917-83, singer, guitarist, songwriter, "16 Tons"
Ernest Tubb, 1914-84, singer
Conway Twitty, 1933-93, singer, songwriter
Hank Williams, Sr., 1923-53, singer, songwriter, "Your Cheatin' Heart"
Bob Wills, 1905-75, singer, bandleader, songwriter, "San Antonio Rose"

Rock and Roll Notables

Since the mid-1950s, rock music has been an important force in American popular culture. The following individuals or groups have made a significant impact. Next to each is an associated "single record" or *record album*.

Paula Abdul: "Forever Your Girl"
AC/DC: "Back in Black"
Ace of Base: "The Sign"
Bryan Adams: "Cuts Like A Knife"
Aerosmith: "Sweet Emotion"

The Allman Brothers Band: "Ramblin' Man"
The Animals: "House of the Rising Sun"
Paul Anka: "Lonely Boy"
Arrested Development: "Mr. Wendal"

The Association: "Cherish"
Frankie Avalon: "Venus"
The Band: "The Weight"
The Beach Boys: "Good Vibrations"

Beastie Boys: "(You Gotta) Fight for Your Right (to Party)"
The Beatles: *Sergeant Pepper's Lonely Hearts Club Band*
The Bee Gees: "Stayin' Alive"
Pat Benatar: "Hit Me With Your Best Shot"
Chuck Berry: "Johnny B. Goode"
The Big Bopper: "Chantilly Lace"
Black Sabbath: "Paranoid"
Blind Faith: "Can't Find My Way Home"
Blondie: "Heart of Glass"
Blood, Sweat, and Tears: "Spinning Wheel"
Gary "U.S." Bonds: "Quarter to Three"
Bon Jovi: "Livin' on a Prayer"
Booker T. and the MGs: "Green Onions"
Earl Bostic: "Flamingo"
David Bowie: "Let's Dance"
James Brown: "Papa's Got a Brand New Bag"
Jackson Browne: "Doctor My Eyes"
Buffalo Springfield: "For What It's Worth"
The Byrds: "Turn! Turn! Turn!"
Mariah Carey: "Vision of Love"
The Cars: "Shake It Up"
Ray Charles: "Georgia on My Mind"
Chubby Checker: "The Twist"
Chicago: "Saturday in the Park"
Eric Clapton: "Tears in Heaven"
The Clash: "Rock the Casbah"
The Coasters: "Yakety Yak"
Eddie Cochran: "Summertime Blues"
Joe Cocker: "With a Little Help From My Friends"
Phil Collins: "Against All Odds (Take a Look at Me Now)"
Sam Cooke: "You Send Me"
Alice Cooper: "School's Out"
Elvis Costello: "Alison"
Counting Crows: "Mr. Jones"
Cream: "Sunshine of Your Love"
Creedence Clearwater Revival: "Proud Mary"
Crosby, Stills, Nash, and Young: "Suite: Judy Blue Eyes"
The Crystals: "Da Doo Ron Ron"
Danny and the Juniors: "At the Hop"
Bobby Darin: "Splish Splash"
Spencer Davis Group: "Gimme Some Lovin'"
Def Leppard: "Photograph"
Depeche Mode: "Strange Love"
Bo Diddley: "Who Do You Love?"
Dion and the Belmonts: "A Teenager in Love"
Dire Straits: "Money for Nothing"
Fats Domino: "Blueberry Hill"
Donovan: "Mellow Yellow"
The Doobie Brothers: "What a Fool Believes"
The Doors: "Light My Fire"
The Drifters: "Save the Last Dance for Me"
Duran Duran: "Hungry Like the Wolf"
Bob Dylan: "Like a Rolling Stone"
The Eagles: "Hotel California"
Earth, Wind, and Fire: "Shining Star"
Emerson, Lake, and Palmer: "From the Beginning"
En Vogue: "Hold On"
The Eurythmics: "Sweet Dreams (Are Made of This)"
Everly Brothers: "Wake Up, Little Susie"
The Five Satins: "In the Still of the Night"
Fleetwood Mac: *Rumours*
The Four Seasons: "Sherry"
The Four Tops: "I Can't Help Myself (Sugar Pie, Honey Bunch)"
Aretha Franklin: "Respect"
Peter Gabriel: "Shock the Monkey"
Marvin Gaye: "I Heard It Through the Grapevine"
Genesis: "No Reply at All"

Grand Funk Railroad: "We're an American Band"
The Grateful Dead: "Uncle John's Band"
Green Day: *Dookie*
Guns N' Roses: "Sweet Child o' Mine"
Bill Haley and the Comets: "Rock Around the Clock"
Hall and Oates: "Kiss on My List"
Heart: "Alone"
Jimi Hendrix: "Purple Haze"
Herman's Hermits: "Mrs. Brown, You've Got a Lovely Daughter"
Buddy Holly and the Crickets: "That'll Be the Day"
Whitney Houston: "I Will Always Love You"
The Impressions: "For Your Precious Love"
INXS: "Need You Tonight"
The Isley Brothers: "It's Your Thing"
The Jackson 5/The Jacksons: "ABC"
Janet Jackson: *Rhythm Nation*
Michael Jackson: *Thriller*
Tommy James & The Shondells: "Crimson and Clover"
Jay and the Americans: "This Magic Moment"
The Jefferson Airplane/Jefferson Starship: "White Rabbit"
Jethro Tull: *Aqualung*
Joan Jett: "I Love Rock 'n' Roll"
Billy Joel: "Piano Man"
Elton John: "Crocodile Rock"
Janis Joplin: "Me and Bobby McGee"
K.C. and the Sunshine Band: "Get Down Tonight"
B. B. King: "The Thrill Is Gone"
Carole King: *Tapestry*
The Kinks: "You Really Got Me"
Kiss: "Rock 'n' Roll All Night"
Gladys Knight and the Pips: "Midnight Train to Georgia"
Kriss Kross: "Jump"
Led Zeppelin: "Stairway to Heaven"
Brenda Lee: "I'm Sorry"
John Lennon: "Imagine"
Jerry Lee Lewis: "Whole Lotta Shakin' Going On"
Little Anthony and the Imperials: "Tears on My Pillow"
Little Richard: "Tutti Frutti"
L. L. Cool J: "Mama Said Knock You Out"
Lovin' Spoonful: "Summer in the City"
Frankie Lymon and the Teenagers: "Why Do Fools Fall in Love?"
Lynyrd Skynyrd: "Free Bird"
Madonna: "Material Girl"
The Mamas and the Papas: "Monday, Monday"
Bob Marley: "Jamming"
Martha and the Vandellas: "Dancin' in the Streets"
The Marvelettes: "Please, Mr. Postman"
Paul McCartney: "Band on the Run"
Don McLean: "American Pie"
Meat Loaf: "Paradise By the Dashboard Light"
John Cougar Mellencamp: "Jack and Diane"
Men at Work: "Who Can It Be Now?"
Metallica: "Enter Sandman"
George Michael: "Don't Let the Sun Go Down on Me"
Joni Mitchell: "Big Yellow Taxi"
The Monkees: "I'm a Believer"
Moody Blues: "Nights in White Satin"
Van Morrison: "Brown-Eyed Girl"
Rick Nelson: "Hello, Mary Lou"
Nirvana: *Nevermind*
Roy Orbison: "Oh, Pretty Woman"
Ozzy Osbourne: "You Can't Kill Rock 'n' Roll"
Pearl Jam: "Jeremy"
Carl Perkins: "Blue Suede Shoes"

Peter, Paul, and Mary: "Leavin' on a Jet Plane"
Tom Petty and the Heartbreakers: "Refugee"
Wilson Pickett: "Land of 1,000 Dances"
Pink Floyd: *The Wall*
Poco: *Deliverin'*
The Police: "Every Breath You Take"
Iggy Pop: "Lust for Life"
Elvis Presley: "Love Me Tender"
The Pretenders: "Back on the Chain Gang"
Lloyd Price: "Stagger Lee"
Prince: "Purple Rain"
Procol Harum: "A Whiter Shade of Pale"
Public Enemy: "Fight the Power"
Queen: "Bohemian Rhapsody"
The Ramones: "Sheena Is a Punk Rocker"
Otis Redding: "(Sittin' on) The Dock of the Bay"
Red Hot Chili Peppers: "Under the Bridge"
Lou Reed: "Walk on the Wild Side"
R.E.M.: "Losing My Religion"
Righteous Brothers: "You've Lost That Lovin' Feeling"
Johnny Rivers: "Poor Side of Town"
Smokey Robinson and the Miracles: "Shop Around"
The Rolling Stones: "Satisfaction"
The Ronettes: "Be My Baby"
Linda Ronstadt: "You're No Good"
Run-D.M.C.: "Raisin' Hell"
Salt-N-Pepa: "Shoop"
Sam and Dave: "Soul Man"
Santana: "Black Magic Woman"
Neil Sedaka: "Breaking Up Is Hard to Do"
The Sex Pistols: "Anarchy in the U.K."
Del Shannon: "Runaway"
The Shirelles: "Soldier Boy"
Carly Simon: "You're So Vain"
Paul Simon: "50 Ways to Leave Your Lover"
Simon and Garfunkel: "Bridge Over Troubled Water"
Sly and the Family Stone: "Everyday People"
Patti Smith: "Because the Night"
Soundgarden: "Black Hole Sun"
Bruce Springsteen: "Hungry Heart"
Steely Dan: "Rikki Don't Lose That Number"
Steppenwolf: "Born to Be Wild"
Rod Stewart: "Maggie Mae"
Sting: "If You Love Somebody, Set Them Free"
Donna Summer: "Bad Girls"
The Supremes: "Stop! In the Name of Love"
Talking Heads: "Once in a Lifetime"
James Taylor: "You've Got a Friend"
The Temptations: "My Girl"
Three Dog Night: "Joy to the World"
Big Joe Turner: "Shake, Rattle & Roll"
Tina Turner: "What's Love Got to Do With It?"
U2: "With or Without You"
Ritchie Valens: "La Bamba"
Van Halen: "Jump"
Dionne Warwick: "I Say a Little Prayer"
Mary Wells: "My Guy"
Whitesnake: "Here I Go Again"
The Who: "My Generation"
Jackie Wilson: "That's Why"
Stevie Wonder: "You Are the Sunshine of My Life"
The Yardbirds: "For Your Love"
Yes: "Owner of a Lonely Heart"
Neil Young: "Down by the River"
The Young Rascals: "Good Lovin'"
Frank Zappa/Mothers of Invention: *Sheik Yerbouti*

Entertainment Personalities — Where and When Born

actors, dancers, musicians, producers, directors, radio-TV performers, singers

(as of mid-1995)

Name	Birthplace	Birthdate	Name	Birthplace	Birthdate
Abbado, Claudio	Milan, Italy	6/26/33	Bacall, Lauren	New York, NY	9/16/24
Abdul, Paula	San Fernando, CA	6/19/62	Bacon, Kevin	Philadelphia, PA.	7/8/58
Abraham, F. Murray	Pittsburgh, PA	10/24/39	Baez, Joan	Staten Island, NY	1/9/41
Adams, Bryan	Kingston, Ontario..	11/5/59	Bain, Conrad	Lethbridge, Alberta.	2/4/23
Adams, Don	New York, NY	4/19/26	Baio, Scott	Brooklyn, NY.	9/22/61
Adams, Edie	Kingston, PA	4/16/29	Baker, Anita	Toledo, OH	1/26/58
Adams, Joey	New York, NY	1/6/11	Baker, Carroll	Johnstown, PA.	5/28/31
Adams, Mason	New York, NY	2/26/19	Baker, Joe Don	Groesbeck, TX	2/12/36
Adjani, Isabelle	W. Germany	6/27/55	Baker, Kathy	Midland, TX.	6/8/50
Agar, John	Chicago, IL	1/31/21	Bakula, Scott	St. Louis, MO	10/9/55
Agutter, Jenny	London, England	12/20/52	Baldwin, Alec	Massapequa, N.Y.	4/3/58
Aiello, Danny	New York, NY	6/20/33	Baldwin, Stephen	Massapequa, N.Y.	1966
Aimee, Anouk	Paris, France.	4/27/34	Baldwin, William	Massapequa, NY	1963
Albanese, Licia.	Bari, Italy	7/22/13	Ballard, Kaye	Cleveland, OH.	11/20/26
Alberghetti, Anna Maria	Pesaro, Italy	5/15/36	Balsam, Martin	New York, NY	11/4/19
Albert, Eddie	Rock Island, IL.	4/22/08	Bancroft, Anne	New York, NY	9/17/31
Albert, Marv	New York, NY	6/12/43	Bandaras, Antonio	Málaga, Spain	1960
Alda, Alan	New York, NY	1/28/36	Bannon, Jack.	Los Angeles, CA	6/14/40
Alexander, Jane	Boston, MA	10/28/39	Baranski, Christine	Buffalo, NY	5/2/52
Alexander, Jason	Newark, NJ	9/23/59	Barbeau, Adrienne	Sacramento, CA	6/11/45
Allen, Debbie	Houston, TX	1/16/50	Bardot, Brigitte.	Paris, France.	9/28/34
Allen, Joan	Rochelle, IL.	8/20/56	Barker, Bob	Darrington, WA	12/12/23
Allen, Karen	Carrollton, TX	10/5/51	Barkin, Ellen	New York, NY	4/16/55
Allen, Mel	Birmingham, AL	2/14/13	Barrie, Barbara	Chicago, IL	5/23/31
Allen, Nancy	New York, NY	6/24/49	Barry, Gene.	New York, NY	6/14/19
Allen, Steve	New York, NY	12/26/21	Barty, Billy.	Millsboro, PA.	10/25/24
Allen, Tim	Denver, CO.	6/13/53	Barrymore, Drew	Los Angeles, CA	2/22/75
Allen, Woody	Brooklyn, NY	12/1/35	Bartolli, Cecilia.	Italy	1967
Alley, Kirstie	Wichita, KS	1/12/55	Bartolucci, Bernardo	Parma, Italy.	3/16/40
Allman, Gregg	Nashville, TN.	12/7/47	Baryshnikov, Mikhail	Riga, Latvia.	1/28/48
Allyson, June	New York, NY	10/7/17	Basinger, Kim	Athens, GA.	12/8/53
Alonso, Maria Conchita	Cuba	1957	Bassey, Shirley	Cardiff, Wales	1/8/37
Alpert, Herb	Los Angeles, CA	3/31/35	Bateman, Jason	Rye, NY.	1/14/69
Altman, Robert.	Kansas City, MO	2/20/25	Bateman, Justine	Rye, NY.	2/19/66
Ames, Ed	Boston, MA	7/9/27	Bates, Alan	Allestree, England	2/17/34
Amos, John	Newark, NJ	12/27/42	Bates, Kathy	Memphis, TN.	6/28/48
Amsterdam, Morey	Chicago, IL	12/14/14	Battle, Kathleen	Portsmouth, OH.	8/13/48
Anderson, Harry	Newport, RI.	10/14/49	Baxter, Meredith.	Los Angeles, CA	6/21/47
Anderson, Ian	Dunfermline, Scotland	8/10/47	Beal, John.	Joplin, MO	8/13/09
Anderson, Kevin.	Illinois	1/13/60	Beasley, Allyce	New York, NY	7/6/54
Anderson, Loni.	St. Paul, MN	8/5/46	Beatty, Ned	Louisville, KY.	7/6/37
Anderson, Lynn	Grand Forks, ND	9/26/47	Beatty, Warren	Richmond, VA.	3/30/37
Anderson, Melissa Sue	Berkeley, CA.	9/26/62	Beck, John	Chicago, IL.	1/28/43
Anderson, Richard	Long Branch, NJ	8/8/26	Bedelia, Bonnie	New York, NY	3/25/48
Anderson, Richard Dean	Minneapolis, MN	1/23/50	Begley, Ed, Jr.	Los Angeles, CA	9/16/49
Andersson, Bibi	Stockholm, Sweden	11/11/35	Belafonte, Harry.	New York, NY	3/1/27
Andress, Ursula	Bern, Switzerland	3/19/36	Bel Geddes, Barbara.	New York, NY	10/31/22
Andrews, Anthony	London, England	1/12/48	Belmondo, Jean-Paul	Neuilly-sur-Seine, France	4/9/33
Andrews, Julie	Walton, England.	10/1/35	Belushi, Jim.	Chicago, IL.	6/15/54
Andrews, Maxene.	Minneapolis, MN	1/3/18	Benatar, Pat	Brooklyn, NY.	1/10/53
Andrews, Patty.	Minneapolis, MN	2/16/20	Benedict, Dirk	Helena, MT.	3/1/45
Aniston, Jennifer	Sherman Oaks, CA.	2/11/69	Bening, Annette	Topeka, KS.	5/29/58
Anka, Paul	Ottawa, Ontario	7/30/41	Benjamin, Richard	New York, NY	5/22/38
Ann-Margret	Stockholm, Sweden	4/28/41	Bennett, Tony	New York, NY	8/3/26
Applegate, Christina	Los Angeles, CA	11/25/72	Benson, George.	Pittsburgh, PA.	3/22/43
Archer, Anne	Los Angeles, CA	8/25/47	Benson, Robby	Dallas, TX.	1/21/55
Arkin, Adam.	Brooklyn, NY.	8/19/56	Beradino, John.	Los Angeles, CA	5/1/17
Arkin, Alan	New York, NY	3/26/34	Berenger, Tom.	Chicago, IL.	5/31/50
Arnaz, Desi, Jr.	Los Angeles, CA	1/19/53	Bergen, Candice	Beverly Hills, CA	5/9/46
Arnaz, Lucie	Los Angeles, CA	7/17/51	Bergen, Polly	Knoxville, TN.	7/14/30
Arness, James	Minneapolis, MN	5/26/23	Bergman, Ingmar	Uppsala, Sweden.	7/14/18
Arnold, Eddy	Henderson, TN	5/15/18	Berle, Milton	New York, NY	7/12/08
Arquette, Patricia	New York, NY	4/8/68	Berlinger, Warren	Brooklyn, NY.	8/31/37
Arquette, Rosanna	New York, NY	8/10/59	Berman, Lazar.	Leningrad, Russia	2/26/30
Arroyo, Martina	New York, NY	2/2/37	Berman, Shelley.	Chicago, IL.	2/3/26
Arthur, Beatrice	New York, NY	5/13/26	Bernard, Crystal	Dallas, TX.	9/30/64
Ashley, Elizabeth	Ocala, FL	8/30/41	Bernhard, Sandra.	Flint, MI	6/6/55
Asner, Ed	Kansas City, MO	11/15/29	Bernsen, Corbin	N. Hollywood, CA.	9/7/54
Assante, Armand	New York, NY	10/4/49	Berry, Chuck	St. Louis, MO	10/18/26
Astin, John	Baltimore, MD	3/30/30	Berry, Halle.	Cleveland, OH.	8/14/68
Atkins, Chet.	Luttrell, TN	6/20/24	Berry, Ken.	Moline, IL	11/3/33
Attenborough, Richard	Cambridge, England.	8/29/23	Bertinelli, Valerie	Wilmington, DE	4/23/60
Auberjonois, Rene	New York, NY	6/1/40	Bialik, Mayim	San Diego, CA.	12/12/75
Aumont, Jean-Pierre	Paris, France.	1/5/09	Bikel, Theodore	Vienna, Austria	5/2/24
Austin, Patti	New York, NY	8/10/48	Billingsley, Barbara	Los Angeles, CA	12/22/22
Autry, Alan	Shreveport, LA.	7/31/52	Birney, David	Washington, DC.	4/23/39
Autry, Gene	Tioga, TX	9/29/07	Bishop, Joey	Bronx, NY.	2/3/18
Avalon, Frankie	Philadelphia, PA.	9/18/39	Bisset, Jacqueline	Weybridge, England.	9/13/44
Ax, Emmanuel	Lvov, Ukraine	6/8/49	Bisset, Josie	Seattle, WA.	10/5/69
Axton, Hoyt	Duncan, OK.	3/25/38	Black, Clint	Katy, TX.	2/4/62
Aykroyd, Dan	Ottawa, Ontario	7/1/52	Black, Karen	Park Ridge, IL.	7/1/42
Ayres, Lew	Minneapolis, MN	12/28/08	Blackstone, Harry, Jr.	Three Rivers, MI	6/30/34
Aznavour, Charles	Paris, France.	5/22/24	Blades, Ruben	Panama City, Panama	7/16/48
			Blaine, Vivian.	Newark, NJ.	11/21/21

Name	Birthplace	Birthdate
Blair, Linda	St. Louis, MO	1/22/59
Blake, Robert	Nutley, NJ	9/18/33
Bledsoe, Tempestt	Chicago, IL	8/1/73
Bloom, Claire	London, England	2/15/31
Blyth, Ann	Mt. Kisco, NY	8/16/28
Bochco, Steven	New York, NY	12/16/43
Bogarde, Dirk	London, England	3/28/20
Bogosian, Eric	Boston, MA	4/24/53
Bogdanovich, Peter	Kingston, NY	7/30/39
Bologna, Joseph	Brooklyn, NY	12/30/38
Bolton, Michael	New Haven, CT	2/26/53
Bonham-Carter, Helena	London, England	5/26/66
Bon Jovi, Jon	Sayreville, NJ	3/2/62
Bono	Dublin, Ireland	5/10/60
Bono, Sonny	Detroit, MI	2/16/35
Boone, Debby	Hackensack, NJ	9/22/56
Boone, Pat	Jacksonville, FL	6/1/34
Borge, Victor	Copenhagen, Denmark	1/3/09
Borgnine, Ernest	Hamden, CT	1/24/17
Bosson, Barbara	Charleroi, PA	11/1/39
Bosco, Philip	Jersey City, NJ	9/26/30
Bosley, Tom	Chicago, IL	10/1/27
Bostwick, Barry	San Mateo, CA	2/24/45
Bottoms, Timothy	Santa Barbara, CA	8/30/51
Bowie, David	London, England	1/8/47
Boxleitner, Bruce	Elgin, IL	5/12/50
Boy George	London, England	6/14/61
Boyle, Peter	Philadelphia, PA	10/18/33
Bracco, Lorraine	Brooklyn, NY	1955
Bracken, Eddie	New York, NY	2/7/20
Branagh, Kenneth	Belfast, No. Ireland	12/10/60
Brando, Marlon	Omaha, NE	4/3/24
Braxton, Toni	Severn, MD	1968
Brennan, Eileen	Los Angeles, CA	9/3/35
Brenner, David	Philadelphia, PA	2/4/45
Brewer, Teresa	Toledo, OH	5/7/31
Brickell, Edie	Oak Cliff, TX	1966
Bridges, Beau	Hollywood, CA	12/9/41
Bridges, Jeff	Los Angeles, CA	12/4/49
Bridges, Lloyd	San Leandro, CA	1/15/13
Brimley, Wilford	Salt Lake City, UT	9/27/34
Brinkley, Christie	Malibu, CA	2/2/54
Broderick, Matthew	New York, NY	3/21/62
Brolin, James	Los Angeles, CA	7/18/40
Bronson, Charles	Ehrenfeld, PA	11/3/22
Brooks, Albert	Beverly Hills, CA	7/22/47
Brooks, Garth	Tulsa, OK	2/7/62
Brooks, James L	North Bergen, NJ	5/9/40
Brooks, Mel	New York, NY	6/28/26
Brosnan, Pierce	Co. Meath, Ireland	5/15/53
Brown, Blair	Washington, DC	1948
Brown, Bobby	Boston, MA	2/5/69
Brown, Bryan	Sydney, Australia	6/23/47
Brown, James	Pulaski, TN	6/17/28
Brown, Les	Reinerton, PA	3/14/12
Browne, Jackson	Heidelberg, Germany	10/9/50
Browne, Roscoe Lee	Woodbury, NJ	5/2/25
Brubeck, Dave	Concord, CA	12/6/20
Buckley, Betty	Ft. Worth, TX	7/3/47
Buffett, Jimmy	Pascagoula, MS	12/25/46
Bujold, Genevieve	Montreal, Quebec	7/1/42
Bullock, Sandra	Arlington, VA	7/26/65
Bumbry, Grace	St. Louis, MO	1/4/37
Burghoff, Gary	Bristol, CT	5/24/40
Burke, Delta	Orlando, FL	7/30/56
Burnett, Carol	San Antonio, TX	4/26/33
Burns, George	New York, NY	1/20/1896
Burrows, Darren E.	Winfield, KS	9/12/66
Burstyn, Ellen	Detroit, MI	12/7/32
Burton, LeVar	Landstuhl, W Germany	2/16/57
Busey, Gary	Goose Creek, TX	6/29/44
Busfield, Timothy	Lansing, MI	6/12/57
Brett Butler	Montgomery, AL	1/30/58
Buttons, Red	New York, NY	2/5/19
Buzzi, Ruth	Westerly, RI	7/24/36
Byrne, David	Dumbarton, Scotland	5/14/52
Caan, James	New York, NY	3/26/39
Caballe, Montserrat	Barcelona, Spain	4/12/33
Caesar, Sid	Yonkers, NY	9/8/22
Cage, Nicolas	Long Beach, CA	1/7/64
Cain, Dean	Mt. Clemmons, MI	7/31/66
Caine, Michael	London, England	3/14/33
Caldwell, Sarah	Maryville, MO	3/6/24
Caldwell, Zoe	Melbourne, Australia	9/14/33
Calhoun, Rory	Los Angeles, CA	8/8/23
Calloway, Cab	Rochester, NY	12/25/07
Cameron, Kirk	Panorama City, CA	10/12/70
Camp, Hamilton	London, England	10/30/34
Campanella, Joseph	New York, NY	11/21/27
Campbell, Glen	Billstown, AR	4/22/36
Campbell, Naomi	London, England	5/22/70
Campion, Jane	Wellington, New Zealand	1955
Cannell, Stephen J.	Los Angeles, CA	2/5/42
Cannon, Dyan	Tacoma, WA	1/4/37
Capshaw, Kate	Ft. Worth, TX	1953
Cara, Irene	New York, NY	3/18/59
Carey, Mariah	Huntington, NY	3/27/70
Cariou, Len	Winnipeg, Canada	9/30/39
Carlin, George	New York, NY	5/12/37
Carlisle, Kitty	New Orleans, LA	9/3/15
Carmen, Eric	Cleveland, OH	8/11/49
Carney, Art	Mt. Vernon, NY	11/4/18
Carpenter, Mary Chapin	Princeton, NJ	1959
Caron, Leslie	Boulogne, France	7/1/31
Carr, Vikki	El Paso, TX	7/19/41
Carradine, David	Hollywood, CA	10/8/36
Carradine, Keith	San Mateo, CA	8/8/49
Carreras, Jose	Barcelona, Spain	12/5/46
Carroll, Diahann	Bronx, NY	7/17/35
Carroll, Pat	Shreveport, LA	5/5/27
Carrey, Jim	Jackson Point, Canada	1/17/62
Carson, Johnny	Corning, IA	10/23/25
Carter, Benny	New York, NY	8/8/07
Carter, Dixie	McLemoresville, TN	5/25/39
Carter, Jack	New York, NY	6/24/23
Carter, June	Maces Spring, VA	6/23/29
Carter, Lynda	Phoenix, AZ	7/24/51
Carter, Nell	Birmingham, AL	9/13/48
Carter, Ron	Royal Oak Twp, MI	5/4/37
Caruso, David	Forest Hills, NY	1/17/56
Carvey, Dana	Missoula, MT	6/6/55
Casadesus, Gaby	Marseilles, France	8/9/01
Cash, Johnny	Kingsland, AR	2/26/32
Cash, Rosanne	Memphis, TN	5/24/55
Cass, Peggy	Boston, MA	5/21/24
Cassidy, David	New York, NY	4/12/50
Cavett, Dick	Gibbon, NE	11/19/36
Chamberlain, Richard	Beverly Hills, CA	3/31/35
Channing, Carol	Seattle, WA	1/31/23
Channing, Stockard	New York, NY	2/13/44
Chaplin, Geraldine	Santa Monica, CA	7/31/44
Chapman, Tracy	Cleveland, OH	3/30/64
Charisse, Cyd	Amarillo, TX	3/8/21
Charles, Ray	Albany, GA	9/23/30
Charo	Murcia, Spain	1/15/51
Chase, Chevy	New York, NY	10/8/43
Checker, Chubby	Philadelphia, PA	10/3/41
Cher	El Centro, CA	5/20/46
Chiklis, Michael	Lowell, MA	8/30/63
Chong, Rae Dawn	Vancouver, Canada	1962
Chong, Thomas	Edmonton, Alberta	5/24/38
Christie, Julie	Assam, India	4/14/40
Christopher, William	Evanston, IL	10/20/32
Church, Thomas Hayden	El Paso, TX	6/17/--
Clapton, Eric	Surrey, England	3/30/45
Clark, Dick	Mt. Vernon, NY	11/30/29
Clark, Petula	Ewell, Surrey, England	11/15/32
Clark, Roy	Meherrin, VA	4/15/33
Clark, Susan	Sarnia, Ontario	3/8/40
Clay, Andrew Dice	Brooklyn, NY	1958
Clayburgh, Jill	New York, NY	4/30/44
Cleese, John	England	10/27/39
Cliburn, Van	Shreveport, LA	7/12/34
Clooney, George	Lexington, KY	5/6/62
Clooney, Rosemary	Maysville, KY	5/23/28
Close, Glenn	Greenwich, CT	3/19/47
Coburn, James	Laurel, NE	8/31/28
Coca, Imogene	Philadelphia, PA	11/18/08
Colbert, Claudette	Paris, France	9/13/03
Cole, Gary	Park Ridge, IL	9/20/57
Cole, Natalie	Los Angeles, CA	2/6/50
Cole, Olivia	Memphis, TN	11/26/42
Coleman, Dabney	Austin, TX	1/3/32
Coleman, Gary	Zion, IL	2/8/68
Coleman, Ornette	Fort Worth, TX	3/9/30
Collins, Joan	London, England	5/23/33
Collins, Judy	Seattle, WA	5/1/39
Collins, Pauline	Exmouth, England	9/3/40
Collins, Phil	London, England	1/30/51
Comden, Betty	Brooklyn, NY	5/3/19
Como, Perry	Canonsburg, PA	5/18/12
Connery, Sean	Edinburgh, Scotland	8/25/30
Connick, Harry, Jr.	New Orleans, LA	9/11/67
Conniff, Ray	Attleboro, MA	11/6/16
Connors, Mike	Fresno, CA	8/15/25

Name	Birthplace	Birthdate
Conrad, Robert	Chicago, IL	3/1/35
Constantine, Michael	Reading, PA	5/22/27
Conti, Tom	Paisley, Scotland	11/22/41
Conway, Tim	Willoughby, OH.	12/15/33
Cook, Barbara	Atlanta, GA	10/25/27
Cooke, Alistair	Manchester, England	11/20/08
Coolidge, Rita	Nashville, TN.	5/1/45
Cooper, Alice	Detroit, MI.	2/4/48
Cooper, Jackie	Los Angeles, CA	9/15/21
Copperfield, David	Metuchen, NJ	9/16/56
Coppola, Francis	Detroit, MI.	4/7/39
Corbin, Barry	Lamesa, TX.	10/16/40
Corby, Ellen.	Racine, WI	6/3/13
Cord, Alex.	New York, NY	8/3/31
Corea, Chick	Chelsea, MA	6/12/41
Corelli, Franco	Ancona, Italy	4/8/23
Corey, Jeff	New York, NY	8/10/14
Corley, Pat	Dallas, TX.	6/1/30
Cosby, Bill.	Philadelphia, PA.	7/12/37
Costas, Bob.	New York, NY	3/22/52
Costello, Elvis	London, England	8/25/54
Costner, Kevin	Compton, CA.	1/18/55
Cougar, John.	Seymour, IN	10/7/51
Courtenay, Tom	Hull, England.	2/25/37
Cox, Courtney	Birmingham, AL	6/15/64
Cox, Ronny.	Cloudcroft, NM.	8/23/38
Crain, Jeanne	Barstow, CA	5/25/25
Crawford, Cindy	DeKalb, IL.	2/20/66
Crawford, Michael.	Salisbury, England	1/19/42
Crenna, Richard.	Los Angeles, CA	11/30/26
Crespin, Regine	Marseilles, France	2/23/26
Cronyn, Hume	London, Ontario.	7/18/11
Crosby, David	Los Angeles, CA	8/14/41
Cross, Ben	London, England	12/16/47
Crouse, Lindsay.	New York, NY	5/12/48
Crow, Sheryl	Kennett, MO	2/11/62
Crowell, Rodney.	Houston, TX	8/17/50
Cruise, Tom.	Syracuse, NY	7/3/62
Crystal, Billy	Long Beach, NY.	3/14/47
Culkin, Macaulay	New York, NY	8/26/80
Cullum, John	Knoxville, TN.	3/2/30
Culp, Robert	Oakland, CA	8/16/30
Cummings, Constance	Seattle, WA.	5/15/10
Curry, Tim	Cheshire, England	4/19/46
Curtin, Jane.	Cambridge, MA	9/6/47
Curtis, Jamie Lee	Los Angeles, CA	11/22/58
Curtis, Keene.	Salt Lake City, UT	2/15/23
Curtis, Tony.	New York, NY	6/3/25
Cusack, Joan.	Evanston, IL	10/11/62
Cusack, John.	Evanston, IL	6/28/66
Cyrus, Billy Ray	Flatwoods, KY	8/25/61
Dafoe, Willem	Appleton, WI	7/22/55
Dahl, Arlene	Minneapolis, MN	8/11/28
Dale, Jim	Rothwell, England	8/15/35
Dalton, Abby	Las Vegas, NV.	8/15/32
Dalton, Timothy	Wales.	3/21/44
Daltrey, Roger	London, England	3/1/44
Daly, Timothy.	Suffern, NY.	3/1/58
Daly, Tyne.	Madison, WI	2/21/47
Damone, Vic	Brooklyn, NY.	6/12/28
D'Angelo, Beverly	Columbus, OH.	11/15/54
Dangerfield, Rodney	Babylon, NY	11/22/22
Daniels, Charlie	Wilmington, NC	10/28/36
Daniels, Jeff	Georgia	2/19/55
Daniels, William	Brooklyn, NY.	3/31/27
Danner, Blythe.	Philadelphia, PA.	2/3/44
Danson, Ted	San Diego, CA.	12/29/47
Danza, Tony	New York, NY	4/21/50
Darby, Kim	Hollywood, CA.	7/8/48
D'Arby, Terence Trent	New York, NY	3/15/62
Davidson, John	Pittsburgh, PA.	12/13/41
Davis, Ann B..	Schenectady, NY.	5/5/26
Davis, Clifton	Chicago, IL	10/4/45
Davis, Geena	Wareham, MA	1/21/57
Davis, Judy	Perth, Australia	1955
Davis, Mac	Lubbock, TX	1/21/42
Davis, Ossie	Cogdell, GA.	12/18/17
Dawber, Pam.	Farmington Hills, MI	10/18/51
Dawson, Richard	Hampshire, England	11/20/32
Day, Doris.	Cincinnati, OH.	4/3/24
Day-Lewis, Daniel.	London, England	4/29/57
Dean, Jimmy	Plainview, TX	8/10/28
De Camp, Rosemary.	Prescott, AZ	11/14/10
DeCarlo, Yvonne	Vancouver, BC	9/1/22
Dee, Frances	Los Angeles, CA	11/26/07
Dee, Ruby.	Cleveland, OH.	10/27/23
Dee, Sandra	Bayonne, NJ	4/23/42

Name	Birthplace	Birthdate
DeFranco, Buddy	Camden, NJ	2/17/23
DeGeneres, Ellen		1958
DeHaven, Gloria.	Los Angeles, CA	7/23/25
De Havilland, Olivia	Tokyo, Japan.	7/1/16
Delany, Dana.	New York, NY	3/13/57
DeLaurentis, Dino.	Torre Annunziata, Italy	8/8/19
Delon, Alain.	Sceaux, France	11/8/35
DeLuise, Dom	Brooklyn, NY.	8/1/33
Demme, Jonathan	Rockville Centre, NY.	2/22/44
DeMornay, Rebecca	Santa Rosa, CA.	11/29/61
Deneuve, Catherine	Paris, France.	10/22/43
De Niro, Robert	New York, NY	8/17/43
Dennehy, Brian	Bridgeport, CT.	7/9/38
Denver, Bob	New Rochelle, NY	1/9/35
Denver, John.	Roswell, NM.	12/31/43
DePalma, Brian	Newark, NJ.	9/11/40
Depardieu, Gerard	Chateauroux, France	12/27/48
Depp, Johnny	Owensboro, KY.	6/9/63
Derek, Bo	Long Beach, CA.	11/20/56
Derek, John.	Hollywood, CA.	8/12/26
Dern, Bruce.	Chicago, IL	6/4/36
Dern, Laura.	Santa Monica, CA	2/1/67
Devane, William	Albany, NY	9/5/37
DeVito, Danny	Neptune, NJ	11/17/44
DeWitt, Joyce	Wheeling, WV	4/23/49
Dey, Susan	Pekin, IL.	12/10/52
Diamond, Neil	Brooklyn, NY.	1/24/41
Dicaprio, Leonardo		1975
Dickinson, Angie	Kulm, ND	9/30/31
Diddley, Bo	McComb, MS	12/20/28
Diller, Phyllis	Lima, OH	7/17/17
Dillman, Bradford	San Francisco, CA.	4/14/30
Dion, Celine.	Charlemagne, Canada	3/30/68
Dillon, Matt	New Rochelle, NY	2/18/64
Dobson, Kevin	New York, NY	3/18/44
Doherty, Shannen	Memphis, TN	4/21/71
Domingo, Placido.	Madrid, Spain	1/21/41
Domino, Fats	New Orleans, LA	2/26/28
Donahue, Phil	Cleveland, OH.	12/21/35
Donahue, Troy	New York, NY	1/27/36
Dotrice, Roy	Guernsey, England.	5/26/23
Douglas, Kirk	Amsterdam, NY.	12/9/16
Douglas, Michael	New Brunswick, NJ	9/25/44
Down, Leslie-Ann	London, England	3/17/54
Downey, Robert, Jr.	New York, NY	4/4/65
Downs, Hugh.	Akron, OH.	2/14/21
Drew, Ellen	Kansas City, MO	11/23/15
Dryer, Fred	Hawthorne, CA	7/6/46
Dreyfuss, Richard.	Brooklyn, NY.	10/29/47
Duchovny, David	New York, NY	1961
Duffy, Julia	Minneapolis, MN	6/27/51
Duffy, Patrick.	Townsend, MT.	3/17/49
Dukakis, Olympia	Lowell, MA	6/20/31
Duke, Patty	New York, NY	12/14/46
Dukes, David	San Francisco, CA.	6/6/45
Dullea, Keir	Cleveland, OH.	5/30/36
Dunaway, Faye	Bascom, FL.	1/14/41
Duncan, Sandy	Henderson, TX	2/20/46
Dunham, Katherine.	Joliet, IL	6/22/10
Dunne, Griffin	New York, NY	6/8/55
Durbin, Deanna	Winnipeg, Manitoba	12/4/21
Durning, Charles	Highland Falls, NY	2/28/23
Dussault, Nancy.	Pensacola, FL.	6/30/36
Dutton, Charles S.	Baltimore, MD	1/30/51
Duvall, Robert	San Diego, CA.	1/5/31
Duvall, Shelley	Houston, TX	7/7/49
Dylan, Bob	Duluth, MN	5/24/41
Dysart, Richard	Augusta, ME	3/30/29
Eastwood, Clint	San Francisco, CA.	5/31/30
Ebert, Roger	Urbana, IL.	6/18/42
Ebsen, Buddy	Belleville, IL.	4/2/08
Edelman, Herb.	Brooklyn, NY.	11/5/33
Eden, Barbara	Tucson, AZ.	8/23/34
Edwards, Anthony	Santa Barbara, CA.	7/19/62
Edwards, Blake	Tulsa, OK.	7/26/22
Edwards, Ralph	Merino, CO.	6/13/13
Eichhorn, Lisa	Reading, PA.	2/4/52
Eikenberry, Jill.	New Haven, CT.	1/21/47
Ekberg, Anita.	Malmo, Sweden.	9/29/31
Ekland, Britt.	Stockholm, Sweden	10/6/42
Elam, Jack	Miami, AZ.	11/13/16
Elizondo, Hector.	New York, NY	12/22/36
Elliott, Bob.	Boston, MA.	3/26/23
Elliott, Sam	Sacramento, CA	8/9/44
Enberg, Dick	Auburn Hills, MI	1/5/35
Englund, Robert.	Hollywood, CA.	6/6/48

Name	Birthplace	Birthdate	Name	Birthplace	Birthdate
Elvira (Cassandra Peterson)	Manhattan, KS	9/17/51	Gabor, Zsa Zsa	Hungary	2/6/17
Enya (Eithne Ni Bhraona)	Gweedore, Ireland	1962	Gabriel, John	Niagara Falls, NY	5/25/31
Ephron, Nora	New York, NY	5/19/41	Gabriel, Peter	London, England	2/13/50
Estefan, Gloria	Havana, Cuba	9/1/58	Gail, Max	Detroit, MI	4/5/43
Estevez, Emilio	New York, NY	5/12/62	Galway, James	Belfast, Ireland	12/8/39
Estrada, Erik	New York, NY	3/16/49	Garagiola, Joe	St. Louis, MO	2/12/26
Etheridge, Melissa	Leavenworth, KS	5/29/61	Garcia, Andy	Havana, Cuba	4/12/56
Evans, Dale	Uvalde, TX	10/31/12	Garfunkel, Art	New York, NY	11/5/41
Evans, Linda	Hartford, CT	11/18/42	Garland, Beverly	Santa Cruz, CA	10/17/26
Evans, Robert	New York, NY	6/29/30	Garner, James	Norman, OK	4/7/28
Everett, Chad	South Bend, IN	6/11/36	Garr, Teri	Lakewood, OH	12/11/45
Everly, Don	Brownie, KY	2/1/37	Garrett, Betty	St. Joseph, MO	5/23/19
Everly, Phil	Chicago, IL	1/19/38	Garson, Greer	Co. Down, N Ireland	9/29/08
Evigan, Greg	S. Amboy, NJ	10/14/53	Garth, Jennie	Champaign, IL	4/3/72
			Gatlin, Larry	Seminole, TX	5/2/48
Fabares, Shelley	Santa Monica, CA	1/19/42	Gayle, Crystal	Paintsville, KY	1/9/51
Fabian (Forte)	Philadelphia, PA	2/6/43	Gaynor, Mitzi	Chicago, IL	9/4/30
Fabio	Milan, Italy	3/15/61	Gazzara, Ben	New York, NY	8/28/30
Fabray, Nanette	San Diego, CA	10/27/20	Geary, Anthony	Coalville, UT	5/29/47
Fairbanks, Douglas, Jr.	New York, NY	12/9/09	Geary, Cynthia	Jackson, MS	3/21/66
Fairchild, Morgan	Dallas, TX	2/3/50	Gedda, Nicolai	Stockholm, Sweden	7/11/25
Falana, Lola	Philadelphia, PA	9/11/46	Geils, J.	New York, NY	2/20/46
Falk, Peter	New York, NY	9/16/27	Gere, Richard	Philadelphia, PA	8/31/49
Farentino, James	Brooklyn, NY	2/24/38	Getty, Estelle	New York, NY	7/25/24
Fargo, Donna	Mt. Airy, NC	11/10/45	Ghostley, Alice	Eve, MO	8/14/26
Farr, Jamie	Toledo, OH	7/1/34	Giannini, Giancarlo	Spezia, Italy	8/1/42
Farrell, Eileen	Willimantic, CT	2/13/20	Gibbons, Leeza		3/26/57
Farrell, Mike	St. Paul, MN	2/6/39	Gibbs, Marla	Chicago, IL	6/14/31
Farrow, Mia	Los Angeles, CA	2/9/45	Gibson, Debbie	New York, NY	8/31/70
Faustino, David	California	3/3/74	Gibson, Henry	Germantown, PA	9/21/35
Fawcett, Farrah	Corpus Christi, TX	2/2/47	Gibson, Mel	Peekskill, NY	1/3/56
Faye, Alice	New York, NY	5/5/12	Gielgud, John	London, England	4/14/04
Feinstein, Michael	Columbus, OH	9/7/56	Gifford, Frank	Santa Monica, CA	8/16/30
Feldon, Barbara	Pittsburgh, PA	3/12/41	Gifford, Kathy Lee	Paris, France	8/16/53
Feliciano, Jose	Lares, Puerto Rico	9/10/45	Gilbert, Sara	Santa Monica, CA	1/29/75
Fell, Norman	Philadelphia, PA	3/24/24	Gilbert, Melissa	Los Angeles, CA	5/8/64
Feldshuh, Tovah	New York, NY	12/27/53	Gilberto, Astrud	Salvador, Brazil	3/30/40
Fenn, Sherilyn	Detroit, MI	2/1/65	Gill, Vince	Norman, OK	4/12/57
Ferrell, Conchata	Charleston, WV	3/28/43	Gillette, Anita	Baltimore, MD	8/16/38
Ferrer, Mel	Elberon, NJ	8/25/17	Gilley, Mickey	Natchez, MS	3/9/36
Fiedler, John	Platville, WI	2/3/25	Gilpin, Peri	Waco, TX	5/27/--
Field, Sally	Pasadena, CA	11/6/46	Ginty, Robert	New York, NY	11/14/48
Fiennes, Ralph	Suffolk, England	12/22/62	Givens, Robin	New York, NY	11/27/64
Finney, Albert	Salford, England	5/9/36	Glaser, Paul Michael	Cambridge, MA	3/25/42
Firkusny, Rudolf	Napajedla, Czechoslovakia	2/11/12	Glenn, Scott	Pittsburgh, PA	1/26/42
Firth, Peter	Yorkshire, England	10/27/53	Gless, Sharon	Los Angeles, CA	5/31/43
Fischer-Dieskau, Dietrich	Berlin, Germany	5/28/25	Glover, Danny	San Francisco, CA	7/22/47
Fishburne, Larry	Augusta, GA	7/30/61	Godard, Jean Luc	Paris, France	12/3/30
Fisher, Carrie	Beverly Hills, CA	10/21/56	Goldberg, Whoopi	New York, NY	11/13/49
Fisher, Eddie	Philadelphia, PA	8/10/28	Goldblum, Jeff	Pittsburgh, PA	10/22/52
Fitzgerald, Ella	Newport News, VA	4/25/18	Goldsboro, Bobby	Marianna, FL	1/18/42
Fitzgerald, Geraldine	Dublin, Ireland	11/24/13	Goldthwait, Bobcat	Syracuse, NY	5/1/62
Flack, Roberta	Black Mountain, NC	2/10/39	Goldwyn, Tony	Los Angeles, CA	5/20/60
Flanagan, Fionnula	Dublin, Ireland	12/10/41	Goodman, John	St. Louis, MO	6/20/53
Fleming, Rhonda	Hollywood, CA	8/10/23	Gorme, Eydie	Bronx, NY	8/16/32
Fletcher, Louise	Birmingham, AL	7/22/34	Gorshin, Frank	Pittsburgh, PA	4/5/34
Foch, Nina	Leyden, Netherlands	4/20/24	Gossett, Louis, Jr.	Brooklyn, NY	5/27/36
Fogelberg, Dan	Peoria, IL	8/13/51	Gould, Elliott	Brooklyn, NY	8/29/38
Fonda, Bridget	Los Angeles, CA	1/27/64	Gould, Harold	Schenectady, NY	12/10/23
Fonda, Jane	New York, NY	12/21/37	Gould, Morton	Richmond Hill, NY	12/10/13
Fonda, Peter	New York, NY	2/23/40	Goulet, Robert	Lawrence, MA	11/26/33
Fontaine, Joan	Tokyo, Japan	10/22/17	Gowdy, Curt	Green River, WY	7/31/19
Ford, Faith	Alexandria, LA	9/14/64	Graham, Virginia	Chicago, IL	7/4/12
Ford, Glenn	Quebec, Canada	5/1/16	Grammer, Kelsey	Virgin Islands	2/20/55
Ford, Harrison	Chicago, IL	7/13/42	Granger, Farley	San Jose, CA	7/1/25
Forsythe, John	Penns Grove, NJ	1/29/18	Grant, Amy	Augusta, GA	12/25/60
Foster, Jodie	New York, NY	11/19/62	Grant, Hugh	London, England	9/9/60
Fox, James	London, England	5/19/39	Grant, Lee	New York, NY	10/31/29
Fox, Michael J.	Edmonton, Alberta	6/9/61	Graves, Peter	Minneapolis, MN	3/18/26
Foxworth, Robert	Houston, TX	11/1/41	Gray, Linda	Santa Monica, CA	9/12/40
Frampton, Peter	Kent, England	4/22/50	Gray, Spaulding	Barrington, RI	6/5/41
Franciosa, Anthony	New York, NY	10/25/28	Grayson, Kathryn	Winston-Salem, NC	2/9/22
Francis, Anne	Ossining, NY	9/16/30	Greco, Jose	Abruzzi, Italy	12/23/18
Francis, Arlene	Boston, MA	10/20/08	Green, Adolph	New York, NY	12/2/15
Francis, Connie	Newark, NJ	12/12/38	Green, Al	Forest City, AR	4/13/46
Frankenheimer, John	Malba, NY	2/19/30	Greene, Shecky	Chicago, IL	4/8/26
Franklin, Aretha	Memphis, TN	3/25/42	Gregory, Cynthia	Los Angeles, CA	7/8/46
Franklin, Bonnie	Santa Monica, CA	1/6/44	Gregory, Dick	St. Louis, MO	10/12/32
Frann, Mary	St. Louis, MO	2/27/43	Gregory, James	Bronx, NY	12/23/11
Franz, Dennis	Maywood, IL	10/28/44	Grey, Jennifer	New York, NY	3/22/60
Freeman, Al, Jr.	San Antonio, TX	3/21/34	Grey, Joel	Cleveland, OH	4/11/32
Freeman, Morgan	Memphis, TN	6/1/37	Grier, David Alan	Detroit, MI	6/30/55
Fricker, Brenda	Dublin, Ireland	2/17/45	Griffin, Merv	San Mateo, CA	7/6/25
Friedkin, William	Chicago, IL	8/29/39	Griffith, Andy	Mount Airy, NC	6/1/26
Frost, David	Tenterden, England	4/7/39	Griffith, Melanie	New York, NY	8/9/57
Funicello, Annette	Utica, NY	10/22/42	Grimes, Tammy	Lynn, MA	1/30/34
Funt, Allen	New York, NY	9/16/14	Grizzard, George	Roanoke Rapids, NC	4/1/28

Name	Birthplace	Birthdate
Grodin, Charles	Pittsburgh, PA	4/21/35
Groh, David	New York, NY	5/21/41
Grosbard, Ulu	Antwerp, Belgium	1/19/29
Gross, Michael	Chicago, IL	6/21/47
Guillaume, Robert	St. Louis, MO	11/30/37
Guinness, Alec	London, England	4/2/14
Gumbel, Greg	New Orleans, LA	5/3/46
Guthrie, Arlo	New York, NY	7/10/47
Guttenberg, Steve	New York, NY	8/24/58
Guy, Buddy	Lettsworth, LA	7/30/36
Guy, Jasmine	Boston, MA	3/10/64
Hackett, Buddy	Brooklyn, NY	8/31/24
Hackman, Gene	San Bernardino, CA	1/30/30
Hagen, Uta	Gottingen, Germany	6/12/19
Haggard, Merle	Bakersfield, CA	4/6/37
Hagman, Larry	Weatherford, TX.	9/21/31
Haid, Charles	San Francisco, CA	6/2/44
Hale, Barbara	DeKalb, IL	4/18/22
Hall, Arsenio	Cleveland, OH	2/12/55
Hall, Daryl	Pottstown, PA	10/11/48
Hall, Deidre	Milwaukee, WI	10/31/48
Hall, Huntz	New York, NY	8/15/19
Hall, Monty	Winnipeg, Manitoba	8/25/25
Hall, Tom T.	Olive Hill, KY	5/25/36
Hamel, Veronica	Philadelphia, PA	11/20/43
Hamill, Mark	Oakland, CA	9/25/51
Hamilton, George	Memphis, TN	8/12/39
Hamilton, Linda	Salisbury, MD	9/26/56
Hamlin, Harry	Pasadena, CA	10/30/51
Hammer	Oakland, CA	3/29/63
Hampton, Lionel	Birmingham, AL	4/12/13
Hancock, Herbie	Chicago, IL	4/12/40
Hanks, Tom	Oakland, CA	7/9/56
Hannah, Daryl	Chicago, IL	1960
Hardison, Kadeem	New York, NY	7/24/66
Harewood, Dorian	Dayton, OH	8/6/51
Harmon, Mark	Burbank, CA	9/2/51
Harper, Jessica	Chicago, IL	10/10/49
Harper, Tess	Mammoth Springs, AR	8/15/50
Harper, Valerie	Suffern, NY	8/22/40
Harrelson, Woody	Midland, TX.	7/23/61
Harrington, Pat	New York, NY	8/13/29
Harris, Barbara	Evanston, IL	7/25/35
Harris, Ed	Englewood, NJ	11/28/50
Harris, Emmylou	Birmingham, AL	4/2/47
Harris, Julie	Grosse Pte. Park, MI	12/2/25
Harris, Neil Patrick	Albuquerque, NM	6/15/73
Harris, Richard	Co. Limerick, Ireland	10/1/33
Harris, Rosemary	Ashby, England	9/19/30
Harrison, George	Liverpool, England	2/25/43
Harrison, Gregory	Avalon, CA	5/31/50
Harry, Deborah	Miami, FL	7/1/45
Hart, Mary	Madison, SD	11/8/51
Hartley, Mariette	New York, NY	6/21/40
Hartman, David	Pawtucket, RI	5/19/35
Hartman, Lisa	Houston, TX	6/1/56
Hartman, Phil	Ontario, Canada	9/24/48
Hasselhoff, David	Baltimore, MD	7/17/52
Hatcher, Teri	Sunnyvale, CA.	12/8/64
Hauer, Rutger	Netherlands	1/23/44
Haver, June	Rock Island, IL	6/10/26
Havoc, June	Seattle, WA.	11/8/16
Hawke, Ethan	Austin, TX.	11/6/70
Hawn, Goldie	Washington, DC	11/21/45
Hayden, Melissa	Toronto, Ontario	4/25/23
Hayes, Isaac	Covington, TN	8/20/42
Hays, Robert	Bethesda, MD	7/24/47
Heard, John	Washington, DC.	3/7/45
Hearn, George	Memphis, TN.	1935
Heckart, Eileen	Columbus, OH	3/29/19
Helmond, Katherine	Galveston, TX	7/5/34
Hemingway, Margaux	Portland, OR	2/19/55
Hemingway, Mariel	Mill Valley, CA.	11/21/61
Hemmings, David	Guildford, England	11/18/41
Hemsley, Sherman	Philadelphia, PA.	2/1/38
Henderson, Florence	Dale, IN	2/14/34
Henderson, Skitch	Halstad, MN	1/27/18
Henley, Don	Gilmer, TX	7/22/47
Henner, Marilu	Chicago, IL	4/6/52
Henning, Doug	Ft. Garry, Manitoba	5/3/47
Hepburn, Katharine	Hartford, CT	5/12/07
Herman, Pee-Wee	Peekskill, NY	8/27/52
Herrmann, Edward	Washington, DC.	7/21/43
Hershey, Barbara	Los Angeles, CA	2/5/48
Hesseman, Howard	Lebanon, OR	2/27/40
Heston, Charlton	Evanston, IL	10/4/24
Hewett, Christopher	Sussex, England	4/5/--

Name	Birthplace	Birthdate
Hildegarde	Adell, WI.	2/1/06
Hill, Arthur	Melfort, Sask.	8/1/22
Hill, Steven	Seattle, WA.	2/24/22
Hill, George Roy	Minneapolis, MN	12/20/22
Hiller, Wendy	Stockport, England	8/15/12
Hillerman, John	Denison, TX	12/30/32
Hines, Gregory	New York, NY	2/14/46
Hines, Roy	Boston, MA.	3/13/26
Hines, Jerome	Hollywood, CA.	11/8/21
Hingle, Pat	Miami, FL	7/19/24
Hirsch, Judd	New York, NY	3/15/35
Hirt, Al	New Orleans, LA	11/7/22
Ho, Don	Kakaako, Oahu, HI.	8/13/30
Hoffman, Dustin	Los Angeles, CA	8/8/37
Hogan, Paul	New South Wales, Australia	10/8/39
Holbrook, Hal.	Cleveland, OH.	2/17/25
Holder, Geoffrey	Trinidad	8/1/30
Holliman, Earl	Delhi, LA.	9/11/28
Holliday, Polly	Jasper, AL.	8/2/37
Holly, Lauren	New York	1964
Holm, Celeste	New York, NY	4/29/19
Hooker, John Lee	Clarksdale, MS	8/22/17
Hooks, Jan	Decatur, GA	4/23/57
Hope, Bob	London, England	5/29/03
Hopkins, Anthony	Port Talbot, South Wales	12/31/37
Hopkins, Bo.	Greenville, SC	2/2/42
Hopkins, Telma	Louisville, KY.	10/28/48
Hopper, Dennis	Dodge City, KS	5/17/36
Horne, Lena	Brooklyn, NY.	6/30/17
Horne, Marilyn	Bradford, PA	1/16/34
Hornsby, Bruce	Williamsburg, VA	11/23/54
Horsley, Lee	Muleshoe, TX	5/15/55
Hoskins, Bob	Suffolk, England.	10/26/42
Houston, Whitney	E Orange, NJ	8/9/63
Howard, Ken	El Centro, CA	3/28/44
Howard, Ron	Duncan, OK	3/1/53
Howell, C. Thomas	Los Angeles, CA	12/7/66
Howes, Sally Ann	London, England	7/20/30
Hughes, Barnard	Bedford Hills, NY	7/16/15
Hulce, Tom	Whitewater, WI	12/6/53
Humperdinck, Engelbert	Madras, India	5/3/36
Hunt, Helen	Los Angeles, CA	6/15/63
Hunt, Linda	Morristown, NJ	4/2/45
Hunter, Holly	Conyers, GA	3/20/58
Hunter, Kim	Detroit, MI.	11/12/22
Hunter, Ross	Cleveland, OH.	5/6/21
Hunter, Tab	New York, NY	7/11/31
Hurt, John	Chesterfield, England	1/22/40
Hurt, Mary Beth	Marshalltown, IA	9/26/46
Hurt, William	Washington, DC.	3/20/50
Hussey, Ruth	Providence, RI.	10/30/14
Huston, Anjelica	Ireland	7/8/51
Hutton, Betty	Battle Creek, MI.	2/26/21
Hutton, Timothy	Malibu, CA	8/16/60
Hyman, Earle	Rocky Mount, NC.	10/11/26
Ian, Janis	New York, NY	4/7/51
Idle, Eric	Durham, England	3/29/43
Idol, Billy	London, England	11/30/55
Iman	Mogadishu, Somalia	7/25/55
Iglesias, Julio	Madrid, Spain	9/23/43
Imus, Don	Riverside, CA	7/23/40
Ireland, Kathy	Santa Barbara, CA	3/8/63
Ingram, James	Akron, OH.	2/16/56
Irons, Jeremy	Cowes, England.	9/19/48
Irving, Amy	Palo Alto, CA.	9/10/53
Irving, George S.	Springfield, MA	11/1/22
Ivey, Judith	El Paso, TX.	9/4/51
Ivory, James	Berkeley, CA.	6/7/28
Jackee	Winston-Salem, NC	8/14/56
Jackson, Anne	Allegheny, PA.	9/3/25
Jackson, Glenda	Liverpool, England	5/9/36
Jackson, Janet	Gary, IN	5/16/66
Jackson, Jermaine	Gary, IN	12/11/54
Jackson, La Toya	Gary, IN	5/29/56
Jackson, Kate	Birmingham, AL	10/29/48
Jackson, Michael	Gary, IN	8/29/58
Jackson, Milt	Detroit, MI.	1/1/22
Jackson, Samuel L.	Tennessee	1949
Jacobi, Derek	London, England	10/22/38
Jaeckel, Richard	Long Beach, NY.	10/10/26
Jagger, Mick	Dartford, England.	7/26/43
James, Etta	Los Angeles, CA	1938
James, Dennis	Jersey City, NJ	8/24/17
Janis, Conrad	New York, NY	2/11/28
Jarreau, Al	Milwaukee, WI.	3/12/40
Jarrette, Keith	Allentown, PA	5/8/45

Name	Birthplace	Birthdate	Name	Birthplace	Birthdate
Jeffreys, Anne	Goldsboro, NC	1/26/23	Kopell, Bernie	New York, NY	6/21/33
Jennings, Waylon	Littlefield, TX	6/15/37	Korman, Harvey	Chicago, IL	2/15/27
Jeter, Michael	Lawrenceburg, TN	8/20/52	Kotto, Yaphet	New York, NY	11/15/37
Jett, Joan	Philadelphia, PA	9/22/60	Kramer, Stanley	New York, NY	9/29/13
Jewison, Norman	Toronto, Ontario	7/21/26	Kristofferson, Kris	Brownsville, TX	6/22/36
Jillian, Ann	Cambridge, MA	1/29/50	Kubelik, Rafael	Bychori, Czechoslovakia	6/29/14
Joel, Billy	Bronx, NY	5/9/49	Kubrick, Stanley	Bronx, NY	7/26/28
John, Elton	Middlesex, England	3/25/47	Kudrow, Lisa	Encino, CA	5/30/63
Johns, Glynis	Durban, S Africa	10/5/23	Kurtz, Swoosie	Omaha, NE	9/6/44
Johnson, Arte	Benton Harbor, MI	1/20/29			
Johnson, Ben	Foraker, OK	6/13/18	LaBelle, Patti	Philadelphia, PA	10/4/44
Johnson, Beverly	Buffalo, NY	10/13/52	Ladd, Cheryl	Huron, SD	7/12/51
Johnson, Don	Flatt Creek, MO	12/15/49	Ladd, Diane	Meridian, MS	11/29/32
Johnson, J. J.	Indianapolis, IN	1/22/24	Lahti, Christine	Detroit, MI	4/5/50
Johnson, Van	Newport, RI	8/25/16	Laine, Cleo	Middlesex, England	10/28/27
Jones, Charlie	Ft. Smith, AK	11/9/30	Laine, Frankie	Chicago, IL	3/30/13
Jones, Davey	Manchester, England	12/30/45	Lake, Ricki	New York, NY	9/21/68
Jones, Dean	Morgan City, AL	1/25/35	Lamarr, Hedy	Vienna, Austria	11/9/13
Jones, Elvin	Pontiac, MI	9/9/27	Lamas, Lorenzo	Santa Monica, CA	1/20/58
Jones, George	Saratoga, TX	9/12/31	Lambert, Christopher	New York, NY	3/29/57
Jones, Grace	Spanishtown, Jamaica	5/19/52	Lamour, Dorothy	New Orleans, LA	12/10/14
Jones, Henry	Philadelphia, PA	8/1/12	Landau, Martin	New York, NY	6/20/34
Jones, Jack	Hollywood, CA	1/14/38	Landis, John	Chicago, IL	8/3/50
Jones, James Earl	Tate Co., MS	1/17/31	Lane, Diane	New York, NY	1/22/63
Jones, Jennifer	Tulsa, OK	3/2/19	lang, k.d.	Consort, Alberta	11/2/61
Jones, Quincy	Chicago, IL	3/14/33	Lang, Stephen	New York, NY	7/11/52
Jones, Shirley	Smithton, PA	3/31/34	Lange, Hope	Redding Ridge, CT	11/28/31
Jones, Tom	Pontypridd, Wales	6/7/40	Lange, Jessica	Cloquet, MN	4/20/49
Jones, Tommy Lee	San Saba, TX	9/15/46	Langella, Frank	Bayonne, NJ	1/1/40
Jordan, Richard	New York, NY	7/19/38	Langford, Frances	Lakeland, FL	4/4/13
Jourdan, Louis	Marseilles, France	6/19/19	Lansbury, Angela	London, England	10/16/25
Judd, Naomi	Ashland, KY	1/11/46	Laredo, Ruth	Detroit, MI	11/20/37
Judd, Wynonna	Ashland, KY	5/3/64	Larroquette, John	New Orleans, LA	11/25/47
Jump, Gordon	Dayton, OH	4/1/32	Lauper, Cyndi	New York, NY	6/20/53
			Laurie, Piper	Detroit, MI	1/22/32
Kahn, Madeline	Boston, MA	9/29/42	Lavin, Linda	Portland, ME	10/15/37
Kanaly, Steve	Burbank, CA	3/14/46	Lawrence, Carol	Melrose Park, IL	9/5/34
Kane, Carol	Cleveland, OH	6/18/52	Lawrence, Joey	Montgomery, PA	4/20/76
Karlen, John	New York, NY	5/28/33	Lawrence, Steve	Brooklyn, NY	7/8/35
Karn, Richard	Seattle, WA	1956	Lawrence, Vicki	Inglewood, CA	3/26/49
Karras, Alex	Gary, IN	7/15/35	Leach, Robin	London, England	8/29/41
Kasem, Casey	Detroit, MI	1933	Leachman, Cloris	Des Moines, IA	4/4/26
Kavner, Julie	Los Angeles, CA	9/7/51	Lear, Norman	New Haven, CT	7/27/22
Kazan, Elia	Istanbul, Turkey	9/7/09	Learned, Michael	Washington, DC	4/9/39
Kazan, Lainie	New York, NY	5/15/42	LeBlanc, Matt	Newton, MA	5/25/68
Keach, Stacy	Savannah, GA	6/2/41	LeBon, Simon	Bushey, England	10/27/58
Keaton, Diane	Santa Ana, CA	1/5/46	Lee, Brenda	Atlanta, GA	12/11/44
Keaton, Michael	Pittsburgh, PA	9/9/51	Lee, Christopher	London, England	5/27/22
Keel, Howard	Gillespie, IL	4/13/17	Lee, Michele	Los Angeles, CA	6/24/42
Keeshan, Bob	Lynbrook, NY	6/27/27	Lee, Peggy	Jamestown, ND	5/26/20
Keitel, Harvey	Brooklyn, NY	5/13/39	Lee, Spike	Atlanta, GA	3/20/57
Keith, Brian	Bayonne, NJ	11/14/21	Leeves, Jane	East Grinstead, England	4/13/63
Keith, David	Knoxville, TN	5/8/54	Legrand, Michel	Paris, France	2/24/32
Kellerman, Sally	Long Beach, CA	6/2/37	Leibman, Ron	New York, NY	10/11/37
Kelley, DeForest	Atlanta, GA	1/20/20	Leigh, Janet	Merced, CA	7/6/27
Kelly, Gene	Pittsburgh, PA	8/23/12	Leigh, Jennifer Jason	Los Angeles, CA	2/5/62
Kennedy, George	New York, NY	2/18/25	Leighton, Laura	Iowa City, IA	3/14/69
Kennedy, Jayne	Washington, DC	11/27/51	Lemmon, Jack	Boston, MA	2/8/25
Kenny G		6/5/56	Leno, Jay	New Rochelle, NY	4/28/50
Kent, Allegra	Los Angeles, CA	8/11/37	Leonard, Robert Sean	Westwood, NJ	2/28/69
Kercheval, Ken	Wolcottville, IN	7/15/35	Leonard, Sheldon	New York, NY	2/22/07
Kerns, Joanna	San Francisco, CA	2/12/53	LaSalle, Eriq	Hartford, CT	6/23/--
Kerr, Deborah	Helensburgh, Scotland	9/30/21	Leslie, Joan	Detroit, MI	1/26/25
Kessel, Barney	Muskogee, OK	1923	Letterman, David	Indianapolis, IN	4/12/47
Khan, Chaka	Great Lakes, IL	3/23/53	Levine, James	Cincinnati, OH	6/23/43
Kidder, Margot	Yellowknife, N.W.T.	10/17/48	Levinson, Barry	Baltimore, MD	6/2/32
Kidman, Nicole	Hawaii	1967	Lewis, Huey	New York, NY	7/5/51
Kiley, Richard	Chicago, IL	3/31/22	Lewis, Jerry	Newark, NJ	3/16/26
Kilmer, Val	Los Angeles, CA	12/31/59	Lewis, Jerry Lee	Ferriday, LA	9/29/35
Kimbrough, Charles	St. Paul, MN	5/23/--	Lewis, John	La Grange, IL	5/30/20
King, Alan	Brooklyn, NY	12/26/27	Lewis, Richard	New York, NY	6/29/47
King, B. B.	Itta Bena, MS	9/16/25	Lewis, Shari	New York, NY	1/17/34
King, Carole	Brooklyn, NY	2/9/42	Lewis, Juliette	San Fernando Valley, CA	6/21/73
King, Larry	New York, NY	11/19/33	Light, Judith	Trenton, NJ	2/9/50
King, Perry	Alliance, OH	4/30/48	Lightfoot, Gordon	Orillia, Ontario	11/17/38
Kingsley, Ben	Yorkshire, England	12/31/43	Limbaugh, Rush	Cape Girardeau, MO	1/12/51
Kinski, Nastassja	Berlin, W Germany	1/24/60	Linden, Hal	New York, NY	3/20/31
Kirby, Bruno	New York, NY	4/28/49	Lindfors, Viveca	Uppsala, Sweden	12/29/20
Kirby, Durward	Covington, KY	8/24/12	Linkletter, Art	Saskatchewan, Canada	7/17/12
Kirkland, Gelsey	Bethlehem, PA	12/29/53	Linn-Baker, Mark	St. Louis, MO	6/17/53
Kitt, Eartha	North, SC	1/26/28	Liotta, Ray	Newark, NJ	12/18/55
Klein, Robert	New York, NY	2/8/42	Lithgow, John	Rochester, NY	10/19/45
Klemperer, Werner	Cologne, Germany	3/22/19	Little, Rich	Ottawa, Ontario	11/26/38
Kline, Kevin	St. Louis, MO	10/24/47	Little Richard	Macon, GA	12/5/32
Klugman, Jack	Philadelphia, PA	4/27/22	L. L. Cool J	New York, NY	1/14/68
Knight, Gladys	Atlanta, GA	5/28/44	Lloyd, Christopher	Stamford, CT	10/22/38
Knotts, Don	Morgantown, WV	7/21/24	Lloyd, Emily	England	9/29/70
Konitz, Lee	Chicago, IL	10/13/27	Lloyd Webber, Andrew	London, England	3/22/48

Name	Birthplace	Birthdate
Locke, Sondra	Shelbyville, TN.	5/28/47
Lockhart, June	New York, NY	6/25/25
Locklear, Heather	Los Angeles, CA	9/25/61
Loggia, Robert	New York, NY	1/3/30
Loggins, Kenny	Everett, WA.	1/17/47
Lollobrigida, Gina	Subiaco, Italy.	7/4/27
Lom, Herbert	Prague, Czechoslovakia	1/9/17
Long, Shelley	Ft. Wayne, IN	8/23/49
Lord, Jack	New York, NY	12/30/22
Loren, Sophia	Rome, Italy	9/20/34
Loring, Gloria	New York, NY	12/10/46
Loudon, Dorothy	Boston, MA	9/17/33
Louis-Dreyfus, Julia	New York, NY	1/13/62
Lovett, Lyle	Klein, TX.	11/1/57
Lovitz, Jon	Tarzana, CA	7/21/57
Loveless, Patty	Pikeville, KY	1/4/57
Lowe, Rob	Charlottesville, VA	3/17/64
Lucas, George	Modesto, CA	5/14/44
Lucci, Susan	Scarsdale, NY	12/23/50
Luckinbill, Laurence	Ft. Smith, AR.	11/21/34
Ludwig, Christa	Berlin, Germany.	3/16/81
Lumet, Sidney	Philadelphia, PA.	6/25/24
LuPone, Patti	Northport, NY	4/21/49
Lynch, David	Missoula, MT.	1/20/46
Lynley, Carol	New York, NY	2/13/42
Lynn, Jeffrey	Auburn, MA.	2/16/09
Lynn, Loretta	Butcher Hollow, KY.	4/14/35
Ma, Yo Yo	Paris, France.	10/7/55
Maazel, Lorin	Paris, France.	3/6/30
MacArthur, James	Los Angeles, CA	12/8/37
MacCorkindale, Simon	Cambridge, England	2/12/52
MacDowell, Andie	Gaffney, SC	4/21/58
MacGraw, Ali	Pound Ridge, NY	4/1/38
MacLachlan, Kyle	Yakima, WA	2/22/59
MacLaine, Shirley	Richmond, VA	4/24/34
MacLeod, Gavin	Mt. Kisco, NY	2/28/30
MacNee, Patrick	London, England	2/6/22
MacNeil, Cornell	Minneapolis, MN	9/24/22
MacPherson, Elle	Sydney, Australia	3/29/64
Macchio, Ralph	Long Island, NY	11/4/62
Macy, Bill	Revere, MA.	5/18/22
Madden, John	Austin, MN	4/10/36
Madigan, Amy	Chicago, IL	9/11/51
Madonna (Ciccone)	Bay City, MI	8/16/58
Mahoney, John	Manchester, England	6/20/40
Majors, Lee	Wyandotte, MI	4/23/40
Malden, Karl	Chicago, IL	3/22/13
Malkovich, John	Christopher, IL.	12/9/53
Malle, Louis	Thumeries, France	10/30/32
Malone, Dorothy	Chicago, IL	1/30/25
Manchester, Melissa	Bronx, NY	2/15/51
Mandel, Howie	Toronto, Ontario.	11/29/55
Mandrell, Barbara	Houston, TX	12/25/48
Mangione, Chuck	Rochester, NY.	11/29/40
Manilow, Barry	New York, NY	6/17/46
Mann, Herbie	New York, NY	4/16/30
Manoff, Dinah	New York, NY	1/25/58
Mantegna, Joe	Chicago, IL	11/13/47
Marceau, Marcel	Strasbourg, France.	3/22/23
Marchand, Nancy	Buffalo, NY	6/19/28
Marin, Cheech	Los Angeles, CA	7/13/46
Marinaro, Ed	New York, NY	3/31/50
Markova, Alicia	London, England	12/1/10
Marriner, Neville	Lincoln, England	4/15/24
Marsalis, Branford	New Orleans, LA	8/26/60
Marsalis, Wynton	New Orleans, LA	10/18/61
Marsh, Jean	London, England	7/1/34
Marshall, E. G.	Owatonna, MN.	6/18/10
Marshall, Penny	New York, NY	10/15/43
Marshall, Peter	Huntington, WV	3/30/27
Martin, Dean	Steubenville, OH	6/17/17
Martin, Dick	Detroit, MI.	1/30/23
Martin, Steve	Waco, TX	4/14/45
Martin, Tony	San Francisco, CA	12/25/13
Martins, Peter	Copenhagen, Denmark	10/27/46
Mason, Jackie	Sheboygan, WI	6/9/31
Mason, Marsha	St. Louis, MO	4/3/42
Masterson, Mary Stuart	Los Angeles, CA	6/28/66
Mastrantonio, Mary Eliz.	Lombard, IL.	11/17/58
Mastroianni, Marcello	Rome, Italy	9/28/23
Masur, Kurt	Brieg, Germany	7/18/27
Masur, Richard	New York, NY	11/20/48
Mathers, Jerry	Sioux City, IA.	6/2/48
Matheson, Tim	Glendale, CA.	12/31/47
Mathis, Johnny	San Francisco, CA	9/30/35
Matlin, Marlee	Morton Grove, IL	8/24/65
Mattea, Kathy	Cross Lanes, W. VA	—

Name	Birthplace	Birthdate
Matthau, Walter	New York, NY	10/1/20
Mature, Victor	Louisville, KY.	1/29/16
May, Elaine	Philadelphia, PA.	4/21/32
Mayfield, Curtis	Chicago, IL.	6/3/42
Mayo, Virginia	St. Louis, MO	11/30/20
Mazursky, Paul	Brooklyn, NY.	4/25/30
McArdle, Andrea	Philadelphia, PA.	11/5/63
McBride, Patricia	Teaneck, NJ	8/23/42
McCallum, David	Glasgow, Scotland	9/19/33
McCambridge, Mercedes	Joliet, IL.	3/17/18
McCarthy, Andrew	Westfield, NJ.	11/29/62
McCarthy, Kevin	Seattle, WA.	2/15/14
McCartney, Paul	Liverpool, England	6/18/42
McCarver, Tim	Memphis, TN.	10/16/41
McClanahan, Rue	Healdton, OK.	2/21/36
McCoo, Marilyn	Jersey City, NJ	9/30/43
McDonnell, Mary	Wilkes-Barre, PA	1952
McDowall, Roddy	London, England	9/28/28
McDowell, Malcolm	Leeds, England	6/13/43
McEntire, Reba	McAlester, OK.	3/28/55
McFerrin, Bobby	New York, NY	3/11/50
McGavin, Darren	Spokane, WA	5/7/22
McGoohan, Patrick	New York, NY	3/19/28
McGovern, Elizabeth	Evanston, IL	7/18/61
McGovern, Maureen	Youngstown, OH	7/27/49
McGuire, Al	New York, NY	9/7/31
McGuire, Dorothy	Omaha, NE.	6/14/19
McKean, Michael	New York, NY	10/17/47
McKechnie, Donna	Pontiac, MI	11/16/42
McKellen, Ian	Burnley, England	5/25/39
McMahon, Ed	Detroit, MI.	3/6/23
McNichol, Kristy	Los Angeles, CA	9/11/62
McParland, Marion	Stough, England	3/20/20
McQueen, Butterfly	Tampa, FL	1/7/11
McRaney, Gerald	Collins, MS	8/19/48
Meadows, Audrey	Wu Chang, China.	2/8/24
Meadows, Jayne	Wu Chang, China.	9/27/20
Meara, Anne	New York, NY	9/20/29
Meat Loaf	Dallas, TX.	9/27/47
Mehta, Zubin	Bombay, India	4/29/36
Mellencamp, John	Seymour, IN	10/7/51
Mendes, Sergio	Niteroi, Brazil.	2/11/41
Menuhin, Yehudi	New York, NY	4/22/16
Mercer, Marian	Akron, OH.	11/26/35
Meredith, Burgess	Cleveland, OH	11/16/09
Merrick, David	St. Louis, MO	11/27/12
Merrill, Dina	New York, NY	12/9/25
Merrill, Robert	Brooklyn, NY.	6/4/19
Messina, Jim	Maywood, CA	12/5/47
Metcalf, Laurie	Carbondale, IL.	6/16/55
Michael, George	Watford, England	6/26/63
Michaels, Al	New York, NY	11/12/44
Michaels, Lorne	Toronto, Canada	11/17/44
Midler, Bette	Paterson, NJ	12/1/45
Midori	Osaka, Japan	10/25/71
Milano, Alyssa	New York, NY	12/19/72
Miles, Sarah	Ingatestone, England	12/31/41
Miles, Vera	near Boise City, OK	8/23/29
Miller, Ann	Houston, TX	4/12/19
Miller, Dennis	Pittsburgh, PA	11/3/53
Miller, Mitch	Rochester, NY.	7/4/11
Miller, Penelope Ann	Los Angeles, CA	1/13/64
Mills, Donna	Chicago, IL	12/11/42
Mills, John	Suffolk, England.	2/22/08
Milner, Martin	Detroit, MI.	12/28/27
Milnes, Sherrill	Downers Grove, IL	1/10/35
Milsap, Ronnie	Robinsville, NC	1/16/44
Minnelli, Liza	Los Angeles, CA	3/12/46
Mitchell, Joni	McLeod, Alberta	11/7/43
Mitchum, Robert	Bridgeport, CT.	8/6/17
Modine, Matthew	Loma Linda, CA.	3/22/59
Moffat, Donald	Plymouth, England	12/26/30
Moffo, Anna	Wayne, PA	6/27/27
Molinaro, Al	Kenosha, WI	6/24/19
Moll, Richard	Pasadena, CA.	1/13/43
Montalban, Ricardo	Mexico City, Mexico	11/25/20
Moody, Ron	London, England	1/8/24
Moore, Clayton	Chicago, IL	9/14/08
Moore, Demi	Roswell, NM	11/11/62
Moore, Dudley	London, England	4/19/35
Moore, Mary Tyler	Brooklyn, NY.	12/29/37
Moore, Melba	New York, NY	10/29/45
Moore, Roger	London, England	10/14/27
Moore, Terry	Los Angeles, CA	1/1/29
Moranis, Rick	Toronto, Ontario.	4/18/53
Moreno, Rita	Humacao, PR	12/11/31
Morgan, Harry	Detroit, MI.	4/10/15
Moriarty, Michael	Detroit, MI.	4/5/41

Name	Birthplace	Birthdate	Name	Birthplace	Birthdate
Morita, Pat	Isleton, CA	6/28/32	Osbourne, Ozzy	Birmingham, England	12/3/46
Morris, Howard	New York, NY	9/4/25	O'Shea, Milo	Dublin, Ireland	6/2/26
Morrison, Van	Belfast, Northern Ireland	8/31/45	Oslin, K.T.	Crosset, AR	1942
Morrissey	Manchester, England	5/22/59	Osmond, Donny	Ogden, UT	12/9/57
Morrow, Rob	New Rochelle, NY	9/21/62	Osmond, Marie	Ogden, UT	10/13/59
Morse, Robert	Newton, MA	5/18/31	O'Sullivan, Maureen	Boyle, Ireland	5/17/11
Morton, Joe	New York, NY	10/18/47	O'Toole, Annette	Houston, TX	4/1/53
Moses, William	Los Angeles, CA	11/17/59	O'Toole, Peter	Connemara, Ireland	8/2/32
Moss, Kate	London, England	1/16/74	Owens, Buck	Sherman, TX	8/12/29
Muldaur, Diana	New York, NY	8/19/38	Oz, Frank	Herford, England	5/25/44
Mulgrew, Kate	Dubuque, IA	4/29/55	Ozawa, Seiji	Shenyang, China	9/1/35
Mulhare, Edward	Ireland	4/8/23			
Mull, Martin	Chicago, IL	8/18/43	Paar, Jack	Canton, OH	5/1/18
Mulligan, Gerry	New York, NY	4/6/27	Pacino, Al	New York, NY	4/25/40
Mulligan, Richard	New York, NY	11/13/32	Packer, Billy	Wellsville, NY	2/25/40
Munsel, Patrice	Spokane, WA	5/14/25	Page, Jimmy	Heston, England	1/9/44
Murphy, Ben	Jonesboro, AR	3/6/42	Page, Patti	Claremore, OK	11/8/27
Murphy, Eddie	Brooklyn, NY	4/3/61	Paige, Janis	Tacoma, WA	9/16/22
Murphy, Michael	Los Angeles, CA	5/5/38	Palance, Jack	Lattimer, PA	2/18/20
Murray, Anne	Springhill, Nova Scotia	6/20/45	Palin, Michael	England	5/5/43
Murray, Bill	Evanston, IL	9/21/50	Palmer, Betsy	East Chicago, IN	11/1/29
Murray, Don	Hollywood, CA	7/31/29	Palmer, Robert	Bately, England	1/19/49
Musburger, Brent	Portland, OR	5/26/39	Papas, Irene	Greece	3/9/26
Muti, Riccardo	Naples, Italy	7/28/41	Paquin, Anna	Wellington, New Zealand	1983
Myers, Mike	Toronto, Ontario	5/23/63	Parker, Alan	London, England	2/14/44
			Parker, Eleanor	Cedarville, OH	6/26/22
Nabors, Jim	Sylacauga, AL	6/12/33	Parker, Fess	Ft. Worth, TX	8/16/25
Nash, Graham	Blackpool, England	2/2/42	Parker, Jameson	Baltimore, MD	11/18/47
Naughton, James	Middletown, CT	7/6/46	Parker, Jean	Deer Lodge, MT	8/11/12
Neal, Patricia	Packard, KY	1/20/26	Parker, Mary-Louise	Fort Jackson, SC	8/2/64
Nealon, Kevin	Bridgeport, CT	11/18/53	Parker, Sarah Jessica	Nelsonville, OH	3/25/65
Neeson, Liam	N. Ireland	6/7/52	Parsons, Estelle	Lynn, MA	11/20/27
Neill, Sam	New Zealand	9/14/47	Parton, Dolly	Sevierville, TN	1/19/46
Nelligan, Kate	London, Ontario	3/16/51	Patinkin, Mandy	Chicago, IL	11/30/52
Nelson, Craig T.	Spokane, WA	4/4/46	Patric, Jason	Queens, NY	1966
Nelson, Ed	New Orleans, LA	12/21/28	Pavarotti, Luciano	Modena, Italy	10/12/35
Nelson, Judd	Portland, ME	11/28/59	Paycheck, Johnny	Greenfield, OH	5/31/41
Nelson, Tracy	Santa Monica, CA	10/25/63	Pearl, Minnie	Centerville, TN	10/25/12
Nelson, Willie	Abbott, TX	4/30/33	Peck, Gregory	La Jolla, CA	4/5/16
Nero, Peter	New York, NY	5/22/34	Pendergrass, Teddy	Philadelphia, PA	3/26/50
Neuwirth, Bebe	Newark, NJ	12/31/--	Penn, Arthur	Philadelphia, PA	9/27/22
Neville, Aaron	New Orleans, LA	1/24/41	Penn, Sean	Burbank, CA	8/17/60
Newhart, Bob	Oak Park, IL	9/29/29	Penny, Joe	London, England	9/14/56
Newley, Anthony	Hackney, England	9/24/31	Perez, Rosie	Brooklyn, NY	—
Newman, Paul	Cleveland, OH	1/26/25	Perkins, Elizabeth	New York, NY	11/18/60
Newman, Randy	Los Angeles, CA	11/28/43	Perlman, Itzhak	Tel Aviv, Israel	8/31/45
Newton, Wayne	Norfolk, VA	4/3/42	Perlman, Rhea	Brooklyn, NY	3/31/48
Newton-John, Olivia	Cambridge, England	9/26/47	Perlman, Ron	New York, NY	4/13/50
Nicholas, Denise	Detroit, MI	7/12/44	Perrine, Valerie	Galveston, TX	9/3/43
Nicholas, Fayard	Philadelphia, PA	10/20/14	Perry, Luke	Fredericktown, OH	10/11/66
Nicholas, Harold	Philadelphia, PA	3/27/24	Perry, Mathew	Williamstown, MA	8/19/70
Nichols, Mike	Berlin, Germany	11/6/31	Persoff, Nehemiah	Jerusalem	8/14/20
Nicholson, Jack	Neptune, NJ	4/28/37	Pesci, Joe	Newark, NJ	2/9/43
Nicks, Stevie	Phoenix, AZ	5/26/48	Peters, Bernadette	New York, NY	2/28/48
Nielsen, Leslie	Regina, Sask.	2/11/26	Peters, Brock	New York, NY	7/2/27
Nilsson, Birgit	Karup, Sweden	5/17/18	Peters, Roberta	New York, NY	5/4/30
Nimoy, Leonard	Boston, MA	3/26/31	Peterson, Oscar	Montreal, Canada	8/15/25
Nolte, Nick	Omaha, NE	2/8/40	Petty, Tom	Gainesville, FL	10/20/53
Norman, Jessye	Augusta, GA	9/15/45	Pfeiffer, Michelle	Santa Ana, CA	4/29/57
Norris, Chuck	Ryan, OK	3/10/40	Philbin, Regis	New York, NY	8/25/34
North, Sheree	Los Angeles, CA	1/17/33	Phillips, Lou Diamond	Philippines	2/17/62
Noth, Christopher	Madison, WI	11/13/--	Phillips, Michelle	Long Beach, CA	6/4/44
Novak, Kim	Chicago, IL	2/13/33	Pickett, Wilson	Prattville, AL	3/18/41
			Pierce, David Hyde	Albany, NY	4/3/59
Oates, John	New York, NY	4/7/48	Pinchot, Bronson	New York, NY	5/20/59
O'Brian, Hugh	Rochester, NY	4/19/25	Piscopo, Joe	Passaic, NJ	6/17/51
O'Brien, Conan	Brookline, MA	4/18/63	Pitt, Brad	Shawnee, OK	12/18/63
O'Brien, Margaret	San Diego, CA	1/15/37	Pleshette, Suzanne	New York, NY	1/31/37
Ocean, Billy	Trinidad	1/21/50	Plowright, Joan	Brigg, England	10/28/29
O'Connor, Carroll	New York, NY	8/2/24	Plummer, Amanda	New York, NY	3/23/57
O'Connor, Donald	Chicago, IL	8/28/25	Plummer, Christopher	Toronto, Ontario	12/13/27
O'Connor, Sinead	Dublin, Ireland	12/8/66	Poitier, Sidney	Miami, FL	2/20/27
Odetta	Birmingham, AL	12/31/30	Polanski, Roman	Paris, France	8/18/33
O'Donnell, Chris	Winnetka, IL	1970	Pollack, Sydney	Lafayette, IN	7/1/34
O'Donnell, Rosie	Commack, NY	1962	Ponti, Carlo	Milan, Italy	12/11/13
O'Hara, Maureen	Dublin, Ireland	8/17/20	Post, Markie	Palo Alto, CA	11/4/50
O'Herlihy, Dan	Wexford, Ireland	5/1/19	Poston, Tom	Columbus, OH	10/17/27
Oldman, Gary	London, England	3/21/58	Potts, Annie	Nashville, TN	10/28/52
Olin, Ken	Chicago, IL	7/30/54	Povich, Maury	Washington, DC	1/17/39
Olin, Lena	Stockholm, Sweden	3/22/55	Powell, Jane	Portland, OR	4/1/28
Olmos, Edward James	E. Los Angeles, CA	2/24/47	Powers, Stefanie	Hollywood, CA	11/2/42
Olsen, Merlin	Logan, UT	9/15/40	Prentiss, Paula	San Antonio, TX	3/4/39
O'Neal, Ryan	Los Angeles, CA	4/20/41	Presley, Priscilla	New York, NY	5/24/46
O'Neal, Tatum	Los Angeles, CA	11/5/63	Preston, Billy	Houston, TX	9/9/46
O'Neill, Ed	Youngstown, OH	4/12/46	Previn, Andre	Berlin, Germany	4/6/29
Ontkean, Michael	Vancouver, B.C.	1/24/46	Price, Leontyne	Laurel, MS	2/10/27
Orbach, Jerry	New York, NY	10/20/35	Price, Ray	Perryville, TX	1/12/26
Orlando, Tony	New York, NY	4/3/44	Pride, Charlie	Sledge, MS	3/18/39

Name	Birthplace	Birthdate
Priestley, Jason	Vancouver, British Columbia.	8/28/69
Prince.	Minneapolis, MN	6/7/58
Principal, Victoria	Fukuoka, Japan	1/3/45
Prosky, Robert.	Philadelphia, PA.	12/13/30
Pryce, Jonathan	Wales.	6/1/47
Pryor, Richard	Peoria, IL	12/1/40
Puente, Tito.	New York, NY	4/20/23
Pulliam, Keshia Knight.	Newark, NJ	4/9/79
Purcell, Sarah	Richmond, IN	10/8/48
Pyle, Denver	Bethune, CO	5/11/20
Quaid, Dennis	Houston, TX	4/9/54
Quaid, Randy.	Houston, TX	10/1/50
Quinn, Aidan	Chicago, IL	3/8/59
Quinn, Anthony	Chihuahua, Mexico.	4/21/15
Quinn, Martha	Albany, NY	5/11/59
Rabb, Ellis.	Memphis, TN.	6/20/30
Rabbitt, Eddie	Brooklyn, NY.	11/27/41
Rachins, Alan	Cambridge, MA	10/10/47
Rae, Charlotte	Milwaukee, WI.	4/22/26
Raffi.	Cairo, Italy	7/8/48
Raitt, Bonnie	Burbank, CA	11/8/49
Ramey, Samuel	Colby, KS	3/28/42
Rampal, Jean-Pierre	Marseilles, France	1/7/22
Randall, Tony	Tulsa, OK	2/26/20
Randolph, John	New York, NY	6/1/15
Randolph, Joyce	Detroit, MI.	10/21/25
Raphael, Sally Jessy	Easton, PA	2/25/43
Rashad, Phylicia	Houston, TX	6/17/48
Ratzenberger, John	Bridgeport, CT.	4/6/47
Rawls, Lou	Chicago, IL	12/1/36
Raymond, Gene	New York, NY	8/13/08
Reddy, Helen.	Melbourne, Australia.	10/25/41
Redford, Robert	Santa Monica, CA	8/18/37
Redgrave, Lynn	London, England	3/8/43
Redgrave, Vanessa	London, England	1/30/37
Reed, Jerry	Atlanta, GA	3/20/37
Reed, Oliver	London, England	2/13/38
Reed, Rex.	Ft. Worth, TX.	10/2/38
Reese, Della	Detroit, MI.	7/6/31
Reeve, Christopher.	New York, NY	9/25/52
Reeves, Keanu	Beirut, Lebanon	9/2/64
Regalbuto, Joe.	New York, NY	8/24/--
Reid, Tim	Norfolk, VA	12/19/44
Reilly, Charles Nelson	New York, NY	1/13/31
Reiner, Carl.	Bronx, NY.	3/20/22
Reiner, Rob.	Bronx, NY.	3/6/45
Reinhold, Judge	Wilmington, DE	5/21/56
Reinking, Ann	Seattle, WA.	11/10/50
Reiser, Paul.	New York, NY	3/30/57
Resnik, Regina.	New York, NY	8/30/24
Reynolds, Burt.	Waycross, GA	2/11/36
Reynolds, Debbie	El Paso, TX.	4/1/32
Richards, Keith	Kent, England	12/18/43
Richards, Michael.	Culver City, CA	7/14/50
Richardson, Miranda.	Lancashire, England	1958
Richardson, Natasha.	London, England	5/11/63
Richie, Lionel.	Tuskegee, AL	6/20/50
Rickles, Don	New York, NY	5/8/26
Rickman, Alan	London, England	1946
Riegert, Peter	New York, NY	4/11/47
Rigg, Diana.	Doncaster, England	7/20/38
Ringwald, Molly	Rosewood, CA.	2/14/68
Ritter, John	Burbank, CA.	9/17/48
Rivera, Chita.	Washington, DC.	1/23/33
Rivera, Geraldo	New York, NY.	7/4/43
Rivers, Joan	Brooklyn, NY.	6/8/37
Roach, Max.	Elizabeth City, NC	1/10/24
Robards, Jason, Jr.	Chicago, IL.	7/26/22
Robbins, Jerome	New York, NY.	10/11/18
Robbins, Tim	W. Covina, CA.	10/16/58
Roberts, Doris	St. Louis, MO	11/4/29
Roberts, Eric	Biloxi, MS	4/18/56
Roberts, Julia	Smyrna, GA	10/25/67
Roberts, Pernell	Waycross, GA	5/18/30
Roberts, Tony	New York, NY	10/22/39
Robertson, Cliff	La Jolla, CA	9/9/25
Robertson, Dale	Harrah, OK	7/14/23
Robinson, Smokey	Detroit, MI.	2/19/40
Roche, Eugene	Boston, MA.	9/22/28
Rodgers, Jimmy	Camas, WA.	9/18/33
Rodriquez, Johnny	Sabinal, TX.	12/10/51
Rogers, Fred	Latrobe, PA.	3/20/28
Rogers, Kenny	Houston, TX	8/21/38
Rogers, Mimi	Coral Gables, FL	1/27/56
Rogers, Roy	Cincinnati, OH.	11/5/12
Rogers, Wayne.	Birmingham, AL	4/7/33

Name	Birthplace	Birthdate
Rolle, Esther	Pompano Beach, FL.	11/8/33
Rollins, Howard	Baltimore, MD.	10/17/50
Rollins, Sonny	New York, NY	9/7/29
Ronstadt, Linda	Tucson, AZ.	7/15/46
Rooney, Mickey	Brooklyn, NY.	9/23/20
Rose, Axl	Lafayette, IN.	2/6/62
Rose Marie	New York, NY	8/15/25
Roseanne	Salt Lake City, UT	11/3/52
Ross, Diana	Detroit, MI.	3/26/44
Ross, Katharine	Hollywood, CA.	1/29/42
Ross, Marion	Albert Lea, MN.	10/25/28
Rossellini, Isabella	Rome, Italy.	6/18/52
Rostropovich, Mstislav	Baku, Azerbaijan	3/12/27
Roth, David Lee	Bloomington, IN.	10/10/55
Rourke, Mickey	Miami, FL	1956
Rowlands, Gena.	Cambria, WI	6/19/34
Ruehl, Mercedes	Queens, NY	—
Rush, Barbara	Denver, CO.	1/4/30
Russell, Jane.	Bemidji, MN	6/21/21
Russell, Ken	Southampton, England	7/3/27
Russell, Kurt	Springfield, MA	3/17/51
Russell, Mark.	Buffalo, NY	8/23/32
Russell, Leon.	Lawton, OK.	4/2/41
Russell, Nipsey	Atlanta, GA	10/13/24
Russell, Theresa	San Diego, CA.	3/20/57
Rutherford, Ann	Toronto, Ontario.	11/2/20
Ruttan, Susan	Oregon City, OR	9/16/50
Ryan, Meg	Fairfield, CT	11/19/63
Ryan, Roz	Detroit, MI.	7/7/51
Rydell, Bobby	Philadelphia, PA.	4/26/42
Ryder, Winona.	Winona, MN	10/29/71
Sade	Ibadan, Nigeria	1/16/59
Sagal, Katie.	Los Angeles, CA	1956
Saget, Bob	Philadelphia, PA.	5/17/56
Sahl, Mort	Montreal, Quebec.	5/11/27
Saint, Eva Marie.	Newark, NJ	7/4/24
St. James, Susan	Los Angeles, CA	8/14/46
St. John, Jill.	Los Angeles, CA	8/19/40
Sajak, Pat	Chicago, IL	10/26/47
Saks, Gene	New York, NY	11/8/21
Sales, Soupy	Franklinton, NC	1/8/26
Samms, Emma	London, England	8/28/60
Sanderson, William.	Memphis, TN.	1/10/48
Sands, Julian	Yorkshire, England	1958
Sandy, Gary	Dayton, OH.	12/25/45
Sanford, Isabel.	New York, NY	8/29/17
Sarandon, Susan	New York, NY	10/4/46
Sarnoff, Dorothy	New York, NY	5/25/17
Sartain, Gailard	Tulsa, OK.	9/18/46
Savage, Fred.	Highland Park, IL	7/9/76
Saxon, John	Brooklyn, NY.	8/5/35
Sayles, John	Schenectady, NY.	9/28/50
Scaggs, Boz	Dallas, TX.	6/8/44
Schallert, William	Los Angeles, CA	7/6/22
Scheider, Roy	Orange, NJ	11/10/32
Schell, Maria	Vienna, Austria	1/15/26
Schell, Maximilian.	Vienna, Austria	12/8/30
Schenkel, Chris	Bippus, IN.	8/21/23
Schiffer, Claudia.	Germany	8/24/71
Schneider, John.	Mt. Kisco, NY	4/8/54
Schroder, Rick.	Staten Island, NY.	4/3/70
Schwarzenegger, Arnold.	Graz, Austria.	7/30/47
Schwarzkopf, Elisabeth	Jarotschin, Poland	12/9/15
Schwimmer, David	Queens, NY	11/1267
Sciorra, Annabella	New York, NY	1964
Scofield, Paul	Hurst, Pierpont, England	1/21/22
Scolari, Peter.	New Rochelle, IL.	9/12/54
Scorsese, Martin	New York, NY.	11/17/42
Scott, George C.	Wise, VA	10/18/27
Scott, Lizabeth	Scranton, PA.	9/29/22
Scott, Martha	Jamesport, MO	9/22/14
Scotto, Renata	Savona, Italy.	2/24/35
Scully, Vin.	New York, NY.	11/29/27
Seagal, Steven	Lansing, MI.	4/10/51
Sedaka, Neil	New York, NY.	3/13/39
Seeger, Pete	New York, NY.	5/3/19
Segal, George	Great Neck, NY.	2/13/34
Seidelman, Susan	Philadelphia, PA.	12/11/52
Seinfeld, Jerry	New York, NY.	4/29/55
Sellecca, Connie	New York, NY.	5/25/55
Selleck, Tom	Detroit, MI.	1/29/45
Severinsen, Doc.	Arlington, OR.	7/7/27
Seymour, Jane.	Middlesex, England	2/15/51
Shackelford, Ted	Oklahoma City, OK.	6/23/46
Shaffer, Paul	Thunder Bay, Ontario	11/28/49
Shandling, Garry	Tucson, AZ.	11/29/49

Name	Birthplace	Birthdate
Shankar, Ravi	India	4/7/20
Sharif, Omar	Alexandria, Egypt	4/10/32
Shatner, William	Montreal, Quebec	3/22/31
Shaver, Helen	St. Thomas, Canada	2/24/51
Shaw, Artie	New York, NY	5/23/10
Shea, John	N. Conway, NH	4/14/49
Shearer, Moira	Scotland	1/17/26
Shearing, George	London, England	8/13/19
Sheedy, Ally	New York, NY	6/12/62
Sheen, Charlie	New York, NY	9/3/65
Sheen, Martin	Dayton, OH	8/3/40
Shelley, Carole	London, England	8/16/39
Shepard, Sam	Ft. Sheridan, IL	11/5/43
Shepherd, Cybill	Memphis, TN	2/18/49
Sheridan, Nicollette	Northington, England	11/21/63
Shields, Brooke	New York, NY	5/31/65
Shire, Talia	New York, NY	4/25/46
Short, Bobby	Danville, IL	9/15/24
Short, Martin	Hamilton, Ontario	3/26/50
Show, Grant	Detroit, MI	4/27/63
Shue, Andrew	South Orange, NJ	2/20/67
Shull, Richard B.	Evanston, IL	2/24/29
Sidney, Sylvia	New York, NY	8/8/10
Siepi, Cesare	Milan, Italy	2/10/23
Sikking, James B.	Los Angeles, CA	3/5/34
Sills, Beverly	Brooklyn, NY	5/25/29
Silver, Ron	New York, NY	7/2/46
Simmons, Gene	Haifa, Israel	8/25/49
Simmons, Jean	London, England	1/31/29
Simmons, Richard	New Orleans, LA	7/12/48
Simon, Carly	New York, NY	6/25/45
Simon, Paul	Newark, NJ	10/13/41
Simone, Nina	Tyron, NC	2/21/33
Sinatra, Frank	Hoboken, NJ	12/12/15
Sinbad	Benton Harbor, MI	11/10/56
Sinclair, Madge	Kingston, Jamaica	4/28/38
Singleton, John	Los Angeles, CA	1/6/68
Siskel, Gene	Chicago, IL	1/26/46
Skelton, Red (Richard)	Vincennes, IN	7/18/13
Skerritt, Tom	Detroit, MI	8/25/33
Slater, Christian	New York, NY	8/19/69
Slater, Helen	Massapequa, NY	12/14/63
Slezak, Erika	Hollywood, CA	8/5/46
Slick, Grace	Chicago, IL	10/30/39
Smirnoff, Yakov	Odessa, Russia	1/24/51
Smith, Allison	New York, NY	12/9/69
Smith, Buffalo Bob	Buffalo, NY	11/27/17
Smith, Jaclyn	Houston, TX	10/26/47
Smith, Keely	Norfolk, VA	3/9/35
Smith, Maggie	Ilford, England	12/28/34
Smith, Will	Philadelphia, PA	9/25/68
Smits, Jimmy	New York, NY	7/9/55
Smothers, Dick	New York, NY	11/20/39
Smothers, Tom	New York, NY	2/2/37
Snipes, Wesley	Orlando, FL	7/31/63
Snow, Hank	Nova Scotia, Canada	5/9/14
Solti, Georg	Budapest, Hungary	10/21/12
Somers, Suzanne	San Bruno, CA	10/16/46
Sommer, Elke	Berlin, Germany	11/5/41
Sorvino, Paul	New York, NY	1939
Sothern, Ann	Valley City, ND	1/22/09
Soul, David	Chicago, IL	8/28/43
Spacek, Sissy	Quitman, TX	12/25/49
Spacey, Kevin	S. Orange, NJ	7/26/59
Spader, James	Boston, MA	2/7/60
Spano, Joe	San Francisco, CA	7/7/46
Spelling, Aaron	Dallas, TX	4/22/28
Spelling, Tori	Los Angeles, CA	5/16/73
Spielberg, Steven	Cincinnati, OH	12/18/47
Springfield, Dusty	London, England	4/16/39
Springfield, Rick	Sydney, Australia	8/23/49
Springsteen, Bruce	Freehold, NJ	9/23/49
Stack, Robert	Los Angeles, CA	1/13/19
Stafford, Jo	Coalinga, CA	11/12/18
Stahl, Richard	Detroit, MI	1/4/32
Stallone, Sylvester	New York, NY	7/6/46
Stamos, John	Cypress, CA	8/19/63
Stamp, Terence	Stepney, England	7/22/39
Stang, Arnold	New York, NY	9/28/25
Stanley, Kim	Tularosa, NM	2/11/25
Stanton, Harry Dean	Kentucky	7/14/26
Stapleton, Jean	New York, NY	1/19/23
Stapleton, Maureen	Troy, NY	6/21/25
Starr, Ringo	Liverpool, England	7/7/40
Steenburgen, Mary	Newport, AZ	2/8/53
Steiger, Rod	W. Hampton, NY	4/14/25
Stephens, James	Mt. Kisco, NY	5/18/51
Stern, Daniel	Stamford, CT	5/28/57

Name	Birthplace	Birthdate
Stern, Howard	New York, NY	1/12/54
Stern, Isaac	Kreminiecz, Russia	7/21/20
Sternhagen, Frances	Washington, DC	1/13/30
Stevens, Andrew	Memphis, TN	6/10/55
Stevens, Cat	London, England	7/21/48
Stevens, Connie	Brooklyn, NY	8/8/38
Stevens, Rise	New York, NY	6/11/13
Stevens, Stella	Yazoo City, MS	10/1/36
Stevenson, McLean	Normal, IL	11/14/29
Stevenson, Parker	Philadelphia, PA	6/4/52
Stewart, James	Indiana, PA	5/20/08
Stewart, Patrick	Mirfield, England	7/13/40
Stewart, Rod	London, England	1/10/45
Stickney, Dorothy	Dickinson, ND	6/21/1896
Stiers, David Ogden	Peoria, IL	10/31/42
Stiller, Jerry	New York, NY	6/8/29
Stills, Stephen	Dallas, TX	1/3/45
Sting	Newcastle, England	10/2/51
Stipe, Michael	Decatur, GA	1/4/60
Stockwell, Dean	Hollywood, CA	3/5/36
Stoltz, Eric	American Samoa	9/30/61
Stone, Dee Wallace	Kansas City, KS	12/14/48
Stone, Oliver	New York, NY	9/15/46
Stone, Sharon	Meadville, PA	3/10/58
Stookey, Paul	Baltimore, MD	12/30/37
Storch, Larry	New York, NY	1/8/23
Storm, Gale	Bloomington, TX	4/5/22
Stowe, Madeleine	Los Angeles, CA	8/18/58
Straight, Beatrice	Old Westbury, NY	8/2/18
Strait, George	Pearsall, TX	5/18/52
Stamos, John	Cypress, CA	8/19/63
Strasser, Robin	New York, NY	5/7/45
Stratas, Teresa	Toronto, Ontario	5/26/38
Strauss, Peter	New York, NY	2/20/47
Streep, Meryl	Summit, NJ	6/22/49
Streisand, Barbra	Brooklyn, NY	4/24/42
Stewart, Patrick	Mirfield, England	7/13/40
Stringfield, Sherry	Colorado Springs, CO	6/24/--
Stritch, Elaine	Detroit, MI	2/2/26
Struthers, Sally	Portland, OR	7/28/48
Stuarti, Enzo	Rome, Italy	3/3/25
Sullivan, Susan	New York, NY	11/18/44
Sumac, Yma	Ichocan, Peru	9/10/27
Summer, Donna	Boston, MA	12/31/48
Sutherland, Donald	St. John, New Brunswick	7/17/34
Sutherland, Joan	Sydney, Australia	11/7/26
Sutherland, Kiefer	London, England	12/20/66
Swayze, Patrick	Houston, TX	8/18/54
Swit, Loretta	Passaic, NJ	11/4/37
Mr. T (Lawrence Tero)	Chicago, IL	5/21/52
Takei, George	Los Angeles, CA	4/20/39
Tallchief, Maria	Fairfax, OK	1/24/25
Tarantino, Quentin		3/27/63
Taylor, Billy	Greenville, SC	7/24/21
Taylor, Elizabeth	London, England	2/27/32
Taylor, James	Boston, MA	3/12/48
Taylor, Rip	Washington, DC	1/13/30
Taylor, Rod	Sydney, Australia	1/11/29
Te Kanawa, Kiri	Gisborne, New Zealand	3/6/44
Tebaldi, Renata	Pesaro, Italy	2/1/22
Temple, Shirley	Santa Monica, CA	4/23/28
Tennant, Victoria	London, England	9/30/50
Tennille, Toni	Montgomery, AL	5/8/43
Tesh, John	Garden City, NY	7/9/52
Tharp, Twyla	Portland, IN	7/1/41
Thicke, Alan	Kirkland Lake, Ontario	3/1/47
Thomas, Jay	New Orleans, LA	7/12/48
Thomas, Jonathan Taylor	Bethlehem, PA	9/8/81
Thomas, Marlo	Detroit, MI	11/21/43
Thomas, Philip Michael	Columbus, OH	5/26/49
Thomas, Richard	New York, NY	6/13/51
Thompson, Emma	London, England	4/15/59
Thompson, Jack	Sydney, Australia	8/31/40
Thompson, Lea	Rochester, MN	5/31/61
Thompson, Sada	Des Moines, IA	9/27/29
Thorne-Smith, Courtney		11/8/68
Thurman, Uma	Boston, MA	4/29/70
Tiegs, Cheryl	Minnesota	9/27/47
Tiffany	Norwalk, CA	10/2/71
Tillis, Mel	Tampa, FL	8/8/32
Tiny Tim	New York, NY	4/12/23
Todd, Richard	Dublin, Ireland	6/11/19
Tomei, Marisa	New York, NY	12/4/64
Tomlin, Lily	Detroit, MI	9/1/39
Tomlinson, David	Scotland	5/7/17
Torme, Mel	Chicago, IL	9/13/25
Torn, Rip	Temple, TX	2/6/31

Name	Birthplace	Birthdate
Townsend, Robert	Chicago, IL	2/6/57
Townsend, Peter	Chiswick, England	5/19/45
Travanti, Daniel J.	Kenosha, WI	3/7/40
Travers, Mary	Louisville, KY.	11/9/36
Travis, Nancy	New York, NY	9/21/61
Travis, Randy	Marshville, NC	5/4/59
Travolta, John	Englewood, NJ	2/18/54
Trebek, Alex	Sudbury, Ontario	7/22/40
Trevor, Claire	New York, NY	3/8/09
Tritt, Travis	Marietta, GA	2/9/63
Tucker, Michael	Baltimore, MD	2/6/44
Tucker, Tanya	Seminole, TX.	10/10/58
Tune, Tommy	Wichita Falls, TX	2/28/39
Turner, Janine	Lincoln, NE	12/6/62
Turner, Kathleen	Springfield, MO	6/19/54
Turner, Tina	Nutbush, TN	11/26/39
Turturro, John	Brooklyn, NY	2/28/57
Twiggy (Leslie Hornby)	London, England	9/19/46
Tyler, Steven	Boston, MA	3/26/48
Tyson, Cicely	New York, NY	12/19/33
Uecker, Bob	Milwaukee, WI	1/26/35
Uggams, Leslie	New York, NY	5/25/43
Ullman, Tracey	Slough, England.	12/30/59
Ullmann, Liv	Tokyo, Japan.	12/16/38
Underwood, Blair	Tacoma, WA	8/25/64
Urich, Robert	Toronto, Ontario	12/19/46
Ustinov, Peter	London, England	4/16/21
Vaccaro, Brenda	Brooklyn, NY	11/18/39
Vale, Jerry	New York, NY	7/8/31
Valente, Caterina	Paris, France.	1/14/31
Valli, Frankie	Newark, NJ	5/3/37
Van Ark, Joan	New York, NY	6/16/43
Vandross, Luther	New York, NY	4/20/51
Van Damme, Jean-Claude	Brussels, Belgium	1961
Van Dyke, Dick	West Plains, MO	12/13/25
Van Dyke, Jerry	Danville, IL	7/27/31
Van Fleet, Jo	Oakland, CA	12/30/22
Van Halen, Eddie	Nijmegen, Netherlands	1/26/57
Van Patten, Dick	New York, NY	12/9/28
Van Peebles, Mario	Mexico	1/15/57
Vaughn, Robert	New York, NY	11/22/32
Vedder, Eddie	Evanston, IL	12/23/66
Verdon, Gwen	Los Angeles, CA	1/13/25
Vereen, Ben	Miami, FL	10/10/46
Verrett, Shirley	New Orleans, LA	5/31/31
Vickers, Jon.	Prince Albert, Sask.	10/26/26
Vincent, Jan-Michael	Denver, CO.	7/15/44
Vinson, Helen	Beaumont, TX	9/17/07
Vinton, Bobby	Canonsburg, PA.	4/16/35
Vitale, Dick	E Rutherford, NJ	6/9/40
Voight, Jon	Yonkers, NY	12/29/38
Von Stade, Frederica	Somerville, NJ	6/1/45
Von Sydow, Max	Lund, Sweden.	4/10/29
Wagner, Jack.	Washington, MO	10/3/59
Wagner, Lindsay	Los Angeles, CA	6/22/49
Wagner, Robert	Detroit, MI.	2/10/30
Wahl, Ken	Chicago, IL	2/14/56
Wain, Bea	Bronx, NY	4/30/17
Waite, Ralph	White Plains, NY	6/22/29
Walden, Robert	New York, NY	9/25/43
Walken, Christopher	New York, NY	3/31/43
Wallach, Eli	Brooklyn, NY.	12/7/15
Walston, Ray	Laurel, MS	11/2/24
Walter, Jessica	New York, NY	1/31/44
Ward, Fred	San Diego, CA.	1943
Ward, Sela	Meridian, MS	8/11/56
Ward, Simon	London, England	10/19/41
Warden, Jack.	Newark, NJ.	9/18/20
Warfield, William	W Helena, AR	1/22/20
Warner, Malcolm-Jamal	Jersey City, NJ	8/18/70
Warren, Lesley Ann	New York, NY	8/16/46
Warrick, Ruth	St. Joseph, MO	6/29/16
Warwick, Dionne	E Orange, NJ	12/12/41
Washington, Denzel	Mt. Vernon, NY	12/28/54
Waterston, Sam	Cambridge, MA	11/15/40
Watts, Andre	Nuremberg, Germany	6/20/46
Wayans, Keenan Ivory	New York, NY	6/8/58
Waxman, Al.	Toronto, Ontario.	3/2/35
Weathers, Carl.	New Orleans, LA	1/14/48
Weaver, Dennis	Joplin, MO	6/4/24
Weaver, Fritz	Pittsburgh, PA.	1/19/26
Weaver, Sigourney	New York, NY	10/8/49
Weir, Peter	Sydney, Australia.	8/8/44
Weitz, Bruce	Norwalk, CT	5/27/43

Name	Birthplace	Birthdate
Welch, Raquel	Chicago, IL	9/5/40
Weld, Tuesday.	New York, NY	8/27/43
Wells, Kitty	Nashville, TN.	8/30/19
Wendt, George	Chicago, IL	10/17/48
West, Adam	Walla Walla, WA	9/19/29
Weston, Jack.	Cleveland, OH.	8/21/24
Wettig, Patricia.	Cincinnati, OH.	12/4/51
Whalley-Kilme, Joanne	Manchester, England	8/25/64
Wheaton, Wil.	Burbank, CA.	7/29/72
Whitaker, Forest.	Longview, TX	7/15/61
White, Barry	Galveston, TX	9/12/44
White, Betty.	Oak Park, IL	1/17/22
White, Jaleel	Los Angeles, CA	11/27/76
White, Jesse	Buffalo, NY	1/3/19
White, Vanna	N Myrtle Beach, SC	2/18/57
Whiting, Margaret.	Detroit, MI.	7/22/24
Whitmore, James	White Plains, NY	10/1/21
Widmark, Richard.	Sunrise, MN	12/26/14
Wiest, Dianne	Kansas City, MO	3/28/48
Wilder, Billy.	Vienna, Austria	6/22/06
Wilder, Gene	Milwaukee, WI.	6/11/35
Williams, Andy.	Wall Lake, IA.	12/3/30
Williams, Billy Dee	New York, NY	4/6/37
Williams, Cindy	Van Nuys, CA	8/22/47
Williams, Esther	Los Angeles, CA	8/8/23
Williams, Hal	Columbus, OH.	12/14/38
Williams, Hank, Jr.	Shreveport, LA.	5/26/49
Williams, JoBeth	Houston, TX	1953
Williams, Montel.	Baltimore, MD	7/3/56
Williams, Paul	Omaha, NE	9/19/40
Williams, Robin	Chicago, IL	7/21/52
Williams, Treat.	Rowayton, CT	12/1/51
Williams, Vanessa	New York, NY	3/18/63
Williamson, Nicol	Hamilton, Scotland	9/14/38
Willis, Bruce	W Germany	3/19/55
Wilson, Demond.	Valdosta, GA.	10/13/46
Wilson, Elizabeth	Grand Rapids, MI.	4/4/25
Wilson, Flip	Jersey City, NJ	12/8/33
Wilson, Nancy	Chillicothe, OH	2/20/37
Windom, William	New York, NY	9/28/23
Winfield, Paul	Los Angeles, CA	5/22/41
Winfrey, Oprah.	Kosciusko, MS.	1/29/54
Winger, Debra	Cleveland, OH.	5/16/55
Winkler, Henry	New York, NY	10/30/45
Winningham, Mare	Phoenix, AZ	5/6/59
Winter, Johnny	Beaumont,TX	2/23/44
Winters, Jonathan	Dayton, OH.	11/11/25
Winters, Shelley	St. Louis, MO	8/18/22
Winwood, Steve.	Birmingham, England	5/12/48
Wiseman, Joseph.	Montreal, Quebec.	5/15/18
Withers, Jane	Atlanta, GA.	4/12/26
Wonder, Stevie	Saginaw, MI	5/13/50
Woodard, Alfre.	Tulsa, OK.	11/2/53
Woods, James.	Vernal, NJ.	4/18/47
Woodward, Edward.	Croyden, England	6/1/30
Woodward, Joanne.	Thomasville, GA	2/27/30
Worth, Irene	Nebraska	6/23/16
Wray, Fay.	Alberta, Canada.	9/10/07
Wright, Martha.	Seattle, WA.	3/23/26
Wright, Max.	Detroit, MI.	8/2/43
Wright, Steven	New York, NY	12/6/55
Wright, Teresa	New York, NY	10/27/18
Wyatt, Jane	Campgaw, NJ	8/10/11
Wyle, Noah	Hollywood, CA.	6/4/--
Wyman, Jane	St. Joseph, MO	1/4/14
Wynette, Tammy	Red Bay, AL	5/5/42
Yankovic, Weird Al	Los Angeles, CA	10/23/59
Yanni	Kalamata, Greece	11/4/54
Yarborough, Glenn	Milwaukee, WI.	1/12/30
Yarrow, Peter	New York, NY	5/31/38
Yoakam, Dwight.	Pikesville, KY	10/23/56
York, Michael	Fulmer, England.	3/27/42
York, Susannah	London, England	1/9/42
Young, Alan.	Northumberland, England	11/19/19
Young, Burt.	New York, NY	4/30/40
Young, Loretta.	Salt Lake City, UT	1/6/13
Young, Neil.	Toronto, Ontario.	11/12/45
Young, Robert.	Chicago, IL.	2/22/07
Young, Sean	Louisville, KY.	11/20/59
Youngman, Henny	Liverpool, England	1/12/06
Zeffirelli, Franco	Florence, Italy.	2/12/23
Zemeckis, Robert.	Chicago, IL.	1952
Zerbe, Anthony	Long Beach, CA.	5/20/36
Zimbalist, Efrem, Jr.	New York, NY	11/30/23
Zimbalist, Stephanie	Encino, CA.	10/8/56
Zukerman, Pinchas.	Tel Aviv, Israel.	7/16/48

Entertainment Personalities of the Past

(as of mid-1995)

Born	Died	Name	Born	Died	Name	Born	Died	Name
1895	1974	Abbott, Bud	1908	1989	Blanc, Mel	1902	1986	Cohen, Myron
1887	1995	Abbott, George	1928	1972	Blocker, Dan	1919	1965	Cole, Nat (King)
1903	1992	Acuff, Roy	1909	1979	Blondell, Joan	1890	1965	Collins, Ray
1872	1953	Adams, Maude	1888	1959	Blore, Eric	1891	1958	Colman, Ronald
1855	1926	Adler, Jacob P.	1901	1975	Blue, Ben	1908	1934	Columbo, Russ
1903	1984	Adler, Luther	1899	1957	Bogart, Humphrey	1921	1992	Connors, Chuck
1898	1933	Adoree, Renee	1880	1965	Boland, Mary	1920	1994	Conrad, William
1902	1986	Aherne, Brian	1895	1969	Boles, John	1917	1982	Conried, Hans
1931	1989	Ailey, Alvin	1904	1987	Bolger, Ray	1911	1975	Conte, Richard
1918	1994	Akins, Claude	1903	1960	Bond, Ward	1914	1984	Coogan, Jackie
1909	1964	Albertson, Frank	1892	1981	Bondi, Beulah	1904	1995	Cook, Elisha
1907	1981	Albertson, Jack	1917	1981	Boone, Richard	1935	1964	Cooke, Sam
1894	1956	Allen, Fred	1833	1893	Booth, Edwin	1901	1961	Cooper, Gary
1906	1964	Allen, Gracie	1796	1852	Booth, Junius Brutus	1888	1971	Cooper, Gladys
1883	1950	Allgood, Sara	1898	1992	Booth, Shirley	1896	1973	Cooper, Melville
1908	1993	Ameche, Don	1905	1965	Bow, Clara	1914	1968	Corey, Wendell
1903	1993	Ames, Leon	1874	1946	Bowes, Maj. Edward	1893	1974	Cornell, Katherine
1902	1993	Anderson, Marian	1928	1977	Boyd, Stephen	1890	1972	Correll, Charles (Andy)
1909	1992	Andrews, Dana	1898	1972	Boyd, William	1905	1979	Costello, Dolores
1913	1967	Andrews, Laverne	1899	1978	Boyer, Charles	1906	1959	Costello, Lou
1887	1933	Arbuckle, Fatty (Roscoe)	1893	1939	Brady, Alice	1905	1994	Cotten, Joseph
1908	1990	Arden, Eve	1894	1974	Brennan, Walter	1899	1973	Coward, Noel
1900	1976	Arlen, Richard	1904	1979	Brent, George	1924	1973	Cox, Wally
1868	1946	Arliss, George	1891	1951	Brice, Fanny	1908	1983	Crabbe, Buster
1888	1945	Armetta, Henry	1916	1994	Brazzi, Rossano	1928	1978	Crane, Bob
1900	1971	Armstrong, Louis	1891	1959	Broderick, Helen	1911	1986	Crawford, Broderick
1917	1986	Arnaz, Desi	1892	1973	Brown, Joe E.	1908	1977	Crawford, Joan
1890	1956	Arnold, Edward	1926	1966	Bruce, Lenny	1880	1942	Crews, Laura Hope
1905	1974	Arquette, Cliff	1895	1953	Bruce, Nigel	1880	1974	Crisp, Donald
1900	1991	Arthur, Jean	1910	1982	Bruce, Virginia	1942	1973	Croce, Jim
1899	1987	Astaire, Fred	1915	1985	Brynner, Yul	1903	1977	Crosby, Bing
1906	1987	Astor, Mary	1903	1979	Buchanan, Edgar	1910	1986	Crothers, Scatman
1885	1946	Atwill, Lionel	1938	1982	Buono, Victor	1908	1990	Cummings, Robert
1905	1967	Auer, Mischa	1885	1970	Burke, Billie	1878	1968	Currie, Finlay
1900	1972	Austin, Gene	1911	1967	Burnette, Smiley			
			1917	1993	Burr, Raymond	1914	1978	Dailey, Dan
1913	1989	Backus, Jim	1925	1984	Burton, Richard	1923	1965	Dandridge, Dorothy
1918	1990	Bailey, Pearl	1897	1946	Busch, Mae	1894	1963	Daniell, Henry
1892	1968	Bainter, Fay	1883	1966	Bushman, Francis X.	1901	1971	Daniels, Bebe
1906	1975	Baker, Josephine	1896	1946	Butterworth, Charles	1936	1973	Darin, Bobby
1904	1983	Balanchine, George	1893	1971	Byington, Spring	1921	1965	Darnell, Linda
1911	1989	Ball, Lucille				1879	1967	Darwell, Jane
1882	1956	Bancroft, George	1904	1972	Cabot, Bruce	1909	1986	Da Silva, Howard
1902	1968	Bankhead, Tallulah	1918	1977	Cabot, Sebastian	1866	1949	Davenport, Harry
1890	1952	Banks, Leslie	1899	1986	Cagney, James	1908	1989	Davis, Bette
1890	1955	Bara, Theda	1895	1956	Calhern, Louis	1907	1961	Davis, Joan
1810	1891	Barnum, Phineas T.	1923	1977	Callas, Maria	1925	1990	Davis, Sammy, Jr.
1879	1959	Barrymore, Ethel	1907	1994	Calloway, Cab	1931	1955	Dean, James
1882	1942	Barrymore, John	1933	1976	Cambridge, Godfrey	1917	1993	Defore, Don
1878	1954	Barrymore, Lionel	1865	1940	Campbell, Mrs. Patrick	1905	1968	Dekker, Albert
1848	1905	Barrymore, Maurice	1950	1994	Candy, John	1908	1983	Del Rio, Dolores
1897	1963	Barthelmess, Richard	1892	1964	Cantor, Eddie	1892	1983	Demarest, William
1914	1984	Basehart, Richard	1897	1991	Capra, Frank	1905	1993	DeMille, Agnes
1904	1984	Basie, Count	1878	1947	Carey, Harry	1881	1959	DeMille, Cecil B.
1923	1985	Baxter, Anne	1913	1994	Carey, Macdonald	1937	1992	Dennis, Sandy
1889	1951	Baxter, Warner	1950	1983	Carpenter, Karen	1891	1967	Denny, Reginald
1904	1965	Beatty, Clyde	1906	1988	Carradine, John	1901	1974	DeSica, Vittorio
1902	1962	Beavers, Louise	1880	1961	Carrillo, Leo	1905	1977	Devine, Andy
1884	1946	Beery, Noah, Sr.	1892	1972	Carroll, Leo G.	1924	1991	Dewhurst, Colleen
1913	1994	Beery, Noah, Jr.	1905	1965	Carroll, Nancy	1942	1972	De Wilde, Brandon
1889	1949	Beery, Wallace	1910	1963	Carson, Jack	1907	1974	De Wolfe, Billy
1901	1970	Begley, Ed	1873	1921	Caruso, Enrico	1920	1985	Diamond, Selma
1904	1991	Bellamy, Ralph	1876	1973	Casals, Pablo	1901	1992	Dietrich, Marlene
1949	1982	Belushi, John	1929	1989	Cassavetes, John	1879	1947	Digges, Dudley
1906	1968	Benaderet, Bea	1893	1969	Castle, Irene	1901	1966	Disney, Walt
1906	1964	Bendix, William	1887	1918	Castle, Vernon	1894	1949	Dix, Richard
1904	1965	Bennett, Constance	1873	1938	Chaliapin, Feodor	1905	1958	Donat, Robert
1910	1990	Bennett, Joan	1919	1980	Champion, Gower	1889	1972	Donlevy, Brian
1943	1987	Bennett, Michael	1918	1961	Chandler, Jeff	1901	1981	Douglas, Melvyn
1894	1974	Benny, Jack	1883	1930	Chaney, Lon	1907	1959	Douglas, Paul
1924	1970	Benzell, Mimi	1905	1973	Chaney, Lon, Jr.	1889	1956	Draper, Ruth
1899	1966	Berg, Gertrude	1942	1981	Chapin, Harry	1881	1965	Dresser, Louise
1903	1978	Bergen, Edgar	1889	1977	Chaplin, Charles	1869	1934	Dressler, Marie
1915	1982	Bergman, Ingrid	1893	1961	Chatterton, Ruth	1820	1897	Drew, Mrs. John
1895	1976	Berkeley, Busby	1888	1972	Chevalier, Maurice	1909	1951	Duchin, Eddy
1923	1986	Bernardi, Herschel	1888	1960	Clark, Bobby	1917	1990	Duff, Howard
1844	1923	Bernhardt, Sarah	1914	1968	Clark, Fred	1890	1974	Dumbrille, Douglass
1893	1943	Bernie, Ben	1920	1966	Clift, Montgomery	1889	1965	Dumont, Margaret
1889	1967	Bickford, Charles	1932	1963	Cline, Patsy	1878	1927	Duncan, Isadora
1934	1993	Bixby, Bill	1892	1967	Clyde, Andy	1905	1967	Dunn, James
1911	1960	Bjoerling, Jussi	1911	1976	Cobb, Lee J.	1898	1990	Dunne, Irene
1895	1973	Blackmer, Sidney	1877	1961	Coburn, Charles	1893	1980	Durante, Jimmy
1931	1989	Blake, Amanda	1878	1942	Cohan, George M.	1907	1968	Duryea, Dan

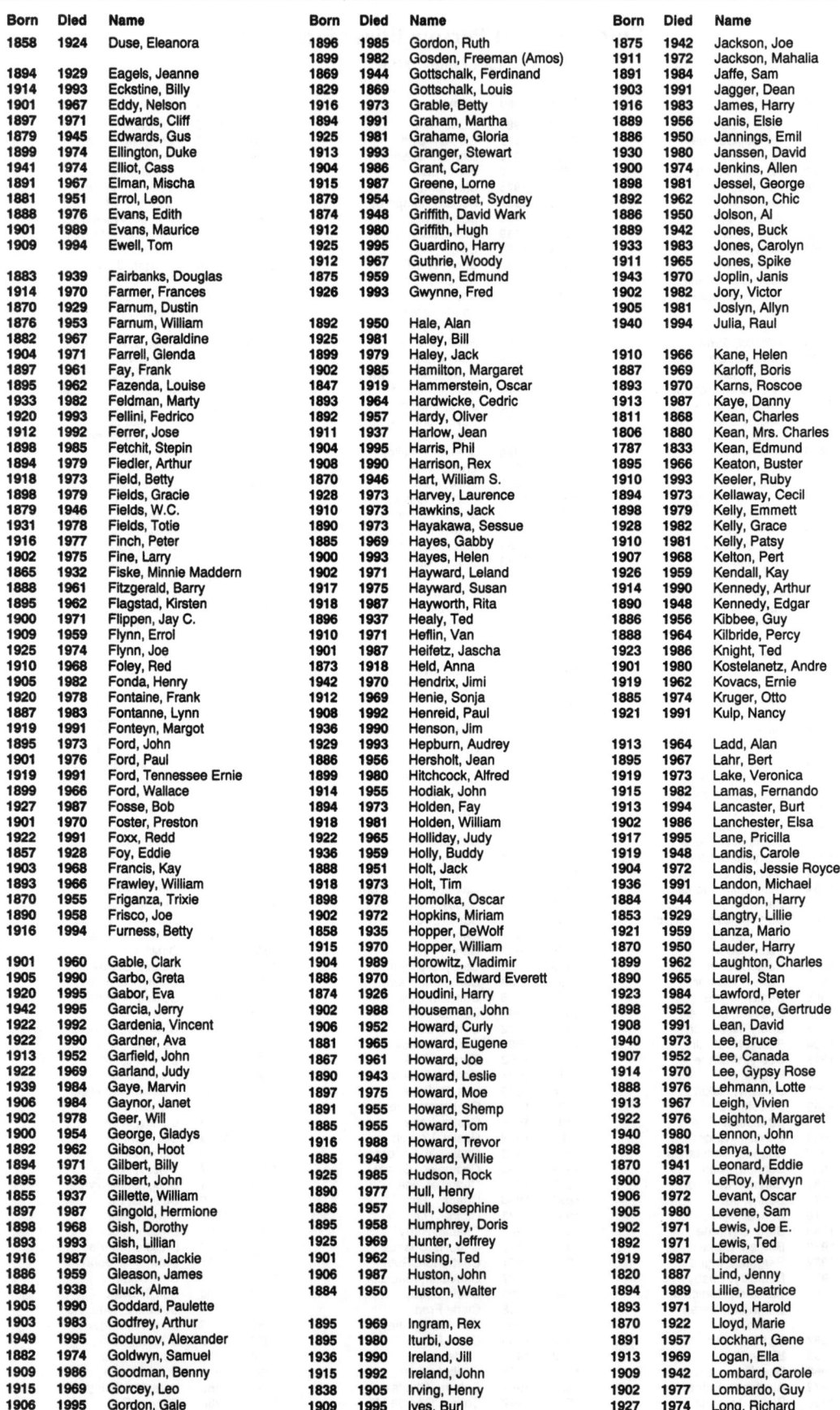

Born	Died	Name	Born	Died	Name	Born	Died	Name
1858	1924	Duse, Eleanora	1896	1985	Gordon, Ruth	1875	1942	Jackson, Joe
			1899	1982	Gosden, Freeman (Amos)	1911	1972	Jackson, Mahalia
1894	1929	Eagels, Jeanne	1869	1944	Gottschalk, Ferdinand	1891	1984	Jaffe, Sam
1914	1993	Eckstine, Billy	1829	1869	Gottschalk, Louis	1903	1991	Jagger, Dean
1901	1967	Eddy, Nelson	1916	1973	Grable, Betty	1916	1983	James, Harry
1897	1971	Edwards, Cliff	1894	1991	Graham, Martha	1889	1956	Janis, Elsie
1879	1945	Edwards, Gus	1925	1981	Grahame, Gloria	1886	1950	Jannings, Emil
1899	1974	Ellington, Duke	1913	1993	Granger, Stewart	1930	1980	Janssen, David
1941	1974	Elliot, Cass	1904	1986	Grant, Cary	1900	1974	Jenkins, Allen
1891	1967	Elman, Mischa	1915	1987	Greene, Lorne	1898	1981	Jessel, George
1881	1951	Errol, Leon	1879	1954	Greenstreet, Sydney	1892	1962	Johnson, Chic
1888	1976	Evans, Edith	1874	1948	Griffith, David Wark	1886	1950	Jolson, Al
1901	1989	Evans, Maurice	1912	1980	Griffith, Hugh	1889	1942	Jones, Buck
1909	1994	Ewell, Tom	1925	1995	Guardino, Harry	1933	1983	Jones, Carolyn
			1912	1967	Guthrie, Woody	1911	1965	Jones, Spike
1883	1939	Fairbanks, Douglas	1875	1959	Gwenn, Edmund	1943	1970	Joplin, Janis
1914	1970	Farmer, Frances	1926	1993	Gwynne, Fred	1902	1982	Jory, Victor
1870	1929	Farnum, Dustin				1905	1981	Joslyn, Allyn
1876	1953	Farnum, William	1892	1950	Hale, Alan	1940	1994	Julia, Raul
1882	1967	Farrar, Geraldine	1925	1981	Haley, Bill			
1904	1971	Farrell, Glenda	1899	1979	Haley, Jack	1910	1966	Kane, Helen
1897	1961	Fay, Frank	1902	1985	Hamilton, Margaret	1887	1969	Karloff, Boris
1895	1962	Fazenda, Louise	1847	1919	Hammerstein, Oscar	1893	1970	Karns, Roscoe
1933	1982	Feldman, Marty	1893	1964	Hardwicke, Cedric	1913	1987	Kaye, Danny
1920	1993	Fellini, Federico	1892	1957	Hardy, Oliver	1811	1868	Kean, Charles
1912	1992	Ferrer, Jose	1911	1937	Harlow, Jean	1806	1880	Kean, Mrs. Charles
1898	1985	Fetchit, Stepin	1904	1995	Harris, Phil	1787	1833	Kean, Edmund
1894	1979	Fiedler, Arthur	1908	1990	Harrison, Rex	1895	1966	Keaton, Buster
1918	1973	Field, Betty	1870	1946	Hart, William S.	1910	1993	Keeler, Ruby
1898	1979	Fields, Gracie	1928	1973	Harvey, Laurence	1894	1973	Kellaway, Cecil
1879	1946	Fields, W.C.	1910	1973	Hawkins, Jack	1898	1979	Kelly, Emmett
1931	1978	Fields, Totie	1890	1973	Hayakawa, Sessue	1928	1982	Kelly, Grace
1916	1977	Finch, Peter	1885	1969	Hayes, Gabby	1910	1981	Kelly, Patsy
1902	1975	Fine, Larry	1900	1993	Hayes, Helen	1907	1968	Kelton, Pert
1865	1932	Fiske, Minnie Maddern	1902	1971	Hayward, Leland	1926	1959	Kendall, Kay
1888	1961	Fitzgerald, Barry	1917	1975	Hayward, Susan	1914	1990	Kennedy, Arthur
1895	1962	Flagstad, Kirsten	1918	1987	Hayworth, Rita	1890	1948	Kennedy, Edgar
1900	1971	Flippen, Jay C.	1896	1937	Healy, Ted	1886	1956	Kibbee, Guy
1909	1959	Flynn, Errol	1910	1971	Heflin, Van	1888	1964	Kilbride, Percy
1925	1974	Flynn, Joe	1901	1987	Heifetz, Jascha	1923	1986	Knight, Ted
1910	1968	Foley, Red	1873	1918	Held, Anna	1901	1980	Kostelanetz, Andre
1905	1982	Fonda, Henry	1942	1970	Hendrix, Jimi	1919	1962	Kovacs, Ernie
1920	1978	Fontaine, Frank	1912	1969	Henie, Sonja	1885	1974	Kruger, Otto
1887	1983	Fontanne, Lynn	1908	1992	Henreid, Paul	1921	1991	Kulp, Nancy
1919	1991	Fonteyn, Margot	1936	1990	Henson, Jim			
1895	1973	Ford, John	1929	1993	Hepburn, Audrey	1913	1964	Ladd, Alan
1901	1976	Ford, Paul	1886	1956	Hersholt, Jean	1895	1967	Lahr, Bert
1919	1991	Ford, Tennessee Ernie	1899	1980	Hitchcock, Alfred	1919	1973	Lake, Veronica
1899	1966	Ford, Wallace	1914	1955	Hodiak, John	1915	1982	Lamas, Fernando
1927	1987	Fosse, Bob	1894	1973	Holden, Fay	1913	1994	Lancaster, Burt
1901	1970	Foster, Preston	1918	1981	Holden, William	1902	1986	Lanchester, Elsa
1922	1991	Foxx, Redd	1922	1965	Holliday, Judy	1917	1995	Lane, Pricilla
1857	1928	Foy, Eddie	1936	1959	Holly, Buddy	1919	1948	Landis, Carole
1903	1968	Francis, Kay	1888	1951	Holt, Jack	1904	1972	Landis, Jessie Royce
1893	1966	Frawley, William	1918	1973	Holt, Tim	1936	1991	Landon, Michael
1870	1955	Friganza, Trixie	1898	1978	Homolka, Oscar	1884	1944	Langdon, Harry
1890	1958	Frisco, Joe	1902	1972	Hopkins, Miriam	1853	1929	Langtry, Lillie
1916	1994	Furness, Betty	1858	1935	Hopper, DeWolf	1921	1959	Lanza, Mario
			1915	1970	Hopper, William	1870	1950	Lauder, Harry
1901	1960	Gable, Clark	1904	1989	Horowitz, Vladimir	1899	1962	Laughton, Charles
1905	1990	Garbo, Greta	1886	1970	Horton, Edward Everett	1890	1965	Laurel, Stan
1920	1995	Gabor, Eva	1874	1926	Houdini, Harry	1923	1984	Lawford, Peter
1942	1995	Garcia, Jerry	1902	1988	Houseman, John	1898	1952	Lawrence, Gertrude
1922	1992	Gardenia, Vincent	1906	1952	Howard, Curly	1908	1991	Lean, David
1922	1990	Gardner, Ava	1881	1965	Howard, Eugene	1940	1973	Lee, Bruce
1913	1952	Garfield, John	1867	1961	Howard, Joe	1907	1952	Lee, Canada
1922	1969	Garland, Judy	1890	1943	Howard, Leslie	1914	1970	Lee, Gypsy Rose
1939	1984	Gaye, Marvin	1897	1975	Howard, Moe	1888	1976	Lehmann, Lotte
1906	1984	Gaynor, Janet	1891	1955	Howard, Shemp	1913	1967	Leigh, Vivien
1902	1978	Geer, Will	1885	1955	Howard, Tom	1922	1976	Leighton, Margaret
1900	1954	George, Gladys	1916	1988	Howard, Trevor	1940	1980	Lennon, John
1892	1962	Gibson, Hoot	1885	1949	Howard, Willie	1898	1981	Lenya, Lotte
1894	1971	Gilbert, Billy	1890	1977	Hull, Henry	1870	1941	Leonard, Eddie
1895	1936	Gilbert, John	1886	1957	Hull, Josephine	1900	1987	LeRoy, Mervyn
1855	1937	Gillette, William	1895	1958	Humphrey, Doris	1906	1972	Levant, Oscar
1897	1987	Gingold, Hermione	1925	1969	Hunter, Jeffrey	1905	1980	Levene, Sam
1898	1968	Gish, Dorothy	1901	1962	Husing, Ted	1902	1971	Lewis, Joe E.
1893	1993	Gish, Lillian	1906	1987	Huston, John	1892	1971	Lewis, Ted
1916	1987	Gleason, Jackie	1884	1950	Huston, Walter	1919	1987	Liberace
1886	1959	Gleason, James				1820	1887	Lind, Jenny
1884	1938	Gluck, Alma	1895	1969	Ingram, Rex	1893	1971	Lloyd, Harold
1905	1990	Goddard, Paulette	1895	1980	Iturbi, Jose	1870	1922	Lloyd, Marie
1903	1983	Godfrey, Arthur	1936	1990	Ireland, Jill	1891	1957	Lockhart, Gene
1949	1995	Godunov, Alexander	1915	1992	Ireland, John	1913	1969	Logan, Ella
1882	1974	Goldwyn, Samuel	1838	1905	Irving, Henry	1909	1942	Lombard, Carole
1909	1986	Goodman, Benny	1909	1995	Ives, Burl	1902	1977	Lombardo, Guy
1915	1969	Gorcey, Leo				1927	1974	Long, Richard
1906	1995	Gordon, Gale						

Born	Died	Name	Born	Died	Name	Born	Died	Name
1895	1975	Lopez, Vincent	1885	1965	Murray, Mae	1873	1943	Reinhardt, Max
1888	1968	Lorne, Marion				1935	1991	Remick, Lee
1904	1964	Lorre, Peter	1896	1970	Nagel, Conrad	1909	1971	Rennie, Michael
1912	1962	Lovejoy, Frank	1900	1973	Naish, J. Carroll	1932	1995	Rich, Charlie
1890	1971	Lowe, Edmund	1898	1961	Naldi, Nita	1902	1983	Richardson, Ralph
1905	1993	Loy, Myrna	1908	1994	Natwick, Mildred	1921	1985	Riddle, Nelson
1892	1947	Lubitsch, Ernst	1914	1994	Nelson, Harriet (Hilliard)	1898	1977	Ritchard, Cyril
1882	1956	Lugosi, Bela	1906	1975	Nelson, Ozzie	1907	1974	Ritter, Tex
1894	1971	Lukas, Paul	1940	1985	Nelson, Rick	1905	1969	Ritter, Thelma
1892	1977	Lunt, Alfred	1885	1967	Nesbit, Evelyn	1901	1965	Ritz, Al
1914	1995	Lupino, Ida	1909	1983	Niven, David	1906	1986	Ritz, Harry
1926	1982	Lynde, Paul	1890	1950	Nijinsky, Vaslav	1903	1985	Ritz, Jimmy
1926	1971	Lynn, Diana	1893	1974	Nilsson, Anna Q.	1925	1982	Robbins, Marty
			1902	1985	Nolan, Lloyd	1898	1976	Robeson, Paul
1903	1965	MacDonald, Jeanette	1894	1930	Normand, Mabel	1878	1949	Robinson, Bill
1902	1969	MacLane, Barton	1899	1968	Novarro, Ramon	1893	1973	Robinson, Edward G.
1908	1991	MacMurray, Fred	1938	1993	Nureyev, Rudolf	1905	1977	Rochester (E. Anderson)
1921	1986	MacRae, Gordon				1897	1933	Rodgers, Jimmie
1909	1973	Macready, George	1903	1978	Oakie, Jack	1911	1995	Rogers, Ginger
1908	1973	Magnani, Anna	1860	1926	Oakley, Annie	1879	1935	Rogers, Will
1924	1994	Mancini, Henry	1928	1982	Oates, Warren	1905	1994	Roland, Gilbert
1890	1975	Main, Marjorie	1911	1979	Oberon, Merle	1907	1994	Romero, Cesar
1932	1967	Mansfield, Jayne	1915	1985	O'Brien, Edmond	1880	1962	Rooney, Pat
1905	1980	Mantovani, Annunzio	1899	1983	O'Brien, Pat	1899	1966	Rose, Billy
1897	1975	March, Fredric	1908	1981	O'Connell, Arthur	1922	1987	Rowan, Dan
1945	1981	Marley, Bob	1921	1993	O'Connell, Helen	1887	1982	Rubinstein, Artur
1890	1966	Marshall, Herbert	1880	1959	O'Connor, Una	1886	1970	Ruggles, Charles
1913	1990	Martin, Mary	1908	1968	O'Keefe, Dennis	1924	1961	Russell, Gail
1920	1981	Martin, Ross	1880	1938	Oland, Warner	1861	1922	Russell, Lillian
1924	1987	Marvin, Lee	1860	1932	Olcott, Chauncey	1911	1976	Russell, Rosalind
1888	1964	Marx, Arthur (Harpo)	1883	1942	Oliver, Edna May	1892	1972	Rutherford, Margaret
1901	1979	Marx, Herbert (Zeppo)	1907	1989	Olivier, Laurence	1903	1973	Ryan, Irene
1890	1977	Marx, Julius (Groucho)	1892	1963	Olsen, Ole	1909	1973	Ryan, Robert
1886	1961	Marx, Leonard (Chico)	1927	1994	O'Neal, Patrick			
1893	1977	Marx, Milton (Gummo)	1849	1920	O'Neill, James	1933	1994	Sargent, Dick
1909	1984	Mason, James	1936	1988	Orbison, Roy	1877	1968	St. Denis, Ruth
1896	1983	Massey, Raymond	1899	1985	Ormandy, Eugene	1884	1955	Sakall, S.Z.
1885	1957	Mayer, Louis B.	1876	1949	Ouspenskaya, Maria	1885	1936	Sale (Chic), Charles
1895	1973	Maynard, Ken	1887	1972	Owen, Reginald	1906	1972	Sanders, George
1935	1995	McClure, Doug				1924	1994	Savalas, Telly
1884	1945	McCormack, John	1860	1941	Paderewski, Ignace	1895	1964	Schildkraut, Joseph
1905	1990	McCrea, Joel	1924	1987	Page, Geraldine	1889	1965	Schipa, Tito
1895	1952	McDaniel, Hattie	1889	1954	Pallette, Eugene	1882	1951	Schnabel, Artur
1899	1981	McHugh, Frank	1914	1986	Palmer, Lilli	1920	1981	Scott, Hazel
1907	1991	McIntire, John	1894	1958	Pangborn, Franklin	1898	1987	Scott, Randolph
1883	1959	McLaglen, Victor	1914	1992	Parks, Bert	1914	1965	Scott, Zachary
1907	1971	McMahon, Horace	1914	1975	Parks, Larry	1843	1896	Scott-Siddons, Mrs.
1930	1980	McQueen, Steve	1881	1940	Pasternack, Josef A.	1938	1979	Seberg, Jean
1920	1980	Medford, Kay	1837	1908	Pastor, Tony	1892	1974	Seeley, Blossom
1880	1946	Meek, Donald	1843	1919	Patti, Adelina	1893	1987	Segovia, Andres
1861	1931	Melba, Nellie	1840	1889	Patti, Carlotta	1925	1980	Sellers, Peter
1890	1973	Melchior, Lauritz	1885	1931	Pavlova, Anna	1902	1965	Selznick, David O.
1890	1963	Menjou, Adolphe	1912	1989	Payne, John	1884	1960	Sennett, Mack
1902	1966	Menken, Helen	1904	1984	Peerce, Jan	1927	1978	Shaw, Robert
1925	1994	Mercouri, Melina	1899	1967	Pendleton, Nat	1891	1972	Shawn, Ted
1908	1984	Merman, Ethel	1905	1941	Penner, Joe	1868	1949	Shean, Al
1905	1986	Milland, Ray	1928	1994	Peppard, George	1902	1983	Shearer, Norma
1904	1944	Miller, Glenn	1932	1992	Perkins, Anthony	1915	1967	Sheridan, Ann
1898	1936	Miller, Marilyn	1915	1963	Piaf, Edith	1917	1994	Shore, Dinah
1903	1955	Minnevitch, Borrah	1893	1979	Pickford, Mary	1875	1953	Shubert, Lee
1939	1976	Mineo, Sal	1897	1984	Pidgeon, Walter	1755	1831	Siddons, Mrs. Sarah
1913	1955	Miranda, Carmen	1892	1957	Pinza, Ezio	1921	1985	Signoret, Simone
1918	1994	Mitchell, Cameron	1898	1963	Pitts, Zasu	1912	1985	Silvers, Phil
1892	1962	Mitchell, Thomas	1904	1976	Pons, Lily	1900	1976	Sim, Alastair
1880	1940	Mix, Tom	1897	1981	Ponselle, Rosa	1858	1942	Skinner, Otis
1926	1962	Monroe, Marilyn	1904	1963	Powell, Dick	1863	1948	Smith, C. Aubrey
1911	1973	Monroe, Vaughn	1912	1982	Powell, Eleanor	1907	1986	Smith, Kate
1917	1951	Montez, Maria	1892	1984	Powell, William	1854	1932	Sousa, John Philip
1938	1995	Montgomery, Elizabeth	1913	1958	Power, Tyrone	1884	1957	Sparks, Ned
1904	1981	Montgomery, Robert	1905	1986	Preminger, Otto	1908	1994	Stander, Lionel
1901	1947	Moore, Grace	1935	1977	Presley, Elvis	1907	1990	Stanwyck, Barbara
1914	1993	Moore, Garry	1918	1987	Preston, Robert	1934	1970	Stevens, Inger
1876	1962	Moore, Victor	1911	1993	Price, Vincent	1882	1977	Stokowski, Leopold
1906	1974	Moorehead, Agnes	1911	1978	Prima, Louis	1879	1953	Stone, Lewis
1910	1994	Morgan, Dennis	1954	1977	Prinze, Freddie	1904	1980	Stone, Milburn
1890	1949	Morgan, Frank				1898	1959	Sturges, Preston
1900	1941	Morgan, Helen	1946	1989	Radner, Gilda	1911	1960	Sullavan, Margaret
1915	1994	Morgan, Henry	1895	1980	Raft, George	1912	1994	Sullivan, Barry
1901	1970	Morris, Chester	1890	1967	Rains, Claude	1902	1974	Sullivan, Ed
1914	1959	Morris, Wayne	1902	1994	Ralson, Esther	1903	1956	Sullivan, Francis L.
1943	1971	Morrison, Jim	1892	1967	Rathbone, Basil	1892	1946	Summerville, Slim
1932	1982	Morrow, Vic	1897	1960	Ratoff, Gregory	1899	1983	Swanson, Gloria
1915	1977	Mostel, Zero	1916	1994	Raye, Martha	1904	1969	Swarthout, Gladys
1897	1969	Mowbray, Alan	1941	1967	Redding, Otis			
1895	1967	Muni, Paul	1908	1985	Redgrave, Michael	1893	1957	Talmadge, Norma
1915	1970	Munshin, Jules	1921	1986	Reed, Donna	1899	1972	Tamiroff, Akim
1924	1971	Murphy, Audie	1932	1992	Reed, Robert	1909	1994	Tandy, Jessica
1902	1992	Murphy, George	1914	1959	Reeves, George	1878	1947	Tanguay, Eva

Born	Died	Name	Born	Died	Name	Born	Died	Name
1885	1966	Taylor, Deems				1891	1967	Whiteman, Paul
1899	1958	Taylor, Estelle	1895	1926	Valentino, Rudolph	1865	1948	Whitty, May
1887	1946	Taylor, Laurette	1901	1986	Vallee, Rudy	1912	1979	Wilding, Michael
1911	1969	Taylor, Robert	1912	1979	Vance, Vivian	1877	1922	Williams, Bert
1847	1928	Terry, Ellen	1924	1990	Vaughan, Sarah	1923	1953	Williams, Hank
1899	1936	Thalberg, Irving	1893	1943	Veidt, Conrad	1905	1975	Wills, Bob
1912	1991	Thomas, Danny	1926	1981	Vera-Ellen	1903	1978	Wills, Chill
1882	1976	Thorndike, Sybil	1885	1957	Von Stroheim, Erich	1917	1972	Wilson, Marie
1896	1960	Tibbett, Lawrence	1906	1981	Von Zell, Harry	1884	1969	Winninger, Charles
1920	1991	Tierney, Gene				1904	1959	Withers, Grant
1909	1958	Todd, Michael	1922	1992	Walker, Nancy	1907	1961	Wong, Anna May
1903	1968	Tone, Franchot	1914	1951	Walker, Robert	1938	1981	Wood, Natalie
1867	1957	Toscanini, Arturo	1887	1980	Walsh, Raoul	1892	1978	Wood, Peggy
1898	1968	Tracy, Lee	1876	1962	Walter, Bruno	1888	1963	Woolley, Monty
1900	1967	Tracy, Spencer	1876	1958	Warner, H. B.	1902	1981	Wyler, William
1903	1972	Traubel, Helen	1924	1963	Washington, Dinah	1886	1966	Wynn, Ed
1894	1975	Treacher, Arthur	1900	1977	Waters, Ethel	1916	1986	Wynn, Keenan
1853	1917	Tree, Herbert Beerbohm	1914	1995	Wayne, David			
1890	1973	Truex, Ernest	1907	1979	Wayne, John	1890	1960	Young, Clara Kimball
1932	1984	Truffaut, Francois	1891	1966	Webb, Clifton	1913	1978	Young, Gig
1919	1986	Tucker, Forrest	1920	1982	Webb, Jack	1887	1953	Young, Roland
1915	1975	Tucker, Richard	1903	1992	Welk, Lawrence			
1884	1966	Tucker, Sophie	1915	1985	Welles, Orson	1902	1979	Zanuck, Darryl F.
1920	1995	Turner, Lana	1896	1975	Wellman, William	1940	1993	Zappa, Frank
1874	1940	Turpin, Ben	1892	1980	West, Mae	1869	1932	Ziegfeld, Florenz
1908	1959	Twelvetrees, Helen	1895	1968	Wheeler, Bert	1873	1976	Zukor, Adolph
1933	1993	Twitty, Conway	1889	1938	White, Pearl			

Original Names of Selected Entertainers

Edie Adams: Elizabeth Edith Enke
Eddie Albert: Edward Albert Heimberger
Alan Alda: Alphonso D'Abruzzo
Fred Allen: John Sullivan
Woody Allen: Allen Konigsberg
Greg Allman: Gregory Lenoir
June Allyson: Ella Geisman
Julie Andrews: Julia Wells
Eve Arden: Eunice Quedens
Beatrice Arthur: Bernice Frankel
Jean Arthur: Gladys Greene
Fred Astaire: Frederick Austerlitz
Alan Autry: Carlos Brown
Lauren Bacall: Betty Joan Perske
Anne Bancroft: Anna Maria Italiano
Brigitte Bardot: Camille Javal
Gene Barry: Eugene Klass
Orson Bean: Dallas Burrows
Pat Benatar: Patricia Andrejewski
Robbie Benson: Robert Segal
Tony Bennett: Anthony Benedetto
Busby Berkeley: William Berkeley Enos
Irving Berlin: Israel Baline
Jack Benny: Benjamin Kubelsky
Joey Bishop: Joseph Gottlieb
Robert Blake: Michael Gubitosi
Bono: Paul Hewson
Victor Borge: Borge Rosenbaum
David Bowie: David Robert Jones
Boy George: George Alan O'Dowd
Fanny Brice: Fanny Borach
Charles Bronson: Charles Buchinski
Albert Brooks: Albert Einstein
Mel Brooks: Melvin Kaminsky
George Burns: Nathan Birnbaum
Ellen Burstyn: Edna Gilhooley
Richard Burton: Richard Jenkins
Red Buttons: Aaron Chwatt
Nicolas Cage: Nicholas Coppola
Michael Caine: Maurice Micklewhite
Maria Callas: Maria Kalogeropoulos
Vikki Carr: Florencia Casillas
Diahann Carroll: Carol Diahann Johnson
Cyd Charisse: Tula Finklea
Ray Charles: Ray Charles Robinson
Chubble Checker: Ernest Evans
Cher: Cherilyn Sarkisian
Patsy Cline: Virginia Patterson Hensley
Lee J. Cobb: Leo Jacoby
Claudette Colbert: Lily Chauchoin
Michael Connors: Kreker Ohanian
Robert Conrad: Conrad Robert Falk

Alice Cooper: Vincent Furnier
David Copperfield: David Kotkin
Howard Cosell: Howard Cohen
Elvis Costello: Declan McManus
Lou Costello: Louis Cristillo
Joan Crawford: Lucille Le Sueur
Michael Crawford: Michael Dumble-Smith
Tom Cruise: Thomas Mapother
Tony Curtis: Bernard Schwartz
Vic Damone: Vito Farinola
Rodney Dangerfield: Jacob Cohen
Bobby Darin: Walden Robert Cassotto
Doris Day: Doris von Kappelhoff
James Dean: James Byron
Yvonne De Carlo: Peggy Middleton
Sandra Dee: Alexandra Zuck
John Denver: Henry John Deutschendorf Jr.
Bo Derek: Mary Cathleen Collins
John Derek: Derek Harris
Danny DeVito: Daniel Michaeli
Angie Dickinson: Angeline Brown
Bo Diddley: Elias Bates
Phyllis Diller: Phyllis Driver
Diana Dors: Diana Fluck
Kirk Douglas: Issur Danielovitch
Melvyn Douglas: Melvyn Hesselberg
Bob Dylan: Robert Zimmerman
Sheena Easton: Sheena Shirley Orr
Barbara Eden: Barbara Huffman
Ron Ely: Ronald Pierce
Dale Evans: Frances Smith
Chad Everett: Raymond Cramton
Tom Ewell: S. Yewell Tompkins
Douglas Fairbanks: Douglas Ullman
Morgan Fairchild: Patsy McClenny
Jamie Farr: Jameel Farah
Alice Faye: Ann Leppert
Stepin Fetchit: Lincoln Perry
Sally Field: Sally Mahoney
W.C. Fields: William Claude Dukenfield
Peter Finch: William Mitchell
Barry Fitzgerald: William Shields
Joan Fontaine: Joan de Havilland
John Ford: Sean O'Fearna
John Forsythe: John Freund
Redd Foxx : John Sanford
Anthony Franciosa: Anthony Papaleo
Arlene Francis: Arlene Kazanjian
Connie Francis: Concetta Franconero
Greta Garbo: Greta Gustafsson
Ava Gardner: Lucy Johnson

Vincent Gardenia: Vincent Scognamiglio
John Garfield: Julius Garfinkle
Judy Garland: Frances Gumm
James Garner: James Bumgarner
Crystal Gayle: Brenda Gayle Webb
Kathy Lee Gifford: Kathie Epstein
Paulette Goddard: Marion Levy
Whoopi Goldberg: Caryn Johnson
Eydie Gorme: Edith Gormezano
Stewart Granger: James Stewart
Cary Grant: Archibald Leach
Lee Grant: Lyova Rosenthal
Joel Grey: Joe Katz
Robert Guillaume: Robert Williams
Buddy Hackett: Leonard Hacker
Hammer: Stanley Kirk Burrell
Jean Harlow: Harlean Carpentier
Rex Harrison: Reginald Carey
Laurence Harvey: Larushka Skikne
Helen Hayes: Helen Brown
Susan Hayward: Edythe Marriner
Rita Hayworth: Margarita Cansino
Pee-Wee Herman: Paul Rubenfeld
Barbara Hershey: Barbara Herzstine
William Holden: William Beedle
Billie Holliday: Eleanora Fagan
Judy Holliday: Judith Tuvim
Harry Houdini: Ehrich Weiss
Leslie Howard: Leslie Stainer
Moe Howard: Moses Horowitz
Rock Hudson: Roy Scherer Jr. (later Fitzgerald)
Engelbert Humperdinck: Arnold Dorsey
Kim Hunter: Janet Cole
Mary Beth Hurt: Mary Supinger
Betty Hutton: Betty Thornberg
Billy Idol: William Board
David Janssen: David Meyer
Anne Jillian: Anne Nauseda
Elton John: Reginald Dwight
Don Johnson: Donald Wayne
Jennifer Jones: Phyllis Isley
Tom Jones: Thomas Woodward
Louis Jourdan: Louis Gendre
Boris Karloff: William Henry Pratt
Danny Kaye: David Kaminsky
Diane Keaton: Diane Hall
Michael Keaton: Michael Douglas
Howard Keel: Harold Leek
Chaka Khan: Yvette Stevens
Carole King: Carole Klein
Larry King: Larry Zeigler
Ben Kingsley: Krishna Banji

Nastassja Kinski: Nastassja Naksyznyski
Ted Knight: Tadeus Wladyslaw Konopka
Cheryl Ladd: Cheryl Stoppelmoor
Veronica Lake: Constance Ockleman
Dorothy Lamour: Mary Kaumeyer
Michael Landon: Eugene Orowitz
Mario Lanza: Alfredo Cocozza
Stan Laurel: Arthur Jefferson
Steve Lawrence: Sidney Leibowitz
Brenda Lee: Brenda Mae Tarpley
Bruce Lee: Lee Yuen Kam
Gypsy Rose Lee: Rose Louise Hovick
Michelle Lee: Michelle Dusiak
Peggy Lee: Norma Egstrom
Janet Leigh: Jeanette Morrison
Vivien Leigh: Vivien Hartley
Huey Lewis: Hugh Cregg
Jerry Lewis: Joseph Levitch
Hal Linden: Harold Lipshitz
Carole Lombard: Jane Peters
Jack Lord: John Joseph Ryan
Sophia Loren: Sophia Scicoloni
Peter Lorre: Laszio Lowenstein
Myrna Loy: Myrna Williams
Bela Lugosi: Bela Ferenc Blasko
Moms Mabley: Loretta Mary Aitken
Shirley MacLaine: Shirley Beaty
Madonna: Madonna Louise Ciccone
Lee Majors: Harvey Lee Yeary 2d
Karl Malden: Malden Sekulovich
Barry Manilow: Barry Alan Pincus
Jayne Mansfield: Vera Jane Palmer
Fredric March: Frederick Bickel
Peter Marshall: Pierre LaCock
Waler Mathau: Walter Matuschanskayasky
Dean Martin: Dino Crocetti
Meat Loaf: Marvin Lee Aday
Ethel Merman: Ethel Zimmerman
George Michael: Georgios Panayiotou
Ray Milland: Reginald Truscott-Jones

Ann Miller: Lucille Collier
Joni Mitchell: Roberta Joan Anderson
Marilyn Monroe: Norma Jean Mortenson, (later) Baker
Yves Montand: Ivo Levi
Ron Moody: Ronald Moodnick
Demi Moore: Demi Guynes
Garry Moore: Thomas Garrison Morfit
Rita Moreno: Rosita Alverio
Harry Morgan: Harry Bratsburg
Paul Muni: Muni Weisenfreund
Mike Nichols: Michael Igor Peschowsky
Chuck Norris: Carlos Ray
Sheree North: Dawn Bethel
Hugh O'Brian: Hugh Krampke
Maureen O'Hara: Maureen Fitzsimmons
Patti Page: Clara Ann Fowler
Jack Palance: Walter Palanuik
Bert Parks: Bert Jacobson
Minnie Pearl: Sarah Ophelia Cannon
Bernadette Peters: Bernadette Lazzaro
Edith Piaf: Edith Gassion
Slim Pickens: Louis Lindley
Mary Pickford: Gladys Smith
Stephanie Powers: Stefania Federkiewicz
Paula Prentiss: Paula Ragusa
Robert Preston: Robert Preston Meservey
Prince: Prince Rogers Nelson
Tony Randall: Leonard Rosenberg
Martha Raye: Margaret O'Reed
Donna Reed: Donna Belle Mullenger
Della Reese: Delloreese Patricia Early
Joan Rivers: Joan Sandra Molinsky
Edward G. Robinson: Emmanuel Goldenberg
Ginger Rogers: Virginia McMath
Roy Rogers: Leonard Slye
Mickey Rooney: Joe Yule Jr.
Lillian Russell: Helen Leonard
Theresa Russell: Theresa Paup
Winona Ryder: Winona Horowitz

Soupy Sales: Milton Hines
Susan Sarandon: Susan Tomaling
Randolph Scott: George Randolph Crane
Jane Seymour: Joyce Frankenberg
Omar Sharif: Michael Shalhoub
Charlie Sheen: Carlos Irwin Estevez
Martin Sheen: Ramon Estevez
Beverly Sills: Belle Silverman
Talia Shire: Talia Coppola
Phil Silvers: Philip Silversmith
Sinbad: David Atkins
Suzanne Somers: Suzanne Mahoney
Ann Sothern: Harriette Lake
Robert Stack: Robert Modini
Barbara Stanwyck: Ruby Stevens
Jean Stapleton: Jeanne Murray
Ringo Starr: Richard Starkey
Connie Stevens: Concetta Ingolia
Sting: Gordon Sumner
Donna Summer: La Donna Gaines
Rip Taylor: Charles Elmer Jr.
Robert Taylor: Spangler Brugh
Danny Thomas: Muzyad Yakhoob, later Amos Jacobs
Randy Travis: Randy Traywick
Sophie Tucker: Sophia Kalish
Tina Turner: Annie Mae Bullock
Conway Twitty: Harold Lloyd Jenkins
Rudolph Valentino: Rudolpho D'Antonguolla
Frankie Valli: Frank Castelluccio
David Wayne: Wayne McMeekan
John Wayne: Marion Morrison
Clifton Webb: Webb Hollenbeck
Raquel Welch: Raquel Tejada
Gene Wilder: Jerome Silberman
Shelley Winters: Shirley Schrift
Stevie Wonder: Stevland Morris
Natalie Wood: Natasha Gurdin
Jane Wyman: Sarah Jane Fulks
Gig Young: Byron Barr

Selected Royal Families of Europe

Name (Birthplace)	Birthdate
Belgium	
King Albert II (Brussels)	6/6/34
Queen Paola (Calabria, Italy)	9/11/37
Prince Philippe (Brussels)	4/15/60
Princess Astrid (Brussels)	6/5/62
Prince Laurent (Brussels)	10/19/63
United Kingdom	
Queen Elizabeth II (London)	4/21/26
Prince Philip (Corfu, Greece)	6/10/21
Prince Charles (London)	11/14/48
Princess Diana (Sandringham, England)	7/1/61
Prince William (London)	6/21/82
Prince Henry (London)	9/15/84
Princess Anne (London)	8/15/50
Prince Andrew (London)	2/19/60
Princess Beatrice (London)	8/8/88
Princess Eugenie (London)	3/23/90
Prince Edward (London)	3/1/64
Princess Margaret (Glamis, Scotland)	8/21/30
Denmark	
Queen Margrethe II (Copenhagen)	4/16/40
Prince Henrik (France)	—
Prince Frederik (Copenhagen)	5/26/68
Prince Joachim (Copenhagen)	6/7/69
Liechtenstein	
Prince Hans-Adam II (Liechtenstein)	2/14/45
Countess Marie	—
Crown Prince Alois (Liechtenstein)	6/11/68
Prince Maximilian (Liechtenstein)	5/16/69
Prince Constantin (Liechtenstein)	3/15/72
Princess Tatjana (Liechtenstein)	4/10/73
Luxembourg	
Grand Duke Jean (Berg Castle, Luxembourg)	1/5/21
Princess Joséphine-Charlotte (Belgium)	10/11/27

Name (Birthplace)	Birthdate
Princess Marie-Astrid (Luxembourg)	2/17/54
Prince Henri (Luxembourg)	4/16/55
Prince Jean (Luxembourg)	5/15/57
Princess Margaretha (Luxembourg)	5/15/57
Prince Guillaume (Luxembourg)	5/1/63
Monaco	
Prince Rainier III (Monaco)	5/31/23
Prince Albert (Monte Carlo)	3/14/58
Princess Caroline (Monte Carlo)	1/23/57
Princess Stephanie (Monaco-Ville, Monaco)	2/1/65
Netherlands	
Queen Beatrix (Baarn, Netherlands)	1/31/38
Prince Claus (Germany)	6/9/26
Prince Willem-Alexander (Netherlands)	4/27/67
Prince Johan Friso (Netherlands)	9/25/68
Prince Constantijn (Netherlands)	10/11/69
Norway	
King Harald V (Skaugum, Norway)	2/21/37
Queen Sonja (Oslo)	7/4/37
Princess Märtha Louise (Oslo)	9/22/71
Crown Prince Haakon (Oslo)	7/20/73
Spain	
King Juan Carlos I (Rome, Italy)	1/5/38
Princess Sofía (Athens, Greece)	11/2/38
Princess Elena (Madrid)	12/20/63
Princess Cristina (Madrid)	6/13/65
Crown Prince Felipe (Madrid)	1/30/68
Sweden	
King Carl XVI Gustav (Stockholm)	4/30/46
Queen Silvia	12/23/43
Princess Victoria (Stockholm)	7/14/77
Prince Carl Philip (Stockholm)	5/13/79
Princess Madeleine (Stockholm)	6/10/82

POPULATION

How America Is Changing — The View From the Census Bureau, 1995

by
Dr. Martha Farnsworth Riche
Director, Bureau of the Census
U.S. Department of Commerce

Gaze a few decades into the future and chances are you would find an America that looks quite a bit different. We at the Census Bureau don't have a crystal ball, but the data we collect give us an idea of what the future may hold—if current trends continue. Here's what we're finding.

We're More Racially and Ethnically Diverse

On Apr. 1, 1995, 9.2 million (4%) of us were Asian or Pacific Islander; blacks numbered 33.0 million, or 13%, of the population; and the American Indian/Eskimo/Aleut populations made up about 2.2 million (1%). An estimated 193.3 million people (74%) considered themselves non-Hispanic white. About 26.8 million of us (10%) were of Hispanic origin (persons of Hispanic origin may be of any race).

Things have changed in a decade and a half. The 1980 census found that 2% of Americans were Asian or Pacific Islander; 12%, black; 1%, American Indian, Eskimo, or Aleut; and 80%, non-Hispanic white. Six percent of all Americans were Hispanic.

Newcomers Arrive Every Day

We have a higher proportion of immigrants than at any time since before World War II. In 1990, about 20 million of us, or 8%, were not born in the U.S., but called it home. This 1990 figure was higher than the 5% in 1970, and the highest percentage since 1940, when it stood at 9%. More than 4 million of us were born in Mexico, making it the most common country of birth among those born in other countries. In 1994, net immigration accounted for 30% of our population growth.

We Speak With Many Voices

In 1990, 31.8 million of us, or 14%, aged 5 years and older, spoke a language other than English at home, more than the 23.1 million, or 11%, a decade earlier. More than half these persons spoke Spanish.

We're Getting Older

Between 1960 and 1994, the total U.S. population grew 45%. The population aged 65 years and older, on the other hand, climbed 100%! The elderly population rose from 17 million, or one in 11 of us, in 1960 to 33 million, or one in 8, in 1994. At the same time, the proportion of Americans 18 years of age or younger declined from 36% to 26%. These changes are reflected in our median age, which increased from 30 years to 34 years during the period.

The Married-Couple Family Is Becoming Less Prevalent

Of our 97 million households in 1994, 71% contained families. Married couples maintained about 78% of families, down from 87% in 1970. In contrast, families maintained by a woman without a husband present in the household rose from 11% of all families in 1970 to 18% in 1994.

These transformations can be explained by changes in our marital status. Back in 1970, 75% of men and 69% of women were married; by 1994, the corresponding percentages had declined to 63% and 59%.

As a result of these changes, children are now less likely to live with 2 parents. About 73% did in 1994, down from 85% in 1970. On the other hand, the percentage of children living only with their mother rose from 11% to 22% during the same period. Likewise, the share who lived only with their father went from 1% to 3%.

With more children living with only one parent, child support awards are more commonplace. In 1992, approximately 5.5 million women and 648,000 men had been awarded child support. Of the 4.9 million women actually due payments in 1991, 76% received at least a portion of the amount they were owed. The corresponding rate for the 443,000 men owed payments was 63%. Women who received child support in 1991 were paid an average of $3,011 that year, one-third more than their male counterparts ($2,292). Overall, of the $17.7 billion due in child support in 1991, $11.9 billion was paid.

More Women Are Moving Into the Labor Force

About 59% of women aged 16 years and older were in the labor force in 1994, up from 52% in 1980; for men, meanwhile, the corresponding proportion declined from 77% in 1980 to 75% in 1994.

As increasing numbers of women move into the labor force, child care is becoming an even greater concern. In 1991, families with employed mothers and preschool-age children spent 7% of their income on child care.

About two-thirds of these children were cared for in a home environment, usually by relatives or neighbors, while their parents were at work. Another 23% received care in an organized facility, such as a nursery school or day-care center. Virtually all the remaining kids (9%) were cared for by their mothers while they worked; most of these mothers worked at home.

The South and West Are Looming Larger

Between 1980 and 1994, the population of the South grew 20% while the West's population increased 32%. Both rates of increase were well above the U.S. average of 15%.

As a result, these two regions combined contained 57% of our population in 1994, up from 52% in 1980. California, with 31.4 million persons, was our most populous state in 1994, followed by Texas (18.4 million), which moved into second place for the first time. New York, with 18.2 million, was third, followed by Florida (14.0 million), and Pennsylvania (12.1 million). Our least populous states were Wyoming (476,000), Vermont (580,000), and Alaska (606,000).

Since 1980, our fastest-growing states have been Nevada, where the population has increased 82%, and Alaska, where the population has risen 51%.

Metro Living Is Now More Common

As recently as 1980, only 76% of Americans lived in metropolitan areas. Twelve years later, the percentage had risen to 80%. At the same time, our metropolitan areas themselves are becoming more suburban. About 61% of metropolitan residents lived outside central cities in 1990, up from 58% in 1980. In 1992, 54% of us lived in a metro area of at least 1 million people. Our 5 most populous metropolitan areas were scattered across the map: New York–Northern New Jersey–Long Island (19.7 million), Los Angeles–Riverside–Orange County (15.0 million), Chicago–Gary–Kenosha (8.4 million), Washington–Baltimore (6.9 million) and San Francisco–Oakland–San Jose (6.4 million).

Metropolitan areas contain central cities. Our 5 most populous cities in 1992 were New York (7.3 million), Los Angeles (3.5 million), Chicago (2.8 million), Houston (1.7 million), and Philadelphia (1.6 million).

Housing Costs Take a Bigger Bite Out of Our Income

In 1993, the U.S. had 107 million housing units, 95 million of which were occupied. People in almost two-thirds (65%) of these households owned their homes. Of the 61 million owner-occupied housing units, 37 million had a mortgage. In 1993, owners with mortgages spent a median of $799 per month, or 22% of their income, on housing costs. Eighteen years earlier, these costs consumed only 18% of their income. Owners without mortgages paid $242, or 13% of their income. In 1975 they spent 11%.

If you lived in one of the 33 million renter-occupied housing units, your housing costs, on average, were $487 per month—29% of your income. Eighteen years earlier, renters spent only 23% of their income on housing.

Overall Our Housing Has Improved

Between 1973 and 1993, the percentage of occupied homes with complete kitchen facilities increased from 98% to 99%; likewise, the percentage with complete plumbing facilities increased from 96% to 98%.

We've also become more likely to have central air conditioning (from 17% to 44%), more than one bathroom (from 31% to 53%), 3 or more bedrooms (from 50% to 56%) and a telephone (87% in 1970, 95% in 1990). And to top that off, our homes are less likely to be crowded, that is, have more than one person to a room. Only 3% were crowded in 1993, down from 6% two decades before.

We're Better Educated Than Ever Before

In 1993, about four-fifths of American adults aged 25 years and older had completed at least high school; more than one in 5 had a bachelor's degree or higher. Both figures are all-time highs. Just a generation ago, in 1970, only slightly more than one-half had received a high school diploma, and about one-tenth were college graduates.

The more education people received, the more money they made. Average annual earnings in 1992 were $12,809 for those without high school diplomas; $18,737 for persons with a diploma only; $32,629 for bachelor's degree holders, $40,368 for those with a master's degree; $54,904 for people with doctorates; and $74,560 for professional degree holders.

Poverty Has Increased Since 1989

In 1993, 39.3 million Americans, or 15.1%, were below the official government poverty level. Back in 1989, 32.4 million, or 13.1%, were poor. At the same time, median household income, adjusted for inflation, declined over the period, from $33,585 to $31,241.

For More of Us, Computers Are Part of Our Lives

In just a decade, the percentage of adults aged 18 years and older who use a computer doubled (from 18% in 1984 to 36% in 1993). This percentage should continue to rise in the future, since 59% of children aged 3 years old to 17 years old used computers in 1993. This number rose from 30% nine years earlier.

Health-Care Costs Are Rising Faster Than Income

Household health-care costs have soared in recent years. Between 1987 and 1993, the amount each household spent on health care (in current dollars) rose 56%. Health insurance costs alone increased 105%. By comparison, household income (again, in current dollar) rose only 28%. From 1987 to 1992, the percentage of persons with health insurance dropped from 87% to 85%.

The 1995 Census Test

Source: Bureau of the Census, U.S. Dept. of Commerce

On Mar. 4, 1995, the Bureau of the Census conducted the 1995 Census Test in preparation for the 22d decennial census that will be taken in the year 2000. Unlike a decennial census, which counts all persons residing in the U.S. and military vessels, the Census Test is a sample survey that was conducted in only 3 areas—2 urban and one rural. The urban sites were Paterson, NJ, and Oakland, CA. The rural site was the 6 parishes that form northwestern Louisiana: Bienville, De Soto, Jackson, Natchitoches, Red River, and Winn.

Although the 1995 Census Test design was not necessarily the design of the 2000 decennial census, it will contribute significantly toward specifying the types of questions that will be asked and the procedures that will be followed to collect data in the 2000 decennial census. New methods aimed at increasing community awareness about the planned census and automating data collection were tried during the testing period. Final results are scheduled to be released before Dec. 31, 1995.

Estimated Population of American Colonies, 1630-1780

Source: Bureau of the Census, U.S. Dept. of Commerce

(in thousands)

Colony	1780	1770	1750	1740	1720	1700	1690	1670	1650	1630
Total	2,780.4	2,148.1	1,170.8	905.6	466.2	250.9	210.4	111.9	50.4	4.6
Maine (counties)[1]	49.1	31.3	...	...	...	...	...	...	1.0	0.4
New Hampshire[2]	87.8	62.4	27.5	23.3	9.4	5.0	4.2	1.8	1.3	0.5
Vermont[3]	47.6	10.0	...	...	...	.:.	...	...	...	...
Plymouth and Massachusetts[1,2,4] . . .	268.6	235.3	188.0	151.6	91.0	55.9	56.9	35.3	15.6	0.9
Rhode Island[2]	52.9	58.2	33.2	25.3	11.7	5.9	4.2	2.2	0.8	...
Connecticut[2]	206.7	183.9	111.3	89.6	58.8	26.0	21.6	12.6	4.1	...
New York[2]	210.5	162.9	76.7	63.7	36.9	19.1	13.9	5.8	4.1	0.4
New Jersey[2]	139.6	117.4	71.4	51.4	29.8	14.0	8.0	1.0	...	...
Pennsylvania[2]	327.3	240.1	119.7	85.6	31.0	18.0	11.4	...	...	...
Delaware[2]	45.4	35.5	28.7	19.9	5.4	2.5	1.5	0.7	0.2	...
Maryland[2]	245.5	202.6	141.1	116.1	66.1	29.6	24.0	13.2	4.5	...
Virginia[2]	538.0	447.0	231.0	180.4	87.8	58.6	53.0	35.3	18.7	2.5
North Carolina[2]	270.1	197.2	73.0	51.8	21.3	10.7	7.6	3.8	...	...
South Carolina[2]	180.0	124.2	64.0	45.0	17.0	5.7	3.9	0.2	...	...
Georgia[2]	56.1	23.4	5.2	2.0	...	...	...	...	...	...
Kentucky[5]	45.0	15.7	...	...	...	...	...	...	...	...
Tennessee[6]	10.0	1.0	...	...	...	...	...	...	...	...

(1) For 1660-1750, Maine counties included with Massachusetts. Maine was part of Massachusetts until it became a separate state in 1820. (2) One of the original 13 states. (3) Admitted to statehood in 1791. (4) Plymouth became a part of the Province of Massachusetts in 1691. (5) Admitted to statehood in 1792. (6) Admitted to statehood in 1796.

U.S. Population by Official

State	1790[1]	1800[1]	1810[1]	1820	1830	1840	1850	1860	1870	1880	1890
AL	....	1	9	127,901	309,527	590,756	771,623	964,201	996,992	1,262,505	1,513,401
AK	....	....	....	....	....	....	....	....	....	33,426	32,052
AZ	....	....	....	....	....	....	....	....	9,658	40,440	88,243
AR	....	....	1	14,273	30,388	97,574	209,897	435,450	484,471	802,525	1,128,211
CA	....	....	....	....	....	....	92,597	379,994	560,247	864,694	1,213,398
CO	....	....	....	....	....	....	....	34,277	39,864	194,327	413,249
CT	238	251	262	275,248	297,675	309,978	370,792	460,147	537,454	622,700	746,258
DE	59	64	73	72,749	76,748	78,085	91,532	112,216	125,015	146,608	168,493
DC	....	8	16	23,336	30,261	33,745	51,687	75,080	131,700	177,624	230,392
FL	....	....	....	....	34,730	54,477	87,445	140,424	187,748	269,493	391,422
GA	83	163	252	340,989	516,823	691,392	906,185	1,057,286	1,184,109	1,542,180	1,837,353
HI	....	....	....	....	....	....	....	....	....	....	....
ID.	....	....	....	....	....	....	....	....	14,999	32,610	88,548
IL	....	....	12	55,211	157,445	476,183	851,470	1,711,951	2,539,891	3,077,871	3,826,352
IN	....	6	25	147,178	343,031	685,866	988,416	1,350,428	1,680,637	1,978,301	2,192,404
IA	....	....	....	....	....	43,112	192,214	674,913	1,194,020	1,624,615	1,912,297
KS	....	....	....	....	....	....	....	107,206	364,399	996,096	1,428,108
KY	74	221	407	564,317	687,917	779,828	982,405	1,155,684	1,321,011	1,648,690	1,858,635
LA	....	....	77	153,407	215,739	352,411	517,762	708,002	726,915	939,946	1,118,588
ME	97	152	229	298,335	399,455	501,793	583,169	628,279	626,915	648,936	661,086
MD	320	342	381	407,350	447,040	470,019	583,034	687,049	780,894	934,943	1,042,390
MA	379	423	472	523,287	610,408	737,699	994,514	1,231,066	1,457,351	1,783,085	2,238,947
MI	....	....	5	8,896	31,639	212,267	397,654	749,113	1,184,059	1,636,937	2,093,890
MN	....	....	....	....	....	....	6,077	172,023	439,706	780,773	1,310,283
MS	....	8	31	75,448	136,621	375,651	606,526	791,305	827,922	1,131,597	1,289,600
MO	....	....	20	66,586	140,455	383,702	682,044	1,182,012	1,721,295	2,168,380	2,679,185
MT	....	....	....	....	....	....	....	....	20,595	39,159	142,924
NE	....	....	....	....	....	....	....	28,841	122,993	452,402	1,062,656
NV	....	....	....	....	....	....	....	6,857	42,491	62,266	47,355
NH	142	184	214	244,161	269,328	284,574	317,976	326,073	318,300	346,991	376,530
NJ	184	211	246	277,575	320,823	373,306	489,555	672,035	906,096	1,131,116	1,444,933
NM	....	....	....	....	....	....	61,547	93,516	91,874	119,565	160,282
NY	340	589	959	1,372,812	1,918,608	2,428,921	3,097,394	3,880,735	4,382,759	5,082,871	6,003,174
NC	394	478	556	638,829	737,987	753,419	869,039	992,622	1,071,361	1,399,750	1,617,949
ND	....	....	....	....	....	....	....	....	2,4052	36,909	190,983
OH	....	45	231	581,434	937,903	1,519,467	1,980,329	2,339,511	2,665,260	3,198,062	3,672,329
OK	....	....	....	....	....	....	....	....	....	....	258,657
OR	....	....	....	....	....	....	12,093	52,465	90,923	174,768	317,704
PA	434	602	810	1,049,458	1,348,233	1,724,033	2,311,786	2,906,215	3,521,951	4,282,891	5,258,113
RI	69	69	77	83,059	97,199	108,830	147,545	174,620	217,353	276,531	345,506
SC	249	346	415	502,741	581,185	594,398	668,507	703,708	705,606	995,577	1,151,149
SD	....	....	....	....	....	....	....	....	4,8372	11,7762	348,600
TN	36	106	262	422,823	681,904	829,210	1,002,717	1,109,801	1,258,520	1,542,359	1,767,518
TX	....	....	....	....	....	....	212,592	604,215	818,579	1,591,749	2,235,527
UT	....	....	....	....	....	....	11,380	40,273	86,786	143,963	210,779
VT	85	154	218	235,981	280,652	291,948	314,120	315,098	330,551	332,286	332,422
VA	692	808	878	938,261	1,044,054	1,025,227	1,119,348	1,219,630	1,225,163	1,512,565	1,655,980
WA	....	....	....	....	....	....	1,201	11,594	23,955	75,116	357,232
WV	56	79	105	136,808	176,924	224,537	302,313	376,688	442,014	618,457	762,794
WI	....	....	....	....	....	30,945	305,391	775,881	1,054,670	1,315,497	1,693,330
WY	....	....	....	....	....	....	....	....	9,118	20,789	62,555
U.S. ...	3,929	5,308	7,240	9,638,453	12,860,702	17,063,353[3]	23,191,876	31,443,321[3]	38,558,371	50,189,209	62,979,766

Note: Where possible, population shown is that of 1990 area of state. Members of the Armed Forces overseas or other U.S. nationals are not included.
(1) Totals for 1790, 1800, and 1810 are in thousands. (2) 1860 figure is for Dakota Territory; 1870 figures are for parts of Dakota Territory. (3) U.S. total includes persons (5,318 in 1830 and 6,100 in 1840) on public ships in the service of the U.S. not credited to any region, division, or state.

Congressional Apportionment

Source: Bureau of the Census, U.S. Dept. of Commerce

State	1990	1980	State	1990	1980	State	1990	1980	State	1990	1980	State	1990	1980
AL	7	7	ID	2	2	MN	8	8	ND	1	1	VT	1	1
AK	1	1	IL	20	22	MS	5	5	OH	19	21	VA	11	10
AZ	6	5	IN	10	10	MO	9	9	OK	6	6	WA	9	8
AR	4	4	IA	5	6	MT	1	2	OR	5	5	WV	3	4
CA	52	45	KS	4	5	NE	3	3	PA	21	23	WI	9	9
CO	6	6	KY	6	7	NV	2	2	RI	2	2	WY	1	1
CT	6	6	LA	7	8	NH	2	2	SC	6	6			
DE	1	1	ME....	2	2	NJ	13	14	SD	1	1	**Totals**	**435**	**435**
FL.....	23	19	MD ...	8	8	NM	3	3	TN	9	9			
GA	11	10	MA....	10	11	NY	31	34	TX	30	27			
HI	2	2	MI	16	18	NC	12	11	UT....	3	3			

The Constitution, in Article 1, Section 2, provided for a census of the population every 10 years to establish a basis for apportionment of representatives among the states. This apportionment largely determines the number of electoral votes allotted to each state.

The number of representatives of each state in Congress is determined by the state's population, but each state is entitled to one representative regardless of population. A congressional apportionment has been made after each decennial census except that of 1920.

Under provisions of a law that became effective Nov. 15, 1941, representatives are apportioned by the method of equal proportions. In the application of this method, the apportionment is made so that the average population per representative has the least possible variation between one state and any other. The first House of Representatives, in 1789, had 65 members, as provided by the Constitution. As the population grew, the number of representatives was increased, but the total membership has been fixed at 435 since the apportionment based on the 1910 census.

Census, 1790-1990

1900	1910	1920	1930	1940	1950	1960	1970	1980	1990
1,828,697	2,138,093	2,348,174	2,646,248	2,832,961	3,061,743	3,266,740	3,444,354	3,894,025	4,040,587
63,592	64,356	55,036	59,278	72,524	128,643	226,167	302,583	401,851	550,043
122,931	204,354	334,162	435,573	499,261	749,587	1,302,161	1,775,399	2,716,546	3,665,228
1,311,564	1,574,449	1,752,204	1,854,482	1,949,387	1,909,511	1,786,272	1,923,322	2,286,357	2,350,725
1,485,053	2,377,549	3,426,861	5,677,251	6,907,387	10,586,223	15,717,204	19,971,069	23,667,764	29,760,021
539,700	799,024	939,629	1,035,791	1,123,296	1,325,089	1,753,947	2,209,596	2,889,735	3,294,394
908,420	1,114,756	1,380,631	1,606,903	1,709,242	2,007,280	2,535,234	3,032,217	3,107,564	3,287,116
184,735	202,322	223,003	238,380	266,505	318,085	446,292	548,104	594,338	666,168
278,718	331,069	437,571	486,869	663,091	802,178	763,956	756,668	638,432	606,900
528,542	752,619	968,470	1,468,211	1,897,414	2,771,305	4,951,560	6,791,418	9,746,961	12,937,926
2,216,331	2,609,121	2,895,832	2,908,506	3,123,723	3,444,578	3,943,116	4,587,930	5,462,982	6,478,216
154,001	191,874	255,881	368,300	422,770	499,794	632,772	769,913	964,691	1,108,229
161,772	325,594	431,866	445,032	524,873	588,637	667,191	713,015	944,127	1,006,749
4,821,550	5,638,591	6,485,280	7,630,654	7,897,241	8,712,176	10,081,158	11,110,285	11,427,409	11,430,602
2,516,462	2,700,876	2,930,390	3,238,503	3,427,796	3,934,224	4,662,498	5,195,392	5,490,214	5,544,159
2,231,853	2,224,771	2,404,021	2,470,939	2,538,268	2,621,073	2,757,537	2,825,368	2,913,808	2,776,755
1,470,495	1,690,949	1,769,257	1,880,999	1,801,028	1,905,299	2,178,611	2,249,071	2,364,236	2,477,574
2,147,174	2,289,905	2,416,630	2,614,589	2,845,627	2,944,806	3,038,156	3,220,711	3,660,324	3,685,296
1,381,625	1,656,388	1,798,509	2,101,593	2,363,880	2,683,516	3,257,022	3,644,637	4,206,116	4,219,973
694,466	742,371	768,014	797,423	847,226	913,774	969,265	993,722	1,125,043	1,227,928
1,188,044	1,295,346	1,449,661	1,631,526	1,821,244	2,343,001	3,100,689	3,923,897	4,216,933	4,781,468
2,805,346	3,366,416	3,852,356	4,249,614	4,316,721	4,690,514	5,148,578	5,689,170	5,737,093	6,016,425
2,420,982	2,810,173	3,668,412	4,842,325	5,256,106	6,371,766	7,823,194	8,881,826	9,262,044	9,295,297
1,751,394	2,075,708	2,387,125	2,563,953	2,792,300	2,982,483	3,413,864	3,806,103	4,075,970	4,375,099
1,551,270	1,797,114	1,790,618	2,009,821	2,183,796	2,178,914	2,178,141	2,216,994	2,520,770	2,573,216
3,106,665	3,293,335	3,404,055	3,629,367	3,784,664	3,954,653	4,319,813	4,677,623	4,916,766	5,117,073
243,329	376,053	548,889	537,606	559,456	591,024	674,767	694,409	786,690	799,065
1,066,300	1,192,214	1,296,372	1,377,963	1,315,834	1,325,510	1,411,330	1,485,333	1,569,825	1,578,385
42,335	81,875	77,407	91,058	110,247	160,083	285,278	488,738	800,508	1,201,833
411,588	430,572	443,083	465,293	491,524	533,242	606,921	737,681	920,610	1,109,252
1,883,669	2,537,167	3,155,900	4,041,334	4,160,165	4,835,329	6,066,782	7,171,112	7,365,011	7,730,188
195,310	327,301	360,350	423,317	531,818	681,187	951,023	1,017,055	1,303,302	1,515,069
7,268,894	9,113,614	10,385,227	12,588,066	13,479,142	14,830,192	16,782,304	18,241,391	17,558,165	17,990,455
1,893,810	2,206,287	2,559,123	3,170,276	3,571,623	4,061,929	4,556,155	5,084,411	5,880,095	6,628,637
319,146	577,056	646,872	680,845	641,935	619,636	632,446	617,792	652,717	638,800
4,157,545	4,767,121	5,759,394	6,646,697	6,907,612	7,946,627	9,706,397	10,657,423	10,797,603	10,847,115
790,391	1,657,155	2,028,283	2,396,040	2,336,434	2,233,351	2,328,284	2,559,463	3,025,487	3,145,585
413,536	672,765	783,389	953,786	1,089,684	1,521,341	1,768,687	2,091,533	2,633,156	2,842,321
6,302,115	7,665,111	8,720,017	9,631,350	9,900,180	10,498,012	11,319,366	11,800,766	11,864,720	11,881,643
428,556	542,610	604,397	687,497	713,346	791,896	859,488	949,723	947,154	1,003,464
1,340,316	1,515,400	1,683,724	1,738,765	1,899,804	2,117,027	2,382,594	2,590,713	3,120,729	3,486,703
401,570	583,888	636,547	692,849	642,961	652,740	680,514	666,257	690,768	696,004
2,020,616	2,184,789	2,337,885	2,616,556	2,915,841	3,291,718	3,567,089	3,926,018	4,591,023	4,877,185
3,048,710	3,896,542	4,663,228	5,824,715	6,414,824	7,711,194	9,579,677	11,198,655	14,225,513	16,986,510
276,749	373,351	449,396	507,847	550,310	688,862	890,627	1,059,273	1,461,037	1,722,850
343,641	355,956	352,428	359,611	359,231	377,747	389,881	444,732	511,456	562,758
1,854,184	2,061,612	2,309,187	2,421,851	2,677,773	3,318,680	3,966,949	4,651,448	5,346,797	6,187,358
518,103	1,141,990	1,356,621	1,563,396	1,736,191	2,378,963	2,853,214	3,413,244	4,132,353	4,866,692
958,800	1,221,119	1,463,701	1,729,205	1,901,974	2,005,552	1,860,421	1,744,237	1,950,186	1,793,477
2,069,042	2,333,860	2,632,067	2,939,006	3,137,587	3,434,575	3,951,777	4,417,821	4,705,642	4,891,769
92,531	145,965	194,402	225,565	250,742	290,529	330,066	332,416	469,557	453,588
76,212,168	92,228,496	106,021,537	123,202,624	132,164,569	151,325,798	179,323,175	203,302,031	226,542,203	248,709,873

U.S. Center of Population, 1790-1990

Source: Bureau of the Census, U.S. Dept. of Commerce

Center of Population is that point which may be considered as center of population gravity of the U.S. or that point upon which the U.S. would balance if it were a rigid plane without weight and the population distributed thereon with each individual being assumed to have equal weight and to exert an influence on a central point proportional to his or her distance from that point. The 1990 center is 818.6 miles from the 1790 center of population and is 39.5 miles SW of the 1980 center.

Year	N Lat ° ′ ″			W Long ° ′ ″			Approximate location
1790	39	16	30	76	11	12	23 miles east of Baltimore, MD
1800	39	16	6	76	56	30	18 miles west of Baltimore, MD
1810	39	11	30	77	37	12	40 miles northwest by west of Washington, DC (in VA)
1820	39	5	42	78	33	0	16 miles east of Moorefield, WV[1]
1830	38	57	54	79	16	54	19 miles west-southwest of Moorefield, WV[1]
1840	39	2	0	80	18	0	16 miles south of Clarksburg, WV[1]
1850	38	59	0	81	19	0	23 miles southeast of Parkersburg, WV[1]
1860	39	0	24	82	48	48	20 miles south by east of Chillicothe, OH
1870	39	12	0	83	35	42	48 miles east by north of Cincinnati, OH
1880	39	4	8	84	39	40	8 miles west by south of Cincinnati, OH (in KY)
1890	39	11	56	85	32	53	20 miles east of Columbus, IN
1900	39	9	36	85	48	54	6 miles southeast of Columbus, IN
1910	39	10	12	86	32	20	In the city of Bloomington, IN
1920	39	10	21	86	43	15	8 miles south-southeast of Spencer, Owen County, IN
1930	39	3	45	87	8	6	3 miles northeast of Linton, Greene County, IN
1940	38	56	54	87	22	35	2 miles southeast by east of Carlisle, Haddon township, Sullivan Co., IN
1950 (Inc. Alaska & Hawaii)	38	48	15	88	22	8	3 miles northeast of Louisville, Clay County, IL
1960	38	35	58	89	12	35	6 1/2 miles northwest of Centralia, Clinton Co., IL
1970	38	27	47	89	42	22	5 miles east southeast of Mascoutah, St. Clair County, IL
1980	38	8	13	90	34	26	1/4 mile west of De Soto, Jefferson Co., MO
1990	37	52	20	91	12	55	9.7 miles northwest of Steelville, MO

(1) West Virginia was set off from Virginia on Dec. 31, 1862, and was admitted as a state on June 20, 1863.

Race and Hispanic Origin for the U.S., 1990 and 1980

Source: Bureau of the Census, U.S. Dept. of Commerce

	1990 Census		1980 Census		Percentage change
	Number	Percent	Number	Percent	1980-1990
Race					
All persons........................	248,709,873	100.0	226,545,805	100.0	9.8
White................................	199,686,070	80.3	188,371,622	83.1	6.0
Black................................	29,986,060	12.1	26,495,025	11.7	13.2
American Indian, Eskimo, or Aleut	1,959,234	0.8	1,420,400	0.6	37.9
American Indian......................	1,878,285	0.8	1,364,033	0.6	37.7
Eskimo............................	57,152	0.0	42,162	0.0	35.6
Aleut.............................	23,797	0.0	14,205	0.0	67.5
Asian-Pacific Islander	7,273,662	2.9	3,500,439[1]	1.5	107.8
Chinese...........................	1,645,472	0.7	806,040	0.4	104.1
Filipino	1,406,770	0.6	774,652	0.3	81.6
Japanese	847,562	0.3	700,974	0.3	20.9
Asian Indian........................	815,447	0.3	361,531	0.2	125.6
Korean	798,849	0.3	354,593	0.2	125.3
Vietnamese........................	614,547	0.2	261,729	0.1	134.8
Hawaiian..........................	211,014	0.1	166,814	0.1	26.5
Samoan...........................	62,964	0.0	41,948	0.0	50.1
Guamanian	49,345	0.0	32,158	0.0	53.4
Other Asian-Pacific Islander	821,692	0.3	(NA)	(NA)	(NA)
Other race	9,804,847	3.9	6,758,319	3.0	45.1
Hispanic origin					
Hispanic origin[2].......................	22,354,059	9.0	14,608,673	6.4	53.0
Mexican...........................	13,495,938	5.4	8,740,439	3.9	54.4
Puerto Rican	2,727,754	1.1	2,013,945	0.9	35.4
Cuban............................	1,043,932	0.4	803,226	0.4	30.0
Other Hispanic......................	5,086,435	2.0	3,051,063	1.3	66.7
Not of Hispanic origin	226,355,814	91.0	211,937,132	93.6	6.8

NA=Not available from 1980 100% tabulations. (1) The 1980 numbers for Asian-Pacific Islanders in this table are not entirely comparable with 1990 counts. The 1980 count of 3,500,439 Asian-Pacific Islanders based on 100% tabulations includes only the 9 specific Asian-Pacific Islander groups listed separately in the 1980 race item. The 1980 total Asian-Pacific Islander population of 3,726,440 from sample tabulations is comparable to the 1990 count; these figures include groups not listed separately in the race item on the 1980 census form. (2) Persons of Hispanic origin may be of any race.

U.S. Population, by Age, Sex, and Household, 1990

Source: Bureau of the Census, U.S. Dept. of Commerce; 1990 Census

Total population.................	**248,709,873**	**Sex**	
Age		Male..............................	121,239,418
Under 5 years	18,354,443	Female	127,470,455
5 to 17 years	45,249,989	**Households by type**	
18 to 20 years	11,726,868	**Total households**.................	**91,947,410**
21 to 24 years	15,010,898	Family households (families)	64,517,947
25 to 44 years	80,754,835	Married-couple families	50,708,322
45 to 54 years	25,223,086	Percentage of total households	55.1
55 to 59 years	10,531,756	Other family, male householder.........	3,143,582
60 to 64 years	10,616,167	Other family, female householder	10,666,043
65 to 74 years	18,106,558	Nonfamily households	27,429,463
75 to 84 years	10,055,108	Percentage of total households........	29.8
85 years and over	3,080,165	Householder living alone	22,580,420
		Householder 65 years and over	8,824,845
Median age...........................	32.9	Persons living in households.............	242,012,129
Under 18 years	63,604,432	Persons per household...............	2.63
Percentage of total population.	25.6	Persons living in group quarters	6,697,744
65 years and over	31,241,831	Institutionalized persons..............	3,334,018
Percentage of total population.	12.6	Other persons in group quarters	3,363,726

Definitions of Race and Hispanic Origin Groups

Source: Bureau of the Census, U.S. Dept. of Commerce

Race

The concept of race as used by the Census Bureau reflects self-identification. It does not denote any clear-cut scientific definition of biological stock. The data for race represent self-classification by people according to the race with which they most closely identify.

Persons identified their race by classifying themselves in one of the categories listed, that is, white, black, American Indian, Eskimo, Aleut, Chinese, Filipino, Japanese, Asian Indian, Korean, Vietnamese, Hawaiian, Samoan, Guamanian, Other API, or Other race. If persons did not identify with any of the given race categories, they were directed to identify as "Other API" (API means Asian-Pacific Islander) or "Other race" and to write in the name of their race in the space provided. Thus, data for the Asian-Pacific Islander groups not listed on the census questionnaire but contained in Census Bureau tables—Cambodian, Hmong, Laotian, Thai, Bangladeshi, Burmese, Indonesian, Malayan, Okinawan, Pakistani, Sri Lankan, Tongan, Tahitian, Northern Mariana Islander, Palauan, and Fijian—were tabulated from write-in responses. The "Other race" category includes persons not included in the race categories described above. Persons reporting in the "Other race" category and providing write-in entries such as a Hispanic origin group (i.e., Mexican, Cuban, Puerto Rican) are included.

Spanish/Hispanic Origin

Persons of Spanish/Hispanic origin or descent are those who classify themselves in one of the specific Hispanic origin categories listed on the census questionnaire—for example, Mexican, Puerto Rican, or Cuban—as well as those who indicated that they were of other Spanish/Hispanic origin.

Persons reporting "Other Spanish/Hispanic" are those whose origins are from other Spanish-speaking countries of the Caribbean, of Central or South America, or from Spain or were persons identifying themselves generally as Spanish, Spanish-American, Hispano, Hispanic, Latino, etc.

Spanish origin and race are distinct; thus, persons of Spanish/Hispanic origin may be of any race.

U.S. Area and Population: 1790-1990

Source: Bureau of the Census, U.S. Dept. of Commerce

Census date	Area (sq mi)			Population		Increase over preceding census	
	Gross	Land	Water	Number	per sq mi of land	Number	%
1990 (Apr. 1)	3,787,428	3,536,344	251,084[1]	248,709,873	70.3	22,164,068	9.8
1980 (Apr. 1)	3,618,770	3,539,289	79,481	226,542,203	64.0	23,240,172	11.4
1970 (Apr. 1)	3,618,770	3,536,855	81,915	203,302,031	57.5	23,978,856	13.4
1960 (Apr. 1)	3,618,770	3,540,911	77,859	179,323,175	50.6	27,997,377	18.5
1950 (Apr. 1)	3,618,770	3,552,206	66,564	151,325,798	42.6	19,161,229	14.5
1940 (Apr. 1)	3,618,770	3,554,608	64,162	132,164,569	37.2	8,961,945	7.3
1930 (Apr. 1)	3,618,770	3,551,608	67,162	123,202,624	34.7	17,181,087	16.2
1920 (Jan. 1)	3,618,770	3,546,931	71,839	106,021,537	29.9	13,793,041	15.0
1910 (Apr. 15)	3,618,770	3,547,045	71,725	92,228,496	26.0	16,016,328	21.0
1900 (June 1)	3,618,770	3,547,314	71,456	76,212,168	21.5	13,232,402	21.0
1890 (June 1)	3,612,299	3,540,705	71,594	62,979,766	17.8	12,790,557	25.5
1880 (June 1)	3,612,299	3,540,705	71,594	50,189,209	14.2	11,630,838	30.2
1870 (June 1)	3,612,299	3,540,705	71,594	38,558,371	10.9	7,115,050	22.6
1860 (June 1)	3,021,295	2,969,640	51,655	31,443,321	10.6	8,251,445	35.6
1850 (June 1)	2,991,655	2,940,042	51,613	23,191,876	7.9	6,122,423	35.9
1840 (June 1)	1,792,552	1,749,462	43,090	17,069,453	9.8	4,203,433	32.7
1830 (June 1)	1,792,552	1,749,462	43,090	12,866,020	7.4	3,227,567	33.5
1820 (June 1)	1,792,552	1,749,462	43,090	9,638,453	5.5	2,398,572	33.1
1810 (Aug. 6)	1,722,685	1,681,828	40,857	7,239,881	4.3	1,931,398	36.4
1800 (Aug. 4)	891,364	864,746	26,618	5,308,483	6.1	1,379,269	35.1
1790 (Aug. 2)	891,364	864,746	26,618	3,929,214	4.5	—	—

(1) Comprises inland, coastal, Great Lakes, and territorial water. Data for prior years cover inland water only.

Note: Percent changes are computed on basis of change in population since preceding census date, and period covered therefore is not always exactly 10 years.

Population density figures given for various years represent the area within the boundaries of the U.S. that was under the jurisdiction on date in question, including in some cases considerable areas not organized or settled and not covered by the census. In 1870, for example, Alaska was not covered by the census.

Revised figure of 39,818,449 for the 1870 population includes adjustments for undernumeration in the southern states. On the basis of the revised figure, the population increased by 8,375,128, or 26.6%, between 1860 and 1870, and by 10,370,760, or 26.1%, between 1870 and 1880.

Resident Population, by Sex, Race, Residence, and Median Age, 1790-1994

Source: Bureau of the Census, U.S. Dept. of Commerce

(in thousands, except as indicated)

Date	Sex		Race				Residence		Median Age (years)		
	Male	Female	White	Black Number	Black Percent	Other	Urban	Rural	All races	White	Black
Conterminous U.S.[1]											
1790 (Aug. 2)	NA	NA	3,172	757	19.3	NA	202	3,728	NA	NA	NA
1810 (Aug. 6)	NA	NA	5,862	1,378	19.0	NA	525	6,714	NA	16.0	NA
1820 (Aug. 7)	4,897	4,742	7,867	1,772	18.4	NA	693	8,945	16.7	16.5	17.2
1840 (June 1)	8,689	8,381	14,196	2,874	16.8	NA	1,845	15,224	17.8	17.9	17.3
1860 (June 1)	16,085	15,358	26,923	4,442	14.1	79	6,217	25,227	19.4	19.7	17.7
1870 (June 1)	19,494	19,065	33,589	4,880	12.7	89	9,902	28,656	20.2	20.4	18.5
1880 (June 1)	25,519	24,637	43,403	6,581	13.1	172	14,130	36,026	20.9	21.4	18.0
1890 (June 1)	32,237	30,711	55,101	7,489	11.9	358	22,106	40,841	22.0	22.5	17.8
1900 (June 1)	38,816	37,178	66,809	8,834	11.6	351	30,160	45,835	22.9	23.4	19.4
1920 (Jan. 1)	53,900	51,810	94,821	10,463	9.9	427	54,158	51,553	25.3	25.6	22.3
1930 (Apr. 1)	62,137	60,638	110,287	11,891	9.7	597	68,955	53,820	26.4	26.9	23.5
1940 (Apr. 1)	66,062	65,608	118,215	12,866	9.8	589	74,424	57,246	29.0	29.5	25.3
United States											
1950 (Apr. 1)	75,187	76,139	135,150	15,045	9.9	1,131	96,847	54,479	30.2	30.7	26.2
1960 (Apr. 1)	88,331	90,992	158,832	18,872	10.5	1,620	125,269	54,054	29.5	30.3	23.5
1970 (Apr. 1)[2]	98,926	104,309	178,098	22,581	11.1	2,557	149,325	53,887	28.0	28.9	22.4
1980 (Apr. 1)[3]	110,053	116,493	194,713	26,683	11.8	5,150	167,051	59,495	30.0	30.9	24.9
1983 (July 1, est)	113,647	120,145	199,420	27,867	11.9	6,505	NA	NA	30.8	31.7	25.9
1985 (July 1, est)	115,730	122,194	202,031	28,569	12.0	7,324	NA	NA	31.4	32.3	26.6
1990 (Apr. 1)	121,239	127,470	199,686	29,986	12.1	19,038	187,053	61,656	32.9	34.4	28.1
1993 (July 1, est)	125,800	131,983	214,789	32,180	12.5	10,814	NA	NA	33.7	34.7	28.7
1994 (July 1, est)	127,076	133,285	216,470	32,672	12.5	11,199	NA	NA	34.0	35.0	29.0

NA=Not available. (1) Excludes Alaska and Hawaii. (2) The revised 1970 resident population count is 203,302,031, which incorporates changes due to errors found after tabulations were completed. The race and sex data shown here reflect the official 1970 census count; the residence data come from the tabulated count. (3) The race data shown for Apr. 1, 1980, have been modified.

Population by State, 1990-94

Source: Bureau of the Census, U.S. Dept. of Commerce

State	1994 population	1990 population	Percentage change 1990-94	State	1994 population	1990 population	Percentage change 1990-94
U.S.	260,340,990	248,709,873	4.7	CO.........	3,655,647	3,294,394	11.0
CA	31,430,697	29,760,021	5.6	CT.........	3,275,251	3,287,116	−0.4
TX	18,378,185	16,986,510	8.2	OK.........	3,258,069	3,145,585	3.6
NY	18,169,051	17,990,455	1.0	OR.........	3,086,188	2,842,321	8.6
FL	13,952,714	12,937,926	7.8	IA	2,829,252	2,776,755	1.9
PA	12,052,367	11,881,643	1.4	MS.........	2,669,111	2,573,216	3.6
IL	11,751,774	11,430,602	2.8	KS.........	2,554,047	2,477,574	3.1
OH	11,102,198	10,847,115	2.4	AR.........	2,452,671	2,350,725	4.3
MI..........	9,496,147	9,295,297	2.2	UT.........	1,907,936	1,722,850	10.7
NJ	7,903,925	7,730,188	2.2	WV	1,822,021	1,793,477	1.6
NC	7,069,836	6,628,637	6.6	NM	1,653,521	1,515,069	9.1
GA	7,055,336	6,478,216	8.9	NE.........	1,622,858	1,578,385	2.8
VA	6,551,522	6,187,358	5.9	NV.........	1,457,028	1,201,833	21.2
MA	6,041,123	6,016,425	0.4	ME.........	1,240,209	1,227,928	1.0
IN..........	5,752,073	5,544,159	3.8	HI	1,178,564	1,108,229	6.3
WA	5,343,090	4,866,692	9.8	NH.........	1,136,820	1,109,252	2.5
MO.........	5,277,640	5,117,073	3.1	ID	1,133,034	1,006,749	12.5
TN	5,175,240	4,877,185	6.1	RI	996,757	1,003,464	−0.7
WI	5,081,658	4,891,769	3.9	MT.........	856,047	799,065	7.1
MD.........	5,006,265	4,781,468	4.7	SD.........	721,164	696,004	3.6
MN.........	4,567,267	4,375,099	4.4	DE.........	706,351	666,168	6.0
LA	4,315,085	4,219,973	2.2	ND.........	637,988	638,800	−0.1
AL	4,218,792	4,040,587	4.4	AK.........	606,276	550,043	10.2
AZ	4,075,052	3,665,228	11.2	VT.........	580,209	562,758	3.1
KY	3,826,794	3,685,296	3.8	DC.........	570,175	606,900	−6.1
SC	3,663,984	3,486,703	5.1	WY	475,981	453,588	4.9

Density of Population by State, 1920-90

Source: Bureau of the Census, U.S. Dept. of Commerce

(per square mile, land area only)

State	1920	1960	1980	1990	State	1920	1960	1980	1990	State	1920	1960	1980	1990
AL ..	45.8	64.2	76.6	79.6	LA ..	39.6	72.2	94.5	96.9	OK..	29.2	33.8	44.1	45.8
AK* .	0.1	0.4	0.7	1.0	ME..	25.7	31.3	36.3	39.8	OR..	8.2	18.4	27.4	29.6
AZ ..	2.9	11.5	23.9	32.3	MD..	145.8	313.5	428.7	489.2	PA ..	194.5	251.4	264.3	265.1
AR ..	33.4	34.2	43.9	45.1	MA..	479.2	657.3	733.3	767.6	RI ..	566.4	819.3	897.8	960.3
CA ..	22.0	100.4	151.4	190.8	MI ..	63.8	137.7	162.6	163.6	SC ..	55.2	78.7	103.4	115.8
CO..	9.1	16.9	27.9	31.8	MN..	29.5	43.1	51.2	55.0	SD..	8.3	9.0	9.1	9.2
CT..	286.4	520.6	637.8	678.4	MS..	38.6	46.0	53.4	54.9	TN..	56.1	86.2	111.6	118.3
DE..	113.5	225.2	307.6	340.8	MO..	49.5	62.6	71.3	74.3	TX ..	17.8	36.4	54.3	64.9
DC..	7,292.9	12,523.9	10,132.3	9,882.8	MT..	3.8	4.6	5.4	5.5	UT ..	5.5	10.8	17.8	21.0
FL ..	17.7	91.5	180.0	239.6	NE..	16.9	18.4	20.5	20.5	VT ..	38.6	42.0	55.2	60.8
GA ..	49.3	67.8	94.1	111.9	NV..	0.7	2.6	7.3	10.9	VA ..	57.4	99.6	134.7	156.3
HI* .	39.9	98.5	150.1	172.5	NH..	49.1	67.2	102.4	123.7	WA ..	20.3	42.8	62.1	73.1
ID ..	5.2	8.1	11.5	12.2	NJ ..	420.0	805.5	986.2	1,042.0	WV .	60.9	77.2	80.8	74.5
IL ..	115.7	180.4	205.3	205.6	NM ..	2.9	7.8	10.7	12.5	WI ..	47.6	72.6	86.5	90.1
IN ..	81.3	128.8	152.8	154.6	NY..	217.9	350.6	370.6	381.0	WY .	2.0	3.4	4.9	4.7
IA...	43.2	49.2	52.1	49.7	NC..	52.5	93.2	120.4	136.1	U.S.	*29.9	50.6	64.0	70.3
KS..	21.6	26.6	28.9	30.3	ND..	9.2	9.1	9.4	9.3					
KY..	60.1	76.2	92.3	92.8	OH..	141.4	236.6	263.3	264.9					

* For purposes of comparison, Alaska and Hawaii are included in above tabulation for 1920, even though not states then.

25 Largest Counties, by Population, 1990-92

Source: Bureau of the Census, U.S. Dept of Commerce

County	1994 population	1990 population	Percentage change, 1990-94	County	1994 population	1990 population	Percentage change, 1990-94
Los Angeles, CA .	9,149,840	8,863,052	3.2	San Bernardino, CA	1,553,608	1,418,380	9.5
Cook, IL	5,141,375	5,105,044	0.7	Philadelphia, PA.	1,524,338	1,585,577	−3.9
Harris, TX......	3,045,212	2,818,101	8.1	New York, NY ..	1,506,430	1,487,536	1.3
San Diego, CA ..	2,632,047	2,498,016	5.4	Middlesex, MA ..	1,403,281	1,398,468	0.3
Orange, CA	2,543,124	2,410,668	5.5	Cuyahoga, OH ..	1,403,239	1,412,140	−0.6
Maricopa, AZ ...	2,346,610	2,122,101	10.6	Broward, FL.....	1,382,983	1,255,531	10.2
Kings, NY	2,271,000	2,300,664	−1.3	Riverside, CA...	1,352,914	1,170,413	15.6
Wayne, MI	2,064,908	2,111,687	−2.2	Suffolk, NY	1,349,191	1,321,768	2.1
Dade, FL	2,025,040	1,937,194	4.5	Allegheny, PA ..	1,320,704	1,336,449	−1.2
Queens, NY	1,964,270	1,951,598	0.6	Alameda, CA ...	1,319,490	1,276,702	3.4
Dallas, TX......	1,942,303	1,852,810	4.8	Nassaua, NY ...	1,302,279	1,287,444	1.2
King, WA	1,587,505	1,507,505	5.3	Bexar, TX	1,280,062	1,185,394	8.0
Santa Clara, CA .	1,557,211	1,497,577	4.0				

Note: The following are the **smallest counties**, by 1994 population: Esmeralda, NV (1,134), Wibaux, MT (1,138), Billings, ND (1,144), Hayes, NE (1,155), Alpine, CA (1,192), Jones, SD (1,307), Terrell, TX (1,309), Prairie, MT (1,331), Eureka, NV (1,375), and Motley, TX (1,378).

Metropolitan Areas, 1990-92

Source: Bureau of the Census, U.S. Dept. of Commerce

(CMSAs and MSAs of more than 600,000 persons listed by 1992 population)

Metropolitan statistical areas (MSAs) are defined for federal statistical use by the Office of Management and Budget (OMB), with technical asistance from the Bureau of the Census. Most individual metropolitan areas over 1 million may, under specified circumstances, be subdivided into component Primary Metropolitan Statistical Areas (PMSAs), in which case the area as a whole is designated a Consolidated Metropolitan Statistical Area (CMSA). Effective June 30, 1993, the OMB designated 253 MSAs, 76 PMSAs, and 19 CMSAs for the U.S. and Puerto Rico based on standards published in the Federal Register on Mar. 30, 1990, as applied to 1990 census data.

CMSAs and MSAs	Population 1990	1992	Percentage change 1990-92
New York–Northern New Jersey–Long Island, NY–NJ–CT–PA CMSA	19,549,649	19,670,175	0.6
Los Angeles–Riverside–Orange County, CA CMSA	14,531,529	15,047,772	3.6
Chicago–Gary–Kenosha, IL–IN–WI CMSA	8,239,820	8,410,402	2.1
Washington–Baltimore, DC–MD–VA–WV CMSA	6,727,050	6,919,572	2.9
San Francisco–Oakland–San Jose, CA CMSA	6,253,311	6,409,891	2.5
Philadelphia–Wilmington–Atlantic City, PA–NJ–DE–MD CMSA	5,892,937	5,938,528	0.8
Boston–Worcester–Lawrence, MA–NH–ME–CT CMSA	5,455,403	5,438,815	–0.3
Detroit–Ann Arbor–Flint, MI CMSA	5,187,171	5,245,906	1.1
Dallas–Fort Worth, TX CMSA	4,037,282	4,214,532	4.4
Houston–Galveston–Brazoria, TX CMSA	3,731,131	3,962,365	6.2
Miami–Fort Lauderdale, FL CMSA	3,192,582	3,309,246	3.7
Atlanta, GA	2,959,950	3,142,857	6.2
Seattle–Tacoma–Bremerton, WA CMSA	2,970,328	3,131,392	5.4
Cleveland, Akron, OH CMSA	2,859,644	2,890,402	1.1
Minneapolis–St. Paul	2,538,834	2,617,973	3.1
San Diego, CA	2,498,016	2,601,055	4.1
St. Louis, MO–IL	2,492,525	2,518,528	1.0
Pittsburgh, PA	2,394,811	2,406,452	0.5
Phoenix–Mesa, AZ	2,238,480	2,330,353	4.1
Tampa–St. Petersburgh–Clearwater, FL	2,067,959	2,107,271	1.9
Denver–Boulder–Greeley, CO CMSA	1,980,140	2,089,321	5.5
Portland–Salem, OR–WA CMSA	1,793,476	1,896,895	5.8
Cincinnati–Hamilton, OH–KY–IN, CMSA	1,817,571	1,865,002	2.6
Milwaukee–Racine, WI CMSA	1,607,183	1,629,420	1.4
Kansas City, MO	1,582,875	1,616,930	2.2
Sacramento–Yolo, CA . CMSA	1,481,102	1,563,374	5.6
Norfolk–Virginia Beach–Newport News, VA–NC	1,443,244	1,496,672	3.7
Indianapolis, IN	1,380,491	1,424,050	3.2
Columbus, OH	1,345,450	1,394,067	3.6
San Antonio, TX	1,324,749	1,378,619	4.1

CMSAs and MSAs	Population 1990	1992	Percentage change 1990-92
Orlando, FL	1,224,852	1,304,700	6.5
New Orleans, LA	1,285,270	1,302,697	1.4
Charlotte–Gastonia–Rock Hill, NC–SC	1,162,093	1,212,393	4.3
Buffalo–Niagara Falls, NY	1,189,288	1,193,901	0.4
Hartford, CT	1,157,585	1,155,725	–0.2
Providence–Fall River–Warwick, RI–MA	1,134,350	1,131,133	–0.3
Salt Lake City–Odgen, UT	1,072,227	1,128,121	5.2
Rochester, NY	1,062,470	1,081,244	1.8
Greensboro–Winston–Salem–High Point, NC	1,050,304	1,078,377	2.7
Memphis, TN–AR–MS	1,007,306	1,033,813	2.6
Nashville, TN	985,026	1,023,315	3.9
Oklahoma City, OK	958,839	983,612	2.6
Las Vegas, NV–AZ	852,737	971,169	13.9
Louisville, KY–IN	948,829	967,587	2.0
Grand Rapids–Muskegon–Holland, MI	937,891	964,352	2.8
Dayton–Springfield, OH	951,270	961,547	1.1
Jacksonville, FL	906,727	952,566	5.1
Raleigh–Durham–Chapel Hill, NC	855,545	909,232	6.3
Austin–San Marcos, TX	846,227	901,048	6.5
West Palm Beach–Boca Raton, FL	863,518	900,655	4.3
Richmond–Petersburg, VA	865,640	896,068	3.5
Albany–Schenectady–Troy, NY	861,424	872,290	1.3
Honolulu, HI	836,231	863,117	3.2
Birmingham, AL	840,140	858,531	2.2
Greenville–Spartanburg–Anderson, SC	830,563	852,962	2.7
Fresno, CA	755,580	804,636	6.5
Syracuse, NY	742,177	752,397	1.4
Tulsa, OK	708,954	731,600	3.2
Tucson, AZ	666,880	690,202	3.5
Omaha, NE–IA	639,580	656,434	2.6
Scranton–Wilkes-Barre–Hazleton, PA	638,466	638,685	0.0
El Paso, TX	591,610	628,472	6.2
Albuquerque, NM	589,131	616,346	4.6
Toledo, OH	614,128	615,308	0.2
Knoxville, TN	585,960	610,482	4.2
Allentown–Bethlehem–Easton, PA	595,081	606,461	1.9
Youngstown–Warren, OH	600,895	605,863	0.8
Harrisburg–Lebanon–Carlisle, PA	587,986	601,371	2.3

Final 1990 census figures showed that the nation had 40 metropolitan areas of at least 1 million population, including 5 that reached that size since 1980. The 40 areas had 128.2 million people, or 51.5% of the U.S. population, in 1990. It is estimated that since 1990, the population of an additional metropolitan area, Nashville, TN, has increased to more than 1 million. By 1992, 54% of the population lived in metropolitan areas that had at least 1 million inhabitants.

It is estimated that 203.2 million people resided in metropolitan areas in 1992. This is an increase of more than 26.2 million (15%) since 1980, and an increase of 5.4 million (2.8%) since 1990. By comparison, the same areas grew by 10.6% in the 1970s. The population living outside metropolitan areas totaled 51.9 million in 1992, an increase of 2.2 million (4.5%) from 1980, and an increase of 920,370 (1.8%) from 1990. The metropolitan population in 1992 constituted 79.7% of the U.S. total, compared with 76.2% in 1980, and 79.4% in 1990.

Population of 100 Largest U.S. Cities

Source: Bureau of the Census, U.S. Dept. of Commerce (100 most populous cities ranked by Apr. 1990 census; revised Apr. 1995)

Rank	City	1990	1980	1970	1960	1950	1900	1850
1	New York, NY	7,322,564	7,071,639	7,895,563	7,781,984	7,891,957	3,437,202	696,115
2	Los Angeles, CA	3,485,557	2,968,528	2,811,801	2,479,015	1,970,358	102,479	1,610
3	Chicago, IL	2,783,726	3,005,072	3,369,357	3,550,404	3,620,962	1,698,575	29,963
4	Houston, TX	1,629,902	1,595,138	1,233,535	938,219	596,163	44,633	2,396
5	Philadelphia, PA	1,585,577	1,688,210	1,949,996	2,002,512	2,071,605	1,293,697	121,376
6	San Diego, CA	1,110,554	875,538	697,471	573,224	334,387	17,700	...
7	Detroit, MI	1,027,974	1,203,368	1,514,063	1,670,144	1,849,568	285,704	21,019
8	Dallas, TX	1,007,618	904,599	844,401	679,684	434,462	42,638	...
9	Phoenix, AZ	983,403	789,704	584,303	439,170	106,818	5,544	...
10	San Antonio, TX	935,393	785,940	654,153	587,718	408,442	53,321	3,488
11	San Jose, CA	782,248	629,400	459,913	204,196	95,280	21,500	...
12	Baltimore, MD	736,014	786,741	905,787	939,024	949,708	508,957	169,054
13	Indianapolis, IN	731,327	700,807	736,856	476,258	427,173	169,164	8,091
14	San Francisco, CA	723,959	678,974	715,674	740,316	775,357	342,782	34,776
15	Jacksonville, FL	635,230	540,920	504,265	201,030	204,517	28,429	1,045
16	Columbus, OH	632,945	565,021	540,025	471,316	375,901	125,560	17,882
17	Milwaukee, WI	628,088	636,297	717,372	741,324	637,392	285,315	20,061
18	Memphis, TN	610,337	646,174	623,988	497,524	396,000	102,320	8,841
19	Washington, DC	606,900	638,432	756,668	763,956	802,178	278,718	40,001
20	Boston, MA	574,283	562,994	641,071	697,197	801,444	560,892	136,881
21	Seattle, WA	516,259	493,846	530,831	557,087	467,591	80,671	...
22	El Paso, TX	515,342	425,259	322,261	276,687	130,485	15,906	...
23	Cleveland, OH	505,616	573,822	750,879	876,050	914,808	381,768	17,034
24	New Orleans, LA	496,938	557,927	593,471	627,525	570,445	287,104	116,375
25	Nashville, TN	488,374	455,651	426,029	170,874	174,307	80,865	10,165
26	Denver, CO	467,610	492,686	514,678	493,887	415,786	133,859	...
27	Austin, TX	465,648	345,890	253,539	186,545	132,459	22,258	629
28	Fort Worth, TX	447,619	385,164	393,455	356,268	278,778	26,688	...
29	Oklahoma City, OK	444,724	404,014	368,164	324,253	243,504	10,037	...
30	Portland, OR	438,802	368,148	379,967	372,676	373,628	90,426	...
31	Kansas City, MO	434,829	448,028	507,330	475,539	456,622	163,752	...
32	Long Beach, CA	429,321	361,498	358,879	344,168	250,767	2,252	...
33	Tucson, AZ	405,323	330,537	262,933	212,892	45,454	7,531	...
34	St. Louis, MO	396,685	452,801	622,236	750,026	856,796	575,238	77,860
35	Charlotte, NC	395,925	315,474	241,420	201,564	134,042	18,091	1,065
36	Atlanta, GA	393,929	425,022	495,039	487,455	331,314	89,872	2,572
37	Virginia Beach, VA	393,089	262,199	172,106	8,091	5,390	...	...
38	Albuquerque, NM	384,619	332,920	244,501	201,189	96,815	6,238	...
39	Oakland, CA	372,242	339,337	361,561	367,548	384,575	66,960	...
40	Pittsburgh, PA	369,879	423,959	520,089	604,332	676,806	321,616	46,601
41	Sacramento, CA	369,365	275,741	257,105	191,667	137,572	29,282	6,820
42	Minneapolis, MN	368,383	370,951	434,400	482,872	521,718	202,718	...
43	Tulsa, OK	367,302	360,919	330,350	261,685	182,740	1,390	...
44	Honolulu, HI	365,272	365,048	324,871	294,194	248,034	39,306	...
45	Cincinnati, OH	364,114	385,409	453,514	502,550	503,998	325,902	115,435
46	Miami, FL	358,648	346,861	334,859	291,688	249,276	1,681	...
47	Fresno, CA	354,091	217,491	165,655	133,929	91,669	12,470	...
48	Omaha, NE	335,719	313,939	346,929	301,598	251,117	102,555	...
49	Toledo, OH	332,943	354,635	383,062	318,003	303,616	131,822	3,829
50	Buffalo, NY	328,175	357,870	462,768	532,759	580,132	352,387	42,261
51	Wichita, KS	304,017	279,838	276,554	254,698	168,279	24,671	...
52	Santa Ana, CA	293,827	204,023	155,710	100,350	45,533	4,933	...
53	Mesa, AZ	288,104	152,404	63,049	33,772	16,790	722	...
54	Colorado Springs, CO	280,430	215,105	135,517	70,194	45,472	21,085	...
55	Tampa, FL	280,015	271,577	277,714	274,970	124,681	15,839	...
56	Newark, NJ	275,221	329,248	381,930	405,220	438,776	246,070	38,894
57	St. Paul, MN	272,235	270,230	309,866	313,411	311,349	163,065	1,112
58	Louisville, KY	269,555	298,694	361,706	390,639	369,129	204,731	43,194
59	Anaheim, CA	266,406	219,494	166,408	104,184	14,556	1,456	...
60	Birmingham, AL	265,347	284,413	300,910	340,887	326,037	38,415	...
61	Arlington, TX	261,717	160,113	90,229	44,775	7,692	1,079	...
62	Norfolk, VA	261,250	266,979	307,951	304,869	213,513	46,624	14,326
63	Las Vegas, NV	258,204	164,674	125,787	64,405	24,624	...	...
64	Corpus Christi, TX	257,428	232,134	204,525	167,690	108,287	4,703	...
65	St. Petersburg, FL	240,318	238,647	216,159	181,298	96,738	1,575	...
66	Rochester, NY	230,356	241,741	295,011	318,611	332,488	162,608	36,403
67	Jersey City, NJ	228,517	223,532	260,350	276,101	299,017	206,433	6,856
68	Riverside, CA	226,546	170,591	140,089	84,332	46,764	7,973	...
69	Anchorage, AK	226,338	174,431	48,081	44,237	11,254	...	...
70	Lexington-Fayette, KY	225,366	204,165	108,137	62,810	55,534	26,369	8,159
71	Akron, OH	223,019	237,177	275,425	290,351	274,605	42,728	3,266
72	Aurora, CO	222,103	158,588	74,974	48,548	11,421	202	...
73	Baton Rouge, LA	219,531	220,394	165,921	152,419	125,629	11,269	3,905
74	Raleigh, NC	212,092	150,255	122,830	93,931	65,679	13,643	4,518
75	Stockton, CA	210,943	148,283	109,963	86,321	70,853	17,506	...
76	Richmond, VA	202,798	219,214	249,332	219,958	230,310	85,050	27,570
77	Shreveport, LA	198,518	205,989	182,064	164,372	127,206	16,013	1,728
78	Jackson, MS	196,637	202,895	153,968	144,422	98,271	7,816	1,881
79	Mobile, AL	196,263	200,452	190,026	194,856	129,009	38,469	20,515
80	Des Moines, IA	193,189	191,003	201,404	208,982	177,965	62,139	...
81	Lincoln, NE	191,972	171,932	149,518	128,521	98,884	40,169	...
82	Madison, WI	190,766	170,616	171,809	126,706	96,056	19,164	1,525
83	Grand Rapids, MI	189,126	181,843	197,649	177,313	176,515	87,565	2,686
84	Yonkers, NY	188,082	195,351	204,297	190,634	152,798	47,931	...
85	Hialeah, FL	188,008	145,254	102,452	66,972	19,676	...	...

Rank	City	1990	1980	1970	1960	1950	1900	1850
86	Montgomery, AL............	187,543	177,857	133,386	134,393	106,525	30,346	8,728
87	Lubbock, TX	186,206	174,361	149,101	126,691	71,747	...	...
88	Greensboro, NC	183,894	155,642	144,076	119,574	74,389	10,035	...
89	Dayton, OH	182,005	193,536	243,023	262,332	243,872	85,333	10,977
90	Huntington Beach, CA	181,519	170,505	115,960	11,492	5,237	...	...
91	Garland, TX	180,635	138,857	81,437	38,501	10,571	819	...
92	Glendale, CA	180,038	139,060	133,000	119,000	96,000	...	...
93	Columbus, GA	178,681	169,441	155,028	116,779	79,611	17,614	9,621
94	Spokane, WA	177,165	171,300	170,516	181,608	161,721	36,848	...
95	Tacoma, WA	176,664	158,501	154,407	147,979	143,673	37,714	...
96	Little Rock, AR	175,727	159,151	132,483	107,813	102,213	38,307	2,167
97	Bakersfield, CA	174,978	105,611	69,515	56,848	...	...	...
98	Fremont, CA	173,339	131,945	100,869	43,790	...	...	...
99	Fort Wayne, IN	172,971	172,391	178,269	161,776	133,607	45,115	4,282
100	Newport News, VA	171,439	144,903	138,000	114,000	42,000	...	...

U.S. Population, by Selected Characteristics, Mar. 1993

Source: Bureau of the Census, U.S. Dept. of Commerce

Characteristic	All Races — Total	Male	Female	Black — Total	Male	Female	White — Total	Male	Female
Age									
Total (thousands) ...	254,241	124,018	130,223	320,36	15,073	16,963	190,532	93,193	97,340
Percentage of the									
population........	100.0	100.0	100.0	100.0	100.0	100.0	100.0	100.0	100.0
Under 5 years	7.8	8.2	7.4	10.2	11.0	9.5	6.9	7.3	6.6
5 to 9 years......	7.4	7.8	7.0	9.1	9.9	8.4	6.8	7.1	6.4
10 to 14 years....	7.2	7.6	6.9	9.1	9.9	8.5	6.7	7.0	6.3
15 to 19 years....	6.5	6.8	6.3	8.2	8.8	7.8	6.0	6.3	5.8
20 to 24 years....	7.0	7.1	6.9	7.8	7.8	7.9	6.6	6.7	6.5
25 to 29 years....	7.7	7.9	7.6	8.2	8.0	8.3	7.4	7.5	7.3
30 to 34 years....	8.8	8.9	8.6	8.7	8.5	8.9	8.7	8.9	8.5
35 to 44 years....	15.9	16.0	15.7	14.5	14.0	14.9	16.2	16.5	15.9
45 to 54 years....	11.2	11.2	11.3	9.1	8.6	9.6	11.9	11.9	11.8
55 to 64 years....	8.4	8.2	8.5	6.8	6.5	7.1	9.0	9.0	9.1
65 to 74 years....	7.2	6.5	7.9	5.3	4.9	5.7	8.1	7.4	8.8
75 years and older.	4.9	3.8	6.0	3.0	2.2	3.6	5.7	4.4	7.0
Marital status									
Total 15 years and									
older (thousands) ...	197,254	94,854	102,400	22,937	10,442	12,495	151,710	73,257	78,452
Percentage of the									
population........	100.0	100.0	100.0	100.0	100.0	100.0	100.0	100.0	100.0
Never married	26.5	30.3	23.0	41.9	45.5	38.9	23.4	27.3	19.8
Married, spouse									
present.......	55.0	57.1	52.9	33.1	37.0	29.8	58.7	60.9	56.7
Married, spouse									
absent........	3.1	2.8	3.5	7.3	5.4	8.8	2.2	2.1	2.4
Widowed........	6.9	2.6	11.0	8.0	4.1	11.2	7.2	2.5	11.5
Divorced........	8.4	7.1	9.7	9.8	8.0	11.3	8.5	7.3	9.7
Region (thousands)									
South...........	87,515	42,381	45,134	17,539	8,299	9,240	61,213	29,795	31,418
North and West	166,726	81,637	85,089	14,497	6,774	7,723	129,319	63,397	65,922
Northeast.........	50,726	24,459	26,267	5,294	2,462	2,832	40,815	19,757	21,059
Midwest..........	60,995	29,698	31,298	6,583	3,022	3,562	51,733	25,306	26,427
West	55,004	27,480	27,525	2,620	1,290	1,329	36,770	18,334	18,436

Geographic Mobility Rates, by Type of Movement, 1960-93

Source: Bureau of the Census, U.S. Dept. of Commerce

(numbers in thousands)

The overall rate of moving for persons aged 1 year old and older declined slightly during the 1992-93 period (16.8%), compared with the 1991-92 period (17.3%). Rates for moving are down from the 1950s and '60s when 20% of the population moved every year. Young adults have the highest rates of moving. More than one in 3 (36%) persons ages 20 to 24 moved in the previous year. About one-third of persons living in renter-occupied housing units in Mar. 1993 had moved in the previous year. In contrast, only 1 in 10 persons in owner-occupied housing units had moved in the same period. If current trends continue, the average American can expect to make 11.7 moves in a lifetime.

The Midwest had a net gain of 233,000 persons from other regions from 1992 to 1993. This is the first statistically significant net change for the Midwest since the region had a run of net losses during the early 1980s. Within metropolitan areas, suburbs gained 2.2 million movers between 1992 and 1993, while central cities lost 2.5 million due to migration.

Mobility period	Total, 1 yr. old and older	Total movers	Residing in the U.S. at the beginning of the period — Total	Different house, same county	Different county — Total	Different house, same state	Different house, different state	Movers from abroad[1]
Number								
1992-93	250,210	42,048	40,743	26,212	14,532	7,735	6,797	1,305
1991-92	247,380	42,800	41,545	26,587	14,957	7,853	7,105	1,255
1990-91	244,884	41,539	40,154	25,151	15,003	7,881	7,122	1,385
1989-90	242,208	43,381	41,821	25,726	16,094	8,061	8,033	1,560
1988-89	239,793	42,620	41,153	26,123	15,030	7,949	7,081	1,467
1987-88	237,431	42,174	40,974	26,201	14,772	7,727	7,046	1,200
1986-87	235,089	43,693	42,551	27,196	15,355	8,762	6,593	1,142
1985-86	232,998	43,237	42,037	26,401	15,636	8,665	6,971	1,200

Mobility period	Total, 1 yr. old and older	Total movers	Residing in the U.S. at the beginning of the period					
					Different county			
			Total	Different house, same county	Total	Different house, same state	Different house, different state	Movers from abroad[1]
1984-85	230,333	46,470	45,043	30,126	14,917	7,995	6,921	1,427
1983-84	228,232	39,379	38,300	23,659	14,641	8,198	6,444	1,079
1982-83	225,874	37,408	36,430	22,858	13,572	7,403	6,169	978
1981-82	223,719	38,127	37,039	23,081	13,959	7,330	6,628	1,088
1980-81	221,641	38,200	36,887	23,097	13,789	7,614	6,175	1,313
1970-71	201,506	37,705	36,161	23,018	13,143	6,197	6,946	1,544
1960-61	177,354	36,533	35,535	24,289	11,246	5,493	5,753	998
Percentage								
1992-93	100.0	16.8	16.3	10.5	5.8	3.1	2.7	0.5
1991-92	100.0	17.3	16.8	10.7	6.0	3.2	2.9	0.5
1990-91	100.0	17.0	16.4	10.3	6.1	3.2	2.9	0.6
1989-90	100.0	17.9	17.3	10.6	6.6	3.3	3.3	0.6
1988-89	100.0	17.8	17.2	10.9	6.3	3.3	3.0	0.6
1987-88	100.0	17.8	17.3	11.0	6.2	3.3	3.0	0.5
1986-87	100.0	18.6	18.1	11.6	6.5	3.7	2.8	0.5
1985-86	100.0	18.6	18.0	11.3	6.7	3.7	3.0	0.5
1984-85	100.0	20.2	19.6	13.1	6.5	3.5	3.0	0.6
1983-84	100.0	17.3	16.8	10.4	6.4	3.6	2.8	0.5
1982-83	100.0	16.6	16.1	10.1	6.0	3.3	2.7	0.4
1981-82	100.0	17.0	16.6	10.3	6.2	3.3	3.0	0.5
1980-81	100.0	17.2	16.6	10.4	6.2	3.4	2.8	0.6
1970-71	100.0	18.7	17.9	11.4	6.5	3.1	3.4	0.8
1960-61	100.0	20.6	20.0	13.7	6.3	3.1	3.2	0.6

(1) Movers from abroad include immigrants and U.S. citizens returning from other countries, including members of the military and their dependents.

Projections of Total Population, by Race, 1995-2050

Source: Bureau of the Census, U.S. Dept. of Commerce

Year	Total population (1,000)				By race (middle series) (1,000)				Percentage distribution			
	Lowest series	Middle series	Highest series	Zero migration	White	Black	American Indian[1]	Asian-Pacific Islander	White	Black	American Indian[1]	Asian-Pacific Islander
1995 ..	262,051	263,434	264,715	260,713	218,334	33,117	2,226	9,756	82.9	12.6	0.8	3.7
1996 ..	263,905	266,096	268,138	262,414	220,023	33,597	2,257	10,219	NA	NA	NA	NA
2000 ..	270,259	276,241	281,957	268,459	226,267	35,469	2,380	12,125	81.9	12.8	0.9	4.4
2005 ..	276,316	288,286	299,941	274,872	233,343	37,793	2,543	14,608	80.9	13.1	0.9	5.1
2010 ..	281,180	300,431	319,536	280,935	240,297	40,224	2,719	17,191	80.0	13.4	0.9	5.7
2015 ..	285,680	313,116	340,794	287,170	247,542	42,797	2,904	19,873	NA	NA	NA	NA
2020 ..	289,553	325,942	363,213	293,166	254,791	45,409	3,309	22,653	78.2	13.9	0.9	8.1
2030 ..	292,902	349,993	410,991	302,280	267,457	50,596	3,473	28,467	76.4	14.5	1.0	9.3
2040 ..	290,351	371,505	463,579	307,356	277,232	55,917	3,894	34,461	74.6	15.1	1.0	10.3
2050 ..	285,502	392,031	522,098	310,418	285,591	61,586	4,346	40,508	72.8	15.7	1.1	11.3

NA = Not available. **Note:** For the series shown, different assumptions were made regarding fertility rates (lifetime births per woman), life expectancy, and immigration in the coming decades. Assumptions were based on a July 1992 estimate of U.S. population consistent with the 1990 decennial census. Yearly net immigration was assumed to be 350,000 for the lowest series, 880,000 for the middle series, and 1,370,000 for the highest series. Immigration is not a factor in the zero migration series. All figures shown are for July 1 of the given year. Resident population only. Percentage distribution may not equal 100 due to rounding. (1) American Indian refers to American Indian, Eskimo, and Aleut.

Persons With Disabilities, by Race and Hispanic Origin, 1992-93

Source: Bureau of the Census, U.S. Dept. of Commerce

(in thousands)

Characteristic	White		Black		Hispanic origin	
	Number	Percentage distribution	Number	Percentage distribution	Number	Percentage Distribution
All ages						
Total	215,875	100.0	32,935	100.0	26,354	100.0
With a disability...........	43,646	20.2	6,462	19.6	4,016	15.2
Severe	21,152	9.8	3,987	12.1	2,224	8.4
Not severe	22,494	10.4	2,475	7.5	1,792	6.8
Persons 0-14 years						
Total	46,678	100.0	9,521	100.0	8,139	100.0
With a disability...........	2,576	5.5	542	5.7	341	4.2
Severe	375	0.8	80	0.8	82	1.0
Not severe	2,201	4.7	462	4.9	259	3.2
Persons 15 years and over						
Total	169,196	100.0	23,414	100.0	18,216	100.0
With a disability...........	41,071	24.3	5,921	25.3	3,675	20.2
Severe	20,777	12.3	3,907	16.7	2,141	11.8
Not severe	20,294	12.0	2,014	8.6	1,534	8.4

Note: A person was considered to have a disability if the person met any of the following criteria: (a) used a wheelchair; (b) used a cane or similar aid for 6 months or longer; (c) had difficulty with a functional activity; (d) had difficulty with an activity of daily living such as bathing or dressing; (e) had difficulty with an instrumental activity of daily living such as using a telephone or keeping track of money or bills; (f) was identified as having a developmental disability or a mental or emotional disability. A person was classified as having a severe disability if they: (a) used a wheelchair or had used another special aid for 6 months or longer; (b) were unable to perform one or more functional activities or needed assistance with an activity of daily living or an instrumental activity of daily living; (c) were prevented from working at a job or doing housework; or (d) had a selected condition including autism, cerebral palsy, Alzheimer's disease, senility or dementia, or mental retardation. Finally, persons who were under 65 years of age and who were covered by Medicare or who received Social Security Insurance and were considered to have a disability (and a severe disability).

Immigrants Admitted for Top 30 Metropolitan Areas of Intended Residence, 1994

Source: Immigration and Naturalization Service, U.S. Dept. of Justice

(fiscal year 1994)

Metropolitan Statistical Area	Number	Percentage	Metropolitan Statistical Area	Number	Percentage
New York, NY	124,423	15.5	Nassau–Suffolk, NY	10,649	1.3
Los Angeles–Long Beach, CA	77,112	9.6	Seattle–Bellevue–Everett, WA	10,504	1.3
Chicago, IL	40,081	5.0	Dallas, TX	9,453	1.2
Miami, FL	29,108	3.6	Riverside–San Bernardino, CA	9,163	1.1
Washington, DC–MD–VA	25,021	3.1	Detroit, MI	8,736	1.1
Boston–Lawrence–Lowell–			Fort Lauderdale, FL	7,846	1.0
Brockton, MA	18,709	2.3	Atlanta, GA	7,825	1.0
San Francisco, CA	18,641	2.3	Jersey City, NJ	7,529	0.9
Houston, TX	17,600	2.2	Sacramento, CA	6,627	0.8
San Jose, CA	16,207	2.0	San Juan, PR	6,546	0.8
Orange County, CA	15,502	1.9	Middlesex–Somerset–Hunterdon, NJ	6,365	0.8
San Diego, CA	14,212	1.8	Honolulu, HI	6,288	0.8
Oakland, CA	13,701	1.7	Fresno, CA	6,232	0.8
Newark, NJ	12,040	1.5	Minneapolis–St. Paul, MN–WI	6,056	0.8
Bergen–Passaic, NJ	11,606	1.4	Portland–Vancouver, OR–WA	5,527	0.7
Philadelphia, PA–NJ	11,535	1.4	Total U.S.[1]	804,416	100.0

(1) Includes metropolitan areas not listed.

Immigrants to U.S., by State of Intended Residence, 1994

Source: Immigration and Naturalization Service, U.S. Dept. of Justice

(fiscal year 1994)

State	Number of immigrants	State	Number of immigrants	State	Number of immigrants	State	Number of immigrants
AL	1,837	KS	2,902	NY	144,354	WV	663
AK	1,129	KY	2,036	NC	6,204	WI	5,328
AZ	9,141	LA	3,366	ND	635	WY	217
AR	1,031	ME	829	OH	9,184	Other:	
CA	208,498	MD	15,937	OK	2,728	Guam	2,531
CO	6,825	MA	22,882	OR	6,784	Marshall Is	1
CT	9,537	MI	12,728	PA	15,971	N Mariana Is	120
DE	984	MN	7,098	RI	2,907	Puerto Rico	10,463
DC	3,204	MS	815	SC	2,110	Virgin Is	1,426
FL	58,093	MO	4,362	SD	570	Armed Service	
GA	10,032	MT	447	TN	3,608	Posts	188
HI	7,746	NE	1,595	TX	56,158	Other or	
ID	1,559	NV	4,051	UT	2,951	unknown	20
IL	42,400	NH	1,144	VT	658	Total	804,416
IN	3,725	NJ	44,083	VA	15,342		
IA	2,163	NM	2,936	WA	18,180		

U.S. Foreign-Born Population, 1994

Source: Bureau of the Census, U.S. Dept. of Commerce

Percentage of U.S. Population That Is Foreign-Born, 1900-1994

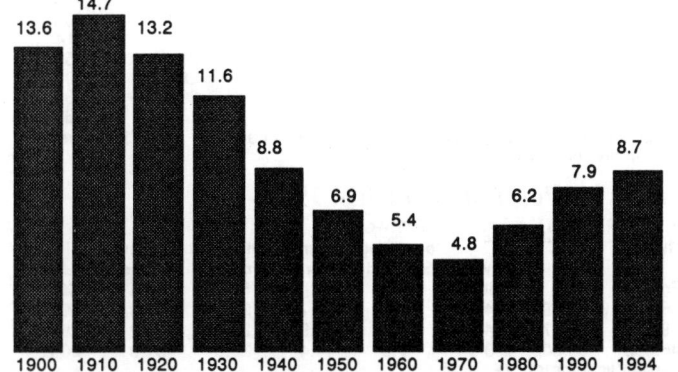

13.6 14.7 13.2 11.6 8.8 6.9 5.4 4.8 6.2 7.9 8.7

1900 1910 1920 1930 1940 1950 1960 1970 1980 1990 1994

Highest Ranking Countries of Birth of U.S. Foreign-Born Population, 1994

Country	Number (in thousands)
Mexico	6,264
Philippines	4,003
Cuba	805
El Salvador	718
Canada	679
Germany	625
China	565
Dominican Republic	556
Korea	533
Vietnam	496
India	494

Poverty Rate

Source: Bureau of the Census, U.S. Dept. of Commerce

The poverty rate is the proportion of the population whose income falls below the government's official poverty level, which is adjusted each year for inflation. The national poverty rate was 15.1% in 1993. Children remained overrepresented among the poor, with a poverty rate of 22.7%. As a group the elderly were slightly underrepresented. Poverty rates for children under 18 years of age and persons aged 18 to 44 years increased between 1990 and 1993.

Poverty, by Family Status, Sex, and Race, 1978-93

Source: Bureau of the Census, U.S. Dept. of Commerce; in thousands

	1993 No.[1]	%[2]	1990 No.[1]	%[2]	1986 No.[1]	%[2]	1978 No.[1]	%[2]
Total poor	39,265	15.1	33,585	13.5	32,370	13.6	24,497	11.4
In families	29,927	13.6	25,232	12.0	24,754	12.0	19,062	10.0
Head of household	8,393	12.3	7,098	10.7	7,023	10.9	5,280	9.1
Related children	14,961	22.0	12,715	19.9	12,257	19.8	9,722	15.7
Unrelated individuals	8,388	22.1	7,446	20.7	6,846	21.6	5,435	22.1
In families with a female householder, no husband present	14,636	38.7	12,578	37.2	11,944	38.3	9,269	35.6
Head of household	4,424	35.6	3,768	33.4	3,613	34.6	2,654	31.4
Related children	8,503	53.7	7,363	53.4	6,943	54.4	5,687	50.6
Unrelated female individuals	5,107	25.7	4,589	24.0	4,311	25.1	3,611	26.0
All other	15,291	8.4	12,654	7.1	12,811	7.3	9,793	5.9
Head of household	3,969	7.1	3,330	6.0	3,410	6.3	2,626	5.3
Related children	6,458	12.4	5,352	10.7	5,313	10.8	4,035	7.9
Unrelated male individuals	3,281	18.1	2,857	16.9	2,536	17.5	1,824	17.1
Total white poor	26,226	12.2	22,326	10.7	22,183	11.0	16,259	8.7
In families	18,968	10.5	15,916	9.0	16,393	9.4	12,050	7.3
Head of household	5,452	9.4	4,622	8.1	4,811	8.6	3,523	6.9
Female	2,376	29.2	2,010	26.8	2,041	28.2	1,391	23.5
Related children	9,123	17.0	7,696	15.1	7,714	15.3	5,674	11.0
Unrelated individuals	6,443	20.1	5,739	18.6	5,198	19.2	4,209	19.8
Total black poor	10,877	33.1	9,837	31.9	8,983	31.1	7,625	30.6
In families	9,242	32.9	8,160	31.0	7,410	29.7	6,493	29.5
Head of household	2,499	31.3	2,193	29.3	1,987	28.0	1,622	27.5
Female	1,908	49.9	1,648	48.1	1,488	50.1	1,208	50.6
Related children	5,030	45.9	4,412	44.2	4,039	42.7	3,781	41.2
Unrelated individuals	1,541	33.4	1,491	35.1	1,431	38.5	1,132	38.6

(1) Beginning in 1980, total includes members of unrelated subfamilies not shown separately. For earlier years, unrelated subfamily members are included in the "in family" category. (2) Percentage of total population in that general category who fell below poverty level. For example, of all black female heads of households in 1993, 49.9% were poor.

Poverty Level by Family Size, 1992-93

Source: Bureau of the Census, U.S. Dept. of Commerce

	1992	1993		1992	1993
1 person	$ 7,143	$ 7,363	3 persons	$ 11,186	$ 11,522
Under 65 years	7,299	7,518	4 persons	14,335	14,763
65 years and over	6,729	6,930	5 persons	16,952	17,449
2 persons	9,137	9,414	6 persons	19,137	19,718
Householder under 65 years	9,443	9,728	7 persons	21,594	22,383
Householder 65 years and over	8,487	8,740	8 persons	24,053	24,838
			9 persons or more	28,745	29,529

Persons Below Poverty Level, 1960-93

Source: Bureau of the Census, U.S. Dept. of Commerce

Year	Number below poverty level (mil) All races[1]	White	Black	Hispanic origin[2]	Percentage below poverty level All races[1]	White	Black	Hispanic origin[2]	Avg. income cutoffs for family of 4 at poverty level[3]
1960	39.9	28.3	NA	NA	22.2	17.8	NA	NA	$3,022
1965	33.2	22.5	NA	NA	17.3	13.3	NA	NA	3,223
1970	25.4	17.5	7.5	NA	12.6	9.9	33.5	NA	3,968
1975	25.9	17.8	7.5	3.0	12.3	9.7	31.3	26.9	5,500
1980[4]	29.3	19.7	8.6	3.5	13.0	10.2	32.5	25.7	8,414
1990	33.6	22.3	9.8	6.0	13.5	10.7	31.9	28.1	13,359
1991	35.7	23.7	10.2	6.3	14.2	11.3	32.7	28.7	13,924
1992	38.0	25.3	10.8	7.6	14.8	11.9	33.4	29.6	14,335
1993	39.3	26.2	10.9	8.1	15.1	12.2	33.1	30.6	14,763

NA = Not available. (1) Includes other races not shown separately. (2) Persons of Hispanic origin may be of any race. (3) Figures for 1960-80 represent only nonfarm families. (4) Data based on revised poverty definition.

Income Distribution by Population Fifths, 1993

Source: Bureau of the Census, U.S. Dept. of Commerce

Families	Upper limit of each fifth[1] Lowest	Second	Third	Fourth	Top 5%[2]	Percentage distribution of total income Lowest fifth	Second fifth	Third fifth	Fourth fifth	Highest fifth	Top 5%
All races	$16,970	$30,000	45,030	66,794	$113,182	4.1	9.9	15.7	23.3	47.0	20.3
White	19,027	32,030	47,300	69,050	117,278	4.6	10.3	15.9	23.0	46.2	20.0
Black	8,000	16,050	27,742	46,502	83,600	3.0	7.8	14.4	23.9	51.0	20.8

(1) The highest fifth does not have an upper limit. (2) Lower limit for top 5%.

Aid to Families With Dependent Children, 1994

Source: Admin. for Children and Families, Office of Family Assistance, U.S. Dept. of Health and Human Services

(in thousands; fiscal year 1994)

State	Total assistance payments[1]	Average monthly caseload	Average monthly recipients	Average monthly children	Average monthly payment per Family	Average monthly payment per Person
Alabama	$ 91,940	50,340	132,067	95,799	$152.20	$58.01
Alaska	112,253	12,759	37,998	24,061	733.17	246.19
Arizona	265,859	71,984	200,809	135,937	307.77	110.33
Arkansas	57,364	26,014	69,333	49,482	183.76	68.95
California	6,088,321	908,999	2,639,214	1,804,077	558.15	192.24
Colorado	158,247	41,614	118,986	80,294	316.89	110.83
Connecticut	397,824	59,201	165,928	111,283	558.86	199.40
Delaware	39,650	11,460	27,488	18,549	288.31	120.20
Dist. of Columbia	126,263	27,117	73,953	50,814	388.02	142.28
Florida	806,235	247,087	669,419	462,564	271.91	100.37
Georgia	427,932	141,451	393,499	274,495	252.11	90.63
Hawaii	163,010	20,420	62,016	41,099	665.25	219.04
Idaho	30,272	8,676	23,170	15,584	290.77	108.87
Illinois	913,544	240,319	712,295	485,846	316.78	106.88
Indiana	228,172	73,803	216,038	145,098	257.64	88.01
Iowa	169,235	39,555	110,268	71,534	356.54	127.90
Kansas	123,087	30,102	86,686	58,737	340.75	118.33
Kentucky	198,307	79,840	208,033	136,690	206.98	79.44
Louisiana	168,357	86,915	248,163	179,697	161.42	56.53
Maine	107,474	22,934	64,333	40,102	390.52	139.22
Maryland	313,799	80,123	221,793	150,628	326.37	117.90
Massachusetts	729,705	111,783	307,082	197,313	543.99	198.02
Michigan	1,132,165	223,950	665,785	438,771	421.29	141.71
Minnesota	379,409	62,979	186,987	124,028	502.03	169.09
Mississippi	81,749	56,785	158,743	115,716	119.97	42.91
Missouri	286,905	92,110	263,452	176,386	259.57	90.75
Montana	48,937	11,908	34,852	22,720	342.48	117.01
Nebraska	61,582	15,934	45,227	30,967	322.06	113.34
Nevada	48,094	14,166	38,128	26,650	282.92	105.12
New Hampshire	61,870	11,475	30,345	19,359	449.31	169.91
New Jersey	531,343	122,427	335,414	227,536	361.67	132.01
New Mexico	143,897	33,633	102,248	66,297	356.54	117.28
New York	2,913,093	454,952	1,254,739	812,994	533.59	193.47
North Carolina	352,505	131,220	332,594	222,618	223.86	88.32
North Dakota	25,553	5,877	16,458	10,826	362.33	129.38
Ohio	1,015,807	250,208	684,519	454,875	338.32	123.66
Oklahoma	165,157	46,971	131,208	90,166	293.01	104.90
Oregon	196,710	42,135	114,043	75,940	389.05	143.74
Pennsylvania	934,769	210,155	619,642	416,843	370.67	125.71
Rhode Island	136,006	22,654	62,843	41,391	500.30	180.35
South Carolina	115,096	51,925	139,694	102,181	184.72	68.66
South Dakota	24,570	6,926	19,105	13,630	295.65	107.17
Tennessee	215,070	110,766	299,686	203,215	161.80	59.80
Texas	544,326	283,744	787,504	549,465	159.86	57.60
Utah	77,253	17,801	49,882	33,140	361.65	129.06
Vermont	64,870	9,883	27,815	17,192	546.99	194.35
Virginia	253,031	74,818	194,603	134,063	281.83	108.35
Washington	609,892	102,952	291,534	186,724	493.67	174.33
West Virginia	125,866	40,729	114,314	71,833	257.53	91.75
Wisconsin	424,665	77,188	226,147	131,873	458.47	156.49
Wyoming	21,415	5,740	16,354	11,078	310.93	109.12
U.S. Total[2]	**$22,797,119**	**5,046,382**	**14,226,009**	**9,590,156**	**$376.46**	**$133.54**

(1) Total assistance payments include AFDC-Basic, AFDC-Unemployed Parent, Title IV-A Payments under JOBS, Home Repair, and payments to Indian tribes. (2) U.S. total includes outlying areas, not shown.

Fertility Characteristics of Mothers Receiving AFDC[1] Payments, Summer 1993

Source: Bureau of the Census, U.S. Dept. of Commerce

(in thousands)

Region	Number of mothers Total	Number of mothers Receiving AFDC	Births per 1,000 mothers	Born out of wedlock	Born before age 18	Born both out of wedlock and before age 18
New England	1,681	185	2,442	63.9	34.1	25.5
Middle Atlantic	4,930	542	2,689	64.3	27.3	22.9
East North Central	6,417	748	2,537	75.1	25.7	24.3
West North Central	2,585	222	3,027	66.1	26.6	24.3
South Atlantic	6,311	591	2,472	76.6	40.5	36.1
East South Central	2,197	191	2,160	74.3	45.7	37.0
West South Central	3,881	369	2,744	66.9	20.3	18.7
Mountain	1,753	119	2,517	65.7	35.0	26.5
Pacific	6,021	787	2,596	59.1	22.7	19.5
Total U.S.	**35,776**	**3,754**	**2,586**	**68.2**	**28.9**	**25.2**

Note: Data are monthly averages collected between June and Sept. 1993 as part of the Bureau of the Census's Survey of Income and Program Participation. Only mothers ages 15 to 44 were included. (1) Aid to Families With Dependent Children.

U.S. Places of 5,000 or More Population—With ZIP and Area Codes

Source: U.S. Bureau of the Census, Dept. of Commerce

The following is a list of places of 5,000 or more inhabitants recognized by the Bureau of the Census, U.S. Dept. of Commerce based on data collected in the 1990 Decennial Census. More recent estimates were not available for all cities as of late 1995. This list includes places that are incorporated under the laws of their respective states as cities, boroughs, towns, and villages, with the following exceptions: boroughs in Alaska and towns in the six New England states (Connecticut, Maine, Massachusetts, New Hampshire, Rhode Island, and Vermont), New York, and Wisconsin. Unincorporated places that the Census Bureau designates as "census designated places (CDPs)" are also included. These communities, marked (u), are statistically compatible with incorporated communities because of their population density. CDP boundaries can change from one census to another. Hawaii is the only state that has no incorporated places recognized by the Census Bureau; all places shown for Hawaii are CDPs.

This list also includes, in *italics*, minor civil divisions (MCDs) for the following states: Connecticut, Maine, Massachusetts, New Hampshire, New Jersey, Rhode Island, Vermont, and Wisconsin. MCDs are areas that are not incorporated under the laws of the state and that are not recognized by the Census Bureau as a CDP but are often the primary political or administrative divisions of a county. These areas may also serve as general-purpose local governments.

The geographical boundaries for places marked with a dagger (†) changed from the 1980 census to the 1990 census.

An asterisk (*) denotes that the ZIP code given is for general delivery; named streets and/or post office boxes within the community may differ. Consult the local postmaster for the correct ZIP code for specific addresses within the community.

Area codes refer only to home and business numbers. Overlay area codes are excluded. When two area codes are listed for one locale, consult local operators for further assistance.

Alabama

ZIP	Place		1990	1980
35007	Alabaster	(205)	14,619	7,079
35950	Albertville	(205)	14,507	12,039
35010	Alexander City	(205)	14,917	13,807
36420	Andalusia	(334)	9,269	10,415
*36201	Anniston	(205)	26,638	29,135
35016	Arab	(205)	6,321	6,053
35611	Athens	(205)	16,901	14,558
*36502	Atmore	(334)	8,046	8,789
35954	Attalla	(205)	6,859	7,737
*36830	Auburn	(334)	33,830	28,471
36507	Bay Minette	(334)	7,168	7,455
*35020	Bessemer	(205)	33,581	31,729
*35203	Birmingham	(205)	265,347	284,413
35957	Boaz	(205)	6,928	7,151
*36426	Brewton	(334)	5,885	6,680
35215	Center Point(u)	(205)	22,658	23,317
36611	Chickasaw	(205)	6,649	7,402
35045	Clanton	(205)	7,669	5,832
*35055	Cullman	(205)	13,367	13,084
36322	Daleville	(334)	5,117	4,250
36526	Daphne	(205)	11,291	3,406
*35601	Decatur	(205)	48,778	42,002
36732	Demopolis	(334)	7,512	7,678
*36302	Dothan	(334)	53,721	48,750
*36330	Enterprise	(334)	20,119	18,033
*36027	Eufaula	(334)	13,220	12,097
35064	Fairfield	(205)	12,200	13,242
36532	Fairhope	(334)	8,490	7,286
*35630	Florence	(205)	36,426	37,029
35214	Forestdale(u)	(205)	10,395	10,814
35967	Fort Payne	(205)	11,838	11,485
36362	Fort Rucker(u)	(205)	7,593	8,932
35068	Fultondale	(205)	6,400	6,217
*35901	Gadsden	(205)	42,523	47,565
35071	Gardendale	(205)	9,251	8,005
36037	Greenville	(334)	7,494	7,807
35976	Guntersville	(205)	7,038	7,041
35570	Hamilton	(205)	5,787	5,093
35640	Hartselle	(205)	10,867	8,858
35209	Homewood	(205)	23,644	21,412
*35244	Hoover	(205)	40,000	18,996
35023	Hueytown	(205)	15,280	13,452
*35801	Huntsville	(205)	159,880	142,513
35210	Irondale	(205)	9,458	6,510
36545	Jackson	(334)	5,819	6,073
36265	Jacksonville	(205)	10,283	9,735
*35501	Jasper	(205)	13,553	11,894
36863	Lanett	(205)	8,985	8,922
35094	Leeds	(205)	10,009	8,638
35758	Madison	(205)	14,792	4,057
35228	Midfield	(205)	5,559	6,182
36054	Millbrook	(205)	6,046	3,101
*36601	Mobile	(334)	196,263	200,452
*36460	Monroeville	(334)	6,993	5,674
*36104	Montgomery	(334)	187,543	177,857
*35223	Mountain Brook	(205)	19,810	19,718
35667	Muscle Shoals	(205)	9,611	8,911
35476	Northport	(205)	17,297	14,291
*36801	Opelika	(334)	22,122	21,896
36467	Opp	(334)	7,011	7,204
36203	Oxford	(205)	9,537	8,939
*36360	Ozark	(334)	13,030	13,188
35124	Pelham	(205)	9,356	6,759
*35125	Pell City	(205)	7,945	6,616
36867	Phenix City	(334)	25,311	26,928
36272	Piedmont	(205)	5,347	5,544
35126	Pinson-Clay-Chalkville(u)	(205)	10,987	....
35127	Pleasant Grove	(205)	8,458	7,102
*36067	Prattville	(334)	19,816	18,647
36610	Prichard	(205)	34,320	39,541
35906	Rainbow City	(205)	7,667	6,299
36274	Roanoke	(334)	6,362	5,809
35653	Russellville	(205)	7,812	8,195
36201	Saks(u)	(205)	11,138	11,118
36571	Saraland	(205)	11,760	9,833
36572	Satsuma	(205)	5,194	3,822
35768	Scottsboro	(205)	13,786	14,758
*36701	Selma	(334)	23,755	26,684
35660	Sheffield	(205)	10,380	11,903
35901	Southside	(205)	5,580	5,141
35150	Sylacauga	(205)	12,520	12,708
35160	Talladega	(205)	18,175	19,128
36078	Tallassee	(334)	5,112	4,763
35217	Tarrant City	(205)	8,046	8,148
*36582	Theodore(u)	(205)	6,509	6,392
36619	Tillman's Corner(u)	(205)	17,988	15,941
36081	Troy	(334)	13,051	13,124
35173	Trussville	(205)	8,283	3,507
*35401	Tuscaloosa	(205)	77,866	75,211
35674	Tuscumbia	(205)	8,413	9,137
36083	Tuskegee	(334)	12,257	13,327
*36854	Valley†	(205)	8,215	8,946
35216	Vestavia Hills	(205)	19,550	15,722

Alaska (907)

ZIP	Place	1990	1980
*99501	Anchorage	226,338	174,431
*99708	College(u)	11,249	4,043
99702	Eielson AFB(u)	5,251	5,232
*99701	Fairbanks	30,843	22,645
*99801	Juneau	26,751	19,528
99611	Kenai	6,327	4,324
*99901	Ketchikan	8,263	7,198
*99615	Kodiak	6,365	4,756
99639	Ninilchik(u)	10,523	341
99835	Sitka	8,588	7,803

Arizona

ZIP	Place		1990	1980
*85220	Apache Junction	(602)	18,092	9,935
85323	Avondale	(602)	16,182	8,168
85603	Bisbee	(520)	6,288	7,154
85326	Buckeye	(602)	4,436	3,434
*86430	Bullhead City†	(520)	21,951	10,719
86322	Camp Verde†	(520)	6,243	3,824
*85222	Casa Grande	(520)	19,076	14,971
*85225	Chandler	(602)	89,862	29,673
86503	Chinle(u)	(520)	5,059	2,815
85228	Coolidge	(520)	6,934	6,851
86326	Cottonwood	(520)	5,918	4,550
86326	Cottonwood-Verde Village(u)	(520)	7,037	....
*85607	Douglas	(520)	13,137	13,058
85335	El Mirage	(602)	5,001	4,307
85231	Eloy	(520)	7,211	6,240
*86004	Flagstaff	(520)	45,857	34,743
85232	Florence	(520)	7,321	3,391
85726	Flowing Wells(u)	(520)	14,013	....
.....	Fortuna Foothills(u)	(520)	7,737	....
*85269	Fountain Hills†	(602)	10,030	2,771
*85234	Gilbert	(602)	29,122	5,717
*85301	Glendale	(602)	147,864	97,172
*85501	Globe	(520)	6,062	6,886

ZIP	Place		1990	1980
85338	Goodyear	(602)	6,258	2,747
*85622	Green Valley(u)	(520)	13,231	7,999
85283	Guadalupe	(602)	5,458	4,506
86401	Kingman	(520)	12,722	9,257
*86403	Lake Havasu City	(520)	24,363	15,909
*85201	Mesa	(602)	288,104	152,404
86440	Mohave Valley(u)	(520)	6,962	....
.....	New Kingman-Butler(u)	(520)	11,627	....
*85621	Nogales	(520)	19,489	15,683
85737	Oro Valley	(520)	6,670	1,489
86040	Page	(520)	6,598	4,907
85253	Paradise Valley	(602)	11,773	11,085
*85541	Payson	(520)	8,377	5,068
85345	Peoria	(602)	50,675	12,171
*85026	Phoenix	(602)	983,403	789,704
*86301	Prescott	(520)	26,592	19,865
*86301	Prescott Valley	(520)	8,904	2,284
*85546	Safford	(520)	7,359	7,010
85251	Scottsdale	(602)	130,075	88,622
*86336	Sedona†	(520)	7,720	5,319
85901	Show Low	(520)	5,020	4,298
*85635	Sierra Vista	(520)	32,983	24,937
85635	Sierra Vista Southeast(u)	(520)	9,237	....
85350	Somerton	(520)	5,282	3,969
85713	South Tucson	(520)	5,171	6,554
*85351	Sun City(u)	(602)	38,126	40,505
85375	Sun City West(u)	(602)	15,997	3,772
85248	Sun Lakes(u)	(602)	6,578	1,925
85374	Surprise	(602)	7,122	3,723
*85282	Tempe	(602)	141,993	106,919
86045	Tuba City(u)	(520)	7,323	5,045
*85726	Tucson	(520)	405,323	330,537
86047	Winslow	(520)	9,279	7,921
*85364	Yuma	(520)	56,966	42,481

Arkansas (501)

ZIP	Place	1990	1980
71923	Arkadelphia	10,014	10,005
71822	Ashdown	5,150	4,218
*72501	Batesville	9,187	8,447
72714	Bella Vista(u)	9,083	2,589
*72015	Benton	18,177	17,717
72712	Bentonville	11,257	8,756
72315	Blytheville	22,523	23,844
72022	Bryant	5,269	2,682
72023	Cabot	8,319	4,806
71701	Camden	14,701	15,356
72830	Clarksville	5,833	5,237
*72032	Conway	26,481	20,375
71635	Crossett	6,282	6,706
71639	Dumas	5,520	6,091
*71730	El Dorado	23,146	25,270
*72701	Fayetteville	42,247	36,608
72335	Forrest City	13,364	13,803
*72901	Fort Smith	72,798	71,626
*72601	Harrison	9,936	9,567
72543	Heber Springs	5,628	4,589
72342	Helena	7,491	9,598
71801	Hope	9,768	10,290
*71901	Hot Springs	32,462	35,781
71909	Hot Springs Village(u)	6,361	2,083
*72076	Jacksonville	29,101	27,589
72401	Jonesboro	46,535	31,530
*72201	Little Rock	175,727	159,151
71753	Magnolia	11,151	11,909
72104	Malvern	9,236	10,163
72360	Marianna	6,033	6,220
72113	Maumelle†	6,714	1,368
71953	Mena	5,475	5,154
71655	Monticello	8,119	8,259
72110	Morrilton	6,551	7,355
72653	Mountain Home	9,027	8,066
72112	Newport	7,459	8,339
*72114	North Little Rock	61,829	64,388
72370	Osceola	8,930	8,881
*72450	Paragould	18,540	15,248
*71601	Pine Bluff	57,140	56,636
72455	Pocahontas	6,151	5,995
*72756	Rogers	24,692	17,429
*72801	Russellville	21,260	14,518
*72143	Searcy	15,180	13,612
72120	Sherwood	18,878	10,423
72761	Siloam Springs	8,151	7,940
*72764	Springdale	29,945	23,458
72160	Stuttgart	10,420	10,941
75502	Texarkana	22,631	21,459
72472	Trumann	6,346	6,395
72956	Van Buren	14,899	12,020
71671	Warren	6,455	7,646
72390	West Helena	10,137	11,367
*72301	West Memphis	28,259	28,138
72396	Wynne	8,817	7,927

California

ZIP	Place		1990	1980
94301	Adelanto	(805)	6,791	2,164
*91376	Agoura Hills†	(818)	20,391	11,399

ZIP	Place		1990	1980
*94501	Alameda	(510)	73,979	63,852
94507	Alamo(u)	(510)	12,277	8,505
94706	Albany	(510)	16,327	15,130
*91802	Alhambra	(818)	82,087	64,767
92656	Aliso Viejo(u)	...	7,612	....
90249	Alondra Park(u)	(310)	12,215	12,189
*91901	Alpine(u) (San Diego)	(619)	9,695	5,368
*91001	Altadena(u)	(818)	42,658	40,983
95945	Alta Sierra(u)	(916)	5,709	2,168
94589	American Canyon(u)	(707)	7,706	5,712
*92803	Anaheim	(714)	266,406	219,494
96007	Anderson	(916)	8,299	7,381
*94509	Antioch	(510)	62,195	42,683
*92307	Apple Valley†	(619)	46,079	16,748
*95003	Aptos(u)	(408)	9,061	7,039
*91006	Arcadia	(818)	48,284	45,993
95521	Arcata	(707)	15,211	12,849
95825	Arden-Arcade(u)	(916)	92,040	87,570
*93420	Arroyo Grande	(805)	14,432	11,290
*90701	Artesia	(310)	15,464	14,301
93203	Arvin	(805)	9,286	6,863
94577	Ashland(u)	(510)	16,590	13,893
93422	Atascadero	(805)	23,138	16,232
94025	Atherton	(415)	7,163	7,797
95301	Atwater	(209)	22,282	17,530
*95603	Auburn	(916)	10,653	7,540
92505	August(u)	(714)	6,376	6,350
93204	Avenal	(209)	9,770	4,137
91746	Avocado Heights(u)	(818)	14,232	11,733
91702	Azusa	(818)	41,203	29,380
*93302	Bakersfield	(805)	174,978	105,611
91706	Baldwin Park	(818)	69,330	50,554
92220	Banning	(909)	20,572	14,020
*92312	Barstow	(619)	21,472	17,690
94565	Bay Point(u)	(510)	17,453	10,244
93402	Baywood-Los Osos(u)	(805)	14,377	10,933
95903	Beale AFB(u)	(916)	6,912	6,329
92223	Beaumont	(714)	9,685	6,818
90201	Bell	(213)	34,365	25,450
*90706	Bellflower	(213)	61,815	53,441
90201	Bell Gardens	(213)/(310)	42,315	34,117
94002	Belmont	(415)	24,165	24,505
94510	Benicia	(707)	24,437	15,376
95005	Ben Lomond(u)	(408)	7,884	7,238
*94704	Berkeley	(510)	102,724	103,328
*90210	Beverly Hills	(213)/(310)	31,971	32,646
92315	Big Bear Lake†	(909)	5,351	4,896
94506	Black Hawk(u)	(510)	6,199	....
92316	Bloomington(u)	(909)	15,116	12,781
*92225	Blythe	(619)	8,448	6,805
93637	Bonadella Ranchos-Madera Ranchos(u)	(209)	5,705	3,272
91902	Bonita(u)	(619)	12,542	6,257
92021	Bostonia(u)	(619)	13,670	....
95006	Boulder Creek(u)	(408)	6,725	5,662
95416	Boyes Hot Springs(u)	(707)	5,973	4,177
92227	Brawley	(619)	18,923	14,946
*92622	Brea	(714)	32,873	27,913
94513	Brentwood	(510)	7,563	4,434
*90622	Buena Park	(714)	68,784	64,165
*91510	Burbank	(818)	93,649	84,625
*94010	Burlingame	(415)	26,666	26,173
*92231	Calexico	(619)	18,633	14,412
*93504	California City	(805)	5,955	2,743
*93010	Camarillo	(805)	52,297	37,797
93428	Cambria(u)	(805)	5,382	3,061
95682	Cameron Park(u)	(916)	11,897	5,607
95008	Campbell	(408)	36,048	26,843
92055	Camp Pendleton North(u)	(714)	10,373	2,065
92055	Camp Pendleton South(u)	(714)	11,299	7,952
92587	Canyon Lake(u)	(909)	7,938	2,039
95010	Capitola	(408)	10,171	9,095
*92008	Carlsbad	(619)	63,292	35,490
*95608	Carmichael(u)	(916)	48,702	43,108
*93013	Carpinteria	(805)	13,747	10,835
*90745	Carson	(310)	83,995	81,221
92077	Casa de Oro-Mt. Helix(u)	(619)	30,727	19,651
*94544	Castro Valley(u)	(510)	48,619	43,810
95012	Castroville	(408)	5,272	4,396
*92235	Cathedral City†	(619)	30,085	11,096
95307	Ceres	(209)	26,413	13,281
90703	Cerritos	(310)	53,244	53,020
91724	Charter Oak(u)	(818)	8,858	6,840
94541	Cherryland(u)	(415)	11,088	9,425
92223	Cherry Valley(u)	(714)	5,945	5,012
*95926	Chico	(916)	39,970	26,716
*91708	Chino	(909)	59,682	40,165
91709	Chino Hills(u)		27,608	....
93610	Chowchilla	(209)	5,930	5,122
*91910	Chula Vista	(619)	135,160	83,927
95610	Citrus(u)	(916)	9,481	12,450
*95621	Citrus Heights(u)	(916)	107,439	85,911
91711	Claremont	(909)	32,610	31,028
94517	Clayton	(510)	7,317	4,325
95422	Clearlake†		11,804	8,343
*93612	Clovis	(209)	50,323	33,021
92236	Coachella	(619)	16,896	9,129
93210	Coalinga	(209)	8,212	6,593
92324	Colton	(714)	40,213	21,310
90022	Commerce	(213)/(310)	12,135	10,509

ZIP	Place	1990	1980
*90221	Compton (310)	90,454	81,350
*94520	Concord (510)	111,308	103,763
93212	Corcoran (209)	13,360	6,454
96021	Corning (916)	5,870	4,745
*91718	Corona (909)	75,943	37,791
*92118	Coronado (619)	26,540	18,790
*94925	Corte Madera (415)	8,272	8,074
*92628	Costa Mesa (714)	96,357	82,562
94931	Cotati (707)	5,714	3,346
94556	Country Club(u) (209)	9,325	9,585
*91722	Covina (818)	43,332	32,746
92325	Crestline(u) (714)	8,594	6,715
90201	Cudahy (213)	22,817	18,275
*90230	Culver City (230)/(310)	38,793	38,139
*95014	Cupertino (408)	39,967	34,297
90630	Cypress (714)	42,655	40,738
*94015	Daly City (415)	92,088	78,519
92629	Dana Point (714)	31,896	21,271†
*94526	Danville (510)	31,306	26,143†
95616	Davis (916)	46,322	36,640
90250	Del Aire(u) (310)	8,040	8,487
*93215	Delano (805)	22,762	16,491
93953	Del Monte Forest(u) (408)	5,069	....
*92240	Desert Hot Springs (619)	11,668	5,941
*91765	Diamond Bar (909)	53,672	....
93618	Dinuba (209)	12,743	9,907
94514	Discovery Bay(u) (510)	5,351	1,326
95620	Dixon (916)	10,417	7,541
*90241	Downey (310)	91,444	82,602
*91009	Duarte (818)	20,716	16,766
94568	Dublin† (510)	23,229	13,496
93219	Earlimart(u) (805)	5,881	4,578
90220	East Compton(u) (310)	7,967	6,435
.....	East Foothills(u)	14,898	16,890
92343	East Hemet(u) (909)	17,611	14,712
90638	East La Mirada(u) (310)	9,367	9,688
90022	East Los Angeles(u) (310)	126,379	110,017
94303	East Palo Alto† (415)	23,451	18,106
91117	East Pasadena(u)	5,910	....
93257	East Porterville(u) (209)	5,790	5,218
.....	East San Gabriel(u)	12,736	....
*93523	Edwards AFB(u) (805)	7,423	8,554
*92020	El Cajon (619)	88,693	73,892
*92244	El Centro (619)	31,405	23,996
94530	El Cerrito (510)	22,869	22,731
95762	El Dorado Hills(u) (916)	6,395	3,453
*95624	Elk Grove(u) (916)	17,483	10,959
*91734	El Monte (818)	106,162	79,494
*93446	El de Paso Robles (310)	18,583	9,163
93030	El Rio(u) (805)	6,419	5,674
90245	El Segundo (310)	15,223	13,752
*94802	El Sobrante(u) (510)	9,852	10,535
92630	El Toro(u) (714)	62,685	38,153
92709	El Toro Station(u) (714)	6,869	7,632
*94612	Emeryville (510)	5,740	3,714
*92024	Encinitas† (619)	55,406	36,550
*92025	Escondido (619)	108,648	64,355
*95501	Eureka (707)	27,025	24,153
93221	Exeter (209)	7,276	5,606
*94930	Fairfax (415)	6,931	7,391
94533	Fairfield (707)	78,650	58,099
95628	Fair Oaks(u) (Sacramento) (916)	26,867	22,602
96052	Fairview(u) (Trinity)	9,045	....
*92028	Fallbrook(u) (619)	22,095	14,041
93223	Farmersville (209)	6,235	5,544
95018	Felton(u) (408)	5,350	4,564
*93015	Fillmore (805)	11,992	9,602
90001	Florence-Graham(u) (213)	57,147	48,662
95828	Florin(u) (916)	24,330	16,523
*95630	Folsom (916)	29,802	11,003
*92334	Fontana (909)	87,535	36,804
95841	Foothill Farms(u) (916)	17,135	13,700
95437	Fort Bragg (707)	6,078	5,019
95540	Fortuna (707)	8,788	7,591
94404	Foster City (415)	28,176	23,287
92728	Fountain Valley (714)	53,691	55,080
95019	Freedom(u) (408)	8,361	6,416
*94537	Fremont (510)	173,339	131,945
*93706	Fresno (209)	354,091	217,491
*92634	Fullerton (714)	114,144	102,246
95632	Galt (209)	8,889	5,514
*90247	Gardena (310)	49,841	45,165
95205	Garden Acres(u) (213)	8,547	7,361
*92642	Garden Grove (714)	143,965	123,307
92394	George AFB(u) (619)	5,085	7,061
*95020	Gilroy (408)	31,487	21,641
92509	Glen Avon(u) (714)	12,663	8,444
*91209	Glendale (818)	180,038	139,060
91741	Glendora (818)	47,832	38,500
93561	Golden Hills(u)	5,423	....
92313	Grand Terrace (714)	10,946	8,498
*95945	Grass Valley (916)	9,048	6,697
93308	Greenacres(u) (805)	7,379	5,381
93927	Greenfield (Monterey) (408)	7,464	4,181
93433	Grover City (805)	11,602	8,827
93434	Guadalupe (805)	5,479	3,629
91745	Hacienda Heights(u) (818)	52,354	49,422
94019	Half Moon Bay (415)	8,886	7,282
*93230	Hanford (209)	30,463	20,958
90716	Hawaiian Gardens (213)	13,639	10,548
*90250	Hawthorne (213)/(310)	71,349	56,437
*94544	Hayward (510)	111,343	93,585
95448	Healdsburg (707)	9,469	7,217
92546	Hemet (909)	36,094	22,531
94547	Hercules (415)	16,829	5,963
90254	Hermosa Beach (310)	18,219	18,070
*92340	Hesperia† (619)	50,418	20,612
92346	Highland† (909)	34,439	21,720
94010	Hillsborough (415)	10,667	10,372
*95023	Hollister (408)	19,318	11,488
91720	Home Gardens(u) (714)	7,780	5,783
*92647	Huntington Beach (714)	181,519	170,505
90255	Huntington Park (213)	56,129	45,932
*91932	Imperial Beach (619)	26,512	22,689
*92201	Indio (619)	36,850	21,611
*90301	Inglewood (213)/(310)	109,602	94,162
.....	Interlaken(u)	6,404	....
95640	Ione (916)	6,516	2,207
*92719	Irvine (714)	110,330	62,134
93117	Isla Vista(u) (805)	20,395	....
94914	Kentfield(u) (415)	6,030	....
93630	Kerman (209)	5,448	4,002
93930	King City (408)	7,634	5,495
93631	Kingsburg (209)	7,245	5,115
*91011	La Canada Flintridge (818)	19,378	20,153
*91224	La Crescenta-Montrose(u) (818)	16,968	16,531
90045	Ladera Heights(u) (310)	6,316	6,647
94549	Lafayette (510)	23,366	20,837
.....	Laguna(u)	9,828	....
*92607	Laguna Beach (714)	23,170	17,858
*92654	Laguna Hills(u) (714)	46,731	33,600
92607	Laguna Niguel† (714)	44,723	12,237
*90631	La Habra (310)	51,263	45,232
90631	La Habra Heights (310)	6,226	4,786
92352	Lake Arrowhead(u) (714)	6,539	6,272
*92531	Lake Elsinore† (714)	18,316	5,982
92530	Lakeland Village(u) (714)	5,159	2,796
93535	Lake Los Angeles(u) (805)	7,977	....
92040	Lakeside(u) (619)	39,412	23,921
*90714	Lakewood (310)	73,553	74,511
*91941	La Mesa (619)	52,911	50,308
*90638	La Mirada (714)	40,452	40,986
93241	Lamont(u) (805)	11,517	9,616
*93539	Lancaster (805)	97,300	48,027
90623	La Palma (714)	15,392	15,399
*91747	La Puente (818)	36,955	30,882
92253	La Quinta† (909)	11,215	4,027
95401	La Riviera(u) (916)	10,986	10,906
95403	Larkfield-Wikiup(u) (707)	6,779	....
*94939	Larkspur (415)	11,068	11,064
95330	Lathrop† (209)	6,841	4,112
91750	La Verne (909)	30,843	23,508
*90260	Lawndale (310)	27,331	23,460
*91945	Lemon Grove (619)	23,984	20,780
93245	Lemoore (209)	13,622	8,832
90304	Lennox(u) (310)	22,757	18,445
95648	Lincoln (916)	7,248	4,132
95901	Linda(u) (916)	13,033	10,225
93247	Lindsay (209)	8,338	6,936
95953	Live Oak(u) (Santa Cruz) (916)	15,212	11,482
*94550	Livermore (510)	56,741	48,349
95334	Livingston (209)	7,317	5,326
*95240	Lodi (209)	51,874	35,221
92354	Loma Linda (714)	18,470	10,694
90717	Lomita (213)	19,442	18,807
*93436	Lompoc (805)	37,649	26,267
*90801	Long Beach (310)	429,321	361,498
95650	Loomis† (916)	5,705	3,663
*90720	Los Alamitos (310)	11,788	11,529
*94022	Los Altos (415)	26,599	25,769
94022	Los Altos Hills (415)	7,514	7,421
*90086	Los Angeles (213)/(310)	3,485,557	2,968,528
93635	Los Banos (209)	14,519	10,341
*95030	Los Gatos (408)	27,357	26,906
91709	Los Serranos(u) (909)	7,099	....
94903	Lucas Valley-Marinwood(u) (415)	5,982	6,409
90262	Lynwood (213)/(310)	61,945	48,289
93250	Mc Farland (805)	7,005	5,151
95521	McKinleyville(u) (707)	10,749	7,772
*93638	Madera (209)	29,282	21,732
93637	Madera Acres(u) (209)	5,245	2,173
95954	Magalia(u) (916)	8,987	....
*90266	Manhattan Beach (310)	32,063	31,542
*95336	Manteca (209)	40,773	24,925
92518	March AFB(u) (714)	5,523	3,607
93933	Marina (408)	26,512	20,647
*90291	Marina Del Rey(u) (310)	7,431	6,336
94553	Martinez (510)	31,808	22,582
95901	Marysville (916)	12,324	9,898
90270	Maywood (213)	27,893	21,810
93640	Mendota (209)	6,821	5,038
*94025	Menlo Park (415)	28,403	26,438
92359	Mentone(u) (909)	5,675	....
*95340	Merced (209)	56,155	36,423
94030	Millbrae (415)	20,414	20,058
*94941	Mill Valley (415)	13,038	12,967
*95035	Milpitas (408)	50,690	37,820
91752	Mira Loma(u) (909)	15,786	7,394
93641	Mira Monte(u) (805)	7,744	....
*92691	Mission Viejo† (714)	72,820	48,503

ZIP	Place		1990	1980
*95350	Modesto	(209)	164,746	106,963
*91017	Monrovia	(818)	35,733	30,531
91763	Montclair	(909)	28,434	22,628
90640	Montebello	(213)	59,564	52,929
93940	Monterey	(408)	31,954	27,558
*91754	Monterey Park	(818)	60,738	54,338
*93021	Moorpark†	(805)	25,494	7,798
*94556	Moraga	(510)	15,987	15,014
*92552	Moreno Valley†	(909)	118,779	28,139
*95037	Morgan Hill	(408)	23,928	17,060
*93442	Morro Bay	(805)	9,664	9,064
*94041	Mountain View	(415)	67,365	58,655
92405	Muscoy(u)	(714)	7,541	6,188
*94558	Napa	(707)	61,865	50,879
*91950	National City	(619)	54,249	48,772
92363	Needles	(619)	5,191	4,120
94560	Newark	(510)	37,861	32,126
*92658	Newport Beach	(714)	66,643	62,556
93444	Nipomo(u)	(805)	7,109	5,247
91760	Norco	(909)	23,302	19,732
95603	North Auburn(u)	(916)	10,301	7,619
94025	North Fair Oaks(u)	(415)	13,912	10,308
95660	North Highlands(u)	(916)	42,105	37,825
90650	Norwalk	(310)	94,279	84,901
*94947	Novato	(415)	47,585	43,916
95361	Oakdale	(209)	11,978	8,474
*94617	Oakland	(510)	372,242	339,337
94561	Oakley(u)	(510)	18,374	2,816
93445	Oceano(u)	(805)	6,169	4,478
*92054	Oceanside	(619)	128,090	76,698
93308	Oildale(u)	(805)	26,553	23,382
*93023	Ojai	(805)	7,613	6,816
95961	Olivehurst(u)	(916)	9,738	8,929
*91761	Ontario	(909)	133,179	88,820
95060	Opal Cliffs(u)	(408)	5,940	5,041
*92613	Orange	(714)	110,658	91,450
93646	Orange Cove	(209)	5,604	4,026
95662	Orangevale(u)	(916)	26,266	20,585
94563	Orinda†	(510)	16,642	17,030
95963	Orland	(916)	5,052	4,031
93647	Orosi(u)	(209)	5,486	4,076
*95965	Oroville	(916)	11,885	8,683
95965	Oroville East(u)	(916)	8,462	....
*93030	Oxnard	(805)	142,560	108,195
94044	Pacifica	(415)	37,670	36,866
93950	Pacific Grove	(408)	16,117	15,755
95968	Palermo(u)		5,260	2,572
93590	Palmdale	(805)	68,946	12,277
92260	Palm Desert	(619)	23,252	11,801
.....	Palm Desert Country(u)	....	5,626	
*92262	Palm Springs	(619)	40,144	32,359
*94303	Palo Alto	(415)	55,900	55,225
90274	Palos Verdes Estates	(310)	13,512	14,376
*95969	Paradise	(916)	25,401	22,571
90723	Paramount	(310)	47,669	36,407
95823	Parkway-So. Sacramento(u)	(916)	31,903	26,815
93648	Parlier	(209)	7,938	2,902
*91109	Pasadena	(818)	131,586	118,072
95363	Patterson	(209)	8,626	3,908
92509	Pedley(u)		8,869	....
*92572	Perris	(909)	21,500	6,827
*94952	Petaluma	(707)	43,166	33,834
*90660	Pico Rivera	(310)	59,177	53,387
*94612	Piedmont	(510)	10,602	10,498
94564	Pinole	(510)	17,460	14,253
*93449	Pismo Beach	(805)	7,669	5,364
94565	Pittsburg	(510)	47,607	33,465
92670	Placentia	(714)	41,259	35,041
95667	Placerville	(916)	8,286	6,739
94523	Pleasant Hill	(510)	31,583	25,547
*94566	Pleasanton	(510)	50,570	35,160
*91769	Pomona	(909)	131,700	92,742
*93257	Porterville	(209)	29,521	19707
*93041	Port Hueneme	(805)	20,322	17,803
92064	Poway†	(619)	43,396	33,439
93907	Prunedale(u)		7,393	....
*93551	Quartz Hill(u)	(805)	9,626	7,421
92065	Ramona(u)	(619)	13,040	8,173
*95670	Rancho Cordova(u)	(916)	48,731	42,881
*91729	Rancho Cucamonga	(714)	101,409	55,250
92270	Rancho Mirage	(619)	9,778	6,281
*90275	Rancho Palos Verdes	(310)	41,667	36,577
.....	Rancho San Diego(u)		6,977	....
92688	Rancho Santa Margarita(u)	....	11,390	....
96080	Red Bluff	(916)	12,363	9,490
*96049	Redding	(916)	66,462	42,103
*92373	Redlands	(909)	60,395	43,619
*90277	Redondo Beach	(310)	60,167	57,102
*94063	Redwood City	(415)	66,072	54,951
93654	Reedley	(209)	15,791	11,071
*92377	Rialto	(909)	72,395	37,862
*94802	Richmond	(510)	86,019	74,676
*93555	Ridgecrest	(619)	28,295	15,929
95003	Rio Del Mar(u)	(408)	8,919	7,067
95673	Rio Linda(u)	(916)	9,481	7,359
95366	Ripon	(209)	7,455	3,509
95367	Riverbank	(209)	8,591	5,695
*92502	Riverside	(909)	226,546	170,591
*95677	Rocklin	(916)	18,806	7,344
94572	Rodeo(u)	(415)	7,589	8,286

ZIP	Place		1990	1980
*94928	Rohnert Park	(707)	36,326	22,965
90274	Rolling Hills Estates	(310)	7,789	7,701
93560	Rosamond(u)	(805)	7,430	2,869
95401	Roseland(u)	(707)	8,779	7,915
91770	Rosemead	(818)	51,638	42,604
95826	Rosemont(u)	(916)	22,851	18,888
*95678	Roseville	(916)	44,685	24,347
90720	Rossmoor(u)	(310)	9,893	10,457
91748	Rowland Heights(u)	(818)	42,647	28,258
92509	Rubidoux(u)	(909)	24,367	17,048
*95814	Sacramento	(916)	369,365	275,741
*93907	Salinas	(408)	108,777	80,479
*94960	San Anselmo	(415)	11,735	12,067
*92401	San Bernardino	(909)	164,676	118,794
*94066	San Bruno	(415)	38,961	35,417
*93001	San Buenaventura (Ventura)	(805)	92,557	73,774
94070	San Carlos	(415)	26,382	24,710
*92674	San Clemente	(714)	41,100	27,325
*92138	San Diego	(619)	1,110,554	875,538
92065	San Diego Country Estates(u)	(619)	6,874	....
91773	San Dimas	(909)	32,398	24,014
*91341	San Fernando	(818)	22,580	17,731
*94142	San Francisco	(415)	723,959	678,974
*91778	San Gabriel	(818)	37,120	30,072
93657	Sanger	(209)	16,839	12,542
*92581	San Jacinto	(909)	16,210	7,098
*95113	San Jose	(408)	782,248	629,400
*92675	San Juan Capistrano	(714)	26,183	18,959
*94577	San Leandro	(510)	68,223	63,952
94580	San Lorenzo(u)	(510)	19,987	20,545
*93401	San Luis Obispo	(805)	41,958	34,252
*92069	San Marcos	(619)	38,974	17,479
*91118	San Marino	(818)	12,959	13,307
*94402	San Mateo	(415)	85,619	77,640
94806	San Pablo	(510)	25,158	19,750
*94915	San Rafael	(415)	48,410	44,700
94583	San Ramon†	(510)	35,303	20,511
*92711	Santa Ana	(714)	293,827	204,023
*93102	Santa Barbara	(805)	85,571	74,414
*95050	Santa Clara	(408)	93,613	87,700
*91380	Santa Clarita†	(805)	110,690	66,730
*95060	Santa Cruz	(408)	49,711	41,483
90670	Santa Fe Springs	(310)	15,520	14,520
93454	Santa Maria	(805)	61,552	39,685
*90401	Santa Monica	(310)	86,905	88,314
*93060	Santa Paula	(805)	25,062	20,658
*95402	Santa Rosa	(707)	113,261	82,658
92071	Santee†	(619)	52,902	40,298
*95070	Saratoga	(408)	28,061	29,261
*94965	Sausalito	(415)	7,152	7,338
*95066	Scotts Valley	(408)	8,667	6,891
90740	Seal Beach	(310)	25,098	25,975
93955	Seaside	(408)	38,826	36,567
*95472	Sebastopol	(707)	7,008	5,595
93662	Selma	(209)	14,757	10,942
93263	Shafter	(805)	8,409	7,010
*91025	Sierra Madre	(818)	10,762	10,837
90806	Signal Hill	(310)	8,371	5,734
*93065	Simi Valley	(805)	100,218	77,500
92075	Solana Beach†	(619)	12,956	12,250
93960	Soledad	(408)	7,161	5,928
95476	Sonoma	(707)	8,168	6,054
95073	Soquel(u)	(408)	9,188	6,212
91733	South El Monte	(213)	20,850	16,623
90280	South Gate	(213)/(310)	86,284	66,784
*96151	South Lake Tahoe	(916)	21,586	20,681
95965	South Oroville(u)	(916)	7,463	7,246
*91030	South Pasadena	(818)	23,936	22,681
*94080	South San Francisco	(415)	54,312	49,393
91770	South San Gabriel(u)	(213)	7,700	5,421
91744	South San Jose Hills(u)	(408)	17,814	16,076
90605	South Whittier(u)	(310)	49,514	43,815
95991	South Yuba(u)	(916)	8,816	7,530
*91977	Spring Valley(u)	(619)	55,331	40,191
94305	Stanford(u)	(415)	18,097	11,045
90680	Stanton	(714)	30,491	23,723
*95208	Stockton	(209)	210,943	148,283
94585	Suisun City	(707)	22,704	11,087
*92586	Sun City(u)	(714)	14,930	8,460
*94086	Sunnyvale	(408)	117,324	106,618
96130	Susanville	(916)	7,279	6,520
93268	Taft	(805)	5,902	5,316
94941	Tamalpais-Homestead Valley(u)	(415)	9,601	8,511
*93581	Tehachapi	(805)	6,182	4,126
*92589	Temecula†	(909)	27,177	4,289
91780	Temple City	(818)	31,153	28,972
95965	Thermalito(u)	(916)	5,646	4,961
*91359	Thousand Oaks	(805)	104,381	77,072
94920	Tiburon	(415)	7,554	6,685
*90503	Torrance	(310)	133,107	129,881
*95376	Tracy	(209)	33,558	18,428
*93274	Tulare	(209)	33,249	22,530
*95380	Turlock	(209)	42,224	26,287
*92681	Tustin	(714)	50,689	32,248
92705	Tustin Foothills(u)	(714)	24,358	26,174
*92277	Twentynine Palms†	(619)	11,821	8,802
92278	Twentynine Palms Base(u)	(619)	10,606	7,079
95060	Twin Lakes(u)	(408)	5,379	4,502
95482	Ukiah	(707)	14,632	12,035

ZIP	Place		1990	1980
94587	Union City	(510)	53,762	39,406
*91785	Upland	(909)	63,374	47,647
*95687	Vacaville	(707)	71,476	43,367
91744	Valinda(u)	(818)	18,735	18,712
*94590	Vallejo	(707)	109,199	80,303
92343	Valle Vista(u)	(714)	8,751	5,474
93437	Vandenberg AFB(u)	(805)	9,846	8,136
93436	Vandenberg Village(u)	(805)	5,971	5,839
	Ventura See San Buenaventura			
*92393	Victorville	(619)	40,674	14,220
90043	View Park-Windsor Hills(u)	(310)	11,769	12,101
92667	Villa Park	(714)	6,299	7,137
.....	Vincent(u)		13,713	....
*93277	Visalia	(209)	75,659	49,729
*92083	Vista	(619)	71,865	35,834
*91788	Walnut	(909)	29,105	12,478
*94596	Walnut Creek	(510)	60,569	54,033
90255	Walnut Park(u)	(310)	14,722	11,811
93280	Wasco	(805)	12,412	9,613
*95076	Watsonville	(408)	31,099	23,662
90044	West Athens(u)	(310)	8,859	8,531
90502	West Carson(u)	(213)	20,143	17,997
90247	West Compton(u)	(310)	5,451	5,907
*91793	West Covina	(818)	96,226	80,292
90069	West Hollywood†	(213/310)	36,118	35,754
91359	Westlake Village†	(805)	7,455	6,130
92684	Westminster	(714)	78,293	71,133
90047	Westmont(u)	(213)	31,044	27,916
91746	West Puente Valley(u)	(818)	20,254	20,445
95691	West Sacramento†	(916)	28,898	24,482
*90606	West Whittier-Los Nietos(u)	(310)	24,164	21,001
*90605	Whittier	(310)	77,671	68,558
92595	Wildomar(u)	(907)	10,411	....
95490	Willits	(707)	5,027	4,008
90222	Willowbrook(u)	(213)	32,772	30,962
95988	Willows	(916)	5,988	4,777
95492	Windsor(u)	(707)	13,371	....
95388	Winton(u)	(209)	7,559	4,995
92502	Woodcrest(u)	(909)	7,796	....
93286	Woodlake	(209)	5,678	4,343
*95695	Woodland	(916)	40,230	30,235
94062	Woodside	(415)	5,034	5,291
*92686	Yorba Linda	(714)	52,422	28,254
96097	Yreka	(916)	6,948	5,916
*95991	Yuba City	(916)	27,385	18,736
92399	Yucaipa†	(909)	32,824	27,654
*92286	Yucca Valley(u)	(619)	13,701	8,294

Colorado

ZIP	Place		1990	1980
*80840	Air Force Academy	(719)	9,062	8,655
81101	Alamosa	(719)	7,579	6,830
80401	Applewood(u)	(303)	11,069	12,040
*80004	Arvada	(303)	89,218	84,576
*81611	Aspen	(970)	5,049	3,678
*80017	Aurora	(303)	222,103	158,588
80908	Black Forest(u)	(719)	8,143	3,372
*80302	Boulder	(303)	83,295	76,685
80601	Brighton	(303)	14,203	12,773
*80020	Broomfield	(303)	24,638	20,730
*81212	Canon City	(719)	12,687	13,037
80104	Castle Rock	(303)	8,710	3,921
80120	Castlewood(u)	(303)	24,392	16,413
80110	Cherry Hills Village	(303)	5,245	5,127
81220	Cimarron Hills(u)	(719)	11,160	6,597
81520	Clifton(u)	(970)	12,671	5,223
*80903	Colorado Springs	(719)	280,430	215,105
80120	Columbine(u)	(303)	23,969	23,523
*80022	Commerce City	(303)	16,466	16,234
81321	Cortez	(970)	7,284	7,095
*81625	Craig	(970)	8,091	8,133
*80202	Denver	(303)	467,610	492,686
80022	Derby(u)	(303)	6,043	8,578
*81301	Durango	(970)	12,439	11,649
*80110	Englewood	(303)	29,396	30,021
80620	Evans	(970)	5,876	5,063
80439	Evergreen(u)	(303)	7,582	6,376
80221	Federal Heights	(303)	9,342	7,838
80913	Fort Carson(u)	(719)	11,309	13,219
*80525	Fort Collins	(970)	87,491	65,092
80621	Fort Lupton	(970)	5,159	4,251
80701	Fort Morgan	(970)	9,068	8,768
80817	Fountain	(719)	10,175	8,324
81504	Fruitvale(u)	(303)	5,222	....
81522	Gateway(u)	(970)	7,510	....
*81601	Glenwood Springs	(970)	6,561	4,637
*80401	Golden	(303)	13,127	12,237
*81501	Grand Junction	(970)	29,255	27,956
*80631	Greeley	(970)	60,454	53,006
*80111	Greenwood Village	(303)	7,589	5,729
80501	Gunbarrel(u)	(303)	9,388	5,172
80126	Highlands Ranch(u)	(303)	10,181	....
80127	Ken Caryl(u)	(303)	24,391	10,661
80026	Lafayette	(303)	14,708	8,985
81050	La Junta	(719)	7,678	8,338
*80226	Lakewood	(303)	126,475	113,808
81052	Lamar	(719)	8,343	7,713

ZIP	Place		1990	1980
*80126	Littleton	(303)	33,711	28,631
*80501	Longmont	(303)	51,529	42,942
80027	Louisville	(303)	12,363	5,593
*80538	Loveland	(970)	37,357	30,215
*81401	Montrose	(970)	8,854	8,722
80233	Northglenn	(303)	27,195	29,847
80649	Orchard Mesa(u)	(303)	5,977	4,876
80134	Parker†	(303)	5,450	290
*81003	Pueblo	(719)	98,640	101,686
	Redlands(u)	(970)	9,355	....
80911	Security-Widefield(u)	(719)	23,822	18,768
80221	Sherrelwood(u)	(303)	16,636	17,629
80122	Southglenn(u)	(303)	43,087	37,787
*80477	Steamboat Springs	(970)	6,695	5,098
80751	Sterling	(970)	10,362	11,385
80906	Stratmoor(u)	(719)	5,854	5,519
80229	Thornton	(303)	55,031	42,054
81082	Trinidad	(719)	8,580	9,663
80229	Welby(u)	(303)	10,218	9,668
80030	Westminster	(303)	74,619	50,211
80221	Westminster East(u)	(303)	5,197	6,002
*80033	Wheat Ridge	(303)	29,419	30,293
80550	Windsor	(970)	5,062	4,277

Connecticut

See note on page 396

ZIP	Place		1990	1980
06401	Ansonia	(203)	18,403	19,039
06001	Avon	(860)	13,937	11,201
06403	Beacon Falls	(203)	5,083	3,995
06037	Berlin	(860)	16,787	15,121
06801	Bethel	(203)	17,541	16,004
06002	Bloomfield	(860)	19,483	18,608
06405	Branford	(203)	27,603	23,363
*06602	Bridgeport	(203)	141,686	142,546
*06010	Bristol	(860)	60,640	57,370
06804	Brookfield	(203)	14,113	12,872
06234	Brooklyn	(860)	6,681	5,691
06013	Burlington	(860)	7,026	5,660
06019	Canton	(860)	8,268	7,635
06040	Central Manchester(u)	(860)	30,934	31,058
06410	Cheshire	(203)	25,684	21,788
06413	Clinton	(860)	12,767	11,195
06415	Colchester	(860)	10,980	7,761
06340	Conning Towers-Nautilus Park(u)	(860)	10,013	9,665
06238	Coventry	(860)	10,063	8,895
06416	Cromwell	(860)	12,286	10,265
*06810	Danbury	(203)	65,585	60,470
06820	Darien	(203)	18,130	18,892
06418	Derby	(203)	12,199	12,346
06422	Durham	(860)	5,732	5,143
06423	East Haddam	(860)	6,676	5,621
06424	East Hampton	(860)	10,428	8,572
*06101	East Hartford(u)	(860)	50,452	52,563
06512	East Haven(u)	(203)	26,144	25,036
06333	East Lyme	(860)	15,340	13,870
06016	East Windsor	(860)	10,081	8,925
06425	Easton	(203)	6,303	5,962
06029	Ellington	(860)	11,197	9,711
*06082	Enfield	(860)	45,532	42,695
06426	Essex	(860)	5,904	5,078
06430	Fairfield	(203)	53,418	54,849
*06032	Farmington	(860)	20,608	16,407
06033	Glastonbury Center(u)	(860)	7,082	7,049
06035	Granby	(860)	9,369	7,956
*06830	Greenwich	(203)	58,441	59,565
06351	Griswold	(860)	10,384	8,967
06340	Groton	(860)	45,144	41,062
06340	Groton Borough	(860)	9,837	10,086
06437	Guilford	(203)	19,848	17,375
06438	Haddam	(860)	6,769	6,383
*06514	Hamden	(203)	52,434	51,071
*06101	Hartford	(860)	139,739	136,392
06791	Harwinton	(860)	5,228	4,889
06082	Hazardville(u)	(860)	5,179	5,436
06248	Hebron	(860)	7,079	5,453
06037	Kensington(u)	(860)	8,306	7,502
06239	Killingly	(860)	15,889	14,519
06249	Lebanon	(860)	6,041	4,762
06339	Ledyard	(860)	14,913	13,735
06759	Litchfield	(860)	8,365	7,605
06443	Madison	(203)	15,485	14,031
06040	Manchester	(860)	51,618	49,761
06250	Mansfield	(860)	21,103	20,634
06447	Marlborough	(860)	5,535	4,746
*06450	Meriden	(203)	59,479	57,118
06762	Middlebury	(203)	6,145	5,995
06457	Middletown	(860)	42,762	39,040
06460	Milford	(203)	49,938	48,168
06468	Monroe	(203)	16,896	14,010
06353	Montville	(860)	16,673	16,455
06770	Naugatuck	(203)	30,625	26,456
*06050	New Britain	(860)	75,491	73,840
06840	New Canaan	(203)	17,864	17,931
06810	New Fairfield	(203)	12,911	11,260
06057	New Hartford	(860)	5,769	4,884

ZIP	Place		1990	1980
*06511	New Haven	(203)	130,474	126,089
*06111	Newington(u)	(860)	29,208	28,841
06320	New London	(860)	28,540	28,842
06776	New Milford	(860)	23,629	19,420
06470	Newtown	(203)	20,779	19,107
06471	North Branford	(203)	12,996	11,554
06473	North Haven(u)	(203)	22,249	22,080
*06856	Norwalk	(203)	78,331	77,767
06360	Norwich	(860)	37,391	38,074
06779	Oakville(u)	(860)	8,741	8,737
06371	Old Lyme	(860)	6,535	6,159
06475	Old Saybrook	(860)	9,552	9,287
06477	Orange	(203)	12,830	13,237
06478	Oxford	(203)	8,685	6,634
06365	Preston	(860)	5,006	4,644
02891	Pawcatuck(u)	(860)	5,289	5,216
06374	Plainfield	(860)	14,363	12,774
06062	Plainville	(860)	17,392	16,401
06782	Plymouth	(860)	11,822	10,732
06480	Portland	(860)	8,418	8,383
06365	Preston	(860)	5,006	4,644
06712	Prospect	(203)	7,775	6,807
06260	Putnam	(860)	6,835	6,855
06260	Putnam†	(860)	9,031	8,580
06898	Redding	(203)	7,927	7,272
06877	Ridgefield Center(u)	(203)	6,363	6,066
06877	Ridgefield	(203)	20,919	20,120
06067	Rocky Hill	(860)	16,554	14,559
06483	Seymour	(203)	14,288	13,434
06484	Shelton	(203)	35,418	31,314
06082	Sherwood Manor(u)	(860)	6,357	6,303
06070	Simsbury	(860)	22,023	21,161
06071	Somers	(860)	9,108	8,473
06488	Southbury	(203)	15,818	14,156
06489	Southington	(860)	38,518	36,879
06074	South Windsor	(860)	22,090	17,198
06082	Southwood Acres(u)	(860)	8,963	9,779
06075	Stafford	(860)	11,091	9,268
*06904	Stamford	(203)	108,056	102,466
06378	Stonington	(860)	16,919	16,220
06268	Storrs(u)	(860)	12,198	11,394
06497	Stratford(u)	(203)	49,389	50,541
06078	Suffield	(860)	11,427	9,294
06786	Terryville(u)	(860)	5,426	5,234
06787	Thomaston	(860)	6,947	6,272
06277	Thompson	(860)	8,668	8,141
06082	Thompsonville(u)	(860)	8,458	8,151
06084	Tolland	(860)	11,001	9,694
06790	Torrington	(860)	33,687	30,987
06611	Trumbull(u)	(203)	32,000	32,989
06066	Vernon	(860)	29,841	27,974
06492	Wallingford	(203)	40,822	37,274
*06701	Waterbury	(203)	108,961	103,266
06385	Waterford	(860)	17,930	17,843
06795	Watertown	(860)	20,456	19,489
06107	West Hartford(u)	(203)	60,110	61,301
06516	West Haven	(203)	54,021	53,184
06498	Westbrook	(860)	5,414	5,216
06883	Weston	(203)	8,648	8,284
*06880	Westport(u)	(203)	24,407	25,290
06109	Wethersfield(u)	(860)	25,651	26,013
06226	Willimantic(u)†	(860)	14,746	14,652
06279	Willington	(860)	5,979	4,694
06897	Wilton	(203)	15,989	15,351
06094	Winchester	(860)	11,524	10,841
06280	Windham	(860)	22,039	21,062
06095	Windsor	(860)	27,817	25,204
06096	Windsor Locks(u)	(860)	12,358	12,190
06098	Winsted	(860)	8,254	8,092
06716	Wolcott	(203)	13,700	13,008
06525	Woodbridge	(203)	7,924	7,761
06798	Woodbury	(203)	8,131	6,942
06281	Woodstock	(860)	6,008	5,117

Delaware (302)

ZIP	Place	1990	1980
19713	Brookside(u)	15,307	15,255
19703	Claymont(u)	9,800	10,022
*19901	Dover	27,630	23,507
19809	Edgemoor(u)	5,853	7,397
19805	Elsmere	5,935	6,493
19963	Milford	6,032	5,366
*19711	Newark	26,463	25,247
19800	Pike Creek(u)	10,163	....
19973	Seaford	5,689	5,256
19977	Smyrna	5,231	4,750
19804	Stanton(u)	5,028	5,495
19803	Talleyville(u)	6,346	6,880
*19899	Wilmington	71,529	70,195
19720	Wilmington Manor	8,568	9,233

District of Columbia (202)

ZIP	Place	1990	1980
*20090	Washington	606,900	638,432

Florida

ZIP	Place		1990	1980
*32714	Altamonte Springs	(407)	35,167	21,105
.....	Andover(u)		6,251	....
33572	Apollo Beach(u)	(813)	6,025	4,014
*32712	Apopka	(407)	13,611	6,019
33821	Arcadia	(941)	6,488	6,002
32233	Atlantic Beach	(904)	11,636	7,847
33823	Auburndale	(941)	8,846	6,501
33280	Aventura(u)	(305)	14,914	9,698
33825	Avon Park	(941)	8,078	8,026
32857	Azalea Park(u)	(407)	8,926	8,301
*33830	Bartow	(941)	14,716	14,780
.....	Bay Hill(u)		5,346	....
34667	Bayonet Point(u)	(813)	21,860	16,455
33505	Bayshore Gardens(u)	(813)	17,062	14,945
33589	Beacon Square(u)	(813)	6,265	6,513
34233	Bee Ridge	(941)	6,406	3,313
32073	Bellair-Meadowbrook Terrace(u)	(813)	15,606	12,144
33430	Belle Glade	(407)	16,177	16,535
*32802	Belle Isle	(407)	5,272	2,848
34420	Belleview(u)	(904)	19,386	15,439
*34464	Beverly Hills(u)	(904)	6,163	5,024
*33509	Bloomingdale(u)	(813)	13,912	....
.....	Boca Del Mar(u)		17,754	....
*33431	Boca Raton	(407)	61,486	49,447
*33923	Bonita Springs(u)	(941)	13,600	5,435
*33436	Boynton Beach	(407)	46,284	35,624
*34206	Bradenton	(941)	43,769	30,228
*33509	Brandon(u)	(813)	57,985	41,826
32503	Brent(u)	(904)	21,624	21,872
33317	Broadview Park(u)	(954)	6,109	6,022
33313	Broadview-Pompano Park(u)	(954)	5,230	5,223
*34601	Brooksville	(904)	7,589	5,582
33311	Browardale(u)	(954)	6,257	7,409
33142	Brownsville(u)	(813)	15,607	18,058
34743	Buena Ventura Lakes(u)		14,148	....
32404	Callaway	(904)	12,253	7,154
32920	Cape Canaveral	(407)	8,014	5,733
*33990	Cape Coral	(941)	74,991	32,103
33055	Carol City(u)	(305)	53,331	47,349
*33688	Carrollwood(u)	(813)	7,195	....
*33601	Carrollwood Village(u)	(813)	15,051	....
*32707	Casselberry	(407)	18,849	15,037
33401	Century Village(u)	(305)	8,363	10,619
*34618	Clearwater	(813)	98,699	85,170
*34711	Clermont	(904)	6,910	5,461
33440	Clewiston	(941)	6,085	5,219
*32922	Cocoa	(407)	17,710	16,096
*32931	Cocoa Beach	(407)	12,123	10,926
32922	Cocoa West(u)	(407)	6,160	6,432
*33063	Coconut Creek	(954)	27,269	6,288
33064	Collier Manor-Cresthaven(u)	(954)	7,322	7,045
33801	Combee Settlement(u)	(813)	5,463	5,400
32809	Conway(u)	(407)	13,159	24,027
33328	Cooper City	(954)	21,335	10,140
33114	Coral Gables	(305)	40,091	43,241
*33060	Coral Springs	(954)	78,864	37,349
33157	Coral Terrace(u)	(305)	23,255	22,702
*32536	Crestview	(904)	9,886	7,617
33803	Crystal Lake(u)	(813)	5,300	6,827
33157	Cutler(u)	(305)	16,201	15,608
33157	Cutler Ridge(u)	(305)	21,268	20,886
33884	Cypress Gardens(u)	(941)	9,188	8,043
33919	Cypress Lake(u)	(941)	10,491	8,721
*33525	Dade City	(904)	5,633	4,923
33004	Dania	(954)	13,183	11,796
33314	Davie	(954)	47,143	20,500
*32114	Daytona Beach	(904)	61,991	54,176
32713	De Bary	(407)	7,176	4,980
*33441	Deerfield Beach	(954)	46,997	39,193
32433	DeFuniak Springs	(904)	5,200	5,563
*32720	De Land	(904)	16,622	15,354
*33444	Delray Beach	(407)	47,184	34,329
33617	Del Rio(u)	(813)	8,248	7,409
*32763	Deltona(u)	(407)	50,828	15,710
*32541	Destin†	(904)	8,090	3,913
.....	Doctor Phillips(u)		7,963	....
*34698	Dunedin	(813)	34,427	30,203
33610	East Lake-Orient Park(u)	(813)	6,171	5,612
33940	East Naples(u)	(941)	22,951	12,127
*32132	Edgewater	(904)	15,351	6,726
32542	Eglin AFB(u)	(904)	8,347	7,574
33614	Egypt Lake(u)	(813)	14,580	11,932
34680	Elfers(u)	(813)	12,356	11,396
*34223	Englewood(u)	(941)	15,025	10,229
32534	Ensley(u)	(904)	16,362	14,422
*32726	Eustis	(904)	12,856	9,453
32804	Fairview Shores(u)	(305)	13,192	10,174
*32034	Fernandina Beach	(904)	8,765	7,224
32730	Fern Park(u)	(407)	8,294	8,904
32514	Ferry Pass(u)	(904)	26,301	16,910
33034	Florida City	(305)	5,978	6,174
32960	Florida Ridge(u)	(407)	12,218	4,988
32714	Forest City(u)	(407)	10,638	6,819
.....	Forest Island Park(u)		5,988	....
*33310	Fort Lauderdale	(954)	149,238	153,279
*33902	Fort Myers	(941)	44,947	36,638

ZIP	Place	1990	1980
*33931	Fort Myers Beach(u) (941)	9,284	5,753
*33922	Fort Myers Shores(u) (941)	5,460	4,426
*34981	Fort Pierce (407)	36,830	33,802
33452	Fort Pierce North(u) (407)	5,833	5,929
34982	Fort Pierce South(u) (407)	5,320	3,324
*32548	Fort Walton Beach (904)	21,407	20,829
*32043	Fruit Cove(u) (904)	5,904	3,906
34230	Fruitville(u) (941)	9,808	2,551
*32602	Gainesville (904)	85,075	81,371
33801	Gibsonia(u) (813)	5,168	5,011
33534	Gibsonton(u) (813)	7,706	....
32960	Gifford(u) (407)	6,278	6,240
33138	Gladeview(u) (954)	15,637	18,919
33143	Glenvar Heights(u) (305)	14,823	13,216
33999	Golden Gate(u) (941)	14,148	4,327
33055	Golden Glades(u) (305)	25,474	23,154
32733	Goldenrod(u) (407)	12,362	13,677
32560	Gonzalez(u) (904)	7,669	6,084
33170	Goulds(u) (305)	7,284	7,078
.....	Greater Northdale(u)	16,318	....
33463	Greenacres City (407)	18,683	8,870
*32561	Gulf Breeze (904)	5,530	5,478
33581	Gulf Gate Estates(u) (813)	11,622	9,248
33707	Gulfport (941)	11,709	11,180
*33844	Haines City (941)	11,683	10,799
*33009	Hallandale (305)/(954)	30,997	36,517
.....	Hammocks(u)	10,897	....
.....	Hamptons at Boca Raton(u)	11,686	....
*33010	Hialeah (305)	188,008	145,254
33016	Hialeah Gardens	7,727	2,700
.....	Highpoint	13,818	....
*33455	Hobe Sound(u) (407)	11,507	6,822
*34689	Holiday(u) (813)	19,360	18,392
32117	Holly Hill (904)	11,141	9,953
*33022	Hollywood (954)	121,720	121,323
*33030	Homestead (305)	26,694	20,668
33039	Homestead AFB(u) (305)	5,153	7,594
34447	Homosassa Springs(u)† (904)	6,271	1,426
*34667	Hudson(u) (813)	7,344	5,799
33934	Immokalee(u) (941)	14,120	11,038
32937	Indian Harbour Beach (407)	6,933	5,967
*34450	Inverness (904)	5,797	4,095
33880	Inwood(u) (941)	6,824	6,668
.....	Iona(u)	9,565	....
33162	Ives Estates(u) (305)	13,531	10,613
*32203	Jacksonville (904)	635,230	540,920
32250	Jacksonville Beach (904)	17,839	15,462
33880	Jan Phyl Village(u) (941)	5,308	2,785
33568	Jasmine Estates(u) (813)	17,136	11,995
*34957	Jensen Beach(u) (407)	9,884	6,642
*33458	Jupiter (407)	24,907	9,868
33183	Kendale Lakes(u) (305)	48,524	32,769
33256	Kendall(u) (305)	87,271	73,758
.....	Kendall Lakes West(u) (305)	6,038	....
33149	Key Biscayne(u) (305)	8,854	6,313
33037	Key Largo(u) (305)	11,336	7,447
*33040	Key West (305)	24,832	24,382
*33573	Kings Point(u) (305)	12,422	8,724
*34744	Kissimmee (407)	30,331	15,487
*32159	Lady Lake (904)	8,071	1,193
*32055	Lake City (904)	9,626	9,257
*33804	Lakeland (941)	70,576	47,406
33801	Lakeland Highlands(u) (941)	9,972	10,426
32569	Lake Lorraine(u) (904)	6,779	5,427
33054	Lake Lucerne(u) (305)	9,478	9,762
33612	Lake Magdalene(u) (813)	15,973	13,256
*32746	Lake Mary (407)	5,929	2,853
33403	Lake Park (407)	6,704	6,909
.....	Lakes by the Bay(u)	5,615	....
32073	Lakeside(u) (904)	29,137	10,534
*33853	Lake Wales (941)	9,670	8,466
34951	Lakewood Park(u) (407)	7,211	3,411
*33461	Lake Worth (407)	28,564	27,048
34639	Land O'Lakes(u) (813)	7,892	4,515
33462	Lantana (407)	8,392	8,048
*34640	Largo (813)	65,910	57,958
33313	Lauderdale Lakes (954)	27,341	25,426
33313	Lauderhill (954)	49,015	37,271
34272	Laurel(u) (941)	8,245	6,368
33714	Lealman(u) (813)	21,748	19,873
*34748	Leesburg (904)	14,783	13,191
*33936	Lehigh Acres(u) (813)	13,611	9,604
33033	Leisure City(u) (305)	19,379	17,905
33074	Lighthouse Point (954)	10,378	11,488
33177	Lindgren Acres(u) (305)	22,290	11,986
32060	Live Oak (904)	6,332	6,732
32860	Lockhart(u) (407)	11,636	10,569
34228	Longboat Key (941)	5,937	4,843
*32750	Longwood (407)	13,316	10,029
33549	Lutz(u) (813)	10,552	5,555
32444	Lynn Haven (904)	9,270	6,239
.....	McGregor(u)	6,504	....
*32751	Maitland (407)	8,932	8,763
33550	Mango(u)† (813)	8,700	6,493
33050	Marathon(u) (305)	8,857	7,568
*33937	Marco(u) (941)	9,493	4,694
33063	Margate (954)	42,985	35,900
*32446	Marianna (904)	6,292	7,006
*32901	Melbourne (407)	60,034	46,536
32666	Melrose Park(u) (904)	6,477	5,672
33561	Memphis(u) (941)	6,760	5,501
*32953	Merritt Island(u) (407)	32,886	30,708
*33101	Miami (305)	358,648	346,681
*33152	Miami Beach (305)	92,639	96,298
33023	Miami Gardens —Utopia-Carver(u) (954)	7,448	8,482
33014	Miami Lakes(u) (305)	12,750	9,809
33153	Miami Shores (305)	10,084	9,244
33166	Miami Springs (305)	13,268	12,350
32976	Micco(u) (407)	8,757	3,585
*32068	Middleburg(u) (407)	6,223	....
*32570	Milton (904)	7,216	7,206
32754	Mims(u) (407)	9,412	7,583
33023	Miramar (954)	40,663	32,813
32757	Mount Dora (904)	7,316	5,883
32526	Myrtle Grove(u) (904)	17,402	14,238
*33940	Naples (941)	19,505	17,581
33940	Naples Park(u) (941)	8,002	5,438
33092	Naranja(u) † (305)	5,790	10,381
32266	Neptune Beach (904)	6,816	5,248
*34653	New Port Richey (813)	14,044	11,196
33552	New Port Richey East(u) (813)	9,683	6,147
*32168	New Smyrna Beach (904)	16,549	13,557
*32578	Niceville (904)	10,509	8,543
33269	Norland(u) (305)	22,109	19,471
33308	North Andrews Gardens(u) (954)	9,002	8,994
33141	North Bay Village (305)	5,383	4,920
33918	North Fort Myers(u) (941)	30,027	22,808
33068	North Lauderdale (954)	26,473	18,653
33961	North Miami (305)	50,001	42,566
33160	North Miami Beach (305)	35,361	36,553
33940	North Naples(u) (941)	13,422	7,950
33408	North Palm Beach (407)	11,284	11,344
34287	North Port (941)	11,973	6,205
34234	North Sarasota(u) (941)	6,702	4,997
33334	Oakland Park (305)	26,326	22,944
33860	Oak Ridge(u) (813)	15,388	15,477
*34478	Ocala (904)	42,045	37,170
32548	Ocean City(u) (904)	5,422	5,582
32761	Ocoee (407)	12,778	7,803
33163	Ojus(u) (305)	15,519	17,344
34677	Oldsmar (813)	8,361	2,608
33265	Olympia Heights(u) (305)	37,792	33,112
*33054	Opa-Locka (305)	15,283	14,460
33054	Opa-Locka North(u) (305)	6,568	5,721
*32763	Orange City (904)	5,347	2,795
*32073	Orange Park (904)	9,488	8,766
*32802	Orlando (407)	164,674	128,291
32861	Orlo Vista(u) (407)	5,990	6,474
*32174	Ormond Beach (904)	29,721	21,436
32074	Ormond By-The-Sea(u) (904)	8,157	7,665
*32765	Oviedo (407)	11,114	3,074
32571	Pace(u) (904)	6,277	5,006
.....	Page Park-Pine Manor(u)	5,116	....
33476	Pahokee (407)	6,822	6,346
*32177	Palatka (904)	10,447	10,175
*32906	Palm Bay (407)	62,543	18,560
33480	Palm Beach (407)	9,814	9,729
33403	Palm Beach Gardens (407)	22,990	14,407
32136	Palm Coast(u) (904)	14,287	2,837
*34221	Palmetto (941)	9,268	8,637
33157	Palmetto Estates(u) (305)	12,293	11,116
*34683	Palm Harbor(u) (813)	50,256	5,215
*33601	Palm River-Clair Mel(u) (813)	13,691	14,447
33460	Palm Springs (407)	9,763	8,166
33012	Palm Springs North(u) (407)	5,300	5,838
32082	Palm Valley(u) (904)	9,960	....
*32401	Panama City (904)	34,396	33,346
33029	Pembroke Pines (954)	65,566	35,776
*32502	Pensacola (904)	59,198	57,619
33257	Perrine(u) (305)	15,576	16,129
32347	Perry (904)	7,151	8,254
32859	Pine Castle(u) (407)	8,276	9,992
32858	Pine Hills(u) (407)	35,322	31,029
.....	Pine Island Ridge	5,244	....
*34665	Pinellas Park (813)	43,571	32,811
33168	Pinewood(u) (305)	15,518	14,346
33318	Plantation (954)	66,814	48,653
*33566	Plant City (813)	22,754	17,064
*33060	Pompano Beach (954)	72,411	52,618
33064	Pompano Beach Highlands(u) (954)	17,915	16,154
*33952	Port Charlotte(u) (941)	41,535	25,770
32124	Port Orange (904)	35,399	18,756
32927	Port St. John(u) (407)	8,933	1,837
*34981	Port St. Lucie (407)	55,761	14,690
34992	Port Salerno(u) (407)	7,786	4,511
33032	Princeton(u) (305)	7,073	....
*33950	Punta Gorda (941)	10,637	6,797
*32351	Quincy (904)	7,452	8,591
33156	Richmond Heights(u) (305)	8,583	8,577
33312	Riverland(u) (954)	5,376	5,919
33569	Riverview(u) (813)	6,478	....
33419	Riviera Beach (407)	27,646	26,489
*32955	Rockledge (407)	16,023	11,877
33411	Royal Palm Beach (407)	15,532	3,423
*33570	Ruskin(u) (813)	6,046	5,117
34695	Safety Harbor (813)	15,120	6,461
*32084	Saint Augustine (904)	11,695	11,985
*34769	Saint Cloud (407)	12,684	7,840
*33733	Saint Petersburg (813)	240,318	238,647

ZIP	Place		1990	1980
33736	Saint Petersburg Beach	(813)	9,200	9,354
33912	San Carlos Park(u)	(941)	11,785	3,590
33432	Sandalfoot Cove(u)	(305)	14,214	5,299
*32771	Sanford	(407)	32,387	23,176
33957	Sanibel	(941)	5,468	3,363
*34230	Sarasota	(941)	50,897	48,868
33577	Sarasota Springs(u)	(941)	16,088	13,860
32937	Satellite Beach	(407)	9,889	9,163
33055	Scott Lake(u)	(305)	14,588	14,154
*32958	Sebastian	(407)	10,248	2,831
*33870	Sebring	(941)	8,841	8,736
33584	Seffner(u)	(813)	5,371	....
*34640	Seminole	(813)	9,251	4,856
33578	Siesta Key(u)	(813)	7,772	7,010
34472	Silver Springs Shores(u)	(904)	6,421	3,983
32809	Sky Lake(u)	(407)	6,202	6,692
32703	South Apopka(u)	(407)	6,360	5,687
33505	South Bradenton(u)	(941)	20,398	14,297
32121	South Daytona	(904)	12,488	11,252
34277	Southgate(u)	(813)	7,324	7,322
34233	South Gate Ridge(u)	(941)	5,924	4,259
33243	South Miami	(305)	10,404	10,895
33157	South Miami Heights(u)	(305)	30,030	23,559
33707	South Pasadena	(813)	5,644	4,188
32937	South Patrick Shores(u)	(407)	10,249	9,816
34230	South Sarasota(u)	(941)	5,298	4,267
33595	South Venice(u)	(813)	11,951	8,075
32401	Springfield	(904)	8,719	7,220
*34601	Spring Hill(u)	(904)	31,117	6,468
32091	Starke	(904)	5,226	5,306
*34994	Stuart	(407)	11,936	9,467
33573	Sun City Center(u)	(813)	8,326	5,605
33160	Sunny Isles(u)	(305)	11,772	12,564
*33322	Sunrise	(954)	65,683	39,681
33283	Sunset(u)	(305)	15,810	13,531
33144	Sweetwater	(305)	13,909	8,067
*32301	Tallahassee	(904)	124,773	81,548
33320	Tamarac	(954)	44,822	29,376
33144	Tamiami(u)	(305)	33,845	17,607
*33602	Tampa	(813)	280,015	271,577
*34689	Tarpon Springs	(813)	17,874	13,251
32778	Tavares	(904)	7,383	4,398
*33601	Temple Terrace	(813)	16,444	11,097
*32780	Titusville	(407)	39,394	31,910
32601	Town 'n' Country(u)	(813)	60,946	37,834
33706	Treasure Island	(813)	7,266	6,316
32867	Union Park(u)	(407)	6,890	19,175
33620	University West(u)†	(904)	23,760	24,514
32401	Upper Grand Lagoon(u)	(904)	7,855	3,314
32580	Valparaiso	(904)	6,316	6,142
*34285	Venice	(941)	17,052	12,153
33595	Venice Gardens(u)	(813)	7,701	6,568
*32960	Vero Beach	(407)	17,350	16,176
32960	Vero Beach South(u)	(407)	16,973	12,636
.....	Villages of Oriole(u)		5,698	....
33901	Villas(u)	(813)	9,898	8,724
32507	Warrington(u)	(904)	16,040	15,792
33314	Washington Park(u)	(954)	6,930	7,240
32703	Wekiva Springs(u)	(407)	23,026	13,386
33414	Wellington(u)	(407)	20,670	4,622
33155	Westchester(u)	(305)	29,883	29,272
.....	Westgate-Belvedere Homes(u)		6,880	....
33138	West Little River(u)	(305)	33,575	32,492
32904	West Melbourne	(407)	8,398	5,078
33144	West Miami	(305)	5,727	6,076
*33406	West Palm Beach	(407)	67,764	63,305
.....	West Park(u)		10,347	9,003
32505	West Pensacola(u)	(904)	22,107	24,371
33168	Westview(u)	(305)	9,668	9,102
33165	Westwood Lakes(u)	(305)	11,522	11,478
.....	Whiskey Creek(u)		5,061	....
33305	Wilton Manors	(954)	11,804	12,742
33803	Winston(u)	(813)	9,118	9,315
*34787	Winter Garden	(407)	9,863	6,789
*33880	Winter Haven	(941)	24,725	21,119
*32789	Winter Park	(407)	22,623	22,339
*32707	Winter Springs	(407)	22,151	10,475
32547	Wright(u)	(904)	18,945	13,011
32097	Yulee(u)	(904)	6,915	3,168
*33540	Zephyrhills	(813)	8,220	5,742

Georgia

ZIP	Place		1990	1980
31620	Adel	(912)	5,093	5,592
*31706	Albany	(912)	78,804	74,425
*30201	Alpharetta	(770)	13,002	3,128
31709	Americus	(912)	16,516	16,120
*30603	Athens	(706)	45,734	42,549
*30301	Atlanta	(404)	393,929	425,022
*30903	Augusta	(706)	44,707	47,532
31717	Bainbridge	(912)	10,803	10,553
30032	Belvedere Park(u)	(404)	18,089	17,766
31723	Blakely	(912)	5,595	5,880
*31520	Brunswick	(912)	16,433	17,605
*30518	Buford	(404)	8,771	6,578
31728	Cairo	(912)	9,035	8,777
*30701	Calhoun	(706)	7,135	5,563
31730	Camilla	(912)	5,124	5,414

ZIP	Place		1990	1980
30032	Candler-McAfee(u)	(404)	29,491	27,306
*30117	Carrollton	(770)	16,029	14,078
30120	Cartersville	(770)	12,037	9,247
30125	Cedartown	(770)	7,976	8,619
30366	Chamblee	(404)	7,668	7,137
30021	Clarkston	(404)	5,385	4,539
30337	College Park	(404)	20,645	24,632
*31908	Columbus	(706)	178,681	169,441
30027	Conley(u)	(404)	5,528	6,033
*30208	Conyers	(404)	7,380	6,567
31015	Cordele	(912)	10,833	11,184
.....	Country Club Estates(u)		7,500	....
30209	Covington	(770)	9,860	10,586
*30720	Dalton	(706)	22,218	20,581
31742	Dawson	(912)	5,295	5,699
*30030	Decatur (DeKalb)	(404)	17,304	18,404
31520	Dock Junction(u)	(912)	7,094	6,189
30362	Doraville	(404)	7,626	7,414
31533	Douglas	(912)	10,464	10,980
*30134	Douglasville	(404)	11,635	7,641
30333	Druid Hills(u)	(404)	12,174	12,700
*31021	Dublin	(912)	16,312	16,083
30136	Duluth	(404)	9,821	2,956
30356	Dunwoody(u)	(404)	26,302	17,768
31023	Eastman	(912)	5,241	5,330
30364	East Point	(404)	34,595	37,486
30635	Elberton	(706)	4,973	5,686
30809	Evans(u)	(706)	13,713	....
30060	Fair Oaks(u)	(404)	6,996	8,486
30535	Fairview(u)	(706)	6,444	6,558
30214	Fayetteville	(404)	5,827	2,715
31750	Fitzgerald	(912)	8,901	10,187
*30050	Forest Park	(404)	16,958	18,782
31905	Fort Benning South(u)	(706)	14,617	15,074
30905	Fort Gordon(u)	(706)	9,140	14,069
30742	Fort Oglethorpe	(706)	5,880	5,443
31314	Fort Stewart(u)	(912)	13,774	15,031
31030	Fort Valley	(912)	8,198	9,000
.....	Gaines School(u)		11,354	....
*30501	Gainesville	(770)	17,885	15,280
31408	Garden City	(912)	7,410	6,895
31754	Georgetown(u)	(912)	5,554	2,785
30316	Gresham Park(u)	(404)	9,000	6,232
*30223	Griffin	(770)	21,325	20,728
30354	Hapeville	(404)	5,483	6,166
31313	Hinesville	(912)	21,596	11,309
31545	Jesup	(912)	8,958	9,418
30144	Kennesaw	(404)	8,936	5,095
31548	Kingsland	(912)	5,474	2,008
30728	La Fayette	(706)	6,313	6,517
*30240	La Grange	(706)	25,574	24,204
30741	Lakeview(u)	(706)	5,237	5,403
*30245	Lawrenceville	(404)	17,250	8,928
*30247	Lilburn	(404)	9,295	3,765
30057	Lithia Springs(u)	(404)	11,403	9,145
30059	Mableton(u)	(404)	25,725	25,111
*31201	Macon	(912)	107,365	116,896
*30060	Marietta	(404)	44,129	30,821
30917	Martinez(u)	(706)	33,731	16,472
31061	Milledgeville	(912)	17,727	12,176
*30655	Monroe	(770)	9,759	8,854
*30260	Morrow	(404)	5,168	3,791
*31768	Moultrie	(912)	14,865	15,105
30087	Mountain Park(u)	(404)	11,025	9,425
*30263	Newnan	(770)	12,497	11,449
*30071	Norcross	(404)	5,947	3,363
30319	North Atlanta(u)	(404)	27,812	30,521
30033	North Decatur(u)	(404)	13,936	11,830
30033	North Druid Hills(u)	(404)	14,170	12,438
30032	Panthersville(u)	(404)	9,874	11,366
30269	Peachtree City	(404)	19,027	6,429
31069	Perry	(912)	9,452	9,453
30073	Powder Springs	(404)	6,862	3,381
31643	Quitman	(912)	5,292	5,188
30074	Redan(u)	(404)	24,376	....
*30274	Riverdale	(404)	9,455	7,121
*30161	Rome	(706)	30,325	28,915
*30077	Roswell	(404)	47,986	23,337
31558	Saint Marys	(912)	8,204	3,596
31522	Saint Simons Island(u)	(912)	12,026	6,566
31082	Sandersville	(912)	6,290	6,137
30358	Sandy Springs(u)	(404)	67,842	46,865
*31402	Savannah	(912)	137,812	141,654
30079	Scottdale(u)	(404)	8,636	8,770
*30080	Smyrna	(404)	30,981	20,312
30278	Snellville	(404)	12,084	8,514
30901	South Augusta(u)	(706)	55,998	51,072
*30458	Statesboro	(912)	15,854	14,866
*30086	Stone Mountain	(404)	6,544	4,867
30747	Summerville	(706)	5,025	4,878
30401	Swainsboro	(912)	7,361	7,602
31791	Sylvester	(912)	6,023	5,860
30286	Thomaston	(706)	9,127	9,682
*31792	Thomasville	(912)	17,554	18,463
30824	Thomson	(706)	6,862	7,001
*31794	Tifton	(912)	14,215	13,749
30577	Toccoa(u)	(706)	8,720	8,869
*30084	Tucker(u)	(404)	25,781	25,399
30291	Union City	(404)	8,887	4,780
*31603	Valdosta	(912)	40,038	37,596

ZIP	Place		1990	1980
30474	Vidalia	(912)	11,118	10,393
30180	Villa Rica	(770)	6,542	3,420
30339	Vinings(u)	(404)	7,417	....
*31088	Warner Robins	(912)	43,861	39,893
*31501	Waycross	(912)	16,410	19,371
30830	Waynesboro	(706)	5,669	5,760
30901	West Augusta(u)	(706)	27,637	24,242
31410	Wilmington Island(u)	(912)	11,230	7,546
30680	Winder	(770)	7,373	6,705

Hawaii (808)

See note on page 396

ZIP	Place		1990	1980
96701	Aiea(u)		8,906	32,879
96818	Aliamanu(u)		8,835	....
96706	Ewa Beach(u)		14,315	14,369
.....	Halawa(u)		13,408	....
96744	Heeia(u)		5,010	5,432
96853	Hickman Housing(u)		6,553	4,425
*96720	Hilo(u)		37,808	35,269
*96820	Honolulu(u)		365,272	365,048
96732	Kahului(u)		16,889	12,978
96734	Kailua(u)		9,126	4,751
96863	Kailua(u)		36,818	35,812
96744	Kaneohe(u)		35,448	29,919
.....	Kaneohe Station(u)		11,662	11,615
96746	Kapaa(u)		8,149	4,467
96753	Kihei(u)		11,107	5,644
*96761	Lahaina(u)		9,073	6,095
96762	Laie(u)		5,577	4,643
96766	Lihue(u)		5,536	4,000
96792	Maili(u)		6,059	5,026
96792	Makaha(u)		7,990	6,582
96706	Makakilo(u)		9,828	7,691
96768	Makawao(u)		5,405	2,900
96789	Mililani Town(u)		29,359	21,365
96792	Nanakuli(u)		9,575	8,185
96782	Pearl City(u)		30,993	42,575
96788	Pukalani(u)		5,879	3,950
96786	Schofield Barracks(u)		19,597	18,851
.....	Village Park(u)		7,407	....
96786	Wahiawa(u)		17,386	16,911
96792	Waianae(u)		8,758	7,941
96793	Wailuku(u)		10,688	10,260
.....	Waimalu(u)		29,967	....
96796	Waimea(u)		5,972	1,179
96797	Waipahu(u)		31,435	29,139
96797	Waipio(u)		11,812	....
96786	Waipio Acres(u)		5,304	4,091

Idaho (208)

ZIP	Place	1990	1980
83401	Ammon	5,002	4,669
83221	Blackfoot	9,646	10,065
*83707	Boise City	125,551	102,249
83318	Burley	8,702	8,761
*83605	Caldwell	18,400	17,699
83202	Chubbuck	7,794	7,052
*83814	Coeur D'Alene	24,561	19,913
83714	Garden City	6,369	4,571
*83402	Idaho Falls	43,973	39,739
83338	Jerome	6,529	6,891
83501	Lewiston	28,082	27,986
*83642	Meridian	9,596	6,658
83843	Moscow	18,398	16,513
83647	Mountain Home	7,913	7,540
83648	Mountain Home AFB(u)	5,936	6,403
*83651	Nampa	28,365	25,112
83661	Payette	5,672	5,448
*83201	Pocatello	46,117	46,340
83854	Post Falls	7,349	5,736
83440	Rexburg	14,298	11,559
83350	Rupert	5,455	5,476
83864	Sandpoint	5,203	4,460
*83301	Twin Falls	27,634	26,209

Illinois

Area code (847) will go into effect on Jan. 20, 1996. Until then, use (708). Area code (630) will go into effect on Aug. 3, 1996. Until then, use (708).

ZIP	Place		1990	1980
60101	Addison	(630)	32,053	29,826
60102	Algonquin	(847)	11,693	5,834
60658	Alsip	(708)	18,227	17,134
62002	Alton	(618)	33,064	34,171
60002	Antioch	(847)	6,105	4,419
*60005	Arlington Heights	(847)	75,463	66,116
*60505	Aurora	(630)	99,556	81,293
*60010	Barrington	(847)	9,538	9,029
60103	Bartlett	(630)	19,395	13,254
61607	Bartonville	(309)	5,671	6,137
60510	Batavia	(630)	17,076	12,574
60085	Beach Park†	(847)	9,492	8,468
62618	Beardstown	(217)	5,270	6,338

ZIP	Place		1990	1980
*62220	Belleville	(618)	42,806	41,580
60104	Bellwood	(708)	20,241	19,811
61008	Belvidere	(815)	15,962	15,176
60106	Bensenville	(630)	17,767	16,106
62812	Benton	(618)	7,216	7,778
60163	Berkeley	(708)	5,137	5,467
60402	Berwyn	(708)	45,426	46,849
62010	Bethalto	(618)	9,507	8,630
60108	Bloomingdale	(630)	16,614	12,656
*61701	Bloomington	(309)	51,889	44,189
60406	Blue Island	(708)	21,203	21,855
60440	Bolingbrook	(630)	40,843	37,261
60538	Boulder Hill(u)	(630)	8,894	9,333
60914	Bourbonnais	(815)	13,929	13,280
60915	Bradley	(815)	10,918	11,015
60455	Bridgeview	(708)	14,402	14,155
60153	Broadview	(708)	8,538	8,618
60513	Brookfield	(708)	18,876	19,395
60089	Buffalo Grove	(847)	36,417	22,230
60459	Burbank	(708)	27,600	28,462
60521	Burr Ridge	(630)	7,684	3,838
62206	Cahokia	(618)	17,550	18,904
60409	Calumet City	(708)	37,840	39,697
60643	Calumet Park	(708)	8,418	8,788
61520	Canton	(309)	13,959	14,626
*62901	Carbondale	(618)	27,033	26,414
62626	Carlinville	(217)	5,416	5,439
62821	Carmi	(618)	5,626	6,107
*60188	Carol Stream	(630)	31,759	15,472
60110	Carpentersville	(847)	23,049	23,272
60013	Cary	(847)	10,043	6,640
62801	Centralia	(618)	14,274	15,126
62206	Centreville	(618)	7,489	9,747
*61821	Champaign	(217)	63,502	58,267
61920	Charleston	(217)	20,398	19,355
62629	Chatham	(217)	6,074	5,597
62233	Chester	(618)	8,204	8,401
*60607	Chicago	(312)	2,783,726	3,005,072
60411	Chicago Heights	(708)	32,966	37,026
60415	Chicago Ridge	(708)	13,643	13,473
61523	Chillicothe	(309)	5,959	6,176
60650	Cicero	(708)	67,436	61,232
60514	Clarendon Hills	(630)	6,994	6,870
61727	Clinton	(217)	7,437	8,014
62234	Collinsville	(618)	22,424	19,475
62236	Columbia	(618)	5,524	4,269
60478	Country Club Hills	(708)	15,431	14,676
60525	Countryside	(708)	5,961	6,242
60435	Crest Hill	(815)	10,999	9,252
60445	Crestwood	(708)	10,823	10,852
60417	Crete	(708)	6,773	5,417
61610	Creve Coeur	(309)	5,938	6,851
*60014	Crystal Lake	(815)	24,696	18,590
*61832	Danville	(217)	33,828	38,985
60561	Darien	(630)	18,148	14,956
*62525	Decatur	(217)	83,900	93,939
60015	Deerfield	(847)	17,327	17,432
60115	De Kalb	(815)	35,076	33,157
*60018	Des Plaines	(847)	53,414	53,568
61021	Dixon	(815)	15,134	15,710
60419	Dolton	(708)	23,956	24,766
*60515	Downers Grove	(630)	46,845	42,259
62832	Du Quoin	(618)	6,697	6,594
62024	East Alton	(618)	7,063	7,096
61244	East Moline	(309)	20,147	20,907
61611	East Peoria	(309)	21,378	22,385
*62201	East St. Louis	(618)	40,944	55,200
62025	Edwardsville	(618)	14,582	12,480
62401	Effingham	(217)	11,927	11,270
*60120	Elgin	(847)	77,010	63,668
*60009	Elk Grove Village	(847)	33,429	28,679
60126	Elmhurst	(630)	42,029	44,276
60635	Elmwood Park	(708)	23,206	24,016
*60201	Evanston	(847)	73,233	73,706
60642	Evergreen Park	(708)	20,874	22,260
62837	Fairfield	(618)	5,442	5,944
62208	Fairview Heights	(618)	14,351	12,111
62839	Flora	(618)	5,093	5,379
60422	Flossmoor	(708)	8,651	8,423
60130	Forest Park	(708)	14,918	15,177
60020	Fox Lake	(847)	7,539	6,831
60423	Frankfort	(815)	7,180	4,357
.....	Frankfort Square(u)	(815)	6,227	....
60131	Franklin Park	(847)	18,485	17,507
61032	Freeport	(815)	25,840	26,266
60030	Gages Lake(u)	(847)	8,349	3,814
*61401	Galesburg	(309)	33,530	35,305
61254	Geneseo	(309)	5,990	6,373
60134	Geneva	(630)	12,625	9,881
62034	Glen Carbon	(618)	7,774	5,197
60022	Glencoe	(847)	8,499	9,200
60139	Glendale Heights	(630)	27,915	23,251
*60137	Glen Ellyn	(630)	24,919	23,691
60025	Glenview	(847)	37,052	32,060
60425	Glenwood	(708)	9,289	10,538
62035	Godfrey(u)	(618)	5,436	....
.....	Goodings Grove(u)	(815)	14,054	....
62040	Granite City	(618)	32,766	36,815
60030	Grayslake	(847)	7,388	5,260
62246	Greenville	(618)	5,108	5,271

ZIP	Place		1990	1980
60031	Gurnee	(847)	13,715	7,179
*60103	Hanover Park	(630)	32,918	28,719
62946	Harrisburg	(618)	9,318	10,410
60033	Harvard	(815)	5,975	5,126
60426	Harvey	(708)	29,771	35,810
60656	Harwood Heights	(708)	7,680	8,228
60429	Hazel Crest	(708)	13,334	13,973
62948	Herrin	(618)	10,857	10,708
60457	Hickory Hills	(708)	13,021	13,778
62249	Highland	(618)	7,546	7,122
*60035	Highland Park	(847)	30,575	30,599
60040	Highwood	(847)	5,331	5,455
60162	Hillside	(708)	7,672	8,279
*60521	Hinsdale	(630)	16,029	16,726
*60195	Hoffman Estates	(847)	46,363	37,272
60430	Homewood	(708)	19,278	19,724
60942	Hoopeston	(217)	5,871	6,411
60067	Inverness	(847)	6,516	4,046
60143	Itasca	(630)	6,947	7,129
*62650	Jacksonville	(217)	19,327	20,284
62052	Jerseyville	(618)	7,382	7,506
*60436	Joliet	(815)	77,217	77,956
60458	Justice	(708)	11,137	10,552
60901	Kankakee	(815)	27,541	29,633
61443	Kewanee	(309)	12,969	14,508
60525	La Grange	(708)	15,362	15,693
60525	La Grange Park	(708)	12,861	13,359
60044	Lake Bluff	(847)	5,486	4,434
60045	Lake Forest	(847)	17,836	15,245
60102	Lake in the Hills	(847)	5,900	5,651
60047	Lake Zurich	(847)	14,927	8,225
60438	Lansing	(708)	28,131	29,039
61301	La Salle	(815)	9,717	10,347
60439	Lemont	(630)	7,359	5,640
*60048	Libertyville	(847)	19,174	16,520
62656	Lincoln	(217)	15,418	16,327
60645	Lincolnwood	(847)	11,365	11,921
60046	Lindenhurst	(847)	8,044	6,220
60532	Lisle	(630)	19,584	13,638
62056	Litchfield	(217)	6,883	7,204
60441	Lockport	(815)	9,401	9,192
60148	Lombard	(630)	39,408	36,879
*61130	Loves Park	(815)	15,457	13,192
60411	Lynwood	(708)	6,535	4,195
60534	Lyons (Cook)	(708)	9,828	9,925
*60050	McHenry	(815)	16,343	10,737
61115	Machesney Park†	(815)	19,042	19,514
61455	Macomb	(309)	19,952	19,863
62959	Marion	(618)	14,545	14,031
60426	Markham (Cook)	(708)	13,136	15,172
62258	Mascoutah	(618)	5,511	4,962
60443	Matteson	(708)	11,378	10,223
61938	Mattoon	(217)	18,441	19,293
*60153	Maywood	(708)	27,139	27,998
*60160	Melrose Park	(708)	20,859	20,735
61342	Mendota	(815)	7,017	7,134
62960	Metropolis	(618)	6,734	7,171
60445	Midlothian	(708)	14,372	14,274
61264	Milan	(309)	5,753	6,371
60448	Mokena	(708)	6,128	4,578
*61265	Moline	(309)	43,080	46,407
61462	Monmouth	(309)	9,489	10,706
60450	Morris	(815)	10,274	8,833
61550	Morton	(309)	13,799	14,178
60053	Morton Grove	(847)	22,373	23,747
62863	Mount Carmel	(618)	8,287	8,908
60056	Mount Prospect	(847)	53,168	52,634
62864	Mount Vernon	(618)	17,082	17,193
60060	Mundelein	(847)	21,224	17,053
62966	Murphysboro	(618)	9,176	9,866
*60540	Naperville	(630)	85,806	42,601
60451	New Lenox	(815)	9,698	5,792
60714	Niles	(847)	28,375	30,363
61761	Normal	(309)	40,023	35,672
60634	Norridge	(708)	14,459	16,483
60542	North Aurora	(630)	6,010	5,205
*60062	Northbrook	(708)	32,572	30,778
60064	North Chicago	(847)	34,978	38,774
60164	Northlake	(708)	12,505	12,166
60546	North Riverside	(708)	6,180	6,764
60521	Oak Brook	(630)	9,087	6,676
60452	Oak Forest	(708)	26,202	25,040
*60455	Oak Lawn	(708)	56,182	60,590
*60303	Oak Park	(708)	53,648	54,887
62269	O'Fallon	(618)	16,064	12,173
62450	Olney	(618)	8,661	9,026
60477	Orland Hills	(708)	5,510	2,784
60462	Orland Park	(708)	35,720	23,045
61350	Ottawa	(815)	17,528	18,166
*60067	Palatine	(847)	38,894	32,171
60463	Palos Heights	(708)	11,478	11,096
60465	Palos Hills	(708)	17,803	16,654
62557	Pana	(217)	5,796	6,040
61944	Paris	(217)	9,016	9,885
60466	Park Forest	(708)	24,656	26,222
60068	Park Ridge	(847)	36,175	38,704
*61554	Pekin	(309)	32,254	33,967
*61601	Peoria	(309)	113,504	124,160
61603	Peoria Heights	(309)	6,930	7,453
61354	Peru	(815)	9,302	10,886

ZIP	Place		1990	1980
60545	Plano	(630)	5,104	4,875
61764	Pontiac	(815)	11,428	11,227
61356	Princeton	(815)	7,197	7,342
60070	Prospect Heights	(847)	15,236	11,823
*62301	Quincy	(217)	39,682	42,554
61866	Rantoul	(217)	17,212	20,161
60471	Richton Park	(708)	10,523	9,403
60627	Riverdale	(708)	13,671	13,233
60305	River Forest	(708)	11,669	12,392
60171	River Grove	(708)	9,961	10,368
60546	Riverside	(708)	8,774	9,236
60472	Robbins	(708)	7,498	8,853
62454	Robinson	(618)	6,740	7,285
61068	Rochelle	(815)	8,769	8,982
61071	Rock Falls	(815)	9,669	10,633
*61125	Rockford	(815)	139,704	139,712
*61201	Rock Island	(309)	40,630	46,821
60008	Rolling Meadows	(847)	22,598	20,167
60446	Romeoville	(815)	14,101	15,519
*60172	Roselle	(630)	20,803	17,034
60073	Round Lake Beach	(847)	16,406	12,921
*60174	Saint Charles	(630)	22,620	17,492
62881	Salem	(618)	7,470	7,813
60548	Sandwich	(815)	5,607	5,356
60411	Sauk Village	(708)	9,926	10,906
*60194	Schaumburg	(847)	68,586	53,355
60176	Schiller Park	(847)	11,189	11,458
62225	Scott AFB(u)	(618)	7,245	8,648
60436	Shorewood	(815)	6,264	4,714
61282	Silvis	(309)	6,926	7,130
*60077	Skokie	(847)	59,432	60,278
60177	South Elgin	(847)	7,474	5,970
60473	South Holland	(708)	22,105	24,977
*62703	Springfield	(217)	105,417	100,054
61362	Spring Valley	(815)	5,246	5,822
60475	Steger	(708)	8,592	9,269
61081	Sterling	(815)	15,142	16,281
60402	Stickney	(708)	5,678	5,893
60107	Streamwood	(630)	31,197	23,456
61364	Streator	(815)	14,121	14,795
60501	Summit	(708)	9,971	10,110
62221	Swansea	(618)	8,201	5,529
60178	Sycamore	(815)	9,896	9,219
62568	Taylorville	(217)	11,133	11,386
60477	Tinley Park	(708)	37,115	26,178
62294	Troy	(618)	6,019	3,772
60466	University Park	(708)	6,204	6,245
61801	Urbana	(217)	36,383	35,978
62471	Vandalia	(618)	6,114	5,338
60061	Vernon Hills	(847)	15,319	9,827
60181	Villa Park	(630)	22,279	23,155
60555	Warrenville	(630)	11,389	7,519
61571	Washington	(309)	10,136	10,364
62204	Washington Park	(618)	7,431	8,223
62298	Waterloo	(618)	5,030	4,646
60970	Watseka	(815)	5,424	5,543
60084	Wauconda	(847)	6,294	5,688
*60085	Waukegan	(847)	69,481	67,653
60154	Westchester	(708)	17,301	17,730
*60185	West Chicago	(630)	14,808	12,550
60558	Western Springs	(708)	11,956	12,876
62896	West Frankfort	(618)	8,526	9,437
60559	Westmont	(630)	21,402	17,353
61604	West Peoria(u)	(309)	5,314	5,219
*60187	Wheaton	(630)	51,441	43,043
*60090	Wheeling	(847)	29,911	23,266
60514	Willowbrook	(630)	8,701	4,953
60091	Wilmette	(847)	26,694	28,221
60190	Winfield	(630)	7,096	4,422
60093	Winnetka	(847)	12,210	12,772
60096	Winthrop Harbor	(847)	6,240	5,427
60097	Wonder Lake(u)	(815)	6,664	5,917
60191	Wood Dale	(630)	12,394	11,251
*60517	Woodridge	(630)	26,359	21,763
62095	Wood River	(618)	11,490	12,446
60098	Woodstock	(815)	14,368	11,725
60482	Worth	(708)	11,208	11,592
60099	Zion	(847)	19,783	17,865

Indiana

ZIP	Place		1990	1980
46001	Alexandria	(317)	5,709	6,028
*46011	Anderson	(317)	59,459	64,695
46703	Angola	(219)	5,851	5,486
46706	Auburn	(219)	9,386	8,122
47421	Bedford	(812)	13,817	14,410
46107	Beech Grove	(317)	13,383	13,196
*47408	Bloomington	(812)	60,633	52,663
46714	Bluffton	(219)	9,104	8,705
47601	Boonville	(812)	6,686	6,300
47834	Brazil	(812)	7,640	7,852
46112	Brownsburg	(317)	7,628	6,242
*46032	Carmel	(317)	25,380	18,272
46303	Cedar Lake	(219)	8,885	8,754
47111	Charlestown	(812)	5,889	5,596
46304	Chesterton	(219)	9,118	8,531

ZIP	Place		1990	1980
47129	Clarksville (Clark Co.)....	(812)	19,838	15,164
47842	Clinton.............	(317)	5,040	5,267
46725	Columbia City........	(219)	5,700	5,091
*47201	Columbus............	(812)	31,802	30,614
47331	Connersville........	(317)	15,550	17,023
47933	Crawfordsville......	(317)	13,584	13,325
46307	Crown Point........	(219)	17,728	16,455
46733	Decatur............	(219)	8,642	8,649
46514	Dunlap(u)..........	(219)	5,705	5,397
46311	Dyer..............	(219)	10,923	9,555
46312	East Chicago.......	(219)	33,892	39,786
*46515	Elkhart...........	(219)	43,627	41,305
46036	Elwood............	(317)	9,494	10,867
*47708	Evansville.........	(812)	126,272	130,496
46038	Fishers...........	(317)	7,189	2,008
*46802	Fort Wayne........	(219)	172,971	172,391
46041	Frankfort.........	(317)	14,754	15,168
46131	Franklin..........	(317)	12,932	11,563
46738	Garrett...........	(219)	5,349	4,751
*46401	Gary.............	(219)	116,646	151,968
46933	Gas City..........	(317)	6,296	6,370
*46526	Goshen...........	(219)	23,794	19,665
46530	Granger(u)........	(219)	20,241	....
46135	Greencastle.......	(317)	8,984	8,403
46140	Greenfield........	(317)	11,657	11,288
47240	Greensburg........	(812)	9,286	9,254
*46142	Greenwood.........	(317)	26,507	19,327
46319	Griffith..........	(219)	17,914	17,026
*46320	Hammond..........	(219)	84,236	93,714
47348	Hartford City......	(317)	6,960	7,622
46322	Highland.........	(219)	23,696	25,935
46342	Hobart...........	(219)	21,822	22,987
47542	Huntingburg.......	(812)	5,236	5,376
46750	Huntington........	(219)	16,389	16,202
*46206	Indianapolis......	(317)	731,327	700,807
*47546	Jasper...........	(812)	10,030	9,097
*47130	Jeffersonville.....	(812)	21,968	21,220
46755	Kendallville......	(219)	7,773	7,299
*46902	Kokomo...........	(317)	44,996	47,808
*47901	Lafayette.........	(317)	43,758	43,011
.....	Lakes of the Four Seasons(u).......	(219)	6,556	....
46405	Lake Station......	(219)	13,899	15,087
*46350	La Porte.........	(219)	21,507	21,796
46226	Lawrence.........	(317)	26,779	25,591
46052	Lebanon..........	(317)	12,059	11,456
47441	Linton...........	(812)	5,814	6,315
46947	Logansport........	(219)	16,865	17,731
46356	Lowell...........	(219)	6,430	5,827
47250	Madison..........	(812)	12,006	12,472
*46952	Marion...........	(317)	32,607	35,874
46151	Martinsville......	(317)	11,677	11,311
46410	Merrillville......	(219)	27,257	27,677
*46360	Michigan City.....	(219)	33,822	36,850
*46544	Mishawaka........	(219)	42,635	40,201
47960	Monticello.......	(219)	5,237	5,162
46158	Mooresville......	(317)	5,541	5,349
47620	Mount Vernon.....	(812)	7,217	7,656
*47302	Muncie..........	(317)	71,170	77,216
46321	Munster.........	(219)	19,949	20,671
46550	Nappanee........	(219)	5,474	4,694
*47150	New Albany......	(812)	36,322	37,103
47362	New Castle......	(317)	17,753	20,056
46774	New Haven......	(219)	9,338	6,714
46060	Noblesville.....	(317)	17,655	12,253
46962	North Manchester......	(219)	6,383	5,998
*47265	North Vernon....	(812)	5,129	5,768
47130	Oak Park(u).....	(812)	5,630	5,871
46970	Peru...........	(317)	12,843	13,764
46168	Plainfield......	(317)	10,438	9,191
46563	Plymouth.......	(219)	8,291	7,693
46368	Portage........	(219)	29,062	27,409
47371	Portland.......	(219)	6,483	7,074
47670	Princeton......	(812)	8,127	8,976
47978	Rensselaer.....	(219)	5,045	4,944
*47374	Richmond......	(317)	38,705	41,349
46975	Rochester.....	(219)	5,969	5,050
46173	Rushville.....	(317)	5,533	6,113
47167	Salem........	(812)	5,619	5,290
46375	Schererville..	(219)	20,155	13,209
47170	Scottsburg....	(812)	5,334	5,068
47172	Sellersburg...	(812)	5,914	3,211
47274	Seymour......	(812)	15,579	15,050
46176	Shelbyville...	(317)	15,347	14,989
*46624	South Bend....	(219)	105,511	109,727
46383	South Haven(u).	(219)	6,112	6,679
46224	Speedway.....	(317)	13,092	12,641
47586	Tell City....	(812)	8,088	8,704
*47808	Terre Haute...	(812)	55,430	61,125
*46383	Valparaiso....	(219)	24,414	22,247
47591	Vincennes....	(812)	19,867	20,857
46992	Wabash......	(219)	12,127	12,985
*46580	Warsaw......	(219)	10,968	10,647
47501	Washington...	(812)	10,864	11,325
*47901	West Lafayette........	(317)	26,144	21,247
46391	Westville....	(219)	5,255	2,887
46394	Whiting.....	(219)	5,155	5,630
47394	Winchester..	(317)	5,095	5,659
46077	Zionsville..	(317)	5,281	3,948

Iowa

ZIP	Place		1990	1980
50511	Algona.............	(515)	6,015	6,289
50009	Altoona............	(515)	7,242	5,764
*50010	Ames............	(515)	47,198	45,775
52205	Anamosa.........	(319)	5,100	4,958
50021	Ankeny.........	(515)	18,482	15,429
50022	Atlantic........	(712)	7,432	7,789
52722	Bettendorf......	(319)	28,139	27,381
50036	Boone.........	(515)	12,392	12,602
52601	Burlington......	(319)	27,208	29,529
51401	Carroll.........	(712)	9,579	9,705
50613	Cedar Falls......	(319)	34,298	36,322
*52401	Cedar Rapids.....	(319)	108,772	110,243
52544	Centerville......	(515)	5,936	6,558
50616	Charles City.....	(515)	7,878	8,778
51012	Cherokee........	(712)	6,026	7,004
51632	Clarinda........	(712)	5,104	5,458
50428	Clear Lake.......	(515)	8,183	7,458
*52732	Clinton.........	(319)	29,201	32,828
50325	Clive..........	(515)	7,462	6,064
52241	Coralville......	(319)	10,347	7,687
*51501	Council Bluffs....	(712)	54,315	56,449
50801	Creston.........	(515)	7,911	8,429
*52802	Davenport.......	(319)	95,333	103,264
52101	Decorah.........	(319)	8,063	7,991
51442	Denison........	(712)	6,604	6,675
*50318	Des Moines......	(515)	193,189	191,003
*52001	Dubuque........	(319)	57,538	62,374
51334	Estherville.....	(712)	6,720	7,518
52556	Fairfield.......	(515)	9,768	9,428
50501	Fort Dodge......	(515)	25,894	29,423
52627	Fort Madison....	(319)	11,614	13,520
50112	Grinnell........	(515)	8,902	8,868
*51537	Harlan.........	(712)	5,148	5,357
50644	Independence.....	(319)	5,972	6,392
50125	Indianola.......	(515)	11,340	10,843
*52240	Iowa City.......	(319)	59,735	50,508
50126	Iowa Falls......	(515)	5,435	6,174
52632	Keokuk.........	(319)	12,451	13,536
50138	Knoxville.......	(515)	8,232	8,143
51031	Le Mars........	(712)	8,454	8,276
52057	Manchester......	(319)	5,137	4,942
52060	Maquoketa......	(319)	6,130	6,313
52302	Marion.........	(319)	20,442	19,474
50158	Marshalltown....	(515)	25,178	26,938
*50401	Mason City......	(515)	29,040	30,144
52641	Mount Pleasant...	(319)	7,959	7,322
52761	Muscatine......	(319)	22,881	23,467
50201	Nevada.........	(515)	6,009	5,912
50208	Newton........	(515)	14,799	15,292
50211	Norwalk.......	(515)	5,726	2,676
50662	Oelwein.......	(319)	6,493	7,564
52577	Oskaloosa.....	(515)	10,600	10,989
52501	Ottumwa.......	(515)	24,488	27,381
50219	Pella.........	(515)	9,270	8,349
50220	Perry.........	(515)	6,652	7,053
*51566	Red Oak.......	(712)	6,264	6,810
51601	Shenandoah.....	(712)	5,572	6,274
51250	Sioux Center...	(712)	5,074	4,588
*51101	Sioux City.....	(712)	80,505	82,003
51301	Spencer.......	(712)	11,066	11,726
50588	Storm Lake.....	(712)	8,769	8,814
50322	Urbandale.....	(515)	23,500	17,869
52349	Vinton........	(319)	5,103	5,040
52353	Washington.....	(319)	7,074	6,584
*50701	Waterloo......	(319)	66,467	75,985
50677	Waverly.......	(319)	8,539	8,444
50595	Webster City....	(515)	7,894	8,572
*50265	West Des Moines......	(515)	31,702	21,894
50311	Windsor Heights....	(515)	5,190	5,474

Kansas

ZIP	Place		1990	1980
67410	Abilene.........	(913)	6,242	6,572
67005	Arkansas City.....	(316)	12,762	13,201
66002	Atchison.......	(913)	10,656	11,407
67010	Augusta........	(316)	7,848	6,968
66012	Bonner Springs....	(913)	6,413	6,266
66720	Chanute.......	(316)	9,488	10,506
67337	Coffeyville.....	(316)	12,917	15,185
67701	Colby.........	(913)	5,510	5,544
66901	Concordia.....	(913)	6,152	6,847
67037	Derby.........	(316)	14,691	9,786
67801	Dodge City.....	(316)	21,129	18,001
67042	El Dorado.....	(316)	11,495	11,551
66801	Emporia.......	(316)	25,512	25,287
66442	Fort Riley North(u).....	(913)	12,848	16,086
66701	Fort Scott.....	(316)	8,362	8,893
67846	Garden City....	(316)	24,097	18,256
67530	Great Bend.....	(316)	15,427	16,608
67601	Hays.........	(913)	17,814	16,301
67060	Haysville.....	(316)	8,364	8,006
*67501	Hutchinson.....	(316)	39,308	40,284
67301	Independence....	(316)	10,030	10,598
66749	Iola.........	(316)	6,351	6,938
66441	Junction City....	(913)	20,642	19,305
*66102	Kansas City.....	(913)	149,800	161,148

ZIP	Place		1990	1980
66043	Lansing	(913)	7,120	5,307
*66044	Lawrence	(913)	65,608	52,738
66048	Leavenworth	(913)	38,495	33,656
66209	Leawood	(913)	19,693	13,360
66210	Lenexa	(913)	34,110	18,639
*67901	Liberal	(316)	16,573	14,911
67460	McPherson	(316)	12,422	11,753
*66502	Manhattan	(913)	37,737	32,644
66202	Merriam	(913)	11,819	10,794
66202	Mission	(913)	9,504	8,643
67114	Newton	(316)	16,700	16,332
*66061	Olathe	(913)	63,402	37,258
66067	Ottawa	(913)	10,667	11,016
66202	Overland Park	(913)	111,790	81,784
67219	Park City†	(316)	5,054	4,056
67357	Parsons	(316)	11,919	12,898
66762	Pittsburg	(316)	17,789	18,770
66202	Prairie Village	(913)	23,186	24,657
67124	Pratt	(316)	6,687	6,885
66205	Roeland Park	(913)	7,706	7,962
*67401	Salina	(913)	42,299	41,843
66203	Shawnee	(913)	37,962	29,653
*66601	Topeka	(913)	119,883	118,690
67880	Ulysses	(316)	5,474	4,653
67152	Wellington	(316)	8,517	8,212
*67209	Wichita	(316)	304,017	279,838
67156	Winfield	(316)	11,931	10,736

Kentucky

ZIP	Place		1990	1980
41001	Alexandria	(606)	5,592	4,735
*41101	Ashland	(606)	23,622	27,064
40004	Bardstown	(502)	6,712	6,155
41073	Bellevue	(606)	6,997	7,678
40403	Berea	(606)	9,129	8,226
*42101	Bowling Green	(502)	41,688	40,450
40261	Buechel(u)	(502)	7,081	6,855
41005	Burlington(u)	(606)	6,070	....
*42718	Campbellsville	(502)	9,592	8,715
42330	Central City	(502)	5,015	5,214
*40701	Corbin	(606)	7,644	8,075
*41011	Covington	(606)	43,646	49,585
41031	Cynthiana	(606)	6,497	5,881
*40422	Danville	(606)	12,559	12,942
41074	Dayton	(606)	6,576	6,979
.....	Douglass Hills	(502)	5,431	4,384
41017	Edgewood	(606)	8,143	7,243
*42701	Elizabethtown	(502)	18,167	15,380
41018	Elsmere	(606)	6,847	7,203
41018	Erlanger	(606)	15,979	14,466
40118	Fairdale(u)	(502)	6,563	7,315
40291	Fern Creek(u)	(502)	16,406	16,866
*41139	Flatwoods	(606)	7,799	8,354
*41042	Florence	(606)	18,586	15,586
42223	Fort Campbell North(u)	(502)	18,861	17,211
40121	Fort Knox(u)	(502)	21,495	31,055
41017	Fort Mitchell	(606)	7,438	7,294
41075	Fort Thomas	(606)	16,032	16,012
41011	Fort Wright	(606)	6,404	4,481
*40601	Frankfort	(502)	26,535	25,973
*42134	Franklin	(502)	7,607	7,738
40324	Georgetown	(502)	11,414	10,972
*42141	Glasgow	(502)	12,351	12,958
40330	Harrodsburg	(606)	7,335	7,265
*41701	Hazard	(606)	5,416	5,371
42420	Henderson	(502)	25,945	24,834
40228	Highview(u)	(502)	14,814	13,286
40229	Hillview	(502)	6,119	5,196
*42240	Hopkinsville	(502)	29,809	27,318
41051	Independence	(606)	10,444	7,998
40269	Jeffersontown	(502)	23,223	15,795
40342	Lawrenceburg	(502)	5,911	5,167
40033	Lebanon	(502)	5,695	6,590
*40507	Lexington	(606)	225,366	204,165
*40741	London	(606)	5,757	4,002
*40232	Louisville	(502)	269,555	298,694
40252	Lyndon	(502)	8,037	1,553
42431	Madisonville	(502)	16,203	16,979
42066	Mayfield	(502)	9,935	10,705
41056	Maysville	(606)	7,169	7,983
40965	Middlesboro	(606)	11,328	12,251
40253	Middletown	(502)	5,016	414
42633	Monticello	(606)	5,357	5,677
40351	Morehead	(606)	8,357	7,789
40353	Mount Sterling	(606)	5,362	5,820
40047	Mount Washington	(502)	5,256	3,997
42071	Murray	(502)	14,442	14,248
40218	Newburg(u)	(502)	21,647	24,612
*41071	Newport	(606)	18,871	21,587
*40356	Nicholasville	(606)	13,603	10,400
40259	Okolona(u)	(502)	18,902	20,039
*42301	Owensboro	(502)	53,577	54,450
*42003	Paducah	(502)	27,256	29,315
*40361	Paris	(606)	8,730	7,935
*41501	Pikeville	(606)	6,324	4,756
40268	Pleasure Ridge Park(u)	(502)	25,131	27,332
42445	Princeton	(502)	6,940	7,073
*40160	Radcliff	(502)	19,Z778	14,656

Louisiana

ZIP	Place		1990	1980
*40475	Richmond	(606)	21,183	21,705
42276	Russellville	(502)	7,454	7,520
.....	Saint Dennis(u)	(502)	10,326	....
40206	Saint Matthews	(502)	15,691	13,519
*40066	Shelbyville	(502)	6,155	5,329
40256	Shively	(502)	15,535	16,645
*42501	Somerset	(606)	10,735	10,649
.....	Taylor Mill	(606)	5,530	4,509
40272	Valley Station(u)	(502)	22,840	24,474
40383	Versailles	(606)	7,269	6,427
....	Villa Hills	(606)	7,370	4,384
41101	Westwoods(u)	(606)	5,300	5,973
40769	Williamsburg	(606)	5,493	5,560
*40391	Winchester	(606)	15,799	15,216

ZIP	Place		1990	1980
*70510	Abbeville	(318)	11,184	12,391
*71301	Alexandria	(318)	49,049	51,648
70032	Arabi(u)	(504)	8,787	10,248
70094	Avondale(u)	(504)	5,813	6,699
*70714	Baker	(504)	13,087	12,865
*71220	Bastrop	(318)	13,916	15,527
*70821	Baton Rouge	(504)	219,531	220,394
70360	Bayou Cane(u)	(504)	15,876	15,723
70037	Belle Chasse(u)	(504)	8,512	5,412
*70427	Bogalusa	(504)	14,280	16,976
*71111	Bossier City	(318)	52,721	50,817
70517	Breaux Bridge	(318)	6,694	5,922
70094	Bridge City(u)	(504)	8,327	....
70811	Brownfields(u)		5,229	....
71291	Brownsville-Bawcomville(u)	(318)	7,397	7,252
71322	Bunkie	(318)	5,044	5,364
70520	Carencro	(318)	5,518	3,712
*70043	Chalmette(u) †	(504)	31,860	33,847
71291	Claiborne(u)	(318)	8,300	6,278
*70433	Covington	(504)	7,691	7,892
*70526	Crowley	(318)	13,983	16,036
70345	Cut Off(u)	(504)	5,325	5,049
*70726	Denham Springs	(504)	8,381	8,563
70634	De Ridder	(318)	9,868	10,337
70047	Destrehan	(504)	8,031	2,382
70346	Donaldsonville	(504)	7,949	7,901
70072	Estelle(u)	(504)	14,091	12,724
70535	Eunice	(318)	11,162	12,479
71459	Fort Polk South	(318)	10,911	12,498
70538	Franklin	(318)	9,004	9,584
70820	Gardere		7,209	....
*70737	Gonzales	(504)	7,208	7,287
71245	Grambling	(318)	5,512	4,226
*70053	Gretna	(504)	17,208	20,615
*70401	Hammond	(504)	15,871	15,226
70123	Harahan	(504)	9,927	11,384
*70058	Harvey(u)	(504)	21,222	22,709
*70360	Houma	(504)	30,495	32,602
70544	Jeanerette	(318)	6,205	6,511
70502	Jefferson(u)	(504)	14,521	15,550
70546	Jennings	(318)	11,305	12,401
*70062	Kenner	(504)	72,033	66,382
70445	Lacombe(u)	(504)	6,523	5,146
*70501	Lafayette	(318)	94,438	80,584
*70601	Lake Charles	(318)	70,580	75,226
71254	Lake Providence	(318)	5,380	6,361
*70068	La Place(u)	(504)	24,194	16,112
70373	Larose(u)	(504)	5,772	5,234
*71446	Leesville	(318)	7,638	9,054
*70448	Mandeville	(504)	7,474	6,076
71052	Mansfield	(318)	5,389	6,485
71351	Marksville	(318)	5,526	5,113
*70072	Marrero(u)	(504)	36,671	36,548
70075	Meraux(u)	(504)	8,849	....
70812	Merrydale(u)	(318)	10,395	....
*70009	Metairie(u)	(504)	149,428	164,160
*71055	Minden	(318)	13,661	15,084
*71203	Monroe	(318)	54,909	57,597
*70380	Morgan City	(504)	14,531	16,114
70612	Moss Bluff(u)	(318)	8,039	7,004
*71457	Natchitoches	(318)	16,609	16,664
*70560	New Iberia	(318)	31,828	32,766
*70140	New Orleans	(504)	496,938	557,920
70760	New Roads	(504)	5,303	3,924
71463	Oakdale	(318)	6,837	7,155
70810	Oak Hills Place		5,479	....
*70570	Opelousas	(318)	19,091	18,903
70392	Patterson	(504)	5,166	4,693
*71360	Pineville	(318)	12,255	12,034
*70764	Plaquemine	(504)	7,101	7,521
70454	Ponchatoula	(504)	5,425	5,469
70767	Port Allen	(504)	6,277	6,114
70601	Prien(u)	(318)	6,448	6,224
70394	Raceland(u)	(504)	5,564	6,302
70578	Rayne	(318)	8,502	9,066
.....	Red Chute(u)		5,431	....
70084	Reserve(u)	(504)	8,847	7,288
70123	River Ridge(u)	(504)	14,800	17,146
*71270	Ruston	(318)	20,071	20,585
70582	Saint Martinville	(318)	7,226	7,965
70087	Saint Rose(u)	(504)	6,259	....

ZIP	Place	1990	1980
70817	Shenandoah(u)	13,429	....
*71102	Shreveport (318)	198,518	206,989
*70458	Slidell (504)	24,124	26,718
71075	Springhill (318/504)	5,668	6,516
*70663	Sulphur (318)	20,125	19,709
*71282	Tallulah (318)	8,526	11,341
70056	Terrytown(u) (504)	23,787	23,548
*70301	Thibodaux (504)	14,125	15,810
70053	Timberlane(u) (504)	12,614	11,579
70809	Village Saint George(u)	6,242	....
70586	Ville Platte (318)	9,037	9,201
70092	Violet(u) (504)	8,574	11,678
70094	Waggaman(u) (504)	9,405	9,004
70669	Westlake (318)	5,007	5,246
*71291	West Monroe (318)	14,096	14,993
*70094	Westwego (504)	11,218	12,663
71483	Winnfield (318)	6,138	7,311
71295	Winnsboro (318)	5,755	5,921
70791	Zachary (504)	9,036	7,297

Maine (207)

See note on page 396

ZIP	Place	1990	1980
*04210	Auburn	24,309	23,128
*04330	Augusta	21,325	21,819
*04401	Bangor	33,181	31,643
04530	Bath	9,799	10,246
04915	Belfast	6,355	6,243
03901	Berwick	5,995	4,149
*04005	Biddeford	20,710	19,638
04412	Brewer	9,021	9,017
04011	Brunswick Center(u)	14,683	10,990
04011	Brunswick	20,906	17,366
04093	Buxton	6,494	5,775
04843	Camden	5,060	4,584
04107	Cape Elizabeth	8,854	7,838
04736	Caribou	9,415	9,916
04021	Cumberland	5,836	5,284
03903	Eliot	5,329	4,948
04605	Ellsworth	5,975	5,179
04937	Fairfield	6,718	6,113
04105	Falmouth	7,610	6,853
04938	Farmington	7,436	6,730
04032	Freeport	6,905	5,863
04345	Gardiner	6,746	6,485
04038	Gorham	11,856	10,101
04039	Gray	5,904	4,344
04444	Hampden	5,974	5,250
*04079	Harpswell	5,012	3,796
04730	Houlton Center(u)	5,627	5,730
04730	Houlton	6,613	6,766
04239	Jay	5,080	5,080
04043	Kennebunk	8,004	6,621
03904	Kittery Center(u)	5,151	5,465
03904	Kittery	9,372	9,314
*04240	Lewiston	39,757	40,481
04750	Limestone	9,922	8,719
04457	Lincoln	5,587	5,066
04250	Lisbon	9,457	8,769
04751	Loring AFB(u)	7,829	6,572
04462	Millinocket Center(u)	6,922	7,567
04462	Millinocket	6,956	7,567
04963	Oakland	5,595	5,162
04064	Old Orchard Beach Ctr.(u)	7,789	6,023
04064	Old Orchard Beach	7,789	6,291
04468	Old Town	8,317	8,422
04473	Orono Center(u)	9,789	9,891
04473	Orono	10,573	10,578
*04101	Portland	64,358	61,572
04769	Presque Isle	10,550	11,172
04841	Rockland	7,972	7,919
04276	Rumford Compact(u)	5,419	6,256
04276	Rumford	7,078	8,240
04072	Saco	15,181	12,921
04073	Sanford Center(u)	10,296	10,268
04073	Sanford	20,463	18,020
*04074	Scarborough	12,518	11,347
04976	Skowhegan Center(u)	6,990	6,517
04976	Skowhegan	8,725	8,098
03908	South Berwick	5877	4,046
*04101	South Portland	23,163	22,712
04084	Standish	7,678	5,946
04086	Topsham	8,746	6,431
*04901	Waterville	17,173	17,779
04090	Wells	7,778	8,211
*04092	Westbrook	16,121	14,976
04062	Windham	13,020	11,282
04901	Winslow Center(u)	5,436	5,903
04901	Winslow	7,997	8,057
04364	Winthrop	5,986	5,889
04096	Yarmouth	7,862	6,585
03909	York	9,818	8,465

Maryland

ZIP	Place	1990	1980
21001	Aberdeen (410)	13,087	11,533
21005	Aberdeen Proving Ground(u) (410)	5,267	5,722
20783	Adelphi(u) (301)	13,524	12,530
20335	Andrews AFB(u) (410)	10,228	10,064
*21401	Annapolis (410)	33,195	31,740
21227	Arbutus(u) (410)	19,750	20,163
21012	Arnold(u) (410)	20,261	12,285
20916	Aspen Hill(u) (301)	45,494	47,455
21220	Ballenger Creek† (410)	5,546	2,659
*21203	Baltimore (410)	736,014	786,741
*21014	Bel Air (410)	8,942	7,814
21050	Bel Air North(u) (410)	14,880	5,043
21014	Bel Air South(u) (410)	26,421	9,140
*20705	Beltsville(u) (301)	14,476	12,760
*20814	Bethesda(u) (301)	62,936	63,022
20710	Bladensburg (301)	8,064	7,691
*20715	Bowie (301)	37,642	33,695
....	Bowleys Quarters(u) (410)	5,595	....
21225	Brooklyn Park(u) (410)	10,987	11,508
21716	Brunswick (301)	5,117	4,572
20866	Burtonsville(u) (410)	5,853	2,046
20818	Cabin John(u) (301)	5,341	5,135
20619	California(u) (410)	7,626	5,770
20705	Calverton(u) (301)	12,046	7,649
21613	Cambridge (410)	11,514	11,703
20748	Camp Springs(u) (301)	16,392	16,118
21401	Cape St. Clair(u) (410)	7,878	6,022
21234	Carney(u) (410)	25,578	21,488
21228	Catonsville(u) (410)	35,233	33,208
20657	Chesapeake Ranch Estates(u) (301)	5,423	....
20784	Cheverly (301)	6,023	5,751
*20815	Chevy Chase(u) (301)	8,559	12,232
20783	Chillum(u) (301)	31,309	32,775
20735	Clinton(u) (301)	19,987	16,438
20904	Cloverly(u) (301)	7,904	5,153
*21030	Cockeysville(u) (410)	18,668	17,013
20914	Colesville(u) (301)	18,819	14,359
*20740	College Park (301)	23,714	23,614
*21045	Columbia(u) (410/301)	75,883	52,518
20743	Coral Hills(u) (410)	11,032	11,602
21114	Crofton(u) (410)	12,781	12,009
*21502	Cumberland (301)	23,712	25,933
20872	Damascus(u) (301)	9,817	4,129
*20747	District Heights (301)	6,711	6,799
21222	Dundalk(u) (410)	65,800	71,293
21601	Easton (410)	9,372	7,536
20737	East Riverdale(u) (301)	14,187	14,104
21219	Edgemere(u) (410)	9,226	9,078
21040	Edgewood(u) (410)	23,903	19,455
21784	Eldersburg(u) (410)	9,720	4,959
21227	Elkridge(u) (410)	12,953	....
*21921	Elkton (410)	9,073	6,468
*21043	Ellicott City(u) (410)	41,396	21,784
21221	Essex(u) (410)	40,872	39,614
20904	Fairland(u) (301)	19,828	5,154
21047	Fallston(u) (410)	5,730	5,572
21061	Ferndale(u) (410)	16,355	14,314
20747	Forestville(u) (301)	16,731	16,401
20755	Fort Meade(u) (301)	12,509	14,083
20744	Fort Washington(u) (301)	24,032	....
*21701	Frederick (301)	40,186	28,086
20744	Friendly(u) (301)	9,028	8,848
21532	Frostburg (301)	8,069	7,715
*20877	Gaithersburg (301)	39,676	26,424
21055	Garrison(u) (410)	5,045	....
*20874	Germantown(u) (301)	41,145	9,721
20706	Glenarden (301)	5,025	4,993
*21061	Glen Burnie(u) (410)	37,305	37,263
20769	Glenn Dale(u) (301)	9,689	4,829
20772	Greater Upper Marlboro	11,528	....
*20770	Greenbelt (301)	20,561	17,332
21122	Green Haven(u) (410)	14,416	6,577
21771	Green Valley(u) (301)	9,424	4,504
*21740	Hagerstown (301)	35,306	34,132
21740	Halfway(u) (301)	8,873	8,659
21078	Havre de Grace (410)	8,952	8,763
20903	Hillandale(u) (301)	10,318	9,686
20748	Hillcrest Heights(u) (301)	17,136	17,021
*20780	Hyattsville (301)	13,864	12,709
20794	Jessup(u) (410)	6,537	4,288
21085	Joppatowne(u) (410)	11,084	11,348
20785	Kentland(u) (301)	7,967	8,596
20772	Kettering(u) (301)	9,901	6,972
21122	Lake Shore(u) (410)	13,269	10,181
20785	Landover(u) (301)	5,052	5,374
20787	Langley Park(u) (301)	17,474	14,038
20706	Lanham-Seabrook(u) (301)	16,792	15,814
21227	Lansdowne-Baltimore Highlands(u)	15,509	16,759
20646	La Plata (301)	5,841	2,484
20772	Largo(u) (301)	9,475	5,557
*20707	Laurel (301)	19,086	12,103
20653	Lexington Park(u) (410)	9,943	10,361
21090	Linthicum(u) (410)	7,547	7,457
21207	Lochearn(u) (410)	25,240	26,908
21037	Londontowne(u) (410)	6,992	6,052
21784	Long Meadow(u)† (410)	5,594	1,203
*21093	Lutherville-Timonium(u) (410)	16,442	16,871
20748	Marlow Heights(u) (301)	5,885	5,824
20772	Marlton(u)	5,523	....
20707	Maryland City(u) (301)	6,813	6,949
21093	Mays Chapel(u) (410)	10,132	5,213

ZIP	Place	1990	1980
21220	Middle River(u) .... (410)	24,616	26,756
21207	Milford Mill(u) .... (410)	22,547	20,354
20717	Mitchellville. .... (301)	12,593	....
20879	Montgomery Village(u) ... (301)	32,315	18,725
20712	Mount Rainier .... (301)	7,954	7,361
21402	Naval Academy(u) .... (410)	5,420	5,367
20784	New Carrollton .... (301)	12,002	12,632
20815	North Bethesda(u) .... (301)	29,656	22,671
20895	North Kensington(u) ..... (301)	8,607	9,039
20707	North Laurel(u) .... (301)	15,008	6,093
20878	North Potomac(u) .... (301)	18,456	....
21842	Ocean City. .... (410)	5,146	4,946
21113	Odenton(u). .... (410)	12,833	13,270
*20832	Olney(u). .... (301)	23,019	13,026
21206	Overlea(u). .... (410)	12,137	12,965
21117	Owings Mills(u) .... (410)	9,474	9,526
*20745	Oxon Hill-Glassmanor(u)†. (301)	35,794	36,267
20785	Palmer Park(u) .... (301)	7,019	7,986
21234	Parkville(u). .... (410)	31,617	35,159
21401	Parole(u) .... (410)	10,054	3,377
21122	Pasadena(u). .... (410)	10,012	7,439
21128	Perry Hall(u) .... (410)	22,723	13,455
21208	Pikesville(u) .... (410)	24,815	22,555
*20850	Potomac(u). .... (301)	45,634	40,313
21227	Pumphrey(u). .... (410)	5,483	5,666
21133	Randallstown(u) .... (410)	26,277	25,927
.....	Redland(u). .... (301)	16,145	10,528
21136	Reisterstown(u). .... (410)	19,314	19,385
*20737	Riverdale. .... (301)	4,843	4,761
21122	Riviera Beach(u) .... (410)	11,376	8,812
*20850	Rockville .... (301)	44,830	43,811
20772	Rosaryville(u) .... (301)	8,976	....
21237	Rosedale(u). .... (410)	18,703	19,956
.....	Rossmoor(u).	6,182	....
21221	Rossville(u). .... (410)	9,492	8,646
20602	Saint Charles(u) .... (301)	28,717	13,921
*21801	Salisbury .... (410)	20,592	16,429
20763	Savage-Guilford(u) ...... (410)	9,669	2,928
20743	Seat Pleasant .... (301)	5,359	5,217
21144	Severn(u). .... (410)	24,499	20,147
21146	Severna Park(u) .... (410)	25,879	21,253
*20907	Silver Spring(u) .... (301)	76,046	72,893
21061	South Gate(u) .... (301)	27,564	24,185
20895	South Kensington(u) ..... (301)	8,777	9,344
20707	South Laurel(u) .... (301)	18,591	18,034
*20746	Suitland-Silver Hills(u) ... (301)	35,111	32,164
*20907	Takoma Park .... (301)	16,724	16,231
*20748	Temple Hills(u) .... (301)	6,865	6,630
21285	Towson(u) .... (410)	49,445	51,083
*20602	Waldorf(u). .... (301)	15,058	9,782
20743	Walker Mill(u) .... (301)	10,920	10,651
*21157	Westminster .... (410)	13,060	8,808
20902	Wheaton-Glenmont(u) ... (301)	53,720	48,598
21162	White Marsh(u) .... (410)	8,183	....
20903	White Oak(u) .... (301)	18,671	13,700
21207	Woodlawn(u) (Baltimore) . (410)	32,907	29,453
21284	Woodlawn(u)		
	(Prince George's) ..... (410)	5,329	5,306

Massachusetts
See note on page 396

ZIP	Place	1990	1980
02351	Abington(u). .... (617)	13,817	13,887
01720	Acton. .... (508)	17,872	17,544
02743	Acushnet .... (508)	9,554	8,704
01220	Adams Center(u) .... (413)	6,356	6,857
01220	Adams. .... (413)	9,445	10,381
01001	Agawam .... (413)	27,323	26,271
01913	Amesbury Center(u). .... (508)	12,109	12,236
01913	Amesbury. .... (508)	14,997	13,971
*01002	Amherst Center(u) ...... (413)	17,824	17,773
*01002	Amherst. .... (413)	35,228	33,229
*01810	Andover(u). .... (508)	8,242	8,445
*01810	Andover. .... (508)	29,151	26,370
02174	Arlington(u) .... (617)	44,630	48,219
01430	Ashburnham. .... (508)	5,433	4,075
01721	Ashland. .... (508)	12,066	9,165
01331	Athol Center(u) .... (508)	8,732	8,708
01331	Athol. .... (508)	11,451	10,634
02703	Attleboro .... (508)	38,383	34,196
01501	Auburn. .... (508)	15,005	14,845
01432	Ayer .... (508)	6,871	6,993
02630	Barnstable .... (508)	40,949	30,898
01730	Bedford .... (617)	12,996	13,067
01007	Belchertown .... (413)	10,579	8,339
02019	Bellingham .... (508)	14,877	14,300
02178	Belmont(u) .... (617)	24,720	26,100
01915	Beverly .... (508)	38,195	37,655
*01821	Billerica .... (508)	37,609	36,727
01504	Blackstone .... (508)	8,023	6,570
*02205	Boston .... (617)	574,283	562,994
02532	Bourne. .... (508)	16,064	13,874
01921	Boxford .... (508)	6,266	5,374
*02205	Braintree(u) .... (617)	33,836	36,337
02631	Brewster .... (508)	8,440	5,226
02324	Bridgewater .... (508)	21,249	17,202
*02403	Brockton .... (508)	92,788	95,172
02146	Brookline(u) .... (617)	54,718	55,062
01803	Burlington. .... (617)	23,302	23,486
*02139	Cambridge .... (617)	95,802	95,322

ZIP	Place	1990	1980
02021	Canton .... (617)	18,530	18,182
02330	Carver. .... (508)	10,590	6,988
*02632	Centerville .... (508)	9,190	3,640
01507	Charlton. .... (508)	9,576	6,719
02633	Chatham .... (508)	6,579	6,071
01824	Chelmsford(u). .... (508)	32,383	31,174
02150	Chelsea. .... (617)	28,710	25,431
*01020	Chicopee. .... (413)	56,632	55,112
01510	Clinton. .... (508)	13,222	12,771
01778	Cochituate(u) .... (508)	6,046	6,126
02025	Cohasset .... (617)	7,075	7,174
01742	Concord. .... (508)	17,076	16,293
*01226	Dalton. .... (413)	7,155	6,797
01923	Danvers(u). .... (508)	24,174	24,100
02714	Dartmouth .... (508)	27,244	23,966
*02026	Dedham(u). .... (617)	23,782	25,298
01342	Deerfield .... (413)	5,018	4,517
02638	Dennis. .... (508)	13,864	12,360
02715	Dighton .... (508)	5,631	5,352
.....	Douglas. .... (508)	5,438	3,730
01826	Dracut .... (508)	25,594	21,249
01571	Dudley. .... (508)	9,540	8,717
*02332	Duxbury .... (617)	13,895	11,807
02333	East Bridgewater .... (508)	11,104	9,945
02536	East Falmouth(u). ...... (508)	5,577	5,181
01027	Easthampton .... (413)	15,537	15,580
01028	East Longmeadow. ...... (413)	13,367	12,905
02334	Easton. .... (508)	19,807	16,623
02149	Everett .... (617)	35,701	37,195
02719	Fairhaven. .... (508)	16,132	15,759
*02722	Fall River. .... (508)	92,703	92,574
*02540	Falmouth .... (508)	27,960	23,640
01420	Fitchburg .... (508)	41,194	39,580
01433	Fort Devens(u) .... (508)	8,973	9,546
02035	Foxborough(u) .... (508)	5,706	5,697
01701	Framingham. .... (508)	64,989	65,113
02038	Franklin Center(u) ...... (508)	9,965	9,296
02038	Franklin. .... (508)	22,095	18,217
02702	Freetown .... (508)	8,522	7,058
01440	Gardner. .... (508)	20,125	17,900
01833	Georgetown .... (508)	6,384	5,687
*01930	Gloucester .... (508)	28,716	27,768
01519	Grafton .... (508)	13,035	11,238
01033	Granby .... (413)	5,565	5,380
01230	Great Barrington .... (413)	7,725	7,405
*01301	Greenfield Center(u) .... (413)	14,016	14,198
01302	Greenfield .... (413)	18,666	18,436
01450	Groton. .... (508)	7,511	6,154
01834	Groveland .... (508)	5,214	5,040
02338	Halifax. .... (617)	6,526	5,513
01936	Hamilton .... (508)	7,280	6,960
02339	Hanover .... (617)	11,912	11,358
02341	Hanson .... (617)	9,028	8,617
01451	Harvard .... (508)	12,329	12,170
02645	Harwich .... (508)	10,275	8,971
*01830	Haverhill .... (508)	51,418	46,865
02043	Hingham .... (617)	19,821	20,339
02343	Holbrook(u) .... (617)	11,041	11,140
01520	Holden. .... (508)	14,628	13,336
01746	Holliston .... (508)	12,926	12,622
*01040	Holyoke(u) .... (413)	43,704	44,678
01747	Hopedale(u) .... (508)	5,666	3,905
01748	Hopkinton .... (508)	9,191	7,114
01749	Hudson Center(u) .... (508)	14,267	14,156
01749	Hudson .... (508)	17,233	16,408
02045	Hull(u) .... (617)	10,466	9,714
02601	Hyannis(u) .... (508)	14,120	9,118
01938	Ipswich .... (508)	11,873	11,158
02364	Kingston .... (617)	9,045	7,362
02347	Lakeville .... (508)	7,785	5,931
01523	Lancaster. .... (508)	6,661	6,334
*01842	Lawrence. .... (508)	70,207	63,175
01238	Lee. .... (413)	5,849	6,247
01524	Leicester .... (508)	10,191	9,446
01240	Lenox .... (413)	5,069	6,523
01453	Leominster .... (508)	38,145	34,508
02173	Lexington(u) .... (617)	28,974	29,479
01773	Lincoln .... (617)	7,666	7,098
01460	Littleton .... (508)	7,051	6,970
*01028	Longmeadow(u) .... (413)	15,467	16,301
*01853	Lowell .... (508)	103,439	92,418
01056	Ludlow. .... (413)	18,820	18,150
01462	Lunenburg .... (508)	9,117	8,405
*01901	Lynn .... (617)	81,245	78,471
01940	Lynnfield(u) .... (617)	11,274	11,267
02148	Malden .... (617)	53,884	53,386
01944	Manchester .... (508)	5,286	5,424
02048	Mansfield. .... (508)	16,568	13,453
01945	Marblehead(u) .... (617)	19,971	20,126
01752	Marlborough .... (508)	31,813	30,617
02050	Marshfield .... (617)	21,531	20,916
02648	Marstons Mills(u). ...... (508)	8,017	....
02649	Mashpee .... (508)	7,884	3,700
02739	Mattapoisett .... (508)	5,850	5,597
01754	Maynard(u). .... (508)	10,325	9,590
02052	Medfield. .... (508)	10,531	10,220
02155	Medford. .... (617)	57,407	58,076
02053	Medway .... (508)	9,931	8,447
*02205	Melrose .... (617)	28,150	30,055
01860	Merrimac .... (508)	5,166	4,451

ZIP	Place		1990	1980
01844	Methuen	(508)	39,990	36,701
02346	Middleborough Center(u)	(508)	6,837	7,012
02346	Middleborough	(508)	17,867	16,404
01757	Milford Center(u)	(508)	23,339	21,730
01757	Milford	(508)	25,355	23,390
01527	Millbury	(508)	12,228	11,808
02054	Millis	(508)	7,613	6,908
02186	Milton(u)	(617)	25,725	25,860
01057	Monson	(413)	7,776	7,315
01351	Montague	(413)	8,316	8,011
*02554	Nantucket	(508)	6,012	5,087
01760	Natick	(508)	30,510	29,461
*02205	Needham(u)	(617)	27,557	27,901
*02740	New Bedford	(508)	99,922	98,478
01951	Newbury	(508)	5,623	4,529
01950	Newburyport(508)		16,317	15,900
*02205	Newton	(617)	82,585	83,622
02056	Norfolk	(508)	9,270	6,363
01247	North Adams	(413)	16,797	18,063
*01002	North Amherst(u)	(413)	6,239	5,616
*01060	Northampton	(413)	29,289	29,286
01845	North Andover	(508)	22,792	20,129
*02760	North Attleborough	(508)	25,038	21,095
01532	Northborough	(508)	11,929	10,568
01534	Northbridge	(508)	13,371	12,246
01864	North Reading	(508)	12,002	11,455
02766	Norton	(508)	14,265	12,690
02061	Norwell	(617)	9,279	9,182
02062	Norwood(u)	(617)	28,700	29,711
01364	Orange	(508)	7,312	6,844
02653	Orleans	(508)	5,838	5,306
01540	Oxford Center(u)	(508)	5,969	6,369
01540	Oxford	(508)	12,588	11,680
01069	Palmer	(413)	12,054	11,389
*01960	Peabody	(508)	47,264	45,976
02359	Pembroke	(617)	14,544	13,487
01463	Pepperell	(508)	10,098	8,061
01866	Pinehurst(u)	(508)	6,614	6,588
*01201	Pittsfield	(413)	48,622	51,974
02762	Plainville	(508)	6,871	5,857
*02360	Plymouth Center(u)	(508)	7,258	7,232
*02360	Plymouth	(508)	45,608	35,913
*02205	Quincy	(617)	84,985	84,743
02368	Randolph(u)	(617)	30,093	28,218
02767	Raynham	(508)	9,867	9,085
01867	Reading(u)	(617)	22,539	22,678
02769	Rehoboth	(508)	8,656	7,570
02151	Revere	(617)	42,786	42,423
02370	Rockland	(617)	16,123	15,695
01966	Rockport	(508)	7,482	6,345
*01970	Salem	(508)	38,091	38,276
01952	Salisbury	(508)	6,882	5,973
02563	Sandwich	(508)	15,489	8,727
01906	Saugus(u)	(617)	25,549	24,746
02066	Scituate	(617)	16,786	17,317
02771	Seekonk	(508)	13,046	12,269
02067	Sharon	(617)	15,517	13,601
01464	Shirley	(508)	6,118	5,124
01545	Shrewsbury	(508)	24,146	22,674
*02722	Somerset(u)	(508)	17,655	18,813
*02205	Somerville(u)	(617)	76,210	77,372
01002	South Amherst	(413)	5,053	4,861
01772	Southborough	(508)	6,628	6,193
01550	Southbridge Center(u)	(508)	13,631	12,882
01550	Southbridge	(508)	17,816	16,665
01075	South Hadley	(413)	16,685	16,399
01077	Southwick	(413)	7,667	7,382
02664	South Yarmouth(u)	(508)	10,358	7,525
01562	Spencer Center(u)	(508)	6,306	6,350
01562	Spencer	(508)	11,645	10,774
*01101	Springfield	(413)	156,983	152,319
01564	Sterling	(508)	6,481	5,440
02180	Stoneham	(617)	22,203	21,424
02072	Stoughton	(617)	26,777	26,710
01775	Stow	(508)	5,328	5,144
01566	Sturbridge	(508)	7,775	5,976
01776	Sudbury	(508)	14,358	14,027
01590	Sutton	(508)	6,824	5,855
01907	Swampscott(u)	(617)	13,650	13,837
02777	Swansea	(508)	15,411	15,461
02780	Taunton	(508)	49,832	45,001
01468	Templeton	(508)	6,438	6,070
01876	Tewksbury	(508)	27,266	24,635
01983	Topsfield	(508)	5,754	5,709
01469	Townsend	(508)	8,496	7,201
01879	Tyngsborough	(508)	8,642	5,683
01569	Uxbridge	(508)	10,415	8,374
01880	Wakefield(u)	(617)	24,825	24,895
02081	Walpole	(508)	20,223	18,859
*02205	Waltham	(617)	57,878	58,200
01082	Ware Center(u)	(413)	6,533	6,806
01082	Ware	(413)	9,808	8,953
02571	Wareham	(508)	19,232	18,457
*02205	Watertown(u)	(617)	33,284	34,384
01778	Wayland	(508)	11,874	12,170
01570	Webster Center(u)	(508)	11,849	11,175
01570	Webster	(508)	16,196	14,480
02181	Wellesley	(617)	26,615	27,209
01581	Westborough	(508)	14,133	13,619
01583	West Boylston	(508)	6,611	6,204

ZIP	Place		1990	1980
02379	West Bridgewater	(508)	6,389	6,359
01742	West Concord(u)	(508)	5,761	5,331
*01085	Westfield	(413)	38,372	36,465
01886	Westford	(508)	16,392	13,434
01473	Westminster	(508)	6,191	5,139
02193	Weston	(617)	10,200	11,169
02790	Westport	(508)	13,852	13,763
*01089	West Springfield(u)	(413)	27,537	27,042
02090	Westwood	(617)	12,557	13,212
02673	West Yarmouth	(508)	5,409	3,852
*02205	Weymouth(u)	(617)	54,063	55,601
01588	Whitinsville(u)	(508)	5,639	5,379
02382	Whitman	(617)	13,240	13,534
01095	Wilbraham	(413)	12,635	12,053
01267	Williamstown	(413)	8,220	8,741
01887	Wilmington(u)	(508)	17,651	17,471
01475	Winchendon	(508)	8,805	7,019
01890	Winchester(u)	(617)	20,267	20,701
02152	Winthrop(u)	(617)	18,127	19,294
*01801	Woburn	(617)	35,943	36,626
*01613	Worcester	(508)	169,759	161,799
02093	Wrentham	(508)	9,006	7,580
02675	Yarmouth	(508)	21,174	18,449

Michigan

ZIP	Place		1990	1980
49221	Adrian	(517)	22,097	21,276
49224	Albion	(517)	10,066	11,059
49401	Allendale(u)	(616)	6,950	....
48101	Allen Park	(313)	31,092	34,196
48801	Alma	(517)	9,034	9,652
49707	Alpena	(517)	11,354	12,214
*48106	Ann Arbor	(313)	109,608	107,969
*48321	Auburn Hills†	(313)	17,076	15,388
*49016	Battle Creek	(616)	53,516	35,724
*48707	Bay City	(517)	38,936	41,593
48505	Beecher(u)	(313)	14,465	17,178
48809	Belding	(616)	5,969	5,634
*49022	Benton Harbor	(616)	12,818	14,707
49022	Benton Heights(u)	(616)	5,465	6,787
48072	Berkley	(313)	16,960	18,637
48025	Beverly Hills	(313)	10,610	11,598
49307	Big Rapids	(616)	12,603	14,361
*48012	Birmingham	(810)	19,997	21,689
48301	Bloomfield(u)	(313)	42,137	42,876
48722	Bridgeport(u)	(517)	8,569	....
48116	Brighton	(810)	5,686	4,268
48601	Buena Vista(u)		8,196	....
*48501	Burton	(810)	27,437	29,976
49601	Cadillac	(616)	10,104	10,199
*48187	Canton(u)	(313)	57,047	....
48724	Carrollton(u)	(517)	6,521	7,482
48015	Center Line	(810)	9,026	9,293
48813	Charlotte	(517)	8,083	8,251
48017	Clawson	(810)	13,874	15,103
*48046	Clinton(u)	(517)	85,866	72,400
49036	Coldwater	(517)	9,607	9,461
49321	Comstock Park(u)	(616)	6,530	5,506
49508	Cutlerville(u)	(616)	11,228	8,256
48423	Davison	(810)	5,693	6,087
*48120	Dearborn	(313)	89,286	90,660
*48127	Dearborn Heights	(313)	60,838	67,706
*48231	Detroit	(313)	1,027,974	1,203,368
49047	Dowagiac	(616)	6,418	6,307
49506	East Grand Rapids	(616)	10,807	10,914
*48826	East Lansing	(517)	50,677	51,392
48021	Eastpointe	(810)	35,283	38,280
49001	Eastwood(u)	(616)	6,340	7,186
48229	Ecorse	(313)	12,180	14,447
49829	Escanaba	(906)	13,659	14,355
49022	Fair Plain(u)	(616)	8,051	8,289
*48333	Farmington	(810)	10,170	11,022
48333	Farmington Hills	(810)	74,614	58,056
48430	Fenton	(313)	8,434	8,098
48220	Ferndale	(313)	25,084	26,227
48134	Flat Rock	(313)	7,290	6,853
*48501	Flint	(810)	140,925	140,925
48433	Flushing	(810)	8,542	8,624
49506	Forest Hills(u)	(616)	16,690	....
48026	Fraser	(810)	13,899	14,560
*48135	Garden City	(313)	31,846	35,640
48439	Grand Blanc	(810)	7,760	6,848
49417	Grand Haven	(616)	11,951	11,763
48837	Grand Ledge	(517)	7,562	6,920
*49501	Grand Rapids	(616)	189,126	181,843
*49418	Grandville	(616)	15,624	12,412
48838	Greenville	(616)	8,101	8,019
48138	Grosse Ile(u)	(313)	9,781	9,320
*48231	Grosse Pointe	(313)	5,681	5,901
48230	Grosse Pointe Farms	(313)	10,092	10,551
48230	Grosse Pointe Park	(313)	12,857	13,562
48230	Grosse Pointe Woods	(313)	17,715	18,886
48212	Hamtramck	(313)	18,372	21,300
48225	Harper Woods	(313)	14,903	16,361
48625	Harrison(u)	(517)	24,685	23,649
48840	Haslett(u)	(517)	10,230	7,025
49058	Hastings	(616)	6,549	6,418
48030	Hazel Park	(810)	20,051	20,914
48203	Highland Park	(313)	20,121	27,909

ZIP	Place		1990	1980
49242	Hillsdale	(517)	8,175	7,432
*49423	Holland	(616)	30,745	26,281
48442	Holly	(810)	5,595	4,874
48842	Holt(u)	(517)	11,744	10,097
49931	Houghton	(906)	7,498	7,512
*48843	Howell	(517)	8,147	6,976
49426	Hudsonville	(616)	6,170	4,844
48070	Huntington Woods	(313)	6,419	6,937
48141	Inkster	(313)	30,772	35,190
48846	Ionia	(616)	5,990	5,920
*49801	Iron Mountain	(906)	8,525	8,341
49938	Ironwood	(906)	6,849	7,741
49849	Ishpeming	(906)	7,200	7,538
*49204	Jackson	(517)	37,425	39,739
*49428	Jenison(u)	(616)	17,882	16,330
*49001	Kalamazoo	(616)	80,277	79,722
49518	Kentwood	(616)	37,826	30,438
49801	Kingsford	(906)	5,480	5,290
49843	K.I. Sawyer AFB(u)	(906)	6,577	7,345
48144	Lambertville(u)	(313)	7,860	6,341
*48901	Lansing	(517)	127,321	130,414
48446	Lapeer	(810)	7,759	6,198
48146	Lincoln Park	(313)	41,832	45,105
*48150	Livonia	(313)	100,850	104,814
49431	Ludington	(616)	8,507	8,937
48071	Madison Heights	(313)	32,196	35,375
49660	Manistee	(616)	6,734	7,665
49855	Marquette	(906)	21,977	23,288
49068	Marshall	(616)	6,941	7,201
48040	Marysville	(810)	8,515	7,345
48854	Mason	(517)	6,768	6,019
48122	Melvindale	(313)	11,216	12,322
49858	Menominee	(906)	9,398	10,099
*48640	Midland	(517)	38,053	37,269
*48381	Milford	(810)	5,500	5,041
48161	Monroe	(313)	22,902	23,531
*48046	Mount Clemens	(810)	18,405	18,991
*48804	Mount Pleasant	(517)	23,299	23,746
*49440	Muskegon	(616)	39,809	40,823
49444	Muskegon Heights	(616)	13,176	14,611
*48047	New Baltimore	(810)	5,798	5,439
49120	Niles	(616)	12,458	13,115
.....	Northview(u)		13,712	11,662
48167	Northville	(313)	6,226	5,698
49441	Norton Shores	(616)	21,755	22,025
*48376	Novi	(810)	32,998	22,525
48237	Oak Park	(313)	30,468	31,537
*48805	Okemos(u)	(517)	20,216	8,882
48867	Owosso	(517)	16,322	16,465
49770	Petoskey	(616)	6,056	6,097
48170	Plymouth	(313)	9,560	9,986
48170	Plymouth Township(u)	(313)	23,646	....
*48343	Pontiac	(810)	71,136	76,715
49081	Portage	(616)	41,042	38,157
*48061	Port Huron	(810)	33,694	33,981
*48231	Redford(u)	(313)	54,387	58,441
48218	River Rouge	(313)	11,314	12,912
48192	Riverview	(313)	13,894	14,569
*48308	Rochester	(810)	7,130	7,203
48306	Rochester Hills†	(810)	61,766	40,704
48174	Romulus	(313)	22,897	24,857
48066	Roseville	(313)	51,412	54,311
*48068	Royal Oak	(810)	65,410	70,893
*48605	Saginaw	(517)	69,512	77,508
48604	Saginaw Township North(u)	(517)	23,018	....
48603	Saginaw Township South(u)	(517)	13,987	....
48079	Saint Clair	(810)	5,116	4,780
*48080	Saint Clair Shores	(810)	68,107	76,210
48879	Saint Johns	(517)	7,392	7,376
49085	Saint Joseph	(616)	9,214	9,622
48176	Saline	(313)	6,663	6,483
49783	Sault Sainte Marie	(906)	14,689	14,448
49455	Shelby(u)	(616)	48,655	....
48609	Shields(u)	(517)	6,634	....
*48037	Southfield	(810)	75,727	75,568
48195	Southgate	(313)	30,771	32,058
49090	South Haven	(616)	5,563	5,943
48178	South Lyon	(810)	6,479	5,214
48161	South Monroe(u)	(313)	5,266	4,232
49015	Springfield	(616)	5,582	5,917
*48311	Sterling Heights	(313)	117,810	108,999
49091	Sturgis	(616)	10,130	9,468
48180	Taylor	(313)	70,811	77,568
49286	Tecumseh	(517)	7,462	7,320
48182	Temperance(u)	(313)	6,542	....
49093	Three Rivers	(616)	7,464	7,015
*49685	Traverse City	(616)	15,155	15,516
48183	Trenton	(313)	20,586	22,762
*48099	Troy	(810)	72,884	67,102
*48318	Utica	(810)	5,081	5,282
49504	Walker	(616)	17,279	15,088
*48390	Walled Lake	(810)	6,278	4,748
*48090	Warren	(810)	144,864	161,134
48329	Waterford(u)	(313)	66,692	64,250
48917	Waverly(u)		15,614	....
48184	Wayne	(313)	19,899	21,159
*48325	West Bloomfield(u)	(313)	54,843	41,962
48185	Westland	(313)	84,724	84,603
49019	Westwood(u)	(616)	8,957	8,519
48393	Wixom	(313)	8,550	6,705
48183	Woodhaven	(313)	11,631	10,902

ZIP	Place		1990	1980
48753	Wurtsmith AFB(u)	(517)	5,080	5,166
*48192	Wyandotte	(313)	30,938	34,006
49509	Wyoming	(616)	63,891	59,616
*48197	Ypsilanti	(313)	24,846	24,031
49464	Zeeland	(616)	5,417	4,764

Minnesota

ZIP	Place		1990	1980
56007	Albert Lea	(507)	18,310	19,200
56308	Alexandria	(612)	8,029	7,608
55304	Andover	(612)	15,216	9,387
*55303	Anoka	(612)	17,192	15,634
55124	Apple Valley	(612)	34,598	21,818
55112	Arden Hills	(612)	9,199	8,012
55912	Austin	(507)	21,926	23,020
56601	Bemidji	(218)	11,165	10,949
55449	Blaine	(612)	38,975	28,558
*55420	Bloomington	(612)	86,335	81,831
56401	Brainerd	(218)	12,353	11,489
55429	Brooklyn Center	(612)	28,887	31,230
55443	Brooklyn Park	(612)	56,381	43,332
55313	Buffalo	(612)	6,856	4,560
*55337	Burnsville	(612)	51,288	35,674
55008	Cambridge	(612)	5,094	3,287
55316	Champlin	(612)	16,849	9,006
55317	Chanhassen	(612)	11,732	6,359
55318	Chaska	(612)	11,339	8,346
55719	Chisholm	(218)	5,290	5,930
55720	Cloquet	(218)	10,885	11,142
55421	Columbia Heights	(612)	18,910	20,029
55433	Coon Rapids	(612)	52,978	35,826
.....	Corcoran	(612)	5,199	4,252
55016	Cottage Grove	(612)	22,935	18,994
56716	Crookston	(218)	8,119	8,628
55428	Crystal	(612)	23,788	25,543
*56501	Detroit Lakes	(218)	6,635	7,106
*55806	Duluth	(218)	85,493	92,811
55121	Eagan	(612)	47,409	20,700
55005	East Bethel	(612)	8,050	6,626
56721	East Grand Forks	(218)	8,658	8,537
*55344	Eden Prairie	(612)	39,311	16,263
55424	Edina	(612)	46,075	46,073
55330	Elk River	(612)	11,143	6,785
56031	Fairmont	(507)	11,265	11,506
55113	Falcon Heights	(612)	5,380	5,291
55021	Faribault	(507)	17,085	16,241
55024	Farmington	(612)	5,940	4,370
*56537	Fergus Falls	(218)	12,362	12,519
55025	Forest Lake	(612)	5,833	4,596
55432	Fridley	(612)	28,335	30,228
55427	Golden Valley	(612)	20,971	22,775
*55744	Grand Rapids	(218)	7,976	7,934
*55304	Ham Lake	(612)	8,924	7,832
55033	Hastings	(612)	15,478	12,827
55810	Hermantown	(218)	6,761	6,759
*55746	Hibbing	(218)	18,046	21,193
*55343	Hopkins	(612)	16,529	15,336
55350	Hutchinson	(612)	11,459	9,244
56649	International Falls	(218)	8,301	5,611
*55075	Inver Grove Heights	(612)	22,477	17,171
55042	Lake Elmo	(612)	5,900	5,296
55044	Lakeville	(612)	24,854	14,790
.....	Lino Lakes	(612)	8,807	4,966
55355	Litchfield	(612)	6,041	5,904
55117	Little Canada	(612)	8,971	7,102
56345	Little Falls	(612)	7,371	7,250
55115	Mahtomedi	(612)	5,633	3,851
*56001	Mankato	(507)	31,405	28,646
55311	Maple Grove	(612)	38,736	20,525
55109	Maplewood	(612)	30,954	26,990
56258	Marshall	(507)	12,023	11,161
55118	Mendota Heights	(612)	9,388	7,288
*55440	Minneapolis	(612)	368,383	370,951
55345	Minnetonka	(612)	48,370	38,683
56265	Montevideo	(612)	5,499	5,845
*55362	Monticello	(612)	5,045	4,693
*56560	Moorhead	(218)	32,295	29,998
56267	Morris	(612)	5,613	5,367
55364	Mound	(612)	9,634	9,280
55112	Mounds View	(612)	12,541	12,593
55112	New Brighton	(612)	22,207	23,269
54427	New Hope	(612)	21,853	23,087
56073	New Ulm	(507)	13,132	13,755
55057	Northfield	(507)	14,684	12,562
56001	North Mankato	(507)	10,662	9,145
55109	North Saint Paul	(612)	12,376	11,921
55128	Oakdale	(612)	18,377	12,123
55323	Orono	(612)	7,285	6,845
55060	Owatonna	(507)	19,386	18,632
55421	Plymouth	(612)	50,889	31,615
55372	Prior Lake	(612)	11,482	7,284
55303	Ramsey	(612)	12,408	10,093
55066	Red Wing	(612)	15,134	13,736
55423	Richfield	(612)	35,710	37,851
55422	Robbinsdale	(612)	14,396	14,422
*55901	Rochester	(507)	70,729	57,906
55068	Rosemount	(612)	8,622	5,083
55113	Roseville	(612)	33,485	35,820
55418	Saint Anthony	(612)	7,727	7,981
*56301	Saint Cloud	(612)	48,812	42,566

ZIP	Place		1990	1980
55426	Saint Louis Park	(612)	43,787	42,931
*55101	Saint Paul	(612)	272,235	270,230
56082	Saint Peter	(507)	9,481	9,056
56377	Sartell	(612)	5,409	3,427
56379	Sauk Rapids	(612)	7,823	5,793
56378	Savage	(612)	9,906	3,954
55379	Shakopee	(612)	11,739	9,941
55126	Shoreview	(612)	24,587	17,300
55331	Shorewood	(612)	5,917	4,646
55075	South Saint Paul	(612)	20,197	21,235
55432	Spring Lake Park	(612)	6,532	6,477
*55082	Stillwater	(612)	13,882	12,290
56701	Thief River Falls	(218)	8,010	9,105
55127	Vadnais Heights	(612)	11,041	5,111
*55792	Virginia	(218)	9,410	11,056
56387	Waite Park	(612)	5,020	3,496
56093	Waseca	(507)	8,385	8,219
55118	West Saint Paul	(612)	19,248	18,527
55110	White Bear Lake	(612)	24,622	22,538
56201	Willmar	(612)	17,531	15,895
55987	Winona	(507)	25,435	25,075
55125	Woodbury	(612)	20,075	10,297
56187	Worthington	(507)	9,977	10,243

Mississippi (601)

ZIP	Place	1990	1980
39730	Aberdeen	6,837	7,184
38821	Amory	7,093	7,307
38606	Batesville	6,403	5,162
*39520	Bay Saint Louis	8,063	7,850
*39530	Biloxi	46,319	49,311
38829	Booneville	7,955	6,199
*39042	Brandon	11,077	9,626
39601	Brookhaven	10,243	10,800
39046	Canton	10,062	11,116
38614	Clarksdale	19,717	21,137
38732	Cleveland	15,384	14,524
*39056	Clinton	21,847	14,660
39429	Columbia	6,815	7,733
*39701	Columbus	23,799	27,503
38834	Corinth	11,820	13,180
39059	Crystal Springs	5,643	4,902
39532	D'Iberville†	6,566	6,236
39074	Forest	5,062	5,229
39553	Gautier†	10,088	10,392
*38701	Greenville	45,226	40,613
*38930	Greenwood	18,906	20,115
*38901	Grenada	10,864	11,508
39564	Gulf Hills(u)	5,004	4,512
*39501	Gulfport	40,775	39,676
*39401	Hattiesburg	41,906	40,829
*38635	Holly Springs	7,261	7,285
38637	Horn Lake	9,069	4,326
38751	Indianola	11,809	8,050
*39205	Jackson	196,637	202,895
39090	Kosciusko	6,986	7,415
*39440	Laurel	18,827	21,897
38756	Leland	6,366	6,667
39560	Long Beach	15,804	14,199
39339	Louisville	7,165	7,323
39648	McComb	11,797	12,331
*39110	Madison	7,471	2,241
*39302	Meridian	41,036	46,577
*39567	Moss Point	17,837	18,998
*39120	Natchez	19,460	22,209
38652	New Albany	6,775	7,072
*39564	Ocean Springs	14,673	14,504
39567	Orange Grove(u)	15,676	13,476
38655	Oxford	10,026	9,882
*39567	Pascagoula	25,899	29,318
39571	Pass Christian	5,557	5,014
39288	Pearl	19,588	18,602
39465	Petal	7,883	8,476
39350	Philadelphia	6,758	6,434
39466	Picayune	10,633	10,361
*39157	Ridgeland	11,714	5,461
38663	Ripley	5,371	4,271
39533	Saint Martin(u)	6,349	....
38671	Southaven†	17,949	16,441
39759	Starkville	18,458	16,139
*38801	Tupelo	30,685	23,905
*39180	Vicksburg	20,909	25,434
39576	Waveland	5,369	4,186
39367	Waynesboro	5,143	5,349
.....	West Hattiesburg(u)	5,450	....
39773	West Point	8,489	8,811
38967	Winona	5,724	6,177
39194	Yazoo City	12,427	12,092

Missouri

Area code (573) will go into effect on Jan. 7, 1996. Until then, use (314).

ZIP	Place		1990	1980
63123	Affton(u)	(314)	21,106	23,181
63010	Arnold	(314)	18,828	19,141
65605	Aurora	(417)	6,459	6,437
*63011	Ballwin	(314)	21,406	12,656
63137	Bellefontaine Neighbors	(314)	10,918	12,082

ZIP	Place		1990	1980
64012	Belton	(816)	18,145	12,708
63134	Berkeley	(314)	12,250	15,922
63031	Black Jack	(314)	6,131	5,293
*64015	Blue Springs	(816)	40,103	25,936
65613	Bolivar	(417)	6,845	5,919
65233	Boonville	(816)	7,095	6,959
63114	Breckenridge Hills	(314)	5,181	5,666
63144	Brentwood	(314)	8,150	8,209
63044	Bridgeton	(314)	17,732	18,445
*63701	Cape Girardeau	(573)	34,475	34,361
64836	Carthage	(417)	10,747	11,104
63830	Caruthersville	(573)	7,389	7,958
63834	Charleston	(573)	5,085	5,230
63017	Chesterfield†	(314)	38,630	28,384
64601	Chillicothe	(816)	8,799	9,089
63105	Clayton	(314)	13,926	14,306
64735	Clinton	(816)	8,703	8,366
*65201	Columbia	(573)	69,133	62,061
63128	Concord(u)	(314)	19,859	20,896
63126	Crestwood	(314)	11,229	12,815
63141	Creve Coeur	(314)	12,289	11,743
63136	Dellwood	(314)	5,245	6,200
63020	De Soto	(314)	5,993	5,993
63131	Des Peres	(314)	8,388	7,953
63841	Dexter	(573)	7,506	7,043
63011	Ellisville	(314)	7,183	6,233
64024	Excelsior Springs	(816)	10,373	10,424
63640	Farmington	(573)	11,596	8,270
63135	Ferguson	(314)	22,290	24,549
63028	Festus	(314)	8,105	7,574
*63033	Florissant	(314)	51,038	55,721
65473	Fort Leonard Wood(u)	(573)	15,863	21,262
65251	Fulton	(573)	10,033	11,046
64118	Gladstone	(816)	26,243	24,990
65254	Glasgow Village(u)	(573)	5,199	....
63122	Glendale	(314)	5,945	6,035
64030	Grandview	(816)	24,973	24,561
63401	Hannibal	(573)	18,004	18,811
64701	Harrisonville	(816)	7,696	6,372
63042	Hazelwood	(314)	15,512	13,098
*64050	Independence	(816)	112,301	111,797
63755	Jackson	(573)	9,256	7,827
*65101	Jefferson City	(573)	35,517	33,619
63136	Jennings	(314)	15,841	16,934
*64801	Joplin	(417)	40,866	39,126
*64108	Kansas City	(816)	434,829	448,028
63857	Kennett	(573)	10,941	10,145
63501	Kirksville	(816)	17,152	17,167
63122	Kirkwood	(314)	27,291	27,739
63124	Ladue (St. Louis Co.)	(314)	8,795	9,369
63367	Lake Saint Louis	(314)	7,536	3,843
65536	Lebanon	(417)	9,983	9,507
*64063	Lee's Summit	(816)	46,418	28,741
63125	Lemay(u)	(314)	18,005	35,424
64068	Liberty	(816)	20,459	16,251
63552	Macon	(816)	5,571	5,680
63863	Malden	(573)	5,123	6,096
63011	Manchester	(314)	6,447	6,351
63143	Maplewood	(314)	9,962	10,960
65340	Marshall	(816)	12,711	12,781
63043	Maryland Heights†	(314)	25,440	26,413
64468	Maryville	(816)	10,663	9,558
63129	Mehlville(u)	(314)	27,557	....
65265	Mexico	(573)	11,290	12,276
65270	Moberly	(816)	12,839	13,418
65708	Monett	(417)	6,529	6,148
63026	Murphy(u)	(314)	9,342	8,121
64850	Neosho	(417)	9,254	9,493
64772	Nevada	(417)	8,597	9,044
63121	Normandy	(314)	5,063	5,174
63121	Northwoods	(314)	5,106	5,831
63129	Oakville(u)	(314)	31,750	....
63366	O'Fallon	(314)	17,427	8,677
63132	Olivette	(314)	7,573	7,952
63114	Overland	(314)	17,987	19,620
63775	Perryville	(573)	6,933	7,343
63120	Pine Lawn	(314)	5,083	6,570
*63901	Poplar Bluff	(573)	16,841	17,139
64083	Raymore	(816)	5,592	3,154
64133	Raytown	(816)	30,601	31,831
65738	Republic	(417)	6,290	4,485
64085	Richmond	(816)	5,738	5,499
63117	Richmond Heights	(314)	10,448	11,516
63124	Rock Hill	(314)	5,217	5,702
65401	Rolla	(573)	14,090	13,303
63074	Saint Ann	(314)	14,449	15,523
*63301	Saint Charles	(314)	50,634	37,379
63114	Saint John	(314)	7,502	7,854
*64501	Saint Joseph	(816)	71,852	76,691
*63166	Saint Louis	(314)	396,685	452,801
63376	Saint Peters	(314)	40,660	15,700
63126	Sappington(u)	(314)	10,917	11,388
*65301	Sedalia	(816)	19,800	20,927
63119	Shrewsbury	(314)	6,416	5,077
63801	Sikeston	(573)	17,641	17,431
63138	Spanish Lake(u)	(314)	20,322	20,632
*65801	Springfield	(417)	140,494	133,116
63080	Sullivan	(573)	5,661	5,461
63006	Town and Country	(314)	9,503	3,187
64683	Trenton	(816)	6,129	6,811

ZIP	Place		1990	1980
63084	Union	(314)	6,048	5,506
63130	University City	(314)	40,087	42,690
64093	Warrensburg	(816)	15,244	13,807
63090	Washington	(314)	10,704	9,251
64870	Webb City	(417)	7,449	7,309
63119	Webster Groves	(314)	22,992	23,097
63385	Wentzville	(314)	4,640	3,193
65775	West Plains	(417)	8,913	7,741

Montana (406)

ZIP	Place	1990	1980
59711	Anaconda	10,356	12,518
*59101	Billings	81,125	66,818
*59715	Bozeman	22,660	21,645
*59701	Butte	33,336	37,205
*59401	Great Falls	55,125	56,884
59501	Havre	10,201	10,891
*59601	Helena	24,609	23,938
.....	Helena Valley West Central(u)	6,327	....
*59901	Kalispell	11,917	10,689
59044	Laurel	5,686	5,481
59457	Lewistown	6,097	7,104
59047	Livingston	6,701	6,994
59402	Malmstrom AFB(u)	5,938	6,675
59301	Miles City	8,461	9,602
*59801	Missoula	42,918	33,351
59801	Orchard Homes(u)	10,317	10,837
59270	Sidney	5,217	5,726

Nebraska

ZIP	Place		1990	1980
69301	Alliance	(308)	9,765	9,920
68310	Beatrice	(402)	12,352	12,891
*68005	Bellevue	(402)	30,948	21,813
*68008	Blair	(402)	6,860	6,418
69337	Chadron	(308)	5,588	5,933
68108	Chalco(u)	(402)	7,337	....
*68601	Columbus	(402)	19,480	17,328
68025	Fremont	(402)	23,680	23,979
69341	Gering	(308)	7,946	7,760
*68802	Grand Island	(308)	39,487	33,180
*68901	Hastings	(402)	22,837	23,045
68949	Holdrege	(308)	5,671	5,624
*68847	Kearney	(308)	24,396	21,158
68128	La Vista	(402)	9,840	9,588
68850	Lexington	(308)	6,600	7,040
*68501	Lincoln	(402)	191,972	171,932
69001	McCook	(308)	8,112	8,404
68410	Nebraska City	(402)	6,547	7,127
*68701	Norfolk	(402)	21,476	19,449
*69101	North Platte	(308)	22,605	24,509
68113	Offutt AFB West(u)	(402)	10,883	8,787
69153	Ogallala	(308)	5,095	5,638
*68108	Omaha	(402)	335,719	313,939
68046	Papillion	(402)	10,378	6,399
68048	Plattsmouth	(402)	6,415	6,295
68127	Ralston	(402)	6,236	5,143
*69361	Scottsbluff	(308)	13,711	14,156
68434	Seward	(402)	5,641	5,713
69162	Sidney	(308)	5,959	6,010
68776	South Sioux City	(402)	9,677	9,339
68787	Wayne	(402)	5,142	5,240
68467	York	(402)	7,940	7,723

Nevada (702)

ZIP	Place	1990	1980
*89005	Boulder City	12,567	9,590
*89701	Carson City	40,443	32,022
89112	East Las Vegas(u)	11,087	6,449
*89801	Elko	14,836	8,758
.....	Enterprise(u)	6,412	....
*89406	Fallon	6,430	4,262
89408	Fernley(u)	5,164	....
89410	Gardnerville Ranchos(u)	7,455	3,542
*89015	Henderson	64,948	24,363
*89450	Incline Village-Crystal Bay(u)	7,119	6,225
*89125	Las Vegas	258,204	164,674
89191	Nellis AFB(u)	8,377	7,476
*89030	North Las Vegas	47,849	42,739
89041	Pahrump(u)	7,424	....
89109	Paradise(u)	124,682	84,818
*89501	Reno	133,850	100,756
*89431	Sparks	53,367	40,780
*89801	Spring Creek(u) †	5,866	4,155
.....	Spring Valley(u)	51,726	....
89110	Sunrise Manor(u)	95,362	44,155
89433	Sun Valley(u)	11,391	8,822
89101	Winchester(u)	23,365	19,728
*89445	Winnemucca	6,102	4,140

New Hampshire (603)

See note on page 396

ZIP	Place	1990	1980
03031	Amherst	9,068	8,243
03811	Atkinson	5,188	4,397
03825	Barrington	6,164	4,404

ZIP	Place	1990	1980
03102	Bedford	12,563	9,481
03220	Belmont	5,796	4,026
03570	Berlin	11,824	13,084
03304	Bow	5,500	4,015
03743	Claremont	13,902	14,557
*03301	Concord	36,006	30,400
03818	Conway	7,940	7,158
03038	Derry Compact(u)	20,446	12,248
03038	Derry	29,603	18,875
*03820	Dover	25,042	22,377
03824	Durham Compact(u)	9,236	8,448
03824	Durham	11,818	10,652
03042	Epping	5,162	3,460
03833	Exeter Compact(u)	9,556	8,947
03833	Exeter	12,481	11,024
03835	Farmington	5,739	4,630
03235	Franklin	8,304	7,901
03246	Gilford	5,867	4,841
03045	Goffstown	14,621	11,315
03841	Hampstead	6,732	3,785
*03842	Hampton Compact(u)	7,989	6,779
*03842	Hampton	12,278	10,493
03755	Hanover Compact(u)	6,538	6,861
03755	Hanover	9,212	9,119
03049	Hollis	5,705	4,679
03106	Hooksett	9,002	7,303
03051	Hudson	19,530	14,022
03452	Jaffrey	5,361	4,349
03431	Keene	22,430	21,449
03848	Kingston	5,591	4,111
*03246	Laconia	15,743	15,575
*03766	Lebanon	12,183	11,134
03501	Litchfield	5,516	4,150
03561	Littleton	5,827	5,558
03053	Londonderry Compact(u)	10,114	....
03053	Londonderry	19,781	13,598
*03103	Manchester	99,332	90,936
03054	Merrimack	22,156	15,406
03055	Milford Compact(u)	8,015	6,269
03055	Milford	11,795	8,685
*03060	Nashua	79,662	67,865
03857	Newmarket	7,157	4,290
03773	Newport	6,110	6,229
03076	Pelham	9,408	8,090
03275	Pembroke	6,561	6,561
03458	Peterborough	5,239	4,895
03865	Plaistow	7,316	5,609
03264	Plymouth	5,811	5,094
*03801	Portsmouth	25,925	26,254
03077	Raymond	8,713	5,453
*03867	Rochester	26,630	21,560
03079	Salem	25,746	24,124
03874	Seabrook	6,503	5,917
03878	Somersworth	11,249	10,350
03275	Suncook(u)	5,214	4,698
*03431	Swanzey	6,236	5,183
03281	Weare	6,193	3,232
03087	Windham	9,000	5,664

New Jersey

See note on page 396

ZIP	Place		1990	1980
08201	Absecon	(609)	7,298	6,859
07401	Allendale	(201)	5,900	5,901
07712	Asbury Park	(908)	16,799	17,015
*08401	Atlantic City	(609)	37,986	40,199
08106	Audubon	(609)	9,205	9,533
07001	Avenel(u)	(908)	15,504	....
08007	Barrington	(609)	6,792	7,418
07002	Bayonne	(201)	61,464	65,047
08722	Beachwood	(908)	9,324	7,687
07109	Belleville(u)†	(201)	34,213	35,367
*08031	Bellmawr	(609)	12,603	13,721
07719	Belmar	(908)	5,877	6,771
07621	Bergenfield	(201)	24,458	25,568
07922	Berkeley Heights Twp.(u)	(908)	11,980	12,549
08009	Berlin	(609)	5,672	5,786
07924	Bernardsville	(908)	6,597	6,715
08012	Blackwood(u)	(609)	5,120	5,219
07003	Bloomfield(u)†	(201)	45,061	47,792
07403	Bloomingdale	(201)	7,530	7,867
07603	Bogota	(201)	7,824	8,344
07005	Boonton	(201)	8,343	8,620
08805	Bound Brook	(908)	9,487	9,710
*08723	Brick Twp. (u)	(201)	66,473	53,629
08302	Bridgeton	(609)	18,942	18,795
08807	Bridgewater Twp.(u)	(908)	32,509	29,175
08203	Brigantine	(609)	11,354	8,318
08015	Browns Mills(u)	(609)	11,429	10,568
07828	Budd Lake(u)	(201)	7,272	6,523
08016	Burlington	(609)	9,835	10,246
07405	Butler	(201)	7,392	7,616
*07006	Caldwell(u)†	(201)	7,549	7,624
*08101	Camden	(609)	87,492	84,910
07072	Carlstadt	(201)	5,510	6,166
08069	Carney's Point Twp. (u)	(609)	8,443	8,396
07008	Carteret	(908)	19,025	20,598

ZIP	Place		1990	1980
07009	Cedar Grove Twp.(u)			
	(Essex)	(201)	12,053	12,600
07928	Chatham	(201)	8,007	8,537
*08034	Cherry Hill Twp.(u)	(609)	69,319	68,785
08077	Cinnaminson Twp.(u)	(609)	14,583	16,072
07066	Clark Twp.(u)	(908)	14,629	16,699
08312	Clayton	(609)	6,155	6,013
08021	Clementon	(609)	5,601	5,764
07010	Cliffside Park	(201)	20,393	21,464
*07015	Clifton	(201)	71,984	74,388
07624	Closter	(201)	8,094	8,164
08108	Collingswood	(609)	15,289	15,838
07067	Colonia(u)	(908)	18,238	
07016	Cranford Twp.(u)	(908)	22,633	24,573
07626	Cresskill	(201)	7,558	7,609
08759	Crestwood Village(u)	(201)	8,030	7,965
*07801	Dover	(201)	15,115	14,681
07628	Dumont	(201)	17,187	18,334
08812	Dunellen	(908)	6,528	6,593
08816	East Brunswick Twp.(u)	(908)	43,548	37,711
07936	East Hanover Twp.(u)	(201)	9,926	9,319
*07019	East Orange	(201)	73,552	77,878
07073	East Rutherford	(201)	7,902	7,849
07724	Eatontown	(908)	13,800	12,703
07020	Edgewater	(201)	5,001	4,628
08010	Edgewater Park Twp.(u)	(609)	8,388	9,273
*08818	Edison Twp.(u)	(908)	88,680	70,193
*07207	Elizabeth	(908)	110,002	106,201
07407	Elmwood Park	(201)	17,623	18,377
07630	Emerson	(201)	6,930	7,793
07631	Englewood	(201)	24,850	23,701
07632	Englewood Cliffs	(201)	5,634	5,698
08618	Ewing Twp.(u)	(609)	34,185	34,842
07004	Fairfield(u)	(201)	7,615	7,987
07704	Fair Haven	(908)	5,270	5,679
07410	Fair Lawn	(201)	30,548	32,229
07022	Fairview (Bergen)	(201)	10,733	10,519
07023	Fanwood	(908)	7,115	7,767
08518	Florence-Roebling(u)	(609)	8,564	7,677
07932	Florham Park	(201)	8,521	9,359
08863	Fords(u)	(908)	14,392	....
08640	Fort Dix(u)	(609)	10,205	14,297
07024	Fort Lee	(201)	31,997	32,449
07417	Franklin Lakes	(201)	9,873	8,769
*08873	Franklin Twp. (Somerset)(u)	(201)	42,780	31,358
07728	Freehold	(908)	10,742	10,020
07026	Garfield	(201)	26,727	26,803
08753	Gilford Park(u)	(908)	8,668	6,528
08028	Glassboro	(609)	15,614	14,574
08029	Glendora(u)	(609)	5,201	5,632
07028	Glen Ridge(u)†	(201)	7,076	7,855
07452	Glen Rock	(201)	10,883	11,497
08030	Gloucester City	(609)	12,649	13,121
07093	Guttenberg	(201)	8,268	7,340
*07602	Hackensack	(201)	37,049	36,039
07840	Hackettstown	(908)	8,120	8,850
08033	Haddonfield	(609)	11,633	12,337
08035	Haddon Heights	(609)	7,860	8,361
*07510	Haledon	(201)	6,951	6,607
*08609	Hamilton Twp. (Mercer)(u)	(609)	86,553	82,801
08037	Hammonton	(609)	12,208	12,298
07981	Hanover Twp.(u)	(201)	11,538	11,846
07029	Harrison	(201)	13,425	12,242
07604	Hasbrouck Heights	(201)	11,488	12,166
*07510	Hawthorne	(201)	17,084	18,200
07730	Hazlet Twp.(u)	(908)	21,976	23,013
08904	Highland Park (Middlesex)	(908)	13,279	13,396
08520	Hightstown	(609)	5,126	4,581
07642	Hillsdale	(201)	9,750	10,495
07205	Hillside Twp.(u)	(908)	21,044	21,440
07030	Hoboken	(201)	33,397	42,460
08753	Holiday City-Berkeley(u)	(908)	14,293	9,019
.....	Holiday City South(u)	(908)	5,452	....
07843	Hopatcong	(201)	15,586	15,531
08525	Hopewell Twp. (Mercer)(u)	(609)	11,590	10,893
07111	Irvington(u)†	(201)	59,774	61,473
08830	Iselin(u)	(908)	16,141	....
*08527	Jackson Twp.(u)	(908)	33,283	25,644
08831	Jamesburg	(908)	5,294	4,114
*07303	Jersey City	(201)	228,517	223,532
07734	Keansburg	(908)	11,069	10,613
07032	Kearny	(201)	34,874	35,735
08824	Kendall Park(u)	(908)	7,127	7,419
07033	Kenilworth	(908)	7,574	8,221
07735	Keyport	(908)	7,586	7,413
07405	Kinnelon	(201)	8,470	7,770
07871	Lake Mohawk(u)	(201)	8,930	8,498
08701	Lakewood(u)	(908)	26,095	22,863
08879	Laurence Harbor(u)	(908)	6,361	6,737
08648	Lawrenceville(u)	(609)	6,446	....
*08733	Leisure Village West-			
	Pine Lake Park(u)	(908)	10,139	....
07605	Leonia	(201)	8,365	8,027
07035	Lincoln Park	(201)	10,978	8,806
07738	Lincroft(u)	(908)	6,193	....
07036	Linden	(908)	36,701	37,836
08021	Lindenwold	(609)	18,734	18,196
08221	Linwood	(609)	6,866	6,144
07424	Little Falls Twp.(u)	(201)	11,294	11,496
07643	Little Ferry	(201)	9,989	9,399

ZIP	Place		1990	1980
07739	Little Silver	(908)	5,721	5,548
07039	Livingston Twp.(u)	(201)	26,609	28,040
07644	Lodi	(201)	22,355	23,956
07740	Long Branch	(908)	28,658	29,819
*07946	Long Hill Twp.(u)	(908)	7,826	7,275
07071	Lyndhurst(u)	(201)	18,262	20,326
08641	McGuire AFB(u)	(609)	7,580	7,853
07940	Madison	(201)	15,850	15,357
08859	Madison Park(u)	(201)	7,490	7,447
*07430	Mahwah Twp.(u)	(201)	17,905	12,127
08736	Manasquan	(908)	5,369	5,354
08835	Manville	(908)	10,567	11,278
08052	Maple Shade Twp.(u)	(609)	19,211	20,525
07040	Maplewood Twp.(u)	(201)	21,756	22,950
08402	Margate City	(609)	8,431	9,179
07746	Marlboro Twp.(u)	(908)	27,974	17,560
08053	Marlton(u)	(609)	10,228	9,411
07747	Matawan	(908)	9,239	8,837
07607	Maywood	(201)	9,536	9,895
08619	Mercerville-Hamilton Sq.(u)	(609)	26,873	25,446
08840	Metuchen	(908)	12,804	13,762
08846	Middlesex	(908)	13,055	13,480
07748	Middletown Twp.(u)	(908)	68,183	62,574
07432	Midland Park	(201)	7,047	7,381
07041	Millburn Twp.(u)	(201)	18,630	19,543
08850	Milltown (Middlesex)	(908)	6,968	7,136
08332	Millville	(609)	25,992	24,815
08094	Monroe Twp. (Gloucester)(u)	(609)	26,703	21,639
*07042	Montclair(u)	(201)	37,729	38,321
07645	Montvale	(201)	6,946	7,318
07045	Montville Twp.(u)	(201)	15,600	14,290
08057	Moorestown-Lenola(u)	(609)	13,242	13,695
07950	Morris Plains	(201)	5,219	5,305
*07960	Morristown	(201)	16,189	16,614
07092	Mountainside	(908)	6,657	7,118
08060	Mount Holly Twp.(u)	(609)	10,639	10,818
08087	Mystic Island(u)	(609)	7,400	4,929
*07753	Neptune Twp.(u)	(609)	28,148	28,366
*07102	Newark	(201)	275,221	329,248
*08901	New Brunswick	(908)	41,711	41,442
07646	New Milford	(201)	15,990	16,876
07974	New Providence	(908)	11,439	12,426
07860	Newton	(201)	7,521	7,748
07031	North Arlington	(201)	13,790	16,587
07047	North Bergen Twp.(u)	(201)	48,414	47,019
08902	North Brunswick Twp.(u)†	(908)	31,287	22,220
07006	North Caldwell(u)†	(201)	6,706	5,832
08225	Northfield	(609)	7,305	7,795
07508	North Haledon	(201)	7,987	8,177
07060	North Plainfield	(908)	18,820	19,108
08260	North Wildwood	(609)	5,017	4,714
07110	Nutley(u)†	(201)	27,099	28,998
07436	Oakland	(201)	11,997	13,443
*08758	Ocean Twp. (Ocean)(u)	(908)	5,416	3,731
*08050	Ocean Acres(u)	(609)	5,587	4,850
08226	Ocean City	(609)	15,512	13,949
07757	Oceanport	(908)	6,146	5,888
08857	Old Bridge(u)	(908)	22,151	21,815
08857	Old Bridge Twp.(u)	(908)	56,493	51,515
07649	Oradell	(201)	8,024	8,658
*07051	Orange(u)†	(201)	29,925	31,136
07650	Palisades Park	(201)	14,536	13,732
08065	Palmyra	(609)	7,056	7,085
07652	Paramus	(201)	25,004	26,474
07656	Park Ridge	(201)	8,102	8,515
07054	Parsippany-Troy Hills Twp.(u)	(201)	48,478	49,868
07055	Passaic	(201)	58,041	52,463
*07510	Paterson	(201)	140,891	137,970
08066	Paulsboro	(609)	6,577	6,944
08110	Pennsauken Twp.(u)	(609)	34,738	33,775
08069	Penns Grove	(609)	5,228	5,760
08070	Pennsville Center(u)	(609)	12,218	12,467
07440	Pequannock Twp.(u)	(201)	12,844	13,776
*08861	Perth Amboy	(908)	41,967	38,951
08865	Phillipsburg	(908)	15,757	16,647
08021	Pine Hill	(609)	9,854	8,684
*08854	Piscataway Twp.(u)	(908)	47,089	42,223
08071	Pitman	(609)	9,365	9,744
*07061	Plainfield	(908)	46,571	45,555
08232	Pleasantville	(609)	16,027	13,435
08742	Point Pleasant	(908)	18,177	17,747
08742	Point Pleasant Beach	(908)	5,112	5,415
07442	Pompton Lakes	(201)	10,539	10,660
*08540	Princeton	(609)	12,016	12,035
07508	Prospect Park	(201)	5,053	5,142
07065	Rahway	(908)	25,325	26,723
08057	Ramblewood(u)	(609)	6,181	6,475
07446	Ramsey	(201)	13,228	12,899
07869	Randolph Twp.(u)	(201)	19,974	17,828
08869	Raritan	(908)	5,798	6,128
07701	Red Bank	(908)	10,636	12,031
07657	Ridgefield	(201)	9,996	10,294
07660	Ridgefield Park	(201)	12,454	12,738
*07451	Ridgewood	(201)	24,152	25,208
07456	Ringwood	(201)	12,623	12,625
07661	River Edge	(201)	10,603	11,111
08075	Riverside Twp.(u)	(609)	7,974	7,941
07675	River Vale(u)	(201)	9,410	9,489
07726	Robertsville(u)	(908)	9,841	8,461

ZIP	Place		1990	1980
07662	Rochelle Park Twp.	(201)	5,587	5,603
07866	Rockaway	(201)	6,243	6,852
07203	Roselle	(908)	20,314	20,641
07204	Roselle Park	(201)	12,805	13,377
07760	Rumson	(908)	6,701	7,623
08078	Runnemede	(609)	9,042	9,461
*07070	Rutherford	(201)	17,790	19,068
07663	Saddle Brook Twp.(u)	(201)	13,296	14,084
08079	Salem	(609)	6,883	6,959
08872	Sayreville	(908)	34,998	29,969
07076	Scotch Plains Twp.(u)	(908)	21,150	20,774
*07094	Secaucus	(201)	14,061	13,719
08753	Silverton	(908)	9,175	7,236
08083	Somerdale	(609)	5,440	5,900
*08873	Somerset(u)	(908)	22,070	21,731
08244	Somers Point	(609)	11,216	10,330
08876	Somerville	(908)	11,632	11,973
08879	South Amboy	(908)	7,851	8,322
07079	South Orange Twp.(u)	(201)	16,390	15,864
07080	South Plainfield	(908)	20,489	20,521
08882	South River	(908)	13,692	14,361
07871	Sparta Twp.(u)	(201)	15,157	13,333
08884	Spotswood	(908)	7,983	7,840
07081	Springfield Twp.(u)	(201)	13,420	13,955
07762	Spring Lake Heights	(908)	5,341	5,424
08084	Stratford	(609)	7,614	8,005
07747	Strathmore(u)	(201)	7,060	....
07876	Succasunna-Kenvil(u)	(201)	11,781	10,931
*07901	Summit	(908)	19,757	21,071
07666	Teaneck Twp.(u)	(201)	37,825	39,007
07670	Tenafly	(201)	13,326	13,552
07724	Tinton Falls	(908)	12,361	7,740
*08753	Toms River(u)	(908)	7,524	7,465
*07512	Totowa	(201)	10,177	11,448
*08650	Trenton	(609)	88,675	92,124
08520	Twin Rivers(u)	(609)	7,715	7,742
07083	Union Twp. (Union)(u)	(908)	50,024	50,184
07735	Union Beach	(908)	6,156	6,354
07087	Union City	(201)	58,012	55,593
07458	Upper Saddle River	(201)	7,198	7,958
08406	Ventnor City	(609)	11,005	11,704
07044	Verona(u)†	(201)	13,597	14,166
08251	Villas(u)	(609)	8,136	5,909
08360	Vineland	(609)	54,780	53,753
07463	Waldwick	(201)	9,757	10,802
07057	Wallington	(201)	10,828	10,741
07465	Wanaque	(201)	9,711	10,025
07882	Washington	(908)	6,474	6,429
07675	Washington Twp.(Bergen)(u)	(201)	9,245	9,550
07060	Watchung	(908)	5,110	5,290
*07470	Wayne Twp.(u)	(201)	47,025	46,474
07087	Weehawken Twp.(u)	(201)	12,385	13,168
07006	West Caldwell(u)†	(201)	10,422	11,407
*07091	Westfield	(908)	28,870	30,447
07728	West Freehold(u)	(908)	11,166	9,929
07764	West Long Branch	(908)	7,690	7,380
07480	West Milford Twp.(u)†	(201)	25,430	22,750
07093	West New York	(201)	38,125	39,194
07052	West Orange(u)†	(201)	39,103	39,510
07424	West Paterson	(201)	10,982	11,293
07675	Westwood	(201)	10,446	10,714
07885	Wharton	(201)	5,405	5,485
08610	White Horse(u)	(609)	9,397	10,098
07886	White Meadow Lake(u)	(201)	8,002	8,429
08094	Williamstown	(609)	10,891	5,768
08046	Willingboro Twp.(u)	(609)	36,291	39,912
08095	Winslow Twp.(u)	(609)	30,087	20,034
07095	Woodbridge(u)	(908)	17,434	....
*07095	Woodbridge Twp.(u)	(908)	93,092	90,074
08096	Woodbury	(609)	10,904	10,353
07675	Woodcliff Lake	(201)	5,303	5,644
07075	Wood-Ridge	(201)	7,506	7,929
07481	Wyckoff Twp.(u)	(201)	15,372	15,500
08620	Yardville-Groveville(u)	(609)	9,248	9,414
07726	Yorketown(u)	(609)	6,313	5,330

New Mexico (505)

ZIP	Place	1990	1980
*88310	Alamogordo	27,596	24,024
*87101	Albuquerque	384,619	332,920
88021	Anthony(u)	5,160	3,285
*88210	Artesia	10,610	10,385
87410	Aztec	5,480	5,512
87002	Belen	6,547	5,617
87004	Bernalillo	5,960	2,988
87413	Bloomfield	5,214	4,881
*88220	Carlsbad	24,952	25,496
*88101	Clovis	30,954	31,194
87048	Corrales	5,453	2,791
*88030	Deming	10,970	9,964
*87532	Espanola	8,389	6,803
*87401	Farmington	33,997	31,222
*87301	Gallup	19,157	18,167
87020	Grants	8,626	11,439
*88240	Hobbs	29,121	29,153
88330	Holloman AFB(u)	5,891	7,245
*88001	Las Cruces	62,360	45,086
87701	Las Vegas	14,753	14,322
87544	Los Alamos(u)	11,455	11,039
87031	Los Lunas	6,013	3,525
88260	Lovington	9,322	9,727
87107	North Valley(u)	12,507	12,984
87114	Paradise Hills(u)	5,513	5,096
88130	Portales	10,690	9,940
87740	Raton	7,372	8,225
*87124	Rio Rancho†	32,512	9,985
*88201	Roswell	44,260	39,676
87115	Sandia(u)	6,742	5,288
*87501	Santa Fe	56,537	49,160
87420	Shiprock(u)	7,687	7,237
*88061	Silver City	10,683	9,887
87801	Socorro	8,159	7,173
87105	South Valley(u)	35,701	38,898
88063	Sunland Park†	8,179	4,313
87901	Truth or Consequences	6,221	5,219
88401	Tucumcari	6,827	6,765
87544	White Rock(u)	6,192	6,560
87327	Zuni Pueblo(u)	5,857	5,551

New York

See note on page 396

ZIP	Place		1990	1980
10901	Airmont(u)	(914)	7,835	....
*12201	Albany	(518)	100,031	101,727
11507	Albertson(u)	(516)	5,166	5,561
14411	Albion	(716)	5,863	4,897
11701	Amityville	(516)	9,286	9,076
12010	Amsterdam	(518)	20,714	21,872
12603	Arlington(u)	(914)	11,948	11,305
*13021	Auburn	(315)	31,258	32,548
*11702	Babylon	(516)	12,249	12,388
11510	Baldwin(u)	(516)	22,719	31,630
11510	Baldwin Harbor(u)	(516)	7,899	....
13027	Baldwinsville	(315)	6,591	6,446
12020	Ballston Spa	(518)	5,194	4,711
14020	Batavia	(716)	16,310	16,703
14810	Bath	(607)	5,801	6,042
11705	Bayport(u)	(516)	7,702	9,282
11706	Bay Shore(u)	(516)	21,279	10,784
11709	Bayville	(516)	7,193	7,034
.....	Baywood(u)		7,351	....
12508	Beacon	(914)	13,243	12,937
11710	Bellmore(u)	(516)	16,438	18,106
11714	Bethpage(u)	(516)	15,761	16,840
*13902	Binghamton	(607)	53,008	55,860
11716	Bohemia(u)	(516)	9,556	9,308
11717	Brentwood(u)	(516)	45,218	44,321
10510	Briarcliff Manor	(914)	7,070	7,115
14610	Brighton (u)	(716)	34,455	35,776
14420	Brockport	(716)	8,749	9,776
10708	Bronxville	(914)	6,028	6,267
*14205	Buffalo	(716)	328,175	357,870
*14424	Canandaigua	(716)	10,725	10,419
13617	Canton	(315)	6,379	7,055
11514	Carle Place(u)	(516)	5,107	5,470
11516	Cedarhurst	(516)	5,716	6,162
11720	Centereach(u)	(516)	26,720	30,136
11934	Center Moriches(u)	(516)	5,987	5,703
11721	Centerport(Suffolk)(u)	(516)	5,333	6,576
11722	Central Islip(u)	(516)	26,028	19,734
*14225	Cheektowaga(u)	(716)	84,387	92,145
10977	Chestnut Ridge†	(914)	7,517	8,217
12065	CliftonPark	(518)	30,117	
12043	Cobleskill	(518)	5,268	5,272
12047	Cohoes	(518)	16,825	18,144
12205	Colonie	(518)	8,019	8,869
11725	Commack(u)	(516)	36,124	34,719
10920	Congers(u)	(914)	8,003	7,123
11726	Copiague(u)	(516)	20,769	20,132
11727	Coram(u)	(516)	30,111	24,752
14830	Corning	(607)	11,938	12,953
13045	Cortland	(607)	19,801	20,138
*10520	Croton-on-Hudson	(914)	7,018	6,889
14437	Dansville	(716)	5,002	4,979
11729	Deer Park(u)	(516)	28,840	30,394
12054	Delmar(u)	(518)	8,360	8,423
14043	Depew	(716)	17,673	19,819
13214	DeWitt(u)	(315)	8,244	9,024
11746	Dix Hills(u)	(516)	25,849	26,693
10522	Dobbs Ferry	(914)	9,940	10,053
14048	Dunkirk	(716)	13,989	15,310
14052	East Aurora	(716)	6,647	6,803
10709	Eastchester(u)	(914)	18,537	20,305
12302	East Glenville(u)	(518)	6,518	6,537
11576	East Hills	(516)	6,746	7,160
11730	East Islip(u)	(516)	14,325	13,852
11758	East Massapequa(u)	(516)	19,550	13,987
11554	East Meadow(u)	(516)	36,909	39,317
11731	East Northport(u)	(516)	20,411	20,187
11772	East Patchogue(u)	(516)	20,195	18,139
14445	East Rochester	(716)	6,932	7,596
11518	East Rockaway	(516)	10,152	10,917
11786	East Shoreham(u)	(516)	5,461	....
*14901	Elmira	(607)	33,724	35,327
11003	Elmont(u)	(516)	28,612	27,592
11731	Elwood(u)	(516)	10,916	11,847
*13760	Endicott	(607)	13,531	14,457
13762	Endwell(u)	(607)	12,602	13,745

ZIP	Place		1990	1980
13219	Fairmount(u)	(315)	12,266	13,415
14450	Fairport	(716)	5,943	5,970
11735	Farmingdale	(516)	8,022	7,946
11738	Farmingville(u)	(516)	14,842	13,398
*11001	Floral Park	(516)	15,947	16,805
13603	Fort Drum(u)	(315)	11,578	....
11768	Fort Salonga(u)	(516)	9,176	9,550
11010	Franklin Square(Nassau)(u)	(516)	28,205	29,051
14063	Fredonia	(716)	10,436	11,126
11520	Freeport	(516)	39,894	38,272
13069	Fulton	(315)	12,929	13,312
*11530	Garden City	(516)	21,675	22,927
11040	Garden City Park(u)	(516)	7,437	7,712
14624	Gates-North Gates(u)	(716)	14,995	15,244
14454	Geneseo	(716)	7,187	6,746
14456	Geneva	(315)	14,143	15,133
11542	Glen Cove	(516)	24,149	24,618
12801	Glens Falls	(518)	15,023	15,897
12801	Glens Falls North(u)	(518)	7,978	6,956
12078	Gloversville	(518)	16,656	17,836
10924	Goshen	(914)	5,255	4,874
*11022	Great Neck	(516)	8,745	9,168
11020	Great Neck Plaza	(516)	5,897	5,604
14616	Greece(u)	(716)	15,632	16,177
11740	Greenlawn(u)	(516)	13,208	13,869
*10583	Greenville(Westchester)(u)	(914)	9,528	8,706
14075	Hamburg	(716)	10,442	10,582
11946	Hampton Bays(u)	(516)	7,893	7,256
10528	Harrison	(914)	23,308	23,046
10530	Hartsdale(u)	(914)	9,587	10,216
10706	Hastings-on-Hudson	(914)	8,000	8,573
*11787	Hauppauge(u)	(516)	19,750	20,960
10927	Haverstraw	(914)	9,438	8,800
*11551	Hempstead	(516)	47,982	40,404
13350	Herkimer	(315)	7,945	8,383
11557	Hewlett(u)	(516)	6,620	6,986
*11802	Hicksville(u)	(516)	40,174	43,245
10977	Hillcrest(u)	(914)	6,447	5,733
14468	Hilton	(716)	5,216	4,151
11741	Holbrook(u)	(516)	25,273	24,382
11742	Holtsville(u)	(516)	14,972	13,515
14843	Hornell	(607)	9,877	10,234
*14845	Horseheads	(607)	6,802	7,348
12534	Hudson	(518)	8,034	7,986
12839	Hudson Falls	(518)	7,651	7,419
11743	Huntington	(516)	18,243	21,727
11746	Huntington Station(u)	(516)	28,247	28,769
13357	Ilion	(315)	8,888	9,450
11696	Inwood(u)	(516)	7,767	8,228
14617	Irondequoit(u)	(716)	52,322	57,648
10533	Irvington	(914)	6,348	5,774
11751	Islip(u)	(516)	18,924	13,438
11752	Islip Terrace(u)	(516)	5,530	5,588
*14850	Ithaca	(607)	29,541	28,732
*14702	Jamestown	(716)	34,681	35,775
10535	Jefferson Valley-Yorktown(u)	(914)	14,118	13,380
11753	Jericho(Nassau)(u)	(516)	13,141	12,739
13790	Johnson City	(607)	16,578	17,126
12095	Johnstown	(518)	9,058	9,360
14217	Kenmore	(716)	17,180	18,474
11754	Kings Park(u)	(516)	17,773	16,131
12401	Kingston	(914)	23,095	24,481
10950	Kiryas Joel(u)	(914)	7,437	2,088
14218	Lackawanna	(716)	20,585	22,701
10512	Lake Carmel(u)	(914)	8,489	7,295
11755	Lake Grove	(516)	9,612	9,692
11779	Lake Ronkonkoma(u)	(516)	18,997	38,336
11552	Lakeview(u)	(516)	5,476	5,276
14086	Lancaster	(716)	11,940	13,056
10538	Larchmont	(914)	6,181	6,308
12110	Latham(u)	(518)	10,131	11,182
11559	Lawrence	(516)	6,513	6,175
11756	Levittown(u)	(516)	53,286	57,045
11757	Lindenhurst	(516)	26,879	26,919
13365	Little Falls	(315)	5,829	6,156
*14094	Lockport	(716)	24,426	24,844
11561	Long Beach	(516)	33,510	34,073
12211	Loudonville(u)	(518)	10,822	11,480
11563	Lynbrook	(516)	19,208	20,424
10541	Mahopac(u)	(914)	7,755	7,681
12953	Malone	(518)	6,777	7,668
11565	Malverne	(516)	9,054	9,262
10543	Mamaroneck	(914)	17,325	17,616
11030	Manhasset(u)	(516)	7,718	8,485
11050	Manorhaven	(516)	5,672	5,384
11949	Manorville(u)	(516)	6,198	....
11758	Massapequa(u)	(516)	22,018	24,454
11762	Massapequa Park	(516)	18,044	19,779
13662	Massena	(315)	11,716	12,851
11950	Mastic(u)	(516)	13,778	10,413
11951	Mastic Beach(u)	(516)	10,293	8,318
13211	Mattydale(u)	(315)	6,418	7,511
12118	Mechanicville	(518)	5,249	5,500
11763	Medford(u)	(516)	21,274	20,418
14103	Medina	(716)	6,686	6,392
11746	Melville(u)	(516)	12,586	8,139
11566	Merrick(u)	(516)	23,042	24,478
11953	Middle Island(u)	(516)	7,848	5,703
*10940	Middletown	(914)	24,160	21,454
11764	Miller Place(u)	(516)	9,315	7,877
11501	Mineola	(516)	19,005	20,757
10950	Monroe	(914)	6,672	5,996
10952	Monsey(u)	(914)	13,986	12,380
12701	Monticello	(914)	6,597	6,306
10970	Mount Ivy(u)	(914)	6,013	....
10549	Mount Kisco	(914)	9,108	8,025
11766	Mount Sinai(u)	(516)	8,023	6,591
*10551	Mount Vernon	(914)	67,153	66,713
12590	Myers Corner(u)	(914)	5,599	5,180
10954	Nanuet(u)	(914)	14,065	12,578
11767	Nesconset(u)	(516)	10,712	10,706
14513	Newark	(315)	9,849	10,017
*12550	Newburgh	(914)	26,454	23,438
11590	New Cassel(u)	(516)	10,257	9,635
10956	New City(u)	(914)	33,673	35,859
*11040	New Hyde Park	(516)	9,728	9,801
12561	New Paltz	(914)	5,470	4,938
*10802	New Rochelle	(914)	67,265	70,794
*12550	New Windsor Center(u)	(914)	8,898	7,812
*10001	New York	(212)/(718)	7,322,564	7,071,639
*14302	Niagara Falls	(716)	61,840	71,384
11701	North Amityville(u)	(516)	13,849	13,140
11703	North Babylon(u)	(516)	18,081	19,019
11706	North Bay Shore(u)	(516)	12,799	35,020
11710	North Bellmore(u)	(516)	19,707	20,630
11713	North Bellport(u)	(516)	8,182	7,432
11757	North Lindenhurst(u)	(516)	10,563	11,511
11758	North Massapequa(u)	(516)	19,365	21,385
11566	North Merrick(u)	(516)	12,113	12,848
11040	North New Hyde Park(u)	(516)	14,359	15,114
11772	North Patchogue(u)	(516)	7,374	7,126
11768	Northport	(516)	7,572	7,651
13212	North Syracuse	(315)	7,363	7,970
10591	North Tarrytown	(914)	8,152	7,994
14120	North Tonawanda	(716)	34,989	35,760
11580	North Valley Stream(u)	(516)	14,574	14,530
11793	North Wantagh(u)	(516)	12,276	12,677
13815	Norwich	(607)	7,613	8,082
10960	Nyack	(914)	6,558	6,428
11769	Oakdale(u)	(516)	7,875	8,090
11572	Oceanside(u)	(516)	32,423	33,639
13669	Ogdensburg	(315)	13,521	12,375
11804	Old Bethpage(u)	(516)	5,610	6,215
14760	Olean	(716)	16,946	18,207
13421	Oneida	(315)	10,850	10,810
13820	Oneonta	(607)	13,954	14,933
12550	Orange Lake(u)	(914)	5,196	5,120
10562	Ossining	(914)	22,582	20,196
13126	Oswego	(315)	19,195	19,793
11771	Oyster Bay(u)	(516)	6,687	6,497
11772	Patchogue	(516)	11,060	11,291
10965	Pearl River(u)	(914)	15,314	15,893
10566	Peekskill	(914)	19,536	18,236
10803	Pelham	(914)	6,413	6,848
10803	Pelham Manor	(914)	5,443	6,130
14527	Penn Yan	(315)	5,257	5,242
11714	Plainedge(u)	(516)	8,739	9,629
11803	Plainview(u)	(516)	26,207	28,037
*12901	Plattsburgh	(518)	21,255	21,057
12903	Plattsburgh AFB(u)	(518)	5,483	5,905
10570	Pleasantville	(914)	6,592	6,749
10573	Port Chester	(914)	24,728	23,565
11777	Port Jefferson	(516)	7,455	6,731
11776	Port Jefferson Station(u)	(516)	7,232	17,009
12771	Port Jervis	(914)	9,060	8,699
11050	Port Washington(u)	(516)	15,387	14,521
13676	Potsdam	(315)	10,251	10,635
*12601	Poughkeepsie	(914)	28,844	29,757
12144	Rensselaer	(518)	8,255	9,047
11961	Ridge(u)	(516)	11,734	8,977
11901	Riverhead(u)	(516)	8,814	6,339
*14692	Rochester	(716)	230,356	241,741
*11571	Rockville Centre	(516)	24,727	25,412
11778	Rocky Point(u)	(516)	8,596	7,012
12205	Roessleville(u)	(518)	10,753	11,685
*13440	Rome	(315)	44,350	43,826
11779	Ronkonkoma(u)	(516)	20,391	....
11575	Roosevelt(u)	(516)	15,030	14,109
11577	Roslyn Heights(u)	(516)	6,405	6,546
12303	Rotterdam(u)	(518)	21,228	22,933
10580	Rye	(914)	14,936	15,083
10573	Rye Brook†	(914)	7,765	7,996
11780	Saint James(u)	(516)	12,703	12,122
14779	Salamanca	(716)	6,566	6,890
13454	Salisbury(u)	(315)	12,226	9,732
12983	Saranac Lake	(518)	5,377	5,578
12866	Saratoga Springs	(518)	25,001	23,906
11782	Sayville(u)	(516)	16,550	12,013
10583	Scarsdale	(914)	16,987	17,650
*12301	Schenectady	(518)	65,566	67,972
10940	Scotchtown(u)	(914)	8,765	7,352
12302	Scotia	(518)	7,359	7,280
11579	Sea Cliff	(516)	5,054	5,364
11783	Seaford(u)	(516)	15,597	16,117
11507	Searingtown(u)	(516)	5,020	....
11784	Selden(u)	(516)	20,608	17,259
13148	Seneca Falls	(315)	7,370	7,466
11733	Setauket-East Setauket(u)	(516)	13,634	10,176
11967	Shirley(Suffolk)(u)	(516)	22,936	18,072
11787	Smithtown(u)	(516)	25,638	30,906

ZIP	Place		1990	1980
13209	Solvay	(315)	6,717	7,140
11789	Sound Beach(u)	(516)	9,102	8,071
11735	South Farmingdale(u)	(516)	15,377	16,439
14850	South Hill(u)	(607)	5,423	5,276
11746	South Huntington(u)	(516)	9,624	14,854
14094	South Lockport(u)	(716)	7,112	3,366
11971	Southold(u)	(516)	5,192	4,770
14904	Southport(u)	(607)	7,753	8,329
11581	South Valley Stream(u)	(516)	5,328	5,462
10977	Spring Valley	(914)	21,802	20,537
11790	Stony Brook(u)	(516)	13,726	16,155
10980	Stony Point(u) (Rockland)	(914)	10,587	8,686
10901	Suffern	(914)	11,055	10,794
11791	Syosset(u)	(516)	18,967	9,818
*13220	Syracuse	(315)	163,860	170,105
10983	Tappan(u)	(914)	6,867	8,267
10591	Tarrytown	(914)	10,739	10,648
11776	Terryville	(516)	10,275	....
10984	Thiells	(914)	5,204	....
10594	Thornwood(u)	(914)	7,025	7,197
*14150	Tonawanda	(716)	17,284	18,693
*14150	Tonawanda(u)	(716)	65,284	72,795
*12180	Troy	(518)	54,269	56,638
10707	Tuckahoe	(914)	6,302	6,076
11553	Uniondale(u)	(516)	20,328	20,016
*13504	Utica	(315)	68,637	75,632
10989	Valley Cottage(u)	(914)	9,007	8,214
*11582	Valley Stream	(516)	33,946	35,769
11792	Wading River(u)	(516)	5,317	....
12586	Walden	(914)	5,836	5,659
11793	Wantagh(u)	(516)	18,567	19,817
10990	Warwick	(914)	5,984	4,320
13165	Waterloo	(315)	5,116	5,303
*13601	Watertown	(315)	29,429	27,861
12189	Watervliet	(518)	11,061	11,354
14580	Webster	(716)	5,464	5,499
14895	Wellsville	(716)	5,241	5,769
*11702	West Babylon(u)	(516)	42,410	41,699
11590	Westbury (Nassau)	(516)	13,060	13,871
14905	West Elmira(u)	(607)	5,218	5,485
12801	West Glens Falls(u)	(518)	5,964	5,331
10993	West Haverstraw	(914)	9,183	9,181
11552	West Hempstead(u)	(516)	17,689	18,536
11743	West Hills(u)	(516)	5,849	6,071
11795	West Islip(u)	(516)	28,419	29,533
12203	Westmere(u)	(518)	6,750	6,881
*10996	West Point(u)	(914)	8,024	8,105
14224	West Seneca(u)	(716)	47,866	51,210
13219	Westvale(u)	(315)	5,952	6,169
11798	Wheatley Heights(u)	(516)	5,027	....
*10602	White Plains	(914)	48,718	46,999
14221	Williamsville	(716)	5,583	6,017
11596	Williston Park	(516)	7,516	8,216
11797	Woodbury(u)	(516)	8,008	7,043
11598	Woodmere(u)	(516)	15,578	17,205
11798	Wyandach(u)	(516)	8,950	13,215
*10702	Yonkers	(914)	188,082	195,351
10598	Yorktown Heights(u)	(914)	7,690	7,696

North Carolina

ZIP	Place		1990	1980
*28001	Albemarle	(704)	14,940	15,110
27263	Archdale	(919)	6,975	5,326
*27203	Asheboro	(910)	16,362	15,252
*28801	Asheville	(704)	61,855	54,022
28012	Belmont	(704)	8,434	4,607
28711	Black Mountain	(704)	5,533	4,083
28607	Boone	(704)	12,949	10,191
28712	Brevard	(704)	5,388	5,323
*27215	Burlington	(910)	39,498	37,266
28547	Camp Lejeune(u)	(919)	36,716	30,764
27510	Carrboro	(919)	12,134	7,336
*27511	Cary	(919)	44,397	21,763
*27514	Chapel Hill	(919)	38,711	32,421
*28204	Charlotte	(704)	395,925	315,474
27012	Clemmons†	(919)	5,982	4,842
28328	Clinton	(910)	8,385	7,552
*28025	Concord	(704)	27,601	16,942
28613	Conover	(704)	5,311	4,245
*28334	Dunn	(910)	8,556	8,962
*27701	Durham	(919)	136,612	101,149
*27288	Eden	(910)	15,238	15,672
27932	Edenton	(919)	5,268	5,357
*27909	Elizabeth City	(919)	14,292	14,004
*28302	Fayetteville	(919)	75,860	59,507
28043	Forest City	(704)	7,475	7,688
28307	Fort Bragg(u)	(919)	34,744	37,834
27529	Garner	(919)	14,716	10,073
*28052	Gastonia	(704)	54,725	47,218
*27530	Goldsboro	(919)	40,709	31,871
27253	Graham	(919)	10,368	8,674
*27420	Greensboro	(919)	183,894	155,642
*27834	Greenville	(919)	46,305	35,740
28540	Half Moon(u)	(910)	6,306	3,592
28345	Hamlet	(919)	6,324	4,720
28532	Havelock	(919)	20,300	17,718
27536	Henderson	(919)	15,655	13,522
*28739	Hendersonville	(704)	7,284	6,862

ZIP	Place		1990	1980
*28603	Hickory	(704)	28,474	20,757
*27260	High Point	(910)	69,428	63,479
28348	Hope Mills	(910)	8,272	5,412
*28540	Jacksonville	(910)	30,398	18,237
*28081	Kannapolis†	(704)	29,709	30,303
*27284	Kernersville	(910)	10,899	5,875
28086	Kings Mountain	(704)	8,768	9,080
*28502	Kinston	(919)	25,295	25,234
*28352	Laurinburg	(919)	11,643	11,480
28645	Lenoir	(704)	14,223	13,748
*27292	Lexington	(704)	16,583	15,711
*28092	Lincolnton	(704)	6,955	4,879
*28358	Lumberton	(910)	18,656	18,241
28403	Masonboro(u)	(910)	7,010	3,729
*28110	Matthews	(704)	13,651	1,648
28227	Mint Hill	(704)	11,615	7,915
*28110	Monroe	(704)	16,385	12,639
28115	Mooresville	(704)	9,317	8,575
28557	Morehead	(919)	6,046	4,359
*28655	Morganton	(704)	15,085	13,763
27030	Mount Airy	(910)	7,156	6,862
28120	Mount Holly	(704)	7,710	4,530
*28562	New Bern	(919)	17,363	14,557
27604	New Hope (Wake)(u)	(704)	5,694	6,745
28540	New River Station(u)	(919)	9,732	5,401
28658	Newton	(704)	9,077	7,624
27565	Oxford	(919)	7,965	7,709
28374	Pinehurst†	(919)	5,091	1,746
28399	Piney Green(u)	(919)	8,999	6,058
*27611	Raleigh	(919)	212,092	150,255
*27320	Reidsville	(910)	12,183	12,492
27870	Roanoke Rapids	(919)	15,722	14,702
28379	Rockingham	(910)	9,399	8,300
*27801	Rocky Mount	(919)	49,438	41,526
27573	Roxboro	(910)	7,332	7,532
28601	Saint Stephens(u)	(704)	8,734	10,797
*28144	Salisbury	(704)	23,626	22,677
*27330	Sanford	(919)	14,755	14,773
28403	Seagate(u)	(910)	5,444	3,421
*28150	Shelby	(704)	14,669	15,310
.....	Smith Creek(u)		7,461	6,562
27577	Smithfield	(919)	7,540	7,288
*28387	Southern Pines	(910)	9,213	8,620
28052	South Gastonia(u)	(704)	5,487	4,767
28390	Spring Lake	(919)	7,552	6,273
*28677	Statesville	(704)	17,567	18,622
27886	Tarboro	(919)	11,037	8,741
*27360	Thomasville	(910)	15,915	14,144
27370	Trinity(u)	(919)	5,469	6,887
*27587	Wake Forest	(919)	5,832	3,780
27889	Washington	(919)	9,160	8,418
28786	Waynesville	(704)	6,760	6,765
28472	Whiteville	(910)	5,078	5,565
27892	Williamston	(919)	5,503	6,159
*28402	Wilmington	(910)	55,530	44,000
*27893	Wilson	(919)	36,930	34,424
*27102	Winston-Salem	(910)	143,532	131,885

North Dakota (701)

ZIP	Place	1990	1980
*58501	Bismarck	49,272	44,485
58301	Devils Lake	7,782	7,442
*58601	Dickinson	16,097	15,924
*58102	Fargo	74,084	61,383
*58201	Grand Forks	49,417	43,765
58204	Grand Forks AFB(u)	9,343	9,390
*58401	Jamestown	15,571	16,280
58554	Mandan	15,177	15,513
*58701	Minot	34,544	32,843
*58704	Minot AFB(u)	9,095	9,880
58072	Valley City	7,163	7,774
*58075	Wahpeton	8,751	9,064
58078	West Fargo	12,287	10,099
*58801	Williston	13,136	13,336

Ohio

Area code (330) will go into effect on Mar. 9, 1996. Until then, use (216).

ZIP	Place		1990	1980
45810	Ada	(419)	5,428	5,669
*44309	Akron	(330)	223,019	237,177
44601	Alliance	(330)	23,376	24,315
44001	Amherst	(216)	10,332	10,638
44805	Ashland	(419)	20,079	20,326
*44004	Ashtabula	(216)	21,633	23,449
45701	Athens	(614)	21,265	19,743
44202	Aurora	(216)	9,192	8,177
44515	Austintown(u)	(330)	32,371	33,636
44011	Avon	(216)	7,337	7,241
44012	Avon Lake	(216)	15,066	13,222
44203	Barberton	(330)	27,623	29,751
44140	Bay Village	(216)	17,000	17,846
44122	Beachwood	(216)	10,644	9,983
45434	Beavercreek	(513)	33,626	31,589
44146	Bedford	(216)	14,822	15,056
44146	Bedford Heights	(216)	12,131	13,214
43906	Bellaire	(614)	6,028	8,241

ZIP	Place		1990	1980
45305	Bellbrook	(513)	6,511	5,174
43311	Bellefontaine.	(513)	12,126	11,888
44811	Bellevue.	(419)	8,157	8,187
45714	Belpre	(614)	6,796	7,193
44017	Berea	(216)	19,051	19,567
43209	Bexley.	(614)	13,088	13,405
43004	Blacklick Estates(u)	(614)	10,080	11,223
45242	Blue Ash	(513)	11,923	9,510
44513	Boardman(u).	(330)	38,596	39,086
43402	Bowling Green	(419)	28,303	25,728
44141	Brecksville	(216)	11,818	10,132
45211	Bridgetown North(u).	(513)	11,748	11,460
44147	Broadview Heights.	(216)	12,219	10,920
44144	Brooklyn	(216)	11,706	12,342
44142	Brook Park.	(216)	22,865	26,195
44212	Brunswick	(330)	28,218	28,104
43506	Bryan	(419)	8,348	7,879
44820	Bucyrus	(419)	13,496	13,433
43725	Cambridge	(614)	11,748	13,573
44405	Campbell	(330)	10,038	11,619
44406	Canfield	(330)	5,409	5,535
*44711	Canton.	(330)	84,161	93,077
45822	Celina	(419)	9,923	9,137
45459	Centerville (Montgomery).	(513)	21,082	18,886
45211	Cheviot	(513)	9,616	9,888
45601	Chillicothe	(614)	21,923	23,420
*45202	Cincinnati.	(513)	364,114	385,409
43113	Circleville	(614)	11,666	11,700
*44101	Cleveland.	(216)	505,616	573,822
44118	Cleveland Heights.	(216)	54,052	56,438
43410	Clyde.	(419)	5,776	5,489
*43216	Columbus.	(614)	632,945	565,021
44030	Conneaut.	(216)	13,241	13,835
44410	Cortland.	(330)	5,652	5,011
43812	Coshocton	(614)	12,193	13,405
45238	Covedale(u)	(513)	6,669	5,830
*44222	Cuyahoga Falls.	(330)	48,950	43,890
*45401	Dayton.	(513)	182,005	193,536
45236	Deer Park.	(513)	6,181	6,745
43512	Defiance	(419)	16,787	16,810
43015	Delaware	(614)	19,966	18,780
45833	Delphos.	(419)	7,093	7,314
45247	Dent(u)	(513)	6,416	....
44622	Dover (Tuscarawas).	(330)	11,329	11,782
45427	Drexel(u)	(513)	5,143	....
45663	Dry Run(u)	(614)	5,389	....
43016	Dublin.	(614)	16,366	3,855
44112	East Cleveland	(216)	33,096	36,957
44095	Eastlake.	(216)	21,161	22,104
43920	East Liverpool.	(330)	13,654	16,687
44413	East Palestine.	(330)	5,168	5,306
45320	Eaton.	(513)	7,396	6,839
44004	Edgewood(u)	(216)	5,189	3,099
*44035	Elyria.	(216)	56,746	57,538
45322	Englewood.	(513)	11,402	11,329
*44101	Euclid.	(216)	54,875	59,999
45324	Fairborn.	(513)	31,300	29,702
45014	Fairfield.	(513)	39,709	30,777
44313	Fairlawn.	(330)	5,779	6,100
44126	Fairview Park	(216)	18,028	19,311
*45839	Findlay.	(419)	35,703	35,594
45224	Finneytown(u)	(513)	13,096	....
45405	Forest Park	(513)	18,621	18,566
45230	Forestville(u).	(513)	9,185	....
45426	Fort McKinley(u)	(513)	9,740	10,161
44830	Fostoria.	(419)	14,971	15,743
45005	Franklin	(513)	11,026	10,711
43420	Fremont.	(419)	17,619	17,834
43230	Gahanna	(614)	23,898	18,001
44833	Galion	(419)	11,859	12,391
44125	Garfield Heights	(216)	31,739	34,938
44041	Geneva	(216)	6,597	6,655
44420	Girard	(330)	11,304	12,517
43212	Grandview Heights	(614)	7,010	7,420
45123	Greenfield	(513)	5,172	5,150
45331	Greenville.	(513)	12,863	12,999
45239	Groesbeck(u)	(513)	6,684	9,594
43123	Grove City	(614)	19,661	16,816
*45011	Hamilton	(513)	61,436	63,189
45030	Harrison.	(513)	7,520	5,855
43056	Heath	(614)	7,231	6,969
44134	Highland Heights.	(216)	6,249	5,739
43026	Hilliard	(614)	11,794	8,131
45133	Hillsboro	(513)	6,235	6,356
44484	Howland Center(u).	(330)	6,732	7,441
44425	Hubbard.	(330)	8,248	9,245
45424	Huber Heights.	(513)	38,696	35,480
43081	Huber Ridge(u)	(614)	5,255	5,835
44236	Hudson.	(216)	5,159	4,615
44839	Huron	(419)	7,067	7,123
44131	Independence (Cuyahoga)	(216)	6,500	6,607
45638	Ironton.	(614)	12,751	14,290
45640	Jackson.	(614)	6,167	6,675
*44240	Kent.	(330)	28,835	26,164
43326	Kenton.	(419)	8,356	8,605
43606	Kenwood(u)	(513)	7,469	9,943
45429	Kettering.	(513)	60,569	61,186
44094	Kirtland.	(216)	5,881	5,969
44107	Lakewood.	(216)	59,718	61,963
43130	Lancaster.	(614)	34,507	34,953
45039	Landen(u)	(513)	9,263	2,870
45036	Lebanon (Warren)	(513)	10,461	9,636
*45802	Lima.	(419)	45,553	47,827
43228	Lincoln Village(u).	(614)	9,958	10,548
43138	Logan	(614)	6,725	6,557
43140	London	(614)	7,807	6,958
*44052	Lorain.	(216)	71,245	75,416
44641	Louisville.	(330)	8,087	7,996
45140	Loveland.	(513)	10,122	9,106
44124	Lyndhurst.	(216)	15,982	18,092
44056	Macedonia.	(216)	7,509	6,571
.....	Mack South(u)		5,767	....
45243	Madeira.	(513)	9,141	9,341
*44901	Mansfield.	(419)	50,627	53,927
44137	Maple Heights.	(216)	27,089	29,735
45750	Marietta.	(614)	15,026	16,467
*43302	Marion.	(614)	34,075	37,040
43935	Martins Ferry.	(614)	8,003	9,331
43040	Marysville	(513)	9,656	7,414
45040	Mason.	(513)	11,450	8,692
*44646	Massillon.	(330)	30,969	30,557
43537	Maumee.	(419)	15,561	15,747
44124	Mayfield Heights.	(216)	19,847	21,550
*44256	Medina.	(330)	19,231	15,268
*44060	Mentor.	(216)	47,491	42,065
44060	Mentor-on-the-Lake.	(216)	8,271	7,919
*45343	Miamisburg.	(513)	17,834	15,304
44130	Middleburg Heights.	(216)	14,702	16,218
*45042	Middletown.	(513)	46,022	43,719
45150	Milford.	(513)	5,660	5,232
45242	Montgomery.	(513)	9,733	10,084
45439	Moraine.	(513)	5,989	5,325
45231	Mount Healthy	(513)	7,580	7,562
43050	Mount Vernon.	(614)	14,550	14,323
44262	Munroe Falls.	(330)	5,359	4,731
43545	Napoleon.	(419)	8,884	8,614
*43055	Newark.	(614)	44,396	41,200
45344	New Carlisle.	(513)	6,049	6,498
43764	New Lexington.	(614)	5,117	5,179
44663	New Philadelphia.	(330)	15,698	16,883
44446	Niles.	(330)	21,128	23,088
45239	Northbrook(u).	(513)	11,471	8,357
44720	North Canton.	(330)	14,904	14,228
45239	North College Hill.	(513)	11,002	11,114
44251	Northgate(u).	(513)	7,864	....
44057	North Madison(u).	(216)	8,699	8,741
44070	North Olmsted	(216)	34,204	36,486
44502	Northridge(u) (Clark).	(513)	5,939	5,559
45414	Northridge(u) (Montgomery)	(513)	9,448	9,720
44039	North Ridgeville.	(216)	21,564	21,522
44133	North Royalton	(216)	23,197	17,671
45322	Northview(u).	(513)	10,337	9,973
43619	Northwood.	(419)	5,506	5,495
44203	Norton.	(330)	11,477	12,242
44857	Norwalk.	(419)	14,731	14,358
45212	Norwood.	(513)	23,674	26,342
44146	Oakwood (Cuyahoga)	(216)	8,957	9,372
44074	Oberlin.	(216)	8,191	8,660
44138	Olmsted Falls.	(216)	6,741	5,868
*43601	Oregon.	(419)	18,334	18,675
44667	Orrville.	(330)	7,712	7,511
45431	Overlook-Page Manor(u).	(513)	13,242	14,825
45056	Oxford.	(513)	18,937	17,655
44077	Painesville.	(216)	15,769	16,391
44129	Parma.	(216)	87,876	92,548
44130	Parma Heights.	(216)	21,448	23,112
44124	Pepper Pike.	(216)	6,185	6,177
44646	Perry Heights(u)	(330)	9,055	9,206
*43551	Perrysburg.	(419)	12,551	10,215
43147	Pickerington.	(513)	5,668	3,917
45356	Piqua.	(513)	20,612	20,480
44319	Portage Lakes(u).	(330)	13,373	11,310
43452	Port Clinton.	(419)	7,106	7,223
45662	Portsmouth.	(614)	22,676	25,943
44266	Ravenna.	(330)	12,069	11,987
45215	Reading.	(513)	12,038	12,843
43068	Reynoldsburg.	(614)	25,748	20,661
44143	Richmond Heights.	(216)	9,611	10,095
44270	Rittman.	(330)	6,147	6,063
44116	Rocky River.	(216)	20,410	21,084
43460	Rossford.	(419)	5,861	5,978
45217	Saint Bernard.	(513)	5,344	5,396
43950	Saint Clairsville.	(614)	5,136	5,452
45885	Saint Marys.	(419)	8,441	8,414
44460	Salem.	(330)	12,233	12,869
*44870	Sandusky.	(419)	29,764	31,360
44870	Sandusky South(u)	(419)	6,336	6,548
44131	Seven Hills.	(216)	12,339	13,650
44120	Shaker Heights.	(216)	30,955	32,487
45241	Sharonville.	(513)	13,121	10,108
44054	Sheffield Lake.	(216)	9,825	10,484
44875	Shelby.	(419)	9,610	9,703
44878	Shiloh(u)	(419)	11,607	11,735
45365	Sidney.	(513)	18,710	17,657
45236	Silverton.	(513)	5,859	6,172
44139	Solon.	(216)	18,548	14,341
44121	South Euclid.	(216)	23,866	25,713

ZIP	Place		1990	1980
45066	Springboro	(513)	6,574	4,962
45246	Springdale	(513)	10,621	10,111
*45501	Springfield	(513)	70,487	72,563
43952	Steubenville	(614)	22,125	26,400
44224	Stow	(330)	27,998	25,303
44241	Streetsboro	(330)	9,932	9,055
44136	Strongsville	(216)	35,308	28,577
44471	Struthers	(330)	12,284	13,624
43560	Sylvania	(419)	17,489	15,527
44278	Tallmadge	(330)	14,870	15,269
45243	The Village of Indian Hill	(513)	5,383	5,521
44883	Tiffin	(419)	18,604	19,549
45371	Tipp City	(513)	6,027	5,595
*43601	Toledo	(419)	332,943	354,635
43964	Toronto	(614)	6,127	6,934
45067	Trenton	(513)	6,189	6,401
45426	Trotwood	(513)	8,816	7,802
45373	Troy	(513)	19,478	19,086
44087	Twinsburg	(216)	9,606	7,632
44683	Uhrichsville	(614)	5,604	6,130
45322	Union	(513)	5,531	5,219
44118	University Heights	(216)	14,787	15,401
43221	Upper Arlington	(614)	34,128	35,648
43351	Upper Sandusky	(419)	5,906	5,967
43078	Urbana	(513)	11,353	10,762
45377	Vandalia	(513)	13,872	13,161
45891	Van Wert	(419)	10,922	11,035
44089	Vermilion	(216)	11,127	11,012
44281	Wadsworth	(330)	15,718	15,166
45895	Wapakoneta	(419)	9,214	8,402
*44481	Warren	(330)	50,793	56,629
44122	Warrensville Heights	(216)	15,745	16,565
43160	Washington Court House	(614)	13,080	12,682
43567	Wauseon	(419)	6,322	6,173
45692	Wellston	(614)	6,049	6,016
45449	West Carrollton City	(513)	14,403	13,148
*43081	Westerville	(614)	30,269	23,414
44145	Westlake	(216)	27,018	19,483
45694	Wheelersburg(u)	(614)	5,113	4,796
43213	Whitehall	(614)	20,572	21,299
45239	White Oak(u)	(513)	12,430	9,563
44092	Wickliffe	(216)	14,558	16,790
44890	Willard	(419)	6,210	5,720
*44094	Willoughby	(216)	20,510	19,329
44094	Willoughby Hills	(216)	8,427	8,612
44095	Willowick	(216)	15,269	17,834
45177	Wilmington	(513)	11,199	10,431
45459	Woodbourne-Hyde Park(u)	(513)	7,837	8,826
44691	Wooster	(330)	22,427	19,289
43085	Worthington	(614)	14,869	15,016
45431	Wright-Patterson AFB(u)	(513)	8,579	9,155
45215	Wyoming	(513)	8,128	8,282
45385	Xenia	(513)	24,836	24,653
*44501	Youngstown	(330)	95,732	115,511
*43701	Zanesville	(614)	26,778	28,655

Oklahoma

ZIP	Place		1990	1980
*74820	Ada	(405)	15,765	15,902
*73521	Altus	(405)	21,910	23,101
73717	Alva	(405)	5,495	6,416
73005	Anadarko	(405)	6,586	6,378
*73401	Ardmore	(405)	23,079	23,689
*74003	Bartlesville	(918)	34,256	34,568
73008	Bethany	(405)	20,075	22,038
74008	Bixby	(918)	9,502	6,969
74631	Blackwell	(405)	7,538	8,400
*74012	Broken Arrow	(918)	58,082	35,761
*73018	Chickasha	(405)	14,988	15,828
*73020	Choctaw	(405)	8,545	7,520
*74017	Claremore	(918)	13,280	12,085
73601	Clinton	(405)	9,298	8,796
74429	Coweta	(918)	6,159	4,554
74023	Cushing	(918)	7,218	7,720
73115	Del City	(405)	23,928	28,523
*73533	Duncan	(405)	21,732	22,517
*74701	Durant	(405)	12,929	11,972
*73034	Edmond	(405)	52,310	34,637
*73644	Elk City	(405)	10,428	9,579
73036	El Reno	(405)	15,414	15,486
*73701	Enid	(405)	45,309	50,363
73503	Fort Sill(u)	(405)	12,107	15,924
73542	Frederick	(405)	5,221	6,153
74033	Glenpool	(918)	6,688	2,706
73044	Guthrie	(405)	10,440	10,312
73942	Guymon	(405)	7,803	8,492
74437	Henryetta	(918)	5,872	6,432
74743	Hugo	(405)	5,978	7,172
74745	Idabel	(405)	6,957	7,622
74037	Jenks	(918)	7,484	5,876
*73501	Lawton	(405)	80,561	80,054
*74501	McAlester	(918)	16,739	17,255
*74354	Miami	(918)	13,142	14,237
73140	Midwest City	(405)	52,267	49,559
73153	Moore	(405)	40,318	35,063

ZIP	Place		1990	1980
*74401	Muskogee	(918)	37,708	40,011
73064	Mustang	(405)	10,434	7,496
*73069	Norman	(405)	80,071	68,020
*73125	Oklahoma City	(405)	444,724	404,014
74447	Okmulgee	(918)	13,441	16,263
74055	Owasso	(918)	11,151	6,149
73075	Pauls Valley	(405)	6,150	5,664
*74601	Ponca City	(405)	26,359	26,238
74953	Poteau	(918)	7,210	7,089
74361	Pryor Creek	(918)	8,327	8,483
74955	Sallisaw	(918)	7,122	6,403
74063	Sand Springs	(918)	15,339	13,121
*74066	Sapulpa	(918)	18,074	15,853
*74868	Seminole	(405)	7,071	8,590
*74801	Shawnee	(405)	26,017	26,506
*74074	Stillwater	(405)	36,676	38,268
*74464	Tahlequah	(918)	10,586	9,708
74873	Tecumseh	(405)	5,570	5,123
*74103	Tulsa	(918)	367,302	360,919
73156	Village	(405)	10,353	11,114
74301	Vinita	(918)	5,804	6,740
*74467	Wagoner	(918)	6,894	6,191
73132	Warr Acres	(405)	9,288	9,940
73096	Weatherford	(405)	10,124	9,640
*73801	Woodward	(405)	12,340	13,781
*73099	Yukon	(405)	20,935	17,112

Oregon

ZIP	Place		1990	1980
97321	Albany	(541)	29,540	26,511
97006	Aloha(u)	(503)	34,284	28,353
97601	Altamont(u)	(541)	18,591	19,805
97520	Ashland	(541)	16,252	14,943
97103	Astoria	(503)	10,069	9,998
97814	Baker City	(541)	9,140	9,471
*97005	Beaverton	(503)	53,307	31,962
*97701	Bend	(541)	20,447	17,263
97013	Canby	(503)	8,990	7,659
97225	Cedar Hills(u)	(503)	9,294	9,619
97291	Cedar Mill(u)†	(503)	9,697	22,118
97502	Central Point	(541)	7,512	6,357
97420	Coos Bay	(541)	15,076	14,424
97113	Cornelius	(503)	6,148	4,462
*97333	Corvallis	(541)	44,757	40,960
97424	Cottage Grove	(541)	7,403	7,148
97338	Dallas	(503)	9,422	8,530
*97401	Eugene	(541)	112,773	105,664
97439	Florence	(541)	5,171	4,411
97116	Forest Grove	(503)	13,559	11,499
97301	Four Corners(u)	(503)	12,156	11,316
97223	Garden Home-Whitford(u)	(503)	6,652	6,911
97027	Gladstone	(503)	10,152	9,500
*97526	Grants Pass	(541)	17,503	15,032
97470	Green(u)	(541)	5,076	3,897
*97030	Gresham	(503)	68,249	33,005
97303	Hayesville(u)	(503)	14,318	9,413
97230	Hazelwood(u)	(503)	11,480	25,541
97838	Hermiston	(541)	10,047	9,408
*97123	Hillsboro	(503)	37,598	27,664
97222	Jennings Lodge(u)	(503)	6,530	....
97303	Keizer†	(503)	21,884	19,785
*97601	Klamath Falls	(541)	17,737	16,661
97850	La Grande	(541)	11,766	11,354
*97034	Lake Oswego	(503)	30,576	22,527
97355	Lebanon	(541)	10,950	10,413
97367	Lincoln City	(541)	5,903	5,469
97128	McMinnville	(503)	17,894	14,080
*97501	Medford	(541)	47,021	39,746
97862	Milton-Freewater	(541)	5,533	5,086
97222	Milwaukie	(503)	18,670	17,931
97361	Monmouth	(503)	6,288	5,594
97132	Newberg	(503)	13,086	10,394
97365	Newport	(541)	8,437	7,519
97459	North Bend	(541)	9,614	9,779
97477	North Springfield(u)	(541)	5,451	6,140
97268	Oak Grove(u)	(503)	12,576	11,640
.....	Oak Hills(u)		6,450	....
.....	Oatfield(u)		15,348	....
97914	Ontario	(541)	9,394	8,814
97045	Oregon City	(503)	14,698	14,673
97801	Pendleton	(541)	15,142	14,521
*97208	Portland	(503)	438,802	368,148
97236	Powellhurst-Centennial(u)	(503)	28,756	20,122
97754	Prineville	(541)	5,355	5,276
97225	Raleigh Hills(u)	(503)	6,066	6,517
97756	Redmond	(541)	7,165	6,452
97404	River Road(u)	(541)	9,443	10,370
.....	Rockcreek(u)		8,282	....
97470	Roseburg	(541)	17,069	16,644
97470	Roseburg North(u)	(541)	6,831	....
97051	Saint Helens	(503)	7,535	7,064
*97301	Salem	(503)	107,793	89,091
97401	Santa Clara(u)	(541)	12,834	14,288
97138	Seaside	(503)	5,359	5,193
97381	Silverton	(503)	5,635	5,168
*97477	Springfield	(541)	44,664	41,621

ZIP	Place		1990	1980
97383	Stayton	(503)	5,011	4,396
97479	Sutherlin	(541)	5,020	4,560
97386	Sweet Home	(541)	6,850	6,921
97058	The Dalles, City of	(541)	11,021	10,820
97223	Tigard	(503)	29,435	14,799
97060	Troutdale	(503)	7,852	5,908
97062	Tualatin	(503)	14,664	7,483
97225	West Haven-Sylvan(u)	(503)	6,009	....
97068	West Linn	(503)	16,389	11,358
97225	West Slope(u)	(503)	7,959	5,364
97503	White City(u)	(541)	5,891	5,445
97070	Wilsonville	(503)	7,106	2,920
97071	Woodburn	(503)	13,404	11,196

Pennsylvania

Communities with area codes marked with a double dagger (‡) are split between area codes (215) and (610); consult local operators. Please also see note on page 396.

ZIP	Place		1990	1980
15001	Aliquippa	(412)	13,374	17,094
*18105	Allentown (Lehigh Co.)	(610)	105,301	103,758
*16603	Altoona	(814)	51,881	57,078
19002	Ambler	(215)‡	6,609	6,628
15003	Ambridge	(412)	8,133	9,575
18403	Archbald	(717)	6,291	6,295
19003	Ardmore(u)	(610)	12,646	
15068	Arnold	(412)	6,113	6,853
19407	Audubon(u)†	(610)	6,328	6,853
15202	Avalon	(412)	5,784	6,240
15005	Baden	(412)	5,074	5,318
15234	Baldwin	(412)	21,923	24,714
18013	Bangor	(610)	5,383	5,006
15009	Beaver	(412)	5,028	5,441
15010	Beaver Falls	(412)	10,687	12,525
16823	Bellefonte	(814)	6,358	6,300
15202	Bellevue	(412)	9,126	10,128
18603	Berwick	(717)	10,976	11,850
15102	Bethel Park	(412)	33,823	34,755
*18016	Bethlehem	(610)	71,427	70,419
18447	Blakely	(717)	7,222	7,438
17815	Bloomsburg	(717)	12,439	11,717
19422	Blue Bell(u)	(215)‡	6,091	....
19061	Boothwyn(u)	(610)	5,069	....
16701	Bradford	(814)	9,625	11,211
15227	Brentwood	(412)	10,823	11,859
15017	Bridgeville	(412)	5,445	6,154
19007	Bristol	(215)	10,405	10,867
19015	Brookhaven	(610)	8,567	7,912
19008	Broomall(u)	(610)	10,930	....
*16001	Butler	(412)	15,714	17,026
15419	California	(412)	5,748	5,703
*17011	Camp Hill	(717)	7,831	8,422
15317	Canonsburg	(412)	9,200	10,459
18407	Carbondale	(717)	10,664	11,255
17013	Carlisle	(717)	18,419	18,314
15106	Carnegie	(412)	9,278	10,099
15108	Carnot-Moon(u)	(412)	10,187	11,102
15234	Castle Shannon	(412)	9,135	10,164
18032	Catasauqua	(610)	6,662	6,711
17201	Chambersburg	(717)	16,647	16,174
15022	Charleroi	(412)	5,014	5,717
*19013	Chester	(610)	41,856	45,794
19013	Chester Twp.(u)	(610)	5,399	5,687
15025	Clairton	(412)	9,656	12,188
16214	Clarion	(814)	6,457	6,198
18411	Clarks Summit	(717)	5,433	5,272
16830	Clearfield	(814)	6,633	7,580
19018	Clifton Heights	(610)	7,111	7,320
19320	Coatesville	(610)	11,038	10,698
19023	Collingdale	(610)	9,175	9,539
17109	Colonial Park(u) (Dauphin)	(717)	13,777	....
17512	Columbia	(717)	10,701	10,466
15425	Connellsville	(412)	9,229	10,319
19428	Conshohocken	(215)‡	8,064	8,591
15108	Coraopolis	(412)	6,747	7,308
16407	Corry	(814)	7,216	7,149
15205	Crafton	(412)	7,188	7,623
19021	Croydon(u)	(215)	9,967	....
17821	Danville	(717)	5,165	5,239
19023	Darby	(610)	11,140	11,513
19036	Darby Twp.(u)	(610)	10,955	12,264
19333	Devon-Berwyn(u)	(610)	5,019	5,246
18519	Dickson City	(717)	6,276	6,699
15033	Donora	(412)	5,928	7,524
15216	Dormont	(412)	9,772	11,275
19335	Downingtown	(610)	7,749	7,650
18901	Doylestown	(215)	8,575	8,717
19026	Drexel Hill(u)	(610)	29,744	....
15801	Du Bois	(814)	8,286	9,290
18512	Dunmore	(717)	15,403	16,781
15110	Duquesne	(412)	8,525	10,094
19401	East Norriton(u)	(215)‡	13,324	12,711
*18042	Easton	(610)	26,276	26,027
18301	East Stroudsburg	(717)	8,781	8,039
17405	East York(u)	(717)	8,487	....
15005	Economy	(412)	9,305	9,538
16412	Edinboro	(814)	7,736	6,324
18704	Edwardsville	(717)	5,399	5,729

ZIP	Place		1990	1980
17022	Elizabethtown	(717)	9,952	8,233
16117	Ellwood City	(412)	8,894	9,998
18049	Emmaus	(610)	11,157	11,001
17025	Enola(u)		5,961	....
17522	Ephrata	(717)	12,133	11,095
*16501	Erie	(814)	108,718	119,123
18643	Exeter	(717)	5,691	5,493
19030	Fairless Hills(u)	(215)	9,026	....
16121	Farrell	(412)	6,835	8,645
19053	Feasterville-Trevose(u)	(215)	6,696	....
16063	Fernway(u)	(412)	9,072	3,843
19032	Folcroft	(610)	7,506	8,231
19033	Folsom(u)	(610)	8,173	....
15221	Forest Hills	(412)	8,173	8,198
18704	Forty Fort	(717)	5,049	5,590
15238	Fox Chapel	(412)	5,319	5,049
16323	Franklin	(814)	7,329	8,146
15143	Franklin Park	(412)	10,109	6,135
18052	Fullerton(u)	(610)	13,127	8,055
17325	Gettysburg	(717)	7,025	7,194
15045	Glassport	(412)	5,582	6,242
19036	Glenolden	(610)	7,260	7,633
19038	Glenside(u)	(215)	8,704	....
15601	Greensburg	(412)	16,318	17,558
16125	Greenville	(412)	6,734	7,730
16127	Grove City	(412)	8,240	8,162
15101	Hampton Twp.(u) (Alleghany)	(412)	15,568	
17331	Hanover	(717)	14,399	14,890
19438	Harleysville(u)	(215)‡	7,405	3,673
*17105	Harrisburg	(717)	52,376	53,264
15065	Harrison Twp.(u) (Alleghany)	(412)	11,763	....
19040	Hatboro	(215)	7,382	7,579
18201	Hazleton	(717)	24,730	27,318
18055	Hellertown	(610)	5,662	6,025
16148	Hermitage†	(412)	15,260	16,365
17033	Hershey(u)	(717)	11,860	13,249
16648	Hollidaysburg	(814)	5,624	5,892
16001	Homeacre-Lyndora(u)	(412)	7,511	8,333
19044	Horsham(u)	(215)	15,051	9,900
16652	Huntingdon	(814)	6,843	7,042
15701	Indiana	(412)	15,174	16,051
15644	Jeannette	(412)	11,221	13,106
15344	Jefferson	(412)	9,533	8,643
18229	Jim Thorpe	(717)	5,048	5,263
*15907	Johnstown	(814)	28,124	35,496
15108	Kennedy Twp.(u)	(412)	7,152	7,159
19348	Kennett Square	(610)	5,218	4,715
19406	King of Prussia(u)	(215)‡	18,406	....
18704	Kingston	(717)	14,507	15,681
16201	Kittanning	(412)	5,120	5,432
19443	Kulpsville(u)	(215)	5,183	....
*17604	Lancaster	(717)	55,551	54,725
19446	Lansdale	(215)	16,362	16,526
19050	Lansdowne	(610)	11,712	11,891
15650	Latrobe	(412)	9,265	10,799
17540	Leacock-Leola-Bareville(u)	(717)	5,685	....
*17042	Lebanon	(717)	24,800	25,711
18235	Lehighton	(610)	5,914	5,826
*19055	Levittown(u)	(215)	55,362	....
17837	Lewisburg	(717)	5,785	5,407
17044	Lewistown (Mifflin)	(717)	9,341	9,830
17112	Linglestown(u)	(717)	5,862	....
19353	Lionville-Marchwood(u)	(610)	6,468	....
17543	Lititz	(717)	8,280	7,590
17745	Lock Haven	(717)	9,230	9,617
17011	Lower Allen(u)	(717)	6,329	....
15068	Lower Burrell	(412)	12,251	13,200
15237	McCandless Twp.(u)	(412)	28,781	26,191
*15134	McKeesport	(412)	26,016	31,012
15136	McKees Rocks	(412)	7,691	8,742
17948	Mahanoy City	(717)	5,209	6,167
17545	Manheim	(717)	5,011	5,015
19002	Maple Glen(u)	(215)	5,881	....
16335	Meadville	(814)	14,318	15,544
17055	Mechanicsburg	(717)	9,452	9,487
*19063	Media	(610)	5,957	6,119
17057	Middletown (Dauphin)	(717)	9,254	10,122
18017	Middletown (Northampton)(u)	(610)	6,866	5,801
17551	Millersville	(717)	8,099	7,668
17847	Milton	(717)	6,746	6,730
15061	Monaca	(412)	6,739	7,661
15062	Monessen	(412)	9,901	11,928
15146	Monroeville	(412)	29,169	30,977
18936	Montgomeryville(u)	(215)	9,114	....
18507	Moosic	(717)	5,397	6,068
19067	Morrisville (Bucks)	(215)	9,765	9,845
17851	Mount Carmel	(717)	7,196	8,190
17552	Mount Joy	(717)	6,398	5,680
15228	Mount Lebanon(u)	(412)	33,362	34,414
15120	Munhall	(412)	13,158	14,535
15668	Murrysville	(412)	17,240	16,036
18634	Nanticoke	(717)	12,267	13,044
18064	Nazareth	(610)	5,713	5,443
....	Nether Providence Twp.(u)	(610)	13,229	12,730
15066	New Brighton	(412)	6,854	7,364
*16108	New Castle	(412)	28,334	33,621
17070	New Cumberland	(717)	7,665	8,051
15068	New Kensington	(412)	15,894	17,660
*19401	Norristown	(610)	30,754	34,684

ZIP	Place		1990	1980
18067	Northampton	(610)	8,717	8,240
15036	North Braddock	(412)	7,036	8,711
15137	North Versailles(u)	(412)	12,302	13,294
16421	Northwest Harborcreek(u)	(814)	6,662	7,485
19074	Norwood (Delaware)	(610)	6,162	6,647
15139	Oakmont (Allegheny)	(412)	6,961	7,039
15238	O'Hara(u)	(412)	9,096	....
16301	Oil City	(814)	11,949	13,881
18518	Old Forge	(717)	8,834	9,304
18447	Olyphant	(717)	5,222	5,204
19075	Oreland(u)	(215)	5,695	....
18071	Palmerton	(610)	5,394	5,455
17078	Palmyra	(717)	6,910	7,228
19301	Paoli(u)	(610)	5,603	5,277
16801	Park Forest Village(u)	(814)	6,703	....
17331	Parkville(u)	(717)	6,014	5,009
15235	Penn Hills(u)	(717)	51,430	57,632
19151	Penn Wynne(u)	(215)	5,807	....
18944	Perkasie	(215)	7,787	5,241
*19104	Philadelphia	(215)	1,585,577	1,688,210
19460	Phoenixville	(610)	15,066	14,165
*15233	Pittsburgh	(412)	369,879	423,959
*18640	Pittston	(717)	9,389	9,903
15236	Pleasant Hills	(412)	8,884	9,604
15239	Plum	(412)	25,609	25,309
18651	Plymouth	(717)	7,134	7,605
19462	Plymouth Meeting(u)	(215)‡	6,241	....
*19464	Pottstown	(610)	21,831	22,729
17901	Pottsville	(717)	16,603	18,195
17109	Progress(u)	(717)	9,654	....
19076	Prospect Park	(610)	6,764	6,593
15767	Punxsutawney	(814)	6,782	7,479
18951	Quakertown	(215)	8,982	8,867
19087	Radnor Twp.(u)	(610)	28,705	27,676
*19612	Reading	(610)	78,380	78,686
17356	Red Lion	(717)	6,130	5,824
18954	Richboro(u)	(215)	5,332	5,141
19078	Ridley Park	(610)	7,592	7,889
15136	Robinson(Alleghany)(u)	(412)	10,830	....
15237	Ross Twp.(u)	(412)	33,482	35,102
15857	Saint Marys	(814)	5,511	6,417
19464	Sanatoga(u)	(610)	5,534	3,723
18840	Sayre	(717)	5,791	6,951
17972	Schuylkill Haven	(717)	5,610	5,977
15683	Scottdale	(412)	5,184	5,833
15106	Scott Twp.(u)	(412)	17,118	20,413
*18505	Scranton	(717)	81,805	88,117
17870	Selinsgrove	(717)	5,384	5,227
15116	Shaler Twp.(u)	(412)	30,533	33,694
17872	Shamokin	(717)	9,184	10,357
16146	Sharon	(412)	17,533	19,057
19079	Sharon Hill	(610)	5,771	6,221
17976	Shenandoah	(717)	6,221	7,589
19607	Shillington	(610)	5,062	5,601
17404	Shiloh(u)	(717)	8,245	5,315
17257	Shippensburg	(717)	5,331	5,261
15501	Somerset	(814)	6,454	6,474
18964	Souderton	(215)	5,957	6,657
15129	South Park Twp.(u)	(814)	14,292	....
17701	South Williamsport	(717)	6,496	6,581
19064	Springfield(Delaware)(u)	(610)	24,160	25,326
*16804	State College	(814)	38,981	36,130
17113	Steelton	(717)	5,152	6,484
15136	Stowe Twp.(u)	(412)	7,681	9,202
18360	Stroudsburg	(717)	5,312	5,148
16323	Sugar Creek	(717)	5,532	5,954
17801	Sunbury	(717)	11,591	12,292
19081	Swarthmore	(610)	6,157	5,950
15218	Swissvale	(412)	10,637	11,345
18704	Swoyersville	(717)	5,630	5,795
18252	Tamaqua	(717)	7,943	8,843
15084	Tarentum	(412)	5,674	6,419
18517	Taylor	(717)	6,941	7,246
16354	Titusville	(814)	6,434	6,884
19401	Trooper(u)	(610)	5,137	7,370
15145	Turtle Creek	(412)	6,556	6,959
16686	Tyrone	(814)	5,743	6,346
15401	Uniontown (Fayette)	(412)	12,034	14,510
19063	Upper Providence Twp.(u)	(610)	9,727	9,477
15241	Upper Saint Clair(u)	(412)	19,692	19,023
15690	Vandergrift	(412)	5,904	6,823
19013	Village Green-Green Ridge(u)	(610)	9,026	....
16365	Warren	(814)	11,122	12,146
15301	Washington	(412)	15,864	18,363
17268	Waynesboro	(717)	9,578	9,726
.....	Weigelstown(u)	(717)	8,665	5,213
*19380	West Chester	(610)	18,041	17,435
19380	West Goshen(u)	(610)	8,948	7,998
*15122	West Mifflin	(412)	23,644	26,322
15905	Westmont	(814)	5,789	6,113
19401	West Norriton(u)	(610)	15,209	14,034
18643	West Pittston	(717)	5,590	5,980
15229	West View	(412)	7,734	7,648
15227	Whitehall (Allegheny)	(412)	14,451	15,143
15131	White Oak	(717)	8,761	9,480
*18703	Wilkes-Barre	(717)	47,523	51,551
15221	Wilkinsburg	(412)	21,080	23,669
15145	Wilkins Twp.(u)	(412)	7,487	8,472
*17701	Williamsport	(717)	31,933	33,401

ZIP	Place		1990	1980
19090	Willow Grove(u) (Montgomery)	(610)	16,325	....
17584	Willow Street(u)	(717)	5,817	....
15025	Wilson	(412)	7,830	7,564
19094	Woodlyn(u)	(610)	10,151	....
19118	Wyndmoor(u)	(215)	5,682	....
19610	Wyomissing	(610)	7,332	6,551
19050	Yeadon	(610)	11,980	11,727
*17405	York	(717)	42,192	44,619

Rhode Island (401)

See note on page 396

ZIP	Place	1990	1980
02806	Barrington(u)	15,849	16,174
02809	Bristol(u)	21,625	20,128
02830	Burrillville	16,230	13,164
02863	Central Falls	17,638	16,995
02813	Charlestown	6,478	4,800
02816	Coventry	31,083	27,065
*02910	Cranston	76,060	71,992
02864	Cumberland	29,038	27,069
02864	Cumberland Hill(u)	6,379	5,421
02818	East Greenwich	11,865	10,211
02914	East Providence	50,380	50,980
02822	Exeter	5,461	4,453
02814	Glocester	9,227	7,550
02828	Greenville(u)	8,303	7,576
02833	Hopkinton	6,873	6,406
02919	Johnston	26,542	24,907
02881	Kingston(u)	6,504	5,479
02865	Lincoln	18,045	16,949
02840	Middletown	19,460	17,216
02882	Narragansett	15,004	12,088
02840	Newport	28,227	29,259
02843	Newport East(u)	11,080	11,030
*02852	North Kingstown	23,786	21,938
02908	North Providence(u)	32,090	29,188
02876	North Smithfield	10,497	9,972
02859	Pascoag(u)	5,011	3,807
*02860	Pawtucket	72,644	71,204
02871	Portsmouth	16,857	14,257
*02904	Providence	160,728	156,804
02812	Richmond	5,351	4,018
02857	Scituate	9,796	8,405
02917	Smithfield	19,163	16,886
02879	South Kingstown	24,631	20,414
02878	Tiverton(u)	7,259	7,653
02878	Tiverton	14,312	13,526
02864	Valley Falls(u)	11,175	10,892
*02879	Wakefield-Peacedale(u)	7,134	6,474
02885	Warren	11,385	10,640
*02886	Warwick	85,427	87,123
02891	Westerly	21,605	18,580
02891	Westerly Center(u)	16,477	14,093
02893	West Warwick (u)	29,268	27,026
02895	Woonsocket	43,877	45,914

South Carolina

Area code (864) will go into effect on Dec. 3, 1995. Until then use (803).

ZIP	Place		1990	1980
29620	Abbeville	(864)	5,778	5,833
*29801	Aiken	(803)	20,386	14,978
*29621	Anderson	(864)	26,385	27,546
29812	Barnwell	(803)	5,255	5,572
*29902	Beaufort	(803)	9,576	8,634
29841	Belvedere(u)	(803)	6,133	6,859
29512	Bennettsville	(803)	10,095	8,774
29611	Berea(u)	(864)	13,535	13,164
29115	Brookdale(u)	(803)	5,339	6,123
29902	Burton(u)	(803)	6,917	3,619
29020	Camden	(803)	6,696	7,462
29033	Cayce	(803)	10,824	11,701
*29402	Charleston	(803)	79,925	69,779
29520	Cheraw	(803)	5,553	5,654
29706	Chester	(803)	7,158	6,820
*29631	Clemson	(864)	11,145	8,118
29325	Clinton	(864)	9,603	8,596
*29201	Columbia	(803)	103,477	101,229
*29526	Conway	(803)	9,819	10,240
*29532	Darlington	(803)	7,310	7,989
29204	Dentsville(u)	(803)	11,839	13,579
29536	Dillon	(803)	6,829	7,060
*29640	Easley	(864)	15,179	14,264
*29501	Florence	(803)	29,913	29,842
29206	Forest Acres	(803)	7,181	6,062
*29341	Gaffney	(864)	13,149	13,453
29605	Gantt(u)	(864)	13,891	13,719
.....	Garden City(u)		6,305	....
*29440	Georgetown	(803)	9,517	10,144
29445	Goose Creek	(803)	24,692	17,811
*29602	Greenville	(864)	58,256	58,242
*29646	Greenwood	(864)	20,807	21,613
*29650	Greer	(864)	10,322	10,525
29406	Hanahan	(803)	13,176	13,224
*29550	Hartsville	(803)	8,372	7,631
*29928	Hilton Head Island†	(803)	23,694	11,239
29621	Homeland Park(u)	(864)	6,569	6,720

ZIP	Place		1990	1980
29063	Irmo	(803)	11,277	3,957
29456	Ladson(u)	(803)	13,540	13,246
29560	Lake City	(803)	7,153	6,731
*29720	Lancaster	(803)	8,914	9,703
29360	Laurens	(864)	9,694	10,587
29571	Marion	(803)	7,658	7,700
29662	Mauldin	(864)	11,662	8,143
29461	Moncks Corner	(803)	5,599	4,179
*29464	Mount Pleasant	(803)	30,108	14,464
29574	Mullins	(803)	5,910	6,068
*29577	Myrtle Beach	(803)	24,848	18,446
29108	Newberry	(803)	10,543	9,866
29841	North Augusta	(803)	15,684	13,593
29405	North Charleston	(803)	70,304	62,479
*29582	North Myrtle Beach	(803)	8,731	3,960
29565	Oak Grove(u)	(803)	7,173	7,092
*29115	Orangeburg	(803)	13,772	14,933
.....	Parker(u)		11,072	....
29905	Parris Island(u)	(803)	7,172	7,752
.....	Red Bank(u)		5,950	....
.....	Red Hill(u)		6,112	....
*29730	Rock Hill	(803)	41,610	35,327
29417	Saint Andrews(u)	(803)	25,692	20,245
29609	Sans Souci(u)	(864)	7,612	8,393
*29678	Seneca	(864)	7,726	7,436
29210	Seven Oaks(u)	(803)	15,722	16,604
*29681	Simpsonville	(864)	11,744	9,037
29577	Socastee(u)	(864)	10,426	1,082
*29306	Spartanburg	(864)	43,479	43,826
*29483	Summerville	(803)	22,519	6,492
*29150	Sumter	(803)	40,977	24,921
29687	Taylors(u)	(864)	19,619	15,801
29379	Union	(864)	9,840	10,523
29607	Wade Hampton(u)	(864)	20,014	20,180
29488	Walterboro	(803)	5,595	6,209
29611	Welcome(u)	(864)	6,560	6,922
*29169	West Columbia	(803)	10,974	10,409
29206	Woodfield(u)	(803)	8,862	9,588
29745	York	(803)	6,709	6,412

South Dakota (605)

ZIP	Place	1990	1980
*57401	Aberdeen	24,995	25,851
57006	Brookings	16,270	14,951
57706	Ellsworth AFB(u)	7,017	4,766
57350	Huron	12,448	13,000
57042	Madison	6,257	6,210
57301	Mitchell	13,798	13,916
57501	Pierre	12,906	11,973
*57701	Rapid City	54,523	46,492
57701	Rapid Valley(u)	5,968	3,265
*57101	Sioux Falls	100,836	81,343
57754	Spearfish Canyon	6,966	5,251
57785	Sturgis	5,330	5,184
57069	Vermillion	10,034	10,136
57201	Watertown	17,632	15,649
57078	Yankton	12,703	12,011

Tennessee

ZIP	Place		1990	1980
37701	Alcoa	(423)	6,400	6,870
*37303	Athens	(423)	12,054	12,080
38134	Bartlett	(901)	26,989	17,170
37660	Bloomingdale(u)	(423)	10,953	12,088
38008	Bolivar	(901)	5,969	6,597
*37027	Brentwood	(615)	16,392	9,431
*37621	Bristol	(423)	23,421	23,986
38012	Brownsville	(901)	10,017	9,307
*37401	Chattanooga	(423)	152,393	169,514
*37040	Clarksville	(615)	75,542	54,777
*37311	Cleveland	(423)	30,354	26,415
*37716	Clinton	(423)	8,960	5,245
37315	Collegedale	(423)	5,048	4,607
*38017	Collierville	(901)	14,501	7,839
37663	Colonial Heights(u)	(423)	6,716	6,744
*38401	Columbia	(615)	28,583	26,571
*38501	Cookeville	(615)	21,744	20,535
38019	Covington	(901)	7,487	6,065
*38555	Crossville	(615)	6,930	6,394
37321	Dayton	(423)	5,671	5,233
*37055	Dickson	(615)	8,783	7,040
*38024	Dyersburg	(901)	16,321	15,856
37801	Eagleton Village(u)	(423)	5,169	5,331
37411	East Brainerd(u)	(423)	11,594	....
37412	East Ridge	(423)	21,101	21,236
*37643	Elizabethton	(423)	11,931	12,431
37650	Erwin	(423)	5,017	4,739
37922	Farragut†	(423)	12,802	5,992
37334	Fayetteville	(615)	7,158	7,559
*37064	Franklin	(615)	20,098	12,407
37066	Gallatin	(615)	18,794	17,191
38138	Germantown	(901)	33,016	21,467
*37072	Goodlettsville	(615)	11,219	8,327
*37743	Greeneville	(423)	13,532	14,097
37215	Green Hills(u)	(615)	6,763	....
38040	Halls(u)	(901)	6,450	10,363
37748	Harriman	(423)	7,119	8,303
37341	Harrison(u)	(423)	7,191	6,206
*37075	Hendersonville	(615)	32,188	26,561

ZIP	Place		1990	1980
38343	Humboldt	(901)	9,651	10,209
*38301	Jackson	(901)	49,145	49,258
37760	Jefferson City	(423)	5,522	5,612
*37601	Johnson City	(423)	49,479	39,753
*37662	Kingsport	(423)	36,353	32,027
*37950	Knoxville	(423)	165,039	175,045
37766	La Follette	(423)	7,201	8,198
37086	La Vergne	(615)	7,499	5,495
38464	Lawrenceburg	(615)	10,397	10,184
*37087	Lebanon	(615)	15,208	11,872
*37771	Lenoir City	(423)	6,147	5,180
37091	Lewisburg	(615)	9,879	8,760
38351	Lexington	(901)	5,810	5,934
38201	McKenzie	(901)	5,168	5,405
37110	McMinnville	(423)	11,194	10,683
37355	Manchester	(615)	7,709	7,250
38237	Martin	(901)	8,588	8,898
*37804	Maryville	(423)	19,208	17,480
37343	Middle Valley(u)	(423)	12,255	11,420
38358	Milan	(901)	7,512	8,083
*38053	Millington	(901)	17,866	20,236
*37813	Morristown	(423)	21,316	19,570
37122	Mount Juliet	(615)	5,389	2,879
*37130	Murfreesboro	(615)	44,922	32,845
*37202	Nashville	(615)	488,374	455,651
37821	Newport	(423)	7,123	7,580
*37830	Oak Ridge	(423)	27,310	27,662
38242	Paris	(901)	9,332	10,728
37148	Portland	(615)	5,165	4,030
37849	Powell(u)	(423)	7,534	7,220
38478	Pulaski	(615)	7,916	7,184
37415	Red Bank	(423)	12,320	13,129
38063	Ripley	(901)	6,188	6,366
37854	Rockwood	(423)	5,348	5,687
38372	Savannah	(901)	6,547	6,992
*37862	Sevierville	(423)	7,178	4,556
37865	Seymour(u)	(423)	7,026	....
37160	Shelbyville	(615)	14,042	13,530
37377	Signal Mountain	(423)	7,034	5,818
37167	Smyrna	(615)	13,647	8,839
37379	Soddy-Daisy	(423)	8,240	8,388
37311	South Cleveland(u)	(423)	5,372	4,360
37172	Springfield	(615)	11,227	10,814
37874	Sweetwater	(423)	5,066	4,725
37388	Tullahoma	(423)	16,761	15,800
*38261	Union City	(901)	10,513	10,436
37398	Winchester	(615)	6,305	5,821

Texas

ZIP	Place		1990	1980
*79604	Abilene	(915)	106,707	98,315
75001	Addison	(214)	8,783	5,553
78516	Alamo	(210)	8,352	5,831
78209	Alamo Heights	(210)	6,502	6,252
77039	Aldine(u)	(713)	11,133	12,623
*78332	Alice	(512)	19,788	20,961
75002	Allen	(214)	19,315	8,314
*79830	Alpine	(915)	5,622	5,465
*77511	Alvin	(713)	19,220	16,515
*79105	Amarillo	(806)	157,571	149,230
78750	Anderson Mill(u)		9,468	....
79714	Andrews	(915)	10,678	11,061
*77515	Angleton	(409)	17,140	13,929
*78336	Aransas Pass	(512)	7,180	7,173
*76004	Arlington	(817)	261,717	160,113
75751	Athens	(903)	10,982	10,197
75551	Atlanta	(214)	6,118	6,272
*78767	Austin	(512)	465,648	345,890
*76020	Azle	(817)	8,868	5,822
77518	Bacliff(u)	(409)	5,549	4,851
75180	Balch Springs	(214)	17,406	13,746
*77414	Bay City	(409)	18,170	17,837
*77520	Baytown	(713)	63,843	56,923
*77707	Beaumont	(409)	114,323	118,102
*76021	Bedford	(817)	43,762	20,821
*78102	Beeville	(512)	13,547	14,574
*77401	Bellaire	(713)	13,844	14,950
76704	Bellmead	(817)	8,336	7,569
76513	Belton	(817)	12,463	10,660
76126	Benbrook	(817)	19,564	13,579
*79720	Big Spring	(915)	23,093	24,804
75418	Bonham	(903)	6,688	7,338
*79007	Borger	(806)	15,675	15,837
76825	Brady	(915)	5,946	5,969
76424	Breckenridge	(817)	5,665	6,921
*77833	Brenham	(409)	11,952	10,966
77611	Bridge City	(409)	8,010	7,667
79316	Brownfield	(806)	9,560	10,387
*78520	Brownsville	(210)	98,962	84,997
*76801	Brownwood	(915)	18,387	19,396
78717	Brushy Creek(u)	(903)	5,833	....
*77801	Bryan	(409)	55,002	44,337
76354	Burkburnett	(817)	10,145	10,668
*76028	Burleson	(817)	16,113	11,734
76520	Cameron	(817)	5,635	5,721
79015	Canyon	(806)	11,365	10,724
78130	Canyon Lake(u)	(210)	9,975	....
78834	Carrizo Springs	(210)	5,745	6,886
*75006	Carrolton	(214)	82,169	40,595

ZIP	Place		1990	1980	ZIP	Place		1990	1980
75633	Carthage	(903)	6,496	6,447	*76248	Keller	(817)	13,683	4,156
*75104	Cedar Hill	(214)	19,988	6,849	79745	Kermit	(915)	6,875	8,015
*78613	Cedar Park	(512)	5,121	3,474	*78028	Kerrville	(210)	17,384	15,276
77530	Channelview(u)	(713)	25,564	17,471	*75662	Kilgore	(903)	11,066	11,331
79201	Childress	(817)	5,055	5,817	*76540	Killeen	(817)	63,535	46,296
*76031	Cleburne	(817)	22,205	19,218	*78363	Kingsville	(512)	25,276	28,808
*77327	Cleveland	(713)	7,124	5,977	77325	Kingwood(u)	(713)	37,397	16,261
77015	Cloverleaf(u)	(713)	18,230	17,317	78219	Kirby	(210)	8,326	6,435
77531	Clute	(409)	9,467	9,577	78236	Lackland AFB(u)	(210)	9,352	14,459
76834	Coleman	(915)	5,410	5,960	77566	Lake Jackson	(409)	22,771	19,102
*77840	College Station	(409)	52,443	37,272	77568	La Marque	(409)	14,120	15,372
76034	Colleyville	(817)	12,724	6,700	79331	Lamesa	(806)	10,809	11,790
*75428	Commerce	(903)	6,825	8,136	76550	Lampasas	(512)	6,382	6,165
*77301	Conroe	(409)	27,675	18,034	*75146	Lancaster	(214)	22,117	14,807
78109	Converse	(512)	8,887	5,150	*77571	La Porte	(713)	27,910	14,062
75019	Coppell	(214)	16,881	3,826	*78041	Laredo	(210)	122,893	91,449
76522	Copperas Cove	(817)	24,079	19,469	*77573	League City	(713)	30,159	16,578
*78469	Corpus Christi	(512)	257,428	232,134	78268	Leon Valley	(210)	9,581	9,088
*75110	Corsicana	(903)	22,911	21,712	*79336	Levelland	(806)	13,986	13,809
75835	Crockett	(409)	7,024	7,405	*75067	Lewisville	(214)	46,521	24,273
76036	Crowley	(817)	6,974	5,852	77575	Liberty	(713)	7,690	7,945
78839	Crystal City	(512)	8,263	8,334	79339	Littlefield	(806)	6,489	7,409
77954	Cuero	(512)	6,700	7,124	78233	Live Oak	(210)	10,023	8,183
79022	Dalhart	(806)	6,246	6,854	77351	Livingston	(409)	5,019	4,928
*75221	Dallas	(214)	1,007,618	904,599	78644	Lockhart	(512)	9,205	7,953
77535	Dayton	(409)	5,042	4,908	*75606	Longview	(903)	70,311	62,762
77536	Deer Park	(713)	27,424	22,648	*79408	Lubbock	(806)	186,206	174,361
*78840	Del Rio	(210)	30,705	30,034	*75904	Lufkin	(409)	30,210	28,562
*75020	Denison	(903)	21,505	23,884	77657	Lumberton	(409)	6,640	2,480
*76201	Denton	(817)	66,270	48,063	*78501	McAllen	(210)	84,021	66,281
79323	Denver City	(512)	5,156	4,704	*75070	McKinney	(214)	21,283	16,256
*75115	De Soto	(214)	30,544	15,538	76063	Mansfield	(817)	15,615	8,102
77539	Dickinson	(713)	9,497	7,505	76661	Marlin	(817)	6,386	7,099
78537	Donna	(210)	12,652	9,952	*75670	Marshall	(903)	23,682	24,921
79029	Dumas	(806)	12,871	12,194	78368	Mathis	(512)	5,423	5,667
*75138	Duncanville	(214)	35,008	27,781	78570	Mercedes	(210)	12,694	11,851
76135	Eagle Mountain(u)	(817)	5,847		*75149	Mesquite	(214)	101,484	67,053
*78852	Eagle Pass	(210)	20,651	21,407	76667	Mexia	(817)	6,933	7,094
*78539	Edinburg	(210)	29,885	24,075	*79701	Midland	(915)	89,343	70,525
77957	Edna	(512)	5,343	5,650	76065	Midlothian	(214)	5,040	3,219
77437	El Campo	(409)	10,511	10,462	*76067	Mineral Wells	(817)	14,935	14,468
*79910	El Paso	(915)	515,342	425,259	*78572	Mission	(210)	28,653	22,653
78543	Elsa	(210)	5,242	5,061	.....	Mission Bend(u)		24,945	....
*75119	Ennis	(214)	13,869	12,110	*77489	Missouri City	(713)	36,178	24,423
*76039	Euless	(817)	38,149	24,002	79756	Monahans	(915)	8,101	8,397
76140	Everman	(817)	5,672	5,387	*75455	Mount Pleasant	(903)	12,291	11,003
79838	Fabens(u)	(915)	5,599	4,285	*75961	Nacogdoches	(409)	30,872	27,149
78355	Falfurrias	(512)	5,788	6,103	77868	Navasota	(409)	6,296	5,971
75234	Farmers Branch	(214)	24,250	24,863	77627	Nederland	(409)	16,192	16,855
.....	First Colony(u)		18,327	....	75570	New Boston	(903)	5,057	4,628
78114	Floresville	(210)	5,247	4,381	*78130	New Braunfels	(210)	27,334	22,402
75028	Flower Mound	(214)	15,527	4,402	76118	North Richland Hills	(817)	45,895	30,592
76119	Forest Hill	(817)	11,482	11,684	*79761	Odessa	(915)	89,699	90,027
79906	Fort Bliss(u)	(915)	13,915	12,687	*77630	Orange	(409)	19,370	23,628
76544	Fort Hood(u)	(817)	35,580	31,250	*75801	Palestine	(903)	18,042	15,948
79735	Fort Stockton	(915)	8,524	8,688	*79065	Pampa	(806)	19,959	21,396
*76161	Fort Worth	(817)	447,619	385,164	*75460	Paris	(903)	24,799	25,498
78624	Fredericksburg	(210)	6,934	6,412	*77501	Pasadena	(713)	119,604	112,560
77541	Freeport	(409)	11,389	13,444	*77581	Pearland	(713)	18,927	13,248
77546	Friendswood	(713)	22,814	10,719	78061	Pearsall	(210)	6,924	7,383
75034	Frisco	(214)	6,138	3,499	78721	Pecan Grove(u)		9,502	....
*76240	Gainesville	(817)	14,256	14,081	79772	Pecos	(915)	12,069	12,855
77547	Galena Park	(713)	10,033	9,879	79070	Perryton	(806)	7,619	7,991
*77550	Galveston	(409)	59,067	61,902	78577	Pharr	(210)	32,921	21,381
*75040	Garland	(214)	180,635	138,857	*79072	Plainview	(806)	21,698	22,187
*76528	Gatesville	(817)	11,492	6,078	*75074	Plano	(214)	127,885	72,331
*78626	Georgetown	(512)	14,840	9,468	78064	Pleasanton	(210)	7,678	6,346
75647	Gladewater	(903)	6,027	6,548	*77640	Port Arthur	(409)	58,551	61,251
78629	Gonzales	(210)	6,527	7,152	78374	Portland	(512)	12,224	12,023
76450	Graham	(817)	8,986	9,170	77979	Port Lavaca	(512)	10,886	10,911
*75051	Grand Prairie	(214)	99,606	71,462	77651	Port Neches	(409)	12,908	13,944
*76051	Grapevine	(817)	29,198	11,801	78580	Raymondville	(210)	8,880	9,493
*75401	Greenville	(903)	23,071	22,161	76028	Rendon(u)	(817)	7,658	....
77619	Groves	(409)	16,744	17,090	*75080	Richardson	(214)	74,840	72,496
76117	Haltom City	(817)	32,856	29,014	76118	Richland Hills	(817)	7,978	7,977
76543	Harker Heights	(817)	12,932	7,345	*77469	Richmond	(713)	10,042	9,692
*78550	Harlingen	(210)	48,746	43,543	78582	Rio Grande City(u)	(210)	9,891	8,930
77859	Hearne	(409)	5,132	5,418	77019	River Oaks	(817)	6,580	6,890
*75652	Henderson	(903)	11,139	11,473	76701	Robinson	(817)	7,111	6,074
79045	Hereford	(806)	14,745	15,853	76380	Robstown	(512)	12,849	12,100
76643	Hewitt	(817)	8,983	5,247	76567	Rockdale	(512)	5,235	5,611
75205	Highland Park	(214)	8,739	8,909	75087	Rockwall	(214)	10,486	5,939
*77562	Highlands(u)	(713)	6,632	6,467	78584	Roma	(210)	8,059	3,384
75067	Highland Village	(214)	7,027	3,246	77471	Rosenberg	(713)	20,183	17,840
76645	Hillsboro	(817)	7,072	7,397	*78681	Round Rock	(512)	30,923	12,740
77563	Hitchcock	(409)	5,868	6,103	*75088	Rowlett	(214)	23,260	7,522
78861	Hondo	(210)	6,018	6,057	75048	Sachse	(214)	5,346	1,640
*77052	Houston	(713)	1,629,902	1,595,138	76179	Saginaw	(817)	8,551	5,736
*77338	Humble	(713)	12,060	6,729	*76902	San Angelo	(915)	84,462	73,240
*77340	Huntsville	(409)	27,925	23,936	*78265	San Antonio	(210)	935,393	785,940
*76053	Hurst	(817)	33,574	31,420	78586	San Benito	(210)	20,125	17,988
78362	Ingleside	(512)	5,696	5,436	78589	San Juan	(210)	10,815	7,608
76367	Iowa Park	(817)	6,072	6,184	*78666	San Marcos	(512)	28,738	23,420
*75015	Irving	(214)	155,037	109,943	*77510	Santa Fe	(713)	8,429	6,172
77029	Jacinto City	(713)	9,343	8,953	78154	Schertz	(210)	10,597	7,262
75766	Jacksonville	(214)	12,765	12,264	77586	Seabrook	(713)	6,685	4,670
75951	Jasper	(409)	7,160	6,959	75159	Seagoville	(214)	8,969	7,304
78729	Jollyville(u)	(512)	15,206	....	*78155	Seguin	(210)	18,692	17,854
*77449	Katy	(713)	8,004	5,660	79360	Seminole	(915)	6,342	6,080
75142	Kaufman	(214)	5,251	4,658	*75090	Sherman	(903)	31,584	30,413

ZIP	Place		1990	1980
77656	Silsbee	(409)	6,368	7,684
78387	Sinton	(512)	5,549	6,044
79364	Slaton	(806)	6,078	6,804
*79549	Snyder	(915)	12,195	12,705
79910	Socorro	(915)	22,995	12,341†
77587	South Houston	(713)	14,207	13,293
76092	Southlake	(817)	7,082	2,808
*77373	Spring(u)	(713)	33,111	....
*77477	Stafford	(713)	8,395	4,755
76401	Stephenville	(817)	13,502	11,881
*77478	Sugar Land	(713)	24,549	8,826
*75482	Sulphur Springs	(903)	14,062	12,804
79556	Sweetwater	(915)	11,967	12,242
76574	Taylor	(512)	11,472	10,619
*76501	Temple	(817)	46,150	42,354
75160	Terrell	(214)	12,490	13,269
*75501	Texarkana	(903)	31,658	31,271
*77590	Texas City	(409)	40,822	41,201
75056	The Colony	(214)	22,113	11,586
77387	The Woodlands(u)	(713)	29,205	8,443
*77335	Tomball	(713)	6,370	3,996
	Town West(u)		6,166	....
*75702	Tyler	(903)	75,450	70,508
*78148	Universal City	(512)	13,057	10,720
76308	University Park	(214)	22,259	22,254
*78801	Uvalde	(210)	14,729	14,178
*76384	Vernon	(817)	12,001	12,695
*77901	Victoria	(512)	55,076	50,695
*77662	Vidor	(409)	10,935	11,834
*76702	Waco	(817)	103,590	101,261
76148	Watauga	(817)	20,009	10,284
75165	Waxahachie	(214)	17,984	14,624
*76086	Weatherford	(817)	14,804	12,049
78728	Wells Branch(u)		7,094	....
*78596	Weslaco	(210)	21,877	19,331
79764	West Odessa(u)	(915)	16,568	....
77005	West University Place	(713)	12,920	12,010
77488	Wharton	(409)	9,011	9,033
75693	White Oak	(903)	5,136	4,415
76108	White Settlement	(817)	15,472	13,508
*76307	Wichita Falls	(817)	96,259	94,201
78239	Windcrest	(210)	5,331	5,332
76712	Woodway	(817)	8,695	7,091
75098	Wylie	(214)	8,716	3,152
77995	Yoakum	(512)	5,611	6,148
78076	Zapata(u)	(512)	7,119	3,831

Utah (801)

ZIP	Place	1990	1980
84003	American Fork	15,722	12,564
*84010	Bountiful	36,147	32,877
84302	Brigham City	15,644	15,596
84109	Canyon Rim(u)	10,527	....
*84720	Cedar City	13,443	10,972
84014	Centerville	11,500	8,069
*84015	Clearfield	21,435	17,982
84015	Clinton	7,945	5,777
84121	Cottonwood Heights(u)	28,766	22,665
84121	Cottonwood West(u)	17,476	11,117
84020	Draper	7,143	5,521
84109	East Millcreek(u)	21,184	24,150
84025	Farmington	9,049	4,691
84003	Highland	5,007	2,435
84117	Holladay-Cottonwood(u)†	14,095	22,189
84037	Kaysville	13,961	9,811
84118	Kearns(u)	28,374	21,353
*84041	Layton	41,784	22,862
84043	Lehi	8,475	6,848
	Little Cottonwood Creek Valley(u)	5,042	....
*84321	Logan	32,771	26,844
84044	Magna(u)	17,829	13,138
84047	Midvale	11,886	10,146
84109	Millcreek(u)	32,230	....
84117	Mount Olympus(u)	7,413	6,068
84107	Murray	31,274	25,750
84404	North Ogden	11,593	9,309
84054	North Salt Lake	6,464	5,548
*84401	Ogden	63,943	64,407
	Oquirrh(u)	7,593	....
*84057	Orem	67,561	52,399
84651	Payson	9,510	8,246
84062	Pleasant Grove	13,476	10,833
84501	Price	8,712	9,086
*84601	Provo	86,835	74,111
84701	Richfield	5,593	5,482
84403	Riverdale	6,419	6,031
84065	Riverton	11,261	7,032
84067	Roy	24,595	19,694
*84770	Saint George	28,572	11,350
*84101	Salt Lake City	159,928	163,034
*84070	Sandy	75,240	52,210
84335	Smithfield	5,566	4,993
84095	South Jordan	12,215	7,492
84403	South Ogden	12,105	11,366
84165	South Salt Lake	10,129	10,413
84660	Spanish Fork	11,272	9,825
84663	Springville	13,950	12,101
84015	Sunset	5,128	5,733
84107	Taylorsville-Bennion(u)†	52,351	17,448
84074	Tooele	13,887	14,335

ZIP	Place	1990	1980
84047	Union(u)	13,684	9,665
*84078	Vernal	6,640	6,600
84403	Washington Terrace	8,189	8,212
*84084	West Jordan	42,915	27,325
*84119	West Valley City†	86,969	72,509
84070	White City(u)	6,506	7,267
84087	Woods Cross	5,384	4,263

Vermont (802)

See note on page 396

ZIP	Place	1990	1980
05641	Barre	9,482	9,824
05641	Barre	7,411	7,090
05201	Bennington	16,451	15,815
05201	Bennington(u)	9,532	9,349
*05301	Brattleboro Center(u)	8,612	8,596
*05301	Brattleboro	12,241	11,886
*05401	Burlington	39,127	37,712
*05446	Colchester	14,731	12,629
05451	Essex	16,498	14,392
*05452	Essex Junction	8,396	7,033
05047	Hartford	9,404	7,963
05849	Lyndon	5,371	5,371
*05753	Middlebury	8,034	7,574
05468	Milton	8,404	6,829
*05602	Montpelier	8,247	8,241
05663	Northfield	5,610	5,435
05101	Rockingham	5,484	5,538
*05701	Rutland	18,230	18,436
05478	Saint Albans	7,339	7,308
05819	Saint Johnsbury(u)	7,608	6,424
05482	Shelburne	5,871	5,000
*05403	South Burlington	12,809	10,679
05156	Springfield	9,579	10,190
05488	Swanton	5,636	5,141
05404	Winooski	6,649	6,318

Virginia

ZIP	Place		1990	1980
*24210	Abingdon	(540)	7,003	4,318
*22313	Alexandria	(703)	111,182	103,217
22003	Annandale(u)	(540)	50,975	49,524
22554	Aquia Harbour(u)	(703)	6,308	2,870
*22210	Arlington(u)	(703)	170,936	152,599
23005	Ashland	(804)	5,864	4,640
22041	Bailey's Crossroads(u)	(703)	19,507	12,564
24523	Bedford	(540)	6,073	5,991
22306	Belle Haven(u)	(804)	6,427	6,520
23234	Bellwood(u)	(804)	6,178	6,439
23234	Bensley(u)	(804)	5,093	5,299
*24060	Blacksburg	(540)	34,590	30,638
24605	Bluefield	(540)	5,363	5,946
23235	Bon Air(u)	(804)	16,413	16,224
*24203	Bristol	(540)	18,426	19,042
24416	Buena Vista	(540)	6,406	6,717
	Bull Run(u)		5,525	....
*22015	Burke(u)	(703)	57,734	33,835
24018	Cave Spring(u)	(540)	24,053	21,682
22020	Centreville(u)	(703)	26,585	7,473
*22021	Chantilly(u)	(703)	29,337	12,259
*22906	Charlottesville	(804)	40,475	39,916
*23320	Chesapeake	(804)	151,982	114,486
23831	Chester(u)	(804)	14,986	11,728
23834	Colonial Heights	(804)	16,064	16,509
22901	Commonwealth(u)	(804)	5,538	3,505
	Countryside(u)		8,349	....
24426	Covington	(540)	6,991	9,063
22701	Culpeper	(540)	8,581	6,621
22193	Dale City(u)	(540)	47,170	33,127
*24541	Danville	(804)	53,056	45,642
23228	Dumbarton(u)	(804)	8,526	8,149
22027	Dunn Loring(u)	(703)	6,509	6,077
23222	East Highland Park(u)	(804)	11,850	11,797
23847	Emporia	(804)	5,479	4,840
23803	Ettrick(u)	(804)	5,290	4,890
*22030	Fairfax	(703)	19,629	19,390
*22046	Falls Church	(703)	9,522	9,515
23901	Farmville	(804)	6,046	6,067
24551	Forest(u)	(804)	5,624	....
22060	Fort Belvoir(u)	(703)	8,590	7,726
22308	Fort Hunt(u)	(703)	12,989	14,294
23801	Fort Lee(u)	(804)	6,895	9,784
22310	Franconia(u)	(703)	19,882	8,476
23851	Franklin	(804)	7,864	7,308
*22404	Fredericksburg	(540)	19,027	15,322
*22630	Front Royal	(540)	11,880	11,126
24333	Galax	(540)	6,670	6,524
*23060	Glen Allen(u)	(804)	9,010	6,202
23062	Gloucester Point(u)	(804)	8,509	5,841
22066	Great Falls(u)	(804)	6,945	2,419
22306	Groveton(u)	(703)	19,997	18,860
*23670	Hampton	(804)	133,811	122,617
22801	Harrisonburg	(540)	30,707	19,671
*22070	Herndon	(703)	16,139	11,449
23075	Highland Springs(u)	(804)	13,823	12,146

ZIP	Place		1990	1980
24019	Hollins(u)	(540)	13,305	12,295
23860	Hopewell	(804)	23,101	23,397
22303	Huntington(u)	(703)	7,489	5,813
22306	Hybla Valley(u)	(703)	15,491	15,533
22043	Idylwood(u)	(703)	14,710	11,982
22042	Jefferson(u)	(804)	25,782	24,342
22041	Lake Barcroft(u)	(703)	8,686	8,725
22191	Lake Ridge(u)	(540)	23,862	11,072
23228	Lakeside(u)	(804)	12,081	12,289
23060	Laurel(u)	(804)	13,011	10,569
22075	Leesburg	(703)	16,202	8,357
24450	Lexington	(540)	6,959	7,292
22312	Lincolnia(u)	(703)	13,041	10,350
*22079	Lorton(u)	(703)	15,385	5,813
*24506	Lynchburg	(804)	66,049	66,743
*22101	McLean(u)	(703)	38,168	35,664
24572	Madison Heights(u)	(804)	11,700	14,146
*22110	Manassas	(703)	27,957	15,438
22110	Manassas Park	(703)	6,734	6,524
22030	Mantua(u)	(703)	6,804	6,523
24354	Marion	(540)	6,630	7,287
*24112	Martinsville	(540)	16,162	18,149
23111	Mechanicsville(u)	(804)	22,027	9,269
*22116	Merrifield(u)	(703)	8,399	7,525
....	Montclair(u)		11,399	4,098
23231	Montrose(u)	(804)	6,405	5,349
22121	Mount Vernon(u)	(703)	27,485	24,058
22122	Newington(u)	(703)	17,965	8,313
*23607	Newport News	(804)	171,439	144,903
*23501	Norfolk	(804)	261,250	266,979
22151	North Springfield(u)	(703)	8,996	9,538
22124	Oakton(u)	(703)	24,610	19,150
*23804	Petersburg	(804)	37,027	41,055
22043	Pimmit Hills(u)	(703)	6,019	6,658
23662	Poquoson	(804)	11,005	8,726
*23705	Portsmouth	(804)	103,910	104,577
24301	Pulaski	(540)	9,985	10,106
22134	Quantico Station(u)	(703)	7,425	7,121
*24141	Radford	(540)	15,940	13,225
*22090	Reston(u)	(703)	48,556	36,407
*23232	Richmond	(804)	202,798	219,214
22901	Rio	(804)	5,133	2,851
*24022	Roanoke	(540)	96,509	100,220
24281	Rose Hill(u)	(540)	12,675	11,926
24153	Salem	(540)	23,797	23,958
22044	Seven Corners(u)	(703)	7,280	6,058
24592	South Boston	(804)	6,997	7,093
*22150	Springfield(u)	(703)	23,706	21,435
*24402	Staunton	(540)	24,461	21,857
*20164	Sterling(u)	(703)	20,512	16,080
24477	Stuarts Draft(u)	(804)	5,087	1,776
23162	Sudley(u)	(540)	7,321	4,674
*23434	Suffolk	(804)	52,143	47,621
22170	Sugarland Run(u)	(703)	9,357	6,258
24502	Timberlake(u)	(804)	10,314	9,697
23229	Tuckahoe(u)	(804)	42,629	39,868
22101	Tysons Corner(u)	(703)	13,124	10,065
22901	University Heights(u)	(804)	6,900	6,736
*22180	Vienna	(703)	14,852	15,469
24179	Vinton	(540)	7,643	8,027
*23458	Virginia Beach	(804)	393,089	262,199
22980	Waynesboro	(540)	18,549	15,329
22110	West Gate(u)	(703)	6,565	7,119
22152	West Springfield(u)	(703)	28,126	25,012
*23185	Williamsburg	(804)	11,409	9,870
*22601	Winchester	(540)	21,947	20,217
24592	Wolf Trap(u)	(804)	13,133	9,875
*22191	Woodbridge(u)	(540)	26,401	24,004
24382	Wytheville	(540)	8,036	7,135
22110	Yorkshire(u)	(703)	5,699	4,940

Washington

ZIP	Place		1990	1980
98520	Aberdeen	(360)	16,565	18,739
98036	Alderwood Manor-Bothell North(u)	(206)	22,945	16,524
98221	Anacortes	(360)	11,451	9,013
98335	Artondale(u)	(206)	7,141	....
*98002	Auburn	(206)	33,650	26,417
*98009	Bellevue	(206)	86,872	73,903
*98225	Bellingham	(360)	52,179	45,794
98390	Bonney Lake	(206)	7,494	5,328
*98011	Bothell	(206)	12,345	7,943
*98337	Bremerton	(206)	38,142	36,208
98036	Brier	(206)	5,633	2,915
98178	Bryn Mawr-Skyway(u)	(206)	12,514	11,754
98166	Burien(u)	(206)	25,089	23,189
98607	Camas	(360)	6,442	5,681
98055	Cascade-Fairwood(u)	(206)	30,107	16,939
98684	Cascade Park East(u)	(206)	6,996	....
98684	Cascade Park West(u)	(206)	6,656	....
98531	Centralia	(360)	12,101	11,555
98532	Chehalis	(360)	6,527	6,100
99004	Cheney	(509)	7,723	7,630
99403	Clarkston	(509)	6,753	6,903
99324	College Place	(509)	6,308	5,771
99218	Country Homes(u)	(509)	5,126	....

ZIP	Place		1990	1980
98042	Covington-Sawyer-Wilderness(u)		24,321	....
98198	Des Moines	(206)	17,283	7,378
99213	Dishman(u)	(509)	9,671	10,169
....	East Hill-Meridian(u)		42,696	....
98366	East Port Orchard(u)		5,409	4,631
98056	East Renton Highlands(u)	(206)	13,218	11,695
98801	East Wenatchee Bench(u)	(509)	12,539	11,410
....	Edgewood-North Hill(u)		9,120	....
*98020	Edmonds	(206)	30,743	27,679
98387	Elk Plain(u)		12,197	....
98926	Ellensburg	(509)	12,360	11,752
....	Ellsworth North(u)		5,796	....
98022	Enumclaw	(360)	7,227	5,427
98823	Ephrata	(509)	5,349	5,359
99210	Esperance(u)	(509)	11,236	11,120
*98201	Everett	(360)	69,974	54,413
98411	Evergreen(u)		11,249	....
98055	Fairwood(u)	(206)	5,807	5,337
*98002	Federal Way	(206)	67,554	....
98248	Ferndale	(360)	5,398	3,855
98466	Fircrest	(206)	5,258	5,477
98597	Five Corners(u)		6,776	....
98433	Fort Lewis(u)	(206)	22,224	23,761
98930	Grandview	(509)	7,169	5,615
....	Harbour Pointe(u)		9,107	....
98660	Hazel Dell North(u)†	(206)	6,924	15,386
98665	Hazel Dell South(u)	(206)	5,796	....
98550	Hoquiam	(206)	8,972	9,719
98011	Inglewood-Finn Hill(u)†.	(206)	29,132	12,467
98027	Issaquah	(206)	7,786	5,536
98626	Kelso	(360)	11,767	11,129
98028	Kenmore(u)	(206)	8,917	7,281
*99336	Kennewick	(509)	42,148	34,397
*98031	Kent	(206)	37,960	22,961
98033	Kingsgate(u)	(206)	14,259	12,652
*98033	Kirkland	(206)	40,059	18,785
98503	Lacey	(360)	19,279	13,940
98155	Lake Forest North(u)	(206)	8,002	7,995
98002	Lakeland North(u)	(206)	14,402	11,648
98002	Lakeland South(u)	(206)	9,027	5,225
98036	Lake Serene-North Lynnwood(u)		14,290	....
98665	Lake Shore(u)	(360)	6,268	....
98259	Lakewood(u)	(206)	58,412	54,533
....	Lea Hill(u)		6,876	....
98632	Longview	(360)	31,499	31,052
98264	Lynden	(360)	5,709	4,022
*98046	Lynnwood	(206)	28,637	22,641
98012	Martha Lake(u)	(206)	10,155	7,022
*98270	Marysville	(360)	10,328	5,080
98040	Mercer Island	(206)	20,816	21,522
....	Midland(u)		5,587	....
98082	Mill Creek†	(206)	7,180	1,803
....	Minnehaha(u)		9,661	....
98837	Moses Lake	(509)	11,235	10,629
98043	Mountlake Terrace	(206)	19,320	16,534
98273	Mount Vernon	(360)	17,647	13,009
98275	Mukilteo	(206)	6,982	1,426
98006	Newport Hills(u)	(206)	14,736	12,245
98166	Normandy Park	(206)	6,709	4,268
98155	North City-Ridgecrest(u)	(206)	13,832	13,551
....	North Creek-Canyon Park(u)		23,236	....
98166	North Hill(u)	(206)	5,706	10,170
98270	North Marysville(u)	(206)	18,711	15,159
98277	Oak Harbor	(360)	17,176	12,271
*98501	Olympia	(360)	33,729	27,447
99214	Opportunity(u)	(509)	22,326	21,241
98662	Orchards North(u)†	(360)	6,479	8,828
98662	Orchards South(u)	(360)	12,956	....
99027	Otis Orchards-East Farms(u)	(360)	5,811	4,597
....	Paine Field-Lake Stickney(u)		18,670	....
98444	Parkland(u)	(206)	20,882	23,355
98366	Parkwood(u)		6,853	4,599
*99301	Pasco	(509)	20,337	18,428
98027	Pine Lake(u)		13,940	....
98362	Port Angeles	(360)	17,710	17,311
98368	Port Townsend	(360)	7,001	6,067
98390	Prairie Ridge(u)		8,278	....
*99163	Pullman	(509)	23,478	23,579
*98371	Puyallup	(206)	23,878	18,251
*98052	Redmond	(206)	35,800	23,318
*98058	Renton	(206)	41,688	31,031
99352	Richland	(509)	32,315	33,578
98160	Richmond Beach-Innis Arden(u)	(206)	7,242	6,700
98113	Richmond Highlands(u)	(206)	26,037	24,463
98188	Riverton-Boulevard Park(u)†.	(206)	15,337	14,182
....	Sahalee(u)		13,951	....
98686	Salmon Creek(u)		11,989	....
*98148	Seatac	(206)	22,694	....
*98101	Seattle	(206)	516,259	493,846
98284	Sedro Woolley	(360)	6,333	6,110
98942	Selah	(509)	5,113	4,500
98584	Shelton	(360)	7,241	7,629
98155	Sheridan Beach(u)	(206)	6,518	6,873
*98383	Silverdale(u)	(360)	7,660	....
98201	Silver Lake-Fircrest(u)	(360)	24,474	10,299
*98290	Snohomish	(360)	6,499	5,294
98373	South Hill(u)		12,963	....
98387	Spanaway(u)	(206)	15,001	8,868

ZIP	Place		1990	1980
*99210	Spokane	(509)	177,165	171,300
98388	Steilacoom	(206)	5,728	4,886
*98371	Summit(u)	(206)	6,312	....
98390	Sumner	(206)	6,459	4,936
98944	Sunnyside	(509)	11,238	9,225
*98402	Tacoma	(206)	176,664	158,501
98501	Tanglewilde-			
	Thompson Place(u)	(360)	6,061	5,910
98948	Toppenish	(509)	7,419	6,517
98138	Tukwila	(206)	11,874	3,578
98501	Tumwater	(360)	9,976	6,705
98464	University Place(u)	(206)	27,701	20,381
*98661	Vancouver	(360)	46,380	42,834
98662	Vancouver Mall(u)	(360)	6,938	....
99037	Veradale(u)	(509)	7,836	7,256
99362	Walla Walla	(509)	26,482	25,618
.....	Waller(u)		6,415	....
*98801	Wenatchee	(509)	21,746	17,257
.....	West Lake Sammamish(u)		6,087	....
98258	West Lake Stevens(u)	(206)	12,453	....
99301	West Pasco(u)	(509)	7,312	5,726
99181	West Valley(u)		6,594	....
98166	White Center-Shorewood(u)	(206)	20,531	19,362
98072	Woodinville(u)	(206)	23,654	....
98032	Woodmont Beach(u)	(206)	7,493	....
*98903	Yakima	(509)	54,843	49,826

West Virginia (304)

ZIP	Place	1990	1980
*25801	Beckley	18,274	20,492
24701	Bluefield	12,756	16,060
26330	Bridgeport	6,695	6,604
26201	Buckhannon	5,909	6,820
*25301	Charleston	57,287	63,968
*26301	Clarksburg	17,970	22,371
25301	Cross Lanes(u)	10,878	....
25064	Dunbar	8,697	9,285
26241	Elkins	7,494	8,536
*26554	Fairmont	20,210	23,863
26354	Grafton	5,524	6,845
*25704	Huntington	54,844	63,684
26726	Keyser	5,870	6,569
25401	Martinsburg	14,073	13,063
*26505	Morgantown	25,879	27,605
26041	Moundsville	10,753	12,419
26155	New Martinsville	6,705	7,109
25143	Nitro	6,851	8,074
25901	Oak Hill	6,812	7,120
*26101	Parkersburg	33,862	39,946
.....	Pea Ridge(u)	6,535	....
24740	Princeton	7,043	7,538
25177	Saint Albans	11,257	12,402
*25301	South Charleston	13,645	15,968
25569	Teays Valley(u)	8,436	....
26105	Vienna	10,862	11,618
26062	Weirton	22,124	25,371
26003	Wheeling	34,882	43,070

Wisconsin

See note on page 396

ZIP	Place		1990	1980
54301	Allouez†	(414)	14,431	14,882
54720	Altoona	(715)	5,889	4,393
54409	Antigo	(715)	8,284	8,653
*59411	Appleton	(414)	65,695	58,913
54806	Ashland	(715)	8,695	9,115
54304	Ashwaubenon	(414)	16,376	14,486
53913	Baraboo	(608)	9,203	8,081
53916	Beaver Dam	(414)	14,196	14,149
54311	Bellevue Town(u)	(414)	7,541	....
*53511	Beloit	(608)	35,571	35,207
54923	Berlin	(414)	5,371	5,478
*53045	Brookfield	(414)	35,184	34,035
53209	Brown Deer	(414)	12,236	12,921
53105	Burlington	(414)	8,855	8,385
53012	Cedarburg	(414)	10,086	9,005
54729	Chippewa Falls	(715)	12,727	12,270
53110	Cudahy	(414)	18,659	19,547
53018	Delafield	(414)	5,347	4,083
53115	Delavan	(414)	6,073	5,684
54115	De Pere	(414)	16,569	14,892
*54703	Eau Claire	(715)	56,806	51,509
53121	Elkhorn	(414)	5,337	4,605
53122	Elm Grove	(414)	6,261	6,735
53714	Fitchburg†	(608)	15,648	11,965
*54935	Fond Du Lac	(414)	37,757	35,863
53538	Fort Atkinson	(414)	10,213	9,785
53217	Fox Point	(414)	7,238	7,649
53132	Franklin	(414)	21,855	16,871
53022	Germantown	(414)	13,658	10,729
53209	Glendale	(414)	14,088	13,882
53024	Grafton	(414)	9,340	8,381
*54303	Green Bay	(414)	96,466	87,899
53129	Greendale	(414)	15,128	16,928
53220	Greenfield	(414)	33,403	31,353

ZIP	Place		1990	1980
53130	Hales Corners	(414)	7,623	7,110
53027	Hartford	(414)	8,188	7,159
53029	Hartland	(414)	6,906	5,559
54303	Howard	(414)	9,874	8,240
54016	Hudson	(715)	6,378	5,434
*53545	Janesville	(608)	52,210	51,071
53549	Jefferson	(414)	6,078	5,647
54130	Kaukauna	(414)	11,982	11,310
*53140	Kenosha	(414)	80,426	77,685
54136	Kimberly	(414)	5,406	5,881
*54601	La Crosse	(608)	51,120	48,347
53147	Lake Geneva	(414)	5,979	5,612
54140	Little Chute	(414)	9,207	7,907
53558	McFarland	(608)	5,232	3,783
*53714	Madison	(608)	190,766	170,616
*54220	Manitowoc	(414)	32,521	32,547
54143	Marinette	(715)	11,843	11,965
54449	Marshfield	(715)	19,291	18,290
54952	Menasha	(414)	14,711	14,728
*53051	Menomonee Falls	(414)	26,840	27,845
54751	Menomonie	(715)	13,547	12,769
53097	Mequon	(414)	18,885	16,193
54452	Merrill	(715)	9,860	9,578
53562	Middleton	(608)	13,785	11,851
*53201	Milwaukee	(414)	628,088	636,297
53716	Monona	(608)	8,637	8,809
53566	Monroe	(608)	10,241	10,027
53150	Muskego	(414)	16,813	15,277
*54956	Neenah	(414)	23,219	22,432
*53151	New Berlin	(414)	33,592	30,529
54961	New London	(414)	6,658	6,210
54017	New Richmond	(715)	5,106	4,306
53154	Oak Creek	(414)	19,513	16,932
53066	Oconomowoc	(414)	10,993	9,909
54650	Onalaska	(608)	11,414	9,249
*54901	Oshkosh	(414)	55,006	49,620
53072	Pewaukee	(414)	5,287	4,637
53818	Platteville	(608)	9,862	9,580
53158	Pleasant Prairie†	(414)	12,037	12,176
54467	Plover	(715)	8,176	5,310
53073	Plymouth	(414)	6,769	6,027
53901	Portage	(608)	8,640	7,896
53074	Port Washington	(414)	9,338	8,612
53821	Prairie du Chien	(608)	5,657	5,859
*53401	Racine	(414)	84,298	85,725
53959	Reedsburg	(608)	5,834	5,038
54501	Rhinelander	(715)	7,382	7,873
54868	Rice Lake	(715)	7,998	7,691
53581	Richland Center	(608)	5,018	4,997
54971	Ripon	(414)	7,241	7,111
54022	River Falls	(715)	10,610	9,019
53207	Saint Francis	(414)	9,245	10,095
54166	Shawano	(715)	7,598	7,013
*53081	Sheboygan	(414)	49,587	48,085
53085	Sheboygan Falls	(414)	5,823	5,253
53211	Shorewood	(414)	14,116	14,327
53172	South Milwaukee	(414)	20,958	21,069
54656	Sparta	(608)	7,788	6,934
54481	Stevens Point	(715)	23,006	22,970
53589	Stoughton	(608)	8,786	7,589
54235	Sturgeon Bay	(414)	9,176	8,847
53590	Sun Prairie	(608)	15,333	12,931
54880	Superior	(715)	27,134	29,571
53089	Sussex	(414)	5,039	3,482
54660	Tomah	(608)	7,570	7,204
54241	Two Rivers	(414)	13,030	13,354
53593	Verona	(608)	5,374	3,336
*53094	Watertown	(414)	19,142	18,113
*53186	Waukesha	(414)	56,958	50,365
53597	Waunakee	(608)	5,897	3,866
53963	Waupun	(414)	8,844	8,132
*54403	Wausau	(715)	37,060	32,426
53213	Wauwatosa	(414)	49,366	51,308
53214	West Allis	(414)	63,221	63,982
53095	West Bend	(414)	24,470	21,484
54476	Weston(u)	(715)	9,714	8,775
53217	Whitefish Bay	(414)	14,272	14,930
53190	Whitewater	(414)	12,636	11,520
*54494	Wisconsin Rapids	(715)	18,245	17,995

Wyoming (307)

ZIP	Place	1990	1980
*82601	Casper	46,765	51,016
*82001	Cheyenne	50,008	47,283
82414	Cody	7,897	6,599
82633	Douglas	5,076	6,030
*82930	Evanston	10,904	6,265
*82716	Gillette	17,545	12,134
82935	Green River	12,711	12,807
82520	Lander	7,023	7,867
*82070	Laramie	26,687	24,410
82435	Powell	5,292	5,310
82301	Rawlins	9,380	11,547
82501	Riverton	9,202	9,562
*82901	Rock Springs	19,050	19,458
82801	Sheridan	13,900	15,146
82240	Torrington	5,651	5,441
82401	Worland	5,742	6,391

Populations and Areas of Counties and States

Source: U.S. Bureau of the Census, Dept. of Commerce; World Almanac research

Population figures listed below are estimates for July 1, 1994.

Alabama

(67 counties, 50,750 sq mi land; pop. 4,218,792)

County	Pop.	County Seat or court house	Land area sq mi
Autauga	38,317	Prattville	596
Baldwin	115,685	Bay Minette	1,596
Barbour	25,544	Clayton	885
Bibb	17,603	Centreville	622
Blount	41,437	Oneonta	645
Bullock	11,222	Union Springs	625
Butler	21,931	Greenville	776
Calhoun	116,875	Anniston	608
Chambers	37,238	Lafayette	597
Cherokee	20,475	Centre	553
Chilton	34,197	Clanton	694
Choctaw	16,082	Butler	913
Clarke	28,131	Grove Hill	1,238
Clay	13,489	Ashland	605
Cleburne	13,238	Heflin	560
Coffee	42,005	Elba	679
Colbert	52,535	Tuscumbia	594
Conecuh	14,102	Evergreen	850
Coosa	11,510	Rockford	652
Covington	36,997	Andalusia	1,034
Crenshaw	13,550	Luverne	609
Cullman	71,578	Cullman	738
Dale	50,632	Ozark	561
Dallas	48,066	Selma	980
De Kalb	57,487	Fort Payne	777
Elmore	55,465	Wetumpka	621
Escambia	36,414	Brewton	947
Etowah	100,428	Gadsden	534
Fayette	18,063	Fayette	627
Franklin	29,023	Russellville	635
Geneva	24,568	Geneva	576
Greene	10,123	Eutaw	645
Hale	16,189	Greensboro	643
Henry	15,725	Abbeville	561
Houston	83,866	Dothan	580
Jackson	49,551	Scottsboro	1,078
Jefferson	656,637	Birmingham	1,112
Lamar	15,736	Vernon	604
Lauderdale	83,152	Florence	669
Lawrence	32,439	Moulton	693
Lee	91,936	Opelika	608
Limestone	58,099	Athens	568
Lowndes	12,844	Hayneville	718
Macon	24,163	Tuskegee	610
Madison	258,035	Huntsville	804
Marengo	23,524	Linden	977
Marion	30,230	Hamilton	741
Marshall	76,715	Guntersville	567
Mobile	396,476	Mobile	1,233
Monroe	24,432	Monroeville	1,025
Montgomery	218,245	Montgomery	789
Morgan	106,177	Decatur	599
Perry	12,600	Marion	719
Pickens	20,939	Carrollton	881
Pike	28,677	Troy	671
Randolph	20,312	Wedowee	581
Russell	51,598	Phenix City	641
Saint Clair	55,930	Ashville & Pell City	633
Shelby	118,242	Columbiana	794
Sumter	16,383	Livingston	904
Talladega	75,965	Talladega	739
Tallapoosa	39,602	Dadeville	718
Tuscaloosa	157,092	Tuscaloosa	1,325
Walker	69,179	Jasper	794
Washington	17,181	Chatom	1,080
Wilcox	13,783	Camden	888
Winston	23,128	Double Springs	614

Alaska

(27 divisions, 570,374 sq mi land; pop. 606,276)

Census Division	Pop.	Land area sq mi
Aleutian East Borough	2,264	6,985
Aleutians West Census Area	7,785	4,402
Anchorage Borough	253,647	1,732
Bethel Census Area	14,985	36,104
Bristol Bay Borough	1,416	531
Denali Borough	1,923	12,719
Dillingham Census Area	4,371	46,042
Fairbanks North Star Borough	85,417	7,404
Haines Borough	2,179	2,374
Juneau Borough	28,758	2,626
Kenai Peninsula Borough	45,215	16,056
Ketchikan Gateway Borough	14,361	1,242
Kodiak Island Borough	14,962	4,796
Lake and Peninsula Borough	1,750	....
Matanuska-Susitna Borough	48,684	24,502
Nome Census Area	8,800	23,871
North Slope Borough	6,794	90,955
Northwest Arctic Borough	6,562	....
Prince of Wales-Outer Ketchikan Census Area	6,941	7,660
Sitka Borough	8,780	2,938
Skagway-Hoonah-Angoon Census Area	3,790	8,012
Southeast Fairbanks Census Area	5,840	25,110
Valdez-Cordova Census Area	10,364	39,229
Wade Hampton Census Area	6,447	17,816
Wrangell-Petersburg Census Area	7,171	6,167
Yakutat Borough	710	4,865
Yukon-Koyukuk Census Area	6,360	145,286

Arizona

(15 counties, 113,642 sq mi land; pop. 4,075,052)

County	Pop.	County Seat or court house	Land area sq mi
Apache	65,516	Saint Johns	11,211
Cochise	106,913	Bisbee	6,218
Coconino	108,276	Flagstaff	18,608
Gila	44,620	Globe	4,752
Graham	28,876	Safford	4,630
Greenlee	9,034	Clifton	1,837
La Paz	14,157	Parker	4,430
Maricopa	2,346,610	Phoenix	9,127
Mohave	116,177	Kingman	13,285
Navajo	85,986	Holbrook	9,955
Pima	731,515	Tucson	9,187
Pinal	126,744	Florence	5,343
Santa Cruz	35,106	Nogales	1,238
Yavapai	127,843	Prescott	8,123
Yuma	127,679	Yuma	5,564

Arkansas

(75 counties, 52,075 sq mi land; pop. 2,452,671)

County	Pop.	County Seat or court house	Land area sq mi
Arkansas	21,153	DeWitt & Stuttgart	1,033
Ashley	24,698	Hamburg	939
Baxter	34,647	Mountain Home	586
Benton	115,265	Bentonville	876
Boone	30,735	Harrison	601
Bradley	11,641	Warren	654
Calhoun	5,831	Hampton	632
Carroll	21,322	Berryville & Eureka Sp.	642
Chicot	15,529	Lake Village	690
Clark	22,128	Arkadelphia	882
Clay	17,733	Corning & Piggott	641
Cleburne	21,338	Heber Springs	591
Cleveland	8,011	Rison	598
Columbia	25,711	Magnolia	766
Conway	19,433	Morrilton	566
Craighead	73,382	Jonesboro & Lake City	713
Crawford	46,493	Van Buren	604
Crittenden	49,937	Marion	636
Cross	19,071	Wynne	622
Dallas	9,483	Fordyce	668
Desha	15,917	Arkansas City	819
Drew	17,618	Monticello	835
Faulkner	69,330	Conway	664
Franklin	15,686	Charleston & Ozark	919
Fulton	10,427	Salem	620
Garland	79,778	Hot Springs	734
Grant	14,831	Sheridan	633
Greene	34,002	Paragould	579
Hempstead	22,117	Hope	741
Hot Spring	27,463	Malvern	622
Howard	13,675	Nashville	595
Independence	32,347	Batesville	771
Izard	12,348	Melbourne	584
Jackson	18,788	Newport	641
Jefferson	84,036	Pine Bluff	913
Johnson	19,859	Clarksville	682
Lafayette	9,283	Lewisville	545
Lawrence	17,447	Walnut Ridge	592
Lee	12,826	Marianna	619
Lincoln	14,031	Star City	572
Little River	13,520	Ashdown	564
Logan	20,950	Booneville & Paris	731
Lonoke	44,117	Lonoke	802
Madison	12,922	Huntsville	837
Marion	13,211	Yellville	640

County	Pop.	County Seat or court house	Land area sq mi
Miller	39,068	Texarkana	637
Mississippi	51,101	Blytheville & Osceola	919
Monroe	10,684	Clarendon	621
Montgomery	8,184	Mount Ida	800
Nevada	10,134	Prescott	620
Newton	7,904	Jasper	823
Ouachita	29,053	Camden	739
Perry	8,642	Perryville	560
Phillips	28,255	Helena	727
Pike	10,079	Murfreesboro	613
Poinsett	24,425	Harrisburg	763
Polk	18,434	Mena	862
Pope	50,203	Russellville	830
Prairie	9,226	Des Arc & De Valls Bluff	675
Pulaski	352,959	Little Rock	807
Randolph	17,286	Pocahontas	656
Saint Francis	28,105	Forrest City	642
Saline	71,142	Benton	730
Scott	10,550	Waldron	898
Searcy	7,603	Marshall	668
Sebastian	103,372	Fort Smith & Greenwood	546
Sevier	14,419	De Queen	581
Sharp	15,816	Ash Flat	606
Stone	10,590	Mountain View	609
Union	46,293	El Dorado	1,055
Van Buren	14,636	Clinton	724
Washington	127,199	Fayetteville	956
White	59,453	Searcy	1,042
Woodruff	9,276	Augusta	594
Yell	18,510	Danville & Dardanelle	948

California

(58 counties, 155,973 sq mi land; pop. 31,430,679)

County	Pop.	County Seat or court house	Land area sq mi
Alameda	1,319,490	Oakland	736
Alpine	1,192	Markleeville	738
Amador	32,798	Jackson	589
Butte	192,250	Oroville	1,646
Calaveras	37,145	San Andreas	1,021
Colusa	17,239	Colusa	1,152
Contra Costa	862,929	Martinez	730
Del Norte	26,867	Crescent City	1,007
El Dorado	144,839	Placerville	1,715
Fresno	729,731	Fresno	5,978
Glenn	25,787	Willows	1,319
Humboldt	121,747	Eureka	3,579
Imperial	137,051	El Centro	4,173
Inyo	18,434	Independence	10,223
Kern	609,326	Bakersfield	8,130
Kings	110,089	Hanford	1,392
Lake	55,765	Lakeport	1,262
Lassen	28,079	Susanville	4,553
Los Angeles	9,149,840	Los Angeles	4,070
Madera	104,923	Madera	2,145
Marin	235,032	San Rafael	523
Mariposa	15,636	Mariposa	1,456
Mendocino	81,894	Ukiah	3,512
Merced	196,847	Merced	1,944
Modoc	9,672	Alturas	4,064
Mono	10,393	Bridgeport	3,018
Monterey	351,921	Salinas	3,303
Napa	114,967	Napa	744
Nevada	85,831	Nevada City	960
Orange	2,543,124	Santa Ana	798
Placer	198,481	Auburn	1,416
Plumas	20,511	Quincy	2,573
Riverside	1,352,914	Riverside	7,214
Sacramento	1,098,143	Sacramento	971
San Benito	40,995	Hollister	1,388
San Bernardino	1,553,608	San Bernardino	20,064
San Diego	2,632,047	San Diego	4,212
San Francisco	734,690	San Francisco	46
San Joaquin	518,165	Stockton	1,415
San Luis Obispo	223,706	San Luis Obispo	3,308
San Mateo	676,232	Redwood City	447
Santa Barbara	380,488	Santa Barbara	2,748
Santa Clara	1,557,211	San Jose	1,293
Santa Cruz	234,968	Santa Cruz	446
Shasta	160,019	Redding	3,786
Sierra	3,352	Downieville	959
Siskiyou	43,928	Yreka	6,281
Solano	367,585	Fairfield	834
Sonoma	410,185	Santa Rosa	1,604
Stanislaus	406,759	Modesto	1,506
Sutter	73,170	Yuba City	602
Tehama	52,875	Red Bluff	2,953
Trinity	13,482	Weaverville	3,190
Tulare	343,252	Visalia	4,808
Tuolumne	51,932	Sonora	2,234
Ventura	702,728	Ventura	1,862
Yolo	146,419	Woodland	1,014
Yuba	62,014	Marysville	640

Colorado

(63 counties, 103,973 sq mi land; pop. 3,655,647)

County	Pop.	County Seat or court house	Land area sq mi
Adams	294,078	Brighton	1,235
Alamosa	14,137	Alamosa	719
Arapahoe	443,318	Littleton	800
Archuleta	6,523	Pagosa Springs	1,353
Baca	4,341	Springfield	2,554
Bent	5,115	Las Animas	1,517
Boulder	249,617	Boulder	742
Chaffee	13,794	Salida	1,008
Cheyenne	2,350	Cheyenne Wells	1,783
Clear Creek	8,520	Georgetown	396
Conejos	7,663	Conejos	1,284
Costilla	3,280	San Luis	1,227
Crowley	4,211	Ordway	790
Custer	2,481	Westcliffe	740
Delta	24,120	Delta	1,141
Denver	493,559	Denver	111
Dolores	1,519	Dove Creek	1,064
Douglas	88,078	Castle Rock	841
Eagle	27,371	Eagle	1,690
Elbert	13,016	Kiowa	1,851
El Paso	452,416	Colorado Springs	2,129
Fremont	35,769	Canon City	1,538
Garfield	34,034	Glenwood Springs	2,952
Gilpin	3,367	Central City	149
Grand	8,735	Hot Sulphur Springs	1,854
Gunnison	11,567	Gunnison	3,238
Hinsdale	598	Lake City	1,115
Huerfano	6,123	Walsenburg	1,584
Jackson	1,652	Walden	1,614
Jefferson	477,194	Golden	768
Kiowa	1,663	Eads	1,758
Kit Carson	7,234	Burlington	2,160
Lake	6,149	Leadville	379
La Plata	36,996	Durango	1,692
Larimer	212,346	Fort Collins	2,604
Las Animas	14,061	Trinidad	4,771
Lincoln	4,548	Hugo	2,586
Logan	17,478	Sterling	1,818
Mesa	103,630	Grand Junction	3,309
Mineral	610	Creede	877
Moffat	11,895	Craig	4,732
Montezuma	20,900	Cortez	2,038
Montrose	27,605	Montrose	2,240
Morgan	23,426	Fort Morgan	1,276
Otero	20,428	La Junta	1,247
Ouray	2,860	Ouray	542
Park	9,450	Fairplay	2,192
Phillips	4,231	Holyoke	688
Pitkin	13,561	Aspen	968
Prowers	13,496	Lamar	1,629
Pueblo	127,664	Pueblo	2,377
Rio Blanco	6,397	Meeker	3,222
Rio Grande	10,996	Del Norte	913
Routt	16,144	Steamboat Springs	2,367
Saguache	5,083	Saguache	3,167
San Juan	550	Silverton	388
San Miguel	4,796	Telluride	1,287
Sedgwick	2,651	Julesburg	540
Summit	16,278	Breckenridge	607
Teller	16,125	Cripple Creek	559
Washington	4,664	Akron	2,520
Weld	144,111	Greeley	3,990
Yuma	9,075	Wray	2,365

Connecticut

(8 counties, 4,845 sq mi land; pop. 3,275,251)

County	Pop.	County Seat or court house	Land area sq mi
Fairfield	829,786	Bridgeport	632
Hartford	839,612	Hartford	739
Litchfield	178,524	Litchfield	921
Middlesex	146,688	Middletown	373
New Haven	796,474	New Haven	610
New London	249,584	Norwich	669
Tolland	130,896	Rockville	412
Windham	103,687	Putnam	515

Delaware

(3 counties, 1,955 sq mi land; pop. 706,351)

County	Pop.	County Seat or court house	Land area sq mi
Kent	119,476	Dover	595
New Castle	462,147	Wilmington	396
Sussex	124,728	Georgetown	942

District of Columbia

(68 sq mi land; pop. 570,175)

Florida

(67 counties, 53,937 sq mi land; pop. 13,952,714)

County	Pop.	County Seat or court house	Land area sq mi
Alachua	193,053	Gainesville	901
Baker	19,776	Macclenny	585
Bay	139,917	Panama City	758
Bradford	23,245	Starke	293
Brevard	443,491	Titusville	995
Broward	1,382,983	Fort Lauderdale	1,211
Calhoun	11,623	Blountstown	568
Charlotte	126,491	Punta Gorda	690
Citrus	104,144	Inverness	629
Clay	120,368	Green Cove Springs	592
Collier	176,419	Naples	1,994
Columbia	46,860	Lake City	796
Dade	2,025,040	Miami	1,955
De Soto	24,791	Arcadia	636
Dixie	11,759	Cross City	701
Duval	703,562	Jacksonville	776
Escambia	271,793	Pensacola	660
Flagler	38,048	Bunnell	491
Franklin	9,657	Apalachicola	545
Gadsden	42,864	Quincy	518
Gilchrist	11,640	Trenton	354
Glades	7,556	Moore Haven	763
Gulf	12,117	Port Saint Joe	559
Hamilton	11,451	Jasper	517
Hardee	20,108	Wauchula	637
Hendry	28,375	La Belle	1,163
Hernando	116,593	Brooksville	477
Highlands	73,450	Sebring	1,029
Hillsborough	874,284	Tampa	1,053
Holmes	16,825	Bonifay	488
Indian River	95,678	Vero Beach	497
Jackson	42,850	Marianna	942
Jefferson	11,894	Monticello	609
Lafayette	5,814	Mayo	545
Lake	173,541	Tavares	954
Lee	367,433	Fort Myers	803
Leon	210,501	Tallahassee	676
Levy	28,860	Bronson	1,100
Liberty	6,030	Bristol	837
Madison	17,197	Madison	710
Manatee	225,528	Bradenton	747
Marion	221,843	Ocala	1,610
Martin	109,117	Stuart	555
Monroe	82,207	Key West	1,034
Nassau	49,601	Fernandina Beach	649
Okaloosa	160,960	Crestview	936
Okeechobee	30,578	Okeechobee	770
Orange	738,103	Orlando	910
Osceola	126,099	Kissimmee	1,350
Palm Beach	954,539	West Palm Beach	1,993
Pasco	298,458	New Port Richey	738
Pinellas	867,189	Clearwater	280
Polk	429,575	Bartow	1,823
Putnam	68,676	Palatka	733
Saint Johns	98,293	Saint Augustine	617
Saint Lucie	169,163	Fort Pierce	581
Santa Rosa	98,966	Milton	1,024
Sarasota	292,400	Sarasota	573
Seminole	323,733	Sanford	298
Sumter	33,340	Bushnell	561
Suwannee	29,568	Live Oak	690
Taylor	17,346	Perry	1,058
Union	10,691	Lake Butler	246
Volusia	402,442	De Land	1,113
Wakulla	16,601	Crawfordville	601
Walton	31,670	De Funiak Springs	1,066
Washington	18,099	Chipley	590

Georgia

(159 counties, 57,919 sq mi land; pop. 7,055,336)

County	Pop.	County Seat or court house	Land area sq mi
Appling	16,169	Baxley	510
Atkinson	6,535	Pearson	344
Bacon	10,379	Alma	286
Baker	3,692	Newton	347
Baldwin	41,310	Milledgeville	257
Banks	11,052	Homer	234
Barrow	34,414	Winder	163
Bartow	61,674	Cartersville	456
Ben Hill	17,149	Fitzgerald	254
Berrien	15,214	Nashville	456
Bibb	154,802	Macon	253
Bleckley	10,753	Cochran	219
Brantley	12,342	Nahunta	445
Brooks	15,582	Quitman	491
Bryan	19,942	Pembroke	441
Bulloch	47,835	Statesboro	678
Burke	21,602	Waynesboro	833
Butts	15,631	Jackson	187
Calhoun	4,940	Morgan	284
Camden	41,662	Woodbine	649
Candler	8,477	Metter	248
Carroll	76,563	Carrollton	501
Catoosa	46,478	Ringgold	162
Charlton	9,232	Folkston	780
Chatham	225,223	Savannah	443
Chattahoochee	15,645	Cusseta	250
Chattooga	22,764	Summerville	313
Cherokee	108,854	Canton	424
Clarke	90,257	Athens	122
Clay	3,455	Fort Gaines	196
Clayton	194,883	Jonesboro	148
Clinch	6,421	Homerville	821
Cobb	508,922	Marietta	343
Coffee	32,038	Douglas	602
Colquitt	37,530	Moultrie	557
Columbia	79,922	Appling	290
Cook	14,009	Adel	233
Coweta	67,799	Newnan	444
Crawford	9,826	Knoxville	328
Crisp	20,634	Cordele	275
Dade	13,911	Trenton	176
Dawson	11,340	Dawsonville	210
Decatur	26,223	Bainbridge	586
De Kalb	577,787	Decatur	270
Dodge	17,849	Eastman	504
Dooly	10,256	Vienna	397
Dougherty	98,008	Albany	330
Douglas	79,863	Douglasville	203
Early	12,084	Blakely	516
Echols	2,187	Statenville	421
Effingham	30,499	Springfield	482
Elbert	19,110	Elberton	367
Emanuel	20,941	Swainsboro	688
Evans	9,275	Claxton	186
Fannin	17,047	Blue Ridge	384
Fayette	75,928	Fayetteville	199
Floyd	83,284	Rome	519
Forsyth	56,827	Cumming	226
Franklin	17,451	Carnesville	264
Fulton	690,534	Atlanta	534
Gilmer	15,154	Ellijay	427
Glascock	2,346	Gibson	144
Glynn	65,020	Brunswick	412
Gordon	37,733	Calhoun	355
Grady	21,165	Cairo	459
Greene	12,646	Greensboro	389
Gwinnett	434,030	Lawrenceville	435
Habersham	29,556	Clarkesville	278
Hall	104,966	Gainesville	379
Hancock	9,077	Sparta	470
Haralson	23,014	Buchanan	283
Harris	19,797	Hamilton	464
Hart	20,430	Hartwell	230
Heard	9,299	Franklin	292
Henry	78,814	McDonough	321
Houston	98,337	Perry	380
Irwin	8,570	Ocilla	362
Jackson	33,077	Jefferson	342
Jasper	8,981	Monticello	371
Jeff Davis	12,272	Hazlehurst	335
Jefferson	17,672	Louisville	529
Jenkins	8,563	Millen	353
Johnson	8,396	Wrightsville	306
Jones	21,651	Gray	394
Lamar	13,646	Barnesville	186
Lanier	6,148	Lakeland	194
Laurens	42,263	Dublin	816
Lee	18,967	Leesburg	358
Liberty	59,042	Hinesville	517
Lincoln	7,916	Lincolnton	196
Long	7,374	Ludowici	402
Lowndes	82,179	Valdosta	507
Lumpkin	16,346	Dahlonega	287
McDuffie	21,217	Thomson	256
McIntosh	9,133	Darien	425
Macon	13,147	Oglethorpe	404
Madison	22,874	Danielsville	285
Marion	6,164	Buena Vista	366
Meriwether	23,001	Greenville	506
Miller	6,234	Colquitt	284
Mitchell	20,687	Camilla	512
Monroe	18,512	Forsyth	397
Montgomery	7,657	Mount Vernon	244
Morgan	13,785	Madison	349
Murray	29,004	Chatsworth	345
Muscogee	187,103	Columbus	218
Newton	48,375	Covington	277
Oconee	20,194	Watkinsville	186
Oglethorpe	10,637	Lexington	442
Paulding	55,718	Dallas	312
Peach	22,748	Fort Valley	152
Pickens	16,286	Jasper	232
Pierce	14,437	Blackshear	344
Pike	10,933	Zebulon	219
Polk	34,606	Cedartown	311
Pulaski	8,238	Hawkinsville	249

County	Pop.	County Seat or court house	Land area sq mi
Putnam	15,619	Eatonton	344
Quitman	2,377	Georgetown	146
Rabun	12,238	Clayton	370
Randolph	8,130	Cuthbert	431
Richmond	196,032	Augusta	326
Rockdale	62,032	Conyers	132
Schley	3,730	Ellaville	169
Screven	14,126	Sylvania	655
Seminole	9,258	Donalsonville	225
Spalding	57,016	Griffin	199
Stephens	24,735	Toccoa	177
Stewart	5,472	Lumpkin	452
Sumter	31,347	Americus	489
Talbot	6,743	Talbotton	395
Taliaferro	1,821	Crawfordville	196
Tattnall	18,167	Reidsville	484
Taylor	7,918	Butler	382
Telfair	11,579	McRae	444
Terrell	10,901	Dawson	337
Thomas	40,336	Thomasville	551
Tift	35,494	Tifton	268
Toombs	24,842	Lyons	371
Towns	7,350	Hiawassee	165
Treutlen	5,960	Soperton	202
Troup	57,611	La Grange	414
Turner	8,905	Ashburn	289
Twiggs	9,892	Jeffersonville	362
Union	13,606	Blairsville	320
Upson	26,762	Thomaston	326
Walker	59,911	La Fayette	446
Walton	44,703	Monroe	330
Ware	35,630	Waycross	907
Warren	6,108	Warrenton	286
Washington	19,815	Sandersville	684
Wayne	24,277	Jesup	647
Webster	2,255	Preston	210
Wheeler	4,817	Alamo	299
White	14,591	Cleveland	242
Whitfield	76,729	Dalton	291
Wilcox	7,084	Abbeville	382
Wilkes	10,562	Washington	470
Wilkinson	10,490	Irwinton	451
Worth	21,213	Sylvester	575

Hawaii

(5 counties, 6,423 sq mi land; pop. 1,178,564)

County	Pop.	County Seat or court house	Land area sq mi
Hawaii	135,499	Hilo	4,034
Honolulu	874,348	Honolulu	596
Kalawas[1]	97		14
Kauai	55,687	Lihue	620
Maui	112,933	Wailuku	1,175

(1) Administered by state government.

Idaho

(44 counties, 82,751 sq mi land; pop. 1,133,034)

County	Pop.	County Seat or court house	Land area sq mi
Ada	243,337	Boise	1,052
Adams	3,850	Council	1,362
Bannock	70,932	Pocatello	1,112
Bear Lake	6,426	Paris	990
Benewah	8,539	Saint Maries	784
Bingham	40,990	Blackfoot	2,096
Blaine	15,990	Hailey	2,634
Boise	4,498	Idaho City	1,901
Bonner	31,890	Sandpoint	1,726
Bonneville	79,213	Idaho Falls	1,840
Boundary	9,189	Bonners Ferry	1,268
Butte	3,044	Arco	2,236
Camas	793	Fairfield	1,071
Canyon	104,431	Caldwell	584
Caribou	7,182	Soda Springs	1,763
Cassia	20,811	Burley	2,560
Clark	814	Dubois	1,763
Clearwater	9,061	Orofino	2,460
Custer	3,984	Challis	4,927
Elmore	22,589	Mountain Home	3,071
Franklin	10,070	Preston	664
Fremont	11,525	Saint Anthony	1,852
Gem	13,467	Emmett	558
Gooding	12,678	Gooding	728
Idaho	14,588	Grangeville	8,497
Jefferson	18,427	Rigby	1,093
Jerome	16,597	Jerome	601
Kootenai	87,277	Coeur d'Alene	1,240
Latah	32,276	Moscow	1,077
Lemhi	7,425	Salmon	4,564
Lewis	3,838	Nezperce	478
Lincoln	3,570	Shoshone	1,205
Madison	23,743	Rexberg	468
Minidoka	20,699	Rupert	757

County	Pop.	County Seat or court house	Land area sq mi
Nez Perce	36,348	Lewiston	845
Oneida	3,657	Malad City	1,200
Owyhee	9,052	Murphy	7,643
Payette	18,956	Payette	405
Power	7,891	American Falls	1,403
Shoshone	13,871	Wallace	2,641
Teton	4,269	Driggs	448
Twin Falls	58,462	Twin Falls	1,944
Valley	7,636	Cascade	3,670
Washington	9,149	Weiser	1,454

Illinois

(102 counties, 55,593 sq mi land; pop. 11,751,774)

County	Pop.	County Seat or court house	Land area sq mi
Adams	67,714	Quincy	862
Alexander	10,309	Cairo	229
Bond	15,250	Greenville	378
Boone	34,785	Belvidere	283
Brown	6,019	Mount Sterling	306
Bureau	36,074	Princeton	866
Calhoun	5,016	Hardin	247
Carroll	16,787	Mount Carroll	456
Cass	13,358	Virginia	371
Champaign	167,485	Urbana	1,000
Christian	34,736	Taylorville	709
Clark	16,244	Marshall	505
Clay	14,408	Louisville	464
Clinton	34,776	Carlyle	434
Coles	52,129	Charleston	506
Cook	5,141,375	Chicago	954
Crawford	19,969	Robinson	443
Cumberland	11,030	Toledo	347
DeKalb	82,058	Sycamore	636
De Witt	16,906	Clinton	399
Douglas	19,646	Tuscola	420
Du Page	843,067	Wheaton	337
Edgar	19,616	Paris	628
Edwards	7,287	Albion	225
Effingham	32,675	Effingham	481
Fayette	20,960	Vandalia	703
Ford	13,920	Paxton	488
Franklin	40,623	Benton	434
Fulton	38,121	Lewiston	877
Gallatin	6,801	Shawneetown	328
Greene	15,357	Carrollton	543
Grundy	34,735	Morris	432
Hamilton	8,453	McLeansboro	435
Hancock	21,447	Carthage	797
Hardin	5,162	Elizabethtown	183
Henderson	8,244	Oquawka	376
Henry	51,520	Cambridge	826
Iroquois	31,428	Watseka	1,122
Jackson	61,741	Murphysboro	605
Jasper	10,638	Newton	495
Jefferson	37,261	Mount Vernon	573
Jersey	20,975	Jerseyville	376
Jo Daviess	22,108	Galena	606
Johnson	11,992	Vienna	345
Kane	348,590	Geneva	520
Kankakee	101,290	Kankakee	678
Kendall	44,091	Yorkville	320
Knox	55,855	Galesburg	728
Lake	559,392	Waukegan	457
La Salle	109,408	Ottawa	1,150
Lawrence	15,941	Lawrenceville	374
Lee	35,489	Dixon	728
Livingston	40,185	Pontiac	1,043
Logan	30,767	Lincoln	622
McDonough	35,581	Macomb	582
McHenry	215,945	Woodstock	610
McLean	137,577	Bloomington	1,173
Macon	116,588	Decatur	578
Macoupin	48,594	Carlinville	872
Madison	255,105	Edwardsville	733
Marion	41,783	Salem	579
Marshall	12,761	Lacon	391
Mason	16,790	Havana	541
Massac	15,189	Metropolis	245
Menard	11,925	Petersburg	312
Mercer	17,452	Aledo	556
Monroe	24,165	Waterloo	382
Montgomery	30,721	Hillsboro	705
Morgan	36,199	Jacksonville	561
Moultrie	14,083	Sullivan	326
Ogle	48,802	Oregon	758
Peoria	183,159	Peoria	623
Perry	21,268	Pinckneyville	439
Piatt	15,967	Monticello	437
Pike	17,162	Pittsfield	828
Pope	4,576	Golconda	381
Pulaski	7,404	Mound City	204
Putnam	5,783	Hennepin	160
Randolph	34,443	Chester	594
Richland	16,846	Olney	364
Rock Island	150,305	Rock Island	424

County	Pop.	County Seat or court house	Land area sq mi
Saint Clair	265,440	Belleville	673
Saline	26,698	Harrisburg	383
Sangamon	183,908	Springfield	879
Schuyler	7,630	Rushville	434
Scott	5,643	Winchester	251
Shelby	22,478	Shelbyville	752
Stark	6,305	Toulon	291
Stephenson	49,095	Freeport	568
Tazewell	126,417	Pekin	652
Union	17,990	Jonesboro	416
Vermilion	87,327	Danville	899
Wabash	12,898	Mount Carmel	222
Warren	18,934	Monmouth	541
Washington	15,055	Nashville	564
Wayne	17,168	Fairfield	715
White	15,914	Carmi	502
Whiteside	60,298	Morrison	687
Will	398,706	Joliet	847
Williamson	59,407	Marion	429
Winnebago	263,122	Rockford	519
Woodford	33,955	Eureka	528

Indiana

(92 counties, 35,870 sq mi land; pop. 5,752,073)

County	Pop.	County Seat or court house	Land area sq mi
Adams	32,123	Decatur	339
Allen	307,685	Fort Wayne	657
Bartholomew	66,965	Columbus	407
Benton	9,594	Fowler	406
Blackford	13,991	Hartford City	165
Boone	40,911	Lebanon	423
Brown	14,809	Nashville	312
Carroll	19,493	Delphi	372
Cass	38,520	Logansport	413
Clark	90,868	Jeffersonville	375
Clay	25,761	Brazil	358
Clinton	32,307	Frankfort	405
Crawford	10,309	English	306
Daviess	28,252	Washington	431
Dearborn	43,255	Lawrenceburg	305
Decatur	24,775	Greensburg	373
DeKalb	37,508	Auburn	363
Delaware	119,243	Muncie	393
Dubois	38,179	Jasper	430
Elkhart	163,992	Goshen	464
Fayette	26,444	Connersville	215
Floyd	69,094	New Albany	148
Fountain	17,996	Covington	396
Franklin	20,280	Brookville	386
Fulton	19,652	Rochester	369
Gibson	32,138	Princeton	489
Grant	73,779	Marion	414
Greene	32,238	Bloomfield	542
Hamilton	134,257	Noblesville	398
Hancock	49,427	Greenfield	306
Harrison	31,891	Corydon	485
Hendricks	84,105	Danville	408
Henry	48,968	New Castle	393
Howard	82,995	Kokomo	293
Huntington	36,408	Huntington	383
Jackson	39,530	Brownstown	509
Jasper	27,375	Rensselaer	560
Jay	21,785	Portland	384
Jefferson	30,536	Madison	361
Jennings	25,512	Vernon	377
Johnson	99,022	Franklin	320
Knox	40,069	Vincennes	516
Kosciusko	67,956	Warsaw	538
Lagrange	31,225	Lagrange	380
Lake	481,635	Crown Point	497
La Porte	109,626	La Porte	598
Lawrence	44,364	Bedford	449
Madison	132,766	Anderson	452
Marion	818,014	Indianapolis	396
Marshall	44,206	Plymouth	444
Martin	10,582	Shoals	336
Miami	34,498	Peru	376
Monroe	113,830	Bloomington	394
Montgomery	35,698	Crawfordsville	505
Morgan	60,999	Martinsville	407
Newton	14,130	Kentland	402
Noble	39,971	Albion	411
Ohio	5,452	Rising Sun	87
Orange	18,848	Paoli	400
Owen	19,223	Spencer	385
Parke	15,867	Rockville	445
Perry	18,997	Cannelton	381
Pike	12,631	Petersburg	336
Porter	138,243	Valparaiso	418
Posey	26,344	Mount Vernon	409
Pulaski	13,003	Winamac	434
Putnam	32,519	Greencastle	480
Randolph	27,143	Winchester	453
Ripley	26,418	Versailles	446
Rush	18,488	Rushville	408
Saint Joseph	255,431	South Bend	457
Scott	22,138	Scottsburg	190
Shelby	42,183	Shelbyville	413
Spencer	20,144	Rockport	399
Starke	22,334	Knox	309
Steuben	29,272	Angola	309
Sullivan	19,297	Sullivan	447
Switzerland	8,136	Vevay	221
Tippecanoe	134,425	Lafayette	500
Tipton	16,347	Tipton	260
Union	7,278	Liberty	162
Vanderburgh	167,445	Evansville	235
Vermillion	16,753	Newport	257
Vigo	107,140	Terre Haute	403
Wabash	34,822	Wabash	413
Warren	8,200	Williamsport	365
Warrick	48,625	Boonville	384
Washington	25,453	Salem	515
Wayne	72,398	Richmond	404
Wells	26,293	Bluffton	370
White	24,202	Monticello	505
Whitley	29,040	Columbia City	336

Iowa

(99 counties, 55,875 sq mi land; pop. 2,829,252)

County	Pop.	County Seat or court house	Land area sq mi
Adair	8,331	Greenfield	570
Adams	4,553	Corning	426
Allamakee	13,941	Waukon	660
Appanoose	13,744	Centerville	515
Audubon	6,957	Audubon	444
Benton	23,683	Vinton	718
Black Hawk	123,701	Waterloo	573
Boone	25,279	Boone	574
Bremer	23,119	Waverly	439
Buchanan	21,303	Independence	573
Buena Vista	20,078	Storm Lake	580
Butler	15,719	Allison	582
Calhoun	11,574	Rockwell City	573
Carroll	21,465	Carroll	570
Cass	15,112	Atlantic	565
Cedar	17,551	Tipton	582
Cerro Gordo	46,560	Mason City	575
Cherokee	13,830	Cherokee	577
Chickasaw	13,382	New Hampton	505
Clarke	8,173	Osceola	431
Clay	17,634	Spencer	573
Clayton	18,846	Elkader	795
Clinton	50,940	Clinton	710
Crawford	16,492	Denison	714
Dallas	32,083	Adel	591
Davis	8,465	Bloomfield	505
Decatur	8,075	Leon	535
Delaware	18,331	Manchester	579
Des Moines	42,866	Burlington	429
Dickinson	15,474	Spirit Lake	404
Dubuque	88,214	Dubuque	616
Emmet	11,268	Estherville	402
Fayette	21,907	West Union	731
Floyd	16,699	Charles City	501
Franklin	11,078	Hampton	583
Fremont	8,213	Sidney	517
Greene	10,045	Jefferson	572
Grundy	12,127	Grundy Center	501
Guthrie	11,285	Guthrie Center	594
Hamilton	16,027	Webster City	577
Hancock	12,138	Garner	573
Hardin	18,592	Eldora	569
Harrison	14,939	Logan	701
Henry	19,703	Mount Pleasant	436
Howard	9,881	Cresco	473
Humboldt	10,374	Dakota City	436
Ida	8,290	Ida Grove	432
Iowa	14,915	Marengo	588
Jackson	20,263	Maquoketa	650
Jasper	35,095	Newton	732
Jefferson	16,856	Fairfield	440
Johnson	100,001	Iowa City	623
Jones	19,950	Anamosa	576
Keokuk	11,515	Sigourney	580
Kossuth	18,179	Algona	976
Lee	39,016	Fort Madison and Keokuk	540
Linn	176,812	Cedar Rapids	724
Louisa	11,689	Wapello	417
Lucas	8,985	Chariton	435
Lyon	11,893	Rock Rapids	588
Madison	13,034	Winterset	563
Mahaska	21,760	Oskaloosa	572
Marion	30,663	Knoxville	575
Marshall	38,147	Marshalltown	573

County	Pop.	County Seat or court house	Land area sq mi
Mills	13,644	Glenwood	441
Mitchell	11,036	Osage	470
Monona	10,065	Onawa	699
Monroe	8,145	Albia	434
Montgomery	12,023	Red Oak	424
Muscatine	41,237	Muscatine	449
O'Brien	15,374	Primghar	574
Osceola	7,141	Sibley	399
Page	16,739	Clarinda	535
Palo Alto	10,421	Emmetsburg	568
Plymouth	24,279	Le Mars	864
Pocahontas	9,129	Pocahontas	578
Polk	345,890	Des Moines	592
Pottawattamie	83,387	Council Bluffs	959
Poweshiek	19,018	Montezuma	586
Ringgold	5,413	Mount Ayr	536
Sac	12,141	Sac City	578
Scott	155,948	Davenport	469
Shelby	13,116	Harlan	591
Sioux	31,027	Orange City	769
Story	74,835	Nevada	574
Tama	17,784	Toledo	722
Taylor	7,118	Bedford	537
Union	12,468	Creston	427
Van Buren	7,717	Keosauqua	489
Wapello	35,917	Ottumwa	436
Warren	38,505	Indianola	573
Washington	20,279	Washington	571
Wayne	6,939	Corydon	527
Webster	39,497	Fort Dodge	718
Winnebago	11,936	Forest City	402
Winneshiek	21,008	Decorah	690
Woodbury	101,187	Sioux City	877
Worth	7,874	Northwood	402
Wright	14,201	Clarion	582

Kansas

(105 counties, 81,823 sq mi land; pop. 2,554,047)

County	Pop.	County Seat or court house	Land area sq mi
Allen	14,794	Iola	505
Anderson	7,905	Garnett	584
Atchison	16,754	Atchison	431
Barber	5,609	Medicine Lodge	1,136
Barton	28,896	Great Bend	895
Bourbon	14,862	Fort Scott	638
Brown	11,031	Hiawatha	572
Butler	55,735	El Dorado	1,443
Chase	2,917	Cottonwood Falls	777
Chautauqua	4,372	Sedan	644
Cherokee	22,054	Columbus	590
Cheyenne	3,266	Saint Francis	1,021
Clark	2,409	Ashland	975
Clay	9,266	Clay Center	632
Cloud	10,516	Concordia	718
Coffey	8,651	Burlington	615
Comanche	2,151	Coldwater	789
Cowley	37,240	Winfield	1,128
Crawford	36,332	Girard	595
Decatur	3,586	Oberlin	894
Dickinson	19,726	Abilene	852
Doniphan	7,625	Troy	388
Douglas	88,031	Lawrence	461
Edwards	3,557	Kinsley	620
Elk	3,332	Howard	650
Ellis	26,015	Hays	900
Ellsworth	6,459	Ellsworth	717
Finney	34,726	Garden City	1,302
Ford	28,477	Dodge City	1,099
Franklin	23,207	Ottawa	577
Geary	31,099	Junction City	377
Gove	3,162	Gove	1,072
Graham	3,390	Hill City	898
Grant	7,676	Ulysses	575
Gray	5,380	Cimarron	868
Greeley	1,803	Tribune	778
Greenwood	7,995	Eureka	1,135
Hamilton	2,311	Syracuse	998
Harper	6,694	Anthony	802
Harvey	31,727	Newton	540
Haskell	3,993	Sublette	578
Hodgeman	2,242	Jetmore	860
Jackson	11,634	Holton	658
Jefferson	16,822	Oskaloosa	535
Jewell	3,943	Mankato	910
Johnson	392,975	Olathe	478
Kearny	4,139	Lakin	868
Kingman	8,469	Kingman	865
Kiowa	3,604	Greensburg	723
Labette	23,148	Oswego	653
Lane	2,322	Dighton	717
Leavenworth	68,852	Leavenworth	463
Lincoln	3,454	Lincoln	720
Linn	8,570	Mound City	601
Logan	3,145	Oakley	1,073
Lyon	34,703	Emporia	844
McPherson	28,101	McPherson	900

County	Pop.	County Seat or court house	Land area sq mi
Marion	13,077	Marion	944
Marshall	11,270	Marysville	878
Meade	4,289	Meade	979
Miami	24,723	Paola	590
Mitchell	7,080	Beloit	717
Montgomery	37,706	Independence	646
Morris	6,321	Council Grove	693
Morton	3,399	Elkhart	731
Nemaha	10,443	Seneca	719
Neosho	16,967	Erie	576
Ness	3,840	Ness City	1,074
Norton	5,744	Norton	873
Osage	16,325	Lyndon	695
Osborne	4,695	Osborne	882
Ottawa	5,634	Minneapolis	721
Pawnee	7,721	Larned	755
Phillips	6,362	Phillipsburg	887
Pottawatomie	17,425	Westmoreland	828
Pratt	9,605	Pratt	735
Rawlins	3,299	Atwood	1,069
Reno	62,551	Hutchinson	1,259
Republic	6,240	Belleville	719
Rice	10,320	Lyons	728
Riley	67,778	Manhattan	593
Rooks	5,936	Stockton	888
Rush	3,566	LaCrosse	718
Russell	7,668	Russell	869
Saline	51,433	Salina	721
Scott	5,157	Scott City	718
Sedgwick	419,367	Wichita	1,007
Seward	19,123	Liberal	640
Shawnee	165,121	Topeka	549
Sheridan	2,825	Hoxie	896
Sherman	6,886	Goodland	1,057
Smith	4,806	Smith Center	897
Stafford	5,231	Saint John	788
Stanton	2,299	Johnson	681
Stevens	5,177	Hugoton	727
Sumner	26,436	Wellington	1,183
Thomas	8,341	Colby	1,075
Trego	3,470	WaKeeney	890
Wabaunsee	6,638	Alma	797
Wallace	1,816	Sharon Springs	914
Washington	6,810	Washington	898
Wichita	2,886	Leoti	719
Wilson	10,292	Fredonia	575
Woodson	4,020	Yates Center	498
Wyandotte	155,075	Kansas City	149

Kentucky

(120 counties, 39,732 sq mi land; pop. 3,826,794)

County	Pop.	County Seat or court house	Land area sq mi
Adair	16,029	Columbia	407
Allen	15,376	Scottsville	346
Anderson	16,671	Lawrenceburg	203
Ballard	8,080	Wickliffe	251
Barren	35,144	Glasgow	491
Bath	10,070	Owingsville	279
Bell	30,766	Pineville	361
Boone	67,491	Burlington	246
Bourbon	19,195	Paris	291
Boyd	50,563	Catlettsburg	160
Boyle	26,476	Danville	182
Bracken	8,149	Brooksville	203
Breathitt	15,396	Jackson	495
Breckinridge	16,525	Hardinsburg	572
Bullitt	54,775	Shepherdsville	299
Butler	11,556	Morgantown	428
Caldwell	13,140	Princeton	347
Calloway	32,193	Murray	386
Campbell	86,258	Newport	152
Carlisle	5,283	Bardwell	193
Carroll	9,539	Carrollton	130
Carter	25,650	Grayson	411
Casey	14,418	Liberty	446
Christian	66,846	Hopkinsville	721
Clark	30,495	Winchester	254
Clay	22,777	Manchester	471
Clinton	9,255	Albany	198
Crittenden	9,407	Marion	362
Cumberland	6,824	Burkesville	306
Daviess	90,138	Owensboro	462
Edmonson	10,472	Brownsville	303
Elliott	6,561	Sandy Hook	234
Estill	15,460	Irvine	254
Fayette	237,611	Lexington	286
Fleming	12,860	Flemingsburg	351
Floyd	44,090	Prestonsburg	394
Franklin	45,605	Frankfort	211
Fulton	7,388	Hickman	209
Gallatin	6,044	Warsaw	99
Garrard	12,679	Lancaster	231
Grant	18,013	Williamstown	260

County	Pop.	County Seat or court house	Land area sq mi
Graves	34,778	Mayfield	556
Grayson	22,538	Leitchfield	504
Green	10,360	Greensburg	289
Greenup	37,110	Greenup	346
Hancock	8,121	Hawesville	189
Hardin	90,389	Elizabethtown	628
Harlan	36,288	Harlan	467
Harrison	16,829	Cynthiana	310
Hart	16,044	Munfordville	416
Henderson	44,210	Henderson	440
Henry	13,870	New Castle	289
Hickman	5,379	Clinton	245
Hopkins	46,307	Madisonville	551
Jackson	12,520	McKee	346
Jefferson	672,311	Louisville	385
Jessamine	33,557	Nicholasville	173
Johnson	23,860	Paintsville	262
Kenton	144,848	Covington	163
Knott	18,337	Hindman	352
Knox	31,137	Barbourville	388
Larue	12,419	Hodgenville	263
Laurel	47,299	London	436
Lawrence	15,072	Louisa	419
Lee	7,749	Beattyville	210
Leslie	13,806	Hyden	404
Letcher	26,991	Whitesburg	339
Lewis	13,254	Vanceburg	485
Lincoln	21,245	Stanford	337
Livingston	9,255	Smithland	316
Logan	25,436	Russellville	556
Lyon	7,570	Eddyville	216
McCracken	64,630	Paducah	251
McCreary	16,239	Whitley City	428
McLean	9,674	Calhoun	254
Madison	61,961	Richmond	441
Magoffin	13,649	Salyersville	310
Marion	16,604	Lebanon	347
Marshall	28,740	Benton	305
Martin	12,930	Inez	231
Mason	17,212	Maysville	241
Meade	26,473	Brandenburg	309
Menifee	5,267	Frenchburg	204
Mercer	19,794	Harrodsburg	251
Metcalfe	9,218	Edmonton	291
Monroe	11,662	Tompkinsville	331
Montgomery	20,304	Mount Sterling	199
Morgan	13,313	West Liberty	381
Muhlenberg	31,064	Greenville	475
Nelson	32,638	Bardstown	423
Nicholas	6,902	Carlisle	197
Ohio	21,492	Hartford	594
Oldham	39,774	La Grange	189
Owen	9,574	Owenton	352
Owsley	5,413	Booneville	198
Pendleton	13,188	Falmouth	280
Perry	31,139	Hazard	342
Pike	73,475	Pikeville	788
Powell	12,153	Stanton	180
Pulaski	53,392	Somerset	662
Robertson	2,200	Mount Olivet	100
Rockcastle	15,312	Mount Vernon	318
Rowan	21,458	Morehead	281
Russell	15,785	Jamestown	254
Scott	26,790	Georgetown	285
Shelby	27,045	Shelbyville	384
Simpson	15,850	Franklin	236
Spencer	7,635	Taylorsville	186
Taylor	22,412	Campbellsville	270
Todd	11,258	Elkton	376
Trigg	11,195	Cadiz	443
Trimble	6,716	Bedford	149
Union	16,469	Morganfield	345
Warren	83,048	Bowling Green	545
Washington	10,569	Springfield	301
Wayne	18,218	Monticello	459
Webster	13,545	Dixon	335
Whitley	34,926	Williamsburg	440
Wolfe	7,099	Campton	223
Woodford	21,233	Versailles	191

Louisiana

(64 parishes, 43,566 sq mi land; pop. 4,315,085)

County	Pop.	County Seat or court house	Land area sq mi
Acadia	56,855	Crowley	657
Allen	23,322	Oberlin	765
Ascension	63,885	Donaldsonville	296
Assumption	22,678	Napoleonville	342
Avoyelles	39,840	Marksville	846
Beauregard	31,400	De Ridder	1,163
Bienville	16,086	Arcadia	816
Bossier	89,369	Benton	845
Caddo	246,787	Shreveport	894
Calcasieu	173,339	Lake Charles	1,082
Caldwell	10,334	Columbia	541
Cameron	8,912	Cameron	1,417
Catahoula	11,260	Harrisonburg	732
Claiborne	17,362	Homer	765
Concordia	20,845	Vidalia	717
De Soto	25,037	Mansfield	880
East Baton Rouge	396,349	Baton Rouge	458
East Carroll	9,468	Lake Providence	426
East Feliciana	20,412	Clinton	455
Evangeline	33,967	Ville Platte	667
Franklin	22,434	Winnsboro	635
Grant	17,775	Colfax	653
Iberia	70,783	New Iberia	589
Iberville	31,018	Plaquemine	638
Jackson	15,683	Jonesboro	579
Jefferson	456,591	Gretna	348
Jefferson Davis	31,380	Jennings	655
Lafayette	176,592	Lafayette	270
Lafourche	86,912	Thibodaux	1,141
La Salle	13,795	Jena	638
Lincoln	43,227	Ruston	472
Livingston	77,863	Livingston	661
Madison	12,472	Tallulah	631
Morehouse	32,062	Bastrop	807
Natchitoches	37,253	Natchitoches	1,264
Orleans	484,194	New Orleans	199
Ouachita	146,449	Monroe	627
Plaquemines	25,454	Pointe a la Hache	1,035
Pointe Coupee	23,016	New Roads	566
Rapides	126,484	Alexandria	1,341
Red River	9,323	Coushatta	394
Richland	20,571	Rayville	563
Sabine	23,473	Many	855
Saint Bernard	66,984	Chalmette	486
Saint Charles	45,749	Hahnville	286
Saint Helena	9,868	Greensburg	409
Saint James	20,999	Convent	248
Saint John The Baptist	41,742	Edgard	213
Saint Landry	82,156	Opelousas	936
Saint Martin	45,741	Saint Martinville	749
Saint Mary	57,185	Franklin	613
Saint Tammany	167,242	Covington	873
Tangipahoa	91,260	Amite	783
Tensas	6,909	Saint Joseph	623
Terrebonne	100,359	Houma	1,367
Union	21,475	Farmerville	884
Vermilion	50,794	Abbeville	1,205
Vernon	57,008	Leesville	1,332
Washington	42,899	Franklinton	676
Webster	42,228	Minden	602
West Baton Rouge	20,057	Port Allen	194
West Carroll	11,999	Oak Grove	360
West Feliciana	13,132	Saint Francisville	406
Winn	16,988	Winnfield	953

Maine

(16 counties, 30,865 sq mi land; pop. 1,240,209)

County	Pop.	County Seat or court house	Land area sq mi
Androscoggin	103,878	Auburn	477
Aroostook	81,917	Houlton	6,721
Cumberland	247,990	Portland	876
Franklin	29,644	Farmington	1,699
Hancock	48,836	Ellsworth	1,537
Kennebec	117,258	Augusta	876
Knox	37,074	Rockland	370
Lincoln	31,023	Wiscasset	458
Oxford	53,030	South Paris	2,053
Penobscot	146,495	Bangor	3,430
Piscataquis	18,548	Dover-Foxcroft	3,986
Sagadahoc	33,868	Bath	257
Somerset	51,216	Skowhegan	3,930
Waldo	35,002	Belfast	730
Washington	35,868	Machias	2,586
York	168,562	Alfred	1,008

Maryland

(23 counties, 1 ind. city, 9,775 sq mi land; pop. 5,006,265)

County	Pop.	County Seat or court house	Land area sq mi
Allegany	73,866	Cumberland	421
Anne Arundel	456,171	Annapolis	418
Baltimore	711,783	Towson	598
Calvert	62,179	Prince Frederick	213
Caroline	28,720	Denton	321
Carroll	136,443	Westminster	452
Cecil	77,037	Elkton	360
Charles	109,295	La Plata	452
Dorchester	30,424	Cambridge	593
Frederick	171,274	Frederick	663
Garrett	29,372	Oakland	657
Harford	201,985	Bel Air	448

County	Pop.	County Seat or court house	Land area sq mi
Howard	212,976	Ellicott City	251
Kent	18,687	Chestertown	278
Montgomery	802,721	Rockville	495
Prince George's	764,053	Upper Marlboro	487
Queen Anne's	36,070	Centreville	372
Saint Mary's	80,323	Leonardtown	373
Somerset	23,727	Princess Anne	338
Talbot	32,015	Easton	259
Washington	126,599	Hagerstown	455
Wicomico	78,473	Salisbury	379
Worcester	39,015	Snow Hill	475
Independent City			
Baltimore	703,057		80

Massachusetts

(14 counties, 7,838 sq mi land; pop. 6,041,123)

County	Pop.	County Seat or court house	Land area sq mi
Barnstable	196,176	Barnstable	400
Berkshire	136,212	Pittsfield	929
Bristol	510,403	Taunton	557
Dukes	12,419	Edgartown	102
Essex	678,155	Salem	495
Franklin	70,712	Greenfield	702
Hampden	446,461	Springfield	618
Hampshire	149,226	Northampton	528
Middlesex	1,403,281	East Cambridge	822
Nantucket	6,794	Nantucket	47
Norfolk	631,338	Dedham	400
Plymouth	449,623	Plymouth	655
Suffolk	633,263	Boston	57
Worcester	717,060	Worcester	1,513

Michigan

(83 counties, 56,809 sq mi land; pop. 9,496,147)

County	Pop.	County Seat or court house	Land area sq mi
Alcona	10,389	Harrisville	679
Alger	9,819	Munising	912
Allegan	96,085	Allegan	832
Alpena	30,814	Alpena	567
Antrim	19,528	Bellaire	480
Arenac	15,953	Standish	367
Baraga	8,061	L'Anse	901
Barry	52,231	Hastings	560
Bay	111,772	Bay City	447
Benzie	13,264	Beulah	322
Berrien	161,734	Saint Joseph	576
Branch	41,990	Coldwater	508
Calhoun	139,991	Marshall	712
Cass	48,920	Cassopolis	496
Charlevoix	22,833	Charlevoix	421
Cheboygan	22,471	Cheboygan	720
Chippewa	36,591	Sault Sainte Marie	1,590
Clare	27,589	Harrison	570
Clinton	60,897	Saint Johns	573
Crawford	13,387	Grayling	559
Delta	38,605	Escanaba	1,173
Dickinson	27,058	Iron Mountain	770
Eaton	96,805	Charlotte	579
Emmet	27,034	Petoskey	468
Genesee	433,300	Flint	642
Gladwin	23,937	Gladwin	505
Gogebic	18,016	Bessemer	1,105
Grand Traverse	69,582	Traverse City	466
Gratiot	39,785	Ithaca	570
Hillsdale	44,829	Hillsdale	603
Houghton	36,375	Houghton	1,014
Huron	35,214	Bad Axe	830
Ingham	278,423	Mason	560
Ionia	59,193	Ionia	577
Iosco	24,034	Tawas City	546
Iron	13,131	Crystal Falls	1,163
Isabella	57,053	Mount Pleasant	577
Jackson	153,287	Jackson	705
Kalamazoo	228,796	Kalamazoo	562
Kalkaska	14,536	Kalkaska	563
Kent	520,123	Grand Rapids	862
Keweenaw	1,880	Eagle River	543
Lake	9,631	Baldwin	568
Lapeer	81,240	Lapeer	658
Leelanau	18,122	Leland	341
Lenawee	95,667	Adrian	753
Livingston	129,080	Howell	574
Luce	5,571	Newberry	904
Mackinac	10,910	Saint Ignace	1,025
Macomb	728,563	Mount Clemens	482
Manistee	22,633	Manistee	543
Marquette	70,683	Marquette	1,821
Mason	27,200	Ludington	494
Mecosta	38,620	Big Rapids	560

County	Pop.	County Seat or court house	Land area sq mi
Menominee	24,532	Menominee	1,045
Midland	79,245	Midland	525
Missaukee	13,347	Lake City	565
Monroe	137,716	Monroe	557
Montcalm	56,886	Stanton	713
Montmorency	9,513	Atlanta	550
Muskegon	163,436	Muskegon	507
Newaygo	42,738	White Cloud	847
Oakland	1,141,997	Pontiac	875
Oceana	23,493	Hart	541
Ogemaw	20,250	West Branch	570
Ontonagon	8,673	Ontonagon	1,311
Osceola	21,375	Reed City	569
Oscoda	8,494	Mio	568
Otsego	20,101	Gaylord	516
Ottawa	205,333	Grand Haven	567
Presque Isle	14,028	Rogers City	656
Roscommon	21,881	Roscommon	528
Saginaw	211,287	Saginaw	815
Saint Clair	152,351	Port Huron	734
Saint Joseph	59,999	Centreville	503
Sanilac	41,567	Sandusky	964
Schoolcraft	8,596	Manistique	1,173
Shiawassee	71,644	Corunna	540
Tuscola	57,017	Caro	812
Van Buren	73,848	Paw Paw	611
Washtenaw	290,542	Ann Arbor	710
Wayne	2,064,908	Detroit	615
Wexford	28,115	Cadillac	566

Minnesota

(87 counties, 79,617 sq mi land; pop. 4,567,267)

County	Pop.	County Seat or court house	Land area sq mi
Aitkin	13,193	Aitkin	1,834
Anoka	270,286	Anoka	430
Becker	28,896	Detroit Lakes	1,312
Beltrami	37,394	Bemidji	2,507
Benton	32,502	Foley	408
Big Stone	6,009	Ortonville	497
Blue Earth	54,021	Mankato	749
Brown	27,049	New Ulm	610
Carlton	30,303	Carlton	864
Carver	56,538	Chaska	351
Cass	23,874	Walker	2,033
Chippewa	13,091	Montevideo	584
Chisago	35,421	Center City	417
Clay	51,872	Moorhead	1,049
Clearwater	8,320	Bagley	999
Cook	4,374	Grand Marais	1,412
Cottonwood	12,504	Windom	640
Crow Wing	48,871	Brainerd	1,008
Dakota	308,562	Hastings	574
Dodge	16,538	Mantorville	439
Douglas	29,999	Alexandria	643
Faribault	16,552	Blue Earth	714
Fillmore	20,755	Preston	862
Freeborn	32,403	Albert Lea	705
Goodhue	42,000	Red Wing	763
Grant	6,131	Elbow Lake	547
Hennepin	1,050,454	Minneapolis	541
Houston	19,115	Caledonia	564
Hubbard	15,924	Park Rapids	936
Isanti	27,844	Cambridge	440
Itasca	42,762	Grand Rapids	2,661
Jackson	11,772	Jackson	699
Kanabec	13,315	Mora	527
Kandiyohi	40,555	Willmar	784
Kittson	5,464	Hallock	1,104
Koochiching	16,067	International Falls	3,108
Lac qui Parle	8,512	Madison	772
Lake	10,534	Two Harbors	2,053
Lake of the Woods	4,367	Baudette	1,296
Le Sueur	24,108	Le Center	446
Lincoln	6,805	Ivanhoe	538
Lyon	24,963	Marshall	714
McLeod	33,103	Glencoe	489
Mahnomen	5,120	Mahnomen	559
Marshall	10,625	Warren	1,760
Martin	22,512	Fairmont	706
Meeker	21,164	Litchfield	624
Mille Lacs	19,673	Milaca	578
Morrison	30,054	Little Falls	1,124
Mower	37,488	Austin	711
Murray	9,581	Slayton	702
Nicollet	29,420	Saint Peter	440
Nobles	20,347	Worthington	714
Norman	7,750	Ada	877
Olmsted	112,908	Rochester	655
Otter Tail	52,572	Fergus Falls	1,973
Pennington	13,389	Thief River Falls	618
Pine	22,749	Pine City	1,421

County	Pop.	County Seat or court house	Land area sq ml
Pipestone	10,398	Pipestone	466
Polk	32,678	Crookston	1,982
Pope	10,954	Glenwood	668
Ramsey	483,399	Saint Paul	154
Red Lake	4,483	Red Lake Falls	433
Redwood	17,090	Redwood Falls	882
Renville	17,308	Olivia	984
Rice	51,565	Faribault	501
Rock	9,871	Luverne	483
Roseau	15,571	Roseau	1,677
Saint Louis	198,022	Duluth	6,125
Scott	67,487	Shakopee	357
Sherburne	50,284	Elk River	435
Sibley	14,598	Gaylord	593
Stearns	124,410	Saint Cloud	1,338
Steele	31,391	Owatonna	431
Stevens	10,382	Morris	560
Swift	10,452	Benson	743
Todd	23,749	Long Prairie	941
Traverse	4,332	Wheaton	575
Wabasha	20,417	Wabasha	537
Wadena	13,090	Wadena	538
Waseca	18,059	Waseca	422
Washington	173,542	Stillwater	390
Watonwan	11,523	Saint James	435
Wilkin	7,400	Breckenridge	751
Winona	48,230	Winona	630
Wright	76,433	Buffalo	672
Yellow Medicine	11,675	Granite Falls	758

County	Pop.	County Seat or court house	Land area sq ml
Pearl River	42,036	Poplarville	819
Perry	11,426	New Augusta	651
Pike	37,660	Magnolia	410
Pontotoc	23,621	Pontotoc	499
Prentiss	23,744	Booneville	417
Quitman	10,130	Marks	406
Rankin	96,280	Brandon	782
Scott	24,767	Forest	610
Sharkey	6,952	Rolling Fork	435
Simpson	24,640	Mendenhall	591
Smith	14,997	Raleigh	635
Stone	11,840	Wiggins	446
Sunflower	36,013	Indianola	707
Tallahatchie	14,701	Charleston & Sumner	651
Tate	22,230	Senatobia	406
Tippah	20,341	Ripley	458
Tishomingo	18,161	Iuka	434
Tunica	8,295	Tunica	460
Union	22,726	New Albany	417
Walthall	14,310	Tylertown	404
Warren	49,034	Vicksburg	597
Washington	66,741	Greenville	733
Wayne	19,660	Waynesboro	813
Webster	10,374	Walthall	424
Wilkinson	9,538	Woodville	678
Winston	19,568	Louisville	610
Yalobusha	12,383	Coffeeville & Water Valley	478
Yazoo	25,354	Yazoo City	933

Mississippi

(82 counties, 46,914 sq mi land; pop. 2,669,111)

County	Pop.	County Seat or court house	Land area sq ml
Adams	34,737	Natchez	456
Alcorn	32,653	Corinth	401
Amite	13,243	Liberty	732
Attala	18,399	Kosciusko	737
Benton	7,925	Ashland	407
Bolivar	41,517	Cleveland & Rosedale	892
Calhoun	14,934	Pittsboro	573
Carroll	9,773	Carrollton & Vaiden	634
Chickasaw	18,151	Houston & Okolona	503
Choctaw	8,981	Ackerman	420
Claiborne	11,284	Port Gibson	494
Clarke	17,542	Quitman	692
Clay	21,550	West Point	415
Coahoma	31,453	Clarksdale	559
Copiah	28,288	Hazlehurst	779
Covington	16,944	Collins	416
De Soto	79,994	Hernando	483
Forrest	70,938	Hattiesburg	469
Franklin	8,380	Meadville	566
George	17,815	Lucedale	483
Greene	11,115	Leakesville	718
Grenada	22,175	Grenada	421
Hancock	36,593	Bay Saint Louis	478
Harrison	176,796	Gulfport	581
Hinds	251,917	Jackson & Raymond	875
Holmes	21,036	Lexington	759
Humphreys	11,717	Belzoni	430
Issaquena	1,732	Mayersville	406
Itawamba	20,650	Fulton	541
Jackson	125,754	Pascagoula	731
Jasper	17,347	Bay Springs & Paulding	678
Jefferson	8,500	Fayette	523
Jefferson Davis	14,030	Prentiss	409
Jones	63,035	Ellisville & Laurel	695
Kemper	10,247	De Kalb	766
Lafayette	32,461	Oxford	669
Lamar	32,740	Purvis	499
Lauderdale	76,495	Meridian	705
Lawrence	12,636	Monticello	435
Leake	18,815	Carthage	584
Lee	70,802	Tupelo	451
Leflore	37,463	Greenwood	605
Lincoln	31,162	Brookhaven	586
Lowndes	60,868	Columbus	517
Madison	63,683	Canton	717
Marion	25,834	Columbia	548
Marshall	31,666	Holly Springs	709
Monroe	37,279	Aberdeen	772
Montgomery	12,337	Winona	408
Neshoba	26,113	Philadelphia	571
Newton	21,071	Decatur	580
Noxubee	12,553	Macon	698
Oktibbeha	38,522	Starkville	459
Panola	31,944	Batesville & Sardis	695

Missouri

(114 cos., 1 ind. city, 68,898 sq mi land; pop. 5,277,640)

County	Pop.	County Seat or court house	Land area sq ml
Adair	24,627	Kirksville	567
Andrew	15,023	Savannah	435
Atchison	7,171	Rockport	542
Audrain	23,583	Mexico	697
Barry	30,307	Cassville	773
Barton	11,687	Lamar	596
Bates	15,289	Butler	849
Benton	15,134	Warsaw	729
Bollinger	11,155	Marble Hill	621
Boone	121,477	Columbia	687
Buchanan	82,962	Saint Joseph	409
Butler	40,199	Poplar Buff	698
Caldwell	8,647	Kingston	430
Callaway	34,572	Fulton	842
Camden	30,594	Camdenton	641
Cape Girardeau	64,506	Jackson	577
Carroll	10,486	Carrollton	695
Carter	5,953	Van Buren	509
Cass	71,383	Harrisonville	701
Cedar	12,548	Stockton	470
Chariton	8,838	Keytesville	758
Christian	40,591	Ozark	564
Clark	7,397	Kahoka	507
Clay	163,330	Liberty	403
Clinton	17,415	Plattsburg	423
Cole	67,046	Jefferson City	392
Cooper	15,680	Boonville	567
Crawford	20,766	Steelville	744
Dade	7,851	Greenfield	491
Dallas	14,233	Buffalo	543
Daviess	7,675	Gallatin	568
De Kalb	10,175	Maysville	425
Dent	13,947	Salem	755
Douglas	12,111	Ava	814
Dunklin	32,895	Kennett	547
Franklin	85,858	Union	922
Gasconade	14,369	Hermann	521
Gentry	6,869	Albany	493
Greene	222,430	Springfield	677
Grundy	10,374	Trenton	437
Harrison	8,348	Bethany	725
Henry	20,763	Clinton	729
Hickory	8,044	Hermitage	379
Holt	5,676	Oregon	457
Howard	9,605	Fayette	465
Howell	33,837	West Plains	928
Iron	10,939	Ironton	552
Jackson	634,742	Kansas City	611
Jasper	94,869	Carthage	641
Jefferson	183,542	Hillsboro	661
Johnson	46,194	Warrensburg	834
Knox	4,349	Edina	507
Laclede	28,682	Lebanon	768
Lafayette	31,946	Lexington	632
Lawrence	31,373	Mount Vernon	613
Lewis	10,155	Monticello	509
Lincoln	31,781	Troy	627
Linn	13,971	Linneus	620
Livingston	14,433	Chillicothe	537
McDonald	18,151	Pineville	540

County	Pop.	County Seat or court house	Land area sq mi
Macon.	15,074	Macon	797
Madison.	11,312	Fredericktown	497
Maries.	8,315	Vienna	528
Marion.	27,851	Palmyra	438
Mercer.	3,969	Princeton	454
Miller.	21,819	Tuscumbia	593
Mississippi	14,039	Charleston	410
Moniteau	12,725	California	417
Monroe	8,764	Paris	670
Montgomery	11,495	Montgomery City	540
Morgan	16,720	Versailles	594
New Madrid	20,784	New Madrid	658
Newton	46,871	Neosho	627
Nodaway	21,091	Maryville	875
Oregon	9,856	Alton	792
Osage	12,202	Linn	606
Ozark	9,228	Gainesville	731
Pemiscot	21,579	Caruthersville.	517
Perry	17,265	Perryville	473
Pettis	36,567	Sedalia	686
Phelps	36,987	Rolla	674
Pike	16,073	Bowling Green	673
Platte	64,786	Platte City	421
Polk	23,822	Bolivar	636
Pulaski	39,802	Waynesville	550
Putnam	5,052	Unionville	520
Ralls	8,795	New London	482
Randolph	24,011	Huntsville	477
Ray	22,012	Richmond	568
Reynolds	6,607	Centerville.	809
Ripley	13,265	Doniphan	631
Saint Charles	239,283	Saint Charles	558
Saint Clair	8,730	Osceola	699
Saint Francois.	51,797	Farmington	451
Saint Louis	1,005,094	Clayton.	506
Sainte Genevieve	16,442	Sainte Genevieve	504
Saline	22,785	Marshall	755
Schuyler	4,263	Lancaster	309
Scotland	4,789	Memphis	438
Scott	40,109	Benton	423
Shannon	7,975	Eminence	1,004
Shelby	6,839	Shelbyville.	501
Stoddard	29,219	Bloomfield	815
Stone	23,973	Galena	451
Sullivan	6,410	Milan	651
Taney	31,036	Forsyth.	608
Texas	22,076	Houston	1,180
Vernon	19,129	Nevada.	837
Warren	21,841	Warrenton	429
Washington	21,481	Potosi.	762
Wayne.	12,622	Greenville	762
Webster.	25,965	Marshfield	594
Worth	2,384	Grant City	266
Wright	17,861	Hartville	682
Independent City			
Saint Louis	368,246		61

Montana

(56 counties, 145,556 sq mi land; pop. 856,047)

County	Pop.	County Seat or court house	Land area sq mi
Beaverhead	8,849	Dillon	5,542
Big Horn	12,061	Hardin	4,995
Blaine	7,054	Chinook	4,226
Broadwater.	3,677	Townsend	1,191
Carbon	8,947	Red Lodge	2,048
Carter	1,531	Ekalaka	3,340
Cascade	81,166	Great Falls	2,698
Chouteau	5,451	Fort Benton	3,973
Custer	12,126	Miles City	3,783
Daniels	2,152	Scobey	1,426
Dawson	8,993	Glendive	2,373
Deer Lodge	10,229	Anaconda	737
Fallon	3,061	Baker	1,620
Fergus.	12,588	Lewistown	4,339
Flathead	67,285	Kalispell	5,099
Gallatin	57,771	Bozeman	2,507
Garfield	1,433	Jordan	4,668
Glacier	12,427	Cut Bank	2,995
Golden Valley	949	Ryegete	1,175
Granite	2,655	Philipsburg	1,728
Hill	17,480	Havre	2,896
Jefferson	8,988	Boulder	1,657
Judith Basin	2,246	Stanford	1,870
Lake	23,653	Polson	1,494
Lewis & Clark	51,523	Helena	3,461
Liberty	2,238	Chester	1,430
Lincoln	18,409	Libby	3,613
McCone.	2,140	Circle	2,643
Madison.	6,384	Virginia City	3,587
Meagher	1,830	White Sulphur Springs	2,392
Mineral	3,633	Superior	1,220
Missoula	85,669	Missoula	2,598
Musselshell	4,422	Roundup	1,867
Park	15,650	Livingston	2,656

County	Pop.	County Seat or court house	Land area sq mi
Petroleum	534	Winnett.	1,654
Phillips	5,039	Malta	5,140
Pondera.	6,218	Conrad	1,625
Powder River	2,006	Broadus	3,297
Powell	6,792	Deer Lodge	2,326
Prairie	1,331	Terry	1,737
Ravalli.	30,700	Hamilton	2,394
Richland	10,380	Sidney	2,084
Roosevelt	11,128	Wolf Point	2,356
Rosebud	10,755	Forsyth.	5,012
Sanders.	9,733	Thompson Falls	2,762
Sheridan	4,434	Plentywood	1,677
Silver Bow	34,813	Butte	718
Stillwater	7,222	Columbus	1,795
Sweet Grass	3,269	Big Timber	1,855
Teton	6,438	Choteau	2,273
Toole	5,087	Shelby	1,911
Treasure	875	Hysham	979
Valley	8,316	Glasgow	4,921
Wheatland	2,355	Harlowton	1,423
Wibaux	1,138	Wibaux	889
Yellowstone	122,762	Billings	2,635

Nebraska

(93 counties, 76,878 sq mi land; pop. 1,622,858)

County	Pop.	County Seat or court house	Land area sq mi
Adams.	29,662	Hastings	564
Antelope	7,617	Neligh.	859
Arthur	444	Arthur.	711
Banner	860	Harrisburg	747
Blaine	668	Brewster	714
Boone	6,511	Albion.	687
Box Butte.	12,891	Alliance.	1,077
Boyd	2,722	Butte	532
Brown	3,626	Ainsworth	1,214
Buffalo.	39,388	Kearney	945
Burt	7,893	Tekamah.	486
Butler	8,567	David City	584
Cass	22,464	Plattsmouth	557
Cedar	10,052	Hartington	740
Chase	4,228	Imperial	894
Cherry	6,367	Valentine.	5,961
Cheyenne	9,574	Sidney	1,196
Clay	7,236	Clay Center.	574
Colfax	9,841	Schuyler	410
Cuming	10,089	West Point	575
Custer	12,400	Broken Bow	2,571
Dakota	17,826	Dakota City	258
Dawes.	9,112	Chadron	1,397
Dawson.	22,075	Lexington	982
Deuel	2,101	Chappell	437
Dixon	6,241	Ponca.	474
Dodge.	34,567	Fremont	534
Douglas.	430,304	Omaha	333
Dundy	2,519	Benkelman	920
Fillmore	6,883	Geneva.	576
Franklin	3,777	Franklin	576
Frontier	3,143	Stockville	976
Furnas.	5,667	Beaver City	721
Gage.	22,834	Beatrice	858
Garden	2,304	Oshkosh	1,680
Garfield	2,068	Burwell	570
Gosper	2,061	Elwood	461
Grant	780	Hyannis	775
Greeley	3,020	Greeley.	570
Hall.	50,694	Grand Island	537
Hamilton	9,147	Aurora	543
Harlan	3,751	Alma	555
Hayes	1,155	Hayes Center.	713
Hitchcock	3,451	Trenton	709
Holt.	12,435	O'Neill	2,406
Hooker	727	Mullen	721
Howard	6,266	Saint Paul	564
Jefferson	8,581	Fairbury	575
Johnson	4,630	Tecumseh	377
Kearney.	6,562	Minden	519
Keith	8,479	Ogallala	1,039
Keya Paha	990	Springview	769
Kimball	4,063	Kimball	952
Knox	9,512	Center	1,105
Lancaster.	225,743	Lincoln	839
Lincoln	33,306	North Platte	2,525
Logan	888	Stapleton	571
Loup	660	Taylor.	574
McPherson	554	Tryon	859
Madison.	33,891	Madison	575
Merrick	8,124	Central City	478
Morrill	5,344	Bridgeport	1,405
Nance	4,275	Fullerton	439
Nemaha.	7,763	Auburn	409
Nuckolls	5,570	Nelson	576
Otoe	14,380	Nebraska City	615
Pawnee.	3,301	Pawnee City	433
Perkins	3,246	Grant	885

County	Pop.	County Seat or court house	Land area sq mi
Phelps	9,869	Holdrege	540
Pierce	7,831	Pierce	575
Platte	30,669	Columbus	669
Polk	5,556	Osceola	437
Red Willow	11,372	McCook	718
Richardson	9,750	Falls City	553
Rock	1,931	Bassett	1,003
Saline	12,898	Wilber	575
Sarpy	109,201	Papillion	238
Saunders	18,706	Wahoo	753
Scotts Bluff	36,946	Gering	725
Seward	16,049	Seward	575
Sheridan	6,669	Rushville	2,453
Sherman	3,611	Loup City	564
Sioux	1,566	Harrison	2,070
Stanton	6,148	Stanton	431
Thayer	6,537	Hebron	575
Thomas	825	Thedford	713
Thurston	7,200	Pender	391
Valley	4,900	Ord	567
Washington	17,445	Blair	386
Wayne	9,564	Wayne	443
Webster	4,190	Red Cloud	575
Wheeler	975	Bartlett	575
York	14,576	York	576

Nevada

(16 counties, 1 ind. city, 109,806 sq mi land; pop. 1,457,028)

County	Pop.	County Seat or court house	Land area sq mi
Churchill	20,300	Fallon	4,913
Clark	938,217	Las Vegas	8,084
Douglas	33,220	Minden	751
Elko	40,399	Elko	17,181
Esmeralda	1,134	Goldfield	3,570
Eureka	1,375	Eureka	4,182
Humboldt	15,261	Winnemucca	9,704
Lander	6,570	Battle Mountain	5,621
Lincoln	3,814	Pioche	10,650
Lyon	24,452	Yerington	2,024
Mineral	5,914	Hawthorne	3,837
Nye	21,861	Tonopah	18,064
Pershing	4,480	Lovelock	6,031
Storey	2,705	Virginia City	262
Washoe	282,932	Reno	6,608
White Pine	9,278	Ely	8,905
Independent City			
Carson City	45,116	Carson City	153

New Hampshire

(10 counties, 8,969 sq mi land; pop. 1,136,820)

County	Pop.	County Seat or court house	Land area sq mi
Belknap	49,814	Laconia	404
Carroll	37,054	Ossipee	933
Cheshire	70,922	Keene	711
Coos	33,902	Lancaster	1,804
Grafton	77,096	Woodsville	1,719
Hillsborough	346,770	Nashua	876
Merrimack	122,135	Concord	936
Rockingham	253,847	Exeter	699
Strafford	106,286	Dover	370
Sullivan	38,994	Newport	540

New Jersey

(21 counties, 7,419 sq mi land; pop. 7,903,925)

County	Pop.	County Seat or court house	Land area sq mi
Atlantic	232,230	Mays Landing	568
Bergen	842,369	Hackensack	237
Burlington	398,807	Mount Holly	808
Camden	506,579	Camden	223
Cape May	97,774	Cape May Court House	263
Cumberland	138,801	Bridgeton	498
Essex	765,363	Newark	127
Gloucester	241,523	Woodbury	327
Hudson	552,384	Jersey City	46
Hunterdon	115,208	Flemington	426
Mercer	329,430	Trenton	227
Middlesex	692,859	New Brunswick	316
Monmouth	578,501	Freehold	472
Morris	438,462	Morristown	470
Ocean	456,511	Toms River	641
Passaic	461,779	Paterson	187
Salem	64,786	Salem	338
Somerset	260,673	Somerville	305
Sussex	138,259	Newton	526
Union	496,227	Elizabeth	103
Warren	95,400	Belvidere	359

New Mexico

(33 counties, 121,364 sq mi land; pop. 1,653,521)

County	Pop.	County Seat or court house	Land area sq mi
Bernalillo	515,570	Albuquerque	1,169
Catron	2,603	Reserve	6,929
Chaves	60,963	Roswell	6,066
Cibola	24,501	Grants	4,468
Colfax	13,760	Raton	3,762
Curry	47,908	Clovis	1,408
De Baca	2,278	Fort Sumner	2,323
Dona Ana	155,466	Las Cruces	3,819
Eddy	52,792	Carlsbad	4,184
Grant	29,332	Silver City	3,969
Guadalupe	4,151	Santa Rosa	3,032
Harding	939	Mosquero	2,122
Hidalgo	6,133	Lordsburg	3,445
Lea	57,112	Lovington	4,390
Lincoln	14,165	Carrizozo	4,832
Los Alamos	18,520	Los Alamos	109
Luna	21,540	Deming	2,965
McKinley	65,511	Gallup	5,442
Mora	4,502	Mora	1,930
Otero	54,306	Alamogordo	6,626
Quay	10,561	Tucumcari	2,874
Rio Arriba	36,297	Tierra Amarilla	5,856
Roosevelt	18,507	Portales	2,453
Sandoval	76,147	Bernalillo	3,707
San Juan	99,252	Aztec	5,522
San Miguel	27,357	Las Vegas	4,709
Santa Fe	112,238	Santa Fe	1,905
Sierra	10,533	Truth or Consequences	4,178
Socorro	15,676	Socorro	6,625
Taos	24,988	Taos	2,204
Torrance	11,969	Estancia	3,335
Union	4,136	Clayton	3,830
Valencia	53,808	Los Lunas	1,068

New York

(62 counties, 47,224 sq mi land; pop. 18,169,051)

County	Pop.	County Seat or court house	Land area sq mi
Albany	291,263	Albany	524
Allegany	51,272	Belmont	1,031
Bronx	1,191,303	Bronx	42
Broome	208,529	Binghamton	707
Cattaraugus	85,571	Little Valley	1,310
Cayuga	83,113	Auburn	693
Chautauqua	142,166	Mayville	1,062
Chemung	94,524	Elmira	408
Chenango	52,342	Norwich	894
Clinton	86,975	Plattsburgh	1,039
Columbia	63,403	Hudson	636
Cortland	49,371	Cortland	500
Delaware	47,736	Delhi	1,446
Dutchess	261,453	Poughkeepsie	802
Erie	967,466	Buffalo	1,045
Essex	37,949	Elizabethtown	1,797
Franklin	49,118	Malone	1,632
Fulton	54,435	Johnstown	496
Genesee	61,289	Batavia	494
Greene	47,331	Catskill	648
Hamilton	5,238	Lake Pleasant	1,721
Herkimer	66,818	Herkimer	1,412
Jefferson	114,885	Watertown	1,272
Kings	2,271,000	Brooklyn	71
Lewis	27,610	Lowville	1,276
Livingston	64,968	Geneseo	632
Madison	71,709	Wampsville	656
Monroe	726,846	Rochester	659
Montgomery	52,094	Fonda	405
Nassau	1,302,279	Mineola	287
New York	1,506,430	New York	28
Niagara	221,599	Lockport	523
Oneida	249,529	Utica	1,213
Onondaga	473,289	Syracuse	780
Ontario	98,773	Canandaigua	644
Orange	320,485	Goshen	816
Orleans	45,617	Albion	391

County	Pop.	County Seat or court house	Land area sq mi
Oswego	125,816	Oswego	953
Otsego	61,585	Cooperstown	1,003
Putnam	89,214	Carmel	232
Queens	1,964,270	Jamaica	109
Rensselaer	156,335	Troy	654
Richmond	397,680	Saint George	59
Rockland	274,834	New City	174
Saint Lawrence	115,487	Canton	2,686
Saratoga	192,881	Ballston Spa	812
Schenectady	149,574	Schenectady	206
Schoharie	33,036	Schoharie	622
Schuyler	19,013	Watkins Glen	329
Seneca	32,638	Ovid & Waterloo	325
Steuben	100,616	Bath	1,393
Suffolk	1,349,191	Riverhead	911
Sullivan	70,627	Monticello	970
Tioga	53,425	Owego	519
Tompkins	96,306	Ithaca	476
Ulster	168,865	Kingston	1,127
Warren	61,335	Queensbury	870
Washington	60,786	Hudson Falls	836
Wayne	92,982	Lyons	604
Westchester	888,815	White Plains	433
Wyoming	44,052	Warsaw	593
Yates	23,910	Penn Yan	338

North Carolina

(100 counties, 48,718 sq mi land; pop. 7,069,836)

County	Pop.	County Seat or court house	Land area sq mi
Alamance	113,454	Graham	433
Alexander	29,435	Taylorsville	259
Alleghany	9,736	Sparta	235
Anson	24,123	Wadesboro	533
Ashe	23,127	Jefferson	426
Avery	15,220	Newland	247
Beaufort	43,872	Washington	826
Bertie	20,642	Windsor	701
Bladen	29,647	Elizabethtown	879
Brunswick	58,362	Bolivia	860
Buncombe	185,914	Asheville	659
Burke	78,892	Morganton	504
Cabarrus	107,485	Concord	364
Caldwell	73,126	Lenoir	471
Camden	6,366	Camden	240
Carteret	46,418	Beaufort	526
Caswell	21,012	Yanceyville	428
Catawba	124,327	Newton	396
Chatham	41,748	Pittsboro	708
Cherokee	21,089	Murphy	452
Chowan	13,902	Edenton	182
Clay	7,623	Hayesville	214
Cleveland	88,512	Shelby	468
Columbus	50,984	Whiteville	938
Craven	83,170	New Bern	701
Cumberland	287,242	Fayetteville	657
Currituck	15,781	Currituck	256
Dare	25,102	Manteo	391
Davidson	133,273	Lexington	548
Davie	29,444	Mocksville	267
Duplin	41,442	Kenansville	819
Durham	192,277	Durham	298
Edgecombe	56,123	Tarboro	506
Forsyth	277,895	Winston-Salem	412
Franklin	40,383	Louisburg	494
Gaston	180,036	Gastonia	357
Gates	9,722	Gatesville	338
Graham	7,572	Robbinsville	289
Granville	40,328	Oxford	534
Greene	16,407	Snow Hill	266
Guilford	368,083	Greensboro	651
Halifax	57,106	Halifax	724
Harnett	73,805	Lillington	601
Haywood	49,066	Waynesville	555
Henderson	75,065	Hendersonville	374
Hertford	22,687	Winton	356
Hoke	26,895	Raeford	391
Hyde	5,325	Swan Quarter	624
Iredell	100,603	Statesville	574
Jackson	28,331	Sylva	491
Johnston	90,911	Smithfield	795
Jones	9,701	Trenton	470
Lee	44,828	Sanford	259
Lenoir	58,658	Kinston	402
Lincoln	55,567	Lincolnton	298
McDowell	37,054	Marion	437
Macon	25,410	Franklin	517
Madison	17,628	Marshall	451
Martin	26,369	Williamston	461
Mecklenburg	563,673	Charlotte	528
Mitchell	14,492	Bakersville	222
Montgomery	23,285	Troy	490
Moore	65,391	Carthage	701
Nash	83,582	Nashville	540
New Hanover	135,057	Wilmington	185
Northampton	20,662	Jackson	538
Onslow	146,325	Jacksonville	763
Orange	105,592	Hillsborough	400
Pamlico	11,935	Bayboro	341
Pasquotank	33,546	Elizabeth City	228
Pender	33,584	Burgaw	875
Perquimans	10,713	Hertford	246
Person	31,684	Roxboro	398
Pitt	116,345	Greenville	657
Polk	15,482	Columbus	238
Randolph	112,771	Asheboro	789
Richmond	45,351	Rockingham	477
Robeson	110,676	Lumberton	949
Rockingham	87,513	Wentworth	569
Rowan	117,155	Salisbury	519
Rutherford	58,889	Rutherfordton	568
Sampson	49,944	Clinton	947
Scotland	34,923	Laurinburg	319
Stanly	53,867	Albemarle	396
Stokes	39,877	Danbury	452
Surry	64,383	Dobson	539
Swain	11,726	Bryson City	526
Transylvania	26,959	Brevard	378
Tyrrell	3,897	Columbia	407
Union	95,186	Monroe	639
Vance	40,444	Henderson	249
Wake	494,228	Raleigh	854
Warren	17,682	Warrenton	427
Washington	14,256	Plymouth	332
Watauga	39,106	Boone	314
Wayne	109,258	Goldsboro	554
Wilkes	60,825	Wilkesboro	752
Wilson	66,986	Wilson	374
Yadkin	32,265	Yadkinville	336
Yancey	16,016	Burnsville	314

North Dakota

(53 counties, 68,994 sq mi land; pop. 637,988)

County	Pop.	County Seat or court house	Land area sq mi
Adams	2,756	Hettinger	988
Barnes	12,085	Valley City	1,498
Benson	7,003	Minnewaukan	1,412
Billings	1,144	Medora	1,152
Bottineau	7,711	Bottineau	1,668
Bowman	3,245	Bowman	1,162
Burke	2,579	Bowbells	1,118
Burleigh	63,897	Bismarck	1,618
Cass	109,716	Fargo	1,767
Cavalier	5,656	Langdon	1,507
Dickey	5,878	Ellendale	1,139
Divide	2,606	Crosby	1,288
Dunn	3,820	Manning	1,993
Eddy	2,858	New Rockford	634
Emmons	4,562	Linton	1,499
Foster	3,890	Carrington	640
Golden Valley	1,945	Beach	1,003
Grand Forks	70,911	Grand Forks	1,440
Grant	3,227	Carson	1,660
Griggs	3,088	Cooperstown	708
Hettinger	3,063	Mott	1,133
Kidder	3,079	Steele	1,362
La Moure	5,135	La Moure	1,150
Logan	2,572	Napoleon	1,000
McHenry	6,220	Towner	1,887
McIntosh	3,691	Ashley	984
McKenzie	5,885	Watford City	2,754
McLean	9,939	Washburn	2,065
Mercer	9,399	Stanton	1,044
Morton	24,220	Mandan	1,921
Mountrail	6,734	Stanley	1,837
Nelson	4,081	Lakota	991
Oliver	2,212	Center	723
Pembina	8,781	Cavalier	1,120
Pierce	4,650	Rugby	1,037
Ramsey	12,665	Devils Lake	1,241
Ransom	5,856	Lisbon	862
Renville	2,927	Mohall	874
Richland	18,326	Wahpeton	1,436
Rolette	13,511	Rolla	914
Sargent	4,450	Forman	857
Sheridan	1,946	McClusky	989
Sioux	4,033	Fort Yates	1,099
Slope	848	Amidon	1,219
Stark	22,908	Dickinson	1,338
Steele	2,296	Finley	713
Stutsman	21,638	Jamestown	2,263
Towner	3,231	Cando	1,035
Traill	8,584	Hillsboro	861
Walsh	12,859	Grafton	1,290
Ward	57,884	Minot	2,041
Wells	5,354	Fessenden	1,288
Williams	20,434	Williston	2,074

Ohio

(88 counties, 40,953 sq mi land; pop. 11,102,198)

County	Pop.	County Seat or court house	Land area sq mi
Adams.........	27,201	West Union	586
Allen........	109,234	Lima..........	405
Ashland.......	49,887	Ashland	424
Ashtabula......	101,937	Jefferson.......	703
Athens........	60,465	Athens	508
Auglaize	46,622	Wapakoneta	398
Belmont........	70,571	Saint Clairsville ..	537
Brown.........	38,270	Georgetown.....	493
Butler.........	312,835	Hamilton.......	470
Carroll........	27,849	Carrollton	393
Champaign......	37,356	Urbana........	429
Clark.........	147,856	Springfield......	398
Clermont	164,012	Batavia........	456
Clinton........	37,666	Wilmington	410
Columbiana	111,406	Lisbon	534
Coshocton	36,004	Coshocton......	566
Crawford	47,496	Bucyrus	403
Cuyahoga	1,403,239	Cleveland	459
Darke	54,141	Greenville	600
Defiance	39,681	Defiance	414
Delaware	76,575	Delaware	443
Erie..........	77,909	Sandusky	264
Fairfield	114,738	Lancaster	506
Fayette	28,215	Washington Court House......	405
Franklin	1,005,161	Columbus	543
Fulton	40,097	Wauseon	407
Gallia	32,180	Gallipolis......	471
Geauga	83,000	Chardon	408
Greene	139,906	Xenia	416
Guernsey	39,852	Cambridge	522
Hamilton	867,728	Cincinnati	412
Hancock	67,683	Findlay	532
Hardin	31,436	Kenton	471
Harrison.......	15,988	Cadiz	400
Henry	29,574	Napoleon	415
Highland	38,479	Hillsboro	553
Hocking.......	27,501	Logan........	423
Holmes	35,069	Millersburg	424
Huron	58,031	Norwalk	494
Jackson.......	31,970	Jackson	420
Jefferson......	78,737	Steubenville....	410
Knox	50,002	Mount Vernon ...	529
Lake	221,418	Painesville.....	231
Lawrence......	63,870	Ironton	457
Licking.......	135,005	Newark.......	686
Logan........	44,705	Bellefontaine ...	458
Lorain	279,405	Elyria	495
Lucas	457,635	Toledo	341
Madison	39,831	London	467
Mahoning......	263,885	Youngstown....	417
Marion........	64,802	Marion	403
Medina	133,052	Medina	422
Meigs	23,870	Pomeroy	432
Mercer........	40,470	Celina........	457
Miami	96,475	Troy	410
Monroe	15,293	Woodsfield	457
Montgomery	572,140	Dayton	458
Morgan	14,452	McConnelsville...	420
Morrow	29,633	Mount Gilead...	406
Muskingum	83,566	Zanesville	654
Noble	11,793	Caldwell	399
Ottawa	40,216	Port Clinton	253
Paulding	20,239	Paulding	419
Perry.........	33,343	New Lexington ..	412
Pickaway	51,547	Circleville	503
Pike	26,090	Waverly	443
Portage	148,887	Ravenna	493
Preble	41,526	Eaton	426
Putnam........	34,806	Ottawa	484
Richland	128,073	Mansfield	497
Ross.........	72,764	Chillicothe	692
Sandusky	62,741	Fremont	409
Scioto	81,858	Portsmouth	613
Seneca	60,403	Tiffin..........	553
Shelby........	46,679	Sidney	409
Stark.........	374,612	Canton	574
Summit	527,920	Akron	412
Trumbull	228,829	Warren	612
Tuscarawas	86,512	New Philadelphia .	570
Union	35,420	Marysville	437
Van Wert	30,265	Van Wert......	410
Vinton	11,780	McArthur......	414
Warren	126,657	Lebanon	403
Washington	63,550	Marietta	640
Wayne	106,168	Wooster	557
Williams.......	37,588	Bryan	422
Wood	116,214	Bowling Green ...	619
Wyandot	22,652	Upper Sandusky..	406

Oklahoma

(77 counties, 68,679 sq mi land; pop. 3,258,069)

County	Pop.	County Seat or court house	Land area sq mi
Adair..........	19,766	Stillwell........	577
Alfalfa	6,187	Cherokee	864
Atoka	13,134	Atoka	980
Beaver	5,876	Beaver	1,808
Beckham	18,544	Sayre	904
Blaine	10,938	Watonga	920
Bryan	33,279	Durant	902
Caddo........	29,777	Anadarko	1,286
Canadian......	80,175	El Reno	901
Carter........	43,809	Ardmore	828
Cherokee......	36,495	Tahlequah......	748
Choctaw	15,596	Hugo........	762
Cimarron	3,105	Boise City	1,842
Cleveland	188,395	Norman	529
Coal	5,938	Coalgate......	520
Comanche	117,627	Lawton	1,076
Cotton	6,714	Walters	656
Craig.........	14,196	Vinita	763
Creek	63,668	Sapulpa	930
Custer........	26,597	Arapaho	981
Delaware	31,283	Jay	720
Dewey........	5,262	Taloga	1,007
Ellis	4,271	Arnett	1,232
Garfield	56,930	Enid........	1,060
Garvin........	26,744	Pauls Valley ...	813
Grady........	43,055	Chickasha....	1,106
Grant	5,559	Medford	1,004
Greer	6,454	Mangum	638
Harmon	3,598	Hollis	537
Harper........	3,821	Buffalo	1,039
Haskell	10,974	Stigler........	570
Hughes	12,837	Holdenville	806
Jackson.......	29,050	Altus........	817
Jefferson	6,994	Waurika	769
Johnston	10,103	Tishomingo ...	639
Kay..........	47,968	Newkirk	921
Kingfisher	13,281	Kingfisher	906
Kiowa	11,089	Hobart	1,019
Latimer	10,336	Wilburton	728
Le Flore.......	44,907	Poteau	1,585
Lincoln	30,070	Chandler.....	964
Logan	29,828	Guthrie	748
Love	8,587	Marietta	519
McClain.......	24,541	Purcell	582
McCurtain	33,972	Idabel.......	1,826
McIntosh	18,074	Eufaula	599
Major	7,730	Fairview	958
Marshall	11,546	Madill	372
Mayes	35,437	Pryor	644
Murray	12,055	Sulphur......	420
Muskogee	69,376	Muskogee	815
Noble	11,269	Perry	736
Nowata	9,824	Nowata......	540
Okfuskee	11,194	Okemah	628
Oklahoma	623,755	Oklahoma City ..	708
Okmulgee	37,348	Okmulgee	698
Osage........	42,546	Pawhuska	2,265
Ottawa	30,995	Miami.......	465
Pawnee	15,825	Pawnee	551
Payne	63,726	Stillwater.....	691
Pittsburg	42,840	McAlester	1,251
Pontotoc	34,348	Ada	717
Pottawatomie ...	60,601	Shawnee	783
Pushmataha....	11,305	Antlers	1,417
Roger Mills....	3,868	Cheyenne	1,146
Rogers	60,690	Claremore.....	683
Seminole	25,018	Wewoka	639
Sequoyah	35,257	Sallisaw	678
Stephens	43,172	Duncan......	884
Texas	16,232	Guymon	2,040
Tillman	9,869	Frederick	904
Tulsa.........	524,609	Tulsa	572
Wagoner	51,592	Wagoner.....	559
Washington	47,634	Bartlesville ...	423
Washita.......	11,557	Cordell	1,006
Woods........	8,662	Alva	1,291
Woodward	18,785	Woodward.....	1,242

Oregon

(36 counties, 96,002 sq mi land; pop. 3,086,188)

County	Pop.	County Seat or court house	Land area sq mi
Baker	16,274	Baker City.....	3,089
Benton	74,492	Corvallis	679
Clackamas.....	310,156	Oregon City....	1,870
Clatsop	35,147	Astoria	873
Columbia	40,879	Saint Helens ...	687
Coos	62,731	Coquille	1,629
Crook	15,895	Prineville.....	2,991
Curry.........	20,805	Gold Beach ...	1,648
Deschutes	90,923	Bend	3,055
Douglas........	98,301	Roseburg	5,071

County	Pop.	County Seat or court house	Land area sq mi
Gilliam	1,851	Condon	1,223
Grant	7,939	Canyon City	4,525
Harney	7,067	Burns	10,228
Hood River	17,989	Hood River	533
Jackson	162,367	Medford	2,801
Jefferson	15,564	Madras	1,791
Josephine	69,420	Grants Pass	1,640
Klamath	60,484	Klamath Falls	6,135
Lake	7,330	Lakeview	8,359
Lane	298,994	Eugene	4,620
Lincoln	43,259	Newport	992
Linn	97,922	Albany	2,296
Malheur	27,421	Vale	9,926
Marion	250,133	Salem	1,194
Morrow	8,647	Heppner	2,094
Multnomah	611,729	Portland	465
Polk	55,649	Dallas	741
Sherman	1,901	Moro	831
Tillamook	23,315	Tillamook	1,125
Umatilla	63,068	Pendleton	3,218
Union	24,950	La Grande	2,038
Wallowa	7,466	Enterprise	3,150
Wasco	22,607	The Dalles	2,396
Washington	359,018	Hillsboro	727
Wheeler	1,578	Fossil	1,713
Yamhill	72,917	McMinnville	718

Pennsylvania

(67 counties, 44,820 sq mi land; pop. 12,052,367)

County	Pop.	County Seat or court house	Land area sq mi
Adams	83,458	Gettysburg	521
Allegheny	1,320,704	Pittsburgh	727
Armstrong	74,599	Kittanning	646
Beaver	188,297	Beaver	436
Bedford	48,984	Bedford	1,017
Berks	347,625	Reading	861
Blair	131,819	Hollidaysburg	527
Bradford	62,056	Towanda	1,152
Bucks	567,238	Doylestown	610
Butler	161,890	Butler	789
Cambria	160,729	Ebensburg	691
Cameron	5,783	Emporium	398
Carbon	58,869	Jim Thorpe	384
Centre	129,833	Bellefonte	1,106
Chester	397,307	West Chester	758
Clarion	42,123	Clarion	607
Clearfield	79,397	Clearfield	1,149
Clinton	37,435	Lock Haven	891
Columbia	63,897	Bloomsburg	486
Crawford	87,984	Meadville	1,011
Cumberland	204,612	Carlisle	547
Dauphin	245,561	Harrisburg	528
Delaware	548,366	Media	184
Elk	35,173	Ridgway	830
Erie	280,318	Erie	804
Fayette	146,534	Uniontown	794
Forest	4,812	Tionesta	428
Franklin	125,998	Chambersburg	774
Fulton	14,262	McConnellsburg	438
Greene	40,169	Waynesburg	577
Huntingdon	44,529	Huntingdon	877
Indiana	90,638	Indiana	829
Jefferson	46,615	Brookville	657
Juniata	21,450	Mifflintown	392
Lackawanna	216,007	Scranton	461
Lancaster	442,679	Lancaster	952
Lawrence	96,580	New Castle	363
Lebanon	116,417	Lebanon	363
Lehigh	297,876	Allentown	348
Luzerne	327,726	Wilkes-Barre	891
Lycoming	120,939	Williamsport	1,237
McKean	48,529	Smethport	979
Mercer	122,160	Mercer	672
Mifflin	47,011	Lewistown	413
Monroe	112,111	Stroudsburg	609
Montgomery	700,308	Norristown	486
Montour	18,218	Danville	131
Northampton	255,007	Easton	376
Northumberland	95,732	Sunbury	461
Perry	43,117	New Bloomfield	557
Philadelphia	1,524,338	Philadelphia	136
Pike	35,489	Milford	550
Potter	17,061	Coudersport	1,081
Schuylkill	153,351	Pottsville	782
Snyder	37,699	Middleburg	329
Somerset	79,030	Somerset	1,073
Sullivan	6,088	Laporte	451
Susquehanna	41,529	Montrose	826
Tioga	41,894	Wellsboro	1,131
Union	37,298	Lewisburg	317
Venango	59,211	Franklin	679
Warren	45,062	Warren	885
Washington	208,119	Washington	958
Wayne	43,111	Honesdale	731
Westmoreland	376,446	Greensburg	1,033
Wyoming	29,353	Tunkhannock	399
York	357,807	York	906

Rhode Island

(5 counties, 1,045 sq mi land; pop. 996,757)

County	Pop.	County Seat or court house	Land area sq mi
Bristol	48,992	Bristol	26
Kent	162,805	East Greenwich	172
Newport	84,708	Newport	107
Providence	584,709	Providence	416
Washington	115,543	West Kingston	333

South Carolina

(46 counties, 30,111 sq mi land; pop. 3,663,984)

County	Pop.	County Seat or court house	Land area sq mi
Abbeville	24,167	Abbeville	508
Aiken	132,060	Aiken	1,092
Allendale	11,690	Allendale	413
Anderson	152,676	Anderson	718
Bamberg	16,702	Bamberg	395
Barnwell	21,418	Barnwell	558
Beaufort	97,120	Beaufort	579
Berkeley	138,839	Moncks Corner	1,108
Calhoun	13,385	Saint Matthews	380
Charleston	293,557	Charleston	938
Cherokee	46,730	Gaffney	396
Chester	32,977	Chester	580
Chesterfield	39,251	Chesterfield	802
Clarendon	29,353	Manning	602
Colleton	36,260	Walterboro	1,052
Darlington	64,710	Darlington	563
Dillon	29,695	Dillon	406
Dorchester	89,888	Saint George	575
Edgefield	19,213	Edgefield	490
Fairfield	22,466	Winnsboro	685
Florence	121,173	Florence	804
Georgetown	50,021	Georgetown	822
Greenville	335,386	Greenville	795
Greenwood	61,431	Greenwood	451
Hampton	18,969	Hampton	561
Horry	152,878	Conway	1,143
Jasper	16,119	Ridgeland	655
Kershaw	46,256	Camden	723
Lancaster	55,944	Lancaster	552
Laurens	59,998	Laurens	712
Lee	18,705	Bishopville	411
Lexington	187,264	Lexington	707
McCormick	9,131	McCormick	350
Marion	35,188	Marion	493
Marlboro	29,968	Bennettsville	483
Newberry	33,817	Newberry	634
Oconee	60,684	Walhalla	629
Orangeburg	88,049	Orangeburg	1,111
Pickens	100,998	Pickens	499
Richland	299,086	Columbia	762
Saluda	16,936	Saluda	456
Spartanburg	237,569	Spartanburg	814
Sumter	106,705	Sumter	665
Union	30,634	Union	515
Williamsburg	37,616	Kingstree	934
York	141,302	York	685

South Dakota

(67 counties, 75,896 sq mi land; pop. 721,164)

County	Pop.	County Seat or court house	Land area sq mi
Aurora	3,008	Plankinton	707
Beadle	18,078	Huron	1,259
Bennett	3,251	Martin	1,182
Bon Homme	6,952	Tyndall	552
Brookings	26,338	Brookings	795
Brown	35,723	Aberdeen	1,722
Brule	5,625	Chamberlain	815
Buffalo	1,781	Gannvalley	475
Butte	8,924	Belle Fourche	2,251
Campbell	1,895	Mound City	732
Charles Mix	9,256	Lake Andes	1,090
Clark	4,350	Clark	953
Clay	13,476	Vermillion	409
Codington	24,530	Watertown	694
Corson	4,119	McIntosh	2,467
Custer	6,590	Custer	1,559
Davison	17,681	Mitchell	436
Day	6,688	Webster	1,022
Deuel	4,489	Clear Lake	631
Dewey	5,601	Timber Lake	2,310
Douglas	3,577	Armour	434
Edmunds	4,262	Ipswich	1,149
Fall River	7,059	Hot Springs	4,742
Faulk	2,566	Faulkton	1,004
Grant	8,303	Milbank	681
Gregory	5,050	Burke	1,013
Haakon	2,527	Philip	1,822
Hamlin	5,239	Hayti	512
Hand	4,199	Miller	1,437

County	Pop.	County Seat or court house	Land area sq mi
Hanson	2,872	Alexandria	433
Harding	1,536	Buffalo	2,678
Hughes	15,522	Pierre	757
Hutchinson	8,090	Olivet	816
Hyde	1,657	Highmore	860
Jackson	2,869	Kadoka	1,872
Jerauld	2,393	Wessington Springs	530
Jones	1,307	Murdo	971
Kingsbury	5,750	De Smet	824
Lake	10,701	Madison	560
Lawrence	22,095	Deadwood	800
Lincoln	16,953	Canton	578
Lyman	3,721	Kennebec	1,679
McCook	5,787	Salem	576
McPherson	3,055	Leola	1,148
Marshall	4,760	Britton	848
Meade	22,909	Sturgis	3,481
Mellette	2,039	White River	1,311
Miner	3,061	Howard	570
Minnehaha	134,338	Sioux Falls	810
Moody	6,611	Flandreau	520
Pennington	86,357	Rapid City	2,783
Perkins	3,760	Bison	2,884
Potter	3,075	Gettysburg	869
Roberts	9,717	Sisseton	1,102
Sanborn	2,762	Woonsocket	569
Shannon	10,966	(Attached to Fall River)	2,094
Spink	7,845	Redfield	1,505
Stanley	2,672	Fort Pierre	1,431
Sully	1,556	Onida	972
Todd	8,743	(Attached to Tripp)	1,388
Tripp	6,827	Winner	1,618
Turner	8,507	Parker	617
Union	10,981	Elk Point	453
Walworth	5,790	Selby	707
Yankton	20,306	Yankton	518
Ziebach	2,137	Dupree	1,969

Tennessee

(95 counties, 41,219 sq mi land; pop. 5,175,240)

County	Pop.	County Seat or court house	Land area sq mi
Anderson	71,216	Clinton	339
Bedford	32,484	Shelbyville	475
Benton	15,512	Camden	392
Bledsoe	9,940	Pikeville	407
Blount	94,565	Maryville	558
Bradley	77,570	Cleveland	327
Campbell	36,445	Jacksboro	479
Cannon	11,172	Woodbury	266
Carroll	28,213	Huntingdon	600
Carter	52,823	Elizabethton	341
Cheatham	31,103	Ashland City	304
Chester	13,492	Henderson	289
Claiborne	28,114	Tazewell	432
Clay	7,115	Celina	227
Cocke	30,801	Newport	432
Coffee	42,853	Manchester	428
Crockett	13,441	Alamo	266
Cumberland	39,289	Crossville	682
Davidson	527,200	Nashville	501
Decatur	10,618	Decaturville	330
De Kalb	14,938	Smithville	291
Dickson	37,919	Charlotte	491
Dyer	35,570	Dyersburg	520
Fayette	26,501	Somerville	705
Fentress	15,386	Jamestown	498
Franklin	35,999	Winchester	543
Gibson	47,167	Trenton	602
Giles	27,660	Pulaski	610
Grainger	18,177	Rutledge	273
Greene	57,280	Greeneville	619
Grundy	13,652	Altamont	361
Hamblen	52,553	Morristown	156
Hamilton	292,772	Chattanooga	539
Hancock	6,846	Sneedville	223
Hardeman	24,137	Bolivar	670
Hardin	24,337	Savannah	578
Hawkins	47,082	Rogersville	486
Haywood	19,374	Brownsville	534
Henderson	22,804	Lexington	520
Henry	29,015	Paris	560
Hickman	18,374	Centerville	610
Houston	7,478	Erin	200
Humphreys	16,267	Waverly	528
Jackson	9,130	Gainesboro	308
Jefferson	36,945	Dandridge	265
Johnson	15,940	Mountain City	297
Knox	357,447	Knoxville	506
Lake	7,379	Tiptonville	169
Lauderdale	23,978	Ripley	474
Lawrence	37,854	Lawrenceburg	617
Lewis	10,072	Hohenwald	282
Lincoln	28,631	Fayetteville	571
Loudon	35,078	Loudon	235
McMinn	44,476	Athens	429
McNairy	23,183	Selmer	562
Macon	16,681	Lafayette	307
Madison	82,559	Jackson	558
Marion	26,116	Jasper	512
Marshall	24,185	Lewisburg	376
Maury	63,888	Columbia	616
Meigs	8,942	Decatur	189
Monroe	32,409	Madisonville	648
Montgomery	119,170	Clarksville	539
Moore	5,113	Lynchburg	129
Morgan	17,921	Wartburg	523
Obion	32,107	Union City	550
Overton	18,242	Livingston	433
Perry	6,892	Linden	412
Pickett	4,532	Byrdstown	159
Polk	14,028	Benton	438
Putnam	55,751	Cookeville	399
Rhea	26,282	Dayton	309
Roane	48,507	Kingston	357
Robertson	46,212	Springfield	476
Rutherford	140,700	Murfreesboro	606
Scott	19,330	Huntsville	528
Sequatchie	9,369	Dunlap	266
Sevier	58,184	Sevierville	590
Shelby	857,651	Memphis	772
Smith	14,742	Carthage	313
Stewart	10,326	Dover	454
Sullivan	147,655	Blountville	415
Sumner	113,560	Gallatin	529
Tipton	42,052	Covington	454
Trousdale	6,318	Hartsville	114
Unicoi	16,743	Erwin	186
Union	14,607	Maynardville	218
Van Buren	5,094	Spencer	273
Warren	34,732	McMinnville	431
Washington	97,411	Jonesboro	326
Wayne	15,525	Waynesboro	734
Weakley	32,344	Dresden	581
White	21,039	Sparta	373
Williamson	97,890	Franklin	584
Wilson	75,064	Lebanon	570

Texas

(254 counties, 261,914 sq mi land; pop. 18,378,185)

County	Pop.	County Seat or court house	Land area sq mi
Anderson	49,050	Palestine	1,077
Andrews	14,452	Andrews	1,501
Angelina	73,925	Lufkin	807
Aransas	20,785	Rockport	280
Archer	7,941	Archer City	907
Armstrong	2,076	Claude	909
Atascosa	32,875	Jourdanton	1,218
Austin	21,780	Bellville	656
Bailey	6,746	Muleshoe	826
Bandera	12,523	Bandera	793
Bastrop	42,587	Bastrop	895
Baylor	4,262	Seymour	862
Bee	23,845	Beeville	880
Bell	215,480	Belton	1,055
Bexar	1,280,062	San Antonio	1,248
Blanco	7,062	Johnson City	714
Borden	767	Gail	900
Bosque	16,166	Meridian	989
Bowie	83,579	Boston	891
Brazoria	211,524	Angleton	1,407
Brazos	130,387	Bryan	589
Brewster	8,761	Alpine	6,169
Briscoe	1,809	Silverton	887
Brooks	8,266	Falfurrias	942
Brown	35,271	Brownwood	936
Burleson	14,678	Caldwell	669
Burnet	25,375	Burnet	994
Caldwell	28,062	Lockhart	546
Calhoun	20,403	Port Lavaca	540
Callahan	12,278	Baird	899
Cameron	299,584	Brownsville	906
Camp	10,458	Pittsburg	203
Carson	6,570	Panhandle	924
Cass	30,393	Linden	937
Castro	8,594	Dimmitt	899
Chambers	21,324	Anahuac	616
Cherokee	40,812	Rusk	1,052
Childress	6,375	Childress	707
Clay	9,976	Henrietta	1,086
Cochran	4,180	Morton	775
Coke	3,497	Robert Lee	908
Coleman	9,662	Coleman	1,277
Collin	326,153	McKinney	851
Collingsworth	3,397	Wellington	909
Colorado	18,591	Columbus	965
Comal	60,829	New Braunfels	555
Comanche	13,449	Comanche	930

County	Pop.	County Seat or court house	Land area sq ml	County	Pop.	County Seat or court house	Land area sq ml
Concho	3,056	Paint Rock	992	Leon	13,570	Centerville	1,079
Cooke	31,269	Gainesville	893	Liberty	58,033	Liberty	1,174
Coryell	71,687	Gatesville	1,057	Limestone	20,913	Groesbeck	930
Cottle	2,065	Paducah	895	Lipscomb	2,951	Lipscomb	933
Crane	4,621	Crane	782	Live Oak	10,172	George West	1,057
Crockett	4,228	Ozona	2,806	Llano	12,495	Llano	939
Crosby	7,277	Crosbyton	899	Loving	137	Mentone	670
Culberson	3,261	Van Horn	3,815	Lubbock	230,525	Lubbock	900
Dallam	5,944	Dalhart	1,505	Lynn	6,625	Tahoka	888
Dallas	1,942,303	Dallas	880	McCulloch	8,481	Brady	1,071
Dawson	14,142	Lamesa	903	McLennan	197,173	Waco	1,031
Deaf Smith	19,250	Hereford	1,497	McMullen	806	Tilden	1,163
Delta	4,808	Cooper	278	Madison	11,352	Madisonville	472
Denton	320,123	Denton	911	Marion	10,069	Jefferson	385
Dewitt	18,438	Cuero	910	Martin	4,937	Stanton	914
Dickens	2,437	Dickens	907	Mason	3,504	Mason	934
Dimmit	10,706	Carrizo Springs	1,307	Matagorda	38,710	Bay City	1,127
Donley	3,703	Clarendon	929	Maverick	44,227	Eagle Pass	1,287
Duval	12,827	San Diego	1,795	Medina	30,446	Hondo	1,331
Eastland	17,866	Eastland	924	Menard	2,333	Menard	902
Ector	123,128	Odessa	903	Midland	114,165	Midland	902
Edwards	2,934	Rocksprings	2,121	Milam	23,473	Cameron	1,019
Ellis	91,850	Waxahachie	939	Mills	4,686	Goldthwaite	748
El Paso	664,800	El Paso	1,014	Mitchell	7,729	Colorado City	912
Erath	29,575	Stephenville	1,080	Montague	17,743	Montague	928
Falls	17,850	Marlin	770	Montgomery	222,157	Conroe	1,047
Fannin	25,083	Bonham	895	Moore	18,890	Dumas	905
Fayette	20,888	La Grange	950	Morris	13,216	Daingerfield	256
Fisher	4,442	Roby	897	Motley	1,378	Matador	959
Floyd	8,224	Floydada	992	Nacogdoches	56,185	Nacogdoches	939
Foard	1,637	Crowell	703	Navarro	40,315	Corsicana	1,068
Fort Bend	280,026	Richmond	876	Newton	13,894	Newton	935
Franklin	8,654	Mount Vernon	294	Nolan	16,439	Sweetwater	915
Freestone	15,762	Fairfield	888	Nueces	310,881	Corpus Christi	847
Frio	15,357	Pearsall	1,133	Ochiltree	8,690	Perryton	919
Gaines	14,471	Seminole	1,504	Oldham	2,233	Vega	1,485
Galveston	234,690	Galveston	399	Orange	84,253	Orange	362
Garza	4,810	Post	895	Palo Pinto	25,098	Palo Pinto	949
Gillespie	18,832	Fredericksburg	1,061	Panola	22,551	Carthage	812
Glasscock	1,442	Garden City	900	Parker	71,303	Weatherford	902
Goliad	6,080	Goliad	859	Parmer	10,245	Farwell	885
Gonzales	17,334	Gonzales	1,068	Pecos	14,432	Fort Stockton	4,777
Gray	23,419	Pampa	921	Polk	37,280	Livingston	1,061
Grayson	97,267	Sherman	934	Potter	102,928	Amarillo	902
Gregg	109,785	Longview	273	Presidio	7,425	Marfa	3,857
Grimes	20,634	Anderson	799	Rains	7,389	Emory	243
Guadalupe	70,584	Seguin	713	Randall	94,107	Canyon	917
Hale	35,676	Plainview	1,005	Reagan	4,523	Big Lake	1,173
Hall	3,750	Memphis	877	Real	2,442	Leakey	697
Hamilton	7,588	Hamilton	836	Red River	13,969	Clarksville	1,054
Hansford	5,403	Spearman	921	Reeves	15,395	Pecos	2,626
Hardeman	4,909	Quanah	688	Refugio	7,814	Refugio	771
Hardin	45,628	Kountze	898	Roberts	996	Miami	915
Harris	3,045,212	Houston	1,734	Robertson	15,432	Franklin	864
Harrison	58,077	Marshall	908	Rockwall	31,398	Rockwall	128
Hartley	3,738	Channing	1,462	Runnels	11,157	Ballinger	1,056
Haskell	6,530	Haskell	901	Rusk	44,229	Henderson	932
Hays	74,221	San Marcos	678	Sabine	10,131	Hemphill	486
Hemphill	3,541	Canadian	903	San Augustine	7,885	San Augustine	524
Henderson	62,121	Athens	888	San Jacinto	18,639	Coldspring	572
Hidalgo	461,015	Edinburg	1,569	San Patricio	64,798	Sinton	693
Hill	28,150	Hillsboro	968	San Saba	5,842	San Saba	1,136
Hockley	24,468	Levelland	908	Schleicher	2,983	Eldorado	1,309
Hood	31,537	Granbury	425	Scurry	18,202	Snyder	900
Hopkins	29,368	Sulphur Springs	789	Shackelford	3,325	Albany	915
Houston	21,670	Crockett	1,234	Shelby	22,322	Center	791
Howard	32,125	Big Spring	901	Sherman	2,868	Stratford	923
Hudspeth	2,911	Sierra Blanca	4,567	Smith	159,000	Tyler	932
Hunt	65,950	Greenville	840	Somervell	5,712	Glen Rose	188
Hutchinson	24,867	Stinnett	872	Starr	49,531	Rio Grande City	1,226
Irion	1,671	Mertzon	1,052	Stephens	8,895	Breckenridge	894
Jack	6,888	Jacksboro	920	Sterling	1,536	Sterling City	923
Jackson	13,579	Edna	844	Stonewall	1,960	Aspermont	925
Jasper	32,321	Jasper	921	Sutton	4,299	Sonora	1,455
Jeff Davis	2,115	Fort Davis	2,257	Swisher	8,293	Tulia	902
Jefferson	242,861	Beaumont	937	Tarrant	1,257,189	Fort Worth	868
Jim Hogg	5,097	Hebbronville	1,136	Taylor	121,902	Abilene	917
Jim Wells	39,390	Alice	867	Terrell	1,309	Sanderson	2,357
Johnson	104,278	Cleburne	730	Terry	12,869	Brownfield	887
Jones	16,010	Anson	931	Throckmorton	1,815	Throckmorton	912
Karnes	12,363	Karnes City	753	Titus	24,469	Mount Pleasant	412
Kaufman	58,271	Kaufman	788	Tom Green	101,243	San Angelo	1,515
Kendall	18,485	Boerne	663	Travis	646,437	Austin	989
Kenedy	427	Sarita	1,389	Trinity	12,236	Groveton	692
Kent	959	Jayton	878	Tyler	18,336	Woodville	922
Kerr	39,553	Kerrville	1,107	Upshur	33,478	Gilmer	587
Kimble	4,137	Junction	1,250	Upton	4,112	Rankin	1,243
King	345	Guthrie	914	Uvalde	24,964	Uvalde	1,564
Kinney	3,242	Brackettville	1,359	Val Verde	42,736	Del Rio	3,150
Kleberg	30,801	Kingsville	853	Van Zandt	40,660	Canton	855
Knox	4,630	Benjamin	845	Victoria	79,437	Victoria	887
Lamar	44,954	Paris	919	Walker	53,492	Huntsville	786
Lamb	14,817	Littlefield	1,013	Waller	25,823	Hempstead	514
Lampasas	15,268	Lampasas	714	Ward	12,257	Monahans	836
La Salle	5,380	Cotulla	1,517	Washington	27,575	Brenham	610
Lavaca	18,594	Hallettsville	971	Webb	163,062	Laredo	3,362
Lee	13,553	Giddings	631	Wharton	39,964	Wharton	1,086
				Wheeler	5,451	Wheeler	904
				Wichita	124,053	Wichita Falls	606

County	Pop.	County Seat or court house	Land area sq mi
Wilbarger	14,557	Vernon	947
Willacy	19,034	Raymondville	589
Williamson	172,666	Georgetown	1,137
Wilson	25,811	Floresville	807
Winkler	8,094	Kermit	840
Wise	37,321	Decatur	902
Wood	31,895	Quitman	689
Yoakum	8,471	Plains	800
Young	17,642	Graham	919
Zapata	10,740	Zapata	999
Zavala	12,331	Crystal City	1,298

Utah
(29 counties, 82,168 sq mi land; pop. 1,907,936)

County	Pop.	County Seat or court house	Land area sq mi
Beaver	5,169	Beaver	2,590
Box Elder	38,730	Brigham City	5,724
Cache	75,664	Logan	1,165
Carbon	20,464	Price	1,479
Daggett	738	Manila	698
Davis	210,943	Farmington	305
Duchesne	13,641	Duchesne	3,238
Emery	10,599	Castle Dale	4,452
Garfield	4,032	Panguitch	5,175
Grand	7,677	Moab	3,682
Iron	24,426	Parowan	3,299
Juab	6,354	Nephi	3,392
Kane	5,815	Kanab	3,992
Millard	11,913	Fillmore	6,590
Morgan	6,318	Morgan	609
Piute	1,391	Junction	758
Rich	1,779	Randolph	1,029
Salt Lake	795,325	Salt Lake City	737
San Juan	13,655	Monticello	7,821
Sanpete	18,931	Manti	1,588
Sevier	16,793	Richfield	1,910
Summit	21,526	Coalville	1,871
Tooele	28,781	Tooele	6,946
Uintah	24,472	Vernal	4,477
Utah	290,983	Provo	1,998
Wasatch	11,403	Heber City	1,181
Washington	66,124	Saint George	2,427
Wayne	2,246	Loa	2,461
Weber	172,044	Ogden	576

Vermont
(14 counties, 9,249 sq mi land; pop. 580,209)

County	Pop.	County Seat or court house	Land area sq mi
Addison	34,398	Middlebury	773
Bennington	36,231	Bennington	676
Caledonia	28,524	Saint Johnsbury	651
Chittenden	137,562	Burlington	540
Essex	6,515	Guildhall	666
Franklin	42,634	Saint Albans	649
Grand Isle	5,747	North Hero	89
Lamoille	20,936	Hyde Park	461
Orange	27,190	Chelsea	690
Orleans	24,853	Newport	697
Rutland	62,572	Rutland	932
Washington	55,991	Montpelier	690
Windham	42,411	Newfane	786
Windsor	54,645	Woodstock	972

Virginia
(95 cos., 41 ind. cities, 39,598 sq mi land; pop. 6,551,522)

County	Pop.	County Seat or court house	Land area sq mi
Accomack	32,375	Accomac	476
Albemarle	71,757	Charlottesville	740
Alleghany	12,650	Covington	444
Amelia	9,542	Amelia Court House	366
Amherst	29,456	Amherst	470
Appomattox	12,644	Appomattox	345
Arlington	174,611	Arlington	26
Augusta	57,875	Staunton	968
Bath	4,854	Warm Springs	540
Bedford	51,171	Bedford	771
Bland	6,777	Bland	369
Botetourt	26,612	Fincastle	549
Brunswick	16,221	Lawrenceville	579
Buchanan	30,822	Grundy	508
Buckingham	13,108	Buckingham	582
Campbell	48,807	Rustburg	511
Caroline	20,620	Bowling Green	549
Carroll	27,432	Hillsville	494
Charles City	6,660	Charles City	208
Charlotte	12,136	Charlotte Court House	471
Chesterfield	234,102	Chesterfield	446
Clarke	12,207	Berryville	174
Craig	4,633	New Castle	336
Culpeper	29,916	Culpeper	389
Cumberland	7,707	Cumberland	292
Dickenson	17,685	Clintwood	335
Dinwiddie	22,356	Dinwiddie	502
Essex	9,165	Tappahannock	264
Fairfax	880,771	Fairfax	399
Fauquier	51,420	Warrenton	660
Floyd	12,556	Floyd	383
Fluvanna	15,228	Palmyra	282
Franklin	42,433	Rocky Mount	721
Frederick	49,925	Winchester	432
Giles	16,409	Pearisburg	369
Gloucester	32,668	Gloucester	257
Goochland	15,858	Goochland	289
Grayson	16,096	Independence	494
Greene	12,564	Stanardsville	153
Greensville	10,752	Emporia	301
Halifax	30,051	Halifax	806
Hanover	71,549	Hanover	436
Henrico	229,206	Henrico	244
Henry	56,588	Martinsville	385
Highland	2,561	Monterey	416
Isle of Wight	27,102	Isle of Wight	319
James City	39,432	Williamsburg	144
King and Queen	6,342	King and Queen Court House	327
King George	16,631	King George	183
King William	12,080	King William	286
Lancaster	11,097	Lancaster	153
Lee	24,375	Jonesville	438
Loudoun	108,123	Leesburg	517
Louisa	22,350	Louisa	514
Lunenburg	11,131	Lunenburg	443
Madison	12,276	Madison	327
Mathews	8,864	Mathews	87
Mecklenburg	30,430	Boydton	675
Middlesex	9,154	Saluda	138
Montgomery	75,632	Christiansburg	395
Nelson	13,360	Lovingston	471
New Kent	11,279	New Kent	221
Northampton	12,994	Eastville	209
Northumberland	11,120	Heathsville	223
Nottoway	15,280	Nottoway	308
Orange	23,445	Orange	355
Page	22,547	Luray	310
Patrick	17,621	Stuart	467
Pittsylvania	56,016	Chatham	985
Powhatan	18,133	Powhatan	272
Prince Edward	18,397	Farmville	357
Prince George	27,900	Prince George	276
Prince William	239,730	Manassas	345
Pulaski	34,486	Pulaski	335
Rappahannock	7,016	Washington	267
Richmond	7,447	Warsaw	203
Roanoke	80,746	Salem	248
Rockbridge	18,816	Lexington	604
Rockingham	60,910	Harrisonburg	865
Russell	29,167	Lebanon	483
Scott	23,233	Gate City	539
Shenandoah	32,991	Woodstock	507
Smyth	32,972	Marion	435
Southampton	17,004	Courtland	599
Spotsylvania	67,086	Spotsylvania	409
Stafford	76,454	Stafford	277
Surry	6,357	Surry	306
Sussex	10,055	Sussex	496
Tazewell	47,047	Tazewell	522
Warren	28,847	Front Royal	219
Washington	47,646	Abingdon	578
Westmoreland	16,257	Montross	250
Wise	39,980	Wise	405
Wythe	26,264	Wytheville	460
York	52,306	Yorktown	122
Independent Cities			
Alexandria	113,522		16
Bedford	6,456		7
Bristol	18,054		12
Buena Vista	6,581		7
Charlottesville	41,138		10
Chesapeake	180,597		353
Clifton Forge	4,450		3
Colonial Heights	16,522		8
Covington	6,980		5
Danville	53,964		44
Emporia	5,958		7
Fairfax	20,526		6
Falls Church	9,570		2
Franklin	8,603		8
Fredericksburg	21,725		10
Galax	6,746		8
Hampton	139,645		57
Harrisonburg	33,024		17
Hopewell	23,113		11
Lexington	7,127		2
Lynchburg	67,030		50

County	Pop.	County Seat or court house	Land area sq mi
Independent Cities			
Manassas	31,785		11
Manassas Park	6,977		3
Martinsville	15,955		11
Newport News	179,149		69
Norfolk	241,472		66
Norton	4,121		7
Petersburg	38,591		23
Poquoson	11,451		10
Portsmouth	103,486		30
Radford	16,162		9
Richmond	201,543		63
Roanoke	97,009		43
Salem	24,261		14
South Boston	7,210		5
Staunton	24,852		20
Suffolk	54,934		430
Virginia Beach	430,317		310
Waynesboro	18,764		14
Williamsburg	12,180		9
Winchester	23,508		9

Washington

(39 counties, 66,581 sq mi land; pop. 5,343,090)

County	Pop.	County Seat or court house	Land area sq mi
Adams	15,046	Ritzville	1,921
Asotin	19,788	Asotin	635
Benton	129,295	Prosser	1,715
Chelan	55,915	Wenatchee	2,916
Clallam	61,787	Port Angeles	1,753
Clark	281,721	Vancouver	627
Columbia	4,102	Dayton	865
Cowlitz	87,614	Kelso	1,140
Douglas	30,372	Waterville	1,817
Ferry	7,033	Republic	2,200
Franklin	42,711	Pasco	1,243
Garfield	2,305	Pomeroy	706
Grant	62,310	Ephrata	2,660
Grays Harbor	66,912	Montesano	1,918
Island	67,673	Coupeville	212
Jefferson	24,094	Port Townsend	1,805
King	1,587,505	Seattle	2,128
Kitsap	220,392	Port Orchard	393
Kittitas	29,726	Ellensburg	2,308
Klickitat	17,821	Goldendale	1,880
Lewis	64,692	Chehalis	2,409
Lincoln	9,428	Davenport	2,310
Mason	45,865	Shelton	961
Okanogan	35,781	Okanogan	5,281
Pacific	20,302	South Bend	908
Pend Oreille	10,317	Newport	1,400
Pierce	638,328	Tacoma	1,675
San Juan	11,454	Friday Harbor	179
Skagit	91,836	Mount Vernon	1,735
Skamania	8,958	Stevenson	1,672
Snohomish	524,326	Everett	2,098
Spokane	395,874	Spokane	1,762
Stevens	36,388	Colville	2,470
Thurston	187,235	Olympia	727
Wahkiakum	3,647	Cathlamet	261
Walla Walla	52,582	Walla Walla	1,261
Whatcom	145,407	Bellingham	2,125
Whitman	38,865	Colfax	2,151
Yakima	207,683	Yakima	4,287

West Virginia

(55 counties, 24,087 sq mi land; pop. 1,822,021)

County	Pop.	County Seat or court house	Land area sq mi
Barbour	16,103	Philippi	343
Berkeley	65,432	Martinsburg	321
Boone	26,276	Madison	503
Braxton	13,166	Sutton	513
Brooke	26,705	Wellsburg	90
Cabell	96,755	Huntington	282
Calhoun	7,932	Grantsville	280
Clay	10,205	Clay	346
Doddridge	7,289	West Union	321
Fayette	48,293	Fayetteville	667
Gilmer	7,466	Glenville	340
Grant	10,926	Petersburg	480
Greenbrier	35,406	Lewisburg	1,025
Hampshire	18,137	Romney	644
Hancock	34,794	New Cumberland	84
Hardy	11,475	Moorefield	585
Harrison	70,718	Clarksburg	417
Jackson	26,664	Ripley	464
Jefferson	38,875	Charles Town	209
Kanawha	206,714	Charleston	901
Lewis	17,509	Weston	389
Lincoln	21,892	Hamlin	439
Logan	42,874	Logan	456
McDowell	33,041	Welch	535
Marion	58,075	Fairmont	312

County	Pop.	County Seat or court house	Land area sq mi
Marshall	37,280	Moundsville	305
Mason	25,335	Point Pleasant	433
Mercer	65,027	Princeton	420
Mineral	27,234	Keyser	329
Mingo	33,935	Williamson	424
Monongalia	78,024	Morgantown	363
Monroe	12,955	Union	473
Morgan	12,943	Berkeley Springs	230
Nicholas	27,369	Summersville	650
Ohio	49,997	Wheeling	106
Pendleton	8,055	Franklin	698
Pleasants	7,493	St. Marys	131
Pocahontas	9,039	Marlinton	942
Preston	29,827	Kingwood	651
Putnam	47,949	Winfield	346
Raleigh	78,103	Beckley	608
Randolph	28,554	Elkins	1,040
Ritchie	10,288	Harrisville	454
Roane	15,228	Spencer	484
Summers	14,126	Hinton	353
Taylor	15,258	Grafton	174
Tucker	7,842	Parsons	421
Tyler	10,029	Middlebourne	258
Upshur	23,674	Buckhannon	355
Wayne	42,466	Wayne	508
Webster	10,413	Webster Springs	556
Wetzel	18,950	New Martinsville	359
Wirt	5,442	Elizabeth	235
Wood	87,988	Parkersburg	367
Wyoming	28,476	Pineville	502

Wisconsin

(72 counties, 54,314 sq mi land; pop. 5,081,658)

County	Pop.	County Seat or court house	Land area sq mi
Adams	17,025	Friendship	648
Ashland	16,458	Ashland	1,048
Barron	42,465	Barron	865
Bayfield	14,739	Washburn	1,462
Brown	207,266	Green Bay	524
Buffalo	13,905	Alma	699
Burnett	13,795	Meenon	818
Calumet	36,858	Chilton	326
Chippewa	54,007	Chippewa Falls	1,017
Clark	32,432	Neillsville	1,218
Columbia	48,373	Portage	771
Crawford	16,267	Prairie du Chien	566
Dane	390,254	Madison	1,205
Dodge	78,264	Juneau	887
Door	26,402	Sturgeon Bay	492
Douglas	42,893	Superior	1,305
Dunn	37,851	Menomonie	853
Eau Claire	87,937	Eau Claire	638
Florence	5,193	Florence	486
Fond du Lac	92,949	Fond du Lac	725
Forest	9,337	Crandon	1,011
Grant	49,705	Lancaster	1,144
Green	31,973	Monroe	583
Green Lake	19,293	Green Lake	357
Iowa	21,268	Dodgeville	760
Iron	6,478	Hurley	751
Jackson	16,954	Black River Falls	998
Jefferson	72,403	Jefferson	562
Juneau	23,173	Mauston	774
Kenosha	137,808	Kenosha	273
Kewaunee	19,275	Kewaunee	343
La Crosse	101,002	La Crosse	457
Lafayette	16,225	Darlington	634
Langlade	20,277	Antigo	873
Lincoln	28,683	Merrill	886
Manitowoc	82,143	Manitowoc	594
Marathon	120,110	Wausau	1,559
Marinette	41,845	Marinette	1,395
Marquette	13,570	Montello	455
Menominee	4,411	Keshena	359
Milwaukee	938,112	Milwaukee	241
Monroe	38,355	Sparta	904
Oconto	31,729	Oconto	1,002
Oneida	34,353	Rhinelander	1,130
Outagamie	147,456	Appleton	642
Ozaukee	78,025	Port Washington	235
Pepin	7,189	Durand	231
Pierce	34,161	Ellsworth	576
Polk	36,667	Balsam Lake	919
Portage	64,038	Stevens Point	810
Price	15,885	Phillips	1,256
Racine	181,702	Racine	334
Richland	17,832	Richland Center	585
Rock	145,956	Janesville	724
Rusk	15,185	Ladysmith	913
Saint Croix	53,993	Hudson	723
Sauk	50,234	Baraboo	838
Sawyer	15,290	Hayward	1,255
Shawano	37,972	Shawano	897
Sheboygan	107,029	Sheboygan	515
Taylor	19,222	Medford	975
Trempealeau	25,807	Whitehall	736

County	Pop.	County Seat or court house	Land area sq mi	County	Pop.	County Seat or court house	Land area sq mi
Vernon	26,754	Viroqua	808	Carbon	16,247	Rawlins	7,877
Vilas	19,711	Eagle River	867	Converse	11,704	Douglas	4,271
Walworth	80,711	Elkhorn	556	Crook	5,612	Sundance	2,855
Washburn	14,788	Shell Lake	815	Fremont	35,128	Lander	9,181
Washington	107,232	West Bend	431	Goshen	12,602	Torrington	2,186
Waukesha	332,200	Waukesha	554	Hot Springs	4,699	Thermopolis	2,005
Waupaca	48,467	Waupaca	754	Johnson	6,503	Buffalo	4,166
Waushara	20,761	Wautoma	628	Laramie	78,038	Cheyenne	2,684
Winnebago	147,867	Oshkosh	449	Lincoln	13,665	Kemmerer	4,070
Wood	75,701	Wisconsin Rapids	801	Natrona	63,885	Casper	5,347
				Niobrara	2,554	Lusk	2,684
				Park	24,928	Cody	6,936

Wyoming

(23 counties, 97,105 sq mi land; pop. 475,981)

County	Pop.	County Seat or court house	Land area sq mi
Albany	31,079	Laramie	4,268
Big Horn	10,844	Basin	3,139
Campbell	30,890	Gillette	4,796
Platte	8,311	Wheatland	2,023
Sheridan	24,828	Sheridan	2,532
Sublette	5,375	Pinedale	4,872
Sweetwater	40,661	Green River	10,352
Teton	13,152	Jackson	4,011
Unita	20,126	Evanston	2,085
Washakie	8,590	Worland	2,243
Weston	6,560	Newcastle	2,402

Population of Outlying Areas

Source: Bureau of the Census, U.S. Dept. of Commerce; World Almanac research

Population estimates for July 1, 1993, are given for Puerto Rican Municipios; all other population counts and all land area figures are from the U.S. census conducted on Apr. 1, 1990. Because only selected areas are shown, the population and land area figures may not equal the total reported. ZIP codes with an asterisk (*) are general delivery ZIP codes. Consult the local postmaster for more specific delivery information. Wake Atoll, Johnson Atoll, and Midway Atoll receive mail through APO and FPO addresses. U.S. outlying areas that are not listed in this table may not receive U.S. mail delivery.

Commonwealth of Puerto Rico

Zip code	Municipio	1993 Pop.	Land area sq mi	Zip code	Municipio	1993 Pop.	Land area sq mi	Zip code	Municipio	1993 Pop.	Land area sq mi
*00601	Adjuntas	19,579	67	00653	Guánica	21,251	37	00723	Patillas	20,218	47
00602	Aguada	37,175	31	*00784	Guayama	41,336	65	00624	Peñuelas	21,879	45
*00605	Aguadilla	64,176	37	00656	Guayanilla	21,554	42	*00732	Ponce	189,734	116
00703	Aguas Buenas	26,281	31	*00970	Guaynabo	97,879	27	00678	Quebradillas	21,653	23
00705	Aibonito	25,469	31	00778	Gurabo	30,948	28	00677	Rincón	12,311	14
00610	Añasco	26,806	39	00659	Hatillo	33,575	42	00721	Río Grande	46,329	61
*00612	Arecibo	94,513	126	00660	Hormigüeros	15,992	11	00637	Sabana Grande	24,196	36
00714	Arroyo	19,230	15	*00792	Humacao	55,954	45	00751	Salinas	29,266	69
00617	Barceloneta	21,940	23	00662	Isabela	39,836	55	00683	San Germán	36,622	55
00794	Barranquitas	26,713	34	00664	Jayuya	16,061	45	*00936	San Juan	443,372	48
*00958	Bayamón	225,338	44	00795	Juana Díaz	46,951	60	00754	San Lorenzo	35,988	53
00623	Cabo Rojo	40,559	70	00777	Juncos	32,272	27	00685	San Sebastián	39,081	70
*00726	Caguas	139,228	59	00667	Lajas	25,433	60	00757	Santa Isabel	19,482	34
00627	Camuy	30,725	46	00669	Lares	29,014	62	*00953	Toa Alta	46,274	27
00729	Canóvanas	39,653	33	00670	Las Marías	10,096	46	*00951	Toa Baja	94,633	23
*00984	Carolina	185,732	45	00771	Las Piedras	29,088	34	*00976	Trujillo Alto	66,992	21
*00962	Cataño	33,485	5	00772	Loíza	30,110	19	00641	Utuado	35,666	114
*00737	Cayey	46,993	52	00773	Luquillo	18,799	26	00692	Vega Alta	35,550	28
00735	Ceiba	17,521	29	00674	Manatí	39,409	45	*00693	Vega Baja	56,914	46
00638	Ciales	18,855	67	00606	Maricao	5,887	37	00765	Vieques	8,582	51
00739	Cidra	36,055	36	00707	Maunabo	12,809	21	00766	Villalba	24,115	36
00769	Coamo	33,402	78	*00681	Mayagüez	102,390	78	00767	Yabucoa	37,667	55
00782	Comerío	19,659	28	00676	Moca	33,456	50	00698	Yauco	41,642	68
00783	Corozal	33,754	43	00687	Morovis	26,926	39	**Total**		**3,622,063**	**3,427**
00775	Culebra	1,724	12	00718	Naguabo	23,079	52				
00646	Dorado	32,198	23	00719	Naranjito	28,359	27				
00738	Fajardo	37,107	30	00720	Orocovis	22,635	64				
00650	Florida	9,008	10								

Commonwealth of the Northern Mariana Islands

Zip code	Municipality	1990 Pop.	Land area sq mi	Zip code	Municipality	1990 Pop.	Land area sq mi		1990 Pop.	Land area sq mi
96950	Northern Islands	36	60	96950	Saipan	38,896	47	**Total**	**43,345**	**179**
96951	Rota	2,295	33	96952	Tinian	2,118	39			

Other U.S. External Territories

American Samoa

Zip code	Area	1990 Pop.	Land area sq mi
96799	American Samoa	46,773	77

Guam

Zip code	Area	1990 Pop.	Land area sq mi	Zip code	Area	1990 Pop.	Land area sq mi	Zip code	Area	1990 Pop.	Land area sq mi
96910	Agaña	1,139	1	*96921	Barrigada	8,846	9	96929	Yigo	14,213	35
96919	Agaña Hts	3,646	1	96924	Chalan-Pago-Ordot	4,451	6	96914	Yona	5,338	20
*96928	Agat	4,960	10	96912	Dededo	31,728	30	**Total**		**133,152**	**210**
96922	Asan	2,070	6	96917	Inarajan	2,469	19				
				96923	Mangilao	10,483	10				
				96916	Merizo	1,742	6				
				96927	Mongmong-Toto-Maite	5,845	2				
				96925	Piti	1,827	7				
				96915	Santa Rita	11,857	17				
				96926	Sinajana	2,658	1				
				96930	Talofofo	2,310	17				
				*96931	Tamuning	16,673	6				
				96918	Umatac	897	6				

Virgin Islands

Zip code	Area	1990 Pop.	Land area sq mi
00820	Saint Croix	50,139	83
*00830	Saint John	3,504	20
*00801	Saint Thomas	48,166	31
00801	Charlotte Amalie	12,331	
*00820	Christiansted	2,555	
*00840	Frederiksted	1,064	
Total		**101,809**	**134**

PRESIDENTIAL ELECTIONS
Popular and Electoral Vote, 1988 and 1992

Source: Voter News Service; Federal Election Commission

States	1992 Electoral Vote Clinton	Bush	Perot	1992 Democrat Clinton	1992 Republican Bush	1992 Ind. Perot	1988 Electoral Vote Dukakis	Bush	1988 Democrat Dukakis	1988 Republican Bush
AL	0	9	0	690,080	804,283	183,109	0	9	549,506	815,576
AK	0	3	0	78,294	102,000	73,481	0	3	72,584	119,251
AZ	0	8	0	543,050	572,086	353,741	0	7	454,029	702,541
AR	6	0	0	505,823	337,324	99,132	0	6	349,237	466,578
CA	54	0	0	5,121,325	3,630,574	2,296,006	0	47	4,702,233	5,054,917
CO	8	0	0	629,681	562,850	366,010	0	8	621,453	728,177
CT	8	0	0	682,318	578,313	348,771	0	8	676,584	750,241
DE	3	0	0	126,054	102,313	59,213	0	3	108,647	139,639
DC	3	0	0	192,619	20,698	9,681	3	0	159,407	27,590
FL	0	25	0	2,071,651	2,171,781	1,052,481	0	21	1,655,851	2,616,597
GA	13	0	0	1,008,966	995,252	309,657	0	12	714,792	1,081,331
HI	4	0	0	179,310	136,822	53,003	4	0	192,364	158,625
ID	0	4	0	137,013	202,645	130,395	0	4	147,272	253,881
IL	22	0	0	2,453,350	1,734,096	840,515	0	24	2,215,940	2,310,939
IN	0	12	0	848,420	989,375	455,934	0	12	860,643	1,297,763
IA	7	0	0	586,353	504,891	253,468	8	0	670,557	545,355
KS	0	6	0	390,434	449,951	312,358	0	7	422,636	554,049
KY	8	0	0	665,104	617,178	203,944	0	9	580,368	734,281
LA	9	0	0	815,971	733,386	211,478	0	10	717,460	883,702
ME	4	0	0	263,420	206,504	206,820	0	4	243,569	307,131
MD	10	0	0	988,571	707,094	281,414	0	10	826,304	876,167
MA	12	0	0	1,318,639	805,039	630,731	13	0	1,401,415	1,194,635
MI	18	0	0	1,871,182	1,554,940	824,813	0	20	1,675,783	1,965,486
MN	10	0	0	1,020,997	747,841	562,506	10	0	1,109,471	962,337
MS	0	7	0	400,258	487,793	85,626	0	7	363,921	557,890
MO	11	0	0	1,053,873	811,159	518,741	0	11	1,001,619	1,084,953
MT	3	0	0	154,507	144,207	107,225	0	4	168,936	190,412
NE	0	5	0	216,864	343,678	174,104	0	5	259,235	397,956
NV	4	0	0	189,148	175,828	132,580	0	4	132,738	206,040
NH	4	0	0	209,040	202,484	121,337	0	4	163,696	281,537
NJ	15	0	0	1,436,206	1,356,865	521,829	0	16	1,317,541	1,740,604
NM	5	0	0	261,617	212,824	91,895	0	5	244,497	270,341
NY	33	0	0	3,444,450	2,346,649	1,090,721	36	0	3,347,882	3,081,871
NC	0	14	0	1,114,042	1,134,661	357,864	0	13	890,167	1,237,258
ND	0	3	0	99,168	136,244	71,084	0	3	127,739	166,559
OH	21	0	0	1,984,942	1,894,310	1,036,426	0	23	1,939,629	2,416,549
OK	0	8	0	473,066	592,929	319,878	0	8	483,423	678,367
OR	7	0	0	621,314	475,757	354,091	7	0	616,206	560,126
PA	23	0	0	2,239,164	1,791,841	902,667	0	25	2,194,944	2,300,087
RI	4	0	0	213,299	131,601	105,045	4	0	225,123	177,761
SC	0	8	0	479,514	577,507	138,872	0	8	370,554	606,443
SD	0	3	0	124,888	136,718	73,295	0	3	145,560	165,415
TN	11	0	0	933,521	841,300	199,968	0	11	679,794	947,233
TX	0	32	0	2,281,815	2,496,071	1,354,781	0	29	2,352,748	3,036,829
UT	0	5	0	183,429	322,632	203,400	0	5	207,352	428,442
VT	3	0	0	133,590	88,122	65,985	0	3	115,775	124,331
VA	0	13	0	1,038,650	1,150,517	348,639	0	12	859,799	1,309,162
WA	11	0	0	993,037	731,234	541,780	10	0	933,516	903,835
WV	5	0	0	331,001	241,974	108,829	5[1]	0	341,016	310,065
WI	11	0	0	1,041,066	930,855	544,479	11	0	1,126,794	1,047,499
WY	0	3	0	68,160	79,347	51,263	0	3	67,113	106,867
Total	**370**	**168**	**0**	**44,908,254**	**39,102,343**	**19,741,065**	**111[1]**	**426**	**41,805,422**	**48,881,221**

(1) Lloyd Bentsen (D, TX) received 1 electoral vote from West Virginia.

Presidential Election Returns by Counties

All 1992 results are official. Results for New England states are for selected cities or towns because county results are not available. Totals are always statewide.

Source: Voter News Service; Federal Election Commission

Alabama

County	1992 Clinton (D)	Bush (R)	Perot (I)	1988 Dukakis (D)	Bush (R)
Autauga	4,819	8,715	1,916	3,667	7,828
Baldwin.	12,195	26,270	7,656	9,271	25,933
Barbour	4,836	4,475	1,020	3,836	4,958
Bibb	2,900	3,124	686	2,244	2,885
Blount	5,433	8,882	1,949	4,485	8,754
Bullock	3,259	1,253	266	3,122	1,421
Butler	4,021	3,494	867	3,465	3,923
Calhoun	16,453	20,623	4,717	12,451	19,806
Chambers . . .	5,938	5,682	1,427	5,103	7,694
Cherokee	4,222	2,745	846	3,176	2,868
Chilton	4,946	8,126	1,363	3,820	8,761
Choctaw	3,941	3,069	489	3,491	3,629
Clarke	5,023	5,495	872	4,217	5,708
Clay	2,073	2,859	652	1,602	3,496
Cleburne	2,144	2,425	630	1,383	3,071
Coffee	5,776	7,591	2,021	4,319	8,890
Colbert	12,206	8,073	2,098	10,397	7,775
Conecuh	3,155	2,463	552	3,022	3,256
Coosa	2,330	1,973	476	1,860	2,405
Covington	5,004	6,840	1,880	3,845	8,130
Crenshaw	2,404	2,339	485	1,836	2,617
Cullman	10,451	14,411	4,113	8,517	14,351
Dale	5,098	8,123	2,423	3,476	9,266
Dallas.	11,053	7,394	1,110	9,660	7,630
DeKalb	8,245	10,519	2,741	7,333	11,478
Elmore	6,223	11,356	2,765	4,501	10,852
Escambia	4,809	5,955	1,616	4,020	6,807
Etowah	20,558	17,467	4,277	17,762	17,828
Fayette	3,830	3,604	1,012	3,186	4,338
Franklin	5,953	4,794	1,075	4,961	5,146
Geneva	3,622	4,843	1,323	2,685	5,703
Greene	3,865	805	194	3,295	1,048
Hale	3,481	2,001	486	3,187	2,414
Henry	2,804	2,970	667	2,206	3,613
Houston	8,857	17,360	3,492	7,001	19,989
Jackson	10,628	5,711	2,462	7,418	6,090
Jefferson.	125,889	149,832	22,191	107,766	148,879
Lamar	2,849	3,262	763	2,274	3,214
Lauderdale . . .	15,936	13,728	4,009	12,862	12,942
Lawrence	6,364	3,576	1,624	4,646	3,616
Lee	13,770	16,885	4,572	9,078	17,180
Limestone. . . .	8,087	9,862	3,584	5,455	9,086
Lowndes	3,500	1,328	284	3,328	1,405
Macon	7,253	1,134	283	6,351	1,304
Madison	38,974	51,444	16,989	25,800	53,575
Marengo	5,632	4,470	919	4,402	4,241
Marion	6,167	5,692	1,389	4,505	5,955
Marshall	10,421	12,249	3,795	7,357	12,148
Mobile	54,962	72,935	15,105	45,524	72,203
Monroe	3,872	4,919	759	3,509	5,379
Montgomery . .	37,342	40,742	7,647	28,709	41,131
Morgan	15,091	21,073	7,683	10,594	18,679
Perry	3,712	1,829	213	3,574	2,107
Pickens.	3,783	3,634	690	3,107	3,851
Pike	4,688	5,423	1,024	3,813	5,897
Randolph	3,318	3,813	919	2,462	4,625
Russell	8,647	5,587	1,360	6,589	6,333
St. Clair	6,517	12,447	2,614	4,335	10,604
Shelby	10,317	32,736	5,022	7,138	27,052
Sumter	4,810	1,807	388	4,390	2,212
Talladega	10,695	12,661	2,629	8,291	12,973
Tallapoosa . . .	5,703	8,140	1,562	4,598	8,502
Tuscaloosa . . .	23,495	27,454	7,011	18,166	27,396
Walker	14,831	11,301	3,344	11,338	11,011
Washington . .	4,046	3,270	829	3,402	3,741
Wilcox	3,439	1,671	174	3,369	1,739
Winston	3,415	5,550	1,110	2,954	6,235
Totals	690,080	804,283	183,109	549,506	815,576

Alabama Vote Since 1944

1944, Roosevelt, Dem., 198,918; Dewey, Rep., 44,540; Watson, Proh., 1,095; Thomas, Soc., 190.

1948, Thurmond, States' Rights, 171,443; Dewey, Rep., 40,930; Wallace, Prog., 1,522; Watson, Proh., 1,085.

1952, Eisenhower, Rep., 149,231; Stevenson, Dem., 275,075; Hamblen, Proh., 1,814.

1956, Stevenson, Dem., 290,844; Eisenhower, Rep., 195,694; Independent electors, 20,323.

1960, Kennedy, Dem., 324,050; Nixon, Rep., 237,981; Faubus, States' Rights, 4,367; Decker, Proh., 2,106; King, Afro-Americans, 1,485; scattering, 236.

1964, Dem. (electors unpledged), 209,848; Goldwater, Rep., 479,085; scattering, 105.

1968, Nixon, Rep., 146,923; Humphrey, Dem., 196,579; Wallace, 3d Party, 691,425; Munn, Proh., 4,022.

1972, Nixon, Rep., 728,701; McGovern, Dem., 219,108 plus 37,815 Natl. Demo. Party of Alabama; Schmitz, Conservative, 11,918; Munn., Proh., 8,551.

1976, Carter, Dem., 659,170; Ford, Rep., 504,070; Maddox, Amer. Ind., 9,198; Bubar, Proh., 6,669; Hall, Com., 1,954; MacBride, Libertarian, 1,481.

1980, Reagan, Rep., 654,192; Carter, Dem., 636,730; Anderson, Independent, 16,481; Rarick, Amer. Ind., 15,010; Clark, Libertarian, 13,318; Bubar, Statesman, 1,743; Hall, Com., 1,629; DeBerry, Soc. Workers, 1,303; McReynolds, Socialist, 1,006; Commoner, Citizens, 517.

1984, Reagan, Rep., 872,849; Mondale, Dem., 551,899; Bergland, Libertarian, 9,504.

1988, Bush, Rep., 815,576; Dukakis, Dem., 549,506; Paul, Lib., 8,460; Fulani, Ind., 3,311.

1992, Bush, Rep., 804,283; Clinton, Dem., 690,080; Perot, Ind., 183,109; Marrou, Libertarian, 5,737; Fulani, New Alliance, 2,161.

Alaska

Election District	1992 Clinton (D)	Bush (R)	Perot (I)	1988 Dukakis (D)	Bush (R)
No. 1.	2,055	2,495	2,120		
No. 2.	2,565	2,916	2,137		
No. 3.	4,064	2,447	1,424		
No. 4.	2,688	2,894	1,561		
No. 5.	2,095	1,844	1,684		
No. 6.	1,546	2,345	1,748		
No. 7.	2,088	2,173	2,244		
No. 8.	1,509	2,499	2,325		
No. 9.	1,540	2,349	2,368		
No. 10.	1,947	3,548	1,899		
No. 11.	2,009	2,730	2,081		
No. 12.	1,831	2,999	2,039		
No. 13.	3,001	2,963	1,907		
No. 14.	1,423	3,013	1,599		
No. 15.	2,389	1,842	1,591		
No. 16.	1,814	1,375	1,320		
No. 17.	1,749	2,623	1,958		
No. 18.	2,483	3,629	2,134		
No. 19.	1,931	2,539	1,840		
No. 20.	2,383	2,914	1,823		
No. 21.	2,386	2,437	1,693		
No. 22.	2,253	3,164	1,713		
No. 23.	1,139	2,127	1,217		
No. 24.	1,876	3,441	1,930		
No. 25.	1,513	3,197	2,122		
No. 26.	1,439	2,675	2,419		
No. 27.	1,625	2,757	2,401		
No. 28.	1,522	2,459	2,825		
No. 29.	3,216	2,205	2,026		
No. 30.	1,860	2,434	1,912		
No. 31.	1,969	2,223	1,992		
No. 32.	1,150	2,339	1,724		
No. 33.	1,712	3,100	2,278		
No. 34.	1,455	3,408	2,201		
No. 35.	1,572	2,525	2,139		
No. 36.	1,748	2,081	1,322		
No. 37.	1,822	1,689	925		
No. 38.	1,897	2,011	850		
No. 39.	1,797	1,777	860		
No. 40.	1,211	1,786	1,122		
Totals.	78,294	102,000	73,481	72,584	119,251

Alaska Vote Since 1960

1960, Kennedy, Dem., 29,809; Nixon, Rep., 30,953.

1964, Johnson, Dem., 44,329; Goldwater, Rep., 22,930.

1968, Nixon, Rep., 37,600; Humphrey, Dem., 35,411; Wallace, 3d Party, 10,024.

1972, Nixon, Rep., 55,349; McGovern, Dem., 32,967; Schmitz, Amer., 6,903.

1976, Carter, Dem., 44,058; Ford, Rep., 71,555; MacBride, Libertarian, 6,785.

1980, Reagan, Rep., 86,112; Carter, Dem., 41,842; Clark, Libertarian, 18,479; Anderson, Ind., 11,155; write-in, 857.

1984, Reagan, Rep., 138,377; Mondale, Dem., 62,007; Bergland, Libertarian, 6,378.

1988, Bush, Rep., 119,251; Dukakis, Dem., 72,584; Paul, Lib., 5,484; Fulani, New Alliance, 1,024.

1992, Bush, Rep., 102,000; Clinton, Dem., 78,294; Perot, Ind., 73,481; Gritz, Populist/America First, 1,379; Marrou, Libertarian, 1,378.

Arizona

County	1992 Clinton (D)	Bush (R)	Perot (I)	1988 Dukakis (D)	Bush (R)
Apache	11,218	4,588	1,979	8,944	5,347
Cochise	12,701	12,202	7,857	11,812	15,815
Coconino . . .	18,888	13,769	9,363	14,660	16,649
Gila	7,571	5,781	4,694	7,147	7,861
Graham	3,391	4,169	1,860	3,407	5,120
Greenlee	1,695	1,451	794	1,733	1,526
La Paz	1,808	1,599	1,488	1,746	2,562
Maricopa . . .	285,457	360,049	221,475	230,952	442,337
Mohave	13,255	13,684	12,706	10,197	17,651
Navajo	10,882	7,994	4,787	9,023	10,393
Pima	128,569	97,036	53,925	113,824	117,899
Pinal	15,468	11,669	9,231	13,850	14,966
Santa Cruz . .	3,512	3,024	1,447	3,268	3,320
Yavapai	18,268	23,419	16,409	14,514	27,842
Yuma	10,367	11,652	5,726	8,952	13,253
Totals	543,050	572,086	353,741	454,029	702,541

Arizona Vote Since 1944

1944, Roosevelt, Dem., 80,926; Dewey, Rep., 56,287; Watson, Proh., 421.

1948, Truman, Dem., 95,251; Dewey, Rep., 77,597; Wallace, Prog., 3,310; Watson, Proh., 786; Teichert, Soc. Labor, 121.

1952, Eisenhower, Rep., 152,042; Stevenson, Dem., 108,528.

1956, Eisenhower, Rep., 176,990; Stevenson, Dem., 112,880; Andrews, Ind. 303.

1960, Kennedy, Dem., 176,781; Nixon, Rep., 221,241; Hass, Soc. Labor, 469.

1964, Johnson, Dem., 237,753; Goldwater, Rep., 242,535; Hass, Soc. Labor, 482.

1968, Nixon, Rep., 266,721; Humphrey, Dem., 170,514; Wallace, 3d Party, 46,573; McCarthy, New Party, 2,751; Halstead, Soc. Workers, 85; Cleaver, Peace and Freedom, 217; Blomen, Soc. Labor, 75.

1972, Nixon, Rep., 402,812; McGovern, Dem., 198,540; Schmitz, Amer., 21,208; Soc. Workers, 30,945. Due to ballot peculiarities in 3 counties (particularly Pima), thousands of voters cast ballots for the Soc. Workers Party *and* one of the major candidates. Court ordered both votes counted as official.

1976, Carter, Dem., 295,602; Ford, Rep., 418,642; McCarthy, Ind., 19,229; MacBride, Libertarian, 7,647; Camejo, Soc. Workers, 928; Anderson, Amer., 564; Maddox, Amer. Ind., 85.

1980, Reagan, Rep., 529,688; Carter, Dem., 246,843; Anderson, Ind., 76,952; Clark, Libertarian, 18,784; De Berry, Soc. Workers, 1,100; Commoner, Citizens, 551; Hall, Com., 25; Griswold, Workers World, 2.

1984, Reagan, Rep., 681,416; Mondale, Dem., 333,854; Bergland, Libertarian, 10,585.

1988, Bush, Rep., 702,541; Dukakis, Dem., 454,029; Paul, Lib., 13,351; Fulani, New Alliance, 1,662.

1992, Bush, Rep., 572,086; Clinton, Dem., 543,050; Perot, Ind., 353,741; Gritz, Populist/America First, 8,141; Marrou, Libertarian, 6,759; Hagelin, Natural Law, 2,267.

Arkansas

County	1992 Clinton (D)	Bush (R)	Perot (I)	1988 Dukakis (D)	Bush (R)
Arkansas	4,709	2,594	639	3,075	4,007
Ashley	5,876	2,686	931	4,466	4,111
Baxter	6,991	5,640	2,938	4,808	8,614
Benton	15,774	21,126	6,128	9,399	24,295
Boone	6,128	6,094	2,079	3,998	7,567
Bradley	2,954	1,482	391	2,167	2,089
Calhoun	1,389	1,047	257	1,024	1,316
Carroll	3,769	3,535	1,500	2,632	4,553
Chicot.	3,504	1,242	347	2,426	1,901
Clark	5,767	2,403	714	4,675	3,389
Clay	4,848	1,647	568	3,442	2,766
Cleburne	5,090	3,580	1,263	3,404	4,932
Cleveland	1,893	1,127	337	1,404	1,462
Columbia	4,747	3,702	1,090	3,706	5,810
Conway	4,898	2,719	803	4,134	4,066
Craighead . . .	13,931	9,104	2,274	9,083	11,887
Crawford. . . .	6,656	6,882	2,442	3,582	9,092
Crittenden	9,683	5,910	848	6,702	7,441

Cross	4,058	2,303	602	2,989	3,186
Dallas.	2,107	1,458	345	1,990	1,947
Desha	3,815	1,279	392	2,859	2,334
Drew	3,748	1,938	596	2,578	2,995
Faulkner	13,000	9,491	2,437	7,302	10,678
Franklin	3,217	2,495	987	2,458	3,588
Fulton	2,827	1,258	631	2,018	1,918
Garland	18,811	12,886	3,475	11,406	19,281
Grant	3,190	2,272	702	2,142	2,717
Greene	7,541	3,510	1,213	5,065	5,161
Hempstead . . .	5,476	2,387	1,022	3,841	3,938
Hot Spring. . . .	6,308	3,036	1,209	5,090	4,181
Howard.	2,764	1,728	466	1,818	2,510
Independence .	7,083	4,232	1,444	4,523	6,637
Izard	3,419	1,532	606	2,652	2,824
Jackson	4,944	1,864	673	4,199	3,049
Jefferson.	21,819	7,525	2,067	16,664	12,520
Johnson	3,951	2,563	1,013	2,818	4,046
Lafayette.	2,273	1,188	504	1,915	1,860
Lawrence	4,146	2,124	636	3,179	3,205
Lee	3,436	1,293	308	2,878	1,863
Lincoln	2,805	1,142	390	2,204	1,557
Little River. . . .	3,327	1,483	890	2,740	2,347
Logan.	3,995	3,408	1,220	1,254	2,203
Lonoke	7,963	6,253	1,554	4,786	7,215
Madison	2,415	2,238	598	2,106	3,067
Marion	2,757	2,023	1,327	2,033	2,993
Miller	7,050	5,273	2,249	5,437	7,110
Mississippi . . .	10,046	4,697	981	6,759	7,841
Monroe	2,578	1,324	355	2,052	1,862
Montgomery . .	1,904	1,205	576	1,362	1,752
Nevada.	2,242	1,217	455	1,732	1,714
Newton	1,765	1,730	608	1,489	2,504
Ouachita	7,411	3,711	1,238	5,229	6,297
Perry	1,906	1,162	412	1,470	1,627
Phillips	6,456	2,695	634	5,580	3,892
Pike	2,168	1,577	472	1,681	2,105
Poinsett	5,341	2,425	761	3,873	3,644
Polk	3,162	2,757	1,225	2,390	4,099
Pope	7,704	8,056	1,989	4,941	10,084
Prairie	2,366	1,154	434	1,688	1,947
Pulaski	79,482	47,789	8,751	55,857	70,562
Randolph	3,921	1,766	578	2,781	2,560
St. Francis . . .	6,548	3,289	766	4,656	4,298
Saline.	12,671	10,105	2,751	8,436	12,353
Scott	2,228	1,695	610	1,707	2,507
Searcy	1,679	1,772	503	1,340	2,743
Sebastian	16,570	16,817	6,023	9,684	24,426
Sevier	2,558	1,592	643	2,037	2,254
Sharp	3,761	2,486	921	2,955	3,623
Stone	2,622	1,672	697	1,728	2,186
Union	8,786	7,305	1,919	5,931	10,581
Van Buren . . .	3,819	2,612	888	2,607	3,562
Washington. . .	22,029	20,292	5,304	12,557	23,601
White	10,494	8,538	2,366	6,957	11,094
Woodruff. . . .	2,589	676	227	1,924	1,097
Yell	4,165	2,506	940	2,763	3,535
Totals	505,823	337,324	99,132	349,237	466,578

Arkansas Vote Since 1944

1944, Roosevelt, Dem., 148,965; Dewey, Rep., 63,551; Thomas, Soc., 438.

1948, Truman, Dem., 149,659; Dewey, Rep., 50,959; Thurmond, States' Rights, 40,068; Thomas, Soc., 1,037; Wallace, Prog., 751; Watson, Proh., 1.

1952, Eisenhower, Rep., 177,155; Stevenson, Dem., 226,300; Hamblen, Proh., 886; MacArthur, Christian Nationalist, 458; Hass, Soc. Labor, 1.

1956, Stevenson, Dem., 213,277; Eisenhower, Rep., 186,287; Andrews, Ind., 7,008.

1960, Kennedy, Dem., 215,049; Nixon, Rep., 184,508; Natl. States' Rights, 28,952.

1964, Johnson, Dem., 314,197; Goldwater, Rep., 243,264; Kasper, Natl. States' Rights, 2,965.

1968, Nixon, Rep., 189,062; Humphrey, Dem., 184,901; Wallace, 3d Party, 235,627.

1972, Nixon, Rep., 445,751; McGovern, Dem., 198,899; Schmitz, Amer., 3,016.

1976, Carter, Dem., 498,604; Ford, Rep., 267,903; McCarthy, Ind., 639; Anderson, Amer., 389.

1980, Reagan, Rep., 403,164; Carter, Dem., 398,041; Anderson, Ind., 22,468; Clark, Libertarian, 8,970; Commoner, Citizens, 2,345; Bubar, Statesman, 1,350; Hall, Com., 1,244.

1984, Reagan, Rep., 534,774; Mondale, Dem., 338,646; Bergland, Libertarian, 2,220.

1988, Bush, Rep., 466,578; Dukakis, Dem., 349,237; Duke, Chr. Pop., 5,146; Paul, Lib., 3,297.

1992, Clinton, Dem., 505,823; Bush, Rep., 337,324; Perot, Ind., 99,132; Phillips, U.S. Taxpayers, 1,437; Marrou, Libertarian, 1,261; Fulani, New Alliance, 1,022.

California

County	1992 Clinton (D)	Bush (R)	Perot (I)	Dukakis (D)	1988 Bush (R)
Alameda	334,224	109,292	81,643	310,283	162,815
Alpine	215	222	186	230	306
Amador	5,286	5,477	4,553	5,197	6,893
Butte	32,489	31,608	20,231	30,406	40,143
Calaveras	5,989	6,006	4,848	5,674	7,640
Colusa	1,798	2,589	1,206	2,022	3,077
Contra Costa	194,960	112,965	72,518	169,411	158,652
Del Norte	3,639	3,083	2,575	3,587	3,714
El Dorado	21,012	25,906	17,503	19,801	30,021
Fresno	92,418	89,137	36,299	92,635	94,835
Glenn	2,666	3,812	2,278	2,894	4,944
Humboldt	28,854	18,299	12,340	29,781	21,460
Imperial	11,109	9,759	4,247	10,243	12,889
Inyo	2,695	3,689	1,999	2,653	5,042
Kern	60,510	80,762	36,891	55,083	90,550
Kings	9,982	10,673	4,899	9,142	12,118
Lake	10,548	6,678	5,797	9,828	9,366
Lassen	3,388	3,836	3,004	3,446	5,157
Los Angeles	1,446,529	799,607	488,624	1,372,352	1,239,716
Madera	10,863	13,066	6,156	10,642	13,255
Marin	76,158	30,479	22,986	69,394	46,855
Mariposa	3,023	2,982	2,211	2,998	3,768
Mendocino	18,344	7,958	9,753	17,152	12,979
Merced	20,133	17,981	10,914	20,105	21,717
Modoc	1,489	1,803	1,269	1,416	2,518
Mono	1,489	1,570	1,248	1,284	2,177
Monterey	54,861	36,461	24,472	48,998	50,022
Napa	24,215	15,662	13,150	22,283	23,235
Nevada	15,433	17,343	11,072	14,980	21,383
Orange	306,930	426,613	232,394	269,013	586,230
Placer	30,783	38,298	21,741	27,516	42,096
Plumas	3,742	3,599	2,551	4,251	4,603
Riverside	166,241	159,457	102,233	133,122	199,979
Sacramento	197,540	160,366	91,412	188,557	201,832
San Benito	5,354	4,112	3,182	4,559	5,578
San Bernardino	183,634	176,563	109,183	151,118	235,167
San Diego	367,397	352,125	259,249	333,264	523,143
San Francisco	233,263	57,352	29,018	201,887	72,503
San Joaquin	63,655	58,355	31,205	61,699	75,309
San Luis Obispo	40,136	36,384	27,314	35,667	46,613
San Mateo	149,232	75,080	50,465	141,859	109,261
Santa Barbara	69,215	57,375	35,105	63,586	77,524
Santa Clara	296,265	170,870	128,895	277,810	254,442
Santa Cruz	66,183	24,916	21,615	63,133	37,728
Shasta	21,605	28,190	17,990	21,171	32,402
Sierra	653	691	519	791	860
Siskiyou	8,254	6,660	5,567	8,365	9,056
Solano	64,320	38,883	27,851	54,344	50,314
Sonoma	104,334	47,619	43,859	91,262	67,725
Stanislaus	52,415	47,275	27,651	44,685	51,648
Sutter	7,883	12,956	4,881	6,557	14,100
Tehama	7,508	7,419	5,884	7,213	9,854
Trinity	1,967	1,886	2,092	2,518	3,267
Tulare	31,188	40,482	16,430	30,711	46,891
Tuolumne	9,216	8,525	6,294	8,717	10,646
Ventura	99,011	94,911	71,844	89,065	147,604
Yolo	33,297	17,574	11,073	30,429	22,358
Yuba	5,785	7,333	3,637	5,444	8,937
Totals	**5,121,325**	**3,630,574**	**2,296,006**	**4,702,233**	**5,054,917**

California Vote Since 1944

1944, Roosevelt, Dem., 1,988,564; Dewey, Rep., 1,512,965; Watson, Proh., 14,770; Thomas, Soc., 3,923; Teichert, Soc. Labor, 327.

1948, Truman, Dem., 1,913,134; Dewey, Rep., 1,895,269; Wallace, Prog., 190,381; Watson, Proh., 16,926; Thomas, Soc., 3,459; Thurmond, States' Rights, 1,228; Teichert, Soc. Labor, 195; Dobbs, Soc. Workers, 133.

1952, Eisenhower, Rep., 2,897,310; Stevenson, Dem., 2,197,548; Hallinan, Prog., 24,106; Hamblen, Proh., 15,653; MacArthur, (Tenny Ticket), 3,326; (Kellems Ticket) 178; Hass, Soc. Labor, 273; Hoopes, Soc., 206; scattered, 3,249.

1956, Eisenhower, Rep., 3,027,668; Stevenson, Dem., 2,420,136; Holtwick, Proh., 11,119; Andrews, Constitution, 6,087; Hass, Soc. Labor, 300; Hoopes, Soc., 123; Dobbs, Soc. Workers, 96; Smith, Christian Natl., 8.

1960, Kennedy, Dem., 3,224,099; Nixon, Rep., 3,259,722; Decker, Proh., 21,706; Hass, Soc. Labor, 1,051.

1964, Johnson, Dem., 4,171,877; Goldwater, Rep., 2,879,108; Hass, Soc. Labor, 489; DeBerry, Soc. Workers, 378; Munn, Proh., 305; Hensley, Universal, 19.

1968, Nixon, Rep., 3,467,664; Humphrey, Dem., 3,244,318; Wallace, 3d Party, 487,270; Peace and Freedom, 27,707; McCarthy, Alternative, 20,721; Gregory, write-in, 3,230;

Mitchell, Com., 260; Munn, Proh., 59; Blomen, Soc. Labor, 341; Soeters, Defense, 17.

1972, Nixon, Rep., 4,602,096; McGovern, Dem., 3,475,847; Schmitz, Amer., 232,554; Spock, Peace and Freedom, 55,167; Hall, Com., 373; Hospers, Libertarian, 980; Munn, Proh., 53; Fisher, Soc. Labor, 197; Jenness, Soc. Workers, 574; Green, Universal, 21.

1976, Carter, Dem., 3,742,284; Ford, Rep., 3,882,244; MacBride, Libertarian, 56,388; Maddox, Amer. Ind., 51,098; Wright, People's, 41,731; Camejo, Soc. Workers, 17,259; Hall, Com., 12,766; write-in, McCarthy, 58,412; other write-in, 4,935.

1980, Reagan, Rep. 4,524,858; Carter, Dem., 3,083,661; Anderson, Ind., 739,833; Clark, Libertarian, 148,434; Commoner, Ind., 61,063; Smith, Peace and Freedom, 18,116; Rarick, Amer. Ind., 9,856.

1984, Reagan, Rep. 5,305,410; Mondale, Dem., 3,815,947; Bergland, Libertarian, 48,400.

1988, Bush, Rep., 5,054,917; Dukakis, Dem., 4,702,233; Paul, Lib., 70,105; Fulani, Ind., 31,181.

1992, Clinton, Dem., 5,121,325; Bush, Rep., 3,630,575; Perot, Ind., 2,296,006; Marrou, Libertarian, 48,139; Daniels, Ind., 18,597; Phillips, U.S. Taxpayers, 12,711.

Colorado

County	1992 Clinton (D)	Bush (R)	Perot (I)	1988 Dukakis (D)	Bush (R)
Adams	45,357	30,856	26,379	49,464	43,163
Alamosa	1,928	1,572	1,089	2,146	2,567
Arapahoe	66,607	72,221	44,363	61,113	95,926
Archuleta	819	1,242	741	795	1,440
Baca	726	1,240	647	851	1,670
Bent	985	759	506	1,088	1,032
Boulder	64,567	33,553	27,762	57,265	48,174
Chaffee	2,284	2,419	1,549	2,548	3,080
Cheyenne	301	615	292	399	760
Clear Creek	1,744	1,356	1,308	1,698	1,820
Conejos	1,705	1,160	578	1,976	1,445
Costilla	1,180	366	199	1,120	454
Crowley	570	602	276	630	862
Custer	343	651	368	310	753
Delta	3,424	4,359	2,627	3,521	5,449
Denver	121,961	55,418	37,298	127,173	77,753
Dolores	242	315	285	230	488
Douglas	9,991	18,592	11,329	6,931	17,035
Eagle	3,870	3,100	3,821	3,314	4,366
Elbert	1,237	2,205	1,567	1,566	2,805
El Paso	45,827	86,044	34,346	39,995	96,965
Fremont	5,356	5,961	3,709	5,278	7,623
Garfield	5,082	4,404	4,408	4,620	6,358
Gilpin	726	462	545	804	728
Grand	1,678	1,763	1,454	1,451	2,306
Gunnison	2,389	1,662	1,671	1,897	2,520
Hinsdale	151	188	136	111	295
Huerfano	1,224	685	385	1,876	1,079
Jackson	216	422	326	294	584
Jefferson	80,834	82,705	58,404	81,824	110,820
Kiowa	290	472	267	398	645
Kit Carson	925	1,801	919	1,196	2,262
Lake	1,426	605	863	1,516	969
La Plata	5,913	5,522	4,083	5,443	7,714
Larimer	38,232	35,995	24,879	35,703	45,967
Las Animas	3,847	1,739	953	4,075	2,162
Lincoln	640	1,079	581	874	1,356
Logan	2,718	3,420	2,184	3,382	4,485
Mesa	15,162	18,169	10,474	14,372	22,150
Mineral	171	159	117	174	217
Moffat	1,386	1,809	1,875	1,634	2,757
Montezuma	2,270	3,124	2,205	2,233	4,208
Montrose	3,713	4,847	3,093	3,748	6,012
Morgan	2,985	3,724	2,175	3,728	4,795
Otero	3,485	3,120	1,590	3,910	4,265
Ouray	461	653	466	439	814
Park	1,307	1,530	1,396	1,343	1,909
Philips	692	1,075	525	923	1,317
Pitkin	3,820	1,686	1,907	3,420	2,801
Prowers	1,770	2,371	1,184	2,207	2,978
Pueblo	30,261	16,210	9,841	32,788	20,119
Rio Blanco	778	1,231	794	803	1,821
Rio Grande	1,541	1,927	1,043	1,545	2,626
Routt	3,188	2,358	2,564	2,922	3,264
Saguache	1,011	675	471	1,033	945
San Juan	147	118	183	192	210
San Miguel	1,380	628	634	961	798
Sedgwick	397	447	295	611	921
Summit	3,344	2,256	2,715	2,595	2,893
Teller	1,873	3,050	1,927	1,656	3,760
Washington	660	1,266	671	958	1,707
Weld	19,295	20,958	13,571	20,548	26,497
Yuma	1,269	2,019	1,197	1,835	2,513
Totals	**629,681**	**52,850**	**366,010**	**621,453**	**728,177**

Colorado Vote Since 1944

1944, Roosevelt, Dem., 234,331; Dewey, Rep., 268,731; Thomas, Soc., 1,977.

1948, Truman, Dem., 267,288; Dewey, Rep., 239,714; Wallace, Prog., 6,115; Thomas, Soc., 1,678; Dobbs, Soc. Workers, 228; Teichert, Soc. Labor, 214.

1952, Eisenhower, Rep., 379,782; Stevenson, Dem., 245,504; MacArthur, Constitution, 2,181; Hallinan, Prog., 1,919; Hoopes, Soc., 365; Hass, Soc. Labor, 352.

1956, Eisenhower, Rep., 394,479; Stevenson, Dem., 263,997; Hass, Soc. Lab., 3,308; Andrews, Ind., 759; Hoopes, Soc., 531.

1960, Kennedy, Dem., 330,629; Nixon, Rep., 402,242; Hass, Soc. Labor, 2,803; Dobbs, Soc. Workers, 572.

1964, Johnson, Dem., 476,024; Goldwater, Rep., 296,767; Hass, Soc. Labor, 302; DeBerry, Soc. Workers, 2,537; Munn, Proh., 1,356.

1968, Nixon, Rep., 409,345; Humphrey, Dem., 335,174; Wallace, 3d Party, 60,813; Blomen, Soc. Labor, 3,016; Gregory, New-party, 1,393; Munn, Proh., 275; Halstead, Soc. Workers, 235.

1972, Nixon, Rep., 597,189; McGovern, Dem., 329,980; Fisher, Soc. Labor, 4,361; Hospers, Libertarian, 1,111; Hall, Com., 432; Jenness, Soc. Workers, 555; Munn, Proh., 467; Schmitz, Amer., 17,269; Spock, Peoples, 2,403.

1976, Carter, Dem., 460,353; Ford, Rep., 584,367; McCarthy, Ind., 26,107; MacBride, Libertarian, 5,330; Bubar, Proh., 2,882.

1980, Reagan, Rep., 652,264; Carter, Dem., 367,973; Anderson, Ind., 130,633; Clark, Libertarian, 25,744; Commoner, Citizens, 5,614; Bubar, Statesman, 1,180; Pulley, Socialist, 520; Hall, Com., 487.

1984, Reagan, Rep., 821,817; Mondale, Dem., 454,975; Bergland, Libertarian, 11,257.

1988, Bush, Rep., 728,177; Dukakis, Dem., 621,453; Paul, Lib., 15,482; Dodge, Proh., 4,604.

1992, Clinton, Dem., 629,681; Bush, Rep., 562,850; Perot, Ind., 366,010; Marrou, Libertarian, 8,669; Fulani, New Alliance, 1,608.

Connecticut

	1992			1988	
City	Clinton (D)	Bush (R)	Perot (I)	Dukakis (D)	Bush (R)
Bridgeport ...	22,321	13,149	6,263	23,831	17,084
Hartford	26,971	6,180	3,390	27,295	8,100
New Britain...	14,159	7,040	4,983	15,843	9,569
New Haven...	29,774	8,931	4,130	31,951	11,616
Norwalk	16,488	14,743	6,046	14,518	18,618
Stamford	23,185	19,809	6,763	20,773	24,877
Waterbury ...	16,366	16,155	9,188	18,202	20,018
West Hartford .	19,623	12,266	5,017	19,311	16,482
Other.......	513,431	480,040	302,991	504,860	623,877
Totals	682,318	578,313	348,771	676,584	750,241

Connecticut Vote Since 1944

1944, Roosevelt, Dem., 435,146; Dewey, Rep., 390,527; Thomas, Soc., 5,097; Teichert, Soc. Labor, 1,220.

1948, Truman, Dem., 423,297; Dewey, Rep., 437,754; Wallace, Prog., 13,713; Thomas, Soc., 6,964; Teichert, Soc. Labor, 1,184; Dobbs, Soc. Workers, 606.

1952, Eisenhower, Rep., 611,012; Stevenson, Dem., 481,649; Hoopes, Soc., 2,244; Hallinan, Peoples, 1,466; Hass, Soc. Labor, 535; write-in, 5.

1956, Eisenhower, Rep., 711,837; Stevenson, Dem., 405,079; scattered, 205.

1960, Kennedy, Dem., 657,055; Nixon, Rep., 565,813.

1964, Johnson, Dem., 826,269; Goldwater, Rep., 390,996; scattered, 1,313.

1968, Nixon, Rep., 556,721; Humphrey, Dem., 621,561; Wallace, 3d Party, 76,650; scattered, 1,300.

1972, Nixon, Rep., 810,763; McGovern, Dem., 555,498; Schmitz, Amer., 17,239; scattered, 777.

1976, Carter, Dem., 647,895; Ford, Rep., 719,261; Maddox, George Wallace Party, 7,101; LaRouche, U.S. Labor, 1,789.

1980, Reagan, Rep., 677,210; Carter, Dem., 541,732; Anderson, Ind., 171,807; Clark, Libertarian, 8,570; Commoner, Citizens, 6,130; scattered, 836.

1984, Reagan, Rep., 890,877; Mondale, Dem., 569,597.

1988, Bush, Rep., 750,241; Dukakis, Dem., 676,584; Paul, Lib., 14,071; Fulani, New Alliance, 2,491.

1992, Clinton, Dem., 682,318; Bush, Rep., 578,313; Perot, Ind., 348,771; Marrou, Libertarian, 5,391; Fulani, New Alliance, 1,363.

Delaware

	1992			1988	
County	Clinton (D)	Bush (R)	Perot (I)	Dukakis (D)	Bush (R)
Kent........	15,364	15,562	8,916	12,996	19,923
New Castle ...	91,516	66,311	37,581	79,147	92,587
Sussex......	19,174	20,440	12,716	16,504	27,129
Totals	126,054	102,313	59,213	108,647	139,639

Delaware Vote Since 1944

1944, Roosevelt, Dem., 68,166; Dewey, Rep., 56,747; Watson, Proh., 294; Thomas, Soc., 154.

1948, Truman, Dem., 67,813; Dewey, Rep., 69,688; Wallace, Prog., 1,050; Watson, Proh., 343; Thomas, Soc., 250; Teichert, Soc. Labor, 29.

1952, Eisenhower, Rep., 90,059; Stevenson, Dem., 83,315; Hass, Soc. Labor, 242; Hamblen, Proh., 234; Hallinan, Prog., 155; Hoopes, Soc., 20.

1956, Eisenhower, Rep., 98,057; Stevenson, Dem., 79,421; Oltwick, Proh., 400; Hass, Soc. Labor, 110.

1960, Kennedy, Dem., 99,590; Nixon, Rep., 96,373; Faubus, States' Rights, 354; Decker, Proh., 284; Hass, Soc. Labor, 82.

1964, Johnson, Dem., 122,704; Goldwater, Rep., 78,078; Hass, Soc. Labor, 113; Munn, Proh., 425.

1968, Nixon, Rep., 96,714; Humphrey, Dem., 89,194; Wallace, 3d Party, 28,459.

1972, Nixon, Rep., 140,357; McGovern, Dem., 92,283; Schmitz, Amer., 2,638; Munn, Proh., 238.

1976, Carter, Dem., 122,596; Ford, Rep., 109,831; McCarthy, non-partisan, 2,437; Anderson, Amer., 645; LaRouche, U.S. Labor, 136; Bubar, Proh., 103; Levin, Soc. Labor, 86.

1980, Reagan, Rep., 111,252; Carter, Dem., 105,754; Anderson, Ind., 16,288; Clark, Libertarian, 1,974; Greaves, Amer., 400.

1984, Reagan, Rep., 152,190; Mondale, Dem., 101,656; Bergland, Libertarian, 268.

1988, Bush, Rep., 139,639; Dukakis, Dem., 108,647; Paul, Lib., 1,162; Fulani, New Alliance, 443.

1992, Clinton, Dem., 126,054; Bush, Rep., 102,313; Perot, Ind., 59,213; Fulani, New Alliance, 1,105.

District of Columbia

	1992			1988	
	Clinton (D)	Bush (R)	Perot (I)	Dukakis (D)	Bush (R)
Totals	192,619	20,698	9,681	159,407	27,590

District of Columbia Vote Since 1964

1964, Johnson, Dem., 169,796; Goldwater, Rep., 28,801.

1968, Nixon, Rep., 31,012; Humphrey, Dem., 139, 566.

1972, Nixon, Rep., 35,226; McGovern, Dem., 127,627; Reed, Soc. Workers, 316; Hall, Com., 252.

1976, Carter, Dem., 137,818; Ford, Rep., 27,873; Camejo, Soc. Workers, 545; MacBride, Libertarian, 274; Hall, Com., 219; LaRouche, U.S. Labor, 157.

1980, Reagan, Rep., 23,313; Carter, Dem., 130,231; Anderson, Ind., 16,131; Commoner, Citizens, 1,826; Clark, Libertarian, 1,104; Hall, Com., 369; DeBerry, Soc. Workers, 173; Griswold, Workers World, 52; write-ins, 690.

1984, Mondale, Dem., 180,408; Reagan, Rep., 29,009; Bergland, Libertarian, 279.

1988, Bush, Rep., 27,590; Dukakis, Dem., 159,407; Fulani, New Alliance, 2,901; Paul, Lib., 554.

1992, Clinton, Dem., 192,619; Bush, Rep., 20,698; Perot, Ind., 9,681; Fulani, New Alliance, 1,459; Daniels, Ind., 1,186.

Florida

	1992			1988	
County	Clinton (D)	Bush (R)	Perot (I)	Dukakis (D)	Bush (R)
Alachua.....	37,876	22,806	15,293	29,375	30,124
Baker	1,974	3,417	1,315	1,353	3,414
Bay........	12,830	22,820	9,702	11,582	31,712
Bradford	3,040	3,671	1,572	2,386	4,218
Brevard.....	61,070	84,545	49,491	42,967	104,721
Broward.....	276,309	164,782	90,923	218,211	220,196
Calhoun.....	1,665	1,721	1,176	1,329	2,420
Charlotte	22,904	24,302	14,711	15,967	28,879
Citrus	15,935	16,402	12,310	12,177	21,052
Clay	10,597	26,313	8,414	7,766	25,882

County					
Collier	18,794	38,447	14,514	12,768	38,910
Columbia	5,526	6,489	2,906	4,072	7,759
Dade	254,444	235,149	53,957	216,847	270,672
De Soto	2,646	3,070	1,687	2,181	4,237
Dixie	1,855	1,401	1,094	1,366	2,027
Duval	92,010	123,480	33,335	74,832	127,875
Escambia	32,018	52,775	19,868	29,934	64,774
Flagler	6,692	6,241	3,387	4,241	6,494
Franklin	1,534	1,660	1,143	1,283	1,911
Gadsden	8,478	3,975	1,871	6,368	5,987
Gilchrist	1,511	1,395	1,090	1,137	1,854
Glades	1,305	1,185	878	1,034	1,546
Gulf	1,938	2,650	1,245	1,687	3,040
Hamilton	1,622	1,402	695	1,314	2,062
Hardee	2,017	2,898	1,498	1,688	3,636
Hendry	2,690	3,279	2,032	2,036	3,962
Hernando	19,171	17,896	11,845	15,432	21,179
Highlands	11,234	14,497	6,592	8,087	16,713
Hillsborough	115,261	130,611	63,037	98,969	150,065
Holmes	1,877	3,196	1,426	1,639	4,221
Indian River	12,359	19,137	12,375	10,447	24,619
Jackson	5,481	6,720	2,447	5,002	8,392
Jefferson	2,270	1,506	894	2,055	2,326
Lafayette	866	1,037	612	722	1,450
Lake	23,199	30,818	15,606	16,762	37,314
Lee	53,656	73,423	38,446	40,709	87,247
Leon	47,770	31,964	17,207	33,446	36,032
Levy	4,330	3,796	2,784	3,433	5,250
Liberty	820	1,126	617	709	1,419
Madison	2,644	2,006	1,174	1,950	2,556
Manatee	33,826	42,708	23,282	26,618	51,160
Marion	30,823	35,438	20,524	20,679	41,488
Martin	14,778	24,768	13,433	11,486	31,270
Monroe	10,435	9,891	8,306	10,151	15,919
Nassau	5,497	9,364	3,251	4,138	8,366
Okaloosa	12,003	32,755	16,649	9,726	40,295
Okeechobee	3,418	3,298	2,645	3,007	4,733
Orange	82,656	108,738	44,827	53,991	117,141
Osceola	15,009	19,139	11,021	9,811	21,350
Palm Beach	187,840	140,317	76,223	144,143	181,408
Pasco	53,125	47,721	34,650	50,369	63,788
Pinellas	160,221	158,733	101,150	152,374	210,971
Polk	51,442	65,952	28,198	38,236	77,065
Putnam	10,707	8,909	5,975	8,569	11,621
St. Johns	12,284	20,173	7,397	7,999	19,164
St. Lucie	23,873	24,397	19,813	17,427	32,241
Santa Rosa	6,526	17,229	8,735	5,251	18,948
Sarasota	54,536	66,831	34,281	42,095	84,585
Seminole	35,649	57,085	24,477	22,627	60,328
Sumter	5,027	4,366	2,901	3,900	5,933
Suwannee	3,985	4,571	2,790	3,126	5,859
Taylor	2,568	2,693	1,929	1,762	4,054
Union	1,247	1,543	770	691	1,643
Volusia	65,213	59,155	30,813	55,437	74,116
Wakulla	2,319	2,586	1,790	1,605	3,157
Walton	3,886	5,719	3,886	3,231	7,481
Washington	2,544	3,694	1,596	2,139	4,366
Totals	2,071,651	2,171,781	1,052,481	1,655,851	2,616,597

Florida Vote Since 1944

1944, Roosevelt, Dem., 339,377; Dewey, Rep., 143,215.
1948, Truman, Dem., 281,988; Dewey, Rep., 194,280; Thurmond, States' Rights, 89,755; Wallace, Prog., 11,620.
1952, Eisenhower, Rep., 544,036; Stevenson, Dem., 444,950; scattered, 351.
1956, Eisenhower, Rep., 643,849; Stevenson, Dem., 480,371.
1960, Kennedy, Dem., 748,700; Nixon, Rep., 795,476.
1964, Johnson, Dem., 948,540; Goldwater, Rep., 905,941.
1968, Nixon, Rep., 886,804; Humphrey, Dem., 676,794; Wallace, 3d Party, 624,207.
1972, Nixon, Rep., 1,857,759; McGovern, Dem., 718,117; scattered, 7,407.
1976, Carter, Dem., 1,636,000; Ford, Rep., 1,469,531; McCarthy, Ind., 23,643; Anderson, Amer., 21,325.
1980, Reagan, Rep., 2,046,951; Carter, Dem., 1,419,475; Anderson, Ind., 189,692; Clark, Libertarian, 30,524; write-ins, 285.
1984, Reagan, Rep., 2,728,775; Mondale, Dem., 1,448,344.
1988, Bush, Rep., 2,616,597; Dukakis, Dem., 1,655,851; Paul, Lib., 19,796, Fulani, New Alliance, 6,655.
1992, Bush, Rep., 2,171,781; Clinton, Dem., 2,071,651; Perot, Ind., 1,052,481; Marrou, Libertarian, 15,068.

Georgia

County	1992 Clinton (D)	Bush (R)	Perot (I)	1988 Dukakis (D)	Bush (R)
Appling	2,455	2,514	1,047	1,837	3,000
Atkinson	1,056	779	342	887	1,126
Bacon	1,423	1,301	604	780	1,407
Baker	864	391	210	707	629
Baldwin	5,813	4,262	1,679	4,008	5,852
Banks	1,530	1,551	583	984	1,590
Barrow	3,991	4,328	1,633	2,442	4,738
Bartow	6,675	7,742	2,500	4,884	8,039
Ben Hill	2,348	1,476	619	1,867	2,005
Berrien	2,103	1,637	796	1,381	2,030
Bibb	28,070	19,847	6,021	22,084	22,179
Bleckley	1,710	1,570	662	1,175	1,950
Brantley	1,883	1,541	840	1,450	1,539
Brooks	1,895	1,779	630	1,500	2,136
Bryan	2,031	2,789	1,095	1,423	2,802
Bulloch	4,903	5,690	2,020	3,417	6,354
Burke	3,647	2,390	807	2,861	2,988
Butts	2,448	1,768	619	1,730	2,184
Calhoun	1,301	464	248	901	644
Camden	2,952	3,517	1,077	2,090	2,913
Candler	1,192	1,014	541	877	1,261
Carroll	8,404	10,750	3,358	4,706	10,754
Catoosa	4,817	7,599	2,290	3,588	9,319
Charlton	1,127	1,333	427	943	1,327
Chatham	31,533	31,925	8,269	25,063	35,623
Chattahoochee	604	413	177	362	454
Chattooga	2,976	2,439	965	2,206	3,665
Cherokee	8,113	16,054	4,950	4,378	14,593
Clarke	15,403	10,459	2,987	11,154	11,150
Clay	778	264	155	595	398
Clayton	25,890	23,965	7,942	14,689	28,225
Clinch	759	790	286	594	863
Cobb	63,960	103,734	28,747	39,297	106,621
Coffee	3,275	3,778	1,256	2,777	4,019
Colquitt	3,891	4,680	1,682	2,998	5,653
Columbia	7,115	16,657	4,379	4,617	16,401
Cook	1,731	1,318	537	1,226	1,555
Coweta	7,093	9,814	3,587	4,212	9,668
Crawford	1,648	974	549	1,340	1,235
Crisp	2,610	2,253	823	1,690	2,916
Dade	1,782	2,191	823	1,120	2,539
Dawson	1,399	1,696	790	761	1,908
Decatur	3,198	3,142	1,068	2,348	3,866
DeKalb	124,559	70,282	19,741	92,521	90,179
Dodge	3,002	2,287	978	2,164	2,677
Dooly	1,993	1,034	350	1,613	1,386
Dougherty	15,236	12,455	3,178	12,579	15,520
Douglas	8,869	13,349	4,362	5,086	13,493
Early	1,970	1,457	652	1,359	1,918
Echols	312	361	238	245	422
Effingham	2,690	3,814	1,443	1,905	3,933
Elbert	3,025	2,372	757	2,118	2,796
Emanuel	2,951	2,662	755	2,387	3,530
Evans	1,230	1,244	480	1,023	1,707
Fannin	2,902	3,255	1,028	2,123	4,271
Fayette	8,430	17,576	5,598	4,593	16,443
Floyd	11,614	12,378	3,779	8,548	14,697
Forsyth	4,936	8,652	3,453	2,347	7,947
Franklin	2,505	2,391	1,014	1,842	2,615
Fulton	147,459	85,451	23,578	120,752	91,785
Gilmer	2,311	2,661	879	1,363	3,353
Glascock	316	516	180	210	580
Glynn	8,581	11,242	3,053	6,339	11,126
Gordon	4,103	5,265	1,818	2,369	6,051
Grady	2,520	2,370	1,126	1,883	2,989
Greene	2,259	1,307	483	1,818	1,432
Gwinnett	44,253	81,822	23,926	20,948	66,372
Habersham	3,098	4,569	1,444	2,114	4,871
Hall	11,214	16,108	5,043	7,782	17,415
Hancock	2,461	506	189	1,947	621
Haralson	3,281	3,142	1,167	2,404	4,529
Harris	2,679	3,316	954	1,905	3,414
Hart	3,614	2,607	1,376	2,476	3,044
Heard	1,456	1,190	617	874	1,551
Henry	7,817	12,634	3,769	4,348	10,882
Houston	12,270	14,119	6,263	8,664	15,748
Irwin	1,366	973	465	918	1,226
Jackson	3,792	3,976	1,381	2,607	4,407
Jasper	1,485	1,153	373	1,188	1,474
Jeff Davis	2,031	1,947	958	1,242	2,050
Jefferson	3,220	2,077	685	2,346	2,788
Jenkins	1,401	929	394	953	1,288
Johnson	1,473	1,314	502	927	1,567
Jones	3,338	2,770	1,159	2,662	3,618
Lamar	2,065	1,707	600	1,416	2,035
Lanier	811	600	298	698	725
Laurens	6,184	6,146	1,602	4,879	6,929
Lee	1,811	3,061	1,024	995	2,875
Liberty	3,853	2,832	1,176	2,906	3,100
Lincoln	1,327	1,149	479	893	1,417
Long	874	719	355	681	858
Lowndes	9,019	10,276	2,864	6,427	10,885
Lumpkin	2,010	1,972	1,035	1,286	2,688
McDuffie	2,640	2,955	860	1,704	3,231
McIntosh	1,925	1,027	550	1,527	1,273
Macon	2,491	944	363	2,268	1,412
Madison	2,393	3,351	1,129	1,639	3,724
Marion	1,145	711	198	844	804
Meriwether	4,002	2,364	942	2,934	3,101
Miller	934	826	455	515	1,105
Mitchell	3,052	1,917	818	2,260	2,590
Monroe	2,774	2,423	949	1,970	2,570
Montgomery	1,185	1,009	416	903	1,228
Morgan	2,057	1,797	596	1,508	2,108
Murray	2,764	3,256	1,186	1,679	3,996
Muscogee	25,476	21,386	4,327	18,772	23,058
Newton	5,811	5,804	1,998	3,111	5,809
Oconee	2,745	4,125	1,182	1,990	4,265

Oglethorpe...	1,491	1,590	620	1,154	1,951
Paulding	5,212	7,180	2,654	2,717	7,329
Peach......	3,677	2,327	947	2,972	2,782
Pickens.....	2,359	2,332	1,037	1,430	3,021
Pierce......	1,852	1,899	708	1,558	1,947
Pike.......	1,651	1,822	623	1,176	2,074
Polk.......	4,872	4,158	1,598	2,977	5,454
Pulaski....	1,756	1,075	614	1,476	1,400
Putnam....	2,149	1,756	775	1,532	2,111
Quitman.....	523	284	113	436	296
Rabun.....	1,878	1,902	825	1,301	2,278
Randolph....	1,756	887	315	1,369	1,319
Richmond ...	28,910	24,227	6,290	20,489	27,566
Rockdale....	7,003	11,945	3,664	4,330	12,413
Schley.....	601	511	180	439	635
Screven....	1,940	1,705	709	1,461	2,178
Seminole....	1,193	850	468	1,171	1,469
Spalding	6,392	7,262	2,044	4,318	7,730
Stephens....	2,976	4,047	1,448	2,185	4,329
Stewart	1,540	1,186	175	1,136	832
Sumter	4,489	3,616	1,046	3,332	4,289
Talbot	1,768	671	238	1,248	802
Taliaferro....	755	269	80	469	306
Tattnall....	2,360	2,566	996	1,694	3,172
Taylor	1,508	1,078	281	1,134	1,145
Telfair.....	2,238	1,324	613	1,765	1,805
Terrell.....	1,942	1,143	384	1,383	1,517
Thomas....	4,841	5,500	1,591	3,530	6,572
Tift	3,930	4,485	1,139	2,446	4,760
Toombs....	2,648	3,609	1,210	1,152	4,433
Towns	1,487	1,674	537	942	1,783
Treutlen....	1,116	898	318	726	970
Troup	6,412	8,118	2,488	4,562	9,484
Turner.....	1,669	936	370	1,122	1,312
Twiggs.....	2,097	853	432	1,730	1,261
Union	2,304	2,533	804	1,258	2,396
Upson	3,740	4,053	1,186	2,666	4,614
Walker.....	6,217	8,489	2,748	4,753	10,487
Walton.....	4,821	5,619	1,923	3,091	5,974
Ware	4,573	4,573	1,263	4,292	4,819
Warren	1,239	751	180	1,091	897
Washington ..	3,508	2,384	820	2,615	2,752
Wayne.....	3,052	3,381	1,107	2,417	3,340
Webster.....	600	208	103	427	361
Wheeler....	880	601	214	658	709
White	1,756	2,477	981	1,028	2,648
Whitfield....	7,335	12,003	2,866	4,618	12,761
Wilcox.....	1,365	916	433	1,079	1,235
Wilkes.....	1,955	1,535	464	1,549	1,810
Wilkinson....	2,286	1,232	520	1,831	1,546
Worth	2,578	2,344	905	1,311	2,668
Totals......	1,008,966	995,252	309,657	714,792	1,081,331

Georgia Vote Since 1944

1944, Roosevelt, Dem., 268,187; Dewey, Rep., 56,506; Watson, Proh., 36.

1948, Truman, Dem., 254,646; Dewey, Rep., 76,691; Thurmond, States' Rights, 85,055; Wallace, Prog., 1,636; Watson, Proh., 732.

1952, Eisenhower, Rep., 198,979; Stevenson, Dem., 456,823; Liberty Party, 1.

1956, Stevenson, Dem., 444,388; Eisenhower, Rep., 222,778; Andrews, Ind., write-in, 1,754.

1960, Kennedy, Dem., 458,638; Nixon, Rep., 274,472; write-in, 239.

1964, Johnson, Dem., 522,557; Goldwater, Rep., 616,600.

1968, Nixon, Rep., 380,111; Humphrey, Dem., 334,440; Wallace, 3d Party, 535,550; write-in, 162.

1972, Nixon, Rep., 881,496; McGovern, Dem., 289,529; scattered, 2,935; Schmitz, Amer., 812.

1976, Carter, Dem., 979,409; Ford, Rep., 483,743; write-in, 4,306.

1980, Reagan, Rep., 654,168; Carter, Dem., 890,955; Anderson, Ind., 36,055; Clark, Libertarian, 15,627.

1984, Reagan, Rep., 1,068,722; Mondale, Dem., 706,628.

1988, Bush, Rep., 1,081,331; Dukakis, Dem., 714,792; Paul, Lib., 8,435; Fulani, New Alliance, 5,099.

1992, Clinton, Dem., 1,008,966; Bush, Rep., 995,252; Perot, Ind., 309,657; Marrou, Libertarian, 7,110.

Hawaii

	1992			1988	
County	Clinton (D)	Bush (R)	Perot (I)	Dukakis (D)	Bush (R)
Hawaii.....	25,725	15,460	8,889	24,091	17,125
Honolulu	123,908	103,937	35,728	138,971	120,258
Kauai	10,715	6,274	1,756	11,770	8,298
Maui	18,962	11,151	6,630	17,532	12,944
Totals......	179,310	136,822	53,003	192,364	158,625

Hawaii Vote Since 1960

1960, Kennedy, Dem., 92,410; Nixon, Rep., 92,295.

1964, Johnson, Dem., 163,249; Goldwater, Rep., 44,022.

1968, Nixon, Rep., 91,425; Humphrey, Dem., 141,324; Wallace, 3d Party, 3,469.

1972, Nixon, Rep., 168,865; McGovern, Dem., 101,409.

1976, Carter, Dem., 147,375; Ford, Rep., 140,003; MacBride, Libertarian, 3,923.

1980, Reagan, Rep., 130,112; Carter, Dem., 135,879; Anderson, Ind., 32,021; Clark, Libertarian, 3,269; Commoner, Citizens, 1,548; Hall, Com., 458.

1984, Reagan, Rep., 184,934; Mondale, Dem., 147,098; Bergland, Libertarian, 2,167.

1988, Bush, Rep., 158,625; Dukakis, Dem., 192,364; Paul, Lib., 1,999; Fulani, New Alliance, 1,003.

1992, Clinton, Dem., 179,310; Bush, Rep., 136,822; Perot, Ind., 53,003; Gritz, Populist/America First, 1,452; Marrou, Libertarian, 1,119.

Idaho

	1992			1988	
County	Clinton (D)	Bush (R)	Perot (I)	Dukakis (D)	Bush (R)
Ada........	31,941	49,000	28,192	30,525	54,951
Adams	457	754	449	643	1,107
Bannock	11,091	12,016	8,116	13,074	14,986
Bear Lake ...	562	1,419	684	867	2,084
Benewah ...	1,270	1,223	1,165	1,518	1,650
Bingham	3,565	7,333	4,144	4,346	10,131
Blaine	2,865	2,243	2,831	2,498	3,130
Boise	623	912	754	620	1,044
Bonner	4,995	3,937	4,645	5,555	5,721
Bonneville ...	7,014	16,557	10,241	7,032	22,613
Boundary ...	1,095	1,479	1,136	1,336	1,800
Butte	433	602	392	521	899
Camas	134	202	145	136	288
Canyon	9,095	19,220	8,974	10,207	21,426
Caribou	562	1,350	1,088	867	2,239
Cassias	1,351	4,052	1,785	1,833	5,345
Clark	95	195	119	133	281
Clearwater...	1,433	1,152	1,098	1,861	1,659
Custer	564	829	729	616	1,253
Elmore	1,858	3,087	1,867	2,078	3,756
Franklin	524	2,115	890	806	2,992
Fremont	903	2,333	1,349	1,178	3,401
Gem	1,609	2,455	1,555	2,064	2,926
Gooding	1,530	2,178	1,591	1,872	2,908
Idaho	1,974	2,709	1,900	2,198	3,541
Jefferson ...	978	3,471	2,164	1,198	5,295
Jerome	1,739	2,972	1,768	1,985	3,830
Kootenai	11,553	13,065	11,261	11,621	15,093
Latah	7,233	5,353	3,602	6,544	6,367
Lemhi	996	1,540	1,175	1,157	2,378
Lewis	674	593	491	807	786
Lincoln	514	656	441	574	918
Madison	741	4,591	1,920	1,009	6,197
Minidoka	1,815	3,304	1,875	2,290	4,623
Nez Perce ...	7,069	5,431	4,363	7,754	7,027
Oneida	351	713	590	508	1,269
Owyhee	686	1,469	862	848	1,707
Payette	1,656	2,895	2,055	1,900	3,786
Power	837	1,352	697	1,095	1,838
Shoshone ...	3,182	1,441	1,878	3,379	2,134
Teton	472	762	608	531	982
Twin Falls ...	6,593	10,335	6,043	7,078	13,243
Valley	1,259	1,548	1,313	1,251	1,897
Washington ..	1,122	1,802	1,204	1,359	2,380
Totals......	137,013	202,645	130,395	147,272	253,881

Idaho Vote Since 1944

1944, Roosevelt, Dem., 107,399; Dewey, Rep., 100,137; Watson, Proh., 503; Thomas, Soc., 282.

1948, Truman, Dem., 107,370; Dewey, Rep., 101,514; Wallace, Prog., 4,972; Watson, Proh., 628; Thomas, Soc., 332.

1952, Eisenhower, Rep., 180,707; Stevenson, Dem., 95,081; Hallinan, Prog., 443; write-in, 23.

1956, Eisenhower, Rep., 166,979; Stevenson, Dem., 105,868; Andrews, Ind., 126; write-in, 16.

1960, Kennedy, Dem., 138,853; Nixon, Rep., 161,597.

1964, Johnson, Dem., 148,920; Goldwater, Rep., 143,557.

1968, Nixon, Rep., 165,369; Humphrey, Dem., 89,273; Wallace, 3d Party, 36,541.

1972, Nixon, Rep., 199,384; McGovern, Dem., 80,826; Schmitz, Amer., 28,869; Spock, Peoples, 903.

1976, Carter, Dem., 126,549; Ford, Rep., 204,151; Maddox, Amer., 5,935; MacBride, Libertarian, 3,558; LaRouche, U.S. Labor, 739.

1980, Reagan, Rep., 290,699; Carter, Dem., 110,192; Anderson, Ind., 27,058; Clark, Libertarian, 8,425; Rarick, Amer., 1,057.

1984, Reagan, Rep., 297,523; Mondale, Dem., 108,510; Bergland, Libertarian, 2,823.
1988, Bush, Rep., 253,881; Dukakis, Dem., 147,272; Paul, Lib., 5,313; Fulani, Ind., 2,502.
1992, Clinton, Dem., 137,013; Bush, Rep., 202,645; Perot, Ind., 130,395; Gritz, Populist/America First, 10,281; Marrou, Libertarian, 1,167.

Illinois

County	1992 Clinton (D)	Bush (R)	Perot (I)	1988 Dukakis (D)	Bush (R)
Adams	11,748	13,529	6,157	13,768	15,831
Alexander	2,566	1,301	474	2,693	1,954
Bond	3,428	2,715	1,373	3,459	3,608
Boone	5,114	5,589	2,880	4,234	6,923
Brown	1,146	1,029	504	1,267	1,373
Bureau	7,551	6,836	3,465	7,354	8,896
Calhoun	1,519	745	532	1,544	1,238
Carroll	2,854	3,297	1,502	2,990	4,464
Cass	3,200	2,162	1,072	3,316	2,916
Champaign	35,003	27,096	13,571	29,733	33,247
Christian	9,042	5,087	3,401	8,295	7,040
Clark	3,338	3,175	1,450	3,275	4,508
Clay	2,962	2,471	1,193	2,761	3,494
Clinton	6,686	5,771	3,315	5,935	7,681
Coles	9,402	8,098	4,707	8,327	11,043
Cook	1,249,533	605,300	281,999	1,129,973	878,582
Crawford	3,964	3,606	2,062	3,555	4,951
Cumberland	2,111	1,860	1,209	1,904	2,667
DeKalb	13,744	12,655	7,680	11,811	17,182
DeWitt	3,009	3,164	1,543	2,660	3,942
Douglas	3,341	3,309	1,600	3,184	4,378
DuPage	114,564	178,271	76,839	94,285	217,907
Edgar	4,014	3,790	1,930	3,880	5,538
Edwards	1,299	1,601	634	1,218	2,212
Effingham	5,221	6,329	3,354	4,553	8,431
Fayette	4,833	3,508	1,730	4,632	5,452
Ford	2,175	3,046	1,222	2,026	4,059
Franklin	12,744	5,504	3,180	11,023	7,677
Fulton	9,725	5,062	2,874	9,046	6,999
Gallatin	2,371	990	568	2,455	1,580
Greene	3,164	2,391	1,461	3,020	3,136
Grundy	6,122	6,346	3,724	5,525	8,743
Hamilton	2,582	1,521	862	2,618	2,622
Hancock	4,213	3,714	2,091	4,740	4,568
Hardin	1,665	985	515	1,308	1,504
Henderson	2,013	1,310	715	2,085	1,726
Henry	11,077	8,989	4,231	11,594	11,358
Iroquois	4,440	6,948	3,073	4,221	9,596
Jackson	13,373	6,899	3,995	11,334	9,687
Jasper	2,284	1,996	1,160	2,135	3,024
Jefferson	8,665	5,497	3,403	7,729	7,624
Jersey	4,749	2,933	2,363	4,376	4,343
JoDaviess	4,044	4,249	2,102	4,141	4,923
Johnson	2,299	2,124	944	1,872	2,797
Kane	44,568	55,684	27,179	36,366	66,283
Kankakee	17,229	15,411	7,264	15,147	20,316
Kendall	5,423	8,521	4,394	4,347	10,653
Knox	12,524	8,331	4,357	12,752	10,842
Lake	81,693	99,000	42,384	64,327	114,115
LaSalle	23,276	16,078	10,434	22,271	22,166
Lawrence	3,270	2,681	1,498	3,140	3,655
Lee	5,530	6,652	3,191	4,608	8,903
Livingston	6,007	8,004	3,029	5,009	10,324
Logan	5,169	6,567	2,420	4,727	8,490
McDonough	5,814	5,297	2,770	5,247	7,173
McHenry	24,783	41,356	21,817	18,919	46,135
McLean	23,090	25,726	10,282	18,659	30,572
Macon	27,449	18,684	9,236	25,364	23,862
Macoupin	12,050	6,518	5,018	12,195	9,362
Madison	58,484	32,167	23,110	54,175	44,907
Marion	9,669	5,764	3,407	8,592	8,695
Marshall	2,819	2,491	1,169	2,742	3,588
Mason	3,969	2,473	1,245	3,406	3,424
Massac	3,347	2,754	892	3,227	3,507
Menard	2,264	2,834	1,179	2,103	3,560
Mercer	3,990	2,983	1,535	4,204	3,683
Monroe	4,894	4,807	2,813	4,529	6,275
Montgomery	7,424	4,407	2,956	7,293	6,388
Morgan	6,351	6,566	3,317	6,032	8,808
Moultrie	3,056	2,065	1,322	3,013	3,167
Ogle	6,512	9,008	4,455	5,641	11,644
Peoria	38,099	30,718	12,195	35,253	37,605
Perry	6,009	3,105	1,955	5,167	4,576
Piatt	3,520	3,076	1,822	3,099	4,137
Pike	4,016	3,342	1,643	4,614	3,965
Pope	1,063	951	391	996	1,202
Pulaski	1,987	1,169	379	1,793	1,666
Putnam	1,574	969	752	1,601	1,516
Randolph	8,529	4,899	3,092	7,844	7,396
Richland	3,286	3,053	1,689	2,843	4,264
Rock Island	37,412	23,212	10,416	40,174	27,412
St. Clair	57,625	31,951	17,592	55,465	41,439
Saline	7,258	3,667	2,302	6,676	5,798
Sangamon	40,052	39,641	16,861	37,729	50,175
Schuyler	1,650	1,512	815	1,866	2,178
Scott	1,057	1,132	588	1,243	1,535
Shelby	5,101	3,631	2,401	4,650	5,370
Stark	1,336	1,384	625	1,274	1,841
Stephenson	7,899	9,005	4,677	7,460	11,342
Tazewell	26,428	23,469	9,927	24,603	28,861
Union	4,681	3,003	1,373	4,197	4,244
Vermilion	18,383	11,703	8,162	17,918	16,943
Wabash	2,436	2,485	1,302	2,241	3,453
Warren	3,661	3,325	1,436	3,617	4,584
Washington	2,986	3,003	1,542	2,689	4,127
Wayne	3,332	3,809	1,702	3,135	5,481
White	4,308	3,057	1,428	4,144	4,354
Whiteside	12,329	10,146	4,589	11,328	12,978
Will	59,633	58,337	32,788	49,816	73,129
Williamson	14,361	9,462	4,779	12,712	12,274
Winnebago	48,298	42,221	21,227	45,280	55,699
Woodford	5,490	8,032	2,733	4,604	9,474
Totals	2,453,350	1,734,096	840,515	2,215,940	2,310,939

Illinois Vote Since 1944

1944, Roosevelt, Dem., 2,079,479; Dewey, Rep., 1,939,314; Teichert, Soc. Labor, 9,677; Watson, Proh., 7,411; Thomas, Soc., 180.
1948, Truman, Dem., 1,994,715; Dewey, Rep., 1,961,103; Watson, Proh., 11,959; Thomas, Soc., 11,522; Teichert, Soc. Labor, 3,118.
1952, Eisenhower, Rep., 2,457,327; Stevenson, Dem., 2,013,920; Hass, Soc. Labor, 9,363; write-in, 448.
1956, Eisenhower, Rep., 2,623,327; Stevenson, Dem., 1,775,682; Hass, Soc. Labor, 8,342; write-in, 56.
1960, Kennedy, Dem., 2,377,846; Nixon, Rep., 2,368,988; Hass, Soc. Labor, 10,560; write-in, 15.
1964, Johnson, Dem., 2,796,833; Goldwater, Rep., 1,905,946; write-in, 62.
1968, Nixon, Rep., 2,174,774; Humphrey, Dem., 2,039,814; Wallace, 3d Party, 390,958; Blomen, Soc. Labor, 13,878; write-in, 325.
1972, Nixon, Rep. 2,788,179; McGovern, Dem., 1,913,472; Fisher, Soc. Labor, 12,344; Schmitz, Amer., 2,471; Hall, Com., 4,541; others, 2,229.
1976, Carter, Dem., 2,271,295; Ford, Rep., 2,364,269; McCarthy, Ind., 55,939; Hall, Com., 9,250; MacBride, Libertarian, 8,057; Camejo, Soc. Workers, 3,615; Levin, Soc. Labor, 2,422; LaRouche, U.S. Labor, 2,018; write-in, 1,968.
1980, Reagan, Rep., 2,358,049; Carter, Dem., 1,981,413; Anderson, Ind., 346,754; Clark, Libertarian, 38,939; Commoner, Citizens, 10,692; Hall, Com., 9,711; Griswold, Workers World, 2,257; DeBerry, Soc. Workers, 1,302; write-ins, 604.
1984, Reagan, Rep., 2,707,103; Mondale, Dem., 2,086,499; Bergland, Libertarian, 10,086.
1988, Bush, Rep., 2,310,939; Dukakis, Dem., 2,215,940; Paul, Lib., 14,944; Fulani, Solid., 10,276.
1992, Clinton, Dem., 2,453,350; Bush, Rep., 1,734,096; Perot, Ind., 840,515; Marrou, Libertarian, 9,218; Fulani, New Alliance, 5,267; Gritz, Populist/America First, 3,577; Hagelin, Natural Law, 2,751; Warren, Soc. Workers, 1,361.

Indiana

County	1992 Clinton (D)	Bush (R)	Perot (I)	1988 Dukakis (D)	Bush (R)
Adams	3,708	6,078	2,865	3,811	8,137
Allen	39,629	55,003	25,809	39,238	74,638
Bartholomew	8,284	13,146	5,882	8,804	17,364
Benton	1,221	2,030	1,056	1,349	2,698
Blackford	2,088	2,347	1,319	2,253	3,336
Boone	3,982	9,485	3,826	4,168	11,608
Brown	2,029	2,633	1,635	2,115	3,348
Carroll	2,561	3,800	2,173	2,952	4,981
Cass	4,757	7,421	3,944	5,784	10,970
Clark	17,460	13,333	5,653	14,528	16,544
Clay	3,306	4,696	2,134	3,724	5,852
Clinton	3,490	6,141	2,535	4,412	8,570
Crawford	2,260	1,903	819	2,036	2,532
Daviess	3,201	5,591	1,695	3,483	6,768
Dearborn	5,116	6,974	3,384	5,066	8,195
Decatur	2,774	5,195	2,299	2,979	6,245
Dekalb	4,652	6,682	3,554	4,657	9,018
Delaware	19,556	20,473	10,453	20,548	27,348
Dubois	5,878	6,785	3,195	5,954	9,995
Elkhart	14,660	27,920	9,450	14,236	33,793
Fayette	3,969	4,376	2,299	4,118	5,949
Floyd	13,166	11,932	4,421	11,024	14,291
Fountain	2,829	3,391	2,162	3,279	5,113
Franklin	2,456	3,831	1,858	2,472	4,777
Fulton	2,552	3,982	1,963	2,788	5,234
Gibson	6,909	5,172	2,680	7,031	7,610
Grant	9,211	13,806	5,597	10,799	18,441
Greene	5,431	5,410	2,610	5,979	7,689

County	Clinton (D)	Bush (R)	Perot (I)	Dukakis (D)	Bush (R)
Hamilton	10,215	34,622	10,365	8,853	36,654
Hancock	4,752	11,072	4,752	5,355	13,374
Harrison	5,768	5,403	2,469	4,933	6,702
Hendricks	7,071	18,373	7,519	7,643	22,090
Henry	6,794	8,720	4,416	7,779	11,280
Howard	10,288	15,306	8,575	11,518	19,971
Huntington	3,855	9,093	2,967	3,873	11,675
Jackson	5,663	7,246	3,148	5,550	9,470
Jasper	3,033	4,809	2,019	3,237	6,009
Jay	3,208	3,609	1,994	3,212	5,363
Jefferson	5,510	4,937	2,565	5,221	6,949
Jennings	3,471	4,392	2,370	3,667	5,636
Johnson	8,712	20,353	8,246	9,001	24,654
Knox	6,718	6,683	3,719	7,006	9,813
Kosciusko	5,307	14,179	5,115	5,321	17,761
LaGrange	2,093	3,584	1,736	2,029	4,495
Lake	102,778	53,867	28,635	105,026	79,929
LaPorte	17,717	14,962	9,641	17,585	20,537
Lawrence	5,557	7,712	3,452	5,787	10,742
Madison	22,276	23,479	13,100	24,443	32,596
Marion	122,234	141,369	57,878	128,627	184,519
Marshall	4,912	8,048	3,522	5,488	10,490
Martin	2,018	2,523	883	2,132	3,066
Miami	3,967	6,416	3,428	4,613	8,533
Monroe	19,712	16,661	6,943	15,855	20,756
Montgomery	3,371	7,602	3,511	3,623	10,793
Morgan	4,690	10,939	5,375	5,375	14,284
Newton	1,757	2,295	1,274	1,744	3,274
Noble	4,411	5,883	3,328	4,143	7,889
Ohio	970	1,009	527	1,113	1,412
Orange	2,948	3,738	1,296	2,739	5,245
Owen	2,207	2,753	1,563	2,484	3,837
Parke	2,429	2,953	1,696	2,563	4,458
Perry	4,829	2,973	1,560	4,804	4,720
Pike	2,960	2,156	1,238	3,037	3,294
Porter	21,022	22,644	13,096	19,390	29,790
Posey	4,632	4,435	2,357	4,468	5,987
Pulaski	1,950	2,712	1,214	2,213	3,677
Putnam	3,487	5,341	3,174	3,850	7,119
Randolph	3,870	4,937	2,939	3,990	6,856
Ripley	3,480	5,033	2,406	3,605	6,414
Rush	2,168	3,873	1,948	2,451	5,112
St. Joseph	46,203	38,934	18,828	48,056	49,481
Scott	4,085	2,649	1,092	3,378	3,455
Shelby	4,560	8,075	3,521	5,382	10,176
Spencer	4,301	3,789	1,464	4,061	4,964
Starke	3,695	3,100	1,885	4,104	4,458
Steuben	3,630	4,868	2,896	3,114	6,855
Sullivan	4,211	3,052	1,857	4,320	4,246
Switzerland	1,535	1,211	636	1,479	1,572
Tippecanoe	17,343	23,050	9,684	16,256	27,897
Tipton	2,125	3,906	1,816	2,485	5,148
Union	898	1,394	664	946	1,814
Vanderburgh	33,799	30,271	12,513	31,270	38,928
Vermillion	3,652	2,360	1,794	4,044	3,674
Vigo	18,050	15,834	8,141	19,192	21,929
Wabash	4,518	7,062	3,424	4,168	9,153
Warren	1,367	1,601	1,020	1,542	2,243
Warrick	8,612	8,087	3,862	7,999	10,504
Washington	4,092	4,043	1,846	3,370	4,998
Wayne	9,960	12,221	5,095	10,209	16,388
Wells	3,282	5,799	2,890	3,437	7,712
White	2,988	4,622	2,582	3,256	6,220
Whitley	3,569	5,217	3,195	3,642	7,679
Totals	848,420	989,375	455,934	860,643	1,297,763

Indiana Vote Since 1944

1944, Roosevelt, Dem., 781,403; Dewey, Rep., 875,891; Watson, Proh., 12,574; Thomas, Soc., 2,223.

1948, Truman, Dem., 807,833; Dewey, Rep., 821,079; Watson, Proh., 14,711; Wallace, Prog., 9,649; Thomas, Soc., 2,179; Teichert, Soc. Labor, 763.

1952, Eisenhower, Rep., 1,136,259; Stevenson, Dem., 801,530; Hamblen, Proh., 15,335; Hallinan, Prog., 1,222; Hass, Soc. Labor, 979.

1956, Eisenhower, Rep., 1,182,811; Stevenson, Dem., 783,908; Holtwick, Proh., 6,554; Hass, Soc. Labor, 1,334.

1960, Kennedy, Dem., 952,358; Nixon, Rep., 1,175,120; Decker, Proh., 6,746; Hass, Soc. Labor, 1,136.

1964, Johnson, Dem., 1,170,848; Goldwater, Rep., 911,118; Munn, Proh., 8,266; Hass, Soc. Labor, 1,374.

1968, Nixon, Rep., 1,067,885; Humphrey, Dem., 806,659; Wallace, 3d Party, 243,108; Munn, Proh., 4,616; Halstead, Soc. Workers, 1,293; Gregory, write-in, 36.

1972, Nixon, Rep., 1,405,154; McGovern, Dem., 708,568; Reed, Soc. Workers, 5,575; Fisher, Soc. Labor, 1,688; Spock, Peace and Freedom, 4,544.

1976, Carter, Dem., 1,014,714; Ford, Rep., 1,185,958; Anderson, Amer., 14,048; Camejo, Soc. Workers, 5,695; LaRouche, U.S. Labor, 1,947.

1980, Reagan, Rep., 1,255,656; Carter, Dem., 844,197; Anderson, Ind., 111,639; Clark, Libertarian, 19,627; Com-

moner, Citizens, 4,852; Greaves, Amer., 4,750; Hall, Com., 702; DeBerry, Soc., 610.

1984, Reagan, Rep., 1,377,230; Mondale, Dem., 841,481; Bergland, Libertarian, 6,741.

1988, Bush, Rep., 1,297,763; Dukakis, Dem., 860,643; Fulani, New Alliance, 10,215.

1992, Bush, Rep., 989,375; Clinton, Dem., 848,420; Perot, Ind., 455,934; Marrou, Libertarian, 7,936; Fulani, New Alliance, 2,583.

Iowa

County	1992 Clinton (D)	1992 Bush (R)	1992 Perot (I)	1988 Dukakis (D)	1988 Bush (R)
Adair	1,655	1,713	814	2,261	1,833
Adams	1,034	863	679	1,283	1,080
Allamakee	2,362	2,627	1,543	2,768	3,186
Appanoose	2,810	2,346	1,161	3,209	2,779
Audubon	1,589	1,373	887	1,863	1,478
Benton	4,467	3,469	2,454	5,873	4,011
Black Hawk	29,584	21,398	10,182	31,657	24,112
Boone	5,913	4,148	2,070	7,232	4,381
Bremer	4,774	4,482	2,338	4,961	5,079
Buchanan	4,166	3,313	2,126	4,778	3,495
Buena Vista	3,374	3,863	1,955	4,580	4,170
Butler	2,548	3,209	1,333	2,593	3,523
Calhoun	2,140	2,169	946	2,990	2,474
Carroll	3,800	3,439	2,192	5,437	3,701
Cass	2,231	3,176	1,608	2,934	3,962
Cedar	3,296	2,965	1,945	4,032	3,373
Cerro Gordo	11,415	8,250	4,498	12,857	9,358
Cherokee	2,590	2,768	1,503	3,574	3,218
Chickasaw	2,913	2,129	1,566	3,530	2,549
Clarke	1,921	1,417	899	2,262	1,631
Clay	3,346	3,011	1,964	4,173	3,641
Clayton	3,742	3,044	2,309	4,320	3,839
Clinton	11,683	8,746	4,414	12,549	10,243
Crawford	3,004	2,693	1,905	3,868	3,375
Dallas	6,554	5,587	2,665	7,501	4,858
Davis	1,962	1,344	718	2,246	1,563
Decatur	1,866	1,316	786	2,192	1,406
Delaware	3,093	3,195	2,144	3,947	3,425
Des Moines	11,309	6,378	3,386	11,593	7,652
Dickinson	3,106	3,196	1,974	3,342	3,678
Dubuque	20,539	14,007	8,208	23,797	14,530
Emmet	2,239	1,749	1,010	2,778	2,173
Fayette	4,412	3,879	2,493	5,304	4,921
Floyd	3,688	2,404	1,611	4,377	3,266
Franklin	2,049	2,137	1,045	2,594	2,320
Fremont	1,422	1,459	1,003	1,547	1,946
Greene	2,422	1,952	956	3,011	2,091
Grundy	1,895	3,160	1,069	2,211	3,433
Guthrie	2,234	1,962	1,216	2,910	2,005
Hamilton	3,262	3,031	1,348	4,156	3,277
Hancock	2,175	2,428	1,170	2,831	2,731
Hardin	3,792	3,590	1,547	5,088	3,856
Harrison	2,349	2,763	1,691	2,883	3,108
Henry	3,544	3,435	1,522	3,754	3,951
Howard	2,099	1,516	1,193	2,330	1,970
Humboldt	1,765	2,299	1,093	2,713	2,594
Ida	1,449	1,714	1,061	1,787	1,951
Iowa	2,560	2,656	1,709	3,338	3,247
Jackson	4,421	2,673	2,096	4,864	3,237
Jasper	8,120	6,866	2,972	8,940	6,703
Jefferson	2,562	2,541	1,241	3,594	3,614
Johnson	28,656	14,041	8,625	28,759	15,453
Jones	3,508	3,071	2,306	4,641	3,496
Keokuk	2,329	1,981	1,238	2,899	2,278
Kossuth	3,660	3,464	1,906	5,088	3,938
Lee	9,366	4,777	2,920	10,911	6,228
Linn	38,567	30,215	19,643	42,993	33,129
Louisa	2,091	1,691	1,044	2,268	2,060
Lucas	2,072	1,734	848	2,454	1,776
Lyon	1,331	3,272	1,068	1,706	3,517
Madison	2,525	2,421	1,168	3,421	2,410
Mahaska	3,714	4,953	1,508	4,451	4,798
Marion	5,531	6,062	1,896	6,922	5,914
Marshall	8,303	6,784	3,100	9,760	7,657
Mills	1,798	2,699	1,638	2,092	3,212
Mitchell	2,177	1,933	1,199	2,870	2,338
Monona	1,939	1,660	1,231	2,408	2,068
Monroe	1,829	1,323	612	2,338	1,313
Montgomery	1,599	2,404	1,341	1,898	3,166
Muscatine	7,089	6,087	3,583	7,059	6,904
O'Brien	2,122	3,869	1,557	2,768	4,241
Osceola	990	1,756	813	1,277	1,951
Page	1,951	3,670	1,669	2,185	4,583
Palo Alto	2,374	1,789	1,186	3,377	2,041
Plymouth	3,171	5,196	2,039	4,220	5,316
Pocahontas	1,919	1,743	942	2,722	1,871
Polk	78,585	63,708	24,155	84,476	57,854
Pottawattamie	13,228	15,671	8,035	14,958	17,193
Poweshiek	4,056	3,245	1,680	4,876	3,683
Ringgold	1,341	967	551	1,609	1,110
Sac	1,896	2,138	1,157	2,613	2,411
Scott	33,765	28,844	11,423	34,415	31,025
Shelby	2,094	2,809	1,614	2,806	3,019

Sioux	2,226	10,637	1,771	2,923	10,270
Story	17,118	12,702	6,275	19,051	13,782
Tama	3,573	2,948	1,748	4,584	3,362
Taylor	1,430	1,200	910	1,671	1,647
Union	2,565	2,224	1,280	3,236	2,751
Van Buren	1,464	1,418	811	1,612	1,692
Wapello	8,670	4,852	2,513	10,177	5,350
Warren	8,612	7,242	3,217	9,627	6,424
Washington	3,384	3,576	1,994	3,776	3,741
Wayne	1,632	1,299	642	1,988	1,467
Webster	8,562	6,992	3,272	10,267	6,926
Winnebago	2,322	2,407	1,329	2,804	2,863
Winneshiek	3,791	3,331	2,416	4,443	4,194
Woodbury	17,398	18,148	7,182	20,153	18,790
Worth	2,009	1,382	1,044	2,440	1,488
Wright	2,776	2,708	1,151	3,353	2,658
Totals	586,353	504,891	253,468	670,557	545,355

Iowa Vote Since 1944

1944, Roosevelt, Dem., 499,876; Dewey, Rep., 547,267; Watson, Proh., 3,752; Thomas, Soc., 1,511; Teichert, Soc. Labor, 193.

1948, Truman, Dem., 522,380; Dewey, Rep., 494,018; Wallace, Prog., 12,125; Teichert, Soc. Labor, 4,274; Watson, Proh., 3,382; Thomas, Soc., 1,829; Dobbs, Soc. Workers, 26.

1952, Eisenhower, Rep., 808,906; Stevenson, Dem., 451,513; Hallinan, Prog., 5,085; Hamblen, Proh., 2,882; Hoopes, Soc., 219; Hass, Soc. Labor, 139; scattering, 29.

1956, Eisenhower, Rep., 729,187; Stevenson, Dem., 501,858; Andrews (A.C.P. of Iowa), 3,202; Hoopes, Soc., 192; Hass, Soc. Labor, 125.

1960, Kennedy, Dem., 550,565; Nixon, Rep., 722,381; Hass, Soc. Labor, 230; write-in, 634.

1964, Johnson, Dem., 733,030; Goldwater, Rep., 449,148; Hass, Soc. Labor, 182; DeBerry, Soc. Workers, 159; Munn, Proh., 1,902.

1968, Nixon, Rep., 619,106; Humphrey, Dem., 476,699; Wallace, 3d Party, 66,422; Munn, Proh., 362; Halstead, Soc. Workers, 3,377; Cleaver, Peace and Freedom, 1,332; Blomen, Soc. Labor, 241.

1972, Nixon, Rep., 706,207; McGovern, Dem., 496,206; Schmitz, Amer., 22,056; Jenness, Soc. Workers, 488; Fisher, Soc. Labor, 195; Hall, Com., 272; Green, Universal, 199; scattered, 321.

1976, Carter, Dem., 619,931; Ford, Rep., 632,863; McCarthy, Ind., 20,051; Anderson, Amer., 3,040; MacBride, Libertarian, 1,452.

1980, Reagan, Rep., 676,026; Carter, Dem., 508,672; Anderson, Ind., 115,633; Clark, Libertarian, 13,123; Commoner, Citizens, 2,273; McReynolds, Socialist, 534; Hall, Com., 298; DeBerry, Soc. Workers, 244; Greaves, Amer., 189; Bubar, Statesman, 150; scattering, 519.

1984, Reagan, Rep., 703,088; Mondale, Dem., 605,620; Bergland, Libertarian, 1,844.

1988, Bush, Rep., 545,355; Dukakis, Dem., 670,557; LaRouche, Ind., 3,526; Paul, Lib., 2,494.

1992, Clinton, Dem., 586,353; Bush, Rep., 504,891; Perot, Ind., 253,468; Hagelin, Natural Law, 3,079; Gritz, Populist/America First, 1,177; Marrou, Libertarian, 1,076.

Kansas

County	1992 Clinton (D)	Bush (R)	Perot (I)	1988 Dukakis (D)	Bush (R)
Allen	2,312	2,351	1,746	2,392	3,429
Anderson	1,178	1,218	1,282	1,466	1,781
Atchison	2,959	2,521	2,020	3,177	3,243
Barber	759	1,225	893	1,118	1,539
Barton	3,846	5,113	4,574	5,024	7,741
Bourbon	2,509	2,876	1,763	2,623	3,660
Brown	1,476	2,203	1,603	1,719	3,059
Butler	7,029	9,166	7,355	7,690	10,976
Chase	470	610	600	538	884
Chautauqua	598	853	607	661	1,247
Cherokee	4,083	3,589	2,067	4,069	4,281
Cheyenne	407	863	477	594	1,105
Clark	293	676	341	409	876
Clay	947	2,198	1,434	1,112	2,997
Cloud	1,720	2,131	1,578	2,022	3,043
Coffey	1,021	1,824	1,443	1,246	2,581
Comanche	325	636	324	375	738
Cowley	5,405	5,422	4,911	6,186	7,778
Crawford	7,366	5,468	3,706	7,783	6,940
Decatur	576	940	565	793	1,291
Dickinson	2,518	3,851	2,833	2,870	5,121
Doniphan	1,177	1,579	1,200	1,312	2,162
Douglas	19,439	12,949	9,630	15,752	16,149
Edwards	567	769	584	792	993
Elk	485	748	503	608	1,075
Ellis	4,544	3,985	3,887	5,289	5,194
Ellsworth	1,010	1,197	1,020	1,219	1,711
Finney	2,612	5,278	3,011	3,408	5,381
Ford	2,635	4,342	3,341	3,817	5,685
Franklin	2,968	3,699	3,184	3,592	4,777
Geary	2,559	2,928	2,057	2,721	3,782
Gove	379	792	532	663	966
Graham	554	752	603	702	1,139
Grant	619	1,561	835	907	1,654
Gray	443	1,039	686	696	1,180
Greeley	191	504	175	317	506
Greenwood	1,262	1,411	1,167	1,421	2,217
Hamilton	386	716	271	517	801
Harper	845	1,371	1,151	1,235	1,941
Harvey	5,047	6,259	3,653	5,503	6,893
Haskell	336	1,023	462	427	964
Hodgeman	258	625	343	439	732
Jackson	1,639	1,970	1,927	2,261	2,759
Jefferson	2,538	2,569	2,642	2,810	3,605
Jewell	546	1,050	698	684	1,546
Johnson	59,573	85,418	49,136	55,183	95,591
Kearny	384	943	376	524	1,073
Kingman	1,100	1,680	1,370	1,420	2,205
Kiowa	355	1,057	475	485	1,276
Labette	4,196	3,368	2,577	4,433	5,125
Lane	265	674	356	450	768
Leavenworth	8,077	7,738	7,306	8,797	9,913
Lincoln	612	893	657	796	1,229
Linn	1,353	1,413	1,358	1,497	2,163
Logan	355	905	446	503	988
Lyon	4,811	5,090	4,717	5,314	6,820
McPherson	3,645	5,745	3,561	4,354	6,563
Marion	1,627	3,142	1,557	2,024	3,685
Marshall	2,022	2,030	1,786	2,560	3,140
Meade	430	1,135	592	664	1,322
Miami	3,835	3,528	3,701	4,427	4,807
Mitchell	938	1,601	1,098	1,145	2,257
Montgomery	5,453	6,848	3,570	5,429	9,067
Morris	957	1,071	1,071	1,165	1,682
Morton	398	915	350	569	1,074
Nemaha	1,580	2,220	1,804	2,261	2,849
Neosho	2,799	2,926	2,136	3,402	3,739
Ness	565	967	678	887	1,230
Norton	779	1,469	815	855	1,923
Osage	2,297	2,561	2,532	2,840	3,496
Osborne	779	1,003	819	943	1,541
Ottawa	764	1,284	762	953	1,836
Pawnee	1,118	1,357	1,097	1,474	1,825
Phillips	843	1,579	955	960	2,316
Pottawatomie	2,099	3,106	2,759	2,544	3,897
Pratt	1,466	1,779	1,528	1,651	2,505
Rawlins	393	1,023	517	612	1,318
Reno	9,257	11,377	7,636	11,545	12,753
Republic	939	1,767	1,084	1,069	2,346
Rice	1,555	2,158	1,543	2,033	2,503
Riley	7,933	8,394	5,387	7,283	9,507
Rooks	771	1,249	1,063	1,012	1,938
Rush	689	756	665	1,020	1,045
Russell	1,178	1,434	1,395	1,448	2,403
Saline	7,890	8,565	7,108	7,998	11,371
Scott	480	1,426	621	717	1,590
Sedgwick	62,670	75,577	47,238	65,618	86,124
Seward	1,488	3,477	1,818	1,655	4,089
Shawnee	31,972	29,344	20,653	33,940	35,489
Sheridan	347	739	546	600	901
Sherman	810	1,630	828	1,082	1,929
Smith	789	1,236	816	1,004	1,951
Stafford	777	1,064	910	1,121	1,532
Stanton	224	556	214	310	592
Stevens	390	1,408	674	612	1,642
Summer	3,564	4,087	3,887	4,417	5,394
Thomas	932	1,849	1,129	1,408	2,342
Trego	608	727	574	795	979
Wabaunsee	851	1,254	1,258	1,166	1,737
Wallace	164	679	219	257	655
Washington	893	1,740	1,054	1,063	2,269
Wichita	241	681	303	399	721
Wilson	1,331	1,925	1,365	1,545	2,743
Woodson	590	662	604	761	1,062
Wyandotte	34,397	12,872	13,620	38,678	19,097
Totals	390,434	449,951	312,358	422,636	554,049

Kansas Vote Since 1944

1944, Roosevelt, Dem., 287,458; Dewey, Rep., 442,096; Watson, Proh., 2,609; Thomas, Soc., 1,613.

1948, Truman, Dem., 351,902; Dewey, Rep., 423,039; Watson, Proh., 6,468; Wallace, Prog., 4,603; Thomas, Soc., 2,807.

1952, Eisenhower, Rep., 616,302; Stevenson, Dem., 273,296; Hamblen, Proh., 6,038; Hoopes, Soc., 530.

1956, Eisenhower, Rep., 566,878; Stevenson. Dem., 296,317; Holtwick, Proh., 3,048.

1960, Kennedy, Dem., 363,213; Nixon, Rep., 561,474; Decker, Proh., 4,138.

1964, Johnson, Dem., 464,028; Goldwater, Rep., 386,579; Munn, Proh., 5,393; Hass, Soc. Labor, 1,901.

1968, Nixon, Rep., 478,674; Humphrey, Dem., 302,996; Wallace, 3d Party, 88,921; Munn, Proh., 2,192.

1972, Nixon, Rep., 619,812; McGovern, Dem., 270,287; Schmitz, Conservative, 21,808; Munn, Proh., 4,188.

1976, Carter, Dem., 430,421; Ford, Rep., 502,752; McCarthy, Ind., 13,185; Anderson, Amer., 4,724; MacBride, Libertarian, 3,242; Maddox, Conservative, 2,118; Bubar, Proh., 1,403.

1980, Reagan, Rep., 566,812; Carter, Dem., 326,150; Anderson, Ind., 68,231; Clark, Libertarian, 14,470; Shelton, Amer., 1,555; Hall, Com., 967; Bubar, Statesman, 821; Rarick, Conservative, 789.

1984, Reagan, Rep., 674,646; Mondale, Dem., 332,471; Bergland, Libertarian, 3,585.

1988, Bush, Rep., 554,049; Dukakis, Dem., 422,636; Paul, Ind., 12,553; Fulani, Ind., 3,806.

1992, Clinton, Dem., 390,434; Bush, Rep., 449,951; Perot, Ind., 312,358; Marrou, Libertarian, 4,314.

Kentucky

County	1992 Clinton (D)	Bush (R)	Perot (I)	1988 Dukakis (D)	Bush (R)
Adair	2,044	3,740	617	1,723	4,346
Allen	2,040	2,747	606	1,573	3,342
Anderson	2,491	2,731	1,219	2,176	3,225
Ballard	2,268	1,108	500	2,162	1,460
Barren	5,688	5,467	1,778	4,799	6,653
Bath	2,229	1,259	694	2,099	1,614
Bell	5,745	4,501	1,193	5,182	5,759
Boone	6,514	12,306	4,676	5,382	12,667
Bourbon	2,895	2,707	1,290	2,793	3,308
Boyd	10,496	7,387	3,195	9,552	9,379
Boyle	3,894	4,019	1,335	3,575	4,746
Bracken	1,259	1,162	500	1,176	1,630
Breathitt	3,496	1,303	515	3,387	2,149
Breckinridge	3,113	2,941	945	2,765	3,841
Bullitt	7,830	7,745	3,333	6,005	8,859
Butler	1,468	2,729	596	1,245	3,278
Caldwell	3,000	1,966	670	2,564	2,952
Calloway	6,181	4,654	1,853	5,287	6,225
Campbell	10,673	16,382	5,659	9,553	19,387
Carlisle	1,383	844	309	1,428	1,104
Carroll	2,119	1,046	566	1,913	1,702
Carter	4,224	3,305	989	4,570	4,325
Casey	1,409	3,317	542	1,216	3,857
Christian	6,709	7,737	1,789	5,704	9,250
Clark	4,892	4,625	1,955	4,252	5,329
Clay	2,012	4,747	648	1,709	4,156
Clinton	1,241	2,830	348	899	3,248
Crittenden	1,740	1,576	495	1,443	2,211
Cumberland	917	1,866	268	753	2,231
Daviess	16,592	14,936	5,112	14,815	17,356
Edmonson	1,653	2,486	438	1,243	2,555
Elliott	1,796	444	273	1,797	550
Estill	1,837	2,453	736	1,692	3,077
Fayette	38,306	41,908	14,215	32,554	48,065
Fleming	2,257	2,045	815	2,086	2,409
Floyd	13,351	3,540	1,723	12,327	5,296
Franklin	9,896	7,591	3,340	9,271	9,805
Fulton	1,813	1,073	306	1,531	1,474
Gallatin	1,171	699	445	1,060	881
Garrard	1,730	2,359	697	1,710	2,681
Grant	2,097	2,128	1,149	1,896	2,835
Graves	8,001	5,311	1,943	7,153	6,274
Grayson	2,909	4,533	993	2,575	5,186
Green	1,760	2,709	500	1,595	3,139
Greenup	7,214	4,975	2,188	6,956	6,559
Hancock	1,714	1,261	551	1,478	1,733
Hardin	9,417	12,299	4,026	7,262	13,240
Harlan	6,796	3,970	1,391	7,341	5,166
Harrison	2,795	2,148	1,225	2,748	2,983
Hart	2,852	2,401	579	2,519	2,927
Henderson	8,270	5,125	2,678	7,648	6,911
Henry	2,838	1,640	720	2,544	2,286
Hickman	1,296	861	294	1,158	1,142
Hopkins	8,881	6,032	2,565	7,453	7,979
Jackson	776	3,398	341	678	3,926
Jefferson	152,728	116,566	39,822	127,936	139,711
Jessamine	3,764	6,474	2,059	2,955	7,057
Johnson	3,669	3,614	1,118	3,538	4,619
Kenton	16,344	27,261	9,336	14,838	30,738
Knott	5,500	1,243	560	5,185	1,691
Knox	3,787	5,011	972	2,919	4,903
Larue	2,190	2,154	582	1,822	2,590
Laurel	4,560	8,583	1,859	3,620	9,296
Lawrence	2,400	2,084	557	2,198	2,294
Lee	1,170	1,617	356	984	1,588
Leslie	1,591	2,879	450	1,105	3,280
Letcher	5,817	3,011	1,206	4,697	3,601
Lewis	1,713	2,493	673	1,568	3,108
Lincoln	2,532	2,624	762	2,677	3,530
Livingston	2,386	1,339	578	2,052	1,834
Logan	4,064	3,710	1,043	3,379	4,295
Lyon	1,583	820	293	1,337	1,077
McCracken	13,341	10,657	3,077	12,208	12,160
McCreary	1,934	3,588	624	1,644	3,477
McLean	2,223	1,355	529	2,269	1,829
Madison	8,005	8,719	3,038	6,672	9,958
Magoffin	3,261	1,992	440	2,895	2,158
Marion	3,403	2,091	805	3,152	2,500
Marshall	6,576	4,368	1,773	5,888	5,256
Martin	1,715	1,961	393	1,581	2,587
Mason	2,657	2,432	916	2,721	3,158
Meade	3,387	2,641	1,298	3,079	3,441
Menifee	1,311	557	254	1,096	670
Mercer	3,010	3,211	1,298	2,832	3,904
Metcalfe	1,703	1,683	409	1,705	2,179
Monroe	1,515	3,776	480	1,025	4,214
Montgomery	3,686	2,590	1,308	3,082	3,435
Morgan	2,655	1,239	498	2,329	1,452
Muhlenberg	7,901	3,551	1,624	6,912	5,369
Nelson	5,437	4,495	1,638	4,788	5,283
Nicholas	1,341	894	513	1,242	1,271
Ohio	4,022	3,385	1,423	3,612	4,910
Oldham	5,457	8,263	2,855	4,025	8,716
Owen	1,830	1,108	613	1,823	1,468
Owsley	678	1,437	209	345	1,266
Pendleton	1,740	1,810	1,086	1,576	2,487
Perry	6,619	4,128	1,308	5,557	5,154
Pike	17,358	8,212	2,444	16,339	9,976
Powell	2,323	1,809	874	2,113	2,128
Pulaski	5,465	11,423	2,449	4,788	13,482
Robertson	439	329	170	515	511
Rockcastle	1,144	3,287	446	1,041	3,880
Rowan	3,558	2,469	1,212	2,968	3,093
Russell	1,950	4,641	673	1,455	4,292
Scott	3,639	3,810	1,800	3,380	4,482
Shelby	4,398	4,550	1,451	3,834	4,998
Simpson	2,834	2,280	708	2,138	2,699
Spencer	1,383	1,305	466	1,121	1,368
Taylor	3,518	4,319	1,044	2,879	5,362
Todd	1,858	1,691	612	1,632	2,282
Trigg	2,438	1,820	573	1,991	2,427
Trimble	1,413	789	413	1,342	1,083
Union	3,325	1,605	794	3,316	2,292
Warren	11,529	14,748	3,533	9,684	16,703
Washington	2,008	2,098	542	1,950	2,445
Wayne	2,516	3,412	560	2,057	3,672
Webster	3,380	1,408	854	3,019	2,159
Whitley	4,600	5,998	1,533	3,794	7,337
Wolfe	1,674	697	297	1,516	916
Woodford	3,161	3,992	1,535	2,653	4,512
Totals	665,104	617,178	203,944	580,368	734,281

Kentucky Vote Since 1944

1944, Roosevelt, Dem., 472,589; Dewey, Rep., 392,448; Watson, Proh., 2,023; Thomas, Soc., 535; Teichert, Soc. Labor, 326.

1948, Truman, Dem., 466,756; Dewey, Rep., 341,210; Thurmond, States' Rights, 10,411; Wallace, Prog., 1,567; Thomas, Soc., 1,284; Watson, Proh., 1,245; Teichert, Soc. Labor, 185.

1952, Eisenhower, Rep., 495,029; Stevenson, Dem., 495,729; Hamblen, Proh., 1,161; Hass, Soc. Labor, 893; Hallinan, Proh., 336.

1956, Eisenhower, Rep., 572,192; Stevenson, Dem., 476,453; Byrd, States' Rights, 2,657; Holtwick, Proh., 2,145; Hass, Soc. Labor, 358.

1960, Kennedy, Dem., 521,855; Nixon, Rep., 602,607.

1964, Johnson, Dem., 669,659; Goldwater, Rep., 372,977; Kasper, Natl. States Rights, 3,469.

1968, Nixon, Rep., 462,411; Humphrey, Dem., 397,547; Wallace, 3d Party, 193,098; Halstead, Soc. Workers, 2,843.

1972, Nixon, Rep., 676,446; McGovern, Dem., 371,159; Schmitz, Amer., 17,627; Jenness, Soc. Workers, 685; Hall, Com., 464; Spock, Peoples, 1,118.

1976, Carter, Dem., 615,717; Ford, Rep., 531,852; Anderson, Amer., 8,308; McCarthy, Ind., 6,837; Maddox, Amer. Ind., 2,328; MacBride, Libertarian, 814.

1980, Reagan, Rep., 635,274; Carter, Dem., 616,417; Anderson, Ind., 31,127; Clark, Libertarian, 5,531; McCormack, Respect For Life, 4,233; Commoner, Citizens, 1,304; Pulley, Socialist, 393; Hall, Com., 348.

1984, Reagan, Rep., 815,345; Mondale, Dem., 536,756.

1988, Bush, Rep., 734,281; Dukakis, Dem., 580,368; Duke, Pop., 4,494; Paul, Lib., 2,118.

1992, Clinton, Dem., 665,104; Bush, Rep., 617,178; Perot, Ind., 203,944; Marrou, Libertarian, 4,513.

Louisiana

County	1992 Clinton (D)	Bush (R)	Perot (I)	1988 Dukakis (D)	Bush (R)
Acadia.........	12,276	9,017	3,145	11,510	11,319
Allen..........	5,626	3,069	1,245	5,204	3,674
Ascension.....	13,036	10,275	4,295	12,147	10,726
Assumption....	5,639	2,928	1,358	5,610	4,017
Avoyelles......	8,696	4,851	2,139	7,353	7,659
Beauregard....	5,037	5,119	2,103	4,704	6,466
Bienville.......	3,899	2,412	832	3,705	3,680
Bossier........	11,313	15,628	4,863	9,035	20,807
Caddo.........	47,733	42,665	11,830	39,204	54,498
Calcasieu......	33,570	24,847	10,980	33,932	29,649
Caldwell.......	2,061	1,752	653	1,423	2,997
Cameron......	1,985	1,329	995	2,257	1,775
Catahoula.....	2,570	1,976	773	1,916	2,862
Claiborne......	3,263	2,599	926	3,158	3,756
Concordia.....	4,283	3,223	1,317	3,461	5,037
DeSoto.......	5,671	3,643	1,358	5,366	5,022
E. Baton Rouge..	68,622	81,072	16,102	59,270	86,791
East Carroll ...	1,835	1,142	283	1,809	1,536
East Feliciana...	4,093	2,813	932	3,659	3,527
Evangeline.....	8,564	5,147	2,124	7,693	7,437
Franklin.......	4,127	3,889	1,311	3,043	5,520
Grant	3,122	3,214	1,174	2,628	4,402
Iberia	13,040	11,905	4,337	12,166	15,438
Iberville	8,218	5,211	1,543	8,678	5,855
Jackson.......	3,370	3,072	882	2,842	4,251
Jefferson......	64,302	100,493	21,278	53,035	110,942
Jefferson Davis..	7,022	4,513	2,221	6,799	5,851
Lafayette.....	28,583	32,406	9,124	24,133	36,648
Lafourche......	16,182	12,744	5,077	15,013	16,152
LaSalle	2,389	3,068	993	1,622	4,559
Lincoln	7,205	7,220	1,751	5,427	8,853
Livingston.....	11,499	14,808	4,971	9,659	15,779
Madison.......	2,773	1,702	469	2,416	2,334
Morehouse.....	6,013	5,364	1,727	4,496	7,335
Natchitoches ...	6,974	5,694	1,606	6,151	7,224
Orleans	133,261	52,019	10,889	116,851	64,763
Ouachita	20,835	27,600	6,612	15,429	33,858
Plaquemines ...	4,467	5,018	1,729	3,997	6,084
Pointe Coupee ..	6,512	3,563	1,157	6,308	4,333
Rapides.......	20,873	22,783	6,599	17,928	29,977
Red River	2,360	1,649	566	2,254	2,266
Richland	3,706	3,808	1,054	2,833	5,226
Sabine........	4,173	3,586	1,219	3,532	4,767
St. Bernard.....	12,305	16,131	4,308	11,406	19,609
St. Charles.....	8,810	9,158	2,593	7,973	9,685
St. Helena	3,416	1,515	589	3,013	2,006
St. James	6,609	3,339	993	6,707	3,799
St. John The Baptist	8,977	6,730	1,922	8,366	7,464
St. Landry	20,383	11,882	4,266	19,091	15,790
St. Martin	11,252	5,909	2,573	10,148	7,541
St. Mary......	10,648	8,792	3,257	10,364	11,540
St. Tammany ...	19,735	37,839	9,005	15,638	38,334
Tangipahoa	15,194	14,128	4,612	13,527	16,669
Tensas	1,666	1,153	353	1,556	1,645
Terrebonne	13,325	14,662	5,505	12,686	18,745
Union	4,005	4,434	1,209	3,210	5,900
Vermilion	12,324	7,062	3,127	12,180	9,224
Vernon	6,005	5,912	2,313	4,998	7,453
Washington	9,095	7,227	2,303	8,369	9,374
Webster.......	8,380	6,640	2,629	7,434	10,204
W. Baton Rouge .	5,131	3,522	1,249	4,686	3,972
West Carroll	2,068	2,082	771	1,607	3,077
West Feliciana ..	2,328	1,501	516	2,146	1,854
Winn	3,537	2,932	843	2,699	4,165
Totals........	815,971	733,386	211,478	717,460	883,702

Louisiana Vote Since 1944

1944, Roosevelt, Dem., 281,564; Dewey, Rep., 67,750.

1948, Thurmond, States' Rights, 204,290; Truman, Dem., 136,344; Dewey, Rep., 72,657; Wallace, Prog., 3,035.

1952, Eisenhower, Rep., 306,925; Stevenson, Dem., 345,027.

1956, Eisenhower, Rep., 329,047; Stevenson, Dem., 243,977; Andrews, States' Rights, 44,520.

1960, Kennedy, Dem., 407,339; Nixon, Rep., 230,890; States' Rights (unpledged), 169,572.

1964, Johnson, Dem., 387,068; Goldwater, Rep., 509,225.

1968, Nixon, Rep., 257,535; Humphrey, Dem., 309,615; Wallace, 3d Party, 530,300.

1972, Nixon, Rep., 686,852; McGovern, Dem., 298,142; Schmitz, Amer., 52,099; Jenness, Soc. Workers, 14,398.

1976, Carter, Dem., 661,365; Ford, Rep., 587,446; Maddox, Amer., 10,058; Hall, Com., 7,417; McCarthy, Ind., 6,588; MacBride, Libertarian, 3,325.

1980, Reagan, Rep., 792,853; Carter, Dem., 708,453; Anderson, Ind., 26,345; Rarick, Amer. Ind., 10,333; Clark, Libertarian, 8,240; Commoner, Citizens, 1,584; DeBerry, Soc. Work., 783.

1984, Reagan, Rep., 1,037,299; Mondale, Dem., 651,586; Bergland, Libertarian, 1,876.

1988, Bush, Rep., 883,702; Dukakis, Dem., 717,460; Duke, Pop., 18,612; Paul, Lib., 4,115.

1992, Clinton, Dem., 815,971; Bush, Rep., 733,386; Perot, Ind., 211,478; Gritz, Populist/America First, 18,545; Marrou, Libertarian, 3,155; Daniels, Ind., 1,663; Phillips, U.S. Taxpayers, 1,552; Fulani, New Alliance, 1,434; LaRouche, Ind., 1,136.

Maine

City	1992 Clinton (D)	Bush (R)	Perot (I)	1988 Dukakis (D)	Bush (R)
Auburn	5,025	3,653	3,964	4,629	5,947
Augusta........	4,657	3,003	3,002	4,576	5,182
Bangor........	6,826	5,185	4,689	6,534	7,194
Bath	1,988	1,630	1,458	1,838	2,543
Bidderford	4,945	2,533	2,717	5,017	4,375
Brewer	1,788	1,907	1,625	1,784	2,908
Gardiner	1,391	1,054	1,115	1,395	1,609
Lewiston	9,265	4,372	6,180	9,225	7,265
Old Town......	2,272	1,173	1,302	2,220	1,640
Portland.......	19,510	8,660	6,910	18,234	11,676
Rockland	1,192	1,081	1,059	1,198	1,850
Saco.........	4,000	2,769	2,303	3,169	3,852
Sanford	3,854	3,030	3,215	3,456	4,541
South Portland ...	5,933	3,999	2,734	5,820	5,744
Waterville......	3,868	1,832	2,257	4,031	3,158
Westbrook	3,665	2,904	2,512	3,648	4,086
Other	183,241	157,719	159,778	166,795	233,561
Totals........	263,420	206,504	206,820	243,569	307,131

Maine Vote Since 1944

1944, Roosevelt, Dem., 140,631; Dewey, Rep., 155,434; Teichert, Soc. Labor, 335.

1948, Truman, Dem., 111,916; Dewey, Rep., 150,234; Wallace, Prog., 1,884; Thomas, Soc., 547; Teichert, Soc. Labor, 206.

1952, Eisenhower, Rep., 232,353; Stevenson, Dem., 118,806; Hallinan, Prog., 332; Hass, Soc. Labor, 156; Hoopes, Soc., 138; scattered, 1.

1956, Eisenhower, Rep., 249,238; Stevenson, Dem., 102,468.

1960, Kennedy, Dem., 181,159; Nixon, Rep., 240,608.

1964, Johnson, Dem., 262,264; Goldwater, Rep., 118,701.

1968, Nixon, Rep., 169,254; Humphrey, Dem., 217,312; Wallace, 3d Party, 6,370.

1972, Nixon, Rep., 256,458; McGovern, Dem., 160,584; scattered, 229.

1976, Carter, Dem., 232,279; Ford, Rep., 236,320; McCarthy, Ind., 10,874; Bubar, Proh., 3,495.

1980, Reagan, Rep., 238,522; Carter, Dem., 220,974; Anderson, Ind., 53,327; Clark, Libertarian, 5,119; Commoner, Citizens, 4,394; Hall, Com., 591; write-ins, 84.

1984, Reagan, Rep., 336,500; Mondale, Dem., 214,515.

1988, Bush, Rep., 307,131; Dukakis, Dem., 243,569; Paul, Lib., 2,700; Fulani, New Alliance, 1,405.

1992, Clinton, Dem., 263,420; Perot, Ind., 206,820; Bush, Rep., 206,504; Marrou, Libertarian, 1,681.

Maryland

County	1992 Clinton (D)	Bush (R)	Perot (I)	1988 Dukakis (D)	Bush (R)
Allegany	11,501	13,862	5,081	11,844	17,462
Anne Arundel	68,629	81,467	35,191	55,440	98,540
Baltimore.......	143,498	126,728	51,757	121,570	163,881
Calvert........	8,619	10,026	4,499	6,376	10,956
Caroline........	2,822	3,856	1,729	2,440	4,661
Carroll........	15,447	28,405	10,965	12,368	31,224
Cecil..........	10,232	10,784	6,115	7,807	13,224
Charles.......	14,498	17,293	6,501	11,823	20,828
Dorchester......	3,933	4,934	2,010	3,709	6,343
Frederick......	21,848	31,290	11,373	17,061	32,575
Garrett	2,856	5,714	1,987	2,557	6,665
Harford	27,164	36,350	17,002	19,803	38,493
Howard	44,763	38,594	16,182	34,007	44,153
Kent	3,093	3,094	1,411	2,925	3,761
Montgomery....	199,757	119,705	41,971	165,187	154,191
Prince George's	168,691	62,955	23,355	133,816	86,545
Queen Anne's....	4,668	6,829	2,958	3,857	7,803
St. Mary's	8,931	11,485	4,550	7,434	12,767
Somerset.......	3,210	3,450	1,230	2,911	4,222
Talbot	4,642	6,774	2,233	3,948	8,170
Washington	16,495	21,977	7,537	14,408	25,912
Wicomico......	11,481	13,560	5,140	9,413	16,272
Worcester	6,040	7,237	3,256	4,787	8,430
City					
Baltimore......	185,753	40,725	17,381	170,813	59,089
Totals......	988,571	707,094	281,414	826,304	876,167

Maryland Vote Since 1944

1944, Roosevelt, Dem., 315,490; Dewey, Rep., 292,949.

1948, Truman, Dem., 286,521; Dewey, Rep., 294,814; Wallace, Prog., 9,983; Thomas, Soc., 2,941; Thurmond, States' Rights, 2,476; Wright, write-in, 2,294.

1952, Eisenhower, Rep., 499,424; Stevenson, Dem., 395,337; Hallinan, Prog., 7,313.

1956, Eisenhower, Rep., 559,738; Stevenson, Dem., 372,613.

1960, Kennedy, Dem., 565,800; Nixon, Rep., 489,538.

1964, Johnson, Dem., 730,912; Goldwater, Rep., 385,495; write-in, 50.

1968, Nixon, Rep., 517,995; Humphrey, Dem., 538,310; Wallace, 3d Party, 178,734.

1972, Nixon, Rep., 829,305; McGovern, Dem., 505,781; Schmitz, Amer., 18,726.

1976, Carter, Dem., 759,612; Ford, Rep., 672,661.

1980, Reagan, Rep., 680,606; Carter, Dem., 726,161; Anderson, Ind., 119,537; Clark, Libertarian, 14,192.

1984, Reagan, Rep., 879,918; Mondale, Dem., 787,935; Bergland, Libertarian, 5,721.

1988, Bush, Rep., 876,167; Dukakis, Dem., 826,304; Paul, Lib., 6,748; Fulani, New Alliance, 5,115.

1992, Clinton, Dem., 988,571; Bush, Rep., 707,094; Perot, Ind., 281,414; Marrou, Libertarian, 4,715; Fulani, New Alliance, 2,786.

Massachusetts

City	1992 Clinton (D)	Bush (R)	Perot (I)	1988 Dukakis (D)	Bush (R)
Boston	114,260	41,868	25,189	122,349	62,202
Brockton	13,209	8,863	7,579	14,776	16,056
Cambridge	30,737	5,847	4,106	32,027	8,770
Fall River	18,652	5,456	6,922	20,184	8,394
Framingham	15,165	8,114	6,089	15,826	12,745
Lawrence	7,698	5,079	3,245	9,255	8,265
Lowell	14,492	8,467	8,893	16,391	13,998
Lynn	15,275	7,350	7,665	18,540	12,182
New Bedford	20,880	5,255	6,965	22,609	9,901
Newton	29,136	9,623	5,685	29,039	13,892
Quincy	18,891	12,306	9,068	20,911	18,403
Somerville	19,792	5,883	4,416	21,612	8,931
Springfield	27,302	12,200	10,361	30,113	16,244
Worcester	32,326	17,228	10,488	34,369	24,355
Other	940,824	651,500	514,060	993,414	960,297
Totals	1,318,639	805,039	630,731	1,401,415	1,194,635

Massachusetts Vote Since 1944

1944, Roosevelt, Dem., 1,035,296; Dewey, Rep., 921,350; Teichert, Soc. Labor, 2,780; Watson, Proh., 973.

1948, Truman, Dem., 1,151,788; Dewey, Rep., 909,370; Wallace, Prog., 38,157; Teichert, Soc. Labor, 5,535; Watson, Proh., 1,663.

1952, Eisenhower, Rep., 1,292,325; Stevenson, Dem., 1,083,525; Hallinan, Prog., 4,636; Hass, Soc. Labor, 1,957; Hamblen, Proh., 886; scattered, 69; blanks, 41,150.

1956, Eisenhower, Rep., 1,393,197; Stevenson, Dem., 948,190; Hass, Soc. Labor, 5,573; Holtwick, Proh., 1,205; others, 341.

1960, Kennedy, Dem., 1,487,174; Nixon, Rep., 976,750; Hass, Soc. Labor, 3,892; Decker, Proh., 1,633; others, 31; blank and void, 26,024.

1964, Johnson, Dem., 1,786,422; Goldwater, Rep., 549,727; Hass, Soc. Labor, 4,755; Munn, Proh., 3,735; scattered, 159; blank, 48,104.

1968, Nixon, Rep., 766,844; Humphrey, Dem., 1,469,218; Wallace, 3d Party, 87,088; Blomen, Soc. Labor, 6,180; Munn, Proh., 2,369; scattered, 53; blanks, 25,394.

1972, Nixon, Rep., 1,112,078; McGovern, Dem., 1,332,540; Jenness, Soc. Workers, 10,600; Fisher, Soc. Labor, 129; Schmitz, Amer., 2,877; Spock, Peoples, 101; Hall, Com., 46; Hospers, Libertarian, 43; scattered, 342.

1976, Carter, Dem., 1,429,475; Ford, Rep., 1,030,276; McCarthy, Ind., 65,637; Camejo, Soc. Workers, 8,138; Anderson, Amer., 7,555; La Rouche, U.S. Labor, 4,922; MacBride, Libertarian, 135.

1980, Reagan, Rep., 1,057,631; Carter, Dem., 1,053,802; Anderson, Ind., 382,539; Clark, Libertarian, 22,038; DeBerry, Soc. Workers, 3,735; Commoner, Citizens, 2,056; McRey-

nolds, Soc., 62; Bubar, Statesman, 34; Griswold, Workers World, 19; scattered, 2,382.

1984, Reagan, Rep., 1,310,936; Mondale, Dem., 1,239,606.

1988, Bush, Rep., 1,194,635; Dukakis, Dem., 1,401,415; Paul, Lib., 24,251; Fulani, New Alliance, 9,561.

1992, Clinton, Dem., 1,318,639; Bush, Rep., 805,039; Perot, Ind., 630,731; Marrou, Libertarian, 9,021; Fulani, New Alliance, 3,172; Phillips, U.S. Taxpayers, 2,218; Hagelin, Natural Law, 1,812; LaRouche, Ind., 1,027.

Michigan

County	1992 Clinton (D)	Bush (R)	Perot (I)	1988 Dukakis (D)	Bush (R)
Alcona	2,383	2,247	1,117	1,918	2,966
Alger	2,144	1,471	941	2,210	1,830
Allegan	12,823	19,077	8,742	10,785	22,163
Alpena	6,894	4,878	3,236	6,341	6,664
Antrim	3,431	3,984	2,528	3,159	5,231
Arenac	3,244	2,330	1,608	3,211	3,064
Baraga	1,695	1,160	754	1,753	1,630
Barry	8,652	9,489	6,303	7,983	12,546
Bay	26,492	16,383	11,258	28,225	20,710
Benzie	2,715	2,438	1,657	2,437	3,240
Berrien	25,840	29,252	14,056	21,948	37,799
Branch	5,850	5,976	4,683	5,231	9,225
Calhoun	25,542	19,791	13,058	22,717	26,771
Cass	8,047	7,391	4,756	7,444	10,229
Charlevoix	4,063	4,017	3,360	3,875	5,802
Cheboygan	4,459	3,864	2,495	3,943	5,395
Chippewa	5,434	5,462	2,706	5,222	6,786
Clare	5,346	3,916	2,812	4,710	5,661
Clinton	10,116	12,216	7,877	9,225	15,497
Crawford	2,252	2,193	1,442	1,825	3,097
Delta	8,387	6,027	3,485	8,891	7,114
Dickinson	5,689	4,273	3,022	6,129	6,158
Eaton	16,752	18,669	12,208	15,322	24,193
Emmet	4,245	5,312	3,576	4,170	7,105
Genesee	105,156	47,834	46,259	104,880	70,922
Gladwin	4,457	3,616	2,649	4,164	4,746
Gogebic	4,792	2,838	1,543	5,151	3,509
Grand Traverse	11,148	13,629	9,495	10,098	17,191
Gratiot	5,678	6,280	3,866	5,719	8,447
Hillsdale	5,244	7,579	4,968	4,763	10,571
Houghton	6,558	5,575	2,945	6,510	7,098
Huron	6,023	6,491	4,064	5,714	9,419
Ingham	61,596	43,926	27,683	55,984	58,363
Ionia	8,370	9,135	6,211	8,160	12,028
Iosco	5,369	4,912	3,131	4,929	7,234
Iron	3,648	1,971	1,344	3,774	2,866
Isabella	8,784	7,706	5,434	7,960	10,362
Jackson	23,686	25,424	15,194	21,865	33,885
Kalamazoo	43,568	38,035	21,666	39,457	50,205
Kalkaska	2,297	2,173	1,915	2,092	3,369
Kent	82,305	115,285	43,707	73,467	131,910
Keweenaw	582	378	212	631	536
Lake	2,351	1,194	981	1,958	1,713
Lapeer	11,982	12,326	10,541	10,736	16,670
Leelanau	3,445	3,993	2,685	3,331	5,215
Lenawee	15,399	14,297	9,517	13,690	19,115
Livingston	17,851	27,539	15,971	13,749	31,331
Luce	972	958	660	864	1,528
Mackinac	2,293	2,278	1,379	2,093	3,127
Macomb	130,732	147,795	67,954	112,856	175,632
Manistee	5,193	3,491	2,923	4,765	5,368
Marquette	16,038	9,665	5,768	15,418	11,704
Mason	4,829	5,102	3,096	4,531	6,800
Mecosta	6,097	6,047	3,612	4,736	8,181
Menominee	4,559	3,995	2,487	4,918	5,440
Midland	13,382	16,149	8,945	13,452	19,994
Missaukee	1,893	2,829	1,306	1,621	3,566
Monroe	24,957	20,250	13,551	21,847	26,189
Montcalm	8,730	8,420	5,504	7,664	10,963
Montmorency	1,903	1,794	1,077	1,563	2,514
Muskegon	32,515	23,769	15,268	28,977	33,567
Newaygo	6,455	7,333	4,056	5,389	9,896
Oakland	214,733	242,160	94,911	174,745	283,359
Oceana	3,846	3,944	2,713	3,356	5,693
Ogemaw	4,016	2,936	2,122	4,012	4,091
Ontonagon	2,451	1,463	805	2,517	2,023
Osceola	3,529	3,606	2,199	2,860	5,218
Oscoda	1,471	1,583	755	1,170	1,972
Otsego	3,129	3,393	2,635	2,635	4,620
Ottawa	22,180	56,862	16,855	18,769	61,515
Presque Isle	3,308	2,398	1,612	3,025	3,614
Roscommon	5,243	4,170	2,551	4,394	5,866
Saginaw	43,819	32,103	20,523	45,616	42,401
St. Clair	23,385	24,508	18,523	20,909	32,336
St. Joseph	7,817	9,836	6,209	7,017	13,084
Sanilac	5,868	7,891	4,894	5,445	10,653
Schoolcraft	2,139	1,253	721	2,071	1,802
Shiawassee	12,629	10,930	8,632	13,056	15,506
Tuscola	9,138	8,636	6,765	9,060	12,093
Van Buren	12,466	10,357	7,255	10,668	14,522
Washtenaw	73,325	41,384	21,889	61,799	55,029
Wayne	508,464	227,002	102,074	450,222	291,996
Wexford	4,894	4,696	2,923	4,287	6,043
Totals	1,871,182	1,554,940	824,813	1,675,783	1,965,486

Michigan Vote Since 1944

1944, Roosevelt, Dem., 1,106,899; Dewey, Rep., 1,084,423; Watson, Proh., 6,503; Thomas, Soc., 4,598; Smith, America First, 1,530; Teichert, Soc. Labor, 1,264.

1948, Truman, Dem., 1,003,448; Dewey, Rep., 1,038,595; Wallace, Prog., 46,515; Watson, Proh., 13,052; Thomas, Soc., 6,063; Teichert, Soc. Labor, 1,263; Dobbs, Soc. Workers, 672.

1952, Eisenhower, Rep., 1,551,529; Stevenson, Dem., 1,230,657; Hamblen, Proh., 10,331; Hallinan, Prog., 3,922; Hass, Soc. Labor, 1,495; Dobbs, Soc. Workers, 655; scattered, 3.

1956, Eisenhower, Rep., 1,713,647; Stevenson, Dem., 1,359,898; Holtwick, Proh., 6,923.

1960, Kennedy, Dem., 1,687,269; Nixon, Rep., 1,620,428; Dobbs, Soc. Workers, 4,347; Decker, Proh., 2,029; Daly, Tax Cut, 1,767; Hass, Soc. Labor, 1,718; Ind. Amer., 539.

1964, Johnson, Dem., 2,136,615; Goldwater, Rep., 1,060,152; DeBerry, Soc. Workers, 3,817; Hass, Soc. Labor, 1,704; Proh. (no candidate listed), 699; scattering, 145.

1968, Nixon, Rep., 1,370,665; Humphrey, Dem., 1,593,082; Wallace, 3d Party, 331,968; Halstead, Soc. Workers, 4,099; Blomen, Soc. Labor, 1,762; Cleaver, New Politics, 4,585; Munn, Proh., 60; scattering, 29.

1972, Nixon, Rep., 1,961,721; McGovern, Dem., 1,459,435; Schmitz, Amer., 63,321; Fisher, Soc. Labor, 2,437; Jenness, Soc. Workers, 1,603; Hall, Com., 1,210.

1976, Carter, Dem., 1,696,714; Ford, Rep., 1,893,742; McCarthy, Ind., 47,905; MacBride, Libertarian, 5,406; Wright, People's, 3,504; Camejo, Soc. Workers, 1,804; LaRouche, U.S. Labor, 1,366; Levin, Soc. Labor, 1,148; scattering, 2,160.

1980, Reagan, Rep., 1,915,225; Carter, Dem., 1,661,532; Anderson, Ind., 275,223; Clark, Libertarian, 41,597; Commoner, Citizens, 11,930; Hall, Com., 3,262; Griswold, Workers World, 30; Greaves, Amer., 21; Bubar, Statesman, 9.

1984, Reagan, Rep., 2,251,571; Mondale, Dem., 1,529,638; Bergland, Libertarian, 10,055.

1988, Bush, Rep., 1,965,486; Dukakis, Dem., 1,675,783; Paul, Lib., 18,336; Fulani, Ind., 2,513.

1992, Clinton, Dem., 1,871,182; Bush, Rep., 1,554,940; Perot, Ind., 824,813; Marrou, Libertarian, 10,175; Phillips, U.S. Taxpayers, 8,263; Hagelin, Natural Law, 2,954.

Minnesota

County	1992 Clinton (D)	1992 Bush (R)	1992 Perot (I)	1988 Dukakis (D)	1988 Bush (R)
Aitkin	3,400	2,151	1,951	3,863	3,011
Anoka	54,621	39,458	35,140	57,953	46,853
Becker	4,958	5,430	3,238	5,787	6,738
Beltrami	7,210	5,204	3,473	7,566	6,652
Benton	5,156	5,053	4,048	5,861	6,060
Big Stone	1,610	1,052	740	2,026	1,469
Blue Earth	11,531	8,813	7,299	12,375	11,959
Brown	4,278	5,390	3,845	5,109	6,898
Carlton	7,736	3,922	3,005	8,790	4,626
Carver	8,349	10,221	7,942	8,439	12,560
Cass	4,901	4,276	2,939	5,127	5,895
Chippewa	2,929	2,143	1,505	3,238	3,190
Chisago	7,077	4,813	5,098	7,875	6,163
Clay	9,845	9,666	3,835	11,186	10,380
Clearwater	1,587	1,315	841	1,769	1,763
Cook	1,005	878	704	1,080	1,078
Cottonwood	2,382	2,481	1,749	3,095	3,390
Crow Wing	8,896	9,112	6,367	9,674	11,017
Dakota	63,660	52,312	40,244	61,942	61,606
Dodge	2,620	3,049	2,231	2,925	3,848
Douglas	5,252	6,356	4,138	5,803	7,898
Faribault	3,339	3,439	2,322	3,879	4,846
Fillmore	3,977	3,583	3,011	4,114	5,004
Freeborn	7,759	5,089	4,878	8,836	7,226
Goodhue	7,916	7,321	5,790	9,438	9,455
Grant	1,561	1,201	885	1,950	1,693
Hennepin	278,648	179,581	123,659	292,909	240,209
Houston	3,744	3,853	2,697	3,936	4,777
Hubbard	3,362	3,227	1,949	3,306	4,365
Isanti	5,386	3,988	3,898	6,075	5,246
Itasca	9,621	5,952	5,147	10,517	8,358
Jackson	2,481	1,824	1,918	3,275	2,629
Kanabec	2,532	1,876	1,836	2,970	2,571
Kandiyohi	7,914	6,784	4,869	8,962	8,634
Kittson	1,307	1,098	558	1,650	1,381
Koochiching	3,474	1,954	1,993	3,867	2,842
LacQuiParle	2,342	1,435	1,163	2,805	2,116
Lake	3,415	1,465	1,437	3,887	1,838
Lake O'Woods	794	762	629	798	984
Le Sueur	4,662	3,858	3,363	5,410	5,415
Lincoln	1,555	1,084	967	1,891	1,479
Lyon	4,481	4,591	3,180	5,657	5,969
McLeod	4,919	5,422	4,933	5,736	7,967
Mahnomen	1,035	854	483	1,277	1,051
Marshall	2,309	2,136	1,306	3,001	2,752
Martin	4,019	4,438	3,089	4,922	5,724
Meeker	3,861	3,497	3,120	4,544	4,999
Mille Lacs	3,648	2,814	2,615	4,327	3,862
Morrison	5,588	5,038	3,710	6,469	6,598
Mower	9,935	5,147	5,001	11,893	6,969
Murray	1,993	1,609	1,588	2,840	2,316
Nicollet	6,055	5,091	3,799	6,786	6,878
Nobles	3,756	3,548	2,586	4,953	4,348
Norman	1,784	1,541	776	2,149	1,789
Olmsted	19,039	23,404	13,806	19,423	27,683
Otter Tail	9,176	11,074	6,274	10,373	14,015
Pennington	2,578	2,155	1,598	3,105	2,920
Pine	4,929	2,841	2,952	5,540	3,857
Pipestone	1,773	1,953	1,429	2,382	2,760
Polk	5,850	5,817	3,176	7,523	7,032
Pope	2,619	1,886	1,390	3,074	2,627
Ramsey	130,932	68,206	50,757	143,767	88,736
Red Lake	1,020	691	472	1,229	918
Redwood	2,740	3,408	2,710	3,178	5,076
Renville	3,414	2,852	2,598	4,454	4,356
Rice	10,908	7,015	6,057	11,570	9,460
Rock	2,006	2,065	1,244	2,435	2,737
Roseau	2,346	2,785	2,099	2,630	3,500
St. Louis	61,813	24,579	21,714	70,344	31,799
Scott	11,225	10,936	9,881	11,405	13,050
Sherburne	7,843	7,339	6,534	7,959	8,360
Sibley	2,421	2,315	2,407	3,154	3,655
Stearns	21,451	22,502	14,834	23,798	27,529
Steele	5,152	5,964	4,542	5,496	7,981
Stevens	2,466	2,229	1,086	2,721	2,679
Swift	2,980	1,603	1,359	3,579	2,156
Todd	4,059	3,990	2,976	5,023	5,633
Traverse	1,053	841	582	1,399	1,061
Wabasha	3,736	3,397	3,012	4,442	4,681
Wadena	2,340	2,492	1,535	2,484	3,733
Waseca	3,146	3,118	2,621	3,721	4,471
Washington	35,820	26,568	22,585	34,952	30,850
Watonwan	2,100	1,871	1,574	2,544	2,821
Wilkin	1,122	1,626	748	1,486	1,933
Winona	9,707	8,585	5,993	10,310	11,012
Wright	12,465	11,650	10,829	14,117	14,987
Yellow Med	2,593	1,909	1,645	3,282	2,925
Totals	1,020,997	747,841	562,506	1,109,471	962,337

Minnesota Vote Since 1944

1944, Roosevelt, Dem., 589,864; Dewey, Rep., 527,416; Thomas, Soc., 5,073; Teichert, Ind. Gov't., 3,176.

1948, Truman, Dem., 692,966; Dewey, Rep., 483,617; Wallace, Prog., 27,866; Thomas, Soc., 4,646; Teichert, Soc. Labor, 2,525; Dobbs, Soc. Workers, 606.

1952, Eisenhower, Rep., 763,211; Stevenson, Dem., 608,458; Hallinan, Prog., 2,666; Hass, Soc. Labor, 2,383; Hamblen, Proh., 2,147; Dobbs, Soc. Workers, 618.

1956, Eisenhower, Rep., 719,302; Stevenson, Dem., 617,525; Hass, Soc. Labor (Ind. Gov.), 2,080; Dobbs, Soc. Workers, 1,098.

1960, Kennedy, Dem., 779,933; Nixon, Rep., 757,915; Dobbs, Soc. Workers, 3,077; Industrial Gov., 962.

1964, Johnson, Dem., 991,117; Goldwater, Rep., 559,624; DeBerry, Soc. Workers, 1,177; Hass, Industrial Gov., 2,544.

1968, Nixon, Rep., 658,643; Humphrey, Dem., 857,738; Wallace, 3d Party, 68,931; scattered, 2,443; Halstead, Soc. Workers, 808; Blomen, Ind. Gov't., 285; Mitchell, Com., 415; Cleaver, Peace, 935; McCarthy, write-in, 585; scattered, 170.

1972, Nixon, Rep., 898,269; McGovern, Dem., 802,346; Schmitz, Amer., 31,407; Spock, Peoples, 2,805; Fisher, Soc. Labor, 4,261; Jenness, Soc. Workers, 940; Hall, Com., 662; scattered, 962.

1976, Carter, Dem., 1,070,440; Ford, Rep., 819,395; McCarthy, Ind., 35,490; Anderson, Amer., 13,592; Camejo, Soc. Workers, 4,149; MacBride, Libertarian, 3,529; Hall, Com., 1,092.

1980, Reagan, Rep., 873,268; Carter, Dem., 954,173; Anderson, Ind., 174,990; Clark, Libertarian, 31,593; Commoner, Citizens, 8,406; Hall, Com., 1,117; DeBerry, Soc. Workers, 711; Griswold, Workers World, 698; McReynolds, Soc., 536; write-ins, 281.

1984, Reagan, Rep., 1,032,603; Mondale, Dem., 1,036,364; Bergland, Libertarian, 2,996.

1988, Bush, Rep., 962,337; Dukakis, Dem., 1,109,471; McCarthy, Minn. Prog., 5,403; Paul, Lib., 5,109.

1992, Clinton, Dem., 1,020,997; Bush, Rep., 747,841; Perot, Ind., 526,506; Marrou, Libertarian, 3,373; Gritz, Populist/America First, 3,363; Hagelin, Natural Law, 1,406.

Mississippi

County	1992 Clinton (D)	Bush (R)	Perot (I)	1988 Dukakis (D)	Bush (R)
Adams.	8,255	5,831	1,753	7,732	8,116
Alcorn	6,373	6,249	1,349	5,335	6,641
Amite	2,608	2,561	498	2,834	3,333
Attala	3,015	3,520	529	2,997	4,524
Benton	2,402	1,253	293	1,718	1,565
Bolivar.	8,801	4,752	593	7,606	6,105
Calhoun.	2,462	3,191	607	2,086	3,375
Carroll	1,182	1,695	200	1,560	2,628
Chickasaw	3,220	3,150	629	2,713	3,390
Choctaw	1,435	2,026	298	1,335	2,297
Claiborne.	3,302	935	161	3,083	1,233
Clarke	2,259	4,207	450	2,576	4,522
Clay	4,620	3,297	626	3,849	3,645
Coahoma.	6,409	4,120	518	6,139	4,939
Copiah	4,397	4,600	409	4,175	5,100
Covington	2,775	3,525	654	2,591	4,005
DeSoto	8,833	16,104	2,569	5,449	14,681
Forrest	8,333	12,432	1,909	6,953	14,249
Franklin	1,587	1,942	393	1,563	2,376
George	2,650	4,141	1,335	2,435	4,545
Greene	1,664	2,406	559	1,637	2,837
Grenada	4,203	4,721	609	3,683	5,352
Hancock	4,651	6,422	2,302	3,760	7,763
Harrison. . . .	15,268	25,049	6,855	14,439	32,892
Hinds	43,434	45,031	5,341	41,058	52,749
Holmes	4,092	1,694	203	5,350	2,737
Humphreys	2,696	1,721	258	2,644	2,018
Issaquena	550	298	79	511	424
Itawamba.	3,635	4,142	918	3,143	4,535
Jackson.	13,017	25,321	6,484	10,328	29,830
Jasper.	3,059	2,789	568	3,184	3,368
Jefferson	2,796	562	156	2,693	702
Jefferson Davis. . .	2,991	2,228	382	2,948	2,745
Jones	8,035	13,824	2,523	7,383	16,764
Kemper	2,243	1,830	278	2,069	2,128
Lafayette	5,224	5,251	861	3,967	5,841
Lamar	3,208	8,259	1,543	2,535	9,145
Lauderdale. . . .	8,489	17,098	1,659	7,967	18,302
Lawrence.	2,582	2,689	765	2,517	3,682
Leake	3,333	3,943	497	2,787	4,168
Lee	7,710	12,231	2,041	6,604	13,767
Leflore	6,374	5,298	611	5,830	6,409
Lincoln	4,744	7,040	1,281	4,534	8,710
Lowndes	6,552	10,509	1,716	5,993	11,258
Madison	9,386	12,810	1,478	8,242	11,399
Marion.	4,654	5,776	1,162	4,240	7,019
Marshall.	7,913	3,847	689	6,982	4,668
Monroe	4,933	5,994	1,255	4,669	6,447
Montgomery	2,076	2,324	370	1,893	2,504
Neshoba	3,090	6,135	794	2,942	6,363
Newton	2,146	5,128	494	2,332	5,658
Noxubee	3,188	1,623	203	2,722	1,870
Oktibbeha	5,726	6,381	984	5,100	7,126
Panola.	6,066	4,644	729	5,222	5,382
Pearl River. . . .	4,683	7,726	2,352	3,939	10,220
Perry.	1,490	2,538	462	1,326	2,983
Pike	6,279	6,005	1,380	6,531	7,637
Pontotoc	2,965	4,595	777	2,772	4,939
Prentiss	3,385	4,317	781	3,429	4,348
Quitman.	2,422	1,451	210	2,497	1,832
Rankin.	8,155	24,537	3,454	6,201	22,937
Scott.	3,349	5,268	691	2,939	5,522
Sharkey.	1,526	1,008	145	1,609	1,277
Simpson	3,213	5,358	726	3,016	6,151
Smith	1,968	4,106	680	1,660	4,573
Stone	1,447	2,295	447	1,452	3,007
Sunflower.	5,050	3,726	600	4,898	4,362
Tallahatchie . . .	2,902	2,213	380	2,881	2,633
Tate	3,519	4,196	634	2,872	4,553
Tippah	3,475	4,444	802	2,958	4,593
Tishomingo	3,910	3,393	751	3,378	3,646
Tunica.	1,451	693	96	1,510	896
Union	3,714	5,173	816	3,044	5,511
Walthall	2,476	2,728	711	2,354	3,103
Warren	8,175	10,209	2,146	7,437	12,507
Washington	10,588	7,598	795	10,222	10,229
Wayne.	3,064	3,874	824	2,889	4,496
Webster.	1,746	2,791	444	1,550	3,061
Wilkinson	3,210	1,399	307	2,678	1,528
Winston.	3,953	4,311	688	3,851	5,317
Yalobusha	2,617	2,179	438	2,402	2,660
Yazoo	4,880	5,113	669	4,989	5,538
Totals.	**400,258**	**487,793**	**85,626**	**363,921**	**557,890**

Mississippi Vote Since 1944

1944, Roosevelt, Dem., 158,515; Dewey, Rep., 3,742; Reg. Dem., 9,964; Ind. Rep., 7,859.

1948, Thurmond, States' Rights, 167,538; Truman, Dem., 19,384; Dewey, Rep., 5,043; Wallace, Prog., 225.

1952, Eisenhower, Ind. vote pledged to Rep. candidate, 112,966; Stevenson, Dem., 172,566.

1956, Eisenhower, Rep., 56,372; Stevenson, Dem., 144,498; Black and Tan Grand Old Party, 4,313; total, 60,685; Byrd, Ind., 42,966.

1960, Kennedy, Dem., 108,362; Democratic unpledged electors, 116,248; Nixon, Rep., 73,561. Mississippi's victorious slate of 8 unpledged Democratic electors cast their votes for Sen. Harry F. Byrd (D, VA).

1964, Johnson, Dem., 52,618; Goldwater, Rep., 356,528.

1968, Nixon, Rep., 88,516; Humphrey, Dem., 150,644; Wallace, 3d Party, 415,349.

1972, Nixon, Rep., 505,125; McGovern, Dem., 126,782; Schmitz, Amer., 11,598; Jenness, Soc. Workers, 2,458.

1976, Carter, Dem., 381,309; Ford, Rep., 366,846; Anderson, Amer., 6,678; McCarthy, Ind., 4,074; Maddox, Ind., 4,049; Camejo, Soc. Workers, 2,805; MacBride, Libertarian, 2,609.

1980, Reagan, Rep., 441,089; Carter, Dem., 429,281; Anderson, Ind., 12,036; Clark, Libertarian, 5,465; Griswold, Workers World, 2,402; Pulley, Soc. Workers, 2,347.

1984, Reagan, Rep., 582,377; Mondale, Dem., 352,192; Bergland, Libertarian, 2,336.

1988, Bush, Rep., 557,890; Dukakis, Dem., 363,921; Duke, Ind., 4,232; Paul, Lib., 3,329.

1992, Bush, Rep., 487,793; Clinton, Dem., 400,258; Perot, Ind., 85,626; Fulani, New Alliance, 2,625; Marrou, Libertarian, 2,154; Phillips, U.S. Taxpayers, 1,652; Hagelin, Natural Law, 1,140.

Missouri

County	1992 Clinton (D)	Bush (R)	Perot (I)	1988 Dukakis (D)	Bush (R)
Adair.	4,232	4,141	2,224	3,571	5,721
Andrew	2,675	2,652	2,151	3,108	3,407
Atchison	1,208	1,140	840	1,468	1,761
Audrain	4,731	3,798	2,099	5,226	5,072
Barry.	4,791	5,565	2,381	4,210	7,231
Barton	1,433	2,775	971	1,603	3,339
Bates	2,993	2,499	2,225	3,332	3,574
Benton	3,195	2,511	1,551	2,654	3,467
Bollinger	2,150	2,289	909	1,883	2,710
Boone.	26,176	19,405	12,040	24,370	22,948
Buchanan	16,570	11,275	9,404	18,601	15,336
Butler	6,602	6,450	2,189	5,751	7,968
Caldwell	1,456	1,295	1,283	1,726	2,074
Callaway	5,799	4,880	3,266	5,209	6,687
Camden	5,140	5,554	3,891	3,930	7,773
Cape Girardeau .	9,605	13,464	5,199	7,904	16,583
Carroll.	2,100	1,774	1,495	2,330	2,811
Carter	1,169	1,101	405	1,087	1,429
Cass.	10,246	10,349	9,216	10,092	12,799
Cedar	2,064	2,085	1,173	1,774	2,966
Chariton	2,141	1,378	1,067	2,347	2,193
Christian	6,242	7,422	3,422	4,724	7,670
Clark	1,815	1,039	725	1,925	1,493
Clay	30,565	23,798	20,951	29,620	30,293
Clinton	3,400	2,391	2,423	3,653	3,282
Cole	10,201	15,270	5,770	8,359	18,023
Cooper	2,709	2,867	1,735	2,510	3,737
Crawford	3,515	2,831	2,002	3,107	3,856
Dade.	1,332	1,577	834	1,315	2,154
Dallas	2,533	2,116	1,392	2,293	2,898
Daviess	1,477	1,107	1,143	1,743	1,765
DeKalb	1,630	1,318	1,207	1,970	1,863
Dent	2,689	2,125	1,049	2,421	2,975
Douglas	2,126	2,569	1,081	1,735	3,225
Dunklin	6,277	4,024	1,166	5,281	5,026
Franklin	13,431	11,477	11,043	11,891	16,611
Gasconade	1,952	2,690	1,672	1,621	4,216
Gentry	1,519	1,272	921	1,872	1,554
Greene	41,137	46,457	17,770	35,475	52,211
Grundy	1,968	1,749	1,372	2,052	2,668
Harrison	1,590	1,563	1,059	1,776	2,271
Henry	4,232	2,681	2,807	4,135	4,167
Hickory	1,929	1,259	864	1,677	2,043
Holt.	1,050	1,202	781	1,258	1,583
Howard	2,085	1,253	1,090	2,446	1,865
Howell	5,492	5,360	2,650	4,324	7,277
Iron.	2,507	1,276	841	2,283	1,877
Jackson.	145,999	78,611	66,142	147,964	107,810
Jasper.	11,727	17,592	6,440	11,159	19,934
Jefferson	32,569	20,637	20,057	27,738	29,279
Johnson	5,546	5,032	4,578	5,373	7,512
Knox.	1,010	724	523	1,255	1,212
Laclede	4,179	5,176	2,852	3,442	6,070
Lafayette	5,213	4,651	3,561	5,654	6,825
Lawrence	4,666	5,608	2,570	4,432	6,911
Lewis	2,196	1,461	892	2,460	1,803
Lincoln	5,453	3,718	3,572	4,605	5,305
Linn	2,916	1,967	1,524	3,150	3,061

Livingston	2,505	2,370	1,976	3,077	3,462	Blaine	1,355	971	699	1,460	1,402
McDonald	2,281	3,010	1,551	2,299	3,812	Broadwater	491	830	505	592	1,054
Macon	3,194	2,256	1,697	3,215	3,406	Carbon	1,549	1,562	1,482	2,039	2,360
Madison	2,501	1,673	899	2,167	2,528	Carter	154	497	220	242	686
Maries	1,732	1,356	915	1,552	1,919	Cascade	14,719	12,494	9,151	15,718	15,946
Marion	5,156	4,762	1,841	5,617	5,034	Chouteau	959	1,380	870	1,166	1,980
Mercer	843	626	378	877	875	Custer	1,968	2,105	1,505	2,343	3,007
Miller	2,905	4,175	2,391	2,555	5,662	Daniels	457	496	402	571	802
Missouri	3,226	1,675	776	2,814	2,218	Dawson	1,785	1,679	1,370	2,120	2,658
Moniteau	2,018	2,566	1,499	1,936	3,502	Deer Lodge	3,174	832	1,207	3,185	1,168
Monroe	2,060	1,153	969	2,461	1,542	Fallon	446	731	427	612	1,002
Montgomery	2,063	1,974	1,266	2,064	2,714	Fergus	1,615	2,736	1,934	2,052	3,948
Morgan	2,906	2,819	2,028	2,604	3,958	Flathead	9,746	11,699	9,109	10,202	14,461
New Madrid	4,883	2,431	962	3,812	3,387	Gallatin	9,535	11,109	7,711	9,527	13,214
Newton	5,987	8,804	3,567	5,798	10,617	Garfield	125	403	281	196	631
Nodaway	3,723	3,147	2,484	4,240	4,103	Glacier	2,076	1,222	997	2,151	1,728
Oregon	2,258	1,402	564	2,042	1,717	Golden Valley	142	192	157	203	335
Osage	1,860	2,784	1,423	1,771	3,885	Granite	358	556	386	511	789
Ozark	1,581	1,772	906	1,329	2,404	Hill	3,618	2,408	2,017	4,219	3,467
Pemiscot	3,924	2,161	670	3,288	3,066	Jefferson	1,415	1,541	1,172	1,746	2,007
Perry	2,525	3,205	1,498	2,136	3,836	Judith Basin	409	610	415	590	902
Pettis	5,314	6,823	4,278	5,486	9,648	Lake	3,938	3,596	2,878	4,109	4,883
Phelps	6,852	6,040	3,774	5,867	8,329	Lewis & Clark	11,117	9,351	5,560	11,932	10,946
Pike	3,609	2,255	1,464	3,816	3,271	Liberty	321	512	363	418	771
Platte	10,920	9,380	9,062	11,225	11,838	Lincoln	2,765	2,799	2,637	3,601	3,500
Polk	3,316	3,465	1,879	3,419	5,030	Madison	779	1,415	1,043	878	2,045
Pulaski	4,113	3,793	2,057	3,446	4,642	McCone	424	528	395	567	814
Putnam	838	1,143	522	803	1,365	Meagher	260	422	310	337	656
Ralls	2,158	1,349	880	2,489	1,494	Mineral	664	403	543	789	616
Randolph	4,951	3,025	2,212	5,291	4,384	Missoula	20,347	12,898	9,735	19,178	15,965
Ray	4,457	2,563	2,567	4,879	3,763	Musselshell	648	876	691	898	1,280
Reynolds	2,014	776	532	1,864	1,162	Park	2,258	2,846	2,182	2,526	3,823
Ripley	2,300	1,814	739	1,961	2,647	Petroleum	61	135	95	91	204
St. Charles	37,263	38,673	30,351	29,286	50,005	Phillips	634	1,026	949	905	1,462
St. Clair	1,965	1,555	1,083	1,864	2,312	Pondera	1,046	1,252	855	1,245	1,795
St. Francois	9,367	5,889	3,635	8,158	7,923	Powder River	258	547	340	395	815
St. Louis	235,760	188,285	109,099	216,534	262,784	Powell	989	1,058	872	1,174	1,574
Ste. Genevieve	3,795	1,780	1,547	3,612	2,532	Prairie	260	412	179	343	541
Saline	4,643	2,688	2,815	5,039	4,625	Ravalli	4,644	5,392	4,573	4,763	7,418
Schuyler	936	742	487	1,013	1,063	Richland	1,440	1,760	1,525	1,824	2,628
Scotland	1,070	798	617	1,117	1,248	Roosevelt	1,827	1,212	1,089	2,083	1,957
Scott	7,452	6,265	2,763	5,914	8,013	Rosebud	1,669	1,130	1,099	1,869	1,822
Shannon	2,135	1,224	579	1,796	1,696	Sanders	1,689	1,361	1,378	1,959	2,152
Shelby	1,435	1,169	786	1,818	1,586	Sheridan	1,077	795	782	1,354	1,381
Stoddard	5,720	4,608	1,977	4,701	5,822	Silver Bow	9,960	3,491	4,570	11,422	5,043
Stone	3,256	4,035	1,884	2,889	5,080	Stillwater	1,178	1,390	1,056	1,407	1,920
Sullivan	1,510	1,326	596	1,562	1,897	Sweet Grass	395	880	507	462	1,242
Taney	4,682	6,081	2,395	3,888	7,043	Teton	1,043	1,364	969	1,303	1,876
Texas	4,597	3,470	1,900	3,887	4,584	Toole	854	943	903	1,070	1,505
Vernon	3,546	2,851	1,890	3,402	4,149	Treasure	157	206	178	231	291
Warren	3,213	2,953	2,471	2,935	4,452	Valley	1,715	1,497	1,320	2,163	2,467
Washington	4,211	2,157	1,618	3,744	3,240	Wheatland	384	478	284	443	667
Wayne	3,073	2,101	837	2,456	2,648	Wibaux	195	234	173	258	358
Webster	4,149	4,361	2,108	3,890	5,123	Yellowstone	20,163	22,822	13,133	21,987	28,069
Worth	599	483	328	732	677	Totals	154,507	144,207	107,225	168,936	190,412
Wright	2,814	3,427	1,425	2,232	4,151						
City											
St. Louis	102,356	25,441	18,864	110,076	40,906						
Totals	1,053,873	811,159	518,741	1,001,619	1,084,953						

Missouri Vote Since 1944

1944, Roosevelt, Dem., 807,357; Dewey, Rep., 761,175; Thomas, Soc., 1,750; Watson, Proh., 1,175; Teichert, Soc. Labor, 221.

1948, Truman, Dem., 917,315; Dewey, Rep., 655,039; Wallace, Prog., 3,998; Thomas, Soc., 2,222.

1952, Eisenhower, Rep., 959,429; Stevenson, Dem., 929,830; Hallinan, Prog., 987; Hamblen, Proh., 885; MacArthur, Christian Nationalist, 302; America First, 233; Hoopes, Soc., 227; Hass, Soc. Labor, 169.

1956, Stevenson, Dem., 918,273; Eisenhower, Rep., 914,299.

1960, Kennedy, Dem., 972,201; Nixon, Rep., 962,221.

1964, Johnson, Dem., 1,164,344; Goldwater, Rep., 653,535.

1968, Nixon, Rep., 811,932; Humphrey, Dem., 791,444; Wallace, 3d Party, 206,126.

1972, Nixon, Rep., 1,154,058; McGovern, Dem., 698,531.

1976, Carter, Dem., 999,163; Ford, Rep., 928,808; McCarthy, Ind., 24,329.

1980, Reagan, Rep., 1,074,181; Carter, Dem., 931,182; Anderson, Ind., 77,920; Clark, Libertarian, 14,422; DeBerry, Soc. Workers, 1,515; Commoner, Citizens, 573; write-ins, 31.

1984, Reagan, Rep., 1,274,188; Mondale, Dem., 848,583.

1988, Bush, Rep., 1,084,953; Dukakis, Dem., 1,001,619; Fulani, New Alliance, 6,656; Paul, write-in, 434.

1992, Clinton, Dem., 1,053,873; Bush, Rep., 811,159; Perot, Ind., 518,741; Marrou, Libertarian, 7,497.

Montana Vote Since 1944

1944, Roosevelt, Dem., 112,556; Dewey, Rep., 93,163; Thomas, Soc., 1,296; Watson, Proh., 340.

1948, Truman, Dem., 119,071; Dewey, Rep., 96,770; Wallace, Prog., 7,313; Thomas, Soc., 695; Watson, Proh., 429.

1952, Eisenhower, Rep., 157,394; Stevenson, Dem., 106,213; Hallinan, Prog., 723; Hamblen, Proh., 548; Hoopes, Soc., 159.

1956, Eisenhower, Rep., 154,933; Stevenson, Dem., 116,238.

1960, Kennedy, Dem., 134,891; Nixon, Rep., 141,841; Decker, Proh., 456; Dobbs, Soc. Workers, 391.

1964, Johnson, Dem., 164,246; Goldwater, Rep., 113,032; Kasper, Natl. States' Rights, 519; Munn, Proh., 499; DeBerry, Soc. Workers, 332.

1968, Nixon, Rep., 138,835; Humphrey, Dem., 114,117; Wallace, 3d Party, 20,015; Halstead, Soc. Workers, 457; Munn, Proh., 510; Caton, New Reform, 470.

1972, Nixon, Rep., 183,976; McGovern, Dem., 120,197; Schmitz, Amer., 13,430.

1976, Carter, Dem., 149,259; Ford, Rep., 173,703; Anderson, Amer., 5,772.

1980, Reagan, Rep., 206,814; Carter, Dem., 118,032; Anderson, Ind., 29,281; Clark, Libertarian, 9,825.

1984, Reagan, Rep., 232,450; Mondale, Dem., 146,742; Bergland, Libertarian, 5,185.

1988, Bush, Rep., 190,412; Dukakis, Dem., 168,936; Paul, Lib., 5,047; Fulani, New Alliance, 1,279.

1992, Clinton, Dem., 154,507; Bush, Rep., 144,207; Perot, Ind., 107,225; Gritz, Populist/America First, 3,658.

Montana

	1992			1988	
County	Clinton (D)	Bush (R)	Perot (I)	Dukakis (D)	Bush (R)
Beaverhead	1,098	1,746	1,202	1,274	2,668
Big Horn	2,154	1,377	840	2,233	1,711

Nebraska

	1992			1988	
County	Clinton (D)	Bush (R)	Perot (I)	Dukakis (D)	Bush (R)
Adams	3,445	6,346	3,273	4,145	8,063
Antelope	650	1,979	1,134	933	2,626

Arthur	18	148	97	58	210
Banner	68	284	128	112	361
Blaine	64	256	130	72	338
Boone	604	1,588	956	976	2,160
Box Butte. . . .	1,935	2,198	1,508	2,466	3,253
Boyd	353	744	468	480	967
Brown	311	999	525	435	1,335
Buffalo.	3,742	9,708	4,083	4,700	9,980
Burt	1,224	1,667	1,009	1,458	2,050
Butler	1,087	1,881	1,157	1,715	2,083
Cass	2,949	4,314	2,657	3,674	4,658
Cedar	1,007	1,981	1,507	1,759	2,462
Chase	398	1,000	674	597	1,446
Cherry.	563	1,707	730	642	2,240
Cheyenne	967	2,197	1,061	1,333	2,862
Clay	802	1,818	952	1,097	2,352
Colfax	1,011	1,915	1,197	1,542	2,329
Cuming	835	2,711	1,192	1,238	3,201
Custer	1,126	3,180	1,492	1,496	4,202
Dakota	2,322	2,771	1,307	2,941	2,744
Dawes.	987	1,961	1,103	1,122	2,618
Dawson	1,739	4,710	2,305	2,184	5,529
Deuel	232	558	327	302	769
Dixon	830	1,484	726	1,166	1,802
Dodge	4,665	7,269	4,432	6,116	8,412
Douglas.	67,003	93,421	38,641	76,444	99,806
Dundy	244	664	332	333	828
Fillmore	988	1,495	993	1,433	1,952
Franklin	477	967	527	768	1,294
Frontier	302	785	479	384	1,057
Furnas.	624	1,365	804	791	1,830
Gage.	3,309	3,995	2,726	4,008	5,114
Garden	212	697	385	366	986
Garfield	221	595	270	234	803
Gosper	254	492	297	331	694
Grant	75	247	124	89	301
Greeley	435	587	395	670	763
Hall.	5,519	9,264	5,822	6,822	12,020
Hamilton	992	2,379	1,213	1,289	3,019
Harlan	488	991	623	725	1,403
Hayes	85	362	207	160	512
Hitchcock. . . .	359	824	540	480	1,132
Holt.	835	3,131	1,714	1,327	4,081
Hooker	70	283	102	91	378
Howard	778	1,138	940	1,186	1,526
Jefferson	1,506	1,783	1,177	1,819	2,470
Johnson.	822	885	642	1,162	1,182
Kearney.	644	1,751	844	1,056	2,120
Keith	731	2,019	1,130	1,067	2,879
Keya Paha . . .	105	368	158	145	446
Kimball	408	931	440	540	1,321
Knox	968	2,112	1,166	1,477	2,644
Lancaster. . . .	41,207	41,400	21,783	44,260	44,605
Lincoln	5,142	7,025	3,384	6,070	8,395
Logan	80	271	98	93	373
Loup	58	233	96	97	295
McPherson. . .	49	217	62	60	229
Madison	2,352	7,851	3,486	2,779	9,135
Merrick	864	1,854	1,072	1,192	2,376
Morrill	577	1,184	752	753	1,554
Nance	559	851	569	794	1,185
Nemaha.	1,110	1,696	1,020	1,457	2,293
Nuckolls	834	1,277	825	1,114	1,750
Otoe	2,038	2,960	1,800	2,616	3,724
Pawnee	566	670	565	767	975
Perkins	300	842	522	467	1,117
Phelps	829	2,748	1,298	1,047	3,316
Pierce	611	1,853	1,084	914	2,474
Platte	2,409	7,712	3,656	3,285	9,029
Polk	661	1,435	812	944	1,768
Red Willow. . .	1,164	2,488	1,660	1,505	3,325
Richardson. . .	1,513	2,050	1,356	1,926	2,702
Rock.	162	588	233	198	756
Saline	2,425	1,740	1,576	3,119	2,352
Sarpy	10,720	20,482	9,270	10,936	20,119
Saunders. . . .	2,509	4,037	2,567	3,524	4,454
Scotts Bluff. . .	4,173	7,213	3,514	4,454	8,594
Seward	2,118	3,044	1,722	2,682	3,467
Sheridan	535	1,698	751	612	2,251
Sherman	568	736	582	839	914
Sioux	148	445	206	194	568
Stanton	496	1,274	786	637	1,709
Thayer.	923	1,387	1,077	1,322	1,981
Thomas.	69	283	115	81	383
Thurston	865	898	487	1,225	1,105
Valley	716	1,173	693	873	1,603
Washington . .	2,108	4,035	2,148	2,552	4,567
Wayne.	921	2,122	1,047	1,111	2,473
Webster.	624	972	657	891	1,314
Wheeler.	88	246	127	141	309
York	1,385	3,783	1,825	1,748	4,744
Totals	**216,864**	**343,678**	**174,104**	**259,235**	**397,956**

Nebraska Vote Since 1944

1944, Roosevelt, Dem., 233,246; Dewey, Rep., 329,880.
1948, Truman, Dem., 224,165; Dewey, Rep., 264,774.
1952, Eisenhower, Rep., 421,603; Stevenson, Dem., 188,057.
1956, Eisenhower, Rep., 378,108; Stevenson, Dem., 199,029.
1960, Kennedy, Dem., 232,542; Nixon, Rep., 380,553.

1964, Johnson, Dem., 307,307; Goldwater, Rep., 276,847.
1968, Nixon, Rep., 321,163; Humphrey, Dem., 170,784; Wallace, 3d Party, 44,904.
1972, Nixon, Rep., 406,298; McGovern, Dem., 169,991; scattered, 817.
1976, Carter, Dem., 233,287; Ford, Rep., 359,219; McCarthy, Ind., 9,383; Maddox, Amer. Ind., 3,378; MacBride, Libertarian, 1,476.
1980, Reagan, Rep., 419,214; Carter, Dem., 166,424; Anderson, Ind., 44,854; Clark, Libertarian, 9,041.
1984, Reagan, Rep., 459,135; Mondale, Dem., 187,475; Bergland, Libertarian, 2,075.
1988, Bush, Rep., 397,956; Dukakis, Dem., 259,235; Paul, Lib., 2,534; Fulani, New Alliance, 1,740.
1992, Bush, Rep., 343,678; Clinton, Dem., 216,864; Perot, Ind., 174,104; Marrou, Libertarian, 1,340.

Nevada

	1992			1988	
	Clinton	Bush	Perot	Dukakis	Bush
County	(D)	(R)	(I)	(D)	(R)
Churchill	1,770	3,789	1,964	1,481	4,578
Clark.	124,586	97,403	75,364	78,359	108,110
Douglas.	3,928	6,182	4,814	3,107	7,074
Elko	2,782	5,208	3,628	2,310	5,722
Esmeralda . . .	118	221	220	143	380
Eureka	129	330	214	151	413
Humboldt. . . .	810	1,505	1,149	1,024	2,378
Lander.	423	885	652	439	1,214
Lincoln	511	890	394	466	1,035
Lyon	2,777	3,509	2,716	2,301	4,390
Mineral	909	918	746	978	1,480
Nye.	2,561	2,743	2,501	1,748	3,619
Pershing	467	643	429	458	867
Storey.	488	458	550	432	651
Washoe.	39,500	42,636	30,974	32,902	52,654
White Pine . . .	1,354	1,206	1,070	1,351	1,774
City					
Carson City . . .	6,035	7,302	5,195	5,088	9,701
Totals	**189,148**	**175,828**	**132,580**	**132,738**	**206,040**

Nevada Vote Since 1944

1944, Roosevelt, Dem., 29,623; Dewey, Rep., 24,611.
1948, Truman, Dem., 31,291; Dewey, Rep., 29,357; Wallace, Prog., 1,469.
1952, Eisenhower, Rep., 50,502; Stevenson, Dem., 31,688.
1956, Eisenhower, Rep., 56,049; Stevenson, Dem., 40,640.
1960, Kennedy, Dem., 54,880; Nixon, Rep., 52,387.
1964, Johnson, Dem., 79,339; Goldwater, Rep., 56,094.
1968, Nixon, Rep., 73,188; Humphrey, Dem., 60,598; Wallace, 3d Party, 20,432.
1972, Nixon, Rep., 115,750; McGovern, Dem., 66,016.
1976, Carter, Dem., 92,479; Ford, Rep., 101,273; MacBride, Libertarian, 1,519; Maddox, Amer. Ind., 1,497; scattered, 5,108.
1980, Reagan, Rep., 155,017; Carter, Dem., 66,666; Anderson, Ind., 17,651; Clark, Libertarian, 4,358.
1984, Reagan, Rep., 188,770; Mondale, Dem., 91,655; Bergland, Libertarian, 2,292.
1988, Bush, Rep., 206,040; Dukakis, Dem., 132,738; Paul, Lib., 3,520; Fulani, New Alliance, 835.
1992, Clinton, Dem., 189,148; Bush, Rep., 175,828; Perot, Ind., 132,580; Gritz, Populist/America First, 2,892; Marrou, Libertarian, 1,835.

New Hampshire

	1992			1988	
	Clinton	Bush	Perot	Dukakis	Bush
City	(D)	(R)	(I)	(D)	(R)
Berlin City . . .	2,680	1,272	1,162	2,271	2,529
Claremont . . .	2,650	1,822	904	2,254	2,513
Concord	8,325	5,651	2,843	6,698	7,439
Dover	5,449	4,197	2,246	4,803	5,357
Keene	5,210	3,257	1,736	4,466	4,535
Laconia	2,390	3,033	1,496	2,111	3,835
Manchester . .	16,627	16,298	7,441	12,567	23,893
Nashua	14,777	12,514	8,306	12,833	19,369
Portsmouth . .	6,132	3,563	2,088	5,377	4,827
Rochester . . .	4,588	4,272	2,541	3,591	5,368
Other	140,212	147,999	90,574	106,725	201,872
Totals	**209,040**	**202,484**	**121,337**	**163,696**	**281,537**

New Hampshire Vote Since 1944

1944, Roosevelt, Dem., 119,663; Dewey, Rep., 109,916; Thomas, Soc., 46.
1948, Truman, Dem., 107,995; Dewey, Rep., 121,299; Wallace, Prog., 1,970; Thomas, Soc., 86; Teichert, Soc. Labor, 83; Thurmond, States' Rights, 7.

1952, Eisenhower, Rep., 166,287; Stevenson, Dem., 106,663.
1956, Eisenhower, Rep., 176,519; Stevenson, Dem., 90,364; Andrews, Const., 111.
1960, Kennedy, Dem., 137,772; Nixon, Rep., 157,989.
1964, Johnson, Dem., 182,065; Goldwater, Rep., 104,029.
1968, Nixon, Rep., 154,903; Humphrey, Dem., 130,589; Wallace, 3d Party, 11,173; New Party, 421; Halstead, Soc. Workers, 104.
1972, Nixon, Rep., 213,724; McGovern, Dem., 116,435; Schmitz, Amer., 3,386; Jenness, Soc. Workers, 368; scattered, 142.
1976, Carter, Dem., 147,645; Ford, Rep., 185,935; McCarthy, Ind., 4,095; MacBride, Libertarian, 936; Reagan, write-in, 388; La Rouche, U.S. Labor, 186; Camejo, Soc. Workers, 161; Levin, Soc. Labor, 66; scattered, 215.
1980, Reagan, Rep., 221,705; Carter, Dem., 108,864; Anderson, Ind., 49,693; Clark, Libertarian, 2,067; Commoner, Citizens, 1,325; Hall, Com., 129; Griswold, Workers World, 76; DeBerry, Soc. Workers, 72; scattered, 68.
1984, Reagan, Rep., 267,051; Mondale, Dem., 120,377; Bergland, Libertarian, 735.
1988, Bush, Rep., 281,537; Dukakis, Dem., 163,696; Paul, Lib., 4,502; Fulani, New Alliance, 790.
1992, Clinton, Dem., 209,040; Bush, Rep., 202,484; Perot, Ind., 121,337; Marrou, Libertarian, 3,548.

New Jersey

	1992			1988	
	Clinton	Bush	Perot	Dukakis	Bush
County	(D)	(R)	(I)	(D)	(R)
Atlantic	39,633	34,279	15,890	34,047	44,748
Bergen	171,104	178,223	52,082	160,655	226,885
Burlington	72,845	63,709	35,322	61,140	87,416
Camden	104,915	67,205	37,144	90,704	100,072
Cape May	17,324	21,502	9,798	15,105	28,738
Cumberland	22,220	19,253	9,901	21,869	26,024
Essex	158,130	89,146	26,961	156,098	111,491
Gloucester	42,425	37,335	24,132	35,479	51,708
Hudson	99,799	66,505	14,569	95,696	81,807
Hunterdon	15,423	25,130	12,736	13,758	31,907
Mercer	71,383	50,473	22,503	68,712	65,384
Middlesex	128,824	108,701	45,055	117,149	143,361
Monmouth	101,750	117,715	45,445	91,844	147,320
Morris	67,593	108,431	32,447	58,721	127,420
Ocean	75,431	95,984	41,668	64,474	124,587
Passaic	70,030	71,147	21,494	66,254	88,070
Salem	10,062	10,363	7,274	9,956	15,240
Somerset	42,867	56,044	21,014	37,406	67,658
Sussex	14,775	29,510	12,537	13,676	36,086
Union	96,671	87,742	23,991	93,158	112,967
Warren	13,002	18,468	9,866	11,640	21,715
Totals	1,436,206	1,356,865	521,829	1,317,541	1,740,604

New Jersey Vote Since 1944

1944, Roosevelt, Dem., 987,874; Dewey, Rep., 961,335; Teichert, Soc. Labor, 6,939; Watson, Natl. Proh., 4,255; Thomas, Soc., 3,385.
1948, Truman, Dem., 895,455; Dewey, Rep., 981,124; Wallace, Prog., 42,683; Watson, Proh., 10,593; Thomas, Soc., 10,521; Dobbs, Soc. Workers, 5,825; Teichert, Soc. Labor, 3,354.
1952, Eisenhower, Rep., 1,373,613; Stevenson, Dem., 1,015,902; Hoopes, Soc., 8,593; Hass, Soc. Labor, 5,815; Hallinan, Prog., 5,589; Krajewski, Poor Man's, 4,203; Dobbs, Soc. Workers, 3,850; Hamblen, Proh., 989.
1956, Eisenhower, Rep., 1,606,942; Stevenson Dem., 850,337; Holtwick, Proh., 9,147; Hass, Soc. Labor, 6,736; Andrews, Cons., 5,317; Dobbs, Soc. Workers, 4,004; Krajewski, Amer. Third Party, 1,829.
1960, Kennedy, Dem., 1,385,415; Nixon, Rep., 1,363,324; Dobbs, Soc. Workers, 11,402; Lee, Cons., 8,708; Hass, Soc. Labor, 4,262.
1964, Johnson, Dem., 1,867,671; Goldwater, Rep., 963,843; DeBerry, Soc. Workers, 8,181; Hass, Soc. Labor, 7,075.
1968, Nixon, Rep., 1,325,467; Humphrey, Dem., 1,264,206; Wallace, 3d Party, 262,187; Halstead, Soc. Workers, 8,667; Gregory, Peace and Freedom, 8,084; Blomen, Soc. Labor, 6,784.
1972, Nixon, Rep., 1,845,502; McGovern, Dem., 1,102,211; Schmitz, Amer., 34,378; Spock, Peoples, 5,355; Fisher, Soc. Labor, 4,544; Jenness, Soc. Workers, 2,233; Mahalchik, Amer. First, 1,743; Hall, Com., 1,263.
1976, Carter, Dem., 1,444,653; Ford, Rep., 1,509,688; McCarthy, Ind., 32,717; MacBride, Libertarian, 9,449; Maddox, Amer., 7,716; Levin, Soc. Labor, 3,686; Hall, Com., 1,662; LaRouche, U.S. Labor, 1,650; Camejo, Soc.

Workers, 1,184; Wright, People's, 1,044; Bubar, Proh., 554; Zeidler, Soc., 469.
1980, Reagan, Rep., 1,546,557; Carter, Dem., 1,147,364; Anderson, Ind., 234,632; Clark, Libertarian, 20,652; Commoner, Citizens, 8,203; McCormack, Right to Life, 3,927; Lynen, Middle Class, 3,694; Hall, Com., 2,555; Pulley, Soc. Workers, 2,198; McReynolds, Soc., 1,973; Gahres, Down With Lawyers, 1,718; Griswold, Workers World, 1,288; Wendelken, Ind., 923.
1984, Reagan, Rep., 1,933,630; Mondale, Dem., 1,261,323; Bergland, Libertarian, 6,416.
1988, Bush, Rep., 1,740,604; Dukakis, Dem., 1,317,541; Lewin, Peace and Freedom, 9,953; Paul, Lib., 8,421.
1992, Clinton, Dem., 1,436,206; Bush, Rep., 1,356,865; Perot, Ind., 521,829; Marrou, Libertarian, 6,822; Fulani, New Alliance, 3,513; Phillips, U.S. Taxpayers, 2,670; LaRouche, Ind., 2,095; Warren, Soc. Workers, 2,011; Daniels, Ind., 1,996; Gritz, Populist/America First, 1,867; Hagelin, Natural Law, 1,353.

New Mexico

	1992			1988	
	Clinton	Bush	Perot	Dukakis	Bush
County	(D)	(R)	(I)	(D)	(R)
Bernalillo	90,863	77,304	31,241	78,346	92,830
Catron	465	771	289	490	925
Chaves	6,360	8,872	3,590	6,730	13,367
Cibola	3,334	2,051	847	3,458	2,640
Colfax	2,607	1,730	871	2,785	2,256
Curry	3,699	6,831	2,056	3,995	8,032
De Baca	451	526	204	480	643
Dona Ana	19,894	16,308	7,682	19,608	21,582
Eddy	7,409	7,313	3,430	8,544	9,805
Grant	5,603	2,917	1,685	5,443	4,196
Guadalupe	1,225	691	173	1,243	861
Harding	268	312	98	291	377
Hidalgo	995	871	442	901	1,100
Lea	5,047	7,921	3,233	5,879	11,309
Lincoln	1,730	2,669	1,431	1,690	3,511
Los Alamos	3,897	4,320	2,339	3,275	6,622
Luna	2,637	2,166	1,445	3,066	3,415
McKinley	9,405	4,720	1,304	9,595	5,694
Mora	1,555	668	188	1,601	923
Otero	5,377	7,481	3,257	5,284	9,984
Quay	1,758	1,759	755	1,901	2,454
Rio Arriba	7,832	2,680	984	7,503	3,024
Roosevelt	2,172	3,215	1,085	2,033	3,589
Sandoval	10,951	8,491	3,954	9,332	9,411
San Juan	11,302	13,415	5,351	11,094	16,202
San Miguel	6,186	2,183	965	6,131	2,763
Santa Fe	27,189	9,684	5,656	23,581	12,891
Sierra	1,771	1,562	1,055	1,595	2,507
Socorro	2,908	2,186	918	2,960	3,114
Taos	7,051	2,260	1,300	6,271	2,897
Torrance	1,662	1,667	810	1,618	2,252
Union	519	975	355	638	1,291
Valencia	7,495	6,305	2,902	7,136	7,874
Totals	261,617	212,824	91,895	244,497	270,341

New Mexico Vote Since 1944

1944, Roosevelt, Dem., 81,389; Dewey, Rep., 70,688; Watson, Proh., 148.
1948, Truman, Dem., 105,464; Dewey, Rep., 80,303; Wallace, Prog., 1,037; Watson, Proh., 127; Thomas, Soc., 83; Teichert, Soc. Labor, 49.
1952, Eisenhower, Rep., 132,170; Stevenson, Dem., 105,661; Hamblen, Proh., 297; Hallinan, Ind. Prog., 225; MacArthur, Christian National, 220; Hass, Soc. Labor, 35.
1956, Eisenhower, Rep., 146,788; Stevenson, Dem., 106,098; Holtwick, Proh., 607; Andrews, Ind., 364; Hass, Soc. Labor, 69.
1960, Kennedy, Dem., 156,027; Nixon, Rep., 153,733; Decker, Proh., 777; Hass, Soc. Labor, 570.
1964, Johnson, Dem., 194,017; Goldwater, Rep., 131,838; Hass, Soc. Labor, 1,217; Munn, Proh., 543.
1968, Nixon, Rep., 169,692; Humphrey, Dem., 130,081; Wallace, 3d Party, 25,737; Chavez, 1,519; Halstead, Soc. Workers, 252.
1972, Nixon, Rep., 235,606; McGovern, Dem., 141,084; Schmitz, Amer., 8,767; Jenness, Soc. Workers, 474.
1976, Carter, Dem., 201,148; Ford, Rep., 211,419; Camejo, Soc. Workers, 2,462; MacBride, Libertarian, 1,110; Zeidler, Soc., 240; Bubar, Proh., 211.
1980, Reagan, Rep., 250,779; Carter, Dem., 167,826; Anderson, Ind., 29,459; Clark, Libertarian, 4,365; Commoner, Citizens, 2,202; Bubar, Statesman, 1,281; Pulley, Soc. Workers, 325.

1984, Reagan, Rep., 307,101; Mondale, Dem., 201,769; Bergland, Libertarian, 4,459.

1988, Bush, Rep., 270,341; Dukakis, Dem., 244,497; Paul, Lib., 3,268; Fulani, New Alliance, 2,237.

1992, Clinton, Dem., 261,617; Bush, Rep., 212,824; Perot, Ind., 91,895; Marrou, Libertarian, 1,615.

New York

County	1992 Clinton (D)	Bush (R)	Perot (I)	1988 Dukakis (D)	Bush (R)
Albany	80,641	49,452	24,064	86,564	59,534
Allegany	4,848	8,976	4,703	5,614	11,880
Bronx	225,038	63,310	15,115	218,245	76,043
Broome	43,444	34,653	21,280	48,130	47,610
Cattaraugus	10,150	13,944	10,662	12,447	19,691
Cayuga	13,088	12,065	10,279	15,044	16,934
Chautauqua	22,645	21,222	18,455	25,814	31,642
Chemung	15,099	16,088	7,493	15,966	20,951
Chenango	8,017	8,114	5,356	8,021	11,727
Clinton	12,881	13,455	5,389	12,670	15,702
Columbia	11,368	11,568	5,829	11,585	15,111
Cortland	7,815	7,782	5,098	7,673	10,934
Delaware	7,152	8,829	4,404	7,463	11,391
Dutchess	41,655	46,709	26,320	38,968	62,165
Erie	196,233	129,444	123,358	238,779	188,796
Essex	6,717	8,278	3,784	6,623	10,350
Franklin	7,654	6,635	3,857	7,928	9,135
Fulton	8,400	9,137	5,120	9,012	11,757
Genesee	8,071	11,663	6,192	9,945	14,182
Greene	6,924	9,390	4,689	7,265	11,874
Hamilton	963	2,038	793	976	2,320
Herkimer	10,880	12,052	6,866	12,694	15,104
Jefferson	13,380	14,227	9,461	14,137	19,304
Kings	411,183	133,344	33,014	363,916	178,961
Lewis	3,676	4,101	3,164	4,252	5,787
Livingston	8,648	12,122	5,775	9,506	14,004
Madison	10,099	11,293	7,391	10,665	14,902
Monroe	141,502	134,021	63,229	153,650	155,271
Montgomery	9,509	8,802	5,020	11,371	11,128
Nassau	282,593	246,881	77,097	250,130	337,430
New York	416,142	84,501	27,689	385,675	115,927
Niagara	35,649	30,401	30,126	43,801	42,537
Oneida	40,966	43,806	22,717	47,665	55,039
Onondaga	90,645	77,642	45,175	94,751	104,080
Ontario	16,064	18,995	9,571	17,341	21,780
Orange	45,946	53,493	22,499	38,465	65,446
Orleans	4,927	7,468	4,275	5,913	9,028
Oswego	16,990	18,530	14,853	18,430	25,362
Otsego	10,471	10,141	5,841	11,069	13,021
Putnam	14,048	18,934	8,011	12,158	24,086
Queens	349,520	157,561	46,014	325,147	217,049
Rensselaer	29,793	28,937	15,198	33,066	35,412
Richmond	56,901	70,707	19,678	47,812	77,427
Rockland	56,759	49,608	15,026	47,634	63,825
St. Lawrence	18,197	13,901	9,758	18,921	20,290
Saratoga	33,011	36,917	19,091	31,684	43,498
Schenectady	32,335	26,258	14,838	36,483	33,364
Schoharie	4,997	5,678	3,327	5,389	7,008
Schuyler	2,859	3,226	2,051	2,900	4,291
Seneca	5,810	5,432	3,660	6,215	7,221
Steuben	12,043	19,761	9,378	12,824	25,359
Suffolk	220,811	229,467	112,973	199,215	311,242
Sullivan	13,717	11,396	6,336	11,635	15,713
Tioga	7,791	9,287	5,867	8,102	12,670
Tompkins	23,197	11,520	6,704	21,455	14,932
Ulster	32,886	29,223	17,952	30,744	41,173
Warren	9,820	12,260	6,401	8,580	15,860
Washington	8,429	10,305	6,143	8,201	14,103
Wayne	11,866	18,019	9,188	12,959	20,613
Westchester	184,300	151,990	39,933	169,860	197,956
Wyoming	4,045	7,324	4,837	5,228	9,451
Yates	3,242	4,366	2,354	3,507	5,488
Totals	3,444,450	2,346,649	1,090,721	3,347,882	3,081,871

New York Vote Since 1944

1944, Roosevelt, Dem., 2,478,598; Amer. Lab., 496,405; Liberal, 329,325; total, 3,304,238; Dewey, Rep., 2,987,647; Teichert, Ind. Gov't., 14,352; Thomas, Soc., 10,553.

1948, Truman, Dem., 2,557,642; Liberal, 222,562; total, 2,780,204; Dewey, Rep., 2,841,163; Wallace, Amer. Lab., 509,559; Thomas, Soc., 40,879; Teichert, Ind. Gov't., 2,729; Dobbs, Soc. Workers, 2,675.

1952, Eisenhower, Rep., 3,952,815; Stevenson, Dem., 2,687,890; Liberal, 416,711; total, 3,104,601; Hallinan, Amer. Lab., 64,211; Hoopes, Soc., 2,664; Dobbs, Soc. Workers, 2,212; Hass, Ind. Gov't., 1,560; scattering, 178; blank and void, 87,813.

1956, Eisenhower, Rep., 4,340,340; Stevenson, Dem., 2,458,212; Liberal, 292,557; total, 2,750,769; write-in votes for Andrews, 1,027; Werdel, 492; Hass, 150; Hoopes, 82; others, 476.

1960, Kennedy, Dem., 3,423,909; Liberal, 406,176; total, 3,830,085; Nixon, Rep., 3,446,419; Dobbs, Soc. Workers, 14,319; scattering, 256; blank and void, 88,896.

1964, Johnson, Dem., 4,913,156; Goldwater, Rep., 2,243,559; Hass, Soc. Labor, 6,085; DeBerry, Soc. Workers, 3,215; scattering, 188; blank and void, 151,383.

1968, Nixon, Rep., 3,007,932; Humphrey, Dem., 3,378,470; Wallace, 3d Party, 358,864; Blomen, Soc. Labor, 8,432; Halstead, Soc. Workers, 11,851; Gregory, Freedom and Peace, 24,517; blank, void, and scattering, 171,624.

1972, Nixon, Rep., 3,824,642; Cons., 368,136; McGovern, Dem., 2,767,956; Liberal, 183,128; Reed, Soc. Workers, 7,797; Fisher, Soc. Labor, 4,530; Hall, Com., 5,641; blank, void, or scattered, 161,641.

1976, Carter, Dem., 3,389,558; Ford, Rep., 3,100,791; MacBride, Libertarian, 12,197; Hall, Com., 10,270; Camejo, Soc. Workers, 6,996; LaRouche, U.S. Labor, 5,413; blank, void, or scattered, 143,037.

1980, Reagan, Rep., 2,893,831; Carter, Dem., 2,728,372; Anderson, Ind., 467,801; Clark, Libertarian, 52,648; McCormack, Right To Life, 24,159; Commoner, Citizens, 23,186; Hall, Com., 7,414; DeBerry, Soc. Workers, 2,068; Griswold, Workers World, 1,416; scattering, 1,064.

1984, Reagan, Rep., 3,664,763; Mondale, Dem., 3,119,609; Bergland, Libertarian, 11,949.

1988, Bush, Rep., 3,081,871; Dukakis, Dem., 3,347,882; Marra, Right to Life, 20,497; Fulani, New Alliance, 15,845.

1992, Clinton, Dem., 3,444,450; Bush, Rep., 2,346,649; Perot, Ind., 1,090,721; Warren, Soc. Workers, 15,472; Marrou, Libertarian, 13,451; Fulani, New Alliance, 11,318; Hagelin, Natural Law, 4,420.

North Carolina

County	1992 Clinton (D)	Bush (R)	Perot (I)	1988 Dukakis (D)	Bush (R)
Alamance	15,521	20,637	6,444	12,642	24,131
Alexander	4,849	6,764	2,002	4,148	7,968
Alleghany	2,271	1,853	600	2,087	2,174
Anson	5,269	2,334	921	4,831	2,782
Ashe	4,624	5,200	1,220	4,034	6,019
Avery	1,755	3,895	1,123	1,367	4,277
Beaufort	6,445	7,337	2,174	5,352	8,190
Bertie	4,382	1,756	600	3,762	2,145
Bladen	5,700	3,214	1,248	5,031	3,770
Brunswick	10,177	8,833	3,349	7,881	10,007
Buncombe	32,955	30,892	11,481	26,964	36,828
Burke	12,565	13,397	4,124	10,848	15,933
Cabarrus	13,513	21,281	6,251	10,686	22,524
Caldwell	9,033	12,543	3,965	7,862	15,176
Camden	1,153	1,039	479	1,081	1,144
Carteret	8,028	10,334	3,401	6,859	11,076
Caswell	4,725	2,793	827	4,189	3,299
Catawba	16,334	25,466	7,523	12,922	28,872
Chatham	9,520	6,568	2,425	7,600	6,999
Cherokee	3,686	4,021	1,040	2,567	4,557
Chowan	2,136	1,661	700	1,756	1,884
Clay	1,600	1,890	465	1,289	2,174
Cleveland	13,037	13,650	3,784	10,321	14,039
Columbus	11,469	5,462	1,963	9,172	6,659
Craven	9,998	11,575	3,679	7,313	12,057
Cumberland	30,291	27,139	6,792	23,789	27,057
Currituck	1,935	2,188	1,163	1,555	2,443
Dare	3,925	4,357	2,388	2,806	5,234
Davidson	16,462	24,869	8,324	13,215	28,374
Davie	3,675	6,796	1,903	3,166	7,988
Duplin	6,816	5,286	1,636	5,945	5,774
Durham	47,331	27,581	7,504	35,441	29,928
Edgecombe	11,174	6,275	2,175	9,044	6,831
Forsyth	49,006	52,787	14,262	39,726	57,688
Franklin	6,517	4,669	2,062	5,438	5,499
Gaston	19,121	34,714	7,490	14,582	34,775
Gates	2,206	1,158	466	2,024	1,451
Graham	1,551	1,919	403	1,313	2,091
Granville	6,178	4,538	1,321	5,280	4,880
Greene	2,768	2,180	780	2,729	2,498
Guilford	66,319	60,140	19,601	50,351	66,060
Halifax	9,960	5,769	2,047	8,726	7,462
Harnett	8,473	9,751	2,684	7,259	9,749
Haywood	10,385	7,292	3,303	9,010	8,957
Henderson	10,747	17,010	5,260	9,338	19,711
Hertford	4,609	2,208	846	4,943	2,977
Hoke	3,730	1,711	887	3,281	2,020
Hyde	1,206	740	340	1,316	940
Iredell	13,263	19,411	6,204	10,530	21,536
Jackson	5,753	4,275	1,516	4,933	5,166
Johnston	11,284	15,418	4,939	8,717	15,563
Jones	1,962	1,438	444	1,946	1,649
Lee	5,852	6,658	2,125	4,231	7,104
Lenoir	8,793	8,932	2,107	7,649	10,669

County	Clinton (D)	Bush (R)	Perot (I)	Dukakis (D)	Bush (R)
Lincoln	8,150	11,018	3,142	6,444	11,651
McDowell	5,309	6,090	1,881	4,449	6,526
Macon	4,624	4,797	1,829	3,773	6,026
Madison	3,980	3,121	857	3,033	3,453
Martin	4,069	2,958	981	3,598	3,149
Mecklenburg	97,065	99,496	31,283	71,907	106,236
Mitchell	1,727	4,405	877	1,377	4,620
Montgomery	4,422	3,543	1,185	3,995	4,504
Moore	9,649	12,448	4,448	7,642	14,543
Nash	10,809	14,446	4,544	8,740	15,906
New Hanover	20,291	24,338	7,401	15,401	23,807
Northampton	5,195	1,845	916	4,599	2,415
Onslow	8,045	11,842	4,387	7,162	12,253
Orange	28,595	13,009	5,535	22,326	14,503
Pamlico	2,229	1,929	809	2,188	2,297
Pasquotank	4,709	3,419	1,434	3,860	4,006
Pender	5,825	4,857	1,725	4,377	4,926
Perquimans	1,818	1,429	624	1,543	1,781
Person	4,323	4,460	1,431	3,777	4,832
Pitt	17,959	16,609	5,262	14,777	18,245
Polk	2,939	3,448	1,134	2,534	3,874
Randolph	11,274	20,697	6,870	8,641	23,881
Richmond	9,163	4,356	2,015	7,151	5,073
Robeson	19,378	7,777	3,277	16,988	9,908
Rockingham	13,880	12,678	4,671	11,551	14,591
Rowan	14,308	21,297	7,053	12,127	23,192
Rutherford	7,855	9,748	2,695	6,926	10,337
Sampson	8,698	8,007	1,852	8,009	8,524
Scotland	5,175	2,980	1,196	3,865	3,199
Stanly	7,735	11,030	2,855	6,627	11,885
Stokes	6,463	7,979	2,183	5,319	8,661
Surry	9,392	10,866	3,164	7,245	11,393
Swain	2,117	1,640	568	1,821	1,795
Transylvania	5,120	5,984	2,006	4,280	7,009
Tyrrell	928	553	189	785	637
Union	10,789	16,542	4,601	8,820	17,015
Vance	6,598	4,747	1,444	5,631	5,625
Wake	88,979	86,798	31,140	61,352	81,613
Warren	4,656	1,767	693	4,249	2,163
Washington	2,902	1,780	563	2,806	2,186
Watauga	8,262	7,899	3,007	6,048	8,662
Wayne	10,307	14,397	2,798	9,135	15,292
Wilkes	7,991	12,547	3,307	7,230	15,231
Wilson	10,105	10,176	2,630	8,214	10,997
Yadkin	3,913	7,311	1,725	3,195	7,918
Yancey	4,285	3,994	917	3,803	4,160
Totals	1,114,042	1,134,661	357,864	890,167	1,237,258

North Carolina Vote Since 1944

1944, Roosevelt, Dem., 527,399; Dewey, Rep., 263,155.

1948, Truman, Dem., 459,070; Dewey, Rep., 258,572; Thurmond, States' Rights, 69,652; Wallace, Prog., 3,915.

1952, Eisenhower, Rep., 558,107; Stevenson, Dem., 652,803.

1956, Eisenhower, Rep., 575,062; Stevenson, Dem., 590,530.

1960, Kennedy, Dem., 713,136; Nixon, Rep., 655,420.

1964, Johnson, Dem., 800,139; Goldwater, Rep., 624,844.

1968, Nixon, Rep., 627,192; Humphrey, Dem., 464,113; Wallace, 3d Party, 496,188.

1972, Nixon, Rep., 1,054,889; McGovern, Dem., 438,705; Schmitz, Amer., 25,018.

1976, Carter, Dem., 927,365; Ford, Rep., 741,960; Anderson, Amer., 5,607; MacBride, Libertarian, 2,219; LaRouche, U.S. Labor, 755.

1980, Reagan, Rep., 915,018; Carter, Dem., 875,635; Anderson, Ind., 52,800; Clark, Libertarian, 9,677; Commoner, Citizens, 2,287; DeBerry, Soc. Workers, 416.

1984, Reagan, Rep., 1,346,481; Mondale, Dem., 824,287; Bergland, Libertarian, 3,794.

1988, Bush, Rep., 1,237,258; Dukakis, Dem., 890,167; Fulani, New Alliance, 5,682; Paul, write-in, 1,263.

1992, Clinton, Dem., 1,114,042; Bush, Rep., 1,134,661; Perot, Ind., 357,864; Marrou, Libertarian, 5,171.

North Dakota

County	1992 Clinton (D)	1992 Bush (R)	1992 Perot (I)	1988 Dukakis (D)	1988 Bush (R)
Adams	469	647	499	708	1,018
Barnes	2,124	2,728	1,568	2,858	3,631
Benson	1,126	874	610	1,691	1,316
Billings	123	279	270	211	437
Bottineau	1,266	1,787	1,036	1,684	2,530
Bowman	506	712	678	737	1,111
Burke	458	551	506	693	971
Burleigh	8,940	16,484	6,780	10,760	18,000
Cass	18,077	25,312	9,513	22,107	26,699
Cavalier	866	1,527	723	1,333	2,096
Dickey	918	1,514	616	1,249	2,064
Divide	634	515	456	875	869
Dunn	667	784	637	892	1,263
Eddy	575	591	432	748	891
Emmons	595	1,047	774	925	1,634

County	Clinton (D)	Bush (R)	Perot (I)	Dukakis (D)	Bush (R)
Foster	565	803	556	837	1,218
Golden Valley	255	503	352	388	781
Grand Forks	10,930	13,705	6,349	12,494	14,801
Grant	415	900	629	654	1,351
Griggs	647	773	330	846	1,020
Hettinger	465	854	500	698	1,395
Kidder	468	739	489	678	1,039
La Moure	797	1,270	679	1,223	1,642
Logan	383	703	390	540	1,111
McHenry	1,173	1,321	886	1,665	1,888
McIntosh	450	1,134	454	598	1,726
McKenzie	787	1,324	969	1,273	1,949
McLean	1,808	2,124	1,330	2,428	2,906
Mercer	1,323	2,274	1,378	1,843	3,013
Morton	3,594	5,042	2,787	4,708	5,588
Mountrail	1,393	1,017	861	1,977	1,443
Nelson	841	864	486	1,151	1,078
Oliver	306	503	407	526	696
Pembina	1,186	1,917	991	1,616	2,471
Pierce	761	1,099	554	1,008	1,422
Ramsey	2,008	2,516	1,507	2,665	3,103
Ransom	1,166	1,102	625	1,459	1,362
Renville	580	655	429	837	893
Richland	2,688	3,873	1,698	3,523	4,670
Rolette	2,002	895	660	2,426	1,126
Sargent	961	816	463	1,306	1,119
Sheridan	276	589	304	428	885
Sioux	463	264	244	701	325
Slope	145	226	162	202	315
Stark	3,003	4,491	3,123	3,678	6,137
Steele	598	503	267	895	690
Stutsman	3,313	4,039	2,580	4,214	5,375
Towner	748	600	402	970	946
Traill	1,638	2,019	875	1,940	2,562
Walsh	1,936	2,544	1,384	2,646	3,250
Ward	7,856	12,056	5,856	9,906	13,179
Wells	888	1,171	850	1,317	1,901
Williams	3,008	3,664	3,180	4,004	5,653
Totals	99,168	136,244	71,084	127,739	166,559

North Dakota Vote Since 1944

1944, Roosevelt, Dem., 100,144; Dewey, Rep., 118,535; Thomas, Soc., 943; Watson, Proh., 549.

1948, Truman, Dem., 95,812; Dewey, Rep., 115,139; Wallace, Prog., 8,391; Thomas, Soc., 1,000; Thurmond, States' Rights, 374.

1952, Eisenhower, Rep., 191,712; Stevenson, Dem., 76,694; MacArthur, Christian Nationalist, 1,075; Hallinan, Prog., 344; Hamblen, Proh., 302.

1956, Eisenhower, Rep., 156,766; Stevenson, Dem., 96,742; Andrews, Amer., 483.

1960, Kennedy, Dem., 123,963; Nixon, Rep., 154,310; Dobbs, Soc. Workers, 158.

1964, Johnson, Dem., 149,784; Goldwater, Rep., 108,207; DeBerry, Soc. Workers, 224; Munn, Proh., 174.

1968, Nixon, Rep., 138,669; Humphrey, Dem., 94,769; Wallace, 3d Party, 14,244; Halstead, Soc. Workers, 128; Munn, Prohibition, 38; Troxell, Ind., 34.

1972, Nixon, Rep., 174,109; McGovern, Dem., 100,384; Jenness, Soc. Workers, 288; Hall, Com., 87; Schmitz, Amer., 5,646.

1976, Carter, Dem., 136,078; Ford, Rep., 153,470; Anderson, Amer., 3,698; McCarthy, Ind., 2,952; Maddox, Amer. Ind., 269; MacBride, Libertarian, 256; scattering, 371.

1980, Reagan, Rep., 193,695; Carter, Dem., 79,189; Anderson, Ind., 23,640; Clark, Libertarian, 3,743; Commoner, Libertarian, 429; McLain, Natl. People's League, 296; Greaves, Amer., 235; Hall, Com., 93; DeBerry, Soc. Workers, 89; McReynolds, Soc., 82; Bubar, Statesman, 54.

1984, Reagan, Rep., 200,336; Mondale, Dem., 104,429; Bergland, Libertarian, 703.

1988, Bush, Rep., 166,559; Dukakis, Dem., 127,739; Paul, Lib., 1,315; LaRouche, Natl. Econ. Recovery, 905.

1992, Clinton, Dem., 99,168; Bush, Rep., 136,244; Perot, Ind., 71,084.

Ohio

County	1992 Clinton (D)	1992 Bush (R)	1992 Perot (I)	1988 Dukakis (D)	1988 Bush (R)
Adams	3,998	4,722	1,993	3,740	5,916
Allen	13,777	25,322	8,131	13,727	31,021
Ashland	5,985	9,864	4,950	6,072	12,726
Ashtabula	18,843	13,254	10,765	20,536	17,654
Athens	13,423	7,184	5,074	10,795	9,314
Auglaize	4,960	10,455	4,840	4,756	13,562

Belmont	18,527	8,614	6,142	19,515	12,214
Brown	5,540	5,912	3,676	5,047	7,539
Butler	39,682	63,375	27,527	33,770	75,725
Carroll	4,731	4,224	3,434	4,667	6,179
Champaign	5,201	7,004	3,992	4,272	8,995
Clark	26,692	24,011	12,551	23,247	32,729
Clermont	17,558	32,065	14,279	15,352	37,417
Clinton	4,638	7,290	3,402	3,746	8,856
Columbiana	19,765	15,016	12,611	21,581	21,175
Coshocton	6,212	5,705	4,081	6,020	8,282
Crawford	6,351	8,618	5,764	6,018	12,472
Cuyahoga	337,548	187,186	112,352	353,401	242,439
Darke	7,016	11,098	6,217	6,851	14,914
Defiance	5,735	7,195	4,187	5,448	9,566
Delaware	9,263	18,225	9,244	7,590	20,693
Erie	14,531	12,459	8,720	15,097	16,670
Fairfield	14,249	24,125	12,246	12,504	29,208
Fayette	2,976	4,916	2,162	2,623	6,186
Franklin	176,656	186,324	79,049	147,585	226,265
Fulton	5,576	8,358	4,798	5,076	10,230
Gallia	5,350	5,776	2,549	4,834	7,399
Geauga	11,466	18,200	10,577	11,874	22,339
Greene	20,139	27,651	11,459	18,025	34,432
Guernsey	6,428	5,749	4,103	5,926	8,507
Hamilton	148,409	192,447	60,145	140,354	227,004
Hancock	7,944	16,821	7,002	7,435	19,896
Hardin	4,364	5,851	2,867	4,145	7,291
Harrison	3,830	2,289	1,679	3,881	3,298
Henry	3,933	6,196	3,178	3,764	8,618
Highland	4,866	7,020	3,315	4,278	8,776
Hocking	3,935	3,761	2,831	3,706	5,426
Holmes	1,969	5,079	1,945	2,179	5,064
Huron	7,930	9,480	6,751	7,794	12,633
Jackson	5,016	5,422	2,389	4,505	6,671
Jefferson	20,978	10,764	6,910	22,095	14,141
Knox	7,259	9,044	5,282	6,882	12,180
Lake	37,682	40,766	26,878	39,667	52,963
Lawrence	12,325	10,044	4,536	11,628	12,937
Licking	18,898	26,918	13,806	16,793	34,540
Logan	4,889	9,364	4,472	4,484	11,099
Lorain	50,962	36,803	30,425	55,600	50,410
Lucas	99,989	63,297	38,108	99,755	83,788
Madison	3,998	6,865	3,170	3,421	8,303
Mahoning	64,731	31,191	29,417	75,524	43,722
Marion	9,444	11,675	6,174	9,596	14,864
Medina	18,995	24,090	17,290	19,505	29,962
Meigs	4,226	3,916	2,098	3,699	5,486
Mercer	4,883	8,683	4,913	4,978	11,162
Miami	12,547	19,741	10,544	11,138	24,915
Monroe	4,235	1,823	1,505	4,269	2,557
Montgomery	108,017	104,751	47,854	95,737	131,596
Morgan	2,402	2,719	1,551	2,085	3,713
Morrow	3,907	5,208	3,623	3,515	7,130
Muskingum	11,670	14,168	8,731	11,691	19,736
Noble	2,201	2,223	1,429	2,079	3,155
Ottawa	8,128	6,782	4,832	8,038	9,352
Paulding	3,293	3,652	2,510	3,114	5,381
Perry	4,972	4,712	3,810	5,011	6,602
Pickaway	5,765	8,690	4,319	4,905	10,796
Pike	5,057	4,094	2,192	5,191	5,611
Portage	26,325	18,447	17,065	25,607	26,334
Preble	5,557	8,023	4,460	4,937	10,297
Putnam	3,962	9,338	3,648	4,004	11,183
Richland	19,606	23,532	13,370	19,617	30,047
Ross	10,452	10,825	5,616	9,271	14,563
Sandusky	9,878	10,772	6,682	9,709	14,203
Scioto	14,715	11,931	6,860	14,442	16,029
Seneca	9,280	9,763	6,967	9,504	13,704
Shelby	5,262	8,854	5,835	5,065	12,198
Stark	70,064	61,863	42,413	69,639	87,087
Summit	107,881	77,530	55,151	112,612	101,155
Trumbull	54,591	25,831	26,791	58,674	38,815
Tuscarawas	14,787	13,179	8,785	14,185	17,145
Union	3,465	7,818	3,433	3,130	8,846
Van Wert	3,822	7,227	3,102	3,848	9,410
Vinton	2,308	1,975	1,050	2,385	2,652
Warren	13,542	27,998	11,115	11,145	31,419
Washington	10,380	12,204	5,415	9,967	14,767
Wayne	13,953	18,350	9,482	13,571	22,320
Williams	4,862	7,614	4,902	4,666	10,782
Wood	20,754	20,579	11,682	18,579	26,013
Wyandot	3,031	4,411	2,929	2,936	6,178
Totals	1,984,942	1,894,310	1,036,426	1,939,629	2,416,549

Ohio Vote Since 1944

1944, Roosevelt, Dem., 1,570,763; Dewey, Rep., 1,582,293.

1948, Truman, Dem., 1,452,791; Dewey, Rep., 1,445,684; Wallace, Prog., 37,596.

1952, Eisenhower, Rep., 2,100,391; Stevenson, Dem., 1,600,367.

1956, Eisenhower, Rep., 2,262,610; Stevenson, Dem., 1,439,655.

1960, Kennedy, Dem., 1,944,248; Nixon, Rep., 2,217,611.

1964, Johnson, Dem., 2,498,331; Goldwater, Rep., 1,470,865.

1968, Nixon, Rep., 1,791,014; Humphrey, Dem., 1,700,586; Wallace, 3d Party, 467,495; Gregory, 372; Munn, Proh., 19; Blomen, Soc. Labor, 120; Halstead, Soc. Workers, 69; Mitchell, Com., 23.

1972, Nixon, Rep., 2,441,827; McGovern, Dem., 1,558,889; Fisher, Soc. Labor, 7,107; Hall, Com., 6,437; Schmitz, Amer., 80,067; Wallace, Ind., 460.

1976, Carter, Dem., 2,011,621; Ford, Rep., 2,000,505; McCarthy, Ind., 58,258; Maddox, Amer. Ind., 15,529; MacBride, Libertarian, 8,961; Hall, Com., 7,817; Camejo, Soc. Workers, 4,717; LaRouche, U.S. Labor, 4,335; scattered, 130.

1980, Reagan, Rep., 2,206,545; Carter, Dem., 1,752,414; Anderson, Ind., 254,472; Clark, Libertarian, 49,033; Commoner, Citizens, 8,564; Hall, Com., 4,729; Congress, Ind., 4,029; Griswold, Workers World, 3,790; Bubar, Statesman, 27.

1984, Reagan, Rep., 2,678,559; Mondale, Dem., 1,825,440; Bergland, Libertarian, 5,886.

1988, Bush, Rep., 2,416,549; Dukakis, Dem., 1,939,629; Fulani, Ind., 12,017; Paul, Ind., 11,926.

1992, Clinton, Dem., 1,984,942; Bush, Rep., 1,894,310; Perot, Ind., 1,036,426; Marrou, Libertarian, 7,252; Fulani, New Alliance, 6,413; Gritz, Populist/America First, 4,699; Hagelin, Natural Law, 3,437; LaRouche, Ind., 2,446.

Oklahoma

	1992			1988	
	Clinton	Bush	Perot	Dukakis	Bush
County	(D)	(R)	(I)	(D)	(R)
Adair	2,645	2,994	914	2,624	3,558
Alfalfa	741	1,567	722	1,117	1,960
Atoka	2,336	1,561	1,255	2,565	1,971
Beaver	580	1,699	565	777	2,013
Beckham	2,947	2,913	1,929	3,388	3,463
Blaine	1,564	2,209	1,258	1,775	2,889
Bryan	6,259	3,452	3,713	6,849	4,615
Caddo	4,861	3,664	2,911	5,387	4,689
Canadian	7,215	16,756	8,985	7,453	17,872
Carter	7,171	5,947	5,188	7,988	8,430
Cherokee	6,794	4,977	3,297	6,483	5,838
Choctaw	3,413	1,641	1,298	3,362	2,217
Cimarron	395	965	254	470	1,153
Cleveland	24,404	35,561	20,352	22,067	36,313
Coal	1,448	714	618	1,365	891
Comanche	12,237	15,704	7,463	11,441	17,464
Cotton	1,314	910	853	1,482	1,266
Craig	2,780	2,106	1,316	2,940	2,463
Creek	9,118	10,055	5,984	9,512	11,308
Custer	3,540	5,362	2,741	3,697	6,735
Delaware	4,842	4,840	2,689	4,889	5,248
Dewey	845	1,244	684	963	1,543
Ellis	594	1,072	632	786	1,422
Garfield	6,720	13,095	5,559	8,067	15,248
Garvin	4,811	3,983	3,014	5,438	5,109
Grady	6,177	6,997	4,528	6,689	7,994
Grant	864	1,311	871	1,249	1,690
Greer	1,162	964	640	1,256	1,225
Harmon	783	496	326	890	611
Harper	486	1,038	501	593	1,281
Haskell	3,069	1,461	995	2,963	1,822
Hughes	2,850	1,522	1,158	3,259	2,037
Jackson	3,273	3,893	2,227	3,542	4,423
Jefferson	1,580	671	758	1,767	1,063
Johnston	2,096	1,191	1,040	2,042	1,518
Kay	6,643	9,115	6,984	7,751	12,646
Kingfisher	1,379	3,479	1,534	1,777	4,011
Kiowa	2,143	1,635	1,114	2,296	2,030
Latimer	2,606	1,212	1,049	2,365	1,830
Le Flore	7,843	5,850	3,021	6,594	6,964
Lincoln	3,904	5,315	3,160	4,225	6,409
Logan	4,453	6,071	3,239	4,603	6,947
Love	1,708	922	1,033	1,889	1,361
McClain	3,378	4,377	2,996	3,594	4,771
McCurtain	5,082	3,519	2,852	4,928	4,920
McIntosh	4,184	2,225	1,469	4,041	2,665
Major	731	2,154	857	982	2,638
Marshall	2,519	1,478	1,486	2,730	1,911
Mayes	6,432	5,445	3,235	6,691	6,115
Murray	2,594	1,536	1,447	2,697	2,056
Muskogee	13,619	8,782	5,454	13,760	11,147
Noble	1,333	2,474	1,449	1,661	3,015
Nowata	1,912	1,531	1,063	2,203	2,000
Okfuskee	2,141	1,580	889	2,209	1,851
Oklahoma	76,271	126,788	56,139	75,812	135,376
Okmulgee	7,767	4,586	3,013	8,262	5,674
Osage	6,894	5,891	4,477	7,778	7,162
Ottawa	6,304	4,141	2,721	6,658	5,026
Pawnee	2,612	2,675	1,656	2,781	3,324
Payne	9,886	13,032	7,852	10,568	16,027
Pittsburg	8,523	5,659	4,594	8,623	7,594
Pontotoc	6,350	5,206	3,916	6,484	6,609

Pottawatomie .	8,616	10,350	6,520	8,873	12,099
Pushmataha. .	2,553	1,319	1,000	2,430	1,841
Roger Mills. . .	767	890	505	866	1,132
Rogers	8,257	12,455	7,101	8,771	12,940
Seminole	4,624	3,253	2,330	4,911	4,078
Sequoyah . . .	6,092	4,925	2,486	4,951	5,710
Stephens . . .	7,644	7,085	5,692	7,833	9,844
Texas	1,487	4,059	1,417	1,717	4,971
Tillman	1,749	1,377	1,039	2,148	1,754
Tulsa.	71,165	117,465	49,760	69,044	127,512
Wagoner	7,041	9,053	5,381	7,378	10,219
Washington . .	6,593	11,342	5,664	6,971	14,613
Washita	1,929	1,912	1,468	2,290	2,402
Woods.	1,361	2,225	1,167	1,735	2,835
Woodward . . .	2,063	4,006	2,411	2,408	4,996
Totals	**473,066**	**592,929**	**319,878**	**483,423**	**678,367**

Oklahoma Vote Since 1944

1944, Roosevelt, Dem., 401,549; Dewey, Rep., 319,424; Watson, Proh., 1,663.

1948, Truman, Dem., 452,782; Dewey, Rep., 268,817.

1952, Eisenhower, Rep., 518,045; Stevenson, Dem., 430,939.

1956, Eisenhower, Rep., 473,769; Stevenson, Dem., 385,581.

1960, Kennedy, Dem., 370,111; Nixon, Rep., 533,039.

1964, Johnson, Dem., 519,834; Goldwater, Rep., 412,665.

1968, Nixon, Rep., 449,697; Humphrey, Dem., 301,658; Wallace, 3d Party, 191,731.

1972, Nixon, Rep., 759,025; McGovern, Dem., 247,147; Schmitz, Amer., 23,728.

1976, Carter, Dem., 532,442; Ford, Rep., 545,708; McCarthy, Ind., 14,101.

1980, Reagan, Rep., 695,570; Carter, Dem., 402,026; Anderson, Ind., 38,284; Clark, Libertarian, 13,828.

1984, Reagan, Rep., 861,530; Mondale, Dem., 385,080; Bergland, Libertarian, 9,066.

1988, Bush, Rep., 678,367; Dukakis, Dem., 483,423; Paul, Lib., 6,261; Fulani, New Alliance, 2,985.

1992, Clinton, Dem., 473,066; Bush, Rep., 592,929; Perot, Ind., 319,878; Marrou, Libertarian, 4,486.

Oregon

	1992			1988	
	Clinton	Bush	Perot	Dukakis	Bush
County	(D)	(R)	(I)	(D)	(R)
Baker	2,395	2,862	2,191	2,896	3,696
Benton	17,966	11,550	8,103	16,930	14,004
Clackamas. . .	60,310	53,724	39,776	59,799	61,381
Clatsop	7,700	4,683	4,316	8,074	5,956
Columbia. . . .	8,298	5,227	5,670	8,983	6,424
Coos.	12,072	9,284	7,989	13,996	10,153
Crook	2,508	2,703	2,024	2,719	3,049
Curry.	3,841	3,809	3,310	4,015	4,761
Deschutes . . .	15,693	15,655	12,293	14,264	16,425
Douglas.	14,137	19,011	12,377	17,255	20,120
Gilliam.	374	377	283	417	470
Grant	1,135	1,496	1,302	1,437	2,264
Harney	973	1,350	1,024	1,379	1,833
Hood River. . .	3,106	2,453	2,283	3,275	3,257
Jackson.	29,146	28,704	18,633	28,028	32,516
Jefferson	2,161	1,962	1,741	2,346	2,509
Josephine	11,007	13,003	8,426	10,646	15,876
Klamath.	7,918	11,864	6,636	8,429	13,484
Lake	1,019	1,791	980	1,237	2,161
Lane	74,083	41,789	34,906	69,883	47,563
Lincoln	9,603	5,716	6,127	9,598	7,364
Linn	15,399	16,461	13,256	17,007	18,312
Malheur.	2,539	5,374	2,654	2,965	6,285
Marion.	41,137	42,145	26,156	41,193	45,292
Morrow	1,174	1,187	1,089	1,375	1,529
Multnomah. . .	165,081	72,326	58,236	161,361	95,561
Polk	9,551	10,082	5,818	9,626	10,553
Sherman	362	424	326	435	555
Tillamook. . . .	5,040	3,359	2,997	5,529	4,297
Umatilla	6,787	7,095	5,581	8,327	10,254
Union	3,990	4,223	3,305	4,682	5,061
Wallowa.	1,203	1,630	1,209	1,425	1,993
Wasco.	4,663	3,242	3,008	5,141	4,462
Washington . .	67,528	57,146	41,575	59,837	67,018
Wheeler.	267	357	227	274	367
Yamhill	11,148	11,693	8,312	11,423	13,321
Totals.	**621,314**	**475,757**	**354,091**	**616,206**	**560,126**

Oregon Vote Since 1944

1944, Roosevelt, Dem., 248,635; Dewey, Rep., 225,365; Thomas, Soc., 3,785; Watson, Proh., 2,362.

1948, Truman, Dem., 243,147; Dewey, Rep., 260,904; Wallace, Prog., 14,978; Thomas, Soc., 5,051.

1952, Eisenhower, Rep., 420,815; Stevenson, Dem., 270,579; Hallinan, Ind., 3,665.

1956, Eisenhower, Rep., 406,393; Stevenson, Dem., 329,204.

1960, Kennedy, Dem., 367,402; Nixon, Rep., 408,060.

1964, Johnson, Dem., 501,017; Goldwater, Rep., 282,779; write-in, 2,509.

1968, Nixon, Rep., 408,433; Humphrey, Dem., 358,866; Wallace, 3d Party, 49,683; write-in, McCarthy, 1,496; N. Rockefeller, 69; others, 1,075.

1972, Nixon, Rep., 486,686; McGovern, Dem., 392,760; Schmitz, Amer., 46,211; write-in, 2,289.

1976, Carter, Dem., 490,407; Ford, Rep., 492,120; McCarthy, Ind., 40,207; write-in, 7,142.

1980, Reagan, Rep., 571,044; Carter, Dem., 456,890; Anderson, Ind., 112,389; Clark, Libertarian, 25,838; Commoner, Citizens, 13,642; scattered, 1,713.

1984, Reagan, Rep., 658,700; Mondale, Dem., 536,479.

1988, Bush, Rep., 560,126; Dukakis, Dem., 616,206; Paul, Lib., 14,811; Fulani, Ind., 6,487.

1992, Clinton, Dem., 621,314; Bush, Rep., 475,757; Perot, Ind., 354,091; Marrou, Libertarian, 4,277; Fulani, New Alliance, 3,030.

Pennsylvania

	1992			1988	
	Clinton	Bush	Perot	Dukakis	Bush
County	(D)	(R)	(I)	(D)	(R)
Adams	9,576	13,552	6,313	8,299	15,650
Allegheny. . . .	324,004	183,035	103,470	348,814	231,137
Armstrong . . .	12,995	9,122	6,166	13,892	11,509
Beaver	44,877	21,361	15,954	50,327	25,764
Bedford	5,840	9,216	3,731	5,754	11,123
Berks	46,031	52,939	31,663	41,040	70,153
Blair	14,857	21,447	8,284	15,588	25,623
Bradford	6,903	10,221	5,452	6,635	13,568
Bucks	97,902	94,584	53,931	82,472	127,563
Butler	22,303	23,656	15,013	22,341	27,777
Cambria	34,334	20,770	11,070	38,517	25,626
Cameron	824	1,173	676	901	1,731
Carbon	9,072	7,243	5,222	9,104	10,232
Centre.	21,177	20,478	9,356	18,357	23,875
Chester	59,643	74,002	34,536	44,853	93,522
Clarion	5,584	6,477	3,619	5,616	8,026
Clearfield	12,247	11,553	6,989	12,235	14,296
Clinton	5,397	4,471	2,654	5,759	5,735
Columbia	8,261	9,742	5,683	7,767	12,114
Crawford	12,813	14,112	7,392	13,021	17,249
Cumberland . .	26,635	43,447	14,344	24,613	47,292
Dauphin	36,990	45,479	16,063	35,079	48,917
Delaware	111,210	108,587	43,728	96,144	147,656
Elk	5,016	4,908	3,885	5,879	6,737
Erie.	56,381	39,283	21,510	53,913	48,306
Fayette	30,577	12,820	10,162	33,098	16,915
Forest	890	801	448	895	1,159
Franklin	13,440	23,387	6,941	12,368	27,086
Fulton	1,588	2,558	869	1,532	3,086
Greene	8,438	3,482	3,186	9,126	4,879
Huntingdon . .	5,153	7,249	3,273	4,752	8,800
Indiana	15,194	10,966	7,089	16,514	14,983
Jefferson	5,998	7,271	4,403	6,235	9,743
Juniata	2,601	3,980	1,819	2,834	4,881
Lackawanna . .	45,054	33,443	15,667	45,591	42,083
Lancaster. . . .	44,255	88,447	26,807	38,982	96,979
Lawrence	20,830	12,359	7,950	21,884	15,829
Lebanon	12,350	21,512	9,005	11,912	24,415
Lehigh	46,711	42,631	24,853	42,801	56,363
Luzerne	56,637	49,285	21,007	58,553	59,059
Lycoming	13,315	20,536	9,170	13,528	24,792
McKean	5,331	6,965	4,019	5,300	9,323
Mercer	23,264	16,081	10,277	24,278	21,301
Mifflin	4,946	6,300	3,382	4,790	8,170
Monroe	13,468	14,557	9,257	9,859	17,185
Montgomery. .	136,572	125,704	53,738	109,834	170,294
Montour.	2,150	3,096	1,373	2,031	3,617
Northampton .	42,203	34,429	20,234	39,264	42,748
Northumberland	12,814	15,057	7,782	14,255	20,207
Perry.	4,086	7,871	3,334	3,910	8,545
Philadelphia . .	434,904	133,328	65,455	449,566	219,053
Pike	4,382	6,084	3,019	3,097	6,659
Potter	1,892	3,452	1,687	2,119	4,432
Schuylkill	23,679	25,780	13,398	24,797	32,666
Snyder	2,952	6,934	2,686	2,658	9,054
Somerset	12,493	13,858	6,333	13,815	16,809
Sullivan	1,030	1,340	731	1,091	1,808
Susquehanna .	5,368	7,356	3,946	4,871	9,077
Tioga	4,868	7,823	3,804	4,807	9,471
Union	3,623	6,362	2,255	3,163	7,912
Venango	8,230	8,545	4,695	8,624	11,468
Warren	6,972	6,585	4,795	6,790	8,991
Washington . .	46,143	21,977	16,083	47,527	28,651
Wayne	4,817	8,184	3,727	3,775	9,926
Westmoreland	69,817	47,315	37,036	76,710	61,472
Wyoming	3,158	5,143	2,525	2,797	6,607
York	46,113	60,130	27,743	37,691	72,408
Totals.	**2,239,164**	**1,791,841**	**902,667**	**2,194,944**	**2,300,087**

Pennsylvania Vote Since 1944

1944, Roosevelt, Dem., 1,940,479; Dewey, Rep., 1,835,054; Thomas, Soc., 11,721; Watson, Proh., 5,750; Teichert, Ind. Gov., 1,789.

1948, Truman, Dem., 1,752,426; Dewey, Rep., 1,902,197; Wallace, Prog., 55,161; Thomas, Soc., 11,325; Watson, Proh., 10,338; Dobbs, Militant Workers, 2,133; Teichert, Ind. Gov., 1,461.

1952, Eisenhower, Rep., 2,415,789; Stevenson, Dem., 2,146,269; Hamblen, Proh., 8,771; Hallinan, Prog., 4,200; Hoopes, Soc., 2,684; Dobbs, Militant Workers, 1,502; Hass, Ind. Gov., 1,347; scattered, 155.

1956, Eisenhower, Rep., 2,585,252; Stevenson, Dem., 1,981,769; Hass, Soc. Labor, 7,447; Dobbs, Militant Workers, 2,035.

1960, Kennedy, Dem., 2,556,282; Nixon, Rep., 2,439,956; Hass, Soc. Labor, 7,185; Dobbs, Soc. Workers, 2,678; scattering, 440.

1964, Johnson, Dem., 3,130,954; Goldwater, Rep., 1,673,657; DeBerry, Soc. Workers, 10,456; Hass, Soc. Labor, 5,092; scattering, 2,531.

1968, Nixon, Rep., 2,090,017; Humphrey, Dem., 2,259,405; Wallace, 3d Party, 378,582; Blomen, Soc. Labor, 4,977; Halstead, Soc. Workers, 4,862; Gregory, Peace and Freedom, 7,821; others, 2,264.

1972, Nixon, Rep., 2,714,521; McGovern, Dem., 1,796,951; Schmitz, Amer., 70,593; Jenness, Soc. Workers, 4,639; Hall, Com., 2,686; others, 2,715.

1976, Carter, Dem., 2,328,677; Ford, Rep., 2,205,604; McCarthy, Ind., 50,584; Maddox, Constitution, 25,344; Camejo, Soc. Workers, 3,009; LaRouche, U.S. Labor, 2,744; Hall, Com., 1,891; others, 2,934.

1980, Reagan, Rep., 2,261,872; Carter, Dem., 1,937,540; Anderson, Ind., 292,921; Clark, Libertarian, 33,263; DeBerry, Soc. Workers, 20,291; Commoner, Consumer, 10,430; Hall, Com., 5,184.

1984, Reagan, Rep., 2,584,323; Mondale, Dem., 2,228,131; Bergland, Libertarian, 6,982.

1988, Bush, Rep., 2,300,087; Dukakis, Dem., 2,194,944; McCarthy, Consumer, 19,158; Paul, Lib., 12,051.

1992, Clinton, Dem., 2,239,164; Bush, Rep., 1,791,841; Perot, Ind., 902,667; Marrou, Libertarian, 21,477; Fulani, New Alliance, 4,661.

Rhode Island

City	1992 Clinton (D)	Bush (R)	Perot (I)	1988 Dukakis (D)	Bush (R)
Cranston	18,589	12,450	8,331	19,711	17,129
East Providence	11,701	5,843	4,661	11,948	8,181
Pawtucket ...	14,177	6,322	6,244	15,985	9,359
Providence...	32,536	11,519	7,816	34,806	15,310
Warwick	20,504	13,348	10,526	21,662	18,052
Other	115,792	82,119	67,467	121,011	109,730
Totals......	213,299	131,601	105,045	225,123	177,761

Rhode Island Vote Since 1944

1944, Roosevelt, Dem., 175,356; Dewey, Rep., 123,487; Watson, Proh., 433.

1948, Truman, Dem., 188,736; Dewey, Rep., 135,787; Wallace, Prog., 2,619; Thomas, Soc., 429; Teichert, Soc. Labor, 131.

1952, Eisenhower, Rep., 210,935; Stevenson, Dem., 203,293; Hallinan, Prog., 187; Hass, Soc. Labor, 83.

1956, Eisenhower, Rep., 225,819; Stevenson, Dem., 161,790.

1960, Kennedy, Dem., 258,032; Nixon, Rep., 147,502.

1964, Johnson, Dem., 315,463; Goldwater, Rep., 74,615.

1968, Nixon, Rep., 122,359; Humphrey, Dem., 246,518; Wallace, 3d Party, 15,678; Halstead, Soc. Workers, 383.

1972, Nixon, Rep., 220,383; McGovern, Dem., 194,645; Jenness, Soc. Workers, 729.

1976, Carter, Dem., 227,636; Ford, Rep., 181,249; MacBride, Libertarian, 715; Camejo, Soc. Workers, 462; Hall, Com., 334; Levin, Soc. Labor, 188.

1980, Reagan, Rep., 154,793; Carter, Dem., 198,342; Anderson, Ind., 59,819; Clark, Libertarian, 2,458; Hall, Com., 218; McReynolds, Soc., 170; DeBerry, Soc. Workers, 90; Griswold, Workers World, 77.

1984, Reagan, Rep., 212,080; Mondale, Dem., 197,106; Bergland, Libertarian, 277.

1988, Bush, Rep., 177,761; Dukakis, Dem., 225,123; Paul, Lib., 825; Fulani, New Alliance, 280.

1992, Clinton, Dem., 213,299; Bush, Rep., 131,601; Perot, Ind., 105,045; Fulani, New Alliance, 1,878.

South Carolina

County	1992 Clinton (D)	Bush (R)	Perot (I)	1988 Dukakis (D)	Bush (R)
Abbeville	3,968	3,317	1,036	3,629	3,738
Aiken	14,802	25,731	6,056	10,598	27,665
Allendale	2,159	1,049	212	1,796	1,295
Anderson....	16,072	24,793	6,966	12,281	25,939
Bamberg	3,426	1,906	360	2,830	2,403
Barnwell	3,344	4,026	752	2,564	4,467
Beaufort	11,466	14,735	4,966	8,691	16,184
Berkeley	12,533	18,048	4,632	9,312	16,779
Calhoun.....	2,770	2,418	564	2,175	2,585
Charleston ...	40,095	47,403	10,354	32,977	49,149
Cherokee....	5,453	6,887	2,186	4,322	7,763
Chester....	5,458	3,451	1,350	3,737	3,968
Chesterfield ..	5,691	4,183	1,315	4,699	4,999
Clarendon ...	6,033	4,147	744	5,030	4,337
Colleton.....	5,455	4,545	1,245	4,508	4,962
Darlington ...	9,090	8,912	1,863	7,625	9,854
Dillon	4,953	3,575	831	3,251	3,793
Dorchester...	9,160	15,004	3,648	7,371	14,756
Edgefield....	3,433	3,339	596	3,020	3,814
Fairfield.....	4,867	2,518	652	3,827	2,714
Florence	15,569	19,802	3,499	12,531	19,490
Georgetown ..	7,494	6,870	1,840	5,402	7,032
Greenville ..	34,651	65,066	13,699	27,188	67,371
Greenwood ..	7,621	9,079	2,101	6,511	9,096
Hampton	4,332	2,402	564	3,435	2,826
Horry	18,896	23,489	8,472	13,316	24,843
Jasper......	3,453	1,725	549	2,894	2,004
Kershaw	6,585	8,499	2,150	4,494	8,877
Lancaster....	8,307	7,757	2,563	6,181	9,152
Laurens.....	6,638	8,347	2,157	5,930	9,731
Lee........	4,454	2,730	611	3,423	2,936
Lexington...	18,312	41,759	8,652	11,366	41,467
McCormick...	1,846	899	295	1,722	1,172
Marion......	5,843	3,647	822	5,008	4,403
Marlboro	5,111	2,526	895	3,937	2,921
Newberry....	4,896	5,980	1,393	3,825	6,427
Oconee.....	6,617	10,379	3,405	4,299	10,184
Orangeburg ..	18,440	11,328	2,383	14,655	13,281
Pickens.....	8,275	17,008	4,128	6,103	17,448
Richland	53,648	43,744	7,918	36,420	43,841
Saluda......	2,393	2,968	833	1,984	3,225
Spartanburg..	25,488	37,707	8,900	22,964	40,801
Sumter.....	11,852	12,576	2,062	9,502	13,161
Union	4,644	4,647	1,371	4,420	6,019
Williamsburg .	8,077	5,289	864	7,343	5,914
York	15,844	21,297	6,418	11,458	21,657
Totals......	479,514	577,507	138,872	370,554	606,443

South Carolina Vote Since 1944

1944, Roosevelt, Dem., 90,601; Dewey, Rep., 4,547; Southern Democrats, 7,799; Watson, Proh., 365; Rep. Tolbert faction, 63.

1948, Thurmond, States' Rights, 102,607; Truman, Dem., 34,423; Dewey, Rep., 5,386; Wallace, Prog., 154; Thomas, Soc., 1.

1952, Eisenhower ran on two tickets. Under state law vote cast for two Eisenhower slates of electors could not be combined. Eisenhower, Ind., 158,289; Rep., 9,793; total, 168,082; Stevenson, Dem., 173,004; Hamblen, Proh., 1.

1956, Eisenhower, Rep., 75,700; Stevenson, Dem., 136,372; Byrd, Ind., 88,509; Andrews, Ind., 2.

1960, Kennedy, Dem., 198,129; Nixon, Rep., 188,558; write-in, 1.

1964, Johnson, Dem., 215,700; Goldwater, Rep., 309,048; write-ins: Nixon, 1, Wallace, 5; Powell, 1; Thurmond, 1.

1968, Nixon, Rep., 254,062; Humphrey, Dem., 197,486; Wallace, 3d Party, 215,430.

1972, Nixon, Rep., 477,044; McGovern, Dem., 184,559; United Citizens, 2,265; Schmitz, Amer., 10,075; write-in, 17.

1976, Carter, Dem., 450,807; Ford, Rep., 346,149; Anderson, Amer., 2,996; Maddox, Amer. Ind., 1,950; write-in, 681.

1980, Reagan, Rep., 439,277; Carter, Dem., 428,220; Anderson, Ind., 13,868; Clark, Libertarian, 4,807; Rarick, Amer. Ind., 2,086.

1984, Reagan, Rep., 615,539; Mondale, Dem., 344,459; Bergland, Libertarian, 4,359.

1988, Bush, Rep., 606,443; Dukakis, Dem., 370,554; Paul, Lib., 4,935; Fulani, United Citizens, 4,077.
1992, Clinton, Dem., 479,514; Bush, Rep., 577,507; Perot, Ind., 138,872; Marrou, Libertarian, 2,719; Phillips, U.S. Taxpayers, 2,680; Fulani, New Alliance, 1,235.

South Dakota

County	1992 Clinton (D)	Bush (R)	Perot (I)	1988 Dukakis (D)	Bush (R)
Aurora	680	594	435	987	856
Beadle	3,925	3,363	1,819	4,523	4,611
Bennett	413	556	221	579	663
Bon Homme	1,294	1,212	836	1,574	1,826
Brookings	4,645	4,698	2,614	4,860	5,394
Brown	7,521	6,665	3,812	8,673	8,537
Brule	1,060	908	687	991	971
Buffalo	282	137	72	334	151
Butte	973	1,674	1,039	1,256	2,291
Campbell	222	574	252	334	909
Chas. Mix	1,639	1,570	886	2,205	1,966
Clark	799	803	761	1,164	1,247
Clay	2,826	1,869	1,303	2,859	2,307
Codington	3,701	3,943	3,262	4,570	5,050
Corson	444	483	321	722	710
Custer	1,078	1,422	845	1,180	1,806
Davison	3,285	3,111	1,706	3,705	4,024
Day	1,578	1,161	973	2,137	1,616
Deuel	880	778	761	1,246	1,251
Dewey	766	642	340	1,007	765
Douglas	481	1,175	403	695	1,438
Edmunds	894	944	415	1,259	1,327
Fall River	1,416	1,533	792	1,380	2,002
Faulk	488	658	281	714	842
Grant	1,484	1,595	1,018	1,988	2,148
Gregory	879	1,027	688	1,138	1,566
Haakon	209	860	245	379	958
Hamlin	826	1,133	774	1,258	1,380
Hand	785	1,130	624	1,101	1,461
Hanson	566	522	341	776	786
Harding	139	515	225	259	633
Hughes	2,578	4,325	1,160	2,853	4,545
Hutchinson	1,211	2,002	920	1,594	2,700
Hyde	301	440	211	436	546
Jackson	351	627	184	450	671
Jerauld	600	518	346	751	777
Jones	166	454	154	261	521
Kingsbury	1,267	1,113	744	1,472	1,592
Lake	2,388	1,890	1,299	2,663	2,439
Lawrence	3,157	3,770	2,673	3,705	5,570
Lincoln	2,943	3,365	1,593	3,190	3,537
Lyman	486	669	311	631	843
McCook	1,167	1,177	617	1,492	1,501
McPherson	478	945	322	571	1,358
Marshall	1,056	810	427	1,372	1,142
Meade	2,694	4,724	2,611	3,212	5,189
Mellette	277	417	140	385	460
Miner	698	543	332	955	795
Minnehaha	27,016	25,081	11,496	29,135	26,765
Moody	1,473	898	715	1,715	1,161
Pennington	11,106	18,052	8,358	12,068	19,510
Perkins	566	872	541	851	1,326
Potter	493	901	375	701	1,175
Roberts	1,716	1,437	954	2,267	2,012
Sanborn	632	595	376	770	815
Shannon	1,267	225	137	1,206	256
Spink	1,732	1,527	839	2,071	1,969
Stanley	427	719	240	511	698
Sully	273	565	167	393	571
Todd	915	456	246	1,117	535
Tripp	1,046	1,459	848	1,219	2,113
Turner	1,507	1,906	867	1,780	2,436
Union	2,210	1,784	1,085	2,612	1,907
Walworth	829	1,439	628	1,094	1,940
Yankton	3,404	3,430	2,511	3,777	4,186
Ziebach	280	328	117	427	362
Totals	124,888	136,718	73,295	145,560	165,415

South Dakota Vote Since 1944

1944, Roosevelt, Dem., 96,711; Dewey, Rep., 135,365.
1948, Truman, Dem., 117,653; Dewey, Rep., 129,651; Wallace, Prog., 2,801.
1952, Eisenhower, Rep., 203,857; Stevenson, Dem., 90,426.
1956, Eisenhower, Rep., 171,569; Stevenson, Dem., 122,288.
1960, Kennedy, Dem., 128,070; Nixon, Rep., 178,417.
1964, Johnson, Dem., 163,010; Goldwater, Rep., 130,108.
1968, Nixon, Rep., 149,841; Humphrey, Dem., 118,023; Wallace, 3d Party, 13,400.
1972, Nixon, Rep., 166,476; McGovern, Dem., 139,945; Jenness, Soc. Workers, 994.

1976, Carter, Dem., 147,068; Ford, Rep., 151,505; MacBride, Libertarian, 1,619; Hall, Com., 318; Camejo, Soc. Workers, 168.
1980, Reagan, Rep., 198,343; Carter, Dem., 103,855; Anderson, Ind., 21,431; Clark, Libertarian, 3,824; Pulley, Soc. Workers, 250.
1984, Reagan, Rep., 200,267; Mondale, Dem., 116,113.
1988, Bush, Rep., 165,415; Dukakis, Dem., 145,560; Paul, Lib., 1,060; Fulani, New Alliance, 730.
1992, Clinton, Dem., 124,888; Bush, Rep., 136,718; Perot, Ind., 73,295.

Tennessee

County	1992 Clinton (D)	Bush (R)	Perot (I)	1988 Dukakis (D)	Bush (R)
Anderson	13,482	11,838	3,149	9,589	15,056
Bedford	5,978	3,836	1,541	4,046	4,856
Benton	3,896	1,625	559	2,826	2,167
Bledsoe	1,884	1,776	352	1,274	1,858
Blount	14,655	18,415	4,468	9,602	20,027
Bradley	9,889	16,528	3,212	6,122	15,829
Campbell	6,756	4,897	1,240	4,188	5,197
Cannon	2,593	1,229	495	1,726	1,604
Carroll	5,741	4,842	1,139	4,151	5,635
Carter	6,502	10,712	1,898	4,634	12,036
Cheatham	4,817	3,496	1,433	3,067	4,132
Chester	2,317	2,834	439	1,757	2,781
Claiborne	4,509	4,065	860	2,977	4,071
Clay	1,922	1,072	223	1,183	1,291
Cocke	3,495	5,298	1,124	2,115	5,430
Coffee	8,534	6,047	2,420	5,686	7,837
Crockett	2,657	2,180	507	1,742	2,214
Cumberland	6,393	7,116	2,200	3,964	7,557
Davidson	106,355	76,567	20,184	89,270	98,599
Decatur	2,633	1,667	351	1,880	2,286
De Kalb	4,382	1,714	608	2,452	2,098
Dickson	7,863	4,450	1,730	5,129	5,343
Dyer	5,845	5,668	1,241	3,690	6,508
Fayette	4,211	3,713	657	3,292	3,573
Fentress	2,730	2,391	606	1,856	3,103
Franklin	7,773	4,507	1,837	5,442	5,381
Gibson	9,555	7,161	1,536	7,542	8,415
Giles	5,601	2,827	1,309	3,918	3,518
Grainger	2,242	2,772	513	1,423	2,734
Greene	7,857	9,912	2,930	5,077	11,947
Grundy	2,997	1,004	366	2,415	1,429
Hamblen	7,114	8,898	1,760	5,061	10,418
Hamilton	46,770	53,476	14,400	40,990	68,111
Hancock	1,000	1,274	151	737	1,303
Hardeman	4,832	3,122	594	3,526	3,547
Hardin	3,922	3,875	734	2,808	4,252
Hawkins	6,623	7,758	1,847	5,212	9,356
Haywood	3,511	2,518	331	2,923	2,687
Henderson	3,502	4,719	785	2,296	5,418
Henry	6,797	3,661	1,588	5,138	4,784
Hickman	4,093	1,820	795	2,643	2,246
Houston	2,012	648	280	1,467	882
Humphreys	3,875	1,641	609	3,037	2,132
Jackson	3,208	708	332	1,962	1,168
Jefferson	4,740	6,184	1,385	3,168	6,832
Johnson	1,781	3,170	574	1,329	3,715
Knox	59,702	66,607	15,669	41,829	73,092
Lake	1,449	680	151	935	806
Lauderdale	4,452	2,928	561	3,296	3,308
Lawrence	6,816	5,608	1,403	4,903	6,273
Lewis	2,491	1,218	434	1,419	1,324
Lincoln	5,063	3,814	1,371	3,672	4,288
Loudon	5,414	6,444	1,602	3,480	7,122
McMinn	6,682	7,453	1,812	4,568	8,462
McNairy	4,691	4,093	774	3,510	4,625
Macon	2,961	2,299	443	1,538	2,962
Madison	13,629	14,869	2,634	11,001	16,952
Marion	5,589	3,262	1,186	4,175	4,407
Marshall	4,491	2,516	1,050	2,795	2,975
Maury	9,997	7,440	2,821	6,280	8,397
Meigs	1,673	1,355	453	1,048	1,507
Monroe	5,384	6,025	936	4,000	6,355
Montgomery	14,507	13,011	3,753	9,145	12,599
Moore	1,151	661	327	731	786
Morgan	3,190	2,306	658	1,941	2,576
Obion	6,497	4,812	1,494	4,785	6,037
Overton	4,489	1,657	468	2,511	1,873
Perry	1,889	708	317	1,208	854
Pickett	1,144	1,094	121	634	1,118
Polk	2,583	1,584	419	2,073	2,297
Putnam	10,858	7,998	2,473	6,606	9,547
Rhea	4,289	4,860	1,163	2,595	5,144
Roane	9,812	8,719	2,396	6,535	10,881
Robertson	8,498	5,271	1,978	5,884	5,714
Rutherford	21,084	18,877	7,005	12,245	20,397
Scott	2,730	3,011	643	1,611	2,562
Sequatchie	1,754	1,381	405	1,196	1,659
Sevier	6,719	11,714	2,760	3,643	11,920
Shelby	191,322	153,310	20,223	149,759	157,457
Smith	5,061	1,482	486	2,522	2,138
Stewart	2,779	1,046	487	1,979	1,302
Sullivan	20,935	28,801	6,730	17,396	32,996

County					
Sumner	19,387	17,401	5,177	11,702	19,523
Tipton	5,652	6,757	1,279	3,824	6,052
Trousdale	1,846	565	243	1,193	969
Unicoi	2,375	3,344	709	1,794	3,664
Union	2,478	2,274	580	1,431	2,110
Van Buren	1,329	555	191	796	780
Warren	7,189	3,704	1,415	4,646	4,529
Washington	13,071	18,206	4,002	10,087	19,615
Wayne	1,868	2,955	424	1,516	3,405
Weakley	5,691	4,800	1,355	4,239	5,701
White	4,102	2,118	821	2,562	2,646
Williamson	13,053	22,015	5,026	7,864	20,847
Wilson	13,861	12,061	3,848	8,360	13,317
Totals	933,521	841,300	199,968	679,794	947,233

Tennessee Vote Since 1944

1944, Roosevelt, Dem., 308,707; Dewey, Rep., 200,311; Watson, Proh., 882; Thomas, Soc., 892.

1948, Truman, Dem., 270,402; Dewey, Rep., 202,914; Thurmond, States' Rights, 73,815; Wallace, Prog., 1,864; Thomas, Soc., 1,288.

1952, Eisenhower, Rep., 446,147; Stevenson, Dem., 443,710; Hamblen, Proh., 1,432; Hallinan, Prog., 885; MacArthur, Christian Nationalist, 379.

1956, Eisenhower, Rep., 462,288; Stevenson, Dem., 456,507; Andrews, Ind., 19,820; Holtwick, Proh., 789.

1960, Kennedy, Dem., 481,453; Nixon, Rep., 556,577; Faubus, States' Rights, 11,304; Decker, Proh., 2,458.

1964, Johnson, Dem., 635,047; Goldwater, Rep., 508,965; write-in, 34.

1968, Nixon, Rep., 472,592; Humphrey, Dem., 351,233; Wallace, 3d Party, 424,792.

1972, Nixon, Rep., 813,147; McGovern, Dem., 357,293; Schmitz, Amer., 30,373; write-in, 369.

1976, Carter, Dem., 825,879; Ford, Rep., 633,969; Anderson, Amer., 5,769; McCarthy, Ind., 5,004; Maddox, Amer. Ind., 2,303; MacBride, Libertarian, 1,375; Hall, Com., 547; LaRouche, U.S. Labor, 512; Bubar, Proh., 442; Miller, Ind., 316; write-in, 230.

1980, Reagan, Rep., 787,761; Carter, Dem., 783,051; Anderson, Ind., 35,991; Clark, Libertarian, 7,116; Commoner, Citizens, 1,112; Bubar, Statesman, 521; McReynolds, Soc., 519; Hall, Com., 503; DeBerry, Soc. Workers, 490; Griswold, Workers World, 400; write-ins, 152.

1984, Reagan, Rep., 990,212; Mondale, Dem., 711,714; Bergland, Libertarian, 3,072.

1988, Bush, Rep., 947,233; Dukakis, Dem., 679,794; Paul, Ind., 2,041; Duke, Ind., 1,807.

1992, Clinton, Dem., 933,521; Bush, Rep., 841,300; Perot, Ind., 199,968; Marrou, Libertarian, 1,847.

Texas

	1992			1988	
	Clinton	Bush	Perot	Dukakis	Bush
County	(D)	(R)	(I)	(D)	(R)
Anderson	5,322	5,598	3,519	6,128	7,858
Andrews	1,081	2,266	875	1,122	3,052
Angelina	10,318	9,722	6,204	10,849	12,738
Aransas	2,246	2,826	1,676	2,305	3,858
Archer	1,284	1,560	1,106	1,627	2,010
Armstrong	278	561	187	314	720
Atascosa	3,766	3,806	2,035	4,657	4,777
Austin	2,278	4,015	1,585	2,593	4,524
Bailey	677	1,308	376	876	1,459
Bandera	1,059	2,674	1,537	1,251	3,435
Bastrop	6,252	4,980	3,240	8,004	5,991
Baylor	990	611	529	1,153	914
Bee	4,083	3,633	1,367	4,616	4,620
Bell	18,684	24,936	11,026	17,751	29,382
Bexar	172,513	168,816	72,110	174,036	193,192
Blanco	891	1,370	830	1,012	1,680
Borden	106	184	87	169	283
Bosque	2,173	2,300	1,999	2,670	3,458
Bowie	11,825	11,776	6,659	12,331	15,454
Brazoria	21,861	30,384	18,954	23,436	34,028
Brazos	14,819	23,943	10,372	14,885	29,369
Brewster	1,383	1,127	712	1,569	1,708
Briscoe	430	360	164	574	464
Brooks	2,856	585	318	2,859	608
Brown	4,264	5,313	3,034	4,763	6,810
Burleson	2,511	2,013	1,179	3,085	2,242
Burnet	3,638	4,272	2,865	4,343	5,120
Caldwell	3,794	2,749	1,776	4,649	3,553
Calhoun	2,550	2,640	1,579	3,314	3,183
Callahan	1,694	2,134	1,452	2,017	2,887
Cameron	29,435	20,123	9,286	30,972	24,263
Camp	1,938	1,219	821	2,121	1,908
Carson	825	1,647	578	1,034	2,100
Cass	5,476	3,999	2,168	5,941	5,305
Castro	1,113	1,307	485	1,436	1,604
Chambers	2,832	3,398	2,122	3,035	3,694
Cherokee	5,003	5,847	3,273	5,604	7,520

County					
Childress	881	1,033	421	1,060	1,201
Clay	1,919	1,586	1,397	2,288	2,043
Cochran	454	750	255	681	771
Coke	580	640	393	674	863
Coleman	1,579	1,462	1,095	1,978	2,340
Collin	24,508	60,514	43,287	22,934	67,776
Collingsworth	635	697	265	809	872
Colorado	2,442	3,286	1,421	2,847	3,723
Comal	6,312	12,651	5,841	5,716	13,994
Comanche	2,296	1,666	1,281	2,622	2,120
Concho	489	414	329	643	617
Cooke	3,105	5,299	4,658	4,217	7,196
Coryell	4,157	6,144	3,974	4,026	7,461
Cottle	542	245	235	690	379
Crane	514	918	412	596	1,219
Crockett	653	623	368	881	932
Crosby	1,010	1,006	313	1,435	1,121
Culberson	424	251	171	557	417
Dallam	434	922	325	645	1,205
Dallas	231,412	256,007	170,571	243,198	347,094
Dawson	1,639	2,691	518	2,155	3,154
Deaf Smith	1,642	3,137	772	1,930	3,744
Delta	864	599	551	1,244	849
Denton	27,891	48,492	39,653	26,204	57,444
DeWitt	2,127	3,238	1,346	2,579	3,628
Dickens	536	373	250	696	435
Dimmit	3,172	844	361	2,735	900
Donley	578	893	260	661	1,043
Duval	4,006	698	326	4,177	907
Eastland	2,738	2,830	1,698	3,215	3,929
Ector	11,130	18,161	6,668	10,825	23,155
Edwards	254	460	171	368	556
Ellis	9,537	13,564	10,303	11,169	16,422
El Paso	67,715	47,224	19,738	62,622	55,573
Erath	3,531	3,835	3,046	4,113	5,427
Falls	2,761	1,826	1,185	2,877	2,344
Fannin	4,164	2,510	2,919	5,163	4,024
Fayette	2,923	3,789	2,088	3,390	4,551
Fisher	1,242	539	442	1,516	721
Floyd	947	1,676	385	1,391	1,741
Foard	435	207	152	513	306
Fort Bend	29,992	41,039	16,853	23,351	39,818
Franklin	1,338	1,058	942	1,453	1,439
Freestone	2,445	2,316	1,596	2,916	3,159
Frio	2,377	1,275	654	3,016	1,505
Gaines	1,095	2,138	696	1,310	2,265
Galveston	38,623	31,303	20,103	38,633	34,913
Garza	558	982	345	989	1,183
Gillespie	1,600	4,712	2,018	1,588	5,662
Glasscock	100	379	93	143	384
Goliad	1,069	1,236	521	1,358	1,427
Gonzales	2,006	2,502	1,018	2,897	2,983
Gray	2,426	6,105	1,810	2,460	7,259
Grayson	12,547	12,322	13,327	14,347	18,825
Gregg	12,797	20,542	8,437	12,486	26,465
Grimes	2,594	2,402	1,213	2,735	2,820
Guadalupe	6,567	10,818	5,618	7,111	13,265
Hale	2,761	6,098	1,357	3,502	6,284
Hall	819	631	263	1,029	714
Hamilton	1,100	1,232	921	1,355	1,718
Hansford	345	1,660	398	443	1,967
Hardeman	954	614	362	1,143	974
Hardin	6,753	5,885	4,129	8,245	6,897
Harris	360,171	406,778	172,922	342,919	464,217
Harrison	9,538	8,733	4,371	8,974	11,957
Hartley	406	1,081	308	505	1,229
Haskell	1,438	852	562	1,715	1,193
Hays	10,842	10,008	6,252	11,187	11,716
Hemphill	479	989	232	527	1,170
Henderson	9,105	8,368	6,746	9,819	11,005
Hidalgo	51,205	26,976	9,757	54,330	29,246
Hill	3,929	3,669	2,752	4,381	4,796
Hockley	2,301	4,261	1,291	2,850	4,368
Hood	4,359	5,313	4,457	4,255	7,400
Hopkins	4,085	3,398	3,147	4,984	5,133
Houston	3,250	3,067	1,690	3,846	3,882
Howard	3,735	5,129	1,984	4,445	6,024
Hudspeth	364	325	178	406	405
Hunt	7,452	9,739	7,387	8,820	12,331
Hutchinson	2,833	6,034	1,993	2,950	7,526
Irion	256	283	290	326	539
Jack	1,254	1,041	1,045	1,521	1,542
Jackson	1,722	2,451	976	2,141	2,954
Jasper	5,658	3,870	2,539	6,613	4,985
Jeff Davis	321	360	187	325	524
Jefferson	48,405	29,622	17,242	55,649	35,754
Jim Hogg	1,520	478	107	1,630	510
Jim Wells	7,812	3,311	1,413	8,495	4,335
Johnson	12,030	13,473	11,573	12,507	17,509
Jones	2,400	2,088	1,436	2,898	3,000
Karnes	1,897	1,990	802	2,529	2,383
Kaufman	6,498	6,578	5,913	7,358	8,466
Kendall	1,374	4,162	1,773	1,446	4,875
Kenedy	87	69	18	119	76
Kent	271	175	163	398	274
Kerr	3,707	8,787	3,790	3,587	11,207
Kimble	467	790	354	551	1,061
King	54	79	56	64	111
Kinney	598	634	299	669	771
Kleberg	5,109	3,897	1,470	5,367	4,443
Knox	854	521	438	1,013	765

Lamar	6,328	5,778	4,093	7,553	8,021	Webb	14,509	7,789	2,517	16,227	7,528
Lamb	1,737	2,998	709	2,230	3,064	Wharton	4,643	5,503	2,624	5,935	6,978
Lampasas	1,508	2,233	1,432	1,954	3,000	Wheeler	938	1,458	367	1,067	1,703
LaSalle	1,522	586	211	1,651	693	Wichita	17,021	17,956	11,478	17,956	23,324
Lavaca	2,700	3,362	1,696	3,531	4,377	Wilbarger	1,924	1,959	1,453	2,248	2,669
Lee	1,847	2,108	1,088	2,527	2,513	Willacy	3,359	1,490	652	3,165	1,750
Leon	2,042	2,212	1,251	2,316	2,778	Williamson	19,437	26,208	15,415	19,589	27,322
Liberty	7,036	6,959	4,311	8,343	8,524	Wilson	3,711	3,766	2,105	3,953	4,436
Limestone	3,188	2,358	1,505	3,476	3,257	Winkler	942	1,173	582	947	1,656
Lipscomb	338	839	270	377	1,111	Wise	4,478	4,555	4,485	5,288	6,064
Live Oak	1,345	1,805	806	1,573	2,277	Wood	4,084	4,708	3,494	4,553	6,216
Llano	2,409	3,056	1,799	2,629	3,550	Yoakum	595	1,486	484	727	1,762
Loving	20	31	45	23	54	Young	2,464	2,894	2,302	3,007	4,156
Lubbock	22,240	48,847	11,618	22,202	50,760	Zapata	2,052	866	326	2,171	958
Lynn	902	1,233	291	1,086	1,279	Zavala	3,058	571	237	3,338	628
McCulloch	1,393	1,108	986	1,665	1,618	Totals	2,281,815	2,496,071	1,354,781	2,352,748	3,036,829
McLennan	25,903	28,473	15,505	27,545	38,606						
McMullen	78	274	89	94	302						
Madison	1,553	1,544	778	1,835	1,896						
Marion	2,156	1,245	882	2,255	1,857						
Martin	641	986	356	632	1,017						
Mason	570	776	364	671	975						
Matagorda	4,759	5,328	3,045	5,675	6,787						
Maverick	4,540	2,002	771	4,395	1,592						
Medina	3,650	4,912	2,167	4,227	5,722						
Menard	553	354	367	614	552						
Midland	9,160	24,143	7,880	8,487	30,618						
Milam	3,542	2,414	1,495	4,865	3,512						
Mills	753	702	530	842	1,043						
Mitchell	1,353	1,128	604	1,773	1,596						
Montague	2,885	2,304	2,330	3,689	3,475						
Montgomery	18,551	39,976	19,203	18,394	40,360						
Moore	1,361	3,147	976	1,537	3,710						
Morris	3,028	1,400	1,138	3,522	2,104						
Motley	256	446	117	262	429						
Nacogdoches	6,937	9,864	4,803	6,886	11,767						
Navarro	6,006	4,897	3,800	6,749	6,445						
Newton	3,249	1,212	1,032	3,640	1,659						
Nolan	2,490	1,993	1,455	2,853	2,734						
Nueces	46,317	36,781	17,374	49,209	46,337						
Ochiltree	557	2,419	576	579	2,928						
Oldham	225	583	177	303	691						
Orange	15,305	9,793	7,321	17,834	11,959						
Palo Pinto	3,392	2,852	3,010	3,930	4,649						
Panola	3,950	3,473	1,906	4,123	4,642						
Parker	7,934	10,321	9,148	8,517	14,090						
Parmer	637	1,829	564	764	2,061						
Pecos	1,778	1,836	895	1,960	2,483						
Polk	5,942	5,390	2,884	5,943	5,831						
Potter	9,527	13,510	4,655	9,563	16,400						
Presidio	1,189	400	290	1,176	586						
Rains	1,108	975	890	1,448	1,281						
Randall	9,119	24,971	6,340	8,492	27,986						
Reagan	337	651	259	418	935						
Real	463	787	386	483	795						
Red River	2,686	1,735	1,228	3,165	2,475						
Reeves	2,569	1,244	734	2,812	1,724						
Refugio	1,531	1,469	716	1,831	1,883						
Roberts	126	391	99	135	441						
Robertson	2,927	1,707	963	3,630	2,184						
Rockwall	2,397	6,427	4,393	2,659	7,214						
Runnels	1,401	1,653	1,279	1,720	2,417						
Rusk	5,391	7,560	3,575	5,140	9,117						
Sabine	2,288	1,490	894	2,053	1,925						
San Augustine	1,737	1,243	667	2,118	1,946						
San Jacinto	2,846	2,494	1,653	2,972	2,691						
San Patricio	8,202	7,456	3,178	9,920	9,159						
San Saba	716	723	660	1,165	1,099						
Schleicher	420	452	355	494	653						
Scurry	1,609	2,670	1,826	2,119	3,749						
Shackelford	484	623	422	681	865						
Shelby	3,986	3,217	1,487	4,261	3,999						
Sherman	261	851	256	340	1,145						
Smith	17,514	27,753	13,569	18,719	34,658						
Somervell	782	872	903	983	1,304						
Starr	7,668	1,209	345	6,958	1,218						
Stephens	1,115	1,573	1,062	1,519	2,342						
Sterling	127	322	182	188	464						
Stonewall	561	242	322	724	421						
Sutton	524	687	387	571	996						
Swisher	1,413	989	541	1,893	1,271						
Tarrant	156,230	183,387	129,998	151,310	242,660						
Taylor	12,382	22,614	10,331	13,073	28,563						
Terrell	325	176	128	390	296						
Terry	1,461	2,309	619	1,941	2,645						
Throckmorton	401	389	228	534	455						
Titus	3,625	3,024	2,146	4,357	4,247						
Tom Green	11,437	14,989	10,244	12,283	21,463						
Travis	130,546	88,105	56,158	127,783	105,915						
Trinity	2,784	1,988	1,133	2,657	2,448						
Tyler	3,465	2,357	1,529	4,198	3,070						
Upshur	4,776	4,511	2,896	5,242	5,991						
Upton	489	908	313	544	1,189						
Uvalde	3,482	3,635	1,387	3,684	4,266						
Val Verde	4,748	4,102	2,093	5,044	5,109						
Van Zandt	5,310	5,810	5,239	6,153	7,371						
Victoria	7,604	13,086	5,136	8,923	15,056						
Walker	5,619	6,662	3,619	5,826	8,473						
Waller	4,270	3,065	1,692	3,957	3,607						
Ward	1,695	1,769	948	1,858	2,709						
Washington	3,283	5,817	1,738	2,960	6,041						

Texas Vote Since 1944

1944, Roosevelt, Dem., 821,605; Dewey, Rep., 191,425; Texas Regulars, 135,439; Watson, Proh., 1,017; Thomas, Soc., 594; America First, 250.

1948, Truman, Dem., 750,700; Dewey, Rep., 282,240; Thurmond, States' Rights, 106,909; Wallace, Prog., 3,764; Watson, Proh., 2,758; Thomas, Soc., 874.

1952, Eisenhower, Rep., 1,102,878; Stevenson, Dem., 969,228; Hamblen, Proh., 1,983; MacArthur, Christian Nationalist, 833; MacArthur, Constitution, 730; Hallinan, Prog., 294.

1956, Eisenhower, Rep., 1,080,619; Stevenson, Dem., 859,958; Andrews, Ind., 14,591.

1960, Kennedy, Dem., 1,167,932; Nixon, Rep., 1,121,699; Sullivan, Constitution, 18,169; Decker, Proh., 3,870; write-in, 15.

1964, Johnson, Dem., 1,663,185; Goldwater, Rep., 958,566; Lightburn, Constitution, 5,060.

1968, Nixon, Rep., 1,227,844; Humphrey, Dem., 1,266,804; Wallace, 3d Party, 584,269; write-in, 489.

1972, Nixon, Rep., 2,298,896; McGovern, Dem., 1,154,289; Schmitz, Amer., 6,039; Jenness, Soc. Workers, 8,664; others, 3,393.

1976, Carter, Dem., 2,082,319; Ford, Rep., 1,953,300; McCarthy, Ind., 20,118; Anderson, Amer., 11,442; Camejo, Soc. Workers, 1,723; write-in, 2,982.

1980, Reagan, Rep., 2,510,705; Carter, Dem., 1,881,147; Anderson, Ind., 111,613; Clark, Libertarian, 37,643; write-in, 528.

1984, Reagan, Rep., 3,433,428; Mondale, Dem., 1,949,276.

1988, Bush, Rep., 3,036,829; Dukakis, Dem., 2,352,748; Paul, Lib., 30,355; Fulani, New Alliance, 7,208.

1992, Clinton, Dem., 2,281,815; Bush, Rep., 2,496,071; Perot, Ind., 1,354,781; Marrou, Libertarian, 19,699.

Utah

	1992			1988	
	Clinton	Bush	Perot	Dukakis	Bush
County	(D)	(R)	(I)	(D)	(R)
Beaver	668	1,040	330	816	1,286
Box Elder	2,186	7,712	4,507	2,736	12,585
Cache	4,973	15,971	8,032	5,871	21,766
Carbon	4,480	2,038	2,002	5,521	3,019
Daggett	122	172	117	132	272
Davis	14,924	39,087	24,105	16,868	50,469
Duchesne	772	1,983	1,229	1,227	3,118
Emery	1,349	1,643	1,138	1,788	2,322
Garfield	309	1,235	355	370	1,470
Grand	1,160	1,100	991	1,287	1,895
Iron	1,537	5,616	1,693	1,736	6,038
Juab	823	1,237	616	974	1,505
Kane	295	1,241	534	398	1,788
Millard	742	2,496	1,064	1,124	3,515
Morgan	520	1,339	851	647	1,889
Piute	169	429	146	206	476
Rich	154	525	187	234	621
Salt Lake	100,082	117,247	91,968	107,453	163,557
San Juan	1,639	2,004	576	1,407	2,377
Sanpete	1,302	2,995	1,742	1,822	4,579
Sevier	1,039	3,160	1,671	1,403	4,747
Summit	3,013	3,133	3,060	2,545	3,881
Tooele	3,270	3,676	3,011	4,166	5,539
Uintah	1,374	3,505	2,250	1,799	5,341
Utah	14,090	61,398	24,558	18,533	68,134
Wasatch	1,042	1,822	1,234	1,451	2,487
Washington	3,364	11,310	4,623	3,054	13,306
Wayne	236	706	251	353	784
Weber	17,795	26,812	20,559	21,431	39,676
Totals	183,429	322,632	203,400	207,352	428,442

Utah Vote Since 1944

1944, Roosevelt, Dem., 150,088; Dewey, Rep., 97,891; Thomas, Soc., 340.

1948, Truman, Dem., 149,151; Dewey, Rep., 124,402; Wallace, Prog., 2,679; Dobbs, Soc. Workers, 73.

1952, Eisenhower, Rep., 194,190; Stevenson, Dem., 135,364.

1956, Eisenhower, Rep., 215,631; Stevenson, Dem., 118,364.

1960, Kennedy, Dem., 169,248; Nixon, Rep., 205,361; Dobbs, Soc. Workers, 100.

1964, Johnson, Dem., 219,628; Goldwater, Rep., 181,785.

1968, Nixon, Rep., 238,728; Humphrey, Dem., 156,665; Wallace, 3d Party, 26,906; Halstead, Soc. Workers, 89; Peace and Freedom, 180.

1972, Nixon, Rep., 323,643; McGovern, Dem., 126,284; Schmitz, Amer., 28,549.

1976, Carter, Dem., 182,110; Ford, Rep., 337,908; Anderson, Amer., 13,304; McCarthy, Ind., 3,907; MacBride, Libertarian, 2,438; Maddox, Amer. Ind., 1,162; Camejo, Soc. Workers, 268; Hall, Com., 121.

1980, Reagan, Rep., 439,687; Carter, Dem., 124,266; Anderson, Ind., 30,284; Clark, Libertarian, 7,226; Commoner, Citizens, 1,009; Greaves, Amer., 965; Rarick, Amer. Ind., 522; Hall, Com., 139; DeBerry, Soc. Workers, 124.

1984, Reagan, Rep., 469,105; Mondale, Dem., 155,369; Bergland, Libertarian, 2,447.

1988, Bush, Rep., 428,442; Dukakis, Dem., 207,352; Paul, Lib., 7,473; Dennis, Amer., 2,158.

1992, Clinton, Dem., 183,429; Bush, Rep., 322,632; Perot, Ind., 203,400; Gritz, Populist/America First, 28,602; Marrou, Libertarian, 1,900; Hagelin, Natural Law, 1,319; LaRouche, Ind., 1,089.

Vermont

City	1992 Clinton (D)	Bush (R)	Perot (I)	1988 Dukakis (D)	Bush (R)
Barre City	1,807	1,508	1,035	2,132	2,100
Bennington	3,646	2,151	1,536	3,180	2,748
Brattleboro	3,519	1,447	847	3,136	2,044
Burlington	12,508	4,462	3,241	9,748	6,382
Montpelier	2,490	1,407	657	2,351	2,013
Rutland City	3,888	2,915	1,722	3,590	3,631
St. Albans City	1,455	887	744	1,441	1,295
St. Johnsbury	1,249	1,243	836	1,188	1,974
South Burlington	3,730	2,131	1,359	3,373	3,136
Winooski	1,462	733	646	1,426	1,014
Other	97,836	69,238	53,362	84,210	97,994
Totals	133,590	88,122	65,985	115,775	124,331

Vermont Vote Since 1944

1944, Roosevelt, Dem., 53,820; Dewey, Rep., 71,527.

1948, Truman, Dem., 45,557; Dewey, Rep., 75,926; Wallace, Prog., 1,279; Thomas, Soc., 585.

1952, Eisenhower, Rep., 109,717; Stevenson, Dem., 43,355; Hallinan, Prog., 282; Hoopes, Soc., 185.

1956, Eisenhower, Rep., 110,390; Stevenson, Dem., 42,549; scattered, 39.

1960, Kennedy, Dem., 69,186; Nixon, Rep., 98,131.

1964, Johnson, Dem., 107,674; Goldwater, Rep., 54,868.

1968, Nixon, Rep., 85,142; Humphrey, Dem., 70,255; Wallace, 3d Party, 5,104; Halstead, Soc. Workers, 295; Gregory, New Party, 579.

1972, Nixon, Rep., 117,149; McGovern, Dem., 68,174; Spock, Liberty Union, 1,010; Jenness, Soc. Workers, 296; scattered, 318.

1976, Carter, Dem., 77,798; Carter, Ind. Vermonter, 991; Ford, Rep., 100,387; McCarthy, Ind., 4,001; Camejo, Soc. Workers, 430; LaRouche, U.S. Labor, 196; scattered, 99.

1980, Reagan, Rep., 94,598; Carter, Dem., 81,891; Anderson, Ind., 31,760; Commoner, Citizens, 2,316; Clark, Libertarian, 1,900; McReynolds, Liberty Union, 136; Hall, Com., 118; DeBerry, Soc. Workers, 75; scattering, 413.

1984, Reagan, Rep., 135,865; Mondale, Dem., 95,730; Bergland, Libertarian, 1,002.

1988, Bush, Rep., 124,331; Dukakis, Dem., 115,775; Paul, Lib., 1,000; LaRouche, Ind., 275.

1992, Clinton, Dem., 133,590; Bush, Rep., 88,122; Perot, Ind., 65,985.

Virginia

County	1992 Clinton (D)	Bush (R)	Perot (I)	1988 Dukakis (D)	Bush (R)
Accomack	4,950	5,666	2,304	4,443	6,926
Albemarle	13,886	13,894	3,855	10,363	15,117
Alleghany	2,396	2,294	926	2,316	2,555
Amelia	1,534	2,062	574	1,359	2,187
Amherst	4,101	5,482	1,268	3,567	6,507
Appomattox	1,919	2,830	801	1,740	3,205
Arlington	47,756	26,376	7,992	40,314	34,191
Augusta	5,190	12,896	3,397	4,170	13,251
Bath	855	1,075	354	881	1,273
Bedford	6,792	10,496	3,251	5,406	10,702
Bland	1,001	1,368	408	937	1,556
Botetourt	4,349	5,904	1,819	3,763	5,687
Brunswick	3,687	2,480	479	3,070	2,742
Buchanan	7,405	3,297	815	6,935	3,912
Buckingham	2,193	2,368	459	1,941	2,481
Campbell	5,999	10,931	2,553	4,574	12,713
Caroline	3,770	2,947	965	3,186	3,065
Carroll	3,790	5,664	1,388	3,190	6,377
Charles City	2,010	729	251	1,839	826
Charlotte	2,098	2,293	640	1,923	2,699
Chesterfield	28,028	56,626	16,898	18,723	58,828
Clarke	1,811	1,994	802	1,478	2,502
Craig	965	1,008	304	864	1,112
Culpeper	3,444	5,226	1,640	2,555	5,896
Cumberland	1,284	1,643	372	1,132	1,978
Dickenson	4,839	2,574	660	4,461	3,091
Dinwiddie	3,624	3,648	1,198	3,405	4,165
Essex	1,583	1,897	382	1,294	2,038
Fairfax	160,186	170,488	53,012	125,711	200,631
Fauquier	6,600	10,497	3,464	4,837	11,733
Floyd	2,026	2,575	672	1,727	2,921
Fluvanna	2,134	2,811	871	1,562	2,447
Franklin	6,590	6,724	2,232	5,734	7,391
Frederick	4,942	9,425	2,981	3,707	9,921
Giles	3,346	3,023	1,142	3,042	3,490
Gloucester	4,058	6,461	2,640	3,372	7,646
Goochland	2,589	3,834	994	2,209	3,765
Grayson	2,615	3,378	860	2,441	3,968
Greene	1,353	2,265	627	899	2,234
Greensville	2,237	1,335	360	2,083	1,610
Halifax	4,752	5,199	1,140	4,282	5,671
Hanover	8,021	20,336	5,674	5,985	20,570
Henrico	36,807	56,910	14,720	26,980	62,284
Henry	9,296	9,005	3,212	7,536	10,871
Highland	494	686	212	456	807
Isle of Wight	4,380	5,370	1,536	3,747	5,779
James City	6,536	8,781	2,675	4,642	8,945
King George	1,363	1,206	323	1,519	2,587
King and Queen	1,811	2,570	918	1,309	1,376
King William	1,822	2,591	758	1,561	2,735
Lancaster	1,812	2,841	739	1,551	3,380
Lee	5,215	3,504	1,002	4,906	4,080
Loudoun	14,462	19,290	7,391	10,101	20,448
Louisa	3,399	3,461	1,381	2,789	3,831
Lunenburg	2,082	2,227	505	1,870	2,530
Madison	1,700	2,341	653	1,427	2,501
Mathews	1,402	2,179	884	1,235	2,752
Mecklenburg	4,273	5,401	1,128	3,275	5,887
Middlesex	1,597	2,224	768	1,361	2,571
Montgomery	10,658	10,606	3,449	8,909	12,326
Nelson	2,586	2,159	748	2,272	2,502
New Kent	1,738	2,708	1,017	1,427	2,917
Northampton	2,568	2,088	844	2,242	2,562
Northumberland	1,862	2,667	729	1,506	2,984
Nottoway	2,411	2,610	606	2,217	3,161
Orange	3,348	4,092	1,425	2,592	4,319
Page	3,010	4,203	1,163	2,499	5,013
Patrick	2,465	3,521	1,026	2,093	3,990
Pittsylvania	7,675	11,467	2,296	6,612	12,229
Powhatan	1,950	3,832	1,232	1,467	4,040
Prince Edward	2,775	2,858	635	2,434	3,147
Prince George	3,087	4,799	1,459	2,469	4,982
Prince William	26,486	35,432	13,190	19,198	39,654
Pulaski	5,633	6,148	2,066	4,686	6,844
Rappahannock	1,273	1,410	487	1,003	1,657
Richmond	1,034	1,609	366	924	1,862
Roanoke	14,704	20,667	5,477	12,938	22,011
Rockbridge	2,908	3,228	1,254	2,412	3,541
Rockingham	5,407	13,016	2,839	4,716	13,241
Russell	6,480	3,891	958	6,222	4,374
Scott	3,979	4,515	957	3,616	4,986
Shenandoah	3,956	7,746	2,063	3,276	8,612
Smyth	4,924	6,128	1,618	3,989	7,446
Southampton	3,199	2,844	754	3,000	3,439
Spotsylvania	8,133	11,829	3,918	5,486	10,978
Stafford	7,718	12,528	4,481	5,380	12,234
Surry	1,823	1,046	364	1,602	1,246
Sussex	2,193	1,527	446	1,958	1,822
Tazewell	8,586	6,375	1,872	8,098	7,165
Warren	3,554	4,319	1,650	2,769	4,700
Washington	7,269	9,150	2,288	5,819	10,722
Westmoreland	2,758	2,554	818	2,311	2,974
Wise	7,681	5,144	1,835	7,017	6,189
Wythe	3,616	5,121	1,557	3,201	5,827

	1992			1988	
	Clinton (D)	Bush (R)	Perot (I)	Dukakis (D)	Bush (R)
York	6,218	10,197	3,426	4,639	11,103
Alexandria	30,784	16,700	4,934	24,358	20,913
Bedford	963	1,091	313	960	1,322
Bristol	2,948	3,616	851	2,446	4,407
Buena Vista	1,023	849	291	828	1,121
Charlottesville	8,685	4,705	1,397	7,671	5,817
Chesapeake	23,495	28,909	9,237	18,828	29,738
Clifton Forge	958	632	251	961	759
Colonial Heights	1,721	5,298	1,312	1,581	6,001
Covington	1,442	995	402	1,567	1,274
Danville	8,134	9,584	1,679	7,353	12,221
Emporia	1,048	1,094	157	977	1,289
Fairfax	3,884	4,333	1,439	3,430	5,576
Falls Church	2,864	1,912	599	2,484	2,470
Franklin	1,696	1,347	272	1,630	1,557
Fredericksburg	3,266	2,819	738	2,683	3,401
Galax	957	1,087	276	907	1,278
Hampton	23,395	19,219	6,581	19,106	24,034
Harrisonburg	3,414	4,935	1,162	2,799	5,376
Hopewell	2,863	3,818	1,227	2,566	4,672
Lexington	1,128	894	228	997	994
Lynchburg	9,587	12,518	2,545	8,279	15,323
Manassas	3,647	5,453	1,971	2,658	5,980
Manassas Park	567	792	356	434	993
Martinsville	3,073	2,690	748	2,794	3,360
Newport News	25,743	26,779	8,217	21,413	32,570
Norfolk	37,602	22,362	8,732	37,778	30,538
Norton	871	472	182	795	608
Petersburg	8,671	3,125	834	8,177	4,231
Poquoson	1,086	3,354	960	877	3,840
Portsmouth	20,416	12,575	4,360	19,698	16,087
Radford	2,183	1,996	582	1,855	2,481
Richmond	47,642	24,341	6,992	42,155	31,586
Roanoke	17,724	13,443	3,753	17,185	15,389
Salem	4,028	5,143	1,430	3,760	5,694
South Boston	1,051	1,435	252	936	1,694
Staunton	2,851	4,989	1,146	2,457	5,775
Suffolk	9,196	8,697	2,150	8,080	9,742
Virginia Beach	44,294	68,936	24,087	33,780	76,481
Waynesboro	2,302	3,758	961	2,038	4,672
Williamsburg	1,856	1,349	445	1,534	1,648
Winchester	2,768	3,833	1,048	2,300	4,497
Totals	1,038,650	1,150,517	348,639	859,799	1,309,162

Virginia Vote Since 1944

1944, Roosevelt, Dem., 242,276; Dewey, Rep., 145,243; Watson, Proh., 459; Thomas, Soc., 417; Teichert, Soc. Labor, 90.

1948, Truman, Dem., 200,786; Dewey, Rep., 172,070; Thurmond, States' Rights, 43,393; Wallace, Prog., 2,047; Thomas, Soc., 726; Teichert, Soc. Labor, 234.

1952, Eisenhower, Rep., 349,037; Stevenson, Dem., 268,677; Hass, Soc. Labor, 1,160; Hoopes, Social Dem., 504; Hallinan, Prog., 311.

1956, Eisenhower, Rep., 386,459; Stevenson, Dem., 267,760; Andrews, States' Rights, 42,964; Hoopes, Soc. Dem., 444; Hass, Soc. Labor, 351.

1960, Kennedy, Dem., 362,327; Nixon, Rep., 404,521; Coiner, Cons., 4,204; Hass, Soc. Labor, 397.

1964, Johnson, Dem., 558,038; Goldwater, Rep., 481,334; Hass, Soc. Labor, 2,895.

1968, Nixon, Rep., 590,319; Humphrey, Dem., 442,387; Wallace, 3d Party, *320,272; Blomen, Soc. Labor, 4,671; Munn, Proh., 601; Gregory, Peace and Freedom, 1,680.
*10,561 votes for Wallace were omitted in the count.

1972, Nixon, Rep., 988,493; McGovern, Dem., 438,887; Schmitz, Amer., 19,721; Fisher, Soc. Labor, 9,918.

1976, Carter, Dem., 813,896; Ford, Rep., 836,554; Camejo, Soc. Workers, 17,802; Anderson, Amer., 16,686; LaRouche, U.S. Labor, 7,508; MacBride, Libertarian, 4,648.

1980, Reagan, Rep., 989,609; Carter, Dem., 752,174; Anderson, Ind., 95,418; Commoner, Citizens, 14,024; Clark, Libertarian, 12,821; DeBerry, Soc. Workers, 1,986.

1984, Reagan, Rep., 1,337,078; Mondale, Dem., 796,250.

1988, Bush, Rep., 1,309,162; Dukakis, Dem., 859,799; Fulani, Ind., 14,312; Paul, Lib., 8,336.

1992, Clinton, Dem., 1,038,650; Bush, Rep., 1,150,517; Perot, Ind., 348,639; LaRouche, Ind., 11,937; Marrou, Libertarian, 5,730; Fulani, New Alliance, 3,192.

Washington

	1992			1988	
County	Clinton (D)	Bush (R)	Perot (I)	Dukakis (D)	Bush (R)
Adams	1,449	2,087	1,010	1,612	2,612
Asotin	3,239	2,425	1,849	3,422	2,874
Benton	16,459	22,883	12,878	14,817	28,688
Chelan	7,860	10,716	4,606	8,183	11,601
Clallam	10,820	9,765	7,775	11,123	11,200
Clark	42,648	36,906	26,163	40,021	37,285
Columbia	668	761	466	730	1,172
Cowlitz	15,052	10,000	9,246	16,090	12,009
Douglas	3,731	4,920	2,315	3,760	5,378
Ferry	963	773	762	972	972
Franklin	3,743	4,486	2,597	4,772	6,488
Garfield	473	620	222	593	714
Grant	7,278	9,503	4,898	7,564	10,859
Grays Harbor	12,599	6,904	7,460	14,097	8,860
Island	9,555	9,526	7,889	8,510	12,552
Jefferson	6,148	3,467	3,168	5,270	4,184
King	391,050	212,986	167,216	349,663	290,574
Kitsap	34,442	29,340	23,873	33,748	34,743
Kittitas	5,432	4,078	2,778	5,318	5,048
Klickitat	2,758	2,085	1,938	2,991	2,920
Lewis	7,810	12,316	6,684	8,629	14,184
Lincoln	1,653	2,152	1,098	1,884	2,689
Mason	8,076	5,776	5,577	7,826	7,426
Okanogan	5,015	4,265	3,541	5,630	5,856
Pacific	4,587	2,243	2,351	5,017	3,073
Pend Oreille	1,798	1,528	1,340	1,925	1,802
Pierce	102,243	77,410	59,523	96,688	94,167
San Juan	3,353	1,901	1,776	3,008	2,660
Skagit	15,936	13,388	10,973	15,159	16,550
Skamania	1,474	1,102	1,050	1,748	1,356
Snohomish	88,643	69,137	65,838	80,694	84,158
Spokane	69,526	59,984	38,251	68,520	68,787
Stevens	4,960	5,706	3,769	5,068	6,576
Thurston	38,293	25,643	19,551	33,860	31,980
Wahkiakum	696	488	584	961	629
Walla Walla	7,325	7,894	4,507	7,448	9,683
Whatcom	26,619	23,801	12,455	25,571	23,820
Whitman	7,637	6,428	3,220	7,403	7,680
Yakima	21,026	25,841	10,583	23,221	30,026
Totals	993,037	731,234	541,780	933,516	903,835

Washington Vote Since 1944

1944, Roosevelt, Dem., 486,774; Dewey, Rep., 361,689; Thomas, Soc., 3,824; Watson, Proh., 2,396; Teichert, Soc. Labor, 1,645.

1948, Truman, Dem., 476,165; Dewey, Rep., 386,315; Wallace, Prog., 31,692; Watson, Proh., 6,117; Thomas, Soc., 3,534; Teichert, Soc. Labor, 1,133; Dobbs, Soc. Workers, 103.

1952, Eisenhower, Rep., 599,107; Stevenson, Dem., 492,845; MacArthur, Christian Nationalist, 7,290; Hallinan, Prog., 2,460; Hass, Soc. Labor, 633; Hoopes, Soc., 254; Dobbs, Soc. Workers, 119.

1956, Eisenhower, Rep., 620,430; Stevenson, Dem., 523,002; Hass, Soc. Labor, 7,457.

1960, Kennedy, Dem., 599,298; Nixon, Rep., 629,273; Hass, Soc. Labor, 10,895; Curtis, Constitution, 1,401; Dobbs, Soc. Workers, 705.

1964, Johnson, Dem., 779,699; Goldwater, Rep., 470,366; Hass, Soc. Labor, 7,772; DeBerry, Freedom Soc., 537.

1968, Nixon, Rep., 588,510; Humphrey, Dem., 616,037; Wallace, 3d Party, 96,990; Blomen, Soc. Labor, 488; Cleaver, Peace and Freedom, 1,609; Halstead, Soc. Workers, 270; Mitchell, Free Ballot, 377.

1972, Nixon, Rep., 837,135; McGovern, Dem., 568,334; Schmitz, Amer., 58,906; Spock, Ind., 2,644; Fisher, Soc. Labor, 1,102; Jenness, Soc. Workers, 623; Hall, Com., 566; Hospers, Libertarian, 1,537.

1976, Carter, Dem., 717,323; Ford, Rep., 777,732; McCarthy, Ind., 36,986; Maddox, Amer. Ind., 8,585; Anderson, Amer., 5,046; MacBride, Libertarian, 5,042; Wright, People's, 1,124; Camejo, Soc. Workers, 905; LaRouche, U.S. Labor, 903; Hall, Com., 817; Levin, Soc. Labor, 713; Zeidler, Soc., 358.

1980, Reagan, Rep., 865,244; Carter, Dem., 650,193; Anderson, Ind., 185,073; Clark, Libertarian, 29,213; Commoner, Citizens, 9,403; DeBerry, Soc. Workers, 1,137; McReynolds, Soc., 956; Hall, Com., 834; Griswold, Workers World, 341.

1984, Reagan, Rep., 1,051,670; Mondale, Dem., 798,352; Bergland, Libertarian, 8,844.

1988, Bush, Rep., 903,835; Dukakis, Dem., 933,516; Paul, Lib., 17,240; LaRouche, Ind., 4,412.

1992, Clinton, Dem., 993,037; Bush, Rep., 731,234; Perot, Ind., 541,780; Marrou, Libertarian, 7,533; Gritz, Populist/America First, 4,854; Hagelin, Natural Law, 2,456; Phillips, U.S. Taxpayers, 2,354; Fulani, New Alliance, 1,776; Daniels, Ind., 1,171.

West Virginia

County	1992 Clinton (D)	Bush (R)	Perot (I)	1988 Dukakis (D)	Bush (R)
Barbour	3,467	2,322	1,153	3,221	3,023
Berkeley	7,159	9,134	3,645	6,313	10,761
Boone	6,576	2,021	1,037	6,539	2,786
Braxton	3,396	1,535	823	3,377	2,024
Brooke	5,693	2,582	2,103	6,258	4,006
Cabell	15,111	13,203	5,311	15,368	17,197
Calhoun	1,627	1,095	537	1,644	1,395
Clay	1,928	1,255	462	2,263	1,536
Doddridge	968	1,500	515	955	1,880
Fayette	9,574	3,991	2,002	11,009	5,143
Gilmer	1,576	1,085	484	1,661	1,387
Grant	1,011	2,762	519	893	3,215
Greenbrier	5,784	4,442	1,898	6,091	5,395
Hampshire	2,365	2,767	1,022	2,085	3,253
Hancock	7,830	3,897	3,267	8,338	5,882
Hardy	1,917	2,144	602	1,689	2,581
Harrison	15,480	9,687	5,131	17,005	13,364
Jackson	5,102	4,192	1,908	4,573	5,696
Jefferson	5,363	4,656	2,114	4,334	5,349
Kanawha	38,315	31,358	11,778	41,144	38,140
Lewis	2,931	2,413	1,197	3,272	3,602
Lincoln	4,502	2,637	787	5,049	3,457
Logan	11,095	3,336	1,835	11,317	4,244
McDowell	7,019	1,941	803	7,204	2,463
Marion	14,042	6,380	4,736	14,441	9,229
Marshall	7,298	4,463	3,402	7,903	6,793
Mason	5,331	3,808	2,045	5,468	5,332
Mercer	9,511	7,888	2,817	10,152	10,221
Mineral	3,992	4,837	1,884	4,059	6,015
Mingo	7,342	2,584	915	7,429	2,896
Monongalia	14,142	9,831	4,576	14,178	12,091
Monroe	2,418	2,311	685	2,427	2,719
Morgan	1,854	2,585	886	1,545	3,002
Nicholas	5,042	2,959	1,495	5,173	3,731
Ohio	9,522	7,421	3,632	10,121	10,341
Pendleton	1,626	1,589	362	1,595	1,901
Pleasants	1,387	1,248	731	1,421	1,761
Pocahontas	1,741	1,401	627	1,958	1,876
Preston	3,933	4,429	2,109	4,357	5,804
Putnam	6,817	7,653	2,910	6,640	8,163
Raleigh	13,171	8,700	3,247	14,302	10,395
Randolph	5,097	3,496	1,582	5,233	4,746
Ritchie	1,474	2,184	745	1,446	2,874
Roane	2,607	2,207	1,009	2,447	2,861
Summers	2,650	1,652	565	3,072	2,231
Taylor	2,843	2,022	1,242	2,852	2,816
Tucker	1,805	1,261	550	1,869	1,699
Tyler	1,587	1,593	1,013	1,501	2,365
Upshur	3,161	3,505	1,558	3,065	4,813
Wayne	8,392	5,729	2,199	8,621	7,123
Webster	2,320	811	436	2,185	1,016
Wetzel	3,753	2,271	1,550	3,928	3,381
Wirt	1,043	939	394	929	1,125
Wood	13,529	15,441	6,998	12,959	19,450
Wyoming	5,782	2,821	996	6,138	3,516
Totals	331,001	241,974	108,829	341,016	310,065

West Virginia Vote Since 1944

1944, Roosevelt, Dem., 392,777; Dewey, Rep., 322,819.

1948, Truman, Dem., 429,188; Dewey, Rep., 316,251; Wallace, Prog., 3,311.

1952, Eisenhower, Rep., 419,970; Stevenson, Dem., 453,578.

1956, Eisenhower, Rep., 449,297; Stevenson, Dem., 381,534.

1960, Kennedy, Dem., 441,786; Nixon, Rep., 395,995.

1964, Johnson, Dem., 538,087; Goldwater, Rep., 253,953.

1968, Nixon, Rep., 307,555; Humphrey, Dem., 374,091; Wallace, 3d Party, 72,560.

1972, Nixon, Rep., 484,964; McGovern, Dem., 277,435.

1976, Carter, Dem., 435,864; Ford, Rep., 314,726.

1980, Reagan, Rep., 334,206; Carter, Dem., 367,462; Anderson, Ind., 31,691; Clark, Libertarian, 4,356.

1984, Reagan, Rep., 405,483; Mondale, Dem., 328,125.

1988, Bush, Rep., 310,065; Dukakis, Dem., 341,016; Fulani, New Alliance, 2,230.

1992, Clinton, Dem., 331,001; Bush, Rep., 241,974; Perot, Ind., 108,829; Marrou, Libertarian, 1,873.

Wisconsin

County	1992 Clinton (D)	Bush (R)	Perot (I)	1988 Dukakis (D)	Bush (R)
Adams	3,539	2,465	2,003	3,598	3,258
Ashland	4,213	2,372	1,746	4,526	2,926
Barron	8,063	6,572	5,479	8,951	8,527
Bayfield	3,873	2,393	1,746	4,323	3,095
Brown	37,513	42,352	22,395	41,788	43,625
Buffalo	2,996	2,029	1,889	3,481	2,783
Burnet	3,172	2,340	1,855	3,537	2,884
Calumet	5,701	7,541	5,055	6,481	8,107
Chippewa	10,487	8,215	6,408	11,447	9,757
Clark	5,540	4,977	4,284	6,642	6,296
Columbia	9,348	9,099	5,439	9,132	10,475
Crawford	3,540	2,390	1,797	3,608	3,238
Dane	114,724	61,957	31,874	105,414	69,143
Dodge	11,438	14,971	9,136	12,663	17,003
Door	4,735	5,468	3,506	5,425	6,907
Douglas	12,319	5,679	4,150	13,907	6,440
Dunn	7,965	5,283	4,809	9,205	7,273
Eau Claire	21,221	15,915	9,783	21,150	17,664
Florence	978	942	719	1,018	1,106
Fond du Lac	13,757	19,785	10,660	15,887	21,985
Forest	1,904	1,393	1,062	2,142	1,845
Grant	8,914	7,678	6,405	9,421	10,049
Green	5,467	4,887	3,735	5,153	6,636
Green Lake	2,772	3,897	2,827	3,033	5,205
Iowa	4,467	3,288	2,341	4,268	4,240
Iron	1,762	1,273	835	2,090	1,599
Jackson	3,681	2,644	2,040	3,924	3,555
Jefferson	11,593	13,072	7,960	11,816	14,309
Juneau	4,177	4,051	2,670	3,734	4,869
Kenosha	27,341	19,854	14,232	30,089	21,661
Kewaunee	4,050	3,570	2,700	4,786	4,330
La Crosse	22,838	18,891	10,224	22,204	21,548
La Fayette	3,143	2,582	2,079	3,521	3,665
Langlade	3,630	3,890	2,444	4,254	4,884
Lincoln	5,297	4,321	3,605	5,819	5,257
Manitowoc	15,903	14,008	11,179	19,680	16,020
Marathon	21,482	20,948	14,600	24,658	24,482
Marinette	7,626	7,984	5,412	8,030	9,637
Marquette	2,533	2,322	1,818	2,463	3,059
Menominee	691	244	221	1,028	381
Milwaukee	235,521	151,314	76,039	268,287	168,363
Monroe	6,427	6,118	4,183	6,437	7,073
Oconto	5,898	5,720	4,405	6,549	7,084
Oneida	7,160	6,725	4,782	7,414	8,130
Outagamie	23,735	30,370	18,479	27,771	33,113
Ozaukee	11,879	22,805	8,002	12,661	22,899
Pepin	1,673	1,098	781	1,906	1,311
Pierce	7,824	4,844	4,492	8,659	6,045
Polk	7,746	5,446	4,753	8,981	6,866
Portage	15,553	10,914	7,083	16,317	12,057
Price	3,575	2,654	2,286	3,987	3,450
Racine	34,875	32,310	20,227	39,631	36,342
Richland	3,458	3,144	1,899	3,643	4,026
Rock	31,154	21,942	15,700	29,576	28,178
Rusk	3,376	2,430	2,085	3,888	3,063
St. Croix	10,281	8,114	7,125	11,392	9,960
Sauk	9,128	8,886	5,280	8,324	10,225
Sawyer	2,796	2,658	1,861	3,231	3,260
Shawano	6,062	7,253	4,540	6,587	8,362
Sheboygan	20,568	22,526	11,295	23,429	23,471
Taylor	3,305	3,415	2,590	3,785	4,254
Trempealeau	6,218	3,577	3,160	6,212	4,902
Vernon	5,673	4,072	2,890	5,754	5,226
Vilas	3,764	4,616	2,827	3,781	5,842
Walworth	11,825	15,727	9,029	12,203	18,259
Washburn	3,080	2,586	1,978	3,393	3,074
Washington	13,339	22,739	13,045	15,907	24,328
Waukesha	50,270	91,461	36,622	57,598	90,467
Waupaca	6,666	10,252	6,088	7,078	11,559
Waushara	3,402	4,045	2,329	3,535	4,953
Winnebago	27,234	33,709	16,140	28,508	35,085
Wood	13,208	13,843	8,822	16,074	16,549
Totals	1,041,066	930,855	544,479	1,126,794	1,047,499

Wisconsin Vote Since 1944

1944, Roosevelt, Dem., 650,413; Dewey, Rep., 674,532; Thomas, Soc., 13,205; Teichert, Soc. Labor, 1,002.

1948, Truman, Dem., 647,310; Dewey, Rep., 590,959; Wallace, Prog., 25,282; Thomas, Soc., 12,547; Teichert, Soc. Labor, 399; Dobbs, Soc. Workers, 303.

1952, Eisenhower, Rep., 979,744; Stevenson, Dem., 622,175; Hallinan, Ind., 2,174; Dobbs, Ind., 1,350; Hoopes, Ind., 1,157; Hass, Ind., 770.

1956, Eisenhower, Rep., 954,844; Stevenson, Dem., 586,768; Andrews, Ind., 6,918; Hoopes, Soc., 754; Hass, Soc. Labor, 710; Dobbs, Soc. Workers, 564.

1960, Kennedy, Dem., 830,805; Nixon, Rep., 895,175; Dobbs, Soc. Workers, 1,792; Hass, Soc. Labor, 1,310.

1964, Johnson, Dem., 1,050,424; Goldwater, Rep., 638,495; DeBerry, Soc. Workers, 1,692; Hass, Soc. Labor, 1,204.

1968, Nixon, Rep., 809,997; Humphrey, Dem., 748,804; Wallace, 3d Party, 127,835; Blomen, Soc. Labor, 1,338; Halstead, Soc. Workers, 1,222; scattered, 2,342.

1972 Nixon, Rep., 989,430; McGovern, Dem., 810,174; Schmitz, Amer., 47,525; Spock, Ind., 2,701; Fisher, Soc. Labor, 998; Hall, Com., 663; Reed, Ind., 506; scattered, 893.

1976, Carter, Dem., 1,040,232; Ford, Rep., 1,004,987; McCarthy, Ind., 34,943; Maddox, Amer. Ind., 8,552;

Zeidler, Soc., 4,298; MacBride, Libertarian, 3,814; Camejo, Soc. Workers, 1,691; Wright, People's, 943; Hall, Com., 749; LaRouche, U.S. Lab., 738; Levin, Soc. Labor, 389; scattered, 2,839.

1980, Reagan, Rep., 1,088,845; Carter, Dem., 981,584; Anderson, Ind., 160,657; Clark, Libertarian, 29,135; Commoner, Citizens, 7,767; Rarick, Constitution, 1,519; McReynolds, Soc., 808; Hall, Com., 772; Griswold, Workers World, 414; DeBerry, Soc. Workers, 383; scattering, 1,337.

1984, Reagan, Rep., 1,198,584; Mondale, Dem., 995,740; Bergland, Libertarian, 4,883.

1988, Bush, Rep., 1,047,499; Dukakis, Dem., 1,126,794; Paul, Lib., 5,157; Duke, Pop., 3,056.

1992, Clinton, Dem., 1,041,066; Bush, Rep., 930,855; Perot, Ind., 544,479; Marrou, Libertarian, 2,877; Gritz, Populist/America First, 2,311; Daniels, Ind., 1,883; Phillips, U.S. Taxpayers, 1,772; Hagelin, Natural Law, 1,070.

Wyoming

	1992			1988	
	Clinton	Bush	Perot	Dukakis	Bush
County	(D)	(R)	(I)	(D)	(R)
Albany.........	5,713	4,176	2,862	5,486	5,653
Big Horn	1,216	2,216	1,236	1,469	3,258
Campbell.......	2,709	5,315	3,133	2,288	6,702
Carbon	2,737	2,320	1,579	2,555	3,336
Converse.......	1,307	2,159	1,260	1,301	2,885
Crook	568	1,377	718	553	1,939
Fremont........	4,765	5,387	3,594	5,020	7,681
Goshen	1,754	2,395	1,144	1,875	3,075
Hot Springs	740	978	652	800	1,490
Johnson........	656	1,614	844	707	2,081
Laramie........	12,177	12,890	6,607	11,851	15,561
Lincoln........	1,430	2,595	1,495	1,592	3,237
Natrona........	9,817	9,717	7,647	9,148	14,005
Niobrara.......	298	635	355	354	825
Park	2,771	5,218	3,145	2,646	6,884
Platte	1,398	1,668	956	1,482	2,253
Sheridan........	4,139	4,303	3,035	4,655	5,980
Sublette	536	1,168	828	576	1,636
Sweetwater......	6,417	4,476	3,879	6,720	6,780
Teton	3,120	2,854	2,340	2,217	3,616
Uinta	2,047	2,701	2,041	1,922	3,464
Washakie	1,118	1,720	1,084	1,197	2,538
Weston.........	727	1,465	829	699	1,988
Totals	68,160	79,347	51,263	67,113	106,867

Wyoming Vote Since 1944

1944, Roosevelt, Dem., 49,419; Dewey, Rep., 51,921.

1948, Truman, Dem., 52,354; Dewey, Rep., 47,947; Wallace, Prog., 931; Thomas, Soc., 137; Teichert, Soc. Labor, 56.

1952, Eisenhower, Rep., 81,047; Stevenson, Dem., 47,934; Hamblen, Proh., 194; Hoopes, Soc., 40; Haas, Soc. Labor, 36.

1956, Eisenhower, Rep., 74,573; Stevenson, Dem., 49,554.

1960, Kennedy, Dem., 63,331; Nixon, Rep., 77,451.

1964, Johnson, Dem., 80,718; Goldwater, Rep., 61,998.

1968, Nixon, Rep., 70,927; Humphrey, Dem., 45,173; Wallace, 3d Party, 11,105.

1972, Nixon, Rep., 100,464; McGovern, Dem., 44,358; Schmitz, Amer., 748.

1976, Carter, Dem., 62,239; Ford, Rep., 92,717; McCarthy, Ind., 624; Reagan, Ind., 307; Anderson, Amer., 290; MacBride, Libertarian, 89; Brown, Ind., 47; Maddox, Amer. Ind., 30.

1980, Reagan, Rep., 110,700; Carter, Dem., 49,427; Anderson, Ind., 12,072; Clark, Libertarian, 4,514.

1984, Reagan, Rep., 133,241; Mondale, Dem., 53,370; Bergland, Libertarian, 2,357.

1988, Bush, Rep., 106,867; Dukakis, Dem., 67,113; Paul, Lib., 2,026; Fulani, New Alliance, 545.

1992, Clinton, Dem., 68,160; Bush, Rep., 79,347; Perot, Ind., 51,263.

1992 Official Presidential General Election Results

Source: State Elections Offices; Voter News Service

Candidate (Party)	Popular Vote	Percent of Popular Vote
Bill Clinton (Democrat)	44,908,254	42.95
George Bush (Republican)	39,102,343	37.40
Ross Perot (Independent)	19,741,065	18.86
Andre Marrou (Libertarian)	291,612	.28
James "Bo" Gritz (Populist/America First)	98,918	.09
Lenora Fulani (New Alliance)	73,248	.07
Howard Phillips (U.S. Taxpayers)	42,960	.04
John Hagelin (Natural Law)	37,137	.04
Ron Daniels (Independent)	27,396	.03
Lyndon LaRouche (Independent)	25,863	.02
James Mac Warren (Socialist Workers)	22,883	.02
Drew Bradford (Independent)	4,749	.00
Jack Herer (Grassroots)	3,875	.00
Helen Halyard (Workers League)	3,050	.00
John Quinn Brisben (Socialist)	2,909	.00
John Yiamouyiannis (Independent)	2,199	.00
Delbert Ehlers (Independent)	1,149	.00
Jim Boren (Apathy)	956	.00
Earl Dodge (Prohibition)	935	.00
Eugene Hem (Third Party)	405	.00
Isabelle Masters (Looking Back Group)	327	.00
Robert J. Smith (American)	292	.00
Gloria Estella La Riva (Workers World)	181	.00
Write-In	177,207	.17
None of the Above (Nevada)	2,537	.00
Total	104,552,736	100

Note: Party designations may vary from one state to another.

Voter Turnout in Presidential Elections, 1932-92

Source: Federal Election Commission; Commission for Study of American Electorate

	Candidates	Voter Participation (% of voting-age population)		Candidates	Voter Participation (% of voting-age population)
1932	Roosevelt-Hoover	52.4	1964	Johnson-Goldwater	61.9
1936	Roosevelt-Landon	56.0	1968	Humphrey-Nixon	60.9
1940	Roosevelt-Willkie.............	58.9	1972	McGovern-Nixon	55.2[1]
1944	Roosevelt-Dewey.............	56.0	1976	Carter-Ford	53.5
1948	Truman-Dewey	51.1	1980	Carter-Reagan	54.0
1952	Stevenson-Eisenhower.........	61.6	1984	Mondale-Reagan	53.1
1956	Stevenson-Eisenhower.........	59.3	1988	Dukakis-Bush	50.2
1960	Kennedy-Nixon	62.8	1992	Clinton-Bush-Perot...........	55.9

(1) The sharp drop in 1972 reflects the expansion of eligibility with the enfranchisement of 18- to 21-year-olds.

Electoral Votes for President
(based on 1990 Census)

The Electoral College

The president and the vice president of the U.S. are the only elective federal officials not elected by direct vote of the people. They are elected by the members of the Electoral College, an institution that was provided for in the U.S. Constitution.

On presidential election day, the first Tuesday after the first Monday in Nov. of every 4th year, each state chooses as many electors as it has senators and representatives in Congress. In 1964, for the first time, as provided by the 23d Amendment to the Constitution, the District of Columbia voted for 3 electors. Thus, with 100 senators and 435 representatives, there are 538 members of the Electoral College, with a majority of 270 electoral votes needed to elect the president and vice president.

Although political parties were not part of the original plan created by the Founding Fathers, today political parties customarily nominate their lists of electors at their respective state conventions. Some states print the names of the candidates for president and vice president at the top of the Nov. ballot; others list only the names of the electors. In either case, the electors of the party receiving the highest vote are elected.

The electors meet on the first Monday after the 2d Wednesday in Dec. in their respective state capitals or in some other place prescribed by state legislatures. By long-established custom, they vote for their party nominees, although this is not required by law.

The Constitution requires electors to cast a ballot for at least one person who is not an inhabitant of that elector's home state. This ensures that presidential and vice presidential candidates from the same party will not be from the same state. Also, an elector cannot be a member of Congress or hold federal office.

Certified and sealed lists of the votes of the electors in each state are sent to the president of the U.S. Senate, who then opens them in the presence of the members of the Senate and House of Representatives in a joint session held on Jan. 6 (the next day if that falls on a Sunday), and the electoral votes of all the states are then counted. If no candidate for president has a majority, the House of Representatives chooses a president from among the 3 highest candidates, with all representatives from each state combining to cast one vote for that state. In 1800 and 1824 the House decided the outcome of the presidential elections. If no candidate for vice president has a majority, the Senate chooses from the top 2, with senators voting as individuals. The Senate chose the vice president following the 1836 election.

Under the electoral college system, a candidate who failed to win a majority of the popular vote can win a majority of electoral votes. This happened in the elections of 1824, 1876, and 1888.

National Political Convention Sites, 1856-1996[1]

Year	Democrats	Republicans	Year	Democrats	Republicans	Year	Democrats	Republicans
1856	Cincinnati	Philadelphia	1904	St. Louis	Chicago	1952	Chicago	Chicago
1860	Baltimore[2]	Chicago	1908	Denver	Chicago	1956	Chicago	San Francisco
1864	Chicago	Baltimore	1912	Baltimore	Chicago	1960	Los Angeles	Chicago
1868	New York City	Chicago	1916	St. Louis	Chicago	1964	Atlantic City	San Francisco
1872	Baltimore	Philadelphia	1920	San Francisco	Chicago	1968	Chicago	Miami Beach
1876	St. Louis	Cincinnati	1924	New York City	Cleveland	1972	Miami Beach	Miami Beach
1880	Cincinnati	Chicago	1928	Houston	Kansas City	1976	New York City	Kansas City, MO
1884	Chicago	Chicago	1932	Chicago	Chicago	1980	New York City	Detroit
1888	St. Louis	Chicago	1936	Philadelphia	Cleveland	1984	San Francisco	Dallas
1892	Chicago	Minneapolis	1940	Chicago	Philadelphia	1988	Atlanta	New Orleans
1896	Chicago	St. Louis	1944	Chicago	Chicago	1992	New York City	Houston
1900	Kansas City, MO	Philadelphia	1948	Philadelphia	Philadelphia	1996	Chicago	San Diego

(1) The first Democratic National Convention was held in 1832. All conventions prior to 1856 were held in Baltimore. The first Republican National Convention was held in 1856. Chicago has hosted more conventions (24) than any other city and is once again the planned site for the 1996 Democratic convention. (2) An earlier convention, held in Charleston, SC, had resulted in a split in the party. The official nomination was made at the Baltimore convention.

Independent Parties and the U.S. Presidency

Although many independent or "third party" candidates have pursued the presidency, only 8 candidates have polled more than a million votes. In most elections since 1860, fewer than one vote in 20 has been cast for a third party candidate. During that same period, in only 5 presidential elections have all third parties combined polled more than 10% of the vote. The major vote-getters in those elections were James B. Weaver, a Populist Party candidate in 1892; Robert M. La Follette, a Progressive Party candidate in 1924; Strom Thurmond, a States' Rights (Dixiecrat) candidate in 1948; George C. Wallace, an American Independent Party candidate in 1968; and H. Ross Perot, an independent candidate in 1992.

In the 1948 presidential election, Thurmond was able to capture 39 electoral votes (from 5 southern states); however,

when combined with the other third party candidates (Henry A. Wallace's Progressives, the Prohibition Party, the Socialist Party, and others), independent parties received only 5.75% of the popular vote in the election. Twenty years later, George Wallace's popularity in the same region allowed him to get 46 electoral votes, but without more national appeal, his candidacy also was unsuccessful. In 1992 Perot was able to capture 19% of the popular vote; however, he did not win a single state and placed second in only Maine and Utah.

Despite the difficulty in winning the presidency, independent candidates are sometimes successful in winning other elected offices and often bring the attention of all presidential candidates to the problems and the concerns that many citizens consider significant.

Notable Independent Party Presidential Candidates

Party	Presidential nominee	Year	Issues	Strength in . . .
Anti-Masonic	William Wirt	1832	Against secret societies and oaths	PA, VT
Liberty	James G. Birney	1844	Anti-slavery	North
Free Soil	Martin Van Buren	1848	Anti-slavery	NY, OH
American (Know-Nothing)	Millard Fillmore	1856	Anti-immigrant	Northeast, South
Greenback	Peter Cooper	1876	For "cheap money," labor rights	National
Greenback	James B. Weaver	1880	For "cheap money," labor rights	National
Prohibition	John P. St. John	1884	Anti-liquor	National
Populist	James B. Weaver	1892	For "cheap money," end of national banks	South, West
Socialist	Eugene V. Debs	1900-12; 1920	For public ownership	National
Progressive (Bull Moose)	Theodore Roosevelt	1912	Against high tariffs	Midwest, West
Progressive	Robert M. La Follete	1924	Farmer and labor rights	Midwest, West
Socialist	Norman Thomas	1928-48	Liberal reforms	National
Union	William Lemke	1936	Anti-"New Deal"	National
States' Rights (Dixiecrats)	Strom Thurmond	1948	For states' rights	South
Progressive	Henry A. Wallace	1948	Anti-Cold War	NY, CA
American Independent	George C. Wallace	1968	For states' rights	South
American	John G. Schmitz	1972	For "law and order"	Far West, OH, LA
None (Independent)	John B. Anderson	1980	A 3d choice	National
None (Independent)	H. Ross Perot	1992	Federal budget deficit	National

Party Nominees for President and Vice President

Asterisk (*) denotes winning ticket

	Democratic		Republican	
Year	President	Vice President	President	Vice President
1856	James Buchanan*	John Breckinridge	John Frémont	William Dayton
1860	Stephen A. Douglas[1]	Herschel V. Johnson	Abraham Lincoln*	Hannibal Hamlin
1864	George McClellan	G.H. Pendleton	Abraham Lincoln*	Andrew Johnson
1868	Horatio Seymour	Francis Blair	Ulysses S. Grant*	Schuyler Colfax
1872	Horace Greeley	B. Gratz Brown	Ulysses S. Grant*	Henry Wilson
1876	Samuel J. Tilden	Thomas Hendricks	Rutherford B. Hayes*	William Wheeler
1880	Winfield Hancock	William English	James A. Garfield*	Chester A. Arthur
1884	Grover Cleveland*	Thomas Hendricks	James Blaine	John Logan
1888	Grover Cleveland	A.G. Thurman	Benjamin Harrison*	Levi Morton
1892	Grover Cleveland*	Adlai Stevenson	Benjamin Harrison	Whitelaw Reid
1896	William J. Bryan	Arthur Sewall	William McKinley*	Garret Hobart
1900	William J. Bryan	Adlai Stevenson	William McKinley*	Theodore Roosevelt
1904	Alton Parker	Henry Davis	Theodore Roosevelt*	Charles Fairbanks
1908	William J. Bryan	John Kern	William H. Taft*	James Sherman
1912	Woodrow Wilson*	Thomas Marshall	William H. Taft	James Sherman[2]
1916	Woodrow Wilson*	Thomas Marshall	Charles Hughes	Charles Fairbanks
1920	James M. Cox	Franklin D. Roosevelt	Warren G. Harding*	Calvin Coolidge
1924	John W. Davis	Charles W. Bryan	Calvin Coolidge*	Charles G. Dawes
1928	Alfred E. Smith	Joseph T. Robinson	Herbert Hoover*	Charles Curtis
1932	Franklin D. Roosevelt*	John N. Garner	Herbert Hoover	Charles Curtis
1936	Franklin D. Roosevelt*	John N. Garner	Alfred M. Landon	Frank Knox
1940	Franklin D. Roosevelt*	Henry A. Wallace	Wendell L. Willkie	Charles McNary
1944	Franklin D. Roosevelt*	Harry S. Truman	Thomas E. Dewey	John W. Bricker
1948	Harry S. Truman*	Alben W. Barkley	Thomas E. Dewey	Earl Warren
1952	Adlai E. Stevenson	John J. Sparkman	Dwight D. Eisenhower*	Richard M. Nixon
1956	Adlai E. Stevenson	Estes Kefauver	Dwight D. Eisenhower*	Richard M. Nixon
1960	John F. Kennedy*	Lyndon B. Johnson	Richard M. Nixon	Henry Cabot Lodge
1964	Lyndon B. Johnson*	Hubert H. Humphrey	Barry M. Goldwater	William E. Miller
1968	Hubert H. Humphrey	Edmund S. Muskie	Richard M. Nixon*	Spiro T. Agnew
1972	George S. McGovern	R. Sargent Shriver Jr.	Richard M. Nixon*	Spiro T. Agnew
1976	Jimmy Carter*	Walter F. Mondale	Gerald R. Ford	Robert J. Dole
1980	Jimmy Carter	Walter F. Mondale	Ronald Reagan*	George Bush
1984	Walter F. Mondale	Geraldine Ferraro	Ronald Reagan*	George Bush
1988	Michael S. Dukakis	Lloyd Bentsen	George Bush*	Dan Quayle
1992	Bill Clinton*	Al Gore	George Bush	Dan Quayle

(1) Douglas and Johnson were nominated at the Baltimore convention. An earlier convention, which had failed to reach a consensus, had nominated John Breckinridge for president and Joseph Lane for vice president. (2) Died Oct. 30; replaced on ballot by Nicholas Butler.

Major Parties' Popular and Electoral Vote for President

(F) Federalist; (D) Democrat; (R) Republican; (DR) Democratic Republican; (NR) National Republican;
(W) Whig; (P) People's; (PR) Progressive; (SR) States' Rights; (LR) Liberal Republican; Asterisk (*)—See notes.

Year	President elected	Popular	Elec.	Losing candidate	Popular	Elec.
1789	George Washington (F)	Unknown	69	No opposition	—	—
1792	George Washington (F)	Unknown	132	No opposition	—	—
1796	John Adams (F)	Unknown	71	Thomas Jefferson (DR)	Unknown	68
1800*	Thomas Jefferson (DR)	Unknown	73	Aaron Burr (DR)	Unknown	73
1804	Thomas Jefferson (DR)	Unknown	162	Charles Pinckney (F)	Unknown	14
1808	James Madison (DR)	Unknown	122	Charles Pinckney (F)	Unknown	47
1812	James Madison (DR)	Unknown	128	DeWitt Clinton (F)	Unknown	89
1816	James Monroe (DR)	Unknown	183	Rufus King (F)	Unknown	34
1820	James Monroe (DR)	Unknown	231	John Quincy Adams (DR)	Unknown	1
1824*	John Quincy Adams (DR)	105,321	84	Andrew Jackson (DR)	155,872	99
				Henry Clay (DR)	46,587	37
				William H. Crawford (DR)	44,282	41
1828	Andrew Jackson (D)	647,231	178	John Quincy Adams (NR)	509,097	83
1832	Andrew Jackson (D)	687,502	219	Henry Clay (NR)	530,189	49
1836	Martin Van Buren (D)	762,678	170	William H. Harrison (W)	548,007	73
1840	William H. Harrison (W)	1,275,017	234	Martin Van Buren (D)	1,128,702	60
1844	James K. Polk (D)	1,337,243	170	Henry Clay (W)	1,299,068	105
1848	Zachary Taylor (W)	1,360,101	163	Lewis Cass (D)	1,220,544	127
				Martin Van Buren (Free Soil)	291,501	—
1852	Franklin Pierce (D)	1,601,474	254	Winfield Scott (W)	1,386,578	42
1856	James Buchanan (D)	1,927,995	174	John C. Fremont (R)	1,391,555	114
				Millard Fillmore (American)	873,053	8
1860	Abraham Lincoln (R)	1,866,352	180	Stephen A. Douglas (D)	1,375,157	12
				John C. Breckinridge (D)	845,763	72
				John Bell (Const. Union)	589,581	39
1864	Abraham Lincoln (R)	2,216,067	212	George McClellan (D)	1,808,725	21
1868	Ulysses S. Grant (R)	3,015,071	214	Horatio Seymour (D)	2,709,615	80
1872*	Ulysses S. Grant (R)	3,597,070	286	Horace Greeley (D-LR)	2,834,079	—
1876*	Rutherford B. Hayes (R)	4,033,950	185	Samuel J. Tilden (D)	4,284,757	184
1880	James A. Garfield (R)	4,449,053	214	Winfield S. Hancock (D)	4,442,030	155
1884	Grover Cleveland (D)	4,911,017	219	James G. Blaine (R)	4,848,334	182
1888*	Benjamin Harrison (R)	5,444,337	233	Grover Cleveland (D)	5,540,050	168
1892	Grover Cleveland (D)	5,554,414	277	Benjamin Harrison (R)	5,190,802	145
				James Weaver (P)	1,027,329	22
1896	William McKinley (R)	7,035,638	271	William J. Bryan (D-P)	6,467,946	176
1900	William McKinley (R)	7,219,530	292	William J. Bryan (D)	6,358,071	155
1904	Theodore Roosevelt (R)	7,628,834	336	Alton B. Parker (D)	5,084,491	140
1908	William H. Taft (R)	7,679,006	321	William J. Bryan (D)	6,409,106	162
1912	Woodrow Wilson (D)	6,286,214	435	Theodore Roosevelt (PR)	4,216,020	88
				William H. Taft (R)	3,483,922	8
1916	Woodrow Wilson (D)	9,129,606	277	Charles E. Hughes (R)	8,538,221	254
1920	Warren G. Harding (R)	16,152,200	404	James M. Cox (D)	9,147,353	127
1924	Calvin Coolidge (R)	15,725,016	382	John W. Davis (D)	8,385,586	136
				Robert M. La Follette (PR)	4,822,856	13
1928	Herbert Hoover (R)	21,392,190	444	Alfred E. Smith (D)	15,016,443	87
1932	Franklin D. Roosevelt (D)	22,821,857	472	Herbert Hoover (R)	15,761,841	59
1936	Franklin D. Roosevelt (D)	27,751,597	523	Alfred Landon (R)	16,679,583	8
1940	Franklin D. Roosevelt (D)	27,243,466	449	Wendell Willkie (R)	22,304,755	82
1944	Franklin D. Roosevelt (D)	25,602,505	432	Thomas E. Dewey (R)	22,006,278	99
1948	Harry S. Truman (D)	24,105,812	303	Thomas E. Dewey (R)	21,970,065	189
				Strom Thurmond (SR)	1,169,021	39
				Henry A. Wallace (PR)	1,157,172	—
1952	Dwight D. Eisenhower (R)	33,936,252	442	Adlai E. Stevenson (D)	27,314,992	89
1956*	Dwight D. Eisenhower (R)	35,585,316	457	Adlai E. Stevenson (D)	26,031,322	73
1960*	John F. Kennedy (D)	34,227,096	303	Richard M. Nixon (R)	34,108,546	219
1964	Lyndon B. Johnson (D)	43,126,506	486	Barry M. Goldwater (R)	27,176,799	52
1968	Richard M. Nixon (R)	31,785,480	301	Hubert H. Humphrey (D)	31,275,166	191
				George C. Wallace (3d party)	9,906,473	46
1972*	Richard M. Nixon (R)	47,165,234	520	George S. McGovern (D)	29,170,774	17
1976*	Jimmy Carter (D)	40,828,929	297	Gerald R. Ford (R)	39,148,940	240
1980	Ronald Reagan (R)	43,899,248	489	Jimmy Carter (D)	35,481,435	49
				John B. Anderson (independent)	5,719,437	—
1984	Ronald Reagan (R)	54,281,858	525	Walter F. Mondale (D)	37,457,215	13
1988*	George Bush (R)	48,881,221	426	Michael S. Dukakis (D)	41,805,422	111
1992	Bill Clinton (D)	44,908,254	370	George Bush (R)	39,102,343	168
				H. Ross Perot (independent)	19,741,065	—

1800—Elected by House of Representatives because of tied electoral vote. **1824**—Elected by House of Representatives. No candidate polled a majority. In 1824, the Democratic Republicans had become a loose coalition of competing political groups. By 1828, the supporters of Jackson were known as Democrats, and the John Q. Adams and Henry Clay supporters as National Republicans. **1872**—Greeley died Nov. 29, 1872. His electoral votes were split among 4 individuals. **1876**—FL, LA, OR, and SC election returns were disputed. Congress in joint session (Mar. 2, 1877) declared Hayes and Wheeler elected president and vice president. **1888**—Cleveland had more votes than Harrison, but the 233 electoral votes cast for Harrison against the 168 for Cleveland elected Harrison president. **1956**—Democrats elected 74 electors, but one from Alabama refused to vote for Stevenson. **1960**—Sen. Harry F. Byrd (D, VA) received 15 electoral votes. **1972**—John Hospers of California and Theodora Nathan of Oregon received one vote from an elector of Virginia. **1976**—Ronald Reagan of CA received one vote from an elector of Washington. **1988**—Sen. Lloyd Bentsen (D, TX) received 1 electoral vote.

Presidents of the U.S.

No.	Name	Politics	Born	In	Inaug.	at age	Died	at age
1	George Washington	Fed.	1732, Feb. 22	VA	1789	57	1799, Dec. 14	67
2	John Adams	Fed.	1735, Oct. 30	MA	1797	61	1826, July 4	90
3	Thomas Jefferson	Dem.-Rep.	1743, Apr. 13	VA	1801	57	1826, July 4	83
4	James Madison	Dem.-Rep.	1751, Mar. 16	VA	1809	57	1836, June 28	85
5	James Monroe	Dem.-Rep.	1758, Apr. 28	VA	1817	58	1831, July 4	73
6	John Quincy Adams	Dem.-Rep.	1767, July 11	MA	1825	57	1848, Feb. 23	80
7	Andrew Jackson	Dem.	1767, Mar. 15	SC	1829	61	1845, June 8	78
8	Martin Van Buren	Dem.	1782, Dec. 5	NY	1837	54	1862, July 24	79
9	William Henry Harrison	Whig	1773, Feb. 9	VA	1841	68	1841, Apr. 4	68
10	John Tyler	Whig	1790, Mar. 29	VA	1841	51	1862, Jan. 18	71
11	James Knox Polk	Dem.	1795, Nov. 2	NC	1845	49	1849, June 15	53
12	Zachary Taylor	Whig	1784, Nov. 24	VA	1849	64	1850, July 9	65
13	Millard Fillmore	Whig	1800, Jan. 7	NY	1850	50	1874, Mar. 8	74
14	Franklin Pierce	Dem.	1804, Nov. 23	NH	1853	48	1869, Oct. 8	64
15	James Buchanan	Dem.	1791, Apr. 23	PA	1857	65	1868, June 1	77
16	Abraham Lincoln	Rep.	1809, Feb. 12	KY	1861	52	1865, Apr. 15	56
17	Andrew Johnson	(1)	1808, Dec. 29	NC	1865	56	1875, July 31	66
18	Ulysses Simpson Grant	Rep.	1822, Apr. 27	OH	1869	46	1885, July 23	63
19	Rutherford Birchard Hayes	Rep.	1822, Oct. 4	OH	1877	54	1893, Jan. 17	70
20	James Abram Garfield	Rep.	1831, Nov. 19	OH	1881	49	1881, Sept. 19	49
21	Chester Alan Arthur	Rep.	1830, Oct. 5	VT	1881	50	1886, Nov. 18	56
22	Grover Cleveland	Dem.	1837, Mar. 18	NJ	1885	47	1908, June 24	71
23	Benjamin Harrison	Rep.	1833, Aug. 20	OH	1889	55	1901, Mar. 13	67
24	Grover Cleveland	Dem.	1837, Mar. 18	NJ	1893	55	1908, June 24	71
25	William McKinley	Rep.	1843, Jan. 29	OH	1897	54	1901, Sept. 14	58
26	Theodore Roosevelt	Rep.	1858, Oct. 27	NY	1901	42	1919, Jan. 6	60
27	William Howard Taft	Rep.	1857, Sept. 15	OH	1909	51	1930, Mar. 8	72
28	Woodrow Wilson	Dem.	1856, Dec. 28	VA	1913	56	1924, Feb. 3	67
29	Warren Gamaliel Harding	Rep.	1865, Nov. 2	OH	1921	55	1923, Aug. 2	57
30	Calvin Coolidge	Rep.	1872, July 4	VT	1923	51	1933, Jan. 5	60
31	Herbert Clark Hoover	Rep.	1874, Aug. 10	IA	1929	54	1964, Oct. 20	90
32	Franklin Delano Roosevelt	Dem.	1882, Jan. 30	NY	1933	51	1945, Apr. 12	63
33	Harry S. Truman	Dem.	1884, May 8	MO	1945	60	1972, Dec. 26	88
34	Dwight David Eisenhower	Rep.	1890, Oct. 14	TX	1953	62	1969, Mar. 28	78
35	John Fitzgerald Kennedy	Dem.	1917, May 29	MA	1961	43	1963, Nov. 22	46
36	Lyndon Baines Johnson	Dem.	1908, Aug. 27	TX	1963	55	1973, Jan. 22	64
37	Richard Milhous Nixon (2)	Rep.	1913, Jan. 9	CA	1969	56	1994, Apr. 22	81
38	Gerald Rudolph Ford	Rep.	1913, July 14	NE	1974	61		
39	Jimmy (James Earl) Carter	Dem.	1924, Oct. 1	GA	1977	52		
40	Ronald Reagan	Rep.	1911, Feb. 6	IL	1981	69		
41	George Bush	Rep.	1924, June 12	MA	1989	64		
42	Bill Clinton	Dem.	1946, Aug. 19	AR	1993	46		

(1) Andrew Johnson was a Democrat, nominated vice president by Republicans, and elected with Lincoln on National Union ticket.
(2) Resigned Aug. 9, 1974.

Presidents, Vice Presidents, Congresses

President	Service	Vice President	Congress
1 George Washington	Apr. 30, 1789—Mar. 3, 1797	1 John Adams	1, 2, 3, 4
2 John Adams	Mar. 4, 1797—Mar. 3, 1801	2 Thomas Jefferson	5, 6
3 Thomas Jefferson	Mar. 4, 1801—Mar. 3, 1805	3 Aaron Burr	7, 8
"	Mar. 4, 1805—Mar. 3, 1809	4 George Clinton	9, 10
4 James Madison	Mar. 4, 1809—Mar. 3, 1813	"(1)	11, 12
"	Mar. 4, 1813—Mar. 3, 1817	5 Elbridge Gerry (2)	13, 14
5 James Monroe	Mar. 4, 1817—Mar. 3, 1825	6 Daniel D. Tompkins	15, 16, 17, 18
6 John Quincy Adams	Mar. 4, 1825—Mar. 3, 1829	7 John C. Calhoun	19, 20
7 Andrew Jackson	Mar. 4, 1829—Mar. 3, 1833	"(3)	21, 22
"	Mar. 4, 1833—Mar. 3, 1837	8 Martin Van Buren	23, 24
8 Martin Van Buren	Mar. 4, 1837—Mar. 3, 1841	9 Richard M. Johnson	25, 26
9 William Henry Harrison (4)	Mar. 4, 1841—Apr. 4, 1841	10 John Tyler	27
10 John Tyler	Apr. 6, 1841—Mar. 3, 1845		27, 28
11 James K. Polk	Mar. 4, 1845—Mar. 3, 1849	11 George M. Dallas	29, 30
12 Zachary Taylor (4)	Mar. 5, 1849—July 9, 1850	12 Millard Fillmore	31
13 Millard Fillmore	July 10, 1850—Mar. 3, 1853		31, 32
14 Franklin Pierce	Mar. 4, 1853—Mar. 3, 1857	13 William R. King (5)	33, 34
15 James Buchanan	Mar. 4, 1857—Mar. 3, 1861	14 John C. Breckinridge	35, 36
16 Abraham Lincoln	Mar. 4, 1861—Mar. 3, 1865	15 Hannibal Hamlin	37, 38
"(4)	Mar. 4, 1865—Apr. 15, 1865	16 Andrew Johnson	39
17 Andrew Johnson	Apr. 15, 1865—Mar. 3, 1869		39, 40
18 Ulysses S. Grant	Mar. 4, 1869—Mar. 3, 1873	17 Schuyler Colfax	41, 42
"	Mar. 4, 1873—Mar. 3, 1877	18 Henry Wilson (6)	43, 44
19 Rutherford B. Hayes	Mar. 4, 1877—Mar. 3, 1881	19 William A. Wheeler	45, 46
20 James A. Garfield (4)	Mar. 4, 1881—Sept. 19, 1881	20 Chester A. Arthur	47
21 Chester A. Arthur	Sept. 20, 1881—Mar. 3, 1885		47, 48
22 Grover Cleveland (7)	Mar. 4, 1885—Mar. 3, 1889	21 Thomas A. Hendricks (8)	49, 50
23 Benjamin Harrison	Mar. 4, 1889—Mar. 3, 1893	22 Levi P. Morton	51, 52
24 Grover Cleveland (7)	Mar. 4, 1893—Mar. 3, 1897	23 Adlai E. Stevenson	53, 54
25 William McKinley	Mar. 4, 1897—Mar. 3, 1901	24 Garret A. Hobart (9)	55, 56
"(4)	Mar. 4, 1901—Sept. 14, 1901	25 Theodore Roosevelt	57
26 Theodore Roosevelt	Sept. 14, 1901—Mar. 3, 1905		57, 58
"	Mar. 4, 1905—Mar. 3, 1909	26 Charles W. Fairbanks	59, 60
27 William H. Taft	Mar. 4, 1909—Mar. 3, 1913	27 James S. Sherman (10)	61, 62
28 Woodrow Wilson	Mar. 4, 1913—Mar. 3, 1921	28 Thomas R. Marshall	63, 64, 65, 66

(continued)

Presidents, Vice Presidents, Congresses (*continued*)

	President	Service		Vice President	Congress
29	Warren G. Harding (4)	Mar. 4, 1921—Aug. 2, 1923	29	Calvin Coolidge	67
30	Calvin Coolidge	Aug. 3, 1923—Mar. 3, 1925			68
	"	Mar. 4, 1925—Mar. 3, 1929	30	Charles G. Dawes	69, 70
31	Herbert C. Hoover	Mar. 4, 1929—Mar. 3, 1933	31	Charles Curtis	71, 72
32	Franklin D. Roosevelt (11)	Mar. 4, 1933—Jan. 20, 1941	32	John N. Garner	73, 74, 75, 76
	"	Jan. 20, 1941—Jan. 20, 1945	33	Henry A. Wallace	77, 78
	"(4)	Jan. 20, 1945—Apr. 12, 1945	34	Harry S. Truman	79
33	Harry S. Truman	Apr. 12, 1945—Jan. 20, 1949			79, 80
	"	Jan. 20, 1949—Jan. 20, 1953	35	Alben W. Barkley	81, 82
34	Dwight D. Eisenhower	Jan. 20, 1953—Jan. 20, 1961	36	Richard M. Nixon	83, 84, 85, 86
35	John F. Kennedy (4)	Jan. 20, 1961—Nov. 22, 1963	37	Lyndon B. Johnson	87, 88
36	Lyndon B. Johnson	Nov. 22, 1963—Jan. 20, 1965			88
	"	Jan. 20, 1965—Jan. 20, 1969	38	Hubert H. Humphrey	89, 90
37	Richard M. Nixon	Jan. 20, 1969—Jan. 20, 1973	39	Spiro T. Agnew (12)	91, 92, 93
	"(13)	Jan. 20, 1973—Aug. 9, 1974	40	Gerald R. Ford (14)	93
38	Gerald R. Ford (15)	Aug. 9, 1974—Jan. 20, 1977	41	Nelson A. Rockefeller (16)	93, 94
39	Jimmy (James Earl) Carter	Jan. 20, 1977—Jan. 20, 1981	42	Walter F. Mondale	95, 96
40	Ronald Reagan	Jan. 20, 1981—Jan. 20, 1989	43	George Bush	97, 98, 99, 100
41	George Bush	Jan. 20, 1989—Jan. 20, 1993	44	Dan Quayle	101, 102
42	Bill Clinton	Jan. 20, 1993—	45	Al Gore	103, 104

(1) Died Apr. 20, 1812. (2) Died Nov. 23, 1814. (3) Resigned Dec. 28, 1832, to become U.S. Senator. (4) Died in office. (5) Died Apr. 18, 1853. (6) Died Nov. 22, 1875. (7) Terms not consecutive. (8) Died Nov. 25, 1885. (9) Died Nov. 21, 1899. (10) Died Oct. 30, 1912. (11) First president to be inaugurated under 20th Amendment, Jan. 20, 1937. (12) Resigned Oct. 10, 1973. (13) Resigned Aug. 9, 1974. (14) First nonelected vice president, chosen under 25th Amendment. (15) First nonelected president. (16) second nonelected vice president, chosen under 25th Amendment procedure.

Vice Presidents of the U.S.

The numerals given vice presidents do not coincide with those given presidents, because some presidents had none and some had more than one.

	Name	Birthplace	Year	Home	Inaug.	Politics	Place of death	Year	Age
1	John Adams	Quincy, MA	1735	MA	1789	Fed.	Quincy, MA	1826	90
2	Thomas Jefferson	Shadwell, VA	1743	VA	1797	Dem.-Rep.	Monticello, VA	1826	83
3	Aaron Burr	Newark, NJ	1756	NY	1801	Dem.-Rep.	Staten Island, NY	1836	80
4	George Clinton	Ulster Co., NY	1739	NY	1805	Dem.-Rep.	Washington, DC	1812	73
5	Elbridge Gerry	Marblehead, MA	1744	MA	1813	Dem.-Rep.	Washington, DC	1814	70
6	Daniel D. Tompkins	Scarsdale, NY	1774	NY	1817	Dem.-Rep.	Staten Island, NY	1825	51
7	John C. Calhoun(1)	Abbeville, SC	1782	SC	1825	Dem.-Rep.	Washington, DC	1850	68
8	Martin Van Buren	Kinderhook, NY	1782	NY	1833	Dem.	Kinderhook, NY	1862	79
9	Richard M. Johnson(2)	Louisville, KY	1780	KY	1837	Dem.	Frankfort, KY	1850	70
10	John Tyler	Greenway, VA	1790	VA	1841	Whig	Richmond, VA	1862	71
11	George M. Dallas	Philadelphia, PA	1792	PA	1845	Dem.	Philadelphia, PA	1864	72
12	Millard Fillmore	Summerhill, NY	1800	NY	1849	Whig	Buffalo, NY	1874	74
13	William R. King	Sampson Co., NC	1786	AL	1853	Dem.	Dallas Co., AL	1853	67
14	John C. Breckinridge	Lexington, KY	1821	KY	1857	Dem.	Lexington, KY	1875	54
15	Hannibal Hamlin	Paris, ME	1809	ME	1861	Rep.	Bangor, ME	1891	81
16	Andrew Johnson	Raleigh, NC	1808	TN	1865	(3)	Carter Co., TN	1875	66
17	Schuyler Colfax	New York, NY	1823	IN	1869	Rep.	Mankato, MN	1885	62
18	Henry Wilson	Farmington, NH	1812	MA	1873	Rep.	Washington, DC	1875	63
19	William A. Wheeler	Malone, NY	1819	NY	1877	Rep.	Malone, NY	1887	68
20	Chester A. Arthur	Fairfield, VT	1830	NY	1881	Rep.	New York, NY	1886	57
21	Thomas A. Hendricks	Muskingum Co., OH	1819	IN	1885	Dem.	Indianapolis, IN	1885	66
22	Levi P. Morton	Shoreham, VT	1824	NY	1889	Rep.	Rhinebeck, NY	1920	96
23	Adlai E. Stevenson(4)	Christian Co., KY	1835	IL	1893	Dem.	Chicago, IL	1914	78
24	Garret A. Hobart	Long Branch, NJ	1844	NJ	1897	Rep.	Paterson, NJ	1899	55
25	Theodore Roosevelt	New York, NY	1858	NY	1901	Rep.	Oyster Bay, NY	1919	60
26	Charles W. Fairbanks	Unionville Centre, OH	1852	IN	1905	Rep.	Indianapolis, IN	1918	66
27	James S. Sherman	Utica, NY	1855	NY	1909	Rep.	Utica, NY	1912	57
28	Thomas R. Marshall	N. Manchester, IN	1854	IN	1913	Dem.	Washington, DC	1925	71
29	Calvin Coolidge	Plymouth, VT	1872	MA	1921	Rep.	Northampton, MA	1933	60
30	Charles G. Dawes	Marietta, OH	1865	IL	1925	Rep.	Evanston, IL	1951	85
31	Charles Curtis	Topeka, KS	1860	KS	1929	Rep.	Washington, DC	1936	76
32	John Nance Garner	Red River Co., TX	1868	TX	1933	Dem.	Uvalde, TX	1967	98
33	Henry Agard Wallace	Adair County, IA	1888	IA	1941	Dem.	Danbury, Conn.	1965	77
34	Harry S. Truman	Lamar, MO	1884	MO	1945	Dem.	Kansas City, MO	1972	88
35	Alben W. Barkley	Graves County, KY	1877	KY	1949	Dem.	Lexington, VA	1956	78
36	Richard M. Nixon	Yorba Linda, CA	1913	CA	1953	Rep.	New York, NY	1994	81
37	Lyndon B. Johnson	Johnson City, TX	1908	TX	1961	Dem.	San Antonio, TX	1973	64
38	Hubert H. Humphrey	Wallace, SD	1911	MN	1965	Dem.	Waverly, MN	1978	66
39	Spiro T. Agnew(5)	Baltimore, MD	1918	MD	1969	Rep.			
40	Gerald R. Ford(6)	Omaha, NE	1913	MI	1973	Rep.			
41	Nelson A. Rockefeller(7)	Bar Harbor, ME	1908	NY	1974	Rep.	New York, NY	1979	70
42	Walter F. Mondale	Ceylon, MN	1928	MN	1977	Dem.			
43	George Bush	Milton, MA	1924	TX	1981	Rep.			
44	Dan Quayle	Indianapolis, IN	1947	IN	1989	Rep.			
45	Al Gore	Washington, DC	1948	TN	1993	Dem.			

(1) John C. Calhoun resigned Dec. 28, 1832, having been elected to the Senate to fill a vacancy. (2) Richard M. Johnson was the first vice president to be chosen by the Senate due to a tied vote in the Electoral College. (3) Andrew Johnson was a Democrat, nominated vice president by Republicans, and elected with Lincoln on the National Union Ticket. (4) Adlai E. Stevenson, 23d vice president, was grandfather of Democratic candidate for president, 1952 and 1956. (5) Resigned Oct. 10, 1973. (6) First nonelected vice president, chosen under the 25th Amendment procedure. (7) Second nonelected vice president, chosen under the 25th Amendment procedure.

AFGHANISTAN ALBANIA ALGERIA ANDORRA ANGOLA

ANTIGUA AND BARBUDA ARGENTINA ARMENIA AUSTRALIA AUSTRIA

AZERBAIJAN THE BAHAMAS BAHRAIN BANGLADESH BARBADOS

BELARUS BELGIUM BELIZE BENIN BHUTAN

BOLIVIA BOSNIA AND HERZEGOVINA BOTSWANA BRAZIL BRUNEI

BULGARIA BURKINA FASO BURUNDI CAMBODIA CAMEROON

CANADA CAPE VERDE CENTRAL AFRICAN REPUBLIC CHAD CHILE

CHINA COLOMBIA COMOROS CONGO COSTA RICA

COTE D'IVOIRE CROATIA CUBA CYPRUS CZECH REPUBLIC

DENMARK DJIBOUTI DOMINICA DOMINICAN REPUBLIC ECUADOR

EGYPT EL SALVADOR EQUATORIAL GUINEA ERITREA ESTONIA

ETHIOPIA
FIJI
FINLAND
FRANCE
GABON

THE GAMBIA
GEORGIA
GERMANY
GHANA
GREECE

GRENADA
GUATEMALA
GUINEA
GUINEA-BISSAU
GUYANA

HAITI
HONDURAS
HUNGARY
ICELAND
INDIA

INDONESIA
IRAN
IRAQ
IRELAND
ISRAEL

ITALY
JAMAICA
JAPAN
JORDAN
KAZAKHSTAN

KENYA
KIRIBATI
NORTH KOREA
SOUTH KOREA
KUWAIT

KYRGYZSTAN
LAOS
LATVIA
LEBANON
LESOTHO

LIBERIA
LIBYA
LIECHTENSTEIN
LITHUANIA
LUXEMBOURG

MACEDONIA
MADAGASCAR
MALAWI
MALAYSIA
MALDIVES

MALI
MALTA
MARSHALL ISLANDS
MAURITANIA
MAURITIUS

MEXICO

MICRONESIA, FEDERATED STATES OF

MOLDOVA

MONACO

MONGOLIA

MOROCCO

MOZAMBIQUE

MYANMAR (BURMA)

NAMIBIA

NAURU

NEPAL

NETHERLANDS

NEW ZEALAND

NICARAGUA

NIGER

NIGERIA

NORWAY

OMAN

PAKISTAN

PALAU

PANAMA

PAPUA NEW GUINEA

PARAGUAY

PERU

PHILIPPINES

POLAND

PORTUGAL

QATAR

ROMANIA

RUSSIA

RWANDA

ST. KITTS AND NEVIS

ST. LUCIA

ST. VINCENT AND THE GRENADINES

SAN MARINO

SAO TOME AND PRINCIPE

SAUDI ARABIA

SENEGAL

SEYCHELLES

SIERRA LEONE

SINGAPORE

SLOVAKIA

SLOVENIA

SOLOMON ISLANDS

SOMALIA

SOUTH AFRICA

SPAIN

SRI LANKA

SUDAN

SURINAME

SWAZILAND

SWEDEN

SWITZERLAND

SYRIA

TAIWAN

TAJIKISTAN	TANZANIA	THAILAND	TOGO	TONGA
TRINIDAD AND TOBAGO	TUNISIA	TURKEY	TURKMENISTAN	TUVALU
UGANDA	UKRAINE	UNITED ARAB EMIRATES	UNITED KINGDOM	UNITED STATES
URUGUAY	UZBEKISTAN	VANUATU	VATICAN CITY	VENEZUELA
VIETNAM	WESTERN SAMOA	YEMEN	YUGOSLAVIA	ZAIRE
ZAMBIA	ZIMBABWE			

INTERNATIONAL TIME ZONES

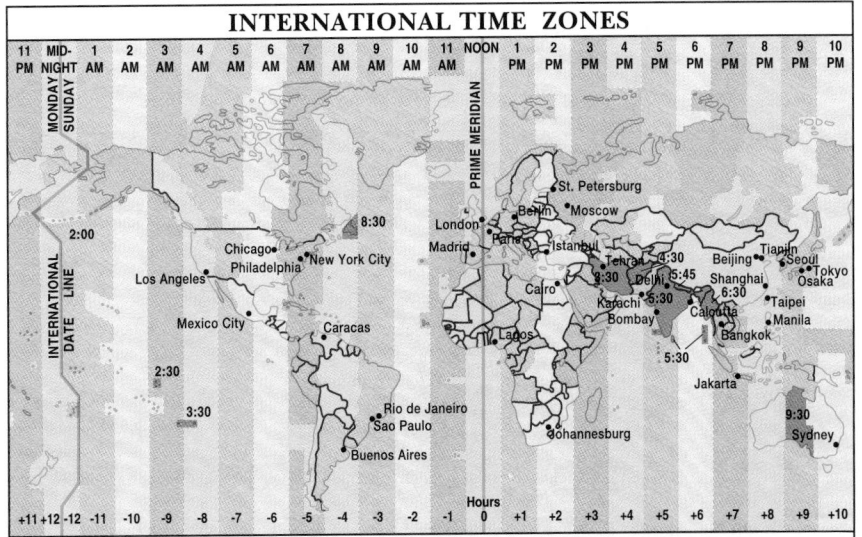

The world is divided into 24 time zones, each 15° longitude wide. The longitudinal meridian passing through Greenwich, England, is the starting point, and is called the *prime meridian*. The 12th zone is divided by the 180th meridian (International Date Line). When the line is crossed going west, the date is advanced one day; when crossed going east, the date becomes a day earlier.

© The World Almanac and Book of Facts

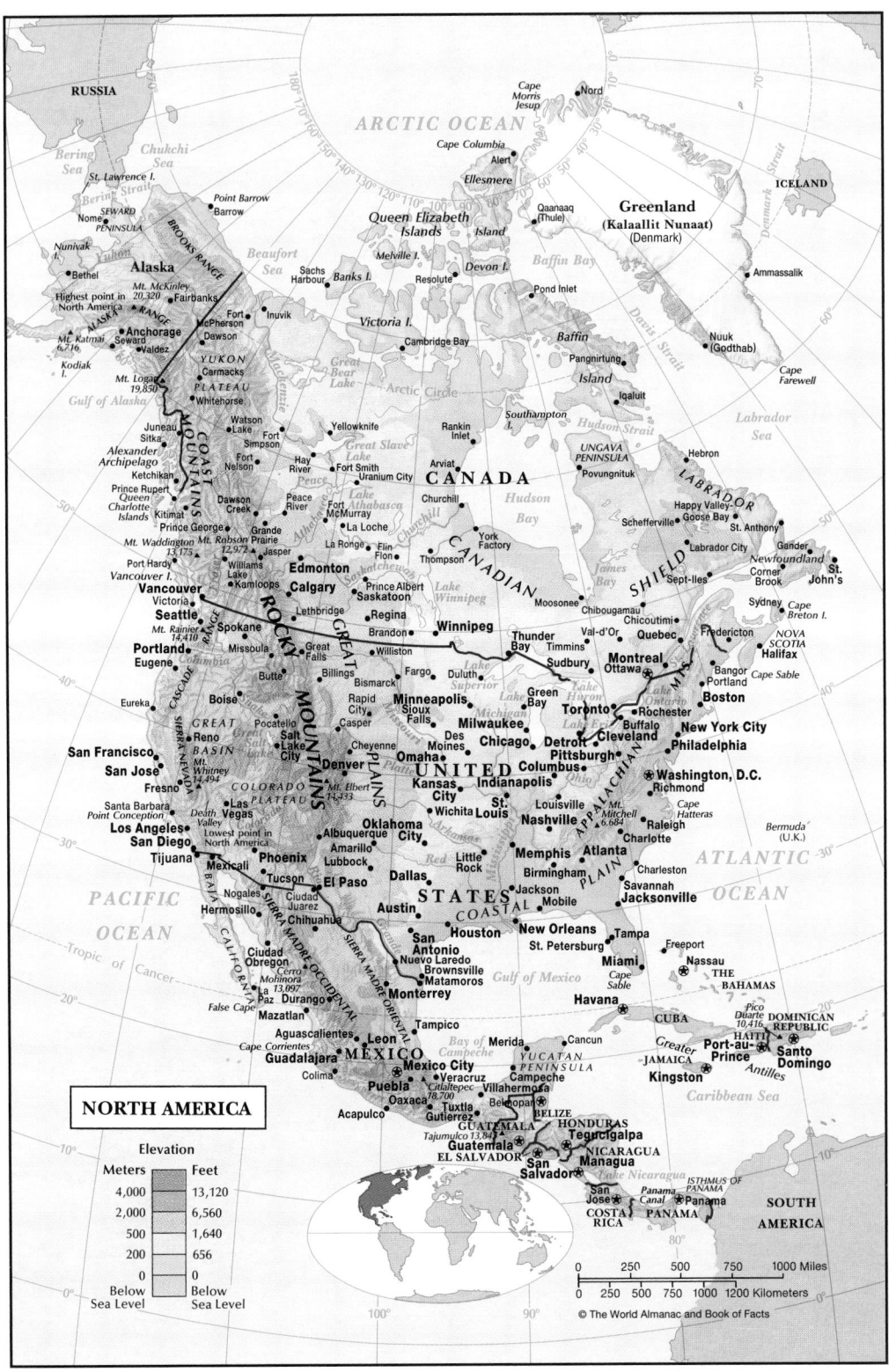

NORTH AMERICA

Elevation

Meters		Feet
4,000		13,120
2,000		6,560
500		1,640
200		656
0		0
Below Sea Level		Below Sea Level

0   250   500   750   1000 Miles

0   250   500   1000   1200 Kilometers

© The World Almanac and Book of Facts

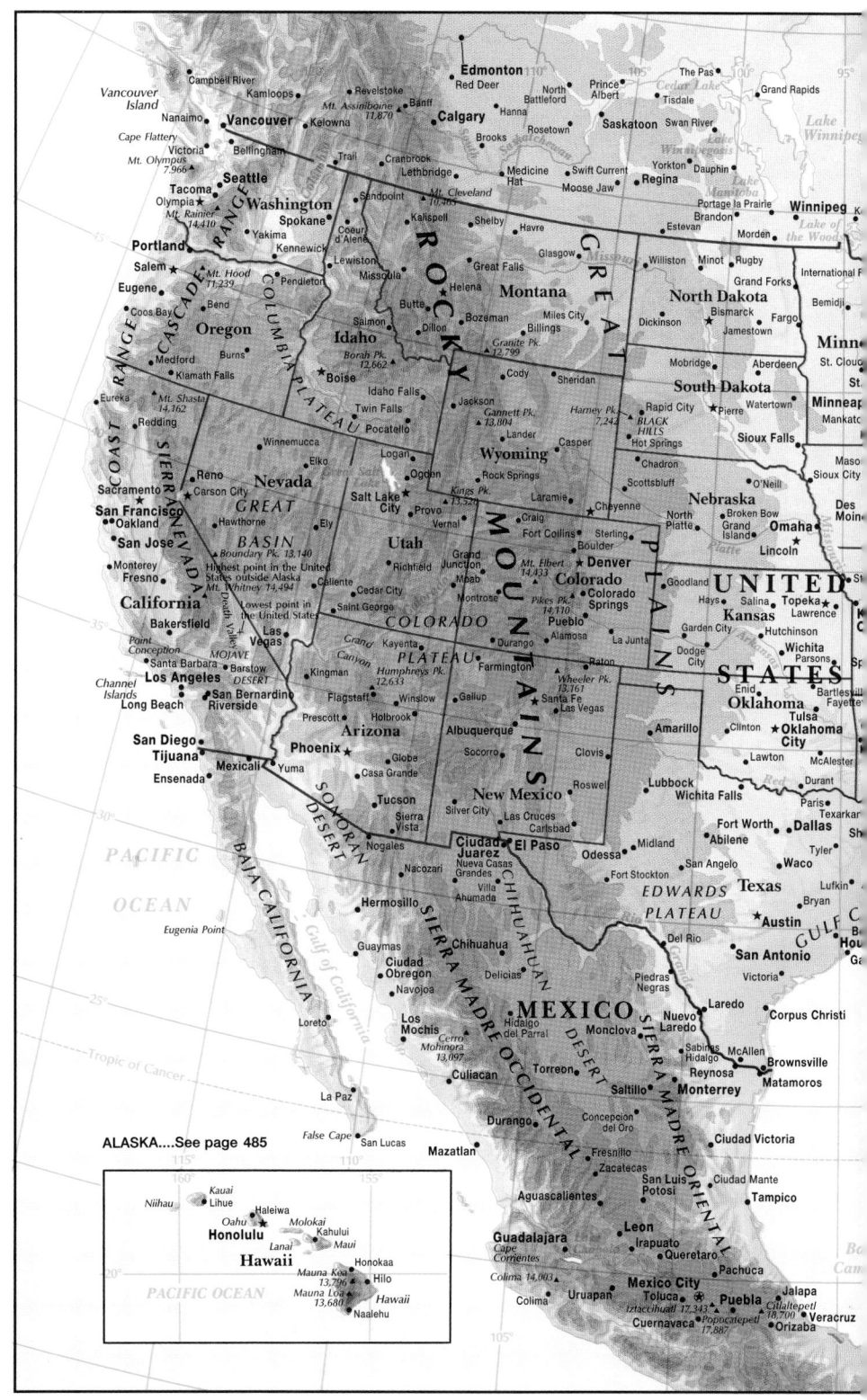

ALASKA....See page 485

UNITED STATES, CANADA, MEXICO

Elevation

Meters		Feet
2,000		6,560
1,000		3,280
500		1,640
200		656
0		0
Below Sea Level		Below Sea Level

© The World Almanac and Book of Facts

0   250   500 Miles

0   250   500   750 Kilometers

(Map labels, reading generally from north to south and west to east:)

CANADIAN SHIELD
NADA
James Bay
Moosonee
Waskaganish
85° 80° 75° 70°
Sept-Iles
Port-Cartier
Anticosti I.
60°
Channel-Port aux Basques
Gulf of St. Lawrence
Gaspé
Cape Breton I.
Baie-Comeau
Matane
Causapscal
Prince Edward I.
Cape Breton I.
Chibougamau
Dalhousie
Bathurst
Charlottetown
Sydney
45°
Geraldton
Hearst
Kapuskasing
Matagami
Mistassini
Alma
Chicoutimi
Rimouski
Newcastle
Edmundston
Grand Falls
Moncton
New Glasgow
Amherst
Canso
pigon
Marathon
Iroquois Falls
Timmins
Rouyn-Noranda
Val-d'Or
Riviere-du-Loup
Caribou
Houlton
Fredericton
Truro
Dartmouth
Wawa
Kirkland Lake
New Liskeard
Quebec
St. Georges
Mt. Katahdin 5,267
Saint John
Calais
Halifax
Chapleau
Mont-Laurier
Shawinigan
Trois-Rivieres
Sherbrooke
Maine
Bangor
Digby
Shelburne
Sault Ste. Marie
Sudbury
North Bay
Deep River
Montreal
Cornwall
Mt. Washington 6,288
Montpelier
Vt. N.H.
Augusta
Bar Harbor
Yarmouth
Cape Sable
Marquette
Elliot Lake
Pembroke
Hull
Ottawa
Burlington
Rutland
Portland
Iron Mountain
Cheboygan
Parry Sound
Bracebridge
Kingston
Peterborough
New York
ADIRONDACK MTS.
Concord
Manchester
Portsmouth
nsin
Wausau
Alpena
Traverse City
Owen Sound
Barrie
Oshawa
Toronto
Syracuse
Albany
Springfield
Boston
Cape Cod
een Bay
Michigan
Kitchener
Hamilton
London
Rochester
Mass.
New Bedford
appleton
Saginaw
Flint
Buffalo
Niagara Falls
Hartford
R.I.
Providence
osse
Grand Rapids
Lansing
Windsor
Binghamton
Scranton
New Haven
Conn.
Madison
Iwaukee
Detroit
Erie
Cleveland
Pa.
Allentown
New York City
Long I.
Long Island Sound
Rockford
Kalamazoo
Youngstown
Trenton N.J.
Chicago
South Bend
Toledo
Akron
Altoona
Harrisburg
Philadelphia
avenport
Gary
Fort Wayne
Mansfield
Wheeling
Pittsburgh
Del.
Wilmington
Rock Island
Peoria
Indiana
Ohio
Dayton
Columbus
Hagerstown
Md.
Dover
Baltimore
Champaign
Muncie
Parkersburg
Spruce Knob 4,861
W.Va.
Washington
Annapolis
Salisbury
Springfield
Indianapolis
Cincinnati
D.C.
Chesapeake Bay
Illinois
Bloomington
Frankfort
Huntington
Richmond
Charlottesville
St. Louis
Louisville
Lexington
Virginia
Newport News
Carbondale
Owensboro
Roanoke
Norfolk
Cape deau
Evansville
Kentucky
Greensboro
Bluff
Paducah
Bowling Green
Johnson City
Raleigh
North Carolina
Cape Hatteras
Nashville
Knoxville
Winston-Salem
Fayetteville
New Bern
Jackson
Asheville
Mt. Mitchell 6,684
Charlotte
Tennessee
Chattanooga
Greenville
Wilmington
Memphis
Huntsville
Columbia
Florence
Tupelo
Gadsden
Athens
South Carolina
Columbus
Birmingham
Atlanta
Augusta
Charleston
Greenville
Tuscaloosa
Macon
Mississippi
Meridian
Montgomery
Georgia
Savannah
Jackson
Alabama
Dothan
Albany
Valdosta
Brunswick
atchez
Hattiesburg
Mobile
Pensacola
Tallahassee
Jacksonville
LAIN
Baton Rouge
Biloxi
Panama City
St. Augustine
ette
New Orleans
Gainesville
Daytona Beach
Morgan City
Orlando
Cape Canaveral
Melbourne
Tampa
St. Petersburg
Florida
West Palm Beach
Sarasota
Lake Okeechobee
Fort Lauderdale
Fort Myers
Miami
ATLANTIC OCEAN
35°
Cape Sable
THE BAHAMAS
ulf of Mexico
Key West
Florida Keys
Straits of Florida
25°
CUBA
20°
DOMINICAN REPUBLIC
HAITI
Cancun
Merida
Cozumel I.
JAMAICA
15°
eche
YUCATAN PENINSULA
90° 85° 80° 75° 70°

APPALACHIAN MOUNTAINS
ATLANTIC COASTAL PLAIN
Lake Superior
Lake Michigan
Lake Huron
Lake Erie
Lake Ontario
NOVA SCOTIA
40°
30°

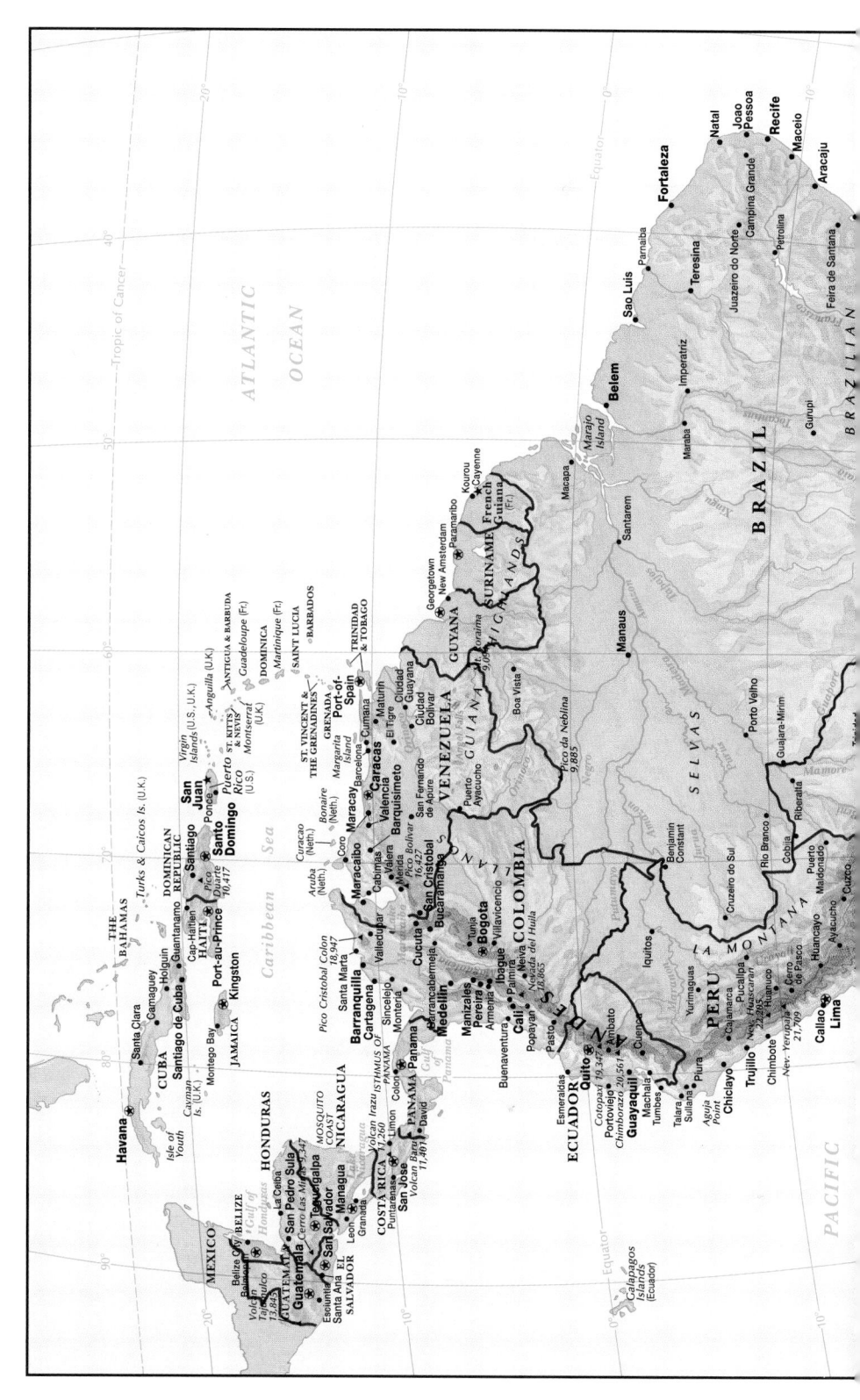

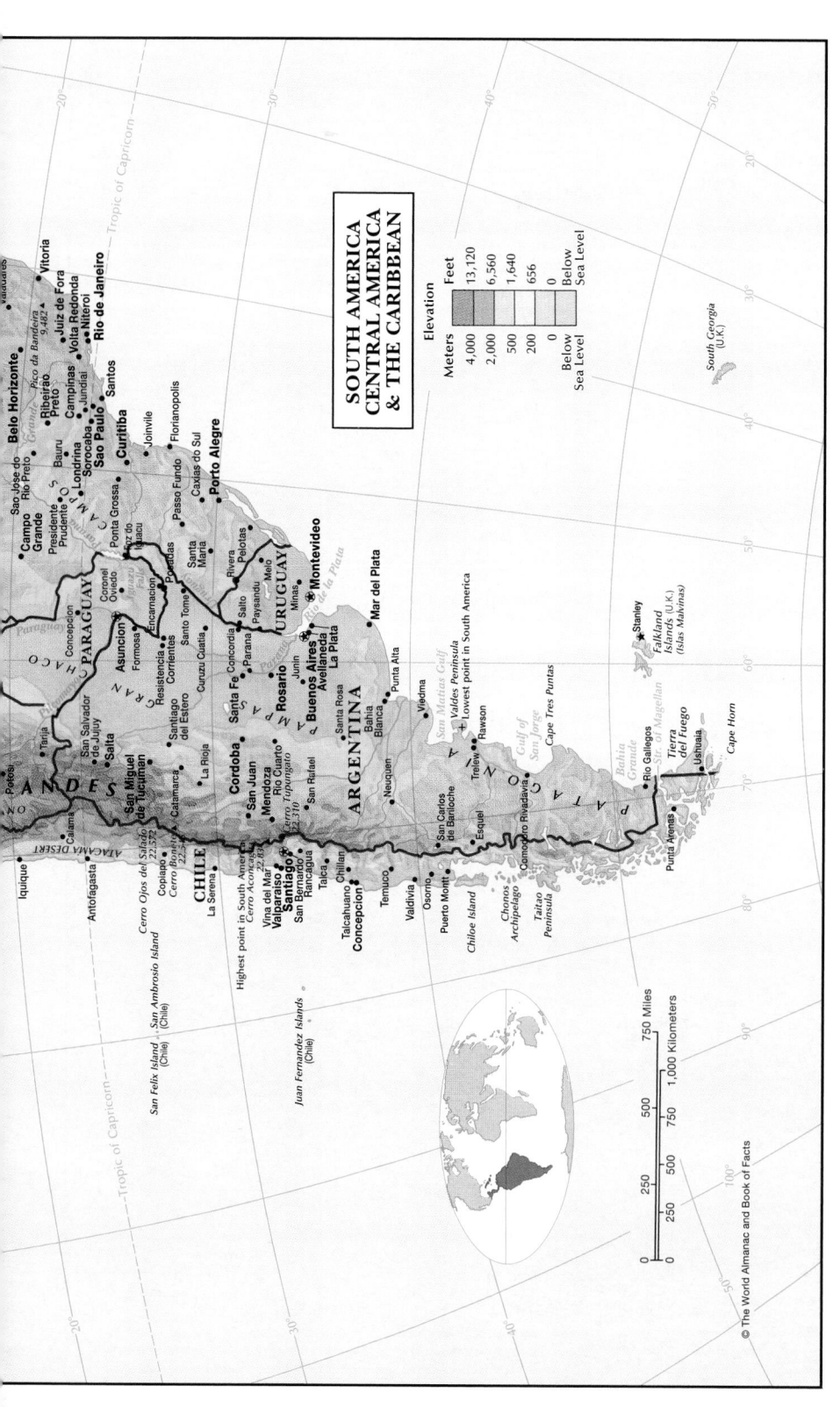

SOUTH AMERICA
CENTRAL AMERICA
& THE CARIBBEAN

Elevation

Meters	Feet
4,000	13,120
2,000	6,560
500	1,640
200	656
0	0
Below Sea Level	Below Sea Level

Tropic of Capricorn

Pico da Bandeira 9,462 ▲

Vitoria
Juiz de Fora
Volta Redonda
Niteroi
Rio de Janeiro
Campinas
Ribeirão
Preto
Jundiai
Sorocaba
Santos
Belo Horizonte
São Paulo
Bauru
Londrina
Curitiba
Sao Jose do Rio Preto
Presidente Prudente
Joinville
Campo Grande
Ponta Grossa
Florianopolis
Porto Alegre
Caxias do Sul
Passo Fundo

PARAGUAY
Concepcion
Asuncion
Coronel Oviedo
Encarnacion
Formosa
Resistencia
Corrientes
Santo Tome
Curuzu Cuatia
Santa Maria
Pelotas
Rivera
Salto
Paysandu
Mercedes
Minas
Santa Fe
Paraná
Concordia
Rosario
Junin
Avellaneda
La Plata
URUGUAY
Montevideo
Mar del Plata

ANDES
Cerro Ojos del Salado 22,572
Cerro Bonete 22,546
Cerro Tupungato 22,310
Cerro Aconcagua
Highest point in South America
Catamarca
La Rioja
San Miguel de Tucuman
Santiago del Estero
Salta
San Salvador de Jujuy
Tarija
Cordoba
San Juan
Mendoza
Rio Cuarto
San Rafael
Santa Rosa
Neuquen
Viedma

CHILE
Iquique
Antofagasta
Copiapo
La Serena
Vina del Mar
Valparaiso
Santiago
San Bernardo
Rancagua
Talca
Chillan
Talcahuano
Concepcion
Temuco
Valdivia
Osorno
Puerto Montt

ARGENTINA
Bahia Blanca
Punta Alta

ATACAMA DESERT
San Felix Island (Chile)
San Ambrosio Island (Chile)

Juan Fernandez Islands (Chile)

PAMPAS
GRAN CHACO

Valdes Peninsula
Lowest point in South America
San Matias Gulf
Gulf of San Jorge
Rawson
Trelew
Comodoro Rivadavia
Esquel
San Carlos de Bariloche
Bahia Grande
PATAGONIA
Cape Tres Puntas
Rio Gallegos
Punta Arenas
Str. of Magellan
Tierra del Fuego
Ushuaia
Cape Horn

Chiloe Island
Chonos Archipelago
Taitao Peninsula

Stanley
Falkland Islands (U.K.)
(Islas Malvinas)

South Georgia (U.K.)

Tropic of Capricorn

| 0 | 250 | 500 | 750 Miles |
| 0 | 250 | 500 | 750 | 1,000 Kilometers |

© The World Almanac and Book of Facts

20°
30°
40°
50°
60°
70°
80°
90°
100°

EUROPE

Elevation

Meters		Feet
4,000		13,120
2,000		6,560
500		1,640
200		656
0		0
Below Sea Level		Below Sea Level

Greenland
(Kalaallit Nunaat)
(Denmark)

ATLANTIC
OCEAN

Arctic Circle

Norwegian
Sea

ICELAND
Keflavik Akureyri
Reykjavik ▲ Hekla
4,892

Faeroe Is.
(Den.)

Shetland Is.
(U.K.)

Orkney Is.

Hebrides

North
Sea

Inverness
Aberdeen
Dundee
Edinburgh

Glasgow
Belfast
IRELAND UNITED
Dublin KINGDOM
Cork Limerick Liverpool Leeds
Manchester Sheffield
Birmingham
Cardiff
Bristol London
Land's End
Plymouth Portsmouth
English Channel
Channel Is. Le Havre
(U.K.) Brest Rouen

Hammerfest
Tromso North Cape
Murmansk
Ivalo
Bodo Kiruna LAPLAND
Rovaniemi Arkhangelsk
Lulea Belomorsk
Oulu
Umea Petrozavodsk
NORWAY Trondheim
FINLAND
Ostersund Kuopio Lake Ladoga
Alesund
Galdhopiggen SWEDEN Vaasa
8,098 Tampere
Bergen Gavle Turku Helsinki
Aland St. Petersburg
Stavanger Oslo Is. Tallinn Novgorod
Skien Uppsala (Fin.) ESTONIA
Kristiansand Stockholm RUSSIA
Linkoping Tartu
Jonkoping Gotland Riga LATVIA
Alborg Goteborg (Swe.) Daugavpils Smolensk
Jutland Klaipeda LITHUANIA
Copenhagen Helsingborg Bornholm RUSSIA Kaunas Vilnius Vitsyebsk
DENMARK Odense Malmo (Den.) Gdansk Kaliningrad Minsk Mahilyow
Hamburg Rostock Szczecin BELARUS Bryansk
Bremen Berlin POLAND Bialystok Homyel
NETHERLANDS Hannover Magdeburg Poznan Warsaw Brest
Amsterdam Bremen Leipzig Lodz Kiev
Hague Essen Dresden Wroclaw Lublin UKRAINE
Rotterdam Cologne GERMANY Katowice Lviv
Antwerp Bonn Prague Kracow Vynnytsya
BELGIUM Frankfurt CZECH REP. Ostrava CARPATHIAN MOUNTAINS
Brussels Luxembourg Brno Kosice MOLDOVA
Paris LUX. Mannheim SLOVAKIA Debrecen Iasi Chisinau
Nurnberg Bratislava Odesa
Strasbourg Stuttgart Linz Miskolc
Orleans Munich Vienna HUNGARY Cluj-Napoca
FRANCE Dijon Zurich Salzburg AUSTRIA Budapest ROMANIA Brasov
Nantes Basel SWITZ. Graz Pecs Timisoara Bucharest
Tours Geneva Mt. Blanc SLOV. CROATIA Belgrade Constanta
Limoges Lyon 15,771 Ljubljana Zagreb BOS. & SERBIA Ruse
Bordeaux Grenoble Milan Trieste HERZ. YUGO. BALKAN Varna
Turin Verona Venice Sarajevo Bucharest Burgas
PYRENEES Nice Genoa Bologna Split MONT. BULGARIA
La Coruna Pico de MONACO APENNINES Dubrovnik Skopje Sofia Plovdiv Black Sea
Vigo Aneto Marseille Florence SAN MACE. Thessaloniki
Oporto 11,168 Corsica MARINO Tirane Larisa TURKEY
Gijon ANDORRA (Fr.) Rome ALBANIA Volos
Coimbra Bilbao Zaragoza Elba ITALY Vlora GREECE
San Sebastian Barcelona Ajaccio Naples Bari Olympus Athens
PORTUGAL Valladolid IBERIAN Vesuvius 9,570 Patras
Lisbon SPAIN Madrid 4,202 Corfu Peloponnesus
PENINSULA Valencia Palma Sardinia Ionian
Cordoba Balearic Is. (It.) Sea Rhodes
Cape Seville Granada (Sp.) Cagliari Tyrrhenian Iraklion
St. Vincent Alicante Sea Palermo Messina Crete
Cadiz Gibraltar Etna Catania
Malaga (U.K.) 11,053 MALTA
Strait of Sicily
Gibraltar Mediterranean Sea

Bay of
Biscay

Gulf of Bothnia

Baltic Sea

Gulf of Finland

Adriatic Sea

Aegean Sea

AFRICA

0		250		500 Miles
0	250		500	750 Kilometers

© The World Almanac and Book of Facts

490

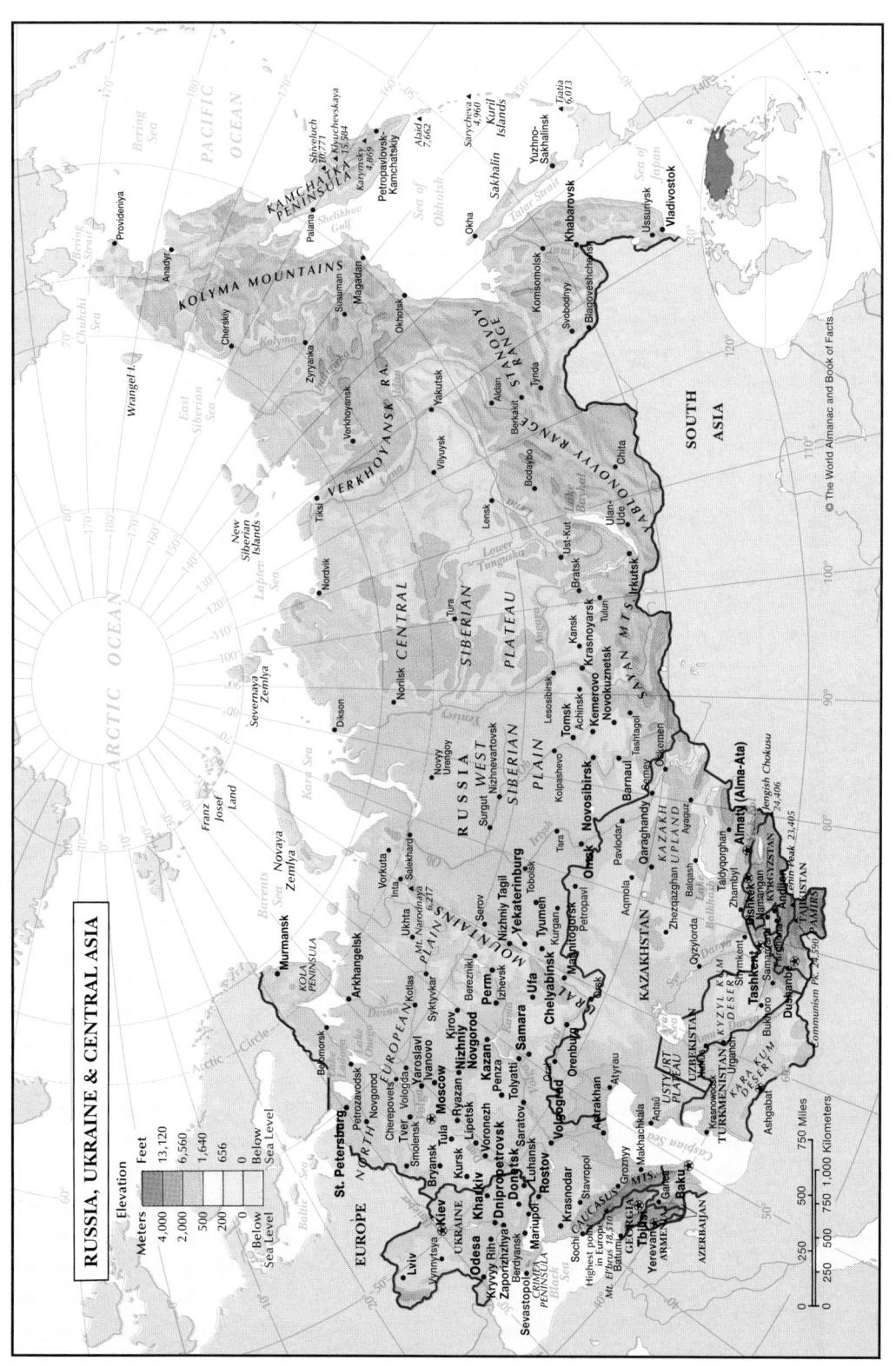

RUSSIA, UKRAINE & CENTRAL ASIA

Elevation

Meters	Feet
4,000	13,120
2,000	6,560
500	1,640
200	656
0	0
Below Sea Level	Below Sea Level

© The World Almanac and Book of Facts.

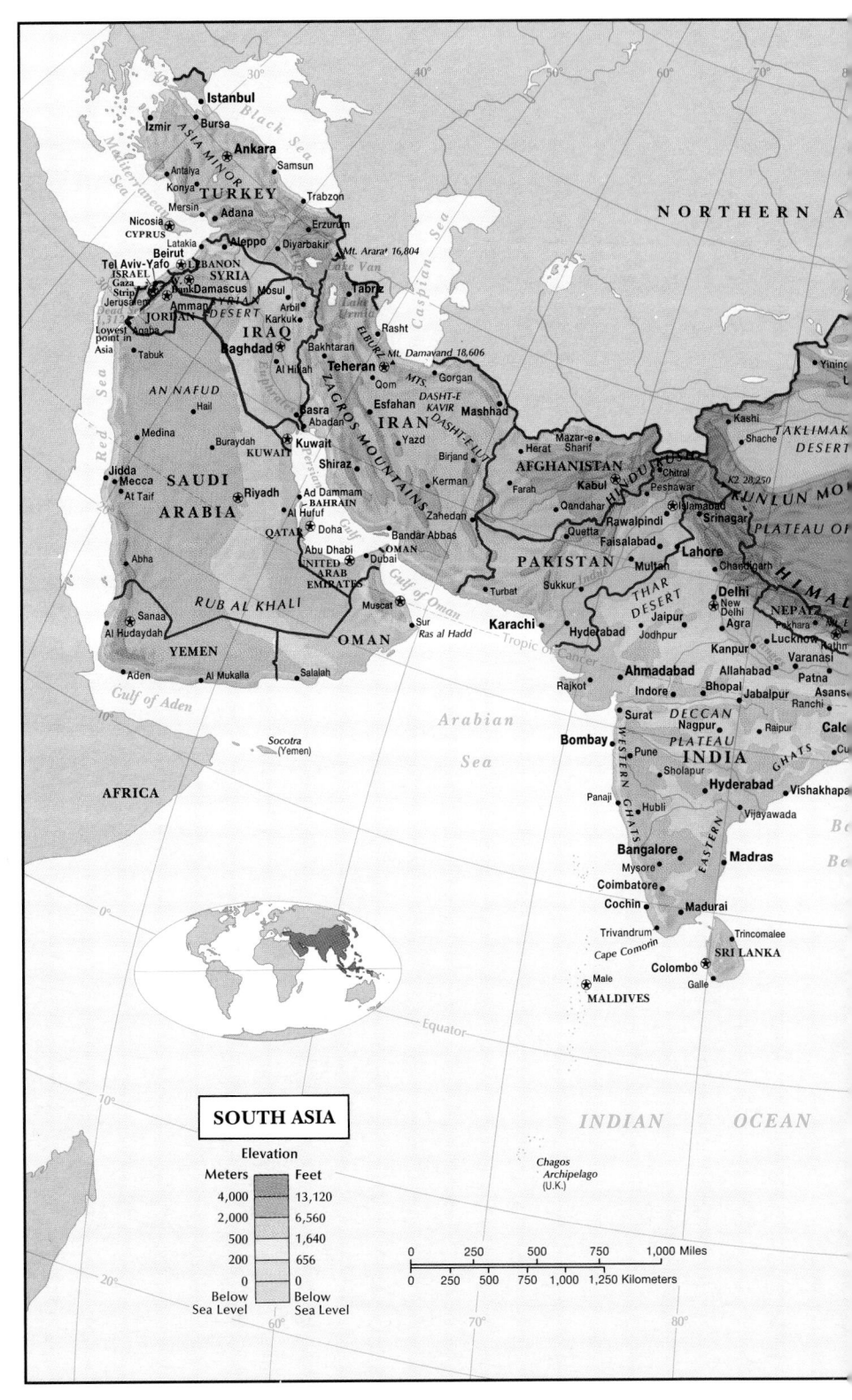

SOUTH ASIA

Elevation

Meters		Feet
4,000		13,120
2,000		6,560
500		1,640
200		656
0		0
Below Sea Level		Below Sea Level

Chagos Archipelago (U.K.)

0   250   500   750   1,000 Miles

0   250   500   750   1,000   1,250 Kilometers

INDIAN   OCEAN

Istanbul
Izmir   Bursa
Ankara   *Black Sea*
Antalya   *ASIA MINOR*   Samsun
Konya   **TURKEY**   Trabzon
Mersin   Adana
Nicosia   Erzurum
CYPRUS   Diyarbakir   *Mt. Ararat 16,804*
Latakia   Aleppo   *Lake Van*
Beirut   *Caspian Sea*
Tel Aviv-Yafo   **LEBANON**   Mosul   **Tabriz**
ISRAEL   **SYRIA**   Arbil   *Lake Urmia*
Gaza Strip   Damascus   Karkuk
Jerusalem   Amman   *SYRIAN DESERT*   Rasht   *ELBURZ MTS.*   *Mt. Damavand 18,606*
Lowest point in Asia   **JORDAN**   **IRAQ**   **Baghdad**   Bakhtaran   **Teheran**   Yining
Aqaba   Tabuk   Al Hillah   Qom   Gorgan   Kashi   *TAKLIMAK*
AN NAFUD   Hail   *MTS.*   Shache   *DESERT*
Medina   Basra   Esfahan   Mashhad   *DASHT-E KAVIR*
Buraydah   Abadan   **IRAN**   *DASHT-E LUT*   Herat   Mazar-e Sharif   *HINDU KUSH*   K2 28,250   *KUNLUN MO*
Jidda   **KUWAIT**   **Kuwait**   Yazd   **AFGHANISTAN**   Chitral   Srinagar   *PLATEAU OF*
Mecca   **Shiraz**   Birjand   Kabul   Peshawar   Islamabad   *HIMAL*
At Taif   **SAUDI**   Riyadh   Ad Dammam   Kerman   Farah   Qandahar   Rawalpindi   Lahore
ARABIA   Al Hufuf   **BAHRAIN**   Zahedan   Quetta   **PAKISTAN**   Chandigarh
Abha   **QATAR**   Doha   Bandar Abbas   Faisalabad   **Delhi**   **NEPAL**
UNITED   ARAB   EMIRATES   Abu Dhabi   Dubai   **OMAN**   Multan   New Delhi   Pokhara
RUB AL KHALI   Muscat   Turbat   *THAR DESERT*   Agra   Kathm
Sur   Sukkur   Jaipur   Kanpur   Lucknow   Varanasi
Sanaa   Ras al Hadd   *Tropic of Cancer*   **Karachi**   **Hyderabad**   Jodhpur   Patna
Al Hudaydah   **OMAN**   Salalah   **Ahmadabad**   Allahabad   Asans
YEMEN   Al Mukalla   Rajkot   Indore   Bhopal   Jabalpur   Ranchi
Aden   *Arabian*   Surat   *DECCAN*   Nagpur   Raipur   Calc   Cu
Gulf of Aden   *Sea*   **Bombay**   *PLATEAU*   **INDIA**
Socotra   Pune   Sholapur   **Hyderabad**   Vishakhapa
(Yemen)   Panaji   Hubli   Vijayawada   *Be*
AFRICA   *WESTERN GHATS*   *EASTERN GHATS*   *Be*
Bangalore   **Madras**
Mysore
Coimbatore
Cochin   Madurai
Trivandrum   Trincomalee
Cape Comorin   **SRI LANKA**
Male   **Colombo**
Galle
MALDIVES

Equator

NORTHERN A

Mediterranean Sea   *Red Sea*   *Gulf of Oman*   *Persian Gulf*   *Euphrates*   *Tigris*   *Dead Sea*

MONGOLIA

Moron · · Darhan Choybalsan
· ❄Ulaanbaatar
MONGOLIAN
Bayanhongor PLATEAU
MOUNTAINS
GOBI DESERT

GREATER KHINGAN RANGE

Amur

Hailar Qiqihar Yichun
Jixi
Harbin
Changchun Jilin
Chongjin
Fushun
Shenyang
Anshan
Hamhung
Luda Inchon Seoul
· Hohhot ❄**Beijing**
Baotou · Datong · **Tianjin**
Taiyuan Shijiazhuang Jinan
Yinchuan Handan

Yumen
· Golmud
Xining · Lanzhou
CHINA Xian
Luoyang
Xuzhou
Zhengzhou
Huainan
Hefei

Nanjing
Shanghai
Hangzhou

Chengdu
Wuhan
Jingdezhen Wenzhou

Zigong
Chongqing
Changsha
Nanchang

Shaoyang Hengyang **Fuzhou**
Guiyang Ganzhou Xiamen
Guilin ❄**Taipei**
TAIWAN
Liuzhou
Kunming
Nanning **Canton**
Macau **(Guangzhou)**
(Port.) **Kaohsiung**
Zhanjiang **Hong Kong**
(U.K.)

Hokkaido
· Sapporo
Hakodate

Akita
· Sendai
Niigata **JAPAN**
Kanazawa **Tokyo**
Yokohama
Fuji-san 12,388
Kyoto **Nagoya**
Kobe **Osaka**
Hiroshima Shikoku
Kitakyushu
Fukuoka
Nagasaki Kyushu
Kagoshima

Sea of
Japan

N. KOREA
Pyongyang
S.KOREA
Taegu
Pusan
Cheju I.

Yellow
Sea

East China
Sea

Ryukyu Is.

PACIFIC

Okinawa
Naha

Tropic of Cancer

OCEAN

Iwo Jima
(Japan)

Philippine
Sea

Laoag Luzon
Baguio

PHILIPPINES
Quezon City
Manila Naga
Samar
Mindoro Tacloban
Iloilo Leyte
Panay **Cebu**
Negros Butuan
Mindanao
Puerto Princesa Davao
Palawan
Zamboanga

BANMAR
Mandalay
Taunggyi

Hsongsali Haiphong
Hanoi Haikou
Louangphrabang Hainan
Vinh (China)
Chiang Hue
Mai Vientiane Da Nang
LAOS
THAILAND
❄**Yangon**
Moulmein
Nakhon Bawan Nakhon
Ratchasima **VIETNAM**
Tavoy Nha Trang
CAMBODIA
Bangkok Batdambang
Sattahip Phnom
Penh
Kompong Som **Ho Chi Minh City**
Can Tho
Phuket
Gulf of
Tonkin

Gulf of
Thailand
Isthmus
of Kra

South

China

Sea

Sandakan

Celebes
Sea

Manado
Ternate
Gorontalo

Halmahera

New
Guinea

equator

Molucccas

Ceram
Ambon

Banda

Sea

Hat Yai
Nicobar
Islands
(India)
Acen
George Town
MALAYSIA Natuna
Medan Is.
Kelang ❄**Kuala Lumpur**
Sibolga **Singapore**
SINGAPORE
Pekanbaru
Padang
Jambi
Sumatra
Bengkulu
Bandar Lampung
Bandand
Bandung

Bandar Seri Begawan
BRUNEI
Tarakan

MALAYSIA
Kuching Sibu

Pontianak
Borneo Balikpapan
Sampit
Banjarmasin
Samarinda

Celebes
Palopo

Parepare
Baubau
Ujungpandang

Java
Sea

I N D O N E S I A

Semarang
❄**Jakarta** Surabaya
Yogyakarta Java Malang Bali
Mataram
Sumba

Ende
Timor
Dili

Kupang

Timor

Sea

AUSTRALIA

Andaman
Sea

100° 110° 120° 130°

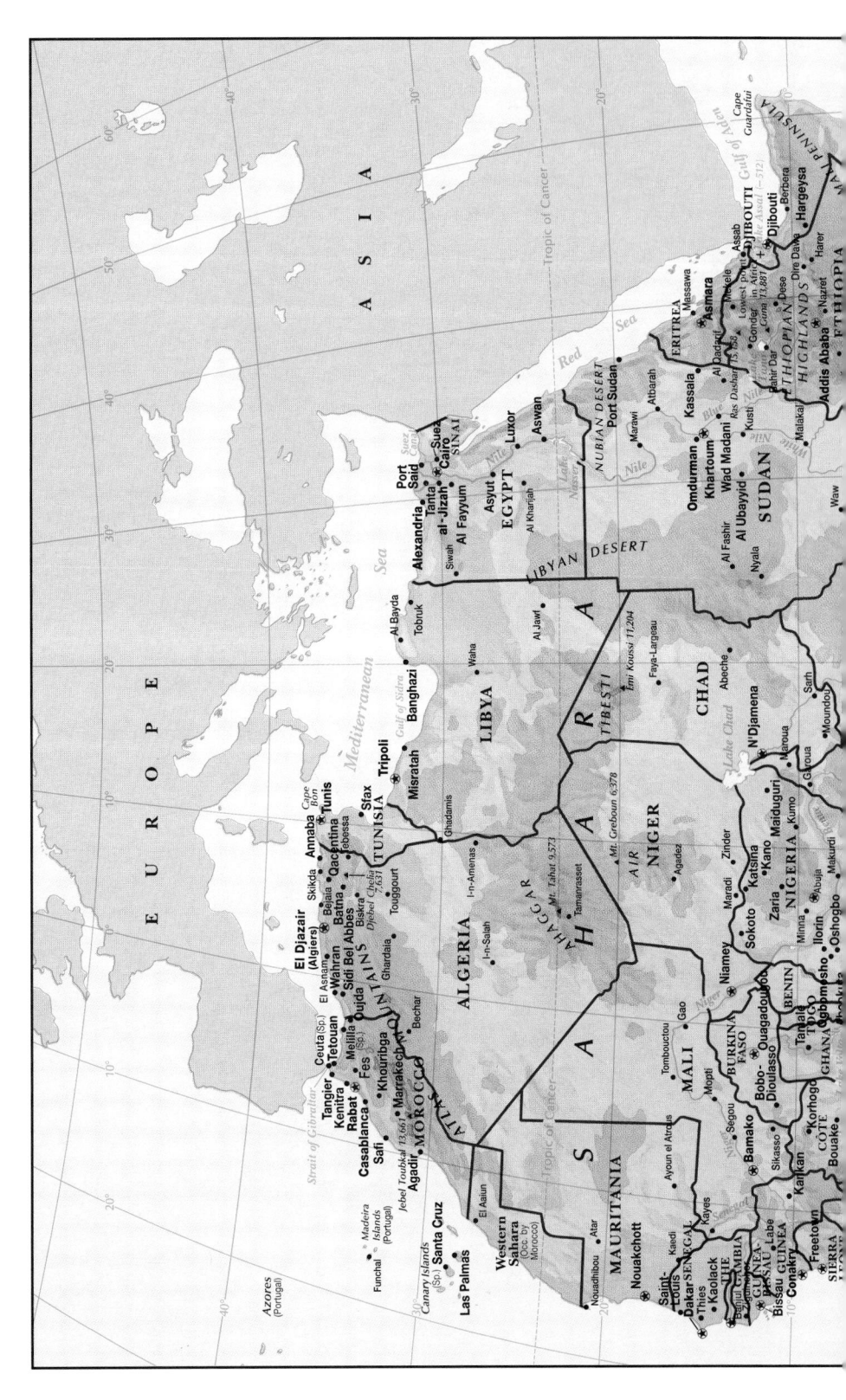

ASIA

EUROPE

Azores
(Portugal)

Madeira
Islands
(Portugal)
Funchal

Canary Islands
(Sp.) Santa Cruz
Las Palmas

Strait of Gibraltar

Tropic of Cancer

Mediterranean Sea

Red Sea

Tangier
Ceuta (Sp.)
Tetouan
Melilla
Kenitra
Rabat
Casablanca
Safi
Khouribga
Marrakech
Agadir
Jebel Toubkal 13,661

ATLAS MOUNTAINS

MOROCCO

El Djazair
(Algiers)
El Asnam
Wahran
Sidi Bel Abbes
Oujda
Fes

Skikda
Bejaïa
Batna
Biskra
Djebel Chélia
7,637
Touggourt

Annaba
Cape
Bon
Constantine
Tebessa

Tunis
TUNISIA

Sfax

Tripoli
Misratah

Ghardaia
Bechar
In-Salah

In-Amenas

Ghadamis

LIBYA

Banghazi

Gulf of Sidra

Waha

Al Bayda
Tobruk

Alexandria
Port
Said
Tanta
al-Jizah
Cairo
Suez
SINAI
Al Fayyum
Asyut
EGYPT
Al Kharijah
Luxor
Aswan

Siwah

Al Jawf

LIBYAN DESERT

NUBIAN DESERT

Lake Nasser

Nile

Blue Nile

White Nile

Suez Canal

Port Sudan

Marawi
Atbarah
Kassala
Omdurman
Khartoum
Wad Madani
Al Ubayyid
Al Fashir
Nyala
SUDAN
Waw

ERITREA
Massawa
Asmara

Gulf of Aden
Cape
Guardafui

DJIBOUTI
Djibouti
Assab
Berbera
Hargeysa

ETHIOPIAN
HIGHLANDS
Ras Dashen
Gonder
Dese
Bahir Dar
Nazret
Addis Ababa
Dire Dawa
Harer

ETHIOPIA

Malakal

ALGERIA

MOUNTAINS

AHAGGAR

Mt. Tahat 9,573
Tamanrasset

HAGGAR

TIBESTI
Emi Koussi 11,204
Mt. Grebour 6,370
Faya-Largeau

S A H A R A

AIR
Agadez

NIGER

CHAD
Abeche
N'Djamena
Maroua
Sarh
Moundou

Lake Chad

Western
Sahara
(Occ. by
Morocco)

El Aaiun

Atar

Nouadhibou

MAURITANIA

Nouakchott

Kaedi

Ayoun el Atrous

Tropic of Cancer

Nioro
Segou
Bamako
Sikasso
Kayes

Tombouctou
Gao
Mopti

Niamey
Maradi
Zinder
Sokoto
Katsina
Kano
Zaria
Maiduguri
Kumo

MALI

BURKINA
FASO
Bobo-
Dioulasso
Ouagadougou

Niger

Koudougou
Tamale
GHANA
Korhogo
Bouaké
CÔTE
D'IVOIRE
Kumasi

BENIN
TOGO
Sokodé
Abomey
Minna
Abuja
Ilorin
Oshogbo
NIGERIA
Makurdi

Saint-
Louis
Dakar
Thies
Kaolack
SENEGAL
Labe
GAMBIA
GUINEA-
BISSAU
Conakry
GUINEA

Freetown
SIERRA
LEONE

Senegal

494

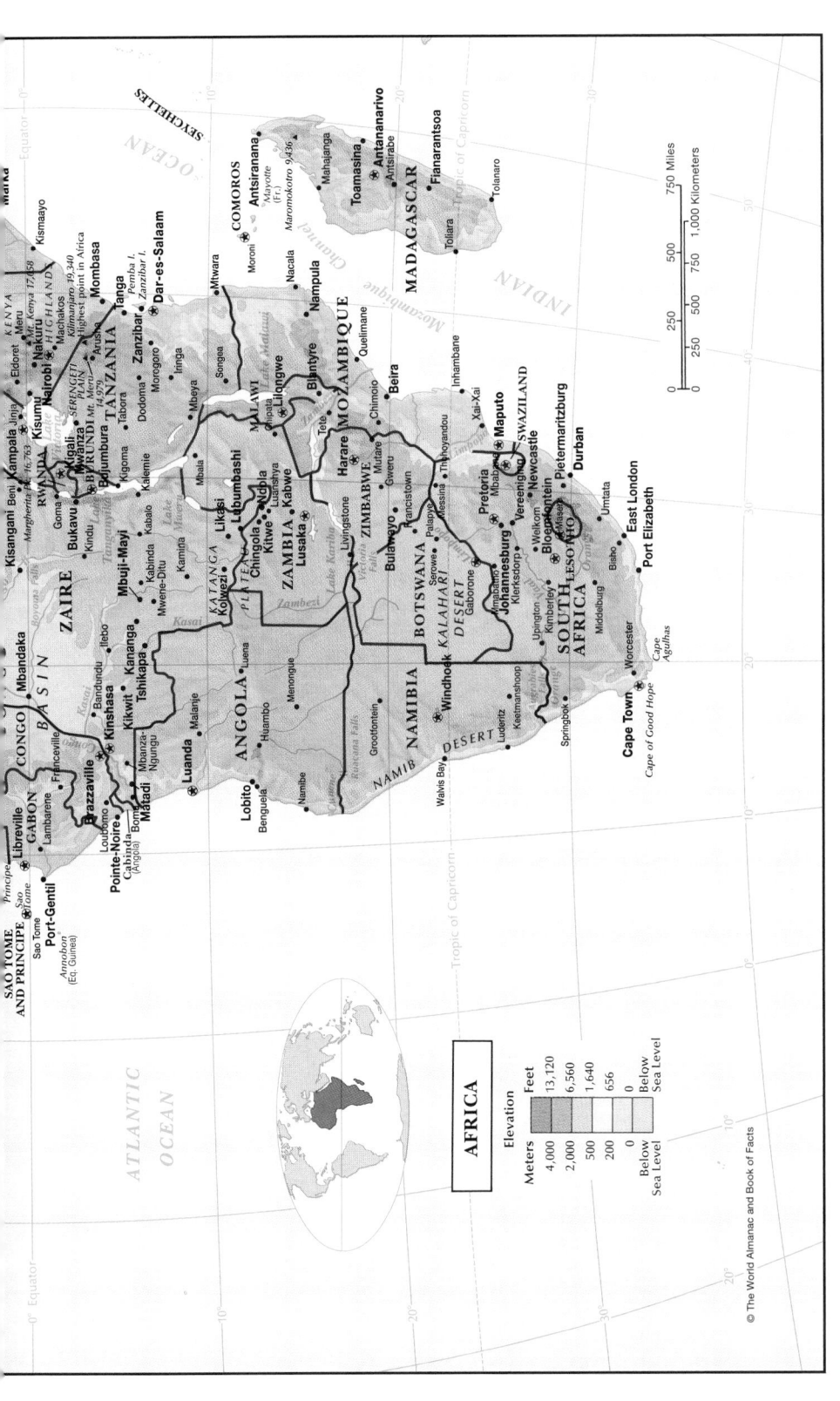

AFRICA

Elevation

Meters	Feet
4,000	13,120
2,000	6,560
500	1,640
200	656
0	0
Below Sea Level	Below Sea Level

© The World Almanac and Book of Facts

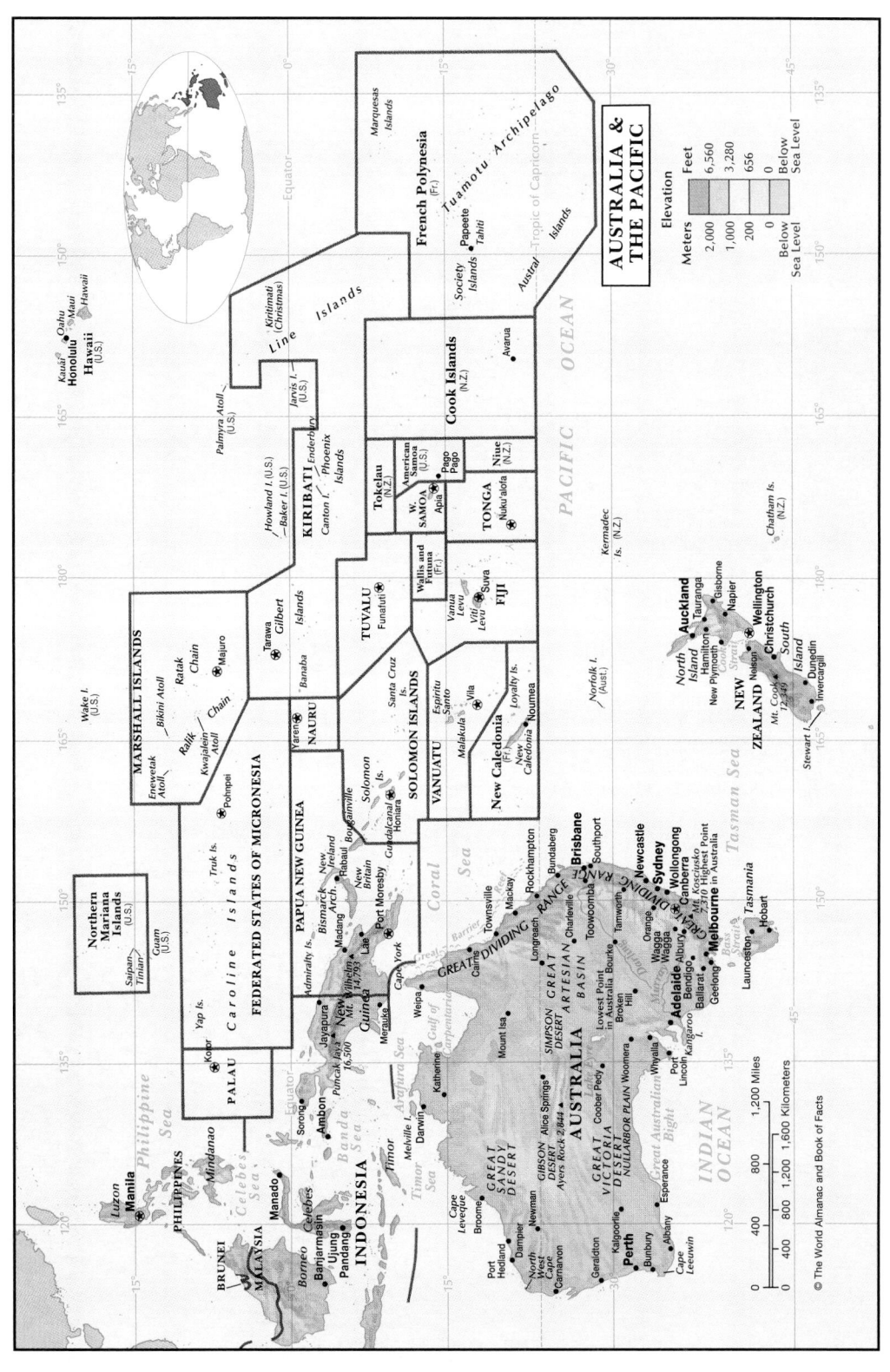

AUSTRALIA & THE PACIFIC

Elevation

Meters	Feet
2,000	6,560
1,000	3,280
200	656
0	0
Below Sea Level	Below Sea Level

© The World Almanac and Book of Facts

UNITED STATES HISTORY

1492
Christopher Columbus and crew sighted land **Oct. 12** in the present-day Bahamas.

1497
John Cabot explored northeast coast to Delaware.

1513
Juan Ponce de León explored Florida coast.

1524
Giovanni da Verrazano led French expedition along coast from Carolina north to Nova Scotia; entered New York harbor.

1539
Hernando de Soto landed in Florida **May 28;** crossed Mississippi River, **1541.**

1540
Francisco Vásquez de Coronado explored Southwest north of Rio Grande. Hernando de Alarcón reached Colorado River, Don Garcia Lopez de Cardenas reached Grand Canyon. Others explored California coast.

1565
St. Augustine, FL, founded by Pedro Menéndez. Razed by Francis Drake **1586.**

1579
Francis Drake entered San Francisco Bay and claimed region for Britain.

1607
Capt. John Smith and 105 cavaliers in 3 ships landed on Virginia coast, started first permanent English settlement in New World at **Jamestown** in May.

1609
Henry Hudson, English explorer of Northwest Passage, employed by Dutch, sailed into New York harbor in **Sept.,** and up Hudson to Albany. The same year, **Samuel de Champlain** explored Lake Champlain just to the north. Spaniards settled **Santa Fe, NM.**

1619
House of Burgesses, first representative assembly in New World, elected **July 30** at Jamestown, VA.
First black laborers—indentured servants—in English N. American colonies, landed by Dutch at Jamestown in **Aug.** Chattel slavery legally recognized, **1650.**

1620
Plymouth Pilgrims, Puritan separatists from Church of England, some living in Holland, left Plymouth, England **Sept. 16** on Mayflower. Original destination Virginia, they reached Cape Cod **Nov. 19,** explored coast; 103 passengers landed **Dec. 26** at Plymouth. Mayflower Compact was agreement to form a government and abide by its laws. Half of colony died during harsh winter.

1624
Dutch colonies started in Albany and in New York area, where New Netherland was established in May.

1626
Peter Minuit bought Manhattan for Dutch from Man-a-hat-a Indians during summer for goods valued at $24; named island New Amsterdam.

1630
Settlement of **Boston** established by Massachusetts colonists led by John Winthrop.

1634
Maryland founded as Catholic colony with religious tolerance.

1636
Roger Williams founded Providence, RI, **June,** as a democratically ruled colony with separation of church and state. Charter was granted, **1644.**
Harvard College founded **Oct. 28,** now oldest in U.S.; Grammar school, compulsory education established at Boston.

1660
British Parliament passed **Navigation Act,** regulating colonial commerce to suit English needs.

1664
Three hundred **British troops Sept. 8 seized New Netherland** from Dutch, who yield peacefully. Charles II granted province of New Netherland and city of New Amsterdam to brother, Duke of York; both renamed New York. The Dutch recaptured the colony **Aug. 9, 1673,** but ceded it to Britain **Nov. 10, 1674.**

1676
Nathaniel Bacon led planters against autocratic British Gov. Berkeley, burned Jamestown, VA. Bacon died, 23 followers executed.
Bloody **Indian war** in New England ended **Aug. 12.** King Philip, Wampanoag chief, and many Narragansett Indians killed.

1682
Robert Cavelier, Sieur de La Salle, claimed lower Mississippi River country for France, called it Louisiana **Apr. 9.** Had French outposts built in Illinois and Texas, **1684.** Killed during mutiny **Mar. 19, 1687.**

1683
William Penn signed treaty with Delaware Indians and made payment for Pennsylvania lands.

1692
Witchcraft delusion at Salem, MA, 20 executed by special court.

1696
Capt. William Kidd, who was born in Scotland and settled in America, was hired by British to fight pirates and take booty, but himself became a pirate. Arrested and sent to England, he was hanged **1701.**

1699
French settlements made in Mississippi, Louisiana.

1704
Indians attacked Deerfield, MA, **Feb. 28-29,** killed 40, carried off 100.
Boston News Letter, first regular newspaper, started by John Campbell, postmaster. (*Publick Occurences* was suppressed after one issue **1690.**)

1709
British-Colonial troops captured French fort, Port Royal, Nova Scotia, in **Queen Anne's War 1701-13.** France yielded Nova Scotia by treaty **1713.**

1712
Slaves revolted in New York **Apr. 6.** Six committed suicide, 21 were executed. Second rising, **1741;** 13 slaves hanged, 13 burned, 71 deported.

1716
First theater in colonies opened in Williamsburg, VA.

1732
Benjamin Franklin published first *Poor Richard's Almanac;* published annually to 1757.

1735
Freedom of the press recognized in New York by acquittal of John Peter Zenger, editor of *Weekly Journal,* on charge of libeling British Gov. Cosby by criticizing his conduct in office.

1740-41
Capt. Vitus Bering, Dane employed by Russians, reached Alaska.

1744
King George's War pitted British and colonials vs. French. Colonials captured Louisburg, Cape Breton Is. **June 17, 1745.** Returned to France **1748** by Treaty of Aix-la-Chapelle.

1752
Benjamin Franklin, flying kite in thunderstorm, proved lightning is electricity **June 15;** invented lightning rod.

1754
French and Indian War (in Europe called 7 Years War, started 1756) began when French occupied Ft. Duquesne (Pittsburgh). British moved Acadian French from Nova Scotia to Louisiana **Oct. 8, 1755.** British captured Québec **Sept. 18, 1759** in battles in which French Gen. Montcalm and British Gen. Wolfe were killed. Peace signed **Feb. 10, 1763.** French lost Canada and American Midwest. British tightened colonial administration in North America.

1764
Sugar Act placed duties on lumber, foodstuffs, molasses and rum in colonies, to pay French and Indian War debts.

1765
Stamp Act required revenue stamps to help defray cost of royal troops. Nine colonies, led by New York and Massachusetts at Stamp Act Congress in New York **Oct. 7-25, 1765,** adopted Declaration of Rights opposing taxation without representation in Parliament and trial without jury by admiralty courts. Stamp Act **repealed Mar. 17, 1766.**

1767
Townshend Acts levied taxes on glass, painter's lead, paper, and tea. In **1770** all duties except on tea were repealed.

1770

British troops fired **Mar. 5** into Boston mob, killed 5 including **Crispus Attucks,** a black man, reportedly leader of group; later called **Boston Massacre.**

1773

East India Co. tea ships turned back at Boston, New York, Philadelphia in **May.** Cargo ship burned at Annapolis **Oct. 14,** cargo thrown overboard at **Boston Tea Party Dec. 16,** to protest the tea tax.

1774

"Intolerable Acts" of Parliament curtailed Massachusetts self-rule; barred use of Boston harbor till tea was paid for.

First Continental Congress held in Philadelphia **Sept. 5-Oct. 26;** protested British measures, called for civil disobedience.

Rhode Island abolished slavery.

1775

Patrick Henry addressed Virginia convention, **Mar. 23,** said "Give me liberty or give me death."

Paul Revere and William Dawes on night of **Apr. 18** rode to alert patriots that British were on way to Concord to destroy arms. At Lexington, MA, **Apr. 19** Minutemen lost 8. On return from Concord, British took 273 casualties.

Col. Ethan Allen (joined by Col. Benedict Arnold) captured **Ft. Ticonderoga, NY, May 10;** also Crown Point. Colonials headed for **Bunker Hill,** fortified Breed's Hill, Charlestown, MA, repulsed British under Gen. William Howe twice before retreating **June 17;** British casualties 1,000; called Battle of Bunker Hill. Continental Congress **June 15** named **George Washington** commander-in-chief.

1776

France and Spain each agreed **May 2** to provide one million livres in arms to Americans.

In Continental Congress **June 7,** Richard Henry Lee (VA) moved "that these united colonies are and of right ought to be free and independent states." Resolution adopted July 2. **Declaration of Independence** approved **July 4.**

Col. Moultrie's batteries at **Charleston, SC,** repulsed British sea attack **June 28.**

Washington, with 10,000 men, lost **Battle of Long Island Aug. 27,** evacuated New York.

Nathan Hale executed as spy by British **Sept. 22.**

Brig. Gen. Arnold's **Lake Champlain** fleet was defeated at Valcour **Oct. 11,** but British returned to Canada. Howe failed to destroy Washington's army at **White Plains Oct. 28.** Hessians captured Ft. Washington, Manhattan, and 3,000 men **Nov. 16;** Ft. Lee, NJ, **Nov. 18.**

Washington in Pennsylvania, recrossed **Delaware River Dec. 25-26,** defeated 1,400 Hessians at Trenton, NJ, **Dec. 26.**

1777

Washington defeated Lord Cornwallis at **Princeton Jan. 3.** Continental Congress adopted Stars and Stripes.

Maj. Gen. John Burgoyne with 8,000 from Canada captured **Ft. Ticonderoga July 6.** Americans beat back Burgoyne at Bemis Heights **Oct. 7** and cut off British escape route. Burgoyne surrendered 5,000 men at **Saratoga, NY, Oct. 17.**

Marquis de Lafayette, aged 20, made major general.

Articles of Confederation and Perpetual Union adopted by Continental Congress **Nov. 15.**

France recognized independence of 13 colonies **Dec. 17.**

1778

France signed treaty of aid with U.S. **Feb. 6.** Sent fleet; British evacuated Philadelphia in consequence **June 18.**

1779

John Paul Jones on the *Bonhomme Richard* defeated *Serapis* in British North Sea waters **Sept. 23.**

1780

Charleston, SC, fell to the British **May 12,** but a British force was defeated near **Kings Mountain, NC, Oct. 7** by militiamen.

Benedict Arnold found to be a traitor **Sept. 23.** Arnold escaped, made brigadier general in British army.

1781

Bank of North America incorporated in Philadelphia **May 26.**

Cornwallis, sapped by patriot victories, retired to **Yorktown, VA.** Adm. De Grasse landed 3,000 French and stopped British fleet in Hampton Roads. Washington and Rochambeau joined forces, arrived near Williamsburg **Sept. 26.** When siege of Cornwallis began **Oct. 6,** British had 6,000, Americans 8,846, French 7,800. **Cornwallis surrendered Oct. 19.**

1782

New **British** cabinet agreed **in March** to **recognize U.S.** independence. Preliminary agreement signed in Paris **Nov. 30.**

1783

Massachusetts Supreme Court **outlawed slavery** in that state, noting the words in the state Bill of Rights "all men are born free and equal."

Britain, U.S. signed **peace treaty Sept. 3** (Congress ratified it **Jan. 14, 1784).**

Washington ordered army disbanded Nov. 3, bade farewell to his officers at Fraunces Tavern, New York City **Dec. 4.**

Noah Webster published *American Spelling Book,* great best-seller.

1784

Jefferson's proposal to **ban slavery** in new territory after 1802 is narrowly defeated **Mar. 1.**

First successful daily newspaper, *Pennsylvania Packet & General Advertiser,* published **Sept. 21.**

1786

Delegates from 5 states at **Annapolis, MD, Sept. 11-14** asked Congress to call convention in Philadelphia to write practical constitution for the 13 states.

1787

Shays's Rebellion, of debt-ridden farmers in Massachusetts, failed **Jan. 25.**

Northwest Ordinance adopted **July 13** by Continental Congress. Determined government of Northwest Territory north of Ohio River, west of New York; 60,000 inhabitants could get statehood. Guaranteed freedom of religion, support for schools, no slavery.

Constitutional convention opened at Philadelphia **May 25** with George Washington presiding. Constitution adopted by delegates **Sept. 17;** ratification by 9th state, New Hampshire, **June 21, 1788,** meant adoption; declared in effect **Mar. 4, 1789.**

1789

George Washington chosen president by all electors voting (73 eligible, 69 voting, 4 absent); John Adams, vice president, 34 votes. **Feb. 4.** First Congress met at Federal Hall, New York City; regular sessions began **Apr. 6.** Washington inaugurated there **Apr. 30.** Supreme Court created by Federal Judiciary Act **Sept. 24.** Congress submitted Bill of Rights to states **Sept. 25.**

1790

Congress passed **Census Act Mar. 1; Naturalization Act** (2-year residency) **Mar. 26.**

Congress met in Philadelphia **Dec. 6,** new temporary Capital.

1791

Bill of Rights went into effect **Dec. 15.**

1792

Coinage Act established **U.S. Mint** in Philadelphia **Apr. 2.**

Gen. **"Mad" Anthony Wayne** made commander in Ohio-Indiana area, trained "American Legion," established string of forts. Routed Indians at Fallen Timbers on Maumee River **Aug. 20, 1794,** checked British at Fort Miami, OH.

White House cornerstone laid **Oct. 13.**

1793

Eli Whitney invented **cotton gin,** reviving southern slavery.

1794

Whiskey Rebellion, west Pennsylvania farmers protesting liquor tax of **1791,** was suppressed by 15,000 militiamen **Sept. 1794.** Alexander Hamilton used incident to establish authority of the new federal government in enforcing its laws.

1795

U.S. bought peace from **Algerian pirates** by paying $1 million ransom for 115 seamen **Sept. 5,** followed by annual tributes.

Gen. Wayne signed peace with Indians at Fort Greenville.

University of North Carolina became first operating state university.

1796

Washington's Farewell Address as president delivered **Sept. 19.** Gave strong warnings against permanent alliances with foreign powers, big public debt, large military establishment, and devices of "small, artful, enterprising minority" to control or change government.

1797

U.S. **frigate United States** launched at Philadelphia **July 10;** Constellation at Baltimore **Sept. 7;** Constitution (Old Ironsides) at Boston **Sept. 20.**

1798

Alien & Sedition Acts passed by Federalists **June-July**; intended to silence political opposition.

War with France threatened over French raids on U.S. shipping and rejection of U.S. diplomats. Congress voided all treaties with France, ordered Navy to capture French armed ships. Navy (45 ships) and 365 privateers captured 84 French ships. *USS Constellation* took French warship *Insurgente* 1799. Napoleon stopped French raids after becoming First Consul.

1800

Federal govt. moves from Philadelphia to **Washington, DC.**

1801

Tripoli declared war June 10 against U.S., which refused added tribute to commerce-raiding Arab corsairs. Land and naval campaigns forced Tripoli to negotiate **peace June 4, 1805.**

1803

Supreme Court, in **Marbury v Madison** case, for the first time overturned a U.S. law **Feb. 24.**

Napoleon, who had recovered Louisiana from Spain by secret treaty, sold all of **Louisiana**, stretching to Canadian border, to U.S., for $11,250,000 in bonds, plus $3,750,000 indemnities to American citizens with claims against France. U.S. took title **Dec. 20.** Purchases doubled U.S. area.

1804

Lewis and Clark expedition ordered by Pres. Jefferson to explore what is now northwest U.S. Started from St. Louis **May 14;** ended **Sept. 23, 1806.** Sacagawea, an Indian woman, served as guide.

Vice Pres. **Aaron Burr,** after long political rivalry, **shot Alexander Hamilton** in a duel **July 11** in Weehawken, NJ; Hamilton died the next day.

1807

Robert Fulton made first practical steamboat trip; left New York City **Aug. 17,** reached Albany, 150 mi, in 32 hr.

Embargo Act bans all trade with foreign countries, forbids ships to set sail for foreign ports **Dec. 22.**

1808

Slave importation outlawed. Some 250,000 slaves were illegally imported **1808-60.**

1811

William Henry Harrison, governor of Indiana, defeated Indians under the Prophet, in battle of Tippecanoe **Nov. 7.**

Cumberland Road begun at Cumberland, MD; became important route to West.

1812

War of 1812 had 3 main causes: Britain seized U.S. ships trading with France; Britain seized 4,000 naturalized U.S. sailors by **1810;** Britain armed Indians who raided western border. U.S. stopped trade with Europe **1807** and **1809.** Trade with Britain only was stopped, **1810.**

Unaware that Britain had raised the blockade against France 2 days before, **Congress declared war June 18** by a small majority. The West favored war, New England opposed it. The British were handicapped by war with France.

U.S. naval victories in 1812 included: *USS Essex* captured *Alert* **Aug. 13;** *USS Constitution* destroyed *Guerriere* **Aug. 19;** *USS Wasp* took *Frolic* **Oct. 18;** *USS United States* defeated *Macedonian* off Azores **Oct. 25;** *Constitution* beat *Java* **Dec. 29.** British captured Detroit **Aug. 16.**

1813

Oliver H. Perry defeated British fleet at Battle of Lake Erie, **Sept. 10.** U.S. victory at Battle of the Thames, Ontario, **Oct. 5,** broke Indian allies of Britain, and made Detroit frontier safe for U.S. But Americans failed in Canadian invasion attempts. York (Toronto) and Buffalo were burned.

1814

British landed in Maryland in August, defeated U.S. force **Aug. 24, burned Capitol** and White House. Maryland militia stopped British advance **Sept. 12.** Bombardment of Ft. McHenry, Baltimore, for 25 hours, **Sept. 13-14,** by British fleet failed; Francis Scott Key wrote words to **"Star Spangled Banner."**

U.S. won naval Battle of **Lake Champlain Sept. 11.** Peace treaty signed at Ghent **Dec. 24.**

1815

Some 5,300 British, unaware of peace treaty, attacked U.S. entrenchments near **New Orleans, Jan. 8.** British had more than 2,000 casualties, Americans lost 71.

U.S. flotilla finally ended piracy by **Algiers, Tunis, Tripoli** by **Aug. 6.**

1816

Second **Bank of the U.S.** chartered.

1817

Rush-Bagot treaty signed **Apr. 28-29;** limited U.S., British armaments on the Great Lakes.

1819

Spain cedes **Florida** to U.S. **Feb. 22.**

American steamship *Savannah* made first part steam-powered, part sail-powered crossing of Atlantic, Savannah, GA, to Liverpool, England, 29 days.

1820

First organized **immigration of blacks to Africa** from U.S. began with 86 free blacks sailing **Feb.** to Sierra Leone, Brit. Colony.

Henry Clay's **Missouri Compromise** bill passed by Congress **March 3.** Slavery was allowed in Missouri, but not elsewhere west of the Mississippi River north of 36° 30′ latitude (the southern line of Missouri). Repealed **1854.**

1821

Emma Willard founded Troy Female Seminary, first U.S. women's college.

1823

Monroe Doctrine enunciated **Dec. 2,** opposing European intervention in the Americas.

1824

Pawtucket, RI, **weavers strike** in first such action by women.

1825

Erie Canal opened; first boat left Buffalo **Oct. 26,** reached NYC **Nov. 4.** Canal cost $7 million but opened Great Lakes area, made NYC chief Atlantic port.

John Stevens, of Hoboken, NJ, built and operated first experimental **steam locomotive** in U.S.

1828

South Carolina **Dec. 19** declared the right of state **nullification of federal laws,** opposing the "Tariff of Abominations."

Noah Webster published his *American Dictionary of the English Language.*

Baltimore & Ohio, 1st U.S. passenger RR, was begun **July 4.**

1830

Mormon church organized by Joseph Smith in Fayette, NY, **Apr. 6.**

1831

William Lloyd Garrison began abolitionist newspaper *The Liberator* **Jan. 1.**

Nat Turner, black slave in Virginia, led local slave rebellion, killed 57 whites in **Aug.** Troops called in, 100 slaves killed, Turner captured, tried, and hanged.

1832

Black Hawk War (IL-WI) **Apr.-Sept.** pushed Sauk and Fox Indians west across Mississippi.

South Carolina convention passed **Ordinance of Nullification** in Nov. against permanent tariff, threatening to withdraw from the Union. Congress **Feb. 1833** passed a compromise tariff act, whereupon South Carolina repealed its act.

1833

Oberlin College, first in U.S. to adopt coeducation; refused to bar students on account of race, **1835.**

1835

Seminole Indians in Florida under Osceola began attacks **Nov. 1,** protesting forced removal. The unpopular 8-year war ended **Aug. 14, 1842;** Indians were sent to Oklahoma. War cost the U.S. 1,500 soldiers.

Texas proclaimed right to secede from Mexico; Sam Houston put in command of Texas army, **Nov. 2-4.**

Gold discovered on **Cherokee land** in Georgia. Indians forced to cede lands **Dec. 20** and to cross Mississippi.

1836

Texans besieged in Alamo in San Antonio by Mexicans under Santa Anna **Feb. 23-Mar. 6;** entire garrison killed. Texas independence declared, **Mar. 2.** At San Jacinto **Apr. 21** Sam Houston and Texans defeated Mexicans.

Marcus Whitman, H. H. Spaulding and wives reached Fort Walla Walla on Columbia River, OR. **First white women to cross plains.**

1838

Cherokee Indians made **"Trail of Tears,"** removed from Georgia to Oklahoma starting **Oct.**

1841

First emigrant **wagon train for California,** 47 persons, left Independence, MO, **May 1,** reached California **Nov. 4.**

Brook Farm commune set up by New England Transcendentalist intellectuals. Lasts to **1846.**

1842

Webster-Ashburton Treaty signed **Aug. 9,** fixing the U.S.-Canada border in Maine and Minnesota.

First use of **anesthetic** (sulphuric ether gas).

Settlement of Oregon begins via **Oregon Trail.**

1843

More than 1,000 settlers left Independence, MO, for Oregon **May 22,** arrived **Oct.**

1844

First message over first **telegraph line** sent **May 24** by inventor Samuel F.B. Morse from Washington to Baltimore: "What hath God wrought!"

1845

Texas Congress **voted for annexation** by U.S. **July 4.** U.S. Congress admits Texas to Union **Dec. 29.**

1846

Mexican War. Pres. James K. Polk ordered Gen. Zachary Taylor to seize disputed Texan land settled by Mexicans. After border clash, U.S. declared war **May 13; Mexico May 23.** Northern Whigs opposed war, southerners backed it.

Bear flag of Republic of California raised by American settlers at Sonoma **June 14.**

About 12,000 U.S. troops took Vera Cruz Mar. 27, 1847, Mexico City Sept. 14, 1847. By **treaty, Feb. 1848,** Mexico ceded claims to Texas, California, Arizona, New Mexico, Nevada, Utah, part of Colorado. U.S. assumed $3 million American claims and paid Mexico $15 million.

Treaty with Great Britain **June 15** set **boundary in Oregon** territory at 49th parallel (extension of existing line). Expansionists had used slogan "54° 40′ or fight."

Mormons, after violent clashes with settlers over polygamy, left Nauvoo, IL, for West under Brigham Young, settled **July 1847 at Salt Lake City, UT.**

Elias Howe invented **sewing machine.**

1847

First **adhesive U.S. postage stamps** on sale **July 1;** Benjamin Franklin 5¢, Washington 10¢.

Ralph Waldo Emerson published first book of poems; **Henry Wadsworth Longfellow** published *Evangeline.*

1848

Gold discovered Jan. 24 in California; 80,000 prospectors emigrate in **1849.**

Lucretia Mott and Elizabeth Cady Stanton lead **Seneca Falls, NY, Women's Rights Convention July 19-20.**

1850

Sen. Henry Clay's **Compromise of 1850** admitted California as 31st state **Sept. 9,** slavery forbidden; made Utah and New Mexico territories without decision on slavery; made Fugitive Slave Law more harsh; ended District of Columbia slave trade.

1851

Herman Melville's *Moby Dick,* **Nathaniel Hawthorne's** *House of the Seven Gables* published.

1852

Uncle Tom's Cabin, by **Harriet Beecher Stowe,** published.

1853

Commodore Matthew C. Perry, U.S.N., received by Lord of Toda, Japan **July 14; negotiated treaty to open Japan** to U.S. ships.

1854

Republican Party formed at Ripon, WI, **Feb. 28.** Opposed Kansas-Nebraska Act (became law **May 30**), which left issue of slavery to vote of settlers.

Henry David Thoreau published *Walden.*

1855

Walt Whitman published *Leaves of Grass.*

First railroad train crossed Mississippi on the river's first bridge, Rock Island, IL, Davenport, IA, **Apr. 21.**

1856

Republican Party's first nominee for president, **John C. Fremont,** defeated. Abraham Lincoln made 50 speeches for him.

Lawrence, KS, sacked **May 21** by proslavery group; abolitionist **John Brown** led antislavery men against Missourians at **Osawatomie, KS, Aug. 30.**

1857

Dred Scott decision by U.S. Supreme Court **Mar. 6** held, 6-3, that a slave did not become free when taken into a free state, Congress could not bar slavery from a territory, and blacks could not be citizens.

1858

First **Atlantic cable** completed by Cyrus W. Field **Aug. 5;** cable failed **Sept. 1.**

Lincoln-Douglas debates in Illinois **Aug. 21-Oct. 15.**

1859

First commercially productive **oil well,** drilled near Titusville, PA, by Edwin L. Drake **Aug. 27.**

Abolitionist **John Brown** with 21 men seized U.S. Armory at **Harpers Ferry (then Virginia) Oct. 16.** U.S. Marines captured raiders, killing several. Brown was hanged for treason by Virginia **Dec. 2.**

1860

Approximately 20,000 **New England shoe workers** strike **Feb. 22** and win higher wages.

Abraham Lincoln, Republican, elected president in 4-way race.

First **Pony Express** between Sacramento, CA, and St. Joseph, MO, started **Apr. 3;** service ended **Oct. 24, 1861,** when first transcontinental telegraph line was completed.

1861

Seven southern states set up **Confederate States of America Feb. 8,** with Jefferson Davis as president, captured federal arsenals and forts. **Civil War** began as Confederates fired on **Ft. Sumter** in Charleston, SC, **Apr. 12;** they captured it **Apr. 14.**

President **Lincoln called for 75,000 volunteers Apr. 15.** By **May,** 11 states had seceded. Lincoln blockaded southern ports **Apr. 19,** cutting off vital exports, aid.

Confederates repelled Union forces at first **Battle of Bull Run July 21.**

First **transcontinental telegraph** was put in operation.

1862

Homestead Act was approved **May 20;** it granted free family farms to settlers.

Land Grant Act approved **July 7,** providing for public land sale to benefit agricultural education; eventually led to establishment of state university systems.

Union forces were victorious in western campaigns, took **New Orleans.** Battles in East were inconclusive.

1863

Lincoln issued **Emancipation Proclamation Jan. 1,** freeing "all slaves in areas still in rebellion."

The entire **Mississippi River** was in Union hands by **July 4.** Union forces won a major victory at **Gettysburg, PA, July 1-3.** Lincoln read his **Gettysburg Address Nov. 19.**

In **draft riots** in New York City about 1,000 were killed or wounded; some blacks were hanged by mobs **July 13-16.** Rioters protested provision allowing money payment in place of service. Such payments were ended 1864.

1864

Gen. Sherman marched through Georgia, taking Atlanta **Sept. 1,** Savannah **Dec. 22.**

Sand Creek massacre of Cheyenne and Arapaho Indians **Nov. 29.** Cavalry attacked Indians who were awaiting surrender terms.

1865

Robert E. Lee surrendered 27,800 Confederate troops to Grant at Appomattox Court House, VA, **Apr. 9.** J. E. Johnston surrendered 31,200 to Sherman at Durham Station, NC, **Apr. 18.** Last rebel troops surrendered **May 26.**

President **Lincoln was shot Apr. 14** by John Wilkes Booth in Ford's Theater, Washington; died the following morning. Booth was reported dead **Apr. 26.** Four coconspirators were hanged **July 7.**

Thirteenth Amendment, abolishing slavery, was ratified **Dec. 6.**

1866

Ku Klux Klan formed secretly in South to terrorize blacks who voted. Disbanded **1869-71.** A second Klan was organized **1915.**

Congress took control of southern Reconstruction, backed freedmen's rights.

1867

Alaska sold to U.S. by Russia for $7.2 million **Mar. 30** through efforts of Sec. of State William H. Seward.
Horatio Alger published first book, *Ragged Dick.*
The **Grange** was organized **Dec. 4,** to protect farmer interests.

1868

The World Almanac, a publication of the *New York World,* appeared for the first time.
Pres. **Andrew Johnson** tried to remove Edwin M. Stanton, secretary of war; was impeached by House **Feb. 24** for violation of Tenure of Office Act; acquitted by Senate **March-May.** Stanton resigned.

1869

Financial **"Black Friday"** in New York **Sept. 24;** caused by attempt to "corner" gold.
Transcontinental railroad completed; golden spike driven at Promontory, UT, **May 10,** marking the junction of Central Pacific and Union Pacific.
Knights of Labor formed in Philadelphia. By **1886,** it had 700,000 members nationally.
Woman suffrage law passed in Territory of Wyoming on **Dec. 10.**

1871

Great fire destroyed Chicago Oct. 8-11; loss est. at $196 million.

1872

Amnesty Act restored civil rights to citizens of the South **May 22** except for 500 Confederate leaders.
Congress founded first national park—**Yellowstone** in Wyoming.

1873

First U.S. **postal card** issued **May 1.**
Banks failed, panic began in **Sept.** Depression lasted 5 years.
"Boss" William Tweed of New York City convicted of stealing public funds. He died in jail in **1878.**
Bellevue Hospital in New York City started the first **school of nursing.**

1875

Congress passed **Civil Rights Act Mar. 1,** giving equal rights to blacks in public accommodations and jury duty. Act invalidated in **1883** by Supreme Court.
First **Kentucky Derby** held **May 17** at Churchill Downs, Louisville, KY.

1876

Samuel J. Tilden, Democrat, received majority of popular votes for president over **Rutherford B. Hayes,** Republican, but 22 electoral votes were in dispute; issue left to Congress. Hayes given presidency **in Feb. 1877** after Republicans agree to end Reconstruction of South.
Col. **George A. Custer** and 264 soldiers of the 7th Cavalry killed **June 25** in "last stand," Battle of the Little Big Horn, MT, in Sioux Indian War.
Mark Twain published *Tom Sawyer.*

1877

Molly Maguires, Irish terrorist society in Scranton, PA, mining areas, broken up by hanging of 11 leaders for murders of mine officials and police.
Pres. Hayes sent troops in violent national **railroad strike.**

1878

First commercial **telephone** exchange opened, New Haven, CT, **Jan. 28.**
Thomas A. Edison founded **Edison Electric Light Co.** on **Oct. 15.**

1879

F. W. Woolworth opened his first five-and-ten store in Utica, NY, **Feb. 22.**
Henry George published *Progress & Poverty,* advocating single tax on land.

1881

Pres. **James A. Garfield shot** in Washington, DC, **July 2;** died **Sept. 19.**
Booker T. Washington founded Tuskegee Institute for blacks.
Helen Hunt Jackson published *A Century of Dishonor* about mistreatment of Indians.

1883

Pendleton Act, passed **Jan. 16,** reformed federal civil service.
Brooklyn Bridge opened **May 24.**

1886

Haymarket riot and bombing, evening of **May 4,** followed bitter labor battles for 8-hour day in Chicago; 7 police and 4 workers died, 66 wounded. Eight anarchists found guilty. Gov. John P. Altgeld denounced trial as unfair.
Geronimo, Apache Indian, finally surrendered **Sept. 4.**
The **Statue of Liberty** was dedicated **Oct. 28.**
American Federation of Labor (AFL) formed **Dec. 8** by 25 craft unions.

1888

Great blizzard in eastern U.S. **Mar. 11-14;** 400 deaths.

1889

U.S. declared Oklahoma open to white settlement **Apr. 22;** within 24 hours **claims for 2 million acres** were staked by 50,000 settlers.
Johnstown, PA, flood May 31; 2,200 lives lost.

1890

First execution by **electrocution:** William Kemmler **Aug. 6** at Auburn Prison, Auburn, NY, for murder.
Battle of **Wounded Knee, SD, Dec. 29,** the last major conflict between Indians and U.S. troops. About 200 Indian men, women, and children and 29 soldiers were killed.
Sherman Antitrust Act begins federal effort to curb monopolies.
Jacob Riis published *How the Other Half Lives,* about city slums.

1891

Forest Reserve Act Mar. 3 let president close public forest land to settlement for establishment of national parks.

1892

Homestead, PA, strike at Carnegie steel mills; 7 guards and 11 strikers and spectators shot to death **July 6;** setback for unions. **Ellis Island** opened as New York immigration depot.

1893

Financial panic began, led to 4-year depression.

1894

Thomas A. **Edison's kinetoscope** (motion pictures) (invented **1887**) given first public showing **Apr. 14.**
Jacob S. Coxey led 500 unemployed from the Midwest into Washington, DC, **Apr. 30.** Coxey was arrested for trespassing on Capitol grounds.

1896

William Jennings Bryan delivered "Cross of Gold" speech **July 7;** wins Democratic Party nomination.
Supreme Court, in **Plessy v Ferguson,** approved racial segregation under the "separate but equal" doctrine.

1898

U.S. **battleship** *Maine* blown up **Feb. 15** at Havana, 260 killed.
U.S. blockaded Cuba Apr. 22 in aid of independence forces. U.S. declared war on Spain, **Apr. 24,** destroyed Spanish fleet in Philippines **May 1,** took Guam **June 20.**
Puerto Rico taken by U.S. **July 25-Aug. 12.** Spain agreed **Dec. 10** to cede Philippines, Puerto Rico, and Guam, and approved independence for Cuba.
U.S. annexed independent republic of **Hawaii.**

1899

Filipino insurgents, unable to get recognition of independence from U.S., started guerrilla war **Feb. 4.** Their leader, Emilio Aguinaldo, captured **May 23, 1901.** Philippine Insurrection ended 1902.
U.S. declared **Open Door Policy** to make China an open international market and to preserve its integrity as a nation.
John Dewey published *School and Society,* backing progressive education.

1900

Carry Nation, Kansas antisaloon agitator, began raiding with hatchet.
U.S. helped suppress **"Boxers"** in Beijing.
International Ladies' Garment Workers Union was founded in New York City in **November.**

1901

Texas had first significant **oil strike,** Jan. 10.
Pres. William **McKinley was shot Sept. 6** by an anarchist, Leon Czolgosz; died **Sept. 14.**

1903

Treaty between U.S. and Colombia to have U.S. dig **Panama Canal** signed **Jan. 22,** rejected by Colombia. Panama declared independence with U.S. support **Nov. 3;** recognized by Pres. Theodore Roosevelt **Nov. 6.** U.S., Panama signed canal treaty **Nov. 18.**

Wisconsin set first **direct primary** voting system **May 23.**

First **automobile trip** across U.S. from San Francisco to New York **May 23-Aug. 1.**

First successful flight in heavier-than-air mechanically propelled airplane by **Orville Wright Dec. 17** near Kitty Hawk, NC, 120 ft in 12 seconds. Fourth flight same day by **Wilbur Wright,** 852 ft in 59 seconds. Improved plane patented **May 22, 1906.**

Jack London published *Call of the Wild.*

Great Train Robbery, pioneering film, produced.

1904
Ida Tarbell published muckraking *History of Standard Oil.*

1905
First **Rotary Club** founded in Chicago **December.**

1906
San Francisco earthquake and fire **Apr. 18-19** left 503 dead, $350 million damages.

Pure Food and Drug Act and Meat Inspection Act both passed **June 30.**

1907
Financial panic and depression started **Mar. 13.**

First round-world cruise of U.S. **"Great White Fleet";** 16 battleships, 12,000 men.

1908
Henry Ford introduced **Model T** car, priced at $850 **Oct. 1.**

1909
Adm. Robert E. Peary reached **North Pole Apr. 6** on 6th attempt, accompanied by Matthew Henson, a black man, and 4 Eskimos.

National Conference on the Negro convened **May 30,** leading to founding of the National Association for the Advancement of Colored People.

1910
Boy Scouts of America founded **Feb. 8.**

1911
Supreme Court dissolved **Standard Oil Co. May 15.**

Building holding NYC's **Triangle Shirtwaist Co.** sweatshop caught fire **Mar. 25;** 146 died, mostly young women; some trapped and killed, others jumped to their deaths.

First **transcontinental airplane flight** (with numerous stops) by C. P. Rodgers, New York to Pasadena, **Sept. 17-Nov. 5;** time in air 82 hr, 4 min.

1912
American Girl Guides founded **Mar. 12;** name changed in 1913 to **Girl Scouts.**

U.S. sent Marines **Aug. 14** to **Nicaragua,** which was in default of loans to U.S. and Europe.

1913
NY Armory Show brought modern art to U.S. **Feb. 17.**

U.S. blockaded Mexico in support of revolutionaries.

Charles Beard published his *Economic Interpretation of the Constitution.*

Federal Reserve System was authorized **Dec. 23,** in a major reform of U.S. banking and finance.

1914
Ford Motor Co. raised basic wage rates from $2.40 for 9-hr day to $5 for 8-hr day **Jan. 5.**

When U.S. sailors were arrested at Tampico, Mexico, **Apr. 9,** Atlantic fleet was sent to **Veracruz,** occupied city.

Pres. Wilson proclaimed **U.S. neutrality** in the European war **Aug. 4.**

Panama Canal was officially opened **Aug. 15.**

The **Clayton Antitrust Act** was passed **Oct. 15,** strengthening federal antimonopoly powers.

1915
First **telephone talk,** New York to San Francisco, **Jan. 25** by Alexander Graham Bell and Thomas A. Watson.

British ship *Lusitania* sunk **May 7** by German submarine; 128 American passengers lost (Germany had warned passengers in advance). As a result of U.S. campaign, Germany issued apology and promise of payments **Oct. 5.** Pres. Wilson asked for a military fund increase **Dec. 7.**

U.S. troops landed in **Haiti July 28.** Haiti became a virtual U.S. protectorate under **Sept. 16** treaty.

1916
Gen. John J. **Pershing entered Mexico** to pursue Francisco (Pancho) Villa, who had raided U.S. border areas. Forces withdrawn **Feb. 5, 1917.**

Rural Credits Act passed **July 17,** followed by Warehouse Act **Aug. 11;** both provided financial aid to farmers.

Bomb exploded during **San Francisco** Preparedness Day parade **July 22,** killed 10. Thomas J. Mooney, labor organizer, and Warren K. Billings, shoe worker, were convicted; both pardoned in **1939.**

U.S. bought **Virgin Islands** from Denmark **Aug. 4.**

Jeannette Rankin, 1st U.S. Congresswoman (R, MT) elected.

U.S. established military government in the **Dominican Republic Nov. 29.**

Trade and loans to **European Allies** soared during the year.

John Dewey published *Democracy and Education.*

Carl Sandburg published *Chicago Poems.*

1917
Germany, suffering from British blockade, declared almost unrestricted **submarine warfare Jan. 31.** U.S. cut diplomatic ties with Germany **Feb. 3,** and formally declared war **Apr. 6.**

Conscription law was passed **May 18.** First U.S. troops arrived in Europe **June 26.**

The 18th **(Prohibition)** Amendment to the Constitution was submitted to the states by Congress **Dec. 18.** On **Jan. 16, 1919,** the 36th state (Nevada) ratified it. Franklin D. Roosevelt, as 1932 presidential candidate, endorsed repeal; 21st Amendment repealed 18th; ratification completed **Dec. 5, 1933.**

1918
Pres. Wilson set out his **14 Points** as basis for peace **Jan. 8.** More than 1 million **American troops** were in Europe by **July.** War ended **Nov. 11.**

Influenza epidemic killed an estimated 20 million worldwide, 548,000 in U.S.

1919
First **transatlantic flight,** by U.S. Navy seaplane, left Rockaway, N,. **May 8,** stopped at Newfoundland, Azores, Lisbon **May 27.**

Boston police strike Sept. 9; National Guard breaks strike.

Sherwood Anderson published *Winesburg, Ohio.*

About 250 **alien radicals** were deported **Dec. 22.**

1920
In national **Red Scare,** some 2,700 Communists, anarchists, and other radicals were arrested **Jan.-May.**

Senate refused **Mar. 19** to ratify the **League of Nations Covenant.**

Nicola Sacco, 29, shoe factory employee and radical agitator, and **Bartolomeo Vanzetti,** 32, fish peddler and anarchist, accused of killing 2 men in Massachusetts payroll holdup **Apr. 15.** Found guilty **1921.** A 6-year worldwide campaign for release on grounds of inconclusive evidence and prejudice failed. Both executed **Aug. 23, 1927.** Vindicated July 19, 1977, by proclamation of Massachusetts Gov. Dukakis.

First regular licensed **radio broadcasting** begun **Aug. 20.**

19th Amendment ratified **Aug. 18,** giving women right to vote.

League of Women Voters founded.

Wall St., New York City, **bomb** explosion killed 30, injured 100, did $2 million damage **Sept. 16.**

Sinclair Lewis's *Main Street,* **F. Scott Fitzgerald's** *This Side of Paradise* published.

1921
Congress sharply curbed **immigration,** set national quota system **May 19.**

Joint congressional resolution declaring **peace with Germany, Austria, and Hungary** signed **July 2** by Pres. Harding; treaties were signed in **August.**

Limitation of Armaments Conference met in Washington **Nov. 12-Feb. 6, 1922.** Major powers agreed to curtail naval construction, outlaw poison gas, restrict submarine attacks on merchant vessels, respect integrity of China.

Ku Klux Klan began revival with violence against Catholics in North, South, and Midwest.

1922
Violence during **coal-mine strike** at Herrin, IL, **June 22-23** cost 36 lives, 21 of them nonunion miners.

Reader's Digest founded.

1923
First **sound-on-film motion picture,** *Phonofilm,* was shown by Lee de Forest at Rivoli Theater, New York City, beginning in **April.**

1924
Law approved by Congress **June 15** making all **Indians citizens.**

Nellie Tayloe Ross elected governor of Wyoming **Nov. 9** after death of her husband **Oct. 2;** installed **Jan. 5, 1925,** first woman governor. **Miriam (Ma) Ferguson** was elected governor of Texas **Nov. 9;** installed **Jan. 20, 1925.**

George Gershwin wrote *Rhapsody in Blue.*

1925

John T. Scopes found guilty of having taught evolution in Dayton, TN, high school, fined $100 and costs **July 24.**

1926

Dr. Robert H. Goddard demonstrated practicality of **rockets Mar. 16** at Auburn, MA, with first liquid fuel rocket; rocket traveled 184 ft in 2.5 seconds.

Congress established **Army Air Corps July 2.**

Air Commerce Act passed **Nov. 2,** providing federal aid for airlines and airports.

1927

About 1,000 **marines landed in China Mar. 5** to protect property in civil war.

Capt. **Charles A. Lindbergh** left Roosevelt Field, NY, **May 20** alone in plane Spirit of St. Louis on first New York-Paris nonstop flight. Reached Le Bourget airfield **May 21,** 3,610 mi in 33 ½ hours.

The Jazz Singer, with **Al Jolson,** demonstrated part-talking pictures in New York City **Oct. 6.**

Show Boat opened in New York **Dec. 27.**

O. E. Rolvaag published *Giants in the Earth.*

1928

Herbert Hoover elected president against **Alfred E. Smith,** the Catholic governor of New York.

Amelia Earhart became first woman to fly the Atlantic **June 17.**

1929

"St. Valentine's Day massacre" in Chicago **Feb. 14;** gangsters killed 7 rivals.

Farm price stability aided by **Agricultural Marketing Act,** passed **June 15.**

Albert B. Fall, former secretary of the interior, was convicted of accepting a bribe of $100,000 in the leasing of the **Elk Hills (Teapot Dome)** naval oil reserve; sentenced **Nov. 1** to a year in prison and fined $100,000.

Stock market crash Oct. 29 marked end of postwar prosperity as stock prices plummeted. Stock losses for 1929-31 estimated at $50 billion; worst American depression began.

Thomas Wolfe published *Look Homeward, Angel.* **William Faulkner** published *The Sound and the Fury.*

1930

London **Naval Reduction Treaty** signed by U.S., Britain, Italy, France, and Japan **Apr. 22;** in effect **Jan. 1, 1931;** expired **Dec. 31, 1936.**

Hawley-Smoot Tariff signed; rate hikes slash world trade.

1931

Empire State Building opened in New York City **May 1.**

Al Capone was convicted of tax evasion **Oct. 17.**

Pearl Buck published *The Good Earth.*

1932

Reconstruction Finance Corp. established **Jan. 22** to stimulate banking and business. Unemployment at 12 million.

Charles Lindbergh Jr. kidnapped Mar. 1; found dead **May 12.**

Bonus March on Washington **May 29** by World War I veterans demanding Congress pay their bonus in full.

1933

Pres. Franklin Roosevelt named **Frances Perkins** U.S. Secretary of Labor; first woman in U.S. Cabinet.

All **banks in the U.S. were ordered closed** by Pres. Roosevelt **Mar. 6.**

In the "100 days" special session, **Mar. 9-June 16,** Congress passed **New Deal** social and economic measures.

Gold standard dropped by U.S.; announced by Pres. Roosevelt **Apr. 19,** ratified by Congress **June 5.**

Prohibition ended in the U.S. as 36th state ratified 21st Amendment **Dec. 5.**

U.S. foreswore armed intervention in **western hemisphere** nations **Dec. 26.**

1934

U.S. troops pull out of **Haiti Aug. 6.**

1935

Comedian **Will Rogers** and aviator Wiley Post **killed Aug. 15** in Alaska plane crash.

Social Security Act passed by Congress **Aug. 14.**

Huey Long, senator from Louisiana and national political leader, was **assassinated Sept. 8.**

Porgy and Bess, **George Gershwin** opera on American theme, opened **Oct. 10** in New York City.

Committee for Industrial Organization (CIO; later Congress of Industrial Organizations) formed to expand industrial unionism **Nov. 9.**

1936

Boulder Dam completed.

Margaret Mitchell published *Gone With the Wind.*

1937

Joe Louis knocked out James J. Braddock, became world heavyweight champ **June 22.**

Amelia Earhart, aviator, and co-pilot Fred Noonan lost **July 2** near Howland Island. in the Pacific.

Pres. Roosevelt asked for 6 additional Supreme Court justices; **"packing" plan** defeated.

Auto, steel labor unions won first big contracts.

1938

Naval Expansion Act passed **May 17.**

National minimum wage enacted **June 25.**

Orson Welles radio dramatization of *War of the Worlds* caused nationwide scare **Oct. 30.**

1939

Pres. Roosevelt asked for **defense budget hike Jan. 5, 12.**

NY World's Fair opened **Apr. 30,** closed **Oct. 31;** re-opened **May 11, 1940,** and finally closed **Oct. 21.**

Einstein alerts Roosevelt to **A-bomb** opportunity in **Aug. 2** letter.

U.S. declares its neutrality in European war **Sept. 5.**

Roosevelt proclaimed a limited **national emergency Sept. 8,** an unlimited emergency **May 27, 1941.** Both ended by Pres. Truman **Apr. 28, 1952.**

John Steinbeck published *Grapes of Wrath.*

1940

U.S. okayed sale of **surplus war material** to Britain **June 3;** announced transfer of 50 overaged destroyers **Sept. 3.**

First **peacetime draft** approved **Sept. 14.**

Richard Wright published *Native Son.*

1941

The **Four Freedoms** termed essential by Pres. Roosevelt in speech to Congress **Jan. 6:** freedom of speech and religion, freedom from want and fear.

Lend-Lease Act signed **Mar. 11,** providing $7 billion in military credits for Britain. Lend-Lease for USSR approved in **November.**

U.S. occupied **Iceland July 7.**

The **Atlantic Charter,** 8-point declaration of principles, issued by Roosevelt and Winston Churchill **Aug. 14.**

Japan attacked **Pearl Harbor,** Hawaii, 7:55 AM. Hawaiian time, **Dec. 7;** 19 ships sunk or damaged, 2,300 dead. U.S. declared war on Japan **Dec. 8,** on Germany and Italy **Dec. 11** after those countries declared war.

1942

Federal government forcibly moved 110,000 **Japanese-Americans** (including 75,000 U.S. citizens) from West Coast to detention camps. Exclusion lasted 3 years.

Battle of **Midway June 4-7** was Japan's first major defeat.

Marines landed on **Guadalcanal Aug. 7;** last Japanese not expelled until **Feb. 9, 1943.**

U.S., Britain invaded North Africa **Nov. 8.**

First **nuclear chain reaction** (fission of uranium isotope U-235) produced at University of Chicago, under physicists Arthur Compton, Enrico Fermi, others **Dec. 2.**

1943

All war contractors barred from **racial discrimination** on **May 27.**

Pres. Roosevelt signed **June 10** the pay-as-you-go income tax bill. Starting **July 1** wage and salary earners were subject to a **paycheck withholding** tax.

Race riot in Detroit June 21; 34 dead, 700 injured. Riot in Harlem section of New York City; 6 killed.

U.S. troops invaded Italy **Sept. 9.**

Marines advanced on **Gilbert Island in Nov.**

1944

U.S., Allied forces invaded Europe at **Normandy June 6.**

G.I. Bill of Rights signed **June 22,** providing veterans benefits.

U.S. forces landed on **Leyte,** Philippines, **Oct. 20.**

1945

Yalta Conference met in the Crimea, USSR, **Feb. 4-11.** Roosevelt, Churchill, and Stalin agreed that the Soviet Union would enter war against Japan.

Marines landed on **Iwo Jima Feb. 19;** U.S. forces invaded **Okinawa Apr. 1.**

Pres. Roosevelt, 63, died of cerebral hemorrhage in Warm Springs, GA, **Apr. 12;** Vice President **Harry S. Truman** became president.

Germany surrendered May 7.

First **atomic bomb,** produced at Los Alamos, NM, exploded at Alamogordo, NM, **July 16.** Bomb dropped on **Hiroshima Aug. 6,** on **Nagasaki Aug. 9.** Japan surrendered **Aug. 14.**

U.S. forces entered **Korea** south of 38th parallel to displace Japanese **Sept. 8.**

Gen. Douglas MacArthur took over supervision of Japan **Sept. 9.**

1946

Strike by 400,000 **mine workers** began **Apr. 1;** other industries followed.

Philippines given independence by U.S. **July 4.**

1947

Truman Doctrine: Pres. Truman asked Congress to aid Greece and Turkey to combat Communist terrorism **Mar. 12.** Approved **May 15.**

United Nations Security Council voted unanimously **Apr. 2** to place under **U.S. trusteeship** the Pacific islands formerly mandated to Japan.

Jackie Robinson joined the Brooklyn Dodgers **Apr. 11,** breaking the color barrier in major league baseball.

Taft-Hartley Labor Act curbing strikes was vetoed by Truman **June 20;** Congress overrode the veto.

Proposals later known as the **Marshall Plan,** under which the U.S. would extend aid to European countries, were made by Secretary of State George C. Marshall **June 5.** Congress authorized some $12 billion in next 4 years.

1948

The USSR began a land **blockade of Berlin's** Allied sectors **Apr. 1.** This blockade and Western counterblockade were lifted **Sept. 30, 1949,** after British and U.S. planes had lifted 2,343,315 tons of food and coal into the city.

Organization of American States founded **Apr. 30.**

Alger Hiss, former State Department official, indicted **Dec. 15** for perjury, after denying he had passed secret documents to Whittaker Chambers for transmission to a Communist spy ring. His second trial ended in conviction **Jan. 21, 1950,** and a sentence of 5 years in prison.

Kinsey Report on sexuality in the human male published.

1949

U.S. troops withdrawn from **Korea June 29.**

North Atlantic Treaty Organization (NATO) established **Aug. 24** by U.S., Canada, and 10 western European nations, agreeing that an armed attack against one or more of them would be considered an attack against all.

Mrs. I. Toguri D'Aquino (**Tokyo Rose** of Japanese wartime broadcasts) was sentenced **Oct. 7** to 10 years in prison for treason. Paroled **1956,** pardoned **1977.**

Eleven leaders of **U.S. Communist Party** convicted **Oct. 14,** after 9-month trial in New York City, of advocating violent overthrow of U.S. government. Ten defendants sentenced to 5 years in prison each, and the 11th to 3 years. Supreme Court upheld the convictions **June 4, 1951.**

1950

U.S. **Jan. 14** recalled all consular officials from **China** after the latter seized the American consulate general in Beijing.

Masked bandits robbed **Brink's, Inc.,** Boston express office, **Jan. 17** of $2.8 million, of which $1.2 million was in cash. Case solved **1956;** 8 sentenced to life.

Pres. Truman authorized production of **H-bomb Jan. 31.**

United Nations asked for troops to restore Korea peace **June 25.**

Truman ordered Air Force and Navy to Korea **June 27** after North Korea invaded South. Truman approved ground forces, air strikes against North **June 30.**

U.S. sent 35 military advisers to **South Vietnam June 27,** and agreed to provide military and economic aid to anti-Communist government.

Army seized all railroads Aug. 27 on Truman's order to prevent a general strike; RR returned to owners in **1952.**

U.S. forces landed at Inchon Sept. 15; UN force took Pyongyang **Oct. 20,** reached China border **Nov. 20,** China sent troops across border **Nov. 26.**

Two members of a **Puerto Rican nationalist** movement tried to kill Pres. Truman **Nov. 1.**

U.S. **Dec. 8** banned shipments to **Communist China** and to Asiatic ports trading with it.

1951

Sen. **Estes Kefauver** led Senate investigation into organized crime. Preliminary report **Feb. 28** said gambling take was more than $20 billion a year.

Julius Rosenberg, his wife, Ethel, and Morton Sobell, all U.S. citizens, were found guilty **Mar. 29** of conspiracy to commit wartime espionage. Rosenbergs sentenced to death, Sobell to 30 years. Rosenbergs **executed June 19, 1953.** Sobell released **Jan. 14, 1969.**

Gen. Douglas MacArthur was removed from his Korea command **Apr. 11** for unauthorized policy statements.

Korea cease-fire talks began in July; lasted 2 years. **Fighting ended July 27, 1953.**

Tariff concessions by the U.S. to the Soviet Union, Communist China, and all Communist-dominated lands were suspended **Aug. 1.**

The U.S., **Australia,** and **New Zealand** signed a mutual security pact **Sept. 1.**

Transcontinental television inaugurated **Sept. 4** with Pres. Truman's address at the Japanese Peace Treaty Conference in San Francisco.

Japanese Peace Treaty signed in San Francisco **Sept. 8** by U.S., Japan, and 47 other nations.

J. D. Salinger published *Catcher in the Rye.*

1952

U.S. **seizure of nation's steel mills** was ordered by Pres. Truman **Apr. 8** to avert a strike. Ruled illegal by Supreme Court **June 2.**

Peace contract between West Germany, U.S., Great Britain, and France was signed **May 26.**

The last racial and ethnic barriers to naturalization were removed, **June 26-27,** with the passage of the **Immigration and Naturalization Act of 1952.**

First **hydrogen device** explosion **Nov. 1** at Eniwetok Atoll in Pacific.

1953

Pres. Eisenhower announced **May 8** that the U.S. had given France $60 million for **Indochina War.** More aid was announced in **September.** In **1954** it was reported that three fourths of the war's costs were met by the U.S.

1954

Nautilus, first atomic-powered submarine, was launched at Groton, CT, **Jan. 21.**

Five members of Congress were wounded in the House **Mar. 1** by **Puerto Rican independence supporters** who fired at random from a spectators' gallery.

Sen. **Joseph McCarthy** led televised hearings **Apr. 22-June 17** into alleged Communist influence in the Army.

Racial segregation in public schools was unanimously ruled unconstitutional by the Supreme Court **May 17,** as a violation of the 14th Amendment clause guaranteeing equal protection of the laws.

Southeast Asia Treaty Organization (SEATO) formed by collective defense pact signed in Manila **Sept. 8** by the U.S., Britain, France, Australia, New Zealand, Philippines, Pakistan, and Thailand.

Condemnation of **Sen. Joseph R. McCarthy** (R, WI) voted by Senate, 67-22, **Dec. 2** for contempt of a Senate elections subcommittee, for abuse of its members, and for insults to the Senate during his Army investigation hearings.

1955

U.S. agreed **Feb. 12** to help train **South Vietnamese** army.

Supreme Court ordered "all deliberate speed" in integration of public schools **May 31.**

A **summit meeting** of leaders of U.S., Britain, France, and USSR took place **July 18-23** in Geneva, Switzerland.

Rosa Parks refused **Dec. 1** to give her seat to a white man on a bus in Montgomery, AL. Bus segregation ordinance declared unconstitutional by a federal court following boycott and NAACP protest.

Merger of America's 2 largest labor organizations was effected **Dec. 5** under the name American Federation of Labor and Congress of Industrial Organizations. The merged **AFL-CIO** had a membership estimated at 15 million.

1956

Massive resistance to Supreme Court desegregation rulings was called for **Mar. 12** by 101 Southern congressmen.

Federal-Aid **Highway Act** signed **June 29,** inaugurating interstate highway system.

First transatlantic **telephone cable** went into operation **Sept. 25.**

1957

Congress approved first **civil rights bill** for blacks since Reconstruction **Apr. 29,** to protect voting rights.

National Guardsmen, called out by Arkansas Gov. Orval Faubus **Sept. 4,** barred 9 black students from entering previously all-white Central High School in **Little Rock.** Faubus complied **Sept. 21** with a federal court order to remove the National Guardsmen. The blacks entered school **Sept. 23** but were ordered to withdraw by local authorities because of fear of mob violence. Pres. Eisenhower sent federal troops **Sept. 24** to enforce the court's order.

Jack Kerouac published *On the Road.*

1958

First U.S. earth satellite to go into orbit, **Explorer I,** launched by Army **Jan. 31** at Cape Canaveral, FL; discovered Van Allen radiation belt.

Five thousand U.S. Marines sent to **Lebanon** to protect elected government from threatened overthrow **July-October.**

First domestic **jet airline** passenger service in U.S. opened by National Airlines **Dec. 10** between New York and Miami.

1959

Alaska admitted as 49th state **Jan. 3; Hawaii** admitted **Aug. 21.**

St. Lawrence Seaway opened **Apr. 25.**

Soviet Premier **Khrushchev** paid unprecedented visit to U.S. **Sept. 15-27,** made transcontinental tour.

1960

Sit-ins began **Feb. 1** when 4 black college students in Greensboro, NC, refused to move from a Woolworth lunch counter when denied service. By **Sept. 1961** more than 70,000 students, whites and blacks, had participated in sit-ins.

Congress approved a strong **voting rights act Apr. 21.**

A **U-2 reconnaisance plane** of the U.S. was shot down in the Soviet Union **May 1.** The incident led to cancellation of an imminent Paris summit conference.

U.S. announced **Dec. 15** it backed rightist group in **Laos,** which took power the next day.

1961

The U.S. severed diplomatic and consular relations with **Cuba Jan. 3,** after disputes over nationalizations of U.S. firms, U.S. military presence at Guantanamo base.

Invasion of Cuba's **"Bay of Pigs" Apr. 17** by Cuban exiles trained, armed, and directed by the U.S., attempting to overthrow the regime of Premier Fidel Castro, failed.

Commander Alan B. Shepard Jr. was rocketed from Cape Canaveral, FL, 116.5 mi above the earth in a Mercury capsule **May 5** in the first U.S.-crewed suborbital space flight.

1962

Lt. Col. John H. Glenn Jr. became the first American in orbit **Feb. 20** when he circled the earth 3 times in the Mercury capsule *Friendship 7.*

Pres. Kennedy said **Feb. 14** U.S. military advisers in Vietnam would fire if fired upon.

Supreme Court **Mar. 26** backed **"one-man one-vote"** apportionment of seats in state legislatures.

First U.S. **communications satellite** launched in **July.**

James Meredith became first black student at University of Mississippi **Oct. 1** after 3,000 troops put down riots.

A Soviet **offensive missile buildup in Cuba** was revealed **Oct. 22** by Pres. Kennedy, who ordered a naval and air quarantine on shipment of offensive military equipment to the island. Kennedy and Soviet Premier Khrushchev reached agreement **Oct. 28** on a formula to end the crisis. Kennedy announced **Nov. 2** that Soviet missile bases in Cuba were being dismantled.

Rachel Carson's *Silent Spring* launched environmentalist movement.

1963

Supreme Court ruled **Mar. 18** that all **criminal defendants** must have counsel and that illegally acquired evidence was not admissible in state as well as federal courts.

Supreme Court ruled, 8-1, **June 17** that laws requiring **recitation of the Lord's Prayer** or Bible verses in public schools were unconstitutional.

A limited **nuclear test-ban treaty** was agreed upon **July 25** by the U.S., the Soviet Union, and Britain barring all nuclear tests except underground.

Washington demonstration by 200,000 persons **Aug. 28** in support of **black demands** for equal rights. Highlight was speech in which Dr. Martin Luther King said: "I have a dream that this nation will rise up and live out the true meaning of its creed, 'We hold these truths to be self-evident: that all men are created equal.' "

South Vietnam Pres. **Ngo Dinh Diem assassinated Nov. 2;** U.S. had earlier withdrawn support.

Pres. John F. Kennedy was shot and fatally wounded by an assassin **Nov. 22** as he rode in a motorcade through downtown Dallas, Tex. Vice Pres. Lyndon B. Johnson was sworn in as president shortly after in Dallas. Lee Harvey Oswald was arrested and charged with the murder. Oswald was shot and fatally wounded **Nov. 24** by Jack Ruby, 52, a Dallas nightclub owner, who was convicted of murder **Mar. 14, 1964,** and sentenced to death. Ruby died of natural causes **Jan. 3, 1967,** while awaiting retrial.

U.S. troops in **Vietnam** totalled more than 15,000 by year-end; aid to South Vietnam was more than $500 million in **1963.**

Betty Friedan's *Feminine Mystique* ignites the women's movement.

1964

Panama suspended relations with U.S. **Jan. 9** after riots. U.S. offered **Dec. 18** to negotiate a new canal treaty.

Supreme Court ordered **Feb. 17** that **congressional districts** have equal populations.

U.S. reported **May 27** it was sending military planes to **Laos.**

Omnibus **civil rights bill** passed **June 29** banning discrimination in voting, jobs, public accommodations.

Three **civil rights workers** were reported missing in Mississippi **June 22;** found buried **Aug. 4.** Twenty-one white men were arrested. On **Oct. 20, 1967,** an all-white federal jury convicted 7 of conspiracy in the slayings.

U.S. Congress **Aug. 7** passed **Tonkin Resolution,** authorizing presidential action in Vietnam, after North Vietnam boats reportedly attacked 2 U.S. destroyers **Aug. 2.**

Congress approved War on Poverty bill **Aug. 11.**

The **Warren Commission** released **Sept. 27** a report concluding that Lee Harvey Oswald was solely responsible for the Kennedy assassination.

1965

Pres. Johnson in **Feb.** ordered continuous **bombing of North Vietnam** below 20th parallel.

Some 14,000 U.S. troops sent to **Dominican Republic** during civil war **Apr. 28.** All troops withdrawn by next year.

New **Voting Rights Act** signed **Aug. 6.**

Los Angeles riot by blacks living in **Watts** area resulted in death of 34 persons and property damage estimated at $200 million **Aug. 11-16.**

National origins quota system of **immigration** abolished **Oct. 3.**

Electric power failure blacked out most of northeastern U.S., parts of 2 Canadian provinces the night of **Nov. 9-10.**

U.S. forces in **S. Vietnam** reached 184,300 by year-end.

1966

U.S. forces began firing into **Cambodia May 1.**

Bombing of Hanoi area of North Vietnam by U.S. planes began **June 29.** By **Dec. 31,** 385,300 U.S. troops were stationed in South Vietnam, plus 60,000 offshore and 33,000 in Thailand.

Medicare, government program to pay part of the medical expenses of citizens over 65, began **July 1.**

Edward Brooke (R, MA) elected **Nov. 8** as first black U.S. senator in 85 years.

1967

Black representative **Adam Clayton Powell** (D, NY) was denied **Mar. 1** his seat in Congress because of charges he misused government funds. Reelected in 1968, he was seated, but fined $25,000 and stripped of his 22 years' seniority.

Pres. Johnson and Soviet Premier Aleksei Kosygin met **June 23 and 25** at **Glassboro State College** in NJ; agreed not to let any crisis push them into war.

Riots by blacks in **Newark, NJ, July 12-17** killed 26, injured 1,500; more than 1,000 arrested. In Detroit, MI, **July 23-30** at least 40 died; 2,000 injured, 5,000 left homeless by rioting, looting, burning in city's black ghetto. Quelled by 4,700 federal paratroopers and 8,000 National Guardsmen.

Thurgood Marshall sworn in **Oct. 2** as first black U.S. Supreme Court Justice. Carl B. Stokes (D, Cleveland) and Richard G. Hatcher (D, Gary, IN) were elected first black mayors of major U.S. cities **Nov. 7.**

By **December** 475,000 U.S. troops were in **South Vietnam.**

1968

USS Pueblo and 83-man crew seized in Sea of Japan **Jan. 23** by North Koreans; 82 men released **Dec. 22.**

"Tet offensive": Communist troops attacked Saigon, 30 province capitals **Jan. 30,** suffer heavy casualties.

Pres. Johnson **curbed bombing** of North Vietnam **Mar. 31.** Peace talks began in Paris **May 10.** All bombing of North halted **Oct. 31.**

Martin Luther King Jr., 39, assassinated Apr. 4 in Memphis, TN. James Earl Ray, an escaped convict, pleaded guilty to the slaying, was sentenced to 99 years.

Sen. Robert F. Kennedy (D, NY), 42, **shot June 5** in Hotel Ambassador, Los Angeles, after celebrating presidential primary victories. Died **June 6.** Sirhan Bishara Sirhan, Jordanian, convicted of murder.

Rep. Shirley Chisholm (D, NY) became the first black woman elected to Congress.

1969

Expanded four-party **Vietnam peace talks** began **Jan. 18.** U.S. force peaked at 543,400 in April. Withdrawal started **July 8.** Pres. Nixon set Vietnamization policy **Nov. 3.**

U.S. astronaut **Neil A. Armstrong,** 38, commander of the Apollo 11 mission, became the first person to **set foot on the moon July 20.**

Woodstock music festival near Bethel, NY, drew 300,000-500,000 people, **Aug. 15-17.**

Anti-Vietnam War **demonstrations reached peak** in U.S.; some 250,000 marched in Washington, DC, **Nov. 15.**

Massacre of hundreds of civilians at **Mylai, South Vietnam,** in 1968 incident was reported **Nov. 16.**

1970

United Mine Workers official **Joseph A. Yablonski,** his wife, and their daughter were found shot **Jan. 5** in their Clarksville, PA, home. UMW chief W. A. (Tony) Boyle was later convicted of the killing.

A federal jury **Feb. 18** found the **"Chicago 7"** innocent of conspiring to incite riots during the 1968 Democratic National Convention. However, 5 were convicted of crossing state lines with intent to incite riots.

Millions of Americans participated in antipollution demonstrations **Apr. 22** to mark the first **Earth Day.**

U.S. and South Vietnamese forces crossed **Cambodian** borders **Apr. 30** to get at enemy bases. Four students were killed **May 4** at **Kent State** University in Ohio by National Guardsmen during a protest against the war.

Two **women generals,** the first in U.S. history, were named by Pres. Nixon **May 15.**

A **postal reform** measure was signed **Aug. 12,** creating an independent U.S. Postal Service, thus relinquishing governmental control of the U.S. mails after almost 2 centuries.

1971

Charles Manson, 36, and 3 of his followers were found guilty **Jan. 26** of first-degree murder in the 1969 slaying of actress Sharon Tate and 6 others.

A constitutional amendment lowering the **voting age to 18** in all elections was approved in the Senate by a vote of 94-0 **Mar. 10.** The proposed 26th Amendment got House approval by a 400-19 vote **Mar. 23.** It was ratified July 1.

A court-martial jury Mar. 29, convicted **Lt. William L. Calley Jr.** of premeditated murder of 22 South Vietnamese at Mylai on **Mar. 16, 1968.** He was sentenced to life imprisonment **Mar. 31.** Sentence was reduced to 20 years **Aug. 20.**

Publication of classified **Pentagon papers** on the U.S. involvement in Vietnam was begun **June 13** by the *New York Times.* In a 6-3 vote, the U.S. Supreme Court **June 30** upheld the right of the *Times* and the *Washington Post* to publish the documents under the protection of the First Amendment.

U.S. bombers struck massively in North Vietnam for 5 days starting **Dec. 26,** in retaliation for alleged violations of agreements reached prior to the 1968 bombing halt. U.S. forces at year-end were down to 140,000.

1972

Pres. Nixon arrived in **Beijing Feb. 21** for an 8-day visit to China, which he called a "journey for peace." The unprecedented visit ended with a joint communique pledging that both powers would work for "a normalization of relations."

By a vote of 84 to 8, the Senate approved **Mar. 22** a constitutional amendment banning **discrimination against women** because of their sex and sent the measure to the states for ratification.

North Vietnamese forces launched the biggest attacks in 4 years across the demilitarized zone **Mar. 30.** The U.S. responded **Apr. 15** by resumption of bombing of Hanoi and Haiphong after a 4-year lull.

Nixon announced **May 8** the mining of **North Vietnam ports.** Last U.S. combat troops left **Aug. 11.**

Alabama Gov. George C. Wallace, campaigning for the presidency at a Laurel, MD, shopping center **May 15, was shot** and seriously wounded. Arthur H. Bremer, 21, was sentenced to 63 years for shooting Wallace and 3 bystanders.

In the first visit of a U.S. president to Moscow, Nixon arrived **May 22** for a week of summit talks with Kremlin leaders that culminated in a landmark **strategic arms pact.**

Five men were arrested **June 17** for breaking into the offices of the Democratic National Committee in the **Watergate** office complex in Washington, DC.

Full-scale bombing of North Vietnam resumed after Paris peace negotiations reached an impasse **Dec. 18.**

1973

Five of seven defendants in the **Watergate** break-in trial pleaded guilty **Jan. 11 and 15,** and the other 2 were convicted **Jan. 30.**

In **Roe v Wade,** the Supreme Court ruled 7-2, **Jan. 22,** that a state may not prevent a woman from having an **abortion** during the **first 3 months of pregnancy** and that a state could regulate but not prohibit abortion during the second trimester; decision in effect overturned antiabortion laws in 46 states.

Four-party **Vietnam peace pacts** were signed in Paris **Jan. 27,** and North Vietnam released some 590 U.S. prisoners by **Apr. 1.** Last U.S. troops left **Mar. 29.**

The **end of the military draft** was announced **Jan. 27.**

Top **Nixon aides** H. R. Haldeman, John D. Ehrlichman, and John W. Dean and Attorney General Richard Kleindienst **resigned Apr. 30** amid charges of White House efforts to obstruct justice in the Watergate case.

John Dean, former Nixon counsel, told Senate hearings **June 25** that Nixon, his staff and campaign aides, and the Justice Department all had conspired to cover up Watergate facts. Nixon refused July 23 to release **tapes** of relevant White House conversations. Some tapes were turned over to the court **Nov. 26.**

The U.S. officially ceased bombing in **Cambodia** at midnight **Aug. 14** in accord with a June congressional action.

Vice President Spiro T. Agnew Oct. 10 resigned and pleaded *nolo contendere* (no contest) to charges of tax evasion on payments made to him by Maryland contractors when he was governor of that state. Gerald Rudolph Ford **Oct. 12** became first appointed vice president under the 25th Amendment; sworn in **Dec. 6.**

A total ban on **oil exports** to the U.S. was imposed by Arab oil-producing nations **Oct. 19-21** after the outbreak of an Arab-Israeli war. The ban was lifted **Mar. 18, 1974.**

Attyorney General Elliot Richardson resigned, and his deputy William D. Ruckelshaus and Watergate Special Prosecutor Archibald Cox were fired by Pres. Nixon **Oct. 20** when Cox threatened to secure a judicial ruling that Nixon was violating a court order to turn tapes over to Watergate case Judge John Sirica.

Leon Jaworski, conservative Texas Democrat, was named **Nov. 1** by the Nixon administration to be special prosecutor to succeed Archibald Cox.

Congress overrode **Nov. 7** Nixon's veto of the **war powers** bill, which curbed the president's power to commit armed forces to hostilities abroad without congressional approval.

1974

Impeachment hearings were opened **May 9** against Pres. Nixon by the House Judiciary Committee.

John D. Ehrlichman and 3 **White House "plumbers"** were found guilty **July 12** of conspiring to violate the civil rights of Dr. Lewis Fielding, formerly psychiatrist to Pentagon Papers leaker Daniel Ellsberg, by breaking into his Beverly Hills, CA, office.

The U.S. Supreme Court ruled, 8-0, **July 24** that Nixon had to turn over **64 tapes** of White House conversations sought by Watergate Special Prosecutor Leon Jaworski.

The House Judiciary Committee, in televised hearings **July 24-30,** recommended 3 **articles of impeachment** against Nixon. The first, voted 27-11 **July 27,** charged Nixon with taking part in a criminal conspiracy to obstruct justice in the Watergate cover-up. The second, voted 28-10 **July 29,** charged he "repeatedly" failed to carry out his constitutional oath in a series of alleged abuses of power. The third, voted 21-17 **July 30,** accused him of unconstitutional defiance of committee subpoenas. The House of Representatives voted without debate **Aug. 20,** by 412-3, to accept the committee report, which included the recommended impeachment articles.

Nixon resigned Aug. 9. Vice President Gerald R. Ford was sworn in as the 38th U.S. president on **Aug. 9.**

An **unconditional pardon** to ex-Pres. Nixon for all federal crimes that he "committed or may have committed" while president was issued by Pres. Gerald Ford **Sept. 8.**

1975

Found guilty of **Watergate** cover-up charges **Jan. 1** were ex-Atty. Gen. John N. Mitchell, ex-presidential advisers H. R. Haldeman and John D. Ehrlichman.

U.S. civilians were evacuated from **Saigon Apr. 29** as Communist forces completed takeover of South Vietnam.

U.S. merchant ship *Mayaguez* and crew of 39 seized by Cambodian forces in Gulf of Siam **May 12.** In rescue operation, U.S. Marines attacked Tang Island, planes bombed air base; Cambodia surrendered ship and crew.

Congress voted $405 million for **South Vietnam refugees May 16;** 140,000 were flown to the U.S.

Illegal **CIA operations,** including records on 300,000 persons and groups, and infiltration of agents into black, antiwar, and political movements, were described by a "blue-ribbon" panel headed by Vice Pres. Rockefeller **June 10.**

FBI agents captured **Patricia (Patty) Hearst,** kidnapped **Feb. 4, 1974,** in San Francisco **Sept. 18** with others. She was indicted for bank robbery; a San Francisco jury convicted her **Mar. 20, 1976.**

1976

The U.S. celebrated its **bicentennial July 4,** marking the 200th anniversary of its independence with festivals, parades, and New York City's Operation Sail, a gathering of tall ships from around the world viewed by 6 million persons.

A mystery ailment **"legionnaire's disease"** killed 29 persons who attended an American Legion convention **July 21-24** in Philadelphia. The cause was found to be a bacterium, it was reported **June 18, 1977.**

The *Viking II* set down on **Mars'** Utopia Plains **Sept. 3,** following the successful landing by *Viking I* **July 20.**

1977

Pres. Jimmy Carter **Jan. 21** pardoned most Vietnam War **draft evaders,** who numbered some 10,000.

Convicted murderer **Gary Gilmore** was executed by a Utah firing squad **Jan. 17,** in the first exercise of capital punishment anywhere in the U.S. since **1967.** Gilmore had opposed all attempts to delay the execution.

Carter signed an act **Aug. 4** creating a new Cabinet-level **Energy Department.**

1978

U.S. Senate voted **Apr. 18** to turn over the **Panama Canal** to Panama on Dec. 31, 1999; **Mar. 16** vote had given approval to a treaty guaranteeing the area's neutrality after the year 2000.

1979

A major accident occurred, **Mar. 28,** at a nuclear reactor on **Three Mile Island** near Middletown, PA.

The federal government announced, **Nov. 1,** a $1.5 billion loan-guarantee plan to aid the nation's 3d largest automaker, **Chrysler Corp.,** which had reported a loss of $460.6 million for the 3d quarter of 1979.

Some 90 people, including 63 Americans, were taken hostage, **Nov. 4,** at the **American embassy in Tehran,** Iran, by militant student followers of Ayatollah Khomeini who demanded the return of former Shah Mohammad Reza Pahlavi, who was undergoing medical treatment in New York City.

1980

Pres. Carter announced, **Jan. 4, punitive measures against the USSR,** including an embargo on the sale of grain and high technology, in retaliation for the Soviet invasion of Afghanistan. At Carter's request, the **U.S. Olympic** Committee voted, **Apr. 12,** not to attend the Moscow Summer Olympics.

Eight Americans were killed and 5 wounded, **Apr. 24,** in an ill-fated attempt to **rescue the hostages** held by Iranian **militants** at the U.S. Embassy in Tehran.

In the state of Washington, **Mt. St. Helens erupted, May 18,** in a violent blast estimated to be 500 times as powerful as the Hiroshima atomic bomb. The blast, followed by others on **May 25** and **June 12,** left about 60 dead and economic losses estimated at nearly $3 billion.

In a sweeping victory, **Nov. 4, Ronald Wilson Reagan** was elected 40th president of the U.S., defeating incumbent Jimmy Carter. The stunning GOP victory extended to the U.S. Congress where Republicans gained control of the Senate and wrested 33 House seats from the Democrats.

Former Beatle **John Lennon** was shot and killed, **Dec. 8,** outside his apartment building in New York City.

1981

Minutes after the **inauguration of Pres. Ronald Reagan, Jan. 20,** the **52 Americans** who had been held **hostage in Iran** for 444 days were flown to freedom following an arrangement in which the U.S. agreed to return to Iran $8 billion in frozen assets.

President Reagan was **shot in the chest** by a would-be assassin, **Mar. 30,** in Washington, DC, as he walked to his limousine following an address.

The world's first reusable spacecraft, the **Space Shuttle** *Columbia,* was sent into space, **Apr. 12,** and completed its successful mission 2 days later.

Both houses of Congress passed, **July 29,** President Reagan's **tax-cut legislation.** The largest tax cut in the nation's history was expected to reduce taxes by $37.6 billion in fiscal 1982 and to save taxpayers $750 billion over the next 5 years.

Federal air traffic controllers, Aug. 3, began an **illegal nationwide strike** after their union rejected the government's final offer for a new contract. Most of the 13,000 striking controllers defied the back-to-work order and were dismissed by President Reagan **Aug. 5.**

In a 99-0 vote, the Senate confirmed, **Sept. 21,** the appointment of **Sandra Day O'Connor** as an **associate justice of the U.S. Supreme Court.** She was the first woman appointed to that body.

1982

The 13-year-old lawsuit against **AT&T** by the **Justice Dept.** was settled **Jan. 8.** AT&T agreed to give up the 22 Bell System companies but in return was allowed to expand into previously prohibited areas including data processing, telephone and computer equipment sales, and computer communication devices.

The Equal Rights Amendment was defeated after a 10-year struggle for ratification.

In December, the **unemployment rate** rose to 10.8%, the highest since 1940.

Lech Walesa, former leader of **Solidarity,** the Polish labor union, was freed **Nov. 13,** after 11 months of internment following the imposition of martial law and the outlawing of Solidarity. Pres. Reagan lifted the **U.S. embargo on sales of oil and gas equipment to the Soviet Union.**

The **Space Shuttle** *Columbia* completed its first operational flight **Nov. 16.**

A retired dentist, **Dr. Barney B. Clark,** 61, became the first recipient of a **permanent artificial heart** during a 7½ hour operation in Salt Lake City **Dec. 2.** The heart was designed by **Dr. Robert Jarvik,** also on the surgical team.

1983

On **Apr. 20, Pres. Reagan** signed a compromise, bipartisan bill designed to rescue the **Social Security System** from bankruptcy.

In an 8-1 decision, **the U.S. Supreme Court** held, **May 24,** that the **Internal Revenue Service** could deny **tax exemptions** to **private schools** that practiced **racial discrimination.**

Sally Ride became the first American **woman** to travel in **space, June 18,** when the **space shuttle** *Challenger* was launched from Cape Canaveral, FL.

On **Oct. 23,** 241 **U.S. Marines and sailors,** members of the multinational **peacekeeping force** in **Lebanon,** were killed when a TNT-laden suicide **terrorist** blew up Marine headquarters at **Beirut** International. Airport. Almost simultaneously, a second truck bomb blew up a **French paratroop** barracks 2 miles away, killing more than 40.

U.S. Marines and Rangers and a small force from 6 Caribbean nations invaded the island of Grenada on Oct. 25, in response to a request from the Organization of Eastern Caribbean States. After a few days, Grenadian militia and Cuban "construction workers" were overcome, hundreds of U.S. citizens evacuated safely, and the Marxist regime deposed. The U.S. Congress applied the War Powers Resolution, requiring U.S. troops to leave Grenada by Dec. 24.

1984

The space shuttle *Challenger* was launched on its 4th trip into space, Feb. 3. On Feb. 7, Navy Capt. Bruce McCandless, followed by Army Lt. Colonel Robert Stewart, became the first humans to fly free of a spacecraft.

On May 7, American Vietnam war veterans reached an out-of-court settlement with 7 chemical companies in their class-action suit regarding the herbicide Agent Orange.

On June 6, former vice president Walter Mondale won the Democratic presidental nomination. In a historic move, July 12, Mondale chose a woman, Rep. Geraldine Ferraro (D, NY) as candidate for vice president.

Ronald Reagan was reelected U.S. President Nov. 6 in the greatest Republican landslide in history, carrying 49 states against Walter F. Mondale.

1985

"Live Aid," a 17-hour rock concert broadcast July 13 on radio and TV from London and Philadelphia to 152 countries, raised $70 million for the starving peoples of Africa.

On Oct. 7, 4 hijackers seized an Italian cruise ship, the *Achille Lauro,* in the open sea as it approached Port Said, Egypt. More than 400 passengers and crew were aboard, including American Leon Klinghoffer, who was killed. The hijackers, members of the Palestine Liberation Front, a faction that had broken away from the PLO, demanded the release of 50 Palestinians held by Israel.

In November, for the first time in 6 years, the leaders of the U.S. and the Soviet Union met at a summit conference. In Geneva, Switzerland, Pres. Reagan and Mikhail Gorbachev, the general secretary of the Soviet Communist Party, talked privately for 5 hours, Nov. 19 and 20.

1986

On Jan. 20, for the first time, the U.S. officially observed Martin Luther King Day.

Moments after liftoff, Jan. 28, the space shuttle *Challenger* exploded, killing 6 astronauts and Christa McAuliffe, a New Hampshire teacher. Subsequent investigations found that NASA had abandoned "good judgment and common sense" regarding safety problems that caused the explosion.

U.S. officials said, June 12, that AIDS cases and deaths would increase tenfold in the next 5 years. At that time, the government had recorded 21,517 cases, 11,713 deaths. An antiviral drug, azidothymidine (AZT) was found to improve the health of some AIDS patient, but was not a cure.

The U.S., via Congress's Sept. override of Pres. Reagan's veto, joined other nations in imposing economic sanctions on S. Africa, pressuring the Botha government to end apartheid.

The U.S. Senate confirmed, Sept. 17, Pres. Reagan's nomination of William Rehnquist as chief justice, Antonin Scalia as associate justice of the Supreme Court.

Congress passed, in late September a comprehensive tax reform law. In effect in 1987, it simplified the system, drastically changing tax brackets, deductions, and more.

In the congressional races, Nov. 4, Democrats won a 55-45 Senate majority, after 6 years of Republican majority, and enlarged their House majority by 5, to 258-177.

Public hearings by the Senate and House committees investigating the Iran-contra affair went on from May-Aug. Lt. Col. Oliver North said he had believed all his activities were authorized by his superiors. Pres. Reagan, Aug. 12, again denied knowing of the funds' diversion to the contras.

The most scandalous year in Wall Street history ended with Ivan Boesky's agreeing, Nov. 14, to plead guilty to an unspecified criminal count, pay a $100 million fine, and return profits; he was barred for life from trading securities.

1987

Pres. Reagan produced the nation's first trillion-dollar budget, Jan. 5.

The stock market continued its phenomenal rise. The Dow closed at 2002.25, Jan. 8, its first finish above 2000.

An Iraqi warplane missile killed 37 sailors on the frigate U.S.S. *Stark* in the Persian Gulf, May 17. Iraq called it an accident. The Stark's officers were found negligent, June 14. The U.S. escorted Kuwaiti oil tankers to the Gulf, reflagging them for the U.S.

Public hearings by the Senate and House committees investigating the Iran-contra affair went on May-Aug. Lt. Col. Oliver North said he had believed all his activities were authorized by his superiors. Pres. Reagan, Aug. 12, again denied knowing of the funds' diversion to the contras.

Wall Street crashed, Oct. 19, the Dow plummeting a record 508 points—22.6%—after a record high of 2722.42, Aug. 25.

Pres. Reagan and Soviet leader Gorbachev met in Wash., Dec. 8, and signed an unprecedented agreement calling for the dismantling of all 1,752 U.S. and 859 Soviet missiles with a 300- to 3,400-mile range.

1988

Federal grand juries in Miami and Tampa returned indictments, Feb. 4, against Gen. Manuel Noriega, ruler of Panama, charging that he had protected and otherwise assisted the Medellín drug cartel.

Nearly 1.4 million illegal aliens met the May 4 deadline for applying for amnesty under a U.S. Immigration and Naturalization Service policy. An estimated 50+% of applications were in California; nationwide, about 71 % of the aliens had entered the U.S. from Mexico.

Much of the U.S. suffered the worst drought in more than 50 years. By June 23, half the nation's agricultural counties had been designated disaster areas.

A missile, fired from the U.S. Navy warship *Vincennes,* in the Persian Gulf, struck and destroyed a commercial Iranian airliner, July 3, killing all 290 persons on the plane. Navy personnel had mistaken the airliner for an Iranian F-14 jet fighter.

George Bush, vice president under Ronald Reagan, was elected 41st U.S. president, Nov. 8. Bush defeated the Democratic nominee, Gov. Michael Dukakis (MA).

Drexel Burnham Lambert agreed, Dec. 21, to plead guilty to 6 violations of federal law, including insider trading, stock manipulation, and falsified records; and to pay penalties of $650 million, by far the largest such settlement.

1989

The Labor Dept. reported, Jan. 6, that unemployment was 5.3% in Dec. 1988, the lowest since July 1974.

The largest oil spill in U.S. history occurred after the *Exxon Valdez* struck Bligh Reef in Alaska's Prince William Sound, Mar. 24. Initially estimated at 240,000 barrels, as of Mar. 29, the spill extended 45 miles.

Former National Security Council staff member Oliver North became the first person, May 4, convicted in a jury trial in connection with the Iran-contra scandal. North received, July 6, a 3-year suspended prison sentence, 2 years' probation, a $150,000 fine, and an order to perform 1,200 hours of community service.

Legislation passed by Congress to rescue the savings and loan industry was signed into law, Aug. 9, by Pres. George Bush. The bill provided $166 billion over 10 years to close or merge insolvent S&Ls. The total cost was put at $400 billion over 30 years, most to be paid by taxpayers.

Army Gen. Colin Powell was nominated by Pres. Bush, Aug. 10, to serve as chairman of the Joint Chiefs of Staff; he became the first black to hold the post.

Minutes before the start of the third game of the 1989 World Series between the San Francisco Giants and the Oakland Athletics, Oct. 17, an earthquake struck the San Francisco Bay area, causing at least 59 deaths and massive property damage.

Democrats won most of the top offices at stake, and black candidates scored major breakthroughs in off-year elections, Nov. 7. Lt. Gov. L. Douglas Wilder, a Democrat, was elected governor of Virginia, the nation's first black governor since Reconstruction. Manhattan Borough Pres. David Dinkins, also a Democrat, became the first black elected mayor of New York City.

Pres. Bush signed into law, Nov. 19, an increase in the minimum wage. Currently $3.35 an hour, the wage would rise to $4.25 an hour by 1991, with a training wage of $3.35 for 16- to 19-year-olds in their first 3 months on a job.

U.S. troops invaded Panama, Dec. 20, overthrowing the government of Manuel Noriega, who eluded capture, took refuge in the Vatican mission, then surrendered to the U.S. Jan. 3, 1990.

1990

The Dow Jones Industrial average pushed to an all-time high, **July 16 and 17,** finishing at 2,999.75.

Pres. Bush signed the **Americans With Disabilities Act** on July 26, barring discrimination against such individuals.

Justice William Brennan announced, **July 20,** his immediate resignation from the U.S. Supreme Court, due to illness. Pres. Bush nominated **Judge David Souter** of the U.S. Court of Appeals for the First Circuit in Boston, **July 23,** and the Senate voted to confirm him, **Sept. 27.**

Operation Desert Shield forces left for **Saudi Arabia, Aug. 7,** to defend that country following the **invasion** of its neighbor **Kuwait by Iraq,** Aug. 2.

Pres. Bush **vetoed, Oct. 22, a civil rights bill** that sought in effect to reverse 6 recent Supreme Court decisions that civil rights organizations contended had weakened antidiscrimination laws on hiring and promoting.

Pres. Bush signed, **Nov. 15,** a bill designed to **reduce budget deficits** by nearly $500 billion over 5 years. The top personal income tax rate would rise from 28 to 31%, and exemptions for upper-income Americans would be phased out; gas, cigarette, liquor taxes would increase; a luxury tax would be imposed on some items.

1991

The **U.S. and its allies defeated Iraq** in **Jan.** and **Feb. 1991** and liberated Kuwait, which Iraq had overrun in Aug. 1990. In **Jan.,** the allies launched an **attack on Iraq from the air.** In a **ground war** in Feb. that lasted just 100 hours, the U.S.-led attackers killed or captured many thousands of Iraqi soldiers and sent the rest into retreat before Pres. George Bush ordered a cease-fire.

The **Dow Jones Industrial Average** finished above 3000 for the first time, **Apr. 17,** closing at 3004.46.

The **case against Oliver North was "terminated,"** with all charges dropped, **Sept. 16.** In 1989, North, a leading figure in the Iran-contra affair, had been convicted of obstructing a congressional investigation, destroying documents, and accepting an illegal gratuity. In 1990, a federal appeals court had overturned one conviction and sent the others back to the federal district court.

The **U.S. Senate approved, Oct. 15, the nomination of Clarence Thomas** to serve as an **associate justice of the Supreme Court,** after investigating an allegation of sexual harassment that had been leveled against him by **Anita Hill, a law professor at the University of Oklahoma.**

Charles Keating was convicted of 17 counts of securities fraud, Dec. 4. The prosecution asserted that as chairman of the Lincoln Savings & Loan Assn. in California, Keating had induced some 17,000 investors to buy $250 million in bonds that were not insured.

1992

R. H. Macy & Co. and **Trans World Airlines** filed for bankruptcy in Jan. Chrysler, Ford, and General Motors announced huge losses in Feb. However, the **Dow Jones Industrial Average** closed, **Feb. 24,** at **3283.32, an all-time high.**

Rioting, looting, and arson swept **South-Central Los Angeles** in late April and early May after a jury that included no blacks acquitted 4 policemen on all but one count in the beating of a black man, Rodney King. The attack on King had been videotaped and shown on TV newcasts across the country. The death toll in the L.A. violence was put at 52; damage was said to run as high as $1 billion.

A **27th Amendment, regarding congressional pay raises,** became part of the **U.S. Constitution** in **May.** Proposed by James Madison, it had been approved by Congress in 1798 and submitted to the states for ratification, which took almost 200 years.

The **Democratic Party** nominated **Gov. Bill Clinton (AR)** as its **candidate for president, July 15,** and **Sen. Al Gore Jr. (TN)** as its **candidate for vice president, July 16,** in New York City. **Texan H. Ross Perot,** who had mounted an independent campaign, announced, **July 16,** that he would **not seek the presidency.**

The **Republican Party** renominated **Pres. George Bush** and **Vice Pres. Dan Quayle** at the convention in Houston, TX, in **early August.**

Gov. Bill Clinton was **elected 42d president of the U.S.** on **Nov. 3,** and his running mate, **Sen. Al Gore Jr.,** was **elected vice president.** The **Democrats** retained control of both houses of Congress.

1993

Bill Clinton was inaugurated **Jan. 20** as the 42d president of the U.S. On **Jan. 25,** he appointed **Hillary Rodham Clinton head of a task force on health-care reform.**

A powerful bomb exploded in an underground parking garage beneath the World Trade Center in New York City, **Feb. 26,** killing 6 people. More than 1,000 people suffered injuries. Five men were arrested in March in connection with the bombing. A 6th man was indicted, **Mar. 31,** but remained at large. A 7th suspect was charged **May 6.**

Four agents of the U.S. Bureau of Alcohol, Tobacco, and Firearms were killed, Feb. 28, during an unsuccessful raid on the **Branch Davidian compound in Waco, TX.** This led to a 51-day siege of the compound. The confrontation ended **Apr. 19,** when, by order of the FBI, armored vehicles pumped tear gas into the compound. Those inside responded with gunfire. Shortly after noon, flames appeared at a window; the compound was leveled by fire in 30 minutes, leaving about 80 cult members dead. The U.S. Treasury Dept., **Sept. 30,** sharply criticized top ATF officials for their handling of the raid.

Janet Reno, a Florida state attorney, became the first woman to serve as attorney general of the U.S. when she took the oath of office **Mar. 12.**

A federal jury, **Apr. 17, found 2 Los Angeles police officers, Sgt. Stacey Koon and Officer Laurence Powell, guilty** and 2 officers not guilty of violating the civil rights of Rodney King, a black motorist whom they had arrested and beaten in 1991. The two officers convicted were sentenced, **Aug. 4,** to 2½ years in prison.

The **"motor-voter" bill** was signed by Pres. Clinton, **May 20.** Under the bill, citizens in any state can register to vote when applying for a driver's license or at some other government offices..

A flood that was worse than anyone in the Midwest could remember surged down the Mississippi River and its tributaries in the summer of 1993. **"The Great Flood of 1993"** inundated 8 million acres of land and left 12 million acres too wet to cultivate. The floods left 50 people dead and some 70,000 homeless. State and federal officials put total damage estimates at $12 billion.

Pres. Clinton, **July 19,** announced circumstances under which homosexual men and women could serve in the U.S. military. An approach of "don't ask, don't tell, don't pursue" was endorsed.

Vincent Foster, the deputy White House counsel and long-time friend of Bill and Hillary Clinton, was found shot to death in a park in northern Virginia **July 20.** An autopsy indicated that he had committed suicide.

Judge Ruth Bader Ginsburg was sworn in, Aug. 10, as the 107th justice of the U.S. Supreme Court, replacing Associate Justice Byron White who announced his retirement, Mar. 19.

After a long and acrimonious debate, **Congress narrowly approved a bill designed to reduce federal budget deficits by $496 billion over 5 years.** The House approved the bill, **Aug. 5,** by a 218-216 margin, and the Senate, divided 50-50, passed the bill, **Aug. 6,** with the tie-breaking vote of Vice Pres. Al Gore. Pres. Clinton signed the bill **Aug. 10.**

Sheikh Omar Abdel Rahman was indicted, Aug. 25, on conspiracy charges of leading a terrorist group responsible for the World Trade Center bombing, a plot to bomb the United Nations and other New York City targets, and the 1990 assassination of Rabbi Meir Kahane.

After extensive debate, the House, **Nov. 17,** approved the North American Free Trade Agreement. The Senate endorsed it **Nov. 20.** NAFTA was to take effect Jan. 1, 1994.

The **"Brady Bill,"** providing for a 5-day waiting period and establishing a national computer network as a means to check the backgrounds of gun buyers, was signed into law by Pres. Clinton **Nov. 30.**

The space shuttle *Endeavour* was launched **Dec. 2.** The mission to repair the Hubble telescope was successful.

Late in the year, federal investigators initiated a probe into the dealings of the Madison Guaranty Savings and Loan, an Arkansas thrift that failed in 1989. Madison's owner James B. McDougal was a partner with Bill and Hillary Rodham Clinton in the **Whitewater** Development Co., a real estate firm. On **Dec. 23,** the Clintons instructed their attorneys to provide federal investigators with all their legal documents and financial records relating to Whitewater.

1994

A predawn **earthquake struck the Los Angeles area, Jan. 17,** claiming 61 lives and causing a widespread devastation. The main jolt lasted 30 seconds and measured 6.8 on the Richter scale. The damage was estimated at $13 billion to $20 billion.

Attorney Gen. Janet Reno on **Jan. 20** appointed Robert Fiske independent counsel to investigate the so-called **Whitewater affair,** named for the Whitewater real estate venture in Arkansas in which the Clintons were partners with **James McDougal,** who also headed a failed savings and loan that had been bailed out with federal funds. Pres. Clinton, **Jan 12,** had asked Reno to appoint an independent counsel to conduct an inquiry into the Clintons' involvement with McDougal. **White House counsel Bernard Nussbaum resigned, Mar. 5,** following a furor over briefings received by White House aides from Treasury Dept. officials concerning Whitewater investigations. Fiske issued his first report **June 30,** in which he said he had not found sufficient evidence that officials had "acted with the intent to corruptly influence" an investigation by the Resolution Trust Corp. into the collapse of McDougal's Madison Guaranty Savings and Loan. The House Banking Committee, **July 26,** and the Senate Banking Committee, **July 29,** began hearings into the Whitewater affair. During those hearings, Treasury and White House officials contradicted one another about details concerning contacts they had with the Resolution Trust Corp. A panel of 3 federal judges, **Aug. 5,** named a new Whitewater prosecutor, who succeeded Fiske. The judges concluded that Fiske was technically an appointee of the administration.

Data released in January showed that **the U.S. inflation rate was at its lowest level in 7 years.** Consumer prices advanced by only 2.7% during 1993, the smallest increase for any year since 1986. The **Dow Jones industrial average** closed, **Jan. 31,** at an all-time high of 3,978.36.

Pres. Bill Clinton announced, **Feb. 3,** that the **U.S. was lifting its trade embargo against Vietnam.** On **Feb. 7,** the Vietnamese government turned over to U.S. officials what were believed to be the remains of 12 U.S. soldiers.

Byron De La Beckwith, a white supremacist, was convicted Feb. 5 of the 1963 murder of **civil rights leader Medgar Evers.** Beckwith was sentenced to life in prison.

On **Feb. 21, Aldrich Ames,** a long-time counterintelligence officer in the CIA, and his wife, **Maria del Rosario Casas Ames, were arrested and charged with selling information to the Soviet Union and Russia.** On **Apr. 28,** Aldrich Ames pleaded guilty to a charge of spying and to a charge of income tax evasion. Under a plea bargain, he received a life sentence in prison and agreed to cooperate with investigators. In return, Rosario Ames, who also pleaded guilty to espionage and tax evasion, was sentenced, **Oct. 21,** to 63 months in prison.

Eleven members of **the Branch Davidian religious cult** were found not guilty, **Feb. 26,** of murder and conspiracy charges related to the deaths of 4 federal agents in a shootout at the cult's compound near Waco, TX, in Feb. 1993.

Four men were found guilty, Mar. 4, of a total of 38 charges related to **the 1993 bombing at the World Trade Center in New York City.** Six people had died in the explosion. On **May 24,** the men received prison terms of 240 years each, with no possibility of parole.

The U.S. Centers for Disease Control and Prevention reported, **Mar. 10,** that **the number of new AIDS cases had more than doubled in the U.S. in 1993,** to 103,500, from 49,016 in 1992. Cases continued to increase more rapidly among women than among men, and blacks and Hispanics continued to be disproportionately represented in the totals.

A former Arkansas state employee filed a suit, May 6, that accused Pres. Bill Clinton of sexual harassment. **Paula Corbin Jones** charged that Clinton, then governor of Arkansas, had made an unwanted sexual advance during a meeting with Jones in a hotel room in Arkansas in 1991. The suit was believed to be the first of its kind ever filed against a sitting president.

Oliver North, whose convictions on several charges in connection with the Iran-contra affair had later been overturned, **won the nomination of the Virginia Republican Party for the U.S. Senate, June 4.** In the Nov. 8 election, however, he lost to Democratic incumbent Charles S. Robb.

O. J. Simpson, one of the most successful running backs in the history of collegiate and professional football, **was charged, June 17, with the murders of his former wife Nicole Brown Simpson and a friend of hers, Ronald Goldman.** After midnight on **June 13,** the 2 victims were found stabbed to death outside Nicole Simpson's condominium in the Brentwood section of Los Angeles. Simpson, **June 20,** entered a plea of not guilty to the murders in Los Angeles Municipal Court. At the pretrial hearing, **July 8,** Simpson was ordered to stand trial on 2 counts of first-degree murder. **At his arraignment,** July 22, Simpson said he was **"absolutely 100% not guilty."** The trail got underway officially, **Sept. 26,** in Los Angeles.

High temperatures and dry conditions created an environment for **forest fires in the western U.S. in July,** and lightning set off blazes that burned 240,000 acres in 11 states. **Fourteen firefighters died** near Glenwood Springs, CO, **July 6,** when they were surrounded by fire.

Major league baseball players went on strike, following the conclusion of the **Aug. 11** games. The principal issue was the attempt by owners to impose a cap on the teams' overall salary levels. The strike interrupted an exciting season during which several players were pursuing records or other major achievements. On **Sept. 14, the remainder of the regular season, the playoffs, and the World Series were canceled because of the strike by players.**

After fierce conflict in both houses, Congress on **Aug. 25** approved **the $30.2 billion 1994 Omnibus Violent Crime Control and Preventions Act.** The bill approved funds to hire 100,000 police officers over 6 years, expanded the federal death penalty to apply to about 60 crimes, banned 19 kinds of semiautomatic weapons, and contained a "3 strikes and you're out" provision to incarcerate repeat offenders for life. The bill was signed by Pres. Bill Clinton on **Sept. 13.**

Pres. Bill Clinton's original **health-care reform proposal gradually lost support** as the business, medical, and insurance industries opposed it. On **Sept. 26** Senate Majority Leader George Mitchell (D, ME) abandoned his effort to get a health-care reform bill through the Senate in 1994.

The regular 1994 session of the 103d Congress ended, **Oct. 8,** amid acrimony as bills failed in the face of Republican filibusters. Barely surviving was the **California Desert Protection Bill,** which passed at the last minute. The bill provided for the upgrading and expansion of Death Valley and Joshua Tree national monuments to national parks, as well as the creation of the Mojave National Preserve and several large wilderness areas in the desert. Affecting 6 million acres, the legislation was **the largest land-conservation bill ever enacted** for the U.S. outside Alaska.

The **National Hockey League did not open its 1994-95 season on Oct. 1** as scheduled. Owners and players could not agree on a new contract.

On **Nov. 3, Susan Smith,** a South Carolina mother, **was charged with murdering her 2 sons, Michael, age 3, and Alexander, 14 months.** Police said that she had driven to the edge of a lake, left the car, and allowed it to roll into the lake with the children inside. On Oct. 25, Smith had appeared on national television, claiming that an armed black man had taken her car and driven off with the boys.

The Republican Party captured control of both houses of Congress in the Nov. 8 elections. In the Senate, Republicans numbered 53, and Democrats, 47. In the House of Representatives, Republicans numbered 230 and Democrats numbered 204; there was 1 independent. Even before the end of the year, the Republican majorities began to increase, as a few Democrats started switching parties. The Republican Party also came out of the voting with a sizable majority of the nation's governorships. In New York, 3-term Democratic Governor Mario Cuomo was defeated by Republican George Pataki. In Texas, Democratic Governor Ann Richards was defeated in her bid for reelection by George W. Bush, son of former Pres. George Bush.

In December, Congress completed its approval of the tariff-cutting provisions of the Uruguay Round of the General Agreement on Tariffs and Trade (GATT; new name, World Trade Organization [WTO]). The House approved the agreement, **Nov. 29,** 288-146, and the Senate, **Dec. 1,** 76-24. Pres. Clinton signed the legislation **Dec. 8.**

The Mayflower Compact

The threat of James I to "harry them out of the land" sent a little band of religious dissenters from England to Holland in 1608. They were known as Separatists because they wished to cut all ties with the established church. In 1620, some of them, known now as the Pilgrims, joined with a larger group in England to set sail on the *Mayflower* for the New World. A joint stock company financed their venture.

In November, they sighted Cape Cod and decided to land an exploring party at Plymouth Harbor. A rebellious group picked up at Southampton and London troubled the Pilgrim leaders, however, and to control their actions 41 Pilgrims drew up the Mayflower Compact and signed it before going ashore. The voluntary agreement to govern themselves was America's first written constitution.

In the name of God, Amen. We, whose names are underwritten, the Loyal Subjects of our dread Sovereign Lord, King *James,* by the Grace of God, of *Great Britain, France and Ireland,* King, *Defender of the Faith,* etc.

Having undertaken for the Glory of God, and Advancement of the Christian Faith, and the Honour of our King and Country, a voyage to plant the first colony in the northern Parts of Virginia; do by these Presents, solemnly and mutually in the Presence of God and one of another, convenant and combine ourselves together into a civil Body Politick, for our better Ordering and Preservation, and Furtherance of the Ends aforesaid; And by Virtue hereof to enact, constitute, and frame, such just and equal Laws, Ordinances, Acts, Constitutions and Offices, from time to time, as shall be thought most meet and convenient for the General good of the Colony; unto which we promise all due Submission and Obedience.

In Witness whereof we have hereunto subscribed our names at *Cape Cod* the eleventh of *November,* in the Reign of our Sovereign Lord, King *James* of *England, France* and *Ireland,* the eighteenth, and of *Scotland* the fifty-fourth. *Anno Domini, 1620.*

The Continental Congress: Meetings, Presidents

Meeting places	Dates of meetings	Congress presidents	Date elected
Philadelphia, PA	Sept. 5 to Oct. 26, 1774	Peyton Randolph, VA ([1])	Sept. 5, 1774
"	"	Henry Middleton, SC	Oct. 22, 1774
Philadelphia, PA	May 10, 1775 to Dec. 12, 1776	Peyton Randolph, VA.	May 10, 1775
"	"	John Hancock, MA	May 24, 1775
Baltimore, MD	Dec. 20, 1776 to Mar. 4, 1777		
Philadelphia, PA	Mar. 5 to Sept. 18, 1777		
Lancaster, PA	Sept. 27, 1777 (one day)		
York, PA	Sept. 30, 1777 to June 27, 1778	Henry Laurens, SC	Nov. 1, 1777(`)
Philadelphia, PA	July 2, 1778 to June 21, 1783	John Jay, NY	Dec. 10, 1778
"	"	Samuel Huntington, CT	Sept. 28, 1779
"	"	Thomas McKean, DE	July 10, 1781
"	"	John Hanson, MD ([2])	Nov. 5, 1781
"	"	Elias Boudinot, NJ	Nov. 4, 1782
Princeton, NJ	June 30 to Nov. 4, 1783	Thomas Mifflin, PA.	Nov. 3, 1783
Annapolis, MD	Nov. 26, 1783 to June 3, 1784		
Trenton, NJ	Nov. 1 to Dec. 24, 1784	Richard Henry Lee, VA	Nov. 30, 1784
New York City, MY	Jan. 11 to Nov. 4, 1785		
"	Nov. 7, 1785 to Nov. 3, 1786	John Hancock, MA ([3])	Nov. 23, 1785
"		Nathaniel Gorham, MA.	June 6, 1786
"	Nov. 6, 1786 to Oct. 30, 1787	Arthur St. Clair, PA	Feb. 2, 1787
"	Nov. 5, 1787 to Oct. 21, 1788	Cyrus Griffin, VA	Jan. 22, 1788
"	Nov. 3, 1788 to Mar. 2, 1789	"	"

(1) Resigned Oct. 22, 1774. (2) Titled "President of the United States in Congress Assembled," John Hanson is considered by some the first U.S. president because he was the first to serve under the Articles of Confederation. He was, however, little more than presiding officer of the Congress, which retained full executive power. He could be considered the head of government, but not head of state. (3) Resigned May 29, 1786, without serving, because of illness. (4) Articles of Confederation agreed upon, Nov. 15, 1777; last ratification from Maryland, Mar. 1, 1781.

Patrick Henry's Speech to the Virginia Convention

The following is an excerpt from Patrick Henry's speech to the Virginia Convention on Mar. 23, 1775:

Gentlemen may cry, peace, peace—but there is no peace. The war is actually begun! The next gale that sweeps from the north will bring to our ears the clash of resounding arms! Our brethren are already in the field! Why stand we here idle? What is it that gentlemen wish? What would they have? Is life so dear, or peace so sweet, as to be purchased at the price of chains and slavery? Forbid it, Almighty God! I know not what course others may take; but as for me, give me liberty, or give me death!

Common Sense

The following is an excerpt from Thomas Paine's *Common Sense.* Paine adopted the doctrine of separation from Britain after the battles of Lexington and Concord and published his pamphlet in Jan. 1776.

The cause of America is in great measure the cause of all mankind. Many circumstances hath, and will arise, which are not local, but universal, and through which principles of all Lovers of Mankind are affected, and in the Event of which, their Affections are interested. The laying a Country desolate with Fire and Sword, declaring war against natural rights of all Mankind, and extirpating the Defenders thereof from the Face of the Earth, is the Concern of every Man to whom Nature hath given the Power of feeling; . . . It is repugnant to reason, to the universal order of things, to all examples from former ages, to suppose, that this continent can longer remain subject to any external power . . .

The last cord is now broken, the people of England are presenting addresses against us. There are injuries which nature cannot forgive; she would cease to be nature if she did . . .

O ye that love mankind! Ye that dare oppose, not only the tyranny, but the tyrant, stand forth! Every spot of the old world is overrun with oppression. Freedom hath been hunted round the globe. Asia, and Africa, have long expelled her—Europe regards her like a stranger, and England hath given her warning to depart. O! Receive the fugitive, and prepare in time an asylum for mankind.

How the Declaration of Independence Was Adopted

On June 7, 1776, Richard Henry Lee, who had issued the first call for a congress of the colonies, introduced in the Continental Congress at Philadelphia a resolution declaring "that these United Colonies are, and of right ought to be, free and independent states, that they are absolved from all allegiance to the British Crown, and that all political connection between them and the state of Great Britain is, and ought to be, totally dissolved."

The resolution, seconded by John Adams on behalf of the Massachusetts delegation, came up again on June 10 when a committee of 5, headed by Thomas Jefferson, was appointed to express the purpose of the resolution in a declaration of independence. The others on the committee were John Adams, Benjamin Franklin, Robert R. Livingston, and Roger Sherman.

Drafting the Declaration was assigned to Jefferson, who worked on a portable desk of his own construction in a room at Market and 7th Sts. The committee reported the result on June 28, 1776. The members of the Congress suggested a number of changes, which Jefferson called "deplorable." They didn't approve Jefferson's arraignment of the British people and King George III for encouraging and fostering the slave trade, which Jefferson called "an execrable commerce." They made 86 changes, eliminating 480 words and leaving 1,337. In the final form, capitalization was erratic. Jefferson had written that men were endowed with "inalienable" rights; in the final copy it came out as "unalienable" and has been thus ever since.

The Lee-Adams resolution of independence was adopted by 12 yeas on July 2—the actual date of the act of independence. The Declaration, which explains the act, was adopted July 4, in the evening.

After the Declaration was adopted, July 4, 1776, it was turned over to John Dunlap, printer, to be printed on broadsides. The original copy was lost and one of his broadsides was attached to a page in the journal of the Congress. It was read aloud July 8 in Philadelphia, PA, Easton, PA, and Trenton, NJ. On July 9 at 6 PM it was read by order of Gen. George Washington to the troops assembled on the Common in New York City (City Hall Park).

The Continental Congress of July 19, 1776, adopted the following resolution:

"Resolved, That the Declaration passed on the 4th, be fairly engrossed on parchment with the title and stile of 'The Unanimous Declaration of the thirteen United States of America' and that the same, when engrossed, be signed by every member of Congress."

Not all delegates who signed the engrossed Declaration were present on July 4. Robert Morris (PA), William Williams (CT), and Samuel Chase (MD) signed on Aug. 2; Oliver Wolcott (CT), George Wythe (VA), Richard Henry Lee (VA), and Elbridge Gerry (MA) signed in August and September; Matthew Thornton (NH) joined the Congress Nov. 4 and signed later. Thomas McKean (DE) rejoined Washington's army before signing and said later that he signed in 1781.

Charles Carroll of Carrollton was appointed a delegate by Maryland on July 4, 1776, presented his credentials July 18, and signed the engrossed Declaration on Aug. 2. Born Sept. 19, 1737, he was 95 years old and the last surviving signer when he died on Nov. 14, 1832.

Two Pennsylvania delegates who did not support the Declaration on July 4 were replaced.

The 4 New York delegates did not have authority from their state to vote on July 4. On July 9, the New York state convention authorized its delegates to approve the Declaration, and the Congress was so notified on July 15, 1776. The 4 signed the Declaration on Aug. 2.

The original engrossed Declaration is preserved in the National Archives Building in Washington.

Declaration of Independence

The Declaration of Independence was adopted by the Continental Congress in Philadelphia on July 4, 1776. John Hancock was president of the Congress, and Charles Thomson was secretary. A copy of the Declaration, engrossed on parchment, was signed by members of Congress on and after Aug. 2, 1776. On Jan. 18, 1777, Congress ordered that "an authenticated copy, with the names of the members of Congress subscribing the same, be sent to each of the United States, and that they be desired to have the same put upon record." Authenticated copies were printed in broadside form in Baltimore,, where the Continental Congress was then in session. The following text is that of the original printed by John Dunlap at Philadelphia for the Continental Congress.

IN CONGRESS, July 4, 1776.

A DECLARATION

By the REPRESENTATIVES of the

UNITED STATES OF AMERICA,

In GENERAL CONGRESS assembled

When in the Course of human Events, it becomes necessary for one People to dissolve the Political Bands which have connected them with another, and to assume among the Powers of the Earth, the separate and equal Station to which the Laws of Nature and of Nature's God entitle them, a decent Respect to the Opinions of Mankind requires that they should declare the causes which impel them to the Separation.

We hold these Truths to be self-evident, that all Men are created equal, that they are endowed by their Creator with certain unalienable Rights, that among these are Life, Liberty, and the Pursuit of Happiness—That to secure these Rights, Governments are instituted among Men, deriving their just Powers from the Consent of the Governed, that whenever any Form of Government becomes destructive of these Ends, it is the Right of the People to alter or to abolish it, and to institute new Government, laying its Foundation on such Principles, and organizing its Powers in such Form, as to them shall seem most likely to effect their Safety and Happiness. Prudence, indeed, will dictate that Governments long established should not be changed for light and transient Causes; and accordingly all Experience hath shewn, that Mankind are more disposed to suffer, while Evils are sufferable, than to right themselves by abolishing the Forms to which they are accustomed. But when a long Train of Abuses and Usurpations, pursuing invariably the same Object, evinces a Design to reduce them under absolute Despotism, it is their Right, it is their Duty, to throw off such Government, and to provide new Guards for their future Security. Such has been the patient Sufferance of these Colonies; and such is now the Necessity which constrains them to alter their former Systems of Government. The History of the present King of Great-Britain is a History of repeated Injuries and Usurpations, all having in direct Object the Establishment of an absolute Tyranny over these States. To prove this, let Facts be submitted to a candid World.

He has refused his Assent to Laws, the most wholesome and necessary for the public Good.

He has forbidden his Governors to pass Laws of immediate and pressing Importance, unless suspended in their Operation till his Assent should be obtained; and when so suspended, he has utterly neglected to attend to them.

He has refused to pass other Laws for the Accommodation of large Districts of People, unless those People would relinquish the Right of Representation in the Legislature, a Right inestimable to them, and formidable to Tyrants only.

He has called together Legislative Bodies at Places unusual, uncomfortable, and distant from the Depository of their Public Records, for the sole Purpose of fatiguing them into Compliance with his Measures.

He has dissolved Representative Houses repeatedly, for opposing with manly Firmness his Invasions on the Rights of the People.

He has refused for a long Time, after such Dissolutions, to cause others to be elected; whereby the Legislative Powers, incapable of Annihilation, have returned to the People at large for their exercise; the State remaining in the mean time exposed to all the Dangers of Invasion from without, and Convulsions within.

He has endeavoured to prevent the Population of these States; for that Purpose obstructing the Laws for Naturalization of Foreigners; refusing to pass others to encourage their Migrations hither, and raising the Conditions of new Appropriations of Lands.

He has obstructed the Administration of Justice, by refusing his Assent to Laws for establishing Judiciary Powers.

He has made Judges dependent on his Will alone, for the Tenure of their Offices, and the Amount and payment of their Salaries.

He has erected a Multitude of new Offices, and sent hither Swarms of Officers to harrass our People, and eat out their Substance.

He has kept among us, in Times of Peace, Standing Armies, without the consent of our Legislatures.

He has affected to render the Military independent of, and superior to the Civil Power.

He has combined with others to subject us to a Jurisdiction foreign to our Constitution, and unacknowledged by our Laws; giving his Assent to their Acts of pretended Legislation:

For quartering large Bodies of Armed Troops among us:

For protecting them, by a mock Trial, from Punishment for any Murders which they should commit on the Inhabitants of these States:

For cutting off our Trade with all Parts of the World:

For imposing Taxes on us without our Consent:

For depriving us, in many Cases, of the Benefits of Trial by Jury:

For transporting us beyond Seas to be tried for pretended Offences:

For abolishing the free System of English Laws in a neighbouring Province, establishing therein an arbitrary Government, and enlarging its Boundaries, so as to render it at once an Example and fit Instrument for introducing the same absolute Rule into these Colonies:

For taking away our Charters, abolishing our most valuable Laws, and altering fundamentally the Forms of our Governments:

For suspending our own Legislatures, and declaring themselves invested with Power to legislate for us in all Cases whatsoever.

He has abdicated Government here, by declaring us out of his Protection and waging War against us.

He has plundered our Seas, ravaged our Coasts, burnt our towns, and destroyed the Lives of our People.

He is, at this Time, transporting large Armies of foreign Mercenaries to complete the works of Death, Desolation, and Tyranny, already begun with circumstances of Cruelty and Perfidy, scarcely paralleled in the most barbarous Ages, and totally unworthy the Head of a civilized Nation.

He has constrained our fellow Citizens taken Captive on the high Seas to bear Arms against their Country, to become the Executioners of their Friends and Brethren, or to fall themselves by their Hands.

He has excited domestic Insurrections amongst us, and has endeavoured to bring on the Inhabitants of our Frontiers, the merciless Indian Savages, whose known Rule of Warfare, is an undistinguished Destruction, of all Ages, Sexes and Conditions.

In every stage of these Oppressions we have Petitioned for Redress in the most humble Terms: Our repeated Petitions have been answered only by repeated Injury. A Prince, whose Character is thus marked by every act which may define a Tyrant, is unfit to be the Ruler of a free People.

Nor have we been wanting in Attentions to our British Brethren. We have warned them from Time to Time of Attempts by their Legislature to extend an unwarrantable Jurisdiction over us. We have reminded them of the Circumstances of our Emigration and Settlement here. We have appealed to their native Justice and Magnanimity, and we have conjured them by the Ties of our common Kindred to disavow these Usurpations, which, would inevitably interrupt our Connections and Correspondence. They too have been deaf to the Voice of Justice and of Consanguinity. We must, therefore, acquiesce in the Necessity, which denounces our Separation, and hold them, as we hold the rest of Mankind, Enemies in War, in Peace, Friends.

We, therefore, the Representatives of the UNITED STATES OF AMERICA, in General Congress, Assembled, appealing to the Supreme Judge of the World for the Rectitude of our Intentions, do, in the Name, and by Authority of the good People of these Colonies, solemnly Publish and Declare, That these United Colonies are, and of Right ought to be, Free and Independent States; that they are absolved from all Allegiance to the British Crown, and that all political Connection between them and the State of Great-Britain, is and ought to be totally dissolved; and that as Free and Independent States, they have full Power to levy War, conclude Peace, contract Alliances, establish Commerce, and to do all other Acts and Things which Independent States may of right do. And for the support of this declaration, with a firm Reliance on the Protection of Divine Providence, we mutually pledge to each other our lives, our Fortunes, and our sacred Honor.

JOHN HANCOCK, President

Attest.
CHARLES THOMSON, Secretary.

Signers of the Declaration of Independence

Delegate (state)	Vocation	Birthplace	Born	Died
Adams, John (MA)	Lawyer	Braintree (Quincy), MA	Oct. 30, 1735	July 4, 1826
Adams, Samuel (MA)	Political leader	Boston, MA	Sept. 27, 1722	Oct. 2, 1803
Bartlett, Josiah (NH)	Physician, judge	Amesbury, MA	Nov. 21, 1729	May 19, 1795
Braxton, Carter (VA)	Farmer	Newington Plantation, VA	Sept. 10, 1736	Oct. 10, 1797
Carroll, Chas. of Carrollton (MD)	Lawyer	Annapolis, MD	Sept. 19, 1737	Nov. 14, 1832
Chase, Samuel (MD)	Judge	Princess Anne, MD	Apr. 17, 1741	June 19, 1811
Clark, Abraham (NJ)	Surveyor	Roselle, NJ	Feb. 15, 1726	Sept. 15, 1794
Clymer, George (PA)	Merchant	Philadelphia, PA	Mar. 16, 1739	Jan. 23, 1813
Ellery, William (RI)	Lawyer	Newport, RI	Dec. 22, 1727	Feb. 15, 1820
Floyd, William (NY)	Soldier	Brookhaven, NY	Dec. 17, 1734	Aug. 4, 1821
Franklin, Benjamin (PA)	Printer, publisher	Boston, MA	Jan. 17, 1706	Apr. 17, 1790
Gerry, Elbridge (MA)	Merchant	Marblehead, MA	July 17, 1744	Nov. 23, 1814
Gwinnett, Button (GA)	Merchant	Down Hatherly, England	c. 1735	May 19, 1777
Hall, Lyman (GA)	Physician	Wallingford, CT	Apr. 12, 1724	Oct. 19, 1790
Hancock, John (MA)	Merchant	Braintree (Quincy), MA	Jan. 12, 1737	Oct. 8, 1793

Delegate (state)	Vocation	Birthplace	Born	Died
Harrison, Benjamin (VA)	Farmer	Berkeley, VA	Apr. 5, 1726	Apr. 24, 1791
Hart, John (NJ)	Farmer	Stonington, CT	c. 1711	May 11, 1779
Hewes, Joseph (NC)	Merchant	Princeton, NJ	Jan. 23, 1730	Nov. 10, 1779
Heyward, Thos. Jr. (SC)	Lawyer, farmer	St. Luke's Parish, SC.	July 28, 1746	Mar. 6, 1809
Hooper, William (NC)	Lawyer	Boston, MA	June 28, 1742	Oct. 14, 1790
Hopkins, Stephen (RI)	Judge, educator	Providence, RI	Mar. 7, 1707	July 13, 1785
Hopkinson, Francis (NJ)	Judge, author	Philadelphia, PA	Sept. 21, 1737	May 9, 1791
Huntington, Samuel (CT)	Judge	Windham County, CT	July 3, 1731	Jan. 5, 1796
Jefferson, Thomas (VA)	Lawyer	Shadwell, VA	Apr. 13, 1743	July 4, 1826
Lee, Francis Lightfoot (VA)	Farmer	Westmoreland County, VA	Oct. 14, 1734	Jan. 11, 1797
Lee, Richard Henry (VA)	Farmer	Westmoreland County, VA	Jan. 20, 1732	June 19, 1794
Lewis, Francis (NY)	Merchant	Llandaff, Wales.	Mar., 1713	Dec. 31, 1802
Livingston, Philip (NY)	Merchant	Albany, NY	Jan. 15, 1716	June 12, 1778
Lynch, Thomas Jr. (SC)	Farmer	Winyah, SC	Aug. 5, 1749	(at sea) 1779
McKean, Thomas (DE)	Lawyer	New London, PA	Mar. 19, 1734	June 24, 1817
Middleton, Arthur (SC)	Farmer	Charleston, SC	June 26, 1742	Jan. 1, 1787
Morris, Lewis (NY)	Farmer	Morrisania (Bronx County), NY.	Apr. 8, 1726	Jan. 22, 1798
Morris, Robert (PA)	Merchant	Liverpool, England	Jan. 20, 1734	May 9, 1806
Morton, John (PA)	Judge	Ridley, PA	1724	Apr., 1777
Nelson, Thos. Jr. (VA)	Farmer	Yorktown, VA	Dec. 26, 1738	Jan. 4, 1789
Paca, William (MD)	Judge	Abingdon, MD	Oct. 31, 1740	Oct. 23, 1799
Paine, Robert Treat (MA)	Judge	Boston, MA	Mar. 11, 1731	May 12, 1814
Penn, John (NC)	Lawyer	Near Port Royal, VA	May 17, 1741	Sept. 14, 1788
Read, George (DE)	Judge	Near North East, MD.	Sept. 18, 1733	Sept. 21, 1798
Rodney, Caesar (DE)	Judge	Dover, DE	Oct. 7, 1728	June 29, 1784
Ross, George (PA)	Judge	New Castle, DE	May 10, 1730	July 14, 1779
Rush, Benjamin (PA)	Physician.	Byberry, PA (Philadelphia)	Dec. 24, 1745	Apr. 19, 1813
Rutledge, Edward (SC)	Lawyer	Charleston, SC	Nov. 23, 1749	Jan. 23, 1800
Sherman, Roger (CT)	Lawyer	Newton, MA	Apr. 19, 1721	July 23, 1793
Smith, James (PA)	Lawyer	Dublin, Ireland	c. 1719	July 11, 1806
Stockton, Richard (NJ)	Lawyer	Near Princeton, NJ	Oct. 1, 1730	Feb. 28, 1781
Stone, Thomas (MD).	Lawyer	Charles County, MD	1743	Oct. 5, 1787
Taylor, George (PA)	Ironmaster.	Ireland	1716	Feb. 23, 1781
Thornton, Matthew (NH)	Physician.	Ireland	1714	June 24, 1803
Walton, George (GA)	Judge	Prince Edward County, VA	1741	Feb. 2, 1804
Whipple, William (NH)	Merchant, judge	Kittery, ME.	Jan. 14, 1730	Nov. 28, 1785
Williams, William (CT)	Merchant.	Lebanon, CT	Apr. 23, 1731	Aug. 2, 1811
Wilson, James (PA)	Judge	Carskerdo, Scotland.	Sept. 14, 1742	Aug. 28, 1798
Witherspoon, John (NJ)	Clergyman, educator.	Gifford, Scotland.	Feb. 5, 1723	Nov. 15, 1794
Wolcott, Oliver (CT)	Judge	Windsor, CT	Dec. 1, 1726	Dec. 1, 1797
Wythe, George (VA)	Lawyer	Elizabeth City Co. (Hampton), VA	1726	June 8, 1806

Origin of the Constitution

The War of Independence was conducted by delegates from the original 13 states, called the Congress of the United States of America and known as the Continental Congress. In 1777 the Congress submitted to the legislatures of the states the Articles of Confederation and Perpetual Union, which were ratified by New Hampshire, Massachusetts, Rhode Island, Connecticut, New York, New Jersey, Pennsylvania, Delaware, Virginia, North Carolina, South Carolina, and Georgia and finally, in 1781, by Maryland.

The first article of the instrument read: "The stile of this confederacy shall be the United States of America." This did not signify a sovereign nation, because the states delegated only those powers they could not handle individually. Taxes for the payment of such debts were levied by the individual states. The president under the Articles signed himself "President of the United States in Congress assembled," but here the United States were considered in the plural, a cooperating group. Canada was invited to join the union on equal terms but did not act.

When the war was won, it became evident that a stronger federal union was needed. The Congress left the initiative to the legislatures. Virginia in Jan. 1786 appointed commissioners to meet with representatives of other states; delegates from Virginia, Delaware, New York, New Jersey, and Pennsylvania met at Annapolis. Alexander Hamilton prepared for their call by asking delegates from all states to meet in Philadelphia in May 1787 "to render the Constitution of the Federal government adequate to the exigencies of the union." Congress endorsed the plan on Feb. 21, 1787. Delegates were appointed by all states except Rhode Island.

The convention met on May 14, 1787. George Washington was chosen president (presiding officer). The states certified 65 delegates, but 10 did not attend. The work was done by 55, not all of whom were present at all sessions. Of the 55 attending delegates, 16 failed to sign, and 39 actually signed Sept. 17, 1787, some with reservations. Some historians have said 74 delegates (9 more than the 65 actually certified) were named and 19 failed to attend. These 9 additional persons refused the appointment, were never delegates, and never counted as absentees. Washington sent the Constitution to Congress, and that body, Sept. 28, 1787, ordered it sent to the legislatures, "in order to be submitted to a convention of delegates chosen in each state by the people thereof."

The Constitution was ratified by votes of state conventions as follows: Delaware, Dec. 7, 1787, unanimous; Pennsylvania, Dec. 12, 1787, 43 to 23; New Jersey, Dec. 18, 1787, unanimous; Georgia, Jan. 2, 1788, unanimous; Connecticut, Jan. 9, 1788, 128 to 40; Massachusetts, Feb. 6, 1788, 187 to 168; Maryland, Apr. 28, 1788, 63 to 11; South Carolina, May 23, 1788, 149 to 73; New Hampshire, June 21, 1788, 57 to 46; Virginia, June 25, 1788, 89 to 79; New York, July 26, 1788, 30 to 27. Nine states were needed to establish the operation of the Constitution "between the states so ratifying the same," and New Hampshire was the 9th state. The government did not declare the Constitution in effect until the first Wednesday in Mar. 1789, which was Mar. 4. After that, North Carolina ratified it on Nov. 21, 1789, 194 to 77; and Rhode Island, May 29, 1790, 34 to 32. Vermont in convention ratified it on Jan. 10, 1791, and by act of Congress approved on Feb. 18, 1791, was admitted into the Union as the 14th state, Mar. 4, 1791.

Constitution of the United States
The Original 7 Articles

The text below (with the exception of Amendment XXVII) is taken from the pocket-size edition of the Constitution published by the U.S. Government Printing Office as a result of a U.S. House and Senate resolution to print the Constitution in its original form as amended through July 5, 1971. Text in **boldface** summarizes an article or amendment and was added by *The World Almanac*. Text in *italic* indicates that an item has been superseded or amended, or provides background information on amendments.

PREAMBLE

We, the People of the United States, in Order to form a more perfect Union, establish Justice, insure domestic Tranquility, provide for the common defence, promote the general Welfare, and secure the Blessings of Liberty to ourselves and our Posterity, do ordain and establish this Constitution for the United States of America.

ARTICLE I.

Section 1—Legislative powers; in whom vested:

All legislative Powers herein granted shall be vested in a Congress of the United States, which shall consist of a Senate and House of Representatives.

Section 2—House of Representatives, how and by whom chosen. Qualifications of a Representative. Representatives and direct taxes, how apportioned. Enumeration. Vacancies to be filled. Power of choosing officers, and of impeachment.

The House of Representatives shall be composed of Members chosen every second Year by the People of the several States, and the Electors in each State shall have the Qualifications requisite for Electors of the most numerous Branch of the State Legislature.

No person shall be a Representative who shall not have attained to the Age of twenty-five Years, and been seven Years a Citizen of the United States, and who shall not, when elected, be an Inhabitant of that State in which he shall be chosen.

(Representatives and direct taxes shall be apportioned among the several States which may be included within this Union, according to their respective Numbers, which shall be determined by adding to the whole Number of free Persons, including those bound to Service for a Term of Years, and excluding Indians not taxed, three-fifths of all other persons.) (The previous sentence was superseded by Amendment XIV, section 2.) The actual Enumeration shall be made within three Years after the first Meeting of the Congress of the United States, and within every subsequent Term of ten Years, in such Manner as they shall by Law direct. The Number of Representatives shall not exceed one for every thirty Thousand, but each State shall have at Least one Representative; and until such enumeration shall be made, the State of New Hampshire shall be entitled to chuse three, Massachusetts eight, Rhode-Island and Providence Plantations one, Connecticut five, New-York six, New Jersey four, Pennsylvania eight, Delaware one, Maryland six, Virginia ten, North Carolina five, South Carolina five, and Georgia three.

When vacancies happen in the Representation from any State, the Executive Authority thereof shall issue Writs of Election to fill such Vacancies.

The House of Representatives shall chuse their Speaker and other Officers; and shall have the sole Power of Impeachment.

Section 3—Senators, how and by whom chosen. How classified. Qualifications of a Senator. President of the Senate, his right to vote. President pro tem., and other officers of the Senate, how chosen. Power to try impeachments. When President is tried, Chief Justice to preside. Sentence.

The Senate of the United States shall be composed of two Senators from each State, *(chosen by the Legislature thereof), (The preceding five words were superseded by Amendment XVII, section 1.)* for six Years; and each Senator shall have one Vote.

Immediately after they shall be assembled in Consequence of the first Election, they shall be divided as equally as may be into three Classes. The Seats of the Senators of the first Class shall be vacated at the Expiration of the second Year, of the second Class at the Expiration of the fourth Year, and of the third Class at the Expiration of the Sixth year, so that one-third may be chosen every second Year; *(and if Vacancies happen by Resignation, or otherwise, during the Recess of the Legislature of any State, the Executive thereof may make temporary Appointments until the next Meeting of the Legislature,*

which shall then fill such Vacancies.) (The words in parentheses were superseded by Amendment XVII, section 2.)

No person shall be a Senator who shall not have attained to the Age of thirty Years, and been nine Years a Citizen of the United States, and who shall not, when elected, be an Inhabitant of that State for which he shall be chosen.

The Vice President of the United States shall be President of the Senate, but shall have no Vote, unless they be equally divided.

The Senate shall chuse their other Officers, and also a President pro tempore, in the absence of the Vice President, or when he shall exercise the Office of President of the United States.

The Senate shall have the sole Power to try all Impeachments. When sitting for that Purpose, they shall be on Oath or Affirmation. When the President of the United States is tried, the Chief Justice shall preside: And no Person shall be convicted without the Concurrence of two thirds of the Members present.

Judgment in Cases of Impeachment shall not extend further than to removal from Office, and disqualification to hold and enjoy any Office of honor, Trust or Profit under the United States: but the Party convicted shall nevertheless be liable and subject to Indictment, Trial, Judgment and Punishment, according to Law.

Section 4—Times, etc., of holding elections, how prescribed. One session each year.

The Times, Places and Manner of holding Elections for Senators and Representatives, shall be prescribed in each State by the Legislature thereof; but the Congress may at any time by Law make or alter such Regulations, except as to the Place of Chusing Senators.

The Congress shall assemble at least once in every Year, and such Meeting shall *(be on the first Monday in December,) (The words in parentheses were superseded by Amendment XX, section 2.)* unless they shall by Law appoint a different Day.

Section 5—Membership, quorum, adjournments, rules. Power to punish or expel. Journal. Time of adjournments, how limited, etc.

Each House shall be the Judge of the Elections, Returns and Qualifications of its own Members, and a Majority of each shall constitute a Quorum to do Business; but a smaller number may adjourn from day to day, and may be authorized to compel the Attendance of absent Members, in such manner, and under such Penalties as each House may provide.

Each House may determine the Rules of its Proceedings, punish its members for disorderly Behavior, and, with the Concurrence of two thirds, expel a Member.

Each House shall keep a Journal of its Proceedings, and from time to time publish the same, excepting such Parts as may in their Judgment require Secrecy; and the Yeas and Nays of the Members of either House on any question shall, at the Desire of one fifth of those Present, be entered on the Journal.

Neither House, during the Session of Congress, shall, without the Consent of the other, adjourn for more than three days, nor to any other Place than that in which the two Houses shall be sitting.

Section 6—Compensation, privileges, disqualifications in certain cases.

The Senators and Representatives shall receive a Compensation for their Services, to be ascertained by Law, and paid out of the Treasury of the United States. They shall in all Cases, except Treason, Felony and Breach of the Peace, be privileged from Arrest during their Attendance at the Session of their respective Houses, and in going to and returning from the same; and for any Speech or Debate in either House, they shall not be questioned in any other Place.

No Senator or Representative shall, during the Time for which he was elected, be appointed to any civil Office under the Authority of the United States, which shall have been created, or the Emoluments whereof shall have been encreased during such time; and no Person holding any Office under the United States, shall be a Member of either House during his Continuance in Office.

Section 7—House to originate all revenue bills. Veto. Bill may be passed by two-thirds of each House, notwithstanding, etc. Bill, not returned in ten days, to become a law. Provisions as to orders, concurrent resolutions, etc.

All bills for raising Revenue shall originate in the House of Representatives; but the Senate may propose or concur with Amendments as on other Bills.

Every Bill which shall have passed the House of Representatives and the Senate, shall, before it become a Law, be presented to the President of the United States; If he approve he shall sign it, but if not he shall return it, with his Objections to that House in which it shall have originated, who shall enter the Objections at large on their Journal, and proceed to reconsider it. If after such Reconsideration two thirds of that House shall agree to pass the Bill, it shall be sent, together with the Objections, to the other House, by which it shall likewise be reconsidered, and if approved by two thirds of that House, it shall become a Law. But in all such Cases the Votes of both Houses shall be determined by Yeas and Nays, and the Names of the Persons voting for and against the Bill shall be entered on the Journal of each House respectively. If any Bill shall not be returned by the President within ten Days (Sundays excepted) after it shall have been presented to him, the Same shall be a Law, in like Manner as if he had signed it, unless the Congress by their Adjournment prevent its Return, in which Case it shall not be a Law.

Every order, Resolution, or Vote to which the Concurrence of the Senate and House of Representatives may be necessary (except on a question of Adjournment) shall be presented to the President of the United States; and before the Same shall take Effect, shall be approved by him, or being disapproved by him, shall be repassed by two thirds of the Senate and House of Representatives, according to the Rules and Limitations prescribed in the Case of a Bill.

Section 8—Powers of Congress.

The Congress shall have Power To lay and collect Taxes, Duties, Imposts and Excises, to pay the Debts and provide for the common Defence and general Welfare of the United States; but all Duties, Imposts and Excises shall be uniform throughout the United States;

To borrow money on the credit of the United States;

To regulate Commerce with foreign Nations, and among the several States, and with the Indian Tribes;

To establish an uniform Rule of Naturalization, and uniform Laws on the subject of Bankruptcies throughout the United States;

To coin Money, regulate the Value thereof, and of foreign Coin, and fix the Standard of Weights and Measures;

To provide for the Punishment of counterfeiting the Securities and current Coin of the United States;

To establish Post Offices and post Roads;

To promote the Progress of Science and useful Arts, by securing for limited Times to Authors and Inventors the exclusive Right to their respective Writings and Discoveries;

To constitute Tribunals inferior to the supreme Court;

To define and punish Piracies and Felonies committed on the high Seas, and Offenses against the Law of Nations;

To declare War, grant Letters of Marque and Reprisal, and make Rules concerning Captures on Land and Water;

To raise and support Armies, but no Appropriation of Money to that Use shall be for a longer Term than two Years;

To provide and maintain a Navy;

To make Rules for the Government and Regulation of the land and naval Forces;

To provide for calling forth the Militia to execute the Laws of the Union, suppress Insurrections and repel Invasions;

To provide for organizing, arming, and disciplining the Militia, and for governing such Part of them as may be employed in the Service of the United States, reserving to the States respectively, the Appointment of the Officers, and the Authority of training the Militia according to the discipline prescribed by Congress;

To exercise exclusive Legislation in all Cases whatsoever, over such District (not exceeding ten Miles square) as may, by Cession of particular States, and the acceptance of Congress, become the Seat of the Government of the United States, and to exercise like Authority over all Places purchased by the Consent of the Legislature of the State in which the Same shall be, for the Erection of Forts, Magazines, Arsenals, dock-Yards, and other needful Buildings;—And

To make all Laws which shall be necessary and proper for carrying into Execution the foregoing Powers, and all other Powers vested by this Constitution in the Government of the United States, or in any Department or Officer thereof.

Section 9—Provision as to migration or importation of certain persons. Habeas corpus, bills of attainder, etc. Taxes, how apportioned. No export duty. No commercial preference. Money, how drawn from Treasury, etc. No titular nobility. Officers not to receive presents, etc.

The Migration or Importation of such Persons as any of the States now existing shall think proper to admit, shall not be prohibited by the Congress prior to the Year one thousand eight hundred and eight, but a tax or duty may be imposed on such Importation, not exceeding ten dollars for each Person.

The privilege of the Writ of Habeas Corpus shall not be suspended, unless when in Cases of Rebellion or Invasion the public Safety may require it.

No Bill of Attainder or ex post facto Law shall be passed.

No capitation, or other direct, Tax shall be laid, unless in Proportion to the Census or Enumeration herein before directed to be taken. *(Modified by Amendment XVI.)*

No Tax or Duty shall be laid on Articles exported from any State.

No Preference shall be given by any Regulation of Commerce or Revenue to the Ports of one State over those of another: nor shall Vessels bound to, or from, one State, be obliged to enter, clear, or pay Duties in another.

No Money shall be drawn from the Treasury, but in Consequence of Appropriations made by Law; and a regular Statement and Account of the Receipts and Expenditures of all public Money shall be published from time to time.

No Title of Nobility shall be granted by the United States: and no Person holding any Office of Profit or Trust under them, shall, without the Consent of the Congress, accept of any present, Emolument, Office, or Title, of any kind whatever, from any King, Prince, or foreign State.

Section 10—States prohibited from the exercise of certain powers.

No State shall enter into any Treaty, Alliance, or Confederation; grant Letters of Marque and Reprisal; coin Money; emit Bills of Credit; make any Thing but gold and silver Coin a Tender in Payment of Debts; pass any Bill of Attainder, ex post facto Law, or Law impairing the Obligation of Contracts, or grant any Title of Nobility.

No State shall, without the Consent of the Congress, lay any Imposts or Duties on Imports or Exports, except what may be absolutely necessary for executing its inspection Laws: and the net Produce of all Duties and Imposts, laid by any State on Imports or Exports, shall be for the Use of the Treasury of the United States; and all such Laws shall be subject to the Revision and Control of the Congress.

No State shall, without the Consent of Congress, lay any duty of Tonnage, keep Troops, or Ships of War in time of Peace, enter into any Agreement or Compact with another State, or with a foreign Power, or engage in War, unless actually invaded, or in such imminent Danger as will not admit of delay.

ARTICLE II.

Section 1—President: his term of office. Electors of President; number and how appointed. Electors to vote on same day. Qualification of President. On whom his duties devolve in case of his removal, death, etc. President's compensation. His oath of office.

The executive Power shall be vested in a President of the United States of America. He shall hold his Office during the Term of four Years, and, together with the Vice President, chosen for the same Term, be elected, as follows.

Each State shall appoint, in such Manner as the Legislature thereof may direct, a Number of Electors, equal to the whole Number of Senators and Representatives to which the State may be entitled in the Congress: but no Senator or Representative, or Person holding an Office of Trust or Profit under the United States, shall be appointed an Elector.

(The Electors shall meet in their respective States, and vote by Ballot for two persons, of whom one at least shall not be an Inhabitant of the same State with themselves. And they shall make a List of all the Persons voted for, and of the Number of Votes for each; which List they shall sign and certify, and transmit sealed to the Seat of the Government of the United States, directed to the President of the Senate. The President of the Senate shall, in the Presence of the Senate and House of Representatives, open all the Certificates, and the Votes shall then be counted. The Person having the greatest Number of Votes shall be the President, if such Number be a Majority of the whole Number of Electors appointed; and if there be more than one who have such Majority, and have an equal Number of Votes, then the House of Representatives shall immediately chuse by Ballot one of them for President; and if no Person have a Majority, then from the five highest on the List the said House shall in like Manner chuse the President. But in chusing the President, the Votes shall be taken by States, the Representation from each State having one Vote; a quorum for this Purpose shall consist of a Member or Members from two thirds of the States, and a Majority of all the States shall be necessary to a Choice. In every Case, after the Choice of the President, the Person having the greatest Number of Votes of the Electors shall be the Vice President. But if there should remain two or more who have equal Votes, the Senate shall chuse from them by Ballot the Vice-President.)

(This clause was superseded by Amendment XII.)

The Congress may detemine the Time of chusing the Electors, and the Day on which they shall give their Votes; which Day shall be the same throughout the United States.

No person except a natural born Citizen, or a Citizen of the United States, at the time of the Adoption of this Constitution, shall be eligible to the Office of President; neither shall any Person be eligible to that Office who shall not have attained to the Age of thirty-five Years, and been fourteen Years a Resident within the United States.

(For qualification of the Vice President, see Amendment XII.)

In Case of the Removal of the President from Office, or of his Death, Resignation, or Inability to discharge the Powers and Duties of the said Office, the same shall devolve on the Vice President, and the Congress may by Law, provide for the Case of Removal, Death, Resignation or Inability, both of the President and Vice President, declaring what Officer shall then act as President, and such Officer shall act accordingly, until the Disability be removed, or a President shall be elected.

(This clause has been modified by Amendments XX and XXV.)

The President shall, at stated Times, receive for his Services, a Compensation, which shall neither be encreased nor diminished during the Period for which he shall have been elected, and he shall not receive within that Period any other Emolument from the United States, or any of them.

Before he enter on the Execution of his Office, he shall take the following Oath or Affirmation:–"I do solemnly swear (or affirm) that I will faithfully execute the Office of President of the United States, and will to the best of my Ability, preserve, protect and defend the Constitution of the United States."

Section 2—President to be Commander-in-Chief. He may require opinions of cabinet officers, etc., may pardon. Treaty-making power. Nomination of certain officers. When President may fill vacancies.

The President shall be Commander in Chief of the Army and Navy of the United States, and of the Militia of the several States, when called into the actual Service of the United States; he may require the Opinion in writing, of the principal Officer in each of the executive Departments, upon any subject relating to the Duties of their respective Offices, and he shall have Power to Grant Reprieves and Pardons for Offenses against the United States, except in Cases of Impeachment.

He shall have Power, by and with the Advice and Consent of the Senate, to make Treaties, provided two-thirds of the Senators present concur; and he shall nominate, and by and with the Advice and Consent of the Senate, appoint Ambassadors, other public Ministers and Consuls, Judges of the supreme Court, and all other Officers of the United States, whose Appointments are not herein otherwise provided for, and which shall be established by Law: but the Congress may by Law vest the Appointment of such inferior Officers, as they think proper, in the President alone, in the Courts of Law, or in the Heads of Departments.

The President shall have Power to fill up all Vacancies that may happen during the Recess of the Senate, by granting Commissions which shall expire at the End of their next Session.

Section 3—President shall communicate to Congress. He may convene and adjourn Congress, in case of disagreement, etc. Shall receive ambassadors, execute laws, and commission officers.

He shall from time to time give to the Congress Information of the State of the Union, and recommend to their Consideration such Measures as he shall judge necessary and expedient; he may, on extraordinary Occasions, convene both Houses, or either of them, and in Case of Disagreement between them, with Respect to the Time of Adjournment, he may adjourn them to such Time as he shall think proper; he shall receive Ambassadors and other public Ministers; he shall take Care that the Laws be faithfully executed, and shall Commission all the Officers of the United States.

Section 4—All civil offices forfeited for certain crimes.

The President, Vice President and all civil Officers of the United States, shall be removed from Office on Impeachment for, and Conviction of, Treason, Bribery, or other high Crimes and Misdemeanors.

ARTICLE III.

Section 1—Judicial powers, Tenure. Compensation.

The judicial Power of the United States, shall be vested in one supreme Court, and in such inferior Courts as the Congress may from time to time ordain and establish. The Judges, both of the supreme and inferior Courts, shall hold their Offices during good Behaviour, and shall, at stated Times, receive for their Services, a Compensation, which shall not be diminished during their Continuance in Office.

Section 2—Judicial power; to what cases it extends. Original jurisdiction of Supreme Court; appellate jurisdiction. Trial by jury, etc. Trial, where.

The judicial Power shall extend to all Cases, in Law and Equity, arising under this Constitution, the Laws of the United States, and Treaties made, or which shall be made, under their Authority;–to all Cases affecting Ambassadors, other public Ministers and Consuls;–to all Cases of admiralty and maritime Jurisdiction;–to Controversies to which the United States shall be a Party;–to Controversies between two or more States;–between a State and Citizens of another State;–between Citizens of different States;–between Citizens of the same State claiming Lands under Grants of different States, and between a State, or the Citizens thereof, and foreign States, Citizens or Subjects.

(This section is modified by Amendment XI.)

In all Cases affecting Ambassadors, other public Ministers and Consuls, and those in which a State shall be Party, the supreme Court shall have original Jurisdiction. In all the other Cases before mentioned, the supreme Court shall have appellate Jurisdiction, both as to Law and Fact, with such Exceptions, and under such Regulations as the Congress shall make.

The trial of all Crimes, except in Cases of Impeachment, shall be by Jury; and such Trial shall be held in the State where the said Crimes shall have been committed; but when not committed within any State, the Trial shall be at such Place or Places as the Congress may by Law have directed.

Section 3—Treason Defined, Proof of, Punishment of.

Treason against the United States, shall consist only in levying War against them, or in adhering to their Enemies, giving them Aid and Comfort. No Person shall be convicted of Treason unless on the Testimony of two Witnesses to the same overt Act, or on Confession in open Court.

The Congress shall have Power to declare the Punishment of Treason, but no Attainder of Treason shall work Corruption of Blood, or Forfeiture except during the Life of the Person attainted.

ARTICLE IV.

Section 1—Each State to give credit to the public acts, etc., of every other State.

Full Faith and Credit shall be given in each State to the public Acts, Records, and judicial Proceedings of every other State. And the Congress may by general Laws prescribe the Manner in which such Acts, Records and Proceedings shall be proved, and the Effect thereof.

Section 2—Privileges of citizens of each State. Fugitives from justice to be delivered up. Persons held to service having escaped, to be delivered up.

The Citizens of each State shall be entitled to all Privileges and Immunities of Citizens in the several States.

A Person charged in any State with Treason, Felony, or other Crime, who shall flee from Justice, and be found in another State, shall on demand of the executive Authority of the State from which he fled, be delivered up, to be removed to the State having Jurisdiction of the Crime.

(No Person held to Service or Labour in one State, under the Laws thereof, escaping into another, shall, in Consequence of any Law or Regulation therein, be discharged from such Service or Labour, but shall be delivered up on Claim of the Party to whom such Service or Labour may be due.) (This clause was superseded by Amendment XIII.)

Section 3—Admission of new States. Power of Congress over territory and other property.

New States may be admitted by the Congress into this Union; but no new State shall be formed or erected within the Jurisdiction of any other State; nor any State be formed by the Junction of two or more States, or parts of States, without the Consent of the Legislatures of the States concerned as well as of the Congress.

The Congress shall have Power to dispose of and make all needful Rules and Regulations respecting the Territory or other Property belonging to the United States; and nothing in this Constitution shall be so construed as to Prejudice any Claims of the United States, or of any particular State.

Section 4—Republican form of government guaranteed. Each state to be protected.

The United States shall guarantee to every State in this Union a Republican Form of Government, and shall protect each of them against Invasion; and on Application of the Legislature, or of the Executive (when the Legislature cannot be convened) against domestic Violence.

ARTICLE V.

Constitution: how amended; proviso.

The Congress, whenever two-thirds of both Houses shall deem it necessary, shall propose Amendments to this Constitution, or, on the Application of the Legislatures of two-thirds of the several States, shall call a Convention for proposing Amendments, which, in either Case, shall be valid to all Intents and Purposes, as part of this Constitution, when ratified by the Legislatures of three-fourths of the several States, or by Conventions in three-fourths thereof, as the one or the other Mode of Ratification may be proposed by the Congress: Provided that no Amendment which may be made prior to the Year One thousand eight hundred and eight shall in any Manner affect the first and fourth Clauses in the Ninth Section of the first Article; and that no State, without its Consent, shall be deprived of its equal Suffrage in the Senate.

ARTICLE VI.

Certain debts, etc., declared valid. Supremacy of Constitution, treaties, and laws of the United States. Oath to support Constitution, by whom taken. No religious test.

All Debts contracted and Engagements entered into, before the Adoption of this Constitution, shall be as valid against the United States under this Constitution, as under the Confederation.

This Constitution, and the Laws of the United States which shall be made in Pursuance thereof; and all Treaties made, or which shall be made, under the Authority of the United States, shall be the supreme Law of the Land; and the Judges in every State shall be bound thereby, any Thing in the Constitution or Laws of any State to the Contrary notwithstanding.

The Senators and Representatives before mentioned, and the Members of the several State Legislatures, and all executive and judicial Officers, both of the United States and of the several States, shall be bound by Oath or Affirmation, to support this Constitution; but no religious Test shall ever be required as a Qualification to any Office or public Trust under the United States.

ARTICLE VII.

What ratification shall establish Constitution.

The Ratification of the Conventions of nine States shall be sufficient for the Establishment of this Constitution between the States so ratifying the Same.

Done in Convention by the Unanimous Consent of the States present the Seventeenth Day of September in the Year of our Lord one thousand seven hundred and Eighty seven and of the Independence of the United States of America the Twelfth.

In Witness whereof We have hereunto subscribed our Names.

Go WASHINGTON, Presidt and deputy from Virginia
New Hampshire—John Langdon, Nicholas Gilman
Massachusetts—Nathaniel Gorham, Rufus King
Connecticut—Wm Saml Johnson, Roger Sherman
New York—Alexander Hamilton
New Jersey—Wil: Livingston, David Brearley, Wm Paterson, Jona: Dayton
Pennsylvania—B Franklin, Thomas Mifflin, Robt. Morris, Geo. Clymer, Thos. FitzSimons, Jared Ingersoll, James Wilson, Gouv Morris
Delaware—Geo: Read, Gunning Bedford jun, John Dickinson, Richard Bassett, Jaco: Broom
Maryland—James McHenry, Dan: of St Thos Jenifer, Danl Carrol
Virginia—John Blair, James Madison Jr.
North Carolina—Wm Blount, Richd. Dobbs Spaight, Hu Williamson
South Carolina—J. Rutledge, Charles Cotesworth Pinckney, Charles Pinckney, Pierce Butler
Georgia—William Few, Abr Baldwin
Attest: William Jackson, Secretary.

Ten Original Amendments: The Bill of Rights

In force Dec. 15, 1791

(The First Congress, at its first session in the City of New York, Sept. 25, 1789, submitted to the states 12 amendments to clarify certain individual and state rights not named in the Constitution. They are generally called the Bill of Rights.

(Influential in framing these amendments was the Declaration of Rights of Virginia, written by George Mason (1725-1792) in 1776. Mason, a Virginia delegate to the Constitutional Convention, did not sign the Constitution and opposed its ratification on the ground that it did not sufficiently oppose slavery or safeguard individual rights.

(In the preamble to the resolution offering the proposed amendments, Congress said: "The conventions of a number of the States having at the time of their adopting the Constitution, expressed a desire, in order to prevent misconstruction or abuse of its powers, that further declaratory and restrictive clauses should be added, and as extending the ground of public confidence in the government will best insure the beneficent ends of its institution, be it resolved," etc.

(Ten of these amendments now commonly known as one to 10 inclusive, but originally 3 to 12 inclusive, were ratified by the states as follows: New Jersey, Nov. 20, 1789; Maryland, Dec. 19, 1789; North Carolina, Dec. 22, 1789; South Carolina, Jan. 19, 1790; New Hampshire, Jan. 25, 1790; Delaware, Jan. 28, 1790; New York, Feb. 27, 1790; Pennsylvania, Mar. 10, 1790; Rhode Island, June 7, 1790; Vermont, Nov. 3, 1791; Virginia, Dec. 15, 1791; Massachusetts, Mar. 2, 1939; Georgia, Mar. 18, 1939; Connecticut, Apr. 19, 1939. These original 10 ratified amendments follow as Amendments I to X inclusive.

(Of the two original proposed amendments that were not ratified promptly by the necessary number of states, the first related to apportionment of Representatives; the second, relating to compensation of members of Congress, was ratified in 1992 and became Amendment 27.)

AMENDMENT I.

Religious establishment prohibited. Freedom of speech, of the press, and right to petition.

Congress shall make no law respecting an establishment of religion, or prohibiting the free exercise thereof; or abridging the freedom of speech, or of the press; or the right of the people peaceably to assemble, and to petition the Government for a redress of grievances.

AMENDMENT II.

Right to keep and bear arms.

A well regulated Militia, being necessary to the security of a free State, the right of the people to keep and bear Arms, shall not be infringed.

AMENDMENT III.

Conditions for quarters for soldiers.

No Soldier shall, in time of peace be quartered in any house, without the consent of the Owner, nor in time of war, but in a manner to be prescribed by law.

AMENDMENT IV.

Right of search and seizure regulated.

The right of the people to be secure in their persons, houses, papers, and effects, against unreasonable searches and seizures, shall not be violated, and no Warrants shall issue, but upon probable cause, supported by Oath or affirmation, and particularly describing the place to be searched, and the persons or things to be seized.

AMENDMENT V.

Provisions concerning prosecution. Trial and punishment—private property not to be taken for public use without compensation.

No person shall be held to answer for a capital, or otherwise infamous crime, unless on a presentment or indictment of a Grand Jury, except in cases arising in the land or naval forces, or in the Militia, when in actual service in time of War or public danger; nor shall any person be subject for the same offence to be twice put in jeopardy of life or limb; nor shall be compelled in any criminal case to be a witness against himself, nor be deprived of life, liberty, or property, without due process of law; nor shall private property be taken for public use, without just compensation.

AMENDMENT VI.

Right to speedy trial, witnesses, etc.

In all criminal prosecutions, the accused shall enjoy the right to a speedy and public trial, by an impartial jury of the State and district wherein the crime shall have been committed, which district shall have been previously ascertained by law, and to be informed of the nature and cause of the accusation; to be confronted with the witnesses against him; to have compulsory process for obtaining witnesses in his favor, and to have the Assistance of Counsel for his defence.

AMENDMENT VII.

Right of trial by jury.

In suits at common law, where the value in controversy shall exceed twenty dollars, the right of trial by jury shall be preserved, and no fact tried by a jury, shall be otherwise reexamined in any Court of the United States, than according to the rules of the common law.

AMENDMENT VIII.

Excessive bail or fines and cruel punishment prohibited.

Excessive bail shall not be required, nor excessive fines imposed, nor cruel and unusual punishments inflicted.

AMENDMENT IX.

Rule of construction of Constitution.

The enumeration in the Constitution, of certain rights, shall not be construed to deny or disparage others retained by the people.

AMENDMENT X.

Rights of States under Constitution.

The powers not delegated to the United States by the Constitution, nor prohibited by it to the States, are reserved to the States respectively, or to the people.

Amendments Since the Bill of Rights

AMENDMENT XI.

Judicial powers construed.

The Judicial power of the United States shall not be construed to extend to any suit in law or equity, commenced or prosecuted against one of the United States by Citizens of another State, or by Citizens or Subjects of any Foreign State.

(This amendment was proposed to the Legislatures of the several States by the Third Congress on March 4, 1794, and was declared to have been ratified in a message from the President to Congress, dated Jan. 8, 1798.

(It was on Jan. 5, 1798, that Secretary of State Pickering received from 12 of the States authenticated ratifications, and informed President John Adams of that fact.

(As a result of later research in the Department of State, it is now established that Amendment XI became part of the Constitution on Feb. 7, 1795, for on that date it had been ratified by 12 States as follows:

(1. New York, Mar. 27, 1794. 2. Rhode Island, Mar. 31, 1794. 3. Connecticut, May 8, 1794. 4. New Hampshire, June 16, 1794. 5. Massachusetts, June 26, 1794. 6. Vermont, between Oct. 9, 1794, and Nov. 9, 1794. 7. Virginia, Nov. 18,

1794. 8. Georgia, Nov. 29, 1794. 9. Kentucky, Dec. 7, 1794. 10. Maryland, Dec. 26, 1794. 11. Delaware, Jan. 23, 1795. 12. North Carolina, Feb. 7, 1795.

(On June 1, 1796, more than a year after Amendment XI had become a part of the Constitution—but before anyone was officially aware of this—Tennessee had been admitted as a State; but not until Oct. 16, 1797, was a certified copy of the resolution of Congress proposing the amendment sent to the Governor of Tennessee, John Sevier, by Secretary of State Pickering, whose office was then at Trenton, New Jersey, because of the epidemic of yellow fever at Philadelphia; it seems, however, that the Legislature of Tennessee took no action on Amendment XI, owing doubtless to the fact that public announcement of its adoption was made soon thereafter.

(Besides the necessary 12 States, one other, South Carolina, ratified Amendment XI, but this action was not taken until Dec. 4, 1797; the two remaining States, New Jersey and Pennsylvania, failed to ratify.)

AMENDMENT XII.
Manner of choosing President and Vice-President.

(Proposed by Congress Dec. 9, 1803; ratified June 15, 1804.)

The Electors shall meet in their respective states and vote by ballot for President and Vice-President, one of whom, at least, shall not be an inhabitant of the same state with themselves; they shall name in their ballots the person voted for as President, and in distinct ballots the person voted for as Vice-President, and they shall make distinct lists of all persons voted for as President, and of all persons voted for as Vice-President, and of the number of votes for each, which lists they shall sign and certify, and transmit sealed to the seat of the government of the United States, directed to the President of the Senate;–The President of the Senate shall, in presence of the Senate and House of Representatives, open all the certificates and the votes shall then be counted;—The person having the greatest number of votes for President, shall be the President, if such number be a majority of the whole number of Electors appointed; and if no person have such majority, then from the persons having the highest numbers not exceeding three on the list of those voted for as President, the House of Representatives shall choose immediately, by ballot, the President. But in choosing the President, the votes shall be taken by states, the representation from each state having one vote; a quorum for this purpose shall consist of a member or members from two-thirds of the states, and a majority of all the states shall be necessary to a choice. *(And if the House of Representatives shall not choose a President whenever the right of choice shall devolve upon them, before the fourth day of March next following, then the Vice-President shall act as President, as in the case of the death or other constitutional disability of the President.) (The words in parentheses were superseded by Amendment XX, section 3.)* The person having the greatest number of votes as Vice-President, shall be the Vice-President, if such number be a majority of the whole number of Electors appointed, and if no person have a majority, then from the two highest numbers on the list, the Senate shall choose the Vice-President; a quorum for the purpose shall consist of two-thirds of the whole number of Senators, and a majority of the whole number shall be necessary to a choice. But no person constitutionally ineligible to the office of President shall be eligible to that of Vice-President of the United States.

THE RECONSTRUCTION AMENDMENTS

(Amendments XIII, XIV, and XV are commonly known as the Reconstruction Amendments, inasmuch as they followed the Civil War, and were drafted by Republicans who were bent on imposing their own policy of reconstruction on the South. Post-bellum legislatures there—Mississippi, South Carolina, Georgia, for example—had set up laws which, it was charged, were contrived to perpetuate Negro slavery under other names.)

AMENDMENT XIII.
Slavery abolished.

(Proposed by Congress Jan. 31, 1865; ratified Dec. 6, 1865. The amendment, when first proposed by a resolution in Con-

gress, was passed by the Senate, 38 to 6, on Apr. 8, 1864, but was defeated in the House, 95 to 66 on June 15, 1864. On reconsideration by the House, on Jan. 31, 1865, the resolution passed, 119 to 56. It was approved by President Lincoln on Feb. 1, 1865, although the Supreme Court had decided in 1798 that the President has nothing to do with the proposing of amendments to the Constitution, or their adoption.)*

1. Neither slavery nor involuntary servitude, except as a punishment for crime whereof the party shall have been duly convicted, shall exist within the United States, or any place subject to their jurisdiction.

2. Congress shall have power to enforce this article by appropriate legislation.

AMENDMENT XIV.
Citizenship rights not to be abridged.

(The following amendment was proposed to the Legislatures of the several states by the 39th Congress, June 13, 1866, ratified July 9, 1868, and declared to have been ratified in a proclamation by the Secretary of State, July 28, 1868.

(The 14th amendment was adopted only by virtue of ratification subsequent to earlier rejections. Newly constituted legislatures in both North Carolina and South Carolina (respectively July 4 and 9, 1868), ratified the proposed amendment, although earlier legislatures had rejected the proposal. The Secretary of State issued a proclamation, which, though doubtful as to the effect of attempted withdrawals by Ohio and New Jersey, entertained no doubt as to the validity of the ratification by North and South Carolina. The following day (July 21, 1868), Congress passed a resolution which declared the 14th Amendment to be a part of the Constitution and directed the Secretary of State so to promulgate it. The Secretary waited, however, until the newly constituted Legislature of Georgia had ratified the amendment, subsequent to an earlier rejection, before the promulgation of the ratification of the new amendment.)

1. All persons born or naturalized in the United States, and subject to the jurisdiction thereof, are citizens of the United States and of the State wherein they reside. No State shall make or enforce any law which shall abridge the privileges or immunities of citizens of the United States; nor shall any State deprive any person of life, liberty, or property, without due process of law; nor deny to any person within its jurisdiction the equal protection of the laws.

2. Representatives shall be apportioned among the several States according to their respective numbers, counting the whole number of persons in each State, excluding Indians not taxed. But when the right to vote at any election for the choice of electors for President and Vice-President of the United States, Representatives in Congress, the Executive and Judicial officers of a State, or the members of the Legislature thereof, is denied to any of the male inhabitants of such State, being twenty-one years of age, and citizens of the United States, or in any way abridged, except for participation in rebellion, or other crime, the basis of representation therein shall be reduced in the proportion which the number of such male citizens shall bear to the whole number of male citizens twenty-one years of age in such State.

3. No person shall be a Senator or Representative in Congress, or elector of President and Vice-President, or hold any office, civil or military, under the United States, or under any State, who, having previously taken an oath, as a member of Congress, or as an officer of the United States, or as a member of any State legislature, or as an executive or judicial officer of any State, to support the Constitution of the United States, shall have engaged in insurrection or rebellion against the same, or given aid or comfort to the enemies thereof. But Congress may by a vote of two-thirds of each House, remove such disability.

4. The validity of the public debt of the United States, authorized by law, including debts incurred for payment of pensions and bounties for services in suppressing insurrection or rebellion, shall not be questioned. But neither the United States nor any State shall assume or pay any debt or obligation incurred in aid of insurrection or rebellion against the United

States, or any claim for the loss or emancipation of any slave; but all such debts, obligations and claims shall be held illegal and void.

The Congress shall have power to enforce, by appropriate legislation, the provisions of this article.

AMENDMENT XV.

Race no bar to voting rights.

(The following amendment was proposed to the legislatures of the several States by the 40th Congress, Feb. 26, 1869, and ratified Feb. 8, 1870.)

1. The right of citizens of the United States to vote shall not be denied or abridged by the United States or by any State on account of race, color, or previous condition of servitude–

2. The Congress shall have power to enforce this article by appropriate legislation.

AMENDMENT XVI.

Income taxes authorized.

(Proposed by Congress July 12, 1909; ratified Feb. 3, 1913.)

The Congress shall have power to lay and collect taxes on incomes, from whatever source derived, without apportionment among the several States, and without regard to any census or enumeration.

AMENDMENT XVII.

United States Senators to be elected by direct popular vote.

(Proposed by Congress May 13, 1912; ratified Apr. 8, 1913.)

The Senate of the United States shall be composed of two Senators from each State, elected by the people thereof, for six years; and each Senator shall have one vote. The electors in each State shall have the qualifications requisite for electors of the most numerous branch of the State legislatures.

When vacancies happen in the representation of any State in the Senate, the executive authority of such State shall issue writs of election to fill such vacancies: *Provided,* That the legislature of any State may empower the executive thereof to make temporary appointments until the people fill the vacancies by election as the legislature may direct.

This amendment shall not be so construed as to affect the election or term of any Senator chosen before it becomes valid as part of the Constitution.

AMENDMENT XVIII.

Liquor prohibition amendment.

(Proposed by Congress Dec. 18, 1917; ratified Jan. 16, 1919. Repealed by Amendment XXI, effective Dec. 5, 1933.)

1. After one year from the ratification of this article the manufacture, sale, or transportation of intoxicating liquors within, the importation thereof into, or the exportation thereof from the United States and all territory subject to the jurisdiction thereof for beverage purposes is hereby prohibited.

2. The Congress and the several States shall have concurrent power to enforce this article by appropriate legislation.

3. This article shall be inoperative unless it shall have been ratified as an amendment to the Constitution by the legislatures of the several States as provided in the Constitution, within seven years from the date of the submission hereof to the States by the Congress.

(The total vote in the Senates of the various States was 1,310 for, 237 against—84.6% dry. In the lower houses of the States the vote was 3,782 for, 1,035 against—78.5% dry.

(The amendment ultimately was adopted by all the States except Connecticut and Rhode Island.)

AMENDMENT XIX.

Giving nationwide suffrage to women.

(Proposed by Congress June 4, 1919; ratified Aug. 18, 1920.)

The right of citizens of the United States to vote shall not be denied or abridged by the United States or by any State on account of sex.

Congress shall have power to enforce this Article by appropriate legislation.

AMENDMENT XX.

Terms of President and Vice President to begin on Jan. 20; those of Senators, Representatives, Jan. 3.

(Proposed by Congress Mar. 2, 1932; ratified Jan. 23, 1933.)

1. The terms of the President and Vice President shall end at noon on the 20th day of January, and the terms of Senators and Representatives at noon on the 3d day of January, of the years in which such terms would have ended if this article had not been ratified; and the terms of their successors shall then begin.

2. The Congress shall assemble at least once in every year, and such meeting shall begin at noon on the 3d day of January, unless they shall by law appoint a different day.

3. If, at the time fixed for the beginning of the term of the President, the President elect shall have died, the Vice President elect shall become President. If a President shall not have been chosen before the time fixed for the beginning of his term, or if the President elect shall have failed to qualify, then the Vice President elect shall act as President until a President shall have qualified; and the Congress may by law provide for the case wherein neither a President elect nor a Vice President elect shall have qualified, declaring who shall then act as President, or the manner in which one who is to act shall be selected, and such person shall act accordingly until a President or Vice President shall have qualified.

4. The Congress may by law provide for the case of the death of any of the persons from whom the House of Representatives may choose a President whenever the right of choice shall have devolved upon them, and for the case of the death of any of the persons from whom the Senate may choose a Vice President whenever the right of choice shall have devolved upon them.

5. Sections 1 and 2 shall take effect on the 15th day of October following the ratification of this article (Oct. 1933).

6. This article shall be inoperative unless it shall have been ratified as an amendment to the Constitution by the legislatures of three-fourths of the several States within seven years from the date of its submission.

AMENDMENT XXI.

Repeal of Amendment XVIII.

(Proposed by Congress Feb. 20, 1933; ratified Dec. 5, 1933.)

1. The eighteenth article of amendment to the Constitution of the United States is hereby repealed.

2. The transportation or importation into any State, Territory, or possession of the United States for delivery or use therein of intoxicating liquors, in violation of the laws thereof, is hereby prohibited.

3. This article shall be inoperative unless it shall have been ratified as an amendment to the Constitution by conventions in the several States, as provided in the Constitution, within seven years from the date of the submission hereof to the States by the Congress.

AMENDMENT XXII.

Limiting Presidential terms of office.

(Proposed by Congress Mar. 24, 1947; ratified Feb. 27, 1951.)

1. No person shall be elected to the office of the President more than twice, and no person who has held the office of President, or acted as President, for more than two years of a term to which some other person was elected President shall be elected to the office of the President more than once. But this Article shall not apply to any person holding the office of

President when this Article was proposed by the Congress, and shall not prevent any person who may be holding the office of President, or acting as President, during the term within which this Article becomes operative from holding the office of President or acting as President during the remainder of such term.

2. This article shall be inoperative unless it shall have been ratified as an amendment to the Constitution by the legislatures of three-fourths of the several States within seven years from the date of its submission to the States by the Congress.

AMENDMENT XXIII.

Presidential vote for District of Columbia.

(Proposed by Congress June 16, 1960; ratified Mar. 29, 1961.)

1. The District constituting the seat of Government of the United States shall appoint in such manner as the Congress may direct:

A number of electors of President and Vice President equal to the whole number of Senators and Representatives in Congress to which the District would be entitled if it were a State, but in no event more than the least populous State; they shall be in addition to those appointed by the States, but they shall be considered, for the purposes of the election of President and Vice President, to be electors appointed by a State; and they shall meet in the District and perform such duties as provided by the twelfth article of amendment.

2. The Congress shall have power to enforce this article by appropriate legislation.

AMENDMENT XXIV.

Barring poll tax in federal elections.

(Proposed by Congress Aug. 27, 1962; ratified Jan. 23, 1964.)

1. The right of citizens of the United States to vote in any primary or other election for President or Vice President, for electors for President or Vice President, or for Senator or Representative in Congress, shall not be denied or abridged by the United States or any State by reason of failure to pay any poll tax or other tax.

2. The Congress shall have power to enforce this article by appropriate legislation.

AMENDMENT XXV.

Presidential disability and succession.

(Proposed by Congress July 6, 1965; ratified Feb. 10, 1967.)

1. In case of the removal of the President from office or of his death or resignation, the Vice President shall become President.

2. Whenever there is a vacancy in the office of the Vice President, the President shall nominate a Vice President who shall take office upon confirmation by a majority vote of both houses of Congress.

3. Whenever the President transmits to the President pro tempore of the Senate and the Speaker of the House of Representatives his written declaration that he is unable to discharge the powers and duties of his office, and until he transmits to them a written declaration to the contrary, such powers and duties shall be discharged by the Vice President as Acting President.

4. Whenever the Vice President and a majority of either the principal officers of the executive departments or of such other body as Congress may by law provide, transmit to the President pro tempore of the Senate and the Speaker of the House of Representatives their written declaration that the President is unable to discharge the powers and duties of his office, the Vice President shall immediately assume the powers and duties of the office as Acting President.

Thereafter, when the President transmits to the President pro tempore of the Senate and the Speaker of the House of Representatives his written declaration that no inability exists, he shall resume the powers and duties of his office unless the Vice President and a majority of either the principal officers of the executive department or of such other body as Congress may by law provide, transmit within four days to the President pro tempore of the Senate and the Speaker of the House of Representatives their written declaration that the President is unable to discharge the powers and duties of his office. Thereupon Congress shall decide the issue, assembling within forty-eight hours for that purpose if not in session. If the Congress, within twenty-one days after receipt of the latter written declaration, or, if Congress is not in session, within twenty-one days after Congress is required to assemble, determines by two-thirds vote of both Houses that the President is unable to discharge the powers and duties of his office, the Vice President shall continue to discharge the same as Acting President; otherwise, the President shall resume the powers and duties of his office.

AMENDMENT XXVI.

Lowering voting age to 18 years.

(Proposed by Congress Mar. 23, 1971; ratified July 1, 1971.)

1. The right of citizens of the United States, who are eighteen years of age or older, to vote shall not be denied or abridged by the United States or by any State on account of age.

2. The Congress shall have the power to enforce this article by appropriate legislation.

AMENDMENT XXVII.

Congressional pay.

(Proposed by Congress Sept. 25, 1789; ratified May 7, 1992.)

No law, varying the compensation for the services of the Senators and Representatives, shall take effect, until an election of Representatives shall have intervened.

How a Bill Becomes a Law

1. A senator or representative introduces a bill by sending it to the clerk of the House or the Senate, who assigns it a number and title. This procedure is termed the first reading. The clerk then refers the bill to the appropriate Senate or House committee.

2. If the committee opposes the bill, it will table, or kill, it. Otherwise, the committee holds hearings to listen to opinions and facts offered by members and other interested people. The committee then debates the bill and possibly offers amendments. A vote is taken, and if favorable, the bill is sent back to the clerk of the House or Senate.

3. The clerk reads the bill to the house—the second reading. Members may then debate the bill and suggest amendments.

4. After debate and possibly amendment, the bill is given a third reading, simply of the title, and put to a voice or roll-call vote.

5. If passed, the bill goes to the other house, where it may be defeated or passed, with or without amendments. If defeated, the bill dies. If passed with amendments, a conference committee made up of members of both houses works out the differences and arrives at a compromise.

6. After passage of the final version by both houses, the bill is sent to the president. If the president signs it, the bill becomes a law. The president may, however, veto the bill by refusing to sign it and sending it back to the house where it originated, with reasons for the veto.

7. The president's objections are then read and debated, and a roll-call vote is taken. If the bill receives less than a two-thirds majority, it is defeated. If it receives at least two-thirds, it is sent to the other house. If that house also passes it by at least a two-thirds majority, the veto is overridden, and the bill becomes a law.

8. If the president neither signs nor vetoes the bill within 10 days—not including Sundays—it automatically becomes a law even without the president's signature. However, if Congress has adjourned within those 10 days, the bill is automatically killed; this indirect rejection is termed a pocket veto.

Confederate States and Secession

The American Civil War (1861-65) grew out of sectional disputes over the continued existence of slavery in the South and the contention of Southern legislators that the states retained many sovereign rights, including the right to secede from the Union.

The war was not fought by state against state but by one federal regime against another, the Confederate government in Richmond assuming control over the economic, political, and military life of the South, under protest from Georgia and South Carolina.

South Carolina voted an ordinance of secession from the Union, repealing its 1788 ratification of the U.S. Constitution on Dec. 20, 1860, to take effect on Dec. 24. Other states seceded in 1861. Their votes in conventions were:

Mississippi, Jan. 9, 84-15; Florida, Jan. 10, 62-7; Alabama, Jan. 11, 61-39; Georgia, Jan. 19, 208-89; Louisiana, Jan. 26, 113-17; Texas, Feb. 1, 166-7, ratified by popular vote Feb. 23 (for 34,794, against 11,325); Virginia, Apr. 17, 88-55, ratified by popular vote on May 23 (for 128,884;

against 32,134); Arkansas, May 6, 69-1; Tennessee, May 7, ratified by popular vote on June 8 (for 104,019, against 47,238); North Carolina, May 21.

Missouri Unionists stopped secession in conventions Feb. 28 and Mar. 9. The legislature condemned secession Mar. 7. Under the protection of Confederate troops, secessionist members of the legislature adopted a resolution of secession at Neosho, Oct. 31. The Confederate Congress seated the secessionists' representatives.

Kentucky did not secede, and its government remained Unionist. In a part of the state occupied by Confederate troops, Kentuckians approved secession, and the Confederate Congress admitted their representatives.

The Maryland legislature voted against secession Apr. 27, 53-13. Delaware did not secede. Western Virginia held conventions at Wheeling, named a pro-Union governor on June 11, 1861; and was admitted to the Union as West Virginia on June 20, 1863. Its constitution provided for gradual abolition of slavery.

Confederate Government

Forty-two delegates from South Carolina, Georgia, Alabama, Mississippi, Louisiana, and Florida met in convention at Montgomery, AL, on Feb. 4, 1861. They adopted a provisional constitution of the Confederate States of America and elected Jefferson Davis (MS) as provisional president and Alexander H. Stephens (GA) as provisional vice president.

A permanent constitution was adopted on Mar. 11; it abolished the African slave trade. The Congress moved to

Richmond, VA, on July 20. Davis was elected president in October and was inaugurated on Feb. 22, 1862.

The Congress adopted a flag, consisting of a red field with a white stripe, and a blue jack with a circle of white stars. Later the more popular flag was the red field with blue diagonal crossbars that held 13 white stars. The stars represented the 11 states actually in the Confederacy plus Kentucky and Missouri.

Lincoln's Address at Gettysburg, 1863

Fourscore and seven years ago our fathers brought forth on this continent a new nation, conceived in liberty and dedicated to the proposition that all men are created equal.

Now we are engaged in a great civil war, testing whether that nation or any nation so conceived and so dedicated can long endure. We are met on a great battle field of that war. We have come to dedicate a portion of that field, as a final resting-place for those who here gave their lives that that nation might live. It is altogether fitting and proper that we should do this.

But, in a larger sense, we can not dedicate—we can not consecrate—we can not hallow—this ground. The brave men, living and dead, who struggled here, have consecrated

it, far above our poor power to add or detract. The world will little note, nor long remember, what we say here, but it can never forget what they did here. It is for us the living, rather, to be dedicated here to the unfinished work which they who fought here have thus far so nobly advanced. It is rather for us to be here dedicated to the great task remaining before us—that from these honored dead we take increased devotion to that cause for which they gave the last full measure of devotion—that we here highly resolve that these dead shall not have died in vain—that this nation, under God, shall have a new birth of freedom—and that government of the people, by the people, for the people, shall not perish from the earth.

Selected Landmark Decisions of the U.S. Supreme Court

1803: Marbury v. Madison. The Court ruled that Congress exceeded its power in the Judiciary Act of 1789; thus, the Court established its power to review acts of Congress and declare invalid those it found in conflict with the Constitution.

1819: McCulloch v. Maryland. The Court ruled that Congress had the authority to charter a national bank, under the Constitution's granting of the power to enact all laws "necessary and proper" to exact the responsibilities of government. The Court also held that the national bank was immune to state taxation.

1819: Trustees of Dartmouth College v. Woodward. The Court ruled that a state could not arbitrarily alter the terms of a college's contract. (In later years the Court widened the implications by using the same principle to limit the states' ability to interfere with business contracts.)

1857: Dred Scott v. Sanford. The Court declared unconstitutional the already-repealed Missouri Compromise of 1820 because it deprived a person of his or her property—a slave—without due process of law. The Court also ruled that slaves were not citizens of any state nor of the

U.S. (The latter part of the decision was overturned by ratification of the 14th Amendment in 1868.)

1896: Plessy v. Ferguson. The Court ruled that a state law requiring federal railroad trains to provide separate but equal facilities for black and white passengers neither infringed upon federal authority to regulate interstate commerce nor violated the 13th and 14th Amendments. (The "separate but equal" doctrine remained effective until the 1954 Brown v. Board of Education decision.)

1904: Northern Securities Co. v. U.S. The Court ruled that a holding company formed solely to eliminate competition between two railroad lines was a combination in restraint of trade, thus a violation of the federal antitrust act.

1908: Muller v. Oregon. The Court ruled to uphold a state law limiting the maximum working hours of women. (Instead of presenting legal arguments, Louis D. Brandeis, counsel for the state, brought forth evidence from social workers, physicians, and factory inspectors that the number of hours women worked affected their health and morals.)

1911: Standard Oil Co. of New Jersey et al. v. U.S. The Court ruled that the Standard Oil Trust must be dissolved because of its unreasonable restraint of trade, not because of its size.

1919: Schenck v. U.S. In its first decision regarding the extent of protection afforded by the First Amendment, the Court sustained the Espionage Act of 1917, maintaining that freedom of speech and press could be constrained if "the words used are in such circumstances and are of such a nature as to create a clear and present danger. . ."

1925: Gitlow v. New York. The Court ruled that the First Amendment prohibition against government abridgement of the freedom of speech applied to the states as well as to the federal government. The decision was the first of a number of rulings holding that the 14th Amendment extended the guarantees of the Bill of Rights to state action.

1935: Schechter Poultry Corp. v. U.S. The Court ruled that Congress exceeded its authority to delegate legislative powers and to regulate interstate commerce when it enacted the National Industrial Recovery Act, which afforded the U.S. president too much discretionary power.

1951: Dennis et al. v. U.S. The Court upheld convictions under the Smith Act of 1940 for speaking about communist theory that advocated the forcible overthrow of the government. (In the 1957 Yates v. U.S. decision, the Court moderated this ruling by allowing such advocacy in the abstract, if not connected to action to achieve the goal.)

1954: Brown v. Board of Education of Topeka. The Court ruled that separate public schools for black and white students were inherently unequal, thus state-sanctioned segregation in public schools violated the equal protection guarantee of the 14th Amendment. And in **Bolling v. Sharpe** the Court ruled that the congressionally mandated segregated public school system in the District of Columbia violated the Fifth Amendment's due process guarantee of personal liberty. (The Brown ruling also led to the abolition of state-sponsored segregation in other public facilities.)

1957: Roth v. U.S., Alberts v. California. The Court ruled that obscene material was not protected by the First Amendment guarantees of freedom of speech and press, defining obscene as "utterly without redeeming social value" and appealing to "prurient interests" in the view of the average person. (This definition, the first offered by the Court, was modified in several subsequent decisions, and the "average person" standard was replaced by the "local community" standard in the **1973 Miller v. California** case.)

1961: Mapp v. Ohio. The Court ruled that evidence obtained in violation of the 4th Amendment guarantee against unreasonable search and seizure must be excluded from use at state as well as federal trials.

1962: Engel v. Vitale. The Court ruled that public school officials could not require pupils to recite a state-composed prayer at the start of each school day, even if the prayer was nondenominational and pupils who so desired could be excused from reciting it, because such official state sanction of religious utterances was an unconstitutional attempt to establish religion.

1962: Baker v. Carr. The Court held that the constitutional challenges to the unequal distribution of voters among legislative districts could be resolved by federal courts, rejecting the doctrine set out in **Colegrove v. Green** in 1946 that such apportionment challenges were "political questions."

1963: Gideon v. Wainwright. The Court ruled that the due process clause of the 14th Amendment extended to state as well as federal defendants, thus all persons charged with serious crimes must be provided with an attorney, and states were required to appoint counsel for defendants unable to pay their own attorneys' fees.

1964: New York Times Co. v. Sullivan. The Court ruled that the First Amendment guarantee of freedom of the press protected the press from libel suits for defamatory reports on public officials unless the officials proved that the reports were made from actual malice. The Court defined malice as "with knowledge that (the defamatory

statement) was false or with reckless disregard of whether it was false or not."

1965: Griswold v. Conn. The Court ruled that a state unconstitutionally interfered with personal privacy in the marriage relationship when it prohibited anyone, including married couples, from using contraceptives.

1966: Miranda v. Arizona. The Court ruled that the guarantee of due process required that before any questioning of suspects in police custody, the suspects must be informed of their right to remain silent, that anything they say may be used against them, and that they have the right to counsel.

1973: Roe v. Wade, Doe v. Bolton. The Court ruled that the right to privacy inherent in the 14th Amendment's due process guarantee of personal liberty protected a woman's decision whether or not to bear a child, and was impermissibly abridged by state laws that made abortion a crime. During the first trimester of pregnancy, the Court maintained, the decision to have an abortion should be left entirely to a woman and her physician.

1974: U.S. v. Nixon. The Court ruled that neither the separation of powers nor the need to preserve the confidentiality of presidential communications could alone justify an absolute executive privilege of immunity from judicial demands for evidence to be used in a criminal trial.

1976: Gregg v. Georgia, Profitt v. Fla., Jurek v. Texas. The Court held that death, as a punishment for persons convicted of first degree murder, was not in and of itself cruel and unusual punishment in violation of the 8th Amendment. The Court also ruled that the amendment required the sentencing judge and jury to consider the individual character of the offender and the circumstances of the particular crime before deciding whether to impose the death sentence. In the associated **Woodson v. N.C., Roberts v. La.,** the Court ruled that states could not make death the mandatory penalty for first-degree murder, since that would fail to meet the constitutional requirement for the consideration of the individual offender and offense.

1978: Regents of Univ. of Calif. v. Bakke. The Court ruled that a special admissions program for a state medical school under which a set number of places were set aside for minority group members, with white applicants denied the opportunity to compete for those seats, violated Title XIV of the 1964 Civil Rights Act, which forbids the exclusion of anyone, because of race, from participation in a federally funded program. The Court also ruled that admissions programs that considered race as one of a complex of factors involved in the decision to admit or reject an applicant were not unconstitutional.

1986: Bowers v. Hardwick. The Court refused to extend the right of privacy inherent in the Constitution to homosexual activity, upholding a Georgia law that made sodomy a crime. (Although the Georgia law covered heterosexual sodomy as well as homosexual sodomy, enforcement in Georgia and most other states had been confined to homosexual activity.)

1990: Cruzan v. Missouri. The Court ruled that a person had the right to refuse life-sustaining medical treatment. However, the Court also ruled that, in the case of a comatose patient, a state could require "clear and convincing evidence" that the patient would not have wanted to live under those conditions before such treatment could be withheld.

1995: Adarand Constructors v. Peña. The Court held that federal programs that classify people by race, unless "narrowly tailored" to accomplish a "compelling governmental interest," may deny individuals the right to equal protection. Such federal programs, the Court maintained, must adhere to the same strict standards required of state-run affirmative action programs.

1995: U.S. Term Limits Inc. v. Thorton. The Court ruled that it is unconstitutional for either the states or Congress to limit the terms of members of Congress, since the Constitution reserves the right to choose federal lawmakers to the people. (This ruling invalidated 23 congressional term-limit laws that had been passed since 1990.)

Presidential Oath of Office

The Constitution (Article II) directs that the president shall take the following oath or affirmation: "I do solemnly swear (affirm) that I will faithfully execute the office of President of the United States, and will, to the best of my ability, preserve, protect, and defend the Constitution of the United States." (Custom decrees the use of the words "So help me God" at the end of the oath when taken by the president-elect, his or her left hand on the Bible for the duration of the oath, with his or her right hand slightly raised.)

Law on Succession to the Presidency

If by reason of death, resignation, removal from office, inability, or failure to qualify there is neither a president nor vice president to discharge the powers and duties of the office of president, then the speaker of the House of Representatives shall upon his resignation as speaker and as representative, act as president. The same rule shall apply in the case of the death, resignation, removal from office, or inability of an individual acting as president.

If at the time when a speaker is to begin the discharge of the powers and duties of the office of president there is no speaker, or the speaker fails to qualify as acting president, then the president pro tempore of the Senate, upon his resignation as president pro tempore and as senator, shall act as president.

An individual acting as president shall continue to act until the expiration of the then current presidential term, except that (1) if his discharge of the powers and duties of the office is founded in whole or in part in the failure of both the president-elect and the vice president-elect to

qualify, then he shall act only until a president or vice president qualifies, and (2) if his discharge of the powers and duties of the office is founded in whole or in part on the inability of the president or vice president, then he shall act only until the removal of the disability of one of such individuals.

If, by reason of death, resignation, removal from office, or failure to qualify, there is no president pro tempore to act as president, then the officer of the United States who is highest on the following list, and who is not under any disability to discharge the powers and duties of president shall act as president; the secretaries of state, treasury, defense, attorney general; secretaries of interior, agriculture, commerce, labor, health and human services, housing and urban development, transportation, energy, education, veterans affairs.

(Legislation approved July 18, 1947; amended Sept. 9, 1965, Oct. 15, 1966, Aug. 4, 1977, and Sept. 27, 1979. See also Constitutional Amendment XXV.)

Origin of the United States National Motto

In God We Trust, designated as the U.S. National Motto by Congress in 1956, originated during the Civil War as an inscription for U. S. coins, although it was used by Francis Scott Key in a slightly different form when he wrote "The Star-Spangled Banner" in 1814. On Nov. 13, 1861, when Union morale had been shaken by battlefield defeats, the Rev. M. R. Watkinson, of Ridleyville, PA, wrote to Secy. of the Treasury Salmon P. Chase. "From my heart I have felt our national shame in disowning God

as not the least of our present national disasters," the minister wrote, suggesting "recognition of the Almighty God in some form on our coins." Secy. Chase ordered designs prepared with the inscription *In God We Trust* and backed coinage legislation that authorized use of this slogan. It first appeared on some U.S. coins in 1864, disappeared and reappeared on various coins until 1955, when Congress ordered it placed on all paper money and all coins.

The Great Seal of the U.S.

On July 4, 1776, the Continental Congress appointed a committee consisting of Benjamin Franklin, John Adams, and Thomas Jefferson "to bring in a device for a seal of the United States of America." The designs submitted by this and a subsequent committee were considered unacceptable. After many delays, a third committee, appointed early in 1782, presented a design prepared by William Barton. Charles Thomson, the secretary of

Congress, suggested certain changes, and Congress finally approved the design on June 20, 1782. The obverse side of the seal shows an American bald eagle. In its mouth is a ribbon bearing the motto *e pluribus unum* (one out of many). In the eagle's talons are the arrows of war and an olive branch of peace. The reverse side shows an unfinished pyramid with an eye (the eye of Providence) above it.

The American's Creed

William Tyler Page, Clerk of the U.S. House of Representatives, wrote "The American's Creed" in 1917.
It was accepted by the House on behalf of the American people on April 3, 1918.

"I believe in the United States of America as a government of the people, by the people, for the people; whose just powers are derived from the consent of the governed; a democracy in a republic; a sovereign Nation of many sovereign States; a perfect union, one and inseparable; established upon those

principles of freedom, equality, justice, and humanity for which American patriots sacrificed their lives and fortunes.

"I therefore believe it is my duty to my country to love it, to support its Constitution, to obey its laws, to respect its flag, and to defend it against all enemies."

The Flag of the U.S.—The Stars and Stripes

The 50-star flag of the United States was raised for the first time officially at 12:01 AM on July 4, 1960, at Fort McHenry National Monument in Baltimore, MD. The 50th star had been added for Hawaii; a year earlier the 49th, for Alaska. Before that, no star had been added since 1912, when New Mexico and Arizona were admitted to the Union.

The true history of the Stars and Stripes has become so cluttered by myth and tradition that the facts are difficult, and in some cases impossible, to establish. For example, it is not certain who designed the Stars and Stripes, who made the first such flag, or even whether it ever flew in any sea fight or land battle of the American Revolution.

All agree, however, that the Stars and Stripes originated as the result of a resolution offered by the Marine Commit-

tee of the Second Continental Congress at Philadelphia and adopted on June 14, 1777. It read:

Resolved: that the flag of the United States be thirteen stripes, alternate red and white; that the union be thirteen stars, white in a blue field, representing a new constellation.

Congress gave no hint as to the designer of the flag, no instructions as to the arrangement of the stars, and no information on its appropriate uses. Historians have been unable to find the original flag law.

The resolution establishing the flag was not even published until Sept. 2, 1777. Despite repeated requests, Washington did not get the flags until 1783, after the American Revolution was over. And there is no certainty that they were the Stars and Stripes.

Early Flags

Many historians consider the first flag of the U.S. to have been the Grand Union (sometimes called Great Union) flag, although the Continental Congress never officially adopted it. This flag was a modification of the British Meteor flag, which had the red cross of St. George and the white cross of St. Andrew combined in the blue canton. For the Grand Union flag, 6 horizontal stripes were imposed on the red field, dividing it into 13 alternating red and white stripes. On Jan. 1, 1776, when the Continental Army came into formal existence, this flag was unfurled on Prospect Hill, Somerville, MA. Washington wrote that "we hoisted the Union Flag in compliment to the United Colonies."

One of several flags about which controversy has raged for years is at Easton, PA. Containing the devices of the national flag in reversed order, this flag has been in the public library at Easton for more than 150 years. Some contend that this flag was actually the first Stars and Stripes, first displayed on July 8, 1776. This flag has 13 red and white stripes in the canton, 13 white stars centered in a blue field.

A flag was hastily improvised from garments by the defenders of Fort Schuyler at Rome, NY, Aug. 3-22, 1777. Historians believe it was the Grand Union Flag.

The Sons of Liberty had a flag of 9 red and white stripes, to signify 9 colonies, when they met in New York in 1765 to oppose the Stamp Tax. By 1775, the flag had grown to 13 red and white stripes, with a rattlesnake on it.

At Concord, Apr. 19, 1775, the minutemen from Bedford, MA, are said to have carried a flag having a silver arm with sword on a red field.

At Cambridge, MA, the Sons of Liberty used a plain red flag with a green pine tree on it.

In June 1775, Washington went from Philadelphia to Boston to take command of the army, escorted to New York by the Philadelphia Light Horse Troop. It carried a yellow flag that had an elaborate coat of arms—the shield charged with 13 knots, the motto "For These We Strive"—and a canton of 13 blue and silver stripes.

In Feb. 1776, Col. Christopher Gadsden, a member of the Continental Congress, gave the South Carolina Provincial Congress a flag "such as is to be used by the commander-in-chief of the American Navy." It had a yellow field, with a rattlesnake about to strike and the words "Don't Tread on Me."

At the Battle of Bennington, Aug. 16, 1777, patriots used a flag of 7 white and 6 red stripes with a blue canton extending down 9 stripes and showing an arch of 11 white stars over the figure 76 and a star in each of the upper corners. The stars are 7-pointed. This flag is preserved in the Historical Museum at Bennington, VT.

At the Battle of Cowpens, Jan. 17, 1781, the 3d Maryland Regiment is said to have carried a flag of 13 red and white stripes, with a blue canton containing 12 stars in a circle around one star.

Who Designed the Flag? No one knows for certain. Francis Hopkinson, designer of a naval flag, declared he also had designed the flag and in 1781 asked Congress to reimburse him for his services. Congress did not do so. Dumas Malone of Columbia University wrote: "This talented man . . . designed the American flag."

Who Called the Flag "Old Glory"? The flag is said to have been named Old Glory by William Driver, a sea captain of Salem, MA. One legend has it that when he raised the flag on his brig, the *Charles Doggett*, in 1824, he said: "I name thee Old Glory." But his daughter, who presented the flag to the Smithsonian Institution, said he named it at his 21st birthday celebration on Mar. 17, 1824, when his mother presented the homemade flag to him.

The Betsy Ross Legend. The widely publicized legend that Mrs. Betsy Ross made the first Stars and Stripes in June 1776, at the request of a committee composed of George Washington, Robert Morris, and George Ross, an uncle, was first made public in 1870, by a grandson of Mrs. Ross. Historians have been unable to find a historical record of such a meeting or committee.

Adding New Stars

The flag of 1777 was used until 1795. Then, on the admission of Vermont and Kentucky to the Union, Congress passed and Pres. Washington signed an act that after May 1, 1795, the flag should have 15 stripes, alternating red and white, and 15 white stars on a blue field.

When new states were admitted, it became evident that the flag would become burdened with stripes. Congress thereupon ordered that after July 4, 1818, the flag should have 13 stripes, symbolizing the 13 original states; that the union have 20 stars, and that whenever a new state was admitted a new star should be added on the July 4 following admission. No law designates the permanent arrangement of the stars. However, since 1912, when a new state has been admitted, the new design has been announced by executive order. No star is specifically identified with any state.

Code of Etiquette for Display and Use of the U.S. Flag

Although the Stars and Stripes originated in 1777, it was not until 146 years later that there was a serious attempt to establish a uniform code of etiquette for the U.S. flag. On Feb. 15, 1923, the War Department issued a circular on the rules of flag usage. These rules were adopted almost in their entirety June 14, 1923, by a conference of 68 patriotic organizations in Washington. Finally, on June 22, 1942, a joint resolution of Congress, amended by Public Law 94-344 July 7, 1976, codified "existing rules and customs pertaining to the display and use of the flag . . ."

When to Display the Flag—The flag should be displayed on all days, especially on legal holidays and other special occasions, on official buildings when in use, in or near polling places on election days, and in or near schools when in session. Citizens may fly the flag at any time. It is customary to display the flag only from sunrise to sunset on buildings and on stationary flagstaffs in the open. It may be displayed at night, however, on special occasions, preferably lighted. In Washington, the flag now flies over the White House both day and night. It flies over the Senate wing of the Capitol when the Senate is in session and over the House wing when that body is in session. It flies day and night over the east and west fronts of the Capitol, without floodlights at night but receiving light from the illuminated Capitol Dome. It flies 24 hours a day at several other places, including the Fort McHenry National Monument in Baltimore, where it inspired Francis Scott Key to write "The Star Spangled Banner." The flag also flies 24 hours a day, properly illuminated, at U.S. Customs ports of entry.

Flying the Flag at Half-Staff—Flying the flag at half-staff, that is, halfway up the staff, is a signal of mourning. The flag should be hoisted to the top of the staff for an instant before being lowered to half-staff. It should be hoisted to the peak again before being lowered for the day or night.

As provided by presidential proclamation, the flag should fly at half-staff for 30 days from the day of death of a president or former president; for 10 days from the day of death of a vice president, chief justice or retired chief justice of the U.S., or speaker of the House of Representatives; from day of death until burial of an associate justice of the Supreme Court, cabinet member, former vice president, or Senate president pro tempore, majority or minority Senate leader, or majority or minority House leader; for a U.S. senator, representative, territorial delegate, or the resident commissioner of Puerto Rico, on day of death and the following day within the metropolitan area of the District of Columbia and from day of death until burial within the decedent's state, congressional district, territory or commonwealth; and for the death of the governor of a state, territory, or possession of the U.S., from day of death until burial within that state, territory, or possession.

On Memorial Day, the flag should fly at half-staff until noon and then be raised to the peak.

How to Fly the Flag—The flag should be hoisted briskly and lowered ceremoniously and should never be allowed to touch the ground or the floor. When the flag is hung over a sidewalk from a rope extending from a building to a pole, the union should be away from the building. When the flag is hung over the center of a street the union should be to the north in an east-west street and to the east in a north-south street. No other flag may be flown above or, if on the same level, to the right of the U.S. flag, except that at the United Nations Headquarters the UN flag may be placed above flags of all member nations and other national flags may be flown with equal prominence or honor with the flag of the U.S. At services by Navy chaplains at sea, the church pennant may be flown above the flag.

When 2 flags are placed against a wall with crossed staffs, the U.S. flag should be at right—its own right, and its staff should be in front of the staff of the other flag; when a number of flags are grouped and displayed from staffs, it should be at the center and highest point of the group.

Church and Platform Use—In an auditorium, the flag may be displayed flat, above and behind the speaker. When displayed from a staff in a church or in a public auditorium, the flag should hold the position of superior prominence, in advance of the audience, and in the position of honor at the speaker's right as she or he faces the audience. Any other flag so displayed should be placed on the left of the speaker or to the right of the audience.

When the flag is displayed horizontally or vertically against a wall, the stars should be uppermost and at the observer's left.

When used to cover a casket, the flag should be placed so that the union is at the head and over the left shoulder. It should not be lowered into the grave nor touch the ground.

How to Dispose of Worn Flags—When the flag is in such condition that it is no longer a fitting emblem for display, it should be destroyed in a dignified way, preferably by burning.

When to Salute the Flag—All persons present should face the flag, stand at attention, and salute on the following occasions: (1) when the flag is passing in a parade or in a review, (2) during the ceremony of hoisting or lowering, (3) when the national anthem is played, and (4) during the Pledge of Allegiance. Those present in uniform should render the military salute. Those not in uniform should place the right hand over the heart. A man wearing a hat should remove it with his right hand and hold it to his left shoulder during the salute.

Prohibited Uses of the Flag—The flag should not be dipped to any person or thing. (An exception—customarily, ships salute by dipping their colors.) It should never be displayed with the union down save as a distress signal. It should never be carried flat or horizontally, but always aloft and free.

It should not be displayed on a float, an automobile, or a boat except from a staff. It should never be used as a covering for a ceiling, nor have placed on it any word, design, or drawing. It should never be used as a receptacle for carrying anything. It should not be used to cover a statue or a monument.

The flag should never be used for advertising purposes, nor be embroidered on such articles as cushions or handkerchiefs,

printed or otherwise impressed on boxes or anything that is designed for temporary use and discard; or used as a costume or athletic uniform. Advertising signs should not be fastened to its staff or halyard.

The flag should never be used as drapery of any sort, never festooned, drawn back, nor up, in folds, but always allowed to fall free. Bunting of blue, white, and red, always arranged with the blue above and the white in the middle, should be used for covering a speaker's desk, draping the front of a platform, and for decoration in general.

An act of Congress approved on Feb. 8, 1917, provided certain penalties for the desecration, mutilation, or improper use of the flag within the District of Columbia. A 1968 federal law provided penalties of as much as a year's imprisonment or a $1,000 fine or both for publicly burning or otherwise desecrating any U.S. flag. In addition, many states have laws against flag desecration. In 1989, the Supreme Court ruled that no laws could prohibit political protesters from burning the flag. The decision had the effect of declaring unconstitutional the flag desecration laws of 48 states, as well as a similar federal statute, in cases of peaceful political expression.

The Supreme Court, June 1990, declared that a new federal law making it a crime to burn or deface the American flag violates the free-speech guarantee of the First Amendment. The 5-4 decision led to renewed calls in Congress for a constitutional amendment to make it possible to prosecute flag burners.

Pledge of Allegiance to the Flag

I pledge allegiance to the flag of the United States of America and to the republic for which it stands, one nation under God, indivisible, with liberty and justice for all.

This, the current official version of the Pledge of Allegiance, has developed from the original pledge, which was first published in the Sept. 8, 1892, issue of *Youth's Companion*, a weekly magazine then published in Boston. The original pledge contained the phrase "my flag," which was changed more than 30 years later to "flag of the United States of America." A 1954 act of Congress added the words "under God."

The authorship of the pledge had been in dispute for many years. The *Youth's Companion* stated in 1917 that the original draft was written by James B. Upham, an executive of the magazine who died in 1910. A leaflet circulated by the magazine later named Upham as the originator of the draft "afterwards condensed and perfected by him and his associates of the Companion force."

Francis Bellamy, a former member of *Youth's Companion* editorial staff, publicly claimed authorship of the pledge in 1923. The United States Flag Association, acting on the advice of a committee named to study the controversy, upheld in 1939 the claim of Bellamy, who had died 8 years earlier. The Library of Congress issued in 1957 a report attributing the authorship to Bellamy.

The History of the National Anthem

"The Star-Spangled Banner" was ordered played by the military and naval services by President Woodrow Wilson in 1916. It was designated the national anthem by Act of Congress, Mar. 3, 1931. It was written by Francis Scott Key, of Georgetown, MD, during the bombardment of Fort McHenry, Baltimore, MD, Sept. 13-14, 1814. Key was a lawyer, a graduate of St. John's College, Annapolis, and a volunteer in a light artillery company. When a friend, Dr. Beanes, a physician of Upper Marlborough, MD, was taken aboard Admiral Cockburn's British squadron for interfering with ground troops, Key and J. S. Skinner, carrying a note from President Madison, went to the fleet under a flag of truce on a cartel ship to ask Beanes's release. Cockburn consented, but as the fleet was about to sail up the Patapsco to bombard Fort McHenry, he detained them, first on HMS *Surprise* and then on a supply ship.

Key witnessed the bombardment from his own vessel. It began at 7 AM, Sept. 13, 1814, and lasted, with intermissions, for 25 hr. The British fired more than 1,500 shells, each weighing as much as 220 lb. They were unable to approach closely because the U.S. had sunk 22 vessels. Only 4 Americans were killed and 24 wounded. A British bomb-ship was disabled.

During the bombardment, Key wrote a stanza on the back of an envelope. Next day at Indian Queen Inn, Baltimore, he wrote out the poem and gave it to his brother-in-law, Judge J. H. Nicholson. Nicholson suggested the tune, Anacreon in Heaven, and had the poem printed on broadsides, of which 2 survive. On Sept. 20 it appeared in the *Baltimore American*. Later Key made 3 copies; one is in the Library of Congress, and one is in the Pennsylvania Historical Society.

The copy that Key wrote in his hotel on Sept. 14, 1814, remained in the Nicholson family for 93 years. In 1907 it was sold to Henry Walters of Baltimore. In 1934 it was bought at auction in New York from the Walters estate by the Walters Art Gallery, Baltimore, for $26,400. The Walters Gallery in 1953 sold the manuscript to the Maryland Historical Society for the same price.

The flag that Key saw during the bombardment is preserved in the Smithsonian Institution, Washington, DC. It is 30 by 42 ft and has 15 alternating red and white stripes and 15 stars, for the original 13 states plus Kentucky and Vermont. It was made by Mary Young Pickersgill. The Baltimore Flag House, a museum, occupies her premises, which were restored in 1953.

The Star-Spangled Banner

I

Oh, say can you see by the dawn's early light
    What so proudly we hailed at the twilight's last gleaming?
Whose broad stripes and bright stars thru the perilous fight,
    O'er the ramparts we watched were so gallantly streaming?
And the rocket's red glare, the bombs bursting in air,
    Gave proof through the night that our flag was still there.
Oh, say does that star-spangled banner yet wave
    O'er the land of the free and the home of the brave?

II

On the shore, dimly seen through the mists of the deep,
    Where the foe's haughty host in dread silence reposes,
What is that which the breeze, o'er the towering steep,
    As it fitfully blows, half conceals, half discloses?
Now it catches the gleam of the morning's first beam,
    In full glory reflected now shines in the stream:
'Tis the star-spangled banner! Oh long may it wave
    O'er the land of the free and the home of the brave!

III

And where is that band who so vauntingly swore
    That the havoc of war and the battle's confusion,
A home and a country should leave us no more!
    Their blood has washed out their foul footsteps' pollution.
No refuge could save the hireling and slave
    From the terror of flight, or the gloom of the grave:
And the star-spangled banner in triumph doth wave
    O'er the land of the free and the home of the brave!

IV

Oh! thus be it ever, when freemen shall stand
    Between their loved home and the war's desolation!
Blest with victory and peace, may the heav'n rescued land
    Praise the Power that hath made and preserved us a
    nation.
Then conquer we must, when our cause it is just,
    And this be our motto: "In God is our trust."
And the star-spangled banner in triumph shall wave
    O'er the land of the free and the home of the brave!

America
(My Country 'Tis of Thee)

First sung in public on July 4, 1831, at a service in the Park Street Church, Boston, the words were written by Rev. Samuel Francis Smith, a Baptist clergyman, who set them to a melody he found in a German songbook, unaware that it was the tune for the British anthem, "God Save the King/Queen."

My country, 'tis of thee,
Sweet land of liberty, Of thee I sing.
Land where my fathers died!
Land of the Pilgrims' pride!
From ev'ry mountainside,
Let freedom ring!

My native country, thee,
Land of the noble free,
Thy name I love.
I love thy rocks and rills,
Thy woods and templed hills;
My heart with rapture thrills
Like that above.

Let music swell the breeze,
And ring from all the trees
Sweet freedom's song.
Let mortal tongues awake;
Let all that breathe partake;
Let rocks their silence break,
The sound prolong.

Our fathers' God, to Thee,
Author of liberty,
To Thee we sing.
Long may our land be bright
With freedom's holy light;
Protect us by Thy might,
Great God, our King!

America, the Beautiful

Composed by Katharine Lee Bates, a Massachusetts educator and author, in 1893. It was inspired by the view Bates experienced atop Pikes Peak. Its final form was established in 1911 and is set to the music of Samuel A. Ward's "Materna."

O beautiful for spacious skies,
For amber waves of grain,
For purple mountain majesties
Above the fruited plain.
America! America!
God shed His grace on thee,
And crown thy good with brotherhood
From sea to shining sea.
O beautiful for pilgrim feet
Whose stern impassion'd stress
A thorough-fare for freedom beat
Across the wilderness.
America! America!
God mend thine ev'ry flaw,
Confirm thy soul in self control,
Thy liberty in law.

O beautiful for heroes prov'd
In liberating strife,
Who more than self their country lov'd
And mercy more than life.
America! America!
May God thy gold refine
Till all success be nobleness,
And ev'ry gain divine.
O beautiful for patriot dream
That sees beyond the years,
Thine alabaster cities gleam,
Undimmed by human tears.
America! America!
God shed His grace on thee,
And crown thy good with brotherhood
From sea to shining sea.

The Liberty Bell: Its History and Significance

The Liberty Bell, in Independence National Historical Park, Philadelphia, is an object of great reverence to Americans because of its association with the historic events of the American Revolution.

The original Province bell was ordered by Assembly Speaker and Chairman of the State House Superintendents Isaac Norris and was ordered from Thomas Lester, Whitechapel Foundry, London. It reached Philadelphia at the end of August 1752. It bore an inscription from Leviticus 25:10: "PROCLAIM LIBERTY THROUGHOUT ALL THE LAND UNTO ALL THE INHABITANTS THEREOF."

The bell was cracked by a stroke of its clapper in Sept. 1752 while it hung on a truss in the State House yard for testing. Pass & Stow, Philadelphia founders, recast the bell, adding 1½ ounces of copper to a pound of the original "Whitechapel" metal to reduce its high tone and brittleness. It was found that the bell contained too much copper, injuring its tone, so Pass & Stow recast it again, this time successfully.

In June 1753 the bell was hung in the old wooden steeple of the State House, erected on top of the brick tower. In use while the Continental Congress was in session in the State House, it rang out in defiance of British tax and trade restrictions, and it proclaimed the Boston Tea Party and the first public reading of the Declaration of Independence.

On Sept. 18, 1777, when the British Army was about to occupy Philadelphia, the bell was moved in a baggage train of the American Army to Allentown, PA, where it was hidden in the Zion Reformed Church until June 27, 1778. It was moved back to Philadelphia after the British left.

In July 1781 the wooden steeple became insecure and had to be taken down. The bell was lowered into the brick section of the tower, where it remained until 1828. Between 1828 and 1844 the old State House bell continued to ring during special occasions. It rang for the last time on Feb. 23, 1846. In 1852 it was placed on exhibition in the Declaration Chamber of Independence Hall.

In 1876, when many thousands of Americans visited Philadelphia for the Centennial Exposition, the bell was placed in its old wooden support in the tower hallway. In 1877 it was hung from the ceiling of the tower by a chain of 13 links. It was returned again to the Declaration Chamber and in 1896 taken back to the tower hall, where it occupied a glass case. In 1915 the case was removed so that the public might touch it. On Jan. 1, 1976, just after midnight to mark the opening of the Bicentennial Year, the bell was moved to a new glass and steel pavilion behind Independence Hall for easier viewing by the larger number of visitors expected during the year.

The measurements of the bell are: circumference around the lip, 12 ft ½ in; circumference around the crown, 6 ft 11¼ in; lip to the crown, 3 ft; height over the crown, 2 ft 3 in; thickness at lip, 3 in; thickness at crown, 1¼ in; weight, 2,080 lb; length of clapper, 3 ft 2 in; cost, £60 14s 5d.

The specific source of the crack in the bell is unknown.

Statue of Liberty National Monument

Since 1886, the Statue of Liberty Enlightening the World has stood as a symbol of freedom in New York harbor. It also commemorates French-American friendship, for it was given by the people of France and designed by French sculptor Frederic Auguste Bartholdi (1834-1904).

Edouard de Laboulaye, French historian and admirer of American political institutions, suggested that the French present a monument to the U.S., the latter to provide pedestal and site. Bartholdi visualized a colossal statue at the entrance of New York harbor, welcoming the peoples of the world with the torch of liberty.

On Washington's Birthday, Feb. 22, 1877, Congress approved the use of a site on Bedloe's Island suggested by Bartholdi. This island of 12 acres had been owned in the 17th century by a Walloon named Isaac Bedloe. It was called Bedloe's until Aug. 3, 1956, when Pres. Eisenhower approved a resolution of Congress changing the name to Liberty Island.

The statue was finished on May 21, 1884, and formally presented to the U.S. minister to France, Levi Parsons Morton, July 4, 1884, by Ferdinand de Lesseps, head of the Franco-American Union, promoter of the Panama Canal, and builder of the Suez Canal.

On Aug. 5, 1884, the Americans laid the cornerstone for the pedestal. This was to be built on the foundations of Fort Wood, which had been erected by the government in 1811. The American committee had raised $125,000, but this was found to be inadequate. Joseph Pulitzer, owner of the *New York World*, appealed on Mar. 16, 1885, for general donations. By Aug. 11, 1885, he had raised $100,000.

The statue arrived dismantled, in 214 packing cases, from Rouen, France, in June 1885. The last rivet of the statue was driven on Oct. 28, 1886, when Pres. Grover Cleveland dedicated the monument.

The statue weighs 450,000 lb, or 225 tons. The copper sheeting weighs 200,000 lb. There are 167 steps from the land level to the top of the pedestal, 168 steps inside the statue to the head, and 54 rungs on the ladder leading to the arm that holds the torch.

A $2.5 million building housing the American Museum of Immigration was opened by Pres. Richard Nixon on Sept. 26, 1972, at the base of the statue. It houses a permanent exhibition of photos, posters, and artifacts tracing the history of American immigration. The Statue of Liberty National Monument is administered by the National Park Service.

Two years of restoration work was completed before the statue's centennial celebration on July 4, 1986. Among other repairs, the multimillion dollar project included replacing the 1,600 wrought iron bands that hold the statue's copper skin to its frame, replacing its torch, and installing an elevator.

A 4-day extravaganza of concerts, tall ships, ethnic festivals, and fireworks celebrated the 100th anniversary. The festivities included Chief Justice Warren E. Burger's swearing-in of 5,000 new citizens on Ellis Island, while 20,000 others across the country were simultaneously sworn in through a satellite telecast.

The ceremonies were followed by others on Oct. 28, 1986, the statue's 100th birthday.

Dimensions of the Statue	Ft.	In.
Height from base to torch (45.3 meters)	151	1
Foundation of pedestal to torch (91.5 meters)	305	1
Heel to top of head	111	1
Length of hand	16	5
Index finger	8	0
Circumference at second joint	3	6
Size of finger nail . . . . 13x10 in.		
Head from chin to cranium	17	3
Head thickness from ear to ear.	10	0
Distance across the eye	2	6
Length of nose	4	6
Right arm, length	42	0
Right arm, greatest thickness.	12	0
Thickness of waist.	35	0
Width of mouth	3	0
Tablet, length	23	7
Tablet, width.	13	7
Tablet, thickness.	2	0

Emma Lazarus' Famous Poem

A poem by Emma Lazarus is graven on a tablet within the pedestal on which the Statue of Liberty stands.

The New Colossus

Not like the brazen giant of Greek fame,
With conquering limbs astride from land to land;
Here at our sea-washed, sunset gates shall stand
A mighty woman with a torch, whose flame
Is the imprisoned lightning, and her name
Mother of Exiles. From her beacon-hand
Glows world-wide welcome; her mild eyes command
The air-bridged harbor that twin cities frame.
"Keep ancient lands, your storied pomp!" cries she
With silent lips. "Give me your tired, your poor,
Your huddled masses yearning to breathe free,
The wretched refuse of your teeming shore.
Send these, the homeless, tempest-tost to me,
I lift my lamp beside the golden door!"

Ellis Island

Ellis Island was the gateway to America for more than 12 million immigrants between 1892 and 1924. In the late 18th century, Samuel Ellis, a New York City merchant, purchased the island and gave it his name. From Ellis, it passed to New York State, and the U.S. government bought it in 1808. In 1892 the government opened an immigration center on the island. The 27½-acre site eventually supported more than 35 buildings, including the Main Building with its Great Hall, in which as many as 5,000 people a day were processed during peak periods. Closed as an immigration station in 1954, Ellis Island was proclaimed part of the National Monument in 1965 by Pres. Lyndon B. Johnson. After an 8-year privately funded $156 million restoration project, Ellis Island was reopened as a museum in 1990. Artifacts, historic photographs and documents, oral histories, and ethnic music depicting 400 years of American immigration are housed in the museum. The museum also includes the American Immigrant Wall of Honor, inscribed with some 420,000 names.

BIOGRAPHIES OF U.S. PRESIDENTS

George Washington (1789-97)

George Washington, first president, was born on Feb. 22, 1732, in Wakefield on Pope's Creek, Westmoreland Co., VA, the son of Augustine and Mary Ball Washington. He spent his early childhood on a farm near Fredericksburg. His father died when George was 11. He studied mathematics and surveying, and when he was 16, he went to live with his elder half brother Lawrence, who built and named Mount Vernon. George surveyed the lands of William Fairfax in the Shenandoah Valley, keeping a diary. He accompanied Lawrence to Barbados, West Indies, where he contracted small pox and was deeply scarred. Lawrence died in 1752, and George inherited his property. He valued land, and when he died, he owned 70,000 acres in Virginia and 40,000 acres in what is now West Virginia.

Washington's military service began in 1753 when Lt. Gov. Robert Dinwiddie of Virginia sent him on missions deep into Ohio country. He clashed with the French and had to surrender Fort Necessity on July 3, 1754. He was an aide to the British general Edward Braddock and at his side when the army was ambushed and defeated (July 9, 1755) on a march to Ft. Duquesne. He helped take Fort Duquesne from the French in 1758.

After Washington's marriage to Martha Dandridge Custis, a widow, in 1759, he managed his family estate at Mount Vernon. Although not at first for independence, he opposed the repressive measures of the British crown and took charge of the Virginia troops before war broke out. He was made commander of the newly created Continental Army by the Continental Congress on June 15, 1775.

The American victory was due to Washington's leadership. He was resourceful, a stern disciplinarian, and the one strong, dependable force for unity. He favored a federal government and became chairman of the Constitutional Convention of 1787. He helped get the Constitution ratified and was unanimously elected president by the Electoral College. He was inaugurated Apr. 30, 1789, on the balcony of New York's Federal Hall.

Washington was reelected in 1792, but refused to consider a 3d term. He retired to Mount Vernon in March 1797. He suffered acute laryngitis after a ride in snow and rain around his estate, was bled profusely, and died Dec. 14, 1799.

John Adams (1797-1801)

John Adams, 2d president, Federalist, was born on Oct. 30, 1735, in Braintree (now Quincy), MA, the son of John and Susanna Boylston Adams. He was a great-grandson of Henry Adams, who came from England in 1636. He graduated from Harvard in 1755 and then taught school and studied law. He married Abigail Smith in 1764. In 1765 he argued against taxation without representation before the royal governor. In 1770 he successfully defended in court the British soldiers who fired on civilians in the Boston Massacre. He was a delegate to the Continental Congress and a signer of the Declaration of Independence. In 1778, Congress sent Adams and John Jay to join Benjamin Franklin as diplomatic respresentatives in Europe. Because he ran second to Washington in Electoral College balloting in 1788, Adams became the nation's first vice president; he was reelected in 1792.

In 1796 Adams was chosen president by the electors. His administration was marked by rivalry with Alexander Hamilton and a crisis in U.S.-France relations. He was extraordinarily unpopular for securing passage of the Alien and Sedition Acts in 1797-98. His foreign policy contributed significantly to the election of Thomas Jefferson in the 1800 election.

Adams lived for a quarter century after he left office, during which time he wrote extensively. He died July 4, 1826, on the same day as Thomas Jefferson (the 50th anniversary of the Declaration of Independence).

Thomas Jefferson (1801-9)

Thomas Jefferson, 3d president, was born on Apr. 13, 1743, in Shadwell in Albemarle Co., VA, the son of Peter and Jane Randolph Jefferson. Peter died when Thomas was 14, leaving him 2,750 acres and his slaves. Jefferson attended (1760-62) the College of William and Mary, read classics in Greek and Latin, and played the violin. In 1769 he was elected to the Virginia House of Burgesses. In 1770 he began building his home, Monticello, and in 1772 he married Martha Wayles Skelton, a wealthy widow. He was a member of the Virginia Committee of Correspondence and the Continental Congress. As a member of the Second Continental Congress he drafted the Declaration of Independence in late June 1776. He was a member of the Virginia House of Delegates (1776-79) and was first elected governor of Virginia in 1779, succeeding Patrick Henry. He was reelected governor in 1780 but resigned in June 1781 amid charges of ineffectual military preparation. During his term he wrote the statute on religious freedom. After his wife's death in 1782, Jefferson again became a delegate to the Congress, and in 1784 he drafted the report that was the basis for the Ordinances of 1784, 1785, and 1787. He was minister to France from 1784 to 1789, when Washington appointed him secretary of state.

Jefferson's strong faith in the consent of the governed, as opposed to executive control, which was favored by Hamilton, secretary of the Treasury, often led to conflict. He resigned on Dec. 31, 1793. In the 1796 election Jefferson was the Democratic Republican candidate for president; John Adams won the election, and Jefferson became vice president. In 1800, Jefferson and Aaron Burr received equal Electoral College votes. The House of Representatives elected Jefferson president. Major events of his first term were the Louisiana Purchase (1803) and the Lewis and Clark Expedition. An important development during his second term was passage of the Embargo Act. Jefferson established the University of Virginia and designed its buildings. He died July 4, 1826, on the same day as John Adams (the 50th anniversary of the Declaration of Independence).

James Madison (1809-17)

James Madison, 4th president, Democratic Republican, was born on Mar. 16, 1751, in Port Conway, King George Co., VA, the son of James and Eleanor Rose Conway Madison. Madison graduated from Princeton in 1771. After serving in the Virginia Constitutional Convention (1776), he became a delegate to the Continental Congress. He was chief recorder at the Constitutional Convention in 1787 and supported ratification in the *Federalist Papers*, written with Alexander Hamilton and John Jay. He was elected to the House of Representatives in 1789, where he helped frame the Bill of Rights and fought against passage of the Alien and Sedition Acts. In the 1790s, he helped found the Democratic Republican Party, which ultimately became the Democratic Party. He became Jefferson's secretary of state in 1801.

Madison was elected president in 1808. His first term was marked by tensions with Great Britain, and his conduct of foreign policy was criticized by the Federalists and by his own party. Nevertheless, he was reelected in 1812, the year war was declared on Great Britain. The war that many considered a second American revolution ended with a treaty that settled none of the issues. Madison's most important action after the war was demilitarizing the U.S.-Canadian border.

In 1817, Madison retired to his estate, Montpelier, where he served as an elder statesman, "the last of the fathers." He edited his famous papers on the Constitutional Convention and helped found the University of Virginia, of which he became rector in 1826. He died June 28, 1836.

James Monroe (1817-25)

James Monroe, 5th president, Democratic Republican, was born on Apr. 28, 1758, in Westmoreland Co., VA, the son of Spence and Eliza Jones Monroe. He entered the College of William and Mary in 1774 but left to serve in the 3d Virginia Regiment during the American Revolution. After the war, he studied law with Thomas Jefferson. In 1782 he was elected to the Virginia House of Delegates, and he served (1783-86) as a delegate to the Continental Congress. He opposed ratification of the Constitution because it lacked a bill of rights. Monroe was elected to the U.S. Senate in 1790. In 1794 President George Washington appointed Monroe minister to France. He served twice as governor of Virginia (1799-1802, 1811). President Jefferson also sent him to France as minister (1803), and then from 1803 to 1807 he was minister to Great Britain.

In 1816 Monroe was elected president; he was re-elected in 1820 with all but one Electoral College vote. His administration became known as the Era of Good Feeling. He obtained Florida from Spain, settled boundaries with Canada, and eliminated border forts. He supported the antislavery position that led to the Missouri Compromise. His most significant contribution was the Monroe Doctrine, which opposed European intervention in Latin America and became a cornerstone of U.S. foreign policy.

Although Monroe retired to Oak Hill, VA, financial problems forced him to sell his property and move to New York City. He died there on July 4, 1831.

John Quincy Adams (1825-29)

John Quincy Adams, 6th president, independent Federalist, later Democratic Republican, was born on July 11, 1767, in Braintree (now Quincy), MA, the son of John and Abigail Adams. His father was the 2d president. He was educated in Paris, in Leyden, and at Harvard, graduating in 1787. In 1803, he was elected to the U.S. Senate. President Monroe chose him as his secretary of state in 1817. In this capacity he negotiated the cession of the Floridas from Spain, supported exclusion of slavery in the Missouri Compromise, and helped formulate the Monroe Doctrine. In 1824 he was elected president by the House of Representatives after he failed to win an Electoral College majority. His expansion of executive powers was strongly opposed, and in the 1828 election he lost to Andrew Jackson. In 1831 he entered the House of Representatives and served 17 years with distinction. He opposed slavery, the annexation of Texas, and the Mexican War. He helped establish the Smithsonian Institution. He suffered a stroke in the House and died in the Speaker's Room on Feb. 23, 1848.

Andrew Jackson (1829-37)

Andrew Jackson, 7th president, Democratic Republican, later a Democrat, was born on Mar. 15, 1767, in the Waxhaws district, New Lancaster Co., SC, the son of Andrew and Elizabeth Hutchinson Jackson. At the age of 13, he joined the militia to fight in the American Revolution and was captured.

Orphaned at the age of 14, Jackson was brought up by a well-to-do uncle. By age 20, he was practicing law, and he later served as prosecuting attorney in Nashville, TN. In 1796 he helped draft the constitution of Tennessee and for a year occupied its one seat in the House of Representatives. The next year he served in the U.S. Senate.

In the War of 1812, Jackson crushed (1814) the Creek Indians at Horseshoe Bend, AL, and, with 6,000 backwoods fighters, defeated (1815) Pakenham's 12,000 British troops at the Battle of New Orleans. In 1818 he briefly invaded Spanish Florida to quell Seminoles and outlaws who harassed frontier settlements. In 1824 he ran for president against John Quincy Adams. Although he won the most popular and electoral votes, he did not have a majority. The House of Representatives decided the election and chose Adams. In the 1828 election, however, Jackson defeated Adams, carrying the West and the South. As president, Jackson introduced what became known as the spoils system—rewarding party members with government posts. Perhaps his most controversial act, however, was depositing federal funds in so-called pet banks, those directed by Democratic bankers, rather than in the Bank of the United States. "Let the people rule" was his slogan. In 1832, Jackson killed the congressional caucus for nominating presidential candidates and substituted the national convention. When South Carolina refused to collect imports under his protective tariff, he ordered army and naval forces to Charleston. After leaving office in 1837, he retired to the Hermitage, outside Nashville, where he died on June 8, 1845.

Martin Van Buren (1837-41)

Martin Van Buren, 8th president, Democrat, was born on Dec. 5, 1782, in Kinderhook, NY, the son of Abraham and Mary Hoes Van Buren. Well educated by private tutors, he became a lawyer at the age of 20. A consummate politician, Van Buren began his career in the New York state senate and then served as state attorney general from 1816 to 1819. He was elected to the U.S. Senate in 1821. He helped swing eastern support to Andrew Jackson in the 1828 election and then served as Jackson's secretary of state from 1829 to 1831. In 1832 he was elected vice president. Known as the Little Magician, Van Buren was extremely influential in Jackson's administration. In the election of 1836 he defeated William Henry Harrison for president and took office as the financial panic of 1837 initiated a 5-year nationwide depression. Although he instituted the independent treasury system, his refusal to spend land revenues led to his defeat by William Henry Harrison in the election of 1840. In 1844, he lost the Democratic nomination to James Knox Polk. In 1848 he again ran for president on the Free Soil ticket but lost. He died in Kinderhook on July 24, 1862.

William Henry Harrison (1841)

William Henry Harrison, 9th president, Whig, who served only 31 days, was born on Feb. 9, 1773, in Berkeley, Charles City Co., VA, the son of Benjamin Harrison, a signer of the Declaration of Independence. He attended Hampden Sydney College. Harrison served as secretary of the Northwest Territory in 1798 and was its delegate to the House of Representatives in 1799. He was the first governor of the Indiana Territory and served as superintendent of Indian affairs. With 900 men he put down a Shawnee uprising at Tippecanoe, IN, on Nov. 7, 1811. A generation later, in 1840, he waged a rousing presidential campaign, using the slogan "Tippecanoe and Tyler too." The Tyler of the slogan was his vice presidential running mate, John Tyler. Although he was born to one of the wealthiest, most prestigious, and most influential families in Virginia, Harrison was elected president with a "log cabin and hard cider" slogan. He caught pneumonia during the inauguration and died Apr. 4, 1841.

John Tyler (1841-45)

John Tyler, 10th president, independent Whig, was born on Mar. 29, 1790, in Greenway, Charles City Co., VA, the son of John and Mary Armistead Tyler. His father was governor of Virginia (1808-11). Tyler graduated from William and Mary in 1807 and in 1811 was elected to the Virginia legislature. In 1816 he was chosen for the U.S. House of Representatives. From 1823 to 1825 he again served in the Virginia legislature, and then in 1825 he was elected governor of Virginia. After a stint in the U.S. Senate (1827-36), he was elected vice president (1840). When William Henry Harrison died only a month after taking office, Tyler succeeded him. Because he was the first person to occupy the presidency without being elected to that office, he was referred to as "His Accidency." His most significant domestic measure was the Preemption Act of 1841, which gave squatters on government land the right to buy 160 acres at the minimum auction price. His last act as president was to sign the resolution annexing Texas. He accepted renomination in 1844 from some Democrats but withdrew in favor of the official party candidate, James K. Polk. He died in Richmond, VA, on Jan. 18, 1862.

James Knox Polk (1845-49)

James Knox Polk, 11th president, Democrat, was born on Nov. 2, 1795, in Mecklenburg Co., NC, the son of Samuel and Jane Knox Polk. He graduated from the University of North Carolina in 1818 and served in the Tennessee state legislature from 1823 to 1825. He served in the U.S. House of Representatives from 1825 to 1839, the last 4 years as Speaker. He was governor of Tennessee from 1839 to 1841. In 1844, after the Democratic National Convention became deadlocked, it nominated Polk, and he thus became the nation's first "dark horse" candidate for president. He was nominated primarily because he was known to favor annexation of Texas. As president, Polk reestablished the independent treasury system originated by Van Buren. He was so intent on acquiring California from Mexico that he sent troops under Zachary Taylor to the Mexican border and, when Mexicans attacked, declared that war existed. The Mexican War ended with the annexation of California and much of the Southwest as part of America's "manifest destiny." Polk compromised on the Oregon boundary ("54-40 or fight!") by accepting the 49th parallel and giving Vancouver to the British.

A few weeks after leaving office, Polk died in Nashville, on June 15, 1849.

Zachary Taylor (1849-50)

Zachary Taylor, 12th president, Whig, who served only 16 months, was born on Nov. 24, 1784, in Orange Co., VA, the son of Richard and Sarah Strother Taylor. He grew up on his father's plantation near Louisville, KY, where he was educated by private tutors. In 1808 Taylor joined the regular army and was commissioned first lieutenant. He fought in the War of 1812, the Black Hawk War (1832), and the second Seminole War (1837). He was called Old Rough and Ready. In 1845 President Polk sent him with an army to the Rio Grande. When the Mexicans attacked him, Polk declared war. Outnumbered 4-1, Taylor defeated (1847) Santa Anna at Buena Vista. A national hero, he received the Whig nomination in 1848 and was elected president, even though he had never bothered to vote. He resumed the spoils system and, though once a slaveholder, worked to admit California as a free state. He fell ill and died in office on July 9, 1850.

Millard Fillmore (1850-53)

Millard Fillmore, 13th president, Whig, was born on Jan. 7, 1800, in Cayuga Co., NY, the son of Nathaniel and Phoebe Millard Fillmore. Although he had little schooling, he became a law clerk at the age of 22 and a year later was admitted to the bar. Entering politics as a member of the Anti-Masonic Party, he was elected to the New York state assembly in 1828 and served until 1831. From 1833 until 1835 and again from 1837 to 1843, he represented his district in the U.S. House of Representatives. He opposed the entrance of Texas as slave territory and voted for a protective tariff. In 1844 he was defeated for governor of New York. In 1848 he was elected vice president, and he succeeded as president after Taylor's death. Fillmore favored the Compromise of 1850 and signed the Fugitive Slave Law. His policies pleased neither expansionists nor slaveholders, and he was not renominated in 1852. In 1856 he was nominated by the American (Know-Nothing) Party, but despite the support of the Whigs, he was defeated by James Buchanan. He died in Buffalo on Mar. 8, 1874.

Franklin Pierce (1853-57)

Franklin Pierce, 14th president, Democrat, was born on Nov. 23, 1804, in Hillsboro, NH, the son of Benjamin Pierce, an American Revolutionary War general and governor of New Hampshire. He graduated from Bowdoin College in 1824 and was admitted to the bar in 1827. He was elected to the New Hampshire state legislature in 1829 and was chosen Speaker in 1831. He went to the U.S. House of Representatives in 1833 and was elected a U.S. senator in 1837. He enlisted in the Mexican War and became brigadier general under Gen. Winfield Scott. In 1852 Pierce was nominated as the Democratic presidential candidate on the 49th ballot. He decisively defeated Gen. Scott, his Whig opponent, in the election. Although against slavery, Pierce was influenced by pro-slavery Southerners. He supported the Kansas-Nebraska Act, which left slavery to popular vote (squatter sovereignty). He signed a reciprocity treaty with Canada and approved the Gadsden Purchase from Mexico. Denied renomination by the Democrats, he spent most of his remaining years in Concord, NH, where he died on Oct. 8, 1869.

James Buchanan (1857-61)

James Buchanan, 15th president, Federalist, later Democrat, was born on Apr. 23, 1791, near Mercersburg, PA, the son of James and Elizabeth Speer Buchanan. He graduated from Dickinson College in 1809 and was admitted to the bar in 1812. He fought in the War of 1812 as a volunteer. He was twice elected to the Pennsylvania general assembly, and in 1821 he entered the U.S. House of Representatives. After briefly serving (1832-33) as minister to Russia, he was elected U.S. senator from Pennsylvania. As Polk's secretary of state (1845-49), he ended the Oregon dispute with Britain and supported the Mexican War and annexation of Texas. As minister to Great Britain, he signed the Ostend Manifesto (1854), which declared the U.S.'s right to take Cuba by force should efforts to purchase the island fail. Nominated by Democrats,

Buchanan was elected president in 1856. On slavery he favored popular sovereignty and choice by state constitutions. He denied the right of states to secede. Buchanan desired to keep peace and found no authority for using force. He died at Wheatland, near Lancaster, PA, on June 1, 1868.

Abraham Lincoln (1861-65)

Abraham Lincoln, 16th president, Republican, was born on Feb. 12, 1809, in a log cabin on a farm then in Hardin Co., KY, now in Larue, the son of Thomas and Nancy Hanks Lincoln.

The Lincolns moved to Spencer Co., IN, near Gentryville, when Abe was 7. After Abe's mother died, his father married (1819) Mrs. Sarah Bush Johnston. In 1830 the family moved to Macon Co., IL. Defeated in 1832 in a race for the state legislature, Lincoln was elected on the Whig ticket 2 years later and served in the lower house from 1834 to 1841.

In 1836 Lincoln was admitted to the bar and became partner in a Springfield, IL, law office. He soon won recognition as an effective and resourceful attorney. In 1846, he was elected to the House of Representatives, where he attracted attention during a single term for his opposition to the Mexican War and his position on slavery. In 1856 he campaigned for the newly founded Republican Party, and in 1858 he became its senatorial candidate against Stephen A. Douglas. Although he lost the election, Lincoln gained national recognition from his debates with Douglas.

In 1860, Lincoln was nominated for president by the Republican Party on an antislavery platform. He ran against Douglas, a northern Democrat; John C. Breckinridge, a Southern proslavery Democrat; and John Bell, the nominee of the Constitutional Union Party. As a result of Lincoln's winning the election, South Carolina seceded from the Union on Dec. 20, 1860, followed in 1861 by 10 other Southern states.

The Civil War erupted when Fort Sumter was attacked on Apr. 12, 1861. On Sept. 22, 1862, 5 days after the Battle of Antietam, Lincoln announced that slaves in territory then in rebellion would be free Jan. 1, 1863, the date of the Emancipation Proclamation. His speeches, including his Gettysburg and Inaugural addresses, are remembered for their eloquence.

Lincoln was reelected, in 1864, over Gen. George B. McClellan, Democrat. Lee surrendered on Apr. 9, 1865. On Apr. 14, Lincoln was shot by actor John Wilkes Booth in Ford's Theater, in Washington, DC. He died the next day.

Andrew Johnson (1865-69)

Andrew Johnson, 17th president, Democrat, was born on Dec. 29, 1808, in Raleigh, NC, the son of Jacob and Mary McDonough Johnson. He was apprenticed to a tailor at the age of 16 but ran away and eventually settled in Greeneville, TN. He became popular with the townspeople and in 1829 was elected councilman and later mayor. In 1835 he was sent to the state general assembly. In 1843 he was elected to the U.S. House of Representatives, where he served for 10 years. Johnson was governor of Tennessee from 1853 to 1857, when he was elected to the U.S. Senate. He supported John C. Breckinridge against Lincoln in the 1860 election. Although Johnson had held slaves, he opposed secession and tried to prevent Tennessee from seceding. In Mar. 1862, Lincoln appointed him military governor of occupied Tennessee. In 1864, in order to balance Lincoln's ticket with a Southern Democrat, the Republicans nominated Johnson for vice president. He was elected vice president with Lincoln and then succeeded to the presidency upon Lincoln's death. In a controversy with Congress over the president's power over the South, he proclaimed, May 26, 1865, an amnesty to all Confederates except certain leaders if they would ratify the 13th Amendment abolishing slavery. States doing so added anti-Negro provisions that enraged Congress, which restored military control over the South. When Johnson removed Edwin M. Stanton, secretary of war, without notifying the Senate, the House impeached him. Ostensibly charging Johnson with violating the Tenure of Office Act, the House was actually responding to his opposition to congressional Reconstruction. He was tried by the Senate and acquitted by only one vote on May 26, 1868. He was reelected to the Senate in 1874. Johnson died July 31, 1875.

Ulysses Simpson Grant (1869-77)

Ulysses S. Grant, 18th president, Republican, was born on Apr. 27, 1822, in Point Pleasant, OH, the son of Jesse R. and Hannah Simpson Grant. The next year the family moved to Georgetown, OH. Grant was named Hiram Ulysses, but on entering West Point in 1839, his name was entered as Ulysses Simpson, and he adopted it. He graduated in 1843. During the Mexican War, Grant served under both Gen. Zachary Taylor and Gen. Winfield Scott. In 1854, he resigned his commission because of loneliness and drinking problems, and in the following years he engaged in generally unsuccessful farming and business ventures. With the start of the Civil War, he was named colonel and then brigadier general of the Illinois Volunteers. He took Forts Henry and Donelson and fought at Shiloh. His brilliant campaign against Vicksburg and his victory at Chattanooga made him so prominent that Lincoln placed him in command of all Union armies. Grant accepted Lee's surrender at Appomattox Court House on Apr. 9, 1865. President Johnson appointed Grant secretary of war when he suspended Stanton, but Grant was not confirmed. He was nominated for president by the Republicans in 1868 and elected over Horatio Seymour, Democrat. The 15th Amendment, amnesty bill, and civil service reform were events of his administration. The Liberal Republicans and Democrats opposed him with Horace Greeley in the 1872 election, but Grant was reelected. His second administration was marked by many scandals, including widespread corruption in the War Department and the Post Office. An attempt by the Stalwarts (Old Guard) to nominate him in 1880 failed. In 1884 the collapse of Grant & Ward, an investment firm in which he was a partner, left him penniless. He wrote his personal memoirs while ill with cancer and completed them 4 days before his death at Mt. McGregor, NY, on July 23, 1885.

Rutherford Birchard Hayes (1877-81)

Rutherford B. Hayes, 19th president, Republican, was born on Oct. 4, 1822, in Delaware, OH, the son of Rutherford and Sophia Birchard Hayes. He was reared by his uncle, Sardis Birchard. Hayes graduated from Kenyon College in 1842 and from Harvard Law School in 1845. He practiced law in Lower Sandusky (now Fremont), OH, and was city solicitor of Cincinnati from 1858 to 1861. During the Civil War, he was major of the 23d Ohio Volunteers. He was wounded several times, and by the end of the war he had risen to the rank of brevet major general. While serving (1864-67) in the U.S. House of Representatives, he supported Reconstruction and Johnson's impeachment. He was twice elected governor of Ohio (1867, 1869). After losing a race for the U.S. House in 1872, he was reelected governor of Ohio in 1875. In 1876 he was nominated for president and believed he had lost the election to Samuel J. Tilden, Democrat. But a few Southern states submitted 2 sets of electoral votes, and the result was in dispute. An electoral commission, appointed by Congress and consisting of 8 Republicans and 7 Democrats, awarded all disputed votes to Hayes, allowing him to become president by one electoral vote. Hayes, keeping a promise to southerners, withdrew troops from areas still occupied in the South, ending the era of Reconstruction. He proceeded to reform the civil service, alienating those favoring the spoils system, and advocated repeal of the Tenure of Office Act. He supported sound money and specie payments. Hayes died in Fremont, OH, on Jan. 17, 1893.

James Abram Garfield (1881)

James A. Garfield, 20th president, Republican, was born on Nov. 19, 1831, in Orange, Cuyahoga Co., OH, the son of Abram and Eliza Ballou Garfield. His father died in 1833, and he was reared in poverty by his mother. He worked as a canal bargeman, a farmer, and a carpenter and managed to secure a college education. He taught at Hiram College and later became principal. In 1859 he was elected to the Ohio legislature. Antislavery and antisecession, he volunteered for military service in the Civil War, becoming colonel of the 42d Ohio Infantry and brigadier in 1862. He fought at Shiloh, was chief of staff for Gen. William Starke Rosecrans, and was made

major general for gallantry at Chickamauga. He entered Congress as a radical Republican in 1863, supporting specie payment as against paper money (greenbacks). On the electoral commission in 1877 he voted for Hayes against Tilden on strict party lines. He was senator-elect in 1880 when he became the Republican nominee for president. He was chosen as a compromise over Gen. Grant, James G. Blaine, and John Sherman. This alienated the Grant following, but Garfield was elected. On July 2, 1881, Garfield was shot by a mentally disturbed office-seeker, Charles J. Guiteau, while entering a railroad station in Washington. He died on Sept. 19, 1881, in Elberon, NJ.

Chester Alan Arthur (1881-85)

Chester A. Arthur, 21st president, Republican, was born on Oct. 5, 1830, in Fairfield, VT, the son of William and Malvina Stone Arthur. He graduated from Union College in 1848, taught school at Pownall, VT, and then studied law and opened a practice in New York City. In 1853 he argued in a fugitive slave case that slaves transported through New York state were thereby freed. In 1871, he was made collector of the Port of New York. President Hayes, reforming the civil service, forced Arthur to resign in 1879. This made the New York machine stalwart enemies of Hayes. Arthur and the Stalwarts tried to nominate Grant for a 3d term in 1880. When Garfield was nominated, Arthur received 2d place in the interests of harmony. Upon Garfield's assassination, Arthur became president. He signed civil service reform legislation and supported the tariff of 1883. He was defeated for renomination in 1884 by James G. Blaine. He died in New York City on Nov. 18, 1886.

Grover Cleveland (1885-89; 1893-97)

(According to a ruling of the State Dept., Grover Cleveland is both the 22d and the 24th president, because his 2 terms were not consecutive. By individuals, he is only the 22d.)

Grover Cleveland, 22d and 24th president, Democrat, was born on Mar. 18, 1837, in Caldwell, NJ, the son of Richard F. and Ann Neale Cleveland. When he was a small boy, his family moved to New York. Prevented by his father's death from attending college, he studied by himself and was admitted to the bar in Buffalo in 1859. In succession he became assistant district attorney (1863), sheriff (1871), mayor (1881), and governor of New York (1882). He was an independent, honest administrator who hated corruption. He was nominated for president over Tammany Hall opposition in 1884 and defeated Republican James G. Blaine. As president, he enlarged the civil service and vetoed many pension raids on the Treasury. In the 1888 election he was defeated by Benjamin Harrison, although his popular vote was larger. Reelected over Harrison in 1892, he faced a money crisis brought about by a lowered gold reserve, circulation of paper, and exorbitant silver purchases under the Sherman Silver Purchase Act. He obtained a repeal of the Sherman Act and a reduced tariff. A severe economic depression and labor troubles racked his administration, but he refused to interfere in business matters and rejected Jacob Coxey's demand for unemployment relief. In 1894, he broke the Pullman strike. In 1896, the Democrats repudiated his administration and chose silverite William Jennings Bryan as their candidate. Cleveland died in Princeton, NJ, on June 24, 1908.

Benjamin Harrison (1889-93)

Benjamin Harrison, 23d president, Republican, was born on Aug. 20, 1833, in North Bend, OH, the son of John Scott and Elizabeth F. Irwin Harrison. His great-grandfather, Benjamin Harrison, was a signer of the Declaration of Independence; his grandfather, William Henry Harrison, was 9th president; his father was a member of Congress. He attended school on his father's farm and graduated from Miami University in Oxford, OH, in 1852. He was admitted to the bar in 1853 and practiced in Indianapolis. During the Civil War, he rose to the rank of brevet brigadier general and fought at Kennesaw Mountain, at Peachtree Creek, at Nashville, and in the Atlanta campaign. He lost the 1876 gubernatorial election in Indiana but succeeded in becoming U.S. senator in 1881. In

1888 he defeated Cleveland for president despite receiving fewer popular votes. As president, he expanded the pension list and signed the McKinley high tariff bill, the Sherman Antitrust Act, and the Sherman Silver Purchase Act. During his administration, 6 states were admitted to the Union. He was defeated for reelection in 1892. He died in Indianapolis on Mar. 13, 1901.

William McKinley (1897-1901)

William McKinley, 25th president, Republican, was born on Jan. 29, 1843, in Niles, OH, the son of William and Nancy Allison McKinley. McKinley attended Allegheny College for a year. When the Civil War broke out in 1861, he enlisted and served for the duration. He rose to captain and in 1865 was made brevet major. After studying law in Albany, NY, he opened (1867) a law office in Canton, OH. He served twice in the U.S. House of Representatives (1877-83; 1885-91) and led the fight there for the McKinley Tariff, which was passed in 1890. However, he was not reelected to the House as a result. He served a term (1892-96) as governor of Ohio. In 1896 he was elected president on a protective tariff, sound money (gold standard) platform over William Jennings Bryan, the Democrat and a proponent of free silver. McKinley was reluctant to intervene in Cuba, but the loss of the battleship *Maine* at Havana crystallized opinion. He demanded Spain's withdrawal from Cuba; Spain made some concessions, but Congress announced a state of war as of Apr. 21, 1898. He was reelected in the 1900 campaign, defeating Bryan's anti-imperialist arguments with the promise of a "full dinner pail." McKinley was respected for his conciliatory nature and for his conservative stance on business issues. On Sept. 6, 1901, while welcoming citizens at the Pan-American Exposition, in Buffalo, NY, he was shot by Leon Czolgosz, an anarchist. He died Sept. 14.

Theodore Roosevelt (1901-9)

Theodore Roosevelt, 26th president, Republican, was born on Oct. 27, 1858, in New York City, the son of Theodore and Martha Bulloch Roosevelt. He was a 5th cousin of Franklin D. Roosevelt and an uncle of Eleanor Roosevelt. Roosevelt graduated from Harvard University in 1880. He attended Columbia Law School briefly but abandoned the study of law to enter politics. He was elected to the New York state assembly in 1881 and served until 1884. He spent the next 2 years ranching and hunting in the Dakota Territory. Back in politics in 1886, he ran unsuccessfully for mayor of New York City. He served as Civil Service commissioner in Washington, DC, from 1889 to 1895. From 1895 to 1897, he served as New York City's police commissioner. He was assistant secretary of the navy under McKinley. The Spanish-American War made Roosevelt a nationally known figure. He organized the 1st U.S. Volunteer Cavalry (Rough Riders) and, as lieutenant colonel, led the charge up Kettle Hill in San Juan. Elected New York governor in 1898, he fought the spoils system and achieved taxation of corporation franchises. Nominated for vice president in 1900, he became the nation's youngest president when McKinley was assassinated. He was reelected in 1904. As president he fought corruption of politics by big business, dissolved the Northern Securities Co. and others for violating antitrust laws, intervened in the 1902 coal strike on behalf of the public, obtained the Elkins Law (1903) forbidding rebates to favored corporations, and helped pass the Hepburn Railway Rate Act of 1905, as well as the Pure Food and Drug Act (1906), the Reclamation Act, and employers' liability laws. He organized conservation efforts, mediated (1905) the peace between Japan and Russia, and won the Nobel Peace Prize. He abetted the 1903 revolution in Panama that led to U.S. acquisition of territory for the Panama Canal.

In 1908 Roosevelt obtained the nomination of William H. Taft, who was elected. Feeling that Taft had abandoned his policies, Roosevelt unsuccessfully sought the nomination in 1912. He bolted the party and ran on the Progressive "Bull Moose" ticket against Taft and Woodrow Wilson, splitting the Republicans and ensuring Wilson's election. He was shot during the campaign but recovered. In 1916 he supported Charles E. Hughes, Republican. A strong friend of Britain, he fought American isolation in World War I. He wrote some 40

books on many topics; his *Winning of the West* is perhaps best known. He died Jan. 6, 1919, at Sagamore Hill, Oyster Bay, NY.

William Howard Taft (1909-13)

William Howard Taft, 27th president, Republican, and 10th chief justice of the U.S., was born on Sept. 15, 1857, in Cincinnati, OH, the son of Alphonso and Louisa Maria Torrey Taft. His father was secretary of war and attorney general in Grant's cabinet and minister to Austria and Russia under Arthur. Taft graduated from Yale in 1878 and from Cincinnati Law School in 1880. After working as a law reporter for Cincinnati newspapers, he served as assistant prosecuting attorney (1881-83), assistant county solicitor (1885), judge, superior court (1887), U.S. solicitor-general (1890), and federal circuit judge (1892). In 1900 he became head of the U.S. Philippines Commission and was the first civil governor of the Philippines (1901-4). In 1904 he served as secretary of war, and in 1906 he was provisional governor of Cuba. He was groomed for the presidency by Theodore Roosevelt and elected over William Jennings Bryan in 1908. His administration dissolved Standard Oil and the tobacco trusts, instituted the Department of Labor, and drafted the amendments calling for direct election of senators and the income tax. His tariff and conservation policies angered progressives. Although renominated in 1912, he was opposed by Roosevelt; the result was Democrat Woodrow Wilson's election. Taft, with some reservations, supported the League of Nations. After leaving office, he was professor of constitutional law at Yale (1913-21) and chief justice of the U.S. (1921-30). Taft was the only person in U.S. history to head 2 branches of the federal government. Illness forced him to resign from the Court in Feb. 1930, and he died in Washington, DC, on Mar. 8, 1930.

Woodrow Wilson (1913-21)

Thomas Woodrow Wilson, 28th president, Democrat, was born on Dec. 28, 1856, in Staunton, VA, the son of Joseph Ruggles and Janet (Jessie) Woodrow Wilson. He grew up in Georgia and South Carolina. He attended Davidson College in North Carolina before graduating from Princeton University in 1879. He studied law at the University of Virginia and then studied political science at Johns Hopkins University, where he received his Ph.D. in 1886. He taught at Bryn Mawr (1885-88) and then at Wesleyan (1888-90) before joining the faculty at Princeton. He was president of Princeton from 1902 until 1910, when he was elected governor of New Jersey. In 1912 he was nominated for president with the aid of William Jennings Bryan, who sought to block James "Champ" Clark and Tammany Hall. Wilson won the election because the Republican vote for Taft was split by the Progressives.

As president, Wilson protected American interests in revolutionary Mexico and fought for American rights on the high seas. He oversaw the creation of the Federal Reserve Board, cut the tariff, and developed a reputation as a reformer. His sharp warnings to Germany led to the resignation of his secretary of state, Bryan, a pacifist. In 1916 he was reelected by a slim margin with the slogan, "He kept us out of war," although his attempts to mediate in the war failed. After 4 American ships had been sunk by the Germans, he secured a declaration of war against Germany on Apr. 6, 1917.

Wilson outlined his peace program on Jan. 8, 1918, in the 14 points, a state paper that had worldwide influence. He enunciated a doctrine of self-determination for the settlement of territorial disputes. The Germans accepted his terms and an armistice on Nov. 11, 1918.

Wilson went to Paris to help negotiate the peace treaty, the crux of which he considered the League of Nations. The Senate demanded reservations that would not make the U.S. subordinate to the votes of other nations in case of war. Wilson refused to consider any reservations and toured the country to get support. He suffered a stroke in Oct. 1919. An invalid for months, he clung to his executive powers while his wife and doctors effectively functioned as president.

Wilson was awarded the 1919 Nobel Peace Prize, but the treaty embodying the League of Nations was rejected by the

Senate in 1920. He left the White House in Mar. 1921. He died in Washington, DC, on Feb. 3, 1924.

Warren Gamaliel Harding (1921-23)

Warren Gamaliel Harding, 29th president, Republican, was born on Nov. 2, 1865, near Corsica (now Blooming Grove), OH, the son of George Tryon and Phoebe Elizabeth Dickerson Harding. He attended Ohio Central College, studied law, and became editor and publisher of a county newspaper. He entered the political arena as state senator (1900-4) and then served as lieutenant governor (1904-6). In 1910 he ran unsuccessfully for governor of Ohio; then in 1915 he was elected to the U.S. Senate. In the Senate he voted for antistrike legislation, woman suffrage, and the Volstead Prohibition Enforcement Act over President Wilson's veto. He opposed the League of Nations. In 1920 he was nominated for president and defeated James M. Cox in the election. The Republicans capitalized on war weariness and fear that Wilson's League of Nations would curtail U.S. sovereignty. Harding stressed a return to "normalcy" and worked for tariff revision and the repeal of excess profits law and high income taxes. Two Harding appointees, Albert B. Fall (secretary of the interior) and Harry Daugherty (attorney general), became involved in the Teapot Dome scandal. As rumors began to circulate about the corruption in his administration, Harding became ill while returning from a trip to Alaska, and he died in San Francisco on Aug. 2, 1923.

Calvin Coolidge (1923-29)

John Calvin Coolidge, 30th president, Republican, was born on July 4, 1872, in Plymouth, VT, the son of John Calvin and Victoria J. Moor Coolidge. Coolidge graduated from Amherst College in 1895. He entered Republican state politics and served as mayor of Northampton, MA, as state senator, as lieutenant governor, and, in 1919, as governor. In Sept. 1919, Coolidge attained national prominence by calling out the state guard in the Boston police strike. He declared: "There is no right to strike against the public safety by anybody, anywhere, anytime." This brought his name before the Republican convention of 1920, where he was nominated for vice president. He succeeded to the presidency on Harding's death. As president, he opposed the League of Nations; approved the World Court; and vetoed the soldiers' bonus bill, which was passed over his veto. In 1924 he was elected by a huge majority. He reduced the national debt by $2 billion in 3 years. He twice vetoed the McNary-Haugen farm bill, which would have provided relief to financially hard-pressed farmers. With Republicans eager to renominate him, he simply announced, Aug. 2, 1927: "I do not choose to run for president in 1928." He died in Northampton, MA, on Jan. 5, 1933.

Herbert Clark Hoover (1929-33)

Herbert Hoover, 31st president, Republican, was born on Aug. 10, 1874, in West Branch, IA, the son of Jesse Clark and Hulda Randall Minthorn Hoover. Hoover grew up in Indian Territory (now Oklahoma) and Oregon and graduated from Stanford University with a degree in engineering in 1891. He worked briefly with the U.S. Geological Survey and then managed mines in Australia, Asia, Europe, and Africa. While chief engineer of imperial mines in China, he directed food relief for victims of the Boxer Rebellion. He gained a reputation not only as an engineer but as a humanitarian as he directed the American Relief Committee, London (1914-15) and the U.S. Commission for Relief in Belgium (1915-19). He was U.S. Food Administrator (1917-19), American Relief Administrator (1918-23), and in charge of Russian Relief (1918-23). He served as secretary of commerce under both Harding and Coolidge. Some historians believe that he was the most effective secretary of commerce ever to hold that office. In 1928 he was elected president over Alfred E. Smith. In 1929 the stock market crashed, and the economy collapsed. During the depression, Hoover inaugurated some government assistance programs. Although opposed to direct federal aid to the unemployed, he reluctantly turned to direct federal spending for welfare purposes. He was defeated in the 1932 election by Franklin D. Roosevelt. President Truman named him coordinator of the European Food Program

(1947) and chairman of the Commission for Reorganization of the Executive Branch (1947-49). He died in New York City on Oct. 20, 1964.

Franklin Delano Roosevelt (1933-45)

Franklin D. Roosevelt, 32d president, Democrat, was born on Jan. 30, 1882, near Hyde Park, NY, the son of James and Sara Delano Roosevelt. He graduated from Harvard University in 1904. He attended Columbia University Law School without taking a degree and was admitted to the New York state bar in 1907. His political career began when he was elected to the New York state senate in 1910. In 1913 President Wilson appointed him assistant secretary of the navy, a post he held during World War I.

In 1920 Roosevelt ran for vice president with James Cox and was defeated. From 1920 to 1928 he worked in his New York law office and was also vice president of Fidelity & Deposit Co. In Aug. 1921, he was stricken with poliomyelitis, which left his legs paralyzed. He learned to walk with leg braces and a cane.

Roosevelt served 2 terms as governor of New York (1929-33). In 1932, W. G. McAdoo, pledged to John N. Garner, threw his votes to Roosevelt, who was nominated for president. The depression and the promise to repeal Prohibition ensured his election. He asked for emergency powers, proclaimed the New Deal, and put into effect a vast number of administrative changes. Foremost was the use of public funds for relief and public works, resulting in deficit financing. He greatly expanded the federal government's regulation of business and by an excess profits tax and progressive income taxes produced a redistribution of earnings on an unprecedented scale. The Wagner Act gave labor many advantages in organizing and collective bargaining. He promoted legislation establishing the Social Security system. He was the last president inaugurated on Mar. 4 (1933) and the first inaugurated on Jan. 20 (1937).

Roosevelt was the first president to use radio for "fireside chats." When the Supreme Court nullified some New Deal laws, he sought power to "pack" the court with additional justices, but Congress refused to give him the authority. He was the first president to break the "no 3d term" tradition (1940) and was elected to a 4th term in 1944, despite failing health. He was openly hostile to fascist governments before World War II and launched a lend-lease program on behalf of the Allies. He wrote the principles of fair dealing into the Atlantic Charter, Aug. 14, 1941 (with Winston Churchill), and urged the Four Freedoms (freedom of speech, of worship, from want, from fear) Jan. 6, 1941. When Japan attacked Pearl Harbor on Dec. 7, 1941, the U.S. entered the war. Roosevelt conferred with allied heads of state at Casablanca (Jan. 1943), Quebec (Aug. 1943), Teheran (Nov.-Dec. 1943), Cairo (Dec. 1943), and Yalta (Feb. 1945). He did not, however, see the end of the war. He died of a cerebral hemorrhage in Warm Springs, GA, on Apr. 12, 1945.

Harry S. Truman (1945-53)

Harry S. Truman, 33d president, Democrat, was born on May 8, 1884, in Lamar, MO, the son of John Anderson and Martha Ellen Young Truman. A family disagreement on whether his middle name should be Shippe or Solomon, after names of 2 grandfathers, resulted in his using only the middle initial S. After graduating from high school in Independence, MO, he worked (1901) for the *Kansas City Star,* as a railroad timekeeper, and as a helper in Kansas City banks until about 1905. He ran his family's farm from 1906 to 1917. He served in France during World War I. After the war he opened a haberdashery shop, was a judge on the Jackson Co. Court (1922-24), and attended Kansas City School of Law (1923-25).

Truman was elected to the U.S. Senate in 1934 and re-elected in 1940. In 1944, with Roosevelt's backing, he was nominated for vice president and elected. On Roosevelt's death in 1945, Truman became president. In 1948 he was elected president.

Truman authorized the first uses of the atomic bomb (Hiroshima and Nagasaki, Aug. 6 and 9, 1945), bringing World War II to a rapid end. He was responsible for creating NATO, the Marshall Plan, and what came to be called the Truman Doctrine (to aid nations such as Greece and Turkey, threatened by communist takeover). In 1948-49, he broke a Soviet blockade of West Berlin with a massive airlift. When communist North Korea invaded South Korea (June 1950), he won UN approval for a "police action" and sent in forces under Gen. Douglas MacArthur. When MacArthur opposed his policy of limited objectives, Truman removed him from command.

Truman was responsible for higher minimum-wage, increased Social Security, and aid-for-housing laws. He died in Kansas City, MO, on Dec. 26, 1972.

Dwight David Eisenhower (1953-61)

Dwight D. Eisenhower, 34th president, Republican, was born on Oct. 14, 1890, in Denison, TX, the son of David Jacob and Ida Elizabeth Stover Eisenhower. He grew up on a small farm in Abilene, KS, and graduated from West Point in 1915. He was on the staff of Gen. Douglas MacArthur in the Philippines from 1935 to 1939. In 1942, he was made commander of Allied forces landing in North Africa; the next year he was made full general. He became supreme Allied commander in Europe that same year and as such led the Normandy invasion (June 6, 1944). He was given the rank of general of the army on Dec. 20, 1944, which was made permanent in 1946. On May 7, 1945, he received the surrender of the Germans at Rheims. He returned to the U.S. to serve as chief of staff (1945-48). In 1948, Eisenhower published *Crusade in Europe,* his war memoirs, which quickly became a best-seller. From 1948 to 1953, he was president of Columbia University, but took a leave of absence in 1950 to command NATO forces.

Eisenhower resigned from the army and was nominated for president by the Republicans in 1952. He defeated Adlai E. Stevenson in the 1952 election and then again in 1956. He called himself a moderate; favored the "free market system" vs. government price and wage controls; kept government out of labor disputes; reorganized the defense establishment; and promoted missile programs. He continued foreign aid; sped the end of the Korean War; endorsed Taiwan and SE Asia defense treaties; backed the UN in condemning the Anglo-French raid on Egypt; and advocated the "open skies" policy of mutual inspection with the USSR. He sent U.S. troops into Little Rock, AR, in Sept. 1957, during the segregation crisis.

Eisenhower died on Mar. 28, 1969, in Washington, DC.

John Fitzgerald Kennedy (1961-63)

John F. Kennedy, 35th president, Democrat, was born on May 29, 1917, in Brookline, MA, the son of Joseph P. and Rose Fitzgerald Kennedy. He graduated from Harvard University in 1940. While serving in the navy (1941-45), he commanded a PT boat in the Solomons and won the Navy and Marine Corps Medal. In 1956, while recovering from spinal surgery, he wrote *Profiles in Courage,* which won a Pulitzer Prize in 1957. He served in the House of Representatives from 1947 to 1953 and was elected to the Senate in 1952 and again in 1958.

In 1960, Kennedy won the Democratic nomination for president and defeated Richard M. Nixon, Republican. He was the youngest president ever elected and the first Roman Catholic.

In Apr. 1961, Kennedy's new administration suffered a severe setback when an invasion force of anti-Castro Cubans, trained and directed by the U.S. Central Intelligence Agency, failed to establish a beachhead at the Bay of Pigs in Cuba.

Kennedy's most important act was his successful demand on Oct. 22, 1962, that the Soviet Union dismantle its missile bases in Cuba. He established a quarantine of arms shipments to Cuba and continued surveillance by air. He defied Soviet attempts to force the Allies out of Berlin. He backed civil rights and expanded medical care for the aged. Space exploration was greatly developed during his administration.

On Nov. 22, 1963, Kennedy was assassinated in Dallas, TX.

Lyndon Baines Johnson (1963-69)

Lyndon B. Johnson, 36th president, Democrat, was born on Aug. 27, 1908, near Stonewall, TX, the son of Sam Ealy and Rebekah Baines Johnson. He graduated from Southwest Texas State Teachers College in 1930 and attended Georgetown University Law School. He taught public speaking in Houston (1930-32) and then served as secretary to Rep. R. M. Kleberg (1932-35). In 1937 Johnson won an election to fill the vacancy caused by the death of a representative and in 1938 was elected to the full term, after which he returned for 4 terms. He was elected U.S. senator in 1948 and reelected in 1954. He became Democratic leader of the Senate in 1953. Johnson had strong support for the Democratic presidential nomination at the 1960 convention, where the nominee, John F. Kennedy, asked him to run for vice president. His campaigning helped overcome religious bias against Kennedy in the South.

Johnson became president when Kennedy was assassinated. He was elected to a full term in 1964. Johnson won passage of major civil rights, anti-poverty, aid to education, and health care (Medicare, Medicaid) legislation—the "Great Society" program. However, his escalation of the war in Vietnam came to overshadow the achievements of his administration.

In the face of increasing division in the nation and in his own party over his handling of the war, Johnson did not seek another term.

Johnson died on Jan. 22, 1973, in San Antonio, TX.

Richard Milhous Nixon (1969-74)

Richard M. Nixon, 37th president, Republican, the only president to resign, was born on Jan. 9, 1913, in Yorba Linda, CA, the son of Francis Anthony and Hannah Milhous Nixon. Nixon graduated from Whittier College in 1934 and from Duke University Law School in 1937. After practicing law in Whittier and serving briefly in the Office of Price Administration in 1942, he entered the navy and served in the South Pacific.

Nixon was elected to the House of Representatives in 1946 and 1948. He achieved prominence as the House Un-American Activities Committee member who forced the showdown that resulted in the Alger Hiss perjury conviction. In 1950 Nixon was elected to the Senate.

He was elected vice president in the Eisenhower landslides of 1952 and 1956. Nixon won the Republican nomination in 1960. He was defeated by Democrat John F. Kennedy, returned to California, and in 1962 was defeated in his race for governor.

In 1968, he won the presidential nomination and went on to defeat Democrat Hubert H. Humphrey.

Nixon was the first U.S. president to visit China (1972). He and his foreign affairs adviser, Henry A. Kissinger, achieved a détente with the Soviet Union. Nixon appointed 4 Supreme Court justices, including the chief justice, thus altering the court's balance in favor of a more conservative view.

Reelected in 1972, Nixon secured a cease-fire agreement in Vietnam.

Nixon's 2d term was cut short by a series of scandals beginning with the burglary of Democratic Party national headquarters in the Watergate office complex on June 17, 1972. On July 16, 1973, a White House aide, under questioning by a Senate committee, revealed that most of Nixon's office conversations and phone calls had been recorded. Nixon claimed executive privilege to keep the tapes secret, and the courts and Congress sought the tapes for criminal proceedings against former White House aides and for a House inquiry into possible impeachment.

On July 24, 1974, the Supreme Court ruled that Nixon's claim of executive privilege must fall before the special prosecutor's subpoenas of tapes relevant to criminal trial proceedings. That same day, the House Judiciary Committee opened debate on impeachment. On July 30, the committee recommended House adoption of 3 articles of impeachment charging Nixon with obstruction of justice, abuse of power, and contempt of Congress.

On Aug. 5, Nixon released transcripts of conversations held 6 days after the Watergate break-in showing that Nixon had known of, approved, and directed Watergate cover-up activities. Nixon resigned from office on Aug. 9.

In later years, Nixon emerged as an elder statesman. He died Apr. 22, 1994, in New York City.

Gerald Rudolph Ford (1974-77)

Gerald R. Ford, 38th president, Republican, was born on July 14, 1913, in Omaha, NE, the son of Leslie and Dorothy Gardner King, and was named Leslie Jr. When he was 2, his parents were divorced, and his mother moved with the boy to Grand Rapids, MI. There she met and married Gerald R. Ford, who formally adopted the boy and gave him his own name.

Ford graduated from the University of Michigan in 1935 and from Yale Law School in 1941. He began practicing law in Grand Rapids, but in 1942 joined the navy and served in the Pacific, leaving the service in 1946 as a lieutenant commander.

He entered the House of Representatives in 1949 and spent 25 years in the House, 8 of them as Republican leader.

On Oct. 12, 1973, after Vice President Spiro T. Agnew resigned, Ford was nominated by President Nixon to replace him. It was the first use of the procedures set out in the 25th Amendment.

When Nixon resigned, Aug. 9, 1974, Ford became president, the only president who was elected neither to the presidency nor to the vice presidency. On Sept. 8 he pardoned Nixon for any federal crimes he might have committed as president. Ford vetoed 48 bills in his first 21 months in office, saying most would prove too costly. He visited China. He was defeated in the 1976 election by Democrat Jimmy Carter.

Jimmy (James Earl) Carter (1977-81)

Jimmy (James Earl) Carter, 39th president, Democrat, was the first president from the Deep South since before the Civil War. He was born on Oct. 1, 1924, in Plains, GA, the son of James and Lillian Gordy Carter.

Carter graduated from the U.S. Naval Academy in 1946 and entered the navy's nuclear submarine program as an aide to Adm. Hyman Rickover. He studied nuclear physics at Union College.

Carter's father died in 1953, and he left the navy to take over the family businesses. He served in the Georgia state senate and as governor of Georgia. In 1976, Carter won the Democratic nomination and defeated President Gerald R. Ford.

On his first full day in office, Carter pardoned all Vietnam draft evaders. He played a major role in the peace negotiations between Israel and Egypt.

However, Carter was widely criticized for the poor state of the economy and high inflation. He was also viewed as weak in his handling of foreign policy. In Nov. 1979, Iranian student militants attacked the U.S. embassy in Teheran and held members of the embassy staff hostage. His failure to obtain the release of the remaining 52 hostages plagued Carter to the end of his term. He reacted to the Soviet invasion of Afghanistan by imposing a grain embargo and boycotting the Moscow Olympic games. He was defeated by Ronald Reagan in the 1980 election. Carter administration efforts finally resulted in the release of the hostages on Inauguration Day, 1981, just after Reagan officially became president.

After leaving office, Carter was hailed for his humanitarian efforts and for his role in mediating international disputes.

Ronald Wilson Reagan (1981-89)

Ronald Wilson Reagan, 40th president, Republican, was born on Feb. 6, 1911, in Tampico, IL, the son of John Edward and Nellie Wilson Reagan. Reagan graduated from Eureka College in 1932, after which he worked as a sports announcer in Des Moines, IA.

Reagan began a successful career as an actor in 1937, starring in numerous movies, and later in television, until the 1960s. He served as president of the Screen Actors Guild from 1947 to 1952 and in 1959.

Reagan was elected governor of California in 1966 and reelected in 1970. In 1980, he gained the Republican nomination and won a landslide victory over Jimmy Carter. He was easily reelected in 1984.

Reagan successfully forged a bipartisan coalition in Congress, which led to enactment of his program of large-scale tax cuts, cutbacks in many government programs, and a major defense buildup. He signed a Social Security reform bill designed to ensure the long-term solvency of the system. In 1986, he signed into law a revolutionary tax-reform bill. He was shot in an assassination attempt in 1981.

In 1983, Reagan sent a task force to lead the invasion of Grenada, and the U.S. joined 3 European nations in maintaining a peacekeeping force in Beirut, Lebanon. His opposition to international terrorism led to the U.S. bombing of Libyan military installations in 1986. He strongly supported El Salvador, the Nicaraguan contras, and other anti-communist governments and forces throughout the world.

Reagan held 4 summit meetings with Soviet leader Mikhail Gorbachev. At the 1987 meeting in Washington, DC, a historic treaty eliminating short- and medium-range missiles from Europe was signed.

Reagan faced a major crisis in 1986-87, when it was revealed that the U.S. had sold weapons to Iran in exchange for the release of U.S. hostages being held in Lebanon and that subsequently some of the money was diverted to the Nicaraguan contras (Congress had barred aid to the contras). The scandal led to the resignation of leading White House aides.

As Reagan left office, the nation was experiencing its 6th consecutive year of economic prosperity. Along with the strong economy, the nation enjoyed low unemployment, energy costs, and inflation. Reagan, however, was unable to control the high budget deficits that plagued him throughout his administration.

In 1994, in a handwritten, personal letter to the American people, Reagan revealed that he was suffering from Alzheimer's disease.

George Herbert Walker Bush (1989-93)

George Herbert Walker Bush, 41st president, Republican, was born on June 12, 1924, in Milton, MA, the son of Prescott and Dorothy Walker Bush. He served as a U.S. Navy pilot in World War II. After graduating from Yale University in 1948, he settled in Texas, where, in 1953, he helped found an oil company.

After losing a bid for a U.S. Senate seat in Texas in 1964, he was elected to the House of Representatives in 1966 and 1968. He lost a 2d U.S. Senate race in 1970. Subsequently he served as U.S. ambassador to the United Nations (1971-73), headed the U.S. Liaison Office in Beijing (1974-75), and was director of central intelligence (1976-77).

Following an unsuccessful bid for the 1980 Republican presidential nomination, Bush was chosen by Ronald Reagan as his vice presidential running mate. He served as U.S. vice president from 1981 to 1989.

In 1988, Bush gained the Republican presidential nomination and defeated Democrat Michael Dukakis. Bush took office faced with the ongoing U.S. budget and trade deficits as well as the rescue of insolvent U.S. savings and loan institutions.

He annually faced a severe budget deficit, struggled with military cutbacks in light of reduced "cold war" tensions, and vetoed congressional actions favorable to freedom of choice on abortion, a minimum-wage law, and an anti-discrimination bill that didn't reflect his own views.

Bush supported Soviet reforms and Eastern Europe democratization. He was criticized, however, for not supporting strongly enough the independence effort of the Baltic republics, for keeping U.S. policy tied for too long to Mikhail Gorbachev as the Soviet leader lost power and his nation broke apart, and for his soft reaction to the Chinese government's violent repression of a pro-democracy movement.

In Dec. 1989, Bush sent military forces to Panama; these forces overthrew the government and captured military strongman Gen. Manuel Noriega.

Bush reacted to Iraq's Aug. 1990 invasion of Kuwait by sending U.S. forces to the Persian Gulf area and assembling a UN-backed coalition, including NATO and Arab League members. After a month-long air war, in Feb. 1991, Allied forces retook Kuwait in a 4-day ground assault. The quick victory gave Bush one of the highest presidential approval ratings in history. His popularity plummeted by the end of 1991, however, as the economy struggled through a prolonged recession and he was perceived as being indifferent to the nation's domestic problems. He was defeated by Bill Clinton in the 1992 election.

Bill (William Jefferson) Clinton (1993-   )

Bill Clinton, 42d president, Democrat, was born on Aug. 19, 1946, in Hope, AR, the son of William Blythe and Virginia Cassidy Blythe, and was named William Jefferson Blythe 3d. Blythe, a traveling salesman, died in an auto accident before his son was born. His mother married Roger Clinton, and several years later, at age 16, William Jefferson Blythe 3d changed his name to Bill Clinton. Clinton attended Georgetown University, Oxford University in England as a Rhodes scholar, and Yale Law School.

Clinton worked on George McGovern's 1972 presidential campaign. He taught at the University of Arkansas from 1973 to 1976. He was elected Arkansas state attorney general in 1976. In 1978, he was elected governor of Arkansas, becoming the nation's youngest governor, but he was defeated for reelection in 1980. He successfully ran for governor again in

1982, 1984, 1986, and 1990. He married Hillary Rodham in 1975.

Despite personal attacks on his character, he won the majority of the 1992 presidential primaries while moving the Democratic Party toward the center, trying to appeal to middle-class suburbanites who had deserted the party during the Reagan era. He defeated Pres. George Bush in the presidential election.

In August 1993, Clinton narrowly won congressional passage of some $500 billion in taxes and spending cuts to reduce the federal budget deficits. Later in the year he proposed major health-care reform legislation, but his plan died in Congress. In late 1993, Clinton achieved a measure of success with the congressional approval of the North American Free Trade Agreement. Following the 1994 midterm elections, Clinton faced Republican majorities in both houses of Congress, which sought swifter and more sweeping action to limit the role of government and reduce federal spending.

Wives and Children of the Presidents

(listed in order of presidential administrations)

Name (Born–died, married)	State	Sons/ daughters	Name (Born–died, married)	State	Sons/ daughters
Martha Dandridge Custis Washington (1732-1802, 1759)	VA	None	Frances Folsom Cleveland (1864-1947, 1886)	NY	2/3
Abigail Smith Adams (1744-1818, 1764)	MA	3/2	Caroline Lavinia Scott Harrison (1832-92, 1853)	OH	1/1
Martha Wayles Skelton Jefferson (1748-82, 1772)	VA	1/5	Mary Scott Lord Dimmick Harrison (1858-1948, 1896)	PA	.../1
Dorothea "Dolley" Payne Todd Madison (1768-1849, 1794)	NC	None	Ida Saxton McKinley (1847-1907, 1871)	OH	.../2
Elizabeth Kortright Monroe (1768-1830, 1786)	NY	.../2 (A)	Alice Hathaway Lee Roosevelt (1861-84, 1880)	MA	.../1
Louisa Catherine Johnson Adams (1775-1852, 1797)	MD(B)	3/1	Edith Kermit Carow Roosevelt (1861-1948, 1886)	CT	4/1
Rachel Donelson Robards Jackson (1767-1828, 1791)	VA	None	Helen Herron Taft (1861-1943, 1886)	OH	2/1
Hannah Hoes Van Buren (1783-1819, 1807)	NY	4/...	Ellen Louise Axson Wilson (1860-1914, 1885)	GA	.../3
Anna Symmes Harrison (1775-1864, 1795)	NJ	6/4	Edith Bolling Galt Wilson (1872-1961, 1915)	VA	None
Letitia Christian Tyler (1790-1842, 1813)	VA	3/5	Florence Kling De Wolfe Harding (1860-1924, 1891)	OH	None
Julia Gardiner Tyler (1820-89, 1844)	NY	5/2	Grace Anna Goodhue Coolidge (1879-1957, 1905)	VT	2/...
Sarah Childress Polk (1803-91, 1824)	TN	None	Lou Henry Hoover (1875-1944, 1899)	IA	2/...
Margaret Smith Taylor (1788-1852, 1810)	MD	1/5	Anna Eleanor Roosevelt Roosevelt (1884-1962, 1905)	NY	4/1 (A)
Abigail Powers Fillmore (1798-1853, 1826)	NY	1/1	Bess Wallace Truman (1885-1982, 1919)	MO	.../1
Caroline Carmichael McIntosh Fillmore (1813-81, 1858)	NJ	None	Mamie Geneva Doud Eisenhower (1896-1979, 1916)	IA	1/... (A)
Jane Means Appleton Pierce (1806-63, 1834)	NH	3/...	Jacqueline Lee Bouvier Kennedy (1929-94, 1953)	NY	1/1 (A)
Mary Todd Lincoln (1818-82, 1842)	KY	4/...	Claudia "Lady Bird" Alta Taylor Johnson (b. 1912, 1934)	TX	.../2
Eliza McCardle Johnson (1810-76, 1827)	TN	3/2	Thelma Catherine Patricia Ryan Nixon (1912-1993, 1940)	NV	.../2
Julia Dent Grant (1826-1902, 1848)	MO	3/1	Elizabeth Bloomer Warren Ford (b. 1918, 1948)	IL	3/1
Lucy Ware Webb Hayes (1831-89, 1852)	OH	7/1	Rosalynn Smith Carter (b. 1927, 1946)	GA	3/1
Lucretia Rudolph Garfield (1832-1918, 1858)	OH	4/1	Anne Frances "Nancy" Robbins Davis Reagan (b. 1921, 1952)	NY	1/1 (C)
Ellen Lewis Herndon Arthur (1837-80, 1859)	VA	2/1	Barbara Pierce Bush (b. 1925, 1945)	NY	4/2
			Hillary Rodham Clinton (b. 1947, 1975)	IL	.../1

James Buchanan, 15th president, was unmarried. (A) plus one infant, deceased. (B) Born London, father a MD citizen. (C) President Reagan married and divorced Jane Wyman. They had a son and a daughter.

First Lady: Hillary Rodham Clinton

The first lady was born in Chicago, Ill., Oct. 26, 1947, the daughter of Hugh and Dorothy Rodham. She graduated from Wellesley College and Yale Law School. She married Bill Clinton in 1975. Their daughter, Chelsea, was born in 1980.

She has been active in the areas of children's rights and education reform. From 1979 to 1992, she was a partner in a Little Rock, AR, law firm and, in 1988 and 1991, was voted one of the "100 Most Influential Lawyers in America" by the National Law Journal.

After Bill Clinton became president, she played a leading role in drafting and promoting sweeping legislation to reform the U.S. health-care system. The plan, however, failed to clear Congress.

Presidential Facts

- **Youngest president**: Theodore Roosevelt, who was 42 when sworn in
- **Oldest president**: Ronald Reagan, who was 78 when he left office
- **Only president to serve more than 2 terms**: Franklin Delano Roosevelt
- **Only president to serve 2 terms that were not back to back**: Grover Cleveland, who was both the 22d and the 24th president
- **Only president to also serve as chief justice of the U.S.**: William Howard Taft
- **First president to live in the White House**: John Adams
- **President who served the shortest term**: William Henry Harrison, who died 31 days after being inaugurated

- **State that has produced the most presidents**: Virginia
- **Only president who was unmarried**: James Buchanan. His niece acted as White House hostess for her uncle.
- **Only president to serve without being elected vice president or president in a national election**: Gerald Ford
- **Presidents who died on July 4**: John Adams, Thomas Jefferson, and James Monroe
- **Presidents who died in office**: Eight presidents have died in office. Four were of them were assassinated: Abraham Lincoln, James Garfield, William McKinley, and John F. Kennedy. The other four were William Henry Harrison, Zachary Taylor, Warren G. Harding, and Franklin Delano Roosevelt.

Burial Places of the Presidents

President	Burial Place	President	Burial Place	President	Burial Place
Washington	Mt. Vernon, VA	Fillmore	Buffalo, NY	T. Roosevelt	Oyster Bay, NY
J. Adams	Quincy, MA	Pierce	Concord, NH	Taft	Arlington Natl. Cem.
Jefferson	Charlottesville, VA	Buchanan	Lancaster, PA	Wilson	Wash. Cathedral
Madison	Montpelier Station, VA	Lincoln	Springfield, IL	Harding	Marion, OH
Monroe	Richmond, VA	A. Johnson	Greeneville, TN	Coolige	Plymouth, VT
J. Q. Adams	Quincy, MA	Grant	New York, NY	Hoover	West Branch, IA
Jackson	Nashville, TN	Hayes	Fremont, OH	F. Roosevelt	Hyde Park, NY
Van Buren	Kinderhook, NY	Garfield	Cleveland, OH	Truman	Independence, MO
W.H. Harrison	North Bend, OH	Arthur	Albany, NY	Eisenhower	Abilene, KS
Tyler	Richmond, VA	Cleveland	Princeton, NJ	Kennedy	Arlington Natl. Cem.
Polk	Nashville, TN	B. Harrison	Indianapolis, IN	L. B. Johnson	Stonewall, TX
Taylor	Louisville, KY	McKinley	Canton, OH	Nixon	Yorba Linda, CA

Presidential Libraries

The presidential libraries listed below, except for that of Richard Nixon (which is a private institution), are coordinated by the National Archives & Records Administration in Washington, DC. It also has custody of the Nixon presidential historical materials and those of George Bush. The Bush presidential library was under construction in 1995 in College Station, TX, at Texas A&M College. Completion was expected some time in 1997. The presidential materials for presidents prior to Herbert Hoover are held by various private institutions around the U.S.

Herbert Hoover Library
Parkside Drive, PO Box 488
West Branch, IA 52358
PHONE: 319-643-5301
FAX: 319-643-5825
Franklin D. Roosevelt Library
511 Albany Post Rd.
Hyde Park, NY 12538
PHONE: 914-229-8114
FAX: 914-229-0872
Harry S. Truman Library
U.S. Hwy. 24 & Delaware St.
Independence, MO 64050-1798
PHONE: 816-833-1400
FAX: 816-833-4368

Dwight D. Eisenhower Library
Southeast Fourth St.
Abilene, KS 67410
PHONE: 913-263-4751
FAX: 913-263-4218
John Fitzgerald Kennedy Library
Columbia Point
Boston, MA 02125
PHONE: 617-929-4545
FAX: 617-929-4538
Lyndon Baines Johnson Library
2313 Red River St.
Austin, TX 78705
PHONE: 512-482-5137
FAX: 512-478-9104
Richard Nixon Library &
   Birthplace
18001 Yorba Linda Blvd.
Yorba Linda, CA 92686
PHONE: 714-993-3393

Gerald R. Ford Library
1000 Beal Ave.
Ann Arbor, MI 48109
PHONE: 313-741-2218
FAX: 313-741-2341
Jimmy Carter Library
441 Freedom Pkwy. &
   One Copenhill Ave.
Atlanta, GA 30307
PHONE: 404-331-3942
FAX: 404-730-2215
Ronald Reagan Library
40 Presidential Dr.
Simi Valley, CA 93065
PHONE: 805-522-8444
FAX: 805-522-9621

UNITED STATES FACTS
Superlative U.S. Statistics

Source: U.S. Geological Survey, Dept. of the Interior; U.S. Bureau of the Census, Dept. of Commerce; World Almanac research

Area for 50 states and Washington, DC....	Total	3,787,319 sq mi
	Land 3,536,278 sq mi— Water 251,041 sq mi	
Largest state	Alaska	656,424 sq mi
Smallest state	Rhode Island	1,545 sq mi
Largest county (excludes Alaska)	San Bernardino County, California	20,064 sq mi
Smallest county	Kalawo, Hawaii	14 sq mi
Northernmost city	Barrow, Alaska	71°17′ N
Northernmost point	Point Barrow, Alaska	71°23′ N
Southernmost city	Hilo, Hawaii	19°43′ N
Southernmost settlement	Naalehu, Hawaii	19°03′ N
Southernmost point	Ka Lae (South Cape), Island of Hawaii	18°55′ N(155°41′ W)
Easternmost city	Eastport, Maine	66°59′ 02″ W
Easternmost settlement[1]	Amchitka Isl., Alaska	179°15′ E
Easternmost point[1]	Semisopochnoi Isl., Alaska	179°52′ E
Westernmost city	Atka, Alaska	174°20′ W
Westernmost settlement	Adak Station, Alaska	176°39′ W
Westernmost point	Amatignak Isl., Alaska	179°06′ W
Highest settlement	Climax, Colorado	11,560 ft
Lowest settlement	Calipatria, California	−185 ft
Highest point on Atlantic coast	Cadillac Mountain, Mount Desert Isl., Maine	1,530 ft
Oldest national park	Yellowstone National Park (1872), Wyoming, Montana, Idaho.	3,468 sq mi
Largest national park	Wrangell-St. Elias, Alaska	13,006 sq mi
Largest national monument	Cape Krusenstern, Alaska	1,031 sq mi
Smallest national monument	Federal Hall, New York, New York	21,780 sq ft
Highest waterfall	Yosemite Falls—Total in three sections.	2,425 ft
	Upper Yosemite Fall	1,430 ft
	Cascades in middle section	675 ft
	Lower Yosemite Fall	320 ft
Longest river	Mississippi-Missouri.	3,710 mi
Highest mountain	Mount McKinley, Alaska.	20,320 ft
Lowest point	Death Valley, California	−282 ft
Deepest lake	Crater Lake, Oregon	1,932 ft
Rainiest spot.	Mt. Waialeale, Hawaii	Annual avg rainfall 460 in
Largest gorge	Grand Canyon, Colorado River, Arizona.	277 mi long, 600 ft
		to 18 mi wide, 1 mi deep
Deepest gorge	Hells Canyon, Snake River, Oregon-Idaho	7,900 ft
Strongest surface wind	Mount Washington, New Hampshire recorded 1934	231 mph
Largest dam	New Cornelia Tailings, Ten Mile Wash,	
	Arizona[2]	274,026,000 cu yds material used
Tallest building	Sears Tower, Chicago, Illinois	1,454 ft
Largest building	Boeing 747 Manufacturing Plant, Everett,	
	Washington	205,600,000 cu ft; covers 47 acres
Tallest structure	TV tower, Blanchard, North Dakota	2,063 ft
Longest bridge span	Verrazano-Narrows, New York.	4,260 ft
Highest bridge	Royal Gorge, Colorado	1,053 ft above water
Deepest well.	Gas well, Washita County, Oklahoma	31,441 ft

The 48 Contiguous States

Area for 48 states and Washington, DC .	Total	3,119,963 sq mi
	Land 2,959,481 sq mi— Water 160,483 sq mi	
Largest state.	Texas.	268,601 sq mi
Northernmost city	Bellingham, Washington	48°46′ N
Northernmost settlement	Angle Inlet, Minnesota	49°21′ N
Northernmost point	Northwest Angle, Minnesota	49°23′ N
Southernmost city	Key West, Florida	24°32′ N
Southernmost mainland city	Florida City, Florida	25°27′ N
Southernmost point	Key West, Florida	24°32′ N
Easternmost settlement	Lubec, Maine	66°58′49″ W
Easternmost point	West Quoddy Head, Maine	66°57′ W
Westernmost town.	La Push, Washington	124°38′ W
Westernmost point	Cape Alava, Washington	124°44′ W
Highest mountain	Mount Whitney, California	14,494 ft

(1) Alaska's Aleutian Islands extend into the eastern hemisphere and therefore technically contain the easternmost point and settlement in the U.S. (2) The New Cornelia Tailings Dam is a privately owned industrial dam composed of tailings, which are remnants of a mining process that once occurred on this site.

Geodetic Datum of North America

In July 1986, the National Oceanic and Atmospheric Administration's National Geodetic Survey (NGS), in cooperation with Canada and Mexico, completed the readjustment and redefinition of the system of latitudes and longitudes. Known as the North American Datum of 1983 (NAD 83), it replaces the North American Datum of 1927, as well as local reference systems for the Hawaiian Islands (the Old Hawaiian Datum) and Puerto Rico and the Virgin Islands (the Puerto Rico Datum). The change was prompted by an increased need for accurate coordinate information. To facilitate the use of satellite surveying and navigation systems, such as the Global Positioning System (GPS), the new datum was redefined using the Geodetic Reference System 1980 as the reference ellipsoid because this model more closely approximates the true size and shape of the earth. In addition, the origin of the coordinate system is referenced to the mass center of the earth to coincide with the orbital orientation of the GPS satellites. Positional changes resulting from the datum redefinition can be as much as 330 ft in the continental U.S., Can., and Mex. Changes that exceed 660 ft can be expected in AK, PR, and the Virgin Islands. Hawaii's coordinates changed approximately 1,300 ft.

Statistical Information About the U.S.

In the *Statistical Abstract of the United States*, the Bureau of the Census, U.S. Dept. of Commerce, annually publishes a summary of social, political, and economic information. A book of more than 1,000 pages, it is prepared under the direction of Glenn W. King, Chief, Statistical Compendia Staff. Information concerning these and other publications may be obtained by writing New Orders, Supt. of Documents, PO Box 371954, Pittsburgh, PA 15250-7954, or by phoning the Census Customer Services Dept. at (301) 457-4100.

Highest and Lowest Altitudes in the U.S. and Territories

Source: U.S. Geological Survey, Dept. of the Interior

(Minus sign means below sea level.)

State	Highest Point Name	County	Elev. (ft)	Lowest Point Name	County	Elev. (ft)
Alabama	Cheaha Mountain	Cleburne	2,405	Gulf of Mexico		Sea level
Alaska	Mount McKinley	Coconino	20,320	Pacific Ocean		Sea level
Arizona	Humphreys Peak	Coconino	12,633	Colorado R	Yuma	70
Arkansas	Magazine Mountain	Logan	2,753	Ouachita R	Ashley-Union	55
California	Mount Whitney	Inyo-Tulare	14,494	Death Valley	Inyo	−282
Colorado	Mount Elbert	Lake	14,433	Arkansas R	Prowers	3,350
Connecticut	Mount Frissell	Litchfield	2,380	Long Island Sound		Sea level
Delaware	On Ebright Road	New Castle	442	Atlantic Ocean		Sea level
Dist. of Col.	Tenleytown	N W part	410	Potomac R		1
Florida	Sec. 30, T6N, R20W	Walton	345	Atlantic Ocean		Sea level
Georgia	Brasstown Bald	Towns-Union	4,784	Atlantic Ocean		Sea level
Guam	Mount Lamlam	Agat District	1,332	Pacific Ocean		Sea level
Hawaii	Mauna Kea	Hawaii	13,796	Pacific Ocean		Sea level
Idaho	Borah Peak	Custer	12,662	Snake R	Nez Perce	710
Illinois	Charles Mound	Jo Daviess	1,235	Mississippi R	Alexander	279
Indiana	Franklin Township	Wayne	1,257	Ohio R	Posey	320
Iowa	Sec. 29, T100N, R41W	Osceola	1,670	Mississippi R	Lee	480
Kansas	Mount Sunflower	Wallace	4,039	Verdigris R	Montgomery	679
Kentucky	Black Mountain	Harlan	4,139	Mississippi R	Fulton	257
Louisiana	Driskill Mountain	Bienville	535	New Orleans	Orleans	−8
Maine	Mount Katahdin	Piscataquis	5,267	Atlantic Ocean		Sea level
Maryland	Backbone Mountain	Garrett	3,360	Atlantic Ocean		Sea level
Massachusetts	Mount Greylock	Berkshire	3,487	Atlantic Ocean		Sea level
Michigan	Mount Arvon	Baraga	1,979	Lake Erie	Monroe	571
Minnesota	Eagle Mountain	Cook	2,301	Lake Superior		600
Mississippi	Woodall Mountain	Tishomingo	806	Gulf of Mexico		Sea level
Missouri	Taum Sauk Mt.	Iron	1,772	St. Francis R	Dunklin	230
Montana	Granite Peak	Park	12,799	Kootenai R	Lincoln	1,800
Nebraska	Johnson Township	Kimball	5,426	Missouri R	Richardson	840
Nevada	Boundary Peak	Esmeralda	13,140	Colorado R	Clark	479
New Hamp.	Mt. Washington	Coos	6,288	Atlantic Ocean	Rockingham	Sea level
New Jersey	High Point	Sussex	1,803	Atlantic Ocean		Sea level
New Mexico	Wheeler Peak	Taos	13,161	Red Bluff Res.	Eddy	2,842
New York	Mount Marcy	Essex	5,344	Atlantic Ocean		Sea level
North Carolina	Mount Mitchell	Yancey	6,684	Atlantic Ocean		Sea level
North Dakota	White Butte	Slope	3,506	Red R	Pembina	750
Ohio	Campbell Hill	Logan	1,549	Ohio R	Hamilton	455
Oklahoma	Black Mesa	Cimarron	4,973	Little R	McCurtain	289
Oregon	Mount Hood	Clackamas-Hood R.	11,239	Pacific Ocean		Sea level
Pennsylvania	Mt. Davis	Somerset	3,213	Delaware R	Delaware	Sea level
Puerto Rico	Cerro de Punta	Ponce District	4,390	Atlantic Ocean		Sea level
Rhode Island	Jerimoth Hill	Providence	812	Atlantic Ocean		Sea level
Samoa	Lata Mountain	Tau Island	3,160	Pacific Ocean		Sea level
South Carolina	Sassafras Mountain	Pickens	3,560	Atlantic Ocean		Sea level
South Dakota	Harney Peak	Pennington	7,242	Big Stone Lake	Roberts	966
Tennessee	Clingmans Dome	Sevier	6,643	Mississippi R	Shelby	178
Texas	Guadalupe Peak	Culberson	8,749	Gulf of Mexico		Sea level
Utah	Kings Peak	Duchesne	13,528	Beaverdam Wash	Washington	2,000
Vermont	Mount Mansfield	Lamoille	4,393	Lake Champlain		95
Virginia	Mount Rogers	Grayson-Smyth	5,729	Atlantic Ocean		Sea level
Virgin Islands	Crown Mountain	St. Thomas Island	1,556	Atlantic Ocean		Sea level
Washington	Mount Rainier	Pierce	14,410	Pacific Ocean		Sea level
West Virginia	Spruce Knob	Pendleton	4,861	Potomac R	Jefferson	240
Wisconsin	Timms Hill	Price	1,951	Lake Michigan		579
Wyoming	Gannett Peak	Fremont	13,804	Belle Fourche R	Crook	3,099

Sec=section; T=township; R=range; N=north; W=west.

U.S. Coastline by States

Source: National Oceanic and Atmospheric Administration, U.S. Dept. of Commerce

(in statute miles)

State	Coastline[1]	Shoreline[2]	State	Coastline[1]	Shoreline[2]
Atlantic coast	**2,069**	**28,673**	**Gulf coast**	**1,631**	**17,141**
Connecticut	0	618	Alabama	53	607
Delaware	28	381	Florida	770	5,095
Florida	580	3,331	Louisiana	397	7,721
Georgia	100	2,344	Mississippi	44	359
Maine	228	3,478	Texas	367	3,359
Maryland	31	3,190			
Massachusetts	192	1,519	**Pacific coast**	**7,623**	**40,298**
New Hampshire	13	131	Alaska	5,580	31,383
New Jersey	130	1,792	California	840	3,427
New York	127	1,850	Hawaii	750	1,052
North Carolina	301	3,375	Oregon	296	1,410
Pennsylvania	0	89	Washington	157	3,026
Rhode Island	40	384			
South Carolina	187	2,876	**Arctic coast, Alaska**	**1,060**	**2,521**
Virginia	112	3,315	**United States**	**12,383**	**88,633**

(1) Figures are lengths of general outline of seacoast. Measurements were made with a unit measure of 30 minutes of latitude on charts as near the scale of 1:1,200,000 as possible. Coastline of sounds and bays is included to a point where they narrow to width of unit measure, and includes the distance across at such point. (2) Figures obtained in 1939-40 with a recording instrument on the largest-scale charts and maps then available. Shoreline of outer coast, offshore islands, sounds, bays, rivers, and creeks is included to the head of tidewater or to a point where tidal waters narrow to a width of 100 feet.

States: Settled, Capitals, Entry Into Union, Area, Rank

The 13 colonies that seceded from Great Britain and fought the War of Independence (American Revolution) became the 13 original states. They were (in the order in which they ratified the Constitution): Delaware, Pennsylvania, New Jersey, Georgia, Connecticut, Massachusetts, Maryland, South Carolina, New Hampshire, Virginia, New York, North Carolina, and Rhode Island.

State	Set-tled[1]	Capital	Entered Union Date		Order	Extent in miles Long (approx. mean)	Wide	Area in square miles Land	Inland Water	Total	Rank in area[2]
AL . .	1702. .	Montgomery	Dec.	14, 1819	22	330	190	50,750	1,673	52,423	30
AK . .	1784. .	Juneau.	Jan.	3, 1959	49	1,480[3]	810[3]	570,374	86,050	656,424	1
AZ . .	1776. .	Phoenix	Feb.	14, 1912	48	400	310	113,642	364	114,006	6
AR . .	1686. .	Little Rock	June	15, 1836	25	260	240	52,075	1,107	53,182	29
CA . .	1769. .	Sacramento	Sept.	9, 1850	31	770	250	155,973	7,734	163,707	3
CO . .	1858. .	Denver.	Aug.	1, 1876	38	380	280	103,729	371	104,100	8
CT . .	1634. .	Hartford	Jan.	9, 1788	5	110	70	4,845	698	5,544	48
DE . .	1638. .	Dover.	Dec.	7, 1787	1	100	30	1,955	535	2,489	49
DC . .	NA . . .	Washington	NA		NA	. . .	. . .	61	7	68	51
FL . .	1565. .	Tallahassee	Mar.	3, 1845	27	500	160	53,937	11, 821	65,756	22
GA . .	1733. .	Atlanta	Jan.	2, 1788	4	300	230	57,919	1,522	59,441	24
HI . .	1820. .	Honolulu	Aug.	21, 1959	50	. . .	. . .	6,423	4,508	10,932	43
ID . .	1842. .	Boise	July	3, 1890	43	570	300	82,751	823	83,574	14
IL . .	1720. .	Springfield	Dec.	3, 1818	21	390	210	55,593	2,325	57,918	25
IN . .	1733. .	Indianapolis	Dec.	11, 1816	19	270	140	35,870	550	36,420	38
IA . .	1788. .	Des Moines	Dec.	28, 1846	29	310	200	55,875	401	56,276	26
KS . .	1727. .	Topeka	Jan.	29, 1861	34	400	210	81,823	459	82,282	15
KY . .	1774. .	Frankfort	June	1, 1792	15	380	140	39,732	679	40,411	37
LA . .	1699. .	Baton Rouge	Apr.	30, 1812	18	380	130	43,566	8,277	51,843	31
ME . .	1624. .	Augusta	Mar.	15, 1820	23	320	190	30,865	4,523	35,387	39
MD . .	1634. .	Annapolis	Apr.	28, 1788	7	250	90	9,775	2,632	12,407	42
MA . .	1620. .	Boston	Feb.	6, 1788	6	190	50	7,838	2,717	10,555	44
MI . .	1668. .	Lansing	Jan.	26, 1837	26	490	240	56,809	39,896	96,705	11
MN . .	1805. .	St. Paul	May	11, 1858	32	400	250	79,617	7,326	86,943	12
MS . .	1699. .	Jackson	Dec.	10, 1817	20	340	170	46,914	1,520	48,434	32
MO . .	1735. .	Jefferson City	Aug.	10, 1821	24	300	240	68,898	811	69,709	21
MT . .	1809. .	Helena	Nov.	8, 1889	41	630	280	145,556	1,490	147,046	4
NE . .	1823. .	Lincoln	Mar.	1, 1867	37	430	210	76,878	481	77,358	16
NV . .	1849. .	Carson City	Oct.	31, 1864	36	490	320	109,806	761	110,567	7
NH . .	1623. .	Concord	June	21, 1788	9	190	70	8,969	382	9,351	46
NJ . .	1660. .	Trenton	Dec.	18, 1787	3	150	70	7,419	1,303	8,722	47
NM . .	1610. .	Santa Fe	Jan.	6, 1912	47	370	343	121,364	234	121,598	5
NY . .	1614. .	Albany	July	26, 1788	11	330	283	47,224	7,247	54,471	27
NC . .	1660. .	Raleigh	Nov.	21, 1789	12	500	150	48,718	5,103	53,821	28
ND . .	1812. .	Bismarck	Nov.	2, 1889	39	340	211	68,994	1,710	70,704	19
OH . .	1788. .	Columbus.	Mar.	1, 1803	17	220	220	40,953	3,875	44,828	34
OK . .	1889. .	Oklahoma City	Nov.	16, 1907	46	400	220	68,679	1,224	69,903	20
OR . .	1811. .	Salem	Feb.	14, 1859	33	360	261	96,002	2,383	98,386	9
PA . .	1682. .	Harrisburg	Dec.	12, 1787	2	283	160	44,820	1,239	46,058	33
RI . .	1636. .	Providence.	May	29, 1790	13	40	30	1,045	500	1,545	50
SC . .	1670. .	Columbia	May	23, 1788	8	260	200	30,111	1,897	32,008	40
SD . .	1859. .	Pierre.	Nov.	2, 1889	40	380	210	75,896	1,225	77,121	17
TN . .	1769. .	Nashville	June	1, 1796	16	440	120	41,219	926	42,146	36
TX . .	1682. .	Austin	Dec.	29, 1845	28	790	660	261,914	6,687	268,601	2
UT . .	1847. .	Salt Lake City	Jan.	4, 1896	45	350	270	82,168	2,736	84,904	13
VT . .	1724. .	Montpelier	Mar.	4, 1791	14	160	80	9,249	366	9,615	45
VA . .	1607. .	Richmond.	June	25, 1788	10	430	200	39,598	3,179	42,777	35
WA . .	1811. .	Olympia	Nov.	11, 1889	42	360	240	66,581	4,721	71,302	18
WV . .	1727. .	Charleston	June	20, 1863	35	240	130	24,087	145	24,231	41
WI . .	1766. .	Madison	May	29, 1848	30	310	260	54,314	11,186	65,499	23
WY .	1834. .	Cheyenne	July	10, 1890	44	360	280	97,105	714	97,818	10

NA=not applicable. (1) First European permanent settlement. (2) Rank is based on total area, including inland water. (3) Aleutian Islands and Alexander Archipelago are not considered in these lengths.

The Continental Divide of the U.S.

The Continental Divide of the U.S., also known as the Great Divide, is located at the watershed that is created by the mountain ranges, or tablelands, of the Rocky Mountains. This watershed separates the waters that drain easterly into the Atlantic Ocean and its marginal seas, such as the Gulf of Mexico, from those waters that drain westerly into the Pacific Ocean. The majority of easterly flowing water drains into the Gulf of Mexico before reaching the Atlantic Ocean. The majority of westerly flowing water, before reaching the Pacific Ocean, either drains through the Columbia R. or through the Colorado R., which flows into the Gulf of California before reaching the Pacific Ocean.

The location and route of the Continental Divide across the U.S. can briefly be described as follows:

Beginning at point of crossing the U.S.-Mexican boundary, near long. 108°45′ W, the Divide, in a northerly direction, crosses New Mexico along the western edge of the Rio Grande drainage basin, entering Colorado near long 106°41′ W.

Thence, by a very irregular route northerly across Colorado along the W summits of the Rio Grande and of the Arkansas, the South Platte, and the North Platte river basins, and across Rocky Mountain National Park, entering Wyoming near long 106°52′ W.

Thence, in a northwesterly direction, forming the W rims of the North Platte, the Big Horn, and the Yellowstone river basins, crossing the SW portion of Yellowstone National Park.

Thence, in a westerly and then a northerly direction forming the common boundary of Idaho and Montana, to a point on said boundary near long 114°00′ W.

Thence, northeasterly and northwesterly through Montana and the Glacier National Park, entering Canada near long 114°04′ W.

Chronological List of Territories and State Admission to Union

Source: National Archives and Records Service

Name of territory	Date of Organic Act	Organic Act effective	Admission as state	Yrs. terr.
Northwest Territory[1]	July 13, 1787	No fixed date	Mar. 1, 1803[2]	16
Territory southwest of River Ohio	May 26, 1790	No fixed date	June 1, 1796[3]	6
Mississippi	Apr. 7, 1798	When president acted	Dec. 10, 1817	19
Indiana	May 7, 1800	July 4, 1800	Dec. 11, 1816	16
Orleans	Mar. 26, 1804	Oct. 1, 1804	Apr. 30, 1812[4]	7
Michigan	Jan. 11, 1805	June 30, 1805	Jan. 26, 1837	31
Louisiana-Missouri[5]	Mar. 3, 1805	July 4, 1805	Aug. 10, 1821	16
Illinois	Feb. 3, 1809	Mar. 1, 1809	Dec. 3, 1818	9
Alabama	Mar. 3, 1817	When MS became a state	Dec. 14, 1819	2
Arkansas	Mar. 2, 1819	July 4, 1819	June 15, 1836	17
Florida	Mar. 30, 1822	No fixed date	Mar. 3, 1845	23
Wisconsin	Apr. 20, 1836	July 3, 1836	May 29, 1848	12
Iowa	June 12, 1838	July 3, 1838	Dec. 28, 1846	8
Oregon	Aug. 14, 1848	Date of act	Feb. 14, 1859	10
Minnesota	Mar. 3, 1849	Date of act	May 11, 1858	9
New Mexico	Sept. 9, 1850	On president's proclamation	Jan. 6, 1912	61
Utah	Sept. 9, 1850	Date of act	Jan. 4, 1896	46
Washington	Mar. 2, 1853	Date of act	Nov. 11, 1889	36
Nebraska	May 30, 1854	Date of act	Mar. 1, 1867	12
Kansas	May 30, 1854	Date of act	Jan. 29, 1861	6
Colorado	Feb. 28, 1861	Date of act	Aug. 1, 1876	15
Nevada	Mar. 2, 1861	Date of act	Oct. 31, 1864	3
Dakota	Mar. 2, 1861	Date of act	Nov. 2, 1889	28
Arizona	Feb. 24, 1863	Date of act	Feb. 14, 1912	49
Idaho	Mar. 3, 1863	Date of act	July 3, 1890	27
Montana	May 26, 1864	Date of act	Nov. 8, 1889	25
Wyoming	July 25, 1868	When officers were qualified	July 10, 1890	22
Alaska[6]	May 17, 1884	No fixed date	Jan. 3, 1959	75
Oklahoma	May 2, 1890	Date of act	Nov. 16, 1907	17
Hawaii	Apr. 30, 1900	June 14, 1900	Aug. 21, 1959	59

(1) Included Ohio, Indiana, Illinois, Michigan, Wisconsin, eastern Minnesota. (2) Admitted as the state of Ohio. (3) Admitted as the state of Tennessee. (4) Admitted as the state of Louisiana. (5) The organic act for Missouri Territory of June 4, 1812, became effective Dec. 7, 1812. (6) Although the May 17, 1884, act actually constituted Alaska as a district, it was often referred to as a territory, and unofficially administered as such. The Territory of Alaska was legally and formally organized by an act of Aug. 24, 1912.

Geographic Centers, U.S. and Each State

Source: U.S. Geological Survey, Dept. of the Interior

There is no generally accepted definition of geographic center, and there is no satisfactory method for determining it. The geographic center of an area may be defined as the center of gravity of the surface or as that point on which the surface of the area would balance if it were a plane of uniform thickness. All localities, therefore, are approximate.

No marked or monumented point has been established by any government agency as the geographic center of either the 50 states, the conterminous U.S., or the North American continent. A monument was erected in Lebanon, KS, the conterminous U.S. center, by a group of citizens. A cairn in Rugby, ND, marks the center of the North American continent.

United States, including Alaska and Hawaii—W of Castle Rock, Butte County, South Dakota; lat. 44°58′N, long. 103°46′W
Conterminous U. S. (48 states)—Near Lebanon, Smith Co., Kansas, lat. 39°50′N, long. 98°35′W
North American continent—6 mi W of Balta, Pierce County, North Dakota; lat. 48°10′N, long. 100°10′W

State—county, locality

Alabama—Chilton, 12 mi SW of Clanton
Alaska—lat. 63°50′N, long. 152°W; approx. 60 mi NW of Mt. McKinley
Arizona—Yavapai, 55 mi E-SE of Prescott
Arkansas—Pulaski, 12 mi NW of Little Rock
California—Madera, 38 mi E of Madera
Colorado—Park, 30 mi NW of Pikes Peak
Connecticut—Hartford, at East Berlin
Delaware—Kent, 11 mi S of Dover
District of Columbia—Near 4th and L Sts. NW
Florida—Hernando, 12 mi N-NW of Brooksville
Georgia—Twiggs, 18 mi SE of Macon
Hawaii—Hawaii, lat. 20°15′N, long. 156°20′W, off Maui Isl.
Idaho—Custer, at Custer, SW of Challis
Illinois—Logan, 28 mi NE of Springfield
Indiana—Boone, 14 mi N-NW of Indianapolis
Iowa—Story, 5 mi NE of Ames
Kansas—Barton, 15 mi NE of Great Bend
Kentucky—Marion, 3 mi N-NW of Lebanon
Louisiana—Avoyelles, 3 mi SE of Marksville
Maine—Piscataquis, 18 mi N of Dover
Maryland—Prince Georges, 4.5 mi NW of Davidsonville
Massachusetts—Worcester, north part of city

Michigan—Wexford, 5 mi N-NW of Cadillac
Minnesota—Crow Wing, 10 mi SW of Brainerd
Mississippi—Leake, 9 mi W-NW of Carthage
Missouri—Miller, 20 mi SW of Jefferson City
Montana—Fergus, 11 mi W of Lewistown
Nebraska—Custer, 10 mi NW of Broken Bow
Nevada—Lander, 26 mi SE of Austin
New Hampshire—Belknap, 3 mi E of Ashland
New Jersey—Mercer, 5 mi SE of Trenton
New Mexico—Torrance, 12 mi S-SW of Willard
New York—Madison, 12 mi S of Oneida and 26 mi SW of Utica
North Carolina—Chatham, 10 mi NW of Sanford
North Dakota—Sheridan, 5 mi SW of McClusky
Ohio—Delaware, 25 mi N-NE of Columbus
Oklahoma—Oklahoma, 8 mi N of Oklahoma City
Oregon—Crook, 25 mi S-SE of Prineville
Pennsylvania—Centre, 2.5 mi SW of Bellefonte
Rhode Island—Kent, 1 mi S-SW of Crompton
South Carolina—Richland, 13 mi SE of Columbia
South Dakota—Hughes, 8 mi NE of Pierre
Tennessee—Rutherford, 5 mi NE of Murfreesboro
Texas—McCulloch, 15 mi NE of Brady
Utah—Sanpete, 3 mi N of Manti
Vermont—Washington, 3 mi E of Roxbury
Virginia—Buckingham, 5 mi SW of Buckingham
Washington—Chelan, 10 mi W-SW of Wenatchee
West Virginia—Braxton, 4 mi E of Sutton
Wisconsin—Wood, 9 mi SE of Marshfield
Wyoming—Fremont, 58 mi E-NE of Lander

International Boundary Lines of the U.S.

The length of the N boundary of the conterminous U.S.—the U.S.-Canadian border, excluding Alaska—is 3,987 mi according to the U.S. Geological Survey, Dept. of the Interior. The length of the Alaskan-Canadian border is 1,538 mi. The length of the U.S.-Mexican border, from the Gulf of Mexico to the Pacific Ocean, is approximately 1,933 mi (1963 boundary agreement).

Origin of the Names of U.S. States

Source: State officials, the Smithsonian Institution, and the Topographic Division, U.S. Geological Survey, Dept. of the Interior

Alabama—Indian for tribal town, later a tribe (Alabamas or Alibamons) of the Creek confederacy.

Alaska—Russian version of Aleutian (Eskimo) word, *alakshak*, for "peninsula," "great lands," or "land that is not an island."

Arizona—Spanish version of Pima Indian word for "little spring place," or Aztec *arizuma*, meaning "silver-bearing."

Arkansas—French variant of Quapaw (downstream people), a Siouan people.

California—Bestowed by the Spanish conquistadors (possibly by Cortez). It was the name of an imaginary island, an earthly paradise, in "Las Serges de Esplandian," a Spanish romance written by Montalvo in 1510. *Baja California* (Lower California, in Mexico) was first visited by Spanish in 1533. The present U.S. state was called *Alta* (Upper) *California.*

Colorado—Spanish, red, first applied to Colorado River.

Connecticut—From Mohican and other Algonquin words meaning "long river place."

Delaware—Named for Lord De La Warr, early governor of Virginia; first applied to river, then to Indian tribe (Lenni-Lenape), and the state.

District of Columbia—For Columbus, 1791.

Florida—Named by Ponce de Leon on *Pascua Florida*, "Flowery Easter," on Easter Sunday, 1513.

Georgia—For King George II of England by James Oglethorpe, colonial administrator, 1732.

Hawaii—Possibly derived from native word for homeland, *Hawaiki* or *Owhyhee.*

Idaho—A coined name with an invented Indian meaning: "gem of the mountains"; originally suggested for the Pikes Peak mining territory (Colorado), then applied to the new mining territory of the Pacific Northwest. Another theory suggests Idaho may be a Kiowa Apache term for the Comanche.

Illinois—French for *Illini* or "land of *Illini,*" Algonquin word meaning men or warriors.

Indiana—Means "land of the Indians."

Iowa—Indian word variously translated as "one who puts to sleep" or "beautiful land."

Kansas—Sioux word for "south wind people."

Kentucky—Indian word variously translated as "dark and bloody ground," "meadowland," and "land of tomorrow."

Louisiana—Part of territory called Louisiana by Sieur de La Salle for French King Louis XIV.

Maine—From Maine, ancient French province. Also: descriptive, referring to the mainland as distinct from the many coastal islands.

Maryland—For Queen Henrietta Maria, wife of Charles I of England.

Massachusetts—From Indian tribe named after "large hill place" identified by Capt. John Smith as being near Milton, MA.

Michigan—From Chippewa words, *mici gama*, meaning "great water," after the lake of the same name.

Minnesota—From Dakota Sioux word meaning "cloudy water" or "sky-tinted water" of the Minnesota River.

Mississippi—Probably Chippewa; *mici zibi*, "great river" or "gathering-in of all the waters." Also: Algonquin word, *messipi.*

Missouri—An Algonquin Indian term meaning "river of the big canoes."

Montana—Latin or Spanish for "mountainous."

Nebraska—From Omaha or Otos Indian word meaning "broad water" or "flat river," describing the Platte River.

Nevada—Spanish, meaning snow-clad.

New Hampshire—Named, 1629, by Capt. John Mason of Plymouth Council for his home county in England.

New Jersey—The Duke of York, 1664, gave a patent to John Berkeley and Sir George Carteret to be called Nova Caesaria, or New Jersey, after England's Isle of Jersey.

New Mexico—Spaniards in Mexico applied term to land north and west of Rio Grande in the 16th century.

New York—For Duke of York and Albany who received patent to New Netherland from his brother Charles II and sent an expedition to capture it, 1664.

North Carolina—In 1619 Charles I gave a large patent to Sir Robert Heath to be called Province of Carolana, from *Carolus*, Latin name for Charles. A new patent was granted by Charles II to Earl of Clarendon and others. Divided into North and South Carolina, 1710.

North Dakota—*Dakota* is Sioux for "friend" or "ally."

Ohio—Iroquois word for "fine or good river."

Oklahoma—Choctaw word meaning "red man," proposed by Rev. Allen Wright, Choctaw-speaking Indian.

Oregon—Origin unknown. One theory holds that the name may have been derived from that of the Wisconsin River shown on a 1715 French map as "Ouaricon-sint."

Pennsylvania—William Penn, the Quaker who was made full proprietor of this area by King Charles II in 1681, suggested "Sylvania," or "woodland," for his tract. The king's government owed Penn's father, Admiral William Penn, £16,000, and the land was granted as partial settlement. Charles II added the "Penn" to Sylvania, against the desires of the modest proprietor, in honor of the admiral.

Puerto Rico—Spanish for "rich port."

Rhode Island—Exact origin is unknown. One theory notes that Giovanni de Verrazano recorded an island about the size of Rhodes in the Mediterranean in 1524, but others believe the state was named Roode Eylandt by Adriaen Block, Dutch explorer, because of its red clay.

South Carolina—See North Carolina.

South Dakota—See North Dakota.

Tennessee—*Tanasi* was the name of Cherokee villages on the Little Tennessee River. From 1784 to 1788 this was the State of Franklin, or Frankland.

Texas—Variant of word used by Caddo and other Indians meaning "friends" or "allies," and applied to them by the Spanish in eastern Texas. Also written *texias, tejas, teysas.*

Utah—From a Navajo word meaning "upper," or "higher up," as applied to a Shoshone tribe called Ute. Spanish form is *Yutta.* The English is *Uta* or *Utah.* Proposed name *Deseret*, "land of honeybees," from Book of Mormon, was rejected by Congress.

Vermont—From French words *vert* (green) and *mont* (mountain). The Green Mountains were said to have been named by Samuel de Champlain. When the state was formed, 1777, Dr. Thomas Young suggested combining *vert* and *mont* into Vermont.

Virginia—Named by Sir Walter Raleigh, who fitted out the expedition of 1584, in honor of Queen Elizabeth, the Virgin Queen of England.

Washington—Named after George Washington. When the bill creating the Territory of Columbia was introduced in the 32d Congress, the name was changed to Washington because of the existence of the District of Columbia.

West Virginia—So named when western counties of Virginia refused to secede from the U.S. in 1863.

Wisconsin—An Indian name, spelled *Ouisconsin* and *Mesconsing* by early chroniclers. Believed to mean "grassy place" in Chippewa. Congress made it Wisconsin.

Wyoming—From the Algonquin words for "large prairie place," or "at the big plains," or "on the great plain."

Territorial Sea of the U.S.

According to a Dec. 27, 1988, proclamation by Pres. Ronald Reagan: "The territorial sea of the United States henceforth extends to 12 nautical miles from the baselines of the United States determined in accordance with international law. In accordance with international law, as reflected in the applicable provisions of the 1982 United Nations Convention on the Law of the Sea, within the territorial sea of the United States, the ships of all countries enjoy the right of innocent passage and the ships and aircraft of all countries enjoy the right of transit passage through international straits."

Accession of Territory by the U.S.

Source: U.S. Dept. of the Interior

	Acquisi-tion date	Total area (sq mi)[1]		Acquisi-tion date	Total area (sq mi)[1]		Acquisi-tion date	Total area (sq mi)[1]
Total U.S.	NA	3,540,558	Texas	1845	388,687	Other areas:		
			Oregon Territory	1846	286,541	Puerto Rico[3]	1898	3,427
United States	NA	3,536,338	Mexican Cession	1848	529,189	Guam[4]	1899	210
Territory in 1790[2]	NA	895,415	Gadsden Purchase	1853	29,670	American Samoa[5]	1900	77
Louisiana Purchase	1803	909,380	Alaska	1867	570,374	U.S. Virgin Islands	1917	134
Purchase of Florida	1819	58,666	Hawaii	1898	6,423	N Mariana Islands[6]	1986	177
						All other[7]	NA	16

NA=not applicable. (1) Area figures from the Bureau of the Census, Apr. 1, 1990. As a result of independent rounding, the sum of these figures do not equal the total. (2) Includes that part of a drainage basin of Red River of the North, S of 49th parallel, sometimes considered part of Louisiana Purchase. (3) Ceded by Spain in 1898, ratified in 1899, and became the Commonwealth of Puerto Rico by Act of Congress on July 25, 1952. (4) Acquired 1899. (5) Acquired 1900. (6) Aquired 1986. (7) Comprises the following islands with gross areas as indicated in sq mi: Midway (2), Wake (3), Palmyra (2), Navassa (3), Baker, Howland, and Jarvis (combined area, 3), Johnson Atoll (combined area, less than 1), and Kingman Reef (less than 0.5).

Federally Owned Land, by State, 1993

Source: Bureau of Land Management, U.S. Dept. of the Interior

(as of Sept. 30, 1993)

State	Total federal acreage	Total state acreage[1]	Percentage of government-owned acreage[2]	State	Total federal acreage	Total state acreage[1]	Percentage of government-owned acreage[2]
AL....	1,079,256.9	32,678,400	3.303	MT ...	26,066,589.5	93,271,040	27.947
AK....	247,998,748.6	365,481,600	67.855	NE ...	710,624.1	49,031,680	1.449
AZ....	34,313,643.0	72,688,000	47.207	NV ...	58,295,286.5	70,264,320	82.966
AR....	2,759,025.0	33,599,360	8.212	NH ...	734,994.0	5,768,960	12.741
CA....	45,210,212.5	100,206,720	45.117	NJ....	162,095.7	4,813,440	3.368
CO....	24,086,131.2	66,485,760	36.228	NM ...	26,253,008.8	77,766,400	33.759
CT....	8,009.2	3,135,360	0.255	NY ...	211,898.4	30,680,960	0.691
DE....	29,150.2	1,265,920	2.303	NC ...	2,005,422.8	31,402,880	6.386
DC....	9,424.8	39,040	24.141	ND ...	1,886,546.4	44,452,480	4.244
FL....	2,976,708.9	34,721,280	8.573	OH ...	339,184.8	26,222,080	1.294
GA....	1,496,734.7	37,295,360	4.013	OK ...	716,397.7	44,087,680	1.625
HI	650,185.9	4,105,600	15.837	OR ...	32,298,251.3	61,598,720	52.433
ID	32,604,814.9	52,933,120	61.596	PA ...	631,020.3	28,804,480	2.191
IL.....	962,307.7	35,795,200	2.688	RI	4,709.8	677,120	0.696
IN	463,730.6	23,158,400	2.002	SC ...	744,380.3	19,374,080	3.842
IA.....	336,004.9	35,860,480	0.937	SD ...	2,805,498.1	48,881,920	5.739
KA....	423,536.1	52,510,720	0.807	TN ...	1,019,238.3	26,727,680	3.813
KY....	1,080,445.0	25,512,320	4.235	TX....	2,276,782.2	168,217,600	1.354
LA....	821,858.3	28,867,840	2.847	UT ...	32,762,451.6	52,696,960	62.171
ME....	163,326.0	19,847,680	0.823	VT....	357,603.0	5,936,640	6.024
MD....	187,997.0	6,319,360	2.975	VA ...	1,813,045.6	25,496,320	7.111
MA....	97,301.7	5,034,880	1.933	WA ...	12,091,189.3	42,693,760	28.321
MI	4,592,220.3	36,492,160	12.584	WV ...	1,022,324.8	15,410,560	6.634
MN....	5,377,366.2	51,205,760	10.502	WI....	3,536,970.0	35,011,200	10.102
MS....	1,304,090.7	30,222,720	4.315	WY ...	30,455,255.3	62,343,040	48.851
MO ...	2,089,399.8	44,248,320	4.722	Total..	650,322,398.7	2,271,343,360	28.632

Note: Data do not include inland water. (1) Bureau of the Census, U.S. Dept. of Commerce figures. (2) Excludes trust properties.

National Recreation Areas Administered by the U.S. Forest Service

Source: U.S. Forest Service, Dept. of Agriculture, 1994

Area name	Location	Estab.	Acres	Area name	Location	Estab.	Acres
Allegheny	PA	1984	23,063	Pine Ridge	NE	1986	6,600
Arapaho	CO	1978	34,928	Rattlesnake	MT	1980	61,000
Ed Jenkins	GA	1991	23,330	Sawtooth	ID	1972	756,019
Flaming Gorge	WY-UT	1968	201,114	Smith River	CA	1990	331,229
Grand Island	MI	1990	12,957	Spring Mts.	NV	1993	316,000
Hells Canyon	ID-OR	1975	541,336	Spruce Knob-Seneca Rocks	WV	1965	100,000
Jemez	NM	1993	57,000	Whiskeytown Shasta-			
Mount Baker	WA	1984	8,473	Trinity	CA	1965	203,587
Mount Rogers	VA	1966	154,816	White Rocks	VT	1984	36,400
Oregon Dunes	OR	1972	31,566	Winding Stair Mt.	OK	1988	26,445

National Parks, Other Areas Administered by National Park Service

Figures given are date area initially protected by Congress or presidential proclamation, date given current designation, and gross area in acres as of Dec. 31, 1994. Approximately 80 mil acres of federal land are administered by the National Park Service.

National Parks

Acadia, ME (1916/1929) 41,819. Includes Mount Desert Island, half of Isle au Haut, Schoodic Peninsula on mainland. Highest elevation on Eastern seaboard.

American Samoa. American Samoa (1988) 9,000. Features a paleotropical rain forest and a coral reef. No federal facilities.

Arches, UT (1929/1971) 73,379. Contains giant red sandstone arches and other products of erosion.

Badlands, SD (1929/1978) 242,756; prairie with bison, bighorn, and antelope. Contains animal fossils from 26 to 37 million years ago.

Big Bend, TX (1935) 801,163. Rio Grande, Chisos Mts.

Biscayne, FL (1968/1980) 172,924. Aquatic park encompasses chain of islands south of Miami.

Bryce Canyon, UT (1923/1928) 35,835. Spectacularly colorful and unusual display of erosion effects.

Canyonlands, UT (1964) 337,570. At junction of Colorado and Green rivers, extensive evidence of prehistoric Indians.

Capitol Reef, UT (1937/1971) 241,904. A 70-mi uplift of sandstone cliffs dissected by high-walled gorges.

Carlsbad Caverns, NM (1923/1930) 46,766. Largest known caverns; not yet fully explored.

Channel Islands, CA (1938/1980) 249,354. Sea lion breeding place, nesting sea birds, unique plants.

Crater Lake, OR (1902) 183,224. Extraordinary blue lake in crater of extinct volcano encircled by lava walls 500 to 2,000 ft high.

Death Valley, CA-NV (1993/1994) 3,367,627. Large desert area includes the lowest point in the Western Hemisphere. Includes Scottys Castle.

Denali, AK (1917/1980) 4,741,910. Name changed from Mt. McKinley NP. Contains highest mountain in U.S.; wildlife.

Dry Tortugas, FL (1935/1992) 64,700. Formerly Ft. Jefferson National Monument.

Everglades, FL (1934) 1,507,850. Largest remaining subtropical wilderness in continental U.S.

Gates of the Arctic, AK (1978/1984) 7,523,888. Vast wilderness in north central region.

Glacier, MT (1910) 1,013,572. Superb Rocky Mt. scenery, numerous glaciers and glacial lakes. Part of Waterton-Glacier Intl. Peace Park established by U.S. and Canada in 1932.

Glacier Bay, AK (1925/1986) 3,225,284. Great tidewater glaciers that move down mountainsides and break up into the sea; much wildlife.

Grand Canyon, AZ (1908/1919) 1,217,158. Most spectacular part of Colorado River's greatest canyon.

Grand Teton, WY (1929) 309,994. Most impressive part of the Teton Mountains, winter feeding ground of largest American elk herd.

Great Basin, NV (1922/1986) 77,180. Includes Wheeler Pk., Lexington Arch, and Lehman Caves.

Great Smoky Mountains, NC-TN (1926) 521,053. Largest eastern mountain range, magnificent forests.

Guadalupe Mountains, TX (1966) 86,416. Extensive Permian limestone fossil reef; tremendous earth fault.

Haleakala, HI (1916/1960) 28,099. Dormant volcano on Maui with large colorful craters.

Hawaii Volcanoes, HI (1916/1961) 209,695. Contains Kilauea and Mauna Loa, active volcanoes.

Hot Springs, AR (1832/1921) 5,549. Bathhouses are furnished with thermal waters from the park's 47 hot springs; these waters are used for bathing and drinking.

Isle Royale, MI (1931) 571,790. Largest island in Lake Superior, noted for its wilderness area and wildlife.

Joshua Tree, CA (1936/1994) 792,749. Desert region includes Joshua trees and other plant and animal life.

Katmai, AK (1918/1980) 3,674,541. "Valley of Ten Thousand Smokes," scene of 1912 volcanic eruption.

Kenai Fjords, AK (1978/1980) 670,643. Abundant marine mammals, birdlife; the Harding Icefield, one of the 4 major icecaps in U.S.

Kings Canyon, CA (1890/1940) 461,901. Mountain wilderness, dominated by Kings River Canyons and High Sierra; contains giant sequoias.

Kobuk Valley, AK (1978/1980) 1,750,736. Contains geological and recreational sites and wildlife.

Lake Clark, AK (1978/1980) 2,636,839. Across Cook Inlet from Anchorage. A scenic wilderness rich in fish and wildlife.

Lassen Volcanic, CA (1907/1916) 106,372. Contains Lassen Peak, recently active volcano, and other volcanic phenomena.

Mammoth Cave, KY (1926/1941) 52,830. 144 mi of surveyed underground passages, beautiful natural formations, river 300 ft below surface.

Mesa Verde, CO (1906) 52,122. Most notable and best preserved prehistoric cliff dwellings in the U.S.

Mount Rainier, WA (1899) 235,613. Greatest single-peak glacial system in the lower 48 states.

North Cascades, WA (1968) 504,781. Spectacular mountainous region with many glaciers, lakes.

Olympic, WA (1909/1938) 922,651. Mountain wilderness containing finest remnant of Pacific Northwest rain forest, active glaciers, Pacific shoreline, rare elk.

Petrified Forest, AZ (1906/1962) 93,533. Extensive petrified wood and Indian artifacts. Contains part of Painted Desert.

Redwood, CA (1968) 110,232. Forty mi of Pacific coastline, groves of ancient redwoods and world's tallest trees.

Rocky Mountain, CO (1915) 265,727. On the continental divide, includes peaks over 14,000 ft.

Saguaro, AZ (1933/1994) 91,116. Part of the Sonoran Desert, includes the giant saguaro cacti, unique to the region.

Sequoia, CA (1890) 402,482. Groves of giant sequoias, highest mountain in conterminous U.S.—Mount Whitney (14,494 ft). World's largest tree.

Shenandoah, VA (1926) 196,466. Portion of the Blue Ridge Mts.; overlooks Shenandoah Valley; Skyline Drive.

Theodore Roosevelt, ND (1947/1978) 70,447. Contains part of T.R.'s ranch and scenic badlands.

Virgin Islands, VI (1956) 14,689. Covers 75% of St. John Island, lush growth, lovely beaches, Indian petroglyphs, evidence of colonial Danes.

Voyageurs, MN (1971) 218,035. Abundant lakes, forests, wildlife, canoeing, boating.

Wind Cave, SD (1903) 28,295. Limestone caverns in Black Hills. Extensive wildlife includes a herd of bison.

Wrangell-St. Elias, AK (1978/1980) 8,323,618. Largest area in park system, most peaks over 16,000 ft, abundant wildlife; day's drive east of Anchorage.

Yellowstone, ID-MT-WY, (1872) 2,219,791. World's first national park. World's greatest geyser area has about 3,000 geysers and hot springs; spectacular falls and impressive canyons of the Yellowstone River; grizzly bear, moose, and bison.

Yosemite, CA (1890) 761,236. Yosemite Valley, the nation's highest waterfall, 1 grove of sequoias, and mountains.

Zion, UT (1909/1919) 146,598. Unusual shapes and landscapes have resulted from erosion and faulting; Zion Canyon, with sheer walls ranging up to 2,640 ft, is readily accessible.

National Historical Parks

Appomattox Court House, VA (1930/1954) 1,594. Where Lee surrendered to Grant.

Boston, MA (1974) 41. Includes Faneuil Hall, Old North Church, Bunker Hill, Paul Revere House.

Cane River Creole (and preserve), LA (1994) 210 (nonfederal). Preserves the Creole culture as it developed along the Cane R.

Chaco Culture, NM (1907/1980) 33,974. Ruins of pueblos built by prehistoric Indians.

Chesapeake and Ohio Canal, MD-WV-DC (1938/1971) 19,237. 184-mi historic canal; DC to Cumberland, MD.

George Rogers Clark, Vincennes, IN (1966) 26. Commemorates American defeat of British in west during Revolution.

Colonial, VA (1930/1936) 9,330. Includes most of Jamestown Island, site of first successful English colony; Yorktown, site of Cornwallis's surrender to George Washington; and the Colonial Parkway.

Cumberland Gap, KY-TN-VA (1940) 20,446. Mountain pass of the Wilderness Road, which carried the first great migration of pioneers into America's interior.

Dayton Aviation, OH (1992) 86. Commemorates the area's aviation heritage.

Harpers Ferry, MD-WV (1944/1963) 2,287. At the confluence of the Shenandoah and Potomac rivers, the site of John Brown's 1859 raid on the Army arsenal.

Hopewell Culture, OH (1923/1992) 1,030. Formerly Mound City Group National Monument.

Independence, PA (1948) 45. Contains several properties in Philadelphia associated with the American Revolution and the founding of the U.S. Includes Independence Hall.

Kalaupapa, HI (1980) 10,779. Molokai's former leper colony site and other historic areas.

Kaloko-Honokohau, HI (1978) 1,161. Preserves the native culture of Hawaii. No federal facilities.

Keweenaw, MI (1992) 1,870. Site of first significant copper mine in U.S.

Klondike Gold Rush, AK-WA (1976) 13,191. Alaskan Trails in 1898 Gold Rush. Museum in Seattle.

Jean Laffite (and preserve), LA (1939/1978) 20,020. Includes Chalmette, site of 1815 Battle of New Orleans; French Quarter.

Lowell, MA (1978) 137. Textile mills, canal, 19th-cent. structures; park shows planned city of Industrial Revolution.

Lyndon B. Johnson, TX (1969/1980) 1,570. President's birthplace, boyhood home, ranch.

Marsh-Billings, VT (1992) 643. Boyhood home of George Perkins Marsh. No federal facilities.

Minute Man, MA (1959) 935. Where the colonial Minute Men battled the British, Apr. 19, 1775. Also contains Nathaniel Hawthorne's home.

Morristown, NJ (1933) 1,684. Sites of important military encampments during the American Revolution; Washington's headquarters 1777, 1779-80.

Natchez, MS (1988) 108. Mansions, townhouses, and villas concerning history of Natchez, MS.

New Orleans Jazz, LA (1994) 194. Preserves, educates, and interprets jazz as it has evolved in New Orleans.

Nez Perce, ID (1965) 2,110. Illustrates the history and culture of the Nez Perce Indian country; with more than 20 separate sites.

Pecos, NM (1965/1990) 6,671. Ruins of ancient Pueblo of Pecos, archaeological sites, and 2 associated Spanish colonial missions from the 17th and 18th centuries.

Pu'uhonua o Honaunau, HI (1955/1978) 182. Until 1819, a sanctuary for Hawaiians vanquished in battle and for those guilty of crimes or breaking taboos.

Salt River Bay, St. Croix, VI (1992) 945. The only site known where, 500 years ago, members of a Columbus party landed on what is now territory of the U.S.

San Antonio Missions, TX (1978) 819. Four of finest Spanish missions in U.S., 18th-cent. irrigation system.

San Francisco Maritime, CA (1988) 31. Artifacts, photographs, and historic vessels related to the development of the Pacific Coast.

San Juan Island, WA (1966) 1,752. Commemorates peaceful relations between the U.S., Canada, and Great Britain since the 1872 boundary disputes.

Saratoga, NY (1938) 3,393. Scene of a major battle that became a turning point in the American Revolution.

Sitka, AK (1910/1972) 107. Scene of last major resistance of the Tlingit Indians to the Russians, 1804.

Tumacacori, AZ (1908/1990) 46. Historic Spanish Catholic mission building stands near the site first visited by Jesuit Father Kino in 1691.

Valley Forge, PA (1976) 3,466. Continental Army campsite in 1777-78 winter.

War in the Pacific, GU (1978) 1,960. Seven distinct units illustrating the Pacific theater of WWII.

Women's Rights, NY (1980) 6. Seneca Falls site where Susan B. Anthony, Elizabeth Cady Stanton began rights movement in 1848.

National Battlefields

Antietam, MD (1890/1978) 3,256. Battle ended first Confederate invasion of North, Sept. 17, 1862.

Big Hole, MT (1910/1963) 656. Site of major battle with Nez Perce Indians.

Cowpens, SC (1929/1972) 842. American Revolution battlefield.

Fort Donelson, TN (1928/1985) 552. Site of first major Union victory.

Fort Necessity, PA (1931/1961) 903. First battle of French and Indian War.

Monocacy, MD (1934/1976) 1,647. Civil War battle in defense of Washington, DC, July 9, 1864.

Moores Creek, NC (1926/1980) 87. 1776 battle between Patriots and Loyalists commemorated here.

Petersburg, VA (1926/1962) 2,744. Scene of 10-month Union campaign 1864-65.

Stones River, TN (1927/1960) 709. Scene of battle that began federal offensive to trisect the Confederacy.

Tupelo, MS (1929/1961) 1. Crucial battle over Sherman's supply line.

Wilson's Creek, MO (1960/1970) 1,750. Civil War battle for control of Missouri.

National Battlefield Parks

Kennesaw Mountain, GA (1917/1935) 2,884. Two major battles of Atlanta campaign in Civil War.

Manassas, VA (1940) 5,072. Two battles in Civil War, 1861 and 1862.

Richmond, VA (1936) 772. Site of battles defending Confederate capital.

National Battlefield Site

Brices Cross Roads, MS (1929) 1. Civil War battlefield.

National Military Parks

Chickamauga and Chattanooga, GA-TN (1890) 8,119. Site of major Confederate victory, 1863.

Fredericksburg and Spotsylvania County, VA (1927) 7,782. Sites of several major Civil War battles and campaigns.

Gettysburg, PA (1895) 5,900. Site of decisive Confederate defeat in North. Gettysburg Address.

Guilford Courthouse, NC (1917) 220. American Revolution battle site.

Horseshoe Bend, AL (1956) 2,040. On Tallapoosa River, where Gen. Andrew Jackson's forces broke the power of the Upper Creek Indian Confederacy.

Kings Mountain, SC (1931) 3,945. American Revolution battle.

Pea Ridge, AR (1956) 4,300. Civil War battle.

Shiloh, TN (1894) 3,973. Major Civil War battle; site includes some well-preserved Indian burial mounds.

Vicksburg, MS (1899) 1,736. Union victory gave North control of the Mississippi and split the Confederacy in two.

National Memorials

Arkansas Post, AR (1960) 389. First permanent French settlement in the lower Mississippi River valley.

Arlington House, the Robert E. Lee Memorial, VA (1925/1972) 28. Lee's home overlooking the Potomac.

Chamizal, El Paso, TX (1966/1974) 55. Commemorates 1963 settlement of 99-year dispute with Mexico.

Coronado, AZ (1941/1952) 4,750. Commemorates first European exploration of the Southwest.

DeSoto, FL (1948) 27. Commemorates 16th-cent. Spanish explorations.

Federal Hall, NY (1939/1955) 0.45. First seat of U.S. government under the Constitution.

Fort Caroline, FL (1950) 138. On St. Johns River, overlooks site of a French Huguenot colony.

Fort Clatsop, OR (1958) 125. Lewis and Clark encampment 1805-6.

General Grant, NY (1958) 0.76. Tombs of pres. and wife.

Hamilton Grange, NY (1962) 0.11. Home of Alexander Hamilton.

Jefferson National Expansion Memorial, St. Louis, MO (1935/1969) 91. Commemorates westward expansion.

Johnstown Flood, PA (1964) 164. Commemorates tragic flood of 1889.

Korean War Veterans, DC (1986) 2.2. Dedicated in 1995, honors those who served in the Korean War.

Lincoln Boyhood, IN (1962) 200. Lincoln grew up here.

Lincoln Memorial, DC (1911) 110. Marble statue of the 16th U.S. president.

Lyndon B. Johnson Grove on the Potomac, DC (1973) 17. Overlooks the Potomac R. vista of the Capital.

Mount Rushmore, SD (1925) 1,278. World-famous sculpture of 4 presidents.

Perry's Victory and International Peace Memorial, Put-in-Bay, OH (1936/1972) 25. The world's most massive Doric column, constructed 1912-15, inculcates the lessons of international peace by arbitration and disarmament.

Roger Williams, RI (1965) 5. Memorial to founder of Rhode Island.

Thaddeus Kosciuszko, PA (1972) 0.02. Memorial to Polish hero of American Revolution.

Theodore Roosevelt Island, DC (1932) 89. Statue of Roosevelt in wooded island sanctuary.

Thomas Jefferson Memorial, DC (1934) 18. Statue of Jefferson in an inscribed circular, colonnaded structure.

USS Arizona, HI (1980). 0.0. Memorializes American losses at Pearl Harbor.

Vietnam Veterans, DC (1980) 2. Black granite wall inscribed with names of those killed in action and missing in the Vietnam War.

Washington Monument, DC (1848) 106. Obelisk honoring the first U.S. president.

Wright Brothers, NC (1927/1953) 428. Site of first powered flight.

National Historic Sites

Abraham Lincoln Birthplace, Hodgenville, KY (1916/1959) 117. Early 17th-cent. cabin.

Adams, Quincy, MA (1946/1952) 14. Home of Presidents John Adams, John Quincy Adams, and celebrated descendants.

Allegheny Portage Railroad, PA (1964) 1,247. Linked the Pennsylvania Canal system and the West.

Andersonville, Andersonville, GA (1970) 495. Noted Civil War prisoner-of-war camp.

Andrew Johnson, Greeneville, TN (1935/1963) 17. Two homes and the tailor shop of the 17th U.S. president.

Bent's Old Fort, CO (1960) 800. Reconstruction of S Plains outpost.

Boston African American, MA (1980) Pre-Civil War black history structures.

Brown v. Board of Education, KS (1992) 2. Commemorates the landmark 1954 U.S. Supreme Court decision.

Carl Sandburg Home, NC (1968) 264. Poet's home.

Charles Pinckney, SC (1988) 28. Statesman's home.

Christiansted, St. Croix, VI (1952/1961) 27. Commemorates Danish colony.

Clara Barton, MD (1974) 9. Home of founder of American Red Cross.

Edgar Allan Poe, PA (1978/1980) 0.52. U.S. writer's home.

Edison, West Orange, NJ (1955/1962) 21. Inventor's home and laboratory.

Eisenhower, Gettysburg, PA (1967) 690. Home of 34th president.

Eleanor Roosevelt, Hyde Park, NY (1977) 181. Personal retreat.

Eugene O'Neill, Danville, CA (1976) 13. Playwright's home.

Ford's Theatre, DC (1866/1970) 0.29. Includes theater, now restored, where Lincoln was assassinated, house where he died, and Lincoln Museum.

Fort Bowie, AZ (1964) 1,000. Focal point of operations against Geronimo and the Apaches.

Fort Davis, TX (1961) 460. Key frontier outpost in West Texas.

Fort Laramie, WY (1938/1960) 833. Military post on Oregon Trail.

Fort Larned, KS (1964/1966) 718. Military post on Santa Fe Trail.

Fort Point, San Francisco, CA (1970) 29. West Coast fortification.

Fort Raleigh, NC (1941) 513. First attempted English settlement in North America.

Fort Scott, KS (1965/1978) 17. Commemorates U.S. frontier of 1840s and '50s.

Fort Smith, AR-OK (1961) 75. Active post during 1817-90.

Fort Union Trading Post, MT-ND (1966) 442. Principal fur-trading post on upper Missouri, 1829-67.

Fort Vancouver, WA (1948/1961) 209. Headquarters for Hudson's Bay Company in 1825. Early political seat.

Frederick Douglass Home, DC (1962/1988) 9. Home of nation's leading black spokesman.

Frederick Law Olmsted, MA (1979) 2. Home of famous city planner.

Friendship Hill, PA (1978) 675. Home of Albert Gallatin, Jefferson's and Madison's secretary of treasury.

Golden Spike, UT (1957) 2,735. Commemorates completion of first transcontinental railroad in 1869.

Grant-Kohrs Ranch, MT (1972) 1,498. Ranch house and part of 19th-cent. ranch.

Hampton, MD (1948) 62. 18th-cent. Georgian mansion.

Harry S. Truman, MO (1983) 7. Home of Pres. Truman after 1919.

Herbert Hoover, West Branch, IA (1965) 187. Birthplace and boyhood home of 31st president.

Home of Franklin D. Roosevelt, Hyde Park, NY (1944) 290. Birthplace, home, and "Summer White House" of 32d president.

Hopewell Furnace, PA (1938/1985) 848. 19th-cent. iron-making village.

Hubbell Trading Post, AZ (1965) 160. Still-active trading post.

James A. Garfield, Mentor, OH (1980) 8. Home of 20th president.

Jimmy Carter, GA (1987) 71. Birthplace and home of 39th president.

John Fitzgerald Kennedy, Brookline, MA (1967) 0.09. Birthplace and childhood home of 35th president.

John Muir, Martinez, CA (1964) 345. Home of early conservationist and writer.

Knife River Indian Villages, ND (1974) 1,758. Remnants of villages last occupied by Hidatsa and Mandan Indians.

Lincoln Home, Springfield, IL (1971) 12. Lincoln's residence at the time he was elected 16th president, 1860.

Longfellow, Cambridge, MA (1972) 2. Longfellow's home, 1837-82, and Washington's headquarters during Boston Siege, 1775-76.

Maggie L. Walker, VA (1978) 1. Richmond home of black leader and bank president; daughter of an ex-slave.

Manzanar, Lone Pine, CA (1992) 500. Commemorates Manzanar War Relocation Ctr., a Japanese-American internment camp during WWII. No federal facilities.

Martin Luther King, Jr., Atlanta, GA (1980) 37. Birthplace, grave, and church of the civil rights leader.

Martin Van Buren, NY (1974) 40. Lindenwald, home of 8th president, near Kinderhook.

Mary McLeod Bethune Council House, DC (1991) 0.07. Commemorates Bethune's leadership in the black women's movement.

Ninety Six, SC (1976) 989. Colonial trading village.

Palo Alto Battlefield, TX (1978) 3,357. First battle of the Mexican War.

Pennsylvania Avenue, DC (1965). Includes area between Capitol and White House, Ford's Theatre.

Puukohola Heiau, HI (1972) 80. Ruins of temple built by King Kamehameha.

Sagamore Hill, Oyster Bay, NY (1962) 83. Home of President Theodore Roosevelt from 1885 until his death in 1919.

Saint-Gaudens, Cornish, NH (1964) 148. Home, studio, and gardens of American sculptor Augustus Saint-Gaudens.

Saint Paul's Church, NY (1943) 6. 18th-cent. site associated with John Peter Zenger's "freedom of press" trial.

Salem Maritime, MA (1938) 9. Only port never seized from the patriots by the British. Major fishing and whaling port.

San Juan, PR (1949) 75. 16th-cent. Spanish fortifications.

Saugus Iron Works, MA (1968) 9. Reconstructed 17th-cent. colonial ironworks.

Springfield Armory, MA (1974) 55. Small-arms manufacturing center for nearly 200 years.

Steamtown, PA (1986) 62. Railyard, roadhouse, and repair shops of former Delaware, Lackawanna, and Western Railroad.

Theodore Roosevelt Birthplace, New York, NY (1962) 0.11. Reconstructed brownstone.

Theodore Roosevelt Inaugural, Buffalo, NY (1966) 1. Wilcox House where he took oath of office, 1901.

Thomas Stone, MD (1978) 328. Home of signer of Declaration of Independence, built in 1771.

Tuskegee Institute, AL (1974) 58. College founded by Booker T. Washington in 1881 for blacks.

Ulysses S. Grant, St. Louis Co., MO (1989) 10. Home of Grant during pre-Civil War years.

Vanderbilt Mansion, Hyde Park, NY (1940) 212. Mansion of 19th-cent. financier.

Weir Farm, Witon, CT (1990) 60. Home and studio of American impressionist painter J. Alden Weir.

Whitman Mission, WA (1936/1963) 98. Site where Dr. and Mrs. Marcus Whitman ministered to the Indians until slain by them in 1847.

William Howard Taft, Cincinnati, OH (1969) 3. Birthplace and early home of the 27th president.

National Monuments

Name	State	Year[1]	Acreage
Agate Fossil Beds	NE	1965	3,055
Alibates Flint Quarries	NM-TX	1965	1,371
Aniakchak**	AK	1978	137,176
Aztec Ruins	NM	1923	320
Bandelier	NM	1916	32,737
Black Canyon of the Gunnison	CO	1933	20,766
Booker T. Washington	VA	1956	224
Buck Island Reef	VI	1961	880
Cabrillo	CA	1913	137
Canyon de Chelly	AZ	1931	83,840
Cape Krusenstern	AK	1978	659,807
Capulin Volcano	NM	1916	793
Casa Grande Ruins	AZ	1892	473
Castillo de San Marcos	FL	1924	21
Castle Clinton	NY	1946	1
Cedar Breaks	UT	1933	6,155
Chiricahua	AZ	1924	11,985
Colorado	CO	1911	20,454
Congaree Swamp	SC	1976	22,200
Craters of the Moon	ID	1924	53,545
Devils Postpile	CA	1911	798
Devils Tower	WY	1906	1,347
Dinosaur	CO-UT	1915	210,844
Effigy Mounds	IA	1949	1,481
El Malpais	NM	1987	114,277
El Morro	NM	1906	1,279
Florissant Fossil Beds**	CO	1969	5,998
Fort Frederica	GA	1936	241
Fort Matanzas	FL	1924	228
Fort McHenry National Monument and Historic Shrine	MD	1925	43
Fort Pulaski	GA	1924	5,623
Fort Stanwix	NY	1935	16
Fort Sumter	SC	1948	195
Fort Union	NM	1954	721
Fossil Butte	WY	1972	8,198
G. Washington Birthplace	VA	1930	550
George Washington Carver	MO	1943	210
Gila Cliff Dwellings	NM	1907	550
Grand Portage	MN	1951	710
Great Sand Dunes	CO	1932	38,662
Hagerman Fossil Beds	ID	1988	4,281
Hohokam Pima*	AZ	1972	1,690
Homestead Natl. Monument of America	NE	1936	195
Hovenweep	CO-UT	1923	785
Jewel Cave	SD	1908	1,274
John Day Fossil Beds	OR	1974	14,014
Lava Beds	CA	1925	46,560
Little Big Horn Battlefield	MT	1879	765
Montezuma Castle	AZ	1906	858
Muir Woods	CA	1908	554
Natural Bridges	UT	1908	7,636
Navajo	AZ	1909	360
Ocmulgee	GA	1934	702
Oregon Caves	OR	1909	488
Organ Pipe Cactus	AZ	1937	330,689
Petroglyph	NM	1990	7,240
Pinnacles	CA	1908	16,265

Name	State	Year[1]	Acreage
Pipe Spring	AZ	1923	40
Pipestone	MN	1937	282
Poverty Point**	LA	1988	911
Rainbow Bridge	UT	1910	160
Russell Cave	AL	1961	310
Salinas Pueblo Missions	NM	1901	1,071
Scotts Bluff	NE	1919	3,003
Statue of Liberty	NJ-NY	1924	58
Sunset Crater	AZ	1930	3,040
Timpanogos Cave	UT	1922	250
Tonto	AZ	1907	1,120
Tuzigoot	AZ	1939	801
Walnut Canyon	AZ	1915	2,249
White Sands	NM	1933	143,733
Wupatki	AZ	1924	35,253
Yucca House*	CO	1919	10

National Preserves

Name	State	Year[1]	Acreage
Aniakchak	AK	1978	465,603
Bering Land Bridge	AK	1978	2,784,960
Big Cypress	FL	1974	716,000
Big Thicket	TX	1974	96,678
Denali	AK	1917	1,334,618
Gates of the Arctic	AK	1978	948,629
Glacier Bay	AK	1925	57,884
Katmai	AK	1918	418,699
Lake Clark	AK	1978	1,407,293
Little River Canyon**	AL	1992	13,669
Mojave	CA	1994	1,489,800
Noatak	AK	1978	6,569,904
Timucuan Ecological & Historic Preserve**	FL	1988	46,000
Wrangell-St. Elias	AK	1978	4,852,773
Yukon-Charley Rivers	AK	1978	2,526,509

National Seashores

Name	State	Year[1]	Acreage
Assateague Island	MD-VA	1965	39,733
Canaveral	FL	1975	57,662
Cape Cod	MA	1961	43,569
Cape Hatteras	NC	1937	30,319
Cape Lookout**	NC	1966	28,243
Cumberland Island	GA	1972	36,415
Fire Island	NY	1964	19,579
Gulf Islands	FL-MS	1971	135,625
Padre Island	TX	1962	130,434
Point Reyes	CA	1962	71,049

National Parkways

Name	State	Year[1]	Acreage
Blue Ridge	VA-NC	1933	87,934
George Washington Memorial	VA-MD	1930	7,248
John D. Rockefeller Jr. Mem.	WY	1972	23,777
Natchez Trace	AL-MS-TN	1938	51,748

National Lakeshores

Name	State	Year[1]	Acreage
Apostle Islands	WI	1970	69,372
Indiana Dunes	IN	1966	15,058
Pictured Rocks	MI	1966	73,228
Sleeping Bear Dunes	MI	1970	71,189

National Reserves

Name	State	Year[1]	Acreage
City of Rocks	ID	1988	14,407
Ebey's Landing	WA	1992	19,000

National Rivers

Name	State	Year[1]	Acreage
	KY-TN	1976	125,000
Big South Fork Natl. R and Recreation Area			
Buffalo	AR	1972	94,309
Mississippi Natl. R and Recreation Area	MN	1988	53,775
New River Gorge	WV	1978	62,144
Niobrara	NE-SD	1991	NA
Ozark	MO	1964	80,790

National Wild and Scenic Rivers

Name	State	Year[1]	Acreage
Alagnak	AK	1980	30,745
Bluestone**	WV	1978	4,268
Delaware	NY-NJ-PA	1978	1,973
Great Egg Harbor	NJ	1992	NA
Missouri	NE-SD	1991	NA
Obed Wild	TN	1976	5,056
Rio Grande**	TX	1978	9,600
Saint Croix	MN-WI	1968	67,456
Upper Delaware	NY-PA	1978	75,000

National Recreation Areas

Name	State	Year[1]	Acreage
Amistad	TX	1965	58,500
Bighorn Canyon	MT-WY	1966	172,924
Chattahoochee R.	GA	1978	9,260
Chickasaw	OK	1902	9,889
Coulee Dam	WA	1946	100,390
Curecanti	CO	1965	42,114
Cuyahoga Valley	OH	1974	32,525
Delaware Water Gap	NJ-PA	1965	67,192
Gateway	NJ-NY	1972	26,579
Gauley R.	WV	1988	11,161
Glen Canyon	AZ-UT	1958	1,236,880
Golden Gate	CA	1972	73,180
Lake Chelan	WA	1968	61,887
Lake Mead	AZ-NV	1936	1,495,666
Lake Meredith	TX	1965	44,978
Ross Lake	WA	1968	117,575
Santa Monica Mts.	CA	1978	150,050
Whiskeytown	CA	1965	42,503

National Scenic Trails

Name	State	Year[1]	Acreage
Appalachian	ME to GA	1968	173,240
Natchez Trace	AL-MS-TN	1983	10,995
Potomac Heritage	MD-DC-VA-PA	1983	***

Parks (no other classification)

Name	State	Year[1]	Acreage
Catoctin Mountain	MD	1954	5,770
Constitution Gardens	DC	1978	52
Fort Washington	MD	1930	341
Greenbelt	MD	1950	1,176
National Capital	DC	1993	6,547
National Mall	DC	1933	146
Piscataway	MD	1961	4,441
Prince William Forest	VA	1948	18,572
Rock Creek	DC	1890	1,754
White House	DC	1933	18
Wolf Trap Farm Park for the Performing Arts	VA	1966	130

International Historic Sites

Name	State	Year[1]	Acreage
Saint Croix Island**	ME	1949	35

NA=Not available. *Not open to the public. **No federal facilities. ***Undetermined. (1) First designated.

Most-Visited Sites in the National Park System, 1994

Source: National Park Service, Dept. of the Interior

Attendance at all areas administered by the National Park Service in 1994 was 268,636,169 recreation visits.

Site (location)	Recreation visits	Site (location)	Recreation visits
Blue Ridge Parkway (NC, VA)	16,928,639	Yosemite National Park (CA)	3,962,117
Golden Gate National Recreation Area (CA)	14,695,771[1]	San Francisco Maritime National Historical Park (CA)	3,733,911
Lake Mead National Recreation Area (AZ, NV)	9,566,725	Castle Clinton National Monument (NY)	3,481,327
Great Smoky Mountains National Park (TN, NC)	8,628,174	Chattahoochee River National Recreation Area (GA)	3,472,026
George Washington Memorial National Parkway (VA, MD)	5,619,821	Olympic National Park (WA)	3,381,573
National Capital Parks (DC)	5,435,837	Colonial National Historical Park (VA)	3,296,242
Natchez Trace National Parkway (MS, AL, TN)	5,287,801	Cuyahoga Valley National Recreation Area (OH)	3,266,401
Cape Cod National Seashore (MA)	5,228,594	Independence National Historical Park (PA)	3,138,276
Gulf Islands National Seashore (FL, MS)	5,069,495	Yellowstone National Park (WY, MT, ID)	3,046,145
Delaware Water Gap National Recreation Area (PA, NJ)	4,773,659	Rocky Mountain National Park (CO)	2,968,450
Grand Canyon National Park (AZ)	4,364,319	Glen Canyon National Recreation Area (AZ, UT)	2,797,734
Statue of Liberty National Monument (NY, NJ)	4,252,823	Acadia National Park (ME)	2,710,749
Gateway National Recreation Area (NY, NJ)	4,192,280		

(1) Estimated.

Federal Indian Reservations and Trust Lands[1]

Source: Tiller Research, Inc., Albuquerque, NM

State	No. of reser.	Tribally owned acreage[2]	Individually owned acreage[2]	No. of persons[3]	Major tribes and/or nations
Alabama.........	1	230	0	16,506	Poarch Creek
Alaska..........	1[4]	86,773	1,265,432	85,698	Aleut, Eskimo, Athapascan,[5] Haida, Tlingit, Tsimpshian
Arizona	23	19,775,959	311,579	203,527	Navajo, Apache, Papago, Hopi, Yavapai, Pima
California	96	520,049	66,769	242,164	Hoopa, Paiute, Yurok, Karok, Cherokee
Colorado	2	764,120	2,805	27,776	Ute
Connecticut	1	1,638	0	6,654	Mashantucket Pequot
Florida	4	153,874	0	36,335	Seminole, Miccosukee, Cherokee
Idaho	4	609,622	327,301	13,780	Shoshone, Bannock, Nez Perce
Iowa	1	3,550	0	7,349	Sac and Fox
Kansas..........	4	7,219	23,763	21,965	Potawatomi, Kickapoo, Iowa
Louisiana........	3	415	0	18,541	Chitimacha, Coushatta, Tunica-Biloxi
Maine...........	3	191,511	0	5,998	Passamaquoddy, Penobscot, Maliseet
Massachusetts....	1	157	0	12,241	Wampanoag
Michigan	8	14,411	9,276	55,638	Chippewa, Potawatomi, Ottawa, Cherokee
Minnesota	14	779,138	50,338	49,909	Chippewa, Sioux
Mississippi	1	20,486	0	8,525	Choctaw
Montana.........	7	2,663,385	2,911,450	47,679	Blackfeet, Crow, Sioux, Assiniboine, Cheyenne
Nebraska........	3	23,792	43,208	12,410	Omaha, Winnebago, Santee Sioux
Nevada	19	1,147,088	78,529	19,637	Paiute, Shoshone, Washoe
New Mexico......	25	7,252,326	630,293	134,355	Apache, Navajo, Pueblo
New York........	8	118,199	0	62,651	Seneca, Mohawk, Onondaga, Oneida
North Carolina	1	56,509	0	80,155	Cherokee, Lumbee
North Dakota	3	214,006	627,289	25,917	Sioux, Chippewa, Mandan, Arikara, Hidatsa
Oklahoma	36[6]	96,839	1,000,165	252,420	Cherokee, Creek, Choctaw, Chickasaw, Osage, Cheyenne, Arapahoe, Kiowa, Comanche
Oregon..........	7	660,367	135,053	38,496	Warm Springs, Wasco, Paiute, Umatilla, Siletz
Rhode Island	1	1,800	0	4,071	Narragansett
South Carolina....	1	639	0	8,246	Catawba
South Dakota.....	9	2,399,531	2,121,188	50,575	Sioux
Texas...........	3	4,726	0	65,877	Alabama-Coushatta, Tiwa, Kickapoo
Utah............	4	2,286,448	32,838	24,283	Ute, Goshute, Southern Paiute, Navajo
Washington	27	2,250,731	467,785	81,483	Yakama, Lummi, Quinault
Wisconsin	11	338,097	80,345	39,387	Chippewa, Oneida, Winnebago
Wyoming	1	1,958,095	101,537	9,479	Shoshone, Arapahoe

(1) In Oct. 1993, the Bureau of Indian Affairs of the U.S. Dept. of the Interior published in the *Federal Register* (vol. 58, no. 202, pp. 54364-69) a comprehensive listing of 552 "Indian Entities Recognized and Eligible To Receive Services From the United States Bureau of Indian Affairs" (328 in the conterminous 48 states, 224 in Alaska). The term *Indian entities* includes Indian tribes, bands, villages, groups, and pueblos; also included are Eskimo and Aleut villages and tribes. All such entities have a government-to-government relationship with the U.S. Some reservation boundaries transcend state lines (e.g., Navajo, which is in Arizona, New Mexico, and Utah). For the purpose of "Number of Reservations," such reservations are counted in the state where their population is predominant and/or tribal headquarters are located. (2) Information provided by the Bureau of Indian Affairs; data current as of 1990. Acreages refer only to lands that are either owned by the tribes and individual members or that are held in trust by the U.S. government. Many of these parcels are located off reservations. Not all lands within reservation boundaries are necessarily trust lands. Many are privately owned by tribes, tribal members, or non-Indians. Others are the property of various governmental agencies. (3) Total Native American (Indian, Eskimo, or Aleut) population in each state with reservation/trust lands, including those persons living outside the Bureau of Indian Affairs service area. Populations as of 1990. (4) The only federally recognized reservation in Alaska is the Annette Island Reserve. In all other cases, the U.S. government's relationship to Native Americans in Alaska is set out by the Alaska Native Claims Settlement Act of 1971. The act provided for the establishment of regional and village corporations to conduct business for profit and nonprofit purposes; these corporations are also landowners. There are 12 regional corporations, each with organized village corporations, plus one regional corporation for Alaska Natives outside the state. (5) Aleuts and Eskimos are racially and linguistically related. Athapascans are related to the Navajo and Apache Indians. (6) There are 36 tribal entities in Oklahoma, each of which owns land in the state. Because of the way in which the state of Oklahoma was formed out of the Oklahoma and Indian territories, the reservation status of land in the state is frequently disputed in both civil and criminal proceedings.

American Indian Population

Source: Bureau of the Census, U.S. Dept. of Commerce, 1990 Census

The Bureau of the Census figures reflect personal self-identification and therefore do not necessarily reflect any designation of a federally or state-recognized tribe.

State	Total	State	Total	State	Total	State	Total	State	Total	State	Total
AL	16,312	FL	35,461	LA	18,361	NE	12,344	OK	252,089	VT	1,650
AK	31,245	GA	12,926	ME	5,945	NV	19,377	OR	37,443	VA	14,893
AZ	203,009	HI	4,738	MD	12,601	NH	2,075	PA	14,210	WA	77,627
AR	12,641	ID	13,594	MA	11,857	NJ	14,500	RI	3,987	WV	2,365
CA	236,078	IL	20,970	MI	56,131	NM	134,097	SC	8,049	WI	38,986
CO	27,271	IN	12,453	MN	49,392	NY	60,855	SD	50,501	WY	9,426
CT	6,472	IA	7,217	MS	8,435	NC	79,825	TN	9,859	**Total**	
DE	1,982	KS	21,767	MO	19,508	ND	25,870	TX	64,349	**U.S.**	**1,878,285**
DC	1,432	KY	5,614	MT	47,524	OH	19,859	UT	24,093		

WORLD HISTORY

Prehistory: Our Ancestors Take Over

Homo sapiens. The precise origins of *Homo sapiens,* the species to which all humans belong, are subject to broad speculation based on a small number of fossils, on genetic and anatomical studies, and on the geological record. Most scientists agree, however, that humans evolved from apelike primate ancestors in a process that began millions of years ago.

Current theories trace the first hominid (humanlike primate) to Africa, where 2 lines of hominids appeared 5 to 7 million years ago. One was *Australopithecus,* a social animal, who lived from perhaps 4 to 3 million years ago, and then apparently became extinct. The other was a human line, *Homo habilis,* a large-brained specimen that walked upright and had a dextrous hand. *Homo habilis* appeared some 2.5 million years ago, lived in semipermanent camps, and had a food-gathering and sharing economy.

Homo erectus, our nearest ancestor, appeared in Africa perhaps 1.75 million years ago and began spreading into Asia and Europe soon after. It had a fairly large brain and a skeletal structure similar to ours. *Homo erectus* learned to control fire and probably had primitive language skills. The final brain development to *Homo sapiens* and then to our subspecies *Homo sapiens sapiens* occurred between 500,000 and 50,000 years ago, either in one place—probably Africa—or virtually simultaneously and independently in different places in Africa, Europe, and Asia. All modern races are unquestionably members of the subspecies *Homo sapiens sapiens.*

The spread of humankind into the remaining habitable continents probably took place near the end of the last Ice Age: from Asia to the Americas, across a land bridge, and to Australia, across the Timor Straits.

Earliest cultures. A variety of cultural modes—in toolmaking, diet, shelter, and possibly social arrangements and spiritual expression—arose as early humankind adapted to different geographic and climatic zones.

Archeologists recognize 3 basic toolmaking traditions as arising and often coexisting from one million years ago to the near past: the *chopper tradition,* found largely in E Asia, producing crude chopping tools and simple flake tools; the *flake tradition,* found in Africa and W Europe, producing a variety of small cutting and flaking tools; and the *biface* tradition, found in all of Africa, W and S Europe, and S Asia, producing pointed hand axes chipped on both faces. Later biface sites yield more refined axes and a variety of other tools, weapons, and ornaments using bone, antler, and wood as well as stone.

Only sketchy evidence remains for the stages in increasing human control over the environment. Traces of 400,000-year-old covered wood shelters have been found at Nice, France. Scraping tools at Neanderthal sites (200,000-30,000 BC in Europe, N Africa, the Middle East, and Central Asia) suggest the treatment of skins for clothing. Sites from all parts of the world show seasonal migration patterns and exploitation of a wide range of plant and animal food sources.

Painting and decoration, for which there is evidence at the Nice site, flourished, along with stone and ivory sculpture, from 25,000 years ago: more than 200 caves in Europe, mainly in S France (Lascaux) and N Spain (Altamira), show remarkable examples of wall painting. Other examples have been found in Africa. Proto-religious rites are suggested by these works, by evidence of ritual cannibalism by Peking Man (500,000 BC), and by evidence of ritual burial with medicinal plants and flowers by Neanderthals at Shanidar in Iraq.

The Neolithic Revolution. Some time after 10,000 BC, among widely separated human communities, a series of dramatic technological and social changes occurred that are summed up as the Neolithic Revolution. The cultivation of previously wild plants encouraged the growth of permanent settlements. Animals were domesticated as a work force and a food source. The manufacture of pottery and cloth began. These techniques permitted a huge increase in world population and in human control over the earth.

No region can safely claim priority as the "inventor" of these techniques. Dispersed sites in Cen. and S America, SE Europe, and the Middle East show roughly contemporaneous (10,000-8000 BC) evidence of one or another "neolithic" trait. Dates near 6000-3000 BC have been given for E and S Asian, W European, and sub-Saharan African neolithic remains. The variety of crops —field grains, rice, maize, and roots—and the varying mix of other traits suggest that the revolution occurred independently in all these regions.

History Begins: 4000-1000 BC

Near Eastern cradle. If history began with writing, the first chapter opened in Mesopotamia, the Tigris-Euphrates river valley. The Sumerians used clay tablets with pictographs to keep records after 4000 BC. A cuneiform (wedge-shaped) script evolved by 3000 BC as a full syllabic alphabet. Neighboring peoples adapted the script to their own language.

Sumerian life centered, from 4000 BC, on large cities (Eridu, Ur, Uruk, Nippur, Kish, and Lagash) organized around temples and priestly bureaucracies, with the surrounding plains watered by vast irrigation works and worked with traction plows. Sailboats, wheeled vehicles, potter's wheels, and kilns were used. Copper was smelted and tempered in Sumeria from c 4000 BC, and bronze was produced not long after. Ores, as well as precious stones and metals, were obtained through long-distance ship and caravan trade. Iron was used from c 2000 BC. Improved ironworking, developed partly by the Hittites, became widespread by 1200 BC.

Sumerian political primacy passed among cities and their kingly dynasties. Semitic-speaking peoples, with cultures derived from the Sumerian, founded a succession of dynasties that ruled in Mesopotamia and neighboring areas for most of 1800 years; among them were the **Akkadians** (first under Sargon I c 2350 BC), the Amorites (whose laws, codified by **Hammurabi,** c 1792-1750 BC, have biblical parallels), and the Assyrians, with interludes of rule by the Hittites, Kassites, and Mitanni, all possibly Indo-Europeans. The political and cultural center of gravity shifted NW with each successive empire.

Mesopotamian learning, maintained by scribes and preserved by successive rulers in vast libraries, was not abstract or theoretical. Algebraic and geometric problems could be solved on a practical basis in construction, commerce, and administration. Systematic lists of astronomical phenomena, plants, animals, and stones were kept; medical texts listed ailments and their herbal cures.

The Sumerians worshiped anthropomorphic gods representing natural forces: Anu, god of heaven, and Enlil (Ea), god of water. Epic poetry related these and other gods in a hierarchy. Sacrifices were made at **ziggurats**—huge stepped temples. Gods were thought to control all events, which could be foretold using oracular materials. This religious pattern persisted into the 1st millennium BC.

The Syria-Palestine area, site of some of the earliest urban remains (Jericho, 7000 BC), and of the recently uncovered **Ebla** civilization (fl 2500 BC), experienced Egyptian cultural and political influence along with Mesopotamian. The **Phoenician** coast was an active commercial center. A phonetic alphabet was invented here before 1600 BC. It became the ancestor of all European, Middle Eastern, Indian, SE Asian, Ethiopian, and many other alphabets.

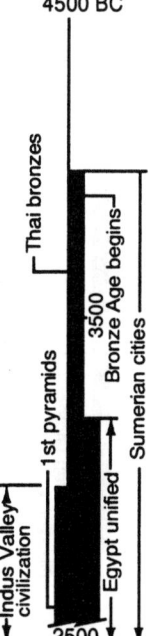

Timeline (left margin, 2500 BC to 1000 BC):

- Ebla civilization
- Bronze-age Minoan civilization emerges on Crete
- Egyptian literature begins
- Peruvian neolithic ceremonial centers
- Phonetic alphabet invented before 1600
- Hammurabi — 1750
- Aryans invade India
- Chinese Shang dynasty
- Mt. Sinai revelations to Moses
- Mexican Olmec civilization established

2500 BC — **1000 BC**

Egypt. Agricultural villages along the Nile were united by 3300 BC into 2 kingdoms, Upper and Lower Egypt, unified (c 3100 BC) under the Pharaoh Menes. A national bureaucracy supervised construction of canals and monuments (**pyramids** starting 2700 BC). Control over Nubia to the S was asserted beginning 2600 BC.

Brilliant Old Kingdom Period achievements in architecture, sculpture, and painting, which reached their height during the 3d and 4th Dynasties, set the standards and forms for all subsequent Egyptian civilization and are still admired. **Hieroglyphic writing** appeared by 3200 BC, recording a sophisticated literature that included religious writings, philosophies, history, and science.

An ordered hierarchy of gods, including totemistic animal elements, was served by a powerful priesthood in Memphis. The pharaoh was identified with the falcon god Horus. Other trends were the belief in an afterlife and the short-lived quasimonotheistic reforms of the pharaoh **Akhenaton** (c 1379-1362 BC).

After a period of dominance by Semitic Hyksos from Asia (c 1700-1550 BC), the New Kingdom established an empire in Syria. Egypt became increasingly embroiled in Asiatic wars and diplomacy. Conquered by Persia in 525 BC, it eventually faded away as an independent culture.

India. An urban civilization with a so-far-undeciphered writing system stretched across the Indus Valley and along the Arabian Sea c 3000-1500 BC. Major sites are Harappa and **Mohenjo-Daro** in Pakistan, well-planned geometric cities with underground sewers and vast granaries. The entire region (600,000 sq mi) may have been ruled as a single state. Bronze was used, and arts and crafts were highly developed. Religious life apparently took the form of fertility cults.

Indus civilization was probably in decline when it was destroyed by **Aryan invaders** from the NW, speaking an Indo-European language from which most of the languages of Pakistan, N India, and Bangladesh descend. Led by a warrior aristocracy whose legendary deeds are in the **Rig Veda**, the Aryans spread E and S, bringing their pantheon of sky gods, elaborate priestly (Brahman) ritual, and the beginnings of the caste system; local customs and beliefs were assimilated by the conquerors.

Europe. On Crete, the Bronze Age **Minoan civilization** emerged c 2500 BC. A prosperous economy and richly decorative art was supported by seaborne commerce. Mycenae and other cities in mainland Greece and in Asia Minor (e.g., **Troy**) preserved elements of the culture until c 1200 BC. Cretan Linear A script (c 2000-1700 BC) remains undeciphered; Linear B script (c 1300-1200 BC) records an early Greek dialect.

Unclear is the possible connection between Mycenaean monumental stonework and the great megalithic monuments and tombs of W Europe, Iberia, and Malta (c 4000-1500 BC).

China. Proto-Chinese neolithic cultures had long covered N and SE China when the first large political state was organized in the north by the **Shang dynasty** (c 1523 BC). Shang kings called themselves Sons of Heaven, and they presided over a cult of human and animal sacrifice to ancestors and nature gods. The Chou dynasty, starting c 1027 BC, expanded the area of the Son of Heaven's dominion, but feudal states exercised most temporal power.

A writing system with 2,000 characters was already in use under the Shang, with **pictographs** later supplemented by phonetic characters. Many of its principles and symbols, despite changes in spoken Chinese, were preserved in later writing systems.

Technical advances allowed urban specialists to create fine ceramic and jade products, and bronze casting after 1500 BC was the most advanced in the world. Bronze artifacts have recently been discovered in northern Thailand dating from 3600 BC, hundreds of years before similar Middle Eastern finds.

Americas. **Olmecs** settled (1500 BC) on the Gulf coast of Mexico and soon developed the first civilization in the western hemisphere. Temple cities and huge stone sculpture date from 1200 BC. A rudimentary calendar and writing system existed. Olmec religion, centering on a jaguar god, and art forms influenced all later Meso-American cultures.

Classical Era of Old World Civilizations

Greece. After a period of decline during the Dorian Greek invasions (1200-1000 BC), Greece and the Aegean area developed a unique civilization. Drawing upon Mycenaean traditions, Mesopotamian learning (weights and measures, lunisolar calendar, astronomy, musical scales), the Phoenician alphabet (modified for Greek), and Egyptian art, the revived **Greek city-states** saw a rich elaboration of intellectual life. Homer's epics the *Iliad* and the *Odyssey* were written in the 8th cent. BC. Long-range commerce was aided by metal coinage (introduced by the Lydians in Asia Minor before 700 BC); colonies were founded around the Mediterranean (Cumae in Italy in 760 BC; Massalia in France c 600 BC) and Black Sea shores.

Philosophy, starting with Ionian speculation on the nature of matter and the universe (Thales, c 634-546 BC) and including mathematical speculation (Pythagoras, c 580-c 500 BC), culminated in Athens in the rationalist idealism of **Plato** (c 428-347 BC), a disciple of **Socrates** (c 469-399 BC); the latter was sentenced to death for alleged impiety. **Aristotle** (384-322 BC) united all fields of study in his system. The arts were highly valued. Architecture culminated in the **Parthenon** (438 BC) in Athens by Phidias (fl 490-430 BC) with his sculpture of Athena; poetry and drama (Aeschylus, 525-456 BC) thrived. Male beauty and strength, a chief artistic theme, were enhanced at the gymnasium and celebrated at the national games at Olympia. Ruled by local tyrants or oligarchies, the Greeks were never politically united, but they managed to resist inclusion in the Persian Empire (Darius defeated at Marathon 490 BC, Xerxes at Salamis, Plataea 479 BC). Local warfare was common; the **Peloponnesian Wars** (431-404 BC) ended in Sparta's victory over Athens. Greek political power waned, but classical Greek cultural forms spread throughout the ancient world from the Atlantic to India.

Hebrews. Nomadic Hebrew tribes entered Canaan before 1200 BC, settling among other Semitic peoples speaking the same language. They brought from the desert a **monotheistic** faith said to have been revealed to Abraham in Canaan c 1800 BC and to Moses at Mt. Sinai c 1250 BC, after the Hebrews' escape from bondage in Egypt. David (ruled 1000-961 BC) and Solomon (ruled 961-922 BC) united the Hebrews in a kingdom that briefly dominated the area. Phoenicians to the N established colonies around the E and W Mediterranean (Carthage, c 814 BC) and sailed into the Atlantic.

(continues on p. 554)

Paleontology: The History of Life

All dates are approximate, and are subject to change based on new fossil finds or new dating techniques; but the sequence of events is generally accepted. Dates are in years before the present.

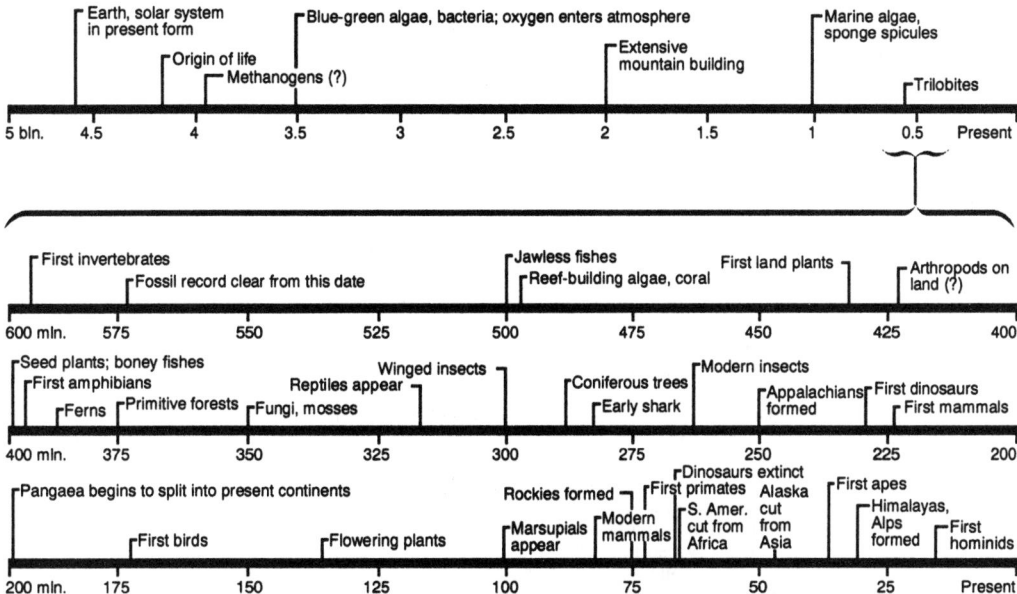

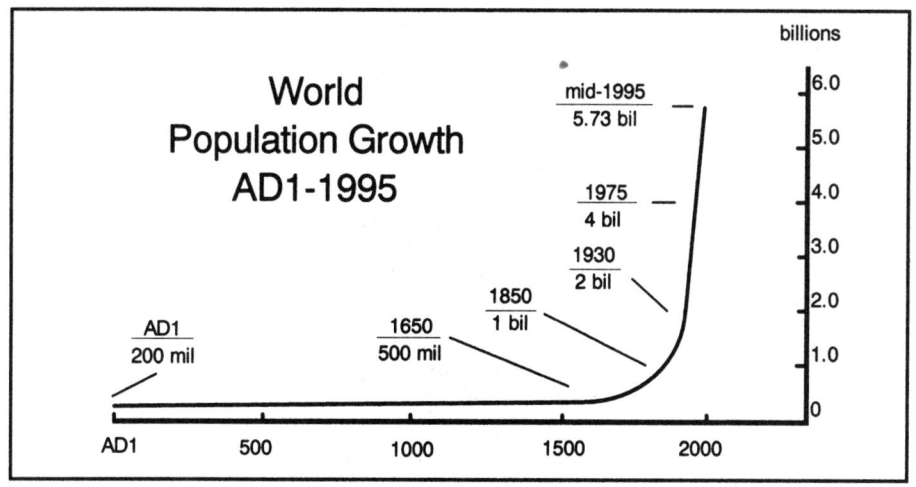

1000 BC

A temple in Jerusalem became the national religious center, with sacrifices performed by a hereditary priesthood. Polytheistic influences, especially of the fertility cult of Baal, were opposed by **prophets** (Elijah, Amos, Isaiah).

Divided into **two kingdoms** after Solomon, the Hebrews were unable to resist the revived Assyrian empire, which conquered Israel, the N kingdom in 722 BC. Judah, the S kingdom, was conquered in 586 BC by the Babylonians under Nebuchadnezzar II. But with the fixing of most of the biblical canon by the mid-4th cent. BC and the emergence of rabbis, Judaism successfully survived the loss of Hebrew autonomy. A Jewish kingdom was revived under the Hasmoneans (168-42 BC).

China. During the **Eastern Chou** dynasty (770-256 BC), Chinese culture spread E to the sea and S to the Yangtze R. Large feudal states on the periphery of the empire contended for preeminence, but continued to recognize the Son of Heaven (king), who retained a purely ritual role enriched with courtly music and dance. In the Age of Warring States (403-221 BC), when the first sections of the **Great Wall** were built, the Ch'in state in the W gained supremacy and finally united all of China.

Iron tools entered China c 500 BC, and casting techniques were advanced, aiding agriculture. Peasants owned their land and owed civil and military service to nobles. Cities grew in number and size, although barter remained the chief trade medium.

Intellectual ferment among noble scribes and officials produced the Classical Age of Chinese literature and philosophy. **Confucius** (551-479 BC) urged a restoration of a supposedly harmonious social order of the past through proper conduct in accordance with one's station and through filial and ceremonial piety. The *Analects* attributed to him are revered throughout E Asia. **Mencius** (d 289 BC) added the view that the Mandate of Heaven can be removed from an unjust dynasty. The Legalists sought to curb the supposed natural wickedness of people through new institutions and harsh laws; they aided the Ch'in rise to power. The Naturalists emphasized the balance of opposites—yin, yang—in the world. **Taoists** sought mystical knowledge through meditation and disengagement.

India. The political and cultural center of India shifted from the Indus to the Ganges River Valley. Buddhism, Jainism, and mystical revisions of orthodox Vedism all developed c 500-300 BC. The *Upanishads,* last part of the *Veda,* urged escape from the physical world. Vedism remained the preserve of the Brahman caste. In contrast, **Buddhism,** founded by Siddarta Gautama (c 563-c 483 BC)—Buddha ("Enlightened One")—appealed to merchants in the urban centers and took hold at first (and most lastingly) on the geographic fringes of Indian civilization. The classic Indian epics were composed in this era: the **Ramayana** perhaps c 300 BC, the **Mahabharata** over a period starting 400 BC.

Northern India was divided into a large number of monarchies and aristocratic republics, probably derived from tribal groupings, when the Magadha kingdom was formed in Bihar c 542 BC. It soon became the dominant power. The **Maurya dynasty,** founded by Chandragupta c 321 BC, expanded the kingdom, uniting most of N India in a centralized bureaucratic empire. The third Mauryan king, **Asoka** (ruled c 274-236 BC), conquered most of the subcontinent: He converted to Buddhism and inscribed its tenets on pillars throughout India. He downplayed the caste system and tried to end expensive sacrificial rites.

Before its final decline in India, Buddhism developed into a popular worship of heavenly Bodhisattvas ("enlightened beings"); and produced a refined architecture (the Great Stupa [shrine] at Sanchi, 100 AD) and sculpture (Gandhara reliefs 1-400 AD).

Persia. Aryan peoples (Persians, Medes) dominated the area of present Iran by the beginning of the 1st millennium BC. The prophet **Zoroaster** (born c 628 BC) introduced a dualistic religion in which the forces of good (Ahura Mazda, "Lord of Wisdom") and evil (Ahriam) battle for dominance; individuals are judged by their actions and earn damnation or salvation. Zoroaster's hymns (*Gathas*) are included in the *Avesta,* the Zoroastrian scriptures. A version of this faith became the established religion of the Persian Empire and probably influenced later monotheistic religions.

Africa. Nubia, periodically occupied by Egypt since about 2600 BC, ruled Egypt c 750-661 BC and survived as an independent Egyptianized kingdom (**Kush;** capital Meroe) for 1,000 years. The Iron Age Nok culture flourished c 500 BC-200 AD on the Benue Plateau of **Nigeria.**

Americas. The Chavin culture controlled N Peru from 900 BC to 200 BC. Its ceremonial centers, featuring the jaguar god, survived long after. Chavin architecture, ceramics, and textiles influenced other Peruvian cultures.

Mayan civilization began to develop in Central America as early as 1500 BC.

Great Empires Unite the Civilized World: 400 BC - AD 400

Persia and Alexander the Great. Cyrus, ruler of a small kingdom in Persia from 559 BC, united the Persians and Medes within 10 years and conquered Asia Minor and Babylonia in another 10. His son Cambyses followed by Darius (ruled 522-486 BC) added vast lands to the E and N as far as the Indus Valley and Central Asia, as well as Egypt and Thrace. The whole empire was ruled by an international bureaucracy and army, with Persians holding the chief positions. The resources and styles of all the subject civilizations were exploited to create a rich syncretic art.

The kingdom of Macedon, which under Phillip II dominated the Greek world and Egypt, passed to his son **Alexander** in 336 BC. Within 13 years, Alexander conquered all the Persian dominions. Imbued by his tutor Aristotle with Greek ideals, Alexander encouraged Greek colonization, and Greek-style cities were founded. After his death in 323 BC, wars of succession divided the empire into 3 parts—**Macedon,** Egypt (ruled by the **Ptolemies**), and the **Seleucid** Empire.

In the ensuing 300 years (the **Hellenistic Era**), a cosmopolitan Greek-oriented culture permeated the ancient world from W Europe to the borders of India, absorbing native elites everywhere.

Hellenistic philosophy stressed the private individual's search for happiness. The Cynics followed Diogenes (c 372-287 BC), who stressed self-sufficiency and restriction of desires and expressed contempt for luxury and social convention. Zeno (c 335-c 263 BC) and the Stoics exalted reason, identified it with virtue, and counseled an ascetic disregard for misfortune. The Epicureans tried to build lives of moderate pleasure without political or emotional involvement. Hellenistic arts imitated life realistically, especially in sculpture and literature (comedies of Menander, 342-292 BC).

(continues on p. 556)

Chavin dynasty begins in Peru

Hebrew kingdom divided

Carthage established

Chou dynasty begins in China
800

Nubia begins rule of Egypt

Metal coins in Asia Minor

Isaiah d.

Zoroaster b.

Pythagoras b.

Indian Buddhism, Jainism begin
Confucius b.   600

Siddarta b.

Aeschylus b.

Socrates b.

Plato b.

Parthenon

Peloponnesian Wars

400 BC

The Seven Wonders of the Ancient World

These ancient works of art and architecture were considered awe-inspiring in splendor and/or size by the Greek and Roman world of the Alexandrian epoch. Later Classical writers disagreed as to which works made up the list of Wonders, but the following were usually included.

The Pyramids of Egypt: The only surviving Wonder, these monumental structures of masonry located at Giza on the W bank of the Nile R above Cairo were built from c 2700 to 2500 BC as royal tombs. Three—Khufu (Cheops), Khafra (Chephren), and Menkaura (Mycerimus)—were often grouped as the first Wonder of the World. The largest, **The Great Pyramid of Khufu,** is a solid mass of limestone blocks covering 13 acres. It is estimated to contain 2.3 million blocks of stone, the stones themselves averaging 2½ tons and some weighing 30 tons. Its construction reputedly took 100,000 laborers 20 years.

The Hanging Gardens of Babylon: These gardens were laid out on a brick terrace about 400 ft square and 75 ft above the ground. To irrigate the trees, shrubs, and flowers, screws were turned to lift water from the Euphrates R. The gardens were probably built by King Nebuchadnezzar II about 600 BC. **The Walls of Babylon,** long, thick, and made of colorfully glazed brick, were considered by some among the Seven Wonders.

The Statue of Zeus (Jupiter) at Olympia: This statue of the king of the gods showed him seated on a throne. His flesh was made of ivory, his robe and ornaments of gold. Reputedly 40 ft high, the statue was made by Phidias and was placed in the great temple of Zeus in the sacred grove of Olympia about 457 BC.

The Colossus of Rhodes: A bronze statue of the sun god Helios, the Colossus was worked on for 12 years in the third century BC by the sculptor Chares. It was probably 120 ft high. A symbol of the city of Rhodes at its height, the statue stood on a promontory overlooking the harbor.

The Temple of Artemis (Diana) at Ephesus: This largest and most complex temple of ancient times was built about 550 BC and was made of marble except for its tile-covered wooden roof. It was begun in honor of a non-Hellenic goddess who later became identified with the Greek goddess of the same name. Ephesus was one of the greatest of the Ionian cities.

The Mausoleum at Halicarnassus: The source of our word *mausoleum*, this marble tomb was built in what is now SE Turkey by Artemisia for her husband Mausolus, king of Caria in Asia Minor, who died in 353 BC. About 135 ft high, the tomb was adorned with the works of 4 sculptors.

The Pharos (Lighthouse) of Alexandria: This structure was designed about 270 BC, during the reign of King Ptolemy II, by the Greek architect Sostratos. Estimates of its height range from 200 to 600 ft.

The Seven Wonders of the Middle Ages

These sites and structures were considered significant by the people of the Middle Ages (from c 5th cent. to c 15th cent.).

The Colosseum of Rome: Erected by the Roman emperor Vespasian, this amphitheater was dedicated by his son and successor Titus in AD 80. It could seat about 50,000 persons and was used for Roman spectacles and contests. It is now in ruins.

The Catacombs of Alexandria, Egypt: This network of subterranean chambers and galleries was used for burial purposes by peoples of the ancient world and as refuge for early Christians.

The Great Wall of China: Begun c 221 BC and completed c 204 BC, this fortification finally reached a length of about 1500 mi. It is built of earth and stone and is faced with brick in the E parts. On average, it is about 20 ft thick at the base and tapers to some 12 ft at the top. The height averages 25 ft, exclusive of the crenellated parapets. Several hundred miles of the Great Wall remain intact in the E reaches.

Stonehenge: This prehistoric ritual monument is situated on Salisbury Plain, N of Salisbury, England, and dates from the late Stone and early Bronze ages (c. 3000-1000 BC). The monument itself consists of 4 concentric ranges of stones. Grouped around the main structure are a number of barrows, some of which contain chips of a blue stone similar to that found in the concentric ranges. In 1964, an American astronomer Gerald S. Hawkins concluded that Stonehenge functioned as a means of predicting the positions of the sun and moon relative to the earth, and thereby the seasons, and perhaps also as a simple daily calendar.

The Leaning Tower of Pisa: Construction on this bell tower began in 1174 but was suspended when the builders became aware that the shallow foundation would be inadequate in the soft soil. The structure was nevertheless complete by the second half of the 14th cent. The Leaning Tower is cylindrical in shape, with 8 arcaded stories, and today slants more than 14 ft from the perpendicular.

The Porcelain Tower of Nanking: This tower in China was built to a height of 260 ft during the 15th cent. and was destroyed in 1853.

The Mosque of Hagia Sophia: Built in the 6th cent., this imposing structure was originally a church (Holy Wisdom). It was converted to a mosque in the 15th cent. and is now a museum.

The Seven Natural Wonders of the World

This list names areas of geological significance and was compiled by world travelers during recent centuries.

Mt. Everest: The highest peak in the world, Mt. Everest is in S central Asia, in the Himalaya range, on the frontier of Nepal and Tibet. Controversy surrounds its actual elevation. A 1954 Indian government survey placed it at 29,028 ft above sea level; however, more recent surveys cast some doubt on this figure. The summit was first scaled in 1953.

Victoria Falls: This 400 ft waterfall is on the Zambezi R in S central Africa on the border between Zimbabwe and Zambia. The river here is about 1 mi wide. A railroad bridge, completed in 1905, spans the gorge below the falls.

The Grand Canyon: This exceptionally deep (more than 1 mi) and extremely beautiful steep-walled chasm in NW Arizona is about 217 mi long and up to 18 mi wide. Excavated by the Colorado R, it is of relatively recent origin; apparently erosion began a little more than a million years ago. The canyon contains towering buttes, mesas, and valleys within its main gorge.

The Great Barrier Reef: This chain of coral reefs is in the Coral Sea, off the E coast of Queensland, Australia. It is the largest known deposit of coral and extends in a NW direction more than 1200 mi. The reef serves as a barrier to disturbances in the Coral Sea, thus affording a sheltered passage for ships.

The Northern Lights: Also known as aurora borealis, the northen lights consists of rapidly shifting patches and dancing columns of light of various hues. The aurora assumes an endless variety of forms, including the arch, the band, filaments and streamers at right angles to the arch or band, the corona, clouds, the glow, and curtains, fans, flames, or streamers of various shapes.

Paricutin: This volcano is one of the world's youngest. It was discovered in 1943 west of Mexico City.

The Harbor at Rio de Janeiro, Brazil (as seen from the sea): One of the world's most beautiful natural harbors, the harbor at Rio is surrounded by low mountain ranges whose spurs extend almost to the waterside, and thus divide the city.

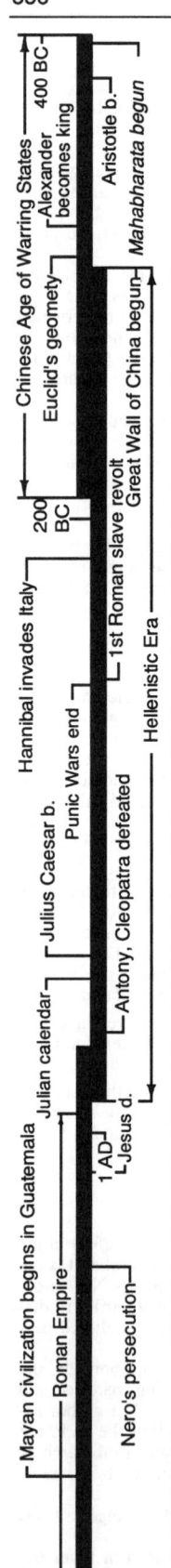

The sciences thrived, especially at Alexandria, where the Ptolemies financed a great library and museum. Fields of study included mathematics (**Euclid's** geometry, c 300 BC; Menelaus non-Euclidean geometry, c 100 AD); astronomy (heliocentric theory of Aristarchus, 310-230 BC; Julian calendar, 45 BC; Ptolemy's *Almagest*, c 150 AD); geography (world map of Eratosthenes, 276-194 BC); hydraulics (**Archimedes**, 287-212 BC); medicine (Galen, 130-200 AD); and chemistry. Inventors refined uses for siphons, valves, gears, springs, screws, levers, cams, and pulleys.

A restored Persian empire under the **Parthians** (N Iranian tribesmen) controlled the eastern Hellenistic world from 250 BC to 229 AD. The Parthians and the succeeding Sassanian dynasty (c 224-651 AD) fought with Rome periodically. The **Sassanians** revived Zoroastrianism as a state religion and patronized a nationalistic artistic and scholarly renaissance.

Rome. The city of Rome was founded, according to legend, by Romulus in 753 BC. Through military expansion and colonization, and by granting citizenship to conquered tribes, the city annexed all of Italy south of the Po in the 100-year period before 268 BC. The Latin and other Italic tribes were annexed first, followed by the Etruscans (founders of a great civilization, N of Rome) and the Greek colonies in the S. With a large standing army and reserve forces of several hundred thousand, Rome was able to defeat Carthage in the 3 **Punic Wars** (264-241, 218-201, 149-146 BC), despite the invasion of Italy (218 BC) by Hannibal, thus gaining Sicily and territory in Spain and North Africa.

New provinces were added in the E, as Rome exploited local disputes to conquer Greece and Asia Minor in the 2d century BC, and Egypt in the 1st (after the defeat and suicide of **Antony and Cleopatra**, 30 BC). All the Mediterranean civilized world up to the disputed Parthian border was now Roman and remained so for 500 years. Less civilized regions were added to the Empire: Gaul (conquered by Julius Caesar, 58-51 BC), Britain (43 AD), and Dacia NE of the Danube (107 AD).

The original aristocratic republican government, with democratic features added in the 5th and 4th centuries BC, deteriorated under the pressures of empire and class conflict (**Gracchus** brothers, social reformers, murdered in 133 BC and 121 BC; slave revolts in 135 BC and 73 BC). After a series of civil wars (Marius vs. Sulla 88-82 BC, Caesar vs. Pompey 49-45 BC, triumvirate vs. Caesar's assassins 44-43 BC, Antony vs. Octavian 32-30 BC), the empire came under the rule of a deified monarch (first emperor, **Augustus**, 27 BC-14 AD). Provincials (nearly all granted citizenship by Caracalla, 212 AD) came to dominate the army and civil service. Traditional Roman law, systematized and interpreted by independent jurists, and local self-rule in provincial cities were supplanted by a vast tax-collecting bureaucracy in the 3d and 4th centuries. The legal rights of women, children, and slaves were strengthened.

Roman innovations in **civil engineering** included water mills, windmills, and rotary mills and the use of cement that hardened under water. Monumental architecture (baths, theaters, temples) relied on the arch and the dome. The network of roads (some still standing) stretched 53,000 mi, passing through mountain tunnels as long as 3.5 mi. Aqueducts brought water to cities; underground sewers removed waste.

Unlike architecture, Roman art and literature were derivative of Greek models. Innovations were made in sculpture (naturalistic busts and equestrian statues), decorative wall painting (as at Pompeii), satire (Juvenal, 60-127 AD), history (Tacitus, 56-120 AD), prose romance (Petronius, d 66 AD). Gladiatorial contests dominated mass public amusements, which were supported by the state.

India. The **Gupta** monarchs reunited N India c 320 AD. Their peaceful and prosperous reign saw a revival of Hindu religious thought and Brahman power. The old Vedic traditions were combined with devotion to a plethora of indigenous deities (who were seen as manifestations of Vedic gods). **Caste lines** were reinforced, and Buddhism gradually disappeared. The art (often erotic), architecture, and literature of the period, patronized by the Gupta court, are considered among India's finest achievements (Kalidasa, poet and dramatist, fl. c 400 AD). Mathematical innovations included the use of the zero and decimal numbers. Invasions by White Huns from the NW destroyed the empire c 550.

Rich cultures also developed in S India in this era. Emotional Tamil religious poetry aided the Hindu revival. The Pallava kingdom controlled much of S India c 350-880 and helped spread Indian civilization to SE Asia.

China. The Ch'in ruler Shih Huang Ti (ruled 221-210 BC), known as the First Emperor, centralized political authority in China, standardized the written language, laws, weights, measures, and coinage, and conducted a census, but tried to destroy most philosophical texts. The **Han dynasty** (202 BC-220 AD) instituted the Mandarin bureaucracy, which lasted for 2,000 years. Local officials were selected by examination in the Confucian classics and trained at the imperial university and at provincial schools. The invention of **paper** facilitated this bureaucratic system. Agriculture was promoted, but the peasants bore most of the tax burden. Irrigation was improved; water clocks and sundials were used; astronomy and mathematics thrived; and landscape painting was perfected.

With the expansion S and W (to nearly the present borders of today's China), trade was opened with India, SE Asia, and the Middle East, over sea and caravan routes. Indian missionaries brought Mahayana Buddhism to China by the 1st century AD and spawned a variety of sects. Taoism was revived and merged with popular superstitions. Taoist and Buddhist monasteries and convents multiplied in the turbulent centuries after the collapse of the Han dynasty.

Monotheism Emerges: 1-750 AD

Christianity. In the Roman Empire polytheism was practiced, and religions indigenous to particular Middle Eastern nations became international in the first 3 centuries of the Roman Empire. Roman citizens worshiped **Isis** of Egypt, **Mithras** of Persia, **Demeter** of Greece, and the great mother **Cybele** of Phrygia. Their cults centered on mysteries (secret ceremonies) and the promise of an afterlife, symbolized by the death and rebirth of the god. The Jews living in the empire preserved their monotheistic religion—Judaism, the world's oldest (c 1200 BC) continuous religion. Its teachings are contained in the Bible (the Old Testament). First-century Judaism embraced several sects, including the **Sadducees**, mostly drawn from the Temple priesthood, who were culturally Hellenized; the **Pharisees**, who upheld the full range of traditional customs and practices as of equal weight to literal scriptural law and elaborated synagogue worship; and the **Essenes**, an ascetic, millennarian sect. Messianic fervor led to repeated,

unsuccessful rebellions against Rome (66-70, 135). As a result, the Temple in Jerusalem was destroyed 200 AD
and the population decimated; this event marked the beginning of the Diaspora (living in exile).

To avoid the dissolution of the faith, a program of codification of law was begun at the academy of Yavneh. The work continued for some 500 years in Palestine and in Babylonia, ending in the final redaction (c 600) of the **Talmud**, a huge collection of legal and moral debates, rulings, liturgy, biblical exegesis, and legendary materials.

Christianity, which emerged as a distinct sect in the second half of the 1st cent. AD, is based on the teachings of **Jesus**, whom believers considered the Savior (Messiah or Christ), and the son of God. The missionary activities of the Apostles and such early leaders as **Paul of Tarsus** spread the faith. Intermittent persecution, as in Rome under Nero in 64 AD, on grounds of suspected disloyalty, failed to disrupt the Christian communities. Each congregation, generally urban and of plebeian character, was tightly organized under a leader (bishop), elders (presbyters or priests), and assistants (deacons). The Gospels (the New Testament), containing the teachings of Jesus, and the Acts of the Apostles were written down in the late 1st and early 2d centuries and circulated along with letters of Paul. An authoritative canon of these writings was not fixed until the 4th century.

A school for priests was established at Alexandria in the 2d century. Its teachers (**Origen** c 182-251) helped define Christian doctrine and promote the faith in Greek-style philosophical works. Pagan Neoplatonism was given Christian coloration in the works of Church Fathers such as Augustine (354-430). Christian hermits, often drawn from the lower classes, began to associate in monasteries, first in Egypt (St. Pachomius c 290-345), then in other E lands, then in the W (**St. Benedict's rule**, 529). Popular devotion to saints, especially Mary, mother of Jesus, spread.

Under **Constantine** (ruled 306-37), Christianity became in effect the established religion of the Empire. Pagan temples were expropriated, state funds were used to build huge churches and support the hierarchy, and laws were adjusted in accordance with Christian notions. Pagan worship was banned by the end of the 4th century, and severe restrictions were placed on Judaism.

The newly established church was rocked by doctrinal disputes, often exacerbated by regional rivalries both within and outside the Empire. Chief heresies (as defined by church councils backed by imperial authority) were **Arianism**, which denied the divinity of Jesus; **Donatism**, which rejected the convergence of church and state and denied the validity of sacraments performed by sinful clergy; and the **Monophysite** position denying the dual nature of Christ.

Islam. The earliest Arab civilization emerged by the end of the 2d millennium BC in the watered highlands of Yemen. Seaborne and caravan trade in frankincense and myrrh connected the area with the Nile and the Fertile Crescent. The Minaean, Sabean (Sheba), and Himyarite states successively held sway. By Mohammed's time (7th cent. AD), the region was a province of Sassanian Persia. In the N, the **Nabataean kingdom** at Petra and the kingdom of Palmyra were first Aramaicized, then Romanized, and finally absorbed, as neighboring Judea had been, into the Roman Empire. Nomads shared the central region with a few trading towns and oases. Wars between tribes and raids on settled communities were common and were celebrated in a poetic tradition that by the 6th century helped establish a classic literary Arabic.

In 611 **Mohammed**, a 40-year-old Arab of Mecca, announced a revelation from the one true God, calling on him to repudiate pagan idolatry. Drawing on elements of Judaism and Christianity, and eventually incorporating some Arab pagan traditions (such as reverence for the black stone at the Kaaba shrine in Mecca), Mohammed's teachings, recorded in the **Koran**, forged a new religion, Islam (submission to Allah). Opposed by the leaders of Mecca, Mohammed made a *hejira* (migration) to Medina to the N in 622, the beginning of the Muslim lunar calendar. He and his followers defeated the Meccans in 624 in the first *jihad* (holy war), and by his death (632) nearly all the Arabian peninsula accepted his religious and secular leadership.

Under the first two **caliphs** (successors), Abu Bakr (632-34) and Omar (634-44), Muslim rule over Arabia was confirmed. Raiding parties into Byzantine and Persian border areas developed into campaigns of conquest against the 2 empires, which had been weakened by wars and by disaffection among subject peoples (including Coptic and Syriac Christians opposed to the Byzantine Orthodox church). Syria, Palestine, Egypt, Iraq, and Persia all fell to the Arab armies. The Arabs at first remained a distinct minority, using non-Muslims in the new administrative system and tolerating Christians, Jews, and Zoroastrians as self-governing "Peoples of the Book," whose taxes supported the empire.

Disputes over the succession, and puritan reaction to the wealth and refinement that empire brought to the ruling strata, led to the growth of schismatic movements. The followers of Mohammed's son-in-law Ali (assassinated 661) and his descendants became the founders of the more mystical **Shi'ite** sect, still the largest non-orthodox Muslim sect. The Karijites, puritanical, militant, and egalitarian, persist as a minor sect to the present.

Under the **Omayyad** caliphs (661-750), the boundaries of Islam were extended across N Africa and into Spain (711). Arab armies in the W were stopped at Tours (France) in 732 by the Frankish King **Charles Martel**. Asia Minor, the Indus Valley, and Transoxiana were conquered in the E. The vast majority of the subject population gradually converted to Islam, encouraged by tax and career privileges. The Arab language supplanted the local tongues in the central and W areas, but Arab soldiers and rulers in the E eventually became assimilated to the indigenous languages.

New Peoples Enter World History: 400-900

Barbarian invasions. Germanic tribes infiltrated S and E from their Baltic homeland during the 1st millennium BC, reaching S Germany by 100 BC and the Black Sea by 214 AD. Organized into large federated tribes under elected kings, most resisted Roman domination and raided the empire in time of civil war (Goths took Dacia in 214 and raided Thrace in 251-69). Germanic troops and commanders came to dominate the Roman armies by the end of the 4th century. **Huns**, invaders from Asia, entered Europe in 372, driving more Germans into the W empire. Emperor Valens allowed Visigoths to cross the Danube in 376. Huns under Attila (d 453) raided Gaul, Italy, and the Balkans. The W empire, weakened by overtaxation and social stagnation, was overrun in the 5th cent. Gaul was effectively lost in 650 AD
406-7, Spain in 409, Britain in 410, and Africa in 429-39. Rome was sacked in 410 by Visigoths under

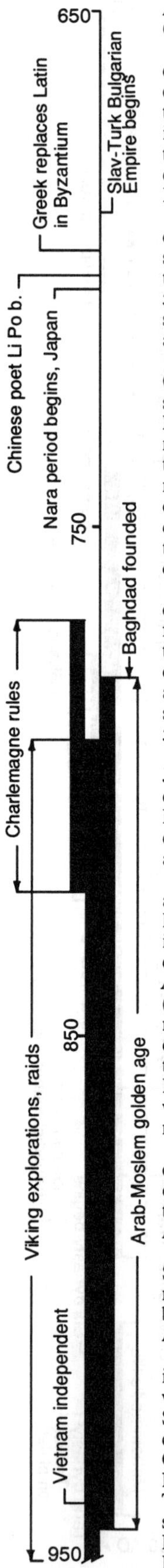
650
Greek replaces Latin in Byzantium
Slav-Turk Bulgarian Empire begins
Chinese poet Li Po b.
Nara period begins, Japan
750
Baghdad founded
Charlemagne rules
850
Viking explorations, raids
Arab-Moslem golden age
Vietnam independent
950

Alaric and in 455 by Vandals. The last western emperor, Romulus Augustulus, was deposed in 476 by the Germanic chief Odovacar.

Celts. Celtic cultures, which in pre-Roman times covered most of W Europe, were confined almost entirely to the British Isles after the Germanic invasions. **St. Patrick** completed (c 457-92) the conversion of Ireland. A strong monastic tradition took hold. Irish monastic missionaries in Scotland, England, and the continent (Columba c 521-97; Columban c 543-615) helped restore Christianity after the Germanic invasions. The monasteries became renowned centers of classic and Christian learning and presided over the recording of a Christianized Celtic mythology, elaborated by secular writers and bards. An intricate decorative art style developed, especially in book illumination (Lindisfarne Gospels, c 700; Book of Kells, 8th cent.).

Successor states. The Visigothic kingdom in Spain (from 419) and much of France (to 507) saw a continuation of much Roman administration, language, and law (Breviary of Alaric, 506) until its destruction by the Muslims in 711. The Vandal kingdom in Africa, from 429, was conquered by the Byzantines in 533. Italy was ruled in succession by an Ostrogothic kingdom under Byzantine suzerainty (489-554), direct Byzantine government, and the German Lombards (568-774). The latter divided the peninsula with the Byzantines and the papacy under the dynamic reformer Pope Gregory the Great (590-604) and his successors.

King Clovis (ruled 481-511) united the Franks on both sides of the Rhine and, after his conversion to Christianity, defeated the Arian heretics, the Burgundians (after 500), and the Visigoths (507) with the support of the native clergy and the papacy. Under the **Merovingian** kings, a feudal system emerged: Power was fragmented among hierarchies of military landowners. Social stratification, which in late Roman times had acquired legal, hereditary sanction, was reinforced. The Carolingians (747-987) expanded the kingdom and restored central power. **Charlemagne** (ruled 768-814) conquered nearly all the Germanic lands, including Lombard Italy, and was crowned Emperor by Pope Leo III in Rome in 800. A centuries-long decline in commerce and the arts was reversed under Charlemagne's patronage. He welcomed Jews to his kingdom, which became a center of Jewish learning (Rashi, 1040-1105). He sponsored the Carolingian Renaissance of learning under the Anglo-Latin scholar Alcuin (c 732-804), who reformed church liturgy.

Byzantine Empire. Under Diocletian (ruled 284-305) the empire had been divided into 2 parts to facilitate administration and defense. Constantine founded (330) **Constantinople** (at old Byzantium) as a fully Christian city. Commerce and taxation financed a sumptuous, orientalized court, a class of hereditary bureaucratic families, and magnificent urban construction (Hagia Sophia, 532-37). The city's fortifications and naval innovations (Greek fire) repelled assaults by Goths, Huns, Slavs, Bulgars, Avars, Arabs, and Scandinavians. Greek replaced Latin as the official language by c 700. Byzantine art, a solemn, sacral, and stylized variation of late classical styles (mosaics at the Church of San Vitale, Ravenna, Italy 526-48), was a starting point for medieval art in E and W Europe.

Justinian (ruled 527-65) reconquered parts of Spain, N Africa, and Italy, codified Roman law (Codex Justinianus [529] was medieval Europe's chief legal text), closed the Platonic Academy at Athens, and ordered all pagans to convert. Lombards in Italy and Arabs in Africa retook most of his conquests. The Isaurian dynasty from Anatolia (from 717) and the Macedonian dynasty (867-1054) restored military and commercial power. The Iconoclast controversy (726-843) over the permissibility of images helped alienate the Eastern Church from the papacy.

Arab Empire. Baghdad (est 762) became the seat of the **Abbasid** Caliphate (est 750), while Ummayads continued to rule in Spain. A brilliant cosmopolitan civilization emerged, inaugurating an Arab-Muslim golden age. Arab lyric poetry revived; Greek, Syriac, Persian, and Sanskrit books were translated into Arabic, often by Syriac Christians and Jews, whose theology and Talmudic law, respectively, influenced Islam. The arts and music flourished at the court of **Harun al-Rashid** (786-809), celebrated in *The Arabian Nights*. The sciences, medicine, and mathematics were pursued at Baghdad, Cordova, and Cairo (est 969). Science and Aristotelian philosophy culminated in the systems of Avicenna (980-1037), Averroes (1126-98), and Maimonides (1135-1204), a Jew; all influenced later Christian scholarship and theology. The Islamic ban on images encouraged a sinuous, geometric decorative tradition, applied to architecture and illumination. A gradual loss of Arab control in Persia (from 874) led to the capture (945) of Baghdad by Persians. By the next century, Spain and N Africa were ruled by Berbers, while Turks prevailed in Asia Minor and the Levant. The loss of political power by the caliphs allowed for the growth of nonorthodox trends, especially the mystical **Sufi** tradition (theologian Ghazali, 1058-1111).

Africa. Immigrants from Saba in S Arabia helped set up the **Axum** kingdom in Ethiopia in the 1st century (their language, Ge'ez, is preserved by the Ethiopian Church). In the 3d century, when the kingdom became Christianized, it defeated Kushite Meroe and expanded its influence into Yemen. Axum was the center of a vast ivory trade and controlled the Red Sea coast until c 1100. Arab conquest in Egypt cut Axum's political and economic ties with Byzantium.

The Iron Age entered W Africa by the end of the 1st millennium BC. **Ghana**, the first known sub-Saharan state, ruled in the upper Senegal-Niger region c 400-1240, controlling the trade of gold from mines in the S to trans-Sahara caravan routes to the N. The **Bantu** peoples, probably of W African origin, began to spread E and S perhaps 2,000 years ago, displacing the Pygmies and Bushmen of central and S Africa during a 1,500-year period.

Japan. The advanced Neolithic Yayoi period, when irrigation, rice farming, and iron and bronze casting techniques were introduced from China or Korea, persisted to c 400 AD. The myriad Japanese states were then united by the **Yamato** clan, under an emperor who acted as the chief priest of the animistic Shinto cult. Japanese political and military intervention by the 6th century in Korea, which was then under strong Chinese influence, quickened a Chinese cultural invasion of Japan, bringing Buddhism, the Chinese language (which long remained a literary and governmental medium), Chinese ideographs, and Buddhist styles in painting, sculpture, literature, and architecture (7th century, Horyu-ji temple at Nara). The Taika Reforms (646) tried to centralize Japan according to Chinese bureaucratic and Buddhist philosophical values, but failed to curb traditional Japanese decentralization. A nativist reaction against the Buddhist **Nara period** (710-94) ushered in the **Heian period** (794-1185) centered at the new capital, Kyoto. Japanese elegance and simplicity modified Chinese styles in architecture, scroll painting, and literature; the writing system was also simplified. The courtly novel *Tale of Genji* (1010-20) testifies to the enhanced role of women.

Southeast Asia. The historic peoples of Southeast Asia began arriving some 2,500 years ago from China and Tibet, displacing scattered aborigines. Their agriculture relied on rice and tubers (yams), which they may have introduced to Africa. Indian cultural influences were strongest; literacy and Hindu and Buddhist ideas followed the southern India-China trade route. From the southern tip of Indochina, the kingdom of **Funan** (1st-7th century) traded as far W as Persia. It was absorbed by Chenla, itself conquered by the **Khmer Empire** (600-1300). The Khmers, under Hindu god-kings (Suryavarman II, 1113-c 1150) built the monumental Angkor Wat temple center for the royal phallic cult. The **Nam-Viet** kingdom in Annam, dominated by China and Chinese culture for 1,000 years, emerged in the 10th century, growing at the expense of the Khmers, who also lost ground in the NW to the new, highly organized **Thai** kingdom. On Sumatra, the **Srivijaya** Empire at Palembang controlled vital sea lanes (7th to 10th century). A Buddhist dynasty, the Sailendras, ruled central **Java** (8th-9th century), building at Borobudur one of the largest stupas in the world.

China. The short-lived Sui dynasty (581-618) ushered in a period of commercial, artistic, and scientific achievement in China, continuing under the **Tang** dynasty (618-906). Such inventions as the magnetic compass, gunpowder, the abacus, and printing were introduced or perfected. Medical innovations included cataract surgery. The state, from the cosmopolitan capital, Chang-an, supervised foreign trade, which exchanged Chinese silks, porcelains, and artworks for spices, ivory, etc. over Central Asian caravan routes and sea routes reaching Africa. A *golden age* of poetry bequeathed tens of thousands of works to later generations (Tu Fu, 712-70; Li Po, 701-62). Landscape painting flourished. Commercial and industrial expansion continued under the **Northern Sung** dynasty (960-1126), facilitated by paper money and credit notes. But commerce never achieved respectability; government monopolies expropriated successful merchants. The population, long stable at 50 million, doubled in 200 years with the introduction of early-ripening rice and the double harvest. In art, native Chinese styles were revived.

Americas. From 300 to 600 a Native American empire stretched from the Valley of Mexico to Guatemala, centering on the huge city **Teotihuacán** (founded 100 BC). To the S, in Guatemala, a high **Mayan** civilization developed (150-900) around hundreds of rural ceremonial centers. The Mayans improved on Olmec writing and the calendar and pursued astronomy and mathematics (using the idea of zero). In South America, a widespread pre-Inca culture grew from **Tiahuanacu,** Bolivia, near Lake Titicaca (Gateway of the Sun, c 700).

Christian Europe Regroups and Expands: 900-1300

Scandinavians. Pagan Danish and Norse (Viking) adventurers, traders, and pirates raided the coasts of the British Isles (Dublin, founded c 831), France, and even the Mediterranean for more than 200 years beginning in the late 8th century. Inland settlement in the W was limited to Great Britain (King Canute, 994-1035) and Normandy, settled (911) under Rollo, as a fief of France. Other Vikings reached Iceland (874), Greenland (c 986), and North America (Leif Eriksson, c 1000). Norse traders (**Varangians**) developed Russian river commerce from the 8th to the 11th century and helped set up a state at Kiev in the late 9th century. Conversion to Christianity occurred during the 10th century, reaching Sweden 100 years later. Eleventh-century Norman bands conquered S Italy and Sicily. Duke **William of Normandy** conquered (1066) England, bringing continental feudalism and the French language, essential elements in later English civilization.

Central and East Europe. Slavs began to expand from about 150 AD in all directions in Europe, and by the 7th cent. they reached as far S as the Adriatic and Aegean seas. In the Balkan Peninsula they dislocated Romanized local populations or assimilated newcomers (Bulgarians, a Turkic people). The first Slavic states were Moravia (628) in Central Europe and the Bulgarian state (680) in the Balkans. Missions of St. Methodius and Cyril (whose Greek-based cyrillic alphabet is still used by some S and E Slavs) converted (863) Moravia. The Eastern Slavs, part-civilized under the overlordship of the Turkish-Jewish **Khazar** trading empire (7th-10th century), gravitated toward Constantinople by the 9th century. The **Kievan state** adopted (989) Eastern Christianity under Prince Vladimir. King Boleslav I (992-1025) began **Poland's** long history of eastern conquest. The Magyars (**Hungarians**), in present-day Hungary since 896, accepted (1001) Latin Christianity.

Germany. The German kingdom that emerged after the breakup of Charlemagne's W Empire remained a confederation of largely autonomous states. Otto I, a Saxon who was king from 936, established the **Holy Roman Empire**—a union of Germany and N Italy—in alliance with Pope John XII, who crowned (962) him emperor; he defeated (955) the Magyars. Imperial power was greatest under the **Hohenstaufens** (1138-1254), despite the growing opposition of the papacy, which ruled central Italy, and the Lombard League cities. Frederick II (1194-1250) improved administration and patronized the arts; after his death, German influence was removed from Italy.

Christian Spain. From its N mountain redoubts, Christian rule slowly migrated S through the 11th century, when Muslim unity collapsed. After the capture (1085) of **Toledo,** the kingdoms of Portugal, Castile, and Aragon undertook repeated crusades of reconquest, finally completed in 1492. Elements of Islamic civilization persisted in recaptured areas, influencing all Western Europe.

Crusades. Pope Urban II called (1095) for a crusade to restore Asia Minor to Byzantium and to regain the Holy Land from the Turks. Some 10 crusades (to 1291) succeeded only in founding 4 temporary Frankish states in the Levant. The 4th crusade sacked (1204) Constantinople. In Rhineland (1096), England (1290), and France (1306), Jews were massacred or expelled, and wars were launched against Christian heretics (**Albigensian** crusade in France, 1229). Trade in eastern luxuries expanded, led by the Venetian naval empire.

Economy. The agricultural base of European life benefited from improvements in **plow design** (c 1000) and by draining of lowlands and clearing of forests, leading to a rural population increase. Towns grew in N Italy, Flanders, and N Germany (Hanseatic League). Improvements in **loom design** permitted factory textile production. **Guilds** dominated urban trades from the 12th century. Banking (centered in Italy, 12th-15th century) facilitated long-distance trade.

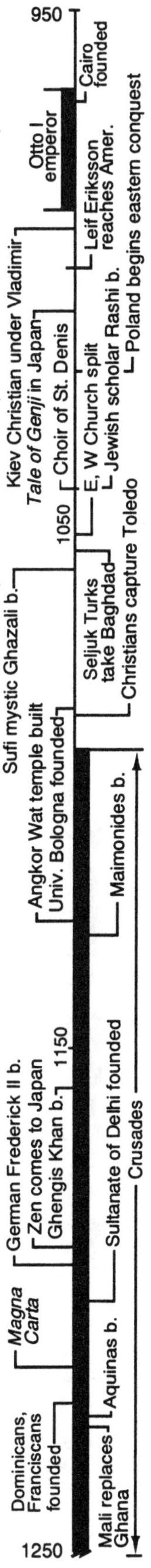

Timeline (right margin, 950–1250):

- 950
- Cairo founded
- Otto I emperor
- Leif Eriksson reaches Amer.
- Poland begins eastern conquest
- Kiev Christian under Vladimir
- *Tale of Genji* in Japan
- Choir of St. Denis
- E, W Church split
- Jewish scholar Rashi b.
- 1050
- Seljuk Turks take Baghdad
- Christians capture Toledo
- Sufi mystic Ghazali b.
- Angkor Wat temple built
- Univ. Bologna founded
- Maimonides b.
- German Frederick II b.
- Zen comes to Japan
- Ghengis Khan b.
- Sultanate of Delhi founded
- Crusades
- 1150
- Magna Carta
- Aquinas b.
- Dominicans, Franciscans founded
- Mali replaces Ghana
- 1250

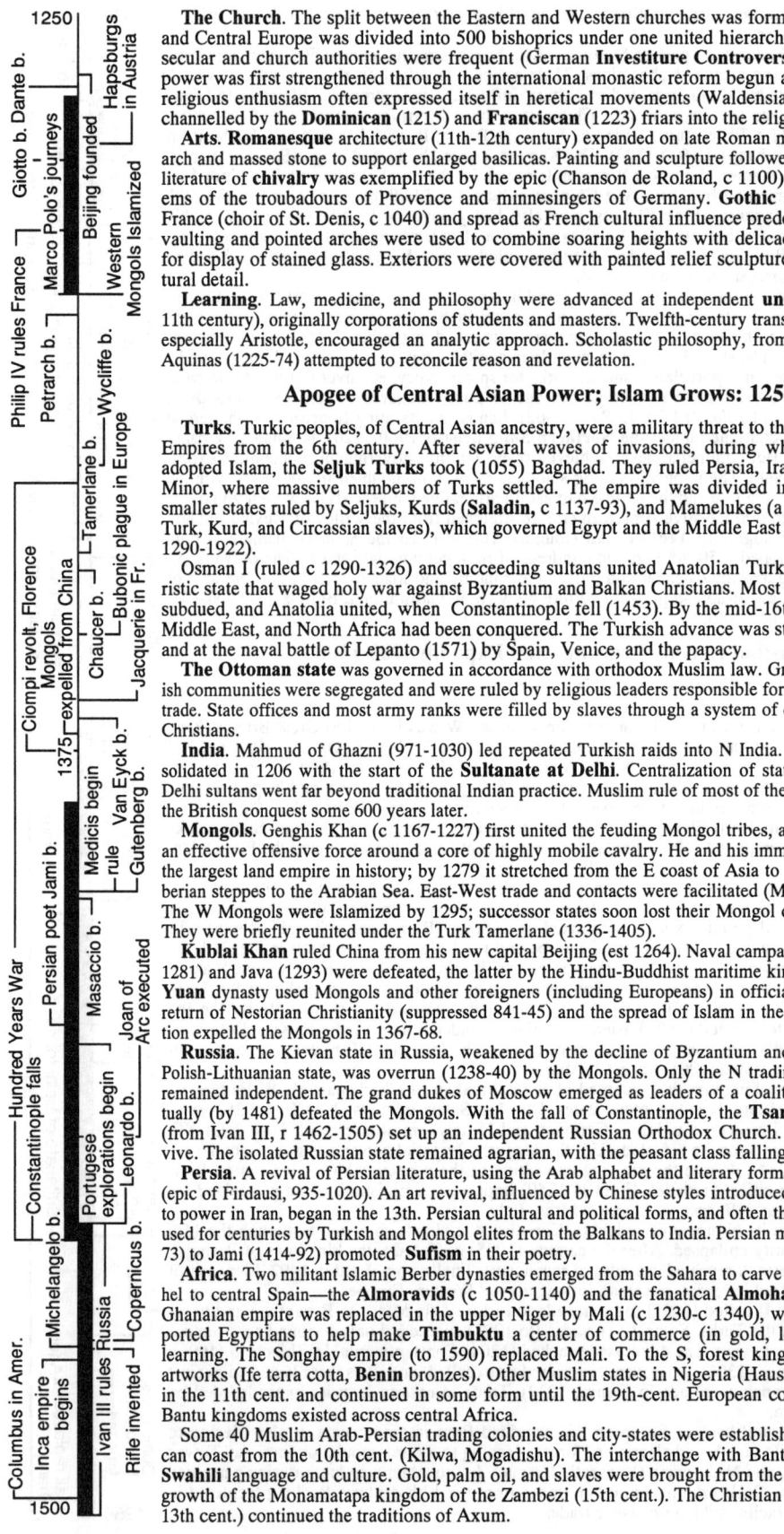

The Church. The split between the Eastern and Western churches was formalized in 1054. Western and Central Europe was divided into 500 bishoprics under one united hierarchy, but conflicts between secular and church authorities were frequent (German **Investiture Controversy**, 1075-1122). Clerical power was first strengthened through the international monastic reform begun at Cluny in 910. Popular religious enthusiasm often expressed itself in heretical movements (Waldensians from 1173), but was channelled by the **Dominican** (1215) and **Franciscan** (1223) friars into the religious mainstream.

Arts. **Romanesque** architecture (11th-12th century) expanded on late Roman models, using the rounded arch and massed stone to support enlarged basilicas. Painting and sculpture followed Byzantine models. The literature of **chivalry** was exemplified by the epic (Chanson de Roland, c 1100) and by courtly love poems of the troubadours of Provence and minnesingers of Germany. **Gothic** architecture emerged in France (choir of St. Denis, c 1040) and spread as French cultural influence predominated in Europe. Rib vaulting and pointed arches were used to combine soaring heights with delicacy, and they freed walls for display of stained glass. Exteriors were covered with painted relief sculpture and elaborate architectural detail.

Learning. Law, medicine, and philosophy were advanced at independent **universities** (Bologna, late 11th century), originally corporations of students and masters. Twelfth-century translations of Greek classics, especially Aristotle, encouraged an analytic approach. Scholastic philosophy, from Anselm (1033-1109) to Aquinas (1225-74) attempted to reconcile reason and revelation.

Apogee of Central Asian Power; Islam Grows: 1250-1500

Turks. Turkic peoples, of Central Asian ancestry, were a military threat to the Byzantine and Persian Empires from the 6th century. After several waves of invasions, during which most of the Turks adopted Islam, the **Seljuk Turks** took (1055) Baghdad. They ruled Persia, Iraq and, after 1071, Asia Minor, where massive numbers of Turks settled. The empire was divided in the 12th century into smaller states ruled by Seljuks, Kurds (**Saladin**, c 1137-93), and Mamelukes (a military caste of former Turk, Kurd, and Circassian slaves), which governed Egypt and the Middle East until the Ottoman era (c 1290-1922).

Osman I (ruled c 1290-1326) and succeeding sultans united Anatolian Turkish warriors in a militaristic state that waged holy war against Byzantium and Balkan Christians. Most of the Balkans had been subdued, and Anatolia united, when Constantinople fell (1453). By the mid-16th century, Hungary, the Middle East, and North Africa had been conquered. The Turkish advance was stopped at Vienna (1529) and at the naval battle of Lepanto (1571) by Spain, Venice, and the papacy.

The Ottoman state was governed in accordance with orthodox Muslim law. Greek, Armenian, and Jewish communities were segregated and were ruled by religious leaders responsible for taxation; they dominated trade. State offices and most army ranks were filled by slaves through a system of child conscription among Christians.

India. Mahmud of Ghazni (971-1030) led repeated Turkish raids into N India. Turkish power was consolidated in 1206 with the start of the **Sultanate at Delhi**. Centralization of state power under the early Delhi sultans went far beyond traditional Indian practice. Muslim rule of most of the subcontinent lasted until the British conquest some 600 years later.

Mongols. Genghis Khan (c 1167-1227) first united the feuding Mongol tribes, and built their armies into an effective offensive force around a core of highly mobile cavalry. He and his immediate successors created the largest land empire in history; by 1279 it stretched from the E coast of Asia to the Danube, from the Siberian steppes to the Arabian Sea. East-West trade and contacts were facilitated (Marco Polo, c 1254-1324). The W Mongols were Islamized by 1295; successor states soon lost their Mongol character by assimilation. They were briefly reunited under the Turk Tamerlane (1336-1405).

Kublai Khan ruled China from his new capital Beijing (est 1264). Naval campaigns against Japan (1274, 1281) and Java (1293) were defeated, the latter by the Hindu-Buddhist maritime kingdom of Majapahit. The **Yuan** dynasty used Mongols and other foreigners (including Europeans) in official posts and tolerated the return of Nestorian Christianity (suppressed 841-45) and the spread of Islam in the S and W. A native reaction expelled the Mongols in 1367-68.

Russia. The Kievan state in Russia, weakened by the decline of Byzantium and the rise of the Catholic Polish-Lithuanian state, was overrun (1238-40) by the Mongols. Only the N trading republic of Novgorod remained independent. The grand dukes of Moscow emerged as leaders of a coalition of princes that eventually (by 1481) defeated the Mongols. With the fall of Constantinople, the **Tsars** (Caesars) at Moscow (from Ivan III, r 1462-1505) set up an independent Russian Orthodox Church. Commerce failed to revive. The isolated Russian state remained agrarian, with the peasant class falling into serfdom.

Persia. A revival of Persian literature, using the Arab alphabet and literary forms, began in the 10th cent. (epic of Firdausi, 935-1020). An art revival, influenced by Chinese styles introduced after the Mongols came to power in Iran, began in the 13th. Persian cultural and political forms, and often the Persian language, were used for centuries by Turkish and Mongol elites from the Balkans to India. Persian mystics from Rumi (1207-73) to Jami (1414-92) promoted **Sufism** in their poetry.

Africa. Two militant Islamic Berber dynasties emerged from the Sahara to carve out empires from the Sahel to central Spain—the **Almoravids** (c 1050-1140) and the fanatical **Almohads** (c 1125-1269). The Ghanaian empire was replaced in the upper Niger by Mali (c 1230-c 1340), whose Muslim rulers imported Egyptians to help make **Timbuktu** a center of commerce (in gold, leather, and slaves) and learning. The Songhay empire (to 1590) replaced Mali. To the S, forest kingdoms produced refined artworks (Ife terra cotta, **Benin** bronzes). Other Muslim states in Nigeria (Hausas) and Chad originated in the 11th cent. and continued in some form until the 19th-cent. European conquest. Less-developed Bantu kingdoms existed across central Africa.

Some 40 Muslim Arab-Persian trading colonies and city-states were established all along the E African coast from the 10th cent. (Kilwa, Mogadishu). The interchange with Bantu peoples produced the **Swahili** language and culture. Gold, palm oil, and slaves were brought from the interior, stimulating the growth of the Monamatapa kingdom of the Zambezi (15th cent.). The Christian Ethiopian empire (from 13th cent.) continued the traditions of Axum.

Southeast Asia. Islam was introduced into Malaya and the Indonesian islands by Arab, Persian, and Indian traders. Coastal Muslim cities and states (starting before 1300), enriched by trade, soon dominated the interior. Chief among these was the **Malacca** state (c 1400-1511), on the Malay peninsula.

Arts and Statecraft Thrive in Europe: 1350-1600

Italian Renaissance & Humanism. Distinctive Italian achievements in the arts in the late Middle Ages (Dante, 1265-1321; Giotto, 1276-1337) led to the vigorous new styles of the Renaissance (14th-16th century). Patronized by the rulers of the quarreling petty states of Italy (Medicis in Florence and the papacy, c 1400-1737), the plastic arts perfected realistic techniques, including **perspective** (Masaccio, 1401-28, Leonardo, 1452-1519). Classical motifs were used in architecture, and increased talent and expense were put into secular buildings. The Florentine dialect was refined as a national literary language (Petrarch, 1304-74). Greek refugees from the E strengthened the respect of humanist scholars for the classic sources (Bruni, 1370-1444). Soon an international movement aided by the spread of **printing** (Gutenberg, c 1400-68), **humanism** was optimistic about the power of human reason (Erasmus of Rotterdam, 1466-1536, Thomas More's *Utopia*, 1516) and valued individual effort in the arts and in politics (Machiavelli, 1469-1527).

France. The French monarchy, strengthened in its repeated struggles with powerful nobles (Burgundy, Flanders, Aquitaine) by alliances with the growing commercial towns, consolidated bureaucratic control under Philip IV (r 1285-1314) and extended French influence into Germany and Italy (popes at Avignon, France, 1309-1417). The **Hundred Years War** (1337-1453) ended English dynastic claims in France (battles of Crécy, 1346, and Poitiers, 1356; Joan of Arc executed, 1431). A French Renaissance, dating from royal invasions (1494, 1499) of Italy, was encouraged at the court of Francis I (r 1515-47), who centralized taxation and law. French vernacular literature consciously asserted its independence (La Pléiade, 1549).

England. The evolution of England's unique political institutions began with the Magna Carta (1215), by which King John guaranteed the privileges of nobles and church against the monarchy and assured jury trial. After the Wars of the Roses (1455-85), the **Tudor dynasty** reasserted royal prerogatives (Henry VIII, r 1509-47), but the trend toward independent departments and ministerial government also continued. English trade (wool exports from c 1340) was protected by the nation's growing maritime power (**Spanish Armada** destroyed, 1588).

English replaced French and Latin in the late 14th cent. in law and literature (Chaucer, c 1340-1400) and English translation of the Bible began (Wycliffe, 1380s). Elizabeth I (r 1558-1603) presided over a confident flowering of poetry (Spenser, 1552-99), drama (**Shakespeare**, 1564-1616), and music.

German Empire. From among a welter of minor feudal states, church lands, and independent cities, the **Hapsburgs** assembled a far-flung territorial domain, based in Austria from 1276. The family held the title Holy Roman Emperor from 1438 to the Empire's dissolution in 1806, but failed to centralize its domains, leaving Germany disunited for centuries. Resistance to Turkish expansion brought Hungary under Austrian control from the 16th cent. The Netherlands, Luxembourg, and Burgundy were added in 1477, curbing French expansion.

The Flemish painting tradition of naturalism, technical proficiency, and bourgeois subject matter began in the 15th cent. (Jan Van Eyck, c 1390-1441), the earliest northern manifestation of the Renaissance. **Dürer** (1471-1528) typified the merging of late Gothic and Italian trends in 16th-cent. German art. Imposing civic architecture flourished in the prosperous commercial cities.

Spain. Despite the unification of Castile and Aragon in 1479, the 2 countries retained separate governments, and the nobility, especially in Aragon and Catalonia, retained many privileges. Spanish lands in Italy (Naples, Sicily) and the Netherlands entangled the country in European wars through the mid-17th cent., while explorers, traders, and conquerors built up a Spanish empire in the Americas and the Philippines.

From the late 15th century, a **golden age** of literature and art produced works of social satire (plays of Lope de Vega, 1562-1635; Cervantes, 1547-1616), as well as spiritual intensity (El Greco, 1541-1614; Velazquez, 1599-1660).

Black Death. The bubonic plague reached Europe from the E in 1348, killing as much as half the population by 1350. Labor scarcity forced a rise in wages and brought greater freedom to the peasantry, making possible **peasant uprisings** (Jacquerie in France, 1358; Wat Tyler's rebellion in England, 1381). In the *ciompi* revolt (1378), Florentine wage earners demanded a say in economic and political power.

Explorations. Organized European maritime exploration began, seeking to evade the Venice-Ottoman monopoly of E trade and to promote Christianity. Beginning in 1418, expeditions from Portugal explored the W coast of Africa, until **Vasco da Gama** rounded the Cape of Good Hope in 1497 and reached India. A Portuguese trading empire was consolidated by the seizure of Goa (1510) and Malacca (1551). Japan was reached in 1542. The voyages of **Columbus** (1492-1504) uncovered a new world, which Spain hastened to subdue. Navigation schools in Spain and Portugal, the development of large sailing ships (carracks), and the invention (c 1475) of the rifle aided European penetration.

Mughals and Safavids. East of the Ottoman Empire, 2 Muslim dynasties ruled unchallenged in the 16th and 17th centuries. The Mughal dynasty of India, founded by Persianized Turkish invaders from the NW under Babur, dates from their 1526 conquest of the Delhi Sultanate. The dynasty ruled most of India for more than 200 years, surviving nominally until 1857. **Akbar** (r 1556-1605) consolidated administration at his glorious court, where the Urdu language (Persian-influenced Hindi) developed. Trade relations with Europe increased. Under Shah Jahan (1629-58), a secularized art fusing Hindu and Muslim element flourished in miniature painting and in architecture (Taj Mahal). Sikhism (founded c 1519) combined elements of both faiths. Suppression of Hindus and Shi'ite Muslims in S India in the late 17th cent. weakened the empire.

Fanatical devotion to the Shi'ite sect characterized the Safavids (1502-1736) of Persia and led to hostilities with the Sunni Ottomans for more than a century. The prosperity and the strength of the empire are evidenced by the mosques at its capital, **Isfahan**. The Safavids enhanced Iranian national consciousness.

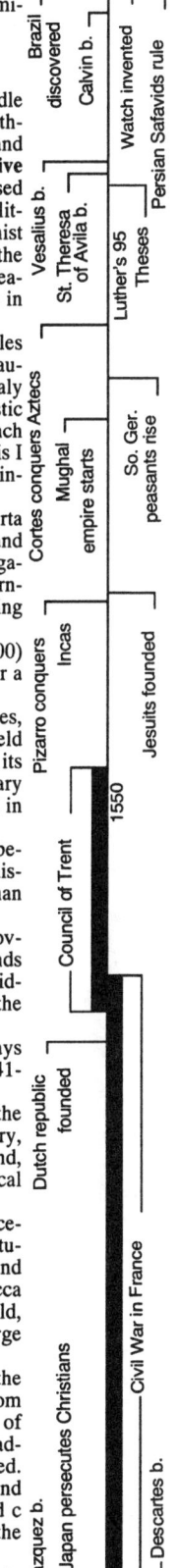

Timeline (1500–1600):
Brazil discovered — Calvin b. — Watch invented — Persian Safavids rule — Vesalius b. — St. Theresa of Avila b. — Luther's 95 Theses — Cortes conquers Aztecs — Mughal empire starts — So. Ger. peasants rise — Pizarro conquers Incas — Jesuits founded — 1550 — Council of Trent — Dutch republic founded — Civil War in France — Japan persecutes Christians — Velazquez b. — Descartes b. — 1600

1600

Jamestown founded

French settle Canada

Bank of Amsterdam

Tokugawa Ieyasu shogun

Thirty Years War

Kepler d.

Galileo d.

Van Dyck d.

Plymouth founded

Manchus rule 1640

Charles I killed

Royal Soc. founded

Fronde

English Revolution

Mazarin d.

Bernini d.

Rembrandt d.

Spinoza d.

Princesse de Cleves

1680

China. The Ming emperors (1368-1644), the last native dynasty in China, wielded unprecedented personal power, while the Confucian bureaucracy began to suffer from inertia. European trade (Portuguese monopoly through **Macao** from 1557) was strictly controlled. Jesuit scholars and scientists (Matteo Ricci, 1552-1610) introduced some Western science; their writings familiarized the West with China. Chinese technological inventiveness declined from this era, but the arts thrived, especially painting and ceramics.

Japan. After the decline of the first hereditary shogunate (chief generalship) at **Kamakura** (1185-1333), fragmentation of power accelerated, as did the consequent social mobility. Under Kamakura and the Ashikaga shogunate (1338-1573), the daimyos (lords) and samurai (warriors) grew more powerful and promoted a martial ideology. Japanese pirates and traders plied the China coast. Popular Buddhist movements included the nationalist Nichiren sect (from c 1250) and **Zen** (brought from China, 1191), which stressed meditation and a disciplined esthetic (tea ceremony, gardening, martial arts, No drama).

Reformed Europe Expands Overseas: 1500-1700

Reformation begun. Theological debate and protests against real and perceived clerical corruption existed in the medieval Christian world, expressed by such dissenters as Wycliffe (c 1320-84) and his followers, the Lollards, in England, and **Huss** (burned as a heretic, 1415) in Bohemia.

Luther (1483-1546) preached that only faith could lead to salvation, without the mediation of clergy or good works. He attacked the authority of the pope, rejected priestly celibacy, and recommended individual study of the Bible (which he translated c 1525). His 95 Theses (1517) led to his excommunication (1521). **Calvin** (1509-64) said that God's elect were predestined for salvation and that good conduct and success were signs of election. Calvin in Geneva and Knox (1505-72) in Scotland established theocratic states.

Henry VIII asserted English national authority and secular power by breaking away (1534) from the Catholic Church. Monastic property was confiscated, and some Protestant doctrines given official sanction.

Religious wars. A century and a half of religious wars began with a South German peasant uprising (1524), repressed with Luther's support. Radical sects—democratic, pacifist, millennarian—arose (Anabaptists ruled Münster in 1534-35) and were suppressed violently. Civil war in France from 1562 between **Huguenots** (Protestant nobles and merchants) and Catholics ended with the 1598 Edict of Nantes tolerating Protestants (revoked 1685). Hapsburg attempts to restore Catholicism in Germany were resisted in 25 years of fighting; the 1555 Peace of Augsburg guarantee of religious independence to local princes and cities was confirmed only after the **Thirty Years War** (1618-48), when much of Germany was devastated by local and foreign armies (Sweden, France).

A Catholic Reformation, or **Counter Reformation**, met the Protestant challenge, clearly defining an official theology at the Council of Trent (1545-63). The **Jesuit** order, founded in 1534 by Loyola (1491-1556), helped reconvert large areas of Poland, Hungary, and S Germany and sent missionaries to the New World, India, and China, while the Inquisition helped suppress heresy in Catholic countries. A revival of piety appeared in the devotional literature (Theresa of Avila, 1515-82) and the grandiose Baroque art (Bernini, 1598-1680) of Roman Catholic countries.

Scientific Revolution. The late nominalist thinkers (Ockham, c 1300-49) of Paris and Oxford challenged Aristotelian orthodoxy, allowing for a freer scientific approach. But metaphysical values, such as the Neoplatonic faith in an orderly, mathematical cosmos, still motivated and directed subsequent inquiry. **Copernicus** (1473-1543) promoted the heliocentric theory, which was confirmed when Kepler (1571-1630) discovered the mathematical laws describing the orbits of the planets. The Christian-Aristotelian belief that heavens and earth were fundamentally different collapsed when Galileo (1564-1642) discovered moving sunspots, irregular moon topography, and moons around Jupiter. He and **Newton** (1642-1727) developed a mechanics that unified cosmic and earthly phenomena. To meet the needs of the new physics, Newton and Leibnitz (1646-1716) invented calculus, Descartes (1596-1650) invented analytic geometry.

An explosion of observational science included the discovery of blood circulation (Harvey, 1578-1657) and microscopic life (Leeuwenhoek, 1632-1723) and advances in anatomy (Vesalius, 1514-64, dissected corpses) and chemistry (Boyle, 1627-91). Scientific research institutes were founded: Florence (1657), London (**Royal Society**, 1660), Paris (1666). Inventions proliferated (Savery's steam engine, 1696).

Arts. Mannerist trends of the High Renaissance (**Michelangelo**, 1475-1564) exploited virtuosity, grace, novelty, and exotic subjects and poses. The notion of artistic genius was promoted, in contrast to the anonymous medieval artisan. Private connoisseurs entered the art market. These trends were elaborated in the 17th cent. **Baroque** era on a grander scale. Dynamic movement in painting and sculpture was emphasized by sharp lighting effects, use of rich materials (colored marble, gilt), and realistic details. Curved facades, broken lines, rich, deep-cut detail, and ceiling decoration characterized Baroque architecture, especially in Germany. Monarchs, princes, and prelates, usually Catholic, used Baroque art to enhance and embellish their authority, as in royal portraits by Velazquez (1599-1660) and Van Dyck (1599-1641).

National styles emerged. In France, a taste for rectilinear order and serenity (Poussin, 1594-1665), linked to the new rational philosophy, was expressed in classical forms. The influence of **classical values** in French literature (tragedies of Racine, 1639-99) gave rise to the "battle of the Ancients and Moderns." New forms included the essay (Montaigne, 1533-92) and novel (*Princesse de Cleves*, La Fayette, 1678).

Dutch painting of the 17th cent. was unique in its wide social distribution. The Flemish tradition of undemonstrative realism reached its peak in **Rembrandt** (1606-69) and Vermeer (1632-75).

Economy. European economic expansion was stimulated by the new trade with the East, by New World gold and silver, and by a doubling of population (50 million in 1450, 100 million in 1600). New business and financial techniques were developed and refined, such as joint-stock companies, insurance, and letters of credit and exchange. The Bank of Amsterdam (1609) and the Bank of England (1694) broke the old monopoly of private banking families. The rise of a business mentality was typified by the spread of clock towers in cities in the 14th cent. By the mid-15th cent., portable clocks were available; the first watch was invented in 1502.

By 1650, most governments had adopted the **mercantile system**, in which they sought to amass metallic wealth by protecting their merchants' foreign and colonial trade monopolies. The rise in prices and the new coin-based economy undermined the craft guild and feudal manorial systems. Expanding industries, such as clothweaving and mining, benefited from technical advances. Coal replaced disappearing wood as the chief fuel; it was used to fuel new 16th-cent. blast furnaces making cast iron.

New World. The **Aztecs** united much of the Meso-American culture area in a militarist empire by 1519, from their capital, Tenochtitlán (pop. 300,000), which was the center of a cult requiring enormous levels of ritual human sacrifice. Most of the civilized areas of South America were ruled by the centralized Inca Empire (1476-1534), stretching 2,000 mi from Ecuador to NW Argentina. Lavish and sophisticated traditions in pottery, weaving, sculpture, and architecture were maintained in both regions.

These empires, beset by revolts, fell in 2 short campaigns to gold-seeking Spanish forces based in the Antilles and Panama. **Cortes** took Mexico (1519-21); **Pizarro,** Peru (1532-35). From these centers, land and sea expeditions claimed most of North and South America for Spain. The Indian high cultures did not survive the impact of Christian missionaries and the new upper class of whites and mestizos. In turn, New World silver and such Indian products as potatoes, tobacco, corn, peanuts, chocolate, and rubber exercised a major economic influence on Europe. Although the Spanish administration intermittently concerned itself with the welfare of Indians, the population remained impoverished at most levels, despite the growth of a distinct South American civilization. European diseases reduced the native population.

Brazil, which the Portuguese reached in 1500 and settled after 1530, and the Caribbean colonies of several European nations developed a plantation economy where sugarcane, tobacco, cotton, coffee, rice, indigo, and lumber were grown commercially by slaves. From the early 16th to the late 19th century, some 10 million Africans were transported to **slavery** in the New World.

Netherlands. The urban, Calvinist N provinces of the Netherlands rebelled (1568) against Hapsburg Spain and founded an oligarchic mercantile republic. Their strategic control of the Baltic grain market enabled them to exploit Mediterranean food shortages. Religious refugees—French and Belgian Protestants, Iberian Jews—added to the cosmopolitan commercial talent pool. After Spain absorbed Portugal in 1580, the Dutch seized Portuguese possessions and created a vast, though generally short-lived commercial empire in Brazil, the Antilles, Africa, India, Ceylon, Malacca, Indonesia, and Taiwan and challenged or supplanted Portuguese traders in China and Japan. Revolution in 1640 restored Portuguese independence.

England. Anglicanism became firmly established under Elizabeth I after a brief Catholic interlude under "Bloody Mary" (1553-58). But religious and political conflicts led to a rebellion (1642) by Parliament. Roundheads (Puritans) defeated Cavaliers (Royalists); Charles I was beheaded (1649). The new **Commonwealth** was ruled as a military dictatorship by Cromwell, who also brutally crushed (1649-51) an Irish rebellion. Conflicts within the Puritan camp (democratic Levelers defeated 1649) aided the Stuart restoration (1660), but Parliament was permanently strengthened and the peaceful "Glorious Revolution" (1688) advanced political and religious liberties (writings of Locke, 1632-1704). British privateers (Drake, 1540-96) challenged Spanish control of the New World and penetrated Asian trade routes (Madras taken, 1639). North American colonies (Jamestown, 1607; Plymouth, 1620) provided an outlet for religious dissenters from Europe.

France. Emerging from the religious civil wars in 1628, France regained military and commercial great power status under the ministries of **Richelieu** (1624-42), Mazarin (1643-61), and Colbert (1662-83). Under Louis XIV (r 1643-1715) royal absolutism triumphed over nobles and local *parlements* (defeat of Fronde, 1648-53). Permanent colonies were founded in Canada (1608), the Caribbean (1626), and India (1674).

Sweden. Sweden seceded from the Scandinavian Union in 1523. The thinly populated agrarian state (with copper, iron, and timber exports) was united by the Vasa kings, whose conquests by the mid-17th cent. made Sweden the dominant Baltic power. The empire collapsed in the Great Northern War (1700-21).

Poland. After the union with Lithuania in 1447, Poland ruled vast territories from the Baltic to the Black Sea, resisting German and Turkish incursions. Catholic nobles failed to gain the loyalty of their Orthodox Christian subjects in the E; commerce and trades were practiced by German and Jewish immigrants. The bloody 1648-49 Cossack uprising began the kingdom's dismemberment.

China. A new dynasty, the Manchus, invaded from the NE, seized power in 1644, and expanded Chinese control to its greatest extent in Central and Southeast Asia. Trade and diplomatic contact with Europe grew, carefully controlled by China. New crops (sweet potato, maize, peanut) allowed an economic and population growth (pop. 300 million, in 1800). Traditional arts and literature were pursued with increased sophistication (*Dream of the Red Chamber*, novel, mid-18th cent.).

Japan. Tokugawa Ieyasu, shogun from 1603, finally unified and pacified feudal Japan. Hereditary daimyos and samurai monopolized government office and the professions. An urban merchant class grew, literacy spread, and a cultural renaissance occurred (haiku, a verse innovation of the poet Basho, 1644-94). Fear of European domination led to persecution of Christian converts from 1597 and to stringent isolation from outside contact from 1640.

Philosophy, Industry, and Revolution: 1700-1800

Science and Reason. Faith in human reason and science as the source of truth and a means to improve the physical and social environment, espoused since the Renaissance (Francis Bacon, 1561-1626), was bolstered by scientific discoveries in spite of theological opposition (Galileo's forced retraction, 1633). Descartes applied the logical method of mathematics to discover "self-evident" scientific and philosophical truths, and Newton emphasized induction from experimental observation.

The challenge of reason to traditional religious and political values and institutions began with **Spinoza** (1632-77), who interpreted the Bible historically and called for political and intellectual freedom.

French philosophers assumed leadership of the **Enlightenment** in the 18th cent. Montesquieu (1689-1755) used British history to support his notions of limited government. Voltaire's (1694-1778) diaries

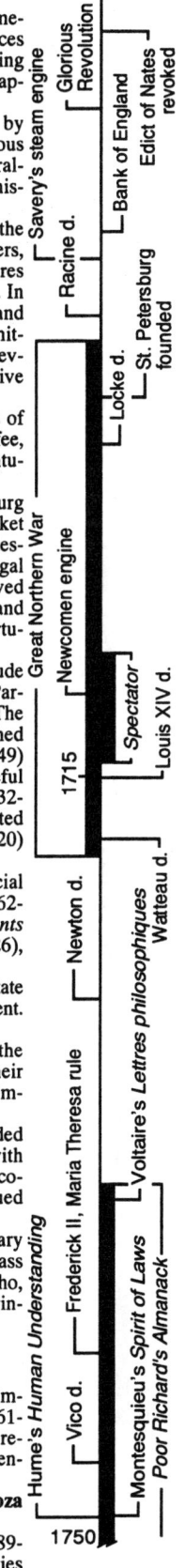

1680

- Savery's steam engine
- Glorious Revolution
- Bank of England
- Edict of Nantes revoked
- Racine d.
- Locke d.
- St. Petersburg founded
- Great Northern War
- Newcomen engine
- Spectator
- Louis XIV d.

1715

- Newton d.
- Watteau d.
- Voltaire's Lettres philosophiques
- Frederick II, Maria Theresa rule
- Montesquieu's Spirit of Laws
- Poor Richard's Almanack
- Hume's Human Understanding
- Vico d.

1750

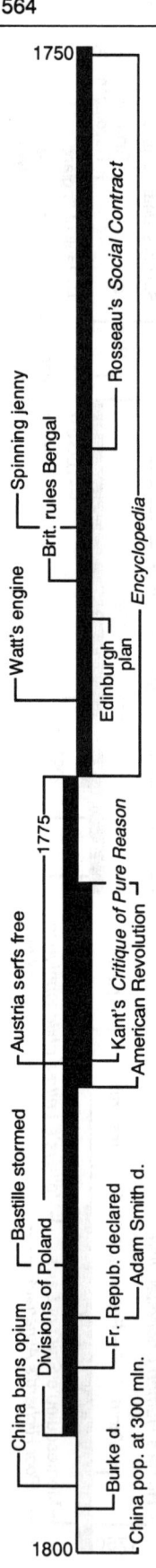

and novels of exotic travel illustrated the intellectual trends toward secular ethics and relativism. Rousseau's (1712-1778) radical concepts of the **social contract** and of the inherent goodness of the common man gave impetus to antimonarchical republicanism. The *Encyclopedia* (1751-72), edited by Diderot and d'Alembert and designed as a monument to reason, was largely devoted to practical technology.

In England, ideals of political and religious liberty were connected with empiricist philosophy and science in the followers of Locke. But the extreme **empiricism of Hume** (1711-76) and Berkeley (1685-1753) posed limits to the identification of reason with absolute truth, as did the evolutionary approach to law and politics of Burke (1729-97) and the utilitarianism of Bentham (1748-1832). Adam Smith (1723-90) and other **physiocrats** called for a rationalization of economic activity by removing artificial barriers to a supposedly natural free exchange of goods.

Despite the political disunity and backwardness of most of Germany, German writers participated in the new philosophical trends popularized by Wolff (1679-1754). **Kant's** (1724-1804) idealism, unifying an empirical epistemology with a priori moral and logical concepts, directed German thought away from skepticism. Italian contributions included work on electricity by Galvani (1737-98) and Volta (1745-1827), the pioneer **historiography of Vico** (1668-1744), and writings on penal reform by Beccaria (1738-94). Benjamin Franklin (1706-90) was celebrated in Europe for his varied achievements.

The growth of the **press** (*Spectator*, 1711-12) and the wide distribution of realistic but sentimental **novels** attested to the increase of a large bourgeois public.

Arts. Rococo art, characterized by extravagant decorative effects, asymmetries copied from organic models, and artificial pastoral subjects, was favored by the continental aristocracy for most of the century (Watteau, 1684-1721) and had musical analogies in the ornamentalized polyphony of late Baroque. The **Neoclassical** art after 1750, associated with the new scientific archeology, was more streamlined and was infused with the supposed moral and geometric rectitude of the Roman Republic (David, 1748-1825). In England, **town planning** on a grand scale began.

Industrial Revolution in England. Agricultural improvements, such as the sowing drill (1701) and livestock breeding, were implemented on the large fields provided by enclosure of common lands by private owners. Profits from agriculture and from colonial and foreign trade (1800 volume, £54 million) were channeled through hundreds of banks and the **Stock Exchange** (est 1773) into new industrial processes.

The Newcomen steam pump (1712) aided coal mining. Coal fueled the new efficient steam engines patented by Watt in 1769, and coke-smelting produced cheap, sturdy iron for machinery by the 1730s. The **flying shuttle** (1733) and **spinning jenny** (c 1764) were used in the large new cotton textile factories, where women and children were much of the work force. Goods were transported cheaply over **canals** (2,000 mi built 1760-1800).

American Revolution. The British colonies in North America attracted a mass immigration of religious dissenters and poor people throughout the 17th and 18th centuries, coming from all parts of the British Isles, Germany, the Netherlands, and other countries. The population reached 3 million nonnatives by the 1770s. The small native population was greatly reduced by European diseases and by wars with and between the various colonies. British attempts to control colonial trade and to tax the colonists to pay for the costs of colonial administration and defense clashed with traditions of local self-government and eventually provoked the colonies to rebellion.

Central and East Europe. The monarchs of the three states that dominated E Europe—Austria, Prussia, and Russia—accepted the advice and legitimation of philosophes in creating more modern, centralized institutions in their kingdoms, enlarged by the division (1772-95) of Poland.

Under **Frederick II** (r 1740-86) Prussia, with its efficient modern army, doubled in size. State monopolies and tariff protection fostered industry, and some legal reforms were introduced. Austria's heterogeneous realms were unified under **Maria Theresa** (r 1740-80) and **Joseph II** (r 1780-90). Reforms in education, law, and religion were enacted, and the Austrian serfs were freed (1781). With its defeat in the Seven Years' War in 1763, Austria failed to regain Silesia and ceased its active role in Germany, but was compensated by expansion to the E and S (Hungary, Slavonia, 1699; Galicia, 1772).

Russia, whose borders continued to expand in all directions, adopted some Western bureaucratic and economic policies under **Peter I** (r 1682-1725) and Catherine II (r 1762-96). Trade and cultural contacts with the West multiplied from the new Baltic Sea capital, **St. Petersburg** (est 1703).

French Revolution. The growing French middle class lacked political power and resented aristocratic tax privileges, especially in light of the successful American Revolution. Peasants lacked adequate land and were burdened with feudal obligations to nobles. Wars with Britain drained the treasury, finally forcing the king to call the **Estates-General** in 1789 (first time since 1614), in an atmosphere of food riots (poor crop in 1788).

Aristocratic resistance to absolutism was soon overshadowed by the reformist Third Estate (middle class), which proclaimed itself the **National Constituent Assembly** June 17 and took the "Tennis Court oath" on June 20 to secure a constitution. The storming of the **Bastille** on July 14 by Parisian artisans was followed by looting and seizure of aristocratic property throughout France. Assembly reforms included abolition of class and regional privileges, a Declaration of Rights, suffrage by taxpayers (75% of males), and the **Civil Constitution of the Clergy** providing for election and loyalty oaths for priests. A republic was declared Sept. 22, 1792, in spite of royalist pressure from Austria and Prussia, which had declared war in April (joined by Britain the next year). Louis XVI was beheaded Jan. 21, 1793, Queen Marie Antoinette was beheaded Oct. 16, 1793.

Royalist uprisings in La Vendée and military reverses led to a **reign of terror** in which tens of thousands of opponents of the Revolution and criminals were executed. Radical reforms in the **Convention** period (Sept. 1793-Oct. 1795) included the abolition of colonial slavery, economic measures to aid the poor, support of public education, and a short-lived de-Christianization.

Division among radicals (execution of Hebert, March 1794; Danton, April; and Robespierre, July) aided the ascendance of a moderate **Directory**, which consolidated military victories. **Napoleon Bonaparte** (1769-1821), a popular young general, exploited political divisions and participated in a coup Nov. 9, 1799, making himself first consul (dictator).

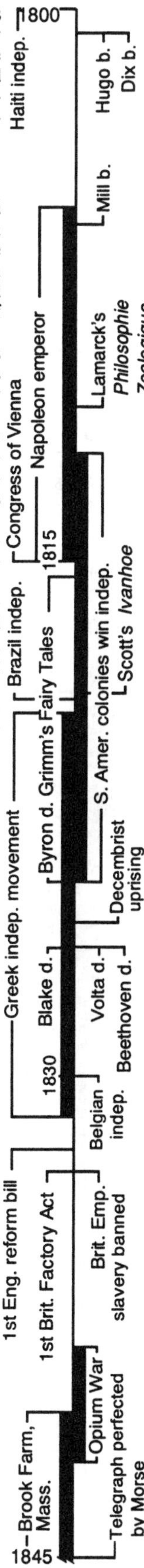

1800
Haiti indep.
Hugo b.
Dix b.
Mill b.
Napoleon emperor
Lamarck's *Philosophie Zoologique*
Congress of Vienna
1815
Brazil indep.
Grimm's Fairy Tales
S. Amer. colonies win indep.
Scott's *Ivanhoe*
Greek indep. movement
Byron d.
Decembrist uprising
Blake d.
Volta d.
Beethoven d.
1830
Belgian indep.
1st Eng. reform bill
1st Brit. Factory Act
Brit. Emp. slavery banned
Opium War
Brook Farm, Mass.
Telegraph perfected by Morse
1845

India. Sikh and Hindu rebels (Rajputs, Marathas) and Afghans destroyed the power of the Mughals during the 18th cent. After France's defeat (1763) in the Seven Years' War, Britain was the primary European trade power in India. Its control of inland **Bengal and Bihar** was recognized (1765) by the Mughal shah, who granted the **British East India Co.** (under Clive, 1725-74) the right to collect land revenue there. Despite objections from Parliament (1784 India Act), the company's involvement in local wars and politics led to repeated acquisitions of new territory. The company exported Indian textiles, sugar, and indigo.

Change Gathers Steam: 1800-40

French ideals and empire spread. Inspired by the ideals of the French Revolution, and supported by the expanding French armies, new republican regimes arose near France: the **Batavian** Republic in the Netherlands (1795-1806), the **Helvetic** Republic in Switzerland (1798-1803), the **Cisalpine** Republic in N Italy (1797-1805), the **Ligurian** Republic in Genoa (1797-1805), and the **Parthenopean** Republic in S Italy (1799). A Roman Republic existed briefly in 1798 after Pope Pius VI was arrested by French troops. In Italy and Germany, new nationalist sentiments were stimulated both in imitation of and in reaction to France (anti-French and anti-Jacobin peasant uprisings in Italy, 1796-99).

From 1804, when Napoleon declared himself emperor, to 1812, a succession of military victories (Austerlitz, 1805; Jena, 1806) extended his control over most of Europe, through puppet states (**Confederation of the Rhine** united W German states for the first time and **Grand Duchy of Warsaw** revived Polish national hopes), expansion of the empire, and alliances.

Among the lasting reforms initiated under Napoleon's absolutist reign were: establishment of the Bank of France, centralization of tax collection, codification of law along Roman models (Code Napoléon), and reform and extension of secondary and university education. In an 1801 concordat, the papacy recognized the effective autonomy of the French Catholic Church. Some 400,000 French soldiers were killed in the Napoleonic Wars, along with 600,000 foreign troops.

Last gasp of old regime. France's coastal blockade of Europe (**Continental System**) failed to neutralize Britain. The disastrous 1812 invasion of Russia exposed Napoleon's overextension. After Napoleon's 1814 exile at Elba, his armies were defeated (1815) at **Waterloo**, by British and Prussian troops.

At the **Congress of Vienna**, the monarchs and princes of Europe redrew their boundaries, to the advantage of Prussia (in Saxony and the Ruhr), Austria (in Illyria and Venetia), and Russia (in Poland and Finland). British conquest of Dutch and French colonies (S Africa, Ceylon, Mauritius) was recognized, and France, under the restored Bourbons, retained its expanded 1792 borders. The settlement brought 50 years of international peace to Europe.

But the Congress was unable to check the advance of liberal ideals and of nationalism among the smaller European nations. The 1825 **Decembrist uprising** by liberal officers in Russia was easily suppressed. But an independence movement in **Greece**, stirred by commercial prosperity and a cultural revival, succeeded in expelling Ottoman rule by 1831, with the aid of Britain, France, and Russia.

A constitutional monarchy was secured in France by the **1830 Revolution**; Louis Philippe became king. The revolutionary contagion spread to **Belgium**, which gained its independence (1830) from the Dutch monarchy, to **Poland**, whose rebellion was defeated (1830-31) by Russia, and to Germany.

Romanticism. A new style in intellectual and artistic life began to replace Neoclassicism and Rococo after the mid-18th cent. By the early 19th cent., this style, Romanticism, had prevailed in the European world.

Rousseau had begun the reaction against excessive rationalism and skepticism; in education (*Émile*, 1762) he stressed subjective spontaneity over regularized instruction. In Germany, Lessing (1729-81) and Herder (1744-1803) favorably compared the German folk song to classical forms and began a cult of Shakespeare, whose passion and "natural" wisdom was a model for the romantic *Sturm und Drang* (Storm and Stress) movement. **Goethe's** *Sorrows of Young Werther* (1774) set the model for the tragic, passionate genius.

A new interest in **Gothic architecture** in England after 1760 (Walpole, 1717-97) spread through Europe, associated with an aesthetic Christian and mystic revival (Blake, 1757-1827). Celtic, Norse, and German mythology and folk tales were revived or imitated (Macpherson's Ossian translation, 1762; Grimm's Fairy Tales, 1812-22). The medieval revival (Scott's *Ivanhoe*, 1819) led to a new interest in history, stressing national differences and organic growth (Carlyle, 1795-1881; Michelet, 1798-1874), corresponding to theories of natural evolution (Lamarck's *Philosophie Zoologique*, 1809; Lyell's *Geology*, 1830-33).

Revolution and war fed an obsession with freedom and conflict, expressed by poets (**Byron**, 1788-1824; **Hugo**, 1802-85) and philosophers (**Hegel**, 1770-1831).

Wild gardens replaced the formal French variety, and painters favored rural, stormy, and mountainous landscapes (**Turner**, 1775-1851; **Constable**, 1776-1837). Clothing became freer, with wigs, hoops, and ruffles discarded. Originality and genius were expected in the life as well as the work of inspired artists (Murger's *Scenes from Bohemian Life*, 1847-49). Exotic locales and themes (as in Gothic horror stories) were used in art and literature (Delacroix, 1798-1863; **Poe**, 1809-49).

Music exhibited the new dramatic style and a breakdown of classical forms (Beethoven, 1770-1827). The use of folk melodies and modes aided the growth of distinct national traditions (Glinka in Russia, 1804-57).

Latin America. Haiti, under the former slave **Toussaint L'Ouverture**, was the first Latin American independent state (1804). All the mainland Spanish colonies won their independence (1810-24), under such leaders as **Bolivar** (1783-1830). Brazil became an independent empire (1822) under the Portuguese prince regent. A new class of military officers divided power with large landholders and the church.

United States. Heavy immigration and exploitation of ample natural resources fueled rapid economic growth. The spread of the franchise, public education, and antislavery sentiment were signs of a widespread democratic ethic.

China. Failure to keep pace with Western arms technology exposed China to greater European influence and hampered efforts to bar imports of opium, which had damaged Chinese society and drained

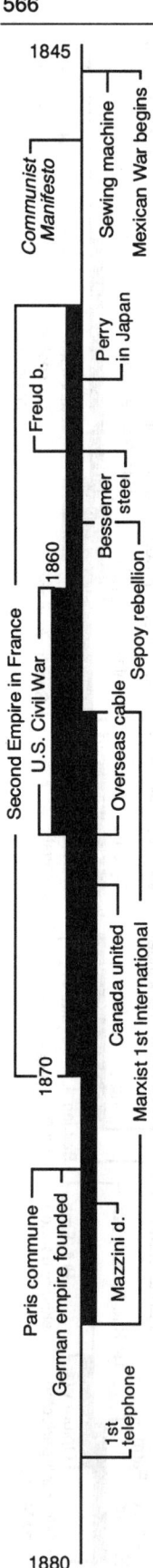

1845

Communist Manifesto

Sewing machine

Mexican War begins

Freud b.

Perry in Japan

Bessemer steel

1860

Second Empire in France

U.S. Civil War

Sepoy rebellion

Overseas cable

Canada united

Marxist 1st International

1870

Paris commune

German empire founded

Mazzini d.

1st telephone

1880

wealth overseas. In the **Opium War** (1839-42), Britain forced China to expand trade opportunities and to cede Hong Kong.

Triumph of Progress: 1840-80

Idea of Progress. As a result of the cumulative scientific, economic, and political changes of the preceding eras, the idea took hold among literate people in the West that continuing growth and improvement was the usual state of human and natural life.

Darwin's statement of the **theory of evolution** and survival of the fittest (*Origin of Species*, 1859), defended by intellectuals and scientists against theological objections, was taken as confirmation that progress was the natural direction of life. The controversy helped define popular ideas of the dedicated scientist and ever-expanding human knowledge of and control over the world (Foucault's demonstration of earth's rotation, 1851; Pasteur's germ theory, 1861).

Liberals following Ricardo (1772-1823) in their faith that unrestrained competition would bring continuous economic expansion sought to adjust political life to the new social realities and believed that unregulated competition of ideas would yield truth (Mill, 1806-73). In England, successive reform bills (1832, 1867, 1884) gave representation to the new industrial towns and extended the franchise to the middle and lower classes and to Catholics, Dissenters, and Jews. On both sides of the Atlantic, reformists tried to improve conditions for the mentally ill (Dix, 1802-87), women (Anthony, 1820-1906), and prisoners. Slavery was barred in the British Empire (1833); the U.S. (1865); and Brazil (1888).

Socialist theories based on ideas of human perfectibility or historical progress were widely disseminated. Utopian socialists such as Saint-Simon (1760-1825) envisaged an orderly, just society directed by a technocratic elite. A model factory town, New Lanark, Scotland, was set up by utopian Robert Owen (1771-1858), and utopian communal experiments were tried in the U.S. (Brook Farm, Mass., 1841-47). Bakunin's (1814-76) anarchism represented the opposite utopian extreme of total freedom. Marx (1818-83) posited the inevitable triumph of socialism in the industrial countries through a historical process of class conflict.

Spread of industry. The technical processes and managerial innovations of the English industrial revolution spread to Europe (especially Germany) and the U.S., causing an explosion of industrial production, demand for raw materials, and competition for markets. Inventors, both trained and self-educated, provided the means for larger-scale production (Bessemer steel, 1856; sewing machine, 1846). Many inventions were shown at the 1851 London Great Exhibition at the Crystal Palace, the theme of which was universal prosperity.

Local specialization and long-distance trade were aided by a revolution in transportation and communication. Railroads were first introduced in the 1820s in England and the U.S. More than 150,000 mi of track had been laid worldwide by 1880, with another 100,000 mi laid in the next decade. Steamships were improved (*Savannah* crossed Atlantic, 1819). The telegraph, perfected by 1844 (Morse), connected the Old and New Worlds by cable in 1866 and quickened the pace of international commerce and politics. The first commercial telephone exchange went into operation in the U.S. in 1878.

The new class of industrial workers, uprooted from their rural homes, lacked job security and suffered from dangerous overcrowded conditions at work and at home. Many responded by organizing trade unions (legalized in England, 1824; France, 1884). The U.S. Knights of Labor had 700,000 members by 1886. The First International (1864-76) tried to unite workers internationally around a Marxist program. The quasi-Socialist Paris Commune uprising (1871) was violently suppressed. Factory Acts to reduce child labor and regulate conditions were passed (1833-50 in England). Social security measures were introduced by the Bismarck regime (1883-89) in Germany.

Revolutions of 1848. Among the causes of the continent-wide revolutions were an international collapse of credit and resulting unemployment, bad harvests in 1845-47, and a cholera epidemic. The new urban proletariat and expanding bourgeoisie demanded a greater political role. Republics were proclaimed in France, Rome, and Venice. Nationalist feelings reached fever pitch in the Hapsburg empire, as Hungary declared independence under Kossuth, as a Slav Congress demanded equality, and as Piedmont tried to drive Austria from Lombardy. A national liberal assembly at Frankfurt called for German unification.

But riots fueled bourgeois fears of socialism (Marx and Engels, *Communist Manifesto*, 1848), and peasants remained conservative. The old establishment—The Papacy, the Hapsburgs with the help of the Czarist Russian army —was able to rout the revolutionaries by 1849. The French Republic succumbed to a renewed monarchy by 1852 (Emperor Napoleon III).

Great nations unified. Using the "blood and iron" tactics of Bismarck from 1862, Prussia controlled N Germany by 1867 (war with Denmark, 1864; Austria, 1866). After defeating France in 1870 (annexation of Alsace-Lorraine), it won the allegiance of S German states. A new **German Empire** was proclaimed (1871). **Italy**, inspired by Mazzini (1805-72) and Garibaldi (1807-82), was unified by the reformed Piedmont kingdom through uprisings, plebiscites, and war.

The **U.S.**, its area expanded after the 1846-48 Mexican War, defeated (1861-65) a secession attempt by slave states. The Canadian provinces were united in an autonomous **Dominion of Canada** (1867). Control in **India** was removed from the East India Co. and centralized under British administration after the 1857-58 Sepoy rebellion, laying the groundwork for the modern Indian State. Queen Victoria was named Empress of India (1876).

Europe dominates Asia. The Ottoman Empire began to collapse in the face of Balkan nationalisms and European imperial incursions in N Africa (Suez Canal, 1869). The Turks had lost control of most of both regions by 1882. Russia completed its expansion S by 1884 (despite the temporary setback of the Crimean War with Turkey, Britain, and France, 1853-56), taking Turkestan, all the Caucasus, and Chinese areas in the E and sponsoring Balkan Slavs against the Turks. A succession of reformist and reactionary regimes presided over a slow modernization (serfs freed, 1861). Persian independence suffered as Russia and British India competed for influence.

China was forced to sign a series of unequal treaties with European powers and Japan. Overpopulation and an inefficient dynasty brought misery and caused rebellions (Taiping, Muslims) leaving tens of millions dead. Japan was forced by the U.S. (Commodore Perry's visits, 1853-54) and Europe to end its isolation. The Meiji restoration (1868) gave power to a Westernizing oligarchy. Intensified empire-building gave Burma to Britain (1824-85) and Indochina to France (1862-95). Christian missionary activity followed imperial and trade expansion in Asia.

Respectability. The fine arts were expected to reflect and encourage the progress of morals and manners among the Victorians. Prudery, exaggerated delicacy, and familial piety were heralded by **Bowdler's** expurgated edition (1818) of Shakespeare. Government-supported mass education inculcated a work ethic as a means to escape poverty (Horatio Alger, 1832-99).

The official **Beaux Arts** school in Paris set an international style of imposing public buildings (Paris Opera, 1861-74; Vienna Opera, 1861-69) and uplifting statues (Bartholdi's *Statue of Liberty*, 1884). Realist painting, influenced by photography (Daguerre, 1837), appealed to a new mass audience with social or historical narrative (Wilkie, 1785-1841; Poynter, 1836-1919) or with serious religious, moral, or social messages (pre-Raphaelites, Millet's *Angelus*, 1858) often drawn from ordinary life. The **Impressionists** (Monet, 1840-1926; Pissarro, 1830-1903; Renoir, 1841-1919) rejected the formalism, sentimentality, and precise techniques of academic art in favor of a spontaneous, undetailed rendering of the world through careful representation of the effect of natural light on objects.

Realistic **novelists** presented the full panorama of social classes and personalities, but retained sentimentality and moral judgment (Dickens, 1812-70; Eliot, 1819-80; Tolstoy, 1828-1910; Balzac, 1799-1850).

Veneer of Stability: 1880-1900

Imperialism triumphant. The vast **African** interior, visited by European explorers (Barth, 1821-65; Livingstone, 1813-73), was conquered by the European powers in rapid, competitive thrusts from their coastal bases after 1880, mostly for domestic political and international strategic reasons. W African Muslim kingdoms (Fulani), Arab slave traders (Zanzibar), and Bantu military confederations (Zulu) were alike subdued. Only Christian Ethiopia (defeat of Italy, 1896) and Liberia resisted successfully. France (W Africa) and Britain ("Cape to Cairo," Boer War, 1899-1902) were the major beneficiaries. The ideology of "the white man's burden" (Kipling, *Barrack Room Ballads*, 1892) or of a "civilizing mission" (France) justified the conquests.

W European foreign capital investment soared to nearly $40 billion by 1914, but most was in E Europe (France, Germany), the Americas (Britain), and the Europeans' colonies. The foundation of the modern interdependent world economy was laid, with cartels dominating raw material trade.

An industrious world. Industrial and technological proficiency characterized the 2 new great powers—Germany and the **U.S.** Coal and iron deposits enabled Germany to reach 2d or 3d place status in iron, steel, and shipbuilding by the 1900s. German electrical and chemical industries were world leaders. The U.S. post-Civil War boom (interrupted by "panics"—1884, 1893, 1896) was shaped by massive immigration from S and E Europe from 1880, government subsidy of railroads, and huge private monopolies (Standard Oil, 1870; U.S. Steel, 1901). The **Spanish-American War**, 1898 (Philippine Insurrection, 1899-1902), and the Open Door policy in China (1899) made the U.S. a world power.

England led in **urbanization** (72% by 1890), with **London** the world capital of finance, insurance, and shipping. Sewer systems (Paris, 1850s), electric subways (London, 1890), parks, and bargain department stores helped improve living standards for most of the urban population of the industrial world.

Westernization of Asia. Asian reaction to European economic, military, and religious incursions took the form of imitation of Western techniques and adoption of Western ideas of progress and freedom. The Chinese "self-strengthening" movement of the 1860s and '70s included rail, port, and arsenal improvements and metal and textile mills. Reformers such as **K'ang Yu-wei** (1858-1927) won liberalizing reforms in 1898, right after the European and Japanese "scramble for concessions."

A universal education system in Japan and importation of foreign industrial, scientific, and military experts aided Japan's unprecedented rapid modernization after 1868, under the authoritarian Meiji regime. Japan's victory in the **Sino-Japanese War** (1894-95) put Formosa and Korea in its power.

In India, the British alliance with the remaining princely states masked reform sentiment among the Westernized urban elite; higher education had been conducted largely in English for 50 years. The **Indian National Congress**, founded in 1885, demanded a larger government role for Indians.

Fin-de-siècle **sophistication.** Naturalist writers pushed realism to its extreme limits, adopting a quasi-scientific attitude and writing about formerly taboo subjects such as sex, crime, extreme poverty, and corruption (Flaubert, 1821-80; Zola, 1840-1902; Hardy, 1840-1928). Unseen or repressed psychological motivations were explored in the clinical and theoretical works of **Freud** (1856-1939) and in the fiction of Dostoyevsky (1821-81), James (1843-1916), Schnitzler (1862-1931), and others.

A contempt for bourgeois life or a desire to shock a complacent audience was shared by the French **symbolist** poets (Verlaine, 1844-96; Rimbaud, 1854-91), by neopagan English writers (Swinburne, 1837-1909), by continental dramatists (Ibsen, 1828-1906) and by satirists (Wilde, 1854-1900). **Nietzsche** (1844-1900) was influential in his elitism and pessimism.

Postimpressionist art neglected long-cherished conventions of representation (Cezanne, 1839-1906) and showed a willingness to learn from primitive and non-European art (Gauguin, 1848-1903; Japanese prints).

Racism. Gobineau (1816-82) gave a pseudobiological foundation to modern racist theories, which spread in the latter 19th cent., along with **Social Darwinism**, the belief that societies are and should be organized as a struggle for survival of the fittest. The medieval period was interpreted as an era of natural Germanic rule (Chamberlain, 1855-1927), and notions of superiority were associated with German national aspirations (Treitschke, 1834-96). **Anti-Semitism**, with a new racist rationale, became a significant political force in Germany (Anti-Semitic Petition, 1880), Austria (Lueger, 1844-1910), and France (Dreyfus case, 1894-1906).

Last Respite: 1900-9

Alliances. While the peace of Europe (and its dependencies) continued to hold (1907 **Hague Conference** extended the rules of war and international arbitration procedures), imperial rivalries, protec-

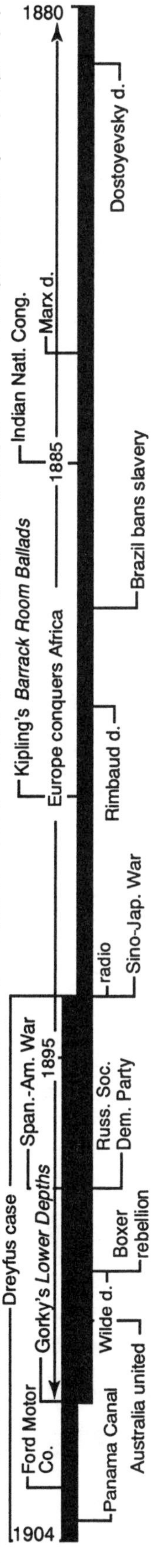

Timeline (right margin)

1880

Dostoyevsky d.

Indian Natl. Cong.

Marx d.

1885

Brazil bans slavery

Kipling's *Barrack Room Ballads*

Europe conquers Africa

Rimbaud d.

radio

Sino-Jap. War

Span.-Am. War

1895

Russ. Soc. Dem. Party

Boxer rebellion

Dreyfus case

Gorky's *Lower Depths*

Wilde d.

Ford Motor Co.

Panama Canal

Australia united

1904

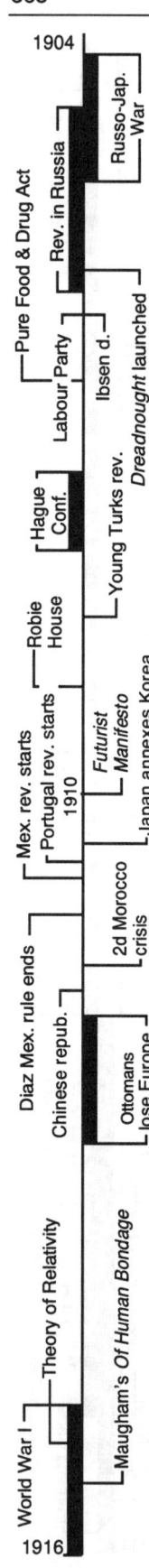

1904

Russo-Jap. War

Rev. in Russia

Pure Food & Drug Act

Ibsen d.

Labour Party

Dreadnought launched

Hague Conf.

Young Turks rev.

Robie House

Japan annexes Korea

Futurist Manifesto

Mex. rev. starts

Portugal rev. starts

1910

2d Morocco crisis

Diaz Mex. rule ends

Chinese repub.

Ottomans lose Europe

Theory of Relativity

Maugham's Of Human Bondage

World War I

1916

tionist trade practices (in Germany and France), and the escalating arms race (British *Dreadnought* battleship launched; Germany widens Kiel canal, 1906) exacerbated minor disputes (German-French Moroccan "crises," 1905, 1911).

Security was sought through alliances: **Triple Alliance** (Germany, Austria-Hungary, Italy; renewed in 1902 and 1907); Anglo-Japanese Alliance (1902), Franco-Russian Alliance (1899), **Entente Cordiale** (Britain, France, 1904), Anglo-Russian Treaty (1907), German-Ottoman friendship.

Ottomans decline. The inefficient, corrupt Ottoman government was unable to resist further loss of territory. Nearly all European lands were lost in 1912 to Serbia, Greece, Montenegro, and Bulgaria. Italy took Libya and the Dodecanese islands the same year, and Britain took Kuwait (1899) and the Sinai (1906). The **Young Turk** revolution in 1908 forced the sultan to restore a constitution, and it introduced some social reform, industrialization, and secularization.

British Empire. British trade and cultural influence remained dominant in the empire, but constitutional reforms presaged its eventual dissolution: The colonies of **Australia** were united in 1901 under a self-governing commonwealth. **New Zealand** acquired dominion status in 1907. The old Boer republics joined Cape Colony and Natal in the self-governing **Union of South Africa** in 1910.

The 1909 Indian Councils Act enhanced the role of elected province legislatures in **India**. The Muslim League (founded 1906) sought separate communal representation.

East Asia. Japan exploited its growing industrial power to expand its empire. Victory in the 1904-5 war against Russia (naval battle of Tsushima, 1905) assured Japan's domination of **Korea** (annexed 1910) and Manchuria (Port Arthur taken, 1905).

In China, central authority began to crumble (empress died, 1908). Reforms (Confucian exam system ended 1905, modernization of the army, building of railroads) were inadequate, and secret societies of reformers and nationalists, inspired by the Westernized **Sun Yat-sen** (1866-1925) fomented periodic uprisings in the S.

Siam, whose independence had been guaranteed by Britain and France in 1896, was split into spheres of influence by those countries in 1907.

Russia. The population of the Russian Empire approached 150 million in 1900. Reforms in education, in law, and in local institutions (*zemstvos*) and an industrial boom starting in the 1880s (oil, railroads) created the beginnings of a modern state, despite the autocratic tsarist regime. Liberals (1903 Union of Liberation), Socialists (Social Democrats founded 1898, Bolsheviks split off 1903), and populists (Social Revolutionaries founded 1901) were periodically repressed, and national minorities were persecuted (anti-Jewish pogroms, 1903, 1905-6).

An industrial crisis after 1900 and harvest failures aggravated poverty among urban workers, and the 1904-5 defeat by Japan (which checked Russia's Asian expansion) sparked the Revolution of 1905-6. A **Duma** (parliament) was created, and an agricultural reform (under Stolypin, prime minister 1906-11) created a large class of landowning peasants (kulaks).

The world shrinks. Developments in transportation and communication and mass population movements helped create an awareness of an interdependent world. Early **automobiles** (Daimler, Benz, 1885) were experimental or were designed as luxuries. Assembly-line mass production (Ford Motor Co., 1903) made the invention practicable, and by 1910 nearly 500,000 motor vehicles were registered in the U.S. alone. **Heavier-than-air flights** began in 1903 in the U.S. (Wright brothers), preceded by glider, balloon, and model plane advances in several countries. Trade was advanced by improvements in **ship design** (gyrocompass, 1910), speed (*Lusitania* crossed Atlantic in 5 days, 1907), and reach (Panama Canal begun, 1904).

The first transatlantic **radio** telegraphic transmission occurred in 1901, 6 years after Marconi discovered radio. Radio transmission of human speech had been made in 1900. Telegraphic transmission of photos was achieved in 1904, lending immediacy to news reports. **Phonographs**, popularized by Caruso's recordings (starting 1902), made for quick international spread of musical styles (ragtime). **Motion pictures**, perfected in the 1890s (Dickson, Lumière brothers), became a popular and artistic medium after 1900; newsreels appeared in 1909.

Emigration from crowded European centers soared in the decade: 9 million migrated to the U.S., and millions more went to Siberia, Canada, Argentina, Australia, South Africa, and Algeria. Some 70 million Europeans emigrated in the century before 1914. Several million Chinese, Indians, and Japanese migrated to Southeast Asia, where their urban skills often enabled them to take a predominant economic role.

Social reform. The social and economic problems of the poor were kept in the public eye by realist fiction writers (Dreiser's *Sister Carrie*, 1900; Gorky's *Lower Depths*, 1902; Sinclair's *Jungle*, 1906), journalists (U.S. muckrakers—Steffens, Tarbell) and artists (Ashcan school). Frequent labor strikes and occasional assassinations by anarchists or radicals (Empress Elizabeth of Austria, 1898; King Umberto I of Italy, 1900; U.S. Pres. McKinley, 1901; Russian Interior Minister Plehve, 1904; Portugal's King Carlos, 1908) added to social tension and fear of revolution.

But democratic reformism prevailed. In Germany, Bernstein's (1850-1932) **revisionist Marxism**, downgrading revolution, was accepted by the powerful Social Democrats and trade unions. The British Fabian Society (the Webbs, Shaw) and the Labour Party (founded 1906) worked for reforms such as Social Security and union rights (1906), while woman suffragists grew more militant. U.S. **progressives** fought big business (Pure Food and Drug Act, 1906). In France, the 10-hour work day (1904) and separation of church and state (1905) were reform victories, as was universal suffrage in Austria (1907).

Arts. An unprecedented period of experimentation, centered in France, produced several new **painting** styles: Fauvism exploited bold color areas (Matisse, *Woman with Hat*, 1905); expressionism reflected powerful inner emotions (the Brücke group, 1905); cubism combined several views of an object on one flat surface (Picasso's *Demoiselles*, 1906-7); futurism tried to depict speed and motion (Italian Futurist Manifesto, 1910). **Architects** explored new uses of steel structures, with facades either neoclassical (Adler and Sullivan in U.S.); curvilinear Art Nouveau (Gaudi's Casa Mila, 1905-10); or functionally streamlined (Wright's Robie House, 1909).

Music and Dance shared the experimental spirit. Ruth St. Denis (1877-1968) and Isadora Duncan (1878-1927) pioneered modern dance, while Diaghilev in Paris revitalized classic ballet from 1909.

Composers explored atonal music (Debussy, 1862-1918) and dissonance (Schoenberg, 1874-1951) or revolutionized classical forms (Stravinsky, 1882-1971), often showing jazz or folk music influences.

War and Revolution: 1910-19

War threatens. Germany under Wilhelm II sought a political and imperial role consonant with its industrial strength, challenging Britain's world supremacy and threatening France, which was still resenting the loss (1871) of Alsace-Lorraine. Austria wanted to curb an expanded Serbia (after 1912) and the threat it posed to its own Slav lands. Russia feared Austrian and German political and economic aims in the Balkans and Turkey. An accelerated arms race resulted: The German standing army rose to more than 2 million men by 1914. Russia and France had more than a million each, and Austria and the British Empire nearly a million each. Dozens of enormous battleships were built by the powers after 1906.

The **assassination of Austrian Archduke Franz Ferdinand** by a Serbian, June 28, 1914, was the pretext for war. The system of alliances made the conflict Europe-wide; Germany's invasion of Belgium to outflank France forced Britain to enter the war. Patriotic fervor was nearly unanimous among all classes in most countries.

World War I. German forces were stopped in France in one month. The rival armies dug **trench networks**. Artillery and improved machine guns prevented either side from any lasting advance despite repeated assaults (600,000 dead at **Verdun**, Feb.-July 1916). Poison gas, used by Germany in 1915, proved ineffective. More than 1 million U.S. troops tipped the balance after mid-1917, forcing Germany to sue for peace the next year. The formal armistice was signed at 5 AM, Nov. 11, 1918.

In the E, the Russian armies were thrown back (battle of **Tannenberg**, Aug. 20, 1914), and the war grew unpopular in Russia. An allied attempt to relieve Russia through Turkey failed (**Gallipoli**, 1915). The **Russian Revolution** (1917) abolished the monarchy. The new Bolshevik regime signed the capitulatory Brest-Litovsk peace in March 1918. Italy entered the war on the allied side in May 1915 but was pushed back by Oct. 1917. A renewed offensive with Allied aid in Oct.-Nov. 1918 forced Austria to surrender.

The British Navy successfully blockaded Germany, which responded with submarine U-boat attacks; **unrestricted submarine warfare** against neutrals after Jan. 1917 helped bring the U.S. into the war. Other battlefields included Palestine and Mesopotamia, both of which Britain wrested from the Turks in 1917, and the African and Pacific colonies of Germany, most of which fell to Britain, France, Australia, Japan, and South Africa.

From 1916, the civilian populations and economies of both sides were mobilized to an unprecedented degree. Hardships intensified among fighting nations in 1917 (French mutiny crushed in May). More than 10 million soldiers died in the war.

Settlement. At the **Paris Peace Conference** (Jan.-June 1919), concluded by the **Treaty of Versailles**, and in subsequent negotiations and local wars (Russian-Polish War, 1920), the map of Europe was redrawn with a nod to U.S. Pres. Wilson's principle of self-determination. Austria and Hungary were separated, and much of their land was given to Yugoslavia (formerly Serbia), Romania, Italy, and the newly independent Poland and Czechoslovakia. Germany lost territory in the W, N, and E, while Finland and the Baltic states were detached from Russia. Turkey lost nearly all its Arab lands to British-sponsored Arab states or to direct French and British rule. Belgium's sovereignty was recognized.

A huge **reparations** burden and partial demilitarization were imposed on Germany. Pres. Wilson obtained approval for a League of Nations, but the U.S. Senate refused to allow the U.S. to join.

Russian revolution. Military defeats and high casualties caused a contagious lack of confidence in Tsar Nicholas, who was forced to abdicate Mar. 1917. A liberal provisional government failed to end the war, and massive desertions, riots, and fighting between factions followed. A moderate socialist government under Kerensky was overthrown in a violent coup by the **Bolsheviks** in Petrograd under Lenin, who disbanded the elected Constituent Assembly in Nov. 1917.

The Bolsheviks brutally suppressed all opposition and ended the war with Germany in Mar. 1918. **Civil war** broke out in the summer between the Red Army, including the Bolsheviks and their supporters, and monarchists, anarchists, nationalities (Ukrainians, Georgians, Poles), and others. Small U.S., British, French, and Japanese units also opposed the Bolsheviks (1918-19; Japan in Vladivostok to 1922). The civil war, anarchy, and pogroms devastated the country until the 1920 Red Army victory. The wartime total monopoly of political, economic, and police power by the Communist Party leadership was retained.

Other European revolutions. An unpopular monarchy in **Portugal** was overthrown in 1910. The new republic took severe anticlerical measures in 1911.

After a century of Home Rule agitation, during which **Ireland** was devastated by famine (1 million dead, 1846-47) and emigration, republican militants staged an unsuccessful uprising in Dublin during Easter 1916. The execution of the leaders and mass arrests by the British won popular support for the rebels. The Irish Free State, comprising all but the 6 N counties, achieved dominion status in 1922.

In the aftermath of the world war, radical revolutions were attempted in Germany (**Spartacist** uprising, Jan. 1919), **Hungary** (Kun regime, 1919), and elsewhere. All were suppressed or failed for lack of support.

Chinese revolution. The Manchu Dynasty was overthrown and a republic proclaimed in Oct. 1911. First president Sun Yat-sen resigned in favor of strongman Yuan Shih-k'ai. Sun organized the parliamentarian **Kuomintang** party.

Students launched protests on May 4, 1919, against League of Nations concessions in China to Japan. Nationalist, liberal, and socialist ideas and political groups spread. The **Communist Party** was founded in 1921. A communist regime took power in Mongolia with Soviet support in 1921.

India restive. Indian objections to British rule erupted in nationalist riots as well as in the nonviolent tactics of Gandhi (1869-1948). Nearly 400 unarmed demonstrators were shot at **Amritsar** in Apr. 1919. Britain approved limited self-rule that year.

Mexican revolution. Under the long Diaz dictatorship (1877-1911) the economy advanced, but Indian and mestizo lands were confiscated, and concessions to foreigners (mostly U.S.) damaged the

Timeline (right margin, 1916–1928): Dada movement; Bolshevik coup; World War I; China May 4 protest; Amritsar riots; Russian Civil War; U.S. prohibition; Iraq, Transjordan; Reza Khan in Persia; Russia's NEP; 1922; Rathenau killed; U.S. women's vote; *Ulysses*; Irish Free State; Fasc. March on Rome; Lenin d.; *Kafka's Trial*; Eng. Labour govt.; Portugal coup; Kellogg-Briand Pact; *Threepenny Opera*; 1928

1928

middle class. A **revolution in 1910** led to civil wars and U.S. intervention (1914, 1916-17). Land reform and a more democratic constitution (1917) were achieved.

The Aftermath of War: 1920-29

U.S. Easy credit, technological ingenuity, and war-related industrial decline in Europe caused a long economic boom, in which ownership of the new products—autos, phones, radios—became democratized. Prosperity, an increase in women workers, woman suffrage (1920), and drastic change in fashion (flappers, mannish bob for women, clean-shaven men) created a wide perception of social change, despite prohibition of alcoholic beverages (1919-33). Union membership and strikes increased. Fear of radicals led to Palmer raids (1919-20) and the Sacco/Vanzetti case (1921-27).

Europe sorts itself out. Germany's liberal **Weimar constitution** (1919) could not guarantee a stable government in the face of rightist violence (Rathenau assassinated, 1922) and Communist refusal to cooperate with Socialists. Reparations and Allied occupation of the Rhineland caused staggering inflation that destroyed middle-class savings, but economic expansion resumed after mid-decade, aided by U.S. loans. A sophisticated, innovative culture developed in architecture and design (Bauhaus, 1919-28), film (Lang, *M*, 1931), painting (Grosz), music (Weill, *Threepenny Opera*, 1928), theater (Brecht, *A Man's a Man*, 1926), criticism (Benjamin), philosophy (Jung), and fashion. This culture was considered decadent and socially disruptive by rightists.

England elected its first labor governments (Jan. 1924, June 1929). A 10-day general strike in support of coal miners failed in May 1926. In **Italy**, strikes, political chaos, and violence by small Fascist bands culminated in the Oct. 1922 Fascist March on Rome, which established Mussolini's dictatorship. Strikes were outlawed (1926), and Italian influence was pressed in the Balkans (Albania a protectorate, 1926). A conservative dictatorship was also established in **Portugal** in a 1926 military coup.

Czechoslovakia, the only stable democracy to emerge from the war in Central or East Europe, faced opposition from Germans (in the Sudetenland), Ruthenians, and some Slovaks. As the industrial heartland of the old Hapsburg empire, it remained fairly prosperous. With French backing, it formed the Little Entente with Yugoslavia (1920) and **Romania** (1921) to block Austrian or Hungarian irredentism. Hungary remained dominated by the landholding classes and expansionist feeling. Croats and Slovenes in **Yugoslavia** demanded a federal state until King Alexander I proclaimed (1929) a royal dictatorship. Poland faced nationality problems as well (Germans, Ukrainians, Jews); Pilsudski ruled as dictator from 1926. The Baltic states were threatened by traditionally dominant ethnic Germans and by Soviet-supported communists.

An economic collapse and famine in **Russia** (1921-22) claimed 5 million lives. The New Economic Policy (1921) allowed landownership by peasants and some private commerce and industry. Stalin was absolute ruler within 4 years of Lenin's death (1924). He inaugurated a brutal collectivization program (1929-32) and used foreign communist parties for Soviet state advantage.

Internationalism. Revulsion against World War I led to pacifist agitation, to the Kellogg-Briand Pact renouncing aggressive war (1928), and to **naval disarmament** pacts (Washington, 1922; London, 1930). But the League of Nations was able to arbitrate only minor disputes (Greece-Bulgaria, 1925).

Middle East. Mustafa Kemal (Ataturk) led **Turkish** nationalists in resisting Italian, French, and Greek military advances (1919-23). The sultanate was abolished (1922), and elaborate reforms were passed, including secularization of law and adoption of the Latin alphabet. Ethnic conflict led to persecution of **Armenians** (more than 1 million dead in 1915, 1 million expelled), Greeks (forced Greek-Turk population exchange, 1923), and Kurds (1925 uprising).

With evacuation of the Turks from **Arab** lands, the puritanical Wahabi dynasty of E Arabia conquered (1919-25) what is now Saudi Arabia. British, French, and Arab dynastic and nationalist maneuvering resulted in the creation of 2 more Arab monarchies in 1921—Iraq and Transjordan (both under British control)—and 2 French mandates—Syria and Lebanon. Jewish immigration into British-mandated **Palestine**, inspired by the Zionist movement, was resisted by Arabs, at times violently (1921, 1929 massacres).

Reza Khan ruled **Persia** after his 1921 coup (shah from 1925), centralized control, and created the trappings of a modern state.

China. The Kuomintang under **Chiang Kai-shek** (1887-1975) subdued the warlords by 1928. The Communists were brutally suppressed after their alliance with the Kuomintang was broken in 1927. Relative peace thereafter allowed for industrial and financial improvements, with some Russian, British, and U.S. cooperation.

Arts. Nearly all bounds of subject matter, style, and attitude were broken in the arts of the period. **Abstract** art first took inspiration from natural forms or narrative themes (Kandinsky from 1911) and then worked free of any representational aims (Malevich's suprematism, 1915-19; Mondrian's geometric style from 1917). The **Dada** movement (from 1916) mocked artistic pretension with absurd collages and constructions (Arp, Tzara, from 1916). Paradox, illusion, and psychological taboos were exploited by **surrealists** by the latter 1920s (Dali, Magritte). Architectural schools celebrated industrial values, whether vigorous abstract constructivism (Tatlin, *Monument to 3rd International*, 1919) or the machined, streamlined **Bauhaus** style, which was extended to many design fields (Helvetica typeface).

Prose writers explored revolutionary narrative modes related to dreams (Kafka's *Trial*, 1925), internal monologue (Joyce's **Ulysses**, 1922), and word play (Stein's *Making of Americans*, 1925). Poets and novelists wrote of modern alienation (Eliot's *Waste Land*, 1922) and aimlessness (Lost Generation).

Sciences. Scientific specialization prevailed by the 20th cent. Advances in knowledge and technological aptitude increased with the geometric rise in the number of practitioners. Physicists challenged common-sense views of causality, observation, and a mechanistic universe, putting science further beyond popular grasp (Einstein's general theory of relativity, 1915; Bohr's quantum mechanics, 1913; Heisenberg's uncertainty principle, 1927).

Rise of Totalitarians: 1930-39

Depression. A worldwide financial panic and economic depression began with the Oct. 1929 U.S. stock market crash and the May 1931 failure of the Austrian Credit-Anstalt. A credit crunch caused in-

1938

Timeline (left margin): Alfonso leaves Spain · India salt march · Stock market crash · Smoot-Hawley Tariff · Japan seizes Manchuria · Gandhi's fast · Hitler dictator · International Style · 1933 · FDR in office · Hitler takes Rhineland · Nuremberg Laws · Long March in China · Fr. Popular Front · Italy takes Ethiopia · Japan invades China · Civil War in Spain

ternational bankruptcies and **unemployment**: 12 million jobless by 1932 in the U.S., 5.6 million in Germany, 2.7 million in England. Governments responded with **tariff restrictions** (Smoot-Hawley Act, 1930; Ottawa Imperial Conference, 1932), which dried up world trade. Government public works programs were vitiated by deflationary budget balancing.

Germany. Years of agitation by violent extremists were brought to a head by the Depression. Nazi leader **Hitler** was named chancellor by Pres. Hindenburg in Jan. 1933 and given dictatorial power by the Reichstag in March. Opposition parties were disbanded, strikes banned, and all aspects of economic, cultural, and religious life were brought under central government and Nazi party control and manipulated by sophisticated propaganda. Severe persecution of Jews began (**Nuremberg Laws,** Sept. 1935). Many Jews, political opponents, and others were sent to concentration camps (Dachau, 1933), where thousands died or were killed. Public works, renewed conscription (1935), arms production, and a 4-year plan (1936) all but ended unemployment.

Hitler's expansionism started with reincorporation of the Saar (1935), occupation of the **Rhineland** (Mar. 1936), and annexation of Austria (Mar. 1938). At **Munich** (Sept. 1938) an indecisive Britain and France sanctioned German dismemberment of Czechoslovakia.

Russia. Urbanization and education advanced. Rapid industrialization was achieved through successive **5-year-plans** starting in 1928, using severe labor discipline and mass forced labor. Industry was financed by a decline in living standards and exploitation of agriculture, which was almost totally collectivized by the early 1930s (*kolkhoz*, collective farm; *sovkhoz*, state farm, often in newly worked lands). Successive **purges** increased the role of professionals and management at the expense of workers. Millions perished in a series of manufactured disasters: elimination (1929-34) of kulaks (peasant landowners), severe famine (1932-33), party purges (Great Purge, 1936-38), suppression of nationalities; and poor conditions in labor camps.

Spain. An industrial revolution during World War I created an urban proletariat, which was attracted to socialism and anarchism; Catalan nationalists challenged central authority. The 5 years after King Alfonso left Spain in Apr. 1931 were dominated by tension between intermittent leftist and anticlerical governments and clericals, monarchists, and other rightists. Anarchist and communist rebellions were crushed, but a July 1936 extreme right rebellion led by Gen. Francisco Franco and aided by Nazi Germany and Fascist Italy succeeded, after a 3-year **civil war** (more than 1 million dead in battles and atrocities). The war polarized international public opinion.

Italy. Despite propaganda for the ideal of the Corporate State, few domestic reforms were attempted. An entente with Hungary and Austria (Mar. 1934), a pact with Germany and Japan (Nov. 1937), and intervention by 50,000-75,000 troops in Spain (1936-39) sealed Italy's identification with the fascist bloc (anti-Semitic laws after Mar. 1938). Ethiopia was conquered (1935-36), and **Albania** annexed (Jan. 1939) in conscious imitation of ancient Rome.

East Europe. Repressive regimes fought for power against an active opposition (liberals, socialists, communists, peasants, Nazis). Minority groups and Jews were restricted within national boundaries that did not coincide with ethnic population patterns. In the destruction of **Czechoslovakia**, **Hungary** occupied S Slovakia (Nov. 1938) and Ruthenia (Mar. 1939), and a pro-Nazi regime took power in the rest of Slovakia. Other boundary disputes (e.g., Poland-Lithuania, Yugoslavia-Bulgaria, Romania-Hungary) doomed attempts to build joint fronts against Germany or Russia. Economic depression was severe.

East Asia. After a period of liberalism in **Japan**, nativist militarists dominated the government with peasant support. Manchuria was seized (Sept. 1931-Feb. 1932), and a puppet state was set up (Manchukuo). Adjacent Jehol (Inner Mongolia) was occupied in 1933. China proper was invaded in July 1937; large areas were conquered by Oct. 1938.

In **China** Communist forces left Kuomintang-besieged strongholds in the S in a Long March (1934-35) to the N. The Kuomintang-Communist civil war was suspended in Jan. 1937 in the face of threatening Japan.

The democracies. The Roosevelt Administration, in office Mar. 1933, embarked on an extensive program of social reform and economic stimulation, including protection for labor unions (heavy industries organized), Social Security, public works, wage-and-hour laws, and assistance to farmers. Isolationist sentiment (1937 Neutrality Act) prevented U.S. intervention in Europe, but military expenditures were increased in 1939.

French political instability and polarization prevented resolution of economic and international security questions. The **Popular Front** government under Blum (June 1936-Apr. 1938) passed social reforms (40-hour week) and raised arms spending. National coalition governments, which ruled Britain from Aug. 1931, brought some economic recovery but failed to define a consistent international policy until Chamberlain's government (from May 1937), which practiced deliberate **appeasement** of Germany and Italy.

India. Twenty years of agitation for autonomy and then for independence (Gandhi's **salt march**, 1930) achieved some constitutional reform (extended provincial powers, 1935) despite Muslim-Hindu strife. Social issues assumed prominence with peasant uprisings (1921), strikes (1928), Gandhi's efforts for untouchables (1932 "fast unto death"), and social and agrarian reform by the provinces after 1937.

Arts. The streamlined, geometric design motifs of Art Deco (from 1925) prevailed through the 1930s. Abstract art flourished (Moore sculptures from 1931) alongside a new realism related to social and political concerns (**Socialist Realism,** the official Soviet style from 1934; Mexican muralist Rivera, 1886-1957; and Orozco, 1883-1949), which were also expressed in fiction and poetry (Steinbeck's *Grapes of Wrath*, 1939; Sandburg's *The People, Yes*, 1936). Modern architecture (International Style, 1932) was unchallenged in its use of artificial materials (concrete, glass), lack of decoration, and monumentality (Rockefeller Center, 1929-40). U.S.-made films captured a worldwide audience with their larger-than-life fantasies *(Gone with the Wind*, 1939).

War, Hot and Cold: 1940-49

War in Europe. The Nazi-Soviet nonaggression pact (Aug. 1939) freed Germany to attack Poland (Sept.). Britain and France, who had guaranteed Polish independence, declared war on Germany. Russia

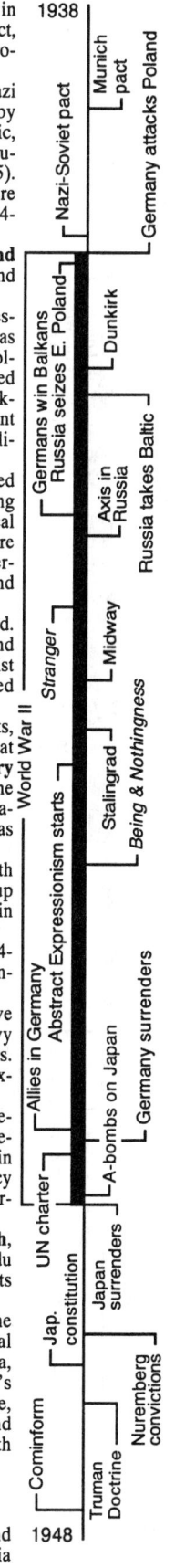

1938

Munich pact

Germany attacks Poland

Nazi-Soviet pact

Germans win Balkans
Russia seizes E. Poland

Dunkirk

Axis in Russia

Russia takes Baltic

World War II

Stranger

Midway

Stalingrad

Being & Nothingness

Abstract Expressionism starts

Allies in Germany

A-bombs on Japan

Germany surrenders

UN charter

Japan surrenders

Jap. constitution

Nuremberg convictions

Cominform

Truman Doctrine

1948

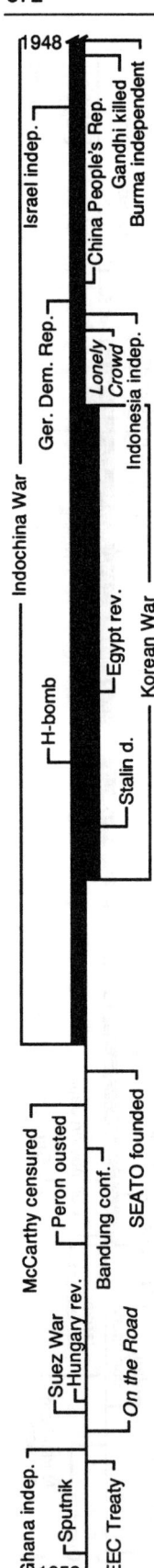

seized E Poland (Sept.), attacked Finland (Nov.), and took the Baltic states (July 1940). Mobile German forces staged *blitzkrieg* attacks during Apr.-June 1940, conquering neutral Denmark, Norway, and the Low Countries and defeating France; 350,000 British and French troops were evacuated at **Dunkirk** (May). The Battle of Britain (June-Dec. 1940) denied Germany air superiority. German-Italian campaigns won the Balkans by Apr. 1941. Three million Axis troops **invaded Russia** in June 1941, marching through Ukraine to the Caucasus, and through White Russia and the Baltic republics to Moscow and Leningrad.

Russian winter counterthrusts (1941-42 and 1942-43) stopped the German advance (Stalingrad, Sept. 1942-Feb. 1943). With British and U.S. Lend-Lease aid and sustaining great casualties, the Russians drove the Axis from all E Europe and the Balkans in the next 2 years. Invasions of N Africa (Nov. 1942), Italy (Sept. 1943), and Normandy (June 1944) brought U.S., British, Free French, and allied troops to Germany by spring 1945. Germany surrendered May 7, 1945.

War in Asia-Pacific. Japan occupied Indochina in Sept. 1940, dominated Thailand in Dec. 1941, and attacked Hawaii, the Philippines, Hong Kong, Malaya on Dec. 7, 1941. Indonesia was attacked in Jan. 1942, and Burma was conquered in Mar. 1942. The Battle of **Midway** (June 1942) turned back the Japanese advance. "Island-hopping" battles (Guadalcanal, Aug. 1942-Jan. 1943; **Leyte Gulf,** Oct. 1944; Iwo Jima, Feb.-Mar. 1945; Okinawa, Apr. 1945) and massive bombing raids on Japan from June 1944 wore out Japanese defenses. Two U.S. atom bombs, dropped Aug. 6 and 9, forced Japan to surrender on Aug. 14, 1945.

Atrocities. The war brought 20th-cent. cruelty to its peak. The Nazi regime systematically killed 5-6 million Jews, including some 3 million who died in death camps (e.g., Auschwitz). Gypsies, political opponents, sick and retarded people, and others deemed undesirable were murdered by the Nazis, as were vast numbers of Slavs, especially leaders.

Civilian deaths. German bombs killed 70,000 British civilians. Some 100,000 Chinese civilians were killed by Japanese forces in the capture of Nanking. Severe retaliation by the Soviet army, E European partisans, Free French, and others took a heavy toll. U.S. and British bombing of Germany killed hundreds of thousands, as did U.S. bombing of Japan (80,000-200,000 at Hiroshima alone). Some 45 million people lost their lives in the war.

Settlement. The United Nations charter was signed in San Francisco on June 26, 1945, by 50 nations. The International Tribunal at Nuremberg convicted 22 German leaders for war crimes in Sept. 1946; 23 Japanese leaders were convicted in Nov. 1948. Postwar border changes included large gains in territory for the USSR, losses for Germany, a shift westward in Polish borders, and minor losses for Italy. Communist regimes, supported by Soviet troops, took power in most of E Europe, including Soviet-occupied Germany (GDR proclaimed Oct. 1949). Japan lost all overseas lands.

Recovery. Basic political and social changes were imposed on Japan and W Germany by the western allies (Japan constitution adopted, Nov. 1946; W German basic law, May 1949). U.S. Marshall Plan aid ($12 billion, 1947-51) spurred W European economic recovery after a period of severe inflation and strikes in Europe and the U.S. The British Labour Party introduced a national health service and nationalized basic industries in 1946.

Cold War. Western fears of further Soviet advances (Cominform formed in Oct. 1947; Czechoslovakia coup, Feb. 1948; Berlin blockade, Apr. 1948-Sept. 1949) led to the formation of NATO. Civil War in Greece and Soviet pressure on Turkey led to U.S. aid under the Truman Doctrine (Mar. 1947). Other anti-Communist security pacts were the Organization of American States (Apr. 1948) and the Southeast Asia Treaty Organization (Sept. 1954). A new wave of Soviet purges and repression intensified in the last years of Stalin's rule, extending to E Europe (Slansky trial in Czechoslovakia, 1951). Only Yugoslavia resisted Soviet control (expelled by Cominform, June 1948; U.S. aid, June 1949).

China, Korea. Communist forces emerged from World War II strengthened by the Soviet takeover of industrial Manchuria. In 4 years of fighting, the Kuomintang was driven from the mainland; the People's Republic was proclaimed Oct. 1, 1949. Korea was divided by USSR and U.S. occupation forces. Separate republics were proclaimed in the 2 zones in Aug.-Sept. 1948.

India. India and Pakistan became independent dominions on Aug. 15, 1947. Millions of Hindu and Muslim refugees were created by the partition; riots (1946-47) took hundreds of thousands of lives; Gandhi was assassinated in Jan. 1948. Burma became completely independent in Jan. 1948; Ceylon took dominion status in Feb.

Middle East. The UN approved partition of Palestine into Jewish and Arab states. Israel was proclaimed on May 14, 1948. Arabs rejected partition, but failed to defeat Israel in war (May 1948-July 1949). Immigration from Europe and the Middle East swelled Israel's Jewish population. British and French forces left Lebanon and Syria in 1946. Transjordan occupied most of Arab Palestine.

Southeast Asia. Communists and others fought against restoration of French rule in Indochina from 1946; a non-Communist government was recognized by France in Mar. 1949, but fighting continued. Both Indonesia and the Philippines became independent; the former in 1949 after 4 years of war with Netherlands, the latter in 1946. Philippine economic and military ties with the U.S. remained strong; a Communist-led peasant rising was checked in 1948.

Arts. New York became the center of the world art market; abstract expressionism was the chief mode (Pollock from 1943, de Kooning from 1947). Literature and philosophy explored existentialism (Camus's *Stranger,* 1942; Sartre's *Being and Nothingness,* 1943). Non-Western attempts to revive or create regional styles (Senghor's Négritude, Mishima's novels) only confirmed the emergence of a universal culture. Radio and phonograph records spread American popular music (swing, bebop) around the world.

The American Decade: 1950-59

Polite decolonization. The peaceful decline of European political and military power in Asia and Africa accelerated in the 1950s. Nearly all of **N Africa** was freed by 1956, but France fought a bitter war to retain Algeria, with its large European minority, until 1962. **Ghana,** independent in 1957, led a parade of new black African nations (more than 2 dozen by 1962), which altered the political character of the UN. Ethnic disputes often exploded in the new nations after decolonization (UN troops in Cyprus, 1964; **Nigeria** civil war, 1967-70). Leaders of the new states, mostly sharing socialist ideologies, tried to create an Afro-Asian bloc (Bandung Conference, 1955), but Western economic influence and U.S. political ties remained strong (Baghdad Pact, 1955).

Trade. World trade volume soared, in an atmosphere of monetary stability assured by international accords (**Bretton Woods,** 1944). In Europe, economic integration advanced (**European Economic Community,** 1957; European Free Trade Association, 1960). Comecon (1949) coordinated the economies of Soviet-bloc countries.

U.S. Economic growth produced an abundance of consumer goods (9.3 million motor vehicles sold, 1955). Suburban housing tracts changed life patterns for middle and working classes (Levittown, 1946-51). **Eisenhower's** landslide election victories (1952, 1956) reflected consensus politics. Censure of McCarthy (Dec. 1954) curbed the political abuse of anti-Communism. A system of alliances and military bases bolstered U.S. influence on all continents. Trade and payments surpluses were balanced by overseas investments and foreign aid ($50 billion, 1950-59).

USSR. In the "thaw" after Stalin's death in 1953, relations with the West improved (evacuation of Vienna, Geneva summit conference, both 1955). Repression of scientific and cultural life eased, and many prisoners were freed or rehabilitated culminating in **de-Stalinization** (1956). Khrushchev's leadership aimed at consumer sector growth, but farm production lagged, despite the virgin lands program (from 1954). The 1956 Hungarian revolution, the 1960 U-2 spy plane episode, and other incidents renewed East-West tension and domestic curbs.

East Europe. Resentment of Russian domination and Stalinist repression combined with nationalist, economic, and religious factors to produce periodic violence. East Berlin workers rioted (1953), Polish workers rioted in Poznan (June 1956), and a broad-based revolution broke out in Hungary (Oct. 1956). All were suppressed by Soviet force or threats (at least 7,000 dead in Hungary). But Poland was allowed to restore private ownership of farms, and a degree of personal and economic freedom returned to Hungary. Yugoslavia experimented with worker self-management and a market economy.

Korea. The 1945 division of Korea left industry in the N, which was organized into a militant regime and armed by the USSR. The S was politically disunited. More than 60,000 North Korean troops invaded the S on June 25, 1950. The U.S., backed by the UN Security Council, sent troops. UN troops reached the Chinese border in Nov. Some 200,000 Chinese troops crossed the Yalu R. and drove back UN forces. A cease-fire in July 1951 found the opposing forces near the original 38th parallel border. After 2 years of sporadic fighting, an armistice was signed on July 27, 1953. U.S. troops remained in the S, and U.S. economic and military aid continued. The war stimulated rapid economic recovery in Japan.

China. Starting in 1952, industry, agriculture, and social institutions were forcibly collectivized. As many as several million people were executed as Kuomintang supporters or as class and political enemies. The Great Leap Forward (1958-60) unsuccessfully tried to force the pace of development by substituting labor for investment.

Indochina. Ho Chi Minh's forces, aided by the USSR and the new Chinese Communist government, fought French and pro-French Vietnamese forces to a standstill and captured the strategic Dienbienphu camp in May 1954. The Geneva Agreements divided Vietnam in half pending elections (never held) and recognized Laos and Cambodia as independent. The U.S. aided the anti-Communist Republic of Vietnam in the S.

Middle East. Arab revolutions placed leftist, militantly nationalist regimes in power in Egypt (1952) and Iraq (1958). But Arab unity attempts failed (United Arab Republic joined Egypt, Syria, Yemen, 1958-61). Arab refusal to recognize Israel (Arab League economic blockade began Sept. 1951) led to a permanent state of war, with repeated incidents (Gaza, 1955). Israel occupied Sinai, and Britain and France took (Oct. 1956) the Suez Canal, but were replaced by the UN Emergency Force. The Mossadegh government in Iran nationalized (May 1951) the British-owned oil industry May, but was overthrown (Aug. 1953) in a U.S.-aided coup.

Latin America. Argentinian Dictator Juan Peron, in office 1946, enforced land reform, some nationalization, welfare state measures, and curbs on the Roman Catholic Church, but crushed opposition. A Sept. 1955 coup deposed Peron. The 1952 revolution in Bolivia brought land reform, nationalization of tin mines, and improvement in the status of Indians, who nevertheless remained poor. The Batista regime in Cuba was overthrown (Jan. 1959) by Fidel Castro, who imposed a Communist dictatorship, aligned Cuba with the USSR, and improved education and health care. A U.S.-backed anti-Castro invasion (Bay of Pigs, Apr. 1961) was crushed. Self-government advanced in the British Caribbean.

Technology. Large outlays on research and development in the U.S. and the USSR focused on military applications (H-bomb in U.S., 1952; USSR, 1953; Britain, 1957; intercontinental missiles, late 1950s). Soviet launching of the Sputnik satellite (Oct. 1957) spurred increases in U.S. science education funds (National Defense Education Act).

Literature and film. Alienation from social and literary conventions reached an extreme in the theater of the absurd (Beckett's *Waiting for Godot,* 1952), the "new novel" (Robbe-Grillet's *Voyeur,* 1955), and avant-garde film (Antonioni's *L'Avventura,* 1960). U.S. Beatniks (Kerouac's *On the Road,* 1957) and others rejected the supposed conformism of Americans (Riesman's *The Lonely Crowd,* 1950).

Rising Expectations: 1960-69

Economic boom. The longest sustained economic boom on record spanned almost the entire decade in the capitalist world; the closely watched GNP figure doubled (1960-70) in the U.S., fueled by Vietnam War-related budget deficits. The **General Agreement on Tariffs and Trade** (1967) stimulated W European prosperity, which spread to peripheral areas (Spain, Italy, E Germany). Japan became a top economic power ($20 billion exports in 1970). Foreign investment aided the industrialization of Brazil. Soviet 1965 economic reform attempts (decentralization, material incentives) were limited, but growth continued.

Reform and radicalization. Pres. John F. Kennedy, inaugurated 1961, emphasized youthful idealism and vigor; he was assassinated Nov. 22, 1963. A series of political and social reform movements took root in the U.S., later spreading to other countries. Blacks demonstrated nonviolently and with

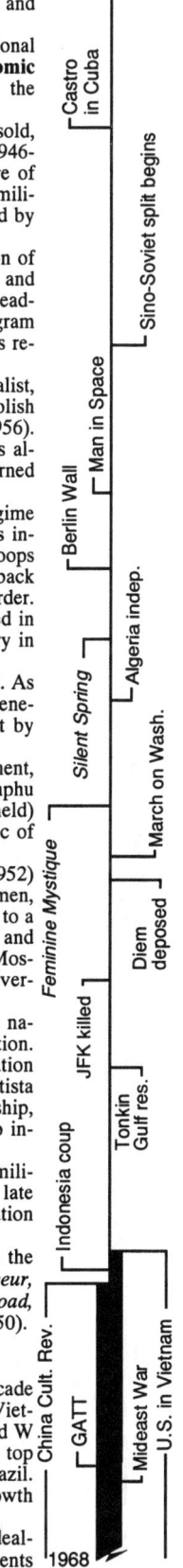

1958

Castro in Cuba

Sino-Soviet split begins

Man in Space

Berlin Wall

Algeria indep.

Silent Spring

March on Wash.

Feminine Mystique

Diem deposed

JFK killed

Tonkin Gulf res.

Indonesia coup

China Cult. Rev.

GATT

Mideast War

U.S. in Vietnam

1968

1968

Sino-Soviet fighting
First Earth Day
Men on moon
Pentagon Papers published
Woodstock festival
Roe v. Wade abortion ruling
U.S. SST barred
Bangladesh indep.
Nixon in Peking
Arab-Israel Yom Kippur War
Worldwide recession
Nixon resigns
Indochina War ends
Mao d.
1 mln. die in Cambodia
Franco d.
U.S. hostages taken in Iran
Khomeini gvt. in Iran
Egypt-Israel treaty
3 Mile Island
USSR invades Afghanistan
18% inflation rate in U.S.

1980

partial success against segregation and poverty (1963 March on Washington; 1964 **Civil Rights Act**), but some urban ghettos erupted in extensive riots (Watts, 1965; Detroit, 1967; King assassination, Apr. 4, 1968). New concern for the poor (Harrington's *Other America*, 1963) led to Pres. Johnson's **"Great Society"** programs (Medicare, Water Quality Act, Higher Education Act, all 1965). Concern with the **environment** surged (Carson's *Silent Spring*, 1962). **Feminism** revived as a cultural and political movement (Friedan's *Feminine Mystique*, 1963; National Organization for Women founded 1966) and a movement for homosexual rights emerged (Stonewall riot in NYC, 1969). Pope John XXIII called Vatican II (1962-65), which liberalized Roman Catholic liturgy.

Opposition to U.S. involvement in Vietnam, especially among university students (**Moratorium** protest, Nov. 1969), turned violent (Weatherman Chicago riots, Oct. 1969). New Left and Marxist theories became popular, and membership in radical groups swelled (Students for a Democratic Society, Black Panthers). Maoist groups, especially in Europe, called for total transformation of society. In France, students sparked a nationwide strike affecting 10 million workers in May-June 1968, but an electoral reaction barred revolutionary change.

Arts and styles. The boundary between fine and popular arts was blurred in the 1960s by Pop Art (Warhol) and rock musicals (*Hair*, 1968). Informality and exaggeration prevailed in fashion (beards, miniskirts). A nonpolitical "counterculture" developed, rejecting traditional bourgeois life goals and personal habits, and use of marijuana and hallucinogens spread (Woodstock festival, Aug. 1969). Indian influence was felt in religion (Ram Dass) and fashion and The Beatles, who brought unprecedented sophistication to rock music, became for many a symbol of the decade.

Science. Achievements in space (men on moon, July 1969) and electronics (lasers, integrated circuits) encouraged a faith in scientific solutions to problems in agriculture ("green revolution"), medicine (heart transplants, 1967), and other areas. The harmful effects of science, it was believed, could be controlled (1963 nuclear weapon test ban treaty, 1968 nonproliferation treaty).

China. Mao's revolutionary militance caused disputes with the USSR under "revisionist" Khrushchev, starting in 1960. The 2 powers exchanged fire in 1969 border disputes. China used force to capture (1962) areas disputed with India. The "Great Proletarian Cultural Revolution" tried to impose a utopian egalitarian program in China and spread revolution abroad; political struggle, often violent, convulsed China in 1965-68.

Indochina. Communist-led guerrillas aided by N Vietnam fought from 1960 against the S Vietnam government of Ngo Dinh Diem (killed 1963). The U.S. military role increased after the 1964 Tonkin Gulf incident. U.S. forces peaked at 543,400 in Apr. 1969. Massive numbers of N Vietnamese troops also fought. Laotian and Cambodian neutrality were threatened by Communist insurgencies, with N Vietnamese aid, and U.S. intrigues.

Third World. A bloc of authoritarian leftist regimes among the newly independent nations emerged in political opposition to the U.S.-led Western alliance and came to dominate the conference of non-aligned nations (Belgrade, 1961; Cairo, 1964; Lusaka, 1970). Soviet political ties and military bases were established in Cuba, Egypt, Algeria, Guinea, and other countries, whose leaders were regarded as revolutionary heroes by opposition groups in pro-Western or colonial countries. Some leaders were ousted in coups by pro-Western groups—Zaire's Lumumba (killed 1961), Ghana's Nkrumah (exiled 1966), and Indonesia's Sukarno (effectively ousted in 1965 after a Communist coup failed).

Middle East. Arab-Israeli tension erupted into a brief war June 1967. Israel emerged as a major regional power. Military shipments before and after the war brought much of the Arab world into the Soviet political sphere. Most Arab states broke U.S. diplomatic ties, while Communist countries cut their ties to Israel. Intra-Arab disputes continued: Egypt and Saudi Arabia supported rival factions in a bloody Yemen civil war 1962-70; Lebanese troops fought Palestinian commandos 1969.

East Europe. To stop the large-scale exodus of citizens, E German authorities built (Aug. 1961) a fortified wall across Berlin. Soviet sway in the Balkans was weakened by Albania's support of China (USSR broke ties in Dec. 1961) and Romania's assertion (1964) of industrial and foreign policy autonomy. Liberalization (spring 1968) in Czechoslovakia was crushed by troops of 5 Warsaw Pact countries. W German treaties (1970) with the USSR and Poland facilitated the transfer of German technology and confirmed postwar boundaries.

Disillusionment: 1970-79

U.S.: Caution and neoconservatism. A relatively sluggish economy, energy and resource shortages (natural gas crunch, 1975; gasoline shortage, 1979), and environmental problems contributed to a **"limits of growth"** philosophy. Suspicion of science and technology killed or delayed major projects (supersonic transport dropped, 1971; Seabrook nuclear power plant protests, 1977-78) and was fed by the Three Mile Island nuclear reactor accident (Mar. 1979).

Mistrust of big government weakened support for government reform plans among liberals. School busing and racial quotas were opposed (Bakke decision, June 1978); the Equal Rights Amendment for women languished; civil rights for homosexuals were opposed (Dade County referendum, June 1977).

Completion of communist forces' takeover of **S Vietnam** (evacuation of U.S. civilians, Apr. 1975), revelations of Central Intelligence Agency misdeeds (Rockefeller Commission report, June 1975), and **Watergate** scandals (Nixon resigned in Aug. 1974) reduced faith in U.S. moral and material capacity to influence world affairs. Revelations of Soviet crimes (Solzhenitsyn's *Gulag Archipelago*, 1974) and Russian intervention in Africa aided a revival of anti-Communist sentiment.

Economy sluggish. The 1960s boom faltered in the 1970s; a severe recession in the U.S. and Europe (1974-75) followed a huge oil price hike (Dec. 1973). Monetary instability (U.S. cut ties to gold in Aug. 1971), the decline of the dollar, and **protectionist** moves by industrial countries (1977-78) threatened trade. Business investment and spending for research declined. Severe inflation plagued many countries (25% in Britain, 1975; 18% in U.S., 1979).

China picks up pieces. After the 1976 deaths of Mao and Zhou, a power struggle for the leadership succession was won by pragmatists. A nationwide purge of orthodox Maoists was carried out, and the **Gang of Four** led by Mao's widow, Chiang Ching, was arrested.

The new leaders freed more than 100,000 political prisoners and reduced public adulation of Mao. Political and trade ties were expanded with Japan, Europe, and the U.S. in the late 1970s, as relations worsened with the USSR, Cuba, and Vietnam (4-week invasion by China, 1979). Ideological guidelines in industry, science, education, and the armed forces, which the ruling faction said had caused chaos and decline, were reversed (bonuses to workers, Dec. 1977; exams for college entrance, Oct. 1977). Severe restrictions on cultural expression were eased (Beethoven ban lifted, Mar. 1977).

Europe. European unity moves (EEC-EFTA trade accord, 1972) faltered as economic problems appeared (Britain floated pound, 1972; France floated franc, 1974). Germany and Switzerland curbed guest workers from S Europe. Greece and Turkey quarreled over Cyprus and Aegean oil rights.

All non-Communist Europe was under democratic rule after free elections were held (June 1976) in **Spain** 7 months after the death of Franco. The conservative, colonialist regime in **Portugal** was overthrown in Apr. 1974. In **Greece** the 7-year-old military dictatorship yielded power in 1974. N Europe, though ruled mostly by Socialists (**Swedish** Socialists unseated in 1976 after 44 years in power), turned conservative. The **British** Labour government imposed (1975) wage curbs and suspended nationalization schemes. Terrorism in **Germany** (1972 Munich Olympics killings) led to laws curbing some civil liberties. **French** "new philosophers" rejected leftist ideologies, and the shaky Socialist-Communist coalition lost a 1978 election bid.

Religion back in politics. The improvement in Muslim countries' political fortunes by the 1950s (with the exception of Central Asia under Soviet and Chinese rule) and the growth of Arab oil wealth were followed by a resurgence of traditional piety. Libyan dictator Qaddafi mixed Islamic laws with socialism and called for Muslim return to Spain and Sicily. The illegal Muslim Brotherhood in **Egypt** was accused of violence, while extreme groups bombed (1977) theaters to protest secular values.

In **Turkey**, the National Salvation Party was the first Islamic group to share (1974) power since secularization in the 1920s. Religious authorities, such as Ayatollah Ruhollah Khomeini, led the **Iranian** revolution, and religiously motivated Muslims took part in the insurrection in Saudi Arabia that briefly seized (1979) the Grand Mosque in Mecca. Muslim puritan opposition to **Pakistan** Pres. Bhutto helped lead to his overthrow in July 1977. Muslim solidarity, however, could not prevent Pakistan's E province (**Bangladesh**) from declaring (Dec. 1971) independence after a bloody civil war.

Muslim and Hindu resentment of coerced sterilization in **India** helped defeat the Gandhi government, which was replaced (Mar. 1977) by a coalition including religious Hindu parties and led by devout Hindu Desai. Muslims in the S **Philippines**, aided by Libya, rebelled against central rule from 1973.

Evangelical Protestant groups grew in numbers and prosperity in the U.S. A revival of interest in Orthodox Christianity occurred among **Russian** intellectuals (Solzhenitsyn). The secularist **Israeli** Labor party, after decades of rule, was ousted in 1977 by conservatives led by Begin, an observant Jew; religious militants founded settlements on the disputed West Bank, part of biblically promised Israel. U.S. Reform Judaism revived many previously discarded traditional practices.

The Buddhist Soka Gakkai movement launched (1964) the Komeito party in Japan, which became a major opposition party in 1972 and 1976 elections.

Old-fashioned religious wars raged intermittently in **N Ireland** (Catholic vs. Protestant, 1969-) and **Lebanon** (Christian vs. Muslim, 1975-) while religious militancy complicated the Israel-Arab dispute (1973 Israel-Arab war). Despite a **1979 peace treaty between Egypt and Israel,** increased religious militancy on the West Bank prevented a quick resolution.

Latin America. Repressive conservative regimes strengthened their hold on most of the continent, with the violent coup against the elected (Sept. 1973) Allende government in **Chile**, the 1976 military coup in **Argentina**, and coups against reformist regimes in **Bolivia** (1971, 1979) and **Peru** (1976). In Central America increasing liberal and leftist militancy led to the ouster (1979) of the Somoza regime of Nicaragua and civil conflict in El Salvador.

Indochina. Communist victories in Vietnam, Cambodia, and Laos by May 1975 did not bring peace. Attempts at radical social reorganization left more than 1 million dead (1975-78) in Cambodia and caused hundreds of thousands of ethnic Chinese and others to flee Vietnam ("boat people," 1979). The Vietnamese invasion of Cambodia swelled the refugee population and contributed to widespread starvation in that devastated country.

Russian expansion. Soviet influence, checked in some countries (troops ousted by Egypt, 1972) was projected further afield, often with the use of Cuban troops (Angola, 1975-89; Ethiopia, 1977-88) and aided by a growing navy, a merchant fleet, and international banking ability. Détente with the West — 1972 Berlin pact, 1972 strategic arms pact (**SALT**)—gave way to a more antagonistic relationship in the late 1970s, exacerbated by the Soviet invasion (1979) of Afghanistan.

Africa. The last remaining European colonies were granted independence (**Spanish Sahara**, 1976; **Djibouti,** 1977) and, after 10 years of civil war and many negotiation sessions, a black government took over (1979) in Zimbabwe (Rhodesia); white domination remained in **S Africa**. Great power involvement in local wars (Russia in **Angola, Ethiopia**; France in **Chad, Zaire, Mauritania**) and the use of tens of thousands of Cuban troops were denounced by some African leaders as neocolonialism. Ethnic or tribal clashes made Africa the chief world locus of sustained warfare in the late 1970s.

Arts. Traditional modes in painting, architecture, and music, pursued in relative obscurity for much of the 20th cent., returned to popular and critical attention in the 1970s. The pictorial emphasis in neo-realist and photorealist painting, the return of many architects to detail, decoration, and natural materials, and the concern with ordered structure in musical composition were, ironically, novel experiences for artistic consumers after the exhaustion of experimental possibilities. These more conservative styles, however, coexisted with modernist works in an atmosphere of variety and tolerance.

Revitalization of Capitalism, Demand for Democracy: 1980-89

USSR, Eastern Europe. A troublesome 1980-85 for the USSR was followed by 5 years of astonishing change: the surrender of the Communist monopoly, remaking of the Soviet state, and disintegration of the Soviet empire. After the deaths of Brezhnev (1982), Andropov (1984), and Chernenko (1985); the harsh treatment of dissent; restriction of emigration; and the invasion (Dec. 1979) of Afghanistan; Gen. Secy. Mikhail Gorbachev (in office 1985-1991) promoted glasnost and perestroika—economic, politi-

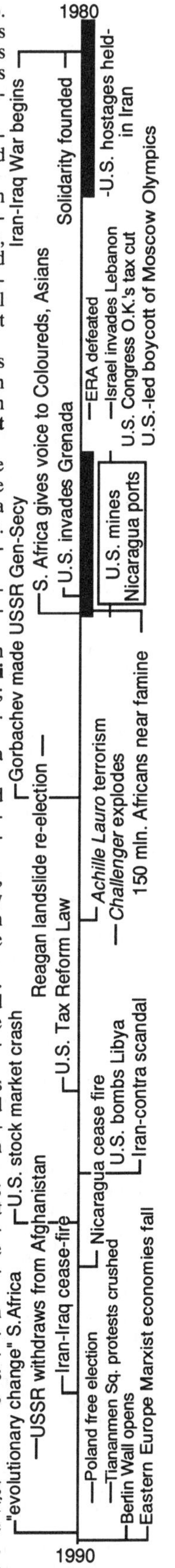
1980
Iran-Iraq War begins
S. Africa gives voice to Coloureds, Asians
Solidarity founded
U.S. hostages held in Iran
ERA defeated
Israel invades Lebanon
U.S. Congress O.K.'s tax cut
U.S.-led boycott of Moscow Olympics
U.S. invades Grenada
U.S. mines Nicaragua ports
Gorbachev made USSR Gen-Secy
Reagan landslide re-election
Achille Lauro terrorism
Challenger explodes
150 mln. Africans near famine
U.S. Tax Reform Law
U.S. stock market crash
Nicaragua cease fire
U.S. bombs Libya
Iran-contra scandal
"evolutionary change" S.Africa
USSR withdraws from Afghanistan
Iran-Iraq cease-fire
Poland free election
Tiananmen Sq. protests crushed
Berlin Wall opens
Eastern Europe Marxist economies fall
1990

cal, and social reform. Supported by the Communist Party (July 1988), he signed (Dec. 1987) the INF treaty. Gorbachev pledged (1988) to cut the military budget; military withdrawal from Afghanistan was completed in Feb.1989; democratization was not hindered in Poland and Hungary; the Soviet people chose (Mar. 1989) part of the new Congress from competing candidates. At decade's end, Gorbachev was widely considered responsible for the 1989 ending of the Cold War.

Poland. Solidarity, the labor union founded (1980) by **Lech Walesa**, was outlawed in 1982 and then legalized in 1988, after years of unrest. Poland's first free election since the Communist takeover brought Solidarity victory (June 1989); Tadeusz Mazowiecki, a Walesa adviser, became (Aug. 1989) prime minister in a government with the Communists.

In the fall of 1989 the failure of Marxist economies in **Hungary, E Germany, Czechoslovakia, Bulgaria, and Romania** brought the fall of the Communist monopoly and the demand for democracy. The **Berlin Wall** was opened in Nov. 1989.

U.S. "The Reagan Years" (1981-88) brought the **longest economic boom** in U.S. history via budget and tax cuts, deregulation, "junk bond" financing, leveraged buyouts, and mergers and takeovers, as well as a **strong anti-Communist stance**, via increased defense spending, aid to anti-Communists in Central America, the invasion of Cuba-threatened Grenada, and a championing of the MX missile system and "Star Wars." Four Reagan-Gorbachev summits (1985-88) climaxed in the INF treaty (1987). Financial scandals mounted (E. F. Hutton, 1985; Ivan Boesky, 1986), the stock market crashed (Oct.1987), the trade imbalance grew (especially with Japan), the budget deficit soared ($3.2 trillion in 1988); and homelessness and drug abuse (esp. "crack") grew. The Iran-contra affair (North's TV testimony, July 1987) was the low point, but Vice Pres. Bush was elected president in 1988.

Middle East. This area remained militarily unstable, with sharp divisions on economic, political, racial, and religious lines. In **Iran**, the revolution (1979-80) and violent political upheavals after, brought a strong anti-U.S. stance. In Sept. 1980, **Iraq** repudiated its border agreement with Iran and began major hostilities that led to an 8-year war in which millions were killed.

Libya's support for international terrorism caused the U.S. to close (May 1981) the diplomatic mission and embargo (Mar. 1982) oil. U.S. accused Muammar al-Qaddafi of aiding (Dec. 1985) terrorists in Rome and of Vienna airport attacks and retaliated by bombing (Apr. 1986) Libya.

Israel affirmed (July 1980) all Jerusalem as its capital, destroyed (1981) an Iraqi atomic reactor, and invaded (1982) Lebanon, forcing the PLO to agree to withdraw. A **Palestinian uprising**, including women and children hurling rocks and bottles at troops, began (Dec.1987) in Israeli-occupied Gaza and spread to the West Bank; troops responded with force, killing 300 by the end of 1988, with 6,000 more in detention camps.

Israeli withdrawal from **Lebanon** began in Feb. 1985 and ended in June 1985, as Lebanon continued torn by military and political conflict. Premier Karami was assassinated in June 1987. Artillery duels (Mar.-Apr. 1989) between Christian East Beirut and Muslim West Beirut left 200 dead and 700 wounded. At decade's end, violence still dominated.

Central America. In **Nicaragua**, the leftist Sandinista National Liberation Front, in power after the 1979 civil war, faced problems as a result of Nicaragua's military aid to leftist guerrillas in El Salvador and U.S. backing of antigovernment contras. The U.S. CIA admitted (1984) directing the mining of Nicaraguan ports, and the U.S. sent humanitarian (1985) and military (1986) aid. Profits from secret arms sales to Iran were found (1987) diverted to contras. Cease-fire talks between the Sandinista government and contras came in 1988, and elections were held in Feb. 1990.

In **El Salvador**, a military coup (Oct. 1979) failed to halt extreme right-wing violence and left-wing activity. Archbishop Oscar Romero was assassinated in Mar. 1980; from Jan. to June some 4,000 civilians reportedly were killed. In 1984, newly elected Pres. Duarte decreased rights abuses. Leftist guerrillas continued their offensive in 1989.

Africa. 1980-85 marked the rapid decline of the economies of virtually all African countries, the result of accelerating desertification, the world economic recession, heavy indebtedness to overseas creditors, rapid population growth, and political instability. Some 60 million Africans faced prolonged hunger in 1981; much of Africa had one of the worst droughts ever in 1983, and by year's end **150 million faced near-famine**. "Live Aid," a marathon rock concert, was presented in July 1985, and the U.S. and Western nations sent aid in Sept. 1985. Economic hardship fueled political unrest and coups. Wars in Ethiopia and Sudan and military strife in 6 other nations continued through 1989. AIDS took a heavy toll.

South Africa. Antiapartheid sentiment gathered force; demonstrations and violent police response grew. South African white voters approved (Nov. 1983) the first constitution to give Coloureds and Asians a voice, while still excluding blacks—70% of the population. The U.S. imposed economic sanctions in Aug. 1985, and 11 Western nations followed in Sept. **P. W. Botha**, 1980s president, was succeeded by **F. W. de Klerk**, in Sept. 1989, on a platform of "evolutionary" change via negotiation with the black population.

China. From 1980 through mid-1989 the Communist Party, under **Chairman Deng Xiaoping**, pursued **far-reaching changes** in political and economic institutions, expanding commercial and technical ties to the industrialized world and increasing the role of market forces in stimulating urban economic development. But Apr. 1989 brought the demand for more changes: students camped out in Tiananmen Sq., Beijing; some 100,000 students and workers marched, and at least 20 other cities saw protests. Martial law was imposed; army troops crushed protests in Tiananmen Sq. on June 3-4, with death toll estimates at 500-7,000, as many as 10,000 injured, as many as 10,000 dissidents arrested, and 31 tried and executed. The conciliatory Communist Party chief was ousted; the Politburo adopted (July) reforms against official corruption.

Japan. Relations with other nations, especially the U.S., were dominated (1980-89) by **trade imbalances favoring Japan**. In 1985 the U.S. trade deficit with Japan was $49.7 billion, one-third of the total U.S. trade deficit. After Japan was found (Apr. 1986) to sell semiconductors and computer memory chips below cost, the U.S. was assured a "fair share" of the market, but charged (Mar. 1987) Japan with failing to live up to the agreement. The **Omnibus Trade Bill** (Aug. 1988) provided for retaliation; Pres. Bush called Japan's practices "unjustifiable," and the law gave Japan 18 months to stop or face trade restrictions.

European Community. With the addition of Greece, Portugal, and Spain, the EC became a **common market of more than 300 million people**, the West's largest trading entity. **Margaret Thatcher** became the first British prime minister in this century to win 3 consecutive terms (1987). France elected (1981) its first socialist president, **François Mitterrand**, who was reelected in 1988. Italy elected (1983) its first socialist premier, **Bettino Craxi**.

International Terrorism. With the 1979 overthrow of the Shah of Iran, terrorism became a prominent political tactic that increased through the '80s, but with fewer high profile attacks after 1985. In 1979-81, Iranian militants held 52 Americans hostage in Iran for 444 days; in 1983 a TNT-laden suicide terrorist blew up U.S. Marine headquarters in Beirut, killing 241 Americans, and a truck bomb blew up a French paratroop barracks, killing 58. The *Achille Lauro* was hijacked (1985), an American passenger killed, and the U.S. subsequently intercepted the Egyptian plane flying the terrorists to safety. Incidents rose to 700 in 1985, and to 1,000 in 1988. The Pentagon reported (Jan. 1989) 52 terrorist groups.

Assassinations included Egypt's Pres. **Anwar al-Sadat** (1981), India's Prime Minister **Indira Gandhi** (1984), Lebanese Premier **Rashid Karami** (1987), and Pakistan's Pres. **Mohammed Zia ul-Haq** (1988).

HISTORICAL FIGURES

Ancient Greeks and Latins

Greeks

Aeschines, orator, 389-314BC.
Aeschylus, dramatist, 525-456BC.
Aesop, fableist, c620-c560BC.
Alcibiades, politician, 450-404BC.
Anacreon, poet, c582-c485BC.
Anaxagoras, philosopher, c500-428BC.
Anaximander, philosopher, 611-546BC.
Antiphon, speechwriter, c480-411BC.
Apollonius, mathematician, c265-170BC.
Archimedes, math. 287-212BC.
Aristophanes, dramatist, c448-380BC.
Aristotle, philosopher, 384-322BC.
Athenaeus, scholar, fl.c200.
Callicrates, architect, fl.5th cent.BC.
Callimachus, poet, c305-240BC.
Cratinus, comic dramatist, 520-421BC.
Democritus, philosopher, c460-370BC.
Demosthenes, orator, 384-322BC.
Diodorus, historian, fl.20BC.

Diogenes, philosopher, 372-c287BC.
Dionysius, historian, d.c7BC.
Empedocles, philosopher, c490-430BC.
Epicharmus, dramatist, c530-440BC.
Epictetus, philosopher, c55-c135.
Epicurus, philosopher, 341-270BC.
Eratosthenes, scientist, 276-194BC.
Euclid, mathematician, fl.c300BC.
Euripides, dramatist, c484-406BC.
Galen, physician, 130-200.
Heraclitus, philosopher, c535-c475BC.
Herodotus, historian, c484-420BC.
Hesiod, poet, 8th cent. BC.
Hippocrates, physician, c460-377BC.
Homer, poet, believed lived c850BC.
Isocrates, orator, 436-338BC.
Menander, dramatist, 342-292BC.
Phidias, sculptor, c500-435BC.
Pindar, poet, c518-c438BC.

Plato, philosopher, c428-347BC.
Plutarch, biographer, c46-120.
Polybius, historian, c200-c118BC.
Praxiteles, sculptor, 400-330BC.
Pythagoras, phil., math., c580-c500BC.
Sappho, poet, c610-c580BC.
Simonides, poet, 556-c468BC.
Socrates, philosopher, 469-399BC.
Solon, statesman, 640-560BC.
Sophocles, dramatist, c496-406BC.
Strabo, geographer, c63BC-AD24.
Thales, philosopher, c634-546BC.
Themistocles, politician, c524-c460BC.
Theocritus, poet, c310-250BC.
Theophrastus, phil., c372-c287BC.
Thucydides, historian, fl.5th cent.BC.
Timon, philosopher, c320-c230BC.
Xenophon, historian, c434-c355BC.
Zeno, philosopher, c495-c430BC.

Latins

Ammianus, historian, c330-395.
Apuleius, satirist, c124-c170.
Boethius, scholar, c480-524.
Caesar, Julius, leader, 100-44BC.
Catilina, politician, c108-62BC.
Cato (Elder), statesman, 234-149BC.
Catullus, poet, c84-54BC.
Cicero, orator, 106-43BC.
Claudian, poet, c370-c404.
Ennius, poet, 239-170BC.
Gellius, author, c130-c165.
Horace, poet, 65-8BC.

Juvenal, satirist, 60-127.
Livy, historian, 59BC-AD17.
Lucan, poet, 39-65.
Lucilius, poet, c180-c102BC.
Lucretius, poet, c99-c55BC.
Martial, epigrammatist, c38-c103.
Nepos, historian, c100-c25BC.
Ovid, poet, 43BC-AD17.
Persius, satirist, 34-62.
Plautus, dramatist, c254-c184BC.
Pliny, scholar, 23-79.
Pliny (Younger), author, 62-113.

Quintilian, rhetorician, c35-c97.
Sallust, historian, 86-34BC.
Seneca, philosopher, 4BC-AD65.
Silius, poet, c25-101.
Statius, poet, c45-c96.
Suetonius, biographer, c69-c122.
Tacitus, historian, 56-120.
Terence, dramatist, 185-c159BC.
Tibullus, poet, c55-c19BC.
Virgil, poet, 70-19BC.
Vitruvius, architect, fl.1st cent.BC.

Rulers of England and Great Britain

England

Name		Began	Died	Age	Rgd
Saxons and Danes					
Egbert	King of Wessex, won allegiance of all English	829	839	—	10
Ethelwulf	Son, King of Wessex, Sussex, Kent, Essex.	839	858	—	19
Ethelbald	Son of Ethelwulf, displaced father in Wessex	858	860	—	2
Ethelbert	2d son of Ethelwulf, united Kent and Wessex	860	866	—	6
Ethelred I	3d son, King of Wessex, fought Danes	866	871	—	5
Alfred	The Great, 4th son, defeated Danes, fortified London	871	899	52	28
Edward	The Elder, Alfred's son, united English, claimed Scotland.	899	924	55	25
Athelstan	The Glorious, Edward's son, King of Mercia, Wessex.	924	940	45	16
Edmund	3d son of Edward, King of Wessex, Mercia	940	946	25	6
Edred	4th son of Edward.	946	955	32	9
Edwy	The Fair, eldest son of Edmund, King of Wessex.	955	959	18	3
Edgar	The Peaceful, 2d son of Edmund, ruled all English	959	975	32	17
Edward	The Martyr, eldest son of Edgar, murdered by stepmother	975	978	17	4
Ethelred II	The Unready, 2d son of Edgar, married Emma of Normandy	978	1016	48	37
Edmund II	Ironside, son of Ethelred II, King of London.	1016	1016	27	0
Canute	The Dane, gave Wessex to Edmund, married Emma.	1016	1035	40	19
Harold I	Harefoot, natural son of Canute	1035	1040	—	5
Hardecanute	Son of Canute by Emma, Danish King	1040	1042	24	2
Edward	The Confessor, son of Ethelred II (Canonized 1161)	1042	1066	62	24
Harold II	Edward's brother-in-law, last Saxon King	1066	1066	44	0
House of Normandy					
William I	The Conqueror, defeated Harold at Hastings	1066	1087	60	21
William II	Rufus, 3d son of William I, killed by arrow.	1087	1100	43	13
Henry I	Beauclerc, youngest son of William I	1100	1135	67	35
House of Blois					
Stephen	Son of Adela, daughter of William I, and Count of Blois	1135	1154	50	19
House of Plantagenet					
Henry II	Son of Geoffrey Plantagenet (Angevin) by Matilda, dau. of Henry I	1154	1189	56	35
Richard I	Coeur de Lion, son of Henry II, crusader.	1189	1199	42	10
John	Lackland, son of Henry II, signed Magna Carta, 1215	1199	1216	50	17
Henry III	Son of John, acceded at 9, under regency until 1227.	1216	1272	65	56
Edward I	Longshanks, son of Henry III	1272	1307	68	35
Edward II	Son of Edward I, deposed by Parliament, 1327.	1307	1327	43	20
Edward III	Of Windsor, son of Edward II	1327	1377	65	50
Richard II	Grandson of Edw. III, minor until 1389, deposed 1399	1377	1400	33	22
House of Lancaster					
Henry IV	Son of John of Gaunt, Duke of Lancaster, son of Edw. III.	1399	1413	47	13
Henry V	Son of Henry IV, victor of Agincourt	1413	1422	34	9
Henry VI	Son of Henry V, deposed 1461, died in Tower.	1422	1471	49	39

Name		Began	Died	Age	Rgd
House of York					
Edward IV.	Great-great-grandson of Edward III, son of Duke of York	1461	1483	41	22
Edward V	Son of Edward IV, murdered in Tower of London.	1483	1483	13	0
Richard III.	Crookback, bro. of Edward IV, fell at Bosworth Field	1483	1485	35	2
House of Tudor					
Henry VII	Son of Edmund Tudor, Earl of Richmond, whose father had married the widow of Henry V; descended from Edward III through his mother, Margaret Beaufort via John of Gaunt. By marriage with dau. of Edward IV he united Lancaster and York	1485	1509	53	24
Henry VIII	Son of Henry VII by Elizabeth, dau. of Edward IV.	1509	1547	56	38
Edward VI.	Son of Henry VIII, by Jane Seymour, his 3d queen. Ruled under regents. Was forced to name Lady Jane Grey his successor. Council of State proclaimed her queen July 10, 1553. Mary Tudor won Council, was proclaimed queen July 19, 1553. Mary had Lady Jane Grey beheaded for treason, Feb., 1554	1547	1553	16	6
Mary I.	Daughter of Henry VIII, by Catherine of Aragon.	1553	1558	43	5
Elizabeth I	Daughter of Henry VIII, by Anne Boleyn	1558	1603	69	44

Great Britain

Name		Began	Died	Age	Rgd
House of Stuart					
James I	James VI of Scotland, son of Mary, Queen of Scots. *First to call himself King of Great Britain. This became official with the Act of Union, 1707.*	1603	1625	59	22
Charles I.	Only surviving son of James I; beheaded Jan. 30, 1649.	1625	1649	48	24
Commonwealth, 1649-1660					
Council of State, 1649; Protectorate, 1653					
The Cromwells. .	Oliver Cromwell, Lord Protector	1653	1658	59	—
	Richard Cromwell, son, Lord Protector, resigned May 25, 1659	1658	1712	86	—
House of Stuart (Restored)					
Charles II	Eldest son of Charles I, died without issue	1660	1685	55	25
James II	2d son of Charles I. Deposed 1688. Interregnum Dec. 11, 1688, to Feb. 13, 1689	1685	1701	68	3
William III	Son of William, Prince of Orange, by Mary, dau. of Charles I	1689	1702	51	13
and Mary II	Eldest daughter of James II and wife of William III		1694	33	6
Anne	2d daughter of James II.	1702	1714	49	12
House of Hanover					
George I.	Son of Elector of Hanover, by Sophia, grand-dau. of James I	1714	1727	67	13
George II	Only son of George I, married Caroline of Brandenburg	1727	1760	77	33
George III.	Grandson of George II, married Charlotte of Mecklenburg	1760	1820	81	59
George IV.	Eldest son of George III, Prince Regent, from Feb., 1811.	1820	1830	67	10
William IV.	3d son of George III, married Adelaide of Saxe-Meiningen.	1830	1837	71	7
Victoria	Dau. of Edward, 4th son of George III; married (1840) Prince Albert of Saxe-Coburg and Gotha, who became Prince Consort	1837	1901	81	63
House of Saxe-Coburg and Gotha					
Edward VII	Eldest son of Victoria, married Alexandra, Princess of Denmark	1901	1910	68	9
House of Windsor					
Name Adopted July 17, 1917					
George V	2d son of Edward VII, married Princess Mary of Teck	1910	1936	70	25
Edward VIII.	Eldest son of George V; acceded Jan. 20, 1936, abdicated Dec. 11	1936	1972	77	1
George VI.	2d son of George V; married Lady Elizabeth Bowes-Lyon	1936	1952	56	15
Elizabeth II	Elder daughter of George VI, acceded Feb. 6, 1952	1952	—	—	—

Rulers of Scotland

Kenneth I MacAlpin was the first Scot to rule both Scots and Picts, 846 AD.

Duncan I was the first general ruler, 1034. Macbeth seized the kingdom 1040, was slain by Duncan's son, Malcolm III MacDuncan (Canmore), 1057.

Malcolm married Margaret, Saxon princess who had fled from the Normans. Queen Margaret introduced English language and English monastic customs. She was canonized, 1250. Her son Edgar, 1097, moved the court to Edinburgh. His brothers Alexander I and David I succeeded. Malcolm IV, the Maiden, 1153, grandson of David I, was followed by his brother, William the Lion, 1165, whose son was Alexander II, 1214. The latter's son, Alexander III, 1249, defeated the Norse and regained the Hebrides. When he died, 1286, his granddaughter, Margaret, child of Eric of Norway and grandniece of Edward I of England, known as the Maid of Norway, was chosen ruler, but died 1290, aged 8.

John Baliol, 1292-1296. (Interregnum, 10 years).

Robert Bruce (The Bruce), 1306-1329, victor at Bannockburn, 1314.

David II, only son of Robert Bruce, ruled 1329-1371.

Robert II, 1371-1390, grandson of Robert Bruce, son of Walter, the Steward of Scotland, was called The Steward, first of the so-called Stuart line.

Robert III, son of Robert II, 1390-1406.

James I, son of Robert III, 1406-1437.

James II, son of James I, 1437-1460.

James III, eldest son of James II, 1460-1488.

James IV, eldest son of James III, 1488-1513.

James V, eldest son of James IV, 1513-1542.

Mary, daughter of James V, born 1542, became queen when one week old; was crowned 1543. Married, 1558, Francis, son of Henry II of France, who became king 1559, died 1560. Mary ruled Scots 1561 until abdication, 1567. She also married (2) Henry Stewart, Lord Darnley, and (3) James, Earl of Bothwell. Imprisoned by Elizabeth I, Mary was beheaded 1587.

James VI, 1566-1625, son of Mary and Lord Darnley, became King of England on death of Elizabeth in 1603. Although the thrones were thus united, the legislative union of Scotland and England was not effected until the Act of Union, May 1, 1707.

Prime Ministers of Great Britain

(W=Whig; T=Tory; Cl=Coalition; P=Peelite; L=Liberal; C=Conservative; La=Labour)

Sir Robert Walpole (W)	1721-1742	George Canning (T)	1827	Sir Henry Campbell-	
Earl of Wilmington (W)	1742-1743	Viscount Goderich (T)	1827-1828	Bannerman (L)	1905-1908
Henry Pelham (W)	1743-1754	Duke of Wellington (T)	1828-1830	Herbert H. Asquith (L)	1908-1915
Duke of Newcastle (W)	1754-1756	Earl Grey (W)	1830-1834	Herbert H. Asquith (Cl)	1915-1916
Duke of Devonshire (W)	1756-1757	Viscount Melbourne (W)	1834	David Lloyd George (Cl)	1916-1922
Duke of Newcastle (W)	1757-1762	Sir Robert Peel (T)	1834-1835	Andrew Bonar Law (C)	1922-1923
Earl of Bute (T)	1762-1763	Viscount Melbourne (W)	1835-1841	Stanley Baldwin (C)	1923-1924
George Grenville (W)	1763-1765	Sir Robert Peel (T)	1841-1846	James Ramsay MacDonald	
Marquess of Rocking-		Lord John Russell (later		(La)	1924
ham (W)	1765-1766	Earl) (W)	1846-1852	Stanley Baldwin (C)	1924-1929
William Pitt the Elder		Earl of Derby (T)	1852	James Ramsay MacDonald	
(Earl of Chatham) (W)	1766-1768	Earl of Aberdeen (P)	1852-1855	(La)	1929-1931
Duke of Grafton (W)	1768-1770	Viscount Palmerston (L)	1855-1858	James Ramsay MacDonald	
Frederick North (Lord		Earl of Derby (C)	1858-1859	(Cl)	1931-1935
North) (T)	1770-1782	Viscount Palmerston (L)	1859-1865	Stanley Baldwin (Cl)	1935-1937
Marquess of Rocking-		Earl Russell (L)	1865-1866	Neville Chamberlain (Cl)	1937-1940
ham (W)	1782	Earl of Derby (C)	1866-1868	Winston Churchill (Cl)	1940-1945
Earl of Shelburne (W)	1782-1783	Benjamin Disraeli (C)	1868	Winston Churchill (C)	1945
Duke of Portland (Cl)	1783	William E. Gladstone (L)	1868-1874	Clement Attlee (La)	1945-1951
William Pitt the		Benjamin Disraeli (C)	1874-1880	Sir Winston Churchill (C)	1951-1955
Younger (T)	1783-1801	William E. Gladstone (L)	1880-1885	Sir Anthony Eden (C)	1955-1957
Henry Addington (T)	1801-1804	Marquess of Salisbury(C)	1885-1886	Harold Macmillan (C)	1957-1963
William Pitt the		William E. Gladstone (L)	1886	Sir Alec Douglas-Home (C)	1963-1964
Younger (T)	1804-1806	Marquess of Salisbury(C)	1886-1892	Harold Wilson (La)	1964-1970
William Wyndham Grenville,		William E. Gladstone (L)	1892-1894	Edward Heath (C)	1970-1974
Baron Grenville (W)	1806-1807	Earl of Rosebery (L)	1894-1895	Harold Wilson (La)	1974-1976
Duke of Portland (T)	1807-1809	Marquess of Salisbury(C)	1895-1902	James Callaghan (La)	1976-1979
Spencer Perceval (T)	1809-1812	Arthur J. Balfour (C)	1902-1905	Margaret Thatcher (C)	1979-1990
Earl of Liverpool (T)	1812-1827			John Major (C)	1990-

Historical Periods of Japan

Yamato	c.300-592	Conquest of Yamato plain c. 300 AD.	Ashikaga	1338-1573	Ashikaga Takauji becomes shogun, 1338.
Asuka	592-710	Accession of Empress Suiko, 592.	Muromachi	1392-1573	Unification of Southern and Northern Courts, 1392.
Nara	710-794	Completion of Heijo (Nara), 710; capital moves to Naga-oka, 784.	Sengoku	1467-1600	Beginning of the Onin war, 1467.
Heian	794-1185	Completion of Heian (Kyoto), 794.	Momoyama	1573-1603	Oda Nobunaga enters Kyoto, 1568; Nobunaga deposes last Ashikaga shogun, 1573; Tokugawa Ieyasu victor at Sekigahara, 1600.
Fujiwara	858-1160	Fujiwara-no-Yoshifusa be-comes regent, 858.			
Taira	1160-1185	Taira-no-Kiyomori assumes control, 1160; Minamoto-no-Yoritomo victor over Taira, 1185.	Edo	1603-1867	Ieyasu becomes shogun, 1603.
			Meiji	1868-1912	Enthronement of Emperor Mutsuhito (Meiji), 1867; Meiji Restoration and Char-ter Oath, 1868.
Kamakura	1192-1333	Yoritomo becomes shogun, 1192.	Taisho	1912-1926	Accession of Emperor Yoshi-hito, 1912.
Namboku	1334-1392	Restoration of Emperor Godaigo, 1334; Southern Court established by Godaigo at Yoshino, 1336.	Showa	1926-1989	Accession of Emperor Hiro-hito, 1926.
			Heisei	1989-	Accession of Emperor Akihito, 1989.

Rulers of France: Kings, Queens, Presidents

Caesar to Charlemagne

Julius Caesar subdued the Gauls, native tribes of Gaul (France) 58 to 51 BC. The Romans ruled 500 years. The Franks, a Teutonic tribe, reached the Somme from the East ca. 250 AD. By the 5th century the Merovingian Franks ousted the Romans. In 451 AD, with the help of Visigoths, Burgundians and others, they defeated Attila and the Huns at Chalons-sur-Marne.

Childeric I became leader of the Merovingians 458 AD. His son Clovis I (Chlodwig, Ludwig, Louis), crowned 481, founded the dynasty. After defeating the Alemanni (Germans) 496, he was baptized a Christian and made Paris his capital. His line ruled until Childeric III was deposed, 751.

The West Merovingians were called Neustrians, the eastern Austrasians. Pepin of Herstal (687-714), major domus, or head of the palace, of Austrasia, took over Neustria as dux (leader) of the Franks. Pepin's son, Charles, called Martel (the Ham-mer), defeated the Saracens at Tours-Poitiers, 732; was suc-ceeded by his son, Pepin the Short, 741, who deposed Childeric III and ruled as king until 768.

His son, Charlemagne, or Charles the Great (742-814) be-came king of the Franks, 768, with his brother Carloman, who died 771. He ruled France, Germany, parts of Italy, Spain, Austria, and enforced Christianity. Crowned Emperor of the Romans by Pope Leo III in St. Peter's, Rome, Dec. 25, 800 AD. Succeeded by son, Louis I the Pious, 814. At death, 840, Louis left empire to sons, Lothair (Roman emperor); Pepin I (king of Aquitaine); Louis II (of Germany); Charles the Bald (France). They quarreled and by the peace of Verdun, 843, divided the empire.

Date in bold is year of accession.

The Carolingians

843   Charles I (the Bald); Roman Emperor, 875
877   Louis II (the Stammerer), son
879   Louis III (died 882) and Carloman, brothers
885   Charles II (the Fat); Roman Emperor, 881
888   Eudes (Odo), elected by nobles
898   Charles III (the Simple), son of Louis II, defeated by
922   Robert, brother of Eudes, killed in war
923   Rudolph (Raoul), Duke of Burgundy
936   Louis IV, son of Charles III
954   Lothair, son, aged 13, defeated by Capet
986   Louis V (the Sluggard), left no heirs

The Capets

987   Hugh Capet, son of Hugh the Great
996   Robert II (the Wise), his son
1031   Henry I, his son
1060   Philip I (the Fair), son
1108   Louis VI (the Fat), son
1137   Louis VII (the Younger), son
1180   Philip II (Augustus), son, crowned at Reims
1223   Louis VIII (the Lion), son
1226   Louis IX, son, crusader; Louis IX (1214-1270) reigned 44 years, arbitrated disputes with English King Henry III; led crusades, 1248 (captured in Egypt 1250) and 1270, when he died of plague in Tunis. Canonized 1297 as St. Louis.
1270   Philip III (the Hardy), son
1285   Philip IV (the Fair), son, king at 17
1314   Louis X (the Headstrong), son. His posthumous son, John I, lived only 7 days
1316   Philip V (the Tall), brother of Louis X
1322   Charles IV (the Fair), brother of Louis X

House of Valois

1328   Philip VI (of Valois), grandson of Philip III
1350   John II (the Good), his son, retired to England
1364   Charles V (the Wise), son
1380   Charles VI (the Beloved), son
1422   Charles VII (the Victorious), son. In 1429 Joan of Arc (Jeanne d'Arc) promised Charles to oust the English, who occupied northern France. Joan won at Orleans and Patay and had Charles crowned at Reims July 17, 1429. Joan was captured May 24, 1430, and executed May 30, 1431, at Rouen for heresy. Charles ordered her rehabilitation, effected 1455.
1461   Louis XI (the Cruel), son, civil reformer
1483   Charles VIII (the Affable), son
1498   Louis XII, great-grandson of Charles V
1515   Francis I, of Angouleme, nephew, son-in-law. Francis I (1494-1547) reigned 32 years, fought 4 big wars, was patron of the arts, aided Cellini, del Sarto, Leonardo da Vinci, Rabelais, embellished Fontainebleau.
1547   Henry II, son, killed at a joust in a tournament. He was the husband of Catherine de Medicis (1519-1589) and the lover of Diane de Poitiers (1499-1566). Catherine was born in Florence, daughter of Lorenzo de Medici. By her marriage to Henry II she became the mother of Francis II, Charles IX, Henry III and Queen Margaret (Reine Margot), wife of Henry IV. She persuaded Charles IX to order the massacre of Huguenots on the Feast of St. Bartholomew, Aug. 24, 1572, the day her daughter was married to Henry of Navarre.
1559   Francis II, son. In 1548, Mary, Queen of Scots since infancy, was betrothed when 6 to Francis, aged 4. They were married 1558. Francis died 1560, aged 16; Mary ruled Scotland, abdicated 1567.
1560   Charles IX, brother
1574   Henry III, brother, assassinated

House of Bourbon

1589   Henry IV, of Navarre, assassinated. Henry IV made enemies when he gave tolerance to Protestants by Edict of Nantes, 1598. He was grandson of Queen Margaret of Navarre, literary patron. He married Margaret of Valois, daughter of Henry II and Catherine de Medicis; was divorced; in 1600 married Marie de Medicis, who became Regent of France, 1610-17, for her son, Louis XIII, but was exiled by Richelieu, 1631.

1610   Louis XIII (the Just), son. Louis XIII (1601-1643) married Anne of Austria. His ministers were Cardinals Richelieu and Mazarin.
1643   Louis XIV (The Grand Monarch), son. Louis XIV was king 72 years. He exhausted a prosperous country in wars for thrones and territory. By revoking the Edict of Nantes (1685) he caused the emigration of the Huguenots. He said: "I am the state."
1715   Louis XV, great-grandson. Louis XV married a Polish princess; lost Canada to the English. His favorites, Mme. Pompadour and Mme. Du Barry, influenced policies. Noted for saying "After me, the deluge."
1774   Louis XVI, grandson; married Marie Antoinette, daughter of Empress Maria Therese of Austria. King and queen beheaded by Revolution, 1793. Their son, called Louis XVII, died in prison, never ruled.

First Republic

1792   National Convention of the French Revolution
1795   Directory, under Barras and others
1799   Consulate, Napoleon Bonaparte, first consul. Elected consul for life, 1802.

First Empire

1804   Napoleon I, emperor. Josephine (de Beauharnais), empress, 1804-09; Marie Louise, empress, 1810-1814. Her son, Francois (1811-1832), titular King of Rome, later Duke de Reichstadt and "Napoleon II," never ruled. Napoleon abdicated 1814, died 1821.

Bourbons Restored

1814   Louis XVIII king; brother of Louis XVI
1824   Charles X, brother; reactionary; deposed by the July Revolution, 1830

House of Orleans

1830   Louis-Philippe, the "citizen king"

Second Republic

1848   Louis Napoleon Bonaparte, president, nephew of Napoleon I. He became:

Second Empire

1852   Napoleon III, emperor; Eugenie (de Montijo), empress. Lost Franco-Prussian war, deposed 1870. Son, Prince Imperial (1856-79), died in Zulu War. Eugenie died 1920.

Third Republic—Presidents

1871   Thiers, Louis Adolphe (1797-1877)
1873   MacMahon, Marshal Patrice M. de (1808-1893)
1879   Grevy, Paul J. (1807-1891)
1887   Sadi-Carnot, M. (1837-1894), assassinated
1894   Casimir-Perier, Jean P. P. (1847-1907)
1895   Faure, François Felix (1841-1899)
1899   Loubet, Emile (1838-1929)
1906   Fallieres, C. Armand (1841-1931)
1913   Poincare, Raymond (1860-1934)
1920   Deschanel, Paul (1856-1922)
1920   Millerand, Alexandre (1859-1943)
1924   Doumergue, Gaston (1863-1937)
1931   Doumer, Paul (1857-1932), assassinated
1932   Lebrun, Albert (1871-1950), resigned 1940
1940   **Vichy govt.** under German armistice: Henri Philippe Petain (1856-1951), Chief of State, 1940-1944.
       Provisional govt. after liberation: Charles de Gaulle (1890-1970) Oct. 1944-Jan. 21, 1946; Felix Gouin (1884-1977) Jan. 23, 1946; Georges Bidault (1899-1983) June 24, 1946.

Fourth Republic—Presidents

1947   Auriol, Vincent (1884-1966)
1954   Coty, Rene (1882-1962)

Fifth Republic—Presidents

1959   de Gaulle, Charles Andre J. M. (1890-1970)
1969   Pompidou, Georges (1911-1974)
1974   Giscard d'Estaing, Valery (1926-   )
1981   Mitterrand, François (1916-   )
1995   Chirac, Jacques (1932-   )

Rulers of Middle Europe; Rise and Fall of Dynasties; Rulers of Germany

Carolingian Dynasty

Charles the Great, or Charlemagne, ruled France, Italy, and Middle Europe; established Ostmark (later Austria); crowned Roman emperor by pope in Rome, 800 AD; died 814.

Louis I (Ludwig) the Pious, son; crowned by Charlemagne 814; died 840.

Louis II, the German, son; succeeded to East Francia (Germany) 843-876.

Charles the Fat, son; inherited East Francia and West Francia (France) 876, reunited empire, crowned emperor by pope, 881, deposed 887.

Arnulf, nephew, 887-899. Partition of empire.

Louis the Child, 899-911, last direct descendant of Charlemagne.

Conrad I, duke of Franconia, first elected German king, 911-918, founded House of Franconia.

Saxon Dynasty; First Reich

Henry I, the Fowler, duke of Saxony, 919-936.

Otto I, the Great, 936-973, son; crowned Holy Roman Emperor by pope, 962.

Otto II, 973-983, son; failed to oust Greeks and Arabs from Sicily.

Otto III, 983-1002, son; crowned emperor at 16.

Henry II, the Saint, duke of Bavaria, 1002-1024, great-grandson of Otto the Great.

House of Franconia

Conrad II, 1024-1039, elected king of Germany.

Henry III, the Black, 1039-1056, son; deposed 3 popes; annexed Burgundy.

Henry IV, 1056-1106, son; regency by his mother, Agnes of Poitou. Banned by Pope Gregory VII, he did penance at Canossa.

Henry V, 1106-1125, son; last of Salic House.

Lothair, duke of Saxony, 1125-1137. Crowned emperor in Rome, 1134.

House of Hohenstaufen

Conrad III, duke of Swabia, 1138-1152. In 2d Crusade.

Frederick I, Barbarossa, 1152-1190; Conrad's nephew.

Henry VI, 1190-1196, took lower Italy from Normans. Son became king of Sicily.

Philip of Swabia, 1197-1208, brother.

Otto IV, of House of Welf, 1198-1215; deposed.

Frederick II, 1215-1250, son of Henry VI; king of Sicily; crowned king of Jerusalem in 5th Crusade.

Conrad IV, 1250-1254, son; lost lower Italy to Charles of Anjou.

Conradin, 1252-1268, son, king of Jerusalem and Sicily, beheaded. Last Hohenstaufen.

Interregnum, 1254-1273, Rise of the Electors.

Transition

Rudolph I of Hapsburg, 1273-1291, defeated King Ottocar II of Bohemia. Bequeathed duchy of Austria to eldest son, Albert.

Adolph of Nassau, 1292-1298, killed in war with Albert of Austria.

Albert I, king of Germany, 1298-1308, son of Rudolph.

Henry VII, of Luxemburg, 1308-1313, crowned emperor in Rome. Seized Bohemia, 1310.

Louis IV of Bavaria (Wittelsbach), 1314-1347. Also elected was Frederick of Austria, 1314-1330 (Hapsburg). Abolition of papal sanction for election of Holy Roman Emperor.

Charles IV, of Luxemburg, 1347-1378, grandson of Henry VII, German emperor and king of Bohemia, Lombardy, Burgundy; took Mark of Brandenburg.

Wenceslaus, 1378-1400, deposed.

Rupert, Duke of Palatine, 1400-1410.

Sigismund, 1411-1437.

Hungary

Stephen I, house of Arpad, 997-1038. Crowned king 1000; converted Magyars; canonized 1083. After several centuries of feuds Charles Robert of Anjou became Charles I, 1308-1342.

Louis I, the Great, son, 1342-1382; joint ruler of Poland with Casimir III, 1370. Defeated Turks.

Mary, daughter, 1382-1395, ruled with husband. Sigismund of Luxemburg, 1387-1437, also king of Bohemia. As bro. of Wenceslaus he succeeded Rupert as Holy Roman Emperor, 1410.

Albert, 1438-1439, son-in-law of Sigismund; also Roman emperor as Albert II. *(see under Hapsburg)*

Ulaszlo I of Poland, 1440-1444.

Ladislaus V, posthumous son of Albert II, 1444-1457. John Hunyadi (Hunyadi Janos), governor (1446-1452), fought Turks, Czechs; died 1456.

Matthias I (Corvinus), son of Hunyadi, 1458-1490. Shared rule of Bohemia, captured Vienna, 1485, annexed Austria, Styria, Carinthia.

Ulaszlo II (king of Bohemia), 1490-1516.

Louis II, son, aged 10, 1516-1526. Wars with Suleiman, Turk. In 1527 Hungary split between Ferdinand I, Archduke of Austria, bro.-in-law of Louis II, and John Zapolya of Transylvania. After Turkish invasion, 1547, Hungary split between Ferdinand, Prince John Sigismund (Transylvania) and the Turks.

House of Hapsburg

Albert V of Austria, Hapsburg, crowned king of Hungary, Jan. 1438, Roman emperor, March 1438, as Albert II; died 1439.

Frederick III, cousin, 1440-1493. Fought Turks.

Maximilian I, son, 1493-1519. Assumed title of Holy Roman Emperor (German), 1493.

Charles V, grandson, 1519-1556. King of Spain with mother co-regent; crowned Roman emperor at Aix, 1520. Confronted Luther at Worms; attempted church reform and religious conciliation; abdicated 1556.

Ferdinand I, king of Bohemia, 1526, of Hungary, 1527; disputed. German king, 1531. Crowned Roman emperor on abdication of brother Charles V, 1556.

Maximilian II, son, 1564-1576.

Rudolph II, son, 1576-1612.

Matthias, brother, 1612-1619, king of Bohemia and Hungary.

Ferdinand II of Styria, king of Bohemia, 1617, of Hungary, 1618, Roman emperor, 1619. Bohemian Protestants deposed him, elected Frederick V of Palatine, starting Thirty Years War.

Ferdinand III, son, king of Hungary, 1625, Bohemia, 1627, Roman emperor, 1637. Peace of Westphalia, 1648, ended war.

Leopold I, 1658-1705; Joseph I, 1705-1711; Charles VI, 1711-1740.

Maria Theresa, daughter, 1740-1780, Archduchess of Austria, queen of Hungary; ousted pretender, Charles VII, crowned 1742; in 1745 obtained election of her husband Francis I as Roman emperor and co-regent (d. 1765). Fought Seven Years' War with Frederick II of Prussia. Mother of Marie Antoinette.

Joseph II, son, 1765-1790, Roman emperor, reformer; powers restricted by Empress Maria Theresa until her death, 1780. First partition of Poland. Leopold II, 1790-1792.

Francis II, son, 1792-1835. Fought Napoleon. Proclaimed first hereditary emperor of Austria, 1804. Forced to abdicate as Roman emperor, 1806; last use of title. Ferdinand I, son, 1835-1848, abdicated during revolution.

Austro-Hungarian Monarchy

Francis Joseph I, nephew, 1848-1916, emperor of Austria, king of Hungary. Dual monarchy of Austria-Hungary formed, 1867. After assassination of heir, Archduke Francis Ferdinand, June 28, 1914, Austrian diplomacy precipitated World War I.

Charles I, grand-nephew, 1916-1918, last emperor of Austria and king of Hungary. Abdicated Nov. 11-13, 1918, died 1922.

Rulers of Prussia

Nucleus of Prussia was the Mark of Brandenburg. First margrave Albert the Bear (Albrecht), 1134-1170. First Hohenzollern margrave was Frederick, burgrave of Nuremberg, 1417-1440.

Frederick William, 1640-1688, the Great Elector. Son, Frederick III, 1688-1713, crowned King Frederick of Prussia, 1701.

Frederick William I, son, 1713-1740.

Frederick II, the Great, son, 1740-1786, annexed Silesia, part of Austria.

Frederick William II, nephew, 1786-1797.

Frederick William III, son, 1797-1840. Napoleonic wars.

Frederick William IV, son, 1840-1861. Uprising of 1848 and first parliament and constitution.

Second and Third Reich

William I, 1861-1888, brother. Annexation of Schleswig and Hanover; Franco-Prussian war, 1870-71, proclamation of German Reich, Jan. 18, 1871, at Versailles; William, German emperor (Deutscher Kaiser), Bismarck, chancellor.

Frederick III, son, 1888.

William II, son, 1888-1918. Led Germany in World War I, abdicated as German emperor and king of Prussia, Nov. 9, 1918. Died in exile in Netherlands June 4, 1941. Minor rulers of Bavaria, Saxony, Wurttemberg also abdicated.

Germany proclaimed republic at Weimar, July 1, 1919. Presidents: Frederick Ebert, 1919-1925; Paul von Hindenburg-Beneckendorff, 1925, reelected 1932, d. Aug. 2, 1934. Adolf Hitler, chancellor, chosen successor as Leader-Chancellor (Fuehrer-Reichskanzler) of Third Reich. Annexed Austria, March, 1938. Precipitated World War II, 1939-1945. Suicide April 30, 1945.

Germany After 1945

Following World War II, Germany was split between democratic West and Soviet-dominated East. Germany was reunited Oct. 3, 1990. Post-reunification Chancellors: Helmut Kohl, 1990- .

Rulers of Poland

House of Piasts

Miesko I, 962?-992; Poland Christianized 966. Expansion under 3 Boleslavs: I, 992-1025, son, crowned king 1024; II, 1058-1079, great-grandson, exiled after killing bishop Stanislav who became chief patron saint of Poland; III, 1106-1138, nephew, divided Poland among 4 sons, eldest suzerain.

1138-1306, feudal division. 1226 founding in Prussia of military order Teutonic Knights. 1226 invasion by Tartars/Mongols.

Vladislav I, 1306-1333, reunited most Polish territories, crowned king 1320. Casimir III the Great, 1333-1370, son, developed economic, cultural life, foreign policy.

House of Anjou

Louis I, 1370-1382, nephew/identical with Louis I of Hungary.

Jadwiga, 1384-1399, daughter, married 1386 Jagiello, Grand Duke of Lituania.

House of Jagelloneans

Vladislav II, 1386-1434, Christianized Lituania, founded personal union between Poland & Lituania. Defeated 1410 Teutonic Knights at Grunwald.

Vladislav III, 1434-1444, son, simultaneously king of Hungary. Fought Turks, killed 1444 in battle of Varna.

Casimir IV, 1446-1492, brother, competed with Hapsburgs, put son Vladislav on throne of Bohemia, later also of Hungary.

Sigismund I, 1506-1548, brother, patronized science & arts, his & son's reign "Golden Age."

Sigismund II, 1548-1572, son, established 1569 real union of Poland and Lituania (lasted until 1795).

Elective kings

Polish nobles proclaimed 1572 Poland a Republic headed by king to be elected by whole nobility.

Stephen Batory, 1576-1586, duke of Transylvania, married Ann, sister of Sigismund II August. Fought Russians.

Sigismund III Vasa, 1587-1632, nephew of Sigismund II. 1592-1598 also king of Sweden. His generals fought Russians, Turks.

Vladislav II Vasa, 1632-1648, son. Fought Russians.

John II Casimir Vasa, 1648-1668, brother. Fought Cossacks, Swedes, Russians, Turks, Tartars (the "Deluge"). Abdicated 1668.

John III Sobieski, 1674-1696. Won Vienna from besieging Turks, 1683.

Stanislav II, 1764-1795, last king. Encouraged reforms; 1791 1st modern Constitution in Europe. 1772, 1793, 1795 Poland partitioned among Russia, Prussia, Austria. Unsuccessful insurrection against foreign invasion 1794 under Kosciuszko, Amer.-Polish gen.

1795-1918 Poland under foreign rule

1807-1815 Grand Duchy of Warsaw created by Napoleon I, Frederick August of Saxony grand duke.

1815 Congress of Vienna proclaimed part of Poland "Kingdom" in personal union with Russia.

Polish uprisings: 1830 against Russia, 1846, 1848 against Austria, 1863 against Russia—all repressed.

1918-1939 Second Republic

1918-1922 Head of State Jozef Pilsudski. Presidents: Gabriel Narutowicz 1922, assassinated. Stanislav Wojciechowski 1922-1926, had to abdicate after Pilsudski's coup d'état. Ignacy Moscicki, 1926-1939, ruled with Pilsudski as (until 1935) virtual dictator.

1939-1945 Poland under foreign occupation

Nazi aggression Sept. 1939. Polish govt.-in-exile, first in France, then in England. Vladislav Raczkiewicz pres., Gen. Vladislav Sikorski, then Stanislav Mikolajczyk, prime ministers. Polish Committee of Natl. Liberation proclaimed at Lublin July 1944, transformed into govt. Jan. 1, 1945.

Rulers of Denmark, Sweden, Norway

Denmark

Earliest rulers invaded Britain; King Canute, who ruled in London 1016-1035, was most famous. The Valdemars furnished kings until the 15th century. In 1282 the Danes won the first national assembly, Danehof, from King Erik V.

Most redoubtable medieval character was Margaret, daughter of Valdemar IV, born 1353, married at 10 to King Haakon VI of Norway. In 1376 she had her first infant son Olaf made king of Denmark. After his death, 1387, she was regent of Denmark and Norway. In 1388 Sweden accepted her as sovereign. In 1389 she made her grand-nephew, Duke Erik of Pomerania, titular king of Denmark, Sweden, and Norway, with herself as regent. In 1397 she effected the Union of Kalmar of the three kingdoms and had Erik VII crowned. In 1439 the three kingdoms deposed him and elected, 1440, Christopher of Bavaria king (Christopher III). On his death, 1448, the union broke up.

Succeeding rulers were unable to enforce their claims as rulers of Sweden until 1520, when Christian II conquered Sweden. He was thrown out 1522, and in 1523 Gustavus Vasa united Sweden. Denmark continued to dominate Norway until the Napoleonic wars, when Frederick VI, 1808-1839, joined the Napoleonic cause after Britain had destroyed the Danish fleet, 1807. In 1814 he was forced to cede Norway to Sweden and Helgoland to Britain, receiving Lauenburg. Successors Christian VIII, 1839; Frederick VII, 1848; Christian IX, 1863; Frederick VIII, 1906; Christian X, 1912; Frederick IX, 1947; Margrethe II, 1972.

Sweden

Early kings ruled at Uppsala, but did not dominate the country. Sverker, c1130-c1156, united the Swedes and Goths. In 1435 Sweden obtained the Riksdag, or parliament. After the Union of Kalmar, 1397, the Danes either ruled or harried the country until Christian II of Denmark conquered it anew, 1520. This led to a rising under Gustavus Vasa, who ruled Sweden 1523-1560, and established an independent kingdom. Charles IX, 1599-1611, crowned 1604, conquered Moscow. Gustavus II Adolphus, 1611-1632, was called the Lion of the North. Later rulers: Christina, 1632; Charles X Gustavus 1654; Charles XI, 1660; Charles XII (invader of Russia and Poland, defeated at Poltava, June 28, 1709), 1697; Ulrika Eleanora, sister, elected queen 1718; Frederick I (of Hesse), her husband, 1720; Adolphus Frederick, 1751; Gustavus III, 1771; Gustavus IV Adolphus, 1792; Charles XIII, 1809. (Union with Norway began 1814.) Charles XIV John, 1818. He was Jean Bernadotte, Napoleon's Prince of Ponte Corvo, elected 1810 to succeed Charles XIII. He founded the present dynasty: Oscar I, 1844; Charles XV, 1859; Oscar II, 1872; Gustavus V, 1907; Gustav VI Adolf, 1950; Carl XVI Gustaf, 1973.

Norway

Overcoming many rivals, Harald Haarfager, 872-930, conquered Norway, Orkneys, and Shetlands; Olaf I, great-grandson, 995-1000, brought Christianity into Norway, Iceland, and Greenland. In 1035 Magnus the Good also became king of Denmark. Haakon V, 1299-1319, had married his daughter to Erik of Sweden. Their son, Magnus, became ruler of Norway and Sweden at 6. His son, Haakon VI, married Margaret of Denmark; their son Olaf IV became king of Norway and Denmark, followed by Margaret's regency and the Union of Kalmar, 1397.

In 1450 Norway became subservient to Denmark. Christian IV, 1588-1648, founded Christiania, now Oslo. After Napoleonic wars, when Denmark ceded Norway to Sweden, a strong nationalist movement forced recognition of Norway as an independent kingdom united with Sweden under the Swedish kings, 1814-1905. In 1905 the union was dissolved and Prince Charles of Denmark became Haakon VII. He died Sept. 21, 1957; succeeded by son, Olav V. Olav V died January 17, 1991; succeeded by son, Harald V.

Rulers of the Netherlands and Belgium

The Netherlands (Holland)

William Frederick, Prince of Orange, led a revolt against French rule, 1813, and was crowned King of the Netherlands, 1815. Belgium seceded Oct. 4, 1830, after a revolt. The secession was ratified by the two kingdoms by treaty Apr. 19, 1839.

Succession: William II, son, 1840; William III, son, 1849; Wilhelmina, daughter of William III and his 2d wife Princess Emma of Waldeck, 1890; Wilhelmina abdicated, Sept. 4, 1948, in favor of daughter, Juliana. Juliana abdicated Apr. 30, 1980, in favor of daughter, Beatrix.

Belgium

A national congress elected Prince Leopold of Saxe-Coburg King; he took the throne July 21, 1831, as Leopold I. Succession: Leopold II, son 1865; Albert I, nephew of Leopold II, 1909; Leopold III, son of Albert, 1934; Prince Charles, Regent 1944; Leopold returned 1950, yielded powers to son Baudouin, Prince Royal, Aug. 6, 1950, abdicated July 16, 1951. Baudouin I took throne July 17, 1951; died July 31, 1993; succeeded by brother, Albert II.

Roman Rulers

From Romulus to the end of the Empire in the West. Rulers of the Roman Empire in the East sat in Constantinople and for a brief period in Nicaea, until the capture of Constantinople by the Turks in 1453, when Byzantium was succeeded by the Ottoman Empire.

BC	Name	AD	Name	AD	Name
	The Kingdom	98	Trajanus	337	Constantinus II, Constans I,
753	Romulus (Quirinus)	117	Hadrianus		Constantius II
716	Numa Pompilius	138	Antoninus Pius	340	Constantius II and Constans I
673	Tullus Hostilius	161	Marcus Aurelius and Lucius Verus	350	Constantius II
640	Ancus Marcius	169	Marcus Aurelius (alone)	361	Julianus II (the Apostate)
616	L. Tarquinius Priscus	180	Commodus	363	Jovianus
578	Servius Tullius	193	Pertinax; Julianus I		
534	L. Tarquinius Superbus	193	Septimius Severus		**West (Rome) and East**
	The Republic	211	Caracalla and Geta		**(Constantinople)**
509	Consulate established	212	Caracalla (alone)	364	Valentinianus I (West) and Valens
509	Quaestorship instituted	217	Macrinus		(East)
498	Dictatorship introduced	218	Elagabalus (Heliogabalus)	367	Valentinianus I with Gratianus
494	Plebeian Tribunate created	222	Alexander Severus		(West) and Valens (East)
494	Plebeian Aedileship created	235	Maximinus I (the Thracian)	375	Gratianus with Valentinianus
444	Consular Tribunate organized	238	Gordianus I and Gordianus II; Pupi-		II (West) and Valens (East)
435	Censorship instituted		enus and Balbinus	378	Gratianus with Valentinianus II
366	Praetorship established	238	Gordianus III		(West), Theodosius I (East)
366	Curule Aedileship created	244	Philippus (the Arabian)	383	Valentinianus II (West) and
362	Military Tribunate elected	249	Decius		Theodosius I (East)
326	Proconsulate introduced	251	Gallus and Volusianus	394	Theodosius I (the Great)
311	Naval Duumvirate elected	253	Aemilianus	395	Honorius (West) and Arcadius
217	Dictatorship of Fabius Maximus	253	Valerianus and Gallienus		(East)
133	Tribunate of Tiberius Gracchus	258	Gallienus (alone)	408	Honorius (West) and Theodosius
123	Tribunate of Gaius Gracchus	268	Claudius Gothicus		II (East)
82	Dictatorship of Sulla	270	Quintillus	423	Valentinianus III (West) and
60	First Triumvirate formed (Caesar,	270	Aurelianus		Theodosius II (East)
	Pompeius, Crassus)	275	Tacitus	450	Valentinianus III (West)
46	Dictatorship of Caesar	276	Florianus		and Marcianus (East)
43	Second Triumvirate formed	276	Probus	455	Maximus (West), Avitus
	(Octavianus, Antonius, Lepidus)	282	Carus		(West); Marcianus (East)
	The Empire	283	Carinus and Numerianus	456	Avitus (West), Marcianus (East)
27	Augustus (Gaius Julius Caesar Oc-	284	Diocletianus	457	Majorianus (West), Leo I (East)
	tavianus)	286	Diocletianus and Maximianus	461	Severus II (West), Leo I (East)
AD		305	Galerius and Constantius I	467	Anthemius (West), Leo I (East)
14	Tiberius I	306	Galerius, Maximius II, Severus I	472	Olybrius (West), Leo I (East)
37	Gaius Caesar (Caligula)	307	Galerius, Maximinus	473	Glycerius (West), Leo I (East)
41	Claudius I		II, Constantinus I, Licinius,	474	Julius Nepos (West), Leo II (East)
54	Nero		Maxentius	475	Romulus Augustulus (West) and
68	Galba	311	Maximinus II, Constantinus I,		Zeno (East)
69	Galba; Otho, Vitellius		Licinius, Maxentius	476	End of Empire in West; Odovacar,
69	Vespasianus	314	Maximinus II, Constantinus I,		King, drops title of Emperor;
79	Titus		Licinius		murdered by King Theodoric of
81	Domitianus	314	Constantinus I and Licinius		Ostrogoths 493 AD
96	Nerva	324	Constantinus I (the Great)		

Rulers of Modern Italy

After the fall of Napoleon in 1814, the Congress of Vienna, 1815, restored Italy as a political patchwork, comprising the Kingdom of Naples and Sicily, the Papal States, and smaller units. Piedmont and Genoa were awarded to Sardinia, ruled by King Victor Emmanuel I of Savoy.

United Italy emerged under the leadership of Camillo, Count di Cavour (1810-1861), Sardinian prime minister. Agitation was led by Giuseppe Mazzini (1805-1872) and Giuseppe Garibaldi (1807-1882), soldier; Victor Em-

manuel I abdicated 1821. After a brief regency for a brother, Charles Albert was King 1831-1849, abdicating when defeated by the Austrians at Novara. Succeeded by Victor Emmanuel II, 1849-1861.

In 1859 France forced Austria to cede Lombardy to Sardinia, which gave rights to Savoy and Nice to France. In 1860 Garibaldi led 1,000 volunteers in a spectacular campaign, took Sicily and expelled the King of Naples. In 1860 the House of Savoy annexed Tuscany, Parma,

Modena, Romagna, the Two Sicilies, the Marches, and Umbria. Victor Emmanuel assumed the title of King of Italy at Turin Mar. 17, 1861. In 1866 he allied with Prussia in the Austro-Prussian War, with Prussia's victory received Venetia. On Sept. 20, 1870, his troops under Gen. Raffaele entered Rome and took over the Papal States, ending the temporal power of the Roman Catholic Church.

Succession: Umberto I, 1878, assassinated 1900; Victor Emmanuel III, 1900, abdicated 1946, died 1947; Humbert II, 1946, ruled a month. In 1921 Benito Mussolini (1883-1945) formed the Fascist party and became prime minister

Oct. 31, 1922. He entered World War II as an ally of Hitler. He was deposed July 25, 1943.

At a plebiscite June 2, 1946, Italy voted for a republic; Premier Alcide de Gasperi became chief of state June 13, 1946. On June 28, 1946, the Constituent Assembly elected Enrico de Nicola, Liberal, provisional president. Successive presidents: Luigi Einaudi, elected May 11, 1948; Giovanni Gronchi, Apr. 29, 1955; Antonio Segni, May 6, 1962; Giuseppe Saragat, Dec. 28, 1964; Giovanni Leone, Dec. 29, 1971; Alessandro Pertini, July 9, 1978; Francesco Cossiga, July 9, 1985; Oscar Luigi Scalfaro, May 28, 1992.

Rulers of Spain

From 8th to 11th centuries Spain was dominated by the Moors (Arabs and Berbers). The Christian reconquest established small kingdoms (Asturias, Aragon, Castile, Catalonia, Leon, Navarre, and Valencia). In 1474 Isabella, b. 1451, became Queen of Castile & Leon. Her husband, Ferdinand, b. 1452, inherited Aragon 1479, with Catalonia, Valencia, and the Balearic Islands, became Ferdinand V of Castile. By Isabella's request Pope Sixtus IV established the Inquisition, 1478. Last Moorish kingdom, Granada, fell 1492. Columbus opened New World of colonies, 1492. Isabella died 1504, succeeded by her daughter, Juana "the Mad," but Ferdinand ruled until his death 1516.

Charles I, b. 1500, son of Juana and grandson of Ferdinand and Isabella, and of Maximilian I of Hapsburg; succeeded later as Holy Roman Emperor, Charles V, 1520; abdicated 1556. Philip II, son, 1556-1598, inherited only Spanish throne; conquered Portugal, fought Turks, persecuted non-Catholics, sent Armada against England. Was married to Mary I of England, 1554-1558. Succession: Philip III, 1598-1621; Philip IV, 1621-1665; Charles II, 1665-1700, left Spain to Philip of Anjou, grandson of Louis XIV, who as Philip V, 1700-1746, founded Bourbon dynasty; Ferdinand VI, 1746-1759; Charles III, 1759-1788; Charles IV, 1788-1808, abdicated.

Napoleon now dominated politics and made his brother Joseph King of Spain 1808, but the Spanish ousted him in 1813. Ferdinand VII, 1808, 1814-1833, lost American colonies; succeeded by daughter Isabella II, aged 3, with wife Maria Christina of Naples regent until 1843. Isabella

deposed by revolution 1868. Elected king by the Cortes, Amadeo of Savoy, 1870; abdicated 1873. First republic, 1873-74. Alphonso XII, son of Isabella, 1875-85. His posthumous son was Alphonso XIII, with his mother, Queen Maria Christina regent; Spanish-American war, Spain lost Cuba, gave up Puerto Rico, Philippines, Sulu Is., Marianas. Alphonso took throne 1902, aged 16, married British Princess Victoria Eugenia of Battenberg. The dictatorship of Primo de Rivera, 1923-30, precipitated the revolution of 1931. Alphonso agreed to leave without formal abdication. The monarchy was abolished and the second republic established, with socialist backing. Presidents were Niceto Alcala Zamora, to 1936, when Manuel Azaña was chosen.

In July, 1936, the army in Morocco revolted against the government and General Francisco Franco led the troops into Spain. The revolution succeeded by Feb. 1939, when Azaña resigned. Franco became chief of state, with provisions that if he was incapacitated the Regency Council by two-thirds vote may propose a king to the Cortes, which must have a two-thirds majority to elect him.

Alphonso XIII died in Rome Feb. 28, 1941, aged 54. His property and citizenship had been restored.

A succession law restoring the monarchy was approved in a 1947 referendum. Prince Juan Carlos, son of the pretender to the throne, was designated by Franco and the Cortes in 1969 as the future king and chief of state. Upon Franco's death, Nov. 20, 1975, Juan Carlos was proclaimed king, Nov. 22, 1975.

Leaders in the South American Wars of Liberation

Simon Bolivar (1783-1830), Jose Francisco de San Martin (1778-1850), and Francisco Antonio Gabriel Miranda (1750-1816), are among the heroes of the early 19th century struggles of South American nations to free themselves from Spain. All three, and their contemporaries, operated in periods of factional strife, during which soldiers and civilians suffered.

Miranda, a Venezuelan, who had served with the French in the American Revolution and commanded parts of the French Revolutionary armies in the Netherlands, attempted to start a revolt in Venezuela in 1806 and failed. In 1810, with British and American backing, he returned and was briefly a dictator, until the British withdrew their support. In 1812 he was overcome by the royalists in Venezuela and taken prisoner, dying in a Spanish prison in 1816.

San Martin was born in Argentina and during 1789-1811 served in campaigns of the Spanish armies in Europe and Africa. He first joined the independence movement in Argentina in 1812 and in 1817 invaded Chile with 4,000 men over the mountain passes. Here he and Gen. Bernardo O'Higgins (1778-1842) defeated the Spaniards at Chacabuco, 1817, and O'Higgins was named Liberator and became first director of Chile, 1817-23. In 1821 San Martin occupied Lima and Callao, Peru, and became protector of Peru.

Bolivar, the greatest leader of South American liberation from Spain, was born in Venezuela, the son of an aristo-

cratic family. He first served under Miranda in 1812 and in 1813 captured Caracas, where he was named Liberator. Forced out next year by civil strife, he led a campaign that captured Bogota in 1814. In 1817 he was again in control of Venezuela and was named dictator. He organized Nueva Granada with the help of General Francisco de Paula Santander (1792-1840). By joining Nueva Granada, Venezuela, and the present terrain of Panama and Ecuador, the republic of Colombia was formed with Bolivar president. After numerous setbacks he decisively defeated the Spaniards in the second battle of Carabobo, Venezuela, June 24, 1821.

In May, 1822, Gen. Antonio Jose de Sucre, Bolivar's lieutenant, took Quito. Bolivar went to Guayaquil to confer with San Martin, who resigned as protector of Peru and withdrew from politics. With a new army of Colombians and Peruvians Bolivar defeated the Spaniards in a battle at Junín in 1824 and cleared Peru.

De Sucre organized Charcas (Upper Peru) as Republica Bolivar (now Bolivia) and acted as president in place of Bolivar, who wrote its constitution. De Sucre defeated the Spanish faction of Peru at Ayacucho, Dec. 19, 1824.

Continued civil strife finally caused the Colombian federation to break apart. Santander turned against Bolivar, but the latter defeated him and banished him. In 1828 Bolivar gave up the presidency he had held precariously for 14 years. He became ill from tuberculosis and died Dec. 17, 1830. He is buried in the national pantheon in Caracas.

Rulers of Russia; Leaders of the USSR

First ruler to consolidate Slavic tribes was Rurik, leader of the Russians who established himself at Novgorod, 862 AD. He and his immediate successors had Scandinavian affiliations. They moved to Kiev after 972 AD and ruled as Dukes of Kiev. In 988 Vladimir was converted and adopted the Byzantine Greek Orthodox service, later modified by Slav influences. Important as organizer and lawgiver was Yaroslav, 1019-1054, whose daughters married kings of Norway, Hungary, and France. His grandson, Vladimir II (Monomakh), 1113-1125, was progenitor of several rulers, but in 1169 Andrew Bogolubski overthrew Kiev and began the line known as Grand Dukes of Vladimir.

Of the Grand Dukes of Vladimir, Alexander Nevsky, 1246-1263, had a son, Daniel, first to be called Duke of Muscovy (Moscow), who ruled 1294-1303. His successors became Grand Dukes of Muscovy. After Dmitri III Donskoi defeated the Tartars in 1380, they also became Grand Dukes of all Russia. Independence of the Tartars and considerable territorial expansion were achieved under Ivan III, 1462-1505.

Tsars of Muscovy—Ivan III was referred to in church ritual as Tsar. He married Sofia, niece of the last Byzantine emperor. His successor, Basil III, died in 1533 when Basil's son Ivan was only 3. He became Ivan IV, "the Terrible"; crowned 1547 as Tsar of all the Russias, ruled till 1584. Under the weak rule of his son, Feodor I, 1584-1598, Boris Godunov had control. The dynasty died, and after years of tribal strife and intervention by Polish and Swedish armies, the Russians united under 17-year-old Michael Romanov, distantly related to the first wife of Ivan IV. He ruled 1613-1645 and established the Romanov line. Fourth ruler after Michael was Peter I.

Tsars, or Emperors of Russia (Romanovs)—Peter I, 1682-1725, known as Peter the Great, took title of Emperor in 1721. His successors and dates of accession were: Catherine, his widow, 1725; Peter II, his grandson, 1727; Anne, Duchess of Courland, 1730, daughter of Peter the Great's brother, Tsar Ivan V; Ivan VI, 1740, great-grandson of Ivan V, child, kept in prison and murdered 1764; Elizabeth, daughter of Peter I, 1741; Peter III, grandson of Peter I, 1761, deposed 1762 for his consort, Catherine II, former princess of Anhalt Zerbst (Germany) who is known as Catherine the Great; Paul I, her son, 1796, killed 1801; Alexander I, son of Paul, 1801, defeated Napoleon; Nicholas I, his brother, 1825; Alexander II, son of Nicholas, 1855, assassinated 1881 by terrorists; Alexander III, son, 1881.

Nicholas II, son, 1894-1917, last Tsar of Russia, was forced to abdicate by the Revolution that followed losses to Germany in WWI. The Tsar, the Empress, the Tsarevich (Crown Prince) and the Tsar's 4 daughters were murdered by the Bolsheviks in Ekaterinburg, July 16, 1918.

Provisional Government—Prince Georgi Lvov and Alexander Kerensky, premiers, 1917.

Union of Soviet Socialist Republics

Bolshevik Revolution, Nov. 7, 1917, displaced Kerensky; council of People's Commissars formed, Lenin (Vladimir Ilyich Ulyanov), premier. Lenin died Jan. 21, 1924. Aleksei Rykov (executed 1938) and V. M. Molotov held the office, but actual ruler was Joseph Stalin (Joseph Vissarionovich Djugashvili), general secretary of the Central Committee of the Communist Party. Stalin became president of the Council of Ministers (premier) May 7, 1941, died Mar. 5, 1953. Succeeded by Georgi M. Malenkov, as head of the Council and premier and Nikita S. Khrushchev, first secretary of the Central Committee. Malenkov resigned Feb. 8, 1955, became deputy premier, was dropped July 3, 1957. Marshal Nikolai A. Bulganin became premier Feb. 8, 1955; was demoted and Khrushchev became premier Mar. 27, 1958. Khrushchev was ousted Oct. 14-15, 1964, replaced by Leonid I. Brezhnev as first secretary of the party and Aleksei N. Kosygin as premier. On June 16, 1977, Brezhnev took office as president. Brezhnev died Nov. 10, 1982; 2 days later the Central Committee unanimously elected former KGB head Yuri V. Andropov president. Andropov died Feb. 9, 1984; on Feb. 13, Konstantin U. Chernenko chosen by Central Committee as its general secretary. Chernenko died Mar. 10, 1985. On Mar. 11, he was succeeded as general secretary by Mikhail Gorbachev, who replaced Andrei Gromyko as president on Oct. 1, 1988. Gorbachev resigned Dec. 25, 1991, and the Soviet Union officially disbanded the next day. A loose Commonwealth of Independent States, made up of most of the 15 former Soviet constituent republics, was created.

Post-Soviet Russia

After adopting a degree of sovereignty, the Russian Republic held elections in June 1991. The winner, Boris Yeltsin, was sworn in, July 10, 1991, as Russia's first elected president. With the December 1991 dissolution of the Soviet Union, Russia (renamed Russian Federation) became a founding member of the Commonwealth of Independent States.

Governments of China

(Until 221 BC and frequently thereafter, China was not a unified state. Where dynastic dates overlap, the rulers or events referred to appeared in different areas of China.)

Hsia	c1994 BC	-	c1523 BC	Sui (reunified China)	581	-	618
Shang	c1523	-	c1028	Tang (a golden age of Chinese culture; capital: Sian)	618	-	906
Western Chou	c1027	-	770	Five Dynasties (Yellow River basin)	902	-	960
Eastern Chou	770	-	256	Ten Kingdoms (southern China)	907	-	979
Warring States	403	-	222	Liao (Khitan Mongols; capital: Peking)	947	-	1125
Ch'in (first unified empire)	221	-	206	Sung	960	-	1279
Han	202 BC	- AD 220	Northern Sung (reunified central and southern China)	960	-	1126
Western Han (expanded Chinese state beyond the Yellow and Yangtze River valleys)	202 BC	-	AD 9	Western Hsai (non-Chinese rulers in northwest)	990	-	1227
Hsin (Wang Mang, usurper)	AD 9	-	AD 23	Chin (Tartars; drove Sung out of central China)	1115	-	1234
Eastern Han (expanded Chinese state into Indo-China and Turkestan)	25	-	220	Yuan (Mongols; Kublai Khan made Peking his capital in 1267)	1271	-	1368
Three Kingdoms (Wei, Shu, Wu)	220	-	265	Ming (China reunified under Chinese rule; capital: Nanking, then Peking in 1420)	1368	-	1644
Chin (western)	265	-	317	Ch'ing (Manchus, descendents of Tartars)	1644	-	1911
(eastern)	317	-	420	Republic (disunity; provincial rulers, warlords)	1912	-	1949
Northern Dynasties (followed several short-lived governments by Turks, Mongols, etc.)	386	-	581	People's Republic of China	1949	-	—
Southern Dynasties (capital: Nanking)	420	-	589				

Leaders of China Since 1949

Mao Zedong	Chairman, Central People's Administrative Council, Communist Party (CPC), 1949-76
Zhou Enlai	Premier, foreign minister, 1949-76
Deng Xiaoping	Vice Premier, 1949-76; 1977-87
Liu Shaoqi	President, 1959-69
Hua Guofeng	Premier, 1976-80; CPC Chairman, 1976-81
Zhao Ziyang	Premier, 1980-88; CPC Chairman, 1987-89
Hu Yaobang	CPC Chairman, 1981-87
Li Xiannian	President, 1983-88
Yong Shang-Kun	President, 1988-93
Li Peng	Premier, 1988-
Jiang Zemin	CPC General Secretary, 1989- ; President, 1993-

WORLD EXPLORATION AND GEOGRAPHY
Early Explorers of the Western Hemisphere

The first people to discover the New World, or Western Hemisphere, are believed to have walked across a "land bridge" from Siberia to Alaska, an isthmus since broken by the Bering Strait. From Alaska, these ancestors of the Native Americans spread through what became known as North, Central, and South America. Anthropologists have placed these crossings at between 18,000 and 14,000 BC, but evidence found in 1967 near Puebla, Mex., indicates people may have reached there as early as 35,000-40,000 years ago.

At first, these people were hunters, using flint weapons and tools. In Mexico, about 7000-6000 BC, they founded farming cultures and developed crops, such as corn and squash. Eventually, they created complex civilizations—the Olmec, Toltec, Aztec, and Maya and, in South America, the Inca. Carbon-14 tests show that humans lived about 8000 BC near what are now Front Royal, VA, Kanawha, WV, and Dutchess Quarry, NY. The Hopewell Culture, based on farming, flourished about 1000 BC; remains of it are seen today in large mounds in Ohio and other states.

Norsemen (Norwegian Vikings sailing out of Iceland and Greenland) are credited by most scholars with being the first Europeans to discover America, with at least 5 voyages occurring about AD 1000 to areas they called Helluland, Markland, Vinland—possibly what are known today as Labrador, Nova Scotia or Newfoundland, and New England.

Christopher Columbus, the most famous explorer, was born Cristoforo Colombo (c1451) in or near Genoa, Italy, but made his voyages of exploration for the Spanish rulers Ferdinand and Isabella. Dates of his voyages, places he reached, and other information follow:

1492—First voyage. Left Palos, Spain, Aug. 3 with 88 (est.) men. His fleet consisted of 3 vessels—the *Niña,* the *Pinta,* and the *Santa María.* Landed San Salvador, (Guanahani or Watling Isl. , Bahamas) Oct. 12. Also Cuba, Hispaniola (Haiti-Dominican Republic); built Fort La Navidad on latter.

1493—Second voyage, first part. Left Sept. 25, with 17 ships, 1,500 men. Travelled to Dominica (Lesser Antilles) Nov. 3. Landed Guadeloupe, Montserrat, Antigua, San Martin, Santa Cruz, Puerto Rico, Virgin Islands. Settled Isabela on Hispaniola. **Second part.** (Columbus having remained in Western Hemisphere) Jamaica, Isle of Pines, La Mona Isl.

1498—Third voyage. Left Spain, May 30, 1498, 6 ships. Landed Trinidad. Saw South American continent, Aug. 1, 1498, but called it Isla Sancta (Holy Island). Entered Gulf of Paria and landed, first time on continental soil. At mouth of Orinoco, Aug. 14, he decided this was the mainland.

1502—Fourth voyage. 4 caravels, 150 men. St. Lucia, Guanaja off Honduras; Cape Gracias a Dios, Honduras; San Juan River, Costa Rica; Almirante, Portobelo, and Laguna de Chiriquí, Panama.

Year	Explorer	Nationality (employer, if different)	Area reached or explored
1497	John Cabot	Italian (English)	Newfoundland or Nova Scotia
1498	John and Sebastian Cabot	Italian (English)	Labrador to Hatteras
1499	Alonso de Ojeda	Spanish	N South American coast, Venezuela
1500, Feb.	Vicente Yáñez Pinzón	Spanish	South American coast, Amazon R.
1500, Apr.	Pedro Alvarez Cabral	Portuguese	Brazil
1500-02	Gaspar Corte-Real	Portuguese	Labrador
1501	Rodrigo de Bastidas	Spanish	Central America
1513	Vasco Núñez de Balboa	Spanish	Panama, Pacific Ocean
1513	Juan Ponce de León	Spanish	Florida, Yucatán Peninsula
1515	Juan de Solis	Spanish	Río de la Plata
1519	Alonso de Pineda	Spanish	Mouth of Mississippi R.
1519	Hernando Cortés	Spanish	Mexico
1519-20	Ferdinand Magellan	Portuguese (Spanish)	Straits of Magellan, Tierra del Fuego
1524	Giovanni da Verrazano	Italian (French)	Atlantic coast, inc. New York harbor
1528	Cabeza de Vaca	Spanish	Texas coast and interior
1532	Francisco Pizarro	Spanish	Peru
1534	Jacques Cartier	French	Canada, Gulf of St. Lawrence
1536	Pedro de Mendoza	Spanish	Buenos Aires
1539	Francisco de Ulloa	Spanish	California coast
1539-41	Hernando de Soto	Spanish	Mississippi R., near Memphis
1539	Marcos de Niza	Italian (Spanish)	SW U.S.
1540	Francisco de Coronado	Spanish	SW U.S.
1540	Hernando Alarcón	Spanish	Colorado R.
1540	Garcia de L. Cardenas	Spanish	Colorado, Grand Canyon
1541	Francisco de Orellana	Spanish	Amazon R.
1542	Juan Rodriguez Cabrillo	Portuguese (Spanish)	W Mexico, San Diego harbor
1565	Pedro Menéndez de Aviles	Spanish	St. Augustine, FL
1576	Sir Martin Frobisher	English	Frobisher's Bay, Canada
1577-80	Sir Francis Drake	English	California coast
1582	Antonio de Espejo	Spanish	SW U.S. (New Mexico)
1584	Amadas & Barlow (for Raleigh)	English	Virginia
1585-87	Sir Walter Raleigh's men	English	Roanoke Isl. , NC
1595	Sir Walter Raleigh	English	Orinoco R.
1603-09	Samuel de Champlain	French	Canadian interior, Lake Champlain
1607	Capt. John Smith	English	Atlantic coast
1609-10	Henry Hudson	English (Dutch)	Hudson R., Hudson Bay
1634	Jean Nicolet	French	Lake Michigan, Wisconsin
1673	Jacques Marquette, Louis Jolliet	French	Mississippi R., S to Arkansas
1682	Robert Cavelier, sieur de La Salle	French	Mississippi R., S to Gulf of Mexico
1789	Sir Alexander Mackenzie	Canadian	NW Canada

Arctic Exploration

Early Explorers

1587 — John Davis (Eng.). Davis Strait to Sanderson's Hope, 72°12′ N.

1596 — Willem Barents and Jacob van Heemskerck (Holland). Discovered Bear Isl., touched NW tip of Spitsbergen, 79°49′ N, rounded Novaya Zemlya, wintered at Ice Haven.

1607 — Henry Hudson (Eng.). North along Greenland's E coast to Cape Hold-with-Hope, 73°30′, then N of Spitsbergen to 80°23′. Returning he explored Hudson's Touches (Jan Mayen).

1616 — William Baffin and Robert Bylot (Eng.). Baffin Bay to Smith Sound.

1728 — Vitus Bering (Russ.). Proved Asia and America were separated by sailing through strait now bearing his name.

1733-40 — Great Northern Expedition (Russ.). Surveyed Siberian Arctic coast.

1741 — Vitus Bering (Russ.). Sighted Alaska from sea, named Mount St. Elias. His lieutenant, Chirikof, explored coast.

1771 — Samuel Hearne (Hudson's Bay Co.). Overland from Prince of Wales Fort (Churchill) on Hudson Bay to mouth of Coppermine R.

1778 — James Cook (Brit.). Through Bering Strait to Icy Cape, AK, and North Cape, Siberia.

1789 — Alexander Mackenzie (North West Co., Brit.). Montreal to mouth of Mackenzie River.

1806 — William Scoresby (Brit.). N of Spitsbergen to 81°30′.

1820-23 — Ferdinand von Wrangel (Russ.). Completed a survey of Siberian Arctic coast. His exploration joined that of James Cook at North Cape, confirming separation of the continents.

1878-79 — (Nils) Adolf Erik Nordenskjöld (Sw.). The first to navigate the Northeast Passage—an ocean route connecting Europe's North Sea, along the Arctic coast of Asia and through the Bering Sea, to the Pacific Ocean.

1881 — The U.S. steamer *Jeannette*, led by Lt. Cmdr. George W. DeLong, was trapped in ice and crushed, June 1881. DeLong and 11 others died; 12 survived.

1888 — Fridtjof Nansen (Nor.) crossed Greenland's ice-cap.

1893-96 — Nansen in *Fram* drifted from New Siberian Isls. to Spitsbergen; tried polar dash in 1895, reached Franz Josef Land, 86°14′ N.

1897 — Salomon A. Andrée (Switz.) and 2 others started in balloon from Spitsbergen, July 11, to drift across pole to U.S., and disappeared. More than 33 yrs. later, Aug. 6, 1930, their frozen bodies were found on White Isl., 82°57′ N, 29°52′ E.

1903-6 — Roald Amundsen (Nor.) first sailed Northwest Passage—an ocean route linking the Atlantic Ocean to the Pacific Ocean via Canada's marine waterways.

North Pole Exploration

Robert E. Peary explored Greenland's coast, 1891-92; tried for North Pole, 1893. In 1900 he reached N limit of Greenland and 83°50′ N; in 1902 he reached 84°06′ N; in 1906 he went from Ellesmere Isl. to 87°06′ N. He sailed in the *Roosevelt*, July 1908, to winter off Cape Sheridan, Grant Land. The dash for the North Pole began Mar. 1 from Cape Columbia, Ellesmere Isl. Peary reached the pole, 90° N, Apr. 6, 1909.

Peary had several supporting groups carrying supplies until the last group turned back at 87°47′ N. Peary, Matthew Henson, and 4 Eskimos proceeded with dog teams and sleds. They crossed the pole several times, finally built an igloo at 90°, remained 36 hours. Started south, Apr. 7 at 4 PM, for Cape Columbia. The Eskimos were Coqueeh, Ootah, Eginwah, and Seegloo.

1914 — Donald MacMillan (U.S.). Northwest, 200 mi, from Axel Heiberg Isl. to seek Peary's Crocker Land.

1915-17 — Vihjalmur Stefansson (Can.). Discovered Borden, Brock, Meighen, and Lougheed Isls.

1918-20 — Amundsen sailed the Northeast Passage.

1925 — Amundsen and Lincoln Ellsworth (U.S.) reached 87°44′ N in attempt to fly to North Pole from Spitsbergen.

1926 — Richard E. Byrd and Floyd Bennett (U.S.) first over North Pole by air, May 9.

1926 — Amundsen, Ellsworth, and Umberto Nobile (It.) flew from Spitsbergen over North Pole May 12, to Teller, AK, in dirigible *Norge*.

1928 — Nobile crossed North Pole in airship, May 24, crashed, May 25. Amundsen died attempting a rescue.

North Pole Exploration Records

On Aug. 3, 1958, the *Nautilus*, under Comdr. William R. Anderson, became the first ship to cross the North Pole beneath the Arctic ice.

In Aug. 1960 the nuclear-powered U.S. submarine *Seadragon* (Comdr. George P. Steele 2d) made the first E-W underwater transit through the Northwest Passage. Traveling submerged for the most part, it took 6 days to make the 850-mi trek from Baffin Bay to the Beaufort Sea.

On Aug. 16, 1977, the Soviet nuclear icebreaker *Arktika* reached the North Pole and became the first surface ship to break through the Arctic ice pack to the top of the world.

On Apr. 30, 1978, Naomi Uemura (Jap.) became the first person to reach the North Pole alone by dog sled. During the 54-day, 600-mi trek over the frozen Arctic, Uemura survived attacks by a marauding polar bear.

In Apr. 1982, Sir Ranulph Fiennes and Charles Burton, Brit. explorers, reached the North Pole and became the first to circle the earth from pole to pole. They had reached the South Pole 16 months earlier. The 52,000-mi trek took 3 years, involved 23 people, and cost an estimated $18 mil. The expedition was also the first to travel down the Scott Glacier and the first to journey up the Yukon and through the Northwest Passage in a single season.

On May 2, 1986, 6 Amer. and Can. explorers reached the North Pole assisted only by dogs. They became the first to reach the pole without mechanical assistance since Robert E. Peary planted a flag there in 1909. The explorers, Amer. Will Steger, Paul Schurke, Anne Bancroft, and Geoff Carroll, and Can. Brent Boddy and Richard Weber, completed the 500-mi journey in 56 days.

On June 15, 1995, Weber and Russ. Mikhail Malakhov became the first pair to make it to the pole and back without any mechanical assistance. The 940-mi trip, made entirely on skis, took 121 days. This was also the longest unsupported stay on the Arctic Ocean.

Antarctic Exploration

Early History

Antarctica has been approached since 1773-75, when Capt. James Cook (Brit.) reached 71° 10′ S. Many sea and landmarks bear names of early explorers. Fabian von Bellingshausen (Russ.) discovered Peter I and Alexander I Islands, 1819-21. Nathaniel Palmer (U.S.) traveled throughout Palmer Peninsula, 60° W, 1820, without realizing that this was a continent. Capt. John Davis (U.S.) made the first known landing on the continent on Feb. 7, 1821. Later, in 1823, James Weddell (Brit.) found Weddell Sea, 74° 15′ S, the southernmost point that had been reached.

First to announce existence of the continent of Antarctica was Charles Wilkes (U.S.), who followed the coast for 1,500 mi, 1840. Adelie Coast, 140° E, was found by Dumont d'Urville (Fr.), 1840. Ross Ice Shelf was found by James Clark Ross (Brit.), 1841-42.

1895 — Leonard Kristensen (Nor.) landed a party on the coast of Victoria Land. They were the first ashore on the main continental mass. C. E. Borchgrevink, a member of that party, returned in 1899 with a Brit. expedition, first to winter on Antarctica.

1902-4 — Robert F. Scott (Brit.) explored Edward VII Peninsula. He reached 82° 17′ S, 146° 33′ E from McMurdo Sound.

1908-9 — Ernest Shackleton (Brit.) introduced the use of Manchurian ponies in Antarctic sledging. He reached 88° 23′ S, discovering a route on to the plateau by way of the Beardmore Glacier and pioneering the way to the pole.

South Pole Exploration

1911 — Roald Amundsen (Nor.) with 4 men and dog teams reached the pole, Dec. 14.

1912 — Scott reached the pole from Ross Isl., Jan. 18, with 4 companions. None of Scott's party survived. Their bodies and expedition notes were found, Nov. 12.

1928 — First person to use an airplane over Antarctica was Sir George Hubert Wilkins (Austral.).

1929 — Richard E. Byrd (U.S.) established Little America on Bay of Whales. On 1,600-mi airplane flight begun Nov. 28, he crossed South Pole, Nov. 29, with 3 others.

1934-35 — Byrd led 2d expedition to Little America, explored 450,000 sq mi, wintered alone at weather station, 80°08′ S.

1934-37 — John Rymill led British Graham Land expedition; discovered that Palmer Penin. is part of Antarctic mainland.

1935 — Lincoln Ellsworth (U.S.) flew S along Palmer Penin.'s E coast, then crossed continent to Little America, making 4 landings on unprepared terrain in bad weather.

1939-41 — U.S. Antarctic Service Expedition built West Base on Ross Ice Shelf under Paul Siple, and East Base on Palmer Peninsula under Richard Black. U.S. Navy plane flights discovered about 150,000 sq mi of new land.

1940 — Byrd charted most of coast between Ross Sea and Palmer Penin.

1946-47 — U.S. Navy undertook Operation Highjump, commanded by Byrd, included 13 ships and 4,000 men. Airplanes photomapped coastline and penetrated beyond pole.

1946-48 — Ronne Antarctic Research Expedition, Comdr. Finn Ronne, USNR, determined the Antarctic to be only one continent with no strait between Weddell Sea and Ross Sea; explored 250,000 sq mi of land by flights to 79° S. Mrs. Ronne and Mrs. H. Darlington were the first women to winter on Antarctica.

1955-57 — U.S. Navy's Operation Deep Freeze led by Adm. Byrd. Supporting U.S. scientific efforts for the International Geophysical Year (IGY), the operation was commanded by Rear Adm. George Dufek. It established 5 coastal stations fronting the Indian, Pacific, and Atlantic oceans and also 3 interior stations; explored more than 1,000,000 sq mi in Wilkes Land.

1957-58 — During the IGY, July 1957 through Dec. 1958, scientists from 12 countries conducted ambitious programs of Antarctic research at a network of some 60 stations on the continent.

Dr. Vivian E. Fuchs led a 12-man Trans-Antarctic Expedition on the first land-crossing of Antarctica. Starting from the Weddell Sea, they reached Scott Station, Mar. 2, 1958, after traveling 2,158 mi in 98 days.

1958 — A group of 5 U.S. scientists led by Edward C. Thiel, seismologist, moving by tractor from Ellsworth Station on Weddell Sea, identified a huge mountain range, 5,000 ft above the ice sheet and 9,000 ft above sea level. The range, originally seen by a Navy plane, was named the Dufek Massif, for Rear Adm. George Dufek.

1959 — Twelve nations — Argentina, Australia, Belgium, Chile, France, Japan, New Zealand, Norway, South Africa, the Soviet Union, the United Kingdom, and the U.S. — signed a treaty suspending any territorial claims for 30 yrs. and reserving the continent, S of 60° S, for research.

1961-62 — Scientists discovered the Bentley Trench, running from Ross Ice Shelf into Marie Byrd Land, near the end of the Ellsworth Mts., toward the Weddell Sea.

1962 — First nuclear power plant began operation at McMurdo Sound.

1963 — On Feb. 22 a U.S. plane made the longest nonstop flight ever in the S Pole area, covering 3,600 mi in 10 hr. The flight was from McMurdo Station S past the geographical S Pole to Shackleton Mts., SE to the "Area of Inaccessibility," and back to McMurdo Station.

1964 — A Brit. survey team was landed by helicopter on Cook Island, the first recorded visit since 1775.

1964 — New Zealanders mapped the mountain area from Cape Adare W some 400 mi to Pennell Glacier.

1985 — Igor A. Zotikov, a Moscow Institute of Geography researcher, discovered sediments in the Ross Ice Shelf that seem to support the continental drift theory. Research by the Ocean Drilling Project off the Queen Maud Land coast indicated the ice sheets of E Antartica are 37 million yr. old.

1989 — Victoria Murden and Shirley Metz both became the first women and the first Americans to reach the South Pole overland when they arrived with 9 others on Jan. 17, 1989. The 51-day trek on skis covered 740 mi.

1991 — Twenty-four nations approved a protocol to the 1959 Antarctia Treaty, Oct. 4. Amendments called for various conservation provisions, including banning oil and other mineral exploration for 50 yr.

Volcanoes

Sources: *Volcanoes of the World*, Geoscience Press; Global Volcanism Network, Smithsonian Institution; as of June 1995

Nearly 75% of the world's approximately 540 historically active volcanoes lie within the Ring of Fire, a zone running along the W coast of the Americas from Chile to Alaska, down the E coast of Asia from Siberia to New Guinea, and continuing to New Zealand. Twenty percent of these volcanoes are in Indonesia. Other prominent groupings are in Japan, the Aleutian Islands, and Central America. Almost all active regions are at the boundaries of the large moving plates that constitute the earth's surface. The Ring of Fire marks the boundary between the plates underlying the Pacific Ocean and those underlying the surrounding continents. Other active regions, such as the Mediterranean and Iceland, are on plate boundaries.

Notable Volcanic Eruptions of the Past

Approximately 7,000 years ago, Mazama, a 9,900-ft volcano in S Oregon, erupted violently, ejecting ash and lava. The ash spread over the entire northwestern U.S. and as far away as Saskatchewan, Can. During the eruption, the top of the mountain collapsed, leaving a caldera 6 mi across and about a half mile deep, which filled with rainwater to form what is now called Crater Lake.

In AD 79, Vesuvio, or Vesuvius, a 4,190-ft volcano overlooking Naples Bay became active after several centuries of quiescence. On Aug. 24 of that year, a heated mud and ash flow swept down the mountain, engulfing the cities of Pompeii, Herculaneum, and Stabiae with debris more than 60 ft deep. About 10% of the population of the 3 towns was killed.

Some of the largest eruptions in recent centuries have been in Indonesia. In 1883, an eruption similar to the Mazama eruption occurred on the island of Krakatau. At least 2,000 people died in pyroclastic flows on Aug. 26. The next day, the 2,640-ft peak of the volcano collapsed to 1,000 ft below sea level, leaving only a small portion of the island standing above the sea and killing more than 3,000 people. A tsunami (tidal wave) generated by the collapse then killed more than 31,000 people in nearby Java and Sumatra and eventually reached England. Ash from the eruption colored sunsets around the world for 2 years. A similar, but even more powerful, eruption had taken place 68 years earlier at Mt. Tambora on the Indonesian island of Sumbawa.

Date	Volcano	Estimated Deaths	Date	Volcano	Estimated Deaths
Aug. 24, 79 AD	Mt. Vesuvius, Italy	16,000	May 8, 1902	Mt. Pelée, Martinique	28,000
1586	Kelut, Java, Indon.	10,000	Jan. 30, 1911	Mt. Taal, Phil.	1,400
Dec. 15, 1631	Mt. Vesuvius, Italy	4,000	May 19, 1919	Mt. Kelud, Java, Indon.	5,000
Aug. 12, 1772	Mt. Papandayan, Java, Idon.	3,000	Jan. 17-21, 1951	Mt. Lamington, New Guinea	3,000
June 8, 1783	Laki, Iceland	9,350	May 18, 1980	Mt. St. Helens, U.S.	57
May 21, 1792	Mt. Unzen, Japan	14,500	Mar. 28, 1982	El Chichon, Mex.	1,880
Apr. 10-12, 1815	Mt. Tambora, Sumbawa, Idon.	92,000[1]	Nov. 13, 1985	Nevado del Ruiz, Colombia	23,000
Aug. 26-28, 1883	Krakatau, Indon.	36,000	Aug. 21, 1986	Lake Nyos, Cameroon	1,700
Apr. 24, 1902	Santa María, Guatemala	1,000[2]	June 15, 1991	Mt. Pinatubo, Luzon, Phil.	800

(1) Of those who died, 10,000 deaths were directly related to the eruption; an additional 82,000 were the result of starvation and disease brought on by the event. (2) An additional 3,000 deaths due to a malaria outbreak are sometimes attributed to the eruption.

Notable Active Volcanoes

Active volcanoes display a wide range of activity. In this table, years are given for the last display of eruptive activity. Eruptions are defined as the explosive ejection of new or old fragmental material, the escape of liquid lava, or both.

Name (latest eruption)	Location	Height (ft)
Africa		
Cameroon (1982)	Cameroon	13,354
Nyiragogo (1994)	Zaire	11,400
Nyamuragira (1994)	Zaire	10,028
Ol Doinyo Lengai (1993)	Tanzania	9,469
Karthala (1991)	Comoros	8,000
Piton de la Fournaise (1992)	Réunion Isl.	5,981
Lake Nyos (1986)	Cameroon	3,011
Erta-Ale (1995)	Ethiopia	1,650
Antarctica		
Erebus (1995)	Ross Isl.	12,450
Deception Island (1970)	S. Shetland Isl.	1,890
Asia-Oceania		
Kliuchevskoi (1995)	Russia	15,584
Kerinci (1970)	Sumatra, Indon.	12,467
Fuji (1708)	Honshu, Japan	12,388
Tolbachik (1876)	Russia	12,080
Semeru (1995)	Java, Indon.	12,060
Slamet (1989)	Java, Indon.	11,247
Raung (1993)	Java, Indon.	10,932
On-take (1980)	Honshu, Japan	10,049
Mayon (1993)	Luzon, Phil.	9,991
Merapi (1994)	Java, Indon.	9,551
Marapi (1993)	Sumatra, Indon.	9,485
Bezymianny (1994)	Russia	9,455
Ruapehu (1995)	New Zealand	9,175
Baitoushan (1702)	China/Korea	9,003
Asama (1990)	Honshu, Japan	8,300
Niigata Yake-yama (1989)	Honshu, Japan	8,111
Canlaon (1993)	Negros, Phil.	8,070
Alaid (1986)	Kuril Isl., Russia	7,662
Ulawun (1993)	Papua New Guinea	7,532
Ngauruhoe (1977)	New Zealand	7,515
Chokai (1974)	Honshu, Japan	7,300
Galunggung (1984)	Java, Indon.	7,113
Azuma (1977)	Honshu, Japan	6,700
Bagana (1993)	Papua New Guinea	6,558
Sangeang Api (1988)	Lesser Sunda Isl., Indon.	6,351
Nasu (1963)	Honshu, Japan	6,210
Tiatia (1981)	Kuril Isl., Russia	6,013
Manam (1995)	Papua New Guinea	6,000
Soputan (1993)	Celebes, Indon.	5,994
Bandai (1888)	Honshu, Japan	5,968
Karangetang (1993)	Sangihe, Indon.	5,853
Kelud (1990)	Java, Indon.	5,679
Gamalama (1993)	Halmahera, Indon.	5,627
Kirishima (1992)	Kyushu, Japan	5,577
Pinatubo (1995)	Luzon, Phil.	5,770
Akita Komaga-take (1971)	Honshu, Japan	5,449
Gamkonora (1987)	Halmahera, Indon.	5,364
Aso (1995)	Kyushu, Japan	5,223
Lokon-Empung (1992)	Celebes, Indon.	5,187
Bulusan (1995)	Luzon, Phil.	5,115
Sarychev Peak(1989)	Kuril Isl., Russia	4,960
Karkar (1979)	Papua New Guinea	4,920
Lopevi (1982)	Vanuatu	4,755
Unzen (1995)	Kyushu, Japan	4,462
Ambrym (1991)	Vanuatu	4,376
Awu (1992)	Sangihe Isl., Indon.	4,350
Sakura-jima (1995)	Kyushu, Japan	3,668
Langila (1995)	Papua New Guinea	3,586
Krakatau (1995)	Indonesia	2,667
Suwanose-jima (1994)	Kyushu, Japan	2,640
Oshima (1990)	Izu Isl., Japan	2,550
Usu (1982)	Hokkaido, Japan	2,400
Rabaul (1995)	Papua New Guinea	2,257
Pagan (1993)	N. Mariana Isl.	1,870
White Island (1994)	New Zealand	1,075
Taal (1977)	Luzon, Phil.	984

Name (latest eruption)	Location	Height (ft)
Central America—Caribbean		
Acatenango (1972)	Guatemala	12,992
Fuego (1987)	Guatemala	12,582
Tacana (1986)	Guatemala	12,400
Santa María (1993)	Guatemala	12,362
Irazú (1965)	Costa Rica	11,260
Turrialba (1866)	Costa Rica	10,650
Póas (1994)	Costa Rica	8,930
Pacaya (1995)	Guatemala	8,346
San Miguel (1986)	El Salvador	6,994
Rincón de la Vieja (1993)	Costa Rica	6,234
San Cristobal (1977)	Nicaragua	5,840
Concepción (1986)	Nicaragua	5,106
Arenal (1995)	Costa Rica	5,092
Pelee (1932)	Martinique	4,583
Momotombo (1905)	Nicaragua	4,199
Soufrière St. Vincent (1979)	St. Vincent	4,048
Masaya (1994)	Nicaragua	2,083
South America		
Llullaillaco (1877)	Chile	22,110
Guallatiri (196087)	Chile	19,882
Lááscar (19954)	Chile	19,652
Cotopaxi (194075)	Ecuador	19,347
El Misti (1870?)	Peru	19,101
Tupungatito (1986)	Chile	18,504
Ruiz (19912)	Colombia	17,716
Sangay (199388)	Ecuador	17,159
Guagua Pichincha (199388)	Ecuador	15,696
Purace (1977)	Colombia	15,601
Galeras (1993)	Colombia	13,996
Llaima (1994)	Chile	10,239
Villarrica (1992)	Chile	9,318
Cerro Hudson (1991)	Chile	8,580
Fernandina (1995)	Galapagos Isl., Ecuador	4,905
Mid-Pacific		
Mauna Loa (1984)	Hawaii, HI	13,680
Kilauea (1995)	Hawaii, HI	4,077
Mid-Atlantic Ridge		
Beerenberg (1985)	Jan Mayen Isl., Norway	7,470
Hekla (1991)	Iceland	4,892
Krafla (1984)	Iceland	2,145
Europe		
Etna (1995)	Italy	11,053
Stromboli (1995)	Italy	3,038
Santorini (1950)	Greece	1,850
North America		
Orizaba (1687)	Mexico	18,405
Popocatépetl (1995)	Mexico	17,930
Rainer (1894?)	Washington	14,410
Wrangell (1907?)	Alaska	14,163
Shasta (1786)	California	14,162
Colima (1994)	Mexico	14,003
Redoubt (1990)	Alaska	10,197
Iliamna (1953)	Alaska	10,016
Shishaldin (1993)	Aleutian Isl., AK.	9,387
St. Helens (1991)	Washington	8,300+
Pavlof (1988)	Alaska	8,261
Veniaminof (1994)	Alaska	8,225
El Chichon (1982)	Mexico	7,300
Novarupta (Katmai) (1912)	Alaska	6,715
Makushin (1987)	Aleutian Isl., AK.	6,680
Great Sitkin (1974)	Aleutian Isl., AK.	5,710
Cleveland (1994)	Aleutian Isl., AK.	5,675
Gareloi (1989)	Aleutian Isl., AK.	5,334
Korovin (1987)	Aleutian Isl., AK.	4,852
Akutan (1992)	Aleutian Isl., AK.	4,275
Kiska (1990)	Aleutian Isl., AK.	4,275
Augustine (1986)	Alaska	3,999
Okmok (1988)	Aleutian Isl., AK.	3,519
Seguam (1993)	Aleutian Isl., AK.	3,458

Mountains

Height of Mount Everest

Mt. Everest was considered 29,002 ft when Edmund Hillary and Tenzing Norgay scaled it in 1953. This triangulation figure had been accepted since 1850. In 1954 the Surveyor General of the Republic of India set the height at 29,028 ft, plus or minus 10 ft because of snow. The National Geographic Society accepts that figure, but many mountaineering groups still use 29,002 ft.

In 1987, new calculations based on satellite measurements indicated that the Himalayan peak K-2 rose 29,064 ft above sea level and that Mt. Everest is 800 ft higher. The National Geographic Society has not accepted the revised figure.

United States, Canada, Mexico

Name	Place	Height (ft)	Name	Place	Height (ft)	Name	Place	Height (ft)
McKinley	AK	20,320	Alverstone	AK-Yukon	14,565	Shavano	CO	14,229
Logan	Yukon	19,850	Browne Tower	AK	14,530	Belford	CO	14,197
Citlaltepec (Orizaba)	Mexico	18,700	Whitney	CA	14,494	Princeton	CO	14,197
St. Elias	AK-Yukon	18,008	University Peak	AK	14,410	Crestone Needle	CO	14,197
Popocatépetl	Mexico	17,930	Elbert	CO	14,433	Yale	CO	14,196
Foraker	AK	17,400	Massive	CO	14,421	Bross	CO	14,172
Iztaccihuatl	Mexico	17,343	Harvard	CO	14,420	Kit Carson	CO	14,165
Lucania	Yukon	17,147	Rainier	WA	14,411	Wrangell	AK	14,163
King	Yukon	16,971	Williamson	CA	14,375	Shasta	CA	14,162
Steele	Yukon	16,644	La Plata Peak	CO	14,361	El Diente Peak	CO	14,159
Bona	AK	16,550	Blanca Peak	CO	14,345	Point Success	WA	14,158
Blackburn	AK	16,390	Uncompahgre Pk.	CO	14,309	Maroon Peak	CO	14,156
Kennedy	AK	16,286	Crestone Peak	CO	14,294	Tabeguache	CO	14,155
Sanford	AK	16,237	Lincoln	CO	14,286	Oxford	CO	14,153
Vancouver	AK-Yukon	15,979	Grays Peak	CO	14,270	Sill	CA	14,153
South Buttress	AK	15,885	Antero	CO	14,269	Sneffels	CO	14,150
Wood	Yukon	15,885	Torreys Peak	CO	14,267	Democrat	CO	14,148
Churchill	AK	15,638	Castle Peak	CO	14,265	Capitol Peak	CO	14,130
Fairweather	AK-Yukon	15,300	Quandary Peak	CO	14,265	Liberty Cap	WA	14,112
Zinantecatl (Toluca)	Mexico	15,016	Evans	CO	14,264	Pikes Peak	CO	14,110
Hubbard	AK-Yukon	15,015	Longs Peak	CO	14,255	Snowmass	CO	14,092
Bear	AK	14,831	McArthur	Yukon	14,253	Russell	CA	14,088
Walsh	Yukon	14,780	Wilson	CO	14,246	Eolus	CO	14,083
East Buttress	AK	14,730	White Mt. Peak	CA	14,246	Windom	CO	14,082
Matlalcueyetl	Mexico	14,636	North Palisade	CA	14,242	Columbia	CO	14,073
Hunter	AK	14,573	Cameron	CO	14,238	Augusta	AK	14,070

South America

Peak, country	Height (ft)	Peak, country	Height (ft)	Peak, country	Height (ft)
Aconcagua, Argentina	22,834	Coropuna, Peru	21,083	Solo, Argentina	20,492
Ojos del Salado, Arg.-Chile	22,572	Laudo, Argentina	20,997	Polleras, Argentina	20,456
Bonete, Argentina	22,546	Ancohuma, Bolivia	20,958	Pular, Chile	20,423
Tupungato, Argentina-Chile	22,310	Ausangate, Peru	20,945	Chani, Argentina	20,341
Pissis, Argentina	22,241	Toro, Argentina-Chile	20,932	Aucanquilcha, Chile	20,295
Mercedario, Argentina	22,211	Illampu, Bolivia	20,873	Juncal, Argentina-Chile	20,276
Huascaran, Peru	22,205	Tres Cruces, Argentina-Chile	20,853	Negro, Argentina	20,184
Llullaillaco, Argentina-Chile	22,057	Huandoy, Peru	20,852	Quela, Argentina	20,128
El Libertador, Argentina	22,047	Parinacota, Bolivia-Chile	20,768	Condoriri, Bolivia	20,095
Cachi, Argentina	22,047	Tortolas, Argentina-Chile	20,745	Palermo, Argentina	20,079
Incahuasi, Argentina-Chile	21,720	Ampato, Peru	20,702	Solimana, Peru	20,068
Yerupaja, Peru	21,709	El Condor, Argentina	20,669	San Juan, Argentina-Chile	20,049
Galan, Argentina	21,654	Salcantay, Peru	20,574	Sierra Nevada, Arg.-Chile	20,023
El Muerto, Argentina-Chile	21,457	Chimborazo, Ecuador	20,561	Antofalla, Argentina	20,013
Sajama, Bolivia	21,391	Huancarhuas, Peru	20,531	Marmolejo, Argentina-Chile	20,013
Nacimiento, Argentina	21,302	Famatina, Argentina	20,505	Chachani, Peru	19,931
Illimani, Bolivia	21,201	Pumasillo, Peru	20,492		

The highest point in the West Indies is in the Dominican Republic, Pico Duarte (10,417 ft).

Africa, Southeast Asian Islands, Australia, New Zealand

Peak, country/island	Height (ft)	Peak, country/island	Height (ft)	Peak, country/island	Height (ft)
Kilimanjaro, Tanzania	19,340	Wilhelm, New Guinea	14,793	Kinabalu, Malaysia	13,455
Kenya, Kenya	17,058	Karisimbi, Zaire-Rwanda	14,787	Cameroon, Cameroon	13,353
Margherita Pk., Uganda-Zaire	16,763	Elgon, Kenya-Uganda	14,178	Kerinci, Sumatra, Indon.	12,467
Jaja, New Guinea	16,500	Batu, Ethiopia	14,131	Cook, New Zealand	12,349
Trikora, New Guinea	15,585	Guna, Ethiopia	13,881	Teide, Canary Islands	12,198
Mandala, New Guinea	15,420	Gughe, Ethiopia	13,780	Semeru, Java, Indon.	12,060
Ras Dashan, Ethiopia	15,158	Toubkal, Morocco	13,661	Kosciusko, Australia	7,310
Meru, Tanzania	14,979				

Europe

Peak, country	Height (ft)	Peak, country	Height (ft)	Peak, country	Height (ft)
Alps		Liskamm, It., Switz.	14,852	Grand Combin, Switz.	14,154
		Weisshom, Switz.	14,780	Lenzpitze, Switz.	14,088
Mont Blanc, Fr.-It.	15,771	Taschhorn, Switz.	14,733	Finsteraarhorn, Switz.	14,022
Monte Rosa (highest peak of group), Switz.	15,203	Matterhorn, It., Switz.	14,690	Castor, Switz.	13,865
		Dent Blanche, Switz.	14,293	Zinalrothorn, Switz.	13,849
Dom, Switz.	14,911	Nadelhorn, Switz.	14,196	Hohberghom, Switz.	13,842

Peak, country	Height (ft)	Peak, country	Height (ft)	Peak, country	Height (ft)
Alphubel, Switz.	13,799	Fiescherhorn, Switz.	13,283	**Pyrenees**	
Rimpfischhom, Switz.	13,776	Grunhorn, Switz.	13,266	Aneto, Sp.	11,168
Aletschorn, Switz.	13,763	Lauteraarhorn, Switz.	13,261	Posets, Sp.	11,073
Strahlhorn, Switz.	13,747	Durrenhorn, Switz.	13,238	Perdido, Sp.	11,007
Dent D'Herens, Switz.	13,686	Allalinhorn, Switz.	13,213	Vignemale, Fr.-Sp.	10,820
Breithorn, It., Switz.	13,665	Weissmies, Switz.	13,199	Long, Sp.	10,479
Bishorn, Switz.	13,645	Lagginhorn, Switz.	13,156	Estats, Sp.	10,304
Jungfrau, Switz.	13,642	Zupo, Switz.	13,120	Montcalm, Sp.	10,105
Ecrins, Fr.	13,461	Fletschhorn, Switz.	13,110		
Monch, Switz.	13,448	Adlerhorn, Switz.	13,081	**Caucasus (Europe-Asia)**	
Pollux, Switz.	13,422	Gletscherhorn, Switz.	13,068	El'brus, Russia	18,510
Schreckhorn, Switz.	13,379	Schalihorn, Switz.	13,040	Shkara, Russia	17,064
Ober Gabelhorn, Switz.	13,330	Scerscen, Switz.	13,028	Dykh Tau, Russia	17,054
Gran Paradiso, It.	13,323	Eiger, Switz.	13,025	Kashtan Tau, Russia	16,877
Bernina, It., Switz.	13,284	Jagerhorn, Switz.	13,024	Dzhangi Tau, Russia	16,565
		Rottalhorn, Switz.	13,022	Kazbek, Russia	16,558

Asia (Mainland)

Peak	Place	Height (ft)	Peak	Place	Height (ft)	Peak	Place	Height (ft)
Everest	Nepal-Tibet	29,028	Kungur	Xinjiang	25,325	Badrinath	India	23,420
K2 (Godwin Austen)	Kashmir	28,250	Tirich Mir	Pakistan	25,230	Nunkun	Kashmir	23,410
Kanchenjunga	India-Nepal	28,208	Makalu II	Nepal-Tibet	25,120	Lenin Peak	Tajikistan	23,405
Lhotse I (Everest)	Nepal-Tibet	27,923	Minya Konka	China	24,900	Pyramid	India-Nepal	23,400
Makalu I	Nepal-Tibet	27,824	Kula Gangri	Bhutan-Tibet	24,784	Api	Nepal	23,399
Lhotse II (Everest)	Nepal-Tibet	27,560	Changtzu (Everest)	Nepal-Tibet	24,780	Pauhunri	India-Tibet	23,385
Dhaulagiri	Nepal	26,810	Muz Tagh Ata	Xinjiang	24,757	Trisul	India	23,360
Manaslu I	Nepal	26,760	Skyang Kangri	Kashmir	24,750	Kangto	India-Tibet	23,260
Cho Oyu	Nepal-Tibet	26,750	Communism Peak	Tajikistan	24,590	Nyenchhe Thanglha	Tibet	23,255
Nanga Parbat	Kashmir	26,660	Jongsang Peak	India-Nepal	24,472	Trisuli	India	23,210
Annapurna I	Nepal	26,504	Jengish Chokusu	Xinjiang-Kyrgyzstan	24,406	Pumori	Nepal-Tibet	23,190
Gasherbrum	Kashmir	26,470	Sia Kangri	Kashmir	24,350	Dunagiri	India	23,184
Broad	Kashmir	26,400	Haramosh Peak	Pakistan	24,270	Lombo Kangra	Tibet	23,165
Gosainthan	Tibet	26,287	Istoro Nal	Pakistan	24,240	Saipal	Nepal	23,100
Annapurna II	Nepal	26,041	Tent Peak	India-Nepal	24,165	Macha Pucchare	Nepal	22,958
Gyachung Kang	Nepal-Tibet	25,910	Chomo Lhari	Bhutan-Tibet	24,040	Numbar	Nepal	22,817
Disteghil Sar	Kashmir	25,868	Chamlang	Nepal	24,012	Kanjiroba	Nepal	22,580
Himalchuli	Nepal	25,801	Kabru	India-Nepal	24,002	Ama Dablam	Nepal	22,350
Nuptse (Everest)	Nepal-Tibet	25,726	Alung Gangri	Tibet	24,000	Cho Polu	Nepal	22,093
Masherbrum	Kashmir	25,660	Baltoro Kangri	Kashmir	23,990	Lingtren	Nepal-Tibet	21,972
Nanda Devi	India	25,645	Mussu Shan	Xinjiang	23,890	Khumbutse	Nepal-Tibet	21,785
Rakaposhi	Kashmir	25,550	Mana	India	23,860	Hlako Gangri	Tibet	21,266
Kamet	India-Tibet	25,447	Baruntse	Nepal	23,688	Mt. Grosvenor	China	21,190
Namcha Barwa	Tibet	25,445	Nepal Peak	India-Nepal	23,500	Thagchhab Gangri	Tibet	20,970
Gurla Mandhata	Tibet	25,355	Amne Machin	China	23,490	Damavand	Iran	18,606
Ulugh Muz Tagh	Xinjiang-Tibet	25,340	Gauri Sankar	Nepal-Tibet	23,440	Ararat	Turkey	16,804

Antarctica

Peak	Height (ft)	Peak	Height (ft)	Peak	Height (ft)	Peak	Height (ft)
Vinson Massif	16,864	Andrew Jackson	13,750	Shear	13,100	Campbell	12,434
Tyree	16,290	Sidley	13,720	Odishaw	13,008	Don Pedro Christophersen	12,355
Shinn	15,750	Ostenso	13,710	Donaldson	12,894	Lysaght	12,326
Gardner	15,375	Minto	13,668	Ray	12,808	Huggins	12,247
Epperly	15,100	Miller	13,650	Sellery	12,779	Sabine	12,200
Kirkpatrick	14,855	Long Gables	13,620	Waterman	12,730	Astor	12,175
Elizabeth	14,698	Dickerson	13,517	Anne	12,703	Mohl	12,172
Markham	14,290	Giovinetto	13,412	Press	12,566	Frankes	12,064
Bell	14,117	Wade	13,400	Falla	12,549	Jones	12,040
Mackellar	14,098	Fisher	13,386	Rucker	12,520	Gjelsvik	12,008
Anderson	13,957	Fridtjof Nansen	13,350	Goldthwait	12,510	Coman	12,000
Bentley	13,934	Wexler	13,202	Morris	12,500		
Kaplan	13,878	Lister	13,200	Erebus	12,450		

Some Notable U.S. Mountains

Name	Place	Height (ft)	Name	Place	Height (ft)	Name	Place	Height (ft)
Gannett Peak	WY	13,804	Adams	WA	12,307	Clingmans Dome	NC-TN	6,643
Grand Teton	WY	13,766	San Gorgonio	CA	11,502	Washington	NH	6,288
Kings	UT	13,528	Hood	OR	11,235	Rogers	VA	5,927
Cloud	WY	13,175	Lassen	CA	10,457	Marcy	NY	5,344
Boundary	NV	13,140	Granite	CA	10,321	Katahdin	ME	5,268
Wheeler	NM	13,065	Guadalupe	TX	8,751	Spruce Knob	WV	4,862
Granite	MT	12,799	Olympus	WA	7,965	Mansfield	VT	4,393
Borah	ID	12,662	Harney	SD	7,242	Black Mountain	KY	4,145
Humphreys	AZ	12,633	Mitchell	NC	6,684			

Important Islands and Their Areas

Source: Bureau of the Census, U.S. Dept. of Commerce; National Atlas Information
Services, Natural Resources Canada; World Almanac research

Figure in parentheses shows rank among the world's 10 largest islands. Because some islands have not been surveyed accurately, estimated areas are shown. Figures are for total land area.

Location-Ownership
Area in square miles

Arctic Ocean
Canadian
Axel Heiberg	16,671
Baffin (5)	195,928
Banks	27,038
Bathurst	6,194
Devon	21,331
Ellesmere (10)	75,767
Melville	16,274
Prince of Wales	12,872
Somerset	9,570
Southampton	15,913
Victoria (9)	83,897

Norwegian
Svalbard	23,940
Nordaustlandet	5,410
Spitsbergen	15,060

Russian
Franz Josef Land	8,000
Novaya Zemlya (two is.)	31,730
Wrangel	2,800

Atlantic Ocean
Anticosti, Canada	3,066
Ascension, UK	34
Azores, Portugal	888
Faial	67
Sao Miguel	291
Bahamas	5,386
Bermuda Isl., UK	20
Bioko Isl., Equatorial Guinea	785
Block, RI	10
Canary Isl., Spain	2,808
Fuerteventura	668
Gran Canaria	592
Tenerife	795
Cape Breton, Canada	3,981
Cape Verde Isl.	1,557
Faeroe Isl., Denmark	540
Falkland Isl., UK	4,700
Fernando de Noronha Archipelago, Brazil	7
Greenland, Denmark (1)	840,000
Iceland	39,769
Long Island, NY	1,320
Madeira Isl. , Portugal	307
Marajo, Brazil	15,444
Martha's Vineyard, MA	89
Mount Desert, ME	104
Nantucket, MA	45
Newfoundland, Canada	42,031
Prince Edward, Canada	2,170
St. Helena, UK	47
South Georgia, UK	1,450
Tierra del Fuego, Chile and Argentina	18,800
Tristan da Cunha, UK	40

British Isles
Great Britain, mainland (8)	84,200
Channel Islands	75
Guernsey	24
Jersey	45
Sark	2
Hebrides	2,744
Ireland	32,599
Irish Republic	27,136
Northern Ireland	5,463

Man	227
Orkney Isl.	390
Scilly Isl.	6
Shetland Isl.	567
Skye	670
Wight	147

Baltic Sea
Aland Isl., Finland	581
Bornholm, Denmark	227
Gotland, Sweden	1,159

Caribbean Sea
Antigua	108
Aruba, Netherlands	75
Barbados	166
Cuba	44,218
Isle of Youth	1,182
Curacao, Netherlands	171
Dominica	290
Guadeloupe, France	687
Hispaniola, Haiti and Dominican Republic	29,371
Jamaica	4,244
Martinique, France	425
Puerto Rico, U.S.	3,339
Tobago	116
Trinidad	1,864
Virgin Isl., UK	59
Virgin Isl., U.S.	134

Indian Ocean
Andaman Isl., India	2,500
Madagascar (4)	226,658
Mauritius	720
Pemba, Tanzania	380
Reunion, France	969
Seychelles	171
Sri Lanka	25,332
Zanzibar, Tanzania	640

Persian Gulf
Bahrain	255

Mediterranean Sea
Balearic Isl., Spain	1,936
Corfu, Greece	229
Corsica, France	3,369
Crete, Greece	3,189
Cyprus	3,572
Elba, Italy	86
Euboea, Greece	1,411
Malta	95
Rhodes, Greece	540
Sardinia, Italy	9,262
Sicily, Italy	9,822

Pacific Ocean
Aleutian Isl., AK	6,912
Adak	275
Amchitka	116
Attu	350
Kanaga	142
Kiska	106
Tanaga	195
Umnak	686
Unalaska	1,051
Unimak	1,571
Canton, Kiribati*	4
Caroline Isl.	472
Christmas, Kiribati*	94
Clipperton, France	2
Diomede, Big, Russia	11
Diomede, Little, U.S.	3
Easter, Chile	69

Fiji	7,056
Vanua Levu	2,242
Viti Levu	4,109
Funafuti, Tuvalu*	2
Galapagos Isl., Ecuador	3,043
Guadalcanal	2,180
Guam	210
Hainan, China	13,000
Hawaiian Isl., HI	6,423
Hawaii	4,028
Oahu	600
Hong Kong	29
Japan	145,809
Hokkaido	30,144
Honshu (7)	87,805
Iwo Jima	8
Kyushu	14,114
Okinawa	459
Shikoku	7,049
Kodiak, AK	3,465
Marquesas Isl., France	492
Marshall Isl.	70
Bikini*	2
Nauru	8
New Caledonia, France	6,530
New Zealand	103,883
Chatham	372
North	44,035
South	58,305
Stewart	674
Northern Mariana Isl.	179
Philippines	115,831
Leyte	2,787
Luzon	40,880
Mindanao	36,775
Mindoro	3,790
Negros	4,907
Palawan	4,554
Panay	4,446
Samar	5,050
Quemoy	56
Sakhalin, Russia	29,500
Samoa Isl.	1,177
American Samoa	77
Tutuila	55
Samoa (Western)	1,133
Savaii	670
Upolu	429
Santa Catalina, CA	75
Tahiti, France	402
Taiwan	13,823
Tasmania, Australia	26,178
Tonga Isl.	270
Vancouver, Canada	12,079
Vanuatu	5,700

East Indies
Bali, Indonesia	2,171
Borneo, Indonesia-Malaysia-Brunei (3)	280,100
Celebes, Indonesia	69,000
Java, Indonesia	48,900
Madura, Indonesia	2,113
Moluccas, Indonesia	32,307
New Britain, Papua New Guinea	14,093
New Guinea, Indonesia-Papua New Guinea (2)	306,000
New Ireland, Papua New Guinea	3,707
Sumatra, Indonesia (6)	165,000
Timor	13,094

* **Atolls:** Bikini (lagoon area 230 sq mi, land area 2 sq mi); Canton (lagoon 20 sq mi, land 4 sq mi), Kiribati; Christmas (lagoon 140 sq mi, land 94 sq mi), Kiribati; Funafuti (lagoon 84 sq mi, land 2 sq mi), Tuvalu. **Australia,** often called an island, is a continent.
Islands in minor waters: Manhattan (22 sq mi), Staten (59 sq mi), and Governors (173 acres), all in New York Harbor, U.S.; Isle Royale (209 sq mi), Lake Superior, U.S.; Manitoulin (1,068 sq mi), Lake Huron, Canada; Pinang (110 sq mi), Strait of Malacca, Malaysia; Singapore (239 sq mi), Singapore Strait, Singapore.

Areas and Average Depths of Oceans, Seas, and Gulfs

Geographers and mapmakers recognize four major bodies of water: the Pacific, the Atlantic, the Indian, and the Arctic oceans. The Atlantic and Pacific oceans are considered divided at the equator into the N and S Atlantic and the N and S Pacific. The Arctic Ocean is the name for waters N of the continental landmasses in the region of the Arctic Circle.

	Area (sq mi)	Avg. depth (ft)		Area (sq mi)	Avg. depth (ft)
Pacific Ocean	64,186,300	12,925	Hudson Bay	281,900	305
Atlantic Ocean	33,420,000	11,730	East China Sea	256,600	620
Indian Ocean	28,350,500	12,598	Andaman Sea	218,100	3,667
Arctic Ocean	5,105,700	3,407	Black Sea	196,100	3,906
South China Sea	1,148,500	4,802	Red Sea	174,900	1,764
Caribbean Sea	971,400	8,448	North Sea	164,900	308
Mediterranean Sea	969,100	4,926	Baltic Sea	147,500	180
Bering Sea	873,000	4,893	Yellow Sea	113,500	121
Gulf of Mexico	582,100	5,297	Persian Gulf	88,800	328
Sea of Okhotsk	537,500	3,192	Gulf of California	59,100	2,375
Sea of Japan	391,100	5,468			

Principal Ocean Depths

Source: Defense Mapping Agency, Hydrographic/Topographic Center, U.S. Dept. of Defense

Name of area	Location (lat.)	Location (long.)	Depth (meters)	Depth (fathoms)	Depth (ft)
Pacific Ocean					
Mariana Trench	11°22′ N	142°36′ E	10,924	5,973	35,840
Tonga Trench	23°16′ S	174°44′ W	10,800	5,906	35,433
Philippine Trench	10°38′ N	126°36′ E	10,057	5,499	32,995
Kermadec Trench	31°53′ S	177°21′ W	10,047	5,494	32,963
Bonin Trench	24°30′ N	143°24′ E	9,994	5,464	32,788
Kuril Trench	44°15′ N	150°34′ E	9,750	5,331	31,988
Izu Trench	31°05′ N	142°10′ E	9,695	5,301	31,808
New Britain Trench	06°19′ S	153°45′ E	8,940	4,888	29,331
Yap Trench	08°33′ N	138°02′ E	8,527	4,663	27,976
Japan Trench	36°08′ N	142°43′ E	8,412	4,600	27,599
Peru-Chile Trench	23°18′ S	71°14′ W	8,064	4,409	26,457
Palau Trench	07°52′ N	134°56′ E	8,054	4,404	26,424
Aleutian Trench	50°51′ N	177°11′ E	7,679	4,199	25,194
New Hebrides Trench	20°36′ S	168°37′ E	7,570	4,139	24,836
North Ryukyu Trench	24°00′ N	126°48′ E	7,181	3,927	23,560
Mid. America Trench	14°02′ N	93°39′ W	6,662	3,643	21,857
Atlantic Ocean					
Puerto Rico Trench	19°55′ N	65°27′ W	8,605	4,705	28,232
S Sandwich Trench	55°42′ S	25°56′ E	8,325	4,552	27,313
Romanche Gap	0°13′ S	18°26′ W	7,728	4,226	25,354
Cayman Trench	19°12′ N	80°00′ W	7,535	4,120	24,721
Brazil Basin	09°10′ S	23°02′ W	6,119	3,346	20,076
Indian Ocean					
Java Trench	10°19′ S	109°58′ E	7,125	3,896	23,376
Ob' Trench	09°45′ S	67°18′ E	6,874	3,759	22,553
Diamantina Trench	35°50′ S	105°14′ E	6,602	3,610	21,660
Vema Trench	09°08′ S	67°15′ E	6,402	3,501	21,004
Agulhas Basin	45°20′ S	26°50′ E	6,195	3,387	20,325
Arctic Ocean					
Eurasia Basin	82°23′ N	19°31′ E	5,450	2,980	17,881
Mediterranean Sea					
Ionian Basin	36°32′ N	21°06′ E	5,150	2,816	16,896

Note: Greater depths have been reported in some of the above areas. They are not official, however, unless confirmed by research vessels.

Latitude, Longitude, and Altitude of World Cities

Source: Defense Mapping Agency, Hydrographic/Topographic Center, U.S. Dept. of Defense

City	Lat. ° ′	Long. ° ′	Alt. (ft)	City	Lat. ° ′	Long. ° ′	Alt. (ft)
Athens, Greece	37 59 N	23 44 E	300	Mexico City, Mexico	19 24 N	99 09 W	7,347
Bangkok, Thailand	13 45 N	100 31 E	0	Moscow, Russia	55 45 N	37 35 E	394
Beijing, China	39 56 N	116 24 E	600	New Delhi, India	28 36 N	77 12 E	770
Berlin, Germany	52 31 N	13 25 E	110	Panama City, Panama	08 58 N	79 32 W	0
Bogotá, Colombia	04 36 N	74 05 W	8,660	Paris, France	48 52 N	02 20 E	300
Bombay, India	18 58 N	72 50 E	27	Quito, Ecuador	00 13 S	78 30 W	9,222
Buenos Aires, Argentina	34 36 S	58 28 W	0	Rio de Janeiro, Brazil	22 43 S	43 13 W	30
Cairo, Egypt	30 03 N	31 15 E	381	Rome, Italy	41 53 N	12 30 E	95
Jakarta, Indonesia	06 10 S	106 48 E	26	Santiago, Chile	33 27 S	70 40 W	4,921
Jerusalem, Israel	31 46 N	35 14 E	2,500	Seoul, South Korea	37 34 N	127 00 E	34
Johannesburg, So. Afr.	26 12 S	28 05 E	5,740	Sydney, Australia	33 53 S	151 12 E	25
Kathmandu, Nepal	27 43 S	85 19 E	4,500	Tehran, Iran	35 40 N	51 26 E	3,937
Kiev, Ukraine	50 26 N	30 31 E	0	Tokyo, Japan	35 42 N	139 46 E	30
London, UK (Greenwich)	51 30 N	00 00	245	Tripoli, Libya	32 54 N	13 11 E	0
Manila, Philippines	14 35 N	120 00 E	0	Warsaw, Poland	52 15 N	21 00 E	360
Mecca, Saudi Arabia	21 27 N	39 49 E	6,562	Wellington, New Zealand	41 18 S	174 47 E	0

Latitude, Longitude, and Altitude of U.S. and Canadian Cities

Source: U.S. geographic positions were provided by National Oceanic Atmospheric Administration, U.S. Dept. of Commerce. U.S. altitudes were provided by Geological Survey, U.S. Dept. of the Interior. Canadian geographic positions were provided by the Geodetic Survey of Canada, Natural Resources Canada. Canadian altitudes were provided by National Atlas Information Service, Natural Resources Canada.

Altitudes are measured in feet at the downtown business areas of U.S. cities or at the city hall of Canadian cities, except where (a) indicates that measurements were made at the tower of a major airport located within the city.

City	Lat. N °	′	″	Long. W °	′	″	Alt. (ft)
Abilene, TX	32	27	05	99	43	51	1,710
Akron, OH	41	05	00	81	30	44	874
Albany, NY	42	39	01	73	45	01	20
Albuquerque, NM	35	05	01	106	39	05	4,945
Alert, N.W.T.	82	29	50	62	21	15	95
Allentown, PA	40	36	11	75	28	06	255
Amarillo, TX	35	12	27	101	50	04	3,685
Anchorage, AK	61	10	00	149	59	00	118
Ann Arbor, MI	42	16	59	83	44	52	880
Asheville, NC	35	35	42	82	33	26	1,985
Ashland, KY	38	28	36	82	38	23	536
Atlanta, GA	33	45	10	84	23	37	1,050
Atlantic City, NJ	39	21	32	74	25	53	10
Augusta, GA	33	28	20	81	58	00	143
Augusta, ME	44	18	53	69	46	29	45
Austin, TX	30	16	09	97	44	37	505
Bakersfield, CA	35	22	31	119	01	18	400
Baltimore, MD	39	17	26	76	36	45	20
Bangor, ME	44	48	13	68	46	18	20
Baton Rouge, LA	30	26	58	91	11	00	57
Battle Creek, MI	42	18	58	85	10	48	820
Bay City, MI	43	36	04	83	53	15	595
Beaumont, TX	30	05	20	94	06	09	20
Belleville, Ont.	44	09	42	77	23	11	257
Bellingham, WA	48	45	34	122	28	36	60
Berkeley, CA	37	52	10	122	16	17	40
Billings, MT	45	47	00	108	30	04	3,120
Biloxi, MS	30	23	48	88	53	00	20
Binghamton, NY	42	06	03	75	54	47	865
Birmingham, AL	33	31	01	86	48	36	600
Bismarck, ND	46	48	23	100	47	17	1,674
Bloomington, IL	40	28	58	88	59	36	800
Boise, ID	43	37	07	116	11	58	2,704
Boston, MA	42	21	24	71	03	25	21
Bowling Green, KY	36	59	41	86	26	33	510
Brandon, Man.	49	51	00	99	57	00	1,343(a)
Brantford, Ont.	43	08	34	80	15	39	705(a)
Brattleboro, VT	42	51	06	72	33	48	300
Bridgeport, CT	41	10	49	73	11	22	10
Brockton, MA	42	05	02	71	01	25	130
Buffalo, NY	42	52	52	78	52	21	585
Burlington, Ont.	43	19	33	79	47	57	284
Burlington, VT	44	28	34	73	12	46	110
Butte, MT	46	01	06	112	32	11	5,765
Calgary, Alta.	51	02	46	114	03	24	3,427
Cambridge, MA	42	22	01	71	06	22	20
Canton, OH	40	47	50	81	22	37	1,030
Carson City, NV	39	10	00	119	46	00	4,680
Cedar Rapids, IA	41	58	01	91	39	53	730
Central Islip, NY	40	47	24	73	12	00	80
Champaign, IL	40	07	05	88	14	48	740
Charleston, SC	32	46	35	79	55	53	9
Charleston, WV	38	21	01	81	37	52	601
Charlotte, NC	35	13	44	80	50	45	720
Charlottetown, P.E.I.	46	14	07	63	07	49	31
Chattanooga, TN	35	02	41	85	18	32	675
Cheyenne, WY	41	08	09	104	49	07	6,100
Chicago, IL	41	52	28	87	38	22	595
Churchill, Man.	58	45	15	94	10	00	94(a)
Cincinnati, OH	39	06	07	84	30	35	550
Cleveland, OH	41	29	51	81	41	50	660
Colorado Springs, CO	38	50	07	104	49	16	5,980
Columbia, MO	38	57	03	92	19	46	730
Columbia, SC	34	00	02	81	02	00	190
Columbus, GA	32	28	07	84	59	24	265
Columbus, OH	39	57	47	83	00	17	780
Concord, NH	43	12	22	71	32	25	290
Corpus Christi, TX	27	47	51	97	23	45	35
Dallas, TX	32	47	09	96	47	37	435
Dartmouth, N.S.	44	39	50	63	34	08	24
Dawson, Yukon	64	03	30	139	26	00	1,050
Dayton, OH	39	45	32	84	11	43	574
Daytona Beach, FL	29	12	44	81	01	10	7
Decatur, IL	39	50	42	88	56	47	682
Denver, CO	39	44	58	104	59	22	5,280
Des Moines, IA	41	35	14	93	37	00	803
Detroit, MI	42	19	48	83	02	57	585
Dodge City, KS	37	45	17	100	01	09	2,480
Dubuque, IA	42	29	55	90	40	08	620
Duluth, MN	46	46	56	92	06	24	610
Durham, NC	36	00	00	78	54	45	405
Eau Claire, WI	44	48	31	91	29	49	790
Edmonton, Alta.	53	32	43	113	29	21	2,186
Elizabeth, NJ	40	39	43	74	12	59	21
El Paso, TX	31	45	36	106	29	11	3,695
Enid, OK	36	23	40	97	52	35	1,240
Erie, PA	42	07	15	80	04	57	685
Eugene, OR	44	03	16	123	05	30	422
Eureka, CA	40	48	08	124	09	46	45
Evansville, IN	37	58	20	87	34	21	385
Fairbanks, AK	64	48	00	147	51	00	448
Fall River, MA	41	42	06	71	09	18	40
Fargo, ND	46	52	30	96	47	18	900
Flagstaff, AZ	35	11	36	111	39	06	6,900
Flint, MI	43	00	50	83	41	33	750
Ft. Smith, AR	35	23	10	94	25	36	440
Ft. Wayne, IN	41	04	21	85	08	26	790
Ft. Worth, TX	32	44	55	97	19	44	670
Fredericton, N.B.	45	57	47	66	38	38	29
Fresno, CA	36	44	12	119	47	11	285
Gadsden, AL	34	00	57	86	00	41	555
Gainesville, FL	29	38	56	82	19	19	175
Gallup, NM	35	31	30	108	44	30	6,540
Galveston, TX	29	18	10	94	47	43	5
Gary, IN	41	36	12	87	20	19	590
Grand Junction, CO	39	04	06	108	33	54	4,590
Grand Rapids, MI	42	58	03	85	40	13	610
Great Falls, MT	47	29	33	111	18	23	3,340
Green Bay, WI	44	30	48	88	00	50	590
Greensboro, NC	36	04	17	79	47	25	839
Greenville, SC	34	50	50	82	24	01	966
Guelph, Ont.	43	32	35	80	14	54	1,065
Gulfport, MS	30	22	04	89	05	36	20
Halifax, N.S.	44	38	54	63	34	30	60
Hamilton, OH	39	23	59	84	33	47	600
Hamilton, Ont.	43	15	20	79	52	30	329
Harrisburg, PA	40	15	43	76	52	59	365
Hartford, CT	41	46	12	72	40	49	40
Helena, MT	46	35	33	112	02	24	4,155
Hilo, HI	19	43	30	155	05	24	40
Honolulu, HI	21	18	22	157	51	35	21
Houston, TX	29	45	26	95	21	37	40
Hull, Que.	45	25	42	75	42	41	185
Huntsville, AL	34	44	18	86	35	19	640
Indianapolis, IN	39	46	07	86	09	46	710
Iowa City, IA	41	39	37	91	31	53	685
Jackson, MI	42	14	43	84	24	22	940
Jackson, MS	32	17	56	90	11	06	298
Jacksonville, FL	30	19	44	81	39	42	20
Jersey City, NJ	40	43	50	74	03	56	20
Johnstown, PA	40	19	35	78	55	03	1,185
Joplin, MO	37	05	26	94	30	00	990
Juneau, AK	58	18	12	134	24	30	50
Kalamazoo, MI	42	17	29	85	35	14	755
Kansas City, KS	39	07	04	94	38	24	750
Kansas City, MO	39	04	56	94	35	20	750
Kenosha, WI	42	35	43	87	50	11	610
Key West, FL	24	33	30	81	48	12	5
Kingston, Ont.	44	13	53	76	28	48	264
Kitchener, Ont.	43	26	58	80	29	12	1,100
Knoxville, TN	35	57	39	83	55	07	890
Lafayette, IN	40	25	11	86	53	39	550
Lancaster, PA	40	02	25	76	18	29	355
Lansing, MI	42	44	01	84	33	15	830
Laredo, TX	27	30	22	99	30	30	440
La Salle, Que.	45	25	30	73	39	30	110
Las Vegas, NV	36	10	20	115	08	37	2,030
Laval, Que.	45	33	05	73	44	42	142
Lawrence, MA	42	42	16	71	10	08	65
Lethbridge, Alta.	49	41	38	112	49	58	2,985
Lexington, KY	38	02	50	84	29	46	955
Lihue, HI	21	58	48	159	22	30	210

City	Lat. N °	'	"	Long. W °	'	"	Alt. (ft)
Lima, OH	40	44	35	84	06	20	865
Lincoln, NE	40	48	59	96	42	15	1,150
Little Rock, AR	34	44	42	92	16	37	286
London, Ont.	42	59	17	81	14	03	822
Los Angeles, CA	34	03	15	118	14	28	340
Louisville, KY	38	14	47	85	45	49	450
Lowell, MA	42	38	25	71	19	14	100
Lubbock, TX	33	35	05	101	50	33	3,195
Macon, GA	32	50	12	83	37	36	335
Madison, WI	43	04	23	89	22	55	860
Manchester, NH.	42	59	28	71	27	41	175
Marshall, TX	32	33	00	94	23	00	410
Memphis, TN.	35	08	46	90	03	13	275
Meriden, CT	41	32	06	72	47	30	190
Miami, FL	25	46	37	80	11	32	10
Milwaukee, WI.	43	02	19	87	54	15	635
Minneapolis, MN	44	58	57	93	15	43	815
Minot, ND	48	14	09	101	17	38	1,550
Mississauga, Ont.	43	33	00	79	35	00	510
Mobile, AL	30	41	36	88	02	33	5
Moncton, N.B.	46	05	18	64	46	41	38
Montgomery, AL	32	22	33	86	18	31	160
Montpelier, VT.	44	15	36	72	34	41	485
Montréal, Que.	45	30	33	73	33	14	90
Moose Jaw, Sask.	50	23	34	105	32	04	1,784
Muncie, IN	40	11	28	85	23	16	950
Nashville, TN.	36	09	33	86	46	55	450
Natchez, MS	31	33	48	91	23	30	210
Newark, NJ	40	44	14	74	10	19	55
New Britain, CT	41	40	08	72	46	59	200
New Haven, CT	41	18	25	72	55	30	40
New Orleans, LA	29	56	53	90	04	10	5
New York, NY	40	45	06	73	59	39	55
Niagara Falls, Ont.	43	06	22	79	03	51	590
Nome, AK	64	30	00	165	25	00	25
Norfolk, VA	36	51	10	76	17	21	10
North Bay, Ont.	46	18	35	79	27	45	670
Oakland, CA	37	48	03	122	15	54	25
Ogden, UT	41	13	31	111	58	21	4,295
Oklahoma City, OK	35	28	26	97	31	04	1,195
Omaha, NE	41	15	42	95	56	14	1,040
Orlando, FL	28	32	42	81	22	38	70
Ottawa, Ont.	45	26	24	75	41	42	185
Paducah, KY.	37	05	13	88	35	56	345
Pasadena, CA	34	08	44	118	08	41	830
Paterson, NJ	40	55	01	74	10	21	100
Pensacola, FL	30	24	51	87	12	56	15
Peoria, IL	40	41	42	89	35	33	470
Peterborough, Ont.	44	18	32	78	19	13	673
Philadelphia, PA	39	56	58	75	09	21	100
Phoenix, AZ	33	27	12	112	04	28	1,090
Pierre, SD.	44	22	18	100	20	54	1,480
Pittsburgh, PA	40	26	19	80	00	00	745
Pittsfield, MA.	42	26	53	73	15	14	1,015
Pocatello, ID	42	51	38	112	27	01	4,460
Pt. Arthur, TX	29	52	30	93	56	15	10
Portland, ME.	43	39	33	70	15	19	25
Portland, OR.	45	31	06	122	40	35	77
Portsmouth, NH.	43	04	30	70	45	24	20
Portsmouth, VA.	36	50	07	76	18	14	10
Prince Rupert, B.C.	54	19	00	130	19	00	125(a)
Providence, RI.	41	49	32	71	24	41	80
Provo, UT	40	14	06	111	39	24	4,550
Pueblo, CO	38	16	17	104	36	33	4,690
Québec City, Que.	46	48	51	71	12	30	163
Racine, WI	42	43	49	87	47	12	630
Raleigh, NC	35	46	38	78	38	21	365
Rapid City, SD.	44	04	52	103	13	11	3,230
Reading, PA	40	20	09	75	55	40	265
Regina, Sask.	50	26	55	104	36	50	1,894(a)
Reno, NV	39	31	27	119	48	40	4,490
Richmond, VA.	37	32	15	77	26	09	160
Roanoke, VA.	37	16	13	79	56	44	905
Rochester, MN	44	01	21	92	28	03	990
Rochester, NY.	43	09	41	77	36	21	515
Rockford, IL	42	16	07	89	05	48	715
Sacramento, CA	38	34	57	121	29	41	30
Saginaw, MI	43	25	52	83	56	05	595
St. Catharines, Ont.	43	09	33	79	14	50	362(a)
St. Cloud, MN	45	34	00	94	10	24	1,040
St. John, N.B.	45	16	22	66	03	48	27
St. John's, Nfld.	47	33	42	52	42	48	200(a)
St. Joseph, MO	39	45	57	94	51	02	850
St. Louis, MO.	38	37	45	90	12	22	455
St. Paul, MN.	44	57	19	93	06	07	780
St. Petersburg, FL	27	46	18	82	38	19	20
Salem, OR	44	56	24	123	01	59	155
Salina, KS	38	50	36	97	36	46	1,229
Salt Lake City, UT	40	45	23	111	53	26	4,390
San Antonio, TX.	29	25	37	98	29	06	650
San Bernardino, CA	34	06	30	117	17	28	1,080
San Diego, CA.	32	42	53	117	09	21	20
San Francisco, CA	37	46	39	122	24	40	65
San Jose, CA	37	20	16	121	53	24	90
San Juan, P.R..	18	27	00	66	04	15	35
Santa Barbara, CA	34	25	18	119	41	55	100
Santa Cruz, CA	36	58	18	122	01	18	20
Santa Fe, NM	35	41	11	105	56	10	6,950
Sarasota, FL	27	20	05	82	32	30	20
Saskatoon, Sask.	52	07	49	106	39	35	1,587
Sault Ste. Marie, Ont.	46	30	24	84	20	04	589
Savannah, GA.	32	04	42	81	05	37	20
Schenectady, NY	42	48	42	73	55	42	245
Seattle, WA.	47	36	32	122	20	12	10
Sheboygan, WI	43	45	03	87	42	52	630
Sherbrooke, Que.	45	24	27	71	51	07	627
Sheridan, WY	44	47	55	106	57	10	3,740
Shreveport, LA.	32	30	46	93	44	58	204
Sioux City, IA.	42	29	46	96	24	30	1,110
Sioux Falls, SD	43	32	35	96	43	35	1,395
South Bend, IN	41	40	33	86	15	01	710
Spartanburg, SC	34	57	03	81	56	06	875
Spokane, WA	47	39	32	117	25	33	1,890
Springfield, IL.	39	47	58	89	38	51	610
Springfield, MA	42	06	21	72	35	32	85
Springfield, MO	37	13	03	93	17	32	1,300
Springfield, OH	39	55	38	83	48	29	980
Stamford, CT.	41	03	09	73	32	24	35
Steubenville, OH	40	21	42	80	36	53	660
Stockton, CA	37	57	30	121	17	16	20
Sudbury, Ont.	46	29	24	80	59	24	879
Superior, WI	46	43	14	92	06	07	630
Sydney, N.S.	46	08	15	60	11	48	25
Syracuse, NY	43	03	04	76	09	14	400
Tacoma, WA	47	14	59	122	26	15	110
Tallahassee, FL	30	26	30	84	16	56	150
Tampa, FL.	27	56	58	82	27	25	15
Terre Haute, IN	39	28	03	87	24	26	496
Texarkana, TX.	33	25	48	94	02	30	324
Thunder Bay, Ont.	48	22	54	89	14	42	616
Toledo, OH	41	39	14	83	32	39	585
Topeka, KS	39	03	16	95	40	23	930
Toronto, Ont.	43	39	10	79	23	00	300
Trenton, NJ	40	13	14	74	46	13	35
Trois-Rivières, Que.	46	20	36	72	32	37	115(a)
Troy, NY	42	43	45	73	40	58	35
Tucson, AZ	32	13	15	110	58	08	2,390
Tulsa, OK	36	09	12	95	59	34	804
Urbana, IL	40	06	42	88	12	06	725
Utica, NY	43	06	12	75	13	33	415
Vancouver, B.C.	49	18	56	123	04	44	141
Victoria, B.C.	48	25	43	123	21	49	57
Waco, TX	31	33	12	97	08	00	405
Walla Walla, WA	46	04	08	118	20	24	936
Washington, DC.	38	53	51	77	00	33	25
Waterloo, IA	42	29	40	92	20	20	850
West Palm Beach, FL.	26	42	36	80	03	07	15
Wheeling, WV	40	04	03	80	43	20	650
Whitehorse, Yukon	60	43	17	135	03	03	2,050
White Plains, NY	41	02	00	73	45	48	220
Wichita, KS	37	41	30	97	20	16	1,290
Wilkes-Barre, PA	41	14	32	75	53	17	640
Wilmington, DE	39	44	46	75	32	51	135
Wilmington, NC	34	14	14	77	56	58	35
Windsor, Ont..	42	18	56	83	02	10	603
Winnipeg, Man.	49	53	56	97	08	23	762
Winston-Salem, NC	36	05	52	80	14	42	860
Worcester, MA.	42	15	37	71	48	17	475
Yakima, WA	46	36	09	120	30	39	1,060
Yellowknife, N.W.T.	62	27	16	114	22	33	674
Youngstown, OH	41	05	57	80	39	02	840
Yuma, AZ	32	42	54	114	37	24	160
Zanesville, OH	39	56	18	82	00	30	720

Principal World Rivers

Source: Geological Survey, U.S. Dept. of the Interior

River	Outflow	Length (mi)	River	Outflow	Length (mi)	River	Outflow	Length (mi)
Albany	James Bay	610	Irrawaddy	Bay of Bengal	1,337	Rhine	North Sea	820
Amazon	Atlantic Ocean	4,000	Japura	Amazon River	1,750	Rhone	Gulf of Lions	505
Amu	Aral Sea	1,578	Jordan	Dead Sea	200	Rio de la Plata	Atlantic Ocean	150
Amur	Tatar Strait	2,744	Kootenay	Columbia R.	485	Rio Grande	Gulf of Mexico	1,900
Angara	Yenisey River	1,151	Lena	Laptev Sea	2,734	Rio Roosevelt	Aripuana	400
Arkansas	Mississippi R.	1,459	Loire	Bay of Biscay	634	Saguenay	St. Lawrence R.	434
Back	Arctic Ocean	605	Mackenzie	Arctic Ocean	1,025	St. John	Bay of Fundy	418
Brahmaputra	Bay of Bengal	1,800	Madeira	Amazon River	2,013	St. Lawrence	Gulf of St. Law.	800
Bug, Southern	Dnieper River	532	Magdalena	Caribbean Sea	956	Salween	Andaman Sea	1,500
Bug, Western	Wisla River	481	Marne	Seine River	326	Sao Francisco	Atlantic Ocean	1,988
Canadian	Arkansas River	906	Mekong	S. China Sea	2,600	Saskatchewan	Lake Winnipeg	1,205
Chang Jiang	E China Sea	3,964	Meuse	North Sea	580	Seine	English Chan.	496
Churchill, Man.	Hudson Bay	1,000	Mississippi	Gulf of Mexico	2,340	Shannon	Atlantic Ocean	230
Churchill, Que.	Atlantic Ocean	532	Missouri	Mississippi R.	2,315	Snake	Columbia River	1,038
Colorado	Gulf of Calif.	1,450	Murray-Darling	Indian Ocean	2,310	Songhua	Amur River	1,150
Columbia	Pacific Ocean	1,243	Negro	Amazon	1,400	Syr	Aral Sea	1,370
Congo	Atlantic Ocean	2,718	Nelson	Hudson Bay	410	Tajo, Tagus	Atlantic Ocean	626
Danube	Black Sea	1,776	Niger	Gulf of Guinea	2,590	Tennessee	Ohio River	652
Dnieper	Black Sea	1,420	Nile	Mediterranean	4,160	Thames	North Sea	236
Dniester	Black Sea	877	Ob-Irtysh	Gulf of Ob	3,362	Tiber	Tyrrhenian Sea	252
Don	Sea of Azov	1,224	Oder	Baltic Sea	567	Tigris	Shatt al-Arab	1,180
Drava	Danube River	447	Ohio	Mississippi	981	Tisza	Danube River	600
Dvina, North	White Sea	824	Orange	Atlantic Ocean	1,300	Tocantins	Para River	1,677
Dvina, West	Gulf of Riga	634	Orinoco	Atantic Ocean	1,600	Ural	Caspian Sea	1,575
Ebro	Mediterranean	565	Ottawa	St. Lawrence R.	790	Uruguay	Rio de la Plata	1,000
Elbe	North Sea	724	Paraguay	Parana River	1,584	Volga	Caspian Sea	2,290
Euphrates	Shatt al-Arab	1,700	Parana	Rio de la Plata	2,485	Weser	North Sea	454
Fraser	Str. of Georgia	850	Peace	Slave River	1,210	Wisla	Bay of Danzig	675
Gambia	Atlantic Ocean	700	Pilcomayo	Paraguay River	1,000	Xi	S. China Sea	1,200
Ganges	Bay of Bengal	1,560	Po	Adriatic Sea	405	Yellow (See Huang)		
Garonne	Bay of Biscay	357	Purus	Amazon River	2,100	Yenisey	Kara Sea	2,543
Huang	Yellow Sea	3,395	Red	Mississippi R.	1,290	Yukon	Bering Sea	1,979
Indus	Arabian Sea	1,800	Red River of N.	Lake Winnipeg	545	Zambezi	Indian Ocean	1,700

Major Rivers in North America

Source: Geological Survey, U.S. Dept. of the Interior

River	Source or upper limit of length	Outflow	Length (mi)
Alabama	Gilmer County, GA	Mobile River	729
Albany	Lake St. Joseph, Ontario	James Bay	610
Allegheny	Potter County, PA	Ohio River	325
Altamaha-Ocmulgee	Junction of Yellow and South Rivers, Newton County, GA	Atlantic Ocean	392
Apalachicola-Chattahoochee	Towns County, GA	Gulf of Mexico	524
Arkansas	Lake County, CO	Mississippi River	1,459
Assiniboine	Eastern Saskatchewan	Red River	450
Attawapiskat	Attawapiskat, Ontario	James Bay	465
Back (N.W.T.)	Contwoyto Lake	Chantrey Inlet	605
Big Black (MS)	Webster County, MS	Mississippi River	330
Brazos	Junction of Salt and Double Mountain Forks, Stonewall County, TX	Gulf of Mexico	923
Canadian	Las Animas County, CO	Arkansas River	906
Cedar (IA)	Dodge County, MN	Iowa River	329
Cheyenne	Junction of Antelope Creek and Dry Fork, Converse County, WY	Missouri River	290
Churchill	Methy Lake, Saskatchewan	Hudson Bay	1,000
Cimarron	Colfax County, NM	Arkansas River	600
Colorado (AZ)	Rocky Mountain National Park, CO (90 mi in Mexico)	Gulf of California	1,450
Colorado (TX)	West Texas	Matagorda Bay	862
Columbia	Columbia Lake, British Columbia	Pacific Ocean, bet. OR and WA	1,243
Columbia, Upper	Columbia Lake, British Columbia	To mouth of Snake River	890
Connecticut	Third Connecticut Lake, NH	Long Island Sound, CT	407
Coppermine (N.W.T.)	Lac de Gras	Coronation Gulf (Arctic Ocean)	525
Cumberland	Letcher County, KY	Ohio River	720
Delaware	Schoharie County, NY	Liston Point, Delaware Bay	390
Fraser	Near Mount Robson (on Continental Divide)	Strait of Georgia	850
Gila	Catron County, NM	Colorado River	649
Green (UT-WY)	Junction of Wells and Trail Creeks, Sublette County, WY	Colorado River	730
Hamilton (Lab.)	Lake Ashuanipi	Atlantic Ocean	532
Hudson	Henderson Lake, Essex County, NY	Upper NY Bay	306
Illinois	St. Joseph County, IN	Mississippi River	420
James (ND-SD)	Wells County, ND	Missouri River	710
James (VA)	Junction of Jackson and Cowpasture Rivers, Botetourt County, VA	Hampton Roads	340
Kanawha-New	Junction of North and South Forks of New River, NC	Ohio River	352
Kentucky	Junction of North and Middle Forks, Lee County, KY	Ohio River	259
Klamath	Lake Ewauna, Klamath Falls, OR	Pacific Ocean	250
Koyukuk	Endicott Mountains, AK	Yukon River	470
Kuskokwim	Alaska Range	Kuskokwim Bay	724
Liard	Southern Yukon, Alaska	Mackenzie River	693

River	Source or upper limit of length	Outflow	Length (mi)
Little Missouri	Crook County, WY	Missouri River	560
Mackenzie	Great Slave Lake, N.W.T.	Arctic Ocean	1,025
Milk	Junction of North and South Forks, Alta.	Missouri River	625
Minnesota	Big Stone Lake, MN	Mississippi River	332
Mississippi	Lake Itasca, MN	Mouth of Southwest Pass	2,340
Mississippi, Upper	Lake Itasca, MN	To mouth of Missouri River	1,171
Mississippi-Missouri-Red Rock	Source of Red Rock, Beaverhead Co., MT	Mouth of Southwest Pass	3,710
Missouri	Junction of Jefferson, Madison, and Gallatin rivers, Madison County, MT	Mississippi River	2,315
Missouri-Red Rock	Source of Red Rock, Beaverhead Co., MT	Mississippi River	2,540
Mobile-Alabama-Coosa	Gilmer County, GA	Mobile Bay	774
Nelson (Man.)	Lake Winnipeg	Hudson Bay	410
Neosho	Morris County, KS	Arkansas River, OK	460
Niobrara	Niobrara County, WY	Missouri River, NE	431
North Canadian	Union County, NM	Canadian River, OK	800
North Platte	Junction of Grizzly and Little Grizzly creeks, Jackson County, CO	Platte River, NE	618
Ohio	Junction of Allegheny and Monongahela rivers, Pittsburgh, PA	Mississippi River	981
Ohio-Allegheny	Potter County, PA	Mississippi River	1,310
Osage	East-central Kansas	Missouri River	500
Ottawa	Lake Capimitchigama	St. Lawrence River	790
Ouachita	Polk County, AR	Red River	605
Peace	Stikine Mountains, B.C.	Slave River	1,210
Pearl	Neshoba County, MS	Gulf of Mexico	411
Pecos	Mora County, NM	Rio Grande	926
Pee Dee-Yadkin	Watauga County, NC	Winyah Bay	435
Pend Oreille-Clark Fork	Near Butte, MT	Columbia River	531
Platte	Junction of North and South Platte Rivers, NE	Missouri River	310
Porcupine	Ogilvie Mountains, AK	Yukon River, Alaska	569
Potomac	Garrett County, MD	Chesapeake Bay	383
Powder	Junction of South and Middle Forks, WY	Yellowstone River	375
Red (OK-TX-LA)	Curry County, NM	Mississippi River	1,290
Red River of the North	Junction of Otter Tail and Bois de Sioux Rivers, Wilkin County, MN	Lake Winnipeg	545
Republican	Junction of North Fork and Arikaree River, NE	Kansas River	445
Rio Grande	San Juan County, CO	Gulf of Mexico	1,900
Roanoke	Junction of North and South Forks, Montgomery County, VA	Albemarle Sound	380
Rock (IL-WI)	Dodge County, WI	Mississippi River	300
Sabine	Junction of South and Caddo Forks, Hunt County, TX	Sabine Lake	380
Sacramento	Siskiyou County, CA	Suisun Bay	377
St. Francis	Iron County, MO	Mississippi River	425
St. Lawrence	Lake Ontario	Gulf of St. Lawrence (Atlantic Ocean)	800
Salmon (ID)	Custer County, ID	Snake River	420
San Joaquin	Junction of South and Middle Forks, Madera County, CA	Suisun Bay	350
San Juan	Silver Lake, Archuleta County, CO	Colorado River	360
Santee-Wateree-Catawba	McDowell County, NC	Atlantic Ocean	538
Saskatchewan, North	Rocky Mountains	Saskatchewan R.	800
Saskatchewan, South	Rocky Mountains	Saskatchewan R.	865
Savannah	Junction of Seneca and Tugaloo rivers, Anderson County, SC	Atlantic Ocean, GA-SC	314
Severn (Ont.)	Sandy Lake	Hudson Bay	610
Smoky Hill	Cheyenne County, CO	Kansas River, KS	540
Snake	Teton County, WY	Columbia River, WA	1,038
South Platte	Junction of South and Middle Forks, Park County, CO	Platte River	424
Susitna	Alaska Range	Cook Inlet	313
Susquehanna	Huyden Creek, Otsego County, NY	Chesapeake Bay	447
Tallahatchie	Tippah County, MS	Yazoo River	301
Tanana	Wrangell Mountains, AK	Yukon River	659
Tennessee	Junction of French Broad and Holston Rivers	Ohio River	652
Tennessee-French Broad	Courthouse Creek, Transylvania County, NC	Ohio River	886
Tombigbee	Prentiss County, MS	Mobile River	525
Trinity	North of Dallas, TX	Galveston Bay	360
Wabash	Darke County, OH	Ohio River	512
Washita	Hemphill County, TX	Red River, OK	500
White (AR-MO)	Madison County, AR	Mississippi River	722
Willamette	Douglas County, OR	Columbia River	309
Wind-Bighorn	Junction of Wind and Little Wind Rivers, Fremont Co., WY (Source of Wind R. is Togwotee Pass, Teton Co., WY)	Yellowstone River	336
Wisconsin	Lac Vieux Desert, Vilas County, WI	Mississippi River	430
Yellowstone	Park County, WY	Missouri River	692
Yukon	McNeil R., Yukon Territory	Bering Sea	1,979

Highest and Lowest Continental Altitudes

Source: National Geographic Society

Continent	Highest point	Elevation (ft)	Lowest point	ft below sea level
Asia	Mount Everest, Nepal-Tibet	29,028	Dead Sea, Israel-Jordan	1,312
South America	Mount Aconcagua, Argentina	22,834	Valdes Peninsula, Argentina	131
North America	Mount McKinley, AK	20,320	Death Valley, California	282
Africa	Kilimanjaro, Tanzania	19,340	Lake Assal, Djibouti	512
Europe	Mount El'brus, Russia	18,510	Caspian Sea, Russia, Azerbaijan	92
Antarctica	Vinson Massif	16,864	Bentley Subglacial Trench	8,327[1]
Australia	Mount Kosciusko, New South Wales	7,310	Lake Eyre, South Australia	52

(1) Estimated. Lower points may exist beneath the ice that have yet to be discovered.

Major Natural Lakes of the World

Source: Geological Survey, U.S. Dept. of the Interior

A lake is a body of water surrounded by land. Although some lakes are called seas (such as the Caspian Sea and the Aral Sea), they are lakes by definition.

Name	Continent	Area (sq mi)	Length (mi)	Maximum depth (ft)	Elevation (ft)
Caspian Sea	Asia-Europe	143,244	760	3,363	-92
Superior	North America	31,700	350	1,330	600
Victoria	Africa	26,828	250	270	3,720
Aral Sea	Asia	24,904[1]	280	220	174
Huron	North America	23,000	206	750	579
Michigan	North America	22,300	307	923	579
Tanganyika	Africa	12,700	420	4,823	2,534
Baykal	Asia	12,162	395	5,315	1,493
Great Bear	North America	12,096	192	1,463	512
Nyasa (Malawi)	Africa	11,150	360	2,280	1,550
Great Slave	North America	11,031	298	2,015	513
Erie	North America	9,910	241	210	570
Winnipeg	North America	9,417	266	60	713
Ontario	North America	7,340	193	802	245
Balkhash	Asia	7,115	376	85	1,115
Ladoga	Europe	6,835	124	738	13
Chad	Africa	6,300	175	24	787
Maracaibo	South America	5,217	133	115	Sea level
Onega	Europe	3,710	145	328	108
Eyre	Australia	3,600[2]	90	4	-52
Volta	Africa	3,276	250	....	....
Titicaca	South America	3,200	122	922	12,500
Nicaragua	North America	3,100	102	230	102
Athabasca	North America	3,064	208	407	700
Reindeer	North America	2,568	143	720	1,106
Rudolf	Africa	2,473	154	240	1,230
Issyk Kul	Asia	2,355	115	2,303	5,279
Torrens	Australia	2,230	130	....	92
Vanern	Europe	2,156	91	328	144
Nettilling	North America	2,140	67	....	95
Winnipegosis	North America	2,075	141	38	830
Albert	Africa	2,075	100	168	2,030
Kariba	Africa	2,050	175	390	1,590
Nipigon	North America	1,872	72	540	1,050
Gairdner	Australia	1,840	90	....	112
Urmia	Asia	1,815	90	49	4,180
Manitoba	North America	1,799	140	12	813

(1) Probably less because of the diversion of feeder rivers. (2) Subject to great seasonal variation.

The Great Lakes

Source: National Ocean Service, U.S. Dept. of Commerce

The Great Lakes form the largest body of fresh water in the world and with their connecting waterways are the largest inland water transportation unit. Draining the great North Central basin of the U.S., they enable shipping to reach the Atlantic via their outlet, the St. Lawrence R., and also the Gulf of Mexico via the Illinois Waterway, from Lake Michigan to the Mississippi R. A third outlet connects with the Hudson R. and then the Atlantic via the New York State Barge Canal System. Traffic on the Illinois Waterway and the New York State Barge Canal System is limited to recreational boating and small shipping vessels.

Only one of the lakes, Lake Michigan, is wholly in the U.S.; the others are shared with Canada. Ships move from the shores of Lake Superior to Whitefish Bay at the E end of the lake, then through the Soo (Sault Ste. Marie) locks, through the St. Mary's R. and into Lake Huron. To reach Gary and the Port of Indiana and South Chicago, IL, ships move W from Lake Huron to Lake Michigan through the Straits of Mackinac.

Lake Superior is 600 ft above mean water level at Point-au-Pere, Quebec, on the International Great Lakes Datum (1955). From Duluth, MN, to the E end of Lake Ontario is 1,156 mi.

	Superior	Michigan	Huron	Erie	Ontario
Length in mi	350	307	206	241	193
Breadth in mi	160	118	183	57	53
Deepest soundings in ft	1,330	923	750	210	802
Volume of water in cu mi	2,900	1,180	850	116	393
Area (sq mi) water surface—U.S.	20,600	22,300	9,100	4,980	3,560
Canada	11,100	.....	13,900	4,930	3,990
Area (sq mi) entire drainage basin—U.S.	16,900	45,600	16,200	18,000	15,200
Canada	32,400	.....	35,500	4,720	12,100
Total Area (sq mi) U.S. and Canada	**81,000**	**67,900**	**74,700**	**32,630**	**34,850**
Mean surface above mean water level at Point-au-Pere, Quebec, avg. level in ft (1900-88)	600.61	578.34	578.34	570.53	244.74
Latitude, North	46° 25'	41° 37'	43° 00'	41° 23'	43° 11'
	49° 00'	46° 06'	46° 17'	42° 52'	44° 15'
Longitude, West	84° 22'	84° 45'	79° 43'	78° 51'	76° 03'
	92° 06'	88° 02'	84° 45'	83° 29'	79° 53'
National boundary line in mi	282.8	None	260.8	251.5	174.6
United States shoreline (mainland only) mi	863	1,400	580	431	300

Famous Waterfalls

Source: National Geographic Society

The earth has thousands of waterfalls, some of considerable magnitude. Their importance is determined not only by height but by volume of flow, steadiness of flow, crest width, whether the water drops sheerly or over a sloping surface, and in one leap or a succession of leaps. A series of low falls flowing over a considerable distance is known as a cascade.

Estimated mean annual flow, in cubic feet per second, of major waterfalls are Niagara, 212,200; Paulo Afonso, 100,000; Urubupunga, 97,000; Iguazu, 61,000; Patos-Maribondo, 53,000; Victoria, 35,400; and Kaieteur, 23,400.

Height = total drop in feet in one or more leaps. † = falls of more than one leap; * = falls that diminish greatly seasonally; ** = falls that reduce to a trickle or are dry for part of each year. If river names not shown, they are the same as the falls. R. = river; L. = lake; (C) = cascade type.

Africa

Name and location	Elevation (ft)
Angola	
Ruacana, Cuene R.	406
Ethiopia	
Fincha	508
Lesotho	
*Maletsunyane	630
Zimbabwe-Zambia	
*Victoria, Zambezi R.	343
South Africa	
*Augrabies, Orange R.	480
† Tugela.	2,014
Tanzania-Zambia	
*Kalambo	726

Asia

Name and location	Elevation (ft)
India—*Cauvery	330
*Jog (Gersoppa), Sharavathi R.	830
Japan	
*Kegon, Daiya R.	330

Australasia

Name and location	Elevation (ft)
Australia	
New South Wales	
Wentworth	614
Wollomombi	1,100
Queensland	
Tully.	885
† Wallaman, Stony Cr.	1,137
New Zealand	
Helena.	890
† Sutherland, Arthur R.	1,904

Europe

Name and location	Elevation (ft)
Austria—† Gastein	492
† Krimml.	1,312
France—*Gavarnie	1,385

Name and location	Elevation (ft)
Great Britain	
Scotland	
Glomach.	370
Wales	
Rhaiadr	240
Italy—Frua, Toce R. (C)	470
Norway	
Mardalsfossen (Northern).	1,535
† Mardalsfossen, (Southern)	2,149
† **Skjeggedal, Nybuai R.	1,378
**Skykje	984
Vetti, Morka-Koldedola R.	900
Sweden	
† Handol.	427
Switzerland	
Giessbach (C).	984
† Reichenbach	656
† Simmen.	459
Staubbach	984
† Trummelbach.	1,312

North America

Name and location	Elevation (ft)
Canada	
Alberta	
Panther, Nigel Cr.	600
British Columbia	
† Della	1,443
† Takakkaw, Daly Glacier.	1,200
Quebec	
Montmorency	274
Canada—United States	
Niagara: American.	182
Horseshoe	173
United States	
California	
*Feather, Fall R.	640
Yosemite National Park	
*Bridalveil	620
*Illilouette	370
*Nevada, Merced R.	594
**Ribbon.	1,612
**Silver Strand, Meadow Br.	1,170
*Vernal, Merced R.	317
† **Yosemite.	2,425
Colorado	
† Seven, South Cheyenne Cr.	300

Name and location	Elevation (ft)
Hawaii	
Akaka, Kolekole Str.	442
Idaho	
**Shoshone, Snake R.	212
Kentucky	
Cumberland	68
Maryland	
*Great, Potomac R. (C)	71
Minnesota	
**Minnehaha.	53
New Jersey	
Passaic	70
New York	
*Taughannock.	215
Oregon	
† Multnomah.	620
Tennessee	
Fall Creek.	256
Washington	
Mt. Rainier Natl. Park	
Sluiskin, Paradise R.	300
**Snoqualmie	268
Wisconsin	
*Big Manitou, Black R. (C)	165
Wyoming	
Yellowstone Natl. Pk. Tower.	132
*Yellowstone (upper)	109
*Yellowstone (lower)	308
Mexico	
El Salto	218

South America

Name and location	Elevation (ft)
Argentina-Brazil	
Iguazu	230
Brazil	
Glass	1,325
Patos-Maribondo, Grande R.	115
Paulo Afonso, Sao Francisco R.	275
Colombia	
Catarata de Candelas, Cusiana R.	984
*Tequendama, Bogota R.	427
Ecuador	
*Agoyan, Pastaza R.	200
Guyana	
Kaieteur, Potaro R.	741
Great, Kamarang R.	1,600
† Marina, Ipobe R.	500
Venezuela	
† *Angel.	3,212
Cuquenan.	2,000

Notable Deserts of the World

Arabian (Eastern), 70,000 sq mi in Egypt between the Nile river and Red Sea, extending southward into Sudan

Atacama, 600 mi. long area rich in nitrate and copper deposits in N Chile

Chihuahuan, 140,000 sq mi in TX, NM, AZ, and Mexico

Dasht-e Kauir, approx. 300 mi long by approx. 100 mi wide in N cen. Iran

Dasht-e Lut, 20,000 sq mi in E Iran

Death Valley, 3,300 sq mi in E CA and SW NV

Gibson, 120,000 sq mi in the interior of W Australia

Gobi, 500,000 sq mi in Mongolia and China

Great Sandy, 150,000 sq mi in W Australia

Great Victoria, 150,000 sq mi in SW Australia

Kalahari, 225,000 sq mi in S Africa

Kara Kum, 120,000 sq mi in Turkmenistan

Kyzyl Kum, 100,000 sq mi in Kazakhstan and Uzbekistan

Libyan, 450,000 sq mi in the Sahara extending from Libya through SW Egypt into Sudan

Mojave, 15,000 sq mi in southern CA

Namib, long narrow area (varies from 30-100 mi wide) extending 800 mi along SW coast of Africa

Nubian, 100,000 sq mi in the Sahara in NE Sudan

Patagonia, 300,000 sq mi in S Argentina

Painted Desert, section of high plateau in N AZ extending 150 mi

Rub al-Khali (Empty Quarter), 250,000 sq mi in the S Arabian Peninsula

Sahara, 3,500,000 sq mi in N Africa extending westward to the Atlantic. Largest desert in the world

Sonoran, 70,000 sq mi in southwestern AZ and southeastern CA extending into NW Mexico

Syrian, 100,000 sq mi arid wasteland extending over much of N Saudi Arabia, E Jordan, S Syria, and W Iraq

Taklimakan, 140,000 sq mi in Xinjiang Province, China

Thar (Great Indian), 100,000 sq mi arid area extending 400 mi along India-Pakistan border

WEIGHTS AND MEASURES

Source: National Institute of Standards and Technology, U.S. Dept. of Commerce

The International System of Units

Two systems of weights and measures exist in the U.S. today: the U.S. Customary System and the International System of Units (SI, after the initials of Système International). SI, commonly referred to as the metric system, is actually a more complete, coherent version of it. Throughout U.S. history, the Customary System (inherited from, but now different from, the British Imperial System) has been customarily used; a plethora of federal and state legislation has given it, through implication, standing as the primary weights and measures system. The metric system, however, is the only system that Congress has ever specifically sanctioned. An 1866 law reads:

It shall be lawful throughout the United States of America to employ the weights and measures of the metric system; and no contract or dealing, or pleading in any court, shall be deemed invalid or liable to objection because the weights or measures expressed or referred to therein are weights or measures of the metric system.

Since that time, use of the metric system in the U.S. has slowly and steadily increased, particularly in the scientific community, in the pharmaceutical industry, and in the manufacturing sector—the last motivated by international commerce, in which the metric system is now predominantly used.

On Feb. 10, 1964, the National Bureau of Standards (now known as the National Institute of Standards and Technology) issued the following bulletin:

Henceforth it shall be the policy of the National Bureau of Standards to use the units of the International System (SI), as adopted by the 11th General Conference on Weights and Measures (October 1960), except when the use of these units would obviously impair communication or reduce the usefulness of a report.

On Dec. 23, 1975, Pres. Gerald R. Ford signed the Metric Conversion Act of 1975. It defines the metric system as being the International System of Units as interpreted in the U.S. by the secretary of commerce. The Trade Act of 1988 and other legislation declare the metric system the preferred system of weights and measures for U.S. trade and commerce, call for the federal government to adopt metric specifications, and mandate the Commerce Dept. to oversee the program. However, the metric system has not become the system of choice for most Americans' daily use.

The following seven units serve as the base for the International System: **length**—meter; **mass**—kilogram; **time**—second; **electric current**—ampere; **thermodynamic temperature**—kelvin; **amount of substance**—mole; and **luminous intensity**—candela.

Prefixes

The following prefixes, in combination with the basic unit names, provide the multiples and submultiples in the International System. For example, the unit name *meter*, with the prefix *kilo* added, produces *kilometer*, meaning "1,000 meters."

Prefix	Symbol	Multiples	Equivalent	Prefix	Symbol	Submultiples	Equivalent
yotta	Y	10^{24}	septillionfold	deci	d	10^{-1}	tenth part
zetta	Z	10^{21}	sextillionfold	centi	c	10^{-2}	hundredth part
exa	E	10^{18}	quintillionfold	milli	m	10^{-3}	thousandth part
peta	P	10^{15}	quadrillionfold	micro	μ	10^{-6}	millionth part
tera	T	10^{12}	trillionfold	nano	n	10^{-9}	billionth part
giga	G	10^{9}	billionfold	pico	p	10^{-12}	trillionth part
mega	M	10^{6}	millionfold	femto	f	10^{-15}	quadrillionth part
kilo	k	10^{3}	thousandfold	atto	a	10^{-18}	quintillionth part
hecto	h	10^{2}	hundredfold	zepto	z	10^{-21}	sextillionth part
deka	da	10	tenfold	yocto	y	10^{-24}	septillionth part

Tables of Metric Weights and Measures

Linear Measure

10 millimeters (mm)	= 1 centimeter (cm)
10 centimeters	= 1 decimeter (dm) = 100 millimeters
10 decimeters	= 1 meter (m) = 1,000 millimeters
10 meters	= 1 dekameter (dam)
10 dekameters	= 1 hectometer (hm) = 100 meters
10 hectometers	= 1 kilometer (km) = 1,000 meters

Area Measure

100 square millimeters (mm²)	= 1 square centimeter (cm²)
10,000 square centimeters	= 1 square meter (m²) = 1,000,000 square millimeters
100 square meters	= 1 are (a)
100 ares	= 1 hectare (ha) = 10,000 square meters
100 hectares	= 1 square kilometer (km²) = 1,000,000 square meters

Fluid Volume Measure

10 milliliters (mL)	= 1 centiliter (cL)
10 centiliters	= 1 deciliter (dL) = 100 milliliters
10 deciliters	= 1 liter (L) = 1,000 milliliters
10 liters	= 1 dekaliter (daL)
10 dekaliters	= 1 hectoliter (hL) = 100 liters
10 hectoliters	= 1 kiloliter (kL) = 1,000 liters

Cubic Measure

1,000 cubic millimeters (mm³)	= 1 cubic centimeter (cm³)
1,000 cubic centimeters	= 1 cubic decimeter (dm³) = 1,000,000 cubic millimeters
1,000 cubic decimeters	= 1 cubic meter (m³) = 1 stere = 1,000,000 cubic centimeters = 1,000,000,000 cubic millimeters

Weight

10 milligrams (mg)	= 1 centigram (cg)
10 centigrams	= 1 decigram (dg) = 100 milligrams
10 decigrams	= 1 gram (g) = 1,000 milligrams
10 grams	= 1 dekagram (dag)
10 dekagrams	= 1 hectogram (hg) = 100 grams
10 hectograms	= 1 kilogram (kg) = 1,000 grams
1,000 kilograms	= 1 metric ton (t)

Table of U.S. Customary Weights and Measures

Linear Measure

12 inches (in)	= 1 foot (ft)
3 feet	= 1 yard (yd)
5 ½ yards	= 1 rod (rd), pole, or perch (16 ½ feet)
40 rods	= 1 furlong (fur)=220 yards= 660 feet
8 furlongs	= 1 statute mile (mi) = 1,760 yards = 5,280 feet
3 miles	= 1 league = 5,280 yards = 15,840 feet
6076.11549 feet	= 1 international nautical mile

Liquid Measure

When necessary to distinguish the liquid pint or quart from the dry pint or quart, the word *liquid* or the abbreviation *liq* should be used in combination with the name or abbreviation of the liquid unit.

4 gills (gi)	= 1 pint (pt) = 28.875 cubic inches
2 pints	= 1 quart (qt) = 57.75 cubic inches
4 quarts	= 1 gallon (gal) = 231 cubic inches = 8 pints = 32 gills

Area Measure

Squares and cubes of units are sometimes abbreviated by using superscripts. For example, ft² means square foot, and ft³ means cubic foot.

144 square inches	= 1 square foot (ft²)
9 square feet	= 1 square yard (yd²) = 1,296 square inches
30 ¼ square yards	= 1 square rod (rd²) = 272 ¼ square feet
160 square rods	= 1 acre = 4,840 square yards = 43,560 square feet
640 acres	= 1 square mile (mi²)
1 mile square	= 1 section (of land)
6 miles square	= 1 township = 36 sections = 36 square miles

Cubic Measure

1 cubic foot (ft³)	= 1,728 cubic inches (in³)
27 cubic feet	= 1 cubic yard (yd³)

Gunter's, or Surveyor's, Chain Measure

7.92 inches (in)	= 1 link
100 links	= 1 chain (ch) = 4 rods = 66 feet
80 chains	= 1 statute mile (mi) = 320 rods = 5,280 feet

Troy Weight

24 grains	= 1 pennyweight (dwt)
20 pennyweights	= 1 ounce troy (oz t) = 480 grains
12 ounces troy	= 1 pound troy (lb t) = 240 pennyweights = 5,760 grains

Dry Measure

When necessary to distinguish the dry pint or quart from the liquid pint or quart, the word *dry* is used in combination with the name or abbreviation of the dry unit.

2 pints (pt)	= 1 quart (qt) = 67.2006 cubic inches
8 quarts	= 1 peck (pk) = 537.605 cubic inches = 16 pints
4 pecks	= 1 bushel (bu) = 2,150.42 cubic inches = 32 quarts

Avoirdupois Weight

When necessary to distinguish the avoirdupois ounce or pound from the troy ounce or pound, the word *avoirdupois* or the abbreviation *avdp* is used in combination with the name or abbreviation of the avoirdupois unit. The *grain* is the same in avoirdupois and troy weight.

27 11/32 grains	= 1 dram (dr)
16 drams	= 1 ounce (oz) = 437 ½ grains
16 ounces	= 1 pound (lb) = 256 drams = 7,000 grains
100 pounds	= 1 hundredweight (cwt)°
20 hundredweights	= 1 ton = 2,000 pounds°

In *gross* or *long* measure, the following values are recognized.

112 pounds	= 1 gross or long hundredweight°
20 gross or long hundredweights	= 1 gross or long ton = 2,240 pounds°

°When the terms *hundredweight* and *ton* are used unmodified, they are commonly understood to mean the 100-pound hundredweight and the 2,000-pound ton, respectively; these units may be designated *net* or *short* when necessary to distinguish them from the corresponding units in gross or long measure.

Tables of Equivalents

In this table it is necessary to distinguish between the *international* and the *survey* foot. The international foot, defined in 1959 as exactly equal to 0.3048 meter, is shorter than the old survey foot by exactly 2 parts in one million. The survey foot is still used in data expressed in feet in geodetic surveys within the U.S. In this table the survey foot is italicized.

When the name of a unit is enclosed in brackets thus, [1 hand], either (1) the unit is not in general current use in the U.S. or (2) the unit is believed to be based on custom and usage rather than on formal definition.

Equivalents involving decimals are, in most instances, rounded to the third decimal place; exact equivalents are so designated.

Lengths

1 angstrom (Å)	0.1 nanometer (exactly) 0.000 1 micrometer (exactly) 0.000 000 1 millimeter (exactly) 0.000 000 004 inch
1 cable's length	120 fathoms (exactly) 720 *feet* (exactly) 219 meters
1 centimeter (cm)	0.3937 inch
1 chain (ch) (Gunter's or surveyor's)	66 *feet* (exactly) 20.1168 meters
1 chain (engineers)	100 feet 30.48 meters (exactly)
1 decimeter (dm)	3.937 inches
1 degree (geographical)	364,566.929 feet 69,047 miles (avg.) 111.123 kilometers (avg.)
-of latitude	68.708 miles at equator 69.403 miles at poles
-of longitude	69,171 miles at equator
1 dekameter (dam)	32.808 feet
1 fathom	6 *feet* (exactly) 1.8288 meters
1 foot (ft)	0.3048 meters (exactly)
1 furlong (fur)	10 chains (surveyors) (exactly) 660 *feet* (exactly) ⅛ statute mile (exactly) 201.168 meters
[1 hand] (height measure for horses from ground to top of shoulders)	4 inches
1 inch (in)	2.54 centimeters (exactly)
1 kilometer (km)	0.621 mile 3,280.8 feet

1 league (land)	3 statute miles (exactly) 4.828 kilometers
1 link (Gunter's or surveyor's)	7.92 inches (exactly) 0.201 meter
1 link (engineer's)	1 foot 0.305 meter
1 meter (m)	39.37 inches 1.094 yards
1 micrometer (μm) [the Greek letter mu]	0.001 millimeter (exactly) 0.000 039 37 inch
1 mil	0.001 inch (exactly) 0.025 4 millimeter (exactly)
1 mile (mi) (statute or land)	5,280 *feet* (exactly) 1.609 kilometers
1 international nautical mile (nmi)	1.852 kilometers (exactly) 1.150779 statute miles 6,076.11549 feet
1 millimeter (mm)	0.039 37 inch
1 nanometer (nm)	0.001 micrometer (exactly) 0.000 000 039 37 inch
1 pica (typography)	12 points
1 point (typography)	0.013 837 inch (exactly) 0.351 millimeter
1 rod (rd), pole, or perch	16 ½ *feet* (exactly) 5.029 meters
1 yard (yd)	0.9144 meter (exactly)

Areas or Surfaces

1 acre	43,560 square *feet* (exactly) 4,840 square yards 0.405 hectare
1 are (a)	119.599 square yards 0.025 acre

1 bolt (cloth measure):
    length . . . .   100 yards (on modern looms)
    width . . . .   45 or 60 inches
1 hectare (ha) . . . .   2.471 acres
[1 square (building)] . . . .   100 square feet
1 square centimeter (cm²) . . . .   0.155 square inch
1 square decimeter (dm²) . . . .   15.500 square inches
1 square foot (ft²) . . . .   929.030 square centimeters
1 square inch (in²) . . . . .   6.4516 square centimeters (exactly)
1 square kilometer (km²) . . . . $\begin{cases} 247.104 \text{ acres} \\ 0.386 \text{ square mile} \end{cases}$
1 square meter (m²) . . . . $\begin{cases} 1.196 \text{ square yards} \\ 10.764 \text{ square feet} \end{cases}$
1 square mile (mi²) . . . .   258.999 hectares
1 square millimeter (mm²) . . . .   0.002 square inch
1 square rod (rd²), sq. pole, or
    sq. perch . . . .   25.293 square meters
1 square yard (yd²) . . . .   0.836 square meter

Capacities or Volumes

1 barrel (bbl), liquid . . . .   31 to 42 gallons°

°There are a variety of "barrels" established by law or usage. For example: federal taxes on fermented liquors are based on a barrel of 31 gallons; many state laws fix the "barrel for liquids" as 31½ gallons; one state fixes a 36-gallon barrel for cistern measurement; federal law recognizes a 40-gallon barrel for "proof spirits"; by custom, 42 gallons constitute a barrel of crude oil or petroleum products for statistical purposes, and this equivalent is recognized "for liquids" by 4 states.

1 barrel (bbl), standard
for fruits, vegetables, $\begin{cases} 7,056 \text{ cubic inches} \\ 105 \text{ dry quarts} \\ 3.281 \text{ bushels, struck} \\ \text{measure} \end{cases}$
and other dry com-
modities except dry
cranberries . . . .
1 barrel (bbl), standard, $\begin{cases} 5,826 \text{ cubic inches} \\ 86\ ^{45}/_{64} \text{ dry quarts} \\ 2.709 \text{ bushels, struck} \\ \text{measure} \end{cases}$
cranberry . . . .
1 board foot (lumber measure) . . a foot-square board 1 inch thick
1 bushel (bu) (U.S.) $\begin{cases} 2,150.42 \text{ cubic inches} \\ \text{(exactly)} \\ 35.239 \text{ liters} \end{cases}$
(struck measure) . . . .
[1 bushel, heaped (U.S.)] . . $\begin{cases} 2,747.715 \text{ cubic inches} \\ 1.278 \text{ bushels, struck} \\ \text{measure}° \end{cases}$

°Frequently recognized as 1¼ bushels, struck measure.

[1 bushel (bu) (British $\begin{cases} 1.032 \text{ U.S. bushels,} \\ \text{struck measure} \\ 2,219.36 \text{ cubic inches} \end{cases}$
Imperial) (struck
measure)]
1 cord (cd) firewood . . . .   128 cubic feet (exactly)
1 cubic centimeter (cm³) . . . .   0.061 cubic inch
1 cubic decimeter (dm³) . . . .   61.024 cubic inches
1 cubic inch (in³) . . . . $\begin{cases} 0.554 \text{ fluid ounce} \\ 4.433 \text{ fluid drams} \\ 16.387 \text{ cubic centimeters} \end{cases}$
1 cubic foot (ft³) . . . . $\begin{cases} 7.481 \text{ gallons} \\ 28.316 \text{ cubic decimeters} \end{cases}$
1 cubic meter (m³) . . . .   1.308 cubic yards
1 cubic yard (yd³) . . . .   0.765 cubic meter
1 cup, measuring . . . . $\begin{cases} 8 \text{ fluid ounces (exactly)} \\ ½ \text{ liquid pint (exactly)} \end{cases}$
[1 drachm, fluid (fl dr) $\begin{cases} 0.961 \text{ U.S. fluid dram} \\ 0.217 \text{ cubic inch} \\ 3.552 \text{ milliliters} \end{cases}$
(British)] . . . .
1 dekaliter (daL) . . . . $\begin{cases} 2.642 \text{ gallons} \\ 1.135 \text{ pecks} \end{cases}$
1 gallon (gal) (U.S.) . . . . $\begin{cases} 231 \text{ cubic inches (exactly)} \\ 3.785 \text{ liters} \\ 0.833 \text{ British gallon} \\ 128 \text{ U.S. fluid ounces (exactly)} \end{cases}$
[1 gallon (gal) $\begin{cases} 277.42 \text{ cubic inches} \\ 1.201 \text{ U.S. gallons} \\ 4.546 \text{ liters} \\ 160 \text{ British fluid ounces (exactly)} \end{cases}$
British Imperial]
1 gill (gi) . . . . $\begin{cases} 7.219 \text{ cubic inches} \\ 4 \text{ fluid ounces (exactly)} \\ 0.118 \text{ liter} \end{cases}$
1 hectoliter (hL) . . . . $\begin{cases} 26.418 \text{ gallons} \\ 2.838 \text{ bushels} \end{cases}$
1 liter (L) (1 cubic decimeter exactly) . . . $\begin{cases} 1.057 \text{ liquid quarts} \\ 0.908 \text{ dry quart} \\ 61.025 \text{ cubic inches} \end{cases}$

1 milliliter (mL) (1 cu cm exactly) . . . . $\begin{cases} 0.271 \text{ fluid dram} \\ 16.231 \text{ minims} \\ 0.061 \text{ cubic inch} \end{cases}$
1 ounce, liquid $\begin{cases} 1.805 \text{ cubic inches} \\ 29.573 \text{ milliliters} \\ 1.041 \text{ British fluid ounces} \end{cases}$
(U.S.) . . . .
[1 ounce, fluid (fl oz) (British)] $\begin{cases} 0.961 \text{ U.S. fluid ounce} \\ 1.734 \text{ cubic inches} \\ 28.412 \text{ milliliters} \end{cases}$
1 peck (pk) . . . .   8.810 liters
1 pint (pt), dry . . . . $\begin{cases} 33.600 \text{ cubic inches} \\ 0.551 \text{ liter} \end{cases}$
1 pint (pt), liquid . . . . $\begin{cases} 28.875 \text{ cubic inches (exactly)} \\ 0.473 \text{ liter} \end{cases}$
1 quart (qt), dry (U.S.) . . . . $\begin{cases} 67.201 \text{ cubic inches} \\ 1.01 \text{ liters} \\ 0.969 \text{ British quart} \end{cases}$
1 quart (qt), liquid (U.S.) . . $\begin{cases} 57.75 \text{ cubic in (exactly)} \\ 0.946 \text{ liter} \\ 0.833 \text{ British quart} \end{cases}$
[1 quart (qt) (British)] . . . . $\begin{cases} 69.354 \text{ cubic inches} \\ 1.032 \text{ U.S. dry quarts} \\ 1.201 \text{ U.S. liquid quarts} \end{cases}$
1 tablespoon . . . . $\begin{cases} 3 \text{ teaspoons°(exactly)} \\ 4 \text{ fluid drams} \\ ½ \text{ fluid ounce (exactly)} \end{cases}$
1 teaspoon . . . . $\begin{cases} ⅓ \text{ tablespoon°(exactly)} \\ 1⅓ \text{ fluid drams°} \end{cases}$

°The equivalent "1 teaspoon=1⅓ fluid drams" has been found by the bureau to correspond more closely with the actual capacities of "measuring" and silver teaspoons than the equivalent "1 teaspoon=1 fluid dram" which is given by many dictionaries.

Weights or Masses

1 assay ton°° (AT) . . . .   29.167 grams

°°Used in assaying. The assay ton bears the same relation to the milligram that a ton of 2,000 pounds avoirdupois bears to the ounce troy; hence, the weight in milligrams of precious metal obtained from one assay ton of ore gives directly the number of troy ounces to the net ton.

1 bale (cotton measure) . . . . $\begin{cases} 500 \text{ pounds in U.S.} \\ 750 \text{ pounds in Egypt} \end{cases}$
1 carat (c) . . . . $\begin{cases} 200 \text{ milligrams (exactly)} \\ 3.086 \text{ grains} \end{cases}$
1 dram avoirdupois (dr avdp) . . $\begin{cases} 27\ ^{11}/_{32}(=27.344) \text{ grains} \\ 1.772 \text{ grams} \end{cases}$
1 gamma (γ) . . . .   1 microgram (exactly), see
    below
1 grain . . . .   64.799 milligrams
1 gram . . . . $\begin{cases} 15.432 \text{ grains} \\ 0.035 \text{ ounce, avoirdupois} \end{cases}$
1 hundredweight, gross or $\begin{cases} 112 \text{ pounds (exactly)} \\ 50.802 \text{ kilograms} \end{cases}$
long°°° (gross cwt) . . . .
1 hundredweight, net or short $\begin{cases} 100 \text{ pounds (exactly)} \\ 45.359 \text{ kilograms} \end{cases}$
(cwt or net cwt) . . . .
1 kilogram (kg) . . . .   2.205 pounds
1 microgram (μg [the Greek letter mu in
combination with the letter g]) . . . .   0.000001 gram (exactly)
1 milligram (mg) . . . .   0.015 grain
1 ounce, avoirdupois $\begin{cases} 437.5 \text{ grains (exactly)} \\ 0.911 \text{ troy ounce} \\ 28.350 \text{ grams} \end{cases}$
(oz avdp) . . . .
1 ounce, troy (oz t) . . . . $\begin{cases} 480 \text{ grains (exactly)} \\ 1.097 \text{ avoirdupois ounces} \\ 31.103 \text{ grams} \end{cases}$
1 pennyweight (dwt) . . . .   1.555 grams
1 pound, avoirdupois $\begin{cases} 7,000 \text{ grains (exactly)} \\ 1.215 \text{ troy pounds} \\ 453.592\ 37 \text{ grams (exactly)} \end{cases}$
(lb avdp) . . . .
1 pound, troy (lb t) . . . . $\begin{cases} 5,760 \text{ grains (exactly)} \\ 0.823 \text{ avoirdupois pound} \\ 373.242 \text{ grams} \end{cases}$
1 ton, gross or long°°° $\begin{cases} 2,240 \text{ pounds (exactly)} \\ 1.12 \text{ net tons (exactly)} \\ 1.016 \text{ metric tons} \end{cases}$
(gross ton) . . . .

°°°The gross or long ton and hundredweight are used commercially in the U.S. to only a limited extent, usually in restricted industrial fields. These units are the same as the British ton and hundredweight.

1 ton, metric (t) . . . . $\begin{cases} 2,204.623 \text{ pounds} \\ 0.984 \text{ gross ton} \\ 1.102 \text{ net tons} \end{cases}$
1 ton, net or short (sh ton) . . $\begin{cases} 2,000 \text{ pounds (exactly)} \\ 0.893 \text{ gross ton} \\ 0.907 \text{ metric ton} \end{cases}$

Tables of Interrelation of Units of Measurement

Units of length and area of the international and survey measures are included in the following tables. Units unique to the survey measure are *italicized*. See Tables of Equivalents, 1st paragraph.

1 international foot	= 0.999 998 survey foot (exactly)
1 survey foot	= 1200/3937 meter (exactly)
1 international foot	= 12 × 0.0254 meter (exactly)

Boldface type indicates exact values.

Units of Length

Units	Inches	Links	Feet	Yards	Rods	Chains	Miles	cm	Meters
1 inch=	1	0.126 263	0.083 333	0.027 778	0.005 051	0.001 263	0.000 016	**2.54**	0.025 4
1 *link*=	7.92	1	**0.66**	0.22	0.04	0.01	0.000 125	20.117	0.201 168
1 foot=	12	1.515 152	1	0.333 333	0.060 606	0.015 152	0.000 189	30.48	0.304 8
1 yard=	36	4.545 45	3	1	0.181 818	0.045 455	0.000 568	91.44	0.914 4
1 *rod*=	198	25	16.5	5.5	1	0.25	0.003 125	502.92	5.029 2
1 *chain*=	792	100	66	22	4	1	0.012 5	2011.68	20.116 8
1 mile=	63 360	8000	5280	1760	320	80	1	160 934.4	1609.344
1 cm=	0.3937	0.049 710	0.032 808	0.010 936	0.001 988	0.000 497	0.000 006	1	0.01
1 meter=	39.37	4.970 960	3.280 840	1.093 613	0.198 838	0.049 710	0.000 621	100	1

Units of Area

Units	Sq. inches	Sq. links	Sq. feet	Sq. yards	Sq. rods	Sq. chains
1 sq. inch=	1	0.015 942 3	0.006 944	0.000 771 605	0.000 025 5	0.000 001 594
1 sq. *link*=	62.726 4	1	0.435 6	0.0484	0.0016	0.000 1
1 sq. foot=	144	2.295 684	1	0.111 111 1	0.003 673 09	0.000 229 568
1 sq. yard=	1296	20.661 16	9	1	0.033 057 85	0.002 066 12
1 sq. *rod*=	39 204	625	272.25	30.25	1	0.062 5
1 sq. *chain*=	627 264	10 000	4 356	484	16	1
1 *acre*=	6 272 640	100 000	43 560	4 840	160	10
1 sq. mile=	4 014 489 600	64 000 000	27 878 400	3 097 600	102 400	6400
1 sq. cm=	0.155 000 3	0.002 471 05	0.001 076	0.000 119 599	0.000 003 954	0.000 000 247
1 sq. meter=	1550.003	24.710 44	10.763 91	1.195 990	0.039 536 70	0.002 471 044
1 *hectare*=	15 500 031	247 104	107 639.1	11 959.90	395.367 0	24.710 44

Units	Acres	Sq. miles	Sq. cm	Sq. meters	Hectares
1 sq. inch=	0.000 000 159 423	0.000 000 000 249 10	**6.451 6**	**0.000 645 16**	0.000 000 065
1 sq. *link*=	**0.000 01**	**0.000 000 015 625**	404.685 642 24	0.040 468 56	0.000 004 047
1 sq. foot=	0.000 022 956 84	0.000 000 035 870 06	929.034 1	0.092 903 41	0.000 009 290
1 sq. yard=	0.000 206 611 6	0.000 000 322 830 6	**8 361.273 6**	**0.836 127 36**	0.000 083 613
1 sq. *rod*=	**0.006 25**	**0.000 009 765 625**	252 929.5	25.292 95	0.002 529 295
1 sq. *chain*=	**0.1**	0.000 156 25		404.687 3	0.040 468 73
1 *acre*=	1	0.001 562 5	4 046 873	40 468 730	0.404 687 3
1 sq. mile=	640	1	25 899 881 103	4 046.873	258.998 811 034
1 sq. cm=	0.000 000 024 711	0.000 000 000 038 610	1	2 589 988.11	**0.000 1**	**0.000 000 01**
1 sq. meter=	0.000 247 104 4	0.000 000 386 102 2	10 000	1	0.0001
1 *hectare*=	2.471 044	0.003 861 006	100 000 000	10 000	1

Units of Mass Not Greater Than Pounds and Kilograms

Units	Grains	Pennyweights	Avdp drams	Avdp ounces
1 grain=	1	0.041 666 67	0.036 571 43	0.002 285 71
1 pennyweight=	24	1	0.877 714 3	0.054 857 14
1 dram avdp=	27.343 75	1.139 323	1	0.062 5
1 ounce avdp=	437.5	18.229 17	16	1
1 ounce troy=	480	20	17.554 29	1.097 143
1 pound troy=	5760	240	210.651 4	13.165 71
1 pound avdp=	7000	291.666 7	256	16
1 milligram=	0.015 432	0.000 643 015	0.000 564 383	0.000 035 274
1 gram=	15.432 36	0.643 014 9	0.564 383 4	0.035 273 96
1 kilogram=	15 432.36	643.014 9	564.383 4	35.273 96

Units	Troy ounces	Troy pounds	Avdp pounds	Milligrams	Grams	Kilograms
1 grain=	0.002 083 33	0.000 173 611	0.000 142 857	64.798 91	**0.064 798 91**	0.000 064 799
1 pennywt.=	0.05	0.004 166 667	0.003 428 571	1555.173 84	1.555 173 84	0.001 555 174
1 dram avdp=	0.056 966 15	0.004 747 179	0.003 906 25	1771.845 195	1.771 845 195	0.001 771 845
1 oz avdp=	0.911 458 3	0.075 954 86	**0.062 5**	28 349.523 125	28.349 523 125	0.028 349 52
1 oz troy=	1	0.083 333 333	0.068 571 43	31 103.476 8	31.103 476 8	0.031 103 48
1 lb troy=	12	1	0.822 857 1	373 241.721 6	373.241 721 6	0.373 241 722
1 lb avdp=	14.583 33	1.215 278	1	453 592.37	453.592 37	0.453 592 37
1 milligram=	0.000 032 151	0.000 002 679	0.000 002 205	1	**0.001**	**0.000 001**
1 gram=	0.032 150 75	0.002 679 229	0.002 204 623	1000	1	**0.001**
1 kilogram=	32.150 75	2.679 229	2.204 623	1 000 000	1000	1

Units of Mass Not Less Than Avoirdupois Ounces

Units	Avdp oz	Avdp lb	Short cwt	Short tons	Long tons	Kilograms	Metric tons
1 oz avdp=	1	**0.0625**	**0.000 625**	**0.000 031 25**	0.000 027 902	0.028 349 523	0.000 028 350
1 lb avdp=	16	1	**0.01**	**0.000 5**	0.000 446 429	**0.453 592 37**	0.000 453 592
1 sh cwt=	1 600	100	1	**0.05**	0.044 642 86	45.359 237	0.045 359 237
1 sh ton=	32 000	2000	20	1	0.892 857 1	907.184 74	0.907 184 74
1 long ton=	35 840	2240	22.4	1.12	1	1 016.046 908 8	1.016 046 909
1 kg=	35.273 96	2.204 623	0.022 046 23	0.001 102 311	0.000 984 207	1	0.001
1 metric ton=	35 273.96	2 204.623	22.046 23	1.102 311	0.984 206 5	1000	1

Units of Volume

Units	Cubic inches	Cubic feet	Cubic yards	Cubic cm	Cubic dm	Cubic meters
1 cubic inch=	1	0.000 578 704	0.000 021 433	16.387 064	0.016 387	0.000 016 387
1 cubic foot=	1728	1	0.037 037 04	28 316.846 592	28.316 847	0.028 316 847
1 cubic yard=	46 656	27	1	764 554.857 984	764.554 858	0.764 554 858
1 cubic cm=	0.061 023 74	0.000 035 315	0.000 001 308	1	0.001	0.000 001
1 cubic dm=	61.023 74	0.035 314 67	0.001 307 951	1 000	1	0.001
1 cubic meter=	61 023.74	35.314 67	1.307 951	1 000 000	1000	1

Units of Capacity (Liquid Measure)

Units	Minims	Fluid drams	Fluid ounces	Gills	Liquid pint
1 minim=	1	0.016 666 7	0.002 083 33	0.000 520 833	0.000 130 208
1 fluid dram=	60	1	0.125	0.031 25	0.007 812 5
1 fluid ounce=	480	8	1	0.25	0.062 5
1 gill=	1920	32	4	1	0.25
1 liquid pint=	7680	128	16	4	1
1 liquid quart=	15 360	256	32	8	2
1 gallon=	61 440	1024	128	32	8
1 cubic inch=	265.974	4.432 900	0.554 112 6	0.138 528 1	0.034 632 03
1 cubic foot=	459 603.1	7 660.052	957.506 5	239.376 6	59.844 16
1 liter=	16 230.73	270.512 18	33.814 02	8.453 506	2.113 376

Units	Liquid quarts	Gallons	Cubic inches	Cubic feet	Liters
1 minim=	0.000 065 104 17	0.000 016 276 04	0.003 759 766	0.000 002 175 790	0.000 061 611 52
1 flu. dram=	0.003 906 25	0.000 976 562 5	0.225 585 9	0.000 130 547 4	0.003 696 691
1 fluid oz=	0.031 25	0.007 812 5	1.804 687 5	0.001 044 379	0.029 573 53
1 gill=	0.125	0.031 25	7.218 75	0.004 177 517	0.118 294 118
1 liquid pt=	0.5	0.125	28.875	0.016 710 07	0.473 176 473
1 liquid qt=	1	0.25	57.75	0.033 420 14	0.946 352 946
1 gallon=	4	1	231	0.133 680 6	3.785 411 784
1 cubic inch=	0.017 316 02	0.004 329 004	1	0.000 578 703 7	0.016 387 064
1 cubic foot=	29.922 08	7.480 519	1728	1	28.316 846 592
1 liter=	1.056 688	0.264 172 05	61.023 74	0.035 314 67	1

Units of Capacity (Dry Measure)

Units	Dry pints	Dry quarts	Pecks	Bushels	Cubic in.	Liters
1 dry pint=	1	0.5	0.062 5	0.015 625	33.600 312 5	0.550 610 47
1 dry quart=	2	1	0.125	0.031 25	67.200 625	1.101 220 9
1 peck=	16	8	1	0.25	537.605	8.809 767 5
1 bushel=	64	32	4	1	2 150.42	35.239 07
1 cubic inch=	0.029 761 6	0.014 880 8	0.001 860 10	0.000 465 025	1	0.016 387 06
1 liter=	1.816 166	0.908 083	0.113 510 37	0.028 377 59	61.023 74	1

Miscellaneous Measures

Caliber—the diameter of a gun bore. In the U.S., caliber is traditionally expressed in hundredths of inches, e.g. .22 or .30. In Britain, caliber is often expressed in thousandths of inches, e.g. .270 or .465. Now, it is commonly expressed in millimeters, e.g. the 5.56 mm M16 rifle. Heavier weapons' caliber has long been expressed in millimeters, e.g. the 81 mm mortar, the 105 mm howitzer (light), the 155 mm howitzer (medium or heavy).

Naval guns' caliber refers to the barrel length as a multiple of the bore diameter. A 5-inch, 50-caliber naval gun has a 5-inch bore and a barrel length of 250 inches.

Carat—a measure of the amount of alloy per 24 parts in gold. Thus 24-carat gold is pure; 18-carat gold is one-fourth alloy.

Decibel (dB)—a measure of the relative loudness or intensity of sound. A 20-decibel sound is 10 times louder than a 10-decibel sound; 30 decibels is 100 times louder; 40 decibels is 1,000 times louder, etc. One decibel is the smallest difference between sounds detectable by the human ear. A 120-decibel sound is painful.

10 decibels	– a light whisper
20	– quiet conversation
30	– normal conversation
40	– light traffic
50	– typewriter, loud conversation
60	– noisy office
70	– normal traffic, quiet train
80	– rock music, subway
90	– heavy traffic, thunder
100	– jet plane at takeoff

Em—a printer's measure designating the square width of any given type size. Thus, an em of 10-point type is 10 points. An en is half an em.

Gauge—a measure of shotgun bore diameter. Gauge numbers originally referred to the number of lead balls of the gun barrel diameter in a pound. Thus, a 16-gauge shotgun's bore was smaller than a 12-gauge shotgun's. Today, an international agreement assigns millimeter measures to each gauge, e.g.:

Gauge	Bore diameter in mm
6	23.34
10	19.67
12	18.52
14	17.60
16	16.81
20	15.90

Horsepower—the power needed to lift 550 pounds one foot in one second or to lift 33,000 pounds one foot in one minute. Equivalent to 746 watts or 2,546.0756 Btu/h.

Knot—a measure of the speed of ships. A knot equals 1 nautical mile per hour.

Quire—25 sheets of paper

Ream—500 sheets of paper

Electrical Units

The **watt** is the unit of power (electrical, mechanical, thermal, etc.). Electrical power is given by the product of the voltage and the current.

Energy is sold by the **joule,** but in common practice the billing of electrical energy is expressed in terms of the **kilowatt-hour,** which is 3,600,000 joules or 3.6 megajoules.

The **horsepower** is a nonmetric unit sometimes used in mechanics. It is equal to 746 watts.

The **ohm** is the unit of electrical resistance and represents the physical property of a conductor that offers a resistance to the flow of electricity, permitting just 1 ampere to flow at 1 volt of pressure.

Compound Interest
Compounded Annually

Principal	Period	4%	5%	6%	7%	8%	9%	10%	12%	14%	16%
$100	1 day	0.011	0.014	0.016	0.019	0.022	0.025	0.027	0.033	0.038	0.044
	1 week	0.077	0.096	0.115	0.134	0.153	0.173	0.192	0.230	0.268	0.307
	6 mos.	2.00	2.50	3.00	3.50	4.00	4.50	5.00	6.00	7.00	8.00
	1 year.	4.00	5.00	6.00	7.00	8.00	9.00	10.00	12.00	14.00	16.00
	2 years . . .	8.16	10.25	12.36	14.49	16.64	18.81	21.00	25.44	29.96	34.56
	3 years . . .	12.49	15.76	19.10	22.50	25.97	29.50	33.10	40.49	48.15	56.09
	4 years	16.99	21.55	26.25	31.08	36.05	41.16	46.41	57.35	68.90	81.06
	5 years	21.67	27.63	33.82	40.26	46.93	53.86	61.05	76.23	92.54	110.03
	6 years	26.53	34.01	41.85	50.07	58.69	67.71	77.16	97.38	119.50	143.64
	7 years	31.59	40.71	50.36	60.58	71.38	82.80	94.87	121.07	150.23	182.62
	8 years	36.86	47.75	59.38	71.82	85.09	99.26	114.36	147.60	185.26	227.84
	9 years . . .	42.33	55.13	68.95	83.85	99.90	117.19	135.79	177.31	225.19	280.30
	10 years . . .	48.02	62.89	79.08	96.72	115.89	136.74	159.37	210.58	270.72	341.14
	12 years . . .	60.10	79.59	101.22	125.22	151.82	181.27	213.84	289.60	381.79	493.60
	15 years . . .	80.09	107.89	139.66	175.90	217.22	264.25	317.72	447.36	613.79	826.55
	20 years . . .	119.11	165.33	220.71	286.97	366.10	460.44	572.75	864.63	1,274.35	1,846.08

Ancient Measures

Biblical			Greek			Roman		
Cubit	=	21.8 inches	Cubit	=	18.3 inches	Cubit	=	17.5 inches
Omer	=	0.45 peck	Stadion	=	607.2 or 622 feet	Stadium	=	202 yards
		3.964 liters	Obolos	=	715.38 milligrams	As, libra,	=	325.971 grams,
Ephah	=	10 omers	Drachma	=	4.2923 grams	pondus		0.71864 pound
Shekel	=	0.497 ounce	Mina	=	0.9463 pound			
		14.1 grams	Talent	=	60 mina			

Weight of Water
at 20°C

1	cubic inch	0.0360 pound	13.45	U.S. gallons	112.0 pounds
12	cubic inches.	0.433 pound	269.0	U.S. gallons	2240.0 pounds
1	cubic foot.	62.4 pounds			
1	cubic foot.	7.48052 U.S. gal		**metric weights, at 4°C (maximum density):**	
1.8	cubic feet.	112.0 pounds	1	cubic centimeter	1 gram
35.96	cubic feet.	2240.0 pounds	1	liter	1 kilogram
1	U.S. gallon.	8.33 pounds	1	cubic meter	1 metric ton

Density of Gases and Vapors
at 0°C and 760 mmHg; kilograms per cubic meter

Gas	Wt.	Gas	Wt.	Gas	Wt.
Acetylene	1.171	Ethylene.	1.260	Methyl fluoride	1.545
Air	1.293	Fluorine	1.696	Mono methylamine	1.38
Ammonia	0.759	Helium	0.178	Neon	0.900
Argon.	1.784	Hydrogen	0.090	Nitric oxide	1.341
Arsine	3.48	Hydrogen bromide.	3.50	Nitrogen	1.250
Butane-iso	2.60	Hydrogen chloride.	1.639	Nitrosyl chloride	2.99
Butane-n	2.519	Hydrogen iodide	5.724	Nitrous oxide.	1.997
Carbon dioxide	1.977	Hydrogen selenide	3.66	Oxygen	1.429
Carbon monoxide	1.250	Hydrogen sulfide	1.539	Phosphine	1.48
Carbon oxysulfide	2.72	Krypton	3.745	Propane.	2.020
Chlorine	3.214	Methane.	0.717	Silicon tetrafluoride	4.67
Chlorine monoxide	3.89	Methyl chloride	2.25	Sulfur dioxide	2.927
Ethane	1.356	Methyl ether	2.091	Xenon	5.897

Temperature Conversion Table

The numbers in **boldface type** refer to the temperature either in degrees Celsius or Fahrenheit that are to be converted. If converting from degrees Fahrenheit to Celsius, the equivalent is in the column on the left; if converting from degrees Celsius to Fahrenheit, the answer is in the column on the right.

For temperatures not shown. To convert Fahrenheit to Celsius, subtract 32 degrees and divide by 1.8; to convert Celsius to Fahrenheit, multiply by 1.8 and add 32 degrees.

Note: Although Centigrade is still frequently used, the International Committee on Weights and Measures and the National Institute of Standards and Technology have recommended since 1948 that this scale be called Celsius.

Celsius		Fahrenheit	Celsius		Fahrenheit	Celsius		Fahrenheit
−273.2	**−459.7**	. . . . . .	−17.8	**0**	32	35.0	**95**	203
−184	**−300**	. . . . . .	−12.2	**10**	50	36.7	**98**	208.4
−169	**−273**	− 459.4	− 6.67	**20**	68	37.8	**100**	212
−157	**−250**	− 418	− 1.11	**30**	86	43	**110**	230
−129	**−200**	− 328	4.44	**40**	104	49	**120**	248
−101	**−150**	− 238	10.0	**50**	122	54	**130**	266
−73.3	**−100**	− 148	15.6	**60**	140	60	**140**	284
−45.6	**−50**	− 58	21.1	**70**	158	66	**150**	302
−40.0	**−40**	− 40	23.9	**75**	167	93	**200**	392
−34.4	**−30**	− 22	26.7	**80**	176	121	**250**	482
−28.9	**−20**	− 4	29.4	**85**	185	149	**300**	572
−23.3	**−10**	14	32.2	**90**	194			

Boiling and Freezing Points of Water

Water boils at 212°F at sea level. For every 550 feet above sea level, boiling point of water is lower by about 1°F. Methyl alcohol boils at 148°F. Average human oral temperature, 98.6°F. Water freezes at 32°F.

Breaking the Sound Barrier; Speed of Sound

The prefix Mach is used to describe supersonic speed. It was named for Ernst Mach (1838-1916), a Czech-born Austrian physicist, who contributed to the study of sound. When a plane moves at the speed of sound, it is Mach 1. When twice the speed of sound, it is Mach 2. When it is near but below the speed of sound, its speed can be designated at less than Mach 1, for example, Mach 0.90. Mach is defined as "the ratio of the velocity of a rocket or a jet to the velocity of sound in the medium being considered."

When a plane passes the sound barrier—flying faster than sound travels—listeners in the area hear thunderclaps, but the pilot of the plane does not hear them.

Sound is produced by vibrations of an object and is transmitted by alternate increase and decrease in pressures that radiate outward through a material media of molecules —somewhat like waves spreading out on a pond after a rock has been tossed into it.

The frequency of sound is determined by the number of times the vibrating waves undulate per second and is measured in cycles per second. The slower the cycle of waves, the lower the frequency. As frequencies increase, the sound is higher in pitch.

Sound is audible to human beings only if the frequency falls within a certain range. The human ear is usually not sensitive to frequencies of fewer than 20 vibrations per second or more than about 20,000 vibrations per second— although this range varies among individuals. Anything at a pitch higher than the human ear can hear is termed ultrasonic.

Intensity, or loudness, is the strength of the pressure of these radiating waves and is measured in decibels. The human ear responds to intensity in a range from zero to 120 decibels. Any sound with pressure more than 120 decibels is painful to the human ear.

The speed of sound is generally placed at 1,088 feet per second at sea level at 32°F. It varies in other temperatures and in different media. Sound travels faster in water than in air, and even faster in iron and steel. It travels a mile in 5 seconds in air, it does a mile under water in 1 second, and it travels through iron in 1/3 second. It travels through ice cold vapor at approximately 4,708 feet per second; ice-cold water, 4,938; granite, 12,960; hardwood, 12,620; brick, 11,960; glass, 16,410 to 19,690; silver, 8,658; gold, 5,717.

Colors of the Spectrum

Color, an electromagnetic wave phenomenon, is a sensation produced through the excitation of the retina of the eye by rays of light. The colors of the spectrum may be produced by viewing a light beam refracted by passage through a prism, which breaks the light into its wavelengths.

Customarily, the primary colors of the spectrum are those 6 monochromatic colors that occupy relatively large areas of the spectrum: red, orange, yellow, green, blue, and violet. However, Sir Isaac Newton named a 7th, indigo, situated between blue and violet on the spectrum. Aubert estimated (1865) the solar spectrum to contain approximately 1,000 distinguishable hues of which according to

Rood (1881) 2 million tints and shades can be distinguished; Luckiesh stated (1915) that 55 distinctly different hues have been seen in a single spectrum.

Many physicists recognize only 3 primary colors: red, yellow, and blue (Mayer, 1775); red, green, and violet (Thomas Young, 1801); red, green, and blue (Clerk Maxwell, 1860).

The color sensation of black is due to complete lack of stimulation of the retina, that of white to complete stimulation. The infrared and ultraviolet rays, below the red (long) end of the spectrum and above the violet (short) end respectively, are invisible to the naked eye. Heat is the principal effect of the infrared rays, and chemical action that of the ultraviolet rays.

Common Fractions Reduced to Decimals

8ths	16ths	32ds	64ths		8ths	16ths	32ds	64ths		8ths	16ths	32ds	64ths	
			1	0.015625				23	0.359375				45	0.703125
		1	2	0.03125	3	6	12	24	0.375			23	46	0.71875
			3	0.046875				25	0.390625				47	0.734375
	1	2	4	0.0625				26	0.40625	6	12	24	48	0.75
			5	0.078125				27	0.421875				49	0.765625
		3	6	0.09375		7	14	28	0.4375			25	50	0.78125
			7	0.109375				29	0.453125				51	0.796875
1	2	4	8	0.125				30	0.46875				52	0.8125
			9	0.140625				31	0.484375			13	26	53	0.828125
		5	10	0.15625	4	8	16	32	0.5				53	0.828125
			11	0.171875				33	0.515625			27	54	0.84375
	3	6	12	0.1875			17	34	0.53125				55	0.859375
			13	0.203125				35	0.546875	7	14	28	56	0.875
		7	14	0.21875			18	36	0.5625				57	0.890625
			15	0.234375				37	0.578125			29	58	0.90625
2	4	8	16	0.25			19	38	0.59375				59	0.921875
			17	0.265625				39	0.609375			15	30	60	0.9375
		9	18	0.28125	5	10	20	40	0.625				60	0.9375
			19	0.296875				41	0.640625				61	0.953125
	5	10	20	0.3125			21	42	0.65625			31	62	0.96875
			21	0.328125				43	0.671875				63	0.984375
		11	22	0.34375		11	22	44	0.6875	8	16	32	64	1.0

Spirits Measures

Pony . . . . 0.5 jigger

Shot . . . . {0.666 jigger / 1.0 ounce

Jigger . . . . 1.5 shots

Pint . . . . {16 shots / 0.625 fifth

Fifth . . . . {25.6 shots / 1.6 pints / 0.8 quart / 0.75706 liter

Quart . . . . {32 shots / 1.25 fifths

Magnum . . . . {2 quarts / 2.49797 bottles (wine)

For champagne and brandy only:

Jeroboam . . . . {6.4 pints / 1.6 magnum / 0.8 gallon

For champagne only:

Rehoboam . . . . 3 magnums
Methuselah . . . . 4 magnums
Salmanazar . . . . 6 magnums
Balthazar . . . . . 8 magnums
Nebuchadnezzar. 10 magnums

Wine bottle (standard) {0.800633 quart / 0.7576778 liter

Mathematical Formulas

To find the CIRCUMFERENCE of a:

Circle — Multiply the diameter by 3.14159265 (usually 3.1416).

To find the AREA of a:

Circle — Multiply the square of the diameter by 0.785398 (usually 0.7854).
Rectangle — Multiply the length of the base by the height.
Sphere (surface) — Multiply the square of the radius by 3.1416 and multiply by 4.

Square — Square the length of one side.
Trapezoid — Add the two parallel sides, multiply by the height, and divide by 2.
Triangle — Multiply the base by the height and divide by 2.

To find the VOLUME of a:

Cone — Multiply the square of the radius of the base by 3.1416, multiply by the height, and divide by 3.
Cube — Cube the length of one edge.
Cylinder — Multiply the square of the radius of the base by 3.1416 and multiply by the height.

Pyramid — Multiply the area of the base by the height and divide by 3.
Rectangular Prism — Multiply the length by the width by the height.
Sphere — Multiply the cube of the radius by 3.1416, multiply by 4, and divide by 3.

Playing Cards and Dice Chances

5-Card Poker Hands

Hand	Number possible	Odds against
Royal flush	4	649,739 to 1
Other straight flush	36	72,192 to 1
Four of a kind	624	4,164 to 1
Full house	3,744	693 to 1
Flush	5,108	508 to 1
Straight	10,200	254 to 1
Three of a kind	54,912	46 to 1
Two pairs	123,552	20 to 1
One pair	1,098,240	4 to 3(1.37 to 1)
Nothing	1,302,540	1 to 1
Total	**2,598,960**	

Dice
(probabilities on 2 dice)

Total	Odds against (single toss)	Total	Odds against (single toss)
2	35 to 1	8	31 to 5
3	17 to 1	9	8 to 1
4	11 to 1	10	11 to 1
5	8 to 1	11	17 to 1
6	31 to 5	12	35 to 1
7	5 to 1		

Dice
(probabilities of consecutive winning plays)

No. consecutive wins	By 7,11, or point	No. consecutive wins	By 7, 11, or point
1	244 in 495	6	1 in 70
2	6 in 25	7	1 in 141
3	3 in 25	8	1 in 287
4	1 in 17	9	1 in 582
5	1 in 34		

Pinochle Auction
(odds against finding in "widow" of 3 cards)

Open places	Odds	Open places	Odds
1	5 to 1 against	4	1½ to 1 for
2	2 to 1 against	5	2 to 1 for
3	Even	6	3 to 1 for

Bridge

The odds — against suit distribution in a hand of 4-4-3-2 are about 4 to 1, against 5-4-2-2 about 8 to 1, against 6-4-2-1 about 20 to 1, against 7-4-1-1 about 254 to 1, against 8-4-1-0 about 2,211 to 1, and against 13-0-0-0 about 158,753,389,899 to 1.

Measures of Force and Pressure

Dyne = force necessary to accelerate a 1-gram mass 1 centimeter per second squared = 0.000072 poundal
Poundal = force necessary to accelerate a 1-pound mass 1 foot per second squared = 13,825.5 dynes = 0.138255 newtons
Newton = force needed to accelerate a 1-kilogram mass 1 meter per second squared

Pascal (pressure) = 1 newton per square meter = 0.020885 pound per square foot
Atmosphere (air pressure at sea level) = 2,116.102 pounds per square foot = 14.6952 pounds per square inch = 1.0332 kilograms per square centimeter = 101,323 newtons per square meter.

Large Numbers

U.S.	Number of zeros	French, British, German	U.S.	Number of zeros	French, British, German
million	6	million	sextillion	21	1,000 trillion
billion	9	milliard	septillion	24	quadrillion
trillion	12	billion	octillion	27	1,000 quadrillion
quadrillion	15	1,000 billion	nonillion	30	quintillion
quintillion	18	trillion	decillion	33	1,000 quintillion

Roman Numerals

I	-	1	VI	-	6	XI	-	11	L	-	50	CD	-	400	$\bar{\text{X}}$	-	10,000
II	-	2	VII	-	7	XIX	-	19	LX	-	60	D	-	500	$\bar{\text{L}}$	-	50,000
III	-	3	VIII	-	8	XX	-	20	XC	-	90	CM	-	900	$\bar{\text{C}}$	-	100,000
IV	-	4	IX	-	9	XXX	-	30	C	-	100	M	-	1,000	$\bar{\text{D}}$	-	500,000
V	-	5	X	-	10	XL	-	40	CC	-	200	$\bar{\text{V}}$	-	5,000	$\bar{\text{M}}$	-	1,000,000

HEALTH
Basic First Aid

First aid experts stress that knowing what to do for an injured person until a doctor or trained person gets to an accident scene can save a life, especially in cases of stoppage of breathing, severe bleeding, and shock.

People with special medical problems, such as diabetes, cardiovascular disease, epilepsy, or allergy, are urged to wear some sort of emblem identifying the problem, as a safeguard against use of medication in an emergency that might be injurious or fatal. Emblems may be obtained from Medic Alert Foundation, Turlock, CA 95380.

Most accidents occur in homes. National Safety Council figures show that home accidents exceed those in other locations, such as in cars, at work, or in public places.

In all cases, get medical assistance as soon as possible.

Animal bite — Wound should be washed with soap under running water and antibiotic ointment and dressing applied. When possible, animal should be caught alive for rabies test.

Asphyxiation — Start rescue breathing immediately after getting patient to fresh air.

Bleeding — Elevate the wound above the heart if possible. Press hard on wound with sterile compress until bleeding stops. Send for doctor if it is severe.

Burn — If mild, with skin unbroken and no blisters, plunge into ice water until pain subsides. Apply a dry dressing if necessary. Send for physician if burn is severe. Apply sterile compresses and keep patient comfortably warm until doctor's arrival. Do not try to clean burn or to break blisters.

Chemical in eye — With patient lying down, pour cupsful of water immediately into corner of eye, letting it run to other side to remove chemicals thoroughly. Cover with sterile compress. Get medical attention immediately.

Choking — See **Abdominal Thrust**.

Convulsions — Place person on back on bed or rug. Loosen clothing. Turn head to side. Do not place a blunt object between the victim's teeth. If convulsions do not stop, get medical attention immediately.

Cut (minor) — Apply mild antiseptic and sterile compress after washing with soap under warm running water.

Fainting — If victim feels faint, lower head to knees. Lay victim down on back with head turned to side if he or she becomes unconscious. Elevate the legs 8 to 10 inches. Loosen clothing and open windows. Keep patient lying quietly for at least 15 minutes after he or she regains consciousness. Call doctor if faint lasts for more than a few minutes.

Foreign body in eye — Touch object with moistened corner of handkerchief if it can be seen. If it cannot be seen or does not come out after a few attempts, take patient to doctor. Do not rub eye.

Frostbite — Handle frostbitten area gently. Do not rub. Soak the affected area in water no warmer than 105°F. Do not allow frostbitten area to touch the container. Soak until frostbitten part looks red and feels warm. Loosely bandage. If fingers or toes are frostbitten, place gauze between them.

Heat Stroke and Heat Exhaustion — Remove the victim from the heat. Loosen any tight clothing and apply cool, wet cloths to the skin. Give the victim cool water, to drink slowly. Call an ambulance if the victim refuses water, vomits, or experiences changes in consciousness.

Hypothermia — Move victim to a warm place. Remove wet clothing and dry victim, if necessary. Warm victim gradually by wrapping the person in warm blankets or clothing. If available, apply heat pads or other heat sources, but not directly to the body. Give the victim warm liquids. Call an ambulance if breathing is slowed or stopped or if the pulse is slow or irregular.

Loss of Limb — If a limb is severed, it is important to properly protect the limb so that it can possibly be reattached to the victim. After the victim is cared for, the limb should be wrapped in a sterile gauze or clean material and placed in a clean plastic bag, garbage can, or other suitable container. Pack ice around the limb on the OUTSIDE of the bag to keep the limb cold. Call ahead to the hospital to alert staff there of the situation.

Poisoning — Call doctor. Use antidote listed on label if container is found. Call local Poison Control Center if possible. Do not give the victim any food or drink or induce vomiting, unless specified on the label or by a medical professional.

Shock (injury-related) — Keep the victim lying down; if uncertain as to his or her injuries, keep the victim flat on the back. Maintain the victim's normal body temperature; if the weather is cold or damp, place blankets or extra clothing over and under the victim; if weather is hot, provide shade.

Snakebite —Wash the injury. Keep the area still and at a lower level than the heart. Keep the victim quiet. If available, use a snakebite kit.

Sprains and fractures — Apply ice to reduce swelling and pain. Do not try to straighten or move broken limbs. Apply a splint to immobilize the injured area if the victim must be transported.

Sting from insect — If possible, remove stinger. Wash the area with soap and water and cover it to keep it clean. Apply a cold pack to reduce pain and swelling. Call physician immediately if body swells or patient collapses.

Unconsciousness — Send for doctor and place person on his or her back. Start rescue breathing if victim stops breathing. Never give food or liquids to an unconscious person.

Abdominal Thrust

The American Red Cross and the American Heart Association both agree that the recommended first aid for choking victims is the abdominal thrust, also known as the Heimlich maneuver, after its creator, Dr. Henry Heimlich. Slaps on the back are no longer advised and may even prove detrimental in an attempt to assist a choking victim.

- Get behind the victim and wrap your arms around him or her above the waist.
- Make a fist with one hand and place it, with the thumb knuckle pressing inward, just below the point of the "v" of the rib cage.
- Grasp the wrist with the other hand and give one or more upward thrusts or hugs.
- Start rescue breathing if breathing stops.

Rescue Breathing

Stressing that your breath can save a life, the American Red Cross gives the following directions for rescue breathing if the victim is not breathing:

- Determine consciousness by tapping the victim on the shoulder and asking loudly, "Are you okay?"
- Tilt the victim's head back so that the chin is pointing upward. Do not press on the soft tissue under the chin, as this might obstruct the airway. If you suspect that an accident victim might have neck or back injuries, open the airway by placing the tips of your index and middle fingers on the corners of the victim's jaw to lift it forward without tilting the head.
- Place your cheek and ear close to the victim's mouth and nose. Look at the victim's chest to see if it rises and falls. Listen and feel for air to be exhaled for about 5 seconds.
- If there is no breathing, pinch the victim's nostrils shut with the thumb and index finger of your hand that is pressing on the victim's forehead. Another way to prevent leakage of air when the lungs are inflated is to press your cheek against the victim's nose.
- Blow air into victim's mouth by taking a deep breath and then sealing your mouth tightly around the victim's mouth. Initially, give two, quick (approx. 1.5 seconds each), full breaths without allowing the lungs to deflate completely between each breath.
- Watch the victim's chest to see if it rises.
- Stop blowing when the victim's chest is expanded. Raise your mouth; turn your head to the side and listen for exhalation.
- Watch the chest to see if it falls.
- Repeat the blowing cycle until the victim starts breathing.

Note: Infants (up to one year) and children (1 to 8 years) should be administered rescue breathing as described above, except for the following:
- Do not tilt the head as far back as an adult's head.
- Both the mouth and nose of an infant should be sealed by the mouth.
- Give breaths to a child once every three seconds.
- Blow into the infant's mouth and nose once every three seconds with less pressure and volume than for a child.

Finding Your Target Heart Rate

Source: Carole Casten, EdD, and Peg Jordan, RN, *Aerobics Today*, Aerobic Fitness Association of America

The target heart rate is the heartbeat rate a person should have during aerobic exercise (such as running, fast walking, cycling, or cross-country skiing) to get the full benefit of the exercise for cardiovascular conditioning.

First, determine the intensity level at which one would like to exercise. A sedentary person may want to begin an exercise regimen at the 60% level and work up gradually to the 70% level. Athletes and highly fit individuals must work at the 85-95% level to receive the benefits of exercise.

Second, calculate the target heart rate. One common way of doing this is by using the American College of Sports Medicine Method.

To obtain cardiovascular fitness benefits from aerobic exercise, it is recommended that an individual participate in an aerobic activity at least 3-5 times a week for 20-30 minutes per session, although cardiac patients and very sedentary individuals can obtain benefits with shorter periods (15-20 minutes). Generally, training changes occur in 4-6 weeks but can occur in as little as 2 weeks.

The American College of Sports Medicine Method

Using the American College of Sports Medicine Method to calculate one's target heart rate, an individual should subtract his or her age from 220, then multiply by the desired intensity level of the workout. Then divide the answer by 6 for a 10-second pulse count. (The 10-second pulse count is useful for checking whether the target heart rate is being achieved during the workout. One can easily check one's pulse—at the wrist or side of the neck—counting the number of beats in 10 seconds.)

For example, a 20-year-old wishing to exercise at 70% intensity, would employ the following steps:

Maximum Heart Rate	220 - 20 = 200
Target Heart Rate	200 × .70 =140
10-second Pulse Count	140 ÷ 6 =23

To work at the desired level of intensity, this 20-year old would strive for a target heart rate of 140 beats per minute, or a 10-second pulse count of 23.

Food and Nutrition

Food contains proteins, carbohydrates, fats, water, vitamins, and minerals. Nutrition is the way your body takes in and uses these ingredients to maintain proper functioning.

The U.S. Dept. of Health and Human Services and the Dept. of Agriculture issued dietary guidelines Nov. 5, 1990, that were the most specific ever and covered children age 2 and over, as well as adults. Recommended were: (1) no more than 30 percent of calories from fat, or about 67 grams of fat in a 2,000-calorie daily diet; and no more than 10 percent of calories, or 22 grams of fat, from saturated fats; (2) maximum alcohol consumption of about 1 drink a day for women, 2 for men; (3) daily consumption of vegetables of 3-5 servings; fruits, 2-4; pastas, cereals, or breads, 6-11; milk, 2-3; meat, poultry, fish, and eggs, 2-3. (For vegetables, 1 serving equals about 1 cup raw leafy greens or one-half cup other kinds; fruit, 1 medium apple, banana, or orange; grains, 1 slice of bread, 1 cup of pasta, or 1 oz. cereal; milk, 1 cup or 1.5 oz. of cheese; meat and poultry, 2-3 oz. cooked lean beef or chicken without skin.)

Protein

Proteins, composed of amino acids, are indispensable in the diet. They build, maintain, and repair the body. Best sources: eggs, milk, fish, meat, poultry, soybeans, nuts. High-quality proteins such as eggs, meat, or fish supply all 8 amino acids needed in the diet. Plant foods can be combined to meet protein needs as well: whole grain breads and cereals, rice, oats, soybeans, other beans, split peas, and nuts.

Fats

Fats provide energy by furnishing calories to the body, and they also carry vitamins A, D, E, and K. They are the most concentrated source of energy in the diet. Best sources of polyunsaturated and monounsaturated fats: margarine, vegetable/plant oils, nuts. Meats, cheeses, butter, cream, egg yolks, lard are concentrated sources of saturated fats.

Carbohydrates

Carbohydrates provide energy for body function and activity by supplying immediate calories. The carbohydrate group includes sugars, starches, fiber, and starchy vegetables. Best sources: grains, legumes, potatoes, vegetables, fruits.

Water

Water dissolves and transports other nutrients throughout the body, aiding the processes of digestion, absorption, circulation, and excretion. It helps regulate body temperature.

Vitamins

Vitamin A—promotes good eyesight and helps keep the skin and mucous membranes resistant to infection. Best sources: liver, sweet potatoes, carrots, kale, cantaloupe, turnip greens, collard greens, broccoli, fortified milk.

Vitamin B$_1$ (thiamine)—prevents beriberi. Essential to carbohydrate metabolism and health of nervous system. Best sources: pork, enriched cereals, grains, soybeans, and nuts.

Vitamin B$_2$ (riboflavin)—protects skin, mouth, eyes, eyelids, and mucous membranes. Essential to protein and energy metabolism. Best sources: milk, meat, poultry, cheese, broccoli, spinach.

Vitamin B$_6$ (pyridoxine)—important in the regulation of the central nervous system and in protein metabolism. Best sources: whole grains, meats, fish, poultry, nuts, brewers' yeast.

Vitamin B$_{12}$ (cobalamin)—needed to form red blood cells. Best sources: meat, fish, poultry, eggs, dairy products.

Niacin—maintains the health of skin, tongue, and digestive system. Best sources: poultry, peanuts, fish, enriched flour and bread.

Folic acid (folacin)—required for normal blood cell formation, growth, and reproduction and for important chemical reactions in body cells. Best sources: yeast, orange juice, green leafy vegetables, wheat germ, asparagus, broccoli, nuts. Other B vitamins—biotin, pantothenic acid.

Vitamin C (ascorbic acid)—maintains collagen, a protein necessary for the formation of skin, ligaments, and bones. It helps heal wounds and mend fractures and aids in resisting some types of viral and bacterial infections. Best sources: citrus fruits and juices, cantaloupe, broccoli, brussels sprouts, potatoes and sweet potatoes, tomatoes, cabbage.

Vitamin D—important for bone development. Best sources: sunlight, fortified milk and milk products, fish-liver oils, egg yolks.

Vitamin E (tocopherol)—helps protect red blood cells. Best sources: vegetable oils, wheat germ, whole grains, eggs, peanuts, margarine, green leafy vegetables.

Vitamin K—necessary for formation of prothrombin, which helps blood to clot. Also made by intestinal bacteria. Best dietary sources: green leafy vegetables, tomatoes.

Minerals

Calcium—the most abundant mineral in the body, works with phosphorus in building and maintaining bones and teeth. Best sources: milk and milk products, cheese, black-strap molasses, tofu.

Phosphorus—the 2d most abundant mineral, performs more functions than any other mineral, and plays a part in nearly every chemical reaction in the body. Best sources: cheese, milk, meats, poultry, fish, tofu.

Iron—Necessary for the formation of myoglobin, which is a reservoir of oxygen for muscle tissue, and hemoglobin, which transports oxygen in the blood. Best sources: lean meats, beans, green leafy vegetables, shellfish, enriched breads and cereals, whole grains.

Other minerals—chromium, cobalt, copper, fluorine, iodine, magnesium, manganese, molybdenum, potassium, selenium, sodium, sulfur, and zinc.

Nutritive Value of Food (Calories, Proteins, etc.)

Source: *Home and Garden Bulletin No. 72*; available from Supt. of Documents, U.S. Government Printing Office, Washington, DC 20402

Food	Measure	Grams	Food Energy (calories)	Protein (grams)	Fat (grams)	Saturated fats (grams)	Carbohydrate (grams)	Calcium (milligrams)	Iron (milligrams)	Sodium (milligrams)	Vitamin A (I.U.)	Ascorbic Acid (milligrams)
Dairy products												
Cheese, cheddar, cut pieces	1 oz.	28	115	7	9	6.0	T	204	0.2	176	300	0
Cheese, cottage, small curd	1 cup	210	215	26	9	6.0	6	126	0.3	850	340	T
Cheese, cream	1 oz.	28	100	2	10	6.2	1	23	0.3	84	400	0
Cheese, Swiss	1 oz.	28	95	7	7	4.5	1	219	0.2	388	230	0
Half-and-half	1 tbsp.	15	20	T	2	1.1	1	16	T	6	70	T
Cream, sour	1 tbsp.	12	25	T	3	1.6	1	14	T	6	90	T
Milk, whole	1 cup	244	150	8	8	5.1	11	291	0.1	120	310	2
Milk, nonfat (skim)	1 cup	245	85	8	T	0.3	12	302	0.1	126	500	2
Milkshake, chocolate	10 oz.	283	355	9	8	4.8	60	374	0.9	314	240	0
Ice cream, hardened	1 cup	133	270	5	14	8.9	32	176	0.1	116	540	1
Sherbet	1 cup	193	270	2	4	2.4	59	103	0.3	88	190	4
Yogurt, fruit-flavored	8 oz.	227	230	10	2	1.6	43	345	0.2	133	100	1
Eggs												
Fried in margarine	1	46	90	6	7	1.9	1	25	0.7	162	390	0
Hard-cooked	1	50	75	6	5	1.6	1	25	0.6	62	280	0
Scrambled (milk added) in margarine	1	61	100	7	7	2.2	1	44	0.7	171	420	T
Fats & oils												
Butter, salted	1 tbsp.	14	100	T	11	7.1	T	3	T	116	430	0
Margarine, salted	1 tbsp.	14	100	T	11	2.2	T	4	T	132	460	T
Olive oil	1 tbsp.	14	125	0	14	1.9	0	0	0	0	0	0
Salad dressing, blue cheese	1 tbsp.	15	75	1	8	1.5	1	12	T	164	30	T
Salad dressing, French, regular	1 tbsp.	16	85	T	9	1.4	1	2	T	188	T	T
Salad dressing, French, low calorie	1 tbsp.	16	25	T	2	0.2	2	6	T	306	T	T
Salad dressing, Italian	1 tbsp.	15	80	T	9	1.3	1	1	T	162	30	T
Mayonnaise	1 tbsp.	14	100	T	11	1.7	T	3	0.1	80	40	0
Fish, meat, poultry												
Clams, raw, meat only	3 oz.	85	65	11	1	0.3	2	59	2.6	102	90	9
Crabmeat, canned	1 cup	135	135	23	3	0.5	1	61	1.1	1,350	50	0
Fish sticks, frozen, reheated	1 fish stick	28	70	6	3	0.8	4	11	0.3	53	20	0
Salmon canned (pink), solids and liquid	3 oz.	85	120	17	5	0.9	0	167	0.7	443	60	0
Sardines, Atlantic, canned in oil, drained solids	3 oz.	85	175	20	9	2.1	0	371	2.6	425	190	0
Shrimp, French fried	3 oz.	85	200	16	10	2.5	11	61	2.0	384	90	0
Trout, broiled, with butter and lemon juice	3 oz.	85	175	21	9	4.1	T	26	1.0	122	230	1
Tuna, canned in oil	3 oz.	85	165	24	7	1.4	0	7	1.6	303	70	0
Bacon, broiled or fried crisp	3 slices	19	110	6	9	3.3	T	2	0.3	303	0	6
Ground beef, broiled, regular	3 oz.	85	245	20	18	6.9	0	9	2.1	70	T	0
Roast beef, relatively lean (lean only)	2.6 oz.	75	135	22	5	1.9	0	3	1.5	46	T	0
Beef steak, lean and fat	3 oz.	85	240	23	15	6.4	0	9	2.6	53	T	0
Beef & vegetable stew	1 cup	245	220	16	11	4.4	15	29	2.9	292	5,690	17
Lamb, chop, broiled loin, lean and fat	2.8 oz.	80	235	22	16	7.3	0	16	1.4	62	T	0
Liver, beef, fried	3 oz.	85	185	23	7	2.5	7	9	5.3	90	30,690	23
Ham, light cure, roasted, lean and fat	3 oz.	85	205	18	14	5.1	0	6	0.7	1,009	0	0
Pork, chop, broiled, lean and fat	3.1 oz.	87	275	24	19	7.0	0	3	0.7	61	10	T
Bologna	2 slices	57	180	7	16	6.1	2	7	0.9	581	0	12
Frankfurter, pork, cooked	1	45	145	5	13	4.8	1	5	0.5	504	0	12
Sausage, pork link, cooked	1 link	13	50	3	4	1.4	T	4	0.2	168	0	T
Veal, cutlet, braised or broiled	3 oz.	85	185	23	9	4.1	0	9	0.8	56	T	0
Chicken, drumstick, fried, bones removed	2.5 oz.	72	195	16	11	3.0	6	12	1.0	194	60	0
Chicken, roasted, half breast, without skin	3 oz.	86	140	27	3	0.9	0	13	0.9	64	20	0
Turkey, roasted, chopped light and dark meat	1 cup	140	240	41	7	2.3	0	35	2.5	98	0	0
Frankfurter, chicken, cooked	1	45	115	6	9	2.5	3	43	0.9	616	60	0
Fruits & fruit products												
Apple, raw, 2-3/4 in. diam.	1	138	80	T	T	0.1	21	10	0.2	T	70	8
Apple juice	1 cup	248	115	T	T	T	29	17	0.9	7	T	2
Apricots, raw	3	106	50	1	T	T	12	15	0.6	1	2,770	11
Banana, raw	1	114	105	1	1	0.2	27	7	0.4	1	90	10
Cherries, sweet, raw	10	68	50	1	1	0.1	11	10	0.3	T	150	5
Cranberry juice cocktail, sweetened	1 cup	253	145	T	T	T	38	8	0.4	10	10	108
Fruit cocktail, canned, in heavy syrup	1 cup	255	185	1	T	T	48	15	0.7	15	520	5
Grapefruit, raw, medium, white	1/2	120	40	1	T	T	10	14	0.1	T	10	41
Grapes, Thompson seedless	10	50	35	T	T	0.1	9	6	0.1	1	40	5
Lemonade, frozen, unsweetened	6 oz.	244	55	1	1	0.1	16	20	0.3	2	30	77
Cantaloupe, 5-in. diam.	1/2	267	95	2	1	0.1	22	29	0.6	24	8,610	113
Orange, 2-5/8 in. diam.	1	131	60	1	T	T	15	52	0.1	T	270	70
Orange juice, frozen, diluted	1 cup	249	110	2	T	T	27	22	0.2	2	190	97
Peach, raw, 2-1/2 in. diam.	1	87	35	1	T	T	10	4	0.1	T	470	6
Raisins, seedless	1 cup	145	435	5	1	0.2	115	71	3.0	17	10	5
Strawberries, whole	1 cup	149	45	1	1	T	10	21	0.6	1	40	84
Watermelon, 4 by 8 in. wedge	1 piece	482	155	3	2	0.3	35	39	0.8	10	1,760	46
Grain products												
Bagel, plain	1	68	200	7	2	0.3	38	29	1.8	245	0	0
Biscuit, 2 in. diam., from home recipe	1	28	100	2	5	1.2	13	47	0.7	195	10	T
Bread, pita, enriched, white, 6-1/2 in. diam	1 pita	60	165	6	1	0.1	12	15	0.7	124	0	0
Bread, white, enriched	1 slice	25	65	2	1	0.3	12	32	0.7	129	T	T
Bread, whole-wheat	1 slice	28	70	3	1	0.4	13	20	1.0	180	T	T
Oatmeal or rolled oats, without added salt	1 cup	234	145	6	2	0.4	25	19	1.6	2	40	0
Bran flakes (40% bran), added sugar, salt, iron, vitamins	1 oz.	28	90	4	1	0.1	22	14	8.1	264	1,250	0
Corn flakes, added sugar, salt, iron, vitamins	1 oz.	28	110	2	T	T	24	1	1.8	351	1,250	15
Rice, puffed, added iron, thiamine, niacin	1 oz.	28	110	2	T	T	25	4	1.8	340	1,250	15
Wheat, shredded, plain, 1 biscuit or 2/3 cup.	1 oz.	28	100	3	1	0.1	23	11	1.2	3	0	0
Bulgur, uncooked	1 cup	170	600	19	3	1.2	129	49	9.5	7	0	0
Cake, angel food, 1/12 of cake	1	53	125	3	T	T	29	44	0.2	269	0	0
Cupcake, 2-1/2 in. diam., with chocolate icing	1	35	120	2	4	1.8	20	21	0.7	92	50	T

Food	Measure	Grams	Food Energy (calories)	Protein (grams)	Fat (grams)	Saturated fats (grams)	Carbohydrate (grams)	Calcium (milligrams)	Iron (milligrams)	Sodium (milligrams)	Vitamin A (I.U.)	Ascorbic Acid (miligrams)
Plain sheet cake with white, uncooked frosting, 1/9 of cake	1	121	445	4	14	4.6	77	61	1.2	275	240	T
Fruitcake, dark, 1/32 of loaf	1	43	165	2	7	1.5	25	41	1.2	67	50	16
Cake, pound, 1/17 of loaf	1	29	110	2	5	3.0	15	8	0.5	108	160	0
Cheesecake, 1/12 of 9-in. diam. cake	1	92	280	5	18	9.9	26	52	0.4	204	230	5
Brownies, with nuts, from commercial recipe	1	25	100	1	4	1.6	16	13	0.6	59	70	T
Cookies, chocolate chip, from home recipe	4	40	185	2	11	3.9	26	13	1.0	82	20	0
Crackers, graham, 2-1/2 in. squares	2	14	60	1	1	0.4	11	6	0.4	86	0	0
Crackers, saltines	4	12	50	1	1	0.5	9	3	0.5	165	0	0
Danish pastry, round piece	1	57	220	4	12	3.6	26	60	1.1	218	60	T
Doughnut, cake type	1	50	210	3	12	2.8	24	22	1.0	192	20	T
Macaroni, firm stage (hot)	1 cup	130	190	7	1	0.1	39	14	2.1	1	0	0
Muffin, bran, commercial mix	1	45	140	3	4	1.3	24	27	1.7	385	100	0
Muffin, corn, from home recipe	1	45	145	3	5	1.5	21	66	0.9	169	80	T
Noodles, enriched, cooked	1 cup	160	200	7	2	0.5	37	16	2.6	3	110	0
Pie, apple, 1/6 of pie	1	158	405	3	18	4.6	60	13	1.6	476	50	2
Pie, cherry, 1/6 of pie	1	158	410	4	18	4.7	61	22	1.6	480	700	0
Pie, lemon meringue, 1/6 of pie	1	140	355	5	14	4.3	53	20	1.4	395	240	4
Pie, pecan, 1/6 of pie	1	138	575	7	32	4.7	71	65	4.6	305	220	0
Popcorn, air-popped, plain	1 cup	8	30	1	T	T	6	1	0.2	T	10	0
Pretzels, stick	10	3	10	T	T	T	2	1	0.1	48	0	0
Rolls, enriched, brown & serve	1	28	85	2	2	0.5	14	33	0.8	155	T	T
Rolls, frankfurter & hamburger	1	40	115	3	2	0.5	20	54	1.2	241	T	T
Tortillas, corn	1	30	65	2	1	0.1	13	42	0.6	1	80	0
Legumes, nuts, seeds												
Beans, Black	1 cup	171	225	15	1	0.1	41	47	2.9	1	T	0
Beans, Great Northern, cooked	1 cup	180	210	14	1	0.1	38	90	4.9	13	0	0
Peanuts, roasted in oil, salted	1 cup	145	840	39	71	9.9	27	125	2.8	626	0	0
Peanut butter	1 tbsp.	16	95	5	8	1.4	3	5	0.3	75	0	0
Refried beans, canned	1 cup	290	295	18	3	0.4	51	141	5.1	1,228	0	17
Tofu	1 piece	120	85	9	5	0.7	3	108	2.3	8	0	0
Sunflower seeds, hulled	1 oz.	28	160	6	14	1.5	5	33	1.9	1	10	T
Mixed foods												
Chop suey with beef and pork, home recipe	1 cup	250	300	26	17	4.3	13	60	4.8	1,053	600	33
Enchilada	1	230	235	20	16	7.7	24	97	3.3	1,332	2,720	T
Pizza, cheese, 1/8 of 15 in.-diam. pie	1	120	290	15	9	4.1	39	220	1.6	699	750	2
Spaghetti with meatballs & tomato sauce	1 cup	248	330	19	12	3.9	39	124	3.7	1,009	1,590	22
Sugars & sweets												
Candy, caramels	1 oz.	28	115	1	3	2.2	22	42	0.4	64	T	T
Candy, milk chocolate	1 oz.	28	145	2	9	5.4	16	50	0.4	23	30	T
Fudge, chocolate	1 oz.	28	115	1	3	2.1	21	22	0.3	54	T	T
Gelatin dessert, from prepared powder	1/2 cup	120	70	2	0	0.0	17	2	T	55	0	0
Candy, hard	1 oz.	28	110	0	0	0.0	28	T	0.1	7	0	0
Honey	1 tbsp.	21	65	T	0	0.0	17	1	0.1	1	0	T
Jams & Preserves	1 tbsp.	20	55	T	T	0.0	14	4	0.2	2	T	T
Popsicle, 3 fl. oz.	1	95	70	0	0	0.0	18	0	T	11	0	0
Sugar, white, granulated	1 tbsp.	12	45	0	0	0.0	12	T	T	T	0	0
Vegetables												
Asparagus, spears, cooked from raw	4 spears	60	15	2	T	T	3	14	0.4	2	500	16
Beans, green, from frozen, cuts	1 cup	135	35	2	T	T	8	61	1.1	18	710	11
Broccoli, cooked from raw	1 spear	180	50	5	1	0.1	10	82	2.1	20	2,540	113
Cabbage, raw, coarsely shredded or sliced	1 cup	70	15	1	T	T	4	33	0.4	13	90	33
Carrots, raw, 7-1/2 by 1-1/8 in.	1	72	30	1	T	T	7	19	0.4	25	20,250	7
Cauliflower, cooked, drained, from raw	1 cup	125	30	2	T	T	6	34	0.5	8	20	69
Celery, raw	1 stalk	40	5	T	T	T	1	14	0.2	35	50	3
Collards, cooked from raw	1 cup	190	25	2	T	0.1	5	148	0.8	36	4,220	19
Corn, sweet, yellow, cooked from raw	1 ear	77	85	3	1	0.2	19	2	0.5	13	170	5
Eggplant, cooked, steamed	1 cup	96	25	1	T	T	6	6	0.3	3	60	1
Lettuce, iceberg, chopped	1 cup	55	5	1	T	T	1	10	0.3	5	180	2
Lettuce, looseleaf (such as romaine)	1 cup	56	10	1	T	T	2	38	0.8	5	1,060	10
Mushrooms, raw	1 cup	70	20	1	T	T	3	4	0.9	3	0	2
Onions, raw, chopped	1 cup	160	55	2	T	0.1	12	40	0.6	3	0	13
Peas, green, frozen, cooked	1 cup	160	125	8	T	0.1	23	38	2.5	139	1,070	16
Potatoes, baked, peeled	1	156	145	3	T	T	34	8	0.5	8	0	20
Potatoes, frozen, French fried (oven-heated)	10	50	110	2	4	2.1	17	5	0.7	16	0	5
Potatoes, mashed, milk added	1 cup	210	160	4	1	0.7	37	55	0.6	636	40	14
Potato chips	10	20	105	1	7	1.8	10	5	0.2	94	0	8
Potato salad	1 cup	250	360	7	21	3.6	28	48	1.6	1,323	520	25
Spinach, drained, cooked from raw	1 cup	180	40	5	T	0.1	7	245	6.4	126	14,740	18
Sweet potatoes, baked in skin, peeled	1	114	115	2	T	T	28	32	0.5	11	24,880	28
Tomatoes, raw	1	123	25	1	T	T	5	9	0.6	10	1,390	22
Vegetable juice cocktail, canned	1 cup	242	45	2	T	T	11	27	1.0	883	2,830	67
Miscellaneous												
Beer, regular	12 fl. oz.	360	150	1	0	0.0	13	14	0.1	18	0	0
Gin, rum, vodka, whisky, 86 proof	1-1/2 fl. oz.	42	105	0	0	0.0	T	T	T	T	0	0
Wine, table, white	3-1/2 fl. oz.	102	80	T	0	0.0	3	9	0.3	5	(¹)	0
Cola-type beverage	12 fl. oz.	369	160	0	0	0.0	41	11	0.2	18	0	0
Ginger ale	12 fl. oz.	366	125	0	0	0.0	32	11	0.1	29	0	0
Coffee, brewed	6 fl. oz.	180	T	T	T	T	T	4	T	2	0	0
Tea, brewed	8 fl. oz.	240	T	T	T	T	T	0	T	1	0	0
Catsup	1 tbsp.	15	15	T	T	T	4	3	0.1	156	210	2
Mustard, prepared, yellow	1 tsp.	5	5	T	T	T	T	4	0.1	63	0	T
Olives, canned, green	4 medium	13	15	T	2	0.2	T	8	0.2	312	40	0
Pickles, dill, whole	1	65	5	T	T	T	1	17	0.7	928	70	4
Relish, finely chopped, sweet	1 tbsp.	15	20	T	T	T	5	3	0.1	107	20	1
Soup, tomato, prepared with milk	1 cup	248	160	6	6	2.9	22	159	1.8	932	850	68
Soup, chicken noodle, prepared with water	1 cup	241	75	4	2	0.7	9	17	0.8	1,106	710	T
Soup, green pea, prepared with water	1 cup	250	165	9	3	1.4	27	28	2.0	988	200	2
Soup, vegetarian, prepared with water	1 cup	241	70	2	2	0.3	12	22	1.1	822	3,010	1

T — Indicates trace (¹) — Value not determined. **Note:** Values shown here for these foods may be from several different manufacturers and, therefore, may differ somewhat from the values provided by one source.

Recommended Daily Dietary Allowances

Source: Food and Nutrition Board, Natl. Academy of Sciences—Natl. Research Council; 1989

Age (years) and sex group		Weight (lbs.)	Protein (grams)	Fat soluble vitamins				Water soluble vitamins							Minerals						
				Vitamin A*	Vitamin D**	Vitamin E†	Vitamin K (micrograms)	Vitamin C (mg.)	Thiamine (mg.)	Riboflavin (mg.)	Niacin (mg.)‡	Vitamin B6 (mg.)	Folate (micrograms)	Vitamin B12 (micrograms)	Calcium (mg.)	Phosphorus (mg.)	Magnesium (mg.)	Iron (mg.)	Zinc (mg.)	Iodine (micrograms)	Selenium (micrograms)
Infants ..	to 5 mos.	13	13	375	7.5	3	5	30	0.3	0.4	5	0.3	25	0.3	400	300	40	6	5	40	10
	to 1 yr.	20	14	375	10	4	10	35	0.4	0.5	6	0.6	35	0.5	600	500	60	10	5	50	15
Children .	1-3	29	16	400	10	6	15	40	0.7	0.8	9	1.0	50	0.7	800	800	80	10	10	70	20
	4-6	44	24	500	10	7	20	45	0.9	1.1	12	1.1	75	1.0	800	800	120	10	10	90	20
	7-10	62	28	700	10	7	30	45	1.0	1.2	13	1.4	100	1.4	800	800	170	10	10	120	30
Males ...	11-14	99	45	1000	10	10	45	50	1.3	1.5	17	1.7	150	2.0	1200	1200	270	12	15	150	40
	15-18	145	59	1000	10	10	65	60	1.5	1.8	20	2.0	200	2.0	1200	1200	400	12	15	150	50
	19-24	160	58	1000	10	10	70	60	1.5	1.7	19	2.0	200	2.0	1200	1200	350	10	15	150	70
	25-50	174	63	1000	5	10	80	60	1.5	1.7	19	2.0	200	2.0	800	800	350	10	15	150	70
	51+	170	63	1000	5	10	80	60	1.2	1.4	15	2.0	200	2.0	800	800	350	10	15	150	70
Females .	11-14	101	46	800	10	8	45	50	1.1	1.3	15	1.4	150	2.0	1200	1200	280	15	12	150	45
	15-18	120	44	800	10	8	55	60	1.1	1.3	15	1.5	180	2.0	1200	1200	300	15	12	150	50
	19-24	128	46	800	10	8	60	60	1.1	1.3	15	1.6	180	2.0	1200	1200	280	15	12	150	55
	25-50	138	50	800	5	8	65	60	1.1	1.3	15	1.6	180	2.0	800	800	280	15	12	150	55
	51+	143	50	800	5	8	65	60	1.0	1.2	13	1.6	180	2.0	800	800	280	10	12	150	55

* Retinol equivalents. ** Micrograms of cholecalciferol. † Milligrams alpha-tocopherol equivalents. ‡ Niacin equivalents.

Recommended Weight Tables

Source: Metropolitan Life Insurance Co., 1983

Weights for people age 25-59 based on lowest mortality. Weight in lbs. according to frame (in indoor clothing weighing 5 lbs. for men, 3 lbs. for women). Heights include shoes with 1-inch heels.

Men					Women				
Height Feet	Inches	Small Frame	Medium Frame	Large Frame	Height Feet	Inches	Small Frame	Medium Frame	Large Frame
5	2	128-134	131-141	138-150	4	10	102-111	109-121	118-131
5	3	130-136	133-143	140-153	4	11	103-113	111-123	120-134
5	4	132-138	135-145	142-156	5	0	104-115	113-126	122-137
5	5	134-140	137-148	144-160	5	1	106-118	115-129	125-140
5	6	136-142	139-151	146-164	5	2	108-121	118-132	128-143
5	7	138-145	142-154	149-168	5	3	111-124	121-135	131-147
5	8	140-148	145-157	152-172	5	4	114-127	124-138	134-151
5	9	142-151	148-160	155-176	5	5	117-130	127-141	137-155
5	10	144-154	151-163	158-180	5	6	120-133	130-144	140-159
5	11	146-157	154-166	161-184	5	7	123-136	133-147	143-163
6	0	149-160	157-170	164-188	5	8	126-139	136-150	146-167
6	1	152-164	160-174	168-192	5	9	129-142	139-153	149-170
6	2	155-168	164-178	172-197	5	10	132-145	142-156	152-173
6	3	158-172	167-182	176-202	5	11	135-148	145-159	155-176
6	4	162-176	171-187	181-207	6	0	138-151	148-162	158-179

Understanding Food Label Claims

Source: Food Labeling Education Information Center, Beltville, Md.

The federal Nutrition Labeling and Education Act of 1990 requires that manufacturers can make certain claims on processed food labels only if they meet the following definitions:

Sugar

Sugar free: less than 0.5 g per serving

No added sugar; Without added sugar; No sugar added:
- No sugars added during processing or packing, including ingredients that contain sugars (for example, fruit juices, applesauce, or dried fruit).
- Processing does not increase the sugar content above the amount naturally present in the ingredients. (A functionally insignificant increase in sugars is acceptable from the processes used for purposes other than increasing sugar content.)
- The compared food normally contains added sugars.

Reduced sugar: at least 25% less sugar than a compared food

Calories

Calorie free: under 5 calories per serving

Low calorie: 40 calories or less per serving; if the serving is 30 g or less or 2 tablespoons or less, 40 calories or less per 50 g of food

Reduced or Fewer calories: at least 25% fewer calories than a compared food

Fat

Fat free: less than 0.5 g of fat per serving

Saturated fat free: less than 0.5 g of saturated fat per serving, and the level of trans fatty acids does not exceed 1% of total fat

Low fat: 3 g or less per serving and, if the serving is 30 g or less or 2 tbs or less, per 50 g of the food

Low saturated fat: 1 g or less per serving and not more than 15% of calories from saturated fatty acids

Reduced or Less fat: at least 25% less per serving than compared food

Cholesterol

Cholesterol free: less than 2 mg of cholesterol and 2 g or less of saturated fat per serving

Low cholesterol: 20 mg or less and 2 g or less of saturated fat per serving and, if the serving is 30 g or less or 2 tbs or less, per 50 g of the food

Reduced or Less cholesterol: at least 25% less than compared food

Sodium

Sodium free: less than 5 mg per serving

Low sodium: 140 mg or less per serving and, if the serving is 30 g or less or 2 tbs or less, per 50 g of the food

Very low sodium: 35 mg or less per serving and, if the serving is 30 g or less or 2 tbs or less, per 50 g of the food

Reduced or Less sodium: at least 25% less per serving than compared food

Fiber

High fiber: 5 g or more per serving. (Also, must meet low-fat definition, or state level of total fat.)

Good source of fiber: 2.5 g to 4.9 g per serving

More or Added fiber: at least 2.5 g more per serving than reference food

Immunization Schedule for Infants and Children

Source: American Academy of Pediatrics, Aug. 1995

By ensuring that your child gets immunized on schedule, you can provide the best defense against dangerous childhood diseases. Childhood immunization means protection from 10 major diseases: hepatitis B, polio, measles, mumps, rubella (German measles), pertussis (whooping cough), diphtheria, tetanus (lockjaw), chickenpox, and *Haemophilus influenzae* type b (a bacterium that can cause such serious infections as meningitis and pneumonia). In 1995 the Food and Drug Administration approved the chickenpox vaccine for use in the U.S. to vaccinate persons against what is currently one of the most common childhood viral infections.

If you do not have a pediatrician, call your local public health department. It usually has supplies of vaccine and may give immunizations free.

	DTP[1]	Polio[2]	Hepatitis B[3]	Measles[4]	Mumps[4]	Rubella[4]	Chicken-pox[5]	Hib[6]	Tetanus-Diphtheria[7]
Birth-2 months			X						
2-4 months			X						
2 months	X	X						X	
4 months	X	X						X	
6 months	X							X	
6-18 months		X	X						
12-15 months				X	X	X		X	
12-18 months	X						X		
4-6 years	X	X		X or	X or	X or			
11-12 years			X	X	X	X	X		X
14-16 years									X

(1) For the best possible protection against diphtheria, tetanus, and pertussis, your child needs a series of five shots of the combination diphtheria-tetanus-pertussis (DTP) vaccine. The first three doses should be given at 2, 4, and 6 months of age. The fourth dose may be given at 12 to 18 months of age, provided the child has received the third dose of DTP six months prior to recieving the fourth dose. A fifth booster dose should be given before school entry (4 to 6 years). After the child has reached 15 months of age, the acellular (DTaP) vaccine may be substituted for the DTP vaccine.

(2) For protection against polio, your child needs a series of four oral polio vaccine doses, the first three at 2, 4, and 6 to 18 months and the final dose before school entry (4 to 6 years).

(3) Infants of mothers with positive blood tests for hepatitis B must receive both the hepatitis B immune globulin (HBIG) and either the Recombivax or the Engerix-B vaccine within 12 hours of birth. In these infants, the second dose is recommended at 1 month and a third hepatitis B vaccine injection at 6 months of age. To be completely protected against hepatitis B, infants born to hepatitis B-negative mothers also need to be vaccinated with a series of three hepatitis B virus (HBV) vaccine shots. The American Academy of Pediatrics recommends that these immunizations be given at birth to 2 months, at 2 to 4 months, and at 6 to 18 months of age (with at least a one-month lapse between doses). Adolescents who have not previously received 3 doses of the vaccine should initiate or complete the 3-dose series at 11-12 years of age.

(4) At 12 to 15 months, your child should have an immunization for measles, mumps, and rubella (the combined MMR vaccine). A second MMR vaccination, primarily to boost measles and mumps immunity, should be given to children either at 4 to 6 years or at 11 to 12 years, consistent with state school or public health authority immunization requirements.

(5) The varicella zoster virus vaccine (VZV) is routinely recommended at 12 to 18 months of age to prevent chickenpox. Children who have not been vaccinated previously and who lack a reliable history of chickenpox should be vaccinated by 13 years of age. VZV can be adminstered to susceptible children any time after 12 months of age. Persons 13 years of age and older should receive two doses of the vaccine 4 to 8 weeks apart.

(6) Several vaccines are available for protection against *Haemophilus influenzae* type b (Hib). However, only three vaccines—HbOC, PRP-T, and PRP-OMP—are approved for children under 15 months of age. The Academy recommends that your child receive either the HbOC or the PRP-T vaccine at 2, 4, and 6 months of age or the PRP-OMP vaccine at 2 and 4 months. Any licensed Hib conjugate vaccine may be used as a booster dose at 12-15 months.

(7) The tetanus and diptheria toxoids (Td) vaccine is recommended at 11-12 years and 14-16 years (must be 5 years from last booster dose of DTP). Repeat every 10 years throughout life.

Some Benefits of Quitting Smoking

Source: American Cancer Society, phone: (800) 227-2345; U.S. Centers for Disease Control and Prevention

Within 20 Minutes
• Blood pressure drops to normal
• Pulse rate drops to normal
• Body temperature of hands and feet increases to normal
Within 8 Hours
• Carbon monoxide level in blood drops to normal
• Oxygen level in blood increases to normal
Within 24 Hours
• Chance of heart attack decreases
Within 48 Hours
• Nerve endings start regrowing
• Ability to smell and taste is enhanced
Within 2 Weeks to 3 Months
• Circulation improves
• Walking becomes easier
• Lung function increases up to 30 percent
Within 1 to 9 Months
• Coughing, sinus congestion, fatigue, shortness of breath decrease

• Cilia regrow in lungs, increasing ability to handle mucus, clean the lungs, reduce infection
• Body's overall energy increases
Within 1 Year
• Excess risk of coronary heart disease is half that of a smoker
Within 5 Years
• Lung cancer death rate for average former smoker (one pack a day) decreases by almost half
• Stroke risk is reduced to that of a nonsmoker 5-15 years after quitting
• Risk of cancer of the mouth, throat, and esophagus is half that of a smoker's
Within 10 Years
• Lung cancer death rate similar to that of nonsmokers
• Precancerous cells are replaced
• Risk of cancer of the mouth, throat, esophagus, bladder, kidney, and pancreas decreases
Within 15 Years
• Risk of coronary heart disease is that of a nonsmoker

Cancer's 7 Warning Signals*

Source: American Cancer Society, 1599 Clifton Road NE, Atlanta, GA 30329-4251; phone: (800) 227-2345

1. A change in bowel or bladder habits.
2. A sore that does not heal.
3. Unusual bleeding or discharge.
4. Thickening or lump in breast or elsewhere.

5. Indigestion or difficulty in swallowing.
6. Obvious change in wart or mole.
7. Nagging cough or hoarseness.
*If you have a warning signal, see your doctor.

Cancer Prevention

Source: American Cancer Society, 1599 Clifton Road NE, Atlanta, GA 30329-4251; phone: (800) 227-2345

PRIMARY PREVENTION: steps that can be taken to avoid those factors that might lead to the development of cancer.

Smoking — Cigarette smoking is responsible for 90% of lung cancer cases among men, 79% among women— about 87% overall. Smoking accounts for about 30% of all cancer deaths. Those who smoke two or more packs of cigarettes a day have lung cancer mortality rates 12-25 times greater than nonsmokers.

Nutrition — Risk for colon, breast, gallbladder, ovarian, prostate, and uterine cancers increases in obese people. High-fat diets may contribute to the development of certain cancers, particularly those of the breast, colon, and prostate. High-fiber foods may help reduce risk of colon cancer. A varied diet containing plenty of vegetables and fruits rich in vitamins A and C may reduce risk for many cancers. Salt-cured, smoked, and nitrite-cured foods have been linked to esophageal and stomach cancer.

Sunlight — Almost all of the more than 800,000 cases of non-melanoma skin cancer diagnosed each year in the U.S. are sun-related. Epidemiological evidence shows that sun exposure is a major factor in the development of melanoma, and the incidence increases for those living near the equator.

Alcohol — Oral cancer and cancers of the larynx, throat, esophagus, and liver occur more frequently among heavy drinkers of alcohol, especially when accompanied by cigarette smoking or use of chewing tobacco.

Smokeless Tobacco — Use of chewing tobacco or snuff increases risk of cancers of the mouth, larynx, throat, and esophagus.

Estrogen — Estrogen treatment to control menopausal symptoms can increase risk of endometrial cancer. However, including progesterone in estrogen replacement therapy helps to minimize this risk. Use of estrogen by menopausal women needs careful discussion by the woman and her physician, while research continues.

Radiation — Excessive exposure to ionizing radiation can increase cancer risk. Most medical and dental X rays are adjusted to deliver the lowest dose possible without sacrificing image quality. Excessive radon exposure in the home may increase lung cancer risk, especially in cigarette smokers. If levels are found to be too high, remedial actions should be taken.

Occupational Hazards — Exposure to several different industrial agents (including nickel, chromate, asbestos, and vinyl chloride) increases risk of various cancers. Risk of lung cancer from asbestos is greatly increased when combined with smoking.

SECONDARY PREVENTION: steps to be taken to diagnose a cancer or precursor as early as possible after it has developed.

Colorectal Tests — The ACS recommends 3 tests for the early detection of colon and rectum cancer in people without symptoms: The digital rectal examination performed by a physician during an office visit, every year after the age of 40; the stool blood test, every year after 50; and the proctosigmoidoscopy examination, every 3 to 5 years after age 50, based on the advice of a physician.

Pap Test — For cervical cancer, women who are or have been sexually active, or have reached 18 years, should have an annual Pap test and pelvic examination. After a woman has had 3 or more consecutive satisfactory normal exams, the Pap test may be performed less frequently at the discretion of her physician.

Breast Cancer Detection — The ACS recommends monthly breast self-examination by women 20 years and older. Examination of the breast by a health-care professional should be done every 3 years from ages 20 to 40, and then every year for women over 40. The ACS recommends a mammogram every year for asymptomatic women age 50 and over. Women age 40-49 should have mammography every 1-2 years, depending on physical and mammographic findings. It is also recommended that women have at least one mammogram prior to age 40.

Prostate Cancer Detection — For early detection of prostate cancer, the ACS recommends that men over age 40 should have an annual digital rectal examination. After age 50, men should have an annual prostate-specific antigen blood test.

Diabetes

Source: American Diabetes Association, 1660 Duke St., Alexandria, VA 22314; phone: (800) 232-3472

Diabetes is a chronic disease in which the body does not produce or properly use insulin, a hormone that is needed to convert sugar, starches, and other foods into energy needed for daily life. Both genetics and environment appear to play roles in the onset of the disease. Diabetes, which has no cure, is the 4th-leading cause of death by disease in the U.S. In 1995, more than 160,000 Americans will die from the disease and its related complications.

There are two major types of diabetes:

Insulin dependent (type I)—The body produces very little or no insulin; disease most often begins in childhood or early adulthood. People with type I diabetes must take daily insulin injections to stay alive.

Non-insulin dependent (type II)—The body does not produce enough or cannot properly use insulin. It is the most common form of the disease (90-95% of cases in people over age 20) and often begins later in life.

Warning Signs of Diabetes

Type I Diabetes (usually occur suddenly):
- frequent urination
- unusual thirst
- extreme hunger
- unusual weight loss
- extreme fatigue
- irritability

Type II Diabetes (occur less suddenly):
- any type I symptoms
- frequent infections
- blurred vision
- cuts/bruises slow to heal
- tingling/numbness in hands or feet
- recurring skin, gum, or bladder infections

Complications of Diabetes

More than half of all individuals with diabetes do not know that they have the disease until one of its life-threatening complications occurs. Potential complications include:

Blindness. Diabetes is the leading cause of blindness in people ages 25-74. Each year, from 15,000 to 39,000 people lose their sight because of diabetes.

Kidney disease. Ten percent of all people with diabetes develop kidney disease. In 1990, more than 13,000 people initiated treatment for end-stage renal disease (kidney failure) because of diabetes.

Amputations. Diabetes is the most frequent cause of nontraumatic lower limb amputations. The risk of a leg amputation is 27.7 times greater for a person with diabetes than for the average American. Each year, 54,000 people lose a foot or leg to complications brought on by diabetes.

Heart disease and stroke. People with diabetes are 2 to 4 times more likely to have heart disease (more than 77,000 deaths due to heart disease annually). And they are 5 times more likely to suffer a stroke (more than 11,000 diabetes-related stroke deaths each year).

Health-care and related costs for the treatment of the disease, as well as the cost of lost productivity, total nearly $92 billion annually in the U.S.

Alzheimer's Disease

Source: Alzheimer's Association, 919 N Michigan Ave., Suite 1000, Chicago, IL 60611-1676; phone: (800) 272-3900

Alzheimer's disease is a progressive, degenerative disease of the brain in which brain cells die and are not replaced. It results in impaired memory, thinking, and behavior, and is the most common form of dementing illness. The debilitating nature of the disease renders patients susceptible to infections (such as pneumonia and urinary tract infections) as they become emaciated, incontinent, immobile, or enter a persistant vegetative state.

Alzheimer's disease afflicts an estimated 4 million Americans, striking equally among men and women of all races. Although most people diagnosed with Alzheimer's are older than age 60, the disease can occur in people in their 40s and 50s. Ten percent of those 65 years of age or older, and almost half of those over age 85, have the disease. It is estimated that the cost of diagnosis, treatment, and long-term care for patients with the disease costs American society $80 billion per year.

The rate of the progression of Alzheimer's disease from the onset of symptoms until death ranges from 3 to 20 years; the average is 8 years. Eventually persons with Alzheimer's disease become totally incapable of caring for themselves.

Diagnosis is complicated by the lack of a single, simple test to identify the disease. Through a series of diagnostic tests by a qualified physician, possible causes of symptoms, such as depression, drug interactions, nutrient imblances, or other forms of dementia, such as those associated with stroke, Huntington's disease, Parkinson's disease, Pick's disease, and infections (AIDS, meningitis, syphilis) are ruled out, yielding a diagnosis (by process of elimination) that is 80-90% accurate. A definitive diagnosis is possible only with a brain biopsy or an autopsy.

No treatment has proven successful in reversing the course of the disease, and providing care for patients with Alzheimer's disease is very physically and psychologically demanding. Nearly 70% of those afflicted with Alzheimer's disease live at home and are cared for by family and friends. In the last stages of the disease, it is often necessary for those afflicted to be cared for in a nursing home. Nearly half of all nursing home patients in the United States suffer from Alzheimer's disease.

People with Alzheimer's disease need a safe, stable environment and should maintain a regular daily schedule. Physical exercise and social activity are important, as is proper nutrition. A medical bracelet identifying the person's name and his or her condition may be helpful in case the person wanders away and becomes disoriented.

The causes of Alzheimer's disease are unknown.

Warning Signs

- Recent memory loss that affects job performance
- Inability to learn new information
- Difficulty with everyday tasks such as cooking or dressing
- Inability to remember simple words
- Use of inappropriate words when communicating
- Disorientation of time and place
- Poor or decreased judgment
- Problems with abstract thinking
- Misplacing objects in inappropriate places
- Rapid changes in mood or behavior
- Increased irritability, anxiety, depression, confusion, and restlessness
- Prolonged loss of initiative

State Laws Regarding the Care of the Critically Ill

Source: Choice In Dying, Inc., 200 Varick Street, 10th Floor, New York, NY 10014-4810; phone: (800) 989-9455; Copyright © 1995

(The specifics of each state's legislation vary)

Living wills authorized—Washington, DC, and all states, except MA, MI, and NY.

Appointment of a health care agent authorized—Washington, DC, and all states, except AL and AK.

Surrogate decisionmaking in the absence of advance directive allowed—AZ, AR, CO, CT, FL, IL, IN, IA, KY, LA, ME, MD, MT, NV, NM, NC, OH, OR, SC, TX, UT, VA, WV, WY, and Washington, DC.

Nonhospital do-not-resuscitate orders authorized—AK, AZ, AR, CA, CO, CT, FL, GA, HI, ID, IL, KS, KY, MD, MT, NM, NY, PA, RI, SC, TN, TX, UT, VA, WA, WV, and WY.

Individuals permitted to refuse artificial nutrition and hydration in their living wills—AK, AZ[1], CA, CO, CT, GA, HI, ID, IL[2], IN, IA, KY, LA, ME, MD, MN, NV, NJ, NH, NM, NC, ND, OH, OK, OR, PA, RI, SC, SD, TN, UT, VA, WA, WI, and WY

Artificial nutrition and hydration required except in very limited circumstances—MO[3]

Health care agents permitted to order the withholding or withdrawal of artificial nutrition and hydration—AZ, CO, CT, GA, HI, ID, IL, IN, IA, KY, LA, MD, MN, MO, NE, NV, NH, NJ, NM, NY, NC, OH, OK, OR, PA, SC, SD, TN, UT, VA, VT, WA, and WI.

Statutes recognize living will documents executed in other states—AK, AZ, AR, CA, FL, HI, IL, IA, LA, ME, MD, MN, MT, NE, NV, NH, NJ, ND, OH, OK, OR, RI, SC, SD, TN, UT, VA, WA, and WV

Statutes recognize health care agents appointed in documents executed in other states—AZ, AR, CA, CO, FL, IN, IA, KS, ME, MD, MA, MN, NE, NH, NJ, NY, ND, OH, OK, OR, RI, SC, TN, TX, UT, VT, VA, WA, and WV.

Statutes define death to include brain death—Washington, DC, and all states, except MA, NY, and WA[4].

(1) The authority to withhold or withdraw artificial nutrition and hydration is explicitly mentioned only in the sample document, not in the text of the Arizona statute. (2) Artificial nutrition and hydration cannot be withheld or withdrawn if the resulting death is due to starvation or dehydration. (3) The medical power of attorney statute in Missouri permits appointed agents to refuse artificial nutrition and hydration on behalf of the principal. (4) Massachusetts and Washington have case law that defines death to include brain death. New York has state regulations that define death to include brain death.

Heart and Blood Vessel Disease

Source: American Heart Association, 7272 Greenville Ave., Dallas, TX 75231-4596; phone: (800) 242-8721

Warning Signs

Of Heart Attack
• Uncomfortable pressure, fullness, squeezing, or pain in the center of the chest lasting two minutes or longer
• Pain may radiate to the shoulder, arm, neck, or jaw
• Sweating may accompany pain or discomfort
• Nausea and vomiting may also occur
• Shortness of breath, dizziness, or fainting may accompany other signs
The American Heart Association advises immediate action at the onset of these symptoms. The association points

out that more than half of heart attack victims die before they reach the hospital and that the average victim waits 2 hours before seeking help.
Of Stroke
• Sudden temporary weakness or numbness of face or limbs on one side of the body
• Temporary loss of speech, or trouble speaking or understanding speech
• Temporary dim or lost vision, especially in one eye
• Unexplained dizziness, unsteadiness, or sudden falls

Some Major Risk Factors

Blood pressure—High blood pressure increases the risk of stroke, heart attack, kidney failure, and congestive heart failure.
Cholesterol—A blood cholesterol level over 240 mg/dl (milligrams of cholesterol per deciliter of blood) approximately doubles the risk of coronary heart disease; about 20% of the U.S. adult population (37.8 mln.) falls into this category. Blood cholesterol levels between 200 and 240 mg/dl are in a zone of moderate and increasing risk. An estimated 27.0 mln. (37% of) youths age 19 and under have levels of

170 mg/dl or higher, comparable to a level of 200 mg/dl in adults.
Cigarettes—Cigarette smokers have more than twice the risk of heart attack and 2-4 times the risk of sudden cardiac death as nonsmokers. Young smokers have a higher risk for early death from stroke.
Obesity—61 mln. adults are 20% or more over their desirable weight (32% of white males, 31.5% of black males, 33.5% of white females, 49.6% of black females).

Understanding Blood Pressure

Source: *Empower Yourself: Control the Pressure. . .and Feel Good!,* Coalition for Hypertension Education and Control; American Heart Association

High blood pressure, or hypertension, affects people of all races, sexes, ethnic origins, and ages. There are a variety of causes that can trigger this often symptomless disease. Since hypertension can increase one's risk for stroke, heart attack, kidney failure, and congestive heart failure, it is recommended that individuals have a blood pressure reading at least once every 2 years (more often if advised by a physician).
A blood pressure reading is really two measurements in one. It is recorded as a fraction. The **upper number** **(systolic pressure)** represents the amount of pressure in the blood vessels when the heart contracts (beats) and pushes blood through the circulatory system. The **lower number** **(diastolic pressure)** represents the pressure in the blood vessels between beats, when the heart is resting. According to National Institutes of Health guidelines, normal blood pressure is below 130/85 and "high normal" is between

130/85 and 139/89. High blood pressure is divided into four stages, based on severity:

• **Stage 1 (mild)** high blood pressure ranges from 140/90 to 159/99
• **Stage 2 (moderate)** is from 160/100 to 179/109
• **Stage 3 (severe)** is from 180/110 to 209/119
• **Stage 4 (very severe)** is 210/120 and up

As these numbers climb higher, the condition becomes more serious. The diagnosis of hypertension can be based on either the systolic or the diastolic reading.
High blood pressure is a chronic disorder, which means it usually cannot be cured, but it can be controlled in a variety of ways, including lifestyle modifications and medication. Treatment should be at the direction and under the supervision of a physician.

Where to Get Help

Source: Reprinted from Health & Medical Year Book 1995, "Where to Get Help," pp. 278-283.
Copyright ©1995 by P.F. Collier, L.P. Reprinted by permission of the publisher.

Listed below are some of the major U.S. and Canadian organizations providing information about good health practices generally or about specific conditions and how to deal with them. (Canadian sources are identified as such.) Where a toll-free number is not available, an address is given when possible.

General Sources

Centers for Disease Control and Prevention Voice Information System
404-332-4555
Tape-recorded information about public health topics, such as AIDS, Lyme disease, and chronic fatigue syndrome. Also, you can request to talk with a CDC expert.
National Health Information Center
800-336-4797; in Maryland, 301-565-4167
Phone numbers for more than 1,000 health-related organizations in the United States and offers printed materials.
National Institutes of Health
Bethesda, MD 20892
301-496-4000
Free information, including the latest research findings, on a wide range of diseases.
Tel-Med
Check the phone book for local listings or call Tel-Med headquarters at 909-825-6034
Tape-recorded information on over 600 health topics. Sponsored by local medical societies, health organizations, or hospitals.

Aging

National Association of Area Agencies on Aging's Eldercare Locator
800-677-1116

Information and assistance on a wide range of services and programs including adult day-care and respite services, consumer fraud, hospital and nursing home information, legal services, elder abuse/protective services, Medicaid/Medigap information, tax assistance, and transportation.
National Institute on Aging Information Center
800-222-2225
Information and publications about disabling conditions, support groups, and community resources.

AIDS

AIDS Clinical Trials Information Service
800-874-2572;
for the hearing impaired, 800-243-7012
Information on federally and privately sponsored clinical trials for patients with AIDS or HIV.
Centers for Disease Control and Prevention National AIDS Hotline
800-342-AIDS 24 hours;
in Spanish, 800-344-SIDA;
for the hearing impaired, 800-AIDS-TTY
Information on the prevention and spread of AIDS, along with referrals.
HIV-AIDS Treatment Information Service
800-HIV-0440; to receive directions for accessing the service's computer data base, 800-272-4787.

Treatment information to people with AIDS, their families, and health care providers.

Alcoholism and Drug Abuse

Alcohol and Drug Helpline
800-821-4357
Referrals to local facilities (24 hours).
American Council on Alcoholism
800-527-5344
Treatment referrals and counseling for recovering alcoholics.
National Cocaine Hotline
800-COCAINE
Answers questions about cocaine and other drugs and provides referrals to treatment centers. Operates 24 hours.
National Council on Alcoholism and Drug Dependence Hopeline
800-622-2255
Information on alcoholism and drug dependence and counseling referrals (24 hours).
National Drug Information, Treatment, and Referral Hotline
800-662-HELP; in Spanish, 800-66-AYUDA
Information on drug/alcohol abuse and on HIV/AIDS as they relate to substance abuse. Makes referrals to support groups and treatment programs.

Alzheimer's Disease

Alzheimer's Association
800-621-0379
Referrals to local chapters and support groups; offers information on publications available from the association.
Alzheimer's Society of Canada
1320 Yonge Street, Suite 201
Toronto, ON M4T 1X2
416-925-3552
Phone numbers for local support chapters. Publishes support materials.

Amyotrophic Lateral Sclerosis

ALS Association
800-782-4747; in the San Fernando Valley, 818-340-7500
Information and educational materials about ALS (Lou Gehrig's Disease) and referrals to ALS specialists; also provides referrals to local chapters and support groups.

Arthritis

Arthritis Foundation
800-283-7800
Information, publications, and referrals to local groups.
Arthritis Society (Canada)
250 Bloor Street East, Suite 901
Toronto, ON M4W 3P2
416-967-1414; in Ontario only, 800-361-1112
Phone numbers for local chapters.
National Arthritis and Musculoskeletal and Skin Diseases Information Clearinghouse
301-495-4484
Subject searches and resource referrals.

Asthma and Allergies

Allergy Foundation of Canada
Box 1904, Saskatoon, SK S7K 3S5
306-373-7591
Information.
Asthma and Allergy Foundation Information Clearinghouse
800-7-ASTHMA
A free packet of information, on request.
American Academy of Allergy and Immunology Referral Line
800-822-ASMA
Written information on asthma and allergies. Operates 24 hours.

Blindness and Eye Care

American Council of the Blind
800-424-8666;
in Washington, DC, 202-467-5081
Information on blindness; referrals to clinics and other organizations.
Canadian National Institute for the Blind
1929 Bayview Avenue
Toronto, ON M4G 3E8
416-480-7594 or contact your local chapter
The national office offers training and a library with braille books and audiotapes. Local chapters provide core services: orientation in mobility, sight enhancement, counseling, referrals, and career development.
Foundation Fighting Blindness
800-683-5555; in Maryland, 410-225-9400; for the hearing impaired, 800-683-5551
Answers questions; written materials.
Library of Congress National Service for the Blind and Physically Handicapped
800-424-9100; in Washington, DC, 202-707-5100
Information on libraries that offer talking books and books in braille.
National Association for Parents of the Visually Impaired
800-562-6265
Support and information for parents of individuals who are visually impaired.

Blood Disorders

Cooley's Anemia Foundation
800-522-7222
Information on patient care and support groups; makes referrals to local chapters.
Sickle Cell Disease Association of America
800-421-8453; in California, 310-216-6363
Genetic counseling and information packet.

Burns

Phoenix Society
800-888-2876
Counseling for burn victims and information on self-help services for burn victims and their families.

Cancer

American Cancer Society Response Line
800-ACS-2345

Publications and information about cancer and coping with cancer; makes referrals to local chapters for support services.
Canadian Cancer Society
10 Alcorn Avenue, Suite 200
Toronto, ON M4V 3B1
416-961-7223
Written materials, videos, support services, and referrals.
National Cancer Institute's Cancer Information Service
800-4-CANCER
Information about clinical trials, treatments, and success rates for any type of cancer.
Y-Me Breast Cancer Support Program
800-221-2141;
in Illinois, 312-986-8228, 24 hours
Information and literature on breast cancer, counseling, and referrals.

Cerebral Palsy

Ontario Federation for Cerebral Palsy
1630 Lawrence Avenue West
Toronto, ON M6L 1C5
416-244-8003
Canada does not have a national cerebral palsy organization, but the provincial organizations (which provide information on housing, services, and coping with life) network and provide contact numbers for the others.
United Cerebral Palsy Associations
800-USA-5UCP;
in Washington, DC, 202-776-0406
Written materials.

Child Abuse

Childhelp's USA National Child Abuse Hotline
800-4-A-CHILD
Crisis intervention, professional counseling, referrals to local groups offering counseling and to shelters for runaways, and literature in English and Spanish. Operates 24 hours.
National Center for Missing and Exploited Children
800-843-5678; for the hearing impaired, 800-826-7653; in Arlington, VA, 703-235-3900
Hotline for reporting missing children and sightings of missing children.

Crisis

National Runaway Switchboard
800-621-4000
Crisis intervention and referrals for runaways. Runaways can leave messages for parents, and vice versa. Operates 24 hours.
National Youth Crisis Hotline
800-HIT-HOME
Counseling for youths dealing with drug abuse, pregnancy, molestation, suicide, and child abuse; makes referrals to local drug treatment centers, shelters, and counseling services. Operates 24 hours.

Cystic Fibrosis

Canadian Cystic Fibrosis Foundation
2221 Yonge Street, Suite 601
Toronto, ON M4S 2B4
416-485-9149
Information and brochures, makes referrals to local chapters.
Cystic Fibrosis Foundation
800-FIGHT-CF; in Maryland, 301-951-4422
Answers questions and offers literature and referrals to local clinics.

Diabetes

American Diabetes Association
800-ADA-DISC; in Virginia and Washington, DC, 703-549-1500
Information about diabetes, nutrition, exercise, and treatment and offers referrals to diabetes specialists.
Canadian Diabetes Association
78 Bond Street, Toronto, ON M5B 2J8
416-363-3373; in Ontario only, 800-361-1306
Information and publications.
Juvenile Diabetes Foundation Hotline
800-223-1138 or 800-533-2873;
in New York City, 212-889-7575
Answers questions, provides literature (some in Spanish), and offers referrals to local chapters, physicians, and clinics.

Digestive Diseases

Crohn's Colitis Foundation of Canada
21 St. Clair Avenue E, Suite 301,
Toronto, ON M4T 1L9
416-920-5035; in Canada only, 800-387-1479
Educational materials.
National Foundation for Ileitis and Colitis
800-932-2432; in New York, 212-685-3440

Educational materials; offer referrals to local chapters which then provide referrals to support groups and physicians.

Disabilities

National Association for the Craniofacially Handicapped
P.O. Box 11082, Chattanooga, TN 37401
615-266-1632
Information on treatment centers, support groups, and financial assistance for individuals with severe facial deformities.
National Information Center for Children and Youth With Disabilities
800-695-0285
Information on how to improve the lives of children and youths with disabilities; referrals.
National Information Clearinghouse for Infants With Life-Threatening Conditions and Severe Disabilities
800-922-9234;
in South Carolina, 800-922-1107
Referrals to support groups and to sources of financial, medical, and legal assistance for developmentally disabled and chronically ill children, aged up to three.

Domestic Violence

National Council on Child Abuse and Family Violence
800-222-2000;
in Washington, DC, 202-429-6695
A recording provides 800 numbers to call for information or referrals.

Down Syndrome

National Down Syndrome Congress
800-232-6372; in Georgia, 404-633-1555
Answers questions on all aspects of Down syndrome; referrals to local organizations.
National Down Syndrome Society Hotline
800-221-4602 and 800-221-4601;
in New York City, 212-460-9330
Information; referrals to local programs for newborns.

Dyslexia

Orton Dyslexia Society
800-ABCD-123; in Maryland, 410-296-0232
Information on testing, tutoring, and computers used to aid people with dyslexia and related disorders.

Endometriosis

Endometriosis Association
800-992-ENDO; in Canada, 800-426-2END
A packet of information (24 hours).

Epilepsy

Epilepsy Foundation of America
800-332-1000
Information and referrals to local chapters.

Grief

Grief Recovery Helpline
800-445-4808
Counseling services on coping with loss.

Headaches

National Headache Foundation
800-843-2256; in Illinois, 800-523-8858
Literature on headaches and treatment.
National Institute of Neurological Disorders and Stroke
800-352-9424
Literature, information, and referrals.

Head Injuries

National Head Injury Foundation Family Helpline
800-444-NHIF
Information on living with head injuries.

Heart Disease

American Heart Association
800-242-8721
Information, publications, and referrals to organizations.

Hospices

Children's Hospice International
800-242-4453; in Virginia, 703-684-0330
Information; referrals to children's hospices.
Hospice Education Institute Hospicelink
800-331-1620
General information about hospice care and makes referrals to local programs.

Huntington's Disease

Huntington's Disease Society of America
800-345-4372; in New York, 212-242-1968
Information and referrals to physicians and support groups.
Huntington Society of Canada
P.O. Box 1269,13 Water Street North, Suite 3
Cambridge, ON N1R 7G6
519-622-1002

Information, including telephone numbers of local services, and publications and referrals.

Impotence

Impotence Information Center
800-843-4315
Information on the causes and treatment of impotence.
Impotence Institute of America Hotline
800-669-1603
Written materials, physician referrals, and telephone phone numbers of local Impotents Anonymous chapters.

Kidney Diseases

Kidney Foundation of Canada
10 Alcorn Avenue, Suite 304
Toronto, ON M4V 3B4
416-925-2836; in Ontario only, 800-268-3740
Educational materials and general information.
National Kidney and Urologic Diseases Information Clearinghouse
3 Information Way
Bethesda, MD 20892-3580
301-654-4415
Information about kidney and urologic diseases and referrals to organizations.
National Kidney Foundation
800-622-9010
Information and referrals.

Lead Exposure

National Lead Information Center Hotline
800-LEAD-FYI
Recommendations (in English and Spanish) for reducing a child's exposure to lead. Referrals to state and local agencies.

Liver Diseases

American Liver Foundation
800-223-0179; in New Jersey, 201-256-2550
Information and physician and support group referrals.

Lung Diseases

American Lung Association
Check the phone book for local listings or call the national office at 800-LUNG-USA for automatic connection to the office nearest you. Answers questions about asthma and lung diseases; publications and referrals.
National Jewish Center for Immunology and Respiratory Medicine Information Service
800-222-LUNG; in Denver, 303-355-LUNG
Answers questions on asthma, emphysema, allergies, smoking, and other respiratory and immune system disorders.

Lupus

American Lupus Society Information Line
800-331-1802
A packet of information. Operates 24 hours.
Lupus Foundation of America
800-558-0121;
in Rockville, MD, 301-670-9292
Answers questions; offers literature about lupus; refers to local affiliates.

Mental Health

Canadian Mental Health Association
2160 Yonge Street, 3d floor
Toronto, ON M4S 2Z3
416-484-7750
Information; referrals to regional branches.
D/ART (Depression awareness, recognition, and treatment)
800-421-4211
Information on seasonal affective disorder and other depressive illnesses. Sponsored by the U.S. National Institute of Mental Health. Operates 24 hours.
National Clearinghouse on Family Support and Children's Mental Health
800-628-1696
Publications, computerized databank, and state-by-state resource file (24 hours).
National Depressive and Manic Depressive Association
800-826-3632
Support for patients and families, answers questions, provides publications, and makes referrals to affiliated organizations.
National Foundation for Depressive Illness
800-248-4344
Recorded message describing the symptoms of depression and offering an address for more information and physician referral (24 hours).
National Institute of Mental Health
5600 Fisher's Lane, Room 7C02
Rockville, MD 20857
301-443-4513

Information on a range of topics, from children's mental disorders to schizophrenia, depression, eating disorders, and others.
National Mental Health Association
800-969-6642
Referrals to mental health groups.

Multiple Sclerosis

Multiple Sclerosis Society of Canada
800-268-7582
Counseling, literature, and referrals to local chapters.
National Multiple Sclerosis Society
800-344-4867
A 24-hour recording allows you to request information.

Nutrition

Meat and Poultry Hotline of the U.S. Department of Agriculture's Food, Safety, and Inspection Service
800-535-4555
Information on proper handling, preparation, storage, and cooking of meat, poultry, and eggs.
Nutrition Hotline of the American Dietetic Association
800-366-1655
General information on nutrition, answers questions, and provides literature.
Seafood Hotline of the U.S.Food and Drug Administration (Department of Health and Human Services)
800-FDA-4010;
in Washington, DC, 202-205-4314
Information on how to buy and use seafood products and on their proper handling and storage. Callers may speak to food specialists on Mon. through Fri., 12 noon to 4 PM.

Organ Donation

Living Bank
800-528-2971
A registry and referral service for people wanting to commit organs to transplantation or research. Operates 24 hours.
Organ Donor Hotline
800-24-DONOR
Information and referrals for organ donation and transplantation; handles requests for organ donor cards. Operates 24 hours.

Osteoporosis

National Osteoporosis Foundation
800-223-9994
Free information packet available on request.

Pain

National Chronic Pain Outreach Association
7979 Old Georgetown Road, Suite 100
Bethesda, MD 20814-2429
301-652-4948
Information clearinghouse, makes referrals, and publishes newsletters.

Parkinson's Disease

National Parkinson Foundation
800-327-4545; in Florida, 800-433-7022;
in Miami, 305-547-6666
Answers questions, makes physician referrals, and provides written information in English and Spanish.
Parkinson's Educational Program
800-344-7872
Written materials, information on support groups, and physician referrals (24 hours).
Parkinson Foundation of Canada
800-565-3000
Information; referrals to support groups.

Polio

International Polio Network
5100 Oakland Avenue, #206
St. Louis, MO 63110
314-534-0475
Information on coping with the late effects of polio; referrals to other organizations.

Prostate Problems

Prostate Information Line
800-543-9632
Advice on treatment.

Rehabilitation

National Rehabilitation Information Center
800-34-NARIC; in Maryland, 301-588-9284
Information on rehabilitation and research on disabilities.

Sexually Transmitted Diseases

American Social Health Association's National STD Hotline
800-227-8922
Information; confidential referrals.

Skin Problems

National Psoriasis Foundation
6600 SW 92nd Avenue, Suite 300
Portland, OR 97223
503-244-7404
Information and referrals.
United Scleroderma Foundation
800-722-4673; in California, 408-728-2202
Referrals to local support groups and treatment centers, as well as information on scleroderma and related skin disorders.

Speech and Hearing

American Speech-Language-Hearing Association Helpline
800-638-8255;
in Maryland call collect, 301-897-0039
Materials on speech and language disorders and hearing impairment; referrals.
Canadian Hard of Hearing Association
2435 Holly Lane, Suite 205
Ottawa, ON K1V 7P2
613-526-1584; TTY 613-526-2692; fax 613-526-4718
Publications; answers general questions.
Dial a Hearing Screening Test
800-222-EARS;
in Pennsylvania, 800-345-EARS
Answers questions on hearing problems and makes referrals to local telephone numbers for a two-minute hearing test. Also makes referrals to ear, nose, and throat specialists and to organizations that can provide specialized ear and hearing aid information.
National Center for Stuttering
800-221-2483
in New York State, 212-532-1460
Information on stuttering in all age groups.
National Hearing Aid Helpline
800-521-5247
Information and distributes a directory of hearing aid specialists certified by the International Hearing Society.
Stuttering Foundation of America
800-992-9392
Referrals to speech pathologists, resource lists, and other publications (24 hours).

Spinal Injuries

American Paralysis Association's Spinal Cord Injury Hotline
800-526-3456
Written materials on spinal cord injuries; referrals to organizations and support groups.
National Spinal Cord Injury Association
800-962-9629;
in Massachusetts, 617-441-8500
Peer counseling; referrals to local chapters and other organizations.

Stroke

Heart and Stroke Foundation of Canada
477 Mount Pleasant Road, 4th Floor
Toronto, ON M4S 2L9
416-489-7100 in Toronto; elsewhere contact your local chapter.
Written material and referrals.
National Stroke Association
800-787-6537
Information on support networks for stroke victims and their families; referrals.

Sudden Infant Death Syndrome

American Sudden Infant Death Syndrome Institute
800-232-SIDS; in Georgia, 800-847-7437
Answers questions; literature; referrals to other organizations (24 hours).
National SIDS Foundation
800-221-SIDS; in Maryland, 410-653-8226
Literature on medical information, referrals, and support groups.

Women's Health

National Women's Health Network
514 10th Street NW, Suite 400
Washington, DC 20004
202-347-1140
Information and referrals on more than 70 women's health topics.
National Women's Health Resource Center
2440 M Street NW, Suite 325
Washington, DC 20037
202-293-6045
Information, primarily written materials.

ASSOCIATIONS AND SOCIETIES

Source: World Almanac questionnaire

Arranged according to **key words** in titles. Founding year of organization in parentheses; last figure after ZIP code indicates membership.

Aaron Burr Assn. (1946), 4520 King Edward Ct., Annandale, VA 22003; 220.

Abortion Federation, Natl. (1977), 1436 U St. NW, Ste. 103, Wash., DC 20009; 300 organizations.

Accountants, Amer. Institute of Certified Public (1887), 1211 Ave. of the Americas, N.Y., NY 10036; 318,000.

Accountants, Institute of Management (1919), 10 Paragon Dr., Box 433, Montvale, NJ 07645-1760; 85,000.

Accountants, Natl. Assn. of Enrolled Federal Tax (1960), PO Box 59-009, Chicago, IL 60659-0009; 450.

Accountants for Cooperatives, Natl. Soc. of (1936), 6320 Augusta Dr., Ste. 800, Springfield, VA 22150; 2,000.

Acoustical Society of America (1929), 500 Sunnyside Blvd., Woodbury, NY 11797; 7,000.

Actors' Equity Assn. (1913), 165 W. 46th St., N.Y., NY 10036.

Actors Guild, Screen (1933), 5757 Wilshire Blvd., Los Angeles, CA 90036; 78,000.

Actuaries, Society of (1949), 475 N. Martingale Rd., Ste. 800, Schaumburg, IL 60173-2226; 16,500.

Advertisers, Assn. of Natl. (1911), 155 E. 44th St., N.Y., NY 10017; 200 cos.

Advertising Agencies, Amer. Assn. of (1917), 666 Third Ave., N.Y., NY 10017; 700 agencies.

Aeronautic Assn., Natl. (1905), 1815 N. Fort Myer Dr., Ste. 700, Arlington, VA 22209-1805; 350,000.

Aerospace Industries Assn. of America (1919), 1250 I St. NW, Wash., DC 20005; 53 cos.

African Violet Soc. of America (1946), 2375 North, Beaumont, TX 77702-1722; 12,000.

Afro-American Life and History, Assn. for the Study of (1915), 1407 14th St. NW, Wash., DC 20005; 2,000.

Aging Assn., Amer. (1970), 2129 Providence Ave., Chester, PA 19013-5506; 400.

Agricultural Economics Assn., Amer. (1919), 1110 Buckeye Ave., Ames, IA 50010-8063; 3,858.

Agricultural History Society (1919), Room 928, 1301 New York Ave. NW, Wash., DC 20005-4788; 1,400.

Agronomy, Amer. Society of (1907), 677 S. Segoe Rd., Madison, WI 53717; 12,600.

Aircraft Assn., Experimental (1953), 3000 Poberezny Rd., PO Box 3086, Oshkosh, WI 54903-3086; 150,000.

Aircraft Owners and Pilots Assn. (1939), 421 Aviation Way, Frederick, MD 21701; 335,000.

Air Force Assn. (1946), 1501 Lee Hwy., Arlington, VA 22209.

Air Force Gunners Assn. (1986), 453 Plaza Circle, Bossier City, LA 71111; 1,700.

Air Line Pilots Assn. (1931), 1625 Massachusetts Ave. NW, Wash., DC 20036; 41,000.

Airmen, Assn. of Independent (1989), 1625 Massachusetts Ave. NW, Wash., DC 20036; 3,000.

Air & Waste Management Assn. (1907), One Gateway Center, Pittsburgh, PA 15222; 17,966.

Al-Anon Family Groups (1950), PO Box 862, Midtown Sta., N.Y., NY 10018; 500,000 worldwide.

Alcoholics Anonymous (1935), 475 Riverside Dr., N.Y., NY 10115; more than 2 mil.

Alcoholism and Drug Dependence, Natl. Council on (1944), 12 W. 21st St., N.Y., NY 10010.

Alcohol Problems, Amer. Council on (1895), 3426 Bridgeland Dr., Bridgeton, MO 63044; 36 state affiliates.

Allergy, Asthma, and Immunology, Amer. Academy of (1943), 611 E. Wells St., Milwaukee, WI 53202; 5,000.

Alpha Delta Kappa (1947), 1615 West 92d St., Kansas City, MO 64114; 60,000.

Alpine Club, Amer. (1902), 710 Tenth St., Ste. 100, Golden, CO 80401; 2,000+.

Alzheimer's Assn. (1980), 919 Michigan Ave., Chicago, IL 60611.

Americares Foundation (1982), 161 Cherry St., New Canaan, CT 06840.

Amnesty Intl. USA (1961), 322 Eighth Ave., N.Y., NY 10001.

Amputation Foundation, Natl. (1919), 73 Church St., Malverne, NY 11565; 2,500.

Animals, Amer. Society for Prevention of Cruelty to (ASPCA) (1866), 424 E. 92d St., N.Y., NY 10128; 350,000.

Animals, People for the Ethical Treatment of (1980), PO Box 42516, Wash., DC 20015; 500,000.

Animal Protection Institute of America (1968), 2831 Fruitridge Rd., Sacramento, CA 95822; 75,000.

Animal Welfare Institute (1951), PO Box 3650, Wash., DC 20007; 4,000.

Anthropological Assn., Amer. (1902), 4350 N. Fairfax Dr., Ste. 640, Arlington, VA 22203; 10,505.

Antiquarian Society, Amer. (1812), 185 Salisbury St., Worcester, MA 01609-1634; 558.

Appalachian Mountain Club (1876), 5 Joy St., Boston, MA 02108; 54,952.

Appalachian Trail Conference (1925), Washington & Jackson Sts., Harpers Ferry, WV 25425; 23,000.

Appraisers, Amer. Society of (1936), 555 Herndon Pkwy., Ste. 125, Herndon, VA 22070; 6,500.

Arab Americans, Natl. Assn. of (1972), 1212 New York Ave. NW, Wash., DC 20005.

Arbitration Assn., Amer. (1926), 140 W. 51st St., N.Y., NY 10020-1203; 6,523.

Arc, The (1950), 500 E. Border St., Ste. 300, Arlington, TX 76010; 140,000.

Archaeological Institute of America (1879), 656 Beacon St., 4th floor, Boston, MA 02215-2010; 10,000.

Archaeology, Institute of Nautical (1972), PO Drawer HG, College Station, TX 77841-5137; 1,950.

Archery Assn., Natl. (1879), One Olympic Plaza, Colorado Springs, CO 80909; 4,000.

Architects, Amer. Institute of (1857), 1735 New York Ave. NW, Wash., DC 20006; 55,000.

Architectural Historians, Society of (1940), 1232 Pine St., Philadelphia, PA 19107-5944; 4,000.

Armed Forces Communications and Electronics Assn. (1946), 4400 Fair Lakes Ct., Fairfax, VA 22033; 40,000.

Army, Assn. of the United States (1950), 2425 Wilson Blvd., Arlington, VA 22201-3385; 117,000.

Arthritis Foundation (1948), 1314 Spring St. NW, Atlanta, GA 30309; 300,000.

Arts, Amer. Council for the (1960), One E. 53d Street, N.Y., NY 10022-4201; 1,500.

Arts, Amer. Federation of (1909), 41 E. 65th St., N.Y., NY 10021; 520+ museums/inst.

Arts and Letters, American Academy of (1898), 633 W. 155 St., N.Y., NY 10032-7599; 250.

Arts and Letters, Natl. Society of (1944), 655 15th St. NW, Wash., DC 20005; 1,600.

Arts and Sciences, Amer. Academy of (1780), Norton's Woods, 136 Irving St., Cambridge, MA 02138; 633.

Association Executives, Amer. Society of (1920), 1575 I St. NW, Wash., DC 20005; 18,000.

Astrologers, Inc., Amer. Federation of (1938), PO Box 22040, Tempe, AZ 85285; 3,000+.

Astronautical Society, Amer. (1954), 6352 Rolling Mill Pl., Ste. 102, Springfield, VA 22152; 1,500.

Astronomical Society, Amer. (1899), 2000 Florida Ave. NW, Ste. 400, Wash., DC 20009; 6,200.

Ataxia Foundation, Natl. (1957), 15500 Wayzata Blvd., Ste. 750, Wayzata, MN 55391; 7,500.

Atheists, Amer. (1963), PO Box 140195, Austin, TX 78714.

Athletic Assn., Natl. Junior College (1938), PO Box 7305, Colorado Springs, CO 80918-7305; 520+.

Athletic Associations, Natl. Federation of State H. S. (1920), 11724 Plaza Circle, Box 20626, Kansas City, MO 64195.

Athletics, Natl. Assn. of Intercollegiate (1940), 6120 S. Yale Ave., Ste. 1450, Tulsa, OK 74136; 392 schools.

Athletic Union of the U.S., Amateur (1888), 3600 W. 86th St., Indianapolis, IN 46268; 300,000.

Auctioneers Assn., Natl. (1949), 8880 Ballentine, Overland Park, KS 66214; 5,800.

Audubon Society, Natl. (1905), 700 Broadway, N.Y., NY 10003; 538,151.

Authors Guild, Inc., The (1913), 330 W. 42d St., 29th Fl., N.Y., NY 10036; 6,500.

Authors League of America (1912), 234 W. 44th St., N.Y., NY 10036; 15,000.

Autism Society of America (1965), 7910 Woodmont Ave., Ste. 650, Bethesda, MD 20814; 17,000.

Autograph Collectors Club, Universal (1965), PO Box 6181, Wash., DC 20044-6181; 2,000.

Automobile Assn., Amer. (1902), 1000 AAA Dr., Heathrow, FL 32779; 37 mil.

Automobile Club of America, Antique (1935), 501 W. Governor Rd., Hershey, PA 17033; 53,000.

Automobile Dealers Assn., Natl. (1917), 8400 Westpark Dr., McLean, VA 22102; 19,000.

Automobile License Plate Collectors Assn. (1954), PO Box 77, Horner, WV 26372; 2,500.

Automotive Hall of Fame (1939), 8225 Cook Rd., PO Box 1727, Midland, MI 48641-1727; 1,500.

Badminton Assn., U.S. (1936), One Olympic Plaza, Colorado Springs, CO 80909; 2,500+.

Bald-Headed Men of America (1973), 102 Bald Dr., Morehead City, NC 28557; 26,000.

Ball Players of Amer., Assn. of Professional (1924), 12062 Valley View St., Ste. 211, Garden Grove, CA 92645; 15,000+.

Band & Choral Directors Hall of Fame, Natl. (1985), 519 N. Halifax Ave., Daytona Beach, FL 32118.

Bankers Assn., Amer. (1875), 1120 Connecticut Ave. NW, Wash., DC 20036.

Bankers Assn. of Amer., Independent (1930), One Thomas Circle NW, Ste. 950, Wash. DC 20005; 5,800 banks.

Bar Assn., Federal (1920), 1815 H St. NW, Wash., DC 20006; 15,200.

Barber Shop Quartet Singing in Amer., Inc., Soc. for the Preservation & Encouragement of (1938), 6315 Third Ave., Kenosha, WI 53143-5199; 34,000.

Baseball Congress, Amer. Amateur (1935), 118 Redfield Plaza, Marshall, MI 49068; 12,650 teams.

Baseball Congress, Natl. (1931), PO Box 1420, Wichita, KS 67201; 6,500.

Baseball Research, Society for Amer. (1971), PO Box 93183, Cleveland, OH 44101; 6,500.

Basketball Assn., Natl. (1946), 645 Fifth Ave., N.Y., NY 10022.

Battleship Assn., Amer. (1964), PO Box 711247, San Diego, CA 92171; 1,350.

Beer Can Collectors of America (1970), 747 Merus Ct., Fenton, MO 63026-2092; 4,100.

Beta Gamma Sigma (1913), 11701 Borman Dr., Ste. 320, St. Louis, MO 63146-4194; 350,000.

Beta Sigma Phi (1931), 1800 W. 91st Pl., Kansas City, MO 64114; 250,000.

Bible Society, Amer. (1816), 1865 Broadway, N.Y., NY 10023; 300,000.

Biblical Literature, Society of (1880), 1549 Clairmont Rd., Ste. 204, Decatur, GA 30033-4635; 6,000+.

Bibliographical Society of America (1904), PO Box 397, Grand Central Station, N.Y., NY 10163; 1,200.

Big Brothers/Big Sisters of America (1902), 230 N. 13th St., Philadelphia, PA 19107; 494 agencies.

Biochemistry and Molecular Biology, Amer. Society for (1906), 9650 Rockville Pike, Bethesda, MD 20814; 9,300.

Biological Sciences, American Institute of (1947), 730 11th St. NW, Wash., DC 20001-4521; 5,000.

Black History Honors & Awards, Contemporary & (1990), 6514 Georgia Rd., Birmingham, AL 35212; 152.

Blind, Amer. Council of the (1961), 1155 15th St. NW, Ste. 720, Wash., DC 20005; 45,000.

Blind, Natl. Federation of the (1940), 1800 Johnson St., Baltimore, MD 21230; 50,000.

Blindness, Natl. Society to Prevent (1908), 500 E. Remington Rd., Schaumburg, IL 60173; 26 affiliates.

Blue Angels Assn. (1982), 4600 Twin Oaks Dr., Apt. 702, Pensacola, FL 32506; 250.

Blueberry Council, North Amer. (1965), PO Box 1036, Folsom, CA 95763-1036.

B'nai B'rith Intl. (1853), 1640 Rhode Island Ave. NW, Wash., DC 20036; 150,000.

Boat Club, Chris Craft Antique (1973), 217 S. Adams St., Tallahassee, FL 32301-1708; 2,175.

Boat Owners Assn. of the U.S. (1966), 880 S. Pickett St., Alexandria, VA 22304; 500,000.

Bodybuilders Assn., Amer. (1981), 6991 Simson St., Oakland, CA 94605-2226; 854.

Bookplate Collectors and Designers, Amer. Soc. of (1922), 605 N. Stoneman Ave., #F, Alhambra, CA 91801; 200.

Booksellers Assn., Amer. (1900), 828 South Broadway, Tarrytown, NY 10591; 8,500.

Bowling Congress, Amer. (1895), 5301 S. 76th St., Greendale, WI 53129; 2.4 mil.

Boy Scouts of America (1910), 1325 Walnut Hill Lane, Irving, TX 75015-2079; 3.8 mil.

Boys & Girls Clubs of America (1906), 1230 W. Peachtree St. NW, Atlanta, GA 30309-3447; 2 mil.+.

Bridge, Tunnel & Turnpike Assn., Intl. (1932), 2120 L St. NW, Ste. 305, Wash., DC 20037; 260 organizations.

Broadcasters, Natl. Assn. of (1922-23), 1771 N St. NW, Wash., DC 20036-2891.

Burroughs Bibliophiles, The (1960), 454 Elaine Dr., Pittsburgh, PA 15236-2417; 632.

Business Bureaus, Council of Better (1970), 4200 Wilson Blvd., Ste. 800, Arlington, VA 22203; 138 bureaus.

Business Clubs, Natl. Assn. of Amer. (1922), 3315 N. Main St., High Point, NC 27262; 7,000.

Business Communicators, Intl. Assn. of (1970), One Hallidie Plaza, Ste. 600, San Francisco, CA 94102; 12,095.

Business Education Assn., Natl. (1946), 1906 Association Dr., Reston, VA 22091; 18,000.

Business Women's Assn., American (1949), 9100 Ward Pkwy., PO Box 8728, Kansas City, MO 64114; 90,000.

Button Society, Natl. (1938), 2733 Juno Pl., Akron, OH 44333-4137; 4,100.

Byron Society, The (1971 England, 1973 in U.S.), 259 New Jersey Ave., Collingswood, NJ 08108; 300.

Campers and RVers, Family (1949), 4804 Transit Rd., Bldg. 2, Depew, NY 14043-4704; 18,000 families.

Camp Fire Boys & Girls (1910), 4601 Madison, Kansas City, MO 64112; 700,000.

Camping Assn., Amer. (1910), 5000 State Rd. 67 N., Martinsville, IN 46131; 5,400.

Cancer Society, Amer. (1913), 1599 Clifton Rd. NE, Atlanta, GA 30329.

Carnegie Hero Fund Commission (1904), 2307 Oliver Bldg., Pittsburgh, PA 15222; 21 members.

Cartoonists Society, Natl. (1946), Columbus Circle Station, PO Box 20267, N.Y., NY 10023; 630.

Cat Fanciers' Assn. (1906), PO Box 1005., Manasquan, NJ 08736-0805; 650 clubs.

Catholic Bishops, Natl. Conference of U.S. (1966), 3211 4th St. NE, Wash., DC 20015.

Catholic Church Extension Society (1905), 35 E. Wacker Dr., #400, Chicago, IL 60601-2105; 169,176.

Catholic Daughters of the Americas (1903), 10 W. 71st St., N.Y., NY 10023; 130,000.

Catholic Educational Assn., Natl. (1904), 1077 30th St. NW, Ste. 100, Wash., DC 20007; 18,353.

Catholic Historical Soc., Amer. (1884), 263 S. Fourth St., PO Box 84, Philadelphia, PA 19106-3819; 800.

Catholic Rural Life Conference, Natl. (1923), 4625 Beaver Ave., Des Moines, IA 50310-2199; 3,000.

Cemetery Assn., Amer. (1887), 1895 Preston White Dr., #220, Reston, VA 22091; 2,200.

Ceramic Society, Amer. (1899), 735 Ceramic Place, Westerville, OH 43081; 14,000.

Cerebral Palsy Assns., United (1948), 1522 K St. NW, Ste. 1112, Wash., DC 20005; 155 affiliates.

Chamber of Commerce of the U.S.A. (1912), 1615 H St. NW, Wash., DC 20062.

Chamber Music Players, Inc., Amateur (1948), 1123 Broadway, Rm. 304, N.Y., NY 10010-2007; 4,000.

Chaplain's Intl. Assn. (1960), Adjutant General Office, 5145 North Farm Rd. #155, Springfield, MO 65803; 1,300.

Checker Federation, Amer. (1948), 220 Lynn Ray Rd., PO Box 365, Petal, MS 39465; 1,000.

Chemical Manufacturers Assn. (1872), 2501 M St. NW, Wash., DC 20037; 185 cos.

Chemical Society, Amer. (1876), 1155 16th St. NW, Wash., DC 20036; 151,000.

Chemists, Amer. Assn. of Cereal (1915), 3340 Pilot Knob Rd., St. Paul, MN 55121; 4,000.

Chemists, Amer. Society of Brewing (1934), 3340 Pilot Knob Rd., St. Paul MN 55121; 730.

Chess Federation, U.S. (1939), 186 Rt. 9W, New Windsor, NY 12553; 82,000.

Chess League of Amer., Correspondence (1897), PO Box 3481, Barrington, IL 60011-3481; 1,200.

Childhood Education, Intl. Assn. for (1892), 11501 Georgia Ave., Ste. 315, Wheaton, MD 20902; 11,300.

Children, Natl. Center for Missing and Exploited (1984), 2101 Wilson Blvd., #550, Arlington, VA 22201.

Children and Adults, Natl. Assn. for Creative (1974), 8080 Springvalley Dr., Cincinnati, OH 45236-1395; 6,000.

Children of the Amer. Revolution, Natl. Society of the (1895), 1776 D St. NW, Wash., DC 20006.

Children's Aid Society (1853), 105 E. 22d St., N.Y., NY 10010; 1,207.

Children's Book Council (1945), 568 Broadway, Ste. 404, N.Y., NY 10012; 75 publishing houses.

Child Welfare League of America (1920), 440 First St. NW, Wash., DC 20001-2085; 730 agencies.

Chiropractic Assn., Amer. (1930), 1710 Clarendon Blvd., Arlington, VA 22209; 20,000.

Christian Endeavor Union, The World's (1895), 3575 Valley Rd., PO Box 820, Liberty Corner, NJ 07938-0820.

Christian Laity Counseling Board (1970), 5901 Plainfield Dr., Charlotte, NC 28215; 38 mil.

Christians and Jews, Natl. Conference of (1927), 71 Fifth Ave., Ste. 1100, N.Y., NY 10003.

Churches, U.S. Conference for the World Council of (1948), 475 Riverside Dr., N.Y., NY 10115; 317 denominations.

Church Federation, Ecumenical (1982), 13014-270 N. Dalemabry, Tampa, FL 33618-2808.

Church Women United (1941), 475 Riverside Dr., Rm. 812, N.Y., NY 10115.

Cincinnati, Society of the (1783), 2118 Massachusetts Ave. NW, Wash., DC 20008; 3,300.

Circulation Managers Assn., Intl. (1889), 11600 Sunrise Valley Dr., Reston, VA 22091; 1,705.

Cities, Natl. League of (1924), 1301 Pennsylvania Ave. NW, Wash., DC 20004-1701; 1,449 cities.

City/County Management Assn., Intl. (1914), 777 N. Capitol St. NE, Ste. 500, Wash., DC 20002-4201.

Civic League, Natl. (1894), 1445 Market St., Ste. 300, Denver, CO 80202-1728; 1,400.

Civil Air Patrol (1941), HQ CAP-USAF, Maxwell AFB, AL 36112-5572; 63,000.

Civil Liberties Union, Amer. (1920), 132 W. 43d St., N.Y. NY 10036; 250,000.

Civitan International (1917), One Civitan Pl., Birmingham, AL 35213-1983; 56,000.

Classical League, Amer. (1919), Hall, Miami Univ., Oxford, OH 45056; 3,604.

CLU & CHFC, Amer. Soc. of (1928), 270 S. Bryn Mawr Ave., Bryn Mawr, PA 19010; 25,500.

Coal Association, Natl. (1917), 1130 17th St. NW, Wash., DC 20036; 150 corporate members.

Coaster Enthusiasts, American (1978), PO Box 8226, Chicago, IL 60680; 4,700+.

Codependents Anonymous (1986), 5150 N. 16th St., Phoenix, AZ 85016.

College Admission Counselors, Natl. Assn. of (1937), 1631 Prince St., Alexandria, VA 22314-2818; 6,003.

College Board, The (1900), 45 Columbus Ave., N.Y., NY 10023; 2,900 institutions.

College Music Society (1958), 202 W. Spruce St., Missoula, MT 59802; 4,000.

Colleges, Amer. Assn. of Community and Jr. (1921), One Dupont Circle NW, Ste. 410, Wash., DC 20036.

Colleges, Assn. of Amer. (1915), 1818 R St. NW, Wash., DC 20009; 640 institutions.

Colleges and Employers, Natl. Assn. of (1956), 62 Highland Ave., Bethlehem, PA 18017; 2,920.

Colleges and Universities, Assn. of Intl. (1973), 1301 S. Noland Rd., Independence, MO 64055; 8,918, 25 inst.

Collegiate Athletic Assn., Natl. (1906), 6201 College Blvd., Overland Park, KS 66211-2422; 1,100 institutions.

Collegiate Schools of Business, Amer. Assembly of (1916), 605 Old Ballas Rd., St. Louis, MO 63141-7077.

Colonial Dames XVII Century, Natl. Society (1915), 1300 New Hampshire Ave. NW, Wash., DC 20036-1595; 14,000.

Colonial Wars, General Society of (1892), 840 Woodbine Ave., Glendale, OH 45246; 4,300.

Commerce, U.S. Junior Chamber of (1915), 4 W. 21st St., Tulsa, OK 74114-1116; 200,000.

Commercial Collectors Assn., Amer. (1970), 4040 W. 70th St., Minneapolis, MN 55435; 3,225.

Commercial Law League of America (1895), 150 N. Michigan, #600, Chicago, IL 60601; 5,000.

Common Cause (1970), 2030 M St. NW, Wash., DC 20036.

Communication, Intl. Training in (1938), 2519 Woodland Dr., Anaheim, CA 92801; 15,000.

Communities, Federation of Egalitarian (1976), E. Wind, Rt. 3, Box 6B2, Tecumseh, MO 65760; 250+.

Community Cultural Center Assn., Amer. (1978), 19 Foothills Dr., Pompton Plains, NJ 07444.

Composers, Authors & Publishers, Amer. Soc. of (ASCAP) (1914), One Lincoln Plaza, N.Y., NY 10023; 24,000.

Composers/USA, Natl. Assn. of (1932), PO Box 49652, Barrington Sta., Los Angeles, CA 90049; 600.

Computer Professionals, Inst. for Certification of (1973), 2200 E. Devon Ave., Ste. 268, Des Plaines, IL 60018-4503.

Computing Machinery, Assn. for (1947), 1515 Broadway, 17th Fl., N.Y., NY 10036; 85,000.

Concrete Institute, Amer. (1904), 22400 W. Seven Mile Rd., Detroit, MI 48219-1849; 20,000.

Conscientious Objectors, Central Committee for (1948), 1515 Cherry St., Philadelphia, PA 19102; 655 Sutter St., #514, San Francisco, CA 94102.

Constantian Society, The (1970), 123 Orr Rd., Pittsburgh, PA 15241-2219; 575.

Construction Industry Manufacturers Assn. (1911), 111 E. Wisconsin Ave., Milwaukee, WI 53202; 150 cos.

Construction Specifications Institute (1948), 601 Madison St., Alexandria, VA 22314-1791; 19,200.

Consulting Organizations, Council of (1989), 521 5th Ave., N.Y., NY 10175.

Consumer Credit Assn., Intl. (1912), 243 N. Lindbergh Blvd., St. Louis, MO 63141; 20,000.

Consumer Federation of America (1968), 1424 16th St. NW, #604, Wash., DC 20036; 240 organizations.

Consumer Interests, Amer. Council on (1953), 240 Stanley Hall, Univ. of Missouri, Columbia, MO 65211; 1,500.

Consumer Protection Institute (1970), 5901 Plainfield Dr., Charlotte, NC 28215.

Consumers Union of the U.S. (1936), 101 Truman Ave., Yonkers, NY 10703; 405,990.

Contract Bridge League, Amer. (1937), 2990 Airways Blvd., Memphis, TN 38116-3847; 153,500.

Contractors of Amer., General (1919), 1957 E St. NW, Wash., DC 20006; 32,000.

Cooperative Business Assn., Natl. (1916), 1401 New York Ave. NW, Ste. 1100, Wash., DC 20005; 540.

Cooperative League of the U.S.A. (1916), 1401 New York Ave. NW, Ste. 1100, Wash., DC 20005; 285 co-ops.

Correctional Assn., Amer. (1870), 8025 Laurel Lakes Court, Laurel, MD 20707; 20,000+.

Correctional Officers, Intl. Assn. of (1977), 8600 Glenarden Pkwy., Glenarden, MD 20706-1599.

Cosmetology Assn., Natl. (1921), 3510 Olive St., St. Louis, MO 63103; 34,000.

Cotton Council of America, Natl. (1932), 1918 N. Parkway, Memphis, TN 38112.

Counseling Assn., Amer. (1952), 5999 Stevenson Ave., Alexandria, VA 22304; 57,000.

Country Music Assn. (1958), One Music Circle S, Nashville, TN 37203; 6,588.

Credit Assn., Intl. (1912), 243 N. Lindberg Blvd., St. Louis, MO 63141; 8,000.

Credit Union Natl. Assn. & Affiliates (1934), 5710 Mineral Point Rd., Madison, WI 53705; 51 state credit union leagues.

Cribbage Congress, American (1978), PO Box 10486, Napa, CA 94581; 7,500+.

Crime and Delinquency, Natl. Council on (1907), 685 Market St., Ste. 620, San Francisco, CA 94105; 500.

Criminology, Amer. Society of (1941), 1314 Kinnear Rd., Ste. 212, Columbus, OH 43212; 2,600.

Crop Protection Assn., American (1933), 1156 15th St. NW, Ste. 900, Wash., DC 20005; 80 cos.

Crop Science Society of America (1955), 677 S. Segoe Rd., Madison, WI 53711; 4,700.

Cryogenic Soc. of Amer. (1964), 1033 South Blvd., Ste. 13, Oak Park, IL 60302; 2,300.

Customs Brokers & Forwarders Assn. of America, Natl. (1897), One World Trade Center, Ste. 1153, N.Y., NY 10048; 612.

Cystic Fibrosis Foundation (1955), 6931 Arlington Rd., Bethesda, MD 20814.

Dairy Council, Natl. (1915), 6300 N. River Rd., Rosemont, IL 60018.

Dairy and Food Industries Supply Assn. (1917), 6245 Executive Blvd., Rockville, MD 20852; 800 cos.

Dairy Goat Assn., American (1904), 209 W. Main St., Spindale, NC 28160; 13,000.

Danish Brotherhood in America (1882), 3717 Harney St., Omaha, NE 68131; 8,600.

Daughters of the American Revolution, Natl. Society (1890), 1776 D St. NW, Wash., DC 20006-5392; 190,000.

Daughters of the British Empire in the U.S.A., Inc. (1909), 839 Elm Way, Edmonds, WA 98020; 5,018.

Daughters of the Confederacy, United (1894), 328 North Blvd., Richmond, VA 23220-4057; 24,000.

Daughters of the Republic of Texas (1891), 510 E. Anderson Ln., Austin, TX 78752; 7,400.

Daughters of Union Veterans of the Civil War (1885), 503 S. Walnut St., Springfield, IL 62704-1932; 3,650.

Deaf, Alexander Graham Bell Assn. for the (1890), 3417 Volta Pl. NW, Wash., DC 20007.

Deaf, Natl. Assn. of the (1880), 814 Thayer Ave., Silver Spring, MD 20910-4500; 22,000.

Defense Preparedness Assn., Amer. (1919), 2101 Wilson Blvd., Ste. 400, Arlington, VA 22201-3061; 23,000.

Delta Kappa Gamma Society Intl. (1929), 416 W. 12th St., Austin, TX 78701; 165,000.

Deltiologists of America (1960), PO Box 8, Norwood, PA 19074-0008; 800+.

Democratic Natl. Committee (1792), 430 S. Capitol St. SE, Wash., DC 20003.

DeMolay International (1919), 10200 N. Executive Hills Blvd., Kansas City, MO 64153-1367; 30,000.

Dental Assn., Amer. (1860), 211 E. Chicago Ave., Chicago, IL 60611; 140,000.

Descendants of the Colonial Clergy, Society of the (1933), 30 Leewood Rd., Wellesley, MA 02181; 1,024.

Descendants of the Signers of the Declaration of Independence (1907), 3300 Binnacle Dr. #210, Naples, FL 33940; 1,024.

Descendants of Washington's Army at Valley Forge, Society of (1976), PO Box 915, Valley Forge, PA 19482-0915; 950.

Desert Protective Council (1955), PO Box 2312, Valley Center, CA 92082-2312; 256.

Diabetes Assn., Amer. (1940), 1660 Duke St., Alexandria, VA 22314.

Dialect Society, Amer. (1889), c/o Allan Metcalf, English Dept., MacMurray College, Jacksonville, IL 62650; 550.

Digital Printing & Imaging Assn. (1993), 10015 Main St., Fairfax, VA 22031; 250 cos.

Direct Marketing Assn. (1917), W. 42d St., N.Y., NY 10036-8096; 3,600.

Directors Guild of America (1936), 7920 Sunset Blvd., Los Angeles, CA 90046; 9,700.

Disabled Amer. Veterans (1920), PO Box 14301, Cincinnati, OH 45250-0301; 1,047,000.

Disabled Collectors' Correspondence Club (1991), PO Box 3113, Fremont, CA 94539.

Disabled Sports USA (1967), 451 Hungerford Dr., Ste. 100, Rockville, MD 20850; 20,000.

Dogs International, Inc., Therapy (1976), 6 Hilltop Rd., Mendham, NJ 07945; 4,000+

Dogs on Stamps Study Unit (1979), 3208 Hana Rd., Edison, NJ 08817-2552; 400.

Dollhouse Museum of the Southwest (1981), 2208 Routh St., Dallas, TX 75201; 250.

Dozenal Society of America (1944), Math Dept., Nassau Community College, Garden City, NY 11530; 144.

Dracula Society, Count (1962), 334 W. 54th St., Los Angeles, CA 90037; 500.

Drug, Chemical and Allied Trades Assn. (1890), 2 Roosevelt Ave., Syosset, NY 11791; 2,018.

Ducks Unlimited (1937), One Waterfowl Way, Memphis, TN 38120; 500,000+.

Dutch Settlers Soc. of Albany (1924), 203 Holmes Dale, Albany, NY 12208; 300.

Eaglehunters (1994), PO Box 1539, Hernando, FL 34442; 500.

Eagles, Fraternal Order of (1898), 12660 W. Capitol Dr., Brookfield, WI 53055; 1.1 mil.

Easter Seal Society, Natl. (1919), 230 W. Monroe, Chicago, IL 60606.

Eastern Star, General Grand Chapter, Order of the (1876), 1618 New Hampshire Ave. NW, Wash., DC 20009; 1.5 mil.

Economic Assn., Amer. (1885), 2014 Broadway, Ste. 305, Nashville, TN 37203; 20,000.

Edsel Club, Intl. (1969), PO Box 371, Sully, IA 50251-0379; 1,090.

Education, Amer. Council on (1918), One Dupont Circle NW, #800, Wash., DC 20036; 1,700.

Education, Council for Advancement & Support of (1974), 11 Dupont Circle NW, Wash., DC 20036; 2,950 schools.

Education, Institute of Intl. (1919), 809 United Nations Plaza, N.Y., NY 10017; 700 U.S colleges, univ.

Education, Natl. Assn. for Family and Community (1936), 5963 Jefferson St., Burlington, KY 41005-9596; 45,000.

Education Assn., National (1857), 1201 16th St. NW, Wash., DC 20036; 2 mil.

Educational Exchange, Council on Intl. (1947), 205 E. 42d St., N.Y., NY 10017; 240 organizations.

Educational Research Assn., Amer. (1916), 1230 17th St. NW, Wash., DC 20036; 22,000.

Education of Young Children, Natl. Assn. for the (1926), 1509 16th St. NW, Wash., DC 20036-1426; 90,000+.

Educators, Assn. of Intl., (1948) 1875 Connecticut Ave., Ste. 1000, Wash., DC 20009; 7,400.

Educators for World Peace, International Assn. of (1969), PO Box 3282, Mastin Lake Station, Huntsville, AL 35810-0282; 25,000.

8th Air Force Historical Society (1975), PO Box 7215, St. Paul, MN 55107; 18,000.

88th Infantry Division Assn., Inc. (1948), PO Box 925, Havertown, PA 19083; 5,200.

82nd Airborne Division Assn., Inc. (1944), NFCS, PO Box 8308, Fayetteville, NC 28311-7694; 23,000 +.

Electrical Manufacturers Assn., Natl. (1926), 2101 L St. NW, Wash., DC 20037; 560 cos.

Electrochemical Society (1902), 10 S. Main St., Pennington, NJ 08534-2896; 6,000.

Electronic Circuits, The Institute for Interconnecting & Packaging (1957), 7380 N. Lincoln, Lincolnwood, IL 60646-1705; 1,900 cos.

Electronic Industries Assn. (1924), 2001 Pennsylvania Ave., Wash., DC 20006-1813; 1,058 cos.

Electronics Technicians, Intl. Society of Certified (1970), 2708 W. Berry, Ft. Worth, TX 76109; 2,000.

Electroplaters' and Surface Finishers' Society, Amer. (1909), 12644 Research Pkwy., Orlando, FL 32826; 8,500.

Elks of the U.S.A., Benevolent and Protective Order of (1868), 2750 N. Lakeview Ave., Chicago, IL 60614; 1.5 mil.

Elvis Presley Burning Love Fan Club (1983), 1904 Williamsburg Dr., Streamwood, IL 60107; 1,500+.

Energy Research Institute, Clean (1974), Univ. of Miami, Coral Gables, FL, 33124.

Engineering, Natl. Academy of (1964), 2101 Constitution Ave. NW, Wash., DC 20418; 1,700.

Engineering, Soc. for the Advancement of Material & Process (1944), 1161 Parkview Dr., Covina, CA 91724-3748; 8,000.

Engineering Society of N. America, Illuminating (1906), 120 Wall St., 17th Floor, N.Y., NY 10005; 9,500.

Engineers, Amer. Inst. of Chemical (1908), 345 E. 47th St., N.Y., NY 10017-2395; 56,800.

Engineers, Amer. Institute of Mining, Metallurgical and Petroleum (1871), 345 E. 47th St., N.Y., NY 10017.

Engineers, Amer. Soc. of Agricultural (ASAE) (1907), 2950 Niles Rd., St. Joseph, MI 49085-9659; 7,500.

Engineers, Amer. Society of Civil (1852), 345 E. 47th St., N.Y., NY 10017; 104,000.

Engineers, Inc., Amer. Soc. of Heating, Refrigerating & Air Conditioning (1894), 1791 Tullie Cir. NE, Atlanta, GA 30329; 50,000.

Engineers, American Soc. of Mechanical (1881), 345 E. 47th St., N.Y., NY 10017; 120,000.

Engineers, Amer. Soc. of Safety (1911), 1800 E. Oakton St., Des Plaines, IL 60018-2187; 28,000.

Engineers, Assn. of Conservation (1961), 64 N. Union St., Rm. 479, Montgomery, AL 36104; 295

Engineers, Assn. of Energy (1977), 4025 Pleasantdale Rd., Ste. 420, Atlanta, GA 30340; 8,500.

Engineers, Assn. of Iron and Steel (1907), Three Gateway Center, Ste. 2350, Pittsburgh, PA 15222; 10,000.

Engineers, Institute of Electrical and Electronics (1884), 345 E. 47th St., N.Y., NY 10017; 320,000.

Engineers, Institute of Industrial (1948), 25 Technology Park, Norcross, GA 30092; 27,000.

Engineers, Inst. of Transportation (1930), 525 School St. SW, Ste. 410, Wash., DC 20024; 12,800.

Engineers, Natl. Society of Professional (1934), 1420 King St., Alexandria, VA 22314; 60,437.

Engineers, Soc. of Fire Protection (1950), One Liberty Sq., Boston, MA 02109-4825; 4,150.

Engineers, Soc. of Logistics (1966), 8100 Professional Dr., Ste. 211, Hyattsville, MD 20785; 8,000.

Engineers, Soc. of Manufacturing (1932), One SME Drive, Dearborn, MI 48121; 70,000.

Engineers, Society of Mining (1871), 8307 Shaffer Pkwy., Littleton, CO 80127; 23,058.

Engineers, Soc. of Motion Picture & Television (1916), 595 West Hartsdale Ave., White Plains, NY 10607; 8,700.

Engineers, Society of Plastics (1942), 14 Fairfield Dr., Brookfield, CT 06804; 37,500.

Engineers, Society of Women (1950), 120 Wall St., 11th Fl., N.Y., NY 10005-3902; 16,500.

English, U.S. (1983), 818 Connecticut Ave. NW, Ste. 200, Wash., DC 20006; 611,000.

English Assn., Inc., The College (1938), English Dept., Winthrop Univ., Rock Hill, SC 29732; 1,350.

English-Speaking Union of the U.S. (1920), 16 E. 69th St., N.Y., NY 10021; 18,000.

Entomological Society of America (1950), 9301 Annapolis Rd., Lanham, MD 20706-3115; 8,500.

Environmental Health Assn., Natl. (1937), 720 S. Colorado Blvd., Ste. 970, Denver, CO 80222; 5,500.

Environmental Information Assn. (1983), 1777 N.E. Expressway, Ste. 150, Atlanta, GA 30329; 2,000.

Environmental Medicine, American Academy of (1965), PO Box 16106, Denver, CO 80216; 450.

Epigraphic Society, Inc., The (1974), 6625 Bamburgh Dr., San Diego, CA 92117; 800.

Esperanto League for North America (1952), PO Box 1129, El Cerrito, CA 94530; 1,000+.

Evangelism Crusades, Intl. (1959), 14617 Victory Blvd., Van Nuys, CA 91411; 1,500.

Exchange Club, Natl. (1911), 3050 Central Ave., Toledo, OH 43606-1700; 37,000.

Fairs & Expositions, Intl. Assn. of (1919), PO Box 985, Springfield, MO 65801; 2,400.

Family Relations, Natl. Council on (1938), 3989 Central Ave. NE, Ste. 550, Minneapolis, MN 55421; 3,900.

Family Service America (1911), 11700 W. Lake Park Dr., Milwaukee, WI 53224; 290 agencies.

Farm Bureau Federation, Amer. (1919), 225 Touhy Ave., Park Ridge, IL 60068; 4 mil.

Farmers of America Org., Natl. Future (1928), 5632 Mt. Vernon Memorial Hwy., Alexandria, VA 22309-0160; 443,428.

Farmers Educational & Co-Operative Union of Amer. (1902), 10065 E. Harvard Ave., Denver, CO 80231; 250,000.

Farmers Union, Natl. (1902), Denver, CO 80251; 250,000.

Fat Acceptance, Natl. Assn. to Advance (NAAFA) (1969), PO Box 188620, Sacramento, CA 95818; 5,000.

Federal Employees, Natl. Fed. of (1917), 1016 16th St. NW, Wash., DC 20036.

Feminists for Life of America (1972), 733 15th St. NW, Wash., DC 20005; 5,000.

Financial Analysts Federation (1945), 5 Boar's Head Lane, Charlottesville, VA 22903; 22,700.

Financial Executives Institute (1931), 10 Madison Ave., PO Box 1938, Morristown, NJ 07962-1938; 14,000.

Financial Women Intl., (1921), 200 North Globe Rd., Ste. 814, Arlington, VA 22203-3728; 10,000.

Financiers, Intl. Society of (1979), PO Box 18508, Asheville, NC 28814; 200.

Fire Chiefs, Intl. Assn. of (1873), 4025 Fair Ridge Dr., Fairfax, VA 22033-2868; 10,000+.

Fire Protection Assn., Natl. (1896), One Batterymarch Park, Quincy, MA 02269; 65,000.

First Amendment Studies, Institute for (1984), 187 Main St., Great Barrington, MA 01230.

Fish Assn., Intl. Game (1939), 1301 E. Atlantic Blvd., Pompano Beach, FL 33060.

Fisheries Soc., American (1870), 5410 Grosvenor Lane, Ste. 110, Bethesda, MD 20814; 9,200.

Fishes, Soc. for the Protection of Old (1967), School of Fisheries, WH-10, Univ. of Washington, Seattle, WA 98195.

Fishing Tackle Manufacturers Assn., Amer. (1933), 1250 Grove Ave., Barrington, IL 60010; 500 cos.

Flag Research Center, The (1962), Box 580, Winchester, MA 01890; 1,300.

Flight Attendants, Assn. of (1973), 1625 Massachusetts Ave. NW, Wash., DC 20036; 28,000.

Fly Fishers, Fed. of (1965), 502 S. 19th, Ste. 1, Bozeman, MT 59715; 11,600.

Flying Disc Fed., World (1985), Gnejsvägen 24, 85357, Sundsvall, Sweden; 15,000.

Food Brokers Assn., Natl. (1904), 1010 Massachusetts Ave. NW, Wash., DC 20001; 1,800 cos.

Food Institute, Amer. Frozen (1942), 1764 Old Meadow Ln., Ste. 350, McLean, VA 22102; 550 firms.

Footwear Industries Assn., Amer. (1869), 1420 K St. NW, Wash. DC 20005; 156 cos.

Foreign Student Affairs, Natl. Assn. for (1948), 1875 Connecticut Ave., Ste. 1000, Wash., DC 20009; 6,800.

Foreign Study, Amer. Institute for (1964), 102 Greenwich Ave., Greenwich, CT 06830; 300,000.

Foreign Trade Council, Inc., Natl. (1914), 1625 K St. NW, Wash., DC 20006; 500 cos.

Forensic Sciences, Amer. Academy of (1948), 410 N. 21st St., Ste. 203, Colorado Springs, CO 80904; 4,100.

Foresters, Society of Amer. (1900), 5400 Grosvenor La., Bethesda, MD 20814; 17,000.

Forest History Society (1946), 701 Vickers Ave., Durham, NC 27701; 1,500.

Forest & Paper Assn., Amer. (1993), 1111 19th St. NW, Wash., DC 20036; 400 cos.

Forest Products Society (1947), 2801 Marshall Ct., Madison, WI 53705-2295; 2,800.

Forestry Assn., Amer. (1875), 1516 P St. NW, Wash., DC 20005; 150,000.

Forests, Amer. (1875), 1516 P St. NW, Wash., DC 20005; 60,000.

Fortean Organization, Intl. (1966), PO Box 367, Arlington, VA 22210-0367; 650.

Founders and Patriots of Amer., The Order of the (1896), 3892 College Ave., Ellicott City, MD 21043; 1,250.

Foundrymen's Society, Amer. (1896), 505 State St., Des Plaines, IL 60016-8399; 14,000

4-H Clubs (1901-1905), Extension Service, U.S. Dept of Agriculture, Wash., DC 20250; 5.8 mil.

458th Service Squadron Assn.-WWII (1991) 2114 W. 29th St., Erie, PA 16508.

Frederick A. Cook Soc., The (1940), PO Box 11421, Pittsburgh, PA 15238; 238.

Freedom of Information Center (1958), 20 Walter Williams Hall, Univ. of Missouri, Columbia, MO 65211.

Freedoms Foundation at Valley Forge (1949), Rt. 23, PO Box 706, Valley Forge, PA 19482-0706; 4,800.

French Institute/Alliance Francaise (1898), 22 E. 60th St., N.Y., NY 10022; 7,000.

Friendship and Good Will, Intl. Soc. of (1978), 9538 Summerville St., Spring Valley, CA 91977-2852; 4,218.

Funeral & Memorial Societies of America (1963), 6900 Lost Lake Rd., Egg Harbor, WI 54209; 500,000.

Gamblers Anonymous (1957), PO Box 17173, Los Angeles, CA 90017.

Garden Club of Amer. (1913), 598 Madison Ave., N.Y., NY 10022; 15,000.

Garden Clubs, Natl. Council of State (1929), 4401 Magnolia Ave., St. Louis, MO 63110; 308,623.

Garden Clubs of America, Men's (1932), 5560 Merle Hay Rd., Johnston, IA 50131; 9,500.

Gas Appliance Manufacturers Assn. (1935), 1901 N. Moore St., Arlington, VA 22209; 205 cos.

Gas Assn., Amer. (1918), 1515 Wilson Blvd., Arlington, VA 22209; 229 cos.; 3,000 individuals.

Gay and Lesbian Task Force, Natl. (1973), 1734 14th St. NW, Wash., DC 20009; 20,000.

Genealogical Society, Natl. (1903), 4527 17th St. N, Arlington, VA 22207-2399; 14,000.

Genetic Assn., Amer. (1905), PO Box 39, Buckeystown, MD 21717; 750.

Geographers, Assn. of Amer. (1904), 1710 16th St. NW, Wash., DC 20009-3198; 7,000.

Geographical Society, Amer. (1851), 156 Fifth Ave., Ste. 600, N.Y., NY 10010-7002; 2,000.

Geographic Education, Natl. Council for (1915), 16A Leo Hall, IUP, Indiana, PA 15705; 2,200.

Geographic Society, Natl. (1888), 1145 17th St. NW, Wash., DC 20036; 9.7 mil.

Geological Society of America (1888), 3300 Penrose Pl., PO Box 9140, Boulder, CO 80301; 15,200.

Geologists, Amer. Assn. of Petroleum (1917), 1444 S. Boulder, Tulsa, OK 74119-3604; 31,961.

Geophysicists, Society of Exploration (1930), PO Box 702740, Tulsa, OK 74170; 14,500.

Geriatrics Society, Amer. (1942), 770 Lexington Ave., Ste. 300, N.Y., NY 10021; 6,000.

Gideons Intl. (1899), 2900 Lebanon Rd., Nashville, TN 37214; 131,000.

Gifted Children, Natl. Assn. for (1953), 1155 15th St. NW, Ste. 1002, Wash., DC 20005; 7,000.

Girl Scouts of the U.S.A. (1912), 420 5th Ave., N.Y., NY 10018; 3.2 mil.

Girls Incorporated (1945), 30 E. 33d St., N.Y., NY 10016; 250,000.

Golf Association, U.S. (1894), Golf House, Far Hills, NJ 07931; 8,000 clubs.

Gospel Music Assn. (1964), 1205 Division St., Nashville, TN 37203; 4,200.

Government Finance Officers Assn. (1906), 180 N. Michigan Ave., Ste. 800, Chicago, IL 60601; 12,500.

Graduate Schools in the U.S., Council of (1961), One Dupont Circle NW, Wash., DC 20036; 412 institutions.

Grandmothers Clubs of America, Natl. Federation of (1934), 203 N. Wabash Ave., Chicago, IL 60601; 10,000.

Graphic Arts, Amer. Institute of (1914), 1059 Third Ave., N.Y., NY 10021; 6,000.

Gray Panthers (1970), 2025 Pennsylvania Ave. NW, Ste. 821, Wash., DC 20006; 15,000.

Green Mountain Club, The (1910), RR1, Box 650, Rt. 100 Waterbury Ctr., VT 05677; 6,000.

Grocers, Natl. Assn. of (1893), 1825 Samuel Morse Dr., Reston, VA 22090.

Grocery Manufacturers of America (1908), 1010 Wisconsin Ave., Ste. 800, Wash., DC 20007; 140 cos.

Guide Dog Foundation for the Blind (1946), 371 E. Jericho Tpk., Smithtown, NY 11787-2976.

Gyro Intl. (1912), 1096 Mentor Ave., Painesville, OH 44077.

Hadassah, the Women's Zionist Organization of America (1912), 50 W. 58th St., N.Y., NY 10019; 385,000.

Hairdressers and Cosmetologists Assn., Natl. (1921), 3510 Olive St., St. Louis, MO 63103; 50,406.

Handball Assn., U.S. (1951), 2333 N. Tucson Blvd., Tucson, AZ 85716; 9,000.

Handicapped, Federation of the (1935), 211 W. 14th St., N.Y., NY 10011; 650.

Handicapped, Natl. Assn. of the Physically (1958), Bethesda Scarlet Oaks, 440 Lafayette Ave., #GA4, Cincinnati, OH 45220-1073; 685.

Health, Physical Education, Recreation and Dance, Amer. Alliance for (1885), 1900 Association Dr., Reston, VA 22091.

Health Council, Natl. (1920), 1730 M St. NW, Ste. 500, Wash., DC 20036.

Health Info. Management Assn., American (1928), 919 N. Michigan Ave., #1400, Chicago, IL 60611-1683; 35,000.

Healthcare Planning and Marketing, Soc. for (1978), One N. Franklin, Chicago, IL 60606; 3,700.

Hearing Society, Intl. (1951), 20361 Middlebelt Rd., Livonia, MI 48152; 3,000.

Hearing and Speech Action, Natl. Assn. for (1910), 10801 Rockville Pike, Rockville, MD 20852.

Heart Assn., Amer. (1924), 7272 Greenville Ave., Dallas, TX 75231.

Hearts, Mended (1951), 7320 Greenville Ave., Dallas, TX 75231; 20,000.

Helicopter Assn. Intl. (1948), 1635 Prince St., Alexandria, VA 22314; 1,800.

Helicopter Society, Amer. (1943), 217 N. Washington St., Alexandria, VA 22314; 6,140.

Hemispheric Affairs, Council on (1975), 724 9th St. NW, Wash., DC 20001; 2,200.

HIAS (Hebrew Immigrant Aid Society) (1880), 333 7th Ave., 17th Floor, N.Y., NY 10001-5004.

Highpointers Club (1987), Box 327, Mtn. Home, AR 72653; 1,050.

High School Assns., Natl. Federation of State (1920), PO Box 20626, Kansas City, MO 64195; 51 state assn.

High Twelve International. (1921), 11155 B2 South Towne Square, St. Louis, MO 63123-7823; 25,000.

Hiking Society, Amer. (1977), PO Box 20160, Wash., DC 20041-2160; 6,000.

Historians, Organization of Amer. (1907), 112 N. Bryan St., Bloomington, IN 47408-4199; 9,200.

Historical Assn., Amer. (1884), 400 A St. SE, Wash., DC 20003; 15,200.

Historic Preservation, Natl. Trust for (1949), 1785 Massachusetts Ave. NW, Wash., DC 20036; 250,000.

History, Amer. Assn. for State & Local (1940), 530 Church St., Ste. 600, Nashville, TN 37219-2325; 5,500.

Hockey, U.S.A. (1937), 4965 N. 30th St., Colorado Springs, CO 80919; 300,000.

Home Builders, Natl. Assn. of (1942), 1201 15th St. NW, Wash., DC 20005; 157,000.

Home Economics Assn., Amer. (1909), 1555 King St., Alexandria, VA 22314; 20,000.

Homemakers of America, Future (1945), 1910 Association Dr., Reston, VA 22091; 281,000+.

Honor Society, Natl. (1921), 1904 Association Dr., Reston, VA 22091; 21,000.

Horatio Alger Soc. (1961), 585 St. Andrews Dr., Media, PA 19063; 250.

Horse Council, American (1969), 1700 K St. NW, #300, Wash., DC 20006; 2,300 members, 200 org.

Horse Protection Assn., Amer. (1966), 1000 29th St. NW, Ste. T-100, Wash., DC 20007; 8,000.

Horse Shows Assn., Amer. (1917), 220 E. 42d St., N.Y., NY 10017-5876; 60,000+.

Hospital Association, Amer. (1899), 1 N. Franklin, Chicago, IL 60606; 5,100 hospitals.

Hospital Marketing and Public Relations, Amer. Society for (1964), 840 N. Lake Shore Dr., Chicago, IL 60611; 3,167.

Hostelling Intl., American Youth Hostels (1934), 733 15th Street NW, Ste. 840, Wash., DC 20005; 128,000.

Hotel & Motel Assn., Amer. (1910), 1201 New York Ave. NW, Wash., DC 20005-3917; 10,000+.

Hot Rod Assn., Natl. (1951), 2035 Financial Way, Glendora, CA 91740; 80,000.

Humane Society of the U.S. (1954), 2100 L St. NW, Wash., DC 20037; 650,000.

Human Resource Management, Society for (1948), 606 N. Washington St., Alexandria, VA 22314.

Husbandry, Natl. Grange of the Order of Patrons of (1867), 1616 H St. NW, Wash., DC 20006; 300,000.

Hydrogen Energy, Intl. Assn. for (1975), PO Box 248266, Coral Gables, FL 33124; 2,500.

Idaho Assn., U.S.S. (BB-42) (1957), PO Box 711247, San Diego, CA 92171; 450.

Identification, Intl. Assn. for (1915), PO Box 2423, Alameda, CA 94501-0247; 4,000.

Illustrators, Society of (1901), 128 E. 63d St., N.Y., NY 10021; 850.

Impotence Inst. of Amer. (1983), 2020 Pennsylvania Ave. NW, Ste. 292, Wash., DC 20006.

Indian Affairs, Assn. on Amer. (1923), 245 Fifth Ave., N.Y., NY 10016-8728; 40,000.

Industrial Designers Society of America (1965), 1142 Walker Rd., Great Falls, VA 22066; 2,300.

Industrial Health Foundation (1935), 34 Penn Circle W, Pittsburgh, PA 15206; 170 cos.

Industrial Security, Amer. Soc. for (1955), 1655 N. Ft. Myer Dr., Ste. 1200, Arlington, VA 22209; 24,000.

Information and Image Management, Assn. for (1943), 1100 Wayne Ave., Ste. 1100, Silver Spring, MD 20910; 11,000.

Information Industry Assn. (1969), 555 New Jersey Ave. NW, Ste. 800, Wash., DC 20001; 500 cos.

Inner Network, The (1991), 300 Darby Hill Rd., RD #1, Delanson, NY 12053; 452.

Insurance Assn., Amer. (1964), 1130 Connecticut Ave. NW, Ste. 1000, Wash., DC 20036; 250+ cos.

Insurance Society, Inc., Intl. (1965), Univ. of Alabama, Rm. 445, Alston Hall, Tuscaloosa, AL 35487; 1,200.

Intellectual Property Owners (1972), 1255 23d St. NW, #850, Wash., DC 20037; 725.

Intelligence Officers, Assn. of Former (1975), 6723 Whittier Ave., Ste. 303A, McLean, VA 22101; 2,700.

Intercultural Programs, Intl. (1947), 220 E. 42d St., N.Y., NY 10017; 475,000.

Interior Designers, Amer. Society of (1931), 608 Massachusetts Ave. NE, Wash., DC 20002; 33,000.

Inventors, Amer. Assn. of (1891), 2020 Pennsylvania Ave. NW, Wash., DC 20006; 5,727.

Investment Clubs, Natl. Assn. of (1951), 1515 E. Eleven Mile Rd., Royal Oak, MI 48067; 140,000.

Investment Management and Research, Assn. for (1990), PO Box 3668, Charlottesville, VA 22903-0668; 26,000.

Investors Corp., Natl. Assn. of (1951), 711 W. Thirteen Mile Rd., Madison Heights, MI 48071; 280,000.

Irish-American Cultural Inst. (1962), 2115 Summit Ave., #5026, St. Paul, MN 55105; 5,000.

Irish Historical Society, American- (1897), 991 5th Ave., N.Y., NY 10028; 700.

Iron Castings Society (1897), 455 State St., Des Plaines, IL 60016; 200 firms.

Iron and Steel Institute, Amer. (1855), 1101 17th St. NW, Ste. 1300, Wash., DC 20036; 1,100.

Italian Historical Society of America (1949), 111 Columbia Heights, Brooklyn, NY 11201.

Izaak Walton League of America, The (1922), 1401 Wilson Blvd., Level B, Arlington, VA 22209; 53,000.

Jamestowne Society (1936), PO Box 14523, Richmond, VA 23221; 3,000.

Jane Austen Society of North Amer. (1979), 207 Pinecroft Dr., Raleigh, NC 27609; 2,800.

Japanese Amer. Citizens League (1929), 1765 Sutter St., San Francisco, CA 94115; 24,000.

Jewish Book Council (1943), 15 E. 26th St., N.Y., NY 10010.

Jewish Committee, Amer. (1906), 165 E. 56th St., N.Y., NY 10022; 50,000.

Jewish Community Centers Assn. (1917), 15 E. 26th St., N.Y., NY 10010.

Jewish Congress, Amer. (1918), 15 E. 84th St., N.Y., NY 10028; 50,000.

Jewish Federations, Council of (1932), 730 Broadway, N.Y., NY 10003; 200 agencies.

Jewish Historical Society, Amer. (1892), 2 Thornton Rd., Waltham, MA 02154; 2,500.

Jewish Women, Natl. Council of (1893), 53 W. 23d St., N.Y., NY 10010; 90,000.

Job's Daughters, Intl. Order of (1920), 233 W. 6th St., Papillion, NE 68046; 21,000.

Jockey Club (1894), 40 E. 52d St., N.Y., NY 10022; 90.

John Birch Society (1958), PO Box 8040, Appleton, WI 54913.

Joseph Diseases Foundation, Intl. (1977), 4047 First St., Ste. 107, Livermore, CA 94550; 3,500.

Journalists, Society of Professional (1909), PO Box 77, Greencastle, IN 46135; 16,000.

Journalists and Authors, Amer. Society of (1948), 1501 Broadway, Ste. 302, N.Y., NY 10036; 900.

Judaism, Amer. Council for (1943), PO Box 9009, Alexandria, VA 22304.

Judicature Society, Amer. (1913), 25 E. Washington, Chicago, IL 60602; 20,000.

Jugglers Assn., Intl. (1947), PO Box 218, Montague, MA 01351; 3,000.

Junior Achievement (1919), One Education Way, Colorado Springs, CO 80906; 300,000.

Junior Auxiliaries, Natl. Assn. of (1941), 845 S. Main St., Greenville, MS 38701; 11,000.

Junior Leagues, Assn. of (1921), 660 First Ave., N.Y., NY 10016; 190,000.

Kennel Club, Amer. (1884), 51 Madison Ave., N.Y., NY 10010; 500+ clubs.

Kidney Fund, Amer. (1971), 6110 Executive Blvd., Ste. 1010, Rockville, MD 20852.

Kiwanis International (1915), 3636 Woodview Trace, Indianapolis, IN 46268-3196; 325,000.

Knights of Columbus (1882), One Columbus Plaza, New Haven, CT 06510; 1,540,324.

Knights of Pythias (1864), 2785 E. Desert Inn Rd., Ste. 150, Las Vegas, NV 89121; 70,000.

Knights Templar U.S.A., Grand Encampment (1816), 5097 N. Elston, Ste. 101, Chicago, IL 60630.

Krishna Consciousness, Intl. Soc. for (ISKON) (1966), 3764 Watseka Ave., Los Angeles, CA 92109; 1 mil.

La Leche League Intl. (1956), 9616 Minneapolis Ave., PO Box 1209, Franklin Park, IL 60131; 48,000.

Lambs, The (1874), 3 W. 51st St., N.Y., NY 10019; 120.

Landscape Architects, Amer. Society of (1899), 4401 Connecticut Ave. NW, Wash., DC 20008-2302; 10,000.

Language Assn. of America, Modern (1883), 10 Astor Pl., N.Y., NY 10003; 32,000.

Language Teachers Assns., Natl. Federation of Modern (1916), Gannon Univ., Erie, PA 16541; 7,200.

Laurel & Hardy Appreciation Soc., Sons of the Desert (1965), PO Box 8341, Universal City, CA 91608; 15,000.

Law, Amer. Society of Intl. (1906), 2223 Massachusetts Ave. NW, Wash., DC 20008; 4,300.

Law Enforcement Officers Assn., Amer. (1966), 1000 Connecticut Ave. NW, Ste. 9, Wash., DC 20036; 50,000.

Law Libraries, Amer. Assn. of (1906), 53 W. Jackson Blvd., #940, Chicago, IL 60604; 5,000.

LCI National Assn., U.S.S. (1990), 134 Lancaster Ave., Columbia, PA 17512; 2,500.

Learned Societies, Amer. Council of (1919), 228 E. 45th St., N.Y., NY 10017; 45 societies.

Lefthanders Intl. (1975), PO Box 8249, Topeka, KS 66608.

Legal Administrators, Assn. of (1971), 175 E. Hawthorn Pkwy., #325, Vernon Hills, IL 60061-1428; 8,000.

Legion, The American (1919), PO Box 1055 Indianapolis, IN 46206; 3.1 mil.

Legion Auxiliary, The American (1919), 777 N. Meridian St., Indianapolis, IN 46204; 1 mil.

Legion of Valor of the U.S.A. (1890), 92 Oak Leaf Lane, Chapel Hill, NC 27516; 800.

Leif Ericson Society (1926), 3 Toft Woods Way, Media, PA 19063; 999.

Leprosy Missions, Amer. (1906), One Alm Way, Greenville, SC 29601.

Leukemia Society of America (1949), 600 Third Ave., N.Y., NY 10016.

Lewis and Clark Trail Heritage Foundation, Inc. (1969), PO Box 3434, Great Falls, MT 59403; 1,493.

Lewis Carroll Society of N. America (1974), 1655 34th St. NW, Wash., DC 20007-2742; 370.

Libertarian Party, The (1971), 1528 Pennsylvania Ave. SE, Wash., DC 20003-3116; 100,000.

Liberty Lobby (1955), 300 Independence Ave. SE, Wash., DC 20003; 20,000.

Libraries Assn., Special (1909), 1700 18th St. NW, Wash., DC 20009; 14,200.

Library Assn., American (1876), 50 E. Huron St., Chicago, IL 60611; 57,000.

Library Assn., American Theological (1947), 820 Church St., Ste. 300, Evanston, IL 60201; 188 libraries.

Library Assn., Medical (1861), 6 N. Michigan Ave., Ste. 300, Chicago, IL 60602; 5,000+.

Life, Americans United for (1971), 343 S. Dearborn St., Ste. 1804, Chicago, IL 60604.

Life Insurance, Amer. Council of (1976), 1001 Pennsylvania Ave. NW, Wash., DC 20004; 616 firms.

Lighter Than Air Society (1952), 1436 Triplett Blvd., Akron, OH 44306; 1,600.

Lions Clubs, Intl (1917), 300 22d St., Oak Brook, IL 60521-8842; 1,425,000.

Liquid Crystal Soc., Intl. (1965), Liquid Crystal Institute, Kent State Univ., Kent, OH 44242-0001; 1,000.

Linguistic Society of America, (1924), 1325 18th St., NW, Ste. 211, Wash., DC 20036; 7,000.

Litchfield Society, The (1984), 6342 Forest Hill Blvd., #350, West Palm Beach, FL 33415-6158; 62.

Literacy Volunteers of America (1962), 5795 Widewaters Pkwy., Syracuse, NY 13214.

Little League Baseball (1939), Rt. 15, S. Williamsport, PA 17701; 2.75 mil. players.

Little People of America (1957), PO Box 9897, Wash., DC 20016; 5,000.

London Club (1975), Rt. 1, Lecompton, KS 66050; 200+.

Lung Assn., Amer. (1904), 1740 Broadway, N.Y., NY 10019.

Lutheran Education Assn. (1942), 7400 Augusta St., River Forest, IL 60305; 3,800.

Magazine Publishers of America (1919), 919 Third Ave., N.Y., NY 10022; 1,200 titles.

Magicians, Intl. Brotherhood of (1922), PO Box 192090, Saint Louis, MO 63119-9998; 14,000.

Magicians, Society of Amer. (1902), PO Box 510260, St. Louis, MO 63151; 5,500.

Management Assn., Amer. (1923), 135 W. 50th St., N.Y., NY 10020; 70,000.

Management Consulting Firms, The Assn. of (1929), 521 5th Ave., 35th Fl., N.Y., NY 10175-3598; 50 firms.

Manufacturers, Natl. Assn. of (1895), 1331 Penna. Ave. NW, Ste. 1500N, Wash., DC 20004-1703; 12,000 cos.

Manufacturers' Agents Natl. Assn. (1947), 23016 Mill Creek Rd., PO Box 3467, Laguna Hills, CA 92654; 6,900.

March of Dimes Birth Defects Foundation (1938), 1275 Mamaroneck Ave., White Plains, NY 10605; 2 mil.+.

Marine Corps League (1937), PO Box 3070, Merrifield, VA 22116-3070; 42,000.

Marine Manufacturers Assn., Natl. (1904), 401 N. Michigan Ave., Chicago, IL 60611; 1,650 cos.

Marketing Assn., Amer. (1934), 250 S. Wacker Dr., Chicago, IL 60606; 40,000.

Market Technicians Assn. (1973), 1 World Trade Center, #4447, N.Y., NY 10048; 900.

Masonic Relief Assn. of U.S. and Canada (1895), 3827 Canal St., New Orleans, LA 70119.

Masons, Royal Arch, General Grand Chapter (1797), PO Box 489, 111 S. 4th St., Danville, KY 40423-0489; 250,000.

Masons, Supreme Council 33°, Ancient and Accepted Scottish Rite, Northern Masonic Jurisdiction (1813), PO Box 519, 33 Marrett Rd., Lexington, MA 02173; 358,479.

Masons, Supreme Council 33°, Ancient and Accepted Scottish Rite, Southern Jurisdiction, (1801), 1733 16th St. NW, Wash., DC 20009-3199; 478,747.

Mathematical Society, Amer. (1888), 201 Charles St., Providence, RI 02904; 28,000.

Mathematical Statistics, Institute of (1935), 3401 Investment Blvd., Ste. 7, Hayward, CA 94545; 4,000.

Mathematics, Society for Industrial and Applied (1952), 3600 Science Ctr., Philadelphia, PA 19104-2688; 9,000+.

Mayflower Descendants, General Society of (1897), 4 Winslow St., PO Box 3297, Plymouth, MA 02361; 30,000+.

Mayors, U.S. Conference of (1932), 1620 I St. NW, Wash., DC 20006.

Mechanics, Amer. Academy of (1969), Dept. of Civil Engineering, Northwestern Univ., Evanston, IL 60201; 1,200.

Medical Assn., Aerospace (1929), 320 S. Henry St., Alexandria, VA 22314-3579; 3,800.

Medical Assn., American (1847), 515 N. State St., Chicago, IL 60610; 300,000.

Medical Assn., Natl. (1895), 1012 Tenth St. NW, Wash., DC 20001; 16,000.

Medical Record Assn., Amer. (1928), 919 N. Michigan Ave., Chicago, IL 60611; 31,000.

Medieval Academy of America (1925), 1430 Massachusetts Ave., Cambridge, MA 02138; 4,100.

Men, Natl. Coalition of Free (1977), PO Box 129, Manhasset, NY 11030.

Mensa, Amer. (1960), 2626 E. 14th St., Brooklyn, NY 11235.

Mental Health Assn., Natl. (1909), 1021 Prince St., Alexandria, VA 22314-2971; 325 affiliates.

Mental Health Program Directors, Natl. Assn. of State (1959), 66 Canal Ctr. Plaza, Ste. 302, Alexandria, VA 22314; 55.

Mentally Ill, Natl. Alliance for the (1979), 2101 Wilson Blvd., Ste. 302, Arlington, VA 22201; 140,000.

Merchants Assn., Natl. Retail (1911), 100 W. 31st St., N.Y., NY 10001; 45,000.

Merrill's Marauders Assn. (1947), 11244 N. 33rd St., Phoenix, AZ 85028-2723; 1,792.

Metallurgy Institute Intl., Amer. Powder (1959), 105 College Rd. East, Princeton, NJ 08540; 2,700.

Metal Powder Industries Federation (1944), 105 College Rd. East, Princeton, NJ 08540; 235 cos.

Metals International (ASM), Amer. Society for (1913), 9639 Kinsman Rd., Materials Park, OH 44073-0002; 47,000.

Meteorological Society, Amer. (1919), 45 Beacon St., Boston, MA 02108; 10,500.

Metric Assn., U.S. (1916), 10245 Andasol Ave., Northridge, CA 91325; 1,200.

Microbiology, Amer. Society for (1899), 1325 Massachusetts Ave. NW, Wash. DC 20005; 40,000.

Mideast Educational & Training Services, Amer. (1951), 1730 M St. NW, Ste. 1100, Wash., DC 20036-4505.

Military Order of the Loyal Legion of the U.S. (1865), 1805 Pine St., Philadelphia, PA 19103; 909.

Military Order of the Purple Heart of the USA (1932), 5413-B Backlick Rd., Springfield, VA 22151; 30,000.

Military Order of the World Wars (1919), 435 N. Lee St., Alexandria, VA 22314; 14,000.

Miniatures Industry Association of America (MIAA) (1979), 1100-H Brandywine Blvd., PO Box 2188, Zanesville, OH 43702-2108; 369.

Mining, Metallurgy and Exploration, Inc., Society for (1871), PO Box 625002, Littleton, CO 80162-5002; 17,000.

Ministerial Assn., Amer. (1929), 2210 Wilshire Blvd., Ste. 582, Santa Monica, CA 90403; 1,000+.

Model Railroad Assn., Natl. (1935), 4121 Cromwell Rd., Chattanooga, TN 37421; 25,000.

Moose Intl., Inc. (1988), Mooseheart, IL 60539; 1.8 mil.

Mothers, Amer., Gold Star (1928), 2128 Leroy Pl. NW, Wash., DC 20008-1893; 2,500.

Mothers, Amer. War (1917), 2615 Woodley Pl. NW, Wash., DC 20008; 1,375.

Mothers, Inc.®, American (1935), 301 Park Ave., N.Y., NY 10022; 6,000+.

Mothers of Twins Clubs, Natl. Organization of (1960), PO Box 23188, Albuquerque, NM 87192-1188; 14,000.

Motion Picture Arts & Sciences, Academy of (1927), 8949 Wilshire Blvd., Beverly Hills, CA 90211; 5,300.

Motion Pictures, Natl. Board of Review of (1909), PO Box 589, Lenox Hill Sta., N.Y., NY 10021.

Motorcyclist Assn., American (1924), 33 Collegeview Rd., Westerville, OH 43081-6114; 200,000.

Motor Fire Apparatus in Amer., Soc. for the Preservation & Appreciation of Antique (1958), PO Box 2005, Syracuse, NY 13220-2005; 3,000.

Motor Vehicle Manufacturers Assn. (1903), 7430 2d Ave., Ste. 300, Detroit, MI 48202; 7 cos.

Multiple Sclerosis Society, Natl. (1945), 733 Third Ave., N.Y., NY 10017; 400,000.

Muscular Dystrophy Assn. (1950), 3300 E. Sunrise Dr., Tucson, AZ 85718.

Museums, Amer. Assn. of (1906), 1225 I St. NW, Ste. 200, Wash., DC 20005; 12,000.

Music Center, Amer. (1939), 30 W. 26th St., N.Y., NY 10010.

Music Council, Natl. (1940), Box 5551, Englewood, NJ 07631-5551; 50 organizations.

Music Educators Natl. Conference (1907), 1902 Association Dr., Reston, VA 22090; 60,000.

Musicological Society, Amer. (1934), 201 S. 34th St., Philadelphia, PA 19104; 3,600.

Music Scholarship Assn., Amer. (1956), 1826 Carew Tower, Cincinnati, OH 45202; 15,000.

Music Teachers Natl. Assn. (1876), The Carew Tower, 441 Vine St., Ste. 505, Cincinnati, OH 44502-2814; 23,277.

Muzzle Loading Rifle Assn., Natl. (1933), PO Box 67, Friendship, IN 47021; 25,000.

Myasthenia Gravis Foundation of America, The (1952), 222 S. Riverside Plaza, Ste. 1540, Chicago, IL 60606; 30,000.

Mystery Writers of Amer., 17 E. 47th St., 6th Fl., N.Y., NY 10017; 2,500.

NAACP (Natl. Assn. for the Advancement of Colored People) (1909), 4805 Mt. Hope Dr., Baltimore, MD 21215.

Na'amat USA (1925), 200 Madison Ave., N.Y., NY 10016.

Narcotics Anonymous (1953), PO Box 9999, Van Nuys, CA 91409; 500,000.

National Guard Assn. of the U.S. (1878), One Massachusetts Ave. NW, Wash., DC 20001; 56,000.

Nature Conservancy (1951), 1815 N. Lynn St., Arlington, VA 22209; 692,000.

Naturist Society, The (1980), 454 Main St., Oshkosh, WI 54901; 20,000.

Naval Architects & Marine Engineers, The Society of (1893), 601 Pavonia Ave., Ste. 400, Jersey City, NJ 07306; 10,000.

Naval Engineers, Amer. Soc. of (1888), 1452 Duke St., Alexandria, VA 22314-3458; 7,000.

Naval Institute, U.S. (1873), 118 Maryland Ave., Annapolis, MD 21402-5035; 90,000.

Naval Reserve Assn. (1954), 1619 King St., Alexandria, VA 22314-2793; 25,000+.

Navigation, Institute of (1945), 1800 Diagonal Rd., Ste. 480, Alexandria, VA 22314; 3,000.

Navy League of the U.S. (1902), 2300 Wilson Blvd., Arlington, VA 22201; 69,000.

Needlework Guild of America (1885), 1007-B Street Rd., Southampton, PA 18966; 100,000.

Negro College Fund, United (1944), 500 E. 62d St., N.Y., NY 10021; 41 institutions.

Neurofibromatosis Foundation, Natl. (1978), 141 Fifth Ave., Ste. 7-S, N.Y., NY 10010; 7,000.

New Age Walkers (1982), 3301 Bellaire Dr., Altadena, CA 91001; 4,700.

Newspaper Assn. of Amer. (1992), NAA, The Newspaper Center, 11600 Sunrise Valley Dr., Reston, VA 22091; 1,800.

Newspaper Marketing Assn., Intl. (1930), 11600 Sunrise Valley Dr., Reston, VA 22091; 1,300+.

Newswomen's Club of N.Y., Inc. (1922), 15 Gramercy Park S., N.Y., NY 10011; 230.

Nikola Tesla Walkers (1982), 10799 Sherman Grove Ave., #18, Sunland, CA 91040; 5,000.

Ninety-Nines (Intl. Organization of Women Pilots) (1929), Box 965, Will Rogers Airport, Oklahoma City, OK 73159; 6,400.

Nobel Laureate Center, Amer. (1941), 1 Morningside Dr. N., Westport, CT 06880;1,000.

Non-Commissioned Officers Assn. (1960), 10635 IH 35 North, San Antonio, TX 78233; 160,000.

Northern Cross Society (1986), Rt. One, Big Springs, KS 66050; 100+.

Notaries, Amer. Society of (1965), 918 16th St. NW, Wash., DC 20006; 20,044.

Nuclear Society, Amer. (1954), 555 N. Kensington Ave., La Grange Park, IL 60525; 16,000.

Nude Recreation, Natl. Society for (1931), 1703 N. Main St., Kissimmee, FL 34744; 45,000.

Numismatic Assn., Amer. (1891), 818 N. Cascade Ave., Colorado Springs, CO 80903-3279; 27,588.

Numismatic Society, Amer. (1858), Broadway at 155th St., N.Y., NY 10032; 2,057.

Nurses Assn., Amer. (1896), 600 Maryland Ave. SW, Ste. 100, SW, Wash., DC 20024-2571; 206,000.

Nursing, Natl. League for (1952), 350 Hudson St., N.Y., NY 10014; 16,000.

Nutrition, Amer. Institute of (1928), 9650 Rockville Pike, Bethesda, MD 20814-3990; 3,500.

Odd Fellows, Independent Order of (1819), 422 Trade St., Winston-Salem, NC 27101-2830; 350,000.

Old Crows, Assn. of (1964), 1000 N. Payne St., Alexandria, VA 22314-1696; 25,000.

Olympic Committee, U.S. (1921), One Olympic Plaza, Colorado Springs, CO 80909.

Opthalmology, Amer. Academy of (1979), 655 Beach St., San Francisco, CA 94109; 21,000.

Optical Society of America (1916), 2010 Massachusetts Ave. NW, Wash., DC 20036; 12,000.

Optimist Intl. (1919), 4494 Lindell Blvd., St. Louis, MO 63108; 155,000.

Optometric Assn., Amer. (1898), 243 N. Lindbergh Blvd., St. Louis, MO 63141; 30,000.

Organists, Amer. Guild of (1896), 475 Riverside Dr., Ste. 1260, N.Y., NY 10115; 20,200.

Oriental Society, Amer. (1842), 329 Sterling Memorial Library, Yale Sta., New Haven, CT 06520; 1,500.

ORT Federation, Amer. (Org. for Rehabilitation through Training) (1924), 817 Broadway, 10th Fl., N.Y., NY 10003; 20,000.

Ornithologists' Union, Amer. (1883), c/o National Museum of Natural History, Division of Birds, MRC-116, Wash., DC 20560; 4,500.

Osteopathic Assn., Amer. (1887), 212 E. Ohio St., Chicago, IL 60611; 23,292.

Ostomy Assn., United (1963), 36 Executive Park, Ste. 120, Irving, CA 92714, 41,009.

Outlaw and Lawman History, Natl. Association for (1974), 1201 Holly Ct., Harker Heights, TX 76543-1538; 400+.

Overeaters Anonymous (1960), World Service Office, 383 Van Ness Ave., #1601, Torrance, CA 90501; 152,000.

Paper Industry, Technical Assn. of the Pulp and (1915), 15 Technology Pkwy. S., Norcross, GA 30092; 33,000.

Parametric Analysts, Intl. Soc. of (1979), PO Box 1056, Germantown, MD 20878; 600.

Parents Without Partners (1957), 401 N. Michigan Ave., Chicago, IL 60611-4267; 70,000.

Parkinson's Disease Foundation, Inc. (1957), 710 W. 168th St., N.Y., NY 10032; 90,000.

Parliamentarians, Natl. Assn. of (1930), 213 S. Main St., Independence, MO 64050-3850; 4,400.

Parliamentary Law, Intl. Organization of Professionals in (1975), 3611 Victoria Ave., Los Angeles, CA 90016; 250.

Pasta Assn., Natl. (1904), 2101 Wilson Blvd., Ste. 920, Arlington, VA 22201; 82 cos.

Pathologists, Amer. Assn. of (1976), 9650 Rockville Pike, Bethesda, MD 20814; 2,000.

Pathologists, Amer. Society of Clinical (1922), 2100 W. Harrison St., Chicago, IL 60612; 70,000.

Pathology, Amer. Soc. for Investigative (1914), 9650 Rockville Pike, Bethesda, MD 20814-3993; 2,600.

Patton Society, The (1970), 3116 Thorn St., San Diego, CA 92104-4618.

Pearl Harbor History Associates (1983), PO Box 205, Sperryville, VA 22740-0205; 498.

PEN American Center (1922), 568 Broadway, N.Y., NY 10012; 2,800.

Pen Friends, Intl. (1967), PO Box 65, Brooklyn, NY 11229; 300,000.

PEN Women, Natl. League of American (1897), 1300 17th St. NW, Wash., DC 20036-1973; 5,000.

P.E.O. (Philanthropic Educational Organization) Sisterhood (1869), 3700 Grand Ave., Des Moines, IA 50312; 242,000.

Personnel Administration, Amer. Society for (1948), 606 N. Washington St., Alexandria, VA 22314; 40,000.

Petroleum Equipment Inst. (1951), 6514 E. 69 St., Tulsa, OK 74133; 1,755 cos.

Petroleum Institute, Amer. (1919), 1220 L St. NW, Wash., DC 20005-2985; 250 corporations.

Pharmaceutical Assn., Amer. (1852), 2215 Constitution Ave. NW, Wash., DC 20037-2985; 46,000.

Phi Delta Kappa (1906), 408 N. Union, PO Box 789, Bloomington, IN 47402-0789; 172,000.

Philatelic Pages & Panels, Amer. Soc. for (1984), 4116 Kilmer Ave., Allentown, PA 18104; 950.

Philatelic Society, Amer. (1886), 100 Oakwood Ave., PO Box 8000, State College, PA 16803-8000; 56,170.

Philological Assn., Amer. (1869), Dept. of Classics, College of the Holy Cross, Worcester, MA 01610-2395; 2,500.

Philosophical Assn., Amer. (1900), Univ. of Delaware, Newark, DE 19716; 8,500.

Philosophical Enquiry, Intl. Soc. For (1974), 5409 Pipers Gap Dr., Memphis, TN 38134; 700+.

Philosophical Society, Amer. (1743), 104 S. 5th St., Philadelphia, PA 19106; 690.

Photogrammetry and Remote Sensing, Amer. Society of (1934), 5410 Grosvenor Ln., Ste. 210, Bethesda, MD 20814.

Photographers of America, Professional (1880), 57 Forsyth St. NW, Ste. 1600, Atlanta, GA 30303; 14,000.

Photographic Society of Amer. (1934), 3000 United Founders Blvd., #103, Oklahoma City, OK 73112.

Physical Therapy Assn., Amer. (1921), 1111 N. Fairfax St., Alexandria, VA 22314; 16,020.

Physicians, Amer. Academy of Family (1947), 8880 Ward Pkwy., Kansas City, MO 64114; 81,964.

Physics, Amer. Inst. of (1931), One Physics Ellipse, College Park, MD 20740-3843; 100,000.

Physiological Society, Amer. (1887), 9650 Rockville Pike, Bethesda, MD 20814; 7,000.

Phytopathological Society, Amer., (1908), 3340 Pilot Knob Rd., St. Paul, MN 55121-2097; 5,000.

Pilgrim Society (1820), 75 Court St., Plymouth, MA 02360-3891; 1,105.

Pilot Intl. & Pilot Intl. Foundation (1921, 1975), 244 College St., Macon, GA 31213; 16,500.

Planetary Society (1980), 65 N. Catalina Ave., Pasadena, CA 91106; 100,000.

Planned Parenthood Federation of America (1916), 810 Seventh Ave., N.Y., NY 10019; 187 affiliates.

Plastic Modelers Society, Intl. (1963), PO Box 6138, Warner Robins, GA 31095-6138; 4,400.

Plastics Industry, Inc., Society of the (1937), 1275 K St. NW, Ste. 400, Wash., DC 20005; 2,000.

Platform Assn., Intl. (1830), Box 250, Winnetka, IL 60093; 5,000.

Poetry Day Committee, Natl. (1947), 1110 N. Venetian Dr., Miami, FL 33139-1019; 17,500.

Poetry Society of America (1910), 15 Gramercy Park, N.Y., NY 10003; 1,700.

Poets, Academy of Amer. (1934), 584 Broadway, Ste. 1208, N.Y., NY 10012; 4,220.

Police, International Assn. of Chiefs of (1893), 515 N. Washington St., #400, Alexandria, VA 22314-2340; 13,920.

Polish Cultural Society of America (1940), PO Box 31, Wall St., N.Y., NY 10005; 115,107.

Political Items Collectors, Amer. (1945), PO Box 340339, San Antonio, TX 78234; 3,200.

Political Science, Academy of (1880), 475 Riverside Dr., Ste. 1274, N.Y., NY 10115-0012; 7,100.

Political Science Assn., Amer. (1903), 1527 New Hampshire Ave. NW, Wash., DC 20036; 16,200.

Political Science Assn., Southern (1928), Dept. of Political Science, Univ. of Mississippi, University, MS 38677; 1,155.

Political & Social Science, Amer. Academy of (1889), 3937 Chestnut St., Philadelphia, PA 19104; 4,000.

Polo Assn., U.S. (1890), 4059 Iron Works Pike, Lexington, KY, 40511; 3,000.

Population Assn. of America (1931), 1722 N St. NW, Wash., DC 20036; 2,700.

Portuguese-American Federation, Inc. (1965), PO Box 694, Bristol, RI 02809; 250.

Portuguese Continental Union of the U.S.A. (1925), 899 Boylston St., Boston, MA 02115.

Postmasters of the U.S., Natl. Assn. of (1898), 8 Herbert St., Arlington, VA 22305-2600; 43,000.

Postmasters of the U.S., Natl. League of (1904), 1023 N. Royal St., Alexandria, VA 22314; 21,874.

Poultry Science Assn. (1908), 309 W. Clark St., Champaign, IL 61820-4690; 2,500.

Power Boat Assn., Amer. (1903), 17640 E. Nine Mile Rd., PO Box 377, Eastpointe, MI 48021; 7,000.

Precancel Collectors, Natl. Assn. of (1951), 5121 Park Blvd., Wildwood, NJ 08260-0121; 7,600.

Press, Associated (1848), 50 Rockefeller Plaza, N.Y., NY 10020; 1,554 newspapers & 6,000 broadcast stations.

Press Club, Natl. (1908), 529 14th St. NW, Wash., DC 20045.

Press Intl., United (1907), 1400 I St. NW, Wash., DC 20005.

Press and Radio Club (1948), 29 Bradley Dr., Montgomery, AL 36109; 770.

Printing Industries of America (1887), 100 Dangerfield Rd., Alexandria, VA 22314; 14,000.

Prisoners of War, Amer. Ex- (1942), 3201 E. Pioneer Pkwy., #40, Arlington, TX 76010-5396; 33,000.

Procrastinators Club of America (1956), Box 712, Bryn Athyn, PA 19009; 10,000.

Production and Inventory Control Soc., American, 500 W. Annandale Rd., Falls Church, VA 22046-4274; 69,114.

Psoriasis Foundation, Natl. (1968), 6600 SW 92nd Ave., Ste. 300, Portland, OR 97223-7195; 35,000.

Psychiatric Assn., Amer. (1844), 1400 K St. NW, Wash., DC 20005; 37,380.

Psychical Research, Amer. Society for (1907), 5 W. 73d St., N.Y., NY 10023; 2,000.

Psychoanalytic Assn., Amer. (1911), 309 E. 49th St., N.Y., NY 10017; 3,000.

Psychological Assn., Amer. (1892), 750 1st St. NE, Wash., DC 20002-4242; 119,000.

Psychological Assn. for Psychoanalysis, Natl. (1948), 150 W. 13th St., N.Y., NY 10011-7891; 355.

Psychological Minorities, Society for the Aid of (1953), 42-25 Hampton St., Elmhurst, NY 11373; 530.

PTA (Natl. Congress of Parents and Teachers), Natl. (1897), 330 N. Wabash, Chicago, IL 60611; 7 mil.

Public Administration, Amer. Soc. for (1939), 1120 G St. NW, Wash., DC 20005; 14,800.

Public Health Assn., World Fed. of (1967), 1015 15th St. NW, Wash., DC 20005; 48 natl. assn.

Public Relations Soc. of Amer. (1947), 33 Irving Pl., N.Y., NY 10003-2376; 15,462.

Publishers, Assn. of Amer. (1970), 220 E. 23d St., N.Y., NY 10010; 230 cos.

Puppeteers of Amer. (1936), 5 Cricklewood Path, Pasadena, CA 91107; 2,400.

Puzzle Buffs Intl. (1978), 1772 State Rd., Cuyahoga Falls, OH 44223; 39,000.

Quality Control, Amer. Society for (1946), 611 E. Wisconsin Ave., Milwaukee, WI 53201-3005; 130,000.

Quota International, Inc. (1919), 1420 21st St. NW, Wash., DC 20036; 11,000+.

Rabbis, Central Conference of Amer. (1889), 192 Lexington Ave., N.Y., NY 10016; 1,540.

Racial Equality (CORE), Congress of (1942), 2111 Nostrand Ave., Brooklyn, NY 11210; 100,000.

Racquetball Assn., American Amateur (1968), 815 N. Weber, Colorado Springs, CO 80903-2947.

Radio, Natl. Assn. of Business and Educational (1965), 1501 Duke St., Alexandria, VA 22314; 2,400.

Radio Relay League, Amer. (1914), 225 Main St., Newington, CT 06111; 172,000.

Radio and Television Society Foundation, Intl. (1939), 420 Lexington Ave., Ste. 1714, N.Y., NY 10170; 1,500.

Radio and TV, Inc., Amer. Women in (1950), 1650 Tyson's Blvd., Ste. 200, McLean, VA 22102.

Radio Union, Intl. Amateur (1925), PO Box AAA, Newington, CT 06111; 126 societies.

Railsplitter Society, 84th Infantry Division (1945), PO Box 827., Sioux Falls, SD 57101-0827; 3,000.

Railway Historical Society, Natl. (1935), PO Box 58153, Philadelphia, PA 19102-8153; 21,000+.

Railway Progress Institute (1908), 700 N. Fairfax St., Ste. 601, Alexandria, VA 22314-2098; 103 cos.

Range Management, Society for (1948), 1839 York St., Denver, CO 80206; 5,300.

Reading Assn., Intl. (1955), 800 Barksdale Rd., Newark, DE 19714; 92,000.

Real Estate Institute, Intl. (1975), 8383 E. Evans Rd., Scottsdale, AZ 85260-3614; 3,000+.

Rebekah Assemblies, Intl. Assn. of (1922), 422 N. Trade St., Winston-Salem, NC 27101; 150,493.

Reconciliation, Fellowship of (1915), 523 N. Broadway, Nyack, NY 10960; 10,000.

Records Managers & Administrators, Assn. of (1975), 4200 Somerset Dr., Ste. 215, Prairie Village, KS 66208; 10,600.

Recreation and Park Assn., Natl. (1965), 2775 S. Quincy St., Ste. 300, Arlington, VA 22206-2204; 23,269

Recycling Coalition, Natl., (1979), 1727 King St., Ste. 105, Alexandria, VA 22514-2720; 3,500.

Red Cross, American (1881), 8111 Gatehouse Rd., Falls Church, VA 22042; 1.5 mil. volunteers.

Red Men, Improved Order of (1765), 4521 Speight Ave., Waco, TX 76711-1708; 28,000.

Redwoods League, Save-the- (1918), 114 Sansome St., Rm. 605, San Francisco, CA 94104-3814; 43,000.

Rehabilitation Assn., Natl. (1925), 633 S. Washington St., Alexandria, VA 22301; 14,200.

Religion, Amer. Academy of (1909), 501 Hall of Languages, Syracuse Univ., Syracuse, NY 13244-1170; 5,600.
Religion Foundation, Freedom from (1978), PO Box 750, Madison, WI 53701; 3,300.
Renaissance Society of America (1954), 24 W. 12th St., N.Y., NY 10011; 3,700.
Republican National Committee (1856), 310 1st St. SE, Wash., DC 20003-1801.
Reserve Officers Assn. of the U.S. (1922), One Constitution Ave. NE, Wash., DC 20002; 123,000.
Restaurant Assn., Natl. (1919), 1200 17th St. NW, Wash., DC 20036; 20,000.
Retail Federation, Natl. (1918), 100 W. 31st St., N.Y., NY 10001; 50,000.
Retired Credit Union People, Natl. Assn. for (1978), PO Box 391, 5910 Mineral Pt. Rd., Madison, WI 53705; 81,180.
Retired Federal Employees, Natl. Assn. of (1921), 1533 New Hampshire Ave. NW, Wash., DC 20036; 500,000.
Retired Officers Assn. (1929), 201 N. Washington St., Alexandria, VA 22314-2539; 400,000.
Retired Persons, Amer. Assn. of (1958), 1909 K St. NW, Wash., DC 20049; 32 mil.
Retired Teachers Assn., Natl. (1947), 1909 K St. NW, Wash., DC 20049; 540,000.
Revolver Assn., U.S. (1900), 40 Larchmont Ave., Taunton, MA 02780-1397; 1,450.
Reye's Syndrome Foundation, Natl. (1974), 426 N. Lewis, Box 829, Bryan, OH 43506; 5,000+.
Richard III Society (1969), PO Box 13786, New Orleans, LA 70185; 700.
Rifle Assn., Natl. (1871), 11250 Waples Mill Rd., Fairfax, VA 22030; 3.4 mil.
Road & Transportation Builders' Assn., Amer. (1902), 1010 Massachusetts Ave. NW, Wash., DC 20001; 4,000.
Rocky Horror Picture Show Preservation Soc. of Terra (1993), One Caddo Ct., Kenner, LA 70064-3920.
Rodeo Cowboys Assn., Professional (1936), 101 Pro Rodeo Dr., Colorado Springs, CO 80919; 9,761.
Roller Skating, U.S. Amateur Confederation of (1937), 4730 South St., PO Box 6579, Lincoln, NE 68506; 30,000.
Rose Society, Amer. (1892), 8877 Jefferson Paige Rd., Shreveport, LA 71119-8817; 23,000.
Rotary Intl. (1905), 1560 Sherman Ave., Evanston, IL 60201; 1,203,726.
Running and Fitness Assn., Amer. (1968), 4405 East West Highway Ste. 405, Bethesda, MD 20877; 15,000.
Ruritan Natl. (1928), Ruritan Natl. Rd., Dublin, VA 24084.

Safety Council, Natl. (1913), 1121 Spring Lake Dr., Itasca, IL 60143; 12,500.
Sailors, Tin Can (1976), PO Box 100, Somerset, MA 02726; 17,000.
Sailors Assn., Destroyer-Escort (1975), PO Box 680085, Orlando, FL 32868-0085; 11,760.
St. Andrew, The Brotherhood of (1883), 1109 Merchant St., PO Box 632, Ambridge, PA 15003; 5,000.
St. Paul, Natl. Guild of (1937), 601 Hill 'n Dale, Lexington, KY 40503; 13,652.
Salespersons, Natl. Assn. of Professional (1970), PO Box 76461, Atlanta, GA 30358; 35,000.
Salt Institute (1914), 700 N. Fairfax St., Ste. 600, Alexandria, VA, 22101; 26 affiliates.
Sand Castle Builders, Intl. Society of (1988), 172 N. Pershing Ave., Akron, OH 44313; 150.
School Administrators, Amer. Assn. of (1865), 1801 N. Moore St., Arlington, VA 22209; 16,409.
School Boards Assn., Natl. (1940), 1680 Duke St., Alexandria, VA 22314.
School Counselor Assn., Amer. (1953), 5999 Stevenson Ave., Alexandria, VA 22304; 13,000.
Schools of Art, Natl. Assn. of (also: School of Art and Design; School of Dance, Music, and Theater) (1944), 11250 Roger Bacon Dr., Reston, VA 22090; 553 institutions.
Schools & Colleges, Amer. Council on (1927), 13014 Dale Mabry Hwy., Ste. 270-B, Tampa, FL 33180-2808; 317
Science, Amer. Assn. for the Advancement of (1848), 1333 H St. NW, Wash., DC 20005; 150.
Science Fiction Society, World (1939), PO Box 1270, Kendall Sq. Sta., Cambridge, MA 02142; 5,000.
Science Service (1921), 1719 N St. NW, Wash., DC 20036.
Sciences, Natl. Academy of (1863), 2101 Constitution Ave. NW, Wash., DC 20418; 1,801.
Science Teachers Assn., Natl. (1944), 1840 Wilson Blvd., Arlington, VA 22201; 52,000.
Science Writers, Natl. Assn. of (1934), PO Box 294, Greenlawn, NY 11740; 1,801.
Scrabble Assn., Natl. (1973), PO Box 700, 120 Front St., Greenport, NY 11944; 10,000.

Screen Printing & Graphic Imaging Assn. Intl. (1948), 10015 Main St., Fairfax, VA 22031; 3,800 cos.
Sculpture Soc., Natl. (1893), 1177 Ave. of the Americas, N.Y., NY 10036; 4,400.
Seamen's Service, United, and the Amer. Merchant Marine Library Assn., (1942, 1921), One World Trade Center, Ste. 2161, N.Y., NY 10048.
2d Air Division Assn. (1947), 06-410 Delaire Landing Rd., Philadelphia, PA 19114; 7,852.
Secondary School Principals, Natl. Assn. of (1916), 1904 Association Dr., Reston, VA 22091; 42,000.
Secretaries, Natl. Assn. of Legal (1920), 2250 E. 73d, Ste. 550, Tulsa, OK 74136-6864; 16,000.
Secretaries Intl., Professional (1942), 10502 N.W. Ambassador Dr., Kansas City, MO 64153; 40,000.
Secular Humanism, Inc., Council for Democratic and (1980), 3965 Rensch Rd., Amherst, NY 14226; 4,000.
Securities Industry Assn. (1972), 120 Broadway, N.Y., NY 10271-0080; 728 firms.
Separation of Church & State, Americans United for (1947), 1816 Jefferson Place NW, Wash., DC 20036; 50,000.
Sertoma International (1912), 1912 E. Meyer Blvd., Kansas City, MO 64132; 30,000.
Sex Information & Education Council of the U.S. (SIECUS) (1964), 130 W. 42d St., Ste. 2500, N.Y., NY 10036; 2,500+.
Sharkhunters Intl. (1983), PO Box 1539, Hernando, FL 34442; 5,000+.
Shipbuilders Council of America (1921), 4301 N. Fairfax Dr., Ste. 330, Arlington, VA 22203; 50 organizations.
Ships-in-Bottles Assn. of Amer. (1983), PO Box 180550, Coronado, CA 92178; 425.
Shore & Beach Preservation Assn., Amer. (1926), PO Box 279, Middletown, CA 95461; 900.
Shrine of North America (1872), 2900 Rocky Point Dr., Tampa, FL 33607-1435; 634,000.
Sierra Club (1892), 730 Polk St., San Francisco, CA 94109; 564,360.
Skeet Shooting Assn., Natl. (1946), PO Box 680007, San Antonio, TX 78268; 15,800.
Ski Assn., U.S. (1904), PO Box 100, Park City, UT 84060.
Small Business United, Natl. (1937), 1155 15th St. NW, Ste. 710, Wash., DC 20005; 65,000.
Smokers' Pollution, Inc., Group Against (1971), PO Box 632, College Park, MD 20741-0632; 10,000+.
Smoking & Health, Natl. Clearinghouse for (1965), Center for Disease Control, 1600 Clifton Rd. NE, Atlanta, GA 30333.
Soccer Federation, U.S. (1913), 1801 S. Prairie Ave., Chicago, IL 60616.
Social Sciences, Natl. Institute of (1865), 1192 Park Ave., 15B, N.Y., NY 10128-1314; 315.
Social Work Education, Council on (1952), 1600 Duke St., Alexandria, VA 22314; 3,000.
Sociological Assn., Amer. (1905), 1722 N St. NW, Wash., DC 20036; 13,000.
Softball Association, Amateur (1933), 2801 N.E. 50th St., Oklahoma City, OK 73111; 5 milllion+.
Soft Drink Assn., Natl. (1921), 1101 16th St. NW, Wash., DC 20036; 1,700.
Soil Science Society of America (1936), 677 S. Segoe Rd., Madison, WI 53711; 5,800.
Soil & Water Conservation Society of America (1945), 7515 N.E. Ankeny Rd., Ankeny, IA 50021-9764; 11,000.
Soldiers' Sailors' and Airmen's Club (1919), 283 Lexington Ave., N.Y., NY 10016.
Songwriters Guild of America, The (1931), 1500 Harbor Blvd., Weehawken, NJ 07087-6732; 4,000+.
Sons of Confederate Veterans (1896), PO Box 59, Columbia, TN 38402-0059.
Sons of Italy in America, Order (1905), 219 E St. NE, Wash. DC 20002; 500,000.
Sons of Norway (1895), 1455 W. Lake St., Minneapolis, MN 55408; 74,000.
Sons of St. Patrick, Society of the Friendly (1784), 80 Wall St., N.Y., NY 10005; 1,500.
Sons of Sherman's March to the Sea (1966), 1725 Farmer Ave., Tempe, AZ 85281-6533; 750.
Sons of the Amer. Legion (1932), Box 1055, Indianapolis, IN 46206; 161,376.
Sons of the American Revolution, Natl. Society of (1889), 1000 S. Fourth St., Louisville, KY 40203; 26,000.
Sons of the Republic of Texas, The (1922), 5942 Abrams Rd., #222, Dallas, TX 75231; 4,500.
Sons of Union Veterans of the Civil War (1881), 7017 Granada Lane, Flint, MI 48532-3023; 4,500.
Soroptimist Intl. of the Americas (1921), Two Penn Center, Ste. 1000, Philadelphia, PA 19102; 47,000.
Southern Christian Leadership Conference (1957), 334 Auburn Ave. NE, Atlanta, GA 30303; 1 mil.

Space Education Assn., U.S. (1973), 231 School Lane, Rheems, PA 17570-0249; 1,500.

Special Olympics Intl. (1968), 1350 New York Ave. NW, Ste. 500, Wash., DC 20005.

Speech Communication Assn. (1914), 5105 Backlick Rd., Annandale, VA 22003; 6,800.

Speech-Language-Hearing Assn., Amer. (1925), 10801 Rockville Pike, Rockville, MD 20852.

Speedskating Union of the U.S., Amateur (1927), 1033 Shady Lane, Glen Ellyn, IL 60137; 3,000.

Speleological Society, Natl. (1941), 2813 Cave Ave., Huntsville, AL 35810-4431; 12,500.

Spiritual Awareness, Assn. for (1984), PO Box 41, Clifton Hill, MO 65244; 1,500.

Sports Car Club of America (1944), 9033 E. Eastern Pl., Englewood, CO 80112; 50,000+.

Sportscasters Assn., Amer. (1980), 5 Beekman St., N.Y., NY 10038; 950+.

Sports Club, Indoor (1930), 1145 Highland St., Napoleon, OH 43545; 950.

State Governments, Council of (1933), PO Box 11910, Lexington, KY 40517; 50 states, 4 territories.

Statistical Assn., Amer. (1839), 1429 Duke St., Alexandria, VA 22314-3402; 19,500.

Steamship Historical Society of America (1940), 300 Ray Dr., Ste. 4, Providence, RI 02906; 3,400.

Steel Construction, Amer. Institute of (1921), 1 E. Wacker Dr., Ste. 3100, Chicago, IL 60601-2001; 2,770.

Stock Car Auto Racing (NASCAR), Natl. Assn. for (1947), PO Box 2875, Daytona Beach, FL 32114; 50,000.

Stock Exchange, Amer. (1911), 86 Trinity Pl., N.Y., NY 10006; 871.

Stock Exchange, N.Y. (1792), 11 Wall St., N.Y., NY 10005.

Stock Exchange, Philadelphia (1790), 1900 Market St., Philadelphia, PA 19103; 505.

Student Councils, Natl. Assn. of (1931), 1904 Association Dr., Reston, VA 22091; 9,000 schools.

Stuttering Project, Natl. (1977), 2151 Irving St., Ste. 208, San Francisco, CA 94122-1609; 4,000.

Sudden Infant Death Syndrome Alliance, Natl. (1987), 10500 Little Patuxent Pkwy., Ste. 420, Columbia, MD 21044.

Sugar Brokers Assn., Natl. (1903), 90 West St., Ste. 706, N.Y., NY 10006; 100.

Surgeons, Amer. College of (1913), 55 E. Erie St., Chicago, IL 60611-2797; 52,000.

Surgeons of the U.S., Assn. of Military (1891), 9320 Old Georgetown Rd., Bethesda, MD 20814; 12,500.

Surveying & Mapping, Amer. Congress on (1941), 5410 Grosvenor Ln., Bethesda, MD 20814-2122; 9,500.

Symphony Orchestra League, Amer. (1942), 1156 Fifteenth St. NW, Ste. 800, Wash., DC 20005; 800+ orchestras.

Systems Management, Assn. for (1947), PO Box 38370, Cleveland, OH 44138; 5,100.

Table Tennis Assn., U.S. (1933), One Olympic Plaza, Colorado Springs, CO 80909; 7,754.

Tailhook Assn., The (1957), 9696 Business Park Ave., PO Box 26700, San Diego, CA 92131.

Tall Buildings and Urban Habitat, Council on (1969), Lehigh Univ., 13 E. Packer Ave., Bethlehem, PA 18015; 3,000.

Tax Administrators, Federation of (1937), 444 N. Capitol St. NW, Wash., DC 20001.

Tax Foundation, Inc. (1957), 1250 H St. NW, Ste. 750, Wash., DC 20005.

Taxpayers Union, Natl. (1969), 713 Maryland Ave., NE, Wash., DC 20002; 300,000.

Tea Assn. of the U.S.A. (1899), 230 Park Ave., Ste. 1460, N.Y., NY 10169; 100 firms.

Teachers of English, Natl. Council of (1911), 1111 W. Kenyon Rd., Urbana, IL 61801-1096; 68,000.

Teachers of English to Speakers of Other Languages (1966), 1600 Cameron St., Ste. 300, Alexandria, VA 22314; 18,700.

Teachers of French, Amer. Assn. of (1927), 57 E. Armory Ave., Champaign, IL 61820; 10,500.

Teachers of Mathematics, Natl. Council of (1920), 1906 Association Dr., Reston, VA 22091-1593; 118,000.

Teachers of Singing, Natl. Assn. of (1944), 2800 Univ. Blvd. N., J.U. Sta., Jacksonville, FL 32211; 5,000.

Teachers of Spanish & Portuguese, Amer. Assn. of (1917), 8 Frasier Hall, Univ. of Northern Colorado, Greeley, CO 80939; 13,000.

Telephone Pioneers of Amer. (1911), 930 15th St., 12th Fl., Denver, CO 80202; 875,000.

Television, Inc., Viewers for Quality (1984), PO Box 195, Fairfax Station, VA 22039; 3,000.

Television Arts & Sciences, Natl. Academy of (1947), 111 W. 57th St., Ste. 1020, N.Y., NY 10019; 12,000.

Television Bureau of Advertising (1954), 850 3rd Ave., 10th Fl., N.Y., NY 10022.

Television & Radio Artists, Amer. Federation of (1937), 260 Madison Ave., 7th Fl., N.Y., NY 10016; 75,000.

Telluride Assn. (1910), 217 West Ave., Ithaca, NY 14850.

Temperance Union, Natl. Women's Christian (1874), 1730 Chicago Ave., Evanston, IL 60201; 12,594.

Tennis Assn., U.S. (1881), 70 W. Red Oak Lane, White Plains, NY 10604.

Terraplane Club, Hudson-Essex (1959), 100 E. Cross St., Ypsilanti, MI 48198; 3,200.

Tesla Memorial Soc., Inc. (1979), 453 Martin Rd., Buffalo, NY 14218; 1,700.

Testing & Materials, Amer. Society for (1898), 1916 Race St., Philadelphia, PA 19103; 35,000+.

Textile Manufacturers Institute, Amer. (1949), 1801 K St. NW, Ste. 900, Wash., DC 20006.

Theodore Roosevelt Assn. (1919), PO Box 719, Oyster Bay, NY 11771; 1,355.

Theological Schools in the U.S. and Canada, Assn. of (1918), 10 Summit Park Dr., Pittsburgh, PA 15275-1103.

Theosophical Society in America, The (1886), 1926 N. Main St., Wheaton, IL 60189-0270; 4,600.

Thoreau Society (1941), 156 Belknap St., Concord, MA 01742; 1,500.

Thoroughbred Racing Assns. (1942), 420 Fair Hill Dr., Ste. 1, Elkton, MD 21921; 41 racing associations.

Tin Can Soldiers, Inc. (1976), 1231 County, PO Box 100, Somerset, MA 02726; 15,000.

Titanic Historical Society (1963), PO Box 51053, Indian Orchard, MA 01151-0053; 5,324.

Toastmasters Intl. (1924), PO Box 9052, Mission Viejo, CA 92690-7052.

Topical Assn., Amer. (1949), PO Box 630, Johnstown, PA 15907; 7,000.

Toy Manufacturers of America (1916), 200 Fifth Ave., N.Y., NY 10010; 265.

Track & Field, USA (1979), PO Box 120, Indianapolis, IN 46206; 200,000.

Trademark Assn., Intl. (1878), 1133 Avenue of the Americas, N.Y., NY 10036-6710; 2,800.

Trail Assn., North Country (1981), 3777 Sparks Dr. SE, Ste. 105, Grand Rapids, MI 49546; 800.

Transit Assn., Amer. Public (1974), 1201 New York Ave. NW, Wash., DC 20005; 1,100 organizations.

Translators Assn., Amer. (1959), 1800 Diagonal Rd., Ste. 220, Alexandria; VA 22314; 6,000.

Trapshooting Assn., Amateur (1923), 601 W. National Rd., Vandalia, OH 45377; 102,360

Travel Agents, Amer. Society of (1931), 1101 King St., Ste. 200, Alexandria, VA 22314; 25,000.

Travelers of America, Order of United, Commercial (1888), 632 N. Park St., Columbus, OH 43215-8419; 130,000.

Travelers Protective Assn. of America (1890), 3755 Lindell Blvd., St. Louis, MO 63108; 148,000.

Trilateral Commission, The (1973), 345 E. 46th St., N.Y., NY 10017; 325.

Truck Historical Soc., Amer. (1971), PO Box 531168, Birmingham, AL 35253; 18,250.

Trucking Assn., Amer. (1933), 2200 Mill Rd., Alexandria, VA 22314-4677; 4,500 cos.

True Sisters, United Order (1846), 212 Fifth Ave., Rm. 1307, N.Y., NY 10010; 10,000.

T. S. Eliot Society (1980), 5007 Waterman Blvd., St. Louis, MO 63108; 148.

Tuberous Sclerosis Assn. of Amer. (1970), 8000 Corporate Dr., Ste. 120, Landover, MD 20785; 3,000+.

UFOs, Natl. Investigation Committee on (1967), 14617 Victory Blvd., Ste. 4, Van Nuys, CA 91411; 750.

UNICEF, U.S. Committee for (1947), 333 E. 38th St., N.Y., NY 10016.

Underwriters, Amer. Soc. of Chartered Life (1927), 270 Bryn Mawr Ave., Bryn Mawr, PA 19010; 30,000.

Underwriters, Natl. Assn. of Life (1890), 1922 F St. NW, Wash., DC 20006; 143,000.

Underwriters (CPCU), Soc. of Chartered Property and Casualty (1944), Kahler Hall, 720 Providence Rd., Malvern, PA 19355-0709; 25,000.

United Nations Assn. of the U.S.A. (1923, as League of Nations Assn.), 485 Fifth Ave., N.Y., NY 10017; 30,000.

United Way of America (1918), 801 N. Fairfax St., Alexandria, VA 22309; 1,200.

Universities, Assn. of Amer. (1914), One Dupont Circle, Ste. 730, Wash., DC 20036; 59 institutions.

Universities & Colleges, Assn. of Governing Bds. of (1921), One Dupont Circle NW, Ste. 400, Wash., DC 20036.

University Continuing Education Assn., Natl. (1915), One Dupont Circle, Ste. 615, Wash., DC 20036; 2,000.

University Extension Assn., Natl. (1915), One Dupont Circle NW, Ste. 400, Wash., DC 20036; 1,100.

University Foundation, Intl. (1973), 1301 S. Noland Rd., Independence, MO 64055; 61,472.

University Professors, Amer. Assn. of (1915), 1012 14th St. NW, Ste. 500, Wash., DC 20005; 41,000.

University Women, Amer. Assn. of (1881), 1111 16th St. NW, Wash., DC 20036; 150,000.

Urban League, Natl. (1910), 500 E. 62d St., N.Y., NY 10020.

Useless Skills, Institute of Totally (1987), Box 181, Temple, NH 03084; 650.

USO (United Service Organizations) (1941), Washington Navy Yard, 901 M St., SE, Bldg. 198, Wash., DC 20374-5096.

Utility Commissioners, Natl. Assn. of Regulatory (1889), 1102 Interstate Commerce Commission Bldg., 12th & Constitution Ave. NW, Wash., DC 20044-0684; 408.

Vampire Research Center (1972), PO Box 252, Elmhurst, NY 11373; 1,250.

Variety Clubs Intl. (1928), 1560 Broadway, N.Y., NY 10036.

VASA Order of America (1896), 65 Bryant Rd., Cranston, RI 02910; 30,000.

Ventriloquists, North American Assn. of (1944), Box 420, Littleton, CO 80160; 1,700.

Veterans, American (AMVETS) (1944); **AMVETS Auxiliary** (1946), 4647 Forbes Blvd., Lanham, MD 20706-9961; 200,000.

Veterans of America, Paralyzed (1947), 801 18th St. NW, Wash., DC 20006; 16,817.

Veterans Assn., Blinded (1945), 477 H St. NW, Wash., DC 20001; 7,900.

Veterans Assn., Coast Guard Combat (1986), 17728 Striley Dr., Ashton, MD 20861-9763; 1,600.

Veterans Assn., Women's Army Corps (1947), Hwy. 21, Anniston, AL 36206; 3,500.

Veterans Assn. of America, Polish Army (1921), 155 Noble St., Brooklyn, NY 11222; 3,500.

Veterans of Foreign Wars of the U.S. (1899), 406 W. 34th St., Kansas City, MO 64111.

Veterans of Foreign Wars of the U.S, Ladies Auxiliary to the (1914), 406 W. 34th St., Kansas City, MO 64111; 770,308.

Veterans of Underage Military Service (1991), 100 Village Lane, Philadelphia, PA 19154; 793.

Veterans of the U.S.A., Catholic War (1935), 419 North Lee St., Alexandria, VA 22314; 30,000.

Veterans of the U.S.A., Jewish War (1896), 1811 R St. NW, Wash., DC 20009; 100,000.

Veterans of the Vietnam War (1980), 760 Jumper Rd., Wilkes-Barre, PA 18702-8033; 30,000.

Veterans of World War I of the USA (1958), PO Box 8027, Alexandria, VA 22306-3027; 17,000.

Veterans of WWII, U.S. Merchant Marine (1945), PO Box 629, San Pedro, CA 90733; 7,612.

Veterans of WWII, U.S. Submarine (1955), 317 N. Palm Ave., Frostproof, FL 33843; 8,250.

Veterans, Women World War (1919), 237 Madison Ave., N.Y., NY 10016; 35,000.

Veterinary Medical Assn., Amer. (1863), 1931 N. Meacham Rd., Schaumburg, IL 60173; 53,512.

Victorian Society in America (1965), 219 S. Sixth St., Philadelphia, PA 19106; 2,300.

Virgil Fox Society, The (1977), 88 Chestnut St., Brooklyn, NY 11208; 450+.

Volleyball Assn., U.S. (1928), 3595 E. Fountain Blvd., Ste. I-2, Colorado Springs, CO 80910-1740; 100,000.

Warrant and Warrant Officers' Assn., Chief, U.S. Coast Guard (1929), c/o Fort McNair Yacht Basin, 200 V St. SW, Wash., DC 20024; 3,346.

Watch & Clock Collectors, Natl. Assn. of (1943), 514 Poplar St., Columbia, PA 17512; 38,000+.

Water Assn., Natl. Ground (1948), 6375 Riverside Dr., Dublin, OH 43017; 24,500.

Watercolor Society, American (1866), 47 Fifth Ave., N.Y., NY 10003; 511.

Water Environment Federation (1928), 601 Wythe St., Alexandria, VA 22314; 40,000.

Water Pollution Control Administration, Assn. of State and Interstate (1961), 750 First St. NE, Ste. 910, Wash., DC 20001.

Water Pollution Control Federation (1928), 601 Wythe St., Alexandria, VA 22314-1994; 32,000.

Water Resources Assn., Amer. (1964), 5410 Grosvenor Ln., Ste. 220, Bethesda, MD 20814-2192; 4,000.

Water Ski Assn., Amer. (1939), 799 Overlook Dr. SE, Winter Haven, FL 33830; 30,000.

Water Works Assn., Amer. (1881), 6666 W. Quincey Ave., Denver, CO 80235; 49,482.

Welding Society, Amer. (1919), 550 N.W. LeJeune Rd., Miami, FL 33126; 41,000+.

Wheelchair Sports, USA (1956), 3595 E. Fountain Blvd., Ste. L-1, Colorado Springs, CO 80910; 4,600.

Widows, Society of Military (1968), 5535 Hemstead Way, Springfield, VA 22151; 2,000.

Wilderness Society (1935), 900 17th St. NW, Wash., DC 20006; 271,268

Wildflower Research Center, Natl. (1982), 4801 La Crosse Ave., Austin, TX 78739; 20,000.

Wildlife, Defenders of (1947), 1244 19th St. NW, Wash., DC 20036; 80,000.

Wildlife Federation, Natl. (1936), 1400 16th St. NW, Wash., DC 20036-2266; 4.7 mil.

Wildlife Fund, World (1961), 1250 24th St. NW, Wash., DC 20037; 1.25 mil.

Wildlife Management Institute (1911), 1101 14th St. NW, Ste. 801, Wash., DC 20005.

William Penn Assn. (1886), 709 Brighton Rd., Pittsburgh, PA 15233; 90,000.

Wireless Pioneers, Society of (1968), PO Box 86, Geyserville, CA 95441; 2,000.

Wizard of Oz Club, Intl. (1957), 220 North 11th St., Escanaba, MI 49829; 2,410.

Women, Natl. Assn. of Bank (1920), 7910 Woodmont Ave. #1430, Bethesda, MD 20814-3015; 30,000.

Women (NOW), Natl. Organization for (1966), 1000 16th St. NW, Ste. 700, Wash., DC 20036; 250,000.

Women for America, Concerned (1979), 370 L'Enfant Promenade SW, #800, Wash., DC 20024; 600,000.

Women Artists, Natl. Assn. of (1889), 41 Union Sq., N.Y., NY 10003; 800.

Women in Communications (1908), 2101 Wilson Blvd., Ste. 417, Arlington, VA 22201; 11,000.

Women's Clubs, General Federation of (1890), 1734 N St. NW, Wash., DC, 20036-2990; 300,000 U.S.

Women's Clubs, Natl. Federation of Business & Professional (1919), 2012 Massachusetts Ave. NW, Wash., DC 20036.

Women's Intl. League for Peace & Freedom (1915), 1213 Race St., Philadelphia, PA 19107-1691; 9,000.

Women's Legal Defense Fund (1971), 1875 Connecticut Ave. NW, Ste. 710, Wash., DC 20009; 2,500.

Women's Overseas Service League (1921), PO Box 39058, Friendship Station, Wash., DC 20016; 1,164.

Women Strike for Peace (1961), 110 Maryland Ave. NE, Ste. 302, Wash., DC 20002; 8,000.

Women of the U.S., Inc., Natl. Council of (1888), 777 UN Plaza, 7th Fl., N.Y., NY 10017; 500 members, 33 affiliate org.

Women Voters of the U.S., League of (1920), 1730 M St. NW, Wash., DC 20036; 90,000.

Woodmen of America, Modern (1883), 1701 1st Ave., Rock Island, IL 61201; 750,000.

Woodmen of the World Life Insurance Soc. (1890), 1700 Farnam St., Omaha, NE 68102; 856,000.

Workmen's Circle (1900), 45 E. 33d St., N.Y., NY 10016.

World Federalist Assn. (1975), 418 7th St. SE, Wash., DC 20003; 9,000.

World Future Society (1966), 7910 Woodmont Ave., Ste. 450, Bethesda, MD 20814; 30,000.

World Learning Inc. (1932), Kipling Rd., PO Box 676, Brattleboro, VT 05153; 2,500.

World's Fair Collectors Soc. (1968), PO Box 20806, Sarasota, FL 34276-3806; 500.

Writers Guild of America, West (1933), 8955 Beverly Blvd., W. Hollywood, CA 90048; 7,500+.

Yachting Assn., Southern California (1921), 5855 Naples Plaza, Ste. 211, Long Beach, CA; 20,000 families.

YM-YWHAs of Greater New York, Associated (1957), 130 E. 59th St., N.Y., NY 10020; 55,100.

Young America's Foundation (1971), 110 Elden St., Herndon, VA 22070.

Young Men's Christian Assns. of the U.S.A. (1851), 101 N. Wacker Dr., Chicago, IL 60606; 13 mil.

Young Women's Christian Assn. of the U.S.A. (1906), 726 Broadway, N.Y., NY 10003; 1.6 mil.

Zero Population Growth (1968), 1400 16th St. NW, Ste. 320, Wash., DC 20036; 50,000.

Zionist Organization of America (1897), 4 E. 34th St., N.Y., NY 10016; 110,000.

Zoo and Aquarium Assn., American (1924), 7970-D Old Georgetown Rd., Bethesda, MD 20814-2493; 6,000.

Zoologists, Amer. Society of (1902), 401 N. Michigan Ave., Chicago, IL 60611; 4,000.

POSTAL INFORMATION
U.S. Postal Service

The Postal Reorganization Act, creating a government-owned postal service under the executive branch and replacing the old Post Office Department, was signed into law by President Richard Nixon on Aug. 12, 1970. The service officially came into being on July 1, 1971.

The U.S. Postal Service is governed by an 11-person Board of Governors. Nine members are appointed to 9-year terms by the president with Senate approval. These 9, in turn, choose a postmaster general. The board and the postmaster general choose the 11th member, who serves as deputy postmaster general. An independent Postal Rate Commission of 5 members, appointed by the president, reviews and rules on proposed postal rate increases submitted by the Board of Governors. As of July 26, 1995, there were 28,322 post offices throughout the U.S.

U.S. Domestic Rates

Postal rates and fees shown below were implemented on Jan. 1, 1995, for domestic mail and on July 8, 1995, for international mail. Domestic rates apply to the U.S., to its territories and possessions, and to APOs and FPOs.

First Class

Letters written and matter sealed against inspection, 32¢ for 1st ounce or fraction, 23¢ for each additional ounce or fraction up to and including 11 oz.

U.S. Postal Service cards, single 20¢, double 40¢; private postcards, same.

First class includes written matter, namely letters, postal cards, postcards (private mailing cards), and all other matter wholly or partly in writing, whether sealed or unsealed, except manuscripts for books, periodical articles and music, manuscript copy accompanying proofsheets or corrected proofsheets of the same, and the writing authorized by law on matter of other classes. Also matter sealed or closed against inspection, bills, and statements of accounts.

Express Mail

Express Mail Service is available for any mailable article up to 70 lb, and guarantees delivery between major U.S. cities or your money back. Articles received by the acceptance time authorized by the postmaster at a postal facility offering Express Mail are delivered by 3 PM the next day to some locations or by noon the next day to other destinations. Or, if you prefer, your shipment can be picked up as early as 10 AM the next business day. Second-day service is available to locations not on the Next Day Delivery Network. Rates include insurance, Shipment Receipt, and Record of Delivery at the destination post office.

The rate for Express Mail weighing up to 8 oz is $10.75. Consult Postmaster for other Express Mail Services and rates. (The Postal Service will refund, upon application to originating office, the postage for any Express Mail shipments not meeting the service standard except for those delayed by strike or work stoppage, delay or cancellation of flights, or government action beyond the control of the Postal Service.)

Second Class

Second class mail includes newspapers and periodicals.

For the general public: The applicable third- or fourth-class postage is paid for this type of mail.

For publishers: Rates vary according to (1) whether the item is printed in the country it is mailed in; (2) the percentage of reading and advertising matter; (3) the item's weight; and (4) the countries to which it may go.

Third Class

Third class: Any mail that weighs less than 16 oz that is not included in first or second class.

Single mailing: Publications, small parcels, printed matter, booklets, and catalogs, first ounce or fraction is 32¢; each additional ounce or fraction up to 11 oz is 23¢; over 11 oz up to 13 oz, each additional 2 oz is 28¢; over 13 oz up to 16 oz, each additional 3 oz is 15¢.

Bulk mailing: At least 200 pieces or 50 lb of such items as solicitations, newsletters, advertising materials, books and cassettes, each item of which individually weighs less than 1 lb. Minimum rate per piece: Basic presort, $0.226 for pieces weighing 3.3067 oz or less; for pieces weighing more than 3.3067 oz, the rate is $0.124 per piece + $0.687 per pound. Contact your post office for the discounts offered for presorted, destination entry, and automation compatible mail.

Separate rates for some nonprofit organizations. Bulk mailing fee, $75 per calendar year. Apply to postmaster for permit. One-time fee for permit imprint, $75.

Parcel Post—Fourth Class

Fourth class or parcel post: Any matter that weighs 16 oz or more that is not included in first or second class. The post office determines fourth (parcel post) class charges according to the weight of the package in pounds and the zone distance it is being shipped. All fractions of a pound are counted as a full pound.

Forwarding Addresses

The mailer, in order to obtain a forwarding address, must endorse the envelope or cover "Address Correction Requested." The destination post office then will determine whether a forwarding address has been left on file and provide it for a fee of 50¢ per manual correction and 20¢ per automated correction.

Priority Mail Flat Rate

The most expeditious handling and transportation available will be used for fastest delivery. If item fits into special Postal Service flat-rate envelope, rate is $3.00 regardless of weight.

Pickup service for Priority Mail is available for $4.95 for each stop (not per package) by the Postal Service.

Priority Mail

Packages weighing up to 70 lb and not exceeding 108 in. in length and girth combined, including written and other material of the first class, whether sealed or unsealed, fractions of a pound being charged as a full pound.

Rates according to zone apply between the U.S. and Puerto Rico and Virgin Islands. The mileage between the specific geographic locations of 3-digit ZIP codes determines the zone number to be used. The mileage range represented by the zone number is: Zone 1—up to 50 mi; 2—51 to 150 mi; 3—151 to 300 mi; 4—301 to 600 mi; 5—601 to 1,000 mi; 6—1,001 to 1,400 mi; 7—1,401 to 1,800 mi; 8—over 1,800 mi.

Parcels weighing less than 15 lb, measuring over 84 in. but not exceeding 108 in. in length and girth combined are chargeable with a minimum rate equal to that for a 15 lb parcel for the zone to which addressed.

Zones	To 2 lb	3 lb	4 lb	5 lb*
1, 2, 3, 4, 5, 6, 7, 8	$3.00	$4.00	$5.00	$6.00

*Consult postmaster for rates for parcels over 5 lb.

Special Handling

Third and fourth class parcels will be handled and delivered as expeditiously as practicable (but not special delivery) upon payment, in addition to the regular postage: up to 10 lb, $5.40; over 10 lb, $7.50. Such parcels must be endorsed "Special Handling."

Special Delivery

First class and priority mail up to 2 lb, $9.95; over 2 lb but not over 10 lb, $10.35; over 10 lb, $11.15. All other classes up to 2 lb, $10.45; over 2 lb but not over 10 lb, $11.25; over 10 lb, $12.10.

Bound Printed Matter Rates

(single piece zone rate)

Fourth Class Mail:
Single-Piece Bound Printed Matter Rates

Weight				Zones				
lb	Local	1&2	3	4	5	6	7	8
1.5	1.11	1.49	1.52	1.58	1.66	1.74	1.84	1.93
2	1.12	1.52	1.56	1.63	1.74	1.85	1.99	2.10
2.5	1.14	1.55	1.60	1.69	1.82	1.96	2.13	2.28
3	1.15	1.57	1.64	1.74	1.90	2.07	2.27	2.45
3.5	1.17	1.60	1.67	1.80	1.98	2.18	2.42	2.62
4	1.18	1.63	1.71	1.85	2.07	2.29	2.56	2.79
4.5	1.20	1.65	1.75	1.91	2.15	2.40	2.71	2.97
5	1.22	1.68	1.79	1.96	2.23	2.51	2.85	3.14
6	1.25	1.73	1.86	2.07	2.39	2.73	3.14	3.49
7	1.28	1.79	1.94	2.18	2.56	2.95	3.43	3.83
8	1.31	1.84	2.01	2.29	2.72	3.17	3.71	4.18
9	1.34	1.90	2.09	2.40	2.89	3.39	4.00	4.52
10	1.37	1.95	2.16	2.51	3.05	3.61	4.29	4.87

(Includes both catalogs and similar bound printed matter.)

(Bound printed matter must weigh at least 1 lb and not more than 10 lb. Bound printed matter includes catalogs, directories, and books not eligible for special 4th class rates.)

Domestic Mail Special Services

Registry—Only matter prepaid with postage at first class postage rates may be registered. Stamps or meter stamps must be attached. The face of the article must be at least 5″ long, 3½″ high. The mailer is required to declare the value of mail presented for registration.

Registered Mail

Value	Insured	Uninsured
$0.00 to $100	$4.95	$4.85
$100.01 to $500	5.40	5.20
$500.01 to $1,000	5.85	5.55
$1,000.01 to $2,000	6.30	5.90
$2,000.01 to $3,000	6.75	6.25
$3,000.01 to $4,000	7.20	6.60
$4,000.01 to $5,000	7.65	6.95
$5,000.01 to $6,000	8.10	7.30
$6,000.01 to $7,000	8.55	7.65
$7,000.01 to $8,000	9.00	8.00
$8,000.01 to $9,000	9.45	8.35
$9,000.01 to $10,000	9.90	8.70

Consult postmaster for registry rates above $10,000.

C.O.D.: Unregistered—is applicable to first, third, fourth class, and Express Mail matter. Such mail must be based on bona fide orders or be in conformity with agreements between senders and addressees. **Registered**—for details, consult postmaster.

Insurance—is applicable to third and fourth class matter. Matter for sale addressed to prospective purchasers who have not ordered it or authorized its sending will not be insured.

Insured Mail Rates

$0.01 to $50	$0.75
50.01 to $100	1.60
100.01 to $200	2.50
200.01 to $300	3.40
300.01 to $400	4.30
400.01 to $500	5.20
500.01 to $600	6.10

Liability for insured mail is limited to $600.

Certified mail—service is available for any matter having no intrinsic value on which first class or air mail postage is paid. Receipt is furnished at time of mailing and evidence of delivery obtained. The fee is $1.10 in addition to postage. Return receipt, restricted delivery, and special delivery are available upon payment of additional fees. No indemnity.

Special Fourth Class Rate

(limit 70 lb)

First pound or fraction, $1.24 (70¢ if 500 pieces or more of special rate matter are presorted to 5 digit ZIP code or $1.04 if 500 pieces or more are presorted to Bulk Mail Centers); each additional pound or fraction through 7 lb, 50¢; each additional pound, 31¢. Only the following specific articles: Books of at least 8 printed pages consisting wholly of reading matter or scholarly bibliography, or reading matter with incidental blank spaces for notations and containing no advertising matter other than incidental announcements of books; 16-mm or narrower width films in final form and catalogs of such films of 24 pages or more (at least 22 of which are printed) except films and film catalogs sent to or from commercial theaters; printed music in bound or sheet form; printed objective test materials; sound recordings, playscripts and manuscripts for books, periodicals, and music; printed educational reference charts; loose-leaf pages and binders thereof consisting of medical information for distribution to doctors, hospitals, medical schools, and medical students; computer-readable media containing prerecorded information and guides for use with such media. Package must be marked "Special 4th Class Rate" stating item contained.

Library Rate

(limit 70 lb)

First pound $1.12, each additional pound through 7 lb, 41¢; each additional pound, 20¢. Books when loaned or exchanged between and sent to or from schools, colleges, public libraries, and certain nonprofit organizations; books, printed music, bound academic theses, periodicals, sound recordings, other library materials, museum materials (specimens, collections), scientific or mathematical kits, instruments or other devices; also catalogs, guides, or scripts for some of these materials. Must be marked "Library Rate."

Also qualifying for library rate are: Books mailed from publishers or distributors to schools, libraries, colleges, or universities or to bookstores owned, operated, and controlled by schools, colleges, or universities.

Parcel Post Rate Schedule

(Inter BMC/ASF ZIP codes only, machinable parcels, no discount, no surcharge)

Weight up to but not exceeding—(pounds)	Local	1 and 2	3	Zones 4	5	6	7	8
2	2.56	2.63	2.79	2.87	2.95	2.95	2.95	2.95
3	2.63	2.76	3.00	3.34	3.68	3.95	3.95	3.95
4	2.71	2.87	3.20	3.78	4.68	4.95	4.95	4.95
5	2.77	2.97	3.38	4.10	5.19	5.56	5.95	5.95
6	2.84	3.07	3.55	4.39	5.67	6.90	7.75	7.95
7	2.90	3.16	3.71	4.67	6.11	7.51	9.15	9.75
8	2.96	3.26	3.85	4.91	6.53	8.08	9.94	11.55
9	3.01	3.33	3.99	5.16	6.92	8.62	10.65	12.95

Weight up to but not exceeding—(pounds)	Local	1 and 2	3	Zones 4	5	6	7	8
10.	3.07	3.42	4.12	5.38	7.29	9.12	11.31	14.00
11.	3.12	3.49	4.25	5.59	7.63	9.59	11.93	15.05
12.	3.17	3.57	4.37	5.79	7.96	10.03	12.52	16.10
13.	3.23	3.64	4.47	5.98	8.26	10.45	13.07	17.15
14.	3.27	3.71	4.59	6.16	8.55	10.84	13.59	18.20
15.	3.32	3.77	4.69	6.34	8.82	11.22	14.08	19.25
16.	3.37	3.83	4.79	6.50	9.09	11.58	14.55	20.30
17.	3.41	3.90	4.88	6.66	9.33	11.92	15.00	21.35
18.	3.45	3.95	4.97	6.81	9.58	12.24	15.42	22.40
19.	3.49	4.02	5.06	6.95	9.80	12.55	15.83	23.25
20.	3.54	4.07	5.14	7.08	10.01	12.84	16.21	23.84
21.	3.57	4.12	5.23	7.21	10.23	13.12	16.59	24.41
22.	3.61	4.18	5.30	7.34	10.43	13.39	16.94	24.96
23.	3.65	4.23	5.39	7.47	10.62	13.66	17.28	25.47
24.	3.69	4.27	5.46	7.58	10.80	13.90	17.60	25.97
25.	3.73	4.32	5.53	7.70	10.98	14.14	17.91	26.45

Postal Union Mail Special Services

Registration—available to practically all countries. Fee $4.85. The maximum indemnity payable—generally only in case of complete loss (of both contents and wrapper)—is $32.35. To Canada only the fee is $4.95 providing indemnity for loss up to $100, $5.40 for loss up to $500, and $5.85 for loss up to $1,000.

Return receipt—showing to whom and date delivered, $1.10.

Special delivery—Available to most countries. Consult post office. Fees for International Special Delivery same for air or surface: for letters, letter packages, and postcards not over 2 lb, $9.95. If over 2 lb, $10.35, for printed matter, matter for the blind, or small packets, $10.45 if not over 2 lb; if over 2 lb, $11.25.

Marking—an article intended for special delivery service must have affixed to the cover near the name of the country of destination "EXPRES" (special delivery) label, obtainable at the post office, or it may be marked on the cover boldly in red "EXPRES" (special delivery).

Special handling—entitles AO surface packages to priority handling between mailing point and U.S. point of dispatch. Fees: $5.40 for packages to 10 lb, and $7.50 for packages over 10 lb.

Airmail—daily air service is available to practically all countries.

Prepayment of replies from other countries—a mailer who wishes to prepay a reply by letter from another country may do so by sending his correspondent one or more international reply coupons, which may be purchased at U.S. post offices. One coupon should be accepted in any country in exchange for stamps to prepay an air mail letter of the first unit of weight to the U.S.

Additional international special services: Insurance: Available to many countries for loss of or damage to items paid at parcel post rate. Consult postmaster for indemnity limits for individual countries.

Limit of Indemnity Not over	Canada	Fees All other countries
$50	$0.75	$1.60
100	1.60	2.45
200	2.50	3.35
300	3.40	4.25
400	4.30	5.15
500	5.20	6.05
600	6.10	6.95
700		7.40
800		7.85
900		8.30
1,000		8.75
1,100		9.20
1,200		9.65

Restricted Delivery: Available to many countries for registered mail, limits who may receive an item. Fee: $2.75.

Post Office-Authorized 2-Letter State Abbreviations

The abbreviations below are approved by the U.S. Postal Service for use in addresses. The official list follows, including the District of Columbia, American Samoa, Guam, Puerto Rico, and the U.S. Virgin Islands (all capital letters are used):

Alabama . . . . AL	Hawaii . . . . HI	Missouri . . . . MO	Puerto Rico . . . . PR
Alaska . . . . AK	Idaho . . . . ID	Montana . . . . MT	Rhode Island . . . . . . RI
American Samoa . . . AS	Illinois IL	Nebraska . . . . NE	South Carolina . . . . . SC
Arizona . . . . AZ	Indiana . . . . IN	Nevada . . . . NV	South Dakota . . . . . . SD
Arkansas . . . . AR	Iowa . . . . IA	New Hampshire . . . . NH	Tennessee . . . . TN
California . . . . CA	Kansas . . . . KS	New Jersey . . . . NJ	Texas . . . . TX
Colorado . . . . CO	Kentucky . . . . KY	New Mexico . . . . NM	Utah . . . . UT
Connecticut . . . . CT	Louisiana . . . . LA	New York . . . . NY	Vermont . . . . VT
Delaware . . . . DE	Maine . . . . ME	North Carolina . . . . . NC	Virginia . . . . VA
Dist. of Col. . . . . . . DC	Marshall Islands[1] . . .	North Dakota . . . . . . ND	Virgin Islands VI
Federated States of	Maryland . . . . MD	Northern Mariana Is. . MP	Washington . . . . . . WA
Micronesia[1] . . . . . . FM	Massachusetts . . . . . MA	Ohio . . . . OH	West Virginia . . . . . WV
Florida . . . . FL	Michigan . . . . MI	Oklahoma . . . . OK	Wisconsin . . . . WI
Georgia . . . . GA	Minnesota . . . . MN	Oregon . . . . OR	Wyoming . . . . WY
Guam . . . . GU	Mississippi . . . . MS	Pennsylvania . . . . . . PA	

(1) Although an independent nation, this country is currently subject to domestic rates and fees.

Canadian Province and Territory Postal Codes

Alberta . . . . AL	Northwest Territories . . . . NT
British Columbia . . . . BC	Ontario . . . . ON
Manitoba . . . . MB	Prince Edward Island . . . . PE
New Brunswick . . . . NB	Quebec . . . . PQ
Newfoundland and Labrador . . . . NF	Saskatchewan . . . . SK
Nova Scotia . . . . NS	Yukon Territory . . . . YT

International Air Mail

Aerogrammes — 50¢ each to all countries.
Air mail postcards (single) — 50¢ to all countries except Canada (40¢ each) and Mexico (35¢ each).
International letters and letter packages: airmail to Canada and Mexico (there are no surface rates to these countries)—weight not over 0.5 oz, 46¢ to Canada, 40¢ to Mexico; not over 1.0 oz, 52¢ to Canada, 46¢ to Mexico; not over 2 oz, 72¢ to Canada, 86¢ to Mexico; not over 3 oz, 95¢ to Canada, $1.26¢ to Mexico.

Air Mail, Letter and Letter Package Rates, Countries Other Than Canada and Mexico

(weight limit: 64 oz [4 lb])

Weight not over	Rate	Weight not over	Rate	Weight not over	Rate	Weight not over	Rate
0.5 oz	$0.60	12.5 oz	$10.20	24.5 oz	$19.80	41 oz	$29.40
1.0	1.00	13.0	10.60	25.0	20.20	42	29.80
1.5	1.40	13.5	11.00	25.5	20.60	43	30.20
2.0	1.80	14.0	11.40	26.0	21.00	44	30.60
2.5	2.20	14.5	11.80	26.5	21.40	45	31.00
3.0	2.60	15.0	12.20	27.0	21.80	46	31.40
3.5	3.00	15.5	12.60	27.5	22.20	47	31.80
4.0	3.40	16.0	13.00	28.0	22.60	48	32.20
4.5	3.80	16.5	13.40	28.5	23.00	49	32.60
5.0	4.20	17.0	13.80	29.0	23.40	50	33.00
5.5	4.60	17.5	14.20	29.5	23.80	51	33.40
6.0	5.00	18.0	14.60	30.0	24.20	52	33.80
6.5	5.40	18.5	15.00	30.5	24.60	53	34.20
7.0	5.80	19.0	15.40	31.0	25.00	54	34.60
7.5	6.20	19.5	15.80	31.5	25.40	55	35.00
8.0	6.60	20.0	16.20	32.0	25.80	56	35.40
8.5	7.00	20.5	16.60	33.0	26.20	57	35.80
9.0	7.40	21.0	17.00	34.0	26.60	58	36.20
9.5	7.80	21.5	17.40	35.0	27.00	59	36.60
10.0	8.20	22.0	17.80	36.0	27.40	60	37.00
10.5	8.60	22.5	18.20	37.0	27.80	61	37.40
11.0	9.00	23.0	18.60	38.0	28.20	62	37.80
11.5	9.40	23.5	19.00	39.0	28.60	63	38.20
12.0	9.80	24.0	19.40	40.0	29.00	64	38.60

Air Mail Parcel Post Rates

Weight steps	Air parcel post rate groups				
	A	B	C	D	E
First pound	$6.50	$8.25	$9.75	$11.20	$12.80
Each additional pound or fraction up to 5 lb	3.36	4.00	5.28	5.76	6.40
Each additional pound or fraction up to 10 lb	2.88	3.20	4.32	5.28	5.44
Each additional pound or fraction up to 20 lb	2.72	2.88	4.00	4.32	4.48
Each additional pound or fraction up to 30 lb	2.24	2.56	3.84	4.16	4.32
Each additional pound or fraction over 30 lb	1.92	2.24	3.68	4.00	4.16

Air Parcel Post Rate Groups

(For further information, consult your local post office.)

Country	Rate group	Maximum weight limit
Afghanistan[1]	D	44
Albania	C	44
Algeria	D	66
Andorra	B	44
Angola	E	22
Anguilla	A	22
Antigua & Barbuda	A	22
Argentina	D	44
Armenia	E	44
Aruba	A	44
Ascension	no air service	44 (surface)
Australia	D	44
Austria	B	44
Azerbaijan	E	22
Azores	C	44
Bahamas	A	44
Bahrain	D	44
Bangladesh	E	22
Barbados	B	44
Belarus	E	44
Belgium	D	44
Belize	A	44
Benin	C	44
Bermuda	A	44
Bhutan	E	44
Bolivia	B	44
Bosnia and Herzegovina	C	33
Botswana	E	44
Brazil	E	44
British Virgin Islands	A	44
Brunei	D	44
Bulgaria	D	44
Burkina Faso	D	44
Burma	see Myanmar	
Burundi	E	44
Cambodia[2]	no parcel post service	
Cameroon	D	44
Canada	separate rate group	66
Cape Verde	D	44
Cayman Islands	A	44
Central African Republic	E	44
Chad[3]	D	44 (air only)
Chile	D	44
China (People's Republic of)	D	44
Colombia	B	44
Comoros	E	44
Congo	D	44
Corsica	E	44
Costa Rica	A	44
Côte d'Ivoire	D	44
Croatia	C	44
Cuba[2]	no parcel post service	
Cyprus	C	44
Czech Republic	C	33
Denmark	C	66
Djibouti	D	44
Dominica	A	44
Dominican Republic	A	44
East Timor	see Indonesia	
Ecuador	C	44

Country	Rate group	Maximum weight limit	Country	Rate group	Maximum weight limit
Egypt	D.	44	Namibia	D	44
El Salvador	B.	44	Nauru	C	44
Equatorial Guinea	D.	44	Nepal	D	44 (surface)
Eritrea	D.	44			11 (air)
Estonia	E.	44	Netherlands	C	44
Ethiopia	D.	44	Netherlands Antilles	A	44
Faeroe Islands	C.	66	New Caledonia	D	44
Falkland Islands[2]	no air PP	44 (surface)	New Zealand	D	44
Fiji	B.	44	Nicaragua	B	44
Finland	D.	44	Niger	D	44
France	E.	44	Nigeria	C	44
French Guiana	C.	44	Norway	D	44
French Polynesia	D.	44	Oman	D	44
Gabon[3]	D.	44	Pakistan	D	44
Gambia	B.	22	Panama	A	44
Georgia, Republic of	E.	22	Papua New Guinea[2]	D	44
Germany	B.	44	Paraguay	D	44
Ghana	D.	44	Peru	B	44
Gibraltar	C.	44	Philippines	D	44
Great Britain and Northern Ireland	C.	66	Pitcairn Island	B	22
Greece	C.	44	Poland	B	33
Greenland	D.	66	Portugal	C	44
Grenada	A.	44	Qatar	C	44
Guadeloupe	A.	44	Reunion	E	44
Guatemala	A.	44	Romania	C	44
Guinea	B.	44	Russia	E	22
Guinea-Bissau	B.	22	Rwanda[2]	D	44
Guyana	B.	44	Saint Helena	C	44
Haiti	A.	44	Saint Kitts & Nevis	A	44
Honduras	B.	44	Saint Lucia	A	44
Hong Kong	C.	44	Saint Pierre & Miquelon	A	44
Hungary	C.	44	Saint Vincent & the Grenadines	A	22
Iceland	C.	44	San Marino	C	44
India	D.	44	São Tomé & Príncipe	D	44
Indonesia[4]	E.	44	Saudi Arabia	D	44
Iran	D.	44	Senegal	D	44
Iraq[2]	D.	44	Seychelles	D	44
Ireland (Eire)	C.	66	Sierra Leone	D	44
Israel	C.	44	Singapore	D	44
Italy	C.	44	Slovakia	C	33
Ivory Coast	see Côte d'Ivoire		Slovenia	C	33
Jamaica	A.	22	Solomon Islands	C	44
Japan	E.	44	Somalia[1]	D	44
Jordan	C.	44	South Africa	D	44
Kazakhstan	E.	44	Spain	C	44
Kenya	D.	44	Sri Lanka	D	44
Kiribati	B.	44	Sudan	D	44
Korea, Democratic People's Rep. of (North)[2]	no parcel post service		Suriname	B	44
Korea, Republic of (South)	C.	44	Swaziland	D	44
Kuwait[3]	C.	44 (air only)	Sweden	D	44
Kyrgyzstan	E.	22	Switzerland	B	66
Laos	E.	44	Syria	C	44
Latvia	E.	44	Taiwan	C	44
Lebanon[2,3]	C.	11 (air only)	Tajikistan	E	22
Lesotho	E.	44	Tanzania	E	44
Liberia[3]	C.	44	Thailand	D	44
Libya[2]	D.	44	Togo	D	44
Liechtenstein	B.	66	Tonga	B	44
Lithuania	E.	44	Trinidad & Tobago	B	22
Luxembourg	B.	44	Tristan da Cunha	E	22
Macao	C.	44	Tunisia	C	44
Macedonia	C.	33	Turkey	C	44
Madagascar	E.	44	Turkmenistan	E	22
Madeira Islands	B.	44	Turks and Caicos Islands	A	22
Malawi	D.	44	Tuvalu	B	44
Malaysia	D.	22	Uganda	D	44
Maldives	D.	22	Ukraine	E	44
Mali	C.	44	United Arab Emirates	D	44
Malta	C.	22	Uruguay	B	44
Martinique	A.	44	Uzbekistan	E	22
Mauritania	D.	44	Vanuatu	B	44
Mauritius	E.	22	Vatican City	C	44
Mexico	A.	44	Venezuela	B	44
Moldova	E.	44	Vietnam	E	44
Monaco	E.	44	Wallis & Futuna Islands	D	44
Mongolia	no parcel post service		Western Samoa	B	44
Montserrat	A.	44	Yemen	E	44
Morocco	C.	44	Yugoslavia[2]	C	33
Mozambique	E.	44	Zaire	E	44
Myanmar	D.	22	Zambia	E	44
			Zimbabwe	E	44

(1) All mail service suspended. (2) Mail service restrictions apply. (3) Surface mail service suspended. (4) Includes East Timor.

LANGUAGE

*New Words in English

Source: Words and definitions from Merriam-Webster Inc., publisher of *Merriam-Webster's Collegiate Dictionary, Tenth Edition*

buzz cut a very short haircut in which the hair resembles the bristle surface of a bush

cocooning the practice of spending leisure time at home in preference to going out

commodify to turn (as a work of art) into a commodity

coulis a thick sauce made with pureed vegetable or fruit and often used as a garnish

cyberpunk (1) science fiction dealing with future urban societies dominated by computer technology (2) an opportunistic computer hacker

cyberspace the online world of computer networks

drive-by carried out from a moving vehicle

ecotourism the practice of touring natural habitats in a manner that minimizes ecological impact

fatwa a legal opinion or decree handed down by an Islamic religious leader

gangbanger a member of a street gang

graphic novel a fictional story for adults that is presented in comic-strip format and published as a trade book

grunge (1) one that is grungy (2) a style of popular music mixing elements of rock and roll, punk rock, and heavy metal; *also* the unkempt working-class fashions typical of fans of grunge

hate crime a crime that violates the victim's civil rights and that is motivated by hostility to the victim's race, religion, creed, national origin, sexual orientation, or gender

hot button a controversial issue or concern that triggers immediate and intense reaction

humvee a diesel-powered multipurpose U.S. military vehicle that replaced the jeep

infomercial a television program that is an extended advertisement often including a discussion or demonstration

infotainment a television program that presents information (as news) in a manner intended to be entertaining

nanotechnology the art of manipulating materials at the atomic or molecular scale esp. to build microscopic devices (as robots)

securitize to consolidate (as mortgage loans) and sell to other investors for resale to the public in the form of securities

shareware software with usu. limited capability or incomplete documentation which is available for trial use at little or no cost but which can be upgraded upon payment of a fee to the author

techno-thriller a thriller whose plot involves modern technology

vogue to strike poses in campy imitation of fashion models

wuss a weak, cowardly, or ineffectual person

Eponyms

(words named for people)

Bloody Mary—a vodka and tomato juice drink; after the nickname of Mary I, Queen of England (1553-58), notorious for her persecution of Protestants.

bloomers—full, loose trousers gathered at the knee; after Amelia Bloomer, an American social reformer who advocated (1851) such clothing.

bobbies—in Great Britain, police officers; after Sir Robert Peel, the statesman who organized the London police force, 1850.

bowdlerize—to delete written matter considered indelicate; after Thomas Bowdler, English editor of an expurgated Shakespeare (1825).

boycott—to combine against in a policy of nonintercourse for economic or political reasons; after Charles C. Boycott, an English land agent in County Mayo, Ireland, ostracized in 1880 for refusing to reduce rents.

Braille—a system of writing for the blind; after Louis Braille, the French teacher of the blind who invented it (1853).

Casanova—a man who is a promiscuous and unscrupulous lover; after Giovanni Giacomo Casanova (1725-98), an Italian adventurer.

chauvinist—excessively patriotic; after Nicolas Chauvin, a character devoted to Napoleon in a 19th-cent. play.

derby—a stiff felt hat with a dome-shaped crown and rather narrow rolled brim; after Edward Stanley, 12th earl of Derby, who in 1780 founded the Derby horse race at Epsom Downs, England, to which these hats are worn.

diesel—a type of internal combustion engine or a vehicle driven by such an engine; after Rudolf Diesel (1858-1913), who built the first successful diesel engine.

gerrymander—to draw an election district in such a way as to favor a political party; after Elbridge Gerry, who created (1812) just such an election district (shaped like a salamander) during his governorship of MA.

guillotine—a machine for beheading; after Joseph Guillotin, a French physician who proposed its use in 1789 as more humane than hanging.

leotard—a close-fitting garment for the torso, worn by dancers, acrobats, and the like; after Julius Leotard, a 19th-century French aerial gymnast.

sandwich—2 or more slices of bread having a filling in between; after John Montagu, 4th earl of Sandwich (1718-92), who supposedly ate food in this form so that he would not have to leave the gaming table.

silhouette—an outline image; from Étienne de Silhouette (1709-67), a close-fisted French finance minister.

Foreign Words and Phrases

(L=Latin; F=French; Y=Yiddish; R=Russian; G=Greek; I=Italian; S=Spanish)

ad hoc (L; ad HOK): for the particular end or purpose at hand

ad infinitum (L; ad in-fi-NITE-um): endless

ad nauseam (L; ad NAWZ-ee-um): to a sickening degree

apropos (F; ap-ruh-POH): being relevant

bête noire (F; BET NWAHR): a thing or person viewed with particular dislike

bon appétit (F; BOH nap-uh-teet): I wish you a good appetite

bona fide (L; BOH nuh-feyed): in good faith

carte blanche (F; kahrt BLANNSH): full discretionary power

cause célèbre (F; kawz suh-LEB-ruh): a notorious incident

c'est la vie (F; se lah VEE): that's life

chutzpah (Y; KHOOT-spuh): amazing nerve bordering on arrogance

coup de grâce (F; kooh duh GRAHS): the final blow

coup d'état (F; kooh duh tah): forceful overthrow of an existing government by a small group

crème de la crème (F; KREM duh luh KREM): the best of the best

cum laude/magna cum laude/summa cum laude (L; KUHM loud-ay; MAHN-ya . . . ; SOO-ma . . .): with praise or honor; with great praise or honor; with the highest praise or honor

de facto (L; di FAK-toh): in fact; generally agreed to without a formal decision

déjà vu (F; DAY-zhah VOOH): the sensation that something happening has happened before

de jure (L; dee JOOR-ee, day YOOR-ay): determined by law, as opposed to de facto

de rigueur (F; duh ree-GUR): necessary according to convention

détente (F; day-TAHNT): an easing or relaxation of strained relations

éminence grise (F; ay-meh-NAHNN-suh GREEZ): one who wields power behind the scenes

enfant terrible (F; ahnn-FAHNN te-REE-bluh): one whose unconventional behavior causes embarrassment

en masse (F; ahn MAHS): in a large body

ergo (L; ER-goh): therefore

esprit de corps (F; es-PREE duh KAWR): group spirit; feeling of camaraderie

eureka (G; YOOR-EE-kuh): I have found it

ex post facto (L; eks pohst FAK-toh): an explanation or regulation concocted after the event

fait accompli (F; fayt uh-kom-PLEE): an accomplished fact

faux pas (F; fowe PAH): a social blunder

hoi polloi (G; hoy puh-LOY): the masses

in loco parentis (L; in LOH-koh puh-REN-tis): in place of a parent

in memoriam (L; in muh-MAWR-ee-uhm): in memory of

in situ (L; in SEYE-tyooh): in the original arrangement

in toto (L; in TOH-toh): totally

je ne sais quoi (F; zhuh nuh say KWAH): I don't know what; the little something that eludes description

joie de vivre (F; zhwah duh VEEV-ruh): joy of living, love of life

mea culpa (L; MAY-uh CUL-puh): my fault

modus operandi (L; MOH-duhs op-uh-RAN-dee): method of operation

noblesse oblige (F; noh-BLES uh-BLEEZH): the obligation of nobility to help the less fortunate

non compos mentis (L; non KOM-puhs MEN-tis): out of control of the mind; insane

nouveau riche (F; nooh-voh REESH): a person newly rich; perhaps one who spends money conspicuously

perestroika (R; PAIR-es TROY-kuh): restructuring

persona non grata (L; per-SOH-nah non GRAH-tah): unacceptable person

postmortem (L; pohst-MORE-tuhm): after death; autopsy; analysis after event

prima donna (I; pree-muh DAH-nuh): a principal female opera singer; temperamental person

pro tempore (L; proh TEM-puh-ree): for the time being

que sera sera (S; keh sair-ah sair-AH): what will be, will be

quid pro quo (L; kwid proh KWOH): something given or received for something else

raison d'être (F; RAY-zohnn DET-ruh): reason for being

savoir faire (F; sav-wahr-FAIR): dexterity in social and practical affairs

schlemiel (Y; shleh-MEEL): an unlucky bungling person

semper fidelis (L; SEM-puhr fee-DAY-lis): always faithful

status quo (L; STAY-tus QWOH): existing order of things

terra firma (L; TER-uh FUR-muh): solid ground

tour de force (F; TOOR duh FAWRS): feat accomplished through great skill

verbatim (L; ver-BAY-tuhm): word for word

vis-à-vis (F; vee-ZUH-VEE): face to face with; compared with

National Spelling Bee Champions

The Scripps Howard National Spelling Bee, conducted by Scripps Howard Newspapers and other leading newspapers since 1939, was instituted by the Louisville (Ky.) *Courier-Journal* in 1925. Children under 16 years of age and not beyond the 8th grade are eligible to compete for cash prizes at the finals, which are held annually in Washington, DC. The 1995 winners were: first prize, **Justin Carroll**, Wynne, AR; second prize, **Marjory Lavery**, Akron, OH; third prize (tie), **Ryan Burke**, Orange, CT; **Jenelle Jindal**, Princeton, NJ; **Vauhini Vara**, Edmond, OK.

Winning Words

These were the last words given in each of the years 1965-95 at the Scripps Howard National Spelling Bee. They were all correctly spelled, thereby determining the national champion.

1965 — eczema	1973 — vouchsafe	1981 — sarcophagus	1989 — spoliator
1966 — ratoon	1974 — hydrophyte	1982 — psoriasis	1990 — fibranne
1967 — chihuahua	1975 — incisor	1983 — purim	1991 — antipyretic
1968 — abalone	1976 — narcolepsy	1984 — luge	1992 — lyceum
1969 — interlocutory	1977 — cambist	1985 — milieu	1993 — kamikaze
1970 — croissant	1978 — deification	1986 — odontalgia	1994 — antediluvian
1971 — shalloon	1979 — maculature	1987 — staphylococci	1995 — xanthosis
1972 — macerate	1980 — elucubrate	1988 — elegiacal	

Common Abbreviations

Usage of periods after abbreviations varies, but recently the tendency has been toward omission. Definitions preceding those in parentheses are in Latin unless otherwise noted.

AA=Alcoholics Anonymous
AAA=American Automobile Association
abbr.=abbreviation
AC=alternating current
AD=*anno Domini* (in the year of the Lord)
AFL=American Federation of Labor
AIDS=acquired immune deficiency syndrome
AM=*ante meridiem* (before noon)
AMA=American Medical Association
anon=anonymous
ASAP=as soon as possible
ASCAP=American Society of Composers, Authors, and Publishers
BA=Bachelor of Arts
bbl=barrel(s)
BC=before Christ
BS=Bachelor of Science
Btu=British thermal unit(s)
bu=bushel(s)
C= Celsius, centigrade
c=*circa* (about), copyright
CEO=chief executive officer
CIA=Central Intelligence Agency
cm=centimeter(s)
COD=Cash (or Collect) on Delivery
CPA=Certified Public Accountant
CPR=cardiopulmonary resuscitation
DA=district attorney
DAR=Daughters of the American Revolution
DC=direct current
DD=Doctor of Divinity
DDS=Doctor of Dental Science (or Surgery)
DNA=deoxyribonucleic acid
DOA=dead on arrival
DWI=driving while intoxicated
ed.=edited, edition, editor
e.g.=*exempli gratia* (for example)
ESP=extrasensory perception
esp.=especially
et al.=*et alii* (and others)
etc.=*et cetera* (and so forth)

F=Fahrenheit
FBI=Federal Bureau of Investigation
FOB=free on board
ft=foot, feet
FYI=for your information
gal=gallon(s)
GB=gigabyte(s)
GDP=gross domestic product
GIGO=garbage in, garbage out
GNP=gross national product
GOP=Grand Old Party (Republican Party)
Hon.=the Honorable
hr=hour(s)
ht=height
HVAC=heating, ventilating, and air-conditioning
i.e.=*id est* (that is)
in.=inch(es)
IQ=Intelligence Quotient
IRA=Individual Retirement Account, Irish Republican Army
IRS=Internal Revenue Service
ISBN=International Standard Book Number
JD=*Juris Doctor* (Doctor of Laws)
JP=Justice of the Peace
K=Kelvin
k=karat
KB=kilobyte(s)
kg=kilogram(s)
km=kilometer(s)
kW=kilowatt(s)
kWh=kilowatt-hour(s)
l=liter(s)
lb=*libra* (pound or pounds)
LLB=Bachelor of Laws
m=meter(s)
MA=Master of Arts
MB=megabyte(s)
MD=*Medicinae Doctor* (Doctor of Medicine)
mfg=manufacturing
mi=mile(s)
MIA=missing in action
min=minute(s)
ml=milliliter(s)

mm=millimeter(s)
mph=miles per hour
MS=Master of Science
MSG=monosodium glutamate
no=*numero* (number)
op=*opus* (work)
oz=ounce(s)
p., pp.=page, pages
PC=personal computer
Ph.D.=Doctor of Philosophy
PM=post meridiem (afternoon)
POW=prisoner of war
PS=*post scriptum* (postscript)
pt=part(s), pint(s), point(s)
qt=quart(s)
REM=rapid eye movement
Rev.=Reverend
RFD=rural free delivery
R.I.P.=*Requiescat in pace* (May he/she rest in peace)
RN=registered nurse
RNA=ribonucleic acid
ROTC=Reserve Officers' Training Corps
rpm=revolutions per minute
RR=railroad
RSVP=Répondez, s'il vous plait (Fr.) (Please reply)
SAD=seasonal affective disorder
SASE=self-addressed stamped envelope
sec=second(s)
SPCA=Society for the Prevention of Cruelty to Animals
SRO=standing room only
St.=saint, street
stat=*statim* (immediately)
t=ton(s)
TGIF=thank God it's Friday
UFO=unidentified flying object
UHF=ultrahigh frequency
USS=United States ship
v (or vs)=*versus* (against)
VCR=videocassette recorder
VHF=very high frequency
W=watt(s)
yd=yard(s)

A Collection of Animal Collectives

The English language boasts an abundance of names to describe groups of things, particularly pairs or aggregations of animals. Some of these words have fallen into comparative disuse, but many of them are still in service, helping to enrich the vocabularies of those who like their language to be precise, who tire of hearing a group referred to as "a bunch of," or who enjoy the sound of words that aren't overworked.

bale of turtles
band of gorillas
bed of clams, oysters
bevy of quail, swans
brace of ducks
brood of chicks
cast of hawks
cete of badgers
charm of goldfinches
cloud of gnats
clowder of cats
clutch of chicks
clutter of cats
colony of ants
congregation of plovers
covey of quail, partridge

crash of rhinoceri
cry of hounds
down of hares
drift of swine
drove of cattle, sheep
exaltation of larks
flight of birds
flock of sheep, geese
gaggle of geese
gam of whales
gang of elks
grist of bees
herd of elephants
horde of gnats
husk of hares
kindle or **kendle** of kittens

knot of toads
leap of leopards
leash of greyhounds, foxes
litter of pigs
mob of kangaroos
murder of crows
muster of peacocks
mute of hounds
nest of vipers
nest, nide of pheasants
pack of hounds, wolves
pair of horses
pod of whales, seals
pride of lions
school of fish
sedge or **siege** of cranes

shoal of fish, pilchards
skein of geese
skulk of foxes
sleuth of bears
sounder of boars, swine
span of mules
spring of teals
swarm of bees
team of ducks, horses
tribe or **trip** of goats
troop of kangaroos, monkeys
volery of birds
watch of nightingales
wing of plovers
yoke of oxen

Young of Animals Have Special Names

The young of many mammals, birds, and fish have come to be called by special names. A young eel, for example, is an elver. Many young animals, of course, are often referred to simply as infants, babies, younglets, or younglings.

bunny: rabbit
calf: cattle, elephant, antelope, rhino, hippo, whale, others
cheeper: grouse, partridge, quail
chick, chicken: fowl
cockerel: rooster
codling, sprag: codfish
colt: horse (male)
cub: lion, bear, shark, fox, others
cygnet: swan
duckling: duck
eaglet: eagle
elver: eel
eyas: hawk, others
fawn: deer
filly: horse (female)

fingerling: fish generally
flapper: wild fowl
fledgling: birds generally
foal: horse, zebra, others
fry: fish generally
gosling: goose
heifer: cow
joey: kangaroo, others
kid: goat
kit: fox, beaver, rabbit, cat
kitten, kitty, catling: cats, other small mammals
lamb, lambkin, cosset, hog: sheep
leveret: hare
nestling: birds generally

owlet: owl
parr, smolt, grilse: salmon
piglet, shoat, farrow, suckling: pig
polliwog, tadpole: frog
poult: turkey
pullet: hen
pup: dog, seal, sea lion, fox
puss, pussy: cat
spike, blinker, tinker: mackerel
squab: pigeon
squeaker: pigeon, others
whelp: dog, tiger, beasts of prey
yearling: cattle, sheep, horse, others

Foreign Idioms

English
Naked as a jaybird
A bird in the hand is worth two in the bush.

To kill two birds with one stone
To eat crow
To eat like a pig
Don't bite off more than you can chew.

Pride goes before a fall.

To go by fits and starts
There is honor among thieves.
Once in a blue moon

English
Don't waste your breath!
To turn up like a bad penny
To talk to yourself
Let's get back to the subject.
To pull a long face
He laughs in your face.
By rule of thumb
To be knock-kneed
Put that in your pipe and smoke it!

It's Greek to me!

English
To hit the ceiling
Go fly a kite!
There's always room for one more.
To have the tables turned
To cut off your nose to spite your face
To slam the door in your face
Give him an inch, he'll take a mile.
To be alive and kicking
You can't make a silk purse out of a sow's ear.

To swear a blue streak

English
Go jump in the lake!
You can only do one thing at a time.

He's as slow as molasses.
He repeats himself.
Where there's smoke, there's fire.
Are you in a hurry?
Drop dead!
He makes a lot of trouble for me.
Go fight City Hall.
Thanks for nothing.

Italian
Naked as a worm (Nudo come un verme)
Better a finch in hand than a thrush on a branch. (Meglio fringuello in man che tordo in frasca.)
To catch two pigeons with one bean (Pigliare due piccioni con una fava)
To swallow the toad (Inghiottire il rospo)
To eat like a buffalo (Mangiare come un bufalo)
Don't take a step longer than your leg. (Non fare il passo piu lungo della gamba.)
Pride rode out on horseback and came back on foot. (La superbia andò a cavallo e tornò a piedi.)
To go by hiccups (Andare a singhiozzo)
A dog doesn't eat a dog. (Cane non mangia cane.)
Every death of a pope (Ad oogni morte di papa)

French
Save your saliva! (Epargne ta salive!)
To arrive like a hair in the soup. (Arriver comme un cheveu sur la soupe.)
To talk to angels (Parler aux anges)
Let's get back to our sheep. (Revenons à nos moutons.)
To make a funny nose (Faire un drôle de nez)
He laughs in your nose. (Il vous rit au nez.)
From the view of the nose (A vue de nez)
To have your legs in an X (Avoir les jambes en X)
Put this in your pocket with your handkerchief on top! (Mets-le dans ta poche avec ton mouchoir dessus!)
It's Chinese! (C'est du chinois!)

Spanish
To scream at the sky (Poner el grito en el cielo)
Go fry asparagus! (Véte a freír esparragos!)
Where six can eat, seven can eat. (Donde comen seis, comen siete.)
To go out for wool and come home shorn (Ir por lana y volver esquilado)
To throw stones at your own roof (Tirar piedras contra su propio tejado)
To slam the door on your nostrils (Cerrarle la puerta en las narices)
Give him a hand and he takes a foot. (Le da la mano y se toma el pie.)
To be alive and wagging your tail (Estar vivo y coleando)
A monkey dressed in silk is still a monkey. (Aunque la mona se vista de seda, mona se queda.)
To toss out toads and snakes (Echar sapos y culebras)

Yiddish
Go whistle in the ocean! (Gai feifen ahfenyam!)
You can't dance at two weddings at the same time. (Me ken nit tantzen auf tsvai chassenes mit ain mol.)
He creeps like a bedbug. (Er kricht vi a vantz.)
He grinds ground flour. (Er molt gemolen mel.)
When bells ring, it's usually a holiday. (Az es klingt, iz misstomeh chogeh.)
Are you standing on one leg? (Bist ahf ain fus?)
You should lie in the earth! (Zolst ligen in drerd!)
He makes my wedding black. (Er macht mir a shvartzeh chasseneh.)
Go fight with God. (Shlog zich mit Got arum.)
Many thanks in your belly button. (A shainem dank dir im pupik.)

Idioms: Their Meaning and Derivation

dyed in the wool: to have traits deeply ingrained; from the fact that if wool is dyed before being made into yarn, or while still raw wool, the color is more firmly fixed.

feet of clay: a blemish in the character of one previously held above reproach; from Daniel's interpretation of Nebuchadnezzar's dream in the Old Testament. The king dreamed of an image made of precious metals, except for feet made of clay and iron. Daniel said that the feet symbolized human vulnerability to weakness and destruction.

hands down: effortlessly; incontestably; from the way a jockey, sure of victory, drops his hands, loosening his grip on the reins.

in seventh heaven: in a state of bliss; especially in Islamic beliefs, the heaven of heavens, the home of God and the highest angels.

kiss of death: something that seems good but is in reality the instrument of one's downfall; from the earlier phrase "Judas kiss," betraying Jesus to the authorities.

mad as a hatter: crazy; from mercury's use in the making of felt hats, thus hatters often were afflicted with a violent twitching of the muscles as a result of its effects.

red herring: a false lead; a herring cured by smoke; from the persistent odor, hence the use, trailed over the ground, for training a dog to follow this scent over any other.

red-letter day: a memorable day; from the custom of using red or purple colors to mark holy days on the calendar.

to bark up the wrong tree: to pursue a false lead; an Americanism that comes from hunting, some say specifically nocturnal racoon hunting, in which dogs often lost track of their quarry.

to buckle down: to adopt an attitude of effort and determination; probably from the act of buckling on armor to prepare for battle.

to go at it with hammer and tongs: no holds barred; from the blacksmith who, with his tongs (long-handled pincers) took a piece of red-hot metal from the forge, laid it on the anvil, and beat it into shape with his hammer.

to hold water: to pass a test for soundness; from testing a pitcher by filling it with water.

to knuckle under: to submit to another; from the time when one knelt before a conquerer, putting the "knuckles" of one's knees (the rounded part of the bone where the joint is bent) on the ground.

to make hay while the sun shines: to seize the opportunity; from hay's composition of mown grass dried for fodder, with the sun as the cheapest and most available drying agent.

to strike while the iron is hot: to seize the opportunity; from the blacksmith's need to swing the hammer while the metal on the anvil is glowing, or he must start up the forge again and reheat the iron.

Names of the Days

English	Russian	Hebrew	French	Italian	Spanish	German	Japanese
Sunday	Voskresenje	Yom rishon	Dimanche	Domenica	domingo	Sonntag	Nichiyo\bi
Monday	Ponedeljnic	Yom sheni	Lundi	Lunedì	lunes	Montag	Getsuyo\bi
Tuesday	Vtornik	Yom shlishi	Mardi	Martedì	martes	Dienstag	Kayo\bi
Wednesday	Sreda	Yom ravii	Mercredi	Mercoledì	miércoles	Mittwoch	Suiyo\bi
Thursday	Chetverg	Yom hamishi	Jeudi	Giovedì	jueves	Donnerstag	Mokuyo\bi
Friday	Pjatnitsa	Yom shishi	Vendredi	Venerdì	viernes	Freitag	Kin-yo\bi
Saturday	Subbota	Shabbat	Samedi	Sabato	sábado	Samstag	Doyo\bi

Commonly Confused English Words

adverse: unfavorable
averse: opposed

affect: to influence
effect: to cause

aggravate: to make worse
annoy: to irritate

allusion: an indirect reference
illusion: an unreal impression

anxious: apprehensive
eager: avid

appraise: to set a value on
apprise: to inform

capital: the seat of government
capitol: the building in which a legislative body meets

complement: to make complete; something that completes
compliment: to praise; praise

denote: to mean
connote: to suggest beyond the explicit meaning

discreet: prudent
discrete: separate

disinterested: impartial
uninterested: without interest

elicit: to draw or bring out
illicit: illegal

emigrate: to leave for another place of residence
immigrate: to come to another place of residence

farther: more distant in space
further: an extension of time or degree

flaunt: to display ostentatiously
flout: to treat with contemptuous disregard

grisly: inspiring horror or intense fear
grizzly: sprinkled or streaked with gray

historic: an important occurrence
historical: any occurrence in the past

imminent: ready to take place
eminent: standing out

imply: to relay information but not explicitly
infer: to understand information that is not relayed explicitly

include: used when the items following are part of a whole
comprise: used when the items following are all of a whole

incredible: unbelievable
incredulous: skeptical

ingenious: clever
ingenuous: innocent

insidious: intended to trick
invidious: detrimental to reputation

literally: actually
figuratively: metaphorically

oral: spoken, as opposed to written
verbal: referring to skill with language, as opposed to other skills

pestilence: a contagious or infectious epidemic disease
petulance: rudeness

prevaricate: to lie
procrastinate: to put off

prostrate: stretched out flat, face down
prostate: of or relating to the prostate gland

qualitative: relating to quality
quantitative: relating to number

Commonly Misspelled English Words

accidentally	convenience	government	miniature
accommodate	deceive	grammar	misspelled
acquainted	describe	harass	mysterious
all right	description	humorous	necessary
already	desirable	hurrying	opportunity
amateur	despair	incidentally	optimistic
appearance	desperate	independent	performance
appropriate	eliminate	inoculate	permanent
bureau	embarrass	irresistible	rhythm
character	fascinating	laboratory	ridiculous
commitment	finally	lightning	similar
conscientious	fluorine	liquefy	sincerely
conscious	foreign	maintenance	transferred
	forty	marriage	

Forms of Address

Addressee	Address	Salutation
Government		
President of the U.S.	The President, The White House, Washington, DC 20500; also, The President and Mrs. _____ or The President and Mr. _____	Dear Sir or Madam; Mr. President or Madam President; Dear Mr. President or Dear Madam President
Vice President of the U.S.	The Vice President, Old Executive Office Building, Washington, DC 20501; also, The Vice President and Mrs. _____ or The Vice President and Mr. _____	Dear Sir or Madam; Mr. Vice President or Madam Vice President; Dear Mr. Vice President or Dear Madam Vice President
Chief Justice	The Hon. *FirstName Surname*, Chief Justice of the U.S., The Supreme Court, Washington, DC 20543	Dear Sir or Madam; Dear Mr. or Madam Chief Justice
Associate Justice	Mr. Justice *Surname*, The Supreme Court, Washington, DC 20543	Dear Sir or Madam; Dear Justice *Surname*
Judge	The Hon. *FirstName Surname*, Associate Judge, U.S. District Court	Dear Judge *Surname*
Attorney General	The Hon. *FirstName Surname*, Attorney General, Dept. of Justice, Constitution Ave. & 10th St. NW, Washington, DC 20530	Dear Sir or Madam; Dear Mr. or Ms. Attorney General
Cabinet Officer	The Hon. *FirstName Surname*, Secretary of _____	Dear Mr. or Madam Secretary; or Dear Mr. or Ms. *Surname*
Senator	The Hon. or Sen. *FirstName Surname*, U.S. Senate, Washington, DC 20510	Dear Mr. or Madam Senator, or Dear Mr. or Ms. *Surname*
Representative	The Hon. or Rep. *FirstName Surname*, House of Representatives, Washington, DC 20515	Dear Mr. or Madam *Surname*
Speaker of the House	The Hon. Speaker of the House of Representatives, House of Representatives, Washington, DC 20515	Dear Mr. or Madam Speaker
Ambassador, U.S.	The Hon. *FirstName Surname*, American Ambassador[1]	Sir or Madam; Dear Mr. or Madam Ambassador
Ambassador, Foreign	His or Her Excellency *FirstName Surname*, Ambassador of _____	Excellency;[2] Dear Mr. or Madam Ambassador
Governor	The Hon. *FirstName Surname*, Governor of *State*; or in some states, His or Her Excellency, the Governor of *State*	Sir or Madam; Dear Governor *Surname*
Mayor	The Hon. *FirstName Surname*, Mayor of *City*	Sir or Madam; Dear Mayor *Surname*
Military Personnel		
All Titles	Full or abbreviated rank + full name + comma + abbreviation for branch of service. Example: Adm. John Smith, USN	Dear *Rank Surname*
Clerical and Religious Orders		
Clergy, Protestant	The Reverend *FirstName Surname*[3]	Dear Ms. or Mr. *Surname*
Pope	His Holiness Pope *Name* or His Holiness the Pope	Your Holiness or Most Holy Father
Priest	The Reverend *FirstName Surname* or The Reverend Father *Surname*	Reverend Father, Dear Father *Surname*, or Dear Father
Rabbi	Rabbi *FirstName Surname*	Dear Rabbi *Surname*
Royalty and Nobility		
King or Queen	His or Her Majesty, King or Queen of *Country*	Sir or Madam, or May it please Your Majesty

(1) If in Canada or Latin America, The Ambassador of the United States of America. (2) An American ambassador is not to be addressed as His or Her Excellency. (3) Any member of the clergy who has a doctorate may be so addressed; for example, The Reverend FirstName Surname, DD, and Dear Dr. Surname.

Pen Names

Alain-Fournier (Henri Fournier)

Shalom Aleichem (Solomon J. Rabinowitz

Woody Allen (Allen Stewart Konigsberg)

Currer, Ellis, and Acton Bell (Charlotte, Emily, and Anne Brontë)

John le Carré (David John Moore Cornwell)

Lewis Carroll (Charles Lutwidge Dodgson)

Colette (Sidonie Gabrielle Colette)

Isak Dinesen (Karen Blixen)

Elia (Charles Lamb)

George Eliot (Mary Ann or Marian Evans)

Maksim Gorky (Aleksey Maksimovich Peshkov)

O. Henry (William Sydney Porter)

James Herriot (James Alfred Wight)

P. D. James (Phyllis Dorothy James White)

[John] Ross Macdonald (Kenneth Millar)

André Maurois (Émile Herzog)

Molière (Jean Baptiste Poquelin)

George Orwell (Eric Arthur Blair)

Ellery Queen (Frederic Dannay and Manfred B. Lee)

Mary Renault (Mary Challans)

Françoise Sagan (Françoise Quoirez)

Saki (Hector Hugh Munro)

George Sand (Amandine Lucie Aurore Dupine)

Dr. Seuss (Theodor Seuss Geisel)

Stendahl (Marie Henri Beyle)

Mark Twain (Samuel Clemens)

Voltaire (François Marie Arouet)

Artemus Ward (Charles Farrar Browne)

Tom Wolfe (Thomas Kennerly, Jr.)

The Principal Languages of the World

Source: S. Culbert, NI-25, University of Washington, Seattle, WA 98195; data as of mid-1995

Languages Spoken by More Than 100,000,000 People

	Speakers (millions) Native	Total		Speakers (millions) Native	Total		Speakers (millions) Native	Total
Mandarin	844	975	Bengali	193	200	Japanese	125	126
Hindi	340	437	Arabic	190	225	German	98	123
Spanish	339	392	Russian	169	284	French	73	125
English	326	478	Portuguese	172	184	Malay-Indonesian	52	159

Languages Spoken by at Least 1 Million People

Total number of speakers (native plus nonnative) of languages spoken by at least one million speakers. A native speaker is one for whom the language is his or her first language. Locations in parentheses are principal areas where language is spoken.

Achinese (N Sumatra, Indonesia)	3	Edo (Bendel, S Nigeria)	1	Kannada (S India)	44
Afghan (see Pashtu)		Efik (incl. Ibibio) (SE Nigeria)	6	Kanuri (Nigeria; Niger; Chad;	
Afrikaans (S Africa)	10	English (see above)	478	Cameroon)	4
Akan (or Twi-Fanti) (Ghana)	7	Estonian (Estonia)	1	Karen (see Sgaw)	
Albanian (Albania; Kosovo,		Ewe (SE Ghana; S Togo)	3	Karo-Dairi (N Sumatra, Indonesia)	2
Yugoslavia)	5	Fang-Bulu (Dialects of Beti, q. v.)		Kashmiri[1] (N India; NE Pakistan)	4
Amharic (Ethiopia)	20	Farsi (see Persian)		Kazakh (Kazakhstan)	8
Arabic (see above)	225	Finnish (Finland; Sweden)	6	Kenuzi-Dongola (S Egypt; Sudan)	1
Armenian (Armenia)	5	Fon (SC Benin; S Togo)	1	Khalka (see Mongolian)	
Assamese[1] (India; Bangladesh)	22	French (see above)	125	Khmer (Cambodia; Vietnam; Thai.)	8
Aymara (Bolivia; Peru)	2	Fula (or Peulh) (Cameroon; Nigeria)	13	Khmer, Northern (Thailand)	1
Azeri (Azerbaijan)	15	Fulakunda (Senegal; Gambia;		Kikuyu (or Gekoyo) (WC Kenya)	5
Balinese (Bali, Indonesia)	3	Guinea-Bissau)	2	Kituba (Bas-Zaire, Bandundu,	
Baluchi (Baluchistan, in SW		Futa Jalon (Guinea; Sierra Leone)	3	Zaire)	4
Pakistan and SE Iran)	5	Galician (Galicia, NW Spain)	4	Kongo (W Zaire; S Congo; NW	
Bashkir (Bashkortostan, Russia)	1	Galla (see Oromo)		Ang.)	3
Batak Toba (Indonesia)	4	Ganda (or Luganda) (S Uganda)	3	Konkani (Maharashtra and SW	
Baule (Côte d'Ivoire)	2	Georgian (Georgia)	4	India)	4
Beja (Kassala, Sudan; Ethiopia)	1	German (see above)	123	Korean (Korea; China; Japan)	75
Bemba (Zambia)	2	Gilaki (Gilan, NW Iran)	2	Kurdish (Iran; Iraq; Turkey)	11
Bengali[1] (see above)	200	Gogo (Riff Valley, Tanzania)	1	Kurukh (or Oraon) (C and E India)	2
Berber[2]		Gondi (Central India)	2	Kyrgyz (Kyrgyzstan)	2
Beti (Cameroon; Gabon; Eq.		Greek (Greece)	12	Lampung (Sumatra, Indonesia)	2
Guinea)	2	Guarani (Paraguay)	4	Lao[5] (Laos)	4
Bhili (India)	3	Gujarati[1] (WC India; S Pakistan)	41	Latvian (Latvia)	2
Bikol (SE Luzon, Philippines)	4	Gusii (Kisii District, Nyanza, Kenya)	2	Lingala (incl. Bangala) (Zaire)	7
Brahui (Pakistan)	2	Gypsy (see Romany)		Lithuanian (Lithuania)	3
Bugis (Indonesia; Malaysia)	4	Hadiyya (Arusi, Ethiopia)	2	Luba-Lulua (or Chiluba) (Zaire)	7
Bulgarian (Bulgaria)	9	Hakka (or Kejia) (SE China)	34	Luba-Shaba (Shaba, Zaire)	1
Burmese (Myanmar)	31	Hani (S China)	1	Lubu (E Sumatra, Indonesia)	1
Buyi (S Guizhou, S China)	2	Hausa (N Nigeria; Niger; Camer-		Luhya (W Kenya)	1
Byelorussian (Belarus)	10	oon)	38	Luo (Kenya; Nyanza, Tanzania)	4
Cantonese (China; Hong Kong)	70	Haya (Kagera, NW Tanzania)	1	Luri (SW Iran; Iraq)	4
Catalan (NE Spain; Balearic Is.;		Hebrew (Israel)	5	Lwena (E Angola; W Zambia)	2
S France; Andorra)	9	Hindi[1,4] (see above)	437	Macedonian (Macedonia)	2
Cebuano (Bohol Sea, Philippines)	13	Hmong (S China; SE Asia)	6	Madurese (Madura, Indonesia)	10
Chagga (Kilimanjaro area,		Ho (Bihar and Orissa States,		Magindanaon (S Philippines)	1
Tanzania)	1	India)	1	Makassar (S Sulawesi, Indonesia)	2
Chiga (Uganda)	1	Hungarian (or Magyar) (Hungary)	14	Makua (S Tanzania;	
Chinese[3]		Iban (Indonesia; Malaysia)	1	N Mozambique)	4
Chuvash (Chuvash, Russia)	2	Ibibio (see Efik)		Malagasy (Madagascar)	12
Czech (Czech Republic)	12	Igbo (or Ibo) (lower Niger, Nigeria)	17	Malay-Indonesian (see above)	159
Danish (Denmark)	5	Ijaw (Niger River delta, Nigeria)	2	Malay, Pattani (SE Thailand)	1
Dimli (EC Turkey)	1	Ilocano (NW Luzon, Philippines)	7	Malayalam[1] (Kerala, S India)	35
Dogri (Jammu-Kashmir, CE		Indonesian (see Malay-Indonesian)		Malinke-Bambara-Dyula	
India)	1	Italian (Italy)	63	(W Africa)	9
Dong (SC China)	2	Japanese (see above)	126	Mandarin (see above)	975
Dutch-Flemish (Netherlands;		Javanese (Java, Indonesia)	64	Marathi[1] (Maharashtra, India)	70
Belg.; NE France)	21	Kabyle (W Kabylia, N Algeria)	3	Mazandarani (S Mazandaran, N	
Dyerma (SW Niger)	2	Kamba (E Kenya)	3	Iran)	2

Mbundu (Benguela, Angola)	4	Ruanda (Rwanda; Uganda; Zaire)	6	Temne (central Sierra Leone) . . .	2
Mbundu (Luanda, Angola)	3	Rundi (Burundi)	6	Thai[5] (Thailand)	51
Meithei (NE India; Bangladesh) . .	1	Russian (see above)	284	Tho (N Vietnam; S China)	2
Mende (Sierra Leone)	2	Samar-Leyte (Central E		Thonga (Mozambique; So. Africa) .	3
Meru (Eastern Province, C		Philippines)	3	Tibetan (SW China; N India;	
Tanzania)	1	Sango (Central African Republic) .	4	Nepal)	5
Mien (China; Viet.; Laos; Thailand) .	2	Santali (E India; Nepal)	5	Tigrinya (S Eritrea; Tigre,	
Min (SE China; Taiwan; Malaysia) .	50	Sasak (Lombok, Alas Strait, Indon.) .	2	Ethiopia)	4
Minangkabau (W Sumatra, Indon.)	6	Serbo-Croatian (Croatia; Serbia;		Tiv (SE Nigeria; Cameroon)	2
Moldavian (included with Romanian)		and other former Yugoslav		Tong (see Dong)	
Mongolian (Mongolia; NE China) .	6	republics and autonomous		Tonga (SW Zambia; NW	
Mordvin (Mordova, Russia)	1	regions)	20	Zimbabwe)	2
Moré (central part of Burkina Faso)	4	Sgaw (SW Myanmar)	2	Tswana (Botswana; So. Africa) .	4
Nepali (Nepal; NE India; Bhutan).	16	Shan (E Myanmar)	3	Tudza (N Vietnam; S China) . . .	1
Ngulu (Mozambique; Malawi) . . .	2	Shilha (W Algeria; S Morocco) . . .	3	Tulu (S India)	2
Nkole (Western Prov., Uganda). .	1	Shona (Zimbabwe)	8	Tumbuka (N Malawi; NE Zambia)	2
Norwegian (Norway)	5	Sidamo (Sidamo, S Ethiopia)	2	Turkish (Turkey)	60
Nung (NE of Hanoi, Vietnam;		Sindhi[1] (SE Pakistan; W India) . . .	18	Turkmen (Turkmenistan;	
China)	2	Sinhalese (Sri Lanka)	13	Afghanistan)	3
Nupe (Kwara, Niger States, Nigeria)	1	Slovak (Slovakia)	5	Twi-Fante (see Akan)	
Nyamwezi-Sukuma (NW		Slovene (Slovenia)	2	Uighur (Xinjiang, NW China) . . .	8
Tanzania)	5	Soga (Busoga, Uganda)	1	Ukrainian (Ukraine; Russia;	
Nyanja (Malawi; Zambia; Zimbabwe)	5	Somali (Som.; Eth.; Ken.; Djibouti)	4	Poland)	47
Oriya[1] (Central and E India)	32	Songye (Kasai Or., NW Shala,		Urdu[1,4] (Pakistan; India)	102
Oromo (West Ethiopia; N Kenya)	9	Zaire)	1	Uzbek (Uzbekistan)	14
Pampangan (NW of Manila, Philip.)	2	Soninke (Mali; countries to W S E)	1	Vietnamese (Vietnam)	65
Panay-Hiligaynon (Philippines) . .	7	Sotho, Northern (So. Africa)	3	Wolaytta (SE Ethiopia)	2
Pangasinan (Lingayen G., Philip.)	2	Sotho, Southern (So. Afr.; Lesotho)	4	Wolof (Senegal)	7
Pashtu (Pakistan; Afghanistan;		Spanish (see above)	392	Wu (Shanghai region, China) . . .	66
Iran)	21	Sundanese (Sunda Strait, Indonesia)	26	Xhosa (SW Cape Prov., So.	
Pedi (see Sotho, Northern)		Swahili (Kenya; Tanz.; Zaire; Ug.) .	49	Africa)	8
Persian (Iran; Afghanistan)	35	Swati (Swaziland; S. Africa)	1	Yao (see Mien)	
Polish (Poland)	44	Swedish (Sweden; Finland)	9	Yao (Malawi; Tanzania; Mo-	
Portuguese (see above)	184	Sylhetti (Bangladesh)	5	zambique)	1
Provençal (S France)	4	Tagalog (Philippines)	54	Yi (S and SW China)	7
Punjabi[1] (Punjab, Pakistan; India) .	95	Tajiki (Tajikistan; Uzbek.; Kyrgyz.) .	5	Yiddish[6]	
Pushto (see Pashtu)		Tamazight (N Morocco; W Algeria) .	3	Yoruba (SW Nigeria; Zou, Benin)	20
Quechua A (Peru; Boliv.; Ec.; Arg.).	8	Tamil[1] (Tamil Nadu, India; Sri Lanka)	71	Zande (NE Zaire; SW Sudan) . .	1
Rejang (SW Sumatra, Indonesia)	1	Tatar (Tatarstan, Russia)	8	Zhuang (S China)	15
Riff (N Morocco; Algerian coast) .	1	Tausug (Philippines; Malaysia) . . .	1	Zulu (N. Natal, South Africa;	
Romanian (Romania; Moldova). .	26	Telugu[1] (Andhra Pradesh, SE		Lesotho)	9
Romany[7].	2	India)	74		

(1) One of the 15 languages of the Constitution of India. (2) See Kabyle, Riff, Shilha, and Tamazight. (3) See Mandarin, Cantonese, Wu, Min, and Hakka. The "common speech" (Putonghua) or the "national language" (Guoyu) is a standardized form of Mandarin as spoken in the area of Beijing. (4) Hindi and Urdu are essentially the same language, Hindustani. As the official language of Pakistan, it is written in a modified Arabic script and called Urdu. As the official language of India, it is written in the Devanagari script and called Hindi. (5) The distinctions between some Thai dialects and Lao are political rather than linguistic. (6) Yiddish is usually considered a variant of German, although it has its own standard grammar and dictionaries, has a highly developed literature, and is written in Hebrew characters. (7) Mainly in central, E, and SE Europe and Turkey; some in the U.S.

American Manual Alphabet

In the American Manual Alphabet, each letter of the alphabet is represented by a position of the fingers. This system was originally developed in France by Abbe Charles Michel De l'Epee in the late 1700s. It was brought to the U.S. by Laurent Clerce (1785-1869), a Frenchman who taught people who were deaf or hearing impaired.

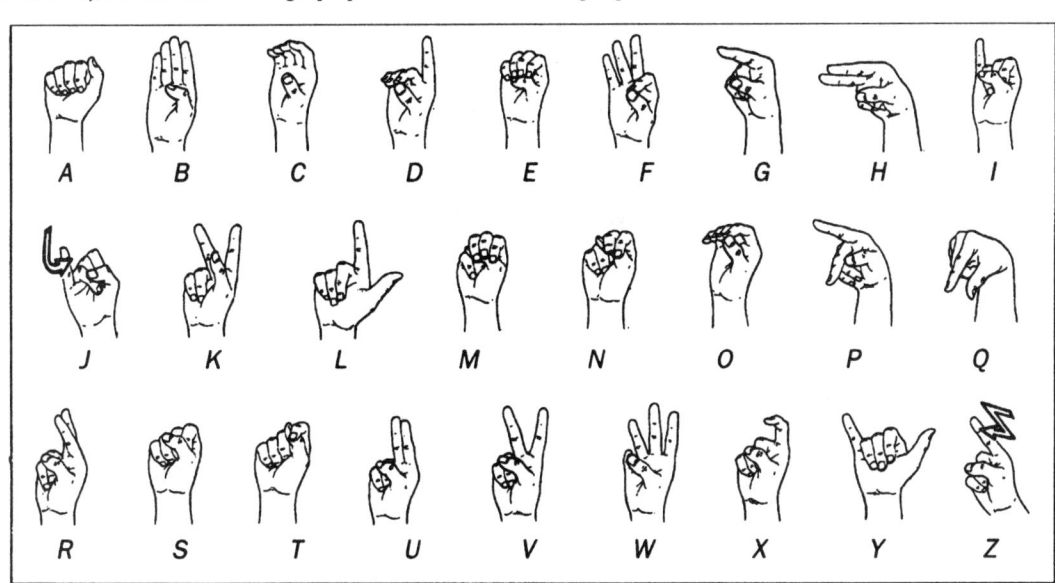

© National Association of the Deaf

RELIGIOUS INFORMATION
Census of Religious Groups in the U.S.

Source: *1995 Yearbook of American & Canadian Churches,* © *National Council of the Churches of Christ in the USA;* World Almanac research

Membership figures generally are based on reports made by group leaders rather than on "head counts" of the population. In many cases, groups keep careful records; others only estimate. Not all groups report annually. Christian church membership figures reported in this table are inclusive and refer to those who are full communicants or confirmed members plus other members baptized, nonconfirmed, or noncommunicant. Only data reported within the past 10 years are included.

The number of churches appears in parentheses. * Indicates that the group declines to publish membership figures.

Religious Group	Members
Adventist churches:	
Advent Christian Ch. (328)	27,300
Ch. of God General Conf. (Oregon, IL) (87)	5,336
Primitive Advent Christian Ch. (10)	345
Seventh-Day Adventists (4,270)	761,703
American Rescue Workers (16)	**35,000**
Apostolic Christian Ch. (Nazarene) (63)	**3,723**
Apostolic Christian Churches of America (80)	**11,450**
Baha'i Faith (1,700)	**125,000**
Baptist churches:	
American Baptist Assn. (1,705)	250,000
American Baptist Chs. in U.S.A. (5,796)	1,516,505
Baptist Bible Fellowship Intl. (3,500)	1,500,000
Baptist General Conference (821)	134,658
Baptist Missionary Assn. of America (1,362)	230,747
Conservative Baptist Assn. of America (1,084)	200,000
Free Will Baptists, Natl. Assn. of (2,513)	214,557
General Assn. of Regular Baptist Chs. (1,505)	154,943
General Baptists, General Assn. of (876)	74,156
Liberty Baptist Fellowship (100)	*
Natl. Baptist Convention of America (2,500)	3,500,000
Natl. Baptist Convention, U.S.A. (33,000)	8,200,000
Natl. Missionary Baptist Convention of America (*)	2,500,000
North American Baptist Conference (267)	43,045
Progressive National Baptist Convention (1,400)	2,500,000
Separate Baptists in Christ (100)	8,000
Seventh-Day Baptist General Conference (90)	5,250
Southern Baptist Convention (38,682)	15,398,642
Sovereign Grace Baptists (300)	3,000
Brethren (German Baptists):	
Brethren Ch. (Ashland, Ohio) (121)	13,117
Fellowship of Grace Brethren (286)	34,702
Old German Baptist Brethren (57)	5,535
Brethren, River:	
Brethren in Christ Ch. (188)	17,986
United Zion Ch. (13)	852
Buddhist Churches of America	**230,000**
Christian Catholic Church (5)	**2,000**
Christian Church (Disciples of Christ) (3,961)	**958,017**
Christian Churches and Churches of Christ (5,579)	**1,070,616**
Christian Congregation (1,437)	**112,437**
Christian and Missionary Alliance (1,943)	**302,414**
Christian Nation Church U.S.A. (5)	**200**
Christian Union, Churches of Christ in (240)	**10,400**
Church of Christ, Scientist (2,400)	*
Churches of Christ (13,013)	**1,651,103**
Churches of God:	
Chs. of God, General Conference (347)	32,488
Ch. of God (Anderson, IN) (2,314)	216,117
Ch. of God (Seventh Day), Denver, CO (168)	5,500
Ch. of God in Christ Which He Purchased With His Own Blood (7)	800
Ch. of God by Faith (145)	8,235
Church of the Nazarene (5,161)	**591,134**
Community Churches, Intl. Council of (423)	**500,000**
Congregational Christian Chs. (405)	**90,000**
Conservative Congregational Christian Conference (201)	**36,864**
Eastern Orthodox churches:	
Albanian Orthodox Diocese of America (2)	1,885
American Carpatho-Russian Orthodox Greek Catholic Ch. (77)	19,101
Antiochian Orthodox Christian Archdiocese of North America (178)	350,000
Apostolic Catholic Assyrian Ch. of the East, N.A. Diocese (22)	120,000
Armenian Apostolic Ch. of America (32)	150,000
Armenian Church of Amer., Diocese of the (72)	414,000
Bulgarian Eastern Orthodox Ch. (9)	1,100
Coptic Orthodox Ch. (85)	180,000
Greek Orthodox Archdiocese of North and South America (555)	1,500,000
Orthodox Ch. in America (700)	600,000
Romanian Orthodox Episcopate of America (37)	65,000

Religious Group	Members
Serbian Orthodox Ch. of U.S.A. & Canada (68)	67,000
Syrian Orthodox Ch. of Antioch (Archdiocese of the U.S.A. and Canada) (17)	32,500
True Orthodox Church of Greece (9)	1,080
Ukrainian Orthodox Ch. in America (Ecumenical Patriarchate) (27)	5,000
Episcopal Church (7,388)	**2,504,682**
Evangelical Church (43)	**3,336**
Evangelical Congregational Church (152)	**23,889**
Evangelical Covenant Church (597)	**89,511**
Evangelical Free Church of America (1,202)	**226,391**
Fellowship of Fundamental Bible Churches (23)	**1,343**
Fire Baptized Holiness Church (Wesleyan) (49)	**692**
Friends:	
Evangelical Friends International, North American (246)	26,322
Friends General Conference (520)	31,500
Friends United Meeting (526)	50,803
Grace Gospel Fellowship (128)	**60,000**
Hindu	**910,000**
Independent Fundamental Churches of America (708)	**71,672**
Islam	**5,500,000[1]**
Jehovah's Witnesses (9,985)	**926,614**
Jewish organizations:	
Union of American Hebrew Congregations (Reform) (853)	1,300,000
Union of Orthodox Jewish Congregations of America (1,200)	1,000,000
United Synagogues of Conservative Judaism, The (800)	2,000,000
Latter-Day Saints:	
Ch. of Jesus Christ (Bickertonites) (63)	2,707
Ch. of Jesus Christ of Latter-Day Saints (Mormon) (10,007)	4,520,000
Reorganized Ch. of Jesus Christ of Latter-Day Saints (1,001)	150,143
Liberal Catholic Ch.-Province of the U.S.A. (34)	**2,800**
Lutheran churches:	
Apostolic Lutheran Ch. of America (60)	9,500
Ch. of the Lutheran Brethren of America (120)	12,527
Ch. of the Lutheran Confession (69)	8,718
Conservative Lutheran Assn. (12)	1,530
Estonian Evangelical Lutheran Ch. (23)	4,079
Evangelical Lutheran Ch. in America (11,023)	5,212,785
Evangelical Lutheran Synod (125)	21,493
Free Lutheran Congregations, Assn. of (230)	29,848
Latvian Evangelical Lutheran Church of America (55)	13,380
Lutheran Ch.—Missouri Synod (6,134)	2,598,935
Lutheran Chs., American Assn. of (94)	22,061
Protestant Conference (Lutheran) (7)	1,150
Wisconsin Evangelical Lutheran Synod (1,220)	416,886
Mennonite churches:	
Beachy Amish Mennonite Chs. (95)	6,968
Church of God in Christ (Mennonite) (86)	10,500
Evangelical Mennonite Ch. (29)	4,228
Fellowship of Evangelical Bible Churches (14)	1,925
Hutterian Brethren (95)	6,700
Mennonite Brethren Chs., The Conf. of (147)	19,218
Mennonite Church (1,058)	95,634
Mennonite Ch., The General Conference (224)	33,629
Old Order Amish Ch. (898)	80,820
Methodist churches:	
African Methodist Episcopal Ch. (8,000)	3,500,000
African Methodist Episcopal Zion Ch. (3,000)	1,200,000
Allegheny Wesleyan Methodist Connection (120)	2,043
Evangelical Methodist Ch. (132)	8,500
Free Methodist Ch. of North America (1,050)	74,585
Fundamental Methodist Ch. (12)	787
Primitive Methodist Ch., U.S.A. (81)	7,360
Southern Methodist Ch. (128)	7,891
United Methodist Ch. (36,771)	8,646,595
The Wesleyan Church (U.S.A.) (1,583)	115,368

Religious Group	Members
Metropolitan Community Churches, Universal Fellowship of (291)	**30,000**
Missionary Church, Inc. (309)	**28,408**
Moravian churches:	
Moravian Ch. in America Southern Province (56)	21,513
Moravian Ch. Northern Province (97)	28,639
Unity of the Brethren (26)	2,602
Natl. Organization of the New Apostolic Ch. of North America (554)	**41,863**
Natl. Spiritualist Assn. of Churches (143)	**3,634**
Old Catholic churches:	
Christ Catholic Ch. (12)	1,558
Pentecostal churches:	
Apostolic Faith Mission (Portland, OR) (54)	4,500
Apostolic Faith Mission Ch. of God (40)	15,400
Apostolic Overcoming Holy Church of God (165)	11,274
Assemblies of God (11,762)	2,271,718
Bible Church of Christ (6)	6,850
Church of God (Cleveland, TN) (5,899)	700,517
Church of God in Christ (15,300)	5,499,875
Church of God of Prophecy (2,044)	72,370
Congregational Holiness Ch. (190)	2,468
Elim Fellowship (66)	*
Intl. Ch. of the Foursquare Gospel (1,638)	217,515
Open Bible Standard Chs. (361)	45,988
Pentecostal Assemblies of the World (1,005)	500,000
Pentecostal Church of God (1,174)	102,760
Pentecostal Free-Will Baptist Ch. (150)	18,000

Religious Group	Members
United Pentecostal Ch. Intl. (3,728)	550,000
Presbyterian churches:	
Associate Reformed Presbyterian Ch. (General Synod) (196)	38,763
Cumberland Presbyterian Ch. (779)	91,489
Evangelical Presbyterian Ch. (175)	56,421
Korean Presbyterian Church in America (203)	26,988
Orthodox Presbyterian Ch. (170)	18,137
Presbyterian Ch. in America (1,212)	239,500
Presbyterian Ch. (U.S.A.) (11,501)	3,796,766
Reformed Presbyterian Ch. of N. America (70)	5,657
Reformed churches:	
Christian Reformed Ch. in N. America (738)	214,545
Hungarian Reformed Ch. in America (27)	9,780
Netherlands Reformed Congregations (15)	4,374
Reformed Ch. in America (923)	316,553
Reformed Ch. in the U.S. (37)	4,204
United Church of Christ (6,225)	1,530,178
Reformed Episcopal Church (83)	**6,565**
Roman Catholic Church (19,787)	**59,858,042**
Salvation Army (1,151)	**446,403**
Schwenkfelder Church (5)	**2,421**
Swedenborgian Church (50)	**2,475**
Unitarian Universalist Assn. (1,020)	**141,315**
United Brethren:	
United Brethren in Christ (239)	24,616
Vedanta Societies (13)	**2,500**

(1) Figure is for Northern America. Estimates vary.

Headquarters of Selected Religious Groups in the United States

Source: *1995 Yearbook of American & Canadian Churches,* © *National Council of the Churches of Christ in the USA;* World Almanac research

Year organized in parentheses

African Methodist Episcopal Church, (1787), 1134 11th St. NW, Washington, DC 20001

African Methodist Episcopal Zion Church (1796), PO Box 32843, Charlotte, NC 28232; Pres., Bishop Milton A. Williams

American Baptist Churches in the U.S.A. (1907), PO Box 851, Valley Forge, PA 19482; Pres., Hector Gonzales

American Rescue Workers (1884), 2827 Frankford Ave., PO Box 4766, Philadelphia, PA 19134; Commander-in-Chief & President, Gen. Paul E. Martin, Reverend

Antiochian Orthodox Christian Archdiocese of North America (1895), 358 Mountain Rd., Englewood, NJ 07631; Primate, Metropolitan Philip Saliba

Armenian Church of America, Diocese of the (1889), **Eastern Diocese**: 630 Second Ave., New York, NY 10016; Primate, Archbishop Khajag Barsamian; **Western Diocese**: 1201 N. Vine St., Hollywood, CA 90038; Primate, His Eminence Archbishop Vatche Hovespian

Assemblies of God (1914), 1445 Boonville Ave., Springfield, MO 65802; General Supt., Thomas E. Trask

Bahá'í Faith, 536 Sheridan Rd., Wilmette, IL 60091

Baptist Bible Fellowship Intl. (1950), PO Box 191, Springfield, MO 65801; Pres., Sam Davison

Baptist General Conference (1852), 2002 S. Arlington Heights Rd., Arlington Heights, IL 60005; President, Dr. Robert Ricker

Brethren in Christ Church (1778), PO Box 290, Grantham, PA 17027; Moderator, Rev. Harvey R. Sider

Buddhist Churches of America (1899), 1710 Octavia St., San Francisco, CA 94109

Christian Church (Disciples of Christ) (1809), 130 E. Washington St., Indianapolis, IN 46206; Gen. Minister, Richard L. Hamm

Christian Churches and Churches of Christ, 4201 Bridgetown Rd., Box 11326, Cincinnati, OH 45211

Christian Congregation, Inc. (1887), 804 W. Hemlock St. LaFollette, TN 37766; General Supt., Rev. Ora W. Eads, D.D.

Christian Methodist Episcopal Church (1870), 4466 Elvis Presley Blvd., Memphis, TN 38116; Executive Secretary, Dr. Clyde W. Williams

Christian and Missionary Alliance (1897), PO Box 35000, Colorado Springs, CO 80935; Pres., Rev. David Rambo, Ph.D

Christian Reformed Church in North America (1857), 2850 Kalamazoo Ave. SE, Grand Rapids, MI 49560; Gen. Secretary, Dr. David H. Engelhard

Church of Christ, Scientist (1879), 175 Huntington Ave., Boston, MA 02115; Pres., Ruth Elizabeth Jenks

Churches of Christ, PO Box 726, Kosciusko, MO 39090

Church of God (Anderson, IN) (1881), Box 2420, Anderson, IN 46018; General Sec., Edward L. Foggs

Church of God (Cleveland, TN) (1886), PO Box 2430, Cleveland, TN 37320; Gen. Overseer, Robert White

Church of God in Christ (1907), Mason Temple, 939 Mason St., Memphis, TN 38126; Presiding Bishop, Rt. Reverend L. H. Ford

Church of Jesus Christ (Bickertonites) (1830), 6th & Linclon Sts., Monongahela, PA 15063; Pres., Dominic R. Thomas

Church of Jesus Christ of the Latter-Day Saints (Mormon) (1830), 50 E. North Temple St., Salt Lake City, UT 84150; Pres., Gordon B. Hinckley

Church of the Nazarene (1907), 6401 The Paseo, Kansas City, MO 64131; General Sec., Jack Stone

Coptic Orthodox Church, 427 West Side Ave., Jersey City, NJ 07304; Archpriest, Very Reverend Fr. John Ramzy, PhD.

Cumberland Presbyterian Church (1810), 1978 Union Ave., Memphis, TN 38104; Moderator, Rev. Donald Alexander

Episcopal Church (1789), 815 Second Ave., New York, NY 10017; Bishop, Most Rev. Edmond L. Browning

Evangelical Free Church of America (1884), 901 E. 78th St., Minneapolis, MN 55420; President, Dr. Paul Cedar

Evangelical Lutheran Church in America (1987), 8765 W. Higgins Rd., Chicago, IL 60631; Bishop, Reverend Dr. Herbert W. Chilstrom

Fellowship of Grace Brethren (1882), PO Box 386, Winona Lake, IN 46590; Moderator, Ed Lewis

Free Methodist Church of North America (1860), World Ministries Center: 770 N. High School Rd., Indianapolis, IN 46214

Friends General Conference (1900), 1216 Arch St., Philadelphia, PA 19107; Gen. Secretary, Bruce Birchard

General Conference Mennonite Church (1860), 722 Main St., Newton, KS 67114; Moderator, Darrell Fast

Greek Orthodox Archdiocese of N. and S. America (1864), 8-10 E. 79th St., New York, NY 10021; Chairperson, Archbishop Iakovos

International Church of the Foursquare Gospel (1927), 1910 W. Sunset Blvd., Ste. 200, Los Angeles, CA 90026; President, Dr. John R. Holland

International Council of Community Churches (1950s), 19115 S. LaGrange Rd., Ste. C, Mokena, IL 60448; Pres., Orsey Malone

Islamic Association in the U.S. and Canada, Federation of, 25351 Five Mile Rd., Redford Township, MI 48239; Sec., Nihad Hamed

Jehovah's Witnesses (1879), 25 Columbia Heights, Brooklyn, NY 11201; Pres., Milton Henschel

Lutheran Church—Missouri Synod (1847), 1333 S. Kirkwood, St. Louis, MO 63122; President, A. L. Barry

Mennonite Church (1525), 421 S. Second St., Elkhart, IN 46516; Moderator, Donella Clemens

Moravian Church (1735), **Northern Province:** 1021 Center St., Bethlehem, PA 18016; Pres., Gordon L. Sommers; **Southern Province:** 459 S. Church St., Winston-Salem, NC 27108; President, Rev. Graham H. Rights

National Baptist Convention, U.S.A. (1880), 1700 Baptist World Center Dr., Nashville, TN 37207; Pres., Dr. T. J. Jemison

(continued)

Headquarters of Selected Religious Groups in the United States (*continued*)

National Baptist Convention of America, Inc. (1880), 777 S.R.L. Thornton Freeway, Ste. 205, Dallas, TX 75203; President, Dr. E. Edward Jones

Natl. Missionary Baptist Convention of America (1988), 6717 Centennial Blvd., Nashville, TN 37209; President, Dr. S. M. Lockridge

Orthodox Church in America (1794), PO Box 675, Syosset, NY 11791; Primate, The Most Blessed Theodosius

Pentecostal Assemblies of the World (c 1900), 3939 Meadows Dr., Indianapolis, IN 46205.

Presbyterian Church (USA), (1983), 100 Witherspoon St., Louisville, KY 40202; Moderator, Robert W. Bohl

Presbyterian Church in America (1973), 1852 Century Pl., Atlanta, GA 30345; Moderator, Dr. William S. Barker

Progressive Natl. Baptist Convention (1961), 601 50th St. NE, Washington, DC 20019; President, Dr. Bennett W. Smith

Reformed Church in America (1628), 475 Riverside Dr., New York, NY 10115; President, I. John Hesslink

Restoration Church of Jesus Christ of Latter-Day Saints (1830), 801 W. 23rd St., Independence, MO 64055; President Marcus L. Juby

Roman Catholic Church, National Conference of Catholic Bishops, 3211 Fourth St., Washington, DC 20017; Pres., William Cardinal Keeler

Romanian Orthodox Episcopate of America (1929), PO Box 309, Grass Lake, MI 49240; Ruling Bishop, His Grace Nathaniel Popp

Salvation Army (1865), 615 Slaters Lane, Alexandria, VA 22313; National Comdr., Commissioner Kenneth Hodder

Seventh-Day Adventists (1863), 12501 Old Columbia Pike, Silver Spring, MD 20904; Pres., Robert Folkenberg

Southern Baptist Convention (1845), 901 Commerce St., Nashville, TN 37203; Pres., Jim Henry

Swedenborgian Church (1792), 48 Sargent St., Newton, MA 02158; President, Rev. Edwin G. Capon

Union of American Hebrew Congregations (Reform), 838 5th Ave., New York, NY; Pres., Rabbi Alexander M. Schindler

Union of Orthodox Jewish Congregations of America 333 7th Ave., New York, NY 10001; Pres., Sheldon Rudoff

Unitarian Universalist Association (1793), 25 Beacon St., Boston, MA 02108

United Church of Christ (1957), 700 Prospect Ave., Cleveland, OH 44115; Pres., Reverend Paul H. Sherry

United Methodist Church (1968), PO Box 320, Nashville, TN 37202; Pres., Bishop Roy A. Sano

United Pentecostal Church Intl. (1925), 8855 Dunn Rd., Hazelwood, MO 63042; General Superintendent, Rev. Nathaniel A. Urshan

United Synagogue of America (Conservative), 155 5th Ave., New York, NY 10010; Pres., Alan Tichnor

Vedanta Societies (1893), 34 W. 71st St., New York, NY 10023

Volunteers of America (1896), 3939 N. Causeway Blvd., Metairie, LA 70002; Chpsn., Walter Faster

Wesleyan Church (1968), PO Box 50434, Indianapolis, IN 46250; General Supts., Dr. Earle L. Wilson; Dr. Lee M. Haines; Dr. H. C. Wilson

Adherents of All Religions by Seven Continental Areas, Mid-1994

Source: *1995 Encyclopaedia Britannica Book of the Year*

	Africa	Asia	Europe	Latin America	Northern America	Oceania	Eurasia	World
Christians	351,682,000	304,887,000	422,159,000	422,140,000	246,319,000	23,240,000	109,747,000	1,900,174,000
Roman Catholics	132,102,000	132,053,000	267,972,000	411,514,000	100,386,000	8,427,000	5,615,000	1,058,069,000
Protestants	93,865,000	87,051,000	75,441,000	17,513,000	99,652,000	7,718,000	9,903,000	391,143,000
Orthodox	30,685,000	3,904,000	36,869,000	1,789,000	6,217,000	591,000	94,129,000	174,184,000
Anglicans	28,873,000	755,000	33,625,000	1,319,000	7,593,000	5,872,000	1,000	78,038,000
Other Christians	66,158,000	81,125,000	8,252,000	10,004,000	33,445,000	623,000	100,000	199,707,000
Muslims	293,993,000	675,297,000	13,194,000	1,395,000	5,500,000	107,000	43,967,000	1,033,453,000
Hindus	1,608,000	759,059,000	725,000	912,000	1,315,000	379,000	2,000	764,000,000
Buddhists	23,000	336,755,000	279,000	559,000	578,000	26,000	401,000	338,621,000
Chinese folk religionists	14,000	149,037,000	61,000	76,000	126,000	21,000	1,000	149,336,000
New-Religionists	23,000	126,869,000	51,000	548,000	1,473,000	10,000	1,000	128,975,000
Tribal religionists	69,872,000	28,197,000	1,000	967,000	42,000	71,000	0	99,150,000
Sikhs	29,000	19,557,000	237,000	8,000	363,000	9,000	1,000	20,204,000
Jews	128,000	4,289,000	1,761,000	458,000	5,907,000	95,000	813,000	13,451,000
Shamanists	1,000	10,754,000	2,000	1,000	1,000	1,000	250,000	11,010,000
Confucians	1,000	6,300,000	2,000	2,000	26,000	1,000	2,000	6,334,000
Baha'is	1,631,000	2,817,000	93,000	827,000	379,000	81,000	7,000	5,835,000
Jains	57,000	3,906,000	15,000	4,000	4,000	1,000	0	3,987,000
Shintoists	0	3,383,000	1,000	1,000	1,000	1,000	0	3,387,000
Other religionists	472,000	12,912,000	1,513,00	3,686,000	1,503,000	4,000	329,000	20,419,000
Nonreligious	2,936,000	733,740,000	58,199,000	19,327,000	23,884,000	3,756,000	82,236,000	924,078,000
Atheists	344,000	167,739,000	16,362,000	3,329,000	1,367,000	563,000	49,407,000	239,111,000
Total Population	**722,814,000**	**3,345,498,000**	**514,655,000**	**474,240,000**	**288,788,000**	**28,366,000**	**287,164,000**	**5,661,525,000**

Continents. These follow current UN demographic terminology. Eurasia is the provisional new term for the former USSR.

Adherents. As defined and enumerated for each of the world's countries in *World Christian Encyclopedia* (1982), projected to mid-1994, adjusted for recent data.

Christians. Followers of Jesus Christ affiliated with churches (church members, including children: 1,759,289,000) plus persons professing in censuses or polls though not so affiliated.

Other Christians. Catholics (non-Roman), marginal Protestants, crypto-Christians, and adherents of African, Asian, black, and Latin-American indigenous churches.

Muslims. 83% Sunnites, 16% Shi'ites, 1% other schools. Up to 1990 the former ethnic Muslims in the USSR who had embraced Communism were not included as Muslims in this table. After the collapse of Communism in 1990-91, these ethnic Muslims are once again enumerated as Muslims where they have returned to Islamic profession and practice.

Hindus. 70% Vaishnavites, 25% Shaivites, 2% neo-Hindus and reform Hindus.

Buddhists. 56% Mahayana, 38% Theravada (Hinayana), 6% Tantrism (Lamaism).

Atheists: Persons professing atheism, skepticism, disbelief, or irreligion, including antireligious (opposed to all religion).

Chinese folk-religionists. Followers of traditional Chinese religion (local deities, ancestor veneration, Confucian ethics, Taoism, universism, divination, some Buddhist elements).

New-Religionists. Followers of Asian 20th-cent. New Religions, New Religious movements, radical new crisis religions, and non-Christian syncretistic mass religions, all founded since 1800 and most since 1945.

Jews. Adherents of Judaism. For detailed data on "core" Jewish population, see the annual "World Jewish Populations" article in the American Jewish Committee's *American Jewish Year Book*.

Confucians. Non-Chinese followers of Confucius and Confucianism, mostly Koreans in Korea.

Other religionists. Including 70 minor world religions and a large number of spiritist religions, New Age religions, quasi religions, pseudo religions, parareligions, religious or mystic systems, and religious and semireligious brotherhoods.

Nonreligious. Persons professing no religion, nonbelievers, agnostics, freethinkers, dereligionized secularists indifferent to all religion.

Atheists. Persons professing atheism, skepticism, disbelief, or irreligion, including antireligious (opposed to all religions).

Total Population. UN medium variant figures for mid-1994, as given in *World Population Prospects* : The 1992 Revision (New York: UN, 1993) pp. 185-91.

Episcopal Church Liturgical Colors and Calendar

Source: The Episcopal Church Center, New York City

White—from Christmas Day through the First Sunday after Epiphany; Maundy Thursday (as an alternative to crimson at the Eucharist); from the Vigil of Easter to the Day of Pentecost (Whitsunday); Trinity Sunday; Feasts of the Lord (except Holy Cross Day); the Confession of St. Peter; the Conversion of St. Paul; St. Joseph; St. Mary Magdalene; St. Mary the Virgin; St. Michael and All Angels; All Saints' Day; St. John the Evangelist; memorials of other saints who were not martyred; Independence Day and Thanksgiving Day; weddings and funerals. **Red**—the Day of Pentecost; Holy Cross Day; feasts of apostles and evangelists (except those listed above); feasts and memorials of martyrs (including Holy Innocents' Day). **Violet**—Advent and Lent. **Crimson** (dark red)—Holy Week. **Green**—the seasons after Epiphany and after Pentecost. **Black**—optional alternative for funerals. Alternative colors used in some churches: **Blue**—Advent; **Lenten White**—Ash Wednesday to Palm Sunday.

In the Episcopal Church the days of fasting are Ash Wednesday and Good Friday. Other days of special devotion (abstinence) are the 40 days of Lent and all Fridays of the year, except those in Christmas and Easter seasons and any Feasts of the Lord that occur on a Friday or during Lent. Ember Days (optional) are days of prayer for the church's ministry. They fall on the Wednesday, Friday, and Saturday after the first Sunday in Lent, the Day of Pentecost, Holy Cross Day, and the Third Sunday of Advent. Rogation Days (also optional) are the 3 days before Ascension Day and are days of prayer for God's blessing on the crops, on commerce and industry, and for the conservation of the earth's resources.

Days, etc.	1995	1996	1997	1998	1999
Golden Number	1	2	3	4	5
Sunday Letter	A	GF	E	D	C
Sundays after Epiphany	8	7	5	7	6
Ash Wednesday	Mar. 1	Feb. 21	Feb. 12	Feb. 25	Feb. 17
First Sunday in Lent	Mar. 5	Feb. 25	Feb. 16	Feb. 29	Feb. 21
Passion/Palm Sunday	Apr. 9	Mar. 31	Mar. 23	Apr. 5	Mar. 28
Good Friday	Apr. 14	Apr. 5	Mar. 28	Apr. 10	Apr. 2
Easter Day	Apr. 16	Apr. 7	Mar. 30	Apr. 12	Apr. 4
Ascension Day	May 25	May 16	May 8	May 21	May 13
The Day of Pentecost	June 4	May 26	May 18	May 31	May 23
Trinity Sunday	June 11	June 2	May 25	June 7	May 30
Numbered Proper of 2 Pentecost	#6	#5	#4	#6	#5
First Sunday of Advent	Dec. 3	Dec. 1	Nov. 30	Nov. 29	Nov. 28

Greek Orthodox Movable Ecclesiastical Dates

This 5-year chart has the dates of Feast Days and fasting days, which are determined annually on the basis of the date of Holy Pascha (Easter). This ecclesiastical cycle begins with the first day of the Triodion and ends with the Sunday of All Saints, a total of 18 weeks.

	1995	1996	1997	1998	1999
Triódion begins	Feb. 12	Feb. 4	Feb. 16	Feb. 8	Jan. 31
Sat. of Souls	Feb. 25	Feb. 17	Mar. 1	Feb. 21	Feb. 13
Meat Fare	Feb. 26	Feb. 18	Mar. 2	Feb. 22	Feb. 14
2d Sat. of Souls	Mar. 4	Feb. 24	Mar. 8	Feb. 28	Feb. 20
Lent Begins	Mar. 6	Feb. 26	Mar. 10	Mar. 2	Feb. 22
St. Theodore 3d Sat. of Souls	Mar. 11	Mar. 2	Mar. 15	Mar. 7	Feb. 27
Sunday of Orthodoxy	Mar. 12	Mar. 3	Mar. 16	Mar. 8	Feb. 28
Sat. of Lazarus	Apr. 15	Apr. 6	Apr. 19	Apr. 11	Apr. 3
Palm Sunday	Apr. 16	Apr. 7	Apr. 20	Apr. 12	Apr. 4
Holy (Good) Friday	Apr. 21	Apr. 12	Apr. 25	Apr. 17	Apr. 9
Western Easter	Apr. 16	Apr. 7	Mar. 30	Apr. 12	Apr. 4
Orthodox Easter	Apr. 23	Apr. 14	Apr. 27	Apr. 19	Apr. 11
Ascension	June 1	May 23	June 5	May 28	May 20
Sat. of Souls	June 10	June 1	June 14	June 6	May 29
Pentecost	June 11	June 2	June 15	June 7	May 30
All Saints	June 18	June 9	June 22	June 14	June 6

Important Islamic Dates, 1996-2000 (1416-20)

The Islamic calendar is a lunar reckoning from the year of the *hegira* AD 622, when Muhammad moved from Mecca to Medina. It runs in cycles of 30 years, of which the 2d, 5th, 7th, 10th, 13th, 16th, 18th, 21st, 24th, 26th, and 29th are leap years; 1416 is the 6th year of the cycle. Common years have 354 days, leap years 355, the extra day being added to the last month, Dhû al-Hijjah. Except for this case, the 12 months beginning with Muharram have alternately 30 and 29 days. Actual Western hemisphere moon sightings may occur a day later, but never earlier, than these dates reflect.

	1416 (1995-96)	1417 (1996-97)	1418 (1997-98)	1419 (1998-99)	1420 (1999-2000)
New Year's Day (Muharram 1)	May 30, 1995	May 18, 1996	May 8, 1997	Apr. 27, 1998	Apr. 17,1999
Ashura (Muharram 10)	June 8, 1995	May 27, 1996	May 17, 1997	May 6, 1998	Apr. 26, 1999
Mawlid (Rabi'l 12)	Aug. 8, 1995	July 28, 1996	July 17, 1997	July 6, 1998	June 26, 1999
Ramadan 1	Jan. 21, 1996	Jan. 10, 1997	Dec. 31, 1997	Dec. 20, 1998	Dec. 9, 1999
al-Fitr (Shawwal 1)	Feb. 20, 1996	Feb. 8, 1997	Jan. 29, 1998	Jan. 19, 1999	Jan. 8, 2000
al-Adha (Dhû al-Hijjah 10)	Apr. 28, 1996	Apr. 17, 1997	Apr. 7, 1998	Mar. 28, 1999	Mar. 16, 2000

Jewish Holy Days, Festivals, and Fasts

	1995 (5755-56)		1996 (5756-57)		1997 (5757-58)		1998 (5758-59)		1999 (5759-60)	
Tu B'Shvat	Jan. 16	Mon.	Feb. 5	Mon.	Jan. 23	Thu.	Feb. 11	Wed.	Feb. 1	Mon.
Ta'anis Esther (Fast of Esther)	Mar. 15	Wed.	Mar. 4	Mon.	Mar. 20	Thu.*	Mar. 11	Wed.	Mar. 1	Mon.
Purim	Mar. 16	Thu.	Mar. 5	Tue.	Mar. 23	Sun.	Mar. 12	Thu.	Mar. 2	Tue.
Passover	Apr. 15	Sat.	Apr. 4	Thu.	Apr. 22	Tue.	Apr. 11	Sat.	Apr. 1	Thu.
	Apr. 22	Sat.	Apr. 11	Thu.	Apr. 29	Tue.	Apr. 18	Sat.	Apr. 8	Thu.
Lag B'Omer	May 18	Thu.	May 7	Tue.	May 25	Sun.	May 14	Thu.	May 4	Tue.
Shavuot	June 4	Sun.	May 24	Fri.	June 11	Sun.	May 31	Sun.	May 21	Fri.
	June 5	Mon.	May 25	Sat.	June 12	Mon.	June 1	Mon.	May 22	Sat.
Fast of the 17th Day of Tammuz	July 16	Sun.*	July 4	Thu.	July 22	Tue.	July 12	Sun.*	July 1	Thu.
Fast of the 9th Day of Av	Aug. 6	Sun.	July 25	Thu.	Aug. 12	Tue.	Aug. 2	Sun.*	July 22	Thu.
Rosh Hashanah	Sept. 25	Mon.	Sept. 14	Sat.	Oct. 2	Thu.	Sept. 21	Mon.	Sept. 11	Sat.
	Sept. 26	Tue.	Sept. 15	Sun.	Oct. 3	Fri.	Sept. 22	Tue.	Sept. 12	Sun.
Fast of Gedalya	Sept. 27	Wed.	Sept. 16	Mon.	Oct. 5	Sun.*	Sept. 23	Wed.	Sept. 13	Mon.
Yom Kippur	Oct. 4	Wed.	Sept 23	Mon.	Oct. 11	Sat.	Sept. 30	Wed.	Sept. 20	Mon.
Sukkot	Oct. 9	Mon.	Sept. 28	Sat.	Oct. 16	Thu.	Oct. 5	Mon.	Sept. 25	Sat.
	Oct. 15	Sun.	Oct. 4	Fri.	Oct. 22	Wed	Oct. 11	Sun.	Oct. 1	Fri.
Shmini Atzeret	Oct. 16	Mon.	Oct. 5	Sat.	Oct. 23	Thu.	Oct. 12	Mon.	Oct. 2	Sat.
	Oct. 17	Tue.	Oct. 6	Sun.	Oct. 24	Fri.	Oct. 13	Tue.	Oct. 3	Sun.
Chanukah	Dec. 18	Mon.	Dec. 6	Fri.	Dec. 24	Wed.	Dec. 14	Mon.	Dec. 4	Sat.
	Dec. 25	Mon.	Dec. 13	Fri.	Dec. 31	Wed.	Dec. 21	Mon.	Dec. 11	Sat.
Fast of the 10th of Tevet	Jan. 2	Tue.	Dec. 20	Fri.	Jan. 8	Thu.	Dec. 29	Tue.	Dec. 19	Sun.

The months of the Jewish year are: 1) Tishri; 2) Cheshvan (also Marcheshvan); 3) Kislev; 4) Tebet (also Tebeth); 5) Shebat (also Shebhat); 6) Adar; 6a) Adar Sheni (II) added in leap years; 7) Nisan; 8) Iyar; 9) Sivan; 10) Tammuz; 11) Av (also Abh); 12) Elul. All Jewish holy days, etc., begin at sunset on the previous day. *Date changed to avoid Sabbath.

Ash Wednesday and Easter Sunday

Year	Ash Wed.	Easter Sunday	Year	Ash Wed.	Easter Sunday	Year	Ash Wed.	Easter Sunday	Year	Ash Wed.	Easter Sunday
1901	Feb. 20	Apr. 7	1951	Feb. 7	Mar. 25	2001	Feb. 28	Apr. 15	2051	Feb. 15	Apr. 2
1902	Feb. 12	Mar. 30	1952	Feb. 27	Apr. 13	2002	Feb. 13	Mar. 31	2052	Mar. 6	Apr. 21
1903	Feb. 25	Apr. 12	1953	Feb. 18	Apr. 5	2003	Mar. 5	Apr. 20	2053	Feb. 19	Apr. 6
1904	Feb. 17	Apr. 3	1954	Mar. 3	Apr. 18	2004	Feb. 25	Apr. 11	2054	Feb. 11	Mar. 29
1905	Mar. 8	Apr. 23	1955	Feb. 23	Apr. 10	2005	Feb. 9	Apr. 27	2055	Mar. 3	Apr. 18
1906	Feb. 28	Apr. 15	1956	Feb. 15	Apr. 1	2006	Mar. 1	Apr. 16	2056	Feb. 16	Apr. 2
1907	Feb. 13	Mar. 31	1957	Mar. 6	Apr. 21	2007	Feb. 21	Apr. 8	2057	Mar. 7	Apr. 22
1908	Mar. 4	Apr. 19	1958	Feb. 19	Apr. 6	2008	Feb. 6	Mar. 23	2058	Feb. 27	Apr. 14
1909	Feb. 24	Apr. 11	1959	Feb. 11	Mar. 29	2009	Feb. 25	Apr. 12	2059	Feb. 12	Mar. 30
1910	Feb. 9	Mar. 27	1960	Mar. 2	Apr. 17	2010	Feb. 17	Apr. 4	2060	Mar. 3	Apr. 18
1911	Mar. 1	Apr. 16	1961	Feb. 15	Apr. 2	2011	Mar. 9	Apr. 24	2061	Feb. 23	Apr. 10
1912	Feb. 21	Apr. 7	1962	Mar. 7	Apr. 22	2012	Feb. 22	Apr. 8	2062	Feb. 8	Mar. 26
1913	Feb. 5	Mar. 23	1963	Feb. 27	Apr. 14	2013	Feb. 13	Mar. 31	2063	Feb. 28	Apr. 15
1914	Feb. 25	Apr. 12	1964	Feb. 12	Mar. 29	2014	Mar. 5	Apr. 20	2064	Feb. 20	Apr. 6
1915	Feb. 17	Apr. 4	1965	Mar. 3	Apr. 18	2015	Feb. 18	Apr. 5	2065	Feb. 11	Mar. 29
1916	Mar. 8	Apr. 23	1966	Feb. 23	Apr. 10	2016	Feb. 10	Mar. 27	2066	Feb. 24	Apr. 11
1917	Feb. 21	Apr. 8	1967	Feb. 8	Mar. 26	2017	Mar. 1	Apr. 16	2067	Feb. 16	Apr. 3
1918	Feb. 13	Mar. 31	1968	Feb. 28	Apr. 14	2018	Feb. 14	Apr. 1	2068	Mar. 7	Apr. 22
1919	Mar. 5	Apr. 20	1969	Feb. 19	Apr. 6	2019	Mar. 6	Apr. 21	2069	Feb. 27	Apr. 14
1920	Feb. 18	Apr. 4	1970	Feb. 11	Mar. 29	2020	Feb. 26	Apr. 12	2070	Feb. 12	Mar. 30
1921	Feb. 9	Mar. 27	1971	Feb. 24	Apr. 11	2021	Feb. 17	Apr. 4	2071	Mar. 4	Apr. 19
1922	Mar. 1	Apr. 16	1972	Feb. 16	Apr. 2	2022	Mar. 2	Apr. 17	2072	Feb. 24	Apr. 10
1923	Feb. 14	Apr. 1	1973	Mar. 7	Apr. 22	2023	Feb. 22	Apr. 9	2073	Feb. 8	Mar. 26
1924	Mar. 5	Apr. 20	1974	Feb. 27	Apr. 14	2024	Feb. 14	Mar. 31	2074	Feb. 28	Apr. 15
1925	Feb. 25	Apr. 12	1975	Feb. 12	Mar. 30	2025	Mar. 5	Apr. 20	2075	Feb. 20	Apr. 7
1926	Feb. 17	Apr. 4	1976	Mar. 3	Apr. 18	2026	Feb. 18	Apr. 5	2076	Mar. 4	Apr. 19
1927	Mar. 2	Apr. 17	1977	Feb. 23	Apr. 10	2027	Feb. 10	Mar. 28	2077	Feb. 24	Apr. 11
1928	Feb. 22	Apr. 8	1978	Feb. 8	Mar. 26	2028	Mar. 1	Apr. 16	2078	Feb. 16	Apr. 3
1929	Feb. 13	Mar. 31	1979	Feb. 28	Apr. 15	2029	Feb. 14	Apr. 1	2079	Mar. 8	Apr. 23
1930	Mar. 5	Apr. 20	1980	Feb. 20	Apr. 6	2030	Mar. 6	Apr. 21	2080	Feb. 21	Apr. 7
1931	Feb. 18	Apr. 5	1981	Mar. 4	Apr. 19	2031	Feb. 26	Apr. 13	2081	Feb. 12	Mar. 30
1932	Feb. 10	Mar. 27	1982	Feb. 24	Apr. 11	2032	Feb. 11	Mar. 28	2082	Mar. 4	Apr. 19
1933	Mar. 1	Apr. 16	1983	Feb. 16	Apr. 3	2033	Mar. 2	Apr. 17	2083	Feb. 17	Apr. 4
1934	Feb. 14	Apr. 1	1984	Mar. 7	Apr. 22	2034	Feb. 22	Apr. 9	2084	Feb. 9	Apr. 26
1935	Mar. 6	Apr. 21	1985	Feb. 20	Apr. 7	2035	Feb. 7	Mar. 25	2085	Feb. 28	Apr. 15
1936	Feb. 26	Apr. 12	1986	Feb. 12	Mar. 30	2036	Feb. 27	Apr. 13	2086	Feb. 13	Mar. 31
1937	Feb. 10	Mar. 28	1987	Mar. 4	Apr. 19	2037	Feb. 18	Apr. 5	2087	Mar. 5	Apr. 20
1938	Mar. 2	Apr. 17	1988	Feb. 17	Apr. 3	2038	Mar. 10	Apr. 25	2088	Feb. 25	Apr. 11
1939	Feb. 22	Apr. 9	1989	Feb. 8	Mar. 26	2039	Feb. 23	Apr. 10	2089	Feb. 16	Apr. 3
1940	Feb. 7	Mar. 24	1990	Feb. 28	Apr. 15	2040	Feb. 15	Apr. 1	2090	Mar. 1	Apr. 16
1941	Feb. 26	Apr. 13	1991	Feb. 13	Mar. 31	2041	Mar. 6	Apr. 21	2091	Feb. 21	Apr. 8
1942	Feb. 18	Apr. 5	1992	Mar. 4	Apr. 19	2042	Feb. 19	Apr. 6	2092	Feb. 13	Mar. 30
1943	Mar. 10	Apr. 25	1993	Feb. 24	Apr. 11	2043	Feb. 11	Mar. 29	2093	Feb. 25	Apr. 12
1944	Feb. 23	Apr. 9	1994	Feb. 16	Apr. 3	2044	Mar. 2	Apr. 17	2094	Feb. 17	Apr. 4
1945	Feb. 14	Apr. 1	1995	Mar. 1	Apr. 16	2045	Feb. 22	Apr. 9	2095	Mar. 9	Apr. 24
1946	Mar. 6	Apr. 21	1996	Feb. 21	Apr. 7	2046	Feb. 7	Mar. 25	2096	Feb. 29	Apr. 15
1947	Feb. 19	Apr. 6	1997	Feb. 12	Mar. 30	2047	Feb. 27	Apr. 14	2097	Feb. 13	Mar. 31
1948	Feb. 11	Mar. 28	1998	Feb. 25	Apr. 12	2048	Feb. 19	Apr. 5	2098	Mar. 5	Apr. 20
1949	Mar. 2	Apr. 17	1999	Feb. 17	Apr. 4	2049	Mar. 3	Apr. 18	2099	Feb. 25	Apr. 12
1950	Feb. 22	Apr. 9	2000	Mar. 8	Apr. 23	2050	Feb. 23	Apr. 10	2100	Feb. 10	Mar. 28

The Ten Commandments

According to Judeo-Christian tradition, as related in the Bible, the Ten Commandments were revealed by God to Moses and form the basic moral component of God's covenant with Israel. The Ten Commandments appear in 2 places in the Old Testament—Exodus 20:1-17 and Deuteronomy 5:6-21; the phrasing is similar but not identical. Most Protestant, Anglican, and Orthodox Christians enumerate the commandments differently from Roman Catholics and Lutherans. Jewish tradition considers the introduction, "I am the Lord..." the first commandment and makes the prohibition against "other gods" and idolatry the second.

Following is abridged text of the Ten Commandments in Exodus 20:1-17:

I. I am the Lord your God, who brought you out of the land of Egypt, out of the house of bondage. You shall have no other gods before me.
II. You shall not make for yourself a graven image. You shall not bow down to them or serve them.
III. You shall not take the name of the Lord your God in vain.
IV. Remember the sabbath day, to keep it holy.
V. Honor your father and your mother.
VI. You shall not kill.
VII. You shall not commit adultery.
VIII. You shall not steal.
IX. You shall not bear false witness against your neighbor.
X. You shall not covet.

Books of the Bible

Old Testament—Standard Protestant English Versions			New Testament—Standard Protestant English Versions		
Genesis	II Chronicles	Daniel	Matthew	Ephesians	Hebrews
Exodus	Ezra	Hosea	Mark	Phillippians	James
Leviticus	Nehemiah	Joel	Luke	Colossians	I Peter
Numbers	Esther	Amos	John	I Thessalonians	II Peter
Deuteronomy	Job	Obadiah	Acts	II Thessalonians	I John
Joshua	Psalms	Jonah	Romans	I Timothy	II John
Judges	Proverbs	Micah	I Corinthians	II Timothy	III John
Ruth	Ecclesiastes	Nahum	II Corinthians	Titus	Jude
I Samuel	Song of Solomon	Habakkuk	Galatians	Philemon	Revelation
II Samuel	Isaiah	Zephaniah			
I Kings	Jeremiah	Haggai			
II Kings	Lamentations	Zechariah			
I Chronicles	Ezekiel	Malachi			

Catholic Versions

All the Catholic books of the Bible (Old Testament and New Testament) have the same names as Protestant Versions. A Catholic Version (and Pre-Reformation Bibles) simply has the books **Tobit, Judith, Wisdom, Sirach (Ecclesiasticus), Baruch, I Maccabees,** and **II Maccabees** as part of the Old Testament. These books are called Deuterocanonical Books.

Roman Catholic Hierarchy

Source: U.S. Catholic Conference; as of mid-1995

Supreme Pontiff

At the head of the Roman Catholic Church is the supreme pontiff, Pope John Paul II, Karol Wojtyla, born at Wadowice (Kraków), Poland, May 18, 1920; ordained priest Nov. 1, 1946; appointed bishop July 4, 1958; promoted to archbishop of Kraków Jan. 13, 1964; proclaimed cardinal June 26, 1967; elected pope as successor of Pope John Paul I Oct. 16, 1978; installed as pope Oct. 22, 1978.

College of Cardinals

Members of the Sacred College of Cardinals are chosen by the pope to be his chief assistants and advisers in the administration of the church. Among their duties is the election of the pope when the Holy See becomes vacant.

In its present form, the College of Cardinals dates from the 12th century. The first cardinals, from about the 6th century, were deacons and priests of the leading churches of Rome and were bishops of neighboring dioceses. The title of cardinal was limited to members of the college in 1567. The number of cardinals was set at 70 in 1586 by Pope Sixtus V. From 1959 Pope John XXIII began to increase the number; however, the number of cardinals eligible to participate in papal elections was limited to 120. There were lay cardinals until 1918, when the Code of Canon Law specified that all cardinals must be priests. Pope John XXIII in 1962 established that all cardinals must be bishops. The first age limits were set in 1971 by Pope Paul VI, who decreed that at age 80 cardinals must retire from curial departments and offices and from participation in papal elections. They continue as members of the college, with all rights and privileges.

North American Cardinals

Name	Office	Born	Named Cardinal
William W. Baum	Major Penitentiary of Apostolic Penitentiary, the Vatican	1926	1976
Joseph L. Bernardin	Archbishop of Chicago	1928	1983
Anthony J. Bevilacqua	Archbishop of Philadelphia	1923	1991
John J. Carberry[1]	Archbishop emeritus of St. Louis	1904	1969
G. Emmett Carter[1]	Archbishop emeritus of Toronto	1912	1979
Ernesto Corripio Ahumada	Archbishop emeritus of Mexico	1919	1979
Edouard Gagnon	Pres. of Pontifical Commission of Intl. Eucharistic Congresses	1918	1985
James A. Hickey	Archbishop of Washington, DC	1920	1988
William Henry Keeler	Archbishop of Baltimore	1931	1994
John J. Krol[1]	Archbishop emeritus of Philadelphia	1910	1967
Bernard F. Law	Archbishop of Boston	1931	1985
Adam Joseph Maida	Archvishop of Detroit	1930	1994
Roger Mahony	Archbishop of Los Angeles	1936	1991
John J. O'Connor	Archbishop of New York	1920	1985
Juan Sandoval Iniquez	Archbishop of Guadalajara	1933	1994
Adolfo Suarez Rivera	Archbishop of Monterrey	1927	1994
Edmund C. Szoka	Pres. of Prefecture of Economic Affairs of Holy See, the Vatican	1927	1988
Jean-Claude Turcotte	Archbishop of Montreal	1936	1994
Louis-Albert Vachon[1]	Archbishop emeritus of Quebec	1912	1985

(1) Ineligible to take part in papal elections.

Chronological List of Popes

Source: Annuario Pontificio. Table lists year of accession of each pope.

The Roman Catholic Church names the Apostle Peter as founder of the church in Rome. He arrived there c 42, was martyred there c 67, and was raised to sainthood.

The pope's temporal title is: Sovereign of the State of Vatican City.

The pope's spiritual titles are: Bishop of Rome, Vicar of Jesus Christ, Successor of St. Peter, Prince of the Apostles, Supreme Pontiff of the Universal Church, Patriarch of the West, Primate of Italy, Archbishop and Metropolitan of the Roman Province.

The names of antipopes are in *italics*. Antipopes were illegitimate claimants of or pretenders to the papal throne.

Year	Pope	Year	Pope	Year	Pope	Year	Pope
	St. Peter	615	St. Deusdedit	983	John XIV	1316	John XXII
67	St. Linus		or Adeodatus	985	John XV	*1328*	*Nicholas V*
76	St. Anacletus	619	Boniface V	996	Gregory V	1334	Benedict XII
	or Cletus	625	Honorius I	*997*	*John XVI*	1342	Clement VI
88	St. Clement I	640	Severinus	999	Sylvester II	1352	Innocent VI
97	St. Evaristus	642	Theodore I	1003	John XVII	1362	Bl. Urban V
105	St. Alexander I	649	St. Martin I, Martyr	1004	John XVIII	1370	Gregory XI
115	St. Sixtus I	654	St. Eugene I	1009	Sergius IV	1378	Urban VI
125	St. Telesphorus	657	St. Vitalian	1012	Benedict VIII	*1378*	*Clement VII*
136	St. Hyginus	672	Adeodatus II	*1012*	*Gregory*	1389	Boniface IX
140	St. Pius I	676	Donus	1024	John XIX	*1394*	*Benedict XIII*
155	St. Anicetus	678	St. Agatho	1032	Benedict IX	1404	Innocent VII
166	St. Soter	682	St. Leo II	1045	Sylvester III	1406	Gregory XII
175	St. Eleutherius	684	St. Benedict II	1045	Benedict IX	*1409*	*Alexander V*
189	St. Victor I	685	John V	1045	Gregory VI	*1410*	*John XXIII*
199	St. Zephyrinus	686	Conon	1046	Clement II	1417	Martin V
217	St. Callistus I	*687*	*Theodore*	1047	Benedict IX	1431	Eugene IV
217	*St. Hippolytus*	*687*	*Paschal*	1048	Damasus II	*1439*	*Felix V*
222	St. Urban I	687	St. Sergius I	1049	St. Leo IX	1447	Nicholas V
230	St. Pontian	701	John VI	1055	Victor II	1455	Callistus III
235	St. Anterus	705	John VII	1057	Stephen IX (X)	1458	Pius II
236	St. Fabian	708	Sisinnius	*1058*	*Benedict X*	1464	Paul II
251	St. Cornelius	708	Constantine	1059	Nicholas II	1471	Sixtus IV
251	*Novatian*	715	St. Gregory II	1061	Alexander II	1484	Innocent VIII
253	St. Lucius I	731	St. Gregory III	*1061*	*Honorius II*	1492	Alexander VI
254	St. Stephen I	741	St. Zachary	1073	St. Gregory VII	1503	Pius III
257	St. Sixtus II	752	Stephen II (III)	*1080*	*Clement III*	1503	Julius II
259	St. Dionysius	757	St. Paul I	1086	Bl. Victor III	1513	Leo X
269	St. Felix I	*767*	*Constantine*	1088	Bl. Urban II	1522	Adrian VI
275	St. Eutychian	*768*	*Philip*	1099	Paschal II	1523	Clement VII
283	St. Caius	768	Stephen III (IV)	*1100*	*Theodoric*	1534	Paul III
296	St. Marcellinus	772	Adrian I	*1102*	*Albert*	1550	Julius III
308	St. Marcellus I	795	St. Leo III	*1105*	*Sylvester IV*	1555	Marcellus II
309	St. Eusebius	816	Stephen IV (V)	1118	Gelasius II	1555	Paul IV
311	St. Melchiades	817	St. Paschal I	*1118*	*Gregory VIII*	1559	Pius IV
314	St. Sylvester I	824	Eugene II	1119	Callistus II	1566	St. Pius V
336	St. Marcus	827	Valentine	1124	Honorius II	1572	Gregory XIII
337	St. Julius I	827	Gregory IV	*1124*	*Celestine II*	1585	Sixtus V
352	Liberius	*844*	*John*	1130	Innocent II	1590	Urban VII
355	*Felix II*	844	Sergius II	*1130*	*Anacletus II*	1590	Gregory XIV
366	St. Damasus I	847	St. Leo IV	*1138*	*Victor IV*	1591	Innocent IX
366	*Ursinus*	855	Benedict III	1143	Celestine II	1592	Clement VIII
384	St. Siricius	*855*	*Anastasius*	1144	Lucius II	1605	Leo XI
399	St. Anastasius I	858	St. Nicholas I	1145	Bl. Eugene III	1605	Paul V
401	St. Innocent I	867	Adrian II	1153	Anastasius IV	1621	Gregory XV
417	St. Zosimus	872	John VIII	1154	Adrian IV	1623	Urban VIII
418	St. Boniface I	882	Marinus I	1159	Alexander III	1644	Innocent X
418	*Eulalius*	884	St. Adrian III	*1159*	*Victor IV*	1655	Alexander VII
422	St. Celestine I	885	Stephen V (VI)	*1164*	*Paschal III*	1667	Clement IX
432	St. Sixtus III	891	Formosus	*1168*	*Callistus III*	1670	Clement X
440	St. Leo I	896	Boniface VI	*1179*	*Innocent III*	1676	Bl. Innocent XI
461	St. Hilary	896	Stephen VI (VII)	1181	Lucius III	1689	Alexander VIII
468	St. Simplicius	897	Romanus	1185	Urban III	1691	Innocent XII
483	St. Felix III (II)	897	Theodore II	1187	Clement III	1700	Clement XI
492	St. Gelasius I	898	John IX	*1187*	*Gregory VIII*	1721	Innocent XIII
496	Anastasius II	900	Benedict IV	1191	Celestine III	1724	Benedict XIII
498	St. Symmachus	903	Leo V	1198	Innocent III	1730	Clement XII
498	*Lawrence*	*903*	*Christopher*	1216	Honorius III	1740	Benedict XIV
	(501-505)	904	Sergius III	1227	Gregory IX	1758	Clement XIII
514	St. Hormisdas	911	Anastasius III	1241	Celestine IV	1769	Clement XIV
523	St. John I, Martyr	913	Landus	1243	Innocent IV	1775	Pius VI
526	St. Felix IV (III)	914	John X	1254	Alexander IV	1800	Pius VII
530	Boniface II	928	Leo VI	1261	Urban IV	1823	Leo XII
530	*Dioscorus*	928	Stephen VII (VIII)	1265	Clement IV	1829	Pius VIII
533	John II	931	John XI	1271	Bl. Gregory X	1831	Gregory XVI
535	St. Agapitus I	936	Leo VII	1276	Bl. Innocent V	1846	Pius IX
536	St. Silverius, Martyr	939	Stephen VIII (IX)	1276	Adrian V	1878	Leo XIII
537	Vigilius	942	Marinus II	1276	John XXI	1903	St. Pius X
556	Pelagius I	946	Agapitus II	1277	Nicholas III	1914	Benedict XV
561	John III	955	John XII	1281	Martin IV	1922	Pius XI
575	Benedict I	963	Leo VIII	1285	Honorius IV	1939	Pius XII
579	Pelagius II	964	Benedict V	1288	Nicholas IV	1958	John XXIII
590	St. Gregory I	965	John XIII	1294	St. Celestine V	1963	Paul VI
604	Sabinian	973	Benedict VI	1294	Boniface VIII	1978	John Paul I
607	Boniface III	*974*	*Boniface VII*	1303	Bl. Benedict XI	1978	John Paul II
608	St. Boniface IV	974	Benedict VII	1305	Clement V		

Census of Religious Groups in Canada

Source: *1995 Yearbook of American and Canadian Churches*; World Almanac research

Number of churches in parentheses; groups with fewer than 1,000 members not included. *Indicates church declines to publish membership figures.

Religious Group	Members
Anglican Church of Canada (1,767)	848,256
Antiochian Orthodox Christian Archdiocese of North America (13)	50,000
Apostolic Church in Canada (14)	1,600
Apostolic Church of Pentecost of Canada Inc. (133)	13,723
Associated Gospel Churches (126)	9,284
Baha'i Faith (398)	27,000
Baptist Convention of Ontario and Quebec (372)	44,713
Baptist General Conference of Canada (70)	6,066
Baptist Union of Western Canada (161)	20,130
Brethren in Christ Church, Canadian Conference (38)	3,194
British Columbia Baptist Conference (23)	2,358
Canadian and American Reformed Churches (46)	13,887
Canadian Baptist Federation (1,150)	131,349
Canadian Convention of Southern Baptists (103)	6,857
Canadian Yearly Meeting of the Religious Society of Friends (22)	1,129
Central Canada Baptist Conference (37)	*
Christian Brethren (also known as Plymouth Brethren) (60)	*
Christian Church (Disciples of Christ) in Canada (34)	3,251
Christian Churches and Churches of Christ in Canada (140)	7,500
Christian and Missionary Alliance in Canada (358)	84,237
Christian Reformed Church in North America (242)	84,910
Churches of Christ in Canada (147)	7,181
Church of God (Anderson, IN) (52)	3,438
Church of God (Cleveland, TN) (99)	6,670
Church of God of Prophecy in Canada (43)	3,009
Church of Jesus Christ of Latter-day Saints in Canada (391)	130,000
Church of the Nazarene (165)	11,359
Conference of Mennonites in Canada (152)	28,000
Coptic Church in Canada (12)	*
Estonian Evangelical Lutheran Church (12)	6,159
Evangelical Baptist Churches in Canada, Fellowship of (500)	61,572
Evangelical Church in Canada (46)	3,688
Evangelical Covenant Church in Canada (22)	1,245
Evangelical Free Church of Canada (133)	13,699
Evangelical Lutheran Church in Canada (652)	199,609
Evangelical Mennonite Conference (49)	6,427
Evangelical Mennonite Mission Conference (26)	3,487
Evangelical Missionary Church of Canada (145)	12,217

Religious Group	Members
Foursquare Gospel Church of Canada (53)	2,531
Free Methodist Church in Canada (146)	7,186
Hindu	80,000
Islam	120,000
Italian Pentecostal Church of Canada (24)	3,500
Jehovah's Witnesses (1,336)	109,303
Jewish Organizations	350,000
Latvian Evangelical Lutheran Church in America (17)	5,117
Lutheran Church–Canada (324)	79,364
Mennonite Brethren Churches, Canadian Conference of (195)	29,413
Metropolitan Community Churches, Universal Fellowship (12)	1,500
Missionary Church of Canada (92)	6,431
Moravian Church in America, Northern Province, Canadian District of (9)	2,007
Netherlands Reformed Congregations of North America (9)	4,634
North American Baptist Conference (118)	17,943
Old Order Amish Church (17)	*
Open Bible Standard Churches of Canada (4)	1,000
Orthodox Church in America (Canada Section) (606)	1,000,000
Pentecostal Assemblies of Canada (976)	194,972
Pentecostal Assemblies of Newfoundland (160)	33,700
Presbyterian Church in Canada (1,107)	215,647
Reformed Church in Canada (43)	6,702
Reformed Doukhobors, Christian Community and Brotherhood of (1)	2,108
Reorganized Church of Jesus Christ of Latter Day Saints (82)	11,111
Roman Catholic Church in Canada (11,286)	11,852,350
Romanian Orthodox Episcopate of America (Jackson, MI) (13)	8,600
Russian Orthodox Church in Canada, Patriarchal Parishes (27)	8,000
Salvation Army in Canada (408)	84,400
Seventh-day Adventist Church in Canada (331)	42,990
Ukrainian Orthodox Church of Canada (258)	120,000
Union D'Eglises Baptistes Francaises Au Canada (24)	1,169
Unitarian Universalist Association (40)	6,003
United Baptist Convention of the Atlantic Provinces (554)	66,625
United Church of Canada (4,001)	1,952,121
United Pentecostal Church in Canada (3,724)	500,000
Wesleyan Church of Canada (82)	5,256

Headquarters of Selected Religious Groups in Canada

Source: *1995 Yearbook of American & Canadian Churches*, © *National Council of the Churches of Christ in the USA;* World Almanac research

(year organized in parentheses)

Anglican Church of Canada (1700), Church House, 600 Jarvis St., Toronto, ON M4Y 2J6; Primate, Most Rev. Michael G. Peters

Bahá'í National Centre of Canada, 7200 Leslie St., Thornhill, ON L3T 6L8

Baptist Ministeries, Canadian, 7185 Millcreek Dr. Mississauga, ON L5N 5R4; Pres., Dr. Bruce Milne

Buddhist Churches, 4860 Garry St., Richmond, BC V7E 2V2

Christian and Missionary Alliance in Canada (1887), 510-105 Gordon Baker Rd., North York, ON M2H 3P8; President, Dr. Arnold Cook

Church of Jesus Christ of Latter-Day Saints (Mormon) (1830), 50 E. North Temple St., Salt Lake City, UT 84150; Pres., Gordon B. Hinckley

Church of the Nazarene (1902), No. 73800-19 St. NE, Calgary, AB T2E 6V2; Executive Admn., Neil Hightower

Council of Muslim Communities in Canada, 1250 Ramsey View Ct., Ste. 504, Sudbury, ON P3E 2E7; Dir., Mir Iqbal Ali

Evangelical Lutheran Church in Canada (1985), 1512 St. James St., Winnipeg, MB R3H OL2; Bishop, Rev. Telmor G. Sartison

Evangelical Missionary Church in Canada, Box 1268, 440 Main St., Steinbach, MB R0A 2A0; Conf. Moderator, Ralph Unger

Fellowship of Evangelical Baptist Churches in Canada (1953), 679 Southgate Dr., Guelph, ON N1G 4S2; Pres., Rev. Terry D. Cuthbert

Greek Orthodox Diocese of Toronto, 27 Teddington Park Ave., Toronto, ON M4N 2C4; Chairperson, Archbishop Iakovos

Jehovah's Witnesses (1879), Canadian office: Box 4100, Halton Hills, ON L7G 4Y4; Pres., Milton Henschel

Jewish Organizations (1768), 3101 Bathurat St. #400, Toronto, ON M6A 2A6

Lutheran Church—Canada (1959), 200-1625 Dublin Ave., Winnipeg, MB R3H OW3; Pres. Dr. Edwin Lehman

Mennonite Church (1898), 421 S. Second St., Ste. 600, Elkhart, IN 46516; Mod., Donella Clemens

Pentecostal Assemblies of Canada (1919), 6745 Century Ave., Mississauga, ON L5N 6P7; General Superintendent, Rev. James M. Mac Knight

Presbyterian Church (1925), 50 Wynford Dr., North York, ON M3C 1J7; Moderator, Dr. George C. Vais

Roman Catholic Church, Canadian Conference of Catholic Bishops, 90 Parent Ave., Ottawa, ON K1N 7B1; Pres., Msgr. Jean-Guy Hamelin

Salvation Army (1865), Salvation Square, PO Box 4021, Postal Sta. A, Toronto, ON M5W 2B1; Territorial Commander, Commissioner Donald O. Kerr

Seventh-Day Adventist Church, 1148 King St., Oshawa, ON L1H 1H8; Pres., Orville Parchment

Ukrainian Orthodox Church (1918), Consistory of the Ukrainian Orthodox Church of Canada, 9 St. John's Ave., Winnipeg, MB R2W; Presidium, Chpsn., Very Rev. William Makarenko

United Church of Canada (1925), The United Church House, 3250 Bloor St. W., Etobicoke, ON M8Xz 2Y4; Mod,. Marion S. Best

Wesleyan Church (1889), The Wesleyan Church Intl. Center, PO Box 50434, Indianapolis, IN 46250-0434

Major Christian Denominations:

Italics indicate that area which, generally speaking, most

Source: Reviewed by Anthony Padovano, Ph.D., S.T.D., prof. of lit.,

Denomination	Origins	Organization	Authority	Special rites
Baptists	In radical Reformation objections to infant baptism, demands for church and state separation; John Smyth, English Separatist in 1609; Roger Williams, 1638, Providence, RI.	Congregational; each local church is autonomous.	Scripture; some Baptists, particularly in the South, interpret the Bible literally.	Baptism, usually early teen years and after, by total immersion; Lord's Supper.
Church of Christ (Disciples)	Among evangelical Presbyterians in KY (1804) and PA (1809), in distress over Protestant factionalism and decline of fervor; organized 1832.	Congregational.	*"Where the Scriptures speak, we speak; where the Scriptures are silent, we are silent."*	Adult baptism; Lord's Supper (weekly).
Episcopalians	Henry VIII separated English Catholic Church from Rome, 1534, for political reasons; Protestant Episcopal Church in U.S. founded 1789.	*Bishops, in apostolic succession, are elected by diocesan representatives; part of Anglican Communion, symbolically headed by the Archbishop of Canterbury.*	Scripture as interpreted by tradition, especially *39 Articles* (1563); not dogmatic; tri-annual convention of bishops, priests, and laypeople.	Infant baptism, Eucharist, and other sacraments; sacrament is symbolic, but has real spiritual effect.
Jehovah's Witnesses	1870 in PA by Charles Taze Russell; incorporated as Watch Tower Bible and Tract Society of PA, 1884; name Jehovah's Witnesses adopted, 1931.	A governing body located in NY coordinates worldwide activities; each congregation cared for by a body of elders; each Witness considered a minister.	The Bible.	Baptism by immersion; annual Lord's Meal ceremony.
Lutherans	By Martin Luther in Wittenberg, Germany, 1517; objection to Catholic doctrine of salvation by merit and sale of indulgences; break complete, 1519.	Varies from congregational to episcopal; in U.S. a combination of regional synods and congregational polities is most common.	*Scripture, and tradition as spelled out in Augsburg Confession (1530) and other creeds; these confessions of faith are binding although interpretations vary.*	Infant baptism; Lord's Supper; Christ's true body and blood present "in, with, and under the bread and wine."
Methodists	Rev. John Wesley began movement, 1738, within Church of England; first U.S. denomination, Baltimore, 1784.	Conference and superintendent system; *in United Methodist Church, general superintendents are bishops—not a priestly order, only an office —who are elected for life.*	Scripture as interpreted by tradition, reason, and experience.	Baptism of infants or adults; Lord's Supper commanded; other rites include marriage, ordination, solemnization of personal commitments.
Mormons	In visions of the Angel Moroni by Joseph Smith, 1827, in NY, in which he received new revelation on golden tablets: The Book of Mormon.	Theocratic; all male adults are in priesthood, which culminates in Council of 12 Apostles and 1st Presidency (1st President, 2 counselors).	The Bible, Book of Mormon, *and other revelations to Smith, and certain pronouncements of the 1st Presidency.*	Baptism, at age 8, laying on of hands (which confers the gift of the Holy Spirit); Lord's Supper; temple rites: baptism for the dead, marriage for eternity, others.
Orthodox	Original Christian proselytizing in 1st century; broke with Rome, 1054, after centuries of doctrinal disputes and diverging traditions.	Synods of bishops in autonomous, usually national, churches elect a patriarch, archbishop or metropolitan; these men, as a group, are the heads of the church.	Scripture, tradition, and the first 7 church councils up to Nicaea II in 787; bishops in council have authority in doctrine and policy.	Seven sacraments: infant baptism and anointing, Eucharist (both bread and wine), ordination, penance, anointing of the sick, and marriage.
Pentecostal	In Topeka, KS (1901) and Los Angeles (1906), in reaction to loss of evangelical fervor among Methodists and other denominations.	Originally a movement, not a formal organization, Pentecostalism now has a variety of organized forms and continues also as a movement.	Scripture; individual charismatic leaders, the teachings of the Holy Spirit.	*Spirit baptism, especially as shown in "speaking in tongues"; healing and sometimes exorcism; adult baptism; Lord's Supper.*
Presbyterians	In 16th-cent. Calvinist Reformation; differed with Lutherans over sacraments, church government; John Knox founded Scotch Presbyterian church about 1560.	*Highly structured representational system of ministers and laypersons (presbyters) in local, regional, and national bodies (synods).*	Scripture.	Infant baptism; Lord's Supper; bread and wine symbolize Christ's spiritual presence.
Roman Catholics	Traditionally, by Jesus who named St. Peter the 1st vicar; historically, in early Christian proselytizing and the conversion of imperial Rome in the 4th century.	Hierarchy with supreme power vested in pope elected by cardinals; councils of bishops advise on matters of doctrine and policy.	*The pope, when speaking for the whole church in matters of faith and morals, and tradition, which is partly recorded in scripture and expressed in church councils.*	Seven sacraments: baptism, reconciliation, confirmation, Eucharist, marriage, ordination, and anointing of the sick (unction).
United Church of Christ	*By ecumenical union, 1957, of Congregationalists and Evangelical & Reformed, representing both Calvinist and Lutheran traditions.*	Congregational; a General Synod, representative of all congregations, sets general policy.	Scripture.	Infant baptism; Lord's Supper.

How Do They Differ?

distinguishes that denomination from any other.

Ramapo College, NJ, adj. prof. of theol. and rel. studies, Fordham U., NYC

Practice	Ethics	Doctrine	Other	Denomination
Worship style varies from staid to evangelistic; extensive missionary activity.	Usually opposed to alcohol and tobacco; sometimes tends toward a perfectionist ethical standard.	*No creed; true church is of believers only, who are all equal.*	Because no authority can stand between the believer and God, the Baptists are strong supporters of church and state separation.	**Baptists**
Tries to avoid any rite or doctrine not explicitly part of the 1st-century church; some congregations may reject instrumental music.	Some tendency toward perfectionism; increasing interest in social action programs.	Simple New Testament faith; avoids any elaboration not firmly based on Scripture.	Highly tolerant in doctrinal and religious matters; strongly supportive of scholarly education.	**Church of Christ (Disciples)**
Formal, based on *Book of Common Prayer* (1549); services range from austerely simple to highly elaborate.	Tolerant, sometimes permissive; some social action programs.	*Apostles' Creed* is basic; otherwise, considerable variation ranges from rationalist and liberal to acceptance of most Roman Catholic dogma.	Strongly ecumenical, holding talks with all other branches of Christendom.	**Episcopalians**
Meetings are held in Kingdom Halls and members' homes for study and worship; extensive door-to-door visitations.	High moral code; stress marital fidelity and family values; avoid tobacco and blood transfusions.	*God, by his first creation, Christ, will soon destroy all wickedness; 144,000 faithful ones will rule in heaven with Christ over others on a paradise earth.*	Total allegiance only to God's kingdom or heavenly government by Christ, thus remain politically neutral; main periodical *The Watchtower* is printed in 115 languages.	**Jehovah's Witnesses**
Relatively simple, formal liturgy with emphasis on the sermon.	Generally, conservative in personal and social ethics; doctrine of "2 kingdoms" (worldly and holy) supports conservatism in secular affairs.	Salvation by faith alone through grace; Lutheranism has made major contributions to Protestant theology.	Though still somewhat divided along ethnic lines (German, Swede, etc.), main divisions are between fundamentalists and liberals.	**Lutherans**
Worship style varies widely by denomination, local church, geography.	Originally pietist and perfectionist; always strong social activist elements.	No distinctive theological development; 25 Articles abridged from Church of England's 39 not binding.	In 1968, The United Methodist Church was formed by the union of The Methodist Church and The Evangelical United Brethren Church.	**Methodists**
Staid service with hymns, sermon; secret temple ceremonies may be more elaborate; strong missionary activity.	Temperance; strict tithing; combine a strong work ethic with communal self-reliance.	God is a material being; he created the universe out of pre-existing matter; all persons can be saved and many will become divine; most other beliefs are traditionally Christian.	Mormons regard mainline churches as apostate and corrupt; reorganized Church (founded 1860) rejects most Mormon doctrine and practice except the Book of Mormon.	**Mormons**
Elaborate liturgy, usually in the vernacular, though extremely traditional; the liturgy is the essence of Orthodoxy; veneration of icons.	Tolerant; very little social action; divorce, remarriage permitted in some cases; bishops are celibate; priests need not be.	Emphasis on Christ's resurrection, rather than crucifixion; the Holy Spirit proceeds from God the Father only.	Orthodox Church in America originally under Patriarch of Moscow, was granted autonomy in 1970; Greek Orthodox do not recognize this autonomy.	**Orthodox**
Loosely structured service with rousing hymns and sermons, culminating in spirit baptism.	Usually, emphasis on perfectionism with varying degrees of tolerance.	Simple traditional beliefs, usually Protestant, with emphasis on the immediate presence of God in the Holy Spirit.	Once confined to lower-class "holy rollers," Pentecostalism now appears in mainline churches and has established middle-class congregations.	**Pentecostal**
A simple, sober service in which the sermon is central.	Traditionally, a tendency toward strictness with firm church- and self-discipline, otherwise tolerant.	Emphasizes the sovereignty and justice of God; no longer doctrinaire.	Although traces of belief in predestination (that God has foreordained salvation for the "elect") remain, this idea is no longer a central element in Presbyterianism.	**Presbyterians**
Relatively elaborate ritual; wide variety of public and private rites, mass, rosary recitation, processions, novenas.	Theoretically very strict; tolerant in practice on most issues; divorce and remarriage not accepted; celibate clergy, except in Eastern rite.	Highly elaborated; salvation by merit gained through faith; dogmatic; unique development of doctrines surrounding Mary, the mother of Jesus Christ.	Roman Catholicism went through a period of relatively rapid change as a result of Vatican Council II.	**Roman Catholics**
Usually simple services with emphasis on the sermon.	Tolerant; some social action emphasis.	Standard Protestant; *Statement of Faith* (1959) is not binding.	The 2 main churches in the 1957 union represented earlier unions with small groups of almost every Protestant denomination.	**United Church of Christ**

The Major World Religions

Source: Reviewed by Anthony Padovano, Ph.D., S.T.D., prof. of lit., Ramapo College, NJ, adj. prof. of theol. and rel. studies, Fordham U., NYC

Buddhism

Founded: About 525 BC, reportedly near Benares, India.

Founder: Gautama Siddhartha (c 563-483 BC), the Buddha, who achieved enlightenment through intense meditation.

Sacred Texts: The Tripitaka, a collection of the Buddha's teachings, rules of monastic life, and philosophical commentaries on the teachings; also a vast body of Buddhist teachings and commentaries, many of which are called *sutras*.

Organization: The basic institution is the *sangha*, or monastic order through which the traditions are passed to each generation. Monastic life tends to be democratic and anti-authoritarian. Large lay organizations have developed in some sects.

Practice: Varies widely according to the sect, and ranges from austere meditation to magical chanting and elaborate temple rites. Many practices, such as exorcism of devils, reflect pre-Buddhist beliefs.

Divisions: A variety of sects grouped into 3 primary branches: Theravada (sole survivor of the ancient Hinayana schools), which emphasizes the importance of pure thought and deed; Mahayana (includes Zen and Soka-gakkai), which ranges from philosophical schools to belief in the saving grace of higher beings or ritual practices and to practical meditative disciplines; and Tantrism, an unusual combination of belief in ritual magic and sophisticated philosophy.

Location: Throughout Asia, from Sri Lanka to Japan. Zen and Soka-gakkai have several thousand adherents in the U.S.

Beliefs: Life is misery and decay, and there is no ultimate reality in it or behind it. The cycle of endless birth and rebirth continues because of desire and attachment to the unreal "self." Right meditation and deeds will end the cycle and achieve Nirvana, the Void, nothingness.

Hinduism

Founded: About 500 BC by Aryan invaders of India where their Vedic religion intermixed with the practices and beliefs of the natives.

Sacred texts: The *Veda,* including the *Upanishads,* a collection of rituals and mythological and philosophical commentaries; a vast number of epic stories about gods, heroes, and saints, including the *Bhagavadgita,* a part of the *Mahabharata,* and the *Ramayana;* and a great variety of other literature.

Organization: None, strictly speaking. Generally, rituals should be performed or assisted by Brahmins, the priestly caste, but in practice simpler rituals can be performed by anyone. Brahmins are the final judges of ritual purity, the vital element in Hindu life. Temples and religious organizations are usually presided over by Brahmins.

Practice: A variety of private rituals, primarily passage rites (for example, initiation, marriage, death, etc.) and daily devotions, and a similar variety of public rites in temples. Of the latter, the *puja,* a ceremonial dinner for a god, is the most common.

Divisions: There is no concept of orthodoxy in Hinduism, which presents a variety of sects, most of them devoted to the worship of one of the many gods. The 3 major living traditions are those devoted to the gods Vishnu and Shiva and to the goddess Shakti; each is divided into further subsects. Numerous folk beliefs and practices, often in amalgamation with the above groups, exist side by side with sophisticated philosophic schools and exotic cults.

Location: Mainly India, Nepal, Malaysia, Guyana, Suriname, Sri Lanka.

Beliefs: There is only one divine principle; the many gods are only aspects of that unity. Life in all its forms is an aspect of the divine, but it appears as a separation from the divine, a meaningless cycle of birth and rebirth (*samsara*) determined by the purity or impurity of past deeds (*karma*). To improve one's *karma* or escape *samsara* by pure acts, thought, and/or devotion is the aim of every Hindu.

Islam

Founded: AD 622 in Medina, Arabian peninsula.

Founder: Muhammad (c 570-632), the Prophet.

Sacred texts: Koran, the words of God; *Hadith,* collections of the sayings of the Prophet.

Organization: Theoretically, the state and religious community are one, administered by a caliph. In practice, Islam is a loose collection of congregations united by a very conservative tradition. Islam is basically egalitarian and nonauthoritarian.

Practice: Every Muslim has 5 duties: to make the profession of faith ("There is no god but Allah ..."), to pray 5 times a day, to give a regular portion of his goods to charity, to fast during the day in the month of Ramadan, and to make at least one pilgrimage to Mecca if possible.

Divisions: The 2 major sects of Islam are the Sunni (orthodox) and the Shia. The Shia believe in 12 *imams,* perfect teachers, who still guide the faithful from Paradise. Shia practice tends toward the ecstatic; however, the Sunni are staid and simple. The Shia affirm human free will; the Sunni are deterministic. The mystic tradition in Islam is Sufism. A Sufi adept is someone who believes he or she has acquired a special inner knowledge direct from Allah.

Location: From the west coast of Africa to the Philippines across a broad band that includes Tanzania, Central Asia and western China, India, Malaysia, and Indonesia. Islam has several million adherents in the U.S.

Beliefs: Strictly monotheistic. God is creator of the universe, omnipotent, just, and merciful. The human being is God's highest creation, but limited and commits sins. Humans are misled by Satan, an evil spirit. God revealed the Koran to Muhammad to guide humans to the truth. Those who repent and sincerely submit to God return to a state of sinlessness. In the end, the sinless go to Paradise, a place of physical and spiritual pleasure, and the wicked burn in Hell.

Judaism

Founded: About 1300 BCE.

Founder: Abraham is regarded as the founding patriarch, but the Torah of Moses is the basic source of the teachings.

Sacred Texts: The 5 books of Moses constitute the written Torah. Special sanctity is also assigned other writings of the Hebrew Bible—the teachings of oral Torah are recorded in the Talmud, in the Midrash, and in various commentaries.

Organization: Originally theocratic, Judaism has evolved a congregational polity. The basic institution is the local synagogue, operated by the congregation and led by a rabbi of their choice. Chief rabbis in France and Great Britain have authority only over those who accept it; in Israel, the 2 chief rabbis have civil authority in family law.

Practice: Among traditional practitioners, almost all areas of life are governed by strict religious discipline. Sabbath and holidays are marked by special observances, and attendance at public worship is regarded as especially important then. The chief annual observances are Passover, celebrating the liberation of the Israelites from Egypt and marked by the ritual Seder meal in the home, and the 10 days from Rosh Hashana (New Year) to Yom Kippur (Day of Atonement), a period of fasting and penitence.

Divisions: Judaism is an unbroken spectrum from ultra conservative to ultra liberal, largely reflecting different points of view regarding the binding character of the prohibitions and duties—particularly the dietary and Sabbath observations—prescribed in the daily life of the Jew.

Location: Almost worldwide, with concentrations in Israel and the U.S.

Beliefs: Strictly monotheistic. God is the creator and absolute ruler of the universe. Men and women are free to choose to rebel against God's rule. God established a particular relationship with the Hebrew people: by obeying a divine law God gave them, they would be a special witness to God's mercy and justice. The emphasis in Judaism is on ethical behavior (and, among the traditional, careful ritual obedience) as the true worship of God.

STATES AND OTHER AREAS OF THE U.S.

Sources: Population: Commerce Dept., Bureau of the Census (July 1994 est., including armed forces personnel in each state but excluding such personnel stationed overseas); area: Bureau of the Census, Geography Division; forested land: Agriculture Dept., Forest Service; lumber production: Bureau of the Census, Industry Division; mineral production: Interior Dept., Bureau of Mines; commercial fishing: Commerce Dept., Natl. Marine Fisheries Service; value of construction: McGraw-Hill Information Systems Co., F.W. Dodge Division; personal per capita income: Commerce Dept., Bureau of Economic Analysis; unemployment: Labor Dept., Bureau of Labor Statistics; finance: Federal Deposit Insurance Corp.; federal employees: Labor Dept., Office of Personnel Management; energy: Energy Dept., Energy Information Administration; education: Education Dept., National Education Assn. Other information from sources in individual states, usually Commerce Dept.

Alabama
Heart of Dixie, Camellia State

People. Population (1994): 4,218,792; **rank: 22; Net change** (1990-94): 4.4%. **Pop. density:** 81.5 per sq mi. **Racial/ethnic distrib.** (1990): 73.6% white; 25.3% black; 0.6% Hispanic.

Geography. Total area: 52,423 sq mi; **rank: 30. Land area:** 50,750 sq mi. **Acres forested land:** 21,974,000. **Location:** East South Central state extending N-S from Tenn. to the Gulf of Mexico; east of the Mississippi River. **Climate:** long, hot summers; mild winters; generally abundant rainfall. **Topography:** coastal plains incl. Prairie Black Belt give way to hills, broken terrain; highest elevation, 2,407 ft. **Capital:** Montgomery.

Economy. Principal industries: pulp and paper, chemicals, electronics, apparel, textiles, primary metals, lumber and wood prods., food processing, fabricated metals, automotive tires, oil and gas exploration. **Principal manufactured goods:** electronics, cast iron and plastic pipe, fabricated steel prods., ships, paper products, chemicals, steel, mobile homes, fabrics, poultry processing, soft drinks, furniture, tires. **Agriculture: Chief crops** (1994): cotton, greenhouse & nursery, peanuts, hay, corn, soybeans, corn, sweet potatoes, spring Irish potatoes, peaches, pecans, wheat, tomatoes, watermelons. **Livestock** (1990): 1.8 mil cattle; 400,000 hogs/pigs; 14.8 mil poultry; 2.7 mil foodsize catfish. **Timber/lumber** (1993): pine, hardwoods; 2.5 bil bd ft. **Nonfuel Minerals** (1994): $576 mil; crushed stone, portland cement, lime, sand & gravel. **Commercial fishing** (1994): $48.3 mil. **Chief ports:** Mobile. **Value of construction** (1994): $4.2 bil. **Employment distribution** (1991): 20% mfg.; 35% trade; 16% serv. **Per capita personal income** (1994): $18,010. **Unemployment** (1994): 6.0%. **Tourism** (1991): tourists spent $3.4 bil.

Finance. FDIC-insured commercial banks & trust companies (1994): 207. **Deposits:** $39.6 bil. **FDIC-insured savings institutions** (1994): 20. **Assets:** $2.3 bil.

Federal government. No. federal civilian employees (Mar. 1994): 44,095. **Avg. salary:** $38,605. **Notable federal facilities:** George C. Marshall NASA Space Center, Huntsville; Gunter Annex & Maxwell AFB, Montgomery; Ft. Rucker, Ozark; Ft. McClellan, Anniston; Natl. Fertilizer Development Center, Muscle Shoals; Navy Station & U.S. Corps of Engineers, Mobile; Redstone Arsenal, Huntsville.

Energy. Electricity production (1994, kWh, by source): Coal: 62.8 bil; Petroleum: 121 mil; Gas: 373 mil; Hydroelectric: 11 bil; Nuclear: 20.5 bil.

Education. Student-teacher ratio (1993): 17.1. **Avg. salary, public school teachers** (1994-95): $31,144.

State data. Motto: We dare defend our rights. **Flower:** Camellia. **Bird:** Yellowhammer. **Tree:** Southern pine. **Song:** Alabama. **Entered union** Dec. 14, 1819; rank, 22d. **State fair** at: Birmingham; early Oct.

History. First Europeans were Spanish explorers in the early 1500s. The French made the first permanent settlement, on Mobile Bay, 1701-2; later, English settled in the northern areas. France ceded the entire region to England at the end of the French and Indian War, 1763, but Spanish Florida claimed the Mobile Bay area until U.S. troops took it, 1813. Gen. Andrew Jackson broke the power of the Creek Indians, 1814, and they were removed to Oklahoma. The Confederate States were organized Feb. 4, 1861, at Montgomery, the first capital.

Tourist attractions. Jefferson Davis's "first White House" of the Confederacy; Montgomery's Civil Rights Memorial; Ivy Green, Helen Keller's birthplace, Tuscumbia; statue of Vulcan, Birmingham; George Washington Carver Museum, Tuskegee Univ.; W. C. Handy Home & Museum, Florence; Alabama Space and Rocket Center, Huntsville; Alabama Shakespeare Festival, Montgomery; Moundville State Monument, Moundville; Pike Pioneer Museum, Troy; USS Alabama Memorial Park, Mobile; 28 hunting areas, 24 public lakes, 82 campgrounds, 21 state parks.

At Russell Cave National Monument, near Bridgeport: a detailed record of occupancy by humans from about 10,000 BC to AD 1650.

Famous Alabamians. Hank Aaron, Tallulah Bankhead, Hugo L. Black, Paul "Bear" Bryant, George Washington Carver, Nat King Cole, William C. Handy, Bo Jackson, Helen Keller, Harper Lee, Joe Louis, Willie Mays, John Hunt Morgan, Jesse Owens, George Wallace, Booker T. Washington, Hank Williams.

Tourist Information. Business Council of Alabama, PO Box 76, Montgomery, AL 36101; 205-834-6000.

Toll-free travel information. 1-800-ALABAMA out of state.

Alaska
The Last Frontier (unofficial)

People. Population (1994): 606,276; **rank: 48; Net change** (1990-94): 10.2%. **Pop. density:** 1.03 per sq mi. **Racial/ethnic distrib.** (1990): 75.5% white; 4.1% black; 15.6% Amer. Indian, Eskimo or Aleut; 3.6% Asian or Pacific Is.; 3.2% Hispanic.

Geography. Total area: 656,424 sq mi; **rank: 1. Land area:** 570,374 sq mi. **Acres forested land:** 129,131,000. **Location:** NW corner of North America, bordered on east by Canada. **Climate:** SE, SW, and central regions, moist and mild; far north extremely dry. Extended summer days, winter nights, throughout. **Topography:** includes Pacific and Arctic mountain systems, central plateau, and Arctic slope. Mt. McKinley, 20,320 ft, is the highest point in North America. **Capital:** Juneau.

Economy. Principal industries: oil, gas, tourism, commercial fishing, mining, forestry. **Principal manufactured goods:** fish products, lumber and pulp, furs. **Agriculture: Chief crops:** barley, oats, hay, silage, potatoes, lettuce. **Livestock** (1995): 9,900 cattle; 1,700 sheep; 33,000 reindeer; (1994) 2,000 poultry. **Timber/lumber:** spruce, yellow cedar, hemlock. **Nonfuel Minerals** (1994): $429 mil; zinc, gold, silver, tin, lead, sand & gravel, crushed stone. **Commercial fishing** (1994): $1.4 bil. **Chief ports:** Anchorage, Dutch Harbor, Kodiak, Seward, Skagway, Juneau, Sitka, Valdez, Wrangell. **International airports at:** Anchorage. **Value of construction** (1994): $833.9 mil. **Employment distribution** (1994): 27% govt.; 40% serv.; 30% trade. **Per capita personal income** (1994): $23,788. **Unemployment** (1994): 7.8%. **Tourism** (1994): out-of-state visitors spend $863 mil.

Finance. FDIC-insured commercial banks & trust companies (1994): 8. **Deposits:** $4.0 bil. **FDIC-insured savings institutions** (1994): 2. **Assets:** $223 mil.

Federal government. No. federal civilian employees (Mar. 1994): 12,633. **Avg. salary:** $39,407.

Energy. Electricity production (1994, kWh, by source): Coal: 295 mil; Petroleum: 441 mil; Gas: 2.7 bil; Hydroelectric: 1.3 bil.

Education. Pupil-teacher ratio(1993): 17.5. **Avg. salary, public school teachers** (1994-95): $47,951.

State data. Motto: North to the future. **Flower:** Forget-Me-Not. **Bird:** Willow ptarmigan. **Tree:** Sitka spruce. **Song:** Alaska's Flag. **Entered union** Jan. 3, 1959; rank, 49th. **State fair** at Palmer; late Aug.–early Sept.

History. Vitus Bering, a Danish explorer working for Russia, was the first European to land in Alaska, 1741. Alexander Baranov, first governor of Russian America, set up headquarters at Archangel, near present Sitka, in 1799. Secretary of State William H. Seward bought

Alaska from Russia for $7.2 million in 1867, a bargain some called "Seward's Folly." In 1896, gold was discovered, and the famed Gold Rush was on.

Tourist attractions. Inside Passage; Portage Glacier; Mendenhall Glacier; Ketchikan Totems; Glacier Bay National Park; Denali National Park, one of N. America's great wildlife sanctuaries, surrounding Mt. McKinley, N. America's highest peak; Transalaska Pipeline; Pribilof Islands fur seal rookeries; restored St. Michael's Russian Orthodox Cathedral, Sitka; Katmai National Park & Preserve.

Famous Alaskans. Tom Bodett, Susan Butcher, Ernest Gruening, Sydney Laurence, Libby Riddles, Jefferson "Soapy" Smith.

Tourist information. Alaska Division of Tourism, PO Box 110801, Juneau, AK 99811-0801; 1-907-465-2010.

Arizona
Grand Canyon State

People. Population (1994): 4,075,052; **rank:** 23; **Net change** (1990-94): 11.2%. **Pop. density:** 33.7 per sq mi. **Racial/ethnic distrib.** (1990): 80.8% white; 3.0% black; 5.6% American Indian; 18.8% Hispanic.

Geography. Total area: 114,006 sq mi; **rank:** 6. **Land area:** 113,642 sq mi. **Acres forested land:** 19,596,000. **Location:** in the southwestern U.S. **Climate:** clear and dry in the southern regions and northern plateau; high central areas have heavy winter snows. **Topography:** Colorado plateau in the N, containing the Grand Canyon; Mexican Highlands running diagonally NW to SE; Sonoran Desert in the SW. **Capital:** Phoenix.

Economy. Principal industries: manufacturing, tourism, mining, agriculture. **Principal manufactured goods:** electronics, printing and publishing, foods, primary and fabricated metals, aircraft and missiles, apparel. **Agriculture: Chief crops:** cotton, lettuce, cauliflower, broccoli, sorghum, barley, corn, wheat, citrus fruits. **Livestock** (1995): 830,000 cattle; 170,000 hogs/pigs; 145,000 sheep; 350,000 poultry. **Timber/lumber** (1993): pine, fir, spruce; 194 mil bd ft. **Nonfuel Minerals** (1994): $3.3 bil; copper, sand and gravel, cement, gold, molybdenum, silver, perlite. **International airports at:** Phoenix, Tucson, Yuma. **Value of construction** (1994): $8.0 bil. **Employment distribution** (1994): 28.5% services; 22.1% trade; 16.9% govt.; 11.4% mfg. **Per capita personal income** (1994): $19,001. **Unemployment** (1994): 6.4%. **Tourism** (1994): tourists spent $10.5 bil.

Finance. FDIC-insured commercial banks & trust companies (1994): 34. **Deposits:** $30.9 bil. **FDIC-insured savings institutions** (1994): 2. **Assets:** $298 mil.

Federal government. No. federal civilian employees (Mar. 1994): 28,863. **Avg. salary:** $35,086. **Notable federal facilities:** Luke, Davis-Monthan AF bases; Ft. Huachuca Army Base; Yuma Proving Grounds.

Energy. Electricity production (1994, kWh, by source): Coal: 38 bil; Petroleum: 128 mil; Gas: 2.5 bil; Hydroelectric: 7.7 mil; Nuclear: 23.2 bil.

Education. Student-teacher ratio (1993): 18.9. **Avg. salary, public school teachers** (1994-95): $32,090.

State data. Motto: Ditat Deus (God enriches). **Flower:** Blossom of the Saguaro cactus. **Bird:** Cactus wren. **Tree:** Paloverde. **Song:** Arizona. **Entered union** Feb. 14, 1912; **rank,** 48th. **State fair** at: Phoenix; late Oct.–early Nov.

History. Marcos de Niza, a Franciscan, and Estevan, a black slave, explored the area, 1539. Eusebio Francisco Kino, Jesuit missionary, taught Indians Christianity and farming, 1690-1711, and left a chain of missions. Spain ceded Arizona to Mexico, 1821. The U.S. took over at the end of the Mexican War, 1848. The area below the Gila River was obtained from Mexico in the Gadsden Purchase, 1854. Long Apache wars did not end until 1886, with Geronimo's surrender.

Tourist attractions. The Grand Canyon of the Colorado, an immense, vari-colored fissure 217 mi long, 4 to 13 mi wide at the brim, 4,000 to 5,500 ft deep; the Painted Desert, extending for 30 mi along U.S. 66; the Petrified Forest; Canyon Diablo, 225 ft deep and 500 ft wide; Meteor Crater, 4,150 ft across, 570 ft deep, made by a prehistoric meteor. Also, London Bridge at Lake Havasu City, Biosphere 2 at Oracle.

Famous Arizonans. Bruce Babbitt, Cochise, Geronimo, Barry Goldwater, Zane Grey, Carl Hayden, George W. P. Hunt, Helen Jacobs, Percival Lowell, Sandra Day O'Connor, William H. Pickering, John J. Rhodes, Morris Udall, Stewart Udall, Frank Lloyd Wright.

Tourist information. Phoenix & Valley of the Sun Visitor and Convention Bureau, 1-602-254-6500.

Arkansas
Land of Opportunity

People. Population (1994): 2,452,671; **rank:** 33; **Net change** (1990-94): 4.3%. **Pop. density:** 46.1 per sq mi. **Racial/ethnic distrib.** (1990): 82.7% white; 15.9% black; 0.8% Hispanic.

Geography. Total area: 53,182 sq mi; **rank:** 29. **Land area:** 52,075 sq mi. **Acres forested land:** 17,864,000. **Location:** in the west south-central U.S. **Climate:** long, hot summers, mild winters; generally abundant rainfall. **Topography:** eastern delta and prairie, southern lowland forests, and the northwestern highlands, which include the Ozark Plateaus. **Capital:** Little Rock.

Economy. Principal industries: manufacturing, agriculture, tourism, forestry. **Principal manufactured goods:** food prods., chemicals, lumber, paper, electric motors, furniture, auto components, airplane parts, apparel, machinery, steel. **Agriculture: Chief crops:** soybeans, rice, cotton, tomatoes, grapes, apples, commercial vegetables, peaches, wheat. **Livestock** (1993): 1.81 mil cattle; 890,000 hogs/pigs; 1,048,800 mil broilers. **Timber/lumber** (1993): oak, hickory, gum, cypress, pine; 2.1 bil bd ft. **Nonfuel Minerals** (1994): $392 mil; crushed stone, bromine, cement, sand & gravel. **Chief ports:** Little Rock, Pine Bluff, Osceola, Helena, Fort Smith, Van Buren, Camden, Dardanelle, North Little Rock, West Memphis, Crossett, McGehee, Morrilton, Helena. **Value of construction** (1994): $2.7 bil. **Employment distribution** (1994): 24.57% mfg.; 22.49% trade; 22.10% serv.; 16.65% govt. **Per capita personal income** (1994): $16,898. **Unemployment** (1994): 5.3%. **Tourism** (1994): travelers spent $2.9 bil.

Finance. FDIC-insured commercial banks & trust companies (1994): 257. **Deposits:** $23.4 bil. **FDIC-insured savings institutions** (1994): 17. **Assets:** $3.3 bil.

Federal government. No. federal civilian employees (Mar. 1994): 11,860. **Avg. salary:** $33,601. **Notable federal facilities:** Nat'l. Center for Toxicological Research, Jefferson; Pine Bluff Arsenal, Little Rock AFB.

Energy. Electricity production (1994, kWh, by source): Coal: 19.8 bil; Petroleum: 96 mil; Gas: 2.3 bil; Hydroelectric: 3.5 bil; Nuclear: 14.0 bil.

Education. Student-teacher ratio (1993): 17.1. **Avg. salary, public school teachers** (1994-95): $28,409.

State data. Motto: Regnat Populus (The people rule). **Flower:** Apple blossom. **Bird:** Mockingbird. **Tree:** Pine. **Song:** Arkansas. **Entered union** June 15, 1836; **rank,** 25th. **State fair** at: Little Rock; late Sept.–early Oct.

History. First European explorers were de Soto, 1541; Jolliet, 1673; La Salle, 1682. First settlement was by the French under Henri de Tonty, 1686, at Arkansas Post. In 1762, the area was ceded by France to Spain, then back again in 1800, and was part of the Louisiana Purchase by the U.S. in 1803. Arkansas seceded from the Union in 1861, only after the Civil War began, and more than 10,000 Arkansans fought on the Union side.

Tourist attractions. 5 natl. parks & 48 state parks, including Hot Springs National Park, water ranging from 95° to 147°F. Eureka Springs, resort since 1879; Blanchard Caverns, near Mountain View, are among the nation's largest; Crater of Diamonds, near Murfreesboro, only U.S. diamond mine; Buffalo Natl. River; Mid-America Museum, Ozark Folk Center.

Famous Arkansans. Daisy Bates, Dee Brown, Glen Campbell, Johnny Cash, Hattie Caraway, Bill Clinton, "Dizzy" Dean, Orval Faubus, James W. Fulbright, John Grisham, Douglas MacArthur, John L. McClellan, James

S. McDonnel, Dick Powell, Winthrop Rockefeller, Mary Steenburgen, Edward Durell Stone, Archibald Yell.

Chamber of Commerce. 410 S. Cross St., Little Rock, AR 72201; 501-374-9225

Toll-free travel information. 1-800-NATURAL.

California
Golden State

People. Population (1994): 31,430,697; **rank:** 1; **Net change** (1990-94): 5.6%. **Pop. density:** 197.9 per sq mi. **Racial/ethnic distrib.** (1990): 69.0% white; 7.4% black; 9.6% Asian; 25.8% Hispanic.

Geography. Total area: 163,707 sq mi; **rank:** 3. **Land area:** 155,973 sq mi. **Acres forested land:** 37,263,000. **Location:** on western coast of the U.S. **Climate:** moderate temperatures and rainfall along the coast; extremes in the interior. **Topography:** long mountainous coastline; central valley; Sierra Nevada on the east; desert basins of the southern interior; rugged mountains of the north. **Capital:** Sacramento.

Economy. Principal industries: agriculture, manufacturing, services, trade. **Principal manufactured goods:** foods, printed material, primary and fabricated metals, machinery, electric and electronic equipment, transportation equipment, instruments. **Agriculture: Chief crops:** grapes, cotton, flowers, oranges, nursery products, hay, tomatoes, lettuce, strawberries, almonds, broccoli, walnuts, sugar beets, peaches, potatoes. **Livestock** (1993): 4.5 mil cattle & calves; 250,000 hogs/pigs; 945,000 sheep and lambs; 31.5 mil chickens exc. broilers. **Timber/lumber** (1993): fir, pine, redwood, oak; 3.6 bil bd ft. **Nonfuel Minerals:** (1994): $2.5 bil; portland cement, sand & gravel, boron, dimension stone, diatomite, gold, silver, tungsten, copper, asbestos. **Commercial fishing** (1994): $159.1 mil. **Chief ports:** Long Beach, Los Angeles, San Diego, Oakland, San Francisco, Sacramento, Stockton. **International airports at:** Los Angeles, San Francisco, San Jose, San Diego. **Value of construction** (1994): $30.4 bil. **Employment distribution** (1993): 28.9% serv.; 23.2% trade; 15% mfg.; 17.3% govt. **Per capita personal income** (1994): $22,493. **Unemployment** (1994): 5.6%. **Tourism** (1992): $52.8 bil.

Finance. FDIC-insured commercial banks & trust companies (1994): 404. **Deposits:** $275.4 bil. **FDIC-insured savings institutions** (1994): 87. **Assets:** $259.2 bil.

Federal government. No. federal civilian employees (Mar. 1994): 190,063. **Avg. salary:** $38,912. **Notable federal facilities:** Vandenberg, Beale, Travis, McClellan AF bases, San Francisco Mint.

Energy. Electricity production (1994, kWh, by source): Petroleum: 1.9 bil; Gas: 61.5 bil; Hydroelectric: 22.8 bil; Nuclear: 33.8 bil.

Education. Student-teacher ratio (1993): 24.0. **Avg. salary, public school teachers** (1994-95): $40,667.

State data. Motto: Eureka (I have found it). **Flower:** Golden poppy. **Bird:** California valley quail. **Tree:** California redwood. **Song:** I Love You, California. **Entered union** Sept. 9, 1850; **rank,** 31st. **State fair** at: Sacramento; late Aug.—early Sept.

History. First European explorers were Cabrillo, 1542, and Drake, 1579. First settlement was the Spanish Alta California mission at San Diego, 1769, first in a string founded by Franciscan Father Junipero Serra. U.S. traders and settlers arrived in the 19th century and staged the abortive Bear Flag Revolt, 1846; later that year U.S. forces occupied California. At the end of the Mexican War, Mexico ceded the province to the U.S., 1848, the same year the Gold Rush began.

Tourist attractions. Scenic regions are Yosemite Valley; Lassen and Sequoia-Kings Canyon national parks; Lake Tahoe; the Mojave and Colorado deserts; San Francisco Bay; Napa Valley; and Monterey Peninsula. Oldest living things on earth are believed to be a stand of Bristlecone pines in the Inyo National Forest, est. to be 4,600 years old. The world's tallest tree, the 365-ft "National Geographic Society" coast redwood, stands in Humboldt Redwoods State Park.

Also, RMS Queen Mary, Spruce Goose, both Long Beach; Palomar Observatory; Disneyland, Anaheim; J. Paul Getty Museum, Malibu; Tournament of Roses and Rose Bowl; Universal Studios, Hollywood; Los Angeles County Art Museum; San Diego Zoo.

Famous Californians. Luther Burbank, John C. Fremont, Bret Harte, William R. Hearst, Jack London, Aimee Semple McPherson, John Muir, Richard M. Nixon, William Saroyan, Junipero Serra, Leland Stanford, John Steinbeck, Earl Warren.

Chamber of Commerce. 1201 K St., Sacramento, CA 95814.

Toll-free travel information. 1-800-862-2543.

Colorado
Centennial State

People. Population (1994): 3,655,647; **rank:** 26; **Net change** (1990-94): 11.0%. **Pop. density:** 33.5 per sq mi. **Racial/ethnic distrib.** (1990): 88.2% white; 4.0% black; 12.9% Hispanic.

Geography. Total area: 104,100 sq mi; **rank:** 8. **Land area:** 103,729 sq mi. **Acres forested land:** 21,338,000. **Location:** in west central U.S. **Climate:** low relative humidity, abundant sunshine, wide daily, seasonal temperatures ranges; alpine conditions in the high mountains. **Topography:** eastern dry high plains; hilly to mountainous central plateau; western Rocky Mountains of high ranges alternating with broad valleys and deep, narrow canyons. **Capital:** Denver.

Economy. Principal industries: manufacturing, government, tourism, agriculture, aerospace, electronics equipment. **Principal manufactured goods:** computer equipment, instruments, foods, machinery, aerospace products. **Agriculture: Chief crops:** corn, wheat, hay, sugar beets, barley, potatoes, apples, peaches, pears, dry edible beans, sorghum, onions, oats. **Livestock** (1992): 3.1 mil cattle; 464,479 hogs/pigs; 4.3 mil poultry. **Timber/lumber** (1993): oak, ponderosa pine, Douglas fir; 129 mil bd ft. **Nonfuel Minerals** (1994): $440 mil; construction sand & gravel, portland cement, crushed stone, gold, lead, zinc, molybdenum. **International airports at:** Denver. **Value of construction** (1994): $6.4 bil. **Employment distribution** (1994): 28.7% serv.; 24.3% trade; 17.1% govt.; 10.9% mfg. **Per capita personal income** (1994): $22,333. **Unemployment** (1994): 4.2%. **Tourism** (1992): $6.4 bil.

Finance. FDIC-insured commercial banks & trust companies (1994): 279. **Deposits:** $29.7 bil. **FDIC-insured savings institutions** (1994): 16. **Assets:** $2.4 bil.

Federal government. No. federal civilian employees (Mar. 1994): 39,666. **Avg. salary:** $39,473. **Notable federal facilities:** U.S. Air Force Academy; U.S. Mint; Ft. Carson; National Renewable Energy Labs; U.S. Rail Transportation Test Center; N. American Aerospace Defense Command; Consolidated Space Operations Center; U.S. Documents Center, Fitzsimons Army Medical Center, Federal Center.

Energy. Electricity production (1994, kWh, by source): Coal: 31.4 bil; Petroleum: 9 mil; Gas: 374 mil; Hydroelectric: 1.5 bil.

Education. Student-teacher ratio (1993): 18.8. **Avg. salary, public school teachers** (1994-95): $34,571.

State data. Motto: Nil Sine Numine (Nothing without Providence). **Flower:** Rocky Mountain columbine. **Bird:** Lark bunting. **Tree:** Colorado blue spruce. **Song:** Where the Columbines Grow. **Entered union** Aug. 1, 1876; **rank** 38th. **State fair** at: Pueblo; last week in Aug.

History. Early civilization centered around Mesa Verde 2,000 years ago. The U.S. acquired eastern Colorado in the Louisiana Purchase, 1803; Lt. Zebulon M. Pike explored the area, 1806, discovering the peak that bears his name. After the Mexican War, 1846-48, U.S. immigrants settled in the east, former Mexicans in the south.

Tourist attractions. 310 or more sunshine days per year; more than 1,000 peaks of 2 or more miles; Rocky Mountain National Park; Garden of the Gods; Great Sand Dunes, Dinosaur, Black Canyon of the Gunnison, and Colorado national monuments; Pikes Peak and Mt. Evans highways; Mesa Verde National Park (ancient

Anasazi Indian cliff dwellings); 35 major ski areas; the Grand Mesa tableland comprises Grand Mesa Forest, 659,584 acres, with 200 lakes stocked with trout. Mining towns of Central City, Silverton, Cripple Creek; Burlington's Old Town; Bent's Fort, outside La Junta; Georgetown Loop Historic Mining Railroad Park, Cumbres & Toltec Scenic Railroad.

Famous Coloradans. Frederick Bonfils, Molly Brown, William N. Byers, M. Scott Carpenter, Jack Dempsey, Mamie Eisenhower, Douglas Fairbanks, Scott Hamilton, "Baby Doe" Tabor, Lowell Thomas, Byron R. White, Paul Whiteman.

Toll-free travel information. 1-800-265-6723.

Connecticut
Constitution State, Nutmeg State

People. Population (1994): 3,275,251; **rank:** 27; **Net change** (1990-94): -0.4%. **Pop. density:** 677.2 per sq mi. **Racial/ethnic distrib.** (1990): 87.0% white; 8.3% black; 6.5% Hispanic.

Geography. Total area: 5,544 sq mi; **rank:** 48. **Land area:** 4,845 sq mi. **Acres forested land:** 1,819,000. **Location:** New England state in the northeastern corner of the U.S. **Climate:** moderate; winters avg. slightly below freezing, warm, humid summers. **Topography:** western upland, the Berkshires, in the NW, highest elevations; narrow central lowland N-S; hilly eastern upland drained by rivers. **Capital:** Hartford.

Economy. Principal industries: manufacturing, retail trade, government, services, finances, insurance, real estate. **Principal manufactured goods:** aircraft engines and parts, submarines, helicopters, instruments, machinery & computer equipment, electronics & electrical equipment, medical instruments, pharmaceuticals. **Agriculture: Chief crops:** nursery stock, Christmas trees, mushrooms, vegetables, sweet corn, tobacco, apples. **Livestock** (1992): 78,000 cattle; 5,800 horses; 5,200 hogs/pigs; 7,500 sheep; 5.6 mil poultry. **Timber/lumber** (1993): oak, birch, beech, maple; 49 mil bd ft. **Nonfuel Minerals** (1994): $97 mil; crushed stone, construction sand & gravel. **Commercial fishing** (1994): $44.3 mil. **Chief ports:** New Haven, Bridgeport, New London. **International airports at:** Windsor Locks. **Value of construction** (1994): $2.9 bil. **Employment distribution** (1995): 21% mfg.; 79% serv. **Per capita personal income** (1994): $29,402. **Unemployment** (1994): 5.6%. **Tourism** (1993): out-of-state visitors spent $3.9 bil.

Finance. FDIC-insured commercial banks & trust companies (1994): 43. **Deposits:** $25.4 bil. **FDIC-insured savings institutions** (1994): 63. **Assets:** $40.0 bil.

Federal Government. No. federal civilian employees (Mar. 1994): 9,838. **Avg. salary:** $40,335. **Notable federal facilities:** U.S. Coast Guard Academy; U.S. Navy Submarine Base.

Energy. Electricity production (1994, kWh, by source): Coal: 2.1 bil; Petroleum: 3.4 bil; Gas: 732 mil; Hydroelectric: 412 mil; Nuclear: 20.2 bil.

Education. Student-teacher ratio (1993): 14.4. **Avg. salary, public school teachers** (1994-95): $51,300.

State data. Motto: Qui Transtulit Sustinet (He who transplanted still sustains). **Flower:** Mountain laurel. **Bird:** American robin. **Tree:** White oak. **Song:** Yankee Doodle. **Fifth** of the 13 original states to ratify the Constitution, Jan. 9, 1788. **State Fair** at: Agawan, MA, Eastern States Exposition, (combined with RI, MA, NH, VT) Sept.

History. Adriaen Block, Dutch explorer, was the first European visitor, 1614. By 1634, settlers from Plymouth Bay started colonies along the Connecticut River and in 1637 defeated the Pequot Indians. In the American Revolution, Connecticut men fought in most major campaigns and turned back British raids on Danbury and other towns, while Connecticut privateers captured British merchant ships.

Tourist attractions. Mark Twain House, Hartford; Yale University's Art Gallery, Peabody Museum, both in New Haven; Mystic Seaport; Mystic Marine Life Aquarium; P. T. Barnum Museum, Bridgeport; Gillette Castle, Hadlyme; U.S.S. Nautilus Memorial, Groton (1st nuclear-powered submarine); Foxwoods Casino, Ledyard.

Famous "Nutmeggers." Ethan Allen, Phineas T. Barnum, Samuel Colt, Jonathan Edwards, Nathan Hale, Katharine Hepburn, Isaac Hull, J. Pierpont Morgan, Israel Putnam, Harriet Beecher Stowe, Mark Twain, Noah Webster, Eli Whitney.

Tourist information. State Dept. of Economic Development, 865 Brook St., Rocky Hill, CT 06067.

Toll-free travel information. 1-800-CTBOUND (282-6863).

Delaware
First State, Diamond State

People. Population (1994): 706,351; **rank:** 46; **Net change** (1990-94): 6.0%. **Pop. density:** 352.5 per sq mi. **Racial/ethnic distrib.** (1990): 80.3% white; 16.9% black; 2.4% Hispanic.

Geography. Total area: 2,489 sq mi; **rank:** 49. **Land area:** 1,955 sq mi. **Acres forested land:** 398,000. **Location:** occupies the Delmarva Peninsula on the Atlantic coastal plain. **Climate:** moderate. **Topography:** Piedmont plateau to the N, sloping to a near sea-level plain. **Capital:** Dover.

Economy. Principal industries: chemistry, agriculture, finance, poultry, shellfish, tourism, auto assembly, food processing, transportation equipment. **Principal manufactured goods:** nylon, apparel, luggage, foods, autos, processed meats and vegetables, railroad and aircraft equipment. **Agriculture: Chief crops:** soybeans, potatoes, corn, mushrooms, lima beans, green peas, barley, cucumbers, snap beans, watermelons, apples, wheat, sweet corn. **Livestock** (1993): 15,000 cattle, 6,600 hogs, 251.4 mil broilers. **Nonfuel Minerals** (1994): $8.7 mil; construction sand & gravel. **Commercial fishing** (1994): $6.1 mil. **Chief ports:** Wilmington. **International airports at:** Philadelphia/Wilmington. **Value of construction** (1994): $714.3 mil. **Employment distribution** (1993): 81% non-manufacturing; 19% mfg. **Per capita personal income** (1994): $22,828. **Unemployment** (1994): 4.9%. **Tourism** (1993): domestic travelers spent $806 mil.

Finance. FDIC-insured commercial banks & trust companies (1994): 38. **Deposits:** $35.1 bil. **FDIC-insured savings institutions** (1994): 4. **Assets:** $1.4 bil.

Federal government. No. federal civilian employees (Mar. 1994): 2,877. **Avg. salary:** $35,186. **Notable federal facilities:** Dover Air Force Base, Federal Wildlife Refuge, Bombay Hook.

Energy. Electricity production (1994, kWh, by source): Coal: 4.8 bil; Petroleum: 1.9 bil; Gas: 2.1 bil.

Education. Student-teacher ratio (1993): 16.5. **Avg. salary, public school teachers** (1994-95): $39,076.

State data. Motto: Liberty and independence. **Flower:** Peach blossom. **Bird:** Blue hen chicken. **Tree:** American holly. **Song:** Our Delaware. **First** of original 13 states to ratify the Constitution, Dec. 7, 1787. **State fair** at: Harrington; end of July.

History. The Dutch first settled in Delaware near present Lewes, 1631, but were wiped out by Indians. Swedes settled at present Wilmington, 1638; Dutch settled anew, 1651, near New Castle and seized the Swedish settlement, 1655, only to lose all Delaware and New Netherland to the British, 1664.

Tourist attractions. Ft. Christina Monument, the site of founding of New Sweden; John Dickinson "Penman of the Revolution" home, Dover; Henry Francis du Pont Winterthur Museum; Hagley Museum, Wilmington; Rehoboth Beach, "nation's summer capitol," Rehoboth; Dover Downs Intl. Speedway, Dover; Old Swedes (Trinity Parish) Church, erected 1698, is the oldest Protestant church in the U.S. still in use.

Famous Delawareans. Thomas F. Bayard, Henry Seidel Canby, E. I. du Pont, John P. Marquand, Howard Pyle, Caesar Rodney.

Chamber of Commerce. One Commerce Center, Wilmington, DE 19801.

Toll-free travel information. 1-800-441-8846.

Florida
Sunshine State

People. Population (1994): 13,952,714; **rank: 4; Net change** (1990-94): 7.8%. **Pop. density:** 249.8 per sq mi. **Racial/ethnic distrib.** (1990): 83.1% white; 13.6% black; 12.2% Hispanic.

Geography. Total area: 65,756 sq mi; **rank: 22. Land area:** 53,937 sq mi. **Acres forested land:** 16,549,000. **Location:** peninsula jutting southward 500 mi bet. the Atlantic and the Gulf of Mexico. **Climate:** subtropical N of Bradenton-Lake Okeechobee-Vero Beach line; tropical S of line. **Topography:** land is flat or rolling; highest point is 345 ft in the NW. **Capital:** Tallahassee.

Economy. Principal industries: tourism, agriculture, manufacturing, construction, services, international trade. **Principal manufactured goods:** electric & electronic equipment, transportation equipment; food; printing & publishing; chemicals, instruments. **Agriculture: Chief crops:** citrus fruits, greenhouse and nursery products, vegetables, potatoes, melons, strawberries, sugarcane. **Livestock** (1994): 2.0 mil cattle, including 170,000 milk cows; 84,000 hogs/pigs; 133 mil broilers, 2.5 bil eggs. **Timber/lumber** (1993): pine, cypress, cedar; 736 mil bd ft. **Nonfuel Minerals** (1994): $1.5 bil; mostly phosphate, cement, sand and gravel, peat, titanium concentrates, crushed stone. **Commercial fishing** (1994): $239 mil. **Chief ports:** Pensacola, Tampa, Manatee, Miami, Port Everglades, Jacksonville, St. Petersburg, Canaveral. **International airports at:** Ft. Lauderdale/Hollywood, Daytona Beach, Ft. Myers, Key West, Jacksonville, Miami, Orlando, St. Petersburg/Clearwater, Panama City, Tampa, Sarasota/Bradenton, West Palm Beach. **Value of construction** (1994): $21.9 bil. **Employment distribution** (1994, total non-agricultural): 33% services, 26% wholesale & retail trade, 16% govt., 8% mfg. **Per capita personal income** (1994): $21,677. **Unemployment** (1994): 6.6% **Tourism** (1994): $33.39 bil.

Finance. FDIC-insured commercial banks & trust companies (1994): 356. **Deposits:** $135.3 bil. **FDIC-insured savings institutions** (1994): 80. **Assets:** $31.0 bil.

Federal government. No. federal civilian employees (Mar. 1994): 63,199. **Avg. salary:** $37,668. **Notable federal facilities:** John F. Kennedy Space Center, NASA-Kennedy Space Center's Spaceport USA; Eglin Air Force Base.

Energy. Electricity production (1994, kWh, by source): Coal: 60.7 bil; Petroleum: 33.3 bil; Gas: 20.7 bil; Hydroelectric: 274 mil; Nuclear: 26.6 bil.

Education. Student-teacher ratio (1993): 18.4. **Avg. salary, public school teachers** (1994-95): $32,588.

State data. Motto: In God we trust. **Flower:** Orange blossom. **Bird:** Mockingbird. **Tree:** Sabal palmetto palm. **Song:** Old Folks at Home. **Entered union** Mar. 3, 1845; rank, 27th. **State fair** at: Tampa; early Feb., call 813-621-7821.

History. First European to see Florida was Ponce de León, 1513. France established a colony, Fort Caroline, on the St. Johns River, 1564; Spain settled St. Augustine, 1565, and Spanish troops massacred most of the French. Britain's Francis Drake burned St. Augustine, 1586. Britain held the area briefly, 1763-83, returning it to Spain. After Andrew Jackson led a U.S. invasion, 1818, Spain ceded Florida to the U.S., 1819. The Seminole War, 1835-42, resulted in removal of most Indians to Oklahoma. Florida seceded from the Union, 1861, was readmitted, 1868.

Tourist attractions. Miami, with a variety of luxury hotels at Miami Beach; St. Augustine, oldest city in U.S., Castillo de San Marcos; Walt Disney World's Magic Kingdom, EPCOT Center, and Disney-MGM Studios, near Orlando; Spaceport USA, the visitors' center at the Kennedy Space Center.

Everglades National Park preserves the beauty of the vast Everglades swamp. Castillo de San Marcos, St. Augustine, is a national monument. Also, the Ringling Museum of Art and the Ringling Museum of the Circus, both in Sarasota; Sea World, Orlando; Cypress Gardens, Winter Haven; Busch Gardens, Tampa; Universal Studios, near Orlando.

Famous Floridians. Henry M. Flagler, James Weldon Johnson, MacKinlay Kantor, Henry B. Plant, Marjorie Kinnan Rawlings, Joseph W. Stilwell, Charles P. Summerall.

Tourist Information. Florida Division of Tourism, 126 Van Buren St., Tallahassee, FL 32399-2000, 1-904-487-1462.

Georgia
Empire State of the South, Peach State

People. Population (1994): 7,055,336; **rank: 11; Net change** (1990-94): 8.9%. **Pop. density:** 116.6 per sq mi. **Racial/ethnic distrib.** (1990): 71.0% white; 27.0% black; 1.7% Hispanic.

Geography. Total area: 59,441 sq mi; **rank: 24. Land area:** 57,919 sq mi. **Acres forested land:** 24,137,000. **Location:** South Atlantic state. **Climate:** maritime tropical air masses dominate in summer; continental polar air masses in winter; east central area drier. **Topography:** most southerly of the Blue Ridge Mts. cover NE and N central; central Piedmont extends to the fall line of rivers; coastal plain levels to the coast flatlands. **Capital:** Atlanta.

Economy. Principal industries: services, manufacturing, govt., retail trade. **Principal manufactured goods** (1994): textiles, food, and kindred prods., pulp and paper products. **Agriculture: Chief crops:** peanuts, cotton, corn, tobacco, hay, soybeans. **Livestock** (1994): 26.3 mil poultry, excluding broilers; 1.54 mil cattle; 1.03 mil hogs/pigs. **Timber/lumber** (1993): pine, hardwood; 3.1 bil bd ft. **Nonfuel Minerals** (1994): $1.5 bil; mostly kaolin and other clays, crushed stone. **Commercial fishing** (1994): $20.3 mil. **Chief ports:** Savannah, Brunswick. **International airports at:** Atlanta. **Value of construction** (1994): $10.7 bil. **Employment distribution** (1993): 23.7% services; 17.6% mfg.; 24.9% retail trade; 17.6% govt. **Per capita personal income** (1994): $20,251. **Unemployment** (1994): 5.2%. **Tourism** (1993): tourists spent $11.2 bil.

Finance. FDIC-insured commercial banks & trust companies (1994): 386. **Deposits:** $66.9 bil. **FDIC-insured savings institutions** (1994): 37. **Assets:** $6.6 bil.

Federal government. No. federal civilian employees (Mar. 1994): 69,338. **Avg. salary:** $36,260. **Notable federal facilities:** Dobbins AFB; Fts. Benning, Gordon, McPherson; Fed. Law Enforcement Training Ctr., Glynco, Warner Robins AFB; Centers for Disease Control, Atlanta.

Energy. Electricity production (1994, kWh, by source): Coal: 64.7 bil; Petroleum: 153 mil; Gas: 80 mil; Hydroelectric: 4.9 bil; Nuclear: 28.9 bil.

Education. Student-teacher ratio (1993): 16.3. **Avg. salary, public school teachers** (1994-95): $32,828.

State data. Motto: Wisdom, justice and moderation. **Flower:** Cherokee rose. **Bird:** Brown thrasher. **Tree:** Live oak. **Song:** Georgia On My Mind. **Fourth** of the 13 original states to ratify the Constitution, Jan. 2, 1788.

History. Gen. James Oglethorpe established the first settlements, 1733, for poor and religiously persecuted Englishmen. Oglethorpe defeated a Spanish army from Florida at Bloody Marsh, 1742. In the American Revolution, Georgians seized the Savannah armory, 1775, and sent the munitions to the Continental Army; they fought seesaw campaigns with Cornwallis's British troops, twice liberating Augusta and forcing final evacuation by the British from Savannah, 1782.

Tourist attractions. Atlanta area: State Capitol, Stone Mt. Park, Six Flags Over Georgia, Kennesaw Mt. Natl. Battlefield Park, Martin Luther King Center, Underground Atlanta, Jimmy Carter Library & Museum, Whitewater Park. NW: Chickamauga Battlefield Park, Chattahoochee Natl. Forest. NE: alpine village of Helen; Dahlonega, site of America's first gold rush; Brasstown Bald Mt., Lake Lanier. SW: Roosevelt's Little White House, Callaway Gardens, Andersonville Natl. Historic Site. SE: Okefenokee Swamp. Coastal: Jekyll Island, St. Simons Island, Cumberland Island Natl. Seashore, historic riverfront district in Savannah, Ft. Pulaski.

Famous Georgians. Griffin Bell, James Bowie, James Brown, Erskine Caldwell, Jimmy Carter, Ray Charles, Lucius D. Clay, Ty Cobb, John C. Fremont, Newt Gingrich, Joel Chandler Harris, Martin Luther King, Jr., Gladys Knight, Sidney Lanier, Juliette Gordon Low, Margaret Mitchell, Flannery O'Connor, Otis Redding, Jackie Robinson, Alice Walker, Joseph Wheeler.

Chamber of Commerce. 235 International Blvd., Atlanta, GA 30303; (404) 880-9000.

Toll-free travel information. 1-800-VISITGA.

Hawai'i
Aloha State

People. Population (1994): 1,178,564; **rank:** 40; **Net change** (1990-94): 6.3%. **Pop. density:** 180.5 per sq mi. **Racial/ethnic distrib.** (1990): 33.4% white; 2.5% black; 61.8% Asian or Pacific Is.; 7.3% Hispanic.

Geography. Total area: 10,932 sq mi; **rank:** 43. **Land area:** 6,423 sq mi. **Acres forested land:** 1,748,000. **Location:** Hawaiian Islands lie in the North Pacific, 2,397 mi SW from San Francisco. **Climate:** subtropical, with wide variations in rainfall; Waialeale, on Kaua'i, wettest spot in U.S. (annual rainfall 444 in.) **Topography:** islands are tops of a chain of submerged volcanic mountains; active volcanoes: Mauna Loa, Kilauea. **Capital:** Honolulu.

Economy. Principal industries: tourism, defense and other government, sugar, pineapple and diversified agriculture, aquaculture, fishing, motion pictures. **Principal manufactured goods:** processed sugar, canned pineapple, clothing, foods, printing and publishing. **Agriculture. Chief crops:** sugar, pineapples, macadamia nuts, fruits, coffee, vegetables, melons, floriculture. **Livestock** (1993): 178,000 cattle and calves; 33,000 hogs/pigs; 1.01 mil chickens. **Nonfuel Minerals** (1994): $137 mil; mostly crushed stone, cement. **Commercial fishing** (1994): $62.5 mil. **Chief ports:** Honolulu, Nawiliwili, Barbers Point, Kahului, Hilo. **International airports at:** Honolulu. **Value of construction** (1994): $2.2 bil. **Employment distribution** (1993): 24.6% trade; 30.3% serv.; 20.7% govt. **Per capita personal income** (1994): $24,057. **Unemployment** (1994): 6.1%. **Tourism** (1993): visitors spent $8.7 bil.

Finance. FDIC-insured commercial banks & trust companies (1994): 16. **Deposits:** $14.0 bil. **FDIC-insured savings institutions** (1994): 5. **Assets:** $5.9 bil.

Federal government. No. federal civilian employees (Mar. 1994): 20,781. **Avg. salary:** $36,975. **Notable federal facilities:** Pearl Harbor Naval Shipyard; Hickam AFB; Schofield Barracks; Ft. Shafter; Marine Corps Base-Kaneohe Bay.

Energy. Electricity production (1994, kWh, by source): Petroleum: 6.0 bil; Hydroelectric: 19 mil.

Education. Student-teacher ratio (1993): 17.8. **Avg. salary, public school teachers** (1994-95): $38,518.

State data. Motto: The life of the land is perpetuated in righteousness. **Flower:** Yellow hibiscus. **Bird:** Hawaiian goose. **Tree:** Kukui (Candlenut). **Song:** Hawai'i Pono'i. **Entered union** Aug. 21, 1959; rank, 50th. **State farm fair** at: Honolulu; late June.

History. Polynesians from islands 2,000 mi to the south settled the Hawaiian Islands, probably between AD 300 and AD 600. First European visitor was British captain James Cook, 1778. Missionaries arrived, 1820, taught religion, reading, and writing. King Kamehameha III and his chiefs created the first constitution and a legislature that set up a public school system. Sugar production began in 1835, and it became the dominant industry. In 1893, Queen Liliuokalani was deposed, followed, 1894, by a republic headed by Sanford B. Dole. Annexation by the U.S. came in 1898.

Tourist attractions. Hawaii Volcanoes, Haleakala National Parks; National Memorial Cemetery of the Pacific; U.S.S. *Arizona* Memorial; Hanauma Bay; Polynesian Cultural Center, Waikiki Beach, Nu'uanu Pali, Bishop Museum, Waimea Canyon, Wailua River State Park.

Famous Islanders. Bernice Pauahi Bishop, John A. Burns, Father Damien de Veuster, Daniel K. Inouye, Duke Kahanamoku, King Kamehameha the Great, Queen Ka'ahumanu, Queen Liliuokalani, Ellison Onizuka.

Chamber of Commerce of Hawaii. 1132 Bishop St., Suite 200, Honolulu, HI 96813.

Toll free travel information. 1-800-257-2999.

Idaho
Gem State

People. Population (1994): 1,133,034; **rank:** 42; **Net change** (1990-94): 12.5%. **Pop. density:** 12.9 per sq mi. **Racial/ethnic distrib.** (1990): 94.4% white; 0.3% black; 5.3% Hispanic.

Geography. Total area: 83,574 sq mi; **rank:** 14. **Land area:** 82,751 sq mi. **Acres forested land:** 21,621,000. **Location:** northwestern Mountain state bordering on British Columbia. **Climate:** tempered by Pacific westerly winds; drier, colder, continental clime in SE; altitude an important factor. **Topography:** Snake R. plains in the S; central region of mountains, canyons, gorges (Hells Canyon, 7,900 ft, deepest in N. America); subalpine northern region. **Capital:** Boise.

Economy. Principal industries: agriculture, manufacturing, tourism, lumber, mining, electronics. **Principal manufactured goods:** processed foods, lumber and wood products, chemical products, primary metals, fabricated metal products, machinery, electronic components, computer equip. **Agriculture. Chief crops:** potatoes, peas, sugar beets, alfalfa seed, wheat, hops, barley, plums and prunes, mint, onions, corn, cherries, apples, hay. **Livestock** (1994): 1.7 mil cattle; 250,000 sheep & lambs; 58,000 hogs; 1.3 mil poultry. **Timber/lumber** (1993): yellow, white pine; Douglas fir; white spruce; 2.0 bil bd ft. **Nonfuel Minerals** (1994): $343 mil; phosphate rock, sand & gravel, gold, molybdenum, silver, lead. **Chief ports:** Lewiston. **Value of construction** (1994) $1.8 bil. **Employment distribution** (1994): 24% trade; 21.2% serv., 14.9% mfg.; 4.6% agric.; 6% constr. **Per capita personal income** (1994): $18,231. **Unemployment** (1994): 5.6%. **Tourism** (1994): $1.4 bil.

Finance. FDIC-insured commercial banks & trust companies (1994): 19. **Deposits:** $8.9 bil. **FDIC-insured savings institutions** (1994): 4. **Assets:** $519 mil.

Federal government. No. federal civilian employees (Mar. 1994): 7,948. **Avg. salary:** $36,554. **Notable federal facilities:** Idaho Nat'l. Engineering Lab, Idaho Falls; Mt. Home Air Force Base, Mt. Home.

Energy. Electricity production (1994, kWh, by source): Hydroelectric: 7.3 bil.

Education. Student-teacher ratio (1993): 19.7. **Avg. salary, public school teachers** (1994-95): $29,783.

State data. Motto: Esto Perpetua (It is perpetual). **Flower:** Syringa. **Bird:** Mountain bluebird. **Tree:** White pine. **Song:** Here We Have Idaho. **Entered union** July 3, 1890; rank, 43d. **State fair** at: Boise, late Aug.; and Blackfoot, early Sept.

History. Exploration of the Idaho area began with Lewis and Clark, 1805-6. Next came fur traders, setting up posts, 1809-34, and missionaries, establishing missions, 1830s-50s. Mormons made their first permanent settlement at Franklin, 1860. Idaho's Gold Rush began that same year and brought thousands of permanent settlers. Strangest of the Indian Wars was the 1,300-mi trek in 1877 of Chief Joseph and the Nez Perce tribe, pursued by troops that caught them a few miles short of the Canadian border. In 1890, Idaho adopted a progressive Constitution and became a state.

Tourist attractions. Hells Canyon, deepest gorge in N. America; World Center for Birds of Prey; Craters of the Moon; Sun Valley, year-round resort in the Sawtooth Mts.; Crystal Falls Cave; Shoshone Falls; Lava Hot Springs; Lake Pend Oreille; Lake Coeur d'Alene; Sawtooth Natl. Recreation Area; River of No Return Wilderness Area.

Famous Idahoans. William E. Borah, Frank Church, Fred T. Dubois, Chief Joseph, Sacagawea.

Tourist information. Department of Commerce, 700 W. State St., Boise, ID 83720.

Toll-free travel information. 1-800-635-7820.

Illinois
Prairie State

People. Population (1994): 11,751,774; **rank: 6; Net change** (1990-94): 2.8%. **Pop. density:** 209.2 per sq mi. **Racial/ethnic distrib.** (1990): 78.3% white; 14.8% black; 7.9% Hispanic.

Geography. Total area: 57,918 sq mi; **rank:** 25. **Land area:** 55,593 sq mi. **Acres forested land:** 4,266,000. **Location:** East North Central state; western, southern, and eastern boundaries formed by Mississippi, Ohio, and Wabash rivers, respectively. **Climate:** temperate; typically cold, snowy winters, hot summers. **Topography:** prairie and fertile plains throughout; open hills in the southern region. **Capital:** Springfield.

Economy. Principal industries: services, manufacturing, travel, wholesale and retail trade, finance, insurance, real estate, construction, health care, agriculture. **Principal manufactured goods:** machinery, electric and electronic equipment, primary and fabricated metals, chemical products, printing and publishing, food and kindred prods. **Agriculture: Chief crops:** corn, soybeans, wheat, sorghum, hay. **Livestock** (1993): 1.98 mil cattle; 5.3 mil hogs/pigs; 95,000 sheep; 3.6 mil poultry. **Timber/lumber** (1993): oak, hickory, maple, cottonwood; 85 mil bd ft. **Nonfuel Minerals** (1994): $770 mil; mostly crushed stone, cement, construction & industrial sand & gravel, lime, zinc. **Commercial fishing** (1994): $566,000. **Chief ports:** Chicago. **International airports at:** Chicago. **Value of construction** (1994): $11.9 bil. **Employment distribution** (1994): 27.7% serv.; 22.8% trade; 17.1% mfg. **Per capita personal income** (1994): $23,784. **Unemployment** (1994): 5.7%. **Tourism** (1993): out-of-state visitors spent $15 bil.

Finance. FDIC-insured commercial banks & trust companies (1994): 906. **Deposits:** $165.0 bil. **FDIC-insured savings institutions** (1994): 161. **Assets:** $44.9 bil.

Federal government. No. federal civilian employees (Mar. 1994): 50,480. **Avg. salary:** $39,501. **Notable federal facilities:** Fermi Nat'l. Accelerator Lab; Argonne Nat'l. Lab; Rock Island Arsenal; Great Lakes, Naval Training Station, Scott AFB.

Energy. Electricity production (1994, kWh, by source): Coal: 61.2 bil; Petroleum: 1.2 bil; Gas: 2.6 bil; Hydroelectric: 45 mil; Nuclear: 72.7 bil.

Education. Student-teacher ratio (1993): 17.1. **Avg. salary, public school teachers** (1994-95): $41,041.

State data. Motto: State sovereignty—national union. **Flower:** Native violet. **Bird:** Cardinal. **Tree:** White oak. **Song:** Illinois. **Entered union** Dec. 3, 1818; rank, 21st. **State fair** at: Springfield, mid-Aug.; DuQuoin, late Aug.

History. Fur traders were the first Europeans in Illinois, followed shortly, 1673, by Jolliet and Marquette, and, 1680, La Salle, who built a fort near present Peoria. First settlements were French, at Fort St. Louis on the Illinois River, 1692, and Kaskaskia, 1700. France ceded the area to Britain, 1763; American General George Rogers Clark, 1778, took Kaskaskia from the British without a shot. Defeat of Indian tribes in Black Hawk War, 1832, and railroads in 1850s, inspired change.

Tourist attractions: Chicago museums, parks; Lincoln shrines at Springfield, New Salem, Sangamon County; Cahokia Mounds, East St. Louis; Starved Rock State Park; Crab Orchard Wildlife Refuge; Mormon settlement at Nauvoo; Fts. Kaskaskia, Chartres, Massac (parks); Shawnee Natl. Forest, Southern Illinois; Illinois State Museum, Springfield; Dickson Mounds Museum, between Havana and Lewistown.

Famous Illinoisans. Jane Addams, Saul Bellow, Jack Benny, Ray Bradbury, Gwendolyn Brooks, William Jennings Bryan, St. Francis Xavier Cabrini, Hillary Rodham Clinton, Clarence Darrow, John Deere, Stephen A. Douglas, James T. Farrell, George W. Ferris, Marshall Field, Betty Friedan, Benny Goodman, Ulysses S. Grant, Ernest Hemingway, Wild Bill Hickok, Abraham Lincoln, Vachel Lindsay, Edgar Lee Masters, Oscar Mayer, Cyrus McCormick, Ronald Reagan, Carl Sandburg, Adlai Stevenson, Frank Lloyd Wright, Philip Wrigley.

Tourist information. Illinois Dept. of Commerce and Community Affairs, 620 E. Adams St., Springfield, IL 62701.

Toll-free travel information: State tourism: 1-800-223-0121; Chicago tourism: 1-800-487-2446.

Indiana
Hoosier State

People. Population (1994): 5,752,073; **rank: 14; Net change** (1990-94): 3.8%. **Pop. density:** 157.8 per sq mi. **Racial/ethnic distrib.** (1990): 90.6% white; 7.8% black; 1.8% Hispanic.

Geography. Total area: 36,420 sq mi; **rank:** 38. **Land area:** 35,870 sq mi. **Acres forested land:** 4,439,000. **Location:** East North Central state; Lake Michigan on northern border. **Climate:** 4 distinct seasons with a temperate climate. **Topography:** hilly southern region; fertile rolling plains of central region; flat, heavily glaciated north; dunes along Lake Michigan shore. **Capital:** Indianapolis.

Economy: Principal industries: manufacturing, services, agriculture, government, wholsesale and retail trade, transportation and public utilities. **Principal manufactured goods:** primary metals, transportation equipment, motor vehicles and equipment, industrial machinery and equipment, electronic and electric equipment. **Agriculture: Chief crops:** corn, wheat, soybeans, nursery and greenhouse products, vegetables, sweet corn, melons, hay. **Livestock** (1994): 1.2 mil cattle; 4.3 mil hogs/pigs; 70,000 sheep; 26.4 mil chickens; 14.6 mil turkeys. **Timber/lumber** (1993): oak, tulip, beech, sycamore; 351 mil bd ft. **Nonfuel Minerals** (1994): $517 mil; mostly crushed stone, cement, construction sand & gravel. **Commercial fishing** (1994): $1.9 mil. **Chief ports:** Burns Harbor, Portage; Southwind Maritime, Mt. Vernon; Clark Maritime, Jeffersonville. **International airports at:** Indianapolis, Ft. Wayne. **Value of construction** (1994): $7.7 bil. **Employment distribution** (1994): 25.5% mfg.; 24.7% trade; 21.5% serv; 12.2% govt. **Per capita personal income** (1994): $20,378. **Unemployment** (1994): 4.9%. **Tourism** (1993): tourists spent $4.4 bil.

Finance. FDIC-insured commercial banks & trust companies (1994): 222. **Deposits:** $50.2 bil. **FDIC-insured savings institutions** (1994): 82. **Assets:** $14.5 bil.

Federal government. No. federal civilian employees (Mar. 1994): 25,069. **Avg. salary:** $36,387. **Notable federal facilities:** Naval Air Warfare Center; Ft. Benjamin Harrison; Del. Grissom AFB; Naval Surface Warfare Center, Crane.

Energy. Electricity production (1994, kWh, by source): Coal: 102.0 bil; Petroleum: 209 mil; Gas: 826 mil; Hydroelectric: 407 mil.

Education. Student-teacher ratio (1993): 17.5. **Avg. salary, public school teachers** (1994-95): $36,516.

State data. Motto: Crossroads of America. **Flower:** Peony. **Bird:** Cardinal. **Tree:** Tulip poplar. **Song:** On the Banks of the Wabash, Far Away. **Entered union** Dec. 11, 1816; rank, 19th. **State fair** at Indianapolis; mid-Aug.

History. Prehistoric Indian Mound Builders of 1,000 years ago were the earliest known inhabitants. A French trading post was built, 1731-32, at Vincennes. La Salle visited the present South Bend area, 1679 and 1681. France ceded the area to Britain, 1763. During the American Revolution, American Gen. George Rogers Clark captured Vincennes, 1778, and defeated British forces 1779. At war's end Britain ceded the area to the U.S. Miami Indians defeated U.S. troops twice, 1790, but were beaten, 1794, at Fallen Timbers by Gen. Anthony Wayne. At Tippecanoe, 1811, Gen. William H. Harrison defeated Tecumseh's Indian confederation.

Tourist attractions. Lincoln boyhood, George Rogers Clark memorials; Wyandotte Cave; Vincennes, Tippecanoe sites; Indiana Dunes; Hoosier Natl. Forest; Benjamin Harrison Home; Indiana Basketball Hall of Fame, New Castle; Dan Quayle Museum, Huntington; Indianapolis 500 race and museum.

Famous "Hoosiers." Larry Bird, Ambrose Burnside, Hoagy Carmichael, Jim Davis, James Dean, Eugene V.

Debs, Theodore Dreiser, Paul Dresser, Gil Hodges, David Letterman, Jane Pauley, Cole Porter, Gene Stratton Porter, Ernie Pyle, James Whitcomb Riley, Oscar Robertson, Red Skelton, Booth Tarkington, Kurt Vonnegut, Lew Wallace, Wendell L. Willkie, Wilbur Wright.

Chamber of Commerce. One North Capital, Suite 200, Indianapolis, IN 46204.

Toll-free travel information. 1-800-289-6646.

Iowa
Hawkeye State

People. Population (1994): 2,829,252; **rank: 30; Net change** (1990-94): 1.9%. **Pop. density:** 50.3 per sq mi. **Racial/ethnic distrib.** (1990): 96.6% white; 1.7% black; 1.2% Hispanic.

Geography. Total area: 56,276 sq mi; **rank: 26. Land area:** 55,875 sq mi. **Acres forested land:** 2,050,000. **Location:** West North Central state bordered by Mississippi R. on the E and Missouri R. on the W. **Climate:** humid, continental. **Topography:** Watershed from NW to SE; soil especially rich and land level in the N central counties. **Capital:** Des Moines.

Economy. Principal industries: agriculture, communications, construction, finance, insurance, trade, services, mfg. **Principal manufactured goods:** tires, farm machinery, electronic products, appliances, household furniture, chemicals, fertilizers, auto accessories. **Agriculture: Chief crops:** silage and grain corn, soybeans, oats, hay. **Livestock** (1994): 4.1 mil cattle; 15.0 mil swine; 320,000 sheep & lambs; 8.8 mil turkeys. **Timber/lumber** (1993): red cedar; 61 mil bd ft. **Nonfuel Minerals** (1994): $426 mil; mostly crushed stone, portland cement, construction sand & gravel, gypsum. **International airports at:** Covington, Louisville. **Value of construction** (1994): 2.7 bil. **Employment distribution** (1994, total non-agricultural): 23.7% trade; 26.3% serv.; 19% mfg.; 17.6% govt. **Per capita personal income** (1994): $17,807. **Unemployment** (1994): 5.4%. **Tourism** (1994): tourists spent $6.8 bil.

Finance. FDIC-insured commercial banks & trust companies (1994): 517. **Deposits:** $31.9 bil. **FDIC-insured savings institutions** (1994): 33. **Assets:** $5.3 bil.

Federal government. No. federal civilian employees (Mar. 1994): 7,848. **Avg. salary:** $35,235.

Energy. Electricity production (1994, kWh, by source): Coal: 26.5 bil; Petroleum: 78 mil; Gas: 199 mil; Hydroelectric: 1.0 bil; Nuclear: 4.1 bil.

Education. Student-teacher ratio (1993): 15.8. **Avg. salary, public school teachers** (1994-95): $31,511.

State data. Motto: Our liberties we prize and our rights we will maintain. **Flower:** Wild rose. **Bird:** Eastern goldfinch. **Tree:** Oak. **Rock:** Geode. **Entered union** Dec. 28, 1846; rank, 29th. **State fair** at: Des Moines; mid-Aug.

History. A thousand years ago several groups of prehistoric Indian Mound Builders dwelt on Iowa's fertile plains. Marquette and Jolliet gave France its claim to the area, 1673. It became U.S. territory through the 1803 Louisiana Purchase. Indian tribes were moved into the area from states further east, but by mid-19th century were forced to move on to Kansas. Before and during the Civil War, Iowans strongly supported Abraham Lincoln and became traditional Republicans.

Tourist attractions. Herbert Hoover birthplace and library, West Branch; Effigy Mounds National Monument, Marquette, a prehistoric Indian burial site; Amana Colonies; Davenport Municipal Art Gallery's collection of Grant Wood's paintings and memorabilia; Living History Farms, Des Moines; Adventureland, Altoona; Boone & Scenic Valley Railroad, Boone; Greyhound Parks in Dubuque, Council Bluffs & Waterloo; Prairie Meadows horse racing, Altoona; riverboat cruises and casino gambling, Mississippi River; Iowa Great Lakes, Okoboji.

Famous Iowans. James A. Van Allen, Marquis Childs, Buffalo Bill Cody, Mamie Dowd Eisenhower, George Gallup, Susan Glaspell, James Norman Hall, Harry Hansen, Herbert Hoover, Glenn Miller, Billy Sunday, Carl Van Vechten, Henry Wallace, John Wayne, Meredith Willson, Grant Wood.

Tourist information. Division of Tourism, Iowa Dept. of Economic Development, 200 E. Grand Ave., Des Moines, IA 50309.

Toll-free travel information. 1-800-345-IOWA.

Kansas
Sunflower State

People. Population (1994): 2,554,047; **rank: 32; Net change** (1990-94): 3.1%. **Pop. density:** 30.8 per sq mi. **Racial/ethnic distrib.** (1990): 90.1% white; 5.8% black; 3.8% Hispanic.

Geography. Total area: 82,282 sq mi; **rank: 15. Land area:** 81,823 sq mi. **Acres forested land:** 1,359,000. **Location:** West North Central state, with Missouri R. on E. **Climate:** temperate but continental, with great extremes between summer and winter. **Topography:** hilly Osage Plains in the E; central region level prairie and hills; high plains in the W. **Capital:** Topeka.

Economy. Principal industries: manufacturing, finance, insurance, real estate, services. **Principal manufactured goods:** transportation equip., machinery and computer equipment, food and kindred products, printing and publishing. **Agriculture: Chief crops:** wheat, sorghum, corn, hay, soybeans. **Chief products:** wheat flour, red meat, sorghum silage, sunflowers. **Livestock** (1994): 6.3 mil cattle; 1.3 mil hogs/pigs; 155,000 sheep & lambs; 1.8 mil poultry. **Timber/lumber** (1994): oak, walnut; 10 mil bd ft. **Nonfuel Minerals** (1994): $495 mil; salt, helium, cement, crushed stone, sand & gravel. **Chief ports:** Kansas City. **International airports at:** Wichita. **Value of construction** (1994): $3.1 bil. **Employment distribution** (1994): 24.2% trade; 23.7% serv.; 20% govt.; 16.1% mfg. **Per capita personal income** (1994): $20,896. **Unemployment** (1994): 5.3%. **Tourism** (1991): out-of-state visitors spent $2.1 bil.

Finance. FDIC-insured commercial banks & trust companies (1994): 458. **Deposits:** $25.5 bil. **FDIC-insured savings institutions** (1994): 24. **Assets:** $7.6 bil.

Federal government. No. federal civilian employees (Mar. 1994): 16,262. **Avg. salary:** $35,979. **Notable federal facilities:** Fts. Riley, Leavenworth, Leavenworth Federal Penitentiary, Colmery-O'Neal Veterans Hospital.

Energy. Electricity production (1994, kWh, by source): Coal: 26.5 bil; Petroleum: 83 mil; Gas: 2.2 bil; Nuclear: 8.5 bil.

Education. Student-teacher ratio (1993): 15.1. **Avg. salary, public school teachers** (1994-95): $34,936.

State data. Motto: Ad Astra per Aspera (To the stars through difficulties). **Flower:** Native sunflower. **Bird:** Western meadowlark. **Tree:** Cottonwood. **Song:** Home on the Range. **Entered union** Jan. 29, 1861; rank, 34th. **State fair** at: Hutchinson; begins Friday after Labor Day.

History. Coronado marched through the Kansas area, 1541; French explorers came next. The U.S. took over in the Louisiana Purchase, 1803. In the pre-war North-South struggle over slavery, so much violence swept the area that it was called Bleeding Kansas. Railroad construction after the war made Abilene and Dodge City terminals of large cattle drives from Texas.

Tourist attractions. Eisenhower Center and "Place of Meditation," Abilene; Agricultural Hall of Fame and National Center, Bonner Springs, displays farm equipment; Dodge City-Boot Hill & Frontier Town; Cowtown historic frontier town, Wichita; Ft. Scott and Ft. Larned, restored 1800s cavalry forts; Kansas Cosmosphere and Space Discovery Center, Hutchinson; Woodlands Racetrack, Kansas City; Wichita Greyhound Park, Wichita; U.S. Cavalry Museum, Ft. Riley; NCAA Visitors Center, Shawnee; Heartland Park Raceway, Topeka.

Famous Kansans. Ed Asner, Thomas Hart Benton, John Brown, Walter P. Chrysler, Glen Cunningham, John Steuart Curry, Robert Dole, Amelia Earhart, Dwight D. Eisenhower, Ron Evans, Wild Bill Hickok, Cyrus Holliday, Dennis Hopper, William Inge, Walter Johnson, Alf Landon, Buster Keaton, Emmett Kelly, Hattie McDaniel, Oscar Micheaux, Carrie Nation, Georgia Neese-Gray, Gordon Parks, Jim Ryun, Barry Sanders, Vivian Vance, William Allen White, Jess Willard.

Tourist Information. Kansas Dept. of Commerce & Housing, Travel and Tourism Div., 700 SW Harrison, Suite 1300, Topeka, KS 66603; 1-913-296-2009. **Toll-free travel information.** 1-800-2KANSAS.

Kentucky
Bluegrass State

People. Population (1994): 3,826,794; **rank:** 24; **Net change** (1990-94): 3.8%. **Pop. density:** 94.5 per sq mi. **Racial/ethnic distrib.** (1990): 92.0% white; 7.1% black; 0.6% Hispanic.

Geography. Total area: 40,411 sq mi; **rank:** 37. **Land area:** 39,732 sq mi. **Acres forested land:** 12,714,000. **Location:** East South Central state, bordered on N by Illinois, Indiana, Ohio; on E by West Virginia and Virginia; on S by Tennessee; on W by Missouri. **Climate:** moderate, with plentiful rainfall. **Topography:** mountainous in E; rounded hills of the Knobs in the N; Bluegrass, heart of state; wooded rocky hillsides of the Pennyroyal; Western Coal Field; the fertile Purchase in the SW. **Capital:** Frankfort.

Economy. Principal industries: manufacturing; finance, insurance and real estate; services; retail trade. **Principal manufactured goods:** industrial machinery, apparel, electic/electronic equip., transportation equip., food products, fabricated metals. **Agriculture: Chief crops:** tobacco, corn, soybeans. **Livestock** (1994): 2.6 mil cattle; 850,000 hogs/pigs; 27,000 sheep; 3.5 mil chickens; 1993 receipts for horse & mule sales, $431 mil. **Timber/lumber** (1993): hardwoods, pines; 761 mil bd ft. **Nonfuel Minerals** (1994): $431 mil; mostly crushed stone, lime, cement, sand & gravel. **Chief ports:** Paducah, Louisville, Covington, Owensboro, Ashland, Henderson County, Lyon County, Hickman-Fulton County. **International airports at:** Covington. **Value of construction** (1994): $4.3 bil. **Employment distribution** (1993): 22.9% serv.; 22.8% trade; 18.5% mfg.; 17.5% govt. **Per capita personal income** (1994): $17,807. **Unemployment** (1994): 5.4%. **Tourism** (1993): tourists spent $6.8 bil.

Finance. FDIC-insured commercial banks & trust companies (1994): 287. **Deposits:** $37.4 bil. **FDIC-insured savings institutions** (1994): 52. **Assets:** $5.9 bil.

Federal government. No. federal civilian employees (Mar. 1994): 26,487. **Avg. salary:** $32,102. **Notable federal facilities:** U.S. Gold Bullion Depository, Fort Knox; Federal Correctional Institution, Lexington.

Energy. Electricity production (1994, kWh, by source): Coal: 79.9 bil; Petroleum: 154 mil; Gas: 31 mil; Hydroelectric: 4.0 bil.

Education. Student-teacher ratio (1993): 17.6. **Avg. salary, public school teachers** (1994-95): $32,257.

State data. Motto: United we stand, divided we fall. **Flower:** Goldenrod. **Bird:** Cardinal. **Tree:** Kentucky coffee tree. **Song:** My Old Kentucky Home. **Entered union** June 1, 1792; **rank**, 15th. **State fair** at: Louisville.

History. Kentucky was the first area west of the Alleghenies settled by American pioneers, first permanent settlement, Harrodsburg, 1774. Daniel Boone blazed the Wilderness Trail through the Cumberland Gap and founded Fort Boonesborough, 1775. Indian attacks, spurred by the British, were unceasing until, during the American Revolution, Gen. George Rogers Clark captured British forts in Indiana and Illinois, 1778. In 1792, after Virginia dropped its claims to the region, Kentucky became the 15th state.

Tourist attractions. Kentucky Derby and accompanying festivities, Louisville; Land Between the Lakes Nat'l. Recreation Area encompassing Kentucky Lake and Lake Barkley; Mammoth Cave National Park with 330 mi of explored passageways, 200-ft high rooms, blind fish, and Echo River, 360 ft below ground; Lake Cumberland in south central Kentucky; Lincoln birthplace, Hodgenville; My Old Kentucky Home, Bardstown; Cumberland Gap Natl. Historical Park, Middlesboro; Kentucky Horse Park, Lexington; Shaker Village, Pleasant Hill.

Famous Kentuckians. Muhammad Ali (Cassius Marcellus Clay), John James Audubon, Alben Barkley, Daniel Boone, Louis D. Brandeis, John C. Breckinridge, Kit Carson, Albert B. "Happy" Chandler, Henry Clay, Jefferson Davis, "Casey" Jones, Abraham Lincoln, Mary Todd Lincoln, Thomas Hunt Morgan, Carrie Nation, Col. Harland Sanders, Diane Sawyer, Jesse Stuart, Adlai Stevenson, Zachary Taylor, Robert Penn Warren, Whitney Young, Jr.

Chamber of Commerce. 452 Versailles Rd., PO Box 817, Frankfort, KY 40602.

Toll-free travel information. 1-800-225-TRIP.

Louisiana
Pelican State

People. Population (1994): 4,315,085; **rank:** 21; **Net change** (1990-94): 2.2%. **Pop. density:** 98.4 per sq mi. **Racial/ethnic distrib.** (1990): 67.3% white; 30.8% black; 2.2% Hispanic.

Geography. Total area: 51,843 sq mi; **rank:** 31. **Land area:** 43,566 sq mi. **Acres forested land:** 13,864,000. **Location:** West South Central state on the Gulf Coast. **Climate:** subtropical, affected by continental weather patterns. **Topography:** lowlands of marshes and Mississippi R. flood plain; Red R. Valley lowlands; upland hills in the Florida Parishes; average elevation, 100 ft **Capital:** Baton Rouge.

Economy. Principal industries: wholesale and retail trade, tourism, government, manufacturing, construction, transportation, mining. **Principal manufactured goods:** chemical products, foods, transportation equipment, electronic equipment, petroleum products, lumber, wood, and paper. **Agriculture: Chief crops:** soybeans, sugarcane, rice, corn, cotton, sweet potatoes, pecans, sorghum, aquaculture. **Livestock** (1994): 930,000 cattle; 45,000 hogs/pigs; 14,500 sheep; 2.5 mil poultry. **Timber/lumber** (1993): pines, hardwoods, oak; 1.39 bil bd ft. **Nonfuel Minerals** (1994): $328 mil; mostly salt, construction sand & gravel, sulfur. **Commercial fishing** (1994): $336.3 mil. **Chief ports:** New Orleans, Baton Rouge, Lake Charles, S. Louisiana Port Commission at La Place, Shreveport. **International airports at:** New Orleans. **Value of construction** (1994): $4.1 bil. **Employment distribution** (June 1995): 23.2% trade; 26.4% service; 19.3% govt.; 10.7% mfg. **Per capita personal income** (1994): $17,651. **Unemployment** (1994): 8.0%. **Tourism** (1992): out-of-state visitors spent $5.2 bil.

Finance. FDIC-insured commercial banks & trust companies (1994): 200. **Deposits:** $35.5 bil. **FDIC-insured savings institutions** (1994): 40. **Assets:** $4.5 bil.

Federal government. No. federal civilian employees (Mar. 1994): 21,698. **Avg. salary:** $34,888. **Notable federal facilities:** Barksdale, Ft. Polk military bases; Strategic Petroleum Reserve, New Orleans; Michoud Assembly Plant, New Orleans; U.S. Public Service Hospital, Carville.

Energy. Electricity production (1994, kWh, by source): Coal: 20.1 bil; Petroleum: 680 mil; Gas: 26.6 bil; Nuclear: 12.4 bil.

Education. Student-teacher ratio (1993): 16.6. **Avg. salary, public school teachers** (1994-95): $26,574.

State data. Motto: Union, justice and confidence. **Flower:** Magnolia. **Bird:** Eastern brown pelican. **Tree:** Cypress. **Song:** Give Me Louisiana. **Entered union** Apr. 30, 1812; **rank**, 18th. **State fair** at: Shreveport; Oct.

History. The area was first visited, 1530, by Cabeza de Vaca and Panfilo de Narvaez. The region was claimed for France by La Salle, 1682. First permanent settlement was by French at Biloxi, now in Mississippi, 1699. France ceded the region to Spain, 1762, took it back, 1800, and sold it to the U.S., 1803, in the Louisiana Purchase. During the American Revolution, Spanish Louisiana aided the Americans. Admitted to statehood, 1812, Louisiana was the scene of the Battle of New Orleans, 1815.

Louisiana Creoles are descendants of early French and/or Spanish settlers. About 4,000 Acadians, French settlers in Nova Scotia, Canada, were forcibly transported by the British to Louisiana in 1755 (an event commemorated in Longfellow's *Evangeline*) and settled near Bayou Teche; their descendants became known as Cajuns. Another group, the Islenos, were descendants of

Canary Islanders brought to Louisiana by a Spanish governor in 1770. Traces of Spanish and French survive in local dialects.

Tourist attractions. Mardi Gras, French Quarter, Superdome, Dixieland jazz, Aquarium of the Americas, all New Orleans; Battle of New Orleans site; Longfellow-Evangeline Memorial Park; Kent House Museum, Alexandria; Hodges Gardens, Natchitoches.

Famous Louisianans. Louis Armstrong, Pierre Beauregard, Judah P. Benjamin, Braxton Bragg, Grace King, Huey Long, Leonidas K. Polk, Henry Miller Shreve, Edward D. White, Jr.

Tourist information. State Dept. of Culture, Recreation & Tourism, PO Box 94291, Baton Rouge, LA 70804-9291.

Toll-free travel information. 1-800-33GUMBO.

Maine
Pine Tree State

People. Population (1994): 1,240,209; **rank:** 39; **Net change** (1990-94): 1.0%. **Pop. density:** 40.0 per sq mi. **Racial/ethnic distrib.** (1990): 98.4% white; 0.4% black; 0.6% Hispanic.

Geography. Total area: 35,387 sq mi; **rank:** 39. **Land area:** 30,865 sq mi. **Acres forested land:** 17,533,000. **Location:** New England state at northeastern tip of U.S. **Climate:** Southern interior and coastal, influenced by air masses from the S and W; northern clime harsher, avg. + 100 in. snow in winter. **Topography:** Appalachian Mts. extend through state; western borders have rugged terrain; long sand beaches on southern coast; northern coast mainly rocky promontories, peninsulas, fjords. **Capital:** Augusta.

Economy. Principal industries: manufacturing, agriculture, fishing, services, trade, government, finance, insurance, real estate, construction. **Principal manufactured goods:** paper and wood products, transportation equipment. **Agriculture: Chief crops:** potatoes, apples, hay, blueberries. **Livestock** (1993): 114,000 cattle; 9,000 hogs/pigs; 18,000 sheep; 5.8 mil poultry. **Timber/lumber** (1993): pine, spruce, fir; 1.06 bil bd ft. **Nonfuel Minerals** (1994): $58 mil; cement, construction sand & gravel, crushed stone. **Commercial fishing** (1994): $243.3 mil. **Chief ports:** Searsport, Portland, Eastport. **International airports at:** Portland, Bangor. **Value of construction** (1994): $1.1 bil. **Employment distribution** (1993): 25.8% serv.; 25.1% trade; 18.3% govt.; 17.6% mfg. **Per capita personal income** (1994): $19,663. **Unemployment** (1994): 7.4%. **Tourism** (1991): $2.75 bil.

Finance. FDIC-insured commercial banks & trust companies (1994): 20. **Deposits:** $6.9 bil. **FDIC-insured savings institutions** (1994): 30. **Assets:** $6.6 bil.

Federal government. No. federal civilian employees (Mar. 1994): 9,558. **Avg. salary:** $35,875. **Notable federal facilities:** Kittery Naval Shipyard; Brunswick Naval Air Station.

Energy. Electricity production (1994, kWh, by source): Petroleum: 702 mil; Hydroelectric: 1.7 bil; Nuclear: 6.6 bil.

Education. Student-teacher ratio (1993): 14.1. **Avg. salary, public school teachers** (1994-95): $31,856.

State data. Motto: Dirigo (I direct). **Flower:** White pine cone and tassel. **Bird:** Chickadee. **Tree:** Eastern white pine. **Song:** State of Maine Song. **Entered union** Mar. 15, 1820; rank, 23d.

History. Maine's rocky coast was explored by the Cabots, 1498-99. French settlers arrived, 1604, at the St. Croix River; English, 1607, on the Kennebec. In 1691, Maine was made part of Massachusetts. In the American Revolution, a Maine regiment fought at Bunker Hill; a British fleet destroyed Falmouth (now Portland), 1775, but the British ship Margaretta was captured near Machiasport. In 1820, Maine broke off from Massachusetts and became a separate state.

Tourist attractions. Acadia National Park, Bar Harbor, on Mt. Desert Island; Old Orchard Beach; Portland's Old Port; Kennebunkport; Common Ground Country Fair;

Portland Headlight; Baxter State Park; Freeport; Camden.

Famous "Down Easters." James G. Blaine, Cyrus H. K. Curtis, Hannibal Hamlin, Stephen King, Henry Wadsworth, Longfellow, Sir Hiram and Hudson Maxim, Edna St. Vincent Millay, Edmund Muskie, Kate Douglas Wiggin, Ben Ames Williams.

Chamber of Commerce and Industry. 126 Sewall St., Augusta, ME 04330.

Toll-free travel information. 1-800-533-9595, out of state only.

Maryland
Old Line State, Free State

People. Population (1994): 5,006,265; **rank:** 19; **Net change** (1990-94): 4.7%. **Pop. density:** 502.1 per sq mi. **Racial/ethnic distrib.** (1990): 71.0% white; 24.9% black; 2.9% Asian; 2.6% Hispanic.

Geography. Total area: 12,407 sq mi; **rank:** 42. **Land area:** 9,775 sq mi. **Acres forested land:** 2,700,000. **Location:** South Atlantic state stretching from the Ocean to the Allegheny Mts. **Climate:** continental in the west; humid subtropical in the east. **Topography:** Eastern Shore of coastal plain and Maryland Main of coastal plain, piedmont plateau, and the Blue Ridge, separated by the Chesapeake Bay. **Capital:** Annapolis.

Economy. Principal industries: manufacturing, biotechnology and information technology, services, tourism. **Principal manufactured goods:** electric and electronic equipment; food and kindred products; chemicals and allied products; printed materials. **Agriculture: Chief crops:** greenhouse and nursery prods., soybeans, corn. **Livestock** (1994): 315,000 cattle; 120,000 hogs/pigs; 25,000 sheep; 3.23 mil layers; 285 mil broilers. **Timber/lumber:** hardwoods; 242 mil bd ft. **Nonfuel Minerals** (1994): $325 mil; crushed stone, sand & gravel, portland cement. **Commercial fishing** (1994): $61.0 mil. **Chief port:** Baltimore. **International airports at:** Baltimore-Washington Intl. **Value of construction** (1994): $6.3 bil. **Employment distribution** (1993): 30.0% service; 24.3% trade; 19.3% govt. **Per capita personal income** (1994): $24,933. **Unemployment** (1994): 5.1%. **Tourism** (1994): tourists spent $5.7 bil.

Finance. FDIC-insured commercial banks & trust companies (1994): 93. **Deposits:** $67.9 bil. **FDIC-insured savings institutions** (1994): 82. **Assets:** $16.5 bil.

Federal government. No. federal civilian employees (Mar. 1994): 107,634. **Avg. salary:** $44,391. **Notable federal facilities:** U.S. Naval Academy, Annapolis; Natl. Agriculture Research Center; Ft. George G. Meade, Aberdeen Proving Ground; Goddard Space Flight Center; Natl. Institutes of Health; Natl. Institute of Standards & Technology; Food & Drug Administration; Bureau of the Census.

Energy. Electricity production (1994, kWh, by source): Coal: 25.4 bil; Petroleum: 4.1 bil; Gas: 993 mil; Hydroelectric: 2.0 bil; Nuclear: 11.2 bil.

Education. Student-teacher ratio (1993): 17.5. **Avg. salary, public school teachers** (1994-95): $40,636.

State data. Motto: Fatti Maschii, Parole Femine (Manly deeds, womanly words). **Flower:** Black-eyed susan. **Bird:** Baltimore oriole. **Tree:** White oak. **Song:** Maryland, My Maryland. **Seventh** of the original 13 states to ratify Constitution, Apr. 28, 1788. **State fair** at: Timonium; late Aug.–early Sept.

History. Capt. John Smith first explored Maryland, 1608. William Claiborne set up a trading post on Kent Island in Chesapeake Bay, 1631. Britain granted land to Cecilius Calvert, Lord Baltimore, 1632; his brother led 200 settlers to St. Marys River, 1634. The bravery of Maryland troops in the American Revolution, as at the Battle of Long Island, won the state its nickname The Old Line State. In the War of 1812, when a British fleet tried to take Fort McHenry, Marylander Francis Scott Key, 1814, wrote "The Star-Spangled Banner."

Tourist attractions. Racing events include the Preakness and Maryland Million, both at Pimlico track, Baltimore, and the International at Laurel Race Course; Baltimore Orioles pro baseball at Oriole Park, Camden

Yards. Also Annapolis yacht races; Ocean City beach resort; restored Ft. McHenry, Baltimore, near which Francis Scott Key wrote "The Star-Spangled Banner;" Antietam Battlefield, 1862, near Hagerstown; South Mountain Battlefield, 1862; Edgar Allan Poe house, Baltimore; National Aquarium, Baltimore Harborplace; The State House, Annapolis, 1772, the oldest still in use in the U.S.; Montgomery & Prince George's County, gateway to Washington, DC.

Famous Marylanders. John Astin, Benjamin Banneker, Tom Clancy, Jonathan Demme, Francis Scott Key, H. L. Mencken, Charles Willson Peale, William Pinkney, Upton Sinclair, Roger B. Taney.

Maryland Dept. of Business & Employment Development. 217 E. Redwood St., Baltimore, MD 21202; (410) 333-6970.

Toll-free travel information. 1-800-543-1036.

Massachusetts
Bay State, Old Colony

People. Population (1994): 6,041,123; **rank:** 13; **Net change** (1990-94): 0.4%. **Pop. density:** 765.3 per sq mi. **Racial/ethnic distrib.** (1990): 89.8% white; 5.0% black; 2.4% Asian; 4.8% Hispanic.

Geography. Total area: 10,555 sq mi; **rank:** 44. **Land area:** 7,838 sq mi. **Acres forested land:** 3,203,000. **Location:** New England state along Atlantic seaboard. **Climate:** temperate, with colder and drier clime in western region. **Topography:** jagged indented coast from Rhode Island around Cape Cod; flat land yields to stony upland pastures near central region and gentle hilly country in west; except in west, land is rocky, sandy, and not fertile. **Capital:** Boston.

Economy. Principal industries: services, trade, manufacturing. **Principal manufactured goods:** electric and electronic equipment, machinery, industrial machinery and equipment, printing and publishing, fabricated metal products. **Agriculture. Chief crops:** cranberries, greenhouse, nursery, vegetables. **Livestock** (1983): 120,000 cattle; 50,000 hogs/pigs; 8,000 sheep; 125,000 horses, ponies; 3.6 mil poultry. **Timber/lumber** (1993): white pine, oak, other hard woods; 99 mil bd ft. **Nonfuel Minerals** (1994): $157 mil; mostly crushed stone, construction sand & gravel. **Commercial fishing** (1994): $206 mil. **Chief ports:** Boston, Fall River, New Bedford, Salem, Gloucester, Plymouth. **International airports at:** Boston. **Value of construction** (1994): $6.5 bil. **Employment distribution** (1994): 23% trade; 33.5% serv.; 15.4% mfg.; 13.5% govt. **Per capita personal income** (1994): $25,616. **Unemployment** (1994): 6.0%. **Tourism** (1993): out-of-state visitors spent $7.35 bil.

Finance. FDIC-insured commercial banks & trust companies (1994): 53. **Deposits:** $77.6 bil. **FDIC-insured savings institutions** (1994): 212. **Assets:** $50.6 bil.

Federal government. No. federal civilian employees (Mar. 1994): 31,286. **Avg. salary:** $39,622. **Notable federal facilities:** Ft. Devens; Thomas P. O'Neill Jr. Federal Bldg., J.W. McCormack Bldg., John Fitzgerald Kennedy Federal Bldg., Boston; Q.M. Laboratory, Natick.

Energy. Electricity production (1994, kWh, by source): Coal: 10.2 bil; Petroleum: 9.6 bil; Gas: 3.7 bil; Hydroelectric: 100 mil; Nuclear: 3.9 bil.

Education. Student-teacher ratio (1993): 14.9. **Avg. salary, public school teachers** (1994-95): $42,078.

State data. Motto: Ense Petit Placidam Sub Libertate Quietem (By the sword we seek peace, but peace only under liberty). **Flower:** Mayflower. **Bird:** Chickadee. **Tree:** American elm. **Song:** All Hail to Massachusetts. **Sixth** of the original 13 states to ratify Constitution, Feb. 6, 1788.

History. Pilgrims settled in Plymouth, 1620; the following year they gave thanks for their survival with the first Thanksgiving Day. Indian opposition reached a high point in King Philip's War, 1675-76, won by the colonists. Demonstrations against British restrictions set off the "Boston Massacre," 1770, and Boston "tea party," 1773. First bloodshed of the American Revolution was at Lexington, 1775.

Tourist attractions. Provincetown artists colony, Cape Cod; Plymouth Rock, Plymouth Plantation, Mayflower II, all Plymouth; Freedom Trail, Museum of Fine Arts, Children's Museum, Museum of Science, New England Aquarium, JFK Library, Boston Ballet, Boston Pops, Boston Symphony Orchestra, all Boston; Tanglewood, Jacob's Pillow Dance Festival, Hancock Shaker Village Berkshire Scenic Railroad, all in the Berkshires; Old Sturbridge Village; Deerfield Historic District; Walden Pond; Naismith Memorial Basketball Hall of Fame, Springfield; Salem.

Famous "Bay Staters." John Adams, John Quincy Adams, Samuel Adams, Louisa May Alcott, Horatio Alger, Susan B. Anthony, Crispus Attucks, Clara Barton, Alexander Graham Bell, Stephen Breyer, Emily Dickinson, Ralph Waldo Emerson, John Hancock, Nathaniel Hawthorne, Oliver W. Holmes, Winslow Homer, Elias Howe, John Fitzgerald Kennedy, Samuel F. B. Morse, Edgar Allan Poe, Paul Revere, Henry David Thoreau, James McNeil Whistler, John Greenleaf Whittier.

Tourist information. Massachusetts Office of Travel & Tourism, 100 Cambridge St., 13th Floor, Boston, MA 02202.

Toll-free travel information. 1-800-447-MASS.

Michigan
Great Lakes State, Wolverine State

People. Population (1994): 9,496,147; **rank:** 8; **Net change** (1990-94): 2.2%. **Pop. density:** 166.1 per sq mi. **Racial/ethnic distrib.** (1990): 83.4% white; 13.9% black; 2.2% Hispanic.

Geography. Total area: 96,705 sq mi; **rank:** 11. **Land area:** 56,809 sq mi. **Acres forested land:** 18,253,000. **Location:** East North Central state bordering on 4 of the 5 Great Lakes, divided into an Upper and Lower Peninsula by the Straits of Mackinac, which link lakes Michigan and Huron. **Climate:** well-defined seasons tempered by the Great Lakes. **Topography:** low rolling hills give way to northern tableland of hilly belts in Lower Peninsula; Upper Peninsula is level in the east, with swampy areas; western region is higher and more rugged. **Capital:** Lansing.

Economy. Principal industries: manufacturing, services, tourism, agriculture, mining. **Principal manufactured goods:** automobiles, transportation equipment, machinery, fabricated metals, food prods., plastics, office furniture. **Agriculture. Chief crops:** corn, winter wheat, soybeans, dry beans, oats, hay, sugar beets, honey, asparagus, sweet corn, apples, cherries, grapes, peaches, blueberries, flowers. **Livestock** (1992): 1.2 mil cattle; 1.3 mil hogs/pigs; 103,000 sheep; 11.5 mil poultry. **Timber/lumber** (1993): maple, oak, aspen; 627 mil bd ft. **Nonfuel Minerals** (1994): $1.6 bil; iron ore, magnesium compounds, portland cement, sand & gravel, crushed stone. **Commercial fishing** (1994): $9.3 mil. **Chief ports:** Detroit, Saginaw River, Escanaba, Muskegon, Sault Ste. Marie, Port Huron, Marine City. **International airports at:** Detroit, Grand Rapids, Flint, Kalamazoo, Lansing, Saginaw. **Value of construction** (1994): $9.6 bil. **Employment distribution** (1992): 23% mfg.; 24% serv. **Per capita personal income** (1994): $22,333. **Unemployment** (1994): 5.9%. **Tourism** (1990): travelers spent $16.5 bil.

Finance. FDIC-insured commercial banks & trust companies (1994): 200. **Deposits:** $87.0 bil. **FDIC-insured savings institutions** (1994): 31. **Assets:** $30.5 bil.

Federal government. No. federal civilian employees (Mar. 1994): 25,183. **Avg. salary:** $38,617. **Notable federal facilities:** Isle Royal, Sleeping Bear Dunes national parks.

Energy. Electricity production (1994, kWh, by source): Coal: 67.5 bil; Petroleum: 556 mil; Gas: 657 mil; Hydroelectric: 725 mil; Nuclear: 14.1 bil.

Education. Student-teacher ratio (1993): 19.9. **Avg. salary, public school teachers** (1994-95): $47,412.

State data. Motto: Si Quaeris Peninsulam Amoenam Circumspice (If you seek a pleasant peninsula, look about you). **Flower:** Apple blossom. **Bird:** Robin. **Tree:** White pine. **Song:** Michigan, My Michigan. **Entered union** Jan. 26, 1837; **rank,** 26th. **State fair** at: Detroit, late

Aug.–early Sept.; Upper Peninsula (Escanaba), mid-Aug; Michigan Festival, mid.-Aug.

History. French fur traders and missionaries visited the region, 1616, set up a mission at Sault Ste. Marie, 1641, and a settlement there, 1668. The whole region went to Britain, 1763. Anthony Wayne defeated their Indian allies at Fallen Timbers, Ohio, 1794. The British returned, 1812, seized Ft. Mackinac and Detroit. Oliver H. Perry's Lake Erie victory and William H. Harrison's troops, who carried the war to the Thames River in Canada, 1813, freed Michigan once more.

Tourist attractions. Henry Ford Museum, Greenfield Village, reconstruction of a typical 19th cent. American village, both in Dearborn; Michigan Space Center, Jackson; Tahquamenon (Hiawatha) Falls; DeZwaan windmill and Tulip Festival, Holland; "Soo Locks," St. Marys Falls Ship Canal, Sault Ste. Marie.

Famous Michiganders. Ralph Bunche, Paul de Kruif, Thomas A. Edison, Gerald R. Ford, Edna Ferber, Henry Ford, Aretha Franklin, Edgar Guest, Lee Iacocca, Robert Ingersoll, Magic Johnson, Will Kellogg, Ring Lardner, Elmore Leonard, Charles Lindbergh, Joe Louis, Madonna, Pontiac, Diana Ross, Tom Selleck, Lily Tomlin, Stewart Edward White, Malcolm X.

Chamber of Commerce. 600 S. Walnut, Lansing, MI 48933.

Toll-free travel information. 1-800-543-2937.

Minnesota
North Star State, Gopher State

People. Population (1994): 4,567,267; **rank:** 20; **Net change** (1990-94): 4.4%. **Pop. density:** 56.3 per sq mi. **Racial/ethnic distrib.** (1990): 94.4% white; 2.2% black; 1.8% Asian; 1.2% Hispanic.

Geography. Total area: 86,943 sq mi; **rank:** 12. **Land area:** 79,617 sq mi. **Acres forested land:** 16,718,000. **Location:** West North Central state bounded on the E by Wisconsin and Lake Superior, on the N by Canada, on the W by the Dakotas, and on the S by Iowa. **Climate:** northern part of state lies in the moist Great Lakes storm belt; the western border lies at the edge of the semi-arid Great Plains. **Topography:** central hill and lake region covering approx. half the state; to the NE, rocky ridges and deep lakes; to the NW, flat plain; to the S, rolling plains and deep river valleys. **Capital:** St. Paul.

Economy. Principal industries: agribusiness, forest products, mining, manufacturing, tourism. **Principal manufactured goods:** food processing, non-electrical machinery, chemicals, paper, electric and electronic equipment, printing and publishing, instruments, fabricated metal products. **Agriculture: Chief crops:** corn, soybeans, wheat, sugar beets, hay, barley, potatoes, sunflowers. **Livestock** (1995): 2.80 mil cattle; 4.85 mil hogs/pigs; 190,000 sheep; 14.2 mil chickens; 41.5 mil turkeys. **Timber/lumber** (1993): needle-leaves and hardwoods; 303 mil bd ft. **Nonfuel Minerals** (1994): $1.35 bil; mostly iron ore, construction sand & gravel, crushed stone. **Commercial fishing** (1994): $236,000. **Chief ports:** Duluth, St. Paul, Minneapolis. **International airports at:** Minneapolis-St. Paul. **Value of construction** (1994): $5.5 bil. **Employment distribution** (1994): 24.2% trade; 27.5% serv.; 18.0% mfg.; 15.5% govt. **Per capita personal income** (1994): $22,453. **Unemployment** (1994): 4.0%. **Tourism** (1994): domestic and international tourists spent about $7 bil.

Finance. FDIC-insured commercial banks & trust companies (1994): 563. **Deposits:** $45.9 bil. **FDIC-insured savings institutions** (1994): 22. **Assets:** $6.6 bil.

Federal government. No. federal civilian employees (Mar. 1994): 14,607. **Avg. salary:** $38,144.

Energy. Electricity production (1994, kWh, by source): Coal: 26.4 bil; Petroleum: 597 mil; Gas: 452 mil; Hydroelectric: 831 mil; Nuclear: 12.2 bil.

Education. Student-teacher ratio (1993): 17.3. **Avg. salary, public school teachers** (1994-95): $37,412.

State data. Motto: L'Etoile du Nord (The star of the north). **Flower:** Pink and white lady's-slipper. **Bird:** Common loon. **Tree:** Red pine. **Song:** Hail! Minnesota.

Entered union May 11, 1858; rank, 32d. **State fair** at: Saint Paul; late Aug.–early Sept.

History. Fur traders and missionaries from French Canada opened the region in the 17th century. Britain took the area east of the Mississippi, 1763. The U.S. took over that portion after the American Revolution and in 1803 bought the western area as part of the Louisiana Purchase. The U.S. built present Ft. Snelling, 1820, bought lands from the Indians, 1837. Sioux Indians staged a bloody uprising, 1862, and were driven from the state.

Tourist attractions. Minnehaha Falls, Minneapolis, inspiration for Longfellow's Hiawatha; more than 15,000 lakes; 66 state parks; 25 historical sites; Minneapolis Aquatennial; Ordway Theater, St. Paul; Guthrie Theater, Minneapolis; professional baseball, football, hockey. Voyageurs Natl. Park, a water wilderness along the Canadian border; Mayo Clinic, Rochester; St. Paul Winter Carnival; North Shore (of Lake Superior).

Famous Minnesotans. William O. Douglas, F. Scott Fitzgerald, Judy Garland, Cass Gilbert, Hubert Humphrey, Garrison Keillor, Sister Elizabeth Kenny, Sinclair Lewis, Paul Manship, E. G. Marshall, William and Charles Mayo, Walter F. Mondale, Charles Schulz, Harold Stassen, Thorstein Veblen.

Tourist information. Minnesota Office of Tourism, 375 Jackson St., 250 Skyway Level, St. Paul, MN 55101.

Toll-free travel information. 1-800-657-3700.

Mississippi
Magnolia State

People. Population (1994): 2,669,111; **rank:** 31; **Net change** (1990-94): 3.6%. **Pop. density:** 55.7 per sq mi. **Racial/ethnic distrib.** (1990): 63.5% white; 35.6% black; 0.6% Hispanic.

Geography. Total area: 48,434 sq mi; **rank:** 32. **Land area:** 46,914 sq mi. **Acres forested land:** 17,000,000. **Location:** East South Central state bordered on the W by the Mississippi R. and on the S by the Gulf of Mexico. **Climate:** semi-tropical, with abundant rainfall, long growing season, and extreme temperatures unusual. **Topography:** low, fertile delta bet. the Yazoo and Mississippi rivers; loess bluffs stretching around delta border; sandy gulf coastal terraces followed by piney woods and prairie; rugged, high sandy hills in extreme NE followed by black prairie belt, Pontotoc Ridge, and flatwoods into the north central highlands. **Capital:** Jackson.

Economy. Principal industries: manufacturing, government, wholesale and retail trade. **Principal manufactured goods:** apparel, food & kindred prods., furniture, lumber and wood products, electrical machinery, transportation equip. **Agriculture: Chief crops:** cotton, catfish, rice, soybeans. **Livestock** (1993): 1.4 mil cattle; 166,000 hogs/pigs; 528.2 mil broilers. **Timber/lumber** (1993): pine, oak, hardwoods; 2.7 bil bd ft. **Nonfuel Minerals** (1994): $112 mil; mostly crushed stone, construction sand & gravel. **Commercial fishing** (1994): $45 mil. **Chief ports:** Pascagoula, Vicksburg, Gulfport, Natchez, Greenville. **Value of construction** (1994): $2.6 bil. **Employment distribution** (1994): 24.7% mfg.; 21% govt.; 21% trade; 20% serv. **Per capita personal income** (1994): $15,838. **Unemployment** (1994): 6.6%. **Tourism** (1993): out-of-state visitors spent $3.3 bil.

Finance. FDIC-insured commercial banks & trust companies (1994): 111. **Deposits:** $21.2 bil. **FDIC-insured savings institutions** (1994): 17. **Assets:** $2.5 bil.

Federal government. No. federal civilian employees (Mar. 1994): 18,298. **Avg. salary:** $35,574. **Notable federal facilities:** Columbus, Keesler AF bases; Meridian Naval Air Station, John C. Stennis Space Center; U.S. Army Corps of Engineers Waterway Experiment Station.

Energy. Electricity production (1994, kWh, by source): Coal: 8.9 bil; Petroleum: 1.1 bil; Gas: 6.6 bil; Nuclear: 9.6 bil.

Education. Student-teacher ratio (1993): 17.8. **Avg. salary, public school teachers** (1994-95): $26,910.

State data. Motto: Virtute et Armis (By valor and arms). **Flower:** Magnolia. **Bird:** Mockingbird. **Tree:** Magnolia. **Song:** Go, Mississippi! **Entered union** Dec. 10, 1817; rank, 20th. **State fair** at: Jackson; fall.

History. Hernando De Soto explored the area, 1540, sighted the Mississippi River, 1541. Robert La Salle traced the river from Illinois to its mouth and claimed the entire valley for France, 1682. First settlement was the French Ft. Maurepas, near Ocean Springs, 1699. The area was ceded to Britain, 1763; American settlers followed. During the American Revolution, Spain seized part of the area and refused to leave even after the U.S. acquired title at the end of the conflict, finally moving out, 1798. Mississippi seceded in 1861. Union forces captured Corinth and Vicksburg and destroyed Jackson and much of Meridian.

Tourist attractions. Vicksburg National Military Park and Cemetery, other Civil War sites; Natchez Trace; Indian mounds; Antebellum homes; pilgrimages in Natchez and some 25 other cities; Jubilee Jam, May, Jackson; Mardi Gras and blessing of the shrimp fleet, June, both in Biloxi.

Famous Mississippians. Dana Andrews, Jimmy Buffett, Hodding Carter III, Bo Diddley, William Faulkner, Shelby Foote, John Grisham, Fannie Lou Hamer, Jim Henson, Robert Johnson, James Earl Jones, B. B. King, L. Q. C. Lamar, Gerald McRaney, Willie Morris, Walter Payton, Elvis Presley, Leontyne Price, Charlie Pride, Margaret Walker, Eudora Welty, Tennessee Williams, Oprah Winfrey, Johnny Winter, Richard Wright, Tammy Wynette.

Dept. of Economic & Community Development. PO Box 849, Jackson, MS 39205-0849.

Toll-free travel information. 1-800-WARMEST.

Missouri
Show Me State

People. Population (1994): 5,277,640; **rank:** 16; **Net change** (1990-94): 3.1%. **Pop. density:** 75.4 per sq mi. **Racial/ethnic distrib.** (1990): 87.7% white; 10.7% black; 1.2% Hispanic.

Geography. Total area: 69,709 sq mi; **rank:** 21. **Land area:** 68,898 sq mi. **Acres forested land:** 14,007,000. **Location:** West North Central state near the geographic center of the conterminous U.S.; bordered on the E by the Mississippi R., on the NW by the Missouri R. **Climate:** continental, susceptible to cold Canadian air, moist, warm gulf air, and drier SW air. **Topography:** rolling hills, open, fertile plains, and well-watered prairie N of the Missouri R.; south of the river land is rough and hilly with deep, narrow valleys; alluvial plain in the SE; low elevation in the west. **Capital:** Jefferson City.

Economy. Principal industries: agriculture, manufacturing, aerospace, tourism. **Principal manufactured goods:** transportation equipment, food and related products, electrical and electronic equipment, chemicals. **Agriculture: Chief crops:** soybeans, corn, wheat, hay. **Livestock** (1994): 4.8 mil cattle; 3.0 mil hogs/pigs; 86,000 sheep; 8.4 mil chickens, 1.6 mil eggs, 21 mil turkeys. **Timber/lumber** (1993): oak, hickory; 518 mil bd ft. **Nonfuel Minerals** (1994): $1 bil; mostly lead, portland cement, crushed stone. **Chief ports:** St. Louis, Kansas City. **International airports at:** St. Louis, Kansas City. **Value of construction** (1994): $5.6 bil. **Employment distribution** (1993): 26.9% services; 23.8% trade; 17.1% mfg.; 15.7% govt. **Per capita personal income** (1994): $20,717. **Unemployment** (1994): 4.9%. **Tourism** (1993): total travelers spent $5 bil.

Finance. FDIC-insured commercial banks & trust companies (1994): 473. **Deposits:** $58.6 bil. **FDIC-insured savings institutions** (1994): 56. **Assets:** $16.2 bil.

Federal government. No. federal civilian employees (Mar. 1994): 42,637. **Avg. salary:** $36,284. **Notable federal facilities:** Federal Reserve banks, St. Louis, Kansas City; Ft. Leonard Wood, Rolla; Jefferson Barracks, St. Louis; Whiteman AFB, Knob Noster.

Energy. Electricity production (1994 kWh, by source): Coal: 48.5 bil; Petroleum: 731 mil; Gas: 338 mil; Hydroelectric: 1.8 bil; Nuclear: 10.0 bil.

Education. Student-teacher ratio (1993): 16.1. **Avg. salary, public school teachers** (1994-95): $31,217.

State data. Motto: Salus Populi Suprema Lex Esto (The welfare of the people shall be the supreme law). **Flower:** Hawthorn. **Bird:** Bluebird. **Tree:** Dogwood. **Song:** Missouri Waltz. **Entered union** Aug. 10, 1821; rank, 24th. **State fair** at: Sedalia; 3d week in Aug.

History. Hernando DeSoto visited the area, 1541. French hunters and lead miners made the first settlement, c1735, at Ste. Genevieve. The U.S. acquired Missouri as part of the Louisiana Purchase, 1803. The fur trade and the Santa Fe Trail provided prosperity; St. Louis became the "jump-off" point for pioneers on their way West. Pro- and anti-slavery forces battled each other there during the Civil War.

Tourist attractions. Branson with 32 indoor theaters, 3 theme parks, 3 outdoor amphitheaters; Mark Twain Area, Hannibal; Pony Express Museum, St. Joseph; Harry S. Truman Library, Independence; Gateway Arch, St. Louis; Silver Dollar City, Branson Worlds of Fun, Kansas City; Lake of the Ozarks, Churchill Memorial, Fulton; State Capitol, Jefferson City.

Famous Missourians. Maya Angelou, Robert Altman, Burt Bacharach, Josephine Baker, Scot Bakula, Thomas Hart Benton, Tom Berenger, Chuck Berry, George Caleb Bingham, Gen. Omar Bradley, Kate Capshaw, Dale Carnegie, George Washington Carver, Bob Costas, Walter Cronkite, Walt Disney, T. S. Eliot, John Goodman, Betty Grable, Jesse James, J. C. Penney, John J. Pershing, Brad Pitt, Joseph Pulitzer, Ginger Rogers, Bess Truman, Harry S. Truman, Kathleen Turner, Tina Turner, Mark Twain, Dick Van Dyke, Tennessee Williams, Shelly Winters, Jane Wyman.

Chamber of Commerce. 428 E. Capitol, Jefferson City, MO 65101.

Toll-free travel information. 1-800-877-1234.

Montana
Treasure State

People. Population (1994): 856,047; **rank:** 44; **Net change** (1990-94): 7.1%. **Pop. density:** 5.66 per sq mi. **Racial/ethnic distrib.** (1990): 92.7% white; 0.3% black; 6.0% Amer. Indian; 1.5% Hispanic.

Geography. Total area: 147,046 sq mi; **rank:** 4. **Land area:** 145,556 sq mi. **Acres forested land:** 22,512,000. **Location:** Mountain state bounded on the E by the Dakotas, on the S by Wyoming, on the SSW by Idaho, and on the N by Canada. **Climate:** colder, continental climate with low humidity. **Topography:** Rocky Mts. in western third of the state; eastern two-thirds gently rolling northern Great Plains. **Capital:** Helena.

Economy. Principal industries: agriculture, timber, mining, tourism, oil & gas. **Principal manufactured goods:** food prods., wood & paper prods., primary metals, printing & publishing, petroleum & coal prods. **Agriculture: Chief crops:** wheat, barley, sugar beets, hay, oats. **Livestock** (1994): 2.5 mil cattle; 180,000 hogs/pigs; 470,000 sheep; 550,000 poultry. **Timber/lumber** (1993): Douglas fir, pines, larch; 1.4 bil bd ft. **Nonfuel Minerals** (1994): $491 mil; platinum, palladium, talc and pyrophylite, copper, gold, zinc, phosphate rock, portland cement. **International airports at:** Great Falls, Billings, Kalispell, Missoula. **Value of construction** (1994): $769.6 mil. **Employment distribution** (1993): 27.5% serv.; 23.1% trade; 17.7% govt.; 6.8% agric.; 5.9% mfg. **Per capita personal income** (1994): $17,865. **Unemployment** (1994): 5.1%. **Tourism** (1994 est.): non-resident visitors spent $1.2 bil.

Finance. FDIC-insured commercial banks & trust companies (1994): 112. **Deposits:** $6.7 bil. **FDIC-insured savings institutions** (1994): 9. **Assets:** $1.6 bil.

Federal government. No. federal civilian employees (Mar. 1994): 8,590. **Avg. salary:** $35,730. **Notable federal facilities:** Malmstrom AFB; Ft. Peck, Hungry Horse, Libby, Yellowtail dams; numerous missile silos.

Energy. Electricity production (1994, kWh, by source): Coal: 16.5 bil; Petroleum: 18 mil; Gas: 61 mil; Hydroelectric: 8.1 bil.

Education. Student-teacher ratio (1993): 16.4. **Avg. salary, public school teachers** (1994-95): $28,785.

State data. Motto: Oro y Plata (Gold and silver). **Flower:** Bitterroot. **Bird:** Western meadowlark. **Tree:** Ponderosa pine. **Song:** Montana. **Entered union** Nov. 8, 1889; rank, 41st. **State fair** at: Great Falls; late July–early Aug.

History. French explorers visited the region, 1742. The U.S. acquired the area partly through the Louisiana Purchase, 1803, and partly through the explorations of Lewis and Clark, 1805-6. Fur traders and missionaries established posts in the early 19th century. Indian uprisings reached their peak with the Battle of the Little Bighorn, 1876. Mining activity and the coming of the Northern Pacific Railway, 1883, brought population growth.

Tourist attractions. Glacier Natl. Park, on the Continental Divide, is a scenic and recreational wonderland, with 60 glaciers, 200 lakes, and many trout streams. Yellowstone Natl. Park has 3 of the 5 entrances in Montana, with 2,221,000 acres of scenic beauty, including geysers, mountains, canyons, streams, lakes, forests, waterfalls.

Also, Museum of the Rockies, Bozeman; Museum of the Plains Indian, Blackfeet Reservation near Browning; Little Bighorn Battlefield Natl. Monument & Custer Natl. Cemetery; Flathead Lake, in the NW; Lewis and Clark Caverns State Park, near Whitehall; 7 Indian reservations, covering more than 5 million acres; state capitol and historical society, Helena.

Famous Montanans. Gary Cooper, Marcus Daly, Chet Huntley, Will James, Myrna Loy, Mike Mansfield, Brent Musberger, Jeannette Rankin, Charles M. Russell, Lester Thurow.

Chamber of Commerce. 2030 11th Ave., PO Box 1730, Helena, MT 59624.

Toll-free travel information. 1-800-VISITMT.

Nebraska
Cornhusker State

People. Population (1994): 1,622,858; **rank:** 37; **Net change** (1990-94): 2.8%. **Pop. density:** 20.9 per sq mi. **Racial/ethnic distrib.** (1990): 93.8% white; 3.6% black; 2.3% Hispanic.

Geography. Total area: 77,358 sq mi; **rank:** 16. **Land area:** 76,878 sq mi. **Acres forested land:** 462,000. **Location:** West North Central state with the Missouri R. for a NE and E border. **Climate:** continental semi-arid. **Topography:** till plains of the central lowland in the eastern third rising to the Great Plains and hill country of the north central and NW. **Capital:** Lincoln.

Economy. Principal industries: agriculture, manufacturing. **Principal manufactured goods:** processed foods, industrial machinery, printed materials, electric and electronic equipment, primary and fabricated metal products, transportation equipment. **Agriculture: Chief crops:** corn, sorghum, soybeans, hay, wheat, beans, oats, potatoes, sugar beets. **Livestock** (1993): 6.1 mil cattle; 4.2 mil hogs/pigs; 92,000 sheep; 9.0 mil chickens, 2.5 mil turkeys. **Timber/lumber** (1993): oak, hickory, and elm; 28 mil bd ft. **Nonfuel Minerals** (1994): $129 mil; mostly construction sand & gravel, portland cement, crushed stone. **Chief ports:** Omaha, Sioux City, Brownville, Blair, Plattsmouth, Nebraska City. **Value of construction** (1994): $1.8 bil. **Employment distribution** (1994): 25.0% trade; 25.4% serv.; 19% govt.; 13.7% mfg. **Per capita personal income** (1994): $20,488. **Unemployment** (1994): 2.9%. **Tourism** (1993): traveler expenditures $1.9 bil.

Finance. FDIC-insured commercial banks & trust companies (1994): 352. **Deposits:** $20.7 bil. **FDIC-insured savings institutions** (1994): 15. **Assets:** $8.0 bil.

Federal government. No. federal civilian employees (Mar. 1994): 8,784. **Avg. salary:** $36,001. **Notable federal facilities:** Offutt AFB, Bellevue.

Energy. Electricity production (1994, kWh, by source): Coal: 14.0 bil; Petroleum: 18 mil; Gas: 259 mil; Hydroelectric: 1.3 mil; Nuclear: 6.3 bil.

Education. Student-teacher ratio (1993): 14.6. **Avg. salary, public school teachers** (1994-95): $30,822.

State data. Motto: Equality before the law. **Flower:** Goldenrod. **Bird:** Western meadowlark. **Tree:** Cottonwood. **Song:** Beautiful Nebraska. **Entered union** Mar. 1, 1867; rank, 37th. **State fair** at: Lincoln; late Aug.–mid-Sept.

History. Spanish and French explorers and fur traders visited the area prior to the Louisiana Purchase, 1803. Lewis and Clark passed through, 1804-6. First permanent settlement was Bellevue, near Omaha, 1823. Many Civil War veterans settled under free land terms of the 1862 Homestead Act; struggles followed between homesteaders and ranchers.

Tourist attractions. Architecturally unique, 400 ft-tall state capitol, Lincoln; Stuhr Museum of the Prairie Pioneer, Grand Island; Museum of the Fur Trade, Chadron; State Museum (Elephant Hall), Lincoln; Joslyn Art Museum, Omaha; Strategic Air Command Museum, Bellevue; Boys Town, founded by Fr. Flanagan, west of Omaha; Arbor Lodge State Park, Nebraska City; Buffalo Bill Ranch State Historical Park, North Platte; Pioneer Village, Minden; Oregon Trail landmarks, Scotts Bluff National Monument, Chimney Rock Historic Site, Ft. Robinson; Hastings Museum, McDonald Planetarium, Hastings.

Famous Nebraskans. Fred Astaire, Marlon Brando, Charles W. Bryan, William Jennings Bryan, Johnny Carson, Willa Cather, Dick Cavett, William F. "Buffalo Bill" Cody, Loren Eiseley, Rev. Edward J. Flanagan, Henry Fonda, Gerald R. Ford, Rollin Kirby, Swoosie Kurtz, Harold Lloyd, Wright Morris, J. Sterling Morton, John Neidhardt, Nick Nolte, George Norris, Gen. John J. Pershing, Roscoe Pound, Chief Red Cloud, Mari Sandoz, Malcolm X.

Division of Travel and Tourism. PO Box 98913, Lincoln, NE 68509-8913.

Toll-free travel information. 1-800-228-4307.

Nevada
Sagebrush State, Battle Born State, Silver State

People. Population (1994): 1,457,028; **rank:** 38; **Net change** (1990-94): 21.2%. **Pop. density:** 12.1 per sq mi. **Racial/ethnic distrib.** (1990): 84.3% white; 6.6% black; 3.2% Asian; 10.4% Hispanic.

Geography. Total area: 110,567 sq mi; **rank:** 7. **Land area:** 109,806 sq mi. **Acres forested land:** 8,938,000. **Location:** Mountain state bordered on N by Oregon and Idaho, on E by Utah and Arizona, on SE by Arizona, and on SW and W by California. **Climate:** semi-arid and arid. **Topography:** rugged N-S mountain ranges; highest elevation, Boundary Peak, 13,140 ft; southern area is within the Mojave Desert; lowest elevation, Colorado River at southern tip of state, 479 ft. **Capital:** Carson City.

Economy. Principal industries: gaming, tourism, mining, manufacturing, government, agriculture, warehousing, trucking. **Principal manufactured goods:** gaming devices, chemicals, aerospace prods., lawn & garden irrigation equip., seismic & machinery-monitoring devices. **Agriculture: Chief crops:** hay, alfalfa seed, potatoes, onions, garlic, barley, wheat. **Livestock** (1993): 470,000 cattle; 9,000 hogs/pigs; 90,000 sheep; 9,000 poultry. **Timber/lumber:** piñon, juniper, other pines. **Nonfuel Minerals** (1994): $2.8 bil; mostly gold, silver, construction sand & gravel. **International airports at:** Las Vegas, Reno. **Value of construction** (1994): $4.8 bil. **Employment distribution** (1993): 43.2% serv.; 19.8% trade, 13.1% govt. **Per capita personal income** (1994): $24,023. **Unemployment** (1994): 6.2%. **Tourism** (1992): out-of-state travelers spent over $15.4 bil.

Finance. FDIC-insured commercial banks & trust companies (1994): 22. **Deposits:** $10.0 bil. **FDIC-insured savings institutions** (1994): 2. **Assets:** $3.4 bil.

Federal government. No. federal civilian employees (Mar. 1994): 7,552. **Avg. salary:** $38,399. **Notable federal facilities:** Nevada Test Site; Hawthorne Army Ammunition Plant, Nellis Air Force Base & Gunnery Range; Fallon Naval Air Station; Palomino Valley Wild Horse & Burro Placement Center.

Energy. Electricity production (1994, kWh, by source): Coal: 15.3 bil; Petroleum: 167 mil; Gas: 3.1 bil; Hydroelectric: 1.9 bil.

Education. Student-teacher ratio (1993): 18.7. **Avg. salary, public school teachers** (1994-95): $34,836.

State data. Motto: All for our country. **Flower:** Sagebrush. **Bird:** Mountain bluebird. **Trees:** Single-leaf piñon and bristlecone pine. **Song:** Home Means Nevada. **Entered union** Oct. 31, 1864; rank, 36th. **State fair** at: Reno; early Sept.

History. Nevada was first explored by Spaniards in 1776. Hudson's Bay Co. trappers explored the north and central region, 1825; trader Jedediah Smith crossed the state, 1826 and 1827. The area was acquired by the U.S., in 1848, at the end of the Mexican War. First settlement, Mormon Station, now Genoa, was established 1849. In the early 20th century, Nevada adopted progressive measures such as the initiative, referendum, recall, and woman suffrage.

Tourist attractions. Legalized casino gambling provided the impetus for the development of resort facilities at Lake Tahoe, Reno, Las Vegas, Laughlin, and elsewhere.

Ghost towns, rodeos, mountain climbing, skiing, golfing, trout fishing, water sports, and hunting. Notable are Hoover Dam, Lake Mead Natl. Recreation Area, Lake Tahoe, Great Basin Natl. Park, Valley of Fire State Park, and Virginia City. Annual events include Helldorado Days & Rodeo, Las Vegas; Reno Rodeo; National Basque Festival, Elko; Nevada Day, Carson City; Cowboy Poetry Gathering, Elko.

Famous Nevadans. Walter Van Tilburg Clark, Sarah Winnemucca Hopkins, Paul Laxalt, Dat So La Lee, John William Mackay, Pat McCarran, Key Pittman, William Morris Stewart.

Tourist information. Commission on Tourism, Capitol Complex, Carson City, NV 89710.

Toll-free travel information. 1-800-638-2328.

New Hampshire
Granite State

People. Population (1994): 1,136,820; **rank:** 41; **Net change** (1990-94): 2.5%. **Pop. density:** 123.8 per sq mi. **Racial/ethnic distrib.** (1990): 98.0% white; 0.6% black; 1.0% Hispanic.

Geography. Total area: 9,351 sq mi; **rank:** 46. **Land area:** 8,969 sq mi. **Acres forested land:** 4,981,000. **Location:** New England state bounded on S by Massachusetts, on W by Vermont, on N and NW by Canada, on E by Maine and the Atlantic Ocean. **Climate:** highly varied, due to its nearness to high mountains and ocean. **Topography:** low, rolling coast followed by countless hills and mountains rising out of a central plateau. **Capital:** Concord.

Economy. Principal industries: tourism, manufacturing, agriculture, trade, mining. **Principal manufactured goods:** machinery, electrical & electronic products, plastics, fabricated metal products. **Agriculture: Chief crops:** dairy products, nursery and greenhouse products, hay, vegetables, fruit, maple syrup & sugar prods. **Livestock** (1993): 52,000 cattle; 9,500 hogs/pigs; 9,000 sheep; 15,500 horses; 214,000 poultry. **Timber/lumber** (1993): white pine, hemlock, oak, birch; 270 mil bd ft. **Nonfuel Minerals** (1994): $37 mil; mostly construction sand & gravel, crushed & dimension stone. **Commercial fishing** (1994): $12.7 mil. **Chief ports:** Portsmouth, Hampton, Rye. **Value of construction** (1994): $1.1 bil. **Employment distribution** (1992): 20.0% mfg.; 25.4% trade; 26.6% serv.; 14.9% govt. **Per capita personal income** (1994): $23,434. **Unemployment** (1994): 4.6%. **Tourism** (1993): out-of-state visitors spent $3.4 bil.

Finance. FDIC-insured commercial banks & trust companies (1994): 24. **Deposits:** $5.8 bil. **FDIC-insured savings institutions** (1994): 31. **Assets:** $11.0 bil.

Federal government. No. federal civilian employees (Mar. 1994): 3,672. **Avg. salary:** $41,574.

Energy. Electricity production (1994, kWh, by source): Coal: 3.2 bil; Petroleum: 1.4 bil; Gas: 115 mil; Hydroelectric: 1.0 bil; Nuclear: 6.2 bil.

Education. Student-teacher ratio (1993): 15.5. **Avg. salary, public school teachers** (1994-95): $34,974.

State data. Motto: Live free or die. **Flower:** Purple lilac. **Bird:** Purple finch. **Tree:** White birch. **Song:** Old New Hampshire. **Ninth** of the original 13 states to ratify the Constitution, June 21, 1788.

History. First explorers to visit the New Hampshire area were England's Martin Pring, 1603, and Champlain, 1605. First settlement was Odiorne's Point (now port of Rye), 1623. Indian raids were halted, 1759, by Robert Rogers' Rangers. Before the American Revolution, New Hampshire men seized a British fort at Portsmouth, 1774, and drove the royal governor out, 1775. Three regiments served in the Continental Army, and scores of privateers raided British shipping.

Tourist attractions. Mt. Washington, highest peak in Northeast, hub of network of trails; Lake Winnipesaukee; White Mt. National Forest; Crawford, Franconia, Pinkham notches in White Mt. region—Franconia famous for the Old Man of the Mountain, described by Hawthorne as the Great Stone Face; the Flume, a spectacular gorge; the aerial tramway on Cannon Mt.; Strawbery Banke, Portsmouth; Shaker Village, Canterbury; Saint-Gaudens, natl. historic site, Cornish; Mt. Monadnock.

Famous New Hampshirites. Salmon P. Chase, Ralph Adams Cram, Mary Baker Eddy, Daniel Chester French, Robert Frost, Horace Greeley, Sarah Buell Hale, Franklin Pierce, Augustus Saint-Gaudens, David H. Souter, Daniel Webster.

Tourist information. Department of Resources and Economic Development, Division of Travel & Tourism Development, PO Box 1856, Concord, NH 03302-1856; 603-271-2666.

Toll-free travel information. 1-800-386-4664, ext. 145.

New Jersey
Garden State

People. Population (1994): 7,903,925; **rank:** 9; **Net change** (1990-94): 2.2%. **Pop. density:** 1,049.9 per sq mi. **Racial/ethnic distrib.** (1990): 79.3% white; 13.4% black; 3.5% Asian; 9.6% Hispanic.

Geography. Total area: 8,722 sq mi; **rank:** 47. **Land area:** 7,419 sq mi. **Acres forested land:** 2,007,000. **Location:** Middle Atlantic state bounded on the N and E by New York and the Atlantic Ocean, on the S and W by Delaware and Pennsylvania. **Climate:** moderate, with marked difference bet. NW and SE extremities. **Topography:** Appalachian Valley in the NW also has highest elevation, High Pt., 1,801 ft; Appalachian Highlands, flat-topped NE-SW mountain ranges; Piedmont Plateau, low plains broken by high ridges (Palisades) rising 400-500 ft; Coastal Plain, covering three-fifths of state in SE, gradually rises from sea level to gentle slopes. **Capital:** Trenton.

Economy. Principal industries: services, trade, manufacturing. **Principal manufactured goods:** chemicals, electronic and electrical equipment, non-electrical machinery, fabricated metals. **Agriculture: Chief crops:** nursery & greenhouse, hay, corn, soybeans, peppers, tomatoes, blueberries, peaches, cranberries. **Livestock** (1994): 65,000 cattle; 26,000 hogs/pigs; 18,000 sheep; 1.9 mil poultry. **Timber/lumber:** pine, cedar, mixed hardwoods; 8 mil bd ft. **Nonfuel Minerals** (1994): $274 mil; mostly crushed stone, construction sand & gravel. **Commercial fishing** (1994): $100 mil. **Chief ports:** Newark, Elizabeth, Hoboken, Camden. **International airports at:** Newark. **Value of construction** (1994): $6.5 bil. **Employment distribution** (1993): 29.1% serv.; 23.3% trade; 14.8% mfg.; 16.2% govt. **Per capita personal income** (1994): $28,038. **Unemployment** (1994): 6.8%. **Tourism** (1994): tourists spent $22.6 bil.

Finance. FDIC-insured commercial banks & trust companies (1994): 89. **Deposits:** $73.0 bil. **FDIC-insured savings institutions** (1994): 95. **Assets:** $40.9 bil.

Federal government. No. federal civilian employees (Mar. 1994): 36,276. **Avg. salary:** $41,461. **Notable federal facilities:** McGuire AFB; Fort Dix; Fort

Monmouth; Picatinny Arsenal; Lakehurst Naval Air Engineering Center.

Energy. Electricity production (1994, kWh, by source): Coal: 4.6 bil; Petroleum: 1.7 bil; Gas: 3.4 bil; Nuclear: 22.1 bil.

Education. Student-teacher ratio (1993): 13.6. **Avg. salary, public school teachers** (1994-95): $46,801.

State data. Motto: Liberty and prosperity. **Flower:** Purple violet. **Bird:** Eastern goldfinch. **Tree:** Red oak. **Third** of the original 13 states to ratify the Constitution, Dec. 18, 1787. **State fair:** usually Aug. in Pennsauken.

History. The Lenni-Lenape (Delaware) Indians had mostly peaceful relations with European colonists who arrived after the explorers Verrazano, 1524, and Hudson, 1609. The Dutch were first; when the British took New Netherland, 1664, the area between the Delaware and Hudson Rivers was given to Lord John Berkeley and Sir George Carteret. New Jersey was the scene of nearly 100 battles, large and small, during the American Revolution, including Trenton, 1776; Princeton, 1777; Monmouth, 1778.

Tourist attractions. 127 miles of beaches; Miss America Pageant and hotel-casinos, Atlantic City; Grover Cleveland birthplace, Caldwell; Cape May Historic District; Edison Labs, W. Orange; Great Adventure amusement park; Liberty State Park; Meadowlands Sports Complex; Pine Barrens wilderness area; Princeton University; numerous Revolutionary War historical sites; State Aquarium, Camden.

Famous New Jerseyans. John Amos, Count Basie, Judy Blume, Jon Bon Jovi, Aaron Burr, Grover Cleveland, James Fenimore Cooper, Stephen Crane, Thomas Edison, Albert Einstein, Alexander Hamilton, Whitney Houston, Joyce Kilmer, Gen. George McClellan, Thomas Paine, Molly Pitcher, Paul Robeson, Philip Roth, Walter Schirra, Frank Sinatra, Bruce Springsteen, Meryl Streep, Walt Whitman, William Carlos Williams, Woodrow Wilson.

Chamber of Commerce. 50 W. State St., Trenton, NJ 08608.

Toll-free travel information. 1-800-JERSEY7.

New Mexico
Land of Enchantment

People. Population (1994): 1,653,521; **rank:** 36; **Net change** (1990-94): 9.1%. **Pop. density:** 13.0 per sq mi. **Racial/ethnic distrib.** (1990): 75.6% white; 2.0% black; 8.9% Amer. Indian; 38.2% Hispanic.

Geography. Total area: 121,598 sq mi; **rank:** 5. **Land area:** 121,364 sq mi. **Acres forested land:** 15,296,000. **Location:** southwestern state bounded by Colorado on the N, Oklahoma, Texas, and Mexico on the E and S, and Arizona on the W. **Climate:** dry, with temperatures rising or falling 5° F with every 1,000 ft elevation. **Topography:** eastern third, Great Plains; central third, Rocky Mts. (85% of the state is over 4,000-ft elevation); western third, high plateau. **Capital:** Santa Fe.

Economy. Principal industries: government, services, trade. **Principal manufactured goods:** foods, machinery, apparel, lumber, printing, transportation equipment. **Agriculture: Chief crops:** hay, onions, wheat, pecans, corn, cotton, sorghum. **Livestock** (1990): 1.34 mil cattle; 27,000 hogs; 462,000 sheep; 1.43 mil poultry. **Timber/lumber** (1993): ponderosa pine, Douglas fir; 146 mil bd ft. **Nonfuel Minerals** (1994): $914 mil; copper, potash, construction sand & gravel. **International airports at:** Albuquerque. **Value of construction** (1994): $1.9 bil. **Employment distribution** (April 1995): 27.1% serv.; 24.2% govt. 23.7% trade. **Per capita personal income** (1994): $17,106. **Unemployment** (1994): 6.3%. **Tourism** (1994): out-of-state visitors spent $2.75 bil.

Finance. FDIC-insured commercial banks & trust companies (1994): 70. **Deposits:** $11.1 bil. **FDIC-insured savings institutions** (1994): 12. **Assets:** $1.3 bil.

Federal government. No. federal civilian employees (Mar. 1994): 23,177. **Avg. salary:** $36,451. **Notable federal facilities:** Kirtland, Cannon, Holloman AF bases; Los Alamos Scientific Laboratory; White Sands Missile

Range; National Solar Observatory; National Radio Astronomy Observatory.

Energy. Electricity production (1994, kWh, by source): Coal: 26.8 bil; Petroleum: 23 mil; Gas: 3.0 bil; Hydroelectric: 213 mil.

Education. Student-teacher ratio (1993): 17.5. **Avg. salary, public school teachers** (1994-95): $28,865.

State data. Motto: Crescit Eundo (It grows as it goes). **Flower:** Yucca. **Bird:** Roadrunner. **Tree:** Piñon. **Song:** O, Fair New Mexico; Asi Es Nuevo Mexico. **Entered union** Jan. 6, 1912; rank, 47th. **State fair** at: Albuquerque; mid-Sept.

History. Franciscan Marcos de Niza and a black slave Estevan explored the area, 1539, seeking gold. First settlements were at San Juan Pueblo, 1598, and Santa Fe, 1610. Settlers alternately traded and fought with the Apache, Comanche, and Navajo. Trade on the Santa Fe Trail to Missouri started 1821. The Mexican War was declared in May 1846; Gen. Stephen Kearny took Santa Fe without firing a shot, Aug.18,1846, declaring New Mexico part of the U.S. In the 1870s, cattlemen staged the famed Lincoln County War in which Billy (the Kid) Bonney played a leading role. Pancho Villa raided Columbus, 1916.

Tourist attractions. Carlsbad Caverns, a national park, has caverns on 3 levels and the largest natural cave "room" in the world, 1,500 ft by 300 ft, 300 ft high; White Sands Natl. Monument, the largest gypsum deposit in the world. Pueblo ruins AD 100, Chaco Canyon; Acoma, the "sky city," built atop a 357-ft mesa; 19 Pueblo, 4 Navajo, and 2 Apache reservations. Also, ghost towns, dude ranches, skiing, hunting, and fishing.

Famous New Mexicans. Billy (the Kid) Bonney, Kit Carson, Peter Hurd, Archbishop Jean Baptiste Lamy, Nancy Lopez, Bill Mauldin, Georgia O'Keeffe, Kim Stanley, Al Unser, Bobby Unser, Lew Wallace.

Tourist information. New Mexico Dept. of Tourism, PO Box 20003, Santa Fe, NM 87503.

Toll-free travel information. 1-800-545-2040.

New York
Empire State

People. Population (1994): 18,169,051; **rank:** 3; **Net change** (1990-94): 1.0%. **Pop. density:** 383.7 per sq mi. **Racial/ethnic distrib.** (1990): 74.4% white; 15.9% black; 3.9% Asian; 12.3% Hispanic.

Geography. Total area: 54,471 sq mi; **rank:** 27. **Land area:** 47,224 sq mi. **Acres forested land:** 18,713,000. **Location:** Middle Atlantic state, bordered by the New England states, Atlantic Ocean, New Jersey and Pennsylvania, Lakes Ontario and Erie, and Canada. **Climate:** variable; the SE region moderated by the ocean. **Topography:** highest and most rugged mountains in the NE Adirondack upland; St. Lawrence-Champlain lowlands extend from Lake Ontario NE along the Canadian border; Hudson-Mohawk lowland follows the flows of the rivers N and W, 10-30 mi wide; Atlantic coastal plain in the SE; Appalachian Highlands, covering half the state westward from the Hudson Valley, include the Catskill Mts., Finger Lakes; plateau of Erie-Ontario lowlands. **Capital:** Albany.

Economy. Principal industries: manufacturing, finance, communications, tourism, transportation, services. **Principal manufactured goods:** books and periodicals, clothing and apparel, pharmaceuticals, machinery, instruments, toys and sporting goods, electronic equipment, automotive and aircraft components. **Agriculture: Chief crops:** apples, grapes, strawberries, cherries, pears, onions, potatoes, cabbage, sweet corn, green beans, cauliflower, field corn, hay, wheat, oats, dry beans. **Products:** milk, cheese, maple syrup, wine. **Livestock** (1995): 1.5 mil cattle; 72,000 hogs/pigs; 72,000 sheep; 7.7 mil poultry. **Timber/lumber** (1993): birch, sugar and red maple, basswood, hemlock, pine, oak, ash; 480 mil bd ft. **Nonfuel Minerals** (1994): $869 mil; mostly salt, crushed stone, construction sand & gravel, portland cement. **Commercial fishing** (1994): $43 mil. **Chief ports:** New York, Buffalo, Albany. **International airports at:** New York, Buffalo, Syracuse,

Massena, Ogdensburg, Watertown, Niagara Falls, Newburgh. **Value of construction** (1994): $13.4 bil. **Employment distribution** (1994): 32% serv.; 20% trade; 18% govt.; 12% mfg. **Per capita personal income** (1994): $25,999. **Unemployment** (1994): 6.9%. **Tourism** (1993): tourists spent $20 bil.

Finance. FDIC-insured commercial banks & trust companies (1994): 167. **Deposits:** $524.0 bil. **FDIC-insured savings institutions** (1994): 120. **Assets:** $117.0 bil.

Federal government. No. federal civilian employees (Mar. 1994): 67,478. **Avg. salary:** $38,391. **Notable federal facilities:** West Point Military Academy; Merchant Marine Academy; Ft. Drum; Griffiss, Plattsburgh AF bases; Watervliet Arsenal.

Energy. Electricity production (1994, kWh, by source): Coal: 20.9 bil; Petroleum: 11.0 bil; Gas: 17.5 bil; Hydroelectric: 25.2 bil; Nuclear: 29.2 bil.

Education. Student-teacher ratio (1993): 15.2. **Avg. salary, public school teachers** (1994-95): $47,250.

State data. Motto: Excelsior (Ever upward). **Flower:** Rose. **Bird:** Bluebird. **Tree:** Sugar maple. **Song:** I Love New York. **Eleventh** of the original 13 states to ratify the Constitution, July 26, 1788. **State fair** at: Syracuse; late Aug.–early Sept.

History. In 1609, Henry Hudson visited the river that bears his name, and Champlain explored the lake, far upstate, that was named for him. Dutch built posts near present-day Albany and New York City in 1624; in 1626 they settled Manhattan. A British fleet seized New Netherland, 1664. Ninety-two of the 300 or more engagements of the American Revolution were fought in New York, including the Battle of Bemis Heights-Saratoga, a turning point of the war.

Tourist attractions. New York City; Adirondack and Catskill Mts.; Finger Lakes, Great Lakes; Long Island beaches; Thousand Islands; Niagara Falls; Saratoga Springs racing and spas; Philipsburg Manor, Sunnyside, the restored home of Washington Irving, The Dutch Church of Sleepy Hollow, all in Tarrytown area; Corning Glass Center and Steuben factory, Corning; Fenimore House, National Baseball Hall of Fame and Museum, both in Cooperstown; Ft. Ticonderoga overlooking Lakes George and Champlain; Albany's Empire State Plaza; Lake Placid Olympic Village.

The Franklin D. Roosevelt National Historic Site, Hyde Park, includes the graves of Pres. and Mrs. Roosevelt, the family home since 1867, and the Roosevelt Library. Sagamore Hill, Oyster Bay, the Theodore Roosevelt estate, includes his home.

Famous New Yorkers. Susan B. Anthony, Lucille Ball, Barbara Bush, Peter Cooper, George Eastman, Millard Fillmore, George and Ira Gershwin, Ruth Bader Ginsberg, Julia Ward Howe, Charles Evans Hughes, Henry and William James, Herman Melville, Franklin Delano Roosevelt, Theodore Roosevelt, J. D. Salinger, Paul Simon, Alfred E. Smith, Elizabeth Cady Stanton, Martin Van Buren, Gore Vidal, Walt Whitman.

Tourist information. N.Y. State Dept. of Economic Development, 1 Commerce Plaza, Albany, NY 12245.

Toll-free travel information. 1-800-CALLNYS from 50 states & U.S. territories; 1-518-474-4116 from other areas and Canada.

North Carolina
Tar Heel State, Old North State

People. Population (1994): 7,069,836; **rank: 10; Net change** (1990-94): 6.6%. **Pop. density:** 140.5 per sq mi. **Racial/ethnic distrib.** (1990): 75.6% white; 22.0% black; 1.2% Amer. Indian; 1.2% Hispanic.

Geography. Total area: 53,821 sq mi; **rank: 28. Land area:** 48,718 sq mi. **Acres forested land:** 19,278,000. **Location:** South Atlantic state bounded by Virginia, South Carolina, Georgia, Tennessee, and the Atlantic Ocean **Climate:** sub-tropical in SE, medium-continental in mountain region; tempered by the Gulf Stream and the mountains in W. **Topography:** coastal plain and tidewater, two-fifths of state, extending to the fall line of the rivers; piedmont plateau, another two-fifths, 200 mi wide of gentle to rugged hills; southern Appalachian Mts. con-

tains the Blue Ridge and Great Smoky Mts. **Capital:** Raleigh.

Economy. Principal industries: manufacturing, agriculture, tobacco, tourism. **Principal manufactured goods:** textiles, rubber/plastics products, electrical and electronic equip., chemicals, furniture, food products, non-electrical machinery. **Agriculture: Chief crops:** tobacco, soybeans, corn, cotton, peanuts, sweet potatoes, feed grains, vegetables, fruits. **Livestock** (1993): 1.1 mil cattle; 5.4 mil hogs/pigs; 19.3 mil chickens, 61 mil turkeys. **Timber/lumber** (1993): yellow pine, oak, hickory, poplar, maple; 2.04 bil bd ft. **Nonfuel Minerals** (1994): $700 mil; mostly, construction sand & gravel, crushed stone, dimension stone, phosphate rock, lithium. **Commercial fishing** (1994): $98 mil. **International airports at:** Charlotte/Douglas, Raleigh/Durham. **Chief ports:** Morehead City, Wilmington. **Value of construction** (1994): $10.1 bil. **Employment distribution** (1994): 25.6% mfg.; 22.7% trade; 21.5% serv.; 16.1% govt. **Per capita personal income** (1994): $19,669. **Unemployment** (1994): 4.4%. **Tourism** (1994): out-of-state visitors spent $8.0 bil.

Finance. FDIC-insured commercial banks & trust companies (1994): 68. **Deposits:** $78.5 bil. **FDIC-insured savings institutions** (1994): 74. **Assets:** $9.7 bil.

Federal government. No. federal civilian employees (Mar. 1994): 31,060. **Avg. salary:** $34,225. **Notable federal facilities:** Ft. Bragg; Camp LeJeune Marine Base; U.S. EPA Research and Development Labs, Cherry Point Marine Corps Air Station; Natl. Humanities Center; Natl. Inst. of Environmental Health Science; Natl. Center for Health Statistics Lab, Research Triangle Park.

Energy. Electricity production (1994, kWh, by source): Coal: 53.2 bil; Petroleum: 199 mil; Gas: 69 mil; Hydroelectric: 5.6 bil; Nuclear: 32.3 bil.

Education. Student-teacher ratio (1993): 16.3. **Avg. salary, public school teachers** (1994-95): $31,079.

State data. Motto: Esse Quam Videri (To be rather than to seem). **Flower:** Dogwood. **Bird:** Cardinal. **Tree:** Pine. **Song:** The Old North State. **Twelfth** of the original 13 states to ratify the Constitution, Nov. 21, 1789. **State fair** at: Raleigh; mid-Oct.

History. The first English colony in America was the first of 2 established by Sir Walter Raleigh on Roanoke Island, 1585 and 1587. The first group returned to England; the second, the "Lost Colony," disappeared without a trace. Permanent settlers came from Virginia, c1660. Roused by British repressions, the colonists drove out the royal governor, 1775; the province's congress was the first to vote for independence. Ten regiments were furnished to the Continental Army. Cornwallis' forces were defeated at Kings Mountain, 1780, and forced out after Guilford Courthouse, 1781.

Tourist attractions. Cape Hatteras and Cape Lookout national seashores; Great Smoky Mts. (half in Tennessee); Guilford Courthouse and Moore's Creek parks, 66 American Revolution battle sites; Bennett Place, NW of Durham, where Gen. Joseph Johnston surrendered the last Confederate army to Gen. William Sherman; Ft. Raleigh, Roanoke Island, where Virginia Dare, first child of English parents in the New World, was born Aug. 18, 1587; Wright Brothers National Memorial, Kitty Hawk; USS *North Carolina* battleship, Wilmington; NC Zoo, Asheboro; NC Symphony, & NC Museum, Raleigh; Carl Sandburg Home, Hendersonville.

Famous North Carolinians. Richard J. Gatling, Billy Graham, Andy Griffith, Andrew Jackson, Andrew Johnson, Michael Jordan, Wm. Rufus King, Charles Kuralt, Dolley Madison, Edward R. Murrow, James K. Polk, Enos Slaughter, Dean Smith, Thomas Wolfe.

Tourist information. Travel & Tourism Division, 430 No. Salisbury St., Raleigh, NC 27603.

Toll-free travel information. 1-800-VISITNC.

North Dakota
Peace Garden State

People. Population (1994): 637,988; **rank: 47; Net change** (1990-94): –0.1%. **Pop. density:** 9.2 per sq mi.

Racial/ethnic distrib. (1990): 94.6% white; 0.6% black; 4.1% Amer. Indian; 0.7% Hispanic.

Geography. Total area: 70,704 sq mi; **rank:** 19. **Land area:** 68,994 sq mi. **Acres forested land:** 722,000. **Location:** West North Central state, situated exactly in the middle of North America, bounded on the N by Canada, on the E by Minnesota, on the S by South Dakota, on the W by Montana. **Climate:** continental, with a wide range of temperature and moderate rainfall. **Topography:** Central Lowland in the E comprises the flat Red River Valley and the Rolling Drift Prairie; Missouri Plateau of the Great Plains on the W. **Capital:** Bismarck.

Economy. Principal industries: agriculture, mining, tourism, manufacturing, telecommunications, energy. **Principal manufactured goods:** farm equipment, processed foods, fabricated metal, high-tech. electronics. **Agriculture: Chief crops:** spring wheat, durum, barley, rye, flaxseed, oats, potatoes, dried edible beans, honey, soybeans, sugar beets, sunflowers, hay. **Livestock** (1994): 1.9 mil cattle; 245,000 hogs/pigs; 166,000 sheep; 235,000 poultry. **Timber/lumber:** oak, ash, cottonwood, aspen; 4 mil bd ft. **Nonfuel Minerals** (1994): $26 mil; mostly construction sand & gravel, lime. **International airports at:** Fargo, Grand Forks, Bismarck, Minot, Pembina, Dunseith. **Value of construction** (1994): $850.6 mil. **Employment distribution** (1995): 26% trade; 28% serv.; 23% govt.; 7.2% mfg. **Per capita personal income** (1994): $18,546. **Unemployment** (1994): 3.9%. **Tourism** (1992): $826 mil.

Finance. FDIC-insured commercial banks & trust companies (1994): 139. **Deposits:** $7.1 bil. **FDIC-insured savings institutions** (1994): 4. **Assets:** $8.5 bil.

Federal government. No. federal civilian employees (Mar. 1994): 5,398. **Avg. salary:** $33,752. **Notable federal facilities:** Strategic Air Command bases at Minot, Grand Forks; Northern Prairie Wildlife Research Center; Garrison Dam; Theodore Roosevelt Natl. Park; Grand Forks Energy Research Center; Ft. Union Natl. Historic Site.

Energy. Electricity production (1994, kWh, by source): Coal: 27.1 bil; Petroleum: 47 bil; Hydroelectric: 1.9 bil.

Education. Student-teacher ratio (1993): 15.4. **Avg. salary, public school teachers** (1994-95): $26,327.

State data. Motto: Liberty and union, now and forever, one and inseparable. **Flower:** Wild prairie rose. **Bird:** Western meadowlark. **Tree:** American elm. **Song:** North Dakota Hymn. **Entered union** Nov. 2, 1889; rank, 39th. **State fair** at: Minot; 3d week in July.

History. Pierre La Verendrye was the first French fur trader in the area, 1738, followed later by the English. The U.S. acquired half the territory in the Louisiana Purchase, 1803. Lewis and Clark built Ft. Mandan, spent the winter of 1804-5 there. In 1818, American ownership of the other half was confirmed by agreement with Britain. First permanent settlement was at Pembina, 1812. Missouri River steamboats reached the area, 1832; the first railroad, 1873, bringing many homesteaders. The state was first to hold a presidential primary, 1912.

Tourist attractions. North Dakota Heritage Center, State Capitol grounds; Bonanzaville, Fargo, restored pioneer town; Ft. Union Trading Post Natl. Historic Site; Lake Sakakawea, 180 mi of fishing, boating, 1,600 mi of shoreline. International Peace Garden, 2,200-acre tract extending across the border into Manitoba; 65,000-acre Theodore Roosevelt National Park, Badlands, contains the president's Elkhorn Ranch; Ft. Abraham Lincoln State Park and Museum, S of Mandan; Dakota Dinosaur Museum, Dickinson.

Famous North Dakotans. Maxwell Anderson, Angie Dickinson, John Bernard Flannagan, Louis L'Amour, Peggy Lee, Eric Sevareid, Vilhjalmur Stefansson, Lawrence Welk.

Chamber of Commerce. PO Box 2639, 2000 Schafer St., Bismarck, ND 58501.

Toll-free travel information. 1-800-437-2077 (out of state), 1-800-472-2100 (in state).

Ohio
Buckeye State

People. Population (1994): 11,102,198; **rank:** 7; **Net change** (1990-94): 2.4%. **Pop. density:** 269.0 per sq mi. **Racial/ethnic distrib.** (1990): 87.8% white; 10.6% black; 1.3% Hispanic.

Geography. Total area: 44,828 sq mi; **rank:** 34. **Land area:** 40,953 sq mi. **Acres forested land:** 7,863,000. **Location:** East North Central state bounded on the N by Michigan and Lake Erie; on the E and S by Pennsylvania, West Virginia, and Kentucky; on the W by Indiana. **Climate:** temperate but variable; weather subject to much precipitation. **Topography:** generally rolling plain; Allegheny plateau in E; Lake Erie plains extend southward; central plains in the W. **Capital:** Columbus.

Economy. Principal industries: manufacturing, trade, services. **Principal manufactured goods:** transportation equipment, machinery, primary and fabricated metal products. **Agriculture: Chief crops:** corn, hay, winter wheat, oats, soybeans. **Livestock** (1993): 1.6 mil cattle; 1.6 mil hogs/pigs; 198,000 sheep and lambs; 27.3 mil broilers, 5.2 mil turkeys. **Timber/lumber** (1993): oak, ash, maple, walnut, beech; 392 mil bd ft. **Nonfuel Minerals** (1994): $893 mil; mostly crushed stone, construction sand & gravel, salt, lime. **Commercial fishing** (1994): $1.4 mil. **Chief ports:** Toledo, Conneaut, Cleveland, Ashtabula. **International airports at:** Cleveland, Cincinnati, Columbus, Dayton. **Value of construction** (1994): $11.9 bil. **Employment distribution** (1995): 21.2% mfg.; 18.7% trade; 26.4% serv.; 14.7% govt. **Per capita personal income** (1994): $20,928. **Unemployment** (1994): 5.5%. **Tourism** (1992): travelers spent $8.8 bil.

Finance. FDIC-insured commercial banks & trust companies (1994): 258. **Deposits:** $106.1 bil. **FDIC-insured savings institutions** (1994): 167. **Assets:** $37.9 bil.

Federal government. No. federal civilian employees (Mar. 1994): 52,972. **Avg. salary:** $39,535. **Notable federal facilities:** Wright Patterson AFB; Defense Construction Supply Center; Lewis Research Ctr.; Portsmouth Gaseous Diffusion Plant; EG&G Mound Applied Tech. Laboratory.

Energy. Electricity production (1994, kWh, by source): Coal: 117.4 bil; Petroleum: 372 mil; Gas: 153 mil; Hydroelectric: 189 mil; Nuclear: 11.0 mil.

Education. Student-teacher ratio (1993): 16.8. **Avg. salary, public school teachers** (1994-95): $36,685.

State data. Motto: With God, all things are possible. **Flower:** Scarlet carnation. **Bird:** Cardinal. **Tree:** Buckeye. **Song:** Beautiful Ohio. **Entered union** Mar. 1, 1803; rank, 17th. **State fair** at: Columbus; August.

History. LaSalle visited the Ohio area, 1669. American furtraders arrived, beginning 1685; the French and Indians sought to drive them out. During the American Revolution, Virginians defeated the Indians, 1774, but hostilities were renewed, 1777. The region became U.S. territory after the American Revolution. First organized settlement was at Marietta, 1788. Indian warfare ended with Anthony Wayne's victory at Fallen Timbers, 1794. In the War of 1812, Oliver Hazard Perry's victory on Lake Erie and William Henry Harrison's invasion of Canada, 1813, ended British incursions.

Tourist attractions. Mound City Group National Monuments, a group of 24 prehistoric Indian burial mounds; Neil Armstrong Air and Space Museum, Wapakoneta; Air Force Museum, Dayton; Pro Football Hall of Fame, Canton; King's Island amusement park, Mason; Cedar Point amusement park, Sandusky; birthplaces, homes of, and memorials to U.S. presidents W. H. Harrison, Grant, Garfield, Hayes, McKinley, Harding, Taft, Benjamin Harrison; Lake Erie Islands, Sandusky; Amish Region, Tuscarawas/Holmes counties; German Village, Columbus; Sea World, Aurora; Jack Nicklaus Sports Center, Mason; Bob Evans Farm, Rio Grande; Rock and Roll Hall of Fame and Museum, Cleveland.

Famous Ohioans. Sherwood Anderson, Neil Armstrong, George Bellows, Johnny Bench, Ambrose Bierce, Erma Bombeck, Clarence Darrow, Paul Laurence

Dunbar, Thomas Edison, Clark Gable, John Glenn, Bob Hope, Jack Nicklaus, Jesse Owens, Eddie Rickenbacker, John D. Rockefeller Sr. and Jr., Pete Rose, Gen. William Sherman, Harriet Beecher Stowe, Charles Taft, Robert A. Taft, William H. Taft, James Thurber, Orville Wright.

Chamber of Commerce. 35 E. Gay St., Columbus, OH 43215-3181.

Toll-free travel information. 1-800-BUCKEYE.

Oklahoma
Sooner State

People. Population (1994): 3,258,069; **rank:** 28; **Net change** (1990-94): 3.6%. **Pop. density:** 46.8 per sq mi. **Racial/ethnic distrib.** (1990): 82.1% white; 7.4% black; 8.0% Amer. Indian; 2.7% Hispanic.

Geography. Total area: 69,903 sq mi; **rank:** 20. **Land area:** 68,679 sq mi. **Acres forested land:** 7,539,000. **Location:** West South Central state bounded on the N by Colorado and Kansas; on the E by Missouri and Arkansas; on the S and W by Texas and New Mexico. **Climate:** temperate; southern humid belt merging with colder northern continental; humid eastern and dry western zones. **Topography:** high plains predominate in the W, hills and small mountains in the E; the east central region is dominated by the Arkansas R. Basin, and the Red R. Plains, in the S. **Capital:** Oklahoma City.

Economy. Principal industries: manufacturing, mineral and energy exploration and production, agriculture, services. **Principal manufactured goods:** non-electrical machinery, transportation equip., food products, fabricated metal products. **Agriculture: Chief crops:** wheat, cotton, hay, peanuts, grain sorghum, soybeans, corn, pecans. **Livestock** (1992): 5.5 mil cattle; 190,000 hogs/pigs; 145,000 sheep; 5.5 mil poultry. **Timber/lumber:** pine, oak, hickory; 204 mil bd ft. **Nonfuel Minerals** (1994): $338 mil; mostly crushed stone, portland cement, sand & gravel, gypsum, iodine. **Chief ports:** Catoosa, Muskogee. **International airports at:** Oklahoma City, Tulsa. **Value of construction** (1994): $3.0 bil. **Employment distribution** (1992): 23.7% serv.; 23.4% trade; 22.3% govt.; 13.4% mfg. **Per capita personal income** (1994): $17,744. **Unemployment** (1994): 5.8%. **Tourism** (1994): tourists spent $3 bil.

Finance. FDIC-insured commercial banks & trust companies (1994): 350. **Deposits:** $27.4 bil. **FDIC-insured savings institutions** (1994): 12. **Assets:** $5.4 bil.

Federal government. No. federal civilian employees (Mar. 1994): 32,119. **Avg. salary:** $35,519. **Notable federal facilities:** Federal Aviation Agency and Tinker AFB, both Oklahoma City; Ft. Sill, Lawton; Altus AFB, Altus; Vance AFB, Enid.

Energy. Electricity production (1994, kWh, by source): Coal: 27.5 bil; Petroleum: 11 mil; Gas: 15.5 bil; Hydroelectric: 2.5 bil.

Education. Student-teacher ratio (1993): 15.5. **Avg. salary, public school teachers** (1994-95): $27,971.

State data. Motto: Labor Omnia Vincit (Labor conquers all things). **Flower:** Mistletoe. **Bird:** Scissor-tailed flycatcher. **Tree:** Redbud. **Song:** Oklahoma! **Entered union** Nov. 16, 1907; **rank,** 46th. **State fair** at: Tulsa; last Thurs. of Sept. through 1st week of Oct.

History. Part of the Louisiana Purchase, 1803, Oklahoma was known as Indian Territory (but was not given territorial government) after it became the home of the "Five Civilized Tribes"—Cherokee, Choctaw, Chickasaw, Creek, and Seminole—1828-46. The land was also used by Comanche, Osage, and other Plains Indians. As white settlers pressed west, land was opened for homesteading by runs and lottery, the first run taking place on Apr. 22, 1889. The most famous run was to the Cherokee Outlet, 1893.

Tourist attractions. State park system—camping, hiking, water sports; Cherokee Heritage Center, Tahlequah; White Water Bay and Frontier City theme pks., both Oklahoma City; Will Rogers Memorial, Claremore; National Cowboy Hall of Fame and Remington Park Race Track, both Oklahoma City; restored Ft. Gibson Stockade, near Muskogee, the Army's largest outpost in

Indian lands; Indian pow-wows; rodeos; fishing; hunting; Ouachita National Forest; Enterprise Square, museum devoted to American economic system; Tulsa's art deco district; Wichita Mts. Wildlife Refuge, Lawton; Woolaroc Museum & Wildlife Preserve, Bartlesville.

Famous Oklahomans. Troy Aikman, Carl Albert, Gene Autry, Johnny Bench, Garth Brooks, William "Hopalong Cassidy" Boyd, L. Gordon Cooper, Jerome "Dizzy" Dean, Ralph Ellison, John Hope Franklin, James Garner, Geronimo, Woody Guthrie, Paul Harvey, Anita Hill, Ron Howard, Gen. Patrick J. Hurley, Jeane Kirkpatrick, Louis L'Amour, Mickey Mantle, Reba McEntire, Carrie Nation, Wiley Post, Tony Randall, Oral Roberts, Will Rogers, Maria Tallchief, Jim Thorpe.

Chamber of Commerce. Chamber of Commerce, 330 NE 10th, Oklahoma City, OK 73104.

Tourism Dept. PO Box 60789, Oklahoma City, OK 73146-0789.

Toll-free travel information. 1-800-652-6552.

Oregon
Beaver State

People. Population (1994): 3,086,188; **rank:** 29; **Net change** (1990-94): 8.6%. **Pop. density:** 31.0 per sq mi. **Racial/ethnic distrib.** (1990): 92.8% white; 1.6% black; 4.0% Hispanic.

Geography. Total area: 98,386 sq mi; **rank:** 9. **Land area:** 96,002 sq mi. **Acres forested land:** 27,997,000. **Location:** Pacific state, bounded on N by Washington; on E by Idaho; on S by Nevada and California; on W by the Pacific. **Climate:** coastal mild and humid climate; continental dryness and extreme temperatures in the interior. **Topography:** Coast Range of rugged mountains; fertile Willamette R. Valley to E and S; Cascade Mt. Range of volcanic peaks E of the valley; plateau E of Cascades, remaining two-thirds of state. **Capital:** Salem.

Economy. Principal industries: manufacturing, forestry, agriculture, tourism, high technology. **Principal manufactured goods:** lumber & wood products, foods, machinery, fabricated metals, paper, printing & publishing, primary metals. **Agriculture: Chief crops:** greenhouse/nursery prods., farm forest prods., hay, wheat, potatoes, onions, grass seed, pears. **Livestock** (1993): 1.4 mil cattle; 70,000 hogs/pigs; 415,000 sheep; 3.3 mil poultry. **Timber/lumber** (1993): Douglas fir, hemlock, ponderosa pine; 5.63 bil bd ft. **Nonfuel Minerals** (1994): $253 mil; mostly crushed stone, construction sand & gravel, portland cement. **Commercial fishing** (1994): $66.3 mil. **Chief ports:** Portland, Astoria, Coos Bay. **International airports at:** Portland, Klamath Falls. **Value of construction** (1994): $4.1 bil. **Employment distribution** (1991): 25.7% trade; 23.2% serv.; 18.0% mfg.; 17.8% govt. **Per capita personal income** (1994): $20,419. **Unemployment** (1994): 5.4%. **Tourism** (1992): travel expenditures, $3.13 bil.

Finance. FDIC-insured commercial banks & trust companies (1994): 44. **Deposits:** $21.3 bil. **FDIC-insured savings institutions** (1994): 10. **Assets:** $6.7 bil.

Federal government. No. federal civilian employees (Mar. 1994): 20,101. **Avg. salary:** $37,413. **Notable federal facilities:** Bonneville Power Administration.

Energy. Electricity production (1994, kWh, by source): Coal: 3.8 bil; Petroleum: 5 mil; Gas: 2.8 bil; Hydroelectric: 30.9 bil.

Education. Student-teacher ratio (1993): 19.5. **Avg. salary, public school teachers** (1994-95): $38,700.

State data. Motto: She flies with her own wings. **Flower:** Oregon grape. **Bird:** Western meadowlark. **Tree:** Douglas fir. **Song:** Oregon, My Oregon. **Entered union** Feb. 14, 1859; **rank,** 33d. **State fair** at: Salem; 12 days ending with Labor Day.

History. American Capt. Robert Gray sighted and sailed into the Columbia River, 1792; Lewis and Clark, traveling overland, wintered at its mouth, 1805-6; fur traders followed. Settlers arrived in the Willamette Valley, 1834. In 1843 the first large wave of settlers arrived via the Oregon Trail. Early in the 20th century, the "Oregon System"—political reforms that included the initiative, referendum, recall, direct primary, and woman suffrage—was adopted.

Tourist attractions. John Day Fossil Beds National Monument; Columbia River Gorge; Mt. Hood & Timberline Lodge; Crater Lake National Park; Oregon Dunes National Recreation Area; Ft. Clatsop National Memorial; Oregon Caves National Monument; Oregon Museum of Science and Industry; Shakespearean Festival, Ashland; High Desert Museum, Bend. Also, skiing, fishing; Annual Albany Timber Carnival, Pendelton Round-Up, Portland Rose Festival.

Famous Oregonians. Ernest Bloch, Ernest Haycox, Chief Joseph, Edwin Markham, Tom McCall, Dr. John McLoughlin, Joaquin Miller, Linus Pauling, John Reed, Alberto Salazar, Mary Decker Slaney, William Simon U'Ren.

Tourist information. Economic Development Department, 775 Summer St. NE, Salem, OR 97310.

Toll-free travel information. 1-800-547-7842.

Pennsylvania
Keystone State

People. Population (1994): 12,052,367; **rank:** 5; **Net change** (1990-94): 1.4%. **Pop. density:** 267.9 per sq mi. **Racial/ethnic distrib.** (1990): 88.5% white; 9.2% black; 2.0% Hispanic.

Geography. Total area: 46,058 sq mi; **rank:** 33. **Land area:** 44,820 sq mi. **Acres forested land:** 16,969,000. **Location:** Middle Atlantic state, bordered on the E by the Delaware R.; on the S by the Mason-Dixon Line; on the W by West Virginia and Ohio; on the N/NE by Lake Erie and New York. **Climate:** continental with wide fluctuations in seasonal temperatures. **Topography:** Allegheny Mts. run SW to NE, with Piedmont and Coast Plain in the SE triangle; Allegheny Front a diagonal spine across the state's center; N and W rugged plateau falls to Lake Erie Lowland. **Capital:** Harrisburg.

Economy. Principal industries: steel, travel, health, apparel, machinery, food & agriculture. **Principal manufactured goods:** primary metals; foods; fabricated metal products; non-electrical machinery; electrical machinery; printing and publishing; stone, clay, and glass products. **Agriculture: Chief crops:** corn, hay, mushrooms, apples, potatoes, winter wheat, oats, vegetables, tobacco, grapes. **Livestock** (1994): 1.8 mil cattle; 1.4 mil hogs/pigs; 139,000 sheep; 21.8 mil poultry. **Timber/lumber** (1993): pine, oak, maple; 1.05 bil bd ft. **Nonfuel Minerals** (1994): $964 mil; mostly crushed stone, portland cement, lime, construction sand & gravel. **Commercial fishing** (1994): $292,000. **Chief ports:** Philadelphia, Pittsburgh, Erie. **International airports at** Allentown, Erie, Harrisburg, Philadelphia, Pittsburgh, Wilkes-Barre/Scranton. **Value of construction** (1994): $9.7 bil. **Employment distribution** (1994): 28% serv.; 26% trade; 20% mfg.; 14% govt. **Per capita personal income** (1994): $22,324. **Unemployment** (1994): 6.2%. **Tourism** (1992): out-of-state visitors spent $10.2 bil.

Finance. FDIC-insured commercial banks & trust companies (1994): 245. **Deposits:** $133.2 bil. FDIC-insured savings institutions (1994): 130. **Assets:** $37.8 bil.

Federal government. No. federal civilian employees (Mar. 1994): 79,183. **Avg. salary:** $35,960. **Notable federal facilities:** Army War College, Carlisle; Ships Control Ctr., Mechanicsburg; New Cumberland Army Depot; Philadelphia Naval Station; Philadelphia Navy Hospital; Indiantown Gap, Annville; Letterkenny Army Depot, Chambersburg; Charles E. Kelly Spt Fac, Pittsburgh; Tobyhanna Army Depot, Tobyhanna; Naval Air Development Center, Warminster; NAS Grove, Willow Grove; Greater Pittsburgh IAP AGS, Corapolis; Willow Grove ARS, Hatboro; Harrisburg Olmsred IAP AGS, Middletown.

Energy. Electricity production (1994, kWh, by source): Coal: 93.9 bil; Petroleum: 5.2 bil; Gas: 1.2 bln; Hydroelectric: 1.5 bil; Nuclear: 67.2 bil.

Education. Student-teacher ratio (1993): 17.2. **Avg. salary, public school teachers** (1994-95): $44,489.

State data. Motto: Virtue, liberty and independence. **Flower:** Mountain laurel. **Bird:** Ruffed grouse. **Tree:**

Hemlock. **Second** of the original 13 states to ratify the Constitution, Dec. 12, 1787. **State fair** at: Harrisburg; 2d week in Jan.

History. First settlers were Swedish, 1643, on Tinicum Is. In 1655, the Dutch seized the settlement but lost it to the British, 1664. The region was given by Charles II to William Penn, 1681. Philadelphia (brotherly love) was the capital of the colonies during most of the American Revolution, and of the U.S., 1790-1800. Philadelphia was taken by the British, 1777; Washington's troops encamped at Valley Forge in the bitter winter of 1777-78. The Declaration of Independence, 1776, and the Constitution, 1787, were signed in Philadelphia.

Tourist attractions. Independence Hall & Natl. Historic Park, Franklin Institute Science Museum, Philadelphia Museum of Art, all in Philadelphia; Valley Forge Natl. Historic Park; Gettysburg Natl. Military Park; Pennsylvania Dutch Country; Hershey; Duquesne Incline, Carnegie Institute, Heinz Hall, all in Pittsburgh; year-round outdoor sports in Pocono Mts., Pine Creek River Gorge, Alleghenies, Laurel Highlands & Presque Isle State Park.

Famous Pennsylvanians. Marian Anderson, Maxwell Anderson, James Buchanan, Andrew Carnegie, Stephen Foster, Benjamin Franklin, George C. Marshall, Andrew W. Mellon, Robert E. Peary, Mary Roberts Rinehart, Betsy Ross.

Chamber of Business and Industry. 417 Walnut St., Harrisburg, PA 17120.

Toll-free travel information. 1-800-VISITPA.

Rhode Island
Little Rhody, Ocean State

People. Population (1994): 996,757; **rank:** 43; **Net change** (1990-94): –0.7%. **Pop. density:** 961.8 per sq mi. **Racial/ethnic distrib.** (1990): 91.4% white; 3.9% black; 4.6% Hispanic.

Geography. Total area: 1,545 sq mi; **rank:** 50. **Land area:** 1,045 sq mi. **Acres forested land:** 401,000. **Location:** New England state. **Climate:** invigorating and changeable. **Topography:** eastern lowlands of Narragansett Basin; western uplands of flat and rolling hills. **Capital:** Providence.

Economy. Principal industries: services, manufacturing. **Principal manufactured goods:** costume jewelry, toys, machinery, textiles, electronics. **Agriculture: Chief crops:** nursery prods., turf, potatoes, apples. **Timber/lumber:** oak; 9 mil bd ft. **Nonfuel Minerals** (1994): $27 mil; construction sand & gravel, crushed stone. **Commercial fishing** (1994): $77 mil. **Chief ports:** Providence, Quonset Point, Newport. **Value of construction** (1994): $673.3 mil. **Employment distribution** (1993): 32% services; 20% mfg.; 22% trade. **Per capita personal income** (1994): $22,251. **Unemployment** (1994): 7.1%. **Tourism** (1993): visitors spent $1.4 bil.

Finance. FDIC-insured commercial banks & trust companies (1994): 9. **Deposits:** $10.3 bil. FDIC-insured savings institutions (1994): 6. **Assets:** $6.1 bil.

Federal government. No. federal civilian employees (Mar. 1994): 5,746. **Avg. salary:** $39,774. **Notable federal facilities:** Naval War College; Naval Underwater Warfare Center, National Marine Fisheries Laboratory, EPA Environmental Research Laboratory.

Energy. Electricity production (1994, kWh, by source): Petroleum: 34 mil; Gas: 35 mil.

Education. Student-teacher ratio (1993): 14.8. **Avg. salary, public school teachers** (1994-95): $40,729.

State data. Motto: Hope. **Flower:** Violet. **Bird:** Rhode Island red. **Tree:** Red maple. **Song:** Rhode Island. **Thirteenth** of original 13 states to ratify the Constitution, May 29, 1790. **State fair** at: Richmond; mid-Aug.

History. Rhode Island is distinguished for its battle for freedom of conscience and action, begun by Roger Williams, founder of Providence, who was exiled from Massachusetts Bay Colony in 1636, and Anne Hutchinson, exiled in 1638. Rhode Island gave protection to Quakers in 1657 and to Jews from Holland in 1658.

The colonists broke the power of the Narragansett Indians in the Great Swamp Fight, 1675, the decisive battle in King Philip's War. British trade restrictions angered the colonists, and they burned the British revenue cutter Gaspee, 1772. The colony declared its independence May 4, 1776. Gen. John Sullivan and Lafayette won a partial victory, 1778, but failed to oust the British.

Tourist attractions. Newport mansions; summer resorts, and water sports; various yachting races including Newport to Bermuda; Block Island; Touro Synagogue, Newport, 1763, oldest in U.S.; first Baptist Church in America, Providence, 1638; Slater Mill Historic Site, including early cottonmill, 1793; Gilbert Stuart birthplace, Saunderstown; Narragansett Indian Fall Festival.

Famous Rhode Islanders. Ambrose Burnside, George M. Cohan, Nelson Eddy, Jabez Gorham, Nathanael Greene, Christopher and Oliver La Farge, Matthew C. and Oliver Hazard Perry, Gilbert Stuart.

Chamber of Commerce. 30 Exchange Terr., Providence, RI 02908.

Toll-free travel information. 1-800-556-2484.

South Carolina
Palmetto State

People. Population (1994): 3,663,984; **rank:** 25; **Net change** (1990-94): 5.1%. **Pop. density:** 119.7 per sq mi. **Racial/ethnic distrib.** (1990): 69.0% white; 29.8% black; 0.9% Hispanic.

Geography. Total area: 32,008 sq mi; **rank:** 40. **Land area:** 30,111 sq mi. **Acres forested land:** 12,257,000. **Location:** South Atlantic state, bordered by North Carolina on the N; Georgia on the SW and W; the Atlantic Ocean on the E, SE, and S. **Climate:** humid sub-tropical. **Topography:** Blue Ridge province in NW has highest peaks; piedmont lies between the mountains and the fall line; coastal plain covers two-thirds of the state. **Capital:** Columbia.

Economy. Principal industries: tourism, agriculture, manufacturing. **Principal manufactured goods:** textiles, chemicals and allied products, machinery & fabricated metal products, apparel and related products. **Agriculture: Chief crops:** tobacco, soybeans, corn, cotton, peaches, hay. **Livestock** (1994): 500,000 cattle; 350,000 hogs/pigs; 6.3 mil chickens, excluding broilers. **Timber/lumber** (1993): pine, oak; 1.39 bil bd ft. **Nonfuel Minerals** (1994): $415 mil; mostly portland cement, crushed stone, construction and masonary sand & gravel. **Commercial fishing** (1994): $28 mil. **Chief ports:** Charleston, Georgetown, Beaufort/ Port Royal. **International airports at:** Charleston. **Value of construction** (1994): $4.2 bil. **Employment distribution** (1993): 23.8% mfg.; 21.2% serv.; 22.4% trade; 6.8% govt. **Per capita personal income** (1994): $17,695. **Unemployment** (1994): 6.3%. **Tourism** (1992): $6.5 bil.

Finance. FDIC-insured commercial banks & trust companies (1994): 75. **Deposits:** $22.3 bil. **FDIC-insured savings institutions** (1994): 37. **Assets:** $8.0 bil.

Federal government. No. federal civilian employees (Mar. 1994): 21,602. **Avg. salary:** $34,221. **Notable federal facilities:** Polaris Submarine Base; Barnwell Nuclear Power Plant; Ft. Jackson; Parris Island; Savannah River Plant.

Energy. Electricity production (1994, kWh, by source): Coal: 26.7 bil.; Petroleum: 101 mil; Gas: 279 mil; Hydroelectric: 2.3 bil; Nuclear: 44.5 bil.

Education. Student-teacher ratio (1993): 16.7. **Avg. salary, public school teachers** (1994-95): $30,341.

State data. Motto: Dum Spiro Spero (While I breathe, I hope). **Flower:** Yellow jessamine. **Bird:** Carolina wren. **Tree:** Palmetto. **Song:** Carolina. **Eighth** of the original 13 states to ratify the Constitution, May 23, 1788. **State fair** at: Columbia; mid-Oct.

History. The first English colonists settled, 1670, on the Ashley River, moved to the site of Charleston, 1680. The colonists seized the government, 1775, and the royal governor fled. The British took Charleston, 1780, but were defeated at Kings Mountain that year, and at Cowpens and Eutaw Springs, 1781. In the 1830s, South Carolinians, angered by federal protective tariffs, adopted the Nullification Doctrine, holding that a state can void an act of Congress. The state was the first to secede in 1861, and Confederate troops fired on and

forced the surrender of U.S. troops at Ft. Sumter, in Charleston Harbor, launching the Civil War.

Tourist attractions. Restored historic Charleston Harbor area and Charleston gardens: Middleton Place, Magnolia, Cypress; other gardens at Brookgreen, Edisto, Glencairn; state parks; coastal islands; shore resorts such as Myrtle Beach and Hilton Head Island; fishing and quail hunting; American Revolution War battle sites; Andrew Jackson State Park & Museum; Ft. Sumter National Monument, in Charleston Harbor; Charleston Museum, est. 1773, the oldest museum in the U.S.; South Carolina State Museum, one of largest museums in the South, Columbia; Riverbanks Zoo, Columbia.

Famous South Carolinians. Charles Bolden, James F. Byrnes, John C. Calhoun, DuBose Heyward, Ernest F. Hollings, Andrew Jackson, Jesse Jackson, James Longstreet, Francis Marion, Ronald McNair, Charles Pinckney, John Rutledge, Thomas Sumter, Strom Thurmond, John B. Watson.

Tourist information. S. Carolina Dept. of Parks, Recreation, & Tourism, 803-734-0122.

South Dakota
Coyote State, Mount Rushmore State

People. Population (1994): 721,164; **rank:** 45; **Net change** (1990-94): 3.6%. **Pop. density:** 9.37 per sq mi. **Racial/ethnic distrib.** (1990): 91.6% white; 0.5% black; 7.3% Amer. Indian; 0.8% Hispanic.

Geography. Total area: 77,121 sq mi; **rank:** 17. **Land area:** 75,896 sq mi. **Acres forested land:** 1,690,000. **Location:** West North Central state bounded on the N by North Dakota; on the E by Minnesota and Iowa; on the S by Nebraska; on the W by Wyoming and Montana. **Climate:** characterized by extremes of temperature, persistent winds, low precipitation and humidity. **Topography:** Prairie Plains in the E; rolling hills of the Great Plains in the W; the Black Hills, rising 3,500 ft, in the SW corner. **Capital:** Pierre.

Economy. Principal industries: agriculture, services, manufacturing. **Principal manufactured goods:** food & kindred prods., machinery, electric & electronic equipment. **Agriculture: Chief crops:** corn, oats, wheat, sunflowers, soybeans, sorghum. **Livestock** (1993): 3.75 mil cattle; 1.75 mil hogs/pigs; 543,000 sheep. **Timber/lumber** (1993): ponderosa pine; 174 mil bd ft. **Nonfuel Minerals** (1994): $322 mil; mostly gold, portland cement, construction sand & gravel. **Value of construction** (1994): $845.6 mil. **Employment distribution** (1994): 24% serv.; 12% mfg. **Per capita personal income** (1994): $19,577. **Unemployment** (1994): 3.3%. **Tourism** (1994): travelers' impact $1.24 bil.

Finance. FDIC-insured commercial banks & trust companies (1994): 120. **Deposits:** $11.4 bil. **FDIC-insured savings institutions** (1994): 6. **Assets:** $757 mil.

Federal government. No. federal civilian employees (Mar. 1994): 7,162. **Avg. salary:** $32,973. **Notable federal facilities:** Bureau of Indian Affairs, Ellsworth AFB, Corp of Engineers, Nat'l Park Service.

Energy. Electricity production (1994, kWh, by source): Coal: 2.8 bil; Petroleum: 19 mil; Gas: 8 mil; Hydroelectric: 5.1 bil.

Education. Student-teacher ratio (1993): 14.9. **Avg. salary, public school teachers** (1994-95): $26,017.

State data. Motto: Under God, the people rule. **Flower:** Pasqueflower. **Bird:** Chinese ring-necked pheasant. **Tree:** Black Hills spruce. **Song:** Hail, South Dakota. **Entered union** Nov. 2, 1889; **rank:** 40th. **State fair** at: Huron; late Aug.-early Sept.

History. The Verendrye brothers (Fr.) explored the region, 1742-43. Lewis and Clark passed through the area, 1804 and 1806. First white American settlement was at Fort Pierre, 1817. Gold was discovered, 1874, on the Great Sioux Reservation; miners rushed in. The U.S. first tried to stop them, then relaxed its opposition. The "Great Dakota Boom" began 1879. Conflicts between the Indian and white communities climaxed in 1890 with the massacre of Indian families at Wounded Knee.

Tourist attractions. Black Hills; Mt. Rushmore, with colossal likenesses of the faces of U.S. Presidents

Washington, Jefferson, Lincoln, and T. Roosevelt carved by sculptor Gutzon Borglum; Needles Highway; Harney Peak, at 7,242 ft, the tallest peak east of the Rockies; Deadwood, an 1876 Gold Rush town; Custer State Park's buffalo and burro herds; Jewel Cave, the 4th longest cave in the world; Badlands Natl. Park's "moonscape"; "Great Lakes of So. Dakota"; Ft. Sisseton, restored 1864 army frontier post; Great Plains Zoo & Museum in Sioux Falls; Corn Palace in Mitchell; Wind Cave; Mammoth Site, ongoing excavation of prehistoric mammoths; Crazy Horse, mountain carving in progress.

Famous South Dakotans. Sparky Anderson, Tom Brokaw, Crazy Horse, Myron Floren, Mary Hart, Cheryl Ladd, Dr. Ernest O. Lawrence, George McGovern, Billy Mills, Allen Neuharth, Pat O'Brien, Sitting Bull.

Tourist Information. South Dakota Tourism, 711 E. Wells Ave., Pierre, SD 57501-3369.

Toll-free travel information. 1-800-SDAKOTA.

Tennessee
Volunteer State

People. Population (1994): 5,175,240; **rank:** 17; **Net change** (1990-94): 6.1%. **Pop. density:** 121.9 per sq mi. **Racial/ethnic distrib.** (1990): 83.0% white; 16.0% black; 0.7% Hispanic.

Geography. Total area: 42,146 sq mi; **rank:** 36. **Land area:** 41,219 sq mi. **Acres forested land:** 13,612,000. **Location:** East South Central state bounded on the N by Kentucky and Virginia; on the E by North Carolina; on the S by Georgia, Alabama, and Mississippi; on the W by Arkansas and Missouri. **Climate:** humid continental to the N; humid sub-tropical to the S. **Topography:** rugged country in the E; the Great Smoky Mts. of the Unakas; low ridges of the Appalachian Valley; the flat Cumberland Plateau; slightly rolling terrain and knobs of the Interior Low Plateau, the largest region; Eastern Gulf Coastal Plain to the W, is laced with meandering streams; Mississippi Alluvial Plain, a narrow strip of swamp and flood plain in the extreme W. **Capital:** Nashville.

Economy. Principal industries: manufacturing, trade, services, tourism, finance, insurance, real estate. **Principal manufactured goods:** chemicals, food, transportation equip., industrial machinery & equip., fabr. metal prods., rubber/plastic prods., paper & allied prods., printing and publishing. **Agriculture: Chief crops:** tobacco, cotton, lint, soybeans, grain, corn. **Livestock** (1994): 2.44 mil cattle; 0.47 mil hogs/pigs; 1.3 mil poultry. **Timber/lumber** (1993): red oak, white oak, yellow poplar, hickory; 879 mil bd ft. **Nonfuel Minerals** (1994): $577 mil; mostly crushed stone, sand & gravel, zinc, cement. **Chief ports:** Memphis, Nashville, Chattanooga, Knoxville. **International airports at:** Memphis, Nashville. **Value of construction** (1994): $6.4 bil. **Employment distribution** (1994): 22.2% mfg.; 23.1% trade; 24.8% serv.; 15.3% govt. **Per capita personal income** (1994): $19,482. **Unemployment** (1994): 4.8%. **Tourism** (1993): out-of-state visitors spent $5.15 bil.

Finance. FDIC-insured commercial banks & trust companies (1994): 251. **Deposit:** $48.5 bil. **FDIC-insured savings institutions** (1994): 30. **Assets:** $7.0 bil.

Federal government. No. federal civilian employees (Mar. 1994): 36,614. **Avg. salary:** $37,608. **Notable federal facilities:** Tennessee Valley Authority; Oak Ridge Nat'l. Laboratories; Arnold Engineering Development Center; Ft. Campbell Army Base; Millington Naval Station.

Energy. Electricity production (1994, kWh, by source): Coal: 52.1 bil; Petroleum: 296 mil; Gas: 95 mil; Hydroelectric: 10.4 bil; Nuclear: 11.9 bil.

Education. Student-teacher ratio (1993): 18.8. **Avg. salary, public school teachers** (1994-95): $31,270.

State data. Motto: Agriculture and commerce. **Flower:** Iris. **Bird:** Mockingbird. **Tree:** Tulip poplar. **Song:** The Tennessee Waltz. **Entered union** June 1, 1796; rank, 16th. **State fair** at: Nashville; mid-Sept.

History. Spanish explorers first visited the area, 1541. English traders crossed the Great Smokies from the east while France's Marquette and Jolliet sailed down the Mississippi on the west, 1673. First permanent settlement was by Virginians on the Watauga River, 1769. During the American Revolution, the colonists helped win the Battle of Kings Mountain, NC, 1780, and joined other eastern campaigns. The state seceded from the Union 1861, and saw many engagements of the Civil War, but 30,000 soldiers fought for the Union.

Tourist attractions. Natural wonders include Reelfoot Lake, the reservoir basin of the Mississippi R. formed by the 1811 earthquake; Lookout Mountain, Chattanooga; Fall Creek Falls, 256 ft high; Great Smoky Mountains National Park; Lost Sea, Sweetwater; Cherokee Natl. Forest; Cumberland Gap Natl. Park.

Also, the Hermitage, 13 mi E of Nashville, home of Andrew Jackson; the homes of presidents Polk and Andrew Johnson; American Museum of Science and Energy, Oak Ridge; the Parthenon, Nashville, a replica of the Parthenon of Athens; the Grand Old Opry, Nashville; Opryland USA, theme park, Nashville; Dollywood, theme park, Pigeon Forge; The Tennessee Aquarium, Chattanooga; Graceland, home of Elvis Presley, Memphis; Alex Haley Home & Museum, Henning; Casey Jones Home & Museum, Jackson.

Famous Tennesseans. Roy Acuff, Davy Crockett, David Farragut, Aretha Franklin, William C. Handy, Sam Houston, Cordell Hull, Grace Moore, Dolly Parton, Minnie Pearl, Dinah Shore, Bessie Smith, Alvin York.

Tourist information. Dept. of Tourist Development, 5th Floor, Rachel Jackson Bldg., 320 6th Ave. N., Nashville, TN 37202.

Toll-free travel information. 1-800-TENN200.

Texas
Lone Star State

People. Population (1994): 18,378,185; **rank:** 2; **Net change** (1990-94): 8.2%. **Pop. density:** 67.4 per sq mi. **Racial/ethnic distrib.** (1990): 75.2% white; 11.9% black; 25.5% Hispanic.

Geography. Total area: 268,601 sq mi; **rank:** 2. **Land area:** 261,914 sq mi; **Acres forested land:** 19,193,000. **Location:** Southwestern state, bounded on the SE by the Gulf of Mexico; on the SW by Mexico, separated by the Rio Grande; surrounding states are Louisiana, Arkansas, Oklahoma, New Mexico. **Climate:** extremely varied; driest region is the Trans-Pecos; wettest is the NE. **Topography:** Gulf Coast Plain in the S and SE; North Central Plains slope upward with some hills; the Great Plains extend over the Panhandle, are broken by low mountains; the Trans-Pecos is the southern extension of the Rockies. **Capital:** Austin.

Economy. Principal industries: trade, oil and gas extraction, services, manufacturing. **Principal manufactured goods:** machinery, transportation equipment, foods, electrical and electronic prods., chemicals and allied prods., apparel. **Agriculture: Chief crops:** cotton, grain sorghum, grains, vegetables, citrus and other fruits, pecans, peanuts. **Livestock** (1995): 1.5 mil cattle; 575,000 hogs/pigs; 1.7 mil sheep; 19.3 mil poultry. **Timber/lumber** (1993): pine, cypress; 1.58 bil bd ft. **Nonfuel Minerals** (1994): $1.4 bil; mostly portland cement, crushed stone, magnesium, gypsum, construction sand & gravel, lime, salt. **Commercial fishing** (1994): $207 mil. **Chief ports:** Houston, Galveston, Brownsville, Beaumont, Port Arthur, Corpus Christi. **Major international airports at:** Houston, Dallas/Ft. Worth, San Antonio. **Value of construction** (1994): $20.8 bil. **Employment distribution** (1994): 24.2% trade; 25.8% serv.; 18.3% govt.; 13.0% mfg. **Per capita personal income** (1994): $19,857. **Unemployment** (1994): 6.4%. **Tourism** (1993): all travel $22.8 bil.

Finance. FDIC-insured commercial banks & trust companies (1994): 980. **Deposits:** $153.4 bil. **FDIC-insured savings institutions** (1994): 60. **Assets:** $56.4 bil.

Federal government. No. federal civilian employees (Mar. 1994): 116,922. **Avg. salary:** $35,978. **Notable federal facilities:** Fort Hood (Killeen); Kelly AFB and Ft. Sam Houston, both San Antonio.

Energy. Electricity production (1994, kWh, by source): Coal: 122.6 bil; Petroleum: 309 mil; Gas: 101.7 bil; Hydroelectric: 1.5 bil; Nuclear: 28.0 bil.

Education. Student-teacher ratio (1993): 16.0. **Avg. salary, public school teachers** (1994-95): $31,310.

State data. Motto: Friendship. **Flower:** Bluebonnet. **Bird:** Mockingbird. **Tree:** Pecan. **Song:** Texas, Our Texas. **Entered union** Dec. 29, 1845; rank, 28th. **State fair** at: Dallas; mid-Oct.

History. Pineda sailed along the Texas coast, 1519; Cabeza de Vaca and Coronado visited the interior, 1541. Spaniards made the first settlement at Ysleta, near El Paso, 1682. Americans moved into the land early in the 19th century. Mexico, of which Texas was a part, won independence from Spain, 1821; Santa Anna became dictator, 1835. Texans rebelled; Santa Anna wiped out defenders of the Alamo, 1836. Sam Houston's Texans defeated Santa Anna at San Jacinto, and independence was proclaimed the same year. In 1845, Texas was admitted to the Union.

Tourist attractions. Padre Island National Seashore; Big Bend, Guadalupe Mts. national parks; The Alamo; Ft. Davis; Six Flags Amusement Park; Sea World and Fiesta Texas, both in San Antonio. Named for Pres. Lyndon B. Johnson are a state park, a natl. historic site marking his birthplace, boyhood home, and ranch, all near Johnson City, and a library in Austin.

Famous Texans. Stephen F. Austin, Lloyd Bentsen, James Bowie, Carol Burnett, J. Frank Dobie, Dwight D. Eisenhower, Sam Houston, Howard Hughes, Lyndon B. Johnson, Mary Martin, Chester Nimitz, Katharine Ann Porter, Sam Rayburn.

Chamber of Commerce. 900 Congress, Suite 501, Austin, TX 78701.

Toll-free travel information. 1-800-8888TEX.

Utah
Beehive State

People. Population (1994): 1,907,936; **rank: 34; Net change** (1990-94): 10.7%. **Pop. density:** 22.1 per sq mi. **Racial/ethnic distrib.** (1990): 93.8% white; 0.7% black; 4.9% Hispanic.

Geography. Total area: 84,904 sq mi; **rank: 13. Land area:** 82,168 sq mi. **Acres forested land:** 16,234,000. **Location:** Middle Rocky Mountain state; its southeastern corner touches Colorado, New Mexico, and Arizona, and is the only spot in the U.S. where 4 states join. **Climate:** arid; ranging from warm desert in SW to alpine in NE. **Topography:** high Colorado plateau is cut by brilliantly colored canyons of the SE; broad, flat, desert-like Great Basin of the W; the Great Salt Lake and Bonneville Salt Flats to the NW; Middle Rockies in the NE run E-W; valleys and plateaus of the Wasatch Front. **Capital:** Salt Lake City.

Economy. Principal industries: services, trade, manufacturing, government, construction. **Principal manufactured goods:** guided missiles and parts, electronic components, food products, fabricated metals, steel, electrical equipment, automobile airbags. **Agriculture: Chief crops:** hay, corn, wheat, barley, apples, potatoes, cherries, onions, peaches, pears. **Livestock:** (1995) 890,000 cattle; 44,000 hogs/pigs; 445,000 sheep; 5.7 mil poultry. **Timber/lumber:** aspen, spruce, pine; 40 mil bd ft. **Nonfuel Minerals** (1994): $1.4 bil; copper, potash, gold, molybdenum, iron ore, magnesium, phosphate rock, salt. **International airports at:** Salt Lake City. **Value of construction** (1994): $3.4 bil. **Employment distribution** (1993): 26.2% serv.; 23.6% trade; 19.7% govt; 13.6% mfg. **Per capita personal income** (1994): $17,043. **Unemployment** (1994): 3.7%. **Tourism** (1986): travelers spent $2.0 bil.

Finance. FDIC-insured commercial banks & trust companies (1994): 44. **Deposits:** $12.0 bil. **FDIC-insured savings institutions** (1994): 4. **Assets:** $927 mil.

Federal government. No. federal civilian employees (Mar. 1994): 27,483. **Avg. salary:** $33,856. **Notable federal facilities:** Hill AFB; Tooele Army Depot; IRS Western Service Center.

Energy. Electricity production (1994, kWh, by source): Coal: 32.8 bil; Petroleum: 30 mil; Gas: 750 mil; Hydroelectric: 716 mil.

Education. Student-teacher ratio (1993): 24.7. **Avg. salary, public school teachers** (1994-95): $28,676.

State data. Motto: Industry. **Flower:** Sego lily. **Bird:** Seagull. **Tree:** Blue spruce. **Song:** Utah, We Love Thee. **Entered union** Jan. 4, 1896; rank, 45th. **State fair** at Salt Lake City; Sept.

History. Spanish Franciscans visited the area, 1776, the first white men to do so. American fur traders followed. Permanent settlement began with the arrival of the Mormons, 1847. They made the arid land bloom and created a prosperous economy, organized the State of Deseret, 1849, and asked admission to the Union. This was not achieved until 1896, after a long period of controversy over the Mormon Church's doctrine of polygamy, which it discontinued in 1890.

Tourist attractions. Temple Square, Mormon Church headdquarters, Salt Lake City; Great Salt Lake; fishing streams, lakes and reservoirs, numerous winter sports; campgrounds. Natural wonders may be seen at Zion, Canyonlands, Bryce Canyon, Arches, and Capitol Reef national parks; Dinosaur, Rainbow Bridge, Timpanogos Cave, and Natural Bridges national monuments. Also Lake Powell and Flaming Gorge reservoirs.

Famous Utahans. Maude Adams, Ezra Taft Benson, John Moses Browning, Mariner Eccles, Philo Farnsworth, James Fletcher, David M. Kennedy, J. Willard Marriott, Merlin Olsen, Osmond family, Ivy Baker Priest, George Romney, Brigham Young, Loretta Young.

Tourist information. Utah Travel Council, Council Hall, Salt Lake City, UT 84114; 801-538-1030.

Vermont
Green Mountain State

People. Population (1994): 580,209; **rank: 49; Net change** (1990-94): 3.1%. **Pop. density:** 61.6 per sq mi. **Racial/ethnic distrib.** (1990): 98.6% white; 0.3% black; 0.6% Asian; 0.7% Hispanic.

Geography. Total area: 9,615 sq mi; **rank: 45. Land area:** 9,249 sq mi. **Acres forested land:** 4,538,000. **Location:** northern New England state. **Climate:** temperate, with considerable temperature extremes; heavy snowfall in mountains. **Topography:** Green Mts. N-S backbone 20-36 mi wide; avg. altitude 1,000 ft. **Capital:** Montpelier.

Economy. Principal industries: manufacturing, tourism, agriculture, trade; finance, insurance, real estate, government. **Principal manufactured goods:** machine tools, furniture, scales, books, computer components, fishing rods. **Agriculture: Chief crops:** dairy products, apples, maple syrup, silage corn, hay. **Livestock** (1992): 310,518 cattle/cows; 3,738 hogs/pigs; 17,145 sheep/lambs; 151,767 hens/pullets; turkeys 1,253. **Timber/lumber** (1993): pine, spruce, fir, hemlock; 225 mil bd ft. **Nonfuel Minerals** (1994): $48 mil; mostly dimension stone, crushed stone, construction sand & gravel, asbestos. **International airports at:** Burlington. **Value of construction** (1994): $553.2 mil. **Employment distribution** (1993): 33% serv.; 29% trade; 21% mfg. **Per capita personal income** (1994): $20,224. **Unemployment** (1994): 4.7%. **Tourism** (1990): visitors spent $1.25 bil.

Finance. FDIC-insured commercial banks & trust companies (1994): 20. **Deposits:** $4.9 bil. **FDIC-insured savings institutions** (1994): 8. **Assets:** $2.4 bil.

Federal government. No. federal civilian employees (Mar. 1994): 2,802. **Avg. salary:** $34,995.

Energy. Electricity production (1994, kWh, by source): Petroleum: 6 mil; Gas: 6 mil; Hydroelectric: 895 mil; Nuclear: 4.3 bil.

Education. Student-teacher ratio (1993): 12.7. **Avg. salary, public school teachers** (1994-95): $36,311.

State data. Motto: Freedom and unity. **Flower:** Red clover. **Bird:** Hermit thrush. **Tree:** Sugar maple. **Song:** Hail, Vermont. **Entered union** Mar. 4, 1791; rank, 14th. **State fair** at: Rutland; early Sept.

History. Champlain explored the lake that bears his name, 1609. First American settlement was Ft. Dummer, 1724, near Brattleboro. Ethan Allen and the Green Mountain Boys captured Ft. Ticonderoga (NY), 1775; John Stark defeated part of Burgoyne's forces near

Bennington, 1777. In the War of 1812, Thomas Mac-Donough defeated a British fleet on Champlain off Plattsburgh (NY), 1814.

Tourist attractions. Year-round outdoor sports: hiking, camping, and skiing; numerous alpine & cross-country ski areas. Shelburne Museum; Rock of Ages Tourist Center, Graniteville; Vermont Marble Exhibit, Proctor; Bennington Battle Monument; Pres. Coolidge homestead, Plymouth; Maple Grove Maple Museum, St. Johnsbury.

Famous Vermonters. Ethan Allen, Chester A. Arthur, Calvin Coolidge, Adm. George Dewey, John Dewey, Stephen A. Douglas, Dorothy Canfield Fisher, James Fisk.

Tourist information. Vermont Dept. of Travel and Tourism, 134 State St., Montpelier, VT 05602; 802-828-3236 .

Toll-free travel information. 1-800-VERMONT

Virginia
Old Dominion

People. Population (1994): 6,551,522; **rank:** 12; **Net change** (1990-94): 5.9%. **Pop. density:** 161.0 per sq mi. **Racial/ethnic distrib.** (1990): 77.4% white; 18.8% black; 2.6% Asian; 2.6% Hispanic.

Geography. Total area: 42,777 sq mi; **rank:** 35. **Land area:** 39,598 sq mi. **Acres forested land:** 15,858,000. **Location:** South Atlantic state bounded by the Atlantic Ocean on the E and surrounded by North Carolina, Tennessee, Kentucky, West Virginia, and Maryland. **Climate:** mild and equable. **Topography:** mountain and valley region in the W, including the Blue Ridge Mts.; rolling piedmont plateau; tidewater, or coastal plain, including the eastern shore. **Capital:** Richmond.

Economy. Principal industries: services, trade, government, manufacturing, tourism, agriculture. **Principal manufactured goods:** textiles, transportation equipment, electric & electronic equipment, food processing, chemicals, printing. **Agriculture: Chief crops:** soybeans, tobacco, peanuts, corn, far grain, tomatoes, apples, summer & sweet potatoes. **Livestock** (1992): 1.78 mil cattle; 390,000 hogs/pigs; 122,000 sheep; 2.38 mil broilers, 19.3 mil turkeys. **Timber/lumber** (1993): pine and hardwoods; 1.24 bil bd ft. **Nonfuel Minerals** (1994): $513 mil; mostly crushed stone, lime, construction sand & gravel. **Commercial fishing** (1994): $101.2 mil. **Chief ports:** Hampton Roads, Richmond, Alexandria. **International airports at:** Norfolk, Dulles, Richmond, Newport News. **Value of construction** (1994): $8.5 bil. **Employment distribution** (1992): 26.6% serv.; 22.3% trade; 20.7% govt.; 14.3% mfg. **Per capita personal income** (1994): $22,594. **Unemployment** (1994): 4.9%. **Tourism** (1992): domestic travelers spent $8.6 bil.

Finance. FDIC-insured commercial banks & trust companies (1994): 164. **Deposits:** $57.9 bil. **FDIC-insured savings institutions** (1994): 38. **Assets:** $13.5 bil.

Federal government. No. federal civilian employees (Mar. 1994): 134,760. **Avg. salary:** $42,552. **Notable federal facilities:** Pentagon; Naval Sta., Norfolk; Naval Air Sta., Norfolk, Virginia Beach; Naval Shipyard, Portsmouth; Marine Corps Base, Quantico; Langley AFB; NASA at Langley.

Energy. Electricity production (1994, kWh, by source): Coal: 22.4 bil; Petroleum: 2.4 bil; Gas: 2.2 bil; Hydroelectric: 289 mil; Nuclear: 25.4 bil.

Education. Student-teacher ratio (1993): 14.9. **Avg. salary, public school teachers** (1994-95): $33,753.

State data. Motto: Sic Semper Tyrannis (Thus always to tyrants). **Flower:** Dogwood. **Bird:** Cardinal. **Tree:** Dogwood. **Song:** Carry Me Back to Old Virginia. **Tenth** of the original 13 states to ratify the Constitution, June 25, 1788. **State fair** at: Richmond; late Sept.-early Oct.

History. English settlers founded Jamestown, 1607. Virginians took over much of the government from royal Gov. Dunmore in 1775, forcing him to flee. Virginians under George Rogers Clark freed the Ohio-Indiana-Illinois area of British forces. Benedict Arnold burned Richmond and Petersburg for the British, 1781. That

same year, Britain's Cornwallis was trapped at Yorktown and surrendered.

Tourist attractions. Colonial Williamsburg; Busch Gardens, Williamsburg; Wolf Trap Farm, near Falls Church; Arlington National Cemetery; Mt. Vernon, home of George Washington; Jamestown Festival Park; Yorktown; Jefferson's Monticello, Charlottesville; Robert E. Lee's birthplace, Stratford Hall, and grave, at Lexington; Appomattox; Shenandoah National Park; Blue Ridge Parkway; Virginia Beach; King's Dominion, near Richmond.

Famous Virginians. Richard E. Byrd, James B. Cabell, William Henry Harrison, Patrick Henry, Thomas Jefferson, Joseph E. Johnston, Robert E. Lee, Meriwether Lewis and William Clark, James Madison, John Marshall, George Mason, James Monroe, Edgar Allan Poe, Walter Reed, Zachary Taylor, John Tyler, Maggie Walker, Booker T. Washington, George Washington, Woodrow Wilson.

Chamber of Commerce. 9 South Fifth St., Richmond, VA 23219.

Toll-free travel information. 1-800-VISITVA.

Washington
Evergreen State

People. Population (1994): 5,343,090; **rank:** 15; **Net change** (1990-94): 9.8%. **Pop. density:** 77.1 per sq mi. **Racial/ethnic distrib.** (1990): 88.5% white; 3.1% black; 4.3% Asian; 4.4% Hispanic.

Geography. Total area: 71,302 sq mi; **rank:** 18. **Land area:** 66,581 sq mi. **Acres forested land:** 20,483,000. **Location:** Pacific state bordered by Canada on the N; Idaho on the E; Oregon on the S; and the Pacific Ocean on the W. **Climate:** mild, dominated by the Pacific Ocean and protected by the Rockies. **Topography:** Olympic Mts. on NW peninsula; open land along coast to Columbia R.; flat terrain of Puget Sound Lowland; Cascade Mts. region's high peaks to the E; Columbia Basin in central portion; highlands to the NE; mountains to the SE. **Capital:** Olympia.

Economy. Principal industries: forest products, aerospace, food products, primary metals, agriculture. **Principal manufactured goods:** aircraft, pulp and paper, lumber and plywood, aluminum, processed fruits and vegetables. **Agriculture: Chief crops:** apples, potatoes, hay, nursery/greenhouse plants, pears, hops, sweet cherries. **Livestock** (1993): 1.4 mil cattle; 46,000 hogs/pigs; 75,000 sheep; 5.6 mil poultry, excluding broilers. **Timber/lumber** (1993): Douglas fir, hemlock, cedar, pine; 4.05 bil bd ft. **Nonfuel Minerals** (1994): $556 mil; mostly construction sand & gravel, crushed stone, magnesium metal, portland cement. **Commercial fishing** (1994): $175.2 mil. **Chief ports:** Seattle, Tacoma, Vancouver, Kelso-Longview. **International airports at:** Seattle/Tacoma, Spokane, Boeing Field. **Value of construction** (1994): $7.8 bil. **Employment distribution** (1993): 24.2% trade; 25.7% serv.; 19.1% govt.; 15.1% mfg. **Per capita personal income** (1994): $22,610. **Unemployment** (1994): 6.4%. **Tourism** (1990): $5.3 bil.

Finance. FDIC-insured commercial banks & trust companies (1994): 86. **Deposits:** $34.7 bil. **FDIC-insured savings institutions** (1994): 27. **Assets:** $34.4 bil.

Federal government. No. federal civilian employees (Mar. 1994): 47,753. **Avg. salary:** $38,143. **Notable federal facilities:** Bonneville Power Admin.; Ft. Lewis; McChord AFB; Hanford Nuclear Reservation; Bremerton Naval Shipyards.

Energy. Electricity production (1994, kWh, by source): Coal: 9.8 bil; Petroleum: 6 mil; Gas: 206 mil; Hydroelectric: 65.1 bil; Nuclear: 6.7 bil.

Education. Student-teacher ratio (1993): 20.1. **Avg. salary, public school teachers** (1994-95): $36,120.

State data. Motto: Alki (By and by). **Flower:** Western rhododendron. **Bird:** Willow goldfinch. **Tree:** Western hemlock. **Song:** Washington, My Home. **Entered union** Nov. 11, 1889; **rank**, 42d. **State fairs** at: many county fairs, mostly in Aug. or Sept.

History. Spain's Bruno Hezeta sailed the coast, 1775. American Capt. Robert Gray sailed up the Columbia

River, 1792. Canadian fur traders set up Spokane House, 1810; Americans under John Jacob Astor established a post at Fort Okanogan, 1811. Missionary Marcus Whitman settled near Walla Walla, 1836. Final agreement on the border of Washington and Canada was made with Britain, 1846, and gold was discovered in the state's northeast, 1855, bringing new settlers.

Tourist attractions. Mt. Rainier, Olympic, and North Cascades national parks; Mt. St. Helens; Pacific beaches; Puget Sound; wineries; Indian cultures; year-round outdoor recreation: Seattle Waterfront, Seattle Center, Space Needle, San Juan Islands, Grand Coulee Dam, Columbia R. Gorge National Scenic Area, Spokane's Riverfront Park.

Famous Washingtonians. Bing Crosby, William O. Douglas, Bill Gates, Henry M. Jackson, Gary Larson, Mary McCarthy, Edward R. Murrow, Theodore Roethke, Marcus Whitman, Minoru Yamasaki.

Tourist information. WA State Tourism Division, PO Box 2500, Olympia, WA 98504-2500.

Toll-free travel information. 1-800-544-1800.

West Virginia
Mountain State

People. Population (1994): 1,822,021; **rank:** 35; **Net change** (1990-94): 1.6%. **Pop. density:** 75.2 per sq mi. **Racial/ethnic distrib.** (1990): 96.2% white; 3.1% black; 0.5% Hispanic.

Geography. Total area: 24,231 sq mi; **rank:** 41. **Land area:** 24,087 sq mi. **Acres forested land:** 12,128,000. **Location:** South Atlantic state bounded on the N by Ohio, Pennsylvania, Maryland; on the S and W by Virginia, Kentucky, Ohio; on the E by Maryland and Virginia. **Climate:** humid continental climate except for marine modification in the lower panhandle. **Topography:** ranging from hilly to mountainous; Allegheny Plateau in the W, covers two-thirds of the state; mountains here are the highest in the state, over 4,000 ft. **Capital:** Charleston.

Economy. Principal industries: manufacturing, services, mining, tourism. **Principal manufactured goods:** machinery, plastic and hardwood prods., fabricated metals, basic organic and inorganic chemicals, aluminum, steel. **Agriculture: Chief crops:** apples, peaches, hay, tobacco, corn, wheat, oats. **Chief products:** dairy prods., eggs. **Livestock** (1993): 500,000 cattle; 31,000 hogs; 62,000 sheep; 2.0 mil chickens. **Timber/lumber** (1993): oak, yellow poplar, hickory, walnut, cherry; 684 mil bd ft. **Nonfuel Minerals** (1994): $176 mil; mostly crushed stone, portland cement, salt. **Chief port:** Huntington. **Value of construction** (1994): $1.2 bil. **Employment distribution** (1993): 23% trade; 20% govt.; 26% serv.; 13% mfg. **Per capita personal income** (1994): $17,208. **Unemployment** (1994): 8.9%. **Tourism** (1992): travel-related expenditures were $2.6 bil.

Finance. FDIC-insured commercial banks & trust companies (1994): 122. **Deposits:** $16.6 bil. **FDIC-insured savings institutions** (1994): 10. **Assets:** $1.4 bil.

Federal government. No. federal civilian employees (Mar. 1994): 11,326. **Avg. salary:** $35,565. **Notable federal facilities:** National Radio Astronomy Observatory, Green Bank; Bureau of Public Debt Bldg., Parkersburg; Natl. Park, Harpers Ferry; Correctional Institution for Women, Alderson.

Energy. Electricity production (1994, kWh, by source): Coal: 77.0 bil; Petroleum: 251 mil; Gas: 25 mil; Hydroelectric: 363 mil.

Education. Student-teacher ratio (1993): 14.9. **Avg. salary, public school teachers** (1994-95): $31,923.

State data. Motto: Montani Semper Liberi (Mountaineers are always free). **Flower:** Big rhododendron. **Bird:** Cardinal. **Tree:** Sugar maple. **Songs:** The West Virginia Hills; This Is My West Virginia; West Virginia, My Home, Sweet Home. **Entered union** June 20, 1863; **rank,** 35th. **State fair** at: Lewisburg (Fairlea); late Aug.

History. Early explorers included George Washington, 1753, and Daniel Boone. The area became part of Virginia and often objected to rule by the eastern part of the

state. When Virginia seceded, 1861, the Wheeling Conventions repudiated the act and created a new state, Kanawha, subsequently changed to West Virginia. It was admitted to the Union as such, 1863.

Tourist attractions. Harpers Ferry National Historic Park has been restored to its condition in 1859, when John Brown seized the U.S. Armory.

Also Science and Cultural Center, Charleston; White Sulphur and Berkeley Springs mineral water spas; Monongahela Natl. Forest; state parks and forests; trout fishing; turkey, deer, and bear hunting; white water rafting; paddleboat tours; skiing; glass tours at Fenton Glass in Williamstown, Viking Glass in New Martinsville, Blenko Glass in Milton; Sternwheel Regatta, Charleston; Mountain State Forest Festival; Mountain State Arts & Crafts Fair, Ripley.

Famous West Virginians. Newton D. Baker, Pearl Buck, John W. Davis, Thomas "Stonewall" Jackson, Don Knotts, Dwight Whitney Morrow, Nick Nolte, Michael Owens, Cyrus Vance, Col. Charles "Chuck" Yeager.

Tourist information. Dept. of Commerce, State Capitol, Charleston WV 25305.

Toll-free travel information. 1-800-CALLWVA.

Wisconsin
Badger State

People. Population (1994): 5,081,658; **rank:** 18; **Net change** (1990-94): 3.9%. **Pop. density:** 92.2 per sq mi. **Racial/ethnic distrib.** (1990): 92.2% white; 5.0% black; 1.9% Hispanic.

Geography. Total area: 65,499 sq mi; **rank:** 23. **Land area:** 54,314 sq mi. **Acres forested land:** 15,513,000. **Location:** East North Central state, bounded on the N by Lake Superior and Upper Michigan; on the E by Lake Michigan; on the S by Illinois; on the W by the St. Croix and Mississippi rivers. **Climate:** long, cold winters and short, warm summers tempered by the Great Lakes. **Topography:** narrow Lake Superior Lowland plain met by Northern Highland, which slopes gently to the sandy crescent Central Plain; Western Upland in the SW; 3 broad parallel limestone ridges running N-S are separated by wide and shallow lowlands in the SE. **Capital:** Madison.

Economy. Principal industries: services, manufacturing, trade, government, agriculture, tourism. **Principal manufactured goods:** industrial machinery, food products, fabricated metals, paper products, printing and publishing, electronic and electrical machinery. **Agriculture: Chief crops:** corn, soybeans, peas, hay, oats, potatoes, sweet corn, snap beans, cranberries. **Chief products:** milk, butter, cheese, canned & frozen vegetables. **Livestock** (1995): 3.85 mil cattle; 1.5 mil milk cows; 1 mil hogs; 4.11 mil poultry; .85 mil sheep. **Timber/lumber** (1993): maple, birch, oak, evergreens; 639 mil bd ft. **Nonfuel Minerals** (1994): $344 mil; mostly crushed stone, construction and industrial sand & gravel, lime. **Commercial fishing** (1994): $5.5 mil. **Chief ports:** Superior, Ashland, Milwaukee, Green Bay, Kewaunee, Pt. Washington, Manitowoc, Sheboygan, Marinette, Kenosha. **International airports at:** Milwaukee. **Value of construction** (1994): $5.5 bil. **Employment distribution** (1994): 22.8% trade; 23.3% mfg.; 25% serv.; 14.8% govt. **Per capita personal income** (1994): $21,019. **Unemployment** (1994): 4.7%. **Tourism** (1994): out-of-state visitors spent $5.7 bil.

Finance. FDIC-insured commercial banks & trust companies (1994): 399. **Deposits:** $45.4 bil. **FDIC-insured savings institutions** (1994): 54. **Assets:** $21.7 bil.

Federal government. No. federal civilian employees (Mar. 1994): 12,532. **Avg. salary:** $35,107. **Notable federal facilities:** Ft. McCoy.

Energy. Electricity production (1994, kWh, by source): Coal: 35.2 bil; Petroleum: 172 mil; Gas: 287 mil; Hydroelectric: 1.9 bil; Nuclear: 11.5 bil.

Education. Student-teacher ratio (1993): 16.0. **Avg. salary, public school teachers** (1994-95): $37,349.

State data. Motto: Forward. **Flower:** Wood violet. **Bird:** Robin. **Tree:** Sugar maple. **Song:** On, Wisconsin!

Entered union May 29, 1848; rank, 30th. **State fair** at West Allis; mid-Aug.

History. Jean Nicolet was the first European to see the Wisconsin area, arriving in Green Bay, 1634; French missionaries and fur traders followed. The British took over, 1763. The U.S. won the land after the American Revolution, but the British were not ousted until after the War of 1812. Lead miners came next, then farmers. Railroads were started in 1851, serving growing wheat harvests and iron mines.

Tourist attractions. Old Wade House and Carriage Museum, Greenbush; Villa Louis, Prairie du Chien; Circus World Museum, Baraboo; Wisconsin Dells; Old World Wisconsin, Eagle; Door County peninsula; Chequamegon and Nicolet national forests; Lake Winnebago; numerous lakes for water sports, ice boating and fishing; skiing and hunting.

Famous Wisconsinites. Edna Ferber, King Camp Gillette, Harry Houdini, Robert La Follette, Alfred Lunt, Georgia O'Keeffe, Donald K. "Deke" Slayton, Spencer Tracy, Thorstein Veblen, Orson Welles, Thornton Wilder, Frank Lloyd Wright.

Tourist information. Wisconsin Dept. of Development, Division of Tourism, 123 W. Washington Ave., Madison, WI 53702.

Toll-free travel information. 1-800-372-2737.

Wyoming
Equality State

People. Population (1994): 475,981; **rank:** 50; **Net change** (1990-94): 4.9%. **Pop. density:** 4.8 per sq mi. **Racial/ethnic distrib.** (1990): 94.2% white; 0.8% black; 2.1% Amer. Indian; 5.7% Hispanic.

Geography. Total area: 97,818 sq mi; **rank:** 10. **Land area:** 97,105 sq mi. **Acres forested land:** 9,966,000. **Location:** Mountain state lying in the high western plateaus of the Great Plains. **Climate:** semi-desert conditions throughout; true desert in the Big Horn and Great Divide basins. **Topography:** the eastern Great Plains rise to the foothills of the Rocky Mts.; the Continental Divide crosses the state from the NW to the SE. **Capital:** Cheyenne.

Economy. Principal industries: mineral extraction, tourism and recreation, agriculture. **Principal manufactured goods:** refined petroleum products, foods, wood products, stone, clay and glass products. **Agriculture: Chief crops:** wheat, beans, barley, oats, sugar beets, hay. **Livestock** (Jan. 1, 1995): 1.4 mil cattle/calves; 790,000 sheep/lambs; (Dec. 1, 1994) 51,000 hogs/pigs. **Timber/lumber** (1993): ponderosa & lodgepole pine, Douglas fir, Engelmann spruce; 225 mil bd ft. **Nonfuel Minerals** (1994): $781 mil; mostly soda ash, clays, helium, gypsum, portland cement, crushed stone. **International airports at:** Casper. **Value of construction** (1994): $561.3 mil. **Employment distribution** (1992): 23% trade; 20% services; 9% mining. **Per capita personal income** (1994): $20,436. **Unemployment** (1994): 5.3%. **Tourism** (1992): out-of-state visitors spent $1.5 bil.

Finance. FDIC-insured commercial banks & trust companies (1994): 53. **Deposits:** $5.3 bil. **FDIC-insured savings institutions** (1994): 5. **Assets:** $342 mil.

Federal government. No. federal civilian employees (Mar. 1994): 4,813. **Avg. salary:** $34,985. **Notable federal facilities:** Warren AFB.

Energy. Electricity production (1994, kWh, by source): Coal: 41.4 bil; Petroleum: 47 mil; Gas: 13 mil; Hydroelectric: 897 mil.

Education. Student-teacher ratio (1993): 15.4. **Avg. salary, public school teachers** (1994-95): $31,300.

State data. Motto: Equal Rights. **Flower:** Indian paintbrush. **Bird:** Meadowlark. **Tree:** Cottonwood. **Song:** Wyoming. **Entered union** July 10, 1890; rank, 44th. **State fair** at: Douglas; late Aug.

History. Frances Francois and Louis La Verendrye were the first Europeans, 1743. John Colter, American, was first to traverse Yellowstone Park, 1807-8. Trappers and fur traders followed in the 1820s. Forts Laramie and Bridger became important stops on the pioneer trail to the West Coast. Indian wars followed massacres of army detachments in 1854 and 1866. Population grew after the Union Pacific crossed the state, 1869. Women won the vote, for the first time in the U.S., from the Territorial Legislature, 1869.

Tourist attractions. Yellowstone National Park, 3,472 sq mi in the NW corner of Wyoming and the adjoining edges of Montana and Idaho, the oldest U.S. national park, established 1872, has some 10,000 geysers, hot springs, mud volcanoes, fossil forests, a volcanic glass (obsidian) mountain, the 1,000-ft-deep canyon and 308-ft-high waterfall of the Yellowstone River, and a wide variety of animals living free in their natural habitat.

Also, Grand Teton National Park, with mountains 13,000 ft high; National Elk Refuge, covering 25,000 acres; Devils Tower, a columnar rock of igneous origin 1,280 ft high; Fort Laramie and surrounding areas of pioneer trails; Buffalo Bill Museum, Cody; Cheyenne Frontier Days Celebration, last full week in July, the state's largest rodeo, and world's largest purse.

Famous Wyomingites. James Bridger, Buffalo Bill Cody, Nellie Tayloe Ross.

Tourist information. Travel Commission, Etchepare Circle, Cheyenne, WY 82002.

Toll-free travel information. 1-800-CALLWYO.

District of Columbia

People. Population (1994): 570,175; **Net Change** (1990-94): -6.1%.

Geography. Total area: 68 sq mi; **rank:** 51. **Land area:** 61 sq mi. **Location:** at the confluence of the Potomac and Anacostia rivers, flanked by Maryland on the N, E, and SE and by Virginia on the SW. **Climate:** hot humid summers, mild winters. **Topography:** low hills rise toward the N away from the Potomac R. and slope to the S; highest elevation, 410 ft, lowest Potomac R., 1 ft.

Economy. Principal industries: government, service, tourism. **Value of Construction** (1994): $789.1 mil. **Employment distribution** (1992) 31.1% govt., 10.3% trade, 33% service. **Per capita personal income** (1994): $31,136; **Unemployment** (1994): 8.2%; **Tourism** (1994):

Finance. FDIC-Insured commercial banks & trust companies (1994): 16 **Deposits:** $7.2 bil. **FDIC-Insured savings institutions** (1994): 1 **Assets:** $256 mil.

Federal Government. No. of federal employees (Mar. 1994): 168,456; **Avg. salary:** $49,727.

Energy. Electricity production (1994, kWh, by source): Petroleum: 274 mil.

Education. Student-teacher ratio (1993): 13.3. **Avg. salary, public school teachers** (1994) $42,959.

District Data. Motto: Justitia omnibus (Justice for all). **Flower:** American beauty rose. **Tree:** Scarlet oak. **Bird:** Wood thrush. The city of Washington is coextensive with the District of Columbia.

The District of Columbia is the seat of the U.S. federal government. It lies on the west central edge of Maryland on the Potomac River, opposite Virginia. Its area was originally 100 sq mi taken from the sovereignty of Maryland and Virginia. Virginia's portion south of the Potomac was given back to that state in 1846.

The 23d Amendment, ratified in 1961, granted residents the right to vote for president and vice president for the first time since 1800 and gave them 3 members in the Electoral College. The first such votes were cast in Nov. 1964.

Congress, which has legislative authority over the District under the Constitution, established in 1874 a government of 3 commissioners appointed by the president. The Reorganization Plan of 1967 substituted a single appointive commissioner (also called mayor), assistant, and 9-member City Council. Funds were still appropriated by Congress; residents had no vote in local government, except to elect school board members.

In Sept. 1970, Congress approved legislation giving the District one delegate to the House of Representatives. The delegate could vote in committee but not on the House floor. The first was elected 1971.

In May 1974 voters approved a congressionally drafted charter giving them the right to elect their own mayor and a 13-member city council; the first took office Jan. 2, 1975. The district won the right to levy its own taxes, but Congress retained power to veto council actions and approve the city's annual budget.

Proposals for a "federal town" for the deliberations of the Continental Congress were made in 1783, 4 years before the adoption of the Constitution. Rivalry between Northern and Southern delegates over the site appeared in the First Congress, 1789. John Adams, presiding officer of the Senate, cast the deciding vote of that body for Germantown, PA. In 1790 Congress compromised by making Philadelphia the temporary capital for 10 years. The Virginia members of the House wanted a capital on the eastern bank of the Potomac; they were defeated by the Northerners, while the Southerners defeated the Northern attempt to have the nation assume the war debts of the 13 original states, the Assumption Bill fathered by Alexander Hamilton. Hamilton and Jefferson arranged a compromise: the Virginia men voted for the Assumption Bill, and the Northerners conceded the capital to the Potomac. President Washington chose the site in Oct. 1790 and persuaded landowners to sell their holdings to the government at £25, then about $66, an acre. The capital was named Washington.

Washington appointed Pierre Charles L'Enfant, a Frenchman, to plan the capital on an area not more than 10 mi square. The L'Enfant plan, for streets 100 to 110 feet wide and one avenue 400 feet wide and a mile long, seemed grandiose and foolhardy, but Washington endorsed it. When L'Enfant ordered a wealthy landowner to remove his new manor house because it obstructed a vista, and demolished it when the owner refused, Washington stepped in and dismissed the architect. Andrew Ellicott, who was working on surveying the area, finished the official map and design of the city. Ellicott was assisted by Benjamin Banneker, a distinguished black architect and astronomer.

On Sept. 18, 1793, Pres. Washington laid the cornerstone of the north wing of the Capitol. On June 3, 1800, Pres. John Adams moved to Washington and on June 10, Philadelphia ceased to be the temporary capital. The City of Washington was incorporated in 1802; the District of Columbia was created as a municipal corporation in 1874, embracing Washington, Georgetown, and Washington County.

Tourist information. 202-789-7000.

OUTLYING U.S. AREAS

American Samoa

Capital: Pago Pago, Island of Tutuila. **Total area:** 84 sq mi. **Population:** (1994 est.) 55,223. **Population growth rate** (1994 est.) -0.52%. **Motto:** Samoa Muamua le Atua (In Samoa, God Is First). **Song:** Amerika Samoa. **Flower:** Paogo (Ula-fala). **Plant:** Ava.

Education. Student-teacher ratio (1993): 22.1.

Blessed with spectacular scenery and delightful South Seas climate, American Samoa is the most southerly of all lands under U.S. sovereignty. It is an unincorporated territory consisting of 7 small islands of the Samoan group: **Tutuila, Aunu'u, Manu'a Group (Ta'u, Olosega and Ofu), Rose,** and **Swains Island.** The islands are 2,300 mi SW of Honolulu.

A tripartite agreement between Great Britain, Germany, and the U.S. in 1899 gave the U.S. sovereignty over the eastern islands of the Samoan group; these islands became American Samoa. Local chiefs officially ceded Tutuila and Aunu'u to the U.S. in April 1900 and the Manu'a group and Rose in July 1904; Swains Island was annexed in 1925.

Samoa (Western), comprising the larger islands of the Samoan group, was a New Zealand mandate and UN Trusteeship until it became an independent nation Jan. 1, 1962.

Tutuila and Aunu'u have an area of 53 sq mi. Ta'u has an area of 17 sq mi, and the islets of Ofu and Olosega, 5 sq mi with a population of a few thousand. Swains Island has nearly 2 sq mi and a population of about 100.

About 70% of the land is bush and mountains. Chief products and exports are fish products. Taro, breadfruit, yams, coconuts, pineapples, oranges, and bananas are also produced.

From 1900 to 1951, American Samoa was under the jurisdiction of the U.S. Navy. Since 1951, it has been under the Interior Dept. On Jan. 3, 1978, the first popularly elected Samoan governor and lieutenant governor were inaugurated. Previously, the governor was appointed by the Secretary of the Interior. American Samoa has a bicameral legislature and elects a delegate to the House of Representatives, who has a voice but no vote, except in committees.

The American Samoans are of Polynesian origin. They are nationals of the U.S.; approximately 20,000 live in Hawaii, 65,000 in California and Washington.

Guam
Where America's Day Begins

People. Population (1994 est.): 149,620. **Population growth rate** (1994): 2.48%. **Pop. density:** 631.6 per sq mi. **Ethnic distribution** (1994 est.): Chamorro 47%, Filipino 25%, Caucasian 10%, Chinese, Japanese, Korean, and other 18%. Native Guamanians, ethnically called Chamorros, are basically of Indonesian stock, with a mixture of Spanish and Filipino. In addition to the official language, they speak the native Chamorro. **Migration** (1990): About 52% of population were born elsewhere; of these, 48% in Asia, 40% in U.S.

Geography. Total area: 210 sq mi land, 30 mi long and 4 to 8.5 mi wide. **Location:** largest and southernmost of the Mariana Islands in the West Pacific, 3,700 mi W of Hawaii. **Climate:** tropical, with temperatures from 70° to 90° F; avg. annual rainfall, about 70 in. **Topography:** coralline limestone plateau in the N; southern chain of low volcanic mountains sloping gently to the W, more steeply to coastal cliffs on the E; general elevation, 500 ft; highest point, Mt. Lamlam, 1,334 ft. **Capital:** Agaña.

Economy. Principal industries: tourism, U.S. military, construction, banking. **Principal manufactured goods:** textiles, foods. **Agriculture:** Chief crops: cabbages, eggplants, cucumber, long beans, tomatoes, bananas, coconuts, watermelon, yams, canteloupe, papayas, maize, sweet potatoes. **Production** (1990) fruits & vegetables, 5.6 mil lb; eggs, 369,000 dz; pork, 215,000 lb; beef, 11,000 lb; poultry, 90,000 lb. **Chief port:** Apra Harbor. **International airport at:** Agaña. **Value of construction** (1980): $80.6 mil. **Employment distribution** (1990): 26.7% govt./defense; 22% service; 17% trade; 12% construction. **Per capita income** (1986): $7,116. **Median household income** (1989): $30,755; persons per household 3.97; persons per family 4.26. **Unemployment** (1992): 2%. **Tourism** (1992): visitors' receipts $1.5 bil.

Finance. Notable industries: insurance, real estate, finance. **FDIC-insured commercial banks & trust companies** (1994): 2. **Deposits:** $562 mil. **FDIC-insured savings institutions** (1994): 2. **Assets:** 225 mil.

Federal government. No. federal employees (1990): 7,200. **Notable federal facilities:** Anderson AFB; naval, air, and port bases.

Education. Student-teacher ratio (1993): 18.8.

Misc. data. Flower: Puti Tai Nobio (Bougainvillea). **Bird:** Toto (Fruit dove). **Tree:** Ifit (Intsiabijuga). **Song:** Stand Ye Guamanians.

History. Guam was probably settled by voyagers from the Indonesian-Philippine archipelago by at least the third century BC. Pottery, rice cultivation, and megalithic technology show strong East Asian cultural influence. Centralized, village clan-based communities engaged in agriculture and offshore fishing. The est. population by the early 16th century was between 50,000 and 75,000 inhabitants. Magellan arrived in the Marianas Mar. 6, 1521. They were colonized in 1668 by Spanish missionaries who named them the Mariana Islands in honor of Maria Anna, queen of Spain. When Spain ceded Guam to the U.S., it sold the other Marianas to Germany. Japan obtained a League of Nations mandate over the German islands in 1919; in Dec. 1941 it seized Guam; the island was retaken by the U.S. in July 1944.

Guam is a self-governing organized unincorporated U.S. territory. The Organic Act of 1950 provides for a governor, elected to a 4-year term, and a 21-member unicameral legislature, elected biennially by the residents, who are American citizens. In 1970, the first governor was elected.

In 1972, a U.S. law gave Guam one delegate to the U.S. House of Representatives who has a voice but no vote, except in committees.

Guam's quest to change its status to a U.S. Commonwealth began in the late 1970s. The Guam Commission on Self-Determination, created in 1984, developed a draft Commonwealth Act. After consultations with a U.S. government representative in late 1993, it was decided that legislation proposing a change of status would be submitted to the U.S. Congress.

In 1994, the U.S. Congress passed legislation transferring 3,200 acres of land on Guam from federal to local control.

General tourist attractions. Tropical climate, oceanic marine environment; annual mid-Aug. Merizo Water Festival; Tarzan Falls; beaches; water sports; duty-free port shopping.

Commonwealth of the Northern Mariana Islands

Located in the perpetually warm climes between Guam and the Tropic of Cancer, the 14 islands of the Northern Marianas form a 300-mile-long archipelago, comprising a total land area of 179 sq miles. The indigenous population, 1990, was 43,345, concentrated on the 3 largest of the 6 inhabited islands: **Saipan,** the seat of government and commerce (38,896), **Rota** (2,295), and **Tinian** (2,118).

The people of the Northern Marianas are predominantly of Chamorro cultural extraction, although numbers of Carolinians and immigrants from other areas of E. Asia and Micronesia have also settled in the islands. English is among the several languages commonly spoken. Pursuant to the Covenant of 1976, which established the Northern Marianas as a commonwealth in political union with the U.S., most of the indigenous population and many domiciliaries of these islands achieved U.S. citizenship on Nov. 3, 1986, when the U.S. terminated its administration of the UN trusteeship as it affected the Northern Marianas. From July 18, 1947, the U.S. had administered the Northern Marianas under a trusteeship agreement with the UN Security Council.

The Northern Mariana Islands has been self-governing since 1978, when both a constitution drafted and adopted by the people became effective and a popularly elected bicameral legislature (2-year term) with offices of governor (4-year term) and lieut. governor was inaugurated.

Commonwealth of Puerto Rico
(Estado Libre Asociado de Puerto Rico)

People. Population (1994 est): 3,801,977 (and about 2.7 mil more Puerto Ricans reside in the mainland U.S.). **Pop. density:** 1,035 per sq mi. **Urban** (1990): 66.8%. **Ethnic distribution** (1990): 99.9% Hispanic. **Language:** On Jan. 28, 1993, the Gov. of Puerto Rico declared Spanish and English joint official languages.

Geography. Total area: 3,492 sq mi. **Land area:** 3,427 sq mi. **Location:** island lying between the Atlantic to the N and the Caribbean to the S; it is easternmost of the West Indies group called the Greater Antilles, of which Cuba, Hispaniola, and Jamaica are the larger islands. **Climate:** mild, with a mean temperature of 77° F. **Topography:** mountainous throughout three-fourths of its rectangular area, surrounded by a broken coastal plain; highest peak is Cerro Puntita, 4,389 ft. **Capital:** San Juan.

Economy. Principal industries: manufacturing. **Principal manufactured goods:** pharmaceuticals, chemicals, machinery and metals, electric machinery and equipment, food products, apparel, petroleum refining. **Agriculture: Chief crops:** coffee, plantains, pineapples, tomatoes, sugarcane, bananas, peppers, pumpkins, lettuce, tobacco, yams. **Livestock** (1993): 552,000 cattle; 115,000 pigs; 13 mil poultry. **Nonfuel Minerals** (1994): $122 mil, mostly portland cement, crushed stone. **Commercial fishing** (1992): $6.2 mil. **Chief ports/river shipping:** San Juan, Ponce, Mayagüez. **Major airports at:** San Juan, Ponce, Mayagüez, Aguadilla. **Value of construction** (1992): $2.7 bil. **Employment distribution** (1993): 42.4% public admin. & defense, 21.3% trade, 17.9% mfg. **Per capita income** (1992): $6,360. **Unemployment** (1994): 14.6%. **Tourism** (1993): Visitors spent $1.6 mil.

Finance. FDIC-insured commercial banks & trust companies (1994): 16. **Deposits:** $19.5 bil. **FDIC-insured savings institutions** (1994): 3. **Assets:** $217 mln.

Federal government. No. federal civilian employees (1992): 10,000. **Notable federal facilities:** U.S. Naval Station at Roosevelt Roads, Ceiba; U.S. Army Training Area and Ft. Allen at Salinas; Sabana SECA Communications Center (U.S. Navy); Ft. Buchanan at Guaynabo.

Energy. Electicity production (1993): 15.3 bil kWh.

Education. Student-teacher ratio (1993): 15.9. **Avg. salary, public school teachers** (1992): $1,000 monthly.

Misc. data. Motto: Joannes Est Nomen Eius (John is his name). **Flower:** Maga. **Bird:** Reinita. **Tree:** Ceiba. **National anthem:** La Borinqueña.

History. Puerto Rico (or Borinquen, after the original Arawak Indian name Boriquen) was visited by Columbus, on his second voyage, Nov. 19, 1493. In 1508, the Spanish arrived.

Sugarcane was introduced, 1515, and slaves were imported 3 years later. Gold mining petered out, 1570. Spaniards fought off a series of British and Dutch attacks; slavery was abolished, 1873. Under the treaty of Paris, Puerto Rico was ceded to the U.S. after the Spanish-American War, 1898. In 1952 the people voted in favor of Commonwealth status.

The Commonwealth of Puerto Rico is a self-governing part of the U.S. with a primarily Hispanic culture. The current commonwealth political status of Puerto Rico gives the island's citizens virtually the same control over their internal affairs as the 50 states of the U.S. However, they do not vote in national elections, although they do vote in national primary elections.

Puerto Rico is represented in the U.S. House of Representatives by a delegate who has a voice but no vote, except in committees.

No federal income tax is collected from residents on income earned from local sources in Puerto Rico. Nevertheless, as part of the U.S. legal system, Puerto Rico is subject to the provisions of the U.S. Constitution; most federal laws apply as they do in the 50 states.

Puerto Rico's famous "Operation Bootstrap," begun in the late 1940s, succeeded in changing the island from "The Poorhouse of the Caribbean" to an area with the highest per capita income in Latin America. This pioneering program encouraged manufacturing and the development of the tourist trade by selective tax exemption, low-interest loans, and other incentives. Despite the marked success of Puerto Rico's development efforts over an extended period of time, per capita income in Puerto Rico is low in comparison to that of the U.S.

General tourist attractions. Ponce Museum of Art; forts El Morro and San Cristobal; Old Walled City of San Juan; Arecibo Observatory; Cordillera Central and state parks; El Yunque Rain Forest; San Juan Cathedral; Porta Coeli Chapel and Museum of Religious Art, Interamerican Univ., San Germán; Condado Convention Center; Casa Blanca, Ponce de León family home, Puerto Rican Family Museum of 16th and 17th centuries, and the Fine Arts Center in San Juan.

Cultural facilities, festivals, etc. Festival Casals classical music concerts, mid-June; Puerto Rico Symphony Orchestra at Music Conservatory; Botanical Garden and Museum of Anthropology, Art, and History at the University of Puerto Rico; Institute of Puerto Rican Culture, at the Dominican Convent; and many popular festivals throughout the island.

Famous Puerto Ricans. Miguel Hernández Agosto, José Celso Barbosa, Julia de Burgos, Pablo Casals, Orlando Cepeda, Roberto Clemente, Rafael Hernández Colón, José de Diego, José Feliciano, Luis A. Ferré, José Ferrer, Doña Felisa Rincón de Gautier, Commodore Diégo E. Hernández, Rafael Hernández (El Jibarito), Marta Casals Istomin, Raúl Julía, Luis Muñoz Marín, René Marqués, Luis Palés Matos, Concha Meléndez, Rita Moreno, Adm. Horacio Rivero.

Chamber of Commerce. 100 Tetuán, PO Box S-3789, San Juan, PR 00902; Ponce & South: El Señorial Bldg., Ponce, PR 00731.

Virgin Islands
St. John, St. Croix, St. Thomas

People. Population (1994 est.): 97,564. **Population growth rate** (1994 est.): -0.52% **Racial distribution:** (1980) 85% black, 15% white. **Major ethnic groups:** West Indian, French, Hispanic.

Geography. Total area: 151 sq mi. **Land area:** 134 sq mi. **Location:** 3 larger and 50 smaller islands and cays in the S and W of the V.I. group (British V.I. colony to the N and E), which is situated 70 mi E of Puerto Rico, located W of the Anegada Passage, a major channel connecting the Atlantic Ocean and the Caribbean Sea. **Climate:** subtropical; the sun tempered by gentle trade winds; humidity is low; average temperature, 78° F. **Topography:** St. Thomas is mainly a ridge of hills running E and W, and has little tillable land; St. Croix rises abruptly in the N but slopes to the S to flatlands and lagoons; St. John has steep, lofty hills and valleys with little level tillable land. **Capital:** Charlotte Amalie, St. Thomas.

Economy. Principal industries: tourism, rum, alumina prod., petroleum refining, watch industry, textiles, electronics. **Principal manufactured goods:** rum, textiles, pharmaceuticals, perfumes. **Gross Domestic Product** (1987): $1.246 bil. **Agriculture: Chief crops:** truck garden produce. **Minerals:** sand, gravel. **Chief ports:** Cruz Bay, St. John; Frederiksted and Christiansted, St. Croix; Charlotte Amalie, St. Thomas. **International airports on:** St. Thomas, St. Croix. **Value of construction** (1987): $167.0 mil. **Per capita income** (1989): $11,052. **Unemployment** (1992): 2.8%. **Tourism** (1992): $792 mil.

Finance. FDIC-insured savings institutions (1994): 1. **Assets:** 48 mil. **No. banks** (1990): 8.

Energy. Electicity production (1992): 565 mil kWh.

Education. Student-teacher ratio (1993): 14.5.

Misc. data. Flower: Yellow elder or yellow trumpet, local designation Ginger Thomas. **Bird:** Yellow breast. **Song:** Virgin Islands March.

History. The islands were visited by Columbus in 1493. Spanish forces, 1555, defeated the Caribes and claimed the territory; by 1596 the native population was annihilated. First permanent settlement in the U.S. territory, 1672, by the Danes; U.S. purchased the islands, 1917, for defense purposes.

The Virgin Islands has a republican form of government, headed by a governor and lieut. governor elected, since 1970, by popular vote for 4-year terms. There is a 15-member unicameral legislature, elected by popular vote for a 2-year term. Residents of the V.I. have been U.S. citizens since 1927. Since 1973 they have elected a delegate to the U.S. House of Representatives, who has a voice but no vote, except in committees.

General tourist attractions. Magens Bay, St. Thomas; duty-free shopping; Virgin Islands National Park, 14,488 acres on St. John of lush growth, beaches, Indian relics, and evidence of colonial Danes.

Tourist information. Dept. of Economic Development & Agriculture: St. Thomas, PO Box 6400, St. Thomas, VI 00801; St. Croix, PO Box 4535, Christiansted, St. Croix 00820.

Other Islands

Navassa lies between Jamaica and Haiti, 100 miles south of Guantanamo Bay, Cuba, in the Caribbean; it covers about 3 sq mi, is reserved by the U.S. for a lighthouse, and is uninhabited. It is administered by the U.S. Coast Guard.

Wake Atoll, and its neighboring atolls, **Wilkes** and **Peale,** lie in the Pacific Ocean on the direct route from Hawaii to Hong Kong, about 2,300 mi W of Honolulu and 1,290 mi E of Guam. The group is 4.5 mi long, 1.5 mi wide, and totals less than 3 sq mi.

The U.S. flag was hoisted over Wake Atoll, July 4, 1898, formal possession taken Jan. 17, 1899; Wake was administered by the U.S. Air Force, 1972-94. The population consists of about 200 persons.

Midway Atoll, acquired in 1867, consist of 2 atolls, **Sand** and **Eastern,** in the North Pacific 1,150 mi. NW of Honolulu, with an area of about 3 sq mi, administered by the U.S. Navy. There is no indigenous population; its population is about 450.

Johnston Atoll, 717 miles WSW of Honolulu, area 1 sq mi, is operated by the Defense Nuclear Agency, and the Fish and Wildlife Service, U.S. Dept. of the Interior; its population is about 1,200. **Kingman Reef,** 920 miles S of Hawaii, is under Navy control.

Howland, Jarvis, and **Baker Islands,** 1,400-1,650 miles SW of Honolulu, uninhabited since World War II, are under the Interior Dept.

Palmyra is an atoll about 1,000 miles south of Hawaii, 2 sq mi. Privately owned, it is under the Interior Dept.

Islands Formerly Under Trusteeship

The U.S. Trust Territory of the Pacific Islands was established in 1947, as the only strategic trusteeship of the 11 trusteeships established by the UN. The territory had a heterogeneous population of about 140,000 people scattered among more than 2,100 islands and atolls in 3 major archipelagos: the Carolines, the Marshalls, and the Marianas. The entire geographic area is sometimes referred to as "Micronesia," meaning "little islands." The area of the Trust Territory covered some 3 million sq miles of the Pacific Ocean, slightly larger than the continental U.S. However, its islands constituted a land area of only 715.8 sq mi—half the size of Rhode Island. It initially consisted of 7 districts and then was reduced to 4 political jurisdictions, whose current names are the Commonwealth of the Northern Mariana Islands, the Federated States of Micronesia, the Republic of the Marshall Islands, and the Republic of Palau. The last three are now independent nations, although with U.S. defense guarantees. The CNMI became a commonwealth of the U.S., effective Nov. 3, 1986. Palau became an independent nation October 1, 1994, ending its status as the last U.S.-administered UN trust territory.

Washington, DC, Capital of the U.S.

Tourism information is available from the Washington, DC, Convention and Visitors Association; phone 202-789-7000.

Bureau of Engraving and Printing

The **Bureau of Engraving and Printing** is the headquarters for the making of U.S. paper money. Twenty-minute self-guided tours Mon. - Fri., 9 AM-2 PM; 3:30 PM-7:30 PM. Closed federal holidays and Dec. 24 - Jan. 3. 14th and C Sts. SW. Phone 202-874-3019.

Capitol

The **United States Capitol** was originally designed by Dr. William Thornton, an amateur architect, who submitted a plan in the spring of 1793 that won him $500 and a city lot.

The south, or House, wing was completed in 1807 under the direction of Benjamin H. Latrobe.

The present Senate and House wings and the iron dome were designed and constructed by Thomas U. Walter, the 4th architect of the Capitol, between 1851 and 1863.

The present cast iron dome at its greatest exterior measures 135 ft 5 in., and it is topped by the bronze Statue of Freedom that stands 19½ ft and weighs 14,985 lb. On its base are the words *E Pluribus Unum* (Out of Many One).

The Capitol is normally open from 9 AM to 4:30 PM; June to Labor Day, to 10 PM. It is closed on Dec. 25, Jan. 1, and Thanksgiving Day. Tours through the Capitol, including the House and Senate galleries, are conducted from 9 AM to 3:45 PM; there is no charge.

To observe the debate in the House or Senate while Congress is in session, individuals living in the U.S. may obtain tickets to the visitor's galleries from their congressperson or senator. Visitors from other countries may obtain passes at the Capitol. Between Constitution & Independence Ave., at Pennsylvania Ave. Phone 202-225-6827.

Federal Bureau of Investigation

The **Federal Bureau of Investigation** offers a tour of its headquarters, beginning with a videotape presentation. Visitors learn about the history of the FBI and see such things as the weapons confiscated from famous gangsters, photos of the most-wanted fugitives, the DNA laboratory, goods forfeited and seized in narcotics operations, and a sharpshooting demonstration.

Tours are conducted Mon. - Fri., 8:45 AM - 4:15 PM, except Jan. 1, Dec. 25, and other federal holidays. Tickets may be obtained at the FBI on the day of the tour or through a congressperson or senator. Admission is free. J. Edgar Hoover Bldg., Pennsylvania Ave., between 9th and 10th Sts. NW. Phone 202-324-3447.

Folger Shakespeare Library

The **Folger Shakespeare Library,** on Capitol Hill, is a research institution holding rare books and manuscripts of the Renaissance period and the largest collection of Shakespearean materials in the world, including 79 copies of the First Folio.

The library's museum and performing arts programs are presented in the Elizabethan Theatre, which resembles an innyard theater of Shakespeare's day.

Exhibit areas may be visited Mon. - Sat., 10 AM - 4 PM. 201 E. Capitol St. Phone 202-544-7077.

Holocaust Memorial Museum

The **U.S. Holocaust Memorial Museum** opened on April 21, 1993. The museum documents, through the use of permanent and temporary displays, interactive videos, and special lectures, the events of the Holocaust beginning in 1933 and continuing until the end of World War II. The permanent exhibition is not recommended for children under the age of 11.

The museum is open daily, 10 AM - 5:30 PM, except Yom Kippur and Dec. 25. Although a limited number of free tickets are available on the day of visit, advance tickets may be ordered for a small fee. 100 Raoul Wallenberg Pl. SW (formerly 15th St. SW), near Independence Ave. Phone 202-488-0400.

Jefferson Memorial

Dedicated in 1943, the **Thomas Jefferson Memorial** stands on the south shore of the Tidal Basin in West Potomac Park. It is a circular stone structure, with Vermont marble on the exterior and Georgia white marble inside, and combines architectural elements of the dome of the Pantheon in Rome and the rotunda designed by Jefferson for the University of Virginia.

The memorial, which is located on the South edge of the Tidal Basin, is open daily, 8 AM - midnight. An elevator and curb ramps for the handicapped are in service. Phone 202-426-6841.

John F. Kennedy Center

The **John F. Kennedy Center for the Performing Arts,** designated by Congress as the National Cultural Center and the official memorial in Washington, DC, to President John F. Kennedy, opened Sept. 8, 1971. Designed by Edward Durell Stone, the center includes an opera house, a concert hall, several theaters, 2 restaurants, and a library.

Free tours are available daily, 10:00 AM - 1:00 PM. New Hampshire Ave. at F St. NW. Phone 202-416-8340.

Korean War Memorial

Dedicated on July 27, 1995, the **Korean War Memorial** honors all Americans who served in the Korean War. Situated at the west end of the Mall, just across the reflecting pool from the Vietnam Memorial, the triangular-shaped stone and steel memorial features a multiservice formation of 19 troops clad in ponchos with the wind at their back, ready for combat. A granite wall, exhibiting real-life images of the men and women who served, juts into a pool of water, the Pool of Remembrance, and is inscribed with the words *Freedom Is Not Free.*

The $18 mil memorial, which was funded by private donations, is open 24 hr daily. Phone 202-426-6841.

Library of Congress

Established by and for Congress in 1800, the **Library of Congress** has extended its services over the years to other government agencies and other libraries, to scholars, and to the general public, and it now serves as the national library. It contains more than 80 million items in 470 languages.

The library's exhibit halls are open to the public Mon. - Fri., 8:30 AM - 9:30 PM; Sat., 8:30 AM - 6:00 PM. The library is closed Jan. 1 and Dec. 25. 10 1st St. SE. Phone 202-707-8000.

Lincoln Memorial

Designed by Henry Bacon, the **Lincoln Memorial** in West Potomac Park, on the axis of the Capitol and the Washington Monument, consists of a large marble hall enclosing a heroic statue of Abraham Lincoln in meditation sitting on a large armchair. The memorial was dedicated on Memorial Day, May 30, 1922. The statue of Lincoln was designed by Daniel Chester French and sculpted by French and the Piccirilli brothers. Murals and ornamentation on the bronze ceiling beams are by Jules Guerin. The text of the Gettysburg Address is in the south chamber, and that of Lincoln's second inaugural speech is in the north chamber. Each is engraved on a stone tablet.

The memorial is open 24 hr daily. An elevator for the handicapped is in service. Phone 202-426-6841.

National Archives

Original copies of the Declaration of Independence, the Constitution of the United States, and the Bill of Rights are on permanent display in the **National Archives** Exhibition Hall. The National Archives also holds other valuable U.S. government records and historic maps, photographs, and manuscripts.

Central Research and Microfilm Research Rooms are also available to the public for genealogical research. Phone 202-502-5400 for hours.

The Exhibition Hall is open daily, 10 AM - 9 PM, Apr. 1- Labor Day; 10AM - 5:30 PM, Labor Day-Mar. 31; closed Jan. 1 and Dec. 25. Pennsylvania Ave. between 7th & 9th Sts. NW. Phone 202-501-5000.

National Gallery of Art

The **National Gallery of Art**, situated on the north side of the Mall facing Constitution Avenue, was established by Joint Resolution of Congress Mar. 24, 1937, and opened Mar. 17, 1941. The original West building was designed by John Russell Pope. The East building, opened in 1978, was designed by I. M. Pei. The National Gallery is separate from, but maintains a relationship with, the Smithsonian Institution.

Normally open daily, 10 AM - 5 PM; Sunday, 11 AM - 6 PM. Closed Jan. 1 and Dec. 25. Constitution Ave. between 3d & 7th Sts. Phone 202-737-4215.

Smithsonian Institution

The **Smithsonian Institution**, established in 1846, is the world's largest museum complex and consists of 14 museums and the National Zoo. It holds some 100 million artifacts and specimens in its trust "for the increase and diffusion of knowledge among men." Nine museums are on the National Mall between the Washington Monument and the Capitol; 5 other museums and the zoo are elsewhere in Washington (the Cooper-Hewitt Museum and the National Museum of the American Indian, administered by the Smithsonian, are in New York City). Most visitors begin their trip with a visit to the **Smithsonian Information Center**, located in "the Castle" on the Mall. Also on the Mall are the **National Museum of American History**, the **National Museum of Natural History**, the **National Air and Space Museum**, the **Hirshhorn Museum and Sculpture Garden**, the **Arthur M. Sackler Gallery**, the **National Museum of African Art**, the **Freer Gallery of Art**, and the **Arts and Industries Building**. Near the Sackler Gallery is the **Enid A. Haupt Garden**. Located nearby are the **National Postal Museum**, the **National Museum of American Art**, the **National Portrait Gallery**, and the **Renwick Gallery**. Farther away, at 1901 Fort Place SE, is the **Anacostia Museum**.

Most museums are open daily, except Dec. 25, - 10 AM to 5:30 PM. Phone 202-357-2700.

Vietnam Veterans Memorial

Originally dedicated on Nov. 13, 1982, the **Vietnam Veterans Memorial** is a symbol of the nation's recognition of the men and women who served in the armed forces in the Vietnam War. On a V-shaped black-granite wall, designed by Maya Ying Lin, are inscribed the names of the more than 58,000 Americans who lost their lives or remain missing.

Since 1982, two additions have been made to the Memorial. The first, dedicated on Nov. 11, 1984, is the Frederick Hart sculpture *Three Servicemen*. On Nov. 11, 1993, the Vietnam Women's Memorial was dedicated, honoring the more than 11,500 women who served in Vietnam. The bronze sculpture, portraying 3 women helping a wounded male soldier, was designed by Glenna Goodacre.

The memorial is open 24 hr daily. Phone 202-426-6841.

Washington Monument

The **Washington Monument**, dedicated in 1885, is a tapering shaft, or obelisk, of white marble, 555 ft, 5⅛ inches in height and 55 ft, 1½ in. square at base. Eight small windows, 2 on each side, are located at the 500-ft level, where points of interest are indicated.

Open daily except Dec. 25, 9 AM - 4:30 PM; 8 AM - midnight, Apr.-Labor Day. Phone 202-426-6841.

The White House

The **White House,** the president's residence, stands on 18 acres on the south side of Pennsylvania Ave., between the Treasury and the old Executive Office Building. The walls are of sandstone, quarried at Aquia Creek, VA. The exterior walls were painted, causing the building to be termed the "White House." On Aug. 24, 1814, during Madison's administration, the house was burned by the British. James Hoban rebuilt it by Oct. 1817.

The White House is normally open for free self-guided tours Tues.-Sat., 10 AM - 12 noon (tickets, necessary Apr. 1 - Labor Day, are available at visitor's booth, 15th St. near E St.). Only the public rooms on the ground floor and state floor may be visited. Free reserved tickets for guided tours can be obtained 8 to 10 weeks in advance from your local congressperson or senator. 1600 Pennsylvania Ave. Phone 202-456-7041.

Other Nearby Attractions

Arlington National Cemetery

Arlington National Cemetery, on the former Custis estate in Arlington, VA, is the site of the **Tomb of the Unknowns** and is the final resting place of John Fitzgerald Kennedy, 35th president of the U.S., who was buried there on Nov. 25, 1963. His wife, Jacqueline Bouvier Kennedy Onassis, is buried at the same site. An eternal flame burns over the grave site. In an adjacent area is the grave of Pres. Kennedy's brother Sen. Robert F. Kennedy (NY), interred on June 8, 1968. Many other famous Americans are also buried at Arlington, as well as more than 200,000 American soldiers from every major war.

North of the National Cemetery, approximately 350 yd, stands the **U.S. Marine Corps War Memorial**, also known as Iwo Jima. The memorial is a bronze statue of the raising of the U.S. flag on Mt. Suribachi, Feb. 23, 1945, during WW2, executed by Felix de Weldon from the photograph by Joe Rosenthal, and presented to the nation by members and friends of the U.S. Marine Corps.

Open daily, 8 AM - 7 PM. Arlington, VA. Phone 703-979-0690.

Mount Vernon

Mount Vernon, George Washington's estate, is on the south bank of the Potomac R., 16 miles below Washington, DC, in northern Virginia.

The present house is an enlargement of one apparently built on the site by Augustine Washington, who lived there 1735-38. His son Lawrence came there in 1743, when he renamed the plantation Mount Vernon in honor of Admiral Vernon, under whom he had served in the West Indies. Lawrence Washington died in 1752 and was succeeded as proprietor of Mount Vernon by his half-brother, George Washington.

The estate has been restored to its 18th-century appearance and includes many original furnishings.

Open 365 days, Apr. - Aug., 8 AM - 5 PM; Sept. - Mar., 9 AM - 5 PM (Nov.-Feb. closes at 4 PM). Phone 703-780-2000.

The Pentagon

The **Pentagon**, headquarters of the Department of Defense, is one of the world's largest office buildings. Situated in Arlington, VA, it houses more than 23,000 employees in offices that occupy 3,707,745 sq ft.

Free tours are available Mon. - Fri. (excluding federal holidays), 9:30 AM - 3:30 PM (June - Aug); 9 AM - 3 PM (Sept. - May). Arlington, VA. 703-695-1776.

CITIES OF THE U.S.

Sources: Bureau of the Census: population (rank) (1990 Census, revised as of April 1995); population growth (1980-90). Geography Division, Bureau of the Census: population density (1990); area (1990). Bureau of Labor Statistics: employment (1994 averages for city proper only). Bureau of Economic Analysis: per capita personal income (Metropolitan Statistical Area, 1993).

Based on 1990 Census, the 100 most populous cities (inc.=incorporated; est.=established).

Akron, Ohio

Population: 223,019 (71); **Pop. density:** 4,055 per sq. mi.; **Pop. growth:** –6.0%. **Area:** 55 sq. mi. **Employment:** 102,984 employed, 7.1% unemployed; **Per capita income:** $19,843; % change 1990-93: 12.1.
History: settled 1825; inc. as city 1865; located on Ohio-Erie Canal and is a port of entry; since 1870 the rubber capital of the U.S.
Transportation: 1 airport; major trucking industry; Conrail; metro transit system. **Communications:** 4 TV, 7 radio stations. **Medical facilities:** 11 hospitals; specialized children's treatment center. **Educational facilities:** 13 universities and colleges; 68 public schools. **Further information:** Akron Regional Development Board or Akron-Summit Convention and Visitors Bureau, Cascade Plaza, Akron, OH 44308.

Albuquerque, New Mexico

Population: 384,619 (38); **Pop. density:** 2,829 per sq. mi.; **Pop. growth:** 15.6%. **Area:** 136 sq. mi. **Employment:** 219,151 employed, 4.5% unemployed; **Per capita income:** $18,899; % change 1990-93: 16.1.
History: founded 1706 by the Spanish; inc. 1890.
Transportation: 1 international airport; 1 railroad; 2 bus lines. **Communications:** 8 TV, 32 radio stations. **Medical facilities:** 10 major hospitals. **Educational facilities:** 1 university, 13 colleges. **Further information:** Convention & Visitors Bureau, 121 Tijeras Ave. NE, Albuquerque, NM 87125.

Anaheim, California

Population: 266,406 (59); **Pop. density:** 6,498 per sq. mi.; **Pop. growth:** 21.4%. **Area:** 41 sq. mi. **Employment:** 138,885 employed, 6.7% unemployed; **Per capita income:** $25,022; % change 1990-93: 3.0.
History: founded 1857; inc. 1870; now known as home of Disneyland (since 1955).
Transportation: 3 municipal airports; 4 railroads; Greyhound buses. **Communications:** 12 TV, 4 radio stations within city limits. **Medical facilities:** 5 hospitals; 4 medical centers. **Educational facilities:** 13 universities and colleges; 22 elementary, 8 junior high, 12 high schools. **Further information:** Chamber of Commerce, 100 South Anaheim Blvd., Suite 300, Anaheim, CA 92805.

Anchorage, Alaska

Population: 226,338 (69); **Pop. density:** 131 per sq. mi.; **Pop. growth:** 29.8%. **Area:** 1,732 sq. mi. **Employment:** 127,386 employed, 5.9% unemployed; **Per capita income:** $26,619; % change 1990-93: 10.4.
History: founded 1914 as a construction camp for railroad; HQ of Alaska Defense Command, WWII; severely damaged in earthquake 1964.
Transportation: 1 international airport, 3 other airports; railroad; transit system. **Communications:** 7 TV, 19 radio stations. **Medical facilities:** 3 hospitals. **Educational facilities:** 2 universities, 1 college, 1 junior college. **Further information:** Chamber of Commerce, 441 W. 5th Ave., Ste. 300, Anchorage, AK 99501-2309.

Arlington, Texas

Population: 261,717 (61); **Pop. density:** 3,313 per sq. mi.; **Pop. growth:** 63.5%. **Area:** 79 sq. mi. **Employment:** 162,395 employed, 4.8% unemployed; **Per capita income:** $20,912; % change 1990-93: 12.0.
History: settled in 1840s between Dallas and Ft. Worth; inc. 1884.
Transportation: Dallas/Ft. Worth airport is 20 minutes away; 11 railway lines; intercity transport system in planning stage. **Communications:** 11 TV, 44 radio stations. **Medical facilities:** 2 hospitals. **Educational facilities:** 1 university; 54 public schools. **Further information:** The Arlington Chamber, 316 W. Main St., Arlington, TX 76010.

Atlanta, Georgia

Population: 393,929 (36); **Pop. density:** 3,008 per sq. mi.; **Pop. growth:** –7.3%. **Area:** 131 sq. mi. **Employment:** 190,490 employed, 7.6% unemployed; **Per capita income:** $22,675; % change 1990-93: 10.9.
History: founded as "Terminus" 1837; renamed Atlanta 1845; inc. 1847; played major role in Civil War; birthplace of Martin Luther King Jr. and civil rights movement; host to 1996 Centennial Olympic Games.
Transportation: 1 international airport; 3 railroad lines; MARTA bus and rapid rail service. **Communications:** 11 TV, 51 radio stations; 26 cable TV companies. **Medical facilities:** 55 hospitals; VA hospital; Natl. Centers for Disease Control and Prevention; American Cancer Society. **Educational facilities:** 40 colleges, universities, seminaries, junior colleges. **Further information:** Chamber of Commerce, 235 International Blvd., Atlanta, GA 30303.

Aurora, Colorado

Population: 222,103 (72); **Pop. density:** 1,645 per sq. mi.; **Pop. growth:** 40.1%. **Area:** 135 sq. mi. **Employment:** 138,459 employed, 3.8% unemployed; **Per capita income:** $23,807; % change 1990-93: 13.4.
History: located 5 miles east of Denver; early growth stimulated by presence of military bases; fast-growing trade center.
Transportation: adjacent to new Denver Intl. Airport; 1 airport; 4 railroads; bus system. **Communications:** 1 TV station. **Medical facilities:** 2 private hospitals, 1 public hospital. **Educational facilities:** 1 university, 1 community college, 2 technical colleges. **Further information:** Aurora Planning Council, 1470 S. Havana St., Rm. 608, Aurora, CO 80012.

Austin, Texas

Population: 465,648 (27); **Pop. density:** 4,014 per sq. mi.; **Pop. growth:** 34.6%. **Area:** 116 sq. mi. **Employment:** 317,134 employed, 4.1% unemployed; **Per capita income:** $19,737; % change 1990-93: 15.7.
History: first permanent settlement 1835; capital of Rep. of Texas 1838; named after Stephen Austin; inc. 1840.
Transportation: 1 international airport; 4 railroads. **Communications:** 7 TV, 20 radio stations. **Medical facilities:** 11 hospitals. **Educational facilities:** 8 universities and colleges. **Further information:** Chamber of Commerce, P.O. Box 1967, Austin, TX 78767.

Bakersfield, California

Population: 174,978 (97); **Pop. density:** 2,033 per sq. mi.; **Pop. growth:** 65.5%. **Area:** 86 sq. mi. **Employment:** 82,514 employed, 10.6% unemployed; **Per capita income:** $16,312; % change 1990-93: 4.3.
History: named after Col. Thomas Baker, an early settler; inc. 1898.
Transportation: 1 airport; 3 railroads; Greyhound buses; local bus system. **Communications:** 4 TV, 34 radio stations. **Medical facilities:** 6 major hospitals; 9 convalescent, 1 psychiatric, 3 physical rehab., 5 urgent care facilities; 3 clinics. **Educational facilities:** 1 university, 1 community college; 9 vocational schools; 1 adult school; 1 college of law. **Further information:** Greater Bakersfield Chamber of Commerce, 1033 Truxtun Avenue, Bakersfield, CA 93301.

Baltimore, Maryland

Population: 736,014 (12); **Pop. density:** 9,200 per sq. mi.; **Pop. growth:** –6.4%. **Area:** 80 sq. mi. **Em-

ployment: 291,231 employed, 8.7% unemployed; **Per capita income:** $23,153; % change 1990-93: 8.9.

History: founded by Maryland legislature 1729; inc. 1797; bombing of its Ft. McHenry 1814 inspired Francis Scott Key to write "Star-Spangled Banner"; rebuilt after fire 1904.

Transportation: 1 major airport; 3 railroads; bus system; subway system; 2 underwater tunnels. **Communications:** 6 TV, 33 radio stations. **Medical facilities:** 29 hospitals; 2 major medical centers. **Educational facilities:** over 30 universities and colleges; 177 public schools. **Further information:** Greater Baltimore Committee, 111 S. Calvert St., Baltimore, MD 21202.

Baton Rouge, Louisiana

Population: 219,531 (73); **Pop. density:** 3,599 per sq. mi.; **Pop. growth:** –0.4%. **Area:** 61 sq. mi. **Employment:** 105,015 employed, 7.6% unemployed; **Per capita income:** $18,308; % change 1990-93: 14.8.

History: claimed by Spain at time of La. Purchase 1803; est. independence by rebellion 1810; inc. as town 1817; held by Union during most of Civil War.

Transportation: 1 airport, 5 airlines; 1 bus line; 3 railroad trunk lines. **Communications:** 5 TV, 19 radio stations. **Medical facilities:** 5 hospitals. **Educational facilities:** 2 universities; 92 public, 39 private schools. **Further information:** Chamber of Commerce, P.O. Box 3217, Baton Rouge, LA 70821.

Birmingham, Alabama

Population: 265,347 (60); **Pop. density:** 2,687 per sq. mi.; **Pop. growth:** –6.5%. **Area:** 99 sq. mi. **Employment:** 118,879 employed, 6.5% unemployed; **Per capita income:** $20,234; % change 1990-93: 15.0.

History: settled as a result of discovery of elements needed for steel production; inc. 1871; named after Great Britain's steel-making center.

Transportation: 1 airport; 4 major rail freight lines, Amtrak; 1 bus line; 75 truck line terminals; 4 interstate highways. **Communications:** 5 TV, 27 radio stations; 1 educational TV, 1 educational radio station. **Medical facilities:** Univ. of Alabama at Birmingham Medical Center; VA hospital with organ transplant program; 15 other hospitals. **Educational facilities:** 1 university, 2 colleges, 2 junior colleges. **Further information:** Chamber of Commerce, 2027 First Ave. N., Birmingham, AL 35202.

Boston, Massachusetts

Population: 574,283 (20); **Pop. density:** 12,484 per sq. mi.; **Pop. growth:** 2.0%. **Area:** 46 sq. mi. **Employment:** 273,486 employed, 5.8% unemployed; **Per capita income:** $24,861; % change 1990-93: 10.1.

History: settled 1630 by John Winthrop; capital of Mass. Bay Colony; figured strongly in Am. Revolution, earning distinction as the "Cradle of Liberty"; inc. 1822.

Transportation: 1 major airport; 2 railroads; city rail and subway system; 3 underwater tunnels; port. **Communications:** 20 TV, 51 radio stations. **Medical facilities:** 16 hospitals; 8 major medical research centers. **Educational facilities:** 19 universities and colleges. **Further information:** Greater Boston Chamber of Commerce, 1 Beacon St., 4th fl., Boston, MA 02108-3114.

Buffalo, New York

Population: 328,175 (50); **Pop. density:** 7,812 per sq. mi.; **Pop. growth:** –8.3%. **Area:** 42 sq. mi. **Employment:** 130,505 employed, 10.0% unemployed; **Per capita income:** $20,013; % change 1990-93: 11.9.

History: founded 1790 by the Dutch; raided twice by British, War of 1812; served as western terminus for Erie Canal, became a center for trade and manufacturing; inc. 1832; last stop on the Underground Railroad; key point for Canada-U.S. political, trade, and social relations.

Transportation: 1 international airport; 6 major railroads; metro rail system; water service to Great Lakes-St. Lawrence seaways system, and Atlantic seaboard. **Communications:** 11 TV, 24 radio stations. **Medical**

facilities: 20 hospitals, 40 research centers. **Educational facilities:** 2 universities, 11 colleges; 428 public, private schools. **Further information:** Greater Buffalo Partnership, 300 Main Place Tower, Buffalo, NY 14202.

Charlotte, North Carolina

Population: 395,925 (35); **Pop. density:** 2,869 per sq. mi.; **Pop. growth:** 25.5%. **Area:** 138 sq. mi. **Employment:** 237,377 employed, 4.0% unemployed; **Per capita income:** $20,856; % change 1990-93: 12.2.

History: settled by Scotch-Irish immigrants 1740s; inc. 1768 and named after Queen Charlotte, George III's wife; scene of first major U.S. gold discovery 1799.

Transportation: 1 airport; 2 major railway lines; 2 bus lines; 238 trucking firms. **Communications:** 6 TV, 20 radio stations. **Medical facilities:** 12 hospitals, 1 medical center. **Educational facilities:** 2 universities, 5 colleges. **Further information:** Chamber of Commerce, P.O. Box 32785, Charlotte, NC 28232.

Chicago, Illinois

Population: 2,783,726 (3); **Pop. density:** 12,209 per sq. mi.; **Pop. growth:** –7.4%. **Area:** 228 sq. mi. **Employment:** 1,218,509 employed, 7.0% unemployed; **Per capita income:** $24,857; % change 1990-93: 12.2.

History: site acquired from Indians 1795; significant white settlement began with opening of Erie Canal 1825; chartered as city 1837; boomed with arrival of railroads from east and canal to Mississippi R.; about one-third of city destroyed by fire 1871; major grain & livestock market.

Transportation: 3 airports; major railroad system; major trucking industry. **Communications:** 9 TV, 31 radio stations. **Medical facilities:** over 123 hospitals. **Educational facilities:** 95 institutions of higher learning. **Further information:** Chicagoland Chamber of Commerce, 1 IBM Plaza, Ste. 2800, Chicago, IL 60611.

Cincinnati, Ohio

Population: 364,114 (45); **Pop. density:** 4,667 per sq. mi.; **Pop. growth:** –5.5%. **Area:** 78 sq. mi. **Employment:** 164,921 employed, 6.8% unemployed; **Per capita income:** $21,116; % change 1990-93: 11.7.

History: founded 1788 and named after the Society of Cincinnati, an organization of Revolutionary War officers; chartered as village 1802; inc. as city 1819.

Transportation: 1 international airport; 3 railroads; 1 bus system. **Communications:** 6 TV, 27 radio stations. **Medical facilities:** 32 hospitals; Children's Hospital Medical Center; VA hospital. **Educational facilities:** 4 universities; 5 colleges, 8 technical & 2-year colleges. **Further information:** Chamber of Commerce, 300 Carew Tower, 441 Vine St., Cincinnati, OH 45202.

Cleveland, Ohio

Population: 505,616 (23); **Pop. density:** 6,400 per sq. mi.; **Pop. growth:** –11.9%. **Area:** 79 sq. mi. **Employment:** 184,182 employed, 11.0% unemployed; **Per capita income:** $22,126; % change 1990-93: 11.2.

History: surveyed in 1796; inc. as village 1814, as city 1836; annexed Ohio City 1854.

Transportation: 1 international airport; rail service; major port; rapid transit system. **Communications:** 9 TV, 26 radio stations. **Medical facilities:** 26 hospitals; research center. **Educational facilities:** 13 universities and colleges; 127 public schools. **Further information:** Greater Cleveland Growth Assn., 200 Tower City Center, 50 Public Square, Cleveland, OH 44113-2291.

Colorado Springs, Colorado

Population: 280,430 (54); **Pop. density:** 2,730 per sq. mi.; **Pop. growth:** 30.7%. **Area:** 103 sq. mi. **Employment:** 155,026 employed, 4.7% unemployed; **Per capita income:** $18,841; % change 1990-93: 12.7.

History: founded 1871 at the foot of Pikes Peak; inc. 1872.

Transportation: 1 municipal airport; 2 railroads; bus line. Communications: 8 TV, 26 radio stations. Medical facilities: 5 hospitals. Educational facilities: 11 universities, 11 colleges. Further information: Chamber of Commerce, P.O. Box B, Colorado Springs, CO 80901.

Columbus, Georgia

Population: 179,280 (93); Pop. density: 822 per sq. mi.; Pop. growth: 5.4%. Area: 218 sq. mi. Employment: 74,021 employed, 6.1% unemployed; Per capita income: $16,612; % change 1990-93: 13.8.
History: settled and inc. 1828; a port city on Chattahoochee R.
Transportation: 1 airport; metro bus system; 2 bus lines; 2 railroads. Communications: 5 TV, 12 radio stations. Medical facilities: 5 hospitals. Educational facilities: 2 colleges; 53 public schools. Further information: Chamber of Commerce, P.O. Box 1200, Columbus, GA 31902.

Columbus, Ohio

Population: 632,945 (16); Pop. density: 3,497 per sq. mi.; Pop. growth: 12.0%. Area: 181 sq. mi. Employment: 353,226 employed, 4.5% unemployed; Per capita income: $20,717; % change 1990-3: 13.4.
History: first settlement 1797; laid out as new capital 1812 with current name; became city 1834.
Transportation: 6 airports; 3 railroads; 4 intercity bus lines. Communications: 8 TV, 25 radio stations. Medical facilities: 18 hospitals. Educational facilities: 13 universities and colleges; 5 technical/2-year schools. Further information: Chamber of Commerce, 37 N. High St., Columbus, OH 43215.

Corpus Christi, Texas

Population: 257,428 (64); Pop. density: 2,476 per sq. mi.; Pop. growth: 10.9%. Area: 104 sq. mi. Employment: 120,615 employed, 8.6% unemployed; Per capita income: $17,093; % change 1990-93: 16.7.
History: settled 1839 and inc. 1852.
Transportation: 1 international airport; 2 bus lines, metro bus system; 3 freight railroads. Communications: 6 TV, 17 radio stations. Medical facilities: 14 hospitals including a children's center. Educational facilities: 1 university, 1 college. Further information: Chamber of Commerce, PO Box 640, Corpus Christi, TX 78403.

Dallas, Texas

Population: 1,007,618 (8); Pop. density: 3,024 per sq. mi.; Pop. growth: 11.3%. Area: 333 sq. mi. Employment: 578,246 employed, 6.6% unemployed; Per capita income: $23,605; % change 1990-93: 15.2.
History: first settled 1841; platted 1846; inc. 1871; developed as the financial and commercial center of Southwest; major distribution center.
Transportation: 1 international airport, 1 regional airport; Amtrak; transit system. Communications: 12 TV, 49 radio stations. Medical facilities: 14 general hospitals; major medical center. Educational facilities: 11 universities and colleges, 3 community college campuses. Further information: Greater Dallas Chamber, 1201 Elm, Suite 2000, Dallas, TX 75270.

Dayton, Ohio

Population: 182,005 (89); Pop. density: 3,793 per sq. mi.; Pop. growth: –5.9%. Area: 48 sq. mi. Employment: 71,807 employed, 8.5% unemployed; Per capita income: $20,093; % change 1990-93: 13.2.
History: settled 1796; inc. 1805; disastrous flood 1913; site where Wright Bros. invented first airplane to sustain flight 1903.
Transportation: 1 international airport, 16 airlines; 3 railroads; 2 bus lines; countywide Dayton Regional Transit Authority. Communications: 5 TV, 17 radio stations. Medical facilities: 11 hospitals including VA facility. Educational facilities: 3 colleges and universities. Further information: Dayton Area Chamber of Commerce, 1 Chamber Plaza, Dayton, OH 45402-2400.

Denver, Colorado

Population: 467,610 (26); Pop. density: 4,213 per sq. mi.; Pop. growth: –5.1%. Area: 111 sq. mi. Employment: 261,889 employed, 4.9% unemployed; Per capita income: $23,807; % change 1990-93: 13.4.
History: settled 1858 by gold prospectors and miners; inc. 1861; growth spurred by gold and silver boom; the financial and industrial center of Rocky Mt. region.
Transportation: 1 international airport; 4 rail freight lines, Amtrak; 1 bus line. Communications: 13 TV, 45 radio stations. Medical facilities: 20 hospitals. Educational facilities: 16 universities and colleges; 8 two-yr. and community colleges. Further information: Denver Metro Chamber of Commerce, 1445 Market St., Denver, CO 80202.

Des Moines, Iowa

Population: 193,189 (80); Pop. density: 2,927 per sq. mi.; Pop. growth: 1.1%. Area: 66 sq. mi. Employment: 114,479 employed, 3.7% unemployed; Per capita income: $22,331; % change 1990-93: 13.2.
History: Fort Des Moines built 1843; settled and inc. 1851; chartered as city 1857.
Transportation: 1 international airport; 4 bus lines; 5 railroads; metro bus system. Communications: 5 TV, 15 radio stations. Medical facilities: 8 hospitals. Educational facilities: 2 universities, 5 colleges. Further information: Greater Des Moines Chamber of Commerce Federation, 601 Locust St., Ste. 100, Des Moines, IA 50309.

Detroit, Michigan

Population: 1,027,974 (7); Pop. density: 7,559 per sq. mi.; Pop. growth: –14.6%. Area: 136 sq. mi. Employment: 345,618 employed, 10.8% unemployed; Per capita income: $22,856; % change 1990-93: 11.6.
History: founded by French 1701; controlled by British 1760; acquired by U.S. 1796; destroyed by fire 1805; inc. as city 1824; capital of state 1837-47; auto manufacturing began 1899.
Transportation: 1 international airport; 10 railroads; major international port; public transit system. Communications: 9 TV, 37 radio stations. Medical facilities: 28 hospitals, major medical center. Educational facilities: 13 universities and colleges. Further information: Greater Detroit Chamber of Commerce, 600 W. Lafayette Blvd., P.O. Box 33840, Detroit, MI 48232.

El Paso, Texas

Population: 515,342 (22); Pop. density: 2,156 per sq. mi.; Pop. growth: 21.2%. Area: 239 sq. mi. Employment: 228,888 employed, 9.6% unemployed; Per capita income: $12,790; % change 1990-93: 11.1.
History: first settled 1827; inc. 1873; arrival of railroad 1881 boosted city's population and industries.
Transportation: 1 international airport; 5 major rail lines; 8 bus lines; 5 major highways; gateway to Mexico. Communications: 10 TV, 23 radio stations. Medical facilities: 15 hospitals; cancer treatment center. Educational facilities: 2 colleges and universities. Further information: Greater El Paso Chamber of Commerce, 10 Civic Center Plaza, El Paso, TX 79901.

Fort Wayne, Indiana

Population: 172,971 (99); Pop. density: 3,328 per sq. mi.; Pop. growth: 0.4%. Area: 52 sq. mi. Employment: 92,133 employed, 5.6% unemployed; Per capita income: $20,299; % change 1990-93: 13.4.
History: French fort 1680; U.S. fort 1794; settled by 1832; inc. 1840 prior to Wabash-Erie canal completion 1843.
Transportation: 2 airports; 3 railroads; 8 bus lines. Communications: 5 TV, 13 radio stations. Medical facilities: 3 major hospitals; VA hospital. Educational facilities: 5 colleges; 82 public schools. Further information: Chamber of Commerce, 826 Ewing Street, Fort Wayne, IN 46802-2182.

Fort Worth, Texas

Population: 447,619 (28); Pop. density: 1,549 per sq. mi.; Pop. growth: 16.2%. Area: 289 sq. mi.

Employment: 229,693 employed, 7.3% unemployed; **Per capita income:** $20,912; % change 1990-93: 12.0.
History: est. as military post 1849; inc. 1873; oil discovered 1917.
Transportation: 1 international airport; 8 major railroads, Amtrak; local bus service; 2 transcontinental, 2 intrastate bus lines. **Communications:** 14 TV, 37 radio stations. **Medical facilities:** 30 hospitals; 2 children's hospitals; 4 government hospitals. **Educational facilities:** 8 universities and colleges. **Further Information:** Chamber of Commerce, 777 Taylor St. #900, Fort Worth, TX 76102.

Fremont, California

Population: 173,339 (98); **Pop. density:** 2,211 per sq. mi.; **Pop. growth:** 31.4%. **Area:** 78.4 sq. mi. **Employment:** 97,502 employed, 4.3% unemployed; **Per capita income:** $25,621; % change 1990-93: 9.7.
History: area first settled by Spanish 1769; inc. 1956 with the consolidation of 5 communities.
Transportation: intracity bus line; Bay Area Rapid Transit System (southern terminal). **Medical facilities:** 2 hospitals. **Educational facilities:** 1 junior college; 43 public schools. **Further Information:** Chamber of Commerce, 2201 Walnut Ave., Ste. 110, Fremont, CA 94538.

Fresno, California

Population: 354,091 (47); **Pop. density:** 5,449 per sq. mi.; **Pop. growth:** 62.9%. **Area:** 65 sq. mi. **Employment:** 163,784 employed, 12.2% unemployed; **Per capita income:** $16,918; % change 1990-93: 6.0.
History: founded 1872; inc. as city 1885.
Transportation: municipal airport; Amtrak; 1 bus line; intracity bus system. **Communications:** 11 TV, 30 radio stations. **Medical facilities:** 6 general hospitals including a VA facility. **Educational facilities:** 9 universities and colleges; 90 public schools. **Further Information:** Chamber of Commerce, 2331 Fresno St., Fresno, CA 93721.

Garland, Texas

Population: 180,635 (91); **Pop. density:** 3,226 per sq. mi.; **Pop. growth:** 30.1%. **Area:** 56 sq. mi. **Employment:** 110,809 employed, 4.3% unemployed; **Per capita income:** $23,605; % change 1990-93: 15.2.
History: settled 1850s; inc. 1891.
Transportation: 30 miles from Dallas/Ft. Worth airport; 2 railroads. **Communications:** 3 TV stations (from Dallas). **Medical facilities:** total of 306 hospital beds. **Educational facilities:** 1 university, 2 community colleges; 56 public schools. **Further Information:** Chamber of Commerce, 914 S. Garland Ave., Garland, TX 75040.

Glendale, California

Population: 180,038 (92); **Pop. density:** 5,886 per sq. mi.; **Pop. growth:** 29.0%. **Area:** 30.59 sq. mi. **Employment:** 82,570 employed, 8.8% unemployed; **Per capita income:** $21,661; % change 1990-93: 4.4.
History: township in 1887, incorporated in 1906. Adjacent to Los Angeles.
Transportation: 1 airport; 1 railroad; in triangle surrounded by 3 freeways; Southern California Rapid Transit system; Glendale Beeline bus. **Communications:** 2 radio stations. **Medical facilities:** 1,100 beds in 3 hospitals. **Educational facilities:** 1 community college. **Further Information:** Chamber of Commerce, 200 S. Louise, Glendale, CA 91205.

Grand Rapids, Michigan

Population: 189,126 (83); **Pop. density:** 4,358 per sq. mi.; **Pop. growth:** 4.0%. **Area:** 43.4 sq. mi. **Employment:** 95,303 employed, 6.2% unemployed; **Per capita income:** $20,062; % change 1990-93: 15.9.
History: originally site of Ottawa Indian village; trading post 1826; became lumbering center and chartered as town 1850.
Transportation: 1 international airport; 4 railroads; 5 bus lines; transit bus system. **Communications:** 6 TV, 25 radio stations. **Medical facilities:** 10 hospitals. **Edu-**cational facilities: 8 colleges; 64 public schools. **Further Information:** Chamber of Commerce, 111 Pearl St., NW, Grand Rapids, MI 49503.

Greensboro, North Carolina

Population: 183,894 (88); **Pop. density:** 3,059 per sq. mi.; **Pop. growth:** 17.9%. **Area:** 60 sq. mi. **Employment:** 106,388 employed, 3.9% unemployed; **Per capita income:** $20,772; % change 1990-93: 12.5.
History: settled 1749; site of Revolutionary War conflict 1781 between Nathanael Greene and Cornwallis; inc. 1807.
Transportation: 1 regional airport; 2 railroads; Trailways/Greyhound bus service. **Communications:** all cable TV stations; 11 radio stations. **Medical facilities:** 4 hospitals. **Educational facilities:** 2 universities, 3 colleges; 56 public schools. **Further Information:** Chamber of Commerce, P.O. Box 3246, Greensboro, NC 27402.

Hialeah, Florida

Population: 188,008 (85); **Pop. density:** 8,545 per sq. mi.; **Pop. growth:** 29.4%. **Area:** 22 sq. mi. **Employment:** 95,170 employed, 8.3% unemployed; **Per capita income:** $19,266; % change 1990-93: 9.2.
History: inc. 1925; industrial and residential city NW of Miami; Hialeah Park horse racing track.
Transportation: Miami Int'l. airport is 5 miles away; Amtrak; 2 rail freight lines. **Medical facilities:** 4 hospitals. **Educational facilities:** 5 universities and colleges. **Further Information:** Hialeah-Dade Development, Inc., 501 Palm Ave., Hialeah, FL 33010.

Honolulu, Hawaii

Population: 365,272 (44); **Pop. density:** 613 per sq. mi.; **Pop. growth:** 0.1%. **Area:** 596 sq. mi. **Employment (MSA):** 403,877 employed, 4.7% unemployed; **Per capita income:** $24,929; % change 1990-93: 13.3.
History: harbor entered by Europeans 1794; declared capital of kingdom by King Kamehameha III 1850; Pearl Harbor naval base attacked by Japanese Dec. 7, 1941.
Transportation: 1 major airport; large, active port for passengers and cargo. **Communications:** 10 TV, 30 radio stations. **Medical facilities:** 39 hospitals. **Educational facilities:** 4 universities, 5 colleges; 165 public schools, 98 private schools. **Further Information:** Hawaii Visitors Bureau, 2270 Kalakaua Avenue, Honolulu, HI 96815.

Houston, Texas

Population: 1,629,902 (4); **Pop. density:** 2,933 per sq. mi.; **Pop. growth:** 2.2%. **Area:** 556 sq. mi. **Employment:** 889,604 employed, 7.8% unemployed; **Per capita income:** $22,433; % change 1990-93: 13.6.
History: founded 1836; inc. 1837; capital of Republic of Texas 1837-39; developed rapidly after completion of canal to Gulf of Mexico 1914; important oil and natural gas center.
Transportation: 3 commercial airports; 4 mainline railroads; major bus transit system; major international port. **Communications:** 11 TV, 53 radio stations. **Medical facilities:** 66 hospitals; major medical center. **Educational facilities:** 26 universities and colleges. **Further Information:** Greater Houston Partnership, 1200 Smith St., Houston, TX 77002-4309.

Huntington Beach, California

Population: 181,519 (90); **Pop. density:** 6,723 per sq. mi.; **Pop. growth:** 6.5%. **Area:** 27 sq. mi. **Employment.** mi.;: 106,058 employed, 4.4% unemployed; **Per capita income:** $21,661; % change 1990-93: 4.4.
History: settled in early 1880s; inc. 1909; oil discovered 1920, led to city's development.
Transportation: 1 railroad; 2 bus lines. **Communications:** 1 TV station. **Medical facilities:** 2 hospitals. **Educational facilities:** 1 junior college; 45 public schools. **Further Information:** Chamber of Commerce, Seacliff Office Park, 2100 Main #200, Huntington Beach, CA 92648.

Indianapolis, Indiana

Population: 731,327 (13); **Pop. density:** 2,108 per sq. mi.; **Pop. growth:** 4.3%. **Area:** 352 sq. mi. **Employment:** 404,079 employed, 4.7% unemployed; **Per capita income:** $22,019; % change 1990-93: 14.5.

History: settled 1820; became capital 1825.

Transportation: 1 international airport; 5 railroads; 3 interstate bus lines. **Communications:** 10 TV, 27 radio stations. **Medical facilities:** 17 hospitals; 1 major medical and research center. **Educational facilities:** 8 universities and colleges; major public library system. **Further information:** Chamber of Commerce, 320 N. Meridian Street, Indianapolis, IN 46204.

Jackson, Mississippi

Population: 196,637 (78); **Pop. density:** 1,852 per sq. mi.; **Pop. growth:** -3.1%. **Area:** 106.2 sq. mi. **Employment:** 98,733 employed, 5.4% unemployed; **Per capita income:** $17,904; % change 1990-93: 16.6.

History: originally known as Le Fleur's Bluff; selected as capital 1822 and named for Andrew Jackson; inc. 1823; scene of secession convention 1861; captured by Sherman 1863.

Transportation: 6 airlines; 3 bus lines; 2 railroads. **Communications:** 5 TV, 18 radio stations. **Medical facilities:** 14 hospitals including a VA facility. **Educational facilities:** 2 universities, 7 colleges; 8 public school districts. **Further information:** Metro Jackson Chamber of Commerce, P.O. Box 22548, Jackson, MS 39225-2548.

Jacksonville, Florida

Population: 635,230 (15); **Pop. density:** 885 per sq. mi.; **Pop. growth:** 17.9%. **Area:** 760 sq. mi. **Employment:** 324,261 employed, 5.3% unemployed; **Per capita income:** $20,102; % change 1990-93: 11.6.

History: settled 1816 as Cowford; renamed after Andrew Jackson 1822; inc. 1832; rechartered 1851; scene of conflicts in Seminole and Civil wars.

Transportation: 1 international airport; 3 railroads; 2 interstate bus lines. **Communications:** 6 TV, 34 radio stations. **Medical facilities:** 11 hospitals. **Educational facilities:** 3 universities, 4 colleges. **Further information:** Chamber of Commerce, 3 Independent Drive, P.O. Box 329, Jacksonville, FL 32201.

Jersey City, New Jersey

Population: 228,517 (67); **Pop. density:** 17,313 per sq. mi.; **Pop. growth:** 2.2%. **Area:** 13.2 sq. mi. **Employment:** 99,244 employed, 11.4% unemployed; **Per capita income:** $21,610; % change 1990-93: 11.1.

History: site bought from Indians 1630; chartered as town by British 1668; scene of Revolutionary War conflict 1779; chartered under present name 1838; important station on Underground Railroad.

Transportation: bus and subway system. **Medical facilities:** 4 hospitals. **Educational facilities:** 3 colleges. **Further information:** Hudson County Chamber of Commerce, 574 Summit Ave., Ste. 404, Jersey City, NJ 07306.

Kansas City, Missouri

Population: 434,829 (31); **Pop. density:** 1,377 per sq. mi.; **Pop. growth:** -2.9%. **Area:** 316 sq. mi. **Employment:** 227,788 employed, 5.5% unemployed; **Per capita income:** $21,639; % change 1990-93: 13.1.

History: settled by 1838 at confluence of the Missouri and Kansas rivers; inc. 1851.

Transportation: 1 international airport; a major rail center; 191 trunk lines; several barge companies. **Communications:** 7 TV, 29 radio stations. **Medical facilities:** 14 hospitals; VA facility. **Educational facilities:** 9 universities and colleges. **Further information:** Greater Kansas City Chamber of Commerce, 911 Main St., Ste. 2600, Kansas City, MO 64105.

Las Vegas, Nevada

Population: 258,204 (63); **Pop. density:** 4,696 per sq. mi.; **Pop. growth:** 56.9%. **Area:** 55 sq. mi. **Employ-

ment: 168,202 employed, 6.0% unemployed; **Per capita income:** $21,232; % change 1990-93: 12.1.

History: occupied by Mormons 1855-57; bought by railroad 1903; city of Las Vegas inc. 1911; gambling legalized 1931.

Transportation: 1 international airport; 2 railroads; bus system. **Communcations:** 9 TV, 30 radio stations. **Medical facilities:** 10 hospitals. **Educational facilities:** 1 university, 1 college; 184 public schools. **Further information:** Chamber of Commerce, 711 E. Desert Inn Rd., Las Vegas, NV 89109.

Lexington, Kentucky

Population: 225,366 (70); **Pop. density:** 794 per sq. mi.; **Pop. growth:** 10.4%. **Area:** 284 sq. mi. **Employment:** 130,059 employed, 3.4% unemployed; **Per capita income:** $19,328; % change 1990-93: 11.4.

History: site was founded and named 1775 by hunters who heard of the Revolutionary War battle at Lexington, Mass.; settled 1779; inc. 1832.

Transportation: 8 airlines; 2 railroads; city buses. **Communications:** 5 TV, 9 radio stations. **Medical facilities:** 5 general, 5 specialized hospitals. **Educational facilities:** 2 universities, 2 colleges. **Further information:** Chamber of Commerce, 330 East Main, Lexington, KY 40507.

Lincoln, Nebraska

Population: 191,972 (81); **Pop. density:** 3,200 per sq. mi.; **Pop. growth:** 11.7%. **Area:** 60 sq. mi. **Employment:** 116,499 employed, 2.8% unemployed; **Per capita income:** $20,130; % change 1990-93: 16.8.

History: originally called Lancaster; chosen state capital 1867 and renamed after Abraham Lincoln; inc. 1869.

Transportation: 1 airport; Greyhound; Amtrak, 2 railroads. **Communications:** 1 TV, 13 radio stations. **Medical facilities:** 4 hospitals including a VA facility. **Educational facilities:** 2 universities, 1 college; 46 public, 15 private schools. **Further information:** Chamber of Commerce, 1221 N St., Lincoln, NE 68508.

Little Rock, Arkansas

Population: 175,727 (96); **Pop. density:** 2,225 per sq. mi.; **Pop. growth:** 10.5%. **Area:** 79 sq. mi. **Employment:** 99,031 employed, 4.0% unemployed; **Per capita income:** $19,192; % change 1990-93: 16.4.

History: founded 1821; inc. as city 1835.

Transportation: 1 airport, 8 airlines; 3 railroads; 1 bus line. **Communications:** 7 TV, 36 radio stations. **Medical facilities:** 20 hospitals; VA center. **Educational facilities:** 8 universities and colleges, Univ. of Arkansas; 100 public schools. **Further information:** Chamber of Commerce, 101 S. Spring St., Little Rock, AR 72201.

Long Beach, California

Population: 429,321 (32); **Pop. density:** 8,589 per sq. mi.; **Pop. growth:** 18.8%. **Area:** 50 sq. mi. **Employment:** 186,840 employed, 8.7% unemployed; **Per capita income:** $21,961; % change 1990-93: 4.4.

History: settled as early as 1769 by Spanish; by 1884 present site developed due to its harbor; inc. 1888; oil discovered 1921.

Transportation: 1 airport; 3 railroads; major international port; 6 bus lines, "lite" rail service. **Communications:** 4 radio stations. **Medical facilities:** 10 hospitals. **Educational facilities:** 1 university, 1 college; 78 public schools. **Further information:** Chamber of Commerce, One World Trade Center, Long Beach, CA 90831.

Los Angeles, California

Population: 3,485,557 (2); **Pop. density:** 7,495 per sq. mi.; **Pop. growth:** 17.4%. **Area:** 465 sq. mi. **Employment:** 1,583,383 employed, 10.6% unemployed; **Per capita income:** $21,661; % change 1990-93: 4.4.

History: founded by Spanish 1781; captured by U.S. 1846; inc. 1850; Hollywood a district of L.A.

Transportation: 1 international airport; 3 railroads; major freeway system; intracity transit system.

Communications: 21 TV, 70 radio stations. **Medical facilities:** 822 hospitals and clinics in metropolitan area. **Educational facilities:** 192 universities and colleges (incl. junior, community, and other); 1,678 public schools; 1,470 private schools. **Further Information:** Chamber of Commerce, 350 S. Bixel St., P.O. Box 3696, Los Angeles, CA 90051-1696.

Louisville, Kentucky

Population: 269,555 (58); **Pop. density:** 4,484 per sq. mi.; **Pop. growth:** −9.9%. **Area:** 60 sq. mi. **Employment:** 126,432 employed, 5.0% unemployed; **Per capita income:** $21,092; % change 1990-93: 15.9.

History: settled 1778; named for Louis XVI of France; inc. 1828; base for Union forces in Civil War.

Transportation: 2 municipal airports; 1 terminal, 4 trunk-line railroads; metro bus line, Greyhound station; 5 barge lines. **Communications:** 5 TV, 21 radio stations, 2 educational. **Medical facilities:** 21 hospitals. **Educational facilities:** 10 universities and colleges, 9 business colleges and technical schools. **Further information:** Louisville Area Chamber of Commerce, 600 W. Main, Louisville, KY 40202.

Lubbock, Texas

Population: 186,206 (87); **Pop. density:** 2,069 per sq. mi.; **Pop. growth:** 6.8%. **Area:** 90 sq. mi. **Employment:** 95,142 employed, 4.5% unemployed; **Per capita income:** $17,947; % change 1990-93: 13.6.

History: settled 1879; inc. 1909 through merger of two towns.

Transportation: 1 international airport; 2 railroads, bus line. **Communications:** 5 TV, 18 radio stations. **Medical facilities:** 7 hospitals. **Educational facilities:** 2 universities, 1 college; 51 public schools. **Further information:** Chamber of Commerce, P.O. Box 561, Lubbock, TX 79408.

Madison, Wisconsin

Population: 190,766 (82); **Pop. density:** 3,188 per sq. mi.; **Pop. growth:** 12.1%. **Area:** 60 sq. mi. **Employment:** 123,046 employed, 2.6% unemployed; **Per capita income:** $23,193; % change 1990-93: 16.9.

History: first white settlement 1832; named after James Madison, who died in 1836; chartered 1856.

Transportation: 1 airport, 9 airlines; 3 rail freight lines; 3 intercity and 1 intracity bus systems. **Communications:** 5 TV, 23 radio stations. **Medical facilities:** 7 hospitals. **Educational facilities:** 4 colleges and universities, Univ. of Wisconsin; 43 public schools. **Further Information:** Chamber of Commerce, P.O. Box 71, Madison, WI 53701.

Memphis, Tennessee

Population: 610,337 (18); **Pop. density:** 2,312 per sq. mi.; **Pop. growth:** −5.5%. **Area:** 264 sq. mi. **Employment:** 281,809 employed, 5.6% unemployed; **Per capita income:** $20,386; % change 1990-93: 14.4.

History: French, Spanish, and U.S. forts by 1797; settled by 1819; inc. as town 1826, as city 1840; surrendered charter to state 1879 after yellow fever epidemics; rechartered as city 1893.

Transportation: 1 international airport; 6 railroads; bus system. **Communications:** 6 TV, 29 radio stations. **Medical facilities:** 23 hospitals. **Educational facilities:** 12 universities and colleges; 205 public, 76 private schools. **Further Information:** Memphis Area Chamber of Commerce, 22 N. Front St., Box 224, Memphis, TN 38101.

Mesa, Arizona

Population: 288,104 (53); **Pop. density:** 4,237 per sq. mi.; **Pop. growth:** 89.0%. **Area:** 68 sq. mi. **Employment:** 156,016 employed, 4.2% unemployed; **Per capita income:** $19,853; % change 1990-93: 10.8.

History: founded by Mormons 1878; inc. 1883; 13 mi. from Phoenix; population boomed fivefold 1960-80.

Transportation: near Sky Harbor intl. airport in Phoenix; 2 railroads; bus line. **Medical facilities:** 4 major

hospitals. **Educational facilities:** 1 university, 1 college; 63 public schools. **Further information:** Convention and Visitor's Bureau, 120 N. Center, Mesa, AZ 85201.

Miami, Florida

Population: 358,648 (46); **Pop. density:** 10,546 per sq. mi.; **Pop. growth:** 3.4%. **Area:** 34 sq. mi. **Employment:** 160,576 employed, 11.5% unemployed; **Per capita income:** $19,266; % change 1990-93: 9.2.

History: site of fort 1836; settlement began 1870; inc. 1896 and modern city developed into resort and recreation center; land speculation in 1920s added to city's growth, as did Cuban, Central and South American, and Haitian immigration since 1960.

Transportation: 1 international airport; Amtrak, transit rail system; 2 bus lines; 65 truck lines. **Communications:** 9 commercial, 2 educational TV stations; 41 radio stations. **Medical facilities:** 36 hospitals, VA hospital. **Educational facilities:** 6 universities and colleges. **Further information:** Metro-Dade Planning Dept., Research Div., 111 NW 1st St., Ste. 1220, Miami, FL 33128.

Milwaukee, Wisconsin

Population: 628,088 (17); **Pop. density:** 6,543 per sq. mi.; **Pop. growth:** −1.3%. **Area:** 96 sq. mi. **Employment:** 280,833 employed, 6.4% unemployed; **Per capita income:** $22,786; % change 1990-93: 14.4.

History: Indian trading post by 1674; settlement began 1835; inc. as city 1848; famous beer industry.

Transportation: 1 international airport; 2 railroads; major port; 4 bus lines. **Communications:** 12 TV, 34 radio stations. **Medical facilities:** 24 hospitals; major medical center. **Educational facilities:** 12 universities and colleges. **Further information:** Metropolitan Milwaukee Association of Commerce, 756 N. Milwaukee Street, Milwaukee, WI 53202.

Minneapolis, Minnesota

Population: 368,383 (42); **Pop. density:** 6,698 per sq. mi.; **Pop. growth:** −0.7%. **Area:** 55 sq. mi. **Employment:** 205,598 employed, 3.7% unemployed; **Per capita income:** $24,145; % change 1990-93: 12.7.

History: site visited by Hennepin 1680; included in area of military reservations 1819; inc. 1867.

Transportation: 1 international airport; 6 railroads; mass transit systems; 5 major barge lines. **Communications:** 6 TV, 39 radio stations. **Medical facilities:** 36 hospitals, including leading heart hospital at Univ. of Minnesota. **Educational facilities:** 13 universities and colleges; 48 public school districts. **Further information:** Greater Minneapolis Chamber of Commerce, 81 S. 9th St., Ste. 200, Minneapolis, MN 55402.

Mobile, Alabama

Population: 196,263 (79); **Pop. density:** 1,596 per sq. mi.; **Pop. growth:** −2.1%. **Area:** 123 sq. mi. **Employment:** 95,652 employed, 7.4% unemployed; **Per capita income:** $16,494; % change 1990-93: 16.7.

History: settled by French 1711; later occupied by U.S. 1813; inc. as town 1814, as city 1819; only seaport of Alabama.

Transportation: 4 rail freight lines, Amtrak; 4 airlines; 65 truck lines; leading river system. **Communications:** 7 TV, 21 radio stations. **Medical facilities:** 9 hospitals. **Educational facilities:** 2 universities, 2 colleges. **Further information:** Chamber of Commerce, P.O. Box 2187, Mobile, AL 36652.

Montgomery, Alabama

Population: 187,543 (86); **Pop. density:** 1,462 per sq. mi.; **Pop. growth:** 5.2%. **Area:** 128 sq. mi. **Employment:** 91,258 employed, 5.2% unemployed; **Per capita income:** $18,716; % change 1990-93: 13.4.

History: inc. as town 1819, as city 1837; first capital of Confederacy 1861.

Transportation: 5 airlines; 2 railroads; 4 bus lines; Alabama River is navigable to Gulf of Mexico. **Communications:** 7 TV, 16 radio stations. **Medical facilities:** 10 hospitals; VA and 32 clinics. **Educational facilities:** 5

universities; 49 public, 31 private schools. **Further information:** Chamber of Commerce, P.O. Box 79, Montgomery, AL 36101.

Nashville, Tennessee

Population: 488,374 (25); **Pop. density:** 984 per sq. mi.; **Pop. growth:** 6.9%. **Area:** 525 sq. mi. **Employment:** 283,720 employed, 3.2% unemployed; **Per capita income:** $21,634; % change 1990-93: 18.0.
History: settled 1779; first chartered 1806; home of the Grand Ole Opry.
Transportation: 1 airport; 1 railroad; bus line; transit system of buses and trolleys. **Communications:** 7 TV, 30 radio stations. **Medical facilities:** 14 hospitals; VA hospital, speech-hearing center. **Educational facilities:** 16 universities and colleges. **Further information:** Chamber of Commerce, 161 4th Ave., Nashville, TN 37219.

Newark, New Jersey

Population: 275,221 (56); **Pop. density:** 11,468 per sq. mi.; **Pop. growth:** −16.4%. **Area:** 24 sq. mi. **Employment:** 98,890 employed, 13.7% unemployed; **Per capita income:** $28,687; % change 1990-93: 12.8.
History: settled by Puritans 1666; used as supply base by Washington 1776; inc. as town 1833, as city 1836.
Transportation: 1 international airport; 2 railroads; bus system; 2 subways. **Communications:** 3 TV, 5 radio stations within city limits. **Medical facilities:** 6 hospitals. **Educational facilities:** 5 universities and colleges; 71 public schools. **Further information:** Regional Business Partnership, 1 Newark Center, Newark, NJ 07102-5265.

New Orleans, Louisiana

Population: 496,938 (24); **Pop. density:** 2,497 per sq. mi.; **Pop. growth:** −10.9%. **Area:** 199 sq. mi. **Employment:** 188,227 employed, 8.1% unemployed; **Per capita income:** $18,882; % change 1990-93: 15.2.
History: founded by French 1718; became major seaport on Mississippi R.; acquired by U.S. as part of La. Purchase 1803; inc. as city 1805; Battle of New Orleans was last battle of War of 1812.
Transportation: 2 airports; major railroad center; major international port. **Communications:** 7 TV, 18 radio stations. **Medical facilities:** numerous hospitals; major research center. **Educational facilities:** 13 universities and colleges. **Further information:** Chamber of Commerce, 301 Camp Street, New Orleans, LA 70130.

Newport News, Virginia

Population: 171,439 (100); **Pop. density:** 2,464 per sq. mi.; **Pop. growth:** 17.4%. **Area:** 69 sq. mi. **Employment:** 80,046 employed, 6.1% unemployed; **Per capita income:** $18,485; % change 1990-93: 10.6.
History: the cities of Warwick and Newport News consolidated in 1958 into the larger city of Newport News; one of the world's major shipbuilding centers.
Transportation: 1 international airport; 2 railroads; Greyhound buses; local bus system. **Communications:** 7 TV, 20 radio stations received in area. **Medical facilities:** 3 hospitals; adolescent psychiatry hospital. **Educational facilities:** 33 public schools. **Further information:** Virginia Peninsula Chamber of Commerce, Six Manhattan Sq., P.O. Box 7269, Hampton, VA 23666.

New York City, New York

Population: 7,322,564 (1); **Pop. density:** 24,327 per sq. mi.; **Pop. growth:** 3.5%. **Area:** 301 sq. mi. **Employment:** 2,923,000 employed, 8.7% unemployed; **Per capita income:** $27,975; % change 1990-93: 13.4.
History: trading post established by H. Hudson 1609; British took control from Dutch 1664 and named New York; briefly capital of U.S.; Washington inaugurated as president 1789; composed of 5 boroughs: The Bronx, Brooklyn, Manhattan, Queens, Staten Island.
Transportation: 2 airports; 2 rail terminals; major subway network; ferry system; 4 underwater tunnels.

Communications: 13 TV, 117 radio stations. **Medical facilities:** 81 hospitals; 5 academic medical centers. **Educational facilities:** 92 universities and colleges; 1,095 public schools, 914 private schools. **Further information:** Convention and Visitors Bureau, 2 Columbus Circle, New York, NY 10019.

Norfolk, Virginia

Population: 261,250 (62); **Pop. density:** 4,929 per sq. mi.; **Pop. growth:** −2.2%. **Area:** 53 sq. mi. **Employment:** 90,699 employed, 6.4% unemployed; **Per capita income:** $18,485; % change 1990-93: 10.6.
History: founded 1682; burned by patriots to prevent capture by British during Revolutionary War; rebuilt and inc. as town 1805, as city 1845; location of world's largest naval base.
Transportation: 1 international airport; Amtrak; bus system. **Communications:** 7 TV, 42 radio stations. **Medical facilities:** 11 hospitals. **Educational facilities:** 2 universities, 1 college, 1 medical school; 58 public schools. **Further information:** Hampton Roads Chamber of Commerce, 420 Bank St., P.O. Box 327, Norfolk, VA 23501.

Oakland, California

Population: 372,242 (39); **Pop. density:** 6,893 per sq. mi.; **Pop. growth:** 9.7%. **Area:** 54 sq. mi. **Employment:** 164,581 employed, 9.7% unemployed; **Per capita income:** $25,621; % change 1990-93: 9.7.
History: area settled by Spanish 1820; inc. as city under present name 1854.
Transportation: 1 international airport; western terminus for 3 railroads; underground, underwater 75-mile subway. **Communications:** 1 TV, 3 radio stations within city limits. **Medical facilities:** 10 hospitals in met. area, including Children's Hospital Oakland, VA hospital. **Educational facilities:** 8 "eastbay" colleges and universities; 94 public schools. **Further information:** Chamber of Commerce, 475 14th St., Oakland, CA 94612-1903.

Oklahoma City, Oklahoma

Population: 444,724 (29); **Pop. density:** 736 per sq. mi.; **Pop. growth:** 10.1%. **Area:** 604 sq. mi. **Employment:** 220,482 employed, 5.3% unemployed; **Per capita income:** $18,328; % change 1990-93: 12.1.
History: settled during land rush in Midwest 1889; inc. 1890; oil discovered 1928.
Transportation: 1 international airport; 3 railroads; public transit system; 5 major bus lines. **Communications:** 8 TV, 24 radio stations. **Medical facilities:** 20 hospitals. **Educational facilities:** 17 universities and colleges; 83 public, 37 private schools. **Further information:** Chamber of Commerce, Economic Development Division, 123 Park Ave., Oklahoma City, OK 73102.

Omaha, Nebraska

Population: 335,719 (48); **Pop. density:** 3,690 per sq. mi.; **Pop. growth:** 7.0%. **Area:** 91 sq. mi. **Employment:** 183,519 employed, 3.4% unemployed; **Per capita income:** $21,281; % change 1990-93: 15.2.
History: founded 1854; inc. 1857; large food-processing and telecommunications center; home for U.S. Strategic Air Command.
Transportation: 11 major airlines; 4 major railroads; intercity bus line. **Communications:** 8 TV, 22 radio stations. **Medical facilities:** 16 hospitals; institute for cancer research. **Educational facilities:** 4 universities, 5 colleges; 216 public, 82 private schools. **Further information:** Chamber of Commerce, 1301 Harney St., Omaha, NE 68102.

Philadelphia, Pennsylvania

Population: 1,585,577 (5); **Pop. density:** 11,659 per sq. mi.; **Pop. growth:** −6.1%. **Area:** 136 sq. mi. **Employment:** 622,062 employed, 7.5% unemployed; **Per capita income:** $24,236; % change 1990-93: 12.7.
History: first settled by Swedes 1640s; by English 1681; named Philadelphia 1682; chartered 1701; Continental Congresses convened 1774, 1775; Dec. of Inde-

pendence signed 1776; national capital 1790-1800; cap. of Penn. 1683-1799.

Transportation: 1 major airport; 3 railroads; major freshwater port; subway, el, rail commuter, bus, and streetcar system. **Communications:** 6 TV, 53 radio stations. **Medical facilities:** 124 hospitals. **Educational facilities:** 88 degree-granting institutions. **Further Information:** Office of City Representative, 1650 Arch St., 19th fl., Philadelphia, PA 19103.

Phoenix, Arizona

Population: 983,403 (9); **Pop. density:** 3,035 per sq. mi.; **Pop. growth:** 24.5%. **Area:** 324 sq. mi. **Employment:** 553,640 employed, 5.4% unemployed; **Per capita Income:** $19,853; % change 1990-93: 10.8.

History: settled 1870; inc. as city 1881.

Transportation: 1 international airport; 5 railroads; 2 transcontinental bus lines; public transit system. **Communications:** 13 TV, 40 radio stations. **Medical facilities:** 42 hospitals, 1 medical research center. **Educational facilities:** 12 institutions of higher learning; 161 public schools. **Further information:** Chamber of Commerce, 201 N. Central Ave. #2700, Phoenix, AZ 85004.

Pittsburgh, Pennsylvania

Population: 369,879 (40); **Pop. density:** 6,725 per sq. mi.; **Pop. growth:** -12.8%. **Area:** 55 sq. mi. **Employment:** 155,602 employed, 6.3% unemployed; **Per capita income:** $21,825; % change 1990-93: 15.1.

History: settled around Ft. Pitt 1758; inc. as city 1816; has one of the largest inland ports; by Civil War, already a center for iron production.

Transportation: 1 international airport; 20 railroads; 2 bus lines; trolley/subway system. **Communications:** 6 TV, 26 radio stations. **Medical facilities:** 35 hospitals; VA installation. **Educational facilities:** 3 universities, 6 colleges; 86 public schools. **Further information:** Chamber of Commerce, 4 Gateway Ctr., Pittsburgh, PA 15222-1259.

Portland, Oregon

Population: 438,802 (30); **Pop. density:** 4,246 per sq. mi.; **Pop. growth:** 18.8%. **Area:** 103 sq. mi. **Employment:** 253,577 employed, 5.1% unemployed; **Per capita income:** $21,651; % change 1990-93: 12.8.

History: settled by pioneers 1845; developed as trading center, aided by California Gold Rush 1849; chartered as city 1851.

Transportation: 1 international airport; 3 major rail freight lines, Amtrak; 2 intercity bus lines; 27-mi. frontage freshwater port; mass transit bus and rail system. **Communications:** 8 TV, 36 radio stations. **Medical facilities:** 23 hospitals; VA hospital. **Educational facilities:** 33 universities and colleges, 3 community colleges. **Further information:** Portland Metropolitan Chamber of Commerce, 221 N.W. 2nd Ave., Portland, OR 97209-3999.

Raleigh, North Carolina

Population: 212,092 (74); **Pop. density:** 3,851 per sq. mi.; **Pop. growth:** 38.4%. **Area:** 54 sq. mi. **Employment:** 137,035 employed, 3.6% unemployed; **Per capita Income:** $22,071; % change 1990-93: 14.0.

History: named after Sir Walter Raleigh; site chosen for capital 1788; laid out 1792; inc. 1795; occupied by Gen. Sherman 1865.

Transportation: 1 international airport, 10 airlines, 4 commuter airlines; 3 railroads; 2 bus lines. **Communications:** 7 TV, 30 radio stations. **Medical facilities:** 8 hospitals. **Educational facilities:** 6 universities and colleges; 1 junior, 1 community college; 95 public schools (county). **Further information:** Chamber of Commerce, 800 S. Salisbury St., P.O. Box 2978, Raleigh, NC 27602.

Richmond, Virginia

Population: 202,798 (76); **Pop. density:** 3,384 per sq. mi.; **Pop. growth:** -7.4%. **Area:** 60 sq. mi. **Employ-**

ment: 99,563 employed, 6.0% unemployed; **Per capita income:** $23,262; % change 1990-93: 9.1.

History: first settled 1607; attacked by British under Benedict Arnold 1781; inc. as city 1782; capital of Confederate States of America, 1861-65.

Transportation: 1 international airport; 4 railroads; 3 intracity bus lines; deepwater terminal accessible to oceangoing ships. **Communications:** 6 TV, 26 radio stations. **Medical facilities:** Medical Coll. of Virginia renowned for heart and kidney transplants; 19 other hospitals incl. VA facility. **Educational facilities:** 9 universities and colleges; 173 public, 45 private schools. **Further information:** Chamber of Commerce, P.O. Box 12280, Richmond, VA 23241-2280.

Riverside, California

Population: 226,546 (68); **Pop. density:** 3,190 per sq. mi.; **Pop. growth:** 32.8%. **Area:** 71 sq. mi. **Employment:** 112,092 employed, 10.5% unemployed; **Per capita income:** $17,180; % change 1990-93: 1.6.

History: founded 1870; inc. 1886; known for its citrus industry.

Transportation: internatl. airport nearby, municipal airport; rail freight lines, commuter line; trolley/bus system. **Communications:** 11 TV, 13 radio stations. **Medical facilities:** 4 hospitals; many clinics. **Educational facilities:** 3 universities, 1 community college. **Further information:** Chamber of Commerce, 3685 Main St., Ste. 350, Riverside, CA 92501.

Rochester, New York

Population: 230,356 (66); **Pop. density:** 6,813 per sq. mi.; **Pop. growth:** -4.2%. **Area:** 34 sq. mi. **Employment:** 105,374 employed, 8.5% unemployed; **Per capita income:** $21,719; % change 1990-93: 8.8.

History: first permanent white settlement 1812; inc. as village 1817, as city 1834; developed as Erie Canal town.

Transportation: 1 internatl. airport; Amtrak; 3 bus lines; intracity transit service; Port of Rochester. **Communications:** 6 TV, 18 radio stations. **Medical facilities:** 8 general hospitals. **Educational facilities:** 10 colleges, 3 community colleges. **Further information:** Chamber of Commerce, 55 St. Paul St., Rochester, NY 14604-1391.

Sacramento, California

Population: 369,365 (41); **Pop. density:** 3,848 per sq. mi.; **Pop. growth:** 34.0%. **Area:** 96 sq. mi. **Employment:** 168,978 employed, 8.9% unemployed; **Per capita income:** $21,073; % change 1990-93: 8.7.

History: settled 1839; important trading center during California Gold Rush 1840s.

Transportation: metropolitan, executive, and cargo airports; 2 mainline transcontinental rail carriers; bus and light rail system; Port of Sacramento. **Communications:** 7 TV, 25 radio stations; 3 cable TV cos. **Medical facilities:** 8 hospitals. **Educational facilities:** 2 universities, 4 community colleges. **Further information:** Chamber of Commerce, 917 7th St., Sacramento, CA 95814.

St. Louis, Missouri

Population: 396,685 (34); **Pop. density:** 6,503 per sq. mi.; **Pop. growth:** -12.4%. **Area:** 61 sq. mi. **Employment:** 160,079 employed, 7.1% unemployed; **Per capita income:** $22,521; % change 1990-93: 12.0.

History: founded 1764 as a fur trading post by French; acquired by U.S. 1803; chartered as city 1822; lies on Mississippi R., near confluence with Missouri R.

Transportation: 1 international airport; major rail center, 17 trunk-line railroads; major inland port; 14 bus lines; 14 barge lines. **Communications:** 7 TV, 35 radio stations. **Medical facilities:** 65 hospitals. **Educational facilities:** 6 universities, 25 colleges and seminaries. **Further information:** City Office, St. Louis Community Development Council, 330 N. 15th St., St. Louis, MO 63103.

St. Paul, Minnesota

Population: 272,235 (57); **Pop. density:** 5,235 per sq. mi.; **Pop. growth:** 0.7%. **Area:** 52 sq. mi. **Employment:** 142,577 employed, 3.8% unemployed; **Per capita income:** $24,145; % change 1990-93: 12.7.

History: founded in early 1840s as "Pig's Eye Landing"; became capital of the Minnesota territory 1849 and chartered as St. Paul.

Transportation: 1 international, 1 business airport; 6 major rail lines; 3 interstate bus lines; public transit system. **Communications:** 6 TV, 35 radio stations. **Medical facilities:** 7 hospitals. **Educational facilities:** 3 universities, 4 colleges; 1 technical, 3 first professional colleges. **Further information:** Chamber of Commerce, 55 E. 5th St., Norwest Ctr., Ste. 101, St. Paul, MN 55101.

St. Petersburg, Florida

Population: 240,318 (65); **Pop. density:** 4,056 per sq. mi.; **Pop. growth:** 0.0%. **Area:** 59 sq. mi. **Employment:** 119,657 employed, 6.0% unemployed; **Per capita income:** $20,004; % change 1990-93: 11.3.

History: founded 1888; inc. 1892.

Transportation: 2 airports (1 international); bus system; 1 full-service port. **Communications:** 12 TV, 22 radio stations. **Medical facilities:** 3 major hospitals, VA hospital. **Educational facilities:** 1 university, 3 colleges; 120 public schools. **Further information:** Chamber of Commerce, P.O. Box 1371, St. Petersburg, FL 33731.

San Antonio, Texas

Population: 935,393 (10); **Pop. density:** 2,681 per sq. mi.; **Pop. growth:** 19.1%. **Area:** 349 sq. mi. **Employment:** 464,239 employed, 5.4% unemployed; **Per capita income:** $17,889; % change 1990-93: 14.8.

History: first Spanish garrison 1718; Battle at the Alamo fought here 1836; city subsequently captured by Texans; inc. 1837.

Transportation: 1 international, 1 municipal airport; 4 railroads; 4 bus lines; public transit system; 25 common-carrier truck lines. **Communications:** 8 TV, 35 radio stations. **Medical facilities:** 27 hospitals; major medical center. **Educational facilities:** 19 universities and colleges; 16 public school districts. **Further information:** Chamber of Commerce, 602 E. Commerce, P.O. Box 1628, San Antonio, TX 78296.

San Diego, California

Population: 1,110,554 (6); **Pop. density:** 3,470 per sq. mi.; **Pop. growth:** 26.8%. **Area:** 320 sq. mi. **Employment:** 525,170 employed, 7.3% unemployed; **Per capita income:** $20,950; % change 1990-93: 6.2.

History: claimed by the Spanish 1542; first mission est. 1769; scene of conflict during Mexican-American War 1846; inc. 1850.

Transportation: 1 major airport; 1 railroad; major freeway system; bus system; trolley system. **Communications:** 8 TV, 22 radio stations. **Medical facilities:** 28 hospitals. **Educational facilities:** 5 universities, 7 colleges. **Further information:** Greater SD Chamber of Commerce, 402 W. Broadway, Suite 1000, San Diego, CA 92101-3585.

San Francisco, California

Population: 723,959 (14); **Pop. density:** 15,403 per sq. mi.; **Pop. growth:** 6.6%. **Area:** 47 sq. mi. **Employment:** 380,795 employed, 6.7% unemployed; **Per capita income:** $32,927; % change 1990-93: 11.0.

History: nearby Farallon Islands sighted by Spanish 1542; city settled by 1776; claimed by U.S. 1846; became a major city during California Gold Rush 1849; inc. as city 1850; earthquake devastated city 1906.

Transportation: 1 major airport; intracity railway system; 2 railway transit systems; bus and railroad service; ferry system; 1 underwater tunnel. **Communications:** 14 TV and cable stations; 69 radio stations. **Medical facilities:** 23 hospitals; 1 major medical center. **Educational**

facilities: 4 universities and colleges. **Further information:** Chamber of Commerce, 465 California Street, San Francisco, CA 94104.

San Jose, California

Population: 782,248 (11); **Pop. density:** 4,951 per sq. mi.; **Pop. growth:** 24.3%. **Area:** 158 sq. mi. **Employment:** 406,075 employed, 7.4% unemployed; **Per capita income:** $27,360; % change 1990-93: 11.5.

History: founded by the Spanish 1777 between San Francisco and Monterey; briefly capital of Calif. 1849-51; inc. 1850.

Transportation: 1 international airport; 2 railroads; bus system. **Communications:** 4 TV, 14 radio stations. **Medical facilities:** 6 hospitals. **Educational facilities:** 3 universities and colleges. **Further information:** Chamber of Commerce, 180 S. Market St., San Jose, CA 95113.

Santa Ana, California

Population: 293,827 (52); **Pop. density:** 10,879 per sq. mi.; **Pop. growth:** 44.0%. **Area:** 27 sq. mi. **Employment:** 137,744 employed, 10.2% unemployed; **Per capita income:** $25,022; % change 1990-93: 3.0.

History: founded 1869; inc. as city 1886.

Transportation: 1 airport; 5 major freeways including main Los Angeles-San Diego artery; Amtrak. **Medical facilities:** 4 hospitals. **Educational facilities:** 1 community college. **Further information:** Chamber of Commerce, 856 N. Ross St., Santa Ana, CA 92701.

Seattle, Washington

Population: 516,259 (21); **Pop. density:** 6,146 per sq. mi.; **Pop. growth:** 4.5%. **Area:** 84 sq. mi. **Employment:** 294,599 employed, 6.5% unemployed; **Per capita income:** $26,121; % change 1990-93: 13.8.

History: settled 1851; inc. 1869; suffered severe fire 1889; played prominent role during Alaska Gold Rush 1897; growth followed opening of Panama Canal 1914; center of aircraft industry WWII.

Transportation: 1 international airport; 2 railroads; ferries serve Puget Sound, Alaska, Canada. **Communications:** 7 TV, 39 radio stations. **Medical facilities:** 40 hospitals. **Educational facilities:** 7 universities, 6 colleges, 11 community colleges. **Further information:** Greater Seattle Chamber of Commerce, 600 University St., Ste. 1200, Seattle, WA 98101-3186.

Shreveport, Louisiana

Population: 198,518 (77); **Pop. density:** 2,482 per sq. mi.; **Pop. growth:** -4.1%. **Area:** 80 sq. mi. **Employment:** 85,323 employed, 7.7% unemployed; **Per capita income:** $17,835; % change 1990-93: 19.1.

History: founded 1833 near site of a 160-mile log jam cleared by Capt. Henry Shreve; inc. 1839; oil discovered 1906.

Transportation: 2 airports; 1 bus line. **Communications:** 6 TV, 16 radio stations. **Medical facilities:** 18 hospitals. **Educational facilities:** 4 universities, 3 colleges. **Further information:** Chamber of Commerce, P.O. Box 20074, Shreveport, LA 71120.

Spokane, Washington

Population: 177,165 (94); **Pop. density:** 3,408 per sq. mi.; **Pop. growth:** 3.4%. **Area:** 52 sq. mi. **Employment:** 85,862 employed, 5.9% unemployed; **Per capita income:** $18,742; % change 1990-93: 14.9.

History: settled 1872; inc. as village of Spokane Falls 1881, destroyed in fire 1889; reinc. as city of Spokane 1891.

Transportation: 1 international airport; 2 railroads; bus system. **Communications:** 5 TV, 25 radio stations. **Medical facilities:** 6 major hospitals. **Educational facilities:** 8 universities and colleges; 14 public school districts, 11 high schools. **Further information:** Chamber of Commerce, W. 1020 Riverside Ave., P.O. Box 2147, Spokane, WA 99210.

Stockton, California

Population: 210,943 (75); **Pop. density:** 5,274 per sq. mi.; **Pop. growth:** 42.3%. **Area:** 40 sq. mi. **Employment:** 86,101 employed, 14.4% unemployed; **Per capita income:** $17,808; % change 1990-93: 10.0.
History: site purchased 1842; settled 1847; inc. 1850; chief distributing point for agricultural products of San Joaquin Valley.
Transportation: 1 airport, 7 railroads; 2 bus lines, county bus system. **Communications:** 5 TV stations. **Medical facilities:** 4 hospitals; regional burn, cancer, and heart centers. **Educational facilities:** 6 universities and colleges; 45 public schools. **Further information:** Chamber of Commerce, 445 W. Weber Ave., Suite 220, Stockton, CA 95203.

Tacoma, Washington

Population: 176,664 (95); **Pop. density:** 3,696 per sq. mi.; **Pop. growth:** 11.5%. **Area:** 47.8 sq. mi. **Employment:** 84,127 employed, 7.4% unemployed; **Per capita income:** $19,010; % change 1990-93: 11.8.
History: first European explorer of area was British Capt. George Vancouver 1792; colonized by Hudson's Bay Co. at Ft. Nisqually 1833; inc. 1884.
Transportation: 1 international airport; 2 railroads; transit system; Port of Tacoma. **Communications:** 6 TV stations. **Medical facilities:** 7 hospitals, Army Medical Center, VA facility. **Educational facilities:** 3 universities, 4 colleges. **Further information:** Chamber of Commerce, P.O. Box 1933, Tacoma, WA 98401-1933.

Tampa, Florida

Population: 280,015 (55); **Pop. density:** 3,334 per sq. mi.; **Pop. growth:** 3.1%. **Area:** 84 sq. mi. **Employment:** 145,358 employed, 6.7% unemployed; **Per capita income:** $20,004; % change 1990-93: 11.3.
History: U.S. army fort on site 1824; inc. 1855.
Transportation: 1 international airport; Port of Tampa; bus system. **Communications:** 7 TV, 27 radio stations. **Medical facilities:** 17 hospitals. **Educational facilities:** 4 universities and colleges; 183 public schools. **Further information:** Chamber of Commerce, 401 E. Jackson St., P.O. Box 420, Tampa, FL 33601.

Toledo, Ohio

Population: 332,943 (49); **Pop. density:** 3,964 per sq. mi.; **Pop. growth:** -6.1%. **Area:** 84 sq. mi. **Employment:** 148,808 employed, 6.8% unemployed; **Per capita income:** $19,920; % change 1990-93: 13.3.
History: site of Ft. Industry 1794; Battles of Ft. Meigs and Ft. Timbers 1812; figured in "Toledo War" 1835-36 between Ohio and Mich. over their borders; inc. 1837.
Transportation: 5 major airlines; 5 railroads; 98 motor freight lines; 2 interstate bus lines. **Communications:** 6 TV, 12 radio stations. **Medical facilities:** 8 major hospital complexes. **Educational facilities:** 6 universities and colleges. **Further information:** Toledo Area Chamber of Commerce, 300 Madison Ave., Ste. 200, Toledo, OH 43604.

Tucson, Arizona

Population: 405,323 (33); **Pop. density:** 4,095 per sq. mi.; **Pop. growth:** 22.6%. **Area:** 99 sq. mi. **Employment:** 208,915 employed, 5.0% unemployed; **Per capita income:** $17,271; % change 1990-93: 13.0.
History: settled 1775 by Spanish as a presidio; acquired by U.S. in Gadsden Purchase 1853; inc. 1877.
Transportation: 1 international airport; 2 railroads; bus system. **Communications:** 8 TV, 27 radio stations. **Medical facilities:** 13 hospitals. **Educational facilities:** 2 universities, 1 college; 165 public schools. **Further information:** Chamber of Commerce, P.O. Box 991, Tucson, AZ 85702.

Tulsa, Oklahoma

Population: 367,302 (43); **Pop. density:** 1,979 per sq. mi.; **Pop. growth:** 1.8%. **Area:** 185.6 sq. mi. **Employment:** 191,643 employed, 5.9% unemployed; **Per capita income:** $19,433; % change 1990-93: 11.7.
History: settled in 1830s by Creek Indians; modern town founded 1882 and inc. 1898; oil discovered early 20th century.
Transportation: 1 international airport; 5 rail lines; 2 bus lines; transit bus system. **Communications:** 43 TV, 25 radio stations. **Medical facilities:** 9 hospitals. **Educational facilities:** 9 universities and colleges; 114 public, 34 private schools. **Further information:** Chamber of Commerce, 616 S. Boston Ave., Ste. 100, Tulsa, OK 74119-1298.

Virginia Beach, Virginia

Population: 393,089 (37); **Pop. density:** 1,541 per sq. mi.; **Pop. growth:** 49.9%. **Area:** 255 sq. mi. **Employment:** 195,732 employed, 4.6% unemployed; **Per capita income:** $18,485; % change 1990-93: 10.6.
History: area founded by Capt. John Smith 1607; formed by merger with Princess Anne Co. 1963.
Transportation: 1 airport; 2 railroads; 2 bus lines; public transit system. **Communications:** 6 TV, 41 radio stations. **Medical facilities:** 2 hospitals. **Educational facilities:** 1 university, 2 colleges; 83 public schools. **Further information:** Virginia Beach Dept. of Economic Development, One Columbus Center, Ste. 300, Virginia Beach, VA 23462.

Washington, District of Columbia

Population: 606,900 (19); **Pop. density:** 9,633 per sq. mi.; **Pop. growth:** -4.9%. **Area:** 61 sq. mi. **Employment:** 289,000 employed, 8.2% unemployed; **Per capita income:** $27,761; % change 1990-93: 10.5.
History: capital of the U.S.; site at Potomac R. chosen by George Washington 1790 on land ceded from Va. and Md. (portion south of Potomac returned to Va. 1846); Congress first met 1800; inc. 1802; sacked by British, War of 1812.
Transportation: 3 airports; rail transit system; extensive local bus service; 1 bus, 2 rail lines. **Communications:** 5 TV, 61 radio stations. **Medical facilities:** 43 hospitals; major medical research center. **Educational facilities:** 10 universities and colleges. **Further information:** DC Chamber of Commerce, 1301 Pennsylvania Ave. NW, Suite 309, Washington, DC 20004.

Wichita, Kansas

Population: 304,017 (51); **Pop. density:** 3,010 per sq. mi.; **Pop. growth:** 8.6%. **Area:** 101 sq. mi. **Employment:** 158,848 employed, 6.7% unemployed; **Per capita income:** $20,692; % change 1990-93: 11.4.
History: founded 1864; inc. 1871.
Transportation: 2 airports; 3 major rail freight lines; 2 bus lines. **Communications:** 5 TV, 26 radio stations. **Medical facilities:** 7 hospitals, 2 psychiatric rehab. centers. **Educational facilities:** 2 universities, 1 college, 1 medical school; 96 public schools. **Further information:** Chamber of Commerce, 350 W. Douglas, Wichita, KS 67202-2970.

Yonkers, New York

Population: 188,082 (84); **Pop. density:** 10,449 per sq. mi.; **Pop. growth:** -3.7%. **Area:** 18 sq. mi. **Employment:** 83,526 employed, 6.8% unemployed; **Per capita income:** $27,975; % change 1990-93: 13.4.
History: founded 1641 by the Dutch; inc. as town 1855; chartered as city 1872; borders NYC to the South.
Transportation: intracity bus system; rail service. **Communications:** see New York City. **Medical facilities:** 3 hospitals. **Educational facilities:** 1 college; 32 public schools. **Further information:** Chamber of Commerce, 540 Nepperhan Ave., Ste. 200, Yonkers, NY 10701.

BUILDINGS, BRIDGES, TUNNELS, AND DAMS
Notable Tall Buildings in North American Cities

Source: World Almanac research

Height from sidewalk to roof, including penthouse and tower if enclosed as integral part of structure; actual number of stories beginning at street level. Asterisk (*) denotes building still under construction. Year is date of completion.

Albany, NY

Building	Ht. ft.	Stories
Erastus Corning II Tower	589	44
State Office Building	388	34

Atlanta, GA

Building	Ht. ft.	Stories
NationsBank Tower (1992)	1,023	55
One Peachtree Center (1992)	880	63
One Atlantic Center (1988)	828	52
191 Peachtree (1990)	770	54
Westin Peachtree Plaza (1973)	723	71
Georgia Pacific Tower (1981)	697	51
Promenade II/AT&T (1989)	691	40
Southern Bell Telephone (1980)	677	47
The Grand/Occidental Hotel (1992)	629	53
Concourse Tower #5 (1988)	570	32
State of Georgia Tower (1968)	556	44
Marriott Marquis (1985)	554	52
Concourse Tower #6 (1991)	553	32
Equitable Building (1967), 100 Peachtree	453	34
101 Marietta Tower (1975)	446	36
Ravinia #3 (1991)	444	34
AT&T Long Line Bldg. (1975)	433	—
Bell South Enterprises (1990)	428	28
Atlanta Plaza I (1986)	425	32
Park Place, 2660 Peachtree (1986)	420	40
Club Towers Apts. (1989)	410	38
One Park Tower (1961)	409	32
Peachtree Summit/Federal Bldg. (1975)	406	31
North Avenue Tower (1979)	403	26
Tower Place (1974), 3361 Piedmont Rd.	401	29
First Union Bank (1987)	396	30
*Atlanta Federal Center (1997)	388	25
Richard B. Russell, Federal Bldg. (1978)	383	26
Atlanta Hilton Hotel (1974)	383	32
Peachtree Center, Harris Bldg. (1975)	382	31
Hewlett-Packard Bldg. (1995)	381	27
Marquis One (1985)	378	30
Marquis Two (1987)	378	30
Sun Trust Bank (1968)	377	28
260 Peachtree (1971)	377	27
Peachtree Center Cain Building (1972)	376	30
Peachtree Center Building (1966)	374	31
One Georgia Center (1966)	371	29
Mayfair Apts. Tower (1990)	370	34
The Campanile (1987), 1145 Peachtree	367	25
Riverwood Tower(1989)	362	26

Austin, TX

Building	Ht. ft.	Stories
One American Center (1982)	395	32
One Congress Plaza (1987)	391	30

Baltimore, MD

Building	Ht. ft.	Stories
U.S. Fidelity & Guaranty Co.	529	40
Maryland National Bank Bldg.	509	34
6 St. Paul Place	493	37
World Trade Center Bldg.	395	32
Tremont Plaza Hotel	395	37
250 W. Pratt St.	360	26
Harbor Court	356	28

Birmingham, AL

Building	Ht. ft.	Stories
Southtrust Tower (1986)	454	34
AmSouth/Harbert Plaza (1989)	390	30
AmSouth/Sonat Tower (1972)	390	30
South Central Bell HQ. Bldg.	390	30

Boston, MA

Building	Ht. ft.	Stories
John Hancock Tower	800	60
Prudential Center	745	52
Boston County Bldg., Court St.	605	41
Federal Reserve Bldg	604	32
Bank of Boston, 100 Federal St.	600	37
One International Place, 100 Oliver St.	600	46
One Financial Center	598	47
Exchange Place, 53 State St.	554	40
John Hancock Bldg.	528	36
Shawmut Bank Bldg.	520	38
One Post Office Sq.	505	40
Sixty State St.	503	38
New England Merch. Bank Bldg.	500	40
U.S. Custom House	496	32
State St. Bank Bldg.	477	34
Two International Place	433	35
Bank of Boston, 100 Summer St	433	33
McCormack Bldg.	401	22
Keystone Custodian Funds	400	32
Harbor Towers (2 bldgs.) 85 E. India	400	40
65 E. India	396	40
125 High St. (1990)	399	30
Saltonstall Office Bldg.	396	22
One Devonshire Place, 250 Wash. St.	396	40
Westin Hotel, Copley Place	395	36
Federal Center (1988)	393	28
75 State St. (1988)	390	31
John F. Kennedy Bldg.	387	24
Marriott Hotel, Copley Place	382	38
One Beacon St.	380	37
Charles River Park, 80 Staniford St.	378	37
100 Staniford St.	338	37
75-101 Federal St. (1988)	360	31

Buffalo, NY

Building	Ht. ft.	Stories
Marine Midland Center (1970)	524	38
Rand Bldg. (1929), (incl. 40-ft. beacon)	351	29

Calgary, Alberta

Building	Ht. ft.	Stories
Petro-Canada Centre, W. Tower (1984)	689	52
Bankers Hall (1989)	645	50
Calgary Tower (1988)	626	—
Canterra Tower (1988)	580	46
First Canadian Centre (1983)	547	44
Western Canadian Place, North Tower	538	41
Calgary Eatons Centre	530	40
Scotia Centre (1976)	504	38
Nova Bldg., 801 7th Ave. SW	500	37
Petro-Canada Centre, E. Tower (1984)	469	33
Two Bow Valley Square (1974)	468	39
Fifth & Fifth Bldg	460	35
Home Oil Tower	463	34
Canada Trust Tower (1991)	462	40
Shell Tower	460	34
Dome Oil Tower	449	33
Four Bow Valley Square (1982)	441	37
Esso Plaza (twin towers)	435	34
Western Canadian Place, South Tower	420	32
Sovereign Life Bldg.	410	33
Pan Canadian Bldg., 150 9th Ave. SW.	410	28
Norcen Tower	408	33
Alberta Stock Exchange Bldg.	407	33
Suncor Building	396	32
Amoco Centre (1988)	396	30
Western Centre	385	40
Calgary Place	385	30
Three Bow Valley Square	382	33

Charlotte, NC

Building	Ht. ft.	Stories
NationsBank Corp. Center (1992)	875	60
One First Union Center (1988)	588	42
NationsBank Plaza (1974)	503	40
Interstate Tower (1990)	459	32
Two First Union Center (1971)	433	32
Wachovia Center (1974)	420	32
Carillon (1991)	394	24
Charlotte Plaza (1982)	388	27

Chicago, IL

Building	Ht. ft.	Stories
Sears Tower (1974)	1,454	110
Amoco (1973)	1,136	82
John Hancock Center (1969)	1,127	100
Two Prudential Plaza (1990)	978	64
311 S. Wacker (1990)	959	65
Prudential Bldg. (1955), 130 E. Randolph, (incl. 311-ft. antenna tower)	912	41
AT&T Corporate Center (1988)	885	60

Building	Ht. ft.	Stories
900 N. Michigan (1989)	871	66
Water Tower Place (1976)	859	74
One First National Plaza (1969)	850	60
Three First National Plaza (1981)	775	57
Olympia Centre (1986)	727	63
Leo Burnett Bldg. (1989)	700	46
IBM Plaza (1991)	695	52
One Magnificent Mile (1983)	673	58
Paine Webber Bldg., 181 W. Madison	644	50
Daley Center (1965)	662	31
1000 Lake Shore Plaza (1964)	648	55
Lake Point Tower (1968)	645	70
Board of Trade (1930), (incl. 81-ft. statue)	605	44
CNA Plaza (1972)	600	44
Huron Apts.	599	56
Marina City Apts., (2 bldgs)	588	61
Mid Continental Plaza (1972)	580	50
Associates Center (1983)	575	41
Pittsfield, 55 E. Washington St. (1927)	572	38
Onterie Center (1985)	570	58
Civic Opera Bldg. (1929)	555	45
Lincoln Tower (1928), 75 E. Wacker Dr.	554	42
Newberry Plaza (1974), State & Oak	553	56
One South Wacker Dr. (1983)	550	40
Harbor Point (1975)	550	54
Madison Plaza (1982)	551	45
190 S. LaSalle (1986)	550	40
LaSalle Natl. Bank (1934)	535	44
One N. LaSalle Street (1930)	530	49
111 E. Chestnut St. (1972)	529	56
Chicago Mercantile Exchange (2 bldgs)	525	40
River Plaza, Rush & Hubbard (1988)	524	56
35 E. Wacker Drive (1926)	523	40
United Ins. Bldg. (1962), 1 E. Wacker Dr.	522	41
Quaker Tower (1987)	518	35
Carbide & Carbon (1929), 230 N. Mich.	503	37
Walton Colonnade (1972)	500	44
Xerox Center (1980)	500	40
One Financial Place (1985)	498	40
LaSalle-Wacker, 221 N. LaSalle St.	491	41
Amer. Nat'l. Bank, 33 N. LaSalle St.	479	40
Bankers (1927), 105 W. Adams St.	476	41
Brunswick Bldg. (1965)	475	37
310 Center (1924)	475	37

Cincinnati, OH

Building	Ht. ft.	Stories
Carew Tower (1930)	574	49
312 Walnut St. (1990)	468	36
Fifth Third Center (1970)	460	31
Atrium Two (1984)	428	30
Chemed Center (1990)	410	32
Central Trust Tower (1913)	408	28
Cincinnati Commerce Center (1984)	402	29
PNC Center (1978)	368	27
Chiquita Center (1984)	365	29
Star Bank Center (1981)	365	28

Cleveland, OH

Building	Ht. ft.	Stories
Society Center (1991)	888	57
Terminal Tower (1930)	708	52
BP America (1985)	658	45
Plaza Tower at Erieview (1964)	529	40
One Cleveland Center (1983)	450	31
Bank One Center (1991)	446	28
Justice Center (1976), 1250 Ontario	420	26
Federal Bldg. (1967)	419	32
National City Center (1980)	410	35
900 Euclid (1971)	383	29
Ohio-Bell (1927)	365	22
J. A. Rhodes Tower (1971), Cleveland St.	363	23
Eaton Center (1983)	360	28

Columbus, OH

Building	Ht. ft.	Stories
James A. Rhodes (State Office Tower)	629	41
LeVeque Tower, 50 W. Broad	555	47
Ohio Bureau of Worker's Compensation & Ind. Comm. (1990)	530	33
Huntington Center, 41 S. High St.	512	37
Verne-Riffe State Office Tower	503	33
One Nationwide Plaza	482	40
Franklin County Courthouse	464	27
One Riverside Plaza	456	31
Borden Bldg., 180 E. Broad	438	34
Three Nationwide Plaza (1989)	408	27
One Columbus	366	26
Columbus Center, 100 E. Broad	357	24

Dallas, TX

Building	Ht. ft.	Stories
NationsBank Plaza (1985)	921	72
Bank One Center (1987)	787	60
Texas Commerce Tower (1987)	738	55
Fountain Place (1986)	721	60
Renaissance Tower (1974)	710	56
Trammell Crow Center (1987)	686	49
1700 Pacific (1983)	655	50
Thanksgiving Tower (1982)	645	50
Elm Place (1965)	625	50
NationsBank Center Tower 2 (1980)	598	50
Lincoln Plaza (1984)	579	45
Harwood @Bryan Corp. Center (1982)	562	36
Cityplace Center East (1989)	560	42
Maxus Energy (1980)	550	34
2001 Bryan Tower. (1973)	512	40
San Jacinto Tower (1982)	456	33
M-Bank Bldg. (1943)	452	31
Stouffer Hotel	451	29
One Dallas Centre (1979)	448	30
One Main Place (1968)	445	34
1600 Pacific Bldg. (1964)	434	32
Magnolia Bldg. (1923)	430	27

Dayton, OH

Building	Ht. ft.	Stories
Kettering Tower (1970), 2d & Main	405	30
Mead World HQ. (1976), 10 W. 2d St.	385	28

Denver, CO

Building	Ht. ft.	Stories
Republic Plaza	714	56
Mountain Bell Center	709	54
United Bank of Denver	698	52
1999 Broadway	544	43
Arco Tower	527	41
Anaconda Tower	507	40
Amoco Bldg., 17th Ave. & Broadway	448	36
17th Street Plaza	438	35
Stellar Plaza	437	31
First Interstate Tower North	434	32
One Denver Place	428	34
Brooks Towers, 1020 15th St.	420	42
Tabor Center, #1	408	32
Manville Plaza	404	29
Colorado Nat'l. Bank, 17th & Curtis	389	26
First Interstate Tower South	385	28
1616 Glenarm Bldg.	384	33
Mellon Financial Center	374	31
Dominion Plaza	368	30
Lincoln Center	366	30
Denver Natl. Bank Plaza	363	29
Bank Western	357	27
Colorado State Bank	352	26

Des Moines, IA

Building	Ht. ft.	Stories
Principal Financial Group Bldg. (1990)	630	44
Ruan Center (1974)	457	35

Detroit, MI

Building	Ht. ft.	Stories
Westin Hotel	720	71
One Detroit Center	620	45
Penobscot Bldg.	557	47
Guardian	485	40
Renaissance Center (4 bldgs.)	479	39
Book Tower	472	35
150 W. Jefferson Bldg.	470	29
Prudential 3000 Town Center	448	32
Cadillac Tower	437	40
David Stott	436	38
ANR Bldg.	430	32
Fisher	420	28
J. L. Hudson Bldg.	397	28
McNamara Federal Office Bldg.	393	27
2000 Prudential Town Ctr.	392	28
American Center	374	27
Top of Troy Bldg.	374	27
Comerica Bldg., 211 N. Fort	370	28
Edison Plaza	365	25
David Broderick Tower	358	34
1st National Bldg.	350	25

Edmonton, Alberta

Building	Ht. ft.	Stories
Manulife Place (1983)	479	36
AGT Tower (1971)	441	33
Canada Trust Tower (1982)	440	31

Building	Ht. ft.	Stories
Commerce Place (1990)	409	30
Metropolitan Place (1980)	397	31
Oxford Tower (1978)	390	27
TD Tower (1975)	386	27
Scotia Place (1983)	366	28
CN Tower (1966)	365	27
Phipps McKinnon (1977)	359	20

Fort Worth, TX

Building	Ht. ft.	Stories
City Center Tower II (1984)	546	38
Burnett Plaza (1983)	538	40
Continental Plaza (1982)	520	40
Texas Commerce Tower(1982)	475	33
Bank One Tower (1974)	457	37
Texas Bldg. (1955)	420	31

Hartford, CT

Building	Ht. ft.	Stories
City Place (1983)	535	38
Travelers Ins. Co. Bldg. (1919)	527	34
Goodwin Square (1990)	522	30
Hartford Plaza (1967)	420	22
Shawmut Bank (1960)	360	26

Honolulu, HI

Building	Ht. ft.	Stories
Imperial Plaza (1992)	400	40
Waterfront Towers (1990)	400	46
Nauru Tower (1991)	400	45
Ala Moana Hotel	396	38
Pacific Tower	350	30
Franklin Towers	350	41
Honolulu Tower.	350	40
Discovery Bay.	350	42
Hyatt Regency Waikiki.	350	39
Maile Court Hotel	350	43
Regency Tower, 2525 Date St..	350	42
Pearlridge Square.	350	43
Yacht Harbor Towers.	350	40
Canterbury Place	350	40
Royal Iolani	350	38
Island Colony	350	44
Century Center	350	41
Pacific Beach Hotel	350	43
Hawaiian Monarch Hotel	350	43
Waikiki Hobron	350	43
Honolulu Tower 2	350	40
Tapa Tower, 2005 Kalia Rd..	350	36
Executive Center, 1088 Bishop St.	350	41
1001 Bishop	350	28

Houston, TX

Building	Ht. ft.	Stories
Texas Commerce Tower (1981)	1,002	75
First Interstate Plaza (1983)	972	71
Transco Tower (1983)	901	64
NationsBank Center (1983)	780	56
Heritage Plaza, 1111 Bagby.	762	53
InterFirst Plaza (1980)	744	55
Houston Industries Plaza	741	53
1600 Smith St. (1984)	729	54
Chevron Tower (1982), 1301 McKinney .	725	52
One Shell Plaza (1970)		
(not incl. 285-ft. TV tower)	714	50
Enron Bldg. (1983)	692	50
Capital Natl. Bank Bldg.	685	50
One Houston Center (1978)	678	47
First City, Tex. Financial Center (1984) . .	662	47
San Felipe Plaza (1984)	620	45
Exxon Bldg. (1962)	606	44
The America Tower.	577	42
Marathon Oil Tower (1983)	572	41
Two Houston Center (1974)	570	40
Kellogg Tower (1973)	550	40
1415 Louisiana Tower (1983)	550	44
Pennzoil, 700 Milam (1975) (2 bldgs.) . . .	523	36
Two Allen Center (1978)	521	36
1201 Louisiana Bldg. (1971)	518	35
Huntington	506	34
Tenneco Bldg. (1962)	502	33
Conoco Tower (1973)	465	32
One Allen Center (1974)	452	34
Summit Tower West (1979)	441	31
Coastal Tower (1978)	441	31
Four Leafs Towers (2 bldgs.)	439	40
Phoenix Tower (1984)	434	34
Chevron Bldg..	428	37
The Spires	426	41

Building	Ht. ft.	Stories
Central Tower, 4 Oaks Place.	420	30
First City Natl. Bank (1960)	410	32
Houston Lighting & Power (1968)	410	27
Niels Esperson Bldg. (1927)	409	31
Hyatt Regency Houston (1972)	401	34

Indianapolis, IN

Building	Ht. ft.	Stories
Bank One Tower (1989)	728	51
AUL Tower (1981)	533	38
Market Tower (1988)	515	32
NBD Bank Tower (1969)	504	35
Riley Towers (2 bldgs.) (1963).	427	30
300 N. Meridian Bldg. (1988).	408	28

Jacksonville, FL

Building	Ht. ft.	Stories
Barnett Center (1990).	617	42
Independent Life Bldg. (1975)	535	37
Southern Bell (1983)	447	32
River Place Tower (1967)	432	28
American Heritage Life (1989).	357	23

Kansas City, MO

Building	Ht. ft.	Stories
One Kansas City Place.	626	42
AT&T Town Pavilion.	590	38
Hyatt Regency.	504	40
Kansas City Power and Light Bldg.	476	32
City Hall	443	29
1201 Walnut	425	30
Federal Office Bldg.	413	35
Commerce Tower.	402	32
City Center Sq.	402	30
Southwest Bell Telephone Bldg.	394	27
2345 Grand Ave.	352	28

Las Vegas, NV

Building	Ht. ft.	Stories
*Stratosphere Tower (1997)	1,010	114
Las Vegas Hilton (1995)	375	30

Little Rock, AK

Building	Ht. ft.	Stories
TCBY Towers (1986)	546	40
First Commercial Bank (1975).	454	30
Worthen Bank & Trust (1969)	375	24
Stephens Bldg. (1985)	365	35
Tower Bldg. (1960).	350	18

Los Angeles, CA

Building	Ht. ft.	Stories
First Interstate World Center (1989)	1,107	72
First Interstate Bank	858	62
Two California Plaza	750	52
Wells Fargo Tower	750	54
The Gas Company Tower (1990).	749	50
333 South Hope Bldg. (1975)	743	55
777 Tower	725	52
Sanwa Bank Plaza (1990).	716	52
Atlantic Richfield Tower	699	52
Bank of America Tower	699	52
444 S. Flower St.	625	48
AT&T Bldg.	620	42
One California Plaza	578	42
Century Plaza Towers (2 bldgs.)	571	44
IBM Tower.	560	45
Citicorp Plaza	534	42
1999 Ave. of the Stars (1989)	533	39
Manulife Tower (1990)	517	37
Union Bank Square	516	41
MCA-Getty	506	36
WTC Bldg..	496	36
Fox Plaza	492	34
ARCO Center	462	33
City Hall	454	28
Equitable Life Bldg.	454	34
Transamerica Center	452	32
Mutual Benefit Life Ins. Bldg..	435	31
Warner Center Plaza III	415	25
Broadway Plaza.	414	33
1900 Ave. of Stars	398	27
One Wilshire Bldg.	395	28
The Evian	390	31
400 S. Hope St.	375	26
Westin Bonaventure Hotel	367	35
Beaudry Center	365	29
California Fed. Savings & Loan Bldg.	363	28
Century City North	363	26
Home Savings Tower	356	25

Louisville, KY

Building	Ht. ft.	Stories
Providian Center (1992), 4th & Market ..	549	35
National City Tower (1972), 4th & Main..	495	40
Humana Bldg (1985), 5th & Main......	417	27
Citizens Plaza (1971), 5th & Jefferson ..	408	30
Meidinger Tower (1982), 462 S. 4th	363	26
Brown & Williamson Tower (1982)	363	26

Memphis, TN

Building	Ht. ft.	Stories
100 N. Main Bldg..................	430	37
Commerce Square	396	31
Sterick Bldg.....................	365	31
Clark, 5100 Poplar	365	32

Miami, FL

Building	Ht. ft.	Stories
First Union Financial Center (1983)	764	55
International Place (1987)	562	35
Metro-Dade Administration Bldg.......	510	30
Florida National Tower (1986)	484	35
One Biscayne Tower...............	456	38
Barnett Tower (1986)	450	33
Courthouse Center (1986)	405	30
Sunbank International Center (1973) ..	375	31
Bristol	371	41
Hotel Inter-Continental Miami........	366	35
Venitia, 1635 Bayshore Dr.	365	42
Dade County Court House...........	357	28

Milwaukee, WI

Building	Ht. ft.	Stories
Firstar Center (1971)..............	625	42
100 East (Faison Bldg.) (1989)........	549	37
Milwaukee Center (1987)............	426	29
411 Bldg., 411 E. Wisconsin (1983)	408	30
Northwestern Mutual Tower (1989).....	395	19
City Hall (1898)..................	350	9

Minneapolis, MN

Building	Ht. ft.	Stories
IDS Center (1973).................	776	51
First Bank Place	775	53
Norwest (1988)...................	773	57
Multifoods Tower (1983)	608	51
Piper Jaffray Tower (1984)...........	627	42
Dain Bosworth Plaza...............	539	40
Pillsbury Center (1981), 200 S. 6th St. ..	530	40
150 South Fifth	498	36
Metropolitan Center (1987), 333 S. 7th ..	496	31
Plaza VII, 45 S. 7th (1987)...........	468	36
Foshay Tower, (1929) (not incl.		
160-ft. antenna tower)	447	31
Hennepin Co. Govt. Center (1974)	413	25
Marriott Hotel (1983)	379	33

Montreal, Quebec

Building	Ht. ft.	Stories
1100 Rue de la Gauchetiere	669	45
1250 Boulevard Rene Levesque	640	45
Place Victoria (1963)	624	47
Place Ville Marie (1962)............	620	45
Canadian Imperial Bank		
of Commerce (1962)	590	45
Le Complexe Desjardins		
La Tour du Sud	498	40
La Tour du L'Est................	428	32
La Tour du Nord	355	27
Les Cooperants (1987)	479	34
Place Montreal Trust (1988)..........	449	32
Chateau Champlain Hotel (1967)	420	38
Port Royal Apts.	400	33
Royal Bank Tower.................	397	22
Sun Life Bldg....................	390	26
500 Place d'Armes	390	32

Nashville, TN

Building	Ht. ft.	Stories
South Central Bell Bldg...........	617	33
Third National Financial Center	490	30
American General Center	452	31
Landmark Center	409	30
Nashville City Center (1987)	402	27
James K. Polk State Office Bldg.	392	32
Stouffer Hotel (1987)	385	35
First American Center	354	28

Newark, NJ

Building	Ht. ft.	Stories
Natl. Newark & Essex Bldg.	465	36
Raymond-Commerce...............	448	37
Park Plaza Bldg.	400	26
Prudential Plaza..................	370	24
Public Service Elec. & Gas	360	26
Prudential Ins. Co., 753 Broad St.	360	26
AT&T Bldg.......................	359	31
Gateway 1......................	355	28

New Orleans, LA

Building	Ht. ft.	Stories
One Shell Square (1972)	697	51
Place St. Charles (1985).............	645	53
Plaza Tower (1969)	531	45
Energy Centre (1984)...............	530	39
LL&E Tower (1987)	481	36
Sheraton Hotel (1985)	478	47
Marriott Hotel (1972)	450	42
Texaco Bldg. (1983)................	442	33
Canal Place One (1979)	439	32
1010 Common (1971)...............	438	31
World Trade Center................	407	33
225 Baronne St. (1965)	362	28
One Poydras Plaza (1983)	360	28
Hibernia Bank Bldg. (1920)	355	23
Hyatt-Regency Hotel (1976)	353	32

New York, NY

Building	Ht. ft.	Stories
One World Trade Center (1972)	1,368	110
Two World Trade Center (1973)	1,362	110
Empire State (1931), 34th St. & 5th Ave. .	1,250	102
(incl. 164-ft. TV tower)	1,414	—
Chrysler (1930), Lexington & 43d	1,046	77
Amer. International (1932), 70 Pine	950	66
40 Wall St. (1929)	927	70
Citicorp Center (1977)	915	59
G.E. Bldg., Rockefeller Center (1933) ...	850	70
Cityspire (1989)	814	72
One Chase Manhattan Plaza (1960)	813	60
MetLife Bldg., 200 Park Ave. (1963)	808	59
Woolworth, 233 Broadway (1913)	792	57
One Worldwide Plaza...............	778	47
Carnegie Tower..................	757	60
Equitable Center Tower West (1985)	752	51
One Penn Plaza (1972)	750	54
1251 Ave. of Americas (1971)	750	54
60 Wall St. (1989)	745	50
One Liberty Plaza (1972)	743	50
Citibank (1907)	741	57
World Financial Center, Tower C (1988)..	739	54
One Astor Plaza (1969)	730	54
Solow Bldg. (1979)................	725	50
Marine Midland Bank	724	52
Metropolitan Tower (1988)...........	716	66
Union Carbide Bldg. (1960)..........	707	52
General Motors Bldg. (1968).........	705	50
Metropolitan Life (1909)............	700	50
500 5th Ave. (1928)	697	58
Chem. Bank, NY. Trust Bldg. (1963)	687	50
55 Water St.	687	53
1585 Broadway	685	42
Four Seasons Hotel (1993)..........	682	52
Chanin (1929), Lexington & 42d	680	56
Trump International Hotel and Tower....	679	45
McGraw Hill (1972), 1221 Ave. of Amer. .	674	51
Citicorp (Queens) (1990)	673	50
Lincoln (1939), 60 E. 42d Street	673	53
1633 Broadway	670	48
Trump Tower (1983), 725 5th Ave.	664	68
599 Lexington Ave. (1988)...........	653	47
Museum Tower Apts. (1985)..........	650	58
712 5th Ave. (1990)	650	56
American Brands, 245 Park Ave.......	648	47
550 Madison Ave. (1983)	648	37
World Financial Center Tower B (1986) ..	645	50
General Electric (1931), 570 Lexington ..	640	50
Irving Trust (1932), 1 Wall St.	640	50
345 Park Ave....................	634	44
Grace Plaza, 1114 Ave. of Amer.	630	50
One New York Plaza (1969)	630	50
Home Insurance Co. Bldg...........	630	44
NYNEX, 1095 Ave. of Amer...........	630	40
Central Park Place (1988)...........	628	56
888 7th Ave.	628	42

Building	Ht. ft.	Stories
One Hammarskjold Plaza	628	50
Waldorf-Astoria (1931), 301 Park Ave.	625	47
Burlington House (1970)	625	50
Olympic Tower (1976), 645 5th Ave.	620	51
10 E. 40th St.	620	48
101 Park Ave.	618	50
750 7th Ave.	615	35
New York Life (1928), 51 Madison Ave.	615	40
Rihga Royal Hotel	610	54
17 State St.	610	41
Penney Bldg., 1301 Ave. of Amer.	609	46
IBM (1983), 590 Madison Ave.	603	41
780 3d Ave.	600	50
Celanese Bldg. (1973)	592	45
U.S. Court House (1976), 505 Pearl St.	590	37
Kalikow Hotel	588	58
Federal Bldg., Foley Square.	587	41
Time & Life (1959), 1271 Ave. of Amer.	587	47
Cooper Bregstein Bldg., 1250 Bway.	580	40
Stevens Tower, 1185 Ave. of Amer.	580	42
Municipal Bldg. (1919)	580	34
520 Madison Ave. (1983)	577	42
One Madison Square Plaza (1968)	576	42
World Financial Center Tower A (1986)	575	42
One Financial Sq. (1987)	575	37
Park Ave. Plaza (1981)	575	44
Westvaco Bldg. 299 Park Ave.	574	42
Marriott Marquis Hotel (1985)	574	42
Socony Mobil Bldg., East 42d St.	572	45
Sperry Rand Bldg., 1290 Ave. of Am.	570	43
600 3d Ave.	570	42
Helmsley Bldg. (1929), 230 Park	565	35
One Bankers Trust Plaza.	565	40
Hemsley Palace Hotel (1980)	563	51
30 Broad St.	562	48
Park Ave Tower (1986)	561	36
Sherry-Netherland, 5th Ave. & 59th St.	560	40
Continental Can (1983), 633 3d Ave.	557	39
Sperry & Hutchinson, 330 Madison.	555	39
Continental Corp., 180 Maiden Lane.	555	41
Galleria (1975), 117 E. 57th St.	552	57
Interchem Bldg., 1133 Ave. of Amer.	552	45
151 E. 44th St.	550	44
NYNEX (1979), 323 Broadway.	550	45
919 3d Ave.	550	47
Burroughs Bldg., 605 3d Ave.	550	44
Bankers Trust. (1963), 33 E. 48 St	547	41
Transportation Bldg., 225 Broadway.	546	45
Equitable (1915), 120 Broadway.	545	42
One Brooklyn Bridge Plaza (1976)	540	42
Paine Webber Bldg. (1961)	540	42
Ritz Tower, Park Ave. & 57th St.	540	41
Bankers Trust, 6 Wall St.	540	39
1166 Ave. of Americas	540	44
1700 Broadway	533	41
Downtown Athletic Club, 19 West St.	530	45
Nelson Towers, 7th Ave. & 34th St.	525	45
767 3d Ave.	525	39
Hotel Pierre (1928), 5th Ave. & 61st St.	525	44
House of Seagram (1958)	525	38
7 World Trade Center (1985)	525	44
Random House, 825 3d Ave.	522	40
3 Park Ave.	522	42
North American Plywood, 800 3d Ave.	520	41
Du Mont Bldg., 515 Madison Ave.	520	42
26 Broadway	520	31
Newsweek Bldg., 444 Madison Ave.	518	43
Sterling Drug Bldg., 90 Park Ave.	515	41
Citibank	515	41
Bank of New York, 48 Wall St.	513	32
Navarre, 512 7th Ave.	513	43
Manhattan Savings Bank (Bklyn.)	512	42
ITT—American, 437 Madison Ave.	512	40
Rockefeller Ctr. International	512	41
1407 Broadway Realty Corp.	512	44
United Nations (1953), 405 E. 42 St.	505	39

Oakland, CA

Building	Ht. ft.	Stories
Ordway Bldg., 1 Kaiser Plaza (1985)	404	28
Kaiser Bldg., 300 Lakeside Dr. (1958)	390	28
Lake Merritt Plaza, 303 20th St. (1988)	371	27
Federal Bldg. (2 bldgs.) (1994), 1301 Clay	368	19
American President Lines, (1990)	360	29

Oklahoma City, OK

Building	Ht. ft.	Stories
Liberty Tower (1971)	500	36
First National Center (1974)	493	28

Building	Ht. ft.	Stories
City Place (1985)	440	33
First Oklahoma Tower (1982)	425	31
Kerr-McGee Center (1973)	393	30
Mid America Tower (1981)	362	19

Omaha, NE

Building	Ht. ft.	Stories
Woodmen Tower (1969)	469	30
Enron Building (1960)	400	18

Orlando, FL

Building	Ht. ft.	Stories
Sun Bank Center Tower (1988)	441	35
*Orange County Courthouse (1997)	416	24
Barnett Bank Center (1988)	404	28

Philadelphia, PA

Building	Ht. ft.	Stories
One Liberty Place (1987)	945	61
Two Liberty Place (1989)	848	58
Mellon Bank Center (1989)	792	54
Bell Atlantic Tower (1991)	739	53
Blue Cross Tower (1990)	700	50
Commerce Sq., #1 (1990).	572	40
Commerce Sq., #2 (1992)	572	40
City Hall Tower (1901), (incl. 37-ft. statue of William Penn.)	548	7
1818 Market St. (1974)	500	40
Meridan Bank (1972)	492	38
Phila. Saving Fund Society (1932).	492	39
Provident Mutual Life (1983)	491	40
Central Penn Natl. Bank (1970).	490	36
Centre Square (2 towers) (1973)	490/416	38/32
Industrial Valley Bank (1968).	482	32
Philadelphia National Bank (1930).	475	25
Two Mellon Plaza (1930)	450	30
2000 Market St. (1973).	435	29
Two Logan Square (1987)	435	34
Two Girard Plaza (1930).	412	30
Fidelity Bank Bldg. (1927)	405	30
Lewis Tower (1929), 15th & Locust	400	33
One Logan Square (1982)	400	32
1500 Locust St. (1973)	390	44
Philadelphia Electric Co. (1970).	384	29
Academy House, 1420 Locust St.	377	37
Penn Mutual Life (1931)	375	20
The Drake, 15th & Spruce (1928)	375	33
INA Annex.	369	27
Medical Tower (1931), 255 S. 17th	364	33

Phoenix, AZ

Building	Ht. ft.	Stories
Bank One Center (1972).	483	40
Bank of America Bldg. (1976)	407	31
Phoenix Plaza I (1989)	397	20
Phoenix Plaza II(1990)	397	20
First Interstate Bank Plaza (1971)	372	26
Phoenix Center (1979)	361	28
Norwest Tower (1980)	356	26

Pittsburgh, PA

Building	Ht. ft.	Stories
USX Towers	841	64
One Mellon Bank Center.	725	54
One PPG Place.	635	40
Fifth Avenue Place (1987).	616	31
One Oxford Centre.	615	45
Gulf, 7th Ave. and Grant St.	582	44
University of Pittsburgh.	535	42
Mellon Bank Bldg.	520	41
One Oliver Plaza	511	37
Grant, Grant St. at 3d Ave.	485	40
Koppers, 7th Ave. and Grant.	475	36
Two PNC Plaza.	445	34
CNG Tower (1987)	430	32
One PNC Plaza.	424	31
Alcoa Bldg., 425 Sixth Ave.	410	30
Liberty Center	358	27
Westinghouse Bldg.	355	23

Portland, OR

Building	Ht. ft.	Stories
First Interstate Tower	546	40
U.S. Bancorp Tower.	536	42
Koin Tower Plaza.	509	35
Standard Insurance Center.	367	29
Pacwest Center	356	30

Providence, RI

Building	Ht. ft.	Stories
Fleet National Bank	420	26
Rhode Island Hospital Trust Tower	410	30

Raleigh, NC

Building	Ht. ft.	Stories
BB & T/2 Hanover Sq. (1991)	431	29
First Union Capitol Center (1991)	390	29

Richmond, VA

Building	Ht. ft.	Stories
James Monroe Bldg.	450	29
City Hall (incl. penthouse)	425	17
Crestar Bank HQ. Bldg.	400	24
Federal Reserve Bank	393	26

Rochester, NY

Building	Ht. ft.	Stories
Xerox Tower (1967)	443	30
Lincoln First Tower (1973)	392	27

Sacramento, CA

Building	Ht. ft.	Stories
Wells Fargo Center	402	30
Park Plaza Tower	373	26
Renaissance Tower	372	28
U.S. Bank	350	25

St. Louis, MO

Building	Ht. ft.	Stories
Gateway Arch (1965)	630	—
Metropolitan Square Tower (1989)	593	42
One Bell Center (1984)	588	44
Mercantile Center Tower (1976)	540	36
Laclede Gas. Bldg. (1970), 8th & Olive	434	31
Boatmen's Plaza	420	30
SW Bell Telephone Bldg.	398	26
Civil Courts Bldg.	390	13
One City Center (1986)	375	25

St. Paul, MN

Building	Ht. ft.	Stories
Minnesota World Trade Center	471	36
Galtier Plaza's Jackson Tower	440	46
First Natl. Bank Bldg.	417	32
Osborn Bldg., 320 Wabasha	368	20
Kellogg Square Apts.	366	32

Salt Lake City, UT

Building	Ht. ft.	Stories
L.D.S. Church Office Bldg.	420	30
Beneficial Life Tower	351	21
Utah One Center (1992)	350	24

San Antonio, TX

Building	Ht. ft.	Stories
Tower of the Americas (1968)	622	—
Marriott Rivercenter (1988)	546	38
Weston Centre (1988)	444	32
Tower Life (1929)	404	30
NationsBank Plaza (1983)	387	28
Nix Professional Bldg. (1931)	375	23

San Diego, CA

Building	Ht. ft.	Stories
One American Plaza (1991)	500	34
Symphony Tower (1989)	499	34
Hyatt Regency San Diego (1992)	495	39
Emerald-Shapery Center (1991)	450	30
One Harbor Drive (1992)	424	41
First Interstate Bank (1985)	398	23
Meridian Condominiums (1985)	395	27
Union Bank (1969)	388	27
First National Bank (1982)	379	27
Imperial Bank	355	24
Executive Complex (1963)	350	25

San Francisco, CA

Building	Ht. ft.	Stories
Transamerica Pyramid (1972)	853	48
Bank of America (1969)	779	52
101 California St. (1986)	600	48
5 Fremont Center (1983)	600	43
Embarcadero Center, No. 4 (1982)	570	45
Security Pacific Bank	569	45
One Market Plaza, Spear St. (1976)	565	43
Wells Fargo Bldg.	561	43
Standard Oil (1975), 575 Market St.	551	39
One Sansome-Citicorp	550	39
Shaklee Bldg., 444 Market	537	38

Building	Ht. ft.	Stories
Aetna Life	529	38
First & Market Bldg. (1973)	529	38
Metropolitan Life (1973)	524	38
Crocker National Bank	500	38
Hilton Hotel	493	46
Pacific Gas & Electric (1970)	492	34
Union Bank (1972)	487	37
Pacific Insurance (1972)	476	34
Bechtel Bldg. (1977), Fremont St.	475	33
333 Market Bldg. (1979)	474	33
Hartford Bldg. (1965)	465	33
Mutual Benefit Life (1969)	438	32
Russ Bldg. (1928)	435	31
Pacific Telephone Bldg. (1925)	435	26
Pacific Gateway (1983)	416	30
Embarcadero Center, No. 3 (1976)	412	31
Embarcadero Center, No. 2 (1974)	412	31
595 Market Bldg. (1979)	410	31
101 Montgomery St.	405	28
California State Automobile Assn. (1974)	399	29
Alcoa Bldg.	398	27
St. Francis Hotel (1970)	395	32
Shell Bldg. (1928)	386	29
Del Monte	378	28
Meridien Hotel (1984)	374	34

Seattle, WA

Building	Ht. ft.	Stories
Columbia Seafirst Center (1985)	943	76
Two Union Square (1989)	740	56
Washington Mutual Tower (1988)	730	55
AT&T Gateway Tower (1990)	722	62
1001 4th Pl. (1969)	609	50
Space Needle (1962)	605	—
Pacific First Center (1989)	580	44
First Interstate Center (1983)	574	48
Seafirst 5th Ave. Plaza (1981)	543	42
Security Pacific Bank Tower (1977)	514	42
Smith Tower (1914)	500	42
520 Pike Tower (1984)	498	29
Key Tower (1986)	493	40
Federal Office Bldg.	487	37
US West Communications	466	33
One Union Square (1981)	456	38
1111 3d Ave. Bldg. (1980)	454	35
Westin Bldg. (1981), 2001 6th Ave.	409	34
Westin Hotel	397	40
Unigard Financial Center (1973)	389	27
Century Square (1986)	379	30
Sheraton Seattle Hotel	371	34

Tampa, FL

Building	Ht. ft.	Stories
100 N. Tampa (1992)	579	42
Barnett Plaza (1986)	577	42
Tampa City Center (1981)	537	38
Landmark Centre (1992)	525	36
First Financial Tower (1973)	458	35
NCNB Plaza (1988)	454	33

Toledo, OH

Building	Ht. ft.	Stories
Owens-Illinois Corp. HQ. (1962)	404	30
Owens-Corning Fiberglas Tower (1970)	400	30
Ohio Citizens Bank Bldg. (1932)	368	27

Toronto, Ontario

Building	Ht. ft.	Stories
CN Tower (1975) (world's tallest self-supporting structure)	1,821	—
First Canadian Place (1975)	952	72
Bay/Adelaide Centre (1991)	945	53
Scotia Plaza (1988)	902	68
Canada Trust Tower (1990)	863	51
Commerce Court West (1972)	784	57
Toronto-Dominion Tower (TD Centre) (1967)	758	56
Bay-Wellington Tower (1990)	705	47
Royal Trust Tower (TD Centre) (1969)	600	46
Royal Bank Plaza—South Tower (1977)	589	41
Manulife Centre (1975)	545	53
IBM Tower (TD Centre) (1986)	520	36
Two Bloor West (1974)	488	34
Exchange Tower (1981)	480	36
Commerce Court North (1930)	476	34
Simpson Tower (1968)	473	33
Eaton Tower (1990)	471	34
Cadillac-Fairview Tower (1982)	466	36
Palace Point (1991)	455	46

Building	Ht. ft.	Stories
Palace Pier (1978)	453	46
Continental Bank Bldg. (1980)	450	35
Sheraton Centre (1972)	443	43
Hudson's Bay Centre (1974)	442	35
Royal York Hotel (1929)	439	26
Ernst & Yonge Tower (1990)	438	31
Old Toronto Exchange Bldg. (1990)	436	31
Leaside Towers (2 bldgs.) (1970)	423	44
Metro Hall (1991)	420	27
Commercial Union Tower (1974)	420	32
Maple Leaf Mills Tower	419	30
Plaza 2 Hotel	415	41
Sun Life Bldg. (1981)	410	28

Tulsa, OK

Building	Ht. ft.	Stories
Bank of Oklahoma Tower	667	52
Cityplex Towers	640	60
1st National Tower	516	41
Mid-Continent Tower	513	36
Bank IV of Tulsa	412	33
320 South Boston Bldg.	400	24
Occidental Place	388	28

Building	Ht. ft.	Stories
Univ. Club Tower	377	32

Vancouver, British Columbia

Building	Ht. ft.	Stories
Granville Square, 200 Granville	466	28
Royal Centre Tower (1973)	466	36
Vancouver Center (1977), 650 W. Georgia	462	36
Bentall IV (1981), 1055 Dunsmuir	450	35
Park Place (1984), 666 Burrard	450	35
Toronto Dominion Bank, 700 W. Georgia	440	30
Harbour Centre (1977), 555 W. Hastings	426	21
Bentall III (1974), 595 Granville	400	31

Winnipeg, Manitoba

Building	Ht. ft.	Stories
Toronto Dominion Centre (1989)	413	33
Richardson Bldg. (1969)	390	34
Commodity Exchange Tower (1980)	384	31

Winston-Salem, NC

Building	Ht. ft.	Stories
Wachovia Bldg. (1995)	460	28
Wachovia Bldg. (1965)	410	27

Other Notable Tall Buildings in North American Cities

Building	City	Ht. ft.	Stories
Skylon	Niagara Falls, Ontario	774	—
Vehicle Assembly Bldg.	Cape Canaveral, FL	552	40
State Capitol (1932)	Baton Rouge, LA	460	34
One Summit Square	Fort Wayne, IN	442	26
State Capitol	Lincoln, NE	432	40
Taj Mahal	Atlantic City, NJ	429	51
First Natl. Bank	Mobile, AL	420	33
Century Twenty One	Hamilton, Ontario	418	43
Lexington Financial Ctr.	Lexington, KY	410	30
United American Bank	Knoxville, TN	400	30
Kanawha Valley Bldg.	Charleson, WV	384	20
American Natl. Bank.	Amarillo, TX	374	33
Valley Bank Tower	Springfield, MA	370	29
Place de Ville, Tower C	Ottawa, Ontario	368	29
Commerical Natl. Tower	Shreveport, LA	365	24
American National Ins.	Galveston, TX	358	20

Notable International Buildings

Source: Council on Tall Buildings and Urban Habitat

Building	Ht. ft.	Stories
Oriental Pearl Television Tower (1995), Shanghai, China	1,535	—
*Petronas Tower I (1996), Kuala Lumpur, Malaysia	1,476	88
*Petronas Tower II (1996), Kuala Lumpur, Malaysia	1,476	88
*Jin Mao Building (1998) Shanghai, China	1,379	88
Central Plaza (1992), Hong Kong	1,227	78
Bank of China Tower (1989), Hong Kong	1,205	70
*T & C Tower (1997), Kaoshiung, Taiwan	1,140	85
Eiffel Tower (1889), Paris	984	—
*Sky Central Plaza (1996), Guangzhou, China	1,056	80
*Baiyoke Tower II (1997), Bangkok, Thailand	1,050	90
*Shenzhen Avic Plaza Building (1997), Shenzhen, China	1,025	63
*Ryugyong Hotel (1995), Pyongyang, N. Korea	984	105
Landmark Tower (1993), Yokohama, Jpn.	971	70
*Jubilee St./Queen's Rd. Central (1997), Hong Kong	958	69
Overseas Union Bank (1986), Singapore	919	66
United Overseas Bank Plaza (1992), Singapore	919	66
Republic Plaza (1995), Singapore	919	66
Commerzbank Tower (1997), Frankfurt, Ger.	850	60
Messeturm. Bldg. (1990), Frankfurt, Ger.	843	63
Gate Tower (1996), Osaka, Jpn.	833	56
Osaka World Trade Center (1995), Osaka, Jpn.	827	55
BNI City Tower (1995), Jakarta, Indonesia	820	46
Korea Life Ins. Co. (1985), Seoul, S. Korea	817	60
Kompleks Tun Abdul Razak Bldg. (1985), (Pinang, Malaysia	804	65
Malayan Bank(1988), Kuala Lumpur, Malaysia	799	50
Hotel de Ville de Tokyo (1991), Tokyo, Jpn.	797	48
Rialto Tower (1985), Melbourne	794	56
JR Central Towers (1999), Nagoya, Jpn.	787	53
Moscow State Univ. (1953), Moscow	784	26
One Canada Sq. (1991), London	777	53
Treasury Bldg., (1986) Singapore	771	52
Shinjuku Park Tower (1994,) Tokyo	764	52
Palace of Science & Culture (1955), Warsaw, Poland	757	42

* desinates under construction

Notable Bridges in North America

Source: Survey of State Highway Engineers (1995)

Asterisk (*) designates railroad bridge. Double asterisk (**) designates under construction.
Span of a bridge is distance (in feet) between its supports.

Suspension

Year	Bridge	Location	Longest span
1964	Verrazano-Narrows	New York, NY	4,260
1937	Golden Gate	San Fran. Bay, CA	4,200
1957	Mackinac	Sts. of Mackinac, MI	3,800
1931	Geo. Washington	Hudson R., NY-NJ	3,500
1950	Tacoma Narrows	Washington	2,800
1936	Transbay[1]	San Fran. Bay, CA	2,310
1939	Bronx-Whitestone	East R., N.Y.C.	2,300
1970	Pierre Laporte	Quebec	2,190
1951	Del. Memorial	Wilmington, DE	2,150
1968	Del. Mem. (new)	Wilmington, DE	2,150
1957	Walt Whitman	Philadelphia, PA	2,000
1929	Ambassador	Detroit-Canada	1,850
1961	Throgs Neck	Long Is. Sound, NY	1,800
1926	Benjamin Franklin	Philadelphia, PA	1,750
1924	Bear Mt., NY	Hudson R.	1,632
1952	William Preston Lane Memorial[2]	Sandy Point, MD	1,600
1903	Williamsburg	East R., N.Y.C.	1,600
1969	Newport	Narragansett Bay, RI	1,600
1883	Brooklyn	East R., N.Y.C.	1,595
1939	Lion's Gate	Burrard Inlet, B.C.	1,550
1930	Mid-Hudson	Poughkeepsie, NY	1,500
1963	Vincent Thomas	Los Angeles Harbor	1,500
1909	Manhattan	East R., N.Y.C.	1,470
1936	Triboro	East R., N.Y.C.	1,380
1931	St. Johns	Portland, OR	1,207
1929	Mount Hope	Rhode Island	1,200
1960	Ogdensburg, NY	St. Lawrence R.	1,150
1939	Deer Isle	Maine	1,080
1931	Simon Kenton Memorial	Ohio R., KY	1,060

Year	Bridge	Location	Longest span
1867	John A. Roebling	Ohio R., KY	1,057
1971	Dent	Clearwater Co., ID	1,050
1900	Miampimi	Mexico	1,030
1849	Wheeling, WV	Ohio R.	1,010

Cantilever

Year	Bridge	Location	Longest span
1917	Quebec	Quebec	1,800
1974	Commodore Barry	Chester, PA	1,622
1958	Mississippi R.	New Orleans, LA	1,575
1988	Mississippi R.	New Orleans, LA	1,575
1995	Mississippi R., LA 3213	Gramercy, LA	1,460
1936	Transbay	San Fran. Bay	1,400
1968	Mississippi R.	Baton Rouge, LA	1,235
1955	Tappan Zee	Hudson R.	1,212
1930	Lewis and Clark	Longview, WA-OR	1,200
1909	Queensboro	East R., N.Y.C.	1,182
1927	Carquinez Strait	California	1,100
1958	Parallel Span	California	1,100
1930	Jacques Cartier	Montreal, Can.	1,097
1968	Isaiah D. Hart	Jacksonville, FL	1,088
1956	Richmond[3]	San Fran. Bay, CA	1,070
1929	Grace Memorial	Charleston, SC	1,050
1980	Newburgh-Beacon	Hudson R., NY	1,000
1963	Newburgh-Beacon	Hudson R., NY	1,000
1949	Martin Luther King	St. Louis, MO	963
1975	Caruthersville, MO	Mississippi R.	920
1977	Saint Marys	Saint Marys, WV, OH	900
1969	Silver Memorial	Pt. Pleasant, WV, OH	900
1981	Ravenswood	WV	900
1987	Carl Perkins	Ohio R., KY	900
1986	Mississippi R.	Natchez, MS	875
1940	Mississippi R.	Natchez, MS	875
1938	Blue Water	Pt. Huron, MI	871
1972	Mississippi R.	Vicksburg, MS	870
1972	N. Fork American R.	Auburn, CA	862
1940	*Baton Rouge	Mississippi R.	848
1899	*Cornwall	St. Lawrence R.	843
1940	Mississippi R.	Greenville, MS	840
1961	Helena, AR.	Mississippi R.	840
1963	Brent Spence	Covington, KY	831
1963	Cincinnati	Ohio R.	830
1963	Mississippi R.	Donaldsonville, LA	825
1940	Mississippi R.	Vicksburg, MS	825
1929	Clark Memorial	Ohio R, KY.	820
1961	Campbellton-Cross Pt.	New Brunswick-Que.	815
1935	Rip Van Winkle	Catskill, NY	800
1938	Cairo	Ohio R., IL-KY	800
1932	Washington Mem.	Seattle, WA	800
1936	McCullough	Coos Bay, OR	793
1935	Huey P. Long[4]	New Orleans	790
1916	*Memphis (Harahan)	Mississippi R.	790
1892	*Memphis	Mississippi R.	790
1949	Memphis-Arkansas	Mississippi R.	790
1904	*Mingo Jct., OH	Ohio R.	769
1910	*P&LE RR Bridge	Ohio R., Beaver, PA	750
1932	Bi-State Vietnam Gold Star	Henderson, KY	720
1992	Jamestown-Verranzzano	Jamestown, RI	636
1943	*Pit River	Redding, CA	620
1941	Columbia R.	Kettle Falls, WA	600
1954	Columbia R.	Umatilla, OR	600
1954	Columbia R.	The Dalles, OR.	573
1968	W. 17th St.	Huntington, WV	562

Simple Truss

Year	Bridge	Location	Longest span
1976	Chester	Chester, WV	745
1917	*Metropolis	Ohio R.	720
1929	Irvin S. Cobb	Ohio R.-IL-KY	716
1922	*Tanana R.	Nenana, Alaska	700
1933	*Henderson	Ohio R.-IN-KY	665
1967	I-77, Ohio R.	Williamstown, WV	650
1917	[4] MacArthur, IL-MO	St. Louis	647
1919	Louisville	Ohio R.	644
1992	St. Charles	Missouri R, MO.	625
1933	Atchafalaya	Morgan City, LA	608
1924	*Castleton	Hudson R., NY.	598
1937	Delaware R.	Easton, PA.	550
1930	Swindell Bridge	Pittsburgh, PA	545
1889	*Cincinnati	Ohio R.	542
1952	Allegheny R., Tpk.	Pittsburgh, PA	534
1930	*Martinez	California	528
1951	Rankin	Pittsburgh, PA	525
1914	Old Brownsville	Brownsville, PA	520
1906	Donora-Webster	Donora-Webster, PA.	515

Year	Bridge	Location	Longest span
1909	Hulton	Pittsburgh, PA	505
1967	Tanana R.	Alaska	500

Steel Truss

Year	Bridge	Location	Longest span
1988	Glade Creek	Raleigh Co., WV	784
1973	Atchafalaya R.	Krotz Springs, LA	780
1972	Piscataqua R.	NH- ME	756
1972	Atchafalaya R.	Simmesport, LA.	720
1957	SR-3, Rappahannock R.	Middlesex Co., VA	648
1978	Atchafalaya R.	Morgan City, LA.	607
1938	US-22	Delaware R., NJ	540
1955	Interstate (I-5)	Columbia R., OR-WA.	531
1910	McKinley, St. Louis[4]	Mississippi R.	517
1972	Mississippi R.	Muscatine, IA	512
1896	Newport	Ohio R., KY.	511
1989	Atchafalaya R., US 190	Krotz Springs, LA	506
1970	Lake Koocanusa	Lincoln Co., MT.	500
1931	Lucy Jefferson Lewis	Cumberland R., KY	500
1958	Lake Oahe	Mobridge, SD	500
1958	Lake Oahe	Gettysburg, SD	500

Continuous Truss

Year	Bridge	Location	Longest span
1966	Columbia R. (Astoria)	OR-WA.	1,232
1977	Francis Scott Key	Baltimore, MD	1,200
1995	**Central	Ohio R., KY-OH	850
1943	Dubuque, IA	Mississippi R.	845
1966	Charles Braga	Fall River, MA	840
1956	Earl C. Clements[5]	Ohio R., Ill-KY	825
1953	John E. Mathews	Jacksonville, FL.	810
1950	Maurice J. Tobin	Boston, MA.	801
1940	Gov. Nice Memorial	Potomac River, MD	800
1957	Kingston-Rhinecliff.	Hudson R., NY	800
1986	Rochester-Monaca.	Rochester-Monaca,PA	780
1918	*Sciotoville	Ohio R.	775
1976	Carroll L. Cropper	Ohio R., IN-KY	750
1981	Sewickley	Sewickley, PA	750
1984	13th St. Bridge, Ohio R.	Ashland, KY	740
1959	Monaca-E. Rochester.	Monaca-E. Rochester, PA	730
1976	Betsy Ross	Philadelphia, PA	729
1929	Madison-Milton	Ohio R., IN-KY	727
1966	Matthew E. Welsh[6]	Mauckport, IN	725
1994	6th St.	Huntington, WV	720
1977	Bert T. Combs-Lambert	Ohio R.	720
1970	Vanport	Vanport, PA	715
1962	Champlain	Montreal, Que.	707
1964	John F. Kennedy[7]	Louisville, KY	700
1973	Girard Point	Philadelphia, PA	700
1954	PA Tpk., Delaware R.	Philadelphia, PA	682
1949	George Platt	Philadelphia, PA	680
1938	Port Arthur-Orange	TX	680
1926	Cape Girardeau, MO	Mississippi R.	677
1929	*Cincinnati	Ohio R.	675
1946	Chester, IL	Mississippi R.	670
1970	Gulfgate	Port Arthur, TX	664
1994	Williamstown-Marietta	Williamstown, WV	650
1955	Jefferson City	Missouri R.	640
1930	Quincy, IL	Mississippi R.	628
1961	Shippingport	Shippingport, PA	620
1959	US 181, over harbor.	Corpus Christi, TX	620
1935	Bourne	Cape Cod Canal, MA.	616
1935	Sagamore	Cape Cod Canal, MA.	616
1965	Clarion R. (I-80)	Clarion, PA	612
1975	Donora-Monesson	Donora-Monesson, PA	608
1991	Hoffstadt Creek	Mt. St. Helens, WA	600
1957	Blatnik	Duluth, MN	600
1965	Rio Grande Gorge	Taos, NM	600
1991	Jefferson City	Missouri R.	596
1962	W. Branch Feather R.	Oroville, CA.	576
1967	Glenwood	Pittsburgh, PA.	567
1936	Meredosia	Illinois R.	567
1936	Mark Twain Mem.	Hannibal, MO	562
1957	Mackinac	Mackinac Straits, MI.	560
1932	Pulaski Skyway	Passaic R.- Hackensack R., NJ	550
1966	Emlenton	Emlenton, PA	540
1936	Homestead High Level	Pittsburgh, PA.	534
1960	Brownsville High Level	Brownsville, PA.	518
1945	Mansfield-Dravosburg	Pittsburgh, PA.	500

Continuous Box and Plate Girder

Year	Bridge	Location	Longest span
1982	Houston Ship Chan.	Houston, TX	750
1967	San Mateo-Hayward #2	San Fran. Bay, CA.	750
1977	Intracoastal Canal	Gibbstown, LA.	750
1976	Intracoastal Canal	Forked Is., LA	750

Year	Bridge	Location	Longest span
1969	San Diego-Coronado[8].	San Diego Bay, CA. .	660
1987	Columbia R.	Umatilla, OR-WA . . .	660
1994	Acosta.	Jacksonville, FL. . . .	630
1981	Douglas	Juneau, AK	620
1976	Wax L. Outlet	Calumet, LA	618
1981	Glenn Jackson (I-205) .	Columbia R., OR-WA	600
1963	Poplar St.	St. Louis, MO	600
1982	Illinois R.	Pekin, IL	550
1982	I-440	Arkansas R.	540
1980	US-64, Tennessee R. .	Savannah, TN	525
1988	Mon City	Monongahela, PA. . .	520
1965	McDonald-Cartier	Ottawa, Ontario	520
1984	Columbia R.	Richland, WA	450
1986	Veterans	Pittsburgh, PA	440
1987	SR 76, Cumberland R.	Dover, TN	440
1987	SR 20, Tennessee R. .	Perryville, TN	440
1970	Willamette R., I-205 . .	West Linn, OR	430
1974	I-430	Arkansas R.	430
1984	FAU 3456, TN R.	Chattanooga, TN	420
1965	I-24, Tennessee R. . . .	Marion Co., TN.	420
1978	Snake R.	Clarkston, WA	420
1975	36th St.	Charleston, WV	420
1974	Dunbar-S. Charleston .	S. Charleston, WV . .	420

Continuous Plate

Year	Bridge	Location	Longest span
1973	Ship Channel (I-610) . .	Houston, TX.	630
1971	W. Atchafalaya	Henderson, LA	573
1981	Illinois 23	Illinois R., IL	510
1968	Trinity R.	Dallas, TX	480
1978	San Joaquin R.	Antioch, CA	460
1977	Thomas Johnson Mem.	Solomons, MD	451
1979	Lewis	St. Louis, MO	450
1975	I-129	Missouri R., IA	450
1967	Mississippi R.	La Crosse, WI	450
1972	Whiskey Bay Pilot	Ramah, LA	425
1966	I-480	Missouri R., IA-NE . .	425
1972	I-435	Missouri R., MO	425
1972	I-80	Missouri R., IA-NE . .	425
1987	I-435	Missouri R., KS-MO .	425
1983	US-36	Missouri R., KS-MO .	425
1972	I-635, Kansas City . . .	Missouri R., KS-MO .	425
1978	I-24	Cumberland R., KY. .	420

Cable-Stayed

Year	Bridge	Location	Longest span
1988	Dames Point	Jacksonville, FL. . . .	1,300
1995	**Houston Ship Channel	Baytowne-LaPorte,TX	1,250
1983	Mississippi R., I-310 . .	Luling, LA	1,222
1987	Sunshine Skyway	Tampa Bay, FL. . . .	1,200
1991	Talmadge Mem.	Savannah, GA	1,100
1979	Columbia River	Pasco-Kennewick, WA	970
1985	E. Huntington	Huntington, WV	900
1985	Mississippi R.	Quincy, IL	900
1980	Veterans Mem'l.	WV-OH	820
1991	Cochrane/Africatown . .	Mobile, AL	780
1995	Chesapeake & Delaware Canal Bridge.	Dover-Wilmington, DE	750
1994	Great River Bridge . . .	Burlington, IA	660
1991	Neches R.	Port Arthur-Orange,TX	640
1990	James R.	Henrico Co., VA	630
1972	Sitka Harbor	Sitka, AK	450

I-Beam Girder

Year	Bridge	Location	Longest span
1980	Interstate 20	Shreveport, LA	438
1988	Route 18	Weston's Mill Pond, NJ	276

Steel Arch

Year	Bridge	Location	Longest span
1977	New R. Gorge.	Fayetteville, WV	1,817
1931	Kill Van Kull	Bayonne, NJ	1,652
1973	Fremont.	Portland, OR	1,255
1964	Port Mann	British Columbia	1,200
1916	*Hell Gate	East R., N.Y.C.	1,038
1959	Glen Canyon	Colorado R., Page, AZ	1,028
1967	Trois-Rivieres	St. Lawrence R., Que.	1,100
1990	Roosevelt Lake.	Arizona	1,080
1962	Lewiston-Queenston . .	Niagara R., Ont. . . .	1,000
1976	Perrine	Twin Falls, ID	993
1941	Rainbow.	Niagara Falls	984
1986	Moundsville	Ohio R., WV	912
1985	I-255	Mississippi R., MO . .	910
1972	I-40, Mississippi R.[9]. . .	Memphis, TN	900
1936	Henry Hudson	Harlem R., N.Y.C. . . .	840
1967	Lincoln Trail	Ohio R., IN-KY	825

Year	Bridge	Location	Longest span
1978	I-57, Cairo, IL	Mississippi R.	821
1980	I-65 Mobile R.	Mobile, AL.	800
1961	Sherman Minton	New Albany, IN	800
1978	I-470 Bridge, Ohio R. . .	Wheeling, WV	780
1930	West End	Pittsburgh, PA.	780

Concrete Arch

Year	Bridge	Location	Longest span
1993	Lake Street Bridge	St. Paul, MN	556
1971	Selah Creek (twin)	Selah, WA.	549
1968	Cowlitz R.	Mossyrock, WA	520
1931	Westinghouse	Pittsburgh, PA.	460
1923	Cappelen	Minneapolis, MN	435

Segmental Concrete

Year	Bridge	Location	Longest span
1988	Zilwaukee Bridge (twin)	Zilwaukee, MI	392
1985	Red River Bridge	Coushatta, LA	370

Twin Concrete Trestle [10]

Year	Bridge	Location	Longest span
1979	I-55/I-10	Manchac, LA.	181,157
1969	L. Pontchartrain Cswy. .	Mandeville, LA.	126,720
1972	Atchafalaya Flwy.	Baton Rouge, LA. . . .	93,984
1963	L. Pontchartrain	Slidell, LA	28,547
1983	Interstate 310	Kenner, LA	25,925

Concrete Slab Dam [10]

Year	Bridge	Location	Longest span
1927	Conowingo Dam	Maryland.	4,611
1952	SR-4, Roanoke R.	Mecklenburg Co., VA.	2,785
1936	Hoover Dam	Lake Mead, AZ-NV . .	1,324

Drawbridges

Vertical Lift

Year	Bridge	Location	Longest span
1959	*Arthur Kill.	NY-NJ	558
1965	Pennsylvania Railroad .	Kirkwood-Mt. Pleasant, DE	548
1935	*Cape Cod Canal.	Massachusetts	544
1960	*Delair, NJ.	Delaware R.	542
1937	Marine Parkway.	Jamaica Bay, N.Y.C. .	540
1931	Burlington, NJ	Delaware R.	534
1908	*Willamette R.	Portland, OR.	521
1968	Second Narrows	Vancouver, B.C.	493
1912	*A-S-B Fratt.	Kansas City.	428
1945	*Harry S Truman	Kansas City.	427
1955	Roosevelt Island	East R., N.Y.C.	418
1980	US-17, James R.	Isle of Wight, Co., VA.	415
1932	*M-K-T R.R.	Missouri R.	414
1969	Cape Fear Mem.	Wilmington, NC	408
1930	Aerial	Duluth, MN	386
1941	Main St.	Jacksonville, FL. . . .	386
1962	Burlington	Ontario	370
1922	*Cincinnati.	Ohio R.	365
1967	SR-156, James R.	Prince George Co., VA	364
1957	Industrial Canal	New Orleans, LA. . . .	360
1950	Red R.	Moncla, LA	360
1936	Tribo.	Harlem R., N.Y.C. . . .	344
1961	Corpus Christi Harbor[4].	Corpus Christi, TX. . .	344
1939	U.S. 1&9, Passaic R. . .	Newark, NJ	333
1930	*Martinez	California	328
1960	St. Andrews Bay	Panama City, FL	327
1929	*Penn-Lehigh	Newark Bay	322
1987	Industrial Canal	New Orleans, LA. . . .	320
1920	*Chattanooga	Tennessee R.	310

Bascule

Year	Bridge	Location	Longest span
1969	E. Pearl R.	Slidell, LA	482
1940	Lorain, OH	Black R.	333
1917	SR-8, Tennessee R. . . .	Chattanooga, TN. . . .	306
1956	Duwamish R.	Seattle, WA.	300
1955	Chehalis R.	Aberdeen, WA.	288
1968	Elizabeth R.	Chesapeake, VA. . . .	280
1913	Broadway	Portland, OR.	278
1954	Fuller Warren	Jacksonville, FL. . . .	224

Swing Bridges

Year	Bridge	Location	Longest span
1927	Fort Madison[4]	Mississippi R.	545
1991	SW. Spokane St.	Seattle, WA.	480
1930	Rigolets Pass	New Orleans, LA. . . .	400
1950	Douglass Memorial . . .	Washington, DC	386
1945	Lord Delaware.	Mattaponi R., VA . . .	252
1957	Eltham	Pamunkey R., VA . . .	237

Year	Bridge	Location	Longest span	Year	Bridge	Location	Longest span
	Swing Span				**Floating Pontoon** [10]		
1903	*East Omaha	Missouri R.	519	1963	Evergreen Pt	Seattle, WA.	7,518
1952	US-17	York R., VA	500	1961	Hood Canal	Pt. Gamble, WA.	6,471
1897	*Duluth, MN	St. Louis Bay	486	1993	Lacey V. Murrow-Lake		
1899	*C.M.&N.R.R.	Chicago	474		Washington.	Seattle, WA	6,543
1913	Rt. 82, Conn-R.	E. Haddam, CT	465	1989	3rd Lake Washington	Seattle, WA.	6,130
1914	*Coos Bay	Oregon	458				

(1) The Transbay Bridge has 2 spans of 2,310 ft. each. (2) A second bridge in parallel was completed in 1973. (3) The Richmond Bridge has twin spans 1,070 ft. each. (4) Railroad and vehicular bridge. (5) Two spans each 825 ft. (6) Two spans each 707 ft. (7) Two spans each 700 ft. (8) Two spans each 660 ft. (9) Two spans each 900 ft. (10) Length listed is total length of bridge.

Oldest U.S. Bridge in Continuous Use

Built in 1697, the stone-arch Frankford Ave. Bridge crosses Pennypack Creek in Philadelphia, PA. A three-span bridge with a total length of 75 ft., it was constructed as part of the King's Road, which eventually connected Philadelphia to New York.

Oldest U.S. Covered Bridge in Continuous Use

Completed in 1827, the double-span 278-ft. Haverhill Bath Bridge spans the Ammonoosuc River, between the towns of Bath and Haverhill, NH.

Notable International Bridges

Span of bridge is distance (in feet) between its supports. Asterisk (*) designates under construction.

Suspension

Year	Bridge	Location	Longest span
1998*	Akashi Kaikyo	Japan	6,529
1996*	Store Bælt (East Bridge)	Denmark	5,328
1981	Humber	England	4,626
1997*	Tsing Ma	Hong Kong	4,518
1988	Minami Bisan-Seto	Japan	3,609
1988	Bosphorus I	Turkey.	3,576
1973	Bosphorus II	Turkey.	3,524
1966	Ponte 25 de Abril.	Portugal.	3,323
1964	Forth (road)	Scotland	3,301
1966	Severn	England	3,241

Cantilever

Year	Bridge	Location	Longest span
1917	Quebec	Canada	1,801
1890	Forth[1] (rail).	Scotland	1,710
1974	Nanko.	Japan.	1,673

Steel Arch

Year	Bridge	Location	Longest span
1932	Sydney Harbour	Australia	1,650

(1) Two spans of 1,710 ft. each.

Concrete Arch

Year	Bridge	Location	Longest span
1980	Krk I	Croatia.	1,280
1964	Gladesville	Australia.	1,001

Steel Plate and Box Girder

Year	Bridge	Location	Longest span
1974	President Costa e Silva	Brazil.	984
1956	Sava I	Yugoslavia	856
1966	Zoobrüke	Germany	850

Cable-Stayed

Year	Bridge	Location	Longest span
1999*	Tatara.	Japan	2,920
1995	Pont de Normandie	France.	2,808
1993	Yangpu	China	1,975
*	Meiko Chuo	Japan	1,936
1991	Skarnsundet	Norway	1,739
1986	Alex Fraser	Canada	1,526
1985	Yokohama.	Japan.	1,509
1987	Hooghly River.	Calcutta	1,499
1996*	Severn.	England	1,496

Underwater Vehicular Tunnels in North America

(more than 5,000 ft. in length)

Name	Location	Waterway	Feet
Brooklyn-Battery (1950)	New York, NY.	East River	9,117
Holland Tunnel (1927) (2 tubes)	New York, NY.	Hudson River.	8,557
Lincoln Tunnel (1937, 1945, 1957) (3 tubes)	New York, NY.	Hudson River.	8,216
Thimble Shoal Channel (1964)	Northampton Co., VA	Chesapeake Bay	8,187
Chesapeake Channel (1964)	Northampton Co., VA	Chesapeake Bay	7,941
Baltimore Harbor Tunnel (1957)	Baltimore, MD	Patapsco River	7,650
Hampton Roads (1957) (twin)	Hampton, VA	Hampton Roads.	7,479
Fort McHenry Tunnel (2 tubes)	Baltimore, MD	Baltimore Harbor.	7,200
Queens Midtown (1940)	New York, NY.	East River	6,414
Sumner Tunnel (1934)	Boston, MA	Boston Harbor	5,650
Louis-Hippolyte Lafontaine Tunnel	Montreal, Quebec.	St. Lawrence River.	5,280
Detroit-Windsor (1930).	Detroit, MI	Detroit River.	5,160
Callahan Tunnel (1961)	Boston, MA	Boston Harbor	5,046

Land Vehicular Tunnels in the U.S.

(more than 3,000 ft. in length; asterisk (*) designates under construction)

Name	Location	Feet	Name	Location	Feet
E. Johnson Memorial	I-70, CO	8,959	Blue Mountain (twin)	PA Turnpike.	4,435
Eisenhower Memorial	I-70, CO	8,941	Lehigh (twin)	PA Turnpike.	4,379
Allegheny (twin)	PA Turnpike	6,072	Wawona	Yosemite Natl. Park	4,233
Liberty Tubes	Pittsburgh, PA.	5,920	Big Walker Mt.	Bland Co., VA	4,229
Zion Natl. Park	Rte. 9, Utah	5,766	Squirrel Hill	Pittsburgh, PA	4,225
East River Mt. (twin)	Bland Co., VA, Mercer Co., WV	5,412	Hanging Lake (twin)	Glenwood Canyon, CO.	4,000
			Caldecott (3 tubes)	Oakland, CA	3,616
Tuscarora (twin)	PA Turnpike	5,400	Fort Pitt	Pittsburgh, PA.	3,560
Tetsuo Harano (twin)	H-3, Hawaii.	5,165	Dingess Tunnel	Mingo Co., WV.	3,400
Kittatinny (twin)	PA Turnpike	4,660	Mall Tunnel	Dist. of Columbia	3,400
*Cumberland Gap	Kentucky	4,600	Cody No. 1	U.S. 14, 16, 20, WY	3,202

World's Longest Railway Tunnels

Source: Railway Directory & Year Book. Tunnels more than 8 mi. in length.

Tunnel	Date	Miles	Operating railway	Country
Seikan	1985	33.50	Japanese Railway	Japan
English Channel Tunnel	1994	31.04	Eurotunnel	UK - France
Dai-shimizu	1979	14.00	Japanese Railway	Japan
Simplon No. 1 and 2	1906, 1922	12.00	Swiss Fed. & Italian St.	Switz.-Italy
Kanmon	1975	12.00	Japanese Railway	Japan
Apennine	1934	11.00	Italian State	Italy
Rokko	1972	10.00	Japanese Railway	Japan
Mt. MacDonald	1989	9.10	Canadian Pacific	Canada
Gotthard	1882	9.00	Swiss Federal	Switzerland
Lotschberg	1913	9.00	Bern-Lotschberg-Simplon	Switzerland
Hokuriku	1962	9.00	Japanese Railway	Japan
Mont Cenis (Frejus)	1871	8.00	Italian State	France-Italy
Shin-Shimizu	1961	8.00	Japanese Railway	Japan
Aki	1975	8.00	Japanese Railway	Japan
Cascade	1929	8.00	Burlington Northern	U.S.
Flathead	1970	8.00	Burlington Northern	U.S.

World's Largest Capacity Hydro Plants

Source: U.S. Committee on Large Dams of the Intl. Commission on Large Dams, 1995

Rank order	Name	Country	Rated capacity now (MW)	Rated capacity planned (MW)	Rank order	Name	Country	Rated capacity now (MW)	Rated capacity planned (MW)
1	Turukhansk (Lower Tunguska)*	Russia		20,000	13 =	Bratsk	Russia	4,500	4,500
					13 =	Ust-Ilim	Russia	3,675	4,500
					15	Cabora Bassa	Mozambique	2,425	4,150
2	Itaipu	Brazil/Paraguay	7,400	13,320	16	Boguchany*	Russia		4,000
3	Grand Coulee	U.S.	6,495	10,830	17 =	Rogun*	Tajikistan		3,600
4	Guri (Raúl Leoni)	Venezuela	10,300	10,300	17 =	Oak Creek	U.S.	3,600	3,600
5	Tucuruí	Brazil	2,640	7,260	19	Paulo Afonso I	Brazil	1,524	3,409
6	Sayano Shu-shensk*	Russia	6,400	6,400	20	Pati*	Argentina		3,300
7 =	Corpus Posadas	Argentina/ Paraguay	4,700	6,000	21 =	Ilha Solteira	Brazil	3,200	3,200
					21 =	Brumley Gap*	U.S.	3,200	3,200
7 =	Krasnoyarsk	Russia	6,000	6,000	23	Chapetón*	Argentina		3,000
9	La Grande 2	Canada	5,328	5,328	24	Gezhouba	China	2,715	2,715
10	Churchill Falls	Canada	5,225	5,225	25	John Day	U.S.	2,160	2,700
11	Xingo	Brazil	3,012	5,020	25 =	Nurek	Tajikistan	900	2,700
12	Tarbela	Pakistan	1,750	4,678	25 =	Yacireta*	Argentina/ Paraguay		2,700

*Planned or under construction; = Equal rank.

Major Dams of the World

Source: U.S. Committee on Large Dams of the Intl. Commission on Large Dams, 1995

World's Highest Dams

Rank order	Name	Country	Height above lowest formation (m)	Rank order	Name	Country	Height above lowest formation (m)
1	Rogun*	Tajikistan	335	11	Mica	Canada	242
2	Nurek	Tajikistan	300	12	Mauvoisin	Switzerland	237
3	Grand Dixence	Switzerland	285	13	Chivor	Colombia	237
4	Inguri	Georgia	272	14	El Cajón	Honduras	234
5	Chicoasén	Mexico	261	15	Chirkei	Russia	233
6	Tehri*	India	261	16	Oroville	U.S.	230
7	Kishau*	India	253	17	Bhakra	India	226
8 =	Ertan	China	245	18	Hoover	U.S.	221
8 =	Sayano-Shushensk*	Russia	245	19	Contra	Switzerland	220
10	Guavio*	Colombia	243	20	Mratinje	Yugoslavia	220

*Under construction; = Equal rank.

World's Largest Volume Embankment Dams

Rank order	Name	Country	Volume cubic meters × 1000	Rank order	Name	Country	Volume cubic meters × 1000
1	Tarbela	Pakistan	148,500	11	Gardiner	Canada	65,000
2	Fort Peck	U.S.	96,050	12	Afsluitdijk	Netherlands	63,400
3	Tucurui	Brazil	85,200	13	Mangla	Pakistan	63,379
4	Ataturk*	Turkey	85,000	14	Oroville	U.S.	59,635
5	Yacireta*	Argentina	81,000	15	San Luis	U.S.	59,559
6	Rogun*	Tajikistan	75,500	16	Nurek	Tajikistan	58,000
7	Oahe	U.S.	70,339	17	Tanda	Pakistan	57,250
8	Guri	Venezuela	70,000	18	Garrison	U.S.	50,843
9	Parambikulam	India	69,165	19	Cochiti	U.S.	50,228
10	High Island West	Hong Kong	67,000	20	Oosterschelde	Netherlands	50,000

*Under construction.

World's Largest Capacity Reservoirs

Rank order	Name	Country	Capacity cubic meters × 1,000,000	Rank order	Name	Country	Capacity cubic meters × 1,000,000
1	Owen Falls	Uganda	204,800	11	Cabora Bassa	Mozambique	63,000
2	Bratsk	Russia	169,000	12	La Grande 2	Canada	61,715
3	Aswan (High)	Egypt	162,000	13	La Grande 3	Canada	60,020
4	Kariba	Zimbabwe/Zambia	160,368	14	Ust-Ilim	Russia	59,300
5	Akosombo	Ghana	147,960	15	Boguchany*	Russia	58,200
6	Daniel Johnson	Canada	141,851	16	Kuibyshev	Russia	58,000
7	Guri	Venezuela	135,000	17	Serra de Mesa	Brazil	54,400
8	Krasnoyarsk	Russia	73,300	18	Caniapiscau Barrage KA 3	Canada	53,790
9	W A C Bennett (Portage Mt.)	Canada	70,309	19	Bukhtarma	Kazakhstan	49,800
10	Zeya	Russia	68,400	20	Ataturk	Turkey	48,700

*Under construction.

Major U.S. Dams and Reservoirs

Source: Committee on Register of Dams, Corps of Engineers, U.S. Army, 1995

Highest U.S. Dams

Order	Dam name	River	State	Type	Height Feet	Height Meters	Year completed
1	Oroville	Feather	California	E	754	230	1968
2	Hoover	Colorado	Nevada	A	725	221	1936
3	Dworshak	N. Fork Clearwater	Idaho	G	718	219	1973
4	Glen Canyon	Colorado	Arizona	A	708	216	1966
5	New Bullards Bar	North Yuba	California	A	636	194	1970
6	New Melones	Stanislaus	California	R	626	191	1979
7	Swift	Lewis	Washington	E	610	186	1958
8	Mossyrock	Cowlitz	Washington	A	607	185	1968
9	Shasta	Sacramento	California	G	600	183	1945
10	Hungry Horse	S. Fork Flathead	Montana	A	564	172	1953
11	Grand Coulee	Columbia	Washington	G	551	168	1942
12	Ross	Skagit	Washington	A	541	165	1949

E= Embankment, Earthfill; R= Embankment, Rockfill; G= Gravity; A= Arch.

Largest U.S. Embankment Dams

Order	Dam name	River	State	Type	Volume Cubic yards X 1000	Volume Cubic meters X 1000	Year completed
1	Fort Peck	Missouri	Montana	E	125,624	96,050	1937
2	Oahe	Missouri	South Dakota	E	91,996	70,339	1958
3	Oroville	Feather	California	E	77,997	59,635	1968
4	San Luis	San Luis Creek	California	E	77,897	59,559	1967
5	Garrison	Missouri	North Dakota	E	66,498	50,843	1953
6	Cochiti	Rio Grande	New Mexico	E	65,693	50,228	1975
7	Earthquake Lake	Madison	Montana	E-G	49,998	38,228	1959
8	Fort Randall	Missouri	South Dakota	E	49,962	38,200	1952
9	Castaic	Castaic Creek	California	E	43,998	33,640	1973
10	Ludington P/S	Lake Michigan	Michigan	E	37,699	28,824	1973
11	Kingsley	N. Platte	Nebraska	E	31,999	24,466	1941
12	Warm Springs	Dry Creek	California	E	29,977	22,920	1982

E= Embankment, Earthfill; G= Gravity.

Largest U.S. Reservoirs

Order	Dam name	Reservoir	Location	Reservoir capacity Acre-Feet	Reservoir capacity Cubic meters X 1000	Year completed
1	Hoover	Lake Mead	Nevada	28,253,000	34,850,000	1936
2	Glen Canyon	Lake Powell	Arizona	26,997,000	33,300,000	1966
3	Garrison	Lake Sakakawea	North Dakota	22,635,000	27,920,000	1953
4	Oahe	Lake Oahe	South Dakota	22,238,000	27,430,000	1958
5	Fort Peck	Fort Peck Lake	Montana	17,933,000	22,120,000	1937
6	Grand Coulee	F D Roosevelt Lake	Washington	9,558,000	11,790,000	1942
7	Libby	Lake Koocanusa	Montana	5,813,000	7,170,000	1973
8	Fort Randall	Lake Francis Case	South Dakota	4,621,000	5,700,000	1952
9	Shasta	Lake Shasta	California	4,548,000	5,610,000	1945
10	Toledo Bend	Toledo Bend Lake	Louisiana	4,475,000	5,520,000	1968
11	Wolf Creek	Cumberland Lake	Kentucky	3,997,000	4,930,000	1951
12	Flaming Gorge	Flaming Gorge Reservoir	Utah	3,786,000	4,670,000	1964

1 acre-foot = 1 acre of water, 1 foot deep

SOCIAL SECURITY

Social Security Programs

Source: Social Security Administration, U.S. Dept. of Health and Human Services; data as of mid-1995

Old-Age, Survivors, and Disability Insurance; Medicare; Supplemental Security Income

Social Security Benefits

Social Security benefits are based on a worker's primary insurance amount (PIA), which is related by law to the average indexed monthly earnings (AIME) on which Social Security contributions have been paid. The full PIA is payable to a retired worker who becomes entitled to benefits at age 65 and to an entitled disabled worker at any age. Spouses and children of retired or disabled workers and survivors of deceased workers receive set proportions of the PIA subject to a family maximum amount. The PIA is calculated by applying varying percentages to succeeding parts of the AIME. The formula is adjusted annually to reflect changes in average annual wages.

Automatic increases in Social Security benefits are initiated for Dec. of a year whenever the Consumer Price Index (CPI) of the Bureau of Labor Statistics for the 3d calendar quarter of a year increases relative to the CPI for the base quarter, which is either the 3d calendar quarter of the preceding year or the quarter in which an increase legislated by Congress becomes effective. The size of the benefit increase is determined by the actual percentage rise of the CPI between the quarters measured.

The average monthly benefit payable to all retired workers was $697.00 in Dec. 1994. The average amount for disabled workers in that month was $661.00.

Minimum and maximum monthly retired-worker benefits payable to individuals who retired at age 65[1]

Year of attainment of age 65[2]	Minimum benefit Payable at time of retirement	Minimum benefit Payable effective Dec.1994	Maximum benefit Payable at time of retirement Men[3]	Maximum benefit Payable at time of retirement Women	Maximum benefit Payable effective Dec. 1994 Men[3]	Maximum benefit Payable effective Dec. 1994 Women
1965 ..	$44.00	$275.10	$131.70	$135.90	$735.90	$759.40
1970 ..	64.00	275.10	189.80	196.40	815.60	844.60
1980 ..	133.90	275.10	572.00	—	1,176.50	—
1990 ..	(4)	(4)	975.00	—	1,157.50	—
1993 ..	(4)	(4)	1,128.80	—	1,190.50	—
1994 ..	(4)	(4)	1,147.50	—	1,179.60	—
1995 ..	(4)	(4)	1,199.10	—	—	—

(1) Assumes retirement at beginning of year. (2) The final benefit amount payable after Supplementary Medical Insurance (SMI) premium or any other deductions is rounded to next lower $1 (if not already a multiple of $1). (3) Benefits for both men and women are shown in men's columns except where women's benefit appears separately. (4) Minimum eliminated for workers who reach age 62 after 1981.

Amount of Work Required

To qualify for benefits, the worker must have worked in covered employment long enough to become insured. Just how long depends on when the worker reaches age 62 or, if earlier, when he or she dies or becomes disabled.

A person is fully insured if he or she has 1 quarter of coverage for every year after 1950 (or year age 21 is reached, if later) up to but not including the year in which the worker reaches age 62, dies, or becomes disabled. In 1995, a person earns 1 quarter of coverage for each $630.00 of annual earnings in covered employment, up to a maximum of 4 quarters per year.

The law permits special monthly payments under the Social Security program to certain very old persons who are not eligible for regular Social Security benefits since they had little or no opportunity to earn Social Security work credits during their working lifetime (so-called special age-72 beneficiaries).

To get disability benefits, in addition to being fully insured, the worker must also have credit for 20 quarters of coverage out of the 40 calendar quarters before he or she becomes disabled. A disabled blind worker need meet only the fully insured requirement. Persons disabled before age 31 can qualify with a briefer period of coverage. Certain survivor benefits are payable if the deceased worker had 6 quarters of coverage in the 13 quarters preceding death.

Work credit for fully insured status for benefits

Born after 1929; die, become disabled, or reach age 62 in	Years needed
1983	8
1984	8¼
1985	8½
1986	8¾
1987	9
1988	9¼
1989	9½
1990	9¾
1991 and after	10

Contribution and benefit base

Calendar year	OASDI[1] Base	HI[2] Base
1984	$37,800	—
1985	39,600	—
1986	42,000	—
1987	43,800	—
1988	45,000	—
1989	48,000	—
1990	51,300	—
1991	53,400	$125,000[3]
1992	55,500	130,200
1993	57,600	135,000
1994	60,600	no limit
1995	61,200	no limit
1996[4]	63,000	no limit

(1) Old-Age, Survivors, and Disability Insurance. (2) Hospital Insurance. (3) Although the OASDI and HI bases were the same prior to 1991, they have differed since that time. (4) Estimate.

Tax-rate schedule
(percentage of covered earnings)

Year	Total Employees and employers, each	OASDI	HI
1979-80	6.13	5.08	1.05
1981	6.65	5.35	1.30
1982-83	6.70	5.40	1.30
1984	7.00	5.70	1.30
1985	7.05	5.70	1.35
1986-87	7.15	5.70	1.45
1988-89	7.51	6.06	1.45
1990 and after	7.65	6.20	1.45
Self-employed			
1979-80	8.10	7.05	1.05
1981	9.30	8.00	1.30
1982-83	9.35	8.05	1.30
1984	14.00	11.40	2.60
1985	14.10	11.40	2.70
1986-87	14.30	11.40	2.90
1988-89	15.02	12.12	2.90
1990 and after	15.30	12.40	2.90

What Aged Workers Get

When a person has enough work in covered employment and reaches retirement age (currently age 65 for full benefit, age 62 for reduced benefit), he or she may retire and get monthly old-age benefits. The age at which unreduced benefits are payable will be increased gradually from ages 65 to 67 over a 21-year period beginning with workers age 62 in the year 2000 (reduced benefits will still be available as early as age 62 but with a larger reduction at age 62). If a person age 65 or older continues to work and has earnings of more than $11,280 in 1995, $1 in benefits will be withheld for every $3 above $11,280. The annual exempt amount for people under age 65 is $8,160 in 1995, and $1 in benefits is withheld for every $2 in earnings above the exempt amount for them. The annual exempt amount is raised automatically as the general earnings level rises. The eligible worker who is age 70 or over receives the full benefit regardless of earnings.

For workers who reach age 65 from 1982 through 1989, the worker's benefit is raised by 3% for each year for which the worker between ages 65 and 70 (72 before 1984) did not receive benefits because of earnings from work or because the worker had not applied for benefits. The delayed retirement credit is 1% per year for workers reaching age 65 before 1982. The delayed retirement credit will gradually rise to 8% per year from 1990 through 2008. The rate for workers reaching age 65 in 1992-93 is 4%. The rate for workers reaching age 65 in 1994-95 is 4.5%. The rate for workers reaching age 65 in 1996-97 is 5%.

Effective Dec. 1994, the special benefit for persons aged 72 or over who do not meet the regular coverage requirements is $188.50 a month. Like the monthly benefits, these payments are subject to cost-of-living increases. The special payment is not made to persons on the public assistance or supplemental security income rolls.

Workers retiring before age 65 have their benefits permanently reduced by ⅚ of 1% for each month they receive benefits before age 65. Thus, workers entitled to benefits in the month they reach age 62 receive 80% of the PIA, while a worker retiring at age 65 receives a benefit equal to 100% of the PIA. The nearer to age 65 the worker is when he or she begins collecting a benefit, the larger the benefit will be.

Benefits for Worker's Spouse

The spouse of a worker who is getting Social Security retirement or disability payments may become entitled to a spouse's insurance benefit when he or she reaches 65 of one-half of the worker's PIA. Reduced spouse's benefits are available at age 62 (²⁵⁄₃₆ of 1% reduction for each month of entitlement before age 65). Benefits are also payable to the aged divorced spouse of an insured worker if he or she was married to the worker for at least 10 yrs.

Benefits for Children of Retired or Disabled Workers

If a retired or disabled worker has a child under age 18, the child will get a benefit that is half of the worker's unreduced benefit, and so will the worker's spouse, even if he or she is under age 62 if he or she is caring for an entitled child of the worker who is under age 16 or who became disabled before age 22. Total benefits paid on a worker's earnings record are subject to a maximum, and if the total that would be paid to a family exceeds that maximum, the individual dependents' benefits are adjusted downward. (Total benefits paid to the family of a worker who retired in Jan. 1995 at age 65 and who always had the maximum amount of earnings creditable under Social Security can be no higher than $2,098.20.)

When entitled children reach age 18, their benefits will generally stop, except that a child disabled before age 22 may get a benefit as long as his or her disability meets the definition in the law. Additionally, benefits will be paid to a child until age 19 if the child is in full-time attendance at an elementary or secondary school.

Benefits may also be paid to a grandchild or step-grandchild of a worker or of his or her spouse, in special circumstances.

OASDI	May 1995	May 1994	May 1993
Monthly beneficiaries, total (in thousands)	**43,068**	**42,461**	**41,784**
Aged 65 and over, total	31,137	30,813	30,484
Retired workers	23,943	23,624	23,303
Survivors and dependents .	7,193	7,186	7,178
Special age-72 beneficiaries	1	2	3
Under age 65, total	11,931	11,649	11,300
Retired workers	2,508	2,520	2,529
Disabled workers	4,049	3,823	3,571
Survivors and dependents .	5,374	5,306	5,200
Total monthly benefits (in millions).	**$27,086**	**$25,814**	**$24,623**

What Disabled Workers Get

A worker who becomes so severely disabled that he or she is unable to work may be eligible to receive a monthly disability benefit. Benefits continue until it is determined that the individual is no longer disabled. Each beneficiary's eligibility is reviewed periodically. When a disabled-worker beneficiary reaches age 65, the disability benefit becomes a retired-worker benefit.

Benefits generally like those provided for dependents of retired-worker beneficiaries may be paid to dependents of disabled beneficiaries. However, the maximum family benefit in disability cases is generally lower than in retirement cases.

Survivor Benefits

If an insured worker should die, one or more types of benefits may be payable to survivors, again subject to a maximum family benefit as described above.

1. If claiming benefits at age 65, the surviving spouse will receive a benefit that is 100% of the deceased worker's PIA. The surviving spouse may choose to get the benefit as early as age 60, but the benefit is then reduced by ¹⁹⁄₄₀ of 1% for each month it is paid before age 65. However, for those whose spouses claimed their benefits before age 65, the benefit is limited to the reduced amount the worker would be getting if alive but not less than 82 ½% of the worker's PIA. Marriage after the worker's death ends the surviving spouse's benefit rights. However, if he or she marries and the marriage is ended, he or she regains benefit rights (A marriage after age 60, age 50 if disabled, is deemed not to have occurred for benefit purposes.). This benefit may also be paid to the divorced spouse if the marriage lasted for at least 10 yrs.

Disabled widows and widowers may under certain circumstances qualify for benefits after attaining age 50 at the rate of 71.5% of the deceased worker's PIA. The widow or widower must have become totally disabled before or within 7 yrs. after the spouse's death or the last month in which he or she received mother's or father's insurance benefits.

2. A benefit for each child until the child reaches age 18. The monthly benefit of each child of a worker who has died is three-quarters of the amount the worker would have received if he or she had lived and drawn full retirement benefits. A child with a disability that began before age 22 may receive benefits. Also, a child may receive benefits until age 19 if he or she is in full-time attendance at an elementary or secondary school.

3. A mother's or father's benefit for the widow(er) if children of the worker under age 16 are in his or her care. The benefit is 75% of the PIA, and he or she draws it until the youngest child reaches age 16, at which time payments stop even if the child's benefit continues. If he or she has a disabled child beneficiary age 16 or over in care, benefits may continue.

4. Dependent parents may be eligible for benefits if they have been receiving at least half their support from the worker before his or her death, have reached age 62, and (except in certain circumstances) have not remarried since the worker's death. Each parent gets 75% of the worker's PIA; if only one parent survives the benefit is 82 ½%.

5. A lump sum cash payment of $255. Payment is made only when there is a spouse who was living with the worker or a spouse or child eligible for immediate monthly survivor benefits.

Self-Employed

A self-employed person who has net earnings of $400 or more in a year must report such earnings for Social Security tax and credit purposes. The person reports net returns from the business. Income from real estate, savings, dividends, loans, pensions, or insurance policies may not be included unless it is part of the business.

A self-employed person gets 1 quarter of coverage for each $630 (for 1995), up to a maximum of 4 quarters of coverage.

The nonfarm self-employed have the option of reporting their earnings as ⅔ of their gross income from self-employment but not more than $1,600 a year and not less than their actual net earnings. This option can be used only if actual net earnings from self-employment income are less than $1,600 and may be used only 5 times. Also, the self-employed person must have actual net earnings of $400 or more in 2 of the 3 taxable years immediately preceding the year in which he or she uses the option.

When a person has both taxable wages and earnings from self-employment, the wages are credited for Social Security purposes first; only as much of the self-employment income as will bring total earnings up to the current taxable maximum is subject to the self-employment tax.

Farm Owners and Workers

Self-employed farmers whose gross annual earnings from farming are $2,400 or less may report ⅔ of their gross earnings instead of net earnings for Social Security purposes. Farmers whose gross income is over $2,400 and whose net earnings are less than $1,600 can report $1,600. Cash or crop shares received from a tenant or share farmer count if the owner participated materially in production or management. The self-employed farmer pays contributions at the same rate as other self-employed persons.

Agricultural employees. A worker's earnings from farm work count toward benefits (1) if the employer pays him $150 or more in cash during the year; or (2) if the employer spends $2,500 or more in the year for agricultural labor. Under these rules a person gets credit for 1 calendar quarter for each $630 in cash pay in 1995 up to 4 quarters.

Foreign farm workers admitted to the U.S. on a temporary basis are not covered.

Household Workers

Anyone age 18 or older employed as maid, cook, laundry worker, nurse, babysitter, chauffeur, gardener, or other worker in the house of another is covered by Social Security if he or she is paid $1,000 or more in cash in a calendar year by any one employer. Room and board do not count, but transportation costs count if paid in cash. The job does not have to be regular or full time. The employee should get a Social Security card at the Social Security office and show it to the employer.

The employer deducts the amount of the employee's Social Security tax from the worker's pay, adds an identical amount as the employer's Social Security tax, and sends the total amount to the federal government, with the employee's Social Security number.

Medicare

The Medicare health insurance program provides acute-care coverage for Social Security and Railroad Retirement beneficiaries age 65 and over, for persons entitled for 24 months to receive Social Security disability benefits, and for certain persons with end-stage kidney disease. The Medicare program cost $178 billion in 1995 and served more than 37 million people.

Persons eligible for Medicare may choose to have their covered services provided through a health maintenance organization (HMO).

Hospital insurance. The hospital insurance program pays the cost of covered services for hospital and posthospital care as follows:
- Medicare pays for all necessary inpatient hospital care for the first 60 days of each benefit period, except for a deductible ($716 in 1995). For days 61-90, Medicare pays for covered services except for a coinsurance amount ($179 per day in 1995). After 90 days, the beneficiary has 60 reserve days for which Medicare helps pay. The coinsurance amount for reserve days was $358 in 1995.
- Up to 100 days' care in a skilled-nursing facility (skilled-nursing home) in each benefit period. Hospital insurance pays for all covered services for the first 20 days; for the 21-100th day, the beneficiary pays coinsurance ($89.50 in 1995).
- Visits by nurses or other health workers (not doctors) from a home health agency.
- Hospice care for terminally ill individuals.

Medical insurance. Aged persons can receive benefits under this supplementary program only if they sign up for them and agree to a monthly premium ($46.10 in 1995). The federal government pays the rest of the cost.

The medical insurance program usually pays 80% of the approved amount (after the first $100 in each calendar year) for the following services:
- Covered services received from a doctor in his or her office, in a hospital, in a skilled-nursing facility, at home, or in other locations.
- Medical and surgical services, including anesthesia.
- Diagnostic tests and procedures that are part of the patient's treatment.

- Radiology and pathology services by doctors while the individual is a hospital inpatient or outpatient.
- Treatment of mental illness. Medicare payments for nonhospital treatment are limited; services may be obtained from doctors, comprehensive outpatient rehabilitation facilities (CORFs), physician assistants, psychologists, and clinical social workers.

The services for nonhospital treatment of a mental illness are subject to a special payment rule. In effect, once the annual deductible is met, Medicare pays only 50% (not 80%) of approved charges for these services. On assigned claims, beneficiaries are responsible for paying the remaining 50%. For unassigned claims, beneficiaries may have to pay more.

Partial hospitalization services for treatment of mental illness are not subject to this special payment rule. Also, brief office visits for the sole purpose of monitoring or changing drug prescriptions used in the treatment of mental illness are not subject to this special payment rule.
- Other services such as:
  — X-rays
  — Services of a doctor's office nurse
  — Drugs and biologicals that cannot be self-administered
  — Transfusions of blood and blood components
  — Medical supplies
  — Physical/occupational therapy and speech pathology services.

To get medical insurance protection, persons approaching age 65 may enroll in the 7-month period that includes 3 months before the 65th birthday, the month of the birthday, and 3 months after the birthday, but if they wish coverage to begin in the month they reach age 65, they must enroll in the 3 months before their birthday. Persons not enrolling within their first enrollment period may enroll later, during the first 3 months of each year (coverage begins July 1), but their premium may be 10% higher for each 12-month period elapsed since they first could have enrolled.

The monthly premium is deducted from the cash benefit for persons receiving Social Security, Railroad Retirement, or Civil Service retirement benefits. Income from the medical premiums and the federal matching payments are put in a Supplementary Medical Insurance Trust Fund, from which benefits and administrative expenses are paid.

Medicare card. Persons qualifying for hospital insurance under Social Security receive a health insurance card similar to cards now used by Blue Cross and other health insurers. The card indicates whether the individual has taken out medical insurance protection. It is to be shown to the hospital, skilled-nursing facility, home health agency, doctor, or whoever provides the covered services.

Payments are made only in the 50 states, Puerto Rico, the Virgin Islands, Guam, and American Samoa, except that, in rare cases, inpatient hospital services may be provided in Canada and Mexico.

Social Security Financing

Social Security is paid for by a tax on earnings (for 1995, on earnings up to $61,200 for Old Age, Survivors, and Disability Insurance and on all earnings [no upper limit] for Hospital Insurance with the Medicare Program; the taxable earnings bases have been adjusted annually to reflect increases in average wages). The employed worker and his or her employer share the tax equally.

Employers remit amounts withheld from employee wages for Social Security and income taxes to the Internal Revenue Service; employer Social Security taxes are also payable at the same time. (Self-employed workers pay their Social Security taxes along with their regular income tax forms.) The Social Security taxes (along with revenues arising from partial taxation of the Social Security benefits of certain high-income people) are transferred to the Social Security Trust Funds—the Federal Old-Age and Survivors Insurance (OASI) Trust Fund, the Federal Disability Insurance (DI) Trust Fund, and the Federal Hospital Insurance (HI) Trust Fund; they can be used only to pay benefits, the cost of rehabilitation services, and administrative expenses. Money not immediately needed for these purposes is by law invested in obligations of the federal government, which must pay interest on the money borrowed and must repay the principal when the obligations are redeemed or mature.

Supplemental Security Income

On Jan. 1, 1974, the Supplemental Security Income (SSI) program established by the 1972 Social Security Act amendments replaced the former federal grants to states for aid to the needy aged, blind, and disabled in the 50 states and the District of Columbia. The program provides both for federal payments based on uniform national standards and eligibility requirements and for state supplementary payments varying from state to state. The Social Security Administration administers the federal payments financed from general funds of the Treasury—and the state supplements as well, if the state elects to have its supplementary program federally administered. The states may supplement the federal payment for all recipients and must supplement it for persons otherwise adversely affected by the transition from the former public assistance programs. In May 1995, the number of persons receiving federal payments and federally administered state payments was 6,432,777, and the amount of these payments was $2.3 billion.

The maximum monthly federal SSI payment for individuals with no other countable income, living in their own household, was $458.00 in 1995. For couples it was $687.00.

Examples of monthly cash benefit awards for selected beneficiary families with first entitlement in 1995, effective January 1995

Beneficiary family	Low earnings ($11,171 in 1995)[1]	Average earnings ($24,825 in 1995)[2]	Maximum earnings ($61,200 in 1995)
Primary insurance amount (worker retiring at 65)	$520.00	$858.00	$1,199.00
Maximum family benefit (worker retiring at 65)	780.20	1,564.40	2,098.20
Disability maximum family benefit (worker disabled at 55; in 1994)*	737.80	1,296.40	1,867.00
Disabled worker: (worker disabled at 55)			
Worker alone	524.00	864.00	1,244.00
Worker, spouse, and 1 child	736.00	1,296.00	1,866.00
Retired worker claiming benefits at age 62:			
Worker alone[3]	419.00	691.00	965.00
Worker with spouse claiming benefits at—			
Age 65 or over	681.00	1,123.00	1,568.00
Age 62[3]	615.00	1,015.00	1,417.00
Widow or widower claiming benefits at—			
Age 65 or over[4]	520.00	858.00	1,199.00
Age 60 (spouse died at 65 without receiving reduced benefits)	372.00	614.00	857.00
Disabled widow or widower claiming benefits at age 50-59[5]	372.00	614.00	857.00
1 surviving child	390.00	644.00	899.00
Widow or widower age 65 or over and 1 child[6]	780.00	1,564.00	2,047.00
Widowed mother or father and 1 child[6]	780.00	1,288.00	1,798.00
Widowed mother or father and 2 children[6]	780.00	1,563.00	2,097.00

*Assumes work beginning at age 22. (1) 45% of average. (2) Estimate. (3) Assumes maximum reduction. (4) A widow(er)'s benefit amount is limited to the amount the spouse would have been receiving if still living but not less than 82.5 % of the PIA. (5) Effective Jan. 1984, disabled widow(er)s claiming benefit at ages 50-59 will receive benefit equal to 71.5 % of the PIA (based on 1983 Social Security Amendment provision). (6) Based on worker dying at age 65.

Social Security Trust Funds

Old-Age and Survivors Insurance Trust Fund, 1940-94

(in millions)

Fiscal year[1]	Income Total	Net contributions[2]	Income from taxation of benefits	Payments from the general fund of the Treasury[3]	Net Interest[4]	Disbursements Total	Benefit payments[5]	Administrative expenses	Transfers to Railroad Retirement program	Interfund borrowing transfers[6]	Net Increase in fund	Fund at end of period
1940	$592	$550	—	—	$42	$28	$16	$12	—	—	$564	$1,745
1950	2,367	2,106	—	$4	257	784	727	57	—	—	1,583	12,893
1960	10,360	9,843	—	—	517	11,073	10,270	202	$600	—	–713	20,829
1970	31,746	29,955	—	442	1,350	27,321	26,268	474	579	—	4,425	32,616
1980	100,051	97,608	—	557	1,886	103,228	100,626	1,160	1,442	—	–3,177	24,566
1985	179,881	175,305	$3,151	105	1,321	169,210	165,310	1,589	2,310	$–4,364	6,308	33,877
1990	278,607	261,506	2,924	34	14,143	218,948	218,948	1,564	2,969	—	55,126	203,445
1991	293,288	270,841	5,790	–2,089	18,746	241,316	236,195	1,746	3,375	—	51,972	255,417
1992	307,102	278,506	6,019	19	22,557	256,239	251,268	1,823	3,148	—	50,862	306,280
1993	319,298	287,569	5,893	14	25,822	269,934	264,561	2,021	3,353	—	49,364	355,644
1994	342,263	308,397	5,351	10	28,505	281,572	276,278	1,874	3,420	—	50,691	415,335

(1) Under the Congressional Budget Act of 1974 (PL 93-344), fiscal years 1977 and later consist of the 12 mos. ending on Sept. 30 of each year. Fiscal years prior to 1977 consisted of the 12 mos. ending on June 30 of each year. (2) Beginning in 1983, includes transfers from general fund of Treasury representing contributions that would have been paid on deemed wage credits for military service in 1957 and later, if such credits were considered covered wages. (3) Includes payments (a) in 1947-52 and in 1967 and later, for costs of noncontributory wage credits for military service performed before 1957; (b) in 1972-83, for costs of deemed wage credits for military service performed after 1956; and (c) in 1969 and later, for costs of benefits to certain uninsured persons who attained age 72 before 1968. (4) Net interest includes net profits or losses on marketable investments. Beginning in 1967, administrative expenses are charged currently to the trust fund on an estimated basis, with a final adjustment, including interest, made in the following fiscal year. The amounts of these interest adjustments are included in net interest. For years prior to 1967, a description of the method of accounting for administrative expenses is contained in the 1970 Annual Report. Beginning in Oct. 1973, the figures shown include relatively small amounts of gifts to the fund. Figures for 1983-86 reflect payments from a borrowing trust fund to a lending trust fund for interest on amounts owed under the interfund borrowing provisions. During 1983-91, interest paid from the trust fund to the general fund on advance tax transfers is reflected. The amounts shown for 1985 and 1986 include interest adjustments of $76.5 mln. and $11.5 mln., respectively, on unnegotiated checks issued before Apr. 1985. (5) Beginning in 1967, includes payments for vocational rehabilitation services furnished to disabled persons receiving benefits because of their disabilities. Beginning in 1983, amounts are reduced by amount of reimbursement for unnegotiated benefit checks. (6) Negative figures represent amounts repaid from the OASI Trust Fund to the DI and HI Trust Funds.

Disability Insurance Trust Fund, 1960-94

(in millions)

Fiscal year[1]	Income					Disbursements				Interfund borrowing transfers[6]	Net Increase in fund	Fund at end of period
	Total	Net contributions[2]	Income from taxation of benefits	Payments from the general fund of the Treasury[3]	Net Interest[4]	Total	Benefit payments[5]	Administrative expenses	Transfers to Railroad Retirement program			
1960	$1,034	$987	—	—	$47	$533	$528	$32	-$27	—	$501	$2,167
1970	4,380	4,141	—	$16	223	2,954	2,795	149	10	—	1,426	5,104
1980	17,376	16,805	—	118	453	15,320	14,998	334	-12	—	2,056	7,680
1985	17,984	16,876	$217	—	891	19,294	18,648	603	43	$2,540	1,230	5,873
1990	28,215	27,291	158	—	766	25,124	24,327	717	80	—	3,091	11,455
1991	29,322	28,953	131	-775	1,014	27,780	26,909	789	82	—	1,543	12,997
1992	31,168	29,871	218	—	1,080	31,285	30,382	845	58	—	-116	12,881
1993	32,056	30,822	268	—	966	34,632	33,615	935	83	—	-2,576	10,305
1994	34,044	33,041	305	—	699	37,979	36,851	1,022	106	—	-3,935	6,370

(1) Under the Congressional Budget Act of 1974 (PL 93-344, fiscal years 1977 and later consist of the 12 mos. ending on Sept. 30 of each year. The act further provides that the calendar quarter Jul.-Sept. 1976 is a period of transition from fiscal year 1976, which ended on Jun. 30, 1976, to fiscal year 1977, which began on Oct. 1, 1976. (2) Beginning in 1983, includes government contributions on deemed wage credits for military service in 1957 and later. (3) Includes payments (a) in 1967 and later, for costs of noncontributory wage credits for military service performed before 1957; and (b) in 1972-83, for costs of deemed wage credits for military service performed after 1956. (4) Net interest includes net profits or losses on marketable investments. Beginning in 1967, administrative expenses are charged currently to the trust fund on an estimated basis, with a final adjustment, including interest, made in the following fiscal year. The amounts of these interest adjustments are included in net interest. For years prior to 1967, a description of the method of accounting for administrative expenses is contained in the 1970 Annual Report of the Board of Trustees of the Federal Old-Age and Survivors Insurance and Disability Insurance Trust Funds. Beginning in 1983, these figures reflect payments from a borrowing trust fund to a lending trust fund for interest on amounts owed under the interfund borrowing provisions. Also, beginning in 1983, interest paid from the trust fund to the general fund on advance tax transfers is reflected. The amount shown for 1985 includes an interest adjustment of $14.8 mln. on unnegotiated checks issued before Apr. 1985. (5) Beginning in 1967, includes payments for vocational rehabilitation services furnished to disabled persons receiving benefits because of their disabilities. Beginning in 1983, amounts are reduced by amount of reimbursement for unnegotiated benefit checks. The amount shown for 1983 is reduced by $48 mln. for all unnegotiated checks issued before 1983; reductions in subsequent years are relatively small. (6) Negative figure represents amounts lent by the DI Trust Fund to the OASI Trust Fund. Positive figures represent repayment of these amounts.

Supplementary Medical Insurance Trust Fund, 1970-94

(in millions)

Fiscal year[1]	Income				Disbursements			Balance in fund at end of year[5]
	Premium from participants	Government contributions[2]	Interest and other income[3]	Total Income	Benefit payments[4]	Administrative expenses	Total disbursements	
1970	$936	$928	$12	$1,876	$1,979	$217	$2,196	$57
1975	1,887	2,330	105	4,322	3,765	405	4,170	1,424
1980	2,928	6,932	415	10,275	10,144	593	10,737	4,532
1985	5,524	17,898	1,155	24,577	21,808	922	22,730	10,646
1990	11,494[5]	33,210	1,434[5]	46,138[5]	41,498	1,524[5]	43,022[5]	14,527[5]
1991	11,807	34,730	1,629	48,166	45,514	1,505	47,019	15,675
1992	12,748	38,684	1,717	53,149	48,627	1,661	50,288	18,535
1993	14,683	44,227	1,889	60,799	54,214[6]	1,845	56,059	23,276
1994	16,895	38,355	2,118	57,368	58,006	1,718	59,724	20,919

(1) For 1967 through 1976, fiscal years cover the interval from Jul. 1 through Jun. 30; fiscal years 1977 and later cover the interval from Oct. 1 through Sept. 30. (2) The payments shown as being from the general fund of the Treasury include certain interest-adjustment items. (3) Other income includes recoveries of amounts reimbursed from the trust fund that are not obligations of the trust fund and other miscellaneous income. (4) Includes the impact of the Medicare Catastrophic Coverage Act of 1988 (PL 100-360). (5) The financial status of the program depends on both the total net assets and the liabilities of the program. (6) Includes $1,805 mln. transfer to the HI trust fund, as provided for by PL 102-394.

Hospital Insurance Trust Fund, 1970-94

(in millions)

Fiscal year[1]	Income								Disbursements			Net increase in fund	Fund at end of year
	Payroll taxes	Income from taxation of benefits	Transfers from railroad retirement acct.	Reimbursement for uninsured persons	Premiums from voluntary enrollees	Pymts. or military wage credits	Interest on investments and other income[2]	Total income	Benefit pymts.[3]	Administrative expense[4]	Total disbursements		
1970	$4,785	—	$64	$617	—	$11	$137	$5,614	$4,804	$149	$4,953	$661	$2,677
1975	11,291	—	132	481	$6	48	609	12,568	10,353	259	10,612	1,956	9,870
1980	23,244	—	244	697	17	141	1,072	25,415	23,790	497	24,288	1,127	14,490
1985	46,490	—	371	766	38	86	3,182	50,933	47,841	813	48,654	4,103[5]	21,277[5]
1990	70,655	—	367	413	113	107	7,908	79,563	65,912	774	66,687	12,876	95,631
1991	74,655	—	352	605	367	-1,011[6]	8,969	83,938	68,705	934	69,638	14,299	109,930
1992	80,978	—	374	621	484	86	10,133	92,677	80,784	1,191	81,974	10,703	120,633
1993	83,147	—	400	367	622	81	12,484[7]	97,101	90,738	866	91,604	5,497	126,131
1994	92,028	$1,639	413	506	852	80	10,676	106,195	101,535	1,235	102,770	3,425	129,555

(1) Fiscal years 1976 and earlier consist of the 12 mos. ending on Jun. 30 of each year; fiscal years 1977 and later consist of the 12 mos. ending on Sept. 30 of each year. (2) Other income includes recoveries of amounts reimbursed from the trust fund that are not obligations of the trust fund and a small amount of miscellaneous income. (3) Includes costs of Peer Review Organizations (beginning with the implementation of the Prospective Payment System on Oct. 1, 1983). (4) Includes costs of experiments and demonstration projects. (5) In fiscal year 1983, $12,437 mln. was loaned to the Old-Age and Survivors Insurance Trust Fund under the interfund borrowing provisions of the Social Security Act. Repayments of $1,824 mln. and $10,613 mln. were made in fiscal years 1985 and 1986, respectively. (6) Includes the lump sum general revenue adjustment of $-1,100 mln., as provided for by section 151 of PL 98-21. (7) Includes $1,805 mln. transfer from the SMI catastrophic coverage reserve fund, as provided for by PL 102-394.   NOTE: Totals do not necessarily equal the sum of rounded components.

CONSUMER INFORMATION

Consumer Information Catalog

Source: Consumer Information Center, U.S. General Services Administration

The *Consumer Information Catalog* is a free listing of more than 200 of the best federal consumer publications. They range from booklets on financial planning to planning a diet, from learning about federal benefits to getting an education, from fixing a car to dealing effectively with consumer problems. Many of these booklets are free.

The *Consumer Information Catalog* is published quarterly by the Consumer Information Center (CIC) of the U.S. General Services Administration. For a free copy of the most current *Consumer Information Catalog,* send your name and address to Consumer Information Center, Pueblo, CO 81009. You can also order a copy of the catalog by phone at 719-948-4000 or by fax at 719-948-9724. Educators, librarians, and members of nonprofit groups who are able to distribute 25 or more copies of the *Consumer Information Catalog* on a quarterly basis should write to the same address for an application to be placed on the mailing list. Costs prevent the Consumer Information Center from maintaining a mailing list for individuals.

Publications listed in the *Consumer Information Catalog* are available online, along with other consumer news, updates, and information. Use your modem or Internet connection to access the Consumer Information Center electronically. Electronic BBS: 202-208-7679; Internet World Wide Web: http://www.gsa.gov/staff/pa/cic/cic.htm

For detailed instructions on connecting to CIC, send e-mail to catalog.pueblo@gsa.gov with the words "SEND INFO" in the body of the message.

The free and low-cost booklets listed below are from the *Consumer Information Catalog* and are available as of fall 1994. Quantities of some may be limited. The handling fee is $1.00. To order, send your name and address, the item numbers of the booklets you want, and the $1.00 fee to: S. James, Consumer Information Center, Pueblo, CO 81009.

At-Home Shopping—Consumer Tips and Rights

Source: Consumer Information Catalog; U.S. Postal Service; U.S. Office of Consumer Affairs

Tips

• Deal only with reliable firms. Check with your local consumer protection agency or the Better Business Bureau (BBB) nearest the business.

• Review the advertising offer carefully.

• If not stated, inquire about warranty, refund, and exchange policies.

• Never send cash. Pay by money order, check, charge, or credit card so that you have a record of your purchase.

• Keep the ad you responded to and a copy of the order form. If there is no order form, record the company's name, address, phone number, date, the item you purchased, amount paid, and the promised delivery date.

• Never give your credit, debit, charge card or bank account number unless you have checked out the company or have done business with it before.

Rights

Late deliveries, delays, canceled orders. By federal law, a company must ship your order within 30 days, unless the advertisement promises a different shipping time. If the company cannot ship within 30 days or the promised time, it must give you an "Option Notice." You can choose to wait longer for your order or to cancel and get a prompt refund. If you cancel and if your order was paid by charge or credit card, the seller has one billing cycle to tell the card issuer to credit your account.

The following are exceptions to this rule:

(1) If a company does not promise a shipping time and if you are applying for credit to pay for your purchase, the company has 50 days after receiving your order to ship.

(2) Spaced deliveries, such as magazine subscriptions (except for 1st shipment), and items that continue until you cancel (for example, book or record clubs), cash on delivery (COD) orders, services, and seeds or growing plants.

Unordered merchandise. If you are shipped a product that you did not order, it's yours. It is illegal for a company to pressure you to pay for it or to return it.

Damaged or spoiled items. If damage is obvious, and if you decide not to accept the package, write "REFUSED" on the wrapper (at time of delivery) and return it unopened to the seller. No new postage is needed, unless the package came by insured, registered, certified, or COD mail and you signed for it.

Disputes or billing errors. If there is a problem with your order—you were billed the wrong amount, you never got the product, the goods arrived in damaged condition, or the merchandise or services were misrepresented—follow these steps:

(1) Write immediately to the company from whom you ordered, explaining the problem and asking for a specific resolution. Be sure to include your name, address, and daytime phone number, your order or invoice number, a copy of the canceled check, or any other helpful information about your purchase.

(2) If you charged your purchase to a charge or credit card account or if you arranged for the payment to be automatically withdrawn from a bank account, send a copy of your letter to the card issuer or bank.

You usually have 60 days after receiving a bill to dispute charges.

Postal regulations allow you to write a check payable to the sender, rather than the delivery company, on COD orders. If, after examining the merchandise, you feel there has been misrepresentation or fraud, you can stop payment on the check and file a complaint with the U.S. Postal Inspector's Office.

For other at-home shopping questions, contact Direct Marketing Assn. (Mail Order Action Line), 1101 17th St. NW, Ste. 705, Washington, DC 20036; 202-347-1222.

Charitable Giving in the U.S., 1984-94, by Sources of Contributions

Source: American Assn. of Fund-Raising Counsel, Inc., AAFRC Trust for Philanthropy

(in billions of inflation-adjusted dollars)

Year	Corporations	Foundations	Bequests	Individuals	Total
1984	$6.84	$6.25	$6.39	$89.34	$108.83
1985	7.24	7.36	7.17	88.12	109.88
1986	7.30	7.74	8.12	96.39	119.55
1987	7.49	8.02	8.98	98.64	123.13
1988	7.30	7.98	8.53	103.92	127.72
1989	7.11	8.08	8.60	108.22	132.00
1990	6.86	8.45	8.93	106.53	130.77
1991	6.68	8.60	8.66	107.00	130.94
1992	6.33	9.23	8.71	104.64	128.90
1993	6.24	9.82	8.80	104.29	129.16
1994	6.11	9.91	8.77	105.09	129.88

Charitable Giving in the U.S., 1994, by Uses of Contributions

Source: American Assn. of Fund-Raising Counsel, Inc., AAFRC Trust for Philanthropy

(in billions of dollars)

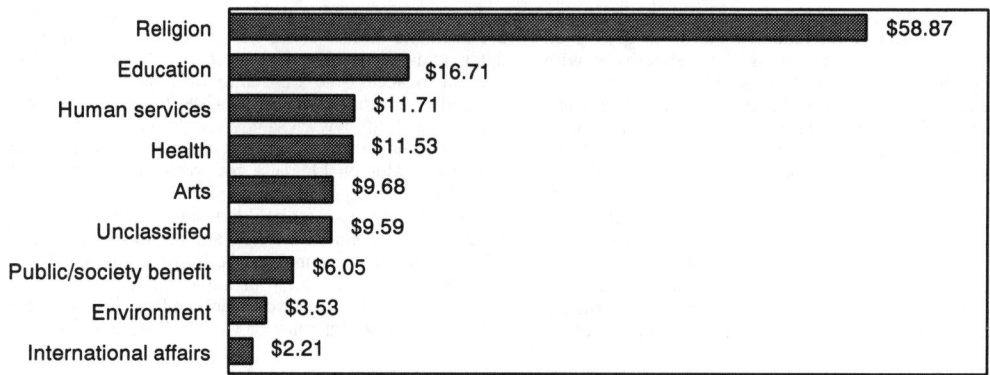

Religion	$58.87
Education	$16.71
Human services	$11.71
Health	$11.53
Arts	$9.68
Unclassified	$9.59
Public/society benefit	$6.05
Environment	$3.53
International affairs	$2.21

Business Directory

Listed below are major U.S. corporations whose operations—products and services—directly concern the American consumer. At the end of each listing is a **representative sample** of the company's products.

Company...Address...Phone number...Top executive ...Business.

Abbott Laboratories...One Abbott Park Rd., North Chicago, IL 60064...(708) 937-6100...D. L. Burnham...health care prods.

Aetna Life & Casualty Co....151 Farmington Ave., Hartford, CT 06156...(203) 273-0123...Ronald E. Compton...insurance, financial services.

H. F. Ahmanson & Co....4900 Rivergrade Rd., Irwindale, CA 91706...(818) 814-7986...R. H. Deihl...operates largest S&L assn. in U.S. (Home Savings of America).

Alberto Culver Co....2525 Armitage Ave., Melrose Park, IL 60160...(708) 450-3000...Leonard H. Lavin...hair care preparations, feminine hygiene products, household and grocery items.

Albertson's Inc....250 Parkcenter Blvd., Boise, ID 83726 ...(208) 385-6200...Gary Michael...supermarkets.

Alexander & Alexander Services Inc....1211 Ave. of the Americas, NY, NY 10036...(212) 840-8500...Frank Zarb...insurance & financial services.

AlliedSignal...Morristown, NJ 07960...(201) 455-2000...Lawrence Bossidy...aerospace, engineered materials, automotive prods.

Aluminum Co. of America (Alcoa)...425 6th Ave., Pittsburgh, PA 15219...(412) 553-4545...Paul O'Neill...mining, refining, & processing of aluminum.

Amerada Hess Corp....1185 Ave. of the Americas, NY, NY 10036...(212) 997-8500...J. B. Hess...integrated petroleum co.

American Brands, Inc....1700 E. Putnam Ave., Old Greenwich, CT 06870...(203) 698-5000...Thomas C. Hays...tobacco, whiskey (Jim Beam), hardware, office prods., golf and leisure products.

American Express Co....200 Vesey St., NY, NY 10285...(212) 640-2000...H. Golub...travelers' checks, credit card services, insurance, investment services.

American Greetings Corp....1 American Rd., Cleveland, OH 44144...(216) 252-7300...Morry Weiss...greeting cards, stationery, gift items.

American Home Products Corp....5 Giralda Farms, Madison, NJ 07940...(201) 660-5000...J. R. Stafford...prescription and over-the-counter drugs (Advil, Anacin, Robitussin), food (Chef Boy-ar-dee).

American Intl. Group...70 Pine St., NY, NY 10270...(212) 770-7000...M. R. Greenberg...insurance, financial services.

American Stores Co....709 E. South Temple, Salt Lake City, UT 84102...(801) 539-0112...Victor Lund ...retail food markets, dept. & drug stores.

Amoco Corp....200 E. Randolph Dr., Chicago, IL 60601...(312) 856-6111...H. L. Fuller...integrated petroleum co.

AMR Corp....PO Box 619616, Dallas/Ft. Worth Airport, TX 75261...(817) 963-1234...Robert Crandall...air transportation (American Airlines).

Anheuser-Busch Cos., Inc....One Busch Place, St. Louis, MO 63118...(314) 577-2000...August A. Busch 3d...brewing (Budweiser, Michelob, Bud Light, Natural Light, Busch), theme parks, snack foods (Eagle).

Apple Computer, Inc....1 Infinite Loop, Cupertino, CA 95014...(408) 996-1010...A. C. Markkula...manuf. personal computers.

Archer Daniels Midland Company...4666 Faires Pkwy., Decatur, IL 62526...(217) 424-5200...Dwayne Andreas...agricultural commodities.

Armstrong World Industries, Inc....PO Box 3001, 313 W. Liberty St., Lancaster, PA 17604...(717) 397-0611...George Lorch...interior furnishings, specialty prods.

Arvin Industries, Inc....1531 13th St., Columbus, IN 47201...(812) 379-3000...J. K. Baker...auto emission & noise control systems.

Ashland Oil, Inc....PO Box 391, Ashland, KY 41101...(606) 329-3333...John R. Hall...petroleum producer and refiner, chemicals, road construction.

Atlantic Richfield Co....515 S. Flower St., Los Angeles, CA 90071-2256...(213) 486-3511...M. R. Bowlin...integrated oil co.

AT&T Corp....32 Ave. of the Americas, NY, NY 10013-2412...(212) 387-5400...Robert Allen...communications, financial services (Co. announced 9/20/95 plans to split into 3 separate cos. handling, respectively, [1] phone service; [2] communications hardware; [3] computer systems.).

Avon Products, Inc....9 West 57th St., NY, NY 10019...(212) 546-6015...James E. Preston...cosmetics, fragrances, toiletries, fashion jewelry, casual apparel, lingerie.

Bally Entertainment Corp....8700 W. Bryn Mawr Ave., Chicago, IL 60631...(312) 399-1300...Arthur M. Goldberg...casino-hotel operator.

BankAmerica Corp....PO Box 37000, San Francisco, CA 94137...(415) 622-3456...R. M. Rosenberg...owns banks.

Bausch & Lomb...One Chase Square, Rochester, NY 14601...(716) 338-6000...Daniel E. Gill...manuf. of vision care products, accessories.

Baxter International Inc....One Baxter Pkwy., Deerfield, IL 60015...(708) 948-2000...Vernon R. Loucks, Jr....health care prods. & services.

Bell Atlantic Corp....1717 Arch St., Philadelphia, PA 19103...(215) 963-6000...Raymond W. Smith...telephone service in mid-Atlantic region.

BellSouth Corp....1155 Peachtree St. NE, Atlanta, GA 30367...(404) 249-2000...John L. Clendenin...telephone service in the South.

Bethlehem Steel Corp....Bethlehem, PA 18016...(215) 694-2424...Curtis H. Barnette...steel & steel prods.

Bic Corporation...500 Bic Dr., Milford, CT 06460...(203) 783-2070...Bruno Bich...writing instruments, disposable lighters, shavers, and correction fluid (wite•out).

Black & Decker Corp....701 E. Joppa Rd., Towson, MD 21204...(410) 716-3900...Nolan D. Archibald...manuf. power tools, household prods., small appliances.

H & R Block, Inc....4410 Main St., Kansas City, MO 64111...(816) 753-6900...Richard H. Brown...tax preparation.

Boeing Company...7755 E. Marginal Way, Seattle, WA 98108...(206) 655-2121...Frank A. Shrontz...aircraft manuf.

Boise Cascade Corp....One Jefferson Square, Boise, ID 83728...(208) 384-6161...George J. Harad...timber, paper, wood prods.

Borden, Inc....180 E. Broad St., Columbus OH 43215-3799...(614) 225-4000...C. Robert Kidder...food, cheese and cheese products, snacks (Cracker Jack), beverages, adhesives (Elmer's, Krazy Glue), pasta (Prince, Creamette), pasta sauce (Aunt Millie's, Classico).

Bristol-Myers Squibb Co....345 Park Ave., NY, NY 10022...(212) 546-4000...Charles A. Heimhold...toiletries (Ban antiperspirant), hair items (Clairol), drugs (Bufferin, Comtrex, Excedrin), infant formula (Enfamil).

Brown-Forman Corp....PO Box 1080, Louisville, KY 40201...(502) 585-1100...Owsley Brown 2d...distilled spirits (Jack Daniel's, Early Times), wines (Bolla, Fontina Candida), champagne (Korbel), liquor (Southern Comfort), Lenox china and crystal.

Brown Group, Inc....8400 Maryland Ave., St. Louis, MO 63105...(314) 854-4000...B. A. Bridgewater, Jr....manuf. and wholesaler of women's, men's, and children's shoes (Buster Brown, Naturalizer); specialty retailing.

Brunswick Corp....One N. Field Ct., Lake Forest, IL 60045-4811...(708) 735-4700...J. F. Reichert...marine, recreation prods., bowling centers & equip., fishing equip.

Burlington Northern Santa Fe Corp....777 Main St., Ft. Worth, TX 76102...(817) 333-2000...Gerald Grinstein...largest U.S. rail transportation co.

Campbell Soup Co....Campbell Pl., Camden, NJ 08103...(609) 342-4800...D. W. Johnson...canned soups, spaghetti (Franco-American), vegetable juice (V-8), pork and beans, pet foods, confections, Swanson frozen dinners, Prego spaghetti sauce, Mrs. Paul's frozen fish, Pepperidge Farm breads.

Capital Cities/ABC, Inc....77 W. 66th St., NY, NY 10023...(212) 456-7777...T. S. Murphy...operates television and radio stations, cable TV (ESPN); newspapers, specialized business and consumer periodicals. (Co. announced 7/31/95 that it had agreed to be acquired by the Walt Disney Co.)

Carter-Wallace, Inc....1345 Ave. of the Americas, NY, NY 10105...(212) 339-5000...H. H. Hoyt, Jr....personal care items, antiperspirant (Arrid), shave lathers (Rise), tooth polish (Pearl Drops), condoms (Trojan), laxative (Carter's Pills), pet prods. (Victory flea collars).

Caterpillar Inc....100 N.E. Adams St., Peoria, IL 61629...(309) 675-1000...Donald Fites...heavy duty earth-moving equip.

CBS Inc....51 W. 52d St., NY, NY 10019...(212) 975-4321...L. A. Tisch...broadcasting. (Co. announced 8/1/95 that it had agreed to be acquired by Westinghouse Electric Corp.)

Chase Manhattan Corp....1 Chase Manhattan Plaza, NY, NY 10081...(212) 552-2222...Thomas Labrecque ...bank holding co. (Co. announced 8/28/95 that it had agreed to merge with Chemical Banking Corp., a move that would make Chase the largest U.S. bank holding co.)

Chevron Corp....225 Bush St., San Francisco, CA 94104...(415) 894-7700...K. T. Derr...integrated oil co.

Chrysler Corp....Highland Pk., MI 48288...(313) 956-3007...Robert J. Eaton...cars, trucks.

Church & Dwight Co., Inc....469 N. Harrison St., Princeton, NJ 08543...(609) 683-5900...D. C. Minton...sodium bicarbonate, consumer prods. (Arm & Hammer).

CIGNA Corp....1 Liberty Pl., Philadelphia, PA 19103...(215) 761-1000...Wilson H. Taylor...insurance holding co.

Circuit City Stores, Inc....9950 Maryland Dr., Richmond, VA 23233-1464...(804) 527-4000...R. L. Sharp...retailer of electronic equip., consumer appliances.

Circus Circus Enterprises, Inc....2880 Las Vegas Blvd. S, Las Vegas, NV 89109...(702) 734-0410...Clyde Turner...casino operator.

Citicorp...399 Park Ave., NY, NY 10043...(212) 559-1000...J. S. Reed...largest U.S. commercial bank.

Clayton Homes...PO Box 15169, Knoxville, TN 37901...(615) 970-7200...J. L. Clayton...produces & sells manufactured homes.

Clorox Co....1221 Broadway, Oakland, CA 94612...(510) 271-7000...G. C. Sullivan...retail consumer prods. (Formula 409, Pine-Sol, Kingsford charcoal briquets, Combat insecticides, Hidden Valley Ranch salad dressing, Soft Scrub cleanser).

Coachman Industries Inc....601 E. Beardsley Ave., Elkhart, IN 46514...(219) 262-0123...T. H. Corson...manuf. recreational vehicles.

Coastal Corp....9 Greenway Plaza, Houston, TX 77046...(713) 877-1400...O. S. Wyatt...oil refineries, natural gas pipeline systems.

Coca-Cola Co....One Coca-Cola Plaza N.W., Atlanta, GA 30313...(404) 676-2121...R. C. Goizueta...soft drinks (Coca-Cola, Sprite, Nestea), syrups, citrus and fruit juices (Minute Maid, Hi-C).

Colgate-Palmolive Co....300 Park Ave., NY, NY 10022...(212) 310-2000...R. Mark...soaps (Palmolive, Irish Spring), detergents (Fab, Ajax, Fresh Start), toothpaste (Colgate, Ultra Brite), household prods. (Handy Wipes, Curad bandages), pet food, crystal.

Columbia/HCA Healthcare Corp....1 Park Plaza, Nashville, TN 37203...(615) 327-9551...T. F. Frist Jr....largest hospital mgmt. co. in the U.S.

Compaq Computer Corp....20555 SH 249, Houston, TX 77070...(713) 370-0670...Benjamin M. Rosen...portable and desktop computers.

ConAgra...1 ConAgra Dr., Omaha, NE 68102...(402) 595-4000...Philip Fletcher...food processor.

Adolph Coors Co....Golden, CO 80401...(303) 279-6565...W. K. Coors...brewery.

Corning, Inc....One Riverfront Plaza, Corning, NY 14831...(607) 974-9000...J. R. Houghton ...glass mfg.

CPC International, Inc....International Plaza, Englewood Cliffs, NJ 07632...(201) 894-4000...Charles Shoemate...branded food items (Hellmann's mayonnaise, Best Foods, Mazola corn oil, Skippy peanut butter, Knorr soups, Thomas' English muffins, Mueller pasta prods., Arnold breads).

Crane Co....100 First Stamford Place, Stamford, CT 06902...(203) 363-7300...R. S. Evans...manuf. fluid control devices, vending machines, fiberglass panels, aircraft brakes.

A. T. Cross Co....One Albion Rd., Lincoln, RI 02865...(401) 333-1200...Bradford R. Boss...writing instruments.

CSX Corp....901 E. Cary St., Richmond, VA 23219...(804)782-1400...John W. Snow...rail freight transportation.

Culbro Corp....387 Park Ave. S, NY, NY 10016...(212) 561-8700...E. M. Cullman...cigars (Corina, Robert Burns, White Owl, Tiparillo's); food, industrial, nursery prods.

Dana Corp....4500 Dorr St., Toledo, OH 43615...(419) 535-4500...S. J. Morcott...truck and auto parts supplies.

Dayton Hudson Corp....777 Nicollet Mall, Minneapolis, MN 55402...(612) 370-6948...Robert J. Ulrich...department, specialty stores.

Deere & Co....John Deere Rd., Moline, IL 61265...(309) 765-8000...Hans W. Becherer...farm, industrial, and outdoor power equip.

Delta Air Lines, Inc....Hartsfield Atlanta Intl. Airport, Atlanta, GA 30320...(404) 715-2600...Ronald W. Allen...air transportation.

Dial Corp....Dial Tower, Phoenix, AZ 85077-2346...(602) 207-4000...J. W. Teets...consumer prods. (Dial, Purex detergents, Armour Star meats, Breck shampoo); contract and fast food services.

Diebold, Inc....PO Box 8230, Canton, OH 44711...(216) 489-4000...R. W. Mahoney...manuf. equip. for financial insts.

Digital Equipment Corp....146 Main St., Maynard, MA 01754-2571...(508) 493-5111...R. B. Palmer...computer systems manuf.

Walt Disney Co....500 S. Buena Vista St., Burbank, CA 91521-7320...(818) 560-1000...M. D. Eisner...motion pictures, cable television, theme parks (Walt Disney World, Disneyland) and resorts, publishing, recordings, retailing (Disney stores). (Co. announced 7/31/95 that it had agreed to acquire Capital Cities/ABC, Inc.)

Dole Food Co....31355 Oak Crest Drive, Westlake Village, CA 91361...(818) 879-6600...David Murdock...food products, fresh fruits and vegetables, real estate.

R. R. Donnelley & Sons Co....77 W. Wacker Dr., Chicago, IL 60601-8375...(312) 326-8000...J. R. Walter...largest commercial printer.

Dow Chemical Co....2030 Dow Center, Midland, MI 48674...(517) 636-1000...F. Popoff...chemicals, plastics, consumer prods. (Ziploc, Saran Wrap, Fantastik).

Dow Jones & Co....200 Liberty St., NY, NY 10281...(212) 416-2000...P. R. Kann...financial news service, publishing (*Wall Street Journal, Barron's*, Ottaway Newspapers).

Dun & Bradstreet Corp....187 Danbury Rd., Wilton, CT 06897...(203) 834-4200...C. W. Moritz...business information and computer services, publishing.

E. I. duPont de Nemours & Co....1007 Market St., Wilmington, DE 19898...(302) 774-1000...Edgar Woolard, Jr....chemicals, petroleum, consumer prods.

Duracell Intl. Inc....Berkshire Industrial Park, Bethel, CT 06801...(203) 796-4000...C. R. Kidder...manuf. batteries.

Eastman Kodak Co....343 State St., Rochester, NY 14650...(716) 724-5492...G. Fisher...photographic prods., information systems.

Eaton Corp....1111 Superior Ave., Cleveland, OH 44114...(216) 523-5000...W. E. Butler...manuf. of electronic, electrical prods., vehicle components.

Emerson Electric Co....8000 W. Florissant Ave., St. Louis, MO 63136...(314) 553-2000...C. F. Knight...electrical, electronics products & systems.

Ethyl Corp....330 S. 4th St., Richmond, VA 23217...(804) 788-5000...Bruce C. Gottwald...petroleum and industrial chemicals.

Exxon Corp....225 E. John W. Carpenter Freeway, Irving, TX 75062-2298...(214) 444-1900...L. R. Raymond...world's largest publicly-owned integrated oil co.

Fabri-Centers of America, Inc....5555 Darrow Rd., Hudson, OH 44236...(216) 656-2600...Alan Rosskamm...specialty fabric stores.

Fedders Corp....PO Box 813, Liberty Corner, NJ 07938...(908) 604-8686...S. Giordano...manuf. of room air conditioners, dehumidifiers.

Federal Express Corp....Box 727, Memphis, TN 38194 ...(901) 369-3600...F. W. Smith...express delivery service.

Federal National Mortgage Assn....3900 Wisconsin Ave. NW, Washington, DC 20016-2899...(202) 752-7115...J. A. Johnson...credit agency.

Federated Dept. Stores...7 W. 7th St., Cincinnati, OH 45202...(513) 579-7000...A. Questrom...Macy's, Bloomingdale's, Stern's.

Fieldcrest Cannon, Inc....Eden, NC 27288...(919) 627-3000...J. M. Fitzgibbons...household textile prods.

First Brands Corp....83 Wooster Hts. Rd., Danbury, CT 06813-1911...(203) 731-2300...A. E. Dudley...consumer prods. (Glad plastic bags, Scoop-Away cat litter, STP auto prods.).

Fleetwood Enterprises, Inc....PO Box 7638, Riverside, CA 92523...(909) 351-3500...John C. Crean...manufactured homes, recreational vehicles.

Fleming Cos., Inc....6301 Waterford Blvd., PO Box 26647, Oklahoma City, OK 73126...(405) 840-7200...Robert E. Stauth...largest U.S. wholesale food distrib.

Fluor Corp....3333 Michelson Dr., Irvine, CA 92730...(714) 975-6961...L. G. McCraw...engineering and construction.

Ford Motor Co....American Rd., Dearborn, MI 48121...(313) 845-8540...Alexander Trotman...motor vehicles (Ford Tractor, Lincoln-Mercury).

Fruit of the Loom, Inc....5000 Sears Tower, Chicago, IL 60606...(312) 876-1724...W. Farley...manuf. of underwear.

Gannett Co., Inc....1100 Wilson Blvd., Arlington, VA 22234...(703) 284-6000...J. J. Curley...newspaper publishing (USA Today), TV and radio stations, outdoor advertising.

The Gap, Inc....1 Harrison, San Francisco, CA 94105...(415) 952-4400...D. G. Fisher...casual and activewear retailer.

GenCorp...175 Ghent Rd., Fairlawn, OH 44333-3300...(216) 869-4200...J. B. Yasinsky...aerospace, auto prods., polymer prods.

General Dynamics Corp....3190 Fairview Park Dr., Falls Church, VA 22042-4523...(703) 876-3000...J. R. Mellor...nuclear submarines, armored vehicles.

General Electric Co....3135 Easton Tpke., Fairfield, CT 06431...(203) 373-2211...J. F. Welch, Jr....electrical, electronic equip., radio and television broadcasting (NBC), aircraft engines, power generation.

General Host Corp....22 Gate House Rd., Stamford, CT 06904...(203) 357-9900...H. J. Ashton...crafts, lawn and garden retail stores (Frank's Nursery & Crafts).

General Mills, Inc....PO Box 1113, Minneapolis, MN 55440...(612) 540-2444...S. W. Sanger...foods (Total, Bisquick, Wheaties, Cheerios, Hamburger Helper, Betty Crocker).

General Motors Corp....3044 W. Grand Blvd., Detroit, MI 48202-3091...(313) 556-5000...John G. Smale....world's largest auto manuf.

Genuine Parts Co....2999 Circle 75 Pkwy., Atlanta, GA 30339...(404) 953-1700...L. L. Prince...distributes auto replacement parts (NAPA).

Georgia-Pacific Corp....133 Peachtree St. NE, Atlanta, GA 30303...(404) 521-5210...A. D. Correll....largest manuf. of paper and wood prods.

Gillette Co....Prudential Tower Bldg., Boston, MA 02199...(617) 421-7000...Alfred Zeieh...razors, pens (Paper Mate), toiletries (Right Guard deodorants, Foamy shaving cream), hair products (Adorn), household appliances (Braun).

Goodyear Tire & Rubber Co....1144 E. Market St., Akron, OH 44316...(216) 796-8576...Stanley Gault...tires and other auto products.

W. R. Grace & Co....One Town Center Rd., Boca Raton, FL 33486...(407) 362-2000...Albert J. Costello...chemicals, health care.

Great Atlantic & Pacific Tea Co. (A&P)...2 Paragon Dr., Montvale, NJ 07645...(201) 573-9700...James Wood...supermarket chain.

GTE Corp....One Stamford Forum, Stamford, CT 06904...(203) 965-2000...Charles R. Lee...large U.S. local exchange telephone co., cellular telephone operator.

Harley-Davidson, Inc....3700 W. Juneau Ave., Milwaukee, WI 53208...(414) 342-4680...V. L. Beals, Jr....manuf. of motorcycles, parts & accessories.

Harrah's Entertainment, Inc....1023 Cherry Rd., Memphis, TN 38117...(901) 762-8852...Michael D. Rose...casino-hotels.

Hartmarx...101 N. Wacker Dr., Chicago, IL 60606...(312) 372-6300...E. O. Hand...apparel manufacturer (Hickey Freeman, Hart Schaffner & Marx, Pierre Cardin).

Hasbro, Inc....1027 Newport Ave., Pawtucket, RI 02862...(401) 431-8697...A. G. Hassenfeld...toy and game manuf. & marketer (Milton Bradley, Playskool, G. I. Joe, Parker Bros., Tonka trucks, Play-Doh).

H. J. Heinz Co....PO Box 57, Pittsburgh, PA 15230...(412) 456-6014...Anthony J. F. O'Reilly...foods (Star-Kist, Ore-Ida, '57 Varieties), pet food (9 Lives), Weight Watchers.

Helene Curtis...325 N. Wells St., Chicago, IL 60610...(312) 661-0222...Gerlad Gidwitz...hair care prods. (Finesse, Suave, Salon Selectives), antiperspirant (Degree).

Hershey Foods Corp....100 Crystal A Dr., Hershey, PA 17033...(717) 534-6799...Kenneth Wolfe...chocolate & confectionery prods. (Reese's peanut butter cups, Kit Kat, Peter Paul Mounds, Almond Joy), pasta (San Giorgio, Ronzoni).

Hewlett-Packard Co....3000 Hanover St., Palo Alto, CA 94304...(415) 857-1501...L. E. Platt...manuf. electronic prods. and systems.

Hillenbrand Industries, Inc....700 State Rte. 46, Batesville, IN 47006-9166...(812) 934-7000...D. A. Hillenbrand...manuf. burial caskets, electronically operated hospital beds, locks.

Home Depot, Inc....2727 Paces Ferry Rd., Atlanta, GA 30339...(404) 433-8211...Bernard Marcus...retailer of building materials & home improvement prods.

Honeywell, Inc....Honeywell Plaza, Minneapolis, MN 55408...(612) 951-1000...Michael Bonsignore...industrial and home control systems, aerospace guidance systems, information systems.

Hormel Foods Corp....PO Box 800, Austin, MN 55912...(507) 437-5611...R. Knowlton...meat packaging, pork and beef prods. (Spam, Dinty Moore, Mary Kitchen).

Houghton Mifflin Co....222 Berkeley St., Boston, MA 02116...(617) 351-5000...Nader F. Darehshori...book publishing.

Household International Inc....2700 Sanders Rd., Prospect Heights, IL 60070...(708) 564-5000...D. C. Clark...financial and insurance services.

Huffy Corp....7701 Byers Rd., Miamisburg, OH 45342...(513) 866-6251...Richard Molen...bicycles, sports and hardware equip. manuf.

Humana, Inc....500 W. Main St., Louisville, KY 40201-1438...(502) 580-1000...D. A. Jones...provides health care plans.

IBP, Inc....IBP Ave., PO Box 515, Dakota City, NE 68731...(402) 494-2061...Robert Peterson...processor of beef and pork.

Ingersoll-Rand Co....Woodcliff Lake, NJ 07675...(201) 573-0123...J. E. Perella...industrial machinery.

Intel Corp....2200 Mission College Blvd., Santa Clara, CA 95052-8119...(408) 765-8080...G. E. Moore...manuf. integrated circuits (Pentium).

International Business Machines Corp....1 Old Orchard Rd., Armonk, NY 10504...(914) 765-1900...Louis Gerstner, Jr. ...information processing systems, equip., and services.

International Paper Co....2 Manhattanville Rd., Purchase, NY 10577...(914) 397-1500...John A. Georges...paper and wood prods., films, chemicals, minerals.

ITT Corp....1330 Ave. of the Americas, NY, NY 10022...(212) 258-1000...R. V. Araskog...manuf., installs communication and electronic equip., auto equip., insurance, hotels (Caesar's World), educational services.

Johnson Controls...5757 N. Green Bay Ave., Milwaukee, WI 53201...(414) 228-1200...James Keyes...fire protection services, auto seats and batteries, beverage containers.

Johnson & Johnson...501 George St., New Brunswick, NJ 08903...(908) 524-0400...Ralph S. Larsen...surgical dressings (Band-Aids), pharmaceuticals (Tylenol), toiletries.

Jostens, Inc....5501 Norman Center Dr., Minneapolis, MN 55437...(612) 830-3300...Robert P. Jensen...school rings, yearbooks.

Kellogg Co....One Kellogg Sq., Battle Creek, MI 49016...(616) 961-2000...Arnold G. Langbo...ready-to-eat cereals & other food prods. (Frosted Flakes, Rice Krispies, Froot Loops, Pop Tarts, Eggo).

Kimberly-Clark Corp....PO Box 619100, Dallas, TX 75261-9100...(214) 281-1200...Wayne R. Sanders...paper and lumber prods., consumer prods. (Kleenex, Huggies, Kotex). (Co. announced 7/17/95 that it had agreed to acquire Scott Paper Co.)

King World Productions, Inc....1700 Broadway, NY, NY 10019...(212) 315-4000...Roger King...syndicator of TV programs (*Oprah Winfrey Show, Wheel of Fortune, Jeopardy!, Inside Edition*).

Kmart Corp....3100 W. Big Beaver Rd., Troy, MI 48084...(810) 643-1000...Floyd Hall...largest U.S. chain of discount stores, book stores (Waldenbooks, Borders), sporting goods stores (Sports Authority), home improvement retail stores.

Knight-Ridder, Inc....One Herold Plaza, Miami, FL 33101...(305) 376-3838...P. A. Ridder...newspaper publishing, book publishing, information services.

Kroger Co....1014 Vine St., Cincinnati, OH 45202...(513) 762-4000...Joseph Pichler...grocery chain.

L.A. Gear, Inc....2850 Ocean Park Blvd., Santa Monica, CA 90405...(310) 822-1995...Stanley P. Gold...athletic & leisure footwear, casual apparel.

La-Z-Boy Chair Co....1284 N. Telegraph Rd., Monroe, MI 48161...(313) 242-1444...C. T. Knabusch...reclining chairs, other furniture.

Lehman Bros. Holdings, Inc....3 World Financial Ctr., NY, NY 10285...(212) 526-7000...R. S. Fuld, Jr.,...investment banker.

Levi Strauss Associates...1155 Battery St., San Francisco, CA 94111...(415)544-6000...Robert D. Haas...blue jeans, casual apparel.

Eli Lilly & Company...Lilly Corp. Center, Indianapolis, IN 46285...(317) 276-2000...R. L. Tobias...mfg. health (Prozac) and agricultural products.

The Limited, Inc....Two Limited Pkwy., Columbus, OH 43216...(614) 479-7000...L. H. Wexner...women's apparel stores (Lane Bryant, Lerner, Victoria's Secret), Abercrombie & Fitch.

Litton Industries, Inc....21240 Burbank Blvd., Woodland Hills, CA 91367...(310) 859-5000...A. J. Brann...industrial systems & services, advanced electronic systems, electronic & electrical prods., marine engineering.

Lockheed Martin Corp....6801 Rockledge Dr., Bethesda, MD 20817...(301) 897-6000...Daniel M. Tellep...commercial and military aircraft, electronics, missiles.

Loews Corp....667 Madison Ave., NY, NY 10021...(212) 545-2000...Laurence A. Tisch...tobacco prods. (Kent, Newport, True), watches, hotels, insurance.

Longs Drug Stores, Inc....141 North Civic Dr., Walnut Creek, CA 94596...(510) 937-1170...R. M. Long...drug store chain.

Lowe's Cos., Inc....Box 1111, N. Wilkesboro, NC 28656...(910) 651-4000...R. L. Strickland...retailer of building materials & related prods.

Luby's Cafeterias, Inc....2211 Northeast Loop 410, San Antonio, TX 78265...(210) 654-9000...J. B. Lahourcade...operates cafeterias in south and southwest U.S.

Manor Care, Inc....10750 Columbia Pike, Silver Spring, MD 20901...(301) 681-9400...S. Bainum, Jr....operates nursing homes, hotels.

Marriott International, Inc....Marriott Dr., Washington, DC 20058...(301) 380-9000...J. Willard Marriott, Jr....hotels, food service.

Mattel, Inc....333 Continental Blvd., El Segundo, CA 90245...(213) 524-2000...J. W. Amerman...toy & hobby prods. (Barbie dolls, Fisher-Price, Hot Wheels).

May Department Stores Co....611 Olive St., St. Louis, MO 63101...(314) 342-6300...David Farrell...department stores (Hecht's, Lord & Taylor, Foley's).

Maytag Corp....Newton, IA 50208...(515) 792-8000...Leonard A. Hadley...manuf. home laundry equip., appliances (Magic Chef, Admiral, Hoover).

McDonald's Corp....1 McDonald's Plaza, Oak Brook, IL 60521 ...(708) 575-7428...M. R. Quinlan...fast-food restaurants.

McDonnell Douglas Corp....PO Box 516, St. Louis, MO 63166-0516...(314) 232-0232...J. F. McDonnell...commercial & military aircraft, space systems & missiles.

McGraw-Hill, Inc....1221 Ave. of the Americas, NY, NY 10020...(212) 512-2000...J. L. Dionne...book, magazine publishing (*Business Week*), information & financial services (Standard and Poor's), TV stations.

MCI Communications Corp....1801 Pennsylvania Ave., Washington, DC 20006...(202) 887-2028...Bert C. Roberts, Jr.,...2d largest U.S. long distance telephone carrier.

McKesson Corp....1 Post St., San Fransicso, CA 94104...(415) 983-8300...Alan Seelenfreund...drugs, toiletries, car-care prods. (Armor All).

Mead Corporation...Courthouse Plaza NE, Dayton, OH 45463 ...(513) 495-6323...Steven C. Mason...printing and writing paper, paperboard, packaging, shipping containers.

Media General, Inc....333 E. Grace St., Richmond, VA 23219...(804) 649-6000...J. S. Bryan 3d...broadcasting, newspaper publishing.

Medtronic, Inc....7000 Central Ave. NE, Minneapolis, MN 55432...(612) 574-4000...Winston R. Wallin...manuf. prosthetic and pacemaker devices.

Melville Corp....1 Theall Rd., Rye, NY 10580...(914) 925-4000...S. P. Goldstein...shoe stores, apparel (Marshalls, Bob's), drug stores (CVS), toy stores (Kay Bee).

Merck & Co., Inc....PO Box 100, Whitehouse Station, NJ 08889-0100...(908) 423-1000...Raymond V. Gilmartin...human & animal health care prods.

Meredith Corp....1716 Locust St., Des Moines, IA 50336...(515) 284-3000...J. D. Rehm...magazine publishing (*Better Homes and Gardens, Ladies Home Journal*), book publishing, broadcasting.

Merrill Lynch & Co., Inc....World Financial Center, N. Tower, NY, NY 10281-1332...(212) 449-1000...Daniel P. Tully...securities broker, financial services.

Metropolitan Life Ins. Co. of NY...1 Madison Ave., NY, NY 10010-3690...(212) 578-2211...H. P. Kamen...insurance, real estate.

Microsoft Corp....One Microsoft Way, Redmond, WA 98052-6399...(206) 882-8080...William H. Gates...the world's largest computer software company.

Minnesota Mining & Manuf. Co....3M Center, St. Paul, MN 55144-1000...(612) 733-1110...L. D. DeSimone...abrasives, adhesives, building services & chemicals, recording materials, electrical, health care, photographic, printing, consumer prods. (Scotch Tape, Post-It).

Mirage Resorts, Inc....3400 Las Vegas Blvd. S, Las Vegas, NV 89109...(702) 385-7111...Stephen A. Wynn...hotel-casino operator (Mirage, Treasure Island, Golden Nugget).

Mobil Corp....3225 Gallows Rd., Fairfax, VA 22037...(703) 846-3000...Lucia A. Noto...integrated international oil co., chemicals.

Monsanto Company...800 N. Lindbergh Blvd., St. Louis, MO 63167...(314) 694-1000...Robert B. Shapiro...chemicals, agricultural prods., pharmaceuticals, consumer prods. (Nutra-Sweet).

Motorola, Inc....1303 E. Algonquin Rd., Schaumburg, IL 60196...(708) 576-5000...W. J. Weisz...electronic equipment and components.

National Semiconductor Corp....2900 Semiconductor Dr., Santa Clara, CA 95052-8090...(408) 721-5000...G. Amelio ...manuf. of semiconductors, integrated circuits.

Nationsbank...1 NCNB Plaza, Charlotte, NC 28255...(704) 386-5000...Hugh L. McColl, Jr....commercial bank.

Navistar Intl. Corp....455 N. Cityfront Plaza Dr., Chicago, IL 60611...(312) 836-2000...J. C. Cotting...manuf. heavy duty trucks, parts.

New York Times Co....229 W. 43d St., NY, NY 10036...(212) 556-3660...A. O. Sulzberger...newspapers, radio, TV stations, magazines (*Tennis, Golf Digest*).

Nike, Inc....One Bowerman Dr., Beaverton, OR 97005...(503) 671-6453...Philip Knight...athletic & leisure footware, apparel.

Norfolk Southern Corp....3 Commercial Place, Norfolk, VA 23510...(804) 629-2640...D. R. Goode...operates Norfolk & Southern railways, freight carrier (North American Van Lines).

Northrop Grumman Corp....1840 Century Park E, Los Angeles, CA 90067...(213) 553-6262...Kent Kresa...aircraft, electronics, communications, missiles.

NYNEX Corp....1095 Ave. of the Americas, NY, NY 10036...(212) 370-7400...W. C. Ferguson...telephone co. in northeast U.S.

Occidental Petroleum Corp....10889 Wilshire Blvd., Los Angeles, CA 90024...(213) 879-1700...Ray Irani...oil, gas, chemicals, coal, agriculture.

Office Depot, Inc....2200 Old Germantown Rd., Delray Beach, FL 33445...(407) 278-4800...David Fuente...retail office supply stores.

Ogden Corp....2 Pennsylvania Plaza, NY, NY 10121...(212) 868-6100...R. E. Ablon...transportation, foods, metals, financial services, waste disposal, energy recovery.

Olsten Corp.... One Merrick Ave., Westbury, NY 11590...(516) 832-8200...F. N. Liguori...provides temporary workers.

Outboard Marine Corp....100 Sea-Horse Dr., Waukegan, IL 60085...(708) 689-6200...H. W. Bowman...outboard motors (Evinrude, Johnson), boats.

Owens-Corning Fiberglas Corp.... Fiberglas Tower, Toledo, OH 43659...(419) 248-8000...Glen H. Hiner...glass fiber and related prods.

Oxford Industries, Inc....222 Piedmont Ave. NE, Atlanta, GA 30308...(404) 659-2424...J. H. Lanier...manuf. men's and women's apparel.

Pacific Telesis Group...130 Kearny St., San Francisco, CA 94108...(415) 394-3000...Philip Quigley...telephone service.

J. C. Penney Co....14841 N. Dallas Pkwy., PO Box 659000, Dallas, TX 75265-9000...(214) 591-1000...James E. Oesterreicher...dept. stores, catalog sales, drug stores, insurance.

Pennzoil Co....PO Box 2967, Houston, TX 77252-8000...(713) 546-4000...J. L. Pate...integrated oil and gas co.

PepsiCo, Inc.... PepsiCo World HQ, Purchase, NY 10577...(914) 253-2000...D. W. Calloway...soft drinks (Pepsi-Cola, Mountain Dew, Slice), snack foods (Ruffles, Lay's, Doritos), restaurants (Pizza Hut, KFC, Taco Bell).

Pfizer, Inc....235 E. 42d St., NY, NY 10017...(212) 573-2323...W. C. Steere, Jr....pharmaceutical, hospital, agricultural, chemical prods., consumer prods. (Visine eye drops, Ben-Gay pain relief).

Philip Morris Cos., Inc....120 Park Ave., NY, NY 10017...(212) 880-5000...Geoffrey Bible...cigarettes (Marlboro, Virginia Slims), beer (Miller, Lowenbrau brands), packaged foods (Jell-O, Entenmann baked goods, Maxwell House coffee, Kool-Aid, Oscar Mayer meats, Tang, Cheez Whiz & Velveeta cheese prods).

Phillips-Van Heusen Corp....1290 Ave. of the Americas, NY, NY 10104...(212) 541-5200...Bruce J. Klatsky...manuf. apparel for men & women; operates retail stores.

Pitney Bowes, Inc.... Wheeler Dr., Stamford, CT 06926...(203) 356-5000...G. B. Harvey...postage meters, mail-handling equip.

Playboy Enterprises, Inc....680 N. Lake Shore Dr., Chicago, IL 60611...(312) 751-8000...Christie Hefner...magazine publishing, CATV, merchandising.

Polaroid Corp.... Technology Sq., Cambridge, MA 02139 ...(617) 386-2000...I. M. Booth...photographic equip., supplies, and optical goods.

PPG Industries, Inc.... One PPG Place, Pittsburgh, PA 15272...(412) 434-3131...Jerry Dempsey...glass prods., paints, chemicals.

Premark Intl., Inc....1717 Deerfield Rd., Deerfield, IL 60015...(708) 405-6000...W. L. Batts...consumer prods. (Tupperware).

Price/Costco, Inc....999 Lake Dr., Issaquah, WA 98207...(206) 313-8100...J. H. Brotman...wholesale cash-and-carry stores.

Procter & Gamble Co.... One Procter & Gamble Plaza, Cincinnati, OH 45202...(513) 983-1100...John Pepper...soap & detergent (Ivory, Cheer, Tide, Mr. Clean, Comet, Spic and Span, Zest), toiletries (Crest toothpaste, Prell, Head and Shoulders shampoos, Noxzema, Oil of Olay, Old Spice), pharmaceuticals (Pepto-Bismol); Pampers disposable diapers, Folger's coffee, Hawaiian Punch, Charmin toilet tissues, Bounty towels, Vicks cough medicines, Crisco shortening, Duncan Hines cakes.

Prudential Ins. Co. of America...751 Broad St., Newark, NJ 07102-3777...(201) 802-6000...A. F. Ryan...insurance, financial services.

Quaker Oats Co.... Quaker Tower, PO Box 9001, Chicago, IL 60604...(312) 222-7818...William D. Smithburg...cereal (Quaker Oat Bran, Life, Cap'n Crunch), foods (Aunt Jemima, Celeste pizza, Van Camp's pork and beans, Gatorade, Snapple), pet foods (Ken-L-Ration, Gaines).

Quaker State Corp....255 Elm St., Oil City, PA 16301...(814) 676-7676...Herbert M. Baum...refining, marketing petroleum prods., filters, antifreeze, quick-change oil centers.

Ralston Purina Co.... Checkerboard Sq., St. Louis, MO 63164...(314) 982-2161...W. K. Stiritz...pet and livestock food (Purina), consumer prods. (Chex cereal, Beech-Nut baby food, Wonder bread, Hostess baked goods, Eveready and Energizer batteries).

Raytheon Company...141 Spring St., Lexington, MA 02173...(617) 862-6600...Dennis J. Picard...electronics, aviation, appliances; Amana Refrigeration, Beech Aircraft.

Reader's Digest Assn., Inc.... Pleasantville, NY 10570...(914) 238-1000...James Schadt...magazines, books.

Reebok Intl., Ltd....100 Technology Ctr. Dr., Stoughton, MA 02072...(617) 341-5000...P. Fireman...athletic & casual footwear, sportswear.

Reynolds Metals Co....6601 W. Broad St., Richmond, VA 23230...(804) 281-2000...Richard G. Holder...aluminum prods.

Rite Aid Corp....PO Box 3165, Harrisburg, PA 17105...(717) 761-2633...Martin Grass...discount drug, beauty aid stores.

RJR Nabisco Holdings Corp....1301 Ave. of the Americas, NY, NY 10019...(212) 258-5600...C. M. Harper...cigarettes (Winston, Salem, Camel), foods (Oreos, Ritz crackers).

Rockwell Intl. Corp....625 Liberty Ave., Pittsburgh, PA 15222...(412) 565-2000...D. R. Beall...aerospace, electronic, automotive prods.

Rubbermaid Inc....1147 Akron Rd., Wooster, OH 44691...(216) 264-6464...Wolfgang R. Schmitt...rubber and plastic consumer prods.

Russell Corp.... Alexander City, AL 35010...(205) 329-4000...J. C. Adams...manuf. leisure apparel, athletic uniforms.

Ryder System, Inc....3600 NW 82d Ave., Miami, FL 33166...(305) 593-3726...M. A. Burns...truck-leasing ser-vice.

Sara Lee Corp....3 First National Plaza, Chicago, IL 60602...(312) 726-2600...J. H. Bryan, Jr....baked goods, fresh and processed meats, fresh and frozen fruits and vegetables and other packaged foods, beverages, tobacco products, hosiery, intimate apparel and knitwear (Hanes, Kiwi, Ball Park, Hillshire Farms, L'eggs, Playtex, Isotoner).

SBC Communications....PO Box 2933, San Antonio, TX 78299...(210) 351-2044...E. Whitacre, Jr....telephone services.

Schering-Plough Corp.... One Giralda Farms, Madison, NJ 07940...(201) 822-7000...R. P. Luciano...pharmaceuticals, consumer prods.

Scott Paper Co.... Scott Plaza, Philadelphia, PA 19113...(215) 522-5000...Albert J. Dunlap...bathroom tissue, paper towels, napkins. (Co. announced 7/17/95 that it had agreed to be acquired by Kimberly-Clark Corp.)

Sears, Roebuck & Co.... Sears Tower, Chicago, IL 60684...(312) 875-2500...Arthur Martinez...department, specialty stores.

Service Merchandise, Inc....PO Box 24600, Nashville, TN 37202-4600...(615) 660-6000...Raymond Zimmerman...operates catalog showrooms.

Shaw Industries, Inc....616 E. Walnut Ave., Dalton, GA 30720...(706) 278-3812...R. E. Shaw...manuf. tufted carpeting (Magee, Philadelphia).

Sherwin-Williams Co....101 Prospect Ave. NW, Cleveland, OH 44115...(216) 566-2000...John G. Breen...paint manuf. (Dutch Boy, Kem-Tone).

Sizzler Intl., Inc....12655 W. Jefferson Blvd., Los Angeles, CA 90066...(310) 827-2300...J. Collins...quick-service restaurants.

Skyline Corp....2520 By-Pass Rd., Elkhart, IN 46515...(219) 294-6521...Arthur J. Decio...mfg. housing and recreational vehicles.

J. M. Smucker Co.... Strawberry Lane, Orrville, OH 44667 ...(216) 682-3000...T. P. Smucker...preserves, jams, jellies, toppings, frozen desserts, juices.

Snap-on, Inc....2801 80th St., Kenosha, WI 53140-1410...(414) 656-5200...R. A. Cornog...manuf. mechanic's tools, equip.

Sprint Corp....PO Box 11315 Plaza Station, Kansas City, MO 64112...(913) 624-3000...W. T. Esrey...long-distance and local telecommunications.

Stride Rite Corp....5 Cambridge Center, Cambridge, MA 02142...(617) 491-8800...Robert Siegel...children's footwear.

Sun Company, Inc....1801 Market St., Philadelphia, PA 19103-1699...(215) 977-3000...R. H. Campbell...energy resources co.

Supervalu, Inc....PO Box 990, Minneapolis, MN 55440...(612) 828-4000...Michael W. Wright...food wholesaler.

Sysco Corp....1390 Enclave Parkway, Houston, TX 77077-2099...(713) 584-1390...John F. Baugh...food distrib.

Tambrands Inc....777 Westchester Ave., White Plains, NY 10604...(914) 696-6000...Howard Wentz...feminine hygiene products (Tampax).

Tandy Corp....1800 One Tandy Center, Fort Worth, TX 76102...(817) 390-3700...J. F. Roach...consumer electronics retailing (Computer City, Radio Shack).

Teledyne, Inc....1901 Ave. of the Stars, Los Angeles, CA 90067-6046...(310) 551-4268...William Rutledge...electronics, aerospace, industrial, consumer prods. (Water Pik).

Tenet Healthcare Corp....2700 Colorado Ave., Santa Monica, CA 90411...(310) 998-8000...J. C. Barbakow...owns, operates hospitals, other health-care facilities.

Tenneco, Inc....PO Box 2511, Houston, TX 77252...(713) 757-2131...Dana Mead...natural gas pipelines, shipbuilding, packaging materials, automotive parts.

Texaco Inc....2000 Westchester Ave., White Plains, NY 10650...(914) 253-4000...A. C. DeCrane, Jr....integrated international oil co.

Texas Instruments Inc....13500 N. Central Expressway, Dallas, TX 75265...(214) 995-3773...J. Junkins...electronics.

Textron, Inc....40 Westminster St., Providence, RI 02903...(401) 421-2800...J. F. Handymon...aerospace, consumer, industrial, metal prods., consumer finance, insurance, management services.

Tiffany & Co....727 5th Ave., NY, NY 10022...(212) 755-8000...W. R. Chaney...designs, manuf., and distributes jewelry & gift items.

Times Mirror Publishing Co....Times Mirror Sq., Los Angeles, CA 90053...(213) 237-3700...R. F. Erburu...newspapers, magazines (*Field & Stream*, *Popular Science*), books.

Time Warner, Inc....75 Rockefeller Plaza, NY, NY 10020...(212) 522-1212...Gerald M. Levin...magazine publishing (*Time*, *Sports Illustrated*, *Fortune*, *Money*, *People*), TV and CATV (WB Network, HBO, Cinemax), book publishing (Little, Brown; Warner Books), motion pictures (Warner Bros.), recordings. (Co. announced 9/22/95 that it had agreed to acquire Turner Broadcasting System, Inc.)

Tootsie Roll Industries, Inc....7401 S. Cicero Ave., Chicago, IL 60629...(312) 838-3400...M. J. Gordon...candy (Tootsie Roll, Mason Dots, Charms, Sugar Daddy, Charleston Chew).

Toro Co....8111 Lyndale Ave. S, Bloomington, MN 55420...(612) 888-8801...Kendrick B. Melrose...lawn and turf maintenance (Lawn-Boy), snow removal equipment.

Toys "R" Us...461 From Rd., Paramus, NJ 07652...(201) 262-7800...Charles Lazarus...toy, clothing stores (Kids "R" Us).

Transamerica Corp....600 Montgomery St., San Francisco, CA 94111...(415) 983-4000...James R. Harvey...insurance, financial services.

Travelers Group, Inc....388 Greenwich St., NY, NY 10022...(212) 816-8000...Sanford I. Weill...insurance, financial services.

Tribune Co....435 N. Michigan Ave., Chicago, IL 60611...(312) 222-9100...C. T. Brumback...newpaper and book publishing, broadcasting, Chicago Cubs baseball team.

Trinity Industries, Inc....2525 Stemmons Freeway, Dallas, TX 75207...(214) 631-4420...W. Ray Wallace...manufactures variety of metal products.

TRW Inc....1900 Richmond Rd., Cleveland, OH 44124...(216) 291-7000...J. T. Gorman...car and truck operations, electronics, and space systems.

Turner Broadcasting System, Inc....1 CNN Center, Atlanta, GA 30303...(404) 827-1700...R. E. Turner...operates cable TV networks: CNN, TBS, TNT; owns MGM film library; owns Atlanta Braves, Hawks. (Co. announced 9/22/95 that it had agreed to be acquired by Time Warner, Inc.)

Tyson Foods, Inc....2210 W. Oaklawn, Springdale, AR 72764...(501) 756-4000...Leland Tollett...fresh and processed poultry and other meat prods. (Holly Farm, Weaver).

UAL Corp....1200 E. Algonquin Rd., Elk Grove Township, IL 60007...(708) 952-4000...Gerald Greenwald...air transportation (United Airlines).

Union Carbide Corp....39 Old Ridgebury Rd., Danbury, CT 06817...(203) 794-2000...R. D. Kennedy...chemicals.

Union Pacific Corp....Martin Tower, 8th & Eaton Aves., Bethlehem, PA 18018...(215) 861-3200...D. Lewis...railroad, trucking, natural resources.

Unisys Corp....PO Box 500, Blue Bell, PA 19424-0001...(215) 986-6999...James Unruh...designs, manuf. computer information systems.

United Parcel Service of America, Inc....55 Glenlake Parkway NE, Atlanta, GA 30328...(404) 913-6000...Kent C. Nelson...courier services.

United Technologies Corp....Hartford, CT 06101...(203) 728-7000...George David... aerospace, industrial prods. & services (Carrier Corp., Otis Elevator, Pratt & Whitney, Sikorsky Aircraft).

Univar Corp....6100 Carillon Pt., Kirkland, WA 98033...(206) 899-3400...James H. Wiborg...industrial chemicals, serves packaging, agricultural, mining, petroleum industries.

Unocal Corp....1201 W. 5th St., Los Angeles, CA 90017...(213) 977-7600...Robert Beach...oil, chemicals, geothermal energy.

Upjohn Co....700 Portage Rd., Kalamazoo, MI 49001...(616) 323-4000...John Zabriskie...pharmaceuticals (Motrin, Rogaine, Halcion), chemicals, agricultural, health-care prods.

USAir Group, Inc....2345 Crystal Dr., Arlington, VA 22202...(703) 418-7000...Seth E. Schofield...air carrier of passengers, property, and mail.

UST Inc....100 W. Putnam Ave., Greenwich, CT 06830...(203) 661-1100...Vincent Gierer, Jr....smokeless tobacco (Copenhagen, Skoal, Happy Days), pipe tobacco, wines.

USX-Marathon Group...600 Grant St., Pittsburgh, PA 15230...(412) 433-1121...Charles A. Corry...integrated oil co.

V.F. Corp....1047 N. Park Rd., Wyomissing, PA 19610...(610) 378-1151...L. R. Pugh...apparel (Vanity Fair, Lee, Wrangler jeans, Jantzen).

Viacom, Inc....200 Elm St., Dedham, MA 02026...(617) 461-1600...Sumner M. Redstone...TV broadcast stations and cable systems, channels (Showtime, MTV); book publishing (Simon & Schuster); produces, dist. movies, TV shows (Paramount); video rental stores (Blockbuster).

Walgreen Co....200 Wilmot Rd., Deerfield, IL 60015...(708) 940-2500...Charles R. Walgreen 3d...retail drug chain.

Wal-Mart Stores, Inc....Box 116, Bentonville, AR 72716...(501) 273-4000...S. Robson Walton...retail dept. stores (Sam's Wholesale Clubs).

Warner-Lambert Co....201 Tabor Rd., Morris Plains, NJ 07950-2693...(201) 540-2000...M. R. Goodes,....health care prods. (Benadryl), consumer prods. (Efferdent dental cleanser, Halls cough tablets, Schick razors, Certs mints, Listerine mouthwash, Trident, Chicklets, Dentyne gums).

Washington Post Co....1150 15th St. NW, Washington, DC 20071...(202) 334-6000...D. E. Graham...newspapers, magazines (*Newsweek*), TV stations.

Weis Markets, Inc....1000 S. 2d St., Sunbury, PA 17801...(717) 286-4571...Robert Weis...operates supermarkets, pet supply stores, distributes frozen foods and grocery items.

Wells Fargo & Co....420 Montgomery St., San Francisco, CA 94163...(415) 396-3606...P. Hazer...banking.

Wendy's Intl., Inc....4288 W. Dublin-Granville Rd., Dublin, OH 43017...(614) 764-3100...J. W. Near...quick-service restaurants.

Westinghouse Electric Corp....Westinghouse Bldg., Gateway Center, Pittsburgh, PA 15222...(412) 244-2000...Michael H. Jordan...manuf. electrical, mechanical equip.; radio and television stations; power generation. (Co. announced 8/1/95 that it had agreed to acquire CBS Inc.)

Westvaco Corp....299 Park Ave., NY, NY 10171...(212) 688-5000...David L. Luke, 3d...manufactures paper for graphic reproduction, communications, and packaging.

Weyerhaeuser Co....Tacoma, WA 98477...(206) 924-2345...G. H. Weyerhaeuser...manuf., distrib. forest prods.

Whirlpool Corp....Benton Harbor, MI 49022...(616) 923-5000...David Whitwam...major home appliances manuf.

Whitman Corp....111 Crossroads of Commerce, 3501 Algonquin Rd., Rolling Meadows, IL 60008...(708) 818-5000...Bruce S. Chelberg...beverage bottler, refrigeration equip., auto prods. (Midas).

Winn-Dixie Stores, Inc....5050 Edgewood Ct., Jacksonville, FL 32205...(904) 783-5000...A. D. Davis....supermarkets.

Winnebago Industries, Inc....PO Box 152, Forest City, IA 50436...(515) 582-3535...J. K. Hanson....manuf. of motor homes, recreation vehicles.

Wolverine World Wide Corp....9341 Courtland Dr., Rockford, MI 49351...(616) 866-5500...Phillip D. Mathews...manuf. footwear (Hush Puppies).

Woolworth Corp....233 Broadway, NY, NY 10279...(212) 553-2000...Roger Farah...variety stores, shoes (Kinney), men's clothing (Richman Brothers), athletic footwear (Foot Locker).

Wm. Wrigley Jr. Co....410 N. Michigan Ave., Chicago, IL 60611...(312) 644-2121...William Wrigley...chewing gum.

Xerox Corp....PO Box 1600, Stamford, CT 06904...(203) 968-3000...Paul Allaire...copiers, printers, document pub. equip.

Zenith Electronics Corp....1000 Milwaukee Ave., Glenview, IL 60025...(708) 391-7000...Jerry K. Pearlman...TVs.

Who Owns What: Familiar Consumer Products

Listed below are consumer products and their parent companies. The parent company address can be found on pp. 714-19.

Admiral appliances: Maytag
Advil: American Home Products
Ajax cleanser: Colgate-Palmolive
Anacin: American Home Products
Arm & Hammer: Church & Dwight
Arrid antiperspirant: Carter-Wallace
Arnold breads: CPC International
Aunt Millie's pasta sauce: Borden
Ban antiperspirant: Bristol-Myers
  Squibb
Barbie dolls: Mattell
Beech Aircraft: Raytheon
Beech-Nut baby food: Ralston Pu-
  rina
Ben-Gay: Pfizer
Betty Crocker products: General
  Mills
Blockbuster video stores: Viacom
Bounce fabric softener: Procter &
  Gamble
Breck shampoo: Dial
Budweiser beer: Anheuser-Busch
Bufferin: Bristol-Myers Squibb
Business Week magazine: McGraw-
  Hill
Buster Brown shoes: Brown Group
BVD underwear: Fruit of the Loom
Cap'n Crunch cereal: Quaker Oats
Carrier air conditioners: United
  Technologies
Celeste Pizza: Quaker Oats
Charmin toilet tissue: Procter &
  Gamble
Cheer detergent: Procter & Gamble
Cheerios cereal: General Mills
Cheez Whiz: Philip Morris
Chef Boy-ar-dee products: American
  Home Products
Cinemax: Time Warner
Clairol hair products: Bristol-Myers
  Squibb
Clorets breath freshener: Warner-
  Lambert
Combat insecticides: Clorox
Comet cleanser: Procter & Gamble
Coppertone sun care products:
  Schering-Plough
Cracker Jack: Borden
Crest toothpaste: Procter & Gamble
Crisco shortening: Procter & Gam-
  ble
Degree antiperspirant: Helene Curtis
Doritos chips: PepsiCo
Dristan: American Home Products
Duncan Hines cakes: Procter &
  Gamble
Efferdent dental cleanser: Warner-
  Lambert
Elmer's glue: Borden
ESPN: Capital Cities/ABC
Eveready batteries: Ralston Purina
Excedrin: Bristol-Myers Squibb
Fab detergent: Colgate-Palmolive
Fantastik spray cleaner: Dow
  Chemical
Foamy shaving cream: Gillette
Folger's coffee: Procter & Gamble
Formula 409 spray cleaner: Clorox
Franco-American foods: Campbell
  Soup
Frito-Lay snacks: PepsiCo
Gatorade: Quaker Oats
Glad plastic wrap: First Brands
Gleem toothpaste: Procter & Gam-
  ble

Halcion: Upjohn
Hamburger Helper: General Mills
Handy Wipes: Colgate-Palmolive
Hanes hosiery: Sara Lee
Hawaiian Punch: Procter & Gamble
HBO: Time Warner
Head and Shoulders shampoo:
  Procter & Gamble
Healthy Request food products:
  Campbell Soup
Hellmann's mayonnaise: CPC Inter-
  national
Hi-C fruit drinks: Coca-Cola
Hillshire Farms meats: Sara Lee
Hostess baked goods: Ralston Pu-
  rina
Huggies: Kimberly-Clark
Hush Puppies shoes: Wolverine
  World Wide
Ivory soap products: Procter &
  Gamble
Jack Daniel's bourbon: Brown-
  Forman
Jell-O: Philip Morris
Jim Beam whiskey: American
  Brands
Ken-L-Ration pet foods: Quaker
  Oats
Kent cigarettes: Loews
Kinney shoe stores: Woolworth
Kleenex: Kimberly-Clark
Knorr soups: CPC International
Kool-Aid: Philip Morris
Krazy Glue: Borden
Ladies Home Journal magazine:
  Meredith
Lee jeans: V.F. Corp.
L'eggs hosiery: Sara Lee
Lenox china: Brown-Forman
Lerner stores: The Limited
Life Savers candy: RJR Nabisco
Listerine mouthwash: Warner-
  Lambert
Log Cabin syrup: Philip Morris
Lord & Taylor dept. stores: May
  Dept. Stores
Marlboro cigarettes: Philip Morris
Mazola oil: CPC International
Maxwell House coffee: Philip Morris
Michelob beer: Anheuser-Busch
Midas automotive centers: Whitman
Miller beer: Philip Morris
Milton Bradley games: Hasbro
Minute Maid beverages: Coca-Cola
Mrs. Paul's frozen fish: Campbell
  Soup
Nature Valley granola bars: General
  Mills
NBC Broadcasting: General Electric
Newsweek magazine: Washington
  Post
9 Lives cat food: H.J. Heinz
North Americ an Van Lines: Norfolk
  Southern
Noxema products: Procter & Gam-
  ble
NutraSweet: Monsanto
Old Spice: Procter & Gamble
Ore-Ida frozen foods: H.J. Heinz
Oreo cookies: RJR Nabisco
Oscar Mayer meats: Philip Morris
Pampers: Procter & Gamble
Paper Mate pens: Gillette
People magazine: Time Warner
Pepto-Bismol: Procter & Gamble

Pepperidge Farm products: Camp-
  bell Soup
Pine-Sol cleaner: Clorox
Pizza Hut restaurants: PepsiCo
Planters nuts: RJR Nabisco
Playskool toys: Hasbro
Playtex apparel: Sara Lee
Post-It stickers: Minn. Min. & Manuf.
Prego spaghetti sauce: Campbell
  Soup
Prell shampoo: Procter & Gamble
Prentice-Hall publishing: Viacom
Prozac: Eli Lilly
Purex detergent: Dial
Radio Shack retail outlets: Tandy
Reese's peanut butter cups: Her-
  shey
Right Guard deodorant: Gillette
Ritz crackers: RJR Nabisco
Robitussin: American Home Prod-
  ucts
Rolaids antacid: Warner-Lambert
Ronzoni pasta: Hershey
Ruffles chips: PepsiCo
San Giorgio pasta: Hershey
Saran Wrap: Dow Chemical
Scholl's foot products: Schering-
  Plough
Scotch tape: Minn. Min. & Manuf.
Simon & Schuster publishing:
  Viacom
Skippy peanut butter: CPC Interna-
  tional
SnackWell's cookies: RJR Nabisco
Snapple beverages: Quaker Oats
Southern Comfort liquor: Brown-
  Forman
Spam meat: Hormel
Sports Authority sporting goods
  stores: Kmart
Sports Illustrated magazine: Time
  Warner
Sprite soda: Coca-Cola
Sugar Twin: Alberto Culver
Swanson frozen dinners: Campbell
  Soup
Taco Bell restaurants: PepsiCo
Thomas' English muffins: CPC In-
  ternational
Tide detergent: Procter & Gamble
Tonka trucks: Hasbro
Trojan condoms: Carter-Wallace
Tupperware: Premark
Tylenol: Johnson & Johnson
Ultra Brite toothpaste: Colgate-
  Palmolive
USA Today newspaper: Gannett
V-8 vegetable juice: Campbell Soup
Vanity Fair apparel: V.F. Corp.
Velveeta cheese prods.: Philip Mor-
  ris
Vicks cough medicines: Procter &
  Gamble
Victoria's Secret stores: The Limited
Victory flea collars: Carter-Wallace
Virginia Slims cigarettes: Philip Mor-
  ris
Visine eye drops: Pfizer
Wall Street Journal: Dow Jones
Weight Watchers: H.J. Heinz
Wheaties cereal: General Mills
White Owl cigars: Culbro
Wise snacks: Borden
Wonder bread: Ralston Purina
Ziploc storage bags: Dow Chemical

Interest Laws and Consumer Finance Loan Rates

Source: Revised by Christian T. Jones, Editor, *Consumer Finance Law Bulletin*, Chicago, IL

All states have laws regulating interest rates. These laws fix a legal or conventional rate, which applies when there is no contract for interest. They also fix a general maximum contract rate, but there are so many exceptions that the general contract maximum actually applies only to exceptional cases. Also, federal law has preempted state limits on first home mortgages, subject to each state's right to reinstate its own law, and has given depository institutions parity with other state lenders.

Legal rate of interest. The legal or conventional rate of interest applies to money obligations when no interest rate is contracted for and also to judgments. The rate is usually somewhat below the general interest rate.

General maximum contract rates. General interest laws in most states set the maximum rate between 8% and 16% per year. In Arkansas, the general maximum is fixed by the state constitution at 5% over the Federal Reserve discount rate. Loans to corporations are frequently exempted or subject to a higher maximum. In recent years, it has also been common to provide special rates for home mortgage loans and variable usury rates that are indexed to market rates.

Specific enabling acts. In many states special statutes permit industrial loan companies, second mortgage lenders, and banks to charge 1.5% a month or more. Laws regulating revolving loans, charge accounts, and credit cards generally limit rates to between 1.5% and 2% per month plus annual fees for credit cards. Rates for installment sales contracts in most states are somewhat higher. Credit unions may generally charge 1% to 1.5% a month. Pawnbrokers' rates vary widely. Savings and loan associations and loans insured by federal agencies are also specially regulated. A number of states allow regulated lenders to charge any rate agreed to with the customer either for all credit or for credit over a certain dollar amount.

Consumer finance loan statutes. Most consumer finance loan statutes are based on early models drafted by the Russell Sage Foundation (1916-42) to provide small loans to wage earners under license and other protective regulations. Since 1969 the model has frequently been the Uniform Consumer Credit Code, which applies to credit sales and loans for consumer purposes. In general, licensed lenders may charge 3% a month and reduced rates for additional amounts. An add-on of 17% ($17 per $100) per year yields about 2.5% per month if paid in equal monthly installments. Discount rates produce higher yields than add-on rates of the same amount. In the table below, unless otherwise stated, monthly and annual rates are based on reducing principal balances, annual add-on rates are based on the original principal for the full term, and 2 or more rates apply to different portions of the balance or original principal.

States (and Puerto Rico) With Consumer Finance Loan Laws and the Rates of Charge as of Aug. 1, 1995

Maximum monthly rates computed on unpaid balances, unless otherwise stated.

AL .... Annual add-on: 15% to $750, 10% to $2,000 (min. 1.5% on unpaid balances). Higher rates for loans up to $749. Over $2,000, any agreed rate. Fee: 4% (max. $25); 5% real estate.

AK .... 3% to $850, 2% to $10,000. Over $10,000, any agreed rate.

AZ .... To $1,000: 3%. Over $1,000: 3% to $500, 2% to $10,000. Over $10,000, any agreed rate. Fee: 4% for real estate credit.

CA .... 2.5% to $225, 2% to $900, 1.5% to $1,650, 1% to $2,500 (1.6% min.). Over $2,500, any agreed rate. 5% fee (max. $50) to $2,500.

CO .... 36% per year to $630, 21% to $2,100, 15% to $25,000 (21% min.).

CT .... Annual add-on: 17% to $600, 11% to $5,000; 11% over $1,800 to $5,000 for certain secured loans. Any agreed rate for 2d mortgages; 8% fee.

DE .... Any agreed rate; 10% fee.

DC .... 24% per year.

FL..... 30% per year to $1,000, 24% to $2,000, 18% to $25,000; $10.00 fee.

GA .... 10% per year discount to 18 months, add-on to 36½ months; 8% fee to $600, 4% on excess plus $2 per month. Over $3,000, any agreed rate.

HI..... 3.5% to $100, 2.5% to $300; 2% on entire balance over $300 or discount rates.

ID..... Any agreed rate.

IL..... Any agreed rate. Fee: 3% real estate.

IN..... 36% per year to $870, 21% to $2,900, 15% to $25,000 (21% min.). Fee: 2% real estate.

IA..... 3% to $1,000, 2% to $2,800, 1.5% to $10,000; or equivalent flat rate. Over $10,000, 21% per year.

KS .... 36% per year to $780, 21% to $2,600, 14.45% to $25,000 (18% min.). Fee: 2% (max. $100); 3% real estate.

KY .... 3% to $1,000, 2% to $3,000. Over $3,000, 2%.

LA .... 36% per year to $1,400, 27% to $4,000, 24% to $7,000, 21% over $7,000, plus $25 fee.

ME .... 30% per year to $1,000, 21% to $2,800, 15% to $25,000 (18% min.).

MD .... 2.75% to $1,000, 2% to $2,000. Over $2,000, 2%.

MA .... 23% per year plus $20 annual fee to $6,000; any agreed rate over $6,000.

MI..... 22% per year to $8,000; 18% for 2d mortgages, plus 2% fee (max. $200).

MN .... 33% per year to $750, 19% over $750 (21.75% min.).

MS .... 36% per year to $1,000, 33% to $1,800, 24% to $5,000, 14% over $5,000. Over $25,000, 18%; 2% fee (max. $50).

MO .... 2.218% to $1,200, 1.67% over $1,200, plus 2% fee (max. $15); 1.67% plus 2% for 2d mortgages.

MT..... Any agreed rate.

NE..... 24% per year to $1,000. 21% over, plus fee of 7% to $2,000 and 5% over (max. $500). Any agreed rate for real estate loans of $7,500 or more.

NV..... Any agreed rate.

NH..... 2% to $600, 1.5% to $1,500; any agreed rate over $1,500 or for real estate mortgages.

NJ..... 30% per year to $5,000 or for 2d mortgages.

NM .... Any agreed rate.

NY..... 25% per year.

NC..... 2.5% to $1,000, 1.5% to $7,500; 1.5% on entire amount to $10,000. 1.5% or variable plus 2% fee for 2d mortgages.

ND..... 2.5% to $250, 2% to $500, 1.75% to $750, 1.5% to $1,000; any agreed rate over $1,000.

OH..... 28% per year to $1,000, 22% to $5,000; 25% on entire amount over $5,000; plus fee.

OK..... 30% per year to $930, 21% to $3,100, 15% to $45,000 (21% min.). Special rates to $500.

OR..... Any agreed rate.

PA..... 9.5% per year discount to 48 months, 6% for remaining time plus 2% fee (max. $100); or 2% on unpaid balances; 1.85% for 2d mortgages over $5,000, plus 2% fee.

PR..... 20.25% per year.

RI ..... 3% to $300, 2.5% for loans between $300 and $800; 2% for larger loans to $5,000. 1.75% over $5,000.

SC..... Any agreed and posted rate.

SD..... Any agreed rate.

TN..... Over $100, 24% per year or discount rates plus fees.

TX..... Annual add-on: 18% to $1,290, 8% to $10,750 or formula rate (18% to 24% per year on unpaid balances)

UT..... Any agreed rate.

VT..... 2% to $1,000, 1% to $3,000 (min. 1.5%); 1.5% for 2d mortgages.

VA..... 3% to $2,500; any agreed rate to $6,000. Any agreed rate for 2d mortgages, plus 5% fee.

WA .... 25% per year plus fees.

WV .... 36% per year to $500, 24% to $1,500, 18% to $2,000. Over $2,000, 27% per year to $2,000, 25% to $10,000, 18% on remainder, plus 2% fee.

WI ..... Any agreed rate.

WY .... 36% per year to $1,000, 21% to $25,000. No limit over $25,000.

How to Check Your Credit File

Any individual can investigate the contents of his or her credit file by directly contacting one or more of the approximately 2,000 credit bureaus, or consumer credit clearinghouses, in the U.S. The nearest ones can be found by calling a local Better Business Bureau or by looking in the telephone Yellow Pages under "Credit Rating or Reporting Agencies."

Although the Fair Credit Reporting Act requires that a bureau give a person no more than an oral or written credit history review, many bureaus will go beyond the technical requirements of the law and furnish the same computer-generated compilation of facts that they give the banks, retailers, and other companies that subscribe to their service. An individual who has been denied credit on the basis of negative information from a credit bureau can obtain this review without charge (or sometimes for a small fee) within 30 days of the denial.

After inspecting this record of past credit behavior, a consumer can question any item believed to be inaccurate, misleading, or vague. The credit bureau must then investigate and remove any item that cannot be substantiated.

When a bureau affirms, rather than removes, a questionable item, an individual can present a 100-word explanation that must be placed in his or her file. And whenever an adverse item is deleted from the file or an explanatory statement is added to one, a consumer may request that the credit bureau inform every credit grantor who received a report within the last 6 months.

Credit Card Rates

Source: Christian T. Jones, Editor, *Consumer Finance Law Bulletin*, Chicago, IL; as of Aug. 1, 1995

Nearly all states have special laws dealing with rates charged for credit cards issued by state banks and other financial institutions. Although some state laws apply only to banks, under federal parity law, the same charges can be made by other financial institutions. A bank can charge the highest rates allowed for revolving credit extended by any other creditor in the state where the bank is located for similar types of credit, and such rates may also be charged to residents of any other state. Maximum rates and fees are shown below; rates are yearly unless otherwise stated.

AL . . No limit.
AK . . 17% plus fee.
AZ . . No limit.
AR . . 5% over FRB discount rate (max. 17%).
CA . . No limit.
CO . . 21%.
CT . . No limit.
DC . . 24%.
DE . . No limit.
FL . . No limit.
GA . . No limit on rate or fee.
HI . . 24%.
ID . . No limit.
IL . . . No limit; plus fee.
IN . . 36-21-15%, @ $870, $2,900; or 21%.
IA . . . No limit.
KS . . 18-14.45% @ $1,000.
KY . . 21%; $20 annual fee.

LA . . 18%; 4% cash advance and $12 annual fee.
ME . . No limit; plus annual fee.
MD . . 24%; 2% fee.
MA . . 18% or formula rate.
MI . . 18%; no limit on annual fee.
MN . . 18%; $50 annual fee.
MS . . 21%; or 18% plus $12 annual fee.
MO . . 22-10% @ $1,000.
MT . . No limit.
NE . . No limit; plus fees.
NV . . No limit.
NH . . No limit.
NJ . . 30%; $15 annual fee or $50 over $5,000.
NM . . No limit.
NY . . 25% plus annual fee.
NC . . 18%; $24 annual fee.
ND . . No limit.

OH . . 25%.
OK . . 30-21-15% @ $930, $3,100; or 21%.
OR . . No limit.
PA . . Variable rate, plus fees.
PR . . 2.17% per mo.
RI . . 18%.
SC . . No limit.
SD . . No limit.
TN . . 24%.
TX . . Set by rule (max. 22%, min. 14%).
UT . . No limit.
VT . . No limit.
VA . . No limit.
WA . . 25% loan; no limit for purchases; fees.
WV . . 18%.
WI . . No limit.
WY . . 36-21% @ $1,000; no limit over $25,000.

The Cost of Raising a Child

Source: Family Economics Research Group, U.S. Dept. of Agriculture

Estimated annual expenditures in 1994 dollars for a child born in 1994, by income group. Estimates are for the younger child in a 2-parent family with 2 children for the overall U.S.

| Year | Age of child | Income group[1] | | | Year | Age of child | Income group[1] | | |
		Low	Middle	High			Low	Middle	High
1994	under 1	$5,100	$7,070	$10,510	2004	10	9,310	12,820	18,800
1995	1	5,410	7,490	11,140	2005	11	9,870	13,590	19,930
1996	2	5,730	7,940	11,810	2006	12	11,370	15,270	22,010
1997	3	6,420	8,880	13,030	2007	13	12,050	16,190	23,330
1998	4	6,800	9,420	13,810	2008	14	12,770	17,160	24,730
1999	5	7,210	9,980	14,640	2009	15	15,390	20,370	29,020
2000	6	8,040	10,870	15,630	2010	16	16,310	21,590	30,760
2001	7	8,530	11,520	16,570	2011	17	17,290	22,890	32,610
2002	8	9,040	12,210	17,560	Total		$175,430	$237,360	$343,630
2003	9	8,790	12,100	17,740					

(1) Low income is less than $32,800 (average=$20,600) in 1994; middle income is $32,800 to $55,500 (average=$43,700); high income is $55,500 or more (average=$81,000). The projected annual inflation rate is 5.7%.

Customs Exemptions and Advice to Travelers

Source: U.S. Dept. of the Treasury, U.S. Customs Service

U.S. residents returning after a stay abroad of at least 48 hr are usually granted customs exemptions of $400 each. The duty-free articles must accompany the traveler at the time of his or her return, be for personal or household use, have been acquired as an incident of the trip, and be properly declared to Customs. Not more than one liter of alcoholic beverages nor more than 100 cigars and 200 cigarettes (one carton) may be included in the $400 exemption. The exemption for alcoholic beverages is accorded only when the returning resident has attained 21 years of age at the time of arrival. Cuban cigars may be included only if purchased in Cuba.

If a U.S. resident arrives directly or indirectly from a U.S. insular possession — American Samoa, Guam, or the U.S. Virgin Islands — a customs exemption of $1,200 is allowed. One thousand cigarettes may be included, but only 200 of them may have been purchased elsewhere. If a U.S. resident returns from any one of the following beneficiary places, the customs exemption is $600, based on fair market value: Antigua and Barbuda, Aruba, Bahamas, Barbados, Belize, British Virgin Islands, Costa Rica, Dominica, Dominican Republic, El Salvador, Grenada, Guatemala, Guyana, Haiti, Honduras, Jamaica, Montserrat, Netherlands Antilles, Nicaragua, Panama, St. Kitts and Nevis, St. Lucia, St. Vincent and the Grenadines, Trinidad and Tobago.

The $400, $600, or $1,200 exemption may be granted only if the exemption or any part of it has not been used within the preceding 30-day period and the stay abroad was for at least 48 hr. The 48-hr absence requirement does not apply to travelers returning from Mexico or the U.S. Virgin Islands. If you cannot claim the $400, $600, or $1,200 exemption because of the 30-day or 48-hr minimum limitations, you may bring in free of duty and tax articles acquired abroad for your personal or household use if the total fair retail value does not exceed $25.

Bona fide gifts of not more than $100 in fair retail value where shipped can be received by friends and relations in the U.S. free of duty and tax if the same person does not receive more than $100 in gift shipments in one day. The amount is increased to $200 if shipped from the U.S. Virgin Islands, American Samoa, or Guam. (Shipping of alcoholic beverages by mail is prohibited by U.S. postal laws. Alcoholic beverages include wine and beer as well as distilled spirits.) These gifts are not declared by you upon your return to the U.S.

A new duty-free exemption for packages sent by mail that are not gifts has also been implemented. Goods shipped for personal use may be imported free of duty and tax if the total value is not more than $200. This exemption does not apply to perfume containing alcohol if it is valued at more than $5 retail, to alcoholic beverages, or to cigars and cigarettes. The $200 mail exemption does not apply to merchandise subject to absolute or tariff-rate quotas unless the item is for personal use. Tailor-made suits ordered from Hong Kong, however, are subject to quota/visa requirements even if imported for personal use.

The U.S. Customs Service booklet *Know Before You Go* answers frequently asked customs questions and is available free by writing U.S. Customs, KBYG, PO Box 7407, Washington, DC 20044.

U.S. Passport, Visa, and Health Requirements
Source: Bureau of Consular Affairs, U.S. Dept. of State, as of Aug. 1995

Passports are issued by the U.S. Department of State to citizens and nationals of the U.S. for the purpose of documenting them for foreign travel and identifying them as U.S. citizens.

How to Obtain a Passport

Applicants who have never been issued a passport in their own name must execute an application in person before (1) a passport agent; (2) a clerk of any federal court or state court of record or a judge or clerk of any probate court accepting applications; (3) a postal employee designated by the postmaster at a post office that has been selected to accept passport applications; or (4) a U.S. diplomatic or consular officer abroad. A DSP-11 is the correct form to use for applicants who must apply in person. All persons are required to obtain individual passports in their own name. An applicant who is 13 years of age or older is required to appear in person before the clerk or agent executing the application. A parent or legal guardian must execute the application for children under 13.

A full validity passport previously issued to the applicant or one in which he or she was included will be accepted as proof of U.S. citizenship. If the applicant has no prior passport and was born in the U.S., a certified copy of his/her birth certificate shall be presented to the agent accepting the passport application. To be acceptable, the certificate must show the given name and surname, the date and place of birth, and that the birth record was filed shortly after birth. A delayed birth certificate (a record filed more than 1 year after the date of birth) is acceptable provided that it shows that acceptable secondary evidence was used for creating this record.

If a birth certificate is not obtainable, a notice from a state registrar shall be submitted stating that no birth record exists. The notice shall be accompanied by the best obtainable secondary evidence, such as a baptismal certificate or a hospital birth record.

A naturalized citizen with no previous passport must present a Certificate of Naturalization. A person born abroad claiming U.S. citizenship through either a native-born or naturalized citizen parent must submit a Certificate of Citizenship issued by the Immigration and Naturalization Service; or a Consular Report of Birth or Certification of Birth Abroad issued by the Dept. of State. If one of the above documents has not been obtained, evidence of citizenship of the parent(s) through whom citizenship is claimed and evidence that would establish the parent/child relationship must be submitted. Additionally, if citizenship is derived through birth to citizen parent(s), the following documents will be required: parents' marriage certificate plus an affidavit from parent(s) showing periods and places of residence or physical presence in the U.S. and abroad, specifying periods spent abroad in the employment of the U.S. government, including the armed forces, or with certain international organizations. If citizenship is derived through naturalization of parents, evidence of admission to the U.S. for permanent residence also will be required.

Persons who possess the most recent passport issued within the last 12 years and after their 18th birthday may be eligible to apply for a new passport by mail. A form DSP-82, Application for Passport by Mail, must be filled out and mailed to the address shown on the form, together with the previous passport, 2 recent identical photographs, and a fee of $55.00. The DSP-82 may not be used if the most recent passport has been altered or mutilated.

Photographs, Fees, and Identity

Photographs—Submit 2 identical photographs that are sufficiently recent (normally not more than 6 months old) and that are a good likeness of and satisfactorily identify the applicant. Photographs should be 2 × 2 in. in size. The image size measured from the bottom of the chin to the top of the head (including hair) should not be less than one in. nor more than 1-3/8 in. Photographs should be portrait-type prints. They must be clear, front view, full face, with a plain white or off-white background. Photographs that depict the applicant as relaxed and smiling are encouraged.

Fees—The fee is $30.00 for passports issued to persons under 18 years of age. These passports are valid for 5 years from the date of issue. The fee is $55.00 for passports issued to persons 18 and older. These passports are valid for 10 years from the date of issuance. An additional fee of $10.00 is charged for the execution of the application. There is no execution fee when using DSP-82, Application for Passport by Mail. Applicants eligible to use this form pay only the $55.00 passport fee.

Identity—Applicants must also establish their identity to the satisfaction of the person accepting the application and to Passport Services. Generally acceptable documents of identity include a previous U.S. passport, a Certificate of Naturalization, a Certificate of Citizenship, a valid driver's license, or a government identification card. Applicants may not use a Social Security card, learner's or temporary driver's license, credit card, or expired identity card. Extremely old documents cannot be used by themselves. Applicants unable to establish identity must present some documentation in their own name and must be accompanied by a person who has known the applicant for at least 2 years and who is a U.S. citizen or legal U.S. permanent resident alien. That person must sign an affidavit before the individual who executes the passport application. The witness will be required to establish his or her own identity.

The loss or theft of a valid passport is a serious matter and should be reported immediately in writing to Passport Services, 1111 19th St., NW, Dept. of State, Washington, DC 20524-1705, telephone: (202) 647-0518, or to the nearest passport agency or the nearest U.S. embassy or consulate when abroad. For more information, the booklet *Passports— Applying for the Easy Way* is available for 50¢ from the Consumer Information Center, Pueblo, CO 81009.

Foreign Regulations

Some countries require that your passport be valid at least 6 months beyond the date of your trip. A visa, usually rubber stamped in a passport by a representative of the country to be visited, indicates that the bearer of the passport is permitted to enter that country for a certain purpose and length of time. In most instances, you must obtain necessary visas before you leave the U.S. Apply directly to the embassy or nearest consulate of each country you plan to visit, or consult a travel agent. The State Dept.'s *Foreign Entry Requirements* contains entry requirements and application instructions for most foreign countries and is also available for 50¢ from the Consumer Information Center. The process may take several weeks, so it is important to apply well in advance and verify requirements with the embassy or nearest consulate of each country before applying.

Copyright Law of the United States

Source: Copyright Office, Library of Congress

What Copyright Is

Copyright is a form of protection provided by the laws of the U.S. (title 17, U.S. Code) to the authors of "original works of authorship," including literary, dramatic, musical, artistic, and certain other intellectual works. This protection is available to both published and unpublished works. Section 106 of the Copyright Act generally gives the owner of copyright the exclusive right to do and to authorize others to do the following:

To reproduce the copyrighted work in copies or phono records;

To prepare derivative works based upon the copyrighted work;

To distribute copies or phono records of the copyrighted work to the public by sale or other transfer of ownership, or by rental, lease, or lending;

To perform the copyrighted work publicly, in the case of literary, musical, dramatic, and choreographic works, pantomimes, and motion pictures and other audiovisual works; and

To display the copyrighted work publicly, in the case of literary, musical, dramatic, and choreographic works, pantomimes, and pictorial, graphic, or sculptural works, including the individual images of a motion picture or other audiovisual work.

It is illegal for anyone to violate any of the rights provided by the act to the owner of copyright. These rights, however, are not unlimited in scope. Sections 107 through 119 of the Copyright Act establish limitations on these rights. In some cases, these limitations are specified exemptions from copyright liability. One major limitation is the doctrine of "fair use," which is given a statutory basis by section 107 of the act. In other instances, the limitation takes the form of a "compulsory license" under which certain limited uses of copyrighted works are permitted upon payment of specified royalties and compliance with statutory conditions.

Copyright protection subsists from the time the work is created in fixed form; that is, it is an incident of the process of authorship. The copyright in the work of authorship *immediately* becomes the property of the author who created it. Only the author or those deriving their rights through the author can rightfully claim copyright.

In the case of works made for hire, the employer and not the employee is presumptively considered the author. Section 101 of the copyright statute defines a "work made for hire" as:

(1) a work prepared by an employee within the scope of his or her employment; or

(2) a work specially ordered or commissioned for use as a contribution to a collective work, as a part of a motion picture or other audiovisual work, as a translation, as a supplementary work, as a compilation, as an instructional text, as a test, as answer material for a test, or as an atlas, if the parties expressly agree in a written instrument signed by them that the work shall be considered a work made for hire.

The authors of a joint work are co-owners of the copyright in the work, unless there is an agreement to the contrary.

Copyright in each separate contribution to a periodical or other collective work is distinct from copyright in the collective work as a whole and vests initially with the author of the contribution.

Copyright protection is available for all unpublished works, regardless of the nationality or domicile of the author.

Published works are eligible for copyright protection in the U.S. if any one of the following conditions is met:

• On the date of 1st publication, one or more of the authors is a national or domiciliary of the U.S. or is a national, domiciliary, or sovereign authority of a foreign nation that is a party to a copyright treaty to which the U.S. is also a party, or is a stateless person wherever that person may be domiciled; or

• The work is 1st published in the U.S. or in a foreign nation that, on the date of 1st publication, is a party to the Universal Copyright Convention; or the work comes within the scope of a Presidential proclamation; or

• The work is 1st published on or after Mar. 1, 1989, in a foreign nation that on the date of 1st publication, is a party to the Berne Convention; or, if the work is *not* 1st published in a country party to the Berne Convention, it is published (on or after Mar. 1, 1989) within 30 days of 1st publication in a country that is party to the Berne Convention; or the work, 1st published on or after Mar. 1, 1989, is a pictorial, graphic, or sculptural work that is incorporated in a permanent structure located in the U.S.; or if the work, 1st published on or after Mar. 1, 1989, is a published audiovisual work, all the authors are legal entities with headquarters in the U.S.

Which Works Are Protected

Copyright protects "original works of authorship" that are fixed in a tangible form of expression. The fixation need not be directly perceptible, as long as it may be communicated with the aid of a machine or device. Copyrightable works include the following categories:

(1) literary works;

(2) musical works, including any accompanying words;

(3) dramatic works, including any accompanying music;

(4) pantomimes and choreographic works;

(5) pictorial, graphic, and sculptural works;

(6) motion pictures and other audiovisual works;

(7) sound recordings; and

(8) architectural works.

These categories should be viewed quite broadly: for example, computer programs and most "compilations" are registrable as "literary works"; maps and architectural plans are registrable as "pictorial, graphic, and sculptural works."

Which Works Are Not Protected

Several categories of material are generally not eligible for statutory copyright protection. These include among others:

• Works that have not been fixed in a tangible form of expression. For example: choreographic works that have not been notated or recorded, or improvisational speeches or performances that have not been written or recorded.

• Titles, names, short phrases, and slogans; familiar symbols or designs; mere variations of typographic ornamentation, lettering, or coloring; mere listings of ingredients or contents.

• Ideas, procedures, methods, systems, processes, concepts, principles, discoveries, or devices, as distinguished from a description, explanation, or illustration.

• Works consisting entirely of information that is common property and containing no original authorship. For example: standard calendars, height and weight charts, tape measures and rulers, and lists or tables taken from public documents or other common sources.

Notice of Copyright

For works first published on and after Mar. 1, 1989, use of the copyright notice is optional, though highly recommended. Before Mar. 1, 1989, the use of the notice was mandatory on all published works, and any work first published before that date *must* bear a notice or risk loss of copyright protection.

Use of the notice is recommended because it informs the public that the work is protected by copyright, identifies the copyright owner, and shows the year of first publication. Furthermore, in the event that a work is infringed, if the work carries a proper notice, the court will not allow a defendant to claim "innocent infringement"—that is, that he or she did not realize that the work is protected. (A successful innocent infringement claim may result in a reduction in damages that the copyright owner would otherwise receive.)

The use of the copyright notice is the responsibility of the copyright owner and does not require advance permission from, or registration with, the Copyright Office.

For visually perceptible copies, the form of the notice consists of the following: © (the letter C in a circle), the word "Copyright," or "Copr.," and the year of first publication, and the name of the owner of copyright in the work. Example: © 1996 Judy Smith. The notice must be affixed in such manner and location as to give reasonable notice of the claim of copyright.

The notice of copyright prescribed for all published phono records of sound recordings consists of the following: ℗ (the letter P in a circle), the year of first publication of the sound recording, and the name of the owner of copyright in the sound recording. Example: ℗ 1996 XYZ Records, Inc. The notice on phono records may appear on the surface of the phono record or on the phono record label or container, provided the manner of placement and location give reasonable notice of the claim.

How Long Copyright Protection Endures

Works Originally Created on or After Jan. 1, 1978

A work that is created (fixed in tangible form for the first time) on or after Jan. 1, 1978, is automatically protected from the moment of its creation and is ordinarily given a term enduring for the author's life, plus an additional 50 yr after the author's death. In the case of "a joint work prepared by 2 or more authors who did not work for hire," the term lasts for 50 yr after the last surviving author's death. For works made for hire and for anonymous and pseudonymous works (unless the author's identity is revealed in Copyright Office records) the duration of copyright is 75 yr from publication or 100 yr from creation, whichever is shorter.

Works that were created but not published or registered for copyright before Jan. 1, 1978, have been automatically brought under the statute and are now given Federal copyright protection. The duration of copyright in these works will generally be computed in the same way as for works created on or after Jan. 1, 1978: the life-plus-50 or 75/100-yr terms will apply to them as well. The law provides that in no case will the term of copyright for works in this category expire before Dec. 31, 2002, and for works published on or before Dec. 31, 2002, the term of copyright will not expire before Dec. 31, 2027.

Works Created and Published or Registered Before Jan. 1, 1978

Under the law in effect before 1978, copyright was secured either on the date a work was published or on the date of registration if the work was registered in unpublished form. In either case, the copyright endured for a first term of 28 yr from the date it was secured. During the last (28th) year of the first term, the copyright was eligible for renewal. The current copyright law has extended the renewal term from 28 to 47 yr for copyrights that were subsisting on Jan. 1, 1978, making these works eligible for a total term of protection of 75 yr. On June 26, 1992, Pres. George Bush signed Public Law 102-307, which amends the Copyright Law to extend automatically the term of copyrights secured between Jan. 1, 1964, and Dec. 31, 1977, to a further term of 47 yr and increases the filing fee from $12.00 to $20.00. This fee increase applies to all renewal applications filed on or after June 29, 1992.

PL 102-307 makes renewal registration optional. An author need not file the renewal in order to extend the original 28-yr copyright term to the full 75 yr. It may be beneficial, however, to file a renewal registration during the 28th year of the original term. (For more information on copyright renewal, request Circular 15 from the Copyright Office.)

International Copyright Protection

There is no such thing as an "international copyright" that will automatically protect an author's writings throughout the world. Protection against unauthorized use in a particular country basically depends on the national laws of that country. However, most countries offer protection to foreign works under certain conditions, which have been greatly simplified by international copyright treaties and conventions. There are 2 principal international copyright conventions, the Berne Union for the Protection of Literary and Artistic Property (Berne Convention) and the Universal Copyright Convention (UCC).

The U.S. became a member of the Berne Convention on Mar. 1, 1989. It has been a member of the UCC since Sept. 16, 1955. Generally, the works of an author who is a national or domiciliary of a country that is a member of these treaties or works 1st published in a member country or published within 30 days of 1st publication in a Berne Union country may claim protection under them. There are no formal requirements in the Berne Convention. Under the UCC, any formality in a national law may be satisfied by the use of a notice of copyright in the form and positions specified in the UCC. A UCC notice should consist of the symbol © (C in a circle) accompanied by the year of 1st publication and the name of the copyright proprietor (©1996 John Doe). This notice must be placed in such a manner and location as to give reasonable notice of the claim to copyright. Since the Berne Convention prohibits formal requirements that affect the "exercise and enjoyment" of the copyright, the U.S. changed its law on Mar. 1, 1989, to make the use of a copyright notice optional. U.S. law, however, still provides certain advantages for use of a copyright notice; for example, the use of a copyright notice can defeat a defense of "innocent infringement."

Even if the work cannot be brought under an international convention, protection may be available in other countries by virtue of a bilateral agreement between the U.S. and other countries or under specific provision of a country's national laws. (Request Circular 38a, International Copyright Relations of the U.S., from the Copyright Office.)

Copyright Registration

Copyright registration is a legal formality intended to make a public record of the basic facts of a particular copyright. Except in specific situations, registration is not a condition for protection, but the copyright law provides several inducements or advantages to encourage copyright owners to register. Among these are the following:

• Registration establishes a public record of the copyright claim.

• Before an infringement suit may be filed in court, registration is necessary for works of U.S. origin and for foreign works not originating in a Berne Union country. (For more information on when a work is of U.S. origin, request Circular 93 from the Copyright Office).

• If made before or within 5 yr of publication, registration will establish prima facie evidence in court of the validity of the copyright and of the facts stated in the certificate.

• If registration is made within 3 months after publication of the work or prior to an infringement of the work, statutory damages and attorney's fees will be available to the copyright owner in court actions. Otherwise, only an award of actual damages and profits is available to the copyright owner.

Copyright registration allows the owner of the copyright to record the registration with the U.S. Customs Service for protection against the importation of infringing copies. For additional information, request Publication No. 563 from Commissioner of Customs, ATTN: IPR Branch, Rm 2104, U.S. Customs Service, 1301 Constitution Avenue, NW, Washington, DC 20229.

Registration may be made at any time within the life of the copyright. When a work has been registered in unpublished form, making another registration when the work becomes published is unnecessary (although the copyright owner may register the published edition, if desired).

The process of registration is simple. Request an appropriate form from the Copyright Office and complete it. Returned it to the Copyright Office along with a $20 nonrefundable filing fee and the appropriate deposit(s) of the work for which registration is sought. In a common example—a published book—the deposit is 2 copies of the best edition of the book. The Copyright Office sends a certificate of registration when the paperwork is completed, a process that usually takes 12 to 16 weeks because of the large volume of registrations the Office must handle (over 500,000 annually).

Although a copyright registration is not required, the Copyright Act establishes a mandatory deposit requirement for works published in the U.S. In general, the owner of copyright or the owner of the exclusive right of publication in the work has a legal obligation to deposit in the Copyright Office, within 3 months of publication in the U.S., 2 copies (or, in the case of sound recordings, 2 phono records) for the use of the Library of Congress. Failure to deposit these copies can result in fines and other penalties but does not affect copyright protection. Certain categories of works are exempt entirely from the mandatory deposit requirements, and the obligation is reduced for certain other categories.

Information on registration and application forms may be obtained free of charge by writing the Copyright Office, Information Section, LM-401, Library of Congress, Washington, DC 20559. Registration application forms and circulars may be ordered on a 24-hr basis by calling (202) 707-9100. Request Circular 1 for additional general information on copyright, including a list of which application forms to use when registering specific types of works.

How to Obtain Birth, Marriage, Death Records

The pamphlet Where to Write for Vital Records: Births, Deaths, Marriages, and Divorces (Stock # 017-022-01196-4) is available from the Superintendent of Documents, Government Printing Office, Washington, DC 20402; advance payment of $2.25 is required. Genealogical Research in the National Archives is sold by the National Archives Trust Fund Board, PO Box 100793, Atlanta, GA 30384.

Birthstones

Source: Jewelry Industry Council

Month	Ancient	Modern	Month	Ancient	Modern
January	Garnet	Garnet	July	Onyx	Ruby
February	Amethyst	Amethyst	August	Carnelian	Sardonyx or Peridot
March	Jasper	Bloodstone or Aquamarine	September	Chrysolite	Sapphire
April	Sapphire	Diamond	October	Aquamarine	Opal or Tourmaline
May	Agate	Emerald	November	Topaz	Topaz
June	Emerald	Pearl, Moonstone, or Alexandrite	December	Ruby	Turquoise or Zircon

Wedding Anniversaries

The traditional names for wedding anniversaries go back many years in social usage. As such names as wooden, crystal, silver, and golden were applied to anniversary years, it was considered proper to present the married couple with gifts made of these products or of something related. The list of traditional gifts, with a few allowable revisions in parentheses, is presented below, followed by modern gifts in boldface.

1st	Paper, **clocks**	9th	Pottery (china), **leather**	25th	Silver, **sterling silver**
2d	Cotton, **china**	10th	Tin, aluminum, **diamond**	30th	Pearl, **diamond**
3d	Leather, **crystal, glass**	11th	Steel, **fashion jewelry**	35th	Coral (jade), **jade**
4th	Linen (silk), **appliances**	12th	Silk, **pearl, colored gems**	40th	Ruby, **ruby**
5th	Wood, **silverware**	13th	Lace, **textiles, furs**	45th	Sapphire, **sapphire**
6th	Iron, **wood**	14th	Ivory, **gold jewelry**	50th	Gold, **gold**
7th	Wool (copper), **desk sets**	15th	Crystal, **watches**	55th	Emerald, **emerald**
8th	Bronze, **linens, lace**	20th	China, **platinum**	60th	Diamond, **diamond**

Mortgage Payment Tables

Source: *The Mortgage Money Guide,* Federal Trade Commission

8% Annual Percentage Rate

Monthly payments (principal and interest)

Amount financed	10 Years	15 Years	20 Years	25 Years	30 Years
$ 25,000	$303.32	$238.91	$209.11	$192.95	$183.44
35,000	424.65	334.48	292.75	270.14	256.82
45,000	545.97	430.04	376.40	347.32	330.19
50,000	606.64	477.83	418.22	385.91	366.88
60,000	727.97	573.39	501.86	463.09	440.26
70,000	849.29	668.96	585.51	540.27	513.64
80,000	970.62	764.52	669.15	617.45	587.01
90,000	1091.95	860.09	752.80	694.63	660.39
100,000	1213.28	955.65	836.44	771.82	733.76
120,000	1455.94	1146.78	1003.72	926.18	880.52
140,000	1698.58	1337.92	1171.02	1080.54	1027.28
160,000	1941.24	1529.04	1338.30	1234.90	1174.02
180,000	2183.90	1720.18	1505.60	1389.26	1320.78
200,000	2426.56	1911.30	1672.88	1543.64	1467.52

10% Annual Percentage Rate

Monthly payments (principal and interest)

Amount financed	10 Years	15 Years	20 Years	25 Years	30 Years
$25,000	$330.38	$268.65	$241.26	$227.18	$219.39
35,000	462.53	376.11	337.76	318.05	307.15
45,000	594.68	483.57	434.26	408.92	394.91
50,000	660.75	537.30	482.51	454.35	438.79
60,000	792.90	644.76	579.01	545.22	526.54
70,000	925.06	752.22	675.52	636.09	614.30
80,000	1057.20	859.68	772.02	726.96	702.06
90,000	1189.36	967.14	868.52	817.83	789.81
100,000	1321.51	1074.61	965.02	908.70	877.57
120,000	1585.80	1289.52	1158.02	1090.44	1053.08
140,000	1850.12	1504.44	1351.04	1272.18	1228.60
160,000	2114.40	1719.36	1544.04	1453.92	1404.12
180,000	2378.72	1934.28	1737.04	1635.66	1579.62
200,000	2643.02	2149.22	1930.04	1817.40	1755.14

9% Annual Percentage Rate

Monthly payments (principal and interest)

Amount financed	10 Years	15 Years	20 Years	25 Years	30 Years
$25,000	$316.69	$253.57	$224.93	$209.80	$201.16
35,000	443.36	354.99	314.90	293.72	281.62
45,000	570.04	456.42	404.88	377.64	362.08
50,000	633.38	507.13	449.86	419.60	402.31
60,000	760.05	608.56	539.84	503.52	482.77
70,000	886.73	709.99	629.81	587.44	563.24
80,000	1013.41	811.41	719.78	671.36	643.70
90,000	1140.08	912.84	809.75	755.28	724.16
100,000	1266.76	1014.27	899.73	839.20	804.62
120,000	1520.10	1217.12	1079.68	1007.04	965.54
140,000	1773.46	1419.98	1259.62	1174.88	1126.48
160,000	2026.82	1622.82	1439.56	1342.72	1287.40
180,000	2280.16	1825.68	1619.50	1510.56	1448.32
200,000	2533.52	2028.54	1799.46	1678.40	1609.24

11% Annual Percentage Rate

Monthly payments (principal and interest)

Amount financed	10 Years	15 Years	20 Years	25 Years	30 Years
$25,000	$344.38	$284.15	$258.05	$245.03	$238.08
35,000	482.13	397.81	361.27	343.04	333.31
45,000	619.88	511.47	464.48	441.05	428.55
50,000	688.75	568.30	516.09	490.06	476.16
60,000	826.50	681.96	619.31	588.07	571.39
70,000	964.25	795.62	722.53	686.08	666.63
80,000	1102.00	909.28	825.75	784.09	761.86
90,000	1239.75	1022.94	928.97	882.10	857.09
100,000	1377.50	1136.60	1032.19	980.11	952.32
120,000	1653.00	1363.92	1238.62	1176.14	1142.78
140,000	1928.50	1591.24	1445.06	1372.16	1333.26
160,000	2204.00	1818.56	1651.50	1568.18	1523.72
180,000	2479.50	2045.88	1857.94	1764.20	1714.18
200,000	2755.00	2273.20	2064.38	1960.22	1904.64

Median Price of Existing Single-Family Homes
Source: National Association of REALTORS®; data as of midyear 1995

City[1]	1993	1994	April 1995	City[1]	1993	1994	April 1995
Akron, OH	$83,200	$84,900	$83,900	Los Angeles, CA[2]	$195,400	$189,100	$177,100
Albuquerque, NM	100,400	110,000	110,800	Louisville, KY/IN	74,500	80,500	82,300
Anaheim/Santa Ana, CA[2]	217,000	211,000	205,100	Madison, WI	104,600	116,000	114,500
Atlanta, GA	91,800	93,600	94,400	Memphis, TN/AR/MS	87,000	86,300	81,600
Austin, TX	91,300	96,200	98,500	Miami, FL	98,800	103,200	102,600
Baltimore, MD	115,700	115,400	109,500	Milwaukee, WI	104,100	109,000	108,800
Baton Rouge, LA	75,900	77,400	79,800	Minneapolis, MN/WI	98,200	101,500	103,700
Birmingham, AL	96,500	100,200	99,700	Mobile, AL	68,200	69,900	68,800
Boise City, ID	91,400	99,000	98,000	Nashville, TN	90,400	96,500	99,500
Boston, MA	173,200	179,300	175,100	New Haven, CT	142,500	139,600	131,900
Bradenton, FL	86,500	88,300	87,600	New Orleans, LA	76,800	76,900	74,400
Buffalo/Niagra Falls, NY	83,500	82,300	82,200	New York, NY	173,200	173,200	167,000
Charleston, SC	89,900	91,600	92,600	Norfolk, VA	98,200	103,800	99,400
Charlotte, NC	106,100	106,500	100,000	Oklahoma City, OK	64,900	66,700	65,600
Chicago, IL	142,000	144,100	143,300	Omaha, NE	72,700	75,600	76,600
Cincinnati, OH/KY/IN	91,400	96,500	94,600	Orlando, FL	90,100	90,700	89,100
Cleveland, OH	95,000	98,500	93,200	Philadelphia, PA/NJ	118,000	119,500	113,400
Colorado Springs, CO	93,700	104,200	104,600	Phoenix, AZ	89,100	91,400	91,600
Columbia, SC	85,100	86,600	86,900	Pittsburgh, PA	82,200	80,700	77,200
Columbus, OH	91,800	94,800	92,800	Portland, OR	106,000	116,900	120,600
Corpus Christi, TX	70,500	74,100	69,400	Providence, RI	116,300	116,400	112,800
Dallas, TX	94,500	95,000	90,600	Raleigh/Durham, NC	109,200	115,200	118,600
Daytona Beach, FL	67,800	69,000	68,200	Sacramento, CA[2]	129,200	124,500	120,200
Denver, CO	104,700	116,800	120,800	St. Louis, MO/IL	84,800	85,000	83,300
Des Moines, IA	78,800	81,700	84,100	Salt Lake City, UT	84,900	98,000	103,000
Detroit, MI	86,000	87,000	90,500	San Antonio, TX	77,000	78,200	76,000
El Paso, TX	71,800	75,300	74,600	San Diego, CA[2]	176,900	176,000	172,100
Eugene, OR	84,400	96,200	99,800	San Francisco, CA[2]	254,400	255,600	244,500
Grand Rapids, MI	76,500	76,900	76,900	Seattle, WA	150,200	155,900	155,100
Hartford, CT	135,300	133,400	126,000	Spokane, WA	85,500	94,600	92,600
Honolulu, HI	358,500	360,000	349,000	Syracuse, NY	84,700	83,100	83,200
Houston, TX	80,900	80,500	77,200	Tampa, FL	75,000	76,200	72,200
Indianapolis, IN	86,600	90,700	88,600	Toledo, OH	72,300	73,800	72,500
Jacksonville, FL	77,100	81,900	80,700	Tucson, AZ	82,200	95,400	97,900
Kansas City, MO/KS	83,600	87,100	88,500	Tulsa, OK	71,300	74,100	72,900
Knoxville, TN	85,300	89,200	88,800	Washington, DC/MD/VA	158,500	157,900	150,100
Las Vegas, NV	108,200	110,500	111,600	Worcester, MA	129,000	130,600	128,900

(1) All areas are metropolitan statistical areas (MSA) as defined by the U.S. Office of Management and Budget as of 1992. They include the named central city and surrounding areas. (2) Data provided by the California Association of REALTORS®.

Housing Affordability
Source: National Association of REALTORS®; data as of midyear 1995

Year	Median-priced existing home	Average mortgage rate[1]	Monthly principal and interest payment	Payment as percentage of median income	Year	Median-priced existing home	Average mortgage rate[1]	Monthly principal and interest payment	Payment as percentage of median income
1984	$72,400	12.49%	$618	28.2%	1990	$97,500	10.04%	$673	22.7%
1985	75,500	11.74	609	26.2	1991	99,700	9.51	671	22.3
1986	80,300	10.25	563	23.0	1992	103,700	8.11	615	20.0
1987	85,600	9.28	565	21.9	1993	106,800	7.16	578	18.8
1988	90,600	9.31	591	22.0	1994	109,800	7.47	612	19.3
1989	93,100	10.11	660	23.1	1995[2]	109,100	8.04	643	19.9

(1) The average mortgage rate is based on the effective rate on loans closed on existing homes monitored by the Federal Housing Finance Board. (2) Preliminary figures for the first quarter of 1995.

Income Needed to Get a Mortgage
Source: National Association of REALTORS®

The following shows the minimum annual gross income needed for various size home loans at different rates. The figures are based on a 30-year loan and assume that the borrower's monthly payments cannot exceed 28% of gross income, the ceiling most lenders use. The figures do not include property taxes and insurance as part of the monthly payment.

Interest rate (percent)	Loan amount				
	$50,000	$75,000	$100,000	$150,000	$200,000
	Income needed				
8	$15,724	$23,586	$31,447	$47,171	$62,895
8½	16,477	24,715	32,954	49,430	65,907
9	17,242	25,863	34,484	51,726	68,968
9½	18,018	27,028	36,037	54,055	72,074
10	18,085	28,208	37,611	56,415	75,221
10½	19,602	29,403	39,203	58,805	78,406
11	20,407	30,611	40,814	61,221	81,628
11½	21,221	31,831	42,441	63,662	84,883
12	22,042	33,063	44,084	66,125	88,167
12½	22,870	34,305	45,740	68,610	91,479
13	23,704	35,556	47,409	71,113	94,817

Marriage Laws

Source: Gary N. Skoloff, Skoloff & Wolfe, Livingston, NJ; as of Sept. 1, 1995

State	Age with parental consent Male	Female	Age without consent Male	Female	Physical exam & blood test for male and female Max. period between exam and license	Scope of medical exam	Waiting period Before license	After license issuance (expiration)
Alabama*	14a,t	14a,t	18	18	—	b	—	30 days
Alaska	16z	16z	18	18	—	—	3 days, w	—
Arizona	16z	16z	18	18	—	—	—	—
Arkansas	17c, z	16c, z	18	18	—	—	v	—
California	aa	aa	18	18	30 days, w, h	jj	—	90 days
Colorado*y	16z	16z	18	18	—	—	—	30 days
Connecticut	16z	16z	18	18	—	bb	4 days, w	65 days
Delaware	18c	16c	18	18	—	—	24 hr, kk	30 days, e
Florida	16a, c	16a, c	18	18	—	—	—	—
Georgia*	16c	16c	16	16	—	bb	3 days, g	30 days
Hawaii	15z	15z	16	16	—	p	—	—
Idaho*	16z	16z	18	18	—	s, zzz	—	—
Illinois	16pp	16pp	18	18	30 days	n	1 day	60 days
Indiana	17c	17c	18	18	—	rr	72 hr, w	60 days
Iowa*	18z	18z	18	18	—	—	3 days	20 days
Kansas*y	18z	18z	18	18	—	—	3 days, w	—
Kentucky	18c, z	18c, z	18	18	—	—	—	—
Louisiana	18z	18z	18	18	10 days	b	72 hr, w	—
Maine	16z	16z	18	18	—	—	3 days, v, w	90 days
Maryland	16c, f	16c, f	18	18	—	—	48 hr, w	6 mo
Massachusetts	14j	12j	18	18	3-60 days, u	—	3 days, v	—
Michigan	16	16	18	18	l	b	3 days, w	—
Minnesota	16z	16z	18	18	—	—	5 days, w	—
Mississippi	aa, j	aa, j	17	15	30 days	b	3 days, w	—
Missouri	15d	15d	18	18	—	b	—	—
Montana*yy	16z	16z	18	18	—	b	—	180 days
Nebraskayy	17	17	19	19	—	bb	—	1 yr
Nevada	16z	16z	18	18	—	—	—	1 yr
New Hampshire	14k	13k	18	18	—	hh	3 days, v, w	90 days
New Jersey	16z, c	16z, c	18	18	30 days	b	72 hr, w	30 days
New Mexico	16d, c	16d, c	18	18	30 days	b	—	—
New York	16k	16k	18	18	—	nn	24 hr, ee	60 days
North Carolina	16c	16c	18	18	—	m	—	—
North Dakota	16	16	18	18	—	—	—	60 days
Ohio	18c, z	16c, z	18	18	30 days	b	5 days,w, r	30 days
Oklahoma*	16c, z	16c, z	18	18	30 days, w	b	ff	30 days
Oregon	17tt	17tt	18	18	—	—	3 days, w	—
Pennsylvania*	16d	16d	18	18	30 days	b	3 days, w	60 days
Puerto Rico	18c, d, z	16c, d, z	21	21	—	b	—	—
Rhode Island*	18d	16d	18	18	—	rrr	—	—
South Carolina*	16c	14c	18	18	—	—	1 day	—
South Dakota	16c	16c	18	18	—	—	—	20 days
Tennessee	16d	16d	18	18	—	—	3 days, cc, w	30 days
Texas*y	14j, k	14j, k	18	18	—	—	—	30 days
Utah*	14a	14a	18x	18x	—	—	—	30 days
Vermont	16z	16z	18	18	30 days, w	b	1 day, w	—
Virginia	16a, c	16a, c	18	18	—	zz	—	60 days
Washington	17d	17d	18	18	—	bbb	3 days	60 days
West Virginia	18c	18c	18	18	—	b	3 days, w	—
Wisconsin	16z	16z	18	18	—	zzz	—	30 days
Wyoming	16d	16d	18	18	—	bb	—	—
Dist. of Columbia*	16a	16a	18	18	30 days	b	3 days, w	—

*Indicates common-law marriage recognized. (a)Parental consent not required if minor was previously married. (aa)No age limits. (b)Venereal diseases. In WV and OK, Circuit Court judge may waive requirement. (bb)Venereal diseases and rubella (for female). (bbb)No exam required, but parties must file affidavit of non-affliction of contagious venereal disease. (c)Younger parties may obtain license in case of pregnancy or birth of child. (cc)Unless parties are over 18 yr of age. (d)Younger parties may obtain license in special circumstances. (e)Residents before expiration of 24-hr waiting period; non-residents formerly residents, before expiration of 96-hr waiting period; others 96 hr. (ee)License effective 1 day after issuance, unless court orders otherwise, valid for 60 days only. (f)If parties are at least 16 yr of age, proof of age and the consent of parents in person is required. If a parent is ill, an affidavit by the incapacitated parent and a physician's affidavit to that effect required. (ff)If one or both parties are below the age for marriage without parental consent, 3-day waiting period. (g)Unless parties are 18 yr of age or more, or female is pregnant, or applicants are the parents of a living child born out of wedlock. (h)When unmarried man and unmarried woman, not minors, have been living together as man and wife, they may, without health certificate, be married upon issuance of appropriate authorization. (hh)Parties must sign affidavit affirming that they have received and discussed brochure prepared by Division of Public Health Services, Dept. of Health and Human Services. (j)Parental consent and/or permission of judge required. (jj)Medical examination for syphilis (and for female, rubella), with required offer of HIV test. (k)Below age of consent parties need parental consent and permission of judge. (kk)Medical examination not required but certificate evidencing HIV counseling required. (l)If both parties are residents, 96 hr. (m)Mental incompetence, infectious tuberculosis, venereal diseases. (n)Venereal diseases; test for sickle cell anemia given at request of examining physician. (nn)Tests for sickle cell anemia may be required for certain applicants. (p)Rubella for female, except under limited circumstances. (pp)Judicial consent may be given when parents refuse to consent. (r)Applicants under age 18 must state that they have had marriage counseling. (rr)Any unsterilized female under 50 must submit with application for license a medical report stating whether she has immunological response to rubella, or written record the rubella vaccine was administered on or after her 1st birthday. Judge may by order dispense with these requirements. (rrr)Physical examination and blood test required; offer of HIV counseling required. (s)Rubella for female; there are certain exceptions, and district judge may waive medical examination on proof that emergency exists. (t)Other statutory requirements apply. (tt)If a party has no parent residing within state, and one party has residence within state for 6 mo, no permission required. (u)Doctor's certificate must be filed 30 days prior to notice of intention. (v)Parties must file notice of intention to marry with local clerk(w)Waiting period may be avoided. (x)Authorizes counties to provide for premarital counseling as a requisite to issuance of license to persons under 19 and persons previously divorced. (y)Marriages by proxy are valid. (yy) Proxy marriages are valid under certain conditions. (z)Younger parties may marry with parental consent and/or permission of judge. In CT, judicial approval. (zz)Required offer of HIV test, and/or must be provided with information on AIDS and tests available. (zzz)Applicants must receive information on AIDS and certify having read it.

Divorce Laws

Source: Gary N. Skoloff, Skoloff & Wolfe, Livingston, NJ; as of Sept. 1, 1995

Important: Almost all states also have other laws as well as qualifications of the laws shown below and proposed divorce-reform laws pending. It would be wise to consult a lawyer in conjunction with the use of this chart.

Some Grounds for Absolute Divorce[1]

	Residence	Adultery	Mental or physical cruelty	Desertion	Alcoholism	Impotency	Non-support	Insanity	Bigamy	Felony conviction or imprisonment	Drug addiction	Fraud, force, duress
PR	1 yr	Yes	Yes	1 yr	Yes	Yes	No	Yes	A	Yes*	Yes	No
AL	6 mo*	Yes	Yes	1 yr	Yes	Yes	2 yr	5 yr	A	2 yr*	Yes	A
AK	*	Yes	Yes	1 yr	1 yr	Yes	No	18 mo	A	Yes	Yes	A
AZ	90 days	No	No	No	No	No	No	No	No	No	No	No
AR	60 days*	Yes	Yes	No	1 yr	Yes	Yes	3 yr	No	Yes	No	A
CA	6 mo*	No	No	No	No	A	No	Yes*	A	No	No	A
CO	90 days	No	No	No	A	A	No	No	A	No	A	A
CT	1 yr*	Yes	Yes	1 yr	No	No	Yes	5 yr	A	life*	No	No
DE	6 mo	Yes	Yes	Yes	Yes	A	No	Yes	Yes	Yes	Yes	A
FL	6 mo	No	No	No	No	No	No	3 yr	No	No	No	A
GA	6 mo	Yes	Yes	1 yr	Yes	Yes	No	2 yr	A	Yes*	Yes	Yes
HI	6 mo	No	No	No	No	No	No	No	A	No	No	A
ID	6 wk	Yes	Yes	Yes	No	A	No	3 yr	A	Yes	No	A
IL	90 days	Yes	Yes	1 yr	2 yr	Yes	No	No	Yes	Yes	2 yr	No
IN	6 mo*	No	No	No	No	Yes	No	2 yr	A	Yes	No	A
IA	1 yr*	No	No	No	No	A	No	A	A	No	No	No
KS	60 days	No	No	No	No	No	Yes	2 yr	A	No	No	A
KY	180 days	No	No	No	No	A	No	No	No	No	No	A
LA	6 mo*	Yes	No	No	No	No	No	No	A	Yes*	No	A
ME	6 mo*	Yes	Yes	3 yr	Yes	Yes	Yes	A	A	No	Yes	No
MD	*	Yes	†	1 yr†	No	No	No	3 yr	A	1 yr*	No	No
MA	1 yr*	Yes	Yes	1 yr	Yes	Yes	No†	A	A	5 yr*	Yes	No
MI	180 days*	No	No	No	No	No	No	No	No	No	No	A
MN	180 days	No	No	No	No	No	No	No	No	No	A	A
MS	6 mo	Yes	Yes	1 yr	Yes	Yes, A	No	3 yr, A	A	Yes	Yes	A
MO	90 days	No	No	No	No	No	No	No	A	No	No	A
MT	90 days	No	No	No	A	A	No	No	A	No	A	A
NE	1 yr*	No	No	No	No	A	No	A	A	No	No	A
NV	6 wk	No	No	No	No	No	No	2 yr	A	No	No	A
NH	1 yr*	Yes	Yes	2 yr	2 yr	Yes	2 yr	No	A	1 yr*	No	No
NJ	1 yr*	Yes	Yes	1 yr	1 yr	A	No	2 yr	A	18 mo	1 yr	A
NM	6 mo	Yes	Yes	Yes	No	No	No	No	No	No	No	No
NY	1 yr*	Yes	Yes	1 yr†	No	No	†	A	A	3 yr†	No	A
NC	6 mo	No	No	No	No	A	No	3 yr	A	No	No	No
ND	6 mo	Yes	Yes	1 yr	No	A	1 yr	5 yr	A	Yes	No	A
OH	6 mo	Yes	Yes	1 yr†	Yes	No	Yes	No	Yes	Yes	No	Yes
OK	6 mo	Yes	Yes	1 yr	Yes	Yes	Yes	5 yr	Yes	Yes	No	Yes
OR	6 mo*	No	No	No	No	No	No	No	No	No	No	No
PA	6 mo	Yes	Yes	1 yr	No	No	No	18 mo*	No	No	No	No
RI	1 yr	Yes	Yes	5 yr*	Yes	Yes	1 yr	No	No	Yes	Yes	No
SC	1 yr*	Yes	Yes	1 yr	Yes	No	No	No	No	No	Yes	No
SD	*	Yes	Yes	1 yr†	1 yr†	A	1 yr†	5 yr	A	Yes	No	A
TN	6 mo*	Yes	Yes	1 yr	Yes	Yes	Yes	No	Yes	Yes	Yes	A
TX	6 mo*	Yes	Yes	1 yr	No	A	No	3 yr	No	1 yr	No	No
UT	3 mo*	Yes	Yes	1 yr	Yes	Yes	Yes	Yes*	A	Yes	No	No
VT	6 mo*	Yes	Yes	7 yr	No	No	Yes	5 yr†	A	3 yr	No	A
VA	6 mo*	Yes	Yes	1 yr†	No	A	†	A	A	1 yr	No	A
WA	bona fide resident	No	No	No	No	No	No	No	A*	No	No	A
WV	1 yr*	Yes	Yes	6 mo	Yes	A	No	3 yr	A	Yes	Yes	No
WI	6 mo	No	No	No	A	A	No	No	A	No	A	A
WY	2 mo*	No	No	No	No	A	No	2 yr	A	No	No	A
DC	6 mo	No	No	No	No	A	No	A	A	No	No	A

(1)Almost all states have "no-fault" divorce laws. Conduct that constitutes "no-fault" divorce may vary from state to state. (*)Indicates qualification; check local statutes. (A)Indicates grounds for annulment. (†)Indicates grounds for divorce or legal separation.

TAXES

Federal Income Tax

Source: George W. Smith III, CPA, Nationally Syndicated Tax Author and Columnist

During the past decade, the U.S. Congress enacted several major tax law changes. Some of the most recent contain provisions that take effect in 1995. A number of further changes in the tax law were under consideration in the 104th Congress in late 1995.

New Tax Provisions Taking Effect in 1995

Self-Employed Health Insurance. On Apr. 11, 1995, President Bill Clinton signed into law the Self-Employment Health Insurance Act. This legislation retroactively reinstates for the 1994 tax year the 25% health insurance premium deduction for the self-employed. Those self-employed taxpayers who filed their 1994 tax returns without taking this allowable deduction could file Form 1040X to amend their returns and request a refund. This law permanently restores the health insurance premium deduction for the self-employed and raises the deduction to 30% beginning in 1995.

Nanny Tax. Congress simplified the tax and paperwork associated with hiring household workers when it passed the Social Security and Domestic and Employment Reform Act of 1994. No longer must an employer withhold employment taxes for household workers who receive less than $1,000 a year.

Starting in 1995, quarterly employment tax returns for household employees also are no longer required. All employment information and withholding tax obligations will now be included in the (employer's) individual income tax return, Form 1040, Schedule H. The previously used Form 942, Employer's Quarterly Tax Return for Household Employees, is no longer valid.

Refunds for Household Employment Taxes. If an individual paid employment taxes to the IRS in 1994 for a household worker who earned less than $1,000 for the calendar year, that individual can claim a refund by using Form 843, Claim for Refund and Request for Abatement.

Household Workers Exclusion. With the recent passage of the "Nanny Tax" act (officially, the Social Security and Domestic and Employment Reform Act of 1994), household workers under the age of 18 are exempt from employment taxes even if they are paid more than $1,000 a year, unless working in a household is their principal occupation.

Social Security Number. Starting in 1995, individuals must obtain a Social Security number for a baby born before Nov. 1, 1995, to claim the child on their tax return.

Empowerment Zones. Generally, a 20% credit is available to all employers against their income tax liability for the first $15,000 of qualified wages paid to full- or part-time employees who are residents of one of 9 empowerment zones (distressed areas designated for economic revitalization by HUD and the USDA) and perform substantially all their employment services within the zone. The maximum credit is $3,000 per employee.

Hardship Distributions. Generally, a 401(k) plan participant now may withdraw funds from the plan without penalty if the distribution is "necessary" to satisfy "immediate and heavy financial needs."

Elective Withholding. After Dec. 31, 1996, taxpayers who receive Social Security benefits and certain other payments from the federal government may elect to have the payor agency withhold federal income tax at a rate of 7%, 15%, 18%, or 31%.

States also will be required to permit elective withholding from unemployment compensation at a rate of 15%.

Installment Payments. Form 9465, Installment Agreement Request, allows many taxpayers to ask the IRS to accept installment payments when they don't have the necessary funds to pay the taxes owed on their return. Penalty and interest will be charged on these installment payments.

Final Estimated Tax Payment. The Omnibus Budget Reconciliation Act of 1993 (OBRA) allowed individual taxpayers to elect to pay in 3 annual interest-free installments any additional 1993 taxes attributable to the newly imposed 36% and 39.6% tax rate brackets. If the taxpayer elected to pay in installments, payment number 2 was due Apr. 17, 1995; payment number 3 is due on or before Apr. 15, 1996. The payments should:

(1) be made payable to the Internal Revenue Service,
(2) include the taxpayer's Social Security number, and
(3) be clearly labeled "1993 OBRA installment."

Other Recent Tax Law Changes and Developments

As there were in 1994, in 1995 there are 5 individual tax rates: 15%, 28%, 31%, 36%, and 39.6%. Both the 1995 Income Tax Tables and the 1995 Tax Rate Schedules were adjusted so that inflation will not increase an individual's tax.

The maximum income tax rate on net long-term capital gains for individuals, estates, and trusts remains at 28%.

Married couples filing jointly and single individuals can file Form 1040EZ if they have no dependents, were not 65 or older or blind, and had taxable income of less than $50,000 from wages, salaries, and tips and not more than $400 of interest income.

Although many dollar amounts in the tax law are adjusted each year for inflation, including the annual limitation on elective deferrals to 401(k) plans, for 1995, the dollar limit for 401(k) plans remains as it was in 1994, $9,240.

For 1995 an individual may not claim an exemption for a dependent child who qualifies as a full-time student and is over age 23 at the end of the year unless the child's gross income is less than $2,500. The amount was $2,450 for 1994.

Interest earned on Series EE bonds issued in 1990 or later may be exempt from federal income tax if used to pay tuition and fees for a taxpayer, a spouse, or a dependent to attend a college, a university, or a qualified technical school during the year the bonds are redeemed. The exclusion is phased out for taxpayers with income over a certain amount.

An individual who buys a new 4-wheel vehicle powered primarily by an electric motor may be eligible for an income tax credit. The credit is 10% of the cost of the vehicle with a maximum credit of $4,000 per qualified electric vehicle. To qualify, the vehicle must be put into service by Dec. 31, 2004.

Parents may elect to include on their income tax return the unearned income of a dependent child under age 14 whose income is more than $500 but less than $5,000. The income must consist solely of interest and dividends. Form 8814, Parent's Election to Report Child's Interest and Dividends, is required to report this income.

If the parents elect to include the child's income on their return, the child is not required to file a return. This election is not available, however, if estimated tax payments were made in the child's name.

If a dependent child with taxable income cannot file an income tax return, a parent, a guardian, or some other legally responsible person must file the return for the child. The parent or guardian may be held liable for any unpaid income tax on the child's taxable income.

For individuals age 55 or older, the 3-out-of-5-year home-use rule for the sale of a principal residence has been expanded. Certain incapacitated individuals who reside in state-licensed facilities may exclude from gross income a maximum of $125,000 of gain resulting from the sale of their home if the house was used as their principal residence for at least one year out of the last 5 years ending on the date of the sale. *Caution:* This is a once-in-a-lifetime exclusion.

The IRS provides videotaped instructions in English and in Spanish for assistance in and completing an individual's tax return. These tapes are available at participating libraries. Individuals also can call their local IRS office for assistance.

Various federal tax forms and tax instructions are now printed in Spanish.

Recent tax legislation made the following 3 important changes to the treatment of distributions from qualified pension plans and annuities:

(1) Most pension plan distributions are now eligible for rollovers;

(2) Plans are required to permit direct rollovers;

(3) Federal withholding of 20% is mandatory on distributions not directly rolled over into another retirement plan.

A business deduction is not allowed for the base rate charged on the first telephone line into a personal residence. This disallowance does not affect the deductibility of long distance calls or optional services such as call waiting, call forwarding, 3-way calling, or extra directory listings as long as they are business related.

The business use of a cellular phone or home computer must be for the convenience of the employer and a condition of employment to be an allowable business deduction for an employee.

The IRS telephone service for hearing-impaired persons is available for taxpayers who have access to TDD equipment. The toll-free number is 1-800-829-4059.

The 1995 wage base for Social Security tax was increased to $61,200. The Social Security tax rate is 6.2%; the Medicare rate is 1.45%. The combined Social Security and Medicare tax rate is 7.65%. The employer and the employee each pay 7.65%.

The tax rate for self-employed individuals is 15.3% (Social Security is 12.4%; Medicare, 2.9%) on all net self-employment income up to a maximum of $61,200.

Congress eliminated the $135,000 ceiling on wages subject to the Medicare tax. All wages (including self-employment income) now are subject to the Medicare tax.

Jury duty pay returned by an employee to an employer in exchange for his or her normal salary is deductible by the employee as an adjustment to income on page 1, Form 1040.

The IRS has affirmed that the buyer can deduct "seller-paid points" on the purchase of a principal residence. Individuals who purchased a home in 1991 or later can file an amended tax return, Form 1040X, for a possible refund.

For 1995, the standard mileage rate for business use of an automobile was increased to 30 cents a mile for all business miles driven. U.S. Postal Service employees who collect or deliver mail on a rural route can use a special standard mileage rate of 45 cents a mile.

The standard mileage rate cannot be used for leased cars.

A maximum of $160 a month for employer-provided parking is tax free to an employee. An employee may exclude up to $60 a month for mass-transit passes.

For 1995, an individual who is under age 65 and collects Social Security can earn $8,160 without losing any benefits. A person who is age 65-69 and collects Social Security can earn $11,280 without losing any benefits. Individuals who are age 70 or over will not lose Social Security benefits regardless of their earnings.

Owners of new diesel-powered highway automobiles not purchased for resale may be entitled to a credit of $102; $198 for the purchase of a diesel-powered light van or truck.

Individuals who file their returns electronically or who use the 1040PC format can instruct the IRS to deposit their refund directly into a checking or savings account.

Expenses paid for business assignments away from home that last for more than one year in a single location are no longer considered "temporary" and are not deductible.

Capital gains can now be included in investment income when figuring the limit on the investment interest deduction. However, the taxpayer will have to reduce the amount of net long-term capital gain that is eligible for the maximum 28% capital gains tax rate in order to offset the additional investment interest deduction.

The election to expense the cost of certain depreciable business assets ("Section 179 Expense") each year remains at $17,500 for 1995.

Goodwill, patents, trademarks, client lists, and certain other intangible assets are amortized over a 15-year period.

Congress reduced the deduction for qualified business meals and entertainment expenses to 50%.

Business expenses for dues paid in business, social, athletic, luncheon, sporting, and country clubs, including airport and hotel clubs, are no longer deductible.

Taxpayers deducting individual charitable contributions of $250 or more must obtain written substantiation from the charity before filing a tax return. The written statement must show the breakdown of the payment if it is for more than $75 and is partly a contribution and partly for goods or services.

The maximum compensation limit allowed in 1995 for a tax-qualified retirement plan participant is $150,000. This includes Profit Sharing, 401(k), Money Purchase Pension, Simplified Employee Pension (SEP), and Defined Benefit plans.

If a taxpayer expects to owe $500 or more of taxes for 1995, he or she is required to file estimated income tax payments unless the current income tax withholding and credits equals 100% of the tax shown on the 1994 return. The percentage increases to 110% of the previous year's tax if the adjusted gross income for 1994 was more than $150,000 ($75,000 if married filing separately). Different rules apply for farmers and people engaged in commercial fishing.

Taxpayers can no longer deduct travel expenses paid for another individual (including a spouse) who accompanies them on a business trip unless the individual (1) is their employee, (2) has a bona fide business purpose for the travel, and (3) would otherwise be allowed to deduct the travel expense.

1995 Individual Tax Rates

The 5 tax rates for 1995 are 15%, 28%, 31%, 36%, and 39.6%. The dollar bracket amounts are adjusted each year for inflation.

Single

Tax Rate	Taxable Income
15%	$0 to $23,350
28%	$23,351 to $56,550
31%	$56,551 to $117,950
36%	$117,951 to $256,500
39.6%	More than $256,500

Married Filing Jointly or Qualifying Widow(er)

Tax Rate	Taxable Income
15%	$0 to $39,000
28%	$39,001 to $94,250
31%	$94,251 to $143,600
36%	$143,601 to $256,500
39.6%	More than $256,500

Married Filing Separately

Tax Rate	Taxable Income
15%	$0 to $19,500
28%	$19,501 to $47,125
31%	$47,126 to $71,800
36%	$71,801 to $128,250
39.6%	More than $128,250

Head of Household

Tax Rate	Taxable Income
15%	$0 to $31,250
28%	$31,251 to $80,750
31%	$80,751 to $130,800
36%	$130,801 to $256,500
39.6%	More than $256,500

Estates and Trusts

Tax Rate	Taxable Income
15%	0 to $1,550
28%	$1,551 to $3,700
31%	$3,701 to $5,600
36%	$5,601 to $7,650
39.6%	More than $7,650

The maximum tax rate on net long-term capital gains for an individual, estate, or trust is 28%. The alternative minimum tax rate for noncorporate taxpayers is 26% for alternative minimum taxable income less the exemption amount up to $175,000 ($87,500 for married individuals filing separately). Above that dollar level, a 28% rate applies.

Standard Deduction

The standard deduction is a flat dollar amount that is subtracted from the adjusted gross income of taxpayers who do not itemize their deductions. The amount of the basic standard deduction depends on the taxpayer's filing status and is adjusted annually for inflation.

1995 Basic Standard Deduction

Single $3,900
Married filing jointly or qualifying widow(er) . . . $6,550
Married filing separately $3,275
Head of household $5,750

These figures are not applicable if someone can claim you as a dependent.

Caution: Taxpayers with itemized deductions such as medical expenses, property taxes, investment and home mortgage interest, charitable contributions, employee business expenses, and gambling losses totaling more than the standard deduction amount should not use the standard deduction. They should itemize their deductions.

An individual claimed as a dependent on another person's income tax return generally may claim on his or her own tax return the larger of $650 or the amount of earned income up to the amount of the basic standard deduction that the taxpayer would normally be allowed.

Earned income includes wages, salaries, commissions, and tips. It also includes net profit from self-employment received as compensation for personal services rendered. Any part of a scholarship or a fellowship grant that must be included in gross income is also considered earned income.

Example 1: During 1995, a dependent mother, age 60, had unearned income (interest and dividends) of $1,700 and no earned income. Her basic standard deduction would be $650. She would have taxable income of $1,050. A dependent cannot claim his or her own personal exemption.

Example 2: A dependent son had $10,000 of unearned income and $100 of earned income. He is limited to a $650 standard deduction because he is a dependent and his earned income is less than $650. He would, therefore, have $9,450 in taxable income.

Example 3: A dependent daughter with $4,000 of earned income and $600 of unearned income would claim the maximum $3,900 standard deduction allowed because her earned income of $4,000 is greater than the standard deduction. She would have taxable income of $700.

Additional Standard Deduction for People Age 65 or Older or Blind

Elderly or blind taxpayers may claim an additional standard deduction in addition to the basic standard deduction. Taxpayers who are age 65 or older or blind at the end of 1995 qualify. Individuals who claim the additional standard deduction because of blindness must attach a doctor's statement to their income tax return.

1994 Additional Standard Deduction

Single or head of household, age 65 or over OR blind	$ 950
Single or head of household, age 65 or over AND blind	$1,900
Married filing jointly or qualifying widow(er), age 65 or over OR blind (per person)	$ 750
Married filing jointly or qualifying widow(er), age 65 or over AND blind (per person)	$1,500
Married filing separately, age 65 or over OR blind	$ 750
Married filing separately, age 65 or over AND blind	$1,500

If someone can claim you as a dependent, different amounts apply.

Example 1: A single, 65-year-old individual would have a standard deduction of $4,850 computed as follows:

Basic standard deduction for a single person	$3,900
Additional standard deduction for age	950
Total	$4,850

Example 2: A 70-year-old husband and a 58-year-old blind wife filing jointly would be entitled to a standard deduction totaling $8,050 computed as follows:

Basic standard deduction for married filing jointly	$6,550
Additional standard deduction for (husband's) age	750
Additional standard deduction for (wife's) blindness	750
Total	$8,050

Caution: Taxpayers who itemize their deductions cannot claim the additional or basic standard deduction.

Dependent and Personal Exemptions

The exemption amount for 1995 has been increased to $2,500. The amount for 1994 was $2,450. The exemption amount is adjusted each year for inflation.

The deduction for each exemption is reduced by 2% for each $2,500 ($1,250 for married filing separately) or fraction thereof by which adjusted gross income for 1995 exceeds the following threshold amount:

Married filing jointly	$172,050
Qualifying widow(er)	$172,050
Head of household	$143,350
Single	$114,700
Married filing separately	$ 86,025

The exemption amount is fully phased out when adjusted gross income is more than $122,500 ($61,250 for married filing separately) over the threshold amount.

Adjustments to Income

Individual Retirement Accounts (IRAs)

Single taxpayers who are not covered by a qualified employer retirement plan may take an IRA deduction up to the lesser of $2,000 or the amount of their earned income, regardless of their total income. Married taxpayers filing jointly also may take an IRA deduction providing neither one is an active participant in a qualified retirement plan. Income earned from IRAs will remain tax-free until the taxpayer makes a withdrawal from the plan.

Taxpayers may contribute to their IRAs even if they are covered by an employer-sponsored qualified retirement plan. However, the amount that can be deducted on their income tax return depends on their total income.

Married taxpayers filing jointly in 1995 with adjusted gross income of $40,000 or less may take the maximum IRA deduction allowed whether or not either is an active participant in a qualified retirement plan. Single taxpayers in a qualified retirement plan also may fully deduct IRA contributions providing their adjusted gross income is $25,000 or less.

The IRA deduction is phased out over the next $10,000 of adjusted gross income if taxpayers are active participants in a qualified retirement plan. Consequently, married couples filing jointly with adjusted gross income of $50,000 or more and single filers with adjusted gross income of $35,000 or more may not deduct any IRA contributions.

Moving Expenses

Taxpayers who change jobs during the year usually can deduct part of their moving expenses. These expenses include the cost of moving household goods and travel to their new home.

To qualify, the move must be for changing job locations or starting a new job and must meet distance and time tests.

Expenses for moving household goods and traveling to a new home now have some additional rules and limitations:

1. The distance test is extended from 35 to at least 50 miles.

2. Premove house-hunting trips, temporary living expenses, and any expenses that pertain to the sale, purchase, or rental of an individual's residence are no longer deductible.

3. Meals while traveling to the new location are no longer deductible.

4. Qualified moving expenses paid or reimbursed by the taxpayer's employer are excludable from gross income.

5. Moving expenses are deductible as an adjustment to income on page 1 of Form 1040 and not as an itemized deduction on Schedule A.

Any reimbursements, directly or indirectly, that are not qualified moving expenses will be included in the employee's gross income as compensation for services and are fully taxable. Moves within the U.S. are reported on Form 3903, Moving Expenses.

Social Security Benefits

As much as 85% of Social Security benefits received by an individual in 1995 could be taxed depending on the amount of the person's total income.

When an individual receives income in addition to Social Security benefits, as much as 50% of these benefits could be included in taxable income if the individual's total income, including 50% of the person's Social Security benefits, is more than the following adjusted base amounts:

$25,000 but less than $34,000 for single, head of household, qualifying widow(er), or married and filing separately and the spouses *lived apart* for all of 1995,

$32,000 but less than $44,000 for married filing jointly.

However, if an individual's income plus 50% of his or her Social Security benefits exceeds the $34,000 or $44,000 base amounts, as much as 85% of Social Security benefits could be included in taxable income.

If the taxpayer is married, filing separately, and *lived with* his or her spouse at any time during 1995, the above base amounts are reduced to zero.

If the only income an individual received during 1995 was from Social Security, generally these benefits will not be taxable, and the individual probably will not have to file a federal income tax return.

Review of Social Security Benefits

Beginning in 1995, individuals age 60 or older who currently are not receiving Social Security benefits, will receive a new unsolicited statement form from the Social Security Administration showing how much Social Security they will receive in retirement, disability, and survivor benefits now or in the future. By 1999, all individuals age 25 and older will automatically receive this annual statement.

To receive a complete earnings history and an estimate of the benefits you can expect to receive at retirement, call the Social Security Administration's toll-free number (800) 772-1213 and ask for Form SSA-7004, *Report for Earnings and Benefit Estimate Statement.*

Itemized Deductions

• Many elective cosmetic surgeries, including hair transplants and other similar procedures, are no longer deductible medical expenses. Cosmetic surgery for congenital abnormality, personal injury resulting from an accident or trauma, or a disfiguring disease is allowed as a medical deduction. Only the total amount of medical expenses that exceeds 7.5% of the taxpayer's adjusted gross income is deductible.

• Investment interest is deductible only to the extent of net investment income. Any excess is carried over to future years.

• Most mortgage interest on a taxpayer's first and second homes remains fully deductible; however, there are limitations.

• Interest on home equity loans is deductible, but only up to the first $100,000 in equity debt.

• State and local income taxes, real estate taxes, and personal property taxes remain fully deductible. Sales taxes are not deductible.

• Casualty and theft losses are deductible subject to the $100 limitation rule for each occurrence and the 10% of adjusted gross income provision.

• Miscellaneous items, such as union and professional dues, tax preparation fees, safe-deposit box rental expense, and employee business expenses, are deductible, but only the amount that exceeds 2% of the taxpayer's adjusted gross income.

• Individuals can deduct on Schedule A gambling losses such as the cost of lottery tickets, but only up to the amount of their gambling winnings reported on page 1, Form 1040.

Employee Business Expenses

All employee business expenses, including travel, automobile, telephone, gifts, and entertainment, are deductible on Schedule A as miscellaneous itemized deductions. Only 50% of the cost of customer meals and entertainment is now deductible. These business expenses are then subject to the 2% of taxpayer's adjusted gross income limitation for miscellaneous deductions. Country club dues are no longer deductible.

Reduction of Itemized Deductions

Many itemized deductions otherwise allowed are further reduced by the lesser of 3% of a taxpayer's adjusted gross income in excess of $114,700 ($57,350 for married taxpayers filing separately) or 80% of the amount of these itemized deductions otherwise allowable for the year. These amounts are adjusted each year for inflation. This provision does not affect medical expenses, investment interest expense, casualty losses, or gambling losses to the extent of gambling winnings.

Earned Income Credit

Low-income workers who have dependent children and maintain a household are eligible for a refundable earned income credit. The credit for 1995 is calculated on earned income such as wages and tips.

The maximum credit for an invidivual with one qualifying child is $2,094. However, the earned income credit is gradually phased out as the person's earned income increases, and it is completely phased out when the adjusted gross income reaches $24,396. For an individual with 2 or more qualifying children, the maximum credit is $3,110 and is phased out when the adjusted gross income reaches $26,673.

If an individual qualifies for the earned income credit, the credit is refundable even if the person is not required to file an income tax return. A tax return must be filed to receive this credit.

To assist individuals, the IRS publishes a chart showing the earned income credit at various levels of income. This chart is available free at any IRS office. The IRS will also assist individuals in preparing this form or will figure the credit for them.

The earned income credit has been extended to include persons who work and do not have a qualifying child. The maximum credit without a child is $314. To qualify:

1. earned income and adjusted gross income must be less than $9,230,

2. an individual or spouse must be at least 25 years old and less than 65, and

3. an individual cannot be claimed as a dependent on another person's return.

Previously, the earned income credit was available only to a taxpayer who had a principal place of abode in the U.S. for more than a half year. Starting in 1995, a member of the U.S. Armed Forces stationed ouside the U.S. while serving on extended active duty is considered maintaining a U.S. place of abode.

Starting in 1996, the credit will not be allowed to taxpayers with more than $2,350 of interest income (whether taxable or tax exempt), dividends, or net income from rents and royalties.

Taxing Children's Unearned Income

Children under age 14 with at least one living parent may use as much as $650 of their standard deduction against unearned income. Unearned income includes interest and dividend income. If the child' unearned income is more than $1,300, that income will be taxed at the child's tax rate or at the parent's rate, whichever is higher.

Parents have the option of including a child's unearned income on their tax return. When this income is included on the parents' tax return, however, all the income over $1,000 is subject to the higher tax rate. Therefore, if the child includes the unearned income on his or her tax return, the child could receive the benefit of a lower tax rate on an additional $300 of unearned income.

A child who may be claimed as a dependent by another taxpayer may not claim his or her own personal exemption even if the exemption is not actually claimed on the other taxpayer's return.

When to File

U.S. individual income tax returns for 1995 are required to be filed with the Internal Revenue Service no later than Monday, Apr. 15, 1996.

An individual who cannot file on time should file Form 4868, Application for Automatic Extension of Time to File U.S. Individual Income Tax Return. Doing so gives the taxpayer an automatic 4-month extension of time to file, until Thursday, Aug. 15, 1996.

This is not, however, an extension of time to pay the tax. The taxpayer will owe interest and may be charged a penalty on any federal income tax owed and not paid to the IRS by Apr. 15, 1996.

Who Must File

Whether a U.S. citizen or resident alien living in the U.S. must file an income tax return depends on the person's gross income, filing status, and age.

Generally, a U.S. citizen or resident alien will have to file an income tax return if the person's gross income for the year is at least as much as the amount shown in the following table:

Filing Status	1995 Gross Income
Single	
• Under 65	$ 6,400
• 65 or older	7,350
Married filing jointly	
• Both spouses under 65	11,500
• One spouse 65 or older	12,300
• Both spouses 65 or older	13,050
Married filing separately	2,500
Head of Household	
• Under 65	8,250
• 65 or older	9,200
Qualifying widow(er)	
• Under 65	9,050
• 65 or older	9,800

Example: John and Mary Smith intend to file a joint return for 1995. John's income is entirely from wages. Mary receives no income subject to tax. Neither John nor Mary is blind. John is 67 years old, but Mary will not be 65 until next year. For 1995, their combined gross income subject to tax will be $12,500. They will have to file a tax return because their gross income will be greater than $12,300.

If Mary were age 65, they would not have to file a 1995 tax return because their gross income would be less than $13,050 as shown in the table.

Some Exceptions to Filing Requirements: A tax return must be filed if:

• Net earnings from self-employment for the year are $400 or more.
• Advance earned income credit payments were received during the year from an employer.
• Taxpayer is entitled to receive an earned income credit.
• Taxpayer expects an income tax refund.
• Gross income is less than the filing requirement amount, but aditional taxes are owed for:

—Social Security tax on unreported tips.
—Alternative minimum tax.
—Recapture of investment credit.
—Tax attributable to qualified retirement distributions (including IRAs), annuities, and modified endowment contracts.

Which Form to File

Most U.S. citizens can use one of 3 basic tax forms: 1040EZ, 1040A, and 1040. Forms 1040EZ and 1040A are shorter and generally easier to complete than Form 1040. Which tax form to use depends on individual circumstances unless the rules specifically say you must file Form 1040.

You may be able to use the shortest of the 3 forms, Form 1040EZ, if:

• You are single or married filing jointly and do not claim any dependents.
• You are not 65 or older or blind.
• You have income from only wages, salaries, tips, and taxable scholarships or fellowships and not more than $400 of income is from interest.
• Your taxable income is less than $50,000.
• You do not itemize deductions, claim any adjustments to income, or have tax credits.
• You did not receive any advance earned income credit payments.
• You did not make any estimated tax payments.
• You file on or before Monday, Apr. 15, 1996. You cannot use Form 1040EZ after Apr. 15 even if you have filed for an extension.

You may be able to use Form 1040A if:

• You have income from wages, salaries, tips, taxable scholarships or fellowships, interest, and dividends.
• You have income from Individual Retirement Account (IRA) distributions, pensions, annuities, unemployment compensation, and taxable Social Security or railroad retirement benefits.
• Your taxable income is less than $50,000.
• You do not itemize deductions.
• You claim a deduction for qualified contributions to an IRA.
• You claim a credit for child and dependent care expenses, credit for the elderly or the disabled, or the earned income credit.
• You take the education exclusion for interest income earned from Series EE U.S. Savings Bonds.
• You have made estimated tax payments.
• You filed for an extension of time to file.

You will have to file Form 1040 if any of the following situations apply:

• Your taxable income is $50,000 or more.
• You itemize deductions.
• You receive any nontaxable dividends or capital gain distributions.
• You have foreign bank accounts and/or foreign trusts.
• You have taxable refunds of state or local income taxes.
• You have business, farm, or rental income.
• You sold or exchanged capital assets or business property.
• You have additional miscellaneous income not allowed on Form 1040EZ or 1040A such as alimony or lottery winnings.
• You have additional adjustments to income such as alimony paid.

- You can claim a foreign tax credit or certain other credits to which you are entitled.
- You have other taxes such as self-employment tax or the alternative minimum tax.
- You are required to file any additional forms such as:
Form 2555, Foreign Earned Income.
Form 3903, Moving Expenses.

Form 4972, Tax on Lump-Sum Distributions.
Form 5329, Return for Additional Taxes Attributable to Qualified Retirement Plans (including IRAs), Annuities, and Modified Endowment Contract.
Form 8814, Parent's Election to Report Child's Interest and Dividends.

Internal Revenue Service Audit

Although probably only about one out of every 100 individual tax returns will be audited in 1995, the IRS is good at selecting returns for audit that will yield additional income taxes. If your return is selected for audit and you feel you are not being treated fairly or that proper attention is not being paid to your statements, you have a right to ask for a hearing at the IRS appellate level. If you are still dissatisfied, you can take your case to the U.S. Tax Court.

If the total amount in question is less than $10,000, your case can be handled under the Small Tax Case procedures. If you are still dissatisfied, your next move would be the U.S. Circuit Court of Appeals.

Your Rights As a Taxpayer

Congress, responding to complaints that taxpayers were not being treated fairly by the IRS, passed a comprehensive law that requires the IRS to explain, in easy-to-understand language, the actions it proposes to take against a taxpayer and to relax some of its audit and collection procedures. This law is called "The Taxpayer Bill of Rights." You can learn more about it by obtaining a free copy of IRS Publication 1, *Your Rights as a Taxpayer*. Call 1-800-TAX-FORM for a copy.

State Government Individual Income Taxes

Source: U.S. Advisory Commission on Intergovernmental Relations

As of November 1994. Only basic rates, brackets, and exemptions are shown. Local income tax rates, even those mandated by the state, are not included. Taxable income rates and brackets listed below apply to single taxpayers and married taxpayers filing "combined separate" returns in states where this is permitted.

State	Tax rates (range in percent)	Taxable income brackets Lowest: Amount under	Taxable income brackets Highest: Amount over	Personal exemptions Single	Personal exemptions Married-Joint return	Personal exemptions Dependents	Standard Deduction[a] Percent	Standard Deduction[a] Single	Standard Deduction[a] Married-Joint return	Federal income tax deductible[b]
AL[*+]	2.0-5.0%	$500	$3,000	$1,500	$3,000	$300	20%	$2,000	$4,000	yes
AK					No state income tax					
AZ[c]	3.25-6.9	10,000	150,000	2,100	4,200	2,300	NA	3,500	7,000	no
AR[*]	1.0-7.0	3,000	25,000	20[d]	40[d]	20[d]	10	1,000	1,000	no
CA[c*]	1.0-11.0	4,722	214,929	65[d]	130[d]	65[d]	NA	2,431	4,862	no
CO					5% of modified federal taxable income					
CT[*]	4.5	Flat rate		12,000	24,000	0	NA	NA	NA	NA
DE[*+]	3.2-7.7	2,000	40,000	1,250	2,500	1,250	NA	1,300	1,600	no
DC	6.0-9.5	10,000	20,000	1,370	2,740	1,370	NA	2,000	2,000	no
FL					No state income tax					no
GA	1.0-6.0	750	7,000	1,500	3,000	1,500	NA	2,300	3,000	no
HI[*]	2.0-10.0	1,500	20,500	1,040	2,080	1,040	NA	1,500	1,900	no
ID[*]	2.0-8.2	1,000	20,000		Same as federal					no
IL[*]	3.0	Flat rate		1,000	2,000	1,000	NA	NA	NA	no
IN[*+]	3.4	Flat rate		1,000	2,000	1,000	NA	NA	NA	no
IA[c*]	0.4-9.98	1,060	47,700	20[d]	40[d]	15[d]	NA	1,340	3,310	yes
KS[*]	4.4-7.75	20,000	30,000	2,000	4,000	2,000	NA	3,000	5,000	no
KY[*+]	2.0-6.0	3,000	8,000	20[d]	40[d]	20[d]	NA	650	650	no
LA	2.0-6.0	10,000	50,000	4,500	9,000	1,000		Combined w/ exemptions		yes
ME[c]	2.0-8.5	4,150	16,500	2,100	4,200	2,100	NA	3,800	6,325	no
MD[*+]	2.0-6.0	1,000	100,000	1,200	2,400	1,200	15	2,000	4,000	no
MA[*]	5.95-12.0	Flat rate		2,200	4,400	1,000	NA	NA	NA	no
MI[*+]	4.4	Flat rate		2,100	4,200	2,100	NA	NA	NA	no
MN	6.0-8.5	15,230	50,030		Same as federal					no
MS	3.0-5.0	5,000	10,000	6,000	9,500	1,500	NA	2,300	3,400	no
MO[*+]	1.5-6.0	1,000	9,000	1,200	2,400	400	NA	Same as federal		yes
MT[c]	2.0-11.0	1,800	62,700	1,430	2,860	1,430	20	2,690	5,380	yes
NE[c*]	2.62-6.99	2,000	46,750	69[d]	138[d]	69[d]	NA	Same as federal		no
NV					No state income tax					
NH[*]					Limited income tax					
NJ[*]	1.9-6.65	20,000	75,000	1,000	2,000	1,500	NA	NA	NA	no
NM	1.7-8.5	5,500	41,600		Same as federal		NA	Same as federal		no
NY[*+]	4.0-7.875	5,500	13,000	0	0	1,000	NA	6,000	9,500	no
NC[*]	6.0-7.75	12,750	60,000	2,000	4,000	2,000	NA	3,000	5,000	no
ND[*]					14% of federal income tax liability (before credits)					yes
OH[*+]	0.743-7.5	5,000	200,000	650	1,300	650	NA	NA	NA	no
OK[*]	0.5-7.0	1,000	9,950	1,000	2,000	1,000	15	2,000	2,000	yes
OR[cd*]	5.0-9.0	2,050	5,150	113	226	113	NA	1,800	3,000	yes
PA[*+]	2.8	Flat rate		NA	NA	NA	NA	NA	NA	no
RI[*]					27.5% of federal income tax liability					no
SC[c]	2.5-7.0	2,190	10,950	2,450	4,900	2,450		Same as federal		no
SD					No state income tax					
TN[*]					Limited income tax					
TX					No state income tax					
UT[*]	2.55-7.2	750	3,750	1,725	3,450	1,725		Same as federal		50%
VT[*]					25% of federal income tax liability					no
VA[*]	2.0-5.75	3,000	17,000	800	1,600	800	NA	3,000	5,000	no
WA					No state income tax					
WV	3.0-6.5	10,000	60,000	2,000	4,000	2,000	NA	NA	NA	no
WI[*]	4.9-6.93	7,500	15,000	0	0	50[d]	NA	5,200	8,900	no
WY					No state income tax					

(notes continued on next page)

Notes: (NA) = not applicable. (+) = states in which one or more local governments levy a local income tax. (a) The lesser of (1) the percentage indicated, multiplied by adjusted gross income (AGI), or (2) the dollar value listed. In some states, when a standard deduction computed using a percentage of AGI is less than the fixed amount shown above, a minimum dollar deduction is allowed. Maryland and Utah have a minimum deduction as well. (b) A state provision that allows the taxpayer to deduct fully the federal income tax reduces the effective marginal tax rate for persons in the highest state and federal tax brackets by approximately 30% of the nominal tax rate—the deduction is of a lesser benefit to other taxpayers with lower federal and state top tax brackets. (c) Indexed by an inflation factor. Iowa indexes the standard deduction and income brackets. California, Maine, Oregon, and South Carolina index personal exemptions and income brackets. The Maine standard deducation is the same as federal. Montana indexes personal exemptions, income brackets, and standard deductions. (d) Exemption is a tax credit.

*State Notes:

Alabama: Social Security taxes are included in itemized deductions. Taxable income brackets for married filing joint over $6,000, taxed at highest rate.

Arkansas: Tax credit per dependent. Taxpayers 65 or older, or blind or deaf receive an additional $20 credit. No tax is imposed on (1) a single taxpayer whose gross income is less than $5,000; (2) a married couple with gross income less than $10,000; and (3) head of household with gross income less than $7,150.

California: Taxpayers 65 and older receive additional $65 credit.

Connecticut: Personal exemption amount is reduced by $1,000 for each $1,000, or fraction thereof, by which the taxpayer's Connecticut AGI exceeds $24,000 (single, married filing separately), $38,000 (head of household), $48,000 (married filing jointly).

Delaware: Lowest personal income tax rate (3.2%) applies to income in the $2,000-$5,000 bracket. Taxable income under $2,000 is not subject to tax and is referred to as the zero bracket amount. Each person age 60 or older may claim an extra personal exemption ($1,250). Each person age 65 or older, or blind, may claim an additional standard deducation ($1,300). Delaware lottery and multi-state (powerball) winnings are exempt.

Hawaii: A refundable food/excise tax credit of at least $55 per exemption is granted; a refundable medical services excise tax credit of 4% of qualified medical expenses, subject to limitation, is granted.

Idaho: Idaho allows a refundable $15 per exemption credit.

Illinois: Effective 1/1/90, an additional $1,000 exemption for taxpayer or spouse 65 years of age or older. An additional $1,000 exemption for taxpayer or spouse who is blind.

Indiana: Additional $1,000 exemption if taxpayer or spouse is over 65 or blind.

Iowa: Tax may not reduce after-tax income of taxpayer below $9,000 (single) or $13,500 (married filing jointly, head of household, surviving spouse). Only limitation for the standard deduction is that the deduction otherwise allowable of $1,340 or $3,310 may not exceed the amount of income remaining after the federal tax deduction. Additional $20 exemption credit is allowed for taxpayers who are legally blind or age 65 and older. Voters within a school district may approve a school district income surtax, which is computed as a percentage of regular state tax liability before refundable credits.

Kansas: A child care credit equal to 25% of the federal child care credit is allowed to taxpayers claiming the federal credit.

Kentucky: Tax credit per dependent. Taxpayers 65 or older receive a $60 credit, as do taxpayers who are blind.

Maryland: For tax years 1992-94 only, the state income tax rate is 6% for taxable income $100,000 or over for single, married filing separately, and dependent taxpayers, $150,000 for all others. All counties have a local income tax surcharge of at least 20% of the state tax liability; most counties have a surcharge of 50%. The maximum local income tax rate is 60% (50% for income taxed at the 6% state rate). Single taxpayers have a minimum standard deduction of $1,500; married taxpayers a minimum standard deduction of $3,000. Blind and elderly get an additional exemption of $1,000. An additional $1,200 exemption is allowed for elderly dependents.

Massachusetts: 12% (flat rate) imposed on net capital gains, interest, and dividends of residents, and Massachusetts business income of nonresidents. All other net income taxed at 5.95%. No tax is imposed on a single person whose gross income is $8,000 or less ($12,000 married). Social Security taxes are deducted from taxable income up to $2,000 per taxpayer.

Michigan: Persons who can be claimed as a dependent on someone else's return get an exemption of $1,000. If their AGI is $1,500 or less, they owe no tax. Rate reduced from 4.6% to 4.4% on May 1, 1994. Annualized rate for 1994 is 4.47%.

Missouri: For taxpayers itemizing deductions, Social Security taxes are deductible. The federal income tax deduction is limited to $5,000 on a single return and $10,000 on a combined return.

Nebraska: Taxable income brackets will vary by filing status. Married individuals filing separate returns: lowest amount under $2,000; highest amount over $23,375. Personal tax credit is phased out for married joint above $93,000 AGI, single above $56,000 AGI, and head of household above $78,000 AGI.

New Hampshire: There is a 5% tax on taxable interest and dividends in excess of $1,200 ($2,400 married). There is no filing requirement for an individual whose total interest and dividend income, after deducting all interest from U.S. obligations, New Hampshire and Vermont banks or credit unions, and dividends from New Hampshire non-holding company banks is less than $1,200 ($2,400 for joint filers) for a taxable period.

New Jersey: The highest taxable income bracket is double for married filing jointly. No taxpayer is subject to tax if gross income is $7,500 or less ($3,750 married, filing separately).

New Mexico: Taxable income brackets will vary by filing status. Married individuals filing jointly: lowest bracket is $8,000, and highest bracket is $64,000 AGI.

New York: A supplemental tax is imposed on taxpayers with New York adjusted gross income in excess of $100,000. Taxpayers must add back the benefit of the lower tax brackets (i.e., 4%, 5%, 6%, and 7%). Taxpayers with New York AGI in excess of $150,000 are taxed at a flat rate of 7.875%.

North Carolina: Breaking points for higher marginal tax rates vary according to filing status. Taxable income brackets shown are for single taxpayers. North Carolina taxable income reflects federal reductions of personal exemptions and itemized deductions for higher income brackets.

North Dakota: Information in table applies to the short-form method, which is used by 95% of taxpayers. As an alternative, taxpayers may use the long-form method with tax rates ranging from 2.67% to 12.0% applied to income brackets ranging from $3,000 to more than $50,000.

Ohio: Taxpayers take a $20 tax credit per exemption.

Oklahoma: These rates and brackets apply to single persons not deducting federal income tax. For individuals deducting the tax, rates range from 0.5% of the first $1,000 to 10% on income over $16,000 (single rate).

Oregon: Federal tax deduction limited to $3,000 ($1,500 if married filing separately). Income brackets are double for married filing jointly.

Pennsylvania: There are eight classes of income: (1) compensation; (2) net profits; (3) interest; (4) dividends; (5) net gain from sale or exchange of property; (6) rents, royalties, patents, and copyrights; (7) income derived through estates or trusts; and (8) gambling and lottery winnings except lottery.

Rhode Island: For tax year 1994 and thereafter, if a taxpayer's federal income tax liability is greater than $15,000, the tax rate is 27.5% of the taxpayer's federal income tax liability in excess of $15,000.

South Carolina: Beginning in tax year 1994, an additional deduction is allowed for each dependent under 6 years of age claimed on the federal income tax return. The deduction is a percentage of the federal income tax exemption allowed, as follows: 35% in 1994, 50% in 1995, 75% in 1996, and 100% after 1996.

Tennessee: Interest and dividends taxed at 6%, but most interest income on bank savings-time accounts is excluded. Persons over 65 having total annual gross income of $9,000 or less, and blind persons, are exempt.

Utah: In determining Utah taxable income, 25% of federal personal exemptions are added back. Exemptions reflect this add-back.

Vermont: Refundable state earned income tax credit (25% of federal credit, maximum $632).

Virginia: An additional exemption of $800 is allowed if the taxpayer or spouse is 65 years of age or older or blind.

Wisconsin: The standard deduction is gradually phased out as income increases; deduction is completely phased out at $50,830 of AGI for single and head of household filers and $55,000 of AGI for joint filers. Taxpayers age 65 and older receive an additional $25 credit.

NATIONS OF THE WORLD

As of mid-1995

The nations of the world are listed in alphabetical order. Initials in the following articles include UN (United Nations), OAS (Org. of American States), NATO (North Atlantic Treaty Org.), EU (European Union, or Common Market), OAU (Org. of African Unity), ILO (Intl. Labor Org.), FAO (Food & Agriculture Org.), WHO (World Health Org.), IMF (Intl. Monetary Fund), WTO (World Trade Organization, formerly GATT), CIS (Commonwealth of Independent States), FY (fiscal year). **Sources:** U.S. Census Bureau: *World Population Profile;* Population Reference Bureau; Central Intelligence Agency: *The World Factbook;* Encyclopaedia Britannica and Encyclopaedia Britannica Book of the Year; International Monetary Fund; International Institute for Strategic Studies: *The Military Balance;* Facts on File; Keesing's Record of World Events; Current History; Collier's Encyclopedia and Collier's Year Book; Encyclopaedia Americana Yearbook; Who's Who in the World; U.S. Dept. of State; UN Statistical Yearbook; UN Demographic Yearbook; The Statesman's Year-Book; The Europa World Year Book; Funk & Wagnalls New Encyclopedia. Population figures are mid-1995 estimates, unless otherwise noted. Gross Domestic Product/Gross National Product: *denotes purchasing power equivalent. Otherwise, exchange rate conversions are used, which may account for significant variation from year to year. National Budget measures expenditures, unless otherwise noted. Tourism figures represent receipts from international tourism. Comm. (commercial) vehicles include trucks and buses. All embassy addresses are Wash., DC; area codes (202), unless otherwise noted. Literacy rates are usually based on the ability to read and write on a lower elementary school level. The concept of literacy is changing in the industrialized countries, where literacy is defined as the ability to read instructions necessary for a job or a license. By these standards, illiteracy may be more common than present rates suggest. Per-person figures in communications and health sections are post-1988.

See pages 481-96 for full-color maps and flags.

Afghanistan
Islamic State of Afghanistan

People: Population: 21,251,821. **Pop. density:** 84 per sq. mi. **Urban:** 18%. **Ethnic groups:** Pashtun 38%, Tajik 25%, Uzbek 6%, Hazara 19%. **Principal languages:** Pashtu 35%, Dari Persian (spoken by Tajiks, Hazaras) 50%, Turkic (incl. Uzbek, Turkmen) 11%. **Religions:** Sunni Muslim 84%, Shi'a Muslim 15%.

Geography: Area: 251,825 sq. mi. **Location:** In SW Asia, NW of the Indian subcontinent. **Neighbors:** Pakistan on E, S, Iran on W, Turkmenistan, Tajikistan, Uzbekistan on N; the NE tip touches China. **Topography:** The country is landlocked and mountainous, much of it over 4,000 ft. above sea level. The Hindu Kush Mts. tower 16,000 ft. above Kabul and reach a height of 25,000 ft. to the E. Trade with Pakistan flows through the 35-mile-long Khyber Pass. The climate is dry, with extreme temperatures, and there are large desert regions, though mountain rivers produce intermittent fertile valleys. **Capital:** Kabul (1993 est.): 700,000.

Government: Type: In transition. **Head of state:** Pres. Burhanuddin Rabbani; b 1940 in office: June 28, 1992. **Local divisions:** 30 provinces. **Defense:** 15% of GDP (1990).

Economy: Industries: Textiles, furniture, cement. **Chief crops:** Nuts, wheat, fruits. **Minerals:** Gas, oil, copper, coal, zinc, iron. **Other resources:** Wool, hides, karakul pelts. **Arable land:** 12%. **Livestock** (1993): cattle: 1.5 mln.; sheep: 14.2 mln. **Electricity prod.** (1992): 1.0 bln. kWh. **Labor force:** Agriculture supports about 68% of the population.

Finance: Monetary unit: Afghani (May 1995: 50.60 = $1 US). **Gross domestic product** (1989): $3 bln. **Per capita GDP:** $200. **Imports** (1991): $874 mln.; partners: CIS 55%, Jap. 8%. **Exports** (1991): $236 mln.; partners: CIS 72%. **International reserves less gold** (Mar. 1992): $227 mln. **Gold:** 965,000 oz t. **Consumer prices** (change in 1991): 57%.

Transport: Motor vehicles: in use: 38,000 passenger cars, 35,000 comm. vehicles. **Civil aviation:** 165 mln. passenger-mi. **Communications: Television sets:** 1 per 203 persons; **Radios:** 1 per 14 persons. **Telephones:** 1 per 443 persons. **Daily newspaper circ.:** 11 per 1,000 pop.

Health: Life expectancy at birth (1995): 46 male; 45 female. **Births** (per 1,000 pop.): 43. **Deaths** (per 1,000 pop.): 19. **Natural increase:** 2.4%. **Hospital beds:** 1 per 2,054 persons. **Physicians:** 1 per 6,866 persons. **Infant mortality** (per 1,000 live births 1995): 153.

Education: Literacy (1990): 29%. Over 88% of adults have no formal schooling.

Major International Organizations: UN (World Bank, IMF). **Embassy:** 2341 Wyoming Ave. NW 20008; 234-3770.

Afghanistan, occupying a favored invasion route since antiquity, has been variously known as Ariana or Bactria (in ancient times) and Khorasan (in the Middle Ages). Foreign empires alternated rule with local emirs and kings until the 18th century, when a unified kingdom was established. In 1973, a military coup ushered in a republic.

Pro-Soviet leftists took power in a bloody 1978 coup and concluded an economic and military treaty with the USSR. In Dec. 1979 the USSR began a massive airlift into Kabul and backed a new coup, leading to installation of a more pro-Soviet leader. Soviet troops fanned out over Afghanistan and became engaged in a protracted guerrilla war with Muslim rebels, in which some 15,000 Soviet troops reportedly died.

A UN-mediated agreement was signed Apr. 14, 1988, providing for withdrawal of Soviet troops, a neutral Afghan state, and repatriation of refugees. Afghan rebels rejected the pact, vowing to continue fighting while "Soviets and their puppets" remained in Afghanistan. The Soviets completed their troop withdrawal Feb. 15, 1989; fighting between Afghan rebels and government forces ensued.

Communist Pres. Najibullah resigned Apr. 16, 1992, as competing guerrilla forces advanced on Kabul. The rebels achieved power Apr. 28, ending 14 years of Soviet-backed regimes. More than 2 million Afghans had been killed and 6 million had left the country since 1979.

Following the rebel victory there were clashes between moderates and Islamic fundamentalist forces. Burhanuddin Rabbani, a guerrilla leader, became president June 28, 1992, but fierce fighting continued around Kabul and elsewhere. Taliban, an insurgent Islamic fundamentalist faction, controlled much of Afghanistan in 1995.

Albania
Republic of Albania
Republika e Shqipërisë

People: Population: 3,413,904. **Pop. density:** 308 per sq. mi. **Urban:** 37%. **Ethnic groups:** Albanians (Gegs in N, Tosks in S) 95%, Greeks 3%. **Principal languages:** Albanian, Greek. **Religions:** Muslim 70%, Greek Orthodox 20%, Roman Catholic 10%.

Geography: Area: 11,100 sq. mi. **Location:** On SE coast of Adriatic Sea. **Neighbors:** Greece on S, Yugoslavia on N, Macedonia on E. **Topography:** Apart from a narrow coastal plain, Albania consists of hills and mountains covered with scrub forest, cut by small E-W rivers. **Capital:** Tiranë. **Cities** (1990 est.): Tiranë 243,000; Durres 85,000; Elbasin 83,000.

Government: Type: Republic. **Head of state:** Pres. Sali Berisha; b 1944; in office: Apr. 9, 1992. **Head of government:** Prem. Alexander Meksi; b 1939; in office: Apr. 13, 1992. **Local divisions:** 26 districts. **Defense:** 8.2% of GNP (1993). **Active troop strength:** 73,000.

Economy: Industries: Cement, textiles, food processing. **Chief crops:** Corn, wheat, cotton, potatoes, tobacco, fruits. **Minerals:** Chromium, coal, oil, gas. **Other resources:** Forests. **Arable land:** 21%. **Livestock** (1993): cattle: 450,000; sheep: 1.2 mln.. **Electricity prod.** (1992): 5.0 bln. kWh. **Labor force:** 60% agric.; 40% ind. & comm.

Finance: Monetary unit: Lek (Oct. 1994: 100 = $1 US). **Gross national product** (1993): $3.3 bln.* **Per capita GNP:** $1,100. **Imports** (1991): $147 mln.; partners: Czech., Yugoslavia, Rom. **Exports** (1991): $80 mln.; partners: Czech., Yugoslavia, Italy. **National budget** (1991): $1.4 bln.

Chief ports: Durres, Vlorne, Sarande.
Communications: Television sets: 1 per 10 persons. **Radios:** 1 per 6 persons. **Daily newspaper circ.:** 42 per 1,000 pop.
Health: Life expectancy at birth (1995): 71 male; 77 female. **Births** (per 1,000 pop.): 22. **Deaths** (per 1,000 pop): 5. **Natural increase:** 1.6%. **Hospital beds:** 1 per 173 persons. **Physicians:** 1 per 585 persons. **Infant mortality** (per 1,000 live births 1995): 28.
Major International Organizations: UN (FAO, WHO).
Education: Literacy (1990): 100%. Free and compulsory ages 7-15.
Embassy: 1511 K St. NW 20005; 223-4942.

Ancient Illyria was conquered by Romans, Slavs, and Turks (15th century); the latter Islamized the population. Independent Albania was proclaimed in 1912, republic was formed in 1920. King Zog I ruled 1925-39, until Italy invaded.

Communist partisans took over in 1944, allied Albania with USSR, then broke with USSR in 1960 over de-Stalinization. Strong political alliance with China followed, leading to several billion dollars in aid, which was curtailed after 1974. China cut off aid in 1978 when Albania attacked its policies after the death of Chinese ruler Mao Zedong. Large-scale purges of officials occurred during the 1970s.

Enver Hoxha, the nation's ruler for 4 decades, died Apr. 11, 1985. Eventually the new regime introduced some liberalization, including measures in 1990 providing for freedom to travel abroad. Efforts were begun to improve ties with the outside world. Mar. 1991 elections left the former Communists in power, but a general strike and urban opposition led to the formation of a coalition cabinet including non-Communists.

Albania's former Communists were routed in elections Mar. 1992, amid economic collapse and social unrest. Sali Berisha was elected as the first non-Communist president since World War II. Voters rejected a draft constitution favored by Berisha in a referendum Nov. 6, 1994.

Algeria
Democratic and Popular Republic of Algeria
Al-Jumhuriya al-Jazairiya ad-Dimuqratiya ash-Shabiya

People: Population: 28,539,321. **Age distrib. (%):** <15: 39; 65+: 4. **Pop. density:** 31 per sq. mi. **Urban:** 50%. **Ethnic groups:** Arab-Berber 99%. **Principal languages:** Arabic (official), French, Berber (indigenous language). **Religions:** Sunni Muslim (state religion) 99%.
Geography: Area: 919,595 sq. mi. **Location:** In NW Africa, from Mediterranean Sea into Sahara Desert. **Neighbors:** Morocco on W, Mauritania, Mali, Niger on S, Libya, Tunisia on E. **Topography:** The Tell, located on the coast, comprises fertile plains 50-100 miles wide, with a moderate climate and adequate rain. Two major chains of the Atlas Mts., running roughly E-W, and reaching 7,000 ft., enclose a dry plateau region. Below lies the Sahara, mostly desert with major mineral resources. **Capital:** Algiers (El Djazair). **Cities** (1987 est.): Algiers 1,507,000; Wahran 610,000; Qacentina 441,000.
Government: Type: Republic. **Head of state:** Pres. Liamine Zeroual; b July 3, 1941; in office: Jan. 31, 1994. **Head of government:** Prime Min. Mokdad Sifi; in office: Apr. 11, 1994. **Local divisions:** 48 provinces. **Defense:** 2.5% of GDP (1993 est.). **Active troop strength:** 121,700.
Economy: Industries: Oil, natural gas, light industry, food processing. **Chief crops:** Grains, wine-grapes, potatoes, olives, oranges. **Minerals:** Iron, zinc, lead. **Crude oil reserves** (1994): 9.2 bln. bbls. **Other resources:** Cork trees. **Arable land:** 3%; **Livestock** (1992): cattle: 1.4 mln.; sheep: 18.6 mln. **Electricity prod.** (1992): 16.4 bln. kWh. **Labor force:** 22% agric.; 27% ind., serv., commerce; 29% govt.
Finance: Monetary unit: Dinar (May 1995: 45.92 = $1 US). **Gross domestic product** (1993): $89 bln.* **Per capita GDP:** $3,300. **Imports** (1991): $9.2 bln.; partners: EEC 64%. **Exports** (1991): $11.7 bln.; partners: EEC 74%. **National budget** (1992 est.): $14.6 bln. **International reserves less gold** (Apr. 1995): $2.3 bln. **Gold:** 5.6 mln. oz t. **Consumer prices** (change in 1994): 29.0%.
Transport: Railroads: Length: 2,941 mi. **Motor vehicles:** in use: 800,000 passenger cars, 600,000 comm. vehicles. **Chief ports:** El Djazair.
Communications: Television sets: 1 per 14 persons. **Radios:** 1 per 7.7 persons. **Telephones:** 1 per 21 persons. **Daily newspaper circ.:** 54 per 1,000 pop.

Health: Life expectancy at birth (1995): 67 male; 69 female. **Births** (per 1,000 pop.): 29. **Deaths** (per 1,000 pop.): 6. **Natural increase:** 2.3%. **Hospital beds:** 1 per 455 persons. **Physicians:** 1 per 1,041 persons. **Infant mortality** (per 1,000 live births 1995): 50.
Education: Literacy (1993): 57%.
Major International Organizations: UN (FAO, IMF, WHO), OAU, Arab League, OPEC.
Embassy: 2118 Kalorama Rd. NW 20008; 265-2800.

Earliest known inhabitants were ancestors of Berbers, followed by Phoenicians, Romans, Vandals, and, finally, Arabs. Turkey ruled 1518 to 1830, when France took control.

Large-scale European immigration and French cultural inroads did not prevent an Arab nationalist movement from launching guerrilla war. Peace, and French withdrawal, was negotiated with French Pres. Charles de Gaulle. One million Europeans left. Independence came July 5, 1962. Ahmed Ben Bella was the victor of infighting and ruled until 1965, when an army coup installed Col. Houari Boumedienne as leader.

In 1967, Algeria declared war on Israel, broke ties with U.S., and moved toward eventual military and political ties with the USSR. Some 500 died in riots protesting economic hardship in 1988. In 1989, voters approved a new constitution, which cleared the way for a multiparty system.

The government canceled Jan. 1992 elections. Islamic fundamentalists were expected to win and banned all nonreligious activities at Algeria's 10,000 mosques. Pres. Mohammed Boudiaf was assassinated June 29, 1992. There were repeated attacks on high-ranking officials, security forces, foreigners, and others by militant Muslim fundamentalists over the next 3 years; pro-government death squads also were active. The overall estimated death toll was 40,000. Presidential elections were scheduled for Nov. 16, 1995.

Andorra
Principality of Andorra
Principat d'Andorra

People: Population: 65,780. **Pop. density:** 363 per sq. mi. **Ethnic groups:** Spanish 61%, Andorran 30%, French 6%. **Principal languages:** Catalan (official), French, Castilian. **Religion:** Roman Catholic.
Geography: Area: 181 sq. mi. **Location:** In Pyrenees Mts. **Neighbors:** Spain on S, France on N. **Topography:** High mountains and narrow valleys over the country. **Capital:** Andorra la Vella.
Government: Type: Parliamentary co-principality. **Heads of State:** President of France & Bishop of Urgel (Spain), as co-princes. **Head of government:** Oscar Ribas Reig; b 1937; in office: May 4, 1992. **Local divisions:** 7 parishes.
Economy: Industries: Tourism, tobacco products. **Labor force:** 76% services; 23% ind.
Finance: Monetary unit: French Franc, Spanish Peseta. **Gross domestic product** (1992): $760 mln.* **Per capita GDP:** $14,000. **National budget** (1993): $177 mln.
Communications: Television sets: 1 per 15 persons. **Radios:** 1 per 4 persons. **Telephones:** 1 per 1.4 persons.
Health: Births (per 1,000 pop.): 13. **Deaths** (per 1,000 pop.): 7. **Natural increase:** 0.6%.
Education: Literacy (1992): 99%. School compulsory to age 16.
Major International Organizations: UN.

Andorra was a co-principality, with joint sovereignty by France and the bishop of Urgel, from 1278 to 1993.

Tourism, especially skiing, is the economic mainstay. A free port, allowing for an active trading center, draws some 10 million tourists annually. The ensuing economic prosperity, accompanied by Andorra's virtual law-free status, gave rise to calls for reform. Andorra voters chose to end a feudal system that had been in place for 715 years and adopt a parliamentary system of government Mar. 14, 1993.

Angola
Republic of Angola
República de Angola

People: Population: 10,069,501. **Pop. density:** 21 per sq. mi. **Urban:** 37%. **Ethnic groups:** Ovimbundu 37%, Kimbundu 25%, Bakongo 13%. **Urban:** 28%. **Principal languages:** Portuguese (official), various Bantu languages. **Religions:** Roman Catholic 38%, Protestant 15%, indigenous beliefs 47%.

Geography: Area: 481,354 sq. mi. **Location:** In SW Africa on Atlantic coast. **Neighbors:** Namibia on S, Zambia on E, Zaire on N; Cabinda, an enclave separated from rest of country by short Atlantic coast of Zaire, borders Congo Republic. **Topography:** Most of Angola consists of a plateau elevated 3,000 to 5,000 feet above sea level, rising from a narrow coastal strip. There is also a temperate highland area in the west-central region, a desert in the S, and a tropical rain forest covering Cabinda. **Capital:** Luanda (1988 est.): 1.1 mln.

Government: Type: Republic. **Head of state:** Pres. José Eduardo dos Santos; b Aug. 28, 1942; in office: Sept. 20, 1979. Prime Min. Marcolino Moco; in office: Dec. 2, 1992. **Local divisions:** 18 provinces. **Defense: Active troop strength:** 82,000 est.

Economy: Industries: Food processing, textiles, mining, tires, petroleum. **Chief crops:** Coffee, bananas. **Minerals:** Iron, diamonds (over 2 mln. carats a year), gold, phosphates, oil. **Livestock** (1993): cattle: 3.2 mln.; goats: 1.5 mln. **Crude oil reserves** (1994): 1.5 bln. bbls. **Arable land:** 2%. **Fish catch** (1991): 75,062 metric tons. **Electricity prod.** (1991): 800 mln. kWh. **Labor force:** 85% agric., 15% industry.

Finance: Monetary unit: New Kwanza (Oct. 1994: 139,294 = $1 US). **Gross domestic product** (1993): $5.7 bln.* **Per capita GDP:** $600. **Imports** (1991): $1.3 bln.; partners: Portugal 29%, Fra. 9%; U.S. 9%. **Exports** (1991): $3.4 bln.; partners: U.S. 56%. **National budget** (1992 est.): $2.5 bln.

Transport: Motor vehicles: in use: 120,000 passenger cars, 40,000 comm. vehicles. **Chief ports:** Cabinda, Lobito, Luanda.

Communications: Television sets: 1 per 216 persons. **Radios:** 1 per 24 persons. **Telephones:** 1 per 132 persons. **Daily newspaper circ.:** 8 per 1,000 pop.

Health: Life expectancy at birth (1995): 44 male; 48 female. **Births** (per 1,000 pop.): 45. **Deaths** (per 1,000 pop.): 18. **Natural increase:** 2.7%. **Hospital beds:** 1 per 845 persons. **Physicians:** 1 per 15,136 persons. **Infant mortality** (per 1,000 live births 1995): 142.

Education: Literacy (1992): 40%.

Major International Organizations: UN (ILO, WHO), OAU.

From the early centuries AD to 1500, Bantu tribes penetrated most of the region. Portuguese came in 1583, allied with the Bakongo kingdom in the north, and developed the slave trade. Large-scale colonization did not begin until the 20th century, when 400,000 Portuguese immigrated.

A guerrilla war begun in 1961 lasted until 1975, when Portugal granted independence. Fighting then erupted between three rival rebel groups —the National Front, based in Zaire, the Soviet-backed Popular Movement for the Liberation of Angola (MPLA), and the National Union for the Total Independence of Angola (UNITA), aided by the U.S. and S Africa. The civil war killed thousands of blacks, drove most whites to emigrate, and completed economic ruin. Cuban troops and Soviet aid helped the MPLA win control of most of the country by 1976 and gain wide recognition as the government of Angola.

An agreement was signed in Dec. 1988 between Angola, Cuba, and S Africa on a timetable for withdrawal of Cuban troops, completed May 25, 1991. The 16-year war was officially ended May 1, 1991, as the government and UNITA signed a peace agreement.

Elections were held in Sept. 1992, but fighting again broke out, as UNITA rejected the presidential election results, and continued into 1993 and 1994, with UNITA forces holding most of the countryside. Large numbers of civilians died from war-related causes, especially starvation. UNITA signed a peace treaty with the government, Nov. 20, 1994. The U.S. formally recognized the government of Angola, May 19, 1993, for the first time since independence.

Antigua and Barbuda

People: Population: 65,176. **Pop. density:** 381 per sq. mi. **Urban:** 31%. **Ethnic groups:** mostly black African. **Principal language:** English (official). **Religion:** predominantly Anglican.

Geography: Area: 171 sq. mi. **Location:** Eastern Caribbean. **Neighbors:** approx. 30 mi. north of Guadeloupe. **Capital:** St. John's (1988 est.): 27,000.

Government: Type: Constitutional monarchy with British-style parliament. **Head of state:** Queen Elizabeth II; represented by Gov.-Gen. James Carlisle; b Aug. 5, 1937; in office: June 10, 1993. **Head of government:** Prime Min. Lester Bird; b 1940; in office: Mar. 9, 1994. **Defense:** 1% of GDP (FY 1990-91).

Economy: Industries: Manufacturing, tourism. **Arable land:** 18%. **Labor force:** 82% commerce & serv.; 11% agric.

Finance: Monetary unit: East Caribbean Dollar (May 1995: 2.70 = $1 US). **Gross domestic product** (1993): $368 mln. **Per capita GDP:** $5,800. **Tourism** (1992): $329 mln. **National budget** (1992): $161 mln.

Health: Births (per 1,000 pop.): 17. **Deaths** (per 1,000 pop.): 5. **Natural increase:** 1.2%.

Education: Literacy (1992): 90%.

Major International Organizations: UN, the Commonwealth.

Embassy: 3400 International Dr. NW 20008; 362-5122.

Columbus landed on Antigua in 1493. The British colonized it in 1632.

The British associated state of Antigua achieved independence as Antigua and Barbuda on Nov. 1, 1981. The government maintains close relations with the U.S., United Kingdom, and Venezuela. The country was hit hard by Hurricane Luis, Sept. 1995.

Argentina
Argentine Republic
República Argentina

People: Population: 34,292,742. **Age distrib.** (%): <15: 30; 65+: 9. **Pop. density:** 32 per sq. mi. **Urban:** 87%. **Ethnic groups:** white 85% (Spanish, Italian), mestizos, Indians. **Principal languages:** Spanish (official), English, Italian. **Religion:** Roman Catholic 90%.

Geography: Area: 1,073,518 sq. mi., second largest country in S America. **Location:** Occupies most of southern S America. **Neighbors:** Chile on W, Bolivia, Paraguay on N, Brazil, Uruguay on NE. **Topography:** The mountains in W: the Andean, Central, Misiones, and Southern. Aconcagua is the highest peak in the western hemisphere, alt. 22,834 ft. E of the Andes are heavily wooded plains, called the Gran Chaco in the N, and the fertile, treeless Pampas in the central region. Patagonia, in the S, is bleak and arid. Rio de la Plata, an estuary in the NE, 170 by 140 mi., is mostly fresh water, from 2,485-mi. Parana and 1,000-mi. Uruguay rivers. **Capital:** Buenos Aires (the Senate has approved the moving of the capital to the Patagonia Region). **Cities** (1991 est.): Buenos Aires 12,582,000 (met.); Cordoba 1.2 mln.; Rosario 1.1 mln. (met.).

Government: Type: Republic. **Head of state:** Pres. Carlos Saúl Menem; b July 2, 1930; in office: July 8, 1989. **Local divisions:** 23 provinces, 1 federal dist. **Defense:** 1.7% of GDP (1992). **Active troop strength:** 69,800.

Economy: Industries: Food processing, chemicals, textiles, machinery, autos. **Chief crops:** Grains, corn, sugar beets, sorghum, soybeans. **Minerals:** Oil, lead, zinc, iron, copper, tin, uranium. **Crude oil reserves** (1994): 1.6 bln. bbls. **Arable land:** 9%. **Livestock** (1993): cattle: 50 mln.; sheep: 24 mln. **Fish catch** (1992): 692,110 metric tons. **Electricity prod.** (1992): 51.3 bln. kWh. **Labor force:** 12% agric.; 31% ind.; 57% services.

Finance: Monetary unit: Peso (May 1995: 1 = $1 US). **Gross domestic product** (1993): $185 bln.* **Per capita GDP:** $5,500. **Imports** (1992): $14.8 bln.; partners: U.S. 22%, Brazil 22%, Ger. 7%, Italy 5%. **Exports** (1992): $12.2 bln.; partners: Brazo; 14%, Neth. 10%, U.S. 11%. **Tourism** (1992): $3.1 bln. **National budget** (1992): $35.8 bln. **International reserves less gold** (May 1995): $9.1 bln. **Gold:** 4.37 mln. oz t. **Consumer prices** (change in 1994): 4.2%.

Transport: Railroads: Length: 21,151 mi. **Motor vehicles:** in use: 4.4 mln. passenger cars, 1.6 mln. comm. vehicles. **Civil aviation:** 5 bln. passenger-mi. **Chief ports:** Buenos Aires, Bahia Blanca, La Plata.

Communications: Television sets: 1 per 4.7 persons. **Radios:** 1 per 1.6 persons. **Telephones:** 1 per 7 persons. **Daily newspaper circ.:** 124 per 1,000 pop.

Health: Life expectancy at birth (1995): 68 male; 75 female. **Births** (per 1,000 pop.): 20. **Deaths** (per 1,000 pop.): 9. **Natural increase:** 1.1%. **Hospital beds:** 1 per 205 persons. **Physicians:** 1 per 326 persons. **Infant mortality** (per 1,000 live births 1994): 29.

Education: Literacy (1992): 95%. **Years compulsory:** to age 14.

Major International Organizations: UN (WHO, IMF, FAO), OAS.

Embassy: 1600 New Hampshire Ave. NW 20009; 939-6400.

Nomadic Indians roamed the Pampas when Spaniards arrived, 1515-16, led by Juan Diaz de Solis. Nearly all the Indians were killed by the late 19th century. The colonists won independence, 1816, and a long period of disorders ended in a strong centralized government.

Large-scale Italian, German, and Spanish immigration in the decades after 1880 spurred modernization. Social reforms were enacted in the 1920s, but military coups prevailed 1930-46, until the election of Gen. Juan Perón as president.

Perón, with his wife, Eva Duarte (d 1952), effected labor reforms, but also suppressed speech and press freedoms, closed religious schools, and ran the country into debt. A 1955 coup exiled Perón, who was followed by a series of military and civilian regimes. Perón returned in 1973, and was once more elected president. He died 10 months later, succeeded by his wife Isabel, who had been elected vice president, and who became the first woman head of state in the western hemisphere.

A military junta ousted Mrs. Perón in 1976 amid charges of corruption. Under a continuing state of siege, the army battled guerrillas and leftists, killed 5,000 people, and jailed and tortured others. On Dec. 9, 1985, after a trial of 5 months and nearly 1,000 witnesses, 5 former junta members were found guilty of murder and human rights abuses.

Argentine troops seized control of the British-held Falkland Islands on Apr. 2, 1982. Both countries had claimed sovereignty over the islands, located 250 miles off the Argentine coast, since 1833. The British dispatched a task force and declared a total air and sea blockade around the Falklands. Fighting began May 1; several hundred lost their lives as the result of the destruction of a British destroyer and the sinking of an Argentine cruiser.

British troops landed on East Falkland Island May 21 and eventually surrounded Stanley, the capital city and Argentine stronghold. The Argentine troops surrendered, June 14; Argentine Pres. Leopoldo Galtieri resigned June 17.

Democratic rule returned to Argentina in 1983 as Raul Alfonsín's Radical Civic Union gained an absolute majority in the presidential electoral college and Congress. By 1989 the nation was plagued by severe financial and political problems, as hyperinflation sparked looting and rioting in several cities. The government of Perónist Pres. Carlos Saúl Menem, installed 1989 and reelected 1995, introduced harsh economic measures to curtail inflation, control government spending, and restructure the foreign debt.

About 100 people were killed in the terrorist bombing of a Jewish cultural center in Buenos Aires, July 18, 1994.

Armenia
Republic of Armenia
Hayastani Hanrapetutyun

People: Population: 3,557,284. **Pop. density:** 309 per sq. mi. **Urban:** 68%. **Ethnic groups:** Armenian 93%, Azeri 3%. **Principal language:** Armenian 96%. **Religion:** Armenian Orthodox 94%.

Geography: Area: 11,500 sq. mi. **Neighbors:** Georgia on N, Azerbaijan on E, Iran on S, Turkey on W. **Topography:** Mountainous with many peaks above 10,000 ft. **Capital:** Yerevan (1991 est.): 1.3 mln.

Government: Type: Republic. **Head of state:** Pres. Levon Ter-Petrosyan; b Jan. 9, 1945; in office: Oct. 16, 1991. **Head of government:** Hrand Bagratyan; b 1958; in office: Feb. 12, 1993. **Defense:** Active troop strength: 32,700 est.

Economy: Industries: Manufacturing, chemicals. **Chief crops:** Cotton, grapes, grain. **Minerals:** Copper, zinc. **Arable land:** 17%. **Electricity prod.** (1992): 9 bln. kWh.

Finance: Monetary unit: Dram (Oct. 1994: 357 = $1 US). **Gross Domestic Product** (1993 est.): $7.1 bln.* **Per capita GDP:** $2,040.

Transport: Vehicles: 230,100 passenger cars.

Communications: Television sets: 1 per 5 persons. **Radios:** 1 per 5.6 persons. **Telephones:** 1 per 5.3 persons. **Daily newspaper circ.:** 469 per 1,000 pop.

Health: Life expectancy at birth (1995): 69 male; 76 female. **Births** (per 1,000 pop.): 23. **Deaths** (per 1,000 pop.): 7. **Natural increase:** 1.6%. **Hospital beds:** 1 per 117 persons. **Physicians:** 1 per 254 persons. **Infant mortality** (per 1,000 live births 1995): 26.

Major International Organizations: UN (IMF), CIS.
Embassy: 1660 L St. NW 20036; 628-5766.

Armenia is an ancient country, parts of which are now in Turkey and Iran. Present-day Armenia was set up as a Soviet Republic Apr. 2, 1921. It joined Georgian and Azerbaijan SSRs Mar. 12, 1922, to form the Transcaucasian SFSR, which became part of the USSR Dec. 30, 1922. Armenia became a constituent republic of the USSR Dec. 5, 1936. An earthquake

struck Armenia Dec. 7, 1988; more than 55,000 were killed and several cities and towns were left in ruins.

Armenia declared independence Sept. 23, 1991, and became an independent state when the USSR disbanded Dec. 26, 1991. Fighting between mostly Christian Armenia and mostly Muslim Azerbaijan escalated in 1992 and continued in 1993 and 1994. Each country claimed Nagorno-Karabakh, an enclave in Azerbaijan that has a majority population of ethnic Armenians. A temporary cease-fire was announced in May 1994, with Armenian forces in control of the enclave. Voters approved, July 5, 1995, a new constitution strengthening presidential powers.

Australia
Commonwealth of Australia

People: Population: 18,322,231. **Age distrib.** (%): <15: 22; 65+: 12. **Pop. density:** 6 per sq. mi. **Urban:** 85%. **Ethnic groups:** Caucasian 95%, Asian 4%, aborigines (including mixed) 1%. **Principal languages:** English, aboriginal languages. **Religions:** Anglican 26%, Roman Catholic 26%, other Christian 24%.

Geography: Area: 2,966,200 sq. mi. **Location:** SE of Asia, Indian O. is W and S, Pacific O. (Coral, Tasman seas) is E; they meet N of Australia in Timor and Arafura seas. Tasmania lies 150 mi. S of Victoria state, across Bass Strait. **Neighbors:** Nearest are Indonesia, Papua New Guinea on N, Solomons, Fiji, and New Zealand on E. **Topography:** An island continent. The Great Dividing Range along the E coast has Mt. Kosciusko, 7,310 ft. The W plateau rises to 2,000 ft., with arid areas in the Great Sandy and Great Victoria deserts. The NW part of Western Australia and Northern Terr. are arid and hot. The NE has heavy rainfall and Cape York Peninsula has jungles. The Murray R. rises in New South Wales and flows 1,600 mi. to the Indian O. **Capital:** Canberra. **Cities** (1993 est.): Sydney 3.7 mln.; Melbourne 3.2 mln.; Brisbane 1.4 mln.; Perth 1.2 mln.; Adelaide 1.1 mln.

Government: Type: Democratic, federal state system. **Head of state:** Queen Elizabeth II, represented by Gov.-Gen. William Hayden; b Jan. 23, 1933; in office: Feb. 16, 1989 (William Deane; named: Aug. 21, 1995; effective: Feb. 15, 1996). **Head of government:** Prime Min. Paul Keating; b Jan. 18, 1944; in office: Dec. 20, 1991. **Local divisions:** 6 states, 2 territories. **Defense:** 2.4% of GDP (FY 1992-93). **Active troop strength:** 61,600.

Economy: Industries: Iron, steel, textiles, electrical equip., chemicals, autos, aircraft, ships, machinery. **Chief crops:** Wheat (a leading export), barley, oats, corn, hay, sugar, wine, fruit, vegetables. **Minerals:** Coal, copper, iron, lead, tin, uranium, zinc. **Crude oil reserves** (1994): 1.6 bln. bbls. **Other resources:** Wool (world's leading exporter). **Arable land:** 6%. **Livestock** (1993): cattle: 24 mln.; sheep: 138 mln.; pigs: 2.6 mln. **Fish catch** (1992): 233,900 metric tons. **Electricity prod.** (1992): 150 bln. kWh. **Labor force:** 6% agric.; 34% finance & services; 36% trade & manuf.

Finance: Monetary unit: Dollar (May 1995: 1.00 = $.71 US). **Gross domestic product** (1993): $339.7 bln.* **Per capita income:** $19,100. **Imports** (1992): $37.8 bln.; partners: U.S. 24%, Jap. 19%, UK 6%. **Exports** (1992): $41.7 bln.; partners: Jap. 26%, U.S. 11%, NZ 6%. **Tourism** (1992): $4.0 bln. **National budget** (1993): $83.1 bln. **International reserves less gold** (May 1995): $12.3 bln. **Gold:** 7.90 mln. oz t. **Consumer prices** (change in 1994): 1.9%.

Transport: Railroads: Length: 23,174 mi. **Motor vehicles:** in use: 7.9 mln. passenger cars, 2.0 mln. comm. vehicles. **Civil aviation:** 25.6 bln. passenger-mi.; 428 airports with scheduled flights. **Chief ports:** Sydney, Melbourne, Newcastle, Port Kembla, Fremantle, Geelong.

Communications: Television sets: 1 per 2.2 persons. **Radios:** 1 per 0.9 persons. **Telephones:** 1 per 2.1 persons. **Daily newspaper circ.:** 249 per 1,000 pop.

Health: Life expectancy at birth (1995): 75 male; 81 female. **Births** (per 1,000 pop.): 14. **Deaths** (per 1,000 pop.): 7. **Natural increase:** 0.7%. **Hospital beds:** 1 per 199 persons. **Physicians:** 1 per 438 persons. **Infant mortality** (per 1,000 live births 1995): 7.

Education: Literacy (1993): 99%. **Years compulsory:** to age 15.

Major International Organizations: UN and all its specialized agencies, OECD, the Commonwealth.
Embassy: 1601 Massachusetts Ave. NW 20036; 797-3000.

Australia harbors many plant and animal species not found elsewhere, including the kangaroo, koalas, platypus, dingo (wild dog), Tasmanian devil (racoon-like marsupial), wombat (bear-like marsupial), and barking and frilled lizards.

Capt. James Cook explored the E coast in 1770, when the continent was inhabited by a variety of different tribes. The first settlers, beginning in 1788, were mostly convicts, soldiers, and government officials. By 1830, Britain had claimed the entire continent, and the immigration of free settlers began to accelerate. The commonwealth was proclaimed Jan. 1, 1901. Northern Terr. was granted limited self-rule July 1, 1978.

State/Territory, Capital	Area (sq. mi.)	Population (1993 est.)
New South Wales, Sydney	309,500	5,998,000
Victoria, Melbourne	87,900	4,465,000
Queensland, Brisbane	666,990	3,116,000
Western Aust., Perth	975,100	1,676,000
South Aust., Adelaide	379,900	1,463,000
Tasmania, Hobart	26,200	471,000
Aust. Capital Terr., Canberra	900	299,000
Northern Terr., Darwin	519,800	169,000

Racially discriminatory immigration policies were abandoned in 1973, after 3 million Europeans (half British) had entered since 1945. The 50,000 aborigines and 150,000 part-aborigines are mostly detribalized, but there are several preserves in the Northern Territory. They remain economically disadvantaged.

Australia's agricultural success makes the country among the top exporters of beef, lamb, wool, and wheat. Major mineral deposits have been developed, largely for export. Industrialization has been completed. The nation endured a deep recession 1990-93 but has rebounded strongly.

The Labor Party won a majority in Feb. 1983 general elections and was reelected in 1984, 1987, 1990, and 1993. Prime Min. Paul Keating announced Sept. 19, 1993, a plan to make Australia a republic by 2001.

Australian External Territories

Norfolk Is., area 13.3 sq. mi., pop. (1990) 1,800, was taken over, 1914. The soil is very fertile, suitable for citrus fruits, bananas, and coffee. Many of the inhabitants are descendants of the Bounty mutineers, moved to Norfolk 1856 from Pitcairn Is. Australia offered the island limited home rule, 1978.

Coral Sea Is. Territory, 1 sq. mi., is administered from Norfolk Is.

Territory of Ashmore and Cartier Is., area 2 sq. mi., in the Indian O. came under Australian authority 1934 and are administered as part of Northern Territory. **Heard** and **McDonald Is.** are administered by the Dept. of Science.

Cocos (Keeling) Is., 27 small coral islands in the Indian O. 1,750 mi. NW of Australia. Pop. (1990) 600, area: 5.5 sq. mi. The residents voted to become part of Australia, Apr. 1984.

Christmas Is. 52 sq. mi., pop. 1,700 (1991), 230 mi. S of Java, was transferred by Britain in 1958. It has phosphate deposits.

Australian Antarctic Territory was claimed by Australia in 1933, including 2,362,000 sq. mi. of territory S of 60th parallel S Lat. and between 160th-45th meridians E Long. It does not include Adelie Coast.

Austria
Republic of Austria
Republik Österreich

People: Population: 7,986,664. Age distrib. (%): <15: 18; 65+: 15. **Pop. density:** 247 per sq. mi. **Urban:** 54%. **Ethnic groups:** German 99%, Croatian, Slovene. **Principal language:** German. **Religions:** Roman Catholic 85%, Protestant 6%.

Geography: Area: 32,378 sq. mi. **Location:** In S Central Europe. **Neighbors:** Switzerland, Liechtenstein on W, Germany, Czech Rep. on N, Slovakia, Hungary on E, Slovenia, Italy on S. **Topography:** Austria is primarily mountainous, with the Alps and foothills covering the western and southern provinces. The eastern provinces and Vienna are located in the Danube River Basin. **Capital:** Vienna (1991 est.): 1,539,000.

Government: Type: Parliamentary democracy. **Head of state:** Pres. Thomas Klestil; b Nov. 4, 1932; in office: July 8, 1992. **Head of government:** Chancellor Franz Vranitzky; b Oct. 4, 1937; in office: June 16, 1986. **Local divisions:** 9 lander (states), each with a legislature. **Defense:** 0.9% of GDP (1993 est.). **Active troop strength:** 51,000 est.

Economy: Industries: Steel, machinery, autos, electrical and optical equip., glassware, sport goods, paper, textiles, chemicals, cement. **Chief crops:** Grains, potatoes, beets. **Minerals:** Iron ore, oil, magnesite. **Other resources:** Forests,

hydro power. **Arable land:** 17%. **Livestock** (1992): cattle: 2.5 mln.; pigs: 3.6 mln. **Electricity prod.** (1992): 49.5 bln. kWh. **Labor force:** 8% agric.; 35% ind. & crafts; 56% service.

Finance: Monetary unit: Schilling (May 1995: 9.75 = $1 US). **Gross domestic product** (1993): $134.4 bln.* **Per capita GDP:** $17,000. **Imports** (1993): $48.5 bln.; partners: EU 67%. **Exports** (1993): $39.9 bln.; partners: EU 64%. **Tourism** (1992): $14.8 bln. **National budget** (1993 est.): $60 bln. **International reserves less gold** (May 1995): $22.3 bln. **Gold:** 12.95 mln. oz t. **Consumer prices** (change in 1994): 3.0%.

Transport: Railroads: Length: 4,136 mi. **Motor vehicles:** in use: 3.2 mln. passenger cars, 279,000 comm. **Civil aviation:** 4.3 bln. passenger-mi.; 6 airports with scheduled flights.

Communications: Television sets: 1 per 2.9 persons. **Radios:** 1 per 1.7 persons. **Telephones:** 1 per 1.6 persons. **Daily newspaper circ.:** 394 per 1,000 pop.

Health: Life expectancy at birth (1995): 74 male; 80 female. **Births** (per 1,000 pop.): 11. **Deaths** (per 1,000 pop.): 10. **Natural increase:** 0.1% **Hospital beds:** 1 per 105 persons. **Physicians:** 1 per 327 persons. **Infant mortality** (per 1,000 live births 1995): 7.

Education: Literacy (1993): 100%. **Years compulsory:** to age 15; attendance 95%.

Major International Organizations: UN and all of its specialized agencies, EU, OECD.

Embassy: 3524 International Court NW 20008; 895-6700.

Rome conquered Austrian lands from Celtic tribes around 15 BC. In 788 the territory was incorporated into Charlemagne's empire. By 1300, the House of Hapsburg had gained control; they added vast territories in all parts of Europe to their realm in the next few hundred years.

Austrian dominance of Germany was undermined in the 18th century and ended by Prussia by 1866. But the Congress of Vienna, 1815, confirmed Austrian control of a large empire in southeast Europe consisting of Germans, Hungarians, Slavs, Italians, and others. The dual Austro-Hungarian monarchy was established in 1867, giving autonomy to Hungary and almost 50 years of peace.

World War I, started after the June 28, 1914, assassination of Archduke Franz Ferdinand, the Hapsburg heir, by a Serbian nationalist, destroyed the empire. By 1918 Austria was reduced to a small republic, with the borders it has today.

Nazi Germany invaded Austria Mar. 13, 1938. The republic was reestablished in 1945, under Allied occupation. Full independence and neutrality were restored in 1955. Austria joined the European Union Jan. 1, 1995.

Azerbaijan
Azerbaijani Republic
Azarbaijchan Respublikasy

People: Population: 7,789,886. **Pop. density:** 233 per sq. mi. **Urban:** 54%. **Ethnic groups:** Azeri 83%, Russian 6%, Armenian 6%. **Principal languages:** Azeri 82%, Russian 7%, Armenian 5%. **Religions:** mostly Muslim.

Geography: Area: 33,400 sq. mi. **Neighbors:** Russia, Georgia on N, Iran on S, Armenia on W, Caspian Sea on E. **Capital:** Baku (1991 est.): 1.1 mln.

Government: Type: in transition. **Head of state:** Pres. Haydar A. Aliyev; b May 10, 1923; in office: June 30, 1993. **Head of government:** Prime Min. Fuad Guliyev; in office: Oct. 6, 1994. **Defense:** 1.9% of GDP (1992). **Active troop strength:** 56,000.

Economy: Industries: Oil refining. **Chief crops:** Grain, cotton, rice, silk. **Minerals:** Oil, gas, iron, copper, lead, zinc. **Crude oil reserves** (1992): 3.3 bln. bbls. **Arable land:** 18%. **Livestock** (1993): cattle: 1.6 mln.; goats & sheep: 5.3 mln. **Electricity prod.** (1992): 22.3 bln. kWh.

Finance: Monetary unit: Manat (Oct. 1994: 293 = $1 US). **Gross Domestic Product** (1993 est.): $15.5 bln.* **Per capita GDP:** $2,040.

Transport: Vehicles: 235,600 passenger cars.

Communications: Daily newspaper circ.: 73 per 1,000 pop.

Health: Life expectancy at birth (1995): 67 male; 75 female. **Births** (per 1,000 pop.): 22. **Deaths** (per 1,000 pop.): 7. **Natural increase:** 1.5%. **Hospital beds:** 1 per 98 persons. **Physicians:** 1 per 251 persons. **Infant mortality** (per 1,000 live births 1995): 34.

Major International Organizations: UN (ILO, IMF, WHO). **Embassy:** 927 15th St. NW 20005; 842-0001.

Azerbaijan was the home of Scythian tribes and part of the Roman Empire. It was overrun by Turks in the 11th century and conquered by Russia in 1806 and 1813. It joined the USSR Dec. 30, 1922, and became a constituent republic in 1936. Azerbaijan declared independence Aug. 30, 1991 and became an independent state when the Soviet Union disbanded Dec. 26, 1991.

Fighting between mostly Muslim Azerbaijan and mostly Christian Armenia escalated in 1992 and continued in 1993 and 1994. Each country claimed Nagorno-Karabakh, an enclave in Azerbaijan with a majority population of ethnic Armenians. A temporary cease-fire was announced in May 1994, with Armenian forces in control of the enclave.

A National Council ousted Communist Pres. Mutaibov and took power May 19, 1992. Abulfez Elchibey became the nation's first democratically elected president June 7, but was ousted from office by Surat Huseynov, commander of a private militia, June 30, 1993. Huseynov became prime minister, and Haydar Aliyev, a pro-Russian former Communist, became president. Huseynov fled the country after his supporters staged an unsuccessful coup attempt Oct. 1994.

The Bahamas
The Commonwealth of The Bahamas

People: Population: 256,616. **Age distrib.** (%): <15: 29; 65+: 5. **Pop. density:** 48 per sq. mi. **Urban:** 84%. **Ethnic groups:** black 85%, white (British, Canadian, U.S.) 15%. **Principal languages:** English, Creole. **Religions:** Baptist 32%, Anglican 20%, Roman Catholic 19%.

Geography: Area: 5,382 sq. mi. **Location:** In Atlantic O., E of Florida. **Neighbors:** Nearest are U.S. on W, Cuba on S. **Topography:** Nearly 700 islands (30 inhabited) and over 2,000 islets in the western Atlantic extend 760 mi. NW to SE. **Capital:** Nassau. **Cities** (1990 est.): Nassau 172,000; Freeport- Lucaya 27,000.

Government: Type: Independent commonwealth. **Head of state:** Queen Elizabeth II, represented by Gov.-Gen. Orville A Turnquest; in office: Jan. 2, 1995. **Head of government:** Prime Min. Hubert Ingraham; b 1947; in office: Aug. 21, 1992. **Local divisions:** 21 districts. **Defense:** 2.1% of GNP (1992). **Active troop strength:** 106,000.

Economy: Industries: Tourism (50% of GDP), rum, banking, pharmaceuticals. **Chief crops:** Fruits, vegetables. **Minerals:** Salt. **Other resources:** Lobsters. **Arable land:** 1%. **Electricity prod.** (1992): 929 mln. kWh. **Labor force:** 5% agric.; 25% tourism; 30% government.

Finance: Monetary unit: Dollar (May 1995: 1 = $1 US). **Gross domestic product** (1993): $4.4 bln.* **Per capita GDP:** $16,500. **Imports** (1992): $1.2 bln.; partners: U.S. 32%, Japan 17%, Nigeria 12%. **Exports** (1992): $310 mln.; partners: U.S. 51%, UK 7%, Norway 7%. **Tourism** (1992): $1.2 bln. **National budget** (1992): $574 mln. **International reserves less gold** (May 1995): $207.9 mln. **Consumer prices** (change in 1994): 1.4%.

Transport: Motor vehicles: in use: 67,000 passenger cars, 14,000 comm. vehicles. **Chief ports:** Nassau, Freeport.

Communications: Radios: 1 per 1.3 persons. **Television sets:** 1 per 4.4 persons. **Telephones:** 1 per 1.8 persons. **Daily newspaper circ.:** 135 per 1,000 pop.

Health: Life expectancy at birth (1995): 67 male; 77 female. **Births** (per 1,000 pop.): 19. **Deaths** (per 1,000 pop.): 6. **Natural increase:** 1.3%. **Infant mortality** (per 1,000 live births 1995): 24.

Education: Literacy (1992): 95%. School compulsory to age 14.

Major International Organizations: UN (World Bank, IMF, WHO), OAS, the Commonwealth.

Embassy: 2220 Massachusetts Ave. NW 20008; 319-2660.

Christopher Columbus first set foot in the New World on San Salvador (Watling I.) in 1492, when Arawak Indians inhabited the islands. British settlement began in 1647; the islands became a British colony in 1783. Internal self-government was granted in 1964; full independence within the Commonwealth was attained July 10, 1973.

International banking and investment management have become major industries alongside tourism.

Bahrain
State of Bahrain
Dawlat al-Bahrayn

People: Population: 575,925. **Age distrib.** (%): <15: 32; 65+: 2. **Pop. density:** 2,149 per sq. mi. **Urban:** 88%. **Ethnic**

groups: Bahraini 63%, Asian 13%, other Arab 10%, Iranian 8%. **Principal languages:** Arabic (official), English, Farsi, Urdu. **Religions:** Shi'a Muslim 70%, Sunni Muslim 30%.

Geography: Area: 268 sq. mi. **Location:** In Persian Gulf. **Neighbors:** Nearest are Saudi Arabia on W, Qatar on E. **Topography:** Bahrain Island, and several adjacent, smaller islands, are flat, hot, and humid, with little rain. **Capital:** Manama (1991 est.): 121,000.

Government: Type: Traditional monarchy. **Head of state:** Emir Isa bin Sulman al-Khalifa; b July 3, 1933; in office: Nov. 2, 1961. **Head of government:** Prime Min. Kahlifa bin Sulman al-Khalifa; b 1935; in office: Jan. 19, 1970. **Local divisions:** 12 districts. **Defense:** 6.0% of GDP (1990). **Active troop strength:** 8,100.

Economy: Industries: Oil products, aluminum smelting. **Chief crops:** Fruits, vegetables. **Minerals:** Oil, gas. **Crude oil reserves** (1994): 70 mln. bbls. **Arable land:** 2%. **Electricity prod.** (1992): 4.7 bln. kWh. **Labor force:** 5% agric.; 85% ind. and commerce; 5% services; 3% govt.

Finance: Monetary unit: Dinar (May 1995: 1.00 = $2.66 US). **Gross domestic product** (1993): $6.8 bln.* **Per capita income:** $12,000. **Imports** (1993): $3.7 bln.; partners: Saudi Arabia 42%, UK 7%, U.S. 14%. **Exports** (1993): $3.5 bln.; partners: UAE 12%, Japan 13%, Pakistan 8%. **National budget** (1992): $1.6 bln. **International reserves less gold** (Apr. 1995): $1.4 bln. **Gold:** 150,000 oz t. **Consumer prices** (change in 1994): 0.8%.

Transport: Motor vehicles: in use: 108,000 passenger cars, 25,000 comm. vehicles. **Chief port:** Sitra.

Communications: Television sets: 1 per 2.0 persons. **Radios:** 1 per 1.7 persons. **Telephones:** 1 per 2.8 persons.

Health: Life expectancy at birth (1995): 71 male; 76 female. **Births** (per 1,000 pop.): 24. **Deaths** (per 1,000 pop.): 3. **Natural increase:** 2.1%. Medical services are free. **Infant mortality** (per 1,000 live births 1995): 18.

Education: Literacy (1992): 77%.

Major International Organizations: UN (WTO, IMF, WHO), Arab League.

Embassy: 3502 International Dr. NW 20008; 342-0741.

Long ruled by the Khalifa family, Bahrain was a British protectorate from 1861 to Aug. 15, 1971, when it regained independence.

Pearls, shrimp, fruits, and vegetables were the mainstays of the economy until oil was discovered in 1932. By the 1970s, oil reserves were depleted; international banking thrived.

Bahrain took part in the 1973-74 Arab oil embargo against the U.S. and other nations. The government bought controlling interest in the oil industry in 1975.

Bangladesh
People's Republic of Bangladesh
Gana Prajatantri Bangladesh

People: Population: 128,094,948. **Age distrib.** (%): <15: 42; 65+: 3. **Pop. density:** 2,236 per sq. mi. **Urban:** 17%. **Ethnic groups:** Bengali 98%, Bihari, tribals. **Principal languages:** Bangla (official), English. **Religions:** Muslim 83%, Hindu 16%.

Geography: Area: 57,295 sq. mi. **Location:** In S Asia, on N bend of Bay of Bengal. **Neighbors:** India nearly surrounds country on W, N, E; Myanmar on SE. **Topography:** The country is mostly a low plain cut by the Ganges and Brahmaputra rivers and their delta. The land is alluvial and marshy along the coast, with hills only in the extreme SE and NE. A tropical monsoon climate prevails, among the rainiest in the world. **Capital:** Dhaka. **Cities** (1991 met. est.): Dhaka 6.1 mln.; Chittagong 2.0 mln.; Khulna 877,000.

Government: Type: Parliamentary democracy. **Head of state:** Pres. Abdur Rahman Biswas; b 1926; in office: Oct. 10, 1991. **Head of government:** Prime Min. Khaleda Zia; b Nov. 1944; in office: Mar. 20, 1991. **Local divisions:** 64 districts. **Defense:** 1.5% of GDP (FY 1992-93). **Active troop strength:** 115,500.

Economy: Industries: Food processing, jute, textiles, fertilizers, steel. **Chief crops:** Jute (most of world output), rice, tea. **Minerals:** Natural gas. **Arable land:** 67%. **Livestock** (1993): cattle: 24 mln.; goats: 26 mln. **Fish catch** (1992): 966,700 metric tons. **Electricity prod.** (1992): 9 bln. kWh. **Labor force:** 65% agric; 14% ind. & mining; 21% services.

Finance: Monetary unit: Taka (May 1995: 40.11 = $1 US). **Gross domestic product** (1993): $122 bln.* **Per capita GDP:** $1,100. **Imports** (FY 1993): $3.5 bln.; partners: Japan 7%, Hong Kong 8%. **Exports** (FY 1993): $2.1 bln.; partners: U.S.

33%; Italy 6%; Germany 8%. **Tourism** (1992): $8.0 mln. **National budget** (1992): $3.7 bln. **International reserves less gold** (May 1995): $3.2 bln. **Gold:** 94,000 oz t. **Consumer prices** (change in 1994): 3.6%.

Transport: Railroads: Length: 1,706 mi. **Motor vehicles:** in use: 67,000 passenger cars, 63,000 comm. vehicles. **Chief ports:** Chittagong, Chalna.

Communications: Radios: 1 per 26 persons. **Television sets:** 1 per 329 persons. **Telephones:** 1 per 427 persons.

Health: Life expectancy at birth (1995): 56 male; 55 female. **Births** (per 1,000 pop.): 35. **Deaths** (per 1,000 pop.): 11. **Natural increase:** 2.3%. **Hospital beds:** 1 per 3,218 persons. **Physicians:** 1 per 5,264 persons. **Infant mortality** (per 1,000 live births 1995): 105.

Education: Literacy (1992): 47%. **Attendance:** 73% primary school; 26% secondary school.

Major International Organizations: UN (WTO, IMF, WHO), the Commonwealth.

Embassy: 2201 Wisconsin Ave. NW 20007; 342-8372.

Muslim invaders conquered the formerly Hindu area in the 12th century. British rule lasted from the 18th century to 1947, when East Bengal became part of Pakistan.

Charging West Pakistani domination, the Awami League, based in the East, won National Assembly control in 1971. Assembly sessions were postponed; riots broke out. Pakistani troops attacked Mar. 25; Bangladesh independence was proclaimed the next day. In the ensuing civil war, one million died and 10 million fled to India.

War between India and Pakistan broke out Dec. 3, 1971. Pakistan surrendered in the East on Dec. 15. Sheikh Mujibur Rahman became prime minister. The country moved into the Indian and Soviet orbits in response to U.S. support of Pakistan, and much of the economy was nationalized.

On May 30, 1981, Pres. Ziaur Rahman was killed in an unsuccessful coup attempt by army rivals. Vice President Abdus Sattar assumed the presidency but was ousted in a coup led by army chief of staff Gen. H.M. Ershad, Mar. 1982. Ershad declared Bangladesh an Islamic Republic in 1988. Bangladesh adopted a parliamentary system of government in 1991.

Bangladesh is subject to devastating storms and floods that kill thousands. A cyclone struck Apr. 1991, killing over 131,000 people and causing $2.7 billion in damages. Chronic destitution in the densely crowded population has been worsened by the decline of jute as a world commodity.

Taslima Nasrin, a Bangladeshi feminist writer charged in court with offending Islam and threatened with death by Islamic militants, left the country for Sweden, Aug. 10, 1994.

Barbados

People: Population: 256,395. **Age distrib.** (%): <15: 24; 65+: 12. **Pop. density:** 1,545 per sq. mi. **Urban:** 38%. **Ethnic groups:** African 80%, mixed 16%, European 4%. **Principal language:** English. **Religions:** Protestant 67%, Roman Catholic 4%.

Geography: Area: 166 sq. mi. **Location:** In Atlantic, farthest E of W Indies. **Neighbors:** Nearest are St. Lucia and St. Vincent and the Grenadines to the W. **Topography:** The island lies alone in the Atlantic almost completely surrounded by coral reefs. Highest point is Mt. Hillaby, 1,115 ft. **Capital:** Bridgetown (1990): 6,000.

Government: Type: Parliamentary democracy. **Head of state:** Queen Elizabeth II, represented by Gov.-Gen. Dame Nita Barrow; b Nov. 15, 1916; in office: June 6, 1990. **Head of government:** Prime Min. Owen Arthur; b 1950; in office: Sept. 7, 1994. **Local divisions:** 11 parishes and Bridgetown. **Defense:** 0.7% of GDP (1989).

Economy: Industries: Sugar, tourism. **Chief crops:** Sugar, cotton. **Minerals:** Oil, gas. **Other resources:** Fish. **Arable land:** 77%. **Electricity prod.** (1992): 540 mln. kWh. **Labor force:** 8% agric.; 22% commerce; 37% serv. & govt.; 22% manuf. & constr.

Finance: Monetary unit: Dollar (May 1995: 2.01 = $1 US). **Gross domestic product** (1993): $2.2 bln.* **Per capita GDP:** $8,700. **Imports** (1992): $465 mln.; partners: U.S. 33%, UK 11%, Trin. & Tob. 11%. **Exports** (1992): $158 mln.; partners: U.S. 13%, UK 13%, Trin. & Tob. 9%. **Tourism** (1992): $463 mln. **National budget** (FY 1992-93): $620 mln. **International reserves less gold** (Apr. 1995): $229 mln. **Consumer prices** (change in 1994): 0.1%.

Transport: Motor vehicles: in use: 39,000 passenger cars; 9,000 comm. vehicles. **Chief port:** Bridgetown.

Communications: Television sets: 1 per 3.7 persons. **Radios:** 1 per 1.3 persons. **Telephones:** 1 per 2.4 persons. **Daily newspaper circ.:** 158 per 1,000 pop.

Health: Life expectancy at birth (1995): 71 male; 77 female. **Births** (per 1,000 pop.): 15. **Deaths** (per 1,000 pop.): 8. **Natural increase:** 0.7%. **Hospital beds:** 1 per 121 persons. **Physicians:** 1 per 1,042 persons. **Infant mortality** (per 1,000 live births 1995): 19.

Education: Literacy (1992): 99%. **Years compulsory:** to age 16.

Major International Organizations: UN (FAO, WTO, ILO, IMF, WHO), OAS, the Commonwealth.

Embassy: 2144 Wyoming Ave. NW 20008; 939-9200.

Barbados was probably named by Portuguese sailors in reference to bearded fig trees. An English ship visited in 1605, and British settlers arrived on the uninhabited island in 1627. Slaves worked the sugar plantations until slavery was abolished in 1834. Self-rule came gradually, with full independence proclaimed Nov. 30, 1966. British traditions have remained.

Belarus
Republic of Belarus
Respublika Belarus

People: Population: 10,437,418. **Pop. density:** 130 per sq. mi. **Urban:** 68%. **Ethnic groups:** Belarussian 78%, Russian 13%. **Principal languages:** Belarussian, Russian. **Religion:** Eastern Orthodox.

Geography: Area: 80,153 sq. mi. **Location:** E Europe. **Neighbors:** Poland on W, Latvia, Lithuania on N, Russia on E, Ukraine on S. **Capital:** Minsk. **Cities** (1992): Minsk 1.7 mln.; Homel 517,000.

Government: Republic. **Head of state:** Pres. Aleksandr Lukashenko; b 1954; in office: July 1994. **Local divisions:** 6 voblastsi and 1 municipality. **Defense:** 1.8% of GNP (1993). **Active troop strength:** 92,500.

Economy: Industries: Manufacturing, chemical fibers, machine-tool & agricultural machinery. **Chief crops:** Grain, flax, potatoes. **Arable land:** 29%. **Livestock** (1993): cattle: 6.2 mln.; pigs: 4.3 mln. **Electricity prod.** (1992): 37.6 bln. kWh. **Labor force:** 40% ind. & const.; 21% agric.

Finance: Monetary unit: Belarusian rubel (Oct. 1994: 5,854 = $1 US). **Gross domestic product** (1993 est.): $61 bln.* **Per capita GDP:** $5,890.

Transport: Railroads: Length: 3,459 mi. **Passenger cars:** 700,000.

Communications: Television sets: 1 per 2.9 persons. **Radios:** 1 per 1.2 persons. **Telephones:** 1 per 5.5 persons. **Daily newspaper circ.:** 286 per 1,000 pop.

Health: Life expectancy at birth (1995): 66 male; 76 female. **Births** (per 1,000 pop.): 13. **Deaths** (per 1,000 pop.): 11. **Natural increase:** 0.2%. **Hospital beds:** 1 per 81 persons. **Physicians:** 1 per 242 persons. **Infant mortality** (per 1,000 live births 1995): 19.

Major International Organizations: UN, CIS.

Embassy: 1619 New Hampshire Ave. NW 20009; 986-1604.

The region was subject to Lithuanians and Poles in medieval times, and was a prize of war between Russia and Poland beginning in 1503. It became part of the USSR in 1922 although the western part of the region was controlled by Poland. Belarus was overrun by German armies in 1941; recovered by Soviet troops in 1944. Following World War II, Belarus increased in area through Soviet annexation of part of NE Poland. Belarus declared independence Aug. 25, 1991. It became an independent state when the Soviet Union disbanded Dec. 26, 1991.

A new constitution was adopted, Mar. 15, 1994, and a new president was chosen in elections concluding July 10. Voters in May 1995 supported economic integration with Russia but failed to elect enough deputies for a new parliament, provoking a constitutional crisis.

Belarussian combat aircraft shot down a sport balloon Sept. 12, 1995, killing the 2 U.S. crew members.

Belgium
Kingdom of Belgium
Koninkrijk België (Dutch)
Royaume de Belgique (French)

People: Population: 10,081,880. **Age distrib.** (%): <15: 18; 65+: 16. **Pop. density:** 855 per sq. mi. **Urban:** 97%. **Ethnic groups:** Fleming 55%, Walloon 33%. **Principal languages:** Flemish (Dutch) 56%, French 32%, German. **Religion:** Roman Catholic 75%.

Geography: Area: 11,787 sq. mi. **Location:** In NW Europe, on N Sea. **Neighbors:** France on W, S, Luxembourg on SE, Germany on E, Netherlands on N. **Topography:** Mostly flat, the country is trisected by the Scheldt and Meuse, major commercial rivers. The land becomes hilly and forested in the SE (Ardennes) region. **Capital:** Brussels. **Cities** (1993 est.): Brussels (met.) 950,000; Antwerp 465,000; Ghent 230,000; Charleroi 207,000; Liege 197,000.

Government: Type: Parliamentary democracy under a constitutional monarch. **Head of state:** King Albert II; b June 6, 1934; in office: Aug. 9, 1993. **Head of government:** Premier Jean-Luc Dehaene; b Aug. 7, 1940; in office: Mar. 7, 1992. **Local divisions:** 9 provinces. **Defense:** 2% of GDP (1992). **Active troop strength:** 63,000.

Economy: Industries: Steel, glassware, diamond cutting, textiles, chemicals. **Chief crops:** Wheat, fruits, sugar beets. **Minerals:** Coal, gas. **Other resources:** Forests. **Arable land:** 24%. **Livestock** (1993): cattle: 3.3 mln.; pigs: 7.0 mln. **Fish catch** (1991): 40,226 metric tons. **Electricity prod.** (1992): 68 bln. kWh. **Labor force:** 2% agric.; 28% industry; 64% services.

Finance: Monetary unit: Franc (May 1995: 28.50 = $1 US). **Gross domestic product** (1993): $177.5 bln.* **Per capita GDP** $17,700. *Note:* The following trade data include Luxembourg. **Imports** (1992): $120 bln.; partners: EU 73%. **Exports** (1992): $118 bln.; partners: EU 74%. **Tourism** (1992): receipts: $4.1 bln. **National budget** (1989): $109.3 bln. **International reserves less gold** (May 1995): $16.8 bln. **Gold:** 19.42 mln. oz t. **Consumer prices** (change in 1994): 2.4%.

Transport: Railroads: Length: 2,132 mi. **Motor vehicles:** in use: 4.1 mln. passenger cars, 390,000 comm. vehicles. **Civil aviation:** 4.0 bln. passenger-mi.; 2 airports with scheduled flights. **Chief ports:** Antwerp, Zeebrugge, Ghent.

Communications: Television sets: 1 per 2.4 persons. **Radios:** 1 per 2.2 persons. **Telephones:** 1 per 1.8 persons. **Daily newspaper circ.:** 305 per 1,000 pop.

Health: Life expectancy at birth (1995): 74 male; 81 female. **Births** (per 1,000 pop.): 11. **Deaths** (per 1,000 pop.): 10. **Natural increase** 0.1%. **Hospital beds:** 1 per 124 persons. **Physicians:** 1 per 278 persons. **Infant mortality** (per 1,000 live births 1995): 7.

Education: Literacy (1992): 98%. **Years compulsory:** to age 18.

Major International Organizations: UN and all of its specialized agencies, NATO, EU, OECD.

Embassy: 3330 Garfield St. NW 20008; 333-6900.

Belgium derives its name from the Belgae, the first recorded inhabitants, probably Celts. The land was conquered by Julius Caesar, and was ruled for 1800 years by conquerors, including Rome, the Franks, Burgundy, Spain, Austria, and France. After 1815, Belgium was made a part of the Netherlands, but it became an independent constitutional monarchy in 1830.

Belgian neutrality was violated by Germany in both world wars. King Leopold III surrendered to Germany, May 28, 1940. After the war, he was forced by political pressure to abdicate in favor of his son, King Baudouin. Baudouin was succeeded by his brother, Albert II, Aug. 9, 1993.

The Flemings of northern Belgium speak Dutch, while French is the language of the Walloons in the south. The language difference has been a perennial source of controversy and led to antagonism between the 2 groups. Parliament has passed measures aimed at transferring power from the central government to 3 regions—Wallonia, Flanders, and Brussels.

Belgium lives by its foreign trade; about 50% of its entire production is sold abroad.

Belize

People: Population: 214,061. **Age distrib.** (%): <15: 44; 65+: 4. **Pop. density:** 24 per sq. mi. **Urban:** 48%. **Ethnic groups:** mestizo 44%, Creole 30%, Maya 11%, Garifuna 7%. **Principal languages:** English (official), Spanish, Maya, Garifuna (Carib). **Religions:** Roman Catholic 62%, Protestant 30%.

Geography: Area: 8,867 sq. mi. **Location:** Eastern coast of Central America. **Neighbors:** Mexico on N, Guatemala on W and S. **Capital:** Belmopan. **Cities** (1992): Belize City 45,000.

Government: Type: Parliamentary democracy. **Head of state:** Queen Elizabeth II, represented by Gov.-Gen. Colville Young; b Nov. 20, 1932; in office: Nov. 17, 1993. **Head of government:** Prime Min. Manuel Esquivel; b May 2, 1940; in office: July 2, 1993. **Local divisions:** 6 districts. **Defense:** 2% of GDP (1992). **Active troop strength:** 950.

Economy: Sugar is the main export.

Finance: Monetary unit: Belize Dollar (May 1995: 2 = $1 US). **Gross domestic product** (1993): $550 mln.* **Per capita GDP:** $2,700. **Imports** (1992): $273 mln.; partners: U.S. 55%, UK 8%. **Exports:** (1992): $102 mln.; partners: U.S. 46%, UK 31%. **National budget** (1991): $123.1 mln. **International reserves less gold** (May 1995): $32.6 mln.

Health: Life expectancy at birth (1995): 66 male; 70 female. **Births** (per 1,000 pop.): 34. **Deaths** (per 1,000 pop.): 6. **Natural increase:** 2.8%. **Hospital beds:** 1 per 332 persons. **Physicians:** 1 per 2,021 persons. **Infant mortality** (per 1,000 live births 1995): 35.

Education: Literacy (1993): 93%. **Years compulsory:** to age 15.

Major International Organizations: OAS, UN (IMF, World Bank), the Commonwealth.

Embassy: 2535 Massachusetts Ave. NW 20008; 332-9636.

Belize (formerly British Honduras) was Britain's last colony on the American mainland. The country achieved independence Sept. 21, 1981. Relations with neighboring Guatemala, initially tense, have improved in recent years.

Benin

Republic of Benin
République du Bénin

People: Population: 5,522,677. **Age distrib.** (%): <15: 47; 65+: 3. **Pop. density:** 127 per sq. mi. **Urban:** 30%. **Ethnic groups:** African (Fon, Adja, Bariba, Yoruba) 99%. **Principal languages:** French (official), Fon, Yoruba. **Religions:** indigenous beliefs 70%, Muslim 15%, Christian 15%.

Geography: Area: 43,500 sq. mi. **Location:** In W Africa on Gulf of Guinea. **Neighbors:** Togo on W, Burkina Faso, Niger on N, Nigeria on E. **Topography:** most of Benin is flat and covered with dense vegetation. The coast is hot, humid, and rainy. **Capital:** Porto-Novo. **Cities** (1992): Cotonou 533,000.

Government: Type: Republic. **Head of state:** Pres. Nicéphore Soglo; b Nov. 29, 1934; in office: Apr. 4, 1991. **Local divisions:** 6 provinces. **Defense:** 2.0% of GNP (1990). **Active troop strength:** 4,800.

Economy: Chief crops: Palm products, peanuts, cotton, corn, rice. **Minerals:** Oil. **Arable land:** 12%. **Livestock** (1993): goats: 1.2 mln.; cattle: 1.1 mln. **Fish catch** (1991): 41,000 metric tons. **Electricity prod.** (1991): 25 mln. kWh. **Labor force:** 60% agric; 38% transport, commerce, public services.

Finance: Monetary unit: CFA Franc (May 1995: 488 = $1 US). **Gross domestic product** (1993): $6.2 bln.* **Per capita GDP:** $1,200. **Imports** (1991): $482 mln.; partners: France 20%. **Exports** (1991): $329 mln.; partners: Germany 36%. **National budget** (1991): $355 bln. **International reserves less gold** (Mar. 1995): $245 mln.

Transport: Railroads: Length: 359 mi. **Chief ports:** Cotonou.

Communications: Radios: 1 per 14 persons. **Televisions:** 1 per 254 persons. **Daily newspaper circ.:** 3 per 1,000 pop.

Health: Life expectancy at birth (1995): 50 male; 54 female. **Births** (per 1,000 pop.): 47. **Deaths** (per 1,000 pop.): 14. **Natural increase:** 3.3%. **Hospital beds:** 1 per 749 persons. **Physicians:** 1 per 11,306 persons. **Infant mortality** (per 1,000 live births 1995): 108.

Education: Literacy (1991): 28%. **Years compulsory:** 6; attendance 43%.

Major International Organizations: UN (FAO, IMF, WHO), OAU.

Embassy: 2737 Cathedral Ave. NW 20008; 232-6656.

The Kingdom of Abomey, rising to power in wars with neighboring kingdoms in the 17th century, came under French domination in the late 19th century and was incorporated into French West Africa by 1904.

Under the name Dahomey, the country became independent Aug. 1, 1960. The name was changed to Benin in 1975. In the fifth coup since independence Col. Ahmed Kerekou took power in 1972; two years later he declared a socialist state with a "Marxist-Leninist" philosophy. In Dec. 1989, Kerekou announced that Marxism-Leninism would no longer be the state ideology.

In Mar. 1991, Kerekou lost to Nicéphore Soglo in Benin's first free presidential election in 30 years.

Bhutan
Kingdom of Bhutan
Druk-Yul

People: Population: 1,780,638. **Age distrib.** (%): <15: 39; 65+: 4. **Pop. density:** 98 per sq. mi. **Ethnic groups:** Bhote 50%, Nepalese 35%. **Principal languages:** Dzongkha (official), Gurung, Assamese. **Religions:** Lamaistic Buddhist (state religion) 75%, Hindu 25%.

Geography: Area: 18,150 sq. mi. **Location:** In eastern Himalayan Mts. **Neighbors:** India on W (Sikkim) and S, China on N. **Topography:** Bhutan is comprised of very high mountains in the N, fertile valleys in the center, and thick forests in the Duar Plain in the S. **Capital:** Thimphu (Paro is administrative capital). **City** (1993 est.): Thimphu 30,000.

Government: Type: Monarchy. **Head of state:** King Jigme Singye Wangchuk; b Nov. 11, 1955; in office: July 21, 1972. **Local divisions:** 18 districts.

Economy: Industries: Cements, wood products. **Chief crops:** Rice, corn, citrus. **Other resources:** Timber. **Arable land:** 2%. **Labor force:** 93% agric.

Finance: Monetary unit: Ngultrum (May 1995: 31.42 = $1 US; Indian Rupee also used). **Gross domestic product** (1993): $500 mln.* **Per capita GDP:** $700. **Tourism** (1990): 2.0 mln. **Imports** (FY 1993): $125 mln.; partners: India 60%. **Exports** (FY 1993): $66 mln.; partners: India 82%. **National budget** (1992 est.): $112 mln.

Communications: Radios: 1 per 26 persons. **Telephones:** 1 per 669 persons.

Health: Life expectancy at birth (1995): 52 male; 50 female. **Births** (per 1,000 pop.): 39. **Deaths** (per 1,000 pop.): 16. **Natural increase:** 2.3%. **Hospital beds:** 1 per 816 persons. **Physicians:** 1 per 5,335 persons. **Infant mortality** (per 1,000 live births 1995): 119.

Education: Literacy (1990): 18%. School attendance: 25%.

Major International Organizations: UN (IMF, World Bank).

The region came under Tibetan rule in the 16th century. British influence grew in the 19th century. A monarchy, set up in 1907, became a British protectorate by a 1910 treaty. The country became independent in 1949, with India guiding foreign relations and supplying aid.

Links to India have been strengthened by airline service and a road network. Most of the population engages in subsistence agriculture.

Bolivia
Republic of Bolivia
República de Bolivia

People: Population: 7,896,254. **Age distrib.** (%): <15: 41; 65+: 4. **Pop. density:** 19 per sq. mi. **Urban:** 58%. **Ethnic groups:** Quechua 30%, Aymara 25%, mestizo 25–30%, European 5–15%. **Principal languages:** Spanish, Quechua, Aymara (all official). **Religion:** Roman Catholic 95%.

Geography: Area: 424,164 sq. mi. **Location:** In central Andes Mts. **Neighbors:** Peru, Chile on W, Argentina, Paraguay on S, Brazil on E and N. **Topography:** The great central plateau, at an altitude of 12,000 ft., over 500 mi. long, lies between two great cordilleras having 3 of the highest peaks in S America. Lake Titicaca, on Peruvian border, is highest lake in world on which steamboats ply (12,506 ft.). The E central region has semitropical forests; the llanos, or Amazon-Chaco lowlands are in E. **Capitals:** La Paz (administrative), Sucre (judicial). **Cities** (1992): La Paz 711,000; Santa Cruz 695,000; El Alto 404,000; Cochabamba 404,000.

Government: Type: Republic. **Head of state:** Pres. Gonzalo Sánchez de Lozada; b 1930; in office: Aug. 6, 1993. **Local divisions:** 9 departments. **Defense:** 2.4% of GNP (1991). **Active troop strength:** 33,500.

Economy: Industry: Textiles, food processing, mining, clothing. **Chief crops:** Coffee, sugar, potatoes, corn, coca (sold for cocaine processing). **Minerals:** Antimony, tin, tungsten, silver, zinc, oil, gas, iron. **Crude oil reserves** (1994): 108 mln. bbls. **Other resources:** rubber, cinchona bark. **Arable land:** 3%. **Livestock** (1992): cattle: 5.8 mln.; sheep: 7.3 mln.; pigs: 2.2 mln. **Electricity prod.** (1992): 1.8 bln. kWh. **Labor force:** 39% agric.; 16% serv. & utilities; 11% manuf. & mining.

Finance: Monetary unit: Boliviano (May 1995: 4.76 = $1 US). **Gross domestic product** (1993): $15.8 bln.* **Per capita**

GDP: $2,100. **Imports** (1993): $1.17 bln.; partners: U.S. 23%. **Exports** (1993): $752 mln.; partners: U.S. 16%. **National budget** (1994 est.): $3.19 bln. **International reserves less gold** (May 1995): $513 mln. **Gold:** 893,000 oz t. **Consumer prices** (change in 1993): 8.5%.

Transport: Railroads: Length: 2,264 mi. **Motor vehicles:** in use: 265,000 passenger cars, 60,000 comm. vehicles. **Civil aviation:** 739 mln. passenger-mi.; 21 airports with scheduled flights.

Communications: Television sets: 1 per 12 persons. **Radios:** 1 per 1.9 persons. **Telephones:** 1 per 38 persons. **Daily newspaper circ.:** 55 per 1,000 pop.

Health: Life expectancy at birth (1995): 61 male; 66 female. **Births** (per 1,000 pop.): 32. **Deaths** (per 1,000 pop.): 8. **Natural increase:** 2.3%. **Hospital beds:** 1 per 1,183 persons. **Physicians:** 1 per 2,561 persons. **Infant mortality** (per 1,000 live births 1995): 71.

Education: Literacy (1991): 78%. **Years compulsory:** ages 6-14; attendance 82%.

Major International Organizations: UN (IMF, FAO, WHO), OAS.

Embassy: 3014 Massachusetts Ave. NW 20008; 483-4410.

The Incas conquered the region from earlier Indian inhabitants in the 13th century. Spanish rule began in the 1530s and lasted until Aug. 6, 1825. The country is named after Simon Bolivar, independence fighter.

In a series of wars, Bolivia lost its Pacific coast to Chile, the oil-bearing Chaco to Paraguay, and rubber-growing areas to Brazil, 1879-1935.

Economic unrest, especially among the militant mine workers, has contributed to continuing political instability. A reformist government under Victor Paz Estenssoro, 1951-64, nationalized tin mines and attempted to improve conditions for the Indian majority but was overthrown by a military junta. A series of coups and countercoups continued through 1981, until the military junta elected Gen. Villa as president.

In July 1982, the military junta assumed power amid a growing economic crisis and foreign debt difficulties. The junta resigned in Oct. and allowed the Congress, elected democratically in 1980, to take power.

U.S. pressure on the government to reduce the country's output of coca, the raw material for cocaine, has led to clashes between police and coca growers and increased anti-U.S. feeling among Bolivians.

Bosnia and Herzegovina
Republic of Bosnia and Herzegovina
Republika Bosna i Hercegovina

People: Population: 3,201,823. **Pop. density:** 162 per sq. mi. **Urban:** 34%. **Ethnic groups:** Muslim 44%, Serbian 31%, Croatian 17%. **Principal languages:** Serbo-Croatian (official) 99%. **Religions:** Muslim 40%, Orthodox 31%, Catholic 15% .

Geography: Area: 19,741 sq. mi. **Location:** On Balkan Peninsula in SE Europe. **Neighbors:** Yugoslavia on E and SE, Croatia on N and W. **Topography:** Hilly with some mountains. About 50% of the land is forested. **Capital:** Sarajevo (1991): 416,000.

Government: Type: In transition. **Head of state:** Pres. Alija Izetbegovic; b 1925; in office: Dec. 1990. **Defense: Active troop strength:** 110,000 est.

Economy: Industries: Textiles, mining, timber. **Chief crops:** Corn, wheat, oats, barley. **Minerals:** Bauxite, iron ore, coal.

Finance: Monetary unit: New Yugoslav Dinar. **Gross domestic product** (1991): $14 bln.* **Per capita GDP:** $3,200.

Health: Births (per 1,000 pop.): 11. **Deaths** (per 1,000 pop.): 8. **Natural increase:** 0.4%. **Hospital beds:** 1 per 219 persons. **Physicians:** 1 per 624 persons. **Infant mortality** (per 1,000 live births 1995): 12.

Education: Literacy (1991): 90%.

Major International Organizations: UN (ILO, WHO).

Bosnia was ruled by Croatian kings c. 958 AD, and by Hungary 1000-1200. It became organized c. 1200 and later took control of Herzegovina. The kingdom disintegrated from 1391, with the southern part becoming the independent duchy Herzegovina. It was conquered by Turks in 1463 and made a Turkish province. The area was placed under control of Austria-Hungary in 1878, and made part of the province of **Bosnia and Herzegovina,** which was formally annexed to Austria-Hungary 1908, and it became a province of Yugoslavia in 1918. It was reunited with Herzegovina as a federated republic in the 1946 Yugoslavian constitution.

The Bosnia and Herzegovina parliament adopted a declaration of sovereignty Oct. 15, 1991. A referendum for independence was passed Feb. 29, 1992. Ethnic Serbs' opposition to the referendum spurred violent clashes and bombings. The U.S. and EU recognized the republic Apr. 7. Fierce three-way fighting continued between Bosnia's Serbs, Muslims, and Croats. Serb forces massacred thousands of Bosnian Muslims and engaged in "ethnic cleansing" (the expulsion of Muslims and other non-Serbs from areas under Bosnian Serb control). The capital, Sarajevo, was surrounded and besieged by Bosnian Serb forces.

Muslims and Croats in Bosnia reached a cease-fire Feb. 23, 1994, and signed an accord, Mar. 18, to create a Muslim-Croat confederation in Bosnia. The Bosnian and Croatian governments agreed to link this confederation loosely with Croatia. Heavy Muslim-Serb fighting continued, with many civilian casualties. By mid-1994, Bosnian Serbs controlled over 70% of the country. They repeatedly rejected an international peace plan giving Serbs 49% of a partitioned Bosnia, and the Muslim-Croat confederation 51%.

As fighting continued in 1995, the balance of power began to shift toward the Muslim-Croat alliance. After NATO air strikes May 26, Bosnian Serbs took more than 350 UN peacekeepers hostage; the Serbian government helped arrange their release. Massive NATO air strikes at Bosnian Serb targets beginning Aug. 30 triggered a new round of peace talks, and the siege of Sarajevo was lifted Sept. 15. The new talks produced an agreement in principle to create autonomous regions within Bosnia, with the Serb region constituting 49% of the country; a Croat-Muslim offensive in Sept. recaptured significant territory, leaving the Bosnian Serbs in control of approximately that percentage. A cease-fire was announced in Oct.

Botswana
Republic of Botswana

People: Population: 1,392,414. **Age distrib.** (%): <15: 43; 65+: 3. **Pop. density:** 6 per sq. mi. **Urban:** 27%. **Ethnic groups:** Batswana 95%, Kalanga, others. **Principal languages:** English (official), Setswana. **Religions:** indigenous beliefs 50%, Christian 50%.

Geography: Area: 224,607 sq. mi. **Location:** In southern Africa. **Neighbors:** Namibia on N and W, South Africa on S, Zimbabwe on NE; Botswana claims border with Zambia on N. **Topography:** The Kalahari Desert, supporting nomadic Bushmen and wildlife, spreads over SW; there are swamplands and farming areas in N, and rolling plains in E where livestock are grazed. **Capital:** Gaborone (1991): 134,000.

Government: Type: Parliamentary republic. **Head of state:** Pres. Quett Ketumile Masire; b July 23, 1925; in office: July 13, 1980. **Local divisions:** 10 districts and 4 town councils. **Defense:** 4.9% of GDP (FY 1993-94). **Active troop strength:** 7,500+.

Economy: Industries: Livestock processing, mining. **Chief crops:** Corn, sorghum, beans. **Minerals:** Copper, coal, nickel, diamonds. **Other resources:** Big game. **Arable land:** 2%. **Electricity prod.** (1992 est.): 901 mln. kWh. **Labor force:** 27% social & personal serv.; 25% agric.; 22% manuf. & constr.

Finance: Monetary unit: Pula (May 1995: 1.00 = $.36 US). **Gross domestic product** (1993): $6.0 bln.* **Per capita GDP:** $4,500. **Imports** (1991): $2.2 bln.; partners: S Africa 88%. **Exports** (1991): $2.7 bln.; partners: Europe 67%, U.S. 17%, S Africa 7%. **Tourism** (1992): $65 mln. **National budget** (1994): $1.99 bln. **International reserves less gold** (Jan. 1995): $4.7 bln. **Consumer prices** (change in 1994): 10.5%.

Transport: Railroads: Length: 551 mi. **Motor vehicles:** in use: 17,000 passenger cars, 30,000 comm. vehicles. **Communications: Radios:** 1 per 1.3 persons. **Telephones:** 1 per 21 persons. **Daily newspaper circ.:** 27 per 1,000 pop. **Health: Life expectancy at birth** (1995): 61 male; 67 female. **Births** (1,000 pop.): 31. **Deaths** (per 1,000 pop.): 7. **Natural increase:** 2.4%. **Hospital beds:** 1 per 395 persons. **Physicians:** 1 per 5,417 persons. **Infant mortality** (per 1,000 live births 1995): 38.

Education: Literacy (1992): 74%.

Major International Organizations: UN (WTO, IMF, WHO), OAU, the Commonwealth.

Embassy: 3400 International Dr. NW 20008; 244-4990.

First inhabited by bushmen, then by Bantus, the region became the British protectorate of Bechuanaland in 1886, halting encroachment by Boers and Germans from the south and southwest. The country became fully independent Sept. 30, 1966, changing its name to Botswana. Cattle raising and mining (diamonds, copper, nickel) have contributed to economic growth. The economy is closely tied to South Africa.

Brazil
Federative Republic of Brazil
República Federativa do Brasil

People: Population: 160,737,489. **Age distrib.** (%): <15: 32; 65+: 5. **Pop. density:** 49 per sq. mi. **Urban:** 77%. **Ethnic groups:** Portuguese, Africans, and mulattoes make up the vast majority; Italians, Germans, Japanese, Amerindians. **Principal languages:** Portuguese (official), Spanish, English, French. **Religion:** Roman Catholic 70%.

Geography: Area: 3,286,500 sq. mi., largest country in South America. **Location:** Occupies eastern half of South America. **Neighbors:** French Guiana, Suriname, Guyana, Venezuela on N, Colombia, Peru, Bolivia, Paraguay, Argentina on W, Uruguay on S. **Topography:** Brazil's Atlantic coastline stretches 4,603 miles. In N is the heavily wooded Amazon basin covering half the country. Its network of rivers navigable for 15,814 mi. The Amazon itself flows 2,093 miles in Brazil, all navigable. The NE region is semiarid scrubland, heavily settled and poor. The S central region, favored by climate and resources, has almost half of the population, produces 75% of farm goods and 80% of industrial output. The narrow coastal belt includes most of the major cities. Almost the entire country has a tropical or semitropical climate. **Capital:** Brasília. **Cities** (1991 est.): São Paulo 15.4 mln.; Rio de Janeiro 9.8 mln.; Salvador 2.1 mln.; Brasília 1.6 mln.

Government: Type: Federal republic. **Head of state:** Pres. Fernando Henrique Cardoso; b June 18, 1931; in office: Jan. 1, 1995. **Local divisions:** 26 states, federal district (Brasília). **Defense:** 1.3% of GNP (1991). **Active troop strength:** 336,800.

Economy: Industries: Steel, autos, textiles, appliances, chemicals, machinery. **Chief crops:** Coffee (largest grower), cotton, soybeans, sugar, cocoa, rice, corn, fruits. **Minerals:** Iron, manganese, phosphates, uranium, gold, nickel, tin, bauxite, oil. **Crude oil reserves** (1994): 3.6 bln. bbls. **Arable land:** 7%. **Livestock** (1992): cattle: 153 mln.; pigs: 33 mln.; sheep: 19.5 mln. **Fish catch** (1992): 790,000 metric tons. **Electricity prod.** (1992): 242.2 bln. kWh. **Labor force:** 42% services; 31% agric.; 27% ind.

Finance: Monetary unit: Real (May 1995: .91 = $1 US). **Gross domestic product** (1993): $785 bln.* **Per capita GDP:** $5,000. **Imports** (1993): $26 bln.; partners: U.S. 23%, EU 23%. **Exports** (1993): $39 bln.; partners: U.S. 17%, EU 27%. **Tourism** (1992): $1.3 bln. **National budget** (1992): $109 bln. **International reserves less gold** (Mar. 1995): $31.9 bln. **Gold:** 4.00 mln. oz t. **Consumer prices** (change in 1994): 2,668.5%.

Transport: Railroads: Length: 18,816 mi. **Motor vehicles:** in use: 13 mln. passenger cars, 1.4 mln. comm. vehicles. **Civil aviation:** 18.5 bln. passenger-mi.; 110 airports with scheduled flights. **Chief ports:** Santos, Rio de Janeiro, Vitoria, Salvador, Rio Grande, Recife.

Communications: Television sets: 1 per 5.2 persons. **Radios:** 1 per 2.6 persons. **Telephones:** 1 per 11 persons. **Daily newspaper circ.:** 54 per 1,000 pop.

Health: Life expectancy at birth (1995): 57 male; 67 female. **Births** (per 1,000 pop.): 21. **Deaths** (per 1,000 pop.): 9. **Natural increase:** 1.2%. **Hospital beds:** 1 per 270 persons. **Physicians:** 1 per 848 persons. **Infant mortality** (per 1,000 live births 1995): 57.

Education: Literacy (1991): 81%.

Major International Organizations: UN and most of its specialized agencies, OAS.

Embassy: 3006 Massachusetts Ave. NW 20008; 745-2700.

Pedro Alvares Cabral, a Portuguese navigator, is generally credited as the first European to reach Brazil, in 1500. The country was thinly settled by various Indian tribes. Only a few have survived to the present, mostly in the Amazon basin.

In the next centuries, Portuguese colonists gradually pushed inland, bringing along large numbers of African slaves. Slavery was not abolished until 1888.

The King of Portugal, fleeing before Napoleon's army, moved the seat of government to Brazil in 1808. Brazil thereupon became a kingdom under Dom Joao VI. After his return to Portugal, his son Pedro proclaimed the independence of Brazil, Sept. 7, 1822, and was acclaimed emperor. The second emperor, Dom Pedro II, was deposed in 1889, and a republic proclaimed, called the United States of Brazil. In 1967 the country was renamed the Federative Republic of Brazil.

A military junta took control in 1930; dictatorial power was assumed by Getulio Vargas, until finally forced out by the military in

1945. A democratic regime prevailed 1945-64, during which time the capital was moved from Rio de Janeiro to Brasília.

In 1964, Pres. Joao Belchoir Marques Goulart instituted economic policies that aggravated Brazil's inflation; he was overthrown by an army revolt. The next 5 presidents were all military leaders. Censorship was imposed, and much of the opposition was suppressed amid charges of torture. In 1974 elections, the official opposition party made gains in the chamber of deputies; some relaxation of censorship occurred.

Since 1930, successive governments have pursued industrial and agricultural growth and the development of interior areas. Exploiting vast mineral resources, fertile soil in several regions, and a huge labor force, Brazil became the leading industrial power of Latin America by the 1970s, while agricultural output soared.

However, income maldistribution and inflation led to severe economic recession. Foreign debt is among the largest in the world. Brazil and its principal commercial bank lenders agreed to restructure the nation's $44 billion commercial debts, July 1992. The 1991 census revealed that population growth dipped below 2 percent for the first time in half a century.

Brazil unveiled a comprehensive environmental program for the Amazon region in 1989, amid an international outcry by environmentalists and others concerned about the ongoing destruction of the Amazon ecosystem. Brazil hosted delegates from 178 countries at the Earth Summit June 3-14, 1992.

Democratic presidential elections were held in 1985 as the nation returned to civilian rule. Fernando Collor de Mello was elected president in Dec. 1989. In Sept. 1992, Pres. Collor was impeached for corruption. He resigned on Dec. 29 as his trial was beginning, and Itamar Franco, who had been acting president, was sworn in as president. In elections held on Oct. 3, 1994, sociology professor and former foreign minister and finance minister Fernando Henrique Cardoso was elected president by the widest popular margin in Brazil since 1945.

Brunei
State of Brunei Darussalam
Negara Brunei Darussalam

People: Population: 292,266. **Pop. density:** 131 per sq. mi. **Ethnic groups:** Malay 64%, Chinese 20%. **Principal languages:** Malay (official), English, Chinese. **Religion:** Muslim (official) 63%, Buddhist 14%, Christian 8%.

Geography: Area: 2,226 sq. mi. **Location:** On the north coast of the island of Borneo; it is surrounded on its landward side by the Malaysian state of Sarawak. **Capital:** Bandar Seri Begawan (1988 est.): 52,000.

Government: Type: Independent sultanate. **Head of government:** Sultan Sir Muda Hassanal Bolkiah Mu'izzadin Waddaulah; b July 15, 1946; in office: Jan. 1, 1984. **Local divisions:** 4 districts. **Defense:** 9% of GDP (1990). **Active troop strength:** 4,400.

Economy: Industries: oil (about 90% of revenue is derived from oil exports). **Chief crops:** rice, bananas, cassava. **Crude oil reserves** (1994): 1.3 bln. bbls.

Finance: Monetary unit: Dollar (Oct. 1994: 1.48 = $1 US). **Gross domestic product** (1991): $2.5 bln. **Per capita GDP:** $9,000.

Transport: Motor vehicles: in use: 122,000 passenger cars, 14,000 commercial vehicles.

Communications: Television sets: 1 per 3.4 persons. **Radios:** 1 per 2.5 persons. **Telephones:** 1 per 4.0 persons.

Education: Literacy (1992): 85%.

Health: Life expectancy at birth: (1995): 70 male; 73 female. **Births** (per 1,000 pop.): 26. **Deaths** (per 1,000 pop.): 5. **Natural increase:** 2.1%. **Infant mortality** (per 1,000 live births 1995): 25.

Major International Organizations: UN and some of its specialized agencies, ASEAN, the Commonwealth.

Embassy: 2600 Virginia Ave. NW 20037; 342-0159.

The Sultanate of Brunei was a powerful state in the early 16th century, with authority over all of the island of Borneo as well as parts of the Sulu Islands and the Philippines. In 1888, a treaty placed the state under the protection of Great Britain.

Brunei became a fully sovereign and independent state on Jan. 1, 1984.

The Sultan of Brunei donated $10 million to the Nicaraguan *contras* in 1986; the subsequent misplacement of the funds generated much media attention in the U.S.

Bulgaria
Republic of Bulgaria
Republika Bulgaria

People: Population: 8,775,198. **Age distrib.** (%): <15: 19; 65+: 14. **Pop. density:** 205 per sq. mi. **Urban:** 67%. **Ethnic groups:** Bulgarian 85%, Turk 8.5%. **Principal language:** Bulgarian. **Religions:** Bulgarian Orthodox 85%, Muslim 13%.

Geography: Area: 42,855 sq. mi. **Location:** In eastern Balkan Peninsula on Black Sea. **Neighbors:** Romania on N, Yugoslavia, Macedonia on W, Greece, Turkey on S. **Topography:** The Stara Planina (Balkan) Mts. stretch E-W across the center of the country, with the Danubian plain on N, the Rhodope Mts. on SW, and Thracian Plain on SE. **Capital:** Sofia. **Cities** (1991 est.): Sofia 1.1 mln.; Plovdiv 379,000; Varna 316,000.

Government: Type: Republic. **Head of state:** Pres. Zhelyu Zhelev; b Mar. 3, 1935; in office: Aug. 1, 1990. **Head of government:** Prime Min. Zhan Videnov; b Mar. 22, 1959; in office: Jan. 1995. **Local divisions:** 9 provinces. **Defense:** 6.0% of GNP (1993). **Active troop strength:** 101,900.

Economy: Industries: Chemicals, machinery, metals, textiles, processed food. **Chief crops:** Grains, fruit, corn, tobacco. **Minerals:** Bauxite, copper, zinc, lead, coal. **Arable land:** 34%. **Livestock** (1994): cattle: 673,000; pigs: 2.0 mln.; sheep: 4.3 mln. **Fish catch** (1993): 27,000 metric tons. **Electricity prod.** (1992): 45 bln. kWh. **Labor force:** 20% agric.; 33% ind.

Finance: Monetary unit: Lev (Oct. 1994: 62.84 = $1 US). **Gross national product** (1993): $33.9 bln.* **Per capita GNP:** $3,800. **Imports** (1991): $2.8 bln.; partners: CIS 43%. **Exports** (1991): $3.5 bln.; partners: CIS 49%. **Tourism** (1992): $49 mln. **National budget** (1993 est.): $17.4 bln.

Transport: Railroads: Length: 4,073 mi. **Motor vehicles:** in use: 1.3 mln. passenger cars, 200,000 commercial vehicles. **Civil aviation:** 2.6 bln. passenger-mi.; 3 airports. **Chief ports:** Burgas, Varna.

Communications: Television sets: 1 per 2.7 persons. **Radios:** 1 per 2.9 persons. **Telephones:** 1 per 3.0 persons. **Daily newspaper circ.:** 267 per 1,000 pop.

Health: Life expectancy at birth (1995): 70 male; 77 female. **Births** (per 1,000 pop.): 12. **Deaths** (per 1,000 pop.): 11. **Natural increase:** 0. **Hospital beds:** 1 per 93 persons. **Physicians:** 1 per 298 persons. **Infant mortality** (per 1,000 live births 1995): 11.

Education: Literacy (1994): 96%.

Major International Organizations: UN.

Embassy: 1621 22d St. NW 20008; 387-7969.

Bulgaria was settled by Slavs in the 6th century. Turkic Bulgars arrived in the 7th century, merged with the Slavs, became Christians by the 9th century, and set up powerful empires in the 10th and 12th centuries. The Ottomans prevailed in 1396 and remained for 500 years.

A revolt in 1876 led to an independent kingdom in 1908. Bulgaria expanded after the first Balkan War but lost its Aegean coastline in World War I, when it sided with Germany. Bulgaria joined the Axis in World War II but withdrew in 1944. Communists took power with Soviet aid; the monarchy was abolished Sept. 8, 1946.

On Nov. 10, 1989, Communist Party leader and head of state Todor Zhivkov, who had held power for 35 years, resigned. Zhivkov was imprisoned, Jan. 1990, and convicted, Sept. 1992, of corruption and abuse of power. In Jan. 1990, Parliament voted to revoke the constitutionally guaranteed dominant role of the Communist Party. A new constitution took effect July 13, 1991.

Burkina Faso

People: Population: 10,422,828. **Pop. density:** 98 per sq. mi. **Urban:** 15%. **Ethnic groups:** Mossi, Gurunsi, Senufo, Lobi, Bobo, Mande, Fulani. **Principal languages:** French (official), Sudanic tribal languages. **Religions:** indigenous beliefs 40%, Muslim 50%, Christian 10%.

Geography: Area: 105,946 sq. mi. **Location:** In W Africa, S of the Sahara. **Neighbors:** Mali on NW, Niger on NE, Benin, Togo, Ghana, Côte d'Ivoire on S. **Topography:** Landlocked Burkina Faso is in the savannah region of W Africa. The N is arid, hot, and thinly populated. **Capital:** Ouagadougou. **Cities** (1990): Ouagadougou 441,000; Bobo-Dioulasso 228,000.

Government: Type: Republic. **Head of state:** Pres. Blaise Compaoré; b 1951; in office: Oct. 15, 1987. **Head of govern-**

ment: Prime Min. Marc-Christian Kabore; in office: Mar. 22, 1994. **Local divisions:** 30 provinces. **Defense:** 4.3% of GDP (1992). **Active troop strength:** 10,000.

Economy: Chief crops: Millet, sorghum, rice, peanuts. **Minerals:** Manganese, limestone, marble, gold. **Arable land:** 10%. **Electricity prod.** (1991): 320 mln. kWh. **Labor force:** 80% agric.; 15% ind.

Finance: Monetary unit: CFA Franc (May 1995: 488 = $1 US). **Gross domestic product** (1993): $7.0 bln.* **Per capita GDP:** $700. **Imports** (1992): $685 mln.; partners: EU 49%. **Exports** (1992): $300 mln.; partners: Côte d'Ivoire 11%, EU 42%, Taiwan 15%. **National budget** (1992): $548 mln. **International reserves less gold** (Mar. 1995): $266 mln. **Gold:** 11,000 oz t. **Consumer prices** (change in 1994): 25.2%.

Transport: Motor vehicles: in use: 12,000 passenger cars, 13,000 comm. vehicles.

Communications: Television sets: 1 per 215 persons. **Radios:** 1 per 49 persons. **Telephones:** 1 per 569 persons.

Health: Life expectancy at birth (1995): 46 male; 48 female. **Births** (per 1,000 pop.): 48. **Deaths** (per 1,000 pop.): 18. **Natural increase:** 3.0%. **Hospital beds:** 1 per 1,837 persons. **Physicians:** 1 per 27,158 persons. **Infant mortality** (per 1,000 live births 1995): 117.

Education: Literacy (1992): 18%. **Years compulsory:** ages 7-14.

Major International Organizations: UN and many of its specialized agencies, OAU.

Embassy: 2340 Massachusetts Ave. NW 20008; 332-5577.

The Mossi tribe entered the area in the 11th to 13th centuries. Their kingdoms ruled until defeated by the Mali and Songhai empires.

French control came by 1896, but Upper Volta (renamed Burkina Faso on Aug. 4, 1984) was not established as a separate territory until 1947. Full independence came Aug. 5, 1960, and a pro-French government was elected. The military seized power in 1980. A 1987 coup established the current regime, which instituted a multiparty democracy in the early 1990s.

Several hundred thousand farm workers migrate each year to Côte d'Ivoire and Ghana. Burkina Faso is heavily dependent on foreign aid.

Burma

(*See Myanmar*)

Burundi

Republic of Burundi

Republika y'Uburundi

People: Population: 6,262,429. **Age distrib.** (%): <15: 46; 65+: 4. **Pop. density:** 583 per sq. mi. **Urban:** 6%. **Ethnic groups:** Hutu 85%, Tutsi 14%, Twa (Pygmy) 1%. **Principal languages:** French, Kirundi (both official), Swahili. **Religions:** Roman Catholic 67%, indigenous beliefs 32%.

Geography: Area: 10,740 sq. mi. **Location:** In central Africa. **Neighbors:** Rwanda on N, Zaire on W, Tanzania on E and S. **Topography:** Much of the country is grassy highland, with mountains reaching 8,900 ft. The southernmost source of the White Nile is located in Burundi. Lake Tanganyika is the second deepest lake in the world. **Capital:** Bujumbura (1991 est.): 240,000.

Government: Type: Republic. **Head of state:** Pres. Sylvestre Ntibantunganya; b 1956; in office: Apr. 8, 1994. **Head of government:** Antoine Nduwayo; in office: Feb. 22, 1995. **Local divisions:** 15 provinces. **Defense:** 2.4% of GNP (1991). **Active troop strength:** 14,600 est.

Economy: Chief crops: Coffee (81% of exports), cotton, tea. **Minerals:** Nickel, uranium. **Arable land:** 43%. **Electricity prod.** (1991): 105 mln. kWh. **Labor force:** 93% agric.

Finance: Monetary unit: Franc (Mar. 1995: 235 = $1 US). **Gross domestic product** (1993): $4.4 bln.* **Per capita GDP:** $700. **Imports** (1992): $188 mln.; partners: Eu 45%. **Exports** (1992): $41 mln.; partners: EU 57%, U.S. 19%. **National budget** (1991 est.): $326 mln. **International reserves less gold** (Mar. 1995): $229 mln. **Gold:** 17,000 oz t. **Consumer prices** (change in 1994): 14.9%.

Transport: Motor vehicles: in use: 14,000 passenger cars, 15,000 comm. vehicles.

Communications: Radios: 1 per 11 persons. **Telephones:** 1 per 259 persons.

Health: Life expectancy at birth (1995): 38 male; 42 female. **Births** (per 1,000 pop.): 43. **Deaths** (per 1,000 pop.): 22. **Natural increase:** 2.2%. **Hospital beds:** 1 per 515 persons. **Physicians:** 1 per 31,777 persons. **Infant mortality** (per 1,000 live births 1995): 112.

Education: Literacy (1992): 74%. **Years compulsory:** 6.

Major International Organizations: UN (FAO, ILO, IMF, WHO), OAU.

Embassy: 2233 Wisconsin Ave. NW 20007; 342-2574.

The pygmy Twa were the first inhabitants, followed by Bantu Hutus, who were conquered in the 16th century by the Tutsi (Watusi), probably from Ethiopia. Under German control in 1899, the area fell to Belgium in 1916, which exercised successively a League of Nations mandate and UN trusteeship over Ruanda-Urundi (now the two countries of Rwanda and Burundi).

Burundi became independent July 1, 1962.

An unsuccessful Hutu rebellion in 1972-73 left 10,000 Tutsi and 150,000 Hutu dead. Over 100,000 Hutu fled to Tanzania and Zaire. In the 1980s, Burundi's Tutsi-dominated regime pledged itself to ethnic reconciliation and democratic reform. In the nation's first democratic presidential election, in June 1993, a Hutu, Melchior Ndadaye, was elected. He was killed in an attempted coup, Oct. 21, 1993, setting off new waves of ethnic violence in which an estimated 50,000 people were killed. Pres. Cyprien Ntaryamira, elected Jan. 1994, was killed with the president of Rwanda in a mysterious plane crash, Apr. 6. The incident sparked massive carnage in Rwanda; violence in Burundi, initially far more limited, intensified in 1995.

Cambodia

Kingdom of Cambodia

Preah Reach Ana Pak Kampuchea

People: Population: 10,561,373. **Pop. density:** 150 per sq. mi. **Urban:** 13%. **Ethnic groups:** Khmer 90%, Vietnamese 5%, Chinese 1%. **Principal languages:** Khmer (official), French. **Religion:** Theravada Buddhism 95%.

Geography: Area: 70,238 sq. mi. **Location:** On Indochina Peninsula. **Neighbors:** Thailand on W and N, Laos on NE, Vietnam on E. **Topography:** The central area, formed by the Mekong R. basin and Tonle Sap lake, is level. Hills and mountains are in SE, a long escarpment separates the country from Thailand on NW. 75% of the area is forested. **Capital:** Phnom Penh (1991 est.): 900,000.

Government: Type: Constitutional monarchy. **Head of state:** King Norodom Sihanouk; b Oct. 31, 1922; in office: Sept. 24, 1993. **Head of government:** First Prime Min. Prince Norodom Ranariddh; b 1944; in office: Sept. 24, 1993. **Local divisions:** 20 provinces. **Defense:** 4.8% of GNP (1992). **Active troop strength:** 88,500 est.

Economy: Industries: Rice milling, wood & rubber. **Chief crops:** Rice, corn. **Minerals:** Gemstones, phosphates, manganese. **Other resources:** Forests, rubber. **Arable land:** 16%. **Livestock** (1993): cattle: 2.5 mln.; pigs: 2.0 mln. **Fish catch** (1991): 110,000 metric tons. **Electricity prod.** (1992): 150 mln. kWh. **Labor force:** 80% agric.

Finance: Monetary unit: Riel (Oct. 1994: 2,587 = $1 US). **Gross domestic product** (1993): $6 bln.* **Per capita GDP:** $600. **Imports** (1992): $360 mln. **Exports** (1992): $70 mln. **National budget** (1994 est.): $350 mln.

Transport: Railroads: Length: 403 mi. **Motor vehicles:** in use: 4,000 passenger cars, 7,000 comm. vehicles. **Chief port:** Kompong Som.

Communications: Television sets: 1 per 133 persons. **Radios:** 1 per 9 persons. **Telephones:** 1 per 1,600 persons.

Health: Life expectancy at birth (1995): 48 male; 51 female. **Births** (per 1,000 pop.): 44. **Deaths** (per 1,000 pop.): 16. **Natural increase:** 2.8%. **Hospital beds:** 1 per 632 persons. **Physicians:** 1 per 14,300 persons. **Infant Mortality** (per 1,000 live births 1995): 110.

Education: Literacy (1993): 74%.

Major International Organizations: UN.

Early kingdoms dating from that of Funan in the 1st century AD culminated in the great Khmer empire which flourished from the 9th century to the 13th, encompassing present-day Thailand, Cambodia, Laos, and southern Vietnam. The peripheral areas were lost to invading Siamese and Vietnamese, and France established a protectorate in 1863. Independence came in 1953.

Prince Norodom Sihanouk, king 1941-1955 and head of state from 1960, tried to maintain neutrality. Relations with the

U.S. were broken in 1965, after South Vietnam planes attacked Vietcong forces within Cambodia. Relations were restored in 1969, after Sihanouk charged Viet Communists with arming Cambodian insurgents.

In 1970, pro-U.S. Prem. Lon Nol seized power, demanding removal of 40,000 North Viet troops; the monarchy was abolished. Sihanouk formed a government-in-exile in Peking, and open war began between the government and Khmer Rouge. The U.S. provided heavy military and economic aid.

Khmer Rouge forces captured Phnom Penh Apr. 17, 1975. The new government evacuated all cities and towns, and shuffled the rural population, sending virtually the entire population to clear jungle, forest, and scrub. Over one million people were killed in executions and enforced hardships.

Severe border fighting broke out with Vietnam in 1978 and developed into a full-fledged Vietnamese invasion. Formation of a backed government was announced, Jan. 8, 1979, one day after the Vietnamese capture of Phnom Penh. Thousands of refugees flowed into Thailand and widespread starvation was reported.

On Jan. 10, 1983, Vietnam launched an offensive against rebel forces in the west. They overran a refugee camp, Jan. 31, driving 30,000 residents into Thailand. In Mar., Vietnam launched a major offensive against camps on the Cambodian-Thailand border, engaged Khmer Rouge guerrillas, and crossed the border instigating clashes with Thai troops. Vietnam announced that it would withdraw all its troops by Sept. 1989.

Following UN-sponsored elections in Cambodia that ended May 28, 1993, the 2 leading parties agreed to share power in an interim government until a new constitution was adopted. On Sept. 21, a constitution reestablishing a monarchy was adopted by the National Assembly. It took effect Sept. 24, with Sihanouk as king. The Khmer Rouge, which had boycotted the elections, opposed the new government, and armed violence continued in 1994 and 1995.

Cameroon
Republic of Cameroon
République du Cameroun

People: Population: 13,521,000. **Age distrib.** (%): <15: 44; 65+: 3. **Pop. density:** 74 per sq. mi. **Urban:** 41%. **Ethnic groups:** Cameroon Highlanders 31%, Equatorial Bantu 19%, Kirdi 11%, Fulani 10%. **Principal languages:** English, French (both official), numerous African groups. **Religions:** indigenous beliefs 51%, Christian 33%, Muslim 16%.

Geography: Area: 183,569 sq. mi. **Location:** Between W and central Africa. **Neighbors:** Nigeria on NW, Chad, Central African Republic on E, Congo, Gabon, Equatorial Guinea on S. **Topography:** A low coastal plain with rain forests in S; plateaus in center lead to forested mountains in W, including Mt. Cameroon, 13,000 ft.; grasslands in N lead to marshes around Lake Chad. **Capital:** Yaoundé. **Cities** (1988 est.): Douala 852,000; Yaoundé 700,000.

Government: Type: Republic. **Head of state:** Pres. Paul Biya; b Feb. 13, 1933; in office: Nov. 6, 1982. **Head of government:** Prime Min. Simon Achidi Achu; in office: Apr. 9, 1992. **Local divisions:** 10 provinces. **Defense:** 1.6% of GNP (1991). **Active troop strength:** 23,600.

Economy: Industries: Oil production and processing, palm products. **Chief crops:** Cocoa, coffee, cotton. **Crude oil reserves** (1994): 400 mln. bbls. **Other resources:** Timber. **Minerals:** Oil, bauxite, iron. **Arable land:** 13%. **Livestock** (1993): cattle: 4.9 mln.; sheep: 3.8 mln.; pigs: 1.4 mln. **Fish catch** (1991): 78,000 metric tons. **Electricity prod.** (1991): 2.2 bln. kWh. **Labor force:** 74% agric.; 11% ind. and transport.

Finance: Monetary unit: CFA Franc (May 1995: 488 = $1 US). **Gross domestic product** (1993): $19.1 bln.* **Per capita GDP:** $1,500. **Imports** (1991): $1.2 bln.; partners: Fr. 41%. **Exports** (1991): $1.8 bln.; partners: EU 50%. **National budget** (1990): $2.4 bln. **International reserves less gold** (Mar. 1995): $2.04 mln. **Gold:** 30,000 oz t.

Transport: Railroads: Length: 686 mi. **Motor vehicles:** in use: 95,000 passenger cars, 80,000 comm. vehicles. **Chief port:** Douala.

Communications: Radios: 1 per 6.3 persons. **Telephones:** 1 per 224 persons.

Health: Life expectancy at birth (1995): 55 male; 60 female. **Births** (per 1,000 pop.): 40. **Deaths** (per 1,000 pop.): 11. **Natural increase:** 2.9%. **Hospital beds:** 1 per 371 persons. **Physicians:** 1 per 11,898 persons. **Infant mortality** (per 1,000 live births 1995): 75.

Education: Literacy (1991): 65%. About 70% attend school.

Major International Organizations: UN, OAU.
Embassy: 2349 Massachusetts Ave. NW 20008; 265-8790.

Portuguese sailors were the first Europeans to reach Cameroon, in the 15th century. The European and American slave trade was very active in the area. German control lasted from 1884 to 1916, when France and Britain divided the territory, later receiving League of Nations mandates and UN trusteeships. French Cameroon became independent Jan. 1, 1960; one part of British Cameroon joined Nigeria in 1961, the other part joined Cameroon. Stability has allowed for development of roads, railways, agriculture, and petroleum production.

Pres. Paul Biya retained his office in Oct. 1992 elections, but the results were widely disputed.

Canada

People: Population: 28,434,545. **Age distrib.** (%): <15: 21; 65+: 12. **Pop. density:** 7 per sq. mi. **Urban:** 77%. **Ethnic groups:** British 40%, French 27%, other European 20%, indigenous Indian and Eskimo 1.5%. **Principal languages:** English, French (both official). **Religions:** Roman Catholic 46%, United Church 16%, Anglican 10%.

Geography: Area: 3,849,674 sq. mi., the largest country in land size in the western hemisphere. Canada stretches 3,426 miles from east to west and extends southward from the North Pole to the U.S. border. Its seacoast includes 36,356 miles of mainland and 115,133 miles of islands, including the Arctic islands almost from Greenland to near the Alaskan border. Climate, while generally temperate, varies from freezing winter cold to blistering summer heat. **Capital:** Ottawa. **Cities** (met. 1994 est.): Toronto 4.1 mln.; Montreal 3.3 mln.; Vancouver 1.7 mln.; Ottawa-Hull 980,000; Edmonton 897,000; Calgary 814,000; Quebec 679,000; Winnipeg 662,000.

Government: Type: Confederation with parliamentary democracy. **Head of state:** Queen Elizabeth II, represented by Gov.-Gen. Roméo A. LeBlanc; b Dec. 18, 1927; in office: Feb. 8, 1995. **Head of government:** Prime Min. Jean Chrétien; b Jan. 11, 1934; in office: Nov. 4, 1993. **Local divisions:** 10 provinces, 2 territories. **Defense:** 2% of GDP (FY 1992-93). **Active troop strength:** 78,100.

Economy: Minerals: Nickel, zinc, copper, gold, lead, molybdenum, potash, silver. **Crude oil reserves** (1994): 5.1 bln. barrels. **Arable land:** 5%. **Livestock** (1993): cattle: 11.8 mln.; pigs: 10.6 mln.; sheep: 662,000. **Fish catch** (1993): 1.1 mln. metric tons. **Electricity prod.** (1992): 493 bln. kWh. **Labor force:** 4% agric., 75% services, 14% manufacturing.

Finance: Monetary unit: Dollar (May 1995: 1.37 = $1 US). **Gross domestic product** (1993): $617.7 bln.* **Per capita GDP:** $22,200. **Imports** (1993): $125 bln.; partners: U.S. 69%, EU 8%, Jap. 5%. **Exports** (1993): $134 bln.; partners: U.S. 75%, EU 9%, Jap. 5%. **Tourism** (1992): $5.7 bln. **National budget** (FY 1993 est.): $123.0 bln. **International reserves less gold** (May 1995): $15.0 bln. **Gold:** 3.61 mln. oz t. **Consumer prices** (change in 1994): 0.2%.

Transport: Railroads: Length: 53,166 mi. **Motor vehicles:** in use: 13.1 mln. passenger cars, 3.7 mln. comm. vehicles. **Civil aviation:** 26 bln. passenger-mi.: 244 airports with scheduled flights.

Communications: Television sets: 1 per 1.6 persons. **Radios:** 1 per 1.3 persons. **Telephones:** 1 per 1.3 persons. **Daily newspaper circ.:** 195 per 1,000 pop.

Health: Life expectancy at birth (1995): 75 male; 82 female. **Births** (per 1,000 pop.): 14. **Deaths** (per 1,000 pop.): 7. **Natural increase:** 0.6%. **Hospital beds:** 1 per 149 persons. **Physicians:** 1 per 464 persons. **Infant mortality** (per 1,000 live births 1995): 7.

Education: Literacy (1994): 96%.
Major International Organizations: UN and all of its specialized agencies, NATO, OECD, the Commonwealth.
Embassy: 501 Pennsylvania Ave. NW 20001; 682-1740.

French explorer Jacques Cartier, who reached the Gulf of St. Lawrence in 1534, is generally regarded as the founder of Canada. But English seaman John Cabot sighted Newfoundland 37 years earlier, in 1497, and Vikings are believed to have reached the Atlantic coast centuries before either explorer.

Canadian settlement was pioneered by the French who established Quebec City (1608) and Montreal (1642) and declared New France a colony in 1663.

Britain acquired Acadia (later Nova Scotia) in 1717 and, through military victory over French forces in Canada, captured Quebec (1759) and obtained control of the rest of New France in 1763. The French, through the Quebec Act of 1774, retained the rights to their own language, religion, and civil law. The

British presence in Canada increased during the American Revolution when many colonials, proudly calling themselves United Empire Loyalists, moved north to Canada.

Fur traders and explorers led Canadians westward across the continent. Sir Alexander Mackenzie reached the Pacific in 1793 and scrawled on a rock by the ocean, "from Canada by land."

In Upper and Lower Canada (later called Ontario and Quebec) and in the Maritimes, legislative assemblies appeared in the 18th century and reformers called for responsible government. But the War of 1812 intervened. The war, a conflict between Great Britain and the United States fought mainly in Upper Canada, ended in a stalemate in 1814.

In 1837 political agitation for more democratic government culminated in rebellions in Upper and Lower Canada. Britain sent Lord Durham to investigate; in a famous report (1839), he recommended union of the 2 parts into one colony called Canada. The union lasted until Confederation, July 1, 1867, when proclamation of the British North America (BNA) Act launched the Dominion of Canada, consisting of Ontario, Quebec, and the former colonies of Nova Scotia and New Brunswick.

Since 1840 the Canadian colonies had held the right to internal self-government. The BNA act, which became the country's written constitution, established a federal system of government on the model of a British parliament and cabinet structure under the crown. Canada was proclaimed a self-governing Dominion within the British Empire in 1931. In 1982 Canada severed its last formal legislative link with Britain by obtaining the right to amend its constitution (the British North America Act of 1867).

The so-called Meech Lake Agreement was signed (subject to provincial ratification) June 3, 1987. The accord would have assured constitutional protection for Quebec's efforts to preserve its French language and culture. Critics charged that it did not make any provision for other minority groups and that it gave Quebec too much power, which might enable Quebec to override the nation's 1982 Charter of Rights and Freedoms. The accord died June 22, 1990.

Its failure sparked a separatist revival in Quebec which culminated in Aug. 1992 in the Charlottetown agreement. This called for changes to the constitution, such as recognition of Quebec as a "distinct society" within the Canadian confederation. It was defeated in a national referendum on Oct. 26, 1992.

In May 1992 voters in the Northwest Territories approved the creation of a self-governing homeland for the 17,500 Inuit living in the territories. The area—to be known as Nunavut, "Our Land"—would cover an area of 136,493 sq. mi. and take effect by 1999.

Canada became the first nation to ratify the North American Free Trade Agreement between Canada, Mexico, and the U.S., June 23, 1993. It went into effect Jan. 1, 1994.

On Feb. 24, 1993, Brian Mulroney resigned as prime minister after more than 8 years in office; he was succeeded by Kim Campbell. In elections Oct. 25, 1993, the ruling Conservatives were defeated in a landslide that left them only 2 of the 295 seats in the House of Commons. Jean Chrétien became prime minister.

Provinces/Territories	Area (sq. mi.)	Population (1994 est.)
Alberta	255,287	2,716,000
British Columbia	365,948	3,668,000
Manitoba	250,947	1,131,000
New Brunswick	28,355	759,000
Newfoundland	156,649	582,000
Nova Scotia	21,425	937,000
Ontario	412,581	10,928,000
Prince Edward Island	2,185	134,000
Quebec	594,860	7,281,000
Saskatchewan	251,866	1,016,000
Northwest Territories	1,322,910	64,000
Yukon Territory	186,661	30,000

Prime Ministers of Canada

Canada is a constitutional monarchy with a parliamentary system of government. It is also a federal state. Canada's official head of state, Queen Elizabeth II, is represented by a resident Governor-General. However, in practice the nation is governed by the Prime Minister, leader of the party that commands the support of a majority of the House of Commons, dominant chamber of Canada's bicameral Parliament.

Name	Party	Term	Name	Party	Term
Sir John A. MacDonald	Conservative	1867-1873	R. B. Bennett	Conservative	1930-1935
		1878-1891	Louis St. Laurent	Liberal	1948-1957
Alexander Mackenzie	Liberal	1873-1878	John G. Diefenbaker	Prog. Cons.	1957-1963
Sir John J. C. Abbott	Conservative	1891-1892	Lester B. Pearson	Liberal	1963-1968
Sir John S. D. Thompson	Conservative	1892-1894	Pierre Elliott Trudeau	Liberal	1968-1979
Sir Mackenzie Bowell	Conservative	1894-1896	Joe Clark	Prog. Cons.	1979-1980
Sir Charles Tupper	Conservative	1896	Pierre Elliott Trudeau	Liberal	1980-1984
Sir Wilfrid Laurier	Liberal	1896-1911	John Turner	Liberal	1984
Sir Robert L. Borden	Cons. Union.	1911-1920	Brian Mulroney	Prog. Cons.	1984-1993
Arthur Meighen	Cons. Union.	1920-1921	Kim Campbell	Prog. Cons.	1993
W. L. Mackenzie King	Liberal	1921-1930[1]	Jean Chrétien	Liberal	1993-
		1935-1948			

(1) King served 2 terms in these years, interrupted June 26-Sept. 25, 1926, when Arthur Meighen served as prime minister.

Cape Verde

Republic of Cape Verde

República de Cabo Verde

People: Population: 435,983. **Age distrib. (%):** <15: 45; 65+: 6. **Pop. density:** 280 per sq. mi. **Urban:** 44%. **Ethnic groups:** Creole (mulatto) 71%, African 28%, European 1%. **Principal languages:** Portuguese (official), Crioulo. **Religions:** Roman Catholic fused with indigenous beliefs.

Geography: Area: 1,557 sq. mi. **Location:** In Atlantic O., off western tip of Africa. **Neighbors:** Nearest are Mauritania, Senegal. **Topography:** Cape Verde Islands are 15 in number, volcanic in origin (active crater on Fogo). The landscape is eroded and stark, with vegetation mostly in interior valleys. **Capital:** Praia. **Cities** (1990 est.): Praia 62,000; Mindelo 47,000.

Government: Type: Republic. **Head of state:** Pres. Antonio Mascarenhas Monteiro; b 1944; in office: Mar. 22, 1991. **Head of government:** Prime Min. Carlos Veiga; b 1949; in office: Apr. 4, 1991. **Local divisions:** 14 administrative districts. **Defense: Active troop strength:** 1,100.

Economy: Chief crops: Bananas, coffee, beets, corn, beans. **Minerals:** Salt. **Other resources:** Fish. **Arable land:** 9%. **Electricity prod.** (1991): 15 mln. kWh.

Finance: Monetary unit: Escudo (Jan. 1995: 79.56 = $1 US). **Gross domestic product** (1991): $415 mln. **Per capita GDP:** $1,070. **Imports** (1990): $145 mln.; partners: Sweden 33%, Spain 11%. **Exports** (1990): $6 mln.; partners: Port. 40%, Algeria 31%. **National budget** (1991): $133 mln.

Transport: Motor vehicles: in use: 10,000 passenger cars, 5,000 comm. vehicles. **Chief ports:** Mindelo, Praia.

Communications: Radios: 1 per 3.5 persons. **Telephones:** 1 per 29 persons.

Health: Life expectancy at birth (1995): 61 male; 65 female. **Births** (per 1,000 pop.): 45. **Deaths** (per 1,000 pop.): 9. **Natural increase:** 3.7%. **Hospital beds:** 1 per 550 persons. **Physicians:** 1 per 4,208 persons. **Infant mortality** (per 1,000 live births 1995): 56.

Education: Literacy (1990): 47%.

Major International Organizations: UN (IMF, WHO), OAU. **Embassy:** 3415 Massachusetts Ave. NW 20007; 965-6820.

The uninhabited Cape Verdes were discovered by the Portuguese in 1456 or 1460. The first Portuguese colonists landed in 1462; African slaves were brought soon after, and most Cape Verdeans descend from both groups. Cape Verde independence came July 5, 1975. Antonio Mascarenhas Monteiro won the nation's first free presidential election Feb. 17, 1991.

Central African Republic
République Centrafricaine

People: Population: 3,209,759. **Pop. density:** 13 per sq. mi. **Urban:** 39%. **Ethnic groups:** Baya 34%, Banda 27%, Mandjia 21%, Sara 10%. **Principal languages:** French (official), Sangho, Arabic. **Religions:** Protestant 25%, Roman Catholic 25%, indigenous beliefs 24%, Muslim 15%.

Geography: Area: 240,324 sq. mi. **Location:** In central Africa. **Neighbors:** Chad on N, Cameroon on W, Congo, Zaire on S, Sudan on E. **Topography:** Mostly rolling plateau, average altitude 2,000 ft., with rivers draining S to the Congo and N to Lake Chad. Open, well-watered savanna covers most of the area, with an arid area in NE, and tropical rainforest in SW. **Capital:** Bangui (1988 est.): 452,000.

Government: Type: Republic. **Head of state:** Pres. Ange-Félix Patassé; b Jan. 25, 1937; in office: Oct. 22, 1993. **Head of government:** Prime Min. Gabriel Koyambounou; in office: Apr. 12, 1995. **Local divisions:** 16 prefectures and 1 commune. **Defense:** 2.2% of GNP (1992). **Active troop strength:** 4,950.

Economy: Industries: Textiles, light manuf., mining. **Chief crops:** Cotton, coffee, corn, tobacco. **Minerals:** Diamonds (chief export), uranium. **Other resources:** Timber. **Arable land:** 3%. **Electricity prod.** (1991): 95 mln. kWh. **Labor force:** 85% agric.

Finance: Monetary unit: CFA Franc (May 1995: 488 = $1 US). **Gross domestic product** (1993): $2.5 bln.* **Per capita GDP:** $800. **Imports** (1992): $165 mln.; partners: Fr. 51%. **Exports** (1992): $124 mln.; partners: Fr. 10%, Belg.-Lux. 57%. **National budget** (1991 est.): $312 mln. **International reserves less gold** (Mar. 1995): $248 mln. **Gold:** 11,000 oz t.

Transport: Motor vehicles: in use: 8,200 passenger cars, 8,500 comm. vehicles. **Communications: Radios:** 1 per 5.4 persons. **Telephones:** 1 per 413 persons.

Health: Life expectancy at birth (1995): 41 male; 44 female. **Births** (per 1,000 pop.): 42. **Deaths** (per 1,000 pop.): 21. **Natural increase:** 2.1%. **Hospital beds:** 1 per 672 persons. **Physicians:** 1 per 18,660 persons. **Infant mortality** (per 1,000 live births 1995): 136.

Education: Literacy (1991): 27%. **Attendance:** primary school 79%; secondary school 18%.

Major International Organizations: UN (WTO, IMF, WHO), OAU.

Embassy: 1618 22d St. NW 20008; 483-7800.

Various Bantu tribes migrated through the region for centuries before French control was asserted in the late 19th century, when the region was named Ubangi-Shari. Complete independence was attained Aug. 13, 1960.

All political parties were dissolved in 1960, and the country became a center for Chinese political influence in Africa. Relations with China were severed after 1965. Pres. Jean-Bedel Bokassa, who seized power in a 1965 military coup, proclaimed himself constitutional emperor of the renamed Central African Empire Dec. 1976.

Bokassa's rule was characterized by ruthless and cruel authoritarianism and human rights violations. He was ousted in a bloodless coup aided by the French government, Sept. 20, 1979. In 1981, Gen. André Kolingba became head of state in another bloodless coup. Multiparty legislative and presidential elections were held in Oct. 1992 but were canceled by the government when Kolingba was losing. New elections were ultimately held in Aug. and Sept. 1993, leading to the installation of a civilian government.

Chad
Republic of Chad
République du Tchad

People: Population: 5,586,505. **Age distrib.** (%): <15: 41; 65+: 3. **Pop. density:** 11 per sq. mi. **Urban:** 22%. **Ethnic groups:** 200 distinct groups. **Principal languages:** French, Arabic (both official), more than 100 other languages. **Religions:** Muslim 50%, Christian 25%, indigenous beliefs 25%.

Geography: Area: 495,755 sq. mi. **Location:** In central N Africa. **Neighbors:** Libya on N, Niger, Nigeria, Cameroon on W, Central African Republic on S, Sudan on E. **Topography:** Wooded savanna, steppe, and desert in the S; part of the Sahara in the N. Southern rivers flow N to Lake Chad, surrounded by marshland. **Capital:** N'Djamena (1992 est.): 688,000.

Government: Type: Republic. **Head of state:** Pres. Idriss Déby; in office: Dec. 4, 1990. **Head of government:** Transitional Prime Min. Koibla Djimasta; in office: Apr. 8, 1995. **Local divisions:** 14 prefectures. **Defense:** 5.2% of GNP (1991). **Active troop strength:** 30,350 est.

Economy: Chief crops: Cotton. **Minerals:** Uranium. **Arable land:** 2%. **Fish catch** (1992): 60,000 metric tons. **Electricity prod.** (1991): 70 mln. kWh. **Labor force:** 85% agric.

Finance: Monetary unit: CFA Franc (May 1995: 488 = $1 US). **Gross domestic product** (1993): $2.7 bln.* **Per capita GDP:** $500. **Imports** (1991): $294 mln.; partners: France 47%. **Exports** (1991): $194 mln.; partners: France. **National budget** (1991 est.): $412 mln. **International reserves less gold** (Mar. 1995): $41 mln. **Gold:** 11,000 oz t.

Transport: Motor vehicles: in use: 9,000 passenger cars, 7,000 comm. vehicles. **Communications: Radios:** 1 per 5.0 persons. **Telephones:** 1 per 678 persons.

Health: Life expectancy at birth (1995): 40 male; 42 female. **Births** (per 1,000 pop.): 42. **Deaths** (per 1,000 pop.): 20. **Natural increase:** 2.2%. **Infant mortality** (per 1,000 live births 1994): 130.

Education: Literacy (1991): 30%.

Major International Organizations: UN, (FAO, IMF, WHO), OAU.

Embassy: 2002 R St. NW 20009; 462-4009.

Chad was the site of paleolithic and neolithic cultures before the Sahara Desert formed. A succession of kingdoms and Arab slave traders dominated Chad until France took control around 1900. Independence came Aug. 11, 1960.

Northern Muslim rebels have fought animist and Christian southern government and French troops from 1966, despite numerous cease-fires and peace pacts.

Libyan troops entered the country at the request of a pro-Libyan Chad government, Dec. 1980. The troops were withdrawn from Chad in Nov. 1981. Rebel forces, led by Hissène Habré, captured the capital and forced Pres. Goukouni Oueddei to flee the country in June 1982.

In 1983, France sent some 3,000 troops to Chad to assist Pres. Habré in opposing Libyan-backed rebels. France and Libya agreed to a simultaneous withdrawal of troops from Chad in Sept. 1984, but Libyan forces remained in the north until Mar. 1987, when Chad forces drove them from their last major stronghold. In Dec. 1990, Habré was overthrown by a Libyan-supported insurgent group, the Patriotic Salvation Movement. Chad's first multiparty democratic elections have been postponed to 1996.

On Feb. 3, 1994, the World Court dismissed a long-standing territorial claim by Libya to the mineral-rich Aozou Strip, on the Libyan border. Libyan troops reportedly withdrew at the end of May.

Chile
Republic of Chile
República de Chile

People: Population: 14,161,216. **Age distrib.** (%): <15: 31; 65+: 6. **Pop. density:** 48 per sq. mi. **Urban:** 85%. **Ethnic groups:** European and European-Indian 95%, Indian 3%. **Principal language:** Spanish. **Religions:** Roman Catholic 89%, Protestant 11%.

Geography: Area: 292,135 sq. mi. **Location:** Occupies western coast of S South America. **Neighbors:** Peru on N, Bolivia on NE, Argentina on E. **Topography:** Andes Mts. are on E border including some of the world's highest peaks; on W is 2,650-mile Pacific coast. Width varies between 100 and 250 miles. In N is Atacama Desert, in center are agricultural regions, in S are forests and grazing lands. **Capital:** Santiago (1993 met. est.): 4.6 mln.

Government: Type: Republic. **Head of state:** Pres. Eduardo Frei Ruíz Tagle; b 1943; in office: Mar. 11, 1994. **Local divisions:** 13 regions. **Defense:** 3.4% of GDP (1991). **Active troop strength:** 93,000.

Economy: Industries: Fish processing, wood products, iron, steel. **Chief crops:** Grain, grapes, beans, potatoes, peas, fruits. **Minerals:** Copper (world's largest producer), molybdenum, nitrates, iodine (half world output), iron, coal, oil, gas, gold, manganese, salt, sulphur. **Other resources:** Forests.

Arable land: 7%. **Livestock** (1992): cattle: 3.3 mln.; sheep: 6.7 mln.; pigs: 1.7 mln. **Fish catch** (1992): 6.3 mln. metric tons. **Electricity prod.** (1992): 22.0 bln. kWh. **Labor force:** 19% agric., forestry, fishing; 34% ind. & commerce; 38% serv.

Finance: Monetary unit: Peso (May 1995: 376 = $1 US). **Gross domestic product** (1993): $96 bln.* **Per capita GDP:** $7,000. **Imports** (1992): $9.2 bln.; partners: U.S. 21%, EU 24%. **Exports** (1992): $10.0 bln.; partners: EU 29%, Japan 17%, U.S. 16%. **Tourism** (1992): $706 mln. **National budget** (1993): $10.9 bln. **International reserves less gold** (Mar. 1995): $13.8 bln. **Gold:** 1.86 mln. oz. t. **Consumer prices** (change in 1994): 11.4%.

Transport: Railroads: Length: 2,778 mi. **Motor vehicles:** in use: 827,000 passenger cars, 438,000 comm. vehicles. **Civil aviation:** 2.2 bln. passenger-mi.; 18 airports with scheduled flights. **Chief ports:** Valparaiso, Arica, Antofagasta.

Communications: Television sets: 1 per 6.8 persons. **Radios:** 1 per 3.2 persons. **Telephones:** 1 per 9.0 persons.

Health: Life expectancy at birth (1995): 72 male; 78 female. **Births** (per 1,000 pop.): 20. **Deaths** (per 1,000 pop.): 5. **Natural increase:** 1.5%. **Hospital beds:** 1 per 312 persons. **Physicians:** 1 per 889 persons. **Infant mortality** (per 1,000 live births 1995): 14.

Education: Literacy (1991): 92%. **Years compulsory:** 8.

Major International Organizations: UN and all of its specialized agencies, OAS.

Embassy: 1732 Massachusetts Ave. NW 20036; 785-1746.

Northern Chile was under Inca rule before the Spanish conquest, 1536-40. The southern Araucanian Indians resisted until the late 19th century. Independence was gained 1810-18, under José de San Martin and Bernardo O'Higgins; the latter, as supreme director 1817-23, sought social and economic reforms until deposed. Chile defeated Peru and Bolivia in 1836-39 and 1879-84, gaining mineral-rich northern land.

In 1970, Salvador Allende Gossens, a Marxist, became president with a third of the national vote. The Allende government improved conditions for the poor. But illegal and violent actions by extremist supporters of the government, the regime's failure to attain majority support, and poorly planned socialist economic programs led to political and financial chaos.

A military junta seized power Sept. 11, 1973, and said Allende had killed himself. The junta named a mostly military cabinet and announced plans to "exterminate Marxism." Repression continued during the 1980s with little sign of any political liberalization.

In a plebiscite held Oct. 5, 1988, voters rejected the incumbent president, Gen. Augusto Pinochet Ugarte. He agreed to presidential elections. In Dec. 1989 voters removed Pinochet from office and elected a civilian president. In Mar. 1994 a Chilean human rights organization announced a revised estimate of more than 3,100 deaths from human rights violations during Pinochet's rule.

Tierra del Fuego is the largest (18,800 sq. mi.) island in the archipelago of the same name at the southern tip of South America, an area of majestic mountains, tortuous channels, and high winds. It was discovered 1520 by Magellan and named the Land of Fire because of its many Indian bonfires. Part of the island is in Chile, part in Argentina. Punta Arenas, on a mainland peninsula, is a center of sheep raising and the world's southernmost city (pop. about 70,000); Puerto Williams is the southernmost settlement.

China

People's Republic of China

Zhonghua Renmin Gonghe Guo

People: Population: 1,203,097,268. **Age distrib.** (%): <15: 27; 65+: 6. **Pop. density:** 326 per sq. mi. **Urban:** 28%. **Ethnic groups:** Han Chinese 92%, Tibetan, Mongol, Korean, Manchu, others. **Principal languages:** Mandarin (official), Yue, Wu, Hakka, Xiang, Gan, Minbei, Minnan. **Religions:** officially atheist; Buddhism, Taoism are traditional.

Geography: Area: 3,696,100 sq. mi. **Location:** Occupies most of the habitable mainland of E Asia. **Neighbors:** Mongolia on N, Russia on NE and NW, Afghanistan, Pakistan, Tajikistan, Kazakhstan on W, India, Nepal, Bhutan, Myanmar, Laos, Vietnam on S, North Korea on NE. **Topography:** Two-thirds of the vast territory is mountainous or desert, and only one-tenth is cultivated. Rolling topography rises to high elevations in the N in the Daxinganlingshanmai separating Manchuria and Mongolia; the Tienshan in Xinjiang; the Himalayan and Kunlunshanmai in the SW and in Tibet. Length is 1,860 mi. from N to S,

width E to W is more than 2,000 mi. The eastern half of China is one of the best-watered lands in the world. Three great river systems, the Changjiang, the Huanghe, and the Xijiang provide water for vast farmlands. **Capital:** Beijing. **Cities** (1990 est.): Shanghai 7.5 mln.; Beijing 5.8 mln.; Tianjin 4.6 mln.; Shenyang 3.6 mln.; Wuhan 3.3 mln.; Canton 2.9 mln.

Government: Type: Communist Party-led state. **Head of state:** Pres. Jiang Zemin; b Aug. 17, 1926; in office: Mar. 27, 1993. **Head of government:** Premier Li Peng; b Oct. 1928; in office: Apr. 9, 1988. **Local divisions:** 23 provinces, 5 autonomous regions, and 3 municipalities. **Defense:** 5.0% of GNP (1992). **Active troop strength:** 2.9 mln. est.

Economy: Industries: Iron and steel, textiles, agriculture implements, consumer goods. **Chief crops:** Grain, rice, cotton, tea. **Minerals:** Tungsten, antimony, coal, oil, mercury, iron, lead, manganese, molybdenum, tin. **Crude oil reserves** (1994): 24 bln. barrels. **Other resources:** Silk. **Arable land:** 10%. **Livestock** (1992): cattle: 83 mln.; pigs: 380 mln.; sheep: 111 mln. **Fish catch** (1991): 13.1 mln. metric tons. **Electricity prod.** (1992): 740 bln. kWh. **Labor force:** 60% agric.; 25% ind. & commerce.

Finance: Monetary unit: Yuan (May 1995): 8.3 = $1 US). **Gross national product** (1993): $2.61 trl.* **Per capita GNP:** $2,200. **Imports** (1992): $80.6 bln.; partners: Jap. 17%, U.S. 11%, Hong Kong 26%. **Exports** (1992): $84.5 bln.; partners: Hong Kong 44%, Jap. 14%, U.S. 10%. **Tourism** (1992): $3.9 bln. **National budget** (1993): $15.6 bln. deficit. **International reserves less gold** (Apr. 1995): $61.4 bln. **Gold:** 12.7 mln. oz t. **Consumer prices** (change in 1993): 17.0%.

Transport: Railroads: Length: 42,564 mi. **Motor vehicles:** in use: 2.3 mln. passenger cars, 4.7 mln. comm. vehicles. **Civil aviation:** 32 bln. passenger-mi., 94 airports with scheduled flights. **Chief ports:** Shanghai, Qinhuangdao, Dalian, Canton.

Communications: Television sets: 1 per 32 persons. **Radios:** 1 per 5.4 persons. **Telephones:** 1 per 77 persons.

Health: Life expectancy at birth (1995): 67 male; 69 female. **Births** (per 1,000 pop.): 18. **Deaths** (per 1,000 pop.): 7. **Natural increase:** 1.0%. **Hospital beds:** 1 per 382 persons. **Physicians:** 1 per 648 persons. **Infant mortality** (per 1,000 live births 1995): 52.

Education: Literacy (1992): 78%. **Years compulsory:** 9; primary school enrollment 96%.

Major International Organizations: UN (IMF, FAO, WHO). **Embassy:** 2300 Conn. Ave. NW 20008; 328-2500.

History. Remains of various humanlike creatures who lived as early as several hundred thousand years ago have been found in many parts of China. Neolithic agricultural settlements dotted the Huanghe basin from about 5000 BC. Their language, religion, and art were the sources of later Chinese civilization.

Bronze metallurgy reached a peak and Chinese pictographic writing, similar to today's, was in use in the more developed culture of the Shang Dynasty (c. 1500 BC-c. 1000 BC), which ruled much of North China.

A succession of dynasties and interdynastic warring kingdoms ruled China for the next 3,000 years. They expanded Chinese political and cultural domination to the south and west, and developed a brilliant technologically and culturally advanced society. Rule by foreigners (Mongols in the Yuan Dynasty, 1271-1368, and Manchus in the Ch'ing Dynasty, 1644-1911) did not alter the underlying culture.

A period of relative stagnation left China vulnerable to internal and external pressures in the 19th century. Rebellions left tens of millions dead, and Russia, Japan, Britain, and other powers exercised political and economic control in large parts of the country. China became a republic Jan. 1, 1912, following the Wuchang Uprising inspired by Dr. Sun Yat-sen.

For a period of 50 years, 1894-1945, China was involved in conflicts with Japan. In 1895, China ceded Korea, Taiwan, and other areas. On Sept. 18, 1931, Japan seized the Northeastern Provinces (Manchuria) and set up a puppet state called Manchukuo. The border province of Jehol was cut off as a buffer state in 1933. Japan invaded China proper July 7, 1937. After its defeat in World War II, Japan gave up all seized land.

Following World War II, internal disturbances arose involving the Kuomintang, Communists, and other factions. China came under domination of Communist armies, 1949-1950. The Kuomintang government moved to Taiwan, 90 mi. off the mainland, Dec. 8, 1949.

The People's Republic of China was proclaimed in Beijing (Peking) Sept. 21, 1949, by the Chinese People's Political Consultative Conference under Mao Zedong. China and the

USSR signed a 30-year treaty of "friendship, alliance and mutual assistance," Feb. 15, 1950. The U.S. refused recognition of the new regime. On Nov. 26, 1950, the People's Republic sent armies into Korea against U.S. troops and forced a stalemate in the Korean War.

By the 1960s, relations with the USSR deteriorated, with disagreements on borders, ideology, and leadership of world Communism. The USSR cancelled aid accords, and China, with Albania, launched anti-Soviet propaganda drives.

On Oct. 25, 1971, the UN General Assembly ousted the Taiwan government from the UN and seated the People's Republic in its place. The U.S. had supported the mainland's admission but opposed Taiwan's expulsion.

U.S. Pres. Richard Nixon visited China Feb. 21-28, 1972, on invitation from Premier Zhou Enlai, ending years of antipathy between the 2 nations. China and the U.S. opened liaison offices in each other's capitals, May-June 1973. The U.S., Dec. 15, 1978, formally recognized the People's Republic of China as the sole legal government of China; diplomatic relations between the 2 nations were established, Jan. 1, 1979.

Internal developments. After an initial period of consolidation, 1949-52, industry, agriculture, and social and economic institutions were forcibly molded according to Maoist ideals. However, frequent drastic changes in policy and violent factionalism interfered with economic development. In 1957, Mao Zedong admitted an estimated 800,000 people had been executed 1949-54; opponents claimed much higher figures.

The Great Leap Forward, 1958-60, tried to force the pace of economic development through intensive labor on huge new rural communes, and through emphasis on ideological purity. The program caused resistance and was largely abandoned.

The Great Proletarian Cultural Revolution, 1965, was an attempt to oppose pragmatism and bureaucratic power and instruct a new generation in revolutionary principles. Massive purges took place. A program of forcibly relocating millions of urban teenagers into the countryside was launched. By 1968 the movement had run its course; many purged officials returned to office in subsequent years, and reforms that had placed ideology above expertise were gradually weakened.

Mao died Sept. 9, 1976. In a continuing "reassessment" of his policies his widow, Jiang Quing, and other "Gang of Four" leftists were convicted of "committing crimes during the 'Cultural Revolution,' " Jan. 25, 1981.

The new ruling group modified Maoist policies in education, culture, and industry, and sought better ties with non-Communist countries. By the mid-1980s, China had enacted far-reaching economic reforms highlighted by the departure from rigid central planning and the stressing of market-oriented socialism.

Some 100,000 students and workers staged a march in Beijing to demand democratic reforms, May 4, 1989. The demonstrations continued during a visit to Beijing by Soviet leader Mikhail Gorbachev May 15-18. It was the first Sino-Soviet summit since 1959. A million people gathered in Beijing to demand reforms and the removal of Deng and other leaders. There were protests in at least 20 other Chinese cities. Martial law was imposed, May 20, but was mostly ignored by protesters.

Chinese army troops entered Beijing, June 3-4, and crushed the pro-democracy protests. Tanks and armored personnel carriers attacked Tiananmen Square, outside the Great Hall of the People, which was the main scene of the demonstrations and hunger strikes. It is estimated that 5,000 died, 10,000 were injured, and hundreds of students and workers were arrested.

Although human rights violations have persisted, the U.S. has continued to renew China's most-favored-nation trading status. Chinese-American Harry Wu, a human rights activist, was detained while trying to enter China June 19, 1995; convicted of spying, he was expelled Aug. 25. China hosted the UN 4th World Conference on Women in Sept.

China's population, the world's largest, is still increasing, but with more couples following the government's one-child policy some experts predict that the nation's population will actually decline after peaking in the early 21st century.

Manchuria. Home of the Manchus, rulers of China 1644-1911, Manchuria has accommodated millions of Chinese settlers in the 20th century. Under Japanese rule 1931-45, the area became industrialized. China no longer uses the name Manchuria for the region, which is divided into the 3 NE provinces of Heilongjiang, Jilin, and Liaoning.

Guangxi is in SE China, bounded on N by Kweichow and Hunan provinces, E and S by Kwangtung, on SW by North Vietnam, and on W by Yunnan. It produces rice in the river valleys and has valuable forest products.

Inner Mongolia was organized by the People's Republic in 1947. Its boundaries have undergone frequent changes, reaching its greatest extent (and restored in 1979) in 1956, with an area of 454,000 sq. mi., allegedly in order to dilute the minority Mongol population. Chinese settlers outnumber the Mongols more than 10 to 1. Pop. (1990 cen.): 21.4 mln. Capital: Hohhot.

Xinjiang, in Central Asia, is 633,802 sq. mi., pop. (1990 cen.): 15.1 mln. (75% Uygurs, a Turkic Muslim group, with a heavy Chinese increase in recent years). Capital: Urumqi. It is China's richest region in strategic minerals.

Tibet, 470,000 sq. mi., is a thinly populated region of high plateaus and massive mountains, the Himalayas on the S, the Kunluns on the N. High passes connect with India and Nepal; roads lead into China proper. Capital: Lhasa. Average altitude is 15,000 ft. Jiachan, 15,870 ft., is believed to be the highest inhabited town on earth. Agriculture is primitive. Pop. (1990 cen.): 2.1 mln. (of whom about 500,000 are Chinese). Another 4 million Tibetans form the majority of the population of vast adjacent areas that have long been incorporated into China.

China ruled all of Tibet from the 18th century, but independence came in 1911. China reasserted control in 1951, and a Communist government was installed in 1953, revising the theocratic Lamaist Buddhist rule. Serfdom was abolished, but all land remained collectivized.

A Tibetan uprising within China in 1956 spread to Tibet in 1959. The rebellion was crushed with Chinese troops, and Buddhism was almost totally suppressed. The Dalai Lama and 100,000 Tibetans fled to India.

Colombia
Republic of Colombia
República de Colombia

People: Population: 36,200,251. **Age distrib.** (%): <15: 33; 65+: 5. **Pop. density:** 82 per sq. mi. **Urban:** 50%. **Ethnic groups:** mestizo 58%, white 20%, mulatto 14%. **Principal language:** Spanish. **Religion:** Roman Catholic 95%.

Geography: Area: 440,831 sq. mi. **Location:** At the NW corner of South America. **Neighbors:** Panama on NW, Ecuador, Peru on S, Brazil, Venezuela on E. **Topography:** Three ranges of Andes, the Western, Central, and Eastern Cordilleras, run through the country from N to S. The eastern range consists mostly of high table lands, densely populated. The Magdalena R. rises in Andes, flows N to Caribbean, through a rich alluvial plain. Sparsely-settled plains in E are drained by Orinoco and Amazon systems. **Capital:** Bogota. **Cities** (1994 est.): Bogota 5.1 mln.; Cali 1.7 mln.; Medellin 1.6 mln.; Barranquilla 1.0 mln.

Government: Type: Republic. **Head of state:** Pres. Ernesto Samper Pizano; b Aug. 3, 1950; in office: Aug. 7, 1994. **Local divisions:** 32 departments, capital district of Bogota. **Defense:** 1.3% of GDP (1993 est.). **Active troop strength:** 146,400.

Economy: Industries: Textiles, food processing, steel, cement, chemicals. **Chief crops:** Coffee (50% of exports), rice, corn, cotton, sugar, tobacco, coca. **Minerals:** Oil, gas, emeralds (50% world output), gold, copper, lead, coal, iron, nickel, salt. **Crude oil reserves** (1994): 1.9 bln. bbls. **Other resources:** Rubber, balsam, dye-woods, copaiba, hydro power. **Arable land:** 4%. **Livestock** (1993): cattle: 25.3 mln.; pigs: 2.6 mln.; sheep: 2.5 mln. **Fish catch** (1991): 108,708 metric tons. **Electricity prod.** (1992): 36 bln. kWh. **Labor force:** 30% agric.; 24% ind.; 46% services.

Finance: Currency: Peso (May 1995: 876 = $1 US). **Gross domestic product** (1993): $192 bln.* **Per capita GDP:** $5,500. **Imports** (1992): $6.7 bln.; partners: U.S. 36%, EU 18%. **Exports** (1992): $6.9 bln.; partners: U.S. 39%, EU 26%. **Tourism** (1992): $705 mln. **National budget** (1993 est.): $12 bln. **International reserves less gold** (Apr. 1995): $8.2 bln. **Gold:** 279,000 oz t. **Consumer prices** (change in 1994): 23.8%.

Transport: Railroads: Length: 2,006 mi. **Motor vehicles:** in use: 854,000 passenger cars, 431,000 comm. vehicles. **Civil aviation:** 2.8 bln. passenger-mi.; 68 airports with scheduled flights. **Chief ports:** Buenaventura, Santa Marta, Barranquilla, Cartagena.

Communications: Television sets: 1 per 6.2 persons. **Radios:** 1 per 1 person. **Telephones:** 1 per 8.7 persons. **Daily newspaper circ.:** 40 per 1,000 pop.

Health: Life expectancy at birth (1995): 70 male; 75 female. **Births** (per 1,000 pop.): 22. **Deaths** (per 1,000 pop.): 5. **Natural increase:** 1.7%. **Hospital beds:** 1 per 693 persons. **Physicians:** 1 per 1,078 persons. **Infant mortality** (per 1,000 live births 1995): 27.

Education: Literacy (1991): 87%. **Years compulsory:** 5.
Major International Organizations: UN (World Bank, WTO), OAS.
Embassy: 2118 Leroy Pl. NW 20008; 387-8338.

Spain subdued the local Indian kingdoms (Funza, Tunja) by the 1530s and ruled Colombia and neighboring areas as New Granada for 300 years. Independence was won by 1819. Venezuela and Ecuador broke away in 1829-30, and Panama withdrew in 1903.

One of the Latin American democracies, Colombia is plagued by rural and urban violence, though scaled down from "La Violencia" of 1948-58, which claimed 200,000 lives. Attempts at land and social reform and progress in industrialization have not succeeded in reducing massive social problems.

The government's increased activity against local drug traffickers sparked a series of retaliation killings. On Aug. 18, 1989, Luis Carlos Galán, the ruling party's presidential hopeful for the 1990 election, was assassinated. In 1990, 2 other presidential candidates were assassinated, as drug traffickers carried on a campaign of intimidation. Pablo Esocobar, head of the Medellín drug cartel, escaped from prison in July 1992, allegedly with aid from military and prison officials. He was killed by government troops Dec. 1, 1993. Charges that Ernesto Samper Pizano's 1994 campaign received money from the Cali drug cartel imperiled his presidency in 1995.

Comoros
Federal Islamic Republic of the Comoros
Jumhur yat al-Qumur al-Itthad yah al-Islam yah

People: Population: 549,338. **Pop. density:** 764 per sq. mi. **Ethnic groups:** Arabs, Africans, Malays. **Principal languages:** Arabic, French, Comorian (all official). **Religions:** Sunni Muslim 86%, Roman Catholic 14%.

Geography: Area: 719 sq. mi. **Location:** 3 islands (Grande Comore, Anjouan, and Moheli) in the Mozambique Channel between NW Madagascar and SE Africa. **Neighbors:** Nearest are Mozambique on W, Madagascar on E. **Topography:** The islands are of volcanic origin, with an active volcano on Grande Comore. **Capital:** Moroni (1992 met. est.): 30,000.

Government: Type: In transition. **Head of government:** Prime Min. Caabi Elyachroutu. **Local divisions:** each of the 3 main islands is a prefecture.

Economy: Industries: Perfume. **Chief crops:** Vanilla, copra, perfume plants, fruits. **Arable land:** 35%. **Electricity prod.** (1991): 25 mln. kWh. **Labor force:** 80% agric.

Finance: Monetary unit: Franc (May 1995: 366 = $1 US). **Gross domestic product** (1993): $360 mln.* **Per capita GDP:** $700. **Imports** (1992): $60 mln.; partners: France 22%. **Exports** (1992): $21 mln.; partners: France 41%, U.S. 53%. **National budget** (1991 est.): $88 mln.
Chief port: Dzaoudzi.
Communications: Radios: 1 per 10 persons. **Telephones:** 1 per 128 persons.
Health: Life expectancy at birth (1995): 56 male; 61 female. **Births** (per 1,000 pop.): 46. **Deaths** (per 1,000 pop.): 11. **Natural increase:** 3.6%. **Infant mortality** (per 1,000 live births 1995): 77.
Education: Literacy (1990): 46%. Less than 20% attend secondary school.
Major International Organizations: UN (IMF, World Bank), OAU, Arab League.
Embassy: 336 E. 45th St., New York, NY 10017; (212) 972-8010.

The islands were controlled by Muslim sultans until the French acquired them 1841-1909. They became a French overseas territory in 1947. A 1974 referendum favored independence, with only the Christian island of Mayotte preferring association with France. The French National Assembly decided to allow each of the islands to decide its own fate. The Comore Chamber of Deputies declared independence July 6, 1975, with Ahmed Abdallah as president. In a referendum in 1976, Mayotte voted to remain French.

A leftist regime that seized power from Abdallah in 1975 was deposed in a pro-French 1978 coup in which he regained the presidency. In Nov. 1989, Pres. Abdallah was assassinated; soon after, a multiparty system was instituted. A Sept. 1995 military coup, assisted by French mercenaries, ousted Pres. Said Mohammed Djohar. French troops invaded, Oct. 4, and forced the surrender of coup leaders.

Congo
Republic of the Congo
République du Congo

People: Population: 2,504,996. **Pop. density:** 19 per sq. mi. **Urban:** 58%. **Ethnic groups:** Kongo 48%, Sangha 20%, Teke 17%, others. **Principal languages:** French (official), African languages. **Religions:** Christian 50% (two-thirds Roman Catholic), indigenous beliefs 48%, Muslim 2%.

Geography: Area: 132,047 sq. mi. **Location:** In W central Africa. **Neighbors:** Gabon, Cameroon on W, Central African Republic on N, Zaire on E, Angola on SW. **Topography:** Much of the Congo is covered by thick forests. A coastal plain leads to the fertile Niari Valley. The center is a plateau; the Congo R. basin consists of flood plains in the lower and savanna in the upper portion. **Capital:** Brazzaville. **Cities** (1992 est.): Brazzaville (met.) 938,000; Pointe-Noire 576,000; Loubomo 84,000.

Government: Type: Republic. **Head of state:** Pres. Pascal Lissouba; b Nov. 15, 1931; in office: Aug. 20, 1992. **Head of government:** Prime Min. Jacques Yhombi-Opango; in office: June 23, 1993. **Local divisions:** 9 regions and 1 commune. **Defense:** 3.8% of GDP (1992). **Active troop strength:** 10,000.

Economy: Chief crops: Cassava, palm oil and kernels, cocoa, coffee. **Minerals:** Gold, lead, copper, zinc. **Crude oil reserves** (1994): 830 mln. bbls. **Arable land:** 2%. **Fish catch** (1991): 45,577 metric tons. **Electricity prod.** (1991): 315 mln. kWh. **Labor force:** 75% agric.

Finance: Monetary unit: CFA Franc (May 1995: 488 = $1 US). **Gross domestic product** (1993): $7 bln.* **Per capita GDP:** $2,900. **Imports** (1990): $621 mln.; partners: France 52%. **Exports** (1990): $981 mln.; partners: U.S. 45%, France 15%. **Tourism** (1992): $6 mln. **National budget** (1990): $952 mln. **International reserves less gold** (Mar. 1995): $59.8 mln. **Gold:** 11,000 oz t.

Transport: Railroads: Length: 494 mi. **Motor vehicles:** in use: 28,000 passenger cars, 17,000 comm. vehicles. **Chief ports:** Pointe-Noire, Brazzaville.

Communications: Television sets: 1 per 326 persons. **Radios:** 1 per 11 persons. **Telephones:** 1 per 85 persons.

Health: Life expectancy at birth (1995): 45 male; 49 female. **Births** (per 1,000 pop.): 40. **Deaths** (per 1,000 pop.): 17. **Natural increase:** 2.3%. **Hospital beds:** 1 per 456 persons. **Physicians:** 1 per 3,873 persons. **Infant mortality** (per 1,000 live births 1995): 109.

Education: Literacy (1991): 57%. **Years compulsory:** 10; attendance 80%.

Major International Organizations: UN (FAO, IMF, WHO), OAU.

Embassy: 4891 Colorado Ave. NW 20011; 726-0825.

The Loango Kingdom flourished in the 15th century, as did the Anzico Kingdom of the Batekes; by the late 17th century they had become weakened. France established control by 1885. Independence came Aug. 15, 1960.

After a 1963 coup sparked by trade unions, the country adopted a Marxist-Leninist stance, with the USSR and China vying for influence. France remained a dominant trade partner and source of technical assistance, however, and French-owned private enterprise retained a major economic role.

In 1990, Marxism was renounced and opposition parties legalized. In 1991 the country's name was changed to Republic of the Congo, and a new constitution was approved. A democratically elected government came into office in 1992; one of its key problems was a resurgence of ethnic and regional hostilities, often erupting into violence.

Costa Rica
Republic of Costa Rica
República de Costa Rica

People: Population: 3,419,114. **Age distrib.** (%): <15: 35; 65+: 5. **Pop. density:** 173 per sq. mi. **Urban:** 49%. **Ethnic groups:** white (with mestizo minority) 96%. **Principal language:** Spanish (official). **Religion:** Roman Catholic 95%.

Geography: Area: 19,730 sq. mi. **Location:** In Central America. **Neighbors:** Nicaragua on N, Panama on S. **Topography:** Lowlands by the Caribbean are tropical. The interior plateau, with an altitude of about 4,000 ft., is temperate. **Capital:** San José (1993 met. est.): 922,000.

Government: Type: Republic. **Head of state:** Pres. José María Figueres; b Dec. 24, 1954; in office: May 8, 1994. **Local**

divisions: 7 provinces. **Defense:** 0.4% of GNP (1991). **Active troop strength:** 7,500.

Economy: Industries: Furniture, food processing, aluminum, textiles, fertilizers, plastics. **Chief crops:** Coffee (chief export), bananas, rice, potatoes. **Minerals:** Gold, salt. **Other resources:** Fish, forests. **Arable land:** 6%. **Livestock** (1992): cattle: 1.7 mln. **Fish catch** (1991): 17,905 metric tons. **Electricity prod.** (1992): 3.6 bln. kWh. **Labor force:** 27% agric.; 35% ind. & commerce; 33% serv. and government.

Finance: Monetary unit: Colon (Apr. 1995: 174 = $1 US). **Gross domestic product** (1993): $19.3 bln.* **Per capita GDP:** $5,900. **Imports** (1992): $2.5 bln.; partners: U.S. 38%, Japan 10%. **Exports** (1992): $1.8 bln.; partners: U.S. 45%, CACM 18%. **Tourism** (1992): $431 mln. **National budget** (1991 est.): $1.34 bln. **International reserves less gold** (May 1995): $922 mln. **Gold:** 35,000 oz t. **Consumer prices** (change in 1994): 13.5%.

Transport: Motor vehicles: in use: 195,000 passenger cars, 100,000 comm. vehicles. **Civil aviation:** 885 mln. passenger-mi.; 13 airports with scheduled flights. **Chief ports:** Limon, Puntarenas, Golfito.

Communications: Television sets: 1 per 9.4 persons. **Radios:** 1 per 12 persons. **Telephones:** 1 per 6.5 persons. **Daily newspaper circ.:** 102 per 1,000 pop.

Health: Life expectancy at birth (1995): 76 male; 80 female. **Births** (per 1,000 pop.): 25. **Deaths** (per 1,000 pop.): 3. **Natural increase:** 2.1%. **Hospital beds:** 1 per 528 persons. **Physicians:** 1 per 962 persons. **Infant mortality** (per 1,000 live births 1995): 10.

Education: Literacy (1992): 93%. **Years compulsory:** 6; attendance 99%.

Major International Organizations: UN (FAO, WTO, ILO, IMF, WHO), OAS.

Embassy: 2114 S St. NW 20008; 234-2945.

Guaymi Indians inhabited the area when Spaniards arrived, 1502. Independence came in 1821. Costa Rica seceded from the Central American Federation in 1838. Since the civil war of 1948-49, there has been little violent social conflict, and free political institutions have been preserved. During 1993 there was an unusual wave of kidnappings and hostage-taking, some of it related to the international cocaine trade.

Costa Rica, though still a largely agricultural country, has achieved a relatively high standard of living and social services, and land ownership is widespread.

Côte d'Ivoire
Republic of Ivory Coast
République de Côte d'Ivoire

People: Population: 14,791,257. **Age distrib.** (%): <15: 47; 65+: 2. **Pop. density:** 119 per sq. mi. **Urban:** 39%. **Ethnic groups:** Baoule 23%, Bete 18%, Senoufou 15%, Malinke 11%, Agni, foreign Africans. **Principal languages:** French (official), Dioula. **Religions:** indigenous 25%, Muslim 60%, Christian 12%.

Geography: Area: 123,847 sq. mi. **Location:** On S coast of W Africa. **Neighbors:** Liberia, Guinea on W, Mali, Burkina Faso on N, Ghana on E. **Topography:** Forests cover the W half of the country, and range from a coastal strip to halfway to the N on the E. A sparse inland plain leads to low mountains in NW. **Capital:** Yamoussoukro (official); Abidjan (de facto). **Cities** (1990 est.): Abidjan 2.7 mln.

Government: Type: Republic. **Head of state:** Henri Konan Bédié; b 1934; in office: Dec. 7, 1993. **Head of government:** Prime Min. Daniel Kablan Duncan; in office: Dec. 1993. **Local divisions:** 50 departments. **Defense:** 0.8% of GNP (1992). **Active troop strength:** 13,900.

Economy: Chief crops: Coffee, cocoa. **Minerals:** Oil, diamonds, manganese. **Other resources:** Timber, rubber, palmkernal oil. **Arable land:** 9%. **Livestock** (1993): goats: 940,000; sheep: 1.2 mln.; cattle: 1.2 mln. **Fish catch** (1992): 87,026 metric tons. **Electricity prod.** (1991): 2.0 bln. kWh. **Labor force:** 85% agric., forestry.

Finance: Monetary unit: CFA Franc (May 1995: 488 = $1 US). **Gross domestic product** (1993): $21 bln.* **Per capita GDP:** $1,500. **Imports** (1990): $1.6 bln.; partners: France 29%, Nigeria 16%, U.S. 4%, Japan 3%. **Exports** (1990): $2.8 bln.; partners: France 14%, Neth. 19%, U.S. 11%, Italy 8%. **Tourism** (1992): $53 mln. **National budget** (1990 est.): $3.6 bln. **International reserves less gold** (Mar. 1995): $198.5 mln. **Gold:** 45,000 oz t. **Consumer prices** (changed in 1993): 2.8%.

Transport: Railroads: Length: 410 mi. **Motor vehicles:** in use: 175,000 passenger cars, 95,000 comm. vehicles. **Chief ports:** Abidjan, Sassandra.

Communications: Television sets: 1 per 17 persons. **Radios:** 1 per 8.9 persons. **Telephones:** 1 per 62 persons.

Health: Life expectancy at birth (1995): 47 male; 51 female. **Births** (per 1,000 pop.): 46. **Deaths** (per 1,000 pop.): 15. **Natural increase:** 3.1%. **Hospital beds:** 1 per 891 persons. **Physicians:** 1 per 11,745 persons. **Infant mortality** (per 1,000 live births 1995): 93.

Education: Literacy (1992): 54%. **Years compulsory:** 6.

Major International Organizations: UN and all of its specialized agencies, OAU.

Embassy: 2424 Massachusetts Ave. NW 20008; 483-2400.

A French protectorate from 1842, Côte d'Ivoire became independent in 1960. It is the most prosperous of the tropical African nations, as a result of diversification of agriculture for export, close ties to France, and encouragement of foreign investment. About 20% of the population are workers from neighboring countries. Côte d'Ivoire officially changed its name from Ivory Coast in Oct. 1985.

Students and workers protested, Feb. 1990, demanding the ouster of longtime Pres. Félix Houphouët-Boigny and multiparty democracy. Côte d'Ivoire held its first multiparty presidential election Oct. 1990, and Houphouët-Boigny retained his office. He died Dec. 7, 1993. The National Assembly named a successor, pending elections scheduled for Oct. 22, 1995.

Croatia
Republic of Croatia
Republika Hrvatska

People: Population: 4,665,821. **Pop. density:** 214 per sq. mi. **Urban:** 54%. **Ethnic groups:** Croatian 78%, Serbian 12%. **Principal languages:** Croatian 96%. **Religions:** Roman Catholic 77%, Orthodox 11%.

Geography: Area: 21,829 sq. mi. **Location:** On the Balkan Peninsula in SE Europe. **Neighbors:** Slovenia, Hungary on the N, Bosnia and Herzegovina, Yugoslavia on the E. **Topography:** Over 33 percent is forested. **Capital:** Zagreb (1991): 707,000.

Government: Type: Parliamentary democracy. **Head of state:** Pres. Franjo Tudjman; b 1922; in office: May 1990. **Head of government:** Prime Min. Nikica Valentic; b 1950; in office: Apr. 3, 1993. **Local divisions:** 21 counties. **Active troop strength:** 105,000 est.

Economy: Industries: Textiles, chemicals, aluminum, steel, paper. **Chief crops:** Olives, fruits. **Minerals:** Bauxite, iron, coal. **Arable land:** 32%. **Electricity prod.** (1992): 11.5 bln. kWh.

Finance: Monetary unit: Kuna (Oct. 1994: 5.68 = $1 US). **Gross domestic product** (1992 est.): $21.8 bln.* **Per capita GDP:** $4,500. **Imports** (1990): $4.4 bln. **Exports** (1990): 2.9 bln.

Transport: Motor vehicles: in use: 670,000 passenger cars, 35,000 comm. vehicles.

Communications: Television sets: 1 per 4.6 persons. **Radios:** 1 per 4.4 persons. **Telephones:** 1 per 4.3 persons. **Daily newspaper circ.:** 150 per 1,000 pop.

Health: Life expectancy at birth (1995): 71 male; 78 female. **Births** (per 1,000 pop.): 11. **Deaths** (per 1,000 pop.): 11. **Natural increase:** 0. **Hospital beds:** 1 per 165 persons. **Physicians:** 1 per 517 persons. **Infant mortality** (per 1,000 live births 1995): 8.

Education: Literacy (1991): 97%.

Major International Organizations: UN (IMF, ILO, WHO).

Embassy: 2343 Massachusetts Ave. NW 20008; 588-5899.

From the 7th century the area was inhabited by Croats, a south Slavic people. It was formed into a kingdom under Tomislav in 924, and joined with Hungary in 1102. The Croats became westernized and separated from Slavs under Austro-Hungarian influence. The Croats retained autonomy under the Hungarian crown. Slavonia was taken by Turks in the 16th century; the northern part was restored by the Treaty of Karlowitz in 1699. Croatia helped Austria put down the Hungarian revolution 1848-49 and as a result was set up with Slavonia as the separate Austrian crownland of Croatia and Slavonia, which was reunited to Hungary as part of *Ausgleich* in 1867. It united with other Yugoslav areas to proclaim the kingdom of Serbs, Croats, and Slovenes in 1918. At the reorganization of

Yugoslavia in 1929, Croatia and Slavonia became Savska co., which in 1939 was united with Primorje co. to form the county of Croatia. A nominally independent state between 1941-45, it became a constituent republic in the 1946 constitution.

On June 25, 1991, Croatia declared independence from Yugoslavia. Fighting began between ethnic Serbs and Croats, with the former gaining control of about 30% of Croatian territory. A cease-fire was declared in Jan. 1992, but new hostilities broke out in 1993. A cease-fire with Serb rebels forming a self-declared republic of Krajina was agreed to Mar. 30, 1994. Croatian government troops recaptured most of the Serb-held territory Aug. 1995.

Cuba
Republic of Cuba
República de Cuba

People: Population: 10,937,635. **Age distrib.** (%): <15: 22; 65+: 9. **Pop. density:** 256 per sq. mi. **Urban:** 74%. **Ethnic groups:** mulatto 51%, white 37%, black 11%. **Principal language:** Spanish. **Religion:** Roman Catholic 85% prior to Castro.

Geography: Area: 42,804 sq. mi. **Location:** Westernmost of West Indies. **Neighbors:** Bahamas, U.S. to N, Mexico to W, Jamaica to S, Haiti to E. **Topography:** The coastline is about 2,500 miles. The N coast is steep and rocky, the S coast low and marshy. Low hills and fertile valleys cover more than half the country. Sierra Maestra, in the E is the highest of 3 mountain ranges. **Capital:** Havana. **Cities** (1989 est.): Havana 2.1 mln.; Santiago de Cuba 397,000; Camagüey 279,000.

Government: Type: Communist state. **Head of state:** Pres. Fidel Castro Ruz; b Aug. 13, 1926; in office: Dec. 3, 1976 (formerly prime min. since Feb. 16, 1959). **Local divisions:** 14 provinces, Havana. **Defense:** 6.0% of GNP (1989). **Active troop strength:** 106,000.

Economy: Industries: Cement, food processing, sugar. **Chief crops:** Sugar (world's largest exporter), tobacco, rice, coffee, fruit. **Minerals:** Cobalt, nickel, iron, copper, manganese, salt. **Other resources:** Forests. **Arable land:** 23%. **Livestock** (1993): cattle: 4.5 mln.; pigs: 1.6 mln. **Fish catch** (1991): 165,236 metric tons. **Electricity prod.** (1992): 16.2 bln. kWh. **Labor force:** 20% agric.; 33% ind. & commerce; 30% services & govt.

Finance: Monetary unit: Peso (Oct. 1994: 1.00 = $1.00 US). **Gross national product** (1993 est.): $13.7 bln.* **Per capita GNP:** $1,250. **Imports** (1993): $1.7 bln. **Exports** (1993): $1.5 bln. **Tourism** (1992): $382 mln. **National budget** (1990 est.): $14.4 bln.

Transport: Railroads: Length: 3,033 mi. **Motor vehicles:** in use: 241,000 passenger cars, 208,000 comm. vehicles. **Civil aviation:** 1.9 bln. passenger-mi.; 12 airports with scheduled flights. **Chief ports:** Havana, Matanzas, Cienfuegos, Santiago de Cuba.

Communications: Television sets: 1 per 4.4 persons. **Radios:** 1 per 5.1 persons. **Telephones:** 1 per 18 persons. **Daily newspaper circ.:** 124 per 1,000 pop.

Health: Life expectancy at birth (1995): 75 male; 79 female. **Births** (per 1,000 pop.): 15. **Deaths** (per 1,000 pop.): 7. **Natural increase:** 0.8%. **Hospital beds:** 1 per 134 persons. **Physicians:** 1 per 231 persons. **Infant mortality** (per 1,000 live births 1995): 8.

Education: Literacy (1992): 96%. 97% attend primary school.

Major International Organizations: UN (WTO, WHO).

Some 50,000 Indians lived in Cuba when it was reached by Columbus in 1492. Its name derives from the Indian Cubanacan. Except for British occupation of Havana, 1762-63, Cuba remained Spanish until 1898. A slave-based sugar plantation economy developed from the 18th century, aided by early mechanization of milling. Sugar remains the chief product and chief export despite government attempts to diversify.

A ten-year uprising ended in 1878 with guarantees of rights by Spain, which Spain failed to carry out. A full-scale movement under Jose Marti began Feb. 24, 1895.

The U.S. declared war on Spain in Apr. 1898, after the sinking of the USS *Maine* in Havana harbor, and defeated it in the Spanish-American War. Spain gave up all claims to Cuba. U.S. troops withdrew in 1902, but under 1903 and 1934 agreements, the U.S. leases a site at Guantánamo Bay in the SE as a naval base. U.S. and other foreign investments acquired a dominant role in the economy. In 1952, former Pres. Fulgencio Batista seized control and established a dictatorship, which grew increasingly harsh and corrupt. Fidel Castro assembled a rebel band in 1956; guerrilla fighting intensified in 1958. Batista fled Jan. 1, 1959, and in the resulting political vacuum Castro took power, becoming premier Feb. 16.

The government began a program of sweeping economic and social changes, without restoring promised liberties. Opponents were imprisoned, and some were executed. Some 700,000 Cubans emigrated in the first years after the Castro takeover, mostly to the U.S.

Cattle and tobacco lands were nationalized, while a system of cooperatives was instituted. By 1960 all banks and industrial companies had been nationalized, including over $1 billion worth of U.S.-owned properties, mostly without compensation.

Poor sugar crops resulted in collectivization of farms, stringent labor controls, and rationing, despite continued aid from the USSR and other Communist countries. The U.S. imposed an export embargo in 1962, severely damaging the economy.

In 1961, some 1,400 Cubans, trained and backed by the U.S. Central Intelligence Agency, unsuccessfully tried to invade and overthrow the regime. In the fall of 1962, the U.S. learned that the USSR had brought nuclear missiles to Cuba. After an Oct. 22 warning from Pres. John F. Kennedy, the missiles were removed.

In 1977, Cuba and the U.S. signed agreements to exchange diplomats, without restoring full ties, and to regulate offshore fishing. In 1978, and again in 1980, the U.S. agreed to accept political prisoners released by Cuba, some of whom were criminals and mental patients. A 1987 agreement provided for 20,000 Cubans to emigrate to the U.S. each year; Cuba agreed to take back some 2,500 jailed in the U.S. since 1980.

In 1975-78, Cuba sent troops to aid one faction in the Angola civil war; the last Cuban troops were withdrawn by May 1991. Cuba's involvement in Central America, Africa, and the Caribbean contributed to poor relations with the U.S.

Cuba resisted the social and economic reforms that took place in the late 1980s and 1990s in the Soviet Union and its successor states and in Eastern Europe. Cuba's economy, formerly propped up by preferential trading status within the Communist bloc, was severely shaken by its collapse. Stiffer trading sanctions enacted by the U.S. in 1992 made things worse. Anti-government demonstrations in Aug. 1994 prompted Castro to loosen emigration restrictions. As the tide of boat refugees rapidly rose, the U.S. announced Aug. 18 that future Cuban refugees would be detained, not granted free entry as in the past. A new U.S.-Cuba emigration agreement in Sept. 1994 ended the exodus of "boat people" after more than 30,000 had left Cuba. In another policy shift, the U.S. announced May 2, 1995, that it would admit 20,000 Cuban refugees held at the Guantánamo base but would forcibly return further boat people to Cuba.

Cyprus
Republic of Cyprus
Kypriaki Dimokratia (Greek)
Kibris Çumhuriyeti (Turkish)

People: Population: 736,636. **Age distrib.** (%): <15: 25; 65+: 11. **Pop. density:** 206 per sq. mi. **Urban:** 68%. **Ethnic groups:** Greeks 78%, Turks 18%. **Principal languages:** Greek, Turkish (both official), English. **Religions:** Greek Orthodox 78%, Muslim 18%.

Geography: Area: 3,572 sq. mi. **Location:** In eastern Mediterranean Sea, off Turkish coast. **Neighbors:** Nearest are Turkey on N, Syria, Lebanon on E. **Topography:** Two mountain ranges run E-W, separated by a wide, fertile plain. **Capital:** Nicosia (1993 met. est.): 177,000.

Government: Type: Republic. **Head of state:** Pres. Glafcos Clerides; b Apr. 24, 1919; in office: Mar. 1, 1993. **Local divisions:** 6 districts. **Defense:** 6.5% of GDP (1993). **Active troop strength:** 10,000.

Economy: Industries: Light manuf. **Chief crops:** Grains, grapes, carobs, citrus fruits, potatoes, olives. **Minerals:** Copper, pyrites, asbestos. **Arable land:** 40%. **Electricity prod.** (1991): 1.8 mln. kWh. **Labor force:** 16% agric., 27% ind., 56% serv.

Finance: Monetary unit: Pound (May 1995: 1.00 = $2.27 US). **Gross domestic product** (1992): $6.7 bln.* **Per capita GDP:** $11,390. **Imports** (1993): $3.3 bln.; partners: UK 11%, Italy 10%, Japan 11%. **Exports** (1993): $1.1 bln.; partners: UK 19%, Greece 8%. **Tourism** (1992): $1.5 bln. **National budget** (1994): $2.2 bln. **International reserves less gold** (Mar. 1995): $1.2 bln. **Gold:** 459,000 oz t. **Consumer prices** (change in 1994): 4.7%.

Transport: Motor vehicles: in use: 198,000 passenger cars, 84,000 comm. vehicles. **Civil aviation:** 1.6 bln. passenger-mi.; 2 airports. **Chief ports:** Famagusta, Limassol.

Communications: Television sets: 1 per 2.5 persons. **Radios:** 1 per 2.5 persons. **Telephones:** 1 per 1.6 persons. **Daily newspaper circ.:** 150 per 1,000 pop.

Health: Life expectancy at birth (1995): 74 male; 79 female. **Births** (per 1,000 pop.): 16. **Deaths** (per 1,000 pop.): 7. **Natural increase:** 0.9%. **Hospital beds:** 1 per 162 persons. **Physicians:** 1 per 677 persons. **Infant mortality** (per 1,000 live births 1995): 9.

Education: Literacy (1992): 94%. **Years compulsory:** 9.

Major International Organizations: UN (IMF, WHO), the Commonwealth.

Embassy: 2211 R St. NW 20008; 462-5772.

Agitation for enosis (union) with Greece increased after World War II, with the Turkish minority opposed, and broke into violence in 1955-56. In 1959, Britain, Greece, Turkey, and Cypriot leaders approved a plan for an independent republic, with constitutional guarantees for the Turkish minority and permanent division of offices on an ethnic basis. Greek and Turkish Communal Chambers dealt with religion, education, and other matters.

Archbishop Makarios III, formerly the leader of the enosis movement, was elected president, and full independence became final Aug. 16, 1960. Further communal strife led the United Nations to send a peacekeeping force in 1964; its mandate has been repeatedly renewed.

The Cypriot National Guard, led by officers from the army of Greece, seized the government July 15, 1974. On July 20, Turkey invaded the island; Greece mobilized its forces but did not intervene. A cease-fire was arranged but collapsed. By Aug. 16, Turkish forces had occupied the NE 40% of the island, despite the presence of UN peacekeeping forces.

Turkish Cypriots voted overwhelmingly, June 8, 1975, to form a separate Turkish Cypriot federated state. A president and assembly were elected in 1976. Some 200,000 Greeks have been expelled from the Turkish-controlled area, replaced by thousands of Turks, some from the mainland.

Turkish Republic of Northern Cyprus

A declaration of independence was announced by Turkish-Cypriot leader Rauf Denktash, Nov. 15, 1983. The state is not internationally recognized, although it does have trade relations with some countries. TRNC contains 1,295 sq mi., pop. (1992 est.): 176,000, 99% Turkish.

Czech Republic
Ceská Republika

(Figures prior to 1993 are for the Czech and Slovak Federal Republic)

People: Population: 10,432,774. **Age distrib.** (%): <15: 21; 65+: 10. **Pop. density:** 343 per sq. mi. **Urban:** 75%. **Ethnic groups:** Czechs 94%, Slovaks 3%. **Principal languages:** Czech, Slovak. **Religions:** atheist 39.8%, Roman Catholic 39.2%, Protestant 4.6%.

Geography: Area: 30,450 sq. mi. **Location:** In E central Europe. **Neighbors:** Poland on N, Germany on N and W, Austria on S, Slovakia on E and SE. **Topography:** Bohemia, in W, is a plateau surrounded by mountains; Moravia is hilly. **Capital:** Prague. **Cities** (1992 est.): Prague 1.2 mln.; Brno 391,000; Ostrava 331,000.

Government: Type: Republic. **Head of state:** Vaclav Havel; b Oct. 5, 1936; in office: Feb. 15, 1993. **Head of government:** Prime Min. Vaclav Klaus; b June 19, 1941; in office: July 1993. **Local divisions:** 8 regions. **Defense:** 2.2% of GDP (1992). **Active troop strength:** 92,900.

Economy: Industries: Machinery, oil products, iron and steel, glass, chemicals, motor vehicles, coal. **Chief crops:** Wheat, sugar beets, potatoes, rye, corn, barley. **Minerals:** Coal, lignite. **Livestock:** (1993): cattle: 2.2 mln.; pigs: 4.1 mln. **Electricity prod.** (1992): 62.2 bln. kWh. **Labor force:** 8% agric.; 38% ind.

Finance: Monetary unit: Koruna (May 1995: 25.96 = $1 US). **Gross domestic product** (1993): $75 bln.* **Per capita GDP:** $7,200. **Imports** (1993): $12.4 bln.; partners: Norway 25%, former USSR 22%, Slovakia 18%. **Exports** (1993): $12.6 bln.; partners: former USSR 18%, Norway 27%, Slovakia 20%. **Tourism** (1992): $1.3 bln. **National budget** (1993 est.): $11.9 bln. **International reserves less gold** (Apr. 1995): $8.5 bln. **Gold:** 1.99 mln. oz t. **Consumer prices** (change in 1994): 10.1%.

Transport: Railroads: Length: 5,865 mi. **Motor vehicles:** in use: 2.5 mln. passenger cars, 363,000 comm. vehicles. **Civil aviation:** 1.6 bln. passenger-mi.; 4 airports.

Communications: Television sets: 1 per 3.2 persons. **Radios:** 1 per 3.6 persons. **Telephones:** 1 per 3.2 persons. **Daily newspaper circ.:** 368 per 1,000 pop.

Health: Life expectancy at birth (1995): 70 male; 77 female. **Births** (per 1,000 pop.): 13. **Deaths** (per 1,000 pop.): 11. **Natural increase:** 0.3%. **Hospital beds:** 1 per 98 persons. **Physicians:** 1 per 323 persons. **Infant mortality** (per 1,000 live births 1995): 9.

Education: Literacy (1993): 100%. **Years compulsory:** 10.

Major International Organizations: UN (WTO, WHO).

Embassy: 3900 Spring of Freedom St. NW 20008; 363-6315.

Bohemia and Moravia were part of the Great Moravian Empire in the 9th century and later became part of the Holy Roman Empire. Under the kings of Bohemia, Prague in the 14th century was the cultural center of Central Europe. Bohemia and Hungary became part of Austria-Hungary.

In 1914-18 Thomas G. Masaryk and Eduard Benes formed a provisional government with the support of Slovak leaders including Milan Stefanik. They proclaimed the Republic of Czechoslovakia Oct. 28, 1918.

Czechoslovakia

By 1938 Nazi Germany had worked up disaffection among German-speaking citizens in Sudetenland and demanded its cession. Prime Min. Neville Chamberlain of Britain, with the acquiescence of France, signed with Hitler at Munich, Sept. 30, 1938, an agreement to the cession, with a guarantee of peace by Hitler and Mussolini. Germany occupied Sudetenland Oct. 1-2.

Hitler on Mar. 15, 1939, dissolved Czechoslovakia, made protectorates of Bohemia and Moravia, and supported the autonomy of Slovakia, proclaimed independent Mar. 14, 1939.

Soviet troops with some Czechoslovak contingents entered eastern Czechoslovakia in 1944 and reached Prague in May 1945; Benes returned as president. In May 1946 elections, the Communist Party won 38% of the votes, and Benes accepted Klement Gottwald, a Communist, as prime minister.

In Feb. 1948, the Communists seized power in advance of scheduled elections. In May 1948 a new constitution was approved. Benes refused to sign it. On May 30 the voters were offered a one-slate ballot and the Communists won full control. Benes resigned June 7 and Gottwald became president. A harsh Stalinist period followed, with complete and violent suppression of all opposition.

In Jan. 1968 a liberalization movement spread explosively through Czechoslovakia. Antonin Novotny, long the Stalinist ruler of the nation, was deposed as party leader and succeeded by Alexander Dubcek, a Slovak, who supported democratic reforms. On Mar. 22 Novotny resigned as president and was succeeded by Gen. Ludvik Svoboda. On Apr. 6, Prem. Joseph Lenart resigned and was succeeded by Oldrich Cernik, a reformer.

In July 1968 the USSR and 4 Warsaw Pact nations demanded an end to liberalization. On Aug. 20, the Soviet, Polish, East German, Hungarian, and Bulgarian armies invaded Czechoslovakia. Despite demonstrations and riots by students and workers, press censorship was imposed, liberal leaders were ousted from office and promises of loyalty to Soviet policies were made by some old-line Communist Party leaders.

On Apr. 17, 1969, Dubcek resigned as leader of the Communist Party and was succeeded by Gustav Husak. In Jan. 1970, Cernik was ousted. Censorship was tightened, and the Communist Party expelled a third of its members. In 1973, amnesty was offered to some of the 40,000 who fled the country after the 1968 invasion, but repressive policies continued.

More than 700 leading Czechoslovak intellectuals and former party leaders signed a human rights manifesto in 1977, called Charter 77, prompting a renewed crackdown by the regime.

The police crushed the largest antigovernment protests since 1968, when tens of thousands of demonstrators took to the streets of Prague, Nov. 17, 1989. As protesters demanded free elections, the Communist Party leadership resigned Nov. 24; millions went on strike Nov. 27.

On Dec. 10, 1989 the first cabinet in 41 years without a Communist majority took power; Vaclav Havel, playwright and human rights campaigner, was chosen president, Dec. 29. Havel failed to win reelection July 3, 1992; his bid was blocked by a Slovak-led coalition.

Slovakia declared sovereignty, July 17. Czech and Slovak leaders agreed, July 23, on a basic plan for a peaceful division of Czechoslovakia into 2 independent states.

Czech Republic

Czechoslovakia split into 2 separate states—the Czech Republic and Slovakia—on Jan. 1, 1993. Havel was elected president, Jan. 26, 1993.

Denmark
Kingdom of Denmark
Kongeriget Danmark

People: Population: 5,199,437. **Age distrib.** (%): <15: 17; 65+: 15. **Pop. density:** 312 per sq. mi. **Urban:** 85%. **Ethnic groups:** Almost all Scandinavian. **Principal languages:** Danish, Faroese. **Religion:** Evangelical Lutheran 91%.

Geography: Area: 16,639 sq. mi. **Location:** In N Europe, separating the North and Baltic seas. **Neighbors:** Germany on S, Norway on NW, Sweden on NE. **Topography:** Denmark consists of the Jutland Peninsula and about 500 islands, 100 inhabited. The land is flat or gently rolling and is almost all in productive use. **Capital:** Copenhagen (1993 met. est.): 1.3 mln.

Government: Type: Constitutional monarchy. **Head of state:** Queen Margrethe II; b Apr. 16, 1940; in office: Jan. 14, 1972. **Head of government:** Prime Min. Poul Nyrup Rasmussen; b June 15, 1943; in office: Jan. 25, 1993. **Local divisions:** 14 counties and one city (Copenhagen). **Defense:** 2% of GDP (1992). **Active troop strength:** 27,000.

Economy: Industries: Machinery, textiles, furniture, electronics. **Chief crops:** Dairy products. **Minerals:** Oil, salt. **Arable land:** 61%. **Livestock** (1987): cattle: 2.3 mln.; pigs: 9.2 mln. **Fish catch** (1992): 1.8 mln. metric tons. **Electricity prod.** (1992): 34.2 bln. kWh. **Labor force:** 6% agric.; 67% serv. & govt.; 20% manuf. & mining.

Finance: Monetary unit: Krone (May 1995: 5.43 = $1 US). **Gross domestic product** (1993): $95.6 bln.* **Per capita GDP:** $18,500. **Imports** (1993): $29.7 bln.; partners: EU 53%, Sweden 11%. **Exports** (1993): $36.7 bln.; partners: EU 54%, Sweden 11%. **Tourism** (1992): $3.8 bln. **National budget** (1993): $55.7 bln. **International reserves less gold** (May 1995): $9.2 bln. **Gold:** 2.0 mln. oz t. **Consumer prices** (change in 1994): 2.0%.

Transport: Railroads: Length: 1,763 mi. **Motor vehicles:** in use: 1.7 mln. passenger cars, 261,000 comm. vehicles. **Civil aviation:** 2.7 bln. passenger-mi.; 12 airports with scheduled flights. **Chief ports:** Copenhagen, Alborg, Arhus, Odense.

Communications: Television sets: 1 per 2.1 persons. **Radios:** 1 per 2.3 persons. **Telephones:** 1 per 1.7 persons. **Daily newspaper circ.:** 332 per 1,000 pop.

Health: Life expectancy at birth (1995): 73 male; 79 female. **Births** (per 1,000 pop.): 12. **Deaths** (per 1,000 pop.): 11. **Natural increase:** 0.1%. **Hospital beds:** 1 per 184 persons. **Physicians:** 1 per 360 persons. **Infant mortality** (per 1,000 live births 1995): 7.

Education: Literacy (1992): 100%. **Years compulsory:** 9.

Major International Organizations: UN and all of its specialized agencies, OECD, EU, NATO.

Embassy: 3200 Whitehaven St. NW 20008; 234-4300.

The origin of Copenhagen dates back to ancient times, when the fishing and trading place named Havn (port) grew up on a cluster of islets, but Bishop Absalon (1128-1201) is regarded as the actual founder of the city.

Danes formed a large component of the Viking raiders in the early Middle Ages. The Danish kingdom was a major north European power until the 17th century, when it lost its land in southern Sweden. Norway was separated in 1815, and Schleswig-Holstein in 1864. Northern Schleswig was returned in 1920.

Voters ratified the Maastricht Treaty on greater European Community unity, May 1993, after having rejected it in 1992.

The **Faeroe Islands** in the North Atlantic, about 300 mi. NW of the Shetlands, and 850 mi. from Denmark proper, 18 inhabited, have an area of 540 sq. mi. and pop. (1987) of 46,000. They are self-governing in most matters.

Greenland
(Kalaallit Nunaat)

Greenland, a huge island between the North Atlantic and the Polar Sea, is separated from the North American continent by Davis Strait and Baffin Bay. Its total area is 840,000 sq. mi., 84% of which is ice-capped. Most of the island is a lofty plateau 9,000 to 10,000 ft. in altitude. The average thickness of the cap is 1,000 ft. The population (1995) is 57,611. Under the 1953 Danish constitution the colony became an integral part of the realm with representatives in the Folketing. The Danish parliament, 1978, approved home rule for Greenland, effective May 1, 1979. Accepting home rule, the islanders elected a socialist-dominated legislature, Apr. 4. With home rule, Greenlandic place names came into official use. The technically correct name for Greenland is now Kalaallit Nunaat; its capital is Nuuk, rather than Gothab. Fish is the principal export.

Djibouti
Republic of Djibouti
Jumhouriyya Djibouti

People: Population: 421,320. **Pop. density:** 47 per sq. mi. **Urban:** 77%. **Ethnic groups:** Somali 60%, Afar 35%. **Principal languages:** French, Arabic (both official); Afar, Somali. **Religions:** Muslim 94%, Christian 6%.

Geography: Area: 8,950 sq. mi. **Location:** On E coast of Africa, separated from Arabian Peninsula by the strategically vital strait of Bab el-Mandeb. **Neighbors:** Ethiopia on W, SW, Eritrea on NW, Somalia on SE. **Topography:** The territory, divided into a low coastal plain, mountains behind, and an interior plateau, is arid, sandy, and desolate. The climate is generally hot and dry. **Capital:** Djibouti (1989 met.): 450,000.

Government: Type: Republic. **Head of state:** Pres. Hassan Gouled Aptidon; b 1916; in office: June 24, 1977. **Head of government:** Prem. Barkat Gourad Hamadou; in office: Sept. 30, 1978. **Local divisions:** 5 districts. **Active troop strength:** 9,600 est.

Economy: Electricity prod. (1991): 200 mln. kWh.

Finance: Monetary unit: Franc (May 1995: 178 = $1 US). **Gross domestic product** (1993): $500 mln.* **Per capita GDP:** $1,200. **Imports** (1992): $334 mln.; partners: Western Europe 48%. **Exports** (1992): $158 mln.; partners: Middle East 40%. **National budget** (1991 est.): $203 mln.

Transport: Motor vehicles: in use: 13,000 passenger cars, 2,000 commercial vehicles. **Chief port:** Djibouti.

Communications: Television sets: 1 per 33 persons. **Radios:** 1 per 19 persons. **Telephones:** 1 per 40 persons.

Health: Life expectancy at birth (1995): 48 male; 52 female. **Births** (per 1,000 pop.): 43. **Deaths** (per 1,000 pop.): 16. **Natural increase:** 2.7%. **Infant mortality** (per 1,000 live births 1995): 109.

Education: Literacy (1991): 48%.

Major International Organizations: UN, OAU, Arab League.

Embassy: 1156 15th St. NW 20005; 331-0270.

France gained control of the territory in stages between 1862 and 1900.

Ethiopia and Somalia have renounced their claims to the area, but each has accused the other of trying to gain control. There were clashes between Afars (ethnically related to Ethiopians) and Issas (related to Somalis) in 1976. Immigrants from both countries continued to enter the country up to independence, which came June 27, 1977.

French aid is the mainstay of the economy, as well as assistance from Arab countries. A peace accord Dec. 1994 ended a 3-year-long uprising by Afar rebels.

Dominica
Commonwealth of Dominica

People: Population: 82,608. **Pop. density:** 285 per sq. mi. **Ethnic groups:** nearly all African, some Caribs. **Principal languages:** English (official), French patois. **Religions:** Roman Catholic 77%, Protestant 15%.

Geography: Area: 290 sq. mi. **Location:** In Eastern Caribbean, most northerly Windward Is. **Neighbors:** Guadeloupe to N, Martinique to S. **Topography:** Mountainous, a central ridge running from N to S, terminating in cliffs; volcanic in origin, with numerous thermal springs; rich deep topsoil on leeward side, red tropical clay on windward coast. **Capital:** Roseau (1991 est.): 16,000.

Government: Type: Parliamentary democracy. **Head of state:** Pres. Crispin Anselm Sorhaindo; in office: Oct. 25, 1993. **Head of government:** Prime Min. Edison James; in office: June 14, 1995. **Local divisions:** 10 parishes.

Economy: Industries: Soap, tourism. **Chief crops:** Bananas, citrus fruits, coconuts. **Minerals:** Pumice. **Other resources:** Forests. **Arable land:** 9%. **Electricity prod.** (1992): 16 mln. kWh. **Labor force:** 40% agric.; 32% ind. & commerce; 28% services.

Finance: Monetary unit: East Caribbean Dollar (May 1995: 2.70 = $1 US). **Gross domestic product** (1992): $185 mln.* **Per capita GDP:** $2,100. **Imports** (1992): $98 mln.; partners: UK 17%, U.S. 25%. **Exports** (1992): $55 mln.; partners: UK 50%. **Tourism** (1992): $25 mln. **National budget** (1991 est.): $84 mln. **Consumer prices** (change in 1994): 1.6%.

Chief port: Roseau.

Communications: Telephones: 1 per 4.2 persons.

Health: Life expectancy at birth (1995): 74 male; 80 female. **Births** (per 1,000 pop.): 19. **Deaths** (per 1,000 pop.): 5. **Natural increase:** 1.3%. **Hospital beds:** 1 per 247 persons. **Physicians:** 1 per 1,889 persons. **Infant mortality** (per 1,000 live births 1995): 10.

Education: Literacy (1992): 94%.

Major International Organizations: UN, OAS, the Commonwealth.

A British colony since 1805, Dominica was granted self-government in 1967. Independence was achieved Nov. 3, 1978.

Hurricane David struck, Aug. 30, 1979, devastating the island and destroying the banana plantations, Dominica's economic mainstay. Coups were attempted in 1980 and 1981.

Dominica participated in the 1983 U.S.-led invasion of Grenada.

Dominican Republic

República Dominicana

People: Population: 7,948,223. **Age distrib.** (%): <15: 35; 65+: 4. **Pop. density:** 425 per sq. mi. **Urban:** 61%. **Ethnic groups:** mixed 73%, white 16%, black 11%. **Principal language:** Spanish. **Religion:** Roman Catholic 95%.

Geography: Area: 18,704 sq. mi. **Location:** In West Indies, sharing I. of Hispaniola with Haiti. **Neighbors:** Haiti on W. **Topography:** The Cordillera Central range crosses the center of the country, rising to over 10,000 ft., highest in the Caribbean. The Cibao Valley to the N is major agricultural area. **Capital:** Santo Domingo. **Cities** (1993 est.): Santo Domingo 2.1 mln.; Santiago de Los Caballeros 690,000.

Government: Type: Republic. **Head of state:** Pres. Joaquín Balaguer; b Sept. 1, 1907; in office: Aug. 16, 1986. **Local divisions:** 29 provinces and Santo Domingo. **Defense:** 0.7% of GDP (1993 est.). **Active troop strength:** 24,500.

Economy: Industries: Sugar refining, cement, tourism. **Chief crops:** sugar, cocoa, coffee, cotton, rice. **Minerals:** Nickel, gold, silver. **Arable land:** 23%. **Livestock** (1991): cattle: 2.2 mln.; pigs: 431,000. **Electricity prod.** (1992): 5 bln. kWh. **Labor force:** 49% agric.; 18% ind.; 33% serv.

Finance: Monetary unit: Peso (May 1995: 13.74 = $1 US). **Gross domestic product** (1993): $23 bln.* **Per capita GDP:** $3,000. **Imports** (1993): $2.2 bln.; partners: U.S. 50%. **Exports** (1993): $769 mln.; partners: U.S. 56%, EU 22%. **Tourism** (1992): $1.1 bln. **National budget** (1993 est.): $1.8 bln. **International reserves less gold** (May 1995): $302 mln. **Gold:** 18,000 oz t. **Consumer prices** (change in 1994): 8.3%.

Transport: Motor vehicles: in use: 150,000 passenger cars, 110,000 comm. vehicles. **Civil aviation:** 889 mln. passenger-mi.; 5 airports. **Chief ports:** Santo Domingo, San Pedro de Macoris, Puerto Plata.

Communications: Television sets: 1 per 11 persons. **Radios:** 1 per 6.7 persons. **Telephones:** 1 per 12 persons. **Daily newspaper circ.:** 31 per 1,000 pop.

Health: Life expectancy at birth (1995): 67 male; 71 female. **Births** (per 1,000 pop.): 24. **Deaths** (per 1,000 pop.): 6. **Natural increase:** 1.8%. **Hospital beds:** 1 per 508 persons. **Physicians:** 1 per 934 persons. **Infant mortality** (per 1,000 live births 1995): 49.

Education: Literacy (1991): 83%. **Years compulsory:** 6; attendance 70%.

Major International Organizations: UN (World Bank, IMF, WTO), OAS.

Embassy: 1715 22d St. NW 20008; 332-6280.

Carib and Arawak Indians inhabited the island of Hispaniola when Columbus landed in 1492. The city of Santo Domingo, founded 1496, is the oldest settlement by Europeans in the hemisphere and has the supposed ashes of Columbus in an elaborate tomb in its ancient cathedral.

The western third of the island was ceded to France in 1697. Santo Domingo itself was ceded to France in 1795. Haitian leader Toussaint L'Ouverture seized it, 1801. Spain returned intermittently 1803-21, as several native republics came and

went. Haiti ruled again, 1822-44, and Spanish occupation occurred 1861-63.

The country was occupied by U.S. Marines from 1916 to 1924, when a constitutionally elected government was installed.

In 1930, Gen. Rafael Leonidas Trujillo Molina was elected president. Trujillo ruled brutally until his assassination in 1961. Pres. Joaquín Balaguer, appointed by Trujillo in 1960, resigned under pressure in 1962.

Juan Bosch, elected president in the first free elections in 38 years, was overthrown in 1963. On Apr. 24, 1965, a revolt was launched by followers of Bosch and others, including a few Communists. Four days later U.S. Marines intervened against the pro-Bosch forces. Token units were later sent by 5 South American countries as a peacekeeping force. A provisional government supervised a June 1966 election, in which Balaguer defeated Bosch. Balaguer remained in office for most of the next 28 years, but his May 1994 reelection was widely denounced as fraudulent, and new elections were scheduled for May 16, 1996.

Continued depressed world prices have affected the main export commodity, sugar.

Ecuador

Republic of Ecuador

República del Ecuador

People: Population: 10,890,950. **Age distrib.** (%): <15: 38; 65+: 4. **Pop. density:** 104 per sq. mi. **Urban:** 58%. **Ethnic groups:** mestizo 55%, Indian 25%, Spanish 10%, African 10%. **Principal languages:** Spanish (official), Quechuan, Jivaroan. **Religion:** Roman Catholic 95%.

Geography: Area: 105,037 sq. mi. **Location:** In NW South America, on Pacific coast, astride the Equator. **Neighbors:** Colombia on N, Peru on E and S. **Topography:** Two ranges of Andes run N and S, splitting the country into 3 zones: hot, humid lowlands on the coast; temperate highlands between the ranges; and rainy, tropical lowlands to the E. **Capital:** Quito. **Cities** (1991 est.): Guayaquil 2.0 mln.; Quito 1.5 mln.

Government: Type: Republic. **Head of state:** Pres. Sixto Durán Ballén; b 1922; in office: Aug. 10, 1992. **Local divisions:** 21 provinces. **Defense:** 2.2% of GDP (1992). **Active troop strength:** 57,500.

Economy: Industries: Petroleum, food processing, wood prods., textiles. **Chief crops:** Bananas and balsawood (world's largest exporter), coffee, rice, sugar, potatoes. **Minerals:** Oil, gas, copper, iron, lead, silver, gold. **Crude oil reserves** (1994): 2.0 bln. bbls. **Other resources:** Rubber, bark. **Arable land:** 6%. **Livestock** (1992): cattle: 4.7 mln.; pigs: 2.4 mln.; sheep: 1.5 mln. **Fish catch** (1991): 383,600 metric tons. **Electricity prod.** (1992): 7.7 bln. kWh. **Labor force:** 35% agric.; 21% manuf.; 28% services.

Finance: Monetary unit: Sucre (Mar. 1995: 2,417 = $1 US). **Gross domestic product** (1993): $41.8 bln.* **Per capita GDP:** $4,000. **Imports** (1992): $2.5 bln.; partners: U.S. 33%. **Exports** (1992): $3.0 bln.; partners: U.S. 53%. **Tourism** (1992): $192 mln. **National budget** (1992): $1.9 bln. **International reserves less gold** (Apr. 1995): $1.8 bln. **Gold:** 414,000 oz t. **Consumer prices** (change in 1994): 27.3%.

Transport: Railroads: Length: 600 mi. **Motor vehicles:** in use: 336,000 passenger cars, 48,000 comm. vehicles. **Civil aviation:** 589 mln. passenger-mi.; 14 airports. **Chief ports:** Guayaquil, Manta, Esmeraldas, Puerto Bolivar.

Communications: Television sets: 1 per 12 persons. **Radios:** 1 per 3.7 persons. **Telephones:** 1 per 20 persons. **Daily newspaper circ.:** 87 per 1,000 pop.

Health: Life expectancy at birth (1995): 68 male; 73 female. **Births** (per 1,000 pop.): 25. **Deaths** (per 1,000 pop.): 6. **Natural increase:** 2.0%. **Hospital beds:** 1 per 598 persons. **Physicians:** 1 per 836 persons. **Infant mortality** (per 1,000 live births 1995): 38.

Education: Literacy (1991): 88%. **Years compulsory:** 6.

Major International Organizations: UN (IMF, WHO), OAS.

Embassy: 2535 15th St. NW 20009; 234-7200.

Spain conquered the region, which was the northern Inca empire, in 1533. Liberation forces defeated the Spanish May 24, 1822, near Quito. Ecuador became part of the Great Colombia Republic but seceded, May 13, 1830.

A peaceful transfer of power from military rule to democratic civilian government took place in 1979.

Since 1972, the economy has revolved around petroleum exports; oil revenues have declined since 1982, causing severe economic problems. Ecuador suspended interest payments for

1987 on its estimated $8.2 billion foreign debt following a Mar. 5-6 earthquake which left 20,000 homeless, and destroyed a stretch of the country's main oil pipeline.

Ecuadoran Indians staged a number of protests in the 1990s to demand greater rights. A border war with Peru flared from Jan. 26, 1995, until a truce took effect Mar. 1.

The **Galapagos Islands,** 600 mi. to the W, are the home of huge tortoises and other unusual animals.

Egypt
Arab Republic of Egypt
Jumhuriyah Misr al-Arabiyah

People: Population: 62,359,623. **Age distrib** (%) <15: 40; 65+: 4. **Pop. density:** 162 per sq. mi. **Urban:** 44%. **Ethnic groups:** Eastern Hamitic stock 99%, Greek, Nubian, Armenian. **Principal languages:** Arabic (official), English, French. **Religion:** Muslim (mostly Sunni) 94%.

Geography: Area: 385,229 sq. mi. **Location:** Northeast corner of Africa. **Neighbors:** Libya on W, Sudan on S, Israel on E. **Topography:** Almost entirely desolate and barren, with hills and mountains in E and along Nile. The Nile Valley, where most of the people live, stretches 550 miles. **Capital:** Cairo. **Cities** (1994 est.): Cairo 6.8 mln.; Alexandria 3.4 mln.; (1991): al-Jizah 2.1 mln.

Government: Type: Republic. **Head of state:** Pres. Hosni Mubarak; b May 4, 1928; in office: Oct. 14, 1981. **Head of government:** Prime Min. Atef Sedki; b 1930; in office: Nov. 10, 1986. **Local divisions:** 26 governorates. **Defense:** 6% of GDP (FY 1992-93). **Active troop strength:** 440,000.

Economy: Industries: Textiles, tourism, chemicals, petrochemicals, food processing, cement. **Chief crops:** Cotton, rice, beans, fruits, grains, vegetables, corn. **Minerals:** Oil, phosphates, gypsum, iron, manganese, limestone. **Crude oil reserves** (1994): 6.3 bln. bbls. **Arable land:** 3%. **Livestock:** cattle (1991): 3.5 mln.; sheep (1993): 3.7 mln. **Fish catch** (1991): 298,000 metric tons. **Electricity prod.** (1992): 47 bln. kWh. **Labor force:** 34% agric.; 36% govt.

Finance: Monetary unit: Pound (May 1995: 3.39 = $1 US). **Gross domestic product** (1993): $139 bln.* **Per capita GDP:** $2,400. **Imports** (1993): $10.5 bln.; partners: U.S. 20%, EU 36%. **Exports** (1993): $3.5 bln.; partners: EU 40%, Arab League 15%. **Tourism** (1992): $2.7 bln. **National budget** (1994 est.): $19.4 bln. **International reserves less gold** (Mar. 1995): $13.8 bln. **Gold:** 2.43 mln. oz t. **Consumer prices** (change in 1994): 8.2%.

Transport: Railroads: Length: 5,484 mi. **Motor vehicles:** in use: 1.1 mln. passenger cars, 467,000 comm. vehicles. **Civil aviation:** 3.3 bln. passenger-mi.; 9 airports. **Chief ports:** Alexandria, Port Said, Suez.

Communications: Television sets: 1 per 11 persons. **Radios:** 1 per 4 persons. **Telephones:** 1 per 22 persons. **Daily newspaper circ.:** 62 per 1,000 pop.

Health: Life expectancy at birth (1995): 59 male; 63 female. **Births** (per 1,000 pop.): 29. **Deaths** (per 1,000 pop.): 9. **Natural increase:** 2.0%. **Hospital beds:** 1 per 504 persons. **Physicians:** 1 per 1,698 persons. **Infant mortality** (per 1,000 live births 1995): 74.

Education: Literacy (1992): 48%. **Years compulsory:** 8.

Major International Organizations: UN (IMF, World Bank, WTO), OAU, Arab League.

Embassy: 3521 International Ct. NW 20008; 895-5400.

Archaeological records of ancient Egyptian civilization date back to 4000 BC. A unified kingdom arose around 3200 BC, and extended its way south into Nubia and north as far as Syria. A high culture of rulers and priests was built on an economic base of serfdom, fertile soil, and annual flooding of the Nile banks.

Imperial decline facilitated conquest by Asian invaders (Hyksos, Assyrians). The last native dynasty fell in 341 BC to the Persians, who were in turn replaced by Greeks (Alexander and the Ptolemies), Romans, Byzantines, and Arabs, who introduced Islam and the Arabic language. The ancient Egyptian language is preserved only in the liturgy of the Coptic Christians.

Egypt was ruled as part of larger Islamic empires for several centuries. The Mamluks, a military caste of Caucasian origin, ruled Egypt from 1250 until defeat by the Ottoman Turks in 1517. Under Turkish sultans the khedive as hereditary viceroy had wide authority. Britain intervened in 1882 and took control of administration, though nominal allegiance to the Ottoman Empire continued until 1914.

The country was a British protectorate from 1914 to 1922. A 1936 treaty strengthened Egyptian autonomy, but Britain retained bases in Egypt and a condominium over the Sudan. Britain fought German and Italian armies from Egypt, 1940-42. In 1951 Egypt abrogated the 1936 treaty. The Sudan became independent in 1956.

The uprising of July 23, 1952, led by the Society of Free Officers, named Maj. Gen. Mohammed Naguib commander in chief and forced King Farouk to abdicate. When the republic was proclaimed June 18, 1953, Naguib became its first president and premier. Lt. Col. Gamal Abdel Nasser removed Naguib and became premier in 1954. In 1956, he was voted president. Nasser died in 1970 and was replaced by Vice Pres. Anwar Sadat.

The Aswan High Dam, completed 1971, provides irrigation for more than a million acres of land. Artesian wells, drilled in the Western Desert, reclaimed 43,000 acres, 1960-66.

When the state of Israel was proclaimed in 1948, Egypt joined other Arab nations invading Israel and was defeated.

After terrorist raids across its border, Israel invaded Egypt's Sinai Peninsula, Oct. 29, 1956. Egypt rejected a cease-fire demand by Britain and France; on Oct. 31 the 2 nations dropped bombs and on Nov. 5-6 landed forces. Egypt and Israel accepted a UN cease-fire; fighting ended Nov. 7.

A UN Emergency Force guarded the 117-mile-long border between Egypt and Israel until May 19, 1967, when it was withdrawn at Nasser's demand. Egyptian troops entered the Gaza Strip and the heights of Sharm el Sheikh and 3 days later closed the Strait of Tiran to all Israeli shipping. Full-scale war broke out June 5; before it ended under a UN cease-fire June 10, Israel had captured Gaza and the Sinai Peninsula, controlled the east bank of the Suez Canal, and reopened the gulf. After sporadic fighting, Israel and Egypt agreed, Aug. 7, 1970, to a new cease-fire.

In a surprise attack Oct. 6, 1973, Egyptian forces crossed the Suez Canal into the Sinai. (At the same time, Syrian forces attacked Israelis on the Golan Heights.) Egypt was supplied by a USSR military airlift; the U.S. responded with an airlift to Israel. Israel counterattacked, crossed the canal, surrounded Suez City. A UN cease-fire took effect Oct. 24.

A disengagement agreement was signed Jan. 18, 1974. Under it, Israeli forces withdrew from the canal's W bank; limited numbers of Egyptian forces occupied a strip along the E bank. A second accord was signed in 1975, with Israel yielding Sinai oil fields. Pres. Sadat's surprise visit to Jerusalem, Nov. 1977, opened the prospect of peace with Israel. On Mar. 26, 1979, Egypt and Israel signed a formal peace treaty, ending 30 years of war, and establishing diplomatic relations. Israel returned control of the Sinai to Egypt in Apr. 1982.

Tension between Muslim fundamentalists and Christians in 1981 caused street riots and culminated in a nationwide security crackdown in Sept. Pres Sadat was assassinated on Oct. 6; he was succeeded by Hosni Mubarak.

Egypt was a political and military supporter of the Allied forces in their defeat of Iraq in the Persian Gulf War, 1991.

Egypt saw a rising tide of Islamic fundamentalist violence in the 1990s. Egyptian security forces conducted raids against Islamic militants, some of whom were executed for terrorism. Naguib Mahfouz, winner of the 1988 Nobel Prize for Literature, was stabbed by Islamic militants Oct. 14, 1994. Pres. Mubarak escaped assassination in Ethiopia, June 26, 1995; Egypt blamed Sudan for the attack.

The **Suez Canal,** 103 mi. long, links the Mediterranean and Red seas. It was built by a French corporation 1859-69, but Britain obtained controlling interest in 1875. The last British troops were removed June 13, 1956. On July 26, Egypt nationalized the canal.

El Salvador
Republic of El Salvador
República de El Salvador

People: Population: 5,870,481. **Age distrib.** (%): <15: 40; 65+: 4. **Pop. density:** 723 per sq. mi. **Urban:** 46%. **Ethnic groups:** mestizo 94%, Indian 5%. **Principal language:** Spanish (official). **Religion:** Roman Catholic 75%.

Geography: Area: 8,124 sq. mi. **Location:** In Central America. **Neighbors:** Guatemala on W, Honduras on N. **Topography:** A hot Pacific coastal plain in the south rises to a cooler plateau and valley region, densely populated. The N is mountainous, including many volcanoes. **Capital:** San Salvador (1993 met. est.): 1.4 mln.

Government: Type: Republic. **Head of state:** Pres. Armando Calderón Sol; in office: June 1, 1994. **Local divisions:**

14 departments. **Defense:** 1.1% of GDP (1994 est.). **Active troop strength:** 30,700.

Economy: Industries: Food and beverages, textiles, petroleum products. **Chief crops:** Coffee, cotton, corn, sugar. **Other resources:** Hydropower. **Arable land:** 27%. **Livestock** (1993): cattle: 1.3 mln.; pigs: 325,000. **Electricity prod.** (1992): 2.2 bln. kWh. **Labor force:** 40% agric.; 16% commerce.

Finance: Monetary unit: Colon (May 1995: 8.75 = $1 US). **Gross domestic product** (1993): $14.2 bln.* **Per capita GDP:** $2,500. **Imports** (1993): $1.9 bln.; partners: U.S. 44%, Guatemala 10%. **Exports** (1993): $730 mln.; partners: U.S. 50%, Guatemala 16%. **Tourism** (1992): $49 mln. **National budget** (1992 est.): $890 mln. **International reserves less gold** (May 1995): $659 mln. **Gold:** 469,000 oz t. **Consumer prices** (change in 1994): 10.6%.

Transport: Railroads: Length: 374 mi. **Motor vehicles:** in use: 222,000 passenger cars, 33,000 comm. vehicles. **Chief ports:** La Union, Acajutla.

Communications: Television sets: 1 per 11 persons. **Radios:** 1 per 2.9 persons. **Telephones:** 1 per 18 persons. **Daily newspaper circ.:** 48 per 1,000 pop.

Health: Life expectancy at birth (1995): 65 male; 70 female. **Births** (per 1,000 pop.): 32. **Deaths** (per 1,000 pop.): 6. **Natural increase:** 2.6%. **Hospital beds:** 1 per 922 persons. **Physicians:** 1 per 2,126 persons. **Infant mortality** (per 1,000 live births 1995): 39.

Education: Literacy (1991): 75%. **Years compulsory:** 6; attendance 82%.

Major International Organizations: UN (IMF, WTO, WHO, ILO), OAS.

Embassy: 2308 California St. NW 20008; 265-9671.

El Salvador became independent of Spain in 1821, and of the Central American Federation in 1839.

A fight with Honduras in 1969 over the presence of 300,000 Salvadoran workers left 2,000 dead.

A military coup overthrew the government of Pres. Carlos Humberto Romero in 1979, but the ruling military-civilian junta failed to quell a rebellion by leftist insurgents, armed by Cuba and Nicaragua. Extreme right-wing death squads organized to eliminate suspected leftists were blamed for thousands of deaths in the 1980s. The Reagan administration staunchly supported the government with military aid.

Voters turned out in large numbers in the May 1984 presidential election. Christian Democrat José Napoleon Duarte, a moderate, was victorious, with 54% of the vote.

The 12-year civil war ended Jan. 16, 1992, as the government and leftist rebels signed a formal peace treaty. The civil war had taken the lives of some 75,000 people. The treaty provided for military and political reforms.

Nine soldiers, including 3 officers, were indicted Jan. 1990 in the Nov. 1989 slaying of 6 Jesuit priests in San Salvador. Two of the officers received maximum 30-year jail sentences. They were released Mar. 20, 1993, when the National Assembly passed a sweeping amnesty.

Equatorial Guinea
Republic of Equatorial Guinea
República de Guinea Ecuatorial

People: Population: 420,293. **Age distrib.** (%): <15: 43; 65+: 4. **Pop. density:** 39 per sq. mi. **Urban:** 37%. **Ethnic groups:** Fangs 80%, Bubi 15%. **Principal languages:** Spanish (official), Fang, Bubi. **Religion:** mostly Roman Catholic.

Geography: Area: 10,831 sq. mi. **Location:** Bioko I. off W Africa coast in Gulf of Guinea, and Rio Muni, mainland enclave. **Neighbors:** Gabon on S, Cameroon on E, N. **Topography:** Bioko I. consists of 2 volcanic mountains and a connecting valley. Rio Muni, with over 90% of the area, has a coastal plain and low hills beyond. **Capital:** Malabo (1989 est.): 38,000.

Government: Type: in transition. **Head of state:** Pres., Supreme Military Council Teodoro Obiang Nguema Mbasogo; b June 5, 1942; in office: Oct. 10, 1979. **Head of government:** Prime Min. Silvestre Siale Bileka; In office: Mar. 4, 1992. **Local divisions:** 7 provinces. **Active troop strength:** 1,320.

Economy: Chief crops: Cocoa, coffee, bananas, sweet potatoes. **Other resources:** Timber. **Arable land:** 8%. **Electricity prod.** (1991): 60 mln. kWh. **Labor force:** 66% agric.; 23% serv.; 11% ind.

Finance: Monetary unit: CFA Franc (May 1995: 488 = $1 US). **Gross domestic product** (1993): $280 mln.* **Per capita**

GDP: $700. **Imports** (1992): $64 mln.; partners: Cameroon 23%, Spain 22%. **Exports** (1992): $53 mln.; partners: Spain 55%. **National budget** (1992 est.): $36 mln.

Chief ports: Malabo, Bata.

Communications: Radios: 1 per 3.8 persons.

Health: Life expectancy at birth (1995): 50 male; 55 female. **Births** (per 1,000 pop.): 40. **Deaths** (per 1,000 pop.): 14. **Natural increase:** 2.6%. **Hospital beds:** 1 per 89 persons. **Physicians:** 1 per 3,532 persons. **Infant mortality** (per 1,000 live births 1995): 100.

Education: Literacy (1991): 55%. About 65% attend primary school.

Major International Organizations: UN (IMF, World Bank), OAU.

Embassy: 57 Magnolia Ave., Mount Vernon, NY 10553; (914) 667-6913.

Fernando Po (now Bioko) Island was reached by Portugal in the late 15th century and ceded to Spain in 1778. Independence came Oct. 12, 1968. Riots occurred in 1969 over disputes between the island and the more backward Rio Muni province on the mainland. Masie Nguema Biyogo, himself from the mainland, became president for life in 1972.

Masie's reign was one of the most brutal in Africa, resulting in a bankrupted nation. Most of the nation's 7,000 Europeans emigrated. He was ousted in a military coup, Aug. 1979, and Teodoro Mbasogo, leader of the coup, became president. His regime eventually agreed to elections, held Nov. 21, 1993. These were nominally won by the ruling party, but boycotted by opposition parties that maintained the rules were rigged.

The nation is heavily dependent on external aid.

Eritrea
State of Eritrea

People: Population: 3,578,709. **Pop. density:** 79 per sq. mi. **Ethnic groups:** Tigrays 50%, Tigre and Kunama 40%, Afar 4%. **Principal languages:** Tigrinya, Tigre. **Religions:** about evenly split between Muslim and Christian.

Geography: Area: 45,300 sq. mi. **Location:** In E Africa. **Neighbors:** Ethiopia on S, Djibouti on SE, Sudan on W, Red Sea on N. **Topography:** Includes many islands of the Dahlak Archipelago, low coastal plains in S, mountain range with peaks to 9,000 ft. in N. **Capital:** Asmara (1992 est.): 400,000.

Government: Type: In transition. **Head of state:** Issaias Afwerki; b 1945; in office: May 24, 1993. **Local divisions:** 8 provinces.

Economy: Industries: Food processing, textiles. **Chief crops:** Cotton, coffee, tobacco, sorghum. **Minerals:** Gold, potash, copper.

Finance: Monetary unit: Ethiopian Birr. **Gross domestic product** (1993): $1.7 bln.* **Per capita GDP:** $500.

Chief ports: Masewa, Assab.

Communications: Telephones: 1 per 275 persons.

Health (1995): **Births** (per 1,000 pop.): 44. **Deaths** (per 1,000 pop.): 16. **Natural increase:** 2.9%.

Education: Literacy (1993): 20%.

Major International Organizations: UN, OAU.

Eritrea was part of the Ethiopian kingdom of Aksum. It was an Italian colony from 1890 to 1941, when it was captured by the British. Following a period of British and UN supervision, Eritrea was awarded to Ethiopia as part of a federation in 1952. Ethiopia annexed Eritrea as a province in 1962. This led to a 31-year struggle for independence, which ended when Eritrea formally declared itself an independent nation May 24, 1993.

Estonia
Republic of Estonia
Eesti Vabariik

People: Population: 1,625,399. **Pop. density:** 93 per sq. mi. **Urban:** 71%. **Ethnic groups:** Estonian 62%, Russian 30%. **Principal languages:** Estonian (official), Latvian, Lithuanian, Russian. **Religion:** Lutheran.

Geography: Area: 17,462 sq. mi. **Neighbors:** Bounded on N, W by the Baltic Sea, E by Russia, S by Latvia. **Capital:** Tallinn (1994 est.): 443,000.

Government: Type: Republic. **Head of state:** Pres. Lennart Meri; b Mar. 29, 1929; in office: Oct. 5, 1992. **Head of government:** Prime Min. Tiit Vahi; b 1947; in office: Apr. 5, 1995.

Local divisions: 15 counties, 6 municipalities. **Defense: Active troop strength:** 2,500..

Economy: Industries: Shipbuilding, electric motors. **Chief crops:** Dairy products, potatoes. **Arable land:** 22%. **Livestock** (1992): cattle: 615,000, pigs: 541,000. **Electricity prod.** (1992): 22.9 bln. kWh. **Labor force:** 42% ind. & const., 20% agric.

Finance: Monetary unit: Kroon (Mar. 1995: 11.01 = $1 US). **Gross domestic product** (1993 est.): $8.8 bln.* **Per capita GDP:** $5,480. **National budget** (1992): $142 mln. **International reserves less gold** (Nov. 1994): $437 mln. **Gold:** 10,000 oz. t.

Transport: Railroads: Length: 633 mi. **Motor vehicles:** in use: 283,000 passenger cars. **Chief port:** Tallinn.

Communications: Television sets: 1 per 2.6 persons. **Radios:** 1 per 1.7 persons. **Telephones:** 1 per 4.0 persons.

Health: Life expectancy at birth (1995): 65 male; 75 female. **Births** (per 1,000 pop.): 14. **Deaths** (per 1,000 pop.): 12. **Natural increase:** 0.2%. **Hospital beds:** 1 per 103 persons. **Physicians:** 1 per 288 persons.

Education: Literacy (1993): 100%. **Years compulsory:** 9. **Major International Organizations:** UN (IMF, WHO). **Embassy:** 1030 15th St. NW 20005; 789-0320.

Estonia was a province of imperial Russia before World War I, was independent between World Wars I and II, but was conquered by the USSR in 1940. Estonia declared itself an "occupied territory," and proclaimed itself a free nation Mar. 1990. During an abortive Soviet coup, Estonia declared immediate full independence, Aug. 20, 1991; the Soviet Union recognized its independence in Sept. 1991. The first free elections in over 50 years were held Sept. 20, 1992. The last occupying Russian troops were withdrawn by Aug. 31, 1994.

Ethiopia
Federal Democratic Republic of Ethiopia
(Figures prior to 1993 include Eritrea)

People: Population: 55,979,018. **Age distrib.** (%): <15: 49; 65+: 3. **Pop. density:** 128 per sq. mi. **Urban:** 15%. **Ethnic groups:** Oromo 40%, Amhara and Tigre 32%, Sidamo 9%. **Principal languages:** Amharic (official), Tigrinya, Galla. **Religions:** Muslim 45–50%, Ethiopian Orthodox 35–40%, animist 12%.

Geography: Area: 437,794 sq. mi. **Location:** In East Africa. **Neighbors:** Sudan on W, Kenya on S, Somalia, Djibouti on E, Eritrea on N. **Topography:** A high central plateau, between 6,000 and 10,000 ft. high, rises to higher mountains near the Great Rift Valley, cutting in from the SW. The Blue Nile and other rivers cross the plateau, which descends to plains on both W and SE. **Capital:** Addis Ababa (1988 est.): 1.7 mln.

Government: Type: Federal republic. **Head of state:** Pres. Negasso Gidada; in office: Aug. 22, 1995. **Head of government:** Prime Meles Zenawi; b 1955; in office: Aug. 23, 1995. **Local divisions:** 9 regions. **Defense:** 8.9% of GDP (1991). **Active troop strength:** 120,000 est.

Economy: Industries: Food processing, chemicals, textiles. **Chief crops:** Coffee (over 50% export earnings), grains. **Minerals:** Platinum, gold, copper, potash. **Arable land:** 12%. **Livestock** (1993): cattle: 29 mln.; sheep: 22 mln. **Electricity prod.** (1991): 650 mln. kWh. **Labor force:** 80% agric.

Finance: Monetary unit: Birr (May. 1995: 5.95 = $1 US). **Gross domestic product** (1993): $22.7 bln.* **Per capita GDP:** $400. **Imports** (1991): $472 mln.; partners: U.S. 7%, Saudi Arabia 6%. **Exports** (1991): $189 mln.; partners: U.S. 20%, Germany 18%, Italy 7%. **National budget** (1992): $1.2 bln. **International reserves less gold** (Apr. 1995): $623 mln. **Gold:** 113,000 oz t. **Consumer prices** (change in 1993): 3.5%.

Transport: Railroads: Length: 486 mi. **Motor vehicles:** in use: 38,000 passenger cars, 21,000 comm. vehicles. **Civil aviation:** 974 mln. passenger-mi.; 25 airports with scheduled flights.

Communications: Television sets: 1 per 518 persons. **Radios:** 1 per 17 persons. **Telephones:** 1 per 326 persons.

Health: Life expectancy at birth (1995): 48 male; 52 female. **Births** (per 1,000 pop.): 47. **Deaths** (per 1,000 pop.): 16. **Natural increase:** 3.1%. **Hospital beds:** 1 per 3,873 persons. **Physicians:** 1 per 30,195 persons. **Infant mortality** (per 1,000 live births 1995): 121.

Education: Literacy (1991): 24%. **Major International Organizations:** UN (IMF, WHO), OAU. **Embassy:** 2134 Kalorama Rd. NW 20008; 234-2281.

Ethiopian culture was influenced by Egypt and Greece. The ancient monarchy was invaded by Italy in 1880 but maintained its independence until another Italian invasion in 1936. British forces freed the country in 1941.

The last emperor, Haile Selassie I, established a parliament and judiciary system in 1931 but barred all political parties.

A series of droughts in the 1970s killed hundreds of thousands. An army mutiny, strikes, and student demonstrations led to the dethronement of Selassie in 1974. The ruling junta pledged to form a one-party socialist state and instituted a successful land reform; opposition was violently suppressed. The influence of the Coptic Church, embraced in 330 AD, was curbed, and the monarchy was abolished in 1975.

The regime, torn by bloody coups, faced uprisings by tribal and political groups in part aided by Sudan and Somalia. Ties with the U.S., once a major ally, deteriorated, while cooperation accords were signed with the USSR in 1977. In 1978, Soviet advisers and Cuban troops helped defeat Somalian forces. Ethiopia and Somalia signed a peace agreement in 1988.

A worldwide relief effort began in 1984, as an extended drought caused millions to face starvation and death. In 1988, victories by Eritrean guerrillas led the government to curtail the work of foreign aid workers in drought-stricken regions. In 1994 Ethiopia again faced possible severe famine as a result of drought.

The Ethiopian People's Revolutionary Democractic Front (EPRDF), an umbrella group of 6 rebel armies, launched a major push against government forces, Feb. 1991. In May, Pres. Mengistu Haile Mariam resigned and left the country. The EPRDF took over and set up a transitional government. Under a new constitution ratified Dec. 8, 1994, Ethiopia's first multiparty general elections were held in 1995.

Eritrea, a province on the Red Sea, declared its independence May 24, 1993.

Fiji
Republic of Fiji

People: Population: 772,891. **Age distrib.** (%): <15: 38; 65+: 3. **Pop. density:** 110 per sq. mi. **Urban:** 39%. **Ethnic groups:** Fijian (Melanesian-Polynesian) 49%, Indian 46%, Europeans. **Principal languages:** English (official), Fijian, Hindustani. **Religions:** Christian 52%, Hindu 38%, Muslim 8%.

Geography: Area: 7,056 sq. mi. **Location:** In western South Pacific O. **Neighbors:** Nearest are Solomons on NW, Tonga on E. **Topography:** 322 islands (106 inhabited), many mountainous, with tropical forests and large fertile areas. Viti Levu, the largest island, has over half the total land area. **Capital:** Suva (1986 est.): 70,000.

Government: Type: Republic. **Head of state:** Pres. Ratu Sir Kamisese Mara; b May 13, 1920; in office: Jan. 18, 1994. **Head of government:** Prime Min. Sitiveni Rabuka; b 1948; in office: June 2, 1992. **Local divisions:** 4 divisions, 1 dependency. **Defense:** 2% of GDP (FY 1991-92). **Active troop strength:** 3,900.

Economy: Industries: Sugar refining, light industry, tourism. **Chief crops:** Sugar, bananas, ginger. **Minerals:** Gold. **Other resources:** Timber. **Arable land:** 8%. **Electricity prod.** (1992): 420 mln. kWh. **Labor force:** 67% subsistence agric.

Finance: Monetary unit: Dollar (May 1995: 1.38 = $1.00 US). **Gross domestic product** (1993): $3 bln.* **Per capita GDP:** $4,000. **Imports** (1992): $517 mln.; partners: Australia 30%, Japan 13%, N.Z. 17%. **Exports** (1992): $417 mln.; partners: EU 26%, Australia 15%. **Tourism** (1992): $223 mln. **National budget** (1993 est.): $546 mln. **International reserves less gold** (Apr. 1995): $251 mln. **Gold:** 1,000 oz t. **Consumer prices** (change in 1994): 0.6%.

Transport: Motor vehicles: in use: 44,000 passenger cars, 31,000 comm. vehicles. **Civil aviation:** 147 mln. passenger-mi.; 13 airports with scheduled flights. **Chief ports:** Suva, Lautoka.

Communications: Television sets: 1 per 73 persons. **Radios:** 1 per 1.7 persons. **Telephones:** 1 per 9.6 persons. **Daily newspaper circ.:** 36 per 1,000 pop.

Health: Life expectancy at birth (1995): 63 male; 68 female. **Births** (per 1,000 pop.): 24. **Deaths** (per 1,000 pop.): 6. **Natural increase:** 1.7%. **Hospital beds:** 1 per 413 persons. **Physicians:** 1 per 2,438 persons. **Infant mortality** (per 1,000 live births 1995): 18.

Education: Literacy (1991): 87%. 95% attend school. **Major International Organizations:** UN (IMF, WHO). **Embassy:** 2233 Wisconsin Ave. NW 20007; 337-8320.

A British colony since 1874, Fiji became an independent parliamentary democracy Oct. 10, 1970.

Cultural differences between the majority Indian community, descendants of contract laborers brought to the islands in the 19th century, and the less modernized native Fijians, who by law own 83% of the land in communal villages, have led to political polarization.

In 1987, a military coup ousted the government; order was restored May 21 under a compromise granting Lt. Col. Sitveni Rabuka, the coup's leader, increased power. Rabuka staged a second coup Sept. 25 and declared Fiji a republic. Civilian government was restored in Dec. A new constitution favoring indigenous Fijians was issued July 25, 1990.

Finland
Republic of Finland
Suomen Tasavalta

People: Population: 5,085,206. **Age distrib.** (%): <15: 19; 65+: 14. **Pop. density:** 39 per sq. mi. **Urban:** 64%. **Ethnic groups:** Finns 94%, Swedes, Lapps. **Principal languages:** Finnish, Swedish (both official). **Religion:** Evangelical Lutheran 89%.

Geography: Area: 130,559 sq. mi. **Location:** In northern Europe. **Neighbors:** Norway on N, Sweden on W, Russia on E. **Topography:** South and central Finland are mostly flat areas with low hills and many lakes. The N has mountainous areas, 3,000-4,000 ft. **Capital:** Helsinki. **Cities** (1993 est.): Helsinki 502,000; Espoo 179,000; Tampere 175,000.

Government: Type: Constitutional republic. **Head of state:** Pres. Martti Ahtisaari; b 1937; in office: Mar. 1, 1994. **Head of government:** Prime Min. Paavo Lipponen; b Apr. 23, 1941; in office: Apr. 13, 1995. **Local divisions:** 12 laanit (provinces). **Defense:** 2% of GDP (1992). **Active troop strength:** 31,200.

Economy: Industries: Machinery, metal, shipbuilding, textiles, clothing. **Chief crops:** Grains, potatoes, dairy prods. **Minerals:** Copper, iron, zinc. **Other resources:** Forests (40% of exports). **Arable land:** 8%. **Livestock** (1992): cattle: 1.3 mln.; pigs: 1.3 mln. **Fish catch** (1991): 82,813 metric tons. **Electricity prod.** (1992): 55.3 bln. kWh. **Labor force:** 9% agric.; 46% ind., commerce & finance.

Finance: Monetary unit: Markka (May 1995: 4.28 = $1 US). **Gross domestic product** (1993): $81.1 bln.* **Per capita GDP:** $16,100. **Imports** (1993): $18 bln.; partners: EU 47%. **Exports** (1993): $23.4 bln.; partners: EU 53%. **Tourism** (1992): $1.3 bln. **National budget** (1992): $40.6 bln. **International reserves less gold** (May 1995): $10.6 bln. **Gold:** 1.6 mln. oz t. **Consumer prices** (change in 1994): 1.1%.

Transport: Railroads: Length: 3,637 mi. **Motor vehicles:** in use: 1.9 mln. passenger cars, 271,000 comm. vehicles. **Civil aviation:** 5.3 bln. passenger-mi.; 25 airports. **Chief ports:** Helsinki, Turku.

Communications: Television sets: 1 per 2.7 persons. **Radios:** 1 per person. **Telephones:** 1 per 1.3 persons. **Daily newspaper circ.:** 524 per 1,000 pop.

Health: Life expectancy at birth (1995): 73 male; 80 female. **Births** (per 1,000 pop.): 12. **Deaths** (per 1,000 pop.): 10. **Natural increase:** 0.2%. **Hospital beds:** 1 per 81 persons. **Physicians:** 1 per 390 persons. **Infant mortality** (per 1,000 live births 1995): 5.

Education: Literacy (1992): 100%. **Years compulsory:** 9.

Major International Organizations: UN (IMF, WTO), EU, OECD.

Embassy: 3216 New Mexico Ave. NW 20016; 363-2430.

The early Finns probably migrated from the Ural area at about the beginning of the Christian era. Swedish settlers brought the country into Sweden, 1154 to 1809, when Finland became an autonomous grand duchy of the Russian Empire. Russian exactions created a strong national spirit; on Dec. 6, 1917, Finland declared its independence and in 1919 became a republic.

On Nov. 30, 1939, the Soviet Union invaded, and the Finns were forced to cede 16,173 sq. mi. of territory. After World War II, further cessions were exacted. In 1948, Finland signed a treaty of mutual assistance with the USSR; Finland and Russia nullified this treaty with a new pact in Jan. 1992.

Following approval by Finnish voters in an advisory referendum Oct. 16, 1994, Finland joined the European Union effective Jan. 1, 1995.

Aland, constituting an autonomous department, is a group of small islands, 590 sq. mi., in the Gulf of Bothnia, 25 mi. from Sweden, 15 mi. from Finland. Mariehamn is the principal port.

France
French Republic
République Française

People: Population: 58,109,160. **Age distrib.** (%): <15: 20; 65+: 15. **Pop. density:** 277 per sq. mi. **Urban:** 74%. **Ethnic groups:** A mixture of various European and Mediterranean groups. **Principal languages:** French (official); minorities speak Breton, Alsatian German, Flemish, Italian, Basque, Catalan. **Religion:** Roman Catholic 90%.

Geography: Area: 210,026 sq. mi. **Location:** In western Europe, between Atlantic O. and Mediterranean Sea. **Neighbors:** Spain on S, Italy, Switzerland, Germany on E, Luxembourg, Belgium on N. **Topography:** A wide plain covers more than half of the country, in N and W, drained to W by Seine, Loire, Garonne rivers. The Massif Central is a mountainous plateau in center. In E are Alps (Mt. Blanc is tallest in W Europe, 15,771 ft.), the lower Jura range, and the forested Vosges. The Rhone flows from Lake Geneva to Mediterranean. Pyrenees are in SW, on border with Spain. **Capital:** Paris. **Cities** (1990 est.): Paris 2.2 mln.; Marseille 801,000; Lyon 415,000; Toulouse 359,000; Nice 342,000; Strasbourg 252,000; Nantes 245,000; Bordeaux 210,000.

Government: Type: Republic. **Head of state:** Pres. Jacques Chirac; b Nov. 29, 1932; in office: May 17, 1995. **Head of government:** Prime Min. Alain Juppe; b Aug. 15, 1945; in office: May 17, 1995. **Local divisions:** 22 administrative regions containing 96 departments. **Defense:** 3.1% of GDP (1993 est.). **Active troop strength:** 409,600.

Economy: Industries: Steel, chemicals, textiles, tourism, wine, perfume, aircraft, electronic equipment. **Chief crops:** Grains, corn, rice, fruits, vegetables. France is largest food producer, exporter, in W Eur. **Minerals:** Bauxite, iron, coal. **Crude oil reserves** (1994): 177 mln. bbls. **Other resources:** Forests. **Arable land:** 32%. **Livestock** (1992): cattle: 20.9 mln.; pigs: 12.4 mln.; sheep: 10.6 mln. **Fish catch** (1991): 813,000 metric tons. **Electricity prod.** (1992): 426 bln. kWh. **Labor force:** 7% agric.; 31% ind.; 62% services.

Finance: Monetary unit: Franc (May 1995: 4.88 = $1 US). **Gross domestic product** (1993): $1.05 trl.* **Per capita GDP:** $18,200. **Imports** (1993): $250 bln.; partners: Germany 18%, Italy 11%, U.S. 10%. **Exports** (1993): $271 bln.; partners: Germany 19%, Italy 11%, Spain 11%, U.S. 6%. **Tourism** (1992): $25.0 bln. **National budget** (1993): $249.1 bln. **International reserves less gold** (Mar. 1995): $26.8 bln. **Gold:** 81.85 mln. oz t. **Consumer prices** (change in 1994): 1.7%.

Transport: Railroads: Length: 21,160 mi. **Motor vehicles:** in use: 24.0 mln. passenger cars, 5.0 mln. comm. vehicles. **Civil aviation:** 26.8 bln. passenger-mi.; 63 airports with scheduled flights. **Chief ports:** Marseille, Le Havre, Nantes, Bordeaux, Rouen.

Communications: Television sets: 1 per 2 persons. **Radios:** 1 per 1.2 persons. **Telephones:** 1 per 1.9 persons. **Daily newspaper circ.:** 210 per 1,000 pop.

Health: Life expectancy at birth (1995): 74 male; 82 female. **Births** (per 1,000 pop.): 13. **Deaths** (per 1,000 pop.): 9. **Natural increase:** 0.4%. **Hospital beds:** 1 per 81 persons. **Physicians:** 1 per 374 persons. **Infant mortality** (per 1,000 live births 1995): 6.

Education: Literacy (1992): 99%. **Years compulsory:** 10.

Major International Organizations: UN and most of its specialized agencies, OECD, EU, NATO.

Embassy: 4101 Reservoir Rd. NW 20007; 944-6000.

Celtic Gaul was conquered by Julius Caesar 58-51 BC; Romans ruled for 500 years. Under Charlemagne, Frankish rule extended over much of Europe. After his death France emerged as one of the successor kingdoms.

The monarchy was overthrown by the French Revolution (1789-93) and succeeded by the First Republic; followed by the First Empire under Napoleon (1804-15), a monarchy (1814-48), the Second Republic (1848-52), the Second Empire (1852-70), the Third Republic (1871-1946), the Fourth Republic (1946-58), and the Fifth Republic (1958 to present).

France suffered severe losses in manpower and wealth in the first World War, 1914-18, when it was invaded by Germany. By the Treaty of Versailles, France exacted return of Alsace and Lorraine, French provinces seized by Germany in 1871. Germany invaded France again in May, 1940, and signed an armistice with a government based in Vichy. After France was liberated by the Allies Sept. 1944, Gen. Charles de Gaulle became head of the provisional government, serving until 1946.

De Gaulle again became premier in 1958, during a crisis over Algeria, and obtained voter approval for a new constitution, ushering in the Fifth Republic. Using strong executive powers, he promoted French economic and technological advances in the context of the European Economic Community and guarded French foreign policy independence.

France had withdrawn from Indochina in 1954, and from Morocco and Tunisia in 1956. Most of its remaining African territories were freed 1958-62. In 1966, France withdrew all its troops from the integrated military command of NATO, though 60,000 remained stationed in Germany.

In May 1968 rebellious students in Paris and other centers rioted, battled police, and were joined by workers who launched nationwide strikes. The government awarded pay increases to the strikers May 26. De Gaulle resigned from office in Apr. 1969, after losing a nationwide referendum on constitutional reform.

On May 10, 1981, France elected François Mitterrand, a Socialist candidate, president. In Sept., the government nationalized 5 major industries and most private banks. From 1986 to 1993, however, France pursued a privatization program in which many state-owned companies were sold. Mitterrand was elected to a 2d 7-year term in 1988.

In 1993, France set tighter rules for entry into the country and made it easier for the government to expel foreigners. In June 1994, France sent troops to Rwanda in an effort to help protect civilians there from ongoing massacres.

The international terrorist known as Carlos the Jackal (Ilich Ramirez Sánchez) was arrested in Sudan Aug. 14, 1994, and extradited to France, where he had been sentenced in absentia to life imprisonment.

Jacques Chirac won the presidency in a runoff election May 7, 1995. A series of terrorist bombings and bombing attempts began in the summer of 1995; Islamic extremists, opposed to France's support of the Algerian government and its struggle with Islamic fundamentalists, were believed responsible. In Sept. 1995, France stirred widespread protests by resuming nuclear tests at Mururoa Atoll, in the South Pacific, after a 3-year moratorium.

The island of **Corsica,** in the Mediterranean W of Italy and N of Sardinia, is an official region of France comprising 2 departments. Area: 3,369 sq. mi.; pop. (1990 cen.): 249,700. The capital is Ajaccio, birthplace of Napoleon.

Overseas Departments

French Guiana is on the NE coast of South America with Suriname on the W and Brazil on the E and S. Its area is 33,399 sq. mi.; pop. (1995 est.): 145,270. Guiana sends one senator and one deputy to the French Parliament. Guiana is administered by a prefect and has a Council General of 16 elected members; capital is Cayenne.

The famous penal colony, Devil's Island, was phased out between 1938 and 1951.

Immense forests of rich timber cover 90% of the land. Placer gold mining is the most important industry. Exports are shrimp, timber, and machinery.

Guadeloupe, in the West Indies' Leeward Islands, consists of 2 large islands, Basse-Terre and Grande-Terre, separated by the Salt River, plus Marie Galante and the Saintes group to the S and, to the N, Desirade, St. Barthelemy and over half of St. Martin (the Netherlands portion is St. Maarten). A French possession since 1635, the department is represented in the French Parliament by 2 senators and 3 deputies; administration consists of a prefect (governor) and an elected general and regional councils.

Area of the islands is 687 sq. mi.; pop. (1995 est.) 403,000, mainly descendants of slaves; capital is Basse-Terre on Basse-Terre Is. The land is fertile; sugar, rum, and bananas are exported; tourism is an important industry.

Martinique, the northernmost of the Windward Islands, in the West Indies, has been a possession since 1635, and a department since Mar. 1946. It is represented in the French Parliament by 2 senators and 3 deputies. The island was the birthplace of Napoleon's Empress Josephine.

It has an area of 436 sq. mi.; pop. (1995 est.) 395,000, mostly descendants of slaves. The capital is Fort-de-France (pop. 1991: 101,000). It is a popular tourist stop. The chief exports are rum, bananas, and petroleum products.

Réunion is a volcanic island in the Indian O. about 420 mi. E of Madagascar, and has belonged to France since 1665. Area, 970 sq. mi.; pop. (1995 est.) 666,000, 30% of French extraction. Capital: Saint-Denis. The chief export is sugar. It elects 3 deputies, 2 senators to the French Parliament.

Territorial Collectivities

Mayotte, claimed by Comoros and administered by France, voted in 1976 to become a territorial collectivity of France. An island NW of Madagascar, area is 144 sq. mi., pop. (1995 est.) 97,000.

St. Pierre and Miquelon, formerly an Overseas Territory (1816-1976) and department (1976-85), made the transition to territorial collectivity in 1985. It consists of 2 groups of rocky islands near the SW coast of Newfoundland, inhabited by fishermen. The exports are chiefly fish products. The St. Pierre group has an area of 10 sq. mi.; Miquelon, 83 sq. mi. Total pop. (1995 est.), 6,757. The capital is St. Pierre. A deputy and a senator are elected to the French Parliament.

Overseas Territories

French Polynesia Overseas Territory comprises 130 islands widely scattered among 5 archipelagos in the South Pacific; administered by a governor. Territorial Assembly and a Council with headquarters at Papeete, Tahiti, one of the **Society Islands** (which include the **Windward** and **Leeward** islands). A deputy and a senator are elected to the French Parliament.

Other groups are the **Marquesas Islands,** the **Tuamotu Archipelago,** including the **Gambier Islands,** and the **Austral Islands.**

Total area of the islands administered from Tahiti is 1,544 sq. mi.; pop. (1995 est.), 220,000, more than half on Tahiti. Tahiti is picturesque and mountainous with a productive coastline bearing coconut, banana and orange trees, sugar cane and vanilla.

Tahiti was visited by Capt. James Cook in 1769 and by Capt. Bligh in the Bounty, 1788-89. Its beauty impressed Herman Melville, Paul Gauguin, and Charles Darwin. Tahitians angered by French nuclear testing rioted Sept. 1995.

French Southern and Antarctic Lands Overseas Territory comprises **Adelie Land,** on Antarctica, and 4 island groups in the Indian O. Adelie, reached 1840, has a research station, a coastline of 185 mi., and tapers 1,240 mi. inland to the South Pole. The U.S. does not recognize national claims in Antarctica. There are 2 huge glaciers, Ninnis, 22 mi. wide, 99 mi. long, and Mentz, 11 mi. wide, 140 mi. long. The Indian O. groups are:

Kerguelen Archipelago, visited 1772, consists of one large and 300 small islands. The chief is 87 mi. long, 74 mi. wide, and has Mt. Ross, 6,429 ft. tall. Principal research station is Port-aux-Français. Seals often weigh 2 tons; there are blue whales, coal, peat, semi-precious stones. **Crozet Archipelago,** reached 1772, covers 195 sq. mi. Eastern Island rises to 6,560 ft. **Saint Paul,** in southern Indian O., has warm springs with earth at places heating to 120° to 390° F. **Amsterdam** is nearby; both produce cod and rock lobster.

New Caledonia and its dependencies, an overseas territory, are a group of islands in the Pacific O. about 1,115 mi. E of Australia and approx. the same distance NW of New Zealand. Dependencies are the **Loyalty Islands,** the **Isle of Pines, Huon Islands,** and the **Chesterfield Islands.**

The largest island, New Caledonia, is 6,530 sq. mi. Total area of the territory is 8,548 sq. mi.; population (1995 est.) 185,000. The group was acquired by France in 1853.

The territory is administered by a governor and government council. There is a popularly elected Territorial Assembly. A deputy and a senator are elected to the French Parliament. Capital: Noumea.

Mining is the chief industry. New Caledonia is one of the world's largest nickel producers. Other minerals found are chrome, iron, cobalt, manganese, silver, gold, lead, and copper. Agricultural products include coffee, copra, cotton, manioc (cassava), corn, tobacco, bananas, and pineapples.

In 1987, New Caledonian voters chose by referendum to remain within the French Republic. There were clashes between French and Melanesians (Kanaks) in 1988.

Wallis and Futuna Islands, 2 archipelagos raised to status of overseas territory July 29, 1961, are in the SW Pacific S of the Equator between Fiji and Samoa. The islands have a total area of 106 sq. mi. and population (1995 est.) of 14,500. **Alofi,** attached to Futuna, is uninhabited. Capital: Mata-Utu. Chief products are copra, yams, taro roots, bananas. A senator and a deputy are elected to the French Parliament.

Gabon
Gabonese Republic
République Gabonaise

People: Population: 1,155,749. **Pop. density:** 11 per sq. mi. **Urban:** 73%. **Ethnic groups:** Fang 25%, Bapounou 10%, other Bantu. **Principal languages:** French (official), Bantu dialects. **Religions:** mostly Christian, some animist.

Geography: Area: 103,347 sq. mi. **Location:** On Atlantic coast of central Africa. **Neighbors:** Equatorial Guinea, Cameroon on N, Congo on E and S. **Topography:** Heavily forested, the country consists of coastal lowlands; plateaus in N, E, and S; mountains in N, SE, and center. The Ogooue R. system covers most of Gabon. **Capital:** Libreville (1991 est.): 275,000.

Government: Type: Republic. **Head of state:** Pres. Omar Bongo; b Dec. 30, 1935; in office: Dec. 2, 1967. **Head of gov-**

ernment: Prime Min. Paulin Obame-Nguema; in office: Nov. 2, 1994. **Local divisions:** 9 provinces. **Defense:** 3.2% of GDP (1990 est.). **Active troop strength:** 4,700.

Economy: Industries: Oil products. **Chief crops:** Cocoa, coffee, rice, palm products. **Minerals:** Manganese, uranium, oil, iron. **Crude oil reserves** (1994): 730 mln. bbls. **Other resources:** Timber. **Arable land:** 1%. **Electricity prod.** (1991): 995 mln. kWh. **Labor force:** 65% agric.; 30% ind. & commerce.

Finance: Monetary unit: CFA Franc (May 1995: 488 = $1 US). **Gross domestic product** (1993): $5.4 bln.* **Per capita income:** $4,800. **Imports** (1992): $702 mln.; partners: France 64%. **Exports** (1992): $2.3 bln.; partners: France 48%, U.S. 15%. **National budget** (1992): $1.5 bln. **Consumer prices** (change in 1992): –0.9%.

Transport: Motor vehicles: in use: 23,000 passenger cars, 17,000 comm. vehicles. **Civil aviation:** 277 mln. passenger-mi.; 16 airports. **Chief ports:** Port-Gentil, Owendo, Mayumba.

Communications: Television sets: 1 per 28 persons. **Radios:** 1 per 4.5 persons. **Telephones:** 1 per 42 persons.

Health: Life expectancy at birth (1995): 52 male; 58 female. **Births** (per 1,000 pop.): 28. **Deaths** (per 1,000 pop.): 14. **Natural increase:** 1.5%. **Hospital beds:** 1 per 103 persons. **Physicians:** 1 per 2,337 persons. **Infant mortality** (per 1,000 live births 1995): 92.

Education: Literacy (1991): 70%. Compulsory to age 16; attendance: 100% primary, 14% secondary.

Major International Organizations: UN (WTO, IMF, World Bank), OAU, OPEC.

Embassy: 2034 20th St. NW 20009; 797-1000.

France established control over the region in the second half of the 19th century. Gabon became independent Aug. 17, 1960. A multiparty political system was introduced in 1990, and a new constitution was enacted Mar. 14, 1991. However, the reelection of longtime Pres. Omar Bongo, on Dec. 5, 1993, prompted rioting and charges of vote fraud. A crackdown on W African immigrants led to the departure of 55,000 foreign workers by mid-Feb. 1995.

Gabon is one of the most prosperous black African countries, thanks to abundant natural resources, foreign private investment, and government development programs.

The Gambia
Republic of The Gambia

People: Population: 989,273. **Age distrib.** (%): <15: 45; 65+: 2. **Pop. density:** 240 per sq. mi. **Urban:** 26%. **Ethnic groups:** Mandinka 42%, Fula 18%, Wolof 16%, others. **Principal languages:** English (official), Mandinka, Wolof. **Religions:** Muslim 90%, Christian 9%.

Geography: Area: 4,127 sq. mi. **Location:** On Atlantic coast near W tip of Africa. **Neighbors:** Surrounded on 3 sides by Senegal. **Topography:** A narrow strip of land on each side of the lower Gambia R. **Capital:** Banjul (1993 est.): 40,000.

Government: Type: Military. **Head of state and government:** Lieut. Yahya Jammeh; in office: July 23, 1994. **Local divisions:** 5 divisions and Banjul. **Defense:** Active troop strength: 800.

Economy: Industries: Tourism, peanut processing. **Chief crops:** Peanuts (main export), rice. **Arable land:** 16%. **Fish catch** (1992): 23,000 metric tons. **Electricity prod.** (1991): 65 mln. kWh. **Labor force:** 75% agric.; 19% ind., comm., serv.

Finance: Monetary unit: Dalasi (May 1995: 9.55 = $1.00 US). **Gross domestic product** (1993): $740 mln.* **Per capita GDP:** $800. **Imports** (1992): $214 mln.; partners: Europe 57%. **Exports** (1992): $164 mln.; partners: Japan 60%. **Tourism** (1992): $56 mln. **National budget** (1990): $80 mln. expenditures. **International reserves less gold** (Feb. 1995): $92.8 mln. **Consumer prices** (change in 1994): 1.7%.

Transport: Motor vehicles: in use: 6,000 passenger cars, 2,500 comm. vehicles. **Chief port:** Banjul.

Communications: Radios: 1 per 5.7 persons. **Telephones:** 1 per 80 persons.

Health: Life expectancy at birth (1995): 48 male; 53 female. **Births** (per 1,000 pop.): 46. **Deaths** (per 1,000 pop.): 15. **Natural increase:** 3.1%. **Physicians:** 1 per 14,536 persons. **Infant mortality** (per 1,000 live births 1995): 121.

Education: Literacy (1993): 30%.

Major International Organizations: UN (IMF, WHO), OAU, the Commonwealth.

Embassy: 1155 15th St. 20005; 785-1399.

The tribes of Gambia were at one time associated with the West African empires of Ghana, Mali, and Songhay. The area became Britain's first African possession in 1588.

Independence came Feb. 18, 1965; republic status within the Commonwealth was achieved in 1970. After a coup attempt in 1981, The Gambia formed the confederation of Senegambia with Senegal that lasted until 1989. The country suffered from severe famine in the 1970s.

On July 23, 1994, after 24 years in power, Pres. Dawda K. Jawara was deposed in a bloodless coup by Lieut. Yahya Jammeh. Jammeh barred political activity, detained potential opponents, and governed by decree. A return to civilian rule has been promised by July 1996.

Georgia
Republic of Georgia
Sakartvelos Respublika

People: Population: 5,725,972. **Pop. density:** 213 per sq. mi. **Urban:** 56%. **Ethnic groups:** Georgian 70%, Armenian 8%, Russian 6%. **Principal languages:** Georgian (official), Russian. **Religions:** Georgian Orthodox 65%, Muslim 11%, Russian Orthodox 10%.

Geography: Area: 26,900 sq. mi. **Location:** In SW Asia, on E coast of Black Sea. **Neighbors:** Russia on N, NE, Turkey, Armenia on S, Azerbaijan on SE. **Topography:** Separated from Russia on NE by main range of the Caucasus Mts. **Capital:** Tbilisi (1991): 1.3 mln.

Government: Type: Republic. **Head of state:** Pres. Eduard A. Shevardnadze; b Jan. 25, 1928; in office: Nov. 6, 1992. **Defense:** 1.5% of GNP (1992).

Economy: Industries: Manganese mining, tourism. **Chief crops:** Citrus fruits, wheat, grapes. **Minerals:** Manganese, iron. **Livestock** (1993): cattle: 1.1 mln.; sheep and goats: 1.4 mln. **Electricity prod.** (1992): 15.8 bln. kWh. **Labor force:** 25% agric.; 31% ind.

Finance: Monetary unit: Coupon (Sept. 1994: 2.5 mln. = $1 U.S.). **Gross domestic product** (1993 est.): $7.8 bln.* **Per capita GDP:** $1,390. **Imports** (1990): $1.5 bln. **Exports** (1990): $176 mln.

Transport: Railroads: Length: 976 mi. **Motor vehicles:** in use: 427,000 passenger cars.

Communications: Telephones: 1 per 5.5 persons. **Daily newspaper circ.:** 671 per 1,000 pop.

Health: Life expectancy at birth (1995): 69 male; 77 female. **Births** (per 1,000 pop.): 16. **Deaths** (per 1,000 pop.): 9. **Natural increase:** 0.7%. **Hospital beds:** 1 per 90 persons. **Physicians:** 1 per 170 persons. **Infant mortality** (per 1,000 live births 1995): 23.

Education: Literacy (1990): 99%.

Major International Organizations: UN, CIS.

Embassy: 1511 K St. NW 20005; 393-6060.

The region contained the ancient kingdoms of Colchis and Iberia. It was Christianized in the 4th century and conquered by Arabs in the 8th century. The region expanded to include area from the Black Sea to Caspian and parts of Armenia and Persia before its disintegration under the impact of Mongol and Turkish invasions. The annexation to Russia in 1801 caused the Russian war with Persia, 1804-1813. Georgia entered the USSR in 1922 and became a constituent republic in 1936.

In 1989, strong nationalist feelings led the USSR to attempts at repression; Soviet troops attacked nationalist demonstrators in April, killing some 20 persons. Georgia declared independence Apr. 9, 1991. It became an independent state when the Soviet Union disbanded Dec. 26, 1991.

There was fighting during 1991 between rebel forces and loyalists of Pres. Zviad Gamsakhurdia, who fled the capital Jan. 6, 1992. The ruling Military Council picked former Soviet Foreign Minister Eduard A. Shevardnadze to chair a newly created State Council. An attempted coup by forces loyal to Gamsakhurdia was crushed June 24, 1992. Shevardnadze was later elected president. Gamsakhurdia died Jan. 1994, reportedly by suicide.

In Abkhazia, an autonomous region within Georgia, ethnic Abkhazis, reportedly aided by Russia, launched a bloody military campaign and, by late 1993, had gained control of much of the region. A cease-fire providing for Russian peacekeepers was signed in Moscow May 14, 1994.

On Feb. 3, 1994, Georgia signed agreements with Russia for economic and military cooperation. On Mar. 1, Georgia's Supreme Council ratified membership by Georgia in the Commonwealth of Independent States.

Shevardnadze was wounded by a car bomb Aug. 29, 1995, while on his way to Parliament to sign a new constitution. Presidential elections were scheduled for Nov. 5.

Germany

Federal Republic of Germany

Bundesrepublik Deutschland

(Figures prior to 1990 for original 11 states)

People: Population: 81,337,541. **Age distrib.** (%): <15: 16; 65+: 15. **Pop. density:** 590 per sq. mi. **Urban:** 85%. **Ethnic groups:** German 95%. **Principal language:** German. **Religions:** Protestant 45%, Roman Catholic 37%.

Geography: Area: 137,823 sq. mi. **Location:** In central Europe. **Neighbors:** Denmark on N, Netherlands, Belgium, Luxembourg, France on W, Switzerland, Austria on S, Czech Rep., Poland on E. **Topography:** Germany is flat in N, hilly in center and W, and mountainous in Bavaria. Chief rivers are Elbe, Weser, Ems, Rhine, and Main, all flowing toward North Sea, and Danube, flowing toward Black Sea. **Capital:** Berlin. **Cities** (1992 est.): Berlin 3.5 mln.; Hamburg 1.7 mln.; Munich 1.2 mln.; Cologne 959,000; Frankfurt 661,000; Essen 628,000; Dortmund 601,000; Stuttgart 597,000; Düsseldorf 577,000; Leipzig 500,000; Nürnberg 498,000; Dresden 483,000.

Government: Type: Federal republic. **Head of state:** Pres. Roman Herzog; b Apr. 5, 1934; in office: July 1, 1994. **Head of government:** Chan. Helmut Kohl; b Apr. 3, 1930; in office: Oct. 1, 1982. **Local divisions:** 16 laender (states) with substantial powers. **Defense:** 2.2% of GDP (1992). **Active troop strength:** 367,300.

Economy: Industries: Steel, ships, vehicles, machinery, electronics, coal, chemicals. **Chief crops:** Grains, potatoes, sugar beets. **Minerals:** Coal, potash, lignite, iron, uranium. **Crude oil reserves** (1994): 449 mln. bbls. **Arable land:** 34%. **Livestock** (1992-93): cattle: 16.2 mln.; pigs: 26.5 mln. **Fish catch** (1992): 258,500 metric tons. **Electricity prod.** (1992): 580 bln. kWh. **Labor force:** 6% agric.; 41% ind.

Finance: Monetary unit: Mark (May 1995: 1.39 = $1 US). **Gross domestic product** (1993): $1,331 trl.* **Per capita GDP:** $16,500. **Imports** (1993): $375 bln.; partners: EU 50%; U.S. 6%. **Exports** (1993): $392 bln.; partners: EU 51%, U.S. 7%. **Tourism** (1992): $10.9 bln. **National budget** (1992): $972 bln. **International reserves less gold** (May 1995): $82 bln. **Gold:** 95.18 mln. oz t. **Consumer prices** (change in 1994): 3.0%.

Transport: Railroads: Length: 56,813. mi. **Motor vehicles:** in use: 32.7 mln. passenger cars, 1.8 mln. comm. vehicles. **Civil aviation:** 12.6 bln. passenger-mi.; 40 airports with scheduled flights. **Chief ports:** Hamburg, Bremen, Bremerhaven, Lubeck.

Communications: Television sets: 1 per 2.5 persons. **Radios:** 1 per 2.3 persons. **Telephones:** 1 per 1.7 persons. **Daily newspaper circ.:** 402 per 1,000 pop.

Health: Life expectancy at birth (1995): 73 male; 80 female. **Births** (per 1,000 pop.): 11. **Deaths** (per 1,000 pop.): 11. **Natural increase:** 0. **Hospital beds:** 1 per 126 persons. **Physicians:** 1 per 313 persons. **Infant mortality** (per 1,000 live births 1995): 6.

Education: Literacy (1993): 100%. **Years compulsory:** 9 or 10; attendance 100%.

Major International Organizations: UN and all of its specialized agencies, EU, OECD, NATO.

Embassy: 4645 Reservoir Rd. NW 20007; 298-4000.

Germany, prior to World War II, was a central European nation composed of numerous states which had a common language and traditions and which had been united in one country since 1871; since World War II until 1990, had been split in 2 parts.

History and government. Germanic tribes were defeated by Julius Caesar, 55 and 53 BC, but Roman expansion N of the Rhine was stopped in 9 AD. Charlemagne, ruler of the Franks, consolidated Saxon, Bavarian, Rhenish, Frankish, and other lands; after him the eastern part became the German Empire. The Thirty Years' War, 1618-1648, split Germany into small principalities and kingdoms. After Napoleon, Austria contended with Prussia for dominance, but lost the Seven Weeks' War to Prussia, 1866. Otto von Bismarck, Prussian chancellor, formed the North German Confederation, 1867.

In 1870 Bismarck maneuvered Napoleon III into declaring war. After the quick defeat of France, Bismarck formed the **German Empire** and on Jan. 18, 1871, in Versailles, proclaimed King Wilhelm I of Prussia German emperor (Deutscher kaiser).

The German Empire reached its peak before World War I in 1914, with 208,780 sq. mi., plus a colonial empire. After that war Germany ceded Alsace-Lorraine to France; West Prussia and Posen (Poznan) province to Poland; part of Schleswig to Denmark; lost all of its colonies and the ports of Memel and Danzig.

Republic of Germany, 1919-1933, adopted the Weimar constitution; met reparation payments and elected Friedrich Ebert and Gen. Paul von Hindenburg presidents.

Third Reich, 1933-1945, Adolf Hitler led the National Socialist German Workers' (Nazi) party after World War I. In 1923 he attempted to unseat the Bavarian government and was imprisoned. Pres. von Hindenburg named Hitler chancellor Jan. 30, 1933; on Aug. 3, 1934, the day after Hindenburg's death, the cabinet joined the offices of president and chancellor and made Hitler fuehrer (leader). Hitler abolished freedom of speech and assembly, and began a long series of persecutions climaxed by the murder of millions of Jews and opponents.

Hitler repudiated the Versailles treaty and reparations agreements. He remilitarized the Rhineland (1936) and annexed Austria (Anschluss, 1938). At Munich he made an agreement with Neville Chamberlain, British prime minister, which permitted Germany to annex part of Czechoslovakia. He signed a nonaggression treaty with the USSR, 1939. He declared war on Poland Sept. 1, 1939, precipitating World War II.

With total defeat near, Hitler committed suicide in Berlin Apr. 1945. The victorious Allies voided all acts and annexations of Hitler's Reich.

Postwar changes. The zones of occupation administered by the Allied Powers and later relinquished gave the USSR Saxony, Saxony-Anhalt, Thuringia, and Mecklenburg, and the former Prussian provinces of Saxony and Brandenburg. The territory E of the Oder-Neisse line within 1937 boundaries, comprising Silesia, Pomerania, and the southern part of East Prussia, was taken by Poland. Northern East Prussia was taken by the USSR.

The Western Allies ended the state of war with Germany in 1951. The USSR did so in 1955.

There was also created the area of Greater Berlin, within but not part of the Soviet zone, administered by the 4 occupying powers under the Allied Command. In 1948 the USSR withdrew, established its single command in East Berlin, and cut off supplies. The Allies utilized a gigantic airlift to bring food to West Berlin, 1948-49. In Aug. 1961 the East Germans built a wall dividing Berlin, after over 3 million E Germans had emigrated.

On Nov. 9, 1989 the E German government announced the decision to open the border with the West, signaling the end of the infamous Berlin Wall.

A New Era: As Communism was being rejected in E Germany, talks began concerning German reunification. At a meeting in Ottawa, Feb. 1990, the foreign ministers of the World War II "Big Four" Allied nations—U.S., USSR, UK, and France—and of E Germany and W Germany reached agreement on a format for high-level talks on German reunification.

In May, NATO ministers adopted a package of proposals on reunification, including the inclusion of the united Germany as a full member of NATO and the barring of the new Germany from having its own nuclear, chemical, or biological weapons. In July, the USSR agreed to conditions that would allow Germany to become a member of NATO.

The 2 nations agreed to monetary unification under the W German mark beginning in July. The merger of the 2 Germanys took place on Oct. 3, 1990, and the first all-German elections since 1932 were held Dec. 2, 1990.

In 1992, neo-Nazi groups intensified their campaign against refugees. Parliament approved constitutional changes to restrict foreigners' rights to seek asylum in Germany, May 1993.

Germany's highest court ruled, July 12, 1994, that German troops could participate in international military missions abroad, when approved by Parliament. Ceremonies were held marking the final withdrawal of Russian troops from Germany, Aug. 31, 1994. Ceremonies were held the following week marking the final withdrawal of American, British, and French troops from Berlin. General elections Oct. 16, 1994, left Chancellor Helmut Kohl's governing coalition with a slim parliamentary majority.

East Germany

The German Democratic Republic was proclaimed in the Soviet sector of Berlin Oct. 7, 1949. It was proclaimed fully sovereign in 1954, but Soviet troops remained on grounds of security and the 4-power Potsdam agreement.

Coincident with the entrance of W Germany into the European defense community in 1952, the E German government decreed a prohibited zone 3 miles deep along its 600-mile border with W Germany and cut Berlin's telephone system in two. Berlin was further divided by erection of a fortified wall in 1961, but an exodus of refugees to the West continued, though on a smaller scale.

E Germany suffered severe economic problems at least until the mid-1960s. Then a "new economic system" was introduced, easing central planning controls and allowing factories to make profits provided they were reinvested in operations or redistributed to workers as bonuses. By the early 1970s, the economy was highly industrialized; and the nation was credited with the highest standard of living among Warsaw Pact countries. But growth slowed in the late 1970s, because of shortages of natural resources and labor, and a huge debt to lenders in the West. Comparison with the lifestyle in the West caused many of the young to leave the country.

The government firmly resisted following the USSR's policy of *glasnost*, but by Oct. 1989, was faced with nationwide demonstrations demanding reform. Pres. Erich Honecker, in office since 1976, was forced to resign, Oct. 18. On Nov. 4, the border with Czechoslovakia was opened and permission granted for refugees to travel on to the West. On Nov. 9, the decision was made to open the border with the West, signaling the end of the "Berlin Wall," which separated the 2 Germanys and was the supreme emblem of the cold war.

On Aug. 23, 1990, the E German Parliament agreed to formal unification with W Germany; this took place on Oct. 3.

West Germany

The Federal Republic of Germany was proclaimed May 23, 1949, in Bonn, after a constitution had been drawn up by a consultative assembly formed by representatives of the 11 laender (states) in the French, British, and American zones. Later reorganized into 9 units, the laender numbered 10 with the addition of the Saar, 1957. Berlin also was granted land (state) status, but the 1945 occupation agreements placed restrictions on it.

The occupying powers, the U.S., Britain, and France, restored the civil status, Sept. 21, 1949. The U.S. resumed diplomatic relations July 2, 1951. The powers lifted controls and the republic became fully independent May 5, 1955.

Dr. Konrad Adenauer, Christian Democrat, was made chancellor Sept. 15, 1949, reelected 1953, 1957, 1961. Willy Brandt, heading a coalition of Social Democrats and Free Democrats, became chancellor Oct. 21, 1969. (He resigned May 1974 because of a spy scandal.)

In 1970 Brandt signed friendship treaties with the USSR and Poland. In 1971, the U.S., Britain, France, and the USSR signed an agreement on Western access to West Berlin. In 1972 E and W Germany signed their first formal treaty, implementing the agreement easing access to West Berlin. In 1973 a W Germany-Czechoslovakia pact normalized relations and nullified the 1938 "Munich Agreement."

W Germany experienced strong economic growth since the 1950s. The country led Europe in provisions for worker participation in the management of industry.

A NATO decision to deploy medium-range nuclear missiles in Western Europe sparked a demonstration by some 400,000 protesters in 1983. In 1989, Chancellor Helmut Kohl's call for early negotiations with the Soviets on reducing short-range missiles caused a rift with NATO allies.

In 1989, the changes in the E German government and the opening of the Berlin Wall sparked talk of reunification of the 2 Germanys. In 1990, under the leadership of Chancellor Kohl, W Germany moved rapidly to reunite with E Germany.

Helgoland, an island of 130 acres in the North Sea, was taken from Denmark by a British Naval Force in 1807 and later ceded to Germany to become a part of Schleswig-Holstein province in return for rights in East Africa. The heavily fortified island was surrendered to UK, May 23, 1945, demilitarized in 1947, and returned to W Germany, Mar 1, 1952. It is a free port.

Ghana
Republic of Ghana

People: Population: 17,763,138. **Age distrib.** (%): <15: 45; 65+: 3. **Pop. density:** 193 per sq. mi. **Urban:** 36%. **Ethnic groups:** Akan 44%, Moshi-Dagomba 16%, Ewe 13%, Ga 8%, others. **Principal languages:** English (official), Akan, Moshi-Dagomba, Ewe, Ga. **Religions:** indigenous beliefs 38%, Muslim 30%, Christian 24%.

Geography: Area: 92,098 sq. mi. **Location:** On southern coast of W Africa. **Neighbors:** Côte D'Ivoire on W, Burkina Faso on N, Togo on E. **Topography:** Most of Ghana consists of low fertile plains and scrubland, cut by rivers and by the artificial Lake Volta. **Capital:** Accra (1988 est.): 949,000.

Government: Type: Republic. **Head of state and government:** Pres. Jerry Rawlings; b 1947; in office: Dec. 31, 1981. **Local divisions:** 10 regions. **Defense:** 0.6% of GNP (1991). **Active troop strength:** 6,850.

Economy: Industries: Aluminum, light industry. **Chief crops:** Cocoa, coffee, rice. **Minerals:** Gold, manganese, indus-

trial diamonds, bauxite. **Other resources:** Timber, rubber. **Arable land:** 5%. **Livestock** (1993): cattle: 1.2 mln.; sheep: 2.2 mln. **Fish catch** (1991): 364,959 metric tons. **Electricity prod.** (1991): 4.5 bln. kWh. **Labor force:** 55% agric.; 19% ind.

Finance: Monetary unit: Cedi (May 1995: 1,149 = $1.00 US). **Gross domestic product** (1993): $25 bln.* **Per capita GDP:** $1,500. **Imports** (1992): $1.5 bln.; partners: UK 22%, Germany 9%, U.S. 11%. **Exports** (1992): $1 bln.; partners: Germany 31%, U.S. 12%. **Tourism** (1992): $167 mln. **National budget** (1991 est.): $905 mln. **International reserves less gold** (Dec. 1994): $584 mln. **Gold:** 275,000 oz t. **Consumer prices** (change in 1994): 24.9%.

Transport: Railroads: Length: 592 mi. **Motor vehicles:** in use: 58,000 passenger cars, 30,000 comm. vehicles. **Civil aviation:** 206 mln. passenger-mi.; 1 airport with scheduled flights. **Chief ports:** Tema, Takoradi.

Communications: Television sets: 1 per 61 persons. **Radios:** 1 per 3.8 persons. **Telephones:** 1 per 187 persons.

Health: Life expectancy at birth (1995): 54 male; 58 female. **Births** (per 1,000 pop.): 44. **Deaths** (per 1,000 pop.): 12. **Natural increase:** 3.2%. **Physicians:** 1 per 22,452 persons. **Infant mortality** (per 1,000 live births 1995): 82.

Education: Literacy (1991): 60%.

Major International Organizations: UN and all of its specialized agencies, OAU, the Commonwealth.

Embassy: 3512 International Dr. NW 20008; 686-4520.

Named for an African empire along the Niger River, 400-1240 AD, Ghana was ruled by Britain for 113 years as the Gold Coast. The UN in 1956 approved merger with the British Togoland trust territory. Independence came March 6, 1957. Republic status within the Commonwealth was attained in 1960.

Pres. Kwame Nkrumah built hospitals and schools, promoted development projects like the Volta R. hydroelectric and aluminum plants but ran the country into debt, jailed opponents, and was accused of corruption. A 1964 referendum gave Nkrumah dictatorial powers and set up a one-party socialist state.

Nkrumah was overthrown in 1966 by a police-army coup, which expelled Chinese and East German teachers and technicians. Elections were held in 1969, but 4 further coups occurred in 1972, 1978, 1979, and 1981. The 1979 and 1981 coups, led by Flight Lieut. Jerry Rawlings, were followed by suspension of the constitution and banning of political parties. A new constitution, which allowed for multiparty politics, was approved in April 1992.

In Feb. 1993 more than 1,000 people were killed in ethnic clashes in northern Ghana.

Greece
Hellenic Republic
Elliniki Dimokratia

People: Population: 10,647,511. **Age distrib.** (%): <15: 19; 65+: 14. **Pop. density:** 209 per sq. mi. **Urban:** 63%. **Ethnic groups:** Greek 98%. **Principal languages:** Greek (official), English, French. **Religion:** Greek Orthodox 98% (official).

Geography: Area: 50,949 sq. mi. **Location:** Occupies southern end of Balkan Peninsula in SE Europe. **Neighbors:** Albania, Macedonia, Bulgaria on N, Turkey on E. **Topography:** About 75% of Greece is nonarable, with mountains in all areas. Pindus Mts. run through the country N to S. The heavily indented coastline is 9,385 mi. long. Of over 2,000 islands, only 169 are inhabited, among them Crete, Rhodes, Milos, Kerkira (Corfu), Chios, Lesbos, Samos, Euboea, Delos, Mykonos. **Capital:** Athens. **Cities** (1991 est.): Athens 748,000; Thessaloníki 378,000.

Government: Type: Parliamentary republic. **Head of state:** Pres. Costis Stefanopoulos; b 1926; in office: Mar. 8, 1995. **Head of government:** Prime Min. Andreas Papandreou; b Feb. 5, 1919; in office: Oct. 13, 1993. **Local divisions:** 52 prefectures. **Defense:** 5.1% of GDP (1992). **Active troop strength:** 159,300.

Economy: Industries: Textiles, chemicals, metals, wine, food processing, tourism. **Chief crops:** Grains, corn, rice, cotton, tobacco, olives, citrus fruits, raisins, figs. **Minerals:** Bauxite, lignite, oil, manganese. **Crude oil reserves** (1994): 41 mln. bbls. **Arable land:** 23%. **Livestock** (1993): sheep: 9.7 mln.; goats: 5.8 mln. **Fish catch** (1991): 149,000 metric tons. **Electricity prod.** (1992): 36.4 bln. kWh. **Labor force:** 24% agric.; 28% ind.; 48% services.

Finance: Monetary unit: Drachma (May 1995: 225 = $1 US). **Gross domestic product** (1993): $93.2 bln.* **Per capita GDP:** $8,900. **Imports** (1992): $23.3 bln.; partners: Germany 20%, Italy 14%, France 8%. **Exports** (1992): $6 bln.; partners:

Germany 23%, Italy 18%, France 7%. **Tourism** (1992): $3.3 bln. **National budget** (1994): $37.6 bln. **International reserves less gold** (Jan. 1995): $14.9 bln. **Gold:** 3.4 mln. oz t. **Consumer prices** (change in 1994): 10.9%.

Transport: Railroads: Length: 1,570 mi. **Motor vehicles:** in use: 2.0 mln. passenger cars, 831,000 comm. vehicles. **Civil aviation:** 4.5 bln. passenger-mi.; 34 airports with scheduled flights. **Chief ports:** Piraeus, Thessaloníki, Patras.

Communications: Television sets: 1 per 4.5 persons. **Radios:** 1 per 2.5 persons. **Telephones:** 1 per 1.9 persons.

Health: Life expectancy at birth (1995): 75 male; 81 female. **Births** (per 1,000 pop.): 11. **Deaths** (per 1,000 pop.): 9. **Natural increase:** 0.1%. **Hospital beds:** 1 per 199 persons. **Physicians:** 1 per 303 persons. **Infant mortality** (per 1,000 live births 1995): 8.

Education: Literacy (1993): 93%. **Years compulsory:** 9.

Major International Organizations: UN (WTO, IMF, WHO, ILO), EU, NATO, OECD.

Embassy: 2221 Massachusetts Ave. NW 20008; 939-5800.

The achievements of ancient Greece in art, architecture, science, mathematics, philosophy, drama, literature, and democracy became legacies for succeeding ages. Greece reached the height of its glory and power, particularly in the Athenian city-state, in the 5th century BC.

Greece fell under Roman rule in the 2d and 1st centuries BC. In the 4th century AD it became part of the Byzantine Empire and, after the fall of Constantinople to the Turks in 1453, part of the Ottoman Empire.

Greece won its war of independence from Turkey 1821-1829, and became a kingdom. A republic was established 1924; the monarchy was restored, 1935, and George II, King of the Hellenes, resumed the throne. In Oct. 1940, Greece rejected an ultimatum from Italy. Nazi support resulted in its defeat and occupation by Germans, Italians, and Bulgarians. By the end of 1944 the invaders withdrew. Communist resistance forces were defeated by Royalist and British troops. A plebiscite again restored the monarchy.

Communists waged guerrilla war 1947-49 against the government but were defeated with the aid of the U.S. A period of reconstruction and rapid development followed, mainly with conservative governments under Premier Constantine Karamanlis. The Center Union, led by George Papandreou, won elections in 1963 and 1964, but King Constantine, who acceded in 1964, forced Papandreou to resign. A period of political maneuvers ended in the military takeover of April 21, 1967, by Col. George Papadopoulos. King Constantine tried to reverse the consolidation of the harsh dictatorship Dec. 13, 1967, but failed and fled to Italy. Papadopoulos was ousted Nov. 25, 1973.

Greek army officers serving in the National Guard of Cyprus staged a coup on the island July 15, 1974. Turkey invaded Cyprus a week later, precipitating the collapse of the Greek junta, which was implicated in the Cyprus coup. Democratic government returned (and in 1975 the monarchy was abolished).

The 1981 electoral victory of the Panhellenic Socialist Movement (Pasok) of Andreas Papandreou brought about substantial changes in Greece's internal and external policies. A scandal centered on George Kostokas, a banker and publisher, led to the arrest or investigation of leading Socialists, implicated Papandreou, and contributed to the defeat of the Socialists at the polls in 1989. However, Papandreou, who was narrowly acquitted Jan. 1992 of corruption charges, led the Socialists to a comeback victory in general elections Oct. 10, 1993.

Tensions between Greece and the Former Yugoslav Republic of Macedonia eased when the 2 countries agreed to normalize relations Sept. 13, 1995.

Grenada

People: Population: 94,486. **Pop. density:** 710 per sq. mi. **Ethnic groups:** mostly black African. **Principal languages:** English (official), French patois. **Religions:** Roman Catholic 64%, Anglican 22%.

Geography: Area: 133 sq. mi. **Location:** 90 mi. N of Venezuela. **Topography:** Main island is mountainous; country includes Carriacon and Petit Martinique islands. **Capital:** Saint George's (1991 est.): 4,400.

Government: Type: Parliamentary democracy. **Head of state:** Queen Elizabeth II, represented by Gov.-Gen. Reginald Palmer; b Feb. 15, 1923; in office: Aug. 6, 1992. **Head of government:** Prime Min.: George Brizan; in office: Feb. 1, 1995. **Local divisions:** 6 parishes and 1 dependency.

Economy: Industries: Tourism, spices. **Chief crops:** Nutmeg, bananas, cocoa, mace. **Arable land:** 15%. **Electricity prod.** (1992): 26 mln. kWh. **Labor force:** 24% agric.; 31% services.

Finance: Monetary unit: East Caribbean dollar (May 1995: 2.70 = $1 US). **Gross domestic product** (1992): $250 mln.* **Per capita GDP:** $3,000. **Imports** (1992): $103 mln.; partners: UK 11%, Trin./Tob. 24%, U.S. 27%. **Exports** (1992): $20 mln.; partners: U.S. 35%, UK 23%. **Tourism** (1992): $38 mln. **National budget** (1991 est.): $51 mln. **International reserves less gold** (Feb. 1995): $26.3 mln.

Chief port: Saint George's.

Communications: Radios: 1 per 1.1 persons. **Telephones:** 1 per 3.8 persons.

Health: Life expectancy at birth (1995): 68 male; 73 female. **Births** (per 1,000 pop.): 30. **Deaths** (per 1,000 pop.): 6. **Natural increase:** 2.4%. **Infant mortality** (per 1,000 live births 1995): 12.

Education: Literacy (1994): 85%; **Years compulsory:** ages 6-14.

Major International Organizations: UN (IMF, WHO), OAS, the Commonwealth.

Embassy: 1701 New Hampshire Ave. NW 20009; 265-2561.

Columbus sighted the island 1498. First European settlers were French, 1650. The island was held alternately by France and England until final British occupation, 1784. Grenada became fully independent Feb. 7, 1974 during a general strike. It is the smallest independent nation in the western hemisphere.

On Oct. 14, 1983, a military coup ousted Prime Minister Maurice Bishop, who was put under house arrest, later freed by supporters, rearrested, and, finally, on Oct. 19, executed. U.S. forces, with a token force from 6 area nations, invaded Grenada, Oct. 25. Resistance from the Grenadian army and Cuban advisors was quickly overcome as most of the population welcomed the invading forces. U.S. troops left Grenada in June 1985.

Guatemala
Republic of Guatemala
República de Guatemala

People: Population: 10,998,602. **Age distrib.** (%): <15: 45; 65+: 3. **Pop. density:** 262 per sq. mi. **Urban:** 38%. **Ethnic groups:** mestizo 56%, Indian 44%. **Principal languages:** Spanish (official), Mayan languages. **Religion:** mostly Roman Catholic.

Geography: Area: 42,042 sq. mi. **Location:** In Central America. **Neighbors:** Mexico on N and W, El Salvador on S, Honduras, Belize on E. **Topography:** The central highland and mountain areas are bordered by the narrow Pacific coast and the lowlands and fertile river valleys on the Caribbean. There are numerous volcanoes in S, more than half a dozen over 11,000 ft. **Capital:** Guatemala City (1994 est.): 1.2 mln.

Government: Type: Republic. **Head of state and government:** Pres. Ramiro de León Carpio; b 1942; in office: June 6, 1993. **Local divisions:** 22 departments. **Defense:** 1% of GDP (1993). **Active troop strength:** 44,200.

Economy: Industries: Furniture, tires, textiles. **Chief crops:** Coffee, sugar, bananas, cotton, corn. **Minerals:** Oil, nickel. **Crude oil reserves** (1994): 207 mln. bbls. **Other resources:** Rare woods, fish, chicle. **Arable land:** 12%. **Electricity prod.** (1992): 2.5 bln. kWh. **Labor force:** 60% agric.; 13% services.

Finance: Monetary unit: Quetzal (May 1995: 5.74 = $1 US). **Gross domestic product** (1993): $311.3 bln.* **Per capita GDP:** $3,000. **Imports** (1993): $2.6 bln.; partners: U.S. 45%. **Exports** (1993): $1.3 bln.; partners: U.S. 37%. **Tourism** (1992): $243 mln. **National budget** (1990 est.): $808 mln. **International reserves less gold** (May 1995): $646 mln. **Gold:** 210,000 oz t. **Consumer prices** (change in 1993): 11.8%.

Transport: Motor vehicles: in use: 145,000 passenger cars, 105,000 comm. vehicles. **Civil aviation:** 143 mln. passenger-mi.; 2 airports with scheduled flights. **Chief ports:** Puerto Barrios, San Jose.

Communications: Television sets: 1 per 21 persons. **Radios:** 1 per 25 persons. **Telephones:** 1 per 36 persons. **Daily newspaper circ.:** 21 per 1,000 pop.

Health: Life expectancy at birth (1995): 62 male; 68 female. **Births** (per 1,000 pop.): 35. **Deaths** (per 1,000 pop.): 7. **Natural increase:** 2.7%. **Physicians:** 1 per 2,356 persons. **Infant mortality** (per 1,000 live births 1995): 52.

Education: Literacy (1991): 55%. **Years compulsory:** 6. **Attendance:** 35%.

Major International Organizations: UN (IMF, World Bank), OAS.

Embassy: 2220 R St. NW 20008; 745-4952.

The old Mayan Indian empire flourished in what is today Guatemala for over 1,000 years before the Spanish.

Guatemala was a Spanish colony 1524-1821; briefly a part of Mexico and then of the U.S. of Central America, the republic was established in 1839.

Since 1945 when a liberal government was elected to replace the long-term dictatorship of Jorge Ubico, the country has seen a variety of military and civilian governments and periods of civil war. More than 100,000 people have been killed since 1961, and another 40,000 "disappeared."

Dissident army officers seized power Mar. 23, 1982, denouncing a presidential election as fraudulent and pledging to restore "authentic democracy" to the nation. Political violence caused large numbers of Guatemalans to seek refuge in Mexico. Another military coup occurred Oct. 8, 1983. The nation returned to civilian rule in 1986.

The crisis-ridden government of Pres. Jorge Serrano Elías was ousted by the military June 1, 1993. Ramiro de León Carpio was elected president by Congress June 6. Limited electoral reforms were approved Jan. 30, 1994, in a referendum. A UN report in March 1995 blamed state authorities for a majority of human rights violations in Guatemala.

Guinea
Republic of Guinea
République de Guinée

People: Population: 6,549,336. **Pop. density:** 69 per sq. mi. **Urban:** 29%. **Ethnic groups:** Fulani 40%, Malinke 30%, Soussou 20%, 15 other tribes. **Principal languages:** French (official), Fulani, Malinke. **Religions:** Muslim 85%, Christian 8%.

Geography: Area: 94,926 sq. mi. **Location:** On Atlantic coast of W Africa. **Neighbors:** Guinea-Bissau, Senegal, Mali on N, Côte d'Ivoire on E, Liberia on S. **Topography:** A narrow coastal belt leads to the mountainous middle region, the source of the Gambia, Senegal, and Niger rivers. Upper Guinea, farther inland, is a cooler upland. The SE is forested. **Capital:** Conakry. **Cities** (1989 est.): Conakry 705,000; Kankan 278,000; Labe 273,000; N'Zerekore 250,000.

Government: Type: Republic. **Head of state and government:** Pres. Brig. Gen. Lansana Conté; b 1944; in office: Apr. 5, 1984. **Local divisions:** 33 administrative regions. **Defense:** 1.3% of GNP (1991). **Active troop strength:** 9,700.

Economy: Chief crops: Bananas, pineapples, rice, corn, palm kernels, coffee, honey. **Minerals:** Bauxite, iron, diamonds. **Arable land:** 6%. **Electricity prod.** (1992) 531 mln. kWh. **Labor force:** 82% agric.; 11% ind. & commerce.

Finance: Monetary unit: Franc (May 1995: 989 = $1 US). **Gross domestic product** (1993): $3.1 bln.* **Per capita GDP:** $500. **Imports** (1992): $768 mln.; partners: France 26%. **Exports** (1992): $622 mln.; partners: U.S. 23%. **National budget** (1990): $708 mln. **International reserves less gold** (Apr. 1995): $100 mln.

Transport: Motor vehicles: in use: 23,000 passenger cars, 13,000 comm. vehicles. **Chief port:** Conakry.

Communications: Radios: 1 per 49 persons. **Telephones:** 1 per 317 persons.

Health: Life expectancy at birth (1995): 42 male; 47 female. **Births** (per 1,000 pop.): 43. **Deaths** (per 1,000 pop.): 19. **Natural increase:** 2.4%. **Physicians:** 1 per 7,445 persons. **Infant mortality** (per 1,000 live births 1995): 137.

Education: Literacy (1993): 28% (in French). **Years compulsory:** 6. **Attendance:** 42% primary, 12% secondary.

Major International Organizations: UN and most of its specialized agencies, OAU.

Embassy: 2112 Leroy Pl. NW 20008; 483-9420.

Part of the ancient West African empires, Guinea fell under French control 1849-98. Under Sékou Touré, it opted for full independence in 1958, and France withdrew all aid.

Touré turned to Communist nations for support and set up a militant one-party state. Thousands of opponents were jailed in the 1970s, in the aftermath of an unsuccessful Portuguese invasion. Many were tortured and killed.

The military took control in a bloodless coup after the March 1984 death of Touré. A new constitution was approved in 1991, but movement toward democracy was slow. When presidential elections were finally held, in Dec. 1993, the incumbent, Gen. Lansana Conté, was the official winner; outside monitors called the elections flawed. Parliamentary elections June 11, 1995, raised similar complaints.

Guinea-Bissau
Republic of Guinea-Bissau
Republica da Guiné-Bissau

People: Population: 1,124,537. **Pop. density:** 81 per sq. mi. **Urban:** 22%. **Ethnic groups:** Balanta 30%, Fula 20%, Manjaca 14%, Mandinga 13%. **Principal languages:** Portuguese (official), Criolo, tribal languages. **Religions:** indigenous beliefs 65%, Muslim 30%, Christian 5%.

Geography: Area: 13,948 sq. mi. **Location:** On Atlantic coast of W Africa. **Neighbors:** Senegal on N, Guinea on E and S. **Topography:** A swampy coastal plain covers most of the country; to the east is a low savanna region. **Capital:** Bissau (1988 est.): 125,000.

Government: Type: Republic. **Head of state:** Pres. Joao Bernardo Vieira; b 1939; in office: Nov. 14, 1980. **Head of government:** Prime Min. Carlos Correia; in office: Dec. 27, 1991. **Local divisions:** 9 regions. **Defense:** 5%-6% of GDP (1987). **Active troop strength:** 9,250.

Economy: Chief crops: Peanuts, cotton, rice. **Minerals:** Bauxite. **Arable land:** 11%. **Electricity prod.** (1991): 30 mln. kWh. **Labor force:** 90% agric.

Finance: Monetary unit: Peso (Mar. 1995: 16,748 = $1 US). **Gross domestic product** (1993): $860 mln.* **Per capita GDP:** $800. **Imports** (1991): $64 mln.; partners: Portugal 23%, Italy 27%. **Exports** (1991): $20 mln.; partners: Portugal 34%. **National budget** (1991 est.): $44.8 mln.

Transport: Motor vehicles: in use: 3,500 passenger cars, 2,500 comm. vehicles.

Communications: Radios: 1 per 26 persons.

Health: Life expectancy at birth (1995): 46 male; 50 female. **Births** (per 1,000 pop.): 40. **Deaths** (per 1,000 pop.): 17. **Natural increase:** 2.4%. **Infant mortality** (per 1,000 live births 1995): 118.

Education: Literacy (1991): 36%. **Years compulsory:** 6.

Major International Organizations: UN, OAU.

Embassy: 918 16th St. NW 20006; 872-4222.

Portuguese mariners explored the area in the mid-15th century; the slave trade flourished in the 17th and 18th centuries, and colonization began in the 19th.

Beginning in the 1960s, an independence movement waged a guerrilla war and formed a government in the interior that achieved international support. Full independence came Sept. 10, 1974, after the Portuguese regime was overthrown.

The November 1980 coup gave Vieira absolute power. Vieira eventually initiated political liberalization; multiparty elections were held July 3, 1994.

Guyana
Co-operative Republic of Guyana

People: Population: 723,774. **Age distrib.** (%): <15: 32; 65+: 4. **Pop. density:** 9 per sq. mi. **Urban:** 33%. **Ethnic groups:** East Indian 51%, black and mixed 43%. **Principal languages:** English (official), Amerindian dialects. **Religions:** Christian 57%, Hindu 33%, Muslim 9%.

Geography: Area: 83,044 sq. mi. **Location:** On N coast of South America. **Neighbors:** Venezuela on W, Brazil on S, Suriname on E. **Topography:** Dense tropical forests cover much of the land, although a flat coastal area up to 40 mi. wide, where 90% of the population lives, provides rich alluvial soil for agriculture. A grassy savanna divides the 2 zones. **Capital:** Georgetown (1985 est.): 195,000.

Government: Type: Republic. **Head of state:** President Cheddi Jagan; b Mar. 22, 1918; in office: Oct. 9, 1992. **Head of Government:** Prime Min. Sam Hinds; in office: Oct. 9, 1992. **Local divisions:** 10 regions. **Defense:** 1.1% of GNP (1991). **Active troop strength:** 1,700.

Economy: Industries: Mining, textiles. **Chief crops:** Sugar, rice, citrus and other fruits. **Minerals:** Bauxite, gold, diamonds. **Other resources:** Timber, shrimp. **Arable land:** 3%. **Electricity prod.** (1992): 276 mln. kWh. **Labor force:** 34% agric.; 45% ind. & commerce; 21% services.

Finance: Monetary unit: Dollar (May 1995: 144 = $1 US). **Gross domestic product** (1993): $1.4 bln.* **Per capita GDP:** $1,900. **Imports** (1993): $520 mln.; partners: U.S. 37%, Trin. & Tob. 13%. **Exports** (1993): $400 mln.; partners: UK 33%, U.S. 31%. **National budget** (1990 est): $225 mln. **International reserves less gold** (Apr. 1995): $250 mln. **Consumer prices** (change in 1992): 2.6%.

Transport: Motor vehicles: in use: 24,000 passenger cars, 9,000 comm. vehicles. **Chief ports:** Georgetown.

Communications: Radios: 1 per 2.4 persons. **Telephones:** 1 per 46 persons. **Daily newspaper circ.:** 106 per 1,000 pop.

Health: Life expectancy at birth (1995): 62 male; 68 female. **Births** (per 1,000 pop.): 19. **Deaths** (per 1,000 pop.): 7. **Natural increase:** 1.2% **Hospital beds:** 1 per 341 persons. **Physicians:** 1 per 2,552 persons. **Infant mortality** (per 1,000 live births 1995): 48.

Education: Literacy (1991): 95%. **Years compulsory:** ages 6-14.

Major International Organizations: UN (WTO, ILO, IMF, World Bank), the Commonwealth, OAS.

Embassy: 2490 Tracy Pl. NW 20008; 265-6900.

Guyana became a Dutch possession in the 17th century, but sovereignty passed to Britain in 1815. Indentured servants from India soon outnumbered African slaves. Ethnic tension has affected political life.

Guyana became independent May 26, 1966. A Venezuelan claim to the western half of Guyana was suspended in 1970 but renewed in 1982. The Suriname border is also disputed. The government has nationalized most of the economy which has remained severely depressed.

The Port Kaituma ambush of U.S. Rep. Leo J. Ryan and others investigating mistreatment of American followers of the Rev. Jim Jones' People's Temple cult triggered a mass suicide-execution of 911 cultists at Jonestown in the Guyana jungle, Nov. 18, 1978.

The People's National Congress, the party in power since Guyana became independent, was voted out of office with the election of Cheddi Jagan in Oct. 1992.

Haiti

Republic of Haiti
République d'Haïti

People: Population: 6,518,159. **Age distrib.** (%): <15: 40; 65+: 4. **Pop. density:** 609 per sq. mi. **Urban:** 31%. **Ethnic groups:** black 95%. **Principal languages:** French (official), Creole. **Religions:** Roman Catholic 80%, Protestant 16%; Voodoo widely practiced.

Geography: Area: 10,695 sq. mi. **Location:** In West Indies, occupies western third of I. of Hispaniola. **Neighbors:** Dominican Republic on E, Cuba on W **Topography:** About two-thirds of Haiti is mountainous. Much of the rest is semiarid. Coastal areas are warm and moist. **Capital:** Port-au-Prince (1992 est.): 752,000.

Government: Type: Republic. **Head of state:** Pres. Jean-Bertrand Aristide; b July 15, 1953; in office Feb. 7, 1991 (ousted in military coup Sept. 30, 1991; restored to office Oct. 15, 1994). **Local divisions:** 9 departments. **Defense:** 2.1% of GDP (1992). **Active troop strength:** 7,300.

Economy: Industries: Sugar refining, textiles. **Chief crops:** Coffee, sugar, mangoes, corn, rice. **Minerals:** Bauxite. **Other resources:** Timber. **Arable land:** 20%. **Livestock** (1993): cattle: 800,000; goats: 910,000. **Fish catch** (1992): 5,000 metric tons. **Electricity prod.** (1992): 480 mln. kWh. **Labor force:** 66% agric.; 9% ind.; 25% services.

Finance: Monetary unit: Gourde (Dec. 1994: 12.95 = $1 US). **Gross domestic product** (1993): $5.2 bln.* **Per capita GDP:** $800. **Imports** (1992): $423 mln.; partners: U.S. 64%. **Exports** (1992): $135 mln.; partners: U.S. 84%. **Tourism** (1992): $46 mln. **National budget** (1990): $416 mln. **Consumer prices** (change in 1994): 42.6%.

Transport: Motor vehicles: in use: 33,000 passenger cars, 22,000 comm. vehicles. **Chief ports:** Port-au-Prince, Les Cayes.

Communications: Television sets: 1 per 255 persons. **Radios:** 1 per 2.1 persons. **Telephones:** 1 per 79 persons. **Daily newspaper circ.:** 7 per 1,000 pop.

Health: Life expectancy at birth (1995): 43 male; 47 female. **Births** (per 1,000 pop.): 39. **Deaths** (per 1,000 pop.): 19. **Natural increase:** 2.0%. **Hospital beds:** 1 per 1,207 persons. **Physicians:** 1 per 10,060 persons. **Infant mortality rate** (per 1,000 live births 1995): 107.

Education: Literacy (1993): 53%. **Years compulsory:** 6.

Major International Organizations: UN and most of its specialized agencies, OAS.

Embassy: 2311 Massachusetts Ave. NW 20008; 332-4090.

Haiti, visited by Columbus, 1492, and a French colony from 1677, attained its independence, 1804, following the rebellion led by former slave Toussaint L'Ouverture. Following a period of political violence, the U.S. occupied the country 1915-34.

Francois Duvalier was voted president in 1957; in 1964 he was named president for life. Upon his death in 1971, he was succeeded by his son, Jean-Claude. Drought in 1975-77 brought famine, and Hurricane Allen in 1980 destroyed most of the rice, bean, and coffee crops. Following several weeks of unrest, President Jean Claude Duvalier fled Haiti aboard a U.S. Air Force jet Feb. 7, 1986, ending the 28-year dictatorship by the Duvalier family.

A military-civilian council headed by Gen. Henri Namphy assumed control. In 1987, voters approved a new constitution, but the Jan. 1988 elections were marred by violence and boycotted by the opposition.

Gen. Namphy seized control, June 20, but was ousted by a military coup in Sept. By mid-1990, there had been 5 governments since Duvalier fled.

Father Jean-Bertrand Aristide was elected president Dec. 1990. A coup led by leaders of the Tonton Macoutes, the private militia of the Duvalier family, was crushed by loyalist army forces, Jan. 1991. The attempted coup sparked riots that left some 70 dead. In Sept. 1991, Aristide was arrested by the military and expelled from the country.

Some 35,000 Haitian refugees were intercepted by the U.S. Coast Guard as they tried to enter the U.S., 1991-92. Most were returned to Haiti. There was a new upsurge of refugees starting in late 1993.

The UN imposed a worldwide oil, arms, and financial embargo on Haiti June 23, 1993. The embargo was suspended when the military agreed to Aristide's return to power on Oct. 30, but the military effectively blocked his return. After renewed sanctions, the UN Security Council authorized, July 31, 1994, an invasion of Haiti by a multinational force. With U.S. invasion forces already en route, an invasion was averted, Sept. 18, by a new agreement for military leaders to step down and Aristide to resume office. As part of the agreement, thousands of U.S. troops began arriving in Haiti, Sept. 19. Aristide returned to Haiti and was restored in office Oct. 15. A UN peacekeeping force took over responsibility for Haiti as of Mar. 31, 1995.

Honduras

Republic of Honduras
República de Honduras

People: Population: 5,459,743. **Age distrib.** (%): <15: 47; 65+: 4. **Pop. density:** 126 per sq. mi. **Urban:** 46%. **Ethnic groups:** mestizo 90%, Indian 7%. **Principal language:** Spanish (official). **Religion:** Roman Catholic 97%.

Geography: Area: 43,277 sq. mi. **Location:** In Central America. **Neighbors:** Guatemala on W, El Salvador, Nicaragua on S. **Topography:** The Caribbean coast is 500 mi. long. The Pacific coast, on Gulf of Fonseca, is 40 mi. long. Honduras is mountainous, with wide fertile valleys and rich forests. **Capital:** Tegucigalpa. **Cities** (1989 est.): Tegucigalpa 608,000; San Pedro Sula 300,000.

Government: Type: Republic. **Head of State:** Pres. Carlos Roberta Reina Idiaquez; b Mar. 13, 1926; in office: Jan. 27, 1994. **Local divisions:** 18 departments. **Defense:** 1.3% of GDP (1993 est.). **Active troop strength:** 16,800.

Economy: Industries: Textiles, wood prods. **Chief crops:** Bananas (chief export), coffee, corn, beans. **Minerals:** Gold, silver, copper, lead, zinc, iron, antimony, coal. **Other resources:** Timber. **Arable land:** 14%. **Livestock** (1992): cattle: 2.4 mln. **Electricity prod.** (1992): 2 bln. kWh. **Labor force:** 62% agric.; 20% services; 9% manuf.

Finance: Monetary unit: Lempira (May 1995: 9.22 = $1 US). **Gross domestic product** (1993): $10 bln.* **Per capita GDP:** $1,950. **Imports** (1993): $1.1 bln.; partners: U.S. 50%, Mexico 8%. **Exports** (1993): $850 mln.; partners: U.S. 53%, Germany 11%. **Tourism** (1992): $32 mln. **National budget** (1990 est.): $1.9 bln. **International reserves less gold** (May 1995): $77 mln. **Gold:** 21,000 oz t. **Consumer prices** (change in 1994): 21.7%.

Transport: Motor vehicles: in use: 65,000 passenger cars, 102,000 comm. vehicles. **Civil aviation:** 321 mln. passenger-mi.; 8 airports with scheduled flights. **Chief ports:** Puerto Cortes, La Ceiba.

Communications: Television sets: 1 per 32 persons. **Radios:** 1 per 2.9 persons. **Telephones:** 1 per 48 persons. **Daily newspaper circ.:** 39 per 1,000 pop.

Health: Life expectancy at birth (1995): 66 male; 71 female. **Births** (per 1,000 pop.): 34. **Deaths** (per 1,000 pop.): 6. **Natural increase:** 2.8%. **Hospital beds:** 1 per 900 persons. **Physicians:** 1 per 1,586 persons. **Infant mortality** (per 1,000 live births 1995): 43.

Education: Literacy (1992): 73%. **Years compulsory:** 6.

Major International Organizations: UN, (IMF, WHO, ILO), OAS.

Embassy: 3007 Tilden St. NW 20008; 966-7702.

Mayan civilization flourished in Honduras in the 1st millennium AD. Columbus arrived in 1502. Honduras became independent after freeing itself from Spain, 1821 and from the Fed. of Central America, 1838.

Gen. Oswaldo Lopez Arellano, president for most of the period 1963-75 by virtue of one election and 2 coups, was ousted by the army in 1975 over charges of pervasive bribery by United Brands Co. of the U.S. The government has resumed land distribution, raised minimum wages, and started a literacy campaign. An elected civilian government took power in 1982.

Some 3,200 U.S. troops were sent to Honduras after the Honduran border was violated by Nicaraguan forces, Mar. 1988.

Honduras is one of the poorest countries in the western hemisphere.

Hungary
Republic of Hungary
Magyar Köztársaság

People: Population: 10,318,838. **Age distrib.** (%): <15: 19; 65+: 14. **Pop. density:** 287 per sq. mi. **Urban:** 63%. **Ethnic groups:** Hungarian 89.9%, Gypsy 4%, German 2.6%. **Principal language:** Hungarian (Magyar). **Religions:** Roman Catholic 67%, Calvinist 20%, Lutheran 5%.

Geography: Area: 35,920 sq. mi. **Location:** In E central Europe. **Neighbors:** Slovakia, Ukraine on N, Austria on W, Slovenia, Yugoslavia, Croatia on S, Romania on E. **Topography:** The Danube R. forms the Slovak border in the NW, then swings S to bisect the country. The eastern half of Hungary is mainly a great fertile plain, the Alfold; the W and N are hilly. **Capital:** Budapest. **Cities** (1993 est.): Budapest 2.0 mln.; Debrecen 217,000; Miskolc 191,000.

Government: Type: Parliamentary democracy. **Head of state:** Pres. Arpad Goncz; b Feb. 10, 1922; in office: May 2, 1990. **Head of government:** Prime Min. Gyula Horn; b July 5, 1932; in office: July 15, 1994. **Local divisions:** 38 counties, 1 capital. **Defense:** 3.5% of GDP (1992). **Active troop strength:** 74,500.

Economy: Industries: Iron and steel, machinery, pharmaceuticals, vehicles, communications equip., milling, distilling. **Chief crops:** Wheat, corn, sunflowers, potatoes, sugar beets. **Minerals:** Bauxite, coal, natural gas. **Arable land:** 51%. **Livestock** (1993): cattle: 1.0 mln.; pigs: 5.0 mln.; sheep: 1.3 mln. **Electricity prod.** (1992): 30 bln. kWh. **Labor force:** 16% agric.; 30% ind.

Finance: Monetary unit: Forint (Apr. 1995: 121 = $1 US). **Gross domestic product** (1993): $57 bln.* **Per capita GDP:** $5,500. **Imports** (1993): $12.5 bln.; partners: EU 43%. **Exports** (1993): $8.9 bln.; partners: EU 50%. **National budget** (1993 est.): $12.5 bln. **Tourism** (1992): $1.2 bln. **International reserves less gold** (Feb. 1995): $6.9 bln. **Gold:** 110,000 oz t. **Consumer prices** (change in 1994): 18.9%.

Transport: Railroads: Length: 8,200 mi. **Motor vehicles:** in use: 2.1 mln. passenger cars, 229,000 comm. vehicles. **Civil aviation:** 924 mln. passenger-mi.; 1 airport with scheduled flights.

Communications: Television sets: 1 per 2.4 persons. **Radios:** 1 per 1.7 persons. **Telephones:** 1 per 5.0 persons. **Daily newspaper circ.:** 266 per 1,000 pop.

Health: Life expectancy at birth (1995): 68 male; 76 female. **Births** (per 1,000 pop.): 13. **Deaths** (per 1,000 pop.): 12. **Natural increase:** 0. **Hospital beds:** 1 per 101 persons. **Physicians:** 1 per 252 persons. **Infant mortality** (per 1,000 live births 1995): 12.

Education: Literacy: (1993): 99%. **Years compulsory:** to age 16.

Major International Organizations: UN (IMF, World Bank, WTO).

Embassy: 3910 Shoemaker St. NW 20008; 362-6730.

Earliest settlers, chiefly Slav and Germanic, were overrun by Magyars from the east. Stephen I (997-1038) was made king by Pope Sylvester II in 1000 AD. The country suffered repeated Turkish invasions in the 15th-17th centuries. After the defeats of the Turks, 1686-1697, Austria dominated, but Hungary obtained concessions until it regained formal independence in 1867, with the emperor of Austria as king of Hungary in a dual monarchy with a single diplomatic service. Defeated with the Central Powers in 1918, Hungary lost Transylvania to Romania, Croatia and Bacska to Yugoslavia, Slovakia and Carpatho-Ruthenia to Czechoslovakia, all of which had large Hungarian minorities. A republic under Michael Karolyi and a bolshevist revolt under Bela Kun were followed by a vote for a monarchy in 1920 with Admiral Nicholas Horthy as regent.

Hungary joined Germany in World War II, and was allowed to annex most of its lost territories. Russian troops captured the country, 1944-1945. By terms of an armistice with the Allied powers Hungary agreed to give up territory acquired by the 1938 dismemberment of Czechoslovakia and to return to its borders of 1937.

A republic was declared Feb. 1, 1946; Zoltan Tildy was elected president. In 1947 the communists forced Tildy out. Premier Imre Nagy, in office since mid-1953, was ousted for his moderate policy of favoring agriculture and consumer production, April 18, 1955.

In 1956, popular demands for the ousting of Erno Gero, Communist Party secretary, and for formation of a government by Nagy, resulted in the latter's appointment Oct. 23; demonstrations against communist rule developed into open revolt. On Nov. 4 Soviet forces launched a massive attack against Budapest with 200,000 troops, 2,500 tanks and armored cars.

About 200,000 persons fled the country. Nagy was executed, and thousands were arrested. In the spring of 1963 the regime freed many captives from the 1956 revolt.

Hungarian troops participated in the 1968 Warsaw Pact invasion of Czechoslovakia. Major economic reforms were launched early in 1968, switching from a central planning system to one in which market forces and profit controlled much of production.

In 1989 Parliament passed legislation legalizing freedom of assembly and association as Hungary shifted away from communism. In Oct. the Communist Party was formally dissolved. The last Soviet troops left Hungary June 19, 1991.

Iceland
Republic of Iceland
Lýdhveldidh Ísland

People: Population: 265,998. **Age distrib.** (%): <15: 25; 65+: 11. **Pop. density:** 7 per sq. mi. **Urban:** 91%. **Ethnic groups:** homogeneous, descendants of Norwegians, Celts. **Principal language:** Icelandic (Islenska). **Religion:** Evangelical Lutheran 96%.

Geography: Area: 39,699 sq. mi. **Location:** At N end of Atlantic O. **Neighbors:** Nearest is Greenland, to W. **Topography:** Iceland is of recent volcanic origin. Three-quarters of the surface is wasteland: glaciers, lakes, a lava desert. There are geysers and hot springs, and the climate is moderated by the Gulf Stream. **Capital:** Reykjavik (1993 est.): 102,000.

Government: Type: Constitutional republic. **Head of state:** Pres. Vigdis Finnbogadottir; b Apr. 15, 1930; in office: Aug. 1, 1980. **Head of government:** Prime Min. David Oddsson; Jan. 17, 1948; in office: Apr. 30, 1991. **Local divisions:** 23 counties, 14 ind. towns.

Economy: Industries: Fish products (some 80% of exports), aluminum. **Chief crops:** Potatoes, turnips, hay. **Arable land:** 1%. **Livestock** (1993): sheep: 488,800. **Fish catch** (1991): 1.1 mln. metric tons. **Electricity prod.** (1992): 5.2 bln. kWh. **Labor force:** 4% agric.; 60% commerce & services; 12% fish.

Finance: Monetary unit: Kron (May 1995: 63.00 = $1 US). **Gross domestic product** (1993): $4.2 bln.* **Per capita GDP:** $16,000. **Imports** (1992): $1.5 bln.; partners: EU 53%. **Exports** (1992): $1.5 bln.; partners: EU 68%. **Tourism** (1992): $129 mln. **National budget** (1992): $1.9 bln. **International reserves less gold** (May 1995): $354 mln. **Gold:** 49,000 oz t. **Consumer prices** (change in 1994): 1.6%.

Transport: Motor vehicles: in use: 116,000 passenger cars, 16,000 comm. vehicles. **Civil aviation:** 1.3 bln. passenger-mi.; 24 airports with scheduled flights. **Chief port:** Reykjavik.

Communications: Television sets: 1 per 3.5 persons. **Radios:** 1 per 1.7 persons. **Telephones:** 1 per 1.9 persons. **Daily newspaper circ.:** 514 per 1,000 pop.

Health: Life expectancy at birth (1995): 77 male; 81 female. **Births** (per 1,000 pop.): 16. **Deaths** (per 1,000 pop.): 7. **Natural increase:** 0.9%. **Hospital beds:** 1 per 80 persons. **Physicians:** 1 per 355 persons. **Infant mortality** (per 1,000 live births 1995): 4.

Education: Literacy (1992): 100%. **Years compulsory:** 10.

Major International Organizations: UN (WTO, IMF, WHO), NATO, EFTA, OECD.

Embassy: 2022 Connecticut Ave. NW 20008; 265-6653.

Iceland was an independent republic from 930 to 1262, when it joined with Norway. Its language has maintained its purity for 1,000 years. Danish rule lasted from 1380-1918; the last ties with the Danish crown were severed in 1941. The Althing, or assembly, is the world's oldest surviving parliament.

India
Republic of India
Bharat

People: Population: 936,545,814. **Age distrib.** (%): <15: 36; 65+: 4. **Pop. density:** 766 per sq. mi. **Urban:** 26%. **Ethnic groups:** Indo-Aryan groups 72%, Dravidians 25%, Mongoloids 3%. **Principal languages:** 16 languages, including Hindi (official) and English (associate official). **Religions:** Hindu 80%, Muslim 14%, Christian 2%, Sikh 2%.

Geography: Area: 1,222,243 sq. mi. **Location:** Occupies most of the Indian subcontinent in S Asia. **Neighbors:** Pakistan on W, China, Nepal, Bhutan on N, Myanmar, Bangladesh on E. **Topography:** The Himalaya Mts., highest in world, stretch across India's northern borders. Below, the Ganges Plain is wide, fertile, and among the most densely populated regions of the world. The area below includes the Deccan Peninsula. Close to one quarter the area is forested. The climate varies from tropical heat in S to near-Arctic cold in N. Rajasthan Desert is in NW; NE Assam Hills get 400 in. of rain a year. **Capital:** New Delhi. **Cities** (1991 met. est.): Bombay 12.6 mln.; Calcutta 11.0 mln.; Delhi 8.4 mln.; Madras 5.4 mln.; Hyderabad 4.3 mln; Bangalore 4.1 mln.

Government: Type: Federal republic. **Head of state:** Pres. Shankar Dayal Sharma; b. Aug. 19, 1918; in office: July 26, 1992. **Head of government:** Prime Min. P. V. Narasimha Rao; b June 28, 1921; in office: June 21, 1991. **Local divisions:** 25 states, 7 union territories. **Defense:** 2.4% of GDP (FY 1993-94). **Active troop strength:** 1.3 mln.

Economy: Industries: Textiles, steel, processed foods, cement, machinery, chemicals, fertilizers, consumer appliances, autos. **Chief crops:** Rice, grains, sugarcane, spices, tea, cashews, cotton, copra, coir, jute, linseed. **Minerals:** Coal, iron, manganese, mica, bauxite, titanium, chromite, oil. **Crude oil reserves** (1994): 5.9 bln. bbls. **Other resources:** Rubber, timber. **Arable land:** 55%. **Livestock** (1992): cattle: 193 mln.; sheep: 44 mln. **Fish catch** (1991): 4.0 mln. metric tons. **Electricity prod.** (1992): 310 bln. kWh. **Labor force:** 65% agric.

Finance: Monetary unit: Rupee (May 1995: 31.42 = $1 US). **Gross domestic product** (1994 est.): $1.7 trl.* **Per capita GDP:** $1,300. **Imports** (1993): $22 bln.; partners: U.S. 10%, Belgium 8%, Germany 8%. **Exports** (1993): $21.4 bln.; partners: U.S. 19%, Germany 8%, Italy 8%. **Tourism** (1992): $1.4 bln. **National budget** (FY 1993): $45.1 bln. **International reserves less gold** (May 1995): $20.6 bln. **Gold:** 12.7 mln. oz t. **Consumer prices** (change in 1994): 10.2%.

Transport: Railroads: Length: 38,800 mi. **Motor vehicles:** in use: 2.8 mln. passenger cars, 2.4 mln. comm. vehicles. **Civil aviation:** 8.9 bln. passenger-mi.; 95 airports with scheduled flights. **Chief ports:** Calcutta, Bombay, Madras, Cochin, Vishakhapatnam.

Communications: Television sets: 1 per 45 persons. **Radios:** 1 per 16 persons. **Telephones:** 1 per 131 persons. **Daily newspaper circ.:** 21 per 1,000 pop.

Health: Life expectancy at birth (1995): 58 male; 60 female. **Births** (per 1,000 pop.): 28. **Deaths** (per 1,000 pop.): 10. **Natural increase:** 1.8%. **Hospital beds:** 1 per 1,357 persons. **Physicians:** 1 per 2,189 persons. **Infant mortality** (per 1,000 live births 1995): 76.

Education: Literacy (1993): 48%. **Years compulsory:** to age 14.

Major International Organizations: UN (IMF, WTO, World Bank), the Commonwealth.

Embassy: 2107 Massachusetts Ave. NW 20008; 939-7000.

India has one of the oldest civilizations in the world. Excavations trace the Indus Valley civilization back for at least 5,000 years. Paintings in the mountain caves of Ajanta, richly carved temples, the Taj Mahal in Agra, and the Kutab Minar in Delhi are among relics of the past.

Aryan tribes, speaking Sanskrit, invaded from the NW around 1500 BC, and merged with the earlier inhabitants to create classical Indian civilization.

Asoka ruled most of the Indian subcontinent in the 3d century BC, and established Buddhism. But Hinduism revived and eventually predominated. During the Gupta kingdom, 4th-6th century AD, science, literature, and the arts enjoyed a "golden age."

Arab invaders established a Muslim foothold in the W in the 8th century, and Turkish Muslims gained control of North India by 1200. The Mogul emperors ruled 1526-1857.

Vasco de Gama established Portuguese trading posts 1498-1503. The Dutch followed. The British East India Co. sent Capt. William Hawkins, 1609, to get concessions from the Mogul emperor for spices and textiles. Operating as the East India Co. the British gained control of most of India. The British parliament assumed political direction; under Lord Bentinck, 1828-35, rule by rajahs was curbed. After the Sepoy troops mutinied, 1857-58, the British supported the native rulers.

Nationalism grew rapidly after World War I. The Indian National Congress and the Muslim League demanded constitutional reform. A leader emerged in Mohandas K. Gandhi (called Mahatma, or Great Soul), born Oct. 2, 1869, assassinated Jan. 30, 1948. He advocated self-rule, non-violence, removal of untouchability. In 1930 he launched "civil disobedience," including boycott of British goods and rejection of taxes without representation.

In 1935 Britain gave India a constitution providing a bicameral federal congress. Mohammed Ali Jinnah, head of the Muslim League, sought creation of a Muslim nation, Pakistan.

The British government partitioned British India into the dominions of India and Pakistan. India became a self-governing member of the Commonwealth and a member of the UN. It became a democratic republic, Jan. 26, 1950.

More than 12 million Hindu & Muslim refugees crossed the India-Pakistan borders in a mass transferral of some of the 2 peoples during 1947; about 200,000 were killed in communal fighting.

After Pakistan troops began attacks on Bengali separatists in East Pakistan, Mar. 25, 1971, some 10 million refugees fled into India. India and Pakistan went to war Dec. 3, 1971, on both the East and West fronts. Pakistan troops in the east surrendered Dec. 16; Pakistan agreed to a cease-fire in the west Dec. 17. In Aug. 1973 India released 93,000 Pakistanis held prisoner since 1971. The 2 countries resumed full relations in 1976.

Mrs. Indira Gandhi, was named prime minister Jan. 19, 1966. Threatened with adverse court rulings and an opposition protest campaign, Gandhi invoked emergency provisions of the constitution June 1975. Thousands of opponents were arrested and press censorship imposed. These and other actions, including the enforcement of coercive birth control measures in some areas, were widely resented. Opposition parties, united in the Janata coalition, turned Gandhi's New Congress Party from power in federal and state parliamentary elections in 1977.

Gandhi became prime minister for the second time, Jan. 14, 1980. She was assassinated by 2 of her Sikh bodyguards Oct. 31, 1984. Widespread rioting followed. Thousands of Sikhs were killed and some 50,000 left homeless.

The assassination was in response to the government suppression of a Sikh uprising in Punjab in June 1984 which included an assault on the Golden Temple, the holiest Sikh shrine. Rajiv, Indira Gandhi's son, replaced her as prime minister. He was swept from office in 1989 amid charges of incompetence and corruption. He was assassinated May 21, 1991 during an election campaign to regain the prime ministership.

Sikhs ignited several violent clashes during the 1980s. The government's May 1987 decision to bring the state of Punjab under the rule of the central government led to violence. Many died during a government siege of the Golden Temple at Amritsar, May 1988. Another trouble spot was Assam in NW India, where thousands were killed in ethnic violence in Feb. 1993; a renewed outburst in July 1994 led to more than 60 deaths there.

In the biggest wave of criminal violence in Indian history, a series of bombings jolted Bombay and Calcutta, Mar. 12-19, 1993, leaving over 300 dead and some 1,200 injured. The explosions came in the wake of nationwide riots prompted by the destruction of a 16th century mosque by Hindu militants in Dec. 1992.

Sikkim, bordered by Tibet, Bhutan, and Nepal, formerly British protected, became a protectorate of India in 1950. Area, 2,740 sq. mi.; pop., 1991 cen., 406,000; capital, Gangtok. In Sept. 1974 India's parliament voted to make Sikkim an associate Indian state, absorbing it into India.

Kashmir, a predominantly Muslim region in the NW, has been in dispute between India and Pakistan since 1947. A cease-fire was negotiated by the UN Jan. 1, 1949; it gave Pakistan control of one-third of the area, in the west and northwest, and India the remaining two-thirds, the Indian state of Jammu and Kashmir, which enjoys internal autonomy.

In the 1990s there were repeated clashes between Indian army troops and pro-independence demonstrators triggered by India's decision to impose central government rule. The clashes strained relations between India and Pakistan, which India charged was aiding the Muslim separatists.

France, 1952-54, peacefully yielded to India its 5 colonies, former French India, comprising Pondicherry, Karikal, Mahe, Yanaon (which became Pondicherry Union Territory, area 190 sq. mi.; pop. 1991, 808,000) and Chandernagor (which was incorporated into the state of West Bengal).

Indonesia
Republic of Indonesia
Republik Indonesia

People: Population: 203,583,886. **Age distrib.** (%): <15: 37; 65+: 4. **Pop. density:** 275 per sq. mi. **Urban:** 31%. **Ethnic groups:** Javanese 45%, Sundanese 14%, Madurese 7.5%, Malay 7.5%. **Principal languages:** Bahasa Indonesian (Malay) (official), English, Dutch, Javanese. **Religions:** Muslim 87%.

Geography: Area: 741,052 sq. mi. **Location:** Archipelago SE of Asia along the Equator. **Neighbors:** Malaysia on N, Papua New Guinea on E. **Topography:** Indonesia comprises some 17,000 islands, including Java (one of the most densely populated areas in the world with 1,500 persons to the sq. mi.), Sumatra, Kalimantan (most of Borneo), Sulawesi (Celebes), and West Irian (Irian Jaya, the W half of New Guinea). Also: Bangka, Billiton, Madura, Bali, Timor. The mountains and plateaus on the major islands have a cooler climate than the tropical lowlands. **Capital:** Jakarta. **Cities** (1990 est.): Jakarta 8.3 mln.; Surabaya 2.4 mln.; Bandung 2.0 mln.; Medan 1.7 mln.

Government: Type: Republic. **Head of state:** Pres. Suharto; b June 8, 1921; in office: Mar. 6, 1967. **Local divisions:** 24 provinces, 2 special regions. **Defense:** 1.5% of GDP (FY 1993-94 est.). **Active troop strength:** 276,000.

Economy: Industries: oil and natural gas, food processing, textiles, cement, light industry. **Chief crops:** Rice, cocoa, sugar. **Minerals:** Nickel, tin, oil, bauxite, copper, natural gas. **Crude oil reserves** (1994): 5.8 bln. bbls. **Other resources:** Rubber. **Arable land:** 8%. **Livestock** (1992): cattle: 11.0 mln.; sheep: 5.9 mln. **Fish catch** (1992): 3.3 mln. metric tons. **Electricity prod.** (1992): 45.8 bln. kWh. **Labor force:** 55% agric.; 10% manuf.

Finance: Monetary unit: Rupiah (May 1995: 2,236 = $1 US). **Gross domestic product** (1993): $571 bln.* **Per capita GDP:** $2,900. **Imports** (1993): $28.3 bln.; partners: Japan 22%, U.S. 14%, Germany 8%. **Exports** (1993): $38.2 bln.; partners: Japan 32%, U.S. 13%, Singapore 9%. **Tourism** (1992): $2.7 bln. **National budget** (1995): $32.8 bln. **International reserves less gold** (Apr. 1995): $12.3 bln. **Gold:** 3.10 mln. oz t. **Consumer prices** (change in 1994): 8.5%.

Transport: Railroads: Length: 4,090 mi. **Motor vehicles:** in use: 1.9 mln. passenger cars, 1.7 mln. comm. vehicles. **Civil aviation:** 9.3 bln. passenger-mi.; 126 airports. **Chief ports:** Jakarta, Surabaya, Medan, Palembang, Semarang.

Communications: Television sets: 1 per 17 persons. **Radios:** 1 per 8.5 persons. **Telephones:** 1 per 114 persons.

Health: Life expectancy at birth (1995): 59 male; 63 female. **Births** (per 1,000 pop.): 24. **Deaths** (per 1,000 pop.): 8. **Natural increase:** 1.6%. **Hospital beds:** 1 per 1,643 persons. **Physicians:** 1 per 6,861 persons. **Infant mortality** (per 1,000 live births 1995): 65.

Education: Literacy (1991): 78%. **Years compulsory:** 9. **Attendance:** 97% attend primary school.

Major International Organizations: UN and all of its specialized agencies, ASEAN, OPEC.

Embassy: 2020 Massachusetts Ave. NW 20036; 775-5200.

Hindu and Buddhist civilization from India reached the peoples of Indonesia nearly 2,000 years ago, taking root especially in Java. Islam spread along the maritime trade routes in the 15th century, and became predominant by the 16th century. The Dutch replaced the Portuguese as the most important European trade power in the area in the 17th century. They secured territorial control over Java by 1750. The outer islands were not finally subdued until the early 20th century, when the full area of present-day Indonesia was united under one rule for the first time.

Following Japanese occupation, 1942-45, nationalists led by Sukarno and Hatta declared independence. The Netherlands ceded sovereignty Dec. 27, 1949, after 4 years of fighting. A republic was declared, Aug. 17, 1950, with Sukarno as president. West Irian, on New Guinea, remained under Dutch control.

After the Dutch in 1957 rejected proposals for new negotiations over West Irian, Indonesia stepped up the seizure of Dutch property. A U.S. mediator's plan was adopted in 1962. In 1963 the UN turned the area over to Indonesia, which promised a plebiscite. In 1969, voting by tribal chiefs favored staying with Indonesia, despite an uprising and widespread opposition.

Sukarno suspended Parliament in 1960, and was named president for life in 1963. He made close alliances with Communist governments. Russian-armed Indonesian troops staged raids in 1964 and 1965 into Malaysia, whose formation Sukarno had opposed.

In 1965 an attempted coup in which several military officers were murdered was successfully put down. The regime blamed the coup on the Communist Party, some of whose members were known to have been involved. In its wake more than 300,000 alleged Communists were killed in army-initiated massacres.

Gen. Suharto, head of the army, was named president in 1968 and was reelected for a 6th consecutive 5-year term in 1993. He developed a strong government party, restricted the opposition, and allied the country with the West. Muslim opposition parties made gains in 1977 elections but lost ground subsequently. The military retained a predominant role.

In 1966 Indonesia and Malaysia signed an agreement ending hostility. In Dec. 1975, Indonesia invaded East Timor as Portuguese rule collapsed there, annexing it in 1976, despite international condemnation.

Oil exports and political stability have spurred economic growth, but Indonesia's foreign debt has ballooned in recent decades.

Iran
Islamic Republic of Iran
Jomhoori-e-Islami-e-Iran

People: Population: 64,625,455. **Age distrib.** (%): <15: 44; 65+: 3. **Pop. density:** 102 per sq. mi. **Urban:** 57%. **Ethnic groups:** Persian 51%, Azerbaijani 24%, Kurd 7%. **Principal languages:** Persian, Turkic, Kurdish, Luri. **Religion:** Shi'a Muslim 95%.

Geography: Area: 632,457 sq. mi. **Location:** Between the Middle East and S Asia. **Neighbors:** Turkey, Iraq on W, Armenia, Azerbaijan, Turkmenistan on N, Afghanistan, Pakistan on E. **Topography:** Interior highlands and plains are surrounded by high mountains, up to 18,000 ft. Large salt deserts cover much of the area, but there are many oases and forest areas. Most of the population inhabits the N and NW. **Capital:** Tehran. **Cities** (1991 cen.): Tehran 6.5 mln.; Mashhad 1.8 mln.; Esfahan 1.1 mln.; Tabriz 1.1 mln.; Shiraz 965,000.

Government: Type: Islamic republic. **Religious head:** Ayatollah Sayyed Ali Khamenei; b 1939; in office: June 4, 1989. **Head of state:** Pres. Hashemi Rafsanjani; in office: Aug. 3, 1989. **Local divisions:** 24 provinces. **Defense:** 15% of GNP (1991). **Active troop strength:** 513,000.

Economy: Industries: Oil, petrochemicals, cement, sugar refining, carpets. **Chief crops:** Grains, rice, fruits, sugar beets, cotton, grapes. **Minerals:** Chromium, oil, gas. **Crude oil reserves** (1994): 93 bln. barrels. **Other resources:** Gums, wool, silk, caviar. **Arable land:** 8%. **Livestock** (1991): cattle: 6.9 mln.; sheep: 45.0 mln. **Fish catch** (1991): 277,444 metric tons. **Electricity prod.** (1992): 43.6 bln. kWh. **Labor force:** 33% agric.; 21% manuf.

Finance: Monetary unit: Rial (May 1995: 1,747 = $1 US). **Gross national product** (1993): $303 bln.* **Per capita GNP** (1991): $4,780. **Imports** (1992): $23.7 bln.; partners: Germany 24%, Japan 13%, Italy 10%. **Exports** (1992): $15.5 bln.; partners: Japan 15%, Italy 10%. **National budget** (1990): $80 bln. **Consumer prices** (change in 1994): 31.5%.

Transport: Motor vehicles: in use: 1.6 mln. passenger cars, 561,000 comm. vehicles. **Civil aviation:** 3.0 bln. passenger-mi.; 19 airports. **Chief port:** Bandar Abbas.

Communications: Television sets: 1 per 26 persons. **Radios:** 1 per 5 persons. **Telephones:** 1 per 16 persons. **Daily newspaper circ.:** 27 per 1,000 pop.

Health: Life expectancy at birth (1995): 66 male; 68 female. **Births** (per 1,000 pop.): 35. **Deaths** (per 1,000 pop.): 7. **Natural increase:** 2.8%. **Hospital beds:** 1 per 650 persons. **Physicians:** 1 per 2,000 persons. **Infant mortality** (per 1,000 live births 1995): 55.

Education: Literacy (1992): 54%.

Major International Organizations: UN (IMF, WHO), OPEC.

Iran was once called Persia. The Iranians, who supplanted an earlier agricultural civilization, came from the E during the 2d millennium BC; they were an Indo-European group related to the Aryans of India.

In 549 BC Cyrus the Great united the Medes and Persians in the Persian Empire, conquered Babylonia in 538 BC, restored Jerusalem to the Jews. Alexander the Great conquered Persia in 333 BC, but Persians regained their independence in the next century under the Parthians, themselves succeeded by

Sassanian Persians in AD 226. Arabs brought Islam to Persia in the 7th century, replacing the indigenous Zoroastrian faith. After Persian political and cultural autonomy was reasserted in the 9th century, the arts and sciences flourished for several centuries.

Turks and Mongols ruled Persia in turn from the 11th century to 1502, when a native dynasty reasserted full independence. The British and Russian empires vied for influence in the 19th century, and Afghanistan was severed from Iran by Britain in 1857.

Reza Khan abdicated as shah, 1941, and was succeeded by his son, Mohammad Reza Pahlavi. Under his rule, Iran underwent economic and social change but political opposition was not tolerated.

Conservative Muslim protests led to 1978 violence. Martial law in 12 cities was declared Sept. 8. A military government was appointed Nov. 6 to deal with striking oil workers. Prime Min. Shahpur Bakhtiar was designated by the shah to head a regency council in his absence. The shah left Iran Jan. 16, 1979.

Exiled religious leader Ayatollah Ruhollah Khomeini named a provisional government council in preparation for his return to Iran, Jan. 31. Clashes between Khomeini's supporters and government troops culminated in a rout of Iran's elite Imperial Guard Feb. 11, leading to the fall of Bakhtiar's government.

The Iranian revolution was marked by revolts among the ethnic minorities and by a continuing struggle between the clerical forces and westernized intellectuals and liberals. The Islamic Constitution established final authority to be vested in a Faghi, the Ayatollah Khomeini.

Iranian militants seized the U.S. embassy, Nov. 4, 1979, and took hostages including 62 Americans. Despite international condemnations and U.S. efforts, including an abortive Apr. 1980 rescue attempt, the crisis continued. The U.S. broke diplomatic relations with Iran, Apr. 7. The shah died in Egypt, July 27. The hostage drama finally ended Jan. 21, 1981, when an accord, involving the release of frozen Iranian assets, was reached.

A dispute over the Shatt al-Arab waterway that divides the two countries brought Iran and Iraq, Sept. 22, 1980, into open warfare. Iraqi planes attacked Iranian air fields including Tehran airport. Iranian planes bombed Iraqi bases. Iraqi troops occupied Iranian territory including the port city of Khorramshahr in October. Iranian troops recaptured the city and drove Iraqi troops back across the border, May 1982. Iraq, and later Iran, attacked several oil tankers in the Persian Gulf during 1984. Saudi Arabian war planes shot down 2 Iranian jets, June 5, which they felt were threatening Saudi shipping. In Aug. 1988, Iran agreed to accept a UN resolution calling for a cease-fire.

In Nov. 1986, senior U.S. officials secretly visited Iran and exchanged arms for Iran's help in obtaining the release of U.S. hostages held by terrorists in Lebanon. The exchange sparked a major scandal in the Reagan administration.

A U.S. Navy warship shot down an Iranian commercial airliner, July 3, 1988, after mistaking it for an F-14 fighter jet; all 290 aboard the plane died.

A major earthquake struck northern Iran June 21, 1990, killing more than 45,000, injuring 100,000, and leaving 400,000 homeless. A U.S. offer of assistance was accepted by the Iranian government.

Some one million Kurdish refugees crossed Iran's border to escape Iraqi forces following the Persian Gulf War.

Iraq
Republic of Iraq
al Jumhouriya al 'Iraqia

People: Population: 20,643,769. **Age distrib.** (%): <15: 47; 65+: 3. **Pop. density:** 123 per sq. mi. **Urban:** 70%. **Ethnic groups:** Arab 75–80%, Kurd 15–20%, Turkoman. **Principal languages:** Arabic (official), Kurdish. **Religions:** Muslim 97% (Shi'a 60–65%, Sunni 32–37%).

Geography: Area: 167,975 sq. mi. **Location:** In the Middle East, occupying most of historic Mesopotamia. **Neighbors:** Jordan, Syria on W, Turkey on N, Iran on E, Kuwait, Saudi Arabia on S. **Topography:** Mostly an alluvial plain, including the Tigris and Euphrates rivers, descending from mountains in N to desert in SW. Persian Gulf region is marshland. **Capital:** Baghdad. **Cities** (1985 est.): Baghdad (met.) 3.8 mln.; Basra 617,000; Mosul 571,000.

Government: Type: Republic. **Head of state:** Pres. Saddam Hussein At-Takriti, b. Apr. 29, 1937; in office: July 16, 1979; also assumed post of prime minister, May 29, 1994. **Local divisions:** 18 provinces. **Defense:** 75% of GNP (1991). **Active troop strength:** 382,000 est.

Economy: Industries: Textiles, petrochemicals, oil refining, cement. **Chief crops:** Grains, rice, dates, cotton. **Minerals:** Oil, gas. **Crude oil reserves** (1994): 100 bln. barrels. **Other resources:** Wool, hides. **Arable land:** 12%. **Livestock** (1993): cattle: 1.2 mln.; sheep: 6 mln. **Fish catch** (1991): 12,000 metric tons. **Electricity prod.** (1992): 12.9 bln. kWh. **Labor force:** 30% agric.; 48% services; 22% ind.

Finance: Monetary unit: Dinar (May 1995: 1.00 = $3.22 US). **Gross national product** (1993): $38 bln.* **Per capita GNP:** $2,000. **Imports** (1990): $6.6 bln.; partners: Tur., U.S. **Exports** (1990): $10.4 bln.; partners: U.S., Tur., Jap. **National budget** (1990): $35 bln.

Transport: Railroads: Length: 1,483 mi. **Motor vehicles:** in use: 672,000 passenger cars, 368,000 comm. vehicles. **Chief port:** Basra.

Communications: Television sets: 1 per 19 persons. **Radios:** 1 per 5.5 persons. **Telephones:** 1 per 25 persons. **Daily newspaper circ.:** 37 per 1,000 pop.

Health: Life expectancy at birth (1995): 66 male; 68 female. **Births** (per 1,000 pop.): 44. **Deaths** (per 1,000 pop.): 7. **Natural increase:** 3.7%. **Hospital beds:** 1 per 568 persons. **Physicians:** 1 per 1,922 persons. **Infant mortality** (per 1,000 live births 1995): 62.

Major International Organizations: UN (IMF, ILO), Arab League, OPEC.

Education: Literacy (1992): 60%. **Years compulsory:** 6.

The Tigris-Euphrates valley, formerly called Mesopotamia, was the site of one of the earliest civilizations in the world. The Sumerian city-states of 3,000 BC originated the culture later developed by the Semitic Akkadians, Babylonians, and Assyrians.

Mesopotamia ceased to be a separate entity after the conquests of the Persians, Greeks, and Arabs. The latter founded Baghdad, from where the caliph ruled a vast empire in the 8th and 9th centuries. Mongol and Turkish conquests led to a decline in population, the economy, cultural life, and the irrigation system.

Britain secured a League of Nations mandate over Iraq after World War I. Independence under a king came in 1932. A leftist, pan-Arab revolution established a republic in 1958, which oriented foreign policy toward the USSR. Most industry has been nationalized, and large land holdings broken up.

A local faction of the international Baath Arab Socialist party has ruled by decree since 1968. Russia and Iraq signed an aid pact in 1972, and arms were sent along with several thousand advisers. The 1978 execution of 21 communists and a shift of trade to the West signalled a more neutral policy, straining relations with the USSR. In the 1973 Arab-Israeli war Iraq sent forces to aid Syria. Within a month of assuming power, Saddam Hussein instituted a bloody purge in the wake of a reported coup attempt against the new regime.

Years of battling with the Kurdish minority resulted in total defeat for the Kurds in 1975, when Iran withdrew support. The fighting led to Iraqi bombing of Kurdish villages in Iran, causing relations with Iran to deteriorate.

After skirmishing intermittently for 10 months over the sovereignty of the disputed Shatt al-Arab waterway that divides the two countries, Iraq and Iran, Sept. 22, 1980, entered into open warfare when Iraqi fighter-bombers attacked 10 Iranian airfields, including Tehran airport, and Iranian planes retaliated with strikes on 2 Iraqi bases. In the following days, there was heavy ground fighting around Abadan and the port of Khorramshahr as Iraq pressed its attack on Iran's oil-rich province of Khuzistan. In May 1982, Iraqi troops were driven back across the border.

Israeli airplanes destroyed a nuclear reactor near Baghdad on June 7, 1981, claiming that it could be used to produce nuclear weapons.

Iraq and Iran expanded their war to the Persian Gulf in Apr. 1984. There were several attacks on oil tankers. An Iraqi warplane launched a missile attack on the U.S.S. *Stark*, a U.S. Navy frigate on patrol in the Persian Gulf, May 17, 1987; 37 U.S. sailors died. Iraq apologized for the attack, claiming it was inadvertent. The fierce war ended Aug. 1988, when Iraq accepted a UN resolution for a cease-fire.

Iraq attacked and overran Kuwait Aug. 2, 1990, sparking an international crisis. The United Nations, Aug. 6, imposed a ban on all trade with Iraq and called on member countries to protect the assets of the legitimate government of Kuwait. Iraq declared Kuwait its 19th province, Aug. 28. A campaign of looting, murder, and pillage was mounted against Kuwaiti civilians. Westerners caught in Iraq and Kuwait were initially held as hostages, but by the end of 1990, all were released.

A U.S.-led coalition launched air and missile attacks on Iraq, Jan. 16, 1991, after the expiration of a UN Security Council deadline for Iraq to withdraw from Kuwait. Iraq retaliated by firing scud missiles at Saudi Arabia and Israel. The coalition began a ground attack to retake Kuwait Feb. 23. Iraqi forces showed little resistance and were soundly defeated in 4 days. Some 175,000 Iraqis were taken prisoner, and casualties were estimated at over 85,000. As part of the cease-fire agreement, Iraq agreed to scrap all poison gas and germ weapons and allow UN observers to inspect the sites. UN trade sanctions would remain in effect until Iraq complied with all terms.

In the aftermath of the war, there were revolts against Pres. Saddam Hussein throughout Iraq. In Feb., Iraqi troops drove Kurdish insurgents and civilians to the Iran and Turkey borders, causing a refugee crisis. The U.S. and allies established havens inside Iraq for the Kurds.

Tensions heightened over the UN's efforts to dismantle Iraq's arms-production program, July 5, 1992, when a UN inspection team was temporarily denied entrance to a ministry building in Baghdad. In Feb. 1994, Iraq agreed to cooperate with the UN in inspection of long-range weapons. Trade sanctions remained in effect, however.

The U.S. launched a missile attack aimed at Iraq's intelligence headquarters in Baghdad June 26, 1993. The U.S. justified the attack by citing evidence that Iraq had sponsored a plot to kill former Pres. George Bush during his visit to Kuwait in Apr. 1993. In Aug. 1955, two of Saddam Hussein's sons-in-law, who held high positions in the Iraqi military, defected to Jordan with their families and aides.

Ireland

Éire

People: Population: 3,550,448. **Age distrib.** (%): <15: 26; 65+: 11. **Pop. density:** 131 per sq. mi. **Urban:** 57%. **Ethnic groups:** Celtic, English minority. **Principal languages:** English predominates, Irish (Gaelic) spoken by minority. **Religions:** Roman Catholic 93%, Anglican 3%.

Geography: Area: 27,137 sq. mi. **Location:** In the Atlantic O. just W of Great Britain. **Neighbors:** United Kingdom (Northern Ireland). **Topography:** Ireland consists of a central plateau surrounded by isolated groups of hills and mountains. The coastline is heavily indented by the Atlantic O. **Capital:** Dublin. **Cities** (1991 est.): Dublin 478,000; Cork 127,000.

Government: Type: Parliamentary republic. **Head of State:** Pres. Mary Robinson; b May 21, 1944; in office: Dec. 3, 1990. **Head of government:** Prime Min. John Bruton; b May 18, 1947; in office: Dec. 15, 1994. **Local divisions:** 26 counties. **Defense:** 1-2% of GDP (1993 est.). **Active troop strength:** 13,000.

Economy: Industries: Food processing, textiles, chemicals, brewing, machinery, tourism. **Chief crops:** Potatoes, grain, sugar beets, turnips. **Minerals:** Zinc, lead, silver, gas. **Arable land:** 14%. **Livestock** (1992): cattle: 7.0 mln.; pigs: 1.4 mln.; sheep: 8.9 mln. **Fish catch** (1991): 241,000 metric tons. **Electricity prod.** (1992): 14.5 bln. kWh. **Labor force:** 14% agric.; 28% manuf.; 57% services.

Finance: Monetary unit: Pound (May 1995: 1.00 = $1.65 US). **Gross domestic product** (1993): $46.3 bln.* **Per capita GDP:** $13,100. **Imports** (1992): $23.3 bln.; partners: UK 41%, U.S. 15%, other EU 25%. **Exports** (1992): $28.3 bln.; partners: UK 32%, other EU 43%, U.S. 9%. **Tourism** (1992): $1.6 bln. **National budget** (1992 est.): $16.6 bln. **International reserves less gold** (May 1995): $7.2 bln. **Gold:** 360,000 oz t. **Consumer prices** (change in 1994): 2.3%.

Transport: Railroads: Length: 1,747 mi. **Motor vehicles:** in use: 858,000 passenger cars, 149,000 comm. vehicles. **Civil aviation:** 2.4 bln. passenger-mi.; 10 airports. **Chief ports:** Dublin, Cork.

Communications: Television sets: 1 per 3.5 persons. **Radios:** 1 per 1.8 persons. **Telephones:** 1 per 3.8 persons. **Daily newspaper circ.:** 186 per 1,000 pop.

Health: Life expectancy at birth (1995): 73 male; 79 female. **Births** (per 1,000 pop.): 14. **Deaths** (per 1,000 pop.): 8. **Natural increase:** 0.6%. **Hospital beds:** 1 per 255 persons. **Physicians:** 1 per 681 persons. **Infant mortality** (per 1,000 live births 1995): 7.

Education: Literacy (1992): 100%. **Years compulsory:** 9; attendance 96%.

Major International Organizations: UN (WTO, IMF, World Bank), EU, OECD.

Embassy: 2234 Massachusetts Ave. NW 20008; 462-3939.

Celtic tribes invaded the islands about the 4th century BC; their Gaelic culture and literature flourished and spread to Scotland and elsewhere in the 5th century AD, the same century in which St. Patrick converted the Irish to Christianity. Invasions by Norsemen began in the 8th century, ended with defeat of the Danes by the Irish King Brian Boru in 1014. English invasions started in the 12th century; for over 700 years the Anglo-Irish struggle continued with bitter rebellions and savage repressions.

The Easter Monday Rebellion (1916) failed but was followed by guerrilla warfare and harsh reprisals by British troops, the "Black and Tans." The Dail Eireann, or Irish parliament, reaffirmed independence in Jan. 1919. The British offered dominion status to Ulster (6 counties) and southern Ireland (26 counties) Dec. 1921. The constitution of the Irish Free State, a British dominion, was adopted Dec. 11, 1922. Northern Ireland remained part of the United Kingdom.

A new constitution adopted by plebiscite came into operation Dec. 29, 1937. It declared the name of the state Eire in the Irish language (Ireland in the English) and declared it a sovereign democratic state.

On Dec. 21, 1948, an Irish law declared the country a republic rather than a dominion and withdrew it from the Commonwealth. The British Parliament recognized both actions, 1949, but reasserted its claim to incorporate the 6 northeastern counties in the United Kingdom. This claim has not been recognized by Ireland. *(See United Kingdom — Northern Ireland.)*

Irish governments have favored peaceful unification of all Ireland. Ireland cooperated with Britain against terrorist groups. On Dec. 15, 1993, the Irish and British governments agreed on outlines of a peace plan to resolve the Northern Ireland issue. Much of it was rejected July 24, 1994, by Sinn Fein, the political wing of the Irish Republican Army, a terrorist group dedicated to the unification of Ireland. On Aug. 31, 1994 however, the I.R.A. issued a cease-fire announcement, saying that it would abandon warfare and would instead rely on peace talks and political means to accomplish its objectives.

Israel

State of Israel

Medinat Israel

People: Population: 5,142,834. **Age distrib.** (%): <15: 30; 65+: 9. **Pop. density:** 643 per sq. mi. **Urban:** 90%. **Ethnic groups:** Jewish 83%, non-Jewish (mostly Arab) 17%. **Principal languages:** Hebrew and Arabic (official). **Religions:** Jewish 82%, Muslim 14%.

Geography: Area: 7,992 sq. mi. **Location:** On eastern end of Mediterranean Sea. **Neighbors:** Lebanon on N, Syria, Jordan on E, Egypt on W. **Topography:** The Mediterranean coastal plain is fertile and well-watered. In the center is the Judean Plateau. A triangular-shaped semi-desert region, the Negev, extends from south of Beersheba to an apex at the head of the Gulf of Aqaba. The eastern border drops sharply into the Jordan Rift Valley, including Lake Tiberias (Sea of Galilee) and the Dead Sea, which is 1,312 ft. below sea level, lowest point on the earth's surface. **Capital:** Jerusalem (most countries maintain their embassy in Tel Aviv). **Cities** (1993 est.): Jerusalem 556,000; Tel Aviv-Yafo 357,000; Haifa 250,000.

Government: Type: Republic. **Head of state:** Pres. Ezer Weizman; b June 15, 1924; in office: May 13, 1993. **Head of government:** Prime Min. Yitzhak Rabin; b Mar. 1, 1922; in office: July 13, 1992. **Local divisions:** 6 districts. **Defense:** 10% of GDP (1993 est.). **Active troop strength:** 172,000 est.

Economy: Industries: Diamond cutting, textiles, electronics, machinery, food processing. **Chief crops:** Citrus fruit, vegetables. **Minerals:** Potash, copper, phosphates, manganese, sulphur. **Arable land:** 17%. **Livestock** (1992): cattle: 349,000; sheep: 360,000. **Fish catch** (1992): 19,200 metric tons. **Electricity prod.** (1992): 21.8 bln. kWh. **Labor force:** 4% agric.; 22% ind.; 29% public services.

Finance: Monetary unit: New Sheqel (May 1995: 3.00 = $1 US). **Gross domestic prod.** (1993): $65.7 bln.* **Per capita GDP:** $13,350. **Imports** (1993): $20.3 bln.; partners: U.S. 18%, Belgium 12%, Germany 10%. **Exports** (1993): $12.1 bln.; partners: U.S. 31%, UK 6%, Belgium 5%. **Tourists** (1992): $1.9 bln. **National budget** (1993): $36.3 bln. **International reserves less gold** (May 1995): $9.6 bln. **Gold:** 9,000 oz t. **Consumer prices** (change in 1994): 12.3%.

Transport: Railroads: Length: 356 mi. **Motor vehicles:** in use: 923,000 passenger cars, 186,000 comm. vehicles. **Civil aviation:** 5.3 bln. passenger-mi.; 7 airports with scheduled flights. **Chief ports:** Haifa, Ashdod, Eilat.

Communications: Television sets: 1 per 4.1 persons. **Radios:** 1 per 2.2 persons. **Telephones:** 1 per 2.0 persons. **Daily newspaper circ.:** 261 per 1,000 pop.

Health: Life expectancy at birth (1995): 76 male; 80 female. **Births** (per 1,000 pop.): 20. **Deaths** (per 1,000 pop.): 6. **Natural increase:** 1.4%. **Hospital beds:** 1 per 177 persons. **Physicians:** 1 per 345 persons. **Infant mortality** (per 1,000 live births 1995): 8.

Education: Literacy (1993): 95%.

Major International Organizations: UN (WTO, IMF).

Embassy: 3514 International Dr. NW 20008; 364-5500.

Occupying the SW corner of the ancient Fertile Crescent, Israel contains some of the oldest known evidence of agriculture and of primitive town life. A more advanced civilization emerged in the 3d millennium BC. The Hebrews probably arrived early in the 2d millennium BC. Under King David and his successors (c.1000 BC-597 BC), Judaism was developed and secured. After conquest by Babylonians, Persians, and Greeks, an independent Jewish kingdom was revived, 168 BC, but Rome took effective control in the next century, suppressed Jewish revolts in 70 AD and 135 AD, and renamed Judea Palestine, after the earlier coastal inhabitants, the Philistines.

Arab invaders conquered Palestine in 636. The Arabic language and Islam prevailed within a few centuries, but a Jewish minority remained. The land was ruled from the 11th century as a part of non-Arab empires by Seljuks, Mamluks, and Ottomans (with a crusader interval, 1098-1291).

After 4 centuries of Ottoman rule, during which the population declined to a low of 350,000 (1785), the land was taken in 1917 by Britain, which in the Balfour Declaration that year pledged to support a Jewish national homeland there, as foreseen by the Zionists. In 1920 a British Palestine Mandate was recognized; in 1922 the land east of the Jordan was detached.

Jewish immigration, begun in the late 19th century, swelled in the 1930s with refugees from the Nazis; heavy Arab immigration from Syria and Lebanon also occurred. Arab opposition to Jewish immigration turned violent in 1920, 1921, 1929, and 1936. The UN General Assembly voted in 1947 to partition Palestine into an Arab and a Jewish state. Britain withdrew in May 1948.

Israel was declared an independent state May 14, 1948; the Arabs rejected partition. Egypt, Jordan, Syria, Lebanon, Iraq, and Saudi Arabia invaded, but failed to destroy the Jewish state, which gained territory. Separate armistices with the Arab nations were signed in 1949; Jordan occupied the West Bank, Egypt occupied Gaza, but neither granted Palestinian autonomy.

After persistent terrorist raids, Israel invaded Egypt's Sinai, Oct. 29, 1956, aided briefly by British and French forces. A UN cease-fire was arranged Nov. 6.

An uneasy truce between Israel and the Arab countries, supervised by a UN Emergency Force, prevailed until May 19, 1967, when the UN force withdrew at the demand of Egypt's Pres. Gamal Abdel Nasser. Egyptian forces reoccupied the Gaza Strip and closed the Gulf of Aqaba to Israeli shipping. In a 6-day war that started June 5, the Israelis took the Gaza Strip, occupied the Sinai Peninsula to the Suez Canal, and captured East Jerusalem, Syria's Golan Heights, and Jordan's West Bank. The fighting was halted June 10 by UN-arranged cease-fire agreements.

Egypt and Syria attacked Israel, Oct. 6, 1973 (Yom Kippur, most solemn day on the Jewish calendar). Israel counterattacked, driving the Syrians back, and crossed the Suez Canal.

A cease-fire took effect Oct. 24; a UN peacekeeping force went to the area. A disengagement agreement was signed Jan. 18, 1974. Israel withdrew from the canal's west bank. A second withdrawal was completed in 1976; Israel returned the Sinai to Egypt in 1982.

Israeli forces raided Entebbe, Uganda, July 3, 1976, and rescued 103 hostages seized by Arab and German terrorists.

In 1977, the conservative opposition, led by Menachem Begin, was voted into office for the first time. Egypt's Pres. Anwar al-Sadat visited Jerusalem Nov. 1977, and on Mar. 26, 1979, Egypt and Israel signed a formal peace treaty, ending 30 years of war and establishing diplomatic relations.

Israel invaded S Lebanon, Mar. 1978, following a Lebanon-based terrorist attack in Israel. Israel withdrew in favor of a 6,000-man UN force, but continued to aid Christian militiamen.

Violence on the Israeli-occupied West Bank rose in 1982 when Israel announced plans to build new Jewish settlements. Israel affirmed the entire city of Jerusalem as its capital, July 1980, encompassing the annexed East Jerusalem.

On June 7, 1981, Israeli jets destroyed an Iraqi atomic reactor near Baghdad that, Israel claimed, would have enabled Iraq to manufacture nuclear weapons.

Israeli jets bombed Palestine Liberation Organization (PLO) strongholds in Lebanon Apr.-May 1982. In reaction to the wounding of the Israeli ambassador to Great Britain, Israeli forces in a coordinated land, sea, and air attack invaded Lebanon, June 6, to destroy PLO strongholds in that country. Israeli forces encircled Beirut June 14. Following massive Israeli bombing of West Beirut, the PLO agreed to evacuate the city.

Israeli troops entered West Beirut after newly elected Lebanese Pres. Bashir Gemayel was assassinated on Sept. 14. Israel received widespread condemnation when Lebanese Christian forces, Sept. 16, entered two West Beirut refugee camps and slaughtered hundreds of Palestinian refugees.

In 1989, violence escalated over the Israeli military occupation of the West Bank and Gaza Strip; Palestinian protesters and Israeli troops clashed frequently. Israeli police and stone-throwing Palestinians clashed, Oct. 8, 1990, around the al-Aqsa mosque on the Temple Mount in Jerusalem. Some 20 Palestinians died.

During the Persian Gulf War, Iraq fired a series of scud missiles at Israel; most were intercepted by U.S. Patriot missiles. Israel agreed in Aug. 1991 to take part in a U.S.-Soviet sponsored Middle East peace conference.

The Labor Party of Yitzhak Rabin won a clear victory in elections held June 23, 1992. Rabin called for peace and reconciliation with Israel's Arab neighbors.

A Jewish gunman opened fire on Arab worshippers at a mosque in Hebron, Feb. 25, 1994, killing at least 29 before he himself was killed.

Ongoing peace talks produced historic agreements between Israel and the Palestine Liberation Organization in Sept. 1993. The latter recognized Israel's right to exist, and Israel recognized the PLO as the representative of the Palestinians; the two sides then signed, Sept. 13, an agreement for limited Palestinian self-rule in Gaza and in the West Bank, beginning with the city of Jericho. An accord formally initiating self-rule was signed in Cairo, May 4, 1994. Israel and Jordan signed, July 25, 1994, in Washington, DC, a declaration ending their 46-year state of war; a formal peace treaty was signed Oct. 26. After intensive negotiations, an Israeli-PLO agreement expanding Palestinian self-rule in the West Bank was signed Sept. 28, 1995.

Gaza: Population (1995 est.): 757,422. **Area:** 140 sq. mi.

West Bank: Population (1995 est.): 1,481,364. **Area:** 2,270 sq. mi.

Italy

Italian Republic

Repubblica Italiana

People: Population: 58,261,971. **Age distrib.** (%): <15: 16; 65+: 16. **Pop. density:** 501 per sq. mi. **Urban:** 68%. **Ethnic groups:** Italians, small minorities of Germans, Slovenes, Albanians. **Principal language:** Italian. **Religion:** predominantly Roman Catholic.

Geography: Area: 116,334 sq. mi. **Location:** In S Europe, jutting into Mediterranean Sea. **Neighbors:** France on W, Switzerland, Austria on N, Slovenia on E. **Topography:** Occupies a long boot-shaped peninsula, extending SE from the Alps into the Mediterranean, with the islands of Sicily and Sardinia offshore. The alluvial Po Valley drains most of N. The rest of the country is rugged and mountainous, except for intermittent coastal plains, like the Campania, S of Rome. Apennine Mts. run down through center of peninsula. **Capital:** Rome. **Cities** (1992 est.): Rome 2.8 mln.; Milan 1.4 mln.; Naples 1.1 mln.; Turin 962,000.

Government: Type: Republic. **Head of state:** Pres. Oscar Luigi Scalfaro; b Sept. 9, 1918; in office: May 28, 1992. **Head of government:** Prime Min. Lamberto Dini; b Mar. 1, 1931; in office: Jan. 13, 1995. **Local divisions:** 20 regions with some autonomy, divided into 95 provinces. **Defense:** 2% of GDP (1992). **Active troop strength:** 322,300.

(continued on page 785)

WAR IN THE BALKANS

Hailed as an American hero, U.S. Air Force Capt. Scott F. O'Grady returns to the U.S. After his F-16 fighter was shot down June 2, 1995, over Bosnia and Herzegovina by Bosnian Serb forces, O'Grady survived for 6 days on a diet of rainwater, plants, and insects before being rescued by U.S. Marines.

More than 200,000 Serb refugees from Croatia fled during August across Bosnia toward Serbia in the wake of a successful Croatian government offensive to recapture Serb-held territory.

WORLD EVENTS

During the morning rush hour of Mar. 20, 1995, a deadly nerve-gas (sarin) attack in Tokyo's subway system killed 12 and injured more than 5,000 commuters. On May 16, Japanese authorities arrested Shoko Asahara (inset), the leader of a religious cult, in connection with the attack.

In a White House ceremony (Sept. 28, 1995), Yitzhak Rabin (left of Pres. Clinton), prime minister of Israel, and Yasir Arafat (right of Clinton), chairman of the PLO, signed an agreement to expand Palestinian self-rule in the West Bank. Witnessing the event were King Hussein of Jordan and Pres. Hosni Mubarak of Egypt (standing behind Clinton).

GAMMA LIAISON

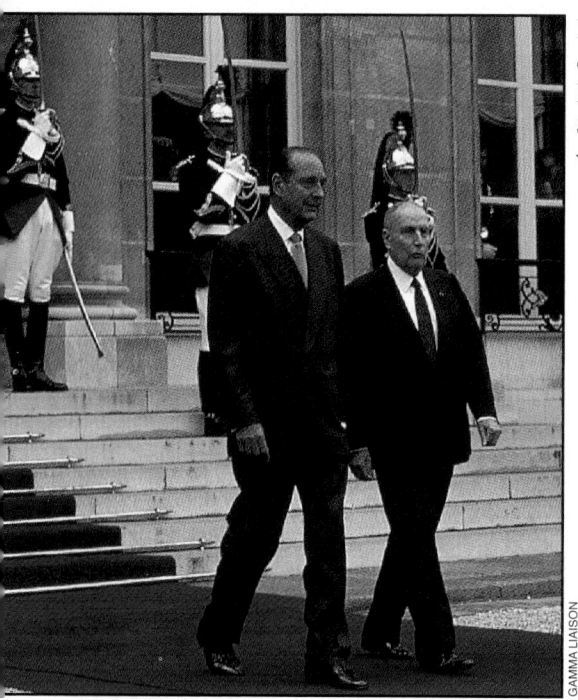

Paris Mayor Jacques Chirac (left), a conservative, was elected president of France on May 7, 1995, succeeding Socialist François Mitterrand (right), who had held the office for 14 years.

PRESSENS BILD/GAMMA LIAISON

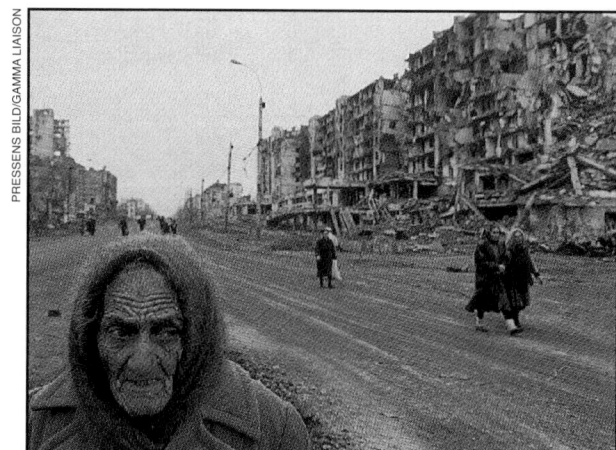

Grozny, capital of the secessionist Russian republic of Chechnya, lay in ruins following fierce fighting between Chechen rebels and Russian troops.

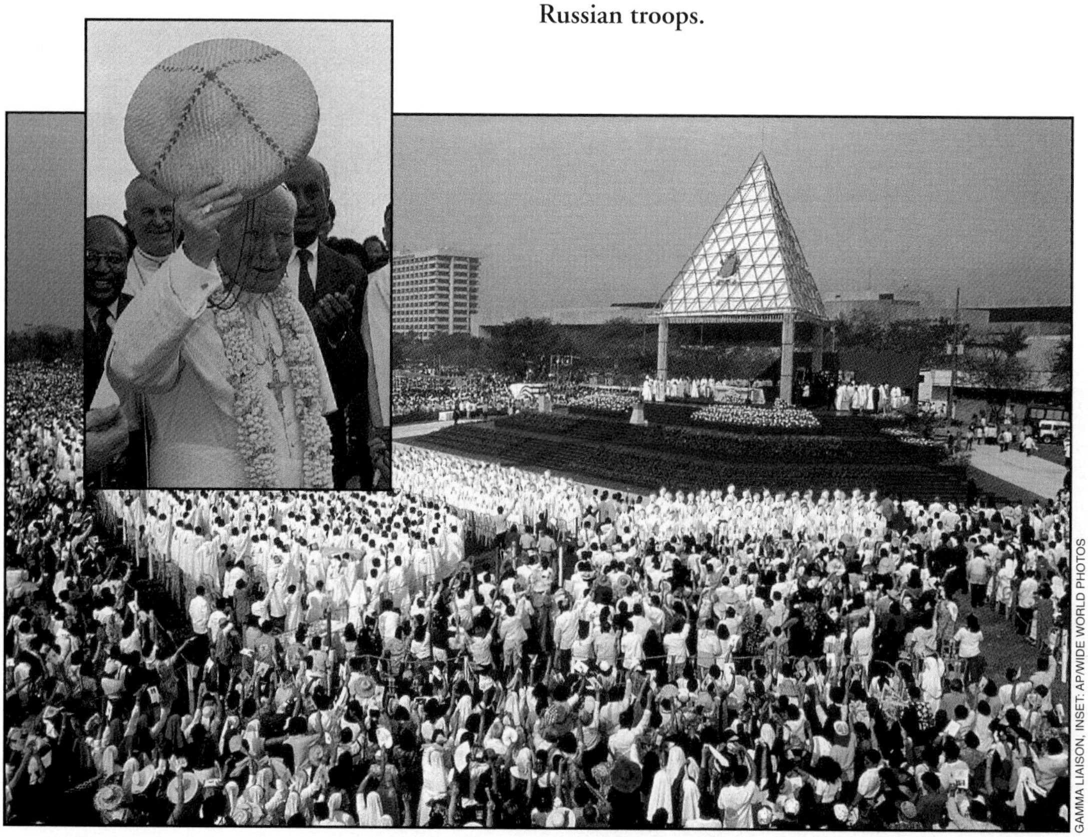

GAMMA LIAISON, INSET: AP/WIDE WORLD PHOTOS

Pope John Paul II celebrated World Youth Day (Jan. 15, 1995) in Manila, the Philippines, as part of an 11-day Asian tour. More than 4 million people were in attendance, the largest gathering for a papal mass during John Paul's tenure.

Arts and Entertainment

At the 37th annual Grammy Awards, held Mar. 1, 1995, singer Sheryl Crow won 3 awards: best record, best female pop vocalist, and best new artist.

Glenn Close took the Tony Award for best leading actress in a musical for her work in *Sunset Boulevard,* the musical adaptation of the 1950 film.

Pocahontas, Disney's animated movie, made its debut under the stars in New York City's Central Park to an audience that could choose the view from any of several giant screens.

Jerry Garcia, lead guitarist of the Grateful Dead and a counterculture icon of the 1960s and '70s, died of a heart attack at the age of 53 on Aug. 9, 1995.

Scenes from two of the hottest new series on TV—(left) *ER*, a medical drama, and (below) *Friends*, a sitcom about friendship.

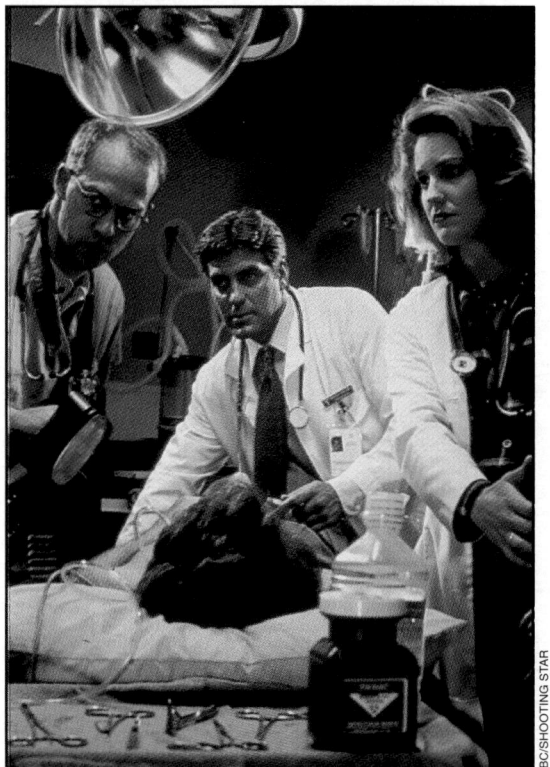

SPORTS HIGHLIGHTS

REUTERS/BETTMANN

One of the greatest power hitters in baseball history, former New York Yankees center fielder Mickey Mantle, died of cancer Aug. 13.

MVP Steve Young pulls back to pass in Super Bowl XXIX, Jan. 29, 1995. He led the San Francisco 49ers to a rout of the San Diego Chargers, 49-26.

FOCUS ON SPORTS

AP/WIDE WORLD PHOTOS

On Sept. 6, 1995, the Baltimore Orioles' Cal Ripken, Jr., broke Lou Gehrig's record of 2130 consecutive games played. A packed Camden Yards stadium and Ripken's teammates celebrate game No. 2131.

782

The NBA finals featured two of the league's most electrifying centers—the Houston Rockets' Hakeem Olajuwon and the Orlando Magic's Shaquille O'Neal. The Rockets swept the Magic in four games.

BEN VAN HOOK/DUOMO

DAVID KLUTHO/SPORTS ILLUSTRATED

Rebecca Lobo (right) led the University of Connecticut Huskies to victory over the Tennessee Lady Volunteers for the NCAA women's championship.

DUOMO

Michael Jordan, the Chicago Bulls' superstar guard, speaks with the media (Mar. 19, 1995) following his first game after coming out of retirement. Jordan rejoined the Bulls in mid-basketball season after a stint as a minor-league baseball player.

SPORTS HIGHLIGHTS

Former heavyweight boxing champion Mike Tyson clobbered Peter McNeeley in an Aug. 19 Las Vegas bout that lasted 89 seconds. It was Tyson's first fight since being released from prison after serving a 3-year sentence for rape.

On July 8, Steffi Graf of Germany won her sixth singles championship at Wimbledon (below). Later in the summer, she took her fourth U.S. Open title.

For only the second time in history, the America's Cup left America in May 1995. It was taken to New Zealand by the team of the yacht *Black Magic*, winners over Dennis Conner's *Stars & Stripes* team.

Economy: Industries: Steel, machinery, autos, textiles, shoes, machine tools, chemicals. **Chief crops:** Grapes, olives, citrus fruits, vegetables, wheat. **Minerals:** Mercury, potash, sulphur. **Crude oil reserves** (1994): 621 mln. bbls. **Arable land:** 32%. **Livestock** (1992): cattle: 8.0 mln.; pigs: 8.5 mln.; sheep: 10.4 mln. **Fish catch** (1992): 355,000 metric tons. **Electricity prod.** (1992): 235 bln. kWh. **Labor force:** 10% agric.; 32% ind.; 58% services.

Finance: Monetary unit: Lira (May 1995: 1,616 = $1 US). **Gross domestic product** (1993): $967.6 mln.* **Per capita GDP:** $16,700. **Imports** (1992): $188.5 bln.; partners: EU 59%, U.S. 6%. **Exports** (1992): $178.2 bln.; partners: EU 58%, U.S. 7%. **Tourism** (1992): $21.5 bln. **National budget** (1993 est.): $391 mln. **International reserves less gold** (May 1995): $30.0 bln. **Gold:** 66.67 mln. oz t. **Consumer prices** (change in 1994): 4.0%.

Transport: Railroads: Length: 12,176 mi. **Motor vehicles:** in use: 28.2 mln. passenger cars, 2.5 mln. comm. vehicles. **Civil aviation:** 15.2 bln. passenger-mi.; 32 airports. **Chief ports:** Genoa, Venice, Trieste, Taranto, Naples, La Spezia.

Communications: Television sets: 1 per 3.4 persons. **Radios:** 1 per 3.9 persons. **Telephones:** 1 per 1.7 persons. **Daily newspaper circ.:** 154 per 1,000 pop.

Health: Life expectancy at birth (1995): 76 male; 80 female. **Births** (per 1,000 pop.): 11. **Deaths** (per 1,000 pop.): 10. **Natural increase:** 0.1%. **Hospital beds:** 1 per 148 persons. **Physicians:** 1 per 193 persons. **Infant mortality** (per 1,000 live births 1995): 7.

Education: Literacy (1993): 97%. **Years compulsory:** 7.

Major International Organizations: UN and all of its specialized agencies, NATO, OECD, EU.

Embassy: 1601 Fuller St. NW 20009; 328-5500.

Rome emerged as the major power in Italy after 500 BC, dominating the more civilized Etruscans to the N and Greeks to the S. Under the Empire, which lasted until the 5th century AD, Rome ruled most of Western Europe, the Balkans, the Near East, and North Africa. In 1988, archaeologists unearthed evidence showing Rome as a dynamic society in the 6th and 7th centuries BC.

After the Germanic invasions, lasting several centuries, a high civilization arose in the city-states of the N, culminating in the Renaissance. But German, French, Spanish, and Austrian intervention prevented the unification of the country. In 1859 Lombardy came under the crown of King Victor Emmanuel II of Sardinia. By plebiscite in 1860, Parma, Modena, Romagna, and Tuscany joined, followed by Sicily and Naples, and by the Marches and Umbria. The first Italian Parliament declared Victor Emmanuel king of Italy Mar. 17, 1861. Mantua and Venetia were added in 1866 as an outcome of the Austro-Prussian war. The Papal States were taken by Italian troops Sept. 20, 1870, on the withdrawal of the French garrison. The states were annexed to the kingdom by plebiscite. Italy recognized the State of Vatican City as independent Feb. 11, 1929.

Fascism appeared in Italy Mar. 23, 1919, led by Benito Mussolini, who took over the government at the invitation of the king Oct. 28, 1922. Mussolini acquired dictatorial powers. He made war on Ethiopia and proclaimed Victor Emmanuel III emperor, defied the sanctions of the League of Nations, sent troops to fight for Franco against the Republic of Spain, and joined Germany in World War II.

After Fascism was overthrown in 1943, Italy declared war on Germany and Japan and contributed to the Allied victory. It surrendered conquered lands and lost its colonies. Mussolini was killed by partisans Apr. 28, 1945. Victor Emmanuel III abdicated May 9, 1946; his son Humbert II was king until June 10, when Italy became a republic after a referendum, June 2-3.

Italy has enjoyed growth in industry and living standards since World War II, in part a result of membership in the European Community.

A wave of left-wing political violence began in the late 1970s with kidnappings and assassinations and continued into the 1980s. Christian Democratic leader and former Prime Min. Aldo Moro was murdered May 1978 by Red Brigade terrorists.

By mid-1991, some 20,000 Albanian refugees had entered Italy as the result of political unrest in their homeland. In Aug. an additional wave of 18,000 Albanians reached Italy. They were rounded up and sent back to Albania.

Italian voters in a referendum and Italy's Parliament approved, in 1993, electoral reforms, as growing corruption scandals implicated some of Italy's most prominent politicians. Under the reforms, most members of Parliament were to be elected from single districts, rather than in a proportional representation system that fragmented power among several major parties. In Mar. 27-28, 1994, elections, right-wing parties won a majority, dislodging Italy's long-powerful Christian Democratic Party.

Sicily, 9,926 sq. mi., pop. (1992) 4,966,000, is an island 180 by 120 mi., seat of a region that embraces the island of **Pantelleria,** 32 sq. mi., and the **Lipari** group, 44 sq. mi., including 2 active volcanoes: **Vulcano,** 1,637 ft., and **Stromboli,** 3,038 ft. From prehistoric times Sicily has been settled by various peoples; a Greek state had its capital at Syracuse. Rome took Sicily from Carthage 215 BC. **Mt. Etna,** 11,053 ft. active volcano, is tallest peak.

Sardinia, 9,301 sq. mi., pop. (1992) 1,647,000, lies in the Mediterranean, 115 mi. W of Italy and 7½ mi. S of Corsica. It is 160 mi. long, 68 mi. wide, and mountainous, with mining of coal, zinc, lead, copper. In 1720 Sardinia was added to the possessions of the Dukes of Savoy in Piedmont and Savoy to form the Kingdom of Sardinia. Giuseppe Garibaldi is buried on the nearby isle of Caprera. **Elba,** 86 sq. mi., lies 6 mi. W of Tuscany. Napoleon I lived in exile on Elba 1814-1815.

Trieste. An agreement, signed Oct. 5, 1954, by Italy and Yugoslavia, confirmed, Nov. 10, 1975, gave Italy provisional administration over the northern section and the seaport of Trieste, and Yugoslavia the part of Istrian peninsula it has occupied.

Jamaica

People: Population: 2,574,291. **Age distrib.** (%): <15: 33; 65+: 8. **Pop. density:** 607 per sq. mi. **Urban:** 53%. **Ethnic groups:** African 76%, Afro-European 15%, white, Chinese, East Indian. **Principal languages:** English (official), Jamaican Creole. **Religion:** Protestant 56%.

Geography: Area: 4,244 sq. mi. **Location:** In West Indies. **Neighbors:** Nearest are Cuba on N, Haiti on E. **Topography:** The country is four-fifths covered by mountains. **Capital:** Kingston (1991 met. est.): 587,000.

Government: Type: Parliamentary democracy. **Head of state:** Queen Elizabeth II, represented by Gov.-Gen. Howard Cooke; in office: Aug. 1, 1991. **Head of government:** Prime Min. Percival J. Patterson; b Apr. 10, 1935; in office: Mar. 30, 1992. **Local divisions:** 13 parishes. **Defense:** 1% of GDP (FY 1991-92). **Active troop strength:** 3,320.

Economy: Industries: Sugar, bauxite, mining, tourism. **Chief crops:** sugarcane, coffee, bananas, potatoes, citrus fruits. **Minerals:** Bauxite, limestone, gypsum. **Arable land:** 19%. **Livestock** (1992): cattle: 320,000; goats: 440,000. **Electricity prod.** (1992): 2.7 bln. kWh. **Labor force:** 23% agric.; 41% services; 19% ind.

Finance: Monetary unit: Dollar (Apr. 1995: 33.45 = $1 US). **Gross domestic product** (1993): $8.0 bln.* **Per capita GDP:** $3,200. **Imports** (1992): $1.5 bln.; partners: U.S. 53%. **Exports** (1992): $1.1 bln.; partners: U.S. 40%. **Tourism** (1992): $858 mln. **National budget** (1991): $736 mln. **International reserves less gold** (Mar. 1995): $783 mln. **Consumer prices** (change in 1994): 35.1%.

Transport: Railroads: Length: 129 mi. **Motor vehicles:** in use: 97,500 passenger cars, 18,000 comm. vehicles. **Civil aviation:** 889 mln. passenger-mi.; 4 airports with scheduled flights. **Chief ports:** Kingston, Montego Bay.

Communications: Television sets: 1 per 5.1 persons. **Radios:** 1 per 1.6 persons. **Telephones:** 1 per 8.8 persons.

Health: Life expectancy at birth (1995): 72 male; 77 female. **Births** (per 1,000 pop.): 22. **Deaths:** (per 1,000 pop.): 6. **Natural increase:** 1.6%. **Hospital beds:** 1 per 462 persons. **Physicians:** 1 per 6,791 persons. **Infant mortality** (per 1,000 live births 1995): 16.

Education: Literacy (1993): 98%.

Major International Organizations: UN (World Bank, WTO), OAS, the Commonwealth.

Embassy: 1850 K St. NW 20006; 452-0660.

Jamaica was visited by Columbus, 1494, and ruled by Spain (under whom Arawak Indians died out) until seized by Britain, 1655. Jamaica won independence Aug. 6, 1962.

In 1974 Jamaica sought an increase in taxes paid by U.S. and Canadian bauxite mines. The socialist government acquired 50% ownership of the companies' Jamaican interests in 1976, and was reelected that year. Rudimentary welfare state measures were passed. Relations with the U.S. improved greatly in the 1980s following the election of Edward Seaga, which marked the beginning of a more conservative era.

Japan
Nippon

People: Population: 125,506,492. **Age distrib.** (%): <15: 16; 65+: 14. **Pop. density:** 861 per sq. mi. **Urban:** 77%. **Ethnic groups:** Japanese 99.4%, other (mostly Korean) 0.6%. **Principal language:** Japanese. **Religions:** Buddhism, Shintoism shared by large majority.

Geography: Area: 145,850 sq. mi. **Location:** Archipelago off E coast of Asia. **Neighbors:** Russia on N, South Korea on W. **Topography:** Japan consists of 4 main islands: Honshu ("mainland"), 87,805 sq. mi.; Hokkaido, 30,144 sq. mi.; Kyushu, 14,114 sq. mi.; and Shikoku, 7,049 sq. mi. The coast, deeply indented, measures 16,654 mi. The northern islands are a continuation of the Sakhalin Mts. The Kunlun range of China continues into southern islands, the ranges meeting in the Japanese Alps. In a vast transverse fissure crossing Honshu E-W rises a group of volcanoes, mostly extinct or inactive, including 12,388 ft. Fuji-San (Fujiyama) near Tokyo. **Capital:** Tokyo. **Cities** (1993 est.): Tokyo 8.1 mln.; Osaka 2.6 mln.; Yokohama 3.3 mln.; Nagoya 2.2 mln.; Sapporo 1.7 mln.; Kyoto 1.5 mln.; Kobe 1.5 mln.; Fukuoka 1.3 mln.; Kawasaki 1.2 mln.; Hiroshima 1.1 mln.

Government: Type: Parliamentary democracy. **Head of state:** Emp. Akihito; b Dec. 23, 1933; in office: Jan. 7, 1989. **Head of government:** Prime Min. Tomiichi Murayama; b Mar. 23, 1924; in office: June 30, 1994. **Local divisions:** 47 prefectures. **Defense:** 0.94% of GDP (FY 1993-94 est.). **Active troop strength:** 237,700.

Economy: Industries: Electrical & electronic equip., autos, machinery, chemicals. **Chief crops:** Rice, grains, vegetables, fruits. **Livestock** (1992): cattle: 5.0 mln.; pigs: 10.9 mln. **Fish catch** (1992): 9.3 mln. metric tons. **Electricity prod.** (1992): 835 bln. kWh. **Labor force:** 7% agric.; 33% manuf. & mining; 54% services & trade.

Finance: Monetary unit: Yen (May 1995: 83.20 = $1 US). **Gross domestic product** (1993): $2.55 trl.* **Per capita GDP:** $20,400. **Imports** (1993): $240.7 bln.; partners: U.S. 23%, SE Asia 25%, China 9%. **Exports** (1993): $360.9 bln.; partners: U.S. 29%, SE Asia 33%. **Tourism** (1992): $3.6 bln. **National budget** (1993): $579 bln. **International reserves less gold** (May 1995): $156 bln. **Gold:** 24.23 mln. oz t. **Consumer prices** (change in 1994): 0.7%.

Transport: Railroads: Length: 23,690 mi. **Motor vehicles:** in use: 39.0 mln. passenger cars, 22.7 mln. comm. vehicles. **Civil aviation:** 65.7 bln. passenger-mi.; 75 airports with scheduled flights. **Chief ports:** Yokohama, Tokyo, Kobe, Osaka, Nagoya, Chiba, Kawasaki, Hakodate.

Communications: Television sets: 1 per 1.2 persons. **Radios:** 1 per 1.3 persons. **Telephones:** 1 per 2.2 persons. **Daily newspaper circ.:** 579 per 1,000 pop.

Health: Life expectancy at birth (1995): 77 male; 82 female. **Births** (per 1,000 pop.): 11. **Deaths** (per 1,000 pop.): 7. **Natural increase:** 0.3%. **Hospital beds:** 1 per 74 persons. **Physicians:** 1 per 570 persons. **Infant mortality** (per 1,000 live births 1995): 4.

Education: Literacy (1992): 100%. **Years compulsory:** 9 (most attend school for 12 years).

Major International Organizations: UN (IMF, WTO, ILO), OECD.

Embassy: 2520 Massachusetts Ave. NW 20008; 939-6700.

According to Japanese legend, the empire was founded by Emperor Jimmu, 660 BC, but earliest records of a unified Japan date from 1,000 years later. Chinese influence was strong in the formation of Japanese civilization. Buddhism was introduced before the 6th century.

A feudal system, with locally powerful noble families and their samurai warrior retainers, dominated from 1192. Central power was held by successive families of shoguns (military dictators), 1192-1867, until recovered by the Emperor Meiji, 1868. The Portuguese and Dutch had minor trade with Japan in the 16th and 17th centuries; U.S. Commodore Matthew C. Perry opened it to U.S. trade in a treaty ratified 1854. Japan fought China, 1894-95, gaining Taiwan. After war with Russia, 1904-05, Russia ceded S half of Sakhalin and gave concessions in China. Japan annexed Korea 1910. In World War I Japan ousted Germany from Shantung, took over German Pacific islands. Japan took Manchuria 1931, started war with China 1932. Japan launched war against the U.S. by attack on Pearl Harbor Dec. 7, 1941. The U.S. dropped atomic bombs on Hiroshima, Aug. 6, and Nagasaki, Aug. 9, 1945. Japan surrendered Aug. 14, 1945. Japan apologized Aug. 15, 1995, for its acts of "colonial rule and aggression" during World War II.

In a new constitution adopted May 3, 1947, Japan renounced the right to wage war; the emperor gave up claims to divinity; the Diet became the sole law-making authority.

The U.S. and 48 other non-communist nations signed a peace treaty and the U.S. a bilateral defense agreement with Japan, in San Francisco Sept. 8, 1951, restoring Japan's sovereignty as of April 28, 1952.

On June 26, 1968, the U.S. returned to Japanese control the Bonin Is., the Volcano Is. (including Iwo Jima) and Marcus Is. On May 15, 1972, Okinawa, the other Ryukyu Is., and the Daito Is. were returned by the U.S.; it was agreed the U.S. would continue to maintain military bases on Okinawa.

Industrialization was begun in the late 19th century. After World War II, Japan emerged as one of the most powerful economies in the world, and as a leader in technology.

The U.S. and EU member nations have criticized Japan for its restrictive policy on imports, which has given Japan a substantial trade surplus.

The Recruit scandal, the nation's worst political scandal since World War II, which involved illegal political donations and stock trading, led to the resignation of Premier Noboru Takeshita in May 1989. A series of scandals rocked Japan's financial sector in 1991.

Following new political scandals, the Liberal Democratic Party was denied a majority in general elections July 18, 1993. The LDP had held power since it was founded in 1955. Morihiro Hosokawa, a reformer, was chosen prime minister Aug. 6; he initiated reforms but resigned Apr. 8, 1994, because of controversy over his financial connections. His replacement, Tsutomu Hata, resigned June 25, to be replaced by Japan's first Socialist premier since 1947-48, Tomiichi Murayama.

An earthquake in the Kobe area, Jan. 17, 1995, claimed more than 5,000 lives. On Mar. 20, a nerve gas attack in the Tokyo subway (blamed on a religious cult) killed 12 and injured thousands.

Jordan
Hashemite Kingdom of Jordan
al Mamlaka al Urduniya al Hashemiyah

Population: 4,100,709. **Age distrib.** (%): <15: 43; 65+: 3. **Pop. density:** 119 per sq. mi. **Urban:** 68%. **Ethnic groups:** Arab 98%. **Principal language:** Arabic (official). **Religions:** Sunni Muslim 92%, Christian 8%.

Geography: Area: 34,342 sq. mi. **Location:** In W Asia. **Neighbors:** Israel on W, Saudi Arabia on S, Iraq on E, Syria on N. **Topography:** About 88% of Jordan is arid. Fertile areas are in W. Only port is on short Aqaba Gulf coast. Country shares Dead Sea (1,312 ft. below sea level) with Israel. **Capital:** Amman. **Cities** (1993 est.): Amman 1.3 mln.; az-Zarqa 605,000; Irbid 385,000.

Government: Type: Constitutional monarchy. **Head of state:** King Hussein I; b Nov. 14, 1935; in office: Aug. 11, 1952. **Head of government:** Prime Min. Sharif Zeid bin Shaker; in office: Jan. 8, 1995. **Local divisions:** 8 governorates. **Defense:** 6.5% of GDP (1993 est.). **Active troop strength:** 98,600.

Economy: Industries: Textiles, cement, food processing. **Chief crops:** Grains, olives, vegetables, fruits. **Minerals:** Phosphates, potash. **Arable land:** 4%. **Electricity prod.** (1992): 3.8 bln. kWh. **Labor force:** 11% ind.; 7% agric.; 52% other services.

Finance: Monetary unit: Dinar (May 1995: 1.00 = $1.45 US). **Gross domestic product** (1993): $11.5 bln.* **Per capita GDP:** $3,000. **Imports** (1993): $3.2 bln.; partners: U.S. 13%, Iraq 13%. **Exports** (1993): $1.4 bln.; partners: Saudi Arabia 12%, India 10%, Iraq 11%. **Tourism** (1992): $462 mln. **National budget** (1993): $1.9 bln. **International reserves less gold** (May 1995): $1.8 bln. **Gold:** 792,000 oz t. **Consumer prices** (change in 1994): 3.5%.

Transport: Motor vehicles: in use: 177,000 passenger cars, 44,000 comm. vehicles. **Civil aviation:** 2.5 bln. passenger-mi.; 2 airports with scheduled flights. **Chief port:** Aqaba.

Communications: Television sets: 1 per 16.4 persons. **Radios:** 1 per 5.8 persons. **Telephones:** 1 per 10.5 persons. **Daily newspaper circ.:** 70 per 1,000 pop.

Health: Life expectancy at birth (1995): 70 male; 74 female. **Births** (per 1,000 pop.): 37. **Deaths** (per 1,000 pop.): 4. **Natural increase:** 3.3%. **Hospital beds:** 1 per 920 persons. **Physicians:** 1 per 574 persons. **Infant mortality** (per 1,000 live births 1995): 32.

Education: Literacy (1992): 80%.

Major International Organizations: UN (WHO, IMF), Arab League.

Embassy: 3504 International Dr. NW 20008; 966-2664.

From ancient times to 1922 the lands to the E of the Jordan River were culturally and politically united with the lands to the W. Arabs conquered the area in the 7th century; the Ottomans took control in the 16th. Britain's 1920 Palestine Mandate covered both sides of the Jordan. In 1921, Abdullah, son of the ruler of Hejaz in Arabia, was installed by Britain as emir of an autonomous Transjordan, covering two-thirds of Palestine. An independent kingdom was proclaimed, 1946.

During the 1948 Arab-Israeli war the West Bank and East Jerusalem were added to the kingdom, which changed its name to Jordan. All these territories were lost to Israel in the 1967 war, which swelled the number of Arab refugees on the East Bank. A 1974 Arab summit conference designated the Palestine Liberation Organization as the sole representative of Arabs on the West Bank. In 1988 Jordan cut legal and administrative ties with the Israeli-occupied West Bank.

Some 700,000 refugees entered Jordan following Iraq's invasion of Kuwait, Aug. 1990. Jordan was viewed as supporting Iraq during the 1990-1991 Persian Gulf crisis.

Jordan and Israel officially agreed, July 25, 1994, to end their state of war; a formal peace treaty was signed Oct. 26.

Kazakhstan
Republic of Kazakhstan
Kazak Respublikasy

People: Population: 17,376,615. **Pop. density:** 17 per sq. mi. **Urban:** 57%. **Ethnic groups:** Kazakh 42%, Russian 37%, Ukrainian 5%, German 5%. **Principal languages:** Kazakh (official), Russian. **Religions:** Muslim 47%, Russian Orthodox 44%.

Geography: Area: 1,049,200 sq. mi. **Location:** In Central Asia. **Neighbors:** Russia on N, China on E, Kyrgyzstan, Uzbekistan, Turkmenistan on S, Caspian Sea on W. **Topography:** Extends from the lower reaches of Volga in Europe to the Altai Mts. on the Chinese border. **Capital:** Almaty (Alma-Ata). **Cities** (1991): Almaty 1.2 mln., Qaraghandy 609,000.

Government: Type: Republic. **Head of state:** Pres. Nursultan A. Nazarbayev; b July 6, 1940. **Head of government:** Prime Min. Arkezhan Kazhgeldin; in office, Oct. 12, 1994. **Local divisions:** 19 oblystar, 1 city. **Defense:** 2.6% of GNP (1993). **Active troop strength:** 40,000.

Economy: Industries: Steel, mining, agricultural machinery. **Chief crops:** Grain, cotton. **Minerals:** Oil, coal, iron, manganese, copper. **Arable land:** 15%. **Livestock** (1993): cattle: 8.3 mln.; sheep and goats: 33.7 mln.; pigs: 2.5 mln. **Electricity prod.** (1992): 81.3 bln. kWh. **Labor force:** 31% ind.; 26% agric.

Finance: Monetary unit: Tenge (Oct. 1994: 57 = $1 US). **Gross domestic product** (1993 est.): $60.3 bln.* **Per capita GDP:** $3,510.

Transport: Railroads: Length: 13,173 mi. **Motor vehicles:** 735,000 passenger cars. **Civil aviation:** 7.8 bln. passenger-mi.; 6 airports with scheduled flights.

Communications: Television: 1 per 3.6 persons. **Radios:** 1 per 4.1 persons. **Telephones:** 1 per 7.8 persons. **Daily newspaper circ.:** 405 per 1,000 pop.

Health: Life expectancy at birth (1995): 64 male; 73 female. **Birth rate** (per 1,000 pop.): 19. **Death rate** (per 1,000 pop.): 8. **Natural increase:** 1.1%. **Hospital beds:** 1 per 75 persons. **Physicians:** 1 per 246 persons. **Infant mortality** (per 1,000 live births 1995): 40.

Education: Literacy (1992): 97%.

Major International Organizations: UN, CIS.

Embassy: 3421 Massachusetts Ave. NW 20007; 333-4504.

The region came under the Mongols in the 13th century and gradually came under Russian rule, 1730-1853. It was admitted to the USSR as a constituent republic 1936. Kazakhstan declared independence Dec. 16, 1991. It became an independent state when the Soviet Union dissolved Dec. 26, 1991. The party chief, Nursultan Nazarbayev, was elected president unopposed. In legislative elections Mar. 7, 1994, criticized by international monitors, his party won a sweeping victory. Kazakhstan agreed, Feb. 14, to dismantle nuclear missiles and adhere to the 1968 Nuclear Nonproliferation Treaty; the U.S. pledged increased aid. A referendum Apr. 29, 1995, extended Nazarbayev's term to Dec. 2000; a new draft constitution was approved in a referendum Aug. 30.

Kenya
Republic of Kenya
Jamhuri ya Kenya

People: Population: 28,817,227. **Age distrib.** (%): <15: 48; 65+: 3. **Pop. density:** 128 per sq. mi. **Urban:** 27%. **Ethnic groups:** Kikuyu 21%, Luhya 14%, Luo 13%, Kalenjin 12%, Kamba 11%, others, including Asians, Arabs, Europeans. **Principal languages:** Swahili, English (both official), Kikuyu, Luhya, Luo, Meru. **Religions:** Roman Catholic 28%, Protestant 26%, indigenous beliefs 18%, Muslim 6%.

Geography: Area: 224,961 sq. mi. **Location:** On Indian O. coast of E Africa. **Neighbors:** Uganda on W, Tanzania on S, Somalia on E, Ethopia, Sudan on N. **Topography:** The northern three-fifths of Kenya is arid. To the S, a low coastal area and a plateau varying from 3,000 to 10,000 ft. The Great Rift Valley enters the country N-S, flanked by high mountains. **Capital:** Nairobi. **Cities** (1987 est.): Nairobi 959,000; Mombasa 401,000.

Government: Type: Republic. **Head of state:** Pres. Daniel arap Moi, b. Sept. 1924; in office: Aug. 22, 1978. **Local divisions:** Nairobi and 7 provinces. **Defense:** 2.8% of GNP (1991 est.). **Active troop strength:** 24,200.

Economy: Industries: Tourism, light industry, petroleum prods. **Chief crops:** Coffee, corn, tea, dairy products. **Minerals:** Gold, limestone, salt, rubies, fluorspar, garnets. **Other resources:** Timber, hides. **Arable land:** 3%. **Livestock** (1993): cattle: 11 mln. **Fish catch** (1993): 176,000 metric tons. **Electricity prod.** (1993): 3.4 bln. kWh. **Labor force:** 19% agric.; 43% services.

Finance: Monetary unit: Shilling (May 1995: 54 = $1 US). **Gross domestic product** (1993): $33.2 bln.* **Per capita GDP:** $1,200. **Imports** (1992): $1.6 bln.; partners: EU 46%. **Exports** (1992): $1.0 bln.; partners: EU 47%. **Tourism** (1992): $442 mln. **National budget** (1990): $2.8 bln. **International reserves less gold** (May 1995): $461 mln. **Gold:** 80,000 oz t. **Consumer prices** (change in 1994): 29.0%.

Transport: Motor vehicles: in use: 157,000 passenger cars, 172,000 comm. vehicles. **Civil aviation:** 828 mln. passenger-mi.; 14 airports with scheduled flights. **Chief port:** Mombasa.

Communications: Television sets: 1 per 102 persons. **Radios:** 1 per 6.3 persons. **Telephones:** 1 per 61 persons.

Health: Life expectancy at birth (1995): 51 male; 54 female. **Births** (per 1,000 pop.): 42. **Deaths** (per 1,000 pop.): 12. **Natural increase:** 3.0%. **Hospital beds:** 1 per 737 persons. **Physicians:** 1 per 7,410 persons. **Infant mortality** (per 1,000 live births 1995): 73.

Education: Literacy (1993): 69%. 86% attend primary school.
Major International Organizations: UN and all of its specialized agencies, OAU, the Commonwealth.
Embassy: 2249 R St. NW 20008; 387-6101.

Arab colonies exported spices and slaves from the Kenya coast as early as the 8th century. Britain obtained control in the 19th century. Kenya won independence Dec. 12, 1963, 4 years after the end of the violent Mau Mau uprising.

Kenya had steady growth in industry and agriculture under a modified private enterprise system, and enjoyed a relatively free political life. But stability was shaken in 1974-75, with opposition charges of corruption and oppression. Jomo Kenyatta, the country's leader since independence, died Aug. 22, 1978. He was succeeded by his vice-president, Daniel arap Moi.

Tribal clashes in the western provinces claimed thousands of lives in the early 1990s and left tens of thousands homeless. The unrest was the worst since independence in 1963. Several western nations issued travel advisories for Kenya.

In the 1990s, Kenya suffered from widespread unemployment and high inflation. Pres. Moi won a third term in Dec. 1992 elections, which were marred by wide-scale violence and charges of corruption.

Kiribati
Republic of Kiribati

People: Population: 79,386. **Pop. density:** 254 per sq. mi. **Ethnic groups:** nearly all Micronesian, some Polynesian. **Principal languages:** English (official), Gilbertese. **Religions:** Roman Catholic 53%, Protestant 41%.
Geography: Area: 313 sq. mi. **Location:** 33 Micronesian islands (the Gilbert, Line, and Phoenix groups) in the mid-Pacific scattered in a 2-mln. sq. mi. chain around the point where the International Date Line cuts the Equator. **Neighbors:** Nearest are Nauru to SW, Tuvalu and Tokelau Is. to S. **Topography:** Except Banaba (Ocean) I., all are low-lying, with soil of coral sand and rock fragments, subject to erratic rainfall. **Capital:** Tarawa (1990): 25,000.
Government: Type: Republic. **Head of state and government:** Pres. Teburoro Tito; in office: Oct. 1, 1994.
Economy: Industries: Copra. **Chief crops:** Taro, breadfruit, sweet potatoes, vegetables. **Other resources:** Fish. **Electricity prod.** (1990): 13 mln. kWh.
Finance: Monetary unit: Australian Dollar. **Gross domestic product** (1990): $36 mln. **Per capita GDP:** $525. **National budget** (1990 est.): $16.3 mln.
Transport: Chief port: Tarawa.
Communications: Radios: 1 per 7.7 persons. **Telephones:** 1 per 47 persons.
Health: Births (per 1,000 pop.): 31. **Deaths** (per 1,000 pop.): 12. **Natural increase:** 1.9%. **Hospital beds:** 1 per 253 persons. **Physicians:** 1 per 4,483 persons.
Education: Literacy (1992): 90%.
Major International Organizations: UN, the Commonwealth.

A British protectorate since 1892, the Gilbert and Ellice Islands colony was completed with the inclusion of the Phoenix Islands, 1937. Self-rule was granted 1971; the Ellice Islands separated from the colony 1975 and became independent Tuvalu, 1978. Kiribati (pronounced *Kiribass)* independence was attained July 12, 1979. Under a treaty of friendship the U.S. relinquished its claims to several of the Line and Phoenix islands, including Christmas (Kiritimati), Canton, and Enderbury.

Tarawa Atoll was the scene of some of the bloodiest fighting in the Pacific during World War II.

Korea, North
Democratic People's Republic of Korea
Chosun Minchu-chui Inmin Konghwa-guk

People: Population: 23,486,550. **Age distrib.** (%): <15: 30; 65+: 4. **Pop. density:** 496 per sq. mi. **Urban:** 61%. **Ethnic groups:** Korean. **Principal languages:** Korean. **Religions:**

activities almost nonexistent; traditionally Buddhism, Confucianism, Chondogyo.
Geography: Area: 47,399 sq. mi. **Location:** In northern E Asia. **Neighbors:** China, Russia on N, South Korea on S. **Topography:** Mountains and hills cover nearly all the country, with narrow valleys and small plains in between. The N and the E coasts are the most rugged areas. **Capital:** Pyongyang (1987 est.): 2.4 mln.
Government: Type: Communist state. **Leader:** Kim Jong Il; b Feb. 16, 1948; in power: July 1994. **Local divisions:** 9 provinces, 3 special cities. **Defense:** 25.5% of GNP (1993). **Active troop strength:** 1.1 mln.
Economy: Industries: Textiles, chemicals, machinery, food processing. **Chief crops:** Corn, potatoes, soybeans, rice. **Minerals:** Coal, lead, tungsten, zinc, graphite, magnesite, iron, copper, gold, salt, fluorspar. **Arable land:** 18%. **Livestock** (1992): cattle: 1.3 mln.; pigs: 3.3 mln. **Fish catch** (1991): 1.7 mln. metric tons. **Electricity prod.** (1992): 26 bln. kWh. **Labor force:** 36% agric.
Finance: Monetary unit: Won (Oct. 1994: 2.15 = $1 US). **Gross national product** (1992): $22 bln.* **Per capita GNP:** $1,000. **Imports** (1992): $1.9 bln.; partners: China 23%, Russia 38%, Japan 10%. **Exports** (1992): $1.3 bln.; partners: Russia 45%, China 7%, Japan 23%. **National budget** (1992): $19.3 bln.
Transport: Chief ports: Chongjin, Hamhung, Nampo.
Communications: Television sets: 1 per 67 persons. **Radios:** 1 per 4.8 persons. **Telephones:** 1 per 20 persons.
Health: Life expectancy at birth (1995): 67 male; 73 female. **Births** (per 1,000 pop.): 23. **Deaths** (per 1,000 pop.): 5. **Natural increase:** 1.8%. **Hospital beds:** 1 per 74 persons. **Physicians:** 1 per 370 persons. **Infant mortality** (per 1,000 live births 1995): 27.
Education: Literacy (1991): 99%. **Years compulsory:** 11.
Major International Organizations: UN.

The Democratic People's Republic of Korea was founded May 1, 1948, in the zone occupied by Russian troops after World War II. Its armies tried to conquer the south, 1950. After 3 years of fighting, with Chinese and U.S. intervention, a cease-fire was proclaimed.

Industry, begun by the Japanese during their 1910-45 occupation, and nationalized in the 1940s, had grown substantially, using North Korea's abundant mineral and hydroelectric resources.

In Mar. 1993, North Korea became the first nation to formally withdraw from the Nuclear Nonproliferation Treaty, the international pact designed to limit the spread of nuclear weapons. The nation suspended its withdrawal in June in reaction to threats of UN economic sanctions, but was widely believed to be developing nuclear weapons. The U.S. and North Korea reached an interim agreement, Aug. 13, 1994, intended to resolve the nuclear issue, and further negotiations followed

Kim Il Sung, who in 1948 had been one of the founders of the state of North Korea and who had ruled over it for more than 40 years, died July 8, 1994. He was apparently succeeded by his son, Kim Jong Il.

Korea, South
Republic of Korea
Daehan Min-kuk

People: Population: 45,553,882. **Age distrib.** (%): <15: 24; 65+: 5. **Pop. density:** 1,188 per sq. mi. **Urban:** 74%. **Ethnic groups:** Korean. **Principal languages:** Korean. **Religions:** Christian 49%, Buddhist 47%.
Geography: Area: 38,330 sq. mi. **Location:** In northern E Asia. **Neighbors:** North Korea on N. **Topography:** The country is mountainous, with a rugged east coast. The western and southern coasts are deeply indented, with many islands and harbors. **Capital:** Seoul. **Cities** (1990 est.): Seoul 10.6 mln.; Pusan 3.8 mln.; Taegu 2.2 mln.; Inchon 1.8 mln.; Kwangju 1.1 mln.
Government: Type: Republic, with power centralized in a strong executive. **Head of state:** Pres. Kim Young Sam; b Dec. 20, 1927; in office: Feb. 25, 1993. **Head of government:** Prime Min. Lee Hong Koo; in office: Dec. 17, 1994. **Local divisions:** 9 provinces and 6 special cities. **Defense:** 3.6% of GNP (1993 est.). **Active troop strength:** 633,000.

Economy: Industries: Electronics, ships, textiles, clothing, motor vehicles. **Chief crops:** Rice, barley, vegetables, wheat. **Minerals:** Tungsten, coal, graphite. **Arable land:** 21%. **Livestock** (1993): cattle: 2.8 mln.; pigs: 5.9 mln. **Fish catch** (1992): 3.3 mln. metric tons. **Electricity prod.** (1992): 105 bln. kWh. **Labor force:** 21% agric.; 27% manuf. & mining; 52% services.

Finance: Monetary unit: Won (May 1995: 760 = $1 US). **Gross national product** (1993): $424 bln.* **Per capita GNP:** $9,500. **Imports** (1993): $78.9 bln.; partners: Japan 26%, U.S. 24%. **Exports** (1993): $81 bln.; partners: U.S. 26%, Japan 17%. **Tourism** (1992): $3.3 bln. **National budget** (1993): $48.4 bln. **International reserves less gold** (May 1995): $27.0 bln. **Gold:** 326,000 oz t. **Consumer prices** (change in 1994): 6.3%.

Transport: Railroads: Length: 4,049 mi. **Motor vehicles:** in use: 3.5 mln. passenger cars, 1.7 mln. comm. vehicles. **Civil aviation:** 12.4 bln. passenger-mi.; 13 airlines with scheduled flights. **Chief ports:** Pusan, Inchon.

Communications: Television sets: 1 per 4.8 persons. **Radios:** 1 per person. **Telephones:** 1 per 2.3 persons.

Health: Life expectancy at birth (1995): 68 male; 74 female. **Births** (per 1,000 pop.): 16. **Deaths** (per 1,000 pop.): 6. **Natural increase:** 0.9%. **Hospital beds:** 1 per 379 persons. **Physicians:** 1 per 902 persons. **Infant mortality** (per 1,000 live births 1995): 21.

Education: Literacy (1993): 96%. **Attendance:** High school 90%, college 14%.

Major International Organizations: UN (WTO, IMF, WHO). **Embassy:** 2450 Massachusetts Ave. NW 20008; 939-5600.

Korea, once called the Hermit Kingdom, has a recorded history since the 1st century BC. It was united in a kingdom under the Silla Dynasty, 668 AD. It was at times associated with the Chinese empire; the treaty that concluded the Sino-Japanese war of 1894-95 recognized Korea's complete independence. In 1910 Japan forcibly annexed Korea as Cho-sun.

At the Potsdam conference, July, 1945, the 38th parallel was designated as the line dividing the Soviet and the American occupation. Russian troops entered Korea Aug. 10, 1945, U.S. troops entered Sept. 8, 1945. The Soviet military organized socialists and Communists and blocked efforts to let the Koreans unite their country. *(See Index for Korean War.)*

The South Koreans formed the Republic of Korea in May 1948 with Seoul as the capital. Dr. Syngman Rhee was chosen president, but a movement spearheaded by college students forced his resignation Apr. 26, 1960.

In an army coup May 16, 1961, Gen. Park Chung Hee became chairman of the ruling junta. He was elected president, 1963; a 1972 referendum allowed him to be reelected for 6-year terms unlimited times. Park was assassinated by the chief of the Korean CIA, Oct. 26, 1979. The calm of the new government was halted by the rise of Gen. Chun Doo Hwan, head of the military intelligence, who reinstated martial law.

In July 1972 South and North Korea agreed on a common goal of reunifying the 2 nations by peaceful means. But there was no sign of a thaw in relations between the two regimes until 1985, when they agreed to discuss economic issues. In 1988, radical students demanding reunification clashed with police.

On June 10, 1987, middle-class office workers, shopkeepers, and business executives joined students in antigovernment protests in Seoul calling for democratic reforms. Following weeks of rioting and violence, Chun, July 1, agreed to permit election of the next president by direct popular vote and other constitutional reforms. In Dec., Roh Tae Woo was elected president. In 1990, the nation's 3 largest political parties merged; some 100,000 students demonstrated, charging that the merger was undemocratic.

Kim Young Sam took office in 1993 as the first civilian president since 1961.

Kuwait
State of Kuwait
Dowlat al-Kuwait

People: Population: 1,817,397. **Age distrib.** (%): <15: 34; 65+: 2. **Pop. density:** 264 per sq. mi. **Ethnic groups:** Kuwaiti 45%, other Arab 35%, Iranians, Indians, Pakistanis. **Principal language:** Arabic (official). **Religion:** Muslim 85%.

Geography: Area: 6,880 sq. mi. **Location:** In Middle East, at N end of Persian Gulf. **Neighbors:** Iraq on N, Saudi Arabia on S. **Topography:** The country is flat, very dry, and extremely hot. **Capital:** Kuwait City. **Cities** (1985 est.): as-Salimiyah 153,000; Hawalli 145,000.

Government: Type: Constitutional monarchy. **Head of state:** Emir Sheikh Jabir al-Ahmad al-Jabir as-Sabah; b 1928; in office: Jan. 1, 1978. **Head of government:** Prime Min. Sheikh Saad Abdulla as-Salim as-Sabah; b 1930; in office: Feb. 8, 1978. **Local divisions:** 5 governorates. **Defense:** 7.3% of GDP (1993). **Active troop strength:** 16,600.

Economy: Industries: Oil products. **Minerals:** Oil, gas. **Crude oil reserves** (1994): 96.5 bln. barrels. **Cultivated land:** 1%. **Electricity prod.** (1992): 12.3 bln. kWh. **Labor force:** 20% construction; 45% services.

Finance: Monetary unit: Dinar (May 1995: 1.00 = $3.36 US). **Gross domestic product** (1993): $25.7 bln. **Per capita GDP:** $15,000. **Imports** (1993): $6 bln.; partners: U.S. 35%, Japan 12%. **Exports** (1993): $10.5 bln.; partners: France 16%, Italy 15%. **Tourism** (1992): $273 mln. **National budget** (1993): $13 bln. **International reserves less gold** (May 1995): $3.7 bln. **Gold:** 2.54 mln. oz t.

Transport: Motor vehicles: in use: 580,000 passenger cars, 127,000 comm. vehicles. **Civil aviation:** 2.5 bln. passenger-mi.; 1 airport with scheduled flights. **Chief port:** Mina al-Ahmadi.

Communications: Television sets: 1 per 1.8 persons. **Radios:** 1 per 1.4 persons. **Telephones:** 1 per 4.0 persons. **Daily newspaper circ.:** 550 per 1,000 pop.

Health: Life expectancy at birth (1995): 73 male; 78 female. **Births** (per 1,000 pop.): 21. **Deaths** (per 1,000 pop.): 2. **Natural increase:** 1.9%. **Hospital beds:** 1 per 347 persons. **Physicians:** 1 per 515 persons. **Infant mortality** (per 1,000 live births 1995): 11.

Education: Literacy (1994): 80%. **Years compulsory:** 8.

Major International Organizations: UN (World Bank, IMF, WTO), Arab League, OPEC.

Embassy: 2940 Tilden St. NW 20008; 966-0702.

Kuwait is ruled by the Al-Sabah dynasty, founded 1759. Britain ran foreign relations and defense from 1899 until independence in 1961. The majority of the population is non-Kuwaiti, with many Palestinians, and cannot vote.

Oil is the fiscal mainstay, providing most of Kuwait's income. Oil pays for free medical care, education, and social security. There are no taxes, except customs duties.

Kuwaiti oil tankers came under frequent attack by Iran because of Kuwait's support of Iraq in the Iran-Iraq War. In July 1987, U.S. Navy warships began escorting Kuwaiti tankers in the Persian Gulf.

Kuwait was attacked and overrun by Iraqi forces Aug. 2, 1990. The emir and senior members of the ruling family fled to Saudi Arabia to establish a government in exile. On Aug. 28, Iraq announced that Kuwait was its 19th province. Following several weeks of aerial attacks on Iraq and Iraqi forces in Kuwait, a U.S.-led coalition began a ground attack Feb. 23, 1991. By Feb. 27, Iraqi forces were routed and Kuwait liberated. Following liberation, there were reports of abuse of Palestinians and others suspected of collaborating with Iraqi occupiers. Kuwait spent more than $5 billion to repair oil installations damaged during 1990–91.

Former U.S. Pres. George Bush visited Kuwait, Apr. 14-16, 1993, and was honored as the leader of the Persian Gulf War alliance that expelled Iraqi troops. Kuwaiti authorities arrested 14 Iraqis and Kuwaitis for allegedly plotting to assassinate Bush during his visit. Thirteen were convicted and sentenced to prison or death, June 4, 1994.

Kyrgyzstan
Republic of Kyrgyzstan
Kyrgyz Respublikasy

People: Population: 4,769,877. **Pop density:** 62 per sq. mi. **Urban:** 36%. **Ethnic groups:** Kirghiz 52%, Russian 22%, Uzbek 13%. **Principal languages:** Kirghiz (official), Russian. **Religion:** Muslim 70%.

Geography: Area: 76,600 sq. mi. **Location:** In Central Asia. **Neighbors:** Kazakhstan on N, China on E, Uzbekistan on W, Tajikistan on S. **Capital:** Bishkek. **Cities** (1991): Bishkek 631,000; Osh 218,000.

Government: Type: Republic. **Head of state:** Pres. Askar Akayev; b 1944; in office: Oct. 28, 1990. **Head of government:** Prime Min. Apas Jumagulov; in office: Dec. 1993. **Local divisions:** 6 oblasts. **Defense: Active troop strength:** 12,000+ est.

Economy: Industries: Tanning, tobacco, textiles, mining. **Chief crops:** Tobacco, cotton, fruits **Minerals:** Gold. **Arable land:** 7%. **Livestock** (1993): cattle: 1.0 mln.; sheep and goats: 9.3 mln. **Electricity prod.** (1992): 11.8 bln. kWh. **Labor force:** 38% agric.; 21% ind.

Finance: Monetary unit: Som (Oct. 1994: 10.20 = $1 US). **Gross domestic prod.** (1993 est.): $11.3 bln.* **Per capita GDP:** $2,440.

Transport: Railroads: Length: 490 mi. **Motor vehicles:** in use: 174,000 passenger cars. **Civil aviation:** 1.6 bln. passenger-mi.; 1 airport.

Communications: Telephones: 1 per 12.8 persons. **Daily newspaper circ.:** 367 per 1,000 pop.

Health: Life expectancy at birth (1995): 64 male; 73 female. **Birth rate** (per 1,000 pop.): 26. **Death rate** (per 1,000 pop.): 7. **Natural increase:** 1.9%. **Hospital beds:** 1 per 85 persons. **Physicians:** 1 per 283 persons. **Infant mortality** (per 1,000 live births 1995): 46.

Education: Literacy (1993): 97%.
Major International Organizations: UN (IMF), CIS.
Embassy: 1511 K St. NW 20005; 347-3732.

The region was inhabited around the 13th century by the Kirghiz. It was annexed to Russia 1864. After 1917, it was nominally a Kara-Kirghiz autonomous area, which was reorganized 1926, and made a constituent republic of the USSR in 1936. Kyrgyzstan declared independence Aug. 31, 1991. It became an independent state when the USSR disbanded Dec. 26, 1991. A constitution was adopted May 5, 1993.

Laos

Lao People's Democratic Republic

Sathalanalat Paxathipatai Paxaxon Lao

People: Population: 4,837,237. **Pop. density:** 53 per sq. mi. **Urban:** 19%. **Ethnic groups:** Lao 50%, tribal Thai 20%, Phoutheung 15%, Meo, Hmong, Yao, others. **Principal languages:** Lao (official), French, English. **Religions:** Buddhist 85%, animist and other 15%.

Geography: Area: 91,429 sq. mi. **Location:** In Indochina Peninsula in SE Asia. **Neighbors:** Myanmar, China on N, Vietnam on E, Cambodia on S, Thailand on W. **Topography:** Landlocked, dominated by jungle. High mountains along the eastern border are the source of the E-W rivers slicing across the country to the Mekong R., which defines most of the western border. **Capital:** Vientiane (1990 met. est.): 442,000.

Government: Type: Communist. **Head of state:** Pres. Nouhak Phoumsavan; b 1914; in office: Nov. 25, 1992. **Head of government:** Prime Min. Khamtai Siphandon; b 1925; in office: Aug. 15, 1991. **Local divisions:** 16 provinces, 1 municipality. **Defense:** 6.1% of GDP (1992). **Active troop strength:** 37,000.

Economy: Industries: Wood products, mining. **Chief crops:** Rice, corn, cotton, opium, vegetables, coffee. **Minerals:** Tin. **Other resources:** Forests. **Arable land:** 4%. **Livestock** (1993): pigs: 1.6 mln. **Fish catch** (1991): 20,000 metric tons. **Electricity prod.** (1992): 990 mln. kWh. **Labor force:** 85% agric.; 6% ind.

Finance: Monetary unit: New Kip (Oct. 1994: 720 = $1 US). **Gross domestic product** (1993): $4.1 bln.* **Per capita GDP:** $900. **Imports** (1992): $266 mln.; partners: Thai. 51%, Japan 15%. **Exports** (1992): $133 mln.; partners: Thai. 34%, China 6%.

Transport: Motor vehicles: in use: 20,000 passenger cars, 13,000 comm. vehicles.

Communications: Radios: 1 per 11 persons.

Health: Life expectancy at birth (1995): 51 male; 54 female. **Births** (per 1,000 pop.): 43. **Deaths** (per 1,000 pop.): 14. **Natural increase:** 2.8%. **Hospital beds:** 1 per 402 persons. **Physicians:** 1 per 3,555 persons. **Infant mortality** (per 1,000 live births 1995): 99.

Education: Literacy (1992): 84%.
Major International Organizations: UN (FAO, IMF, WHO).
Embassy: 2222 S St. NW 20008; 332-6416.

Laos became a French protectorate in 1893, but regained independence as a constitutional monarchy July 19, 1949.

Conflicts among neutralist, communist, and conservative factions created a chaotic political situation. Armed conflict increased after 1960.

The 3 factions formed a coalition government in June 1962, with neutralist Prince Souvanna Phouma as premier. A 14-nation conference in Geneva signed agreements, 1962, guaranteeing neutrality and independence. By 1964 the Pathet Lao had withdrawn from the coalition, and, with aid from N Vietnamese troops, renewed sporadic attacks. U.S. planes bombed the Ho Chi Minh trail, supply line from N Vietnam to Communist forces in Laos and S Vietnam.

In 1970 the U.S. stepped up air support and military aid. After Pathet Lao military gains, Souvanna Phouma in May 1975 ordered government troops to cease fighting; the Pathet Lao took control. The Lao People's Democratic Republic was proclaimed Dec. 3, 1975. From the mid-1970s through the 1980s, the Laotian government relied on Vietnam for military and financial aid.

Latvia

Republic of Latvia

Latvijas Republika

People: Population: 2,762,899. **Pop density:** 111 per sq. mi. **Urban:** 69%. **Ethnic groups:** Latvian 52%, Russian 34%. **Principal languages:** Latvian (official), Lithuanian, Russian. **Religions:** Lutheran, Roman Catholic, Russian Orthodox.

Geography: Area: 24,946 sq. mi. **Location:** E Europe, on the Baltic Sea. **Neighbors:** Estonia on N, Lithuania, Belarus on S, Russia on E. **Capital:** Riga (1993): 874,000.

Government: Type: Republic. **Head of state:** Pres. Guntis Ulmanis; in office: July 1993. **Head of government:** Prime Min. Maris Gailis; in office: Sept. 15, 1994. **Local divisions:** 26 counties, 7 municipalities. **Defense: Active troop strength:** 6,850.

Economy: Industries: Machinery, vehicles, electric railway passenger cars. **Chief crops:** oats, barley, potatoes. **Arable land:** 27%. **Livestock** (1993): cattle 1.1 mln. **Fish catch** (1991): 370,000 metric tons. **Electricity prod.** (1992): 5.8 bln. kWh. **Labor force:** 16% agric. & forestry; 41% ind.

Finance: Monetary unit: Lat (Oct. 1994: 0.55 = $1 US). **Gross domestic product** (1993 est.): $13.2 bln.* **Per capita GDP:** $4,810. **Imports** (1990): $9.0 bln. **Exports** (1990): $239 mln.

Transport: Railroads: Length: 1,489 mi. **Motor vehicles:** in use: 340,000 passenger cars, 87,000 comm. vehicles. **Civil aviation:** 1.9 bln. passenger-mi.; 1 airport. **Chief port:** Riga.

Communications: Television sets: 1 per 2.4 persons. **Radios:** 1.9 per household. **Telephones:** 1 per 3.6 persons. **Daily newspaper circ.:** 1,377 per 1,000 pop.

Health: Life expectancy at birth (1995): 65 male, 75 female. **Births** (per 1,000 pop.): 14. **Deaths** (per 1,000 pop.): 13. **Natural increase:** 0.1%. **Hospital beds:** 1 per 78 persons. **Physicians:** 1 per 246 persons. **Infant mortality rates** (per 1,000 live births 1995): 21.

Major International Organizations: UN.
Embassy: 4325 17th St. NW 20011; 726-8213.

Prior to 1918, Latvia was occupied by the Russians and Germans. It was an independent republic, 1918-39. The Aug. 1939 Soviet-German agreement assigned it to the Soviet sphere of influence. It was officially accepted as part of the USSR on Aug. 5, 1940. It was overrun by the German army, but retaken in 1945.

During an abortive Soviet coup, Latvia declared independence, Aug. 21, 1991. The Soviet Union recognized Latvia's independence in Sept. 1991. The last Russian troops in Latvia withdrew by Aug. 31, 1994.

Lebanon

Republic of Lebanon
al-Jumhouriya al-Lubnaniya

People: Population: 3,695,921. **Age distrib.** (%): <15: 33; 65+: 5. **Pop. density:** 936 per sq. mi. **Urban:** 86%. **Ethnic groups:** Arab 95%, Armenian 4%. **Principal languages:** Arabic, French (both official). **Religions:** Muslim 70%, Christian 30%.

Geography: Area: 3,950 sq. mi. **Location:** On E end of Mediterranean Sea. **Neighbors:** Syria on E, Israel on S. **Topography:** There is a narrow coastal strip, and 2 mountain ranges running N-S enclosing the fertile Beqaa Valley. The Litani R. runs S through the valley, turning W to empty into the Mediterranean. **Capital:** Beirut. **Cities** (1991 est.): Beirut 1.1 mln.; Tripoli 240,000.

Government: Type: Republic. **Head of state:** Pres. Elias Hrawi; b 1930; in office: Nov. 24, 1989. **Head of government:** Prime Min. Rafiq al-Hariri; b 1944; in office: Oct. 31, 1992. **Local divisions:** 5 governorates. **Defense:** 4.4% of GDP (1993). **Active troop strength:** 44,300.

Economy: Industries: Banking, food products, textiles, cement, oil products. **Chief crops:** Fruits, olives, tobacco, grapes, vegetables. **Minerals:** Limestone, iron. **Arable land:** 21%. **Livestock** (1993): goats: 450,000; sheep: 250,000. **Electricity prod.** (1992): 3.4 bln. kWh. **Labor force:** 11% agric.; 79% ind., commerce, services.

Finance: Monetary unit: Pound (May 1995: 1,624 = $1 US). **Gross domestic product** (1993): $6.1 bln. **Per capita GDP:** $1,720. **Imports** (1993): $4.1 bln.; partners: Italy 14%, France 12%, U.S. 6%. **Exports** (1993): $925 mln.; partners: Saudi Arabia 21%, Switzerland 10%, Jordan 6%. **National budget** (1993): $2.0 bln. **International reserves less gold** (May 1995): $3.1 bln. **Gold:** 9.22 mln. oz t.

Transport: Motor vehicles: in use: 300,000 passenger cars, 50,000 comm. vehicles. **Civil aviation:** 798 mln. passenger-mi.; 1 airport with scheduled flights. **Chief ports:** Beirut, Tripoli, Sidon.

Communications: Television sets: 1 per 2.6 persons. **Radios:** 1 per 1.3 persons. **Telephones:** 1 per 8.3 persons.

Health: Life expectancy at birth (1995): 67 male; 72 female. **Births** (per 1,000 pop.): 28. **Deaths** (per 1,000 pop.): 6. **Natural increase:** 2.1%. **Hospital beds:** 1 per 263 persons. **Physicians:** 1 per 407 persons. **Infant mortality** (per 1,000 live births 1995): 38.

Education: Literacy (1991): 75%. **Years compulsory:** 5; attendance 93%.

Major International Organizations: UN, Arab League.

Embassy: 2560 28th St. NW 20008; 939-6300.

Formed from 5 former Turkish Empire districts, Lebanon became an independent state Sept. 1, 1920, administered under French mandate 1920-41. French troops withdrew in 1946.

Under the 1943 National Covenant, all public positions were divided among the various religious communities, with Christians in the majority. By the 1970s, Muslims became the majority and demanded a larger political and economic role.

U.S. Marines intervened, May-Oct. 1958, during a Syrian-aided revolt. Continued raids against Israeli civilians, 1970-75, brought Israeli attacks against guerrilla camps and villages. Israeli troops occupied S Lebanon, Mar. 1978, and again in Apr. 1980.

An estimated 60,000 were killed and billions of dollars in damage inflicted in a 1975-76 civil war. Palestinian units and leftist Muslims fought against the Maronite militia, the Phalange, and other Christians. Several Arab countries provided political and arms support to the various factions, while Israel aided Christian forces. Up to 15,000 Syrian troops intervened in 1976, and fought Palestinian groups. Arab League troops from several nations tried to impose a cease-fire.

Clashes between Syrian troops and Christian forces erupted, Apr. 1, 1981, bringing to an end the cease-fire. By Apr. 22, fighting had also broken out between two Muslim factions. In July, Israeli air raids on Beirut killed or wounded some 800 persons.

Israeli forces invaded Lebanon June 6, 1982, in a coordinated land, sea, and air attack aimed at crushing strongholds of the Palestine Liberation Organization (PLO). Israeli and Syrian forces engaged in the Bekaa Valley. By June 14, Israeli troops had encircled Beirut. On Aug. 21, the PLO evacuated west Beirut following massive Israeli bombings of the city. Israeli troops entered west Beirut following the Sept. 14 assassination of newly elected Lebanese Pres. Bashir Gemayel. On Sept. 16, Lebanese Christian troops entered 2 refugee camps and massacred hundreds of Palestinian refugees. Israeli troops withdrew from Lebanon in June 1985.

In 1983, terrorist bombings became a way of life in Beirut as some 50 people were killed in an explosion at the U.S. Embassy, Apr. 18; 241 U.S. servicemen and 58 French soldiers died in separate Muslim suicide attacks, Oct. 23.

There was heavy fighting between Shiite militiamen and Palestinian guerrillas in May 1985. In June, Beirut Airport was the scene of a hostage crisis where Shiite terrorists held U.S. citizens for 17 days. Fierce artillery duels between Christian east Beirut and Muslim west Beirut, Mar.-Apr. 1989, left some 200 dead and 700 wounded.

Kidnapping of foreign nationals by Islamic militants became common in the 1980s. U.S., British, French, and Soviet citizens were victims. All were released by 1992.

A treaty signed May 22, 1991, between Lebanon and Syria recognized Lebanon as a separate, independent state for the first time since the 2 countries gained independence in 1943. At least 20,000 Syrian troops remained in Lebanon, however.

Israeli forces conducted air raids and artillery strikes against guerrilla bases and villages in S Lebanon, causing over 200,000 to flee their homes July 25-29, 1993.

Lesotho

Kingdom of Lesotho

People: Population: 1,992,960. **Age distrib.** (%): <15: 41; 65+: 4. **Pop. density:** 170 per sq. mi. **Urban:** 22%. **Ethnic groups:** Sotho 99.7%. **Principal languages:** English (official), Sesotho. **Religion:** Christian 80%.

Geography: Area: 11,720 sq. mi. **Location:** In southern Africa. **Neighbors:** Completely surrounded by Republic of South Africa. **Topography:** Landlocked and mountainous, with altitudes ranging from 5,000 to 11,000 ft. **Capital:** Maseru (1990 est.): 109,000.

Government: Type: Constitutional monarchy. **Head of state:** King Moshoeshoe II; b May 2, 1938; in office: Jan. 25, 1995. **Head of government:** Ntsu Mokhehle; in office: Sept. 14, 1994. **Local divisions:** 10 districts. **Defense:** 13% of GDP (1990 est.). **Active troop strength:** 2,000.

Economy: Industries: Food processing. **Chief crops:** Corn, grains, peas, beans. **Other resources:** Diamonds. **Arable land:** 10%. **Labor force:** 86% subsistence agric.

Finance: Monetary unit: Loti (May 1995: 1.00 = $.27 US). **Gross domestic product** (1993): $2.8 bln.* **Per capita GDP:** $1,500. **Imports** (1992): $964 mln.; partners: Mostly South Africa. **Exports** (1992): $109 mln.; partners: South Africa 42%, EU 28%. **National budget** (1994): $430 mln.

Transport: Motor vehicles: in use: 6,000 passenger cars, 14,000 comm. vehicles.

Communications: Radios: 1 per 4.4 persons. **Daily newspaper circ.:** 19 per 1,000 pop.

Health: Life expectancy at birth (1995): 61 male; 64 female. **Births** (per 1,000 pop.): 33. **Deaths** (per 1,000 pop.): 9. **Natural increase:** 2.4%. **Hospital beds:** 1 per 765 persons. **Physicians:** 1 per 13,209 persons. **Infant mortality** (per 1,000 live births 1995): 67.

Education: Literacy (1992): 74%.

Major International Organizations: UN (IMF, WTO, WHO), OAU, the Commonwealth.

Embassy: 2511 Massachusetts Ave. NW 20008; 797-5533.

Lesotho (once called Basutoland) became a British protectorate in 1868 when Chief Moshesh sought protection against the Boers. Independence came Oct. 4, 1966. Elections were suspended in 1970. Most of Lesotho's GNP is provided by citizens working in S Africa. Livestock raising is the chief industry; diamonds are the chief export.

S Africa imposed a blockade, Jan. 1, 1986, because of Lesotho's giving sanctuary to rebel groups fighting to overthrow the

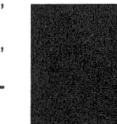

S African government. The blockade sparked a Jan. 20 military coup, and was lifted, Jan. 25, when the new leaders agreed to expel the rebels.

In Mar. 1990, King Moshoeshoe was exiled by the military government. Letsie III became king Nov. 12. In Mar. 1993, Ntsu Mokhehle, a civilian, was elected prime minister, ending 23 years of military rule. After a series of violent disturbances, the king dismissed the Mokhele government Aug. 17, 1994; constitutional rule was restored Sept. 14. Letsie abdicated and Moshoeshoe was reinstated Jan. 25, 1995.

Liberia

Republic of Liberia

People: Population: 3,073,245. **Age distrib.** (%): <15: 46; 65+: 4. **Pop. density:** 80 per sq. mi. **Urban:** 44%. **Ethnic groups:** indigenous tribes 95%, Americo-Liberians 5%. **Principal languages:** English (official), tribal languages. **Religions:** traditional beliefs 70%, Muslim 20%, Christian 10%.

Geography: Area: 38,250 sq. mi. **Location:** On SW coast of W Africa. **Neighbors:** Sierra Leone on W, Guinea on N, Côte d'Ivoire on E. **Topography:** Marshy Atlantic coastline rises to low mountains and plateaus in the forested interior; 6 major rivers flow in parallel courses to the ocean. **Capital:** Monrovia (1987 est.): 400,000.

Government: Type: In transition. **Head of state:** Wilton Sankawulo, head of transitional Council of State; in office: Sept. 1, 1995. **Local divisions:** 13 counties. **Defense:** 4.4% of GNP (1988).

Economy: Industries: Food processing, mining. **Chief crops:** Rice, cassava, coffee, cocoa, sugar. **Minerals:** Iron, diamonds, gold. **Other resources:** Rubber, timber. **Arable land:** 1%. **Fish catch** (1991): 9,620 metric tons. **Electricity prod.** (1991): 750 mln. kWh. **Labor force:** 71% agric.

Finance: Monetary unit: Dollar (May 1995: 1.00 = $1 US). **Gross national product** (1993): $2.3 bln.* **Per capita GNP:** $800. **Imports** (1989): $394 mln.; partners: U.S. 32%, W Germany 10%, Japan 6%, Neth. 7%. **Exports** (1989): $505 mln.; partners: W Germany 31%, U.S. 20%, Italy 14%, France 9%. **National budget** (1989): $435 mln.

Transport: Motor vehicles: in use: 22,000 passenger cars, 18,000 comm. vehicles. **Chief ports:** Monrovia, Buchanan, Greenville.

Communications: Television sets: 1 per 53 persons. **Radios:** 1 per 3.9 persons. **Telephones:** 1 per 252 persons. **Daily newspaper circ.:** 14 per 1,000 pop.

Health: Life expectancy at birth (1995): 56 male; 61 female. **Births** (per 1,000 pop.): 43. **Deaths** (per 1,000 pop.): 12. **Natural increase:** 3.1%. **Infant mortality** (per 1,000 live births 1995): 111.

Education: Literacy (1990): 40%; 35% attend primary school.

Major International Organizations: UN and most of its specialized agencies, OAU.

Embassy: 5303 Colorado Ave. NW 20011; 723-0437.

Liberia was founded in 1822 by U.S. black freedmen who settled at Monrovia with the aid of colonization societies. It became a republic July 26, 1847, with a constitution modeled on that of the U.S. Descendants of freedmen dominated politics.

Charging rampant corruption, an Army Redemption Council of enlisted men staged a bloody predawn coup, April 12, 1980, in which Pres. Tolbert was killed and replaced as head of state by Sgt. Samuel Doe. Doe was chosen president in a disputed election, and survived a subsequent coup, in 1985.

A civil war began Dec. 1989. Rebel forces seeking to depose Pres. Doe made major territorial gains and advanced on the capital, June 1990. In Sept., Doe was captured and put to death. Despite the introduction of peacekeeping forces from several countries, factional fighting intensified, and a series of cease-fires failed to hold. A new accord Aug. 19, 1995, called for leaders of rival factions to share power pending national elections. A transitional Council of State was instituted Sept. 1, 1995. More than half of the nation's population became refugees as a result of the civil war.

Libya

Socialist People's Libyan Arab Republic

al-Jamahiriyah al-Arabiya al-Libya al-Shabiya al-Ishtirakiya

People: Population: 5,248,401. **Age distrib.** (%): <15: 48; 65+: 3. **Pop. density:** 8 per sq. mi. **Urban:** 85%. **Ethnic groups:** Arab-Berber 97%. **Principal language:** Arabic (official). **Religion:** Sunni Muslim 97%.

Geography: Area: 678,400 sq. mi. **Location:** On Mediterranean coast of N Africa. **Neighbors:** Tunisia, Algeria on W, Niger, Chad on S, Sudan, Egypt on E. **Topography:** Desert and semidesert regions cover 92% of the land, with low mountains in N, higher mountains in S, and a narrow coastal zone. **Capital:** Tripoli (1988 est.): 591,000.

Government: Type: Islamic Arabic Socialist "Mass-State." **Leader:** Col. Muammar al-Qaddafi; b Sept. 1942; in power: Sept. 1969. **Local divisions:** 25 municipalities. **Defense:** 15% of GDP (1989 est.). **Active troop strength:** 70,000.

Economy: Industries: Carpets, textiles, petroleum. **Chief crops:** Dates, olives, citrus and other fruits, grapes, wheat. **Minerals:** Gypsum, oil, gas. **Crude oil reserves** (1994): 22.8 bln. bbls. **Arable land:** 2%. **Livestock** (1993): sheep: 5.6 mln.; goats: 1.3 mln. **Electricity prod.** (1992): 14.4 bln. kWh. **Labor force:** 18% agric.; 31% ind.; 27% services; 24% govt.

Finance: Monetary unit: Dinar (May 1995: 1.00 = $3.00 US). **Gross domestic product** (1993): $32.0 bln.* **Per capita GDP:** $6,600. **Imports** (1993): $8.3 bln.; partners: Italy 13%, Germany 9%, UK 5%. **Exports** (1993): $7.7 bln.; partners: Italy 49%, Germany 22%, Spain 11%. **National budget** (1989): $9.8 bln. **International reserves less gold** (Jun. 1993): $5.9 bln. **Gold:** 3.6 mln. oz t.

Transport: Motor vehicles: in use: 450,000 passenger cars, 330,000 comm. vehicles. **Chief ports:** Tripoli, Benghazi.

Communications: Television sets: 1 per 10.1 persons. **Radios:** 1 per 5.0 persons. **Daily newspaper circ.:** 8.2 per 1,000 pop.

Health: Life expectancy at birth (1995): 62 male; 67 female. **Births** (per 1,000 pop.): 45. **Deaths** (per 1,000 pop.): 8. **Natural increase:** 3.7%. **Physicians:** 1 per 956 persons. **Infant mortality** (per 1,000 live births 1995): 61.

Education: Literacy (1992): 64%. **Years compulsory:** 7. **Attendance:** 90%.

Major International Organizations: UN, Arab League, OAU, OPEC.

First settled by Berbers, Libya was ruled in succession by Carthage, Rome, the Vandals, and the Ottomans. Italy ruled from 1912, and Britain and France after WW II. Libya became an independent constitutional monarchy Jan. 2, 1952. In 1969 a junta led by Col. Muammar al-Qaddafi seized power.

Libya and Egypt fought several air and land battles along their border in July 1977. Chad charged Libya with military occupation of its uranium-rich northern region in 1977. Libyan troops were driven from their last major stronghold by Chad forces in 1987, leaving over $1 billion in military equipment behind.

Libya reportedly helped arm violent revolutionary groups in Egypt and Sudan and aided terrorists of various nationalities.

On Jan. 7, 1986, the U.S., in response, imposed economic sanctions against Libya, ordered all Americans to leave that country, and froze all Libyan assets in the U.S. The U.S. commenced flight operations over the Gulf of Sidra, Jan. 27, and a U.S. Navy task force began conducting exercises in the Gulf, Mar. 23. When Libya fired antiaircraft missiles at American warplanes, the U.S. responded by sinking 2 Libyan ships and bombing a missile installation by Libya in the Gulf, Mar. 27. The U.S. withdrew from the Gulf, Mar. 27.

The U.S. accused Qaddafi of having ordered the Apr. 5, 1986, bombing of a West Berlin discotheque, which killed 3, including a U.S. serviceman. In response, the U.S. sent warplanes to attack terrorist-related targets in Tripoli and Benghazi, Libya, Apr. 14.

The UN imposed limited sanctions, Apr. 15, 1992, for Libya's failure to extradite 2 intelligence agents linked to the 1988 bombing of Pan American World Airways Flight 103 over Lockerbie, Scotland, and 4 others linked to an airplane bombing over Niger. Sanctions were tightened as of Dec. 1, 1993.

Liechtenstein
Principality of Liechtenstein
Fürstentum Liechtenstein

People: Population: 30,654. **Age distrib.** (%): <15: 19; 65+: 10. **Pop. density:** 494 per sq. mi. **Ethnic groups:** Alemannic 95%. **Principal languages:** German (official), Alemannic dialect. **Religions:** Roman Catholic 87%, Protestant 8%.

Geography: Area: 62 sq. mi. **Location:** In the Alps. **Neighbors:** Switzerland on W, Austria on E. **Topography:** The Rhine Valley occupies one-third of the country, the Alps cover the rest. **Capital:** Vaduz. **Cities** (1993 est.): Vaduz 5,100; Schaan 5,100.

Government: Type: Hereditary constitutional monarchy. **Head of state:** Prince Hans-Adam II; b Feb 14, 1945; in office: Nov. 13, 1989. **Head of government:** Mario Frick; b 1965; in office: Dec. 15, 1993. **Local divisions:** 11 communes.

Economy: Industries: Machines, instruments, chemicals, furniture, ceramics. **Arable land:** 25%. **Labor force:** 53% industry, trade, and building; 45% services; 2% agric., fishing, forestry.

Finance: Monetary unit: Swiss Franc. **Gross domestic product** (1990): $630 mln.* **Per capita GDP:** $22,300.* **National budget** (1990): $292 mln.

Communications: Radios: 1 per 2.7 persons. **Telephones:** 1 per 1.6 persons. **Daily newspaper circ.:** 611 per 1,000 pop.

Health: Births (per 1,000 pop.): 13. **Deaths** (per 1,000 pop.): 7. **Natural increase:** 0.6%. **Infant mortality** (per 1,000 live births 1995): 5.

Education: Literacy (1993): 100%. **Years compulsory:** 9; attendance 100%.

Major International Organizations: UN, EFTA.

Liechtenstein became sovereign in 1866. Austria administered Liechtenstein's ports up to 1920; Switzerland has administered its postal services since 1921. Liechtenstein is united with Switzerland by a customs and monetary union. Taxes are low; many international corporations have headquarters there. Foreign workers comprise a third of the population.

Lithuania
Republic of Lithuania
Lietuvos Respublika

People: Population: 3,876,396. **Pop. density:** 154 per sq. mi. **Urban:** 68%. **Ethnic groups:** Lithuanian 80%, Russian 9%, Polish 8%. **Principal languages:** Lithuanian (official), Polish, Russian. **Religion:** mostly Roman Catholic.

Geography: Area: 25,213 sq. mi. **Location:** In E Europe, on SE coast of Baltic. **Neighbors:** Latvia on N, Belarus on E, S, Poland, Russia on W. **Capital:** Vilnius. **Cities** (1993): Vilnius 590,000; Kaunas 429,000.

Government: Type: Republic. **Head of state:** Pres. Algirdas Brazauskas; in office: Feb. 25, 1993. **Head of government:** Prime Min. Adolfas Slezevicius; in office: Mar. 1993. **Local divisions:** 44 regions, 11 municipalities. **Defense:** 5.5% of GDP (1993 est.). **Active troop strength:** 8,900 est.

Economy: Industries: Machinery, shipbuilding. **Chief crops:** grain, potatoes, vegetables. **Arable land:** 49%. **Livestock** (1993): cattle: 1.7 mln., pigs: 1.4 mln. **Electricity prod.** (1992): 25 bln. kWh. **Labor force:** 18% agric.; 42% ind.

Finance: Monetary unit: Litas (Oct. 1994: 4.00 = $1 US). **Gross domestic product** (1993 est.): $12.4 bln. **Per capita GDP:** $3,240. **National budget** (1992 est.): $270.2 mln.

Transport: Railroads: Length: 1,862 mi. **Motor vehicles:** in use: 565,000 passenger cars, 92,000 comm. vehicles. **Civil aviation:** 569 mln. passenger-mi.; 3 airports. **Chief port:** Klaipeda.

Communications: Television sets: 1 per 2.7 persons. **Radios:** 1 per 2.6 persons. **Telephones:** 1 per 4.3 persons.

Health: Life expectancy at birth (1995): 67 male; 76 female. **Births** (per 1,000 pop.): 14. **Deaths** (per 1,000 pop.): 11. **Natural increase:** 0.4%. **Hospital beds:** 1 per 85 persons.

Physicians: 1 per 274 persons. **Infant mortality rate** (per 1,000 live births 1995): 16.

Major International Organizations: UN.

Embassy: 2622 16th St. NW 20009; 234-5860.

Lithuania, was occupied by the German Army, 1914-18. It was annexed by the Soviet Russian army, but the Soviets were overthrown, 1919. Lithuania was a democratic republic until 1926 when the regime was ousted by a coup. In 1939, the Soviet-German treaty assigned most of Lithuania to the Soviet sphere of influence. It was annexed by the USSR Aug. 3, 1940. Lithuania formally declared its independence from the Soviet Union Mar. 11, 1990. During an abortive Soviet coup in Aug., the Western nations recognized Lithuania's independence, which was recognized by the Soviet Union in Sept. 1991. The last Russian troops withdrew on Aug. 31, 1993.

In 1992 elections, former Communists won an absolute majority in the legislature.

Luxembourg
Grand Duchy of Luxembourg
Grand-Duché de Luxembourg

People: Population: 404,660. **Age distrib.** (%): <15: 18; 65+: 14. **Pop. density:** 405 per sq. mi. **Urban:** 86%. **Ethnic groups:** Mixture of French and Germans predominates. **Principal languages:** French, German, Luxembourgisch. **Religions:** Roman Catholic 97%.

Geography: Area: 999 sq. mi. **Location:** In W Europe. **Neighbors:** Belgium on W, France on S, Germany on E. **Topography:** Heavy forests (Ardennes) cover N, S is a low, open plateau. **Capital:** Luxembourg (1991 est.): 75,000.

Government: Type: Constitutional monarchy. **Head of state:** Grand Duke Jean; b Jan. 5, 1921; in office: Nov. 12, 1964. **Head of government:** Prime Min. Jean-Claude Juncker; b Dec. 9, 1954; in office: Jan. 19, 1995. **Local divisions:** 3 districts. **Defense:** 1.2% of GDP (1992). **Active troop strength:** 800.

Economy: Industries: Steel, chemicals, beer, tires, banking, engineering, metal products, cement. **Chief crops:** Grains, wine. **Arable land:** 24%. **Electricity prod.** (1990): 1.4 bln. kWh. **Labor force:** 3% agric.; 32% ind.; 65% services.

Finance: Monetary unit: Franc (May 1995: 28.50 = $1 US). **Gross domestic product** (1993): $8.7 bln.* **Per capita GDP:** $22,600. **Tourism** (1992): $287 mln. **National budget** (1992): $3.5 bln. **Consumer prices** (change in 1994): 2.2%.

Transport: Railroads: Length: 171 mi. **Motor vehicles:** in use: 209,000 passenger cars, 22,000 comm. vehicles.

Communications: Television sets: 1 per 2.9 persons. **Radios:** 1 per 1.7 persons. **Telephones:** 1 per 1.9 persons. **Daily newspaper circ.:** 382 per 1,000 pop.

Health: Life expectancy at birth (1995): 73 male; 81 female. **Births** (per 1,000 pop.): 13. **Deaths** (per 1,000 pop.): 9. **Natural increase:** 0.3%. **Hospital beds:** 1 per 87 persons. **Physicians:** 1 per 486 persons. **Infant mortality** (per 1,000 live births 1995): 7.

Education: Literacy (1992): 100%. **Years compulsory:** 9; attendance 100%.

Major International Organizations: UN, OECD, EU, NATO.

Embassy: 2200 Massachusetts Ave. NW 20008; 265-4171.

Luxembourg, founded about 963, was ruled by Burgundy, Spain, Austria, and France from 1448 to 1815. It left the Germanic Confederation in 1866. Overrun by Germany in 2 world wars, Luxembourg ended its neutrality in 1948, when a customs union with Belgium and Netherlands was adopted.

Macedonia
The Former Yugoslav Republic of Macedonia
Republika Makedonija

People: Population: 2,159,503. **Pop. density:** 218 per sq. mi. **Urban:** 58%. **Ethnic groups:** Macedonian 65%, Albanian 22%. **Principal languages:** Macedonian, Albanian, Turkish,

Serbo-Croatian. **Religions:** Eastern Orthodox 67%, Muslim 30%.

Geography: Area: 9,928 sq. mi. **Location:** In SE Europe. **Neighbors:** Bulgaria on E, Greece on S, Albania on W, Yugoslavia on N. **Capital:** Skopje. **Cities** (1991 met. est.): Skopje 563,000; Tetova 181,000.

Government: Type: Republic. **Head of state:** Interim Pres. Stojan Andov; in office: Oct. 4, 1995. **Head of government:** Prime Min. Branko Crvenkovski; b 1962. **Local divisions:** 34 counties. **Defense: Active troop strength:** 10,400.

Economy: Industries: Light industry. **Chief crops:** Wheat, cotton, tobacco. **Minerals:** Chromium, lead, zinc. **Arable land:** 5%. **Livestock** (1993): sheep: 2.4 mln.. **Electricity prod.** (1992): 6.3 bln. kWh. **Labor force:** 8% agric.; 40% manuf. & mining.

Finance: Monetary unit: Denar (Oct. 1994: 82 = $1 US). **Gross domestic product** (1993): $2.2 bln.* **Per capita GDP:** $1,000.

Transport: Railroads: Length: 573 mi. **Vehicles:** in use: 280,000 passenger cars, 23,000 comm. vehicles. **Civil aviation:** 1 airport.

Communications: Television sets: 1 per 5.2 persons. **Radios:** 1 per 4.5 persons. **Telephones:** 1 per 5.7 persons. **Daily newspaper circ.:** 26 per 1,000 pop.

Health: Births (per 1,000 pop.): 16. **Deaths** (per 1,000 pop.): 7. **Natural increase:** 0.9%. **Hospital beds:** 1 per 171 persons. **Physicians:** 1 per 464 persons. **Infant mortality** (per 1,000 live births 1995): 24.

Education: Literacy (1991): 89%.
Major International Organizations: UN.

Macedonia, as part of a larger region also called Macedonia, was ruled by Muslim Turks from 1389 to 1912, when native Greeks, Bulgarians, and Slavs won independence. Serbia received the largest part of the territory, with the rest going to Greece and Bulgaria. The area was incorporated in Serbia in 1918. Macedonia declared its independence from Yugoslavia, Sept. 8, 1991, and was admitted to the UN under a provisional name in 1993. A UN force, which included several hundred U.S. troops, was deployed there to deter the warring factions in Bosnia from carrying their dispute into other areas of the Balkans. In Feb. 1994 both Russia and the U.S. recognized Macedonia. Greece, which objected to Macedonia's use of what it considered a Hellenic name and symbols, imposed a trade blockade on the landlocked nation; the 2 countries agreed to normalize relations Sept. 13, 1995. A car bombing, Oct. 3, seriously injured Pres. Kiro Gligorov; an interim pres. was named the next day.

Madagascar
Republic of Madagascar
Repoblikan'i Madagasikara

People: Population: 13,862,325. **Pop. density:** 61 per sq. mi. **Urban:** 22%. **Ethnic groups:** 18 Malayan-Indonesian tribes (Merina 26%), with Arab and African presence. **Principal languages:** Malagasy, French (both official). **Religions:** indigenous beliefs 52%, Christian 41%, Muslim 7%.

Geography: Area: 226,658 sq. mi. **Location:** In the Indian O., off the SE coast of Africa. **Neighbors:** Comoro Is., Mozambique (across Mozambique Channel). **Topography:** Humid coastal strip in the E, fertile valleys in the mountainous center plateau region, and a wider coastal strip on the W. **Capital:** Antananarivo (1993 est.): 1.1 mln.

Government: Type: Republic. **Head of state:** Pres. Albert Zafy; in office: Feb. 10, 1993. **Head of government:** Prime Min. Francisque Ravony; in office: Aug. 1993. **Local divisions:** 6 provinces. **Defense:** 2.2% of GDP (1991 est.). **Active troop strength:** 21,000.

Economy: Industries: Food processing, textiles. **Chief crops:** Coffee (over 45% of exports), cloves, vanilla, rice, sugar, tobacco, peanuts. **Minerals:** Chromite, graphite, coal, bauxite. **Arable land:** 4%. **Livestock** (1993): cattle: 10.3 mln.; pigs: 1.5 mln. **Fish catch** (1992): 120,000 metric tons. **Electricity prod.** (1991): 450 mln. kWh. **Labor force:** 76% agric.

Finance: Monetary unit: Franc (Apr. 1995: 4,113 = $1 US). **Gross domestic product** (1993): $10.4 bln.* **Per capita GDP:** $800. **Imports** (1992): $350 mln.; partners: France 30%, Ger-

many 6%, U.S. 6%. **Exports** (1992): $312 mln.; partners: France 27%, U.S. 16%. **Tourism** (1992): $39 mln. **National budget** (1991): $265 mln. **International reserves less gold** (Jan. 1993): $89 mln. **Consumer prices** (change in 1994): 38.9%.

Transport: Railroads: Length: 640 mi. **Motor vehicles:** in use: 50,000 passenger cars, 35,000 comm. vehicles. **Civil aviation:** 268 mln. passenger-mi.; 18 airports with scheduled flights. **Chief ports:** Tamatave, Diego-Suarez, Mahajanga, Toliara.

Communications: Television sets: 1 per 102 persons. **Radios:** 1 per 8.8 persons. **Telephones:** 1 per 189 persons.

Health: Life expectancy at birth (1995): 52 male; 56 female. **Births** (per 1,000 pop.): 45. **Deaths** (per 1,000 pop.): 13. **Natural increase:** 3.2%. **Physicians:** 1 per 8,628 persons. **Infant mortality** (per 1,000 live births 1995): 87.

Education: Literacy (1991): 80%. **Years compulsory:** 5; attendance 83%.

Major International Organizations: UN (WHO, IMF), OAU.
Embassy: 2374 Massachusetts Ave. NW 20008; 265-5525.

Madagascar was settled 2,000 years ago by Malayan-Indonesian people, whose descendants still predominate. A unified kingdom ruled the 18th and 19th centuries. The island became a French protectorate, 1885, and a colony 1896. Independence came June 26, 1960.

Discontent with inflation and French domination led to a coup in 1972. The new regime nationalized French-owned financial interests, closed French bases and a U.S. space tracking station, and obtained Chinese aid. The government conducted a program of arrests, expulsion of foreigners, and repression of strikes, 1979.

In 1990, Madagascar ended a ban on multiparty politics that had been in place since 1975. Albert Zafy was elected president in 1993, ending the 17-year rule of Adm. Didier Ratsiraka.

Malawi
Republic of Malawi

People: Population: 9,808,384. **Age distrib.** (%): <15: 48; 65+: 3. **Pop. density:** 214 per sq. mi. **Urban:** 17%. **Ethnic groups:** Chewa, Nyanja, Lomwe, other Bantu tribes. **Principal languages:** English, Chichewa (both official). **Religions:** Christian 75%, Muslim 20%.

Geography: Area: 45,747 sq. mi. **Location:** In SE Africa. **Neighbors:** Zambia on W, Mozambique on SE, Tanzania on N. **Topography:** Malawi stretches 560 mi. N-S along Lake Malawi (Lake Nyasa), most of which belongs to Malawi. High plateaus and mountains line the Rift Valley the length of the nation. **Capital:** Lilongwe. **Cities** (1987 est.): Blantyre 333,000; Lilongwe 223,000.

Government: Type: Republic. **Head of state and government:** Pres. Bakili Muluzi; b Mar. 17, 1943; in office: May 21, 1994. **Local divisions:** 24 districts. **Defense:** 1.1% of GNP (1991). **Active troop strength:** 10,400.

Economy: Industries: Agricultural processing, cement. **Chief crops:** Tea, tobacco, sugar, coffee, corn, potatoes. **Arable land:** 25%. **Fish catch** (1991): 63,000 metric tons. **Electricity prod.** (1992): 620 mln. kWh. **Labor force:** 43% agric.; 25% ind. & commerce; 15% personal services.

Finance: Monetary unit: Kwacha (May 1995: 15.30 = $1 US). **Gross domestic product** (1993): $6.0 bln.* **Per capita GDP:** $600. **Imports** (1992): $720 mln.; partners: South Africa 29%, UK 24%, Japan 6%. **Exports** (1992): $392 mln.; partners: UK 27%, South Africa 8%, Germany 10%. **National budget** (1992): $498 mln. **International reserves less gold** (May 1995): $37.6 mln. **Gold:** 13,000 oz t. **Consumer prices** (change in 1993): 19.7%.

Transport: Railroads: Length: 495 mi. **Motor vehicles:** in use: 16,000 passenger cars, 17,000 comm. vehicles.

Communications: Radios: 1 per 9.7 persons. **Telephones:** 1 per 180 persons.

Health: Life expectancy at birth (1995): 38 male; 40 female. **Births** (per 1,000 pop.): 50. **Deaths** (per 1,000 pop.): 24. **Natural increase:** 2.6%. **Hospital beds:** 1 per 627 persons. **Physicians:** 1 per 27,094 persons. **Infant mortality** (per 1,000 live births 1995): 140.

Education: Literacy (1990): 42%. About 45% attend school.
Major International Organizations: UN (World Bank, WTO, IMF), OAU, the Commonwealth.
Embassy: 2408 Massachusetts Ave. NW 20008; 797-1007.

Bantus came in the 16th century, Arab slavers in the 19th. The area became the British protectorate Nyasaland in 1891. It became independent July 6, 1964, and a republic in 1966. After 3 decades as a one-party state under Pres. Hastings Kamuzu Banda, the country adopted a new constitution and, in multiparty elections May 17, 1994, chose a new leader.

Malaysia

People: Population: 19,723,587. **Age distrib.** (%): <15: 36; 65+: 4. **Pop. density:** 155 per sq. mi. **Urban:** 51%. **Ethnic groups:** Malay and other indigenous 59%, Chinese 32%, Indian 9%. **Principal languages:** Malay (official), English, Chinese, Indian languages. **Religions:** Muslim, Hindu, Buddhist, Confucian, Christian, Taoist, local religions.

Geography: Area: 127,584 sq. mi. **Location:** On the SE tip of Asia, plus the N coast of the island of Borneo. **Neighbors:** Thailand on N, Indonesia on S. **Topography:** Most of W Malaysia is covered by tropical jungle, including the central mountain range that runs N-S through the peninsula. The western coast is marshy, the eastern, sandy. E Malaysia has a wide, swampy coastal plain, with interior jungles and mountains. **Capital:** Kuala Lumpur (1991 est.): 1.1 mln.

Government: Type: Federal parliamentary democracy with a constitutional monarch. **Head of state:** Paramount Ruler Sultan Jaafar bin Abdul Rahman; in office: Apr. 26, 1994. **Head of government:** Prime Min. Datuk Seri Mahathir bin Mohamad; b Dec. 20, 1925; in office: July 16, 1981. **Local divisions:** 13 states and 2 federal terr. **Defense:** 5% of GDP (1992). **Active troop strength:** 114,500.

Economy: Industries: Rubber goods, steel, electronics. **Chief crops:** Palm oil, rice, pepper. **Minerals:** Tin (a leading producer), oil, bauxite, iron. **Crude oil reserves** (1994): 4.3 bln. bbls. **Other resources:** Rubber (35% world output). **Arable land:** 3%. **Livestock** (1992): pigs: 2.5 mln. **Fish catch** (1991): 620,000 metric tons. **Electricity prod.** (1992): 30 bln. kWh. **Labor force:** 21% agric.; 25% services & trade; 23% manuf.

Finance: Monetary unit: Ringgit (May 1995: 2.47 = $1 US). **Gross domestic product** (1993): $141 bln.* **Per capita GDP:** $7,500. **Imports** (1993): $40.4 bln.; partners: Japan 26%, U.S. 16%, Singapore 21%. **Exports** (1993): $46.8 bln.; partners: Japan 13%, U.S. 15%, Singapore 23%. **Tourism** (1992): $1.7 bln. **National budget** (1994 est.): $18.0 bln. **International reserves less gold** (Mar. 1995): $25.0 bln. **Gold:** 2.39 mln. oz t. **Consumer prices** (change in 1994): 3.7%.

Transport: Railroads: Length: 1,381 mi. **Motor vehicles:** in use: 2.1 mln. passenger cars, 472,000 comm. vehicles. **Civil aviation:** 9.3 bln. passenger-mi.; 40 airports with scheduled flights. **Chief ports:** George Town, Kelang, Melaka, Kuching.

Communications: Television sets: 1 per 9.5 persons. **Radios:** 1 per 5.4 persons. **Telephones:** 1 per 8.9 persons. **Daily newspaper circ.:** 140 per 1,000 pop.

Health: Life expectancy at birth (1995): 67 male; 73 female. **Births** (per 1,000 pop.): 28. **Deaths** (per 1,000 pop.): 6. **Natural increase:** 2.2%. **Hospital beds:** 1 per 482 persons. **Physicians:** 1 per 2,412 persons. **Infant mortality** (per 1,000 live births 1995): 25.

Education: Literacy (1992): 78%. **Attendance:** 96% primary, 65% secondary.

Major International Organizations: UN (World Bank, IMF, WTO), ASEAN, the Commonwealth.

Embassy: 2401 Massachusetts Ave. NW 20008; 328-2700.

European traders appeared in the 16th century; Britain established control in 1867. Malaysia was created Sept. 16, 1963. It included Malaya (which had become independent in 1957 after the suppression of Communist rebels), plus the formerly-British Singapore, Sabah (N Borneo), and Sarawak (NW Borneo). Singapore was separated in 1965, in order to end tensions between Chinese, the majority in Singapore, and Malays in control of the Malaysian government.

A monarch is elected by a council of hereditary rulers of the Malayan states every 5 years.

Abundant natural resources have assured prosperity, and foreign investment has aided industrialization. Work on a new federal capital south of Kuala Lumpur began in 1995.

Maldives
Republic of Maldives
Divehi Jumhuriyya

People: Population: 261,310. **Age distrib.** (%): <15: 47; 65+: 3. **Pop. density:** 2,272 per sq. mi. **Urban:** 26%. **Ethnic groups:** Sinhalese, Dravidian, Arab, African. **Principal language:** Divehi (Sinhalese dialect). **Religion:** Sunni Muslim.

Geography: Area: 115 sq. mi. **Location:** In the Indian O. SW of India. **Neighbors:** Nearest is India on N. **Topography:** 19 atolls with 1,087 islands, about 200 inhabited. None of the islands are over 5 sq. mi. in area, and all are nearly flat. **Capital:** Male (1991 est.): 55,000.

Government: Type: Republic. **Head of state:** Pres. Maumoon Abdul Gayoom; b Dec. 29, 1939; in office: Nov. 11, 1978. **Local divisions:** 19 districts.

Economy: Industries: Fish processing, tourism. **Chief crops:** Coconuts, fruit, millet. **Other resources:** Shells. **Arable land:** 10%. **Fish catch** (1991): 81,000 metric tons. **Electricity prod.** (1991): 28 mln. kWh. **Labor force:** 25% fishing & agric.; 15% manuf.; 16% trade.

Finance: Monetary unit: Rufiyaa (May 1995: 11.77 = $1 US). **Gross domestic product** (1991): $140 mln. **Per capita GDP:** $620. **Imports** (1993): $174 mln.; partners: Singapore, Germany, Sri Lanka. **Exports** (1993): $56 mln.; partners: U.S., UK. **Tourism** (1992): $113 mln. **National budget** (1993 est.): $143 mln.

Transport: Chief ports: Male Atoll.

Communications: Radios: 1 per 9.5 persons. **Telephones:** 1 per 27 persons.

Health: Life expectancy at birth (1995): 64 male; 67 female. **Births** (per 1,000 pop.): 43. **Deaths** (per 1,000 pop.): 7. **Natural increase:** 3.6%. **Infant morality** (per 1,000 live births 1995): 50.

Education: Literacy (1989): 93%. Only 6% of those aged 11-15 attend school.

Major International Organizations: UN, the Commonwealth.

The islands had been a British protectorate since 1887. The country became independent July 26, 1965. Long a sultanate, the Maldives became a republic in 1968. Natural resources and tourism are being developed; however, it remains one of the world's poorest countries.

Mali
Republic of Mali
République du Mali

People: Population: 9,375,132. **Age distrib.** (%): <15: 46; 65+: 4. **Pop. density:** 19 per sq. mi. **Urban:** 22%. **Ethnic groups:** Mande (Bambara, Malinke, Sarakole) 50%, Peul 17%, Voltaic 12%, Songhai 6%, Tuareg and Moor 10%. **Principal languages:** French (official), Bambara, Senufo. **Religion:** Muslim 90%.

Geography: Area: 482,077 sq. mi. **Location:** In the interior of W Africa. **Neighbors:** Mauritania, Senegal on W, Guinea, Côte d'Ivoire, Burkina Faso on S, Niger on E, Algeria on N. **Topography:** A landlocked grassy plain in the upper basins of the Senegal and Niger rivers, extending N into the Sahara. **Capital:** Bamako (1989 met. est.): 800,000.

Government: Type: Republic. **Head of state:** Pres. Alpha Oumar Konare; b 1946; in office: June 8, 1992. **Head of government:** Prime Min. Ibrahim Boubakar Keita; in office: Feb. 4, 1994. **Local divisions:** 8 regions. **Defense:** 2% of GDP (1989). **Active troop strength:** 7,350.

Economy: Chief crops: Millet, rice, peanuts, cotton. **Minerals:** Bauxite, iron, gold. **Arable land:** 2%. **Livestock** (1993): sheep and goats: 13.9 mln.; cattle: 5.6 mln. **Fish catch** (1991): 60,000 metric tons. **Electricity prod.** (1991): 750 mln. kWh. **Labor force:** 80% agric.; 19% services.

Finance: Monetary unit: CFA Franc (May 1995: 488 = $1 US). **Gross domestic product** (1993): $5.8 bln.* **Per capita GDP:** $650. **Imports** (1992): $682 mln.; partners: France 27%, Côte d'Ivoire 19%. **Exports** (1992): $330 mln.; partners: Western Europe, Fr. 15%. **Tourism** (1992): $45 mln. **National budget** (1992): $697 mln. **International reserves less gold** (Mar. 1995): $280 mln. **Gold:** 19,000 oz t. **Consumer prices** (change in 1993): -0.1%.

Transport: Railroads: Length: 399 mi. **Motor vehicles:** in use: 23,000 passenger cars, 10,000 comm. vehicles.
Communications: Radios: 1 per 58 persons. **Telephones:** 1 per 730 persons.
Health: Life expectancy at birth (1995): 45 male; 48 female. **Births** (per 1,000 pop.): 52. **Deaths** (per 1,000 pop.): 20. **Natural increase:** 3.2%. **Hospital beds:** 1 per 2,253 persons. **Physicians:** 1 per 67,789 persons. **Infant mortality** (per 1,000 live births 1995): 104.
Education: Literacy (1992): 19%. **Attendance:** 21% attend primary school.
Major International Organizations: UN and most of its specialized agencies, OAU.
Embassy: 2130 R St. NW 20008; 332-2249.

Until the 15th century the area was part of the great Mali Empire. Timbuktu was a center of Islamic study. French rule was secured, 1898. The Sudanese Rep. and Senegal became independent as the Mali Federation June 20, 1960, but Senegal withdrew, and the Sudanese Rep. was renamed Mali.

Mali signed economic agreements with France and, in 1963, with Senegal. In 1968, a coup ended the socialist regime. Famine struck in 1973-74, killing as many as 100,000 people. Drought conditions returned in the 1980s.

The military, Mar. 26, 1991, overthrew the government of Pres. Amadou Toumani Traoré, who had been in power since 1968. Oumar Konare, a leader in the coup, was elected president, Apr. 26, 1992.

Malta
Republic of Malta
Repubblika ta' Malta

People: Population: 369,609. **Age distrib.** (%): <15: 23; 65+: 11. **Pop. density:** 3,030 per sq. mi. **Ethnic groups:** Italian, Arab, French, Spanish. **Principal languages:** Maltese, English (both official). **Religion:** Roman Catholic 98%.
Geography: Area: 122 sq. mi. **Location:** In center of Mediterranean Sea. **Neighbors:** Nearest is Italy on N. **Topography:** Island of Malta is 95 sq. mi.; other islands in the group: Gozo, 26 sq. mi.; Comino, 1 sq. mi. The coastline is heavily indented. Low hills cover the interior. **Capital:** Valletta. **Cities** (1994 est.): Birkirkara 22,000; Qormi 20,000.
Government: Type: Parliamentary democracy. **Head of state:** Pres. Ugo Mifsud Bonnici; b July 17, 1933; in office: Apr. 4, 1994. **Head of government:** Prime Min. Edward Fenech-Adami; b Feb. 7, 1934; in office: May 12, 1987. **Defense:** 0.8% of GNP (1991). **Active troop strength:** 1,850.
Economy: Industries: Textiles, machinery, food & beverages, tourism. **Chief crops:** Potatoes, tomatoes. **Arable land:** 38%. **Electricity prod.** (1992): $1.1 bln. kWh. **Labor force:** 2% agric.; 22% manuf.; 26% services; 37% gov.
Finance: Monetary unit: Maltese Lira (May 1995: 1.00 = $2 US). **Gross domestic product** (1992): $2.4 bln. **Per capita GDP:** $6,600. **Imports** (1992): $1.9 bln.; partners: UK 16%, Italy 30%, Germany 13%, U.S. 4%. **Exports** (1992): $1.3 bln.; partners: Germany 22%, UK 11%, Italy 30%. **Tourism** (1992): $568 mln. **National budget** (1994): $1.2 bln. **International reserves less gold** (Apr. 1995): 1.8 bln. **Gold:** 105,000 oz t. **Consumer prices** (change in 1994): 4.1%.
Transport: Motor vehicles: in use: 120,000 passenger cars, 28,000 comm. vehicles. **Civil aviation:** 630 mln. passenger-mi.; 1 airport. **Chief port:** Valletta.
Communications: Television sets: 1 per 2.5 persons. **Radios:** 1 per 4.0 persons. **Telephones:** 1 per 1.8 persons.
Health: Life expectancy at birth (1995): 75 male; 79 female. **Births** (per 1,000 pop.): 13. **Deaths** (per 1,000 pop.): 7. **Natural increase:** 0.6%. **Hospital beds:** 1 per 107 persons. **Physicians:** 1 per 424 persons. **Infant mortality** (per 1,000 live births 1995): 8.
Education: Literacy (1992): 96%. **Years compulsory:** until age 16.
Major International Organizations: UN (WTO, WHO, IMF), the Commonwealth.
Embassy: 2017 Connecticut Ave. NW 20008; 462-3611.

Malta was ruled by Phoenicians, Romans, Arabs, Normans, the Knights of Malta, France, and Britain (since 1814). It be-

came independent Sept. 21, 1964. Malta became a republic in 1974. The withdrawal of the last British sailors, Apr. 1, 1979, ended 179 years of British military presence on the island.

Marshall Islands
Republic of the Marshall Islands

People: Population: 56,157. **Pop. density:** 802 per sq. mi. **Ethnic groups:** Micronesian. **Principal languages:** English (official), Marshallese, Japanese. **Religions:** Protestant 90%.
Geography: Area: 70 sq. mi. **Location:** In central Pacific Ocean; comprised of two 800-mi-long parallel chains of coral atolls. **Capital:** Majuro.
Government: Type: Republic. **Head of state:** Pres. Amata Kabua; in office: 1980.
Economy: Agriculture and tourism are mainstays of the economy. **Electricity prod.** (1990): 80 mln. kWh.
Finance: Monetary unit: U.S. Dollar. **Gross domestic product** (1989): $63 mln. **Per capita GDP:** $1,500. **Imports** (1992): $63 mln. **Exports** (1992): $4 mln.
Transport: 23 airports with scheduled flights. **Chief port:** Majuro.
Communications: Telephones: 1 per 51 persons.
Health: Life expectancy at birth (1995): 62 male; 65 female. **Births** (per 1,000 pop.): 46. **Deaths** (per 1,000 pop.): 7. **Natural increase:** 3.9%. **Infant mortality** (per 1,000 live births 1995): 48.
Education: Literacy (1992): 91%.
Major International Organizations: UN.
Embassy: 2433 Massachusetts Ave. NW 20008; 234-5414.

The Marshall Islands were a German possession until World War I and were administered by Japan between the World Wars. After WW II, they were administered as part of the UN Trust Territory of the Pacific Islands by the U.S.

The Marshall Islands secured international recognition as an independent nation on Sept. 17, 1991.

Mauritania
Islamic Republic of Mauritania
République Islamique de Mauritanie

People: Population: 2,263,202. **Age distrib.** (%): <15: 45; 65+: 4. **Pop. density:** 6 per sq. mi. **Urban:** 39%. **Ethnic groups:** mixed Maur/black 40%, Maur 30%, black 30%. **Principal languages:** Hasaniya Arabic, Wolof (both official), Pular, Soninke. **Religions:** Muslim.
Geography: Area: 398,000 sq. mi. **Location:** In W Africa. **Neighbors:** Morocco on N, Algeria, Mali on E, Senegal on S. **Topography:** The fertile Senegal R. valley in the S gives way to a wide central region of sandy plains and scrub trees. The N is arid and extends into the Sahara. **Capital:** Nouakchott. **Cities** (1992 est.): Nouakchott 480,000; Nouadhibou 72,000; Kaedi 35,000.
Government: Type: Islamic republic. **Head of state:** Pres. Maaouya Ould Sidi Ahmed Taya; b 1943; in office: Apr. 18, 1992. **Head of government:** Prime Min. Sidi Mohamed Ould Boubacar; in office: Apr. 18, 1992. **Local divisions:** 12 regions, 1 capital district. **Defense:** 3.1% of GNP (1992). **Active troop strength:** 15,650 est.
Economy: Industries: Fish processing, iron mining. **Chief crops:** Dates, grain. **Minerals:** Iron ore, gypsum. **Livestock** (1992): sheep: 5.4 mln.; goats: 3.6 mln.; cattle: 1.4 mln. **Fish catch** (1992): 107,000 metric tons. **Electricity prod.** (1991): 135 mln. kWh. **Labor force:** 47% agric.; 14% ind. & commerce, 29% services.
Finance: Monetary unit: Ouguiya (May 1995: 129 = $1 US). **Gross domestic product** (1992): $2.2 bln.* **Per capita GDP:** $1,050. **Imports** (1992): $413 mln.; partners: EU 60%. **Exports** (1992): $432 mln.; partners: EU 43%, Japan 27%. **International reserves less gold** (May 1995): $48 mln. **Gold:** 12,000 oz t.
Transport: Motor vehicles: in use: 10,000 passenger cars, 5,000 comm. vehicles. **Chief ports:** Nouakchott, Nouadhibou.
Communications: Radios: 1 per 7.2 persons. **Telephones:** 1 per 120 persons.

Health: Life expectancy at birth (1995): 46 male; 52 female. **Births** (per 1,000 pop.): 47. **Deaths** (per 1,000 pop.): 16. **Natural increase:** 3.2%. **Hospital beds:** 1 per 1,217 persons. **Physicians:** 1 per 14,259 persons. **Infant mortality** (per 1,000 live births 1995): 83.
Education: Literacy (1992): 34%. **Attendance:** 79% in primary school, 18% in secondary school.
Major International Organizations: UN (WTO, IMF, WHO), OAU, Arab League.
Embassy: 2129 Leroy Pl. NW 20008; 232-5700.

Mauritania was a French protectorate from 1903. It became independent Nov. 28, 1960. It annexed the south of former Spanish Sahara in 1976. Saharan guerrillas stepped up attacks in 1977; 8,000 Moroccan troops and French bomber raids aided the government. Mauritania signed a peace treaty with the Polisario Front, 1980, resumed diplomatic relations with Algeria while breaking a defense treaty with Morocco, and renounced sovereignty over its share of former Spanish Sahara. Opposition parties were legalized and a new constitution approved in 1991.

Mauritius
Republic of Mauritius

People: Population: 1,127,068. **Age distrib.** (%): <15: 30; 65+: 6. **Pop. density:** 1,430 per sq. mi. **Urban:** 44%. **Ethnic groups:** Indo-Mauritian 68%, Creole 27%. **Principal languages:** English (official), French, Creole, Hindi, Bhojpoori. **Religions:** Hindu 52%, Christian 28%, Muslim 17%.
Geography: Area: 788 sq. mi. **Location:** In the Indian O., 500 mi. E of Madagascar. **Neighbors:** Nearest is Madagascar on W. **Topography:** A volcanic island nearly surrounded by coral reefs. A central plateau is encircled by mountain peaks. **Capital:** Port Louis (1992 est.): 143,000.
Government: Type: Republic. **Head of state:** Pres. Cassam Uteem; b Mar. 22, 1941; in office: June 30, 1992. **Head of government:** Prime Min. Aneerood Jugnauth; b Mar. 29, 1930; in office: June 12, 1982. **Local divisions:** 9 districts, 3 dependencies. **Defense: Active troop strength:** 1,300 (paramilitary).
Economy: Industries: Tourism, textiles, food processing. **Chief crops:** sugarcane, tea. **Arable land:** 54%. **Electricity prod.** (1992): 630 mln. kWh. **Labor force:** 27% agric. & fishing; 22% manuf.; 29% govt. services.
Finance: Monetary unit: Rupee (May 1995: 17.06 = $1 US). **Gross domestic product** (1993): $8.6 bln.* **Per capita GDP:** $7,800. **Imports** (1992): $1.6 bln.; partners: France 13%, South Africa 13%. **Exports** (1992): $1.3 bln.; partners: UK 35%, France 21%, U.S. 13%. **Tourists** (1992): $299 mln. **National budget** (1990): $607 mln. **International reserves less gold** (May 1995): $685 mln. **Gold:** 62,000 oz t. **Consumer prices** (change in 1994): 7.3%.
Transport: Motor vehicles: in use: 33,000 passenger cars. **Chief port:** Port Louis.
Communications: Television sets: 1 per 7.1 persons. **Radios:** 1 per 4.4 persons. **Telephones:** 1 per 11 persons. **Daily newspaper circ.:** 87 per 1,000 pop.
Health: Life expectancy at birth (1995): 67 male; 75 female. **Births** (per 1,000 pop.): 19. **Deaths** (per 1,000 pop.): 6. **Natural increase:** 1.3%. **Hospital beds:** 1 per 351 persons. **Physicians:** 1 per 1,098 persons. **Infant mortality** (per 1,000 live births 1995): 18.
Education: Literacy (1992): 80%. **Attendance:** almost all children attend school.
Major International Organizations: UN and all of its specialized agencies, OAU, the Commonwealth.
Embassy: 4301 Connecticut Ave. NW 20008; 244-1491.

Mauritius was uninhabited when settled in 1638 by the Dutch, who introduced sugarcane. France took over in 1721, bringing African slaves. Britain ruled from 1810 to Mar. 12, 1968, bringing Indian workers for the sugar plantations.
Mauritius formally severed its association with the British crown Mar. 12, 1992.

Mexico
United Mexican States
Estados Unidos Mexicanos

People: Population: 93,985,848. **Age distrib.** (%): <15: 36; 65+: 4. **Pop. density:** 124 per sq. mi. **Urban:** 71%. **Ethnic groups:** mestizo 60%, Amerindian 30%, white 9%. **Principal languages:** Spanish (official), Amerindian languages. **Religions:** Roman Catholic 89%.
Geography: Area: 756,066 sq. mi. **Location:** In southern North America. **Neighbors:** U.S. on N, Guatemala, Belize on S. **Topography:** The Sierra Madre Occidental Mts. run NW-SE near the west coast; the Sierra Madre Oriental Mts., run near the Gulf of Mexico. They join S of Mexico City. Between the 2 ranges lies the dry central plateau, 5,000 to 8,000 ft. alt., rising toward the S, with temperate vegetation. Coastal lowlands are tropical. About 45% of land is arid. **Capital:** Mexico City. **Cities** (1991 met. est.): Mexico City 20 mln.; Guadalajara 3 mln.; Monterrey 2.7 mln.
Government: Type: Federal republic. **Head of state:** Pres. Ernesto Zedillo Ponce de León; b Dec. 27, 1951; in office: Dec. 1, 1994. **Local divisions:** 31 states, federal district. **Defense:** 0.5% of GDP (1992). **Active troop strength:** 175,000.
Economy: Industries: Steel, chemicals, electric goods, textiles, rubber, petroleum, tourism. **Chief crops:** Cotton, coffee, wheat, rice, sugarcane, vegetables, corn. **Minerals:** Silver, lead, zinc, gold, oil, natural gas. **Crude oil reserves** (1994): 51 bln. barrels. **Arable land:** 12%. **Livestock** (1993): cattle: 31 mln.; pigs: 11 mln.; sheep: 6 mln. **Fish catch** (1992): 1.1 mln. metric tons. **Electricity prod.** (1992): 120.7 bln. kWh. **Labor force:** 28% agric.; 11% manuf.; 32% services; 15% commerce.
Finance: Monetary unit: New Peso (May 1995: 6.18 = $1 US). **Gross domestic product** (1993): $740 bln.* **Per capita GDP:** $8,200. **Imports** (1993): $65.5 bln.; partners: U.S. 74%, Japan 11%. **Exports** (1993): $50.5 bln.; partners: U.S. 74%, Japan 8%. **Tourism** (1992): $6.0 bln. **National budget** (1992): $53.0 bln. **International reserves less gold** (May 1995): $11.0 bln. **Gold:** 503,000 oz t. **Consumer prices** (change in 1994): 7.0%.
Transport: Railroads: Length: 12,747 mi. **Motor vehicles:** in use: 7.5 mln. passenger cars, 3.6 mln. comm. vehicles. **Civil aviation:** 11.9 bln. passenger-mi.; 57 airports. **Chief ports:** Veracruz, Tampico, Mazatlan, Coatzacoalcos.
Communications: Television sets: 1 in 6.7 persons. **Radios:** 1 in 5.5 persons. **Telephones:** 1 in 7.6 persons. **Daily newspaper circ.:** 142 per 1,000 pop.
Health: Life expectancy at birth (1995): 70 male; 77 female. **Births** (per 1,000 pop.): 27. **Deaths** (per 1,000 pop.): 5. **Natural increase:** 2.2%. **Hospital beds:** 1 per 1,367 persons. **Physicians:** 1 per 885 persons. **Infant mortality** (per 1,000 live births 1995): 26.
Education: Literacy (1993): 90%. **Years compulsory:** 8.
Major International Organizations: UN (IMF, WTO), OAS, OECD.
Embassy: 1911 Pennsylvania Ave. NW 20006; 728-1600.

Mexico was the site of advanced Indian civilizations. The Mayas, an agricultural people, moved up from Yucatan, built immense stone pyramids, invented a calendar. The Toltecs were overcome by the Aztecs, who founded Tenochtitlan AD 1325, now Mexico City. Hernando Cortes, Spanish conquistador, destroyed the Aztec empire, 1519-21.
After 3 centuries of Spanish rule the people rose, under Fr. Miguel Hidalgo y Costilla, 1810, Fr. Morelos y Payon, 1812, and Gen. Agustin Iturbide, who made himself emperor as Agustin I, 1821. A republic was declared in 1823.
Mexican territory extended into the present American Southwest and California until Texas revolted and established a republic in 1836; the Mexican legislature refused recognition but was unable to enforce its authority there. After numerous clashes, the U.S.-Mexican War, 1846-48, resulted in the loss by Mexico of the lands north of the Rio Grande.
French arms supported an Austrian archduke on the throne of Mexico as Maximilian I, 1864-67, but pressure from the U.S. forced France to withdraw. A dictatorial rule by Porfirio Diaz, president 1877-80, 1884-1911, led to fighting by rival forces until the new constitution of Feb. 5, 1917, provided social

reform. Since then Mexico has developed large-scale programs of social security, labor protection, and school improvement. A constitutional provision requires management to share profits with labor.

The Institutional Revolutionary Party (PRI) has been dominant in politics since 1929. Radical opposition, including some guerrilla activity, has been contained by strong measures.

Some gains in agriculture, industry, and social services have been achieved. The land is rich, but the rugged topography and lack of sufficient rainfall are major obstacles. Economic prospects brightened with the discovery of vast oil reserves, perhaps the world's greatest. But much of the work force is jobless or underemployed. Inflation and a drop in world oil prices aggravated the country's economic problems in the 1980s. An antipoverty program was launched in 1989.

Mexico reached agreement with the U.S. and Canada on the North American Free Trade Agreement Aug. 12, 1992; it went into effect Jan. 1, 1994.

Guerrillas of the Zapatista National Liberation Army (EZLN) launched an uprising, Jan. 1, 1994, in southern Mexico. A tentative peace accord was reached Mar. 2.

The presidential candidate of the governing PRI, Luis Donaldo Colosio Murrieta, was assassinated at a political rally in Tijuana, Mar. 23, 1994. The new PRI candidate, Ernesto Zedillo Ponce de León, won election Aug. 21 and was inaugurated Dec. 1. An austerity plan and pledges of U.S. aid saved Mexico's currency from collapse in early 1995.

Micronesia
Federated States of Micronesia

People: Population: 122,950. **Pop. density:** 454 per sq. mi. **Urban:** 26%. **Ethnic groups:** 9 ethnic Micronesian and Polynesian groups. **Principal languages:** English (official). **Religions:** mostly Christian.

Geography: Area: 271 sq. mi. The Federation consists of 607 islands in the W Pacific Ocean. **Capital:** Palikir.

Government: Type: Republic. **Head of state:** Bailey Olter; b 1932; in office: May 21, 1991. **Local divisions:** 4 states.

Economy: Chief crops: Tropical fruits, vegetables, pepper.

Finance: Monetary unit: U.S. Dollar. **Gross national product** (1989): $150 mln.* **Per capita GDP:** $1,500. **Imports** (1988): $67 mln. **Exports** (1988): $2 mln.

Transport: 4 airports with scheduled flights.

Communications: Television sets: 1 per 15 persons. **Radios:** 1 per 1.5 persons. **Telephones:** 1 per 18 persons.

Health: Life expectancy at birth (1995): 66 male; 70 female. **Births** (per 1,000 pop.): 28. **Deaths** (per 1,000 pop.): 6. **Natural increase:** 2.2%. **Hospital beds:** 1 per 309 persons. **Physicians:** 1 per 2,227 persons. **Infant mortality** (per 1,000 live births 1995): 37.

Education: Literacy (1991): 90%.

Major International Organizations: UN.

Embassy: 1725 N St. NW 20036; 223-4383.

The Federated States of Micronesia, formerly known as the Caroline Islands, was ruled successively by Spain, Germany, Japan, and the U.S. It was internationally recognized as an independent nation Sept. 17, 1991.

Moldova
Republic of Moldova
Republica Moldova

People: Population: 4,489,657. **Pop. density:** 345 per sq. mi. **Urban:** 47%. **Ethnic groups:** Moldovan/Romanian 65%, Ukrainian 14%, Russian 13%. **Principal languages:** Moldovan (official), Russian. **Religions:** Eastern Orthodox 99%.

Geography: Area: 13,012 sq. mi. **Location:** In E Europe. **Neighbors:** Romania on W, Ukraine on N, E, and S. **Capital:** Chisinau. **Cities** (1991): Chisinau 753,000; Tiraspol 186,000.

Government: Type: Republic. **Head of state:** Pres. Mircea Snegur; b Jan. 17, 1940; in office: Sept. 1990. **Head of government:** Prime Min. Andre Sangheli; in office: July 1, 1992. **Defense: Active troop strength:** 11,100.

Economy: Industries: Canning, wine making, textiles. **Chief crops:** Grain, grapes. **Minerals:** Lignite, gypsum. **Arable land:** 50%. **Livestock** (1993): cattle: 900,000; pigs: 1.6 mln.; sheep: 1.1 mln. **Electricity prod.** (1992): 11.1 bln. kWh.

Finance: Monetary unit: Lei (May 1995: 4.56 = $1 US). **Gross domestic product** (1993 est.): $16.3 bln.* **Per capita GDP:** $3,650. **International reserves less gold** (Mar. 1995): $169 mln.

Transport: Railroads: Length: 715 mi. **Motor vehicles:** in use: 222,000 passenger cars. **Civil aviation:** 1.5 bln. passenger-mi.; 1 airport.

Communications: Telephones: 1 per 7.9 persons. **Daily newspaper circ.:** 561 per 1,000 pop.

Health: Life expectancy at birth (1995): 65 male; 72 female. **Births** (per 1,000 pop.): 16. **Deaths** (per 1,000 pop.): 10. **Natural increase:** 0.6%. **Hospital beds:** 1 per 77 persons. **Physicians:** 1 per 251 persons. **Infant mortality** (per 1,000 live births 1995): 30.

Education: Literacy (1992): 96%.

Major International Organizations: UN, CIS.

In 1918, Romania annexed all of Bessarabia which Russia had acquired from Turkey in 1812 by the Treaty of Bucharest. In 1924, the Soviet Union established the Moldavian Autonomous Soviet Socialist Republic on the eastern bank of the Dniester. It was merged with the Romanian-speaking districts of Bessarabia in 1940 to form the Moldavian SSR.

During World War II, Romania, allied with Germany, occupied the area. It was recaptured by the USSR in 1944. Moldova declared independence Aug. 27, 1991. It became an independent state when the Soviet Union disbanded Dec. 26, 1991. Fighting erupted between Moldovan security forces and Slavic separatists—ethnic Russians and ethnic Ukrainians—Mar. 1992. The Slavs feared that Moldovans, who are Romanian in language and culture, would merge with neighboring Romania. In a plebiscite on Mar. 6, 1994, however, the electorate supported independence, without unification with Romania.

Monaco
Principality of Monaco
Principanté de Monaco

People: Population: 31,515. **Pop. density:** 42,020 per sq. mi. **Ethnic groups:** French 47%, Italian 16%, Monegasque 16%. **Principal languages:** French (official). **Religions:** Roman Catholic 95%.

Geography: Area: 0.75 sq. mi. **Location:** On the NW Mediterranean coast. **Neighbors:** France to W, N, E. **Topography:** Monaco-Ville sits atop a high promontory, the rest of the principality rises from the port up the hillside. **Capital:** Monaco.

Government: Type: Constitutional monarchy. **Head of state:** Prince Rainier III; b May 31, 1923; in office: May 9, 1949. **Head of government:** Min. of State Jacques Dupont. **Local divisions:** 4 quarters.

Economy: Industries: Tourism, gambling, chemicals, precision instruments, plastics.

Finance: Monetary unit: French Franc or Monégasque Franc. **Gross domestic product** (1991): $475 mln. **Per capita GDP:** $16,000. **National budget** (1991): $424 mln. revenues.

Transport: Chief port: La Condamine.

Communications: Television sets: 1 per 1.5 persons. **Telephones:** 1 per 0.5 persons.

Health: Births (per 1,000 pop.): 11. **Deaths** (per 1,000 pop.): 12. **Natural increase:** -0.1%. **Infant mortality** (per 1,000 live births 1995): 7.

Education: Literacy (1989): 99%. **Years compulsory:** 10; attendance 99%.

Major International Organizations: UN.

An independent principality for over 300 years, Monaco has belonged to the House of Grimaldi since 1297, except during the French Revolution. It was placed under the protectorate of Sardinia in 1815, and under that of France, 1861. The Prince of Monaco was an absolute ruler until a 1911 constitution.

Monaco's fame as a tourist resort is widespread. It is noted for its mild climate and magnificent scenery.

Mongolia

Mongol Uls

People: Population: 2,493,615. **Pop. density:** 4 per sq. mi. **Urban:** 55%. **Ethnic groups:** Mongol 90%. **Principal languages:** Khalka Mongolian (official). **Religions:** traditionally Tibetan Buddhist.

Geography: Area: 604,800 sq. mi. **Location:** In E Central Asia. **Neighbors:** Russia on N, China on S. **Topography:** Mostly a high plateau with mountains, salt lakes, and vast grasslands. Arid lands in the S are part of the Gobi Desert. **Capital:** Ulaanbaatar. **Cities** (1991 est.): Ulaanbaatar 537,000; Darhan 80,000.

Government: Type: Republic. **Head of state:** Pres. Punsalmaagiyn Ochirbat; b 1942; in office: Mar. 21, 1990. **Head of government:** Prime Min. Puntsagiyn Jasray; in office: July 21, 1992. **Local divisions:** 18 provinces, 3 municipalities. **Defense:** 2.4% of GNP (1993). **Active troop strength:** 21,250.

Economy: Industries: Food processing, mining, cement. **Chief crops:** Grain. **Minerals:** Coal, oil, tungsten, copper, molybdenum, gold, tin. **Arable land:** 1%. **Livestock** (1993): sheep: 14.7 mln.; cattle: 2.8 mln. **Electricity prod.** (1992): 3.7 bln. kWh. **Labor force:** 28% agric.; 18% manuf. & mining; 27% services.

Finance: Monetary unit: Tugrik (Mar. 1995: 433 = $1 US). **Gross domestic product** (1993): $2.8 bln.* **Per capita GDP:** $1,200. **Imports** (1991): $360 mln.; partners: CIS 91%. **Exports** (1991): $279 mln.; partners: CIS 80%.

Transport: Railroads: Length: 1,438 mi.

Communications: Television sets: 1 per 19 persons. **Radios:** 1 per 11 persons. **Telephones:** 1 per 31 persons. **Daily newspaper circ.:** 74 per 1,000 pop.

Health: Life expectancy at birth (1995): 64 male; 69 female. **Births** (per 1,000 pop.): 33. **Deaths** (per 1,000 pop.): 7. **Natural increase:** 2.6%. **Hospital beds:** 1 per 83 persons. **Physicians:** 1 per 340 persons. **Infant mortality** (per 1,000 live births 1995): 42.

Education: Literacy (1991): 98%.

Major International Organizations: UN (ILO, WHO).

Embassy: 2833 M St. NW 20007; 333-7117.

One of the world's oldest countries, Mongolia reached the zenith of its power in the 13th century when Genghis Khan and his successors conquered all of China and extended their influence as far west as Hungary and Poland. In later centuries, the empire dissolved and Mongolia became a province of China.

With the advent of the 1911 Chinese revolution, Mongolia, with Russian backing, declared its independence. A Communist regime was established July 11, 1921.

In 1990, the Mongolian Communist Party yielded its monopoly on power. Free elections in July 1990 were won by the Communists. A new constitution took effect Feb. 12, 1992.

Morocco

Kingdom of Morocco

al-Mamlaka al-Maghrebia

People: Population: 29,168,848. **Age distrib.** (%): <15: 40; 65+: 4. **Pop. density:** 165 per sq. mi. **Urban:** 47%. **Ethnic groups:** Arab-Berber 99%. **Principal languages:** Arabic (official), Berber. **Religions:** Sunni Muslim 99%.

Geography: Area: 177,117 sq. mi. **Location:** On NW coast of Africa. **Neighbors:** Western Sahara on S, Algeria on E. **Topography:** Consists of 5 natural regions: mountain ranges (Riff in the N, Middle Atlas, Upper Atlas, and Anti-Atlas); rich plains in the W; alluvial plains in SW; well-cultivated plateaus in the center; a pre-Sahara arid zone extending from SE. **Capital:** Rabat. **Cities** (1984): Casablanca 2.6 mln.; Fes 852,000; Rabat 556,000.

Government: Type: Constitutional monarchy. **Head of state:** King Hassan II; b July 9, 1929; in office: Mar. 3, 1961. **Head of government:** Prime Min. Abdellatif Filali; in office: May 25, 1994. **Local divisions:** 37 provinces, 5 municipalities. **Defense:** 3.3% of GDP (1993). **Active troop strength:** 195,000.

Economy: Industries: Carpets, clothing, leather goods, mining, tourism. **Chief crops:** Grain, fruits, dates, grapes. **Minerals:** Iron ore, manganese, phosphates, lead, zinc. **Arable land:** 18%. **Livestock** (1993): cattle: 2.9 mln.; sheep: 16.3 mln.; goats: 4.8 mln. **Fish catch** (1993): 607,000 metric tons.

Electricity prod. (1992): 8.9 bln. kWh. **Labor force:** 50% agric.; 26% services; 15% ind.

Finance: Monetary unit: Dirham (May 1995: 8.39 = $1 US). **Gross domestic product** (1993): $70.3 bln.* **Per capita GDP:** $2,500. **Imports** (1992): $8.4 bln.; partners: EU 63%, U.S. 6%. **Exports** (1992): $5.7 bln.; partners: EU 64%. **Tourism** (1992): $1.3 bln. **National budget** (1992): $7.7 bln. **International reserves less gold** (May 1995): $3.8 bln. **Gold:** 704,000 oz t. **Consumer prices** (change in 1994): 5.1%.

Transport: Railroads: Length: 1,176 mi. **Motor vehicles:** in use: 812,000 passenger cars, 292,000 comm. vehicles. **Civil aviation:** 1.7 bln. passenger-mi.; 16 airports. **Chief ports:** Tangier, Casablanca, Kenitra.

Communications: Television sets: 1 per 22 persons. **Radios:** 1 per 5.9 persons. **Telephones:** 1 per 36 persons. **Daily newspaper circ.:** 13 per 1,000 pop.

Health: Life expectancy at birth (1995): 67 male; 71 female. **Births** (per 1,000 pop.): 28. **Deaths** (per 1,000 pop.): 6. **Natural increase:** 2.2%. **Hospital beds:** 1 per 937 persons. **Physicians:** 1 per 4,148 persons. **Infant mortality** (per 1,000 live births 1995): 46.

Education: Literacy (1991): 49%.

Major International Organizations: UN (ILO, WTO, IMF, WHO), Arab League.

Embassy: 1601 21st St. NW 20009; 462-7979.

Berbers were the original inhabitants, followed by Carthaginians and Romans. Arabs conquered in 683. In the 11th and 12th centuries, a Berber empire ruled all NW Africa and most of Spain from Morocco.

Part of Morocco came under Spanish rule in the 19th century; France controlled the rest in the early 20th. Tribal uprisings lasted from 1911 to 1933. The country became independent Mar. 2, 1956. Tangier, an internationalized seaport, was turned over to Morocco, 1956. Ifni, a Spanish enclave, was ceded in 1969.

Morocco annexed over 70,000 sq. mi. of phosphate-rich land Apr. 14, 1976, two-thirds of former Spanish Sahara, with the remainder annexed by Mauritania. Spain had withdrawn in February. Polisario, a guerrilla movement, proclaimed the region independent Feb. 27, and launched attacks with Algerian support. When Mauritania signed a treaty with the Polisario Front and gave up its portion of the former Spanish Sahara, Morocco occupied the area, 1980.

After years of bitter fighting, Morocco controlled the main urban areas, but the Polisario Front's guerrillas moved freely in the vast, sparsely populated deserts. The 2 sides signed a cease-fire agreement in 1990. The UN planned to conduct a referendum in Western Sahara on whether the territory should become independent or remain part of Morocco.

Mozambique

Republic of Mozambique

República de Moçambique

People: Population: 18,115,250. **Age distrib.** (%): <15: 46; 65+: 2. **Pop. density:** 58 per sq. mi. **Urban:** 33%. **Ethnic groups:** Bantu tribes. **Principal languages:** Portuguese (official), Makua, Malawi, Shona, Tsonga. **Religions:** indigenous beliefs 60%, Christian 30%, Muslim 10%.

Geography: Area: 313,661 sq. mi. **Location:** On SE coast of Africa. **Neighbors:** Tanzania on N, Malawi, Zambia, Zimbabwe on W, South Africa, Swaziland on S. **Topography:** Coastal lowlands comprise nearly half the country with plateaus rising in steps to the mountains along the western border. **Capital:** Maputo. **Cities** (1991 est.): Maputo 933,000; Beira 299,000.

Government: Type: Republic. **Head of state:** Pres. Joaquim Chissano; b Oct. 22, 1939; in office: Oct. 19, 1986. **Head of government:** Mario de Graca Machungo; in office: July 17, 1986. **Local divisions:** 10 provinces. **Defense:** 8% of GDP (1993 est.). **Active troop strength:** 2,000 est.

Economy: Industries: Cement, petroleum products, textiles. **Chief crops:** Cashews, cotton, sugar, corn, tea. **Minerals:** Coal, titanium. **Arable land:** 4%. **Livestock** (1993): cattle: 1.2 mln. **Fish catch** (1991): 34,000 metric tons. **Electricity prod.** (1991): 1.7 bln. kWh. **Labor force:** 90% agric.

Finance: Monetary unit: Metical (Feb. 1995: 7,193 = $1 US). **Gross domestic product** (1993): $9.8 bln.* **Per capita**

GDP: $600. **Imports** (1993): $1.0 bln.; partners: South Africa 23%, U.S. 7%. **Exports** (1993): $164 mln.; partners: Spain 18%, U.S. 12%, Jap. 10%. **National budget** (1992 est.): $607 mln.

Transport: Railroads: Length: 1,857 mi. **Motor vehicles:** in use: 35,000 passenger cars, 35,000 comm. vehicles. **Chief ports:** Maputo, Beira, Nacala, Quelimane.

Communications: Television sets: 1 per 435 persons. **Radios:** 1 per 25 persons. **Telephones:** 1 per 198 persons.

Health: Life expectancy at birth (1995): 47 male; 51 female. **Births** (per 1,000 pop.): 45. **Deaths** (per 1,000 pop.): 16. **Natural increase:** 2.9%. **Hospital beds:** 1 per 1,227 persons. **Physicians:** 1 per 36,428 persons. **Infant mortality** (per 1,000 live births 1995): 126.

Education: Literacy (1992): 33%.

Major International Organizations: UN (IMF, World Bank), OAU.

Embassy: 1990 M St. NW 20036; 293-7146.

The first Portuguese post on the Mozambique coast was established in 1505, on the trade route to the East. Mozambique became independent June 25, 1975, after a ten-year war against Portuguese colonial domination. The 1974 revolution in Portugal had paved the way for the orderly transfer of power to Frelimo (Front for the Liberation of Mozambique). Frelimo took over local administration Sept. 20, 1974, over the opposition, in part violent, of some blacks and whites.

The new government, led by Maoist Pres. Samora Machel, provided for a gradual transition to a communist system. Economic problems included the emigration of most of the country's whites, a politically untenable economic dependence on white-ruled South Africa, and a large external debt.

In the 1980s, severe drought and civil war caused famine and heavy loss of life.

The ruling party formally abandoned Marxist-Leninism in 1989, and a new constitution, effective Nov. 30, 1990, provided for multiparty elections and a free-market economy.

On Oct. 4, 1992, a peace agreement was signed aimed at ending hostilities between the government and the rebel Mozambique National Resistance (MNR). Elections took place Oct. 27-28, 1994. Repatriation of 1.7 million Mozambican refugees officially ended June 1995.

Myanmar (*formerly* Burma)

Union of Myanmar

Pyidaungzu Myanma Naingngandaw

People: Population: 45,103,809. **Age distrib.** (%): <15: 36; 65+: 4. **Pop. density:** 173 per sq. mi. **Urban:** 25%. **Ethnic groups:** Burmese (related to Tibetans) 68%, Shan 9%, Karen 7%, Rakhine 4%. **Principal languages:** Burmese (official), Karen, Shan. **Religions:** Buddhist 89%, Christian, Muslim.

Geography: Area: 261,228 sq. mi. **Location:** Between S and SE Asia, on Bay of Bengal. **Neighbors:** Bangladesh, India on W, China, Laos, Thailand on E. **Topography:** Mountains surround Myanmar on W, N, and E, and dense forests cover much of the nation. N-S rivers provide habitable valleys and communications, especially the Irrawaddy, navigable for 900 miles. The country has a tropical monsoon climate. **Capital:** Yangôn (Rangoon). **Cities** (1983 est.): Yangôn 2.5 mln.; Mandalay 533,000.

Government: Type: Military. **Head of state and government:** Gen. Than Shwe; b 1933; in office: Apr. 24, 1992. **Local divisions:** 7 states and 7 divisions. **Defense:** 3.1% of GDP (1992). **Active troop strength:** 286,000 est.

Economy: Industries: mining, textiles, footwear, wood products, petroleum, refining. **Chief crops:** Rice, sugarcane, corn, pulses. **Minerals:** Oil, lead, copper, tin, tungsten, precious stones. **Crude oil reserves** (1994): 50 mln. bbls. **Other resources:** Rubber, teakwood. **Arable land:** 15%. **Livestock** (1993): cattle: 9.6 mln.; pigs: 2.5 mln. **Fish catch** (1991): 769,000 metric tons. **Electricity prod.** (1992): 2.8 bln. kWh. **Labor force:** 65% agric.; 14% ind.

Finance: Monetary unit: Kyat (May 1995: 5.45 = $1 US). **Gross domestic product** (1993): $41 bln.* **Per capita GDP:** $950. **Imports** (1993): $1.0 bln.; partners: Japan 50%, EU 20%. **Exports** (1993): $613 mln.; partners: SE Asian countries

30%; EU 12%. **Tourism** (1992): $8 mln. **National budget** (1992): $11.6 bln. **International reserves less gold** (Apr. 1995): $594 mln. **Gold:** 251,000 oz t. **Consumer prices** (change in 1994): 24.1%.

Transport: Railroads: Length: 1,949 mi. **Motor vehicles:** in use: 35,000 passenger cars, 35,000 comm. vehicles. **Civil aviation:** 138 mln. passenger-mi.; 20 airports with scheduled flights. **Chief ports:** Yangôn, Bassein, Moulmein.

Communications: Television sets: 1 per 45 persons. **Radios:** 1 per 14 persons. **Telephones:** 1 per 501 persons.

Health: Life expectancy at birth (1995): 58 male; 63 female. **Births** (per 1,000 pop.): 28. **Deaths** (per 1,000 pop.): 10. **Natural increase:** 1.8%. **Hospital beds:** 1 per 1,586 persons. **Physicians:** 1 per 3,306 persons. **Infant mortality** (per 1,000 live births 1995): 62.

Education: Literacy (1993): 78%. **Years compulsory:** 4. **Attendance:** 84%.

Major International Organizations: UN (World Bank, IMF, WTO).

Embassy: 2300 S St. NW 20008; 332-9044.

The Burmese arrived from Tibet before the 9th century, displacing earlier cultures, and a Buddhist monarchy was established by the 11th. Burma was conquered by the Mongol dynasty of China in 1272, then ruled by Shans as a Chinese tributary, until the 16th century.

Britain subjugated Burma in 3 wars, 1824-84, and ruled the country as part of India until 1937, when it became self-governing. Independence outside the Commonwealth was achieved Jan. 4, 1948.

Gen. Ne Win dominated politics from 1962 to 1988, first as military ruler then as constitutional president. His regime drove Indians from the civil service and Chinese from commerce. Socialization of the economy was advanced, isolation from foreign countries enforced. In 1987 Burma, once the richest nation in SE Asia, was granted less developed status by the UN.

Ne Win resigned July 1988, following waves of antigovernment riots. Rioting and street violence continued, and in Sept. the military seized power, under Gen. Saw Maung. In 1989 the country's name was changed to Myanmar.

The first free multiparty elections in 30 years took place May 27, 1990, with the main opposition party winning a decisive victory, but the military refused to hand over power. A key opposition leader, Aung San Suu Kyi, awarded the Nobel Peace Prize in 1991, was held under house arrest from July 20, 1989, to July 10, 1995.

Namibia

Republic of Namibia

People: Population: 1,651,545. **Pop density:** 5 per sq. mi. **Urban:** 32%. **Ethnic groups:** Ovambo 47%, Kavango 9%, Herero 7%, Damara 7%, white 6%. **Principal languages:** Afrikaans, English (official), German, indigenous languages. **Religions:** Lutheran 50%, other Christian 30%.

Geography: Area: 318,580 sq. mi. **Location:** In S Africa on the coast of the Atlantic Ocean. **Neighbors:** Angola on N, Botswana on E, and South Africa on S. **Capital:** Windhoek (1990 est.): 125,000.

Government: Type: Republic. **Head of state:** Pres. Sam Nujoma; b May 12, 1929; in office: Mar. 21, 1990. **Head of government:** Prime Min. Hage Geingob. **Local divisions:** 13 regions. **Defense:** 3.4% of GDP (1992). **Active troop strength:** 8,100.

Economy: Mining accounts for 25% of GDP. **Minerals:** Diamonds, copper, gold, zinc, lead, uranium. **Fish catch** (1991): 205,000 metric tons. **Electricity prod.** (1991): 1.3 mln. kWh.

Finance: Monetary unit: Dollar (May 1995: 3.68 = $1 US). **Gross domestic product** (1993): $3.8 bln.* **Per capital GDP:** $2,500. **Imports** (1992): $1.2 bln. **Exports** (1992): $1.3 bln. **Tourism** (1992): $91 mln. **National budget** (1993): $1.1 bln. **International reserves less gold** (Apr. 1995): $219 mln.

Transport: Railroads: Length: 1,481 mi.

Communications: Television sets: 1 per 40 persons. **Radios:** 1 per 5.6 persons. **Telephones:** 1 per 16 persons.

Health: Life expectancy at birth (1995): 59 male; 65 female. **Births** (per 1,000 pop.): 43. **Deaths** (per 1,000 pop.): 9.

Natural increase: 3.4%. **Hospital beds:** 1 per 216 persons. **Physicians:** 1 per 4,594 persons. **Infant mortality** (per 1,000 live births 1995): 60.

Education: Literacy (1990): 72%.

Major International Organizations: UN, OAU, the Commonwealth.

Embassy: 1605 New Hampshire Ave. NW 20009; 986-0540.

Namibia was declared a protectorate by Germany in 1890 and officially called South-West Africa. South Africa seized the territory from Germany in 1915 during World War I; the League of Nations gave South Africa a mandate over the territory in 1920. In 1966, the Marxist South-West Africa People's Organization (SWAPO) launched a guerrilla war for independence.

In 1968 the UN General Assembly gave the area the name Namibia.

After many years of guerrilla warfare and failed diplomatic efforts, S Africa, Angola, and Cuba signed a U.S.-mediated agreement Dec. 22, 1988, to end S African administration of Namibia and provide for a cease-fire and transition to independence, in accordance with a 1978 UN plan. A separate accord between Cuba and Angola provided for a phased withdrawal of Cuban troops from Namibia. SWAPO later endorsed the plan. Elections were held for a constituent assembly, and a constitution providing for multiparty government was adopted Feb. 9, 1990. Namibia became an independent nation Mar. 21, 1990.

Walvis Bay, the principal deepwater port, had been turned over to S African administration in 1922. It remained in S African hands after independence, but S Africa turned control of the port back to Namibia, as of Mar. 1, 1994.

Nauru

Republic of Nauru

People: Population: 10,149. **Pop density:** 1,238 per sq. mi. **Ethnic groups:** Nauruan 58%, other Pacific Islander 26%, Chinese 8%, European 8%. **Principal languages:** Nauruan (official). **Religions:** predominantly Christian.

Geography: Area: 8.2 sq. mi. **Location:** In Western Pacific O. just S of the Equator. **Neighbors:** Nearest are Solomon Is. **Topography:** Mostly a plateau bearing high grade phosphate deposits, surrounded by a coral cliff and a sandy shore in concentric rings. **Capital:** Yaren.

Government: Type: Republic. **Head of state:** Pres. Bernard Dowiyogo; b Feb. 14, 1946; in office: Dec. 12, 1989. **Local divisions:** 14 districts.

Economy: Phosphate mining. **Electricity prod.** (1990): 50 mln. kWh.

Finance: Monetary unit: Australian Dollar. **Gross national product** (1989): $90 mln.

Communications: Radios: 1 per 2.5 persons. **Telephones:** 1 per 5.9 persons.

Health: Births (per 1,000 pop.): 18. **Deaths** (per 1,000 pop.): 5. **Natural increase:** 1.3%. **Infant mortality** (per 1,000 live births 1995): 41.

Education: Literacy (1989): 99%. **Years compulsory:** ages 6-16.

The island was discovered in 1798 by the British but was formally annexed to the German Empire in 1886. After World War I, Nauru became a League of Nations mandate administered by Australia. During World War II the Japanese occupied the island and shipped 1,200 Nauruans to the fortress island of Truk as slave laborers.

In 1947 Nauru was made a UN trust territory, administered by Australia. Nauru became an independent republic Jan. 31, 1968.

Phosphate exports provide Nauru with per capita revenues that are among the highest in the Third World. Phosphate reserves, however, are expected to be depleted by 2000.

Nepal

Kingdom of Nepal

Nepal Adhirajya

People: Population: 21,560,869. **Age distrib.** (%): <15: 42; 65+: 3. **Pop. density:** 379 per sq. mi. **Urban:** 10%. **Ethnic groups:** The many tribes are descendants of Indian, Tibetan, and Central Asian migrants. **Principal languages:** Nepali (official) (an Indic language), many others. **Religions:** Hindu (official) 90%, Buddhist 5%, Muslim 3%.

Geography: Area: 56,827 sq. mi. **Location:** Astride the Himalaya Mts. **Neighbors:** China on N, India on S. **Topography:** The Himalayas stretch across the N, the hill country with its fertile valleys extends across the center, while the S border region is part of the flat, subtropical Ganges Plain. **Capital:** Kathmandu. **Cities** (1991 met. est.): Kathmandu 419,000; Biratnagar 130,000; Lalitpur 117,000; Pokhara 95,000.

Government: Type: Constitutional monarchy. **Head of state:** King Birendra Bir Bikram Shah Dev; b Dec. 28, 1945; in office: Jan. 31, 1972. **Head of government:** Prime Min. Sher Bahadur Deuba; in office: Sept. 11, 1995. **Local divisions:** 14 zones. **Defense:** 2% of GDP (1992). **Active troop strength:** 35,000.

Economy: Industries: Sugar, jute mills, tourism. **Chief crops:** Jute, rice, grain. **Minerals:** Quartz. **Other resources:** Forests. **Arable land:** 17%. **Livestock** (1992): cattle: 6.2 mln. **Electricity prod.** (1992): 1 bln. kWh. **Labor force:** 93% agric.

Finance: Monetary unit: Rupee (May 1995: 50 = $1 US). **Gross domestic product** (1993): $20.5 bln.* **Per capita GDP:** $1,000. **Imports** (1993): $789 mln.; partners: India 32%, Singapore 14%, Japan 13%. **Exports** (1993): $369 mln.; partners: Germany 36%, India 22%. **Tourism** (1992): $110 mln. **National budget** (1993): $725 mln. **International reserves less gold** (Mar. 1995): $720 mln. **Gold:** 153,000 oz t. **Consumer prices** (change in 1994): 9.1%.

Transport: Civil aviation: 439 mln. passenger-mi.

Communications: Radios: 1 per 32 persons. **Telephones:** 1 per 275 persons.

Health: Life expectancy at birth (1995): 53 male; 53 female. **Births** (per 1,000 pop.): 37. **Deaths** (per 1,000 pop.): 13. **Natural increase:** 2.4%. **Hospital beds:** 1 per 3,898 persons. **Physicians:** 1 per 12,623 persons. **Infant mortality** (per 1,000 live births 1995): 81.

Education: Literacy (1991): 38%. **Years compulsory:** 3; attendance: 79% primary, 22% secondary.

Major International Organizations: UN (IMF).

Embassy: 2131 Leroy Pl. NW 20008; 667-4550.

Nepal was originally a group of petty principalities, the inhabitants of one of which, the Gurkhas, became dominant about 1769. In 1951 King Tribhubana Bir Bikram, member of the Shah family, ended the system of rule by hereditary premiers of the Ranas family, who had kept the kings virtual prisoners, and established a cabinet system of government.

Virtually closed to the outside world for centuries, Nepal is now linked to India and Pakistan by roads and air service and to Tibet by road. Polygamy, child marriage, and the caste system were officially abolished in 1963.

The government announced the legalization of political parties in 1990. Elections on Nov. 15, 1994, led to the installation of Nepal's first Communist government, which held power until a no-confidence vote Sept. 10, 1995.

Netherlands

Kingdom of the Netherlands

Koninkrijk der Nederlanden

People: Population: 15,452,903. **Age distrib.** (%): <15: 18; 65+: 13. **Pop. density:** 964 per sq. mi. **Urban:** 89%. **Ethnic groups:** Dutch 96%. **Principal language:** Dutch. **Religions:** Roman Catholic 34%, Protestant 25%.

Geography: Area: 16,033 sq. mi. **Location:** In NW Europe on North Sea. **Topography:** The land is flat, an average alt. of 37 ft. above sea level, with much land below sea level reclaimed and protected by some 1,500 miles of dikes. Since 1920 the government has been draining the IJsselmeer, formerly the Zuider Zee. **Capital:** Amsterdam. **Cities** (1993): Amsterdam 720,000; Rotterdam 596,000; The Hague 445,000.

Government: Type: Parliamentary democracy under a constitutional monarch. **Head of state:** Queen Beatrix; b Jan. 31, 1938; in office: Apr. 30, 1980. **Head of government:** Prime Min. Wim Kok; b Sept. 29, 1938; in office: Aug. 22, 1994. **Seat of govt.:** The Hague. **Local divisions:** 12 provinces. **Defense:** 3% of GDP (1992). **Active troop strength:** 70,900.

Economy: Industries: Metals, machinery, chemicals, oil refinery, diamond cutting, electronics, tourism. **Chief crops:**

Grains, potatoes, sugar beets, vegetables, fruits, flowers. **Minerals:** Natural gas, oil. **Crude oil reserves** (1994): 132 mln. bbls. **Arable land:** 26%. **Livestock** (1993): cattle: 4.8 mln.; pigs: 15.0 mln. **Fish catch** (1991): 443,000 metric tons. **Electricity prod.** (1992): 63.5 bln. kWh. **Labor force:** 6% agric.; 50% services; 16% govt.; 28% manuf.

Finance: Monetary unit: Guilder (May 1995: 1.55 = $1 US). **Gross domestic product** (1993): $262.8 bln.* **Per capita GDP:** $17,200. **Imports** (1992): $156 bln.; partners: Germany 26%, Belgium 14%, U.S. 9%, UK 9%. **Exports** (1992): $160 bln.; partners: Germany 26%, Belgium 14%, France 10%, UK 9%. **Tourism** (1992): $5.0 bln. **National budget** (1992): $122.1 bln. **International reserves less gold** (May 1995): $37.1 bln. **Gold:** 34.77 mln. oz t. **Consumer prices** (change in 1994): 2.8%.

Transport: Railroads: Length: 1,711 mi. **Motor vehicles:** in use: 5.7 mln. passenger cars, 797,000 comm. vehicles. **Civil aviation:** 19.8 bln. passenger-mi.; 5 airports. **Chief ports:** Rotterdam, Amsterdam, IJmuiden.

Communications: Television sets: 1 per 2.7 persons. **Radios:** 1 per 1.3 persons. **Telephones:** 1 per 1.4 persons. **Daily newspaper circ.:** 311 per 1,000 pop.

Health: Life expectancy at birth (1995): 75 male; 81 female. **Births** (per 1,000 pop.): 12. **Deaths** (per 1,000 pop.): 8. **Natural increase:** 0.4%. **Hospital beds:** 1 per 172 persons. **Physicians:** 1 per 400 persons. **Infant mortality** (per 1,000 live births 1995): 6.

Education: Literacy (1993): 100%. **Years compulsory:** 10; attendance: 100%.

Major International Organizations: UN and all of its specialized agencies, NATO, EU, OECD.

Embassy: 4200 Linnean Ave. NW 20008; 244-5300.

Julius Caesar conquered the region in 55 BC, when it was inhabited by Celtic and Germanic tribes.

After the empire of Charlemagne fell apart, the Netherlands (Holland, Belgium, Flanders) split among counts, dukes and bishops, passed to Burgundy and thence to Charles V of Spain. His son, Philip II, tried to check the Dutch drive toward political freedom and Protestantism (1568-1573). William the Silent, prince of Orange, led a confederation of the northern provinces, called Estates, in the Union of Utrecht, 1579. The Estates retained individual sovereignty, but were represented jointly in the States-General, a body that had control of foreign affairs and defense. In 1581 they repudiated allegiance to Spain. The rise of the Dutch republic to naval, economic, and artistic eminence came in the 17th century.

The United Dutch Republic ended 1795 when the French formed the Batavian Republic. Napoleon made his brother Louis king of Holland, 1806; Louis abdicated 1810 when Napoleon annexed Holland. In 1813 the French were expelled. In 1815 the Congress of Vienna formed a kingdom of the Netherlands, including Belgium, under William I. In 1830, the Belgians seceded and formed a separate kingdom.

The constitution, promulgated 1814, and subsequently revised, provides for a hereditary constitutional monarchy.

The Netherlands maintained its neutrality in World War I, but was invaded and brutally occupied by Germany, 1940-45.

In 1949, after several years of fighting, the Netherlands granted independence to Indonesia. In 1963, West New Guinea was turned over to Indonesia.

The independence of former Dutch colonies has instigated mass emigrations to the Netherlands.

Though the Netherlands has been heavily industrialized, its small farms export large quantities of pork and dairy foods. Rotterdam, located along the principal mouth of the Rhine, handles the most cargo of any ocean port in the world. Canals, of which there over 3,400 miles, are important in transportation.

Netherlands Antilles

The **Netherlands Antilles,** constitutionally on a level of equality with the Netherlands homeland within the kingdom, consist of 2 groups of islands in the West Indies. **Curacao, Aruba,** and **Bonaire** are near the South American coast; **St. Eustatius, Saba,** and the southern part of **St. Maarten** are SE of Puerto Rico. Northern two-thirds of St. Maarten belong to French Guadeloupe; the French call the island St. Martin. Total area of the 2 groups is 385 sq. mi., including: Aruba 75, Bonaire 111, Curacao 171, St. Eustatius 11, Saba 5, St. Maarten (Dutch part) 13. St. Maarten suffered extensive damage from Hurricane Luis, Sept. 1995.

Aruba was separated from The Netherlands Antilles on Jan. 1, 1986; it is an autonomous member of The Netherlands, the same status as the Netherland Antilles.

Total pop. (1995 est.) was 207,000. Willemstad, on Curacao, is the capital. Principal industry is the refining of crude oil from Venezuela. Tourism is an important industry, as is shipbuilding.

New Zealand

People: Population: 3,407,277. **Age distrib.** (%): <15: 23; 65+: 12 **Pop. density:** 33 per sq. mi. **Urban:** 85%. **Ethnic groups:** European (mostly British) 88%, Maori 9%. **Principal languages:** English (official), Maori. **Religions:** Anglican 24%, Presbyterian 18%, Roman Catholic 15%.

Geography: Area: 104,454 sq. mi. **Location:** In SW Pacific O. **Neighbors:** Nearest are Australia on W, Fiji, Tonga on N. **Topography:** Each of the 2 main islands (North and South Is.) is mainly hilly and mountainous. The east coasts consist of fertile plains, especially the broad Canterbury Plains on South I. A volcanic plateau is in center of North I. South I. has glaciers and 15 peaks over 10,000 ft. **Capital:** Wellington. **Cities** (1992 est.): Auckland 317,000; Christchurch 294,000; Manukau 230,000; Wellington 150,000.

Government: Type: Parliamentary democracy. **Head of state:** Queen Elizabeth II, represented by Gov.-Gen. Dame Catherine Tizard; b Apr. 4, 1931; in office: Nov. 20, 1990. **Head of government:** Prime Min. Jim Bolger; b 1935; in office: Oct. 27, 1990. **Local divisions:** 93 counties, 12 towns & districts. **Defense:** 1.5% of GNP (1993). **Active troop strength:** 10,000.

Economy: Industries: Food processing, textiles, machinery, fish, forest prods. **Chief crops:** Grains, fruits. **Minerals:** Oil, gas, iron, coal. **Crude oil reserves** (1994): 156 mln. bbls. **Other resources:** Wool, timber. **Arable land:** 2%. **Livestock** (1993): cattle: 8.7 mln.; sheep: 51 mln. **Fish catch** (1993): 581,000 metric tons. **Electricity prod.** (1992): 31 bln. kWh. **Labor force:** 20% manuf.; 67% services.

Finance: Monetary unit: Dollar (May 1995: 1.00 = $.67 US). **Gross domestic product** (1993): $53 bln.* **Per capita GDP:** $15,700. **Imports** (1993): $9.4 bln.; partners: Australia 21%, U.S. 20%, Japan 15%. **Exports** (1993): $10.3 bln.; partners: Australia 19%, U.S. 13%, Japan 15%. **Tourism** (1992): $1.0 bln. **National budget** (1992): $15.2 bln. **International reserves less gold** (Apr. 1995): $3.7 bln. **Consumer prices** (change in 1994): 1.7%.

Transport: Railroads: Length: 2,627 mi. **Motor vehicles:** in use: 1.6 mln. passenger cars; 325,000 comm. vehicles. **Civil aviation:** 8.3 bln. passenger-mi.; 36 airports. **Chief ports:** Auckland, Wellington, Lyttleton, Tauranga.

Communications: Television sets: 1 per 3.2 persons. **Radios:** 1 per 1.1 persons. **Telephones:** 1 per 1.4 persons. **Daily newspaper circ.:** 324 per 1,000 pop.

Health: Life expectancy at birth (1995): 73 male; 80 female. **Births** (per 1,000 pop.): 15. **Deaths** (per 1,000 pop.): 8. **Natural increase:** 0.7%. **Hospital beds:** 1 per 114 persons. **Physicians:** 1 per 359 persons. **Infant mortality** (per 1,000 live births 1995): 9.

Education: Literacy (1991): 99%. **Years compulsory:** ages 6-15; attendance: 100%.

Major International Organizations: UN (WTO, World Bank, IMF), the Commonwealth, OECD.

Embassy: 37 Observatory Cir. NW 20008; 328-4800.

The Maoris, a Polynesian group from the eastern Pacific, reached New Zealand before and during the 14th century. The first European to sight New Zealand was Dutch navigator Abel Janszoon Tasman, but Maoris refused to allow him to land. British Capt. James Cook explored the coasts, 1769-1770.

British sovereignty was proclaimed in 1840, with organized settlement beginning in the same year. Representative institutions were granted in 1853. Maori Wars ended in 1870 with British victory. The colony became a dominion in 1907, and is an independent member of the Commonwealth.

In July 1985, the *Rainbow Warrior,* flagship of the Greenpeace organization, was bombed and sunk in Auckland harbor by French secret service agents.

A progressive tradition in politics dates back to the 19th century, when New Zealand was internationally known for social experimentation. Private ownership is basic to the economy, but state ownership or regulation affects many industries. In recent years, the Labor and National parties have had alternating periods in power. The National Party, led by Jim Bolger, won general elections in 1990 and 1993.

The native Maoris number about 325,000. Four of 99 members of the House of Representatives are elected directly by the Maori people.

New Zealand comprises **North Island,** 44,035 sq. mi.; **South Island,** 58,304 sq. mi.; **Stewart Island,** 674 sq. mi.; **Chatham Islands,** 372 sq. mi.

In 1965, the **Cook Islands** (pop. 1986 est., 17,185; area 93 sq. mi.) became self-governing although New Zealand retains responsibility for defense and foreign affairs. **Niue** attained the same status in 1974; it lies 400 mi. to W (pop. 1987 est., 2,500; area 100 sq. mi.). **Tokelau Is.** (pop. 1987 est., 1,600; area 4 sq. mi.) are 300 mi. N of Samoa.

Ross Dependency, administered by New Zealand since 1923, comprises 160,000 sq. mi. of Antarctic territory.

Nicaragua
Republic of Nicaragua
República de Nicaragua

People: Population: 4,206,353. **Age distrib.** (%): <15: 46; 65+: 3. **Pop. density:** 83 per sq. mi. **Urban:** 62%. **Ethnic groups:** mestizo 69%, white 17%, black 9%, Indian 5%. **Principal languages:** Spanish (official). **Religions:** Roman Catholic 95%.

Geography: Area: 50,838 sq. mi. **Location:** In Central America. **Neighbors:** Honduras on N, Costa Rica on S. **Topography:** Both Atlantic and Pacific coasts are over 200 mi. long. The Cordillera Mts., with many volcanic peaks, run NW-SE through the middle of the country. Between this and a volcanic range to the E lie Lakes Managua and Nicaragua. **Capital:** Managua (1992 met. est.): 974,000.

Government: Type: Republic. **Head of state and government:** Pres. Violeta Barrios de Chamorro; b 1929; in office Apr. 25, 1990. **Local divisions:** 17 departments. **Defense:** 2.7% of GDP (1993). **Active troop strength:** 15,200.

Economy: Industries: Oil refining, food processing, chemicals, textiles. **Chief crops:** Bananas, cotton, fruit, coffee, sugar, corn, rice. **Minerals:** Gold, silver, copper, tungsten. **Other resources:** Forests, shrimp. **Arable land:** 9%. **Livestock** (1993): cattle: 1.7 mln.; pigs: 709,000. **Electricity prod.** (1993): 1.1 bln. kWh. **Labor force:** 44% agric.; 13% ind.; 43% services.

Finance: Monetary unit: Cordoba (Dec. 1994: 7.11 = $1 US). **Gross domestic product** (1993): $6.4 bln.* **Per capita GDP:** $1,600. **Imports** (1992): $907 mln.; partners: U.S. 26%, Latin Amer. 30%, EU 20%. **Exports** (1992): $228 mln.; partners: EU 26%, U.S. 26%. **National budget** (1991): $410 mln. **International reserves less gold** (Feb. 1995): $168 mln. **Consumer prices** (change in 1992): 20%.

Transport: Railroads: Length: 186 mi. **Motor vehicles:** in use: 35,000 passenger cars, 35,000 comm. vehicles. **Chief ports:** Corinto, Puerto Somoza, San Juan del Sur.

Communications: Television sets: 1 per 20 persons. **Radios:** 1 per 4.7 persons. **Telephones:** 1 per 81 persons. **Daily newspaper circ.:** 65 per 1,000 pop.

Health: Life expectancy at birth (1995): 62 male; 68 female. **Births** (per 1,000 pop.): 34. **Deaths** (per 1,000 pop.): 6. **Natural increase:** 2.7%. **Hospital beds:** 1 per 804 persons. **Physicians:** 1 per 1,882 persons. **Infant mortality** (per 1,000 live births 1995): 50.

Education: Literacy (1991): 74%. **Years compulsory:** 11 years or 16 years old.

Major International Organizations: UN and most of its specialized agencies, OAS.

Embassy: 1627 New Hampshire Ave. NW 20009; 939-6570.

Nicaragua, inhabited by various Indian tribes, was conquered by Spain in 1552. After gaining independence from Spain, 1821, Nicaragua was united for a short period with Mexico, then with the United Provinces of Central America, finally becoming an independent republic, 1838.

U.S. Marines occupied the country at times in the early 20th century, the last time from 1926 to 1933.

Gen. Anastasio Somoza Debayle was elected president 1967. He resigned 1972, but was elected president again in 1974. Martial law was imposed in Dec. 1974, after officials

were kidnapped by the Marxist Sandinista guerrillas. Violent opposition spread to nearly all classes in 1978; nationwide strikes called against the government touched off a state of civil war. Months of simmering civil war ended when Somoza fled, July 19, 1979.

Relations with the U.S. were strained as a result of Nicaragua's aid to leftist guerrillas in El Salvador and U.S. backing of anti-Sandinista contra guerrilla groups.

In 1983, the contras launched their first major offensive; the Sandinistas imposed rule by decree. In 1985, the U.S. House rejected Pres. Reagan's request for military aid to the contras. The subsequent diversion of funds to the contras from the proceeds of a secret arms sale to Iran caused a major scandal in the U.S.

In a stunning upset, Violeta Barrios de Chamorro defeated Sandinista leader Daniel Ortega Saavedra in national elections, Feb. 25, 1990.

Niger
Republic of Niger
République du Niger

People: Population: 9,280,208. **Age distrib.** (%): <15: 49; 65+: 3. **Pop. density:** 19 per sq. mi. **Urban:** 15%. **Ethnic groups:** Hausa 56%, Djerma 22%, Fula 9%, Tuareg 8%. **Principal languages:** French (official), Hausa, Djerma. **Religions:** Sunni Muslim 80%.

Geography: Area: 496,900 sq. mi. **Location:** In the interior of N Africa. **Neighbors:** Libya, Algeria on N, Mali, Burkina Faso on W, Benin, Nigeria on S, Chad on E. **Topography:** Mostly arid desert and mountains. A narrow savanna in the S and the Niger R. basin in the SW contain most of the population. **Capital:** Niamey (1988 est.): 392,000.

Government: Type: Republic. **Head of state:** Pres. Mahamane Ousmane; in office: Apr. 16, 1993. **Head of government:** Prime Min. Amadou Hama; in office: Feb. 21, 1995. **Local divisions:** 7 departments. **Defense:** 1.0% of GNP (1992). **Active troop strength:** 5,300.

Economy: Chief crops: Peanuts, cotton. **Minerals:** Uranium, coal, iron. **Arable land:** 3%. **Livestock** (1993): cattle: 1.8 mln.; sheep: 3.5 mln.; goats: 5.4 mln. **Electricity prod.** (1991): 230 mln. kWh. **Labor force:** 90% agric.

Finance: Monetary unit: CFA Franc (Apr. 1995: 488 = $1 US). **Gross domestic product** (1993): $5.4 bln.* **Per capita GDP:** $650. **Imports** (1991): $346 mln.; partners: Germany 26%, Côte d'Ivoire 11%. **Exports** (1991): $294 mln.; partners: France 77%, Nigeria 8%. **National budget** (1991): $355 mln. **International reserves less gold** (Mar. 1995): $144 mln. **Gold:** 11,000 oz t. **Consumer prices** (change in 1994): 36.0%.

Transport: Motor vehicles: in use: 31,000 passenger cars, 9,000 comm. vehicles.

Communications: Television sets: 1 per 341 persons. **Radios:** 1 per 21 persons. **Telephones:** 1 per 589 persons.

Health: Life expectancy at birth (1995): 43 male; 47 female. **Births** (per 1,000 pop.): 55. **Deaths** (per 1,000 pop.): 21. **Natural increase:** 3.4%. **Physicians:** 1 per 52,900 persons. **Infant mortality** (per 1,000 live births 1994): 109.

Education: Literacy (1991): 28%. **Years compulsory:** 6; attendance: 15%.

Major International Organizations: UN (IMF, WHO, FAO), OAU.

Embassy: 2204 R St. NW 20008; 483-4224.

Niger was part of ancient and medieval African empires. European explorers reached the area in the late 18th century. The French colony of Niger was established 1900-22, after the defeat of Tuareg fighters, who had invaded the area from the N a century before. The country became independent Aug. 3, 1960. The next year it signed a bilateral agreement with France.

In 1993, Niger held its first free and open elections since independence; an opposition leader, Mahamane Ousmane, won the presidency. A peace accord Apr. 24, 1995, ended a Tuareg rebellion that began in 1990.

Nigeria
Federal Republic of Nigeria

People: Population: 101,232,251. **Age distrib.** (%): <15: 45; 65+: 3. **Pop. density:** 284 per sq. mi. **Urban:** 16%. **Ethnic**

groups: Hausa 21%, Yoruba 20%, Ibo 17%, Fulani 9%, others. **Principal languages:** English (official), Hausa, Yoruba, Ibo. **Religions:** Muslim 50% (in N), Christian 40% (in S).

Geography: Area: 356,669 sq. mi. **Location:** On the S coast of W Africa. **Neighbors:** Benin on W, Niger on N, Chad, Cameroon on E. **Topography:** 4 E-W regions divide Nigeria: a coastal mangrove swamp 10-60 mi. wide, a tropical rain forest 50-100 mi. wide, a plateau of savanna and open woodland, and semidesert in the N. **Capital:** Abuja. **Cities:** (1992) Lagos 1.3 mln.; Ibadan 1.3 mln.

Government: Type: In transition. **Head of state and government:** Pres. Gen. Sani Abacha; b 1943; in office: Nov. 17, 1993. **Local divisions:** 30 states plus federal capital territory. **Defense:** 1% of GDP (1992). **Active troop strength:** 76,500.

Economy: Industries: Crude oil (95% of export), food processing, textiles. **Chief crops:** Cocoa (main export crop), palm products, corn, rice, cotton, soybeans. **Minerals:** Oil, gas, coal, iron, limestone, columbite, tin. **Crude oil reserves** (1994): 17.9 bln. bbls. **Other resources:** Timber, rubber, hides. **Arable land:** 31%. **Livestock** (1993): cattle: 16.3 mln.; goats: 24.5 mln.; sheep: 14 mln. **Fish catch** (1991): 267,000 metric tons. **Electricity prod.** (1991): 8.3 bln. kWh. **Labor force:** 54% agric.; 19% ind., commerce, and serv.

Finance: Monetary unit: Naira (Apr. 1995: 21.88 = $1 US). **Gross domestic product** (1993): $95.1 bln.* **Per capita GDP:** $1,000. **Imports** (1992): $8.3 bln.; partners: EU 64%, U.S. 10%. **Exports** (1992): $11.9 bln.; partners: U.S. 54%, EU 23%. **Tourism receipts** (1992): $29 mln. **National budget** (1992 est.): $10.8 bln. **International reserves less gold** (Feb. 1995): $1.8 bln. **Gold:** 687,000 oz t. **Consumer prices** (change in 1993): 57.2%.

Transport: Motor vehicles: in use: 800,000 passenger cars, 625,000 comm. vehicles. **Civil aviation:** 619 mln. passenger-mi.; 12 airports. **Chief ports:** Port Harcourt, Lagos, Warri, Calabar.

Communications: Television sets: 1 per 21 persons. **Radios:** 1 per 9 persons. **Telephones:** 1 per 118 persons. **Daily newspaper circ.:** 16 per 1,000 pop.

Health: Life expectancy at birth (1995): 55 male; 57 female. **Births** (per 1,000 pop.): 43. **Deaths** (per 1,000 pop.): 12. **Natural increase:** 3.1%. **Hospital beds:** 1 per 844 persons. **Physicians:** 1 per 5,006 persons. **Infant mortality** (per 1,000 live births 1995): 73.

Education: Literacy (1992): 42%. **Primary school attendance:** 42%.

Major International Organizations: UN (WTO, IMO, WHO), OPEC, OAU, the Commonwealth.

Embassy: 1333 16th St. NW 20036; 822-1500.

Early cultures in Nigeria date back to at least 700 BC. From the 12th to the 14th centuries, more advanced cultures developed in the Yoruba area, at Ife, and in the north, where Muslem influence prevailed.

Portuguese and British slavers appeared from the 15th-16th centuries. Britain seized Lagos, 1861, and gradually extended control inland until 1900. Nigeria became independent Oct. 1, 1960, and a republic Oct. 1, 1963.

On May 30, 1967, the Eastern Region seceded, proclaiming itself the Republic of Biafra, plunging the country into civil war. Casualties in the war were estimated at over 1 million, including many "Biafrans" (mostly Ibos) who died of starvation despite international efforts to provide relief. The secessionists, after steadily losing ground, capitulated Jan. 12, 1970.

Oil revenues have made possible a massive economic development program, largely using private enterprise, but agriculture has lagged.

After 13 years of military rule, the nation experienced a peaceful return to civilian government, Oct., 1979. However, military rule resumed, Dec. 31, 1983, as a coup ousted the democratically elected government. A second coup came in 1985. The new regime, headed by Gen. Ibrahim Babangida, promised elections but voided the result of a presidential election on June 23, 1993; riots followed in which many were killed.

Babangida resigned and appointed a civilian to head an interim government, Aug, 26, 1993, but that government was ousted in a military coup, Nov. 17. On June 11, 1994, the presumed winner of the 1993 presidential election, Moshood Abiola, declared himself president; he was jailed June 23. Criticism of human rights abuses in Nigeria mounted during 1995.

Norway

Kingdom of Norway

Kongeriket Norge

People: Population: 4,330,951. **Age distrib.** (%): <15: 19; 65+: 16. **Pop. density:** 35 per sq. mi. **Urban:** 73%. **Ethnic groups:** Germanic (Nordic, Alpine, Baltic), minority Lapps. **Principal languages:** Norwegian (official). **Religions:** Evangelical Lutheran 88%.

Geography: Area: 125,050 sq. mi. **Location:** Occupies the W part of Scandinavian peninsula in NW Europe (extends farther north than any European land). **Neighbors:** Sweden, Finland, Russia on E. **Topography:** A highly indented coast is lined with tens of thousands of islands. Mountains and plateaus cover most of the country, which is only 25% forested. **Capital:** Oslo. **Cities** (1994 met. est.): Oslo 478,000; Bergen 220,000.

Government: Type: Hereditary constitutional monarchy. **Head of state:** King Harald V; b Feb. 21, 1937; in office: Jan. 17, 1991. **Head of government:** Prime Min. Gro Harlem Brundtland; b Apr. 20, 1939; in office: Nov. 3, 1990. **Local divisions:** Oslo and 18 fylker (counties). **Defense:** 3.4% of GDP (1992). **Active troop strength:** 33,500.

Economy: Industries: Paper, shipbuilding, engineering, metals, chemicals, food processing, fish, oil, gas. **Chief crops:** Grains, potatoes, fruits. **Minerals:** Oil, copper, pyrites, nickel, iron, zinc, lead. **Crude oil reserves** (1994): 9.3 bln. bbls. **Other resources:** Timber. **Arable land:** 3%. **Livestock** (1993): sheep: 937,000; cattle: 976,000; pigs: 745,000. **Fish catch** (1993): 2.4 mln. metric tons. **Electricity prod.** (1992): 111 bln. kWh. **Labor force:** 6% agric.; 47% ind., banking, commerce; 39% services.

Finance: Monetary unit: Krone (May 1995: 6.18 = $1 US). **Gross domestic product** (1993): $89.5 bln.* **Per capita GDP:** $20,800. **Imports** (1993): $24.8 bln.; partners: EU 49%. **Exports** (1993): $32.1 bln.; partners: EU 66%. **Tourism** (1992): $1.9 bln. **National budget** (1993): $52 bln. **International reserves less gold** (May 1995): $21.5 bln. **Gold:** 1.18 mln. oz t. **Consumer prices** (change in 1994): 1.4%.

Transport: Railroads: Length: 2,502 mi. **Motor vehicles:** in use: 1.6 mln. passenger cars, 396,000 comm. vehicles. **Civil aviation:** 5.6 bln. passenger-mi.; 48 airports. **Chief ports:** Bergen, Stavanger, Oslo, Tonsberg.

Communications: Television sets: 1 per 2.9 persons. **Radios:** 1 per 1.3 persons. **Telephones:** 1 per 1.9 persons. **Daily newspaper circ.:** 614 per 1,000 pop.

Health: Life expectancy at birth (1995): 74 male; 81 female. **Births** (per 1,000 pop.): 13. **Deaths** (per 1,000 pop.): 10. **Natural increase:** 0.3%. **Hospital beds:** 1 per 183 persons. **Physicians:** 1 per 299 persons. **Infant mortality** (per 1,000 live births 1995): 6.

Education: Literacy (1993): 100%. **Years compulsory:** 9.

Major International Organizations: UN and all of its specialized agencies, NATO, OECD, EFTA.

Embassy: 2720 34th St. NW 20008; 333-6000.

The first ruler of Norway was Harald the Fairhaired, who came to power in 872 AD. Between 800 and 1000, Norway's Vikings raided and occupied widely dispersed parts of Europe.

The country was united with Denmark 1381-1814, and with Sweden, 1814-1905. In 1905, the country became independent with Prince Charles of Denmark as king.

Norway remained neutral during World War I. Germany attacked Norway Apr. 9, 1940, and held it until liberation May 8, 1945. The country abandoned its neutrality after the war, and joined NATO. In a referendum Nov. 28, 1994, Norwegian voters rejected European Union membership.

Abundant hydroelectric resources provided the base for Norway's industrialization, producing one of the highest living standards in the world.

Norway's merchant marine is one of the world's largest.

Svalbard is a group of mountainous islands in the Arctic O., c. 23,957 sq. mi., pop. varying seasonally from 1,500 to 3,600. The largest, Spitsbergen (formerly called West Spitsbergen), 15,060 sq. mi., seat of governor, is about 370 mi. N of Norway. By a treaty signed in Paris, 1920, major European powers recognized the sovereignty of Norway, which incorporated it in 1925.

Oman

Sultanate of Oman

Saltanat 'Uman

People: Population: 2,125,089. **Pop. density:** 18 per sq. mi. **Urban:** 12%. **Ethnic groups:** Omani Arab 74%, Pakistani 21%. **Principal languages:** Arabic (official). **Religions:** Ibadhi Muslim 75%, other Muslim, Hindu.

Geography: Area: 118,150 sq. mi. **Location:** On SE coast of Arabian peninsula. **Neighbors:** United Arab Emirates, Saudi Arabia, Yemen on W. **Topography:** Oman has a narrow coastal plain up to 10 mi. wide, a range of barren mountains reaching 9,900 ft., and a wide, stony, mostly waterless plateau, avg. alt. 1,000 ft. Also the tip of the Ruus-al-Jebal peninsula controls access to the Persian Gulf. **Capital:** Muscat (1982 est.): 85,000.

Government: Type: Absolute monarchy. **Head of state and government:** Sultan Qabus bin Said; b Nov. 18, 1942; in office: July 23, 1970. **Defense:** 16% of GDP (1993 est.). **Active troop strength:** 42,900.

Economy: Chief crops: Dates, fruits, vegetables, wheat, bananas. **Minerals:** Oil (85% of exports). **Crude oil reserves** (1994): 4.7 bln. bbls. **Fish catch** (1992): 112,000 metric tons. **Electricity prod.** (1992): 5.1 bln. kWh. **Labor force:** 40% agric.

Finance: Monetary unit: Rial Omani (May 1995: .38 = $1 US). **Gross domestic product** (1993): $16.4 bln. **Per capita GDP:** $10,000. **Imports** (1993): $3.7 bln.; partners: Japan 20%, UAE 14%, UK 19%. **Exports** (1993): $5.0 bln.; partners: Japan 27%, UAE 30%. **Tourism** (1992): $85 mln. **National budget** (1994): $5.2 bln. **International reserves less gold** (Feb. 1995): $977 mln. **Gold:** 291,000 oz t.

Transport: Motor vehicles: in use: 175,000 passenger cars, 91,000 comm. vehicles. **Civil aviation:** 1.2 bln. passenger-mi.; 6 airports. **Chief ports:** Matrah, Muscat.

Communications: Television sets: 1 per 1.3 persons. **Radios:** 1 per 2.2 persons. **Telephones:** 1 per 6.1 persons.

Health: Life expectancy at birth (1995): 68 male; 72 female. **Births** (per 1,000 pop.): 38. **Deaths** (per 1,000 pop.): 5. **Natural increase:** 3.3%. **Hospital beds:** 1 per 380 persons. **Physicians:** 1 per 1,078 persons. **Infant mortality** (per 1,000 live births 1995): 34.

Education: Literacy (1992): 41%. **Attendance:** 80% primary, 30% secondary.

Major International Organizations: UN (World Bank, IMF), Arab League.

Embassy: 2535 Belmont Rd. NW 20008; 387-1980.

A long history of rule by other lands, including Portugal in the 16th century, ended with the ouster of the Persians in 1744. By the early 19th century, Muscat and Oman was one of the most important countries in the region, controlling much of the Persian and Pakistan coasts, and ruling far-away Zanzibar, which was separated in 1861 under British mediation.

British influence was confirmed in a 1951 treaty, and Britain helped suppress an uprising by traditionally rebellious interior tribes against control by Muscat in the 1950s.

On July 23, 1970, Sultan Said bin Taimur was overthrown by his son, who changed the nation's name to Sultanate of Oman. Oil is the major source of income.

Oman opened its air bases to Western forces following the Iraqi invasion of Kuwait on Aug. 2, 1990.

Pakistan

Islamic Republic of Pakistan

Islami Jamhuriyae Pakistan

People: Population: 131,541,920. **Age distrib.** (%): <15: 41; 65+: 3. **Pop. density:** 387 per sq. mi. **Urban:** 32%. **Ethnic groups:** Punjabi, Sindhi, Pathan, Urdu, Balochi, others. **Principal languages:** Urdu, English (both official), Punjabi, Sindhi, Pashtu, Balochi. **Religions:** Sunni Muslim 77%, Shi'a Muslim 20%.

Geography: Area: 339,697 sq. mi. **Location:** In W part of South Asia. **Neighbors:** Iran on W, Afghanistan, China on N, India on E. **Topography:** The Indus R. rises in the Hindu Kush and Himalaya Mts. in the N (highest is K2, or Godwin Austen, 28,250 ft., 2d highest in world), then flows over 1,000 mi. through fertile valley and empties into Arabian Sea. Thar Desert, Eastern Plains flank Indus Valley. **Capital:** Islamabad. **Cities** (1992 est.): Karachi 7.0 mln.; Lahore 3.5 mln.; Faisalabad 2.0 mln.; Hyderabad 795,000; Rawalpindi 928,000.

Government: Type: Parliamentary democracy in a federal setting. **Head of state:** Pres. Farooq Ahmed Leghari; in office: Nov. 14, 1993. **Head of government:** Prime Min. Benazir Bhutto; b June 21, 1953; in office: Oct. 19, 1993. **Local divisions:** 4 provinces, federal capital, tribal areas. **Defense:** 6% of GDP (1992). **Active troop strength:** 587,000.

Economy: Industries: Textiles, food processing, chemicals, petroleum prods. **Chief crops:** Rice, wheat, cotton. **Minerals:** Natural gas, iron ore. **Crude oil reserves** (1994): 203 mln. bbls. **Other resources:** Wool. **Arable land:** 26%. **Livestock** (1992-93): cattle: 17.8 mln.; sheep: 27.7 mln.; goats: 40.2 mln. **Fish catch** (1992): 553,000 metric tons. **Electricity prod.** (1992): 43 bln. kWh. **Labor force:** 54% agric.; 13% mining & manuf.; 33% services.

Finance: Monetary unit: Rupee (May 1995: 30.97 = $1 US). **Gross national product** (1993): $239 bln.* **Per capita GNP:** $1,900. **Imports** (1992): $9.1 bln.; partners: Japan 16%, U.S. 9%, Germany 8%. **Exports** (1992): $6.8 bln.; partners: U.S. 14%, Germany 8%, UK 7%. **Tourism** (1992): $120 mln. **National budget** (1993): $10.9 bln. **International reserves less gold** (May 1995): $2.5 bln. **Gold:** 2.1 mln. oz t. **Consumer prices** (change in 1994): 12.5%.

Transport: Railroads: Length: 5,453 mi. **Motor vehicles:** in use: 721,000 passenger cars, 200,000 comm. vehicles. **Civil aviation:** 6.3 bln. passenger-mi.; 34 airports with scheduled flights. **Chief port:** Karachi.

Communications: Television sets: 1 per 62 persons. **Radios:** 1 per 13 persons. **Telephones:** 1 per 85 persons. **Daily newspaper circ.:** 15 per 1,000 persons.

Health: Life expectancy at birth (1995): 57 male; 59 female. **Births** (per 1,000 pop.): 42. **Deaths** (per 1,000 pop.): 12. **Natural increase:** 3.0%. **Hospital beds:** 1 per 1,619 persons. **Physicians:** 1 per 2,242 persons. **Infant mortality** (per 1,000 live births 1995): 99.

Education: Literacy (1993): 26%.

Major International Organizations: UN (WTO, ILO, IMF, WHO), the Commonwealth.

Embassy: 2315 Massachusetts Ave. NW 20008; 939-6200.

Present-day Pakistan shares the 5,000-year history of the India-Pakistan subcontinent. At present day Harappa and Mohenjo Daro, the Indus Valley Civilization, with large cities and elaborate irrigation systems, flourished c. 4,000-2,500 BC.

Aryan invaders from the NW conquered the region around 1,500 BC, forging a Hindu civilization that dominated Pakistan as well as India for 2,000 years.

Beginning with the Persians in the 6th century BC, and continuing with Alexander the Great and with the Sassanians, successive nations to the west ruled or influenced Pakistan, eventually separating the area from the Indian cultural sphere.

The first Arab invasion, 712 AD, introduced Islam. Under the Mogul empire (1526-1857), Muslims ruled most of India, yielding to British encroachment and resurgent Hindus.

After World War I the Muslims of British India began agitation for minority rights in elections. Mohammad Ali Jinnah (1876-1948) was the principal architect of Pakistan. A leader of the Muslim League from 1916, he worked for dominion status for India; from 1940 he advocated a separate Muslim state.

When the British withdrew Aug. 14, 1947, the Islamic majority areas of India acquired self-government as Pakistan, with dominion status in the Commonwealth. Pakistan was divided into 2 sections, West Pakistan and East Pakistan. The 2 areas were nearly 1,000 mi. apart on opposite sides of India. Pakistan became a republic in 1956.

In Oct. 1958, Gen. Mohammad Ayub Khan took power in a coup. He was elected president in 1960, reelected in 1965. He resigned Mar. 25, 1969, after several months of violent rioting and unrest, most of it in East Pakistan, which demanded autonomy. The government was turned over to Gen. Agha Mohammad Yahya Khan and martial law was declared.

The Awami League, which sought regional autonomy for East Pakistan, won a majority in Dec. 1970 elections to a constituent assembly. In March 1971 Yahya postponed the assembly. Rioting and strikes broke out in the East.

On Mar. 25, 1971, government troops launched attacks in the East. The Easterners, aided by India, proclaimed the independent nation of Bangladesh. In months of widespread fighting, countless thousands were killed. Some 10 million Easterners fled into India.

Full-scale war between India and Pakistan had spread to both the East and West fronts by Dec. 3. Pakistan troops in the East surrendered Dec. 16; Pakistan agreed to a cease-fire in the West Dec. 17. On July 3, 1972, Pakistan and India signed a pact agreeing to withdraw troops from their borders and seek peaceful solutions to all problems.

Zulfikar Ali Bhutto, leader of the Pakistan People's Party, which had won the most West Pakistan votes in the Dec. 1970 elections, became president Dec. 20.

Bhutto was overthrown in a military coup July 1977. Convicted of complicity in a 1974 political murder, he was executed Apr. 4, 1979. More than 3 million Afghan refugees flooded into Pakistan after the USSR invaded Afghanistan Dec. 1979; over 1.4 million remained in the mid-1990s.

Pres. Mohammad Zia ul-Haq was killed when his plane exploded in Aug. 1988. Following Nov. elections, Benazir Bhutto, the daughter of Zulfikar Ali Bhutto, was named prime minister, becoming the first woman leader of a Muslim nation. She was accused of corruption and dismissed by the president, Aug. 1990, and her party was soundly defeated in the Oct. 1990 elections. However, she was returned to power after elections in Oct. 1993.

Palau

Republic of Palau

Belu'u era Belau

Population: 16,661. **Pop. density:** 88 per sq. mi. **Ethnic groups:** Polynesian, Malayan, Melanesian. **Principal languages:** English, Palauan (both official), other local languages. **Religions:** Roman Catholic, Protestant, Modeknegi.

Geography: Area: 188 sq. mi. **Location:** Archipelago (26 islands, more than 300 islets) in the W Pacific Ocean, about 530 mi SE of the Philippines. **Neighbors:** Micronesia to E, Indonesia to S. **Capital:** Koror (Note: a new capital is being built on the island of Babelthuap).

Government: Type: Republic. **Head of state:** Pres. Kuniwo Nakamura; in office: Nov. 4, 1992.

Economy: Chief crops: Coconuts, copra, cassava, sweet potatoes. **Fish catch** (1992): 4,000 metric tons.

Finance: Gross domestic product (1986): $31.6 mln.* **Per capita GDP:** $2,260.

Communications: Television sets: 1 per 9.4 persons. **Radios:** 1 per 67 persons.

Health: Life expectancy at birth (1995): 69 male; 73 female. **Births** (per 1,000 pop.): 22. **Deaths** (per 1,000 pop.): 7. **Infant mortality** (per 1,000 live births 1995): 25.

Major International Organizations: UN.

Spain acquired the Palau Islands in 1886 and sold them to Germany in 1899. Japan seized them in 1914. American forces occupied the islands in 1944; in 1947, they became part of the U.S.-administered UN Trust Territory of the Pacific Islands. In 1981 Palau became an autonomous republic; in 1993 the republic ratified a compact of free association with the U.S., which provides financial aid in return for U.S. use of Palauan military facilities over 15 years. Palau became an independent nation on Oct. 1, 1994.

Panama

Republic of Panama

República de Panamá

People: Population: 2,680,903. **Age distrib.** (%): <15: 34; 65+: 5. **Pop. density:** 92 per sq. mi. **Urban:** 54%. **Ethnic groups:** mestizo 70%, West Indian 14%, white 10%, Indian 6%. **Principal languages:** Spanish (official), English. **Religions:** Roman Catholic 85%, Protestant 15%.

Geography: Area: 29,157 sq. mi. **Location:** In Central America. **Neighbors:** Costa Rica on W, Colombia on E. **To-**pography: 2 mountain ranges run the length of the isthmus. Tropical rain forests cover the Caribbean coast and eastern Panama. **Capital:** Panama City (1990 est.): 414,000.

Government: Type: Constitutional democracy. **Head of state and government:** Pres. Ernesto Pérez Balladares; b 1946; in office: Sept. 1, 1994. **Local divisions:** 9 provinces, 1 territory. **Defense:** 1.0% of GDP (1993 est.). **Active troop strength:** 11,700.

Economy: Industries: Oil refining, international banking. **Chief crops:** Bananas, pineapples, rice, corn, sugar. **Minerals:** Copper. **Other resources:** Forests (mahogany), shrimp. **Arable land:** 6%. **Livestock** (1992): cattle: 1.4 mln.; pigs: 257,000. **Electricity prod.** (1992): 4.4 bln. kWh. **Labor force:** 27% agric. & fishing; 32% govt. & community services.

Finance: Monetary unit: Balboa (May 1995: 1.00 = $1 US). **Gross domestic product** (1993): $11.6 bln.* **Per capita GDP:** $4,500. **Imports** (1993): $2.5 bln.; partners: U.S. 35%. **Exports** (1993): $545 mln.; partners: U.S. 38%. **Tourism** (1992): $207 mln. **National budget** (1992 est.): $1.9 bln. **International reserves less gold** (Apr. 1995): $696 mln. **Consumer prices** (change in 1994): 1.3%.

Transport: Motor vehicles: in use: 151,000 passenger cars, 73,000 comm. vehicles. **Civil aviation:** 209 mln. passenger-mi.; 8 airports with scheduled flights. **Chief ports:** Balboa, Cristobal.

Communications: Television sets: 1 per 12 persons. **Radios:** 1 per 5.6 persons. **Telephones:** 1 per 8.8 persons. **Daily newspaper circ.:** 70 per 1,000 pop.

Health: Life expectancy at birth (1995): 73 male; 78 female. **Births** (per 1,000 pop.): 24. **Deaths** (per 1,000 pop.): 5. **Natural increase:** 1.9%. **Hospital beds:** 1 per 335 persons. **Physicians:** 1 per 844 persons. **Infant mortality** (per 1,000 live births 1995): 16.

Education: Literacy (1992): 88%. **Primary school attendance:** almost 100%.

Major International Organizations: UN (IMF, IMO, World Bank), OAS.

Embassy: 2862 McGill Terrace NW 20008; 483-1407.

The coast of Panama was sighted by Rodrigo de Bastidas, sailing with Columbus for Spain in 1501, and was visited by Columbus in 1502. Vasco Nunez de Balboa crossed the isthmus and "discovered" the Pacific O. Sept. 13, 1513. Spanish colonies were ravaged by Francis Drake, 1572-95, and Henry Morgan, 1668-71. Morgan destroyed the old city of Panama which had been founded in 1519. Freed from Spain, Panama joined Colombia in 1821.

Panama declared its independence from Colombia Nov. 3, 1903, with U.S. recognition. U.S. naval forces deterred action by Colombia. Panama granted use, occupation, and control of the Canal Zone to the U.S. by treaty, ratified Feb. 26, 1904. In 1978, a new treaty provided for a gradual takeover by Panama of the canal, and withdrawal of U.S. troops, to be completed by 1999. U.S. payments were substantially increased in the interim.

President Delvalle was ousted by the National Assembly, Feb. 26, 1988, after he tried to fire the head of the Panama Defense Forces, Gen. Manuel Antonio Noriega. Noriega had been indicted by 2 U.S. federal grand juries on drug charges. A general strike followed. Despite U.S.-imposed economic sanctions Noriega remained in power. Voters went to the polls to elect a new president May 7, 1989. Noriega claimed victory, but foreign observers said that the opposition had won overwhelmingly. The government voided the election May 10, charging foreign interference. There was an attempted coup against Noriega Oct. 3.

U.S. troops invaded Panama Dec. 20, 1989, following a series of incidents, including the killing of a U.S. Marine by Panamanian soldiers. The operation had as its chief objective the capture of Noriega. He took refuge in the Vatican diplomatic mission, but surrendered to U.S. officials Jan. 3, 1990. He was convicted on 8 counts of racketeering and drug trafficking in a U.S. District Court in Miami, FL, Apr. 9, 1992.

Papua New Guinea

Independent State of Papua New Guinea

People: Population: 4,294,750. **Age distrib.** (%): <15: 40; 65+: 4. **Pop. density:** 24 per sq. mi. **Urban:** 15%. **Ethnic**

groups: Papuan (in S and interior), Melanesian (N,E). **Principal languages:** English (official), Melanesian languages, Papuan languages. **Religions:** Protestant 44%, Roman Catholic 22%, local religions 34%.

Geography: Area: 178,704 sq. mi. **Location:** Occupies eastern half of island of New Guinea. **Neighbors:** Indonesia (West Irian) on W, Australia on S. **Topography:** Thickly forested mts. cover much of the center of the country, with lowlands along the coasts. Included are some of the nearby islands of Bismarck and Solomon groups, including Admiralty Is., New Ireland, New Britain, and Bougainville. **Capital:** Port Moresby. **Cities** (1991): Port Moresby 193,000; Lae 80,000.

Government: Type: Parliamentary democracy. **Head of state:** Queen Elizabeth II, represented by Gov. Gen. Wiwa Korowi; in office: Oct. 4, 1991. **Head of government:** Prime Min. Julius Chan; b Aug. 29, 1939; in office: Aug. 30, 1994. **Local divisions:** 20 provinces. **Defense:** approx. 1.8% of GDP (1993 est.). **Active troop strength:** 3,800.

Economy: Chief crops: Coffee, coconuts, cocoa. **Minerals:** Gold, copper, silver. **Arable land:** 0%. **Livestock** (1992): pigs: 1.0 mln. **Electricity prod.** (1992): 1.6 bln. kWh. **Labor force:** 82% agric., 3% ind. and commerce, 8% services.

Finance: Monetary unit: Kina (Mar. 1995: 1.00 = $.82 US). **Gross domestic product** (1993): $8.2 bln.* **Per capita GDP:** $2,000. **Imports** (1992): $1.5 bln.; partners: Australia 40%, Japan 17%; U.S. 9%. **Exports** (1992): $1.8 bln.; partners: Japan 26%, W Germany 36%, Australia 8%. **Tourism** (1992): $49 mln. **National budget** (1993 est.): $1.49 bln. **International reserves less gold** (Mar. 1995): $35.5 mln. **Gold:** 14,000 oz t. **Consumer prices** (change in 1993): 5.0%.

Transport: Motor vehicles: in use: 13,000 passenger cars, 24,000 comm. vehicles. **Chief ports:** Port Moresby, Lae.

Communications: Television sets: 1 per 415 persons. **Radios:** 1 per 18 persons. **Telephones:** 1 per 59 persons. **Daily newspaper circ.:** 13 per 1,000 pop.

Health: Life expectancy at birth (1995): 56 male; 58 female. **Births** (per 1,000 pop.): 33. **Deaths** (per 1,000 pop.): 10. **Natural increase:** 2.3%. **Hospital beds:** 1 per 234 persons. **Physicians:** 1 per 12,874 persons. **Infant mortality** (per 1,000 live births 1995): 62.

Education: Literacy (1991): 52%. **Attendance:** 65% primary school; 13% secondary school.

Major International Organizations: UN, the Commonwealth.

Embassy: 1615 New Hampshire Ave. NW 20009; 745-3680.

Human remains have been found in the interior of New Guinea dating back at least 10,000 years and possibly much earlier. Successive waves of peoples probably entered the country from Asia through Indonesia. Europeans visited in the 15th century, but land claims did not begin until the 19th century, when the Dutch took control of the western half of the island.

The southern half of eastern New Guinea was first claimed by Britain in 1884, and transferred to Australia in 1905. The northern half was claimed by Germany in 1884, but captured in World War I by Australia, which was granted a League of Nations mandate and then a UN trusteeship over the area. The 2 territories were administered jointly after 1949, given self-government Dec. 1, 1973, and became independent Sept. 16, 1975.

The indigenous population consists of a huge number of tribes, many living in almost complete isolation with mutually unintelligible languages. Secessionist rebels have clashed with government forces on Bougainville since 1988.

Paraguay
Republic of Paraguay
República del Paraguay

People: Population: 5,358,198. **Age distrib.** (%): <15: 40; 65+: 4. **Pop. density:** 34 per sq. mi. **Urban:** 51%. **Ethnic groups:** mestizo 95%, small white, Indian, black minorities. **Principal languages:** Spanish (official), Guarani. **Religions:** Roman Catholic (official) 90%.

Geography: Area: 157,048 sq. mi. **Location:** One of the 2 landlocked countries of South America. **Neighbors:** Bolivia on N, Argentina on S, Brazil on E. **Topography:** Paraguay R. bisects the country. To E are fertile plains, wooded slopes, grasslands. To W is the Chaco plain, with marshes and scrub trees. Extreme W is arid. **Capital:** Asunción (1992 est.): 502,000.

Government: Type: Republic. **Head of state:** Pres. Juan Carlos Wasmosy; b 1942; in office: Aug. 15, 1993. **Local divisions:** 19 departments. **Defense:** 1.1% of GNP (1991). **Active troop strength:** 16,500.

Economy: Industries: Food processing, wood products, textiles, cement. **Chief crops:** Corn, cotton, soybeans, sugarcane. **Minerals:** Iron, manganese, limestone. **Other resources:** Forests. **Arable land:** 20%. **Livestock** (1992): cattle: 7.8 mln.; pigs: 2.6 mln. **Electricity prod.** (1992): 16.2 bln. kWh. **Labor force:** 44% agric.; 34% ind. and commerce; 18% services.

Finance: Monetary unit: Guarani (Apr. 1995: 1,975 = $1 US). **Gross domestic product** (1993): $15.2 bln.* **Per capita GDP:** $3,000. **Imports** (1993): $1.4 bln.; partners: Brazil 30%, EU 20%. **Exports** (1993): $728 mln.; partners: EU 37%, Brazil 25%. **Tourism** (1992): $153 mln. **National budget** (1992): $1.4 bln. **International reserves less gold** (Dec. 1994): $1.02 bln. **Gold:** 35,000 oz t. **Consumer prices** (change in 1993): 18.3%.

Transport: Motor vehicles: in use: 117,000 passenger cars, 3,000 comm. vehicles. **Civil aviation:** 700 mln. passenger-mi.; 1 airport with scheduled flights. **Chief port:** Asunción.

Communications: Television sets: 1 per 13 persons. **Radios:** 1 per 6.0 persons. **Telephones:** 1 per 30 persons. **Daily newspaper circ.:** 39 per 1,000 pop.

Health: Life expectancy at birth (1995): 72 male; 75 female. **Births** (per 1,000 pop.): 32. **Deaths** (per 1,000 pop.): 4. **Natural increase:** 2.7%. **Hospital beds:** 1 per 835 persons. **Physicians:** 1 per 1,423 persons. **Infant mortality** (per 1,000 live births 1995): 24.

Education: Literacy (1992): 90%. **Years compulsory:** 7; attendance: 83%.

Major International Organizations: UN (IMF, WHO, WTO), OAS.

Embassy: 2400 Massachusetts Ave. NW 20008; 483-6960.

The Guarani Indians were settled farmers speaking a common language before the arrival of Europeans.

Visited by Sebastian Cabot in 1527 and settled as a Spanish possession in 1535, Paraguay gained its independence from Spain in 1811. It lost much of its territory to Brazil, Uruguay, and Argentina in the War of the Triple Alliance, 1865-1870. Large areas were won from Bolivia in the Chaco War, 1932-35.

Gen. Alfredo Stroessner, who ruled since 1954, was ousted in a military coup led by Gen. Andrés Rodríguez on Feb. 3, 1989. Rodríguez was elected president May 1. Juan Carlos Wasmosy was elected president May 9, 1993, becoming the nation's first civilian head of state in many years.

Peru
Republic of Peru
República del Perú

People: Population: 24,087,372. **Age distrib.** (%): <15: 36; 65+: 4. **Pop. density:** 49 per sq. mi. **Urban:** 70%. **Ethnic groups:** Indian 45%, mestizo 37%, white 15%, black, Asian. **Principal languages:** Spanish, Quechua (both official), Aymara. **Religions:** Roman Catholic 90%.

Geography: Area: 496,225 sq. mi. **Location:** On the Pacific coast of South America. **Neighbors:** Ecuador, Colombia on N, Brazil, Bolivia on E, Chile on S. **Topography:** An arid coastal strip, 10 to 100 mi. wide, supports much of the population thanks to widespread irrigation. The Andes cover 27% of land area. The uplands are well-watered, as are the eastern slopes reaching the Amazon basin, which covers half the country with its forests and jungles. **Capital:** Lima. **Cities** (1993 est.): Lima (met.) 5.8 mln.; Callao 638,000; Arequipa 620,000.

Government: Type: in transition. **Head of state:** Pres. Alberto Fujimori; b July 28, 1938; in office: July 28, 1990. **Head of government:** Prime Min. Dante Cordova; in office: July 28, 1995. **Local divisions:** 24 departments, 1 constitutional province. **Defense:** 2% of GDP (1991). **Active troop strength:** 115,000.

Economy: Industries: Fishing, mineral processing, light industry, textiles. **Chief crops:** Cotton, sugar, coffee, rice. **Minerals:** Copper, silver, gold, iron, oil. **Crude oil reserves** (1994):

381 mln. bbls. **Other resources:** Wool, sardines. **Arable land:** 3%. **Livestock** (1993): cattle: 3.9 mln.; pigs: 2.4 mln.; sheep: 11.9 mln. **Fish catch** (1992): 6.8 mln. metric tons. **Electricity prod.** (1992): 17.4 bln. kWh. **Labor force:** 37% agric.; 19% ind.; 44% govt. and other services.

Finance: Monetary unit: New Sol (May 1995: 2.25 = $1 US). **Gross domestic product** (1993): $70 bln.* **Per capita GDP:** $3,000. **Imports** (1993): $4.5 bln.; partners: U.S. 30%, EU 17%. **Exports** (1993): $3.7 bln.; partners: U.S. 25%, Japan 9%. **Tourism** (1992): $237 mln. **National budget** (1992 est.): $1.7 bln. **International reserves less gold** (Apr. 1995): $7.1 bln. **Gold:** 1.1 mln. oz t. **Consumer prices** (change in 1994): 23.7%.

Transport: Railroads: Length: 2,157 mi. **Motor vehicles:** in use: 402,000 passenger cars, 258,000 comm. vehicles. **Civil aviation:** 803 mln. passenger-mi.; 25 airports. **Chief ports:** Callao, Chimbote, Mollendo.

Communications: Television sets: 1 per 12 persons. **Radios:** 1 per 5.2 persons. **Telephones:** 1 per 28 persons. **Daily newspaper circ.:** 79 per 1,000 pop.

Health: Life expectancy at birth (1995): 64 male; 68 female. **Births** (per 1,000 pop.): 25. **Deaths** (per 1,000 pop.): 7. **Natural increase:** 1.8%. **Hospital beds:** 1 per 625 persons. **Physicians:** 1 per 997 persons. **Infant mortality** (per 1,000 live births 1995): 52.

Education: Literacy (1991): 89%. **Years compulsory:** 10.

Major International Organizations: UN and all of its specialized agencies, OAS.

Embassy: 1700 Massachusetts Ave. NW 20036; 833-9860.

The powerful Inca empire had its seat at Cuzco in the Andes covering most of Peru, Bolivia, and Ecuador, as well as parts of Colombia, Chile, and Argentina. Building on the achievements of 800 years of Andean civilization, the Incas had a high level of skill in architecture, engineering, textiles, and social organization.

A civil war had weakened the empire when Francisco Pizarro, Spanish conquistador, began raiding Peru for its wealth, 1532. In 1533 he had the seized ruling Inca, Atahualpa, filled a room with gold as a ransom, then executed him and enslaved the natives.

Lima was the seat of Spanish viceroys until the Argentine liberator, José de San Martin, captured it in 1821; Spanish forces were ultimately routed by Simón Bolívar, 1824.

On Oct. 3, 1968, a military coup ousted Pres. Fernando Belaunde Terry. In 1968-74, the military government started socialist programs. Food shortages, escalating foreign debt, and strikes led to another coup, Aug. 29, 1976.

After 12 years of military rule, Peru returned to democratic leadership in 1980 but was plagued by economic problems and terrorism by left-wing Sendero Luminosa (Shining Path) guerrillas. Pres. Alberto Fujimori, elected in June 1990, dissolved the National Congress, suspended parts of the constitution, and initiated press censorship, Apr. 5, 1992. The leader of Sendero Luminosa was captured Sept. 12, 1992. With the economy booming and guerrilla activity curtailed, Fujimori won reelection by a landslide, Apr. 9, 1995.

Philippines

Republic of the Philippines

Republika ng Pilipinas

People: Population: 73,265,584. **Age distrib.** (%): <15: 40; 65+: 3. **Pop. density:** 632 per sq. mi. **Urban:** 49%. **Ethnic groups:** Malays the large majority, Chinese, Americans, Spanish are minorities. **Principal languages:** Pilipino (based on Tagalog), English (both official), Cebuano, Bicol, Ilocano, Pampango, many others. **Religions:** Roman Catholic 83%, Protestant 9%, Muslim 5%.

Geography: Area: 115,860 sq. mi. **Location:** An archipelago off the SE coast of Asia. **Neighbors:** Nearest are Malaysia, Indonesia on S, Taiwan on N. **Topography:** The country consists of some 7,100 islands stretching 1,100 mi. N-S. About 95% of area and population are on 11 largest islands, which are mountainous, except for the heavily indented coastlines and for the central plain on Luzon. **Capital:** Manila. **Cities** (1990 est.): Quezon City 1.7 mln.; Manila 1.6 mln.; Cebu 610,000.

Government: Type: Republic. **Head of state:** Pres. Fidel V. Ramos; b Mar. 18, 1928; in office: June 30, 1992. **Local divi-**

sions: 15 regions, divided into 76 provinces. **Defense:** 1.9% of GNP (1991). **Active troop strength:** 106,500.

Economy: Industries: Food processing, textiles, clothing, pharmaceuticals, wood prods., appliances. **Chief crops:** Sugar, rice, corn, pineapple, coconut. **Minerals:** Cobalt, copper, gold, nickel, silver, oil. **Other resources:** Forests (40% of area). **Arable land:** 26%. **Livestock** (1992): buffalo: 2.6 mln.; cattle: 1.7 mln.; pigs: 8.0 mln. **Fish catch** (1991): 2.3 mln. metric tons. **Electricity prod.** (1992): 28 bln. kWh. **Labor force:** 46% agric.; 16% ind. and comm.; 19% services.

Finance: Monetary unit: Peso (Apr. 1995: 26.02 = $1 US). **Gross national product** (1993): $171 bln.* **Per capita GNP:** $2,500. **Imports** (1993): $17.1 bln.; partners: U.S. 18%, Japan 21%. **Exports** (1993): $11.1 bln.; partners: U.S. 39%, Japan 18%. **Tourism** (1992): $1.6 bln. **National budget** (1994 est.): $13 bln. **International reserves less gold** (Mar. 1995): $5.6 bln. **Gold:** 3.01 mln. oz t. **Consumer prices** (change in 1994): 9.1%.

Transport: Railroads: Length: 658 mi. **Motor vehicles:** in use: 481,000 passenger cars, 917,000 comm. vehicles. **Civil aviation:** 8.0 bln. passenger-mi.; 20 airports with scheduled flights. **Chief ports:** Cebu, Manila, Iloilo, Davao.

Communications: Television sets: 1 per 9.5 persons. **Radios:** 1 per 17 persons. **Telephones:** 1 per 55 persons. **Daily newspaper circ.:** 54 per 1,000 pop.

Health: Life expectancy at birth (1995): 63 male; 68 female. **Births** (per 1,000 pop.): 30. **Deaths** (per 1,000 pop.): 7. **Natural increase:** 2.3%. **Hospital beds:** 1 per 780 persons. **Physicians:** 1 per 1,062 persons. **Infant mortality** (per 1,000 live births 1995): 50.

Education: Literacy (1992): 89%. **Attendance:** 97% in elementary, 55% secondary.

Major International Organizations: UN (World Bank, IMF, WTO), ASEAN.

Embassy: 1600 Massachusetts Ave. NW 20036; 467-9300.

The Malay peoples of the Philippine Islands, whose ancestors probably migrated from Southeast Asia, were mostly hunters, fishers, and unsettled cultivators when first visited by Europeans.

The archipelago was visited by Magellan, 1521. The Spanish founded Manila, 1571. The islands, named for King Philip II of Spain, were ceded by Spain to the U.S. for $20 million, 1898, following the Spanish-American War. U.S. troops suppressed a guerrilla uprising in a brutal 6-year war, 1899-1905.

Japan attacked the Philippines Dec. 8, 1941 and occupied the islands during WW II. On July 4, 1946, independence was proclaimed in accordance with an act passed by the U.S. Congress in 1934. A republic was established.

Riots by radical youth groups and terrorism by leftist guerrillas and outlaws increased from 1970. On Sept. 21, 1972, Pres. Ferdinand Marcos declared martial law. Ruling by decree, he ordered some land reform and stabilized prices. But opposition was suppressed, and a high population growth rate aggravated poverty and unemployment. Political corruption was widespread. On Jan. 17, 1973, Marcos proclaimed a new constitution with himself as president. His wife, Imelda, received wide powers in 1978 to supervise planning and development.

Government troops battled Muslim (Moro) secessionists, 1973-76, in southern Mindanao. Fighting resumed, 1977, after a Libyan-mediated agreement on autonomy was rejected by the region's mainly Christian voters.

Martial law was lifted Jan. 17, 1981, but Marcos retained broad emergency powers. He was reelected in June to a new 6-year term as president.

The assassination of prominent opposition leader Benigno S. Aquino Jr, Aug. 21, 1983, sparked demonstrations calling for the resignation of Marcos. A bitter presidential election campaign ended Feb. 7, 1986, as elections were held amid allegations of widespread fraud. On Feb. 16, Marcos was declared the victor over Corazon Aquino, widow of the slain opposition leader. She proclaimed herself president and announced a nonviolent "active resistance" to overthrow the Marcos government.

On Feb. 24, Marcos declared a state of emergency as his military and religious support eroded. He ended his 20-year tenure as president Feb. 26 and fled the country. Aquino was recognized as president by the U.S. and other nations.

In 1987, Aquino announced the start of land reforms. Candidates endorsed by Aquino won large majorities in legislative elections held in May. She was plagued, however, by a weak economy, widespread poverty, Communist insurgents, and lukewarm support from the military. Rebel troops seized military bases, TV stations, and bombed the presidential palace, Dec. 1, 1989. Government forces defeated the attempted coup with the aid of air cover provided by U.S. F-4s. Aquino endorsed Fidel Ramos in the May 1992 presidential election, which he won.

The U.S. vacated the Subic Bay Naval Station at the end of 1992, ending its long military presence in the Philippines.

The government signed a cease-fire agreement, Jan. 30, 1994, with Muslim separatist guerrillas, but some rebels refused to abide by the accord.

The archipelago has a coastline of 10,850 mi. Manila Bay, with an area of 770 sq. mi. and a circumference of 120 mi., is the finest harbor in the Far East.

Poland
Republic of Poland
Rzeczpospolita Polska

People: Population: 38,792,442. **Age distrib.** (%): <15: 24; 65+: 11. **Pop. density:** 321 per sq. mi. **Urban:** 62%. **Ethnic groups:** Polish 98%, Germans, Ukrainians, Belarussians. **Principal languages:** Polish. **Religions:** Roman Catholic 95%.

Geography: Area: 120,728 sq. mi. **Location:** On the Baltic Sea in E Central Europe. **Neighbors:** Germany on W, Czech Rep., Slovakia on S, Lithuania, Belarus, Ukraine on E, Russia on N. **Topography:** Mostly lowlands forming part of the Northern European Plain. The Carpathian Mts. along the southern border rise to 8,200 ft. **Capital:** Warsaw. **Cities** (1993 est.): Warsaw 1.6 mln.; Lodz 839,000; Krakow 744,000.

Government: Type: Democratic state. **Head of state:** Pres. Lech Walesa; b Sept. 29, 1943; in office: Dec. 22, 1990. **Head of government:** Prime Min. Jozef Oleksy; named: Feb. 7, 1995. **Local divisions:** 49 provinces. **Defense:** 1.8% of GNP (1993 est.). **Active troop strength:** 283,600.

Economy: Industries: Shipbuilding, chemicals, metals, machinery, food processing. **Chief crops:** Grains, potatoes, sugar beets, tobacco, flax. **Minerals:** Coal, copper, silver, lead, sulphur, natural gas. **Arable land:** 46%. **Livestock** (1993): cattle: 8.2 mln.; pigs: 22.1 mln. **Fish catch** (1991): 457,000 metric tons. **Electricity prod.** (1992): 137 bln. kWh. **Labor force:** 28% agric.; 32% ind. & constr.

Finance: Monetary unit: Zloty (Apr. 1995: 2.40 = $1 US). **Gross domestic product** (1993): $180.4 bln.* **Per capita GDP:** $4,680. **Imports** (1993): $15.6 bln.; partners: Germany 24%, Russia 9%. **Exports** (1993): $13.5 bln.; partners: Germany 31%, Netherlands 6%. **Tourism** (1992): $183 mln. **National budget** (1993 est.): $27.1 bln. **International reserves less gold** (Apr. 1995): $8.9 bln. **Gold:** 473,000. **Consumer prices** (change in 1994): 33.3%.

Transport: Railroads: Length: 16,061 mi. **Motor vehicles:** in use: 6.1 mln. passenger cars, 1.3 mln. comm. vehicles. **Civil aviation:** 2.2 bln. passenger-mi.; 12 airports. **Chief ports:** Gdansk, Gdynia, Szczecin.

Communications: Television sets: 1 per 3.9 persons. **Radios:** 1 per 3.7 persons. **Telephones:** 1 per 6.6 persons. **Daily newspaper circ.:** 127 per 1,000 pop.

Health: Life expectancy at birth (1995): 69 male; 77 female. **Births** (per 1,000 pop.): 13. **Deaths** (per 1,000 pop.): 9. **Natural increase:** 0.4%. **Hospital beds:** 1 per 177 persons. **Physicians:** 1 per 459 persons. **Infant mortality** (per 1,000 live births 1995): 12.

Education: Literacy (1993): 99%. **Years compulsory:** 8; attendance 97%.

Major International Organizations: UN (WTO, WHO). **Embassy:** 2640 16th St. NW 20009; 234-3800.

Slavic tribes in the area were converted to Latin Christianity in the 10th century. Poland was a great power from the 14th to the 17th centuries. In 3 partitions (1772, 1793, 1795) it was apportioned among Prussia, Russia, and Austria. Overrun by the Austro-German armies in World War I, it declared its independence on Nov. 11, 1918, and was recognized as independent by the Treaty of Versailles, June 28, 1919. Large territories to the east were taken in a war with Russia, 1921.

Germany and the USSR invaded Poland Sept. 1-27, 1939, and divided the country. During the war, some 6 million Polish citizens, half of them Jews, were killed by the Nazis. With Germany's defeat, a Polish government-in-exile in London was recognized by the U.S., but the USSR pressed the claims of a rival group. The election of 1947 was completely dominated by the Communists.

In compensation for 69,860 sq. mi. ceded to the USSR, 1945, Poland received approx. 40,000 sq. mi. of German territory E of the Oder-Neisse line comprising Silesia, Pomerania, West Prussia, and part of East Prussia.

In 12 years of rule by Stalinists, large estates were abolished, industries nationalized, schools secularized, and Roman Catholic prelates jailed. Farm production fell off. Harsh working conditions caused a riot in Poznan, June 28-29, 1956. A new Politburo, committed to a more independent Polish Communism, was named Oct. 1956, with Wladyslaw Gomulka as first secretary of the party. Collectivization of farms was ended.

In Dec. 1970 workers in port cities rioted because of price rises and new incentive wage rules. On Dec. 20 Gomulka resigned as party leader; he was succeeded by Edward Gierek. The incentive rules were dropped; price rises were revoked. In 1956 Gomulka agreed to permit religious liberty and religious publications, provided the church kept out of politics.

After 2 months of labor turmoil had crippled the country, the Polish government, Aug. 30, 1980, met the demands of striking workers at the Lenin Shipyard, Gdansk. Among the 21 concessions granted were the right to form independent trade unions and the right to strike. By 1981, 9.5 mln. workers had joined the independent trade union (Solidarity). Solidarity leaders proposed, Dec. 12, a nationwide referendum on establishing a non-Communist government if the government failed to agree to a series of demands.

Spurred by the fear of Soviet intervention, the government, Dec. 13, imposed martial law. Lech Walesa and other Solidarity leaders were arrested. The U.S. imposed economic sanctions, which were lifted when martial law was suspended Dec. 1982. On Apr. 5, 1989, an accord was reached between the government and opposition factions on a broad range of political and economic reforms including free elections. Candidates endorsed by Solidarity swept the parliamentary elections, June 4. Lech Walesa became president, 1990.

A radical economic program designed to transform the economy into a free-market system drew protests from unions, farmers, and miners because it resulted in inflation and unemployment. In Sept. 1993 elections, former Communists and other leftists won a majority of seats in the lower house of Parliament. Poland has sought to join the European Union and NATO.

Portugal
Portuguese Republic
República Portuguesa

People: Population: 10,562,388. **Age distrib.** (%): <15: 18; 65+: 14. **Pop. density:** 297 per sq. mi. **Urban:** 34%. **Ethnic groups:** homogeneous Mediterranean stock with small African minority. **Principal languages:** Portuguese. **Religions:** Roman Catholic 97%.

Geography: Area: 35,574 sq. mi., incl. the Azores and Madeira Islands. **Location:** At SW extreme of Europe. **Neighbors:** Spain on N, E. **Topography:** Portugal N of Tajus R, which bisects the country NE-SW, is mountainous, cool and rainy. To the S there are drier, rolling plains, and a warm climate. **Capital:** Lisbon. **Cities** (1988 met. est.): Lisbon 2 mln.; Oporto 1.5 mln.

Government: Type: Parliamentary democracy. **Head of state:** Pres. Mario Soares; b Dec. 7, 1924; in office: Mar. 9, 1986. **Head of government:** Prime Min. Antonio Guterres; in office: Oct. 1995. **Local divisions:** 18 districts, 2 autonomous regions, one dependency. **Defense:** 2.9% of GDP (1992). **Active troop strength:** 50,700.

Economy: Industries: Textiles, footwear, cork, chemicals, fish canning, wine, paper. **Chief crops:** Grains, potatoes, rice, grapes, olives, fruits. **Minerals:** Tungsten, uranium, iron. **Other resources:** Forests (world leader in cork production). **Arable land:** 32%. **Livestock** (1993): sheep: 5.6 mln.; pigs: 2.5 mln.; cattle: 1.3 mln. **Fish catch** (1991): 325,000 metric tons. **Electricity prod.** (1992): 26.4 bln. kWh. **Labor force:** 20% agric.; 35% ind.; 45% services.

Finance: Monetary unit: Escudo (May 1995: 146 = $1 US). **Gross domestic product** (1993): $91.5 bln.* **Per capita GDP:** $8,700. **Imports** (1993): $28.0 bln.; partners: EU 72%. **Exports** (1993): $17.5 bln.; partners: EU 75%. **Tourism** (1992): $3.7 bln. **National budget** (1991): $33.2 bln. **International reserves less gold** (Apr. 1995): $14.4 bln. **Gold:** 16.1 mln. oz t. **Consumer prices** (change in 1994): 4.9%.

Transport: Railroads: Length: 2,066 mi. **Motor vehicles:** in use: 2.0 mln. passenger cars, 696,000 comm. vehicles. **Civil aviation:** 4.9 bln. passenger-mi.; 14 airports. **Chief ports:** Lisbon, Setubal, Leixoes.

Communications: Television sets: 1 per 5.6 persons. **Radios:** 1 per 4.0 persons. **Telephones:** 1 per 2.9 persons. **Daily newspaper circ.:** 38 per 1,000 pop.

Health: Life expectancy at birth (1995): 72 male; 79 female. **Births** (per 1,000 pop.): 12. **Deaths** (per 1,000 pop.): 10. **Natural increase:** 0.2%. **Hospital beds:** 1 per 235 persons. **Physicians:** 1 per 344 persons. **Infant mortality** (per 1,000 live births 1995): 9.

Education: Literacy (1993): 87%. **Years compulsory:** 6; attendance 60%.

Major International Organizations: UN (WTO, IMF, WHO), NATO, EU, OECD.

Embassy: 2125 Kalorama Rd. NW 20008; 328-8610.

Portugal, an independent state since the 12th century, was a kingdom until a revolution in 1910 drove out King Manoel II and a republic was proclaimed.

From 1932 a strong, repressive government was headed by Premier Antonio de Oliveira Salazar. Illness forced his retirement in Sept. 1968.

On Apr. 25, 1974, the government was seized by a military junta led by Gen. Antonio de Spinola, who was named president.

The new government reached agreements providing independence for Guinea-Bissau, Mozambique, Cape Verde Islands, Angola, and São Tomé and Príncipe. Despite a 64% victory for democratic parties in Apr. 1975, the Soviet-supported Communist Party increased its influence. Banks, insurance companies, and other industries were nationalized.

Parliament approved, June 1, 1989, a package of reforms that did away with the socialist economy and created a "democratic" economy, denationalizing industries.

Azores Islands, in the Atlantic, 740 mi. W of Portugal, have an area of 868 sq. mi. and a pop. (1992) of 236,000. A 1951 agreement gave the U.S. rights to use defense facilities in the Azores. The **Madeira Islands,** 350 mi. off the NW coast of Africa, have an area of 306 sq. mi. and a pop. (1992) of 253,000. Both groups were offered partial autonomy in 1976.

Macau, area of 6 sq. mi., is an enclave, a peninsula and 2 small islands, at the mouth of the Canton R. in China. Portugal granted broad autonomy in 1976. In 1987, Portugal and China agreed that Macau would revert to China in 1999. Macau, like Hong Kong, was guaranteed 50 years of noninterference in its way of life and capitalist system. Pop. (1995 est.): 491,000.

Qatar

State of Qatar

Dawlat Qatar

People: Population: 533,916. **Pop. density:** 121 per sq. mi. **Urban:** 91%. **Ethnic groups:** Arab 40%, Pakistani 18%, Indian 18%, Iranian 10%. **Principal languages:** Arabic (official), English. **Religions:** Muslim 95%.

Geography: Area: 4,412 sq. mi. **Location:** Occupies peninsula on W coast of Persian Gulf. **Neighbors:** Saudi Arabia on W, United Arab Emirates on S. **Topography:** Mostly a flat desert, with some limestone ridges, vegetation of any kind is scarce. **Capital:** Doha (1987 est.): 236,000.

Government: Type: Traditional monarchy. **Head of state and head of government:** Emir & Prime Min. Hamad bin Khalifa ath-Thani; b 1950; in office: as emir, June 27, 1995; as prime min., July 11, 1995. **Defense:** 4.1% of GNP (1992). **Active troop strength:** 10,100.

Economy: Industries: Oil production and refining. **Crude oil reserves** (1994): 3.7 bln. bbls. **Electricity prod.** (1992): 4.8 bln. kWh. **Labor force:** 2% agric; 25% manuf. & constr.; 51% services.

Finance: Monetary unit: Riyal (May 1995: 3.64 = $1 US). **Gross domestic product** (1993): $8.8 bln.* **Per capita GDP:** $17,500. **Imports** (1993): $1.8 bln.; partners: Japan 14%, UK

12%, U.S. 12%. **Exports** (1993): $3.4 bln.; partners: Japan 61%. **National budget** (1992): $3.0 bln.

Transport: Chief ports: Doha, Musayid.

Communications: Television sets: 1 per 1.8 persons. **Radios:** 1 per 1.8 persons. **Telephones:** 1 per 2.9 persons.

Health: Life expectancy at birth (1995): 70 male; 75 female. **Births** (per 1,000 pop.): 23. **Deaths** (per 1,000 pop.): 4. **Natural increase:** 1.9%. **Hospital beds:** 1 per 481 persons. **Physicians:** 1 per 671 persons. **Infant mortality** (per 1,000 live births 1995): 20.

Education: Literacy (1992): 76%. **Years compulsory:** ages 6-16; attendance: 98%.

Major International Organizations: UN (FAO, IMF, World Bank), Arab League, OPEC.

Embassy: 600 New Hampshire Ave. NW 20037; 338-0111.

Qatar was under Bahrain's control until the Ottoman Turks took power, 1872 to 1915. In a treaty signed 1916, Qatar gave Great Britain responsibility for its defense and foreign relations. After Britain announced it would remove its military forces from the Persian Gulf area by the end of 1971, Qatar sought a federation with other British protected states in the area; this failed and Qatar declared itself independent, Sept. 1, 1971. Crown Prince Hamad bin Khalifa ath-Thani ousted his father, Emir Khalifa bin Hamad ath-Thani, June 27, 1995.

Oil revenues give Qatar a per capita income among the highest in the world, but lack of skilled labor hampers development.

Romania

People: Population: 23,198,330. **Age distrib.** (%): <15: 22; 65+: 11. **Pop. density:** 253 per sq. mi. **Urban:** 55%. **Ethnic groups:** Romanian 89%, Hungarian 9%. **Principal languages:** Romanian (official), Hungarian, German. **Religions:** Romanian Orthodox 70%, Roman Catholic 6%, Protestant 6%.

Geography: Area: 91,699 sq. mi. **Location:** In SE Europe on the Black Sea. **Neighbors:** Moldova on E, Ukraine on N, Hungary, Yugoslavia on W, Bulgaria on S. **Topography:** The Carpathian Mts. encase the north-central Transylvanian plateau. There are wide plains S and E of the mountains, through which flow the lower reaches of the rivers of the Danube system. **Capital:** Bucharest. **Cities** (1992 est.): Bucharest 2.1 mln.; Constanta 350,000; Iasi 343,000; Timisoara 334,000.

Government: Type: Republic. **Head of state:** Pres. Ion Iliescu; b Mar. 30, 1930; in office: Dec. 25, 1989. **Head of government:** Prime Min. Nicolae Vacaroiu; b 1943; in office; Nov. 4, 1992. **Local divisions:** Bucharest and 40 counties. **Defense:** 3% of GDP (1993). **Active troop strength:** 230,500.

Economy: Industries: Steel, metals, machinery, oil products, chemicals, food processing, beverages. **Chief crops:** Grains, sunflower, vegetables, potatoes. **Minerals:** Oil, gas, coal. **Crude oil reserves** (1994): 1.6 bln. bbls. **Other resources:** Timber. **Arable land:** 43%. **Livestock** (1993): cattle: 3.7 mln.; pigs: 9.9 mln.; sheep: 12.1 mln. **Fish catch** (1991): 125,000 metric tons. **Electricity prod.** (1992): 59 bln. kWh. **Labor force:** 28% agric.; 38% ind.

Finance: Monetary unit: Lei (May 1995: 1,936 = $1 US). **Gross domestic product** (1993): $63.7 bln.* **Per capita GDP:** $2,700. **Imports** (1993): $5.4 bln.; partners: EU 46%, Russia 11%. **Exports** (1993): $4.0 bln.; partners: Eu 36%, Russia 5%. **Tourism** (1992): $262 mln. **National budget** (1991): $20 bln. **International reserves less gold** (Apr. 1995): $1.8 bln. **Gold:** $2.65 mln. oz t. **Consumer prices** (change in 1994): 136.8%.

Transport: Railroads: Length: 6,887 mi. **Motor vehicles:** in use: 1.3 mln. passenger cars; 332,000 comm. vehicles. **Civil aviation:** 2.3 bln. passenger-mi.; 14 airports. **Chief ports:** Constanta, Galati, Braila.

Communications: Television sets: 1 per 5.7 persons. **Radios:** 1 per 7.6 persons. **Telephones:** 1 per 7.1 persons.

Health: Life expectancy at birth (1995): 69 male; 75 female. **Births** (per 1,000 pop.): 14. **Deaths** (per 1,000 pop.): 10. **Natural increase:** 0.4%. **Hospital beds:** 1 per 105 persons. **Physicians:** 1 per 469 persons. **Infant mortality** (per 1,000 live births 1995): 190.

Education: Literacy (1992): 97%. **Years compulsory:** 10; attendance 98%.

Major International Organizations: UN (World Bank, IMF, WTO).

Embassy: 1607 23d St. NW 20008; 332-4846.

Romania's earliest known people merged with invading Proto-Thracians, preceding by centuries the Dacians. The Dacian kingdom was occupied by Rome, 106 AD-271 AD; people and language were Romanized. The principalities of Wallachia and Moldavia, dominated by Turkey, were united in 1859, became Romania in 1861. In 1877 Romania proclaimed independence from Turkey, became an independent state by the Treaty of Berlin, 1878, a kingdom, 1881, under Carol I. In 1886 Romania became a constitutional monarchy with a bicameral legislature.

Romania helped Russia in its war with Turkey, 1877-78. After World War I it acquired Bessarabia, Bukovina, Transylvania, and Banat. In 1940 it ceded Bessarabia and Northern Bukovina to the USSR, part of southern Dobrudja to Bulgaria, and northern Transylvania to Hungary.

In 1941, Romanian Prem. Marshal Ion Antonescu led his country in support of Germany against the USSR. In 1944 he was overthrown by King Michael and Romania joined the Allies.

After occupation by Soviet troops a People's Republic was proclaimed, Dec. 30, 1947; Michael was forced to abdicate. Land owners were dispossessed; most banks, factories and transportation units were nationalized.

On Aug. 22, 1965, a new constitution proclaimed Romania a Socialist, rather than a People's Republic.

Internal policies were oppressive. Ethnic Hungarians protested cultural and job discrimination, which led to strained relations with Hungary. Romania became industrialized, but lagged in consumer goods and in personal freedoms. All industry was state owned, and state farms and cooperatives owned almost all the arable land.

On Dec. 16, 1989, security forces opened fire on antigovernment demonstrators in Timisoara; hundreds were buried in mass graves. President Nicolae Ceausescu declared a state of emergency as protests spread to other cities. On Dec. 21, in Bucharest, security forces fired on protesters. Army units joined the rebellion, Dec. 22, and a group known as the Council of National Salvation announced that it had overthrown the government. Fierce fighting took place between the army, which backed the new government, and forces loyal to Ceausescu.

Ceausescu and his wife were captured and, following a trial in which they were found guilty of genocide, were executed Dec. 25, 1989. Former Communists dominated the government in succeeding years. A new constitution providing for a multiparty system took effect Dec. 8, 1991.

Russia
Russian Federation
Rossiyskaya Federatsiya

(Figures prior to 1992 are for the former USSR)

People: Population: 149,909,089. **Age distrib.** (%): <15: 22; 65+: 11. **Pop. density:** 23 per sq. mi. **Urban:** 73%. **Ethnic groups:** Russians 82%, Tatar 4%. **Principal languages:** Russian (official), Ukrainian, Belarussian, Uzbek, Armenian, Azerbaijani, Georgian, many others. **Religions:** Russian Orthodox 25%, nonreligious 60%.

Geography: Area: 6,592,800 sq. mi., more than 76% of the total area of the former USSR and the largest country in the world. **Location:** Stretches from E Europe across N Asia to the Pacific O. **Neighbors:** Finland, Poland, Norway, Estonia, Belarus, Ukraine on W, Georgia, Azerbaijan, Kazakhstan, China, Mongolia, North Korea on S. **Topography:** Russia contains every type of climate except the distinctly tropical, and has a varied topography.

The European portion is a low plain, grassy in S, wooded in N, with Ural Mts. on the E, and Caucasus Mts. on the S. Urals stretch N-S for 2,500 mi. The Asiatic portion is also a vast plain, with mountains on the S and in the E; tundra covers extreme N, with forest belt below; plains, marshes are in W, desert in SW. **Capital:** Moscow. **Cities** (1993 est.): Moscow 8.8 mln.; St. Petersburg 4.4 mln.; Nizhniy Novgorod 1.4 mln.; Novosibirsk 1.4 mln.

Government: Type: Federation. **Head of state:** Pres. Boris Yeltsin; b Feb. 1, 1931; in office: July 10, 1991. **Head of government:** Prime Min. Viktor Chernomyrdin; b 1938; in office: Dec. 14, 1992. **Local divisions:** 21 autonomous republics, 49 oblasts, 6 krays. **Defense:** 9.9% of GNP (1992). **Active troop strength:** 1.7 mln. est.

Economy: Industries: Steel, machinery, machine tools, vehicles, chemicals, mining, cement, textiles, appliances, paper. **Chief crops:** Grain, cotton, sugar beets, potatoes, vegetables, sunflowers. **Minerals:** Manganese, mercury, potash, bauxite, cobalt, chromium, copper, coal, gold, lead, molybdenum, nickel, phosphates, silver, tin, tungsten, zinc, oil, gas, potassium salts. **Crude oil reserves** (1994): 157 bln. bbls. **Other resources:** Forests. **Arable land:** 8%. **Livestock** (1993): cattle: 52 mln.; sheep: 48 mln.; pigs: 31 mln.; goats: 3.2 mln. **Fish catch** (1992): 5.3 mln. metric tons. **Electricity prod.** (1992): 956 bln. kWh. **Labor force:** 84% production & serv.; 16% govt.

Finance: Monetary unit: Ruble (Oct. 1994: 2,927 = $1 US). **Gross domestic product** (1993 est.): $975.4 bln.* **Per capita GNP:** $5,190. **Imports** (1993): $27 bln.; partners: EU, CIS. **Exports** (1993): $43 bln.; partners: EU, CIS. **National budget** (1989): $310 bln. **Tourism** (1988): $216 mln.

Transport: Railroads: Length: 98,239 mi. **Motor vehicles:** in use: 10.5 mln. passenger cars, 407,000 comm. vehicles. **Civil aviation:** 73 bln. passenger-mi.; 58 airports with scheduled flights. **Chief ports:** St. Petersburg, Murmansk, Tver, Arkhangelsk.

Communications: Television sets: 1 per 2.7 persons. **Radios:** 1 per 1.7 persons. **Telephones:** 1 per 6.0 persons. **Daily newspaper circ.:** 1,119 per 1,000 pop.

Health: Life expectancy at birth (1995): 64 male; 74 female. **Births** (per 1,000 pop.): 13. **Deaths** (per 1,000 pop.): 11. **Natural increase:** 0.1%. **Hospital beds:** 1 per 74 persons. **Physicians:** 1 per 225 persons. **Infant mortality** (per 1,000 live births 1995): 26.

Education: Literacy (1993): 98%. Most receive 11 years of schooling.

Major International Organizations: UN (ILO, IMF, WHO), CIS.

Embassy: 1125 16th St. NW 20036; 628-7551.

History. Slavic tribes began migrating into Russia from the W in the 5th century AD. The first Russian state, founded by Scandinavian chieftains, was established in the 9th century, centering in Novgorod and Kiev. In the 13th century the Mongols overran the country. It recovered under the grand dukes and princes of Muscovy, or Moscow, and by 1480 freed itself from the Mongols. Ivan the Terrible was the first to be formally proclaimed Tsar (1547). Peter the Great (1682-1725) extended the domain and, in 1721, founded the Russian Empire.

Western ideas and the beginnings of modernization spread through the huge Russian empire in the 19th and early 20th centuries. But political evolution failed to keep pace.

Military reverses in the 1905 war with Japan and in World War I led to the breakdown of the Tsarist regime. The 1917 Revolution began in March with a series of sporadic strikes for higher wages by factory workers. A provisional democratic government under Prince Georgi Lvov was established but was quickly followed in May by the second provisional government, led by Alexander Kerensky. The Kerensky government and the freely-elected Constituent Assembly were overthrown in a Communist coup led by Vladimir Ilyich Lenin Nov. 7.

Soviet Union

Lenin's death Jan. 21, 1924, resulted in an internal power struggle from which Joseph Stalin eventually emerged on top. Stalin secured his position at first by exiling opponents, but from the 1930s to 1953, he resorted to a series of "purge" trials, mass executions, and mass exiles to work camps. These measures resulted in millions of deaths, according to most estimates.

Germany and the Soviet Union signed a non-aggression pact Aug. 1939; Germany launched a massive invasion of the Soviet Union, June 1941. Notable heroic episode was the "900 days" siege of Leningrad, lasting to Jan. 1944, and causing a million deaths; the city was never taken. Russian winter counterthrusts, 1941-42 and 1942-43, stopped the German advance. Turning point was the failure of German troops to take and hold Stalingrad, Sept. 1942 to Feb. 1943. With British and U.S. Lend-Lease aid sustaining great casualties, the Russians drove the German forces from eastern Europe and the Balkans in the next 2 years.

After Stalin died, Mar. 5, 1953, Nikita Khrushchev was elected first secretary of the Central Committee. In 1956 he condemned Stalin. "De-Stalinization" of the country was begun.

Under Khrushchev the open antagonism of Poles and Hungarians toward domination by Moscow was brutally suppressed in 1956. He advocated peaceful co-existence with the capitalist countries, but continued arming the Soviet Union with nuclear weapons. He aided the Cuban revolution under Fidel Castro but withdrew Soviet missiles from Cuba during confrontation by U.S. Pres. Kennedy, Sept.-Oct. 1962. Khrushchev was suddenly deposed, Oct. 1964, and replaced by Leonid I. Brezhnev.

In Aug. 1968 Russian, Polish, East German, Hungarian, and Bulgarian military forces invaded Czechoslovakia to put a curb on liberalization policies of the Czech government.

Massive Soviet military aid to North Vietnam in the late 1960s and early 1970s helped assure Communist victories throughout Indo-China. Soviet arms aid and advisers were sent to several African countries in the 1970s.

In 1979, Soviet forces entered Afghanistan to support that government against rebels. In 1988, the Soviets announced withdrawal of their troops, ending a futile 8-year war.

Mikhail Gorbachev was chosen gen. secy. of the Communist Party, Mar. 1985. He was the youngest member of the Politburo and signaled a change in Soviet leadership. He held 4 summit meetings with U.S. Pres. Reagan. In 1987, in Washington, a treaty was signed eliminating intermediate–range nuclear missiles from Europe.

In 1987, Gorbachev initiated a program of reforms, including expanded freedoms and the democratization of the political process, through openness (*glasnost*) and restructuring (*perestroika*). The reforms were opposed by some Eastern bloc countries and many old-line Communists in the USSR. Gorbachev faced economic problems as well as ethnic and nationalist unrest in the republics.

On Aug. 19, 1991, it was announced that the vice president had taken over the country because of Gorbachev's ilness. A state of emergency was imposed for 6 months. The Russian republic's pres. Boris Yeltsin denounced the coup and called for a general strike. Some 50,000 demonstrated at the Russian Parliament in support of Yeltsin. By Aug. 21, the coup had failed and Gorbachev was restored as pres. On Aug. 24, Gorbachev resigned as leader of the Communist Party and recommended that its central committee be disbanded. Several republics declared their independence, including Russia, Ukraine, and Kazakhstan. On Aug. 29, the Soviet Parliament voted to suspend all activities of the Communist Party.

On Sept. 2, Gorbachev declared that the nation was "on the brink of catastrophe," and proposed to transfer all central authority to himself, the leaders of 10 republics, and an appointed legislative council in order to form a new kind of Soviet Union.

The Soviet Union officially broke up Dec. 26, 1991, one day after Gorbachev resigned. The Soviet hammer and sickle flying over the Kremlin was lowered and replaced by the flag of Russia, ending the domination of the Communist Party over all areas of national life since 1917.

Russian Federation

In a first major step in radical economic reform, Russia eliminated state subsidies of most goods and services, Jan. 1992. The effect was to allow prices to soar far beyond the means of ordinary workers. In June 1992, Pres. Yeltsin and then-U.S. Pres. George Bush agreed to massive arms reductions.

Russia launched a drive to privatize thousands of large and medium-sized state-owned enterprises in 1993. Pres. Yeltsin narrowly survived an impeachment vote by the Congress of People's Deputies, Mar. 28. He received strong support from voters in a countrywide referendum Apr. 25, but he continued to face a legislature dominated by conservatives and former Communists.

On Sept. 21, 1993, Yeltsin called early elections and dissolved Parliament, which in turn declared him deposed. Anti-Yeltsin legislators then barricaded themselves in the Parliament building. On Oct. 3, anti-Yeltsin forces attacked some facilities in Moscow and broke into the Parliament building. Yeltsin ordered the army to attack and seize the building. About 140 people were killed in the fighting, according to medical authorities. More than 150 were arrested.

In elections Dec. 12, 1993, a Yeltsin-supported constitution was approved, but ultranationalists and Communist hard-liners made strong showings in legislative contests. In Dec. 1994 the Russian government sent troops into the breakaway republic of

Chechnya; Grozny, the Chechen capital, fell in Feb. 1995 after heavy fighting, but Chechen rebels continued to resist.

Rwanda

Republic of Rwanda
Republika y'u Rwanda

People: Population: 8,605,307. **Age distrib.** (%): <15: 48; 65+: 3. **Pop. density:** 846 per sq. mi. **Urban:** 5%. **Ethnic groups:** Hutu 90%, Tutsi 9%, Twa (Pygmies) 1%. **Principal languages:** French, Kinyarwanda (both official). **Religions:** Christian 74%, indigenous 25%, Muslim 1%.

Geography: Area: 10,169 sq. mi. **Location:** In E central Africa. **Neighbors:** Uganda on N, Zaire on W, Burundi on S, Tanzania on E. **Topography:** Grassy uplands and hills cover most of the country, with a chain of volcanoes in the NW. The source of the Nile R. has been located in the headwaters of the Kagera (Akagera) R., SW of Kigali. **Capital:** Kigali (1991 est.): 238,000.

Government: Type: In transition. **Head of state:** Pres. Pasteur Bizimungu; in office: July 19, 1994. **Head of government:** Prime Min. Pierre Claver Rwigema; in office: Aug. 31, 1995. **Local divisions:** 10 prefectures. **Defense:** 7.5% of GNP (1991). **Active troop strength:** 5,000.

Economy: Chief crops: Coffee, tea. **Minerals:** Tin, gold, wolframite. **Arable land:** 29%. **Electricity prod.** (1991): 130 mln. kWh. **Labor force:** 93% agric.

Finance: Monetary unit: Franc (Feb. 1994: 144 = $1 US). **Gross domestic product** (1993): $6.8 bln.* **Per capita GDP:** $800. **Imports** (1992): $259.5 mln.; partners: Kenya 13%, Belgium 17%, France 7%. **Exports** (1992): $66.6 mln.; partners: Germany 21%, Netherlands 19%. **National budget** (1992 est.): $453.7 mln. **International reserves less gold** (Feb. 1994): $47.5 mln. **Consumer prices** (change in 1993): 12.4%.

Transport: Motor vehicles: in use: 8,000 passenger cars, 2,000 comm. vehicles.

Communications: Radios: 1 per 12 persons. **Telephones:** 1 per 335 persons.

Health: Life expectancy at birth (1995): 38 male; 40 female. **Births** (per 1,000 pop.): 49. **Deaths** (per 1,000 pop.): 22. **Natural increase:** 2.7%. **Hospital beds:** 1 per 649 persons. **Physicians:** 1 per 24,697 persons. **Infant mortality** (per 1,000 live births 1995): 118.

Education: Literacy (1992): 50%. **Years compulsory:** 8; attendance: 70%.

Major International Organizations: UN (IMF, WHO), OAU.

Embassy: 1714 New Hampshire Ave. NW 20009; 232-2882.

For centuries, the Tutsi (an extremely tall people) dominated the Hutu (90% of the population). A civil war broke out in 1959 and Tutsi power was ended. Many Tutsi went into exile. A referendum in 1961 abolished the monarchic system. Rwanda, which had been part of the Belgian UN trusteeship of Rwanda-Urundi, became independent July 1, 1962.

In 1963 Tutsi exiles invaded in an unsuccessful coup; a large-scale massacre of Tutsi followed. Rivalries among Hutu led to a bloodless coup July 1973 in which Juvénal Habyarimana took power. After an invasion and coup attempt by Tutsi exiles in 1990, a multiparty democracy was established.

Renewed ethnic strife led to an Aug. 1993 peace accord between the government and rebels of the Tutsi-led Rwandan Patriotic Front (RPF). But after Habyarimana and the president of Burundi were killed Apr. 6, 1994, in a suspicious plane crash, massive violence broke out. An estimated 200,000 or more died in massacres, mainly of Tutsi by Hutu militias, and in civil warfare as the RPF sought power. An estimated 2 million Tutsi and Hutu fled to camps in Zaire and other countries, where many died of cholera and other natural causes. French troops under a UN mandate moved into SW Rwanda June 23 to establish a so-called safe zone. The RPF claimed victory, installing a government in July led by a moderate Hutu president. French troops pulled out Aug. 22; a small African peacekeeping force remained. A UN tribunal for Rwanda convened June 1995 to try those responsible for genocide.

Saint Kitts and Nevis

Federation of Saint Kitts and Nevis

People: Population: 40,992. **Pop. density:** 394 per sq. mi. **Urban:** 42%. **Ethnic groups:** black African 95%. **Principal languages:** English. **Religions:** Protestant 76%.

Geography: Area: 104 sq. mi. in the N part of the Leeward group of the Lesser Antilles in the eastern Caribbean Sea. **Neighbors:** Antigua and Barbuda to E. **Capital:** Basseterre (1990): 15,000.

Government: Constitutional monarchy. **Head of state:** Queen Elizabeth II, represented by Sir Clement Arrindell. **Head of government:** Prime Min. Kennedy A. Simmonds; b Apr. 12, 1936; in office: Sept. 19, 1983. **Local divisions:** 14 parishes.

Economy: Sugar is the principal industry.

Finance: Monetary unit: East Caribbean Dollar (May 1995: 2.70 = $1 US). **Gross domestic product** (1992): $163 mln. **Tourism** (1990): $63 mln. receipts.

Communications: Telephones: 1 per 4.6 persons.

Health: Births (per 1,000 pop.): 23. **Deaths** (per 1,000 pop.): 10. **Natural increase:** 1.4%. **Infant mortality** (per 1,000 live births 1995): 19.

Education: Literacy (1992): 98%.

Embassy: 2100 M St. NW 20037; 833-3550.

St. Kitts (known by the natives as Liamuiga) and Nevis were reached (and named) by Columbus in 1493. They were settled by Britain in 1623, but ownership was disputed with France until 1713. They were part of the Leeward Islands Federation, 1871-1956, and the Federation of the W Indies, 1958-62. The colony achieved self-government as an Associated State of the UK in 1967, and became fully independent Sept. 19, 1983.

Saint Lucia

People: Population: 156,050. **Age distrib.** (%): <15: 37; 65+: 7. **Pop. density:** 656 per sq. mi. **Ethnic groups:** African descent 90%. **Principal languages:** English (official), French patois. **Religions:** Roman Catholic 90%.

Geography: Area: 238 sq. mi. **Location:** In E Caribbean, 2d largest of the Windward Is. **Neighbors:** Martinique to N, St. Vincent to SW. **Topography:** Mountainous, volcanic in origin; Soufriere, a volcanic crater, in the S. Wooded mountains run N-S to Mt. Gimie, 3,145 ft., with streams through fertile valleys. **Capital:** Castries (1992 met. est.): 14,000.

Government: Type: Parliamentary democracy. **Head of state:** Queen Elizabeth II, represented by Gov.-Gen. S.A. James; b Nov. 13, 1919; in office: Oct. 10, 1988. **Head of government:** Prime Min. John Compton; b 1926 in office: May 3, 1982. **Local divisions:** 11 quarters.

Economy: Industries: Agriculture, tourism, manufacturing. **Chief crops:** Bananas, coconuts, cocoa, citrus fruits. **Other resources:** Forests. **Arable land:** 8%. **Electricity prod.** (1992): 112 mln. kWh. **Labor force:** 43% agric.; 18% ind. & commerce; 39% services.

Finance: Monetary unit: East Caribbean Dollar (May 1995: 2.70 = $1 US). **Gross domestic product** (1993): $433 mln. **Per capita GDP:** $3,000. **Imports** (1992): $276 mln.; partners: U.S. 34%, UK 14%, Japan 7%. **Exports** (1992): $123 mln.; partners: UK 56%, U.S. 22%. **Tourism** (1992): $67 mln.

Transport: Motor vehicles: in use: 10,000 passenger cars, 9,000 comm. vehicles. **Chief ports:** Castries, Vieux Fort.

Communications: Television sets: 1 per 5.6 persons. **Radios:** 1 per 1.6 persons. **Telephones:** 1 per 3.8 persons.

Health: Life expectancy at birth (1995): 66 male; 74 female. **Births** (per 1,000 pop.): 22. **Deaths** (per 1,000 pop.): 6. **Natural increase:** 1.6%. **Hospital beds:** 1 per 318 persons. **Physicians:** 1 per 2,235 persons. **Infant mortality** (per 1,000 live births 1995): 20.

Education: Literacy (1993): 80%; **Years compulsory:** ages 5-15; attendance: 80%.

Major International Organizations: UN (IMF, WTO, ILO), the Commonwealth, OAS.

Embassy: 2100 M St. NW 20037; 463-7378.

St. Lucia was ceded to Britain by France at the Treaty of Paris, 1814. Self-government was granted with the West Indies Act, 1967. Independence was attained Feb. 22, 1979.

Saint Vincent and the Grenadines

People: Population: 117,580. **Pop. density:** 784 per sq. mi. **Urban:** 25%. **Ethnic groups:** mainly African descent. **Principal languages:** English, French patois. **Religions:** Methodist, Anglican, Roman Catholic.

Geography: Area: 150 sq. mi. **Location:** In the E Caribbean, St. Vincent (133 sq. mi.) and the northern islets of the Grenadines form a part of the Windward chain. **Neighbors:** St. Lucia to N, Barbados to E, Grenada to S. **Topography:** St. Vincent is volcanic, with a ridge of thickly wooded mountains running its length. **Capital:** Kingstown (1991 est.): 15,000.

Government: Type: Constitutional monarchy. **Head of state:** Queen Elizabeth II, represented by Gov.-Gen. David Jack; b July 16, 1918; in office: Sept. 20, 1989. **Head of government:** Prime Min. James Mitchell; b May 15, 1931; in office: July 30, 1984. **Local divisions:** 6 parishes.

Economy: Industries: Agriculture, tourism. **Chief crops:** Bananas, arrowroot, coconuts. **Arable land:** 38%. **Electricity prod.** (1992): 64 mln. kWh. **Labor force:** 30% agric.

Finance: Monetary unit: East Caribbean Dollar (May 1995: 2.70 = $1 US). **Gross domestic product** (1992): $215 mln. **Per capita GDP:** $2,000. **Tourism** (1992): $54 mln. **National budget** (1990): $67 mln.

Transport: Motor vehicles: in use: 5,000 passenger cars, 2,000 comm. vehicles. **Chief port:** Kingstown.

Communications: Telephones: 1 per 5.4 persons.

Health: Life expectancy at birth (1995): 71 male; 74 female. **Births** (per 1,000 pop.): 20. **Deaths** (per 1,000 pop.): 5. **Natural increase:** 1.4%. **Infant mortality** (per 1,000 live births 1995): 17.

Education: Literacy (1992): 85%.

Major International Organizations: UN, OAS, the Commonwealth.

Embassy: 1717 Massachusetts Ave. NW 20036; 462-7806.

Columbus landed on St. Vincent on Jan. 22, 1498 (St. Vincent's Day). Britain and France both laid claim to the island in the 17th and 18th centuries; the Treaty of Versailles, 1783, finally ceded it to Britain. Associated State status was granted 1969; independence was attained Oct. 27, 1979.

San Marino
Most Serene Republic of San Marino
Serenissima Repubblica di San Marino

People: Population: 24,313. **Age distrib.** (%): <15: 15; 65+: 14. **Pop. density:** 1,013 per sq. mi. **Urban:** 90%. **Ethnic groups:** Sanmarinese 78%, Italian 21%. **Principal languages:** Italian. **Religions:** mostly Roman Catholic.

Geography: Area: 24 sq. mi. **Location:** In N central Italy near Adriatic coast. **Neighbors:** Completely surrounded by Italy. **Topography:** The country lies on the slopes of Mt. Titano. **Capital:** San Marino (1994 est.): 2,399.

Government: Type: Republic. **Head of state:** Two co-regents appt. every 6 months. **Local divisions:** 9 municipalities. **Defense:** 1% of GDP (1992 est.).

Economy: Industries: Tourism, woolen goods, wine, cement, ceramics. **Arable land:** 17%.

Finance: Monetary unit: Italian Lira. **Gross domestic product** (1992): $370 mln.*

Communications: Television sets: 1 per 2.9 persons. **Radios:** 1 per 1.9 persons. **Telephones:** 1 per 0.6 persons.

Health: Births (per 1,000 pop.): 11. **Deaths** (per 1,000 pop.): 8. **Natural increase:** 0.3%. **Infant mortality** (per 1,000 live births 1995): 6.

Education: Literacy (1994): 98%. **Years compulsory:** 8; attendance: 93%.

Major International Organizations: UN.

San Marino claims to be the oldest state in Europe and to have been founded in the 4th century. A Communist-led coalition ruled 1947-57; a similar coalition ruled 1978-86. It has had a treaty of friendship with Italy since 1862.

São Tomé and Príncipe
Democratic Republic of São Tomé and Príncipe
República Democrática de São Tomé e Príncipe

People: Population: 140,423. **Pop. density:** 364 per sq. mi. **Urban:** 46%. **Ethnic groups:** Portuguese-African mixture, African minority (Angola, Mozambique immigrants). **Principal languages:** Portuguese (official). **Religions:** mostly Christian.

Geography: Area: 386 sq. mi. **Location:** In the Gulf of Guinea about 125 miles off W Central Africa. **Neighbors:** Gabon, Equatorial Guinea to E. **Topography:** São Tomé and Príncipe islands, part of an extinct volcano chain, are both covered by lush forests and croplands. **Capital:** São Tomé (1993 est.): 43,000.

Government: Type: Republic. **Head of state:** Pres. Miguel Trovoada; b 1946; in office: Apr. 3, 1991. **Head of government:** Prime Min. Carlos da Graca; in office: Oct. 25, 1994. **Local divisions:** 2 districts.

Economy: Chief crops: Cocoa (78% of exports), coconut products. **Arable land:** 1%; **Permanent crops:** 20%. **Electricity prod.** (1991): 10 mln. kWh.

Finance: Monetary unit: Dobra (Oct. 1994: 812 = $1 US). **Gross domestic product** (1992): $41.4 mln. **Per capita GDP:** $315.

Transport: Chief ports: São Tomé, Santo Antonio.

Communications: Radios: 1 per 4.0 persons.

Health: Births (per 1,000 pop.): 35. **Deaths** (per 1,000 pop.): 9. **Natural increase:** 2.6%. **Physicians:** 1 per 1,881 persons. **Infant mortality** (per 1,000 live births 1995): 62.

Education: Literacy (1989): 54%.

Major International Organizations: UN, OAU.

The islands were discovered in 1471 by the Portuguese, who brought the first settlers — convicts and exiled Jews. Sugar planting was replaced by the slave trade as the chief economic activity until coffee and cocoa were introduced in the 19th century.

Portugal agreed, 1974, to turn the colony over to the Gabon-based Movement for the Liberation of São Tomé and Príncipe, which proclaimed as first president its East German-trained leader, Manuel Pinto da Costa. Independence came July 12, 1975. Democratic reforms were instituted in 1987. In 1991 Miguel Trovoada won the first free presidential election following the withdrawal of Pres. da Costa. A military coup that ousted Trovoada Aug. 15, 1995, was reversed a week later after Angolan mediation.

Saudi Arabia
Kingdom of Saudi Arabia
al-Mamlaka al-'Arabiya as-Sa'udiya

People: Population: 18,729,576. **Age distrib.** (%): <15: 43; 65+: 2. **Pop. density:** 22 per sq. mi. **Urban:** 79%. **Ethnic groups:** Arab 90%, Afro-Asian 10%. **Principal languages:** Arabic. **Religions:** Muslim 100%.

Geography: Area: 865,000 sq. mi. **Location:** Occupies most of Arabian Peninsula in Middle East. **Neighbors:** Kuwait, Iraq, Jordan on N, Yemen, Oman on S, United Arab Emirates, Qatar on E. **Topography:** The highlands on W, up to 9,000 ft., slope as an arid, barren desert to the Persian Gulf. **Capital:** Riyadh. **Cities** (1986 est.): Riyadh 1.3 mln.; Jidda 1.2 mln.; Mecca 463,000.

Government: Type: Monarchy with council of ministers. **Head of state and government:** King Fahd ibn Abdul Aziz; b 1922; in office: June 13, 1982 (prime min. since 1982). **Local divisions:** 14 emirates. **Defense:** 13% of GDP (1993). **Active troop strength:** 104,000.

Economy: Industries: Oil products. **Chief crops:** Dates, wheat, barley, fruit. **Minerals:** Oil, gas, gold, copper, iron. **Crude oil reserves** (1994): 261 bln. barrels. **Arable land:** 1%. **Livestock** (1993): sheep: 7.1 mln.; goats: 3.4 mln. **Electricity prod.** (1992): 63 bln. kWh. **Labor force:** 16% agric.; 34% govt.; 28% industry & oil; 22% services.

Finance: Monetary unit: Riyal (May 1995: 3.74 = $1 US). **Gross domestic product** (1993): $194 bln.* **Per capita GDP:** $11,000. **Imports** (1993): $26.0 bln.; partners: US 18%, Japan 10%, UK 12%. **Exports** (1993): $42.3 bln.; partners: U.S. 21%, Japan 18%. **Tourism** (1992): $1.0 bln. **National budget** (1993 est.): $52.5 bln. **International reserves less gold** (Apr. 1995): $8.9 bln. **Gold:** 4.60 mln. oz t. **Consumer prices** (change in 1994): 0.6%.

Transport: Railroads: Length: 864 mi. **Motor vehicles:** in use: 2.8 mln. passenger cars, 2.3 mln. comm. vehicles. **Civil aviation:** 10.9 bln. passenger-mi.; 24 airports. **Chief ports:** Jidda, Ad Dammam, Ras Tannurah.

Communications: Television sets: 1 per 3.9 persons.

Radios: 1 per 3.5 persons. **Telephones:** 1 per 11 persons. **Daily newspaper circ.:** 42 per 1,000 pop.

Health: Life expectancy at birth (1995): 67 male; 70 female. **Births** (per 1,000 pop.): 39. **Deaths** (per 1,000 pop.): 6. **Natural increase:** 3.3%. **Hospital beds:** 1 per 359 persons. **Physicians:** 1 per 523 persons. **Infant mortality** (per 1,000 live births 1995): 49.

Education: Literacy (1990): 62%.

Major International Organizations: UN (IMF, WHO, FAO), Arab League, OPEC.

Embassy: 601 New Hampshire Ave. NW 20037; 342-3800.

Arabia was united for the first time by Muhammad, in the early 7th century. His successors conquered the entire Near East and North Africa, bringing Islam and the Arabic language. But Arabia itself soon returned to its former status.

Nejd, long an independent state and center of the Wahhabi sect, fell under Turkish rule in the 18th century, but in 1913 Ibn Saud, founder of the Saudi dynasty, overthrew the Turks and captured the Turkish province of Hasa; took the Hejaz in 1925 and by 1926, most of Asir. The discovery of oil in the 1930s transformed the new country.

Crown Prince Khalid was proclaimed king on Mar. 25, 1975, after the assassination of King Faisal. Fahd became king on June 13, 1982, following Khalid's death. There is no constitution and no parliament. The king exercises authority together with a Council of Ministers. The Islamic religious code is the law of the land. Alcohol and public entertainments are restricted, and women have an inferior legal status.

Saudi units fought against Israel in the 1948 and 1973 Arab-Israeli wars. Billions of dollars of advanced arms have been purchased from Britain, France, and the U.S. Beginning with the 1967 Arab-Israeli war, Saudi Arabia provided large annual financial gifts to Egypt; aid was later extended to Syria, Jordan, and Palestinian guerrilla groups, as well as to other Muslim countries.

Faisal played a leading role in the 1973-74 Arab oil embargo against the U.S. and other nations in an attempt to force them to adopt an anti-Israel policy. Saudi Arabia joined most other Arab states, 1979, in condemning Egypt's peace treaty with Israel.

In the 1980s, Saudi Arabia's moderate position on crude oil prices often prevailed at OPEC meetings.

Two Saudi oil tankers were attacked May 1984, as Iran and Iraq began air attacks against shipping in the Persian Gulf. On May 29, the U.S., citing grave concern over the growing escalation of the Iran-Iraq war in the Persian Gulf, authorized the sale of 400 Stinger antiaircraft missiles.

The Hejaz contains the holy cities of Islam—Medina, where the Mosque of the Prophet enshrines the tomb of Muhammad, and Mecca, his birthplace. More than 600,000 Muslims from 60 nations pilgrimage to Mecca annually.

In 1987, Iranians making a pilgrimage to Mecca clashed with anti-Iranian pilgrims and Saudi police; more than 400 were killed. Saudi Arabia broke diplomatic relations with Iran in 1988. Some 1,426 Muslim pilgrims died July 2, 1990, in a stampede in a pedestrian tunnel leading to Mecca. Nearly 300 pilgrims were killed in a stampede in Mecca, May 26, 1994.

Following Iraq's attack on Kuwait, Aug. 2, 1990, Saudi Arabia accepted the Kuwait royal family and more than 400,000 Kuwaiti refugees. King Fahd invited Western and Arab troops to deploy on its soil in support of Saudi defense forces. During the Persian Gulf War, Iraq fired a series of Scud missiles at Saudi Arabia; most were intercepted by U.S. Patriot missiles, although 28 U.S. soldiers were killed when a Scud hit their barracks in Dhahran, Feb. 25, 1991. The nation's northern Gulf coastline suffered severe pollution as a result of Iraqi sabotage of the Kuwaiti oil fields.

Senegal
Republic of Senegal
République du Sénégal

People: Population: 9,007,080. **Age distrib.** (%): <15: 45; 65+: 3. **Pop. density:** 119 per sq. mi. **Urban:** 39%. **Ethnic groups:** Wolof 36%, Serer 17%, Fulani 17%, Diola 9%, Toucouleur 9%, Mandingo 9%. **Principal languages:** French (official), Wolof, Pulaar, Diola, Mandingo, others. **Religions:** Muslim 92%, indigenous 6%, Christian 2%.

Geography: Area: 75,951 sq. mi. **Location:** At W extreme of Africa. **Neighbors:** Mauritania on N, Mali on E, Guinea, Guinea-Bissau on S, surrounds Gambia on three sides. **Topography:** Low rolling plains cover most of Senegal, rising somewhat in the SE. Swamp and jungles are in SW. **Capital:** Dakar. **Cities** (1992): Dakar 1.7 mln.; Thies 201,000; Kaolack 180,000.

Government: Type: Republic. **Head of state:** Pres. Abdou Diouf; b Sept. 7, 1935; in office: Jan. 1, 1981. **Head of government:** Prime Min. Habib Thiam; b Jan 21, 1933; in office: Apr. 8, 1991. **Local divisions:** 10 regions. **Defense:** 2.1% of GNP (1992). **Active troop strength:** 13,350.

Economy: Industries: Food processing, fishing. **Chief crops:** Peanuts, millet, rice. **Minerals:** Phosphates. **Arable land:** 27%. **Livestock** (1993): cattle: 2.7 mln.; sheep: 4.4 mln.; goats: 3.1 mln. **Fish catch** (1991): 338,000 metric tons. **Electricity prod.** (1991): 760 mln. kWh. **Labor force:** 77% subsistence agric.

Finance: Monetary unit: CFA Franc (May 1995: 488 = $1 US). **Gross domestic product** (1993): $11.8 bln.* **Per capita GDP:** $1,400. **Imports** (1991): $1.2 bln.; partners: France 37%, U.S. 6%. **Exports** (1991): $904 mln.; partners: France 25%, UK 6%. **Tourism** (1992): $172 mln. **National budget** (1989): $1.2 bln. **International reserves less gold** (Mar. 1995): $255 mln. **Gold:** 29,000 oz t. **Consumer prices** (change in 1994): 32.3%.

Transport: Railroads: Length: 562 mi. **Motor vehicles:** in use: 100,000 passenger cars, 45,000 comm. vehicles. **Chief ports:** Dakar, Saint-Louis.

Communications: Television sets: 1 per 130 persons. **Radios:** 1 per 9.3 persons. **Telephones:** 1 per 154 persons.

Health: Life expectancy at birth (1995): 56 male; 59 female. **Births** (per 1,000 pop.): 43. **Deaths** (per 1,000 pop.): 12. **Natural increase:** 3.1%. **Hospital beds:** 1 per 1,041 persons. **Physicians:** 1 per 15,350 persons. **Infant mortality** (per 1,000 live births 1995): 74.

Education: Literacy (1991): 29%. **Attendance:** 48% primary, 11% secondary.

Major International Organizations: UN and all of its specialized agencies, OAU.

Embassy: 2112 Wyoming Ave. NW 20008; 234-0540.

Portuguese settlers arrived in the 15th century, but French control grew from the 17th century. The last independent Muslim state was subdued in 1893. Dakar became the capital of French West Africa.

Independence as part, along with the Sudanese Rep., of the Mali Federation, came June 20, 1960. Senegal withdrew Aug. 20. French political and economic influence remained strong.

Senegal, Dec. 17, 1981, signed an agreement with The Gambia for confederation of the 2 countries, without loss of individual sovereignty, under the name of Senegambia. The confederation collapsed in 1989, although in 1991 the 2 nations signed a friendship and cooperation treaty.

Separatists in Casamance Province of S Senegal have clashed with government forces since 1982.

Seychelles
Republic of Seychelles

People: Population: 72,709. **Age distrib.** (%): <15: 32; 65+: 7. **Pop. density:** 413 per sq. mi. **Urban:** 50%. **Ethnic groups:** Seychellois (mixture of Asians, Africans, and French) predominate. **Principal languages:** English, French (both official). **Religions:** Roman Catholic 90%.

Geography: Area: 176 sq. mi. **Location:** In the Indian O. 700 miles NE of Madagascar. **Neighbors:** Nearest are Madagascar on SW, Somalia on NW. **Topography:** A group of 86 islands, about half of them composed of coral, the other half granite, the latter predominantly mountainous. **Capital:** Victoria (1987): 24,000.

Government: Type: Republic. **Head of state:** Pres. France-Albert René, b. Nov. 16, 1935; in office: June 5, 1977. **Local divisions:** 23 districts. **Defense:** 4% of GDP (1990 est.). **Active troop strength:** 800.

Economy: Industries: Tourism, food processing. **Chief crops:** Coconut products, cinnamon, vanilla. **Electricity prod.** (1991): 80 mln. kWh. **Labor force:** 12% agric.; 31% industry & comm.; 20% govt; 21% services.

Finance: Monetary unit: Rupee (May 1995: 4.59 = $1 US). **Gross domestic product** (1992): $407 mln. **Per capita GDP:** $5,900. **Imports** (1992): $192 mln.. **Exports** (1992): $47 mln. **National budget** (1991): $181 mln. **Tourism** (1992): $117 mln. **International reserves less gold** (Apr. 1995): $31 mln. **Consumer prices** (change in 1994): 1.8%.

Transport: Motor vehicles: in use: 4,700 passenger cars, 1,600 comm. vehicles. **Chief port:** Victoria.

Communications: Radios: 1 per 1.8 persons. **Telephones:** 1 per 3.9 persons. **Daily newspaper circ.:** 47 per 1,000 pop.

Health: Life expectancy at birth (1995): 67 male; 74 female. **Births** (per 1,000 pop.): 21. **Deaths** (per 1,000 pop.): 7. **Natural increase:** 1.5%. **Hospital beds:** 1 per 168 persons. **Physicians:** 1 per 1,019 persons. **Infant mortality** (per 1,000 live births 1995): 11.

Education: Literacy (1993): 84%. **Years compulsory:** 9; attendance 98%.

Major International Organizations: UN, OAU, the Commonwealth.

The islands were occupied by France in 1768, and seized by Britain in 1794. Ruled as part of Mauritius from 1814, the Seychelles became a separate colony in 1903. The ruling party had opposed independence as impractical, but pressure from the OAU and the UN became irresistible, and independence was declared June 29, 1976. The first president was ousted in a coup a year later by a socialist leader.

A new constitution, approved June 1993, provided for a multiparty state.

Sierra Leone
Republic of Sierra Leone

People: Population: 4,753,120. **Age distrib.** (%): <15: 44; 65+: 3. **Pop. density:** 172 per sq. mi. **Urban:** 35%. **Ethnic groups:** Temne 30%, Mende 30%, other tribes 39%. **Principal languages:** English (official), tribal languages. **Religions:** Muslim 60%, indigenous beliefs 30%, Christian 10%.

Geography: Area: 27,699 sq. mi. **Location:** On W coast of W Africa. **Neighbors:** Guinea on N, E, Liberia on S. **Topography:** The heavily-indented, 210-mi. coastline has mangrove swamps. Behind are wooded hills, rising to a plateau and mountains in the E. **Capital:** Freetown. **Cities** (1985 est.): Freetown 475,000; Koidu-New Sembehun 80,000; Bo, Kenema, Makeni.

Government: Type: Military. **Head of government:** Capt. Valentine E. M. Strasser; b 1966; in office: May 7, 1992. **Local divisions:** 4 provinces. **Defense:** 2.3% of GNP (1991). **Active troop strength:** 6,150.

Economy: Industries: Mining. **Chief crops:** Cocoa, coffee, palm kernels, rice, ginger. **Minerals:** Diamonds, bauxite. **Arable land:** 25%. **Fish catch** (1991): 50,000 metric tons. **Electricity prod.** (1991): 185 mln. kWh. **Labor force:** 65% agric.; 35% ind. & serv.

Finance: Monetary unit: Leone (May 1995: 650 = $1 US). **Gross domestic product** (1993): $4.5 bln.* **Per capita GDP:** $1,000. **Imports** (1992): $131 mln.; partners: UK 22%, France 11%. **Exports** (1992): $145 mln.; partners: Netherlands 31%; UK 15%, U.S. 9%. **National budget** (1992 est.): $118 mln. **International reserves less gold** (May 1995): $34.4 mln. **Consumer prices** (change in 1994): 24.2%.

Transport: Motor vehicles: in use: 32,000 passenger cars, 12,000 comm. vehicles. **Chief ports:** Freetown, Bonthe.

Communications: Television sets: 1 per 180 persons. **Radios:** 1 per 4.5 persons. **Telephones:** 1 per 125 persons.

Health: Life expectancy at birth (1995): 44 male; 50 female. **Births** (per 1,000 pop.): 45. **Deaths** (per 1,000 pop.): 18. **Natural increase:** 2.6%. **Hospital beds:** 1 per 980 persons. **Physicians:** 1 per 10,832 persons. **Infant mortality** (per 1,000 live births 1995): 139.

Education: Literacy (1992): 21%.

Major International Organizations: UN (IMF, WHO), the Commonwealth, OAU.

Embassy: 1701 19th St. NW 20009; 939-9261.

Freetown was founded in 1787 by the British government as a haven for freed slaves. Their descendants, known as Creoles, number more than 60,000.

Successive steps toward independence followed the 1951 constitution. Full independence arrived Apr. 27, 1961. Sierra

Leone became a republic Apr. 19, 1971. A one-party state approved by referendum 1978, brought political stability, but the economy has been plagued by inflation, corruption, and dependence upon the International Monetary Fund and creditors.

Mutinous soldiers ousted Pres. Joseph Momoh Apr. 30, 1992. The new military regime faced continued armed opposition from the Revolutionary United Front.

Singapore

Republic of Singapore

People: Population: 2,890,468. **Age distrib.** (%): <15: 23; 65+: 7. **Pop. density:** 11,702 per sq. mi. **Urban:** 100%. **Ethnic groups:** Chinese 77%, Malay 15%, Indian 6%. **Principal languages:** Chinese, Malay, Tamil, English (all official). **Religions:** Buddhist 29%, Christian 19%, Muslim 16%, Taoist 13%.

Geography: Area: 247 sq. mi. **Location:** Off tip of Malayan Peninsula in SE Asia. **Neighbors:** Nearest are Malaysia on N, Indonesia on S. **Topography:** Singapore is a flat, formerly swampy island. The nation includes 40 nearby islets. **Capital:** Singapore.

Government: Type: Republic. **Head of state:** Pres. Ong Teng Cheong; b Jan 22, 1936; in office: Sept. 2, 1993. **Head of government:** Prime Min. Goh Chok Tong; b May 20, 1941; in office: Nov. 28, 1990. **Defense:** 6% of GDP (1993 est.). **Active troop strength:** 54,000.

Economy: Industries: Shipbuilding; oil refining; electronics; banking; textiles; food; rubber and lumber processing, biotechnology. **Arable land:** 4%. **Fish catch** (1992): 9,000 metric tons. **Electricity prod.** (1992): 18 bln. kWh. **Labor force:** 59% ind. & comm.; 30% services.

Finance: Monetary unit: Dollar (May 1995: 1.39 = $1 US). **Gross domestic product** (1993): $42.4 bln.* **Per capita GDP:** $15,000. **Imports** (1992): $66.4 bln.; partners: Japan 21%, Malaysia 15%, U.S. 16%, Saudi Arabia 5%. **Exports** (1992): $61.5 bln.; partners: U.S. 21%, Malaysia 12%, Japan 8%, Hong Kong 8%. **Tourism** (1992): $5.2 bln. **National budget** (1994): $10.5 bln. **International reserves less gold** (Mar. 1995): $61.3 bln. **Consumer prices** (change in 1994): 3.1%.

Transport: Motor vehicles: in use: 322,000 passenger cars, 132,000 comm. vehicles. **Civil aviation:** 23 bln. passenger-mi.; 1 airport.

Communications: Television sets: 1 per 4.4 persons. **Radios:** 1 per 3.0 persons. **Telephones:** 1 per 2.5 persons. **Daily newspaper circ.:** 280 per 1,000 pop.

Health: Life expectancy at birth (1995): 73 male; 79 female. **Births** (per 1,000 pop.): 16. **Deaths** (per 1,000 pop.): 5. **Natural increase:** 1.1%. **Hospital beds:** 1 per 295 persons. **Physicians:** 1 per 725 persons. **Infant mortality** (per 1,000 live births 1995): 6.

Education: Literacy (1992): 91%. **Years compulsory:** none; attendance 94%.

Major International Organizations: UN (WTO, IMF, WHO), the Commonwealth, ASEAN.

Embassy: 3501 International Pl. NW 20008; 537-3100.

Founded in 1819 by Sir Thomas Stamford Raffles, Singapore was a British colony until 1959, when it became autonomous within the Commonwealth. On Sept. 16, 1963, it joined with Malaya, Sarawak, and Sabah to form the Federation of Malaysia. Tensions between Malayans, dominant in the federation, and ethnic Chinese, dominant in Singapore, led to an agreement under which Singapore became a separate nation, Aug. 9, 1965.

Singapore is one of the world's largest ports. Standards in health, education, and housing are high. International banking has grown. The government, dominated by a single party, has taken strong actions to suppress dissent.

Slovakia

Slovak Republic

Slovenská Republika

People: Population: 5,432,383. **Pop. density:** 287 per sq. mi. **Urban:** 57%. **Ethnic groups:** Slovak 86%, Hungarian 11%. **Principal languages:** Slovak (official), Hungarian. **Religions:** Roman Catholic 60%, Protestant 8%.

Geography: Area: 18,933 sq. mi. **Location:** In E central Europe. **Neighbors:** Poland on N, Hungary on S, Austria, Czech Rep. on W, Ukraine on E. **Topography:** mountains (Carpathians) in N, fertile Danube plane in S. **Capital:** Bratislava. **Cities** (1993 est.): Bratislava 447,000; Kosice 237,000.

Government: Type: Republic. **Head of state:** Pres. Michal Kovac; b 1931; in office: Feb. 2, 1993. **Head of government:** Prime Min. Vladimir Meciar; b July 26, 1942; in office: Dec. 13, 1994. **Local divisions:** 4 departments. **Defense: Active troop strength:** 47,000.

Economy: Industries: Iron and steel, glass, chemicals, coal, plastics. **Chief crops:** Grains, potatoes, hops, fruit. **Electricity prod.** (1992): 24 bln. kWh. **Labor force:** 33% ind.; 12% agric.

Finance: Monetary unit: Koruna (Mar. 1995: 29.00 = $1 US). **Gross domestic product** (1993): $31 bln.* **Per capita GDP:** $5,800. **Imports** (1993): $5.9 bln. **Exports** (1993): $5.1 bln. **International reserves less gold** (Mar. 1995): 1.9 bln. **Gold:** 1.3 mln. oz t.

Transport: Railroads: Length: 2,275 mi. **Motor vehicles:** in use: 953,000 passenger cars, 81,000 comm. vehicles.

Communications: Radios: 1 per 5.0 persons. **Telephones:** 1 per 3.9 persons.

Health: Births (per 1,000 pop.): 15. **Deaths** (per 1,000 pop.): 9. **Natural increase:** 0.5%. **Infant mortality** (per 1,000 live births 1995): 10.

Education: Literacy (1993): 100%.

Major International Organizations: UN.

Embassy: 2201 Wisconsin Ave. NW 20007; 965-5161.

Slovakia was originally settled by Illyrian, Celtic, and Germanic tribes and was incorporated into Great Moravia in the 9th century. It became part of Hungary in the 11th century. Overrun by Czech Hussites in the 15th century, it was restored to Hungarian rule in 1526. The Slovaks disassociated themselves from Hungary following World War I and joined the Czechs of Bohemia to form the Republic of Czechoslovakia, Oct. 28, 1918.

Germany invaded Czechoslovakia, 1939, and declared Slovakia independent. Slovakia rejoined Czechoslovakia in 1945.

Czechoslovakia split into 2 separate states—the Czech Republic and Slovakia—on Jan. 1, 1993. Slovakia, with its less developed economy, applied to join the European Union in 1995.

Slovenia

Republic of Slovenia

Republika Slovenija

People: Population: 2,051,522. **Pop. density:** 262 per sq. mi. **Urban:** 50%. **Ethnic groups:** Slovene 91%. **Principal languages:** Slovenian, Serbo-Croatian. **Religions:** Roman Catholic 96%.

Geography: Area: 7,821 sq. mi. **Location:** In SE Europe. **Neighbors:** Italy on W, Austria on N, Hungary on NE, Croatia on SE, S. **Topography:** Mostly hilly; 42% of the land is forested. **Capital:** Ljubljana (1991): 276,000.

Government: Type: Republic. **Head of state:** Pres. Milan Kucan; b Jan. 14, 1941; in office: Apr. 1990. **Head of government:** Prime Min. Janez Drnovsek; b 1950; in office: May 14, 1992. **Local divisions:** 60 provinces. **Defense:** 4.5% of GDP (1993). **Active troop strength:** 8,100.

Economy: Industries: Steel, textiles. **Minerals:** Coal, mercury. **Chief crops:** Potatoes, hops, hemp. **Arable land:** 10%. **Livestock** (1992): cattle: 504,000; pigs: 602,000. **Electricity prod.** (1992): 10 bln. kWh.

Finance: Monetary unit: Tolar (Apr. 1995: 112 = $1 US). **Gross domestic product** (1993): $15 bln.* **Per capita GDP:** $7,600. **Imports** (1993): $5.3 bln.; partners: Germany 23%, Croatia 14%, Italy 14%. **Exports** (1993): $5.1 bln.; partners: Germany 27%, Croatia 14%.

Transport: Motor vehicles: in use: 602,000 passenger cars.

Communications: Television sets: 1 per 4.4 persons. **Radios:** 1 per 3.3 persons. **Telephones:** 1 per 3.4 persons. **Daily newspaper circ.:** 154 per 1,000 pop.

Health: Life expectancy at birth (1995): 71 male; 79 female. **Births** (per 1,000 pop.): 12. **Deaths** (per 1,000 pop.): 9. **Natural increase:** 0.3%. **Hospital beds:** 1 per 167 persons.

Physicians: 1 per 489 persons. **Infant mortality** (per 1,000 live births 1995): 8.
Education: Literacy (1992): 99%.
Major International Organizations: UN.
Embassy: 1525 New Hampshire Ave. NW 20036; 667-5363.

The Slovenes settled in their current territory during the period from the 6th to the 8th century. They fell under German domination as early as the 9th century. Modern Slovenian political history began after 1848 when the Slovenes, who were divided among several Austrian provinces, began their struggle for political and national unification. With the establishment of Yugoslavia in 1918, this unification was largely achieved when the majority of the Slovenes entered the new state, which became the Kingdom of the Serbs, Croats, and Slovenes.

Slovenia declared independence June 25, 1991, and was admitted to the UN May 22, 1992.

Solomon Islands

People: Population: 399,206. **Pop. density:** 36 per sq. mi. **Urban:** 13%. **Ethnic groups:** Melanesian 93%, Polynesian 4%. **Principal languages:** English (official), Papuan, Melanesian, Polynesian languages. **Religions:** Anglican 34%, Roman Catholic 19%, Baptist 17%, other Christian 26%.
Geography: Area: 10,954 sq. mi. **Location:** Melanesian Archipelago in the W Pacific O. **Neighbors:** Nearest is Papua New Guinea on W. **Topography:** 10 large volcanic and rugged islands and 4 groups of smaller ones. **Capital:** Honiara (1990): 35,000.
Government: Type: Parliamentary democracy within the Commonwealth of Nations. **Head of state:** Queen Elizabeth II, represented by Gov.-Gen. Moses Pitakaka; in office: June 1994. **Head of government:** Prime Min. Solomon Mamaloni; b 1943; in office: Nov. 7, 1994. **Local divisions:** 7 provinces and Honiara.
Economy: Industries: Fish canning. **Chief crops:** Coconuts, rice, cocoa, beans. **Other resources:** Forests. **Arable land:** 1%. **Fish catch** (1993): 32,000 metric tons. **Electricity prod.** (1993): 48.9 mln. kWh. **Labor force:** 32% agric.; 25% services; 12% ind. & comm.
Finance: Monetary unit: Dollar (Sept. 1994: 3.32 = $1 US). **Gross domestic product** (1991): $900 mln.* **Per capita GDP:** $2,500. **Imports** (1991): $110 mln.; partners: Australia 34%, Japan 16%. **Exports** (1991): $84 mln.; partners: Japan 39%, UK 23%.
Communications: Radios: 1 per 9.2 persons. **Telephones:** 1 per 46 persons.
Health: Life expectancy at birth (1995): 68 male; 73 female. **Births** (per 1,000 pop.): 38. **Deaths** (per 1,000 pop.): 5. **Natural increase:** 3.4%. **Infant mortality** (per 1,000 live births 1995): 27.
Education: Literacy (1993): 54%. **Attendence:** primary school 78%, secondary school 21%.
Major International Organizations: UN, the Commonwealth.

The Solomon Islands were sighted in 1568 by an expedition from Peru. Britain established a protectorate in the 1890s over most of the group, inhabited by Melanesians. The islands saw major World War II battles. Self-government came Jan. 2, 1976, and independence was formally attained July 7, 1978.

Somalia

Soomaaliya

People: Population: 7,347,554. **Pop. density:** 30 per sq. mi. **Urban:** 24%. **Ethnic groups:** mainly Somali. **Principal languages:** Somali (official), Arabic, Italian, English. **Religions:** Sunni Muslim 99%.
Geography: Area: 246,000 sq. mi. **Location:** Occupies the eastern horn of Africa. **Neighbors:** Djibouti, Ethiopia, Kenya on W. **Topography:** The coastline extends for 1,700 mi. Hills cover the N; the center and S are flat. **Capital:** Mogadishu (1986 est.): 700,000.
Government: Type: In transition. **Local divisions:** 16 regions.
Economy: Chief crops: Sugar, bananas, sorghum, corn, mangoes. **Minerals:** Iron, tin, gypsum, bauxite, uranium. **Arable land:** 2%. **Livestock** (1993): cattle: 1.5 mln.; goats: 12.5 mln.; sheep: 6.5 mln. **Fish catch** (1991): 16,000 metric tons. **Labor force:** 71% agric.

Finance: Monetary unit: Shilling (Oct. 1994: 2,622 = $1 US). **Gross domestic product** (1993): $3.4 bln.* **Per capita GDP:** $500. **Imports** (1990): $249 mln.; partners: Italy 29%, France 18%. **Exports** (1990): $58 mln.; partners: Italy 17%.
Transport: Motor vehicles: in use: 10,500 passenger cars, 11,500 comm. vehicles. **Chief ports:** Mogadishu, Berbera.
Communications: Radios: 1 per 16 persons.
Health: Life expectancy at birth (1995): 55 male; 56 female. **Births** (per 1,000 pop.): 46. **Deaths** (per 1,000 pop.): 13. **Natural increase:** 3.2%. **Hospital beds:** 1 per 1,053 persons. **Physicians:** 1 per 19,071 persons. **Infant mortality** (per 1,000 live births 1995): 119.
Education: Literacy (1990): 24%. **Attendance:** 50% attend primary school, 7% attend secondary school.
Major International Organizations: UN, OAU, Arab League.

The UN in 1949 approved eventual creation of Somalia as a sovereign state, and in 1950 Italy took over the trusteeship held by Great Britain since World War II.

British Somaliland was formed in the 19th century in the NW. Britain gave it independence June 26, 1960; on July 1 it joined with the former Italian part to create the independent Somali Republic.

On Oct. 21, 1969, a Supreme Revolutionary Council seized power in a bloodless coup, named a Council of Secretaries of State, and abolished the Assembly. In May 1970, several foreign companies were nationalized.

Somalia has laid claim to Ogaden, the huge eastern region of Ethiopia, peopled mostly by Somalis. Ethiopia battled Somali rebels in 1977. Some 11,000 Cuban troops with Soviet arms defeated Somali army troops and ethnic Somali rebels in Ethiopia, 1978. As many as 1.5 mln. refugees entered Somalia. Guerrilla fighting in Ogaden continued until 1988, when a peace agreement was reached with Ethiopia.

Twenty-one years of one-man rule ended in Jan. 1991 with the flight of Gen. Muhammad Siyad Barre from the capital. Fighting between rival factions caused 40,000 casualties in 1991 and 1992, and by mid-1992 the civil war, drought, and banditry combined to produce a famine that threatened some 1.5 million people with starvation. In July 1992 the UN secretary general declared Somalia to be a country without a government.

In Dec. 1992 the UN accepted a U.S. offer of troops to safeguard the delivery of food to the starving. The UN took control of the multinational relief effort from the U.S. May 4, 1993. While the operation helped alleviate the famine, efforts to reestablish order foundered, and there were significant U.S. and other casualties. The U.S. withdrew its peacekeeping forces Mar. 25, 1994. When the last UN troops pulled out Mar. 3, 1995, Mogadishu still had no functioning government, and armed factions controlled different parts of the country.

South Africa

Republic of South Africa

People: Population: 45,095,459. **Age distrib.** (%): <15: 37; 65+: 5. **Pop. density:** 96 per sq. mi. **Urban:** 63%. **Ethnic groups:** black 75%, white 14%, Coloured 9%, Indian 3%. **Principal languages:** 11 official languages incl. Afrikaans, English, Ndebele, Sotho. **Religions:** mainly Christian; Hindu, Muslim minorities.
Geography: Area: 472,281 sq. mi. **Location:** At the southern extreme of Africa. **Neighbors:** Namibia, Botswana, Zimbabwe on N, Mozambique, Swaziland on E; surrounds Lesotho. **Topography:** The large interior plateau reaches close to the country's 2,700-mi. coastline. There are few major rivers or lakes; rainfall is sparse in W, more plentiful in E. **Capitals:** Cape Town (legislative), Pretoria (executive), and Bloemfontein (judicial). **Cities** (1991 met.): Cape Town 2.4 mln.; Johannesburg (met.) 1.9 mln.; Durban 1.1 mln.; Pretoria 1.1 mln.
Government: Type: Federal republic with bicameral Parliament and universal suffrage. **Head of state and government:** Pres. Nelson Mandela; b July 1918; in office: May 10, 1994. Deputy presidents: Thabo Mbeki, F.W. de Klerk. **Local divisions:** 9 provinces. **Defense:** 2.5% of GDP (1993). **Active troop strength:** 78,500.
Economy: Industries: Mining, steel, tires, motors, textiles, plastics. **Chief crops:** Corn, dairy products, grain, tobacco, sugar, fruit, peanuts, grapes. **Minerals:** Gold (largest producer), chromium, antimony, coal, iron, manganese, nickel, phosphates, tin, uranium, gem diamonds, platinum, copper, vanadium. **Other resources:** Wool. **Arable land:** 10%.

Livestock (1993): cattle: 13.2 mln.; sheep: 30 mln. **Fish catch** (1991): 499,000 metric tons. **Electricity prod.** (1991): 180 bln. kWh. **Labor force:** 30% agric.; 20% ind.; 35% services.

Finance: Monetary unit: Rand (May 1995: 1.00 = $.27 US). **Gross domestic product** (1993): $171 bln.* **Per capita GDP** $4,000. **Imports** (1993): $18.1 bln.; partners: Germany 15%, U.S. 13%, UK 10%. **Exports** (1993): $24.3 bln.; partners: Italy 8%, Germany 6%, Japan 6%, U.S. 5%. **Tourism** (1992): $1.2 bln. **National budget** (1994): $34 bln. **International reserves less gold** (May 1995): $1.9 bln. **Gold:** 4.41 mln. oz t. **Consumer prices** (change in 1994): 9.0%.

Transport: Railroads: Length: 13,432 mi. **Motor vehicles:** in use: 3.5 mln. passenger cars, 1.9 mln. comm. vehicles. **Civil aviation:** 6.5 bln. passenger-mi.; 31 airports. **Chief ports:** Durban, Cape Town, East London, Port Elizabeth.

Communications: Television sets: 1 per 12 persons. **Radios:** 1 per 4.1 persons. **Telephones:** 1 per 7.6 persons. **Daily newspaper circ.:** 38 per 1,000 pop.

Health: Life expectancy at birth (1995): 63 male; 68 female. **Births** (per 1,000 pop.): 33. **Deaths** (per 1,000 pop.): 7. **Natural increase:** 2.6%. **Hospital beds:** 1 per 222 persons. **Physicians:** 1 per 1,264 persons. **Infant mortality** (per 1,000 live births 1995): 46.

Education: Literacy (1992): 76%.

Major International Organizations: UN (WTO), OAU, the Commonwealth.

Embassy: 3051 Massachusetts Ave. NW 20008; 232-4400.

Bushmen and Hottentots were the original inhabitants. Bantus, including Zulu, Xhosa, Swazi, and Sotho, had occupied the area from Transvaal to south of Transkei before the 17th century.

The Cape of Good Hope area was settled by Dutch, beginning in the 17th century. Britain seized the Cape in 1806. Many Dutch trekked north and founded 2 republics, the Transvaal and the Orange Free State. Diamonds were discovered, 1867, and gold, 1886. The Dutch (Boers) resented encroachments by the British and others; the Anglo-Boer War followed, 1899-1902. Britain won and, effective May 31, 1910, created the Union of South Africa, incorporating the British colonies of Cape and Natal, the Transvaal and the Orange Free State. After a referendum, the Union became the Republic of South Africa, May 31, 1961, and withdrew from the Commonwealth.

With the election victory of Daniel Malan's National Party in 1948, the policy of separate development of the races, or apartheid, already existing unofficially, became official. This called for separate development, separate residential areas, and ultimate political independence for the whites, Bantus, Asians, and Coloureds. In 1959 the government passed acts providing the eventual creation of several Bantu nations or Bantustans on 13% of the country's land area, though most black leaders opposed the plan.

Under apartheid, blacks were severely restricted to certain occupations, and paid far lower wages than whites for similar work. Only whites could vote or run for public office. There was an advisory Indian Council, partly elected, partly appointed. In 1969, a Coloured People's Representative Council was created.

At least 600 persons, mostly Bantus, were killed in 1976 riots protesting apartheid. Black protests continued as violence broke out in several black townships. A new constitution was approved by referendum, Nov. 1983, which extended the parliamentary franchise to the Coloured and Asian minorities. Laws banning interracial sex and marriage were repealed in 1985.

In 1963, the Transkei, an area in the SE, became the first of the partially self-governing black territories or "Homelands." Transkei became independent on Oct. 26, 1976, Bophuthatswana on Dec. 6, 1977, and Venda on Sept. 13, 1979; none received international recognition.

In 1981, South Africa launched military operations in Angola and Mozambique to combat terrorists groups; South African troops attacked the South West African People's Organization (SWAPO) guerrillas in Angola, Mar. 1982. South Africa and Mozambique signed a non-aggression pact in 1984.

In 1986, Nobel Peace Prize winner Bishop Desmond Tutu called for Western nations to apply sanctions against South Africa to force an end to apartheid. President Botha announced in Apr. the end to the nation's system of racial pass laws and

offered blacks an advisory role in government. On May 19, South Africa attacked 3 neighboring countries—Zimbabwe, Botswana, Zambia—to strike at guerrilla strongholds of the black nationalist African National Congress. A nationwide state of emergency was declared June 12, giving almost unlimited power to the security forces. As confrontation between blacks and government increased, there was widespread support in Western nations for a complete trade embargo on South Africa.

Some 2 million South African black workers staged a massive strike, June 6-8, 1988. P.W. Botha, head of the government since 1978, resigned Aug. 14, 1989, and was replaced by Frederik W. de Klerk.

In 1990, the government lifted its ban on the ANC. On Feb. 11, black nationalist leader Nelson Mandela was freed after more than 27 years in prison. In Oct. the Separate Amenities Act was repealed, ending the legal basis of segregation in public places. In Feb. 1991, Pres. de Klerk announced plans to end all apartheid laws. In June the race registration law was repealed.

A band of marauders swept through the township of Boipatong, June 17, 1992, killing some 40 blacks and prompting the ANC to temporarily break off constitutional talks with the white-minority government. Violence involving rival black groups continued later in the year. Violence flared in several black townships following the assassination of Chris Hani, head of the South African Communist Party, Apr. 10, 1993.

In 1993 the nation's negotiating parties, led by the ANC and the National Party, agreed on basic principles for a new constitution, with elections in which all races could vote. A multiracial transition committee was instituted in Dec. to oversee certain government operations prior to elections. Voters would determine party composition of a National Assembly and provincial assemblies. The former would elect the president, enact legislation, and approve a permanent constitution. Under the new system, South Africa's homelands were abolished as such, incorporated into the national system of 9 provinces.

In elections Apr. 26-29, 1994, the ANC won 62.7% of the vote, enabling Mandela to become president. The National Party won 20.4%. The Inkatha Freedom Party won 10.5% and control of the legislature in a predominantly Zulu province.

Spain
Kingdom of Spain
Reino de España

People: Population: 39,404,348. **Age distrib.** (%): <15: 17; 65+: 15. **Pop. density:** 202 per sq. mi. **Urban:** 64%. **Ethnic groups:** Spanish (Castilian, Valencian, Andalusian, Asturian) 72.3%, Catalan 16.3%, Galician 8.1%, Basque 2.3%. **Principal languages:** Castilian Spanish (official), Catalan, Galician, Basque. **Religions:** Roman Catholic 99%.

Geography: Area: 194,898 sq. mi. **Location:** In SW Europe. **Neighbors:** Portugal on W, France on N. **Topography:** The interior is a high, arid plateau broken by mountain ranges and river valleys. The NW is heavily watered, the south has lowlands and a Mediterranean climate. **Capital:** Madrid. **Cities** (1991 met. est.): Madrid 2.9 mln.; Barcelona 1.6 mln.; Valencia 753,000; Seville 659,000.

Government: Type: Constitutional monarchy. **Head of state:** King Juan Carlos I de Borbon y Borbon, b. Jan. 5, 1938; in office: Nov. 22, 1975. **Head of government:** Prime Min. Felipe González Márquez; b Mar. 5, 1942; in office: Dec. 2, 1982. **Local divisions:** 17 autonomous communities. **Defense:** 1.26% of GDP (1994). **Active troop strength:** 206,500.

Economy: Industries: Machinery, metals, textiles, shoes, autos, processed foods, tourism. **Chief crops:** Grains, olives, grapes, citrus fruits, vegetables. **Minerals:** Lignite, uranium, lead, iron, copper, zinc, coal. **Other resources:** Forests. **Arable land:** 31%. **Livestock** (1993): cattle: 4.8 mln.; pigs: 18 mln.; sheep: 24.8 mln. **Fish catch** (1992): 895,000 metric tons. **Electricity prod.** (1992): 157 bln. kWh. **Labor force:** 14% agric.; 24% ind.; 53% serv.

Finance: Monetary unit: Peseta (May 1995: 120.72 = $1 US). **Gross domestic product** (1993): $498 bln.* **Per capita GDP:** $12,700. **Imports** (1993): $92.5 bln.; partners: EU 61%, U.S. 7%. **Exports** (1993): $72.8 bln.; partners: EU 71%, U.S. 5%. **Tourism** (1992): $22.1 bln. **National budget** (1993 est.): $128 bln. **International reserves less gold** (May 1995): $33.3 bln. **Gold:** 15.62 mln. oz t. **Consumer prices** (change in 1994): 4.7%.

Transport: Railroads: Length: 8,109 mi. **Motor vehicles:** in use: 13.1 mln. passenger cars, 2.7 mln. comm. vehicles.

Civil aviation: 16.6 bln. passenger-mi.; 23 airports with scheduled flights. **Chief ports:** Barcelona, Bilbao, Valencia, Cartagena, Gijon.

Communications: Television sets: 1 per 2.3 persons. **Radios:** 1 per 3.1 persons. **Telephones:** 1 per 2.5 persons. **Daily newspaper circ.:** 82 per 1,000 pop.

Health: Life expectancy at birth (1995): 75 male; 81 female. **Births** (per 1,000 pop.): 11. **Deaths** (per 1,000 pop.): 9. **Natural increase:** 0.2%. **Hospital beds:** 1 per 234 persons. **Physicians:** 1 per 257 persons. **Infant mortality** (per 1,000 live births 1995): 7.

Education: Literacy (1991): 97%. **Years compulsory:** to age 16.

Major International Organizations: UN and all of its specialized agencies, NATO, OECD, EU.

Embassy: 2700 15th St. NW 20009; 265-0190.

Spain was settled by Iberians, Basques, and Celts, partly overrun by Carthaginians, conquered by Rome c. 200 BC. The Visigoths, in power by the 5th century AD, adopted Christianity but by 711 AD lost to the Islamic invasion from Africa. Christian reconquest from the N led to a Spanish nationalism. In 1469 the kingdoms of Aragon and Castile were united by the marriage of Ferdinand II and Isabella I, and the last Moorish power was broken by the fall of the kingdom of Granada, 1492.

Spain obtained a colonial empire with the discovery of America by Columbus, 1492, the conquest of Mexico by Cortes, and Peru by Pizarro. It also controlled the Netherlands and parts of Italy and Germany. Spain lost its American colonies in the early 19th century. It lost Cuba, the Philippines, and Puerto Rico during the Spanish-American War, 1898.

Primo de Rivera became dictator in 1923. King Alfonso XIII revoked the dictatorship, 1930, but was forced to leave the country 1931. A republic was proclaimed which disestablished the church, curtailed its privileges, and secularized education. A conservative reaction occurred 1933 but was followed by a Popular Front (1936-1939) composed of socialists, Communists, republicans, and anarchists.

Army officers under Francisco Franco revolted against the government, 1936. In a destructive 3-year war, in which some one million died, Franco received massive help and troops from Italy and Germany, while the USSR, France, and Mexico supported the republic. War ended Mar. 28, 1939. Franco was named caudillo, leader of the nation. Spain was neutral in World War II, but its relations with fascist countries caused its exclusion from the UN until 1955.

In July 1969, Franco and the Cortes (Parliament) designated Prince Juan Carlos as the future king and chief of state. After Franco's death, Nov. 20, 1975, Juan Carlos was sworn in as king. He presided over the formal dissolution of the institutions of the Franco regime. In free elections June 1977, moderates and democratic socialists emerged as the largest parties.

In 1981 a coup attempt by right-wing military officers was thwarted by the king. The Socialist Workers' Party, under Felipe González Márquez, won 4 consecutive general elections, from 1982 to 1993, but showed weakness in nationwide municipal elections May 28, 1995.

Catalonia and the Basque country were granted autonomy, Jan. 1980, following overwhelming approval in home-rule referendums. Basque extremists, however, have continued their campaign for independence.

The **Balearic Islands** in the western Mediterranean, 1,935 sq. mi., are a province of Spain; they include **Majorca** (Mallorca), with the capital, Palma; **Minorca, Cabrera, Ibiza** and **Formentera.** The **Canary Islands,** 2,807 sq. mi., in the Atlantic W of Morocco, form 2 provinces, including the islands of **Tenerife, Palma, Gomera, Hierro, Grand Canary, Fuerteventura,** and **Lanzarote** with Las Palmas and Santa Cruz thriving ports. **Ceuta** and **Melilla,** small enclaves on Morocco's Mediterranean coast, are part of Metropolitan Spain.

Spain has sought the return of Gibraltar, in British hands since 1704.

Sri Lanka
Democratic Socialist Republic of Sri Lanka
Sri Lanka Prajathanthrika Samajavadi Janarajaya

People: Population: 18,342,660. **Age distrib.** (%): <15: 35; 65+: 4. **Pop. density:** 724 per sq. mi. **Urban:** 22%. **Ethnic**
groups: Sinhalese 74%, Tamil 18%, Moor 7%. **Principal languages:** Sinhalese (official), Tamil. **Religions:** Buddhist 69%, Hindu 15%, Christian 8%, Muslim 8%.

Geography: Area: 25,332 sq. mi. **Location:** In Indian O. off SE coast of India. **Neighbors:** India on NW. **Topography:** The coastal area and the northern half are flat; the S-central area is hilly and mountainous. **Capital:** Colombo (1990): 615,000.

Government: Type: Republic. **Head of state:** Pres. Chandrika Bandaranaike Kumaratunga; b June 29, 1945; in office: Nov. 12, 1994. **Head of government:** Prime Min. Sirimavo Bandaranaike; b Apr. 17, 1916; in office: Nov. 14, 1994. **Local divisions:** 9 provinces, 25 districts. **Defense:** 4.7% of GDP (1992). **Active troop strength:** 126,000.

Economy: Industries: Clothing, milling, chemicals, textiles. **Chief crops:** Tea, coconuts, rice. **Minerals:** Graphite, limestone, gems, phosphates. **Other resources:** Forests, rubber. **Arable land:** 16%. **Livestock** (1993): cattle: 1.6 mln. **Fish catch** (1991): 198,000 metric tons. **Electricity prod.** (1992): 3.6 bln. kWh. **Labor force:** 46% agric.; 13% mining & manuf.

Finance: Monetary unit: Rupee (May 1995: 50 = $1 US). **Gross domestic product** (1993): $53.5 bln.* **Per capita GDP:** $3,000. **Imports** (1992): $3.0 bln.; partners: Japan 15%, UK 7%. **Exports** (1992): $2.3 bln.; partners: U.S. 22%, UK 7%. **Tourism** (1992): $199 mln. **National budget** (1992): $3.6 bln. **International reserves less gold** (May 1995): $2.1 bln. **Gold:** 145,000 oz t. **Consumer prices** (change in 1994): 8.4%.

Transport: Railroads: Length: 887 mi. **Motor vehicles:** in use: 189,000 passenger cars, 154,000 comm. vehicles. **Civil aviation:** 2.3 bln. passenger-mi.; 1 airport. **Chief ports:** Colombo, Trincomalee, Galle.

Communications: Television sets: 1 per 25 persons. **Radios:** 1 per 8.0 persons. **Telephones:** 1 per 92 persons.

Health: Life expectancy at birth (1995): 70 male; 75 female. **Births** (per 1,000 pop.): 18. **Deaths** (per 1,000 pop.): 6. **Natural increase:** 1.2%. **Hospital beds:** 1 per 362 persons. **Physicians:** 1 per 5,203 persons. **Infant mortality** (per 1,000 live births 1995): 21.

Education: Literacy (1991): 87%. **Years compulsory:** to age 12; attendance 98%.

Major International Organizations: UN (World Bank, WTO, IMF), the Commonwealth.

Embassy: 2148 Wyoming Ave. NW 20008; 483-4025.

The island was known to the ancient world as Taprobane (Greek for copper-colored) and later as Serendip (from Arabic). Colonists from northern India subdued the indigenous Veddahs about 543 BC; their descendants, the Buddhist Sinhalese, still form most of the population. Hindu descendants of Tamil immigrants from southern India account for one-fifth of the population. Parts were occupied by the Portuguese in 1505 and by the Dutch in 1658. The British seized the island in 1796. As Ceylon it became an independent member of the Commonwealth in 1948. On May 22, 1972, Ceylon became the Republic of Sri Lanka.

Prime Min. W. R. D. Bandaranaike was assassinated Sept. 25, 1959. In new elections, the Freedom Party was victorious under Mrs. Sirimavo Bandaranaike, widow of the former prime minister.

After May 1970 elections, Mrs. Bandaranaike became prime minister again. In 1971 the nation suffered economic problems and terrorist activities by ultra-leftists, thousands of whom were executed. Massive land reform and nationalization of foreign-owned plantations was undertaken in the mid-1970s. Mrs. Bandaranaike was ousted in 1977 elections. The powers of the presidency were increased in 1978 in an effort to restore stability.

Tension between the Sinhalese and Tamil separatists erupted into violence repeatedly in the 1980s. In 1987, hundreds died in an attack by Tamil rebels Apr. 17. Sri Lankan government forces retaliated in June with attacks on the rebel-held Jaffna peninsula. Over 35,000 have died in the civil war, which continued in the 1990s. Pres. Ranasinghe Premadasa was assassinated May 1, 1993, by a Tamil rebel.

Mrs. Bandaranaike's daughter, Chandrika Bandaranaike Kumaratunga, became prime minister after the Aug. 16, 1994, general elections. Elected president Nov. 9, Kumaratunga appointed her mother prime minister.

Sudan

Republic of the Sudan

Jamhuryat as-Sudan

People: Population: 30,120,420. **Age distrib.** (%): <15: 35; 65+: 4. **Pop. density:** 31 per sq. mi. **Urban:** 27%. **Ethnic groups:** black 52%, Arab 39%, Beja 6%. **Principal languages:** Arabic (official), Dinka, Nubian, Nuer, Beja, others. **Religions:** Sunni Muslim 70%, indigenous beliefs 25%, Christians 5%.

Geography: Area: 966,757 sq. mi., the largest country in Africa. **Location:** At the E end of Sahara desert zone. **Neighbors:** Egypt on N, Libya, Chad, Central African Republic on W, Zaire, Uganda, Kenya on S, Ethiopia and Eritrea on E. **Topography:** The N consists of the Libyan Desert in the W, and the mountainous Nubia Desert in E, with narrow Nile valley between. The center contains large, fertile, rainy areas with fields, pasture, and forest. The S has rich soil, heavy rain. **Capitals:** Khartoum (executive), Omdurman (legislative). **Cities** (1983 est.): Omdurman 526,000; Khartoum 476,000; North Khartoum 341,000; Port Sudan 206,000.

Government: Type: Military. **Head of state and government:** Pres. Gen. Omar Hassan Ahmad Al-Bashir; in office: June 30, 1989. **Local divisions:** 9 states. **Defense:** 8.6% of GNP (1991). **Active troop strength:** 118,500.

Economy: Industries: Textiles, food processing. **Chief crops:** Gum arabic, sorghum, cotton (main export), wheat. **Minerals:** Chromium, copper. **Crude oil reserves** (1994): 300 mln. bbls. **Arable land:** 5%. **Livestock** (1992): cattle: 21.6 mln.; sheep: 22.6 mln.; goats: 18.7 mln. **Electricity prod.** (1991): 905 mln. kWh. **Labor force:** 80% agric.; 10% ind., comm.

Finance: Monetary unit: Pound (May 1995: 521 = $1 US). **Gross domestic product** (1993): $21.5 bln.* **Per capita GDP:** $750. **Imports** (1993): $1.1 bln.; partners: EU 32%, U.S. 13%. **Exports** (1993): $350 mln.; partners: EU 46%. **National budget** (1993): $1.2 bln. **International reserves less gold** (Mar. 1995): $78 mln. **Consumer prices** (change in 1993): 101.4%.

Transport: Railroads: Length: 2,960 mi. **Motor vehicles:** in use: 116,000 passenger cars, 57,000 comm. vehicles. **Civil aviation:** 360 mln. passenger-mi.; 12 airports with scheduled flights. **Chief port:** Port Sudan.

Communications: Television sets: 1 per 100 persons. **Radios:** 1 per 3.3 persons. **Telephones:** 1 per 269 persons. **Daily newspaper circ.:** 24 per 1,000 pop.

Health: Life expectancy at birth (1995): 54 male; 56 female. **Births** (per 1,000 pop.): 41. **Deaths** (per 1,000 pop.): 12. **Natural increase:** 3.0%. **Hospital beds:** 1 per 1,222 persons. **Physicians:** 1 per 9,439 persons. **Infant mortality** (per 1,000 live births 1995): 78.

Education: Literacy (1992): 27%. **Years compulsory:** 9; attendance 50%.

Major International Organizations: UN (IMF, WHO, FAO), Arab League, OAU.

Embassy: 2210 Massachusetts Ave. NW 20008; 338-8565.

Northern Sudan, ancient Nubia, was settled by Egyptians in antiquity, and was converted to Coptic Christianity in the 6th century. Arab conquests brought Islam in the 15th century.

In the 1820s Egypt took over Sudan, defeating the last of earlier empires, including the Fung. In the 1880s a revolution was led by Mohammed Ahmed, who called himself the Mahdi (leader of the faithful), and his followers, the dervishes.

In 1898 an Anglo-Egyptian force crushed the Mahdi's successors. In 1951 the Egyptian Parliament abrogated its 1899 and 1936 treaties with Great Britain and amended its constitution to provide for a separate Sudanese constitution. Sudan voted for complete independence as a parliamentary government effective Jan. 1, 1956.

In 1969, a Revolutionary Council took power, but a civilian premier and cabinet were appointed; the government announced it would create a socialist state. The northern 12 provinces are predominantly Arab-Muslim and have been dominant in the central government. The 3 southern provinces are populated largely by black Christians and animists. The 2 halves of the nation began a civil war in 1988.

Economic problems plagued the nation in the 1980s and 1990s, aggravated by continuing civil war and influxes of refugees from neighboring countries. After 16 years in power, Pres. Jaafar al-Nimeiry was overthrown in a bloodless military coup,

Apr. 6, 1985. Sudan held its first democratic parliamentary elections in 18 years in 1986, but the elected government was overthrown in a bloodless coup June 30, 1989.

Close to 300,000 people died as a result of drought and famine in 1988. Sudan agreed to allow large-scale UN relief efforts in 1991, as millions were threatened with famine. The UN suspended aid to southern Sudan in 1992 because of the fighting. In 1993, Amnesty International accused Sudan of practicing "ethnic cleansing" against the Nuba people in the South, and Sudan was among several countries cited for human rights violations by the UN Human Rights Commission Mar. 9, 1994. Egypt publicly blamed Sudan for an attempted assassination of Egyptian President Hosni Mubarak in Ethiopia, June 26, 1995.

Suriname

Republic of Suriname

Republiek Suriname

People: Population: 429,544. **Pop. density:** 7 per sq. mi. **Urban:** 49%. **Ethnic groups:** Hindustani 37%, Creole 31%, Javanese 15%. **Principal languages:** Dutch (official), Sranan Tonga, English. **Religions:** Christian 48%, Hindu 27%, Muslim 20%.

Geography: Area: 63,251 sq. mi. **Location:** On N shore of South America. **Neighbors:** Guyana on W, Brazil on S, French Guiana on E. **Topography:** A flat Atlantic coast, where dikes permit agriculture. Inland is a forest belt; to the S, largely unexplored hills cover 75% of the country. **Capital:** Paramaribo (1993): 201,000.

Government: Type: Republic. **Head of state:** Pres. Roland Venetiaan; b 1936; in office: Sept. 16, 1991. **Head of government:** Prime Min. Jules Adjodhia; in office: Sept. 16, 1991. **Local divisions:** 10 districts. **Defense: Active troop strength:** 1,800.

Economy: Industries: Aluminum. **Chief crops:** Rice, bananas, fruits. **Minerals:** Bauxite. **Other resources:** Forests, shrimp. **Arable land:** 0%. **Electricity prod.** (1992): 2.0 bln. kWh.

Finance: Monetary unit: Guilder (Apr. 1995: 492 = $1 US). **Gross domestic product** (1993): $1.17 bln.* **Per capita GDP:** $2,800. **Imports** (1993): $250 mln.; partners: U.S. 42%, Netherlands 22%, Trin./Tob. 10%. **Exports** (1993): $290 mln.; partners: Norway 33%, U.S. 13%, Netherlands 26%. **Tourism** (1992): $11 mln. **National budget** (1990): $716 mln. **Gold:** 54,000 oz t.

Transport: Motor vehicles: in use: 43,000 passenger cars, 16,000 comm. vehicles. **Chief ports:** Paramaribo, Nieuw-Nickerie.

Communications: Television sets: 1 per 9.7 persons. **Radios:** 1 per 1.7 persons. **Telephones:** 1 per 6.5 persons. **Daily newspaper circ.:** 95 per 1,000 pop.

Health: Life expectancy at birth (1995): 67 male; 72 female. **Births** (per 1,000 pop.): 25. **Deaths** (per 1,000 pop.): 6. **Natural increase:** 1.9%. **Infant mortality** (per 1,000 live births 1995): 30.

Education: Literacy (1992): 95%. **Years compulsory:** ages 6–12.

Major International Organizations: UN (WHO, WTO, ILO, FAO, World Bank, IMF), OAS.

Embassy: 4301 Connecticut Ave. NW 20008; 244-7488.

The Netherlands acquired Suriname in 1667 from Britain, in exchange for New Netherlands (New York). The 1954 Dutch constitution raised the colony to a level of equality with the Netherlands and the Netherlands Antilles. Independence was granted Nov. 25, 1975, despite objections from East Indians. Some 40% of the population (mostly East Indians) emigrated to the Netherlands in the months before independence.

The National Military Council took over control of the government, Feb. 1982. Civilian rule was restored in 1987, but political turmoil continued for another 5 years, disrupting the nation's economy.

Swaziland

Kingdom of Swaziland

People: Population: 966,977. **Age distrib.** (%): <15: 46; 65+: 2. **Pop. density:** 144 per sq. mi. **Urban:** 30%. **Ethnic**

groups: African 97%, European 3%. **Principal languages:** siSwati, English (both official). **Religions:** Christians 60%, indigenous beliefs 40%.

Geography: Area: 6,704 sq. mi. **Location:** In southern Africa, near Indian O. coast. **Neighbors:** South Africa on N, W, S, Mozambique on E. **Topography:** The country descends from W-E in broad belts, becoming more arid in the low veld region, then rising to a plateau in the E. **Capital:** Mbabane. **Cities** (1990 est.): Manzini 53,000; Mbabane 47,000.

Government: Type: Constitutional monarchy. **Head of state:** King Mswati 3d; b 1968; in office: Apr. 25, 1986. **Head of government:** Prime Min. Prince Jameson Mbilini Dlamini; in office: Feb. 16, 1994. **Local divisions:** 4 districts.

Economy: Industries: Wood pulp. **Chief crops:** Sugar, corn, cotton, rice, pineapples, sugar, citrus fruits. **Minerals:** Asbestos, clay, coal. **Other resources:** Forests. **Arable land:** 8%. **Electricity prod.** (1991): 198 mln. kWh. **Labor force:** 36% agric.; 20% community & social services.

Finance: Monetary unit: Lilangeni (May 1995: 1.00 = $.27 US). **Gross domestic product** (1993): $2.3 bln.* **Per capita GDP:** $2,500. **Imports** (1993): $734 mln.; partners: South Africa, 90%. **Exports** (1993): $632 mln.; partners: South Africa 50%. **Tourism** (1992): $32 mln. **National budget** (1994 est.): $410 mln. **International reserves less gold** (May 1995): $235 mln. **Consumer prices** (change in 1994): 14.3%.

Transport: Motor vehicles: in use: 25,000 passenger cars, 7,000 comm. vehicles.

Communications: Radios: 1 per 13 persons. **Telephones:** 1 per 32 persons.

Health: Life expectancy at birth (1995): 53 male; 61 female. **Births** (per 1,000 pop.): 43. **Deaths** (per 1,000 pop.): 11. **Natural increase:** 3.2%. **Infant mortality rate** (per 1,000 live births 1995): 91.

Education: Literacy (1991): 67%. 82% attend primary school.

Major International Organizations: UN (IMF, WTO, WHO, FAO), OAU, the Commonwealth.

Embassy: 3400 International Dr. NW 20008; 362-6683.

The royal house of Swaziland traces back 400 years, and is one of Africa's last ruling dynasties. The Swazis, a Bantu people, were driven to Swaziland from lands to the N by the Zulus in 1820. Their autonomy was later guaranteed by Britain and Transvaal, with Britain assuming control after 1903. Independence came Sept. 6, 1968. In 1973 the king repealed the constitution and assumed full powers.

A new constitution banning political parties took effect Oct. 13, 1978. Swaziland was moving toward a multiparty system in the 1990s.

Sweden
Kingdom of Sweden
Konungariket Sverige

People: Population: 8,821,759. **Age distrib.** (%): <15: 19; 65+: 18. **Pop. density:** 51 per sq. mi. **Urban:** 83%. **Ethnic groups:** Swedish 90%, Finnish 2%, Lapps, European immigrants. **Principal languages:** Swedish. **Religions:** Evangelical Lutheran (official) 94%.

Geography: Area: 173,732 sq. mi. **Location:** On Scandinavian Peninsula in N Europe. **Neighbors:** Norway on W, Denmark on S (across Kattegat), Finland on E. **Topography:** Mountains along NW border cover 25% of Sweden, flat or rolling terrain covers the central and southern areas, which include several large lakes. **Capital:** Stockholm. **Cities** (1994): Stockholm 693,000; Göteborg 437,000; Malmö 237,000.

Government: Type: Constitutional monarchy. **Head of state:** King Carl XVI Gustaf; b Apr. 30, 1946; in office: Sept. 19, 1973. **Head of government:** Prime Min. Ingvar Carlsson; b Nov. 9, 1934; in office: Oct. 7, 1994. **Local divisions:** 24 provinces. **Defense:** 3.8% of GDP (1993). **Active troop strength:** 64,000.

Economy: Industries: Steel, machinery, instruments, autos, shipbuilding, shipping, paper. **Chief crops:** Grains, potatoes, sugar beets. **Minerals:** Zinc, iron, lead, copper, silver. **Other resources:** Forests (half the country); yield one-fourth exports. **Arable land:** 7%. **Livestock** (1993): cattle: 1.8 mln.; pigs: 2.3 mln. **Fish catch** (1993): 334,000 metric tons. **Electricity prod.** (1992): 142 bln. kWh. **Labor force:** 3% agric.; 21% manuf. & mining; 38% social services.

Finance: Monetary unit: Krona (May 1995: 7.23 = $1 US). **Gross domestic product** (1993): $153.7 bln.* **Per capita**

GDP: $17,600. **Imports** (1993): $42.3 bln.; partners: EU 54%; U.S. 8%. **Exports** (1993): $49.7 bln.; partners: EU 56%, U.S. 8%. **Tourism** (1992): $3.1 bln. **National budget** (1994): $73.1 bln. **International reserves less gold** (Mar. 1995): $24.5 bln. **Gold:** 6.07 mln. oz t. **Consumer prices** (change in 1994): 2.2%.

Transport: Railroads: Length: 6,863 mi. **Motor vehicles:** in use: 3.6 mln. passenger cars, 316,000 comm. vehicles. **Civil aviation:** 5.0 bln. passenger-mi.; 45 airports. **Chief ports:** Göteborg, Stockholm, Malmö.

Communications: Television sets: 1 per 2.3 persons. **Radios:** 1 per 1.2 persons. **Telephones:** 1 per 1.1 persons. **Daily newspaper circ.:** 533 per 1,000 pop.

Health: Life expectancy at birth (1995): 76 male; 81 female. **Births** (per 1,000 pop.): 13. **Deaths** (per 1,000 pop.): 11. **Natural increase:** 0.2%. **Hospital beds:** 1 per 177 persons. **Physicians:** 1 per 394 persons. **Infant mortality** (per 1,000 live births (1995): 6.

Education: Literacy (1994): 100%. **Years compulsory:** 12; attendance 100%.

Major International Organizations: UN and all of its specialized agencies, EU, OECD.

Embassy: 600 New Hampshire Ave. NW 20037; 944-5600.

The Swedes have lived in present-day Sweden for at least 5,000 years, longer than nearly any other European people. Gothic tribes from Sweden played a major role in the disintegration of the Roman Empire. Other Swedes helped create the first Russian state in the 9th century.

The Swedes were Christianized from the 11th century, and a strong centralized monarchy developed. A parliament, the Riksdag, was first called in 1435, the earliest parliament on the European continent, with all classes of society represented.

Swedish independence from rule by Danish kings (dating from 1397) was secured by Gustavus I in a revolt, 1521-23; he built up the government and military and established the Lutheran Church. In the 17th century Sweden was a major European power, gaining most of the Baltic seacoast, but its international position subsequently declined.

The Napoleonic wars, in which Sweden acquired Norway (it became independent 1905), were the last in which Sweden participated. Armed neutrality was maintained in both world wars.

Over 4 decades of Social Democratic rule ended in the 1976 parliamentary elections; the party returned to power in the 1982 elections. After Prime Min. Olof Palme was shot to death in Stockholm, Feb. 28, 1986, Ingvar Carlsson took office. Carl Bildt, a non-Socialist, became prime minister Oct. 1991, with a mandate to restore Sweden's economic competitiveness. The Social Democrats returned to power following 1994 elections. Swedish voters approved membership in the European Union Nov. 13, 1994, and Sweden entered the EU as of Jan. 1, 1995.

Switzerland
Swiss Confederation

People: Population: 7,084,984. **Age distrib.** (%): <15: 16; 65+: 15. **Pop. density:** 444 per sq. mi. **Urban:** 68%. **Ethnic groups:** mixed European stock. **Principal languages:** German, French, Italian (all official). **Religions:** Roman Catholic 48%, Protestant 44%.

Geography: Area: 15,940 sq. mi. **Location:** In the Alps Mts. in central Europe. **Neighbors:** France on W, Italy on S, Austria on E, Germany on N. **Topography:** The Alps cover 60% of the land area; the Jura, near France, 10%. Running between, from NE to SW, are midlands, 30%. **Capitals:** Bern (administrative), Lausanne (judicial). **Cities** (1993): Zurich 345,000; Basel 175,000; Geneva 170,000; Bern 130,000.

Government: Type: Federal republic. **Head of government:** The president is elected by the Federal Assembly to a nonrenewable 1-year term. **Local divisions:** 20 full cantons, 6 half cantons. **Defense:** 1.7% of GDP (1993 est.). **Active troop strength:** 1,800.

Economy: Industries: Machinery, machine tools, steel, instruments, watches, textiles, foodstuffs (cheese, chocolate), banking, tourism. **Chief crops:** Dairy products. **Minerals:** Salt. **Other resources:** Hydropower potential. **Arable land:** 10%. **Livestock** (1992): cattle: 1.8 mln.; pigs: 1.7 mln. **Electricity prod.** (1992): 56 bln. kWh. **Labor force:** 33% ind. and crafts; 6% agric.; 50% serv.

Finance: Monetary unit: Franc (May 1995: 1.14 = $1 US). **Gross domestic product** (1993): $149.1 bln.* **Per capita GDP:** $21,300. **Imports** (1993): $60.7 bln.; partners: EU 72%. **Exports** (1993): $63.0 bln.; partners: EU 56%; U.S. 9%. **Tourism** (1992): $7.6 bln. **National budget** (1993): $26.9 bln. **International reserves less gold** (May 1995): $31.9 bln. **Gold:** 83.28 mln. oz t. **Consumer prices** (change in 1994): 0.8%.

Transport: Railroads: Length: 3,125 mi. **Motor vehicles:** in use: 3.1 mln. passenger cars, 291,000 comm. vehicles. **Civil aviation:** 10.0 bln. passenger-mi.; 6 airports with scheduled flights.

Communications: Television sets: 1 per 3.0 persons. **Radios:** 1 per 2.6 persons. **Telephones:** 1 per 1.1 persons. **Daily newspaper circ.:** 463 per 1,000 pop.

Health: Life expectancy at birth (1995): 75 male; 82 female. **Births** (per 1,000 pop.): 12. **Deaths** (per 1,000 pop.): 9. **Natural increase:** 0.3%. **Physicians:** 1 per 311 persons. **Infant mortality** (per 1,000 live births 1995): 6.

Education: Literacy (1993): 100%. **Years compulsory:** 9; attendance 100%.

Major International Organizations: Many UN specialized agencies (though not a member), EFTA, OECD. **Embassy:** 2900 Cathedral Ave. NW 20008; 745-7900.

Switzerland, the Roman province of Helvetia, is a federation of 23 cantons (20 full cantons and 6 half cantons), 3 of which in 1291 created a defensive league and later were joined by other districts. Voters in the French-speaking part of Canton Bern voted for self-government, 1978; Canton Jura was created Jan. 1, 1979.

In 1648 the Swiss Confederation obtained its independence from the Holy Roman Empire. The cantons were joined under a federal constitution in 1848, with large powers of local control retained by each canton.

Switzerland has maintained an armed neutrality since 1815, and has not been involved in a foreign war since 1515. It is the seat of many UN and other international agencies.

Switzerland is a leading world banking center; stability of the currency brings funds from many quarters. The nation's famed secret bank accounts were phased out in 1992.

Syria
Syrian Arab Republic
al-Jumhuriyah al-Arabiyah as-Suriyah

People: Population: 15,451,917. **Age distrib.** (%): <15: 49; 65+: 4. **Pop. density:** 216 per sq. mi. **Urban:** 51%. **Ethnic groups:** Arab 90%, Kurd, Armenian, others. **Principal languages:** Arabic (official), Kurdish, Armenian. **Religions:** Sunni Muslim 74%, other Muslim 16%, Christian 10%.

Geography: Area: 71,498 sq. mi. **Location:** At E end of Mediterranean Sea. **Neighbors:** Lebanon, Israel on W, Jordan on S, Iraq on E, Turkey on N. **Topography:** Syria has a short Mediterranean coastline, then stretches E and S with fertile lowlands and plains, alternating with mountains and large desert areas. **Capital:** Damascus. **Cities** (1993 est.): Damascus 1.5 mln.; Aleppo 1.5 mln.; Homs 537,000.

Government: Type: Republic (under military regime). **Head of state:** Pres. Hafez al-Assad; b Mar. 1930; in office: Feb. 22, 1971. **Head of government:** Prime Min. Mahmoud Zuabi; in office: Nov. 1, 1987. **Local divisions:** Damascus and 13 provinces. **Defense:** 6% of GDP (1992). **Active troop strength:** 408,000.

Economy: Industries: Oil products, textiles, tobacco, glassware, brassware. **Chief crops:** Cotton, grain, olives, lentils, chickpeas. **Minerals:** Oil, phosphates, gypsum. **Crude oil reserves** (1994): 1.7 bln. bbls. **Other resources:** Wool. **Arable land:** 28%. **Livestock** (1993): sheep: 16 mln., goats: 950,000. **Electricity prod.** (1992): 11.9 bln. kWh. **Labor force:** 32% agric.; 32% ind. & constr.; 36% services.

Finance: Monetary unit: Pound (May 1995: 11.22 = $1 US). **Gross domestic product** (1993): $81.7 bln.* **Per capita GDP:** $5,700. **Imports** (1993): $4.1 bln.; partners: EU 37%. **Exports** (1993): $3.4 bln.; partners: EU 48%. **Tourism** (1992): $600 mln. **National budget** (1993): $9.5 bln. **Gold:** 833,000 oz t. **Consumer prices** (change in 1993): 11.8%.

Transport: Railroads: Length: 1,097 mi. **Motor vehicles:** in use: 118,000 passenger cars, 153,000 comm. vehicles. **Civil**

aviation: 719 mln. passenger-mi.; 5 airports with scheduled flights. **Chief ports:** Latakia, Tartus.

Communications: Television sets: 1 per 19 persons. **Radios:** 1 per 4.5 persons. **Telephones:** 1 per 18 persons. **Daily newspaper circ.:** 22 per 1,000 pop.

Health: Life expectancy at birth (1995): 66 male; 68 female. **Births** (per 1,000 pop.): 43. **Deaths** (per 1,000 pop.): 6. **Natural increase:** 3.7%. **Hospital beds:** 1 per 891 persons. **Physicians:** 1 per 1,037 persons. **Infant mortality** (per 1,000 live births 1995): 41.

Education: Literacy (1992): 64%. **Years compulsory:** 6; attendance: 94%.

Major International Organizations: UN (IMF, WHO, FAO), Arab League.

Embassy: 2215 Wyoming Ave. NW 20008; 232-6313.

Syria contains some of the most ancient remains of civilization. It was the center of the Seleucid empire, but later became absorbed in the Roman and Arab empires. Ottoman rule prevailed for 4 centuries, until the end of World War I.

The state of Syria was formed from former Turkish districts, separated by the Treaty of Sevres, 1920, and divided into the states of Syria and Greater Lebanon. Both were administered under a French League of Nations mandate 1920-1941.

Syria was proclaimed a republic by the occupying French Sept. 16, 1941, and exercised full independence effective Apr. 17, 1946. Syria joined in the Arab invasion of Israel in 1948. Syria joined Egypt Feb. 1958 in the United Arab Republic but seceded Sept. 1961. The Socialist Baath party and military leaders seized power Mar. 1963. The Baath, a pan-Arab organization, became the only legal party. The government has been dominated by members of the minority Alawite sect.

In the Arab-Israeli war of June 1967, Israel seized and occupied the Golan Heights area inside Syria, from which Israeli settlements had for years been shelled by Syria. On Oct. 6, 1973, Syria joined Egypt in an attack on Israel. Arab oil states agreed in 1974 to give Syria $1 billion a year to aid anti-Israel moves. Some 30,000 Syrian troops entered Lebanon in 1976 to mediate in a civil war. They fought Palestinian guerrillas and, later, Christian militiamen. Syrian troops again battled Christian forces in Lebanon, Apr. 1981, ending a cease-fire that had been in place.

Following the June 6, 1982 Israeli invasion of Lebanon, Israeli planes destroyed 17 Syrian antiaircraft missile batteries in the Bekka Valley, June 9. Some 25 Syrian planes were downed during the engagement. Israel and Syria agreed to a cease-fire June 11. In 1983, Syria backed the PLO rebels who ousted Yasir Arafat's forces from Tripoli.

Syria's role in promoting international terrorism led to the breaking of diplomatic relations with Great Britain and to limited sanctions by the European Community in 1986.

Syria condemned the Aug. 1990 Iraqi invasion of Kuwait and sent troops to help Allied forces in the Gulf War. In 1991, Syria accepted U.S. proposals for the terms of an Arab-Israeli peace conference. Syria subsequently participated in peace negotiations with Israel. In Jan. 1994, Syria held out the prospect that the 2 countries might normalize relations.

Taiwan
Republic of China
Chung-hua Min-kuo

People: Population: 21,500,583. **Age distrib.** (%): <15: 25; 65+: 7. **Pop. density:** 1,539 per sq. mi. **Urban:** 75%. **Ethnic groups:** Taiwanese 84%, Chinese 14%. **Principal languages:** Mandarin Chinese (official), Taiwanese, Hakka dialects. **Religions:** Buddhism, Taoism, Confucianism prevail.

Geography: Area: 13,969 sq. mi. **Location:** Off SE coast of China, between East and South China seas. **Neighbors:** Nearest is China. **Topography:** A mountain range forms the backbone of the island; the eastern half is very steep and craggy, the western slope is flat, fertile, and well cultivated. **Capital:** Taipei. **Cities** (1993): Taipei 2.7 mln.; Kaohsiung 1.4 mln.; Taichung 805,000; Tainan 698,000.

Government: Type: Democracy. **Head of state and Nationalist Party chmn.:** Pres. Lee Teng-hui; b Jan. 15, 1923; in office: Jan. 13, 1988. **Head of government:** Prime Min. Lien Chan; b 1936; in office: Feb. 10, 1993. **Local divisions:** 16 counties, 5 municipalities, Taipei & Kaohsiung. **Defense:** 5.4%

of GNP (FY 1993-94 est.). **Active troop strength:** 425,000.

Economy: Industries: Textiles, clothing, electronics, processed foods, chemicals, clothing. **Chief crops:** vegetables, rice, fruit, tea, sugarcane. **Minerals:** Coal, limestone, marble. **Arable land:** 24%. **Livestock** (1993): pigs: 9.8 mln. **Fish catch** (1993): 1.2 mln. metric tons. **Electricity prod.** (1992): 98.5 bln. kWh. **Labor force:** 16% agric.; 53% ind. & comm.; 22% services.

Finance: Monetary unit: New Taiwan Dollar (Oct. 1994: 26.16 = $1 US). **Gross domestic product** (1993): $224 bln.* **Per capita GNP:** $10,600. **Imports** (1993): $77.1 bln.; partners: U.S. 22%, Japan 30%. **Exports** (1993): $85 bln.; partners: U.S. 28%, EU 15%, Hong Kong 22%. **Tourism** (1990): $1.7 bln. **National budget** (1991): $30.1 bln.

Transport: Motor vehicles: in use: 3.4 mln. passenger cars, 791,000 commercial vehicles. **Civil aviation:** 17.5 bln. passenger-mi.; 12 airports. **Chief ports:** Kaohsiung, Keelung, Hualien, Taichung.

Communications: Television sets: 1 per 3.1 persons. **Radios:** 1 per 1.5 persons. **Telephones:** 1 per 2.4 persons. **Daily newspaper circ.:** 202 per 1,000 pop.

Health: Life expectancy at birth (1995): 72 male; 79 female. **Births** (per 1,000 pop.): 15. **Deaths** (per 1,000 pop.): 6. **Natural increase:** 1.0%. **Hospital beds:** 1 per 215 persons. **Physicians:** 1 per 829 persons. **Infant mortality** (per 1,000 live births 1995): 6.

Education: Literacy (1994): 93%. **Years compulsory:** 9; attendance 99%.

Large-scale Chinese immigration began in the 17th century. The island came under mainland control after an interval of Dutch rule, 1620-62. Taiwan (also called Formosa) was ruled by Japan 1895-1945. Two million Kuomintang supporters fled to Taiwan in 1949. Both the Taipei and Beijing governments consider Taiwan an integral part of China. Taiwan has rejected Beijing's efforts at reunification, but unofficial dealings with the mainland have grown more flexible.

The U.S., upon its recognition of the People's Republic of China, Dec. 15, 1978, severed diplomatic ties with Taiwan. It maintains the unofficial American Institute in Taiwan, while Taiwan has established the Coordination Council for North American Affairs in Washington, DC.

Land reform, government planning, U.S. aid and investment, and free universal education have brought huge advances in industry, agriculture, and mass living standards. In 1987, martial law was lifted after 38 years, and in 1991, the 43-year period of emergency rule ended. The ruling Nationalist Party has faced increasing challenge from opposition parties.

Taiwan has one of the world's strongest economies and is among the 10 leading capital exporters.

The Penghu (Pescadores), 50 sq. mi., pop. 120,000, lie between Taiwan and the mainland. **Quemoy** and **Matsu,** pop. (1990) 70,000 lie just off the mainland.

Tajikistan
Republic of Tajikistan
Jumhurii Tojikiston

People: Population: 6,155,474. **Age distrib.** (%): <15: 43; 65+: 4. **Pop. density:** 111 per sq. mi. **Urban:** 31%. **Ethnic groups:** Tajik 65%, Uzbek 25%, Russian 4%. **Principal languages:** Tajik (official). **Religions:** Sunni Muslim 80%.

Geography: Area: 55,300 sq. mi. **Neighbors:** Uzbekistan and Kyrgyzstan on N and W, China on E, Afghanistan on S and E. **Topography:** Mountainous region that contains the Pamirs, Trans Alai mountain system. **Capital:** Dushanbe (1989 est.): 582,000.

Government: Type: Republic. **Head of state:** Pres. Imomali Rakhmonov; in office: Nov. 16, 1994. **Local divisions:** 2 oblasts, 1 autonomous oblast. **Defense:** 3.7% of GDP (1992). **Active troop strength:** 2-3,000.

Economy: Industries: Textiles, knitwear, mining. **Chief crops:** Cotton, barley, wheat, vegetables. **Minerals:** Coal, lead, zinc. **Arable land:** 6%. **Livestock** (1993): cattle: 1.2 mln.; sheep and goats: 3.3 mln. **Electricity prod.** (1992): 16.8 bln. kWh. **Labor force:** 43% agric.; 24% serv. & govt.

Finance: Monetary unit: Russian Ruble. **Gross domestic product** (1993 est.): $6.9 bln.* **Per capita GDP:** $1,180. **Imports** (1990): 1.3 bln. **Exports** (1990): $706 mln.

Transportation: Railroads: Length: 554 mi. **Civil aviation:**

3.2 bln. passenger-mi.; 1 airport.

Communications: Television sets: 1 per 6.3 persons. **Radios:** 1 per 6.4 persons. **Telephones:** 1 per 19 persons. **Daily newspaper circ.:** 309 per 1,000 pop.

Health: Life expectancy at birth (1995): 66 male; 72 female. **Births** (per 1,000 pop.): 34. **Deaths** (per 1,000 pop.): 7. **Natural increase:** 2.7%. **Hospital beds:** 1 per 93 persons. **Physicians:** 1 per 412 persons. **Infant mortality** (per 1,000 live births 1995): 60.

Major International Organizations: UN, CIS.

There were settled societies in the region from about 3000 BC. Throughout history, the region has undergone invasions by Iranians (Arabs who converted the population to Islam), Mongols, Uzbeks, Afghans, and Russians. In 1924, the Tadzhik ASSR was created within the Uzbek SSR. The Tadzhik SSR was proclaimed in 1929.

Tajikistan declared independence Sept. 9, 1991. It became an independent state when the Soviet Union disbanded Dec. 26, 1991. Conservative Communist Pres. Rakhmon Nabiyev was forced to resign, Sept. 1992, by a coalition of Islamic, nationalist, and Western-oriented parties.

Factional fighting led to the installation of a pro-Communist regime, Jan. 1993. A new constitution establishing a presidential system was approved by referendum Nov. 6, 1994. Muslim rebels, reportedly armed by Afghanistan, continued to fight the regime, which had Russian support.

Tanzania
United Republic of Tanzania
Jamhuri ya Muungano wa Tanzania

People: Population: 28,701,077. **Age distrib.** (%): <15: 47; 65+: 3. **Pop. density:** 79 per sq. mi. **Urban:** 21%. **Ethnic groups:** African. **Principal languages:** Swahili, English (both official), many others. **Religions:** Christians 40%, Muslims 40%, indigenous beliefs 20%.

Geography: Area: 364,017 sq. mi. **Location:** On coast of E Africa. **Neighbors:** Kenya, Uganda on N, Rwanda, Burundi, Zaire on W, Zambia, Malawi, Mozambique on S. **Topography:** Hot, arid central plateau, surrounded by the lake region in the W, temperate highlands in N and S, the coastal plains. Mt. Kilimanjaro, 19,340 ft., is highest in Africa. **Capital:** Dar-es-Salaam. **Cities** (1992 est.): Dar-es-Salaam 1.4 mln.

Government: Type: Republic. **Head of state:** Pres. Ali Hassan Mwinyi; b May 8, 1925; in office: Nov. 5, 1985. **Head of government:** Prime Min. Cleopa Msuya; in office: Dec. 7, 1994. **Local divisions:** 25 regions. **Defense:** 3.9% of GDP (1992). **Active troop strength:** 49,600.

Economy: Industries: Food processing, clothing. **Chief crops:** Sisal, cotton, coffee, tea, tobacco, corn. **Minerals:** Tin, diamonds, gold, nickel. **Other resources:** Pyrethrum (insecticide made from chrysanthemums). **Arable land:** 5%. **Livestock** (1993): cattle: 13.3 mln.; goats: 9.4 mln.; sheep: 3.8 mln. **Fish catch** (1992): 332,000 metric tons. **Electricity prod.** (1991): 600 mln. kWh. **Labor force:** 90% agric.; 10% ind., comm.

Finance: Monetary unit: Shilling (Apr. 1995: 551 = $1 US). **Gross domestic product** (1993): $16.7 bln.* **Per capita GDP:** $600. **Imports** (1992): $1.5 bln.; partners: UK 14%, Japan 12%, Germany 10%. **Exports** (1992): $418 mln.; partners: Ger. 15%, UK 13%. **Tourism** (1990): $63 mln. **National budget** (1990): $631 mln. **International reserves less gold** (Jan. 1994): $191 mln. **Consumer prices** (change in 1993): 23.5%.

Transport: Motor vehicles: in use: 50,000 passenger cars; 40,000 comm. vehicles. **Civil aviation:** 97 mln. passenger-mi.; 12 airports. **Chief ports:** Dar-es-Salaam, Mtwara, Tanga.

Communications: Radios: 1 per 6.6 persons. **Telephones:** 1 per 171 persons.

Health: Life expectancy at birth (1995): 41 male; 44 female. **Births** (per 1,000 pop.): 45. **Deaths** (per 1,000 pop.): 20. **Natural increase:** 2.5%. **Hospital beds:** 1 per 924 persons. **Physicians:** 1 per 19,775 persons. **Infant mortality** (per 1,000 live births 1995): 109.

Education: Literacy (1991): 94%. **Attendance:** 87% attend primary school.

Major International Organizations: UN and all of its specialized agencies, OAU, the Commonwealth.

Embassy: 2139 R. St. NW 20008; 939-6125.

The Republic of Tanganyika in E Africa and the island Republic of Zanzibar, off the coast of Tanganyika, both of which had recently gained independence, joined into a single nation, the United Republic of Tanzania, Apr. 26, 1964. Zanzibar retains internal self-government.

Until resigning as president in 1985, Julius K. Nyerere, a former Tanganyikan independence leader, dominated Tanzania's politics, which emphasized government planning and control of the economy, with single-party rule. In 1992 the constitution was amended to allow opposition parties to participate in elections. Privatization of the economy was undertaken in the 1990s.

Tanganyika. Arab colonization and slaving began in the 8th century AD; Portuguese sailors explored the coast by about 1500. Other Europeans followed.

In 1885 Germany established German East Africa of which Tanganyika formed the bulk. It became a League of Nations mandate and, after 1946, a UN trust territory, both under Britain. It became independent Dec. 9, 1961, and a republic within the Commonwealth a year later.

Zanzibar, the Isle of Cloves, lies 23 mi. off the coast of Tanganyika; its area is 621 sq. mi. The island of **Pemba,** 25 mi. to the NE, area 380 sq. mi., is included in the administration. The total population (1990 est.) is 375,000.

Chief industry is the production of cloves and clove oil, of which Zanzibar and Pemba produce the bulk of the world's supply.

Zanzibar was for centuries the center for Arab slave-traders. Portugal ruled for 2 centuries until ousted by Arabs around 1700. Zanzibar became a British Protectorate in 1890; independence came Dec. 10, 1963. Revolutionary forces overthrew the Sultan Jan. 12, 1964. The new government ousted Western diplomats and newsmen, slaughtered thousands of Arabs, and nationalized farms. Union with Tanganyika followed.

Thailand
Kingdom of Thailand
Muang Thai *or* Prathet Thai

People: Population: 60,271,300. **Age distrib.** (%): <15: 31; 65+: 4. **Pop. density:** 304 per sq. mi. **Urban:** 19%. **Ethnic groups:** Thai 75%, Chinese 14%. **Principal languages:** Thai (official), Chinese, Malay, regional dialects. **Religions:** Buddhist 95%, Muslim 4%.

Geography: Area: 198,115 sq. mi. **Location:** On Indochinese and Malayan peninsulas in SE Asia. **Neighbors:** Myanmar on W, Laos on N, Cambodia on E, Malaysia on S. **Topography:** A plateau dominates the NE third of Thailand, dropping to the fertile alluvial valley of the Chao Phraya R. in the center. Forested mountains are in N, with narrow fertile valleys. The S peninsula region is covered by rain forests. **Capital:** Bangkok (1992 est.): 5.6 mln.

Government: Type: Constitutional monarchy. **Head of state:** King Bhumibol Adulyadej; b Dec. 5, 1927; in office: June 9, 1946. **Head of government:** Prime Min. Banharn Silpaarcha; b July 20, 1932; in office: July 13, 1995. **Local divisions:** 73 provinces. **Defense:** 2% of GNP (FY 1992-93). **Active troop strength:** 256,000.

Economy: Industries: Textiles, mining, wood prods., tourism. **Chief crops:** Rice (a major export), corn, tapioca, sugarcane. **Minerals:** Among world's largest producers of tin and tungsten. **Other resources:** Forests (teak is exported), rubber. **Arable land:** 34%. **Livestock** (1992): cattle: 6.8 mln.; pigs: 5.1 mln. **Fish catch** (1991): 3.1 mln. metric tons. **Electricity prod.** (1992): 43.7 bln. kWh. **Labor force:** 62% agric.; 24% ind. & comm.; 14% serv. & govt.

Finance: Monetary unit: Baht (May 1995: 24.63 = $1 US). **Gross national product** (1993): $323 bln.* **Per capita GNP:** $5,500. **Imports** (1992): $37.6 bln.; partners: Japan 29%, U.S. 11%. **Exports** (1992): $28.4 bln.; partners: Japan 18%, U.S. 22%. **Tourism** (1992): $4.8 bln. **National budget** (1993 est.): $22.4 bln. **International reserves less gold** (May 1995): $32.2 bln. **Gold:** 2.47 mln. oz t. **Consumer prices** (change in 1994): 5.3%.

Transport: Railroads: Length: 2,405 mi. **Motor vehicles:** in use: 891,000 passenger cars, 2.2 mln. comm. vehicles. **Civil**

aviation: 12.7 bln. passenger-mi.; 26 airports with scheduled flights. **Chief ports:** Bangkok, Sattahip.

Communication: Television sets: 1 per 17 persons. **Radios:** 1 per 5.7 persons. **Telephones:** 1 per 36 persons. **Daily newspaper circ.:** 72 per 1,000 pop.

Health: Life expectancy at birth (1995): 65 male; 72 female. **Births** (per 1,000 pop.): 19. **Deaths** (per 1,000 pop.): 6. **Natural increase:** 1.2%. **Hospital beds:** 1 per 604 persons. **Physicians:** 1 per 4,327 persons. **Infant mortality** (per 1,000 live births 1995): 36.

Education: Literacy (1991): 89%. **Years compulsory:** 6; attendance 96%.

Major International Organizations: UN (WTO, World Bank), ASEAN.

Embassy: 2300 Kalorama Rd. NW 20008; 483-7200.

Thais began migrating from southern China during the 11th century.

Thailand is the only country in SE Asia never taken over by a European power, thanks to King Mongkut and his son King Chulalongkorn—who ruled from 1851 to 1910, modernized the country, and signed trade treaties with both Britain and France. A bloodless revolution in 1932 limited the monarchy.

Japan occupied the country in 1941.

The military took over the government in a bloody 1976 coup. Kriangsak Chomanan, prime minister resigned, Feb. 1980, because of soaring inflation, oil price increases, labor unrest, and growing crime. Vietnamese troops crossed the border but were repulsed by Thai forces in the 1980s.

Chatichai Choonhavan was chosen prime minister in a democratic election, Aug. 1988. In Feb. 1991, the military ousted Choonhavan in a bloodless coup. A violent crackdown on street demonstrations in May 1992 led to more than 50 deaths. After general elections July 2, 1995, Banharn Silpaarcha succeeded Chuan Leekpai as prime minister.

Togo
Republic of Togo
République Togolaise

People: Population: 4,410,370. **Age distrib.** (%): <15: 49; 65+: 2. **Pop. density:** 201 per sq. mi. **Urban:** 30%. **Ethnic groups:** Ewe, Mina, Kabye, 34 other tribes. **Principal languages:** French (official), Ewe, Mina, Dagomba, Kabye. **Religions:** indigenous beliefs 70%, Christian 20%, Muslim 10%.

Geography: Area: 21,925 sq. mi. **Location:** On S coast of W Africa. **Neighbors:** Ghana on W, Burkina Faso on N, Benin on E. **Topography:** A range of hills running SW-NE splits Togo into 2 savanna plains regions. **Capital:** Lomé (1990 met. est.): 513,000.

Government: Type: Republic. **Head of state:** Pres. Gnassingbé Eyadéma; b Dec. 26, 1937; in office: Apr. 14, 1967. **Head of government:** Prime Min. Edem Kodjo; in office: Apr. 23, 1994. **Local divisions:** 23 circumscriptions. **Defense:** 3% of GNP (1991). **Active troop strength:** 6,950.

Economy: Industries: Textiles, shoes. **Chief crops:** Coffee, cocoa, yams, cotton, millet, rice. **Minerals:** Phosphates. **Arable land:** 25%. **Electricity prod.** (1990): 209 mln. kWh. **Labor force:** 78% agric.; 22% industry.

Finance: Monetary unit: CFA Franc (May 1995: 488 = $1 US). **Gross domestic product** (1993): $3.3 bln.* **Per capita GDP:** $800. **Imports** (1991): $636 mln.; partners: EU 57%. **Exports** (1991): $558 mln.; partners: EU 40%. **Tourism** (1992): $39 mln. **National budget** (1991 est.): $407 mln. **International reserves less gold** (Mar. 1995): $104 mln. **Gold:** 13,000 oz t. **Consumer prices** (change in 1993): –1.0%.

Transport: Railroads: Length: 326 mi. **Chief port:** Lomé.

Communications: Television sets: 1 per 165 persons. **Radios:** 1 per 5.4 persons. **Telephones:** 1 per 119 persons.

Health: Life expectancy at birth (1994): 55 male; 60 female. **Births** (per 1,000 pop.): 47. **Deaths** (per 1,000 pop.): 11. **Natural increase:** 3.6%. **Hospital beds:** 1 per 625 persons. **Physicians:** 1 per 12,299 persons. **Infant mortality** (per 1,000 live births 1995): 86.

Education: Literacy (1990): 43%.

Major International Organizations: UN (WTO, IMF), OAU.

Embassy: 2208 Massachusetts Ave. NW 20008; 234-4212.

The Ewe arrived in southern Togo several centuries ago. The country later became a major source of slaves. Germany took control in 1884. France and Britain administered Togoland as UN trusteeships. The French sector became the republic of Togo Apr. 27, 1960.

The population is divided between Bantus in the S and Hamitic tribes in the N. Togo has actively promoted regional integration, as a means of stimulating the economy.

In Jan. 1993 police fired on antigovernment demonstrators, killing at least 22. Some 25,000 people fled to Ghana and Benin as a result of civil unrest. In Jan. 1994 at least 40 people were killed when gunmen reportedly attacked an army base. Further violence marred Togo's first multiparty legislative elections, held Feb. 1994.

Tonga
Kingdom of Tonga
Pule'anga Fakatu'i 'o Tonga

People: Population: 105,600. **Pop. density:** 364 per sq. mi. **Ethnic groups:** Polynesian, European. **Principal languages:** Tongan, English (both official). **Religions:** Free Wesleyan 43%, Roman Catholic 16%, Mormon 12%, Free Church of Tonga 11%, Church of Tonga 7%.

Geography: Area: 290 sq. mi. **Location:** In western S Pacific O. **Neighbors:** Nearest are Fiji on W, New Zealand on S. **Topography:** Tonga comprises 169 volcanic and coral islands, 45 inhabited. **Capital:** Nuku'alofa (1990 est.): 34,000.

Government: Type: Constitutional monarchy. **Head of state:** King Taufa'ahau Tupou IV; b July 4, 1918; in office: Dec. 16, 1965. **Head of government:** Prime Min. Baron Vaea; b May 15, 1921; in office: Aug. 21, 1991. **Local divisions:** 3 main island groups.

Economy: Industries: Tourism. **Chief crops:** Coconut products, bananas, vanilla. **Other resources:** Fish. **Arable land:** 25%. **Electricity prod.** (1990): 8 mln. kWh. **Labor force:** 70% agric.

Finance: Monetary unit: Pa'anga (Apr. 1995: 1.27 = $1 US). **Gross domestic product** (1993): $200 mln.* **Imports** (1992): $68 mln.; partners: NZ 33%, Australia 22%. **Exports** (1992): $19 mln.; partners: Japan 34%, U.S. 17%. **Tourism** (1992): $9 mln.

Transport: Motor vehicles: in use: 3,300 passenger cars, 3,800 comm. vehicles. **Chief ports:** Nuku'alofa.

Communications: Radios: 1 per 1.5 persons. **Telephones:** 1 per 14 persons.

Health: Life expectancy at birth (1992): 66 male; 71 female. **Births** (per 1,000 pop.): 24. **Deaths** (per 1,000 pop.): 7. **Natural increase:** 1.8%. **Infant mortality** (per 1,000 live births 1995): 20.

Education: Literacy (1992): 93%. **Years compulsory:** 8; attendance: 77%.

The islands were first visited by the Dutch in the early 17th century. A series of civil wars ended in 1845 with establishment of the Tupou dynasty. In 1900 Tonga became a British protectorate. On June 4, 1970, Tonga became independent and a member of the Commonwealth.

Trinidad and Tobago
Republic of Trinidad and Tobago

People: Population: 1,271,159. **Age distrib. (%):** <15: 31; 65+: 6. **Pop. density:** 642 per sq. mi. **Urban:** 65%. **Ethnic groups:** blacks 43%, East Indian 40%, mixed 14%. **Principal languages:** English (official). **Religions:** Roman Catholic 32%, Protestant 28%, Hindu 24%, Muslim 6%.

Geography: Area: 1,980 sq. mi. **Location:** Off eastern coast of Venezuela. **Neighbors:** Nearest is Venezuela on SW. **Topography:** Three low mountain ranges cross Trinidad E-W, with a well-watered plain between N and central ranges. Parts of E and W coasts are swamps. Tobago, 116 sq. mi., lies 20 mi. NE. **Capital:** Port-of-Spain (1991 est.): 51,000.

Government: Type: Parliamentary democracy. **Head of state:** Pres. Noor Hassanali; b Aug. 13, 1918; in office: Mar. 19, 1987. **Head of government:** Prime Min. Patrick Manning; b Aug. 17, 1946; in office: Dec. 17, 1991. **Local divisions:** 8 counties, 3 municipalities, 1 ward. **Defense:** 0.6% of GNP (1991). **Active troop strength:** 2,600.

Economy: Industries: Oil products, chemicals, tourism.

Chief crops: Sugar, cocoa, coffee, citrus fruits, bananas. **Minerals:** Asphalt, oil, gas. **Crude oil reserves** (1994): 466 mln. bbls. **Arable land:** 14%. **Electricity prod.** (1992): 3.5 bln. kWh. **Labor force:** 18% constr. & util.; 15% manuf. & mining; 11% agric.

Finance: Monetary unit: Dollar (May 1995: 5.88 = $1 US). **Gross domestic product** (1993): $10.4 bln.* **Per capita GDP:** $8,000. **Imports** (1993): $900 mln.; partners: U.S. 41%, Venezuela 10%. **Exports** (1993): $1.4 bln.; partners: U.S. 47%. **Tourism** (1992): $111 mln. **National budget** (1993 est.): $1.6 bln. **International reserves less gold** (Apr. 1995): $334 mln. **Gold:** 54,000 oz t. **Consumer prices** (change in 1994): 8.8%.

Transport: Motor vehicles: in use: 150,000 passenger cars, 60,000 comm. vehicles. **Civil aviation:** 2.0 bln. passenger-mi.; 2 airports. **Chief ports:** Port-of-Spain.

Communications: Television sets: 1 per 5.0 persons. **Radios:** 1 per 1.8 persons. **Telephones:** 1 per 5.1 persons. **Daily newspaper circ.:** 77 per 1,000 pop.

Health: Life expectancy at birth (1995): 68 male; 73 female. **Births** (per 1,000 pop.): 17. **Deaths** (per 1,000 pop.): 7. **Natural increase:** 1.0%. **Hospital beds:** 1 per 285 persons. **Physicians:** 1 per 1,275 persons. **Infant mortality** (per 1,000 live births 1995): 18.

Education: Literacy (1992): 96%. **Years compulsory:** 8.

Major International Organizations: UN (WTO, IMF, WHO), the Commonwealth, OAS.

Embassy: 1708 Massachusetts Ave. NW 20036; 467-6490.

Columbus sighted Trinidad in 1498. A British possession since 1802, Trinidad and Tobago won independence Aug. 31, 1962. It became a republic in 1976. The People's National Movement party has held control of the government since 1956.

The nation is one of the most prosperous in the Caribbean. Oil production has increased with offshore finds. Middle Eastern oil is refined and exported, mostly to the U.S.

In July 1990, some 120 Muslim extremists captured the Parliament building and TV station and took about 50 hostages, including Prime Min. Arthur Robinson, who was beaten, shot in the legs, and tied to explosives. After a 6-day siege, the rebels surrendered.

Tunisia
Republic of Tunisia
al-Jumhuriyah at-Tunisiyah

People: Population: 8,879,845. **Age distrib. (%):** <15: 37; 65+: 5. **Pop. density:** 140 per sq. mi. **Urban:** 60%. **Ethnic groups:** Arab-Berber 98%. **Principal languages:** Arabic (official), French. **Religions:** Muslim 98%.

Geography: Area: 63,378 sq. mi. **Location:** On N coast of Africa. **Neighbors:** Algeria on W, Libya on E. **Topography:** The N is wooded and fertile. The central coastal plains are given to grazing and orchards. The S is arid, approaching Sahara Desert. **Capital:** Tunis. **Cities** (1989 est.): Tunis 620,000, Sfax 222,000.

Government: Type: Republic. **Head of state:** Pres. Gen. Zine al-Abidine Ben Ali; b Sept 3, 1936; in office: Nov. 7, 1987. **Head of government:** Prime Min. Hamed Karoui; in office: Sept. 27, 1989. **Local divisions:** 23 governorates. **Defense:** 3.7% of GDP (1993 est.). **Active troop strength:** 35,500.

Economy: Industries: Food processing, textiles, oil products, mining, construction materials. **Chief crops:** Grains, dates, olives, vegetables, grapes. **Minerals:** Phosphates, iron, oil, lead, zinc. **Crude oil reserves** (1994): 1.7 bln. bbls. **Arable land:** 20%. **Livestock** (1992): sheep: 6.4 mln.; goats: 1.3 mln. **Fish catch** (1991): 91,000 metric tons. **Electricity prod.** (1992): 5.1 bln. kWh. **Labor force:** 32% agric.

Finance: Monetary unit: Dinar (May 1995: 0.93 = $1 US). **Gross domestic product** (1993): $34.3 bln.* **Per capita GDP:** $4,000. **Imports** (1993): $6.4 bln.; partners: EU 70%. **Exports** (1993): $4.1 bln.; partners: EU 75%. **Tourism** (1992): $1.1 bln. **National budget** (1993 est.): $5.5 bln. **International reserves less gold** (Apr. 1995): $1.6 bln. **Gold:** 216,000 oz t. **Consumer prices** (change in 1994): 4.7%.

Transport: Railroads: Length: 1,404 mi. **Motor vehicles:** in use: 321,000 passenger cars, 209,000 comm. vehicles. **Civil aviation:** 1.0 bln. passenger-mi.; 5 airports. **Chief ports:** Tunis, Sfax, Bizerte.

Communications: Television sets: 1 per 13 persons. **Radios:** 1 per 5.1 persons. **Telephones:** 1 per 18 persons. **Daily newspaper circ.:** 37 per 1,000 pop.
Health: Life expectancy at birth (1995): 71 male; 75 female. **Births** (per 1,000 pop.): 23. **Deaths** (per 1,000 pop.): 5. **Natural increase:** 1.8%. **Hospital beds:** 1 per 521 persons. **Physicians:** 1 per 1,799 persons. **Infant mortality** (per 1,000 live births 1995): 32.
Education: Literacy (1993): 65%. **Years compulsory:** 8; attendance 85%.
Major International Organizations: UN, Arab League, OAU.
Embassy: 1515 Massachusetts Ave. NW 20005; 862-1850.

Site of ancient Carthage and a former Barbary state under the suzerainty of Turkey, Tunisia became a protectorate of France under a treaty signed May 12, 1881. The nation became independent Mar. 20, 1956, and ended the monarchy the following year. Habib Bourguiba, an independence leader, served as president until 1987, when he was deposed by his prime minister, Zine al-Abidine Ben Ali.
Tunisia has actively repressed Islamic fundamentalism.

Turkey
Republic of Turkey
Turkiye Cumhuriyeti

People: Population: 63,405,526. **Age distrib.** (%): <15: 33; 65+: 4. **Pop. density:** 211 per sq. mi. **Urban:** 51%. **Ethnic groups:** Turk 80%, Kurd 20%. **Principal languages:** Turkish (official), Kurdish, Arabic. **Religions:** Muslim 99.8%.
Geography: Area: 300,948 sq. mi. **Location:** Occupies Asia Minor, and stretches into continental Europe; borders on Mediterranean and Black seas. **Neighbors:** Bulgaria, Greece on W, Georgia, Armenia on N, Iran on E, Iraq, Syria on S. **Topography:** Central Turkey has wide plateaus, with hot, dry summers and cold winters. High mountains ring the interior on all but W, with more than 20 peaks over 10,000 ft. Rolling plains are in W; mild, fertile coastal plains are in S, W. **Capital:** Ankara. **Cities** (1990 est.): Istanbul 6.6 mln.; Ankara 2.6 mln.; Izmir 1.8 mln.; Adana 916,000.
Government: Type: Republic. **Head of state:** Pres. Suleyman Demirel; b 1924; in office: May 16, 1993. **Head of government:** Prime Min. Tansu Ciller; b 1946; in office: July 5, 1993. **Local divisions:** 73 provinces. **Defense:** 5.6% of GDP (1994). **Active troop strength:** 503,800.
Economy: Industries: Iron, steel, machinery, metal prods., oil, processed foods. **Chief crops:** Tobacco, cereals, cotton, barley, corn, fruits, potatoes, sugar beets. **Minerals:** Antimony, chromium, mercury, copper, coal. **Crude oil reserves** (1994): 488 mln. bbls. **Other resources:** Wool, silk, forests. **Arable land:** 30%. **Livestock** (1992): cattle: 12.0 mln.; sheep: 40.4 mln. **Fish catch** (1991): 365,000 metric tons. **Electricity prod.** (1991): 44 bln. kWh. **Labor force:** 48% agric.; 20% ind.; 32% serv.
Finance: Monetary unit: Lira (Apr. 1995: 42,374 = $1 US). **Gross domestic product** (1993): $312.4 bln.* **Per capita GDP:** $5,100. **Imports** (1992): $22.9 bln.; partners: EU 44%, U.S. 11%. **Exports** (1992): $14.9 bln.; partners: EU 53%. **Tourism** (1992): $3.6 bln. **National budget** (1994): $47.6 bln. **International reserves less gold** (Apr. 1995): $12.3 bln. **Gold:** 3.7 mln. oz t. **Consumer prices** (change in 1994): 106.3%.
Transport: Railroads: Length: 5,238 mi. **Motor vehicles:** in use: 2.2 mln. passenger cars, 816,000 comm. vehicles. **Civil aviation:** 4.5 bln. passenger-mi.; 22 airports with scheduled flights. **Chief ports:** Istanbul, Izmir, Mersin, Samsun.
Communications: Television sets: 1 per 5.7 persons. **Radios:** 1 per 8.4 persons. **Telephones:** 1 per 5.0 persons.
Health: Life expectancy at birth (1995): 69 male; 74 female. **Births** (per 1,000 pop.): 25. **Deaths** (per 1,000 pop.): 6. **Natural increase:** 2.0%. **Hospital beds:** 1 per 463 persons. **Physicians:** 1 per 1,974 persons. **Infant mortality** (per 1,000 live births 1995): 46.
Education: Literacy (1992): 79%. **Years compulsory:** 6; attendance 95%.
Major International Organizations: UN (WTO, WHO, IMF), NATO, OECD.
Embassy: 1714 Massachusetts Ave. NW 20036; 659-8200.

Ancient inhabitants of Turkey were among the worlds first agriculturalists. Such civilizations as the Hittite, Phrygian, and Lydian flourished in Asiatic Turkey (Asia Minor), as did much of Greek civilization. After the fall of Rome in the 5th century, Constantinople was the capital of the Byzantine Empire for 1,000 years. It fell in 1453 to Ottoman Turks, who ruled a vast empire for over 400 years.
Just before World War I, Turkey, or the Ottoman Empire, ruled what is now Syria, Lebanon, Iraq, Jordan, Israel, Saudi Arabia, Yemen, and islands in the Aegean Sea.
Turkey joined Germany and Austria in World War I and its defeat resulted in loss of much territory and fall of the sultanate. A republic was declared Oct. 29, 1923. The Caliphate (spiritual leadership of Islam) was renounced 1924.
Long embroiled with Greece over Cyprus, off Turkey's south coast, Turkey invaded the island July 20, 1974, after Greek officers seized the Cypriot government as a step toward unification with Greece. Turkey sought a new government for Cyprus, with Greek Cypriot and Turkish Cypriot zones. In reaction to Turkey's moves, the U.S. cut off military aid in 1975. Turkey, in turn, suspended the use of most U.S. bases. Aid was restored in 1978. There was a military takeover, Sept. 12, 1980.
Religious and ethnic tensions and active left and right extremists have caused endemic violence. Martial law, imposed in 1978, was lifted in 1984. The military formally transferred power to an elected Parliament in 1983.
Turkey was a member of the Allied forces which ousted Iraq from Kuwait, 1991. In the aftermath of the war, millions of Kurdish refugees fled to Turkey's border to escape Iraqi forces. The Turkish government mounted sporadic offensives against separatist Kurds in this border area and in N Iraq, causing heavy casualties among guerrillas and civilians.
Kurdish militants raided Turkish diplomatic missions in some 25 Western European cities June 24, 1993. The militants were demanding an independent state for the Kurds. Tansu Ciller officially became Turkey's first woman prime min. July 5, 1993.

Turkmenistan
Republic of Turkmenistan

People: Population: 4,075,316. **Pop. density:** 22 per sq. mi. **Urban:** 45%. **Ethnic groups:** Turkmen 73%, Russian 10%, Uzbek 9%. **Principal languages:** Turkmen, Russian, Uzbek. **Religions:** Muslim 87%, Eastern Orthodox 11%.
Geography: Area: 188,500 sq. mi. **Neighbors:** Uzbekistan, Kazakhstan on N, NE, Afghanistan and Iran on S. The Kara Kum Desert occupies 80% of the area. **Capital:** Ashgabat (1991): 416,000.
Government: Type: Republic. **Head of state:** Pres. Saparmurad Niyazov; b 1940; in office: Oct. 27, 1990. **Local divisions:** 5 regions.
Economy: Industries: Mining, oil, natural gas, textiles. **Chief crops:** Grain, cotton, grapes. **Minerals:** Coal, sulfur, salt. **Crude oil reserves** (1992): 740 mln. bbls. **Arable land:** 3%. **Livestock** (1992): sheep and goats: 5.6 mln. **Electricity prod.** (1992): 13.1 bln. kWh. **Labor force:** 44% agric.; 20% ind.
Finance: Monetary unit: Manat (Oct. 1994: 10 = $1 US). **Gross domestic product** (1993 est.): $13 bln.* **Per capita GDP:** $3,330. **Imports** (1990): $970 mln. **Exports** (1990): $239 mln.
Transport: Railroads: Length: 1,317 mi.
Communications: Telephones: 1 per 14 persons.
Health: Life expectancy at birth (1995): 62 male; 69 female. **Births** (per 1,000 pop.): 30. **Deaths** (per 1,000 pop.): 7. **Natural increase:** 2.3%. **Hospital beds:** 1 per 92 persons. **Physicians:** 1 per 412 persons. **Infant mortality** (per 1,000 live births 1995): 68.
Major International Organizations: UN, CIS.
Embassy: 1511 K St. NW 20005; 737-4800.

The region has been inhabited by Turki tribes since the 10th century. It became part of Russian Turkistan 1881, and a constituent republic of the USSR 1925. Turkmenistan declared independence Oct. 27, 1991, and became an independent state when the Soviet Union disbanded Dec. 26, 1991.
Extensive oil and gas reserves place Turkmenistan in a more favorable economic position than other former Soviet republics. Power remained mainly with the former Communist Party apparatus; Pres. Saparmurad Niyazov became the object of a strong personality cult.

Tuvalu

People: Population: 9,991. **Pop. density:** 1,063 per sq. mi. **Ethnic groups:** Polynesian 96%. **Principal languages:** Tuvaluan, English. **Religions:** Church of Tuvalu (Congregationalist) 97%.

Geography: Area: 9.4 sq. mi. **Location:** 9 islands forming a NW-SE chain 360 mi. long in the SW Pacific O. **Neighbors:** Nearest are Samoa to SE, Fiji to S. **Topography:** The islands are all low-lying atolls, nowhere rising more than 15 ft. above sea level, composed of coral reefs. **Capital:** Fongafale, on Funafuti Atoll (1990 est.): 3,400.

Government: Head of state: Queen Elizabeth II, represented by Gov.-Gen. Tulaga Manuella; in office: June 1994. **Head of government:** Prime Min. Kamuta Laatasi; in office: Dec. 1993.

Economy: Industries: Copra. **Chief crops:** Coconuts. **Other resources:** fish. **Labor force:** Approx. 1,500 Tuvaluans work overseas in the Gilberts' phosphate industry, or as overseas seamen.

Finance: Monetary unit: Tuvalu Dollar, Australian Dollar. **Transport: Chief port:** Funafuti.

Health: Life expectancy at birth (1995): 62 male; 64 female. **Births** (per 1,000 pop.): 25. **Deaths** (per 1,000 pop.): 9. **Natural increase:** 1.6%. **Infant mortality** (per 1,000 live births 1995): 28.

Education: Literacy (1990): 96%.

The Ellice Islands separated from the British Gilbert and Ellice Islands colony in 1975 and became independent Tuvalu, Oct. 1, 1978.

Uganda
Republic of Uganda

People: Population: 19,573,262. **Age distrib.** (%): <15: 47; 65+: 3. **Pop. density:** 210 per sq. mi. **Urban:** 11%. **Ethnic groups:** Bantu, Nilotic, Nilo-Hamitic, Sudanic tribes. **Principal languages:** English (official), Luganda, Swahili. **Religions:** Christian 66%, Muslim 16%, indigenous beliefs 18%.

Geography: Area: 93,070 sq. mi. **Location:** In E Central Africa. **Neighbors:** Sudan on N, Zaire on W, Rwanda, Tanzania on S, Kenya on E. **Topography:** Most of Uganda is a high plateau 3,000-6,000 ft. high, with high Ruwenzori range in W (Mt. Margherita 16,750 ft.), volcanoes in SW; NE is arid, W and SW rainy. Lakes Victoria, Edward, Albert form much of borders. **Capital:** Kampala (1991): 773,000.

Government: Type: Republic. **Head of state:** Pres. Yoweri Kaguta Museveni; b 1944; in office: Jan. 29, 1986. **Head of government:** Prime Min. Kintu Mosoke; in office: Nov. 18, 1994. **Local divisions:** 10 provinces. **Defense:** 15% of budget (FY 1989-90). **Active troop strength:** 50,000 est.

Economy: Chief crops: Coffee, cotton, tea, corn, tobacco. **Minerals:** Copper, cobalt. **Arable land:** 23%. **Livestock** (1993): cattle: 5.2 mln.; goats: 3.4 mln.; sheep: 1.8 mln. **Fish catch** (1991): 255,000 metric tons. **Electricity prod.** (1991): 610 mln. kWh. **Labor force:** 80% agric.

Finance: Monetary unit: Shilling (Apr. 1995: 931 = $1 US). **Gross domestic product** (1993): $24.1 bln.* **Per capita GDP:** $1,200. **Imports** (1992): $513 mln.; partners: Kenya 25%, UK 14%. **Exports** (1992): $150 mln.; partners: U.S. 25%, UK 18%, France 11%. **National budget** (1989 est.): $545 mln. **International reserves less gold** (Mar. 1995): $345 mln. **Consumer prices** (change in 1994): 9.7%.

Transport: Motor vehicles: in use: 18,000 passenger cars, 25,000 comm. vehicles.

Communications: Television sets: 1 per 154 persons. **Radios:** 1 per 5.1 persons. **Telephones:** 1 per 314 persons.

Health: Life expectancy at birth (1995): 36 male; 37 female. **Births** (per 1,000 pop.): 48. **Deaths** (per 1,000 pop.): 24. **Natural increase:** 2.4%. **Hospital beds:** 1 per 817 persons. **Physicians:** 1 per 20,720 persons. **Infant mortality** (per 1,000 live births 1995): 112.

Education: Literacy (1989): 48%. About 50% attend primary school.

Major International Organizations: UN (WTO, WHO, IMF), OAU, the Commonwealth.

Embassy: 5909 16th St. NW 20011; 726-7100.

Britain obtained a protectorate over Uganda in 1894. The country became independent Oct. 9, 1962, and a republic within the Commonwealth a year later. In 1967, the traditional kingdoms, including the powerful Buganda state, were abolished and the central government strengthened. (In 1993 the government authorized restoration of the Buganda and other monarchies, but as ceremonial only.)

Gen. Idi Amin seized power from Prime Min. Milton Obote in 1971. As many as 300,000 of his opponents were reported killed in subsequent years. Amin was named president for life in 1976.

In 1972 Amin expelled nearly all of Uganda's 45,000 Asians. In 1973 the U.S. withdrew all diplomatic personnel. Amid worsening economic and domestic crises, Uganda's troops exchanged invasion attacks with long-standing foe Tanzania, 1978 to 1979. Tanzanian forces, coupled with Ugandan exiles and rebels, ended the dictatorial rule of Amin, Apr. 11, 1979.

A draft constitution was issued in late 1992, but a promised transition to multiparty democracy was postponed.

Ukraine
Ukrayina

People: Population: 51,867,828. **Age distrib.** (%): <15: 21; 65+: 13. **Pop. density:** 223 per sq. mi. **Urban:** 68%. **Ethnic groups:** Ukrainian 73%, Russian 22%. **Principal languages:** Ukrainian, Russian. **Religions:** mostly Ukrainian Orthodox, some Ukrainian Catholic.

Geography: Area: 233,100 sq. mi. **Location:** In SE Europe. **Neighbors:** Belarus on N, Russia on NE and E, Moldova and Romania on SW, Hungary, Slovakia, and Poland on W. **Topography:** Part of the E European plain. Mountainous areas include the Carpathians in the SW and the Crimean chain in the S. Arable black soil constitutes a large part of the country. **Climate:** Average temperature range from 21°F in Jan. to 66°F in July. Annual precipitation averages 27.5 in. in the W part of the country and less than 11 in. in the E. **Capital:** Kiev. **Cities** (1993 est.): Kiev 2.6 mln.; Kharkiv 1.6 mln.; Dnipropetrovsk 1.2 mln.; Donetsk 1.1 mln.; Odesa 1.1 mln.

Government: Type: Constitutional republic. **Head of state:** Pres. Leonid J. Kuchma; b Aug. 9, 1938; in office: July 19, 1994. **Head of government:** Yevhen Marchuk; in office: 1995. **Local divisions:** 24 oblasts, 2 municipalities, 1 autonomous republic. **Defense:** 3.9% of GNP (1993). **Active troop strength:** 517,000.

Economy: Industries: Steel, chemicals, machinery, vehicles, food processing. **Chief crops:** Grains, sugar beets, vegetables. **Minerals:** Iron, manganese, coal, gas, oil, sulphur, nickel, salt. **Other resources:** Forests. **Arable land:** 56%. **Livestock** (1993): cattle: 22.5 mln.; pigs: 16.2 mln. **Fish catch** (1992): 1.3 mln. metric tons. **Electricity prod.** (1992): 281 bln. kWh. **Labor force:** 21% agric.; 33% ind. & constr.

Finance: Monetary unit: Karbovanets (Oct. 1994: 30,028 = $1 US). **Gross domestic product** (1993 est.): $205.4 bln.* **Per capita GDP:** $3,960. **Imports** (1990): $16.7 bln. **Exports** (1990): $13.5 bln. **National budget** (1990): $8 bln.

Transport: Railroads: Length: 14,167 mi. **Motor vehicles:** in use: 2.9 mln. passenger cars. **Civil aviation:** 5.2 bln. passenger-mi.; 20 airports. **Chief ports:** Odesa, Kherson, Mariupol, Sevastopol, Berdyansk.

Communications: Television sets: 1 per 3 persons. **Radios:** 1 per 3.5 persons. **Telephones:** 1 per 6.2 persons. **Daily newspaper circ.:** 251 per 1,000 pop.

Health: Life expectancy at birth (1995): 66 male; 75 female. **Births** (per 1,000 pop.): 12. **Deaths** (per 1,000 pop.): 13. **Natural increase:** 0. **Hospital beds:** 1 per 75 persons. **Physicians:** 1 per 228 persons. **Infant mortality** (per 1,000 live births 1995): 20.

Education: Literacy (1993): 98%.

Major International Organizations: UN, CIS.

Embassy: 3350 M St. NW 20007; 333-0606.

The ancient ancestors of Ukrainians, the Trypilians, flourished along the Dnipro River, Ukraine's main artery, from 6000-1000 BC. The Slavic ancestors of the Ukrainians inhabited modern Ukrainian territory well before the first century AD.

The princes of Kyyiv established a strong state called Kyyivan Rus in the 9th century. A strong dynasty was established, with ties to virtually all major European royal families. St. Volodymyr the Great, ruler of Kyyivan Ukraine, accepted Christianity as the national faith in 988. At the crossroads of European trade routes, Kyyivan Rus reached its zenith under Iaroslav the Wise (1019-1054). While directly absorbing most of the Asian invasion of Europe in the 13th century, the Ukrainian state slowly disintegrated and was divided mainly between Russia and Poland.

The Ukrainian Cossack State, founded in the late 16th century, waged numerous wars of liberation against the occupiers of Ukraine: Russia, Poland, and Turkey. By the late 18th century, Ukrainian independence was lost. Ukraine's neighbors once again divided its territory. At the turn of the last century, Ukraine was occupied by Russia and Austria-Hungary.

An independent Ukrainian National Republic was proclaimed on January 22, 1918. In 1921, Ukraine's neighbors occupied and divided Ukrainian territory. In 1932-33, the Soviet government engineered a man-made famine in eastern Ukraine, resulting in the deaths of 7-10 million Ukrainians.

In March 1939, independent Carpatho-Ukraine was the first European state to wage war against Nazi-led aggression in the region. During WW2 the Ukrainian nationalist underground and its Ukrainian Insurgent Army (UPA) fought both Nazi German and Soviet forces. The restoration of Ukrainian independence was declared on June 30, 1941. Over 5 million Ukrainians lost their lives during the war. With the reoccupation of Ukraine by Soviet troops in 1944 came a renewed wave of mass arrests, executions, and deportations of Ukrainians.

The world's worst nuclear power plant disaster occurred in Chernobyl, Ukraine, in April 1986.

Ukrainian independence was restored in Dec. 1991 with the dissolution of the Soviet Union. In the post-Soviet period Ukraine was burdened with a deteriorating economy.

The Ukrainian Parliament ratified Feb. 3, 1994, a Jan. 14 agreement with Russia and the U.S. calling for deactivation of Ukraine's large nuclear arsenal. Russia and Ukraine reached agreement June 9, 1995, on the disputed Black Sea fleet at Sevastopol.

United Arab Emirates
al-Imarata al-Arabiyah al-Muttahidah

People: Population: 2,924,594. **Pop. density:** 97 per sq. mi. **Urban:** 82%. **Ethnic groups:** Arab, Iranian, Pakistani, Indian. **Principal languages:** Arabic (official), several others. **Religions:** Muslim 96%, Christian, Hindu.

Geography: Area: 30,000 sq. mi. **Location:** On the S shore of the Persian Gulf. **Neighbors:** Qatar on N, Saudi Arabia on W, S, Oman on E. **Topography:** A barren, flat coastal plain gives way to uninhabited sand dunes on the S. Hajar Mts. are on E. **Capital:** Abu Dhabi. **Cities** (1990 est.): Abu Dhabi 722,000; Dubai 266,000.

Government: Type: Federation of emirates. **Head of state:** Pres. Zaid ibn Sultan an-Nahayan b. 1923; in office: Dec. 2, 1971. **Head of government:** Prime Min. Sheikh Maktum ibn Rashid al-Maktum; in office: Nov. 20, 1990. **Local divisions:** 7 autonomous emirates: Abu Dhabi, Ajman, Dubai, Fujaira, Ras al-Khaimah, Sharjah, Umm al-Qaiwain. **Defense:** 6% of GNP (1992). **Active troop strength:** 61,500.

Economy: Chief crops: Vegetables, dates. **Minerals:** Oil, natural gas. **Crude oil reserves** (1994): 98 bln. barrels. **Arable land:** 0%. **Electricity prod.** (1992): 17.8 bln. kWh. **Labor force:** 5% agric.; 85% ind. and commerce; 5% serv.; 5% gvt.

Finance: Monetary unit: Dirham (May 1995: 3.67 = $1 US). **Gross domestic product** (1993): $63.8 bln.* **Per capita GDP:** $24,000. **Imports** (1993): $18.0 bln.; partners: Japan 14%, UK 9%, U.S. 8%. **Exports** (1993): $22.6 bln.; partners: Japan 39%. **National budget** (1993): $4.8 bln. **International reserves less gold** (Apr. 1995): $7.5 bln. **Gold:** 796,000 oz t.

Transport: Motor vehicles: in use: 353,000 passenger cars, 188,000 comm. vehicles. **Civil aviation:** 1.9 bln. passenger-mi.; 4 airports with scheduled flights. **Chief ports:** Dubai, Abu Dhabi.

Communications: Television sets: 1 per 12 persons. **Radios:** 1 per 5 persons. **Telephones:** 1 per 1.9 persons.

Health: Life expectancy at birth (1995): 70 male; 75 female. **Births** (per 1,000 pop.): 27. **Deaths** (per 1,000 pop.): 3. **Natural increase:** 2.4%. **Hospital beds:** 1 per 292 persons. **Physicians:** 1 per 618 persons. **Infant mortality** (per 1,000 live births 1995): 21.

Education: Literacy (1992): 73%. **Years compulsory:** ages 6-12.

Major International Organizations: UN (World Bank, IMF, ILO), Arab League, OPEC.

Embassy: 3000 K St. NW 20007; 338-6500.

The 7 "Trucial Sheikdoms" gave Britain control of defense and foreign relations in the 19th century. They merged to become an independent state Dec. 2, 1971.

The Abu Dhabi Petroleum Co. was fully nationalized in 1975. Oil revenues have given the UAE one of the highest per capita GDPs in the world. International banking has grown in recent years.

United Kingdom
United Kingdom of Great Britain and Northern Ireland

People: Population: 58,295,119. **Age distrib.** (%): <15: 19; 65+: 16. **Pop. density:** 619 per sq. mi. **Urban:** 92%. **Ethnic groups:** English 81.5%, Scottish 9.6%, Irish 2.4%, Welsh 1.9%, Ulster 1.8%; West Indian, Indian, Pakistani, others 2.8%. **Principal languages:** English, Welsh, Scottish, Gaelic. **Religions:** Church of England, Roman Catholic.

Geography: Area: 94,251 sq. mi. **Location:** Off the NW coast of Europe, across English Channel, Strait of Dover, and North Sea. **Neighbors:** Ireland to W, France to SE. **Topography:** England is mostly rolling land, rising to Uplands of southern Scotland; Lowlands are in center of Scotland, granite Highlands are in N. Coast is heavily indented, especially on W. British Isles have milder climate than N Europe due to the Gulf Stream and ample rainfall. Severn, 220 mi., and Thames, 215 mi., are longest rivers. **Capital:** London. **Cities** (1994 est.): London 6.9 mln. (1992); Birmingham 1.0 mln.; Leeds 721,000; Glasgow 681,000; Sheffield 524,000; Bradford 481,000; Liverpool 461,000; Edinburgh 442,000; Manchester 432,000; Bristol 374,000.

Government: Type: Constitutional monarchy. **Head of state:** Queen Elizabeth II; b Apr. 21, 1926; in office: Feb. 6, 1952. **Head of government:** Prime Min. John Major; b Mar. 29, 1943; in office: Nov. 28, 1990. **Local divisions:** England and Wales: 47 counties, 7 metropolitan counties; Scotland: 9 regions, 3 island areas; Northern Ireland: 26 districts. **Defense:** 3.8% of GDP (FY 1992-93). **Active troop strength:** 254,300.

Economy: Industries: Steel, metals, vehicles, shipbuilding, banking, textiles, chemicals, electronics, aircraft, machinery, distilling. **Chief crops:** Grains, sugar beets, fruits, vegetables. **Minerals:** Coal, tin, oil, gas, limestone, iron, salt, clay. **Crude oil reserves** (1994): 4.6 bln. bbls. **Arable land:** 29%. **Livestock** (1993): cattle: 11.7 mln.; pigs: 7.0 mln.; sheep: 29.3 mln. **Fish catch** (1991): 823,000 metric tons. **Electricity prod.** (1992): 317 bln. kWh. **Labor force:** 1% agric.; 25% manuf. & constr.; 63% services.

Finance: Monetary unit: Pound (May 1995: 1.00 = $1.60 US). **Gross domestic product** (1993): $980.2 bln.* **Per capita GDP:** $16,900. **Imports** (1993): $222 bln.; partners: EU 52%, U.S. 12%. **Exports** (1993): $190 bln.; partners: EU 57%, U.S. 11%. **Tourism** (1992): $13.7 bln. **National budget** (FY 1993 est.): $400.9 bln. **International reserves less gold** (Feb. 1995): $40.8 bln. **Gold:** 18.44 mln. oz t. **Consumer prices** (change in 1994): 2.5%.

Transport: Railroads: Length: 23,518 mi. **Motor vehicles:** in use: 20.3 mln. passenger cars, 2.8 mln. comm. vehicles. **Civil aviation:** 54 bln. passenger-mi.; 54 airports with scheduled flights. **Chief ports:** London, Liverpool, Glasgow, Southampton, Cardiff, Belfast.

Communications: Television sets: 1 per 2.9 persons. **Radios:** 1 per 0.8 person. **Telephones:** 1 per 1.9 persons. **Daily newspaper circ.:** 395 per 1,000 pop.

Health: Life expectancy at birth (1995): 74 male; 80 female. **Births:** (per 1,000 pop.): 13. **Deaths:** (per 1,000 pop.): 11. **Natural increase:** 0.3%. **Hospital beds:** 1 per 146 persons. **Physicians:** 1 per 611 persons. **Infant mortality** (per 1,000 live births 1995): 7.

Education: Literacy (1992): 100%. **Years compulsory:** 12; attendance 99%.

Major International Organizations: UN and all of its specialized agencies, NATO, EU, OECD, the Commonwealth.

Embassy: 3100 Massachusetts Ave. NW 20008; 462-1340.

The United Kingdom of Great Britain and Northern Ireland comprises England, Wales, Scotland, and Northern Ireland.

Queen and Royal Family. The ruling sovereign is Elizabeth II of the House of Windsor, born Apr. 21, 1926, elder daughter of King George VI. She succeeded to the throne Feb. 6, 1952, and was crowned June 2, 1953. She was married Nov. 20, 1947, to Lt. Philip Mountbatten, born June 10, 1921, former Prince of Greece. He was created Duke of Edinburgh, Earl of Merioneth, and Baron Greenwich, and given the style H.R.H., Nov. 19, 1947; he was given the title Prince of the United Kingdom and Northern Ireland Feb. 22, 1957. Prince Charles Philip Arthur George, born Nov. 14, 1948, is the Prince of Wales and heir apparent. His son, William Philip Arthur Louis, born June 21, 1982, is second in line to the throne.

Parliament is the legislative governing body for the United Kingdom, with certain powers over dependent units. It consists of 2 houses: The **House of Lords** includes 763 hereditary and 314 life peers and peeresses, certain judges, 2 archbishops and 24 bishops of the Church of England. Total membership is over 1,000. The **House of Commons** has 650 members, who are elected by direct ballot and divided as follows: England 516; Wales 36; Scotland 71; Northern Ireland 12.

Resources and Industries. Great Britain's major occupations are manufacturing and trade. Metals and metal-using industries contribute more than 50% of the exports. Of about 60 million acres of land in England, Wales, and Scotland, 46 million are farmed, of which 17 million are arable, the rest pastures.

Large oil and gas fields have been found in the North Sea. Commercial oil production began in 1975. There are large deposits of coal.

Britain imports all of its cotton, rubber, sulphur, about 80% of its wool, half of its food and iron ore, also certain amounts of paper, tobacco, chemicals. Manufactured goods made from these basic materials have been exported since the industrial age began. Main exports are machinery, chemicals, woolen and synthetic textiles, clothing, autos and trucks, iron and steel, locomotives, ships, jet aircraft, farm machinery, drugs, radio, TV, radar and navigation equipment, scientific instruments, arms, whisky.

Religion and Education. The Church of England is Protestant Episcopal. The queen is its temporal head, with rights of appointments to archbishoprics, bishoprics, and other offices. There are 2 provinces, Canterbury and York, each headed by an archbishop. The most famous church is Westminster Abbey (1050-1760), site of coronations, tombs of Elizabeth I, Mary, Queen of Scots, kings, poets, and of the Unknown Warrior.

The most celebrated British universities are Oxford and Cambridge, each dating to the 13th century. There are about 40 other universities.

History. Britain was part of the continent of Europe until about 6,000 BC, but migration of peoples across the English Channel continued long afterward. Celts arrived 2,500 to 3,000 years ago. Their language survives in Welsh, and Gaelic enclaves.

England was added to the Roman Empire in 43 AD. After the withdrawal of Roman legions in 410, waves of Jutes, Angles, and Saxons arrived from German lands. They contended with Danish raiders for control from the 8th through 11th centuries. The last successful invasion was by French speaking Normans in 1066, who united the country with their dominions in France.

Opposition by nobles to royal authority forced King John to sign the Magna Carta in 1215, a guarantee of rights and the rule of law. In the ensuing decades, the foundations of the parliamentary system were laid.

English dynastic claims to large parts of France led to the Hundred Years War, 1338-1453, and the defeat of England. A long civil war, the War of the Roses, lasted 1455-85, and ended with the establishment of the powerful Tudor monarchy. A distinct English civilization flourished. The economy prospered over long periods of domestic peace unmatched in continental Europe. Religious independence was secured when the Church of England was separated from the authority of the pope in 1534.

Under Queen Elizabeth I, England became a major naval power, leading to the founding of colonies in the new world and the expansion of trade with Europe and the Orient. Scotland was united with England when James VI of Scotland was crowned James I of England in 1603.

A struggle between Parliament and the Stuart kings led to a bloody civil war, 1642-49, and the establishment of a republic under the Puritan Oliver Cromwell. The monarchy was restored in 1660, but the "Glorious Revolution" of 1688 confirmed the sovereignty of Parliament: a Bill of Rights was granted 1689.

In the 18th century, parliamentary rule was strengthened. Technological and entrepreneurial innovations led to the Industrial Revolution. The 13 North American colonies were lost, but replaced by growing empires in Canada and India. Britain's role in the defeat of Napoleon, 1815, strengthened its position as the leading world power.

The extension of the franchise in 1832 and 1867, the formation of trade unions, and the development of universal public education were among the drastic social changes which accompanied the spread of industrialization and urbanization in the 19th century. Large parts of Africa and Asia were added to the empire during the reign of Queen Victoria, 1837-1901.

Though victorious in World War I, Britain suffered huge casualties and economic dislocation. Ireland became independent in 1921, and independence movements became active in India and other colonies. The country suffered major bombing damage in World War II, but held out against Germany singlehandedly for a year after the fall of France in 1940.

Industrial growth continued in the postwar period, but Britain lost its leadership position to other powers. Labor governments passed socialist programs nationalizing some basic industries and expanding social security. The Conservative government of Prime Min. Margaret Thatcher, however, tried to increase the role of private enterprise. In 1987, Thatcher became the first British leader in 160 years to be elected to a 3d consecutive term as prime minister. Falling on unpopular times, she resigned as prime minister in Nov. 1990. Her successor, John Major, led Conservatives to an upset victory at the polls, Apr. 9, 1993.

The UK supported the UN resolutions against Iraq and sent military forces to the Persian Gulf War.

The Channel Tunnel linking Britain to the Continent was officially inaugurated May 6, 1994.

Wales

The Principality of Wales in western Britain has an area of 8,019 sq. mi. and a population (1992 est.) of 2,899,000. Cardiff is the capital, pop. (1994 est.) 299,000.

England and Wales are administered as a unit. Less than 20% of the population of Wales speak both English and Welsh; about 32,000 speak Welsh solely. A 1979 referendum rejected, 4-1, the creation of an elected Welsh Assembly.

Early Anglo-Saxon invaders drove Celtic peoples into the mountains of Wales, terming them Waelise (Welsh, or foreign). There they developed a distinct nationality. Members of the ruling house of Gwynedd in the 13th century fought England but were crushed, 1283. Edward of Caernarvon, son of Edward I of England, was created Prince of Wales, 1301.

Scotland

Scotland, a kingdom now united with England and Wales in Great Britain, occupies the northern 37% of the main British island, and the Hebrides, Orkney, Shetland, and smaller islands. Length, 275 mi., breadth approx. 150 mi., area, 30,418 sq. mi., population (1992 est.) 5,111,000.

The Lowlands, a belt of land approximately 60 mi. wide from the Firth of Clyde to the Firth of Forth, divide the farming region of the Southern Uplands from the granite Highlands of the North, contain 75% of the population and most of the industry. The Highlands, famous for hunting and fishing, have been opened to industry by many hydroelectric power stations.

Edinburgh, pop. (1994 est.) 442,000, is the capital. Glasgow, pop. (1994 est.) 681,000, is Britain's greatest industrial center. It is a shipbuilding complex on the Clyde and an ocean port. Aberdeen, pop. (1994 est.) 218,000, NE of Edinburgh, is a major port, center of granite industry, fish processing, and North Sea oil exploration. Dundee, pop. (1993 est.) 170,000, NE of Edinburgh, is an industrial and fish processing center. About 90,000 persons speak Gaelic as well as English.

History. Scotland was called Caledonia by the Romans who battled early Celtic tribes and occupied southern areas from the 1st to the 4th centuries. Missionaries from Britain introduced Christianity in the 4th century; St. Columba, an Irish monk, converted most of Scotland in the 6th century.

The Kingdom of Scotland was founded in 1018. William Wallace and Robert Bruce both defeated English armies 1297 and 1314, respectively.

In 1603 James VI of Scotland, son of Mary, Queen of Scots, succeeded to the throne of England as James I, and effected the Union of the Crowns. In 1707 Scotland received representation in the British Parliament, resulting from the union of former separate Parliaments. Its executive in the British cabinet is the Secretary of State for Scotland. The growing Scottish National Party urges independence. A 1979 referendum on the creation of an elected Scotland Assembly was defeated.

Memorials of Robert Burns, Sir Walter Scott, John Knox, Mary, Queen of Scots draw many tourists, as do the beauties of the Trossachs, Loch Katrine, Loch Lomond, and abbey ruins.

Industries. Engineering products are the most important industry, with growing emphasis on office machinery, autos, electronics, and other consumer goods. Oil has been discovered offshore in the North Sea, stimulating on-shore support industries.

Scotland produces fine woolens, worsteds, tweeds, silks, fine linens, and jute. It is known for its special breeds of cattle and sheep. Fisheries have large hauls of herring, cod, whiting. Whisky is the biggest export.

The Hebrides are a group of c. 500 islands, 100 inhabited, off the W coast. The Inner Hebrides include **Skye, Mull,** and **Iona,** the last famous for the arrival of St. Columba, 563 AD. The Outer Hebrides include **Lewis** and **Harris.** Industries include sheep raising and weaving. The **Orkney Islands,** c. 90, are to the NE. The capital is Kirkwall, on Pomona Is. Fish curing, sheep raising, and weaving are occupations. NE of the Orkneys are the 200 **Shetland Islands,** 24 inhabited, home of Shetland pony. The Orkneys and Shetlands have become centers for the North Sea oil industry.

Northern Ireland

Six of the 9 counties of Ulster, the NE corner of Ireland, constitute Northern Ireland, with the parliamentary boroughs of Belfast and Londonderry. Area 5,452 sq. mi., pop. (1992 est.) 1,610,000, capital and chief industrial center, Belfast, pop. (1994 est.) 281,000.

Industries. Shipbuilding, including large tankers, has long been an important industry, centered in Belfast, the largest port. Linen manufacture is also important, along with apparel, rope, and twine. Growing diversification has added engineering products, synthetic fibers, and electronics. There are large numbers of cattle, hogs, and sheep. Potatoes, poultry, and dairy foods are also produced.

Government. An act of the British Parliament, 1920, divided Northern from Southern Ireland, each with a parliament and government. When Ireland became a dominion, 1921, and later a republic, Northern Ireland chose to remain a part of the United Kingdom. It elects 12 members to the British House of Commons.

During 1968-69, large demonstrations were conducted by Roman Catholics who charged they were discriminated against in voting rights, housing, and employment. The Catholics, a minority comprising about a third of the population, demanded abolition of property qualifications for voting in local elections. Violence and terrorism intensified, involving branches of the Irish Republican Army (outlawed in the Irish Republic), Protestant groups, police, and British troops.

A succession of Northern Ireland prime ministers pressed reform programs but failed to satisfy extremists on both sides. Over 2,000 were killed in over 15 years of bombings and shootings through 1990, many in England itself. Britain suspended the Northern Ireland parliament Mar. 30, 1972, and imposed direct British rule. A coalition government was formed in 1973 when moderates won election to a new one-house Assembly. But a Protestant general strike overthrew the government in 1974 and direct rule was resumed.

The turmoil and agony of Northern Ireland was dramatized in 1981 by the deaths of 10 imprisoned Irish nationalist hunger strikers in Maze Prison near Belfast. The inmates had starved themselves to death in an attempt to achieve status as political

prisoners, but the British government refused to yield to their demands. In 1985, the Hillsborough agreement gave the Rep. of Ireland a voice in the governing of Northern Ireland; the accord was strongly opposed by Ulster loyalists. On Dec. 12, 1993, Britain and Ireland announced a declaration of principles aimed at leading to a political settlement of the Northern Ireland issue. On Aug. 31, 1994, the IRA announced a cease-fire, saying it would rely on political means to achieve its objectives.

Education and Religion. Northern Ireland is 2/3 Protestant, 1/3 Roman Catholic. Education is compulsory through age 15.

Channel Islands

The Channel Islands, area 75 sq. mi., pop. (1986 est.) 145,000, off the NW coast of France, the only parts of the one-time Dukedom of Normandy belonging to England, are **Jersey, Guernsey** and the dependencies of Guernsey — **Alderney, Brechou, Great Sark, Little Sark, Herm, Jethou and Lihou.** Jersey and Guernsey have separate legal existences and lieutenant governors named by the Crown. The islands were the only British soil occupied by German troops in World War II.

Isle of Man

The Isle of Man, area 227 sq. mi., pop. (1991 est.) 69,788, is in the Irish Sea, 20 mi. from Scotland, 30 mi. from Cumberland. It is rich in lead and iron. The island has its own laws and a lieutenant governor appointed by the Crown. The Tynwald (legislature) consists of the Legislative Council, partly elected, and House of Keys, elected. Capital: Douglas. Farming, tourism, fishing (kippers, scallops) are chief occupations. Man is famous for the Manx tailless cat.

Gibraltar

Gibraltar, a dependency on the southern coast of Spain, guards the entrance to the Mediterranean. The Rock has been in British possession since 1704. The Rock is 2.75 mi. long, 3/4 of a mi. wide and 1,396 ft. in height; a narrow isthmus connects it with the mainland. Pop. (1995 est.) 31,874.

Gibraltar has historically been an object of contention between Britain and Spain. Residents voted with near unanimity to remain under British rule, in a 1967 referendum held in pursuance of a UN resolution on decolonization. A new constitution, May 30, 1969, increased Gibraltarian control of domestic affairs (the UK continues to handle defense and internal security matters). Following a 1984 agreement between Britain and Spain, the border, closed by Spain in 1969, was fully reopened in Feb. 1985. A UN General Assembly resolution requested Britain to end Gibraltar's colonial status by Oct. 1, 1996. No settlement has been reached.

British West Indies

Swinging in a vast arc from the coast of Venezuela NE, then N and NW toward Puerto Rico are the Leeward Islands, forming a coral and volcanic barrier sheltering the Caribbean from the open Atlantic. Many of the islands are self-governing British possessions. Universal suffrage was instituted 1951-54; ministerial systems were set up 1956-1960.

The **Leeward Islands,** still associated with the UK are **Montserrat,** area 32 sq. mi., pop. (1995 est.) 12,700; capital Plymouth, the small **British Virgin Islands,** pop. 13,000, and **Anguilla** pop. (1992) 8,960, the most northerly of the Leeward Islands.

The three **Cayman Islands,** a dependency, lie S of Cuba, NW of Jamaica. Pop. (1995 est.) 33,200, most of it on Grand Cayman. It is a free port; in the 1970s Grand Cayman became a tax-free refuge for foreign funds and branches of many Western banks were opened there. Total area 102 sq. mi., capital Georgetown.

The **Turks and Caicos Islands,** at the SE end of the Bahama Islands, are a separate possession. There are about 30 islands, only 6 inhabited; area 193 sq. mi., pop. (1995 est.) 13,900; capital Grand Turk. Salt, crayfish, and conch shells are the main exports.

Bermuda

Bermuda is a British dependency governed by a royal governor and an assembly, dating from 1620, the oldest legislative body among British dependencies. Capital is Hamilton.

It is a group of 360 small islands of coral formation, 20 inhabited, comprising 20.6 sq. mi. in the western Atlantic, 580 mi. E of North Carolina. Pop. (1995 est.) 61,600 (about 61% of African descent). Density is high.

The U.S. has air and naval bases under long-term lease, and a NASA tracking facility.

Bermuda boasts many resort hotels. The government raises most revenue from import duties. Exports: petroleum products, medicine. In a referendum Aug. 15, 1995, voters rejected independence by nearly a 3-to-1 majority.

South Atlantic

Falkland Islands and Dependencies, a British dependency, lies 300 mi. E of the Strait of Magellan at the southern end of South America.

The Falklands or Islas Malvinas include about 200 islands, area 4,700 sq. mi., pop. (1991 cen.) 2,121. Sheep-grazing is the main industry; wool is the principal export. There are indications of large oil and gas deposits. The islands are also claimed by Argentina though 97% of inhabitants are of British origin. Argentina invaded the islands Apr. 2, 1982. The British responded by sending a task force to the area, landing their main force on the Falklands, May 21, and forcing an Argentine surrender at Port Stanley, June 14.

British Antarctic Territory, south of 60° S lat., was made a separate colony in 1962 and comprises mainly the **South Shetland Islands,** the **South Orkneys** and **Graham's Land.** A chain of meteorological stations is maintained.

St. Helena, an island 1,200 mi. off the W coast of Africa and 1,800 E of South America, has 47 sq. mi. and est. pop., 1995, of 6,800. Flax, lace, and rope making are the chief industries. After Napoleon Bonaparte was defeated at Waterloo the Allies exiled him to St. Helena, where he lived from Oct. 16, 1815, to his death, May 5, 1821. Capital is Jamestown.

Tristan da Cunha is the principal of a group of islands of volcanic origin, total area 40 sq. mi., halfway between the Cape of Good Hope and South America. A volcanic peak 6,760 ft. high erupted in 1961. The 262 inhabitants were removed to England, but most returned in 1963. The islands are dependencies of St. Helena. Pop. (1988) 313.

Ascension is an island of volcanic origin, 34 sq. mi. in area, 700 mi. NW of St. Helena, through which it is administered. It is a communications relay center for Britain, and has a U.S. satellite tracking center. Pop. (1993) was 1,117, half of them communications workers. The island is noted for sea turtles.

Hong Kong

A Crown Colony at the mouth of the Canton R. in China, 90 mi. S of Canton. Its nucleus is Hong Kong Is., 35½ sq. mi., acquired from China 1841, on which is located Victoria, the capital. Opposite is Kowloon Peninsula, 3 sq. mi. and Stonecutters Is., ¼ sq. mi., added, 1860. An additional 355 sq. mi. known as the New Territories, a mainland area and islands, were leased from China, 1898, for 99 years. Britain and China, Dec. 19, 1984, signed an agreement under which Hong Kong would be allowed to keep its capitalist system for 50 years after 1997, the year that the 99-year lease will expire. During 1994 the Hong Kong legislature approved democratic reforms, which were opposed by China. Total area of the colony is 415 sq. mi., with a population, 1995 est., of 5.5 million, including fewer than 20,000 British. From 1949 to 1962 Hong Kong absorbed more than a million refugees from China.

Hong Kong harbor was long an important British naval station and one of the world's great trans-shipment ports.

Principal industries are textiles and apparel; also tourism, $4.9 bln. expenditures (1991), shipbuilding, iron and steel, fishing, cement, and small manufactures.

Spinning mills, among the best in the world, and low wages compete with textiles elsewhere and have resulted in the protective measures in some countries. Hong Kong also has a booming electronics industry.

British Indian Ocean Territory

Formed Nov. 1965, embracing islands formerly dependencies of Mauritius or Seychelles: the Chagos Archipelago (including Diego Garcia), Aldabra, Farquhar and Des Roches. The latter 3 were transferred to Seychelles, which became independent in 1976. Area 22 sq. mi. No civilian population remains.

Pacific Ocean

Pitcairn Island is in the Pacific, halfway between South America and Australia. The island was discovered in 1767 by Carteret but was not inhabited until 23 years later when the mutineers of the Bounty landed there. The area is 1.7 sq. mi. and 1993 pop. was 65. It is a British colony and is administered by a British Representative in New Zealand and a local Council. The uninhabited islands of **Henderson, Ducie,** and **Oeno** are in the Pitcairn group.

United States of America

People: Population: 263,814,032 (incl. 50 states & Dist. of Columbia). **Age distrib.** (%): <15: 22; 65+: 13. **Pop. density:** 72 per sq. mi. **Urban:** 75%.

Geography: 3,679,192 sq. mi. (incl. 50 states and D. of C.). Vast central plain, mountains in west, hills and low mountains in east.

Government: Federal republic, strong democratic tradition. **Head of state:** Pres. Bill Clinton; b Aug. 19, 1946; in office: Jan. 20, 1993. **Administrative divisions:** 50 states and Dist. of Columbia. **Defense:** 5.3% of GDP (1992). **Active troop strength:** 1.65 mln.

Economy: Minerals: Coal, copper, lead, molybdenum, phosphates, uranium, bauxite, gold, iron, mercury, nickel, potash, silver, tungsten, zinc. **Crude oil reserves** (1994): 24 bln. barrels. **Arable land:** 20%. **Livestock** (1992): cattle: 99.6 mln.; pigs: 57.7 mln.; sheep: 10.7 mln. **Fish catch** (1992): 3.3 mln. metric tons. **Electricity prod.** (1992): 3,230 bln. kWh.

Finance: Gross domestic product (1993): 6.38 trl.* **Per capita GDP:** $24,700. **Imports** (1993): $582 bln.; partners: Canada 19%, Japan 19%, Mexico 7%. **Exports** (1993): $465 bln.; partners: Canada 22%, Japan 10%, Mexico 9%, UK 6%. **Tourism** (1992): $53.8 bln. **International reserves less gold** (May 1995): $79.5 bln. **Gold:** 261.81 mln. oz t. **Consumer prices** (change in 1994): 2.6%.

Transport: Railroads: Length: 136,000 mi. **Motor vehicles:** in use: 144 mln. passenger cars, 46 mln. comm. vehicles. **Civil aviation:** 480 bln. passenger-mi.; 834 airports with scheduled flights.

Communications: Television sets: 1 per 1.2 persons. **Radios:** 1 per 0.5 persons. **Telephones:** 1 per 1.3 persons. **Daily newspaper circ.:** 250 per 1,000 pop.

Health: Life expectancy at birth (1995): 73 male; 80 female. **Births** (per 1,000 pop.): 15. **Deaths** (per 1,000 pop.): 8. **Natural increase:** 0.7%. **Hospital beds:** 1 per 218 persons. **Physicians:** 1 per 391 persons. **Infant mortality** (per 1,000 live births 1995): 8.

Education: Literacy (1991): 96%.

Major International Organizations: UN (WTO, ILO, IMF, WHO, FAO), OAS, NATO, OECD.

Uruguay
Oriental Republic of Uruguay
República Oriental del Uruguay

People: Population: 3,222,716. **Age distrib.** (%): <15: 26; 65+: 12. **Pop. density:** 47 per sq. mi. **Urban:** 90%. **Ethnic groups:** white (Iberians, Italians) 88%, mestizo 8%, black 4%. **Principal languages:** Spanish. **Religions:** Roman Catholic 66%.

Geography: Area: 68,037 sq. mi. **Location:** In southern South America, on the Atlantic O. **Neighbors:** Argentina on W, Brazil on N. **Topography:** Uruguay is composed of rolling, grassy plains and hills, well-watered by rivers flowing W to Uruguay R. **Capital:** Montevideo (1992 est.): 1.4 mln.

Government: Type: Republic. **Head of state:** Pres. Julio María Sanguinetti Cairolo; Jan. 6, 1936; in office: Mar. 1, 1995. **Local divisions:** 19 departments. **Defense:** 2.3% of GDP (1991 est.). **Active troop strength:** 25,600.

Economy: Industries: Meat packing, textiles, wine, oil products. **Chief crops:** Corn, wheat, citrus fruits, rice, oats, linseed. **Arable land:** 8%. **Livestock** (1992): cattle: 9.5 mln.; sheep: 25.7 mln. **Fish catch** (1992): 126,000 metric tons. **Electricity prod.** (1992): 6.0 bln. kWh. **Labor force** 11% agric.; 19% manuf.; 33% serv.; 25% govt.; 12% comm.

Finance: Monetary unit: Peso (Apr. 1995: 6.04 = $1 US). **Gross domestic product** (1993): $19 bln.* **Per capita GDP:** $6,000. **Imports** (1993): $2.3 bln.; partners: EU 27%, Brazil

27%, Argentina 21%, U.S. 10%. **Exports** (1993): $1.6 bln.; partners: Brazil 22%, Argentina 19%, U.S. 9%. **Tourism** (1992): $381 mln. **National budget** (1991): $3.0 bln. **International reserves less gold** (Mar. 1995): $1.0 bln. **Gold:** 1.71 mln. oz t. **Consumer prices** (change in 1994): 44.7%

Transport: Railroads: Length: 1,865 mi. **Motor vehicles:** in use: 311,000 passenger cars, 149,000 comm. vehicles. **Civil aviation:** 293 mln. passenger-mi.; 7 airports. **Chief port:** Montevideo.

Communications: Television sets: 1 per 5.2 persons. **Radios:** 1 per 1.8 persons. **Telephones:** 1 per 5.4 persons. **Daily newspaper circ.:** 233 per 1,000 pop.

Health: Life expectancy at birth (1995): 71 male; 78 female. **Births** (per 1,000 pop.): 18. **Deaths** (per 1,000 pop.): 9. **Natural increase:** 0.8%. **Hospital beds:** 1 per 215 persons. **Physicians:** 1 per 295 persons. **Infant mortality** (per 1,000 live births 1995): 16.

Education: Literacy (1992): 95%.

Major International Organizations: UN (WTO, IMF, WHO), OAS.

Embassy: 1918 F St. NW 20006; 331-1313.

Spanish settlers did not begin replacing the indigenous Charrua Indians until 1624. Portuguese from Brazil arrived later, but Uruguay was attached to the Spanish Viceroyalty of Rio de la Plata in the 18th century. Rebels fought against Spain beginning in 1810. An independent republic was declared Aug. 25, 1825.

Socialist measures were adopted as far back as 1911. The state owns the power, telephone, railroad, cement, oil-refining, and other industries.

Uruguay's standard of living was one of the highest in South America, and political and labor conditions among the freest. Economic stagnation, inflation, floods and drought, and a general strike in the late 1960s brought government attempts to strengthen the economy through devaluation of the peso and wage and price controls.

Terrorist activities led to Pres. Juan Maria Bordaberry agreeing to military control of his administration Feb. 1973. In June he abolished Congress and set up a Council of State in its place. Bordaberry was removed by the military in a 1976 coup. Civilian government was restored to the country in 1985.

Uzbekistan
Republic of Uzbekistan
Ozbekiston Republikasy

People: Population: 23,089,261. **Age distrib.** (%): <15: 41; 65+: 4. **Pop. density:** 134 per sq. mi. **Urban:** 41%. **Ethnic groups:** Uzbek 71%, Russian 8%. **Principal languages:** Uzbek, Russian. **Religions:** mostly Sunni Muslim.

Geography: Area: 172,700 sq. mi. **Neighbors:** Kazakhstan on N and W, Kyrgyzstan and Tajikistan on E, Afghanistan and Turkmenistan on S. **Topography:** Mostly plains and desert. **Capital:** Tashkent (1992 est.): 2.1 mln.

Government: Type: Republic. **Head of state:** Pres. Islam A. Karimov; b 1938; in office: March 24, 1990. **Head of government:** Prime Min. Abdulkhashim Mutalov; in office: Jan. 8, 1992. **Local divisions:** 12 regions, 1 autonomous republic, and Tashkent. **Defense: Active troop strength:** 45,000.

Economy: Industries: Steel, tractors, natural gas, textiles. **Chief crops:** Cotton, rice. **Minerals:** Gas, oil, coal, copper. **Arable land:** 10%. **Livestock** (1994): cattle: 5.3 mln.; sheep: 9.4 mln. **Electricity prod.** (1992): 51.0 bln. kWh. **Labor force:** 43% agric. & forestry; 22% ind. & constr.

Finance: Monetary unit: Sum (Oct. 1994: 16 = $1 US). **Gross domestic product** (1993 est.): $53.7 bln.* **Per capita GDP:** $2,430. **Imports** (1992): $929 mln. **Exports** (1992): $869 mln.

Transport: Railroads: Length: 4,200 mi. **Civil aviation:** 6.5 bln. passenger-mi.; 1 airport.

Communications: Television sets: 1 per 6.3 persons. **Telephones:** 1 per 14 persons.

Health: Life expectancy at birth (1995): 65 male; 72 female. **Births** (per 1,000 pop.): 29. **Deaths** (per 1,000 pop.): 6. **Natural increase:** 2.3%. **Hospital beds:** 1 per 83 persons. **Physicians:** 1 per 282 persons. **Infant mortality** (per 1,000 live births 1995): 52.

Education: Literacy (1992): 97%.

Major International Organizations: UN, CIS.

Embassy: 1511 K St. NW 20005; 638-4266.

The region was overrun by the Mongols under Genghis Khan in 1220. In the 14th century, Uzbekistan became the center of a native empire—that of the Timurids. In later centuries Muslim feudal states emerged. Russian military conquest began in the 19th century.

The Uzbek SSR became a Soviet Union republic in 1925. Uzbekistan declared independence Aug. 29, 1991. It became an independent republic when the Soviet Union disbanded Dec. 26, 1991. Subsequently, the government of Uzbekistan was dominated by former Communists.

Vanuatu
Republic of Vanuatu
Ripablik blong Vanuatu

People: Population: 173,648. **Pop. density:** 37 per sq. mi. **Urban:** 18%. **Ethnic groups:** mainly Melanesian, some European, Asian, Pacific Islander. **Principal languages:** French, English (both official), Bislama. **Religions:** Presbyterian 37%, Anglican 15%, Roman Catholic 15%, other Christian 10%, indigenous beliefs 8%.

Geography: Area: 4,707 sq. mi. **Location:** SW Pacific, 1,200 mi. NE of Brisbane, Australia. **Topography:** Dense forest with narrow coastal strips of cultivated land. **Capital:** Vila (1990): 19,000.

Government: Type: Republic. **Head of state:** Pres. Jean-Marie Leye; b 1932; in office: Mar. 2, 1994. **Head of gov't:** Prime Min. Maxime Carlot Korman; in office: Dec. 16, 1991. **Local divisions:** 11 island councils.

Economy: Industries: Fish-freezing, meat canneries, tourism. **Chief crops:** Copra, cocoa, coffee. **Minerals:** Manganese. **Other resources:** Forests, cattle. **Fish catch** (1991): 3,200 metric tons.

Finance: Monetary unit: Vatu (May 1995): 113 = $1 US). **Gross domestic product** (1990): $142 mln. **Imports** (1991): $74 mln. **Exports** (1991): $15 mln. **Tourism** (1992): $27 mln.

Communications: Radios: 1 per 2.9 persons.

Health: Life expectancy at birth (1995): 58 male; 62 female. **Births** (per 1,000 pop.): 31. **Deaths** (per 1,000 pop.): 9. **Natural increase:** 2.2%. **Infant mortality** (per 1,000 live births 1995): 66.

Education: Literacy (1992): 53%. Education not compulsory, but 85-90% of children of primary school age attend primary schools.

Major International Organizations: UN, the Commonwealth.

The Anglo-French condominium of the New Hebrides, administered jointly by France and Great Britain since 1906, became the independent Republic of Vanuatu on July 30, 1980.

Vatican City (The Holy See)
Città del Vaticano (Santa Sede)

People: Population: 811. **Ethnic groups:** Italian, Swiss. **Principal languages:** Latin, Italian.

Geography: Area: 108.7 acres. **Location:** In Rome, Italy. **Neighbors:** Completely surrounded by Italy.

Monetary unit: Vatican Lira, Italian Lira.

Apostolic Nunciature in U.S.: 3339 Massachusetts Ave. NW 20008; 333-7121.

The popes for many centuries, with brief interruptions, held temporal sovereignty over mid-Italy (the so-called Papal States), comprising an area of some 16,000 sq. mi., with a population in the 19th century of more than 3 million. This territory was incorporated in the new Kingdom of Italy, the sovereignty of the pope being confined to the palaces of the Vatican and the Lateran in Rome and the villa of Castel Gandolfo, by an Italian law, May 13, 1871. This law also guaranteed to the pope and his successors a yearly indemnity of over $620,000. The allowance, however, remained unclaimed.

A Treaty of Conciliation, a concordat and a financial convention were signed Feb. 11, 1929, by Cardinal Gasparri and Premier Mussolini. The documents established the independent state of Vatican City, and gave the Catholic religion special status in Italy. The treaty (Lateran Agreement) was made part of the Constitution of Italy (Article 7) in 1947. Italy and the Vatican reached preliminary agreement in 1976 on revisions of the concordat, that would eliminate Roman Catholicism as the state religion and end required religious education in Italian schools.

Vatican City includes St. Peter's, the Vatican Palace and Museum covering over 13 acres, the Vatican gardens, and neighboring buildings between Viale Vaticano and the Church. Thirteen buildings in Rome, outside the boundaries, enjoy extraterritorial rights; these buildings house congregations or officers necessary for the administration of the Holy See.

The legal system is based on the code of canon law, the apostolic constitutions, and the laws especially promulgated for the Vatican City by the pope. The Secretariat of State represents the Holy See in its diplomatic relations. By the Treaty of Conciliation the pope is pledged to a perpetual neutrality unless his mediation is specifically requested. This, however, does not prevent the defense of the Church whenever it is persecuted.

The present sovereign of the State of Vatican City is the Supreme Pontiff John Paul II, Karol Wojtyla, born in Wadowice, Poland, May 18, 1920, elected Oct. 16, 1978 (the first non-Italian to be elected Pope in 456 years).

The U.S. restored formal relations in 1984 after the U.S. Congress repealed an 1867 ban on diplomatic relations with the Vatican. The Vatican and Israel agreed to establish formal relations Dec. 30, 1993.

Venezuela

Republic of Venezuela

República de Venezuela

People: Population: 21,004,773. **Age distrib.** (%): <15: 38; 65+: 4. **Pop. density:** 60 per sq. mi. **Urban:** 84%. **Ethnic groups:** mestizo 67%, white (Spanish, Portuguese, Italian) 21%, black 10%, Indian 2%. **Principal languages:** Spanish (official). **Religions:** Roman Catholic 96%.

Geography: Area: 352,144 sq. mi. **Location:** On the Caribbean coast of South America. **Neighbors:** Colombia on W, Brazil on S, Guyana on E. **Topography:** Flat coastal plain and Orinoco Delta are bordered by Andes Mts. and hills. Plains, called llanos, extend between mountains and Orinoco. Guyana Highlands and plains are S of Orinoco, which stretches 1,600 mi. and drains 80% of Venezuela. **Capital:** Caracas. **Cities** (1990 est.): Caracas 1.3 mln.; Maracaibo 1.2 mln.; Valencia 955,000; Barquisimeto 724,000.

Government: Type: Federal republic. **Head of state:** Pres. Rafael Caldera Rodríguez; b Jan. 24, 1916; in office: Feb. 2, 1994. **Local divisions:** 21 states, territory, federal district, federal dependency. **Defense:** 4% of GDP (1991). **Active troop strength:** 79,000.

Economy: Industries: Steel, oil products, textiles. **Chief crops:** Coffee, rice, corn, fruits, sugar. **Minerals:** Oil, gas, iron (extensive reserves and production), gold. **Crude oil reserves** (1994): 63 bln. barrels. **Arable land:** 3%. **Livestock** (1992): cattle: 14.1 mln. **Fish catch** (1991): 353,000 metric tons. **Electricity prod.** (1992): 58.5 bln. kWh. **Labor force:** 16% agric.; 28% ind.; 56% services.

Finance: Monetary unit: Bolivar (May 1995: 170 = $1 US). **Gross domestic product** (1993): $161 bln.* **Per capita GDP:** $8,000. **Imports** (1993): $11.0 bln.; partners: U.S. 50%. **Exports** (1993): $14.2 bln.; partners: U.S. 42%. **Tourism** (1992): $432 mln. **National budget** (1993): $11.9 bln. **International reserves less gold** (May 1995): $7.9 bln. **Gold:** 11.46 mln. oz t. **Consumer prices** (change in 1994): 60.8%.

Transport: Railroads: Length: 226 mi. **Motor vehicles:** in use: 1.6 mln. passenger cars, 456,000 comm. vehicles. **Civil aviation:** 4.2 bln. passenger-mi.; 25 airports with scheduled flights. **Chief ports:** Maracaibo, La Guaira, Puerto Cabello.

Communications: Television sets: 1 per 5.5 persons. **Radios:** 1 per 2.5 persons. **Telephones:** 1 per 9.4 persons. **Daily newspaper circ.:** 142 per 1,000 pop.

Health: Life expectancy at birth (1995): 70 male; 76 female. **Births** (per 1,000 pop.): 25. **Deaths** (per 1,000 pop.): 5. **Natural increase:** 2.1%. **Hospital beds:** 1 per 382 persons. **Physicians:** 1 per 576 persons. **Infant mortality** (per 1,000 live births 1995): 26.

Education: Literacy (1992): 92%. **Years compulsory:** 8; attendance 82%.

Major International Organizations: UN (IMF, WTO, WHO, FAO), OAS, OPEC.

Embassy: 1099 30th St. NW 20007; 342-2214.

Columbus first set foot on the South American continent on the peninsula of Paria, Aug. 1498. Alonso de Ojeda, 1499, found Lake Maracaibo, called the land Venezuela, or Little Venice, because natives had houses on stilts. Venezuela was under Spanish domination until 1821. The republic was formed after secession from the Colombian Federation in 1830.

Military strongmen ruled Venezuela for most of the 20th century. They promoted the oil industry; some social reforms were implemented. Since 1959, the country has had democratically elected governments.

Venezuela helped found the Organization of Petroleum Exporting Countries (OPEC). The government, Jan. 1, 1976, nationalized the oil industry with compensation. Oil accounts for much of total export earnings and the economy suffered a severe cash crisis in the 1980s and 1990s as a result of falling oil revenues. The government has attempted to reduce dependence on oil.

A coup attempt, led by midlevel military officers, was thwarted by loyalist troops Feb. 4, 1992. A second coup attempt was thwarted in Nov. Pres. Carlos Andrés Pérez was suspended from office and charged with misappropriating government funds, May 1993. Citing an economic crisis, Pres. Rafael Caldera Rodríguez, a populist elected Dec. 5, 1993, suspended many civil liberties June 27, 1994; constitutional rights were restored in most regions July 6, 1995.

Vietnam

Socialist Republic of Vietnam

Cong Hoa Xa Hoi Chu Nghia Viet Nam

People: Population: 74,393,324. **Age distrib.** (%): <15: 39; 65+: 5. **Pop. density:** 585 per sq. mi. **Urban:** 21%. **Ethnic groups:** Vietnamese 85–90%, Chinese 3%, Muong, Thai, Meo, Khmer, Man, Cham. **Principal languages:** Vietnamese (official), French, Chinese. **Religions:** mainly Buddhist and Taoist, also Roman Catholic, indigenous beliefs, Muslim, Protestant.

Geography: Area: 127,246 sq. mi. **Location:** On the E coast of the Indochinese Peninsula in SE Asia. **Neighbors:** China on N, Laos, Cambodia on W. **Topography:** Vietnam is long and narrow, with a 1,400-mi. coast. About 24% of country is readily arable, including the densely settled Red R. valley in the N, narrow coastal plains in center, and the wide, often marshy Mekong R. Delta in the S. The rest consists of semiarid plateaus and barren mountains, with some stretches of tropical rain forest. **Capital:** Hanoi. **Cities** (1992): Ho Chi Minh City 4.2 mln.; Hanoi 2.1 mln.

Government: Type: Communist. **Head of state:** Pres. Le Duc Anh; b 1920; in office: Sept. 23, 1992. **Head of government:** Prime Min. Vo Van Kiet; b 1922; in office: Aug. 8, 1991. **Local divisions:** 50 provinces, 3 municipalities. **Defense:** 11% of GNP (1992). **Active troop strength:** 572,000.

Economy: Industries: Food processing, textiles, cement, chemical fertilizers. **Chief crops:** Rice, rubber, fruits and vegetables, soybeans, coffee, tea, bananas. **Minerals:** Phosphates, coal, manganese, bauxite, chromate, oil. **Crude oil reserves** (1994): 500 mln. bbls. **Other resources:** Forests. **Arable land:** 22%. **Livestock** (1993): cattle: 3.3 mln.; pigs: 14.9 mln. **Fish catch** (1992): 1.1 mln. metric tons. **Electricity prod.** (1992): 9 bln. kWh. **Labor force:** 65% agric.; 35% ind. and services.

Finance: Monetary unit: Dong (Oct. 1994: 11,053 = $1 US). **Gross national product** (1993): $72 bln.* **Per capita GNP:** $1,000. **Imports** (1993): $3.1 bln.; partners: Singapore 28%, Japan 14%. **Exports** (1993): $2.6 bln.; partners: Japan

34%, Singapore 18%. **Tourism** (1992): $80 mln. **National budget** (1992): $2 bln.

Transport: Railroads: Length: 2,001 mi. **Civil aviation:** 54 mln. passenger-mi.; 12 airports with scheduled flights. **Chief ports:** Ho Chi Minh City, Haiphong, Da Nang.

Communications: Television sets: 1 per 28 persons. **Radios:** 1 per 8.8 persons. **Telephones:** 1 per 563 persons. **Daily newspaper circ.:** 9 per 1,000 pop.

Health: Life expectancy at birth (1995): 64 male; 68 female. **Births** (per 1,000 pop.): 26. **Deaths** (per 1,000 pop.): 8. **Natural increase:** 1.9%. **Hospital beds:** 1 per 329 persons. **Physicians:** 1 per 2,617 persons. **Infant mortality** (per 1,000 live births 1995): 45.

Education: Literacy (1994): 88%.

Major International Organizations: UN (IMF, WHO).

Vietnam's recorded history began in Tonkin before the Christian era. Settled by Viets from central China, Vietnam was held by China, 111 BC-939 AD, and was a vassal state during subsequent periods. Vietnam defeated the armies of Kublai Khan, 1288. Conquest by France began in 1858 and ended in 1884 with the protectorates of Tonkin and Annam in the N and the colony of Cochin-China in the S.

In 1940 Vietnam was occupied by Japan; nationalist aims gathered force. A number of groups formed the Vietminh (Independence) League, headed by Ho Chi Minh, Communist guerrilla leader. In Aug. 1945 the Vietminh forced out Bao Dai, former emperor of Annam, head of a Japan-sponsored regime. France, seeking to reestablish colonial control, battled Communist and nationalist forces, 1946-1954, and was finally defeated at Dienbienphu, May 8, 1954. Meanwhile, on July 1, 1949, Bao Dai had formed a State of Vietnam, with himself as chief of state, with French approval. China backed Ho Chi Minh.

A cease-fire signed in Geneva July 21, 1954, provided for a buffer zone, withdrawal of French troops from the North, and elections to determine the country's future. Under the agreement the Communists gained control of territory north of the 17th parallel, with its capital at Hanoi and Ho Chi Minh as president. South Vietnam came to comprise the 39 southern provinces. Some 900,000 North Vietnamese fled to South Vietnam.

On Oct. 26, 1955, Ngo Dinh Diem, premier of the interim government of South Vietnam, proclaimed the Republic of Vietnam and became its first president.

The North, adopted a constitution Dec. 31, 1959, based on Communist principles and calling for reunification of all Vietnam. North Vietnam sought to take over South Vietnam beginning in 1954. Fighting persisted from 1956, with the Communist Vietcong, aided by North Vietnam, pressing war in the South. Northern aid to Vietcong guerrillas was intensified in 1959, and large-scale troop infiltration began in 1964, with Soviet and Chinese arms assistance. Large Northern forces were stationed in border areas of Laos and Cambodia.

A serious political conflict arose in the South in 1963 when Buddhists denounced authoritarianism and brutality. This paved the way for a military coup Nov. 1-2, 1963, which overthrew Diem. Several other military coups followed.

In 1964, the U.S. began air strikes against North Vietnam. Beginning in 1965, the raids were stepped up and U.S. troops became combatants. U.S. troop strength in Vietnam, which reached a high of 543,400 in Apr. 1969, was ordered reduced by President Nixon in a series of withdrawals, beginning in June 1969. U.S. bombings were resumed in 1972-73.

A cease-fire agreement was signed in Paris Jan. 27, 1973 by the U.S., North and South Vietnam, and the Vietcong. It was never implemented.

North Vietnamese forces launched attacks against remaining government outposts in the Central Highlands in the first months of 1975. Government retreats turned into a rout, and the Saigon regime surrendered April 30. North Vietnam assumed control, and began transforming society along Communist lines.

The war's toll included — Combat deaths: U.S. 47,369; South Vietnam over 200,000; other allied forces 5,225. Total U.S. fatalities numbered more than 58,000. Vietnamese civilian casualties were over a million. Displaced war refugees in South Vietnam totaled over 6.5 million.

The country was officially reunited July 2, 1976. The Northern capital, flag, anthem, emblem, and currency were applied to the new state. Nearly all major government posts went to officials of the former Northern government.

Heavy fighting with Cambodia took place, 1977-80, amid mutual charges of aggression and atrocities against civilians. Increasing numbers of Vietnamese civilians, ethnic Chinese, escaped the country, via the sea, or the overland route across Cambodia. Vietnam launched an offensive against Cambodian refugee strongholds along the Thai-Cambodian border in 1985; they also engaged Thai troops.

Relations with China soured as 140,000 ethnic Chinese left Vietnam charging discrimination; China cut off economic aid. Reacting to Vietnam's invasion of Cambodia, China attacked 4 Vietnamese border provinces, Feb. 1979, instigating heavy fighting.

Vietnam announced a package of reforms aimed at reducing central control of the economy in 1987, as many of the old revolutionary followers of Ho Chi Minh were removed from office.

Citing Vietnamese cooperation in returning remains of U.S. soldiers killed in the Vietnam War, the U.S. announced an end Feb. 3, 1994, to a 19-year-old U.S. embargo on trade with Vietnam. The U.S. extended full diplomatic recognition to Vietnam July 11, 1995.

Western Samoa
Independent State of Western Samoa
Malotuto'atasi o Samoa i Sisifo

People: Population: 209,360. **Age distrib.** (%): <15: 41; 65+: 4. **Pop. density:** 192 per sq. mi. **Urban:** 21%. **Ethnic groups:** Samoan (Polynesian) 93%, Euronesian (mixed) 7%, European, other Pacific Islanders. **Principal languages:** Samoan, English (both official). **Religions** Christian 99.7%.

Geography: Area: 1,093 sq. mi. **Location:** In the S Pacific O. **Neighbors:** Nearest are Fiji on W, Tonga on S. **Topography:** Main islands, Savai'i (670 sq. mi.) and Upolu (429 sq. mi.), both ruggedly mountainous, and small islands Manono and Apolima. **Capital:** Apia (1991 est.): 33,000.

Government: Type: Constitutional monarchy. **Head of state:** Malietoa Tanumafili II; b Jan. 4, 1913; in office: Jan. 1, 1962. **Head of government:** Prime Min. Tofilau Eti Alesana; in office: Apr. 11, 1988. **Local divisions:** 11 districts.

Economy: Chief crops: Coconuts, yams, bananas. **Other resources:** Hardwoods, fish. **Arable land:** 19%. **Electricity prod.** (1990): 45 mln. kWh. **Labor force:** 58% agric.

Finance: Monetary unit: Tala (May 1995: 1.00 = $.41 US). **Gross domestic product** (1993): $400 mln.* **Per capita GDP:** $2,000. **Imports** (1992): $11.5 mln.; partners: NZ 37%. **Exports** (1992): $5.7 mln.; partners: NZ 34%. **International reserves less gold** (Apr. 1995): $50 mln. **Consumer prices** (change in 1994): 18.3%.

Transport: Motor vehicles: in use: 2,300 passenger cars, 3,300 comm. vehicles. **Chief ports:** Apia, Asau.

Communications: Radios: 1 per 2.2 persons. **Telephones:** 1 per 18 persons.

Health: Life expectancy at birth (1995): 66 male; 71 female. **Births** (per 1,000 pop.): 32. **Deaths** (per 1,000 pop.): 6. **Natural increase:** 2.6%. **Hospital beds:** 1 per 255 persons. **Physicians:** 1 per 3,183 persons. **Infant mortality** (per 1,000 live births 1995): 35.

Education: Literacy (1989): 90%. 95% attend elementary school.

Major International Organizations: UN (IMF, World Bank), the Commonwealth.

Embassy: 820 2d Ave. New York, NY 10017; (212) 599-6196.

Western Samoa was a German colony, 1899 to 1914, when New Zealand landed troops and took over. It became a New Zealand mandate under the League of Nations and, in 1945, a New Zealand UN Trusteeship.

An elected local government took office in Oct. 1959 and the country became fully independent Jan. 1, 1962.

Yemen
Republic of Yemen
al-Jumhuriyah al-Yamaniyah

People: Population: 14,728,474. **Pop. density:** 72 per sq. mi. **Urban:** 25%. **Ethnic groups:** Arab, some Afro-Arab, South Asian. **Principal languages:** Arabic. **Religions:** Muslim (Sha'fi-Sunni, Zaydi-Shi'a).

Geography: Area: 205,356 sq. mi. **Location:** On the S coast of the Arabian Peninsula. **Neighbors:** Saudi Arabia on NE, Oman on the E. **Topography:** A sandy coastal strip leads to well-watered fertile mountains in interior. **Capital:** Sanaa. **Cities:** Sanaa (1986 est.) 427,000; Aden (1984 est.) 318,000.

Government: Type: Republic. **Head of state:** Pres. Ali Abdullah Saleh, b. 1942; in office: July 17, 1978. **Head of government:** Prime Min. Abd al-Aziz al-Ghani; in office: Oct. 6, 1994. **Local divisions:** 17 governorates, Sanaa. **Defense:** 10% of GDP (1992). **Active troop strength:** N Yemen 38,500; S Yemen 27,500.

Economy: Industries: Food processing, mining, petroleum refining. **Chief crops:** Wheat, sorghum, fruits, coffee, cotton. **Minerals:** Oil, salt. **Crude oil reserves** (1994): 4 bln. bbls. **Arable land:** 6%. **Livestock** (1993): goats: 3.3 mln.; sheep: 3.7 mln. **Fish catch** (1991): 85,000 metric tons. **Electricity prod.** (1992): 1.2 bln. kWh. **Labor force:** 45% agric.; 11% ind.; 21% services.

Finance: Monetary unit: Rial (May 1995: 50.04 = $1 US). **Gross domestic product** (1993): $9 bln. **Per capita GDP:** $800. **Imports** (1993): $1.6 bln.; partners: Saudi Arabia 6%, UAE 6%, Japan 6%. **Exports** (1993): $695 mln.; partners: Italy 55%, U.S. 32%, Jordan 5%.

Transport: Motor vehicles: in use: 186,000 passenger cars, 254,000 commercial vehicles. **Civil aviation:** 641 mln. passenger-mi.; 12 airports with scheduled flights. **Chief ports:** Al Hudaydah, Al Mukalla, Aden.

Communications: Television sets: 1 per 34 persons. **Radios:** 1 per 39 persons. **Telephones:** 1 per 83 persons.

Health: Life expectancy at birth (1995): 62 male; 63 female. **Births** (per 1,000 pop.): 45. **Deaths** (per 1,000 pop.): 8. **Natural increase:** 3.7%. **Hospital beds:** 1 per 995 persons. **Physicians:** 1 per 5,531 persons. **Infant mortality** (per 1,000 live births 1995): 58.

Education: Literacy (1991): 38%. **Primary school attendance:** 59%.

Major International Organizations: UN (IMF, WHO), Arab League.

Embassy: 2600 Virginia Ave. NW 20037; 965-4760.

Yemen's territory once was part of the ancient Kindgom of Sheba, or Saba, a prosperous link in trade between Africa and India. A Biblical reference speaks of its gold, spices, and precious stones as gifts borne by the Queen of Sheba to King Solomon.

Yemen became independent in 1918, after years of Ottoman Turkish rule, but remained politically and economically backward. Imam Ahmed ruled 1948-1962. Army officers headed by Brig. Gen. Abdullah al-Salal declared the country to be the Yemen Arab Republic.

The Imam Ahmed's heir, the Imam Mohamad al-Badr, fled to the mountains where tribesmen joined royalist forces; internal warfare between them and the republican forces continued. About 150,000 people died in the fighting.

There was a bloodless coup Nov. 5, 1967. In April 1970 hostilities ended with an agreement between Yemen and Saudi Arabia. On June 13, 1974, an army group, led by Col. Ibrahim al-Hamidi, seized the government. He was assassinated in 1977.

Meanwhile, South Yemen won independence from Britain in 1967, formed out of the British colony of Aden and the British protectorate of South Arabia. It became the Arab world's only Marxist state, taking the name People's Democratic Republic of Yemen in 1970 and signing a friendship treaty with the USSR in 1979 that allowed for the stationing of Soviet troops.

More than 300,000 Yemenis fled from the south to the north after independence, contributing to 2 decades of hostility between the 2 states that flared into warfare twice in the 1970s.

An Arab League-sponsored agreement between North and South Yemen on unification of the 2 countries was signed Mar.

29, 1979. An agreement providing for widespread political and economic cooperation was signed in 1988.

The 2 countries were formally united on May 21, 1990, but regional clan-based rivalries led to full-scale civil war in 1994. Secessionists declared a breakaway state in S Yemen, May 21, 1994. However, northern troops captured the former southern capital of Aden in July. A new constitution was approved Sept. 28.

Yugoslavia
Federal Republic of Yugoslavia
Federativna Republika Jugoslavija

(Data prior to 1992 include former republics Croatia, Slovenia, Bosnia and Herzegovina, and Macedonia)

People: Population: 11,101,833. **Age distrib.** (%): <15: 23; 65+: 10. **Pop. density:** 281 per sq. mi. **Urban:** 47%. **Ethnic groups:** Serbs 63%, Albanians 14%. **Principal languages:** Serbo-Croatian (official) 95%, Albanian 5%. **Religions:** Orthodox 65%, Muslim 19%, Roman Catholic 4%.

Geography: Area: 39,449 sq. mi. **Location:** On the Balkan Peninsula in SE Europe. Present-day Yugoslavia consists of the former republics of Serbia and Montenegro. **Neighbors:** Croatia, Bosnia and Herzegovina on W, Hungary on N, Romania, Bulgaria on E, Greece, Albania, Macedonia on S. **Capital:** Belgrade (1993 est.): 1.2 mln.

Government: Type: Republic. **Head of state:** Pres. Zoran Lilic; b 1954; in office: June 25, 1993. **Head of government:** Prime Min. Radoje Kontic; b 1936; in office: Dec. 29, 1992. **Local divisions:** 2 republics, 2 autonomous provinces. **Defense:** 4%-6% of GDP (1992 est.). **Active troop strength:** 126,500.

Economy: Industries: Steel, machinery, consumer goods, mining, wood products. **Chief crops:** Corn, grains, tobacco, cotton, vegetables. **Minerals:** Oil, gas, coal, antimony, lead, nickel, gold, copper, chrome. **Arable land:** 30%. **Livestock** (1993): cattle: 2.0 mln.; pigs: 4.1 mln.; sheep: 2.8 mln. **Fish catch:** (1991): 37,000 metric tons. **Electricity prod.** (1992): 42 bln. kWh. **Labor force:** 5% agric.; 40% ind. & mining.

Finance: Monetary unit: New Dinar (Oct. 1994: 1.56 = $1 US). **Gross national product** (1993): $10 bln. **Per capita GNP:** $1,000. **Imports** (1990): $19.1 bln.; partners: EU 54%, USSR 15%. **Exports** (1990): $14.6 bln.; partners: EU 54%, USSR 17%. **Tourism** (1992): $200 mln. **National budget:** NA. **International reserves less gold** (Mar. 1993): $1.4 bln. **Gold:** 1.90 mln. oz t. **Consumer prices** (change in 1991): 117.4%.

Transport: Motor vehicles: in use: 1.4 mln. passenger cars, 132,000 comm. vehicles. **Civil aviation:** 5 airports.

Communications: Television sets: 1 per 6.4 persons. **Radios:** 1 per 3.9 persons. **Telephones:** 1 per 4.8 persons. **Daily newspaper circ.:** 98 per 1,000 pop.

Health: Life expectancy at birth (1995): 72 male; 77 female. **Births** (per 1,000 pop. 1991): 14. **Deaths** (per 1,000 pop. 1991): 9. **Natural increase:** 0.6%. **Hospital beds:** 1 per 179 persons. **Physicians:** 1 per 402 persons. **Infant mortality** (per 1,000 live births 1995): 18.

Education: Literacy (1993): 89%. Almost all attend primary school.

Major International Organizations: Some UN agencies (though not a member).

Embassy: 2410 California St. NW 20008; 462-6566.

Serbia, which had since 1389 been a vassal principality of Turkey, was established as an independent kingdom by the Treaty of Berlin, 1878. Montenegro, independent since 1389, also obtained international recognition in 1878. After the Balkan wars Serbia's boundaries were enlarged by the annexation of Old Serbia and Macedonia, 1913.

When the Austro-Hungarian empire collapsed after World War I, the Kingdom of the Serbs, Croats, and Slovenes was formed from the former provinces of Croatia, Dalmatia, Bosnia, Herzegovina, Slovenia, Voyvodina, and the independent state of Montenegro. The name was later changed to Yugoslavia.

Nazi Germany invaded in 1941. Many Yugoslav partisan troops continued to operate. Among these were the Chetniks led by Draja Mikhailovich, who fought other partisans led by Josip Broz, known as Marshal Tito. Tito, backed by the USSR and Britain from 1943, was in control by the time the Germans had been driven from Yugoslavia in 1945. Mikhailovich was executed July 17, 1946, by the Tito regime.

A constituent assembly proclaimed Yugoslavia a republic Nov. 29, 1945. It became a federated republic Jan. 31, 1946, and Marshal Tito, a Communist, became head of the government. The Stalin policy of dictating to all Communist nations was rejected by Tito. He accepted economic aid and military equipment from the U.S. and received aid in foreign trade also from France and Great Britain. Tito also supported the liberal government of Czechoslovakia in 1968 before the Soviet invasion.

A separatist movement among Croatians brought arrests and a change of leaders in the Croatian Republic in Jan. 1972. Violence by Croatian nationalists and fears of Soviet political intervention led to restrictions on political and intellectual dissent.

Beginning in 1965, reforms designed to decentralize the administration of economic development and to force industries to produce more efficiently were introduced, and considerable trade with the West was developed.

Pres. Tito died May 4, 1980; with his death, the post as head of the Collective Presidency and also that as head of the League of Communists became a rotating system of succession among the members representing each republic.

On Jan. 22, 1990, a Communist Party conference renounced its constitutionally guaranteed leading role in society and called on Parliament to enact "political pluralism, including a multiparty system."

Croatia and Slovenia formally declared independence June 25, 1991. In Croatia, fighting began between Croats and ethnic Serbs. Serbia sent arms and medical supplies to the Serb rebels in Croatia. There were numerous clashes between Croatian forces and Yugoslavian army units and their Serb supporters.

The republics of Serbia and Montenegro proclaimed a new "Federal Republic of Yugoslavia" Apr. 17, 1992. Serbia, under Pres. Slobodan Milosevic, was the main supplier of arms to the ethnic Serb fighters in Bosnia and Herzegovina. The UN imposed sweeping international sanctions on the new Yugoslavia (Serbia and Montenegro) as a means of ending the bloodshed in Bosnia, May 30, 1992. On Aug. 4, 1994, Yugoslavia said it was cutting off support for Bosnian Serbs because they rejected an international partition plan for Bosnia. This prompted the UN to vote for a conditional easing of sanctions, Sept. 23, 1994.

Kosovo: An area in southern Serbia (4,203 sq. mi.), with a population of about 2,000,000, mostly Albanians. The capital is Pristina. The Albanian majority has declared its independence, which Serbia has not recognized.

Vojvodina: An area in northern Serbia (8,304 sq. mi.), with a population of about 2,000,000, mostly Serbian. The capital is Novi Sad.

Zaire

Republic of Zaire

République du Zaïre

People: Population: 44,060,636. **Age distrib.** (%): <15: 48; 65+: 3. **Pop. density:** 49 per sq. mi. **Urban:** 29%. **Ethnic groups:** Bantu tribes 80%, over 200 other tribes. **Principal languages:** French (official), Kongo, Luba, Mongo, Rwanda, others. **Religions:** Christian 70%, Muslim 10%, Kimbanguist 10%.

Geography: Area: 905,446 sq. mi. **Location:** In central Africa. **Neighbors:** Congo on W, Central African Republic, Sudan on N, Uganda, Rwanda, Burundi, Tanzania on E, Zambia, Angola on S. **Topography:** Zaire includes the bulk of the Zaire (Congo) R. basin. The vast central region is a low-lying plateau covered by rain forest. Mountainous terraces in the W, savannas in the S and SE, grasslands toward the N, and the high Ruwenzori Mts. on the E surround the central region. A short strip of territory borders the Atlantic O. The Zaire R. is 2,718 mi. long. **Capital:** Kinshasa. **Cities** (1991 est.): Kinshasa 3.8 mln.; Lubumbashi 739,000.

Government: Type: Republic with strong presidential authority (in transition). **Head of state:** Pres. Mobutu Sese

Seko; b Oct. 14, 1930; in office: Nov. 25, 1965. **Head of government:** Prime Min. Kengo Wa Dondo; in office: July 6, 1994. **Local divisions:** 10 regions, Kinshasa. **Defense:** 0.8% of GDP (1988). **Active troop strength:** 49,100.

Economy: Chief crops: Coffee, rice, bananas, plantains, cassavas, bananas, quinine, palm oil. **Minerals:** Cobalt (60% of world reserves), copper, cadmium, oil, diamonds, gold, silver, tin, germanium, zinc, iron, manganese, uranium, radium. **Crude oil reserves** (1994): 187 mln. bbls. **Other resources:** Forests, rubber, ivory. **Arable land:** 3%. **Livestock** (1993): cattle: 1.6 mln.; goats: 4.1 mln. **Fish catch** (1992): 150,000 metric tons. **Electricity prod.** (1991): 6 bln. kWh. **Labor force:** 75% agric.

Finance: Monetary unit: New Zaire (Mar. 1995: 3,600 = $1 US). **Gross domestic product** (1993): $2.1 bln.* **Per capita GDP:** $500. **Imports** (1992): $1.2 bln.; partners: Belgium 21%, France 12%, Germany 12%, China 7%. **Exports** (1992): $1.5 bln.; partners: Belgium 45%, U.S. 18%. **National budget** (1990): $1.1 bln. **International reserves less gold** (Feb. 1995): $116 mln. **Gold:** 28,000 oz t. **Consumer prices** (change in 1994): 23,773%.

Transport: Railroads: Length: 3,275 mi. **Motor vehicles:** in use: 105,000 passenger cars, 95,000 comm. vehicles. **Civil aviation:** 90 mln. passenger-mi.; 24 airports with scheduled flights. **Chief ports:** Matadi, Boma.

Communications: Television sets: 1 per 1,929 persons. **Radios:** 1 per 13 persons. **Telephones:** 1 per 1,026 persons. **Daily newspaper circ.:** 1 per 1,000 pop.

Health: Life expectancy at birth (1995): 46 male; 49 female. **Births** (per 1,000 pop.): 48. **Deaths** (per 1,000 pop.): 17. **Natural increase:** 3.2%. **Hospital beds:** 1 per 487 persons. **Physicians:** 1 per 15,584 persons. **Infant mortality** (per 1,000 live births 1995): 109.

Education: Literacy (1990): 72%.

Major International Organizations: UN and most of its specialized agencies, OAU.

Embassy: 1800 New Hampshire Ave. NW 20009; 234-7690.

The earliest inhabitants of Zaire may have been the pygmies, followed by Bantus from the E and Nilotic tribes from the N. The large Bantu Bakongo kingdom ruled much of Zaire and Angola when Portuguese explorers visited in the 15th century.

Leopold II, king of the Belgians, formed an international group to exploit the Congo in 1876. In 1877 Henry M. Stanley explored the Congo, and in 1878 the king's group sent him back to organize the region and win over the native chiefs. The Conference of Berlin, 1884-85, organized the Congo Free State with Leopold as king and chief owner. Exploitation of native laborers on the rubber plantations caused international criticism and led to granting of a colonial charter, 1908.

Belgian and Congolese leaders agreed Jan. 27, 1960, that the Congo would become independent June 30. In the first general elections, May 31, the National Congolese movement of Patrice Lumumba won 35 of 137 seats in the National Assembly. He was appointed premier June 21, and formed a coalition cabinet.

Widespread violence caused Europeans and others to flee. The UN Security Council Aug. 9, 1960, called on Belgium to withdraw its troops and sent a UN contingent. President Kasavubu removed Lumumba as premier; he was murdered in 1961.

The last UN troops left the Congo June 30, 1964, and Moise Tshombe became president.

On Sept. 7, 1964, leftist rebels set up a "People's Republic" in Stanleyville. Tshombe hired foreign mercenaries and sought to rebuild the Congolese Army. In Nov. and Dec. 1964 rebels killed scores of white hostages and thousands of Congolese; Belgian paratroops, dropped from U.S. transport planes, rescued hundreds. By July 1965 the rebels had lost their effectiveness.

In 1965 Gen. Joseph D. Mobutu was named president. He later changed his name to Mobutu Sese Seko. The country changed its name to Republic of Zaire on Oct. 27, 1971.

Economic difficulties, amid charges of corruption by government officials, plagued Zaire in the 1980s and worsened in the 1990s. In 1990, Pres. Mobutu announced an end to a 20-year ban on multiparty politics. He sought to retain power despite economic collapse, outside pressure, and widespread internal opposition.

During 1994, Zaire was inundated with refugees from the massive ethnic bloodshed in Rwanda. At least 200 people died in 1995 from an Ebola virus outbreak in Kikwit, W Zaire.

Zambia
Republic of Zambia

People: Population: 9,445,723. **Age distrib.** (%): <15: 50; 65+: 2. **Pop. density:** 33 per sq. mi. **Urban:** 42%. **Ethnic groups:** mostly Bantu tribes. **Principal languages:** English (official), Bantu dialects. **Religions:** Christian 50–75%, Hindu and Muslim 24-49%.

Geography: Area: 290,586 sq. mi. **Location:** In S central Africa. **Neighbors:** Zaire on N, Tanzania, Malawi, Mozambique on E, Zimbabwe, Namibia on S, Angola on W. **Topography:** Zambia is mostly high plateau country covered with thick forests, and drained by several important rivers, including the Zambezi. **Capital:** Lusaka. **Cities** (1990): Lusaka 982,000; Ndola 376,000; Kitwe 349,000.

Government: Type: Republic. **Head of state:** Pres. Frederick Chiluba; b 1943; in office: Nov. 2, 1991. **Local divisions:** 9 provinces. **Defense:** 1% of GDP (1992 est.). **Active troop strength:** 24,000.

Economy: Chief crops: Corn, tobacco, peanuts, cotton, sugar. **Minerals:** Cobalt, copper, zinc, emerald, gold, lead, silver, uranium, coal. **Arable land:** 7%. **Livestock** (1993): cattle: 3.2 mln. **Fish catch** (1991): 66,000 metric tons. **Electricity prod.** (1991): 12 bln. kWh. **Labor force:** 85% agric.; 15% ind. and commerce.

Finance: Monetary unit: Kwacha (May 1995: 1.00 = $.001 US). **Gross domestic product** (1993): $7.3 bln.* **Per capita GDP:** $800. **Imports** (1992): $1.2 bln.; South Africa 13%, Germany 6%, U.S. 7%. **Exports** (1992): $1.0 bln.; partners: Japan 4%, UK 3%, U.S. 10%, Germany 9%. **National budget** (1991 est.): $767 mln. **International reserves less gold** (Mar. 1994): $207 mln. **Consumer prices** (change in 1993): 189.0%.

Transport: Motor vehicles: in use: 100,000 passenger cars, 75,000 comm. vehicles. **Civil aviation:** 313 mln. passenger-mi.; 8 airports with scheduled flights.

Communications: Television sets: 1 per 44 persons. **Radios:** 1 per 5.0 persons. **Telephones:** 1 per 76 persons. **Daily newspaper circ.:** 12 per 1,000 pop.

Health: Life expectancy at birth (1995): 43 male; 43 female. **Births** (per 1,000 pop.): 45. **Deaths** (per 1,000 pop.): 18. **Natural increase:** 2.7%. **Hospital beds:** 1 per 349 persons. **Physicians:** 1 per 8,437 persons. **Infant mortality** (per 1,000 live births 1995): 86.

Education: Literacy (1991): 54%. **Attendance:** less than 50% in grades 1–7.

Major International Organizations: UN (WTO, IMF, WHO), OAU, the Commonwealth.

Embassy: 2419 Massachusetts Ave. NW 20008; 265-9717.

As Northern Rhodesia, the country was under the administration of the South Africa Company, 1889 until 1924, when the office of governor was established, and, subsequently, a legislature. The country became an independent republic within the Commonwealth Oct. 24, 1964.

After the white minority government of Rhodesia declared its independence from Britain Nov. 11, 1965, relations between Zambia and Rhodesia became strained.

As part of a program of government participation in major industries, a government corporation in 1970 took over 51% of the ownership of 2 foreign-owned copper mining companies. Privately-held land and other enterprises were nationalized in 1975. In the 1980s and 1990s lowered copper prices hurt the economy and severe drought caused famine.

Food riots erupted in June 1990, as the nation suffered its worst violence since independence.

Elections held Oct. 1991 resulted in an end to one-party rule. The new government made efforts to sell off state enterprises.

Zimbabwe
Republic of Zimbabwe

People: Population: 11,139,961. **Age distrib.** (%): <15: 44; 65+: 3. **Pop. density:** 74 per sq. mi. **Urban:** 27%. **Ethnic groups:** Shona 71%, Ndebele 16%. **Principal languages:** English (official), Shona, Sindebele. **Religions:** syncretic (Christian-indigenous mix) 50%, Christian 25%, indigenous beliefs 24%.

Geography: Area: 150,872 sq. mi. **Location:** In southern Africa. **Neighbors:** Zambia on N, Botswana on W, South Africa on S, Mozambique on E. **Topography:** Zimbabwe is high plateau country, rising to mountains on eastern border, sloping down on the other borders. **Capital:** Harare. **Cities** (1992 est.): Harare 1.2 mln.; Bulawayo 621,000.

Government: Type: Republic. **Head of state:** Pres. Robert Mugabe; b Feb. 21, 1924; in office: Jan. 1, 1988. **Local divisions:** 8 provinces. **Defense:** 6% of GDP (1991 est.). **Active troop strength:** 46,900.

Economy: Industries: Clothing, mining, chemicals, light industries. **Chief crops:** Tobacco, sugar, cotton, corn, wheat. **Minerals:** Chromium, gold, nickel, asbestos, copper, iron, coal. **Arable land:** 7%. **Livestock** (1993): cattle: 4 mln.; goats: 2.5 mln. **Electricity prod.** (1992): 8.2 bln. kWh. **Labor force:** 74% agric.; 16% serv.

Finance: Monetary unit: Dollar (May 1995: 1.00 = $.12 US). **Gross domestic product** (1993): $15.9 bln.* **Per capita GDP:** $1,400. **Imports** (1992): $1.8 bln.; partners: South Africa 25%, UK 15%. **Exports** (1992): $1.5 bln.; partners: UK 14%, Germany 11%, South Africa 10%. **Tourism** (1992): $105 mln. **National budget** (1993): $2.2 bln. **Total reserves less gold** (May 1995): $595 mln. **Gold:** 37,000 oz t. **Consumer prices** (change in 1994): 22.3%.

Transport: Motor vehicles: in use: 310,000 passenger cars, 30,000 comm. vehicles. **Civil aviation:** 508 mln. passenger-mi.; 5 airports with scheduled flights.

Communications: Television sets: 1 per 78 persons. **Radios:** 1 per 20 persons. **Telephones:** 1 per 31 persons. **Daily newspaper circ.:** 21 per 1,000 pop.

Health: Life expectancy at birth (1995): 40 male; 43 female. **Births** (per 1,000 pop.): 36. **Deaths** (per 1,000 pop.): 19. **Natural increase:** 1.8%. **Physicians:** 1 per 7,371 persons. **Infant mortality** (per 1,000 live births 1995): 73.

Education: Literacy (1992): 76%. **Attendance:** 90% primary, 15% secondary for Africans; higher for whites, Asians.

Major International Organizations: UN (IMF, WTO, World Bank), OAU, the Commonwealth.

Embassy: 1608 New Hampshire Ave. NW 20009; 332-7100.

Britain took over the area as Southern Rhodesia in 1923 from the British South Africa Co. (which, under Cecil Rhodes, had conquered the area by 1897) and granted internal self-government. Under a 1961 constitution, voting was restricted to maintain whites in power. On Nov. 11, 1965, Prime Min. Ian D. Smith announced his country's unilateral declaration of independence. Britain termed the act illegal and demanded that Zimbabwe (known as Rhodesia until 1980) broaden voting rights to provide for eventual rule of the country by the majority Africans.

Urged by Britain, the UN imposed sanctions, including embargoes on oil shipments to Zimbabwe. Some oil and gasoline reached Zimbabwe, however, from South Africa and Mozambique, before the latter became independent in 1975. In May 1968, the UN Security Council ordered a trade embargo.

A new constitution came into effect, Mar. 2, 1970. The election law effectively prevented full black representation through income tax requirements.

Intermittent negotiations between the government and various black nationalist groups failed to prevent increasing guerrilla warfare. An "internal settlement" signed Mar. 1978 in which Smith and 3 popular black leaders would share control of the government until a transfer of power to the black majority was rejected by guerrilla leaders.

In the country's first universal-franchise election, Apr. 21, 1979, Bishop Abel Muzorewa's United African National Council gained a bare majority control of the black-dominated Parliament. Britain, 1979, began efforts to normalize its relationship with Zimbabwe. A British cease-fire was accepted by all parties, Dec. 5. Independence was finally achieved Apr. 18, 1980.

Pres. Robert Mugabe declared Zimbabwe's drought a national disaster and appealed to foreign donors for food, money, and medicine, Mar. 6, 1992. An economic adjustment program caused widespread hardship.

Area and Population of the World

Source: Bureau of the Census, U.S. Dept. of Commerce; prior to 1950, Rand McNally & Co.

| Continent or Region | Area (1,000 sq. mi.) | % of Earth | Population (est., thousands) | | | | | | | % World |
			1650	1750	1850	1900	1950	1980	1995	Total, 1995
North America	9,400	16.2	5,000	5,000	39,000	106,000	166,000	252,000	292,000	5.1
South America	6,900	11.9	8,000	7,000	20,000	38,000	—	—	—	—
Latin America, Caribbean	—	—	—	—	—	—	166,000	362,000	481,000	8.4
Europe	3,800	6.6	100,000	140,000	265,000	400,000	392,000	484,000	509,000	8.9
Asia	17,400	30.1	335,000	476,000	754,000	932,000	1,368,000	2,501,000	3,247,000	56.62
Africa	11,700	20.2	100,000	95,000	95,000	118,000	272,000	570,000	878,000	15.3
Former USSR	—	—	—	—	—	—	180,000	266,000	298,000	5.2
Oceania, incl. Australia	3,300	5.7	2,000	2,000	2,000	6,000	12,000	23,000	29,000	0.5
Antarctica	5,400	9.3	Uninhabited							
World	57,900	—	550,000	725,000	1,175,000	1,600,000	2,556,000	4,458,000	5,734,000	—

Figures may not add to total because of independent rounding.

Leading Countries in Population and Area in 1995

China had the highest population in the world, with 1.2 billion inhabitants, more than one-fifth of the world's population. India had more than 936 million people and was expected to reach 1 billion by the end of the decade. The United States had the third-largest population, with over 263 million, followed by Indonesia, Brazil, and Russia. Russia is the largest country in area, with over 6.5 million square miles, followed by Canada, China, the United States, and Brazil.

Population of the World's Largest Cities

Source: United Nations, Dept. for Economic and Social Information and Policy Analysis

The figures are United Nations estimates and projections, as revised in 1994, for "urban agglomerations"—that is, contiguous densely populated urban areas, without regard to administrative boundaries. Therefore, population figures in this table may not correspond to figures in other parts of *The World Almanac*.

Rank	City, Country	Pop. (thousands) 1994	Pop. (thousands, projected) 2015	Annual growth rate (percent) 1990-1995	Percentage increase between: 1975-1995	Percentage increase between: 1995-2015	Pop. of city as percentage of: Total pop.[1]	Pop. of city as percentage of: Urban pop.[2]
1.	Tokyo, Japan	26,518	28,700	1.4	35.7	7.0	21.2	27.4
2.	New York City, U.S.	16,271	17,600	0.3	2.8	8.0	6.2	8.2
3.	Sao Paulo, Brazil	16,110	20,800	2.0	66.0	26.6	10.1	13.0
4.	Mexico City, Mexico	15,525	18,800	0.7	39.2	20.1	16.9	22.6
5.	Shanghai, China	14,709	23,400	2.3	31.8	55.0	1.2	4.1
6.	Bombay, India	14,496	27,400	4.2	120.1	81.4	1.6	6.0
7.	Los Angeles, U.S.	12,232	14,300	1.6	39.0	15.0	4.7	6.2
8.	Beijing, China	12,030	19,400	2.6	44.7	57.1	1.0	3.4
9.	Calcutta, India	11,485	17,600	1.7	48.0	51.0	1.3	4.7
10.	Seoul, South Korea	11,451	13,100	1.9	71.2	12.9	25.7	32.1
11.	Jakarta, Indonesia	11,017	21,200	4.4	138.9	84.1	5.7	16.4
12.	Buenos Aires, Argentina	10,914	12,400	0.7	20.3	12.6	31.9	36.4
13.	Osaka, Japan	10,585	10,600	0.2	7.7	0.0	8.5	10.9
14.	Tianjin, China	10,376	17,000	2.9	73.5	59.0	0.9	2.9
15.	Rio de Janeiro, Brazil	9,817	11,600	0.8	25.6	16.9	6.2	8.0

(1) Denotes percentage of the total population of the country in which the corresponding city is located. (2) Denotes the percentage of the total urban population of the country in which the corresponding city is located.

Current Population and Projections for All Countries: 1995, 2010, and 2020

Source: Bureau of the Census, U.S. Dept. of Commerce

(in thousands)

Country	1995	2010	2020	Country	1995	2010	2020
Afghanistan	21,252	38,516	49,570	Belarus	10,437	10,864	11,047
Albania	3,414	4,016	4,424	Belgium	10,082	10,135	10,015
Algeria	28,539	38,479	44,783	Belize	214	299	356
Andorra	66	79	78	Benin	5,523	8,955	11,920
Angola	10,070	14,982	19,272	Bhutan	1,781	2,474	3,035
Antigua and Barbuda	65	74	80	Bolivia	7,896	10,671	12,547
Argentina	34,293	39,947	43,190	Bosnia and Herzegovina	3,202	3,641	3,685
Armenia	3,557	3,854	3,959	Botswana	1,392	1,871	2,187
Australia	18,322	21,151	22,724	Brazil	160,737	183,742	197,466
Austria	7,987	8,259	8,329	Brunei	292	410	490
Azerbaijan	7,790	8,995	9,689	Bulgaria	8,775	8,757	8,642
Bahamas	257	293	314	Burkina Faso	10,423	14,478	18,123
Bahrain	576	759	870	Burundi	6,262	8,382	10,734
Bangladesh	128,095	176,902	210,248	Cambodia	10,561	15,679	20,208
Barbados	256	272	284	Cameroon	13,521	21,165	28,329

Country	1995	2010	2020	Country	1995	2010	2020
Canada	28,435	32,265	34,347	Mozambique	18,115	27,381	35,240
Cape Verde	436	646	812	Myanmar	45,104	57,720	65,914
Central African Republic	3,210	3,898	4,561	Namibia	1,652	2,705	3,638
Chad	5,587	7,680	9,396	Nauru	10	11	12
Chile	14,161	17,266	19,225	Nepal	21,561	30,783	37,767
China	1,203,097	1,348,429	1,424,725	Netherlands	15,453	16,140	16,222
Colombia	36,200	44,504	49,266	New Zealand	3,407	3,543	3,586
Comoros	549	919	1,249	Nicaragua	4,206	5,864	6,945
Congo	2,505	3,219	3,775	Niger	9,280	15,311	21,148
Costa Rica	3,419	4,537	5,257	Nigeria	101,232	161,969	215,893
Côte d'Ivoire	14,791	22,924	29,705	Norway	4,331	4,424	4,446
Croatia	4,666	4,805	4,727	Oman	2,125	3,576	4,782
Cuba	10,937	11,839	12,266	Pakistan	131,542	195,108	251,330
Cyprus	737	829	883	Palau	17	20	21
Czech Republic	10,433	10,892	10,991	Panama	2,681	3,422	3,886
Denmark	5,199	5,311	5,307	Papua New Guinea	4,295	5,925	7,044
Djibouti	421	588	751	Paraguay	5,358	7,730	9,474
Dominica	83	89	96	Peru	24,087	30,483	34,340
Dominican Republic	7,948	9,928	11,152	Philippines	73,266	98,726	115,988
Ecuador	10,891	13,990	15,894	Poland	38,792	41,332	42,474
Egypt	62,360	80,689	92,350	Portugal	10,562	10,997	11,038
El Salvador	5,870	7,603	8,763	Qatar	534	660	735
Equatorial Guinea	420	615	783	Romania	23,198	23,950	24,337
Eritrea	3,579	6,018	7,674	Russia	149,909	155,933	159,263
Estonia	1,625	1,776	1,880	Rwanda	8,605	11,755	15,006
Ethiopia	55,979	86,962	114,402	Saint Kitts and Nevis	41	50	57
Fiji	773	933	1,037	Saint Lucia	156	183	202
Finland	5,085	5,246	5,283	Saint Vincent and the			
France	58,109	61,001	61,793	Grenadines	118	132	146
Gabon	1,156	1,445	1,675	San Marino	24	26	27
Gambia, The	989	1,561	2,073	São Tomé and Príncipe	140	196	232
Georgia	5,726	6,253	6,506	Saudi Arabia	18,730	31,198	43,255
Germany	81,338	82,837	82,385	Senegal	9,007	14,318	19,127
Ghana	17,763	27,305	35,877	Seychelles	73	81	86
Greece	10,648	10,920	10,689	Sierra Leone	4,753	7,041	9,036
Grenada	94	115	141	Singapore	2,890	3,206	3,335
Guatemala	10,999	15,284	18,131	Slovakia	5,432	5,883	6,078
Guinea	6,549	9,303	11,664	Slovenia	2,051	2,094	2,078
Guinea-Bissau	1,125	1,579	1,925	Solomon Islands	399	620	767
Guyana	724	767	833	Somalia	7,348	12,588	16,832
Haiti	6,518	7,989	9,351	South Africa	45,095	65,850	82,502
Honduras	5,460	7,643	9,042	Spain	39,404	40,682	40,241
Hungary	10,319	10,477	10,449	Sri Lanka	18,343	21,331	22,877
Iceland	266	293	306	Sudan	30,120	46,167	58,090
India	936,546	1,173,621	1,320,746	Suriname	430	534	598
Indonesia	203,584	250,033	276,474	Swaziland	967	1,566	2,128
Iran	64,625	88,231	104,282	Sweden	8,822	9,228	9,469
Iraq	20,644	34,545	46,260	Switzerland	7,085	7,519	7,696
Ireland	3,550	3,846	4,034	Syria	15,452	25,768	34,309
Israel	5,143	6,242	6,935	Taiwan	21,501	24,092	25,122
Italy	58,262	59,089	57,844	Tajikistan	6,155	8,619	10,429
Jamaica	2,574	2,896	3,208	Tanzania	28,701	38,651	48,526
Japan	125,506	129,361	126,062	Thailand	60,271	64,181	62,941
Jordan	4,101	6,112	7,529	Togo	4,410	7,401	10,146
Kazakhstan	17,377	18,794	19,404	Tonga	106	119	128
Kenya	28,817	37,990	44,240	Trinidad and Tobago	1,271	1,323	1,409
Kiribati	79	95	98	Tunisia	8,880	11,050	12,413
Korea, North	23,487	28,491	30,969	Turkey	63,405	81,790	93,362
Korea, South	45,554	51,677	54,014	Turkmenistan	4,075	5,277	6,116
Kuwait	1,817	3,160	3,560	Tuvalu	10	12	15
Kyrgyzstan	4,770	5,810	6,490	Uganda	19,573	24,584	29,882
Laos	4,837	7,168	8,923	Ukraine	51,868	52,280	52,337
Latvia	2,763	3,009	3,194	United Arab Emirates	2,925	4,873	6,080
Lebanon	3,696	4,973	5,748	United Kingdom	58,295	59,617	60,042
Lesotho	1,993	2,771	3,314	United States	263,814	300,811	326,322
Liberia	3,073	4,903	6,449	Uruguay	3,223	3,594	3,822
Libya	5,248	8,913	12,391	Uzbekistan	23,089	30,380	35,422
Liechtenstein	31	34	36	Vanuatu	174	230	266
Lithuania	3,876	4,263	4,505	Venezuela	21,005	27,407	31,312
Luxembourg	405	428	436	Vietnam	74,393	91,729	102,359
Macedonia	2,160	2,394	2,499	Western Samoa	209	288	341
Madagascar	13,862	22,064	29,362	Yemen	14,728	26,504	37,449
Malawi	9,808	13,233	16,697	Yugoslavia	11,102	11,727	11,917
Malaysia	19,724	26,589	31,681	Zaire	44,061	69,079	92,860
Maldives	261	423	554	Zambia	9,446	12,614	15,828
Mali	9,375	14,966	20,427	Zimbabwe	11,140	12,990	14,620
Malta	370	404	420	**Regions**			
Marshall Islands	56	100	144	Africa	878,323	1,290,745	1,638,261
Mauritania	2,263	3,630	4,859	Asia	3,246,600	3,934,703	4,360,221
Mauritius	1,127	1,322	1,428	Latin America and			
Mexico	93,986	120,115	136,096	Caribbean	481,365	586,262	651,163
Micronesia	123	141	143	North America	292,375	333,218	360,820
Moldova	4,490	4,738	4,880	Europe	509,254	526,848	528,823
Monaco	32	33	34	Former Soviet Union	297,508	320,844	335,119
Mongolia	2,494	3,545	4,309	Oceania inc. Australia	28,680	34,109	37,369
Morocco	29,169	38,442	44,519	**World**[1]	**5,734,106**	**7,026,729**	**7,911,776**

(1) Figures may not add to total due to rounding and exclusion of certain pseudo-national entities.

Estimated HIV Infection and Reported AIDS Cases

Source: World Health Organization

The interval between infection with the human immunodeficiency virus (HIV) and development of acquired immune deficiency syndrome (AIDS) is estimated to be 7-10 years. The actual number of AIDS cases worldwide is estimated to be more than 4.5 million—4 times the number of reported cases—because of underdiagnosis, underreporting, and the use of different definitions of AIDS in different countries. As of June 30, 1995, a total of 1,169,811 AIDS cases had been reported to the World Health Organization, a 19% increase from the 985,119 reported on July 1, 1994.

Estimated Total HIV[1] Cases by Region, Mid-1995

Region	Est. cases	Region	Est. cases	Region	Est. cases
Sub-Saharan Africa	11,000,000+	North America	1,100,000	E. Europe/Central Asia	50,000+
South/Southeast Asia	3,500,000	Western Europe	600,000	Australasia	25,000+
				East Asia/Pacific	50,000+
Latin America/Caribbean	2,000,000	North Africa/Middle East	150,000	**World**	**18,500,000+**

(1) Estimated cumulative HIV prevalence in adults. The WHO estimated more than 1.5 million children had also been infected with HIV by mid-1995.

Cumulative Reported AIDS Cases by Continent, 1980-95

Year	Africa	America[1]	Asia	Europe	Oceania[2]	World
1980	0	187	1	17	0	205
1985	744	24,379	46	2,457	315	27,941
1990	130,100	245,385	1,226	58,713	3,030	438,454
1995 (midyear)	418,051	580,129	23,912	141,275	6,444	1,169,811

(1) Includes North and South America and the Caribbean. (2) Includes Australia.

The World's Refugees

Source: *World Refugee Survey 1995*, U.S. Committee for Refugees, a nonprofit corp. The refugees in this table include only those who are in need of protection and/or assistance and do not include refugees who have permanently settled in other countries.

(as of Dec. 31, 1994)

Place of asylum	Mostly from	Number
Total Africa		**5,880,000**
Algeria	Western Sahara, Mali, Niger	130,000[1]
Burundi	Rwanda, Zaire	165,000[1]
Côte d'Ivoire	Liberia	320,000
Ethiopia	Somalia, Sudan, Djibouti	250,000[1]
Ghana	Togo, Liberia	110,000
Guinea	Liberia, Sierra Leone	580,000[1]
Kenya	Somalia, Sudan, Ethiopia	257,000[1]
Liberia	Sierra Leone	100,000[1]
Malawi	Mozambique	70,000
South Africa	Mozambique	200,000[1]
Sudan	Eritrea, Ethiopia, Chad	550,000[1]
Tanzania	Rwanda, Burundi, Mozambique	752,000[1]
Uganda	Sudan, Zaire, Rwanda	323,000
Zaire	Rwanda, Angola, Burundi, Sudan, Uganda	1,527,000[1]
Zambia	Angola, Zaire	123,000
Total East Asia/Pacific		**444,000**
China	Vietnam, Myanmar	297,100[1]
Thailand	Myanmar, Laos	83,050
Total Europe & No. America		**2,625,000**
Armenia	Azerbaijan	295,800[1]
Azerbaijan	Armenia, Uzbekistan	279,000[1]

Place of asylum	Mostly from	Number
Croatia	Bosnia and Herzegovina, other	188,000
Germany	Bosnia and Herzegovina, Croatia, other	430,000[1]
Russia	Former USSR, other	451,000[1]
United States	Cuba, Haiti, other	181,700
Yugoslavia[2]	Croatia, Bosnia and Herzegovina	300,000[1]
Total Latin America/Caribbean		**94,000**
Total Middle East		**5,448,000**
Gaza Strip	Palestinians	644,000
Iran	Afghanistan, Iraq	2,220,000[1]
Iraq	Palestinians, Iran, Turkey	120,500
Jordan	Palestinians	1,232,150
Lebanon	Palestinians	338,200
Syria	Palestinians, Iraq	332,900
West Bank	Palestinians	504,000
Total South & Central Asia		**1,776,000**
Bangladesh	Myanmar	116,200
India	Tibet, Sri Lanka, Bangladesh, Bhutan, Afghanistan	327,850[1]
Nepal	Bhutan, Tibet	104,600
Pakistan	Afghanistan	1,202,650[1]
Total Refugees		**16,267,000**

(1) Significant variance among sources in number reported. (2) Serbia/Montenegro.

Principal Sources of Refugees

Palestinians	3,136,800	Somalia	457,400[1]	Sierra Leone	260,000[1]
Afghanistan	2,835,300[1]	Eritrea	384,500[1]	Armenia	229,000[1]
Rwanda	1,715,000[1]	Azerbaijan	374,000[1]	Myanmar	203,300[1]
Bosnia and Herzegovina	863,300[1]	Angola	344,000	Ethiopia	190,750[1]
Liberia	784,000[1]	Burundi	330,000[1]	Tajikistan	165,000[1]
Iraq	635,900[1]	Mozambique	325,000[1]	Togo	140,000
Sudan	510,000	Vietnam	294,900	Tibet	139,000

(1) Significant variance among sources in number reported.

U.S. Immigration Law

Source: Immigration and Naturalization Service, U.S. Dept. of Justice

(Note: As of late 1995, legislation to revise existing U.S. immigration law was pending in the 104th Congress.)

The Immigration Act of 1990 became law when it was signed by Pres. George Bush on Nov. 29, 1990. Bush called the bill the "most comprehensive reform of U.S. immigration laws in 66 years." Most of its provisions amend the Immigration and Nationality Act, which remains the basic law. The new law raised the total number of numerically limited immigrants entering the U.S. annually in FY 1992-94 to 700,000 (excluding refugees whose admission numbers are announced annually and some others not subject to limitation). The visas would be distributed as follows:

- 465,000 for family immigrants;
- 55,000 for the spouses and children of aliens legalized under IRCA (see below);
- 140,000 for employment-based immigrants;
- 40,000 for nationals from "adversely affected" countries.

Beginning in FY 1995 the number drops from 700,000 to 675,000. These visas would be distributed as follows:

- 480,000 for family immigrants;
- 140,000 for employment-based immigrants;
- 55,000 for "diversity immigrants."

Family Immigrants

Fiscal year 1992-94: 465,000 minus the number of "immediate relatives" admitted the previous fiscal year, plus any numbers unused by the employment-based preference system. During this period, the number of family-sponsored visas could not fall below 226,000 (10,000 visas higher than the previous allocation). If visa availability dipped below this new floor, the shortfall would be made up from the category below.

During this period, 55,000 additional visas would be made available to the spouses and children of aliens legalized under the Immigration Reform and Control Act (IRCA) of 1986.

Fiscal year 1995 and beyond: 480,000 minus the number of "immediate relatives" admitted during the previous fiscal year, plus any unused numbers under the employment-based preference system. The number of family-sponsored visas cannot drop below a floor of 226,000.

New Family Preference System

First preference—unmarried sons and daughters of U.S. citizens: 23,400 visas plus unused visas from the 4th preference.

Second preference—spouses and unmarried children of Lawful Permanent Residents (LPRs): 114,200 visas, plus any visas available above the floor of 226,000 family preference visas, plus any unused visas from the previous preference.

The category is subdivided as follows: A minimum of 77% of the visas allocated to the category goes to the spouses and minor children of LPRs; 75% of the visas are issued without regard to per country ceilings; these visas are distributed in the order in which the petitions were filed; a maximum of 23% of the category visa allocation goes to the unmarried sons and daughters of LPRs. This group of visas continues to be subject to per country ceilings.

Third preference—married sons and daughters of U.S. citizens; 23,400 visas plus unused visas from all earlier preferences.

Fourth preference—brothers and sisters of U.S. citizens: 65,000 plus unused visas from all earlier preferences.

Employment-Based Immigrants

A total of 140,000 plus, beginning in 1994, any unused numbers under the family-sponsored system. These visas would be distributed as follows:

First preference—Priority Workers—28.6% of the employment-based limit plus visas unused by the fourth and fifth employment-based preferences "investors" and "special immigrants." The category is subdivided as follows: (1) extraordinary ability, demonstrated by sustained national or international acclaim, in the sciences, arts, education, business, and athletics; no U.S. employer required; (2) outstanding, internationally recognized and with at least 3 years of experience, professors and researchers seeking to enter in senior positions; U.S. employer required; (3) executives and managers of multinationals—requires one year of prior service with the firm during the preceding 3 years; terms are extensively defined; U.S. employer required.

Second preference—Professionals with advanced degrees and aliens of exceptional ability—28.6% of the employment-based limit plus any unused "priority worker" visas. A U.S. employer and labor certification are required—although the Attorney General can waive both requirements. Members of the professions with advanced degrees or

exceptional ability in the sciences, arts, or business. The possession of a degree, certificate, or license is not by itself considered sufficient evidence of exceptional ability.

Third preference—Skilled workers, professionals, and "other workers"—40,000 visas plus any visas unused by the 2 previous categories. Requires a U.S. employer and labor certification. Skilled workers must be in an occupation that requires at least 2 years training or experience. Professionals need a bachelor's degree. "Other workers" refers to unskilled workers. Their numbers are limited to no more than 10,000 visas per year.

Fourth preference—Special immigrants—7.1% of the employment-based limit. This category includes ministers of religion and persons working for religious organizations for at least 2 years, foreign medical graduates, employees of the U.S. government abroad including certain employees of the U.S. mission in Hong Kong who file for admission as special immigrants before Jan. 1, 2002, retired employees of international organizations, etc.

Fifth preference—7.1% of the employment-based limit—7,000 for investors of $1 million in urban areas and 3,000 for investors of no less than $500,000 in rural or high-unemployment areas. The Attorney General may increase the required investment amount up to $3 million for high employment areas. Investment must create employment for at least 10 U.S. workers.

Diversity Immigrant (DV) Category

The Immigration and Nationality Act provides 55,000 immigrant visas each fiscal year (beginning with FY 1995) to provide immigration opportunities for persons from countries other than the principal sources of current immigration to the U.S. DV visas are divided among six geographic regions. Not more than 3,850 visas (7% of the 55,000 visa limit) may be provided to immigrants from any one country.

The allotment of FY 1995 visa numbers for each region is as follows: Africa, 20,200; Asia, 6,837; Europe, 24,549; North America (Bahamas), 8; South America, Central America, and the Caribbean, 2,589; and Oceania, 817.

Diversity Immigrant Visa Lottery (DV) Drawing

On Aug. 12, 1994, the National Visa Center in Portsmouth, NH, began the selection of winners of the DV lottery. The first notices were sent to the winners in September.

The DV registration mail-in was held June 1-30, 1994. During this one-month period, the National Visa Center received approximately 6.5 million qualified entries. An additional 1.5 million entries received during those dates were disqualified for not providing the requested information or following published guidelines.

In order to issue all 55,000 visas in FY 1995, the National Visa Center planned to notify 110,000 principal applicants. Persons whose entries were not selected were not notified. Winners were sent instructions on how to apply for an immigrant visa. During the visa interview, applicants must provide proof of a high school education or its equivalent or must show two years of work experience within the past five years in an occupation that requires at least two years of training or experience.

Those selected needed to act on their immigrant visa applications quickly. As soon as 55,000 visas were issued, the program for FY 1995 would end.

Naturalization: How to Become an American Citizen

Source: Federal Statutes

A person who desires to be naturalized as a citizen of the United States may obtain the necessary application form as well as detailed information from the nearest office of the Immigration and Naturalization Service or from the clerk of a court handling naturalization cases.

An applicant must be at least 18 years old and must have been a lawful resident of the United States continuously for 5 years. For husbands and wives of U.S. citizens the period is 3 years in most instances. Special provisions apply to certain veterans of the armed forces.

An applicant must have been physically present in the country for at least half of the required 5 years' residence.

Every applicant for naturalization must:

(1) demonstrate an understanding of the English language, including an ability to read, write, and speak words in ordinary usage in the English language (persons physically unable to do so and persons who, on the date of their examinations, are over 55 years of age and have been lawful permanent residents of the United States for 15 years or more are exempt);

(2) have been a person of good moral character, attached to the principles of the Constitution, and well disposed to the good order and happiness of the United States for 5 years just before filing the petition or for whatever

other period of residence is required in the particular case and continue to be such a person until admitted to citizenship; and

(3) demonstrate a knowledge and understanding of the fundamentals of the history, and the principles and form of government, of the United States. This can be done at private, designated testing entities or at the interview before an immigration examiner.

At the interview the applicant may be represented by a lawyer or social service agency. There is a 30-day wait. If action is favorable, there is a swearing in ceremony conducted administratively or judicially. At that ceremony the following oath of allegiance is administered:

I hereby declare, on oath, that I absolutely and entirely renounce and abjure all allegiance and fidelity to any foreign prince, potentate, state or sovereignty, to whom or which I have heretofore been a subject or citizen; that I will support and defend the Constitution and laws of the United States of America against all enemies, foreign and domestic; that I will bear true faith and allegiance to the same; that I will bear arms on behalf of the United States when required by the law; that I will perform noncombatant service in the armed forces of the United States when required by the law; that I will perform work of national importance under civilian direction when required by the law; and that I take this obligation freely without any mental reservation or purpose of evasion; so help me God.

Major International Organizations

As of mid-1995

Asia-Pacific Economic Cooperation Group (APEC), founded Nov. 1989 as a forum to further cooperation on trade and investment between nations of the region and the rest of the world. Members in 1995 were Australia, Brunei, Canada, Chile, China, Hong Kong, Indonesia, Japan, Malaysia, Mexico, New Zealand, Papua New Guinea, Philippines, Singapore, South Korea, Taiwan, Thailand, and United States. Headquarters is in Singapore.

Association of Southeast Asian Nations (ASEAN), formed in 1967 to promote economic, social, and cultural cooperation and development among states of the Southeast Asian region. Members in 1995 were Brunei, Indonesia, Malaysia, Philippines, Singapore, Thailand, and Vietnam (the first Communist nation to be admitted to ASEAN). Annual ministerial meetings set policy; a central Secretariat in Jakarta and specialized intergovernmental committees work in trade, transportation, communications, agriculture, science, finance, and culture.

Caribbean Community and Common Market (CARICOM), established July 4, 1973. Its function is to further cooperation in economics, health, education, culture, science and technology, and tax administration, as well as the coordination of foreign policy. Members in 1995 were Antigua and Barbuda, Bahamas, Barbados, Belize, Dominica, Grenada, Guyana, Jamaica, Montserrat, Saint Kitts and Nevis, Saint Lucia, Saint Vincent and the Grenadines, Suriname, and Trinidad and Tobago.

Commonwealth of Independent States (CIS), created Dec. 1991 upon the disbanding of the Soviet Union. It is made up of 12 of the 15 former Soviet constituent republics. Members in 1995 were Armenia, Azerbaijan, Belarus, Georgia, Kazakhstan, Kyrgyzstan, Moldova, Russia, Tajikistan, Turkmenistan, Ukraine, and Uzbekistan. The commonwealth is not in itself a state but an alliance of fully independent states. Commonwealth policy is set through coordinating bodies such as a Council of Heads of State and Council of Heads of Government. The capital of the commonwealth is Minsk, Belarus.

The Commonwealth, originally called the British Commonwealth of Nations, and then the Commonwealth of Nations, an association of nations and dependencies loosely joined by a common interest based on having been parts of the old British Empire. The British monarch is the symbolic head of the Commonwealth.

There are 51 self-governing independent nations in the Commonwealth, plus various colonies and protectorates. As of 1995, the members were the United Kingdom of Great Britain and Northern Ireland and 15 other nations recognizing the British monarch, represented by a governor-general, as their head of state: Antigua and Barbuda, Australia, The Bahamas, Barbados, Belize, Canada, Grenada, Jamaica, New Zealand, Papua New Guinea, Saint Kitts and Nevis, Saint Lucia, Saint Vincent and the Grenadines, Solomon Islands, and Tuvalu (special member); and 35 countries with their own heads of state: Bangladesh, Botswana, Brunei, Cyprus, Dominica, The Gambia, Ghana, Guyana, India, Kenya, Kiribati, Lesotho, Malawi, Malaysia, The Maldives, Malta, Mauritius, Namibia, Nauru (special member), Nigeria, Pakistan, Seychelles, Sierra Leone, Singapore, South Africa, Sri Lanka, Swaziland, Tanzania, Tonga, Trinidad and Tobago, Uganda, Vanuatu, Western Samoa, Zambia, and Zimbabwe.

The Commonwealth facilitates consultation among member states through meetings of prime ministers and finance ministers, and through a permanent Secretariat. Members consult on economic, scientific, educational, financial, legal, and military matters, and try to coordinate policies.

European Union (EU)—known as the European Community (EC) until 1994—the collective designation of three organizations with common membership: the European Economic Community (Common Market), the European Coal and Steel Community, and the European Atomic Energy Community (Euratom). The 15 full members in 1995 were Austria, Belgium, Denmark, Finland, France, Germany, Greece, Ireland, Italy, Luxembourg, Netherlands, Portugal, Spain, Sweden, and United Kingdom. Austria, Finland, and Sweden entered the EU on Jan. 1, 1995; Norway was scheduled to join at the same time, but Norwegian citizens in a Nov. 1994 referendum, voted against membership. Some 70 nations in Africa, the Caribbean, and the Pacific are affiliated under the Lomé Convention.

A merger of the 3 communities' executives went into effect July 1, 1967, though the component organizations date back to 1951 and 1958. The Council of Ministers, the European Commission, the European Parliament, and the European Court of Justice comprise the permanent structure. The EU aims to integrate the economies, coordinate social developments, and bring about political union of the democratic states of Europe. Effective Dec. 31, 1992, there are no restrictions on the movement of goods, services, capital, workers, and tourists within the EU. There are also common agricultural, fisheries, and nuclear research policies.

Leaders of the member nations (12 at the time) met Dec. 9–11, 1991, in Maastricht, the Netherlands. Treaties on monetary union and political union and accompanying protocols agreed upon by the leaders:

- Committed the organization to launching a common currency for at least some nations by 1999. Britain and, later, Denmark were allowed to "opt out" of joining.
- Sought to establish common foreign policies for the members.
- Laid the groundwork for a common defense policy.
- Expanded the policy issues in which the organization would have a voice.
- Gave the organization a leading role in social policy. Britain was not included in this plan.
- Pledged increased aid for the 4 poorest member nations—Ireland, Greece, Spain, and Portugal.
- Slightly increased the powers of the 567-member European Parliament.

The treaties went into effect Nov. 1, 1993, following ratification by all 12 members.

European Free Trade Association (EFTA), created May 3, 1960, to promote expansion of free trade. By Dec. 31, 1966, tariffs and quotas between member nations had been eliminated. Members of the EFTA entered into free trade agreements with the EU in 1972 and 1973. In 1992 the EFTA and EU concluded an agreement to create a single market—with free flow of goods, services, capital, and labor—encompassing the nations of the two organizations. Members in 1995 were Iceland, Liechtenstein, Norway, and Switzerland. Austria, Finland, and Sweden left the EFTA and joined the EU Jan. 1, 1995.

Group of Seven (G-7), organization of seven major industrial democracies who meet periodically to discuss world economic and other issues. Established Sept. 22, 1985. Members are Canada, France, Germany, Italy, Japan, United Kingdom, and United States.

International Criminal Police Organization (Interpol), created June 13, 1956, to ensure and promote the widest possible mutual assistance between all police authorities within the limits of the law existing in the different countries and in the spirit of the Universal Declaration of Human Rights. There were 176 members (independent nations), plus 13 subbureaus (dependencies), in 1995.

Arab League (League of Arab States), created Mar. 22, 1945. Members in 1995 were Algeria, Bahrain, Comoros, Djibouti, Egypt, Iraq, Jordan, Kuwait, Lebanon, Libya, Mauritania, Morocco, Oman, the Palestine Liberation Org., Qatar, Saudi Arabia, Somalia, Sudan, Syria, Tunisia, United Arab Emirates, and Yemen. The League promotes economic, social, political, and military cooperation and mediates disputes among the Arab states; it represents Arab states in certain international matters. The league's headquarters is in Cairo.

North Atlantic Treaty Organization (NATO), created by treaty (signed Apr. 4, 1949; in effect Aug. 24, 1949). Members in 1995 were Belgium, Canada, Denmark, France, Germany, Greece, Iceland, Italy, Luxembourg, Netherlands, Norway, Portugal, Spain, Turkey, United Kingdom, and United States. The members agreed to settle disputes by peaceful means; to develop their individual and collective capacity to resist armed attack; to regard an attack on one as an attack on all; and to take necessary action to repel an attack under Article 51 of the United Nations Charter.

The NATO structure consists of a Council and a Military Committee of 3 commands (Allied Command Europe, Allied Command Atlantic, Allied Command Channel) and the Canada-U.S. Regional Planning Group.

With the dissolution of the Soviet Union and the end of the cold war in the early 1990s, NATO members sought to modify the organization's mission, putting greater stress on political action and creating a rapid deployment force to react to local crises. Former Warsaw Pact members were no longer considered adversaries, and Hungary gained associate membership in 1991. By June 1995, 25 nations, including former Soviet republics had joined with NATO in the Partnership for Peace (PFP) agreement, which provided for limited joint military exercises, peacekeeping missions, and information exchange. On June 1, 1995, Russia became an active member in the PFP, but prospects for its continued participation were uncertain due to conflicts over NATO's role in the war in the former Yugoslav republics and concern with NATO's attempts to expand into Eastern Europe.

Organization of African Unity (OAU), formed May 25, 1963, by 32 African countries (53 members in 1995) to promote peace and security as well as economic and social development. It holds annual conferences of heads of state. Headquarters is in Addis Ababa, Ethiopia.

Organization of American States (OAS), formed in Bogotá, Colombia, Apr. 30, 1948. Headquarters is in Washington, DC. It has a Permanent Council, Inter-American Economic and Social Council, Inter-American Council for Education, Science, and Culture, Juridical Committee, and Commission on Human Rights. The Permanent Council can call meetings of foreign ministers to deal with urgent security matters. A General Assembly meets annually. A secretary general and assistant are elected for 5-year terms. There are 35 members, each with one vote in the various organizations: Antigua and Barbuda, Argentina, The Bahamas, Barbados, Belize, Bolivia, Brazil, Canada, Chile, Colombia, Costa Rica, Cuba, Dominica, Dominican Republic, Ecuador, El Salvador, Grenada, Guatemala, Guyana,

Haiti, Honduras, Jamaica, Mexico, Nicaragua, Panama, Paraguay, Peru, Saint Kitts and Nevis, Saint Lucia, Saint Vincent and the Grenadines, Suriname, Trinidad and Tobago, United States, Uruguay, and Venezuela. In 1962, the OAS excluded Cuba from OAS activities but not from membership.

Organization for Economic Cooperation and Development (OECD), established Sept. 30, 1961, to promote economic and social welfare in member countries, and to stimulate and harmonize efforts on behalf of developing nations. The OECD collects and disseminates economic and environmental information. Members in 1995 were Australia, Austria, Belgium, Canada, Denmark, Finland, France, Germany, Greece, Iceland, Ireland, Italy, Japan, Luxembourg, Mexico, Netherlands, New Zealand, Norway, Portugal, Spain, Sweden, Switzerland, Turkey, United Kingdom, and United States. Headquarters is in Paris.

Organization of Petroleum Exporting Countries (OPEC), created Sept. 14, 1960. The group attempts to set world oil prices by controlling oil production. It is also involved in advancing members' interests in trade and development dealings with industrialized oil-consuming nations. Members in 1995 were Algeria, Gabon, Indonesia, Iran, Iraq, Kuwait, Libya, Nigeria, Qatar, Saudi Arabia, United Arab Emirates, and Venezuela. Headquarters is in Vienna.

Organization for Security and Cooperation in Europe (OSCE), established 1972 as the Conference on Security and Cooperation in Europe; current name adopted Jan. 1, 1995. The group, formed by NATO and Warsaw Pact members, is interested in furthering East-West relations through a commitment to nonaggression and human rights as well as cooperation in economics, science and technology, cultural exchange, and environmental protection. There were 53 member states in 1995. Headquarters is in Vienna.

United Nations

The 50th regular session of United Nations General Assembly opened in September 1995.

UN headquarters is in New York, NY, between First Ave. and Roosevelt Drive and E. 42d St. and E. 48th St. The General Assembly Bldg., Secretariat, Conference and Library bldgs. are interconnected.

A European office at Geneva includes Secretariat and agency staff members. Other offices of UN bodies and related organizations with a staff of some 23,000 from some 150 countries are scattered throughout the world.

The UN has a post office originating its own stamps.

Proposals to establish an organization of nations for maintenance of world peace led to the United Nations Conference on International Organization at San Francisco, Apr. 25-June 26, 1945, where the charter of the United Nations was drawn up. It was signed June 26 by 50 nations, and by Poland, one of the original 51 UN members, on Oct. 15, 1945. The charter

came into effect Oct. 24, 1945, upon ratification by the permanent members of the Security Council and a majority of other signatories.

Purposes: To maintain international peace and security; to develop friendly relations among nations; to achieve international cooperation in solving economic, social, cultural, and humanitarian problems and in promoting respect for human rights and fundamental freedoms; to be a center for harmonizing the actions of nations in attaining these common ends.

Visitors to the UN: Headquarters is open to the public every day of the year except Christmas and New Year's Day. Guided tours are given approximately every half hour from 9:15 AM to 4:15 PM daily. Groups of 15 or more persons should write to the Group Program Unit, Visitors' Service, Room GA-56, United Nations, New York, NY 10017, or telephone (212) 963-4440. Children under 5 are not permitted on tours.

Roster of the United Nations

The 185 members of the United Nations, with the years in which they became members; as of Sept. 1995

Member	Year	Member	Year	Member	Year	Member	Year
Afghanistan	1946	Brunei	1984	Ecuador	1945	India	1945
Albania	1955	Bulgaria	1955	Egypt[3]	1945	Indonesia[4]	1950
Algeria	1962	Burkina Faso	1960	El Salvador	1945	Iran	1945
Andorra	1993	Burundi	1962	Equatorial Guinea	1968	Iraq	1945
Angola	1976	Cambodia	1955	Eritrea	1993	Ireland	1955
Antigua and Barbuda	1981	Cameroon	1960	Estonia	1991	Israel	1949
Argentina	1945	Canada	1945	Ethiopia	1945	Italy	1955
Armenia	1992	Cape Verde	1975	Fiji	1970	Jamaica	1962
Australia	1945	Central African Rep.	1960	Finland	1955	Japan	1956
Austria	1955	Chad	1960	France	1945	Jordan	1955
Azerbaijan	1992	Chile	1945	Gabon	1960	Kazakhstan	1992
Bahamas	1973	China[1]	1945	Gambia, The	1965	Kenya	1963
Bahrain	1971	Colombia	1945	Georgia	1992	Korea, North	1991
Bangladesh	1974	Comoros	1975	Germany	1973	Korea, South	1991
Barbados	1966	Congo	1960	Ghana	1957	Kuwait	1963
Belarus	1945	Costa Rica	1945	Greece	1945	Kyrgyzstan	1992
Belgium	1945	Côte d'Ivoire	1960	Grenada	1974	Laos	1955
Belize	1981	Croatia	1992	Guatemala	1945	Latvia	1991
Benin	1960	Cuba	1945	Guinea	1958	Lebanon	1945
Bhutan	1971	Cyprus	1960	Guinea-Bissau	1974	Lesotho	1966
Bolivia	1945	Czech Republic[2]	1993	Guyana	1966	Liberia	1945
Bosnia and		Denmark	1945	Haiti	1945	Libya	1955
Herzegovina	1992	Djibouti	1977	Honduras	1945	Liechtenstein	1990
Botswana	1966	Dominica	1978	Hungary	1955	Lithuania	1991
Brazil	1945	Dominican Republic	1945	Iceland	1946	Luxembourg	1945

Member	Year	Member	Year	Member	Year	Member	Year
Macedonia[5]	1993	Nicaragua	1945	Samoa (Western)	1976	Tanzania[9]	1961
Madagascar	1960	Niger	1960	San Marino	1992	Thailand	1946
Malawi	1964	Nigeria	1960	São Tomé and		Togo	1960
Malaysia[6]	1957	Norway	1945	Príncipe	1975	Trinidad and Tobago	1962
Maldives	1965	Oman	1971	Saudi Arabia	1945	Tunisia	1956
Mali	1960	Pakistan	1947	Senegal	1960	Turkey	1945
Malta	1964	Palau	1994	Seychelles	1976	Turkmenistan	1992
Marshall Islands	1991	Panama	1945	Sierra Leone	1961	Uganda	1962
Mauritania	1961	Papua New Guinea	1975	Singapore[6]	1965	Ukraine	1945
Mauritius	1968	Paraguay	1945	Slovakia[2]	1993	United Arab Emirates	1971
Mexico	1945	Peru	1945	Slovenia	1992	United Kingdom	1945
Micronesia	1991	Philippines	1945	Solomon Islands	1978	United States	1945
Moldova	1992	Poland	1945	Somalia	1960	Uruguay	1945
Monaco	1993	Portugal	1955	South Africa[8]	1945	Uzbekistan	1992
Mongolia	1961	Qatar	1971	Spain	1955	Vanuatu	1981
Morocco	1956	Romania	1955	Sri Lanka	1955	Venezuela	1945
Mozambique	1975	Russia[7]	1945	Sudan	1956	Vietnam	1977
Myanmar (Burma)	1948	Rwanda	1962	Suriname	1975	Yemen[10]	1947
Namibia	1990	Saint Kitts and Nevis	1983	Swaziland	1968	Yugoslavia[11]	1945
Nepal	1955	Saint Lucia	1979	Sweden	1946	Zaire	1960
Netherlands	1945	Saint Vincent and		Syria[3]	1945	Zambia	1964
New Zealand	1945	the Grenadines	1980	Tajikistan	1992	Zimbabwe	1980

(1) The General Assembly voted in 1971 to expel the Chinese government on Taiwan and admit the Beijing government in its place. (2) Czechoslovakia, which split into the separate nations of the Czech Republic and Slovakia on Jan. 1, 1993, was a UN member from 1945 to 1992. (3) Egypt and Syria were original members of the UN. In 1958, the United Arab Republic was established by a union of Egypt and Syria and continued as a single member of the UN. In 1961, Syria resumed its separate membership. (4) Indonesia withdrew from the UN in 1965 and rejoined in 1966. (5) Admitted under the provisional name of The Former Yugoslav Republic of Macedonia. (6) Malaya joined the UN in 1957. In 1963, its name was changed to Malaysia following the accession of Singapore, Sabah, and Sarawak. Singapore became an independent UN member in 1965. (7) The Union of Soviet Socialist Republics was an original member of the UN from 1945. After the USSR's dissolution in 1991, Russia informed the UN that it would be continuing the USSR's membership in the Security Council and all other UN organs with the support of the Commonwealth of Independent States (comprised of most of the former Soviet republics). (8) In 1994, the General Assembly accepted the credentials of the South African delegation, which had been rejected for 24 years because of the country's former apartheid policies. (9) Tanganyika was a member of the UN from 1961 and Zanzibar was a member from 1963. Following the ratification in 1964 of Articles of Union between Tanganyika and Zanzibar, the United Republic of Tanganyika and Zanzibar continued as a single member of the UN, later changing its name to United Republic of Tanzania. (10) The Yemen Arab Republic was admitted in 1947; the People's Republic of Yemen, in 1967. The two nations merged in 1990. (11) The Socialist Federal Republic of Yugoslavia became a member in 1945. After four of its six republics (Bosnia and Herzegovina, Croatia, Macedonia, and Slovenia) declared independence in 1991-92, the two remaining republics, Montenegro and Serbia, reconstituted themselves as the Federal Republic of Yugoslavia, which assumed Yugoslavia's UN seat Apr. 8, 1992. The General Assembly suspended Yugoslavia in Sept. 1992 for violating UN resolutions relating to the civil wars in the former Yugoslav republics.

United Nations Secretaries General

Year	Secretary, Nation	Year	Secretary, Nation	Year	Secretary, Nation
1946	Trygve Lie, Norway	1961	U Thant, Burma	1982	Javier Perez de Cuellar, Peru
1953	Dag Hammarskjold, Sweden	1972	Kurt Waldheim, Austria	1992	Boutros Boutros-Ghali, Egypt

U.S. Representatives to the United Nations

The U.S. Representative to the United Nations is the Chief of the U.S. Mission to the United Nations in New York and holds the rank and status of Ambassador Extraordinary and Plenipotentiary (A.E.P.).

Year	Representative	Year	Representative	Year	Representative
1946	Edward R. Stettinius, Jr.	1968	George W. Ball	1977	Andrew Young
1946	Herschel V. Johnson (act.)	1968	James Russell Wiggins	1979	Donald McHenry
1947	Warren R. Austin	1969	Charles W. Yost	1981	Jeane J. Kirkpatrick
1953	Henry Cabot Lodge, Jr.	1971	George Bush	1985	Vernon A. Walters
1960	James J. Wadsworth	1973	John A. Scali	1989	Thomas R. Pickering
1961	Adlai E. Stevenson	1975	Daniel P. Moynihan	1992	Edward J. Perkins
1965	Arthur J. Goldberg	1976	William W. Scranton	1993	Madeleine K. Albright

Organization of the United Nations

The text of the UN Charter may be obtained from the Office of Public Information, United Nations, New York, NY 10017.

General Assembly. The General Assembly is composed of representatives of all the member nations. Each nation is entitled to one vote.

The General Assembly meets in regular annual sessions and in special session when necessary. Special sessions are convoked by the Secretary General at the request of the Security Council or of a majority of the members of the UN.

On important questions a two-thirds majority of members present and voting is required; on other questions a simple majority is sufficient.

The General Assembly must approve the budget and apportion expenses among members. A member in arrears will have no vote if the amount of arrears equals or exceeds the amount of the contributions due for the preceding 2 full years.

Security Council. The Security Council consists of 15 members, 5 with permanent seats. The remaining 10 are elected for 2-year terms by the General Assembly; they are not eligible for immediate reelection.

Permanent members of the Council are: China, France, Russia, United Kingdom, United States.

Nonpermanent members are: (with terms expiring Dec. 31, 1995) Argentina, Czech Republic, Nigeria, Oman, Rwanda; (with terms expiring Dec. 31, 1996) Botswana, Germany, Honduras, Indonesia, Italy.

The Security Council has the primary responsibility within the UN for maintaining international peace and security. The Council may investigate any dispute that threatens international peace and security.

Any member of the UN at UN headquarters may participate in its discussions and a nation not a member of the UN may appear if it is a party to a dispute.

Decisions on procedural questions are made by an affirmative vote of 9 members. On all other matters the affirmative vote of 9 members must include the concurring votes of all permanent members; it is this clause which gives rise to the so-called veto power of permanent members. A party to a dispute must refrain from voting.

The Security Council directs the various peacekeeping forces deployed throughout the world.

Economic and Social Council. The Economic and Social Council consists of 54 members elected by the General Assembly for 3-year terms of office. The council is responsible under the General Assembly for carrying out the functions of the United Nations with regard to international economic, social, cultural, educational, health, and related matters. The council meets once a year.

Trusteeship Council. The administration of trust territories is under UN supervision.

Secretariat. The Secretary General is the chief administrative officer of the UN. He may bring to the attention of the Security Council any matter that threatens international peace. He reports to the General Assembly.

Budget: The General Assembly approved a total budget for 1994-95 of $2.58 billion, later revised to $2.61 billion.

International Court of Justice (World Court). The International Court of Justice is the principal judicial organ of the United Nations. All members are *ipso facto* parties to the statute of the Court. Other states may become parties to the Court's statute.

The jurisdiction of the Court comprises cases which the parties submit to it and matters especially provided for in the charter or in treaties. The Court gives advisory opinions and renders judgments. Its decisions are binding only between the parties concerned and in respect to a particular dispute. If any party to a case fails to heed a judgment, the other party may have recourse to the Security Council.

The 15 judges are elected for 9-year terms by the General Assembly and the Security Council. Retiring judges are eligible for reelection. The Court remains permanently in session, except during vacations. All questions are decided by majority. The Court sits in The Hague, Netherlands.

Selected Specialized and Related Agencies

These agencies are autonomous, with their own memberships and organs, and have a functional relationship or working agreement with the UN (headquarters), except for UNICEF and UNHCR, which report directly to the Economic and Social Council and to the General Assembly.

Food and Agriculture Organization (FAO), aims to increase production from farms, forests, and fisheries; improve food distribution and marketing, nutrition, and the living conditions of rural people. (Viale delle Terme di Caracalla, 00100 Rome, Italy.)

International Atomic Energy Agency (IAEA), aims to promote the safe, peaceful uses of atomic energy. (Vienna International Centre, PO Box 100, A-1400, Vienna, Austria.)

International Bank for Reconstruction and Development (IBRD) (World Bank), provides loans and technical assistance for economic development projects in developing member countries; encourages cofinancing for projects from other public and private sources. The IBRD has 3 affiliates: (1) The **International Development Association (IDA)** provides funds for development projects on concessionary terms to the poorer developing member countries. (2) The **International Finance Corporation (IFC)** promotes the growth of the private sector in developing member countries; encourages the development of local capital markets; stimulates the international flow of private capital. (3) The **Multilateral Investment Guarantee Agency (MIGA)** promotes private investment in developing countries; guarantees investments to protect investors from noncommercial risks, such as war or nationalization; advises governments on attracting private investment. (1818 H St., NW, Washington, DC 20433.)

International Civil Aviation Org. (ICAO), promotes international civil aviation standards and regulations. (1000 Sherbrooke St. W., Montreal, Quebec, Canada H3A 2R2.)

International Fund for Agricultural Development (IFAD), aims to mobilize funds for agricultural and rural projects in developing countries. (107 Via del Serafico, Rome, Italy.)

International Labor Org. (ILO), aims to promote employment; improve labor conditions and living standards. (4 route de Morillons, CH-1211 Geneva 22, Switzerland.)

International Maritime Org. (IMO), aims to promote cooperation on technical matters affecting international shipping. (4 Albert Embankment, London SE1 7SR, England.)

International Monetary Fund (IMF), aims to promote international monetary cooperation and currency stabilization and expansion of international trade. (700 19th St., NW, Washington, DC 20431.)

International Telecommunication Union (ITU), establishes international regulations for radio, telegraph, telephone, and space radio-communications, allocates radio frequencies. (Place des Nations, 1211 Geneva 20, Switzerland.)

United Nations Children's Fund (UNICEF), provides aid and development assistance to programs for children and mothers in developing countries. (1 UN Plaza, New York, NY 10017.)

United Nations Educational, Scientific, and Cultural Org. (UNESCO), aims to promote collaboration among nations through education, science, and culture. (7 Place de Fontenoy, 75352 Paris 07SP, France.)

United Nations High Commissioner for Refugees (UNHCR), provides essential assistance for refugees. (Place des Nations, 1211 Geneva 10, Switzerland.)

Universal Postal Union (UPU), aims to perfect postal services and promote international collaboration. (Weltpoststrasse 4, 3000 Berne, 15 Switzerland.)

World Health Org. (WHO), aims to aid the attainment of the highest possible level of health. (1211 Geneva 27, Switzerland.)

World Intellectual Property Org. (WIPO), seeks to protect, through international cooperation, literary, industrial, scientific, and artistic works. (34, Chemin des Colom Bettes, 1211 Geneva, Switzerland.)

World Meteorological Org. (WMO), aims to coordinate and improve world meteorological work. (Case Postale 5, CH-1211 Geneva 20, Switzerland.)

World Trade Org. (WTO), replacing the General Agreement on Tariffs and Trade (GATT), is the major body overseeing international trade. The WTO administers trade agreements and treaties, examines the trade regimes of members, keeps track of various trade measures and statistics, and attempts to settle trade disputes. (Centre William Rappard, 154 rue de Lausanne, 1211 Geneva 21, Switzerland.)

Geneva Conventions

The Geneva Conventions are 4 international treaties governing the protection of civilians in time of war, the treatment of prisoners of war, and the care of the wounded and sick in the armed forces. The first convention, covering the sick and wounded, was concluded in Geneva, Switzerland, in 1864; it was amended and expanded in 1906. A third convention, in 1929, covered prisoners of war. Outrage at the treatment of prisoners and civilians during World War II by some belligerents, notably Germany and Japan, prompted the conclusion, in August 1949, of 4 new conventions. Three of these restated and strengthened the previous conventions, and the fourth codified general principles of international law governing the treatment of civilians in wartime.

The 1949 convention for civilians provided for special safeguards for the wounded, children under 15, pregnant women, and the elderly. Discrimination was forbidden on racial, religious, national, or political grounds. Torture, collective punishment, reprisals, the unwarrented destruction of property, and the forced use of civilians for an occupier's armed forces were also prohibited.

Also included in the new 1949 treaties was a pledge to treat prisoners humanely, feed them adequately, and deliver relief supplies to them. They were not to be forced to disclose more than minimal information.

Most countries have formally accepted all or most of the humanitarian conventions as binding. A nation is not free to withdraw its ratification of the conventions during wartime. However, there is no permanent machinery in place to apprehend, try, or punish violators.

Ambassadors and Envoys

"Envoys from the United States" as of Oct. 1995. "Envoys to the United States" as of Sept. 1995. The address of U.S. embassies abroad is the appropriate foreign capital. The U.S. does not have diplomatic relations with the following countries: Cuba[1], Iran[2], Iraq[3], Libya[4], Liechtenstein, North Korea, and Taiwan[5]. There are informal relations with Bhutan.

Countries	Envoys from United States	Envoys to United States
Afghanistan	Vacancy	Yar Mohammad Mohabbat, Chargé
Albania	Joseph E. Lake, Amb.	Lublin Dilja, Amb.
Algeria	Ronald E. Neumann, Amb.	Hadj Osmane Bencherif, Amb.
Angola	Donald K. Steinberg, Amb.	Antonio Franca, Amb.
Antigua & Barbuda	Jeanette W. Hyde, Amb.	Patrick Albert Lewis, Amb.
Argentina	James R. Cheek, Amb.	Raul Enrique Granillo Ocampo, Amb.
Armenia	Peter Tomsen, Amb.	Rouben Robert Shugarian, Amb.
Australia	Edward J. Perkins, Amb.	Donald Eric Russell, Amb.
Austria	Swanee G. Hunt, Amb.	Helmut Tuerk, Amb.
Azerbaijan	Richard D. Kauzlarich, Amb.	Hafiz Mir Jalal Oglu Pashayev, Amb.
Bahamas	Sidney Williams, Amb.	Timothy Baswell Donaldson, Amb.
Bahrain	David M. Ransom, Amb.	Muhammad Abdul Ghaffar Abdulla, Amb.
Bangladesh	David N. Merrill, Amb.	Humayun Kabir, Amb.
Barbados	Jeanette W. Hyde, Amb.	Courtney N. M. Blackman, Amb.
Belarus	Kenneth S. Yalowitz, Amb.	Serguei Nikolaevich Martynov, Amb.
Belgium	Alan J. Blinken, Amb.	Andre Adam, Amb.
Belize	George C. Bruno, Amb.	Dean Russell Lindo, Amb.
Benin	Ruth A. Davis, Amb.	Lucien Edgar Tonoukouin, Amb.
Bolivia	Curt W. Kamman, Amb.	Andres Petricevic, Amb.
Bosnia and Herzegovina	John K. Menzies, Amb.	Sven Alkalaj, Amb.
Botswana	Howard F. Jeter, Amb.	Mustaq Ahmed Moorad, Chargé
Brazil	Melvyn Levitsky, Amb.	Paulo Tarso Flecha de Lima, Amb.
Brunei	Theresa A. Tull, Amb.	Haji Jaya bin Abdul Latif, Amb.
Bulgaria	William D. Montgomery, Amb.	Snejana Damianova Botoucharova, Amb.
Burkina Faso	Donald J. McConnell, Amb.	Gaetan R. Ouedraogo, Amb.
Burundi	Robert Krueger, Amb.	Severin Ntahomvukiye, Amb.
Cambodia	Charles H. Twining Jr., Amb.	Var Huoth, Amb.
Cameroon	Harriet W. Isom, Amb.	Jerome Mendouga, Amb.
Canada	James J. Blanchard, Amb.	Raymond A. J. Chretien, Amb.
Cape Verde	Joseph M. Segars, Amb.	Corentino Virgillio Santos, Amb.
Central African Republic	Mosina H. Jordan, Amb.	Henry Koba, Amb.
Chad	Laurence E. Pope II, Amb.	Ahmat Mahamat-Saleh, Amb.
Chile	Gabriel Guerra-Mondragon, Amb.	John Biehl, Amb.
China	Vacancy	Li Daoyu, Amb.
Colombia	Myles R. R. Frechette, Amb.	Carlos Lleras, Amb.
Comoros	Leslie M. Alexander, Amb.	Amini Ali Moumin, Amb.
Congo	William C. Ramsay, Amb.	Vacancy
Costa Rica	Peter Jon de Vos, Chargé	Sonia Picado, Amb.
Côte d'Ivoire	Lannon Walker, Amb.	Koffi Moise Koumoue, Amb.
Croatia	Peter W. Galbraith, Amb.	Petar Sarcevic, Amb.
Cyprus	Richard A. Boucher, Amb.	Andrew J. Jacovides, Amb.
Czech Republic	Jenonne R. Walker, Amb.	Michael Zantovsky, Amb.
Denmark	Edward E. Elson, Amb.	K. Erik Tygesen, Amb.
Djibouti	Martin L. Cheshes, Amb.	Roble Olhaye, Amb.
Dominica	Jeanette W. Hyde, Amb.	Vacancy
Dominican Republic	Donna J. Hrinak, Amb.	Jose del Carmen Ariza, Amb.
Ecuador	Peter F. Romero, Amb.	Edgar Teran-Teran, Amb.
Egypt	Edward S. Walker, Amb.	Ahmed Maher El Sayed, Amb.
El Salvador	Alan H. Flanigan, Amb.	Ana Cristina Sol, Amb.
Equatorial Guinea	Vacancy	Pastor Micha Ondo Bile, Amb.
Eritrea	Robert G. Houdek, Amb.	Amdemicael Kahsai, Amb.
Estonia	Lawrence P. Taylor, Amb.	Toomas Hendrik Ilves, Amb.
Ethiopia	Irvin Hicks, Amb.	Berhane Gebre-Christos, Amb.
Fiji	Vacancy	Pita Kewa Nacuva, Amb.
Finland	Derek Shearer, Amb.	Jukka Valtasaari, Amb.
France	Pamela Harriman, Amb.	Patrick Villemur, Chargé
Gabon	Elizabeth Raspolic, Amb.	Paul Boundoukou-Latha, Amb.
Gambia, The	Vacancy	Tombong Saidy, Chargé
Georgia	William H. Courtney, Amb.	Tedo Djaparidze, Amb.
Germany	Charles E. Redman, Amb.	Juergen Chrobog, Amb.
Ghana	Edward Brynn, Amb.	Ekwow Spio-Garbrah, Amb.
Greece	Thomas M. T. Niles, Amb.	Loucas Tsilas, Amb.
Grenada	Jeanette W. Hyde, Amb.	Denneth Modeste, Amb.
Guatemala	Marilyn McAfee, Amb.	Edmond A. Mulet, Amb.
Guinea	Joseph A. Saloom III, Amb.	Elhadj Boubacar Barry, Amb.
Guinea-Bissau	Peggy Blackford, Amb.	Alfredo Lopes Cabral, Amb.
Guyana	David L. Hobbs, Amb.	Mohammed Ali Odeen Ishmael, Amb.
Haiti	William L. Swing, Amb.	Jean Casimir, Amb.
Honduras	William T. Pryce, Amb.	Roberto Flores Bermudez, Amb.
Hungary	Donald M. Blinken, Amb.	Gyorgy Banlaki, Amb.
Iceland	Parker W. Borg, Amb.	Einar Benediktsson, Amb.
India	Frank G. Wisner, Amb.	Siddhartha Shankar Ray, Amb.
Indonesia	Vacancy	Arifin Mohamad Siregar, Amb.
Ireland	Jean Kennedy Smith, Amb.	Dermot A. Gallagher, Amb.
Israel	Martin S. Indyk, Amb.	Itamar Rabinovich, Amb.
Italy	Reginald Bartholomew, Amb.	Boris Biancheri, Amb.
Jamaica	Jerome G. Cooper, Amb.	Richard Leighton Bernal, Amb.
Japan	Walter F. Mondale, Amb.	Takakazu Kuriyama, Amb.
Jordan	Wesley W. Egan, Amb.	Fayez A. Tarawneh, Amb.
Kazakhstan	A. Elizabeth Jones, Amb.	Touleoutai S. Souleimenov, Amb.
Kenya	Aurelia E. Brazeal, Amb.	Benjamin Edgar Kipkorir, Amb.
Kiribati	Vacancy	Vacancy

Countries	Envoys from United States	Envoys to United States
Korea, South	James T. Laney, Amb.	Kun Woo Park, Amb.
Kuwait	Ryan C. Crocker, Amb.	Mohammed Sabah Salim Al-Sabah, Amb.
Kyrgyzstan	Eileen A. Malloy, Amb.	Almas Chukin, Chargé
Laos	Victor L. Tomseth, Amb.	Hiem Phommachanh, Amb.
Latvia	Larry C. Napper, Amb.	Ojars E. Kalnins, Amb.
Lebanon	Vacancy	Riad Tabbarah, Amb.
Lesotho	Bismarck Myrick, Amb.	Eunice M. Bulane, Amb.
Liberia	Vacancy	Konah Blackett, Chargé
Lithuania	James W. Swihart Jr., Amb.	Alfonsas Eidintas, Amb.
Luxembourg	Clay Constantinou, Amb.	Alphonse Berns, Amb.
Madagascar	Dennis P. Barrett, Amb.	Pierrot J. Rajaonarivelo, Amb.
Malawi	Peter R. Chaveas, Amb.	W. Chokani, Amb.
Malaysia	Vacancy	Dato Mohamed Abdul Majid, Amb.
Maldives	Vacancy	Vacancy
Mali	Vacancy	Siragatou Ibrahim Cisse, Amb.
Malta	Joseph R. Paolino Jr., Amb.	Albert Borg Olivier de Puget, Amb.
Marshall Islands	Vacancy	Wilfred I. Kendall, Amb.
Mauritania	Dorothy Myers Sampas, Amb.	Ismail Ould Iyahi, Amb.
Mauritius	Leslie M. Alexander, Amb.	Anund Priyay Neewoor, Amb.
Mexico	James R. Jones, Amb.	Jesus Silva Herzog, Amb.
Micronesia	March Fong Eu, Amb.	Jesse B. Marehalau, Amb.
Moldova	John T. Stewart, Amb.	Nicolae Tau, Amb.
Mongolia	Donald C. Johnson, Amb.	Khalzkhuu Narankuu, Chargé
Morocco	Marc C. Ginsberg, Amb.	Mohamed Benaissa, Amb.
Mozambique	Dennis C. Jett, Amb.	Hipolito Pereira Zozimo Patricio, Amb.
Myanmar	Franklin P. Huddle Jr., Chargé	U Thaung, Amb.
Namibia	Marshall F. McCallie, Amb.	Tuliameni Kalomoh, Amb.
Nauru	Vacancy	Vacancy
Nepal	Sandra L. Vogelgesang, Amb.	Basudev Prasad Dhungana, Amb.
Netherlands	K. Terry Dornbush, Amb.	Adriaan P. R. Jacobovits de Szeged, Amb.
New Zealand	Josiah Horton Beeman, Amb.	L. John Wood, Amb.
Nicaragua	John F. Maisto, Amb.	Roberto G. Mayorga-Cortes, Amb.
Niger	John S. Davison, Amb.	Adamou Seydou, Amb.
Nigeria	Walter C. Carrington, Amb.	Zubair Mahmud Kazaure, Amb.
Norway	Thomas A. Loftus, Amb.	Kjeld Vibe, Amb.
Oman	Vacancy	Abdulla Moh'd. Aqeel Al- Dhahab, Amb.
Pakistan	Vacancy	Maleeha Lodhi, Amb.
Palau	Richard G. Watkins, Chargé	Isaac Ngewakl Soaladaob, Chargé
Panama	William J. Hughes, Amb.	Ricardo Alberto Arias, Amb.
Papua New Guinea	Richard W. Teare, Amb.	Kepas Isimel Watangia, Amb.
Paraguay	Robert E. Service, Amb.	Jorge G. Prieto, Amb.
Peru	Alvin P. Adams Jr., Amb.	Ricardo V. Luna, Amb.
Philippines	John D. Negroponte, Amb.	Raul Ch. Rabe, Amb.
Poland	Nicholas Andrew Rey, Amb.	Jerzy Kozminski, Amb.
Portugal	Elizabeth Frawley Bagley, Amb.	Fernando Andresen Guimaraes, Amb.
Qatar	Patrick N. Theros, Amb.	Sheikh Abdulrahman bin Saud al-Thani, Amb.
Romania	Alfred H. Moses, Amb.	Ion Gorita, Chargé
Russia	Thomas R. Pickering, Amb.	Yuli M. Vorontsov, Amb.
Rwanda	David P. Rawson, Amb.	Joseph W. Mutaboba, Chargé
St. Kitts & Nevis	Jeanette W. Hyde, Amb.	Erstein Mallet Edwards, Amb.
St. Lucia	Jeanette W. Hyde, Amb.	Dr. Joseph Edsel Edmunds, Amb.
St. Vincent and the Grenadines	Jeanette W. Hyde, Amb.	Kingsley C.A. Layne, Amb.
São Tomé and Príncipe	Elizabeth Raspolic, Amb.	Vacancy
Saudi Arabia	Raymond E. Mabus Jr., Amb.	Prince Bandar Bin Sultan, Amb.
Senegal	Mark Johnson, Amb.	Mamadou Mansour Seck, Amb.
Seychelles	Carl B. Stokes, Amb.	Marc R. Marengo, Amb.
Sierra Leone	John L. Hirsch, Amb.	Thomas Kahota Kargbo, Amb.
Singapore	Timothy A. Chorba, Amb.	S. R. Nathan, Amb.
Slovakia	Theodore E. Russell, Amb.	Branislav Lichardus, Amb.
Slovenia	Victor Jackovich, Amb.	Ernest Petric, Amb.
Solomon Islands	Richard W. Teare, Amb.	Vacancy
South Africa	Princeton N. Lyman, Amb.	Franklin Sonn, Amb.
Spain	Richard N. Gardner, Amb.	Jaime de Ojeda, Amb.
Sri Lanka	Vacancy	Jayantha Cudah Bandara Dhanapala, Amb.
Sudan	Timothy M. Carney, Amb.	Mirghani Mohamed Salih, Chargé
Suriname	Roger R. Gamble, Amb.	Willem A. Udenhout, Amb.
Swaziland	John T. Sprott, Amb.	Mary M. Kanya, Amb.
Sweden	Thomas L. Siebert, Amb.	Carl Henrik Sihver Liljegren, Amb.
Switzerland	M. Larry Lawrence, Amb.	Carlo Jagmetti, Amb.
Syria	Christopher W. S. Ross, Amb.	Walid Al-Moualem, Amb.
Tajikistan	R. Grant Smith, Amb.	Vacancy
Tanzania	Brady Anderson, Amb.	Mustafa Salim Nyang'anyi, Amb.
Thailand	Vacancy	Manaspas Xuto, Amb.
Togo	Johnny Young, Amb.	Kossivi Osseyi,Amb.
Tonga	Vacancy	Sione Kite, Amb.
Trinidad and Tobago	Brian J. Donnelly, Amb.	Corinne Averille McKnight, Amb.
Tunisia	Mary Ann Casey, Amb.	Azouz Ennifar, Amb.
Turkey	Marc Grossman, Amb.	Nuzhet Kandemir, Amb.
Turkmenistan	Michael W. Cotter, Amb.	Halil Ugur, Amb.
Tuvalu	Vacancy	Vacancy
Uganda	E. Michael Southwick, Amb.	Stephen Kapimpina Katenta-Apuli, Amb.
Ukraine	William Green Miller, Amb.	Yuri M. Shcherbak, Amb.
United Arab Emirates	David C. Litt, Amb.	Mohammad bin Hussein Al-Shaali, Amb.
United Kingdom	William J. Crowe Jr., Amb.	John Kerr, Amb.
Uruguay	Thomas J. Dodd, Amb.	Alvaro Diez de Medina, Amb.
Uzbekistan	Stanley Tuemler Escudero, Amb.	Fatikh Teshabaev, Amb.
Vanuatu	Richard W. Teare, Amb.	Vacancy
Vatican City	Raymond Leo Flynn, Amb.	Agostino Cacciavillan, Pro-Nuncio

Countries	Envoys from United States	Envoys to United States
Venezuela	Jeffrey Davidow, Amb.	Pedro Luis Echeverria, Amb.
Vietnam	Vacancy	Bang Van Le, Chargé
Western Samoa	Josiah Horton Beeman, Amb.	Tuiloma Neroni Slade, Amb.
Yemen	David G. Newton, Amb.	Mohsin Y. Alaini, Amb.
Yugoslavia	Vacancy	Zoran Popovic, Chargé
Zaire	Daniel H. Simpson, Amb.	Mukendi Tambo a Kabila, Chargé
Zambia	Roland K. Kuchel, Amb.	Dunstan Weston Kamana, Amb.
Zimbabwe	Johnny Carson, Amb.	Amos Bernard Muvengwa Midzi, Amb.

Special Missions

U.S. Mission to NATO, Brussels—Robert E. Hunter, A.E.P.; U.S. Mission to the European Union, Brussels—Stuart E. Eizenstat, A.E.P.; U.S. Mission to the UN, New York—Madeleine K. Albright, A.E.P.; U.S. Mission to the European Office of the UN, Geneva—Daniel L. Spiegel, Amb.; U.S. Mission to the OECD, Paris—David L. Aaron, Amb.; U.S. Mission to the Organization of American States, Washington—Harriet C. Babbit, Amb.; U.S. Mission to the Vienna Office of the UN—John B. Ritch III, Amb.

(1) Relations severed in 1961; limited ties restored in 1977. (2) U.S. severed relations on Apr. 7, 1980. (3) Operations temporarily suspended. (4) Embassy closed on May 2, 1980. U.S. closed the Libyan mission on May 6, 1981. (5) U.S. severed relations in 1978; unofficial relations are maintained.

Codes for International Direct Dial Calling From the U.S.

Station-to-station: 011 + country code (below) + city code (if required) + local number.
Person-to-person (operator-assisted, collect calls, credit card calls, and calls billed to another number): 01 + country code (below) + city code (if required) + local number.
For countries not listed, contact your long distance company.

Country/Territory	Code	Country/Territory	Code	Country/Territory	Code	Country/Territory	Code
Afghanistan[1]	93	Cayman Islands	809*	Jamaica	809*	Puerto Rico	809*
Albania	355	Central African		Japan	81	Qatar	974
Algeria	213	Republic	236	Jordan	962	Romania	40
American Samoa	684	Chad	235	Kazakhstan	7	Russia	7
Andorra	376	Chile	56	Kenya	254	Rwanda	250
Angola	244	China	86	Kiribati	686	St. Kitts & Nevis	809*
Anguilla	809*	Colombia	57	Korea, North	850	St. Lucia	809*
Antarctica (Scott		Comoros	269	Korea, South	82	St. Vincent & the	
Base)	672	Congo	242	Kuwait	965	Grenadines	809*
Antigua & Barbuda	809*	Costa Rica	506	Kyrgyzstan	7	San Marino	378
Argentina	54	Côte d'Ivoire	225	Laos	856	São Tomé & Prín-	
Armenia	374	Croatia	385	Latvia	371	cipe	239
Aruba	297	Cuba	53	Lebanon	961	Saudi Arabia	966
Ascension Island	247	Cyprus	357	Lesotho	266	Senegal	221
Australia	61	Czech Republic	42	Liberia	231	Seychelles	248
Austria	43	Denmark	45	Libya	218	Sierra Leone	232
Azerbaijan	994	Djibouti	253	Liechtenstein	4175	Singapore	65
Bahamas	809*	Dominica	809*	Lithuania	370	Slovakia	42
Bahrain	973	Dominican Republic	809*	Luxembourg	352	Slovenia	386
Bangladesh	880	Ecuador	593	Macau	853	Solomon Islands	677
Barbados	809*	Egypt	20	Macedonia	389	Somalia[1]	252
Belarus	375	El Salvador	503	Madagascar	261	South Africa	27
Belgium	32	Equatorial Guinea	240	Malawi	265	Spain	34
Belize	501	Eritrea	291	Malaysia	60	Sri Lanka	94
Benin	229	Estonia	372	Maldives	960	Sudan	249
Bermuda	809*	Ethiopia	251	Mali	223	Suriname	597
Bhutan	975	Falkland Islands	500	Malta	356	Swaziland	268
Bolivia	591	Fiji	679	Marshall Islands	692	Sweden	46
Bosnia & Herze-		Finland	358	Mauritania	222	Switzerland	41
govina	387	France	33	Mauritius	230	Syria	963
Botswana	267	French Antilles	596	Mexico	52	Taiwan	886
Brazil	55	French Guiana	594	Micronesia	691	Tajikistan	7
British Virgin Islands	809*	French Polynesia	689	Moldova	373	Tanzania	255
Brunei	673	Gabon	241	Monaco	33	Thailand	66
Bulgaria	359	Gambia, The	220	Mongolia	976	Togo	228
Burkina Faso	226	Georgia	7	Montserrat	809*	Tonga	676
Burundi	257	Germany	49	Morocco	212	Trinidad & Tobago	809*
Cambodia	855	Ghana	233	Mozambique	258	Tunisia	216
Cameroon	237	Gibraltar	350	Myanmar	95	Turkey	90
Canada		Greece	30	Namibia	264	Turmenistan	7
Alberta	403*	Greenland	299	Nauru	674	Turks & Caicos Is-	
British Columbia	604*	Grenada	809*	Nepal	977	lands	809*
Manitoba	204*	Guadeloupe	590	Netherlands	31	Tuvalu	688
New Brunswick	506*	Guam	671	New Caledonia	687	Uganda	256
Newfoundland	709*	Guantanamo Bay	5399	New Zealand	64	Ukraine	380
Nova Scotia	902*	Guatemala	502	Nicaragua	505	United Arab Emir-	
Ontario		Guinea	224	Niger	227	ates	971
London	519*	Guinea-Bissau	245	Nigeria	234	United Kingdom	44
North Bay	705*	Guyana	592	Northern Mariana		Uruguay	598
Ottawa	613*	Haiti	509	Islands	670	Uzbekistan	7
Thunder Bay	807*	Honduras	504	Norway	47	Vanuatu	678
Toronto Metro	416*	Hong Kong	852	Oman	968	Vatican City	39
Toronto Vicinity	905*	Hungary	36	Pakistan	92	Venezuela	58
Prince Edward		Iceland	354	Palau	680	Vietnam	84
Island	902*	India	91	Panama	507	Virgin Islands, U.S.	809*
Quebec		Indonesia	62	Papua New Guinea	675	Western Samoa	685
Montreal	514*	Iran	98	Paraguay	595	Yemen	967
Quebec City	418*	Iraq	964	Peru	51	Yugoslavia	381
Sherbrooke	819*	Ireland	353	Philippines	63	Zaire	243
Saskatchewan	306*	Israel	972	Poland	48	Zambia	260
Cape Verde	238	Italy	39	Portugal	351	Zimbabwe	263

* These numbers are area codes. Follow Domestic Dialing instructions: dial "1" + area code + number you're calling. (1) Direct dial not available as of July 1995.

SPORTS

Ten Most Dramatic Sports Events, Nov. 1994-Oct. 1995

Baltimore Orioles shortstop Cal Ripken, Jr., played in his 2,131st consecutive game, Sept. 6, to surpass New York Yankee great Lou Gehrig's "unbreakable" record, which had stood for over 56 years. Ripken's streak began on May 30, 1982, and at season's end stood at 2,153 games.

America mourned the loss of one of baseball's legends, former N.Y. Yankee slugger Mickey Mantle, who died of liver cancer, Aug. 13. In his last weeks, Mantle underwent a highly publicized and controversial liver transplant and showed great public remorse for the years of alcohol abuse that contributed to his condition.

The San Francisco 49ers racked up an unprecedented fifth Super Bowl victory, Jan. 29, by defeating the San Diego Chargers, 49-26, at Joe Robbie Stadium in Miami, FL. The Niners were led by quarterback Steve Young, who was named the MVP of Super Bowl XXIX.

The New Jersey Devils beat the Detroit Red Wings 5-2, on June 24, to complete an impressive four-game sweep and win the Stanley Cup. Devils goalie Martin Brodeur allowed a meager 7 goals by the Red Wings, who were the NHL's best team during the regular season, and Devils right wing Claude Lemieux was named MVP of the playoffs.

The Houston Rockets took their second consecutive National Basketball Association title, June 14, by decisively beating the Orlando Magic, 113-101, to complete a four-game sweep. After a mediocre regular season, the Rockets were seeded only sixth in the playoffs, but caught fire and went on to beat some of the NBA's finest teams—the Utah Jazz, Phoenix Suns, San Antonio Spurs, and the Magic. Rockets center Hakeem Olajuwon was playoff MVP for the second year in a row.

"I'm back," read the statement by Chicago Bulls superstar guard Michael Jordan, who announced that he was coming out of retirement, March 18. Jordan had retired before the start of the 1993-94 NBA season to pursue a professional baseball career in the Chicago White Sox organization. Jordan had only moderate success as a baseball player, and the extended players strike coupled with his love for basketball prompted him to return to the NBA.

"March Madness" saw the crowning of dominant men's and women's NCAA Division I basketball champions. On April 2 in Minneapolis, MN, the University of Connecticut Huskies defeated the Tennessee Lady Volunteers, 70-64, to win the NCAA women's championship, capping a 35-0 season. On April 3 in Seattle, WA, the top-seeded UCLA Bruins defeated the defending champion Arkansas Razorbacks, 89-78, to take the men's title; UCLA finished the season with a 31-2 record.

The University of Nebraska Cornhuskers came from behind to defeat the Miami Hurricanes, 24-17, in the Orange Bowl in Miami, Jan. 1. The victory gave the Huskers a 13-0 record and clinched for them a number one ranking in the final NCAA Division I football polls.

Steffi Graf defeated Monica Seles, 7-6, 0-6, 6-3, to capture the U.S. Open women's singles title, Sept. 9. Seles was playing in her first major tennis tournament since being stabbed at a match by a deranged fan of Graf's in 1993; the loss was her first since returning to the game in August 1995. The victory gave Graf 3 of 4 grand slam titles for 1995.

The World Series was played for the first time since 1993. The Atlanta Braves, appearing for the third time in the last four Series, defeated the power-hitting Cleveland Indians 4 games to 2. In a series that was dominated by pitching, Braves lefty ace Tom Glavine—winner of two Series games—was named MVP; in the sixth and decisive game, Glavine combined with reliever Mark Wohlers for a 1-hit shutout.

OLYMPICS

Winter Olympic Games Champions, 1924-94

Sites of Games

1924	Chamonix, France	1960	Squaw Valley, California	1984	Sarajevo, Yugoslavia
1928	St. Moritz, Switzerland	1964	Innsbruck, Austria	1988	Calgary, Alberta
1932	Lake Placid, New York	1968	Grenoble, France	1992	Albertville, France
1936	Garmisch-Partenkirchen, Germany	1972	Sapporo, Japan	1994	Lillehammer, Norway
1948	St. Moritz, Switzerland				
1952	Oslo, Norway	1976	Innsbruck, Austria	1998	Nagano, Japan
1956	Cortina d'Ampezzo, Italy	1980	Lake Placid, New York	2002	Salt Lake City, Utah

In 1992, the Unified Team represented the former Soviet republics of Russia, Ukraine, Belarus, Kazakhstan, and Uzbekistan.

Bobsledding

(Driver in parentheses)

	4-Man Bob	Time
1924	Switzerland (Eduard Scherrer)	5:45.54
1928	United States (William Fiske) (5-man)	3:20.50
1932	United States (William Fiske)	7:53.68
1936	Switzerland (Pierre Musy)	5:19.85
1948	United States (Francis Tyler)	5:20.10
1952	Germany (Andreas Ostler)	5:07.84
1956	Switzerland (Franz Kapus)	5:10.44
1964	Canada (Victor Emery)	4:14.46
1968	Italy (Eugenio Monti) (2 races)	2:17.39
1972	Switzerland (Jean Wicki)	4:43.07
1976	E. Germany (Meinhard Nehmer)	3:40.43
1980	E. Germany (Meinhard Nehmer)	3:59.92
1984	E. Germany (Wolfgang Hoppe)	3:20.22
1988	Switzerland (Ekkehard Fasser)	3:47.51

		Time
1992	Austria (Ingo Appelt)	3:53.90
1994	Germany (Wolfgang Hoppe)	3:27.28
	2-Man Bob	**Time**
1932	United States (Hubert Stevens)	8:14.74
1936	United States (Ivan Brown)	5:29.29
1948	Switzerland (F. Endrich)	5:29.20
1952	Germany (Andreas Ostler)	5:24.54
1956	Italy (Dalla Costa)	5:30.14
1964	Great Britain (Anthony Nash)	4:21.90
1968	Italy (Eugenio Monti)	4:41.54
1972	W. Germany (Wolfgang Zimmerer)	4:57.07
1976	E. Germany (Meinhard Nehmer)	3:44.42
1980	Switzerland (Erich Schaerer)	4:09.36
1984	E. Germany (Wolfgang Hoppe)	3:25.56
1988	USSR (Janis Kipours)	3:54.19
1992	Switzerland (Gustav Weber)	4:03.26
1994	Switzerland (Gustav Weber)	3:30.81

Luge

Men's Singles

		Time
1964	Thomas Keohler, Germany	3:26.77
1968	Manfred Schmid, Austria	2:52.48
1972	Wolfgang Scheidel, E. Germany.....	3:27.58
1976	Detlef Guenther, E. Germany.......	3:27.688
1980	Bernhard Glass, E. Germany.......	2:54.796
1984	Paul Hildgartner, Italy	3:04.258
1988	Jens Mueller, E. Germany	3:05.548
1992	Georg Hackl, Germany	3:02.363
1994	Georg Hackl, Germany	3:21.571

Men's Pairs

		Time
1964	Austria	1:41.62
1968	E. Germany	1:35.85
1972	Italy, E. Germany (tie)	1:28.35
1976	E. Germany	1:25.604
1980	E. Germany	1:19.331
1984	W. Germany.................	1:23.620
1988	E. Germany	1:31.940
1992	Germany	1:32.053
1994	Italy	1:36.720

Women's Singles

		Time
1964	Ortun Enderlein, Germany	3:24.67
1968	Erica Lechner, Italy	2:28.66
1972	Anna M. Muller, E. Germany	2:59.18
1976	Margit Schumann, E. Germany.....	2:50.621
1980	Vera Zozulya, USSR	2:36.537
1984	Steffi Martin, E. Germany..........	2:46.570
1988	Steffi Walter, E. Germany.........	3:03.973
1992	Doris Neuner, Austria	3:06.696
1994	Gerda Weissensteiner, Italy	3:15.517

Biathlon

Men's 10 Kilometers

		Time
1980	Frank Ullrich, E. Germany	32:10.69
1984	Eirik Kvalfoss, Norway..........	30:53.80
1988	Frank-Peter Roetsch, E. Germany	25:08.10
1992	Mark Kirchner, Germany	26:02.30
1994	Serguei Tchepikov, Russia.........	28:07.00

Men's 20 Kilometers

		Time
1960	Klas Lestander, Sweden	1:33:21.6
1964	Vladimir Melanin, USSR	1:20:26.8
1968	Magnar Solberg, Norway..........	1:13:45.9
1972	Magnar Solberg, Norway..........	1:15:55.50
1976	Nikolai Kruglov, USSR............	1:14:12.26
1980	Anatoly Aljabiev, USSR...........	1:08:16.31
1984	Peter Angerer, W. Germany........	1:11:52.7
1988	Frank-Peter Roetsch, E. Germany	0:56:33.33
1992	Yevgeny Redkine, Unified Team	0:57:34.4
1994	Serguei Tarasov, Russia	0:57:25.3

Men's 30-Kilometer Relay

		Time
1968	USSR, Norway, Sweden (40 km)	2:13:02.4
1972	USSR, Finland, E. Germany (40 km)...	1:51:44.92
1976	USSR, Finland, E. Germany (40 km)...	1:57:55.64
1980	USSR, E. Germany, W. Germany.....	1:34:03.27
1984	USSR, Norway, W. Germany	1:38:51.70
1988	USSR, W. Germany, Italy	1:22:30.00
1992	Germany, Unified Team, Sweden.....	1:24:43.50
1994	Germany, Russia, France	1:30:22.1

Women's 7.5 Kilometers

		Time
1992	Anfissa Restsova, Unified Team	24:29.20
1994	Myriam Bedard, Canada	26:08.8

Women's 15 Kilometers

		Time
1992	Antje Misersky, Germany..........	51:47.2
1994	Myriam Bedard, Canada	52:06.6

Women's 22.5 Kilometer Relay

		Time
1992	France, Germany, Unified Team......	1:15:55.6

Women's 30 Kilometer Relay

		Time
1994	Russia, Germany, France	1:47:19.5

Figure Skating

Men's Singles

1908	Ulrich Salchow, Sweden
1920	Gillis Grafstrom, Sweden
1924	Gillis Grafstrom, Sweden
1928	Gillis Grafstrom, Sweden
1932	Karl Schaefer, Austria
1936	Karl Schaefer, Austria
1948	Richard Button, U.S.
1952	Richard Button, U.S.
1956	Hayes Alan Jenkins, U.S.
1960	David W. Jenkins, U.S.
1964	Manfred Schnelldorfer, Germany
1968	Wolfgang Schwartz, Austria
1972	Ondrej Nepela, Czechoslovakia
1976	John Curry, Great Britain
1980	Robin Cousins, Great Britain
1984	Scott Hamilton, U.S.
1988	Brian Boitano, U.S.
1992	Viktor Petrenko, Unified Team
1994	Aleksei Urmanov, Russia

Women's Singles

1908	Madge Syers, Great Britain
1920	Magda Julin-Mauroy, Sweden
1924	Herma von Szabo-Planck, Austria
1928	Sonja Henie, Norway
1932	Sonja Henie, Norway
1936	Sonja Henie, Norway
1948	Barbara Ann Scott, Canada
1952	Jeanette Altwegg, Great Britain
1956	Tenley Albright, U.S.
1960	Carol Heiss, U.S.
1964	Sjoukje Dijkstra, Netherlands
1968	Peggy Fleming, U.S.
1972	Beatrix Schuba, Austria
1976	Dorothy Hamill, U.S.
1980	Anett Poetzsch, E. Germany
1984	Katarina Witt, E. Germany
1988	Katarina Witt, E. Germany
1992	Kristi Yamaguchi, U.S.
1994	Oksana Baiul, Ukraine

Pairs

1908	Anna Hubler & Heinrich Burger, Germany
1920	Ludovika & Walter Jakobsson, Finland
1924	Helene Engelman & Alfred Berger, Austria
1928	Andree Joly & Pierre Brunet, France
1932	Andree Joly & Pierre Brunet, France
1936	Maxi Herber & Ernst Baier, Germany
1948	Micheline Lannoy & Pierre Baugniet, Belgium
1952	Ria and Paul Falk, Germany
1956	Elisabeth Schwartz & Kurt Oppelt, Austria
1960	Barbara Wagner & Robert Paul, Canada
1964	Ludmila Beloussova & Oleg Protopopov, USSR
1968	Ludmila Beloussova & Oleg Protopopov, USSR
1972	Irina Rodnina & Alexei Ulanov, USSR
1976	Irina Rodnina & Aleksandr Zaitzev, USSR
1980	Irina Rodnina & Aleksandr Zaitzev, USSR
1984	Elena Valova & Oleg Vassiliev, USSR
1988	Ekaterina Gordeeva & Sergei Grinkov, USSR
1992	Natalia Mishkutienok & Artur Dimitriev, Unified Team
1994	Ekaterina Gordeeva & Sergei Grinkov, Russia

Ice Dancing

1976	Ludmila Pakhomova & Aleksandr Gorschkov, USSR
1980	Natalya Linichuk & Gennadi Karponosov, USSR
1984	Jayne Torvill & Christopher Dean, Great Britain
1988	Natalia Bestemianova & Andrei Bukin, USSR
1992	Marina Klimova & Sergei Ponomarenko, Unified Team
1994	Oksana Grichtchuk & Yevgeny Platov, Russia

Ice Hockey

1920	Canada, U.S., Czechoslovakia
1924	Canada, U.S., Great Britain
1928	Canada, Sweden, Switzerland
1932	Canada, U.S., Germany
1936	Great Britain, Canada, U.S.
1948	Canada, Czechoslovakia, Switzerland
1952	Canada, U.S., Sweden
1956	USSR, U.S., Canada
1960	U.S., Canada, USSR
1964	USSR, Sweden, Czechoslovakia
1968	USSR, Czechoslovakia, Canada
1972	USSR, U.S., Czechoslovakia,
1976	USSR, Czechoslovakia, W. Germany
1980	U.S., USSR, Sweden
1984	USSR, Czechoslovakia, Sweden
1988	USSR, Finland, Sweden
1992	Unified Team, Canada, Czechoslovakia
1994	Sweden, Canada, Finland

Alpine Skiing

Men's Downhill

Year	Name	Time
1948	Henri Oreiller, France	2:55.0
1952	Zeno Colo, Italy	2:30.8
1956	Anton Sailer, Austria	2:52.2
1960	Jean Vuarnet, France	2:06.0
1964	Egon Zimmermann, Austria	2:18.16
1968	Jean-Claude Killy, France	1:59.85
1972	Bernhard Russi, Switzerland	1:51.43
1976	Franz Klammer, Austria	1:45.73
1980	Leonhard Stock, Austria	1:45.50
1984	Bill Johnson, U.S.	1:45:59
1988	Pirmin Zurbriggen, Switzerland	1:59.63
1992	Patrick Ortlieb, Austria	1:50.37
1994	Tommy Moe, U.S.	1:45.75

Men's Super Giant Slalom

Year	Name	Time
1988	Franck Piccard, France	1:39.66
1992	Kjetil-Andre Aamodt, Norway	1:13.04
1994	Markus Wasmeier, Germany	1:32.53

Men's Giant Slalom

Year	Name	Time
1952	Stein Eriksen, Norway	2:25.0
1956	Anton Sailer, Austria	3:00.1
1960	Roger Staub, Switzerland	1:48.3
1964	Francois Bonlieu, France	1:46.71
1968	Jean-Claude Killy, France	3:29.28
1972	Gustavo Thoeni, Italy	3:09.62
1976	Heini Hemmi, Switzerland	3:26.97
1980	Ingemar Stenmark, Sweden	2:40.74
1984	Max Julen, Switzerland	2:41.18
1988	Alberto Tomba, Italy	2:06:37
1992	Alberto Tomba, Italy	2:06.98
1994	Markus Wasmeier, Germany	2:52.46

Men's Slalom

Year	Name	Time
1948	Edi Reinalter, Switzerland	2:10.3
1952	Othmar Schneider, Austria	2:00.0
1956	Anton Sailer, Austria	3:14.7
1960	Ernst Hinterseer, Austria	2:08.9
1964	Josef Stiegler, Austria	2:11.13
1968	Jean-Claude Killy, France	1:39.73
1972	Francisco Fernandez Ochoa, Spain	1:49.27
1976	Piero Gros, Italy	2:03.29
1980	Ingemar Stenmark, Sweden	1:44.26
1984	Phil Mahre, U.S.	1:39.41
1988	Alberto Tomba, Italy	1:39.47
1992	Finn Christian Jagge, Norway	1:44.39
1994	Thomas Stangassinger, Austria	2:02.02

Men's Combined

Year	Name	Time
1988	Hubert Strolz, Austria	36.55 (pts.)
1992	Josef Polig, Italy	14.58 (pts.)
1994	Lasse Kjus, Norway	3:17.53

Women's Downhill

Year	Name	Time
1948	Hedi Schlunegger, Switzerland	2:28.3
1952	Trude Jochum-Beiser, Austria	1:47.1
1956	Madeleine Berthod, Switzerland	1:40.7
1960	Heidi Biebl, Germany	1:37.6
1964	Christl Haas, Austria	1:55.39
1968	Olga Pall, Austria	1:40.87
1972	Marie Therese Nadig, Switzerland	1:36.68
1976	Rosi Mittermaier, W. Germany	1:46.16
1980	Annemarie Proell Moser, Austria	1:37.52
1984	Michela Figini, Switzerland	1:13.36
1988	Marina Kiehl, W. Germany	1:25.86
1992	Kerrin Lee-Gartner, Canada	1:52.55
1994	Katja Seizinger, Germany	1:35.93

Women's Super Giant Slalom

Year	Name	Time
1988	Sigrid Wolf, Austria	1:19.03
1992	Deborah Compagnoni, Italy	1:21.22
1994	Diann Roffe-Steinrotter, U.S.	1:22.15

Women's Giant Slalom

Year	Name	Time
1952	Andrea Mead Lawrence, U.S.	2:06.8
1956	Ossi Reichert, Germany	1:56.5
1960	Yvonne Ruegg, Switzerland	1:39.9
1964	Marielle Goitschel, France	1:52.24
1968	Nancy Greene, Canada	1:51.97
1972	Marie Therese Nadig, Switzerland	1:29.90
1976	Kathy Kreiner, Canada	1:29.13
1980	Hanni Wenzel, Liechtenstein (2 runs)	2:41.66

Year	Name	Time
1984	Debbie Armstrong, U.S.	2:20.98
1988	Vreni Schneider, Switzerland	2:06.49
1992	Pernilla Wiberg, Sweden	2:12.74
1994	Deborah Compagnoni, Italy	2:30.97

Women's Slalom

Year	Name	Time
1948	Gretchen Fraser, U.S.	1:57.2
1952	Andrea Mead Lawrence, U.S.	2:10.6
1956	Renee Colliard, Switzerland	1:52.3
1960	Anne Heggtveigt, Canada	1:49.6
1964	Christine Goitschel, France	1:29.86
1968	Marielle Goitschel, France	1:25.86
1972	Barbara Cochran, U.S.	1:31.24
1976	Rosi Mittermaier, W. Germany	1:30.54
1980	Hanni Wenzel, Liechtenstein	1:25.09
1984	Paoletta Magoni, Italy	1:36.47
1988	Vreni Schneider, Switzerland	1:36.69
1992	Petra Kronberger, Austria	1:32.68
1994	Vreni Schneider, Switzerland	1:56.01

Women's Combined

Year	Name	Time
1988	Anita Wachter, Austria	29.25 (pts.)
1992	Petra Kronberger, Austria	2.55 (pts.)
1994	Pernilla Wiberg, Sweden	3:05.16

Freestyle Skiing

Men's Moguls

Year	Name	Points
1992	Edgar Grospiron, France	25.81
1994	Jean-Luc Brassard, Canada	27.24

Men's Aerials

Year	Name	Points
1994	Andreas Schoenbaechler, Switzerland	234.67

Women's Moguls

Year	Name	Points
1992	Donna Weinbrecht, U.S.	23.69
1994	Stine Lise Hattestad, Norway	25.97

Women's Aerials

Year	Name	Points
1994	Lina Tcherjazova, Uzbekistan	166.84

Nordic Skiing

Cross-Country Events

Men's 10 kilometers (6.2 miles)

Year	Name	Time
1992	Vegard Ulvang, Norway	27:36.0
1994	Bjorn Daehlie, Norway	24:20.1

Men's 15 kilometers (9.3 miles)

Year	Name	Time
1924	Thorleif Haug, Norway	1:14:31
1928	Johan Grottumsbraaten, Norway	1:37:01
1932	Sven Utterstrom, Sweden	1:23:07
1936	Erik-August Larsson, Sweden	1:14:38
1948	Martin Lundstrom, Sweden	1:13:50
1952	Hallgeir Brenden, Norway	1:01:34
1956	Hallgeir Brenden, Norway	49:39.0
1960	Haakon Brusveen, Norway	51:55.5
1964	Eero Maentyranta, Finland	50:54.1
1968	Harald Groenningen, Norway	47:54.2
1972	Sven-Ake Lundback, Sweden	45:28.24
1976	Nikolai Balukov, USSR	43:58.47
1980	Thomas Wassberg, Sweden	41:57.63
1984	Gunde Svan, Sweden	41:25.6
1988	Mikhail Deviatiarov, USSR	41:18.9
1992	Bjorn Daehlie, Norway	38:01.9
1994	Bjorn Daehlie, Norway	35:48.8

(Note: approx. 18-km course 1924-1952)

Men's 30 kilometers (18.6 miles)

Year	Name	Time
1956	Veikko Hakulinen, Finland	1:44:06.0
1960	Sixten Jernberg, Sweden	1:51:03.9
1964	Eero Maentyranta, Finland	1:30:50.7
1968	Franco Nones, Italy	1:35:39.2
1972	Vyacheslav Vedenine, USSR	1:36:31.15
1976	Sergei Saveliev, USSR	1:30:29.38
1980	Nikolai Zimyatov, USSR	1:27:02.80
1984	Nikolai Zimyatov, USSR	1:28:56.3
1988	Aleksei Prokourorov, USSR	1:24:26.3
1992	Vegard Ulvang, Norway	1:22:27.8
1994	Thomas Alsgaard, Norway	1:12:26.4

Men's 50 kilometers (31.2 miles)

Year	Name	Time
1924	Thorleif Haug, Norway	3:44:32.0
1928	Per Erik Hedlund, Sweden	4:52:03.0
1932	Veli Saarinen, Finland	4:28:00.0

(continued)

1936	Elis Wiklund, Sweden	3:30:11.0
1948	Nils Karlsson, Sweden.	3:47:48.0
1952	Veikko Hakulinen, Finland	3:33:33.0
1956	Sixten Jernberg, Sweden.	2:50:27.0
1960	Kalevi Hamalainen, Finland	2:59:06.3
1964	Sixten Jernberg, Sweden.	2:43:52.6
1968	Ole Ellefsaeter, Norway.	2:28:45.8
1972	Paal Tyldum, Norway	2:43:14.75
1976	Ivar Formo, Norway.	2:37:30.05
1980	Nikolai Zimyatov, USSR	2:27:24.60
1984	Thomas Wassberg, Sweden	2:15:55.8
1988	Gunde Svan, Sweden	2:04:30.9
1992	Bjorn Daehlie, Norway.	2:03:41.5
1994	Vladimir Smirnov, Kazakhstan	2:07:20.3

Men's 40-kilometer Relay — Time

1936	Finland, Norway, Sweden	2:41:33.0
1948	Sweden, Finland, Norway	2:32:08.0
1952	Finland, Norway, Sweden	2:20:16.0
1956	USSR, Finland, Sweden	2:15:30.0
1960	Finland, Norway, USSR.	2:18:45.6
1964	Sweden, Finland, USSR	2:18:34.6
1968	Norway, Sweden, Finland	2:08:33.5
1972	USSR, Norway, Switzerland.	2:04:47.94
1976	Finland, Norway, USSR.	2:07:59.72
1980	USSR, Norway, Finland.	1:57:03.46
1984	Sweden, USSR, Finland	1:55:06.30
1988	Sweden, USSR, Czechoslovakia	1:43:58.60
1992	Norway, Italy, Finland	1:39:26.00
1994	Italy, Norway, Finland	1:41:15.00

Women's 5 kilometers (approx. 3.1 miles) — Time

1964	Claudia Boyarskikh, USSR	17:50.5
1968	Toini Gustafsson, Sweden.	16:45.2
1972	Galina Koulacova, USSR.	17:00.50
1976	Helena Takalo, Finland	15:48.69
1980	Raisa Smetanina, USSR	15:06.92
1984	Marja-Liisa Haemaelainen, Finland.	17:04.0
1988	Marjo Matikainen, Finland	15:04.0
1992	Marjut Lukkarinen, Finland.	14:13.8
1994	Ljubov Egorova, Russia.	14:08.8

Women's 10 kilometers (6.2 miles) — Time

1952	Lydia Wideman, Finland	41:40.0
1956	Lyubov Kosyreva, USSR	38:11.0
1960	Maria Gusakova, USSR.	39:46.6
1964	Claudia Boyarskikh, USSR	40:24.3
1968	Toini Gustafsson, Sweden.	36:46.5
1972	Galina Koulacova, USSR.	34:17.82
1976	Raisa Smetanina, USSR	30:13.41
1980	Barbara Petzold, E. Germany.	30:31.54
1984	Marja-Liisa Haemaelainen, Finland.	31:44.2
1988	Vida Ventsene, USSR.	30:08.3
1992	Lyubov Egorova, Unified Team	25:53.7
1994	Lyubov Egorova, Russia.	27:30.1

Women's 15 kilometers (9.3 miles) — Time

1992	Lyubov Egorova, Unified Team	42:20.8
1994	Manuela Di Centa, Italy	39:44.5

Women's 30 kilometers (18.6 miles) — Time

1992	Stefania Belmondo, Italy	1:22:30.1
1994	Manuela Di Centa, Italy	1:25:41.6

Women's 20-kilometer Relay — Time

1956	Finland, USSR, Sweden (15 km.)	1:09:01.0
1960	Sweden, USSR, Finland (15 km.)	1:04:21.4
1964	USSR, Sweden, Finland (15 km.)	59:20.2
1968	Norway, Sweden, USSR (15 km.)	57:30.0
1972	USSR, Finland, Norway (15 km.)	48:46.15
1976	USSR, Finland, E. Germany	1:07:49.75
1980	E. Germany, USSR, Norway	1:02:11.1
1984	Norway, Czechoslovakia, Finland.	1:06:49.7
1988	USSR, Norway, Finland.	59:51.1
1992	United Team, Norway, Italy	59:34.8
1994	Russia, Norway, Italy.	57:12.5

Combined Cross-Country & Jumping (Men)

Nordic Combined — Points

1924	Thorleif Haug, Norway.	453.800
1928	Johan Grottumsbraaten, Norway	427.800
1932	Johan Grottumsbraaten, Norway	446.000
1936	Oddbjorn Hagen, Norway	430.300
1948	Heikki Hasu, Finland	448.800
1952	Simon Slattvik, Norway	451.621
1956	Sverre Stenersen, Norway	455.000
1960	Georg Thoma, Germany	457.952
1964	Tormod Knutsen, Norway	469.280
1968	Franz Keller, W. Germany	449.040

1972	Ulrich Wehling, E. Germany	413.340
1976	Ulrich Wehling, E. Germany	423.390
1980	Ulrich Wehling, E. Germany	432.200
1984	Tom Sandberg, Norway	422.595
1988	Hippolyt Kempf, Switzerland	235.8
1992	Fabrice Guy, France.	426.470
1994	Fred Barre Lundberg, Norway.	457.970

Team Nordic Combined — Time

1988	W. Germany, Switzerland, Austria	1:20:46.0
1992	Japan, Norway, Austria.	1:23:36.5
	Japan, Norway, Switzerland	1,368.860 (pts.)

Ski Jumping (Men)

90 meters — Points

1924	Jacob Thams, Norway	227.5
1928	Alfred Andersen, Norway	230.5
1932	Birger Ruud, Norway	228.1
1936	Birger Ruud, Norway	232.0
1948	Petter Hugsted, Norway	228.1
1952	Arnfinn Bergmann, Norway	226.0
1956	Antti Hyvarinen, Finland	227.0
1960	Helmut Recknagel, Germany	227.2
1964	Toralf Engan, Norway.	230.7
1968	Vladimir Beloussov, USSR	231.3
1972	Wojiech Fortuna, Poland	219.9
1976	Karl Schnabl, Austria	234.8
1980	Jouko Tormanen, Finland	271.0
1984	Matti Nykaenen, Finland	231.2
1988	Matti Nykaenen, Finland	224.0
1992	Ernst Vettori, Austria	222.8
1994	Espen Bredesen, Norway	282.0

120 meters — Points

1992	Toni Nicminen, Finland.	239.5
1994	Jens Weissflog, Germany.	274.5

Team (90 meters) — Points

1988	Finland, Yugoslavia, Norway.	634.4
1992	Finland, Austria, Czechoslovakia.	644.4
1994	Germany, Japan, Austria	970.1

Speed Skating

Men's 500 meters — Time

1924	Charles Jewtraw, U.S.	0:44.0
1928	Thunberg, Finland & Evensen, Norway (tie)	0:43.4
1932	John A. Shea, U.S.	0:43.4
1936	Ivar Ballangrud, Norway	0:43.4
1948	Finn Helgesen, Norway	0:43.1
1952	Kenneth Henry, U.S.	0:43.2
1956	Evgeniy Grishin, USSR.	0:40.2
1960	Evgeniy Grishin, USSR.	0:40.2
1964	Terry McDermott, U.S.	0:40.1
1968	Erhard Keller, W. Germany.	0:40.3
1972	Erhard Keller, W. Germany	0:39.44
1976	Evgeny Kulikov, USSR.	0:39.17
1980	Eric Heiden, U.S.	0:38.03
1984	Sergei Fokichev, USSR	0:38.19
1988	Uwe-Jens Mey, E. Germany	0:36.45
1992	Uwe-Jens Mey, Germany	0:37.14
1994	Aleksandr Golubev, Russia.	0:36.33

Men's 1,000 meters — Time

1976	Peter Mueller, U.S.	1:19.32
1980	Eric Heiden, U.S.	1:15.18
1984	Gaetan Boucher, Canada	1:15.80
1988	Nikolai Guiliaev, USSR.	1:13.03
1992	Olaf Zinke, Germany	1:14.85
1994	Dan Jansen, U.S.	1:12.43

Men's 1,500 meters — Time

1924	Clas Thunberg, Finland	2:20.8
1928	Clas Thunberg, Finland	2:21.1
1932	John A. Shea, U.S.	2:57.5
1936	Charles Mathiesen, Norway	2:19.2
1948	Sverre Farstad, Norway	2:17.6
1952	Hjalmar Andersen, Norway	2:20.4
1956	Grishin, & Mikhailov, both USSR (tie)	2:08.6
1960	Aas, Norway & Grishin, USSR (tie)	2:10.4
1964	Ants Anston, USSR	2:10.3
1968	Cornetis Verkerk, Netherlands	2:03.4
1972	Ard Schenk, Netherlands	2:02.96
1976	Jan Egil Storholt, Norway	1:59.38
1980	Eric Heiden, U.S.	1:55.44
1984	Gaetan Boucher, Canada	1:58.36
1988	Andre Hoffmann, E. Germany	1:52.06
1992	Johann Koss, Norway.	1:54.81
1994	Johann Koss, Norway.	1:51.29

Men's 5,000 meters		Time
1924	Clas Thunberg, Finland	8:39.0
1928	Ivar Ballangrud, Norway	8:50.5
1932	Irving Jaffee, U.S.	9:40.8
1936	Ivar Ballangrud, Norway	8:19.6
1948	Reidar Liaklev, Norway	8:29.4
1952	Hjalmar Andersen, Norway	8:10.6
1956	Boris Shilkov, USSR	7:48.7
1960	Viktor Kosichkin, USSR	7:51.3
1964	Knut Johannesen, Norway	7:38.4
1968	F. Anton Maier, Norway	7:22.4
1972	Ard Schenk, Netherlands	7:23.61
1976	Sten Stensen, Norway	7:24.48
1980	Eric Heiden, U.S.	7:02.29
1984	Sven Tomas Gustafson, Sweden	7:12.28
1988	Tomas Gustafson, Sweden	6:44.63
1992	Geir Karlstad, Norway	6:59.97
1994	Johann Koss, Norway	6:34.96

Men's 10,000 meters		Time
1924	Julius Skutnabb, Finland	18:04.8
1928	Event not held, thawing of ice	
1932	Irving Jaffee, U.S.	19:13.6
1936	Ivar Ballangrud, Norway	17:24.3
1948	Ake Seyffarth, Sweden	17:26.3
1952	Hjalmar Andersen, Norway	16:45.8
1956	Sigvard Ericsson, Sweden	16:35.9
1960	Knut Johannesen, Norway	15:46.6
1964	Jonny Nilsson, Sweden	15:50.1
1968	Jonny Hoeglin, Sweden	15:23.6
1972	Ard Schenk, Netherlands	15:01.35
1976	Piet Kleine, Netherlands	14:50.59
1980	Eric Heiden, U.S.	14:28.13
1984	Igor Malkov, USSR	14:39.90
1988	Tomas Gustafson, Sweden	13:48.20
1992	Bart Veldkamp, Netherlands	14:12.12
1994	Johann Koss, Norway	13:30.55

Women's 500 meters		Time
1960	Helga Haase, Germany	0:45.9
1964	Lydia Skoblikova, USSR	0:45.0
1968	Ludmila Titova, USSR	0:46.1
1972	Anne Henning, U.S.	0:43.33
1976	Sheila Young, U.S.	0:42.76
1980	Karin Enke, E. Germany	0:41.78
1984	Christa Rothenburger, E. Germany	0:41.02
1988	Bonnie Blair, U.S.	0:39.10
1992	Bonnie Blair, U.S.	0:40.33
1994	Bonnie Blair, U.S.	0:39.25

Women's 1,000 meters		Time
1960	Klara Guseva, USSR	1:34.1
1964	Lydia Skoblikova, USSR	1:33.2
1968	Carolina Geijssen, Netherlands	1:32.6
1972	Monika Pflug, W. Germany	1:31.40

1976	Tatiana Averina, USSR	1:28.43
1980	Natalya Petruseva, USSR	1:24.10
1984	Karin Enke, E. Germany	1:21.61
1988	Christa Rothenburger, E. Germany	1:17.65
1992	Bonnie Blair, U.S.	1:21.90
1994	Bonnie Blair, U.S.	1:18.74

Women's 1,500 meters		Time
1960	Lydia Skoblikova, USSR	2:52.2
1964	Lydia Skoblikova, USSR	2:22.6
1968	Kaija Mustonen, Finland	2:22.4
1972	Dianne Holum, U.S.	2:20.85
1976	Galina Stepanskaya, USSR	2:16.58
1980	Anne Borckink, Netherlands	2:10.95
1984	Karin Enke, E. Germany	2:03.42
1988	Yvonne van Gennip, Netherlands	2:00.68
1992	Jacqueline Boerner, Germany	2:05.87
1994	Emese Hunyady, Austria	2:02.19

Women's 3,000 meters		Time
1960	Lydia Skoblikova, USSR	5:14.3
1964	Lydia Skoblikova, USSR	5:14.9
1968	Johanna Schut, Netherlands	4:56.2
1972	Christina Baas-Kaiser, Netherlands	4:52.14
1976	Tatiana Averina, USSR	4:45.19
1980	Bjoerg Eva Jensen, Norway	4:32.13
1984	Andrea Schoene, E. Germany	4:24.79
1988	Yvonne van Gennip, Netherlands	4:11.94
1992	Gunda Niemann, Germany	4:19.90
1994	Svetlana Bazhanova, Russia	4:17.43

Women's 5,000 meters		Time
1988	Yvonne van Gennip, Netherlands	7:14.13
1992	Gunda Niemann, Germany	7:31.57
1994	Claudia Pechstein, Germany	7:14.37

Short Track Speed Skating

Men's 1,000 meters		Time
1992	Kim Ki-Hoon, S. Korea	1:30.76
1994	Kim Ki-Hoon, S. Korea	1:34.57

Men's 5,000-meter relay		Time
1992	S. Korea, Canada, Japan	7:14.02
1994	Italy, U.S., Australia	7:11.74

Women's 500 meters		Time
1992	Cathy Turner, U.S.	47:04
1994	Cathy Turner, U.S.	45.98

Women's 3,000-meter relay		Time
1992	Canada, U.S., Unified Team	4:36.62
1994	S. Korea, Canada, U.S.	4:26.64

Winter Olympic Games in 1994

Lillehammer, Norway, Feb. 12-27, 1994

The 1994 Olympic Winter Games were held only 2 years after the 1992 games, due to an International Olympic Committee decision to switch to a 2-year cycle between summer and winter Olympics. The next Summer Games will be held in 1996 (in Atlanta, GA), and the next Winter Games in 1998 (in Nagano, Japan). The 17th Olympic Winter Games, held in Lillehammer, Norway, featured 1,884 athletes from 67 countries, including 11 former Soviet republics now competing as independent countries. Athletes from host-country Norway, whose speed skater Johann Olav Koss broke 3 Olympic records, won a games-high 26 medals. U.S. speed skater Bonnie Blair took home 2 gold medals, giving her a career total of 5 gold medals, the most of any female American Olympian. Team USA captured 13 medals, more than in any previous Olympic Winter Games.

For the first time, the U.S. Olympic Committee rewarded athletes' superior performances by handing out prizes of $15,000 for a gold medal, $10,000 for a silver, $7,500 for a bronze, and $5,000 for a fourth-place finish.

Final Medal Standings

	Gold	Silver	Bronze	Total		Gold	Silver	Bronze	Total
Norway	10	11	5	26	France	0	1	4	5
Germany	9	7	8	24	Netherlands	0	1	3	4
Russia	11	8	4	23	Sweden	2	1	0	3
Italy	7	5	8	20	Kazakhstan	1	2	0	3
U.S.	6	5	2	13	China	0	1	2	3
Canada	3	6	4	13	Slovenia	0	0	3	3
Switzerland	3	4	2	9	Ukraine	1	0	1	2
Austria	2	3	4	9	Belarus	0	2	0	2
S. Korea	4	1	1	6	Great Britain	0	0	2	2
Finland	0	1	5	6	Uzbekistan	1	0	0	1
Japan	1	2	2	5	Australia	0	0	1	1

Summer Olympic Games in 1992

Barcelona, Spain, July 25-Aug. 9, 1992

More than 14,000 athletes gathered in Barcelona, Spain, in July and August, 1992, for 16 days to compete in the Games of the XXV Olympiad. The athletes represented a record 172 nations, 11 more than had participated in any previous Olympics, and competed for medals in 257 events.

The 1992 games will be remembered mostly for the appearance of the Dream Team—the U.S. basketball team—featuring, for the first time, the stars of the National Basketball Association. As expected, the team crushed all its opponents on the way to a gold medal. Other notable events at the games were the victory in the long jump for Carl Lewis, his third consecutive gold medal in the event; the successful defense in the heptathlon by Jackie Joyner-Kersee; and the domination in men's gymnastics by Vitaly Shcherbo of the Unified Team. Perhaps the biggest surprise was the failure of world-record holder Sergei Bubka (Ukraine) to win a medal in the pole vault. Also notable was the appearance of South African athletes after missing 7 consecutive Olympiads.

The Unified Team, made up of athletes of 12 republics of the former Soviet Union, won the most gold medals, 45, and the most medals, 112. The U.S. finished second with 37 gold medals and 108 medals overall.

Final Medal Standings

	Gold	Silver	Bronze	Total		Gold	Silver	Bronze	Total
Unified Team[1]	45	38	29	112	Ethiopia	1	0	2	3
United States	37	34	37	108	Latvia	0	2	1	3
Germany	33	21	28	82	Croatia	0	1	2	3
China	16	22	16	54	Belgium	0	1	2	3
Cuba	14	6	11	31	Iran	0	1	2	3
Hungary	11	12	7	30	I.O.P.[2]	0	1	2	3
South Korea	12	5	12	29	Greece	2	0	0	2
France	8	5	16	29	Ireland	1	1	0	2
Australia	7	9	11	27	Algeria	1	0	1	2
Spain	13	7	2	22	Estonia	1	0	1	2
Japan	3	8	11	22	Lithuania	1	0	1	2
Britain	5	3	12	20	Austria	0	2	0	2
Italy	6	5	8	19	Namibia	0	2	0	2
Poland	3	6	10	19	South Africa	0	2	0	2
Canada	6	5	7	18	Israel	0	1	1	2
Romania	4	6	8	18	Mongolia	0	0	2	2
Bulgaria	3	7	6	16	Slovenia	0	0	2	2
Netherlands	2	6	7	15	Switzerland	1	0	0	1
Sweden	1	7	4	12	Mexico	0	1	0	1
New Zealand	1	4	5	10	Peru	0	1	0	1
North Korea	4	0	5	9	Taiwan	0	1	0	1
Kenya	2	4	2	8	Argentina	0	0	1	1
Czechoslovakia	4	2	1	7	Bahamas	0	0	1	1
Norway	2	4	1	7	Colombia	0	0	1	1
Turkey	2	2	2	6	Ghana	0	0	1	1
Denmark	1	1	4	6	Malaysia	0	0	1	1
Indonesia	2	2	1	5	Pakistan	0	0	1	1
Finland	1	2	2	5	Philippines	0	0	1	1
Jamaica	0	3	1	4	Puerto Rico	0	0	1	1
Nigeria	0	3	1	4	Qatar	0	0	1	1
Brazil	2	1	0	3	Suriname	0	0	1	1
Morocco	1	1	1	3	Thailand	0	0	1	1

(1) Athletes from 12 former Soviet republics. (2) Independent Olympic Participants (athletes from Serbia, Montenegro, Macedonia).

Summer Olympic Games Records

The modern Olympic Games, first held in Athens, Greece, in 1896, were the result of efforts by Baron Pierre de Coubertin, a French educator, to promote interest in education and culture, and to foster better international understanding through the universal medium of youth's love of athletics.

His source of inspiration for the Olympic Games was the ancient Greek Olympic Games, most notable of the 4 Panhellenic celebrations. The games were combined patriotic, religious, and athletic festivals held every 4 years. The first such recorded festival was held in 776 BC, the date from which the Greeks began to keep their calendar by "Olympiads," or 4-year spans between the games.

The first Olympiad is said to have consisted merely of a 200-yd foot race near the small city of Olympia, but the games gained in scope and became demonstrations of national pride. Only Greek citizens—amateurs—were permitted to participate. Winners received laurel, wild olive, and palm wreaths and were accorded many special privileges. Under the Roman emperors, the games deteriorated into professional carnivals and circuses. Emperor Theodosius banned them in AD 394.

Baron de Coubertin enlisted 13 nations to send athletes to the first modern Olympics in 1896; now more than 170 nations compete. Winter Olympic Games were started in 1924.

Sites of Summer Olympic Games

1896	Athens, Greece	1920	Antwerp, Belgium	1952	Helsinki, Finland	1976	Montreal, Canada
1900	Paris, France	1924	Paris, France	1956	Melbourne, Australia	1980	Moscow, USSR
1904	St. Louis, U.S.	1928	Amsterdam, Netherlands	1960	Rome, Italy	1984	Los Angeles, U.S.
1906	Athens,* Greece	1932	Los Angeles, U.S.	1964	Tokyo, Japan	1988	Seoul, S. Korea
1908	London, England	1936	Berlin, Germany	1968	Mexico City, Mexico	1992	Barcelona, Spain
1912	Stockholm, Sweden	1948	London, England	1972	Munich, W. Germany	1996	Atlanta, U.S.
						2000	Sydney, Australia

* Games not recognized by International Olympic Committee. Games 6 (1916), 12 (1940), and 13 (1944) were not celebrated. The 1980 games were boycotted by 62 nations, including the U.S. The 1984 games were boycotted by the USSR and by most Eastern bloc nations. East and West Germany competed separately 1968-88. The 1992 Unified Team consisted of 12 former Soviet republics. The 1992 Independent Olympic Participants (I.O.P.) were athletes from Serbia, Montenegro, and Macedonia.

Summer Olympic Games Champions, 1896-1992

(*Indicates Olympic Record)

Track and Field — Men

100-Meter Run

1896	Thomas Burke, United States	12s
1900	Francis W. Jarvis, United States	11.0s
1904	Archie Hahn, United States	11s
1908	Reginald Walker, South Africa	18s
1912	Ralph Craig, United States	10.8s
1920	Charles Paddock, United States	10.8s
1924	Harold Abrahams, Great Britain	10.6s
1928	Percy Williams, Canada	10.8s
1932	Eddie Tolan, United States	10.3s
1936	Jesse Owens, United States	10.3s
1948	Harrison Dillard, United States	10.3s
1952	Lindy Remigino, United States	10.4s
1956	Bobby Morrow, United States	10.5s
1960	Armin Hary, Germany	10.2s
1964	Bob Hayes, United States	10.0s
1968	Jim Hines, United States	9.95s
1972	Valery Borzov, USSR	10.14s
1976	Hasely Crawford, Trinidad	10.06s
1980	Allan Wells, Great Britain	10.25s
1984	Carl Lewis, United States	9.99s
1988	Carl Lewis, United States	9.92s*
1992	Linford Christie, Great Britain	9.96s

200-Meter Run

1900	Walter Tewksbury, United States	22.2s
1904	Archie Hahn, United States	21.6s
1908	Robert Kerr, Canada	22.6s
1912	Ralph Craig, United States	21.7s
1920	Allan Woodring, United States	22s
1924	Jackson Scholz, United States	21.6s
1928	Percy Williams, Canada	21.8s
1932	Eddie Tolan, United States	21.2s
1936	Jesse Owens, United States	20.7s
1948	Mel Patton, United States	21.1s
1952	Andrew Stanfield, United States	20.7s
1956	Bobby Morrow, United States	20.6s
1960	Livio Berruti, Italy	20.5s
1964	Henry Carr, United States	20.3s
1968	Tommie Smith, United States	19.83s
1972	Valeri Borzov, USSR	20.00s
1976	Donald Quarrie, Jamaica	20.23s
1980	Pietro Mennea, Italy	20.19s
1984	Carl Lewis, United States	19.80s
1988	Joe DeLoach, United States	19.75s*
1992	Mike Marsh, United States	20.01s

400-Meter Run

1896	Thomas Burke, United States	54.2s
1900	Maxey Long, United States	49.4s
1904	Harry Hillman, United States	49.2s
1908	Wyndham Halswelle, Great Britain, walkover	50s
1912	Charles Reidpath, United States	48.2s
1920	Bevil Rudd, South Africa	49.6s
1924	Eric Liddell, Great Britain	47.6s
1928	Ray Barbuti, United States	47.8s
1932	William Carr, United States	46.2s
1936	Archie Williams, United States	46.5s
1948	Arthur Wint, Jamaica	46.2s
1952	George Rhoden, Jamaica	45.9s
1956	Charles Jenkins, United States	46.7s
1960	Otis Davis, United States	44.9s
1964	Michael Larrabee, United States	45.1s
1968	Lee Evans, United States	43.8s
1972	Vincent Matthews, United States	44.66s
1976	Alberto Juantorena, Cuba	44.26s
1980	Viktor Markin, USSR	44.60s
1984	Alonzo Babers, United States	44.27s
1988	Steven Lewis, United States	43.87s
1992	Quincy Watts, United States	43.50s*

800-Meter Run

1896	Edwin Flack, Australia	2m. 11s
1900	Alfred Tysoe, Great Britain	2m. 1.2s
1904	James Lightbody, United States	1m. 56s
1908	Mel Sheppard, United States	1m. 52.8s
1912	James Meredith, United States	1m. 51.9s
1920	Albert Hill, Great Britain	1m. 53.4s
1924	Douglas Lowe, Great Britain	1m. 52.4s
1928	Douglas Lowe, Great Britain	1m. 51.8s
1932	Thomas Hampson, Great Britain	1m. 49.8s
1936	John Woodruff, United States	1m. 52.9s
1948	Mal Whitfield, United States	1m. 49.2s
1952	Mal Whitfield, United States	1m. 49.2s
1956	Thomas Courtney, United States	1m. 47.7s
1960	Peter Snell, New Zealand	1m. 46.3s
1964	Peter Snell, New Zealand	1m. 45.1s
1968	Ralph Doubell, Australia	1m. 44.3s
1972	Dave Wottle, United States	1m. 45.9s
1976	Alberto Juantorena, Cuba	1m. 43.50s
1980	Steve Ovett, Great Britain	1m. 45.40s
1984	Joaquim Cruz, Brazil	1m. 43.00s*
1988	Paul Ereng, Kenya	1m. 43.45s
1992	William Tanui, Kenya	1m. 43.66s

1,500-Meter Run

1896	Edwin Flack, Australia	4m. 33.2s
1900	Charles Bennett, Great Britain	4m. 6.2s
1904	James Lightbody, United States	4m. 5.4s
1908	Mel Sheppard, United States	4m. 3.4s
1912	Arnold Jackson, Great Britain	3m. 56.8s
1920	Albert Hill, Great Britain	4m. 1.8s
1924	Paavo Nurmi, Finland	3m. 53.6s
1928	Harry Larva, Finland	3m. 53.2s
1932	Luigi Beccali, Italy	3m. 51.2s
1936	Jack Lovelock, New Zealand	3m. 47.8s
1948	Henri Eriksson, Sweden	3m. 49.8s
1952	Joseph Barthel, Luxemburg	3m. 45.2s
1956	Ron Delany, Ireland	3m. 41.2s
1960	Herb Elliott, Australia	3m. 35.6s
1964	Peter Snell, New Zealand	3m. 38.1s
1968	Kipchoge Keino, Kenya	3m. 34.9s
1972	Pekka Vasala, Finland	3m. 36.3s
1976	John Walker, New Zealand	3m. 39.17s
1980	Sebastian Coe, Great Britain	3m. 38.4s
1984	Sebastian Coe, Great Britain	3m. 32.53s*
1988	Peter Rono, Kenya	3m. 35.96s
1992	Fermin Cacho Ruiz, Spain	3m. 40.12s

3,000-Meter Steeplechase

1920	Percy Hodge, Great Britain	10m. 0.4s
1924	Willie Ritola, Finland	9m. 33.6s
1928	Toivo Loukola, Finland	9m. 21.8s
1932	Volmari Iso-Hollo, Finland	10m. 33.4s
	(About 3,450 m; extra lap by error.)	
1936	Volmari Iso-Hollo, Finland	9m. 3.8s
1948	Thore Sjoestrand, Sweden	9m. 4.6s
1952	Horace Ashenfelter, United States	8m. 45.4s
1956	Chris Brasher, Great Britain	8m. 41.2s
1960	Zdzislaw Krzyszkowiak, Poland	8m. 34.2s
1964	Gaston Roelants, Belgium	8m. 30.8s
1968	Amos Biwott, Kenya	8m. 51s
1972	Kipchoge Keino, Kenya	8m. 23.6s
1976	Anders Garderud, Sweden	8m. 08.2s
1980	Bronislaw Malinowski, Poland	8m. 09.7s
1984	Julius Korir, Kenya	8m. 11.8s
1988	Julius Kariuki, Kenya	8m. 05.51s*
1992	Matthew Birir, Kenya	8m. 08.84s

5,000-Meter Run

1912	Hannes Kolehmainen, Finland	14m. 36.6s
1920	Joseph Guillemot, France	14m. 55.6s
1924	Paavo Nurmi, Finland	14m. 31.2s
1928	Willie Ritola, Finland	14m. 38s
1932	Lauri Lehtinen, Finland	14m. 30s
1936	Gunnar Hockert, Finland	14m. 22.2s
1948	Gaston Reiff, Belgium	14m. 17.6s
1952	Emil Zatopek, Czechoslovakia	14m. 6.6s
1956	Vladimir Kuts, USSR	13m. 39.6s
1960	Murray Halberg, New Zealand	13m. 43.4s
1964	Bob Schul, United States	13m. 48.8s
1968	Mohamed Gammoudi, Tunisia	14m. 05.0s
1972	Lasse Viren, Finland	13m. 26.4s
1976	Lasse Viren, Finland	13m. 24.76s
1980	Miruts Yifter, Ethiopia	13m. 21.0s
1984	Said Aouita, Morocco	13m. 05.59s*
1988	John Ngugi, Kenya	13m. 11.70s
1992	Dieter Baumann, Germany	13m. 12.52s

10,000-Meter Run

1912	Hannes Kolehmainen, Finland	31m. 20.8s
1920	Paavo Nurmi, Finland	31m. 45.8s
1924	Willie Ritola, Finland	30m. 23.2s
1928	Paavo Nurmi, Finland	30m. 18.8s
1932	Janusz Kusocinski, Poland	30m. 11.4s
1936	Ilmari Salminen, Finland	30m. 15.4s
1948	Emil Zatopek, Czechoslovakia	29m. 59.6s
1952	Emil Zatopek, Czechoslovakia	29m. 17.0s
1956	Vladimir Kuts, USSR	28m. 45.6s
1960	Pyotr Bolotnikov, USSR	28m. 32.2s
1964	Billy Mills, United States	28m. 24.4s
1968	Naftali Temu, Kenya	29m. 27.4s
1972	Lasse Viren, Finland	27m. 38.4s
1976	Lasse Viren, Finland	27m. 40.38s
1980	Miruts Yifter, Ethiopia	27m. 42.7s
1984	Alberto Cova, Italy	27m. 47.54s
1988	Brahim Boutaib, Morocco	27m. 21.46s*
1992	Khalid Skah, Morocco	27m. 46.70s

Marathon

1896	Spiridon Loues, Greece	2h. 58m. 50s
1900	Michel Theato, France	2h. 59m. 45s
1904	Thomas Hicks, United States	3h. 28m. 63s
1908	John J. Hayes, United States	2h. 55m. 18.4s
1912	Kenneth McArthur, South Africa	2h. 36m. 54.8s
1920	Hannes Kolehmainen, Finland	2h. 32m. 35.8s
1924	Albin Stenroos, Finland	2h. 41m. 22.6s
1928	A.B. El Ouafi, France	2h. 32m. 57s
1932	Juan Zabala, Argentina	2h. 31m. 36s
1936	Kijung Son, Japan (Korean)	2h. 29m. 19.2s
1948	Delfo Cabrera, Argentina	2h. 34m. 51.6s
1952	Emil Zatopek, Czechoslovakia	2h. 23m. 03.2s
1956	Alain Mimoun, France	2h. 25m.
1960	Abebe Bikila, Ethiopia	2h. 15m. 16.2s
1964	Abebe Bikila, Ethiopia	2h. 12m. 11.2s
1968	Mamo Wolde, Ethiopia	2h. 20m. 26.4s
1972	Frank Shorter, United States	2h. 12m. 19.8s
1976	Waldemar Cierpinski, E. Germany	2h. 09m. 55s
1980	Waldemar Cierpinski, E. Germany	2h. 11m. 03s
1984	Carlos Lopes, Portugal	2h. 09m. 21 s*
1988	Gelindo Bordin, Italy	2h. 10m. 32s
1992	Hwang Young-Cho, S. Korea	2h. 13m. 23s

20-Kilometer Walk

1956	Leonid Spirin, USSR	1h. 31m. 27.4s
1960	Vladimir Golubnichy, USSR	1h. 33m. 7.2s
1964	Kenneth Mathews, Great Britain	1h. 29m. 34.0s
1968	Vladimir Golubnichy, USSR	1h. 33m. 58.4s
1972	Peter Frenkel, E. Germany	1h. 26m. 42.4s
1976	Daniel Bautista, Mexico	1h. 24m. 40.6s
1980	Maurizio Damilano, Italy	1h. 23m. 35.5s
1984	Ernesto Canto, Mexico	1h. 23m. 13.0s
1988	Josef Pribilinec, Czechoslovakia	1h. 19m. 57.0s*
1992	Daniel Plaza Montero, Spain	1h. 21m. 45.0s

50-Kilometer Walk

1932	Thomas W. Green, Great Britain	4h. 50m. 10s
1936	Harold Whitlock, Great Britain	4h. 30m. 41.4s
1948	John Ljunggren, Sweden	4h. 41m. 52s
1952	Giuseppe Dordoni, Italy	4h. 28m. 07.8s
1956	Norman Read, New Zealand	4h. 30m. 42.8s
1960	Donald Thompson, Great Britain	4h. 25m. 30s
1964	Abdon Pamich, Italy	4h. 11m. 12.4s
1968	Christoph Hohne, E. Germany	4h. 20m. 13.6s
1972	Bern Kannenberg, W. Germany	3h. 56m. 11.6s
1980	Hartwig Gauter, E. Germany	3h. 49m. 24.0s
1984	Raul Gonzalez, Mexico	3h. 47m. 26.0s
1988	Vayachselav Ivanenko, USSR	3h. 38m. 29.0s*
1992	Andrei Perlov, Unified Team	3h. 50m. 13.0s

110-Meter Hurdles

1896	Thomas Curtis, United States	17.6s
1900	Alvin Kraenzlein, United States	15.4s
1904	Frederick Schule, United States	16s
1908	Forrest Smithson, United States	15s
1912	Frederick Kelly, United States	15.1s
1920	Earl Thomson, Canada	14.8s
1924	Daniel Kinsey, United States	15s
1928	Sydney Atkinson, South Africa	14.8s
1932	George Saling, United States	14.6s
1936	Forrest Towns, United States	14.2s
1948	William Porter, United States	13.9s

1952	Harrison Dillard, United States	13.7s
1956	Lee Calhoun, United States	13.5s
1960	Lee Calhoun, United States	13.8s
1964	Hayes Jones, United States	13.6s
1968	Willie Davenport, United States	13.3s
1972	Rod Milburn, United States	13.24s
1976	Guy Drut, France	13.30s
1980	Thomas Munkelt, E. Germany	13. 39s
1984	Roger Kingdom, United States	13.20s
1988	Roger Kingdom, United States	12.98s*
1992	Mark McCoy, Canada	13.12s

400-Meter Hurdles

1900	J.W.B. Tewksbury, United States	57.6s
1904	Harry Hillman, United States	53s
1908	Charles Bacon, United States	55s
1920	Frank Loomis, United States	54s
1924	F. Morgan Taylor, United States	52.6s
1928	Lord Burghley, Great Britain	53.4s
1932	Robert Tisdall, Ireland	51.7s
1936	Glenn Hardin, United States	52.4s
1948	Roy Cochran, United States	51.1s
1952	Charles Moore, United States	50.8s
1956	Glenn Davis, United States	50.1s
1960	Glenn Davis, United States	49.3s
1964	Rex Cawley, United States	49.6s
1968	Dave Hemery, Great Britain	48.12s
1972	John Akii-Bua, Uganda	47.82s
1976	Edwin Moses, United States	47.64s
1980	Volker Beck, E. Germany	48.70s
1984	Edwin Moses, United States	47.75s
1988	Andre Phillips, United States	47.19s
1992	Kevin Young, United States	46.78s*

High Jump

1896	Ellery Clark, United States	5ft. 11 1-4 in.
1900	Irving Baxter, United States	6ft. 2 4-5 in.
1904	Samuel Jones, United States	5ft. 11 in.
1908	Harry Porter, United States	6ft. 3 in.
1912	Alma Richards, United States	6ft. 4 in.
1920	Richmond Landon, United States	6ft. 4 in.
1924	Harold Osborn, United States	6ft. 6 in.
1928	Robert W. King, United States	6ft. 4 1-2 in.
1932	Duncan McNaughton, Canada	6ft. 5 5-8 in.
1936	Cornelius Johnson, United States	6ft. 8 in.
1948	John L. Winter, Australia	6ft. 6 in.
1952	Walter Davis, United States	6ft. 8.32 in.
1956	Charles Dumas, United States	6ft. 11 1-2 in.
1960	Robert Shavlakadze, USSR	7ft. 1 in.
1964	Valery Brumel, USSR	7ft. 1 3-4 in.
1968	Dick Fosbury, United States	7ft. 4 1-4 in.
1972	Yuri Tarmak, USSR	7ft. 3 3-4 in.
1976	Jacek Wszola, Poland	7ft. 4 1-2 in.
1980	Gerd Wessig, E. Germany	7ft. 8 3-4 in.
1984	Dietmar Mogenburg, W. Germany	7ft. 8 1-2 in.
1988	Guennadi Avdeenko, USSR	7ft. 9 1-2 in.*
1992	Javier Sotomayor, Cuba	7ft. 8 in.

Long Jump

1896	Ellery Clark, United States	20ft. 10 in.
1900	Alvin Kraenzlein, United States	23ft. 6 3-4 in.
1904	Myer Prinstein, United States	24ft. 1 in.
1908	Frank Irons, United States	24ft. 6 1-2 in.
1912	Albert Gutterson, United States	24ft. 11 1-4 in.
1920	William Petersson, Sweden	23ft. 5 1-2 in.
1924	DeHart Hubbard, United States	24ft. 5 in.
1928	Edward B. Hamm, United States	25ft. 4 1-2 in.
1932	Edward Gordon, United States	25ft. 3-4 in.
1936	Jesse Owens, United States	26ft. 5 1-2 in.
1948	William Steele, United States	25ft. 8 in.
1952	Jerome Biffle, United States	24ft. 10 in.
1956	Gregory Bell, United States	25ft. 8 1-4 in.
1960	Ralph Boston, United States	26ft. 7 3-4 in.
1964	Lynn Davies, Great Britain	26ft. 5 3-4 in.
1968	Bob Beamon, United States	29ft. 2 1-2 in.*
1972	Randy Williams, United States	27ft. 1-2 in.
1976	Arnie Robinson, United States	27ft. 4 1-2 in.
1980	Lutz Dombrowski, E. Germany	28ft. 1-4 in.
1984	Carl Lewis, United States	28ft. 1-4 in.
1988	Carl Lewis, United States	28ft. 7 1-4 in.
1992	Carl Lewis, United States	28ft. 5 1-2 in.

400-Meter Relay

1912	Great Britain	42.4s
1920	United States	42.2s
1924	United States	41s

1928	United States	41s
1932	United States	40s
1936	United States	39.8s
1948	United States	40.6s
1952	United States	40.1s
1956	United States	39.5s
1960	Germany (U.S. disqualified)	39.5s
1964	United States	39.0s
1968	United States	38.2s
1972	United States	38.19s
1976	United States	38.33s
1980	USSR	38.26s
1984	United States	37.83s
1988	USSR (U.S. disqualified)	38.19s
1992	United States	37.40s*

1,600-Meter Relay

1908	United States	3m. 29.4s
1912	United States	3m. 16.6s
1920	Great Britain	3m. 22.2s
1924	United States	3m. 16s
1928	United States	3m. 14.2s
1932	United States	3m. 8.2s
1936	Great Britain	3m. 9s
1948	United States	3m. 10.4s
1952	Jamaica	3m. 03.9s
1956	United States	3m. 04.8s
1960	United States	3m. 02.2s
1964	United States	3m. 00.7s
1968	United States	2m. 56.16s
1972	Kenya	2m. 59.8s
1976	United States	2m. 58.65s
1980	USSR	3m. 01.1s
1984	United States	2m. 57.91s
1988	United States	2m. 56.16s
1992	United States	2m. 55.74s*

Pole Vault

1896	William Hoyt, United States	10ft. 10 in.
1900	Irving Baxter, United States	10ft. 10 in.
1904	Charles Dvorak, United States	11ft. 5 3-4 in.
1908	A. C. Gilbert, United States	
	Edward Cook Jr., United States	12ft. 2 in.
1912	Harry Babcock, United States	12ft. 11 1-2 in.
1920	Frank Foss, United States	13ft. 5 in.
1924	Lee Barnes, United States	12ft. 11 1-2 in.
1928	Sabin W. Carr, United States	13ft. 9 1-4 in.
1932	William Miller, United States	14ft. 1 3-4 in.
1936	Earle Meadows, United States	14ft. 3 1-4 in.
1948	Guinn Smith, United States	14ft. 1 1-4 in.
1952	Robert Richards, United States	14ft. 11 in.
1956	Robert Richards, United States	14ft. 11 1-2 in.
1960	Don Bragg, United States	15ft. 5 in.
1964	Fred Hansen, United States	16ft. 8 3-4 in.
1968	Bob Seagren, United States	17ft. 8 1-2 in.
1972	Wolfgang Nordwig, E. Germany	18ft. 1-2 in.
1976	Tadeusz Slusarski, Poland	18ft. 1-2 in.
1980	Wladyslaw Kozakiewicz, Poland	18ft. 11 1-2 in.
1984	Pierre Quinon, France	18ft. 10 1-4 in.
1988	Sergei Bubka, USSR	19ft. 9 1-4 in.*
1992	Maksim Tarassov, Unified Team	19ft. 1-4 in.

Hammer Throw

1900	John Flanagan, United States	163ft. 1 in.
1904	John Flanagan, United States	168ft. 1 in.
1908	John Flanagan, United States	170ft. 4 1-4 in.
1912	Matt McGrath, United States	179ft. 7 1-8 in.
1920	Pat Ryan, United States	173ft. 5 5-8 in.
1924	Fred Tootell, United States	174ft. 10 1-8 in.
1928	Patrick O'Callaghan, Ireland	168ft. 7 1-2 in.
1932	Patrick O'Callaghan, Ireland	176ft. 11 1-8 in.
1936	Karl Hein, Germany	185ft. 4 in.
1948	Imre Nemeth, Hungary	183ft. 11 1-2 in.
1952	Jozsef Csermak, Hungary	197ft. 11 9-16 in.
1956	Harold Connolly, United States	207ft. 3 1-2 in.
1960	Vasily Rudenkov, USSR	220ft. 1 5-8 in.
1964	Romuald Klim, USSR	228ft. 9 1-2 in.
1968	Gyula Zsivotsky, Hungary	240ft. 8 in.
1972	Anatoli Bondarchuk, USSR	247ft. 8 in.
1976	Yuri Syedykh, USSR	254ft. 4 in.
1980	Yuri Syedykh, USSR	268ft. 4 1-2 in.
1984	Juha Tiainen, Finland	256ft. 2 in.
1988	Sergei Litinov, USSR	278ft. 2 1-2 in.*
1992	Andrey Abduvaliyev, Unified Team	270ft. 9 1-2 in.

Discus Throw

1896	Robert Garrett, United States	95ft. 7 1-2 in.
1900	Rudolf Bauer, Hungary	118ft. 3 in.
1904	Martin Sheridan, United States	128ft. 10 1-2 in.
1908	Martin Sheridan, United States	134ft. 2 in.
1912	Armas Taipale, Finland	148ft. 3 in.
	Both hands—Armas Taipale, Finland	271ft. 10 1-4 in.
1920	Elmer Niklander, Finland	146ft. 7 in.
1924	Clarence Houser, United States	151ft. 4 in.
1928	Clarence Houser, United States	155ft. 3 in.
1932	John Anderson, United States	162ft. 4 in.
1936	Ken Carpenter, United States	165ft. 7 in.
1948	Adolfo Consolini, Italy	173ft. 2 in.
1952	Sim Iness, United States	180ft. 6.85 in.
1956	Al Oerter, United States	184ft. 10 1-2 in.
1960	Al Oerter, United States	194ft. 2 in.
1964	Al Oerter, United States	200ft. 1 1-2 in.
1968	Al Oerter, United States	212ft. 6 1-2 in.
1972	Ludvik Danek, Czechoslovakia	211ft. 3 in.
1976	Mac Wilkins, United States	221ft. 5.4 in.
1980	Viktor Rashchupkin, USSR	218ft. 8 in.
1984	Rolf Dannenberg, W. Germany	218ft. 6 in.
1988	Jurgen Schult, E. Germany	225ft. 9 1-4 in.*
1992	Romas Ubartas, Lithuania	213ft. 7 3-4 in.

Triple Jump

1896	James Connolly, United States	44ft. 11 3-4 in.
1900	Myer Prinstein, United States	47ft. 5 3-4 in.
1904	Myer Prinstein, United States	47 ft.
1908	Timothy Ahearne, Great Britain, Ireland	48ft. 11 1-4 in.
1912	Gustaf Lindblom, Sweden	48ft. 5 1-4 in.
1920	Vilho Tuulos, Finland	47ft. 7 in.
1924	Anthony Winter, Australia	50ft. 11 1-4 in.
1928	Mikio Oda, Japan	49ft. 11 in.
1932	Chuhei Nambu, Japan	51ft. 7 in.
1936	Naoto Tajima, Japan	52ft. 6 in.
1948	Arne Ahman, Sweden	50ft. 6 1-4 in.
1952	Adhemar da Silva, Brazil	53ft. 2 3-4 in.
1956	Adhemar da Silva, Brazil	53ft. 7 3-4 in.
1960	Jozef Schmidt, Poland	55ft. 2 in.
1964	Jozef Schmidt, Poland	55ft. 3 1-2 in.
1968	Viktor Saneev, USSR	57ft. 3-4 in.
1972	Viktor Saneev, USSR	56ft. 11 in.
1976	Viktor Saneev, USSR	56ft. 8 3-4 in.
1980	Jaak Uudmae, USSR	56ft. 11 1-4 in.
1984	Al Joyner, United States	56ft. 7 1-2 in.
1988	Hristo Markov, Bulgaria	57ft. 9 1-4 in.
1992	Mike Conley, United States	59ft. 7 1-2 in.*

16-lb. Shot Put

1896	Robert Garrett, United States	36ft. 9 3-4 in.
1900	Richard Sheldon, United States	46ft. 3 1-4 in.
1904	Ralph Rose, United States	48ft. 7 in.
1908	Ralph Rose, United States	46ft. 7 1-2 in.
1912	Pat McDonald, United States	50ft. 4 in.
	Both hands—Ralph Rose, United States	90ft. 5 1-2 in.
1920	Ville Porhola, Finland	48ft. 7 1-4 in.
1924	Clarence Houser, United States	49ft. 2 1-4 in.
1928	John Kuck, United States	52ft. 3-4 in.
1932	Leo Sexton, United States	52ft. 6 in.
1936	Hans Woellke, Germany	53ft. 1 3-4 in.
1948	Wilbur Thompson, United States	56ft. 2 in.
1952	Parry O'Brien, United States	57ft. 1-2 in.
1956	Parry O'Brien, United States	60ft. 11 1-4 in.
1960	William Nieder, United States	64ft. 6 3-4 in.
1964	Dallas Long, United States	66ft. 8 1-2 in.
1968	Randy Matson, United States	67ft. 4 3-4 in.
1972	Wladyslaw Komar, Poland	69ft. 6 in.
1976	Udo Beyer, E. Germany	69ft. 3-4 in.
1980	Vladimir Kiselyov, USSR	70ft. 1-2 in.
1984	Alessandro Andrei, Italy	69ft. 9 in.
1988	Ulf Timmermann, E. Germany	73ft. 8 3-4 in.*
1992	Michael Stulce, United States	71ft. 2 1-4 in.

Javelin

1908	Erik Lemming, Sweden	178ft. 7 1-2 in.
	Held in middle—Erik Lemming,	
	Sweden	179ft. 10 1-2 in.
1912	Erik Lemming, Sweden	198ft. 11 1-4 in.
	Both hands, Julius Saaristo, Finland	358ft. 11 7-8 in.
1920	Jonni Myyra, Finland	215ft. 9 3-4 in.
1924	Jonni Myyra, Finland	206ft. 6 3-4 in.
1928	Eric Lundkvist, Sweden	218ft. 6 1-8 in.
1932	Matti Jarvinen, Finland	238ft. 6 in.

(continued)

1936	Gerhard Stoeck, Germany	235ft. 8 5-16 in.
1948	Tapio Rautavaara, Finland	228ft. 10 1-2 in.
1952	Cy Young, United States	242ft. 0.79 in.
1956	Egil Danielson, Norway	281ft. 2 1-4 in.
1960	Viktor Tsibulenko, USSR	277ft. 8 3-8 in.
1964	Pauli Nevala, Finland	271ft. 2 1-2 in.
1968	Janis Lusis, USSR	295ft. 7 1-4 in.
1972	Klaus Wolfermann, W. Germany	296ft. 10 in.
1976	Miklos Nemeth, Hungary	310ft. 4 in.
1980	Dainis Kula, USSR	299ft. 2 3-8 in.
1984	Arto Haerkoenen, Finland	284ft. 8 in.
1988	Tapio Korjus, Finland	276ft. 6 in.
1992	Jan Zelezny, Czechoslavakia	294ft. 2 in.

Decathlon

1912	Hugo Wieslander, Sweden	7,724.49 pts.(a)
1920	Helge Lovland, Norway	6,804.35 pts.
1924	Harold Osborn, United States	7,710.77 pts.
1928	Paavo Yrjola, Finland	8,053.29 pts.
1932	James Bausch, United States	8,462.23 pts.

1936	Glenn Morris, United States	7,900 pts.
1948	Robert Mathias, United States	7,139 pts.
1952	Robert Mathias, United States	7,887 pts.
1956	Milton Campbell, United States	7,937 pts.
1960	Rafer Johnson, United States	8,392 pts.
1964	Willi Holdorf, Germany	7,887 pts.(b)
1968	Bill Toomey, United States	8,193 pts.
1972	Nikolai Avilov, USSR	8,454 pts.
1976	Bruce Jenner, United States	8,617 pts.
1980	Daley Thompson, Great Britain	8,495 pts.
1984	Daley Thompson, Great Britain	8,798 pts.*(c)
1988	Christian Schenk, E. Germany	8,488 pts.
1992	Robert Zmelik, Czechoslavakia	8,611 pts.

(a) Jim Thorpe of the U.S. won the 1912 Decathlon with 8,413 pts. but was disqualified and had to return his medals because he had played professional baseball prior to the Olympic games. The medals were restored posthumously in 1982. (b) Former point systems used prior to 1964. (c) Scoring change effective Apr. 1985.

Track and Field—Women

100-Meter Run

1928	Elizabeth Robinson, United States	12.2s
1932	Stella Walsh, Poland	11.9s
1936	Helen Stephens, United States	11.5s
1948	Francina Blankers-Koen, Netherlands	11.9s
1952	Marjorie Jackson, Australia	11.5s
1956	Betty Cuthbert, Australia	11.5s
1960	Wilma Rudolph, United States	11.0s
1964	Wyomia Tyus, United States.	11.4s
1968	Wyomia Tyus, United States.	11.0s
1972	Renate Stecher, E. Germany	11.07s
1976	Annegret Richter, W. Germany.	11.08s
1980	Lyudmila Kondratyeva, USSR	11.6s
1984	Evelyn Ashford, United States	10.97s
1988	Florence Griffith-Joyner, United States	10.54s*
1992	Gail Devers, United States	10.82s

200-Meter Run

1948	Francina Blankers-Koen, Netherlands	24.4s
1952	Marjorie Jackson, Australia	23.7s
1956	Betty Cuthbert, Australia.	23.4s
1960	Wilma Rudolph, United States.	24.0s
1964	Edith McGuire, United States	23.0s
1968	Irena Szewinska, Poland	22.5s
1972	Renate Stecher, E. Germany	22.40s
1976	Barbel Eckert, E. Germany	22.37s
1980	Barbel Wockel, E. Germany	22.03s
1984	Valerie Brisco-Hooks, United States	21.81s
1988	Florence Griffith-Joyner, United States	21.34s*
1992	Gwen Torrence, United States	21.81s

400-Meter Run

1964	Betty Cuthbert, Australia	52s
1968	Colette Besson, France.	52s
1972	Monika Zehrt, E. Germany	51.08s
1976	Irena Szewinska, Poland	49.29s
1980	Marita Koch, E. Germany	48.88s
1984	Valerie Brisco-Hooks, United States.	48.83s
1988	Olga Bryzgina, USSR	48.65s*
1992	Marie-Jose Perec, France	48.83s

800-Meter Run

1928	Lina Radke, Germany	2m. 16.8s
1960	Ludmila Shevtsova, USSR	2m. 4.3s
1964	Ann Packer, Great Britain	2m. 1.1s
1968	Madeline Manning, United States	2m. 0.9s
1972	Hildegard Falck, W. Germany	1m. 58.6s
1976	Tatyana Kazankina, USSR	1m. 54.94s
1980	Nadezhda Olizayrenko, USSR	1m. 53.5s*
1984	Doina Melinte, Romania	1m. 57.6s
1988	Sigrun Wodars, E. Germany	1m. 56.10s
1992	Ellen Van Langen, Netherlands	1m. 55.54s

1,500-Meter Run

1975	Lyudmila Bragina, USSR	4m. 01.4s
1976	Tatyana Kazankina, USSR	4m. 05.48s
1980	Tatyana Kazankina, USSR	3m. 56.6s
1984	Gabriella Dorio, Italy	4m. 03.25s
1988	Paula Ivan, Romania	3m. 53.96s*
1992	Hassiba Boulmerka, Algeria	3m. 55.30s

3,000-Meter Run

1984	Maricica Puica, Romania	8m. 35.96s
1988	Tatyana Samolenko, USSR.	8m. 26.53s*
1992	Elena Romanova, Unified Team	8m. 46.04s

10,000-Meter Run

1988	Olga Boldarenko, USSR	31m. 44.69s
1992	Derartu Tulu, Ethiopia	31m. 06.02s*

400-Meter Relay

1928	Canada	48.4s
1932	United States	46.9s
1936	United States	46.9s
1948	Netherlands	47.5s
1952	United States	45.9s
1956	Australia	44.5s
1960	United States	44.5s
1964	Poland	43.6s
1968	United States	42.8s
1972	West Germany	42.81s
1976	East Germany	42.55s
1980	East Germany	41.60s*
1984	United States	41.65s
1988	United States	41.98s
1992	United States	42.11s

1,600-Meter Relay

1972	East Germany	3m. 23s
1976	East Germany	3m. 19.23s
1980	USSR	3m. 20.02s
1984	United States	3m. 18.29s
1988	USSR	3 m. 15.18s*
1992	Unified Team	3m. 20.20s

100-Meter Hurdles

1972	Annelie Ehrhardt, E. Germany	12.59s
1976	Johanna Schaller, E. Germany	12.77s
1980	Vera Komisova, USSR	12.56s
1984	Benita Brown-Fitzgerald, United States.	12.84s
1988	Jordanka Donkova, Bulgaria	12.38s*
1992	Paraskevi Patoulidou, Greece.	12.64s

400-Meter Hurdles

1984	Nawal el Moutawakii, Morocco	54.61s
1988	Debra Flintoff-King, Australia.	53.17s*
1992	Sally Gunnell, Great Britain	53.23s

Heptathlon

1984	Glynis Nunn, Australia	6,390 pts.
1988	Jackie Joyner-Kersee, United States	7,215 pts.*
1992	Jackie Joyner-Kersee, United States	7,044 pts.

High Jump

1928	Ethel Catherwood, Canada	5ft. 2 1-2 in.
1932	Jean Shiley, United States	5ft. 5 1-4 in.
1936	Ibolya Csak, Hungary	5ft. 3 in.
1948	Alice Coachman, United States	5ft. 6 1-8 in.
1952	Esther Brand, South Africa	5ft. 5 3-4 in.
1956	Mildred L. McDaniel, United States	5ft. 9 1-4 in.
1960	Iolanda Balas, Romania	6ft. 3-4 in.
1964	Iolanda Balas, Romania	6ft. 2 3-4 in.
1968	Miloslava Reskova, Czechoslovakia	5ft. 11 1-2 in.
1972	Ulrike Meyfarth, W. Germany	6ft. 4 in.
1976	Rosemarie Ackermann, E. Germany	6ft. 3 3-4 in.

1980	Sara Simeoni, Italy .... 6ft. 5 1-2 in.
1984	Ulrike Meyfarth, W. Germany .... 6ft. 7 1-2 in.
1988	Louise Ritter, United States .... 6ft. 8 in.*
1992	Heike Henkel, Germany .... 6ft. 7 1-2 in.

Discus Throw

1928	Helena Konopacka, Poland .... 129ft. 11 3-4 in.
1932	Lillian Copeland, United States .... 133ft. 2 in.
1936	Gisela Mauermayer, Germany .... 156ft. 3 in.
1948	Micheline Ostermeyer, France .... 137ft. 6 1-2 in.
1952	Nina Romaschkova, USSR .... 168ft. 8 in.
1956	Olga Fikotova, Czechoslovakia .... 176ft. 1 in.
1960	Nina Ponomareva, USSR .... 180ft. 8 1-4 in.
1964	Tamara Press, USSR .... 187ft. 10 in.
1968	Lia Manoliu, Romania .... 191ft. 2 in.
1972	Faina Melnik, USSR .... 218ft. 7 in.
1976	Evelin Schlaak, E. Germany .... 226ft. 4 in.
1980	Evelin Jahl, E. Germany .... 229ft. 6 in.
1984	Ria Stalman, Netherlands .... 214ft. 5 in.
1988	Martina Hellmann, E. Germany ... 237ft. 2 1-4 in.*
1992	Maritza Marten Garcia, Cuba .... 222ft. 10 in.

Javelin Throw

1932	"Babe" Didrikson, United States .... 143ft. 4 in.
1936	Tilly Fleischer, Germany .... 148ft. 2 3-4 in.
1948	Herma Bauma, Austria .... 149ft. 6 in.
1952	Dana Zatopkova, Czechoslovakia .... 165ft. 7 in.
1956	Inese Jaunzeme, USSR .... 176ft. 8 in.
1960	Elvira Ozolina, USSR .... 183ft. 8 in.
1964	Mihaela Penes, Romania .... 198ft. 7 1-2 in.
1968	Angela Nemeth, Hungary .... 198ft. 1-2 in.
1972	Ruth Fuchs, E. Germany .... 209ft. 7 in.
1976	Ruth Fuchs, E. Germany .... 216ft. 4 in.
1980	Maria Colon, Cuba .... 224ft. 5 in.
1984	Tessa Sanderson, Great Britain .... 228ft. 2 in.
1988	Petra Felke, E. Germany .... 245ft.*
1992	Silke Renke, Germany .... 224ft. 2 1-2 in.

Shot Put (8lb., 13oz.)

1948	Micheline Ostermeyer, France .... 45ft. 1 1-2 in.
1952	Galina Zybina, USSR .... 50ft. 1 3-4 in.
1956	Tamara Tishkyevich, USSR .... 54ft. 5 in.
1960	Tamara Press, USSR .... 56ft. 10 in.
1964	Tamara Press, USSR .... 59ft. 6 1-4 in.
1968	Margitta Gummel, E. Germany .... 64ft. 4 in.
1972	Nadezhda Chizova, USSR .... 69ft.
1976	Ivanka Hristova, Bulgaria .... 69ft. 5 1-4 in.
1980	Ilona Slupianek, E. Germany....... 73ft. 6 1-4 in.*
1984	Claudia Losch, W. Germany .... 67ft. 2 1-4 in.
1988	Natalya Lisovskaya, USSR .... 72ft. 11 1-2 in.
1992	Svetlana Kriveleva, Unified Team .... 69ft. 1 1-2in.

Long Jump

1948	Olga Gyarmati, Hungary .... 18ft. 8 1-4 in.
1952	Yvette Williams, New Zealand .... 20ft. 5 3-4 in.
1956	Elzbieta Krzeskinska, Poland .... 20ft. 9 3-4 in.
1960	Vyera Krepkina, USSR .... 20ft. 10 3-4 in.
1964	Mary Rand, Great Britain .... 22ft. 2 1-4 in.
1968	Viorica Viscopoleanu, Romania .... 22ft. 4 1-2 in.
1972	Heidemarie Rosendahl, W. Germany ... 22ft. 3 in.
1976	Angela Voigt, E. Germany .... 22ft. 3-4 in.
1980	Tatyana Kolpakova, USSR .... 23ft. 2 in.
1984	Anisoara Stanciu, Romania .... 22ft. 10 in.
1988	Jackie Joyner-Kersee, United States ... 24ft. 3 1-2 in.
1992	Helke Drechsler, Germany .... 23ft. 5 1-4 in.*

Marathon

1984	Joan Benoit, United States 2h. 24m. 52s*
1988	Rosa Mota, Portugal.................. 2h. 25m. 40s
1992	Valentina Yegorova, Unified Team...... 2h. 32m. 41s

Swimming and Diving—Men

50-Meter Freestyle

1988	Matt Biondi, U.S. 22.14
1992	Alexandre Popov, Unified Team 21.91*

100-Meter Freestyle

1896	Alfred Hajos, Hungary........................ 1:22.2
1904	Zoltan de Halmay, Hungary (100 yards) 1:02.8
1908	Charles Daniels, U.S. 1:05.6
1912	Duke P. Kahanamoku, U.S. 1:03.4
1920	Duke P. Kahanamoku, U.S. 1:01.4
1924	John Weissmuller, U.S. 59.0
1928	John Weissmuller, U.S. 58.6
1932	Yasuji Miyazaki, Japan 58.2
1936	Ferenc Csik, Hungary 57.6
1948	Wally Ris, U.S. 57.3
1952	Clark Scholes, U.S. 57.4
1956	Jon Henricks, Australia 55.4
1960	John Devitt, Australia........................ 55.2
1964	Don Schollander, U.S. 53.4
1968	Mike Wenden, Australia 52.2
1972	Mark Spitz, U.S. 51.22
1976	Jim Montgomery, U.S. 49.99
1980	Jorg Woithe, E. Germany 50.40
1984	Rowdy Gaines, U.S. 49.80
1988	Matt Biondi, U.S. 48.63*
1992	Alexandre Popov, Unified Team 49.02

200-Meter Freestyle

1968	Mike Wenden, Australia 1:55.2
1972	Mark Spitz, U.S. 1:52.78
1976	Bruce Furniss, U.S. 1:50.29
1980	Sergei Kopliakov, USSR...................... 1:49.81
1984	Michael Gross, W. Germany 1:47.44
1988	Duncan Armstrong, Australia................ 1:47.25
1992	Yevgeny Sadovyi, Unified Team 1:46.70*

400-Meter Freestyle

1904	C. M. Daniels, U.S. (440 yards) 6:16.2
1908	Henry Taylor, Great Britain 5:36.8
1912	George Hodgson, Canada.................... 5:24.4
1920	Norman Ross, U.S. 5:26.8
1924	John Weissmuller, U.S. 5:04.2
1928	Albert Zorilla, Argentina 5:01.6
1932	Clarence Crabbe, U.S. 4:48.4
1936	Jack Medica, U.S. 4:44.5
1948	William Smith, U.S. 4:41.0
1952	Jean Boiteux, France 4:30.7
1956	Murray Rose, Australia....................... 4:27.3
1960	Murray Rose, Australia....................... 4:18.3
1964	Don Schollander, U.S. 4:12.2
1968	Mike Burton, U.S. 4:09.0
1972	Brad Cooper, Australia...................... 4:00.27
1976	Brian Goodell, U.S. 3:51.93
1980	Vladimir Salnikov, USSR 3:51.31
1984	George DiCarlo, U.S........................ 3:51.23
1988	Ewe Dassler, E. Germany 3:46.95
1992	Yevgeny Sadovyi, Unified Team............. 3:45.00*

1,500-Meter Freestyle

1908	Henry Taylor, Great Britain 22:48.4
1912	George Hodgson, Canada 22:00.0
1920	Norman Ross, U.S. 22:23.2
1924	Andrew Charlton, Australia 20:06.6
1928	Arne Borg, Sweden 19:51.8
1932	Kusuo Kitamura, Japan 19:12.4
1936	Noboru Terada, Japan 19:13.7
1948	James McLane, U.S. 19:18.5
1952	Ford Konno, U.S. 18:30.3
1956	Murray Rose, Australia 17:58.9
1960	Jon Konrads, Australia 17:19.6
1964	Robert Windle, Australia 17:01.7
1968	Mike Burton, U.S. 16:38.9
1972	Mike Burton, U.S. 15:52.58

(continued)

1976	Brian Goodell, U.S.	15:02.40
1980	Vladimir Salnikov, USSR	14:58.27
1984	Michael O'Brien, U.S.	15:05.20
1988	Vladimir Salnikov, USSR	15:00.40
1992	Kieren Perkins, Australia	14:43.48*

400-Meter Medley Relay

1960	United States	4:05.4
1964	United States	3:58.4
1968	United States	3:54.9
1972	United States	3:48.16
1976	United States	3:42.22
1980	Australia	3:45.70
1984	United States	3:39.30
1988	United States	3:36.93*
1992	United States	3:36.93*

400-Meter Freestyle Relay

1964	United States	3:31.2
1968	United States	3:31.7
1972	United States	3:26.42
1984	United States	3:19.03
1988	United States	3:16.53*
1992	United States	3:16.74

800-Meter Freestyle Relay

1908	Great Britain	10:55.6
1912	Australia	10:11.6
1920	United States	10:04.4
1924	United States	9:53.4
1928	United States	9:36.2
1932	Japan	8:58.4
1936	Japan	8:51.5
1948	United States	8:46.0
1952	United States	8:31.1
1956	Australia	8:23.6
1960	United States	8:10.2
1964	United States	7:52.1
1968	United States	7:52.33
1972	United States	7:35.78
1976	United States	7:23.22
1980	USSR	7:23.50
1984	United States	7:15.69
1988	United States	7:12.51
1992	Unified Team	7:11.95*

100-Meter Backstroke

1904	Walter Brack, Germany (100 yds.)	1:16.8
1908	Arno Bieberstein, Germany	1:24.6
1912	Harry Hebner, U.S.	1:21.2
1920	Warren Kealoha, U.S.	1:15.2
1924	Warren Kealoha, U.S.	1:13.2
1928	George Kojac, U.S.	1:08.2
1932	Masaji Kiyokawa, Japan	1:08.6
1936	Adolph Kiefer, U.S.	1:05.9
1948	Allen Stack, U.S.	1:06.4
1952	Yoshi Oyakawa, U.S.	1:05.4
1956	David Thiele, Australia	1:02.2
1960	David Thiele, Australia	1:01.9
1968	Roland Matthes, E. Germany	58.7
1972	Roland Matthes, E. Germany	56.58
1976	John Naber, U.S.	55.49
1980	Bengt Baron, Sweden	56.33
1984	Rick Carey, U.S.	55.79
1988	Daichi Suzuki, Japan	55.05
1992	Mark Tewksbury, Canada	53.98*

200-Meter Backstroke

1964	Jed Graef, U.S.	2:10.3
1968	Roland Matthes, E. Germany	2:09.6
1972	Roland Matthes, E. Germany	2:02.82
1976	John Naber, U.S.	1:59.19
1980	Sandor Wladar, Hungary	2:01.93
1984	Rick Carey, U.S.	2:00.23
1988	Igor Polianski, USSR	1:59.37
1992	Martin Lopez-Zubero, Spain	1:58.47*

100-Meter Breaststroke

1968	Don McKenzie, U.S.	1:07.7
1972	Nobutaka Taguchi, Japan	1:04.94
1976	John Hencken, U.S.	1:03.11
1980	Duncan Goodhew, Great Britain	1:03.44
1984	Steve Lundquist, U.S.	1:01.65
1988	Adrian Moorhouse, Great Britain	1:02.04
1992	Nelson Diebel, U.S.	1:01.50*

200-Meter Breaststroke

1908	Frederick Holman, Great Britain	3:09.2
1912	Walter Bathe, Germany	3:01.8
1920	Haken Malmroth, Sweden	3:04.4
1924	Robert Skelton, U.S.	2:56.6
1928	Yoshiyuki Tsuruta, Japan	2:48.8
1932	Yoshiyuki Tsuruta, Japan	2:45.4
1936	Tetsuo Hamuro, Japan	2:41.5
1948	Joseph Verdeur, U.S.	2:39.3
1952	John Davies, Australia	2:34.4
1956	Masura Furukawa, Japan	2:34.7
1960	William Mulliken, U.S.	2:37.4
1964	Ian O'Brien, Australia	2:27.8
1968	Felipe Munoz, Mexico	2:28.7
1972	John Hencken, U.S.	2:21.55
1976	David Wilkie, Great Britain	2:15.11
1980	Robertas Zhulpa, USSR	2:15.85
1984	Victor Davis, Canada	2:13.34
1988	Jozsef Szabo, Hungary	2:13.52
1992	Mike Barrowman, U.S.	2:10.16*

100-Meter Butterfly

1968	Doug Russell, U.S.	55.9
1972	Mark Spitz, U.S.	54.27
1976	Matt Vogel, U.S.	54.35
1980	Par Arvidsson, Sweden	54.92
1984	Michael Gross, W. Germany	53.08
1988	Anthony Nesty, Suriname	53.00*
1992	Pablo Morales, U.S.	53.32

200-Meter Butterfly

1956	William Yorzyk, U.S.	2:19.3
1960	Michael Troy, U.S.	2:12.8
1964	Kevin J. Berry, Australia	2:06.6
1968	Carl Robie, U.S.	2:08.7
1972	Mark Spitz, U.S.	2:00.70
1976	Mike Bruner, U.S.	1:59.23
1980	Sergei Fesenko, USSR	1:59.76
1984	Jon Sieben, Australia	1:57.04
1988	Michael Gross, W. Germany	1:56.94
1992	Mel Stewart, U.S.	1:56.26*

200-Meter Individual Medley

1968	Charles Hickcox, U.S.	2:12.0
1972	Gunnar Larsson, Sweden	2:07.17
1984	Alex Baumann, Canada	2:01.42
1988	Tamas Darnyi, Hungary	2:00.17*
1992	Tamas Darnyi, Hungary	2:00.76

400-Meter Individual Medley

1964	Dick Roth, U.S.	4:45.4
1968	Charles Hickcox, U.S.	4:48.4
1972	Gunnar Larsson, Sweden	4:31.98
1976	Rod Strachan, U.S.	4:23.68
1980	Aleksandr Sidorenko, USSR	4:22.89
1984	Alex Baumann, Canada	4:17.41
1988	Tamas Darnyi, Hungary	4:14.75
1992	Tamas Darnyi, Hungary	4:14.23*

Springboard Diving — Points

1908	Albert Zurner, Germany	85.5
1912	Paul Guenther, Germany	79.23
1920	Louis Kuehn, U.S.	675.40
1924	Albert White, U.S.	97.46
1928	Pete Desjardins, U.S.	185.04
1932	Michael Galitzen, U.S.	161.38
1936	Richard Degener, U.S.	163.57
1948	Bruce Harlan, U.S.	163.64
1952	David Browning, U.S.	205.29
1956	Robert Clotworthy, U.S.	159.56
1960	Gary Tobian, U.S.	170.00
1964	Kenneth Sitzberger, U.S.	159.90
1968	Bernie Wrightson, U.S.	170.15
1972	Vladimir Vasin, USSR	594.09
1976	Phil Boggs, U.S.	619.52
1980	Aleksandr Portnov, USSR	905.02
1984	Greg Louganis, U.S.	754.41
1988	Greg Louganis, U.S.	730.80
1992	Mark Lenzi, U.S.	676.530

Platform Diving — Points

1904	Dr. G.E. Sheldon, U.S.	12.75
1908	Hjalmar Johansson, Sweden	83.75
1912	Erik Adlerz, Sweden	73.94

1920	Clarence Pinkston, U.S.	100.67
1924	Albert White, U.S.	97.46
1928	Pete Desjardins, U.S.	98.74
1932	Harold Smith, U.S.	124.80
1936	Marshall Wayne, U.S.	113.58
1948	Sammy Lee, U.S.	130.05
1952	Sammy Lee, U.S.	156.28
1956	Joaquin Capilla, Mexico	152.44
1960	Robert Webster, U.S.	165.56

1964	Robert Webster, U.S.	148.58
1968	Klaus Dibiasi, Italy	164.18
1972	Klaus Dibiasi, Italy	504.12
1976	Klaus Dibiasi, Italy	600.51
1980	Falk Hoffmann, E. Germany	835.65
1984	Greg Louganis, U.S.	710.91
1988	Greg Louganis, U.S.	638.61
1992	Sun Shuwei, China	677.310

Swimming and Diving—Women

50-Meter Freestyle

1988	Kristin Otto, E. Germany	25.49
1992	Yang Wenyi, China	24.76*

100-Meter Freestyle

1912	Fanny Durack, Australia	1:22.2
1920	Ethelda Bleibtrey, U.S.	1:13.6
1924	Ethel Lackie, U.S.	1:12.4
1928	Albina Osipowich, U.S.	1:11.0
1932	Helene Madison, U.S.	1:06.8
1936	Hendrika Mastenbroek, Holland	1:05.9
1948	Greta Andersen, Denmark	1:06.3
1952	Katalin Szoke, Hungary	1:06.8
1956	Dawn Fraser, Australia	1:02.0
1960	Dawn Fraser, Australia	1:01.2
1964	Dawn Fraser, Australia	59.5
1968	Jan Henne, U.S.	1:00.0
1972	Sandra Neilson, U.S.	58.59
1976	Kornelia Ender, E. Germany	55.65
1980	Barbara Krause, E. Germany	54.79
1984	(tie) Carrie Steinseifer, U.S.	55.92
	Nancy Hogshead, U.S.	55.92
1988	Kristin Otto, E. Germany	54.93
1992	Zhuang Yong, China	54.64*

200-Meter Freestyle

1968	Debbie Meyer, U.S.	2:10.5
1972	Shane Gould, Australia	2:03.56
1976	Kornelia Ender, E. Germany	1:59.26
1980	Barbara Krause, E. Germany	1:58.33
1984	Mary Wayte, U.S.	1:59.23
1988	Heike Friedrich, E. Germany	1:57.65*
1992	Nicole Haislett, U.S.	1:57.90

400-Meter Freestyle

1924	Martha Norelius, U.S.	6:02.2
1928	Martha Norelius, U.S.	5:42.8
1932	Helene Madison, U.S.	5:28.5
1936	Hendrika Mastenbroek, Netherlands	5:26.4
1948	Ann Curtis, U.S.	5:17.8
1952	Valerie Gyenge, Hungary	5:12.1
1956	Lorraine Crapp, Australia	4:54.6
1960	Susan Chris von Saltza, U.S.	4:50.6
1964	Virginia Duenkel, U.S.	4:43.3
1968	Debbie Meyer, U.S.	4:31.8
1972	Shane Gould, Australia	4:19.44
1976	Petra Thuemer E. Germany	4:09.89
1980	Ines Diers, E. Germany	4:08.76
1984	Tiffany Cohen, U.S.	4:07.10
1988	Janet Evans, U.S.	4:03.85*
1992	Dagmar Hase, Germany	4:07.18

800-Meter Freestyle

1968	Debbie Meyer, U.S.	9:24.0
1972	Keena Rothhammer, U.S.	8:53.68
1976	Petra Thuemer, E. Germany	8:37.14
1980	Michelle Ford, Australia	8:28.90
1984	Tiffany Cohen, U.S.	8:24.95
1988	Janet Evans, U.S.	8:20.20*
1992	Janet Evans, U.S.	8:25.52

100-Meter Backstroke

1924	Sybil Bauer, U.S.	1:23.2
1928	Marie Braun, Netherlands	1:22.0
1932	Eleanor Holm, U.S.	1:19.4
1936	Dina Senff, Netherlands	1:18.9
1948	Karen Harup, Denmark	1:14.4
1952	Joan Harrison, South Africa	1:14.3

1956	Judy Grinham, Great Britain	1:12.9
1960	Lynn Burke, U.S.	1:09.3
1964	Cathy Ferguson, U.S.	1:07.7
1968	Kaye Hall, U.S.	1:06.2
1972	Melissa Belote, U.S.	1:05.78
1976	Ulrike Richter, E. Germany	1:01.83
1980	Rica Reinisch, E. Germany	1:00.86
1984	Theresa Andrews, U.S.	1:02.55
1988	Kristin Otto, E. Germany	1:00.89
1992	Krisztina Egerszegi, Hungary	1:00.68*

200-Meter Backstroke

1968	Pokey Watson, U.S.	2:24.8
1972	Melissa Belote, U.S.	2:19.19
1976	Ulrike Richter, E. Germany	2:13.43
1980	Rica Reinisch, E. Germany	2:11.77
1984	Jolanda De Rover, Netherlands	2:12.38
1988	Krisztina Egerszegi, Hungary	2:09.29
1992	Krisztina Egerszegi, Hungary	2:07.06*

100-Meter Breaststroke

1968	Djurdjica Bjedov, Yugoslavia	1:15.8
1972	Cathy Carr, U.S.	1:13.58
1976	Hannelore Anke, E. Germany	1:11:16
1980	Ute Geweniger, E. Germany	1:10.22
1984	Petra Van Staveren, Netherlands	1:09.88
1988	Tania Dangalakova, Bulgaria	1:07.95*
1992	Elena Roudkovskaia, Unified Team	1:08.00

200-Meter Breaststroke

1924	Lucy Morton, Great Britain	3:33.2
1928	Hilde Schrader, Germany	3:12.6
1932	Clare Dennis, Australia	3:06.3
1936	Hideko Maehata, Japan	3:03.6
1948	Nelly Van Vliet, Netherlands	2:57.2
1952	Eva Szekely, Hungary	2:51.7
1956	Ursula Happe, Germany	2:53.1
1960	Anita Lonsbrough, Great Britain	2:49.5
1964	Galina Prozumenschikova, USSR	2:46.4
1968	Sharon Wichman, U.S.	2:44.4
1972	Beverly Whitfield, Australia	2:41.71
1976	Marina Koshevaia, USSR	2:33.35
1980	Lina Kachushite, USSR	2:29.54
1984	Anne Ottenbrite, Canada	2:30.38
1988	Silke Hoerner, E. Germany	2:26.71
1992	Kyoko Iwasaki, Japan	2:26.65*

200-Meter Individual Medley

1968	Claudia Kolb, U.S.	2:24.7
1972	Shane Gould, Australia	2:23.07
1984	Tracy Caulkins, U.S.	2:12.64
1988	Daniela Hunger, E. Germany	2:12.59
1992	Lin Li, China	2:11.65*

400-Meter Individual Medley

1964	Donna de Varona, U.S.	5:18.7
1968	Claudia Kolb, U.S.	5:08.5
1972	Gail Neall, Australia	5:02.97
1976	Ulrike Tauber, E. Germany	4:42.77
1980	Petra Schneider, E. Germany	4:36.29*
1984	Tracy Caulkins, U.S.	4:39.24
1988	Janet Evans, U.S.	4:37.76
1992	Krisztina Egerszegi, Hungary	4:36.54

100-Meter Butterfly

1956	Shelley Mann, U.S.	1:11.0
1960	Carolyn Schuler, U.S.	1:09.5
1964	Sharon Stouder, U.S.	1:04.7

(continued)

1968	Lynn McClements, Australia	1:05.5
1972	Mayumi Aoki, Japan	1:03.34
1976	Kornelia Ender, E. Germany	1:00.13
1980	Caren Metschuck, E. Germany	1:00.42
1984	Mary T. Meagher, U.S.	59.26
1988	Kristin Otto, E. Germany	59.00
1992	Qian Hong, China	58.62*

200-Meter Butterfly

1968	Ada Kok, Netherlands	2:24.7
1972	Karen Moe, U.S.	2:15.57
1976	Andrea Pollack, E. Germany	2:11.41
1980	Ines Geissler, E. Germany	2:10.44
1984	Mary T. Meagher, U.S.	2:06.90*
1988	Kathleen Nord, E. Germany	2:09.51
1992	Summer Sanders, U.S.	2:08.67

400-Meter Medley Relay

1960	United States	4:41.1
1960	United States	4:33.9
1968	United States	4:28.3
1972	United States	4:20.75
1976	East Germany	4:07.95
1980	East Germany	4:06.67
1984	United States	4:08.34
1988	East Germany	4:03.74
1992	United States	4:02.54*

400-Meter Freestyle Relay

1912	Great Britain	5:52.8
1920	United States	5:11.6
1924	United States	4:58.8
1928	United States	4:47.6
1932	United States	4:38.0
1936	Netherlands	4:36.0
1948	United States	4:29.2
1952	Hungary	4:24.4
1956	Australia	4:17.1
1960	United States	4:08.9
1964	United States	4:03.8
1968	United States	4:02.5
1972	United States	3:55.19
1976	United States	3:44.82

1980	East Germany	3:42.71
1984	United States	3:43.43
1988	East Germany	3:40.63
1992	United States	3:39.46*

Springboard Diving — Points

1920	Aileen Riggin, U.S.	539.90
1924	Elizabeth Becker, U.S.	474.50
1928	Helen Meany, U.S.	78.62
1932	Georgia Coleman U.S.	87.52
1936	Marjorie Gestring, U.S.	89.27
1948	Victoria M. Draves, U.S.	108.74
1952	Patricia McCormick, U.S.	147.30
1956	Patricia McCormick, U.S.	142.36
1960	Ingrid Kramer, Germany	155.81
1964	Ingrid Engel-Kramer, Germany	145.00
1968	Sue Gossick, U.S.	150.77
1972	Micki King, U.S.	450.03
1976	Jenni Chandler, U.S.	506.19
1980	Irina Kalinina, USSR	725.91
1984	Sylvie Bernier, Canada	530.70
1988	Gao Min, China	580.23
1992	Gao Min, China	572.400

Platform Diving — Points

1912	Greta Johansson, Sweden	39.90
1920	Stefani Fryland-Clausen, Denmark	34.60
1924	Caroline Smith, U.S.	33.20
1928	Elizabeth B. Pinkston, U.S.	31.60
1932	Dorothy Poynton, U.S.	40.26
1936	Dorothy Poynton Hill, U.S.	33.93
1948	Victoria M. Draves, U.S.	68.87
1952	Patricia McCormick, U.S.	79.37
1956	Patricia McCormick, U.S.	84.85
1960	Ingrid Kramer, Germany	91.28
1964	Lesley Bush, U.S.	99.80
1968	Milena Duchkova, Czech.	109.59
1972	Ulrika Knape, Sweden	390.00
1976	Elena Vaytsekhouskaya, USSR	406.59
1980	Martina Jaschke, E. Germany	596.25
1984	Zhou Jihong, China	435.51
1988	Xu Yanmei, China	445.20
1992	Fu Mingxia, China	461.430

Boxing

Light Flyweight (106 lbs)

1968	Francisco Rodriguez, Venezuela
1972	Gyorgy Gedo, Hungary
1976	Jorge Hernandez, Cuba
1980	Shamil Sabyrov, USSR
1984	Paul Gonzalez, U.S.
1988	Ivailo Hristov, Bulgaria
1992	Rogelio Marcelo, Cuba

Flyweight (112 lbs)

1904	George Finnegan, U.S.
1920	William Di Gennara, U.S.
1924	Fidel LaBarba, U.S.
1928	Antal Kocsis, Hungary
1932	Istvan Enekes, Hungary
1936	Willi Kaiser, Germany
1948	Pascual Perez, Argentina
1952	Nathan Brooks, U.S.
1956	Terence Spinks, Great Britain
1960	GyulaTorok, Hungary
1964	Fernando Atzori, Italy
1968	Ricardo Delgado, Mexico
1972	Georgi Kostadinov, Bulgaria
1976	Leo Randolph, U.S.
1980	Peter Lessov, Bulgaria
1984	Steve McCrory, U.S.
1988	Kim Kwang Sun, S. Korea
1992	Su Choi Choi, N. Korea

Bantamweight (119 lbs)

1904	Oliver Kirk, U.S.
1908	A Henry Thomas, Great Britain
1920	Clarence Walker, South Africa

1924	William Smith, South Africa
1928	Vittorio Tamagnini, Italy
1932	Horace Gwynne, Canada
1936	Ulderico Sergo, Italy
1948	Tibor Csik, Hungary
1952	Pentti Hamalainen, Finland
1956	Wolfgang Behrendt, E. Germany
1960	Oleg Grigoryev, USSR
1964	Takao Sakurai, Japan
1968	Valery Sokolov, USSR
1972	Orlando Martinez, Cuba
1976	Yong-Jo Gu, N. Korea
1980	Juan Hernandez, Cuba
1984	Maurizio Stecca, Italy
1988	Kennedy McKinney, U.S.
1992	Joel Casamayor, Cuba

Featherweight (126 lbs)

1904	Oliver Kirk, U.S.
1908	Richard Gunn, Great Britain
1920	Paul Fritsch, France
1924	John Fields, U.S.
1928	Lambertus van Klaveren, Netherlands
1932	Carmelo Robledo, Argentina
1936	Oscar Casanovas, Argentina
1948	Ernesto Formenti, Italy
1952	Jan Zachara, Czechoslovakia
1956	Vladimir Safronov, USSR
1960	Francesco Musso, Italy
1964	Stanislav Stephashkin, USSR
1968	Antonin Roldan, Mexico
1972	Boris Kousnetsov, USSR
1976	Angel Herrera, Cuba
1980	Rudi Fink, E. Germany

1984	Meldrick Taylor, U.S.
1988	Giovanni Parisi, Italy
1992	Andreas Tews, Germany

Lightweight (132 lbs)

1904	Harry Spanger, U.S.
1908	Frederick Grace, Great Britain
1920	Samuel Mosberg, U.S.
1924	Hans Nielsen, Denmark
1928	Carlo Orlandi, Italy
1932	Lawrence Stevens, South Africa
1936	Imre Harangi, Hungary
1948	Gerald Dreyer, South Africa
1952	Aureliano Bolognesi, Italy
1956	Richard McTaggart, Great Britain
1960	Kazimierz Pazdzior, Poland
1964	Jozef Grudzien, Poland
1968	Ronald Harris, U.S.
1972	Jan Szczepanski, Poland
1976	Howard Davis, U.S.
1980	Angel Herrera, Cuba
1984	Pernell Whitaker, U.S.
1988	Andreas Zuelow, E. Germany
1992	Oscar De La Hoya, U.S.

Light Welterweight (140 lbs)

1952	Charles Adkins, U.S.
1956	Vladimir Yengibaryan, USSR
1960	Bohumil Nemecek, Czechoslavakia
1964	Jerzy Kulej, Poland
1968	Jerzy Kulej, Poland
1972	Ray Seales, U.S.
1976	Ray Leonard, U.S.
1980	Patrizio Oliva, Italy

1984	Jerry Page, U.S.			1980	Slobodan Kacar, Yugoslavia
1988	Viatcheslav Janovski, USSR			1984	Anton Josipovic, Yugoslavia
1992	Hector Vinent, Cuba			1988	Andrew Maynard, U.S.

Middleweight (165 lbs)

1904	Charles Mayer, U.S.
1908	John Douglas, Great Britain
1920	Harry Mallin, Great Britain
1924	Harry Mallin, Great Britain
1928	Piero Toscani, Italy
1932	Carmen Barth, U.S.
1936	Jean Despeaux, France
1948	Laszio Papp, Hungary
1952	Floyd Patterson, U.S.
1956	Gennady Schatkov, USSR
1960	Edward Crook, U.S.
1964	Valery Popenchenko, USSR
1968	Christopher Finnegan, Great Britain
1972	Vyacheslav Lemechev, USSR
1976	Michael Spinks, U.S.
1980	Jose Gomez, Cuba
1984	Joon-Sup Shin, S. Korea
1988	Henry Maske, E. Germany
1992	Ariel Hernandez, Cuba

Welterweight (147 lbs)

1904	Albert Young, U.S.
1920	Albert Schneider, Canada
1924	Jean Delarge, Belgium
1928	Edward Morgan, New Zealand
1932	Edward Flynn, U.S.
1936	Sten Suvio, Finland
1948	Julius Torma, Czechoslavakia
1952	Zygmunt Chychia, Poland
1956	Nicolae Linca, Romania
1960	Giovanni Benvenuti, Italy
1964	Marian Kasprzyk, Poland
1968	Manfred Wolke, E. Germany
1972	Emilio Correa, Cuba
1976	Jochen Bachfeld, E. Germany
1980	Andres Aldama, Cuba
1984	Mark Breland, U.S.
1988	Robert Wangila, Kenya
1992	Michael Carruth, Ireland

Light Heavyweight (179 lbs)

1920	Edward Eagan, U.S.
1924	Harry Mitchell, Great Britain
1928	Victor Avendano, Argentina
1932	David Carstens, South Africa
1936	Roger Michelot, France
1948	George Hunter, South Africa
1952	Norvel Lee, U.S.
1956	James Boyd, U.S.
1960	Cassius Clay, U.S.
1964	Cosimo Pinto, Italy
1968	Dan Poznyak, USSR
1972	Mate Parlov, Yugoslavia
1976	Leon Spinks, U.S.

Light Middleweight (157 lbs)

1952	Laszlo Papp, Hungary
1956	Laszlo Papp, Hungary
1960	Wilbert McClure, U.S.
1964	Boris Lagutin, USSR
1968	Boris Lagutin, USSR
1972	Dieter Kottysch, W. Germany
1976	Jerzy Rybicki, Poland
1980	Armando Martinez, Cuba
1984	Frank Tate, U.S.
1988	Park Si Hun, S. Korea
1992	Juan Lemus, Cuba

1992	Torsten May, Germany

Heavyweight (201 lbs)

1984	Henry Tillman, U.S.
1988	Ray Mercer, U.S.
1992	Felix Savon, Cuba

Super Heavyweight (Unlimited)
(known as heavyweight from 1904-80)

1904	Samuel Berger, U.S.
1908	Albert Oldham, Great Britain
1920	Ronald Rawson, Great Britain
1924	Otto von Porat, Norway
1928	Arturo Rodriguez Jurado, Argentina
1932	Santiago Lovell, Argentina
1936	Herbert Runge, Germany
1948	Rafael Inglesias, Argentina
1952	H. Edward Sanders, U.S.
1956	T. Peter Rademacher, U.S.
1960	Franco De Piccoli, Italy
1964	Joe Frazier, U.S.
1968	George Foreman, U.S.
1972	Teofilo Stevenson, Cuba
1976	Teofilo Stevenson, Cuba
1980	Teofilo Stevenson, Cuba
1984	Tyrell Biggs, U.S.
1988	Lennox Lewis, Canada
1992	Roberto Balado, Cuba

Other Summer Olympics Gold Medalists in 1992

Archery

Men's 70-Meter Individual—Sebastien Flute, France.
Men's Team—Spain.
Women's 70-Meter Individual—Cho Youn Jeong, S. Korea.
Women's Team—S. Korea.

Badminton

Men's Singles—Alan Budi Kusuma, Indonesia.
Men's Doubles—Kim Moon Soo and Park Joo Bong, S. Korea.
Women's Singles—Susi Susanti, Indonesia.
Women's Doubles—Hwang Hye Young and Chung So-Young, S. Korea.

Baseball

G-Cuba; S-Taiwan; B-Japan.

Basketball

Men—G-U.S.; S-Croatia; B-Lithuania.
Women—G-Cuba; S-China; B-U.S.

Canoe/Kayak

Men

Single Kayak Slalom—Pierpaolo Ferrazzi, Italy.
Kayak 500M Singles—Mikko Yrjoe Kolehmainen, Finland.
Kayak 500M Doubles—Germany.
Kayak 1,000M Singles—Clint Robinson, Australia.
Kayak 1,000M Doubles—Germany.
Kayak 1,000M Fours—Germany.
Double Canoe Slalom—U.S.
Canoe Slalom—Lukas Pollert, Czechoslovakia.
Canoe 500M Singles—Nikolai Boukhalov, Bulgaria.
Canoe 500M Doubles—Unified Team.
Canoe 1,000M Singles—Nikolai Boukhalov, Bulgaria.
Canoe 1,000M Doubles—Germany.

Women

Kayak Slalom—Elisabeth Micheler, Germany.
Kayak 500M Singles—Birgit Schmidt, Germany.

Kayak 500M Doubles—Germany.
Kayak 500M Fours—Hungary.

Cycling

Men

Individual Road Race—Fabio Casartelli, Italy.
Sprint—Jens Fiedler, Germany.
Individual Points Race—Giovanni Lombardi, Italy.
4,000 Team Pursuit—Germany.
4K Individual Pursuit—Chris Boardman, Great Britain.
1 KM Time Trial—Jose Moreno, Spain.
Road Race—Germany.

Women

Sprint—Erika Salumae, Estonia.
Individual Pursuit—Petra Rossner, Germany.
Individual Road Race—Kathryn Watt, Australia.

Diving

Men's Platform—Sun Shuwei, China.
Men's Springboard—Mark Lenzi, U.S.
Women's Platform—Fu Mingxia, China.
Women's Springboard—Gao Min, China.

Equestrian

Ind. Three-Day Event—Matthew Ryan, Australia.
Team Three-Day Event—Australia.
Individual Dressage—Nicole Uphoff, Germany.
Team Dressage—Germany.
Individual Jumping—Ludger Beerbaum, Germany.
Team Jumping—Netherlands.

Fencing

Men

Individual Foil—Philippe Omnes, France.
Team Foil—Germany.
Individual Saber—Bence Szabo, Hungary.
Team Saber—Unified Team.
Individual Épée—Eric Srecki, France.
Team Épée—Germany.

(continued)

Women
Individual Foil—Giovanna Trillini, Italy.
Team Foil—Italy.

Field Hockey

Men—G-Germany; S-Australia; B-Pakistan.
Women—G-Spain; S-Germany; B-Great Britain.

Gymnastics

Men
Floor Exercise—Li Xiaosahuang, China.
Horizontal Bar—Trent Dimas, U.S.
Parallel Bars—Vitaly Shcherbo, Unified Team.
Pommel Horse—(tie) Vitaly Shcherbo, Unified Team; Pae Gil Su, N. Korea.
Rings—Vitaly Shcherbo, Unified Team.
Vault—Vitaly Shcherbo, Unified Team.
Individual All-Around—Vitaly Shcherbo, Unified Team.
Team—Unified Team.

Women
Balance Beam— Tatiana Lisenko, Unified Team.
Floor Exercise—Lavinia Corina Milosovici, Romania.
Uneven Bars—Lu Li, China.
Vault—(tie) Henrietta Onodi, Hungary; Lavinia Corina Milosovici, Romania.
All-Around—Tatiana Gutsu, Unified Team.
Team Artistic—Unified Team.

Rhythmic Gymnastics

Alexandra Timoshenko, Unified Team.

Judo

Men
132 Pounds—Nazim Gousseinov, Unified Team.
143 Pounds—Rogerio Sampalo Cardoso, Brazil.
157 Pounds—Toshihiko Koga, Japan.
172 Pounds—Hidehiko Yoshida, Japan.
198 Pounds—Waldemar Legien, Poland.
209 Pounds—Antal Kovacs, Hungary.
Heavyweight—David Khakhaleichvili, Unified Team.

Women
106 Pounds—Cecile Nowak, France.
115 Pounds—Almudena Munoz Martinez, Spain.
123 Pounds—Miriam Blasco Soto, Spain.
134 Pounds—Catherine Fleury, France.
146 Pounds—Odalis Reve Jimenez, Cuba.
159 Pounds—Kim Mi Jung, S. Korea.
Over 159 Pounds—Zhuang Xiaoyan, China.

Modern Pentathlon

Individual—Arkadiusz Skrzypaszek, Poland.
Team—Poland.

Rowing

Men
Single Sculls—Thomas Lange, Germany.
Double Sculls—Australia.
Coxless Pairs—Great Britain.
Coxed Pairs—Great Britain.
Coxed Fours—Romania.
Coxless Fours—Australia.
Quadruple Sculls—Germany.
Coxed Eights—Canada.

Women
Single Sculls—Elisabeta Lipa, Romania.
Double Sculls—Germany.
Coxless Pairs—Canada.
Coxless Fours—Canada.
Quadruple Sculls—Germany.
Coxed Eights—Canada.

Shooting

Men
Running Game Target—Michael Jakosits, Germany.
Rapid Fire Pistol—Ralf Schumann, Germany.

Three-Position Rifle—Gratchia Petikiane, Unified Team.
Free Rifle—Lee Eun Chul, S. Korea.
Air Pistol—Wang Yifu, China.
Air Rifle—Iouri Fedkine, Unified Team.
Free Pistol—Konstantine Loukachik, Unified Team.

Women
Air Pistol—Marina Logvinenko, Unified Team.
Three-Position Rifle—Launi Meili, U.S.
Sport Pistol—Marina Logvinenko, Unified Team.
Air Rifle—Yeo Kab Soon, S. Korea.

Mixed
Trap—Petr Hrdlicka, Czechoslovakia.
Skeet—Zhang Shan, China.

Soccer

G-Spain; S-Poland; B-Ghana.

Synchronized Swimming

Solo—Kristen Babb-Sprague, U.S.
Duet—Karen Josephson and Sarah Josephson, U.S.

Table Tennis

Men's Singles—Jan Waldner, Sweden.
Men's Doubles—Lu Lin and Wang Tao, China.
Women's Singles—Deng Yaping, China.
Women's Doubles—Deng Yaping and Qiao Hong, China.

Team Handball

Men—G-Unified Team; S-Sweden; B-France.
Women—G-S. Korea; S-Norway; B-Unified Team.

Tennis

Men's Singles—Marc Rosset, Switzerland.
Men's Doubles—Boris Becker and Michael Stich, Germany.
Women's Singles—Jennifer Capriati, U.S.
Women's Doubles—Gigi Fernandez and Mary Joe Fernandez, U.S.

Volleyball

Men—G-Brazil; S-Netherlands; B-U.S.
Women—G-Cuba; S-Unified Team; B-U.S.

Water Polo

G-Italy; S-Spain; B-Unified Team.

Weight Lifting

115 Pounds—Ivan Ivanov, Bulgaria.
123 Pounds—Chun Byung Kwan, S. Korea.
132 Pounds—Naim Suleymanoglu, Turkey.
148 Pounds—Israel Militossian, Unified Team.
165 Pounds—Fedor Kassapu, Unified Team.
180 Pounds—Pyrros Dimas, Greece.
198 Pounds—Kakhi Kakhiachvili, Unified Team.
220 Pounds—Victor Tregoubov, Unified Team.
243 Pounds—Ronny Weller, Germany.
Over 243 Pounds—Aleksandr Kourlovitch, Unified Team.

Wrestling

Freestyle
106 Pounds—Kim Il, N. Korea.
115 Pounds—Li Hak Son, S. Korea.
126 Pounds—Alejandro Puerto Diaz, Cuba.
137 Pounds—John Smith, U.S.
150 Pounds—Arsen Fadzaev, Unified Team.
163 Pounds—Park Jang Soon, S. Korea.
182 Pounds—Kevin Jackson, U.S.
198 Pounds—Makharbek Khadartsev, Unified Team.
220 Pounds—Leri Khabelov, Unified Team.
286 Pounds—Bruce Baumgartner, U.S.

Greco-Roman

106 Pounds—Oleg Koutherenko, Unified Team.
115 Pounds—Jon Ronningen, Norway.
126 Pounds—An Han Bong, S. Korea.
137 Pounds—M. Akif Pirim, Turkey.
150 Pounds—Attila Repka, Hungary.
163 Pounds—Mnatsakan Iskandarian, Unified Team.
181 Pounds—Peter Farkas, Hungary.
198 Pounds—Maik Bullmann, Germany.
220 Pounds—Hector Milian Perez, Cuba.
286 Pounds—Aleksandr Karelin, Unified Team.

Yachting

Soling—Denmark.
Finn—Jose Van Der Ploeg, Spain.
Tornado—France.
Europe—Linda Anderson, Norway.
Flying Dutchman—Spain.
Star—U.S.
Men's Sailboard—Franck David, France.
Women's Sailboard—Barbara Kendall, New Zealand.
Men's 470—Spain.
Women's 470—Spain.

Olympic Information

Symbol: Five rings or circles, linked together to represent the sporting friendship of all peoples. The rings also symbolize 5 geographic areas—Europe, Asia, Africa, Australia, and America. Each ring is a different color—blue, yellow, black, green, and red.

Flag: The symbol of the 5 rings on a plain white background.

Motto: "Citius, Altius, Fortius." Latin meaning "faster, higher, braver," or the modern interpretation "swifter, higher, stronger." The motto was coined by Father Didon, a French educator, in 1895.

Creed: "The most important thing in the Olympic Games is not to win but to take part, just as the most important thing in life is not the triumph but the struggle. The essential thing is not to have conquered but to have fought well."

Oath: An athlete of the host country recites the following at the opening ceremony. "In the name of all competitors I promise that we will take part in these Olympic Games, respecting and abiding by the rules which govern them, in the true spirit of sportsmanship for the glory of sport and the honor of our teams." Both the oath and the creed were composed by Baron Pierre de Coubertin, the founder of the modern Games.

Flame: Symbolizes the continuity between the ancient and modern Games. The modern version of the flame was adopted in 1936. The torch used to kindle the flame is first lit by the sun's rays at Olympia, Greece, and then carried to the site of the Games by relays of runners. Ships and planes are used when necessary.

TRACK AND FIELD

World Track and Field Records

As of Oct. 1, 1995

The International Amateur Atheletic Federation, the world body of track and field, recognizes only records in metric distances except for the mile.

Men's Records

Running

Event	Record	Holder	Country	Date	Where made
100 meters	9.85 s.	Leroy Burrell	U.S.	July 6, 1994	Lausanne, Switz.
200 meters	19.72 s.	Pietro Mennea	Italy	Sept. 12, 1979	Mexico City
400 meters	43.29 s.	Butch Reynolds	U.S.	Aug. 16, 1988	Zurich
800 meters	1 m., 41.73 s.	Sebastian Coe	Gr. Britain	June 10, 1981	Florence, Italy
1,000 meters	2 m., 12.18 s.	Sebastian Coe	Gr. Britain	July 11, 1981	Oslo
1,500 meters	3 m., 27.37 s.	Noureddine Morceli	Algeria	July 12, 1995	Nice France
1 mile	3 m., 44.39 s.	Noureddine Morceli	Algeria	Sept. 5, 1993	Rieti, Italy
2,000 meters	4 m., 47.88 s.	Noureddine Morceli	Algeria	July 3, 1995	Paris
3,000 meters	7 m., 25.11 s.	Noureddine Morceli	Algeria	Aug. 2, 1994	Monte Carlo
5,000 meters	12 m., 44.39 s.	Haile Gebreselasie	Ethiopia	Aug. 16, 1995	Zurich
10,000 meters	26 m., 43.63 s.	Haile Gebreselasie	Ethiopia	June 5,1995	Netherlands
20,000 meters	56 m., 55.6 s.	Arturo Barrios	Mexico	Mar. 30, 1991	France
25,000 meters	1 hr., 13 m., 55.8 s.	Toshihiko Seko	Japan	Mar. 22, 1981	New Zealand
3,000 meter stpl.	7 m., 59.18 s.	Moses Kiptanui	Kenya	Aug. 18, 1995	Zurich
Marathon	2 hr., 6 m., 50 s.	Belayneh Densimo	Ethiopia	Apr. 17, 1988	Rotterdam

Hurdles

Event	Record	Holder	Country	Date	Where made
110 meters	12.91 s.	Colin Jackson	Gr. Britain	Aug. 20, 1993	Stuttgart
400 meters	46.78 s.	Kevin Young	U.S.	Aug. 6, 1992	Barcelona

Relay Races

Event	Record	Holder	Country	Date	Where made
400 mtrs. (4x100)	37.40 s.	(Marsh, Burrell, Mitchell, Lewis)	U.S.	Aug. 8, 1992	Barcelona
		(Drummond, Cason, Mitchell, Burrell)	U.S.	Aug. 22, 1993	Stuttgart
800 mtrs. (4×200)	1 m., 18.68 s.	(Marsh, Burrell, Heard, Lewis)	U.S.	Apr. 17, 1994	Walnut, Calif.
1,600 mtrs. (4×400)	2 m., 54.29 s.	(Valmon, Watts, Reynolds, Johnson)	U.S.	Aug. 22, 1993	Stuttgart
3,200 mtrs. (4×800)	7 m., 03.89 s.	(Elliott, Cook, Cram, Coe)	Gr. Britain	Aug. 30, 1982	London

Field Events

Event	Record	Holder	Country	Date	Where made
High jump	8 ft., ½ in.	Javier Sotomayor	Cuba	July 27, 1993	Salamanca, Spain
Long jump	29 ft., 4½ in.	Mike Powell	U.S.	Aug. 30, 1991	Tokyo
Triple jump	60 ft., ¼ in.	Jonathan Edwards	Gr. Britain	June 16, 1985	Indianapolis
Pole vault	20 ft., 1¾ in.	Sergei Bubka	Ukraine	July 31, 1994	Sestriere, Italy
16 lb. shot put	75 ft., 10¼ in.	Randy Barnes	U.S.	May 20, 1990	Los Angeles
Discus	243 ft.	Juergen Schult	E. Germany	June 6, 1986	E. Germany
Javelin	313 ft., 10 in.	Jan Zelezny	Czech Rep.	Aug. 29, 1993	Sheffield, England
16 lb. hammer	284 ft., 7 in.	Yuri Sedykh	USSR	Aug. 30, 1986	Stuttgart
Decathlon	8,891 pts.	Dan O'Brien	U.S.	Sept. 4-5, 1992	Talence, France

Women's Records

Running

Event	Record	Holder	Country	Date	Where made
100 meters	**10.49 s.**	Florence Griffith Joyner	U.S.	July 16, 1988	Indianapolis
200 meters	**21.34 s.**	Florence Griffith Joyner	U.S.	Sept. 29, 1988	Seoul
400 meters	**47.60 s.**	Marita Koch	E. Germany	Oct. 6, 1985	Canberra
800 meters	**1 m., 53.28 s.**	Maria Mutola	Mozambique	Aug. 25, 1995	Brussels
1,000 meters	**2 m., 29.34 s.**	Christine Wachtel	E. Germany	Aug. 17, 1990	Berlin
1,500 meters	**3 m., 50.46 s.**	Qu Yunxia	China	Sept. 11, 1993	Beijing
1 mile	**4 m., 15.61 s.**	Paula Ivan	Romania	July 10, 1989	Nice, France
2,000 meters	**5 m., 25.36 s.**	Sonia O'Sullivan	Ireland	July 9, 1994	Edinburgh
3,000 meters	**8 m., 06.11 s.**	Wang Junxia	China	Sept. 13, 1993	Beijing
5,000 meters	**14 m., 37.33 s.**	Ingrid Kristiansen	Norway	Aug. 5, 1986	Stockholm
10,000 meters	**29 m., 31.78 s.**	Wang Junxia	China	Sept. 8, 1993	Beijing
Marathon	**2 h., 21 m., 06 s.**	Ingrid Kristiansen	Norway	Apr. 21, 1985	London

Hurdles

Event	Record	Holder	Country	Date	Where made
100 meters	**12.21 s.**	Yordanka Donkova	Bulgaria	Aug. 21, 1988	Bulgaria
400 meters	**52.61 s.**	Kim Batten	U.S.	Aug. 11, 1995	Göteborg, Sweden

Field Events

Event	Record	Holder	Country	Date	Where made
High jump	**6 ft., 10¼ in.**	Stefka Kostadinova	Bulgaria	Aug. 30, 1987	Rome
Long jump	**24 ft., 8¼ in.**	Galina Chistyakova	USSR	June 11, 1988	Leningrad
Triple jump	**50 ft., 10¼ in.**	Inessa Kravets	Ukraine	Aug. 8, 1995	Göteborg, Sweden
Pole vault	**13 ft., 10¾ in.**	Daniela Bartova	Czech Republic	Sept. 11, 1995	Hungary
Shot put	**74 ft., 3 in.**	Natalya Lisovskaya	USSR	June 7, 1987	Moscow
Discus	**252 ft.**	Gabriele Reinsch	E. Germany	July 9, 1988	E. Germany
Javelin	**262 ft., 5 in.**	Petra Felke	E. Germany	Sept. 9, 1988	E. Germany
Heptathlon	**7,291 pts.**	Jackie Joyner-Kersee	U.S.	Sept. 23-24, 1988	Seoul

Relay Races

Event	Record	Holder	Country	Date	Where made
400 mtrs. (4×100)	**41.37 s.**	National team	E. Germany	Oct. 6, 1985	Canberra
800 mtrs. (4×200)	**1 m., 28.15 s.**	National team	E. Germany	Aug. 9, 1980	E. Germany
1,600 mtrs. (4×400)	**3 m., 15.17 s.**	National team	USSR	Oct. 1, 1988	Seoul
3,200 mtrs. (4×800)	**7 m., 50.17 s.**	National team	USSR	Aug. 5, 1984	Moscow

World Track and Field Indoor Records

As of Oct. 1, 1995

The International Amateur Athletic Federation began recognizing world indoor track and field records as official on Jan. 1, 1987. Prior to that, there were only unofficial world indoor bests. World indoor bests set prior to Jan. 1, 1987, are subject to approval as world records providing they meet the prescribed IAAF world records criteria, including drug testing. To be accepted as a world indoor record, a performance must meet the same criteria as a world record outdoors except that a track performance cannot be set on an indoor track larger than 200 meters. *Record pending.

Men

Event	Record	Holder	Country	Date	Where made
50 meters	**5.61**	Manfred Kokot	E. Germany	Feb. 4, 1973	E. Berlin
		James Sanford	U.S.	Feb. 20, 1981	San Diego
60 meters	**6.41**	Andre Cason	U.S.	Feb. 14, 1992	Madrid
200 meters	**20.36**	Bruno Marie-Rose	France	Feb. 22, 1987	Lievin, France
400 meters	**45.02**	Danny Everett	U.S.	Feb. 2, 1992	Stuttgart
800 meters	**1:44.84**	Paul Ereng	Kenya	Mar. 4, 1989	Budapest
1,000 meters	**2:15.26**	Noureddine Morceli	Algeria	Feb. 22, 1992	Birmingham, England
1,500 meters	**3:34.16**	Noureddine Morceli	Algeria	Feb. 28, 1991	Seville, Spain
1 mile	**3:49.78**	Eamonn Coghlan	Ireland	Feb. 27, 1983	E. Rutherford, N.J.
3,000 meters	**7:37.31**	Moses Kiptanui	Kenya	Feb. 20, 1992	Seville, Spain
5,000 meters	**13:20.40**	Suleiman Nyambui	Tanzania	Feb. 6, 1981	New York
50-meter hurdles	**6.25**	Mark McKoy	Canada	Mar. 5, 1986	Kobe, Japan
60-meter hurdles	***7.30**	Colin Jackson	Gr. Britain	Mar. 6, 1994	Germany
High jump	**7 ft., 11¼ in.**	Javier Sotomayor	Cuba	Mar. 4, 1989	Budapest
Pole vault	**20 ft., 2 in.**	Sergei Bubka	Ukraine	Feb. 21, 1993	Ukraine
Long jump	**28 ft., 10¼ in.**	Carl Lewis	U.S.	Jan. 27, 1984	New York
Triple jump	***58 ft., 3¾ in.**	Leonid Voloshin	Russia	Feb. 6, 1994	Grenoble, France
Shot put	**74 ft., 4¼ in.**	Randy Barnes	U.S.	Jan. 20, 1989	Los Angeles

Women

Event	Record	Holder	Country	Date	Where made
50 meters	**6.00**	Merlene Ottey	Jamaica	Feb. 4, 1994	Moscow
60 meters	**6.92**	Irina Privalova	Russia	Feb. 11, 1993	Madrid
200 meters	**21.87**	Merlene Ottey	Jamaica	Feb. 13, 1993	Lievin, France
400 meters	**49.59**	Jarmila Kratochvilova	Czechoslovakia	Mar. 7, 1982	Milan
800 meters	**1:56.40**	Christine Wachtel	E. Germany	Feb. 13, 1988	Vienna
1,000 meters	**2:34.8**	Brigitte Kraus	W. Germany	Feb. 19, 1978	W. Germany
1,500 meters	**4:00.27**	Doina Melinte	Romania	Feb. 9, 1990	E. Rutherford, N.J.
1 mile	**4:17.14**	Doina Melinte	Romania	Feb. 9, 1990	E. Rutherford, N.J.
3,000 meters	**8:33.82**	Elly van Hulst	Netherlands	Mar. 4, 1989	Budapest
5,000 meters	**15:03.17**	Liz McColgan	Gr. Britain	Feb. 22, 1992	Birmingham, England
50-meter hurdles	**6:58**	Cornelia Oschkenat	E. Germany	Feb. 20, 1988	Berlin
60-meter hurdles	**7.69**	Lyudmila Narozhilenko	USSR	Feb 4, 1990	Chelyabinsk, USSR
High jump	**6 ft., 9½ in.**	Heike Henkel	Germany	Feb. 8, 1992	Germany
Long jump	**24 ft., 2¼ in.**	Heike Drechsler	E. Germany	Feb. 13, 1988	Vienna
Triple jump	***48 ft., 10¾ in.**	Inna Lasovskaya	Russia	Feb. 13, 1994	Lievin, France
Shot put	**73 ft., 10 in.**	Helena Fibingerova	Czechoslovakia	Feb. 19, 1977	Czechoslovakia

NATIONAL FOOTBALL LEAGUE
1995 Preview: Franchise Shifts and Expansion Teams

Before the start of the 1995 season, Los Angeles lost both its NFL franchises. The Rams moved to St. Louis, and the Raiders returned to Oakland, where they had played from 1960 to 1981. Two expansion teams began play in 1995: the Jacksonville Jaguars joined the Central Division of the American Football Conference, and the Carolina Panthers (based in Charlotte, NC) joined the Western Division of the National Football Conference.

Final 1994 Standings

American Football Conference

Eastern Division

	W	L	T	Pct.	Pts.	Opp.
Miami	10	6	0	.625	389	327
New England	10	6	0	.625	351	312
Indianapolis	8	8	0	.500	307	320
Buffalo	7	9	0	.438	340	356
N.Y. Jets	6	10	0	.375	264	320

Central Division

	W	L	T	Pct.	Pts.	Opp.
Pittsburgh	12	4	0	.750	316	234
Cleveland	11	5	0	.688	340	204
Cincinnati	3	13	0	.188	276	406
Houston	2	14	0	.125	226	352

Western Division

	W	L	T	Pct.	Pts.	Opp.
San Diego	11	5	0	.688	381	306
Kansas City	9	7	0	.563	319	298
L.A. Raiders	9	7	0	.563	303	327
Denver	7	9	0	.438	347	396
Seattle	6	10	0	.375	287	323

National Football Conference

Eastern Division

	W	L	T	Pct.	Pts.	Opp.
Dallas	12	4	0	.750	414	248
N.Y. Giants	9	7	0	.563	279	305
Arizona	8	8	0	.500	235	267
Philadelphia	7	9	0	.438	308	308
Washington	3	13	0	.188	320	412

Central Division

	W	L	T	Pct.	Pts.	Opp.
Minnesota	10	6	0	.625	356	314
Detroit	9	7	0	.563	357	342
Green Bay	9	7	0	.563	382	287
Chicago	9	7	0	.563	271	307
Tampa Bay	6	10	0	.375	251	351

Western Division

	W	L	T	Pct.	Pts.	Opp.
San Francisco	13	3	0	.813	505	296
New Orleans	7	9	0	.438	348	407
Atlanta	7	9	0	.438	313	389
L.A. Rams	4	12	0	.250	286	365

AFC Playoffs—Miami 27, Kansas City 17; Cleveland 20, New England 13; Pittsburgh 29, Cleveland 9; San Diego 22, Miami 21; San Diego 17, Pittsburgh 13.
NFC Playoffs—Green Bay 16, Detroit 12; Chicago 35, Minnesota 18; San Francisco 44, Chicago 15; Dallas 35, Green Bay 9; San Francisco 38, Dallas 28.
Super Bowl—San Francisco 49, San Diego 26.

National Football League Champions

Year	East Winner (W-L-T)	West Winner (W-L-T)	Playoff
1933	New York Giants (11-3-0)	Chicago Bears (10-2-1)	Chicago Bears 23, New York 21
1934	New York Giants (8-5-0)	Chicago Bears (13-0-0)	New York 30, Chicago Bears 13
1935	New York Giants (9-3-0)	Detroit Lions (7-3-2)	Detroit 26, New York 7
1936	Boston Redskins (7-5-0)	Green Bay Packers (10-1-1)	Green Bay 21, Boston 6
1937	Washington Redskins (8-3-0)	Chicago Bears (9-1-1)	Washington 28, Chicago Bears 21
1938	New York Giants (8-2-1)	Green Bay Packers (8-3-0)	New York 23, Green Bay 17
1939	New York Giants (9-1-1)	Green Bay Packers (9-2-0)	Green Bay 27, New York 0
1940	Washington Redskins (9-2-0)	Chicago Bears (8-3-0)	Chicago Bears 73, Washington 0
1941	New York Giants (8-3-0)	Chicago Bears (10-1-1)(a)	Chicago Bears 37, New York 9
1942	Wash. Redskins (10-1-1)	Chicago Bears (11-0-0)	Washington 14, Chicago Bears 6
1943	Wash. Redskins (6-3-1)(a)	Chicago Bears (8-1-1)	Chicago Bears, 41, Washington 21
1944	New York Giants (8-1-1)	Green Bay Packers (8-2-0)	Green Bay 14, New York 7
1945	Wash. Redskins (8-2-0)	Cleveland Rams (9-1-0)	Cleveland 15, Washington 14
1946	New York Giants (7-3-1)	Chicago Bears (8-2-1)	Chicago Bears 24, New York 14
1947	Philadelphia Eagles (8-4-0)(a)	Chicago Cardinals (9-3-0)	Chicago Cardinals 28, Philadelphia 21
1948	Philadelphia Eagles (9-2-1)	Chicago Cardinals (11-1-0)	Philadelphia 7, Chicago Cardinals 0
1949	Philadelphia Eagles (11-1-0)	Los Angeles Rams (8-2-2)	Philadelphia 14, Los Angeles 0
1950	Cleveland Browns (10-2-0)(a)	Los Angeles Rams (9-3-0)(a)	Cleveland 30, Los Angeles 28
1951	Cleveland Browns (11-1-0)	Los Angeles Rams (8-4-0)	Los Angeles 24, Cleveland 17
1952	Cleveland Browns (8-4-0)	Detroit Lions (9-3-0)(a)	Detroit 17, Cleveland 7
1953	Cleveland Browns (11-1-0)	Detroit Lions (10-2-0)	Detroit 17, Cleveland 16
1954	Cleveland Browns (9-3-0)	Detroit Lions (9-2-1)	Cleveland 56, Detroit 10
1955	Cleveland Browns (9-2-1)	Los Angeles Rams (8-3-1)	Cleveland 38, Los Angeles 14
1956	New York Giants (8-3-1)	Chicago Bears (9-2-1)	New York 47, Chicago Bears 7
1957	Cleveland Browns (9-2-1)	Detroit Lions (8-4-0)(a)	Detroit 59, Cleveland 14
1958	New York Giants (9-3-0)(a)	Baltimore Colts (9-3-0)	Baltimore 23, New York 17(b)
1959	New York Giants (10-2-0)	Baltimore Colts (9-3-0)	Baltimore 31, New York 16
1960	Philadelphia Eagles (10-2-0)	Green Bay Packers (8-4-0)	Philadelphia 17, Green Bay 13
1961	New York Giants (10-3-1)	Green Bay Packers (11-3-0)	Green Bay 37, New York 0
1962	New York Giants (12-2-0)	Green Bay Packers (13-1-0)	Green Bay 16, New York 7
1963	New York Giants (11-3-0)	Chicago Bears (11-1-2)	Chicago 14, New York 10
1964	Cleveland Browns (10-3-1)	Baltimore Colts (12-2-0)	Cleveland 27, Baltimore 0
1965	Cleveland Browns (11-3-0)	Green Bay Packers (10-3-1)(a)	Green Bay 23, Cleveland 12
1966	Dallas Cowboys (10-3-1)	Green Bay Packers (12-2-0)	Green Bay 34, Dallas 27

(a) Won divisional playoff. (b) Won at 8:15 of sudden death overtime period.

Year	Conference	Division	Winner (W-L-T)	Playoff
1967	East	Century	Cleveland (9-5-0)	Dallas 52, Cleveland 14
		Capitol	Dallas (9-5-0)	
	West	Central	Green Bay (9-4-1)	Green Bay 28, Los Angeles 7
		Coastal	Los Angeles (11-1-2)(a)	Green Bay 21, Dallas 17
1968	East	Century	Cleveland (10-4-0)	Cleveland 31, Dallas 20
		Capitol	Dallas (12-2-0)	
	West	Central	Minnesota (8-6-0)	Baltimore 24, Minnesota 14
		Coastal	Baltimore (13-1-0)	Baltimore 34, Cleveland 0

(continued)

Year	Conference	Division	Winner (W-L-T)	Playoff
1969	East	Century	Cleveland (10-3-1)	Cleveland 38, Dallas 14
		Capitol	Dallas (11-2-1)	
	West	Central	Minnesota (12-2-0)	Minnesota 23, Los Angeles 20
		Coastal	Los Angeles (11-3-0)	Minnesota 27, Cleveland 7
1970	American	Eastern	Baltimore (11-2-1)	Baltimore 17, Cincinnati 0
		Central	Cincinnati (8-6-0)	Oakland 21, Miami 14
		Western	Oakland (8-4-2)	Baltimore 27, Oakland 17
	National	Eastern	Dallas (10-4-0)	Dallas 5, Detroit 0
		Central	Minnesota (12-2-0)	San Francisco 17, Minnesota 14
		Western	San Francisco (10-3-1)	Dallas 17, San Francisco 10
1971	American	Eastern	Miami (10-3-1)	Miami 27, Kansas City 24
		Central	Cleveland (9-5-0)	Baltimore 20, Cleveland 3
		Western	Kansas City (10-3-1)	Miami 21, Baltimore 0
	National	Eastern	Dallas (11-3-0)	Dallas 20, Minnesota 12
		Central	Minnesota (11-3-0)	San Francisco 24, Washington 20
		Western	San Francisco (9-5-0)	Dallas 14, San Francisco 3
1972	American	Eastern	Miami (14-0-0)	Miami 20, Cleveland 14
		Central	Pittsburgh (11-3-0)	Pittsburgh 13, Oakland 7
		Western	Oakland (10-3-1)	Miami 21, Pittsburgh 17
	National	Eastern	Washington (11-3-0)	Washington 16, Green Bay 3
		Central	Green Bay (10-4-0)	Dallas 30, San Francisco 28
		Western	San Francisco (8-5-1)	Washington 26, Dallas 3
1973	American	Eastern	Miami (12-2-0)	Miami 34, Cincinnati 16
		Central	Cincinnati (10-4-0)	Oakland 33, Pittsburgh 14
		Western	Oakland (9-4-1)	Miami 27, Oakland 10
	National	Eastern	Dallas (10-4-0)	Dallas 27, Los Angeles 16
		Central	Minnesota (12-2-0)	Minnesota 27, Washington 20
		Western	Los Angeles (12-2-0)	Minnesota 27, Dallas 10
1974	American	Eastern	Miami (11-3-0)	Oakland 28, Miami 26
		Central	Pittsburgh (10-3-1)	Pittsburgh 32, Buffalo 14
		Western	Oakland (12-2-0)	Pittsburgh 24, Oakland 13
	National	Eastern	St. Louis (10-4-0)	Minnesota 30, St. Louis 14
		Central	Minnesota (10-4-0)	Los Angeles 19, Washington 10
		Western	Los Angeles (10-4-0)	Minnesota 14, Los Angeles 10
1975	American	Eastern	Baltimore (10-4-0)	Pittsburgh 28, Baltimore 10
		Central	Pittsburgh (12-2-0)	Oakland 31, Cincinnati 28
		Western	Oakland (11-3-0)	Pittsburgh 16, Oakland 10
	National	Eastern	St. Louis (11-3-0)	Dallas 17, Minnesota 14
		Central	Minnesota (12-2-0)	Los Angeles 35, St. Louis 23
		Western	Los Angeles (12-2-0)	Dallas 37, Los Angeles 7
1976	American	Eastern	Baltimore (11-3-0)	Pittsburgh 40, Baltimore 14
		Central	Pittsburgh (10-4-0)	Oakland 24, New England 21
		Western	Oakland (13-1-0)	Oakland 24, Pittsburgh 7
	National	Eastern	Dallas (11-3-0)	Minnesota 35, Washington 20
		Central	Minnesota (11-2-1)	Los Angeles 14, Dallas 12
		Western	Los Angeles (10-3-1)	Minnesota 24, Los Angeles 13
1977	American	Eastern	Baltimore (10-4-0)	Oakland 37, Baltimore 31
		Central	Pittsburgh (9-5-0)	Denver 34, Pittsburgh 21
		Western	Denver (12-2-0)	Dallas 37, Chicago 7
	National	Eastern	Dallas (12-2-0)	Minnesota 14, Los Angeles 7
		Central	Minnesota (9-5-0)	Denver 20, Oakland 17
		Western	Los Angeles (10-4-0)	Dallas 23, Minnesota 6
1978	American	Eastern	New England (11-5-0)	Pittsburgh 33, Denver 10
		Central	Pittsburgh (14-2-0)	Houston 31, New England 14
		Western	Denver (10-6-0)	Pittsburgh 34, Houston 5
	National	Eastern	Dallas (12-4-0)	Dallas 27, Atlanta 20
		Central	Minnesota (8-7-1)	Los Angeles 34, Minnesota 10
		Western	Los Angeles (12-4-0)	Dallas 28, Los Angeles 0
1979	American	Eastern	Miami (10-6-0)	Houston 17, San Diego 14
		Central	Pittsburgh (12-4-0)	Pittsburgh 34, Miami 14
		Western	San Diego (12-4-0)	Pittsburgh 27, Houston 13
	National	Eastern	Dallas (11-5-0)	Tampa Bay 24, Philadelphia 17
		Central	Tampa Bay (10-6-0)	Los Angeles 21, Dallas 19
		Western	Los Angeles (9-7-0)	Los Angeles 9, Tampa Bay 0
1980	American	Eastern	Buffalo (11-5-0)	San Diego 20, Buffalo 14
		Central	Cleveland (11-5-0)	Oakland 14, Cleveland 12
		Western	San Diego (11-5-0)	Oakland 34, San Diego 27
	National	Eastern	Philadelphia (12-4-0)	Philadelphia 31, Minnesota 16
		Central	Minnesota (9-7-0)	Dallas 30, Atlanta 27
		Western	Atlanta (12-4-0)	Philadelphia 20, Dallas 7
1981	American	Eastern	Miami (11-4-1)	San Diego 41, Miami 38
		Central	Cincinnati (12-4-0)	Cincinnati 28, Buffalo 21
		Western	San Diego (10-6-0)	Cincinnati 27, San Diego 7
	National	Eastern	Dallas (12-4-0)	Dallas 38, Tampa Bay 0
		Central	Tampa Bay (9-7-0)	San Francisco 38, N.Y. Giants 24
		Western	San Francisco (13-3-0)	San Francisco 28, Dallas 27
1982	American		L.A. Raiders (8-1-0)	
	National		Washington (8-1-0)	Strike-shortened season

AFC playoffs—Mia. 28, N.E. 13; L.A. Raiders 27, Cleve. 10; N.Y. Jets 44, Cin. 17; S.D. 31, Pitt. 28; N.Y. Jets 17, L.A. Raiders 14; Mia. 34, S.D. 13; Mia. 14, N.Y. Jets 0. **NFC playoffs**—Wash. 31, Det. 7; G.B. 41, St.L. 16; Dal. 30, T.B. 17; Minn. 30, Atl. 24; Wash. 21, Minn. 7; Dal. 37, G.B. 26; Wash. 31, Dal. 17.

Year	Conference	Division	Winner (W-L-T)	Playoff
1983	American	Eastern	Miami (12-4-0)	Seattle 27, Miami 20
		Central	Pittsburgh (10-6-0)	L.A. Raiders 38, Pittsburgh 10
		Western	L.A. Raiders (12-4-0)	L.A. Raiders 30, Seattle 14
	National	Eastern	Washington (14-2-0)	Washington 51, L.A. Rams 7
		Central	Detroit (9-7-0)	San Francisco 24, Detroit 23
		Western	San Francisico (10-6-0)	Washington 24, San Francisco 21

Year	Conference	Division	Winner (W-L-T)	Playoff
1984	American	Eastern	Miami (14-2-0)	Miami 31, Seattle 10
		Central	Pittsburgh (9-7-0)	Pittsburgh 24, Denver 17
		Western	Denver (13-3-0)	Miami 45, Pittsburgh 28
	National	Eastern	Washington (11-5-0)	Chicago 23, Washington 19
		Central	Chicago (10-6-0)	San Francisco 21, N.Y. Giants 10
		Western	San Francisco (15-1-0)	San Francisco 23, Chicago 0
1985	American	Eastern	Miami (12-4-0)	New England 27, L.A. Raiders 20
		Central	Cleveland (8-8-0)	Miami 24, Cleveland 21
		Western	L.A. Raiders (12-4-0)	New England 31, Miami 14
	National	Eastern	Dallas (10-6-0)	Chicago 21, N.Y. Giants 0
		Central	Chicago (15-1-0)	L.A. Rams 20, Dallas 0
		Western	L.A. Rams (11-5-0)	Chicago 24, L.A. Rams 0
1986	American	Eastern	New England (11-5-0)	Denver 22, New England 17
		Central	Cleveland (12-4-0)	Cleveland 23, N.Y. Jets 20
		Western	Denver (11-5-0)	Denver 23, Cleveland 20
	National	Eastern	N.Y. Giants (14-2-0)	N.Y. Giants 49, San Francisco 3
		Central	Chicago (14-2-0)	Washington 27, Chicago 13
		Western	San Francisco (10-5-1)	N.Y. Giants 17, Washington 0
1987	American	Eastern	Indianapolis (9-6-0)	Cleveland 38, Indianapolis 21
		Central	Cleveland (10-5-0)	Denver 34, Houston 10
		Western	Denver (10-4-1)	Denver 38, Cleveland 33
	National	Eastern	Washington (11-4-0)	Washington 21, Chicago 17
		Central	Chicago (11-4-0)	Minnesota 36, San Francisco 24
		Western	San Francisco (13-2-0)	Washington 17, Minnesota 10
1988	American	Eastern	Buffalo (12-4-0)	Buffalo 17, Houston 10
		Central	Cincinnati (12-4-0)	Cincinnati 21, Seattle 13
		Western	Seattle (9-7-0)	Cincinnati 21, Buffalo 10
	National	Eastern	Philadelphia (10-6-0)	Chicago 20, Philadelphia 12
		Central	Chicago (12-4-0)	San Francisco 34, Minnesota 9
		Western	San Francisco (10-6-0)	San Francisco 28, Chicago 3
1989	American	Eastern	Buffalo (9-7-0)	Cleveland 34, Buffalo 30
		Central	Cleveland (9-6-1)	Denver 24, Pittsburgh 23
		Western	Denver (11-5-0)	Denver 37, Cleveland 21
	National	Eastern	N.Y. Giants (12-4-0)	San Francisco 41, Minnesota 13
		Central	Minnesota (10-6-0)	L.A. Rams 19, N.Y. Giants 13
		Western	San Francisco (14-2-0)	San Francisco 30, L.A. Rams 3
1990	American	Eastern	Buffalo (13-3-0)	L.A. Raiders 20, Cincinnati 10
		Central	Cincinnati (9-7-0)	Buffalo 44, Miami 34
		Western	L.A. Raiders (12-4-0)	Buffalo 51, L.A. Raiders 3
	National	Eastern	N.Y. Giants (13-3-0)	San Francisco 28, Washington 10
		Central	Chicago (11-5-0)	N.Y. Giants 31, Chicago 3
		Western	San Francisco (14-2-0)	N.Y. Giants 15, San Francisco 13
1991	American	Eastern	Buffalo (13-3-0)	Denver 26, Houston 24
		Central	Houston (11-5-0)	Buffalo 37, Kansas City 14
		Western	Denver (12-4-0)	Buffalo 10, Denver 7
	National	Eastern	Washington (14-2-0)	Washington 24, Atlanta 7
		Central	Detroit (12-4-0)	Detroit 38, Dallas 6
		Western	New Orleans (11-5-0)	Washington 41, Detroit 10
1992	American	Eastern	Miami (11-5-0)	Miami 31, San Diego 0
		Central	Pittsburgh (11-5-0)	Buffalo 24, Pittsburgh 3
		Western	San Diego (11-5-0)	Buffalo 29, Miami 10
	National	Eastern	Dallas (13-3-0)	Dallas 34, Philadelphia 10
		Central	Minnesota (11-5-0)	San Francisco 20, Washington 13
		Western	San Francisco (14-2-0)	Dallas 30, San Francisco 20
1993	American	Eastern	Buffalo (12-4-0)	Buffalo 29, L.A. Raiders 23
		Central	Houston (12-4-0)	Kansas City 28, Houston 20
		Western	Kansas City (11-5-0)	Buffalo 30, Kansas City 13
	National	Eastern	Dallas (12-4-0)	Dallas 27, Green Bay 17
		Central	Detroit (10-6-0)	San Francisco 44, N.Y. Giants 3
		Western	San Francisco (10-6-0)	Dallas 38, San Francisco 21
1994	American	Eastern	Miami (10-6-0)	Pittsburgh 29, Cleveland 9
		Central	Pittsburgh (12-4-0)	San Diego 22, Miami 21
		Western	San Diego (11-5-0)	San Diego 17, Pittsburgh 13
	National	Eastern	Dallas (12-4-0)	San Francisco 44, Chicago 15
		Central	Minnesota (10-6-0)	Dallas 35, Green Bay 9
		Western	San Francisco (13-3-0)	San Francisco 38, Dallas 28

NFL Head Coaches at Start of 1995 Season

AFC

Buffalo—Marv Levy
Cincinnati—David Shula
Cleveland—Bill Belichick
Denver—Mike Shanahan
Houston—Jeff Fisher
Indianapolis—Ted Marchibroda
Jacksonville—Jeff Coughlin

Kansas City—Marty Schottenheimer
Miami—Don Shula
New England—Bill Parcells
N.Y. Jets—Rich Kotite
Oakland—Mike White
Pittsburgh—Bill Cowher
San Diego—Bobby Ross
Seattle—Dennis Erickson

NFC

Arizona—Buddy Ryan
Atlanta—June Jones
Carolina—Dom Capers
Chicago—Dave Wannstedt
Dallas—Barry Switzer
Detroit—Wayne Fontes
Green Bay—Mike Holmgren
Minnesota—Dennis Green

New Orleans—Jim Mora
N.Y. Giants—Dan Reeves
Philadelphia—Ray Rhodes
St. Louis—Rich Brooks
San Francisco—George Seifert
Tampa Bay—Sam Wyche
Washington—Norv Turner

49ers Defeat Chargers in Super Bowl

The San Francisco 49ers scored early and often and defeated the San Diego Chargers 49-26 in Super Bowl XXIX on Jan. 29, 1995, in Miami. San Francisco scored its first touchdown 1:24 into the game and widened a 28-10 halftime lead to 42-10 on the way to the rout. The 49ers became the first team to win the Super Bowl 5 times. Quarterback Steve Young threw a Super Bowl record 6 touchdown passes, breaking Joe Montana's mark of 5, and was named the game's MVP.

Score by Quarters

San Diego	7	3	8	8—26
San Francisco	14	14	14	7—49

Scoring

San Francisco—Rice, 44 yd pass from Young (Brien kick)
San Francisco—Watters, 51 yd pass from Young (Brien kick)
San Diego—Means, 1 yd run (Carney kick)
San Francisco—Floyd, 5 yd pass from Young (Brien kick)
San Francisco—Watters, 8 yd pass from Young (Brien kick)
San Diego—Carney, 31 yd field goal
San Francisco—Watters, 9 yd run (Brien kick)
San Francisco—Rice, 15 yd pass from Young (Brien kick)
San Diego—Coleman, 98 yd kickoff return (Seay, pass from Humphries for 2 points)
San Francisco—Rice, 7 yd pass from Young (Brien kick)
San Diego—Martin, 30 yd pass from Humphries (Pupunu, pass from Humphries for 2 points)

Individual Statistics

Rushing —San Diego, Means 13-33, Jefferson 1-10, Harmon 2-10, Gilbert 1-8, Bieniemy 1-3, Humphries 1-3. San Francisco, Young 5-49, Watters 15-47, Floyd 9-32, Rice 1-10, Carter 2 for minus 5.

Passing —San Diego, Humphries 24-49-2-275, Gilbert 3-6-1-30. San Francisco, Young 24-36-0-325, Grbac 0-1-0-0, Musgrave 1-1-0-6.

Receiving —San Diego, Harmon 8-68, Seay 7-75, Pupunu 4-48, Martin 3-59, Jefferson 2-15, Bieniemy 1-33, Means 1-4, Young 1-3. San Francisco, Rice 10-149, Taylor 4-43, Floyd 4-26, Watters 3-61, Jones 2-41, Popson 1-6, McCaffrey 1-5.

Team Statistics

	Chargers	49ers
First downs	20	28
Rushes-yards	19-67	32-133
Passing yards	287	316
Punt returns-yards	3-1	2-12
Kickoff returns-yards	8-242	4-48
Interception returns-yards. . . .	0-0	3-16
Comp.-att.-int.	27-55-3	25-38-0
Sacked-yards lost	2-18	3-15
Punts-average.	4-49	5-40
Fumbles-lost	1-0	2-0
Penalties-yards	6-63	3-18
Time of possession	28:29	31:31

Super Bowls

	Year	Winner	Loser	Winning coach	Site
I	1967	Green Bay Packers, 35	Kansas City Chiefs, 10	Vince Lombardi	Los Angeles Coliseum
II	1968	Green Bay Packers, 33	Oakland Raiders, 14	Vince Lombardi	Orange Bowl, Miami
III	1969	New York Jets, 16	Baltimore Colts, 7	Weeb Ewbank	Orange Bowl, Miami
IV	1970	Kansas City Chiefs, 23	Minnesota Vikings, 7	Hank Stram	Tulane Stadium, New Orleans
V	1971	Baltimore Colts, 16	Dallas Cowboys, 13	Don McCafferty	Orange Bowl, Miami
VI	1972	Dallas Cowboys, 24	Miami Dolphins, 3	Tom Landry	Tulane Stadium, New Orleans
VII	1973	Miami Dolphins, 14	Washington Redskins, 7	Don Shula	Los Angeles Coliseum
VIII	1974	Miami Dolphins, 24	Minnesota Vikings, 7	Don Shula	Rice Stadium, Houston
IX	1975	Pittsburgh Steelers, 16	Minnesota Vikings, 6	Chuck Noll	Tulane Stadium, New Orleans
X	1976	Pittsburgh Steelers, 21	Dallas Cowboys, 17	Chuck Noll	Orange Bowl, Miami
XI	1977	Oakland Raiders, 32	Minnesota Vikings, 14	John Madden	Rose Bowl, Pasadena
XII	1978	Dallas Cowboys, 27	Denver Broncos, 10	Tom Landry	Superdome, New Orleans
XIII	1979	Pittsburgh Steelers, 35	Dallas Cowboys, 31	Chuck Noll	Orange Bowl, Miami
XIV	1980	Pittsburgh Steelers, 31	Los Angeles Rams, 19	Chuck Noll	Rose Bowl, Pasadena
XV	1981	Oakland Raiders, 27	Philadelphia Eagles, 10	Tom Flores	Superdome, New Orleans
XVI	1982	San Francisco 49ers, 26	Cincinnati Bengals, 21	Bill Walsh	Silverdome, Pontiac, Mich.
XVII	1983	Washington Redskins, 27	Miami Dolphins, 17	Joe Gibbs	Rose Bowl, Pasadena
XVIII	1984	Los Angeles Raiders, 38	Washington Redskins, 9	Tom Flores	Tampa Stadium
XIX	1985	San Francisco 49ers, 38	Miami Dolphins, 16	Bill Walsh	Stanford Stadium, Palo Alto, Cal.
XX	1986	Chicago Bears, 46	New England Patriots, 10	Mike Ditka	Superdome, New Orleans
XXI	1987	New York Giants, 39	Denver Broncos, 20	Bill Parcells	Rose Bowl, Pasadena
XXII	1988	Washington Redskins, 42	Denver Broncos, 10	Joe Gibbs	San Diego Stadium
XXIII	1989	San Francisco 49ers, 20	Cincinnati Bengals, 16	Bill Walsh	Joe Robbie Stadium, Miami
XXIV	1990	San Francisco 49ers, 55	Denver Broncos, 10	George Seifert	Superdome, New Orleans
XXV	1991	New York Giants, 20	Buffalo Bills, 19	Bill Parcells	Tampa Stadium
XXVI	1992	Washington Redskins, 37	Buffalo Bills, 24	Joe Gibbs	Metrodome, Minneapolis
XXVII	1993	Dallas Cowboys, 52	Buffalo Bills, 17	Jimmy Johnson	Rose Bowl, Pasadena
XXVIII	1994	Dallas Cowboys, 30	Buffalo Bills, 13	Jimmy Johnson	Georgia Dome, Atlanta
XXIX	1995	San Francisco, 49	San Diego, 26	George Seifert	Joe Robbie Stadium, Miami

Super Bowl MVPs

1967	Bart Starr, Green Bay	1977	Fred Biletnikoff, Oakland	1987	Phil Simms, N.Y. Giants
1968	Bart Starr, Green Bay	1978	Randy White, Harvey Martin, Dallas	1988	Doug Williams, Washington
1969	Joe Namath, N.Y. Jets	1979	Terry Bradshaw, Pittsburgh	1989	Jerry Rice, San Francisco
1970	Len Dawson, Kansas City	1980	Terry Bradshaw, Pittsburgh	1990	Joe Montana, San Francisco
1971	Chuck Howley, Dallas	1981	Jim Plunkett, Oakland	1991	Ottis Anderson, N.Y. Giants
1972	Roger Staubach, Dallas	1982	Joe Montana, San Francisco	1992	Mark Rypien, Washington
1973	Jake Scott, Miami	1983	John Riggins, Washington	1993	Troy Aikman, Dallas
1974	Larry Csonka, Miami	1984	Marcus Allen, L.A. Raiders	1994	Emmitt Smith, Dallas
1975	Franco Harris, Pittsburgh	1985	Joe Montana, San Francisco	1995	Steve Young, San Francisco
1976	Lynn Swann, Pittsburgh	1986	Richard Dent, Chicago		

American Football League

Year	Eastern Division	Western Division	Playoff
1960	Houston Oilers (10-4-0)	L. A. Chargers (10-4-0)	Houston 24, Los Angeles 16
1961	Houston Oilers (10-3-1)	San Diego Chargers (12-2-0)	Houston 10, San Diego 3
1962	Houston Oilers (11-3-0)	Dallas Texans (11-3-0)	Dallas 20, Houston 17(b)
1963	Boston Patriots (8-6-1)(a)	San Diego Chargers (11-3-0)	San Diego 51, Boston 10
1964	Buffalo Bills (12-2-0)	San Diego Chargers (8-5-1)	Buffalo 20, San Diego 7
1965	Buffalo Bills (10-3-1)	San Diego Chargers (9-2-3)	Buffalo 23, San Diego 0
1966	Buffalo Bills (9-4-1)	Kansas City Chiefs (11-2-1)	Kansas City 31, Buffalo 7
1967	Houston Oilers (9-4-1)	Oakland Raiders (13-1-0)	Oakland 40, Houston 7
1968	New York Jets (11-3-0)	Oakland Raiders (12-2-0)(a)	New York 27, Oakland 23
1969	New York Jets (10-4-0)	Oakland Raiders (12-1-1)	Kansas City 17, Oakland 7(c)

(a) Won divisional playoff. (b) Won at 2:45 of second overtime. (c) Kansas City defeated Jets to make playoffs.

American Football Conference Leaders

(American Football League, 1960-69)

Passing / Pass-Receiving

Player, team	Atts	Com	YG	TD	Year	Player, team	Ct	YG	TD
Jack Kemp, Los Angeles	406	211	3,018	20	1960	Lionel Taylor, Denver	92	1,235	12
George Blanda, Houston	362	187	3,330	36	1961	Lionel Taylor, Denver	100	1,176	4
Len Dawson, Dallas	310	189	2,759	29	1962	Lionel Taylor, Denver	77	908	4
Tobin Rote, Kansas City	286	170	2,510	20	1963	Lionel Taylor, Denver	78	1,101	10
Len Dawson, Kansas City	354	199	2,879	30	1964	Charley Hennigan, Houston	101	1,546	8
John Hadl, San Diego	348	174	2,798	20	1965	Lionel Taylor, Denver	85	1,131	6
Len Dawson, Kansas City	284	159	2,527	26	1966	Lance Alworth, San Diego	73	1,383	13
Daryle Lamonica, Oakland	425	220	3,228	30	1967	George Sauer, N.Y. Jets	75	1,189	6
Len Dawson, Kansas City	224	131	2,109	17	1968	Lance Alworth, San Diego	68	1,312	10
Greg Cook, Cincinnati	197	106	1,854	15	1969	Lance Alworth, San Diego	64	1,003	4
Daryle Lamonica, Oakland	356	179	2,516	22	1970	Marlin Briscoe, Buffalo	57	1,036	8
Bob Griese, Miami	263	145	2,089	19	1971	Fred Biletnikoff, Oakland	61	929	9
Earl Morrall, Miami	150	83	1,360	11	1972	Fred Biletnikoff, Oakland	58	802	7
Ken Stabler, Oakland	260	163	1,997	14	1973	Fred Willis, Houston	57	371	1
Ken Anderson, Cincinnati	328	213	2,667	18	1974	Lydell Mitchell, Baltimore	72	544	2
Ken Anderson, Cincinnati	377	228	3,169	21	1975	Reggie Rucker, Cleveland	60	770	3
						Lydell Mitchell, Baltimore	60	554	4
Ken Stabler, Oakland	291	194	2,737	27	1976	MacArthur Lane, Kansas City	66	686	1
Bob Griese, Miami	307	180	2,252	22	1977	Lydell Mitchell, Baltimore	71	620	4
Terry Bradshaw, Pittsburgh	368	207	2,915	28	1978	Steve Largent, Seattle	71	1,168	8
Dan Fouts, San Diego	530	332	4,082	24	1979	Joe Washington, Baltimore	82	750	3
Brian Sipe, Cleveland	554	337	4,132	30	1980	Kellen Winslow, San Diego	89	1,290	9
Ken Anderson, Cincinnati	479	300	3,754	29	1981	Kellen Winslow, San Diego	88	1,075	10
Ken Anderson, Cincinnati	309	218	2,495	12	1982	Kellen Winslow, San Diego	54	721	6
Dan Marino, Miami	296	173	2,210	20	1983	Todd Christensen, L.A. Raiders	92	1,247	12
Dan Marino, Miami	564	362	5,084	48	1984	Ozzie Newsome, Cleveland	89	1,001	5
Ken O'Brien, N.Y. Jets	488	297	3,888	25	1985	Lionel James, San Diego	86	1,027	6
Dan Marino, Miami	623	378	4,746	44	1986	Todd Christensen, L.A. Raiders	95	1,153	8
Bernie Kosar, Cleveland	389	241	3,033	22	1987	Al Toon, N.Y. Jets	68	976	5
Boomer Esiason, Cincinnati	388	223	3,572	28	1988	Al Toon, N.Y. Jets	93	1,067	5
Boomer Esiason, Cincinnati	455	258	3,525	28	1989	Andre Reed, Buffalo	88	1,312	9
Jim Kelly, Buffalo	346	219	2,829	24	1990	Haywood Jeffires, Houston	74	1,048	8
						Drew Hill, Houston	74	1,019	5
Jim Kelly, Buffalo	474	304	3,844	33	1991	Haywood Jeffires, Houston	100	1,181	7
Warren Moon, Houston	346	224	2,521	18	1992	Haywood Jeffires, Houston	90	913	9
John Elway, Denver	551	348	4,030	25	1993	Reggie Langhorne, Indianapolis	85	1,038	3
Dan Marino, Miami	615	385	4,453	30	1994	Ben Coates, New England	96	1,174	7

Scoring / Rushing

Player, team	TD	PAT	FG	Pts	Year	Player, team	Yds	Atts	TD
Gene Mingo, Denver	6	33	18	123	1960	Abner Haynes, Dallas	875	156	9
Gino Cappelletti, Boston	8	48	17	147	1961	Billy Cannon, Houston	948	200	6
Gene Mingo, Denver	4	32	27	137	1962	Cookie Gilchrist, Buffalo	1,096	214	13
Gino Cappelletti, Boston	2	35	22	113	1963	Clem Daniels, Oakland	1,099	215	3
Gino Cappelletti, Boston	7	36	25	155	1964	Cookie Gilchrist, Buffalo	981	230	6
Gino Cappelletti, Boston	9	27	17	132	1965	Paul Lowe, San Diego	1,121	222	7
Gino Cappelletti, Boston	6	35	16	119	1966	Jim Nance, Boston	1,458	299	11
George Blanda, Oakland	0	56	20	116	1967	Jim Nance, Boston	1,216	269	7
Jim Turner, N.Y. Jets	0	43	34	145	1968	Paul Robinson, Cincinnati	1,023	238	8
Jim Turner, N.Y. Jets	0	33	32	129	1969	Dick Post, San Diego	873	182	6
Jan Stenerud, Kansas City	0	26	30	116	1970	Floyd Little, Denver	901	209	3
Garo Yepremian, Miami	0	33	28	117	1971	Floyd Little, Denver	1,133	284	6
Bobby Howfield, N.Y. Jets	0	40	27	121	1972	O.J. Simpson, Buffalo	1,251	292	6
Roy Gerela, Pittsburgh	0	36	29	123	1973	O.J. Simpson, Buffalo	2,003	332	12
Roy Gerela, Pittsburgh	0	33	20	93	1974	Otis Armstrong, Denver	1,407	263	9
O.J. Simpson, Buffalo	23	0	0	138	1975	O.J. Simpson, Buffalo	1,817	329	16
Toni Linhart, Baltimore	0	49	20	109	1976	O.J. Simpson, Buffalo	1,503	290	8
Errol Mann, Oakland	0	39	20	99	1977	Mark van Eeghen, Oakland	1,273	324	7
Pat Leahy, N.Y. Jets	0	41	22	107	1978	Earl Campbell, Houston	1,450	302	13
John Smith, New England	0	46	23	115	1979	Earl Campbell, Houston	1,697	368	19
John Smith, New England	0	51	26	129	1980	Earl Campbell, Houston	1,934	373	13
Jim Breech, Cincinnati	0	49	22	115	1981	Earl Campbell, Houston	1,376	361	10
Marcus Allen, L.A. Raiders	14	0	0	84	1982	Freeman McNeil, N.Y. Jets	786	151	6
Gary Anderson, Pittsburgh	0	38	27	119	1983	Curt Warner, Seattle	1,446	335	13
Gary Anderson, Pittsburgh	0	45	24	117	1984	Earnest Jackson, San Diego	1,179	296	8
Gary Anderson, Pittsburgh	0	40	33	139	1985	Marcus Allen, L.A. Raiders	1,759	380	11
Tony Franklin, New England	0	44	32	140	1986	Curt Warner, Seattle	1,481	319	13
Jim Breech, Cincinnati	0	25	24	97	1987	Eric Dickerson, L.A. Rams-Ind.	1,288*	283	6
Scott Norwood, Buffalo	0	33	32	129	1988	Eric Dickerson, Indianapolis	1,659	388	14
David Treadwell, Denver	0	39	27	120	1989	Christian Okoye, Kansas City	1,480	370	12
Nick Lowery, Kansas City	0	37	34	139	1990	Thurman Thomas, Buffalo	1,297	271	11
Pete Stoyanovich, Miami	0	28	31	121	1991	Thurman Thomas, Buffalo	1,407	288	7
Pete Stoyanovich, Miami	0	34	30	124	1992	Barry Foster, Pittsburgh	1,690	390	11
Jeff Jaeger, L.A. Raiders	0	27	35	132	1993	Thurman Thomas, Buffalo	1,315	355	6
John Carney, San Diego	0	33	34	135	1994	Chris Warren, Seattle	1,545	333	9

* 1,011 AFC yards led conference.

National Football Conference Leaders

(National Football League, 1960-69)

Passing

Player, team	Atts	Com	YG	TD
Milt Plum, Cleveland	250	151	2,297	21
Milt Plum, Cleveland	302	177	2,416	18
Bart Starr, Green Bay	285	178	2,438	12
Y.A. Tittle, N.Y. Giants	367	221	3,145	36
Bart Starr, Green Bay	272	163	2,144	15
Rudy Bukich, Chicago	312	176	2,641	20
Bart Starr, Green Bay	251	156	2,257	14
Sonny Jurgensen, Washington	508	288	3,747	31
Earl Morrall, Baltimore	317	182	2,909	26
Sonny Jurgensen, Washington	442	274	3,102	22
John Brodie, San Francisco	378	223	2,941	24
Roger Staubach, Dallas	211	126	1,882	15
Norm Snead, N.Y. Giants	325	196	2,307	17
Roger Staubach, Dallas	286	179	2,428	23
Sonny Jurgensen, Washington	167	107	1,185	11
Fran Tarkenton, Minnesota	425	273	2,294	25
James Harris, Los Angeles	158	91	1,460	8
Roger Staubach, Dallas	361	210	2,620	18
Roger Staubach, Dallas	413	231	3,190	25
Roger Staubach, Dallas	461	267	3,586	27
Ron Jaworski, Philadelphia	451	257	3,529	27
Joe Montana, San Francisco	488	311	3,565	19
Joe Thiesmann, Washington	252	161	2,033	13
Steve Bartkowski, Atlanta	423	274	3,167	22
Joe Montana, San Francisco	432	279	3,630	28
Joe Montana, San Francisco	494	303	3,653	27
Tommy Kramer, Minnesota	372	208	3,000	24
Joe Montana, San Francisco	398	266	3,054	31
Wade Wilson, Minnesota	332	204	2,746	15
Joe Montana, San Francisco	386	271	3,521	26
Phil Simms, N.Y. Giants	311	184	2,284	15
Steve Young, San Francisco	279	180	2,517	17
Steve Young, San Francisco	402	268	3,465	25
Steve Young, San Francisco	462	314	4,023	29
Steve Young, San Francisco	461	324	3,969	35

Pass-Receiving

Year	Player, team	Ct	YG	TD
1960	Raymond Berry, Baltimore	74	1,298	10
1961	Jim Phillips, L.A. Rams	78	1,092	5
1962	Bobby Mitchell, Washington	72	1,384	11
1963	Bobby Joe Conrad, St. Louis	73	967	10
1964	Johnny Morris, Chicago	93	1,200	10
1965	Dave Parks, San Francisco	80	1,344	12
1966	Charley Taylor, Washington	72	1,119	12
1967	Charley Taylor, Washington	70	990	9
1968	Clifton McNeil, San Francisco	71	994	7
1969	Dan Abramowicz, New Orleans	73	1,015	7
1970	Dick Gordon, Chicago	71	1,026	13
1971	Bob Tucker, Giants	59	791	4
1972	Harold Jackson, Philadelphia	62	1,048	4
1973	Harold Carmichael, Philadelphia	67	1,116	9
1974	Charles Young, Philadelphia	63	696	3
1975	Chuck Foreman, Minnesota	73	691	9
1976	Drew Pearson, Dallas	58	806	6
1977	Ahmad Rashad, Minnesota	51	681	2
1978	Rickey Young, Minnesota	88	704	5
1979	Ahmad Rashad, Minnesota	80	1,156	9
1980	Earl Cooper, San Francisco	83	567	4
1981	Dwight Clark, San Francisco	85	1,105	4
1982	Dwight Clark, San Francisco	60	913	5
1983	Roy Green, St. Louis	78	1,227	14
	Charlie Brown, Washington	78	1,225	8
	Earnest Gray, N.Y. Giants	78	1,139	5
1984	Art Monk, Washington	106	1,372	7
1985	Roger Craig, San Francisco	92	1,016	6
1986	Jerry Rice, San Francisco	86	1,570	15
1987	J.T. Smith, St. Louis	91	1,117	8
1988	Henry Ellard, L.A. Rams	86	1,414	10
1989	Sterling Sharpe, Green Bay	90	1,423	12
1990	Jerry Rice, San Francisco	100	1,502	13
1991	Michael Irvin, Dallas	93	1,523	8
1992	Sterling Sharpe, Green Bay	108	1,461	13
1993	Sterling Sharpe, Green Bay	112	1,274	11
1994	Cris Carter, Minnesota	122	1,256	7

Scoring

Player, team	TD	PAT	FG	Pts
Paul Hornung, Green Bay	15	41	15	176
Paul Hornung, Green Bay	10	41	15	146
Jim Taylor, Green Bay	19	0	0	114
Don Chandler, N.Y. Giants	0	52	18	106
Lenny Moore, Baltimore	20	0	0	120
Gale Sayers, Chicago	22	0	0	132
Bruce Gossett, L.A. Rams	0	29	28	113
Jim Bakken, St. Louis	0	36	27	117
Leroy Kelly, Cleveland	20	0	0	120
Fred Cox, Minnesota	0	43	26	121
Fred Cox, Minnesota	0	35	30	125
Curt Knight, Washington	0	27	29	114
Chester Marcol, Green Bay	0	29	33	128
David Ray, Los Angeles	0	40	30	130
Chester Marcol, Green Bay	0	19	25	94
Chuck Foreman, Minnesota	22	0	0	132
Mark Moseley, Washington	0	31	22	97
Walter Payton, Chicago	16	0	0	96
Frank Corrall, Los Angeles	0	31	29	118
Mark Moseley, Washington	0	39	25	114
Ed Murray, Detroit	0	35	27	116
Ed Murray, Detroit	0	46	25	121
Wendell Tyler, L.A. Rams	13	0	0	78
Mark Moseley, Washington	0	62	33	161
Ray Wersching, San Francisco	0	56	25	131
Kevin Butler, Chicago	0	51	31	144
Kevin Butler, Chicago	0	36	28	120
Jerry Rice, San Francisco	23	0	0	138
Mike Cofer, San Francisco	0	40	27	121
Mike Cofer, San Francisco	0	49	29	136
Chip Lohmiller, Washington	0	41	30	131
Chip Lohmiller, Washington	0	56	31	149
Morten Andersen, New Orleans	0	33	29	120
Chip Lohmiller, Washington	0	30	30	120
Jason Hanson, Detroit	0	28	34	130
Fuad Reveiz, Minnesota	0	30	34	132
Emmitt Smith, Dallas	22	0	0	132

Rushing

Year	Player, team	Yds	Atts	TD
1960	Jim Brown, Cleveland	1,257	215	9
1961	Jim Brown, Cleveland	1,408	305	8
1962	Jim Taylor, Green Bay	1,474	272	19
1963	Jim Brown, Cleveland	1,863	291	12
1964	Jim Brown, Cleveland	1,446	280	7
1965	Jim Brown, Cleveland	1,544	289	17
1966	Gale Sayers, Chicago	1,231	229	8
1967	Leroy Kelly, Cleveland	1,205	235	11
1968	Leroy Kelly, Cleveland	1,239	248	16
1969	Gale Sayers, Chicago	1,032	236	8
1970	Larry Brown, Washington	1,125	237	5
1971	John Brockington, Green Bay	1,105	216	4
1972	Larry Brown, Washington	1,216	285	8
1973	John Brockington, Green Bay	1,144	265	3
1974	Lawrence McCutcheon, Los Angeles	1,109	236	3
1975	Jim Otis, St. Louis	1,076	269	5
1976	Walter Payton, Chicago	1,390	311	13
1977	Walter Payton, Chicago	1,852	339	14
1978	Walter Payton, Chicago	1,395	333	11
1979	Walter Payton, Chicago	1,610	369	14
1980	Walter Payton, Chicago	1,460	317	15
1981	George Rogers, New Orleans	1,674	378	13
1982	Tony Dorsett, Dallas	745	177	5
1983	Eric Dickerson, L.A. Rams	1,808	390	18
1984	Eric Dickerson, L.A. Rams	2,105	379	14
1985	Gerald Riggs, Atlanta	1,719	397	10
1986	Eric Dickerson, L.A. Rams	1,821	404	11
1987	Charles White, L.A. Rams	1,374	324	11
1988	Herschel Walker, Dallas	1,514	361	5
1989	Barry Sanders, Detroit	1,470	280	14
1990	Barry Sanders, Detroit	1,304	255	13
1991	Emmitt Smith, Dallas	1,563	365	12
1992	Emmitt Smith, Dallas	1,713	373	18
1993	Emmitt Smith, Dallas	1,486	283	9
1994	Barry Sanders, Detroit	1,883	331	7

1994 NFL Individual Leaders

American Football Conference

Passing

	Att	Comp	Pct comp	Yds	Avg gain	TD	Pct TD	Int	Rating points
Marino, Dan, Miami	615	385	62.6	4,453	7.24	30	4.9	17	89.2
Elway, John, Denver	494	307	62.1	3,490	7.06	16	3.2	10	85.7
Kelly, Jim, Buffalo	448	285	63.6	3,114	6.95	22	4.9	17	84.6
Montana, Joe, Kansas City	493	299	60.6	3,283	6.66	16	3.2	9	83.6
Humphries, Stan, San Diego	453	264	58.3	3,209	7.08	17	3.8	12	81.6
Hostetler, Jeff, L.A. Raiders	455	263	57.8	3,334	7.33	20	4.4	16	80.8
O'Donnell, Neil, Pittsburgh	370	212	57.3	2,443	6.60	13	3.5	9	78.9
Esiason, Boomer, N.Y. Jets	440	255	58.0	2,782	6.32	17	3.9	13	77.3
Blake, Jeff, Cincinnati	306	156	51.0	2,154	7.04	14	4.6	9	76.9
Bledsoe, Drew, New England	691	400	57.9	4,555	6.59	25	3.6	27	73.6
Testaverde, Vinny, Cleveland	376	207	55.1	2,575	6.85	16	4.3	18	70.7
Mirer, Rick, Seattle	381	195	51.2	2,151	5.65	11	2.9	7	70.2

Rushing

	Att	Yds	Avg	Long	TD
Warren, Chris, Seattle	333	1,545	4.6	41	9
Means, Natrone, San Diego	343	1,350	3.9	25	12
Faulk, Marshall, Indianapolis.	314	1,282	4.1	52	11
Thomas, Thurman, Buffalo	287	1,093	3.8	29	7
Williams, Harvey, L.A. Raiders . . .	282	983	3.5	28	4
Johnson, Johnny, N.Y. Jets	240	931	3.9	90	3
Hoard, Leroy, Cleveland.	209	890	4.3	39	5
Parmalee, Bernie, Miami	216	868	4.0	42td	6
Foster, Barry, Pittsburgh	216	851	3.9	29	5
Morris, Bam, Pittsburgh	198	836	4.2	20	7

Pass Receiving

	No	Yds	Avg	Long	TD
Coates, Ben, New England.	96	1,174	12.2	62td	7
Reed, Andre, Buffalo	90	1,303	14.5	83td	6
Brown, Tim, L.A. Raiders	89	1,309	14.7	77td	9
Sharpe, Shannon, Denver	87	1,010	11.6	44	4
Blades, Brian, Seattle	81	1,086	13.4	45	4
Moore, Rob, N.Y. Jets	78	1,010	12.9	41td	6
Milburn, Glyn, Denver	77	549	7.1	33	3
Timpson, Michael, New England . .	74	941	12.7	37	3
Fryar, Irving, Miami	73	1,270	17.4	54td	7
Pickens, Carl, Cincinnati	71	1,127	15.9	70td	11

Scoring—Non-Kickers

	TD	Rush	Pass	2 Pt	Pts
Means, Natrone, San Diego . . .	12	12	0	0	72
Faulk, Marshall, Indianapolis. . .	12	11	1	0	72
Warren, Chris, Seattle	11	9	2	1	68
Pickens, Carl, Cincinnati	11	0	11	0	66
Brown, Tim, L.A. Raiders	9	0	9	0	54
Hoard, Leroy, Cleveland.	9	5	4	0	54
Russell, Leonard, Denver	9	9	0	0	54
Thomas, Thurman, Buffalo	9	7	2	0	54

Scoring—Kickers

	PAT	FG	Pts
Carney, John, San Diego	33/33	34/38	135
Elam, Jason, Denver	29/29	30/37	119
Bahr, Matt, New England	36/36	27/34	117
Stover, Matt, Cleveland	32/32	26/28	110
Christie, Steve, Buffalo.	38/38	24/28	110

Interceptions

	No	Yds	Avg	Long	TD
Turner, Eric, Cleveland	9	199	22.1	93td	1
Buchanan, Ray, Indianapolis . . .	8	221	27.6	90td	3
Hurst, Maurice, New England . . .	7	68	9.7	24	0
McDaniel, Terry, L.A. Raiders . . .	7	103	14.7	35	2
Perry, Darren, Pittsburgh	7	112	16.0	42	0

Kickoff Returns

	No	Yds	Avg	Long	TD
Baldwin, Randy, Cleveland. . .	28	753	26.9	85td	1
Coleman, Andre, San Diego . .	49	1,293	26.4	90td	2
Vaughn, Jon, Sea.-K.C.	33	829	25.1	93td	2
By'not'e, Butler, Denver	24	545	22.7	41	0
Dickerson, Ron, Kansas City . .	21	472	22.5	62	0

Punt Returns

	No	FC	Yds	Avg	Long	TD
Gordon, Darrien, San Diego .	36	19	475	14.1	78td	2
Brown, Tim, L.A. Raiders . . .	40	14	487	12.2	48	0
Sawyer, Corey, Cincinnati . . .	26	16	307	11.8	82td	1
Burris, Jeff, Buffalo	32	6	332	10.4	57	0
Metcalf, Eric, Cleveland	35	6	348	9.9	92td	2

Punting

	No	Yds	Long	Avg
Gossett, Jeff, L.A. Raiders . . .	77	3,377	65	43.9
Johnson, Lee, Cincinnati	79	3,461	64	43.8
Tuten, Rick, Seattle.	91	3,905	64	42.9
Rouen, Tom, Denver	76	3,258	59	42.9
Camarillo, Rich, Houston	96	4,115	58	42.9

Sacks

	No
Greene, Kevin, Pittsburgh	14.0
O'Neal, Leslie, San Diego	12.5
Smith, Neil, Kansas City	11.5
Mims, Chris, San Diego	11.0
Thomas, Derrick, Kansas City	11.0

National Football Conference

Passing

	Att	Comp	Pct comp	Yds	Avg gain	TD	Pct TD	Int	Rating points
Young, Steve, San Francisco	461	324	70.3	3,969	8.61	35	7.6	10	112.8
Favre, Brett, Green Bay	582	363	62.4	3,882	6.67	33	5.7	14	90.7
Everett, Jim, New Orleans	540	346	64.1	3,855	7.14	22	4.1	18	84.9
Aikman, Troy, Dallas	361	233	64.5	2,676	7.41	13	3.6	12	84.9
George, Jeff, Atlanta	524	322	61.5	3,734	7.13	23	4.4	18	83.3
Erickson, Craig, Tampa Bay	399	225	56.4	2,919	7.32	16	4.0	10	82.5
Moon, Warren, Minnesota	601	371	61.7	4,264	7.09	18	3.0	19	79.9
Walsh, Steve, Chicago.	343	208	60.6	2,078	6.06	10	2.9	8	77.9
Cunningham, Randall, Philadelphia	490	265	54.1	3,229	6.59	16	3.3	13	74.4
Miller, Chris, L.A. Rams	317	173	54.6	2,104	6.64	16	5.0	14	73.6
Brown, Dave, N.Y. Giants	350	201	57.4	2,536	7.25	12	3.4	16	72.5
Schroeder, Jay, Arizona.	238	133	55.9	1,510	6.34	4	1.7	7	68.4

(continued)

Rushing

	Att	Yds	Avg	Long	TD
Sanders, Barry, Detroit	331	1,883	5.7	85	7
Smith, Emmitt, Dallas	368	1,484	4.0	46	21
Hampton, Rodney, N.Y. Giants	327	1,075	3.3	27td	6
Allen, Terry, Minnesota	255	1,031	4.0	45	8
Bettis, Jerome, L.A. Rams	319	1,025	3.2	19	3
Rhett, Errict, Tampa Bay	284	1,011	3.6	27	7
Tillman, Lewis, Chicago	275	899	3.3	25td	7
Watters, Ricky, San Francisco	239	877	3.7	23	6
Moore, Ron, Arizona	232	780	3.4	24	4
Heyward, Craig, Atlanta	183	779	4.3	17	7

Receiving

	No	Yds	Avg	Long	TD
Carter, Cris, Minnesota	122	1,256	10.3	65td	7
Rice, Jerry, San Francisco	112	1,499	13.4	69td	13
Mathis, Terance, Atlanta	111	1,342	12.1	81	11
Sharpe, Sterling, Green Bay	94	1,119	11.9	49	18
Reed, Jake, Minnesota	85	1,175	13.8	59	4
Early, Quinn, New Orleans	82	894	10.9	33	4
Rison, Andre, Atlanta	81	1,088	13.4	69td	8
Irvin, Michael, Dallas	79	1,241	15.7	65td	6
Barnett, Fred, Philadelphia	78	1,127	14.4	54	5
Bennett, Edgar, Green Bay	78	546	7.0	40	4

Scoring—Non-Kickers

	TD	Rush	Pass	2 Pt	Pts
Smith, Emmitt, Dallas	22	21	1	0	132
Sharpe, Sterling, Green Bay	18	0	18	0	108
Rice, Jerry, San Francisco	15	2	13	1	92
Mathis, Terance, Atlanta	11	0	11	2	70
Moore, Herman, Detroit	11	0	11	0	66
Watters, Ricky, San Francisco	11	6	5	0	66
Jones, Brent, San Francisco	9	0	9	1	56
Bennett, Edgar, Green Bay	9	5	4	0	54

Scoring—Kickers

	PAT	FG	Pts
Reveiz, Fuad, Minnesota	30/30	34/39	132
Andersen, Morten, New Orleans	32/32	28/39	116
Boniol, Chris, Dallas	48/48	22/29	114
Brien, Doug, San Francisco	60/62	15/20	105
Jacke, Chris, Green Bay	41/43	19/26	98

Interceptions

	No	Yds	Avg	Long	TD
Williams, Aeneas, Arizona	9	89	9.9	43	0
Hanks, Merton, San Francisco	7	93	13.3	38	0
Jackson, Greg, Philadelphia	6	86	14.3	55td	1
Sanders, Deion, San Francisco	6	303	50.5	93td	3
7 tied with 5					

Kickoff Returns

	No	Yds	Avg	Long	TD
Gray, Mel, Detroit	45	1,276	28.4	102td	3
Walker, Herschel, Philadelphia	21	581	27.7	94td	1
Williams, Kevin, Dallas	43	1,148	26.7	87td	1
Mitchell, Brian, Washington	58	1,478	25.5	86	0
Lewis, Nate, Chicago	35	874	25.0	55	0

Punt Returns

	No	FC	Yds	Avg	Long	TD
Mitchell, Brian, Washington	32	24	452	14.1	78td	2
Meggett, David, N.Y. Giants	26	14	323	12.4	68td	2
Gray, Mel, Detroit	21	12	233	11.1	24	0
Turner, Vernon, Tampa Bay	21	4	218	10.4	80td	1
Sydner, Jeff, Philadelphia	40	17	381	9.5	49	0

Punting

	No	Yds	Long	Avg
Landeta, Sean, L.A. Rams	78	3,494	62	44.8
Roby, Reggie, Washington	82	3,639	65	44.4
Montgomery, Greg, Detroit	63	2,782	64	44.2
Barnhardt, Tommy, New Orleans	67	2,920	57	43.6
Saxon, Mike, Minnesota	77	3,301	67	42.9

Sacks

	No
Harvey, Ken, Washington	13.5
Randle, John, Minnesota	13.5
Haley, Charles, Dallas	12.5
Smith, Chuck, Atlanta	11.0
Conner, Darion, New Orleans	10.5
Jones Sean Green Bay	10.5

NFL MVP, Defensive Player of the Year, and Rookie of the Year

The Jim Thorpe Trophy goes to the most valuable player as chosen by the Jim Thorpe Academy, a panel of distinguished sports journalists and former players. The George Halas Trophy is awarded to the outstanding defensive player as chosen by a panel of sports experts. Rookie of the Year is one of many awards given out annually by the *Sporting News*. Many other organizations give out annual awards honoring the NFL's finest players.

MVP

1955	Harlon Hill, Chicago
1956	Frank Gifford, N.Y. Giants
1957	John Unitas, Baltimore
1958	Jim Brown, Cleveland
1959	Charley Conerly, N.Y. Giants
1960	Norm Van Brocklin, Philadelphia
1961	Y.A. Tittle, N.Y. Giants
1962	Jim Taylor, Green Bay
1963	Jim Brown, Cleveland
	Y.A. Tittle, N.Y. Giants
1964	Lenny Moore, Baltimore
1965	Jim Brown, Cleveland
1966	Bart Starr, Green Bay
1967	John Unitas, Baltimore
1968	Earl Morrall, Baltimore
1969	Roman Gabriel, L.A. Rams
1970	John Brodie, San Francisco
1971	Bob Griese, Miami
1972	Larry Brown, Washington
1973	O.J. Simpson, Buffalo
1974	Ken Stabler, Oakland
1975	Fran Tarkenton, Minnesota
1976	Bert Jones, Baltimore
1977	Walter Payton, Chicago
1978	Earl Campbell, Houston
1979	Earl Campbell, Houston
1980	Earl Campbell, Houston
1981	Ken Anderson, Cincinnati
1982	Dan Fouts, San Diego
1983	Joe Theismann, Washington
1984	Dan Marino, Miami
1985	Walter Payton, Chicago
1986	Phil Simms, N.Y. Giants
1987	Jerry Rice, San Francisco
1988	Roger Craig, San Francisco
1989	Joe Montana, San Francisco
1990	Warren Moon, Houston
1991	Thurman Thomas, Buffalo
1992	Steve Young, San Francisco
1993	Emmitt Smith, Dallas
1994	Steve Young, San Francisco

Defensive Player of the Year

1966	Larry Wilson, St. Louis
1967	Deacon Jones, Los Angeles
1968	Deacon Jones, Los Angeles
1969	Dick Butkus, Chicago
1970	Dick Butkus, Chicago
1971	Carl Eller, Minnesota
1972	Joe Greene, Pittsburgh
1973	Alan Page, Minnesota
1974	Joe Greene, Pittsburgh
1975	Curley Culp, Houston
1976	Jerry Sherk, Cleveland
1977	Harvey Martin, Dallas
1978	Randy Gradishar, Denver
1979	Lee Roy Selmon, Tampa Bay
1980	Lester Hayes, Oakland
1981	Joe Klecko, N.Y. Jets
1982	Mark Gastineau, N.Y. Jets
1983	Jack Lambert, Pittsburgh
1984	Mike Haynes, L.A. Raiders
1985	Howie Long, L.A. Raiders
	Andre Tippett, New England
1986	Lawrence Taylor, N.Y. Giants
1987	Reggie White, Philadelphia
1988	Mike Singletary, Chicago
1989	Tim Harris, Green Bay
1990	Bruce Smith, Buffalo
1991	Pat Swilling, New Orleans
1992	Junior Seau, San Diego
1993	Bruce Smith, Buffalo
1994	Deion Sanders, San Francisco

Rookie of the Year

1964	Charley Taylor, Washington
1965	Gale Sayers, Chicago
1966	Tommy Nobis, Atlanta
1967	Mel Farr, Detroit
1968	Earl McCullouch, Detroit
1969	Calvin Hill, Dallas
1970	NFC: Bruce Taylor, San Francsico
	AFC: Dennis Shaw, Buffalo
1971	NFC: John Brockington, Green Bay
	AFC: Jim Plunkett, New England
1972	NFC: Chester Marcol, Green Bay
	AFC: Franco Harris, Pittsburgh
1973	NFC: Chuck Foreman, Minnesota
	AFC: Boobie Clark, Cincinnati
1974	NFC: Wilbur Jackson, San Francisco
	AFC: Don Woods, San Diego
1975	NFC: Steve Bartkowski, Atlanta
	AFC: Robert Brazile, Houston
1976	NFC: Sammy White, Minnesota
	AFC: Mike Haynes, New England
1977	NFC: Tony Dorsett, Dallas
	AFC: A. J. Duhe, Miami
1978	NFC: Al Baker, Detroit
	AFC: Earl Campbell, Houston
1979	NFC: Ottis Anderson, St. Louis
	AFC: Jerry Butler, Buffalo
1980	Billy Sims, Detroit
1981	George Rogers, New Orleans
1982	Marcus Allen, L.A. Raiders
1983	Dan Marino, Miami
1984	Louis Lipps, Pittsburgh
1985	Eddie Brown, Cincinnati
1986	Rueben Mayes, New Orleans
1987	Robert Awalt, St. Louis
1988	Keith Jackson, Philadelphia
1989	Barry Sanders, Detroit
1990	Richmond Webb, Miami
1991	Mike Croel, Denver
1992	Santana Dotson, Tampa Bay
1993	Jerome Bettis, L.A. Rams
1994	Marshall Faulk, Indianapolis

Number One NFL Draft Choices, 1936-95

Year	Team	Player, Pos., College	Year	Team	Player, Pos., College
1936	Philadelphia	Jay Berwanger, HB, Chicago	1966	Atlanta	Tommy Nobis, LB, Texas
1937	Philadelphia	Sam Francis, FB, Nebraska	1967	Baltimore	Bubba Smith, DT, Michigan St.
1938	Cleve.Rams	Corbett Davis, FB, Indiana	1968	Minnesota	Ron Yary, T, USC
1939	Chi. Cards	Ki Aldrich, C, TCU	1969	Buffalo	O.J. Simpson, RB, USC
1940	Chi. Cards	George Cafego, HB, Tennessee	1970	Pittsburgh	Terry Bradshaw, QB, La.Tech
1941	Chi. Bears	Tom Harmon, HB, Michigan	1971	New England	Jim Plunkett, QB, Stanford
1942	Pittsburgh	Bill Dudley, HB, Virginia	1972	Buffalo	Walt Patulski, DE, Notre Dame
1943	Detroit	Frank Sinkwich, HB, Georgia	1973	Houston	John Matuszak, DE, Tampa
1944	Boston Yanks	Angelo Bertelli, QB, Notre Dame	1974	Dallas	Ed "Too Tall" Jones, Tenn.St.
1945	Chi. Cards	Charley Trippi, HB, Georgia	1975	Atlanta	Steve Bartkowski, QB, Cal.
1946	Boston Yanks	Frank Dancewicz, QB, Notre Dame	1976	Tampa Bay	Lee Roy Selmon, DE, Oklahoma
1947	Chi. Bears	Bob Fenimore, HB, Okla. A&M	1977	Tampa Bay	Ricky Bell, RB, USC
1948	Washington	Harry Gilmer, QB, Alabama	1978	Houston	Earl Campbell, RB, Texas
1949	Philadelphia	Chuck Bednarik, C, Penn	1979	Buffalo	Tom Cousineau, LB, Ohio St.
1950	Detroit	Leon Hart, E, Notre Dame	1980	Detroit	Billy Sims, RB, Oklahoma
1951	N.Y. Giants	Kyle Rote, HB, SMU	1981	New Orleans	George Rogers, RB, S.Carolina
1952	L.A. Rams	Bill Wade, QB, Vanderbilt	1982	New England	Kenneth Sims, DT, Texas
1953	San Francisco	Harry Babcock, E, Georgia	1983	Baltimore	John Elway, QB, Stanford
1954	Cleveland	Bobby Garrett, QB, Stanford	1984	New England	Irving Fryar, WR, Nebraska
1955	Baltimore	George Shaw, QB, Oregon	1985	Buffalo	Bruce Smith, DE, Va.Tech
1956	Pittsburgh	Gary Glick, DB, Col. A&M	1986	Tampa Bay	Bo Jackson, RB, Auburn
1957	Green Bay	Paul Hornung, QB, Notre Dame	1987	Tampa Bay	Vinny Testaverde, QB, Miami (FL)
1958	Chi. Cards	King Hill, QB, Rice	1988	Atlanta	Aundray Bruce, LB, Auburn
1959	Green Bay	Randy Duncan, QB, Iowa	1989	Dallas	Troy Aikman, QB, UCLA
1960	L.A. Rams	Billy Cannon, HB, LSU	1990	Indianapolis	Jeff George, QB, Illinois
1961	Minnesota	Tommy Mason, HB, Tulane	1991	Dallas	Russell Maryland, DL, Miami (FL)
1962	Washington	Ernie Davis, HB, Syracuse	1992	Indianapolis	Steve Emtman, DL, Washington
1963	L.A. Rams	Terry Baker, QB, Oregon St.	1993	New England	Drew Bledsoe, QB, Washington St.
1964	San Francisco	Dave Parks, E, Texas Tech	1994	Cincinnati	Dan Wilkinson, DT, Ohio St.
1965	N.Y. Giants	Tucker Frederickson, HB, Auburn	1995	Cincinnati	Ki-Jana Carter, RB, Penn State

First-Round Selections in the 1995 NFL Draft

Team	Player	Pos	College	Team	Player	Pos	College
1. Cincinnati	Ki-Jana Carter	RB	Penn St.	17. N.Y. Giants	Tyrone Wheatley	RB	Michigan
2. Jacksonville	Tony Boselli	T	Southern Cal	18. Oakland	Napoleon Kaufman	RB	Washington
3. Houston	Steve McNair	QB	Alcorn St.	19. Jacksonville	James Stewart	RB	Tennessee
4. Washington	Michael Westbrook	WR	Colorado	20. Detroit	Luther Elliss	DT	Utah
5. Carolina	Kerry Collins	QB	Penn St.	21. Chicago	Rashaan Salaam	RB	Colorado
6. St. Louis	Kevin Carter	DE	Florida	22. Carolina	Tyrone Poole	DB	Ft. Valley (GA) St.
7. Philadelphia	Mike Mamula	DE	Boston College	23. New Enlgand	Ty Law	DB	Michigan
8. Seattle	Joey Galloway	WR	Ohio St.	24. Minnesota	Korey Stringer	T	Ohio St.
9. N.Y. Jets	Kyle Brady	TE	Penn St.	25. Miami	Billy Milner	T	Houston
10. San Francisco	J.J. Stokes	WR	UCLA	26. Atlanta	Devin Bush	DB	Florida St.
11. Minnesota	Derrick Alexander	DE	Florida St.	27. Pittsburgh	Mark Bruener	TE	Washington
12. Tampa Bay	Warren Sapp	DT	Miami (FL)	28. Tampa Bay	Derrick Brooks	LB	Florida St.
13. New Orleans	Mark Fields	LB	Washington St.	29. Carolina	Blake Brockermeyer	T	Texas
14. Buffalo	Ruben Brown	G	Pittsburgh	30. Cleveland	Craig Powell	LB	Ohio St.
15. Indianapolis	Ellis Johnson	DT	Florida	31. Kansas City	Trezelle Jenkins	T	Michigan
16. N.Y. Jets	Hugh Douglas	DE	Central St. (OH)	32. Green Bay	Craig Newsome	DB	Arizona St.

Pro Football Hall of Fame, Canton, Ohio

Herb Adderley	Tony Dorsett	Ken Houston	George McAfee	Joe Schmidt
Lance Alworth	Paddy Driscoll	Cal Hubbard	Mike McCormack	Tex Schramm
Doug Atkins	Bill Dudley	Sam Huff	Hugh McElhenny	Lee Roy Selmon
Morris "Red" Badgro	Turk Edwards	Lamar Hunt	John "Blood" McNally	Art Shell
Lem Barney	Weeb Ewbank	Don Hutson	Mike Michalske	O.J. Simpson
Cliff Battles	Tom Fears	Jimmy Johnson	Wayne Millner	Jackie Smith
Sammy Baugh	Jim Finks	John Henry Johnson	Bobby Mitchell	Bart Starr
Chuck Bednarik	Ray Flaherty	Deacon Jones	Ron Mix	Roger Staubach
Bert Bell	Len Ford	Stan Jones	Lenny Moore	Ernie Stautner
Bobby Bell	Dr. Daniel Fortmann	Henry Jordan	Marion Motley	Jan Stenerud
Raymond Berry	Dan Fouts	Sonny Jurgensen	George Musso	Ken Strong
Charles Bidwell	Frank Gatski	Leroy Kelly	Bronko Nagurski	Joe Stydahar
Fred Biletnikoff	Bill George	Walt Kiesling	Joe Namath	Fran Tarkenton
George Blanda	Frank Gifford	Frank "Bruiser" Kinard	Greasy Neale	Charlie Taylor
Mel Blount	Sid Gillman	Curly Lambeau	Ernie Nevers	Jim Taylor
Terry Bradshaw	Otto Graham	Jack Lambert	Ray Nitschke	Jim Thorpe
Jim Brown	Red Grange	Tom Landry	Chuck Noll	Y.A. Tittle
Paul Brown	Joe Greene	Dick "Night Train" Lane	Leo Nomellini	George Trafton
Roosevelt Brown	Forrest Gregg	Jim Langer	Merlin Olsen	Charlie Trippi
Willie Brown	Bob Griese	Willie Lanier	Jim Otto	Emlen Tunnell
Buck Buchanan	Lou Groza	Steve Largent	Steve Owen	Clyde "Bulldog" Turner
Dick Butkus	Joe Guyon	Yale Lary	Alan Page	Johnny Unitas
Earl Campbell	George Halas	Dante Lavelli	Clarence "Ace" Parker	Gene Upshaw
Tony Canadeo	Jack Ham	Bobby Layne	Jim Parker	Norm Van Brocklin
Joe Carr	John Hannah	Tuffy Leemans	Walter Payton	Steve Van Buren
Guy Chamberlin	Franco Harris	Bob Lilly	Joe Perry	Doak Walker
Jack Christiansen	Ed Healey	Larry Little	Pete Pihos	Bill Walsh
Dutch Clark	Mel Hein	Vince Lombardi	Hugh "Shorty" Ray	Paul Warfield
George Connor	Ted Hendricks	Sid Luckman	Dan Reeves	Bob Waterfield
Jim Conzelman	Pete Henry	Link Lyman	John Riggins	Arnie Weinmeister
Larry Csonka	Arnold Herber	John Mackey	Jim Ringo	Randy White
Al Davis	Bill Hewitt	Tim Mara	Andy Robustelli	Bill Willis
Willie Davis	Clarke Hinkle	Gino Marchetti	Art Rooney	Larry Wilson
Len Dawson	Elroy "Crazy Legs"	George Marshall	Pete Rozelle	Kellen Winslow
Mike Ditka	Hirsch	Ollie Matson	Bob St. Clair	Alex Wojciechowicz
Art Donovan	Paul Hornung	Don Maynard	Gale Sayers	Willie Wood

All-Time NFL Coaching Victories

(at start of 1995 season; *active through 1994)

Coach	Years	Teams	Regular Season				Career			
			W	L	T	Pct	W	L	T	Pct
Don Shula*	32	Colts, Dolphins	319	149	6	.679	338	165	6	.670
George Halas	40	Bears	318	148	31	.671	324	151	31	.671
Tom Landry	29	Cowboys	250	162	6	.605	270	178	6	.601
Curly Lambeau	33	Packers, Cardinals, Redskins	226	132	22	.624	229	134	22	.623
Chuck Noll	23	Steelers	193	148	1	.566	209	156	1	.572
Chuck Knox*	22	Rams, Bills, Seahawks	186	147	1	.558	193	158	1	.550
Paul Brown	21	Browns, Bengals	166	100	6	.621	170	109	6	.607
Bud Grant	18	Vikings	158	96	5	.620	168	109	5	.605
Steve Owen	23	Giants	151	100	17	.595	154	108	17	.582
Joe Gibbs	12	Redskins	124	60	0	.674	140	65	0	.683
Dan Reeves*	14	Broncos, Giants	130	85	1	.604	138	92	1	.600
Hank Stram	17	Chiefs, Saints	131	97	10	.571	136	100	10	.573
Weeb Ewbank	20	Colts, Jets	130	129	7	.502	134	130	7	.507
Marv Levy*	14	Chiefs, Bills	117	90	0	.565	127	96	0	.570
Sid Gillman	18	Rams, Chargers, Oilers	122	99	7	.550	123	104	7	.541
George Allen	12	Rams, Redskins	116	47	5	.705	120	54	5	.684
Don Coryell	14	Cardinals, Chargers	111	83	1	.572	114	89	1	.561
Mike Ditka	11	Bears	106	62	0	.631	112	68	0	.622
John Madden	10	Raiders	103	32	7	.750	112	39	7	.731
M. Schottenheimer*	11	Browns, Chiefs	103	63	1	.620	108	72	1	.599

All-Time Professional (NFL and AFL) Football Records

(at start of 1995 season; *active through 1994)

Leading Lifetime Rushers

Player	League	Yrs	Att	Yards	Avg	Player	League	Yrs	Att	Yards	Avg
Walter Payton	NFL	13	3,838	16,726	4.4	Thurman Thomas*	NFL	7	2,018	8,724	4.3
Eric Dickerson	NFL	11	2,996	13,259	4.4	Barry Sanders*	NFL	6	1,763	8,672	4.9
Tony Dorsett	NFL	12	2,936	12,739	4.3	Jim Taylor	NFL	10	1,941	8,597	4.4
Jim Brown	NFL	9	2,359	12,312	5.2	Joe Perry	NFL	14	1,737	8,378	4.8
Franco Harris	NFL	13	2,949	12,120	4.1	Roger Craig	NFL	11	1,991	8,189	4.1
John Riggins	NFL	14	2,916	11,352	3.9	Gerald Riggs	NFL	10	1,989	8,188	4.1
O.J. Simpson	AFL-NFL	11	2,404	11,236	4.7	Larry Csonka	AFL-NFL	11	1,891	8,081	4.3
Ottis Anderson	NFL	14	2,562	10,273	4.0	Freeman McNeil	NFL	12	1,798	8,074	4.5
Marcus Allen*	NFL	13	2,485	10,018	4.0	Herschel Walker*	NFL	9	1,907	7,996	4.2
Earl Campbell	NFL	8	2,187	9,407	4.3	James Brooks	NFL	12	1,685	7,962	4.7

Most Yards Gained, Season — 2,105, Eric Dickerson, Los Angeles Rams, 1984.
Most Yards Gained, Game — 275, Walter Payton, Chicago Bears vs. Minnesota Vikings, Nov. 20, 1977.
Most Touchdowns Rushing, Career — 110, Walter Payton, Chicago Bears, 1975-1987.
Most Touchdowns Rushing, Season — 24, John Riggins, Washington Redskins, 1983.
Most Touchdowns Rushing, Game — 6, Ernie Nevers, Chicago Cardinals vs. Chicago Bears, Nov. 8, 1929.
Most Rushing Attempts, Game — 45, Jamie Morris, Washington Redskins vs. Cincinnati Bengals, Dec. 17, 1988 (overtime).
Longest Run From Scrimmage — 99 yds., Tony Dorsett, Dallas vs. Minnesota, Jan. 3, 1983 (scored touchdown).

Leading Lifetime Passers

(minimum 1,500 attempts)

Player	League	Yrs	Att	Comp	Yds	Pts†	Player	League	Yrs	Att	Comp	Yds	Pts†
Steve Young*	NFL	10	2,429	1,546	19,869	96.8	Ken Anderson	NFL	16	4,475	2,654	32,838	81.9
Joe Montana*	NFL	15	5,391	3,409	40,551	92.3	Bernie Kosar*	NFL	10	3,225	1,896	22,394	81.8
Dan Marino*	NFL	12	6,049	3,604	45,173	88.2	Jeff Hostetler*	NFL	9	1,505	864	10,985	81.8
Jim Kelly*	NFL	9	3,942	2,397	29,527	85.8	Danny White	NFL	13	2,950	1,761	21,959	81.7
Roger Staubach	NFL	11	2,958	1,685	22,700	83.4	Boomer Esiason*	NFL	11	4,291	2,440	31,874	81.6
Dave Krieg*	NFL	15	4,390	2,562	32,114	83.0	Troy Aikman*	NFL	6	2,281	1,424	16,303	81.6
Neil Lomax	NFL	8	3,153	1,817	22,771	82.7	Bart Starr	NFL	16	3,149	1,808	24,718	80.5
Sonny Jurgensen	NFL	18	4,262	2,433	32,224	82.6	Ken O'Brien	NFL	11	3,602	2,110	25,094	80.4
Len Dawson	NFL-AFL	19	3,741	2,136	28,711	82.6	Fran Tarkenton	NFL	18	6,467	3,686	47,003	80.4
Brett Favre*	NFL	4	1,580	983	10,412	82.2	Warren Moon*	NFL	11	5,147	3,003	37,949	80.3

†Rating points based on performances in the following categories: Percentage of completions, percentage of touchdown passes, percentage of interceptions, and average gain per pass attempt.

Most Yards Gained, Career — 47,003, Fran Tarkenton, Minnesota Vikings, 1961-66, 1972-78; New York Giants, 1967-71.
Most Yards Gained, Season — 5,084, Dan Marino, Miami Dolphins, 1984.
Most Yards Gained, Game — 554, Norm Van Brocklin, Los Angeles Rams vs. New York Yankees, Sept. 18, 1951 (27 completions in 41 attempts).
Most Touchdowns Passing, Career — 342, Fran Tarkenton, Minnesota Vikings, 1961-66, 1972-78; New York Giants, 1967-71.
Most Touchdowns Passing, Season — 48, Dan Marino, Miami Dolphins, 1984.
Most Touchdowns Passing, Game — 7, Sid Luckman, Chicago Bears vs. New York Giants, Nov. 14, 1943; Adrian Burk, Philadelphia Eagles vs. Washington Redskins, Oct. 17, 1954; George Blanda, Houston Oilers vs. New York Titans, Nov. 19, 1961; Y.A. Tittle, New York Giants vs. Washington Redskins, Oct. 28, 1962; Joe Kapp, Minnesota Vikings vs. Baltimore Colts, Sept. 28, 1969.
Most Passes Completed, Season — 404, Warren Moon, Houston Oilers, 1991.
Most Passes Completed, Game — 45, Drew Bledsoe, New England Patriots vs. Minnesota Vikings, Nov. 13, 1994 (overtime).

Leading Lifetime Receivers

Player	League	Yrs	No	Yds	Avg	Player	League	Yrs	No	Yds	Avg
Art Monk*	NFL	15	934	12,607	13.5	Drew Hill	NFL	14	634	9,831	15.5
Jerry Rice*	NFL	10	820	13,275	16.2	Don Maynard	AFL-NFL	15	633	11,834	18.7
Steve Largent	NFL	14	819	13,089	16.0	Raymond Berry	NFL	13	631	9,275	14.7
James Lofton	NFL	16	764	14,004	18.3	Sterling Sharpe*	NFL	7	595	8,134	13.7
Charlie Joiner	AFL-NFL	18	750	12,146	16.2	Harold Carmichael	NFL	14	590	8,985	15.2
Andre Reed*	NFL	10	676	9,536	14.1	Fred Biletnikoff	AFL-NFL	14	589	8,974	15.2
Henry Ellard*	NFL	12	667	11,158	16.7	Mark Clayton	NFL	11	582	8,974	15.4
Gary Clark*	NFL	10	662	10,331	15.6	Harold Jackson	NFL	16	579	10,372	17.9
Ozzie Newsome	NFL	13	662	7,980	12.1	Lionel Taylor	AFL-NFL	10	567	7,195	12.7
Charley Taylor	NFL	13	649	9,110	14.0	Roger Craig	NFL	11	566	4,911	8.7

Most Yards Gained, Season — 1,746, Charley Hennigan, Houston Oilers, 1961.
Most Yards Gained, Game — 336, Flipper Anderson, Los Angeles Rams vs. New Orleans, Nov. 26, 1989 (overtime).
Most Pass Receptions, Season — 122, Cris Carter, Minnesota Vikings, 1994.
Most Pass Receptions, Game — 18, Tom Fears, Los Angeles Rams vs. Green Bay Packers, Dec. 3, 1950 (189 yards).
Most Touchdown Passes, Season — 22, Jerry Rice, San Francisco 49ers, 1987.
Most Touchdown Passes, Game — 5, Bob Shaw, Chicago Cardinals vs. Baltimore Colts, Oct. 2, 1950; Kellen Winslow, San Diego Chargers vs. Oakland Raiders, Nov. 22, 1981; Jerry Rice, San Francisco 49ers vs. Atlanta Falcons, Oct. 14, 1990.

Leading Lifetime Scorers

Player	League	Yrs	TD	PAT	FG	Total	Player	League	Yrs	TD	PAT	FG	Total
George Blanda	AFL-NFL	26	9	943	335	2,002	Gary Anderson*	NFL	13	0	416	309	1,343
Jan Stenerud	AFL-NFL	19	0	580	373	1,699	Matt Bahr*	NFL	16	0	495	277	1,326
Nick Lowery*	NFL	16	0	512	349	1,559	Morten Anderson*	NFL	13	0	412	302	1,318
Pat Leahy	NFL	18	0	558	304	1,470	Jim Breech	NFL	14	0	517	243	1,246
Jim Turner	AFL-NFL	16	1	521	304	1,439	Chris Bahr	NFL	14	0	490	241	1,213
Mark Moseley	NFL	16	0	482	300	1,382	Norm Johnson*	NFL	13	0	476	243	1,205
Jim Bakken	NFL	17	0	534	282	1,380	Gino Cappelletti	AFL	11	42	350	176	1,130
Fred Cox	NFL	15	0	519	282	1,365	Ray Wersching	NFL	15	0	456	222	1,122
Eddie Murray*	NFL	15	0	465	298	1,359	Don Cockroft	NFL	13	0	432	216	1,080
Lou Groza	NFL	17	1	641	234	1,349	Garo Yepremian	AFL-NFL	14	0	444	210	1,074

Most Points, Season — 176, Paul Hornung, Green Bay Packers, 1960 (15 TD's, 41 PAT's, 15 FG's).
Most Points, Game — 40, Ernie Nevers, Chicago Cardinals vs. Chicago Bears, Nov. 28, 1929 (6 TD's, 4 PAT's).
Most Touchdowns, Career — 139, Jerry Rice, San Francisco 49ers, 1985-94 (8 rushing, 131 pass receptions).
Most Touchdowns, Season — 24, John Riggins, Washington Redskins, 1984 (24 rushing).
Most Touchdowns, Game — 6, Ernie Nevers, Chicago Cardinals vs. Chicago Bears, Nov. 28, 1929 (6 rushing); Dub Jones, Cleveland Browns vs. Chicago Bears, Nov. 25, 1951 (4 rushing, 2 pass receptions); Gale Sayers, Chicago Bears vs. San Francisco 49ers, Dec. 12, 1965 (4 rushing, 1 pass reception, 1 punt return).
Most Points After Touchdown, Season — 66, Uwe von Schamann, Miami Dolphins, 1984.
Most Consecutive Points After Touchdown — 234, Tommy Davis, San Francisco 49ers, 1959-69.
Most Field Goals, Game — 7, Jim Bakken, St. Louis Cardinals vs. Pittsburgh Steelers, Sept. 24, 1967; Rich Karlis, Minnesota Vikings vs. Los Angeles Rams, Nov. 5, 1989 (overtime).
Longest Field Goal — 63 yds., Tom Dempsey, New Orleans Saints vs. Detroit Lions, Nov. 8, 1970.

NFL Stadiums

Team—Stadium, Location, Turf (Year Built)	Capacity	Team—Stadium, Location, Turf (Year Built)	Capacity
Bears—Soldier Field, Chicago, Ill., G (1924)	66,944	Giants—Giants Stad., E. Rutherford, N.J., A (1976)	78,148
Bengals—Riverfront Stad., Cincinnati, Oh., A (1970)	60,389	Jaguars—Jacksonville Municipal Stad., Fla., G (1995)[2]	73,000
Bills—Rich Stad., Buffalo, N.Y., A (1973)	80,091	Jets—Giants Stad., E. Rutherford, N.J., A (1976)	77,716
Broncos—Mile High Stad., Denver, Col., G (1948)	76,273	Lions—Pontiac Silverdome, Mich., A (1975)	80,368
Browns—Cleveland Stad., Oh., G (1931)	78,512	Oilers—Astrodome, Houston, Tex., A (1965)	59,969
Buccaneers—Tampa Stad., Fla., G (1967)	74,321	Packers—Lambeau Field, Green Bay, Wis., G (1957)	60,790
Cardinals—Sun Devil Stad., Tempe, Ariz., G (1958)	73,400	Panthers—Carolinas Stad., Charlotte, N.C., G (1996)[3]	72,500
Chargers—San Diego Jack Murphy Stad., G (1967)	60,794	Patriots—Foxboro Stad., Mass., G (1971)	60,292
Chiefs—Arrowhead Stad., Kansas City, Mo., G (1972)	79,101	Raiders—Oakland Coliseum, Cal., G (1966)	50,000
Colts—RCA Dome, Indianapolis, Ind., A (1984)	60,272	Rams—Trans World Dome, St. Louis, Mo., A (1995)[4]	65,000
Cowboys—Texas Stad., Irving, Tex., A (1971)	65,812	Redskins—R. F. Kennedy Stad., Wash., D.C., G (1961)	56,454
Dolphins—Joe Robbie Stad., Miami, Fla., G (1987)	74,196	Saints—Louisiana Superdome, New Orleans, A (1975)	69,056
Eagles—Veterans Stad., Philadelphia, Pa., A (1971)	64,899	Seahawks—Kingdome, Seattle, Wash., A (1976)	66,400
Falcons—Georgia Dome, Atlanta, A (1992)	71,280	Steelers—Three Rivers Stad., Pittsburgh, Pa., A (1970)	59,600
49ers—3Com Park, San Francisco, Cal., G (1960)[1]	69,497	Vikings—Metrodome, Minneapolis, Minn., A (1982)	64,035

G=Grass. A=Artificial turf. Stad.=Stadium. (1) Formerly Candlestick Park. (2) Formerly the Gator Bowl. (3) The Panthers played home games during the 1995 season at Clemson Memorial Stad., Clemson, S.C., G (1942), 76,055. (4) Before the Trans World Dome was completed in late 1995, the Rams played home games at Busch County Stad., St. Louis, Mo., A (1966), 57,191.

The *Sporting News* 1994 NFL All-Pro Team

Offense—QB: Steve Young, San Francisco; RB: Barry Sanders, Detroit, and Emmitt Smith, Dallas; WR: Jerry Rice, San Francisco, and Cris Carter, Minnesota; TE: Ben Coates, New England; T: William Roaf, New Orleans, and Richmond Webb, Miami; G: Randall McDaniel, Minnesota, and Steve Wisniewski, L.A. Raiders; C: Dermontii Dawson, Pittsburgh. **Defense**—OLB: Kevin Greene, Pittsburgh, and Greg Lloyd, Pittsburgh; ILB: Junior Seau, San Diego, and Chris Spielman, Detroit; DE: Charles Haley, Dallas, and Bruce Smith, Buffalo; DT: Chester McGlockton, L.A. Raiders, and John Randle, Minnesota; CB: Deion Sanders, San Francisco, and Rod Woodson, Pittsburgh; SS: Darren Woodson, Dallas; FS: Merton Hanks, San Francisco. **Special Teams**—K: John Carney, San Diego; P: Reggie Roby, Washington; PR: Eric Metcalf, Cleveland; KR: Mel Gray.

Future Sites of the Super Bowl

No.	Site	Date
XXX	Sun Devil Stadium, Tempe, Arizona	Jan. 28, 1996
XXXI	Superdome, New Orleans, Louisiana	Jan. 26, 1997
XXXII	San Diego Jack Murphy Stadium, California	Jan. 25, 1998
XXXIII	3Com (Candlestick) Park, San Francisco, California	Jan. 31, 1999

CANADIAN FOOTBALL LEAGUE
Grey Cup Championship Game

1954 Edmonton Eskimos 26, Montreal Alouettes 25	1975 Edmonton Eskimos 9, Montreal Alouettes 8
1955 Edmonton Eskimos 34, Montreal Alouettes 19	1976 Ottawa Rough Riders 23, Saskatchewan Roughriders 20
1956 Edmonton Eskimos 50, Montreal Alouettes 27	1977 Montreal Alouettes 41, Edmonton Eskimos 6
1957 Hamilton Tiger-Cats 32, Winnipeg Blue Bombers 7	1978 Edmonton Eskimos 20, Montreal Alouettes 13
1958 Winnipeg Blue Bombers 35, Hamilton Tiger-Cats 28	1979 Edmonton Eskimos 17, Montreal Alouettes 9
1959 Winnipeg Blue Bombers 21, Hamilton Tiger-Cats 7	1980 Edmonton Eskimos 48, Hamilton Tiger-Cats 10
1960 Ottawa Rough Riders 16, Edmonton Eskimos 6	1981 Edmonton Eskimos 26, Ottawa Rough Riders 23
1961 Winnipeg Blue Bombers 21, Hamilton Tiger-Cats 14	1982 Edmonton Eskimos 32, Toronto Argonauts 16
1962 Winnipeg Blue Bombers 28, Hamilton Tiger-Cats 27	1983 Toronto Argonauts 18, B.C. Lions 17
1963 Hamilton Tiger-Cats 21, British Columbia Lions 10	1984 Winnipeg Blue Bombers 47, Hamilton Tiger-Cats 17
1964 British Columbia Lions 34, Hamilton Tiger-Cats 24	1985 B.C. Lions 37, Hamilton Tiger-Cats 24
1965 Hamilton Tiger-Cats 22, Winnipeg Blue Bombers 16	1986 Hamilton Tiger-Cats 39, Edmonton Eskimos 15
1966 Saskatchewan Roughriders 29, Ottawa Rough Riders 14	1987 Edmonton Eskimos 38, Toronto Argonauts 36
1967 Hamilton Tiger-Cats 24, Saskatchewan Roughriders 1	1988 Winnipeg Blue Bombers 22, B.C. Lions 21
1968 Ottawa Rough Riders 24, Calgary Stampeders 21	1989 Saskatchewan Roughriders 43, Hamilton Tiger-Cats 40
1969 Ottawa Rough Riders 29, Saskatchewan Roughriders 11	1990 Winnipeg Blue Bombers 50, Edmonton Eskimos 11
1970 Montreal Alouettes 23, Calgary Stampeders 10	1991 Toronto Argonauts 36, Calgary Stampeders 21
1971 Calgary Stampeders 14, Toronto Argonauts 11	1992 Calgary Stampeders 24, Winnipeg Blue Bombers 10
1972 Hamilton Tiger-Cats 13, Saskatchewan Roughriders 10	1993 Edmonton Eskimos 33, Winnipeg Blue Bombers 23
1973 Ottawa Rough Riders 22, Edmonton Eskimos 18	1994 B.C. Lions 26, Baltimore Football Club* 23
1974 Montreal Alouettes 20, Edmonton Eskimos 7	1995 Nov. 19, 1995, in Regina, Saskatchewan

*Baltimore's team nickname had not been determined at this time.

CFL Teams and Divisions, 1995

The CFL was realigned before the start of the 1995 season. The league formerly had an Eastern and a Western Division, both with 6 teams. In 1995, with the addition of U.S.-based expansion teams in Birmingham and Memphis, the CFL split into the North Division (Canadian teams) and the South Division (U.S. teams). The Sacramento Gold Miners moved to San Antonio. The Las Vegas Posse suspended operations after its fledgling 1994 season, pending possible relocation.

North Division
British Columbia Lions
Calgary Stampeders
Edmonton Eskimos
Hamilton Tiger-Cats
Ottawa Rough Riders
Saskatchewan Roughriders
Toronto Argonauts
Winnipeg Blue Bombers

South Division
Baltimore Stallions
Birmingham Barracudas
Memphis Mad Dogs
San Antonio Texans
Shreveport Pirates

All-Time CFL Records
(through 1994 season)

Longest Run—The Canadian Football League features 3 downs, 12 players on a side, and a field that is 110 yards long. George Dixon of the Montreal Alouettes made full use of the field with a 109-yard run against Ottawa on Sept. 2, 1963. Willie Fleming of the British Columbia Lions did the same against Edmonton on Oct. 17, 1964.

Leading Lifetime Rushers

	Yrs	No	Yds	Avg	Long	TDs		Yrs	No	Yds	Avg	Long	TDs
George Reed, Sask.	13	3,243	16,116	5.0	71	134	Jim Everson, B.C.-Ott.	7	1,460	7,060	4.8	68	37
Johnny Bright, Calg.-Edm. . . .	13	1,969	10,909	5.5	90	69	Earl Lunsford, Calg.	6	1,199	6,994	5.8	85	55
Normie Kwong, Calg.-							Dick Shatto, Tor.	12	1,322	6,958	5.3	67	39
Edm.	13	1,745	9,022	5.2	60	78	Lovell Coleman, Calg.-Ott.-						
Leo Lewis, Wpg.	11	1,351	8,861	6.5	92	48	B.C.	10	1,135	6,566	5.8	85	42
Dave Thelen, Ott.-Tor.	9	1,530	8,463	5.5	77	47	Willie Burden, Calg.	8	1,242	6,234	5.0	71	32

Leading Lifetime Passers
(ranked by total yards passing)

	Yrs	Att	Comp	Yds	Pct	Avg	Long	TDs
Ron Lancaster, Ott.-Sask.	19	6,233	3,384	50,535	54.3	14.9	102	333
Tom Clements, Ott.-Sask.-Ham.-Wpg. . .	12	4,657	2,807	39,041	60.3	13.9	105	252
Matt Dunigan, Edm.-B.C.-Tor.-Wpg.	12	4,622	2,581	37,221	55.8	14.4	89	257
Dieter Brock, Wpg.-Ham.	11	4,535	2,602	34,830	57.4	13.4	98	210
Kent Austin, Sask.-B.C.	8	3,964	2,281	30,819	57.5	13.5	107	176
Tom Burgess, Ott.-Sask.-Wpg.	9	3,766	1,982	28,706	52.6	14.5	104	178
Damon Allen, Edm.-Ott.-Ham.	10	3,614	1,842	27,575	51.0	15.0	102	170
Doug Flutie, B.C.-Calg.	5	3,172	1,888	27,342	59.5	14.5	106	178
Tracy Ham, Edm.-Tor-Balt.	8	3,154	1,642	25,735	52.0	15.7	85	180
Sam Etcheverry, Mtl.	7	2,829	1,630	25,582	57.6	15.7	109	183
Condredge Holloway, Ott.-Tor.-B.C.	13	3,013	1,710	25,193	56.8	14.7	80	166
Russ Jackson, Ott.	12	2,530	1,356	24,592	53.6	18.1	107	185
Bernie Faloney, Edm.-Ham.-Mtl.-B.C.	12	2,876	1,493	24,264	51.9	16.3	96	161
Roy Dewalt, B.C.-Wpg.-Ott.	9	3,130	1,803	24,147	57.6	13.4	90	132
Joe Kapp, Calg.-B.C.	8	2,709	1,476	22,725	54.5	16.4	106	136

Leading Lifetime Receivers

	Yrs	No	Yds		Yrs	No	Yds
Ray Elgaard, Sask.	12	765	12,353	Terry Evanshen, Mtl.-Calg.-Tor.	14	600	9,697
Rocky DiPietro, Ham.	14	706	9,762	Craig Ellis, Wpg.-Calg.-Sask.-Tor.-Edm. .	10	580	7,757
Tommy Joe Coffey, Edm.-Ham.-Tor. . .	14	650	10,320	Brian Kelly, Edm.	9	575	11,169
Tom Scott, Wpg.-Edm.-Calg.	11	649	10,837	James Murphy, Wpg.	8	573	9,036
Tony Gabriel, Ham.-Ont.	11	614	9,832	Tom Forzani, Calg.	11	553	8,285

COLLEGE FOOTBALL

Annual Results of Major Bowl Games

(Dates indicate the year that the game was played.)

Rose Bowl, Pasadena

1902	(Jan.) Michigan 49, Stanford 0	1942*	Oregon St. 20, Duke 16	1969	Ohio State 27, Southern Cal 16
1916	Wash. State 14, Brown 0	1943	Georgia 9, UCLA 0	1970	Southern Cal 10, Michigan 3
1917	Oregon 14, Pennsylvania 0	1944	Southern Cal 29, Washington 0	1971	Stanford 27, Ohio State 17
1918	Service teams	1945	Southern Cal 25, Tennessee 0	1972	Stanford 13, Michigan 12
1919	Service teams	1946	Alabama 34, Southern Cal 14	1973	Southern Cal 42, Ohio State 17
1920	Harvard 7, Oregon 6	1947	Illinois 45, UCLA 14	1974	Ohio State 42, Southern Cal 21
1921	California 28, Ohio State 0	1948	Michigan 49, Southern Cal 0	1975	Southern Cal 18, Ohio State 17
1922	Wash. & Jeff. 0, California 0	1949	Northwestern 20, California 14	1976	UCLA 23, Ohio State 10
1923	Southern Cal 14, Penn State 3	1950	Ohio State 17, California 14	1977	Southern Cal 14, Michigan 6
1924	Navy 14, Washington 14	1951	Michigan 14, California 6	1978	Washington 27, Michigan 20
1925	Notre Dame 27, Stanford 10	1952	Illinois 40, Stanford 7	1979	Southern Cal 17, Michigan 10
1926	Alabama 20, Washington 19	1953	Southern Cal 7, Wisconsin 0	1980	Southern Cal 17, Ohio State 16
1927	Alabama 7, Stanford 7	1954	Mich. State 28, UCLA 20	1981	Michigan 23, Washington 6
1928	Stanford 7, Pittsburgh 6	1955	Ohio State 20, Southern Cal 7	1982	Washington 28, Iowa 0
1929	Georgia Tech 8, California 7	1956	Mich. State 17, UCLA 14	1983	UCLA 24, Michigan 14
1930	Southern Cal 47, Pittsburgh 14	1957	Iowa 35, Oregon St. 19	1984	UCLA 45, Illinois 9
1931	Alabama 24, Wash. State 0	1958	Ohio State 10, Oregon 7	1985	Southern Cal 20, Ohio State 17
1932	Southern Cal 21, Tulane 12	1959	Iowa 38, California 12	1986	UCLA 45, Iowa 28
1933	Southern Cal 35, Pittsburgh 0	1960	Washington 44, Wisconsin 8	1987	Arizona St. 22, Michigan 15
1934	Columbia 7, Stanford 0	1961	Washington 17, Minnesota 7	1988	Mich. State 20, Southern Cal 17
1935	Alabama 29, Stanford 13	1962	Minnesota 21, UCLA 3	1989	Michigan 22, Southern Cal 14
1936	Stanford 7, So. Methodist 0	1963	Southern Cal 42, Wisconsin 37	1990	Southern Cal. 17, Michigan 10
1937	Pittsburgh 21, Washington 0	1964	Illinois 17, Washington 7	1991	Washington 46, Iowa 34
1938	California 13, Alabama 0	1965	Michigan 34, Oregon St. 7	1992	Washington 34, Michigan 14
1939	Southern Cal 7, Duke 3	1966	UCLA 14, Mich. State 12	1993	Michigan 38, Washington 31
1940	Southern Cal 14, Tennessee 0	1967	Purdue 14, Southern Cal 13	1994	Wisconsin 21, UCLA 16
1941	Stanford 21, Nebraska 13	1968	Southern Cal. 14, Indiana 3	1995	Penn St. 38, Oregon 20

*Played at Durham, NC

Orange Bowl, Miami

1935	(Jan.)Bucknell 26, Miami (FL) 0	1956	Oklahoma 20, Maryland 6	1977	Ohio State 27, Colorado 10
1936	Catholic U. 20, Mississippi 19	1957	Colorado 27, Clemson 21	1978	Arkansas 31, Oklahoma 6
1937	Duquesne 13, Miss. State 12	1958	Oklahoma 48, Duke 21	1979	Oklahoma 31, Nebraska 24
1938	Auburn 6, Mich. State 0	1959	Oklahoma 21, Syracuse 6	1980	Oklahoma 24, Florida St. 7
1939	Tennessee 17, Oklahoma 0	1960	Georgia 14, Missouri 0	1981	Oklahoma 18, Florida St. 17
1940	Georgia Tech 21, Missouri 7	1961	Missouri 21, Navy 14	1982	Clemson 22, Nebraska 15
1941	Miss. State 14, Georgetown 7	1962	LSU 25, Colorado 7	1983	Nebraska 21, Louisiana St. 20
1942	Georgia 40, TCU 26	1963	Alabama 17, Oklahoma 0	1984	Miami (FL) 31, Nebraska 30
1943	Alabama 37, Boston Coll. 21	1964	Nebraska 13, Auburn 7	1985	Washington 28, Oklahoma 17
1944	LSU 19, Texas A&M 14	1965	Texas 21, Alabama 17	1986	Oklahoma 25, Penn State 10
1945	Tulsa 26, Georgia Tech 12	1966	Alabama 39, Nebraska 28	1987	Oklahoma 42, Arkansas 8
1946	Miami (FL) 13, Holy Cross 6	1967	Florida 27, Georgia Tech 12	1988	Miami (FL) 20, Oklahoma 14
1947	Rice 8, Tennessee 0	1968	Oklahoma 26, Tennessee 24	1989	Miami (FL) 23, Nebraska 3
1948	Georgia Tech 20, Kansas 14	1969	Penn State 15, Kansas 14	1990	Notre Dame 21, Colorado 6
1949	Texas 41, Georgia 28	1970	Penn State 10, Missouri 3	1991	Colorado 10, Notre Dame 9
1950	Santa Clara 21, Kentucky 13	1971	Nebraska 17, Louisiana St. 12	1992	Miami (FL) 22, Nebraska 0
1951	Clemson 15, Miami (FL) 14	1972	Nebraska 38, Alabama 6	1993	Florida St. 27, Nebraska 14
1952	Georgia Tech 17, Baylor 14	1973	Nebraska 40, Notre Dame 6	1994	Florida St. 18, Nebraska 16
1953	Alabama 61, Syracuse 6	1974	Penn State 16, Louisiana St. 9	1995	Nebraska 24, Miami (FL) 17
1954	Oklahoma 7, Maryland 0	1975	Notre Dame 13, Alabama 11		
1955	Duke 34, Nebraska 7	1976	Oklahoma 14, Michigan 6		

Sugar Bowl, New Orleans

1935	(Jan.) Tulane 20, Temple 14	1955	Navy 21, Mississippi 0	1975	Alabama 13, Penn St. 6
1936	TCU 3, LSU 2	1956	Georgia Tech 7, Pittsburgh 0	1977	(Jan.) Pittsburgh 27, Georgia 3
1937	Santa Clara 21, LSU 14	1957	Baylor 13, Tennessee 7	1978	Alabama 35, Ohio State 6
1938	Santa Clara 6, LSU 0	1958	Mississippi 39, Texas 7	1979	Alabama 14, Penn State 7
1939	TCU 15, Carnegie Tech 7	1959	LSU 7, Clemson 0	1980	Alabama 24, Arkansas 9
1940	Texas A&M 14, Tulane 13	1960	Mississippi 21, LSU 0	1981	Georgia 17, Notre Dame 10
1941	Boston Col. 19, Tennessee 13	1961	Mississippi 14, Rice 6	1982	Pittsburgh 24, Georgia 20
1942	Fordham 2, Missouri 0	1962	Alabama 10, Arkansas 3	1983	Penn State 27, Georgia 23
1943	Tennessee 14, Tulsa 7	1963	Mississippi 17, Arkansas 13	1984	Auburn 9, Michigan 7
1944	Georgia Tech 20, Tulsa 18	1964	Alabama 12, Mississippi 7	1985	Nebraska 28, Louisiana St. 10
1945	Duke 29, Alabama 26	1965	LSU 13, Syracuse 10	1986	Tennessee 35, Miami (FL) 7
1946	Oklahoma A&M 33, St. Mary's 13	1966	Missouri 20, Florida 18	1987	Nebraska 30, Louisiana St. 15
1947	Georgia 20, N. Carolina 10	1967	Alabama 34, Nebraska 7	1988	Syracuse 16, Auburn 16
1948	Texas 27, Alabama 7	1968	LSU 20, Wyoming 13	1989	Florida St. 13, Auburn 7
1949	Oklahoma 14, N. Carolina 6	1969	Arkansas 16, Georgia 2	1990	Miami 33, Alabama 25
1950	Oklahoma 35, LSU 0	1970	Mississippi 27, Arkansas 22	1991	Tennessee 23, Virginia 22
1951	Kentucky 13, Oklahoma 7	1971	Tennessee 34, Air Force 13	1992	Notre Dame 39, Florida 28
1952	Maryland 28, Tennessee 13	1972	Oklahoma 40, Auburn 22	1993	Alabama 34, Miami (FL) 13
1953	Georgia Tech 24, Mississippi 7	1972*	(Dec.) Okla. 14, Penn State 0	1994	Florida 41, West Virginia 7
1954	Georgia Tech 42, West Virginia 19	1973	Notre Dame 24, Alabama 23	1995	Florida St. 23, Florida 17
		1974	Nebraska 13, Florida 10		

* Penn St. awarded game by forfeit

Fiesta Bowl, Tempe

1971	(Dec.)Arizona St. 45, Florida St. 38	1979	Pittsburgh 16, Arizona 10	1988	Florida St. 31, Nebraska 28
1972	Arizona St. 49, Missouri 35	1980	Penn St. 31, Ohio St. 19	1989	Notre Dame 34, W. Virginia 21
1973	Arizona St. 28, Pittsburgh 7	1982	(Jan.) Penn St. 26, USC 10	1990	Florida St. 41, Nebraska 17
1974	Okla. St. 16, Brigham Young 6	1983	Arizona St. 32, Oklahoma 21	1991	Louisville 34, Alabama 7
1975	Arizona St. 17, Nebraska 14	1984	Ohio State 28, Pittsburgh 23	1992	Penn St. 42, Tennessee 17
1976	Oklahoma 41, Wyoming 7	1985	UCLA 39, Miami (FL) 37	1993	Syracuse 26, Colorado 22
1977	Penn St. 42, Arizona St. 30	1986	Michigan 27, Nebraska 23	1994	Arizona 29, Miami (FL) 0
1978	UCLA 10, Arkansas 10	1987	Penn St. 14, Miami (FLla.) 10	1995	Colorado 41, Notre Dame 24

Hall of Fame Bowl, Tampa

1986	(Dec.) Boston Coll. 27, Georgia 24	1990	Auburn 31, Ohio St. 14	1993	Tennessee 38, Boston Coll. 23
1988	(Jan.) Michigan 28, Alabama 24	1991	Clemson 30, Illinois 0	1994	Michigan 42, N.C. St. 7
1989	Syracuse 23, LSU 10	1992	Syracuse 24, Ohio St. 17	1995	Wisconsin 34, Duke 20

Cotton Bowl, Dallas

1937	(Jan.) TCU 16, Marquette 6	1957	TCU 28, Syracuse 27	1977	Houston 30, Maryland 21
1938	Rice 28, Colorado 14	1958	Navy 20, Rice 7	1978	Notre Dame 38, Texas 10
1939	St. Mary's 20, Texas Tech 13	1959	TCU 0, Air Force 0	1979	Notre Dame 35, Houston 34
1940	Clemson 6, Boston Col. 3	1960	Syracuse 23, Texas 14	1980	Houston 17, Nebraska 14
1941	Texas A&M 13, Fordham 12	1961	Duke 7, Arkansas 6	1981	Alabama 30, Baylor 2
1942	Alabama 29, Texas A&M 21	1962	Texas 12, Mississippi 7	1982	Texas 14, Alabama 12
1943	Texas 14, Georgia Tech 7	1963	LSU 13, Texas 0	1983	SMU 7, Pittsburgh 3
1944	Randolph Field 7, Texas 7	1964	Texas 28, Navy 6	1984	Georgia 10, Texas 9
1945	Oklahoma A&M 34, TCU 0	1965	Arkansas 10, Nebraska 7	1985	Boston Coll. 45, Houston 28
1946	Texas 40, Missouri 27	1966	LSU 14, Arkansas 7	1986	Texas A&M 36, Auburn 16
1947	Arkansas 0, LSU 0	1966	(Dec.) Georgia 24, SMU 9	1987	Ohio St. 28, Texas A&M 12
1948	So. Methodist 13, Penn State 13	1968	(Jan.) Texas A&M 20, Ala. 16	1988	Texas A&M 35, Notre Dame 10
1949	So. Methodist 21, Oregon 13	1969	Texas 36, Tennessee 13	1989	UCLA 17, Arkansas 3
1950	Rice 27, No. Carolina 13	1970	Texas 21, Notre Dame 17	1990	Tennessee 31, Arkansas 27
1951	Tennessee 20, Texas 14	1971	Notre Dame 24, Texas 11	1991	Miami (FL) 46, Texas 3
1952	Kentucky 20, TCU 7	1972	Penn State 30, Texas 6	1992	Florida St. 10, Texas A&M 2
1953	Texas 16, Tennessee 0	1973	Texas 17, Alabama 13	1993	Notre Dame 28, Texas A&M 3
1954	Rice 28, Alabama 6	1974	Nebraska 19, Texas 3	1994	Notre Dame 24, Texas A&M 21
1955	Georgia Tech 14, Arkansas 6	1975	Penn State 41, Baylor 20	1995	Southern Cal. 55, Tex. Tech 14
1956	Mississippi 14, TCU 13	1976	Arkansas 31, Georgia 10		

Sun Bowl, El Paso (John Hancock Bowl, 1989-93)

1936	(Jan.) Hardin-Simmons 14, New Mexico St. 14	1954	Texas Western 37, Southern Miss. 14	1973	Missouri 34, Auburn 17
				1974	Mississippi St. 26, N. Carolina 24
1937	Hardin-Simmons 34, Texas Mines 6	1955	Texas Western 47, Florida St. 20	1975	Pittsburgh 33, Kansas 19
		1956	Wyoming 21, Texas Tech 14	1977	(Jan.) Texas A&M 37, Florida 14
1938	West Virginia 7, Texas Tech 6	1957	Geo. Washington 13, Texas Western 0	1977	(Dec.) Stanford 24, LSU 14
1939	Utah 26, New Mexico 0			1978	Texas 42, Maryland 0
1940	Catholic U. 0, Arizona St. 0	1958	Louisville 34, Drake 20	1979	Washington 14, Texas 7
1941	Western Reserve 26, Arizona St. 13	1958	(Dec.) Wyoming 14, Hardin-Simmons 6	1980	Nebraska 31, Mississippi St. 17
1942	Tulsa 6, Texas Tech 0			1981	Oklahoma 40, Houston 14
1943	2d Air Force 13, Hardin-Simmons 7	1959	New Mexico St. 28, N. Texas St. 8	1982	North Carolina 26, Texas 10
1944	Southwestern (TX) 7, New Mexico 0	1960	New Mexico St. 20, Utah State 13	1983	Alabama 28, SMU 7
		1961	Villanova 17, Wichita 9	1984	Maryland 28, Tennessee 27
1945	Southwestern (TX) 35, U. of Mexico 0	1962	West Texas St. 15, Ohio U. 14	1985	Georgia 13, Arizona 13
		1963	Oregon 21, So. Methodist 14	1986	Alabama 28, Washington 6
1946	New Mexico 34, Denver 24	1964	Georgia 7, Texas Tech 0	1987	Oklahoma St. 35, West Virginia 33
1947	Cincinnati 18, Virginia Tech 6	1965	Texas Western 13, TCU 12	1988	Alabama 29, Army 28
1948	Miami (OH) 13, Texas Tech 12	1966	Wyoming 28, Florida St. 20	1989	Pittsburgh 31, Texas A&M 28
1949	West Virginia 21, Texas Mines 12	1967	UTex El Paso 14, Mississippi 7	1990	Michigan St. 17, USC 16
1950	Texas Western 33, Georgetown 20	1968	Auburn 34, Arizona 10	1991	UCLA 6, Illinois 3
1951	West Texas St. 14, Cincinnati 13	1969	Nebraska 45, Georgia 6	1992	Baylor 20, Arizona 15
1952	Texas Tech 25, Pacific (CA) 14	1970	Georgia Tech. 17, Texas Tech 9	1993	Oklahoma 41, Texas Tech 10
1953	Pacific (CA) 26, Southern Miss. 7	1971	LSU 33, Iowa State 15	1994	Texas 35, North Carolina 31
		1972	North Carolina 32, Texas Tech 28		

Gator Bowl, Jacksonville

1946	(Jan.) Wake Forest 26, S.C. 14	1962	Florida 17, Penn State 7	1978	Clemson 17, Ohio State 15
1947	Oklahoma 34, NC State 13	1963	N. Carolina 35, Air Force 0	1979	N. Carolina 17, Michigan 15
1948	Maryland 20, Georgia 20	1965	(Jan.) Florida St. 36, Okla.19	1980	Pittsburgh 37, S. Carolina 9
1949	Clemson 24, Missouri 23	1965	(Dec.) Georgia Tech 31, Texas Tech 21	1981	N. Carolina 31, Arkansas 27
1950	Maryland 20, Missouri 7			1982	Florida St. 31, West Virginia 12
1951	Wyoming 20, Wash. & Lee 7	1966	Tennessee 18, Syracuse 12	1983	Florida 14, Iowa 6
1952	Miami (FL) 14, Clemson 0	1967	Penn State 17, Florida St. 17	1984	Oklahoma St. 21, S. Carolina 14
1953	Florida 14, Tulsa 13	1968	Missouri 35, Alabama 10	1985	Florida St. 34, Oklahoma St. 23
1954	Texas Tech 35, Auburn 13	1969	Florida 14, Tennessee 13	1986	Clemson 27, Stanford 21
1954	(Dec.) Auburn 33, Baylor 13	1971	(Jan.) Auburn 35, Mississippi 28	1987	LSU 30, S. Carolina 13
1955	Vanderbilt 25, Auburn 13	1971	(Dec.) Georgia 7, N. Carolina 3	1989	(Jan.) Georgia 34, Michigan St. 27
1956	Georgia Tech 21, Pittsburgh 14	1972	Auburn 24, Colorado 3	1989	(Dec.) Clemson 27, W. Va. 7
1957	Tennessee 3, Texas A&M 0	1973	Texas Tech 28, Tenn. 19	1991	(Jan.) Michigan 35, Mississippi 3
1958	Mississippi 7, Florida 3	1974	Auburn 27, Texas 3	1991	(Dec.) Oklahoma 48, Virginia 14
1960	(Jan.) Arkansas 14, Ga.Tech 7	1975	Maryland 13, Florida 0	1992	Florida 27, NC State 10
1960	(Dec.) Florida 13, Baylor 12	1976	Notre Dame 20, Penn State 9	1993	Alabama 24, N. Carolina 10
1961	Penn State 30, Georgia Tech 15	1977	Pittsburgh 34, Clemson 3	1994	Tennessee 45, Virginia Tech 23

Liberty Bowl, Memphis

1959	(Dec.) Penn State 7, Alabama 0	1971	Tennessee 14, Arkansas 13	1983	Notre Dame 19, Boston Coll. 18

1959 (Dec.) Penn State 7, Alabama 0
1960 Penn State 41, Oregon 12
1961 Syracuse 15, Miami 14
1962 Oregon State 6, Villanova 0
1963 Miss. State 16, NC State 12
1964 Utah 32, West Virginia 6
1965 Mississippi 13, Auburn 7
1966 Miami (FL) 14, Virginia Tech 7
1967 N.C. State 14, Georgia 7
1968 Mississippi 34, Virginia Tech 17
1969 Colorado 47, Alabama 33
1970 Tulane 17, Colorado 3

1971 Tennessee 14, Arkansas 13
1972 Georgia Tech 31, Iowa State 30
1973 N. Carolina St. 31, Kansas 18
1974 Tennessee 7, Maryland 3
1975 USC 20, Texas A&M 0
1976 Alabama 36, UCLA 6
1977 Nebraska 21, N. Carolina 17
1978 Missouri 20, Louisiana St. 15
1979 Penn St. 9, Tulane 6
1980 Purdue 28, Missouri 25
1981 Ohio State 31, Navy 28
1982 Alabama 21, Illinois 15

1983 Notre Dame 19, Boston Coll. 18
1984 Auburn 21, Arkansas 15
1985 Baylor 21, Louisiana St. 7
1986 Tennessee 21, Minnesota 14
1987 Georgia 20, Arkansas 17
1988 Indiana 34, S. Carolina 10
1989 Mississippi 42, Air Force 29
1990 Air Force 23, Ohio State 11
1991 Air Force 38, Mississippi St. 15
1992 Mississippi 13, Air Force 0
1993 Louisville 18, Michigan St. 7
1994 Illinois 30, East Carolina 0

Freedom Bowl, Anaheim

1984 (Dec.) Iowa 55, Texas 17
1985 Washington 20, Colorado 17
1986 UCLA 31, Brigham Young 10
1987 Arizona St. 33, Air Force 28

1988 Brigham Young 20, Colorado 17
1989 Washington 34, Florida 7
1990 Colorado St. 32, Oregon 31
1991 Tulsa 28, San Diego St. 17

1992 Fresno St. 24, USC 7
1993 Southern Cal 28, Utah 21
1994 Utah 16, Arizona 13

Copper Bowl, Tucson

1989 (Dec.) Arizona 17, N.C. St. 10
1990 California 17, Wyoming 15

1991 Indiana 24, Baylor 0
1992 Washington St. 31, Utah 28

1993 Kansas St. 52, Wyoming 17
1994 Brigham Young 31, Oklahoma 6

Independence Bowl, Shreveport

1976 (Dec.)McNeese St. 20, Tulsa 16
1977 Louisiana Tech 24, Louisville 14
1978 E. Carolina 35, La. Tech 13
1979 Syracuse 31, McNeese St. 7
1980 So. Miss. 16, McNeese St. 14
1981 Texas A&M 33, Oklahoma St. 16

1982 Wisconsin 14, Kansas St. 3
1983 Air Force 9, Mississippi 3
1984 Air Force 23, Virginia Tech 7
1985 Minnesota 20, Clemson 13
1986 Mississippi 20, Texas Tech 17
1987 Washington 24, Tulane 12
1988 So. Mississippi 38, UTEP 18

1989 Oregon 27, Tulsa 24
1990 Louisiana Tech 34, Maryland 34
1991 Georgia 24, Arkansas 15
1992 Wake Forest 39, Oregon 35
1993 Virginia Tech 45, Indiana 20
1994 Virginia 20 Texas Christian 10

Florida Citrus Bowl, Orlando (Tangerine Bowl until 1983)

1947 (Jan.) Catawba 31, Maryville 6
1948 Catawba 7, Marshall 0
1949 Murray State 21, Sul Ross St. 21
1950 St. Vincent 7, Emory & Henry 6
1951 Morris Harvey 35, Emory & Henry 14
1952 Stetson 35, Arkansas St. 20
1953 East Texas St. 33, Tenn. Tech 0
1954 East Texas St. 7, Arkansas St. 7
1955 Neb.-Omaha 7, E. Kentucky 6
1956 Juniata 6, Missouri Valley 6
1957 West Texas St. 20, So. Miss. 13
1958 East Texas St. 10, So. Miss. 9
1958 (Dec.) East Texas St. 26, Missouri Valley 7
1960 (Jan.) Middle Tenn. 21, Presbyterian 12
1960 (Dec.) Citadel 27, Tenn. Tech 0

1961 Lamar 21, Middle Tennessee 14
1962 Houston 49, Miami (OH) 21
1963 Western Ky. 27, Coast Guard 0
1964 E. Carolina 14, Massachusetts 13
1965 East Carolina 31, Maine 0
1966 Morgan State 14, West Chester 6
1967 Tenn.-Martin 25, West Chester 8
1968 Richmond 49, Ohio U. 42
1969 Toledo 56, Davidson 33
1970 Toledo 40, William & Mary 12
1971 Toledo 28, Richmond 3
1972 Tampa 21, Kent State 18
1973 Miami (OH) 16, Florida 7
1974 Miami (OH) 21, Georgia 10
1975 Miami (OH) 20, S. Carolina 7
1976 Okla. St. 49, Brigham Young 21
1977 Florida St. 40, Texas Tech 17

1978 N.C. State 30, Pittsburgh 17
1979 LSU 34, Wake Forest 10
1980 Florida 35, Maryland 20
1981 Missouri 19, Southern Miss. 17
1982 Auburn 33, Boston College 26
1983 Tennessee 30, Maryland 23
1984 Georgia 17, Florida St. 17
1985 Ohio St. 10, Brigham Young 7
1987 (Jan.) Auburn 16, USC 7
1988 Clemson 35, Penn St. 10
1989 Clemson 13, Oklahoma 6
1990 Illinois 31, Virginia 21
1991 Georgia Tech 45, Nebraska 21
1992 California 37, Clemson 13
1993 Georgia 21, Ohio St. 14
1994 Penn St. 31, Tennessee 13
1995 Alabama 24, Ohio St. 17

Peach Bowl, Atlanta

1968 (Dec.) LSU 31, Florida St. 27
1969 West Virginia 14, S. Carolina 3
1970 Arizona St. 48, N. Carolina 26
1971 Mississippi 41, Georgia Tech 18
1972 N. Carolina St. 49, W. Va. 13
1973 Georgia 17, Maryland 16
1974 Vanderbilt 6, Texas Tech 6
1975 W. Virginia 13, N. Carolina St. 10
1976 Kentucky 21, North Carolina 0
1977 N. Carolina St. 24, Iowa St. 14

1978 Purdue 41, Georgia Tech. 21
1979 Baylor 24, Clemson 18
1981 (Jan.) Miami (FL) 20, Virginia Tech 10
1981 (Dec.) West Virginia 26, Florida 6
1982 Iowa 28, Tennessee 22
1983 Florida St. 28, North Carolina 3
1984 Virginia 27, Purdue 22
1985 Army 31, Illinois 29
1986 Va. Tech 25, N.C. State 24

1988 (Jan.) Tennessee 28, Indiana 22
1988 (Dec.) N.C. State 28, Iowa 23
1989 Syracuse 19, Georgia 18
1990 Auburn 27, Indiana 23
1992 (Jan.) E. Carolina 37, N.C. St. 34
1993 North Carolina 21, Mississippi St. 17
1993 (Dec.) Clemson 14, Kentucky 13
1995 (Jan.) N.C. St. 28, Miss. St. 24

Holiday Bowl, San Diego

1978 (Dec.) Navy 23, Brig. Young 16
1979 Indiana 38, Brigham Young 37
1980 Brigham Young 46, SMU 45
1981 Brigham Young 38, Wash. St. 36
1982 Ohio State 47, Brigham Young 17
1983 Brigham Young 21, Missouri 17

1984 Brigham Young 24, Michigan 17
1985 Arkansas 18, Arizona St. 17
1986 Iowa 39, San Diego St. 38
1987 Iowa 20, Wyoming 19
1988 Oklahoma St. 62, Wyoming 14
1989 Penn St. 50, Brigham Young 39

1990 Texas A&M 65, Brigham Young 14
1991 Iowa 13, Brigham Young 13
1992 Hawaii 27, Illinois 17
1993 Ohio St. 28, Brigham Young 21
1994 Michigan 24, Colorado St. 14

Aloha Bowl, Honolulu

1982 (Dec.) Washington 21, Md. 20
1983 Penn State 13, Washington 10
1984 SMU 27, Notre Dame 20
1985 Alabama 24, USC 3

1986 Arizona 30, North Carolina 21
1987 UCLA 20, Florida 16
1988 Washington St. 24, Houston 22
1989 Michigan St. 33, Hawaii 13

1990 Syracuse 28, Arizona 0
1991 Georgia Tech 18, Stanford 17
1992 Kansas 23, Brigham Young 20
1993 Colorado 41, Fresno St. 30
1994 Boston Coll. 12, Kansas St. 7

Carquest Bowl, Miami (Blockbuster Bowl until 1993)

1990 (Dec.) Florida St. 24, Penn St. 17

1991 Alabama 30, Colorado 25
1993 (Jan.) Stanford 24, Penn St. 3

1994 Boston College 31, Virginia 13
1995 S. Carolina 24, W. Virginia 21

Las Vegas Bowl, Las Vegas

1992 (Dec.) Bowling Green 35, Nevada 34

1993 Utah St. 42, Ball St. 33

1994 UNLV 52, Central Michigan 24

Selected College Division I Football Teams

Team	Nickname	Team colors	Conference	Coach	1994 record (W-L-T)
Air Force	Falcons	Blue & silver	Western Athletic	Fisher De Berry	8-4-0
Akron	Zips	Blue & gold	Mid-American	Lee Owens	1-10-0
Alabama	Crimson Tide	Crimson & white	Southeastern	Gene Stallings	11-1-0
Arizona	Wildcats	Cardinal & navy	Pacific Ten	Dick Tomey	8-3-0
Arizona State	Sun Devils	Maroon & gold	Pacific Ten	Bruce Snyder	3-8-0
Arkansas	Razorbacks	Cardinal & white	Southeastern	Danny Ford	4-7-0
Arkansas State	Indians	Scarlet & black	Big West	John Bobo	1-10-0
Army	Cadets	Black, gold, gray	Independent	Bob Sutton	4-7-0
Auburn	Tigers	Burnt orange & navy	Southeastern	Terry Bowden	9-1-1
Ball State	Cardinals	Cardinal & white	Mid-American	Bill Lynch	5-5-1
Baylor	Bears	Green & gold	Southwest	Chuck Reedy	7-4-0
Boston College	Eagles	Maroon & gold	Big East	Dan Henning	6-4-1
Boston University	Terriers	Scarlet & white	Yankee	Dan Allen	9-2-0
Bowling Green	Falcons	Orange & brown	Mid-American	Gary Blackney	9-2-0
Brigham Young	Cougars	Royal blue & white	Western Athletic	LaVell Edwards	9-3-0
Brown	Bears	Brown, cardinal, white	Ivy	Mark Whipple	7-3-0
California	Golden Bears	Blue & gold	Pacific Ten	Keith Gilbertson	4-7-0
Central Michigan	Chippewas	Maroon & gold	Mid-American	Dick Flynn	9-2-0
Cincinnati	Bearcats	Red & black	Independent	Rick Minter	2-8-1
Citadel	Bulldogs	Blue & white	Southern	Charles Taaffe	6-5-0
Clemson	Tigers	Purple & orange	Atlantic Coast	Tommy West	5-6-0
Colgate	Red Raiders	Maroon	Patriot	Ed Sweeney	3-8-0
Colorado	Buffaloes	Silver, gold & black	Big Eight	Rick Neuheisel	10-1-0
Colorado State	Rams	Green & gold	Western Athletic	Sonny Lubick	10-1-0
Cornell	Big Red	Carnelian & white	Ivy	Jim Hofher	6-4-0
Dartmouth	Big Green	Dartmouth green & white	Ivy	John Lyons	4-6-0
Delaware	Fightin' Blue Hens	Blue & gold	Yankee	Harold Raymond	7-3-1
Delaware State	Hornets	Red & blue	Mid-Eastern	William Collick	7-4-0
Duke	Blue Devils	Royal blue & white	Atlantic Coast	Fred Goldsmith	8-3-0
East Carolina	Pirates	Purple & gold	Independent	Steve Logan	7-4-0
East Tennessee State	Buccaneers	Blue & gold	Southern	Mike Cavan	6-5-0
Eastern Illinois	Panthers	Blue & gray	Gateway	Bob Spoo	6-5-0
Eastern Kentucky	Colonels	Maroon & white	Ohio Valley	Roy Kidd	9-2-0
Eastern Michigan	Eagles	Dark green & white	Mid-American	Rick Rasnick	5-6-0
Eastern Washington	Eagles	Red & white	Big Sky	Mike Kramer	4-7-0
Florida	Gators	Orange & blue	Southeastern	Steve Spurrier	10-1-1
Florida A&M	Rattlers	Orange & green	Mid-Eastern	Billy Joe	6-5-0
Florida State	Seminoles	Garnet & gold	Atlantic Coast	Bobby Bowden	9-1-1
Fresno State	Bulldogs	Cardinal & blue	Western Athletic	Jim Sweeney	5-7-1
Furman	Paladins	Purple & white	Southern	Bobby Johnson	3-8-0
Georgia	Bulldogs	Red & black	Southeastern	Ray Goff	6-4-1
Georgia Southern	Eagles	Blue & white	Southern	Tim Stowers	6-5-0
Georgia Tech	Yellow Jackets	Old gold & white	Atlantic Coast	George O'Leary	1-10-0
Grambling	Tigers	Black & gold	Southwestern	Eddie Robinson	9-2-0
Harvard	Crimson	Crimson, black, white	Ivy	Tim Murphy	4-6-0
Hawaii	Rainbow Warriors	Green & white	Western Athletic	Bob Wagner	3-8-1
Holy Cross	Crusaders	Royal purple	Patriot	Peter Vaas	3-8-0
Houston	Cougars	Scarlet & white	Southwest	Kim Helton	1-10-0
Howard	Bison	Blue, white & red	Mid-Eastern	Steve Wilson	4-7-0
Idaho	Vandals	Silver & gold	Big Sky	Chris Tormey	9-2-0
Idaho State	Bengals	Orange & black	Big Sky	Brian McNeely	6-5-0
Illinois	Fighting Illini	Orange & blue	Big Ten	Lou Tepper	6-5-0
Illinois State	Redbirds	Red & white	Gateway	Jim Heacock	5-5-1
Indiana	Fightin' Hoosiers	Cream & crimson	Big Ten	Bill Mallory	6-5-0
Indiana State	Sycamores	Blue & white	Gateway	Dennis Raetz	5-6-0
Iowa	Hawkeyes	Old gold & black	Big Ten	Hayden Fry	5-5-1
Iowa State	Cyclones	Cardinal & gold	Big Eight	Dan McCarney	0-10-1
Jackson State	Tigers	Blue & white	Southwestern	James Carson	7-4-0
James Madison	Dukes	Purple & gold	Yankee	Alex Wood	9-2-0
Kansas	Jayhawks	Crimson & blue	Big Eight	Glen Mason	6-5-0
Kansas State	Wildcats	Purple & white	Big Eight	Bill Snyder	9-2-0
Kent	Golden Flashes	Navy blue & gold	Mid-American	Jim Corrigall	2-9-0
Kentucky	Wildcats	Blue & white	Southeastern	Bill Curry	1-10-0
Lafayette	Leopards	Maroon & white	Patriot	Bill Russo	5-6-0
Lehigh	Engineers	Brown & white	Patriot	Kevin Higgins	5-5-1
Liberty	Flames	Red, white & blue	Independent	Sam Rutigliano	5-6-0
Louisiana State (LSU)	Fighting Tigers	Purple & gold	Southeastern	Gerry DiNardo	4-7-0
Louisiana Tech	Bulldogs	Red & blue	Big West	Joe Raymond Peace	3-8-0
Louisville	Cardinals	Red, black & white	Independent	Ron Cooper	6-5-0
Maine	Black Bears	Blue & white	Yankee	Jack Cosgrove	3-8-0
Marshall	Thundering Herd	Green & white	Southern	Jim Donnan	10-1-0
Maryland	Terrapins	Red, white, black, gold	Atlantic Coast	Mark Duffner	4-7-0
Massachusetts	Minutemen	Maroon & white	Yankee	Mike Hodges	5-6-0
McNeese State	Cowboys	Blue & gold	Southland	Bobby Keasler	9-2-0

Team	Nickname	Team colors	Conference	Coach	1994 record (W-L-T)
Memphis	Tigers	Blue & gray	Independent	Rip Scherer	6-5-0
Miami (Florida)	Hurricanes	Orange, green, white	Big East	Butch Davis	10-1-0
Miami (Ohio)	Redskins	Red & white	Mid-American	Randy Walker	5-5-1
Michigan	Wolverines	Maize & blue	Big Ten	Lloyd Carr	7-4-0
Michigan State	Spartans	Green & white	Big Ten	Nick Saban	5-6-0
Middle Tennessee St.	Blue Raiders	Blue & white	Ohio Valley	Boots Donnelly	8-2-1
Minnesota	Golden Gophers	Maroon & gold	Big Ten	Jim Wacker	3-8-0
Mississippi	Rebels	Cardinal red & navy	Southeastern	Tommy Tuberville	4-7-0
Mississippi State	Bulldogs	Maroon & white	Southeastern	Jackie Sherrill	8-3-0
Mississippi Valley	Delta Devils	Green & white	Southwestern	Larry Dorsey	3-7-0
Missouri	Tigers	Old gold & black	Big Eight	Larry Smith	3-8-1
Montana	Grizzlies	Copper, silver, gold	Big Sky	Don Read	9-2-0
Montana State	Bobcats	Blue & gold	Big Sky	Cliff Hysell	3-8-0
Morehead State	Eagles	Blue & gold	Ohio Valley	Matt Ballard	0-11-0
Morgan State	Bears	Blue & orange	Mid-Eastern	Ricky Diggs	3-8-0
Murray State	Racers	Blue & gold	Ohio Valley	Houston Nutt	5-6-0
Navy	Midshipmen	Navy blue & gold	Independent	Charlie Weatherbie	3-8-0
Nebraska	Cornhuskers	Scarlet & cream	Big Eight	Tom Osborne	12-0-0
Nev.-Las Vegas (UNLV)	Rebels	Scarlet & gray	Big West	Jeff Horton	6-5-0
Nevada-Reno	Wolf Pack	Silver & blue	Big West	Chris Ault	9-2-0
New Hampshire	Wildcats	Blue & white	Yankee	Bill Bowes	10-1-0
New Mexico	Lobos	Cherry & silver	Western Athletic	Dennis Franchione	5-7-0
New Mexico State	Aggies	Crimson & white	Big West	Jim Hess	3-8-0
Nicholls St.	Colonels	Red & gray	Southland	Darren Barbier	5-6-0
North Carolina	Tar Heels	Carolina blue & white	Atlantic Coast	Mack Brown	8-3-0
North Carolina A & T	Aggies	Blue & gold	Mid-Eastern	Bill Hayes	6-5-0
North Carolina State	Wolfpack	Red & white	Atlantic Coast	Mike O'Cain	8-3-0
North Texas	Eagles	Green & white	Independent	Matt Simon	7-3-1
Northeast Louisiana	Indians	Maroon & gold	Independent	Ed Zaunbrecher	3-8-0
Northeastern	Huskies	Red & black	Yankee	Barry Gallup	2-9-0
Northern Arizona	Lumberjacks	Blue & gold	Big Sky	Steve Axman	7-4-0
Northern Illinois	Huskies	Cardinal & black	Big West	Charlie Sadler	4-7-0
Northern Iowa	Panthers	Purple & old gold	Gateway	Terry Allen	8-3-0
Northwestern	Wildcats	Purple & white	Big Ten	Gary Barnett	3-7-1
Northwestern State	Demons	Purple & white	Southland	Sam Goodwin	5-6-0
Notre Dame	Fighting Irish	Gold & blue	Independent	Lou Holtz	6-4-1
Ohio	Bobcats	Green & white	Mid-American	Jim Grobe	0-11-0
Ohio State	Buckeyes	Scarlet & gray	Big Ten	John Cooper	9-3-0
Oklahoma	Sooners	Crimson & cream	Big Eight	Howard Schnellenberger	6-5-0
Oklahoma State	Cowboys	Orange & black	Big Eight	Bob Simmons	3-7-1
Oregon	Ducks	Green & yellow	Pacific Ten	Mike Bellotti	9-3-0
Oregon State	Beavers	Orange & black	Pacific Ten	Jerry Pettibone	4-7-0
Pacific	Tigers	Orange & black	Big West	Chuck Shelton	6-5-0
Penn State	Nittany Lions	Blue & white	Big Ten	Joe Paterno	11-0-0
Pennsylvania	Red & Blue, Quakers	Red & blue	Ivy	Al Bagnoli	9-0-0
Pittsburgh	Panthers	Gold & blue	Big East	Johnny Majors	3-8-0
Princeton	Tigers	Orange & black	Ivy	Steve Tosches	7-3-0
Purdue	Boilermakers	Old gold & black	Big Ten	Jim Colletto	4-5-2
Rhode Island	Rams	Blue & white	Yankee	Floyd Keith	2-9-0
Rice	Owls	Blue & gray	Southwest	Ken Hatfield	5-6-0
Richmond	Spiders	Red & blue	Yankee	Jim Reid	3-8-0
Rutgers	Scarlet Knights	Scarlet	Big East	Doug Graber	5-5-1
Sam Houston State	Bearkats	Orange & white	Southland	Ron Randleman	6-5-0
Samford	Bulldogs	Crimson & blue	Independent	Pete Hurt	4-6-1
San Diego State	Aztecs	Scarlet & black	Western Athletic	Ted Tollner	4-7-0
San Jose State	Spartans	Gold, white & blue	Big West	John Ralston	3-8-0
South Carolina	Fighting Gamecocks	Garnet & black	Southeastern	Brad Scott	6-5-0
South Carolina State	Bulldogs	Garnet & blue	Mid-Eastern	Willie Jeffries	9-2-0
SE Missouri State	Indians	Red & black	Ohio Valley	John Mumford	7-5-0
Southern-Baton Rouge	Jaguars	Blue & gold	Southwestern	Pete Richardson	6-5-0
Southern California (USC)	Trojans	Cardinal & gold	Pacific Ten	John Robinson	7-3-1
Southern Illinois	Salukis	Maroon & white	Gateway	Shawn Watson	1-10-0
So. Methodist (SMU)	Mustangs	Red & blue	Southwest	Tom Rossley	1-9-1
Southern Mississippi	Golden Eagles	Black & gold	Independent	Jeff Bower	6-5-0
SW Missouri State	Bears	Maroon & white	Gateway	Del Miller	4-7-0
SW Texas State	Bobcats	Maroon & gold	Southland	Jim Bob Helduser	4-7-0
SW Louisiana	Ragin' Cajuns	Vermillion & white	Big West	Nelson Stokley	6-5-0
Stanford	Cardinal	Cardinal & white	Pacific Ten	Tyrone Willingham	3-7-1
Stephen F. Austin State	Lumberjacks	Purple & white	Southland	John Pearce	6-3-2
Syracuse	Orangemen	Orange	Big East	Paul Pasqualoni	7-4-0
Temple	Owls	Cherry & white	Big East	Ron Dickerson	2-9-0
Tennessee	Volunteers	Orange & white	Southeastern	Phillip Fulmer	7-4-0
Tenn.-Chattanooga	Moccasins	Navy blue & gold	Southern	Buddy Green	3-8-0
Tenn.-Martin	Pacers	Orange, white, blue	Ohio Valley	Don McLeary	5-6-0
Tennessee State	Tigers	Royal blue & white	Ohio Valley	Bill Davis	5-6-0
Tennessee Tech	Golden Eagles	Purple & gold	Ohio Valley	Jim Ragland	5-6-0
Texas	Longhorns	Burnt orange & white	Southwest	John Mackovic	7-4-0

(continued)

Team	Nickname	Team colors	Conference	Coach	1994 record (W-L-T)
Texas A & M	Aggies	Maroon & white	Southwest	R.C. Slocum	10-0-1
Texas Christian (TCU)	Horned Frogs	Purple & white	Southwest	Pat Sullivan	7-4-0
Texas Southern	Tigers	Maroon & gray	Southwestern	Bill Thomas	4-7-0
Texas Tech	Red Raiders	Scarlet & black	Southwest	Spike Dykes	6-5-0
Toledo	Rockets	Blue & gold	Mid-American	Gary Pinkel	6-4-1
Towson State	Tigers	Gold & white	Eastern College	Gordy Combs	8-2-0
Tulane	Green Wave	Olive green & sky blue	Independent	Buddy Teevens	1-10-0
Tulsa	Golden Hurricane	Blue & gold	Independent	David Rader	3-8-0
UCLA	Bruins	Blue & gold	Pacific Ten	Terry Donahue	5-6-0
Utah	Utes	Crimson & white	Western Athletic	Ron McBride	9-2-0
Utah State	Aggies	Navy blue & white	Big West	John L. Smith	3-8-0
UTEP	Miners	Orange, blue, white	Western Athletic	Charlie Bailey	3-7-1
Vanderbilt	Commodores	Black & gold	Southeastern	Rod Dowhower	5-6-0
Villanova	Wildcats	Blue & white	Yankee	Andy Talley	5-6-0
Virginia	Cavaliers	Orange & blue	Atlantic Coast	George Welsh	8-3-0
VMI	Keydets	Red, white & yellow	Southern	Bill Stewart	1-10-0
Virginia Tech	Gobblers, Hokies	Orange & maroon	Big East	Frank Beamer	8-3-0
Wake Forest	Demon Deacons	Old gold & black	Atlantic Coast	Jim Caldwell	3-8-0
Washington	Huskies	Purple & gold	Pacific Ten	Jim Lambright	7-4-0
Washington State	Cougars	Crimson & gray	Pacific Ten	Mike Price	7-4-0
Weber State	Wildcats	Royal purple & white	Big Sky	Dave Arslanian	5-6-0
West Virginia	Mountaineers	Old gold & blue	Big East	Don Nehlen	7-5-0
Western Carolina	Catamounts	Purple & gold	Southern	Steve Hodgin	6-5-0
Western Illinois	Leathernecks	Purple & gold	Gateway	Randy Ball	8-3-0
Western Kentucky	Hilltoppers	Red & white	Independent	Jack Harbaugh	5-6-0
Western Michigan	Broncos	Brown & gold	Mid-American	Al Molde	7-4-0
William & Mary	Tribe	Green, gold & silver	Yankee	Jimmye Laycock	8-3-0
Wisconsin	Badgers	Cardinal & white	Big Ten	Barry Alvarez	6-4-1
Wyoming	Cowboys	Brown & yellow	Western Athletic	Joe Tiller	6-6-0
Yale	Bulldogs, Elis	Yale blue & white	Ivy	Carmen Cozza	5-5-0
Youngstown State	Penguins	Red & white	Independent	Jim Tressel	10-0-1

Heisman Trophy Winners

Awarded annually to the nation's outstanding college football player.

1935	Jay Berwanger, Chicago, HB
1936	Larry Kelley, Yale, E
1937	Clinton Frank, Yale, HB
1938	David O'Brien, Texas Christian, QB
1939	Nile Kinnick, Iowa, HB
1940	Tom Harmon, Michigan, HB
1941	Bruce Smith, Minnesota, HB
1942	Frank Sinkwich, Georgia, HB
1943	Angelo Bertelli, Notre Dame, QB
1944	Leslie Horvath, Ohio State, QB
1945	Felix Blanchard, Army, FB
1946	Glenn Davis, Army, HB
1947	John Lujack, Notre Dame, QB
1948	Doak Walker, SMU, HB
1949	Leon Hart, Notre Dame, E
1950	Vic Janowicz, Ohio State, HB
1951	Richard Kazmaier, Princeton, HB
1952	Billy Vessels, Oklahoma, HB
1953	John Lattner, Notre Dame, HB
1954	Alan Ameche, Wisconsin, FB
1955	Howard Cassady, Ohio St., HB
1956	Paul Hornung, Notre Dame, QB
1957	John Crow, Texas A & M, HB
1958	Pete Dawkins, Army, HB
1959	Billy Cannon, La. State, HB
1960	Joe Bellino, Navy, HB
1961	Ernest Davis, Syracuse, HB
1962	Terry Baker, Oregon State, QB
1963	Roger Staubach, Navy, QB
1964	John Huarte, Notre Dame, QB
1965	Mike Garrett, USC, HB
1966	Steve Spurrier, Florida, QB
1967	Gary Beban, UCLA, QB
1968	O. J. Simpson, USC, RB
1969	Steve Owens, Oklahoma, RB
1970	Jim Plunkett, Stanford, QB
1971	Pat Sullivan, Auburn, QB
1972	Johnny Rodgers, Nebraska, RB-WR
1973	John Cappelletti, Penn State, RB
1974	Archie Griffin, Ohio State, RB
1975	Archie Griffin, Ohio State, RB
1976	Tony Dorsett, Pittsburgh, RB
1977	Earl Campbell, Texas, RB
1978	Billy Sims, Oklahoma, RB
1979	Charles White, USC, RB
1980	George Rogers, S. Carolina, RB
1981	Marcus Allen, USC, RB
1982	Herschel Walker, Georgia, RB
1983	Mike Rozier, Nebraska, RB
1984	Doug Flutie, Boston College, QB
1985	Bo Jackson, Auburn, RB
1986	Vinny Testaverde, Miami, QB
1987	Tim Brown, Notre Dame, WR
1988	Barry Sanders, Oklahoma St., RB
1989	Andre Ware, Houston, QB
1990	Ty Detmer, BYU, QB
1991	Desmond Howard, Michigan, WR
1992	Gino Torretta, Miami, QB
1993	Charlie Ward, Florida St., QB
1994	Rashaan Salaam, Colorado, RB

Outland Award

Honoring the outstanding interior lineman selected by the Football Writers Association of America.

1946	George Connor, Notre Dame, T
1947	Joe Steffy, Army, G
1948	Bill Fischer, Notre Dame, G
1949	Ed Bagdon, Michigan St., G
1950	Bob Gain, Kentucky, T
1951	Jim Weatherall, Oklahoma, T
1952	Dick Modzelewski, Maryland, T
1953	J. D. Roberts, Oklahoma, G
1954	Bill Brooks, Arkansas, G
1955	Calvin Jones, Iowa, G
1956	Jim Parker, Ohio State, G
1957	Alex Karras, Iowa, T
1958	Zeke Smith, Auburn, G
1959	Mike McGee, Duke, T
1960	Tom Brown, Minnesota, G
1961	Merlin Olsen, Utah State, T
1962	Bobby Bell, Minnesota, T
1963	Scott Appleton, Texas, T
1964	Steve Delong, Tennessee, T
1965	Tommy Nobis, Texas, G
1966	Loyd Phillips, Arkansas, T
1967	Ron Yary, Southern Cal, T
1968	Bill Stanfill, Georgia, T
1969	Mike Reid, Penn State, DT
1970	Jim Stillwagon, Ohio State, MG
1971	Larry Jacobson, Nebraska, DT
1972	Rich Glover, Nebraska, MG
1973	John Hicks, Ohio State, OT
1974	Randy White, Maryland, DE
1975	Lee Roy Selmon, Oklahoma, DT
1976	Ross Browner, Notre Dame, DE
1977	Brad Shearer, Texas, DT
1978	Greg Roberts, Oklahoma, G
1979	Jim Ritcher, N. Carolina St., C
1980	Mark May, Pittsburgh, OT
1981	Dave Rimington, Nebraska, C
1982	Dave Rimington, Nebraska, C
1983	Dean Steinkuhler, Nebraska, G
1984	Bruce Smith, Virginia Tech, DT
1985	Mike Ruth, Boston College, NG
1986	Jason Buck, BYU, DT
1987	Chad Hennings, Air Force, DT
1988	Tracy Rocker, Auburn, DT
1989	Mohammed Elewonibi, BYU, G
1990	Russell Maryland, Miami (FL) DT
1991	Steve Emtman, Washington, DT
1992	Will Shields, Nebraska, G
1993	Rob Waldrop, Arizona, NG
1994	Zach Wiegert, Nebraska, OT

All-Time Division I-A Percentage Leaders

(Classified as Division I-A for the last 10 years; record includes bowl games; ties computed as half won and half lost)

	Years	Won	Lost	Tied	Pct.	Bowl Games W	Bowl Games L	Bowl Games T
Notre Dame	106	729	216	42	.760	13	7	0
Michigan	115	747	246	36	.746	13	13	0
Alabama	100	703	238	44	.736	27	17	3
Oklahoma	100	665	246	52	.718	20	11	1
Texas	102	695	277	32	.708	17	16	2
Ohio St.	105	668	269	53	.702	13	14	0
USC	102	638	257	53	.701	24	13	0
Nebraska	105	686	290	40	.695	15	18	0
Penn St.	108	686	291	41	.694	19	10	2
Tennessee	98	644	280	53	.686	19	16	0
Central Michigan . . .	94	489	258	36	.648	3	2	0
Florida St.	48	326	177	17	.643	15	7	2
Washington	105	569	314	49	.637	12	8	1
Army	105	592	334	50	.632	2	1	0
Miami (Ohio)	106	551	313	43	.631	5	2	0
Georgia	101	595	337	54	.631	15	13	3
Louisiana St.	101	577	332	46	.628	11	16	1
Arizona St	82	447	263	24	.625	9	5	1
Auburn	102	567	336	47	.622	12	9	2
Colorado	105	568	349	36	.615	7	12	0
Miami (Florida)	68	421	262	19	.613	10	11	0
Bowling Green	76	398	244	52	.611	2	3	0
Michigan St.	98	526	334	43	.606	5	6	0
Texas A&M	100	559	361	48	.602	10	10	0
UCLA	76	442	286	37	.602	10	8	1

National College Football Champions

The unofficial national champion as selected each year by the AP poll of writers and the USA Today-CNN (until 1992 the UPI) poll of coaches. When the polls disagree, both teams are listed. The AP poll originated in 1936, and the UPI poll in 1950.

1936 Minnesota	1951 Tennessee	1966 Notre Dame	1981 Clemson
1937 Pittsburgh	1952 Michigan State	1967 Southern Cal	1982 Penn State
1938 Texas Christian	1953 Maryland	1968 Ohio State	1983 Miami (FL)
1939 Texas A&M	1954 Ohio State, UCLA	1969 Texas	1984 Brigham Young
1940 Minnesota	1955 Oklahoma	1970 Nebraska, Texas	1985 Oklahoma
1941 Minnesota	1956 Oklahoma	1971 Nebraska	1986 Penn State
1942 Ohio State	1957 Auburn, Ohio State	1972 Southern Cal	1987 Miami (FL)
1943 Notre Dame	1958 Louisiana State	1973 Notre Dame, Alabama	1988 Notre Dame
1944 Army	1959 Syracuse	1974 Oklahoma, Southern Cal	1989 Miami (FL)
1945 Army	1960 Minnesota	1975 Oklahoma	1990 Colorado, Georgia Tech
1946 Notre Dame	1961 Alabama	1976 Pittsburgh	1991 Miami (FL), Washington
1947 Notre Dame	1962 Southern Cal	1977 Notre Dame	1992 Alabama
1948 Michigan	1963 Texas	1978 Alabama, Southern Cal	1993 Florida St.
1949 Notre Dame	1964 Alabama	1979 Alabama	1994 Nebraska
1950 Oklahoma	1965 Alabama, Mich. State	1980 Georgia	

College Football Coach of the Year

The Division I-A Coach of the Year has been selected by the American Football Coaches Assn. since 1935 and selected by the Football Writers Assn. of America since 1957. When polls disagree, both winners are indicated.

1935 Lynn Waldorf, Northwestern		Darrell Royal, Texas (FWAA)	1976 Johnny Majors, Pittsburgh
1936 Dick Harlow, Harvard	1962 John McKay, USC	1977 Don James, Washington
1937 Edward Mylin, Lafayette	1963 Darrell Royal, Texas	(AFCA);
1938 Bill Kern, Carnegie Tech	1964 Ara Parseghian, Notre Dame, &	Lou Holtz, Arkansas (FWAA)
1939 Eddie Anderson, Iowa	Frank Broyles, Arkansas(AFCA);	1978 Joe Paterno, Penn St.
1940 Clark Shaughnessy, Stanford	Ara Parseghian (FWAA)	1979 Earle Bruce, Ohio St.
1941 Frank Leahy, Notre Dame	1965 Tommy Prothro, UCLA (AFCA);	1980 Vince Dooley, Georgia
1942 Bill Alexander, Georgia Tech	Duffy Daugherty, Michigan St.	1981 Danny Ford, Clemson
1943 Amos Alonzo Stagg, Pacific	(FWAA)	1982 Joe Paterno, Penn St.
1944 Carroll Widdoes, Ohio St.	1966 Tom Cahill, Army	1983 Ken Hatfield, Air Force (AFCA);
1945 Bo McMillin, Indiana	1967 John Pont, Indiana	Howard Schnellenberger, Miami
1946 Earl "Red" Blaik, Army	1968 Joe Paterno, Penn St. (AFCA);	(FL) (FWAA)
1947 Fritz Crisler, Michigan	Woody Hayes, Ohio St. (FWAA)	1984 LaVell Edwards, Brigham Young
1948 Bennie Oosterbaan, Michigan	1969 Bo Schembechler, Michigan	1985 Fisher De Berry, Air Force
1949 Bud Wilkinson, Oklahoma	1970 Charles McClendon, LSU, &	1986 Joe Paterno, Penn St.
1950 Charlie Caldwell, Princeton	Darrell Royal, Texas (AFCA);	1987 Dick MacPherson, Syracuse
1951 Chuck Taylor, Stanford	Alex Agase, Northwestern	1988 Don Nehlen, W. Virginia (AFCA);
1952 Biggie Munn, Michigan St.	(FWAA)	Lou Holtz, Notre Dame (FWAA)
1953 Jim Tatum, Maryland	1971 Paul "Bear" Bryant, Alabama	1989 Bill McCartney, Colorado
1954 Henry "Red" Sanders, UCLA	(AFCA);	1990 Bobby Ross, Georgia Tech
1955 Duffy Daugherty, Michigan St.	Bob Devaney, Nebraska (FWAA)	1991 Don James, Washington
1956 Bowden Wyatt, Tennessee	1972 John McKay, USC	1992 Gene Stallings, Alabama
1957 Woody Hayes, Ohio St.	1973 Paul "Bear" Bryant, Alabama	1993 Barry Alvarez, Wisconsin
1958 Paul Dietzel, LSU	(AFCA);	(AFCA);
1959 Ben Schwartzwalder, Syracuse	Johnny Majors, Pittsburgh (FWAA)	Terry Bowden, Auburn (FWAA)
1960 Murray Warmath, Minnesota	1974 Grant Teaff, Baylor	1994 Tom Osborne, Nebraska
1961 Paul "Bear" Bryant, Alabama	1975 Frank Kush, Arizona St. (AFCA);	(AFCA)
(AFCA);	Woody Hayes, Ohio St. (FWAA)	Rich Brooks, Oregon (FWAA)

All-Time Division I-A Coaching Victories (Incl. Bowl Games)

Paul "Bear" Bryant	323	Jess Neely	207	Howard Jones	194
Glenn "Pop" Warner	319	*Hayden Fry	205	*Jim Sweeney	191
Amos Alonzo Stagg	314	Warren Woodson	203	John Vaught	190
*Joe Paterno	269	Eddie Anderson	201	John Heisman	185
*Bobby Bowden	249	Vince Dooley	201	Darrell Royal	184
Woody Hayes	238	*Lou Holtz	199	Gil Dobie	180
Bo Schembechler	234	Dana Bible	198	Carl Snavely	180
*Tom Osborne	219	Dan McGugin	197	Jerry Claiborne	179
*LaVell Edwards	207	Fielding Yost	196	*Johnny Majors	179

Active coaches are denoted by an asterisk (*). Eddie Robinson of Grambling State Univ. holds the record for most college football victories with 397 at the start of the 1995 season.

Longest Division I-A Winning Streaks
(includes bowl games)

Wins	Team	Years	Ended by	Score
47	Oklahoma	1953-57	Notre Dame	7-0
39	Washington	1908-14	Oregon State	0-0
37	Yale	1890-93	Princeton	6-0
37	Yale	1887-89	Princeton	10-0
35	Toledo	1969-71	Tampa	21-0
34	Pennsylvania	1894-96	Lafayette	6-4
31	Oklahoma	1948-50	Kentucky	13-7
31	Pittsburgh	1914-18	Cleveland Naval Reserve	10-9
31	Pennsylvania	1896-98	Harvard	10-0
30	Texas	1968-70	Notre Dame	24-11
29	Miami (FL)	1990-93	Alabama	34-13
29	Michigan	1901-03	Minnesota	6-6
28	Alabama	1991-93	Tennessee	17-17
28	Alabama	1978-80	Mississippi State	6-3
28	Oklahoma	1973-75	Kansas	23-3
28	Michigan State	1950-53	Purdue	6-0

College Football Conference Champions

	Atlantic Coast		Ivy		Big Eight		Big Ten
1979	N. Carolina St.	1979	Yale	1979	Oklahoma	1979	Ohio State
1980	North Carolina	1980	Yale	1980	Oklahoma	1980	Michigan
1981	Clemson	1981	Yale, Dartmouth	1981	Nebraska	1981	Iowa, Ohio State
1982	Clemson	1982	Harvard, Dartmouth, Penn	1982	Nebraska	1982	Michigan
1983	Maryland	1983	Harvard, Penn	1983	Nebraska	1983	Illinois
1984	Maryland	1984	Penn	1984	Nebraska, Oklahoma	1984	Ohio State
1985	Maryland	1985	Penn	1985	Oklahoma	1985	Iowa
1986	Clemson	1986	Penn	1986	Oklahoma	1986	Michigan, Ohio State
1987	Clemson	1987	Harvard	1987	Oklahoma	1987	Michigan St.
1988	Clemson	1988	Penn, Cornell	1988	Nebraska	1988	Michigan
1989	Virginia, Duke	1989	Yale, Princeton	1989	Colorado	1989	Michigan
1990	Georgia Tech	1990	Dartmouth	1990	Colorado	1990	Iowa, Illinois, Michigan, Michigan St.
1991	Clemson	1991	Dartmouth	1991	Nebraska, Colorado	1991	Michigan
1992	Florida St.	1992	Dartmouth, Princeton	1992	Nebraska	1992	Michigan
1993	Florida St.	1993	Penn	1993	Nebraska	1993	Ohio St., Wisconsin
1994	Florida St.	1994	Penn	1994	Nebraska	1994	Penn St.

	Mid-American		Southern		Southeastern		Southwest
1979	Central Michigan	1979	Tenn.-Chattanooga	1979	Alabama	1979	Houston, Arkansas
1980	Central Michigan	1980	Furman	1980	Georgia	1980	Baylor
1981	Toledo	1981	Furman	1981	Georgia, Alabama	1981	SMU
1982	Bowling Green	1982	Furman	1982	Georgia	1982	SMU
1983	Northern Illinois	1983	Furman	1983	Auburn	1983	Texas
1984	Toledo	1984	Tenn.-Chattanooga	1984	Florida (title vacated)	1984	SMU, Houston
1985	Bowling Green	1985	Furman	1985	Tennessee	1985	Texas A&M
1986	Miami	1986	Appalachian St.	1986	LSU	1986	Texas A&M
1987	E. Michigan	1987	Appalachian St.	1987	Auburn	1987	Texas A&M
1988	W. Michigan	1988	Marshall, Furman	1988	Auburn, LSU	1988	Arkansas
1989	Ball State	1989	Furman	1989	Alabama, Tennessee, Auburn	1989	Arkansas
1990	Central Michigan	1990	Furman	1990	Tennessee	1990	Texas
1991	Bowling Green	1991	Appalachian St.	1991	Florida	1991	Texas A&M
1992	Bowling Green	1992	Citadel	1992	Alabama	1992	Texas A&M
1993	Ball State	1993	Georgia Southern	1993	Florida, Auburn	1993	Texas A&M
1994	Central Michigan	1994	Marshall	1994	Florida	1994	Baylor, Rice, Tex., Tex. Christian, Tex. Tech

	Pacific Ten		Western Athletic		Big West
1979	USC	1979	Brigham Young	1979	San Jose St.
1980	Washington	1980	Brigham Young	1980	Long Beach State
1981	Washington	1981	Brigham Young	1981	San Jose State
1982	UCLA	1982	Brigham Young	1982	Fresno State
1983	UCLA	1983	Brigham Young	1983	Cal State-Fullerton
1984	USC	1984	Brigham Young	1984	Nevada-Las Vegas
1985	UCLA	1985	Brigham Young, Air Force	1985	Fresno State
1986	Arizona State	1986	San Diego State	1986	San Jose State
1987	UCLA, USC	1987	Wyoming	1987	San Jose State
1988	USC	1988	Wyoming	1988	Fresno State
1989	USC	1989	Brigham Young	1989	Fresno State
1990	Washington	1990	Brigham Young	1990	San Jose State
1991	Washington	1991	Brigham Young	1991	San Jose St., Fresno St.
1992	Washington, Stanford	1992	Hawaii, Brigham Young, Fresno St.	1992	Nevada-Reno
1993	UCLA	1993	Wyoming, Fresno St., Brigham Young	1993	SW Louisiana, Utah St.
1994	Oregon	1994	Colorado St.	1994	Nevada-Reno, SW Louisiana, Nevada-Las Vegas

HOCKEY
National Hockey League, 1994-95
1994-95 NHL Review: Lockout Shortens Season; Quebec Moves

A 103-day lockout by NHL team owners postponed the start of the 1994-95 season from Oct. 1, 1994, to Jan. 20, 1995; the regular season schedule was shortened from 84 to 48 games. Following the season, the Quebec Nordiques were sold and moved to Denver, CO; they were renamed the Colorado Avalanche and now play in the Pacific Division.

Final Standings

Eastern Conference

Northeast Division

	W	L	T	GF	GA	PTS
Quebec..........	30	13	5	185	134	65
Pittsburgh......	29	16	3	181	158	61
Boston	27	18	3	150	127	57
Buffalo	22	19	7	130	119	51
Hartford........	19	24	5	127	141	43
Montreal	18	23	7	125	148	43
Ottawa	9	34	5	117	174	23

Atlantic Division

	W	L	T	GF	GA	PTS
Philadelphia	28	16	4	150	132	60
New Jersey.....	22	18	8	136	121	52
Washington.....	22	18	8	136	120	52
N.Y. Rangers....	22	23	3	139	134	47
Florida	20	22	6	115	127	46
Tampa Bay	17	28	3	120	144	37
N.Y. Islanders ...	15	28	5	126	158	35

Western Conference

Central Division

	W	L	T	GF	GA	PTS
Detroit	33	11	4	180	117	70
St. Louis.......	28	15	5	178	135	61
Chicago........	24	19	5	156	115	53
Toronto	21	19	8	135	146	50
Dallas	17	23	8	136	135	42
Winnipeg	16	25	7	157	177	39

Pacific Division

	W	L	T	GF	GA	PTS
Calgary	24	17	7	163	135	55
Vancouver	18	18	12	153	148	48
San Jose	19	25	4	129	161	42
Los Angeles....	16	23	9	142	174	41
Edmonton	17	27	4	136	183	38
Anaheim	16	27	5	125	164	37

Devils Win Stanley Cup Championship

The New Jersey Devils won the 1995 Stanley Cup by sweeping the Detroit Red Wings in 4 games. Devils right wing Claude Lemieux won the Conn Smythe Trophy as the most valuable player in the playoffs.

Stanley Cup Playoff Results

Eastern Conference

N.Y. Rangers defeated Quebec 4-2
Pittsburgh defeated Washington 4-3
Philadelphia defeated Buffalo 4-1
New Jersey defeated Boston 4-1
New Jersey defeated Pittsburgh 4-1
Philadelphia defeated N.Y. Rangers 4-0
New Jersey defeated Philadelphia 4-2

Western Conference

Detroit defeated Dallas 4-1
Vancouver defeated St. Louis 4-3
Chicago defeated Toronto 4-3
San Jose defeated Calgary 4-3
Detroit defeated San Jose 4-0
Chicago defeated Vancouver 4-0
Detroit defeated Chicago 4-1

Finals
New Jersey defeated Detroit 4-0

Stanley Cup Champions Since 1927

Year	Champion	Coach	Final opponent	Year	Champion	Coach	Final opponent
1927	Ottawa	Dave Gill	Boston	1962	Toronto	Punch Imlach	Chicago
1928	N.Y. Rangers	Lester Patrick	Montreal	1963	Toronto	Punch Imlach	Detroit
1929	Boston	Cy Denneny	N.Y. Rangers	1964	Toronto	Punch Imlach	Detroit
1930	Montreal	Cecil Hart	Boston	1965	Montreal	Toe Blake	Chicago
1931	Montreal	Cecil Hart	Chicago	1966	Montreal	Toe Blake	Detroit
1932	Toronto	Dick Irvin	N.Y. Rangers	1967	Toronto	Punch Imlach	Montreal
1933	N.Y. Rangers	Lester Patrick	Toronto	1968	Montreal	Toe Blake	St. Louis
1934	Chicago	Tommy Gorman	Detroit	1969	Montreal	Claude Ruel	St. Louis
1935	Montreal Maroons	Tommy Gorman	Toronto	1970	Boston	Harry Sinden	St. Louis
1936	Detroit	Jack Adams	Toronto	1971	Montreal	Al MacNeil	Chicago
1937	Detroit	Jack Adams	N.Y. Rangers	1972	Boston	Tom Johnson	N.Y. Rangers
1938	Chicago	Bill Stewart	Toronto	1973	Montreal	Scotty Bowman	Chicago
1939	Boston	Art Ross	Toronto	1974	Philadelphia	Fred Shero	Boston
1940	N.Y. Rangers	Frank Boucher	Toronto	1975	Philadelphia	Fred Shero	Buffalo
1941	Boston	Cooney Weiland	Detroit	1976	Montreal	Scotty Bowman	Philadelphia
1942	Toronto	Hap Day	Detroit	1977	Montreal	Scotty Bowman	Boston
1943	Detroit	Jack Adams	Boston	1978	Montreal	Scotty Bowman	Boston
1944	Montreal	Dick Irvin	Chicago	1979	Montreal	Scotty Bowman	N.Y. Rangers
1945	Toronto	Hap Day	Detroit	1980	N.Y. Islanders	Al Arbour	Philadelphia
1946	Montreal	Dick Irvin	Boston	1981	N.Y. Islanders	Al Arbour	Minnesota
1947	Toronto	Hap Day	Montreal	1982	N.Y. Islanders	Al Arbour	Vancouver
1948	Toronto	Hap Day	Detroit	1983	N.Y. Islanders	Al Arbour	Edmonton
1949	Toronto	Hap Day	Detroit	1984	Edmonton	Glen Sather	N.Y. Islanders
1950	Detroit	Tommy Ivan	N.Y. Rangers	1985	Edmonton	Glen Sather	Philadelphia
1951	Toronto	Joe Primeau	Montreal	1986	Montreal	Jean Perron	Calgary
1952	Detroit	Tommy Ivan	Montreal	1987	Edmonton	Glen Sather	Philadelphia
1953	Montreal	Dick Irvin	Boston	1988	Edmonton	Glen Sather	Boston
1954	Detroit	Tommy Ivan	Montreal	1989	Calgary	Terry Crisp	Montreal
1955	Detroit	Jimmy Skinner	Montreal	1990	Edmonton	John Muckler	Boston
1956	Montreal	Toe Blake	Detroit	1991	Pittsburgh	Bob Johnson	Minnesota
1957	Montreal	Toe Blake	Boston	1992	Pittsburgh	Scotty Bowman	Chicago
1958	Montreal	Toe Blake	Boston	1993	Montreal	Jacques Demers	Los Angeles
1959	Montreal	Toe Blake	Toronto	1994	N.Y. Rangers	Mike Keenan	Vancouver
1960	Montreal	Toe Blake	Toronto	1995	New Jersey	Jacques Lemaire	Detroit
1961	Chicago	Rudy Pilous	Detroit				

Individual Leaders, 1994-95

Points
Jaromir Jagr, Pittsburgh, 70; Eric Lindros, Philadelphia, 70; Alexei Zhamnov, Winnipeg, 65; Joe Sakic, Quebec, 62; Ron Francis, Pittsburgh, 59.

Goals
Peter Bondra, Washington, 34; Jaromir Jagr, Pittsburgh, 32; Owen Nolan, Quebec, 30; Ray Sheppard, Detroit, 30; Alexei Zhamnov, Winnipeg, 30.

Assists
Ron Francis Pittsburgh, 48; Paul Coffey, Detroit, 44; Joe Sakic, Quebec, 43; Eric Lindros, Philadelphia, 41; Adam Oates, Boston, 41.

Power-play goals
Cam Neely, Boston, 16; Donald Audette, Buffalo, 13; Owen Nolan, Quebec,13; Peter Bondra, Washington, 12; Alexander Mogilny, Buffalo, 12.

Shorthanded goals
Peter Bondra, Washington, 6; Wayne Presley, Buffalo, 5; 8 players tied with 3.

Shooting percentage
(minimum 48 shots)
Ian Laperrierre, St. Louis, 24.5; Ray Sheppard, Detroit, 24.0; Roman Oksiuta, Edmonton-Vancouver, 23.9; Ray Ferraro, N.Y. Islanders, 23.4; Andrei Kovalenko, Quebec, 22.2.

Plus/Minus
Ron Francis, Pittsburgh, 30; Steve Duchesne, St. Louis, 29; Curtis Leschyshyn, Quebec, 29; Eric Lindros, Philadelphia, 27; Jaromir Jagr, Pittsburgh, 23.

GOALTENDING LEADERS
(minimum 13 games)

Goals against average
Dominik Hasek, Buffalo, 2.111; Rick Tabaracci, Washington-Calgary, 2.114; Jim Carey, Washington, 2.13; Chris Osgood, Detroit, 2.26; Ed Balfour, Chicago, 2.28.

Wins
Ken Wregget, Pittsburgh, 25; Ed Belfour, Chicago, 22; Trevor Kidd, Calgary, 22; Curtis Joseph, St. Louis, 20; 4 players tied with 19.

Save percentage
Dominik Hasek, Buffalo, .930; Chris Osgood, Detroit, .917; Jocelyn Thibault, Quebec, .917; Damian Rhodes, Toronto, .916; Andy Moog, Dallas, .915.

Shutouts
Ed Belfour, Chicago, 5; Dominik Hasek, Buffalo, 5; Jim Carey, Washington, 4; Arturs Irbe, San Jose, 4; Blaine Lacher, Boston, 4; John Vanbiesbrouck, Florida, 4.

Individual Scoring, 1994-95

(24 or more games played)

Mighty Ducks of Anaheim

	GP	G	A	Pts	PIM	+/-
Paul Kariya	47	18	21	39	4	-17
Shaun Van Allen	45	8	21	29	32	-4
Stephan Lebeau	38	8	16	24	12	6
Todd Krygier	35	11	11	22	10	1
Peter Douris	46	10	11	21	12	4
Patrick Carnback	41	6	15	21	32	-8
Bobby Dollas	45	7	13	20	12	-3
Bob Corkum	44	10	9	19	25	-7
Joe Sacco	41	10	8	18	23	-8
Steve Rucchin	43	6	11	17	23	7
Mike Sillinger	28	4	11	15	8	4
Oleg Tverdovsky	36	3	9	12	14	-6
Valeri Karpov	30	4	7	11	6	-4
Milos Holan	25	2	8	10	14	4
Jason York	25	1	10	11	14	4
Garry Valk	36	3	6	9	34	-4
Randy Ladouceur	44	2	4	6	36	2
Dave Karpa	28	1	5	6	91	-1
Robert Dirk	38	1	3	4	56	-3
Todd Ewen	24	0	0	0	90	-2
Guy Hebert	39	0	0	0	2	0

Coach—Ron Wilson

Boston Bruins

	GP	G	A	Pts	PIM	+/-
Adam Oates	48	12	41	53	8	-11
Ray Bourque	46	12	31	43	20	3
Cam Neely	42	27	14	41	72	7
Bryan Smolinksi	44	18	13	31	31	-3
Mariusz Czerkawski	47	12	14	26	31	4
Mats Naslund	34	8	14	22	4	-4
Don Sweeney	47	3	19	22	24	6
Ted Donato	47	10	10	20	10	3
Jozef Stumpel	44	5	13	18	8	4
Steve Heinze	36	7	9	16	23	0
Alexei Kasatonov	44	2	14	16	33	-2
Brent Hughes	44	6	6	12	139	6
Stephen Leach	35	5	6	11	68	-3
Jon Rohloff	34	3	8	11	39	1
Dave Reid	38	5	5	10	10	8
Glen Murray	35	5	2	7	46	-11
David Shaw	44	3	4	7	36	-9
Jamie Huscroft	34	0	6	6	103	-3
John Grunden	38	0	6	6	22	3
Blaine Lacher	35	0	1	1	4	0

Coach—Brian Sutter

Buffalo Sabres

	GP	G	A	Pts	PIM	+/-
Alexander Mogilny	44	19	28	47	36	0
Donald Audette	46	24	13	37	27	-3
Garry Galley	47	3	29	32	30	4
Yuri Khmylev	48	8	17	25	14	8
Derek Plante	47	3	19	22	12	-4
Doug Bodger	44	3	17	20	47	-3
Wayne Presley	46	14	5	19	41	5
Dave Hannan	42	4	12	16	32	3
Alexei Zhitnik	32	4	10	14	61	-6
Jason Dawe	42	7	4	11	19	-6
Craig Simpson	24	4	7	11	26	-5
Richard Smehlik	39	4	7	11	46	5
Bob Sweeney	45	5	4	9	18	-6
Charlie Huddy	41	2	5	7	42	-7
Brad May	33	3	3	6	87	5
Craig Muni	40	0	6	6	36	-4
Petr Svoboda	37	0	8	8	70	-5
Scott Pearson	42	3	5	8	74	-14
Doug Houda	28	1	2	3	68	1
Rob Ray	47	0	3	3	173	-4
Dominik Hasek	41	0	0	0	2	0

Coach—John Muckler

Calgary Flames

	GP	G	A	Pts	PIM	+/-
Theoren Fleury	47	29	29	58	112	6
Joe Nieuwendyk	46	21	29	50	33	11
Phil Housley	43	8	35	43	18	17
Robert Reichel	48	18	17	35	28	-2
Zarley Zalapski	48	4	24	28	46	9
Steve Chiasson	45	2	23	25	39	10
German Titov	40	12	12	24	16	6
Joel Otto	47	8	13	21	130	8
Wes Walz	39	6	12	18	11	7
Paul Kruse	45	11	5	16	141	13
Sheldon Kennedy	30	7	8	15	45	5
Ronnie Stern	39	9	4	13	163	4
Kevin Dahl	34	4	8	12	38	8
Mike Sullivan	38	4	7	11	14	-2
Nikolai Borschevsky	27	0	10	10	0	10
James Patrick	43	0	10	10	14	-3
Sandy McCarthy	37	5	3	8	101	1
Dan Keczmer	28	2	3	5	10	7
Alan May	34	2	3	5	119	3
Frank Musil	35	0	5	5	61	6
Trent Yawney	37	0	2	2	108	-4
Trevor Kidd	43	0	1	1	2	0

Coach—Dave King

Chicago Blackhawks

	GP	G	A	Pts	PIM	+/-
Bernie Nicholls	48	22	29	51	32	4
Joe Murphy	40	23	18	41	89	6
Chris Chelios	48	5	33	38	72	17
Gary Suter	48	10	27	37	42	14
Tony Amonte	48	15	20	35	41	9
Jeremy Roenick	33	10	24	34	14	5

	GP	G	A	Pts	PIM	+/-
Patrick Poulin	45	15	15	30	53	13
Denis Savard	43	10	15	25	18	-3
Sergei Krivokrasov	41	12	7	19	33	9
Jeff Shantz	45	6	12	18	33	11
Brent Sutter	47	7	8	15	51	6
Dirk Graham	40	4	9	13	42	2
Eric Weinrich	48	3	10	13	33	1
Steve Smith	48	1	12	13	128	6
Brent Grieve	24	1	5	6	23	2
Jim Cummins	37	4	1	5	158	-6
Gerald Diduck	35	2	3	5	63	-5
Cam Russell	33	1	3	4	88	4
Ed Belfour	42	0	3	3	11	0

Coach—Darryl Sutter

Dallas Stars

	GP	G	A	Pts	PIM	+/-
Dave Gagner	48	14	28	42	42	2
Mike Modano	30	12	17	29	8	7
Kevin Hatcher	47	10	19	29	66	-4
Mike Donnelly	44	12	15	27	33	-4
Corey Millen	45	5	18	23	36	6
Trent Klatt	47	12	10	22	26	-2
Greg Adams	43	8	13	21	16	-3
Todd Harvey	40	11	9	20	67	-3
Mike Kennedy	44	6	12	18	33	4
Grant Ledyard	38	5	13	18	20	6
Paul Broten	47	7	9	16	36	-7
Derian Hatcher	43	5	11	16	105	3
Dean Evason	47	8	7	15	48	3
Brent Gilchrist	32	9	4	13	16	-3
Paul Cavallini	44	1	11	12	28	8
Peter Zezel	30	6	5	11	19	-6
Craig Ludwig	47	2	7	9	61	-6
Doug Zmolek	42	0	5	5	67	-6
Shane Churla	27	1	3	4	186	0
Andy Moog	31	0	1	1	14	0

Coach—Bob Gainey

Detroit Red Wings

	GP	G	A	Pts	PIM	+/-
Paul Coffey	45	14	44	58	72	18
Sergei Fedorov	42	20	30	50	24	6
Dino Ciccarelli	42	16	27	43	39	12
Keith Primeau	45	15	27	42	99	17
Ray Sheppard	43	30	10	40	17	11
Steve Yzerman	47	12	26	38	40	6
Vyacheslav Kozlov	46	13	20	33	45	12
Nicklas Lidstrom	43	10	16	26	6	15
Doug Brown	45	9	12	21	16	14
Bob Errey	43	8	13	21	58	13
Shawn Burr	42	6	8	14	60	13
Vladimir Konstantinov	47	3	11	14	101	10
Darren McCarty	31	5	8	13	88	5
Martin Lapointe	39	4	6	10	73	1
Kris Draper	36	2	6	8	22	1
Bob Rouse	48	1	7	8	36	14
Mike Ramsey	33	1	2	3	23	11
Stu Grimson	42	0	1	1	147	-11
Mike Vernon	30	0	0	0	8	0

Coach—Scotty Bowman

Edmonton Oilers

	GP	G	A	Pts	PIM	+/-
Doug Weight	48	7	33	40	69	-17
Jason Arnott	42	15	22	37	128	-14
Shayne Corson	48	12	24	36	86	-17
David Oliver	44	16	14	30	20	-11
Todd Marchant	45	13	14	27	32	-3
Kelly Buchberger	48	7	17	24	82	0
Scott Thornton	47	10	12	22	89	-4
Igor Kravchuk	36	7	11	18	29	-15
Mike Stapleton	46	6	11	17	21	-12
Luke Richardson	46	3	10	13	40	-6
Jiri Slegr	31	2	10	12	46	-5
Kirk Maltby	47	8	3	11	49	-11
Dean Kennedy	40	2	8	10	25	2
Fredrik Olausson	33	0	10	10	20	-4
Boris Mironov	29	1	7	8	40	-9
Ken Sutton	24	4	3	7	42	-3
Bryan Marchment	40	1	5	6	184	-11
Louie Debrusk	34	2	0	2	93	-4
Bill Ranford	40	0	2	2	2	0

Coach—George Burnett, Ron Low

Florida Panthers

	GP	G	A	Pts	PIM	+/-
Jesse Belanger	47	15	14	29	18	-5
Stu Barnes	41	10	19	29	8	7
Scott Mellanby	48	13	12	25	90	-16
Gord Murphy	46	6	16	22	24	-14
Dave Lowry	45	10	10	20	25	-3
Jody Hull	46	11	8	19	8	-1
Bill Lindsay	48	10	9	19	46	1
Tom Fitzgerald	48	3	13	16	31	-3
Gaetan Duchesne	46	3	9	12	16	-3
Brian Skrudland	47	5	9	14	88	0
Johan Garpenlov	40	4	10	14	2	1
Mike Hough	48	6	7	13	38	1
Jason Woolley	34	4	9	13	18	-1
Rob Niedermayer	48	4	6	10	36	-13
Bob Kudelski	26	6	3	9	2	2
Brian Benning	24	1	7	8	18	-6
Andrei Lomakin	31	1	6	7	6	-5
Paul Laus	37	0	7	7	138	12
Geoff Smith	47	2	4	6	22	-5
John Vanbiesbrouck	37	0	1	1	6	0

Coach—Roger Neilson

Hartford Whalers

	GP	G	A	Pts	PIM	+/-
Andrew Cassels	46	7	30	37	18	-3
Darren Turcotte	47	17	18	35	22	1
Geoff Sanderson	46	18	14	32	24	-10
Steven Rice	40	11	10	21	61	2
Paul Ranheim	47	6	14	20	10	-3
Frantisek Kucera	48	3	17	20	30	3
Jimmy Carson	38	9	10	19	29	5
Robert Kron	37	10	8	18	10	-3
Andrei Nikolishin	39	8	10	18	10	7
Adam Burt	46	7	11	18	65	0
Glen Wesley	48	2	14	16	50	-6
Chris Pronger	43	5	9	14	54	-12
Jocelyn Lemieux	41	6	5	11	32	-7
Ted Drury	34	3	6	9	21	-3
Mark Janssens	46	2	5	7	93	-8
Brian Glynn	43	1	6	7	32	-2
Kelly Chase	28	0	4	4	141	1
Brad McCrimmon	33	0	1	1	42	7
Sean Burke	42	0	1	1	8	0

Coach—Paul Holmgren

Los Angeles Kings

	GP	G	A	Pts	PIM	+/-
Wayne Gretzky	48	11	37	48	6	-20
Rick Tocchet	36	18	17	35	70	-8
Dan Quinn	44	14	17	31	32	-3
Jari Kurri	38	10	19	29	24	-17
Tony Granato	33	13	11	24	68	9
Darryl Sydor	48	4	19	23	36	-2
Marty McSorley	41	3	18	21	83	-14
John Druce	43	15	5	20	20	-3
Randy Burridge	40	4	15	19	10	-4
Michel Petit	40	5	12	17	84	4
Eric Lacroix	45	9	7	16	54	2
Pat Conacher	48	7	9	16	12	-9
Robert Lang	36	4	8	12	4	-7
Rob Blake	24	4	7	11	38	-16
Kevin Todd	33	3	8	11	12	-5
Rob Cowie	32	2	7	9	20	-6
Chris Snell	32	2	7	9	22	-7
Yanic Perreault	26	2	5	7	20	3
Troy Crowder	29	1	2	3	99	0
Denis Tsygurov	25	0	0	0	15	-3
Kelly Hrudey	35	0	0	0	0	0

Coach—Barry Melrose, Rogie Vachon

Montreal Canadiens

	GP	G	A	Pts	PIM	+/-
Mark Recchi	49	16	32	48	28	-9
Pierre Turgeon	49	24	23	47	14	0
Vincent Damphousse	48	10	30	40	42	15
Benoit Brunet	45	7	18	25	16	7
Vladimir Malakhov	40	4	17	21	46	-3
Mike Keane	48	10	10	20	15	5
Brian Savage	37	12	7	19	27	5
Brian Bellows	41	8	8	16	8	-7
Patrice Brisebois	35	4	8	12	26	-2
Yves Racine	47	4	7	11	42	-1
Lyle Odelein	48	3	7	10	152	-13
J.J. Daigneault	45	3	5	8	40	2
Turner Stevenson	41	6	1	7	86	0
Ed Ronan	30	1	4	5	12	-7
Peter Popovic	33	0	5	5	8	-10
Valeri Bure	24	3	1	4	6	-1
Mark Lamb	47	1	2	3	20	-12
Patrick Roy	43	0	1	1	20	0

Coach—Jacques Demers

New Jersey Devils

	GP	G	A	Pts	PIM	+/-
Stephane Richer	45	23	16	39	10	8
Neal Broten	47	8	24	32	24	1
John MacLean	46	17	12	29	32	13
Bill Guerin	48	12	13	25	72	6
Scott Stevens	48	2	20	22	56	4
Shawn Chambers	45	4	17	21	12	2
Bobby Holik	48	10	10	20	18	9
Claude Lemieux	45	6	13	19	86	2
Scott Niedermayer	48	4	15	19	18	19
Tom Chorske	42	10	8	18	16	-4
Brian Rolston	40	7	11	18	17	5
Bob Carpenter	41	5	11	16	19	-1
Bruce Driver	41	4	12	16	18	-1
Tommy Albelin	48	5	10	15	20	9
Danton Cole	38	4	5	9	14	-1
Sergei Brylin	26	6	8	14	8	12
Randy McKay	33	5	7	12	44	10
Mike Peluso	46	2	9	11	167	5
Ken Daneyko	25	1	2	3	54	4
Chris McAlpine	24	0	3	3	17	4
Martin Brodeur	40	0	2	2	2	0

Coach—Jacques Lemaire

New York Islanders

	GP	G	A	Pts	PIM	+/-
Ray Ferraro	47	22	21	43	30	1
Mathieu Schneider	43	8	21	29	79	-8
Patrick Flatley	45	7	20	27	12	9
Kirk Muller	45	11	16	27	47	-18
Steve Thomas	47	11	15	26	60	-14
Derek King	43	10	16	26	41	-5
Zigmund Palffy	33	10	7	17	6	3
Marty McInnis	41	9	7	16	8	-1
Scott Lachance	26	6	7	13	26	2
Travis Green	42	5	7	12	25	-10
Dennis Vaske	41	1	11	12	53	3
Brent Severyn	28	2	4	6	71	-2
Ron Sutter	27	1	4	5	21	-8
Brett Lindros	33	1	3	4	100	-8
Chris Luongo	47	1	3	4	36	-2
Dean Chynoweth	32	0	2	2	77	9
Mick Vukota	40	0	2	2	109	1
Tommy Soderstrom	26	0	0	0	2	0

Coach—Lorne Henning

New York Rangers

	GP	G	A	Pts	PIM	+/-
Mark Messier	46	14	39	53	40	8
Brian Leetch	48	9	32	41	18	0
Sergei Zubov	38	10	26	36	18	-2
Adam Graves	47	17	14	31	51	9
Steve Larmer	47	14	15	29	16	8
Alexei Kovalev	48	13	15	28	30	-6
Brian Noonan	45	14	13	27	26	-3
Petr Nedved	46	11	12	23	26	-1
Pat Verbeek	48	17	16	33	71	-2
Sergei Nemchinov	47	7	6	13	16	-6
Alexander Karpovtsev	47	4	8	12	30	-4
Jay Wells	43	2	7	9	36	0
Troy Loney	30	5	4	9	23	-2
Stephane Matteau	41	3	5	8	25	-8
Kevin Lowe	44	1	7	8	58	-2
Nathan Lafayette	39	4	4	8	2	3
Mark Osborne	37	1	3	4	19	-2
Nick Kypreos	40	1	3	4	93	0
Jeff Beukeboom	44	1	3	4	70	3
Joey Kocur	48	1	2	3	71	-4
Dan Lacroix	24	1	0	1	38	-2
Mike Richter	35	0	0	0	2	0

Coach—Colin Campbell

Ottawa Senators

	GP	G	A	Pts	PIM	+/-
Alexei Yashin	47	21	23	44	20	-20
Alexandre Daigle	47	16	21	37	14	-22
Sylvain Turgeon	33	11	8	19	29	-1
Martin Straka	37	5	13	18	16	-1
Sean Hill	45	1	14	15	30	-11
Rob Gaudreau	36	5	9	14	8	-16
Michel Picard	24	5	8	13	14	-1
Scott Levins	24	5	6	11	51	4
Dave McLlwain	43	5	6	11	22	-26
Radek Bonk	42	3	8	11	28	-5
Randy Cunneyworth	48	5	5	10	68	-19

	GP	G	A	Pts	PIM	+/-
Pat Elynuik	41	3	7	10	51	-11
Chris Dahlquist	46	1	7	8	36	-30
Phil Bourque	38	4	3	7	20	-17
Kerry Huffman	37	2	4	6	46	-17
Stanislav Neckar	48	1	3	4	37	-20
Dennis Vial	27	0	4	4	65	0
Jim Paek	29	0	2	2	28	-5
Don Beaupre	38	0	0	0	10	0

Coach—Rick Bowness

Philadelphia Flyers

	GP	G	A	Pts	PIM	+/-
Eric Lindros	46	29	41	70	60	27
Mikael Renberg	47	26	31	57	20	20
John LeClair	46	26	28	54	30	20
Rod Brind'Amour	48	12	27	39	33	-4
Eric Desjardins	43	5	24	29	14	12
Dimitri Yushkevich	40	5	9	14	47	-4
Kevin Dineen	40	8	5	13	39	-1
Chris Therien	48	3	10	13	38	8
Brent Fedyk	30	8	4	12	14	-2
Craig MacTavish	45	3	9	12	23	2
Shjon Podein	44	3	7	10	33	-2
Anatoli Semenov	41	4	6	10	10	-12
Kevin Haller	36	2	8	10	48	16
Gilbert Dionne	26	0	9	9	4	-4
Petr Svoboda	37	0	8	8	70	-5
Karl Dykhuis	33	2	6	8	37	7
Patrik Juhlin	42	4	3	7	6	-13
Rob DiMaio	36	3	1	4	53	8
Dave Brown	28	1	2	3	53	-1
Rob Zettler	32	0	1	1	34	-3
Shawn Antoski	32	0	0	0	107	-4
Ron Hextall	31	0	0	0	13	0

Coach—Terry Murray

Pittsburgh Penguins

	GP	G	A	Pts	PIM	+/-
Jaromir Jagr	48	32	38	70	37	23
Ron Francis	44	11	48	59	18	30
Tomas Sandstrom	47	21	23	44	42	1
Luc Robitaille	46	23	19	42	37	10
Larry Murphy	48	13	25	38	18	12
Joe Mullen	45	16	21	37	6	15
John Cullen	46	13	24	37	66	-4
Kevin Stevens	27	15	12	27	51	0
Shawn McEachern	44	13	13	26	22	4
Norm Maciver	41	4	16	20	16	-2
Troy Murray	46	4	12	16	39	-2
	44	1	15	16	113	11
Chris Joseph	33	5	10	15	46	3
Len Barrie	48	3	11	14	66	-4
Mike Hudson	40	2	9	11	34	-1
Kjell Samuelsson	41	1	6	7	54	8
Jim McKenzie	39	2	1	3	63	-7
Chris Tamer	36	2	0	2	82	0
Francois Leroux	40	0	2	2	114	7
Drake Berehowsky	29	0	2	2	28	-9
Ken Wregget	38	0	0	0	14	0

Coach—Eddie Johnston

Quebec Nordiques

	GP	G	A	Pts	PIM	+/-
Joe Sakic	47	19	43	62	30	7
Peter Forsberg	47	15	35	50	16	17
Owen Nolan	46	30	19	49	46	21
Scott Young	48	18	21	39	14	9
Mike Ricci	48	15	21	36	40	5
Wendel Clark	37	12	18	30	45	-1
Valeri Kamensky	40	10	20	30	22	3
Bob Bassen	47	12	15	27	33	14
Andrei Kovalenko	45	14	10	24	31	-4
Uwe Krupp	44	6	17	23	20	14
Adam Deadmarsh	48	9	8	17	56	16
Curtis Leschyshyn	44	2	13	15	20	29
Sylvain Lefebvre	48	2	11	13	17	13
Claude Lapointe	29	4	8	12	41	5
Chris Simon	29	3	9	12	106	14
Craig Wolanin	40	3	6	9	40	12
Adam Foote	35	0	7	7	52	17
Bill Huard	33	3	3	6	77	0
Stephane Fiset	32	0	3	3	2	0
Steven Finn	40	0	3	3	64	1

Coach—Marc Crawford

St. Louis Blues

	GP	G	A	Pts	PIM	+/-
Brett Hull	48	29	21	50	10	13
Brendan Shanahan	45	20	21	41	136	7
Steve Duchesne	47	12	26	38	36	29
Esa Tikkanen	43	12	23	35	22	13
Adam Creighton	48	14	20	34	74	17
Jeff Norton	48	3	27	30	72	22
Al MacInnis	32	8	20	28	43	19
Ian Laperriere	37	13	14	27	85	12
Glenn Anderson	36	12	14	26	37	9
Greg Gilbert	46	11	14	25	11	22
Todd Elik	35	9	14	23	22	8
Bill Houlder	41	5	13	18	20	16
Denis Chasse	47	7	9	16	133	12
Guy Carbonneau	42	5	11	16	16	11
Patrice Tardif	27	3	10	13	29	4
Vitali Karamnov	26	3	7	10	14	7
Doug Lidster	37	2	7	9	12	9
Murray Baron	39	0	5	5	93	9
Tony Twist	28	3	0	3	89	0
Curtis Joseph	36	0	1	1	0	0
Coach—Mike Keenan						

San Jose Sharks

	GP	G	A	Pts	PIM	+/-
Ulf Dahlen	46	11	23	34	11	-2
Craig Janney	35	7	20	27	10	-1
Jeff Friesen	48	15	10	25	14	-8
Ray Whitney	39	13	12	25	14	-7
Sandis Ozolinsh	48	9	16	25	30	-6
Sergei Makarov	43	10	14	24	40	-4
Igor Larionov	33	4	20	24	14	-3
Kevin Miller	36	8	12	20	13	4
Pat Falloon	46	12	7	19	25	-4
Tom Pederson	47	5	11	16	31	-14
Chris Tancill	26	3	11	14	10	1
Jamie Baker	43	7	4	11	22	-7
Mike Rathje	42	2	7	9	29	-1
Andrei Nazarov	26	3	5	8	94	-1
Jeff Odgers	48	4	3	7	117	-8
Jay More	45	0	6	6	71	7
Shawn Cronin	29	0	2	2	61	0
Arturs Irbe	38	0	0	0	4	0
Coach—Kevin Constantine						

Tampa Bay Lightning

	GP	G	A	Pts	PIM	+/-
Brian Bradley	46	13	27	40	42	-6
Paul Ysebaert	44	12	16	28	18	3
Chris Gratton	46	7	20	27	89	-2
Petr Klima	47	13	13	26	26	-13
John Tucker	46	12	13	25	14	-10
Roman Hamrlik	48	12	11	23	86	-18
Alexander Semak	41	7	11	18	25	-7
Alexander Selivanov	43	10	6	16	14	-2
Rob Zamuner	43	9	6	15	24	-3
Marc Bureau	48	2	12	14	30	-8
Mikael Andersson	36	4	7	11	4	-3
Enrico Ciccone	41	2	4	6	225	3
Marc Bergevin	44	2	4	6	51	-6
Cory Cross	43	1	5	6	41	-6
Jason Wiemer	36	1	4	5	44	-2
Eric Charron	45	1	4	5	26	1
Bob Halkidis	31	1	4	5	46	-10
Ben Hankinson	26	0	2	2	13	-5
Rudy Poeschek	25	1	1	2	92	0
Daren Puppa	36	0	1	1	2	0
Coach—Terry Crisp						

Toronto Maple Leafs

	GP	G	A	Pts	PIM	+/-
Mats Sundin	47	23	24	47	14	-5
Dave Andreychuk	48	22	16	38	34	-7
Mike Ridley	48	10	27	37	14	1
Doug Gilmour	44	10	23	33	26	-5
Todd Gill	47	7	25	32	64	-8
Randy Wood	48	13	11	24	34	7
Mike Gartner	38	12	8	20	6	0
Dmitri Mironov	33	5	12	17	28	6
Benoit Hogue	45	9	7	16	34	0
Dave Ellett	33	5	10	15	26	-6
Paul Dipietro	34	5	6	11	10	-9
Mike Craig	37	5	5	10	12	-21
Jamie Macoun	46	2	8	10	75	-6
Tie Domi	40	4	5	9	159	-5

	GP	G	A	Pts	PIM	+/-
Kenny Jonsson	39	2	7	9	16	-8
Garth Butcher	45	1	7	8	59	-5
Warren Rychel	33	1	6	7	120	-4
Grant Jennings	35	0	6	6	43	-4
Bill Berg	32	5	1	6	26	-11
Rich Sutter	37	0	3	3	38	-6
Kent Manderville	36	0	1	1	22	-2
Felix Potvin	36	0	0	0	4	0
Coach—Pat Burns						

Vancouver Canucks

	GP	G	A	Pts	PIM	+/-
Pavel Bure	44	20	23	43	47	-8
Trevor Linden	48	18	22	40	40	-5
Russ Courtnall	45	11	24	35	17	2
Geoff Courtnall	45	16	18	34	81	2
Josef Beranek	51	13	18	31	30	-7
Jeff Brown	33	8	23	31	16	-2
Sergio Momesso	48	10	15	25	65	-2
Cliff Ronning	41	6	19	25	27	-4
Martin Gelinas	46	13	10	23	36	8
Roman Oksiuta	38	16	4	20	10	-12
Christian Ruuttu	45	7	11	18	29	14
Jyrki Lumme	36	5	12	17	26	4
Dave Babych	40	3	11	14	18	-13
Bret Hedican	45	2	11	13	34	-3
Mike Peca	33	6	6	12	30	-6
Dana Murzyn	40	0	8	8	129	14
Tim Hunter	34	3	2	5	120	1
John McIntyre	28	0	4	4	37	-3
Jassen Cullimore	34	1	2	3	39	-2
Kirk McLean	40	0	1	1	4	0
Coach—Rick Ley						

Washington Capitals

	GP	G	A	Pts	PIM	+/-
Peter Bondra	47	34	9	43	24	9
Joe Juneau	44	5	38	43	8	-1
Michal Pivonka	46	10	23	33	50	3
Calle Johansson	46	5	26	31	35	-6
Dimitri Khristich	48	12	14	26	41	0
Steve Konowalchuk	46	11	14	25	44	7
Kelly Miller	48	10	13	23	6	5
Dale Hunter	45	8	15	23	101	-4
Keith Jones	40	14	6	20	65	-2
Sylvain Cote	47	5	14	19	53	2
Jim Johnson	47	0	13	13	43	6
Mark Tinordi	42	3	9	12	71	-5
Dave Poulin	29	4	5	9	10	2
Mike Eagles	40	3	4	7	48	-11
Sergei Gonchar	31	2	5	7	22	4
Joe Reekie	48	1	6	7	97	10
Craig Berube	43	2	4	6	173	-5
Rob Pearson	32	0	6	6	96	-6
Kevin Kaminski	27	1	1	2	102	-6
Jim Carey	28	0	0	0	0	0
Coach—Jim Schoenfeld						

Winnipeg Jets

	GP	G	A	Pts	PIM	+/-
Alexei Zhamnov	48	30	35	65	20	5
Keith Tkachuk	48	22	29	51	152	-4
Teemu Selanne	45	22	26	48	2	1
Nelson Emerson	48	14	23	37	26	-12
Igor Korolev	45	8	22	30	10	1
Dallas Drake	43	8	18	26	30	-6
Stephane Quintal	43	6	17	23	78	0
Teppo Numminen	42	5	16	21	16	12
Mike Eastwood	49	8	11	19	36	-9
Dave Manson	44	3	15	18	139	-20
Thomas Steen	31	5	10	15	14	-13
Darryl Shannon	40	5	9	14	48	1
Ed Olczyk	33	4	9	13	12	-1
Randy Gilhen	44	5	6	11	52	-17
Kris King	48	4	2	6	85	0
Neil Wilkinson	40	1	4	5	75	-26
Michal Grosek	24	2	2	4	21	-3
Oleg Mikulchik	25	0	2	2	12	10
Nikolai Khabibulin	26	0	1	1	4	0
Tim Cheveldae	30	0	1	1	2	0
Brent Thompson	29	0	0	0	78	-17
Coach—John Paddock, Terry Simpson						

Individual Goaltending, 1994-95

(top goalie for each team by games played)

Player	GP	GAA	W	L	T	SO	SV%	Player	GP	GAA	W	L	T	SO	SV%
Hebert, Ana.	39	3.13	12	20	4	2	.904	Soderstrom, N.Y.I.	26	3.11	8	12	3	1	.902
Lacher, Bos.	35	2.41	19	11	2	4	.902	Richter, N.Y.R.	35	2.92	14	17	2	2	.890
Hasek, Buf.	41	2.11	19	14	7	5	.930	Beaupre, Ott.	38	3.36	8	25	3	1	.896
Kidd, Cgy.	43	2.61	22	14	6	3	.909	Hextall, Phila.	31	2.89	17	9	4	1	.890
Belfour, Chi.	42	2.28	22	15	3	5	.906	Wregget, Pitts.	38	3.21	25	9	2	0	.903
Moog, Dal.	31	2.44	10	12	7	2	.915	Fiset, Que.	32	2.78	17	10	3	2	.910
Vernon, Det.	30	2.52	19	6	4	1	.893	Joseph, St.L.	36	2.79	20	10	1	1	.902
Ranford, Edm.	40	3.62	15	20	3	2	.883	Irbe, S.J.	38	3.26	14	19	3	4	.895
Vanbiesbrouck, Fla.	37	2.47	14	15	4	4	.914	Puppa, T.B.	36	2.68	14	19	2	1	.905
Burke, Hfd.	42	2.68	17	19	4	0	.912	Potvin, Tor.	36	2.91	15	13	7	0	.907
Hrudey, L.A.	35	3.14	14	13	5	0	.910	McLean, Van.	40	2.75	18	12	10	1	.904
Roy, Mon.	43	2.97	17	20	6	1	.906	Carey, Wash.	28	2.13	18	6	3	4	.913
Brodeur, N.J.	40	2.45	19	11	6	3	.902	Cheveldae, Winn.	30	3.70	8	16	3	0	.881

All-Time Leading Scorers

Player	Goals	Assists	Points	Player	Goals	Assists	Points
Wayne Gretzky*	814	1,692	2,506	Gilbert Perreault.	512	814	1,326
Gordie Howe.	801	1,049	1,850	Dale Hawerchuk*	489	825	1,314
Marcel Dionne.	731	1,040	1,771	Jari Kurri*	565	731	1,296
Phil Esposito.	717	873	1,590	Alex Delvecchio	456	825	1,281
Stan Mikita	541	926	1,467	Jean Ratelle	491	776	1,267
Bryan Trottier	524	901	1,425	Denis Savard*	451	812	1,263
John Bucyk.	556	813	1,369	Peter Stastny*	450	789	1,239
Mark Messier*.	492	877	1,369	Ray Bourque*	323	908	1,231
Guy Lafleur.	560	793	1,353	Norm Ullman	490	739	1,229
Paul Coffey*	358	978	1,336	Jean Beliveau	507	712	1,219

*Player was active at end of 1994-95 season.

Art Ross Trophy (Leading Scorer)

1927	Bill Cook, N.Y. Rangers	1950	Ted Lindsay, Detroit
1928	Howie Morenz, Montreal	1951	Gordie Howe, Detroit
1929	Ace Bailey, Toronto	1952	Gordie Howe, Detroit
1930	Cooney Weiland, Boston	1953	Gordie Howe, Detroit
1931	Howie Morenz, Montreal	1954	Gordie Howe, Detroit
1932	Harvey Jackson, Toronto	1955	Bernie Geoffrion, Montreal
1933	Bill Cook, N.Y. Rangers	1956	Jean Beliveau, Montreal
1934	Charlie Conacher, Toronto	1957	Gordie Howe, Detroit
1935	Charlie Conacher, Toronto	1958	Dickie Moore, Montreal
1936	Dave Schriner, N.Y. Americans	1959	Dickie Moore, Montreal
1937	Dave Schriner, N.Y. Americans	1960	Bobby Hull, Chicago
1938	Gordie Drillon, Toronto	1961	Bernie Geoffrion, Montreal
1939	Toe Blake, Montreal	1962	Bobby Hull, Chicago
1940	Milt Schmidt, Boston	1963	Gordie Howe, Detroit
1941	Bill Cowley, Boston	1964	Stan Mikita, Chicago
1942	Bryan Hextall, N.Y. Rangers	1965	Stan Mikita, Chicago
1943	Doug Bentley, Chicago	1966	Bobby Hull, Chicago
1944	Herbie Cain, Boston	1967	Stan Mikita, Chicago
1945	Elmer Lach, Montreal	1968	Stan Mikita, Chicago
1946	Max Bentley, Chicago	1969	Phil Esposito, Boston
1947	Max Bentley, Chicago	1970	Bobby Orr, Boston
1948	Elmer Lach, Montreal	1971	Phil Esposito, Boston
1949	Roy Conacher, Chicago	1972	Phil Esposito, Boston

1973	Phil Esposito, Boston
1974	Phil Esposito, Boston
1975	Bobby Orr, Boston
1976	Guy Lafleur, Montreal
1977	Guy Lafleur, Montreal
1978	Guy Lafleur, Montreal
1979	Bryan Trottier, N.Y. Islanders
1980	Marcel Dionne, Los Angeles
1981	Wayne Gretzky, Edmonton
1982	Wayne Gretzky, Edmonton
1983	Wayne Gretzky, Edmonton
1984	Wayne Gretzky, Edmonton
1985	Wayne Gretzky, Edmonton
1986	Wayne Gretzky, Edmonton
1987	Wayne Gretzky, Edmonton
1988	Mario Lemieux, Pittsburgh
1989	Mario Lemieux, Pittsburgh
1990	Wayne Gretzky, Los Angeles
1991	Wayne Gretzky, Los Angeles
1992	Mario Lemieux, Pittsburgh
1993	Mario Lemieux, Pittsburgh
1994	Wayne Gretzky, Los Angeles
1995	Jaromir Jagr, Pittsburgh

James Norris Memorial Trophy (Outstanding Defenseman)

1954	Red Kelly, Detroit	1968	Bobby Orr, Boston	1982	Doug Wilson, Chicago
1955	Doug Harvey, Montreal	1969	Bobby Orr, Boston	1983	Rod Langway, Washington
1956	Doug Harvey, Montreal	1970	Bobby Orr, Boston	1984	Rod Langway, Washington
1957	Doug Harvey, Montreal	1971	Bobby Orr, Boston	1985	Paul Coffey, Edmonton
1958	Doug Harvey, Montreal	1972	Bobby Orr, Boston	1986	Paul Coffey, Edmonton
1959	Tom Johnson, Montreal	1973	Bobby Orr, Boston	1987	Ray Bourque, Boston
1960	Doug Harvey, Montreal	1974	Bobby Orr, Boston	1988	Ray Bourque, Boston
1961	Doug Harvey, Montreal	1975	Bobby Orr, Boston	1989	Chris Chelios, Montreal
1962	Doug Harvey, N.Y. Rangers	1976	Denis Potvin, N.Y. Islanders	1990	Ray Bourque, Boston
1963	Pierre Pilote, Chicago	1977	Larry Robinson, Montreal	1991	Ray Bourque, Boston
1964	Pierre Pilote, Chicago	1978	Denis Potvin, N.Y. Islanders	1992	Brian Leetch, N.Y. Rangers
1965	Pierre Pilote, Chicago	1979	Denis Potvin, N.Y. Islanders	1993	Chris Chelios, Chicago
1966	Jacques Laperriere, Montreal	1980	Larry Robinson, Montreal	1994	Ray Bourque, Boston
1967	Harry Howell, N.Y. Rangers	1981	Randy Carlyle, Pittsburgh	1995	Paul Coffey, Detroit

Vezina Trophy (Outstanding Goalie)*

1927	George Hainsworth, Montreal	1952	Terry Sawchuk, Detroit	1975	Bernie Parent, Philadelphia
1928	George Hainsworth, Montreal	1953	Terry Sawchuk, Detroit	1976	Ken Dryden, Montreal
1929	George Hainsworth, Montreal	1954	Harry Lumley, Toronto	1977	Dryden, Larocque, Montreal
1930	Tiny Thompson, Boston	1955	Terry Sawchuk, Detroit	1978	Dryden, Larocque, Montreal
1931	Roy Worters, N.Y. Americans	1956	Jacques Plante, Montreal	1979	Dryden, Larocque, Montreal
1932	Charlie Gardiner, Chicago	1957	Jacques Plante, Montreal	1980	Sauve, Edwards, Buffalo
1933	Tiny Thompson, Boston	1958	Jacques Plante, Montreal	1981	Sevigny, Larocque, Herron,
1934	Charlie Gardiner, Chicago	1959	Jacques Plante, Montreal		Montreal
1935	Lorne Chabot, Chicago	1960	Jacques Plante, Montreal	1982	Bill Smith, N.Y. Islanders
1936	Tiny Thompson, Boston	1961	John Bower, Toronto	1983	Pete Peeters, Boston
1937	Normie Smith, Detroit	1962	Jacques Plante, Montreal	1984	Tom Barrasso, Buffalo
1938	Tiny Thompson, Boston	1963	Glenn Hall, Chicago	1985	Pelle Lindbergh, Philadelphia
1939	Frank Brimsek, Boston	1964	Charlie Hodge, Montreal	1986	John Vanbiesbrouck, N.Y.
1940	Dave Kerr, N.Y. Rangers	1965	Sawchuk, Bower, Toronto		Rangers
1941	Turk Broda, Toronto	1966	Worsley, Hodge, Montreal	1987	Ron Hextall, Philadelphia
1942	Frank Brimsek, Boston	1967	Hall, DeJordy, Chicago	1988	Grant Fuhr, Edmonton
1943	Johnny Mowers, Detroit	1968	Worsley, Vachon, Montreal	1989	Patrick Roy, Montreal
1944	Bill Durnan, Montreal	1969	Hall, Plante, St. Louis	1990	Patrick Roy, Montreal
1945	Bill Durnan, Montreal	1970	Tony Esposito, Chicago	1991	Ed Belfour, Chicago
1946	Bill Durnan, Montreal	1971	Giacomin, Villemure, N.Y.	1992	Patrick Roy, Montreal
1947	Bill Durnan, Montreal		Rangers	1993	Ed Belfour, Chicago
1948	Turk Broda, Toronto	1972	Esposito, Smith, Chicago	1994	Dominik Hasek, Buffalo
1949	Bill Durnan, Montreal	1973	Ken Dryden, Montreal	1995	Dominik Hasek, Buffalo
1950	Bill Durnan, Montreal	1974	Bernie Parent, Philadelphia;		
1951	Al Rollins, Toronto		Tony Esposito, Chicago		

*1927-81, awarded to the goalie who played a minimum 25 games for the team that allowed the fewest goals; since 1982, awarded to the outstanding goalie.

Calder Memorial Trophy (Rookie of the Year)

1933	Carl Voss, Detroit	1953	Gump Worsley, N.Y. Rangers	1975	Eric Vail, Atlanta
1934	Russ Blinco, Montreal	1954	Camille Henry, N.Y. Rangers	1976	Bryan Trottier, N.Y. Islanders
	Maroons	1955	Ed Litzenberger, Chicago	1977	Willi Plett, Atlanta
1935	Dave Schriner, N.Y. Americans	1956	Glenn Hall, Detroit	1978	Mike Bossy, N.Y. Islanders
1936	Mike Karakas, Chicago	1957	Larry Regan, Boston	1979	Bobby Smith, Minnesota
1937	Syl Apps, Toronto	1958	Frank Mahovlich, Toronto	1980	Ray Bourque, Boston
1938	Cully Dahlstrom, Chicago	1959	Ralph Backstrom, Montreal	1981	Peter Stastny, Quebec
1939	Frank Brimsek, Boston	1960	Bill Hay, Chicago	1982	Dale Hawerchuk, Winnipeg
1940	Kilby Macdonald, N.Y.	1961	Dave Keon, Toronto	1983	Steve Larmer, Chicago
	Rangers	1962	Bobby Rousseau, Montreal	1984	Tom Barrasso, Buffalo
1941	John Quilty, Montreal	1963	Kent Douglas, Toronto	1985	Mario Lemieux, Pittsburgh
1942	Grant Warwick, N.Y. Rangers	1964	Jacques Laperriere, Montreal	1986	Gary Suter, Calgary
1943	Gaye Stewart, Toronto	1965	Roger Crozier, Detroit	1987	Luc Robitaille, Los Angeles
1944	Gus Bodnar, Toronto	1966	Brit Selby, Toronto	1988	Joe Nieuwendyk, Calgary
1945	Frank McCool, Toronto	1967	Bobby Orr, Boston	1989	Brian Leetch, N.Y. Rangers
1946	Edgar Laprade, N.Y. Rangers	1968	Derek Sanderson, Boston	1990	Sergei Makarov, Calgary
1947	Howie Meeker, Toronto	1969	Danny Grant, Minnesota	1991	Ed Belfour, Chicago
1948	Jim McFadden, Detroit	1970	Tony Esposito, Chicago	1992	Pavel Bure, Vancouver
1949	Pentti Lund, N.Y. Rangers	1971	Gilbert Perreault, Buffalo	1993	Teemu Selanne, Winnipeg
1950	Jack Gelineau, Boston	1972	Ken Dryden, Montreal	1994	Martin Brodeur, New Jersey
1951	Terry Sawchuk, Detroit	1973	Steve Vickers, N.Y. Rangers	1995	Peter Forsberg, Quebec
1952	Bernie Geoffrion, Montreal	1974	Denis Potvin, N.Y. Islanders		

Lady Byng Memorial Trophy (Most Gentlemanly Player)

1925	Frank Nighbor, Ottawa	1949	Bill Quackenbush, Detroit	1973	Gil Perreault, Buffalo
1926	Frank Nighbor, Ottawa	1950	Edgar Laprade, N.Y. Rangers	1974	John Bucyk, Boston
1927	Billy Burch, N.Y. Americans	1951	Red Kelly, Detroit	1975	Marcel Dionne, Detroit
1928	Frank Boucher, N.Y. Rangers	1952	Sid Smith, Toronto	1976	Jean Ratelle, N.Y. R.–Boston
1929	Frank Boucher, N.Y. Rangers	1953	Red Kelly, Detroit	1977	Marcel Dionne, Los Angeles
1930	Frank Boucher, N.Y. Rangers	1954	Red Kelly, Detroit	1978	Butch Goring, Los Angeles
1931	Frank Boucher, N.Y. Rangers	1955	Sid Smith, Toronto	1979	Bob MacMillan, Atlanta
1932	Joe Primeau, Toronto	1956	Earl Reibel, Detroit	1980	Wayne Gretzky, Edmonton
1933	Frank Boucher, N.Y. Rangers	1957	Andy Hebenton, N.Y. Rangers	1981	Rick Kehoe, Pittsburgh
1934	Frank Boucher, N.Y. Rangers	1958	Camille Henry, N.Y. Rangers	1982	Rick Middleton, Boston
1935	Frank Boucher, N.Y. Rangers	1959	Alex Delvecchio, Detroit	1983	Mike Bossy, N.Y. Islanders
1936	Doc Romnes, Chicago	1960	Don McKenney, Boston	1984	Mike Bossy, N.Y. Islanders
1937	Marty Barry, Detroit	1961	Red Kelly, Toronto	1985	Jari Kurri, Edmonton
1938	Gordie Drillon, Toronto	1962	Dave Keon, Toronto	1986	Mike Bossy, N.Y. Islanders
1939	Clint Smith, N.Y. Rangers	1963	Dave Keon, Toronto	1987	Joe Mullen, Calgary
1940	Bobby Bauer, Boston	1964	Ken Wharram, Chicago	1988	Mats Naslund, Montreal
1941	Bobby Bauer, Boston	1965	Bobby Hull, Chicago	1989	Joe Mullen, Calgary
1942	Syl Apps, Toronto	1966	Alex Delvecchio, Detroit	1990	Brett Hull, St. Louis
1943	Max Bentley, Chicago	1967	Stan Mikita, Chicago	1991	Wayne Gretzky, Los Angeles
1944	Clint Smith, Chicago	1968	Stan Mikita, Chicago	1992	Wayne Gretzky, Los Angeles
1945	Bill Mosienko, Chicago	1969	Alex Delvecchio, Detroit	1993	Pierre Turgeon, N.Y. Islanders
1946	Toe Blake, Montreal	1970	Phil Goyette, St. Louis	1994	Wayne Gretzky, Los Angeles
1947	Bobby Bauer, Boston	1971	John Bucyk, Boston	1995	Ron Francis, Pittsburgh
1948	Buddy O'Connor, N.Y. Rangers	1972	Jean Ratelle, N.Y. Rangers		

Frank J. Selke Trophy (Best Defensive Forward)

1978	Bob Gainey, Montreal	1984	Doug Jarvis, Washington	1990	Rick Meagher, St. Louis
1979	Bob Gainey, Montreal	1985	Craig Ramsay, Buffalo	1991	Dirk Graham, Chicago
1980	Bob Gainey, Montreal	1986	Troy Murray, Chicago	1992	Guy Carbonneau, Montreal
1981	Bob Gainey, Montreal	1987	Dave Poulin, Philadelphia	1993	Doug Gilmour, Toronto
1982	Steve Kasper, Boston	1988	Guy Carbonneau, Montreal	1994	Sergei Fedorov, Detroit
1983	Bobby Clarke, Philadelphia	1989	Guy Carbonneau, Montreal	1995	Ron Francis, Pittsburgh

Hart Memorial Trophy (MVP)

1927	Herb Gardiner, Montreal	1949	Sid Abel, Detroit	1973	Bobby Clarke, Philadelphia
1928	Howie Morenz, Montreal	1950	Chuck Rayner, N.Y. Rangers	1974	Phil Esposito, Boston
1929	Roy Worters, N.Y. Americans	1951	Milt Schmidt, Boston	1975	Bobby Clarke, Philadelphia
1930	Nels Stewart, Montreal Maroons	1952	Gordie Howe, Detroit	1976	Bobby Clarke, Philadelphia
		1953	Gordie Howe, Detroit	1977	Guy Lafleur, Montreal
1931	Howie Morenz, Montreal	1954	Al Rollins, Chicago	1978	Guy Lafleur, Montreal
1932	Howie Morenz, Montreal	1955	Ted Kennedy, Toronto	1979	Bryan Trottier, N.Y. Islanders
1933	Eddie Shore, Boston	1956	Jean Beliveau, Montreal	1980	Wayne Gretzky, Edmonton
1934	Aurel Joliat, Montreal	1957	Gordie Howe, Detroit	1981	Wayne Gretzky, Edmonton
1935	Eddie Shore, Boston	1958	Gordie Howe, Detroit	1982	Wayne Gretzky, Edmonton
1936	Eddie Shore, Boston	1959	Andy Bathgate, N.Y. Rangers	1983	Wayne Gretzky, Edmonton
1937	Babe Siebert, Montreal	1960	Gordie Howe, Detroit	1984	Wayne Gretzky, Edmonton
1938	Eddie Shore, Boston	1961	Bernie Geoffrion, Montreal	1985	Wayne Gretzky, Edmonton
1939	Toe Blake, Montreal	1962	Jacques Plante, Montreal	1986	Wayne Gretzky, Edmonton
1940	Ebbie Goodfellow, Detroit	1963	Gordie Howe, Detroit	1987	Wayne Gretzky, Edmonton
1941	Bill Cowley, Boston	1964	Jean Beliveau, Montreal	1988	Mario Lemieux, Pittsburgh
1942	Tom Anderson, N.Y. Americans	1965	Bobby Hull, Chicago	1989	Wayne Gretzky, Los Angeles
		1966	Bobby Hull, Chicago	1990	Mark Messier, Edmonton
1943	Bill Cowley, Boston	1967	Stan Mikita, Chicago	1991	Brett Hull, St. Louis
1944	Babe Pratt, Toronto	1968	Stan Mikita, Chicago	1992	Mark Messier, N.Y. Rangers
1945	Elmer Lach, Montreal	1969	Phil Esposito, Boston	1993	Mario Lemieux, Pittsburgh
1946	Max Bentley, Chicago	1970	Bobby Orr, Boston	1994	Sergei Fedorov, Detroit
1947	Maurice Richard, Montreal	1971	Bobby Orr, Boston	1995	Eric Lindros, Philadelphia
1948	Buddy O'Connor, N.Y. Rangers	1972	Bobby Orr, Boston		

Conn Smythe Trophy (MVP in Playoffs)

1965	Jean Beliveau, Montreal	1975	Bernie Parent, Philadelphia	1986	Patrick Roy, Montreal
1966	Roger Crozier, Detroit	1976	Reg Leach, Philadelphia	1987	Ron Hextall, Philadelphia
1967	Dave Keon, Toronto	1977	Guy Lafleur, Montreal	1988	Wayne Gretzky, Edmonton
1968	Glenn Hall, St. Louis	1978	Larry Robinson, Montreal	1989	Al MacInnis, Calgary
1969	Serge Savard, Montreal	1979	Bob Gainey, Montreal	1990	Bill Ranford, Edmonton
1970	Bobby Orr, Boston	1980	Bryan Trottier, N.Y. Islanders	1991	Mario Lemieux, Pittsburgh
1971	Ken Dryden, Montreal	1981	Butch Goring, N.Y. Islanders	1992	Mario Lemieux, Pittsburgh
1972	Bobby Orr, Boston	1982	Mike Bossy, N.Y. Islanders	1993	Patrick Roy, Montreal
1973	Yvan Cournoyer, Montreal	1983	Billy Smith, N.Y. Islanders	1994	Brian Leetch, N.Y. Rangers
1974	Bernie Parent, Philadelphia	1984	Mark Messier, Edmonton	1995	Claude Lemieux, New Jersey
		1985	Wayne Gretzky, Edmonton		

Most NHL Goals in a Season

Player	Team	Season	Goals	Player	Team	Season	Goals
Wayne Gretzky	Edmonton	1981-82	92	Jari Kurri	Edmonton	1985-86	68
Wayne Gretzky	Edmonton	1983-84	87	Phil Esposito	Boston	1971-72	66
Brett Hull	St. Louis	1990-91	86	Lanny McDonald	Calgary	1982-83	66
Mario Lemieux	Pittsburgh	1988-89	85	Steve Yzerman	Detroit	1988-89	65
Phil Esposito	Boston	1970-71	76	Mike Bossy	N.Y. Islanders	1981-82	64
Alexander Mogilny	Buffalo	1992-93	76	Luc Robitaille	Los Angeles	1992-93	63
Teemu Selanne	Winnipeg	1992-93	76	Wayne Gretzky	Edmonton	1986-87	62
Wayne Gretzky	Edmonton	1984-85	73	Steve Yzerman	Detroit	1989-90	62
Brett Hull	St. Louis	1989-90	72	Mike Bossy	N.Y. Islanders	1985-86	61
Wayne Gretzky	Edmonton	1982-83	71	Phil Esposito	Boston	1974-75	61
Jari Kurri	Edmonton	1984-85	71	Reggie Leach	Philadelphia	1975-76	61
Mario Lemieux	Pittsburgh	1987-88	70	Mike Bossy	N.Y. Islanders	1982-83	60
Bernie Nicholls	Los Angeles	1988-89	70	Guy Lafleur	Montreal	1977-78	60
Bret Hull	St. Louis	1991-92	70	Steve Shutt	Montreal	1976-77	60
Mike Bossy	N.Y. Islanders	1978-79	69	Dennis Maruk	Washington	1981-82	60
Mario Lemieux	Pittsburgh	1992-93	69	Pavel Bure	Vancouver	1992-93	60
Phil Esposito	Boston	1973-74	68	Pavel Bure	Vancouver	1993-94	60
Mike Bossy	N.Y. Islanders	1980-81	68				

NCAA Hockey Champions

In Jan. 1995, former members of the 1969-70 Cornell hockey team gathered for a reunion in Ithaca, NY. The Big Red went 29-0 that season to become the only NCAA Division I hockey team to finish without a loss or a tie.

1948	Michigan	1960	Denver	1972	Boston Univ.	1984	Bowling Green
1949	Boston College	1961	Denver	1973	Wisconsin	1985	RPI
1950	Colorado College	1962	Michigan Tech	1974	Minnesota	1986	Michigan State
1951	Michigan	1963	North Dakota	1975	Michigan Tech	1987	North Dakota
1952	Michigan	1964	Michigan	1976	Minnesota	1988	Lake Superior St.
1953	Michigan	1965	Michigan Tech	1977	Wisconsin	1989	Harvard
1954	RPI	1966	Michigan State	1978	Boston Univ.	1990	Wisconsin
1955	Michigan	1967	Cornell	1979	Minnesota	1991	N. Michigan
1956	Michigan	1968	Denver	1980	North Dakota	1992	Lake Superior St.
1957	Colorado College	1969	Denver	1981	Wisconsin	1993	Maine
1958	Denver	1970	Cornell	1982	North Dakota	1994	Lake Superior St.
1959	North Dakota	1971	Boston Univ.	1983	Wisconsin	1995	Boston Univ.

THOROUGHBRED RACING

Triple Crown Winners

Since 1920, colts have carried 126 lb in triple crown events; fillies, 121 lb

(Kentucky Derby, Preakness, and Belmont Stakes)

Year	Horse	Jockey	Trainer	Year	Horse	Jockey	Trainer
1919	Sir Barton	J. Loftus	H. G. Bedwell	1946	Assault	W. Mehrtens	M. Hirsch
1930	Gallant Fox	E. Sande	J. Fitzsimmons	1948	Citation	E. Arcaro	H. A. Jones
1935	Omaha	W. Sanders	J. Fitzsimmons	1973	Secretariat	R. Turcotte	L. Laurin
1937	War Admiral	C. Kurtsinger	G. Conway	1977	Seattle Slew	J. Cruguet	W. H. Turner Jr.
1941	Whirlaway	E. Arcaro	B. A. Jones	1978	Affirmed	S. Cauthen	L. S. Barrera
1943	Count Fleet	J. Longden	G. D. Cameron				

Kentucky Derby

Churchill Downs, Louisville, KY; inaugurated 1875; distance 1-1/4 mi; 1-1/2 mi until 1896. 3-year olds.
Best time: 1:59.2, Secretariat, 1973.

Year	Winner	Jockey	Year	Winner	Jockey	Year	Winner	Jockey
1875	Aristides	O. Lewis	1916	George Smith	J. Loftus	1957	Iron Liege	W. Hartack
1876	Vagrant	R. Swim	1917	Omar Khayyam	C. Borel	1958	Tim Tam	I. Valenzuela
1877	Baden Baden	W. Walker	1918	Exterminator	W. Knapp	1959	Tomy Lee	W. Shoemaker
1878	Day Star	J. Carter	1919	Sir Barton	J. Loftus	1960	Venetian Way	W. Hartack
1879	Lord Murphy	C. Schauer	1920	Paul Jones	T. Rice	1961	Carry Back	J. Sellers
1880	Fonso	G. Lewis	1921	Behave Yourself	C. Thompson	1962	Decidedly	W. Hartack
1881	Hindoo	J. McLaughlin	1922	Morvich	A. Johnson	1963	Chateaugay	B. Baeza
1882	Apollo	B. Hurd	1923	Zev	E. Sande	1964	Northern Dancer	W. Hartack
1883	Leonatus	W. Donohue	1924	Black Gold	J. D. Mooney	1965	Lucky Debonair	W. Shoemaker
1884	Buchanan	I. Murphy	1925	Flying Ebony	E. Sande	1966	Kauai King	D. Brumfield
1885	Joe Cotton	E. Henderson	1926	Bubbling Over	A. Johnson	1967	Proud Clarion	R. Ussery
1886	Ben Ali	P. Duffy	1927	Whiskery	L. McAtee	1968	Dancer's Image (a)	R. Ussery
1887	Montrose	I. Lewis	1928	Reigh Count	C. Lang	1969	Majestic Prince	W. Hartack
1888	Macbeth II	G. Covington	1929	Clyde Van Dusen	L. McAtee	1970	Dust Commander	M. Manganello
1889	Spokane	T. Kiley	1930	Gallant Fox	E. Sande	1971	Canonero II	G. Avila
1890	Riley	I. Murphy	1931	Twenty Grand	C. Kurtsinger	1972	Riva Ridge	R. Turcotte
1891	Kingman	I. Murphy	1932	Burgoo King	E. James	1973	Secretariat	R. Turcotte
1892	Azra	A. Clayton	1933	Brokers Tip	D. Meade	1974	Cannonade	A. Cordero
1893	Lookout	E. Kunze	1934	Cavalcade	M. Garner	1975	Foolish Pleasure	J. Vasquez
1894	Chant	F. Goodale	1935	Omaha	W. Saunders	1976	Bold Forbes	A. Cordero
1895	Halma	J. Perkins	1936	Bold Venture	I. Hanford	1977	Seattle Slew	J. Cruguet
1896	Ben Brush	W. Simms	1937	War Admiral	C. Kurtsinger	1978	Affirmed	S. Cauthen
1897	Typhoon II	F. Garner	1938	Lawrin	E. Arcaro	1979	Spectacular Bid	R. Franklin
1898	Plaudit	W. Simms	1939	Johnstown	J. Stout	1980	Genuine Risk*	J. Vasquez
1899	Manuel	F. Taral	1940	Gallahadion	C. Bierman	1981	Pleasant Colony	J. Velasquez
1900	Lieut. Gibson	J. Boland	1941	Whirlaway	E. Arcaro	1982	Gato del Sol	E. Delahoussaye
1901	His Eminence	J. Winkfield	1942	Shut Out	W. D. Wright	1983	Sunny's Halo	E. Delahoussaye
1902	Alan-a-Dale	J. Winkfield	1943	Count Fleet	J. Longden	1984	Swale	L. Pincay
1903	Judge Himes	H. Booker	1944	Pensive	C. McCreary	1985	Spend a Buck	A. Cordero
1904	Elwood	F. Prior	1945	Hoop, Jr.	E. Arcaro	1986	Ferdinand	W. Shoemaker
1905	Agile	J. Martin	1946	Assault	W. Mehrtens	1987	Alysheba	C. McCarron
1906	Sir Huon	R. Troxler	1947	Jet Pilot	E. Guerin	1988	Winning Colors*	G. Stevens
1907	Pink Star	A. Minder	1948	Citation	E. Arcaro	1989	Sunday Silence	P. Valenzuela
1908	Stone Street	A. Pickens	1949	Ponder	S. Brooks	1990	Unbridled	C. Perret
1909	Wintergreen	V. Powers	1950	Middleground	W. Boland	1991	Strike the Gold	C. Antley
1910	Donau	F. Herbert	1951	Count Turf	C. McCreary	1992	Lil E. Tee	P. Day
1911	Meridian	G. Archibald	1952	Hill Gail	E. Arcaro	1993	Sea Hero	J. Bailey
1912	Worth	C.H. Shilling	1953	Dark Star	H. Moreno	1994	Go for Gin	C. McCarron
1913	Donerail	R. Goose	1954	Determine	R. York	1995	Thunder Gulch	G. Stevens
1914	Old Rosebud	J. McCabe	1955	Swaps	W. Shoemaker			
1915	Regret*	J. Notter	1956	Needles	D. Erb			

(a) Dancer's Image was disqualified from purse money after tests disclosed that he had run with a pain-killing drug, phenylbutazone, in his system. All wagers were paid on Dancer's Image. Forward Pass was awarded first place money.
The Kentucky Derby has been won 5 times by 2 jockeys, Eddie Arcaro, 1938, 1941, 1945, 1948, and 1952; and Bill Hartack, 1957, 1960, 1962, 1964, and 1969; four times by Willie Shoemaker, 1955, 1959, 1965, and 1986; and 3 times by each of 3 jockeys, Isaac Murphy, 1884, 1890, and 1891; Earle Sande, 1923, 1925, and 1930; and Angel Cordero in 1974, 1976, and 1985.
* Regret, Genuine Risk, and Winning Colors are the only fillies to win the Derby.

Preakness

Pimlico, Baltimore, MD; inaugurated 1873; distance 1-3/16 mi. 3-year olds. Best time: 1:53.2, Tank's Prospect, 1985.

Year	Winner	Jockey	Year	Winner	Jockey	Year	Winner	Jockey
1873	Survivor	G. Barbee	1887	Dunboyne	W. Donohue	1904	Bryn Mawr	E. Hildebrand
1874	Culpepper	M. Donohue	1888	Refund	F. Littlefield	1905	Cairngorm	W. Davis
1875	Tom Ochiltree	L. Hughes	1889	Buddhist	G. Anderson	1906	Whimsical	W. Miller
1876	Shirley	G. Barbee	1890	Montague	W. Martin	1907	Don Enrique	G. Mountain
1877	Cloverbrook	C. Holloway	1894	Assignee	F. Taral	1908	Royal Tourist	E. Dugan
1878	Duke of Magenta	C. Holloway	1895	Belmar	F. Taral	1909	Effendi	W. Doyle
1879	Harold	L. Hughes	1896	Margrave	H. Griffin	1910	Layminster	R. Estep
1880	Grenada	L. Hughes	1897	Paul Kauvar	C. Thorpe	1911	Watervale	E. Dugan
1881	Saunterer	W. Costello	1898	Sly Fox	W. Simms	1912	Colonel Holloway	C. Turner
1882	Vanguard	W. Costello	1899	Half Time	R. Clawson	1913	Buskin	J. Butwell
1883	Jacobus	W. Donohue	1900	Hindus	H. Spencer	1914	Holiday	A. Schuttinger
1884	Knight of Ellerslie	S. H. Fisher	1901	The Parader	F. Landry	1915	Rhine Maiden	D. Hoffman
1885	Tecumseh	J. McLaughlin	1902	Old England	L. Jackson	1916	Damrosch	L. McAtee
1886	The Bard	S. H. Fisher	1903	Flocarline	W. Gannon	1917	Kalitan	E. Haynes

(continued)

Year	Winner	Jockey	Year	Winner	Jockey	Year	Winner	Jockey
1918	War Cloud	J. Loftus	1943	Count Fleet	J. Longden	1970	Personality	E. Belmonte
	Jack Hare Jr.	C. Peak	1944	Pensive	C. McCreary	1971	Canonero II	G. Avila
1919	Sir Barton	J. Loftus	1945	Polynesian	W.D. Wright	1972	Bee Bee Bee	E. Nelson
1920	Man o' War	C. Kummer	1946	Assault	W. Mehrtens	1973	Secretariat	R. Turcotte
1921	Broomspun	F. Coltiletti	1947	Faultless	D. Dodson	1974	Little Current	M. Rivera
1922	Pillory	L. Morris	1948	Citation	E. Arcaro	1975	Master Derby	D. McHargue
1923	Vigil	B. Marinelli	1949	Capot	T. Atkinson	1976	Elocutionist	J. Lively
1924	Nellie Morse	J. Merimee	1950	Hill Prince	E. Arcaro	1977	Seattle Slew	J. Cruguet
1925	Coventry	C. Kummer	1951	Bold	E. Arcaro	1978	Affirmed	S. Cauthen
1926	Display	J. Malben	1952	Blue Man	C. McCreary	1979	Spectacular Bid	R. Franklin
1927	Bostonian	A. Abel	1953	Native Dancer	E. Guerin	1980	Codex	A. Cordero
1928	Victorian	R. Workman	1954	Hasty Road	J. Adams	1981	Pleasant Colony	J. Velasquez
1929	Dr. Freeland	L. Schaefer	1955	Nashua	E. Arcaro	1982	Aloma's Ruler	J. Kaenel
1930	Gallant Fox	E. Sande	1956	Fabius	W. Hartack	1983	Deputed Testamony	D. Miller
1931	Mate	G. Ellis	1957	Bold Ruler	E. Arcaro	1984	Gate Dancer	A. Cordero
1932	Burgoo King	E. James	1958	Tim Tam	I. Valenzuela	1985	Tank's Prospect	P. Day
1933	Head Play	C. Kurtsinger	1959	Royal Orbit	W. Harmatz	1986	Snow Chief	A. Solis
1934	High Quest	R. Jones	1960	Bally Ache	R. Ussery	1987	Alysheba	C. McCarron
1935	Omaha	W. Saunders	1961	Carry Back	J. Sellers	1988	Risen Star	E. Delahoussaye
1936	Bold Venture	G. Woolf	1962	Greek Money	J.L. Rotz	1989	Sunday Silence	P. Valenzuela
1937	War Admiral	C. Kurtsinger	1963	Candy Spots	W. Shoemaker	1990	Summer Squall	P. Day
1938	Dauber	M. Peters	1964	Northern Dancer	W. Hartack	1991	Hansel	J. Bailey
1939	Challedon	G. Seabo	1965	Tom Rolfe	R. Turcotte	1992	Pine Bluff	C. McCarron
1940	Bimelech	F.A. Smith	1966	Kauai King	D. Brumfield	1993	Prairie Bayou	M. Smith
1941	Whirlaway	E. Arcaro	1967	Damascus	W. Shoemaker	1994	Tabasco Cat	P. Day
1942	Alsab	B. James	1968	Forward Pass	I. Valenzuela	1995	Timber Country	P. Day
			1969	Majestic Prince	W. Hartack			

Belmont Stakes

Belmont Park, Elmont, NY; inaugurated 1867; distance 1-1/2 mi. 3-year olds. Best time: 2:24, Secretariat, 1973.

Year	Winner	Jockey	Year	Winner	Jockey	Year	Winner	Jockey
1867	Ruthless	J. Gilpatrick	1910	Sweep	J. Butwell	1955	Nashua	E. Arcaro
1868	General Duke	R. Swim	1913	Prince Eugene	R. Troxler	1956	Needles	D. Erb
1869	Fenian	C. Miller	1914	Luke McLuke	M. Buxton	1957	Gallant Man	W. Shoemaker
1870	Kingfisher	W. Dick	1915	The Finn	G. Byrne	1958	Cavan	P. Anderson
1871	Harry Bassett	W. Miller	1916	Friar Rock	E. Haynes	1959	Sword Dancer	W. Shoemaker
1872	Joe Daniels	J. Rowe	1917	Hourless	J. Butwell	1960	Celtic Ash	W. Hartack
1873	Springbok	J. Rowe	1918	Johren	F. Robinson	1961	Sherluck	B. Baeza
1874	Saxon	G. Barbee	1919	Sir Barton	J. Loftus	1962	Jaipur	W. Shoemaker
1875	Calvin	R. Swim	1920	Man o' War	C. Kummer	1963	Chateaugay	B. Baeza
1876	Algerine	W. Donohue	1921	Grey Lag	E. Sande	1964	Quadrangle	M. Ycaza
1877	Cloverbrook	C. Holloway	1922	Pillory	C. H. Miller	1965	Hail to All	J. Sellers
1878	Duke of Magenta	L. Hughes	1923	Zev	E. Sande	1966	Amberoid	W. Boland
1879	Spendthrift	S. Evans	1924	Mad Play	E. Sande	1967	Damascus	W. Shoemaker
1880	Grenada	L. Hughes	1925	American Flag	A. Johnson	1968	Stage Door Johnny	H. Gustines
1881	Saunterer	T. Costello	1926	Crusader	A. Johnson	1969	Arts and Letters	B. Baeza
1882	Forester	J. McLaughlin	1927	Chance Shot	E. Sande	1970	High Echelon	J. L. Rotz
1883	George Kinney	J. McLaughlin	1928	Vito	C. Kummer	1971	Pass Catcher	W. Blum
1884	Panique	J. McLaughlin	1929	Blue Larkspur	M. Garner	1972	Riva Ridge	R. Turcotte
1885	Tyrant	P. Duffy	1930	Gallant Fox	E. Sande	1973	Secretariat	R. Turcotte
1886	Inspector B.	J. McLaughlin	1931	Twenty Grand	C. Kurtsinger	1974	Little Current	M. Rivera
1887	Hanover	J. McLaughlin	1932	Faireno	T. Malley	1975	Avatar	W. Shoemaker
1888	Sir Dixon	J. McLaughlin	1933	Hurryoff	M. Garner	1976	Bold Forbes	A. Cordero
1889	Eric	W. Hayward	1934	Peace Chance	W. D. Wright	1977	Seattle Slew	J. Cruguet
1890	Burlington	S. Barnes	1935	Omaha	W. Saunders	1978	Affirmed	S. Cauthen
1891	Foxford	E. Garrison	1936	Granville	J. Stout	1979	Coastal	R. Hernandez
1892	Patron	W. Hayward	1937	War Admiral	C. Kurtsinger	1980	Temperence Hill	E. Maple
1893	Comanche	W. Simms	1938	Pasteurized	J. Stout	1981	Summing	G. Martens
1894	Henry of Navarre	W. Simms	1939	Johnstown	J. Stout	1982	Conquistador Cielo	L. Pincay
1895	Belmar	F. Taral	1940	Bimelech	F. A. Smith	1983	Caveat	L. Pincay
1896	Hastings	H. Griffin	1941	Whirlaway	E. Arcaro	1984	Swale	L. Pincay
1897	Scottish Chieftain	J. Scherrer	1942	Shut Out	E. Arcaro	1985	Creme Fraiche	E. Maple
1898	Bowling Brook	F. Littlefield	1943	Count Fleet	J. Longden	1986	Danzig Connection	C. McCarron
1899	Jean Bereaud	R. R. Clawson	1944	Bounding Home	G. L. Smith	1987	Bet Twice	C. Perret
1900	Ildrim	N. Turner	1945	Pavot	E. Arcaro	1988	Risen Star	E. Delahoussaye
1901	Commando	H. Spencer	1946	Assault	W. Mehrtens	1989	Easy Goer	P. Day
1902	Masterman	J. Bullman	1947	Phalanx	R. Donoso	1990	Go and Go	M. Kinane
1903	Africander	J. Bullman	1948	Citation	E. Arcaro	1991	Hansel	J. Bailey
1904	Delhi	G. Odom	1949	Capot	T. Atkinson	1992	A.P. Indy	E. Delahoussaye
1905	Tanya	E. Hildebrand	1950	Middleground	W. Boland	1993	Colonial Affair	J. Krone
1906	Burgomaster	L. Lyne	1951	Counterpoint	D. Gorman	1994	Tabasco Cat	P. Day
1907	Peter Pan	G. Mountain	1952	One Count	E. Arcaro	1995	Thunder Gulch	G. Stevens
1908	Colin	J. Notter	1953	Native Dancer	E. Guerin			
1909	Joe Madden	E. Dugan	1954	High Gun	E. Guerin			

Annual Leading Jockey—Money Won

Year	Jockey	Dollars	Year	Jockey	Dollars	Year	Jockey	Dollars
1957	Bill Hartack	$3,060,501	1970	Laffit Pincay, Jr.	$2,626,526	1983	Angel Cordero, Jr.	$10,116,697
1958	Willie Shoemaker	2,961,693	1971	Laffit Pincay, Jr.	3,784,377	1984	Chris McCarron	12,045,813
1959	Willie Shoemaker	2,843,133	1972	Laffit Pincay, Jr.	3,225,827	1985	Laffit Pincay, Jr.	13,353,299
1960	Willie Shoemaker	2,123,961	1973	Laffit Pincay, Jr.	4,093,492	1986	Jose Santos	11,329,297
1961	Willie Shoemaker	2,690,819	1974	Laffit Pincay, Jr.	4,251,060	1987	Jose Santos	12,375,433
1962	Willie Shoemaker	2,916,844	1975	Braulio Baeza	3,695,198	1988	Jose Santos	14,877,298
1963	Willie Shoemaker	2,526,925	1976	Angel Cordero, Jr.	4,709,500	1989	Jose Santos	13,838,389
1964	Willie Shoemaker	2,649,553	1977	Steve Cauthen	6,151,750	1990	Gary Stevens	13,881,198
1965	Braulio Baeza	2,582,702	1978	Darrel McHargue	6,029,885	1991	Chris McCarron	14,441,083
1966	Braulio Baeza	2,951,022	1979	Laffit Pincay, Jr.	8,193,535	1992	Kent Desormeaux	14,193,006
1967	Braulio Baeza	3,088,888	1980	Chris McCarron	7,663,300	1993	Mike Smith	14,024,815
1968	Braulio Baeza	2,835,108	1981	Chris McCarron	8,397,604	1994	Mike Smith	15,979,820
1969	Jorge Velasquez	2,542,315	1982	Angel Cordero, Jr.	9,483,590			

Breeders' Cup

The Breeders' Cup was inaugurated in 1984 and consists of 7 races at one track on one day late in the year to determine thoroughbred racing's champion contenders.

Juvenile

Distances: one mi 1984-85, 87; 1-1/16 mi 1986 and since 1988

Year		Jockey	Year		Jockey	Year		Jockey
1984	Chief's Crown	Don MacBeth	1988	Is It True	Laffit Pincay Jr.	1992	Gilded Time	Chris McCarron
1985	Tasso	Laffit Pincay, Jr.	1989	Rhythm	Craig Perre	1993	Brocco	Gary Stevens
1986	Capote	Laffit Pincay, Jr.	1990	Fly So Free	Jose Santos	1994	Timber Country	Pat Day
1987	Success Express	Jose Santos	1991	Arazi	Pat Valenzuela	1995	Unbridled's Song	Mike Smith

Juvenile Fillies

Distances: one mi 1984-85, 87; 1-1/16 mi 1986 and since 1988

Year		Jockey	Year		Jockey	Year		Jockey
1984	*Outstandingly	Walter Guerra	1988	Open Mind	Angel Cordero, Jr.	1992	Eliza	Pat Valenzuela
1985	Twilight Ridge	Jorge Velasquez	1989	Go for Wand	Randy Romero	1993	Phone Chatter	Laffit Pincay, Jr.
1986	Brave Raj	Pat Valenzuela	1990	Meadow Star	Jose Santos	1994	Flanders	Pat Day
1987	Epitome	Pat Day	1991	Pleasant Stage	Eddie Delahoussaye	1995	My Flag	Jerry Bailey

*By disqualification.

Sprint

Distance: six furlongs

Year		Jockey	Year		Jockey	Year		Jockey
1984	Eillo	Craig Perret	1988	Gulch	Angel Cordero, Jr.	1992	Thirty Slews	Eddie Delahoussaye
1985	Precisionist	Chris McCarron	1989	Dancing Spree	Angel Cordero, Jr.	1993	Cardmania	Eddie Delahoussaye
1986	Smile	Jacinto Vasquez	1990	Safely Kept	Craig Perret	1994	Cherokee Run	Mike Smith
1987	Very Subtle	Pat Valenzuela	1991	Sheikh Albadou	Pat Eddery	1995	Desert Stormer	Kent Desormeaux

Mile

Year		Jockey	Year		Jockey	Year		Jockey
1984	Royal Heroine	Fernando Toro	1989	Steinlen	Jose Santos	1993	Lure	Mike Smith
1985	Cozzene	Walter Guerra	1990	Royal Academy	Lester Piggott	1994	Barathea	Lanfranco Dettori
1986	Last Tycoon	Yves St.-Martin	1991	Opening Verse	Pat Valenzuela	1995	Ridgewood	John Murtagh
1987	Miesque	Freddie Head	1992	Lure	Mike Smith		Pearl	
1988	Miesque	Freddie Head						

Distaff

Distances: 1-1/4 mi 1984-87; 1-1/8 mi since 1988

Year		Jockey	Year		Jockey	Year		Jockey
1984	Princess Rooney	Eddie Delahoussaye	1988	Personal Ensign	Randy Romero	1992	Paseana	Chris McCarron
1985	Life's Magic	Angel Cordero, Jr.	1989	Bayakoa	Laffit Pincay, Jr.	1993	Hollywood Wildcat	Eddie Delahoussaye
1986	Lady's Secret	Pat Day	1990	Bayakoa	Laffit Pincay, Jr.	1994	One Dreamer	Gary Stevens
1987	Sacahuista	Randy Romero	1991	Dance Smartly	Pat Day	1995	Inside Information	Mike Smith

Turf

Distance: 1-1/2 mi

Year		Jockey	Year		Jockey	Year		Jockey
1984	Lashkari	Yves St.-Martin	1988	Great Communicator	Ray Sibille	1991	Miss Alleged	Eric Legrix
1985	Pebbles	Pat Eddery	1989	Prized	Eddie Delahoussaye	1992	Fraise	Pat Valenzuela
1986	Manila	Jose Santos				1993	Kotashaan	Kent Desormeaux
1987	Theatrical	Pat Day	1990	In The Wings	Gary Stevens	1994	Tikkanen	Mike Smith
						1995	Northern Spur	Chris McCarron

Classic

Distance: 1-1/4 mi

Year		Jockey	Year		Jockey	Year		Jockey
1984	Wild Again	Pat Day	1989	Sunday Silence	Chris McCarron	1992	A.P. Indy	Eddie Delahoussaye
1985	Proud Truth	Jorge Velasquez				1993	Arcangues	Jerry Bailey
1986	Skywalker	Laffit Pincay, Jr.	1990	Unbridled	Pat Day	1994	Concern	Jerry Bailey
1987	Ferdinand	Willie Shoemaker	1991	Black Tie Affair	Jerry Bailey	1995	Cigar	Jerry Bailey
1988	Alysheba	Chris McCarron						

Eclipse Awards

The Eclipse Awards, honoring the Horse of the Year and other champions of the sport, began in 1971 and are sponsored by the *Daily Racing Form,* the Thoroughbred Racing Associations, and the National Turf Writers Assn. Prior to 1971, the DRF (1936-70) and the TRA (1950-70) issued separate selections for horse of the year.

Eclipse Awards for 1994

Horse of the Year—Holy Bull
2-year-old colt or gelding—Timber Country
2-year-old filly—Flanders
3-year-old colt or gelding—Holy Bull
3-year-old filly—Heavenly Prize
Older male (4-year-olds & up)—The Wicked North
Older female (4-year-olds & up)—Sky Beauty
Male turf horse—Paradise Creek

Turf filly or mare—Hatoof
Sprinter—Cherokee Run
Steeplechase horse—Warm Spell
Trainer—D. Wayne Lukas
Jockey—Mike Smith
Apprentice jockey—Dale Beckner
Breeder—William T. Young

Horse of the Year

Year	Horse	Year	Horse	Year	Horse	Year	Horse
1936	Granville	1952	One Count (DRF)		Moccasin (TRA)	1980	Spectacular Bid
1937	War Admiral		Native Dancer (TRA)	1966	Buckpasser	1981	John Henry
1938	Seabiscuit	1953	Tom Fool	1967	Damascus	1982	Conquistador Cielo
1939	Challedon	1954	Native Dancer	1968	Dr. Fager	1983	All Along
1940	Challedon	1955	Nashua	1969	Arts and Letters	1984	John Henry
1941	Whirlaway	1956	Swaps	1970	Fort Marcy (DRF)	1985	Spend A Buck
1942	Whirlaway	1957	Bold Ruler (DRF)		Personality (TRA)	1986	Lady's Secret
1943	Count Fleet		Dedicate (TRA)	1971	Ack Ack	1987	Ferdinand
1944	Twilight Tear	1958	Round Table	1972	Secretariat	1988	Alysheba
1945	Busher	1959	Sword Dancer	1973	Secretariat	1989	Sunday Silence
1946	Assault	1960	Kelso	1974	Forego	1990	Criminal Type
1947	Armed	1961	Kelso	1975	Forego	1991	Black Tie Affair
1948	Citation	1962	Kelso	1976	Forego	1992	A.P. Indy
1949	Capot	1963	Kelso	1977	Seattle Slew	1993	Kotashaan
1950	Hill Prince	1964	Kelso	1978	Affirmed	1994	Holy Bull
1951	Counterpoint	1965	Roman Brother (DRF)	1979	Affirmed		

HARNESS RACING

Harness Horse of the Year

(Chosen by the U.S. Trotting Assn. and the U.S. Harness Writers Assn.)

Year	Horse	Year	Horse	Year	Horse	Year	Horse
1951	Pronto Don	1962	Su Mac Lad	1973	Sir Dalrae	1984	Fancy Crown
1952	Good Time	1963	Speedy Scot	1974	Delmonica Hanover	1985	Nihilator
1953	Hi Lo's Forbes	1964	Bret Hanover	1975	Savior	1986	Forrest Skipper
1954	Stenographer	1965	Bret Hanover	1976	Keystone Ore	1987	Mack Lobell
1955	Scott Frost	1966	Bret Hanover	1977	Green Speed	1988	Mack Lobell
1956	Scott Frost	1967	Nevele Pride	1978	Abercrombie	1989	Matt's Scooter
1957	Torpid	1968	Nevele Pride	1979	Niatross	1990	Beach Towel
1958	Emily's Pride	1969	Nevele Pride	1980	Niatross	1991	Precious Bunny
1959	Bye Bye Byrd	1970	Fresh Yankee	1981	Fan Hanover	1992	Artsplace
1960	Adios Butler	1971	Albatross	1982	Cam Fella	1993	Staying Together
1961	Adios Butler	1972	Albatross	1983	Cam Fella	1994	Cam's Card Shark

The Hambletonian (3-year-old trotters)

Year	Winner	Driver	Year	Winner	Driver
1965	Egyptian Candor	Del Cameron	1981	Shiaway St. Pat	Ray Remmen
1966	Kerry Way	Frank Ervin	1982	Speed Bowl	Tommy Haughton
1967	Speedy Streak	Del Cameron	1983	Duenna	Stanley Dancer
1968	Nevele Pride	Stanley Dancer	1984	Historic Freight	Ben Webster
1969	Lindy's Pride	Howard Beissinger	1985	Prakas	Bill O'Donnell
1970	Timothy T	John Simpson, Sr.	1986	Nuclear Kosmos	Ulf Thoresen
1971	Speedy Crown	Howard Beissinger	1987	Mack Lobell	John Campbell
1972	Super Bowl	Stanley Dancer	1988	Armbro Goal	John Campbell
1973	Flirth	Ralph Baldwin	1989	Park Avenue Joe	Ron Waples
1974	Christopher T	Bill Haughton	1990	Harmonious	John Campbell
1975	Bonefish	Stanley Dancer	1991	Giant Victory	Jack Moiseyev
1976	Steve Lobell	Bill Haughton	1992	Alf Palema	Mickey McNicholl
1977	Green Speed	Bill Haughton	1993	American Winner	Ron Pierce
1978	Speedy Somolli	Howard Beissinger	1994	Victory Dream	Michael La Chance
1979	Legend Hanover	George Sholty	1995	Tagliabue	John Campbell
1980	Burgomeister	Bill Haughton			

BOWLING

Professional Bowlers Association

Hall of Fame

Performance			Meritorious service	
Bill Allen	Mike Durbin	David Ozio	Dick Weber	Lou Frantz
Glenn Allison	Buzz Fazio	George Pappas	Billy Welu	Harry Golden
Earl Anthony	Skee Foremsky	Johnny Petraglia	Walter Ray Williams, Jr.	Ted Hoffman, Jr.
Barry Asher	Jim Godman	Dick Ritger	Wayne Zahn	John Jowdy
Ray Bluth	Johnny Guenther	Mark Roth	**Meritorious service**	Joe Kelley
Roy Buckley	Billy Hardwick	Jim St. John	Joe Antenora	Steve Nagy
Nelson Burton, Jr.	Tommy Hudson	Carmen Salvino	John Archibald	Chuck Pezzano
Don Carter	Don Johnson	Bob Strampe	Chuck Clemens	Jack Reichert
Pat Colwell	Joe Joseph	Harry Smith	Eddie Elias	Joe Richards
Steve Cook	Larry Laub	Dave Soutar	Frank Esposito	Chris Schenkel
Dave Davis	Mike Limongello	Jim Stefanich	Dick Evans	Lorraine Stilzlein
Gary Dickinson	Don McCune	Brian Voss	Raymond Firestone	Al Thompson
	Mike McGrath	Wayne Webb	E. A. "Bud" Fisher	Roger Zeller

Tournament of Champions

Year	Winner	Year	Winner	Year	Winner	Year	Winner
1965	Billy Hardwick	1973	Jim Godman	1980	Wayne Webb	1988	Mark Williams
1966	Wayne Zahn	1974	Earl Anthony	1981	Steve Cook	1989	Del Ballard, Jr.
1967	Jim Stefanich	1975	Dave Davis	1982	Mike Durbin	1990	Dave Ferraro
1968	Dave Davis	1976	Marshall Holman	1983	Joe Berardi	1991	David Ozio
1969	Jim Godman	1977	Mike Berlin	1984	Mike Durbin	1992	Marc McDowell
1970	Don Johnson	1978	Earl Anthony	1985	Mark Williams	1993	George Branham 3d
1971	Johnny Petraglia	1979	George Pappas	1986	Marshall Holman	1994	Norm Duke
1972	Mike Durbin			1987	Pete Weber	1995	Mike Aulby

PBA Leading Money Winners

Total winnings are from PBA, ABC Masters, and BPAA All-Star tournaments only, and do not include numerous other tournaments or earnings from special television shows and matches.

Year	Bowler	Amount	Year	Bowler	Amount	Year	Bowler	Amount
1962	Don Carter	$49,972	1974	Earl Anthony	$99,585	1986	Walter Ray Williams Jr.	$145,550
1963	Dick Weber	46,333	1975	Earl Anthony	107,585			
1964	Bob Strampe	33,592	1976	Earl Anthony	110,833	1987	Pete Weber	175,491
1965	Dick Weber	47,674	1977	Mark Roth	105,583	1988	Brian Voss	225,485
1966	Wayne Zahn	54,720	1978	Mark Roth	134,500	1989	Mike Aulby	298,237
1967	Dave Davis	54,165	1979	Mark Roth	124,517	1990	Amleto Monacelli	204,775
1968	Jim Stefanich	67,377	1980	Wayne Webb	116,700	1991	David Ozio	225,585
1969	Billy Hardwick	64,160	1981	Earl Anthony	164,735	1992	Marc McDowell	174,215
1970	Mike McGrath	52,049	1982	Earl Anthony	134,760	1993	Walter Ray Williams Jr.	296,370
1971	Johnny Petraglia	85,065	1983	Earl Anthony	135,605			
1972	Don Johnson	56,648	1984	Mark Roth	158,712	1994	Norm Duke	273,753
1973	Don McCune	69,000	1985	Mike Aulby	201,200			

Leading PBA Averages by Year

Year	Bowler	Average	Year	Bowler	Average	Year	Bowler	Average
1962	Don Carter	212.844	1974	Earl Anthony	219.394	1985	Mark Baker	213.718
1963	Billy Hardwick	210.346	1975	Earl Anthony	219.060	1986	John Gant	214.378
1964	Ray Bluth	210.512	1976	Mark Roth	215.970	1987	Marshall Holman	216.801
1965	Dick Weber	211.895	1977	Mark Roth	218.174	1988	Mark Roth	218.036
1966	Wayne Zahn	208.663	1978	Mark Roth	219.834	1989	Pete Weber	215.432
1967	Wayne Zahn	212.342	1979	Mark Roth	221.662	1990	Amleto Monacelli	218.158
1968	Jim Stefanich	211.895	1980	Earl Anthony	218.535	1991	Norm Duke	218.208
1969	Bill Hardwick	212.957	1981	Mark Roth	216.699	1992	Dave Ferraro	219.702
1970	Nelson Burton Jr.	214.908	1982	Marshall Holman	212.844	1993	Walter Ray Williams Jr.	222.980
1971	Don Johnson	213.977	1983	Earl Anthony	216.645			
1972	Don Johnson	215.290	1984	Marshall Holman	213.911	1994	Norm Duke	222.830
1973	Earl Anthony	215.799						

American Bowling Congress

ABC Masters Tournament Champions

Year	Winner	Year	Winner	Year	Winner
1980	Neil Burton, St. Louis, MO	1985	Steve Wunderlich, St. Louis, MO	1991	Doug Kent, Canandaigua, NY
1981	Randy Lightfoot, St. Charles, MO	1986	Mark Fahy, Chicago, IL	1992	Ken Johnson, N. Richmond Hills, TX
1982	Joe Berardi, Brooklyn, NY	1987	Rick Steelsmith, Wichita, KS		
1983	Mike Lastowski, Havre de Grace, MD	1988	Del Ballard Jr., Richardson, TX	1993	Norm Duke, Oklahoma City, OK
		1989	Mike Aulby, Indianapolis, IN	1994	Steve Fehr, Cincinnati, OH
1984	Earl Anthony, Dublin, CA	1990	Chris Warren, Dallas, TX	1995	Mike Aulby, Indianapolis, IN

Champions in 1995

Singles—Matt Surina, Mead, WA
Doubles Event—Michael Wambold and Scott Kruppenbacher, Rochester, NY

All Events—Jeff Kwiatkowski, Maumee, OH
Regular Team—Arden Lanes, Seattle, WA
Booster Team—First Texas Bank, Killeen, TX

Most Sanctioned 300 Games

Mike Whalin, Cincinnati, OH	51	Doug Spicer, W. Bloomfield, MI	30	Dave Soutar, Kansas City, MO	24
Bob Learn, Jr., Erie, PA	48	Bob Johnson, Dayton, OH	28	Tony Torrice, Wolcott, CT	24
Jim Johnson, Jr., Wilmington, DE	48	Jim Ewald, Jr., Louisville, KY	27	Gary Barney, St. Louis, MO	23
Jerry Kessler, Dayton, OH	39	Steve Gehringer, Reading, PA	27	Mitch Jabczenski, Detroit, MI	23
Joe Jimenez, Saginaw, MI	37	Elvin Mesger, Sullivan, MO	27	Steve Levering, Landisville, PA	23
Jeff Jensen, Wichita, KS	36	Randy Choat, Granite City, IL	26	Jerome Penxa, Detroit, MI	23
Bob Buckery, McAdoo, PA	34	Alan Hulsizer, Reading, PA	25	Teata Semiz, Fairfield, NJ	23
Ralph Burley, Jr., Dayton, OH	33	Anthony Juliano, Margate, FL	25	Don Anthony, Columbus, OH	22
Ron Woolet, Louisville, KY	33	Mark Stibora, Cleveland, OH	25	Steve Carson, Oklahoma City, OK	22
John Wilcox, Jr., Shavertown, PA	32	John Chako, Jr., Larksville, PA	24	Bob Goike, Belleville, MI	21
Eric Roddy, New Orleans, LA	30	Jason Hurd, Tulare, CA	24	Dave Heller, Highland Falls, NY	21

Women's International Bowling Congress

Champions in 1995

Queens Tournament—Sandra Postma, Lansing, IL
Singles Event—Beth Owen, Dallas, TX
All Events—Beth Owen, Dallas, TX

Doubles Event—Carol Harsh and Debbie Villani, Las Vegas, NV
Team—Contour Power Grips, Detroit, MI

Most Sanctioned 300 Games

Tish Johnson, Panorama City, CA	25	Vicki Fischel, Wheat Ridge, CO	16	Cindy Coburn-Carroll, Tonawanda, NY	12
Jeanne Maiden-Naccarato, Tacoma, WA	21	Leanne Barrette, Youkon, OK	15	Donna Adamek, Apple Valley, CA	11
Aleta Sill, Dearborn, MI	17	Cheryl Daniels, Detroit, MI	13	Robin Romeo, Van Nuys, CA	9
		Betty Morris, Stockton, CA	12		

Figure Skating Champions

	U.S. Champions			World Champions	
Men	**Women**	**Year**	**Men**		**Women**
Dick Button	Tenley Albright	1952	Dick Button, U.S.		Jacqueline du Bief, France
Hayes Jenkins	Tenley Albright	1953	Hayes Jenkins, U.S.		Tenley Albright, U.S.
Hayes Jenkins	Tenley Albright	1954	Hayes Jenkins, U.S.		Gundi Busch, W. Germany
Hayes Jenkins	Tenley Albright	1955	Hayes Jenkins, U.S.		Tenley Albright, U.S.
Hayes Jenkins	Tenley Albright	1956	Hayes Jenkins, U.S.		Carol Heiss, U.S.
Dave Jenkins	Carol Heiss	1957	Dave Jenkins, U.S.		Carol Heiss, U.S.
Dave Jenkins	Carol Heiss	1958	Dave Jenkins, U.S.		Carol Heiss, U.S.
Dave Jenkins	Carol Heiss	1959	Dave Jenkins, U.S.		Carol Heiss, U.S.
Dave Jenkins	Carol Heiss	1960	Alain Giletti, France		Carol Heiss, U.S.
Bradley Lord	Laurence Owen	1961	none		none
Monty Hoyt	Barbara Roles Pursley	1962	Don Jackson, Canada		Sjoukje Dijkstra, Neth.
Tommy Litz	Lorraine Hanlon	1963	Don McPherson, Canada		Sjoukje Dijkstra, Neth.
Scott Allen	Peggy Fleming	1964	Manfred Schnelldorfer, W. Germany		Sjoukje Dijkstra, Neth.
Gary Visconti	Peggy Fleming	1965	Alain Calmat, France		Petra Burka, Canada
Scott Allen	Peggy Fleming	1966	Emmerich Danzer, Austria		Peggy Fleming, U.S.
Gary Visconti	Peggy Fleming	1967	Emmerich Danzer, Austria		Peggy Fleming, U.S.
Tim Wood	Peggy Fleming	1968	Emmerich Danzer, Austria		Peggy Fleming, U.S.
Tim Wood	Janet Lynn	1969	Tim Wood, U.S.		Gabriele Seyfert, E. Germany
Tim Wood	Janet Lynn	1970	Tim Wood, U.S.		Gabriele Seyfert, E. Germany
John Misha Petkevich	Janet Lynn	1971	Ondrej Nepela, Czech.		Beatrix Schuba, Austria
Ken Shelley	Janet Lynn	1972	Ondrej Nepela, Czech.		Beatrix Schuba, Austria
Gordon McKellen Jr.	Janet Lynn	1973	Ondrej Nepela, Czech.		Karen Magnussen, Canada
Gordon McKellen Jr.	Dorothy Hamill	1974	Jan Hoffmann, E. Germany		Christine Errath, E. Germany
Gordon McKellen Jr.	Dorothy Hamill	1975	Sergei Volkov, USSR		Dianne de Leeuw, Neth.-U.S.
Terry Kubicka	Dorothy Hamill	1976	John Curry, Gr. Britain		Dorothy Hamill, U.S.
Charles Tickner	Linda Fratianne	1977	Vladimir Kovalev, USSR		Linda Fratianne, U.S.
Charles Tickner	Linda Fratianne	1978	Charles Tickner, U.S.		Anett Poetzsch, E. Germany
Charles Tickner	Linda Fratianne	1979	Vladimir Kovalev, USSR		Linda Fratianne, U.S.
Charles Tickner	Linda Fratianne	1980	Jan Hoffmann, E. Germany		Anett Poetzsch, E. Germany
Scott Hamilton	Elaine Zayak	1981	Scott Hamilton, U.S.		Denise Biellmann, Switzerland
Scott Hamilton	Rosalynn Sumners	1982	Scott Hamilton, U.S.		Elaine Zayak, U.S.
Scott Hamilton	Rosalynn Sumners	1983	Scott Hamilton, U.S.		Rosalynn Sumners, U.S.
Scott Hamilton	Rosalynn Sumners	1984	Scott Hamilton, U.S.		Katarina Witt, E. Germany
Brian Boitano	Tiffany Chin	1985	Aleksandr Fadeev, USSR		Katarina Witt, E. Germany
Brian Boitano	Debi Thomas	1986	Brian Boitano, U.S.		Debi Thomas, U.S.
Brian Boitano	Jill Trenary	1987	Brian Orser, Canada		Katarina Witt, E. Germany
Brian Boitano	Debi Thomas	1988	Brian Boitano, U.S.		Katarina Witt, E. Germany
Christopher Bowman	Jill Trenary	1989	Kurt Browning, Canada		Midori Ito, Japan
Todd Eldredge	Jill Trenary	1990	Kurt Browning, Canada		Jill Trenary, U.S.
Todd Eldredge	Tonya Harding	1991	Kurt Browning, Canada		Kristi Yamaguchi, U.S.
Christopher Bowman	Kristi Yamaguchi	1992	Viktor Petrenko, Ukraine		Kristi Yamaguchi, U.S.
Scott Davis	Nancy Kerrigan	1993	Kurt Browning, Canada		Oksana Baiul, Ukraine
Scott Davis	vacant[1]	1994	Elvis Stojko, Canada		Yuka Sato, Japan
Todd Eldredge	Nicole Bobek	1995	Elvis Stojko, Canada		Chen Lu, China

(1) Tonya Harding was stripped of title.

James E. Sullivan Memorial Trophy Winners

The James E. Sullivan Memorial Trophy, named after the former president of the AAU and inaugurated in 1930, is awarded annually by the AAU to the athlete who "by his or her performance, example and influence as an amateur, has done the most during the year to advance the cause of sportsmanship."

Year	Winner	Sport	Year	Winner	Sport	Year	Winner	Sport
1930	Bobby Jones	Golf	1953	Dr. Sammy Lee	Diving	1977	John Naber	Swimming
1931	Barney Berlinger	Track	1954	Mal Whitfield	Track	1978	Tracy Caulkins	Swimming
1932	Jim Bausch	Track	1955	Harrison Dillard	Track	1979	Kurt Thomas	Gymnastics
1933	Glenn Cunningham	Track	1956	Patricia McCormick	Diving	1980	Eric Heiden	Speed Skating
1934	Bill Bonthron	Track	1957	Bobby Joe Morrow	Track			
1935	Lawson Little	Golf	1958	Glenn Davis	Track	1981	Carl Lewis	Track
1936	Glenn Morris	Track	1959	Parry O'Brien	Track	1982	Mary Decker	Track
1937	Don Budge	Tennis	1960	Rafer Johnson	Track	1983	Edwin Moses	Track
1938	Don Lash	Track	1961	Wilma Rudolph Ward	Track	1984	Greg Louganis	Diving
1939	Joe Burk	Rowing				1985	Joan Benoit Samuelson	Marathon
1940	Greg Rice	Track	1962	James Beatty	Track			
1941	Leslie MacMitchell	Track	1963	John Pennel	Track	1986	Jackie Joyner-Kersee	Track
1942	Cornelius Warmerdam	Track	1964	Don Schollander	Swimming	1987	Jim Abbott	Baseball
1943	Gilbert Dodds	Track	1965	Bill Bradley	Basketball	1988	Florence Griffith Joyner	Track
1944	Ann Curtis	Swimming	1966	Jim Ryun	Track			
1945	Doc Blanchard	Football	1967	Randy Matson	Track	1989	Janet Evans	Swimming
1946	Arnold Tucker	Football	1968	Debbie Meyer	Swimming	1990	John Smith	Wrestling
1947	John Kelly Jr.	Rowing	1969	Bill Toomey	Track	1991	Mike Powell	Track
1948	Robert Mathias	Track	1970	John Kinsella	Swimming	1992	Bonnie Blair	Speed Skating
1949	Dick Button	Skating	1971	Mark Spitz	Swimming			
1950	Fred Wilt	Track	1972	Frank Shorter	Track	1993	Charlie Ward	Football, Basketball
1951	Rev. Robert Richards	Track	1973	Bill Walton	Basketball			
			1974	Rick Wohlhutter	Track	1994	Dan Jansen	Speed Skating
1952	Horace Ashenfelter	Track	1975	Tim Shaw	Swimming			
			1976	Bruce Jenner	Track			

Professional Sports Directory
Major League Baseball

Commissioner's Office
350 Park Ave.
New York, NY 10022

National League

National League Office
350 Park Ave.
New York, NY 10022

Atlanta Braves
521 Capitol Ave. SW
Atlanta, GA 30312

Chicago Cubs
Wrigley Field
Chicago, IL 60613

Cincinnati Reds
100 Riverfront Stadium
Cincinnati, OH 45202

Colorado Rockies
1700 Broadway
Denver, CO 80290

Florida Marlins
2267 NW 199th St.
Miami, FL 33056

Houston Astros
PO Box 288
Houston, TX 77001

Los Angeles Dodgers
Dodger Stadium
Los Angeles, CA 90012

Montreal Expos
PO Box 500, Station M
Montreal, Que. H1V 3P2

New York Mets
Shea Stadium
Flushing, NY 11368

Philadelphia Phillies
PO Box 7575
Philadelphia, PA 19101

Pittsburgh Pirates
Three Rivers Stadium
Pittsburgh, PA 15212

St. Louis Cardinals
Busch Memorial Stadium
St. Louis, MO 63102

San Diego Padres
PO Box 2000
San Diego, CA 92112

San Francisco Giants
3Com (Candlestick) Park
San Francisco, CA 94124

American League

American League Office
350 Park Ave.
New York, NY 10022

Baltimore Orioles
333 W. Camden St.
Baltimore, MD 21202

Boston Red Sox
24 Yawkey Way
Boston, MA 02215

California Angels
Anaheim Stadium
Anaheim, CA 92803

Chicago White Sox
333 W. 35th St.
Chicago, IL 60616

Cleveland Indians
2401 Ontario St.
Cleveland, OH 44115

Detroit Tigers
Tiger Stadium
Detroit, MI 48216

Kansas City Royals
P.O. Box 419969
Kansas City, MO 64141

Milwaukee Brewers
Milwaukee County Stadium
Milwaukee, WI 53214

Minnesota Twins
501 Chicago Ave. South
Minneapolis, MN 55415

New York Yankees
Yankee Stadium
Bronx, NY 10451

Oakland Athletics
Oakland Coliseum
Oakland, CA 94621

Seattle Mariners
PO Box 4100
Seattle, WA 98104

Texas Rangers
PO Box 90111
Arlington, TX 76004

Toronto Blue Jays
1 Blue Jays Way
Toronto, Ont. M5V 1J1

National Basketball Association

League Office
645 5th Ave.
New York, NY 10022

Atlanta Hawks
One CNN Center
Atlanta, GA 30303

Boston Celtics
151 Merrimac St.
Boston, MA 02114

Charlotte Hornets
100 Hive Dr.
Charlotte, NC 28217

Chicago Bulls
1901 W. Madison St.
Chicago, IL 60612

Cleveland Cavaliers
1 Center Court
Cleveland, OH 44115-4001

Dallas Mavericks
777 Sports St.
Dallas, TX 75207

Denver Nuggets
1635 Clay St.
Denver, CO 80204

Detroit Pistons
Two Championship Dr.
Auburn Hills, MI 48362

Golden State Warriors
7000 Coliseum Way
Oakland, CA 94621-1918

Houston Rockets
Ten Greenway Plaza
Houston, TX 77046-3865

Indiana Pacers
300 E. Market St.
Indianapolis, IN 46204

Los Angeles Clippers
3939 S. Figueroa St.
Los Angeles, CA 90037

Los Angeles Lakers
3900 W. Manchester Blvd.
Inglewood, CA 90306

Miami Heat
Miami Arena
Miami, FL 33136-4102

Milwaukee Bucks
1001 N. 4th St.
Milwaukee, WI 53203-1312

Minnesota Timberwolves
600 1st Ave. N
Minneapolis, MN 55403

New Jersey Nets
405 Murray Hill Parkway
E. Rutherford, NJ 07073

New York Knickerbockers
Two Pennsylvania Plaza
New York, NY 10121-0091

Orlando Magic
One Magic Place
Orlando, FL 32801

Philadelphia 76ers
Veterans Stadium
Philadelphia, PA 19147-0240

Phoenix Suns
201 E. Jefferson
Phoenix, AZ 85004

Portland Trail Blazers
One Center Ct., Ste. 200
Portland, OR 97227

Sacramento Kings
One Sports Parkway
Sacramento, CA 95834

San Antonio Spurs
100 Montana St.
San Antonio, TX 78203-1031

Seattle SuperSonics
190 Queen Ann Ave. N
Seattle, WA 98109-9711

Toronto Raptors
20 Bay St., Ste. 1702
Toronto, Ont. M5J 2N8

Utah Jazz
301 W. South Temple
Salt Lake City, UT 84101

Vancouver Grizzlies
800 Griffiths Way
Vancouver, B.C. V6B 6G1

Washington Bullets
USAir Arena
Landover, MD 20785

National Hockey League

League Headquarters
1251 Ave. of the Americas
New York, NY 10020

Mighty Ducks of Anaheim
2695 E. Katella Ave.
Anaheim, CA 92803-6177

Boston Bruins
FleetCenter
Boston, MA 02114

Buffalo Sabres
140 Main St.
Buffalo, NY 14202

Calgary Flames
PO Box 1540
Calgary, Alta. T2P 3B9

Chicago Blackhawks
1901 W. Madison St.
Chicago, IL 60612

Colorado Avalanche
1635 Clay St.
Denver, CO 80204

Dallas Stars
211 Cowboys Parkway
Irving, TX 75063

Detroit Red Wings
600 Civic Center Dr.
Detroit, MI 48226

Edmonton Oilers
Edmonton Coliseum
Edmonton, Alta. T5B 4M9

Florida Panthers
100 NE Third Ave.
Ft. Lauderdale, FL 33301

Hartford Whalers
242 Trumbull St.
Hartford, CT 06103

(continued)

Los Angeles Kings
3900 W. Manchester Blvd.
Inglewood, CA 90305

New York Rangers
4 Pennsylvania Plaza
New York, NY 10001

St. Louis Blues
1401 Clark
St. Louis, MO 63103

Vancouver Canucks
800 Griffiths Way
Vancouver, B.C. V6B 6G1

Montreal Canadiens
2313 St. Catherine St. W
Montreal, Que. H3H 1N2

Ottawa Senators
301 Moodie Dr.
Nepean, Ont. K2H 9C4

San Jose Sharks
525 W. Santa Clara St.
San Jose, CA 95113

Washington Capitals
USAir Arena
Landover, MD 20785

New Jersey Devils
PO Box 504
E. Rutherford, NJ 07073

Philadelphia Flyers
3601 S. Broad St.
Philadelphia, PA 19148

Tampa Bay Lightning
501 E. Kennedy Blvd.
Tampa, FL 33602

Winnipeg Jets
15-1430 Maroons Rd.
Winnipeg, Man. R3G 0L5

New York Islanders
Nassau Coliseum
Uniondale, NY 11553

Pittsburgh Penguins
Civic Arena
Pittsburgh, PA 15219

Toronto Maple Leafs
60 Carlton St.
Toronto, Ont. M5B 1L1

National Football League

League Office
410 Park Avenue
New York, NY 10022

Dallas Cowboys
One Cowboys Parkway
Irving, TX 75063

Los Angeles Raiders
332 Center St.
El Segundo, CA 90245

Pittsburgh Steelers
300 Stadium Circle
Pittsburgh, PA 15212

Arizona Cardinals
PO Box 888
Phoenix, AZ 85001-0888

Denver Broncos
13655 Broncos Parkway
Englewood, CO 80112

Miami Dolphins
7500 SW 30th St.
Davie, FL 33314

St. Louis Rams
Matthews Dickey Boys Club
4245 N. Kings Highway
St. Louis, MO 63115

Atlanta Falcons
2745 Burnett Road
Suwanee, GA 30174

Detroit Lions
1200 Featherstone Rd.
Pontiac, MI 48342

Minnesota Vikings
9520 Viking Dr.
Eden Prairie, MN 55344

San Diego Chargers
PO Box 609609
San Diego, CA 92160-9609

Buffalo Bills
One Bills Drive
Orchard Park, NY 14127

Green Bay Packers
PO Box 10628
Green Bay, WI 54307-0628

New England Patriots
60 Washington St.
Foxboro, MA 02035

San Francisco 49ers
4949 Centennial Blvd.
Santa Clara, CA 95054-1229

Carolina Panthers
227 W. Trade St., Ste. 1600
Charlotte, NC 28202

Houston Oilers
6910 Fannin St.
Houston, TX 77030

New Orleans Saints
6928 Saints Dr.
Metairie, LA 70003

Seattle Seahawks
11220 NE 53d St.
Kirkland, WA 98033

Chicago Bears
250 N. Washington Rd.
Lake Forest, IL 60045

Indianapolis Colts
PO Box 535000
Indianapolis, IN 46253

New York Giants
Giants Stadium
E. Rutherford, NJ 07073

Tampa Bay Buccaneers
One Buccaneer Place
Tampa, FL 33607

Cincinnati Bengals
200 Riverfront Stadium
Cincinnati, OH 45202

Jacksonville Jaguars
One Stadium Pl.
Jacksonville, FL 32202

New York Jets
1000 Fulton Ave.
Hempstead, NY 11550

Cleveland Browns
80 First Ave.
Berea, OH 44017-0679

Kansas City Chiefs
One Arrowhead Drive
Kansas City, MO 64129

Philadelphia Eagles
3501 S. Broad St.
Philadelphia, PA 19148

Washington Redskins
PO Box 17247
Washington, DC 20041

Other Sports Organizations

Amateur Athletic Union
3400 W. 86th St.
Indianapolis, IN 46268

Intl. Game Fish Assn.
1301 E. Atlantic Blvd.
Pompano Beach, FL 33060

Pro Bowlers Assn.
1720 Merriman Rd.
Akron, OH 44334

U.S. Figure Skating Assn.
20 First St.
Colorado Springs, CO 80906

Amateur Softball Assn.
2801 NE 50th St.
Oklahoma City, OK 73111

LPGA
2570 Intl. Speedway Blvd.
Daytona Beach, FL 32114

PGA
100 Ave. of the Champions
Palm Beach Gardens, FL 33418

U.S. Olympic Committee
One Olympic Plaza
Colorado Springs, CO 80909

American Horse Shows Assn.
220 E. 42d St.
New York, NY 10017

Little League Baseball
PO Box 3485
Williamsport, PA 17701

Pro Rodeo Cowboys Assn.
101 Pro Rodeo Dr.
Colorado Springs, CO 80919

U.S. Skiing Assn.
PO Box 100
Park City, UT 84060

American Kennel Club
51 Madison Ave.
New York, NY 10010

National Archery Assn.
One Olympic Plaza
Colorado Springs, CO 80909

Special Olympics
1325 G St., NW
Washington, DC 20005

U.S. Soccer Federation
1801 S. Prairie Ave.
Chicago, IL 60616

American Water Ski Assn.
799 Overlook Dr. SE
Winter Haven, FL 33884

NASCAR
PO Box 2875
Daytona Beach, FL 32120

Thoroughbred Racing Assns.
420 Fair Hill Dr.
Elkton, MD 21921

U.S. Tennis Assn.
70 W. Red Oak Lane
White Plains, NY 10604

Canadian Football League
110 Eglinton Ave. W
Toronto, Ont. M4R 1A3

NCAA
6201 College Blvd.
Overland Park, KS 66211

USA Track & Field
PO Box 120
Indianapolis, IN 46206

IndyCar
755 W. Big Beaver Rd.
Troy, MI 48084

National Rifle Assn.
11250 Waples Mill Rd.
Fairfax, VA 22030

U.S. Auto Club
4910 W. 16th St.
Speedway, IN 46224

U.S. Trotting Assn.
750 Michigan Ave.
Columbus, OH 43215

NCAA Wrestling Champions

Year	Champion	Year	Champion	Year	Champion	Year	Champion	Year	Champion
1964	Oklahoma State	1970	Iowa State	1977	Iowa State	1984	Iowa	1990	Oklahoma State
1965	Iowa State	1971	Oklahoma State	1978	Iowa	1985	Iowa	1991	Iowa
1966	Oklahoma State	1972	Iowa State	1979	Iowa	1986	Iowa	1992	Iowa
1967	Michigan State	1973	Iowa State	1980	Iowa	1987	Iowa State	1993	Iowa
1968	Oklahoma State	1974	Oklahoma	1981	Iowa	1988	Arizona State	1994	Oklahoma State
1969	Iowa State	1975	Iowa	1982	Iowa	1989	Oklahoma State	1995	Iowa
		1976	Iowa	1983	Iowa				

World Swimming Records
As of Aug. 1995

Men's Records

Distance	Time	Holder	Country	Where made	Date
		Freestyle			
50 meters	0:21.81	Tom Jager	U.S.	Nashville, TN	Mar. 24, 1990
100 meters	0:48.21	Alexander Popov	Russia	Monte Carlo	June 18, 1994
200 meters	1:46.69	Giorgio Lamberti	Italy	Bonn	Aug. 15, 1989
400 meters	3:43.80	Kieren Perkins	Australia	Rome	Sept. 9, 1994
800 meters	7:46.00	Kieren Perkins	Australia	Victoria, Canada	Aug. 24, 1994
1,500 meters	14:41.66	Kieren Perkins	Australia	Victoria, Canada	Aug. 24, 1994
		Breaststroke			
100 meters	1:00.95	Karolyi Guttler	Hungary	Sheffield, Gr. Britain	Aug. 5, 1994
200 meters	2:10.16	Mike Barrowman	U.S.	Barcelona	July 29, 1992
		Butterfly			
100 meters	0:52.32	Denis Pankratov	Russia	Vienna	Aug. 23, 1995
200 meters	1:55.22	Denis Pankratov	Russia	Canet, France	June 14, 1995
		Backstroke			
100 meters	0:53.86	Jeff Rouse	U.S.	Barcelona	July 29, 1992
200 meters	1:56.57	Martin Lopez-Zubero	Spain	Tuscaloosa, AL	Nov. 23, 1991
		Individual Medley			
200 meters	1:58.16	Jani Sievinen	Finland	Rome	Sept. 11, 1994
400 meters	4:12.30	Tom Dolan	U.S.	Rome	Sept. 6, 1994
		Freestyle Relays			
400 m. (4×100)	3:15.11	(Fox, Hudepohl, Olsen, Hall)	U.S.	Atlanta, GA	Aug. 12, 1995
800 m. (4×200)	7:11.95	(Lepikov, Pychenko, Taianovitch, Sadovyi)	Unified Team	Barcelona	July 27, 1992
		Medley Relay			
400 m. (4×100)	3:36.93	(Berkoff, Schroeder, Jacobs, Biondi)	U.S.	Seoul	Sept. 25, 1988
		(Rouse, Diebel, Morales, Olsen)	U.S.	Barcelona	July 31, 1992

Women's Records

Distance	Time	Holder	Country	Where made	Date
		Freestyle			
50 meters	0:24.51	Jingyi Le	China	Rome	Sept. 11, 1994
100 meters	0:54.01	Jingyi Le	China	Rome	Sept. 5, 1994
200 meters	1:56.78	Franziska Van Almsick	Germany	Rome	Sept. 6, 1994
400 meters	4:03.85	Janet Evans	U.S.	Seoul	Sept. 22, 1988
800 meters	8:16.22	Janet Evans	U.S.	Tokyo	Aug. 20, 1989
1,500 meters	15:52.10	Janet Evans	U.S.	Orlando, FL	Mar. 26, 1988
		Breaststroke			
100 meters	1:07.69	Samatha Riley	Australia	Rome	Sept. 9, 1994
200 meters	2:24.76	Rebecca Brown	Australia	Queensland, Australia	Mar. 16, 1994
		Butterfly			
100 meters	0:57.93	Mary T. Meagher	U.S.	Brown Deer, WI	Aug. 16, 1981
200 meters	2:05.96	Mary T. Meagher	U.S.	Brown Deer, WI	Aug. 13, 1981
		Backstroke			
100 meters	1:00.16	Cihong He	China	Rome	Sept. 10, 1994
200 meters	2:06.62	Krisztina Egerszegi	Hungary	Athens	Aug. 25, 1991
		Individual Medley			
200 meters	2:11.65	Li Lin	China	Barcelona	July 30, 1992
400 meters	4:36.10	Petra Schneider	E. Germany	Ecuador	Aug. 1, 1982
		Freestyle Relays			
400 m. (4×100)	3:37.91	(Jingyi Le, Ying Shan, Ying Le, Lu Bin)	China	Rome	Sept. 7, 1994
		Medley Relays			
400 m. (4×100)	4:01.67	(Cihong He, Guohong. Dai, Limin Liu, Jingyi Le)	China	Rome	Sept. 10, 1994

NATIONAL BASKETBALL ASSOCIATION

1995-96 NBA Preview: Canadian Expansion Teams; 1994-95 Review

The NBA became an international league in 1995-96 with the addition of two Canadian-based expansion teams: the Toronto Raptors (Central Division) and the Vancouver Grizzlies (Midwest Division). Notable news items and achievements in 1994-95: Michael Jordan returned from retirement after a brief stab at professional baseball to lead the Chicago Bulls into the playoffs; John Stockton of the Utah Jazz became the all-time NBA assists leader, overtaking the great Magic Johnson; and Atlanta Hawks coach Lenny Wilkens became the all-time leader in coaching victories, surpassing Red Auerbach.

Final Standings, 1994-95 Season

Eastern Conference

Atlantic Division

	W	L	Pct	GB
Orlando	57	25	.695	—
New York	55	27	.671	2
Boston	35	47	.427	22
Miami	32	50	.390	25
New Jersey	30	52	.366	27
Philadelphia	24	58	.293	33
Washington	21	61	.256	36

Central Division

	W	L	Pct	GB
Indiana	52	30	.634	—
Charlotte	50	32	.610	2
Chicago	47	35	.573	5
Cleveland	43	39	.524	9
Atlanta	42	40	.512	10
Milwaukee	34	48	.415	18
Detroit	28	54	.341	24

Western Conference

Midwest Division

	W	L	Pct	GB
San Antonio	62	20	.756	—
Utah	60	22	.732	2
Houston	47	35	.573	15
Denver	41	41	.500	21
Dallas	36	46	.439	26
Minnesota	21	61	.256	41

Pacific Division

	W	L	Pct	GB
Phoenix	59	23	.720	—
Seattle	57	25	.695	2
L.A. Lakers	48	34	.585	11
Portland	44	38	.537	15
Sacramento	39	43	.476	20
Golden State	26	56	.317	33
L.A. Clippers	17	65	.207	42

NBA Regular Season Individual Highs in 1994-95

Most minutes played, season — 3,361: Vin Baker, Milwaukee.

Most points, game — 56: Glen Rice, Miami v. Orlando, Apr. 15.

Most field goals made, game — 21: Cedric Ceballos, L.A. Lakers v. Minnesota, Dec. 20; Hakeem Olajuwon, Houston v. San Antonio, Jan. 13; Dana Barros, Philadelphia v. Houston, Mar. 14; Michael Jordan, Chicago v. New York, Mar. 28.

Most field goal attempts, game — 37: Michael Jordan, Chicago v. New York, Mar. 28; Jamal Mashburn, Dallas v. Houston, Apr. 11 (OT).

3-point field goals made, highest percentage (min. 50 made), season — .524: Steve Kerr, Chicago.

Most free throws made, game — 24: Willie Burton, Philadelphia v. Miami, Dec. 13.

Most rebounds, game — 30: Dennis Rodman, San Antonio v. Houston, Feb. 21.

Most offensive rebounds, season — 329: Popeye Jones, Dallas.

Most defensive rebounds, season — 715: Karl Malone, Utah.

Most assists, game — 22: Tim Hardaway, Golden State v. Orlando, Dec. 16 (OT); Non-overtime — 20: John Stockton, Utah v. Philadelphia, Jan. 7.

Most steals, game — 8: Scottie Pippen, Chicago v. Milwaukee, Mar. 17; Latrell Sprewell, Golden State v. Orlando, Mar. 26; Pooh Richardson, L.A. Clippers v. Orlando, Dec. 30 (OT).

Most blocked shots, game — 11: Dikembe Mutombo, Denver v. Dallas, Nov. 8.

Most personal fouls, season — 338: Shawn Bradley, Philadelphia.

Most games disqualified, season — 18: Shawn Bradley, Philadelphia.

Rockets Win Second Consecutive Championship by Sweeping the Magic 4 Games to 0

The Houston Rockets won their second consecutive National Basketball Association championship by defeating the Orlando Magic 4 games to 0. The lowest-seeded playoff team ever to win a championship, the Rockets became the first team in league history to eliminate 4 teams that won 50 or more regular-season games and the first defending champions to sweep their opponents in the finals. Houston center Hakeem Olajuwon won Finals MVP honors for the second year in a row.

Houston Rockets

	FG A-M	FT A-M	Reb O-D	Ast	Avg
Olajuwon	116-56	26-18	11-35	22	32.8
Drexler	60-27	38-30	13-25	27	21.5
Horry	53-23	21-14	9-31	15	17.8
Elie	37-24	10-9	4-13	13	16.3
Cassell	35-15	24-20	1-6	12	14.3
Smith	29-11	0-0	2-5	16	7.5
Brown	11-5	2-2	3-8	0	3.0
Jones	2-1	2-2	1-6	0	1.0
Chilcutt	0-0	0-0	0-0	0	0.0

Orlando Magic

	FG A-M	FT A-M	Reb O-D	Ast	Avg
O'Neal	74-44	42-24	11-39	25	28.0
Hardaway	70-35	23-21	6-13	32	25.5
Grant	47-25	5-4	19-29	6	13.5
Shaw	47-20	0-0	4-9	13	12.5
Anderson	50-18	10-3	6-28	17	12.3
Scott	42-13	9-9	2-12	9	10.5
Bowie	10-6	0-0	0-2	6	3.3
Turner	10-2	0-0	0-4	2	1.5
Royal	0-0	0-0	0-0	0	0.0

1995 NBA Playoff Results

Eastern Conference

Orlando defeated Boston 3 games to 1
Indiana defeated Atlanta 3 games to 0
New York defeated Cleveland 3 games to 1
Chicago defeated Charlotte 3 games to 1
Indiana defeated New York 4 games to 3
Orlando defeated Chicago 4 games to 2
Orlando defeated Indiana 4 games to 3

Western Conference

San Antonio defeated Denver 3 games to 0
Phoenix defeated Portland 3 games to 0
Houston defeated Utah 3 games to 2
L.A. Lakers defeated Seattle 3 games to 1
San Antonio defeated L.A. Lakers 4 games to 2
Houston defeated Phoenix 4 games to 3
Houston defeated San Antonio 4 games to 2

Championship

Houston defeated Orlando 4 games to 0

MVP in Playoffs

1969 Jerry West, Los Angeles	1978 Wes Unseld, Washington	1987 Magic Johnson, L.A. Lakers
1970 Willis Reed, New York	1979 Dennis Johnson, Seattle	1988 James Worthy, L.A. Lakers
1971 Lew Alcindor, Milwaukee	1980 Magic Johnson, Los Angeles	1989 Joe Dumars, Detroit
1972 Wilt Chamberlain, Los Angeles	1981 Cedric Maxwell, Boston	1990 Isiah Thomas, Detroit
1973 Willis Reed, New York	1982 Magic Johnson, Los Angeles	1991 Michael Jordan, Chicago
1974 John Havlicek, Boston	1983 Moses Malone, Philadelphia	1992 Michael Jordan, Chicago
1975 Rick Barry, Golden State	1984 Larry Bird, Boston	1993 Michael Jordan, Chicago
1976 Jo Jo White, Boston	1985 Kareem Abdul-Jabbar, L.A. Lakers	1994 Hakeem Olajuwon, Houston
1977 Bill Walton, Portland	1986 Larry Bird, Boston	1995 Hakeem Olajuwon, Houston

NBA Scoring Leaders

Year	Scoring champion	Pts	Avg	Year	Scoring champion	Pts	Avg
1947	Joe Fulks, Philadelphia	1,389	23.2	1972	Kareem Abdul-Jabbar (Alcindor), Milwaukee	2,822	34.8
1948	Max Zaslofsky, Chicago	1,007	21.0				
1949	George Mikan, Minneapolis	1,698	28.3	1973	Nate Archibald, Kansas City-Omaha	2,719	34.0
1950	George Mikan, Minneapolis	1,865	27.4				
1951	George Mikan, Minneapolis	1,932	28.4	1974	Bob McAdoo, Buffalo	2,261	30.6
1952	Paul Arizin, Philadelphia	1,674	25.4	1975	Bob McAdoo, Buffalo	2,831	34.5
1953	Neil Johnston, Philadelphia	1,564	22.3	1976	Bob McAdoo, Buffalo	2,427	31.1
1954	Neil Johnston, Philadelphia	1,759	24.4	1977	Pete Maravich, New Orleans	2,273	31.1
1955	Neil Johnston, Philadelphia	1,631	22.7	1978	George Gervin, San Antonio	2,232	27.2
1956	Bob Pettit, St. Louis	1,849	25.7	1979	George Gervin, San Antonio	2,365	29.6
1957	Paul Arizin, Philadelphia	1,817	25.6	1980	George Gervin, San Antonio	2,585	33.1
1958	George Yardley, Detroit	2,001	27.8	1981	Adrian Dantley, Utah	2,452	30.7
1959	Bob Pettit, St. Louis	2,105	29.2	1982	George Gervin, San Antonio	2,551	32.3
1960	Wilt Chamberlain, Philadelphia	2,707	37.9	1983	Alex English, Denver	2,326	28.4
1961	Wilt Chamberlain, Philadelphia	3,033	38.4	1984	Adrian Dantley, Utah	2,418	30.6
1962	Wilt Chamberlain, Philadelphia	4,029	50.4	1985	Bernard King, New York	1,809	32.9
1963	Wilt Chamberlain, San Francisco	3,586	44.8	1986	Dominique Wilkins, Atlanta	2,366	30.3
1964	Wilt Chamberlain, San Francisco	2,948	36.5	1987	Michael Jordan, Chicago	3,041	37.1
1965	Wilt Chamberlain, San Fran., Phila.	2,534	34.7	1988	Michael Jordan, Chicago	2,868	35.0
1966	Wilt Chamberlain, Philadelphia	2,649	33.5	1989	Michael Jordan, Chicago	2,633	32.5
1967	Rick Barry, San Francisco	2,775	35.6	1990	Michael Jordan, Chicago	2,753	33.6
1968	Dave Bing, Detroit	2,142	27.1	1991	Michael Jordan, Chicago	2,580	31.5
1969	Elvin Hayes, San Diego	2,327	28.4	1992	Michael Jordan, Chicago	2,404	30.1
1970	Jerry West, Los Angeles	2,309	31.2	1993	Michael Jordan, Chicago	2,541	32.6
1971	Lew Alcindor, Milwaukee	2,596	31.7	1994	David Robinson, San Antonio	2,383	29.8
				1995	Shaquille O'Neal, Orlando	2,315	29.3

NBA Most Valuable Player

1956 Bob Pettit, St. Louis	1975 Bob McAdoo, Buffalo
1957 Bob Cousy, Boston	1976 Kareem Abdul-Jabbar, Los Angeles
1958 Bill Russell, Boston	1977 Kareem Abdul-Jabbar, Los Angeles
1959 Bob Pettit, St. Louis	1978 Bill Walton, Portland
1960 Wilt Chamberlain, Philadelphia	1979 Moses Malone, Houston
1961 Bill Russell, Boston	1980 Kareem Abdul-Jabbar, Los Angeles
1962 Bill Russell, Boston	1981 Julius Erving, Philadelphia
1963 Bill Russell, Boston	1982 Moses Malone, Houston
1964 Oscar Robertson, Cincinnati	1983 Moses Malone, Philadelphia
1965 Bill Russell, Boston	1984 Larry Bird, Boston
1966 Wilt Chamberlain, Philadelphia	1985 Larry Bird, Boston
1967 Wilt Chamberlain, Philadelphia	1986 Larry Bird, Boston
1968 Wilt Chamberlain, Philadelphia	1987 Magic Johnson, L.A. Lakers
1969 Wes Unseld, Baltimore	1988 Michael Jordan, Chicago
1970 Willis Reed, New York	1989 Magic Johnson, L.A. Lakers
1971 Lew Alcindor, Milwaukee	1990 Magic Johnson, L.A. Lakers
1972 Kareem Abdul-Jabbar (Alcindor), Milwaukee	1991 Michael Jordan, Chicago
	1992 Michael Jordan, Chicago
1973 Dave Cowens, Boston	1993 Charles Barkley, Phoenix
1974 Kareem Abdul-Jabbar, Milwaukee	1994 Hakeem Olajuwon, Houston
	1995 David Robinson, San Antonio

NBA Champions 1947-95

	Regular season			Playoffs	
Year	Eastern Conference	Western Conference	Winner	Coach	Runner-up
1947	Washington	Chicago	Philadelphia	Ed Gottlieb	Chicago
1948	Philadelphia	St. Louis	Baltimore	Buddy Jeannette	Philadelphia
1949	Washington	Rochester	Minneapolis	John Kundla	Washington
1950	Syracuse	Minneapolis	Minneapolis	John Kundla	Syracuse
1951	Philadelphia	Minneapolis	Rochester	Lester Harrison	New York
1952	Syracuse	Rochester	Minneapolis	John Kundla	New York
1953	New York	Minneapolis	Minneapolis	John Kundla	New York
1954	New York	Minneapolis	Minneapolis	John Kundla	Syracuse
1955	Syracuse	Ft. Wayne	Syracuse	Al Cervi	Ft. Wayne
1956	Philadelphia	Ft. Wayne	Philadelphia	George Senesky	Ft. Wayne
1957	Boston	St. Louis	Boston	Red Auerbach	St. Louis
1958	Boston	St. Louis	St. Louis	Alex Hannum	Boston
1959	Boston	St. Louis	Boston	Red Auerbach	Minneapolis
1960	Boston	St. Louis	Boston	Red Auerbach	St. Louis
1961	Boston	St. Louis	Boston	Red Auerbach	St. Louis

(continued)

	Regular season		Playoffs		
Year	Eastern Conference	Western Conference	Winner	Coach	Runner-up
1962	Boston	Los Angeles	Boston	Red Auerbach	Los Angeles
1963	Boston	Los Angeles	Boston	Red Auerbach	Los Angeles
1964	Boston	San Francisco	Boston	Red Auerbach	San Francisco
1965	Boston	Los Angeles	Boston	Red Auerbach	Los Angeles
1966	Philadelphia	Los Angeles	Boston	Red Auerbach	Los Angeles
1967	Philadelphia	San Francisco	Philadelphia	Alex Hannum	San Francisco
1968	Philadelphia	St. Louis	Boston	Bill Russell	Los Angeles
1969	Baltimore	Los Angeles	Boston	Bill Russell	Los Angeles
1970	New York	Atlanta	New York	Red Holzman	Los Angeles

Year	Atlantic	Central	Midwest	Pacific	Winner	Coach	Runner-up
1971	New York	Baltimore	Milwaukee	Los Angeles	Milwaukee	Lady Costello	Baltimore
1972	Boston	Baltimore	Milwaukee	Los Angeles	Los Angeles	Bill Sharman	New York
1973	Boston	Baltimore	Milwaukee	Los Angeles	New York	Red Holzman	Los Angeles
1974	Boston	Capital	Milwaukee	Los Angeles	Boston	Tom Heinsohn	Milwaukee
1975	Boston	Washington	Chicago	Golden State	Golden State	Al Attles	Washington
1976	Boston	Cleveland	Milwaukee	Golden State	Boston	Tom Heinsohn	Phoenix
1977	Philadelphia	Houston	Denver	Los Angeles	Portland	Jack Ramsay	Philadelphia
1978	Philadelphia	San Antonio	Denver	Portland	Washington	Dick Motta	Seattle
1979	Washington	San Antonio	Kansas City	Seattle	Seattle	Len Wilkens	Washington
1980	Boston	Atlanta	Milwaukee	Los Angeles	Los Angeles	Paul Westhead	Philadelphia
1981	Boston	Milwaukee	San Antonio	Phoenix	Boston	Bill Fitch	Houston
1982	Boston	Milwaukee	San Antonio	Los Angeles	Los Angeles	Pat Riley	Philadelphia
1983	Philadelphia	Milwaukee	San Antonio	Los Angeles	Philadelphia	Billy Cunningham	Los Angeles
1984	Boston	Milwaukee	Utah	Los Angeles	Boston	K.C. Jones	Los Angeles
1985	Boston	Milwaukee	Denver	L.A. Lakers	L.A. Lakers	Pat Riley	Boston
1986	Boston	Milwaukee	Houston	L.A. Lakers	Boston	K.C. Jones	Houston
1987	Boston	Atlanta	Dallas	L.A. Lakers	L.A. Lakers	Pat Riley	Boston
1988	Boston	Detroit	Denver	L.A. Lakers	L.A. Lakers	Pat Riley	Detroit
1989	New York	Detroit	Utah	L.A. Lakers	Detroit	Chuck Daly	L. A. Lakers
1990	Philadelphia	Detroit	San Antonio	L.A. Lakers	Detroit	Chuck Daly	Portland
1991	Boston	Chicago	San Antonio	Portland	Chicago	Phil Jackson	L. A. Lakers
1992	Boston	Chicago	Utah	Portland	Chicago	Phil Jackson	Portland
1993	New York	Chicago	Houston	Phoenix	Chicago	Phil Jackson	Phoenix
1994	New York	Atlanta	Houston	Seattle	Houston	Rudy Tomjanovich	New York
1995	Orlando	Indiana	San Antonio	Phoenix	Houston	Rudy Tomjanovich	Orlando

NBA Coach of the Year, 1963-95

1963 Harry Gallatin, St. Louis Hawks
1964 Alex Hannum, San Francisco Warriors
1965 Red Auerbach, Boston Celtics
1966 Dolph Schayes, Philadelphia 76ers
1967 Johnny Kerr, Chicago Bulls
1968 Richie Guerin, St. Louis Hawks
1969 Gene Shue, Baltimore Bullets
1970 Red Holzman, New York Knicks
1971 Dick Motta, Chicago Bulls
1972 Bill Sharman, Los Angeles Lakers
1973 Tom Heinsohn, Boston Celtics
1974 Ray Scott, Detroit Pistons

1975 Phil Johnson, Kansas City-Omaha Kings
1976 Bill Fitch, Cleveland Cavaliers
1977 Tom Nissalke, Houston Rockets
1978 Hubie Brown, Atlanta Hawks
1979 Cotton Fitzsimmons, Kansas City Kings
1980 Bill Fitch, Boston Celtics
1981 Jack McKinney, Indiana Pacers
1982 Gene Shue, Washington Bullets
1983 Don Nelson, Milwaukee Bucks
1984 Frank Layden, Utah Jazz
1985 Don Nelson, Milwaukee Bucks
1986 Mike Fratello, Atlanta Hawks

1987 Mike Schuler, Portland Trail Blazers
1988 Doug Moe, Denver Nuggets
1989 Cotton Fitzsimmons, Phoenix Suns
1990 Pat Riley, Los Angeles Lakers
1991 Don Chaney, Houston Rockets
1992 Don Nelson, Golden State Warriors
1993 Pat Riley, New York Knicks
1994 Lenny Wilkens, Atlanta Hawks
1995 Del Harris, L.A. Lakers

NBA All-League Team 1994-95

First team	Position	Second team
Scottie Pippen, Chicago	Forward	Shawn Kemp, Seattle
Karl Malone, Utah	Forward	Charles Barkley, Phoenix
David Robinson, San Antonio	Center	Shaquille O'Neal, Orlando
John Stockton, Utah	Guard	Mitch Richmond, Sacramento
Anfernee Hardaway, Orlando	Guard	Gary Payton, Seattle

NBA Statistical Leaders, 1994-95

Scoring
(Minimum 70 games or 1,400 pts.)

	G	FG	FT	Pts	Avg
O'Neal, Orlando	79	930	455	2,315	29.3
Olajuwon, Houston	72	798	406	2,005	27.8
D. Robinson, San Antonio	81	788	656	2,238	27.6
K. Malone, Utah	82	830	516	2,187	26.7
Mashburn, Dallas	80	683	447	1,926	24.1
Ewing, New York	79	730	420	1,886	23.9
Barkley, Phoenix	68	554	379	1,561	23.0
Richmond, Sacramento	82	668	375	1,867	22.8
Rice, Miami	82	667	312	1,831	22.3
G. Robinson, Milwaukee	80	636	397	1,755	21.9

Rebounds per Game
(Minimum 70 games or 800 rebounds)

	G	Off	Def	Tot	Avg
Rodman, San Antonio	49	274	549	823	16.8
Mutombo, Denver	82	319	710	1,029	12.5
O'Neal, Orlando	79	328	573	901	11.4
Ewing, New York	79	157	710	867	11.0
Kemp, Seattle	82	318	575	893	10.9
Hill, Cleveland	70	269	496	765	10.9
D. Robinson, San Antonio	81	234	643	877	10.8
Olajuwon, Houston	72	172	603	775	10.8
K. Malone, Utah	82	156	715	871	10.6
Jones, Dallas	80	329	515	844	10.6

(continued)

Field Goal Percentage
(Minimum 300 field goals made)

	FG	FGA	Pct
Gatling, Golden State	324	512	.633
O'Neal, Orlando	930	1,594	.583
Grant, Orlando	401	707	.567
Thorpe, Houston-Portland	385	681	.565
Davis, Indiana	324	576	.563
Muresan, Washington	303	541	.560
Mutombo, Denver	349	628	.556
Kemp, Seattle	545	997	.547
Manning, Phoenix	340	622	.547
Polynice, Sacramento	376	691	.544

Free Throw Percentage
(Minimum 125 free throws made)

	FTM	FTA	Pct
Webb, Sacramento	226	242	.934
Price, Cleveland	148	162	.914
Barros, Philadelphia	347	386	.899
Miller, Indiana	383	427	.897
Bogues, Charlotte	160	180	.889
Skiles, Washington	179	202	.886
Abdul-Rauf, Denver	138	156	.885
Armstrong, Chicago	206	233	.884
Hornacek, Utah	284	322	.882
Jennings, Golden State	134	153	.876

3-Point Field Goal Percentage
(Minimum 50 goals made)

	FG	FGA	Pct
Kerr, Chicago	89	170	.524
Schrempf, Seattle	93	181	.514
Barros, Philadelphia	197	425	.464
Davis, New York	131	288	.455
Stockton, Utah	102	227	.449
Hawkins, Charlotte	131	298	.440
Person, Phoenix	116	266	.436
Smith, Houston	142	331	.429
Curry, Charlotte	154	361	.427
Armstrong, Chicago	108	253	.427

Assists
(Minimum 70 games or 400 assists)

	G	No	Avg
Stockton, Utah	82	1,011	12.3
Anderson, New Jersey	72	680	9.4
Hardaway, Golden State	62	578	9.3
Strickland, Portland	64	562	8.8
Bogues, Charlotte	78	675	8.7
Van Exel, L.A. Lakers	80	660	8.3
Johnson, San Antonio	82	670	8.2
Richardson, L.A. Clippers	80	632	7.9
Blaylock, Atlanta	80	616	7.7
Kidd, Dallas	79	607	7.7

Steals
(Minimum 70 games or 125 steals)

	G	No	Avg
Pippen, Chicago	79	232	2.94
Blaylock, Atlanta	80	200	2.50
Payton, Seattle	82	204	2.49
Stockton, Utah	82	194	2.37
McMillan, Seattle	80	165	2.06
Jones, L.A. Lakers	64	131	2.05
Kidd, Dallas	79	151	1.91
Perry, Phoenix	82	156	1.90
Olajuwon, Houston	72	133	1.85
Barros, Philadelphia	82	149	1.82

Blocked Shots
(Minimum 70 games or 100 blocked shots)

	G	Blk	Avg
Mutombo, Denver	82	321	3.91
Olajuwon, Houston	72	242	3.36
Bradley, Philadelphia	82	274	3.34
D. Robinson, San Antonio	81	262	3.23
Mourning, Charlotte	77	225	2.92
O'Neal, Orlando	79	192	2.43
Divac, L.A. Lakers	80	174	2.18
Ewing, New York	79	159	2.01
Outlaw, L.A. Clippers	81	151	1.86
Campbell, L.A. Lakers	73	132	1.81
Miller, Detroit	64	116	1.81

NBA Rookie of the Year

Year	Player
1953	Don Meineke, Ft. Wayne
1954	Ray Felix, Baltimore
1955	Bob Pettit, Milwaukee
1956	Maurice Stokes, Rochester
1957	Tom Heinsohn, Boston
1958	Woody Sauldsberry, Philadelphia
1959	Elgin Baylor, Minneapolis
1960	Wilt Chamberlain, Philadelphia
1961	Oscar Robertson, Cincinnati
1962	Walt Bellamy, Chicago
1963	Terry Dischinger, Chicago
1964	Jerry Lucas, Cincinnati
1965	Willis Reed, New York
1966	Rick Barry, San Francisco
1967	Dave Bing, Detroit
1968	Earl Monroe, Baltimore

Year	Player
1969	Wes Unseld, Baltimore
1970	Lew Alcindor, Milwaukee
1971	Dave Cowens, Boston; Geoff Petrie, Portland (tie)
1972	Sidney Wicks, Portland
1973	Bob McAdoo, Buffalo
1974	Ernie DiGregorio, Buffalo
1975	Keith Wilkes, Golden State
1976	Alvan Adams, Phoenix
1977	Adrian Dantley, Buffalo
1978	Walter Davis, Phoenix
1979	Phil Ford, Kansas City
1980	Larry Bird, Boston
1981	Darrell Griffith, Utah
1982	Buck Williams, New Jersey

Year	Player
1983	Terry Cummings, San Diego
1984	Ralph Sampson, Houston
1985	Michael Jordan, Chicago
1986	Patrick Ewing, New York
1987	Chuck Person, Indiana
1988	Mark Jackson, New York
1989	Mitch Richmond, Golden State
1990	David Robinson, San Antonio
1991	Derrick Coleman, New Jersey
1992	Larry Johnson, Charlotte
1993	Shaquille O'Neal, Orlando
1994	Chris Webber, Golden State
1995	Grant Hill, Detroit; Jason Kidd, Dallas (tie)

Individual Statistics, 1994-95
(more than 600 minutes played)

Atlanta Hawks

	Min	FG%	FT%	Reb	Ast	Pts	Avg
Blaylock	3069	.425	.729	393	616	1373	17.2
Smith	2665	.426	.841	276	274	1305	16.3
Augmon	2362	.453	.728	368	197	1053	13.9
Norman	1879	.453	.457	362	94	938	12.7
Long	2641	.478	.751	606	131	939	11.6
Ehlo	1166	.453	.620	147	113	477	9.7
Lang	2340	.473	.809	456	72	794	9.7
Corbin	1389	.442	.684	262	67	502	6.2
Anderson	622	.548	.479	188	17	148	2.9
Koncak	943	.412	.542	184	52	179	2.9

Coach—Lenny Wilkens

Boston Celtics

	Min	FG%	FT%	Reb	Ast	Pts	Avg
Wilkins	2423	.424	.782	401	166	1370	17.8
Radja	2147	.490	.759	573	111	1133	17.2
Brown	2792	.447	.852	249	301	1236	15.6
Douglas	2048	.475	.689	170	446	954	14.7

	Min	FG%	FT%	Reb	Ast	Pts	Avg
Montross	2315	.534	.635	566	36	781	10.0
Fox	1039	.481	.772	155	139	464	8.8
McDaniel	1430	.451	.712	300	108	587	8.6
Wesley	1380	.409	.755	117	266	378	7.4
Ellison	1083	.507	.717	309	34	375	6.8
Strong	1344	.453	.820	375	44	441	6.3
Minor	945	.515	.833	137	66	377	6.0

Coach—Chris Ford

Charlotte Hornets

	Min	FG%	FT%	Reb	Ast	Pts	Avg
Mourning	2941	.519	.761	761	111	1643	21.3
Johnson	3234	.480	.774	585	369	1525	18.8
Hawkins	2731	.482	.867	314	262	1172	14.3
Curry	1718	.441	.856	168	113	935	13.6
Burrell	2014	.467	.694	368	161	750	11.5
Bogues	2629	.477	.889	257	675	862	11.1
Sutton	690	.409	.711	56	91	263	5.0
Parish	1352	.427	.703	350	44	389	4.8

Coach—Allan Bristow

Chicago Bulls

	Min	FG%	FT%	Reb	Ast	Pts	Avg
Jordan	668	.411	.801	117	90	457	26.9
Pippen	3014	.480	.716	639	409	1692	21.4
Kukoc	2584	.504	.748	440	372	1271	15.7
Armstrong	2577	.468	.884	186	244	1150	14.0
Kerr	1839	.527	.778	119	151	674	8.2
Perdue	1592	.553	.582	522	90	621	8.0
Harper	1536	.426	.618	180	157	530	6.9
Longley	1001	.447	.822	263	73	358	6.5
Wennington	956	.492	.810	190	40	363	5.0
Myers	1270	.415	.614	139	148	318	4.5
Buechler	605	.492	.564	98	50	217	3.8
Blount	889	.476	.567	240	60	238	3.5

Coach—Phil Jackson

Cleveland Cavaliers

	Min	FG%	FT%	Reb	Ast	Pts	Avg
Price	1375	.413	.914	112	335	757	15.8
Hill	2397	.504	.662	765	55	963	13.8
Brandon	1961	.448	.855	186	363	889	13.3
Williams	2641	.452	.685	507	192	929	12.6
Mills	2814	.420	.817	366	154	986	12.3
Phills	2500	.414	.779	265	180	878	11.0
Ferry	1290	.446	.881	143	96	614	7.5
Campbell	1128	.411	.830	153	69	469	6.0
Cage	2040	.521	.602	564	56	407	5.0
Colter	752	.396	.761	59	101	196	3.4

Coach—Mike Fratello

Dallas Mavericks

	Min	FG%	FT%	Reb	Ast	Pts	Avg
Jackson	1982	.472	.805	260	191	1309	25.7
Mashburn	2980	.436	.739	331	298	1926	24.1
Tarpley	1354	.479	.836	449	58	691	12.6
Kidd	2668	.385	.698	430	607	922	11.7
Jones	2385	.443	.645	844	163	825	10.3
McCloud	802	.439	.833	147	53	402	9.6
Harris	1695	.459	.800	220	132	751	9.5
Brooks	808	.458	.810	66	116	341	5.8
Smith	826	.417	.760	144	44	320	5.1
Dumas	613	.384	.649	62	57	264	4.6
Williams	2383	.477	.376	690	124	328	4.0
Hodge	633	.407	.765	122	41	209	3.9

Coach—Dick Motta

Denver Nuggets

	Min	FG%	FT%	Reb	Ast	Pts	Avg
Abdul-Rauf	2082	.470	.885	137	263	1165	16.0
R. Williams	2198	.459	.759	329	231	993	13.4
Rogers	2142	.488	.651	385	161	979	12.2
Pack	1144	.430	.783	113	290	507	12.1
Mutombo	3100	.556	.654	1029	113	946	11.5
D. Ellis	1996	.453	.866	222	57	918	11.3
Stith	2329	.472	.824	268	153	911	11.2
Rose	1798	.454	.739	217	389	663	8.2
B. Williams	1261	.589	.654	298	53	498	7.9
Hammonds	956	.535	.746	222	36	410	5.9

Coach—Bernie Bickerstaff

Detroit Pistons

	Min	FG%	FT%	Reb	Ast	Pts	Avg
Hill	2678	.477	.732	445	353	1394	19.9
Dumars	2544	.430	.805	158	368	1214	18.1
Mills	2514	.447	.799	558	160	1118	15.5
Houston	1996	.463	.860	167	164	1101	14.5
Miller	1558	.555	.629	475	93	545	8.5
Addison	1776	.476	.747	242	109	656	8.3
Hunter	944	.374	.727	75	159	314	7.5
West	1543	.556	.478	408	18	500	7.5
Dawkins	1170	.463	.909	113	205	325	6.5
Macon	721	.381	.794	76	63	276	5.0
Knight	708	.397	.720	61	127	199	4.2
Leckner	623	.527	.708	174	14	225	3.9

Coach—Don Chaney

Golden State Warriors

	Min	FG%	FT%	Reb	Ast	Pts	Avg
Sprewell	2771	.418	.781	256	279	1420	20.6
Hardaway	2321	.427	.760	190	578	1247	20.1
Mullin	890	.489	.879	115	125	476	19.0
Gatling	1470	.633	.592	443	51	796	13.7
Marshall	2086	.394	.662	405	105	906	12.6
Pierce	673	.437	.877	64	40	338	12.5
Seikaly	1035	.516	.694	266	45	435	12.1
Alexander	1237	.515	.600	291	60	502	10.0
Rogers	1017	.529	.521	278	37	438	8.9
Jennings	1722	.447	.876	148	373	589	7.4
Lorthridge	672	.475	.684	71	101	272	7.4
Rozier	1494	.485	.447	486	45	448	6.8
Wood	1336	.469	.778	241	65	428	5.5

Coach—Bob Lanier

Houston Rockets

	Min	FG%	FT%	Reb	Ast	Pts	Avg
Olajuwon	2853	.517	.756	775	255	2005	27.8
Drexler	2728	.461	.824	480	362	1653	21.8
Maxwell	2038	.394	.688	164	274	854	13.3
Smith	2030	.484	.851	155	323	842	10.4
Horry	2074	.447	.761	324	216	652	10.2
Cassell	1882	.427	.843	211	405	783	9.5
Elie	1896	.499	.842	196	189	710	8.8
Herrera	1331	.523	.624	278	44	415	6.8
Brown	814	.603	.613	189	30	249	6.1
Chilcutt	1347	.445	.738	317	66	358	5.3

Coach—Rudy Tomjanovich

Indiana Pacers

	Min	FG%	FT%	Reb	Ast	Pts	Avg
Miller	2665	.462	.897	210	242	1588	19.6
Smits	2381	.526	.753	601	111	1400	17.9
McKey	2805	.493	.744	394	276	1075	13.3
D. Davis	2346	.563	.533	696	58	786	10.6
Scott	1528	.455	.850	151	108	802	10.0
A. Davis	1030	.445	.672	280	25	335	7.6
Jackson	2402	.422	.778	306	616	624	7.6
Mitchell	1377	.487	.724	243	61	529	6.5
Fleming	686	.495	.722	88	109	251	4.6
Workman	1028	.375	.743	111	194	292	4.2
Ferrell	607	.480	.753	88	31	231	4.1

Coach—Larry Brown

Los Angeles Clippers

	Min	FG%	FT%	Reb	Ast	Pts	Avg
Vaught	2966	.514	.710	772	139	1401	17.5
Murray	2556	.402	.754	354	133	1142	14.1
Sealy	1604	.435	.780	214	107	778	13.0
Richardson	2864	.394	.648	261	632	874	10.9
Dehere	1774	.407	.784	152	225	835	10.4
Massenburg	2127	.469	.753	455	67	741	9.3
Piatkowski	1208	.441	.783	133	77	566	7.0
Outlaw	1655	.523	.441	313	84	422	5.2
Ellis	656	.481	.590	88	40	252	3.7

Coach—Bill Fitch

Los Angeles Lakers

	Min	FG%	FT%	Reb	Ast	Pts	Avg
Ceballos	2029	.509	.716	464	105	1261	21.7
Van Exel	2944	.420	.783	223	660	1348	16.9
Divac	2807	.507	.777	829	329	1277	16.0
Jones	1981	.460	.722	249	128	897	14.0
Campbell	2076	.459	.666	445	92	913	12.5
Peeler	1559	.432	.797	168	122	756	10.4
Threatt	1384	.497	.793	124	248	558	9.5
Daniels	604	.383	.815	63	40	208	6.9
Lynch	953	.468	.721	184	62	341	6.1
Smith	1024	.427	.698	107	102	340	5.6
Bowie	1225	.442	.764	288	118	306	4.6

Coach—Del Harris

Miami Heat

	Min	FG%	FT%	Reb	Ast	Pts	Avg
Rice	3014	.475	.855	378	192	1831	22.3
Willis	2390	.466	.690	732	86	1154	17.2
Owens	2296	.491	.620	502	246	1002	14.3
Coles	2207	.430	.810	191	416	679	10.0
Reeves	1462	.443	.714	186	288	619	9.2
Geiger	1712	.536	.650	413	55	617	8.3
Gamble	1223	.489	.784	122	119	566	7.4
Eackles	898	.439	.722	95	72	395	7.3
Miner	871	.403	.726	117	69	329	7.3
Salley	1955	.499	.739	336	123	547	7.3
Askins	854	.391	.807	198	39	229	4.6
Lohaus	730	.420	.667	102	43	267	4.4

Coach—Alvin Gentry

Milwaukee Bucks

	Min	FG%	FT%	Reb	Ast	Pts	Avg
Robinson	2958	.451	.796	513	197	1755	21.9
Baker	3361	.483	.593	846	296	1451	17.7
Day	2717	.424	.754	322	134	1310	16.0
Murdock	2158	.415	.790	214	482	977	13.0
Conlon	2064	.532	.613	426	110	815	9.9
Newman	1896	.463	.801	173	91	634	7.7
Mayberry	1744	.422	.699	82	276	474	5.8
Mobley	587	.591	.489	153	21	180	3.9
Barry	602	.425	.763	49	85	191	3.7
Lister	776	.493	.500	236	12	167	2.8
Pinckney	835	.495	.710	211	21	140	2.3

Coach—Mike Dunleavy

Minnesota Timberwolves

	Min	FG%	FT%	Reb	Ast	Pts	Avg
Rider	2645	.447	.817	249	245	1532	20.4
Laettner . . .	2770	.489	.818	613	234	1322	16.3
West	2328	.461	.837	227	185	919	12.9
Gugliotta . . .	2568	.443	.690	572	279	976	12.7
Rooks	2405	.470	.761	486	97	868	10.9
Martin	803	.408	.877	64	133	254	7.5
Garland	1931	.415	.795	168	318	448	6.1
King	792	.467	.667	165	26	266	5.3
Durham	852	.494	.656	94	53	302	5.1
Smith	1073	.439	.651	73	146	320	5.0
Foster	1144	.472	.703	259	39	385	4.9

Coach—Bill Blair

New Jersey Nets

	Min	FG%	FT%	Reb	Ast	Pts	Avg
Coleman . . .	2103	.424	.767	591	187	1146	20.5
Anderson . .	2689	.399	.841	250	680	1267	17.6
Gilliam	2472	.503	.770	613	99	1212	14.8
Morris	2131	.410	.728	402	147	950	13.4
Benjamin . . .	1598	.510	.760	440	38	675	11.1
Brown	2466	.446	.671	487	135	651	8.1
Walters	1435	.439	.769	93	121	523	6.5
Childs	1021	.380	.753	69	219	308	5.8
Williams . . .	982	.461	.533	425	35	363	4.8
Higgins	735	.385	.875	77	29	268	4.7
Floyd	831	.335	.698	54	126	197	4.1
Mahorn	630	.523	.796	162	26	198	3.4

Coach—Alfred "Butch" Beard

New York Knickerbockers

	Min	FG%	FT%	Reb	Ast	Pts	Avg
Ewing	2920	.503	.750	867	212	1886	23.9
Starks	2725	.395	.737	219	411	1223	15.3
Smith	2150	.471	.792	324	120	966	12.7
Harper . . .	2716	.446	.724	194	458	919	11.5
Oakley . . .	1567	.489	.793	445	126	506	10.1
Davis	1697	.480	.808	110	150	820	10.0
Mason	2496	.566	.641	650	240	765	9.9
Anthony . . .	943	.437	.789	64	160	372	6.1
Bonner . . .	1126	.456	.657	262	80	221	3.8
H. Williams	743	.456	.622	132	27	187	3.3

Coach—Pat Riley

Orlando Magic

	Min	FG%	FT%	Reb	Ast	Pts	Avg
O'Neal	2923	.583	.533	901	214	2315	29.3
Hardaway . . .	2901	.512	.769	336	551	1613	20.9
Anderson . . .	2588	.476	.704	335	314	1200	15.8
Scott	1499	.439	.754	146	131	802	12.9
Grant	2693	.567	.692	715	173	948	12.8
Royal	1841	.475	.746	279	198	635	9.1
Shaw	1836	.389	.737	241	406	502	6.4
Bowie	1261	.480	.836	139	159	427	5.5
Avent	1066	.430	.640	293	41	258	3.6

Coach—Brian Hill

Philadelphia 76ers

	Min	FG%	FT%	Reb	Ast	Pts	Avg
Barros	3318	.490	.899	274	619	1686	20.6
Malone	660	.507	.864	55	29	350	18.4
Weatherspoon	2991	.439	.751	526	215	1373	18.1
Burton	1564	.401	.824	164	96	812	15.3
Wright	2044	.465	.645	472	48	904	11.4
Bradley	2365	.455	.638	659	53	778	9.5
Grayer	1098	.428	.699	149	74	389	8.3
Williams	1781	.475	.738	485	59	491	6.4
Graham	775	.426	.753	62	66	251	5.0
Alston	1032	.465	.492	219	33	299	4.7
Tyler	809	.381	.700	62	174	195	3.5

Coach—John Lucas

Phoenix Suns

	Min	FG%	FT%	Reb	Ast	Pts	Avg
Barkley	2382	.486	.748	756	276	1561	23.0
Manning . . .	1510	.547	.673	276	154	822	17.9
Majerle	3091	.425	.730	375	340	1281	15.6
Johnson . . .	1352	.470	.810	115	360	730	15.5
Green	2687	.504	.732	669	127	916	11.2
Person	1800	.484	.792	201	105	814	10.4
Tisdale	1276	.484	.770	247	45	650	10.0
Perry	1977	.520	.810	151	394	795	9.7
Ainge	1374	.460	.808	109	210	571	7.7
Schayes . . .	823	.508	.725	208	89	303	4.4
Kleine	968	.449	.857	259	39	280	3.7

Coach—Paul Westphal

Portland Trail Blazers

	Min	FG%	FT%	Reb	Ast	Pts	Avg
C. Robinson .	2725	.452	.694	423	198	1601	21.3
Strickland . . .	2267	.466	.745	317	562	1211	18.9
Thorpe	2096	.565	.594	558	112	937	13.4
Williams	2422	.512	.673	669	78	757	9.2
J. Robinson . .	1539	.409	.591	132	180	651	9.2
Grant	1771	.461	.705	284	82	683	9.1
Porter	770	.393	.707	81	133	312	8.9
Kersey	1143	.415	.766	256	82	508	8.1
McKie	827	.444	.685	129	89	293	6.5
Dudley	2245	.406	.464	764	34	447	5.5
Bryant	658	.526	.651	161	28	244	5.0

Coach—P.J. Carlesimo

Sacramento Kings

	Min	FG%	FT%	Reb	Ast	Pts	Avg
Richmond . .	3172	.446	.843	357	311	1867	22.8
Williams . . .	2739	.446	.731	345	316	1259	16.4
Grant	2289	.511	.636	598	99	1058	13.2
Webb	2458	.438	.934	174	468	878	11.6
Polynice . . .	2534	.544	.639	725	62	877	10.8
M. Smith . .	1736	.542	.485	486	67	567	6.9
Simmons . .	1064	.420	.702	196	89	327	5.6
Brown	1086	.432	.671	108	133	317	4.7
Hurley	1105	.363	.763	70	226	285	4.2
Causwell . .	820	.517	.582	174	15	209	3.6

Coach—Garry St. Jean

San Antonio Spurs

	Min	FG%	FT%	Reb	Ast	Pts	Avg
Robinson . .	3074	.530	.774	877	236	2238	27.6
Elliott	2858	.468	.807	287	206	1466	18.1
Johnson . . .	3011	.519	.685	208	670	1101	13.4
Del Negro . .	2360	.486	.790	192	226	938	12.5
Person	2033	.423	.647	258	106	872	10.8
Rodman . . .	1568	.571	.676	823	97	349	7.1
Reid	1566	.508	.687	393	55	563	7.0
Cummings .	1273	.483	.585	378	59	520	6.8
Rivers	989	.358	.732	109	162	321	5.1

Coach—Bob Hill

Seattle SuperSonics

	Min	FG%	FT%	Reb	Ast	Pts	Avg
Payton	3015	.509	.716	281	583	1689	20.6
Schrempf . . .	2886	.523	.839	509	310	1572	19.2
Kemp	2679	.547	.749	893	149	1530	18.7
Gill	2125	.457	.742	290	192	1002	13.7
Perkins	2356	.466	.799	398	135	1043	12.7
Askew	1721	.492	.739	181	176	703	9.9
Marciulionis	1194	.473	.732	68	110	612	9.3
McMillan . . .	2070	.418	.586	302	421	419	5.2
Johnson . . .	907	.443	.630	289	16	199	3.1

Coach—George Karl

Utah Jazz

	Min	FG%	FT%	Reb	Ast	Pts	Avg
Malone	3126	.536	.742	871	285	2187	26.7
Hornacek . . .	2696	.514	.882	210	347	1337	16.5
Stockton . . .	2867	.542	.804	251	1011	1206	14.7
Benoit	1841	.486	.841	368	58	740	10.4
Carr	1677	.531	.821	265	67	746	9.6
Spencer	905	.488	.793	260	17	317	9.3
Edwards	1112	.461	.833	130	77	459	6.9
Chambers . .	1240	.457	.807	213	73	503	6.2
Keefe	1270	.577	.676	327	30	461	6.1
Russell	860	.437	.667	141	34	283	4.5
Crotty	1019	.403	.810	97	205	295	3.7
Watson	673	.500	.679	74	59	195	3.3
Donaldson . .	613	.595	.710	107	14	110	2.6

Coach—Jerry Sloan

Washington Bullets

	Min	FG%	FT%	Reb	Ast	Pts	Avg
Webber . . .	2067	.495	.502	518	256	1085	20.1
Howard . . .	2348	.489	.664	545	165	1104	17.0
Cheaney . . .	2651	.453	.812	321	177	1293	16.6
Chapman . .	1468	.397	.862	113	128	731	16.2
Skiles	2077	.455	.886	159	452	805	13.0
MacLean . .	1052	.438	.765	165	51	430	11.0
Muresan . . .	1720	.560	.709	488	38	730	10.0
Butler	1554	.421	.665	170	91	597	7.9
Duckworth .	818	.442	.643	195	20	283	7.1
Overton . . .	1704	.416	.872	143	246	576	7.0
Tucker	982	.457	.614	170	68	243	3.9

Coach—Jim Lynam

1995 NBA Player Draft, First Round Picks

Golden State—Joe Smith, Maryland
L.A. Clippers—Antonio McDyess, Alabama
Philadelphia—Jerry Stackhouse, North Carolina
Washington—Rasheed Wallace, North Carolina
Minnesota—Kevin Garnett, no college
Vancouver—Bryant Reeves, Oklahoma State
Toronto—Damon Stoudamire, Arizona
Portland—Shawn Respert, Michigan State
New Jersey—Ed O'Bannon, UCLA
Miami—Kurt Thomas, Texas Christian
Milwaukee—Gary Trent, Ohio University
Dallas—Cherokee Parks, Duke
Sacramento—Corliss Williamson, Arkansas
Boston—Eric Williams, Providence
Denver—Brent Barry, Oregon State

Atlanta—Alan Henderson, Indiana
Cleveland—Bob Sura, Florida State
Detroit—Theo Ratliff, Wyoming
Detroit—Randolph Childress, Wake Forest
Chicago—Jason Caffey, Alabama
Phoenix—Michael Finley, Wisconsin
Charlotte—George Zidek, UCLA
Indiana—Travis Best, Georgia Tech
Dallas—Loren Meyer, Iowa State
Orlando—David Vaughn, Memphis
Seattle—Sherell Ford, Illinois-Chicago
Phoenix—Mario Bennett, Arizona State
Utah—Greg Ostertag, Kansas
San Antonio—Cory Alexander, Virginia

Number One First Round NBA Draft Picks, 1966-95

Year	Team	Player, college	Year	Team	Player, college
1966	New York	Cazzie Russell, Michigan	1981	Dallas	Mark Aguirre, DePaul
1967	Detroit	Jimmy Walker, Providence	1982	L.A. Lakers	James Worthy, N. Carolina
1968	Houston	Elvin Hayes, Houston	1983	Houston	Ralph Sampson, Virginia
1969	Milwaukee	Lew Alcindor,[1] UCLA	1984	Houston	Akeem Olajuwon, Houston
1970	Detroit	Bob Lanier, St. Bonaventure	1985	New York	Patrick Ewing, Georgetown
1971	Cleveland	Austin Carr, Notre Dame	1986	Cleveland	Brad Daugherty, N. Carolina
1972	Portland	LaRue Martin, Loyola-Chicago	1987	San Antonio	David Robinson, Navy
1973	Philadelphia	Doug Collins, Illinois St.	1988	L.A. Clippers	Danny Manning, Kansas
1974	Portland	Bill Walton, UCLA	1989	Sacramento	Pervis Ellison, Louisville
1975	Atlanta	David Thompson,[2] N.C. State	1990	New Jersey	Derrick Coleman, Syracuse
1976	Houston	John Lucas, Maryland	1991	Charlotte	Larry Johnson, UNLV
1977	Milwaukee	Kent Benson, Indiana	1992	Orlando	Shaquille O'Neal, LSU
1978	Portland	Mychal Thompson, Minnesota	1993	Orlando	Chris Webber,[3] Michigan
1979	L.A. Lakers	Magic Johnson, Michigan St.	1994	Milwaukee	Glenn Robinson, Purdue
1980	Golden State	Joe Barry Carroll, Purdue	1995	Golden State	Joe Smith, Maryland

(1) Later Kareem Abdul-Jabbar. (2) Signed with Denver of the ABA. (3) Traded to Golden State.

NBA All-Defensive Team 1994-95

First team	Position	Second team
Scottie Pippen, Chicago	Forward	Horace Grant, Orlando
Dennis Rodman, San Antonio	Forward	Derrick McKey, Indiana
David Robinson, San Antonio	Center	Dikembe Mutombo, Denver
Gary Payton, Seattle	Guard	John Stockton, Utah
Mookie Blaylock, Atlanta	Guard	Nate McMillan, Seattle

All-Time NBA Statistical Leaders

(At the start of the 1995-96 season. *Player active in 1994-95 season.)

Scoring Average
(Minimum 400 games or 10,000 points)

	G	Pts.	Avg
*Michael Jordan	684	21,998	32.2
Wilt Chamberlain	1,045	31,419	30.1
Elgin Baylor	846	23,149	27.4
Jerry West	932	25,192	27.0
Bob Pettit	792	20,880	26.4
George Gervin	791	20,708	26.2
*Karl Malone	816	21,237	26.0
*Dominique Wilkins	984	25,389	25.8
*David Robinson	475	12,209	25.7
Oscar Robertson	1,040	26,710	25.7

Field Goal Percentage
(Minimum 2,000 field goals made)

	FGA	FGM	Pct.
Artis Gilmore	9,570	5,732	.599
*Mark West	3,958	2,330	.589
*Shaquille O'Neal	4,489	2,616	.583
Steve Johnson	4,965	2,841	.572
Darryl Dawkins	6,079	3,477	.572
*James Donaldson	5,442	3,105	.571
Jeff Ruland	3,734	2,105	.564
Kareem Abdul-Jabbar	28,307	15,837	.559
*Otis Thorpe	9,515	5,283	.555
*Charles Barkley	12,285	6,813	.555

Free Throw Percentage
(Minimum 1,200 free throws made)

	FTA	FTM	Pct.
*Mark Price	2,078	1,883	.906
Rick Barry	4,243	3,818	.900
Calvin Murphy	3,864	3,445	.892
*Scott Skiles	1,731	1,540	.890
Larry Bird	4,471	3,960	.886
Bill Sharman	3,559	3,143	.883
*Reggie Miller	3,624	3,186	.879
*Ricky Pierce	3,459	3,033	.877
Kiki Vandeweghe	3,997	3,484	.872
*Jeff Malone	3,351	2,918	.871

Points

Kareem Abdul-Jabbar	38,387
Wilt Chamberlain	31,419
*Moses Malone	27,409
Elvin Hayes	27,313
Oscar Robertson	26,710
John Havlicek	26,395
Alex English	25,613
*Dominique Wilkins	25,389
Jerry West	25,192
Adrian Dantley	23,177

Games Played

Kareem Abdul-Jabbar	1,560
*Robert Parish	1,494
*Moses Malone	1,329
Elvin Hayes	1,303
John Havlicek	1,270
Paul Silas	1,254
Alex English	1,193
*Tree Rollins	1,156
*James Edwards	1,140
Hal Greer	1,122
*Buck Williams	1,122

Assists

*John Stockton	10,394
Magic Johnson	9,921
Oscar Robertson	9,887
Isiah Thomas	9,061
Maurice Cheeks	7,392
Len Wilkens	7,211
Bob Cousy	6,955
Guy Rodgers	6,917
Nate Archibald	6,476
John Lucas	6,454

Field Goals Made

Kareem Abdul-Jabbar	15,837
Wilt Chamberlain	12,681
Elvin Hayes	10,976
Alex English	10,659
John Havlicek	10,513
*Dominique Wilkins	9,516
Oscar Robertson	9,508
*Moses Malone	9,435
*Robert Parish	9,424
Jerry West	9,016

Rebounds

Wilt Chamberlain	23,924
Bill Russell	21,620
Kareem Abdul-Jabbar	17,440
Elvin Hayes	16,279
*Moses Malone	16,212
Nate Thurmond	14,464
*Robert Parish	14,323
Walt Bellamy	14,241
Wes Unseld	13,769
Jerry Lucas	12,942

Basketball Hall of Fame, Springfield, Mass.

Players

Abdul-Jabbar, Kareem	Hayes, Elvin	Schmidt, Ernest	Julian, Alvin	Bee, Clair
Archibald, Nate	Heinsohn, Tom	Schommer, John	Keaney, Frank	Brown, Walter
Arizin, Paul	Holman, Nat	Sedran, Barney	Keogan, George	Bunn, John
Barlow, Thomas	Houbregs, Bob	Semyonova, Ulyona	Knight, Bob	Douglas, Bob
Barry, Rick	Hyatt, Chuck	Sharman, Bill	Kundla, John	Duer, Al O.
Baylor, Elgin	Issel, Dan	Steinmetz, Christian	Lambert, Ward	Fagan, Cliff
Beckman, John	Jeannette, Buddy	Thompson, Cat	Litwack, Harry	Fisher, Harry
Bellamy, Walt	Johnson, William	Thurmond, Nate	Loeffler, Kenneth	Fleisher, Larry
Belov, Sergei	Johnston, Neil	Twyman, Jack	Lonborg, Dutch	Gottlieb, Edward
Bing, Dave	Jones, K.C.	Unseld, Wes	McCutchan, Arad	Gulick, Dr. L. H.
Blazejowski, Carol	Jones, Sam	Vandivier, Fuzzy	McGuire, Al	Harrison, Lester
Borgmann, Bennie	Krause, Moose	Wachter, Edward	McGuire, Frank	Hepp, Dr. Ferenc
Bradley, Bill	Kurland, Bob	Walton, Bill	Meanwell, Dr. W.E.	Hickox, Edward
Brennan, Joseph	Lanier, Bob	Wanzer, Bobby	Meyer, Ray	Hinkle, Tony
Cervi, Al	Lapchick, Joe	West, Jerry	Miller, Ralph	Irish, Ned
Chamberlain, Wilt	Lovellette, Clyde	White, Nera	Ramsay, Jack	Jones, R. W.
Cooper, Charles	Lucas, Jerry	Wilkens, Lenny	Rupp, Adolph	Kennedy, Walter
Cousy, Bob	Luisetti, Hank	Wooden, John	Sachs, Leonard	Liston, Emil
Cowens, Dave	Macauley, Ed		Shelton, Everett	McLendon, John
Cunningham, Billy	Maravich, Pete	**Coaches**	Smith, Dean	Mokray, Bill
Davies, Bob	Martin, Slater	Anderson, Harold	Taylor, Fred	Morgan, Ralph
DeBernardi, Forrest	McCracken, Branch	Auerbach, Red	Teague, Bertha	Morgenweck, Frank
DeBusschere, Dave	McCracken, Jack	Barry, Sam	Wade, Margaret	Naismith, Dr. James
Dehnert, Dutch	McDermott, Bobby	Blood, Ernest	Watts, Stan	Newell, Pete
Donovan, Anne	McGuire, Dick	Cann, Howard	Wooden, John	O'Brien, John
Endacott, Paul	Meyers, Ann	Carlson, Dr. H. C.	Woolpert, Phil	O'Brien, Larry
Erving, Julius	Mikan, George	Carnesecca, Lou		Olsen, Harold
Foster, Bud	Mikkelsen, Vern	Carnevale, Ben	**Referees**	Podoloff, Maurice
Frazier, Walt	Miller, Cheryl	Case, Everett	Enright, James	Porter, H. V.
Friedman, Max	Monroe, Earl	Crum, Denny	Hepburn, George	Reis, William
Fulks, Joe	Murphy, Calvin	Daly, Chuck	Hoyt, George	Ripley, Elmer
Gale, Lauren	Murphy, Stretch	Dean, Everett	Kennedy, Matthew	St. John, Lynn
Gallatin, Harry	Page, Pat	Diddle, Edgar	Leith, Lloyd	Saperstein, Abe
Gates, Pop	Pettit, Bob	Drake, Bruce	Mihalik, Red	Schabinger, Arthur
Gola, Tom	Phillip, Andy	Gaines, Clarence	Nucatola, John	Stagg, Amos Alonzo
Greer, Hal	Pollard, Jim	Gardner, Jack	Quigley, Ernest	Stankovich, Boris
Gruenig, Ace	Ramsey, Frank	Gill, Slats	Shirley, J. Dallas	Steitz, Edward
Hagan, Cliff	Reed, Willis	Gomelsky, Aleksandr	Strom, Earl	Taylor, Chuck
Hanson, Victor	Robertson, Oscar	Harshman, Marv	Tobey, David	Tower, Oswald
Harris, Luisa	Roosma, John S.	Hickey, Edgar	Walsh, David	Trester, Arthur
Havlicek, John	Russell, Bill	Hobson, Howard		Wells, Clifford
Hawkins, Connie	Russell, Honey	Holzman, Red	**Contributors**	Wilke, Lou
	Schayes, Adolph	Iba, Hank	Abbott, Senda B.	
			Allen, Phog	

All-Time NBA Coaching Victories
(*Active through 1994-95 season)

Coach	W-L	Pct.	Coach	W-L	Pct.
Lenny Wilkens*	968-814	.543	Larry Costello	430-300	.589
Red Auerbach	938-479	.662	Tom Heinsohn	427-263	.619
Dick Motta*	892-909	.495	John Kundla	423-302	.583
Jack Ramsay	864-783	.525	Mike Fratello*	414-327	.559
Bill Fitch*	862-942	.478	Del Harris*	380-375	.503
Don Nelson*	817-604	.575	Phil Jackson*	342-150	.695
Cotton Fitzsimmons	805-745	.519	Hubie Brown	341-410	.454
Gene Shue	784-861	.477	Bill Russell	341-290	.540
Pat Riley*	756-299	.717	Bill Sharman	333-240	.581
John MacLeod	707-657	.518	Richie Guerin	327-291	.529
Red Holzman	696-604	.535	Al Cervi	326-241	.575
Doug Moe	628-529	.543	Joe Lapchick	326-247	.569
Chuck Daly	564-379	.598	George Karl*	321-262	.551
Alvin Attles	557-518	.518	Fred Schaus	315-245	.563
Larry Brown*	533-407	.567	Stan Albeck	307-267	.535
K.C. Jones	522-252	.674	Lester Harrison	295-181	.620
Kevin Loughery*	474-662	.417	Rick Adelman	291-154	.654
Alex Hannum	471-412	.533	Frank Layden	277-294	.485
Jerry Sloan*	458-314	.593	Paul Seymour	271-241	.529
Billy Cunningham	454-196	.698	Jim Lynam*	267-325	.451

NBA Home Courts

Team	Name (built)	Capacity	Team	Name (built)	Capacity
Atlanta	The Omni (1972)	16,378	Milwaukee	Bradley Center (1988)	18,633
Boston	FleetCenter (1995)	18,600	Minnesota	Target Center (1990)	19,006
Charlotte	Charlotte Coliseum (1988)	24,042	New Jersey	Meadowlands Arena (1981)	20,039
Chicago	United Center (1994)	21,711	New York	Madison Square Garden (1968)	19,763
Cleveland	Gund Arena (1994)	20,562	Orlando	Orlando Arena (1989)	16,010
Dallas	Reunion Arena (1980)	17,502	Philadelphia	CoreStates Spectrum (1967)	18,168
Denver	McNichols Sports Arena (1975)	17,171	Phoenix	America West Arena (1992)	19,023
Detroit	Palace of Auburn Hills (1988)	21,454	Portland	The Rose Garden (1995)	21,400
Golden State	Oakland Coliseum Arena (1966)	15,025	Sacramento	ARCO Arena (1988)	17,317
Houston	The Summit (1975)	16,611	San Antonio	Alamodome (1993)	20,662
Indiana	Market Square Arena (1974)	16,530	Seattle	Key Arena (1995)	17,100
L.A. Clippers	L.A. Memorial Sports Arena (1959); Arrowhead Pond of Anaheim (1992)	16,021 18,211	Toronto	SkyDome (1989)	22,911
			Utah	Delta Center (1991)	19,911
L.A. Lakers	The Great Western Forum (1967)	17,505	Vancouver	General Motors Place (1995)	20,004
Miami	Miami Arena (1988)	15,200	Washington	USAir Arena (1973)	18,756

COLLEGE BASKETBALL
Final NCAA Division I Conference Standing, 1994-95
(*conference tournament champion; †conference does not hold a tournament)

American West
Team	Conf W	Conf L	Overall W	Overall L
Southern Utah*	6	0	17	11
Cal St. Northridge	4	2	8	20
Cal St. Sacramento	2	4	6	21
Cal Poly SLO	0	6	1	26

Atlantic Coast
Team	Conf W	Conf L	Overall W	Overall L
Wake Forest*	12	4	26	6
North Carolina	12	4	28	6
Maryland	12	4	26	8
Virginia	12	4	25	9
Georgia Tech	8	8	18	12
Clemson	5	11	15	13
Florida St.	5	11	12	15
North Carolina St.	4	12	12	15
Duke	2	14	13	18

Atlantic 10
Team	Conf W	Conf L	Overall W	Overall L
Massachusetts*	13	3	29	5
George Washington	10	6	18	14
Temple	10	6	19	11
St. Bonaventure	9	7	18	13
St. Joseph's (Pa.)	9	7	17	12
West Virginia	7	9	13	13
Rutgers	7	9	13	15
Duquesne	5	11	10	18
Rhode Island	2	14	7	20

Big East
Team	Conf W	Conf L	Overall W	Overall L
Connecticut	16	2	28	5
Villanova*	14	4	25	8
Syracuse	12	6	20	10
Georgetown	11	7	21	10
Miami (Fla.)	9	9	15	13
Providence	7	11	17	13
Seton Hall	7	11	16	14
St. John's (N.Y.)	7	11	14	14
Pittsburgh	5	13	10	18
Boston College	2	16	9	19

Big Eight
Team	Conf W	Conf L	Overall W	Overall L
Kansas	11	3	25	6
Oklahoma St.*	10	4	27	10
Oklahoma	9	5	23	9
Missouri	8	6	20	9
Iowa St.	6	8	23	11
Colorado	5	9	15	13
Nebraska	4	10	18	14
Kansas St.	3	11	12	15

Big Sky
Team	Conf W	Conf L	Overall W	Overall L
Weber St.*	11	3	21	9
Montana	11	3	21	9
Montana St.	8	6	21	8
Boise St.	7	7	17	10
Idaho St.	7	7	18	10
Idaho	6	8	12	15
Northern Arizona	4	10	8	18
E. Washington	2	12	6	20

Big South
Team	Conf W	Conf L	Overall W	Overall L
N.C.-Greensboro	14	2	23	6
Charleston So.*	12	4	19	10
Md.-Balt. County	10	6	13	14
Radford	9	7	16	12
Liberty	7	9	12	16
N.C.-Asheville	7	9	11	16
Towson St.	6	10	12	15
Winthrop	4	12	7	20
Coastal Carolina	3	13	6	20

Big Ten†
Team	Conf W	Conf L	Overall W	Overall L
Purdue	15	3	25	7
Michigan St.	14	4	22	6
Indiana	11	7	19	12
Michigan	11	7	17	14
Illinois	10	8	19	12
Minnesota	10	8	19	12
Iowa	9	9	21	12
Penn St.	9	9	21	11
Wisconsin	7	11	13	14
Ohio St.	2	16	6	22
Northwestern	1	17	5	22

Big West
Team	Conf W	Conf L	Overall W	Overall L
Utah St.	14	4	21	8
New Mexico St.	13	5	25	10
Long Beach St.*	13	5	20	10
Nevada	12	6	18	11
Pacific (Cal.)	9	9	14	13
UC Santa Barbara	8	10	13	14
UNLV	7	11	12	16
UC Irvine	6	12	13	16
Cal St. Fullerton	5	13	7	20
San Jose St.	3	15	4	23

Colonial Athletic
Team	Conf W	Conf L	Overall W	Overall L
Old Dominion*	12	2	21	12
N.C.-Wilmington	10	4	16	11
James Madison	9	5	16	13
East Carolina	7	7	18	11
American	7	7	9	19
William & Mary	6	8	8	19
Richmond	3	11	8	20
George Mason	2	12	7	20

Great Midwest
Team	Conf W	Conf L	Overall W	Overall L
Memphis	9	3	24	10
St. Louis	8	4	23	8
Marquette	7	5	21	12
Cincinnati*	7	5	22	12
DePaul	6	6	17	11
Ala.-Birmingham	5	7	14	16
Dayton	0	12	7	20

Ivy League†
Team	Conf W	Conf L	Overall W	Overall L
Pennsylvania	14	0	22	6
Princeton	10	4	16	10
Dartmouth	10	4	13	13
Brown	8	6	13	13
Yale	5	9	9	17
Cornell	4	10	9	17
Harvard	4	10	6	20
Columbia	1	13	4	22

Metropolitan
Team	Conf W	Conf L	Overall W	Overall L
N.C.-Charlotte	8	4	19	9
Louisville*	7	5	19	14
Tulane	7	5	23	10
Virginia Tech	6	6	25	10
Southern Miss.	6	6	17	13
South Florida	5	7	18	12
Va. Commonwealth	3	9	16	14

Metro Atlantic Athletic
Team	Conf W	Conf L	Overall W	Overall L
Manhattan	12	2	26	5
St. Peter's*	10	4	19	11
Canisius	10	4	21	14
Fairfield	6	8	13	15
Iona	6	8	10	17
Loyola (Md.)	5	9	9	18
Siena	5	9	8	19
Niagara	2	12	5	25

Mid-American
Team	Conf W	Conf L	Overall W	Overall L
Miami (Ohio)	16	2	23	7
Ohio	13	5	24	10
Eastern Michigan	12	6	20	10
Ball St.*	11	7	19	11
Bowling Green	10	8	16	11
Toledo	10	8	16	11
Western Michigan	9	9	14	13
Kent	5	13	8	19
Akron	4	14	8	18
Central Michigan	0	18	3	23

Mid-Continent
Team	Conf W	Conf L	Overall W	Overall L
Valparaiso*	14	4	20	8
Western Illinois	13	5	20	8
Buffalo	12	6	18	10
Youngstown St.	10	8	18	10
Troy St.	10	8	11	16
Eastern Illinois	10	8	16	13
Mo.-Kansas City	7	11	7	19
Central Conn. St.	6	12	8	18
Chicago St.	6	12	6	20
Northeastern Illinois	2	16	4	23

Mid-Eastern Athletic
Team	Conf W	Conf L	Overall W	Overall L
Coppin St.	15	1	21	10
South Carolina St.	11	5	15	13
North Carolina A&T*	10	6	15	15
Bethune-Cookman	9	7	12	16
Md.-East. Shore	9	7	13	14
Howard	8	8	9	18
Morgan St.	5	11	5	22
Delaware St.	3	13	7	21
Florida A&M	2	14	5	22

Midwestern Collegiate
Team	Conf W	Conf L	Overall W	Overall L
Xavier (Ohio)	14	0	23	5
Wis.-Green Bay*	11	4	22	8
Ill.-Chicago	11	4	18	9
Detroit.	9	5	13	15
Butler*	8	7	15	12
La Salle	7	7	13	14
Northern Ill.	7	8	19	10
Wright St.	6	8	13	17
Cleveland St.	3	11	10	17
Loyola (Ill.)	2	13	5	22
Wis.-Milwaukee	2	13	3	24

Missouri Valley
Team	Conf W	Conf L	Overall W	Overall L
Tulsa	15	3	24	8
Southern Illinois*	13	5	23	9
Illinois St.	13	5	20	13
Bradley	12	6	20	10
Evansville	11	7	18	9
Southwest Mo. St.	9	9	16	11
Drake	9	9	12	15
Wichita St.	6	12	13	14
Northern Iowa	4	14	8	20
Creighton	4	14	7	19
Indiana St.	3	15	7	19

North Atlantic
Team	Conf W	Conf L	Overall W	Overall L
Drexel*	12	4	22	8
New Hampshire	11	5	19	9
Northeastern	10	6	18	11
Hartford	7	9	11	16
Boston U.	7	9	15	16
Vermont	7	9	14	13
Delaware	7	9	12	15
Maine	6	10	11	16
Hofstra	5	11	10	18

Northeast
Team	Conf W	Conf L	Overall W	Overall L
Rider	13	5	18	11
Mt. St. Mary's (Md.)*.	12	6	17	13
Marist	12	6	17	11
Monmouth (N.J.)	11	7	13	14
FDU-Teaneck	11	7	16	12
Wagner	9	9	10	17
LIU-Brooklyn	8	10	11	17
St. Francis (Pa.)	7	11	12	16
St. Francis (N.Y.)	5	13	9	18
Robert Morris	2	16	4	23

Ohio Valley
Team	Conf W	Conf L	Overall W	Overall L
Murray St.*	11	5	21	9
Tennessee St.	11	5	17	10
Morehead St.	10	6	15	12
Tennessee Tech	9	7	13	14
Austin Peay	8	8	13	16
Southeast Mo. St.	7	9	13	14
Eastern Kentucky.	6	10	9	19
Middle Tenn. St.	5	11	12	15
Tennessee-Martin	5	11	7	20

Pacific-10†
Team	Conf W	Conf L	Overall W	Overall L
UCLA	16	2	31	2
Arizona	13	5	23	8
Arizona St.	12	6	24	9
Oregon	11	7	19	9
Stanford	10	8	20	9
Washington St.	10	8	18	12
Oregon St.	6	12	9	18
California	5	13	13	14
Washington	5	13	9	18
Southern Cal.	2	16	7	21

Patriot

	Conference W	L	Overall Record W	L
Colgate*	11	3	17	13
Bucknell	11	3	13	14
Navy	10	4	20	9
Holy Cross	9	5	15	12
Fordham	6	8	11	17
Lehigh	5	9	11	16
Army	4	10	12	16
Lafayette	0	14	2	25

Southeastern

Eastern Division

	Conference W	L	Overall Record W	L
Kentucky*	14	2	28	5
Georgia	9	7	18	10
Florida	8	8	17	13
Vanderbilt	6	10	13	15
South Carolina	5	11	10	17
Tennessee	4	12	11	16

Western Division

	W	L	W	L
Arkansas	12	4	32	7
Mississippi St.	12	4	22	8
Alabama	10	6	23	10
Auburn	7	9	16	13
Louisiana St.	6	10	12	15
Mississippi	3	13	8	19

Southern

Northern Division

	W	L	W	L
Marshall	10	4	18	9
East Tennessee St.	9	5	14	14
Davidson	7	7	14	13
Virginia Military	6	8	10	17
Appalachian St.	4	10	9	20

Southern Division

	W	L	W	L
Tenn.-Chattanooga*	11	3	19	11
Western Carolina	8	6	14	14
Citadel	6	8	11	16
Furman	6	8	10	17
Georgia Southern	3	11	8	20

Southland

	Conference W	L	Overall Record W	L
Nicholls St.*	17	1	24	6
Northeast Lousiana	11	7	14	18
Texas-San Antonio	11	7	15	13
Stephen F. Austin	9	9	14	14
North Texas	9	9	14	13
Northwestern St.	8	10	13	14
Texas-Arlington	7	11	10	17
McNeese St.	7	11	11	16
Southwest Tex. St.	7	11	12	14
Sam Houston St.	4	14	7	19

Southwest

	W	L	W	L
Texas*	11	3	23	7
Texas Tech	11	3	20	10
Texas Christian	8	6	16	11
Rice	8	6	15	13
Texas A&M	7	7	14	16
Houston	5	9	9	19
Baylor	3	11	9	19
Southern Methodist	3	11	7	20

Southwestern Athletic

	W	L	W	L
Texas Southern*	12	2	22	7
Mississippi Val.	10	4	17	11
Alabama St.	8	6	11	15
Southern-B. R.	7	7	13	13
Jackson St.	7	7	12	19
Grambling	5	9	11	17
Alcorn St.	4	10	7	19
Prairie View	3	11	6	21

Sun Belt

	W	L	W	L
Western Kentucky*	17	1	27	4
New Orleans	13	5	20	11
Jacksonville	12	6	18	9
Tex.-Pan American	10	8	14	14
Louisiana Tech	9	9	14	13
Ark.-Little Rock	9	9	17	12
South Alabama	7	11	9	18
Lamar	6	12	11	16
Southwestern La.	4	14	7	22
Arkansas St.	3	15	8	20

Trans America Athletic

	Conference W	L	Overall Record W	L
Charleston (S.C.)	15	1	23	6
Samford	11	5	16	11
Stetson	11	5	15	12
Mercer	8	8	15	14
Southeastern La.	7	9	12	16
Central Florida	7	9	11	16
Centenary	7	9	10	17
Georgia St.	6	10	11	17
Florida Int'l.*	4	12	11	19
Campbell*	4	12	8	18
Florida Atlantic	-	-	9	18

West Coast

	W	L	W	L
Santa Clara	12	2	21	7
Portland	10	4	21	8
St. Mary's (Cal.)	10	4	18	10
Gonzaga*	7	7	21	9
San Diego	5	9	11	16
San Francisco	4	10	10	19
Pepperdine	4	10	8	19
Loyola Marymount	4	10	13	15

Western Athletic

	W	L	W	L
Utah*	15	3	28	6
Brigham Young	13	5	22	10
UTEP	13	5	20	10
Wyoming	9	9	13	15
New Mexico	9	9	15	15
Hawaii	8	10	16	13
Colorado St.	7	11	17	14
Fresno St.	7	11	13	15
San Diego St.	5	13	11	17
Air Force	4	14	8	20

Independents

	W	L
Notre Dame	15	12
Oral Roberts	10	17

All-Time Winningest College Teams by Percentage

School	Years	Won	Lost	Pct.	School	Years	Won	Lost	Pct.
Kentucky	92	1,616	518	.757	Arkansas	72	1,230	635	.660
UNLV	37	779	268	.744	Notre Dame	90	1,389	730	.655
North Carolina	85	1,626	577	.738	Louisville	81	1,277	675	.654
UCLA	76	1,351	588	.697	Indiana	95	1,369	732	.652
St. John's (NY)	88	1,508	666	.694	Weber State	33	605	328	.648
Kansas	97	1,567	702	.691	Temple	99	1,435	780	.648
Western Kentucky	76	1,331	621	.682	La Salle	65	1,069	589	.645
Syracuse	94	1,403	661	.680	Utah	87	1,290	717	.643
Duke	90	1,474	727	.670	Illinois	90	1,281	713	.642
DePaul	72	1,166	582	.667	Purdue	97	1,311	732	.642

Major College Basketball Tournaments

The National Invitation Tournament (NIT), first played in 1938, is the nation's oldest basketball tournament. The National Collegiate Athletic Association's (NCAA) national championship tournament was first played a year later. Selections for both tournaments are made in March, with the NCAA selecting first from among the top Division I teams.

National Invitation Tournament Champions

Year	Champion	Year	Champion	Year	Champion	Year	Champion
1938	Temple	1953	Seton Hall	1967	Southern Illinois	1982	Bradley
1939	Long Island Univ.	1954	Holy Cross	1968	Dayton	1983	Fresno State
1940	Colorado	1955	Duquesne	1969	Temple	1984	Michigan
1941	Long Island Univ.	1956	Louisville	1970	Marquette	1985	UCLA
1942	West Virginia	1957	Bradley	1971	North Carolina	1986	Ohio State
1943	St. John's	1958	Xavier (Ohio)	1972	Maryland	1987	Southern Mississippi
1944	St. John's	1959	St. John's	1973	Virginia Tech	1988	Connecticut
1945	De Paul	1960	Bradley	1974	Purdue	1989	St. John's
1946	Kentucky	1961	Providence	1975	Princeton	1990	Vanderbilt
1947	Utah	1962	Dayton	1976	Kentucky	1991	Stanford
1948	St. Louis	1963	Providence	1977	St. Bonaventure	1992	Virginia
1949	San Francisco	1964	Bradley	1978	Texas	1993	Minnesota
1950	CCNY	1965	St. John's	1979	Indiana	1994	Villanova
1951	Brigham Young	1966	Brigham Young	1980	Virginia	1995	Virginia Tech
1952	LaSalle			1981	Tulsa		

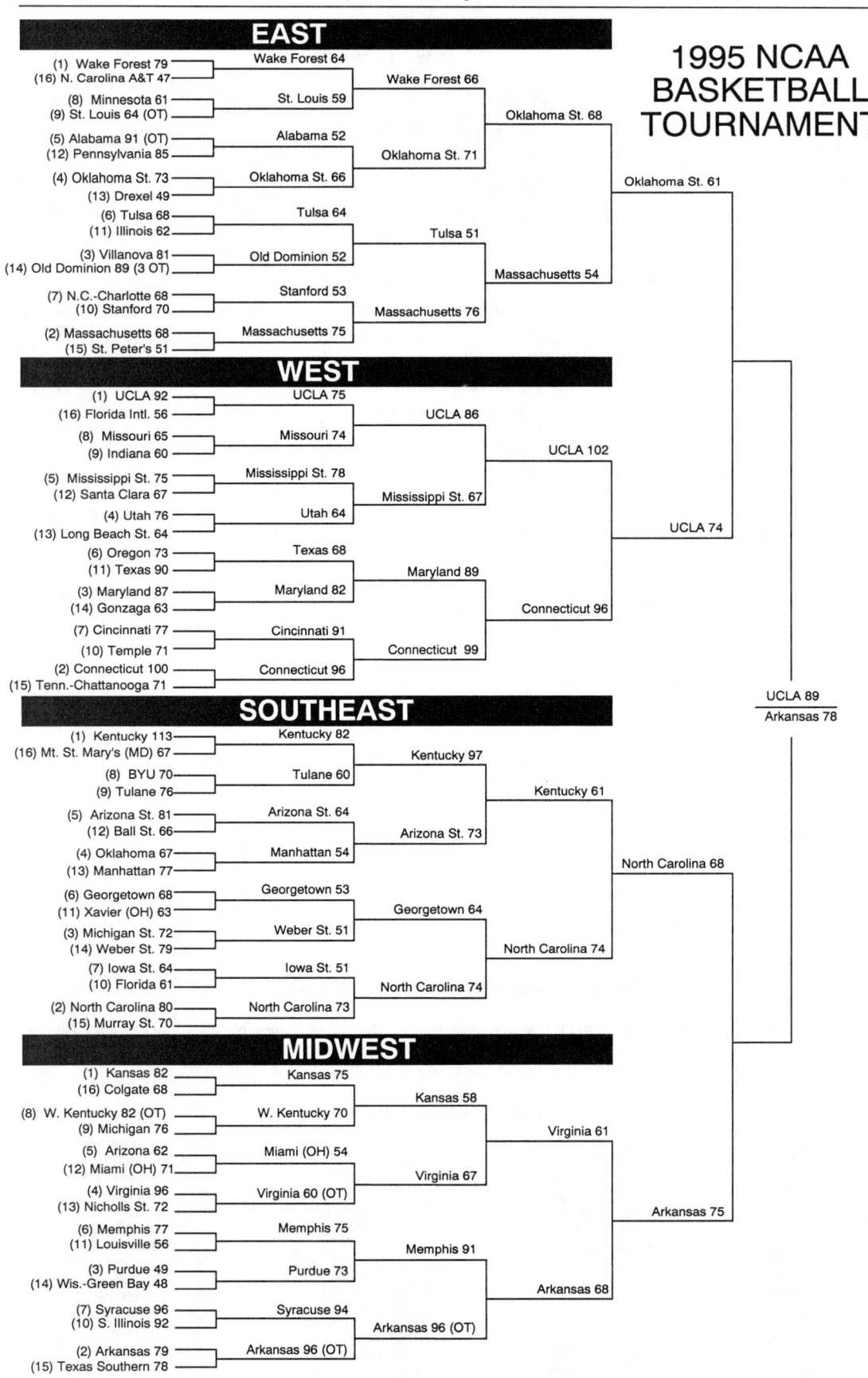

1995 NCAA BASKETBALL TOURNAMENT

EAST

- (1) Wake Forest 79 / (16) N. Carolina A&T 47 → Wake Forest 64
- (8) Minnesota 61 / (9) St. Louis 64 (OT) → St. Louis 59
  - Wake Forest 66
- (5) Alabama 91 (OT) / (12) Pennsylvania 85 → Alabama 52
- (4) Oklahoma St. 73 / (13) Drexel 49 → Oklahoma St. 66
  - Oklahoma St. 71
    - Oklahoma St. 68
- (6) Tulsa 68 / (11) Illinois 62 → Tulsa 64
- (3) Villanova 81 / (14) Old Dominion 89 (3 OT) → Old Dominion 52
  - Tulsa 51
- (7) N.C.-Charlotte 68 / (10) Stanford 70 → Stanford 53
- (2) Massachusetts 68 / (15) St. Peter's 51 → Massachusetts 75
  - Massachusetts 76
    - Massachusetts 54

Oklahoma St. 61

WEST

- (1) UCLA 92 / (16) Florida Intl. 56 → UCLA 75
- (8) Missouri 65 / (9) Indiana 60 → Missouri 74
  - UCLA 86
- (5) Mississippi St. 75 / (12) Santa Clara 67 → Mississippi St. 78
- (4) Utah 76 / (13) Long Beach St. 64 → Utah 64
  - Mississippi St. 67
    - UCLA 102
- (6) Oregon 73 / (11) Texas 90 → Texas 68
- (3) Maryland 87 / (14) Gonzaga 63 → Maryland 82
  - Maryland 89
- (7) Cincinnati 77 / (10) Temple 71 → Cincinnati 91
- (2) Connecticut 100 / (15) Tenn.-Chattanooga 71 → Connecticut 96
  - Connecticut 99
    - Connecticut 96

UCLA 74

SOUTHEAST

- (1) Kentucky 113 / (16) Mt. St. Mary's (MD) 67 → Kentucky 82
- (8) BYU 70 / (9) Tulane 76 → Tulane 60
  - Kentucky 97
- (5) Arizona St. 81 / (12) Ball St. 66 → Arizona St. 64
- (4) Oklahoma 67 / (13) Manhattan 77 → Manhattan 54
  - Arizona St. 73
    - Kentucky 61
- (6) Georgetown 68 / (11) Xavier (OH) 63 → Georgetown 53
- (3) Michigan St. 72 / (14) Weber St. 79 → Weber St. 51
  - Georgetown 64
- (7) Iowa St. 64 / (10) Florida 61 → Iowa St. 51
- (2) North Carolina 80 / (15) Murray St. 70 → North Carolina 73
  - North Carolina 74
    - North Carolina 74

North Carolina 68

MIDWEST

- (1) Kansas 82 / (16) Colgate 68 → Kansas 75
- (8) W. Kentucky 82 (OT) / (9) Michigan 76 → W. Kentucky 70
  - Kansas 58
- (5) Arizona 62 / (12) Miami (OH) 71 → Miami (OH) 54
- (4) Virginia 96 / (13) Nicholls St. 72 → Virginia 60 (OT)
  - Virginia 67
    - Virginia 61
- (6) Memphis 77 / (11) Louisville 56 → Memphis 75
- (3) Purdue 49 / (14) Wis.-Green Bay 48 → Purdue 73
  - Memphis 91
- (7) Syracuse 96 / (10) S. Illinois 92 → Syracuse 94
- (2) Arkansas 79 / (15) Texas Southern 78 → Arkansas 96 (OT)
  - Arkansas 96 (OT)
    - Arkansas 68

Arkansas 75

UCLA 89 / Arkansas 78

NCAA Division I Champions

Year	Champion	Coach	Final opponent	Score	Outstanding player	Site
1939	Oregon	Howard Hobson	Ohio St.	46-33	None	Evanston, IL
1940	Indiana	Branch McCracken	Kansas	60-42	Marvin Huffman, Indiana	Kansas City, MO
1941	Wisconsin	Harold Foster	Washington St.	39-34	John Kotz, Wisconsin	Kansas City, MO
1942	Stanford	Everett Dean	Dartmouth	53-38	Howard Dallmar, Stanford	Kansas City, MO
1943	Wyoming	Everett Shelton	Georgetown	46-34	Ken Sailors, Wyoming	New York, NY
1944	Utah	Vadal Peterson	Dartmouth	42-40[1]	Arnold Ferrin, Utah	New York, NY
1945	Oklahoma St.[2]	Henry Iba	NYU	49-45	Bob Kurland, Oklahoma St.	New York, NY
1946	Oklahoma St.[2]	Henry Iba	N. Carolina	43-40	Bob Kurland, Oklahoma St.	New York, NY
1947	Holy Cross	Alvin Julian	Oklahoma	58-47	George Kaftan, Holy Cross	New York, NY
1948	Kentucky	Adolph Rupp	Baylor	58-42	Alex Groza, Kentucky	New York, NY
1949	Kentucky	Adolph Rupp	Oklahoma St.	46-36	Alex Groza, Kentucky	Seattle, WA
1950	CCNY	Nat Holman	Bradley	71-68	Irwin Dambrot, CCNY	New York, NY
1951	Kentucky	Adolph Rupp	Kansas St.	68-58	None	Minneapolis, MN
1952	Kansas	Forrest Allen	St. John's	80-63	Clyde Lovellette, Kansas	Seattle, WA
1953	Indiana	Branch McCracken	Kansas	69-68	B.H. Born, Kansas	Kansas City, MO
1954	La Salle	Kenneth Loeffler	Bradley	92-76	Tom Gola, La Salle	Kansas City, MO
1955	San Francisco	Phil Woolpert	LaSalle	77-63	Bill Russell, San Francisco	Kansas City, MO
1956	San Francisco	Phil Woolpert	Iowa	83-71	Hal Lear, Temple	Evanston, IL
1957	N. Carolina	Frank McGuire	Kansas	54-53[1]	Wilt Chamberlain, Kansas	Kansas City, MO
1958	Kentucky	Adolph Rupp	Seattle	84-72	Elgin Baylor, Seattle	Louisville, KY
1959	California	Pete Newell	W. Virginia	71-70	Jerry West, W. Virginia	Louisville, KY
1960	Ohio St.	Fred Taylor	California	75-55	Jerry Lucas, Ohio St.	San Francisco, CA
1961	Cincinnati	Edwin Jucker	Ohio St.	70-65[1]	Jerry Lucas, Ohio St.	Kansas City, MO
1962	Cincinnati	Edwin Jucker	Ohio St.	71-59	Paul Hogue, Cincinnati	Louisville, KY
1963	Loyola (Ill.)	George Ireland	Cincinnati	60-58[1]	Art Heyman, Duke	Louisville, KY
1964	UCLA	John Wooden	Duke	98-83	Walt Hazzard, UCLA	Kansas City, MO
1965	UCLA	John Wooden	Michigan	91-80	Bill Bradley, Princeton	Portland, OR
1966	Texas-El Paso[3]	Don Haskins	Kentucky	72-65	Jerry Chambers, Utah	College Park, MD
1967	UCLA	John Wooden	Dayton	79-64	Lew Alcindor, UCLA	Louisville, KY
1968	UCLA	John Wooden	N. Carolina	78-55	Lew Alcindor, UCLA	Los Angeles, CA
1969	UCLA	John Wooden	Purdue	92-72	Lew Alcindor, UCLA	Louisville, KY
1970	UCLA	John Wooden	Jacksonville	80-69	Sidney Wicks, UCLA	College Park, MD
1971	UCLA	John Wooden	Villanova*	68-62	Howard Porter, Villanova*	Houston, TX
1972	UCLA	John Wooden	Florida St.	81-76	Bill Walton, UCLA	Los Angeles, CA
1973	UCLA	John Wooden	Memphis St.	87-66	Bill Walton, UCLA	St. Louis, MO
1974	N. Carolina St.	Norm Sloan	Marquette	76-64	David Thompson, N.C. St.	Greensboro, NC
1975	UCLA	John Wooden	Kentucky	92-85	Richard Washington, UCLA	San Diego, CA
1976	Indiana	Bob Knight	Michigan	86-68	Kent Benson, Indiana	Philadelphia, PA
1977	Marquette	Al McGuire	N. Carolina	67-59	Butch Lee, Marquette	Atlanta, GA
1978	Kentucky	Joe Hall	Duke	94-88	Jack Givens, Kentucky	St. Louis, MO
1979	Michigan St.	Jud Heathcote	Indiana St.	75-64	Magic Johnson, Michigan St.	Salt Lake City, UT
1980	Louisville	Denny Crum	UCLA*	59-54	Darrell Griffith, Louisville	Indianapolis, IN
1981	Indiana	Bob Knight	N. Carolina	63-50	Isiah Thomas, Indiana	Philadelphia, PA
1982	N. Carolina	Dean Smith	Georgetown	63-62	James Worthy, N. Carolina	New Orleans, LA
1983	N. Carolina St.	Jim Valvano	Houston	54-52	Hakeem Olajuwon, Houston	Albuquerque, NM
1984	Georgetown	John Thompson	Houston	84-75	Patrick Ewing, Georgetown	Seattle, WA
1985	Villanova	Rollie Massimino	Georgetown	66-64	Ed Pinckney, Villanova	Lexington, KY
1986	Louisville	Denny Crum	Duke	72-69	Pervis Ellison, Louisville	Dallas, TX
1987	Indiana	Bob Knight	Syracuse	74-73	Keith Smart, Indiana	New Orleans, LA
1988	Kansas	Larry Brown	Oklahoma	83-79	Danny Manning, Kansas	Kansas City, MO
1989	Michigan	Steve Fisher	Seton Hall	80-79[1]	Glen Rice, Michigan	Seattle, WA
1990	UNLV	Jerry Tarkanian	Duke	103-73	Anderson Hunt, UNLV	Denver, CO
1991	Duke	Mike Krzyzewski	Kansas	72-65	Christian Laettner, Duke	Indianapolis, IN
1992	Duke	Mike Krzyzewski	Michigan	71-51	Bobby Hurley, Duke	Minneapolis, MN
1993	N. Carolina	Dean Smith	Michigan	77-71	Donald Williams, N. Carolina	New Orleans, LA
1994	Arkansas	Nolan Richardson	Duke	76-72	Corliss Williamson, Arkansas	Charlotte, NC
1995	UCLA	Jim Harrick	Arkansas	89-78	Ed O'Bannon, UCLA	Seattle, WA

*Declared ineligible subsequent to the tournament. (1) Overtime. (2) Known as Oklahoma A&M at that time. (3) Known as Texas Western at that time.

Top Career Scorers

Player, school	Years	Points	Avg.	Player, school	Years	Points	Avg.
Pete Maravich, LSU	1968-70	3,667	44.2	Frank Selvy, Furman	1952-54	2,538	32.5
Austin Carr, Notre Dame	1969-71	2,560	34.6	Rick Mount, Purdue	1968-70	2,323	32.3
Oscar Robertson, Cincinnati	1958-60	2,973	33.8	Darrell Floyd, Furman	1954-56	2,281	32.1
Calvin Murphy, Niagara	1968-70	2,548	33.1	Nick Werkman, Seton Hall	1962-64	2,273	32.0
Dwight Lamar, SW Louisiana	1972-73	1,862	32.7	Willie Humes, Idaho State	1970-71	1,510	31.5

John R. Wooden Award

Awarded annually to the nation's outstanding college basketball player by the United States Basketball Writers Assn.

1977	Marques Johnson, UCLA	1984	Michael Jordan, North Carolina	1990	Lionel Simmons, La Salle
1978	Phil Ford, North Carolina	1985	Chris Mullin, St. John's	1991	Larry Johnson, UNLV
1979	Larry Bird, Indiana State	1986	Walter Berry, St. John's	1992	Christian Laettner, Duke
1980	Darrell Griffith, Louisville	1987	David Robinson, Navy	1993	Calbert Cheaney, Indiana
1981	Danny Ainge, Brigham Young	1988	Danny Manning, Kansas	1994	Glenn Robinson, Purdue
1982	Ralph Sampson, Virginia	1989	Sean Elliott, Arizona	1995	Ed O'Bannon, UCLA
1983	Ralph Sampson, Virginia				

Selected Division I Basketball Coaches in 1994

College	Coach	College	Coach	College	Coach
Akron	Dan Hipsher	Indiana St.	Sherman Dillard	Rice	Willis Wilson
Alabama	David Hobbs	Iowa	Tom Davis	Richmond	Bill Dooley
Ala.-Birmingham	Gene Bartow	Iowa St.	Tim Floyd	Rutgers	Bob Wenzel
American	Chris Knoche	James Madison	Lefty Driesell	St. Bonaventure	Jim Baron
Arizona	Lute Olson	Kansas	Roy Williams	St. John's (N.Y.)	Brian Mahoney
Arizona St.	Bill Frieder	Kansas St.	Tom Asbury	St. Joseph's (Pa.)	Phil Martelli
Arkansas	Nolan Richardson	Kent	Dave Grube	St. Louis	Charlie Spoonhour
Army	Dino Gaudio	Kentucky	Rick Pitino	St. Mary's (Cal.)	Ernie Kent
Auburn	Cliff Ellis	Long Beach St.	Seth Greenberg	St. Peter's	Rodger Blind
Austin Peay	Dave Loos	LSU	Dale Brown	San Diego	Brad Holland
Ball St.	Ray McCallum	Louisville	Denny Crum	San Diego St.	Fred Trenkle
Baylor	Harry Miller	Loyola (California)	John Olive	San Francisco	Phil Matthews
Boise St.	Rod Jensen	Loyola (Illinois)	Ken Burmeister	San Jose St.	Stan Morrison
Boston Coll.	Jim O'Brien	Manhattan	Fran Fraschilla	Santa Clara	Dick Davey
Bowling Green	Jim Larranaga	Marquette	Mike Deane	Seton Hall	George Blaney
Bradley	Jim Molinari	Maryland	Gary Williams	South Carolina	Eddie Fogler
Brigham Young	Roger Reid	Massachusetts	John Calipari	South Florida	Bobby Paschal
Brown	Frank Dobbs	Memphis	Larry Finch	SE Missouri St.	Ron Shumate
Butler	Barry Collier	Miami (Florida)	Leonard Hamilton	USC	Charlie Parker
California	Todd Bozeman	Miami (Ohio)	Herb Sendek	Southern Illinois	Rick Herrin
Cal. St. Fullerton	Bob Hawking	Michigan	Steve Fisher	SMU	Mike Dement
UC Irvine	Rod Baker	Michigan St.	Tom Izzo	Southern Mississippi	M. K. Turk
UC Santa Barbara	John H. Wade	Middle Tenn. St.	David Farrar	SW Missouri St.	Steve Alford
Central Mich.	Leonard Drake	Minnesota	Clem Haskins	Stanford	Mike Montgomery
Cincinnati	Bob Huggins	Mississippi	Rob Evans	Syracuse	Jim Boeheim
Clemson	Rick Barnes	Mississippi St.	Richard Williams	Temple	John Chaney
Cleveland St.	Mike Boyd	Missouri	Norm Stewart	Tennessee	Kevin O'Neill
Colgate	Jack Bruen	Montana	Blaine Taylor	Tennessee St.	Frankie Allen
Colorado	Joe Harrington	Montana St.	Mick Durham	Tennessee Tech	Frank Harrell
Colorado St.	Stew Morrill	Morehead St.	Dick Fick	Tenn.-Chattanooga	Mack McCarthy
Columbia	Armond Hill	Mt. St. Mary's (MD)	James Phelan	Tennessee-Martin	Calvin C. Luther
Connecticut	Jim Calhoun	Murray St.	Mark Gottfried	Texas	Tom Penders
Cornell	Al Walker	Nebraska	Danny Nee	Texas A&M	Tony Barone
Creighton	Dana Altman	Nevada	Pat Foster	Texas Christian	Billy Tubbs
Dartmouth	Dave Faucher	UNLV	Bill Bayno	Texas-Arlington	Eddie McCarter
Dayton	Oliver Purnell	New Mexico	Dave Bliss	UTEP	Don Haskins
DePaul	Joey Meyer	New Mexico St.	Neil McCarthy	Texas Southern	Robert Moreland
Detroit Mercy	Perry Watson	Nicholls St.	Rickey Broussard	Toledo	Larry Gipson
Drake	Rudy Washington	North Carolina	Dean Smith	Tulane	Perry Clark
Drexel	Bill Herrion	North Carolina A&T	Roy Thomas	Tulsa	Steve Robinson
Duke	Mike Krzyzewski	North Carolina St.	Les Robinson	UCLA	Jim Harrick
E. Carolina	Joe Dooley	N.C.-Charlotte	Jeff Mullins	Utah	Rick Majerus
E. Illinois	Rick Samuels	N.C.-Greensboro	Randy Peele	Utah St.	Larry Eustachy
E. Kentucky	Mike Calhoun	N.C.-Wilmington	Jerry Wainwright	Valparaiso	Homer Drew
E. Michigan	Ben Braun	N. Arizona	Ben Howland	Vanderbilt	Jan van Breda Kolff
E. Washington	Steve Aggers	N. Illinois	Brian Hammel	Villanova	Steve Lappas
Evansville	Jim Crews	N. Iowa	Eldon Miller	Virginia	Jeff Jones
Florida	Lon Kruger	Northwestern	Ricky Byrdsong	Va. Commonwealth	Sonny Smith
Florida International	Shakey Rodriguez	Notre Dame	John MacLeod	Virginia Tech	Bill Foster
Florida St.	Pat Kennedy	Ohio	Larry Hunter	Wake Forest	Dave Odom
Fresno St.	Jerry Tarkanian	Ohio St.	Randy Ayers	Washington	Bob Bender
George Mason	Paul Westhead	Oklahoma	Kelvin Sampson	Washington St.	Kevin Eastman
Geo. Washington	Mike Jarvis	Oklahoma St.	Eddie Sutton	Weber St.	Ron Abegglen
Georgetown	John Thompson	Old Dominion	Jeff Capel	West Virginia	Gale Catlett
Georgia	Tubby Smith	Oregon	Jerry Green	W. Illinois	Jim Kerwin
Georgia Tech	Bobby Cremins	Oregon St.	Eddie Payne	W. Kentucky	Matt Kilcullen
Gonzaga	Dan Fitzgerald	Pacific (California)	Bob Thomason	W. Michigan	Bob Donewald
Harvard	Frank Sullivan	Pennsylvania	Fran Dunphy	Wichita St.	Scott Thompson
Hawaii	Riley Wallace	Penn St.	Jerry Dunn	William & Mary	Charlie Woollum
Houston	Alvin Brooks	Pepperdine	Tony Fuller	Wisconsin	Dick Bennett
Idaho	Joe Cravens	Pittsburgh	Ralph Willard	Wis.-Green Bay	Mike Heideman
Idaho St.	Herb Williams	Portland	Rob Chavez	Wright St.	Ralph Underhill
Illinois	Lou Henson	Princeton	Pete Carril	Wyoming	Joby Wright
Illinois St.	Kevin Stallings	Providence	Pete Gillen	Xavier (Ohio)	Skip Prosser
Illinois-Chicago	Bob Hallberg	Purdue	Gene Keady	Yale	Dick Kuchen
Indiana	Bob Knight	Rhode Island	Al Skinner		

Most Coaching Victories in the NCAA Tournament Through 1994

Coach, school(s), years	Wins	Tournaments	Coach, school(s), years	Wins	Tournaments
Dean Smith, North Carolina, 1967-95	60	25	Adolph Rupp, Kentucky, 1942-72	30	20
John Wooden, UCLA, 1950-75	47	16	Guy Lewis, Houston, 1961-84	26	14
Bob Knight, Indiana, 1973-95	40	19	Eddie Sutton, Creighton, Arkansas,		
Mike Krzyzewski, Duke, 1984-94	39	11	Kentucky, Oklahoma St., 1974-95	25	17
Denny Crum, Louisville, 1972-95	37	19	Jim Boeheim, Syracuse, 1976-95	22	16
Jerry Tarkanian, Long Beach State and			Nolan Richardson, Tulsa and		
UNLV, 1970-91	31	13	Oklahoma, 1982-95	22	11
John Thompson, Georgetown, 1975-95	31	18			

NCAA Division I Basketball Statistical Trends

Averages and percentages are for both teams, per game.

Year	Games	FG Made	FG Att.	Pct.	FT Made	FT Att.	Pct.	PF	Pts.
1948	3945	40.6	138.7	29.3	25.3	42.2	59.8	36.9	106.5
1950	3659	43.2	136.8	31.6	28.7	46.5	61.8	39.0	115.1
1952	4009	47.5	140.6*	33.7	31.6	50.5	62.6	44.9*	126.6
1953	3754	48.0	138.1	34.7	42.1	65.8*	64.0	42.5	138.1
1955	3829	51.1	138.6	36.9	43.1*	64.7	66.5	37.9	145.3
1958	4153	51.6	134.2	38.4	33.6	50.5	66.4	36.4	136.8
1960	4295	52.6	132.3	39.8	34.7	51.5	67.4	36.7	139.9
1963	4180	53.2	127.6	41.7	32.6	47.8	68.2	36.4	139.0
1965	4520	58.3	135.4	43.1	34.7	50.3	69.0	38.5	151.4
1971	5232	60.2	135.6	44.4	35.0	51.3	68.1	38.5	155.4*
1973	5582	62.3*	139.2	44.8	26.2	38.3	68.4	38.4	150.9
1975	6147	62.9	136.7	46.0	27.4	39.7	69.0	40.3	153.1
1979	7131	59.2	124.1	47.7	29.5	42.2	69.7*	41.1	147.9
1983	7957	54.3	114.0	47.7	29.0	42.3	68.5	39.7	138.7
1985	8269	54.5	113.9	47.9*	29.3	42.5	68.9	39.3	138.3
1986	8360	54.7	114.6	47.7	29.4	42.5	69.1	39.1	138.7
1987	8580	54.4	117.3	46.6	29.7	43.0	69.1	39.3	145.5
1988	8587	54.8	116.6	47.0	30.2	43.8	68.9	39.4	147.8
1989	8677	55.7	118.5	47.0	31.1	45.0	69.1	40.2	151.4
1990	8646	54.7	118.9	46.0	31.1	45.1	68.9	39.6	149.8
1991	8720	55.6	121.3	45.8	31.7	46.3	68.5	39.2	152.9
1992	8803*	53.0	116.6	45.5	31.6	46.4	68.1	40.0	147.6
1993	8528	52.9	117.2	45.2	30.8	45.5	67.7	39.1	147.2
1994	8630	53.7	121.1	44.3	31.2	46.4	67.1	39.7	150.0
1995	8662	52.7	119.1	44.2	30.4	45.0	67.6	39.4	147.6

*All-time high

Women's College Basketball

Connecticut Huskies Go Unbeaten in Winning the NCAA Women's Championship

The University of Connecticut Huskies defeated the U. of Tennessee Lady Volunteers, 70-64, to win the NCAA Division I Women's Basketball Championship, April 2, 1995, in Minneapolis, MN. The victory capped an unbeaten 35-0 season for UConn, setting the mark for the most victories in a season by any NCAA basketball team—men's or women's. UConn trailed 38-32 at halftime and did not regain the lead for good until there were less than 2 minutes left in the game. The Huskies' all-American forward Rebecca Lobo led all scorers with 17 points. She was named the outstanding player in the tournament.

NCAA Division I Women's Champions

Year	Champion	Coach	Final opponent	Score	Outstanding player	Site
1982	Louisiana Tech	Sonja Hogg	Cheyney	76-62	Janice Lawrence, La. Tech	Norfolk, VA
1983	USC	Linda Sharp	Louisiana Tech	69-67	Cheryl Miller, USC	Norfolk, VA
1984	USC	Linda Sharp	Tennessee	72-61	Cheryl Miller, USC	Los Angeles, CA
1985	Old Dominion	Marianne Stanley	Georgia	70-65	Tracy Claxton, Old Dominion	Austin, TX
1986	Texas	Jody Conradt	USC	97-81	Clarissa Davis, Texas	Lexington, KY
1987	Tennessee	Pat Summitt	Louisiana Tech	67-44	Tonya Edwards, Tennessee	Austin, TX
1988	Louisiana Tech	Leon Barmore	Auburn	56-54	Erica Westbrooks, La. Tech	Tacoma, WA
1989	Tennessee	Pat Summitt	Auburn	76-60	Bridgette Gordon, Tennessee	Tacoma, WA
1990	Stanford	Tara VanDerveer	Auburn	88-81	Jennifer Azzi, Stanford	Knoxville, TN
1991	Tennessee	Pat Summitt	Virginia	70-67*	Dawn Staley, Virginia	New Orleans, LA
1992	Stanford	Tara VanDerveer	W. Kentucky	78-62	Molly Goodenbour, Stanford	Los Angeles, CA
1993	Texas Tech	Marsha Sharp	Ohio St.	84-82	Sheryl Swoopes, Texas Tech	Atlanta, GA
1994	North Carolina	Sylvia Hatchell	Louisiana Tech	60-59	Charlotte Smith, North Carolina	Richmond, VA
1995	Connecticut	Geno Auriemma	Tennessee	70-64	Rebecca Lobo, Connecticut	Minneapolis, MN

* Overtime.

Wade Trophy

Awarded by the National Assn. for Girls and Women in Sport for academics, community service, and player performance in basketball.

Year	Player, school	Year	Player, school	Year	Player, school
1978	Carol Blazejowski, Montclair St.	1984	Janice Lawrence, Louisiana Tech	1989	Clarissa Davis, Texas
1979	Nancy Lieberman, Old Dominion			1990	Jennifer Azzi, Stanford
1980	Nancy Lieberman, Old Dominion	1985	Cheryl Miller, USC	1991	DaedraCharles, Tennessee
1981	Lynette Woodard, Kansas	1986	Kamie Ethridge, Texas	1992	Susan Robinson, Penn St.
1982	Pam Kelly, Louisiana Tech	1987	Shelly Pennefeather, Villanova	1993	Karen Jennings, Nebraska
1983	LaTaunya Pollard, Long Beach St.	1988	Teresa Weatherspoon, Louisiana Tech	1994	Carol Ann Shudlick, Minnesota
				1995	Rebecca Lobo, Connecticut

Top Women's Career Scorers

Player, school	Years	Points	Avg.	Player, school	Years	Points	Avg.
Patricia Hoskins, Mississippi Valley State	1985-89	3,122	28.4	Joyce Walker, LSU	1981-84	2,906	24.8
Sandra Hodge, New Orleans	1981-84	2,860	26.7	Tarcha Hollis, Grambling	1988-91	2,058	24.2
Lorri Bauman, Duke	1981-84	3,115	26.0	Karen Pelphrey, Marshall	1983-86	2,746	24.1
Valorie Whiteside, Appalachian State	1984-88	2,944	25.4	Erma Jones, Bethune-Cookman	1982-84	2,095	24.1
				Cheryl Miller, USC	1983-86	3,018	23.6
				Chris Starr, Nevada-Reno	1983-86	2,356	23.3

LACROSSE

Lacrosse Champions in 1995

World Lacrosse Championship (1994; held every 4 years)—Manchester, England, July 30: U.S. 21, Australia 7.
U.S. Club Lacrosse Association Championship—Baltimore, MD, June 24: Mount Washington 20, Long Island L.C. 11.
NCAA Division I Championship—College Park, MD, May 29: Syracuse 13, Maryland 9.
NCAA Division II Championship—Springfield, MA, May 13: Adelphi 12, Springfield College 10.
NCAA Division III Championship—College Park, MD, May 28: Salisbury State (MD) 22, Nazareth 13.
USILA Division I All-Star Game—Baltimore, MD, June 9: North 19, South 18.
National Junior College Championship—Garden City, NY, May 13: Herkimer (NY) C.C. 15, Essex (MD) C.C. 11.

NCAA Women's Division I Championship—Ewing Township, NJ, May 21: Maryland 13, Princeton 5.
NCAA Women's Division III Championship— Ewing Township, NJ, May 21: Trenton State 14, William Smith 13.

USILA Division I All America Team

Attack: Brian Piccola, Johns Hopkins; Terry Riordan, Johns Hopkins; David Evans, Brown.
Midfield: Peter Jacobs, Johns Hopkins; Matt Dwan, Loyola (MD); Matt Ogelsby, Duke; Roy Colsey, Syracuse.
Defense: Todd Higgins, Princeton; Ric Beardsley, Syracuse; Dan Radebaugh, Maryland.
Goal: Brian Dougherty, Maryland.
Coach of the Year: Dick Edell, Maryland.
Note: 4 midfielders selected for the 3 midfield positions.

NCAA Division I Champions

Year	Champion	Year	Champion	Year	Champion	Year	Champion
1972	Virginia	1978	Johns Hopkins	1984	Johns Hopkins	1990	Syracuse
1973	Maryland	1979	Johns Hopkins	1985	Johns Hopkins	1991	North Carolina
1974	Johns Hopkins	1980	Johns Hopkins	1986	North Carolina	1992	Princeton
1975	Maryland	1981	North Carolina	1987	Johns Hopkins	1993	Syracuse
1976	Cornell	1982	North Carolina	1988	Syracuse	1994	Princeton
1977	Cornell	1983	Syracuse	1989	Syracuse	1995	Syracuse

SKIING

World Cup Alpine Champions

Men

1967	Jean Claude Killy, France	1978	Ingemar Stenmark, Sweden	1987	Pirmin Zurbriggen, Switzerland
1968	Jean Claude Killy, France	1979	Peter Luescher, Switzerland	1988	Pirmin Zurbriggen, Switzerland
1969	Karl Schranz, Austria	1980	Andreas Wenzel, Liechtenstein	1989	Marc Girardelli, Luxembourg
1970	Karl Schranz, Austria	1981	Phil Mahre, U.S.	1990	Pirmin Zurbriggen, Switzerland
1971	Gustavo Thoeni, Italy	1982	Phil Mahre, U.S.	1991	Marc Girardelli, Luxembourg
1972	Gustavo Thoeni, Italy	1983	Phil Mahre, U.S.	1992	Paul Accola, Switzerland
1973	Gustavo Thoeni, Italy	1984	Pirmin Zurbriggen, Switzerland	1993	Marc Girardelli, Luxembourg
1974	Piero Gros, Italy	1985	Marc Girardelli, Luxembourg	1994	Kjetil Andre Aamodt, Norway
1975	Gustavo Thoeni, Italy	1986	Marc Girardelli, Luxembourg	1995	Alberto Tomba, Italy
1976	Ingemar Stenmark, Sweden				
1977	Ingemar Stenmark, Sweden				

Women

1967	Nancy Greene, Canada	1977	Lise-Marie Morerod, Switzerland	1987	Maria Walliser, Switzerland
1968	Nancy Greene, Canada	1978	Hanni Wenzel, Liechtenstein	1988	Michela Figini, Switzerland
1969	Gertrud Gabl, Austria	1979	Annemarie Proell Moser, Austria	1989	Vreni Schneider, Switzerland
1970	Michele Jacot, France	1980	Hanni Wenzel, Liechtenstein	1990	Petra Kronberger, Austria
1971	Annemarie Proell, Austria	1981	Marie-Theres Nadig, Switzerland	1991	Petra Kronberger, Austria
1972	Annemarie Proell, Austria	1982	Erika Hess, Switzerland	1992	Petra Kronberger, Austria
1973	Annemarie Proell, Austria	1983	Tamara McKinney, U.S.	1993	Anita Wachter, Austria
1974	Annemarie Proell, Austria	1984	Erika Hess, Switzerland	1994	Vreni Schneider, Switzerland
1975	Annemarie Proell, Austria	1985	Michela Figini, Switzerland	1995	Vreni Schneider, Switzerland
1976	Rose Mittermaier, W. Germany	1986	Maria Walliser, Switzerland		

DOGS

Westminster Kennel Club

Year	Best-in-show	Breed	Owner
1986	Ch. Marjetta National Acclaim	Pointer	Mrs. Alan Robson & Michael Zollo
1987	Ch. Covy Tucker Hill's Manhattan	German shepherd	Shirley Braunstein & Jane Firestone
1988	Ch. Great Elms Prince Charming II	Pomeranian	Skip Piazza & Olga Baker
1989	Ch. Royal Tudor's Wild As The Wind	Doberman	Sue & Art Kemp, Richard & Carolyn Vida, Beth Wilhite
1990	Ch. Wendessa Crown Prince	Pekingese	Ed Jenner
1991	Ch. Whisperwind on a Carousel	Poodle	Joan & Frederick Hartsock
1992	Ch. Registry's Lonesome Dove	Fox terrier	Marion & Sam Lawrence
1993	Ch. Salilyn's Condor	English springer spaniel	Donna & Roger Herzig
1994	Ch. Chidley Willum	Norwich terrier	Ruth Cooper & Patricia Lussier
1995	Ch. Gaelforce Post Script	Scottish terrier	Dr. Vandra Huber & Dr. Joe Kinnarney

Iditarod Trail Sled Dog Race in 1995

Doug Swingley of Simms, MT, won the 1995 Iditarod Trail Sled Dog Race, March 14, in a record time of 9 days 2 hours 43 minutes. By winning the 1,049-mile race from Anchorage to Nome, Swingley received $52,500 in prize money and a pickup truck. Swingley was the first non-Alaskan to win the race.

IGFA Saltwater & Freshwater All-Tackle World Records

Source: International Game Fish Association; records confirmed to Sept. 1995

Saltwater Fish Records

Species	Weight	Where caught	Date	Angler
Albacore	88 lbs. 2 oz.	Gran Canaria, Canary Islands	Nov. 19, 1977	Siegfried Dickemann
Amberjack, greater	155 lbs. 10 oz.	Challenger Bank, Bermuda	June 24, 1981	Joseph Dawson
Barracuda, great	85 lbs.	Christmas Island, Kiribati	Apr. 11, 1992	John Helfrich
Barracuda, Mexican	21 lbs.	Phantom Isle, Costa Rica	Mar. 27, 1987	E. Greg Kent
Barracuda, Pacific	7 lbs. 11 oz.	Catalina Island, Cal.	May 22, 1994	Jim Kingsmill
Bass, barred sand	13 lbs. 3 oz.	Huntington Beach, Cal.	Aug. 29, 1988	Robert Halal
Bass, black sea	9 lbs. 8 oz.	Virginia Beach, Va.	Jan. 9, 1987	Joe Mizelle Jr.
		Virginia Beach, Va.	Dec. 22, 1990	Jack G. Stallings
Bass, giant sea	563 lbs. 8 oz.	Anacaba Island, Cal.	Aug. 20, 1968	James D. McAdam Jr.
Bass, redeye	8 lbs. 12 oz.	Apalatchicola River, Fla.	Jan. 28, 1995	Carl W. Davis
Bass, striped	78 lbs. 8 oz.	Atlantic City, N.J.	Sept. 21, 1982	Albert McReynolds
Bluefish	31 lbs. 12 oz.	Hatteras Inlet, N.C.	Jan. 30, 1972	James M. Hussey
Bonefish	19 lbs.	Zululand, South Africa	May 26, 1962	Brian W. Batchelor
Bonito, Atlantic	18 lbs. 4 oz.	Faial I., Azores	July 8, 1953	D. Gama Higgs
Bonito, Pacific	14 lbs. 12 oz.	San Benitos Island, Mexico	Oct. 12, 1980	Jerome Rilling
Cabezon	23 lbs.	Juan De Fuca Strait, Wash.	Aug. 4, 1990	Wesley Hunter
Cobia	135 lbs. 9 oz.	Shark Bay, Australia	July 9, 1985	Peter W. Goulding
Cod, Atlantic	98 lbs. 12 oz.	Isle of Shoals, N.H.	June 8, 1969	Alphonse Bielevich
Cod, Pacific	30 lbs.	Andrew Bay, Alaska	June 7, 1984	Donald Vaughn
Conger	133 lbs. 4 oz.	Berry Head, S. Devon, England	June 5, 1995	Vic Evans
Dolphin	87 lbs.	Papagallo Gulf, Costa Rica	Sept. 25, 1976	Manuel Salazar
Drum, black	113 lbs. 1 oz.	Lewes, Del.	Sept. 15, 1975	Gerald Townsend
Drum, red	94 lbs. 2 oz.	Avon, N.C.	Nov. 7, 1984	David Deuel
Eel, American	8 lbs. 8 oz.	Cliff Pond, Brewster, Mass.	May 17, 1992	Gerald LaPierre
Eel, marbled	36 lbs. 1 oz.	Hazelwood Dam, South Africa	June 10, 1984	Ferdie van Nooten
Flounder, southern	20 lbs. 9 oz.	Nassau Sound, Fla.	Dec. 23, 1983	Larenza Mungin
Flounder, summer	22 lbs. 7 oz.	Montauk, N.Y.	Sept. 15, 1975	Charles Nappi
Grouper, Warsaw	436 lbs. 12 oz.	Gulf of Mexico, Destin, Fla.	Dec. 22, 1985	Steve Haeusler
Halibut, Atlantic	255 lbs. 4 oz.	Gloucester, Mass.	July 28, 1989	Sonny Manley
Halibut, California	53 lbs. 4 oz.	Santa Rosa Island, Cal.	July 7, 1988	Russell Harmon
Halibut, Pacific	368 lbs.	Gustavus, Alaska	July 5, 1991	Celia Dueitt
Jack, crevalle	57 lbs. 5 oz.	Barra do Kwanza, Angola	Oct. 10, 1992	Cam Nicolson`
Jack, horse-eye	24 lbs. 8 oz.	Miami, Fla.	Dec. 20, 1982	Tito Schnau
Jack, Pacific crevalle	29 lbs. 8 oz.	Playa Zancudo, Costa Rica	Jan. 1, 1994	Ronald C. Snody
Jewfish	680 lbs.	Fernandina Beach, Fla.	May 20, 1961	Lynn Joyner
Kawakawa	29 lbs.	Clarion Island, Mexico	Dec. 17, 1986	Ronald Nakamura
Lingcod	69 lbs.	Langara Island, B.C.	June 16, 1992	Murray Romer
Mackerel, cero	17 lbs. 2 oz.	Islamorada, Fla.	Apr. 5, 1986	G. Michael Mills
Mackerel, king	90 lbs.	Key West, Fla.	Feb. 16, 1976	Norton Thomton
Mackerel, Spanish	13 lbs.	Ocracoke Inlet, N.C.	Nov. 4, 1987	Robert Cranton
Marlin, Atlantic blue	1,402 lbs. 2 oz.	Vitoria, Brazil	Feb. 29, 1992	Paulo Amorim
Marlin, black	1,560 lbs.	Cabo Blanco, Peru	Aug. 4, 1953	Alfred C. Glassell Jr.
Marlin, Pacific blue	1,376 lbs.	Kaaiwi Pt., Kona, Hawaii	May 31, 1982	Jay W. deBeaubien
Marlin, striped	494 lbs.	Tutukaka, New Zealand	Jan. 16, 1986	Bill Boniface
Marlin, white	181 lbs. 14 oz.	Vitoria, Brazil	Dec. 8, 1979	Evandro Luiz Coser
Permit	53 lbs. 4 oz.	Lake Worth Inlet, Fla.	March 25, 1994	Roy Brooker
Pollack, European	27 lbs. 6 oz.	Salcombe, Devon, England	Jan. 16, 1986	Robert Milkins
Pollock	46 lbs. 10 oz.	Perkins Cove, Ogunquit, Me.	Oct. 24, 1990	Linda Paul
Pompano, African	50 lbs. 8 oz.	Daytona Beach, Fla.	Apr. 21, 1990	Tom Sargent
Roosterfish	114 lbs.	La Paz, Baja Cal., Mexico	June 1, 1960	Abe Sackheim
Runner, blue	8 lbs. 7 oz.	Port Aransas, Tex.	Feb. 13, 1995	Allen E. Windecker
Runner, rainbow	37 lbs. 9 oz.	Clarion Island, Mexico	Nov. 21, 1991	Tom Pfleger
Sailfish, Atlantic	135 lbs. 5 oz.	Lagos, Nigeria	Nov. 10, 1991	Ron King
Sailfish, Pacific	221 lbs.	Santa Cruz Island, Ecuador	Feb. 12, 1947	C. W. Stewart
Seabass, white	83 lbs. 12 oz.	San Felipe, Mexico	Mar. 31, 1953	L. C. Baumgardner
Seatrout, spotted	16 lbs.	Mason's Beach, Va.	May 28, 1977	William Katko
Shark, bigeye thresher	802 lbs.	Tutukaka, New Zealand	Feb. 8, 1981	Dianne North
Shark, bignose	369 lbs. 14 oz.	Markham R., Papua New Guinea	Oct. 23, 1993	Lester Rohrlach
Shark, blue	437 lbs.	Catherine Bay, N.S.W., Australia	Oct. 2, 1976	Peter Hyde
Shark, great hammerhead	991 lbs.	Sarasota, Fla.	May 30, 1982	Allen Ogle
Shark, Greenland	1,708 lbs. 9 oz.	Trondheimsfjord, Norway	Oct. 18, 1987	Terje Nordtvedt
Shark, man-eater or white	2,664 lbs.	Ceduna, S.A., Australia	Apr. 21, 1959	Alfred Dean
Shark, porbeagle	507 lbs.	Caithness, Scotland	Mar. 9, 1993	Christopher Bennet
Shark, shortfin mako	1,115 lbs.	Black River, Mauritius	Nov. 16, 1988	Patrick Guillanton
Shark, tiger	1,780 lbs.	Cherry Grove, S.C.	June 14, 1964	Walter Maxwell
Shark, tope	72 lbs. 12 oz.	Parengarenga Harbor, New Zealand	Dec. 19, 1986	Melanie Feldman
Sheepshead	21 lbs. 4 oz.	New Orleans, La.	Apr. 16, 1982	Wayne Deselle
Skipjack, black	26 lbs.	Thetis Bank, Baja Cal., Mexico	Oct. 23, 1991	Clifford Hamaishi
Snapper, cubera	121 lbs. 8 oz.	Cameron, La.	July 5, 1982	Mike Hebert
Snapper, red	46 lbs. 8 oz.	Destin, Fla.	Oct. 1, 1985	E. Lane Nichols 3d
Snook	53 lbs. 10 oz.	Parismina Ranch, Costa Rica	Oct. 18, 1978	Gilbert Ponzi
Spearfish, Mediterranean	90 lbs. 13 oz.	Madeira Island, Portugal	June 2, 1980	Joseph Larkin
Swordfish	1,182 lbs.	Iquique, Chile	May 7, 1953	L. Marron
Tarpon	283 lbs. 4 oz.	Sherbro Island, Sierra Leone	Apr. 16, 1991	Yvon Sebag
Tautog	24 lbs.	Wachapreague, Va.	Aug. 25, 1987	Gregory Bell
Trevally, bigeye	18 lbs. 1 oz.	Clipperton Island, France	May 12, 1990	Rebecca Mills
Trevally, giant	145 lbs. 8 oz.	Makena, Maui, Hawaii	Mar. 28, 1991	Russell Mori
Tuna, Atlantic bigeye	375 lbs. 8 oz.	Ocean City, Md.	Aug. 26, 1977	Cecil Browne
Tuna, blackfin	42 lbs.	Bermuda	June 2, 1978	Alan J. Card
		Challenger Bank, Bermuda	July 18, 1989	Gilbert Pearman

(continued)

Species	Weight	Where caught	Date	Angler
Tuna, bluefin	1,496 lbs.	Aulds Cove, Nova Scotia	Oct. 26, 1979	Ken Fraser
Tuna, longtail	79 lbs. 2 oz.	Montague I., N.S.W., Australia	Apr. 12, 1982	Tim Simpson
Tuna, Pacific bigeye	435 lbs.	Cabo Blanco, Peru	Apr. 17, 1957	Dr. Russel Lee
Tuna, skipjack	41 lbs. 14 oz.	Pearl Beach, Mauritius	Nov. 12, 1985	Edmund Heinzen
Tuna, southern bluefin	348 lbs. 5 oz.	Whakatane, New Zealand	Jan. 16, 1981	Rex Wood
Tuna, yellowfin	388 lbs. 12 oz.	San Benedicto Island, Mexico	Apr. 1, 1977	Curt Wiesenhutter
Tunny, little	35 lbs. 2 oz.	Cap de Garde, Algeria	Dec. 14, 1988	Jean Yves Chatard
Wahoo	155 lbs. 8 oz.	San Salvador, Bahamas	Apr. 3, 1990	William Bourne
Weakfish	19 lbs. 2 oz.	Jones Beach Inlet, N.Y.	Oct. 11, 1984	Dennis Rooney
		Delaware Bay, Del.	May 20, 1989	William Thomas
Yellowtail, California	79 lbs. 4 oz.	Alijos Rocks, Baja Cal., Mexico	July 2, 1991	Robert Walker
Yellowtail, southern	114 lbs. 10 oz.	Tauranga, New Zealand	Feb. 5, 1984	Mike Godfrey

Freshwater Fish Records

Species	Weight	Where caught	Date	Angler
Barramundi	63 lbs. 2 oz.	Normah River, Australia	Apr. 28, 1991	Scott Barnsley
Bass, largemouth	22 lbs. 4 oz.	Montgomery Lake, Ga.	June 2, 1932	George W. Perry
Bass, peacock	27 lbs.	Rio Negro, Brazil	Dec. 4, 1994	Gerald "Doc" Lawson
Bass, rock	3 lbs.	York River, Ont.	Aug. 1, 1974	Peter Gulgin
Bass, smallmouth	11 lbs. 15 oz.	Dale Hollow Lake, Ky.	July 9, 1955	David L. Hayes
Bass, Suwannee	3 lbs. 14 oz.	Suwannee River, Fla.	Mar. 2, 1985	Ronnie Everett
Bass, white	6 lbs. 13 oz.	Lake Orange, Va.	July 31, 1989	Ronald Sprouse
Bass, whiterock	24 lbs. 3 oz.	Leesville Lake, Va.	May 12, 1989	David Lambert
Bass, yellow	2 lbs. 4 oz.	Lake Monroe, Ind.	Mar. 27, 1977	Donald L. Stalker
Bluegill	4 lbs. 12 oz.	Ketona Lake, Ala.	Apr. 9, 1950	T. S. Hudson
Bowfin	21 lbs. 8 oz.	Florence, S.C.	Jan. 29, 1980	Robert Harmon
Buffalo, bigmouth	70 lbs. 5 oz.	Bussey Brake, Bastrop, La.	Apr. 21, 1980	Delbert Sisk
Buffalo, black	55 lbs. 8 oz.	Cherokee Lake, Tenn.	May 3, 1984	Edward McLain
Buffalo, smallmouth	68 lbs. 8 oz.	Lake Hamilton, Ark.	May 16, 1984	Jerry Dolezal
Bullhead, brown	5 lbs. 11 oz.	Cedar Creek, Fla.	Mar. 28, 1995	Robert Bengis
Bullhead, yellow	4 lbs. 4 oz.	Mormon Lake, Ariz.	May 11, 1984	Emily Williams
Burbot	18 lbs. 4 oz.	Pickford, Mich.	Jan. 31, 1980	Thomas Courtemanche
Carp, common	75 lbs. 11 oz.	Lac de St. Cassien, France	May 21, 1987	Leo van der Gugten
Catfish, blue	109 lbs. 4 oz.	Cooper River, S.C.	Mar. 14, 1991	George Lijewski
Catfish, channel	58 lbs.	Santee-Cooper Res., S.C.	July 7, 1964	W. B. Whaley
Catfish, flathead	91 lbs. 4 oz.	Lake Lewisville, Tex.	Mar. 28, 1982	Mike Rogers
Catfish, white	18 lbs. 14 oz.	Withlacoochee River, Fla.	Sept. 21, 1991	Jim Miller
Char, Arctic	32 lbs. 9 oz.	Tree River, Canada	July 30, 1981	Jeffrey Ward
Crappie, white	5 lbs. 3 oz.	Enid Dam, Miss.	July 31, 1957	Fred L. Bright
Dolly Varden	18 lbs. 9 oz.	Mashutuk River, Alaska	July 13, 1993	Richard B. Evans
Dorado	51 lbs. 5 oz.	Toledo (Corrientes), Argentina	Sept. 27, 1984	Armando Giudice
Drum, freshwater	54 lbs. 8 oz.	Nickajack Lake, Tenn.	Apr. 20, 1972	Benny E. Hull
Gar, alligator	279 lbs.	Rio Grande, Tex.	Dec. 2, 1951	Bill Valverde
Gar, Florida	21 lbs. 3 oz.	Boca Raton, Fla.	June 3, 1981	Jeff Sabol
Gar, longnose	50 lbs. 5 oz.	Trinity River, Tex.	July 30, 1954	Townsend Miller
Gar, shortnose	5 lbs.	Sally Jones Lake, Okla.	Apr. 26, 1985	Buddy Croslin
Gar, spotted	9 lbs. 12 oz.	Lake Mexia, Tex.	Apr. 7, 1994	Rick Rivard
Grayling, Arctic	5 lbs. 15 oz.	Katseyedie River, N.W.T.	Aug. 16, 1967	Jeanne P. Branson
Inconnu	53 lbs.	Pah River, Alaska	Aug. 20, 1986	Lawrence Hudnall
Kokanee	9 lbs. 6 oz.	Okanagan Lake, Vernon, B.C.	June 18, 1988	Norm Kuhn
Muskellunge	67 lbs. 8 oz.	Lake Court Oreilles, Wis.	July 24, 1949	Cal Johnson
Muskellunge, tiger	51 lbs. 3 oz.	Lac Vieux-Desert, Wis.-Mich.	July 16, 1919	John Knobla
Perch, Nile	191 lbs. 8 oz.	Lake Victoria, Kenya	Sept. 5, 1991	Andy Davison
Perch, white	4 lbs. 12 oz.	Messalonskee Lake, Me.	June 4, 1949	Mrs. Earl Small
Perch, yellow	4 lbs. 3 oz.	Bordentown, N.J.	May, 1865	Dr. C. C. Abbot
Pickerel, chain	9 lbs. 6 oz.	Homerville, Ga.	Feb. 17, 1961	Baxley McQuaig Jr.
Pike, northern	55 lbs. 1 oz.	Lake of Grefeern, W. Germany	Oct. 16, 1986	Lothar Louis
Redhorse, greater	9 lbs. 3 oz.	Salmon River, Pulaski, N.Y.	May 11, 1985	Jason Wilson
Redhorse, silver	11 lbs. 7 oz.	Plum Creek, Wis.	May 29, 1985	Neal Long
Salmon, Atlantic	79 lbs. 2 oz.	Tana River, Norway	1928	Henrik Henriksen
Salmon, chinook	97 lbs. 4 oz.	Kenai River, Alaska	May 17, 1985	Les Anderson
Salmon, chum	32 lbs.	Behm Canal, Alaska	June 7, 1985	Fredrick Thynes
Salmon, coho	33 lbs. 4 oz.	Salmon River, Pulaski, N.Y.	Sept. 27, 1989	Jerry Lifton
Salmon, pink	13 lbs. 1 oz.	St. Mary's River, Ont.	Sept. 23, 1992	Ray Higaki
Salmon, sockeye	15 lbs. 3 oz.	Kenai River, Alaska	Aug. 9, 1987	Stan Roach
Sauger	8 lbs. 12 oz.	Lake Sakakawea, N.D.	Oct. 6, 1971	Mike Fischer
Shad, American	11 lbs. 4 oz.	Connecticut River, Mass.	May 19, 1986	Bob Thibodo
Sturgeon, beluga	224 lbs. 13 oz.	Guryev, Kazakhstan	May 3, 1993	Merete Lehne
Sturgeon, white	468 lbs.	Benicia, Cal.	July 9, 1983	Joey Pallotta 3d
Sunfish, green	2 lbs. 2 oz.	Stockton Lake, Mo.	June 18, 1971	Paul M. Dilley
Sunfish, redbreast	1 lb. 12 oz.	Suwannee River, Fla.	May 29, 1984	Alvin Buchanan
Sunfish, redear	5 lbs. 3 oz.	Sacramento, Cal.	June 27, 1994	Anthony H. White
Tigerfish, giant	97 lbs.	Zaire River, Kinshasa, Zaire	July 9, 1988	Raymond Houtmans
Tilapia	6 lbs. 5 oz.	Lake Aranal, Costa Rica	Feb. 10, 1995	Marvin C. Smith
Trout, Apache	5 lbs. 3 oz.	Apache Res., Ariz.	May 29, 1991	John Baldwin
Trout, brook	14 lbs. 8 oz.	Nipigon River, Ont.	July 1916	Dr. W. J. Cook
Trout, brown	40 lbs. 4 oz.	Little Red River, Ark.	May 9, 1992	Howard "Rip" Collins
Trout, bull	32 lbs.	Lake Pond Oreille, Ida.	Oct. 27, 1949	N. L. Higgins
Trout, cutthroat	41 lbs.	Pyramid Lake, Nev.	Dec. 1925	John Skimmerhorn
Trout, golden	11 lbs.	Cooks Lake, Wyo.	Aug. 5, 1948	Charles S. Reed
Trout, lake	66 lbs. 8 oz.	Great Bear Lake, N.W.T.	July 19, 1991	Rodney Harback
Trout, rainbow	42 lbs. 2 oz.	Bell Island, Alaska	June 22, 1970	David Robert White
Trout, tiger	20 lbs. 13 oz.	Lake Michigan, Wis.	Aug. 12, 1978	Pete Friedland
Walleye	25 lbs.	Old Hickory Lake, Tenn.	Aug. 2, 1960	Mabry Harper
Warmouth	2 lbs. 7 oz.	Yellow River, Holt, Fla.	Oct. 19, 1985	Tony D. Dempsey
Whitefish, lake	14 lbs. 6 oz.	Meaford, Ont.	May 21, 1984	Dennis Laycock
Whitefish, mountain	5 lbs. 6 oz.	Rioh River, Sask.	June 15, 1988	John Bell
Whitefish, round	6 lbs.	Putahow River, Manitoba	June 14, 1984	Allen Ristori
Zander	25 lbs. 2 oz.	Trosa, Sweden	June 12, 1986	Harry Lee Tennison

GOLF

United States Open Winners

Year	Winner	Year	Winner	Year	Winner	Year	Winner
1903	Willie Anderson	1927	Tommy Armour	1953	Ben Hogan	1975	Lou Graham
1904	Willie Anderson	1928	John Farrell	1954	Ed Furgol	1976	Jerry Pate
1905	Willie Anderson	1929	Bobby Jones*	1955	Jack Fleck	1977	Hubert Green
1906	Alex Smith	1930	Bobby Jones*	1956	Cary Middlecoff	1978	Andy North
1907	Alex Ross	1931	Wm. Burke	1957	Dick Mayer	1979	Hale Irwin
1908	Fred McLeod	1932	Gene Sarazen	1958	Tommy Bolt	1980	Jack Nicklaus
1909	George Sargent	1933	John Goodman*	1959	Billy Casper	1981	David Graham
1910	Alex Smith	1934	Olin Dutra	1960	Arnold Palmer	1982	Tom Watson
1911	John McDermott	1935	Sam Parks, Jr.	1961	Gene Littler	1983	Larry Nelson
1912	John McDermott	1936	Tony Manero	1962	Jack Nicklaus	1984	Fuzzy Zoeller
1913	Francis Ouimet*	1937	Ralph Guldahl	1963	Julius Boros	1985	Andy North
1914	Walter Hagen	1938	Ralph Guldahl	1964	Ken Venturi	1986	Ray Floyd
1915	Jerome Travers*	1939	Byron Nelson	1965	Gary Player	1987	Scott Simpson
1916	Chick Evans*	1940	Lawson Little	1966	Billy Casper	1988	Curtis Strange
1917-18	(Not played)	1941	Craig Wood	1967	Jack Nicklaus	1989	Curtis Strange
1919	Walter Hagen	1942-45	(Not played)	1968	Lee Trevino	1990	Hale Irwin
1920	Edward Ray	1946	Lloyd Mangrum	1969	Orville Moody	1991	Payne Stewart
1921	Jim Barnes	1947	L. Worsham	1970	Tony Jacklin	1992	Tom Kite
1922	Gene Sarazen	1948	Ben Hogan	1971	Lee Trevino	1993	Lee Janzen
1923	Bobby Jones*	1949	Cary Middlecoff	1972	Jack Nicklaus	1994	Ernie Els
1924	Cyril Walker	1950	Ben Hogan	1973	Johnny Miller	1995	Corey Pavin
1925	Willie MacFarlane	1951	Ben Hogan	1974	Hale Irwin		
1926	Bobby Jones*	1952	Julius Boros				

* Amateur

Professional Golfer's Association Championship Winners

Year	Winner	Year	Winner	Year	Winner	Year	Winner
1922	Gene Sarazen	1941	Victor Ghezzi	1961	Jerry Barber	1979	David Graham
1923	Gene Sarazen	1942	Sam Snead	1962	Gary Player	1980	Jack Nicklaus
1924	Walter Hagen	1944	Bob Hamilton	1963	Jack Nicklaus	1981	Larry Nelson
1925	Walter Hagen	1945	Byron Nelson	1964	Bob Nichols	1982	Ray Floyd
1926	Walter Hagen	1946	Ben Hogan	1965	Dave Marr	1983	Hal Sutton
1927	Walter Hagen	1947	Jim Ferrier	1966	Al Geiberger	1984	Lee Trevino
1928	Leo Diegel	1948	Ben Hogan	1967	Don January	1985	Hubert Green
1929	Leo Diegel	1949	Sam Snead	1968	Julius Boros	1986	Bob Tway
1930	Tommy Armour	1950	Chandler Harper	1969	Ray Floyd	1987	Larry Nelson
1931	Tom Creavy	1951	Sam Snead	1970	Dave Stockton	1988	Jeff Sluman
1932	Olin Dutra	1952	James Turnesa	1971	Jack Nicklaus	1989	Payne Stewart
1933	Gene Sarazen	1953	Walter Burkemo	1972	Gary Player	1990	Wayne Grady
1934	Paul Runyan	1954	Melvin Harbert	1973	Jack Nicklaus	1991	John Daly
1935	Johnny Revolta	1955	Doug Ford	1974	Lee Trevino	1992	Nick Price
1936	Denny Shute	1956	Jack Burke	1975	Jack Nicklaus	1993	Paul Azinger
1937	Denny Shute	1957	Lionel Hebert	1976	Dave Stockton	1994	Nick Price
1938	Paul Runyan	1958	Dow Finsterwald	1977	Lanny Wadkins	1995	Steve Elkington
1939	Henry Picard	1959	Bob Rosburg	1978	John Mahaffey		
1940	Byron Nelson	1960	Jay Hebert				

Masters Golf Tournament Winners

Year	Winner	Year	Winner	Year	Winner	Year	Winner
1934	Horton Smith	1951	Ben Hogan	1966	Jack Nicklaus	1981	Tom Watson
1935	Gene Sarazen	1952	Sam Snead	1967	Gay Brewer, Jr.	1982	Craig Stadler
1936	Horton Smith	1953	Ben Hogan	1968	Bob Goalby	1983	Seve Ballesteros
1937	Byron Nelson	1954	Sam Snead	1969	George Archer	1984	Ben Crenshaw
1938	Henry Picard	1955	Cary Middlecoff	1970	Billy Casper	1985	Bernhard Langer
1939	Ralph Guldahl	1956	Jack Burke	1971	Charles Coody	1986	Jack Nicklaus
1940	Jimmy Demaret	1957	Doug Ford	1972	Jack Nicklaus	1987	Larry Mize
1941	Craig Wood	1958	Arnold Palmer	1973	Tommy Aaron	1988	Sandy Lyle
1942	Byron Nelson	1959	Art Wall Jr.	1974	Gary Player	1989	Nick Faldo
1943-45	(Not played)	1960	Arnold Palmer	1975	Jack Nicklaus	1990	Nick Faldo
1946	Herman Keiser	1961	Gary Player	1976	Ray Floyd	1991	Ian Woosnam
1947	Jimmy Demaret	1962	Arnold Palmer	1977	Tom Watson	1992	Fred Couples
1948	Claude Harmon	1963	Jack Nicklaus	1978	Gary Player	1993	Bernhard Langer
1949	Sam Snead	1964	Arnold Palmer	1979	Fuzzy Zoeller	1994	Jose Maria Olazabal
1950	Jimmy Demaret	1965	Jack Nicklaus	1980	Seve Ballesteros	1995	Ben Crenshaw

British Open Winners

Year	Winner	Year	Winner	Year	Winner	Year	Winner
1931	Tommy Armour	1951	Max Faulkner	1966	Jack Nicklaus	1981	Bill Rogers
1932	Gene Sarazen	1952	Bobby Locke	1967	Roberto de Vicenzo	1982	Tom Watson
1933	Denny Shute	1953	Ben Hogan	1968	Gary Player	1983	Tom Watson
1934	Henry Cotton	1954	Peter Thomson	1969	Tony Jacklin	1984	Seve Ballesteros
1935	Alf Perry	1955	Peter Thomson	1970	Jack Nicklaus	1985	Sandy Lyle
1936	Alf Padgham	1956	Peter Thomson	1971	Lee Trevino	1986	Greg Norman
1937	T.H. Cotton	1957	Bobby Locke	1972	Lee Trevino	1987	Nick Faldo
1938	R.A. Whitcombe	1958	Peter Thomson	1973	Tom Weiskopf	1988	Seve Ballesteros
1939	Richard Burton	1959	Gary Player	1974	Gary Player	1989	Mark Calcavecchia
1940-45	(Not played)	1960	Kel Nagle	1975	Tom Watson	1990	Nick Faldo
1946	Sam Snead	1961	Arnold Palmer	1976	Johnny Miller	1991	Ian Baker-Finch
1947	Fred Daly	1962	Arnold Palmer	1977	Tom Watson	1992	Nick Faldo
1948	Henry Cotton	1963	Bob Charles	1978	Jack Nicklaus	1993	Greg Norman
1949	Bobby Locke	1964	Tony Lema	1979	Seve Ballesteros	1994	Nick Price
1950	Bobby Locke	1965	Peter Thomson	1980	Tom Watson	1995	John Daly

Professional Golf Tournaments in 1995
Men

Date	Event	Winner	Score	Prize
Jan. 8	Mercedes Championships, Carlsbad, CA.	Steve Elkington	*278	$180,000
Jan. 15	United Airlines Hawaiian Open, Honolulu, HI	John Morse	269	216,000
Jan. 22	Northern Telecom Open, Tucson, AZ	Phil Mickelson	269	225,000
Jan. 29	Phoenix Open, Scottsdale, AZ	Vijay Singh	*269	234,000
Feb. 5	AT&T National Pro-Am, Pebble Beach, CA	Peter Jacobsen	271	252,000
Feb. 12	Buick Invitational of CA, La Jolla, CA.	Peter Jacobsen	269	216,000
Feb. 19	Bob Hope Chrysler Classic, Bermuda Dunes, CA.	Kenny Perry	335	216,000
Feb. 26	Nissan Open, Pacific Palisades, CA	Corey Pavin	268	216,000
Mar. 5	Doral-Ryder Open, Miami, FL.	Nick Faldo	273	270,000
Mar. 12	Honda Classic, Ft. Lauderdale, FL	Mark O'Meara	275	216,000
Mar. 19	Nestle Invitational, Orlando, FL.	Loren Roberts	272	216,000
Mar. 26	THE PLAYERS Championship, Ponte Vedra Beach, FL	Lee Janzen	283	540,000
Apr. 2	Freeport-McMoRan Classic, New Orleans, LA	Davis Love III.	*274	216,000
Apr. 9	The Masters Tournament, Augusta, GA.	Ben Crenshaw	274	396,000
Apr. 16	MCI Classic, Hilton Head Island, SC	Bob Tway	*275	234,000
Apr. 23	Kmart Greater Greensboro Open, NC	Jim Gallagher, Jr.	274	270,000
Apr. 30	Shell Houston Open, The Woodlands, TX	Payne Stewart	*276	252,000
May 7	BellSouth Classic, Marietta, GA	Mark Calcavecchia	271	234,000
May 14	GTE Byron Nelson Classic, Irving, TX	Ernie Els	263	234,000
May 21	Buick Classic, Rye, NY	Vijay Singh	*278	216,000
May 28	Colonial National Invitation, Ft. Worth, TX	Tom Lehman	271	252,000
June 4	Memorial Tournament, Dublin, OH	Greg Norman	269	306,000
June 11	Kemper Open, Potomac, MD.	Lee Janzen	*272	252,000
June 18	U.S. Open, Southampton, NY.	Corey Pavin	280	350,000
June 25	Canon Greater Hartford Open, Cromwell, CT.	Greg Norman	267	216,000
July 2	FedEx St. Jude Classic, Memphis, TN.	Jim Gallagher, Jr.	267	225,000
July 9	Motorola Western Open, Lemont, IL	Billy Mayfair	279	360,000
July 16	Anheuser-Busch Golf Classic, Williamsburg, VA	Ted Tryba	272	198,000
July 23	British Open, Fife, Scotland	John Daly	*282	199,375
July 23	Deposit Guaranty Golf Classic, Madison, MS	Ed Dougherty	272	126,000
July 30	Ideon Classic, Sutton, MA	Fred Funk	268	180,000
Aug. 6	Buick Open, Grand Blanc, MI	Woody Austin	*270	216,000
Aug. 13	PGA Championship, Los Angeles, CA.	Steve Elkington	*267	360,000
Aug. 20	The Sprint International, Castle Rock, CO	Lee Janzen	34 pts	270,000
Aug. 27	NEC World Series of Golf, Akron, OH	Greg Norman	*278	360,000
Sept. 3	Greater Milwaukee Open, WI	Scott Hoch	269	180,000
Sept. 10	Bell Canadian Open, Oakville, Ontario	Mark O'Meara	*274	234,000
Sept. 17	B.C. Open, Endicott, NY.	Hal Sutton	269	180,000
Sept. 24	Quad City Classic, Coal Valley, IL.	D. A. Weibring	†197	180,000
Oct. 1	Buick Challenge, Pine Mountain, GA.	Fred Funk	272	180,000

Women

Date	Event	Winner	Score	Prize
Jan. 15	Chrysler-Plymouth Tournament of Champions, Orlando, FL	Dawn Coe-Jones	281	$115,000
Jan. 22	HEALTHSOUTH Inaugural, Lake Buena Vista, FL.	Pat Bradley	211	67,500
Feb. 18	Cup Noodles Hawaiian Ladies Open, Honolulu, HI	Barb Thomas	204	82,500
Mar. 12	PING/Welch's Championship, Tucson, AZ	Dottie Mochrie	278	67,500
Mar. 19	Standard Register PING Classic, Phoenix, AZ.	Laura Davies	280	105,000
Mar. 26	Nabisco Dinah Shore Classic, Rancho Mirage, CA	Nanci Bowen	285	127,500
Apr. 16	Pinewild Women's Championship, Pinehurst, NC	Rosie Jones	*211	97,500
Apr. 23	Chick-fil-A Charity Championship, Stockbridge, GA	Laura Davies	201	75,000
Apr. 30	Sprint Championship, Daytona, FL	Val Skinner	273	180,000
May 7	Sara Lee Classic, Old Hickory, TN	Michelle McGann	202	78,750
May 14	McDonald's LPGA Championship, Wilmington, DE	Kelly Robbins	274	180,000
May 21	The Star Bank LPGA Classic, Dayton, OH	Chris Johnson	210	75,000
May 28	LPGA Corning Classic, Corning, NY.	Alison Nicholas	275	82,500
May 28	JCPenney/LPGA Skins Game, Frisco, TX.	Dottie Mochrie	8 skins	290,000
June 4	Oldsmobile Classic, East Lansing, MI	Dale Eggeling	274	90,000
June 11	First Bank-Edina Realty Classic, Brooklyn Park, MN	Julie Larsen	205	75,000
June 18	Rochester International, Pittsford, NY.	Patty Sheehan	278	82,500
June 25	ShopRite LPGA Classic, Somers Pt., NJ.	Betsy King	204	97,500
July 2	Youngstown-Warren LPGA Classic, Warren, OH.	Michelle McGann	*205	82,500
July 9	Jamie Farr Toledo Classic, Sylvania, OH	Kathryn Marshall	205	75,000
July 16	U.S. Women's Open, Colorado Springs, CO	Annika Sorenstam	278	175,000
July 23	JAL Big Apple Classic, New Rochelle, NY.	Tracy Kerdyk	273	105,000
July 30	Friendly's Classic, Agawam, MA	Becky Iverson	276	75,000
Aug. 6	McCall's LPGA Classic, Stratton Mountain, VT	Dottie Mochrie	204	75,000
Aug. 13	PING/Welch's Championship, Canton, MA	Beth Daniel	271	67,500
Aug. 20	Weetabix Women's British Open, Milton Keynes, Eng.	Karrie Webb.	278	92,400
Aug. 27	Du Maurier Ltd. Classic, Pointe-Claire, Que.	Jenny Lidback	280	150,000
Sept. 4	State Farm Rail Classic, Springfield, IL.	Mary Beth Zimmerman	*206	82,500
Sept. 10	PING-AT&T Wireless Servs. Championship, Portland, OR	Alison Nicholas	207	75,000
Sept. 17	SAFECO Classic, Kent, WA.	Patty Sheehan	274	75,000
Sept. 24	GHP Heartland Classic, St. Louis, MO	Annika Sorenstam	278	78,750
Oct. 1	Fieldcrest Cannon Classic, Huntersville, NC	Gail Graham	273	75,000

* Won playoff. † Shortened due to weather.

Ryder Cup in 1995

A team of professional golfers from Europe defeated the U.S. team, 14½-13½, at Oak Hill Country Club in Rochester, NY, to take the Ryder Cup, Sept. 22-24. Europe overcame deficits of 5-3 and 9-7. It was the first time Europe had won the biennial match-play competition since 1989, and only the second time it had won on U.S. soil.

U.S. Women's Open Golf Champions

Year	Winner	Year	Winner	Year	Winner	Year	Winner
1948	"Babe" Zaharias	1960	Betsy Rawls	1972	Susie Maxwell Berning	1984	Hollis Stacy
1949	Louise Suggs	1961	Mickey Wright	1973	Susie Maxwell Berning	1985	Kathy Baker
1950	"Babe" Zaharias	1962	Murle Lindstrom	1974	Sandra Haynie	1986	Jane Geddes
1951	Betsy Rawls	1963	Mary Mills	1975	Sandra Palmer	1987	Laura Davies
1952	Louise Suggs	1964	Mickey Wright	1976	JoAnne Carner	1988	Liselotte Neumann
1953	Betsy Rawls	1965	Carol Mann	1977	Hollis Stacy	1989	Betsy King
1954	"Babe" Zaharias	1966	Sandra Spuzich	1978	Hollis Stacy	1990	Betsy King
1955	Fay Crocker	1967	Catherine Lacoste*	1979	Jerilyn Britz	1991	Meg Mallon
1956	Mrs. K. Cornelius	1968	Susie Maxwell Berning	1980	Amy Alcott	1992	Patty Sheehan
1957	Betsy Rawls	1969	Donna Caponi	1981	Pat Bradley	1993	Lauri Merten
1958	Mickey Wright	1970	Donna Caponi	1982	Janet Alex	1994	Patty Sheehan
1959	Mickey Wright	1971	JoAnne Carner	1983	Jan Stephenson	1995	Annika Sorenstam

*Amateur

PGA Leading Money Winners

Year	Player	Dollars	Year	Player	Dollars	Year	Player	Dollars
1946	Ben Hogan	$42,556	1963	Arnold Palmer	$128,230	1979	Tom Watson	$462,636
1947	Jimmy Demaret	27,936	1964	Jack Nicklaus	113,284	1980	Tom Watson	530,808
1948	Ben Hogan	36,812	1965	Jack Nicklaus	140,752	1981	Tom Kite	375,699
1949	Sam Snead	31,593	1966	Billy Casper	121,944	1982	Craig Stadler	446,462
1950	Sam Snead	35,758	1967	Jack Nicklaus	188,988	1983	Hal Sutton	426,668
1951	Lloyd Mangrum	26,088	1968	Billy Casper	205,168	1984	Tom Watson	476,260
1952	Julius Boros	37,032	1969	Frank Beard	175,223	1985	Curtis Strange	542,321
1953	Lew Worsham	34,002	1970	Lee Trevino	157,037	1986	Greg Norman	653,296
1954	Bob Toski	65,819	1971	Jack Nicklaus	244,490	1987	Curtis Strange	925,941
1955	Julius Boros	65,121	1972	Jack Nicklaus	320,542	1988	Curtis Strange	1,147,644
1956	Ted Kroll	72,835	1973	Jack Nicklaus	308,362	1989	Tom Kite	1,395,278
1957	Dick Mayer	65,835	1974	Johnny Miller	353,201	1990	Greg Norman	1,165,477
1958	Arnold Palmer	42,407	1975	Jack Nicklaus	323,149	1991	Corey Pavin	979,430
1959	Art Wall, Jr.	53,167	1976	Jack Nicklaus	266,438	1992	Fred Couples	1,344,188
1960	Arnold Palmer	75,262	1977	Tom Watson	310,653	1993	Nick Price	1,478,557
1961	Gary Player	64,540	1978	Tom Watson	362,429	1994	Nick Price	1,499,927
1962	Arnold Palmer	81,448						

LPGA Leading Money Winners

Year	Player	Dollars	Year	Player	Dollars	Year	Player	Dollars
1954	Patty Berg	$16,011	1968	Kathy Whitworth	$48,379	1982	JoAnne Carner	$310,399
1955	Patty Berg	16,492	1969	Carol Mann	49,152	1983	JoAnne Carner	291,404
1956	Marlene Hagge	20,235	1970	Kathy Whitworth	30,235	1984	Betsy King	266,771
1957	Patty Berg	16,272	1971	Kathy Whitworth	41,181	1985	Nancy Lopez	416,472
1958	Beverly Hanson	12,629	1972	Kathy Whitworth	65,063	1986	Pat Bradley	492,021
1959	Betsy Rawls	26,774	1973	Kathy Whitworth	82,854	1987	Ayako Okamoto	466,034
1960	Louise Suggs	16,892	1974	JoAnne Carner	87,094	1988	Sherri Turner	347,255
1961	Mickey Wright	22,236	1975	Sandra Palmer	94,805	1989	Betsy King	654,132
1962	Mickey Wright	21,641	1976	Judy Rankin	150,734	1990	Beth Daniel	863,578
1963	Mickey Wright	31,269	1977	Judy Rankin	122,890	1991	Pat Bradley	763,118
1964	Mickey Wright	29,800	1978	Nancy Lopez	189,813	1992	Dottie Mochrie	693,335
1965	Kathy Whitworth	28,658	1979	Nancy Lopez	215,987	1993	Betsy King	595,992
1966	Kathy Whitworth	33,517	1980	Beth Daniel	231,000	1994	Laura Davies	687,201
1967	Kathy Whitworth	32,937	1981	Beth Daniel	206,977			

Rifle and Pistol Individual Championships in 1995

Source: National Rifle Association

National Outdoor Rifle and Pistol Championships

Smallbore Rifle Prone—SGT Thomas A. Tamas, USA, Ft. Benning, GA, 6393-524X

Civilian Smallbore Rifle Prone—T.R. Bishop, Lenoir, NC, 6389-487X

Woman Smallbore Rifle Prone—Edie P. Reynolds, Raleigh, NC, 6387-502X

Smallbore Rifle NRA 3-Position—CPL Kenneth Johnson, USA, Columbus, GA, 2294-97X

Civilian Smallbore Rifle NRA 3-Position—Kenneth Benyo, New Tripoli, PA, 2269-79X

Woman Smallbore Rifle NRA 3-Position—Jean A. Foster, Bozeman, MT, 2259-78X

High Power Rifle—Mitchell Maxberry, Philport, KY, 2374-110X

Civilian High Power Rifle—Mitchell Maxberry, Philport, KY, 2374-110X

Woman High Power Rifle—Sandy L. Pagel, Mazomanie, WI, 2360-84X

Pistol—James R. Lenardson, Toledo, OH, 2639-113X

Civilian Pistol—James R. Lenardson, Toledo, OH, 2639-113X

Woman Pistol—SFC Ruby Fox, USAR, Parker, AZ, 2592-100X

National Indoor Rifle and Pistol Championships

Smallbore Rifle 4-Position—Jordan Daniel, Franktown, CO 800

Woman Smallbore Rifle 4-Position—Wanda R. Jewel, Columbus, GA, 797

Smallbore Rifle NRA 3-Position—Matthew P. Suggs, Columbus, GA, 1188

Woman Smallbore Rifle NRA 3-Position—Karen E. Monez, Weatherford, TX, 1178

International Smallbore Rifle—David Johnson, Colorado Springs, CO, 1185

Woman International Smallbore Rifle—Elizabeth S. Bourland, Wichita Falls, KS, 1177

Air Rifle—David Johnson, Colorado Springs, CO, 591

Woman Air Rifle— Elizabeth S. Bourland, Wichita Falls, KS, 590

Conventional Pistol—Gregory J. Derr, Marshfield, MA 885

Woman Conventional Pistol—Rosemary H. Lyman, Whitefish, MT, 863

International Free Pistol—Richard D. McConnell, Clifton Park, NY, 542

Woman International Free Pistol—Janine Lavallee, New London, CT, 486

International Standard Pistol—Scott Lorenz, Lynwood, WA, 573

Woman International Standard Pistol— Janine Lavallee, New London, CT, 531

Air Pistol—Warren M. Kelly, Charleston AFB, SC, 574

Woman Air Pistol—Rhonda Barush, Columbus GA, 566

NRA Bianchi Cup National Action Pistol Championships

Action Pistol—John H. Pride, La Verne, CA, 1920

Woman Action Pistol—Dewi Hazeltine, Lyons, Australia, 1908

Junior Action Pistol—Lee M. Healey, Hay, Australia, 1895

Notable Sports Personalities

Henry (Hank) Aaron, b. 1934: Milwaukee-Atlanta outfielder hit record 755 home runs; led NL 4 times.

Kareem Abdul-Jabbar, b. 1947: Milwaukee, L.A. Lakers center; MVP 6 times; leading scorer twice; playoff MVP, 1971, 1985; all-time leading NBA scorer.

Grover Cleveland Alexander, (1887-1950): pitcher won 374 NL games; pitched 16 shutouts, 1916.

Muhammad Ali, b. 1942: 3-time heavyweight champion.

Mario Andretti, b. 1940: won Indy 500, 1969; Grand Prix champ, 1978.

Eddie Arcaro, b. 1916: jockey rode 4,779 winners including the Kentucky Derby 5 times; the Preakness and Belmont Stakes 6 times each.

Henry Armstrong, (1912-1988): boxer held feather-, welter-, lightweight titles simultaneously, 1937-38.

Arthur Ashe, (1943-1993): U.S. singles champ, 1968; Wimbledon champ, 1975.

Red Auerbach, b. 1917: coached Boston Celtics to 9 NBA championships.

Ernie Banks, b. 1931: Chicago Cubs slugger hit 512 NL homers; twice MVP.

Roger Bannister, b. 1929: Briton ran first sub 4-minute mile, May 6, 1954.

Rick Barry, b. 1944: NBA scoring leader, 1967; ABA, 1969.

Sammy Baugh, b. 1914: Washington Redskins quarterback held numerous records upon retirement after 16 pro seasons.

Elgin Baylor, b. 1934: L.A. Lakers forward; 1st team all-star 10 times.

Boris Becker, b. 1967: German tennis star; won U.S. Open 1989; Wimbledon champ 3 times.

Jean Beliveau, b. 1931: Montreal Canadiens center scored 507 goals; twice MVP.

Johnny Bench, b. 1947: Cincinnati Reds catcher; MVP twice; led league in home runs twice, RBIs 3 times.

Patty Berg, b. 1918: won more than 80 golf tournaments; AP Woman Athlete-of-the-Year 3 times.

Yogi Berra, b. 1925: N.Y. Yankees catcher; MVP 3 times; played in 14 World Series.

Raymond Berry, b. 1933: Baltimore Colts receiver caught 631 passes.

Matt Biondi, b. 1965: swimmer won 5 gold medals at 1988 Olympics.

Larry Bird, b. 1956: Boston Celtics forward; chosen MVP 1984-86; Playoff MVP, 1984, 1986.

George Blanda, b. 1927: quarterback, kicker; 26 years as active player, scoring record 2,002 points.

Wade Boggs, b. 1958: AL batting champ, 1983, 1985-88.

Barry Bonds, b. 1964: outfielder was NL MVP 3 times.

Bjorn Borg, b. 1956: led Sweden to first Davis Cup, 1975; Wimbledon champion 5 times.

Mike Bossy, b. 1957: N.Y. Islanders right wing scored more than 50 goals 8 times.

Ray Bourque, b. 1960: Boston Bruins defenseman won Norris Trophy 4 times.

Terry Bradshaw, b. 1948; Pittsburgh Steelers quarterback led team to 4 Super Bowl titles.

George Brett, b. 1953: Kansas City Royals infielder led AL in batting, 1976, 1980, 1990; MVP, 1980.

Lou Brock, b. 1939: St. Louis Cardinals outfielder stole NL record 118 bases, 1974; led NL 8 times.

Jim Brown, b. 1936: Cleveland Browns fullback ran for 12,312 career yards; MVP 3 times.

Paul Brown, (1908-1991), football owner, coach; led Cleveland Browns to 3 NFL championships.

Paul "Bear" Bryant, (1913-1983), college football coach with 323 victories.

Sergei Bubka, b. 1963: Ukrainian pole vaulter; first to clear 20 feet both indoors and outdoors.

Maria Bueno, b. 1939: U.S. singles champ 4 times; Wimbledon champ 3 times.

Dick Butkus, b. 1942: Chicago Bears linebacker twice chosen best NFL defensive player.

Dick Button, b. 1929: figure skater won 1948, 1952 Olympic gold medals; world titlist, 1948-52.

Walter Camp, (1859-1925): Yale football player, coach, athletic director; established many rules; promoted All-America designations.

Roy Campanella, (1921-1993): Brooklyn Dodgers catcher; MVP 3 times.

Earl Campbell, b. 1955: NFL running back; MVP 1978-80.

Rod Carew, b. 1945: AL infielder won 7 batting titles; MVP, 1977.

Steve Carlton, b. 1944: NL pitcher won 20 games 5 times, Cy Young award 4 times.

Billy Casper, b. 1931: PGA Player-of-the-Year 3 times; U.S. Open champ twice.

Wilt Chamberlain, b. 1936: center was NBA leading scorer 7 times; MVP 4 times.

Bobby Clarke, b. 1949: Philadelphia Flyers center led team to 2 Stanley Cup championships; MVP 3 times.

Roger Clemens, b. 1962: Boston Red Sox pitcher; AL MVP 1986; Cy Young award 1986, 1987, 1991.

Roberto Clemente, (1934-1972): Pittsburgh Pirates outfielder won 4 batting titles; MVP, 1966.

Ty Cobb, (1886-1961): Detroit Tigers outfielder had record .367 lifetime batting average, 12 batting titles.

Sebastian Coe, b. 1956: Briton won Olympic 1,500-meter run, 1980, 1984.

Nadia Comaneci, b. 1961: Romanian gymnast won 3 gold medals, achieved 7 perfect scores, 1976 Olympics.

Maureen Connolly, (1934-1969): won tennis "grand slam," 1953; AP Woman-Athlete-of-the-Year 3 times.

Jimmy Connors, b. 1952: U.S. singles champ 5 times; Wimbledon champ twice.

James J. Corbett, (1866-1933): heavyweight champion, 1892-97; credited with being the first "scientific" boxer.

Angel Cordero, b. 1942: leading money winner, 1976, 1982-83; rode 3 Kentucky Derby winners.

Margaret Smith Court, b. 1942: Australian won U.S. singles championship 5 times; Wimbledon champ 3 times.

Bob Cousy, b. 1928: Boston Celtics guard led team to 6 NBA championships; MVP, 1957.

Dizzy Dean, (1911-1974): colorful pitcher for St. Louis Cardinals "Gashouse Gang" in the '30s; MVP, 1934.

Jack Dempsey, (1895-1983): heavyweight champ, 1919-26.

Eric Dickerson, b. 1960: running back ran for NFL record 2,105 yds., 1984; led NFC 3 times, AFC twice.

Joe DiMaggio, b. 1914: N.Y. Yankees outfielder hit safely in record 56 consecutive games, 1941; AL MVP 3 times.

Leo Durocher, (1906-1991): manager won 3 NL pennants.

Stefan Edberg, b. 1966: U.S. singles champ 1991, 1992; Wimbledon champ 1988, 1990.

Gertrude Ederle, b. 1906: first woman to swim English Channel, broke existing men's record, 1926.

Julius Erving, b. 1950: MVP and leading scorer in ABA 3 times; NBA MVP, 1981.

Phil Esposito, b. 1942: NHL scoring leader 5 times.

Chris Evert, b. 1954: U.S. singles champ 6 times, Wimbledon champ 3 times.

Patrick Ewing, b. 1962: center led Georgetown Univ. to 1984 NCAA championship.

Ray Ewry, (1873-1937): track and field star won 8 gold medals, 1900, 1904, and 1908 Olympics.

Nick Faldo, 1957: British golfer won Masters, 1989-90; British Open 3 times.

Juan Fangio, (1911-1995): World Grand Prix champion 5 times.

Bob Feller, b. 1918: Cleveland Indians pitcher won 266 games; pitched 3 no-hitters, 12 one-hitters.

Peggy Fleming, b. 1948: world figure skating champion, 1966-68; gold medalist 1968 Olympics.

Whitey Ford, b. 1928: N.Y. Yankees pitcher won record 10 World Series games.

George Foreman, b. 1949: heavyweight champion, 1973-74, 1994-95; at 45, the oldest to win a heavyweight title.

Dick Fosbury, b. 1947: high jumper won 1968 Olympic gold medal; developed the "Fosbury Flop."

Jimmie Foxx, (1907-1967): Red Sox, Athletics slugger; MVP 3 times; triple crown, 1933.

A.J. Foyt, b. 1935: won Indy 500 4 times; U.S. Auto Club champ 7 times.

Joe Frazier, b. 1944: heavyweight champion, 1970-73.

Lou Gehrig, (1903-1941): N.Y. Yankees 1st baseman played 2,130 consecutive games; MVP, 1927, 1936; triple crown, 1934; AL record 184 RBIs, 1931.

George Gervin, b. 1952: leading NBA scorer, 1978-80, 1982.

Althea Gibson, b. 1927: twice U.S. and Wimbledon singles champ.

Bob Gibson, b. 1935: St. Louis Cardinals pitcher won Cy Young award twice; struck out 3,117 batters.

Frank Gifford, b. 1930: N.Y. Giants back; MVP, 1956.

Pancho Gonzales, (1928-1995): tennis great was U.S. singles champ, 1947-48.

Steffi Graf, b. 1969: German won tennis "grand slam," 1988; U.S. champ 4 times; Wimbledon champ 6 times.

Otto Graham, b. 1921: Cleveland Browns quarterback; all-pro 4 times.

Red Grange, (1903-1991): All-America at Univ. of Illinois 1923-25; played for Chicago Bears, 1925-35.

Joe Greene, b. 1946: Pittsburgh Steelers lineman; twice NFL outstanding defensive player.

Wayne Gretzky, b. 1961: all-time leading scorer in NHL history; MVP, 1980-87, 1989.

Florence Griffith Joyner, b. 1959: sprinter won 3 gold medals at 1988 Olympics.

Lefty Grove, (1900-1975): pitcher won 300 AL games; 20-game winner 8 times.

Tony Gwynn, b. 1960: 6-time NL batting champ, 1984, 1987-89, 1994-95.

Walter Hagen, (1892-1969): won PGA championship 5 times; British Open 4 times.

George Halas, (1895-1983): founder-coach of Chicago Bears; won 5 NFL championships.

Bill Hartack, b. 1932: jockey rode 5 Kentucky Derby winners.

John Havlicek, b. 1940: Boston Celtics forward scored more than 26,000 NBA points.

Rickey Henderson, b. 1958: AL outfielder stole record 130 bases, 1982; record lifetime steals; AL MVP, 1990.

Sonja Henie, (1912-1969): world champion figure skater, 1927-36; Olympic gold medalist, 1928, 1932, 1936.

Ben Hogan, b. 1912: won 4 U.S. Open championships, 2 PGA, 2 Masters.

Rogers Hornsby, (1896-1963): NL 2d baseman batted record .424 in 1924; twice won triple crown; batting leader, 1920-25.

Paul Hornung, b. 1935: Green Bay Packers runner-placekicker scored record 176 points, 1960.

Gordie Howe, b. 1928: hockey forward; NHL MVP 6 times.

Carl Hubbell, (1903-1988): N.Y. Giants pitcher; 20-game winner 5 consecutive years, 1933-37.

Bobby Hull, b. 1939: NHL all-star 10 times.

Brett Hull, b. 1964: St. Louis Blues forward led NHL in goals, 1990-92; MVP 1991.

Catfish Hunter, b. 1946: pitched perfect game, 1968; 20-game winner 5 times.

Don Hutson, b. 1913: Green Bay Packers receiver caught 99 NFL touchdown passes.

Reggie Jackson, b. 1946: slugger led AL in home runs 4 times; MVP, 1973; hit 5 World Series home runs, 1977.

Jack Johnson, (1878-1946): heavyweight champion, 1910-15.

Jimmy Johnson, b. 1943: football coach, led Univ. of Miami (FL) to national championship in 1987, and Dallas Cowboys to consecutive Super Bowl wins, 1993-94.

Magic Johnson, b. 1959: NBA MVP 1987, 1989, 1990; Playoff MVP 1980, 1982, 1987; 2d in career assists.

Walter Johnson, (1887-1946): Washington Senators pitcher won 416 games; record 110 shutouts.

Bobby Jones, (1902-1971): won "grand slam of golf" 1930; U.S. Amateur champ 5 times, U.S. Open champ 4 times.

Deacon Jones, b. 1938: L.A. Rams lineman; twice NFL outstanding defensive player.

Michael Jordan, b. 1963: NBA leading scorer, 1987-93; MVP, 1988, 1991, 1992; Playoff MVP, 1991, 1992, 1993.

Jackie Joyner-Kersee, b. 1962; Olympic gold medalist in heptathlon, 1988, 1992.

Sonny Jurgensen, b. 1934: quarterback named all-pro 5 times.

Duke Kahanamoku, (1890-1968): swimmer won 1912, 1920 Olympic gold medals in 100-meter freestyle; surfing pioneer.

Harmon Killebrew, b. 1936: Minnesota Twins slugger led AL in home runs 6 times; 573 lifetime.

Jean Claude Killy, b. 1943: French skier won 3 1968 Olympic gold medals.

Ralph Kiner, b. 1922: Pittsburgh Pirates slugger led NL in home runs 7 consecutive years, 1946-52.

Billie Jean King, b. 1943: U.S. singles champ 4 times; Wimbledon champ 6 times.

Bob Knight, b. 1940: Indiana U. basketball coach led team to NCAA championships, 1976, 1981, 1987.

Olga Korbut, b. 1955: Soviet gymnast won 3 1972 Olympic gold medals.

Sandy Koufax, b. 1935: Dodgers pitcher won Cy Young award 3 times; lowest ERA in NL, 1962-66; pitched 4 no-hitters, one a perfect game.

Mike Krzyzewski, b. 1947: basketball coach, led Duke Univ. to consecutive national championships, 1991-92.

Guy Lafleur, b. 1951: forward led NHL in scoring 3 times; MVP, 1977, 1978.

Tom Landry, b. 1924: Dallas Cowboys head coach 1960-88.

Rod Laver, b. 1938: Australian won tennis "grand slam," 1962, 1969; Wimbledon champ 4 times.

Mario Lemieux, b. 1965: NHL leading scorer, 1988-89, 1992-93; MVP, 1988, 1993; Playoff MVP, 1991, 1992.

Ivan Lendl, b. 1960: U.S. singles champ, 1985-87.

Sugar Ray Leonard, b. 1956: boxer held titles in 5 different weight classes.

Carl Lewis, b. 1961: track and field star won 8 Olympic gold medals in sprinting and the long jump.

Vince Lombardi, (1913-1970): Green Bay Packers coach led team to 5 NFL championships and 2 Super Bowl victories.

Joe Louis, (1914-1981): heavyweight champion, 1937-49.

Sid Luckman, b. 1916: Chicago Bears quarterback led team to 4 NFL championships; MVP, 1943.

Connie Mack, (1862-1956): Philadelphia Athletics manager, 1901-50; won 9 pennants, 5 championships.

Greg Maddux, b. 1966: first pitcher ever to win 3 consecutive Cy Young awards, 1992-94.

Bill Madlock, b. 1951: NL batting leader 4 times.

Moses Malone, b. 1955: NBA center was MVP 1979, 1982, 1983.

Mickey Mantle, (1931-1995): N.Y. Yankees outfielder; triple crown, 1956; 18 World Series home runs; MVP 3 times.

Pete Maravich (1948-1988): guard scored NCAA record 44.2 ppg during collegiate career; led NBA in scoring, 1977.

Rocky Marciano, (1923-1969): heavyweight champion, 1952-56; retired undefeated.

Dan Marino, b. 1961: Miami Dolphins quarterback passed for NFL record 5,084 yds and 48 touchdowns, 1984.

Roger Maris, (1934-1985): N.Y. Yankees outfielder hit record 61 home runs, 1961; MVP, 1960 and 1961.

Eddie Mathews, b. 1931: Milwaukee-Atlanta 3d baseman hit 512 career home runs.

Christy Mathewson, (1880-1925): N.Y. Giants pitcher won 373 games.

Bob Mathias, b. 1930: decathlon gold medalist, 1948, 1952.

Don Mattingly, b. 1961: N.Y. Yankees 1st baseman won 1984 AL batting title; MVP, 1985.

Willie Mays, b. 1931: N.Y.-S.F. Giants center fielder hit 660 home runs; led NL 4 times; twice MVP.

Willie McCovey, b. 1938: S.F. Giants slugger hit 521 home runs; led NL 3 times; MVP, 1969.

John McEnroe, b. 1959: U.S. singles champ, 1979-81, 1984; Wimbledon champ, 1981, 1983-84.

John McGraw, (1873-1934): N.Y. Giants manager led team to 10 pennants, 3 championships.

Mark Messier, b. 1961: center chosen NHL MVP, 1990 and 1992; Conn Smythe Trophy, 1984.

George Mikan, b. 1924: Minn. Lakers center considered the best basketball player of the first half of the century.

Stan Mikita, b. 1940: Chicago Black Hawks center led NHL in scoring 4 times; MVP twice.

Joe Montana, b. 1956: S.F. 49ers quarterback was Super Bowl MVP, 1982, 1985, 1990.

Archie Moore, b. 1913: world light-heavyweight champion, 1952-62.

Howie Morenz, (1902-1937): Montreal Canadiens forward considered the best hockey player of the first half of the century.

Joe Morgan, b. 1943: National League MVP, 1975, 1976.

Thurman Munson, (1947-1979): N.Y. Yankees catcher; MVP, 1976.

Eddie Murray, b. 1956: slugger led AL in home runs and RBIs, 1981; 3,000+ lifetime hits; 475+ lifetime home runs.

Stan Musial, b. 1920: St. Louis Cardinals star won 7 NL batting titles; MVP 3 times.

Bronko Nagurski, (1908-1990): Chicago Bears fullback and tackle; gained more than 4,000 yds. rushing.

Joe Namath, b. 1943: N.Y. Jets quarterback was Super Bowl MVP, 1969.

Martina Navratilova, b. 1956: Wimbledon champ 9 times, U.S. champ 1983-84, 1986-87.

Byron Nelson, b. 1912: won 11 consecutive golf tournaments in 1945; twice Masters and PGA titlist.

Ernie Nevers, (1903-1976): Stanford star selected the best college fullback to play between 1919-69.

John Newcombe, b. 1943: Australian twice U.S. singles champ; Wimbledon titlist 3 times.

Jack Nicklaus, b. 1940: PGA Player-of-the-Year, 1967, 1972; leading money winner 8 times; won Masters 6 times.

Chuck Noll, b. 1931: coach led Pittsburgh Steelers to 4 Super Bowl titles.

Paavo Nurmi, (1897-1973): Finnish distance runner won 6 Olympic gold medals, 1920, 1924, 1928.

Al Oerter, b. 1936: discus thrower won gold medal at 4 consecutive Olympics, 1956-68.

Hakeem Olajuwon, b. 1963: Houston Rockets center was NBA MVP 1994, Playoffs MVP 1994-95

Bobby Orr, b. 1948: Boston Bruins defenseman; Norris Trophy 8 times; led NHL in scoring twice, assists 5 times.

Mel Ott, (1909-1958): N.Y. Giants outfielder hit 511 home runs; led NL 6 times.

Jesse Owens, (1913-1980): track and field star won 4 1936 Olympic gold medals.

Satchel Paige, (1906-1982): pitcher starred in Negro leagues, 1924-48; entered major leagues at age 42.

Arnold Palmer, b. 1929: golf's first $1 million winner; won 4 Masters, 2 British Opens.

Jim Palmer, b. 1945: Baltimore Orioles pitcher; Cy Young award 3 times; 20-game winner 8 times.

Floyd Patterson, b. 1935: twice heavyweight champion.

Walter Payton, b. 1954: Chicago Bears running back has most rushing yards in NFL history; leading NFC rusher, 1976-80.

Pele, b. 1940: Brazilian soccer star scored 1,281 goals during 22-year career.

Bob Pettit, b. 1932: first NBA player to score 20,000 points; twice NBA scoring leader.

Richard Petty, b. 1937: NASCAR national champ 7 times; 7-time Daytona 500 winner.

Laffit Pincay Jr., b. 1946: leading money-winning jockey, 1970-74, 1979.

Jacques Plante, (1929-1986): goalie, 7 Vezina trophies; first goalie to wear a mask in a game.

Kirby Puckett, b. 1961: Minn. Twins outfielder won AL batting title, 1989; led AL in hits, 1987-89, 1992; RBIs, 1994.

Willis Reed, b. 1942: N.Y. Knicks center; MVP, 1970; Playoff MVP, 1970, 1973.

Jerry Rice, b. 1962: S.F. 49ers receiver; Super Bowl MVP, 1989; NFL record for career touchdowns.

Jim Rice, b. 1953: Boston Red Sox outfielder led AL in home runs, 1977-78, 1983; MVP 1978.

Maurice Richard, b. 1921: Montreal Canadiens forward scored 544 regular season goals, 82 playoff goals.

Branch Rickey, (1881-1965): executive helped break baseball's color barrier, 1947; initiated farm system, 1919.

Pat Riley, b. 1945: coached L.A. Lakers to 4 NBA titles.

Cal Ripken Jr., b. 1960: Baltimore Orioles shortstop; AL MVP 1983, 1991; broke Lou Gehrig's record for most consecutive games played, 1995.

Oscar Robertson, b. 1938: guard averaged career 25.7 points per game; 3d most career assists; MVP, 1964.

Brooks Robinson, b. 1937: Baltimore Orioles 3d baseman played in 4 World Series; MVP, 1964.

Frank Robinson, b. 1935: slugger was MVP in both NL and AL; triple crown, 1966; 586 lifetime home runs; first black manager in majors.

Jackie Robinson, (1919-1972): broke baseball's color barrier with Brooklyn Dodgers, 1947; MVP, 1949.

Sugar Ray Robinson, (1920-1989): middleweight champion 5 times, welterweight champion.

Knute Rockne, (1888-1931): Notre Dame football coach, 1918-31; revolutionized game by stressing forward pass.

Pete Rose, b. 1941: won 3 NL batting titles; hit safely in 44 consecutive games, 1978; has most major league hits.

Wilma Rudolph, (1940-1994): sprinter won 3 1960 Olympic gold medals.

Bill Russell, b. 1934: Boston Celtics center led team to 11 NBA titles; MVP 5 times; first black coach of major pro sports team.

Babe Ruth, (1895-1948): N.Y. Yankees outfielder hit 60 home runs, 1927; 714 lifetime; led AL 12 times.

Johnny Rutherford, b. 1938: auto racer won Indy 500 3 times.

Nolan Ryan, b. 1947: pitcher struck out record 383 batters, 1973; record 5,714 career; pitched record 7 no-hitters; won 324 major league games.

Bret Saberhagen, b. 1964: pitcher won AL Cy Young award, 1985, 1989; World Series MVP, 1985.

Pete Sampras, b. 1971: won U.S. Open and Wimbledon 3 times each.

Gene Sarazen, b. 1902: won PGA championship 3 times, U.S. Open twice; developer of sand wedge.

Gale Sayers, b. 1943: Chicago Bears back twice led NFL in rushing.

Mike Schmidt, b. 1949: Phillies 3d baseman led NL in home runs 8 times; 548 lifetime; NL MVP, 1980, 1981, 1986.

Tom Seaver, b. 1944: pitcher won NL Cy Young award 3 times; won 311 major league games.

Monica Seles, b. 1973; U.S. Open champ 1991, 1992.

Bill Shoemaker, b. 1931: jockey rode 3 Kentucky Derby and 5 Belmont Stakes winners; leading career money winner.

Eddie Shore, (1902-1985): Boston Bruins defenseman; MVP 4 times, first-team all-star 7 times.

Don Shula, b. 1930: all-time winningest NFL coach.

Al Simmons, (1902-1956): AL outfielder batted .334 lifetime.

O.J. Simpson, b. 1947: running back rushed for 2,003 yds., 1973; AFC leading rusher 4 times.

George Sisler, (1893-1973): St. Louis Browns 1st baseman had record 257 hits, 1920; batted .340 lifetime.

Billy Smith, b. 1950: N.Y. Islanders goalie led team to 4 Stanley Cup championships.

Dean Smith, b. 1931: U. of North Carolina basketball coach has most career NCAA Division I victories.

Emmitt Smith, b. 1969: Dallas Cowboys running back led NFL in rushing, 1991-93; NFL and Super Bowl MVP, 1993.

Lee Smith, b. 1957: relief pitcher, all-time saves leader.

Sam Snead, b. 1912: PGA and Masters champ 3 times each.

Warren Spahn, b. 1921: pitcher won 363 NL games; 20-game winner 13 times; Cy Young award, 1957.

Tris Speaker, (1885-1958): AL outfielder batted .344 over 22 seasons; hit record 793 career doubles.

Mark Spitz, b. 1950: swimmer won 7 1972 Olympic gold medals.

Amos Alonzo Stagg, (1862-1965): coached Univ. of Chicago football team for 41 years, including 5 undefeated seasons; introduced huddle, man-in-motion, and end-around play.

Bart Starr, b. 1934: Green Bay Packers quarterback led team to 5 NFL titles and 2 Super Bowl victories.

Roger Staubach, b. 1942: Dallas Cowboys quarterback; leading NFC passer 5 times.

Casey Stengel, (1890-1975): managed Yankees to 10 pennants, 7 championships, 1949-60.

Jackie Stewart, b. 1939: Scot auto racer retired with 27 Grand Prix victories.

John L. Sullivan, (1858-1918): last bareknuckle heavyweight champion, 1882-1892.

Fran Tarkenton, b. 1940: quarterback holds career passing records for touchdowns, yardage.

Lawrence Taylor, b. 1959: linebacker led N.Y. Giants to 2 Super Bowl titles; played in 10 Pro Bowls.

Gustavo Thoeni, b. 1951: Italian 4-time world alpine ski champ.

Jim Thorpe, (1888-1953): football All-America, 1911, 1912; won pentathlon and decathlon, 1912 Olympics.

Bill Tilden, (1893-1953): U.S. singles champ 7 times; played on 11 Davis Cup teams.

Y.A. Tittle, b. 1926: N.Y. Giants quarterback; MVP, 1961, 1963.

Lee Trevino, b. 1939: won the U.S. and British Open championships twice.

Bryan Trottier, b. 1956: center played on 6 Stanley Cup championship teams.

Wyomia Tyus, b. 1945: sprinter won 1964, 1968 Olympic 100-meter dash.

Johnny Unitas, b. 1933: Baltimore Colts quarterback passed for more than 40,000 yds.; MVP, 1957, 1967.

Al Unser, b. 1939: Indy 500 winner 4 times.

Bobby Unser, b. 1934: Indy 500 winner 3 times.

Norm Van Brocklin, (1926-1983): quarterback passed for game record 554 yds., 1951; MVP, 1960.

Honus Wagner, (1874-1955): Pittsburgh Pirates shortstop won 8 NL batting titles.

Tom Watson, b. 1949: golfer won British Open 5 times.

Johnny Weissmuller, (1903-1984): swimmer won 52 national championships, 5 Olympic gold medals; set 67 world records.

Jerry West, b. 1938: L.A. Lakers guard had career average 27 points per game; first team all-star 10 times.

Kathy Whitworth, b. 1939: women's golf leading money winner 8 times; first woman to earn more than $300,000.

Ted Williams, b. 1918: Boston Red Sox outfielder won 6 batting titles; last major leaguer to hit over .400: .406 in 1941; twice won triple crown; .344 lifetime batting average.

Katarina Witt, b. 1965: German figure skater; won Olympic gold medal, 1984, 1988.

John Wooden, b. 1910: coached UCLA basketball team to 10 national championships.

Mickey Wright, b. 1935: won LPGA championship 4 times, Vare Trophy 5 times; twice AP Woman-Athlete-of-the-Year.

Carl Yastrzemski, b. 1939: Boston Red Sox slugger won 3 batting titles; triple crown, 1967.

Cy Young, (1867-1955): pitcher won record 511 major league games.

Steve Young, b. 1961: San Francisco 49ers quarterback led NFL in passing, 1991-94; Super Bowl MVP, 1995.

Babe Didrikson Zaharias, (1914-1956): track star won 2 1932 Olympic gold medals; won numerous golf tournaments.

Tour de France in 1995

On July 23, Miguel Indurain of Spain won the Tour de France, the world's most prestigious bicycle race, for the fifth consecutive year. His margin of victory in the 82d Tour de France was 4 minutes 35 seconds, and he completed the 20-day, 2,270-mile (3,635-km) race in a total time of 92 hours, 44 minutes, 59 seconds. Alex Zuelle of Switzerland finished second.

World Gymnastics Championships in 1995

On October 8, Lilia Podkopayeva of Ukraine won the women's all-around title at the World Gymnastics Championship in Sabae, Japan; it was her first major international competition. Li Xiaoshuang of China won the men's all-around title.

TENNIS
U.S. Open Champions

Men's Singles

Year	Champion	Final opponent	Year	Champion	Final opponent
1910	William Larned	T. C. Bundy	1953	Tony Trabert	E. Victor Seixas Jr.
1911	William Larned	Maurice McLoughlin	1954	E. Victor Seixas Jr.	Rex Hartwig
1912	Maurice McLoughlin	Wallace Johnson	1955	Tony Trabert	Ken Rosewall
1913	Maurice McLoughlin	Richard Williams	1956	Ken Rosewall	Lewis Hoad
1914	Richard Williams	Maurice McLoughlin	1957	Malcolm Anderson	Ashley Cooper
1915	William Johnston	Maurice McLoughlin	1958	Ashley Cooper	Malcolm Anderson
1916	Richard Williams	William Johnston	1959	Neale A. Fraser	Alejandro Olmedo
1917	R. L. Murray	N. W. Niles	1960	Neale A. Fraser	Rod Laver
1918	R. L. Murray	Bill Tilden	1961	Roy Emerson	Rod Laver
1919	William Johnston	Bill Tilden	1962	Rod Laver	Roy Emerson
1920	Bill Tilden	William Johnston	1963	Rafael Osuna	F. A. Froehling 3d
1921	Bill Tilden	Wallace Johnson	1964	Roy Emerson	Fred Stolle
1922	Bill Tilden	William Johnston	1965	Manuel Santana	Cliff Drysdale
1923	Bill Tilden	William Johnston	1966	Fred Stolle	John Newcombe
1924	Bill Tilden	William Johnston	1967	John Newcombe	Clark Graebner
1925	Bill Tilden	William Johnston	1968	Arthur Ashe	Tom Okker
1926	Rene Lacoste	Jean Borotra	1969	Rod Laver	Tony Roche
1927	Rene Lacoste	Bill Tilden	1970	Ken Rosewall	Tony Roche
1928	Henri Cochet	Francis Hunter	1971	Stan Smith	Jan Kodes
1929	Bill Tilden	Francis Hunter	1972	Ilie Nastase	Arthur Ashe
1930	John Doeg	Francis Shields	1973	John Newcombe	Jan Kodes
1931	H. Ellsworth Vines	George Lott	1974	Jimmy Connors	Ken Rosewall
1932	H. Ellsworth Vines	Henri Cochet	1975	Manuel Orantes	Jimmy Connors
1933	Fred Perry	John Crawford	1976	Jimmy Connors	Bjorn Borg
1934	Fred Perry	Wilmer Allison	1977	Guillermo Vilas	Jimmy Connors
1935	Wilmer Allison	Sidney Wood	1978	Jimmy Connors	Bjorn Borg
1936	Fred Perry	Don Budge	1979	John McEnroe	Vitas Gerulaitis
1937	Don Budge	Baron G. von Cramm	1980	John McEnroe	Bjorn Borg
1938	Don Budge	C. Gene Mako	1981	John McEnroe	Bjorn Borg
1939	Robert Riggs	S. Welby Van Horn	1982	Jimmy Connors	Ivan Lendl
1940	Don McNeill	Robert Riggs	1983	Jimmy Connors	Ivan Lendl
1941	Robert Riggs	F. L. Kovacs	1984	John McEnroe	Ivan Lendl
1942	F. R. Schroeder Jr.	Frank Parker	1985	Ivan Lendl	John McEnroe
1943	Joseph Hunt	Jack Kramer	1986	Ivan Lendl	Miloslav Mecir
1944	Frank Parker	William Talbert	1987	Ivan Lendl	Mats Wilander
1945	Frank Parker	William Talbert	1988	Mats Wilander	Ivan Lendl
1946	Jack Kramer	Thomas Brown Jr.	1989	Boris Becker	Ivan Lendl
1947	Jack Kramer	Frank Parker	1990	Pete Sampras	Andre Agassi
1948	Pancho Gonzales	Eric Sturgess	1991	Stefan Edberg	Jim Courier
1949	Pancho Gonzales	F. R. Schroeder Jr.	1992	Stefan Edberg	Pete Sampras
1950	Arthur Larsen	Herbert Flam	1993	Pete Sampras	Cedric Pioline
1951	Frank Sedgman	E. Victor Seixas Jr.	1994	Andre Agassi	Michael Stich
1952	Frank Sedgman	Gardnar Mulloy	1995	Pete Sampras	Andre Agassi

Women's Singles

Year	Champion	Final opponent	Year	Champion	Final opponent
1926	Molla B. Mallory	Elizabeth Ryan	1961	Darlene Hard	Ann Haydon
1927	Helen Wills	Betty Nuthall	1962	Margaret Smith	Darlene Hard
1928	Helen Wills	Helen Jacobs	1963	Maria Bueno	Margaret Smith
1929	Helen Wills	M. Watson	1964	Maria Bueno	Carole Graebner
1930	Betty Nuthall	L. A. Harper	1965	Margaret Smith	Billie Jean Moffitt
1931	Helen Wills Moody	E. B. Whittingstall	1966	Maria Bueno	Nancy Richey
1932	Helen Jacobs	Carolin A. Babcock	1967	Billie Jean King	Ann Haydon Jones
1933	Helen Jacobs	Helen Wills Moody	1968	Virginia Wade	Billie Jean King
1934	Helen Jacobs	Sarah H. Palfrey	1969	Margaret Smith Court	Nancy Richey
1935	Helen Jacobs	Sarah Palfrey Fabyan	1970	Margaret Smith Court	Rosemary Casals
1936	Alice Marble	Helen Jacobs	1971	Billie Jean King	Rosemary Casals
1937	Anita Lizana	Jadwiga Jedrzejowska	1972	Billie Jean King	Kerry Melville
1938	Alice Marble	Nancye Wynne	1973	Margaret Smith Court	Evonne Goolagong
1939	Alice Marble	Helen Jacobs	1974	Billie Jean King	Evonne Goolagong
1940	Alice Marble	Helen Jacobs	1975	Chris Evert	Evonne Goolagong
1941	Sarah Palfrey Cooke	Pauline Betz	1976	Chris Evert	Evonne Goolagong
1942	Pauline Betz	Louise Brough	1977	Chris Evert	Wendy Turnbull
1943	Pauline Betz	Louise Brough	1978	Chris Evert	Pam Shriver
1944	Pauline Betz	Margaret Osborne	1979	Tracy Austin	Chris Evert Lloyd
1945	Sarah Palfrey Cooke	Pauline Betz	1980	Chris Evert Lloyd	Hana Mandlikova
1946	Pauline Betz	Doris Hart	1981	Tracy Austin	Martina Navratilova
1947	Louise Brough	Margaret Osborne	1982	Chris Evert Lloyd	Hana Mandlikova
1948	Margaret Osborne duPont	Louise Brough	1983	Martina Navratilova	Chris Evert Lloyd
1949	Margaret Osborne duPont	Doris Hart	1984	Martina Navratilova	Chris Evert Lloyd
1950	Margaret Osborne duPont	Doris Hart	1985	Hana Mandlikova	Martina Navratilova
1951	Maureen Connolly	Shirley Fry	1986	Martina Navratilova	Helena Sukova
1952	Maureen Connolly	Doris Hart	1987	Martina Navratilova	Steffi Graf
1953	Maureen Connolly	Doris Hart	1988	Steffi Graf	Gabriela Sabatini
1954	Doris Hart	Louise Brough	1989	Steffi Graf	Martina Navratilova
1955	Doris Hart	Patricia Ward	1990	Gabriela Sabatini	Steffi Graf
1956	Shirley Fry	Althea Gibson	1991	Monica Seles	Martina Navratilova
1957	Althea Gibson	Louise Brough	1992	Monica Seles	Arantxa Sanchez Vicario
1958	Althea Gibson	Darlene Hard	1993	Steffi Graf	Helena Sukova
1959	Maria Bueno	Christine Truman	1994	Arantxa Sanchez Vicario	Steffi Graf
1960	Darlene Hard	Maria Bueno	1995	Steffi Graf	Monica Seles

All-England Champions, Wimbledon

Men's Singles

Year	Champion	Final opponent	Year	Champion	Final opponent
1933	Jack Crawford	Ellsworth Vines	1967	John Newcombe	Wilhelm Bungert
1934	Fred Perry	Jack Crawford	1968	Rod Laver	Tony Roche
1935	Fred Perry	Gottfried von Cramm	1969	Rod Laver	John Newcombe
1936	Fred Perry	Gottfried von Cramm	1970	John Newcombe	Ken Rosewall
1937	Donald Budge	Gottfried von Cramm	1971	John Newcombe	Stan Smith
1938	Donald Budge	Wilfred Austin	1972	Stan Smith	Ilie Nastase
1939	Bobby Riggs	Elwood Cooke	1973	Jan Kodes	Alex Metreveli
1940-45	not held		1974	Jimmy Connors	Ken Rosewall
1946	Yvon Petra	Geoff E. Brown	1975	Arthur Ashe	Jimmy Connors
1947	Jack Kramer	Tom P. Brown	1976	Bjorn Borg	Ilie Nastase
1948	Bob Falkenburg	John Bromwich	1977	Bjorn Borg	Jimmy Connors
1949	Ted Schroeder	Jaroslav Drobny	1978	Bjorn Borg	Jimmy Connors
1950	Budge Patty	Frank Sedgman	1979	Bjorn Borg	Roscoe Tanner
1951	Dick Savitt	Ken McGregor	1980	Bjorn Borg	John McEnroe
1952	Frank Sedgman	Jaroslav Drobny	1981	John McEnroe	Bjorn Borg
1953	Vic Seixas	Kurt Nielsen	1982	Jimmy Connors	John McEnroe
1954	Jaroslav Drobny	Ken Rosewall	1983	John McEnroe	Chris Lewis
1955	Tony Trabert	Kurt Nielsen	1984	John McEnroe	Jimmy Connors
1956	Lew Hoad	Ken Rosewall	1985	Boris Becker	Kevin Curren
1957	Lew Hoad	Ashley Cooper	1986	Boris Becker	Ivan Lendl
1958	Ashley Cooper	Neale Fraser	1987	Pat Cash	Ivan Lendl
1959	Alex Olmedo	Rod Laver	1988	Stefan Edberg	Boris Becker
1960	Neale Fraser	Rod Laver	1989	Boris Becker	Stefan Edberg
1961	Rod Laver	Chuck McKinley	1990	Stefan Edberg	Boris Becker
1962	Rod Laver	Martin Mulligan	1991	Michael Stich	Boris Becker
1963	Chuck McKinley	Fred Stolle	1992	Andre Agassi	Goran Ivanisevic
1964	Roy Emerson	Fred Stolle	1993	Pete Sampras	Jim Courier
1965	Roy Emerson	Fred Stolle	1994	Pete Sampras	Goren Ivanisevic
1966	Manuel Santana	Dennis Ralston	1995	Pete Sampras	Boris Becker

Women's Singles

Year	Champion	Year	Champion	Year	Champion	Year	Champion
1946	Pauline Betz	1959	Maria Bueno	1972	Billie Jean King	1984	Martina Navratilova
1947	Margaret Osborne	1960	Maria Bueno	1973	Billie Jean King	1985	Martina Navratilova
1948	Louise Brough	1961	Angela Mortimer	1974	Chris Evert	1986	Martina Navratilova
1949	Louise Brough	1962	Karen Hantze-Susman	1975	Billie Jean King	1987	Martina Navratilova
1950	Louise Brough	1963	Margaret Smith	1976	Chris Evert	1988	Steffi Graf
1951	Doris Hart	1964	Maria Bueno	1977	Virginia Wade	1989	Steffi Graf
1952	Maureen Connolly	1965	Margaret Smith	1978	Martina Navratilova	1990	Martina Navratilova
1953	Maureen Connolly	1966	Billie Jean King	1979	Martina Navratilova	1991	Steffi Graf
1954	Maureen Connolly	1967	Billie Jean King	1980	Evonne Goolagong	1992	Steffi Graf
1955	Louise Brough	1968	Billie Jean King	1981	Chris Evert Lloyd	1993	Steffi Graf
1956	Shirley Fry	1969	Ann Haydon-Jones	1982	Martina Navratilova	1994	Conchita Martinez
1957	Althea Gibson	1970	Margaret Smith Court	1983	Martina Navratilova	1995	Steffi Graf
1958	Althea Gibson	1971	Evonne Goolagong				

Davis Cup Challenge Round

Year	Result	Year	Result	Year	Result
1900	United States 5, British Isles 0	1932	France 3, United States 2	1966	Australia 4, India 1
1901	(not played)	1933	Great Britain 3, France 2	1967	Australia 4, Spain 1
1902	United States 3, British Isles 2	1934	Great Britain 4, United States 1	1968	United States 4, Australia
1903	British Isles 4, United States 1	1935	Great Britain 5, United States 0	1969	United States 5, Romania 0
1904	British Isles 5, Belgium 0	1936	Great Britain 3, Australia 2	1970	United States 5, W. Germany 0
1905	British Isles 5, United States 0	1937	United States 4, Great Britain 1	1971	United States 3, Romania 2
1906	British Isles 5, United States 0	1938	United States 3, Australia 2	1972	United States 3, Romania 2
1907	Australia 3, British Isles 2	1939	Australia 3, United States 2	1973	Australia 5, United States 0
1908	Australasia 3, United States 2	1940-45	(not played)	1974	South Africa (default by India)
1909	Australasia 5, United States 0	1946	United States 5, Australia 0	1975	Sweden 3, Czechoslovakia 2
1910	(not played)	1947	United States 4, Australia 1	1976	Italy 4, Chile 1
1911	Australasia 5, United States 0	1948	United States 5, Australia 0	1977	Australia 3, Italy 1
1912	British Isles 3, Australasia 2	1949	United States 4, Australia 1	1978	United States 4, Great Britain 1
1913	United States 3, British Isles 2	1950	Australia 4, United States 1	1979	United States 5, Italy 0
1914	Australasia 3, United States 2	1951	Australia 3, United States 2	1980	Czechoslovakia 4, Italy 1
1915-18	(not played)	1952	Australia 4, United States 1	1981	United States 3, Argentina 1
1919	Australasia 4, British Isles 1	1953	Australia 3, United States 2	1982	United States 3, France, 0
1920	United States 5, Australasia 0	1954	United States 3, Australia 2	1983	Australia 3, Sweden 1
1921	United States 5, Japan 0	1955	Australia 5, United States 0	1984	Sweden 3, United States 0
1922	United States 4, Australasia 1	1956	Australia 5, United States 0	1985	Sweden 3, W. Germany 2
1923	United States 4, Australasia 1	1957	Australia 3, United States 2	1986	Australia 3, Sweden 2
1924	United States 5, Australasia 0	1958	United States 3, Australia 2	1987	Sweden 5, India 0
1925	United States 5, France 0	1959	Australia 3, United States 2	1988	W. Germany 4, Sweden 1
1926	United States 4, France 1	1960	Australia 4, Italy 1	1989	W. Germany 3, Sweden 2
1927	France 3, United States 2	1961	Australia 5, Italy 0	1990	United States 3, Australia 2
1928	France 4, United States 1	1962	Australia 5, Mexico 0	1991	France 3, United States 1
1929	France 3, United States 2	1963	United States 3, Australia 2	1992	United States 3, Switzerland 1
1930	France 4, United States 1	1964	Australia 3, United States 2	1993	Germany 4, Australia 1
1931	France 3, Great Britain 2	1965	Australia 4, Spain 1	1994	Sweden 4, Russia 1

French Open Singles Champions

Year	Men	Women	Year	Men	Women
1969	Rod Laver	Margaret Smith Court	1983	Yannick Noah	Chris Evert Lloyd
1970	Jan Kodes	Margaret Smith Court	1984	Ivan Lendl	Martina Navratilova
1971	Jan Kodes	Evonne Goolagong	1985	Mats Wilander	Chris Evert Lloyd
1972	Andres Gimeno	Billie Jean King	1986	Ivan Lendl	Chris Evert Lloyd
1973	Ilie Nastase	Margaret Smith Court	1987	Ivan Lendl	Steffi Graf
1974	Bjorn Borg	Chris Evert	1988	Mats Wilander	Steffi Graf
1975	Bjorn Borg	Chris Evert	1989	Michael Chang	Arantxa Sanchez Vicario
1976	Adriano Panatta	Sue Barker	1990	Andres Gomez	Monica Seles
1977	Guillermo Vilas	Mima Jausovec	1991	Jim Courier	Monica Seles
1978	Bjorn Borg	Virginia Ruzici	1992	Jim Courier	Monica Seles
1979	Bjorn Borg	Chris Evert Lloyd	1993	Sergi Bruguera	Steffi Graf
1980	Bjorn Borg	Chris Evert Lloyd	1994	Sergi Bruguera	Arantxa Sanchez Vicario
1981	Bjorn Borg	Hana Mandlikova	1995	Thomas Muster	Steffi Graf
1982	Mats Wilander	Martina Navratilova			

Australian Open Singles Champions

Year*	Men	Women	Year*	Men	Women
1969	Rod Laver	Margaret Smith Court	1982	Johan Kriek	Chris Evert Lloyd
1970	Arthur Ashe	Margaret Smith Court	1983	Mats Wilander	Martina Navratilova
1971	Ken Rosewall	Margaret Smith Court	1984	Mats Wilander	Chris Evert Lloyd
1972	Ken Rosewall	Virginia Wade	1985	Stefan Edberg	Martina Navratilova
1973	John Newcombe	Margaret Smith Court	1986	Not held	Not held
1974	Jimmy Connors	Evonne Goolagong	1987	Stefan Edberg	Hana Mandlikova
1975	John Newcombe	Evonne Goolagong	1988	Mats Wilander	Steffi Graf
1976	Mark Edmondson	Evonne Goolagong	1989	Ivan Lendl	Steffi Graf
1977	Roscoe Tanner	Kerry Reid	1990	Ivan Lendl	Steffi Graf
	Vitas Gerulaitis	Evonne Goolagong	1991	Boris Becker	Monica Seles
1978	Guillermo Vilas	Chris O'Neill	1992	Jim Courier	Monica Seles
1979	Guillermo Vilas	Barbara Jordan	1993	Jim Courier	Monica Seles
1980	Brian Teacher	Hana Mandlikova	1994	Pete Sampras	Steffi Graf
1981	Johan Kriek	Martina Navratilova	1995	Andre Agassi	Mary Pierce

* Two tournaments were held in 1977 (Jan. & Dec.). Tournament moved back to Jan. in 1987, so no championship was decided in 1986.

AUTO RACING

Indianapolis 500 Winners

Year	Winner, Car	MPH	Year	Winner, Car	MPH
1911	Ray Harroun, Marmon Wasp	74.59	1959	Rodger Ward, Leader Card Special	135.857
1912	Joe Dawson, National	78.72	1960	Jim Rathmann, Ken Paul Special	138.767
1913	Jules Goux, Peugeot	75.933	1961	A.J. Foyt, Bowes Seal Fast	139.130
1914	Rene Thomas, Delage	82.47	1962	Rodger Ward, Leader Card Special	140.293
1915	Ralph DePalma, Mercedes	89.84	1963	Parnelli Jones, Agajanian Special	143.137
1916	Dario Resta, Peugeot	84.00	1964	A.J. Foyt, Sheraton-Thompson	
1917-18	race not held			Special	147.350
1919	Howdy Wilcox, Peugeot	88.05	1965	Jim Clark, Lotus-Ford	150.686
1920	Gaston Chevrolet, Monroe	88.16	1966	Graham Hill, American Red Ball	144.317
1921	Tommy Milton, Frontenac	89.62	1967	A.J. Foyt, Sheraton-Thompson	
1922	Jimmy Murphy, Murphy Special	94.48		Special	151.207
1923	Tommy Milton, H.C.S.	90.95	1968	Bobby Unser, Rislone Special	152.882
1924	L.L. Corum-Joe Boyer, Duesenberg	98.23	1969	Mario Andretti, STP Oil Treatment	
1925	Pete DePaolo, Duesenberg	101.13		Special	156.867
1926	Frank Lockhart, Miller	95.904	1970	Al Unser, Johnny Lightning Special	155.749
1927	George Souders, Duesenberg	97.545	1971	Al Unser, Johnny Lightning Special	157.735
1928	Louis Meyer, Miller	99.482	1972	Mark Donohue, Sunoco McLaren	162.962
1929	Ray Keech, Simplex	97.585	1973	Gordon Johncock, STP Double Oil	
1930	Billy Arnold, Miller-Hartz	100.448		Filter	159.036
1931	Louis Schneider, Bowes Seal Fast	96.629	1974	Johnny Rutherford, McLaren	158.589
1932	Fred Frame, Miller-Hartz	104.144	1975	Bobby Unser, Jorgenson Eagle	149.213
1933	Louis Meyer, Tydol	104.162	1976	Johnny Rutherford, Hygain McLaren	148.725
1934	Bill Cummings, Boyle Products	104.863	1977	A.J. Foyt, Gilmore Coyote-Ford	161.331
1935	Kelly Petillo, Gilmore Speedway	106.240	1978	Al Unser, Lola Cosworth	161.363
1936	Louis Meyer, Ring Free	109.069	1979	Rick Mears, Penske-Cosworth	158.899
1937	Wilbur Shaw, Shaw-Gilmore	113.580	1980	Johnny Rutherford, Chaparral-	
1938	Floyd Roberts, Burd Piston Ring	117.200		Cosworth	142.862
1939	Wilbur Shaw, Boyle	115.035	1981	Bobby Unser, Penske-Cosworth	139.085
1940	Wilbur Shaw, Boyle	114.277	1982	Gordon Johncock, Wildcat-Cosworth	162.026
1941	Floyd Davis-Mauri Rose, Knock-Out-		1983	Tom Sneva, March-Cosworth	162.117
	Hose Clip	115.117	1984	Rick Mears, March-Cosworth	163.621
1942-45	race not held		1985	Danny Sullivan, March-Cosworth	152.982
1946	George Robson, Thorne Engineering	114.820	1986	Bobby Rahal, March-Cosworth	170.722
1947	Mauri Rose, Blue Crown Special	116.338	1987	Al Unser, March-Cosworth	162.175
1948	Mauri Rose, Blue Crown Special	119.814	1988	Rick Mears, Penske-Chevy V8	144.809
1949	Bill Holland, Blue Crown Special	121.327	1989	Emerson Fittipaldi, Penske PC 18-	
1950	Johnny Parsons, Wynn Kurtis Kraft	124.002		Chevy	167.581
1951	Lee Wallard, Belanger	126.224	1990	Arie Luyendyk, Lola-Chevy	185.984
1952	Troy Ruttman, Agajanian	128.922	1991	Rick Mears, Penske-Chevy	176.457
1953	Bill Vukovich, Fuel Injection	128.740	1992	Al Unser Jr., Galmer-Chevy A	134.477
1954	Bill Vukovich, Fuel Injection	130.840	1993	Emerson Fittipaldi, Penske-Chevy C	157.207
1955	Bob Sweikert, John Zink Special	128.209	1994	Al Unser Jr., Penske-Mercedes	160.872
1956	Pat Flaherty, John Zink Special	128.490	1995	Jacques Villeneuve, Reynard-Ford	153.616
1957	Sam Hanks, Belond Exhaust	135.601			
1958	Jimmy Bryan, Belond A.P.	133.791			

The race was less than 500 mi in the following years: 1916 (300 mi), 1926 (400 mi), 1950 (345 mi), 1973 (332.5 mi), 1975 (435 mi), 1976 (255 mi). Race record —185.984 mph, Arie Luyendyk, 1990.

Notable One-Mile Speed Records

Date	Driver	Car	MPH	Date	Driver	Car	MPH
1/26/06	Marriott......	Stanley (Steam)	127.659	9/3/35	Campbell	Bluebird Special	301.13
3/16/10	Oldfield......	Benz	131.724	11/19/37	Eyston	Thunderbolt 1	311.42
4/23/11	Burman......	Benz	141.732	9/16/38	Eyston	Thunderbolt 1	357.5
2/12/19	DePalma.....	Packard	149.875	8/23/39	Cobb	Railton	368.9
4/27/20	Milton.......	Dusenberg	155.046	9/16/47	Cobb	Railton-Mobil	394.2
4/28/26	Parry-Thomas .	Thomas Spl.	170.624	8/5/63	Breedlove....	Spirit of America	407.45
3/29/27	Seagrave	Sunbeam	203.790	10/27/64	Arfons	Green Monster	536.71
4/22/28	Keech.......	White Triplex	207.552	11/15/65	Breedlove....	Spirit of America	600.601
3/11/29	Seagrave	Irving-Napier	231.446	10/23/70	Gabelich.....	Blue Flame	622.407
2/5/31	Campbell	Napier-Campbell	246.086	10/9/79	Barrett	Budweiser Rocket	638.637*
2/24/32	Campbell	Napier-Campbell	253.96	10/4/83	Noble.......	Thrust 2	633.6
2/22/33	Campbell	Napier-Campbell	272.109				

*Not recognized as official by sanctioning bodies.

IndyCar Champions

(U.S. Auto Club Champions prior to 1979; CART Champions, 1979-95)

Year	Driver	Year	Driver	Year	Driver	Year	Driver
1960	A. J. Foyt	1969	Mario Andretti	1978	Tom Sneva	1987	Bobby Rahal
1961	A. J. Foyt	1970	Al Unser	1979	Rick Mears	1988	Danny Sullivan
1962	Rodger Ward	1971	Joe Leonard	1980	Johnny Rutherford	1989	Emerson Fittipaldi
1963	A. J. Foyt	1972	Joe Leonard	1981	Rick Mears	1990	Al Unser Jr.
1964	A. J. Foyt	1973	Roger McCluskey	1982	Rick Mears	1991	Michael Andretti
1965	Mario Andretti	1974	Bobby Unser	1983	Al Unser	1992	Bobby Rahal
1966	Mario Andretti	1975	A. J. Foyt	1984	Mario Andretti	1993	Nigel Mansell
1967	A. J. Foyt	1976	Gordon Johncock	1985	Al Unser	1994	Al Unser Jr.
1968	Bobby Unser	1977	Tom Sneva	1986	Bobby Rahal	1995	Jacques Villeneuve

Le Mans 24-Hour Race in 1995

Yannick Dalmas (France), J. J. Lehto (Finland), and Masanori Sekiya (Japan) drove their McLaren F1-GTR to victory in the 1995 Le Mans 24-hr race. They traveled the 2,518.1 mi at an average of 105.01 mph.

World Grand Prix Champions

Year	Driver	Year	Driver	Year	Driver
1951	Juan Fangio, Argentina	1966	Jack Brabham, Australia	1981	Nelson Piquet, Brazil
1952	Alberto Ascari, Italy	1967	Denis Hulme, New Zealand	1982	Keke Rosberg, Finland
1953	Alberto Ascari, Italy	1968	Graham Hill, England	1983	Nelson Piquet, Brazil
1954	Juan Fangio, Argentina	1969	Jackie Stewart, Scotland	1984	Niki Lauda, Austria
1955	Juan Fangio, Argentina	1970	Jochen Rindt, Austria	1985	Alain Prost, France
1956	Juan Fangio, Argentina	1971	Jackie Stewart, Scotland	1986	Alain Prost, France
1957	Juan Fangio, Argentina	1972	Emerson Fittipaldi, Brazil	1987	Nelson Piquet, Brazil
1958	Mike Hawthorne, England	1973	Jackie Stewart, Scotland	1988	Ayrton Senna, Brazil
1959	Jack Brabham, Australia	1974	Emerson Fittipaldi, Brazil	1989	Alain Prost, France
1960	Jack Brabham, Australia	1975	Niki Lauda, Austria	1990	Ayrton Senna, Brazil
1961	Phil Hill, United States	1976	James Hunt, England	1991	Ayrton Senna, Brazil
1962	Graham Hill, England	1977	Niki Lauda, Austria	1992	Nigel Mansell, Britain
1963	Jim Clark, Scotland	1978	Mario Andretti, U.S.	1993	Alain Prost, France
1964	John Surtees, England	1979	Jody Scheckter, So. Africa	1994	Michael Schumacher, Germany
1965	Jim Clark, Scotland	1980	Alan Jones, Australia	1995	Michael Schumacher, Germany

Grand Prix Races for Formula 1 Cars in 1995

Grand Prix	Winner, car	Grand Prix	Winner, car
Argentinian	Damon Hill, Williams-Renault	Hungarian	Damon Hill, Williams-Renault
Belgian	Michael Schumacher, Benetton-Renault	Italian	Johnny Herbert, Benetton-Renault
Brazilian	Michael Schumacher, Benetton-Renault	Monaco...........	Michael Schumacher, Benetton-Renault
British	Johnny Herbert, Benetton-Renault	Pacific	Michael Schumacher, Benetton-Renault
Canadian	Jean Alesi, Ferrari 412T2	Portuguese	David Coulthard, Williams-Renault
European........	Michael Schumacher, Benetton-Renault	San Marino	Damon Hill, Williams-Renault
French..........	Michael Schumacher, Benetton-Renault	Spanish..........	Michael Schumacher, Benetton-Renault
German.........	Michael Schumacher, Benetton-Renault		

Winston Cup Champions (NASCAR)

Year	Driver	Year	Driver	Year	Driver	Year	Driver
1949	Red Byron	1961	Ned Jarrett	1973	Benny Parsons	1984	Terry Labonte
1950	Bill Rexford	1962	Joe Weatherly	1974	Richard Petty	1985	Darrell Waltrip
1951	Herb Thomas	1963	Joe Weatherly	1975	Richard Petty	1986	Dale Earnhardt
1952	Tim Flock	1964	Richard Petty	1976	Cale Yarborough	1987	Dale Earnhardt
1953	Herb Thomas	1965	Ned Jarrett	1977	Cale Yarborough	1988	Bill Elliott
1954	Lee Petty	1966	David Pearson	1978	Cale Yarborough	1989	Rusty Wallace
1955	Tim Flock	1967	Richard Petty	1979	Richard Petty	1990	Dale Earnhardt
1956	Buck Baker	1968	David Pearson	1980	Dale Earnhardt	1991	Dale Earnhardt
1957	Buck Baker	1969	David Pearson	1981	Darrell Waltrip	1992	Alan Kulwicki
1958	Lee Petty	1970	Bobby Isaac	1982	Darrell Waltrip	1993	Dale Earnhardt
1959	Lee Petty	1971	Richard Petty	1983	Bobby Allison	1994	Dale Earnhardt
1960	Rex White	1972	Richard Petty				

Daytona 500 Winners

Year	Driver, car	Avg. MPH	Year	Driver, car	Avg. MPH
1959	Lee Petty, Oldsmobile	135.521	1978	Bobby Allison, Ford	159.730
1960	Junior Johnson, Chevrolet	124.740	1979	Richard Petty, Oldsmobile	143.977
1961	Marvin Panch, Pontiac	149.601	1980	Buddy Baker, Oldsmobile	177.602
1962	Fireball Roberts, Pontiac	152.529	1981	Richard Petty, Buick	169.651
1963	Tiny Lund, Ford	151.566	1982	Bobby Allison, Buick	153.991
1964	Richard Petty, Plymouth	154.334	1983	Cale Yarborough, Pontiac	155.979
1965	Fred Lorenzen, Ford (a)	141.539	1984	Cale Yarborough, Chevrolet	150.994
1966	Richard Petty, Plymouth (b)	160.627	1985	Bill Elliott, Ford	172.265
1967	Mario Andretti, Ford	146.926	1986	Geoff Bodine, Chevrolet	148.124
1968	Cale Yarborough, Mercury	143.251	1987	Bill Elliott, Ford	176.263
1969	Lee Roy Yarborough, Ford	160.875	1988	Bobby Allison, Buick	137.531
1970	Pete Hamilton, Plymouth	149.601	1989	Darrell Waltrip, Chevrolet	148.466
1971	Richard Petty, Plymouth	144.456	1990	Derrike Cope, Chevrolet	165.761
1972	A. J. Foyt, Mercury	161.550	1991	Ernie Irvan, Chevrolet	148.148
1973	Richard Petty, Dodge	157.205	1992	Davey Allison, Ford	160.256
1974	Richard Petty, Dodge (c)	140.894	1993	Dale Jarrett, Chevrolet	154.972
1975	Benny Parsons, Chevrolet	153.649	1994	Sterling Marlin, Chevrolet	156.931
1976	David Pearson, Mercury	152.181	1995	Sterling Marlin, Chevrolet	141.710
1977	Cale Yarborough, Chevrolet	153.218			

(a) 322.5 mi. (b) 495 mi. (c) 450 mi.

NASCAR Racing in 1995

Winston Cup Races

Date	Race, site	Winner	Car
Feb. 19	Daytona 500, Daytona Beach, FL	Sterling Marlin	Chevrolet
Feb. 26	Goodwrench 500, Rockingham, NC	Jeff Gordon	Chevrolet
Mar. 5	Pontiac Excitement 400, Richmond, VA	Terry Labonte	Chevrolet
Mar. 12	Purolator 500, Atlanta, GA	Jeff Gordon	Chevrolet
Mar. 26	Transouth Finanacial 400, Darlington, SC	Sterling Marlin	Chevrolet
Apr. 2	Food City 500, Bristol, TN	Jeff Gordon	Chevrolet
Apr. 9	First Union 400, N. Wilkesboro, NC	Dale Earnhardt	Chevrolet
Apr. 23	Hanes 500, Martinsville, VA	Rusty Wallace	Ford
Apr. 30	Winston Select 500, Talladega, AL	Mark Martin	Ford
May 7	Save Mart Supermarkets 300, Sonoma, CA	Dale Earnhardt	Chevrolet
May 28	Coca Cola 600, Charlotte, NC	Bobby Labonte	Chevrolet
June 4	Miller Genuine Draft 500, Dover, DE	Kyle Petty	Chevrolet
June 11	UAW-GM Teamwork 500, Pocono, PA	Terry Labonte	Chevrolet
June 18	Miller Genuine Draft 400, Brooklyn, MI	Bobby Labonte	Chevrolet
July 1	Pepsi 400, Daytona Beach, FL	Jeff Gordon	Chevrolet
July 9	Slick 50 300, Loudon, NH	Jeff Gordon	Chevrolet
July 16	Miller Genuine Draft 500, Pocono, PA	Dale Jarrett	Ford
July 23	Die-Hard 500, Talladega, AL	Sterling Marlin	Chevrolet
Aug. 5	Brickyard 400, Indianapolis, IN	Dale Earnhardt	Chevrolet
Aug. 13	The Bud at The Glen, Watkins Glen, NY	Mark Martin	Ford
Aug. 20	GM Goodwrench Dealer 400, Brooklyn, MI	Boby Labonte	Chevrolet
Aug. 26	Goody's 500, Bristol, TN	Terry Labonte	Chevrolet
Sept. 3	Mountain Dew Southern 500, Darlington, SC	Jeff Gordon	Chevrolet
Sept. 9	Miller Genuine Draft 400, Richmond, VA	Rusty Wallace	Ford
Sept. 17	MBNA 500, Dover, DE	Jeff Gordon	Chevrolet
Sept. 24	Goody's 500, Martinsville, VA	Dale Earnhardt	Chevrolet
Oct. 1	Tyson Holly Farms 400, N. Wilkesboro, NC	Mark Martin	Ford
Oct. 8	UAW-GM 500, Charlotte, NC	Mark Martin	Ford

MOTORCYCLE RACING

1995 American Motorcyclist Assn. Racing Champions

Road Racing

AMA Superbike—Miguel Duhamel, Repentigny, Que., Honda RC45

AMA 250cc Grand Prix—Rich Oliver, Fresno, CA, Yamaha TZ250

AMA 600cc SuperSport—Miguel Duhamel, Repentigny, Que., Honda CBR600

AMA 750cc SuperSport—Tom Kipp, Mentor, OH, Yamaha YZF750

AMA SuperTwins—Scott Zampach, West Bend, WI, Harley-Davidson 883

AMA SuperTeams—Cycle Motion Racing, Birmingham, AL, Suzuki GSXR1100

AMA 125cc Grand Prix—Rodney Fee, Los Angeles, CA, Honda RS125

Motocross

AMA 250cc Motocross—Jeremy McGrath, Murrieta, CA, Honda CR250R

AMA 125cc Motocross—Steve Lamson, Pollock Pines, CA, Honda CR125R

Supercross

AMA Supercross—Jeremy McGrath, Murrieta, CA, Honda CR250R

Grand National Dirt Track

AMA Grand National—Scott Parker, Swartz Creek, MI, Harley-Davidson XR750

AMA 883cc Dirt Track—Mike Hacker, Prince George, VA, Harley-Davidson 883

1995 World Motorcycle Racing Champions

Road Racing

500cc Grand Prix—Michael Doohan, Australia, Honda
250cc Grand Prix—Max Biaggi, Italy, Aprilia
125cc Grand Prix—Haruchika Aoki, Japan, Honda
World Superbike—Carl Fogerty, England, Ducati

Motocross

500cc—Joel Smets, Belgium, Husaberg
250cc—Stefan Everts, Belgium, Suzuki
125cc—Alessandro Puzar, Italy, Honda

Speedway

World Individual—Hans Nielsen, Denmark

BOXING
Champions by Classes

There are numerous governing bodies in boxing, including the World Boxing Council, World Boxing Assn., International Boxing Federation, World Boxing Organization, United States Boxing Assn., North American Boxing Federation, and European Boxing Union. Other organizations are recognized by TV networks and the print media. All the governing bodies have their own champions and assorted boxing divisions. The following are the recognized champions—generally as of Aug. 1995, heavyweights as of Oct. 1995—in the principal divisions of the WBC, WBA, and IBF.

Class, Weight limit	WBC	WBA	IBF
Heavyweight	Frank Bruno, U.K.	Bruce Seldon, U.S.	Vacant
Cruiserweight (195 lb)	Anaclet Wamba, France	Nate Miller, U.S.	Al Cole, U.S.
Light Heavyweight (175 lb)	Fabrice Tiozzo, France	Virgil Hill, U.S.	Henry Maske, Germany
Super Middleweight (168 lb)	Nigel Benn, U.K.	Frank Liles, U.S.	Roy Jones, U.S.
Middleweight (160 lb)	Julian Jackson, U.S.	Jorge Castro, Argentina	Bernard Hopkins, U.S.
Jr. Middleweight (154 lb)	Luis Santana, Dominican Rep.	Carl Daniels, U.S.	Vincent Pettway, U.S.
Welterweight (147 lb)	Pernell Whitaker, U.S.	Ike Quartey, Ghana	Felix Trinidad, Puerto Rico
Jr. Welterweight (140 lb)	Julio Cesar Chavez, Mexico	Frankie Randall, U.S.	Kostya Tszyu, Australia
Lightweight (135 lb)	Miguel Angel Gonzalez, Mexico	Orzubek Nazarov, Japan	Vacant
Jr. Lightweight (130 lb)	Gabriel Ruelas, U.S.	Vacant	Tracy Patterson, U.S.
Featherweight (126 lb)	Alejandro Gonzalez, Mexico	Eloy Rojas, Venezuela	Tom Johnson, U.S.
Jr. Featherweight (122 lb)	Hector Acero-Sanchez, U.S.	Antonio Cermeno, Venezuela	Vuyani Bungu, South Africa
Bantamweight (118 lb)	Wayne McCullough, U.S.	Daorung Chuvatana, Thailand	Mbulelo Botile, South Africa
Jr. Bantamweight (115 lb)	Hiroshi Kawashima, Japan	Alimi Goitia, Venezuela	Harold Grey, Colombia
Flyweight (112 lb)	Yuri Arbachakov, Russia	Saen Sow Ploenchit, Thailand	Danny Romero, U.S.
Jr. Flyweight (108 lb)	Saman Sorjaturong, Thailand	Hi Yong Choi, South Korea	Saman Sorjaturong, Thailand

Ring Champions by Years
(*abandoned the title or was stripped of it)

Heavyweights

1882-1892	John L. Sullivan (a)
1892-1897	James J. Corbett (b)
1897-1899	Robert Fitzsimmons
1899-1905	James J. Jeffries* (c)
1905-1906	Marvin Hart
1906-1908	Tommy Burns
1908-1915	Jack Johnson
1915-1919	Jess Willard
1919-1926	Jack Dempsey
1926-1928	Gene Tunney*
1928-1930	Vacant
1930-1932	Max Schmeling
1932-1933	Jack Sharkey
1933-1934	Primo Carnera
1934-1935	Max Baer
1935-1937	James J. Braddock
1937-1949	Joe Louis*
1949-1951	Ezzard Charles
1951-1952	Joe Walcott
1952-1956	Rocky Marciano*
1956-1959	Floyd Patterson
1959-1960	Ingemar Johansson
1960-1962	Floyd Patterson
1962-1964	Sonny Liston
1964-1967	Cassius Clay* (Muhammad Ali) (d)
1970-1973	Joe Frazier
1973-1974	George Foreman
1974-1978	Muhammad Ali
1978	Leon Spinks (e); Ken Norton (WBC); Larry Holmes (WBC) (f); Muhammad Ali* (WBA)
1979	John Tate (WBA)
1980	Mike Weaver (WBA)
1982	Michael Dokes (WBA)
1983	Gerrie Coetzee (WBA)
1984	Tim Witherspoon (WBC); Pinklon Thomas (WBC); Greg Page (WBA)
1985	Tony Tubbs (WBA); Michael Spinks (IBF)
1986	Tim Witherspoon (WBA); Trevor Berbick (WBC); Mike Tyson (WBC); James "Bone-crusher" Smith (WBA)
1987	Mike Tyson (WBC, WBA)
1988	Mike Tyson (WBC, WBA, IBF)
1990	James "Buster" Douglas (WBA, WBC, IBF); Evander Holyfield (WBA, WBC, IBF)
1992	Riddick Bowe (WBA, IBF, WBC*); Lennox Lewis (WBC)
1993	Evander Holyfield (WBA, IBF)
1994	Michael Moorer (WBA, IBF); Oliver McCall (WBC); George Foreman (WBA*, IBF*)
1995	Bruce Seldon (WBA); Frank Bruno (WBC)

(a) London Prize Ring (bare knuckle champion).
(b) First Marquis of Queensberry champion.
(c) Jeffries abandoned the title (1905) and designated Marvin Hart and Jack Root as logical contenders. Hart defeated Root in 12 rounds (1905) and in turn was defeated by Tommy Burns (1906), who laid claim to the title. Jack Johnson defeated Burns (1908) and was recognized as champion. He clinched the title by defeating Jeffries in an attempted comeback (1910).
(d) Title declared vacant by the WBA and other groups in 1967 after Ali's refusal to fulfill his military obligation. Joe Frazier was recognized as champion by 6 states, Mexico, and So. America. Jimmy Ellis was declared champion by the WBA. Frazier KOd Ellis, Feb. 16, 1970.
(e) After Spinks defeated Ali, the WBC recognized Ken Norton as champion. Ali defeated Spinks in a rematch to win the WBA title and subsequently retired in 1979.
(f) Holmes was stripped of his WBC title in 1984. He was the IBF champion when he lost to Michael Spinks in 1985.

Light Heavyweights

1903	Jack Root, George Gardner
1903-1905	Bob Fitzsimmons
1905-1912	Philadelphia Jack O'Brien*
1912-1916	Jack Dillon
1916-1920	Battling Levinsky
1920-1922	George Carpentier
1922-1923	Battling Siki
1923-1925	Mike McTigue
1925-1926	Paul Berlenbach
1926-1927	Jack Delaney*
1927-1929	Tommy Loughran*
1930-1934	Maxey Rosenbloom
1934-1935	Bob Olin
1935-1939	John Henry Lewis*
1939	Melio Bettina
1939-1941	Billy Conn*
1941	Anton Christoforidis (won NBA title)
1941-1948	Gus Lesnevich, Freddie Mills
1948-1950	Freddie Mills
1950-1952	Joey Maxim
1952-1960	Archie Moore
1961-1962	Vacant
1962-1963	Harold Johnson
1963-1965	Willie Pastrano
1965-1966	Jose Torres
1966-1968	Dick Tiger
1968-1974	Bob Foster*
1974-1977	John Conteh (WBC); Victor Galindez (WBA)
1977	Miguel Cuello (WBC)
1978	Mike Rossman (WBA); Mate Parlov (WBC); Marvin Johnson (WBC)
1979	Matthew Saad Muhammad (WBC); Victor Galindez (WBA); Marvin Johnson (WBA)
1980	Eddie Mustafa Muhammad (WBA)
1981	Michael Spinks (WBA); Dwight Braxton (WBC)
1983-1985	Michael Spinks*
1985	J. B. Williamson (WBC)
1986	Marvin Johnson (WBA); Dennis Andries (WBC)
1987	Thomas Hearns* (WBC); Leslie Stewart (WBA); Virgil Hill (WBA); Don Lalonde (WBC)
1988	Ray Leonard* (WBC)
1989	Dennis Andries (WBC); Jeff Harding (WBC)
1990	Dennis Andries (WBC)
1991	Thomas Hearns (WBA); Jeff Harding (WBC)
1992	Iran Barkley* (WBA); Virgil Hill (WBA)

1994	Mike McCallum (WBC)
1995	Fabrice Tiozzo (WBC)

Middleweights

1884-1891	Jack "Nonpareil" Dempsey
1891-1897	Bob Fitzsimmons*
1897-1907	Tommy Ryan*
1907-1908	Stanley Ketchel, Billy Papke
1908-1910	Stanley Ketchel
1911-1913	vacant
1913	Frank Klaus; George Chip
1914-1917	Al McCoy
1917-1920	Mike O'Dowd
1920-1923	Johnny Wilson
1923-1926	Harry Greb
1926-1931	Tiger Flowers; Mickey Walker
1931-1932	Gorilla Jones (NBA)
1932-1937	Marcel Thil
1938	Al Hostak (NBA); Solly Krieger (NBA)
1939-1940	Al Hostak (NBA)
1941-1947	Tony Zale
1947-1948	Rocky Graziano
1948	Tony Zale; Marcel Cerdan
1949-1951	Jake LaMotta
1951	Ray Robinson; Randy Turpin; Ray Robinson*
1953-1955	Carl (Bobo) Olson
1955-1957	Ray Robinson
1957	Gene Fullmer; Ray Robinson; Carmen Basilio
1958	Ray Robinson
1959	Gene Fullmer (NBA); Ray Robinson (N.Y.)
1960	Gene Fullmer (NBA); Paul Pender (New York and Mass.)
1961	Gene Fullmer (NBA); Terry Downes (New York, Mass., Europe)
1962	Gene Fullmer; Dick Tiger (NBA); Paul Pender (New York and Mass.)*
1963	Dick Tiger (universal)
1963-1965	Joey Giardello
1965-1966	Dick Tiger
1966-1967	Emile Griffith
1967	Nino Benvenuti
1967-1968	Emile Griffith
1968-1970	Nino Benvenuti
1970-1977	Carlos Monzon*
1977-1978	Rodrigo Valdez
1978-1979	Hugo Corro
1979-1980	Vito Antuofermo
1980	Alan Minter; Marvin Hagler
1987	Ray Leonard* (WBC); Thomas Hearns (WBC); Sumbu Kalambay (WBA)
1988	Iran Barkley (WBC)
1989	Mike McCallum* (WBA); Roberto Duran (WBC)
1991	Julian Jackson (WBC)
1992	Reggie Johnson (WBA)
1993	Gerald McClellan (WBC); John David Jackson* (WBA)
1994	Jorge Castro (WBA)
1995	Julian Jackson (WBC)

Welterweights

1892-1894	Mysterious Billy Smith
1894-1896	Tommy Ryan
1896	Kid McCoy*
1900	Rube Ferns; Matty Matthews
1901	Rube Ferns
1901-1904	Joe Walcott
1904-1906	Dixie Kid; Joe Walcott; Honey Mellody
1907-1911	Mike Sullivan
1911-1915	Vacant
1915-1919	Ted Lewis
1919-1922	Jack Britton
1922-1926	Mickey Walker
1926	Pete Latzo
1927-1929	Joe Dundee
1929	Jackie Fields
1930	Jack Thompson; Tommy Freeman
1931	Freeman; Thompson; Lou Brouillard
1932	Jackie Fields
1933	Young Corbett; Jimmy McLarnin
1934	Barney Ross; Jimmy McLarnin
1935-1938	Barney Ross
1938-1940	Henry Armstrong
1940-1941	Fritzie Zivic
1941-1946	Fred Cochrane
1946-1946	Marty Servo*; Ray Robinson (a)
1946-1950	Ray Robinson*
1951	Johnny Bratton (NBA)
1951-1954	Kid Gavilan
1954-1955	Johnny Saxton

1955	Tony De Marco; Carmen Basilio
1956	Carmen Basilio; Johnny Saxton; Basilio
1957	Carmen Basilio*
1958-1960	Virgil Akins, Don Jordan
1960	Benny Paret
1961	Emile Griffith; Benny Paret
1962	Emile Griffith
1963	Luis Rodriguez; Emile Griffith
1964-1966	Emile Griffith*
1966-1969	Curtis Cokes
1969-1970	Jose Napoles; Billy Backus
1971-1975	Jose Napoles
1975-1976	John Stracey (WBC); Angel Espada (WBA)
1976-1979	Carlos Palomino (WBC); Jose Cuevas (WBA)
1979	Wilfredo Benitez (WBC); Sugar Ray Leonard (WBC)
1980	Roberto Duran (WBC); Thomas Hearns (WBA); Sugar Ray Leonard (WBC)
1981-1982	Sugar Ray Leonard*
1983	Donald Curry (WBA); Milton McCrory (WBC)
1985	Donald Curry
1986	Lloyd Honeyghan (WBC)
1987	Mark Breland (WBA); Marlon Starling (WBA); Jorge Vaca (WBC).
1988	Tomas Molinares (WBA); Lloyd Honeyghan (WBC)
1989	Marlon Starling (WBC); Mark Breland (WBA)
1990	Maurice Blocker (WBC); Aaron Davis (WBA)
1991	Meldrick Taylor (WBA); Simon Brown (WBC); Buddy McGirt (WBC)
1992	Crisanto Espana (WBA)
1993	Pernell Whitaker (WBC)
1994	Ike Quartey (WBA)

(a) Robinson gained the title by defeating Tommy Bell in an elimination agreed to by the NY Commission and the NBA. Both claimed Robinson waived his title when he won the middleweight crown from LaMotta in 1951.

Lightweights

1896-1899	Kid Lavigne
1899-1902	Frank Erne
1902-1908	Joe Gans
1908-1910	Battling Nelson
1910-1912	Ad Wolgast
1912-1914	Willie Ritchie
1914-1917	Freddie Welsh
1917-1925	Benny Leonard*
1925	Jimmy Goodrich; Rocky Kansas
1926-1930	Sammy Mandell
1930	Al Singer; Tony Canzoneri
1930-1933	Tony Canzoneri
1933-1935	Barney Ross*
1935-1936	Tony Canzoneri
1936-1938	Lou Ambers
1938	Henry Armstrong
1939	Lou Ambers
1940	Lew Jenkins
1941-1943	Sammy Angott
1944	S. Angott (NBA); J. Zurita (NBA)
1945-1951	Ike Williams (NBA: later universal)
1951-1952	James Carter
1952	Lauro Salas; James Carter
1953-1954	James Carter
1954	Paddy De Marco; James Carter
1955	James Carter; Bud Smith
1956	Bud Smith; Joe Brown
1956-1962	Joe Brown
1962-1965	Carlos Ortiz
1965	Ismael Laguna
1965-1968	Carlos Ortiz
1968-1969	Teo Cruz
1969-1970	Mando Ramos
1970	Ismael Laguna; Ken Buchanan (WBA)
1971	Mando Ramos (WBC); Pedro Carrasco (WBC)
1972-1979	Roberto Duran* (WBA)
1972	Pedro Carrasco; Mando Ramos; Chango Carmona; Rodolfo Gonzalez (all WBC)
1974-1976	Guts Ishimatsu (WBC)
1976-1977	Esteban De Jesus (WBC)
1979	Jim Watt (WBC); Ernesto Espana (WBA)
1980	Hilmer Kenty (WBA)
1981	Alexis Arguello (WBC); Sean O'Grady (WBA); Arturo Frias (WBA)
1982-1984	Ray Mancini (WBA)
1983	Edwin Rosario (WBC)
1984	Livingstone Bramble (WBA); Jose Luis Ramirez (WBC)
1985	Hector (Macho) Camacho (WBC)
1986	Edwin Rosario (WBA); Jose Luis Ramirez (WBC)

(continued)

1987	Julio Cesar Chavez (WBA)
1989	Edwin Rosario (WBA); Pernell Whitaker (WBC)
1990	Juan Nazario (WBA); Pernell Whitaker* (WBA)
1992	Joey Gamache (WBA); Miguel Angel Gonzalez (WBC); Tony Lopez (WBA)
1993	Dingaan Thobela (WBA); Orzubek Nazarov (WBA)

Featherweights

1892-1900	George Dixon (disputed)
1900-1901	Terry McGovern; Young Corbett*
1901-1912	Abe Attell
1912-1923	Johnny Kilbane
1923	Eugene Criqui; Johnny Dundee
1923-1925	Johnny Dundee*
1925-1927	Kid Kaplan*
1927-1928	Benny Bass; Tony Canzoneri
1928-1929	Andre Routis
1929-1932	Battling Battalino*
1932-1934	Tommy Paul (NBA)
1933-1936	Freddie Miller
1936-1937	Petey Sarron
1937-1938	Henry Armstrong*
1938-1940	Joey Archibald (a)
1940-41	Harry Jeffra
1942-1948	Willie Pep
1948-1949	Sandy Saddler
1949-1950	Willie Pep
1950-1957	Sandy Saddler*
1957-1959	Hogan (Kid) Bassey
1959-1963	Davey Moore

1963-1964	Sugar Ramos
1964-1967	Vicente Saldivar*
1968-1971	Paul Rojas (WBA); Sho Saijo (WBA)
1971	Antonio Gomez (WBA); Kuniaki Shibada (WBC)
1972	Ernesto Marcel* (WBA); Clemente Sanchez* (WBC); Jose Legra (WBC)
1973	Eder Jofre (WBC)
1974	Ruben Olivares (WBA); Alexis Arguello (WBA); Bobby Chacon (WBC)
1975	Ruben Olivares (WBC); David Kotey (WBC)
1976	Danny Lopez (WBC)
1977	Rafael Ortega (WBA)
1978	Cecilio Lastra (WBA); Eusebio Pedrosa (WBA)
1980	Salvador Sanchez (WBC)
1982	Juan LaPorte (WBC)
1984	Wilfredo Gomez (WBC); Azumah Nelson (WBC)
1985	Barry McGuigan (WBA)
1986	Steve Cruz (WBA)
1987	Antonio Esparragoza (WBA)
1988	Jeff Fenech (WBC)
1990	Marcos Villasana (WBC)
1991	Park Yung Kyun (WBA); Paul Hodkinson (WBC)
1993	Goyo Vargas (WBC); Kevin Kelley (WBC); Eloy Rojas (WBA)
1995	Alejandro Gonzalez (WBC)

(a) After Petey Scalzo knocked out Archibald in an overweight match and was refused a title bout, the NBA named Scalzo champion. NBA title succession: Scalzo, 1938-1941; Richard Lemos, 1941; Jackie Wilson, 1941-1943; Jackie Callura, 1943; Phil Terranova, 1943-1944; Sal Bartolo, 1944-1946.

History of Heavyweight Championship Bouts
(bouts in which title changed hands)

1889—July 8—John L. Sullivan def. Jake Kilrain, 75, Richburg, Miss. Last championship bare knuckles bout.

1892—Sept. 7—James J. Corbett def. John L. Sullivan, 21, New Orleans. Big gloves used for first time.

1897—Bob Fitzsimmons def. James J. Corbett, 14, Carson City, Nev.

1899—June 9—James J. Jeffries def. Bob Fitzsimmons, 11, Coney Island, N.Y.

1905—James J. Jeffries retired, July 3—Marvin Hart KOd Jack Root, 12, Reno. Jeffries refereed and presented the title to the victor. Jack O'Brien also claimed the title.

1906—Feb. 23—Tommy Burns def. Marvin Hart, 20, Los Angeles.

1908—Dec. 26—Jack Johnson KOd Tommy Burns, 14, Sydney, Australia. Police halted contest.

1915—April 5—Jess Willard def. Jack Johnson, 26, Havana. Cuba.

1919—July 4—Jack Dempsey KOd Jess Willard, Toledo, Oh. Willard failed to answer bell for 4th round.

1926—Sept. 23—Gene Tunney def. Jack Dempsey, 10, Philadelphia.

1930—June 12—Max Schmeling def. Jack Sharkey, 4, New York. Sharkey fouled Schmeling in a bout which was generally considered to have resulted in the election of a successor to Gene Tunney.

1932—June 21—Jack Sharkey def. Max Schmeling, 15, New York.

1933—June 29— Primo Carnera KOd Jack Sharkey, 6, New York.

1934—June 14—Max Baer KOd Primo Carnera, 11, New York.

1935—June 13—James J. Braddock def. Max Baer, 15, New York.

1937—June 22—Joe Louis KOd James J. Braddock, 8, Chicago.

1949—June 22—Following Joe Louis' retirement Ezzard Charles def. Joe Walcott, 15, Chicago; NBA recognition only.

1951—July 18—Joe Walcott KOd Ezzard Charles, 7, Pittsburgh.

1952—Sept. 23—Rocky Marciano KOd Joe Walcott, 13, Philadelphia.

1956—Nov. 30—Floyd Patterson KOd Archie Moore, 5, Chicago.

1959—June 26—Ingemar Johansson KOd Floyd Patterson, 3, New York.

1960—June 20—Floyd Patterson KOd Ingemar Johansson, 5, New York. First heavyweight in boxing history to regain title.

1962—Sept. 25—Sonny Liston KOd Floyd Patterson, 1, Chicago.

1964—Feb. 25—Cassius Clay (Muhammad Ali) KOd Sonny Liston, 7, Miami Beach. (In 1967, Ali was stripped of his title by the WBA and others for refusing military service.)

1970—Feb. 16—Joe Frazier KOd Jimmy Ellis, 5, New York.

1971—Mar. 8—Joe Frazier def. Muhammad Ali, 15, New York.

1973—Jan. 22—George Foreman KOd Joe Frazier, 2, Kingston, Jamaica.

1974—Oct. 30—Muhammad Ali KOd George Foreman, 8, Zaire.

1978—Feb. 15—Leon Spinks def. Muhammad Ali, 15, Las Vegas.

1978—June 9—(WBC) Larry Holmes def. Ken Norton, 15, Las Vegas.

1978—Sept. 15—(WBA) Muhammad Ali def. Leon Spinks, 15, New Orleans. (Ali retired in 1979.)

1980—Mar. 31—(WBA) Mike Weaver KOd John Tate, 15, Knoxville.

1982—Dec. 10—(WBA) Michael Dokes KOd Mike Weaver, 1, Las Vegas.

1983—Sept. 23—(WBA) Gerrie Coetzee KOd Michael Dokes, 10, Richfield, Oh.

1984—Mar. 10—(WBC) Tim Witherspoon def. Greg Page, 12, Las Vegas, Nev.

1984—Aug. 31—(WBC) Pinklon Thomas def. Tim Witherspoon, 12, Las Vegas, Nev.

1984—Dec. 2—(WBA) Greg Page KOd Gerrie Coetzee, 8, Sun City, Bophuthatswana

1985—Apr. 29—(WBA) Tony Tubbs def. Greg Page, 15, Buffalo, N.Y.

1985—Sept. 21—(IBF) Michael Spinks def. Larry Holmes, 15, Las Vegas, Nev.

1986—Jan. 17—(WBA) Tim Witherspoon def. Tony Tubbs, 15, Atlanta, Ga.

1986—Mar. 23—(WBC) Trevor Berbick def. Pinklon Thomas, 12, Miami, Fla.

1986—Nov. 22—(WBC) Mike Tyson KOd Trevor Berbick, 2, Las Vegas.

1986—Dec. 12—(WBA) James (Bonecrusher) Smith KOd Tim Witherspoon, 1, New York.

1987—Mar. 7—(WBA) Mike Tyson def. James (Bonecrusher) Smith, 12, Las Vegas.

1988—June 27—(IBF) Mike Tyson KOd Michael Spinks, 1, Atlantic City.

1990—Feb. 11—(WBA, WBC, IBF) James "Buster" Douglas KOd Mike Tyson, 10, Tokyo.

1990—Oct. 25—(WBA, WBC, IBF) Evander Holyfield KOd James "Buster" Douglas, 3, Las Vegas.

1992—Nov. 13—(WBA, WBC, IBF) Riddick Bowe def. Evander Holyfield, 12, Las Vegas. (Lennox Lewis was later named WBC champion when Bowe refused to fight him.)

1993—Nov. 6—(WBA, IBF) Evander Holyfield def. Riddick Bowe, 12, Las Vegas.

1994—Apr. 22—(WBA, IBF) Michael Moorer def. Evander Holyfield, 12, Las Vegas.

1994—Sept. 24—(WBC) Oliver McCall KOd Lennox Lewis, 2, London.

1994—Nov. 5—(WBA, IBF) George Foreman KOd Michael Moorer, 10, Las Vegas. (In March 1995, Foreman was stripped of the WBA title, which was awarded to Bruce Seldon. In July, Foreman relinquished the IBF title.)

1995—Sept. 2— (WBC) Frank Bruno def. Oliver McCall, 12, London.

Pro Rodeo Championship Standings in 1994

Event	Winner	Money won	Event	Winner	Money won
All Around	Ty Murray, Stephenville, TX	$246,170	Steer Roping	Guy Allen, Lovington, NM.	$57,338
Saddle Bronc	Dan Mortenson, Manhattan, MT. . .	177,664	Team Roping	Jake Barns, Cave Creek, AZ &	
Bareback	Marvin Garrett, Belle Fourch, SD . . .	124,001		Clay O'Brien Cooper, Higley, AZ . . .	94,461
Bull Riding	Daryl Mills, Pink Mountain, B.C. . . .	105,178			
Calf Roping	Herbert Theriot, Wiggins, MS	151,922	Women's Barrel		
Steer Wrestling	Blaine Pederson, Amisk, Alta.	102,301	Racing	Kristie Peterson, Elbert, CO	110,341

Pro Rodeo Cowboy All-Around Champions

Year	Winner	Money won	Year	Winner	Money won
1972	Phil Lyne, George West, TX	$60,852	1983	Roy Cooper, Durant, OK	$153,391
1973	Larry Mahan, Dallas, TX.	64,447	1984	Dee Pickett, Caldwell, ID.	122,618
1974	Tom Ferguson, Miami, OK	66,929	1985	Lewis Feild, Elk Ridge, UT.	130,347
1975	Leo Camarillo, Oakdale, CA	50,300	1986	Lewis Feild, Elk Ridge, UT.	166,042
	Tom Ferguson, Miami, OK	50,300	1987	Lewis Feild, Elk Ridge, UT.	144,335
1976	Tom Ferguson, Miami, OK	87,908	1988	Dave Appleton, Arlington, TX.	121,546
1977	Tom Ferguson, Miami, OK	76,730	1989	Ty Murray, Odessa, TX.	134,806
1978	Tom Ferguson, Miami, OK	103,734	1990	Ty Murray, Stephenville, TX	213,772
1979	Tom Ferguson, Miami, OK	96,272	1991	Ty Murray, Stephenville, TX	244,230
1980	Paul Tierney, Rapid City, SD	105,568	1992	Ty Murray, Stephenville, TX	225,992
1981	Jimmie Cooper, Monument, NM . . .	105,862	1993	Ty Murray, Stephenville, TX	297,896
1982	Chris Lybbert, Coyote, CA.	123,709	1994	Ty Murray, Stephenville, TX	246,170

The America's Cup

In the 1995 America's Cup match, the New Zealand yacht *Black Magic 1* defeated the U.S. yacht *Young America* 5-0 in the waters off San Diego, CA. It was only the 2d time since 1851 that the U.S. lost the Cup. *Black Magic 1* was skippered by Russell Coutts. The next America's Cup competition is scheduled for 1999-2000 in New Zealand.

Competition for the America's Cup grew out of the first contest to establish a world yachting championship, one of the carnival features of the London Exposition of 1851. The race, open to all classes of yachts from all over the world, covered a 60-mi course around the Isle of Wight; the prize was a cup worth about $500, donated by the Royal Yacht Squadron of England, known as the "America's Cup" because it was first won by the U.S. yacht *America*.

Winners of the America's Cup

1851	America	1937	Ranger defeated Endeavour II, England, (4-0)
1870	Magic defeated Cambria, England, (1-0)	1958	Columbia defeated Sceptre, England, (4-0)
1871	Columbia (first three races) and Sappho (last two races)	1962	Weatherly defeated Gretel, Australia, (4-1)
	defeated Livonia, England, (4-1)	1964	Constellation defeated Sovereign, England, (4-0)
1876	Madeline defeated Countess of Dufferin, Canada, (2-0)	1967	Intrepid defeated Dame Pattie, Australia, (4-0)
1881	Mischief defeated Atalanta, Canada, (2-0)	1970	Intrepid defeated Gretel II, Australia, (4-1)
1885	Puritan defeated Genesta, England, (2-0)	1974	Courageous defeated Southern Cross, Australia, (4-0)
1886	Mayflower defeated Galatea, England, (2-0)	1977	Courageous defeated Australia, Australia, (4-0)
1887	Volunteer defeated Thistle, Scotland, (2-0)	1980	Freedom defeated Australia, Australia, (4-1)
1893	Vigilant defeated Valkyrie II, England, (3-0)	1983	Australia II, Australia, defeated Liberty, (4-3)
1895	Defender defeated Valkyrie III, England, (3-0)	1987	Stars & Stripes defeated Kookaburra III, Australia, (4-0)
1899	Columbia defeated Shamrock, England, (3-0)	1988	Stars & Stripes defeated New Zealand, New Zealand,
1901	Columbia defeated Shamrock II, England, (3-0)		(2-0)
1903	Reliance defeated Shamrock III, England, (3-0)	1992	America[3] defeated Il Moro di Venezia, Italy, (4-1)
1920	Resolute defeated Shamrock IV, England, (3-2)	1995	Black Magic 1, New Zealand, defeated Young America
1930	Enterprise defeated Shamrock V, England, (4-0)		(5-0)
1934	Rainbow defeated Endeavour, England, (4-2)		

American Power Boat Assn. Gold Cup Champions

Year	Boat	Driver	Year	Boat	Driver
1975	Pay 'N Pak	George Henley	1986	Miller American.	Chip Hanauer
1976	Miss U.S.	Tom D'Eath	1987	Miller American.	Chip Hanauer
1977	Atlas Van Lines	Bill Muncey	1988	Miller American.	Chip Hanauer
1978	Atlas Van Lines	Bill Muncey	1989	Miss Budweiser	Tom D'Eath
1979	Atlas Van Lines	Bill Muncey	1990	Miss Budweiser	Tom D'Eath
1980	Miss Budweiser	Dean Chenoweth	1991	Winston Eagle	Mark Tate
1981	Miss Budweiser	Dean Chenoweth	1992	Miss Budweiser	Chip Hanauer
1982	Atlas Van Lines	Chip Hanauer	1993	Miss Budweiser	Chip Hanauer
1983	Atlas Van Lines	Chip Hanauer	1994	Smokin' Joe's	Mark Tate
1984	Atlas Van Lines	Chip Hanauer	1995	Miss Budweiser	Chip Hanauer
1985	Miller American	Chip Hanauer			

The World Cup

In 1994 the World Cup, emblematic of international soccer supremacy, was held in the U.S. for the first time. Brazil captured an unprecedented 4th World Cup by defeating Italy on July 17, 1994, at the Rose Bowl in Pasadena CA. For the first time ever, the final was decided in the tie-breaking, penalty-kick round, in which Brazil outscored Italy 3-2, after neither team had been able to score in 90 minutes of regulation time and an additional 30 minutes of extra time. The 1998 World Cup is scheduled to be held in France. Winners and sites of all World Cup tournaments follow:

Year	Winner	Final opponent	Site	Year	Winner	Final opponent	Site
1930	Uruguay	Argentina	Uruguay	1970	Brazil	Italy	Mexico
1934	Italy	Czechoslovakia	Italy	1974	W. Germany	Netherlands	W. Germany
1938	Italy	Hungary	France	1978	Argentina	Netherlands	Argentina
1950	Uruguay	Brazil	Brazil	1982	Italy	W. Germany	Spain
1954	W. Germany	Hungary	Switzerland	1986	Argentina	W. Germany	Mexico
1958	Brazil	Sweden	Sweden	1990	W. Germany	Argentina	Italy
1962	Brazil	Czechoslovakia	Chile	1994	Brazil	Italy	U.S.
1966	England	W. Germany	England				

BASEBALL

1995 Review: Strike Settled, Attendance Down, Cal Is the New "Iron Man"

On April 2, 1995, the longest work stoppage in the history of professional sports came to an end when major league baseball owners accepted the players' offer to return to work, although the issues that led to the strike remained unresolved. The 234-day strike, which began on Aug. 12, 1994, caused the cancellation of the 1994 postseason and shortened the 1995 season to 144 games. Before the strike ended, major league teams had held spring training with replacement players. Baseball fans showed their displeasure with the game by staying away from the ballpark; attendance was generally down in 1995. By the end of the 1995 season there was still no collective bargaining agreement between the two sides. There were bright spots, however. Baltimore Orioles shortstop Cal Ripken, Jr., broke Lou Gehrig's record for most consecutive games played, Sept. 6, and the first "full" season with the new divisional alignment and extra tier of playoffs led to exciting pennant races in both leagues. In other baseball news, two new teams are scheduled to join the major leagues in 1998, the Arizona Diamondbacks (Phoenix) and the Tampa Bay Devil Rays; league designations had yet to be determined as of Oct. 1995.

Major League Pennant Winners, 1901–1995

	National League						American League				
Year	Winner	Won	Lost	Pct	Manager	Year	Winner	Won	Lost	Pct	Manager
1901	Pittsburgh	90	49	.647	Clarke	1901	Chicago	83	53	.610	Griffith
1902	Pittsburgh	103	36	.741	Clarke	1902	Philadelphia	83	53	.610	Mack
1903	Pittsburgh	91	49	.650	Clarke	1903	Boston	91	47	.659	Collins
1904	New York	106	47	.693	McGraw	1904	Boston	95	59	.617	Collins
1905	New York	105	48	.686	McGraw	1905	Philadelphia	92	56	.622	Mack
1906	Chicago	116	36	.763	Chance	1906	Chicago	93	58	.616	Jones
1907	Chicago	107	45	.704	Chance	1907	Detroit	92	58	.613	Jennings
1908	Chicago	99	55	.643	Chance	1908	Detroit	90	63	.588	Jennings
1909	Pittsburgh	110	42	.724	Clarke	1909	Detroit	98	54	.645	Jennings
1910	Chicago	104	50	.675	Chance	1910	Philadelphia	102	48	.680	Mack
1911	New York	99	54	.647	McGraw	1911	Philadelphia	101	50	.669	Mack
1912	New York	103	48	.682	McGraw	1912	Boston	105	47	.691	Stahl
1913	New York	101	51	.664	McGraw	1913	Philadelphia	96	57	.627	Mack
1914	Boston	94	59	.614	Stallings	1914	Philadelphia	99	53	.651	Mack
1915	Philadelphia	90	62	.592	Moran	1915	Boston	101	50	.669	Carrigan
1916	Brooklyn	94	60	.610	Robinson	1916	Boston	91	63	.591	Carrigan
1917	New York	98	56	.636	McGraw	1917	Chicago	100	54	.649	Rowland
1918	Chicago	84	45	.651	Mitchell	1918	Boston	75	51	.595	Barrow
1919	Cincinnati	96	44	.686	Moran	1919	Chicago	88	52	.629	Gleason
1920	Brooklyn	93	60	.604	Robinson	1920	Cleveland	98	56	.636	Speaker
1921	New York	94	56	.614	McGraw	1921	New York	98	55	.641	Huggins
1922	New York	93	61	.604	McGraw	1922	New York	94	60	.610	Huggins
1923	New York	95	58	.621	McGraw	1923	New York	98	54	.645	Huggins
1924	New York	93	60	.608	McGraw	1924	Washington	92	62	.597	Harris
1925	Pittsburgh	95	58	.621	McKechnie	1925	Washington	96	55	.636	Harris
1926	St. Louis	89	65	.578	Hornsby	1926	New York	91	63	.591	Huggins
1927	Pittsburgh	94	60	.610	Bush	1927	New York	110	44	.714	Huggins
1928	St. Louis	95	59	.617	McKechnie	1928	New York	101	53	.656	Huggins
1929	Chicago	98	54	.645	McCarthy	1929	Philadelphia	104	46	.693	Mack
1930	St. Louis	92	62	.597	Street	1930	Philadelphia	102	52	.662	Mack
1931	St. Louis	101	53	.656	Street	1931	Philadelphia	107	45	.704	Mack
1932	Chicago	90	64	.584	Grimm	1932	New York	107	47	.695	McCarthy
1933	New York	91	61	.599	Terry	1933	Washington	99	53	.651	Cronin
1934	St. Louis	95	58	.621	Frisch	1934	Detroit	101	53	.656	Cochrane
1935	Chicago	100	54	.649	Grimm	1935	Detroit	93	58	.616	Cochrane
1936	New York	91	62	.597	Terry	1936	New York	102	51	.667	McCarthy
1937	New York	95	57	.625	Terry	1937	New York	102	52	.662	McCarthy
1938	Chicago	89	63	.586	Hartnett	1938	New York	99	53	.651	McCarthy
1939	Cincinnati	97	57	.630	McKechnie	1939	New York	106	45	.702	McCarthy
1940	Cincinnati	100	53	.654	McKechnie	1940	Detroit	90	64	.584	Baker
1941	Brooklyn	100	54	.649	Durocher	1941	New York	101	53	.656	McCarthy
1942	St. Louis	106	48	.688	Southworth	1942	New York	103	51	.669	McCarthy
1943	St. Louis	105	49	.682	Southworth	1943	New York	98	56	.636	McCarthy
1944	St. Louis	105	49	.682	Southworth	1944	St. Louis	89	65	.578	Sewell
1945	Chicago	98	56	.636	Grimm	1945	Detroit	88	65	.575	O'Neill
1946	St. Louis	98	58	.628	Dyer	1946	Boston	104	50	.675	Cronin
1947	Brooklyn	94	60	.610	Shotton	1947	New York	97	57	.630	Harris
1948	Boston	91	62	.595	Southworth	1948	Cleveland	97	58	.626	Boudreau
1949	Brooklyn	97	57	.630	Shotton	1949	New York	97	57	.630	Stengel
1950	Philadelphia	91	63	.591	Sawyer	1950	New York	98	56	.636	Stengel
1951	New York	98	59	.624	Durocher	1951	New York	98	56	.636	Stengel
1952	Brooklyn	96	57	.627	Dressen	1952	New York	95	59	.617	Stengel
1953	Brooklyn	105	49	.682	Dressen	1953	New York	99	52	.656	Stengel
1954	New York	97	57	.630	Durocher	1954	Cleveland	111	43	.721	Lopez
1955	Brooklyn	98	55	.641	Alston	1955	New York	96	58	.623	Stengel
1956	Brooklyn	93	61	.604	Alston	1956	New York	97	57	.630	Stengel
1957	Milwaukee	95	59	.617	Haney	1957	New York	98	56	.636	Stengel
1958	Milwaukee	92	62	.597	Haney	1958	New York	92	62	.597	Stengel
1959	Los Angeles	88	68	.564	Alston	1959	Chicago	94	60	.610	Lopez
1960	Pittsburgh	95	59	.617	Murtaugh	1960	New York	97	57	.630	Stengel
1961	Cincinnati	93	61	.604	Hutchinson	1961	New York	109	53	.673	Houk
1962	San Francisco	103	62	.624	Dark	1962	New York	96	66	.593	Houk
1963	Los Angeles	99	63	.611	Alston	1963	New York	104	57	.646	Houk
1964	St. Louis	93	69	.574	Keane	1964	New York	99	63	.611	Berra
1965	Los Angeles	97	65	.599	Alston	1965	Minnesota	102	60	.630	Mele
1966	Los Angeles	95	67	.586	Alston	1966	Baltimore	97	63	.606	Bauer
1967	St. Louis	101	60	.627	Schoendienst	1967	Boston	92	70	.568	Williams
1968	St. Louis	97	65	.599	Schoendienst	1968	Detroit	103	59	.636	Smith

National League

Year	East Winner	W	L	Pct	Manager	West Winner	W	L	Pct	Manager	Pennant winner
1969	N.Y. Mets	100	62	.617	Hodges	Atlanta	93	69	.574	Harris	New York
1970	Pittsburgh	89	73	.549	Murtaugh	Cincinnati	102	60	.630	Anderson	Cincinnati
1971	Pittsburgh	97	65	.599	Murtaugh	San Francisco . . .	90	72	.556	Fox	Pittsburgh
1972	Pittsburgh	96	59	.619	Virdon	Cincinnati	95	59	.617	Anderson	Cincinnati
1973	N.Y. Mets	82	79	.509	Berra	Cincinnati	99	63	.611	Anderson	New York
1974	Pittsburgh	88	74	.543	Murtaugh	Los Angeles.	102	60	.630	Alston	Los Angeles
1975	Pittsburgh	92	69	.571	Murtaugh	Cincinnati	108	54	.667	Anderson	Cincinnati
1976	Philadelphia . .	101	61	.623	Ozark	Cincinnati	102	60	.630	Anderson	Cincinnati
1977	Philadelphia . .	101	61	.623	Ozark	Los Angeles.	98	64	.605	Lasorda	Los Angeles
1978	Philadelphia . .	90	72	.556	Ozark	Los Angeles.	95	67	.586	Lasorda	Los Angeles
1979	Pittsburgh	98	64	.605	Tanner	Cincinnati	90	71	.559	McNamara	Pittsburgh
1980	Philadelphia . .	91	71	.562	Green	Houston	93	70	.571	Virdon	Philadelphia
1981(a)	Philadelphia . .	34	21	.618	Green	Los Angeles.	36	21	.632	Lasorda	(c)
1981(b)	Montreal	30	23	.566	Williams, Fanning	Houston	33	20	.623	Virdon	Los Angeles
1982	St. Louis	92	70	.568	Herzog	Atlanta	89	73	.549	Torre	St. Louis
1983	Philadelphia . .	90	72	.556	Corrales, Owens	Los Angeles.	91	71	.562	Lasorda	Philadelphia
1984	Chicago	96	65	.596	Frey	San Diego	92	70	.568	Williams	San Diego
1985	St. Louis	101	61	.623	Herzog	Los Angeles.	95	67	.586	Lasorda	St. Louis
1986	N.Y. Mets	108	54	.667	Johnson	Houston	96	66	.593	Lanier	New York
1987	St. Louis	95	67	.586	Herzog	San Francisco . . .	90	72	.556	Craig	St. Louis
1988	N.Y. Mets	100	60	.625	Johnson	Los Angeles.	94	67	.584	Lasorda	Los Angeles
1989	Chicago	93	69	.571	Zimmer	San Francisco . . .	92	70	.568	Craig	San Francisco
1990	Pittsburgh	95	67	.586	Leyland	Cincinnati	91	71	.562	Piniella	Cincinnati
1991	Pittsburgh	98	64	.605	Leyland	Atlanta	94	68	.580	Cox	Atlanta
1992	Pittsburgh	96	66	.593	Leyland	Atlanta	98	64	.605	Cox	Atlanta
1993	Philadelphia . .	97	65	.599	Fregosi	Atlanta	104	58	.642	Cox	Philadelphia

Year	Division	Winner	W	L	Pct.	Playoffs	Pennant Winner	Manager
1994(d)	East	Montreal	74	40	.649	—	—	—
	Central	Cincinnati	66	48	.579			
	West	Los Angeles	58	56	.509			
1995	East	Atlanta	90	54	.625	Atlanta 3, Colorado* 1	Atlanta	Cox
	Central	Cincinnati	85	59	.590	Cincinnati 3, Los Angeles 0		
	West	Los Angeles	78	66	.542	Atlanta 4, Cincinnati 0		

American League

Year	East Winner	W	L	Pct	Manager	West Winner	W	L	Pct	Manager	Pennant winner
1969	Baltimore . . .	109	53	.673	Weaver	Minnesota. . . .	97	65	.599	Martin	Baltimore
1970	Baltimore . . .	108	54	.667	Weaver	Minnesota. . . .	98	64	.605	Rigney	Baltimore
1971	Baltimore . . .	101	57	.639	Weaver	Oakland	101	60	.627	Williams	Baltimore
1972	Detroit	86	70	.551	Martin	Oakland	93	62	.600	Williams	Oakland
1973	Baltimore . . .	97	65	.599	Weaver	Oakland	94	68	.580	Williams	Oakland
1974	Baltimore . . .	91	71	.562	Weaver	Oakland	90	72	.556	Dark	Oakland
1975	Boston	95	65	.594	Johnson	Oakland	98	64	.605	Dark	Boston
1976	New York . . .	97	62	.610	Martin	Kansas City. .	90	72	.556	Herzog	New York
1977	New York . . .	100	62	.617	Martin	Kansas City. .	102	60	.630	Herzog	New York
1978	New York . . .	100	63	.613	Martin, Lemon	Kansas City. .	92	70	.568	Herzog	New York
1979	Baltimore . . .	102	57	.642	Weaver	California	88	74	.543	Fregosi	Baltimore
1980	New York . . .	103	59	.636	Howser	Kansas City. .	97	65	.599	Frey	Kansas City
1981(a)	New York . . .	34	22	.607	Michael	Oakland	37	23	.617	Martin	(c)
1981(b)	Milwaukee . .	31	22	.585	Rodgers	Kansas City. .	30	23	.566	Frey, Howser	New York
1982	Milwaukee . .	95	67	.586	Rodgers, Kuenn	California	93	69	.574	Mauch	Milwaukee
1983	Baltimore . . .	98	64	.605	Altobelli	Chicago	99	63	.611	LaRussa	Baltimore
1984	Detroit	104	58	.642	Anderson	Kansas City. .	84	78	.519	Howser	Detroit
1985	Toronto.	99	62	.615	Cox	Kansas City. .	91	71	.562	Howser	Kansas City
1986	Boston	95	66	.590	McNamara	California	92	70	.568	Mauch	Boston
1987	Detroit	98	64	.605	Anderson	Minnesota. . . .	85	77	.525	Kelly	Minnesota
1988	Boston	89	73	.549	McNamara, Morgan	Oakland	104	58	.642	LaRussa	Oakland
1989	Toronto.	89	73	.549	Williams, Gaston	Oakland	99	63	.611	LaRussa	Oakland
1990	Boston	88	74	.543	Morgan	Oakland	103	59	.636	LaRussa	Oakland
1991	Toronto.	91	71	.562	Gaston	Minnesota. . . .	95	67	.586	Kelly	Minnesota
1992	Toronto.	96	66	.593	Gaston	Oakland	96	66	.593	LaRussa	Toronto
1993	Toronto.	95	67	.586	Gaston	Chicago	94	68	.580	Lamont	Toronto

Year	Division	Winner	W	L	Pct.	Playoffs	Pennant Winner	Manager
1994(d)	East	New York	70	43	.619	—	—	—
	Central	Chicago	67	46	.593			
	West	Texas	52	62	.456			
1995	East	Boston	86	58	.597	Cleveland 3, Boston 0	Cleveland	Hargrove
	Central	Cleveland	100	44	.694	Seattle 3, New York* 2		
	West	Seattle	79	66	.545	Cleveland 4, Seattle 2		

*Wild card team. (a) First half. (b) Second half. (c) Montreal, L.A., N.Y. Yankees, and Oakland won the divisional playoffs. (d) In Aug. 1994, a players strike began that caused the cancellation of the remainder of the season, the playoffs, and the World Series.

Cal Ripken, Jr., Breaks Lou Gehrig's Consecutive Games Record

On Sept. 6, 1995, Baltimore Orioles shortstop Cal Ripken, Jr., played in his 2,131st consecutive game to break Lou Gehrig's record, which had stood for over 56 years and was thought by many to be unbreakable. Here is a comparison of some of their statistics during their respective streaks:

Lou Gehrig		Cal Ripken, Jr.
June 1, 1925	Streak began	May 30, 1982
April 30, 1939	Streak ended	—
2,130	Consecutive games played	2,153*
7,938	At bats	8,387
2,700	Hits	2,330
492	Home Runs	324
1,984	Runs Batted In	1,247
.340	Batting Average	.278

*As of the end of the 1995 season.

The Sporting News Gold Glove Awards in 1994

National League	**American League**
Greg Maddux, Atlanta, pitcher	Mark Langston, California, pitcher
Tom Pagnozzi, St. Louis, catcher	Ivan Rodriguez, Texas, catcher
Jeff Bagwell, Houston, first base	Don Mattingly, New York, first base
Craig Biggio, Houston, second base	Roberto Alomar, Toronto, second base
Matt Williams, San Francisco, third base	Wade Boggs, New York, third base
Barry Larkin, Cincinnati, shortstop	Omar Vizquel, Cleveland, shortstop
Barry Bonds, San Francisco, outfield	Ken Griffey, Jr., Seattle, outfield
Marquis Grissom, Montreal,	Kenny Lofton, Cleveland, outfield
Darren Lewis, San Francisco, outfield	Devon White, Toronto, outfield

The following are the players at each position who have won the most Gold Gloves since the award was instituted in 1957.

Pitcher:	Jim Kaat	16	Second base:	Ryne Sandberg	9	Outfield:	Roberto Clemente	12
	Bob Gibson	9		Bill Mazeroski	8		Willie Mays	12
Catcher:	Johnny Bench	10		Frank White	8		Al Kaline	10
	Bob Boone	7	Third base:	Brooks Robinson	16		Paul Blair	8
First base:	Keith Hernandez	11		Mike Schmidt	10		Dwight Evans	8
	Don Mattingly	9	Shortstop:	Ozzie Smith	13		Garry Maddox	8
				Luis Aparicio	9			

Home Run Leaders

National League				**American League**	
Year	**Player, Club**	**HR**	**Year**	**Player, Club**	**HR**
1901	Sam Crawford, Cincinnati	16	1901	Napoleon Lajoie, Philadelphia	14
1902	Thomas Leach, Pittsburgh	6	1902	Socks Seybold, Philadelphia	16
1903	James Sheckard, Brooklyn	9	1903	Buck Freeman, Boston	13
1904	Harry Lumley, Brooklyn	9	1904	Harry Davis, Philadelphia	10
1905	Fred Odwell, Cincinnati	9	1905	Harry Davis, Philadelphia	8
1906	Timothy Jordan, Brooklyn	12	1906	Harry Davis, Philadelphia	12
1907	David Brain, Boston	10	1907	Harry Davis, Philadelphia	8
1908	Timothy Jordan, Brooklyn	12	1908	Sam Crawford, Detroit	7
1909	Red Murray, New York	7	1909	Ty Cobb, Detroit	9
1910	Fred Beck, Bos., Frank Schulte, Chi.	10	1910	Jake Stahl, Boston	10
1911	Frank Schulte, Chicago	21	1911	J. Franklin Baker, Philadelphia	11
1912	Henry Zimmerman, Chicago	14	1912	J. Franklin Baker, Philadelphia, Tris Speaker, Boston	10
1913	Gavvy Cravath, Philadelphia	19	1913	J. Franklin, Baker, Philadelphia	12
1914	Gavvy Cravath, Philadelphia	19	1914	J. Franklin, Baker, Philadelphia	9
1915	Gavvy Cravath, Philadelphia	24	1915	Robert Roth, Chicago-Cleveland	7
1916	Dave Robertson, N.Y., Fred (Cy) Williams, Chi.	12	1916	Wally Pipp, New York	12
1917	Dave Robertson, N.Y., Gavvy Cravath, Phil.	12	1917	Wally Pipp, New York	9
1918	Gavvy Cravath, Philadelphia	8	1918	Babe Ruth, Bos., Tilly Walker, Phil.	11
1919	Gavvy Cravath, Philadelphia	12	1919	Babe Ruth, Boston	29
1920	Cy Williams, Philadelphia	15	1920	Babe Ruth, New York	54
1921	George Kelly, New York	23	1921	Babe Ruth, New York	59
1922	Rogers Hornsby, St. Louis	42	1922	Ken Williams, St. Louis	39
1923	Cy Williams, Philadelphia	41	1923	Babe Ruth, New York	41
1924	Jacques Fournier, Brooklyn	27	1924	Babe Ruth, New York	46
1925	Rogers Hornsby, St. Louis	39	1925	Bob Meusel, New York	33
1926	Hack Wilson, Chicago	21	1926	Babe Ruth, New York	47
1927	Hack Wilson, Chicago; Cy Williams, Philadelphia	30	1927	Babe Ruth, New York	60
1928	Hack Wilson, Chicago; Jim Bottomley, St. Louis	31	1928	Babe Ruth, New York	54
1929	Chuck Klein, Philadelphia	43	1929	Babe Ruth, New York	46
1930	Hack Wilson, Chicago	56	1930	Babe Ruth, New York	49
1931	Chuck Klein, Philadelphia	31	1931	Babe Ruth, Lou Gehrig, New York	46
1932	Chuck Klein, Philadelphia, Mel Ott, New York	38	1932	Jimmie Foxx, Philadelphia	58
1933	Chuck Klein, Philadelphia	28	1933	Jimmie Foxx, Philadelphia	48
1934	Rip Collins, St. Louis; Mel Ott, New York	35	1934	Lou Gehrig, New York	49
1935	Walter Berger, Boston	34	1935	Jimmie Foxx, Philadelphia, Hank Greenberg, Detroit	36
1936	Mel Ott, New York	33	1936	Lou Gehrig, New York	49
1937	Mel Ott, New York; Joe Medwick, St. Louis	31	1937	Joe DiMaggio, New York	46
1938	Mel Ott, New York	36	1938	Hank Greenberg, Detroit	58
1939	John Mize, St. Louis	28	1939	Jimmie Foxx, Boston	35
1940	John Mize, St. Louis	43	1940	Hank Greenberg, Detroit	41
1941	Dolph Camilli, Brooklyn	34	1941	Ted Williams, Boston	37
1942	Mel Ott, New York	30	1942	Ted Williams, Boston	36
1943	Bill Nicholson, Chicago	29	1943	Rudy York, Detroit	34
1944	Bill Nicholson, Chicago	33	1944	Nick Etten, New York	22
1945	Tommy Holmes, Boston	28	1945	Vern Stephens, St. Louis	24
1946	Ralph Kiner, Pittsburgh	23	1946	Hank Greenberg, Detroit	44
1947	Ralph Kiner, Pittsburgh; John Mize, New York.	51	1947	Ted Williams, Boston	32
1948	Ralph Kiner, Pittsburgh; John Mize, New York.	40	1948	Joe DiMaggio, New York	39
1949	Ralph Kiner, Pittsburgh	54	1949	Ted Williams, Boston	43
1950	Ralph Kiner, Pittsburgh	47	1950	Al Rosen, Cleveland	37
1951	Ralph Kiner, Pittsburgh	42	1951	Gus Zernial, Chicago-Philadelphia	33
1952	Ralph Kiner, Pittsburgh; Hank Sauer, Chicago.	37	1952	Larry Doby, Cleveland	32
1953	Ed Mathews, Milwaukee	47	1953	Al Rosen, Cleveland	43
1954	Ted Kluszewski, Cincinnati	49	1954	Larry Doby, Cleveland	32
1955	Willie Mays, New York	51	1955	Mickey Mantle, New York	37
1956	Duke Snider, Brooklyn	43	1956	Mickey Mantle, New York	52
1957	Hank Aaron, Milwaukee	44	1957	Roy Sievers, Washington	42
1958	Ernie Banks, Chicago	47	1958	Mickey Mantle, New York	42
1959	Ed Mathews, Milwaukee	46	1959	Rocky Colavito, Cleve., Harmon Killebrew, Wash.	42
1960	Ernie Banks, Chicago	41	1960	Mickey Mantle, New York	40
1961	Orlando Cepeda, San Francisco	46	1961	Roger Maris, New York	61

National League

Year	Player, Club	HR
1962	Willie Mays, San Francisco	49
1963	Hank Aaron, Milwaukee, Willie McCovey, S.F.	44
1964	Willie Mays, San Francisco	47
1965	Willie Mays, San Francisco	52
1966	Hank Aaron, Atlanta	44
1967	Hank Aaron, Atlanta	39
1968	Willie McCovey, San Francisco	36
1969	Willie McCovey, San Francisco	45
1970	Johnny Bench, Cincinnati	45
1971	Willie Stargell, Pittsburgh	48
1972	Johnny Bench, Cincinnati	40
1973	Willie Stargell, Pittsburgh	44
1974	Mike Schmidt, Philadelphia	36
1975	Mike Schmidt, Philadelphia	38
1976	Mike Schmidt, Philadelphia	38
1977	George Foster, Cincinnati	52
1978	George Foster, Cincinnati	40
1979	Dave Kingman, Chicago	48
1980	Mike Schmidt, Philadelphia	48
1981	Mike Schmidt, Philadelphia	31
1982	Dave Kingman, New York	37
1983	Mike Schmidt, Philadelphia	40
1984	Mike Schmidt, Phil.; Dale Murphy, Atlanta	36
1985	Dale Murphy, Atlanta	37
1986	Mike Schmidt, Philadelphia	37
1987	Andre Dawson, Chicago	49
1988	Darryl Strawberry, New York	39
1989	Kevin Mitchell, San Francisco	47
1990	Ryne Sandberg, Chicago	40
1991	Howard Johnson, New York	38
1992	Fred McGriff, San Diego	35
1993	Barry Bonds, San Francisco	46
1994	Matt Williams, San Francisco	43
1995	Dante Bichette, Colorado	40

American League

Year	Player, Club	HR
1962	Harmon Killebrew, Minnesota	48
1963	Harmon Killebrew, Minnesota	45
1964	Harmon Killebrew, Minnesota	49
1965	Tony Conigliaro, Boston	32
1966	Frank Robinson, Baltimore	49
1967	Carl Yastrzemski, Boston, Harmon Killebrew, Minn.	44
1968	Frank Howard, Washington	44
1969	Harmon Killebrew, Minnesota	49
1970	Frank Howard, Washington	44
1971	Bill Melton, Chicago	33
1972	Dick Allen, Chicago	37
1973	Reggie Jackson, Oakland	32
1974	Dick Allen, Chicago	32
1975	George Scott, Milwaukee; Reggie Jackson, Oakland	36
1976	Graig Nettles, New York	32
1977	Jim Rice, Boston	39
1978	Jim Rice, Boston	46
1979	Gorman Thomas, Milwaukee	45
1980	Reggie Jackson, New York; Ben Oglivie, Milwaukee	41
1981	Bobby Grich, California; Tony Armas, Oakland; Dwight Evans, Boston; Eddie Murray, Baltimore	22
1982	Gorman Thomas, Milwaukee; Reggie Jackson, Cal.	39
1983	Jim Rice, Boston	39
1984	Tony Armas, Boston	43
1985	Darrell Evans, Detroit	40
1986	Jesse Barfield, Toronto	40
1987	Mark McGwire, Oakland	49
1988	Jose Canseco, Oakland	42
1989	Fred McGriff, Toronto	36
1990	Cecil Fielder, Detroit	51
1991	Cecil Fielder, Detroit; Jose Canseco, Oakland	44
1992	Juan Gonzalez, Texas	43
1993	Juan Gonzalez, Texas	46
1994	Ken Griffey Jr., Seattle	40
1995	Albert Belle, Cleveland	50

Runs Batted In Leaders

National League

Year	Player, Club	RBI
1907	Honus Wagner, Pittsburgh	91
1908	Honus Wager, Pittsburgh	106
1909	Honus Wager, Pittsburgh	102
1910	Sherwood Magee, Philadelphia	116
1911	Frank Schulte, Chicago	121
1912	Henry Zimmerman, Chicago	98
1913	Gavvy Cravath, Philadelphia	118
1914	Sherwood Magee, Philadelphia	101
1915	Gavvy Cravath, Philadelphia	118
1916	Hal Chase, Cincinnati	94
1917	Henry Zimmerman, New York	100
1918	Frederick Merkle, Chicago	71
1919	Hi Myers, Boston	72
1920	George Kelly, N.Y., Rogers Hornsby, St. Louis	94
1921	Rogers Hornsby, St. Louis	126
1922	Rogers Hornsby, St. Louis	152
1923	Emil Meusel, New York	125
1924	George Kelly, New York	136
1925	Rogers Hornsby, St. Louis	143
1926	Jim Bottomley, St. Louis	120
1927	Paul Waner, Pittsburgh	131
1928	Jim Bottomley, St. Louis	136
1929	Hack Wilson, Chicago	159
1930	Hack Wilson, Chicago	190
1931	Chuck Klein, Philadelphia	121
1932	Don Hurst, Philadelphia	143
1933	Chuck Klein, Philadelphia	120
1934	Mel Ott, New York	135
1935	Walter Berger, Boston	130
1936	Joe Medwick, St. Louis	138
1937	Joe Medwick, St. Louis	154
1938	Joe Medwick, St. Louis	122
1939	Frank McCormick, Cincinnati	128
1940	John Mize, St. Louis	137
1941	Adolph Camilli, Brooklyn	120
1942	John Mize, New York	110
1943	Bill Nicholson, Chicago	128
1944	Bill Nicholson, Chicago	122
1945	Dixie Walker, Brooklyn	124
1946	Enos Slaughter, St. Louis	130
1947	John Mize, New York	138
1948	Stan Musial, St. Louis	131
1949	Ralph Kiner, Pittsburgh	127
1950	Del Ennis, Philadelphia	126
1951	Monte Irvin, New York	121

American League

Year	Player, Club	RBI
1907	Ty Cobb, Detroit	116
1908	Ty Cobb, Detroit	101
1909	Ty Cobb, Detroit	115
1910	Sam Crawford, Detroit	115
1911	Ty Cobb, Detroit	144
1912	J. Franklin Baker, Philadelphia	133
1913	J. Franklin Baker, Philadelphia	126
1914	Sam Crawford, Detroit	112
1915	Sam Crawford, Detroit	116
1916	Wally Pipp, New York	99
1917	Robert Veach, Detroit	115
1918	George Burns, Phila., Robert Veach, Detroit	74
1919	Babe Ruth, Boston	112
1920	Babe Ruth, New York	137
1921	Babe Ruth, New York	171
1922	Ken Williams, St. Louis	155
1923	Babe Ruth, New York	131
1924	Goose Goslin, Washington	129
1925	Bob Meusel, New York	138
1926	Babe Ruth, New York	145
1927	Lou Gehrig, New York	175
1928	Babe Ruth, N.Y., Lou Gehrig, N.Y.	142
1929	Al Simmons, Philadelphia	157
1930	Lou Gehrig, New York	174
1931	Lou Gehrig, New York	184
1932	Jimmie Foxx, Philadelphia	169
1933	Jimmie Foxx, Philadelphia	163
1934	Lou Gehrig, New York	165
1935	Hank Greenberg, Detroit	170
1936	Hal Trosky, Cleveland	162
1937	Hank Greenberg, Detroit	183
1938	Jimmie Foxx, Boston	175
1939	Ted Williams, Boston	145
1940	Hank Greenberg, Detroit	150
1941	Joe DiMaggio, New York	125
1942	Ted Williams, Boston	137
1943	Rudy York, Detroit	118
1944	Vern Stephens, St. Louis	109
1945	Nick Etten, New York	111
1946	Hank Greenberg, Detroit	127
1947	Ted Williams, Boston	114
1948	Joe DiMaggio, New York	155
1949	Ted Williams, Bos., Vern Stephens, Bos.	159
1950	Walt Dropo, Bos., Vern Stephens, Bos.	144
1951	Gus Zernial, Chicago-Philadelphia	129

(continued)

National League		American League	
Year **Player, Club**	**RBI**	**Year** **Player, Club**	**RBI**
1952 Hank Sauer, Chicago	121	1952 Al Rosen, Cleveland	105
1953 Roy Campanella, Brooklyn	142	1953 Al Rosen, Cleveland	145
1954 Ted Kluszewski, Cincinnati	141	1954 Larry Doby, Cleveland	126
1955 Duke Snider, Brooklyn	136	1955 Ray Boone, Detroit, Jackie Jensen, Boston	116
1956 Stan Musial, St. Louis	109	1956 Mickey Mantle, New York	130
1957 Hank Aaron, Milwaukee	132	1957 Roy Sievers, Washington	114
1958 Ernie Banks, Chicago	129	1958 Jackie Jensen, Boston	122
1959 Ernie Banks, Chicago	143	1959 Jackie Jensen, Boston	112
1960 Hank Aaron, Milwaukee	126	1960 Roger Maris, New York	112
1961 Orlando Cepeda, San Francisco	142	1961 Roger Maris, New York	142
1962 Tommy Davis, Los Angeles	153	1962 Harmon Killebrew, Minnesota	126
1963 Hank Aaron, Milwaukee	130	1963 Dick Stuart, Boston	118
1964 Ken Boyer, St. Louis	119	1964 Brooks Robinson, Baltimore	118
1965 Deron Johnson, Cincinnati	130	1965 Rocky Colavito, Cleveland	108
1966 Hank Aaron, Atlanta	127	1966 Frank Robinson, Baltimore	122
1967 Orlando Cepeda, St. Louis	111	1967 Carl Yastrzemski, Boston	121
1968 Willie McCovey, San Francisco	105	1968 Ken Harrelson, Boston	109
1969 Willie McCovey, San Francisco	126	1969 Harmon Killebrew, Minnesota	140
1970 Johnny Bench, Cincinnati	148	1970 Frank Howard, Washington	126
1971 Joe Torre, St. Louis	137	1971 Harmon Killebrew, Minnesota	119
1972 Johnny Bench, Cincinnati	125	1972 Dick Allen, Chicago	113
1973 Willie Stargell, Pittsburgh	119	1973 Reggie Jackson, Oakland	117
1974 Johnny Bench, Cincinnati	129	1974 Jeff Burroughs, Texas	118
1975 Greg Luzinski, Philadelphia	120	1975 George Scott, Milwaukee	109
1976 George Foster, Cincinnati	121	1976 Lee May, Baltimore	109
1977 George Foster, Cincinnati	149	1977 Larry Hisle, Minnesota	119
1978 George Foster, Cincinnati	120	1978 Jim Rice, Boston	139
1979 Dave Winfield, San Diego	118	1979 Don Baylor, California	139
1980 Mike Schmidt, Philadelphia	121	1980 Cecil Cooper, Milwaukee	122
1981 Mike Schmidt, Philadelphia	91	1981 Eddie Murray, Baltimore	78
1982 Dale Murphy, Atlanta; Al Oliver, Montreal	109	1982 Hal McRae, Kansas City	133
1983 Dale Murphy, Atlanta	121	1983 Cecil Cooper, Milwaukee; Jim Rice, Boston	126
1984 Mike Schmidt, Phil.; Gary Carter, Montreal	106	1984 Tony Armas, Boston	123
1985 Dave Parker, Cincinnati	125	1985 Don Mattingly, New York	145
1986 Mike Schmidt, Philadelphia	119	1986 Joe Carter, Cleveland	121
1987 Andre Dawson, Chicago	137	1987 George Bell, Toronto	134
1988 Will Clark, San Francisco	109	1988 Jose Canseco, Oakland	124
1989 Kevin Mitchell, San Francisco	125	1989 Ruben Sierra, Texas	119
1990 Matt Williams, San Francisco	122	1990 Cecil Fielder, Detroit	132
1991 Howard Johnson, New York	117	1991 Cecil Fielder, Detroit	133
1992 Darren Daulton, Philadelphia	109	1992 Cecil Fielder, Detroit	124
1993 Barry Bonds, San Francisco	123	1993 Albert Belle, Cleveland	129
1994 Jeff Bagwell, Houston	116	1994 Kirby Puckett, Minnesota	112
1995 Dante Bichette, Colorado	128	1995 Albert Belle, Cleveland; Mo Vaughn, Boston	126

Batting Champions

National League				American League		
Year	**Player**	**Club**	**Avg.**	**Year** **Player**	**Club**	**Avg.**
1901	Jesse C. Burkett	St. Louis	.382	1901 Napoleon Lajoie	Philadelphia	.422
1902	Clarence Beaumont	Pittsburgh	.357	1902 Ed Delahanty	Washington	.376
1903	Honus Wagner	Pittsburgh	.355	1902 Napoleon Lajoie	Cleveland	.355
1904	Honus Wagner	Pittsburgh	.349	1904 Napoleon Lajoie	Cleveland	.381
1905	James Seymour	Cincinnati	.377	1905 Elmer Flick	Cleveland	.308
1906	Honus Wagner	Pittsburgh	.339	1906 George Stone	St. Louis	.358
1907	Honus Wagner	Pittsburgh	.350	1907 Ty Cobb	Detroit	.350
1908	Honus Wagner	Pittsburgh	.354	1908 Ty Cobb	Detroit	.324
1909	Honus Wagner	Pittsburgh	.339	1909 Ty Cobb	Detroit	.377
1910	Sherwood Magee	Philadelphia	.331	1910 Ty Cobb	Detroit	.385
1911	Honus Wagner	Pittsburgh	.334	1911 Ty Cobb	Detroit	.420
1912	Henry Zimmerman	Chicago	.372	1912 Ty Cobb	Detroit	.410
1913	Jacob Daubert	Brooklyn	.350	1913 Ty Cobb	Detroit	.390
1914	Jacob Daubert	Brooklyn	.329	1914 Ty Cobb	Detroit	.368
1915	Larry Doyle	New York	.320	1915 Ty Cobb	Detroit	.369
1916	Hal Chase	Cincinnati	.339	1916 Tris Speaker	Cleveland	.386
1917	Edd Roush	Cincinnati	.341	1917 Ty Cobb	Detroit	.383
1918	Zach Wheat	Brooklyn	.335	1918 Ty Cobb	Detroit	.382
1919	Edd Roush	Cincinnati	.321	1919 Ty Cobb	Detroit	.384
1920	Rogers Hornsby	St. Louis	.370	1920 George Sisler	St. Louis	.407
1921	Rogers Hornsby	St. Louis	.397	1921 Harry Heilmann	Detroit	.394
1922	Rogers Hornsby	St. Louis	.401	1922 George Sisler	St. Louis	.420
1923	Rogers Hornsby	St. Louis	.384	1923 Harry Heilmann	Detroit	.403
1924	Rogers Hornsby	St. Louis	.424	1924 Babe Ruth	New York	.378
1925	Rogers Hornsby	St. Louis	.403	1925 Harry Heilmann	Detroit	.393
1926	Eugene Hargrave	Cincinnati	.353	1926 Henry Manush	Detroit	.378
1927	Paul Waner	Pittsburgh	.380	1927 Harry Heilmann	Detroit	.398
1928	Rogers Hornsby	Boston	.387	1928 Goose Goslin	Washington	.379
1929	Lefty O'Doul	Philadelphia	.398	1929 Lew Fonseca	Cleveland	.369
1930	Bill Terry	New York	.401	1930 Al Simmons	Philadelphia	.381
1931	Chick Hafey	St. Louis	.349	1931 Al Simmons	Philadelphia	.390
1932	Lefty O'Doul	Brooklyn	.368	1932 Dale Alexander	Detroit-Boston	.367
1933	Chuck Klein	Philadelphia	.368	1933 Jimmie Foxx	Philadelphia	.356
1934	Paul Waner	Pittsburgh	.362	1934 Lou Gehrig	New York	.363
1935	Arky Vaughan	Pittsburgh	.385	1935 Buddy Myer	Washington	.349
1936	Paul Waner	Pittsburgh	.373	1936 Luke Appling	Chicago	.388
1937	Joe Medwick	St. Louis	.374	1937 Charlie Gehringer	Detroit	.371
1938	Ernie Lombardi	Cincinnati	.342	1938 Jimmie Foxx	Boston	.349
1939	John Mize	St. Louis	.349	1939 Joe DiMaggio	New York	.381

National League / American League

Year	Player	Club	Avg.	Year	Player	Club	Avg.
1940	Debs Garms	Pittsburgh	.355	1940	Joe DiMaggio	New York	.352
1941	Pete Reiser	Brooklyn	.343	1941	Ted Williams	Boston	.406
1942	Ernie Lombardi	Boston	.330	1942	Ted Williams	Boston	.356
1943	Stan Musial	St. Louis	.357	1943	Luke Appling	Chicago	.328
1944	Dixie Walker	Brooklyn	.357	1944	Lou Boudreau	Cleveland	.327
1945	Phil Cavarretta	Chicago	.355	1945	George Stirnweiss	New York	.309
1946	Stan Musial	St. Louis	.365	1946	Mickey Vernon	Washington	.353
1947	Harry Walker	Philadelphia	.363	1947	Ted Williams	Boston	.343
1948	Stan Musial	St. Louis	.376	1948	Ted Williams	Boston	.369
1949	Jackie Robinson	Brooklyn	.342	1949	George Kell	Detroit	.343
1950	Stan Musial	St. Louis	.346	1950	Billy Goodman	Boston	.354
1951	Stan Musial	St. Louis	.355	1951	Ferris Fain	Philadelphia	.344
1952	Stan Musial	St. Louis	.336	1952	Ferris Fain	Philadelphia	.327
1953	Carl Furillo	Brooklyn	.344	1953	Mickey Vernon	Washington	.337
1954	Willie Mays	New York	.345	1954	Roberto Avila	Cleveland	.341
1955	Richie Ashburn	Philadelphia	.338	1955	Al Kaline	Detroit	.340
1956	Hank Aaron	Milwaukee	.328	1956	Mickey Mantle	New York	.353
1957	Stan Musial	St. Louis	.351	1957	Ted Williams	Boston	.388
1958	Richie Ashburn	Philadelphia	.350	1958	Ted Williams	Boston	.328
1959	Hank Aaron	Milwaukee	.355	1959	Harvey Kuenn	Detroit	.353
1960	Dick Groat	Pittsburgh	.325	1960	Pete Runnels	Boston	.320
1961	Roberto Clemente	Pittsburgh	.351	1961	Norm Cash	Detroit	.361
1962	Tommy Davis	Los Angeles	.346	1962	Pete Runnels	Boston	.326
1963	Tommy Davis	Los Angeles	.326	1963	Carl Yastrzemski	Boston	.321
1964	Roberto Clemente	Pittsburgh	.339	1964	Tony Oliva	Minnesota	.323
1965	Roberto Clemente	Pittsburgh	.329	1965	Tony Oliva	Minnesota	.321
1966	Matty Alou	Pittsburgh	.342	1966	Frank Robinson	Baltimore	.316
1967	Roberto Clemente	Pittsburgh	.357	1967	Carl Yastrzemski	Boston	.326
1968	Pete Rose	Cincinnati	.335	1968	Carl Yastrzemski	Boston	.301
1969	Pete Rose	Cincinnati	.348	1969	Rod Carew	Minnesota	.332
1970	Rico Carty	Atlanta	.366	1970	Alex Johnson	California	.328
1971	Joe Torre	St. Louis	.363	1971	Tony Oliva	Minnesota	.337
1972	Billy Williams	Chicago	.333	1972	Rod Carew	Minnesota	.318
1973	Pete Rose	Cincinnati	.338	1973	Rod Carew	Minnesota	.350
1974	Ralph Garr	Atlanta	.353	1974	Rod Carew	Minnesota	.364
1975	Bill Madlock	Chicago	.354	1975	Rod Carew	Minnesota	.359
1976	Bill Madlock	Chicago	.339	1976	George Brett	Kansas City	.333
1977	Dave Parker	Pittsburgh	.338	1977	Rod Carew	Minnesota	.388
1978	Dave Parker	Pittsburgh	.334	1978	Rod Carew	Minnesota	.333
1979	Keith Hernandez	St. Louis	.344	1979	Fred Lynn	Boston	.333
1980	Bill Buckner	Chicago	.324	1980	George Brett	Kansas City	.390
1981	Bill Madlock	Pittsburgh	.341	1981	Carney Lansford	Boston	.336
1982	Al Oliver	Montreal	.331	1982	Willie Wilson	Kansas City	.332
1983	Bill Madlock	Pittsburgh	.323	1983	Wade Boggs	Boston	.361
1984	Tony Gwynn	San Diego	.351	1984	Don Mattingly	New York	.343
1985	Willie McGee	St. Louis	.353	1985	Wade Boggs	Boston	.368
1986	Tim Raines	Montreal	.334	1986	Wade Boggs	Boston	.357
1987	Tony Gwynn	San Diego	.369	1987	Wade Boggs	Boston	.363
1988	Tony Gwynn	San Diego	.313	1988	Wade Boggs	Boston	.366
1989	Tony Gwynn	San Diego	.336	1989	Kirby Puckett	Minnesota	.339
1990	Willie McGee	St. Louis	.335	1990	George Brett	Kansas City	.329
1991	Terry Pendleton	Atlanta	.319	1991	Julio Franco	Texas	.342
1992	Gary Sheffield	San Diego	.330	1992	Edgar Martinez	Seattle	.343
1993	Andres Galarraga	Colorado	.370	1993	John Olerud	Toronto	.363
1994	Tony Gwynn	San Diego	.394	1994	Paul O'Neill	New York	.359
1995	Tony Gwynn	San Diego	.368	1995	Edgar Martinez	Seattle	.356

Cy Young Award Winners

Year	Player, Club	Year	Player, Club	Year	Player, Club
1956	Don Newcombe, Dodgers	1973	(NL) Tom Seaver, Mets	1984	(NL) Rick Sutcliffe, Cubs
1957	Warren Spahn, Braves		(AL) Jim Palmer, Orioles		(AL) Willie Hernandez, Tigers
1958	Bob Turley, Yankees	1974	(NL) Mike Marshall, Dodgers	1985	(NL) Dwight Gooden, Mets
1959	Early Wynn, White Sox		(AL) Jim (Catfish) Hunter, A's		(AL) Bret Saberhagen, Royals
1960	Vernon Law, Pirates	1975	(NL) Tom Seaver, Mets	1986	(NL) Mike Scott, Astros
1961	Whitey Ford, Yankees		(AL) Jim Palmer, Orioles		(AL) Roger Clemens, Red Sox
1962	Don Drysdale, Dodgers	1976	(NL) Randy Jones, Padres	1987	(NL) Steve Bedrosian, Phillies
1963	Sandy Koufax, Dodgers		(AL) Jim Palmer, Orioles		(AL) Roger Clemens, Red Sox
1964	Dean Chance, Angels	1977	(NL) Steve Carlton, Phillies	1988	(NL) Orel Hershiser, Dodgers
1965	Sandy Koufax, Dodgers		(AL) Sparky Lyle, Yankees		(AL) Frank Viola, Twins
1966	Sandy Koufax, Dodgers	1978	(NL) Gaylord Perry, Padres	1989	(NL) Mark Davis, Padres
1967	(NL) Mike McCormick, Giants		(AL) Ron Guidry, Yankees		(AL) Bret Saberhagan, Royals
	(AL) Jim Lonborg, Red Sox	1979	(NL) Bruce Sutter, Cubs	1990	(NL) Doug Drabek, Pirates
1968	(NL) Bob Gibson, Cardinals		(AL) Mike Flanagan, Orioles		(AL) Bob Welch, A's
	(AL) Dennis McLain, Tigers	1980	(NL) Steve Carlton, Phillies	1991	(NL) Tom Glavine, Braves
1969	(NL) Tom Seaver, Mets		(AL) Steve Stone, Orioles		(AL) Roger Clemens, Red Sox
	(AL) (tie) Dennis McLain, Tigers	1981	(NL) Fernando Valenzuela, Dodgers	1992	(NL) Greg Maddux, Cubs
	Mike Cuellar, Orioles		(AL) Rollie Fingers, Brewers		(AL) Dennis Eckersley, A's
1970	(NL) Bob Gibson, Cardinals	1982	(NL) Steve Carlton, Phillies	1993	(NL) Greg Maddux, Braves
	(AL) Jim Perry, Twins		(AL) Pete Vuckovich, Brewers		(AL) Jack McDowell, White Sox
1971	(NL) Ferguson Jenkins, Cubs	1983	(NL) John Denny, Phillies	1994	(NL) Greg Maddux, Braves
	(AL) Vida Blue, A's		(AL) LaMarr Hoyt, White Sox		(AL) David Cone, Royals
1972	(NL) Steve Carlton, Phillies				
	(AL) Gaylord Perry, Indians				

Pitchers With 300 Major League Wins

Cy Young	511	Warren Spahn	363	Steve Carlton	329	Nolan Ryan	324	Mickey Welch	311
Walter Johnson	416	Pud Galvin	361	Eddie Plank	327	Phil Niekro	318	Old Hoss Radbourn	308
Christy Mathewson	373	Kid Nichols	360	John Clarkson	326	Gaylord Perry	314	Lefty Grove	300
Grover Alexander	373	Tim Keefe	344	Don Sutton	324	Tom Seaver	311	Early Wynn	300

Most Valuable Player
Baseball Writers' Association

National League

Year	Player, team	Year	Player, team	Year	Player, team
1931	Frank Frisch, St. Louis	1953	Roy Campanella, Brooklyn	1974	Steve Garvey, Los Angeles
1932	Charles Klein, Philadelphia	1954	Willie Mays, New York	1975	Joe Morgan, Cincinnati
1933	Carl Hubbell, New York	1955	Roy Campanella, Brooklyn	1976	Joe Morgan, Cincinnati
1934	Dizzy Dean, St. Louis	1956	Don Newcombe, Brooklyn	1977	George Foster, Cincinnati
1935	Gabby Hartnett, Chicago	1957	Hank Aaron, Milwaukee	1978	Dave Parker, Pittsburgh
1936	Carl Hubbell, New York	1958	Ernie Banks, Chicago	1979	(tie)Willie Stargell, Pittsburgh
1937	Joe Medwick, St. Louis	1959	Ernie Banks, Chicago		Keith Hernandez, St. Louis
1938	Ernie Lombardi, Cincinnati	1960	Dick Groat, Pittsburgh	1980	Mike Schmidt, Philadelphia
1939	Bucky Walters, Cincinnati	1961	Frank Robinson, Cincinnati	1981	Mike Schmidt, Philadelphia
1940	Frank McCormick, Cincinnati	1962	Maury Wills, Los Angeles	1982	Dale Murphy, Atlanta
1941	Dolph Camilli, Brooklyn	1963	Sandy Koufax, Los Angeles	1983	Dale Murphy, Atlanta
1942	Mort Cooper, St. Louis	1964	Ken Boyer, St. Louis	1984	Ryne Sandberg, Chicago
1943	Stan Musial, St. Louis	1965	Willie Mays, San Francisco	1985	Willie McGee, St. Louis
1944	Martin Marion, St. Louis	1966	Roberto Clemente, Pittsburgh	1986	Mike Schmidt, Philadelphia
1945	Phil Cavarretta, Chicago	1967	Orlando Cepeda, St. Louis	1987	Andre Dawson, Chicago
1946	Stan Musial, St. Louis	1968	Bob Gibson, St. Louis	1988	Kirk Gibson, Los Angeles
1947	Bob Elliott, Boston	1969	Willie McCovey, San Francisco	1989	Kevin Mitchell, San Francisco
1948	Stan Musial, St. Louis	1970	Johnny Bench, Cincinnati	1990	Barry Bonds, Pittsburgh
1949	Jackie Robinson, Brooklyn	1971	Joe Torre, St. Louis	1991	Terry Pendleton, Atlanta
1950	Jim Konstanty, Philadelphia	1972	Johnny Bench, Cincinnati	1992	Barry Bonds, Pittsburgh
1951	Roy Campanella, Brooklyn	1973	Pete Rose, Cincinnati	1993	Barry Bonds, San Francisco
1952	Hank Sauer, Chicago			1994	Jeff Bagwell, Houston

American League

Year	Player, team	Year	Player, team	Year	Player, team
1931	Lefty Grove, Philadelphia	1953	Al Rosen, Cleveland	1974	Jeff Burroughs, Texas
1932	Jimmie Foxx, Philadelphia	1954	Yogi Berra, New York	1975	Fred Lynn, Boston
1933	Jimmie Foxx, Philadelphia	1955	Yogi Berra, New York	1976	Thurman Munson, New York
1934	Mickey Cochrane, Detroit	1956	Mickey Mantle, New York	1977	Rod Carew, Minnesota
1935	Hank Greenberg, Detroit	1957	Mickey Mantle, New York	1978	Jim Rice, Boston
1936	Lou Gehrig, New York	1958	Jackie Jensen, Boston	1979	Don Baylor, California
1937	Charley Gehringer, Detroit	1959	Nellie Fox, Chicago	1980	George Brett, Kansas City
1938	Jimmie Foxx, Boston	1960	Roger Maris, New York	1981	Rollie Fingers, Milwaukee
1939	Joe DiMaggio, New York	1961	Roger Maris, New York	1982	Robin Yount, Milwaukee
1940	Hank Greenberg, Detroit	1962	Mickey Mantle, New York	1983	Cal Ripken, Jr., Baltimore
1941	Joe DiMaggio, New York	1963	Elston Howard, New York	1984	Willie Hernandez, Detroit
1942	Joe Gordon, New York	1964	Brooks Robinson, Baltimore	1985	Don Mattingly, New York
1943	Spurgeon Chandler, New York	1965	Zoilo Versalles, Minnesota	1986	Roger Clemens, Boston
1944	Hal Newhouser, Detroit	1966	Frank Robinson, Baltimore	1987	George Bell, Toronto
1945	Hal Newhouser, Detroit	1967	Carl Yastrzemski, Boston	1988	Jose Canseco, Oakland
1946	Ted Williams, Boston	1968	Denny McLain, Detroit	1989	Robin Yount, Milwaukee
1947	Joe DiMaggio, New York	1969	Harmon Killebrew, Minnesota	1990	Rickey Henderson, Oakland
1948	Lou Boudreau, Cleveland	1970	John (Boog) Powell, Baltimore	1991	Cal Ripken, Jr., Baltimore
1949	Ted Williams, Boston	1971	Vida Blue, Oakland	1992	Dennis Eckersley, Oakland
1950	Phil Rizzuto, New York	1972	Dick Allen, Chicago	1993	Frank Thomas, Chicago
1951	Yogi Berra, New York	1973	Reggie Jackson, Oakland	1994	Frank Thomas, Chicago
1952	Bobby Shantz, Philadelphia				

Rookie of the Year
Baseball Writers' Association

1947—Combined selection—Jackie Robinson, Brooklyn, 1b; 1948—Combined selection—Alvin Dark, Boston, N.L., ss

National League

Year	Player, team	Year	Player, team	Year	Player, team
1949	Don Newcombe, Brooklyn, p	1965	Jim Lefebvre, Los Angeles, 2b	1980	Steve Howe, Los Angeles, p
1950	Sam Jethroe, Boston, of	1966	Tommy Helms, Cincinnati, 2b	1981	Fernando Valenzuela, Los
1951	Willie Mays, New York, of	1967	Tom Seaver, New York, p		Angeles, p
1952	Joe Black, Brooklyn, p	1968	Johnny Bench, Cincinnati, c	1982	Steve Sax, Los Angeles, 2b
1953	Jim Gilliam, Brooklyn, 2b	1969	Ted Sizemore, Los Angeles, 2b	1983	Darryl Strawberry, New York, of
1954	Wally Moon, St. Louis, of	1970	Carl Morton, Montreal, p	1984	Dwight Gooden, New York, p
1955	Bill Virdon, St. Louis, of	1971	Earl Williams, Atlanta, c	1985	Vince Coleman, St. Louis, of
1956	Frank Robinson, Cincinnati, of	1972	Jon Matlack, New York, p	1986	Todd Worrell, St. Louis, p
1957	Jack Sanford, Philadelphia, p	1973	Gary Matthews, S.F., of	1987	Benito Santiago, San Diego, c
1958	Orlando Cepeda, S.F., 1b	1974	Bake McBride, St. Louis, of	1988	Chris Sabo, Cincinnati, 3b
1959	Willie McCovey, S.F., 1b	1975	John Montefusco, S.F., p	1989	Jerome Walton, Chicago, of
1960	Frank Howard, Los Angeles, of	1976	(tie)John Montefusco, San Diego, p	1990	Dave Justice, Atlanta, 1b
1961	Billy Williams, Chicago, of		Pat Zachry, Cincinnati, p	1991	Jeff Bagwell, Houston, 1b
1962	Ken Hubbs, Chicago, 2b	1977	Andre Dawson, Montreal, of	1992	Eric Karros, Los Angeles, 1b
1963	Pete Rose, Cincinnati, 2b	1978	Bob Horner, Atlanta, 3b	1993	Mike Piazza, Los Angeles, c
1964	Richie Allen, Philadelphia, 3b	1979	Rick Sutcliffe, Los Angeles, p	1994	Raul Mondesi, Los Angeles, of

American League

Year	Player, team	Year	Player, team	Year	Player, team
1949	Roy Sievers, St. Louis, of	1965	Curt Blefary, Baltimore, of	1980	Joe Charboneau, Cleveland, of
1950	Walt Dropo, Boston, 1b	1966	Tommie Agee, Chicago, of	1981	Dave Righetti, New York, p
1951	Gil McDougald, New York, 3b	1967	Rod Carew, Minnesota, 2b	1982	Cal Ripken, Jr., Baltimore, ss
1952	Harry Byrd, Philadelphia, p	1968	Stan Bahnsen, New York, p	1983	Ron Kittle, Chicago, of
1953	Harvey Kuenn, Detroit, ss	1969	Lou Piniella, Kansas City, of	1984	Alvin Davis, Seattle, 1b
1954	Bob Grim, New York, p	1970	Thurman Munson, New York, c	1985	Ozzie Guillen, Chicago, ss
1955	Herb Score, Cleveland, p	1971	Chris Chambliss, Cleveland, 1b	1986	Jose Canseco, Oakland, of
1956	Luis Aparicio, Chicago, ss	1972	Carlton Fisk, Boston, c	1987	Mark McGwire, Oakland, 1b
1957	Tony Kubek, New York, if-of	1973	Al Bumbry, Baltimore, of	1988	Walt Weiss, Oakland, ss
1958	Albie Pearson, Washington, of	1974	Mike Hargrove, Texas, 1b	1989	Gregg Olson, Baltimore, p
1959	Bob Allison, Washington, of	1975	Fred Lynn, Boston, of	1990	Sandy Alomar, Jr., Cleveland, c
1960	Ron Hansen, Baltimore, ss	1976	Mark Fidrych, Detroit, p	1991	Chuck Knoblauch, Minnesota, 2b
1961	Don Schwall, Boston, p	1977	Eddie Murray, Baltimore, dh	1992	Pat Listach, Milwaukee, ss
1962	Tom Tresh, New York, if-of	1978	Lou Whitaker, Detroit, 2b	1993	Tim Salmon, California, of
1963	Gary Peters, Chicago, p	1979	(tie)John Castino, Minnesota, 3b	1994	Bob Hamelin, Kansas City, dh
1964	Tony Oliva, Minnesota, of		Alfredo Griffin, Toronto, ss		

National League Records, 1995
Final standings for strike-shortened season

Eastern Division

	W	L	Pct.	GB	Home	vs. RHP	Grass	Night
Atlanta	90	54	.625	—	44-28	67-41	65-44	65-40
New York.....	69	75	.479	21	40-32	48-51	55-57	52-52
Philadelphia	69	75	.479	21	35-37	49-48	20-25	53-50
Florida	67	76	.469	22½	37-34	46-48	52-54	53-61
Montreal	66	78	.458	24	31-41	48-59	22-23	45-58

Central Division

	W	L	Pct.	GB	Home	vs. RHP	Grass	Night
Cincinnati......	85	59	.590	—	44-28	62-47	17-23	62-43
Houston	76	68	.528	9	36-36	52-51	21-19	56-48
Chicago.......	73	71	.507	12	34-38	49-51	57-56	36-33
St. Louis	62	81	.434	22½	39-33	49-58	14-30	45-54
Pittsburgh	58	86	.403	27	31-41	45-58	16-29	44-60

Western Division

	W	L	Pct.	GB	Home	vs. RHP	Grass	Night
Los Angeles	78	66	.542	—	39-33	56-48	62-51	61-51
Colorado*......	77	67	.535	1	44-28	49-50	63-52	45-49
San Diego	70	74	.486	8	40-32	53-51	56-56	46-51
San Francisco ...	67	77	.465	11	37-35	57-57	55-56	30-43

*Wild card team.

Division Series
Atlanta defeated Colorado 3 games to 1
Cincinnati defeated Los Angeles 3 games to 0

Championship Series
Atlanta 2, Cincinnati 1 (11)   Atlanta 5, Cincinnati 2
Atlanta 6, Cincinnati 2 (10)   Atlanta 6, Cincinnati 0

(Atlanta defeated Cincinnati 4 games to 0)

Team Batting

	Avg	AB	R	H	HR	RBI
Colorado	.282	4994	785	1406	200	749
Houston	.275	5097	747	1403	109	694
San Diego	.272	4950	668	1345	116	618
Cincinnati.....	.270	4903	747	1326	161	694
New York	.267	4958	657	1323	125	617
Chicago......	.265	4963	693	1315	158	648
Los Angeles ..	.264	4942	634	1303	140	593
Philadelphia ...	.262	4950	615	1296	94	576
Florida	.262	4886	673	1278	144	636
Pittsburgh	.259	4937	629	1281	125	587
Montreal	.259	4905	621	1268	118	572
San Francisco ..	.253	4971	652	1256	152	610
Atlanta	.250	4814	645	1202	168	618
St. Louis	.247	4779	563	1182	107	533

Team Pitching

	ERA	IP	H	BB	SO	Sv
Atlanta....	3.44	1291.2	1184	436	1087	34
Los Angeles	3.66	1295.0	1188	462	1060	36
New York ..	3.88	1291.0	1296	401	901	36
Cincinnati ..	4.03	1289.1	1270	424	903	38
Houston...	4.06	1320.1	1357	460	1056	32
St. Louis ...	4.09	1265.2	1290	445	842	38
Montreal...	4.11	1283.2	1286	416	950	42
Chicago ...	4.13	1301.0	1313	518	926	45
San Diego ..	4.13	1284.2	1242	512	1047	35
Philadelphia.	4.21	1290.1	1241	538	980	41
Florida....	4.27	1286.0	1299	562	994	29
Pittsburgh..	4.70	1275.1	1407	477	871	29
San Francisco	4.86	1293.2	1368	505	801	34
Colorado ..	4.97	1288.1	1443	512	891	43

Individual Batting (at least 155 at-bats); Individual Pitching (at least 63 innings or 8 saves)

Atlanta Braves

Batting	AB	R	H	HR	RBI	SB	Avg
Lopez........	333	37	105	14	51	0	.315
Klesko........	329	48	102	23	70	5	.310
McGriff.......	528	85	148	27	93	3	.280
Jones	524	87	139	23	86	8	.265
Grissom	551	80	142	12	42	29	.258
Lemke........	399	42	101	5	38	2	.253
Justice	411	73	104	24	78	4	.253
O'Brien	198	18	45	9	23	0	.227
Belliard	180	12	40	0	7	2	.222
Blauser.......	431	60	91	12	31	8	.211

Pitching	W	L	ERA	IP	H	BB	SO	Sv
Maddux....	19	2	1.63	209.2	147	23	181	0
Wohlers ...	7	3	2.09	64.2	51	24	90	25
McMichael..	7	2	2.79	80.2	64	32	74	2
Glavine	16	7	3.08	198.2	182	66	127	0
Smoltz	12	7	3.18	192.2	166	72	193	0
Clontz.....	8	1	3.65	69.0	71	22	55	4
Mercker....	7	8	4.15	143.0	140	61	102	0
Avery	7	13	4.67	173.1	165	52	141	0

Manager—Bobby Cox

Chicago Cubs

Batting	AB	R	H	HR	RBI	SB	Avg
Grace	552	97	180	16	92	6	.326
Dunston......	477	58	141	14	69	10	.296
McRae.......	580	92	167	12	48	27	.288
Sanchez......	428	57	119	3	27	6	.278
Gonzalez.....	471	69	130	13	69	6	.276
Sosa	564	89	151.	36	119	34	.268
Servais	264	38	70	13	47	2	.265
Timmons	171	30	45	8	28	3	.263
Zeile........	426	50	105	14	52	1	.246
Hernandez....	245	37	60	13	40	1	.245
Parent	265	30	62	18	38	0	.234
Johnson......	169	26	33	7	22	1	.195

Pitching	W	L	ERA	IP	H	BB	SO	Sv
Castillo.....	11	10	3.21	188.0	179	52	135	0
Navarro	14	6	3.28	200.1	194	56	128	0
Perez......	2	6	3.66	71.1	72	27	49	2
Myers......	1	2	3.88	55.2	49	28	59	38
Bullinger ...	12	8	4.14	150.0	152	65	93	0
Foster	12	11	4.51	167.2	149	65	146	0
Trachsel....	7	13	5.15	160.2	174	76	117	0

Manager—Jim Riggleman

Cincinnati Reds

Batting	AB	R	H	HR	RBI	SB	Avg
M. Lewis	171	25	58	3	30	0	.339
Larkin	496	98	158	15	66	51	.319
R. Sanders	484	91	148	28	99	36	.306
Howard	281	42	85	3	26	17	.302
Walton	162	32	47	8	22	10	.290
Duncan	265	36	76	6	36	1	.287
Santiago	266	40	76	11	44	2	.286
Taubensee	218	32	62	9	44	2	.284
Morris	359	53	100	11	51	1	.279
Gant	410	79	113	29	88	23	.276
Boone	513	63	137	15	68	5	.267
Branson	331	43	86	12	45	2	.260
D. Lewis	472	66	118	1	24	32	.250
Harris	197	32	41	2	16	10	.208

Pitching	W	L	ERA	IP	H	BB	SO	Sv
Brantley	3	2	2.82	70.1	53	20	62	28
Schourek	18	7	3.22	190.1	158	45	160	0
Wells	6	5	3.59	72.2	74	16	50	0
Smiley	12	5	3.46	176.2	173	39	124	0
Pugh	6	5	3.84	98.1	100	32	38	0
Burba	10	4	3.97	106.2	90	51	96	0
Portugal	11	10	4.01	181.2	185	56	96	0
Carrasco	2	7	4.12	87.1	86	46	64	5
Rijo	5	4	4.17	69.0	76	22	62	0
Hernandez	7	2	4.60	90.0	95	31	84	3
Jarvis	3	4	5.70	79.0	91	32	33	0

Manager—Davey Johnson

Colorado Rockies

Batting	AB	R	H	HR	RBI	SB	Avg
Bichette	579	102	197	40	128	13	.340
Young	366	68	116	6	36	35	.317
Castilla	527	82	163	32	90	2	.309
Walker	494	96	151	36	101	16	.306
Galarraga	554	89	155	31	106	12	.280
Kingery	350	66	94	8	37	13	.269
Bates	322	42	86	8	46	3	.267
Burks	278	41	74	14	49	7	.266
Girardi	462	63	121	8	55	3	.262
Weiss	427	65	111	1	25	15	.260

Pitching	W	L	ERA	IP	H	BB	SO	Sv
Ruffin	0	1	2.12	34.0	26	19	23	11
Reed	5	2	2.14	84.0	61	21	79	3
Holmes	6	1	3.24	66.2	59	28	61	14
Leskanic	6	3	3.40	98.0	83	33	107	10
Saberhagen	7	6	4.18	153.0	165	33	100	0
Ritz	11	11	4.21	173.1	171	65	120	2
Swift	9	3	4.94	105.2	122	43	68	0
Rekar	4	6	4.98	85.0	95	24	60	0
Bailey	7	6	4.98	81.1	88	39	33	0
Reynoso	7	7	5.32	93.0	116	36	40	0
Freeman	3	7	5.89	94.2	122	41	61	0

Manager—Don Baylor

Florida Marlins

Batting	AB	R	H	HR	RBI	SB	Avg
Sheffield	213	46	69	16	46	19	.324
Conine	483	72	146	25	105	2	.302
Tavarez	189	31	55	2	13	7	.291
Pendleton	513	70	149	14	78	1	.290
Colbrunn	528	70	146	23	89	11	.277
Arias	216	22	58	3	26	1	.269
Veras	440	86	115	5	32	56	.261
Dawson	226	30	58	8	37	0	.257
Browne	184	21	47	1	17	1	.255
Abbott	420	60	107	17	60	4	.255
Johnson	315	40	79	11	39	0	.251
Gregg	156	20	37	6	20	3	.237
Carr	308	54	70	2	20	25	.227

Pitching	W	L	ERA	IP	H	BB	SO	Sv
Nen	0	7	3.29	65.2	62	23	68	23
Mathews	4	4	3.38	82.2	70	27	72	3
Rapp	14	7	3.44	167.1	158	76	102	0
Hammond	9	6	3.80	161.0	157	47	126	0
Witt	2	7	3.90	110.2	104	47	95	0
Burkett	14	14	4.30	188.1	208	57	126	0
Gardner	5	5	4.49	102.1	109	43	87	1
Banks	2	6	5.66	90.2	106	58	62	0
Weathers	4	5	5.98	90.1	104	52	60	0

Manager—Rene Lachemann

Houston Astros

Batting	AB	R	H	HR	RBI	SB	Avg
Bell	452	63	151	8	86	27	.334
Cangelosi	201	46	64	2	18	21	.318
Magadan	348	44	109	2	51	2	.313
Hunter	321	52	97	2	28	24	.302
Biggio	553	123	167	22	77	33	.302
May	206	29	62	8	41	5	.301
Eusebio	368	46	110	6	58	0	.299
Bagwell	448	88	130	21	87	12	.290
Gutierrez	156	22	43	0	12	5	.276
Shipley	232	23	61	3	24	6	.263
Miller	324	36	85	5	36	3	.262
Mouton	298	42	78	4	27	25	.262
Wilkins	202	30	41	7	19	0	.203

Pitching	W	L	ERA	IP	H	BB	SO	Sv
Veres	5	1	2.26	103.1	89	30	94	1
Henneman	0	1	3.00	21.0	21	4	19	8
Jones	6	5	3.07	99.2	89	52	96	15
Hampton	9	8	3.35	150.2	141	49	115	0
Reynolds	10	11	3.47	189.1	196	37	175	0
Brocail	6	4	4.19	77.1	87	22	39	1
Swindell	10	9	4.47	153.0	180	39	96	0
Drabek	10	9	4.77	185.0	205	54	143	0
Dougherty	8	4	4.92	67.2	76	25	49	0
Kile	4	12	4.96	127.0	114	73	113	0

Manager—Terry Collins

Los Angeles Dodgers

Batting	AB	R	H	HR	RBI	SB	Avg
Piazza	434	82	150	32	93	1	.346
Butler	513	78	154	1	38	32	.300
Karros	551	83	164	32	105	4	.298
Hansen	181	19	52	1	14	0	.287
Offerman	429	69	123	4	33	2	.287
Mondesi	536	91	153	26	88	27	.285
Fonville	320	43	89	0	16	20	.278
Kelly	504	58	140	7	57	19	.278
Wallach	327	24	87	9	38	0	.266
DeShields	425	66	109	8	37	39	.256
Ashley	215	17	51	8	27	0	.237

Pitching	W	L	ERA	IP	H	BB	SO	Sv
Worrell	4	1	2.02	62.1	50	19	61	32
Nomo	13	6	2.54	191.1	124	78	236	0
Valdes	13	11	3.05	197.2	168	51	150	1
Candiotti	7	14	3.50	190.1	187	58	141	0
Martinez	17	7	3.66	206.1	176	81	138	0
Astacio	7	8	4.24	104.0	103	29	80	0

Manager—Tommy Lasorda

Montreal Expos

Batting	AB	R	H	HR	RBI	SB	Avg
Berry	314	38	100	14	55	3	.318
Segui	456	68	141	12	68	2	.309
R. White	474	87	140	13	57	25	.295
Cordero	514	64	147	10	49	9	.286
Fletcher	350	42	100	11	45	0	.286
Alou	344	48	94	14	58	4	.273
Lansing	467	47	119	10	62	27	.255
Tarasco	438	64	109	14	40	24	.249
Grudzielanek	269	27	66	1	20	8	.245
Andrews	220	27	47	8	31	1	.214

Pitching	W	L	ERA	IP	H	BB	SO	Sv
Henry	7	9	2.84	126.2	133	28	60	0
Martinez	14	10	3.47	194.2	158	66	174	0
Perez	10	8	3.69	141.1	142	28	106	0
Scott	2	0	3.98	63.1	52	23	57	2
Rojas	1	4	4.12	67.2	69	29	61	30
Heredia	5	6	4.31	119.0	137	21	74	1
Fassero	13	14	4.33	189.0	207	74	164	0

Manager—Felipe Alou

New York Mets

Batting	AB	R	H	HR	RBI	SB	Avg
Bonilla.......	317	49	103	18	53	0	.325
Brogna.......	495	72	143	22	76	0	.289
Vizcaino......	509	66	146	3	56	8	.287
Orsulak.......	290	41	82	1	37	1	.283
C. Jones......	182	33	51	8	31	2	.280
Hundley......	275	39	77	15	51	1	.280
Alfonzo.......	335	26	93	4	41	1	.278
Kent.........	472	65	131	20	65	3	.278
Everett	289	48	75	12	54	2	.260
Thompson.....	267	39	67	7	31	3	.251
Stinnett.......	196	23	43	4	18	2	.219

Pitching	W	L	ERA	IP	H	BB	SO	Sv
Franco	5	3	2.44	51.2	48	17	41	29
Isringhausen	9	2	2.81	93.0	88	31	55	0
Henry	3	6	2.96	67.0	48	25	62	4
Harnisch ...	2	8	3.68	110.0	111	24	82	0
DiPoto.....	4	6	3.78	78.2	77	29	49	2
Pulsipher...	5	7	3.98	126.2	122	45	81	0
B. Jones ...	10	10	4.19	195.2	209	53	127	0
Mlicki	9	7	4.26	160.2	160	54	123	0
Cornelius...	3	7	5.54	66.2	75	30	39	0
Acevedo ...	4	6	6.44	65.2	82	20	40	0

Manager—Dallas Green

St. Louis Cardinals

Batting	AB	R	H	HR	RBI	SB	Avg
Mabry	388	35	119	5	41	0	.307
Gilkey	480	73	143	17	69	12	.298
Jordan........	490	83	145	22	81	24	.296
Lankford......	483	81	134	25	82	24	.277
Sheaffer......	208	24	48	5	30	0	.231
Cooper.......	374	29	86	3	40	0	.230
Cromer.......	345	36	78	5	18	0	.226
Pagnozzi.....	219	17	47	2	15	0	.215
Oquendo	220	31	46	2	17	1	.209
Smith........	156	16	31	0	11	4	.199
Oliva	183	15	26	7	20	0	.142

Pitching	W	L	ERA	IP	H	BB	SO	Sv
Henke	1	1	1.82	54.1	42	18	48	36
DeLucia	8	7	3.39	82.1	63	36	76	0
Morgan	7	7	3.56	131.1	133	34	61	0
Parrett	4	7	3.64	76.2	71	28	71	0
Urbani	3	5	3.70	82.2	99	21	52	0
Osborne	4	6	3.81	113.1	112	34	82	0
Petkovsek ..	6	6	4.00	137.1	136	35	71	0
Watson	7	9	4.96	114.1	126	41	49	0
Hill.........	6	7	5.06	110.1	125	45	50	0
Jackson	2	12	5.90	100.2	120	48	52	0

Manager—Joe Torre, Mike Jorgensen

Philadelphia Phillies

Batting	AB	R	H	HR	RBI	SB	Avg
Gallagher	157	12	50	1	12	0	.318
Eisenreich.....	377	46	119	10	55	10	.316
Jefferies	480	69	147	11	56	9	.306
Morandini	494	65	140	6	49	9	.283
Hayes........	529	58	146	11	85	5	.276
Whiten	212	38	57	11	37	7	.269
Dykstra.......	254	37	67	2	18	10	.264
Daulton......	342	44	85	9	55	3	.249
Van Slyke	214	26	52	3	16	7	.243
Hollins.......	205	46	47	7	25	1	.229
Stocker	412	42	90	1	32	6	.218

Pitching	W	L	ERA	IP	H	BB	SO	Sv
Bottalico ...	5	3	2.46	87.2	50	42	87	1
Slocumb ...	5	6	2.89	65.1	64	35	63	32
Williams ...	3	3	3.29	87.2	78	29	57	0
Fernandez..	6	1	3.34	64.2	48	21	79	0
Schilling ...	7	5	3.57	116.0	96	26	114	0
Borland....	1	3	3.77	74.0	81	37	59	6
Mimbs.....	9	7	4.15	136.2	127	75	93	1
Quantrill ..	11	12	4.67	179.1	212	44	103	0
Green.....	8	9	5.31	140.2	157	66	85	0

Manager—Jim Fregosi

San Diego Padres

Batting	AB	R	H	HR	RBI	SB	Avg
Gwynn........	535	82	197	9	90	17	.368
Livingstone....	196	26	66	5	32	2	.337
Roberts......	296	40	90	2	25	20	.304
Caminiti.....	526	74	159	26	94	12	.302
Finley........	562	104	167	10	44	36	.297
Ausmus......	328	44	96	5	34	16	.293
E. Williams	296	35	77	12	47	0	.260
Reed	445	58	114	4	40	6	.256
Plantier	216	33	55	9	34	1	.255
Johnson.....	207	20	52	3	29	0	.251
Cedeno	390	42	82	6	31	5	.210
Nieves	234	32	48	14	38	2	.205

Pitching	W	L	ERA	IP	H	BB	SO	Sv
Ashby	12	10	2.94	192.2	180	62	150	0
Florie......	2	2	3.01	68.2	49	38	68	1
Hamilton ..	6	9	3.08	204.1	189	56	123	0
Hoffman....	7	4	3.88	53.1	48	14	52	31
Benes	4	7	4.17	118.2	121	45	126	0
Sanders....	5	5	4.30	90.0	79	31	88	0
Blair......	7	5	4.34	114.0	112	45	83	0
Valenzuela..	8	3	4.98	90.1	101	34	57	0
Dishman ...	4	8	5.01	97.0	104	34	43	0
B. Williams ..	3	10	6.00	72.0	79	38	75	0

Manager—Bruce Bochy

Pittsburgh Pirates

Batting	AB	R	H	HR	RBI	SB	Avg
Merced.......	487	75	146	15	83	7	.300
C. Garcia......	367	41	108	6	50	8	.294
Liriano........	259	29	74	5	38	2	.286
Martin........	439	70	124	13	41	20	.282
Clark........	196	30	55	4	24	3	.281
Brumfield......	402	64	109	4	26	22	.271
King.........	445	61	118	18	87	7	.265
Bell..........	530	79	139	13	55	2	.262
Pegues	171	17	42	6	16	1	.246
Young.......	181	13	42	6	22	1	.232
Encarnacion ...	159	18	36	2	10	1	.226
Johnson......	221	32	46	13	28	5	.208

Pitching	W	L	ERA	IP	H	BB	SO	Sv
Neagle	13	8	3.43	209.2	221	45	150	0
Dyer	4	5	4.34	74.2	81	30	53	0
Ericks	3	9	4.58	106.0	108	50	80	0
Miceli	4	4	4.66	58.0	61	28	56	21
Wagner....	5	16	4.80	165.0	174	72	120	1
Loaiza.....	8	9	5.16	172.2	205	55	85	0
Parris	6	6	5.38	82.0	89	33	61	0
Lieber....	4	7	6.32	72.2	103	14	45	0

Manager—Jim Leyland

San Francisco Giants

Batting	AB	R	H	HR	RBI	SB	Avg
Williams	283	53	95	23	65	2	.336
Carreon	396	53	119	17	65	0	.301
Bonds	506	109	149	33	104	31	.294
Sanders......	343	48	92	6	28	24	.268
Scarsone	233	33	62	11	29	3	.266
Hill..........	497	71	131	24	86	25	.264
Manwaring	379	21	95	4	36	1	.251
Clayton	509	56	124	5	58	24	.244
Thompson	336	51	75	8	23	1	.223
Benjamin	186	19	41	3	12	11	.220
Patterson	205	27	42	1	14	4	.205
Phillips........	231	27	45	9	28	1	.195

Pitching	W	L	ERA	IP	H	BB	SO	Sv
VanLandingham	6	3	3.67	122.2	124	40	95	0
Leiter	10	12	3.82	195.2	185	55	129	0
Wilson	3	4	3.92	82.2	82	38	38	0
Beck	5	6	4.45	58.2	60	21	42	33
Brewington ..	6	4	4.54	75.1	68	45	45	0
S. Valdez ...	4	5	4.75	66.1	78	17	29	0
Mulholland ..	5	13	5.80	149.0	190	38	65	0
Bautista.....	3	8	6.44	100.2	120	26	45	0

Manager—Dusty Baker

American League Records, 1995

Final standings for strike-shortened season

Eastern Division

	W	L	Pct.	GB	Home	vs. RHP	Grass	Night
Boston	86	58	.597	—	42-30	66-41	76-51	60-40
New York*	79	65	.549	7	46-26	54-37	71-57	53-40
Baltimore	71	73	.493	15	36-36	49-56	62-64	51-53
Detroit	60	84	.417	26	35-37	45-63	51-74	39-54
Toronto	56	88	.389	30	29-43	41-59	22-44	33-62

Central Division

	W	L	Pct.	GB	Home	vs. RHP	Grass	Night
Cleveland.	100	44	.694	—	54-18	73-30	89-38	71-31
Kansas City	70	74	.486	30	35-37	56-47	60-66	50-56
Chicago	68	76	.472	32	38-34	53-51	61-65	48-57
Milwaukee	65	79	.451	35	33-39	52-50	56-73	45-52
Minnesota	56	88	.389	44	29-43	37-62	24-39	44-62

Western Division

	W	L	Pct.	GB	Home	vs. RHP	Grass	Night
Seattle	79	66	.545	—	46-27	54-47	27-36	59-46
California	78	67	.538	1	39-33	55-49	66-59	55-50
Texas	74	70	.514	4½	41-31	49-48	66-60	60-53
Oakland	67	77	.465	11½	38-34	40-55	61-66	37-49

*Wild card team.

Division Series

Cleveland defeated Boston 3 games to 0
Seattle defeated New York 3 games to 2

Championship Series

Seattle 3, Cleveland 2	Seattle 5, Cleveland 2 (11)	Cleveland 3, Seattle 2
Cleveland 5, Seattle 2	Cleveland 7, Seattle 0	Cleveland 4, Seattle 0

(Cleveland defeated Seattle 4 games to 2)

Team Batting

	Avg	AB	R	H	HR	RBI
Cleveland. .	.291	5028	840	1461	207	803
Chicago. . .	.280	5060	755	1417	146	712
Boston . . .	.280	4997	791	1399	175	754
Minnesota .	.279	5005	703	1398	120	662
California .	.277	5019	801	1390	186	761
New York . .	.276	4947	749	1365	122	709
Seattle . . .	.276	4996	796	1377	182	767
Milwaukee .	.266	5000	740	1329	128	700
Texas . . .	.265	4913	691	1304	138	651
Oakland . .	.264	4915	730	1296	169	694
Baltimore . .	.262	4837	704	1267	173	668
Kansas City	.260	4903	629	1275	119	578
Toronto . . .	.260	5036	642	1309	140	613
Detroit . . .	.247	4865	654	1204	159	619

Team Pitching

	ERA	IP	H	BB	SO	Sv
Cleveland .	3.83	1301.0	1261	445	926	50
Baltimore. .	4.31	1267.0	1165	523	930	29
Boston . . .	4.39	1292.2	1338	476	888	39
Kansas City	4.49	1288.0	1323	503	763	37
Seattle . . .	4.50	1289.1	1343	591	1068	39
California. .	4.52	1284.1	1310	486	901	42
New York .	4.56	1284.2	1286	535	908	35
Texas . . .	4.66	1285.0	1385	514	838	34
Milwaukee .	4.82	1286.0	1391	603	699	31
Chicago . .	4.85	1284.2	1374	617	892	36
Toronto . .	4.88	1292.2	1336	654	894	22
Oakland . .	4.93	1273.0	1320	556	890	38
Detroit . . .	5.49	1275.0	1509	536	729	38
Minnesota .	5.76	1272.2	1450	533	790	27

Individual Batting (at least 155 at-bats); Individual Pitching (at least 63 innings or 8 saves)

Baltimore Orioles

Batting	AB	R	H	HR	RBI	SB	Avg
Bonilla.	237	47	79	10	46	0	.333
Palmeiro	554	89	172	39	104	3	.310
Baines	385	60	115	24	63	0	.299
Goodwin	289	40	76	1	24	22	.263
Ripken	550	71	144	17	88	0	.262
Anderson	554	108	145	16	64	26	.262
Manto	254	31	65	17	38	0	.256
Hoiles	352	53	88	19	58	1	.250
Huson.	161	24	40	1	19	5	.248
Bass	295	32	72	5	32	8	.244
Hammonds	178	18	43	4	23	4	.242
Barberie	237	32	57	2	25	3	.241
Alexander	242	35	57	3	23	11	.236

Pitching	W	L	ERA	IP	H	BB	SO	Sv
Mussina . . .	19	9	3.29	221.2	187	50	158	0
K. Brown. . .	10	9	3.60	172.1	155	48	117	0
McDonald . .	3	6	4.16	80.0	67	38	62	0
Krivda.	2	7	4.54	75.1	76	25	53	0
Erickson . . .	13	10	4.81	196.1	213	67	106	0
Jones	0	4	5.01	46.2	55	16	42	22
Moyer	8	6	5.21	115.2	117	30	65	0
Rhodes	2	5	6.21	75.1	68	48	77	0

Manager—Phil Regan

Boston Red Sox

Batting	AB	R	H	HR	RBI	SB	Avg
O'Leary	399	60	123	10	49	5	.308
Naehring	433	61	133	10	57	0	.307
Canseco	396	64	121	24	81	4	.306
Vaughn	550	68	165	39	126	11	.300
Valentin	520	108	155	27	102	20	.298
Greenwell.	481	67	143	15	76	9	.297
McGee.	200	32	57	2	15	5	.285
Tinsley	341	61	97	7	41	18	.284
Alicea	419	64	113	6	44	13	.270
Macfarlane.	364	45	82	15	51	2	.225

Pitching	W	L	ERA	IP	H	BB	SO	Sv
Aguilera	3	3	2.60	55.1	46	13	52	32
Wakefield. . .	16	8	2.95	195.1	163	68	119	0
Belinda	8	1	3.10	69.2	51	28	57	10
Maddux	4	1	3.61	89.2	86	15	65	1
Cormier	7	5	4.07	115.0	131	31	69	0
Clemens . . .	10	5	4.18	140.0	141	60	132	0
Hanson	15	5	4.24	186.2	187	59	139	0
Eshelman. . .	6	3	4.85	81.2	86	36	41	0
Smith.	8	8	5.61	110.2	144	23	47	0

Manager—Kevin Kennedy

California Angels

Batting	AB	R	H	HR	RBI	SB	Avg
Salmon	537	111	177	34	105	5	.330
G. Anderson .	374	50	120	16	69	6	.321
Davis	424	81	135	20	86	3	.318
DiSarcina .	362	61	111	5	41	7	.307
Edmonds. . . .	558	120	162	33	107	1	.290
Snow	544	80	157	24	102	2	.289
Hudler.	223	30	59	6	27	12	.265
Phillips	525	119	137	27	61	13	.261
Myers	273	35	71	9	38	0	.260
Fabregas. . . .	227	24	56	1	22	0	.247
Owen	218	17	50	1	28	3	.229
Easley.	357	35	77	4	35	5	.216

Pitching	W	L	ERA	IP	H	BB	SO	Sv
Percival.	3	2	1.95	74.0	37	26	94	3
L. Smith	0	5	3.47	49.1	42	25	43	37
Abbott.	11	8	3.70	197.0	209	64	86	0
Finley	15	12	4.21	203.0	192	93	195	0
Langston. . . .	15	7	4.63	200.1	212	64	142	0
Harkey	8	9	5.44	127.1	155	47	56	0
Boskie	7	7	5.64	111.2	127	25	51	0
B. Anderson .	6	8	5.87	99.2	110	30	45	0
Bielecki.	4	6	5.97	75.1	80	31	45	0

Manager—Marcel Lachemann

Chicago White Sox

Batting	AB	R	H	HR	RBI	SB	Avg
F. Thomas.	493	102	152	40	111	3	.308
Kruk	159	13	49	2	23	0	.308
Martinez	303	49	93	5	37	8	.307
Johnson	607	98	186	10	57	40	.306
Devereaux.	333	48	102	10	55	6	.306
Mouton	179	23	54	5	27	1	.302
Ventura.	492	79	145	26	93	4	.295
Raines	502	81	143	12	67	13	.285
Martin	160	17	43	2	17	5	.269
Durham.	471	68	121	7	51	18	.257
Guillen	415	50	103	1	41	6	.248
Karkovice	323	44	70	13	51	2	.217

Pitching	W	L	ERA	IP	H	BB	SO	Sv
Fernandez. .	12	8	3.80	203.2	200	65	159	0
Hernandez .	3	7	3.92	59.2	63	28	84	32
Alvarez	8	11	4.32	175.0	171	93	118	0
McCaskill . .	6	4	4.89	81.0	97	33	50	2
Keyser	5	6	4.97	92.1	114	27	48	0
DeLeon. . . .	5	3	5.19	67.2	60	28	53	0
Bere	8	15	7.19	137.2	151	106	110	0

Manager— Gene Lamont, Terry Bevington

Cleveland Indians

Batting	AB	R	H	HR	RBI	SB	Avg
Murray	436	68	141	23	82	5	.323
Belle.	546	121	173	50	126	5	.317
Perry	162	23	51	3	23	1	.315
Baerga	557	87	175	15	90	11	.314
Thome	452	92	142	25	73	4	.314
Lofton.	481	93	149	7	53	54	.310
Ramirez	484	85	149	31	107	6	.308
Alomar	203	32	61	10	35	3	.300
Vizquel	542	87	144	6	56	29	.266
Pena.	263	25	69	5	28	1	.262
Sorrento	323	50	76	25	79	1	.235
Kirby	188	29	39	1	14	10	.207

Pitching	W	L	ERA	IP	H	BB	SO	Sv
Mesa	3	0	1.13	64.0	49	17	58	46
Tavarez. . . .	10	2	2.44	85.0	76	21	68	0
Plunk	6	2	2.67	64.0	48	27	71	2
Ogea	8	3	3.05	106.1	95	29	57	0
Martinez . .	12	5	3.08	187.0	174	46	99	0
Hershiser . .	16	6	3.87	167.1	151	51	111	0
Hill	4	1	3.98	74.2	77	32	48	0
Nagy.	16	6	4.55	178.0	194	61	139	0
Clark.	9	7	5.27	124.2	143	42	68	0

Manager—Mike Hargrove

Detroit Tigers

Batting	AB	R	H	HR	RBI	SB	Avg
Whitaker	249	36	73	14	44	4	.293
Fryman	567	79	156	15	81	4	.275
Trammell	223	28	60	2	23	3	.269
Curtis.	586	96	157	21	67	27	.268
Gibson.	227	37	59	9	35	9	.260
Flaherty	354	39	86	11	40	0	.243
Fielder	494	70	120	31	82	0	.243
Fletcher	182	19	42	1	17	1	.231
Higginson. . . .	410	61	92	14	43	6	.224
Gomez.	431	49	96	11	50	4	.223
Bautista	271	28	55	7	27	4	.203

Pitching	W	L	ERA	IP	H	BB	SO	Sv
Henneman . .	0	1	1.53	29.1	24	9	24	18
Wells	10	3	3.04	130.1	120	37	83	0
Lira	9	13	4.31	146.1	151	56	89	1
Doherty	5	9	5.10	113.0	130	37	46	6
Bergman . . .	7	10	5.12	135.1	169	67	86	0
Bohanon . . .	1	1	5.54	105.2	121	41	63	1
Lima	3	9	6.11	73.2	85	18	37	0
Boever.	5	7	6.39	98.2	128	44	71	3
Moore	5	15	7.53	132.2	179	68	64	0

Manager—Sparky Anderson

Kansas City Royals

Batting	AB	R	H	HR	RBI	SB	Avg
Lockhart.	274	41	88	6	33	8	.321
Joyner	465	69	144	12	83	3	.310
Goodwin	480	72	138	4	28	50	.288
Damon.	188	32	53	3	23	7	.282
Samuel	205	31	54	12	39	6	.263
Gaetti.	514	76	134	35	96	3	.261
Tucker	177	23	46	4	17	2	.260
Gagne	430	58	110	6	49	3	.256
Mayne	307	23	77	1	27	0	.251
Nunnally.	303	51	74	14	42	6	.244
Howard	255	23	62	0	19	6	.243
Hamelin	208	20	35	7	25	0	.168

Pitching	W	L	ERA	IP	H	BB	SO	Sv
Montgomery .	2	3	3.43	65.2	60	25	49	31
Haney	3	4	3.65	81.1	78	33	31	0
Gubicza	12	14	3.75	213.1	222	62	81	0
Appier	15	10	3.89	201.1	163	80	185	0
Pichardo	8	4	4.36	64.0	66	30	43	1
Gordon	12	12	4.43	189.0	204	89	119	0
Jacome	4	6	5.36	84.0	101	21	39	0
Fleming	1	6	5.96	80.0	84	53	40	0

Manager—Bob Boone

Milwaukee Brewers

Batting	AB	R	H	HR	RBI	SB	Avg
Surhoff.	415	72	133	13	73	7	.320
Jaha	316	59	99	20	65	2	.313
Seitzer.	492	56	153	5	69	2	.311
Nilsson.	263	41	73	12	53	2	.278
Cirillo.	328	57	91	9	39	7	.277
Oliver.	337	43	92	12	51	2	.273
Hamilton	398	54	108	5	44	11	.271
Vina.	288	46	74	3	29	6	.257
Mieske.	267	42	67	12	48	2	.251
Hulse.	339	46	85	3	47	15	.251
Matheny	166	13	41	0	21	2	.247
Vaughn	392	67	88	17	59	10	.224
Valentin	338	62	74	11	49	16	.219
Listach.	334	35	73	0	25	13	.219

Pitching	W	L	ERA	IP	H	BB	SO	Sv
Fetters	0	3	3.38	34.2	40	20	33	22
Karl	6	7	4.14	124.0	141	50	59	0
Bones	10	12	4.63	200.1	218	83	77	0
Sparks	9	11	4.63	202.0	210	86	96	0
Givens	5	7	4.95	107.1	116	54	73	0
Miranda	4	5	5.23	74.0	83	49	45	1
Wegman	5	7	5.35	70.2	89	21	50	2
Roberson . . .	6	4	5.76	84.1	102	37	40	0
Scanlan	4	7	6.59	83.1	101	44	29	0

Manager—Phil Garner

Minnesota Twins

Batting	AB	R	H	HR	RBI	SB	Avg
Knoblauch.....	538	107	179	11	63	46	.333
Puckett.......	538	83	169	23	99	3	.314
Munoz........	376	45	113	18	58	0	.301
Reboulet......	216	39	63	4	23	1	.292
Merullo	195	19	55	1	27	0	.282
Cordova	512	81	142	24	84	20	.277
Meares	390	57	105	12	49	10	.269
Stahoviak	263	28	70	3	23	5	.266
Walbeck	393	40	101	1	44	3	.257
Leius.........	372	51	92	4	45	2	.247
Masteller	198	21	47	3	21	1	.237
Becker	392	45	93	2	33	8	.237

Pitching	W	L	ERA	IP	H	BB	SO	Sv
Tapani	6	11	4.92	133.2	155	34	88	0
Stevens....	5	4	5.07	65.2	74	32	47	10
Guardado ..	4	9	5.12	91.1	99	45	71	2
Radke.....	11	14	5.32	181.0	195	47	75	0
Trombley ..	4	8	5.62	97.2	107	42	68	0
Rodriguez ..	5	8	6.13	105.2	114	57	59	0
Mahomes ..	4	10	6.37	94.2	100	47	67	3
Klingenbeck	2	4	7.12	79.2	101	42	42	0

Manager— Tom Kelly

New York Yankees

Batting	AB	R	H	HR	RBI	SB	Avg
Boggs........	460	76	149	5	63	1	.324
B. Williams	563	93	173	18	82	8	.307
O'Neill........	460	82	138	22	96	1	.300
Mattingly......	458	59	132	7	49	0	.288
James........	209	22	60	2	26	4	.287
Velarde.......	367	60	102	7	46	5	.278
Leyritz.......	264	37	71	7	37	1	.269
Stanley	399	63	107	18	83	1	.268
Sierra	479	73	126	19	86	5	.263
Polonia	238	37	62	2	15	10	.261
G. Williams	182	33	45	6	28	4	.247
Fernandez.....	384	57	94	5	45	6	.245
Kelly.........	270	32	64	4	29	8	.237

Pitching	W	L	ERA	IP	H	BB	SO	Sv
Wetteland ..	1	5	2.93	61.1	40	14	66	31
Cone.......	18	8	3.57	229.1	195	88	191	0
McDowell ..	15	10	3.93	217.2	211	78	157	0
Kamieniecki.	7	6	4.01	89.2	83	49	43	0
Wickman...	2	4	4.05	80.0	77	33	51	1
Pettitte	12	9	4.17	175.0	183	63	114	0
Hitchcock ..	11	10	4.70	168.1	155	68	121	0
Rivera.....	5	3	5.51	67.0	71	30	51	0
Perez	5	5	5.58	69.1	70	31	44	0

Manager—Buck Showalter

Oakland Athletics

Batting	AB	R	H	HR	RBI	SB	Avg
Henderson	407	67	122	9	54	32	.300
Berroa........	546	87	152	22	88	7	.278
Steinbach	406	43	113	15	65	1	.278
Javier	442	81	123	8	56	36	.278
McGwire	317	75	87	39	90	1	.274
Bordick	428	46	113	8	44	11	.264
Brosius	389	69	102	17	46	4	.262
Giambi	176	27	45	6	25	2	.256
Gates	524	60	133	5	56	3	.254
Tartabull	280	34	66	8	35	0	.236
Paquette	283	42	64	13	49	5	.226

Pitching	W	L	ERA	IP	H	BB	SO	Sv
Ontiveros ..	9	6	4.37	129.2	144	38	77	0
Stottlemyre .	14	7	4.55	209.2	228	80	205	0
Eckersley ..	4	6	4.83	50.1	53	11	40	29
Van Poppel .	4	8	4.88	138.1	125	56	122	0
Reyes.....	4	6	5.09	69.0	71	28	48	0
Darling	4	7	6.23	104.0	124	46	69	0
Stewart	3	7	6.89	81.0	101	39	58	0

Manager— Tony LaRussa

Seattle Mariners

Batting	AB	R	H	HR	RBI	SB	Avg
E. Martinez....	511	121	182	29	113	4	.356
Cora........	427	64	127	3	39	18	.297
T. Martinez....	519	92	152	31	111	0	.293
Sojo........	339	50	98	7	39	4	.289
Coleman	455	66	131	5	29	42	.288
Amaral.......	238	45	67	2	19	21	.282
Wilson.......	399	40	111	9	51	2	.278
Strange	155	19	42	2	21	0	.271
Buhner......	470	86	123	40	121	0	.262
Newson	157	34	41	5	15	2	.261
Griffey	260	52	67	17	42	4	.258
Blowers	439	59	113	23	96	2	.257
Diaz........	270	44	67	3	27	18	.248
Fermin.......	200	21	39	0	15	2	.195

Pitching	W	L	ERA	IP	H	BB	SO	Sv
Charlton......	2	1	1.51	47.2	23	16	58	14
Nelson......	7	3	2.17	78.2	58	27	96	2
R. Johnson...	18	2	2.48	214.1	159	65	294	0
Ayala........	6	5	4.44	71.0	73	30	77	19
Belcher	10	12	4.52	179.1	188	88	96	0
Bosio.......	10	8	4.92	170.0	211	69	85	0
Wells	4	3	5.75	76.2	88	39	38	0
Benes	7	2	5.86	63.0	72	33	45	0
Torres.......	3	8	6.00	72.0	87	42	45	0

Manager—Lou Piniella

Texas Rangers

Batting	AB	R	H	HR	RBI	SB	Avg
Rodriguez	492	56	149	12	67	0	.303
Clark........	454	85	137	16	92	0	.302
Gonzalez	352	57	104	27	82	0	.295
Nixon........	589	87	174	0	45	50	.295
Frye........	313	38	87	4	29	3	.278
Greer........	417	58	113	13	61	3	.271
Maldonado ...	190	28	50	9	30	1	.263
McLemore	467	73	122	5	41	21	.261
Tettleton.....	429	76	102	32	78	0	.238
Pagliarulo.....	241	27	56	4	27	0	.232
Gil	415	36	91	9	46	2	.219

Pitching	W	L	ERA	IP	H	BB	SO	Sv
Russell.....	1	0	3.03	32.2	36	9	21	20
Rogers.....	17	7	3.38	208.0	192	76	140	0
McDowell ...	7	4	4.02	85.0	86	34	49	4
Pavlik.....	10	10	4.37	191.2	174	90	149	0
Tewksbury ..	8	7	4.58	129.2	169	20	53	0
Gross......	9	15	5.54	183.2	200	89	106	0
Darwin.....	3	10	7.45	99.0	131	31	58	0

Manager— Johnny Oates

Toronto Blue Jays

Batting	AB	R	H	HR	RBI	SB	Avg
Alomar.......	517	71	155	13	66	30	.300
Olerud	492	72	143	8	54	0	.291
Green	379	52	109	15	54	1	.288
White.......	427	61	121	10	53	11	.283
Molitor	525	63	142	15	60	12	.270
Carter	558	70	141	25	76	12	.253
Sprague......	521	77	127	18	74	0	.244
Gonzalez	367	51	89	10	42	4	.243
Martinez......	191	12	46	2	25	0	.241
Cedeno	161	18	38	4	14	0	.236
Parrish.......	178	15	36	4	22	0	.202

Pitching	W	L	ERA	IP	H	BB	SO	Sv
Castillo.....	1	5	3.22	72.2	64	24	38	13
Leiter......	11	11	3.64	183.0	162	108	153	0
Menhart	1	4	4.92	78.2	72	47	50	0
Hentgen....	10	14	5.11	200.2	236	90	135	0
Hurtado	5	2	5.45	77.2	81	40	33	0
Guzman...	4	14	6.32	135.1	151	73	94	0

Manager—Cito Gaston

National Baseball Hall of Fame and Museum, Cooperstown, N.Y.

Aaron, Hank
Alexander, Grover Cleveland
Alston, Walt
Anson, Cap
Aparicio, Luis
Appling, Luke
Ashburn, Richie
Averill, Earl
Baker, Home Run
Bancroft, Dave
Banks, Ernie
Barlick, Al
Barrow, Edward G.
Beckley, Jake
Bell, Cool Papa
Bench, Johnny
Bender, Chief
Berra, Yogi
Bottomley, Jim
Boudreau, Lou
Bresnahan, Roger
Brock, Lou
Brouthers, Dan
Brown, Mordecai (Three Finger)
Bulkeley, Morgan C.
Burkett, Jesse C.
Campanella, Roy
Carew, Rod
Carey, Max
Carlton, Steve
Cartwright, Alexander
Chadwick, Henry
Chance, Frank
Chandler, Happy
Charleston, Oscar
Chesbro, John
Clarke, Fred
Clarkson, John
Clemente, Roberto
Cobb, Ty
Cochrane, Mickey
Collins, Eddie
Collins, James
Combs, Earle
Comiskey, Charles A.

Conlan, Jocko
Connolly, Thomas H.
Connor, Roger
Coveleski, Stan
Crawford, Sam
Cronin, Joe
Cummings, Candy
Cuyler, Kiki
Dandridge, Ray
Day, Leon
Dean, Dizzy
Delahanty, Ed
Dickey, Bill
DiHigo, Martin
DiMaggio, Joe
Doerr, Bobby
Drysdale, Don
Duffy, Hugh
Durocher, Leo
Evans, Billy
Evers, John
Ewing, Buck
Faber, Urban
Feller, Bob
Ferrell, Rick
Fingers, Rollie
Flick, Elmer H.
Ford, Whitey
Foster, Andrew
Foxx, Jimmie
Frick, Ford
Frisch, Frank
Galvin, Pud
Gehrig, Lou
Gehringer, Charles
Gibson, Bob
Gibson, Josh
Giles, Warren
Gomez, Lefty
Goslin, Goose
Greenberg, Hank
Griffith, Clark
Grimes, Burleigh
Grove, Lefty
Hafey, Chick

Haines, Jesee
Hamilton, Bill
Harridge, Will
Harris, Bucky
Hartnett, Gabby
Heilmann, Harry
Herman, Billy
Hooper, Harry
Hornsby, Rogers
Hoyt, Waite
Hubbard, Cal
Hubbell, Carl
Huggins, Miller
Hulbert, William
Hunter, Catfish
Irvin, Monte
Jackson, Reggie
Jackson, Travis
Jenkins, Ferguson
Jennings, Hugh
Johnson, Byron
Johnson, William (Judy)
Johnson, Walter
Joss, Addie
Kaline, Al
Keefe, Timothy
Keeler, William
Kell, George
Kelley, Joe
Kelly, George
Kelly, King
Killebrew, Harmon
Kiner, Ralph
Klein, Chuck
Klem, Bill
Koufax, Sandy
Lajoie, Napoleon
Landis, Kenesaw M.
Lazzeri, Tony
Lemon, Bob
Leonard, Buck
Lindstrom, Fred
Lloyd, Pop
Lombardi, Ernie
Lopez, Amos

Lyons, Ted
Mack, Connie
MacPhail, Larry
Mantle, Mickey
Manush, Henry
Maranville, Rabbit
Marichal, Juan
Marquard, Rube
Mathews, Eddie
Mathewson, Christy
Mays, Willie
McCarthy, Joe
McCarthy, Thomas
McCovey, Willie
McGinnity, Joe
McGowan, Bill
McGraw, John
McKechnie, Bill
Medwick, Joe
Mize, Johnny
Morgan, Joe
Musial, Stan
Newhouser, Hal
Nichols, Kid
O'Rourke, James
Ott, Mel
Paige, Satchel
Palmer, Jim
Pennock, Herb
Perry, Gaylord
Plank, Ed
Radbourn, Charlie
Reese, Pee Wee
Rice, Sam
Rickey, Branch
Rixey, Eppa
Rizzuto, Phil (Scooter)
Roberts, Robin
Robinson, Brooks
Robinson, Frank
Robinson, Jackie
Robinson, Wilbert
Roush, Edd
Ruffing, Red
Rusie, Amos

Ruth, Babe
Schalk, Ray
Schmidt, Mike
Schoendienst, Red
Seaver, Tom
Sewell, Joe
Simmons, Al
Sisler, George
Slaughter, Enos
Snider, Duke
Spahn, Warren
Spalding, Albert
Speaker, Tris
Stargell, Willie
Stengel, Casey
Terry, Bill
Thompson, Sam
Tinker, Joe
Traynor, Pie
Vance, Dazzy
Vaughan, Arky
Veeck, Bill
Waddell, Rube
Wagner, Honus
Wallace, Roderick
Walsh, Ed
Waner, Lloyd
Waner, Paul
Ward, John
Weiss, George
Welch, Mickey
Wheat, Zach
Wilhelm, Hoyt
Williams, Billy
Williams, Ted
Williams, Vic
Wilson, Hack
Wright, George
Wright, Harry
Wynn, Early
Yastrzemski, Carl
Yawkey, Tom
Young, Cy
Youngs, Ross

Hall of Famers Chosen in First Year of Eligibility

Year	Name	Year	Name	Year	Name	Year	Name
1962	Jackie Robinson, Bob Feller	1977	Ernie Banks	1985	Lou Brock	1991	Rod Carew
1966	Ted Williams	1979	Willie Mays	1986	Willie McCovey	1992	Tom Seaver
1969	Stan Musial	1980	Al Kaline	1988	Willie Stargell	1993	Reggie Jackson
1972	Sandy Koufax	1981	Bob Gibson	1989	Johnny Bench, Carl Yastrzemski	1994	Steve Carlton
1973	Warren Spahn	1982	Hank Aaron, Frank Robinson	1990	Jim Palmer, Joe Morgan	1995	Mike Schmidt
1974	Mickey Mantle	1983	Brooks Robinson				

All-Star Baseball Games, 1933-1995

Year	Winner	Score	Location	Year	Winner	Score	Location
1933	American	4-2	Chicago	1963	National	5-3	Cleveland
1934	American	9-7	New York	1964	National	7-4	New York
1935	American	4-1	Cleveland	1965	National	6-5	Minnesota
1936	National	4-3	Boston	1966	National (3)	2-1	St. Louis
1937	American	8-3	Washington	1967	National (4)	2-1	Anaheim
1938	National	4-1	Cincinnati	1968*	National	1-0	Houston
1939	American	3-1	New York	1969	National	9-3	Washington
1940	National	4-0	St. Louis	1970*	National (2)	5-4	Cincinnati
1941	American	7-5	Detroit	1971*	American	6-4	Detroit
1942	American	3-1	New York	1972*	National	4-3	Atlanta
1943*	American	5-3	Philadelphia	1973*	National	7-1	Kansas City
1944*	National	7-1	Pittsburgh	1974*	National	7-2	Pittsburgh
1945	Not played			1975*	National	6-3	Milwaukee
1946	American	12-0	Boston	1976*	National	7-1	Philadelphia
1947	American	2-1	Chicago	1977*	National	7-5	New York
1948	American	5-2	St. Louis	1978*	National	7-3	San Diego
1949	American	11-7	New York	1979*	National	7-6	Seattle
1950	National (1)	4-3	Chicago	1980*	National	4-2	Los Angeles
1951	National	8-3	Detroit	1981*	National	5-4	Cleveland
1952	National	3-2	Philadelphia	1982*	National	4-1	Montreal
1953	National	5-1	Cincinnati	1983*	American	13-3	Chicago
1954	American	11-9	Cleveland	1984*	National	3-1	San Francisco
1955	National (2)	6-5	Milwaukee	1985*	National	6-1	Minneapolis
1956	National	7-3	Washington	1986*	American	3-2	Houston
1957	American	6-5	St. Louis	1987*	National (5)	2-0	Oakland
1958	American	4-3	Baltimore	1988*	American	2-1	Cincinnati
1959	National	5-4	Pittsburgh	1989*	American	5-3	Anaheim
1959	American	5-3	Los Angeles	1990*	American	2-0	Chicago
1960	National	5-3	Kansas City	1991*	American	4-2	Toronto
1960	National	6-0	New York	1992*	American	13-6	San Diego
1961	National (3)	5-4	San Francisco	1993*	American	9-3	Baltimore
1961	Called-rain	1-1	Boston	1994*	National	8-7	Pittsburgh
1962	National (3)	3-1	Washington	1995*	National	3-2	Texas
1962	American	9-4	Chicago				

(1) 14 innings. (2) 12 innings. (3) 10 innings. (4) 15 innings. (5) 13 innings. * Night game.

Major League Leaders in 1995
Final statistics for strike-shortened season

American League

Batting
E. Martinez, Seattle, .356; Knoblauch, Minnesota, .333; Salmon, California, .330; Boggs, New York, .324; Murray, Cleveland, .323.

Runs
Belle, Cleveland, 121; E. Martinez, Seattle, 121; Edmonds, California, 120; Phillips, California, 119; Salmon, California, 111.

Runs Batted In
Belle, Cleveland, 126; Vaughn, Boston 126; Buhner, Seattle, 121; E. Martinez, Seattle, 113; T. Martinez, Seattle, 111; F. Thomas, Chicago, 111.

Hits
L. Johnson, Chicago, 186; E. Martinez, Seattle, 182; Knoblauch, Minnesota, 179; Salmon, California, 177; Baerga, Cleveland, 175.

Doubles
Belle, Cleveland, 52; E. Martinez, Seattle, 52; Puckett, Minnesota, 39; Valentin, Boston, 37; T. Martinez, Seattle, 35.

Triples
Lofton, Cleveland, 13; L. Johnson, Chicago, 12; Anderson, Baltimore, 10; B. Williams, New York, 9.

Home Runs
Belle, Cleveland, 50; Buhner, Seattle, 40; F. Thomas, Chicago, 40; McGwire, Oakland, 39; Palmeiro, Baltimore, 39; Vaughn, Boston, 39.

Stolen Bases
Lofton, Cleveland, 54; Goodwin, Kansas City, 50; Nixon, Texas, 50; Knoblauch, Minnesota, 46; Coleman, Kansas City-Seattle, 42.

Pitching (15 Decisions)
R. Johnson, Seattle, 18-2, .900; Hanson, Boston, 15-5, .750; Hershiser, Cleveland, 16-6, .727; Nagy, Cleveland, 16-6, .727; Rogers, Texas; 17-7, .708.

Strikeouts
R. Johnson, Seattle, 294; Stottlemyre, Oakland, 205; Finley, California, 195; Cone, Toronto-New York, 191; Appier, Kansas City, 185.

Saves
Mesa, Cleveland, 46; L. Smith, California, 37; Aguilera, Minnesota-Boston, 32; Hernandez, Chicago, 32; Montgomery, Kansas City, 31; Wetteland, New York, 31.

National League

Batting
Gwynn, San Diego, .368; Piazza, Los Angeles, .346; Bichette, Colorado, .340; D. Bell, Houston, .334; Grace, Chicago, .326.

Runs
Biggio, Houston, 123; Bonds, San Francisco, 109; Finley, San Diego, 104; Bichette, Colorado, 102; Larkin, Cincinnati, 98.

Runs Batted In
Bichette, Colorado, 128; Sosa, Chicago, 119; Galarraga, Colorado, 106; Conine, Florida, 105; Karros, Los Angeles, 105.

Hits
Bichette, Colorado, 197; Gwynn, San Diego, 197; Grace, Chicago, 180; Biggio, Houston, 167; Finley, San Diego, 167; McRae, Chicago, 167.

Doubles
Grace, Chicago, 51; Bichette, Colorado, 38; McRae, Chicago, 38; R. Sanders, Cincinnati, 36; Cordero, Montreal, 35; Lankford, St. Louis, 35.

Triples
Butler, New York-Los Angeles, 9; E. Young, Colorado, 9; Finley, San Diego, 8; Gonzalez, Houston-Chicago, 8; D. Sanders, Cincinnati-San Francisco, 8.

Home Runs
Bichette, Colorado, 40; Sosa, Chicago, 36; Walker, Colorado, 36; Bonds, San Francisco, 33; Castilla, Colorado, 32; Karros, Los Angeles, 32; Piazza, Los Angeles, 32.

Stolen Bases
Veras, Florida, 56; Larkin, Cincinnati, 51; DeShields, Los Angeles, 39; Finley, San Diego, 36; R. Sanders, Cincinnati, 36.

Pitching (15 Decisions)
Maddux, Atlanta, 19-2, .905; Schourek, Cincinnati, 18-7, .720; R. Martinez, Los Angeles, 17-7, .708; Smiley, Cincinnati, 12-5, .706; Navarro, Chicago, 14-6, .700.

Strikeouts
Nomo, Los Angeles, 236; Smoltz, Atlanta, 193; Maddux, Atlanta, 181; Reynolds, Houston, 175; P.J. Martinez, Montreal, 174.

Saves
Myers, Chicago, 38; Henke, St. Louis, 36; Beck, San Francisco, 33; Slocumb, Philadelphia, 32; Worrell, Los Angeles, 32.

Earned Run Average Leaders

	National League					American League			
Year	Player, club	G	IP	ERA	Year	Player, club	G	IP	ERA
1972	Steve Carlton, Philadelphia	41	346	1.98	1972	Luis Tiant, Boston	43	179	1.91
1973	Tom Seaver, New York	36	290	2.07	1973	Jim Palmer, Baltimore	38	296	2.40
1974	Buzz Capra, Atlanta	39	217	2.28	1974	Catfish Hunter, Oakland	41	318	2.49
1975	Randy Jones, San Diego	37	285	2.24	1975	Jim Palmer, Baltimore	39	323	2.09
1976	John Denny, St. Louis	30	207	2.52	1976	Mark Fidrych, Detroit	31	250	2.34
1977	John Candelaria, Pittsburgh	33	231	2.34	1977	Frank Tanana, California	31	241	2.54
1978	Craig Swan, New York	29	207	2.43	1978	Ron Guidry, New York	35	274	1.74
1979	J. R. Richard, Houston	38	292	2.71	1979	Ron Guidry, New York	33	236	2.78
1980	Don Sutton, Los Angeles	32	212	2.21	1980	Rudy May, New York	41	175	2.47
1981	Nolan Ryan, Houston	21	149	1.69	1981	Steve McCatty, Oakland	22	186	2.32
1982	Steve Rogers, Montreal	35	277	2.40	1982	Rick Sutcliffe, Cleveland	34	216	2.96
1983	Atlee Hammaker, San Francisco	23	172	2.25	1983	Rick Honeycutt, Texas	25	174	2.42
1984	Alejandro Pena, Los Angeles	28	199	2.48	1984	Mike Boddicker, Baltimore	34	261	2.79
1985	Dwight Gooden, New York	35	276	1.53	1985	Dave Stieb, Toronto	36	265	2.48
1986	Mike Scott, Houston	37	275	2.22	1986	Roger Clemens, Boston	33	254	2.48
1987	Nolan Ryan, Houston	34	211	2.76	1987	Jimmy Key, Toronto	36	261	2.76
1988	Joe Magrane, St. Louis	24	165	2.18	1988	Allan Anderson, Minnesota	30	202	2.45
1989	Scott Garrelts, San Francisco	30	193	2.28	1989	Bret Saberhagen, Kansas City	36	262	2.16
1990	Danny Darwin, Houston	48	162	2.21	1990	Roger Clemens, Boston	31	228	1.93
1991	Dennis Martinez, Montreal	31	222	2.39	1991	Roger Clemens, Boston	35	271	2.62
1992	Bill Swift, San Francisco	30	164	2.08	1992	Roger Clemens, Boston	32	246	2.41
1993	Greg Maddux, Atlanta	36	267	2.36	1993	Kevin Appier, Kansas City	34	238	2.56
1994	Greg Maddux, Atlanta	25	202	1.56	1994	Steve Ontiveros, Oakland	27	115	2.65
1995	Greg Maddux, Atlanta	28	209	1.63	1995	Randy Johnson, Seattle	30	214	2.48

ERA is computed by multiplying earned runs allowed by 9, then dividing by innings pitched.

All-Time Major League Leaders

(*player active at end of 1995 season)

Games		At Bats		Runs Batted In		Stolen Bases (since 1898)	
Pete Rose	3,562	Pete Rose	14,043	Hank Aaron	2,297	Rickey Henderson*	1,149
Carl Yastrzemski	3,308	Hank Aaron	12,364	Babe Ruth	2,211	Lou Brock	938
Hank Aaron	3,298	Carl Yastrzemski	11,988	Lou Gehrig	1,990	Ty Cobb	892
Ty Cobb	3,034	Ty Cobb	11,429	Ty Cobb	1,961	Tim Raines*	777
Stan Musial	3,026	Robin Yount	11,008	Stan Musial	1,951	Eddie Collins	742
Willie Mays	2,992	Dave Winfield*	11,003	Jimmie Foxx	1,921	Vince Coleman*	740
Dave Winfield*	2,973	Stan Musial	10,972	Willie Mays	1,903	Max Carey	738
Rusty Staub	2,951	Willie Mays	10,881	Mel Ott	1,861	Honus Wagner	703
Brooks Robinson	2,896	Brooks Robinson	10,654	Carl Yastrzemski	1,844	Joe Morgan	689
Robin Yount	2,856	Eddie Murray*	10,603	Ted Williams	1,839	Willie Wilson	668

Runs		Strikeouts		Shutouts		Saves	
Ty Cobb	2,245	Nolan Ryan	5,714	Walter Johnson	110	Lee Smith*	471
Hank Aaron	2,174	Steve Carlton	4,136	Grover C. Alexander	90	Jeff Reardon	367
Babe Ruth	2,174	Bert Blyleven	3,701	Christy Mathewson	83	Rollie Fingers	341
Pete Rose	2,165	Tom Seaver	3,640	Cy Young	77	Dennis Eckersley*	323
Willie Mays	2,062	Don Sutton	3,574	Eddie Plank	69	Tom Henke*	311
Stan Musial	1,949	Gaylord Perry	3,534	Warren Spahn	63	Rich Gossage	310
Lou Gehrig	1,888	Walter Johnson	3,508	Mordecai Brown	63	Bruce Sutter	300
Tris Speaker	1,882	Phil Niekro	3,340	Tom Seaver	61	John Franco*	295
Mel Ott	1,859	Ferguson Jenkins	3,192	Nolan Ryan	61	Dave Righetti*	252
Frank Robinson	1,829	Bob Gibson	3,117	Bert Blyleven	60	Dan Quisenberry	244

All-Time Home Run Leaders

Player	HR	Player	HR	Player	HR	Player	HR
Hank Aaron	755	Ted Williams	521	Dave Winfield*	465	Graig Nettles	390
Babe Ruth	714	Willie McCovey	521	Carl Yastrzemski	452	Johnny Bench	389
Willie Mays	660	Ed Mathews	512	Dave Kingman	442	Dwight Evans	385
Frank Robinson	586	Ernie Banks	512	Andre Dawson*	436	Frank Howard	382
Harmon Killebrew	573	Mel Ott	511	Billy Williams	426	Jim Rice	382
Reggie Jackson	563	Lou Gehrig	493	Darrell Evans	414	Orlando Cepeda	379
Mike Schmidt	548	Eddie Murray*	479	Duke Snider	407	Tony Perez	379
Mickey Mantle	536	Stan Musial	475	Al Kaline	399		
Jimmy Foxx	534	Willie Stargell	475	Dale Murphy	398		

Players With 3,000 Major League Hits

Player	Hits	Player	Hits	Player	Hits
Pete Rose	4,256	Eddie Collins	3,312	Eddie Murray*	3,071
Ty Cobb	4,191	Willie Mays	3,283	Rod Carew	3,053
Hank Aaron	3,771	Nap Lajoie	3,242	Lou Brock	3,023
Stan Musial	3,630	George Brett	3,154	Al Kaline	3,007
Tris Speaker	3,514	Paul Waner	3,152	Cap Anson	3,000
Carl Yastrzemski	3,419	Robin Yount	3,142	Roberto Clemente	3,000
Honus Wagner	3,415	Dave Winfield*	3,110		

Baseball Stadiums

National League

Team	Stadium (year opened)	Surface	Home run distances (ft.) LF	Center	RF	Seating capacity
Atlanta Braves	Atlanta-Fulton County Stadium (1966)	Grass	330	402	330	52,710
Chicago Cubs	Wrigley Field (1914)	Grass	355	400	353	38,765
Cincinnati Reds	Riverfront Stadium (1970)	Artificial	330	404	330	52,952
Colorado Rockies	Coors Field (1995)	Grass	347	415	350	50,000
Florida Marlins	Joe Robbie Stadium (1987)	Grass	335	410	345	48,000
Houston Astros	The Astrodome (1965)	Artificial	325	400	325	53,821
Los Angeles Dodgers	Dodger Stadium (1962)	Grass	330	395	330	56,000
Montreal Expos	Olympic Stadium (1976)	Artificial	325	404	325	46,500
New York Mets	Shea Stadium (1964)	Grass	338	410	338	55,601
Philadelphia Phillies	Veterans Stadium (1971)	Artificial	330	408	330	62,530
Pittsburgh Pirates	Three Rivers Stadium (1970)	Artificial	335	400	335	47,972
St. Louis Cardinals	Busch Stadium (1966)	Artificial	330	402	330	57,000
San Diego Padres	San Diego/Jack Murphy Stadium (1967)	Grass	327	405	327	46,510
San Francisco Giants	3Com (Candlestick) Park (1960)	Grass	335	400	328	63,000

American League

Team	Stadium (year opened)	Surface	Home run distances (ft.) LF	Center	RF	Seating capacity
Baltimore Orioles	Oriole Park at Camden Yards (1992)	Grass	333	400	318	48,282
Boston Red Sox	Fenway Park (1912)	Grass	315	420	302	33,871
California Angels	Anaheim Stadium (1966)	Grass	333	404	333	64,593
Chicago White Sox	Comiskey Park (1991)	Grass	347	400	347	44,321
Cleveland Indians	Jacobs Field (1994)	Grass	325	405	325	42,400
Detroit Tigers	Tiger Stadium (1912)	Grass	340	440	325	52,416
Kansas City Royals	Kauffman Stadium (1973)	Artificial	330	400	330	40,625
Milwaukee Brewers	County Stadium (1953)	Grass	315	402	315	53,192
Minnesota Twins	Hubert H. Humphrey Metrodome (1982)	Artificial	343	408	327	56,783
New York Yankees	Yankee Stadium (1923)	Grass	312	410	310	57,545
Oakland A's	Oakland-Alameda County Coliseum (1968)	Grass	330	400	330	47,313
Seattle Mariners	The Kingdome (1976)	Artificial	331	405	312	59,166
Texas Rangers	The Ballpark in Arlington (1994)	Grass	332	400	325	49,292
Toronto Blue Jays	SkyDome (1989)	Artificial	330	400	330	50,516

1995 World Series

The Atlanta Braves defeated the Cleveland Indians, 1-0, in Game 6 on Oct. 28, on a combined one-hit shutout by Tom Glavine and Mark Wohlers, to take the 1995 World Series 4 games to 2. The Indians had the best record in baseball (100-44) and were the best-hitting team (207 home runs, .291 batting average), but the Braves' pitching staff, with an ERA of 2.67 during the Series, was just too tough. Glavine, who won 2 games and had an ERA of 1.29, was named the Series' most valuable player.

First Game

Cleveland	ab	r	h	bi	Atlanta	ab	r	h	bi
Lofton, cf	4	2	1	0	Grissom, cf	4	0	1	0
Vizquel, ss	4	0	0	0	Lemke, 2b	3	0	1	0
Baerga, 2b	4	0	0	1	CpJones, 3b	4	0	0	0
Belle, lf	3	0	0	0	McGriff, 1b	3	2	1	1
Murray, 1b	3	0	0	0	Justice, rf	1	1	0	0
Tavarez, p	0	0	0	0	Klesko, lf	2	0	0	0
Embree, p	0	0	0	0	Dever'x, ph-lf	0	0	0	0
Thome, 3b	3	0	1	0	O'Brien, c	2	0	0	0
MRamirez, rf	3	0	0	0	Polonia, ph	1	0	0	1
SAlomar, c	3	0	0	0	JLopez, c	0	0	0	0
Hershiser, p	2	0	0	0	Belliard, ss	2	0	0	1
Assnmchr, p	0	0	0	0	GMaddux, p	3	0	0	0
Sorrento, 1b	1	0	0	0	Totals	25	3	3	3
Totals	30	2	2	1					

Cleveland	1	0	0	0	0	0	0	0	1—2
Atlanta	0	1	0	0	0	0	2	0	x—3

	ip	h	r	er	bb	so
Cleveland						
Hershiser L, 0-1	6.0	3	3	3	3	7
Assenmacher	0.0	0	0	0	1	0
Tavarez	1.1	0	0	0	1	0
Embree	0.2	0	0	0	0	2
Atlanta						
GMaddux W, 1-0	9.0	2	2	0	0	4

E - Belliard (1), McGriff (1). LOB - Cleveland 1, Atlanta 4. HR - McGriff (1). RBI - Baerga (1), McGriff (1), Polonia (1), Belliard (1). SB - Lofton 2 (2). S - Belliard.

How runs were scored—One in Indians first: Lofton safe at first on Belliard's fielding error. Lofton stole second. Lofton stole third. Baerga grounded out scoring Lofton.

One in Braves second: McGriff hit a home run.

Two in Braves seventh: McGriff walked. Justice walked. Devereaux walked. Polonia safe at first on fielder's choice scoring McGriff and moving Justice to third. Belliard sacrificed scoring Justice.

One in Indians ninth: Lofton singled. Vizquel grounded out moving Lofton to second. Lofton scored on McGriff's throwing error.

Second Game

Cleveland	ab	r	h	bi	Atlanta	ab	r	h	bi
Lofton, cf	5	1	1	0	Grissom, cf	3	1	1	0
Vizquel, ss	4	0	1	0	Lemke, 2b	3	1	1	0
Baerga, 2b	4	0	0	0	CpJones, 3b	3	0	2	1
Belle, lf	3	1	1	0	McGriff, 1b	4	0	0	0
Murray, 1b	3	1	1	2	Justice, rf	3	1	2	1
MRamirez, rf	4	0	2	0	Wohlers, p	0	0	0	0
Thome, 3b	3	0	0	0	Klesko, rf	3	0	0	0
Pena, c	3	0	0	0	Dever'x, lf-rf	1	0	0	0
Sorrento, ph	1	0	0	0	JLopez, c	3	1	1	2
SAlomar, c	0	0	0	0	Belliard, ss	4	0	0	0
DMartinez, p	2	0	0	0	Glavine, p	1	0	0	0
Embree, p	0	0	0	0	DwSmith, ph	1	0	1	0
Kirby, ph	1	0	0	0	McMichael, p	0	0	0	0
Poole, p	0	0	0	0	Pena, p	0	0	0	0
Tavarez, p	0	0	0	0	Polonia, lf	0	0	0	0
Amaro, ph	1	0	0	0	Totals	29	4	8	4
Totals	34	3	6	2					

Cleveland	0	2	0	0	0	0	1	0	0—3
Atlanta	0	0	2	0	0	2	0	0	x—4

	ip	h	r	er	bb	so
Cleveland						
DMartinez L, 1-0	5.2	8	4	4	3	3
Embree	0.1	0	0	0	0	0
Poole	1.0	0	0	0	0	0
Tavarez	1.0	0	0	0	0	0
Atlanta						
Glavine W, 1-0	6.0	3	2	2	3	3
McMichael H, 1	0.2	1	1	0	1	1
Pena H, 1	1.0	1	0	0	1	0
Wohlers S, 1	1.1	1	0	0	0	1

E - DMartinez (1), Belle (1), CpJones (1), Devereaux (1). LOB - Cleveland 9, Atlanta 7. 2B - CpJones (1). HR - Murray (1), JLopez (1). RBI - Murray 2 (2), CpJones (1), Justice (1), JLopez 2 (2). SB - Lofton 2 (4), Vizquel (1). SF - CpJones.

Third Game

Atlanta	ab	r	h	bi	Cleveland	ab	r	h	bi
Grissom, cf	6	1	2	0	Lofton, cf	3	3	3	0
Polonia, lf	4	1	1	1	Vizquel, ss	6	2	2	1
CpJones, 3b	3	2	1	0	Baerga, 2b	6	0	3	3
McGriff, 1b	5	1	3	2	Espinoza, pr	0	1	0	0
Justice, rf	5	0	0	0	Belle, lf	4	0	1	1
Klesko, dh	3	1	2	1	Murray, dh	6	0	1	1
Dever'x, ph-dh	2	0	1	1	Thome, 3b	4	0	0	0
JLopez, c	5	0	0	0	MRamirez, rf	2	1	0	0
Lemke, 2b	5	0	2	0	Sorrento, 1b	4	0	1	0
Belliard, ss	2	0	0	0	Kirby, pr	0	0	0	0
DwSmith, ph	1	0	0	0	HPerry, 1b	1	0	0	0
Mordecai, ss	1	0	0	0	SAlomar, c	5	0	1	0
Totals	42	6	12	6	Totals	41	7	12	7

Atlanta	1	0	0	0	0	1	1	3	0	0	0—6
Cleveland	2	0	2	0	0	0	1	1	0	0	1—7

	ip	h	r	er	bb	so
Atlanta						
Smoltz	2.1	6	4	4	2	4
Clontz	2.1	1	0	0	0	1
Mercker	2.0	1	1	1	2	2
McMichael	0.2	1	1	1	1	1
Wohlers BS, 1	2.2	1	0	0	3	2
Pena L, 0-1	0.0	2	1	1	1	0
Cleveland						
Nagy	7.0	8	5	5	1	4
Assenmacher BS, 1	0.1	0	1	1	1	0
Tavarez	0.2	1	0	0	0	0
Mesa W, 1-0	3.0	3	0	0	1	3

E - Belliard (2), Sorrento (1), Baerga (1). LOB - Atlanta 7, Cleveland 12. 2B - CpJones (2), Grissom (1), Lofton (1), SAlomar (1), Baerga (1). 3B - Vizquel (1). HR - McGriff (2), Klesko (1). RBI - McGriff 2 (3), Klesko (1), Polonia (2), Justice (2), Devereaux (1), Vizquel (1), Baerga 3 (4), Belle (1), Alomar (1), Murray (3). SB - Polonia (1), McGriff (1), Lofton (5), MRamirez (1). CS - Grissom (1), Lofton (1). S - Mordecai.

How runs were scored—One in Braves first: Jones doubled. McGriff singled scoring Jones.

Two in Indians first: Lofton singled. Vizquel tripled scoring Lofton. Baerga grounded out scoring Vizquel.

Two in Indians third: Lofton doubled. Vizquel hit a bunt single moving Lofton to third. Baerga singled scoring Lofton. Belle singled scoring Vizquel.

One in Braves sixth: McGriff hit a home run.

One in Braves seventh: Klesko hit a home run.

One in Indians seventh: Lofton walked. Vizquel grounded out moving Lofton to second. Lofton stole third. Baerga hit an infield single scoring Lofton.

Three in Braves eighth: Grissom doubled. Polonia singled scoring Grissom. Polonia stole second. Jones walked. McGriff flied out moving Polonia to third and Jones to second. Justice safe at first on Baerga's fielding error scoring Polonia and moving Jones to third. Devereaux singled scoring Jones.

One in Indians eighth: Ramirez walked. Sorrento singled moving Ramirez to third. Alomar doubled scoring Ramirez.

One in Indians eleventh: Baerga doubled. Espinoza ran for Baerga. Belle intentionally walked. Murray singled scoring Espinoza.

Fourth Game

Atlanta	ab	r	h	bi	Cleveland	ab	r	h	bi
Grissom, cf	4	1	3	0	Lofton, cf	5	0	0	0
Polonia, lf	4	1	2	1	Vizquel, ss	3	0	0	0
Dever'x, lf	0	0	0	0	Baerga, 2b	4	0	1	0
CpJones, 3b	4	1	0	0	Belle, lf	3	1	1	1
McGriff, 1b	3	1	1	0	Murray, dh	2	0	0	0
Justice, rf	5	0	1	2	MRamirez, rf	3	1	1	1
Klesko, dh	3	1	1	1	HPerry, 1b	3	0	0	0
Mordecai, ph	1	0	0	0	Sorrento, ph	1	0	1	0
JLopez, c	5	0	2	1	Espinoza, 3b	2	0	1	0
Lemke, 2b	5	0	1	0	Thome, ph-3b	2	0	1	0
Belliard, ss	3	0	0	0	SAlomar, c	4	0	0	0
Totals	37	5	11	5	Totals	32	2	6	2

Atlanta	0	0	0	0	0	1	3	0	1—5
Cleveland	0	0	0	0	0	1	0	0	1—2

	ip	h	r	er	bb	so
Atlanta						
Avery W, 1-0	6.0	3	1	1	5	3
McMichael H, 2	2.0	1	0	0	0	0
Wohlers	0.0	2	1	1	0	0
Borbon S, 1	1.0	0	0	0	0	2
Cleveland						
Hill L, 0-1	6.1	6	3	3	4	1
Assenmacher	0.2	1	1	0	1	2
Tavarez	0.2	2	0	0	1	1
Embree	1.1	2	1	1	0	0

E - Lemke (1). LOB - Atlanta 12, Cleveland 8. 2B - JLopez 2 (2), Polonia (1), McGriff (1), Thome (1), Sorrento (1). 3B - Vizquel (1). HR - Klesko (2), Belle (1), MRamirez (1). RBI - Klesko (2), Polonia (3), Justice 2 (4), JLopez (3), Belle (2), MRamirez, (1). SB - Grissom 2 (2). CS - Espinoza (1). S - Belliard.

How runs were scored—One in Braves sixth: Klesko hit a home run.

One in Indians sixth: Belle hit a home run.

Three in Braves seventh: Grissom walked. Polonia doubled scoring Grissom. Jones intentionally walked. Polonia to third, Jones to second on Alomar passed ball. Justice singled scoring Polonia and Jones.

One in Braves ninth: McGriff doubled. Lopez doubled scoring McGriff.

One in Indians ninth: Ramirez hit a home run.

Fifth Game

Atlanta	ab	r	h	bi	Cleveland	ab	r	h	bi
Grissom, cf	4	0	1	1	Lofton, cf	4	0	0	0
Polonia, lf	4	1	1	1	Vizquel, ss	3	1	1	0
CpJones, 3b	4	0	1	0	Baerga, 2b	4	1	1	0
McGriff, 1b	4	1	1	0	Belle, lf	3	2	1	2
Justice, rf	4	0	0	0	Murray, dh	3	0	0	0
Klesko, dh	4	2	2	2	Thome, 3b	4	1	2	2
Lemke, 2b	4	0	0	0	MRamirez, rf	3	0	1	1
O'Brien, c	1	0	0	0	HPerry, 1b	1	0	0	0
JLopez, ph-c	1	0	0	0	Sorrento, 1b	3	0	0	0
Belliard, ss	1	0	0	0	Kirby, rf	3	0	0	0
DwSmith, ph	0	0	0	0	SAlomar, c	3	0	2	0
Mordecai, ph	1	0	1	0	Totals	31	5	8	5
Totals	32	4	7	4					

Atlanta	0	0	0	1	1	0	0	0	2—4
Cleveland	2	0	0	0	0	2	0	1	x—5

Mickey Mantle, Oct. 20, 1931–Aug. 13, 1995

Mickey Mantle, the former New York Yankee slugger who had been a hero to millions of baseball fans since the early 1950s, died on Aug. 13, 1995, at the age of 63. Here are some of his records and achievements:

Led AL in home runs 3 times (1956, 1958, 1960).
Led AL in runs scored 6 times.
Won the Triple Crown, 1956 (52 HRs, 130 RBIs, .353 batting average).
Named AL MVP 3 times (1956, 1957, 1962).

Most career home runs by a switch hitter (536—ranks 8th on the all-time home run list).
World Series records: most home runs (18); most runs batted in (40); most runs scored (42); most total bases (123); most walks (43).

Atlanta

	ip	h	r	er	bb	so
GMaddux L, 1-1	7.0	7	4	4	3	4
Clontz	1	1	1	1	0	1
Cleveland						
Hershiser W, 1-1	8.0	5	2	1	1	6
Mesa S, 1	1.0	2	2	2	0	1

E - Hershiser (1). LOB - Atlanta 3, Cleveland 5. 2B - CpJones (3), McGriff (2), Baerga (2), SAlomar (2). HR - Polonia (3), Belle (2), Thome (1). RBI - Polonia (4), Grissom (1), Klesko 2 (4), Belle 2 (4), Thome 2 (2), MRamirez, (2). S - O'Brien.

How runs were scored—Two in Indians first: Vizquel walked. Belle hit a home run scoring Vizquel.

One in Braves fourth: Polonia hit a home run.

One in Braves fifth: Klesko singled. Lemke safe on fielder's choice and Hershiser's throwing error moving Klesko to second. O'Brien sacrificed. Smith intentionally walked. Grissom hit an infield single scoring Klesko.

Two in Indians sixth: Baerga doubled. Belle intentionally walked. Murray flied out moving Baerga to third. Thome singled scoring Baerga, moving Belle to third. Ramirez singled scoring Belle.

One in Indians eighth: Thome hit a home run.

Two in Braves ninth: McGriff doubled. Klesko hit a home run scoring McGriff.

Sixth Game

Cleveland	ab	r	h	bi	Atlanta	ab	r	h	bi
Lofton, cf	4	0	0	0	Grissom, cf	4	0	1	0
Vizquel, ss	3	0	0	0	Lemke, 2b	2	0	1	0
Sorrento, ph	1	0	0	0	CpJones, 3b	3	0	2	0
Baerga, 2b	4	0	0	0	McGriff, 1b	4	0	0	0
Belle, lf	1	0	0	0	Justice, rf	2	1	2	1
Murray, 1b	2	0	0	0	Klesko, lf	1	0	0	0
MRamirez, rf	3	0	0	0	Dever'x, lf	1	0	0	0
Embree, p	0	0	0	0	JLopez, c	3	0	0	0
Tavarez, p	0	0	0	0	Belliard, ss	4	0	0	0
Assnmchr, p	0	0	0	0	Glavine, p	3	0	0	0
Thome, 3b	3	0	0	0	Polonia, ph	1	0	0	0
Pena, c	3	0	1	0	Wohlers, p	0	0	0	0
DMartinez, p	1	0	0	0	Totals	28	1	6	1
Poole, p	1	0	0	0					
Hill, p	0	0	0	0					
Amaro, rf	1	0	0	0					
Totals	27	0	1	0					

Cleveland	0	0	0	0	0	0	0	0	0—0
Atlanta	0	0	0	0	0	1	0	0	x—1

	ip	h	r	er	bb	so
Cleveland						
DMartinez	4.2	4	0	0	5	2
Poole L, 0-1	1.1	1	1	1	0	1
Hill	0.0	1	0	0	0	0
Embree	1.0	0	0	0	2	0
Tavarez	0.2	0	0	0	0	0
Assenmacher	0.1	0	0	0	0	1
Atlanta						
Glavine W, 2-0	8.0	1	0	0	3	8
Wohlers S, 2	1.0	0	0	0	0	0

E - Thome (1). LOB - Cleveland 3, Atlanta 11. 2B - Justice (1). HR - Justice (1). RBI - Justice (5). SB - Lofton (6), Grissom (3). CS - Belle (1), Lemke (1). S - Lemke.

How runs were scored—One in Braves sixth: Justice hit a home run.

World Series Results, 1903-1995

1903	Boston AL 5, Pittsburgh NL 3	1934	St. Louis NL 4, Detroit AL 3	1965	Los Angeles NL 4, Minnesota AL 3
1904	No series	1935	Detroit AL 4, Chicago NL 2	1966	Baltimore AL 4, Los Angeles NL 0
1905	New York NL 4, Philadelphia AL 1	1936	New York AL 4, New York NL 2	1967	St. Louis NL 4, Boston AL 3
1906	Chicago AL 4, Chicago NL 2	1937	New York AL 4, New York NL 1	1968	Detroit AL 4, St. Louis NL 3
1907	Chicago NL 4, Detroit AL 0, 1 tie	1938	New York AL 4, Chicago NL 0	1969	New York NL 4, Baltimore AL 1
1908	Chicago NL 4, Detroit AL 1	1939	New York AL 4, Cincinnati NL 0	1970	Baltimore AL 4, Cincinnati NL 1
1909	Pittsburgh NL 4, Detroit AL 3	1940	Cincinnati NL 4, Detroit AL 3	1971	Pittsburgh NL 4, Baltimore AL 3
1910	Philadelphia AL 4, Chicago NL 1	1941	New York AL 4, Brooklyn NL 1	1972	Oakland AL 4, Cincinnati NL 3
1911	Philadelphia AL 4, New York NL 2	1942	St. Louis NL 4, New York AL 1	1973	Oakland AL 4, New York NL 3
1912	Boston AL 4, New York NL 3, 1 tie	1943	New York AL 4, St. Louis NL 1	1974	Oakland AL 4, Los Angeles NL 1
1913	Philadelphia AL 4, New York NL 1	1944	St. Louis NL 4, St. Louis AL 2	1975	Cincinnati NL 4, Boston AL 3
1914	Boston NL 4, Philadelphia AL 0	1945	Detroit AL 4, Chicago NL 3	1976	Cincinnati NL 4, New York AL 0
1915	Boston AL 4, Philadelphia NL 1	1946	St. Louis NL 4, Boston AL 3	1977	New York AL 4, Los Angeles NL 2
1916	Boston AL 4, Brooklyn NL 1	1947	New York AL 4, Brooklyn NL 3	1978	New York AL 4, Los Angeles NL 2
1917	Chicago AL 4, New York NL 2	1948	Cleveland AL 4, Boston NL 2	1979	Pittsburgh NL 4, Baltimore AL 3
1918	Boston AL 4, Chicago NL 2	1949	New York AL 4, Brooklyn NL 1	1980	Philadelphia NL 4, Kansas City AL 2
1919	Cincinnati NL 5, Chicago AL 3	1950	New York AL 4, Philadelphia NL 0	1981	Los Angeles NL 4, New York AL 2
1920	Cleveland AL 5, Brooklyn NL 2	1951	New York AL 4, New York NL 2	1982	St. Louis NL 4, Milwaukee AL 3
1921	New York NL 5, New York AL 3	1952	New York AL 4, Brooklyn NL 3	1983	Baltimore AL 4, Philadelphia NL 1
1922	New York NL 4, New York AL 0, 1 tie	1953	New York AL 4, Brooklyn NL 2	1984	Detroit AL 4, San Diego NL 1
1923	New York AL 4, New York NL 2	1954	New York NL 4, Cleveland AL 0	1985	Kansas City AL 4, St. Louis NL 3
1924	Washington AL 4, New York NL 3	1955	Brooklyn NL 4, New York AL 3	1986	New York NL 4, Boston AL 3
1925	Pittsburgh NL 4, Washington AL 3	1956	New York AL 4, Brooklyn NL 3	1987	Minnesota AL 4, St. Louis NL 3
1926	St. Louis NL 4, New York AL 3	1957	Milwaukee NL 4, New York AL 3	1988	Los Angeles NL 4, Oakland AL 1
1927	New York AL 4, Pittsburgh NL 0	1958	New York AL 4, Milwaukee NL 3	1989	Oakland AL 4, San Francisco NL 0
1928	New York AL 4, St. Louis NL 0	1959	Los Angeles NL 4, Chicago AL 2	1990	Cincinnati NL 4, Oakland AL 0
1929	Philadelphia AL 4, Chicago NL 1	1960	Pittsburgh NL 4, New York AL 3	1991	Minnesota AL 4, Atlanta NL 3
1930	Philadelphia AL 4, St. Louis NL 2	1961	New York AL 4, Cincinnati NL 1	1992	Toronto AL 4, Atlanta NL 2
1931	St. Louis NL 4, Philadelphia AL 3	1962	New York AL 4, San Francisco NL 3	1993	Toronto AL 4, Philadelphia NL 2
1932	New York AL 4, Chicago NL 0	1963	Los Angeles NL 4, New York AL 0	1994	No series
1933	New York NL 4, Washington AL 1	1964	St. Louis NL 4, New York AL 3	1995	Atlanta NL 4, Cleveland AL 2

Major League Franchise Shifts and Additions

1953—Boston Braves (NL) became Milwaukee Braves.
1954—St. Louis Browns (AL) became Baltimore Orioles.
1955—Philadelphia Athletics (AL) became Kansas City Athletics.
1958—New York Giants (NL) became San Francisco Giants.
1958—Brooklyn Dodgers (NL) became Los Angeles Dodgers.
1961—Washington Senators (AL) became Minnesota Twins.
1961—Los Angeles Angels (later renamed the California Angels) enfranchised by the American League.
1961—Washington Senators enfranchised by the American League (a new team, replacing the former Washington club, whose franchise was moved to Minneapolis-St. Paul).
1962—Houston Colt .45's (later renamed the Houston Astros) enfranchised by the National League.
1962—New York Mets enfranchised by the National League.

1966—Milwaukee Braves (NL) became Atlanta Braves.
1968—Kansas City Athletics (AL) became Oakland Athletics.
1969—Kansas City Royals and Seattle Pilots enfranchised by the American League; Montreal Expos and San Diego Padres enfranchised by the National League.
1970—Seattle Pilots became Milwaukee Brewers.
1971—Washington Senators became Texas Rangers (Dallas-Fort Worth area).
1977—Toronto Blue Jays and Seattle Mariners enfranchised by the American Leaue.
1993—Colorado Rockies (Denver) and Florida Marlins (Miami) enfranchised by the National League.
1998—Arizona Diamondbacks (Phoenix) and Tampa Bay Devil Rays scheduled to begin play (enfranchised in 1995); leagues to be determined.

Little League World Series

The Little League World Series is played annually in Williamsport, PA. The team from Taiwan won the 1995 Little League World Series by defeating the team from Spring, TX, 17-3, on Aug. 26.

Year	Winning / Losing Team	Score	Year	Winning / Losing Team	Score	Year	Winning / Losing Team	Score
1947	Williamsport, PA; Lock Haven, PA	16-7	1962	San Jose, CA; Kankakee, IL	3-0	1980	Taiwan; Tampa, FL	4-3
1948	Lock Haven, PA; St. Petersburg, FL	6-5	1963	Granada Hills, CA; Stratford, CT	2-1	1981	Taiwan; Tampa, FL	4-2
1949	Hammonton, NJ; Pensacola, FL	5-0	1964	Staten Island, NY; Mexico	4-0	1982	Kirkland, WA; Taiwan	6-0
1950	Houston, TX; Bridgeport, CT	2-1	1965	Windsor Locks, CT; Ontario, Canada	3-1	1983	Marietta, GA; Dominican Rep.	3-1
1951	Stamford, CT; Austin, TX	3-0	1966	Houston, TX; W. New York, NJ	8-2	1984	South Korea; Altamonte Springs, FL	6-2
1952	Norwalk, CT; Monongahela, PA	4-3	1967	Tokyo, Japan; Chicago, IL	4-1	1985	South Korea; Mexico	7-1
1953	Birmingham, AL; Schenectady, NY	1-0	1968	Osaka, Japan; Richmond, VA	1-0	1986	Taiwan; Tucson, AZ	12-0
1954	Schenectady, NY; Colton, CA	7-5	1969	Taiwan; Santa Clara, CA	5-0	1987	Chinese Taipei; Irvine, CA	21-1
1955	Morrisville, PA; Merchantville, NJ	4-3	1970	Wayne, NJ; Campbell, CA	2-0	1988	Chinese Taipei; Pearl City, HI	10-0
1956	Roswell, NM; Delaware, NJ	3-1	1971	Taiwan; Gary, IN	12-3	1989	Trumbull, CT; Chinese Taipei	5-2
1957	Mexico; La Mesa, CA	4-0	1972	Taiwan; Hammond, IN	6-0	1990	Chinese Taipei; Shippensburg, PA	9-0
1958	Mexico; Kankakee, IL	10-1	1973	Taiwan; Tucson, AZ	12-0	1991	Chinese Taipei; Danville, CA	11-0
1959	Hamtramck, MI; Auburn, CA	12-0	1974	Taiwan; Red Bluff, CA	12-1	1992	Long Beach, CA; Philippines	6-0
1960	Levittown, PA; Ft. Worth, TX	5-0	1975	Lakewood, NJ; Tampa, FL	4-3	1993	Long Beach, CA; Panama	3-2
1961	El Cajon, CA; El Campo, TX	4-2	1976	Tokyo, Japan; Campbell, CA	10-3	1994	Venezuela; Northridge, CA	4-3
			1977	Taiwan; El Cajon, CA	7-2	1995	Taiwan; Spring, TX	17-3
			1978	Taiwan; Danville, CA	11-1			
			1979	Taiwan; Campbell, CA	2-1			

NCAA Baseball Champions

1960	Minnesota	1969	Arizona St.	1978	USC	1987	Stanford
1961	USC	1970	USC	1979	Cal. St.-Fullerton	1988	Stanford
1962	Michigan	1971	USC	1980	Arizona	1989	Wichita St.
1963	USC	1972	USC	1981	Arizona St.	1990	Georgia
1964	Minnesota	1973	USC	1982	Miami, Fla.	1991	LSU
1965	Arizona St.	1974	USC	1983	Texas	1992	Pepperdine
1966	Ohio St.	1975	Texas	1984	Cal. St.-Fullerton	1993	LSU
1967	Arizona St.	1976	Arizona	1985	Miami, Fla.	1994	Oklahoma
1968	USC	1977	Arizona St.	1986	Arizona	1995	Cal. St.-Fullerton

Chess

World Chess Champions

Source: U.S. Chess Federation

Chess dates back to antiquity, its exact origin unknown. The best players of their time, regarded by later generations as world champions, were François Philidor, Alexandre Deschappelles, Louis de la Bourdonnais, all France; Howard Staunton, England; Adolph Anderssen, Germany; and Paul Morphy, U.S. In 1866 Wilhelm Steinitz defeated Adolph Anderssen and claimed the world champion title. Official world champions since the title was first used follow:

1866-1894	Wilhelm Steinitz, Austria	1948-1957	Mikhail Botvinnik, USSR	1972-1975	Bobby Fischer, U.S. (b)
1894-1921	Emanuel Lasker, Germany	1957-1958	Vassily Smyslov, USSR	1975-1985	Anatoly Karpov, USSR
1921-1927	Jose R. Capablanca, Cuba	1958-1959	Mikhail Botvinnik, USSR	1985-1993	Gary Kasparov,
1927-1935	Alexander A. Alekhine, France	1960-1961	Mikhail Tal, USSR		USSR/Russia (c)
1935-1937	Max Euwe, Netherlands	1961-1963	Mikhail Botvinnik, USSR	1993-	Gary Kasparov, Russia (PCA)
1937-1946	Alexander A. Alekhine, France (a)	1963-1969	Tigran Petrosian, USSR	1993-	Anatoly Karpov, Russia (FIDE)
		1969-1972	Boris Spassky, USSR		

(a) After Alekhine died in 1946, the title was vacant until 1948, when Botvinnik won the first championship match sanctioned by the International Chess Federation (FIDE). (b) Defaulted championship after refusal to accept FIDE rules 'for a championship match, April 1975. (c) Kasparov broke with FIDE, Feb. 26, 1993. FIDE stripped Kasparov of his title Mar. 23. Kasparov defeated Nigel Short of Great Britain in a world championship match played Sept.-Oct. 1993 under the auspices of a new organization the two had founded, the Professional Chess Association (PCA). FIDE held a championship match between Anatoly Karpov (Russia) and Jan Timman (the Netherlands), which Karpov won in Nov. 1993. Kasparov completed a successful defense of the PCA title on Oct. 10, 1995, defeating Viswanathan Anand of India, 10½ to 7½. Karpov was scheduled to defend the FIDE title in late 1995 against 1991 U.S. chess champion Gata Kamsky of New York City. The PCA and FIDE agreed to hold a reunification match sometime in 1996.

United States Chess Champions

Unofficial champions		1906-1909	vacant	1973-1974	Lubomir Kavalek, John Grefe	1986	Yasser Seirawan
1857-1871	Paul Morphy	1909-1936	Frank Marshall			1987	(tie) Joel Benjamin,
1871-1876	George Mackenzie	1936-1944	Samuel Reshevsky	1974-1977	Walter Browne		Nick DeFirmian
1876-1880	James Mason	1944-1946	Arnold Denker	1978-1980	Lubomir Kavalek	1988	Michael Wilder
1880-1889	George Mackenzie	1946-1948	Samuel Reshevsky	1980-1981	(tie) Larry Evans, Larry Christiansen, Walter Browne	1989	(tie) Stuart Rachels, Yasser Seirawan, Roman Dzindzichashvili
1889-1890	S. Lipschutz	1948-1951	Herman Steiner				
1890	Jackson Showalter	1951-1954	Larry Evans				
Official champions		1954-1957	Arthur Bisguier	1981-1983	(tie) Walter Browne, Yasser Seirawan	1990	Lev Alburt
1891-1892	Jackson Showalter	1957-1961	Bobby Fischer			1991	Gata Kamsky
1892-1894	S. Lipschutz	1961-1962	Larry Evans	1983	(tie) Walter Browne, Larry Christiansen, Roman Dzindzichashvili	1992	Patrick Wolff
1894	Jackson Showalter	1962-1968	Bobby Fischer			1993	(tie) Alexander Shabaloz, Alex Yermolinsky
1894-1895	Albert Hodges	1968-1969	Larry Evans				
1895-1897	Jackson Showalter	1969-1972	Samuel Reshevsky	1984-1985	Lev Alburt	1994	Boris Gulko
1897-1906	Harry Pillsbury	1972-1973	Robert Byrne				

Special Olympics

Special Olympics is an international program of year-round sports training and athletic competition for children and adults with mental retardation. All 50 U.S. states, Washington, DC, and Guam have chapter offices. In addition, there are accredited Special Olympics programs in more than 100 countries. Persons wishing to volunteer or find out more about Special Olympics can contact Special Olympics International Headquarters, 1350 New York Ave. NW, Washington, DC 20005.

1995 Special Olympic World Games/1997 World Winter Special Olympic Games

The ninth Special Olympic World Games were held July 1-9, 1995, in New Haven, CT. A total of 6,500 athletes and coaches from 120 countries participated. Athletes competed in 21 sports.

The sixth World Winter Special Olympic Games will be held February 1-8, 1997, in Toronto and Collingwood, Ontario, Canada. About 2,000 athletes from more than 80 countries are expected to participate, along with 500 coaches, 1,500 volunteers, and 2,000 family members and friends. Athletes will compete in the following sports: Alpine Skiing, Nordic Skiing, Floor Hockey, Figure Skating, and Speed Skating.

Marathons

Boston Marathon in 1995

Cosmos N'Deti of Kenya won the Boston Marathon for the third straight year, April 17, with a time of 2 hours 9 minutes 22 seconds. Uta Pippig of Germany was the first woman to finish for the second consecutive year, with a time of 2:25:11. It was the first time that a man and woman had consecutive victories in the marathon in the same year.

New York Marathon in 1994

German Silva of Mexico overcame a wrong turn late in the 1994 New York Marathon, held Nov. 6, to win in the closest finish in race history. Silva's time of 2 hours 11 minutes 21 seconds was only 2 seconds ahead of second-place finisher Benjamin Paredes, also of Mexico. Tegla Loroupe of Kenya had no trouble finding the finish line, winning the women's race in 2:27:37.

CRIME

Crime Down Overall in 1994

Serious crimes reported to law enforcement agencies in the U.S. decreased 3% in 1994 compared with 1993, according to preliminary *Uniform Crime Reports* figures released by the Federal Bureau of Investigation. The decrease continued the trend from 1993, when overall crime was down 2% from the previous year.

Serious crime is measured by the Crime Index, composed of 4 violent and 4 property crimes. Violent crime dropped 4% in 1994, and property crime decreased 3%.

All 4 violent crimes in the Crime Index declined. Robbery declined 6%, murder and forcible rape both declined 5%, and aggravated assault declined 2%.

In the property crime category, burglary was down 5%, motor vehicle theft fell 2%, and both larceny-theft and arson were down 1%.

Declines in overall Crime Index totals occurred in all regions: 5% in the northeast, 2% in the south, and 1% in the midwest and west.

There were Crime Index decreases in the nation's cities during 1994 except in cities with a population of 10,000 to 24,999. The greatest decline—6%—was recorded in cities with populations of more than 1 million. Rural county law enforcement agencies reported a Crime Index increase of 1%, while suburban county law enforcement agencies reported no change.

Crime Index Trends

Source: FBI, *Uniform Crime Reports*, 1994 Preliminary Annual Release

(percentage change 1994 over 1993, offenses known to the police)

Population group and area	No. of agen-cies[1]	Popula-tion (thou-sands)	Crime Index (total)	Vio-lent crime	Prop-erty crime[2]	Mur-der	Forc-ible rape	Rob-bery	Aggra-vated assault	Bur-glary	Lar-ceny/theft	Motor ve-hicle theft	Ar-son
Total U.S.	10,576	212,873	−3	−4	−3	−5	−5	−6	−2	−5	−1	−2	−1
Cities:													
Over 1,000,000	9	21,338	−6	−7	−5	−8	−8	−10	−4	−7	−4	−6	−11
500,000 to 999,999	19	12,329	−4	−5	−4	−12	−5	−9	0	−7	−3	−5	+4
250,000 to 499,999	37	13,153	−1	−2	−1	−3	−4	−4	−1	−4	+1	−2	+2
100,000 to 249,999	135	19,935	−1	−2	−1	+4	−6	−2	−3	−5	0	+3	+1
50,000 to 99,999	313	21,505	−2	−2	−2	+3	−3	−1	−3	−5	−2	−3	+4
25,000 to 49,999	565	19,592	−1	−1	−1	−12	−1	−1	−2	−4	−1	0	+4
10,000 to 24,999	1,295	20,402	0	+1	0	−2	−8	+2	0	−5	+1	0	+3
Under 10,000	4,917	17,165	−1	−4	0	−16	−3	−6	−5	−4	+1	+1	+4
Counties:													
Suburban[3]	1,148	45,915	0	0	0	−4	−7	−4	+1	−5	+1	+1	+1
Rural[4]	2,138	21,538	+1	+6	+1	−12	+1	+3	+3	−2	+2	+6	−5
Areas:													+2
Suburban area[5]	5,269	84,720	−1	−1	−1	−6	−6	−3	0	−5	+1	+1	
Cities outside met-ropolitan areas	2,656	18,354	−1	−2	0	−11	−4	+1	−3	−3	0	+2	+5

(1) Law-enforcement agencies. (2) Data for arson not included. (3) Includes crimes reported to sheriffs' departments, county police departments, and state police within Metropolitan Statistical Areas. (4) Includes crimes reported to sheriffs' departments, county police departments, and state police outside Metropolitan Statistical Areas. (5) Includes crimes reported to city, county, and state law enforcement agencies within Metropolitan Statistical Areas but outside the central cities.

Crime Index Trends by Geographic Region

Source: FBI, *Uniform Crime Reports*, 1994 Preliminary Annual Release

(percentage change 1994 over 1993, offenses known to the police)

Region	Crime Index (total)	Violent crime	Property crime[1]	Mur-der	Forcible rape	Rob-bery	Aggra-vated assault	Burglary	Larceny-theft	Motor vehicle theft	Arson
Total U.S.	−3	−4	−3	−5	−5	−6	−2	−5	−1	−2	−1
Northeast	−5	−5	−5	−7	−5	−5	−4	−8	−4	−8	+8
Midwest	−1	−1	−1	−1	−3	−3	+1	−2	0	−1	+5
South	−2	−4	−2	−6	−5	−6	−3	−6	−1	−2	−2
West	−1	−4	0	−7	−7	−8	0	−4	+1	+2	−5

(1) Data for arson not included.

Crime Index Trends, 1991-94

Source: FBI, *Uniform Crime Reports*, 1994 Preliminary Annual Release

(percentage change over previous year)

Year	Crime Index (total)	Violent crime	Property crime[1]	Murder	Forcible rape	Rob-bery	Aggra-vated assault	Burglary	Larceny-theft	Motor vehicle theft	Arson
1990	+2	+11	0	+9	+9	+11	+11	−3	+1	+5	+3
1991	+3	+5	+2	+5	+4	+8	+4	+3	+2	+2	+1
1992	−3	+1	−4	−4	+2	−2	+3	−6	−3	−3	0
1993	−2	0	−2	+3	−4	−2	+1	−5	−1	−3	−5
1994	−3	−4	−3	−5	−5	−6	−2	−5	−1	−2	−1

(1) Data for arson not included.

Crime in the U.S., 1974-93
Source: FBI, *Uniform Crime Reports*, 1993

Population[1]	Crime Index (total)[2]	Violent crime	Property crime[3]	Murder and non-negligent man-slaughter	Forcible rape	Robbery	Burglary	Larceny-theft
Population by year				**Number of offenses**				
1974–211,392,000...	10,253,400	974,720	9,278,700	20,710	55,400	442,400	3,039,200	5,262,500
1975–213,124,000...	11,292,400	1,039,710	10,252,700	20,510	56,090	470,500	3,265,300	5,977,700
1976–214,659,000...	11,349,700	1,004,210	10,345,500	18,780	57,080	427,810	3,108,700	6,270,800
1977–216,332,000...	10,984,500	1,029,580	9,955,000	19,120	63,500	412,610	3,071,500	5,905,700
1978–218,059,000...	11,209,000	1,085,550	10,123,400	19,560	67,610	426,930	3,128,300	5,991,000
1979–220,099,000...	12,249,500	1,208,030	11,041,500	21,460	76,390	480,700	3,327,700	6,601,000
1980–225,349,264...	13,408,300	1,344,520	12,063,700	23,040	82,990	565,840	3,795,200	7,136,900
1981–229,146,000...	13,423,800	1,361,820	12,061,900	22,520	82,500	592,910	3,779,700	7,194,400
1982–231,534,000...	12,974,400	1,322,390	11,652,000	21,010	78,770	553,130	3,447,100	7,142,500
1983–233,981,000...	12,108,600	1,258,090	10,850,500	19,310	78,920	506,570	3,129,900	6,712,800
1984–236,158,000...	11,881,800	1,273,280	10,608,500	18,690	84,230	485,010	2,984,400	6,591,900
1985–238,740,000...	12,431,400	1,328,800	11,102,600	18,980	88,670	497,870	3,073,300	6,926,400
1986–241,077,000...	13,211,900	1,489,170	11,722,700	20,610	91,460	542,780	3,241,400	7,257,200
1987–243,400,000...	13,508,700	1,484,000	12,024,700	20,100	91,110	517,700	3,236,200	7,499,900
1988–245,807,000...	13,923,100	1,566,220	12,356,900	20,680	92,490	542,970	3,218,100	7,705,900
1989–248,239,000...	14,251,400	1,646,040	12,605,400	21,500	94,500	578,330	3,168,200	7,872,400
1990–248,709,873...	14,475,600	1,820,130	12,655,500	23,440	102,560	639,270	3,073,900	7,945,700
1991–252,177,000...	14,872,900	1,911,770	12,961,100	24,700	106,590	687,730	3,157,200	8,142,200
1992–255,082,000...	14,438,200	1,932,270	12,505,900	23,760	109,060	672,480	2,979,900	7,915,200
1993–257,908,000...	14,141,000	1,924,190	12,216,800	24,530	104,810	659,760	2,834,800	7,820,900
Percent change: number of offenses								
1993/1992.........	−2.1	−0.4	−2.3	+3.2	−3.9	−1.9	−4.9	−1.2
1993/1989.........	−0.8	+16.9	−3.1	+14.1	+10.9	+14.1	−10.5	−0.7
1993/1984.........	+19.0	+51.1	+15.2	+31.2	+24.4	+36.0	−5.0	+18.6
Year				**Rate per 100,000 inhabitants**				
1974.............	4,850.4	461.1	4,389.3	9.8	26.2	209.3	1,437.7	2,489.5
1975.............	5,298.5	487.8	4,810.7	9.6	26.3	220.8	1,532.1	2,804.8
1976.............	5,287.3	467.8	4,819.5	8.8	26.6	199.3	1,448.2	2,921.3
1977.............	5,077.6	475.9	4,601.7	8.8	29.4	190.7	1,419.8	2,729.9
1978.............	5,140.3	497.8	4,642.5	9.0	31.0	195.8	1,434.6	2,747.4
1979.............	5,565.5	548.9	5,016.6	9.7	34.7	218.4	1,511.9	2,999.1
1980.............	5,950.0	596.6	5,353.3	10.2	36.8	251.1	1,684.1	3,167.0
1981.............	5,858.2	594.3	5,263.9	9.8	36.0	258.7	1,649.5	3,139.7
1982.............	5,603.6	571.1	5,032.5	9.1	34.0	238.9	1,488.8	3,084.8
1983.............	5,175.0	537.7	4,637.4	8.3	33.7	216.5	1,337.7	2,868.9
1984.............	5,031.3	539.2	4,492.1	7.9	35.7	205.4	1,263.7	2,791.3
1985.............	5,207.1	556.6	4,650.5	7.9	37.1	208.5	1,287.3	2,901.2
1986.............	5,480.4	617.7	4,862.6	8.6	37.9	225.1	1,344.6	3,010.3
1987.............	5,550.0	609.7	4,940.3	8.3	37.4	212.7	1,329.6	3,081.3
1988.............	5,664.2	637.2	5,027.1	8.4	37.6	220.9	1,309.2	3,134.9
1989.............	5,741.0	663.1	5,077.9	8.7	38.1	233.0	1,276.3	3,171.3
1990.............	5,820.3	731.8	5,088.5	9.4	41.2	257.0	1,235.9	3,194.8
1991.............	5,897.8	758.1	5,139.7	9.8	42.3	272.7	1,252.0	3,228.8
1992.............	5,660.2	757.5	4,902.7	9.3	42.8	263.6	1,168.2	3,103.0
1993.............	5,482.9	746.1	4,736.9	9.5	40.6	255.8	1,099.2	3,032.4
Percent change: rate per 100,000 inhabitants								
1993/1992.........	−3.1	−1.5	−3.4	+2.2	−5.1	−3.0	−5.9	−2.3
1993/1989.........	−4.5	+12.5	−6.7	+9.2	+6.6	+9.8	−13.9	−4.4
1993/1984.........	+9.0	+38.4	+5.4	+20.3	+13.7	+24.5	−13.0	+8.6

(1) Populations are Bureau of the Census provisional estimates as of July 1, except 1980 and 1990, which are the decennial census counts. (2) Because of rounding, the offenses may not add to totals. (3) Data for arson not included.

Note: All rates were calculated on the offenses before rounding.

Law Enforcement Officers
Source: FBI, *Uniform Crime Reports*, 1993

The U.S. law enforcement community employed an average of 2.3 full-time officers for every 1,000 inhabitants as of October 31, 1993. Considering full-time civilians, the overall law enforcement employee rate was 3.1 per 1,000 inhabitants according to 13,041 city, county, and state police agencies. These agencies collectively offered law enforcement service to a population of more than 244 million, employing 553,773 officers and 212,353 civilians.

The law enforcement employee average for all cities nationwide was 2.8 per 1,000 inhabitants. City law enforcement employee averages were 3.5 per 1,000 inhabitants in cities with populations of less than 10,000 and 3.6 in those with populations of 250,000 or more. Rural and suburban counties averaged full-time law enforcement employee rates of 3.9 and 3.6 per 1,000 population, respectively.

Regionally, the highest law enforcement employee rate was in the South, with 3.3, and lowest in the West, 2.4.

Nationally, males constituted 91 percent of all sworn employees. Ninety-three percent of the officers in rural counties were males, and in suburban counties males accounted for 88 percent.

Civilians made up 28 percent of the total U.S. law enforcement employee force. They represented 22 percent of the police employees in cities, 34 percent of those in rural counties, and 37 percent in suburban counties.

Seventy law enforcement officers were feloniously slain in the line of duty in 1993, 7 more than in 1992. Another 59 officers were killed due to accidents occurring while performing official duties.

Crime Rates by Region, Geographic Division, and State, 1993

Source: FBI, *Uniform Crime Reports*, 1993

(rate per 100,000)

Area	Total	Violent crime[1]	Property crime[2]	Murder	Rape	Robbery	Aggravated assault	Burglary	Larceny-theft	Motor vehicle theft
United States Total	**5,482.9**	**746.1**	**4,736.9**	**9.5**	**40.6**	**255.8**	**440.1**	**1,099.2**	**3,032.4**	**605.3**
Northeast	**4,612.6**	**713.0**	**3,899.6**	**8.2**	**28.4**	**322.6**	**353.9**	**878.2**	**2,357.6**	**663.8**
New England	**4,431.2**	**537.6**	**3,893.6**	**4.1**	**31.4**	**140.9**	**361.2**	**925.3**	**2,366.2**	**602.1**
Connecticut	4,650.4	456.2	4,194.2	6.3	24.4	196.7	228.7	978.1	2,620.6	595.5
Maine	3,153.9	125.7	3,028.2	1.6	26.6	21.3	76.3	719.0	2,174.7	134.4
Massachusetts	4,893.9	804.9	4,089.0	3.9	33.4	175.7	592.0	1,001.7	2,271.3	816.1
New Hampshire	2,905.0	137.8	2,767.2	2.0	44.4	27.3	64.1	515.1	2,058.0	194.0
Rhode Island	4,499.0	401.7	4,097.3	3.9	29.6	101.1	268.1	1,040.9	2,410.1	646.3
Vermont	3,972.4	114.2	3,858.2	3.6	39.8	9.0	61.8	874.3	2,851.2	132.6
Middle Atlantic	**4,675.6**	**773.9**	**3901.7**	**9.6**	**27.3**	**385.6**	**351.4**	**861.8**	**2,354.7**	**685.2**
New Jersey	4,800.8	626.9	4,174.0	5.3	28.1	296.0	297.5	974.0	2,486.1	714.0
New York	5,551.3	1,073.5	4,477.8	13.3	27.5	561.2	471.5	998.6	2,644.2	835.0
Pennsylvania	3,271.4	417.5	2,853.9	6.8	26.5	179.0	205.1	582.0	1,831.7	440.2
Midwest	**4,805.8**	**601.6**	**4,204.3**	**7.6**	**42.3**	**204.0**	**347.7**	**899.6**	**2,850.4**	**454.3**
East North Central	**4,953.2**	**661.3**	**4,291.9**	**8.3**	**45.9**	**235.1**	**372.0**	**909.9**	**2,882.8**	**499.2**
Illinois	5,617.9	959.7	4,658.2	11.4	34.6	381.2	532.6	1,015.5	3,084.0	558.7
Indiana	4,465.1	489.1	3,976.0	7.5	39.1	119.8	322.6	852.0	2,695.9	428.1
Michigan	5,452.5	791.5	4,661.0	9.8	71.1	238.5	472.1	982.7	3,063.2	615.0
Ohio	4,485.3	504.1	3,981.2	6.0	49.1	192.7	256.3	878.1	2,667.7	435.3
Wisconsin	4,054.1	264.4	3,789.7	4.4	25.2	113.4	121.4	663.0	2,762.0	364.7
West North Central	**4,454.4**	**459.3**	**3,995.1**	**5.9**	**33.8**	**129.8**	**289.8**	**875.1**	**2,772.8**	**347.2**
Iowa	3,846.4	325.5	3,521.0	2.3	24.4	53.9	244.8	730.7	2,599.4	190.8
Kansas	4,975.3	496.4	4,478.8	6.4	40.1	123.6	326.3	1,132.2	3,024.0	322.7
Minnesota	4,386.2	327.2	4,059.0	3.4	35.2	112.7	175.8	844.5	2,872.0	342.6
Missouri	5,095.4	744.4	4,351.0	11.3	36.2	241.8	455.2	1,028.5	2,777.8	547.7
Nebraska	4,117.1	339.1	3,778.0	3.9	27.8	55.4	252.0	663.5	2,912.9	201.6
North Dakota	2,820.3	82.2	2,738.1	1.7	23.5	7.3	8.3	48.7	373.2	2,216.2	148.7
South Dakota	2,958.2	208.4	2,749.8	3.4	44.5	15.0	145.6	549.2	2,086.0	114.5
South	**5,983.3**	**802.0**	**5,181.3**	**11.3**	**45.2**	**235.8**	**509.7**	**1,285.6**	**3,339.2**	**556.5**
South Atlantic	**6,333.5**	**871.6**	**5,461.9**	**10.8**	**42.8**	**276.0**	**541.9**	**1,361.5**	**3,528.0**	**572.5**
Delaware	4,872.1	685.9	4,186.3	5.0	77.0	186.7	417.1	892.0	2,979.0	315.3
District of Columbia	11,761.1	2,921.8	8,839.3	78.5	56.1	1,229.6	1,557.6	1,995.5	5,449.0	1,394.8
Florida	8,351.0	1,206.0	7,145.0	8.9	53.8	357.6	785.7	1,835.4	4,413.9	895.7
Georgia	6,193.0	723.1	5,469.8	11.4	35.4	248.0	428.3	1,307.3	3,568.7	593.8
Maryland	6,106.5	997.8	5,108.7	12.7	44.0	434.7	506.4	1,132.8	3,292.5	683.4
North Carolina	5,652.3	679.3	4,973.0	11.3	34.3	192.4	441.3	1,515.8	3,168.8	288.5
South Carolina	5,903.4	1,023.4	4,880.0	10.3	52.3	187.3	773.4	1,309.2	3,226.8	344.0
Virginia	4,115.5	372.2	3,743.3	8.3	32.1	142.0	189.8	667.7	2,790.1	285.5
West Virgina	2,532.6	208.4	2,324.2	6.9	20.1	43.0	138.5	599.1	1,563.5	161.5
East South Central	**4,528.4**	**640.8**	**3,887.5**	**10.3**	**41.0**	**159.1**	**430.5**	**1,068.3**	**2,429.0**	**390.2**
Alabama	4,878.8	780.4	4,098.4	11.6	35.1	159.5	574.3	1,088.6	2,672.0	337.8
Kentucky	3,259.7	462.7	2,797.0	5.6	34.3	90.4	331.4	740.1	1,840.7	216.2
Mississippi	4,418.3	433.9	3,984.4	13.5	42.6	139.3	238.4	1,285.8	2,363.5	335.1
Tennessee	5,239.5	765.8	4,473.8	10.2	49.9	220.1	485.5	1,182.6	2,700.2	591.0
West South Central	**6,227.9**	**778.7**	**5,449.2**	**12.7**	**51.3**	**213.0**	**501.7**	**1,283.7**	**3,541.7**	**623.8**
Arkansas	4,810.7	593.3	4,217.5	10.2	42.4	127.9	415.8	1,099.3	2,795.7	322.5
Louisiana	6,846.6	1,061.7	5,784.9	20.3	42.3	283.6	715.4	1,368.3	3,802.9	613.7
Oklahoma	5,294.3	634.8	4,659.4	8.4	49.3	121.8	455.3	1,235.0	2,943.7	480.7
Texas	6,439.1	762.1	5,677.0	11.9	55.0	224.4	470.8	1,297.3	3,687.3	692.3
West	**6,220.0**	**844.6**	**5,375.3**	**9.9**	**42.9**	**283.1**	**508.7**	**1,221.5**	**3,359.8**	**794.1**
Mountain	**5,929.4**	**589.3**	**5,340.0**	**6.4**	**43.5**	**129.7**	**409.8**	**1,116.9**	**3,707.7**	**515.5**
Arizona	7,431.7	715.0	6,716.7	8.6	37.8	162.9	505.7	1,465.5	4,387.4	863.8
Colorado	5,526.8	567.3	4,959.5	5.8	45.8	116.7	399.0	1,009.8	3,499.4	450.3
Idaho	3,845.1	281.8	3,563.3	2.9	35.3	16.9	226.7	668.8	2,711.1	183.4
Montana	4,790.0	177.5	4,612.5	3.0	27.9	32.4	114.2	714.2	3,652.1	246.2
Nevada	6,180.1	875.2	5,304.9	10.4	60.9	340.1	463.9	1,245.0	3,321.6	738.3
New Mexico	6,266.1	929.7	5,336.4	8.0	52.1	138.4	731.1	1,421.2	3,510.1	405.1
Utah	5,237.4	301.0	4,936.3	3.1	44.6	58.6	194.7	790.8	3,903.4	242.2
Wyoming	4,163.0	286.2	3,876.8	3.4	34.3	17.2	231.3	643.2	3,078.7	154.9
Pacific	**6,323.8**	**936.0**	**5,387.8**	**11.2**	**42.6**	**338.1**	**544.2**	**1,258.9**	**3,235.1**	**893.8**
Alaska	5,567.9	760.8	4,807.2	9.0	83.8	122.4	545.6	816.9	3,539.4	450.9
California	6,456.9	1,077.5	5,379.1	13.1	37.7	405.1	621.8	1,327.0	3,029.1	1,023.0
Hawaii	6,277.0	261.2	6,015.8	3.8	33.6	103.6	120.1	1,135.7	4,429.4	450.8
Oregon	5,765.6	503.1	5,262.5	4.6	51.3	129.6	317.6	1,024.8	3,656.9	580.7
Washington	5,952.3	514.6	5,437.7	5.2	64.4	137.1	307.9	1,067.2	3,914.4	456.1

(1) Violent crimes are murder, forcible rape, robbery, and aggravated assault. (2) Property crimes are burglary, larceny-theft, and motor vehicle theft. Data are not included for the property crime of arson.

State and Federal Prison Population; Death Penalty

Source: Prison population: Bureau of Justice Statistics, U.S. Dept. of Justice, Dec. 31, 1994;
Death penalty: Bureau of Justice Statistics, as of Dec. 31, 1993

The number of prisoners under the jurisdiction of federal or state correctional authorities at year-end 1994 reached a record high of 1,053,738. The states and the District of Columbia added 78,847 prisoners in 1994; the federal system, 5,447. Although the 1994 growth rate of 8.6% nearly equaled the average annual percent increase since 1980, the total increase (83,294) was the 2d largest yearly increase on record. The 1994 growth rate was greater than the percentage increase recorded during 1993 (7.4%), and translated into a nationwide need to confine an additional 1,602 inmates per week compared with 1,254 per week in 1993. Prisoners serving a drug-related sentence increased from 8% of the state and federal prison population in 1980 to 26% in 1993. During the same period, the percentage of prisoners serving for a violent offense fell from 57% to 45% and those serving for a property offense fell from 30% to 22%. Prisoners with a sentence of more than 1 year accounted for 96% of the total prison population at the end of 1994.

| | Sentenced to more than 1 yr | | % change 1993–94 | Under sentence of death | Death penalty 1993 | |
	Final 1993	Advance 1994			Executions	Death penalty
Total	932,266	1,012,463	8.6%	2,716	38	—
Federal institutions	74,399	79,795	7.3	6	0	Yes
State institutions	857,867	932,668	8.7	2,710	38	36
Northeast	140,941	146,754	4.1	181	0	—
Connecticut	10,508	10,500	−0.1	5	0	Yes
Maine	1,446	1,464	1.2	0	0	No
Massachusetts	10,145	10,340	1.9	0	0	No
New Hampshire	1,775	2,021	13.9	0	0	Yes
New Jersey	23,831	24,544	3.0	7	0	Yes
New York	64,569	66,760	3.4	0	0	No
Pennsylvania	26,055	28,301	8.6	169	0	Yes
Rhode Island	1,719	1,853	7.8	0	0	No
Vermont	893	981	9.9	0	0	No
Midwest	172,709	182,768	5.8	421	4	—
Illinois	34,495	36,531	5.9	152	0	Yes
Indiana	14,364	14,925	3.9	47	0	Yes
Iowa	4,898	5,437	11.0	0	0	No
Kansas	5,727	6,373	11.3	0	0	No
Michigan	39,318	40,775	3.7	0	0	No
Minnesota	4,200	4,572	8.9	0	0	No
Missouri	16,178	17,898	10.6	80	4	Yes
Nebraska	2,467	2,590	5.0	11	0	Yes
North Dakota	446	501	12.3	0	0	No
Ohio	40,641	41,913	3.1	129	0	Yes
South Dakota	1,553	1,734	11.7	2	0	Yes
Wisconsin	8,422	9,519	13.0	0	0	No
South	364,551	412,309	13.1	1,500	30	—
Alabama	18,169	19,074	5.0	120	0	Yes
Arkansas	7,984	8,711	9.1	33	0	Yes
Delaware	2,781	2,788	0.3	15	2	Yes
District of Columbia	8,908	8,962	0.6	0	0	No
Florida	52,883	57,129	8.0	324	3	Yes
Georgia	27,079	32,523	20.1	96	2	Yes
Kentucky	10,440	11,066	6.0	30	0	Yes
Louisiana	22,468	22,956	2.2	45	1	Yes
Maryland	19,121	19,854	3.8	15	0	Yes
Mississippi	9,769	10,950	12.1	50	0	Yes
North Carolina	21,367	22,983	7.6	99	0	Yes
Oklahoma	16,409	16,631	1.4	122	0	Yes
South Carolina	17,896	18,168	1.5	47	0	Yes
Tennessee	12,824	14,474	12.9	98	0	Yes
Texas	92,013	118,094	28.3	357	17	Yes
Virginia	22,635	26,016	14.9	49	5	Yes
West Virginia	1,805	1,930	6.9	0	0	No
West	179,666	190,837	6.2	608	4	—
Alaska	1,954	1,934	−1.0	0	0	No
Arizona	17,160	19,005	10.8	112	2	Yes
California	115,573	121,084	4.8	363	1	Yes
Colorado	9,462	10,717	13.3	3	0	Yes
Hawaii	2,330	2,392	2.7	0	0	No
Idaho	2,606	2,964	13.7	22	0	Yes
Montana	1,541	1,680	9.0	6	0	Yes
Nevada	6,138	6,877	12.0	42	0	Yes
New Mexico	3,373	3,679	9.1	1	0	Yes
Oregon	5,111	5,458	6.8	12	0	Yes
Utah	2,871	2,997	4.4	9	0	Yes
Washington	10,419	10,833	4.0	7	1	Yes
Wyoming	1,128	1,217	7.9	0	0	Yes

Note: Prisoner counts for 1993 may differ from those reported previously. Counts for 1994 are subject to revision.

Sentences vs. Time Served for Selected Crimes

Source: Bureau of Justice Statistics, *National Corrections Reporting Program, 1992,* October 1994

The following is a comparison of the average maximum sentence lengths (excluding both life and death sentences) and the actual time served for selected state-court convictions, based on 1992 data.

Crime	Sentence	Time served	Crime	Sentence	Time served
Murder	19 years, 11 months	8 years, 2 months	Burglary	5 years, 6 months	1 years, 10 months
Rape	9 years, 9 months	4 years, 11 months	Drug Offenses	4 years, 5 months	1 year, 4 months
Robbery	7 years, 11 months	3 years, 2 months	Weapons Offenses	3 years, 4 months	1 year, 5 months

Prison Situation Among the States, 1994

Source: *Prisoners in 1994*, Bureau of Justice Statistics, U.S. Dept. of Justice; year-end 1994.

10 states with the largest total 1994 prison populations	Number of inmates	10 states with the highest incarceration rates, 1994[1]	Prisoners per 100,000 residents	10 states with the largest % increases in prison population			
				1993–94	% increase	1989–94	% increase
California	125,605	Texas	636	Texas	20.1	New Hampshire	73.3
Texas	118,195	Louisiana	530	Georgia	16.2	Connecticut	66.4
New York	66,750	Oklahoma	508	Nevada	15.5	Georgia	65.8
Florida	57,139	South Carolina	494	Virginia	15.2	Texas	60.5
Ohio	41,913	Nevada	460	Wisconsin	10.7	Virginia	59.9
Michigan	40,775	Arizona	459	New Hampshire	9.9	Vermont	56.7
Illinois	36,531	Georgia	456	Idaho	9.8	Washington	56.4
Georgia	33,425	Alabama	450	Colorado	9.5	Colorado	55.1
Pennsylvania	28,302	Michigan	428	Tennessee	9.0	Iowa	51.7
Virginia	26,192	Mississippi	408	Mississippi	8.4	Arizona	49.3

Note: The District of Columbia as a wholly urban jurisdiction is excluded. (1) Prisoners with sentences of more than 1 year.

Executions, by State and Method, 1977-93

Source: Bureau of Justice Statistics, *Capital Punishment 1993*, Dec. 1994

State	No.	Lethal Injection	Electrocution	Lethal gas	Firing squad	Hanging	State	No.	Lethal Injection	Electrocution	Lethal gas	Firing squad	Hanging
Total U.S.	226	108	108	8	1	1	South						
Texas	71	71					Carolina	4		4			
Florida	32		32				Utah	4	3			1	
Virginia	22		22				Arkansas	4	3	1			
Louisiana	21	1	20				Oklahoma	3	3				
Georgia	17		17				Arizona	3	2		1		
Missouri	11	11					Delaware	3	3				
Alabama	10		10				California	2			2		
Nevada	5	4		1			Indiana	2	2				
North							Illinois	1	1				
Carolina	5	5					Wyoming	1	1				
Mississippi	4			4			Washington	1					1

Note: This table shows the distribution of execution methods used since 1977. Electrocution and lethal injection were each used in about 48% of the executions carried out. Five states—Arizona, Arkansas, Louisiana, Nevada, and Utah—employed 2 methods.

Total Estimated Arrests,[1] 1993

Source: FBI, *Uniform Crime Reports*, 1993

Total[2]	10,448,491	Vandalism	235,170
Murder and nonnegligent manslaughter	18,856	Weapons: carrying, possessing, etc.	204,433
Forcible rape	29,432	Prostitution and commercialized vice	83,346
Robbery	143,877	Sex offenses (except forcible rape and prostitution)	80,332
Aggravated assault	408,148	Drug abuse violations	884,771
Burglary	308,849	Gambling	14,121
Larceny–theft	1,131,768	Offenses against family and children	71,119
Motor vehicle theft	156,711	Driving under the influence	1,059,517
Arson	14,504	Liquor laws	357,116
Violent crimes[3]	**600,313**	Drunkenness	558,833
Property crime[4]	**1,611,832**	Disorderly conduct	542,837
Crime Index total[5]	**2,212,145**	Vagrancy	23,000
Other assaults	870,146	All other offenses	2,531,244
Forgery and counterfeiting	80,989	Suspicion (not included in totals)	7,412
Fraud	296,737	Curfew and loitering law violations	73,502
Embezzlement	10,092	Runaways	136,785
Stolen Property: buying, receiving, possesseing	122,256		

(1) Arrest totals are based on all reporting agencies and estimates for unreported areas. (2) Because of rounding, figures may not add to totals. (3) Violent crimes are murder, forcible rape, robbery, and aggravated assault. (4) Property crimes are burglary, larceny–theft, motor vehicle theft, and arson. (5) Includes arson.

Terrorist Incidents[1] in the U.S., 1990-94

Source: FBI, *Terrorism in the United States, 1994*

Date	Location	Incident type	Group
1/12/90	Santurce, PR	pipe bombing	Eugenio Maria de Hostos International Brigade of the Pedro Albizu Campos Revolutionary Forces
1/12/90	Carolina, PR	pipe bombing	same as above
2/22/90	Los Angeles, CA	bombing	Up the IRS, Inc.
4/22/90	Santa Cruz Cty., CA	malicious destruction of property	Earth Night Action Group
5/27/90	Mayaguez, PR	arson	Unknown Puerto Rican group
9/17/90	Arecibo, PR	bombing	Pedro Albizu Group Revolutionary Forces
9/17/90	Vega Baja, PR	bombing	Pedro Albizu Group Revolutionary Forces
2/3/91	Mayaguez, PR	arson	Popular Liberation Army (PLA)
2/18/91	Sabana Grande, PR	arson	PLA
3/17/91	Carolina, PR	arson	Unknown Puerto Rican group
4/1/91	Fresno, CA	bombing	Up the IRS, Inc.
7/6/91	Punta Borinquen, PR	bombing	PLA
4/5/92	New York City	hostile takeover	Mujahedin-E-Khalq (MEK)
11/19/92	Urbana, IL	attempted firebombing	Mexican Revolutionary Movement
12/10/92	Chicago	car fire and attempted bombing	Boricua Revolutionary Front (2 incidents)
2/26/93	New York City	car bombing	International Radical Terrorists
7/20/93	Tacoma, WA	pipe bombing	American Front Skinheads
7/22/93	Tacoma, WA	bombing	American Front Skinheads
11/27-28/93	Chicago	firebombing	Animal Liberation Front (9 incidents)
1994		no incidents	

(1) The FBI defines "domestic terrorism" as the unlawful use of force or violence committed by a group(s) of 2 or more individuals, against persons or property to intimidate or coerce a government, the civilian population, or any segment thereof, in furtherance of political or social objectives.

VITAL STATISTICS

Births, Deaths, Marriages, and Divorces in the U.S., First Quarter 1995

Source: National Center for Health Statistics, U.S. Dept. of Health and Human Services

Births

According to provisional statistics for the first quarter of 1995, there were 971,000 births, a decrease from the number reported for the same 3-month period in 1994 (996,000). The birthrate declined by 4%, from 15.6 per 1,000 population in the first quarter of 1994 to 15.0 in the first quarter of 1995.

During the 12 months ending Mar. 1995, there were an estimated 3,954,000 live births, 2% less than reported for the comparable period ending a year earlier (4,043,000). The birthrate was 15.1 per 1,000 population, 3% below the rate for the 12 months ending Mar. 1994 (15.6). These lower rates continue the generally downward trend observed since early 1991.

Marriages

The total number of marriages for the first quarter of 1995 was 402,000, a decrease of 2% from the number for the comparable period in 1994 (410,000). The marriage rate was 6.4 per 1,000 population, also a 2% decrease from the first quarter of 1994.

During the 12 months ending Mar. 1995, an estimated 2,354,000 couples married, an increase of 1% from the previous 12-month period (2,329,000). The 12-month marriage rate remained unchanged at 9.0.

Divorces

A total of 288,000 couples divorced during the first quarter of 1995, a 2% decrease compared with the first quarter of 1994 (283,000). The divorce rate was 4.4 per 1,000 population, a decrease of less than 1% from the first quarter of 1994 (4.5).

During the 12 months ending Mar. 1995, an estimated 1,187,000 couples divorced, a slight increase over the number for the same period a year earlier (1,183,000). Despite the increase in number, the divorce rate for the 12-month period (4.5) was 2% lower than the rate for the period ending Mar. 1994 (4.6).

Deaths

According to provisional statistics, there were 620,000 deaths during the first quarter of 1995, 1% lower than for the first quarter of 1994 (627,000). The death rate was 9.6 per 1,000 population, 2% lower than the Jan.-Mar. 1994 rate (9.8). Among the deaths for the first quarter of 1995 were 7,700 deaths at ages under 1 year, yielding an infant mortality rate of 8.0 per 1,000 live births, compared with a rate of 8.2 for the first quarter of 1994. This change in infant mortality was not statistically significant.

The death rate for the 12 months ending Mar. 1995 (8.7 deaths per 1,000 population) was 2% lower than the rate of 8.9 for the comparable 12-month period a year earlier. The infant mortality rate for this 12-month period was 7.9 per 1,000 live births, 4% lower than the rate of 8.2 for the 12 months ending Mar. 1994.

Provisional Statistics
12 months ending with Mar.

	Number 1995	Number 1994	Rate* 1995	Rate* 1994
Live births	3,954,000	4,043,000	15.1	15.6
Deaths	2,279,000	2,293,000	8.7	8.9
Natural increase.	1,675,000	1,750,000	6.4	6.7
Marriages	2,354,000	2,329,000	9.0	9.0
Divorces	1,187,000	1,183,000	4.5	4.6
Infant deaths . . .	31,000	32,800	7.9	8.2

*Per 1,000 population. **Note:** Figures include revisions.

Annual Report for the Year 1994 (Provisional Statistics)

Source: National Center for Health Statistics, U.S. Dept. of Health and Human Services

Highlights

The lowest U.S. infant mortality rate ever (791.7 per 100,000 live births) was recorded in 1994.

Births

An estimated 3,979,000 babies were born in the U.S. in 1994, a decline of 1% from the 4,039,000 births in 1993. The birthrate of 15.3 per 1,000 population was 3% lower than the provisional rate of 15.7 for the preceding year. The fertility rate (the number of live births per 1,000 women aged 15-44 years) for 1994 was 67.1, 2% lower than the rate for 1993 (68.3).

Deaths

The provisional count of deaths during 1994 was 2,286,000, about 1% more than in the previous year (2,268,000). The death rate of 876.9 deaths per 100,000 population was slightly lower than the 1993 provisional death rate of 879.3 for 1993. The small, but significant decrease in the death rate reflects lower mortality from heart disease, homicide, and certain perinatal conditions. The infant mortality rate was 791.7 per 100,000 live births, 4% lower than the rate of 828.8 for 1993.

Natural Increase

As a result of natural increase, the excess of births over deaths, an estimated 1,693,000 persons were added to the population in 1994. This rate was 6.5 per 1,000 population, 6% lower than the rate of 6.9 for 1993, and was the lowest rate since 1978 (6.3). The decline in the rate of natural increase reflects a decrease in the birthrate and no change in the death rate.

Marriages

An estimated 2,362,000 marriages were performed in 1994. This was 1% higher than in 1993 (2,334,000). The marriage rate for 1994 (9.1 per 1,000 population) was slightly higher than in 1993 (9.0), but lower than any rate during 1965-92.

Divorces

Approximately 1,191,000 divorces were granted in the U.S. in 1994, 4,000 more than in 1993 (1,187,000), but 2% fewer than the all-time high of 1,215,000 in 1992. The divorce rate per 1,000 population in 1994 was unchanged from 1993 (4.6), which continued a general leveling of the divorce rate since the late 1980s.

Births and Deaths in the U.S.

Source: National Center for Health Statistics, U.S. Dept. of Health and Human Services

	Births Total number	Births Rate	Deaths Total number	Deaths Rate
Year				
1960	4,257,850	23.7	1,711,982	9.5
1970	3,731,386	18.4	1,921,031	9.5
1980	3,612,258	15.9	1,989,841	8.7
1990	4,158,212	16.7	2,148,463	8.6
1991	4,110,907	16.3	2,169,518	8.6
1992	4,065,014	15.9	2,175,613	8.5
1993	4,000,240	15.5	2,268,000	8.8
1994 (P)	3,979,000	15.3	2,286,000	8.8

Note: Refers only to events occurring within the U.S. Excludes fetal deaths. Rates per 1,000 population enumerated as of Apr. 1 for 1960 and 1970; estimated as of July 1 for all other years. Beginning 1970 excludes births and deaths occurring to nonresidents of the U.S. Data include revisions. (P) provisional data

Births and Deaths by States and Regions, 1993-94

Source: National Center for Health Statistics, U.S. Dept. of Health and Human Services

Area	Live births 1993 Number	1993 Rate	1994 Number	1994 Rate	Deaths 1993 Number	1993 Rate	1994 Number	1994 Rate[1]
New England	**183,678**	**13.9**	**175,080**	**13.2**	**120,492**	**9.1**	**117,309**	
Maine	15,027	12.1	14,320	11.5	11,479	9.3	11,386	
New Hampshire ...	14,952	13.3	14,605	12.8	8,919	7.9	8,907	
Vermont	7,286	12.6	7,158	12.3	4,868	8.5	4,573	
Massachusetts ...	86,317	14.4	83,449	13.8	56,460	9.4	54,558	
Rhode Island	14,275	14.3	13,440	13.5	9,709	9.7	9,333	
Connecticut	45,821	14.0	42,108	12.9	29,057	8.9	28,552	
Middle Atlantic	**560,516**	**14.7**	**553,536**	**14.5**	**369,956**	**9.7**	**368,532**	
New York	278,307	15.3	279,187	15.4	170,203	9.4	167,977	
New Jersey	123,020	15.6	117,289	14.8	72,776	9.2	72,391	
Pennsylvania	159,189	13.2	157,060	13.0	126,977	10.5	128,164	
East North Central ..	**645,299**	**15.0**	**643,455**	**14.9**	**387,135**	**9.0**	**394,562**	
Ohio	156,748	14.1	162,059	14.6	100,678	9.1	105,603	
Indiana	84,644	14.8	83,381	14.5	52,210	9.1	53,290	
Illinois	191,042	16.3	189,228	16.1	107,563	9.2	107,611	
Michigan	143,576	15.1	139,931	14.7	82,651	8.7	83,312	
Wisconsin	69,289	13.8	68,856	13.5	44,033	8.7	44,746	
West North Central ..	**258,692**	**14.3**	**251,531**	**13.8**	**172,679**	**9.5**	**169,968**	
Minnesota	63,761	14.1	64,681	14.2	36,236	8.0	36,417	
Iowa	37,044	13.2	35,926	12.7	28,612	9.9	26,352	
Missouri	77,424	14.8	75,366	14.3	56,305	10.8	55,985	
North Dakota	8,746	13.8	8,639	13.5	5,925	9.3	6,107	
South Dakota	10,830	15.1	10,615	14.7	6,863	9.6	6,851	
Nebraska	22,847	14.2	23,032	14.2	15,401	9.6	14,732	
Kansas	38,040	15.0	33,272	13.0	23,337	9.2	23,524	
South Atlantic	**673,147**	**14.7**	**661,731**	**14.3**	**423,762**	**9.3**	**428,153**	
Delaware	10,555	15.1	10,361	14.7	6,116	8.7	6,185	
Maryland	75,526	15.2	71,553	14.3	43,087	8.7	40,600	
District of Columbia	9,780	16.9	9,669	17.0	6,713	11.6	6,445	
Virginia	95,161	14.7	95,865	14.6	51,773	8.0	53,829	
West Virginia	22,044	12.1	21,554	11.8	19,929	11.0	20,221	
North Carolina	100,597	14.5	101,911	14.4	62,580	9.0	64,512	
South Carolina ...	53,997	14.8	50,907	13.9	31,404	8.6	31,570	
Georgia	112,400	16.2	108,908	15.4	55,851	8.1	56,377	
Florida	193,087	14.1	191,000	13.7	146,309	10.7	148,414	
East South Central ..	**231,361**	**14.7**	**231,741**	**14.6**	**154,664**	**9.8**	**156,124**	
Kentucky	52,256	13.8	51,926	13.6	36,921	9.7	37,407	
Tennessee	73,613	14.4	75,688	14.6	49,628	9.7	49,645	
Alabama	63,332	15.1	60,745	14.4	41,540	9.9	42,138	
Mississippi	42,160	16.0	43,382	16.3	26,575	10.1	26,934	
West South Central .	**481,374**	**17.2**	**470,975**	**16.6**	**234,665**	**8.4**	**237,175**	
Arkansas	34,248	14.1	34,571	14.1	26,371	10.9	26,667	
Louisiana	69,819	16.3	68,454	15.9	40,117	9.3	40,418	
Oklahoma	46,711	14.5	45,682	14.0	32,574	10.1	32,452	
Texas	330,596	18.3	322,268	17.5	135,603	7.5	137,638	
Mountain	**246,110**	**16.7**	**243,362**	**16.0**	**108,143**	**7.3**	**113,122**	
Montana	11,450	13.6	11,032	12.9	7,502	8.9	7,346	
Idaho	17,162	15.6	17,358	15.3	8,345	7.6	8,552	
Wyoming	6,662	14.2	6,385	13.4	3,544	7.5	3,512	
Colorado	54,817	15.4	54,144	14.8	23,722	6.7	24,416	
New Mexico	27,658	17.1	27,981	16.9	11,861	7.3	12,305	
Arizona	70,770	18.0	66,143	16.2	32,090	8.2	34,677	
Utah	36,462	19.6	38,808	20.3	10,193	5.5	10,545	
Nevada	21,129	15.2	21,511	14.8	10,886	7.8	11,769	
Pacific	**733,461**	**17.8**	**734,658**	**17.6**	**296,347**	**7.2**	**300,700**	
Washington	71,437	13.6	79,296	14.8	41,986	8.0	39,648	
Oregon	42,195	13.9	42,276	13.7	27,275	9.0	27,303	
California	589,685	18.9	581,763	18.5	217,559	7.0	224,082	
Alaska	10,555	17.6	12,079	19.9	2,247	3.8	2,431	
Hawaii	19,589	16.7	19,244	16.3	7,280	6.2	7,236	

Note: Data are provisional estimates, reported by state of residence. Figures include revisions, and so may differ from those previously published. Rates for births and deaths are per 1,000 population. (1) Data not available for 1994.

Deaths Under 1 Year and Infant Mortality Rates, for 10 Selected Causes, 1994-95

Source: National Center for Health Statistics, U.S. Dept. of Health and Human Services

Age and cause of death	1995 Number	1995 Rate	1994 Number	1994 Rate	Age and cause of death	1995 Number	1995 Rate	1994 Number	1994 Rate
Total, under 1 year ...	31,100	786.2	33,100	825.4	Birth trauma	180	4.6	180	4.5
Under 28 days	19,630	496.5	21,420	534.3	Intrauterine hypoxia and birth asphyxia	520	13.2	670	16.7
28 days to 11 months ..	11,450	289.6	11,670	291.1	Respiratory distress syndrome	1,460	36.9	2,070	51.6
Certain gastrointestinal diseases	240	6.1	220	5.5	Other conditions originating in the peri-natal period	7,810	197.5	8,340	208.0
Pneumonia and influenza	450	11.4	430	10.7					
Congenital anomalies ..	6,740	170.5	6,700	167.1	Sudden infant death syndrome	3,370	85.2	4,280	106.8
Disorders relating to short gestation and unspecified low birth-weight	3,870	97.9	4,130	103.0	All other causes	6,420	162.4	6,070	151.4

Notes: Data are provisional, estimated from a 10% sample of deaths for a 12-month period ending in Feb. of the year cited. Rates are on an annual basis per 100,000 live births. Due to rounding of estimates, figures may not add to totals.

Infant Mortality Rates, by Race and Sex, 1960-92[1]

Source: National Center for Health Statistics, U.S. Dept. of Health and Human Services

	All races			White			Black		
Year	Both sexes	Male	Female	Both sexes	Male	Female	Both sexes	Male	Female
1960	26.0	29.3	22.6	22.9	26.0	19.6	44.3	49.1	39.4
1970	20.0	22.4	17.5	17.8	20.0	15.4	32.6	36.2	29.0
1980	12.6	13.9	11.2	11.0	12.3	9.6	21.4	23.3	19.4
1981	11.9	13.1	10.7	10.5	11.7	9.2	20.0	21.7	18.3
1982	11.5	12.8	10.2	10.1	11.2	8.9	19.6	21.5	17.7
1983	11.2	12.3	10.0	9.7	10.8	8.6	19.2	21.1	17.2
1984	10.8	11.9	9.6	9.4	10.5	8.3	18.4	19.8	16.9
1985	10.6	11.9	9.3	9.3	10.6	8.0	18.2	19.9	16.5
1986	10.4	11.5	9.1	8.9	10.0	7.8	18.0	20.0	16.0
1987	10.1	11.2	8.9	8.6	9.6	7.6	17.9	19.6	16.0
1988	10.0	11.0	8.9	8.5	9.5	7.4	17.6	19.0	16.1
1989	9.8	10.8	8.8	8.1	9.0	7.1	18.6	20.0	17.2
1990	9.2	10.3	8.1	7.6	8.5	6.6	18.0	19.6	16.2
1991	8.9	10.0	7.8	7.3	8.3	6.3	17.6	19.4	15.7
1992	8.5	9.4	7.6	6.9	7.7	6.1	16.8	18.4	15.3

(1) Final data. Rates per 1,000 live births.

The 10 Leading Causes of Death, 1994[1]

Source: National Center for Health Statistics, U.S. Dept. of Health and Human Services

Rank	Cause of death	Number	Death rate[2]	Percentage of total deaths
	All causes	2,286,000	876.9	100.0
1.	Heart Disease	734,090	281.6	32.1
2.	Cancer	536,860	206.0	23.5
3.	Stroke	154,350	59.2	6.8
4.	Chronic obstructive lung diseases and allied conditions	101,870	39.1	4.5
5.	Accidents and adverse effects	90,140	34.6	3.9
	Motor vehicle accidents	42,170	NA	1.8
	All other accidents and adverse effects	47,980	NA	2.1
6.	Pneumonia and influenza	82,090	31.5	3.6
7.	Diabetes mellitus	55,390	21.2	2.4
8.	Human immunodeficiency virus (HIV) infection[3]	41,930	16.1	1.8
9.	Suicide	32,410	12.4	1.4
10.	Chronic liver disease and cirrhosis	25,730	9.9	1.1

NA=Not available. (1) Data are provisional, estimated from a 10% sample of deaths. Figures may not add to totals due to rounding. Rates have been recomputed based on revised population estimates. (2) Per 100,000 population. (3) HIV is the virus that causes AIDS.

U.S. Abortions, by State, 1988-92

Source: Alan Guttmacher Institute, New York, NY

State	Number of reported abortions[1]			Rate per 1,000 women[2]			Percentage change 1988-92
	1988	1991	1992	1988	1991	1992	
Total	1,590,750	1,556,510	1,528,930	27.3	26.3	25.9	−5
Alabama	18,220	17,400	17,450	18.7	18.2	18.2	−3
Alaska	2,390	2,400	2,370	18.2	16.9	16.5	−10
Arizona	23,070	19,690	20,600	28.8	23.2	24.1	−16
Arkansas	6,250	7,150	7,130	11.6	13.6	13.5	16
California	311,720	320,960	304,230	45.9	44.4	42.1	−8
Colorado	18,740	21,010	19,880	22.4	25.3	23.6	6
Connecticut	23,630	20,530	19,720	31.2	26.7	26.2	−16
Delaware	5,710	5,720	5,730	35.7	34.9	35.2	−1
District of Columbia	26,120	21,510	21,320	163.3	136.1	138.4	−15
Florida	82,850	84,570	84,680	31.5	29.9	30.0	−5
Georgia	36,720	39,720	39,680	23.5	24.2	24.0	2
Hawaii	11,170	12,130	12,190	43.0	45.9	46.0	7
Idaho	1,920	1,740	1,710	8.2	7.5	7.2	−12
Illinois	72,570	64,990	68,420	26.4	24.1	25.4	−4
Indiana	15,760	15,940	15,840	11.9	12.1	12.0	1
Iowa	9,420	7,200	6,970	14.6	11.7	11.4	−22
Kansas	11,440	12,770	12,570	20.1	22.9	22.4	11
Kentucky	11,520	8,270	10,000	13.0	9.5	11.4	−12
Louisiana	17,340	13,930	13,600	16.3	13.7	13.4	−18
Maine	4,620	4,210	4,200	16.2	14.7	14.7	−9
Maryland	32,670	33,000	31,260	28.6	27.5	26.4	−8
Massachusetts	43,720	44,150	40,660	30.2	30.2	28.4	−6
Michigan	63,410	55,800	55,580	28.5	25.1	25.2	−11
Minnesota	18,580	16,880	16,180	18.2	16.3	15.6	−14
Mississippi	5,120	8,160	7,550	8.4	13.5	12.4	48
Missouri	19,490	15,770	13,510	16.4	13.5	11.6	−29
Montana	3,050	3,680	3,300	16.5	20.6	18.2	11
Nebraska	6,490	6,230	5,580	17.7	17.5	15.7	−11
Nevada	10,190	14,450	13,300	40.3	49.0	44.2	10
New Hampshire	4,710	4,260	3,890	17.5	15.7	14.6	−17

(continued)

U.S. Abortions, by State (continued)

State	Number of reported abortions[1]			Rate per 1,000 women[2]			Percentage change
	1988	1991	1992	1988	1991	1992	1988-92
New Jersey	63,900	55,800	55,320	35.1	30.9	31.0	−12
New Mexico	6,810	6,190	6,410	19.1	17.2	17.7	−7
New York	183,980	190,410	195,390	43.3	44.5	46.2	7
North Carolina	39,720	37,210	36,180	25.4	23.2	22.4	−12
North Dakota	2,230	1,600	1,490	14.9	11.4	10.7	−28
Ohio	53,400	52,030	49,520	21.0	20.4	19.5	−7
Oklahoma	12,120	9,130	8,940	16.2	12.8	12.5	−23
Oregon	15,960	16,580	16,060	23.9	24.9	23.9	0
Pennsylvania	51,830	51,780	49,740	18.9	19.2	18.6	−2
Rhode Island	7,190	7,500	6,990	30.6	31.5	30.0	−2
South Carolina	14,160	13,520	12,190	16.7	15.8	14.2	−15
South Dakota	900	980	1,040	5.7	6.4	6.8	19
Tennessee	22,090	19,840	19,060	18.9	16.9	16.2	−14
Texas	100,690	95,930	97,400	24.8	23.0	23.1	−7
Utah	5,030	4,250	3,940	12.8	10.4	9.3	−27
Vermont	3,580	3,110	2,900	25.8	22.7	21.2	−18
Virginia	35,420	35,170	35,020	23.7	22.8	22.7	−5
Washington	31,220	32,640	33,190	27.6	27.6	27.7	0
West Virginia	3,270	2,590	3,140	7.5	6.3	7.7	2
Wisconsin	18,040	15,510	15,450	16.0	13.6	13.6	−15
Wyoming	600	520	460	5.1	4.9	4.3	−16

(1) Numbers of abortions are rounded to the nearest 10. (2) Only women aged 15-44 years old.

Suicides by Age, Race, and Sex, 1994

Source: National Center for Health Statistics, U.S. Dept. of Health and Human Services

	All ages	1-14 yrs.	15-24 yrs.	25-34 yrs.	35-44 yrs.	45-54 yrs.	55-64 yrs.	65-74 yrs.	75-84 yrs.	85 yrs. & over	Age not stated
All races, both sexes[1] .	32,410	390	5,350	6,610	6,430	3,940	3,050	3,040	2,620	950	40
Male	26,710	300	4,770	5,530	5,240	2,900	2,420	2,500	2,200	800	40
Female	5,700	100	570	1,080	1,190	1,040	620	540	410	150	(—)
White, both sexes	28,850	330	4,370	5,560	5,790	3,690	2,840	2,820	2,530	900	20
Male	23,760	240	3,910	4,650	4,710	2,730	2,280	2,330	2,130	760	20
Female	5,090	80	470	910	1,080	960	560	490	400	140	(—)
Black, both sexes	2,350	30	710	600	460	170	150	130	40	50	10
Male	2,080	30	620	550	400	140	120	120	40	40	10
Female	280	(—)	80	50	50	30	30	10	(—)	10	(—)

(—) = Data represent zero. **Note:** Data are provisional, estimated from a 10% sample of deaths. Due to rounding of estimates, figures may not add to totals. (1) All races includes races other than white and black.

Living Arrangements of Children, 1970-93

Source: Bureau of the Census, U.S. Dept. of Commerce

(as of Mar.; excludes persons under 18 years of age who maintained households or resided in group quarters)

Race, Hispanic origin, and year	Number (1,000)	Both parents	Percent living with— Mother only					Father only	Neither parent
			Total	Divorced	Married spouse absent	Single[1]	Widowed		
White									
1970	58,790	90	8	3	3	Z	2	1	2
1980	52,242	83	14	7	4	1	2	2	2
1990	51,390	79	16	8	4	3	1	3	2
1991	51,918	79	17	8	5	3	1	3	2
1993	53,042	77	17	8	4	4	1	4	2
Black									
1970	9,422	59	30	5	16	4	4	2	10
1980	9,375	42	44	11	16	13	4	2	12
1990	10,018	38	51	10	12	27	2	4	8
1991	10,209	36	54	10	11	31	2	4	7
1993	10,649	36	54	10	12	31	1	3	7
Hispanic[2]									
1970	4,006[3]	78	NA	NA	NA	NA	NA	NA	NA
1980	5,459	75	20	6	8	4	2	2	4
1990	7,174	67	27	7	10	8	2	3	3
1991	7,462	66	27	7	10	9	2	3	4
1993	7,773	64	28	7	9	11	1	4	4

NA=Not available. Z=Less than 0.5%. (1) Never married. (2) Hispanic persons may be of any race. (3) All persons under 18 years old.

Living Arrangements of the Elderly, 1992

Source: Bureau of the Census, U.S. Dept. of Commerce

There were slightly more than 32 mil elderly persons (aged 65 years or older) in the U.S. in 1992. Approximately 30.6 mil lived in the community. Of these elderly, 9.52 mil lived alone, 16.54 mil lived with a spouse, and the remaining 4.53 mil lived with other relatives or nonrelatives. Data from the 1990 census show 3.3 mil persons of all ages lived in institutional group quarters in 1990 and 1.6 mil of these were elderly persons living in nursing homes.

Of those elderly who lived alone, 8 in 10 were women. Persons aged 65 to 74 were one and a half times more likely to live with a spouse (63%) than were those aged 75 and over (41%).

Drug Use: America's Students

Source: Univ. of Michigan Inst. for Social Research, National Institute on Drug Abuse

Middle and High School Students

Drug use among American young people continued to rise in 1994, according to the results of the University of Michigan's 20th annual survey of American high school seniors and 4th annual survey of 8th and 10th graders. Although drug use was still not at the peak levels reached in the 1970s, evidence supported a reversal of the declines recorded for more than a decade. Researchers reported a continued rise in marijuana use throughout the U.S. at all 3 grade levels, as well as an increase in the use of stimulants, LSD and other hallucinogens, inhalants, stimulants, barbiturates, and, in the most recent survey, cocaine and crack.

Marijuana remained the most popular of illegal drugs among the 10th graders and seniors. In 1994, the proportion of students that reported using marijuana in the past year rose to 13% of 8th graders, 25% of 10th graders, and 31% of seniors.

The use of alcohol showed slight (although not statistically significant) increases for all grade levels in 1994. One in 7 eighth-graders, nearly 1 in 4 tenth graders, and more than 1 in 4 twelfth-graders had five or more drinks in a row during the 2 weeks prior to completing the survey.

Cigarette smoking remained high among all 3 grade levels in 1994. Nearly 19% of 8th graders, 25% of 10th graders, and 31% of 12th graders reported having smoked during the 30 days before they responded to the survey.

Although the surveys missed the 15-20% of a class group that drops out of school early, investigators said there was little reason to believe trends would differ among this group, although it would undoubtedly have higher rates of use overall.

In 1994, about 16,000 seniors in 139 public and private high schools participated in the survey, along with 16,000 10th graders in 130 schools and 18,000 8th graders in 150 schools.

College Students

A 1993 survey of 1,500 college students found that the increase in overall drug usage that occurred from 1991 to 1992 had halted and there was virtually no change in drug use from the previous year. Of those surveyed, 30.6% used some illicit drugs at least once in the prior 12 months. Use of marijuana among college students in the prior 12 months increased 0.2% from the 1992 level of 27.7%.

Usage of an illicit drug other than marijuana decreased slightly, from 13.1% to 12.5%. Although use of hallucinogens had been rising, a small decrease was seen for the first time since 1989, with 6% of those surveyed reporting use of hallucinogens. LSD usage, which is included in the hallucinogen category, decreased slightly to its 1991 level, 5.1%; however, usage was still high compared with the 1989 level of 3.4%.

The popularity of cocaine (excluding crack) continued to decline, with use dropping from 3.0% of college students surveyed in 199 to 2.7% of the 1993 students.

Crack, stimulants, barbiturates, tranquilizers, inhalants, heroin, opiates other than heroine, and other illicitly used drugs showed little or no further decline in active use among college students in 1993, although a number of them had been declining previously.

Drug Use: America's High School Seniors

Source: Univ. of Michigan Inst. for Social Research

Percentage ever used

	Class of 1975	Class of 1980	Class of 1986	Class of 1987	Class of 1988	Class of 1990	Class of 1991	Class of 1992	Class of 1993	Class of 1994	'93-'94 change
Marijuana/hashish	47.3	60.3	50.9	50.2	47.2	40.7	36.7	32.6	35.3	38.2	+2.9
Inhalants	NA	11.9	15.9	17.0	16.7	18.0	17.6	16.6	17.4	17.7	+0.3
Inhalants adjusted[1]	NA	17.3	20.1	18.6	17.5	18.5	18.0	17.0	17.7	18.3	+0.6
Amyl & butyl nitrites	NA	11.1	8.6	4.7	3.2	2.1	1.6	1.5	1.4	1.7	+0.3
Hallucinogens	16.3	13.3	9.7	10.3	8.9	9.4	9.6	9.2	10.9	11.4	+0.5
Hallucinogens adjusted[2]	NA	15.6	11.9	10.6	9.2	9.7	10.0	9.4	11.3	11.7	+0.4
LSD	11.3	9.3	7.2	8.4	7.7	8.7	8.8	8.6	10.3	10.5	+0.2
PCP	NA	9.6	4.8	3.0	2.9	2.8	2.9	2.4	2.9	2.8	−0.1
Cocaine	9.0	15.7	16.9[5]	15.2	12.1	9.4	7.8	6.1	6.1	5.9	−0.2
"Crack"	NA	NA	NA	5.4	4.8	3.5	3.1	2.6	2.6	3.0	+0.4
Heroin	2.2	1.1	1.1	1.2	1.1	1.3	0.9	1.2	1.1	1.2	+0.1
Other opiates[3]	9.0	9.8	9.0	9.2	8.6	8.3	6.6	6.1	6.4	6.6	+0.2
Stimulants[3,4]	22.3	26.4	23.4	21.6	19.8	17.5	15.4	13.9	15.1	15.7	+0.6
Sedatives[3]	18.2	14.9	10.4	8.7	7.8	7.5	6.7	6.1	6.4	7.3	+0.9
Barbiturates[3]	16.9	11.0	8.4	7.4	6.7	6.8	6.2	5.5	6.3	7.0	+0.7
Methaqualone[3]	8.1	9.5	5.2	4.0	3.3	2.3	1.3	1.6	0.8	1.4	+0.6
Tranquilizers[3]	17.0	15.2	10.9	10.9	9.4	7.2	7.2	6.0	6.4	6.6	+0.2
Alcohol	90.4	93.2	91.3	92.2	92.0	89.5	88.0	87.5	87.0	NA	NA
Cigarettes	73.6	71.0	67.6	67.2	66.4	64.4	63.1	61.8	61.9	6.2	NA

NA=Not available. (1) Adjusted for underreporting of amyl and butyl nitrites. (2) Adjusted for underreporting of PCP. (3) Only drug use that was not under a doctor's orders. (4) Adjusted for overreporting of the nonprescription stimulants. (5) In 1986, three-fourths of those who used cocaine used it in powder form; the remainder used the "crack" form.

Drug Use in the General U.S. Population

Source: Bureau of Justice Statistics, U.S. Dept. of Justice

According to the Substance Abuse and Mental Health Administration's 1993 National Household Survey on Drug Abuse, an estimated 77 mil (37.2%) Americans 12 years of age and older had used an illicit drug at least once during their lifetimes, 11.8% used one during the previous year, and 5.6% used one in the month before the survey was conducted. Among those 25 years of age and under, an estimated 1.6 mil used cocaine (including crack), and 8.6 mil used marijuana at least once within the previous year.

Among those 26 years of age and over, 2.9 mil used cocaine (including crack), and 10 mil used marijuana at least once within the previous year.

The National Institute on Drug Abuse's Drug Abuse Warning Network reported an estimated 433,493 admissions to hospital emergency rooms nationwide that involved drug abuse in 1992. A total of 7,532 drug-abuse-related deaths were reported in 1992 by 137 medical examiners in 38 metropolitan areas.

Principal Types of Accidental Deaths, 1970-94

Source: National Safety Council

Year	Motor vehicle	Falls	Poison (solid, liquid)	Drowning	Fires, burns	Ingestion of food, object	Firearms	Poison (gases)
1970.......	54,633	16,926	3,679	7,860	6,718	2,753	2,406	1,620
1975.......	45,853	14,896	4,694	8,000	6,071	3,106	2,380	1,577
1980.......	53,172	13,294	3,089	7,257	5,822	3,249	1,955	1,242
1985.......	45,901	12,001	4,091	5,316	4,938	3,551	1,649	1,079
1990.......	46,300	12,400	5,700	5,200	4,300	3,200	1,400	800
1991.......	43,500	12,200	5,600	4,600	4,200	2,900	1,400	800
1992.......	40,300	12,400	5,200	4,300	4,000	2,700	1,400	700
1993.......	42,000	13,500	6,500	4,800	4,000	2,900	1,600	700
1994.......	43,000	13,300	8,000	4,000	4,200	3,000	1,500	700
Death rates per 100,000 population								
1970.......	26.8	8.3	1.8	3.9	3.3	1.4	1.2	0.8
1975.......	21.3	6.9	2.2	3.7	2.8	1.4	1.1	0.7
1980.......	23.4	5.9	1.4	3.2	2.6	1.4	0.9	0.5
1985.......	19.2	5.0	1.7	2.2	2.1	1.5	0.7	0.5
1990.......	18.8	5.0	2.3	2.1	1.7	1.3	0.6	0.3
1991.......	17.2	4.8	2.2	1.8	1.7	1.1	0.6	0.3
1992.......	15.8	4.9	2.0	1.7	1.6	1.1	0.5	0.3
1993.......	16.3	5.2	2.5	1.9	1.6	1.1	0.6	0.3
1994.......	16.5	5.1	3.1	1.5	1.6	1.2	0.6	0.3

Note: There were 14,500 other accidental deaths in 1994; the most frequently occurring types were medical complications, machinery, air transport, water transport, mechanical suffocation, and excessive cold.

Motor Vehicle Accidents

Source: National Safety Council

Motor vehicle deaths increased 2% in 1994 compared with 1993. Of the 175,128,000 licensed drivers in 1994, about 89 mil (51%) were males and 86,128,000 (49%) were females.

Male drivers were involved in more fatal accidents than female drivers in 1994. About 38,200 men and 14,600 women drivers were involved in fatal accidents.

About 12.4 mil male drivers and 7.6 mil female drivers were involved in all types of accidents in 1994. However, since males account for about 64% of the miles driven each year, according to the latest estimates, and females for 36%, women have higher accident involvement rates. At least part of the difference in accident involvement rates between men and women may be due to differences in the time, place, and circumstance of driving experienced by both groups of drivers. Accident rates were 82 per ten million miles driven for men and 90 per ten million miles driven for women.

About 44% of all traffic fatalities in 1993 involved an intoxicated or alcohol-impaired driver or nonoccupant. Of these 17,461 alcohol-related traffic fatalities, an estimated 13,984 occurred in accidents in which a driver or nonoccupant was intoxicated, and the remainder involved a driver or nonoccupant who had been drinking but was not legally intoxicated. Alcohol was also a factor in about 7% of all traffic accidents, both fatal and nonfatal, in 1993. In 1983 alcohol-related fatalities accounted for 56% of all traffic deaths.

	Death total 1994	Percentage change from 1993	Death rate 1994[1]
All motor vehicle accidents	43,000	+2	16.5
Collision between motor vehicles	19,300	+5	7.4
Collision with fixed object	12,400	+2	4.8
Pedestrian accidents	5,600	-8	2.1
Noncollision accidents	4,300	+2	1.6
Collision with pedalcycle	800	0	0.3
Collision with railroad train	500	-17	0.2
Other collision (animal, animal-drawn vehicles, street cars)	100	0	(2)

(1) Deaths per 100,000 population. (2) Death rate was less than 0.05.

Improper Driving Reported in Accidents, 1994

Source: National Safety Council

Type	Percentage of fatal accidents 1993	1994	Percentage of injury accidents 1993	1994	Percentage of all accidents 1993	1994
Improper driving	57.7	63.7	72.7	65.7	68.6	67.3
Speed too fast or unsafe	16.5	19.5	13.5	11.2	12.2	11.9
Right of way	12.7	15.1	25.0	24.1	20.6	21.3
Failed to yield	7.8	9.1	17.3	15.0	15.1	14.5
Passed stop sign	2.7	2.6	2.7	3.1	2.0	2.5
Disregarded signal	2.2	3.4	5.0	6.0	3.5	4.3
Drove left of center	7.6	9.4	2.1	2.5	1.8	2.3
Improper overtaking	1.2	1.6	1.0	1.2	1.3	1.4
Made improper turn	2.9	2.6	3.4	2.9	4.5	4.1
Followed too closely	0.5	0.5	6.2	5.9	5.5	5.6
Other improper driving	16.3	15.0	21.5	17.9	22.7	20.6
No improper driving stated	42.3	36.3	27.3	34.3	31.4	32.7

Note: Based on reports from 11 state traffic authorities. When a driver was under the influence of alcohol or drugs, the accident was considered a result of the driver's physical condition—not a driving error. For this reason, accidents in which the driver was reported to be under the influence are classified under "no improper driving."

Deaths Involving Firearms, by Age, 1992

Source: National Safety Council

The following table contains final data for 1992. Provisional data indicate that there were 40,230 deaths due to firearms in 1993 and 39,720 deaths due to firearms in 1994. As with the final 1992 data, early estimates for 1993 and 1994 show the greatest number of firearms deaths for both males and females for the age groups 15-24 and 25-34 years.

	All ages	Under 5	5-14	15-24	25-44	45-64	65-74	75 & over
Total firearms deaths[1]	37,474	117	776	10,425	15,028	6,218	2,502	2,308
Male	32,130	68	602	9,328	12,737	5,167	2,148	2,080
Female	5,344	49	174	1,097	2,391	1,051	354	228
Accidents	1,409	36	180	519	413	166	50	45
Male	1,238	22	155	476	364	141	44	36
Female	171	14	25	43	496	25	6	9
Suicides	18,169	0	175	3,073	6,437	4,249	2,166	2,069
Male	15,802	0	137	2,756	5,492	3,586	1,907	1,924
Female	2,367	0	38	317	945	663	259	145
Homicides	17,488	80	402	6,701	8,085	1,769	268	183
Male	14,747	46	294	5,975	6,728	1,410	182	112
Female	2,741	34	108	726	1,357	359	86	71
Undetermined[2]	408	1	19	132	193	34	18	11
Male	343	0	16	121	153	30	15	8
Female	65	1	3	11	40	4	3	3

(1) Excludes firearms deaths by legal intervention. These deaths totaled 302 in 1992. (2) Undetermined means the intentionality of the death (accident, suicide, homicide) cannot be determined.

Home Accident Deaths, 1950-94

Source: National Safety Council

Year	Total	Falls	Poison (solid, liquid)	Fires, burns[1]	Suffo., ingesting object	Firearms	Suffo., mechanical	Poison (gases)	All other[2]
1950	29,000	14,800	1,300	5,000	[3]	950	1,600	1,250	4,100
1960	28,000	12,300	1,350	6,350	1,850	1,200	1,500	900	2,550
1970	27,000	9,700	3,000	5,600	1,800[4]	1,400[4]	1,100[4]	1,100	3,300[4]
1980	22,800	7,100	2,500	4,800	2,000	1,100	500	700	4,100[5]
1990	21,500	6,700	4,000	3,400	2,300	800	600	500	3,200
1991	22,100	6,900	4,500	3,400	2,200	800	700	500	3,100
1992[6]	24,000	7,700	4,800	3,700	1,500	1,000	700	400	4,200
1993[6]	26,100	8,600	5,600	3,700	1,600	1,000	700	500	4,400
1994[7]	26,700	8,500	6,400	3,900	1,400	900	700	500	4,400

(1) Includes deaths resulting from conflagration, regardless of nature of injury. (2) Includes drowning in swimming pools and bathtubs. (3) Included in All other. (4) Data for this year and subsequent years not comparable with previous years due to classification changes. (5) Includes about 1,000 excessive deaths due to summer heat wave. (6) Revised. The National Safety Council adopted the Bureau of Labor Statistics Census of Fatal Occupational Injuries count for work-related unintentional injuries retroactive to 1992 data. (7) Data are preliminary.

Worldwide Airline Fatalities, 1980-94

Source: National Safety Council

Year	Aircraft accidents[1]	Passenger deaths	Death rate[2]	Year	Aircraft accidents[1]	Passenger deaths	Death rate[2]
1980	22	814	0.14	1988	25	699	0.08
1981	21	362	0.06	1989	27	817	0.08
1982	26	764	0.13	1990	22	440	0.04
1983	20	809	0.13	1991	25	510	0.05
1984	16	223	0.03	1992	25	990	0.09
1985	22	1,066	0.15	1993	31	801	0.07
1986	17	331	0.04	1994[3]	24	732	0.09
1987	24	890	0.10				

(1) Involving a passenger fatality. (2) Passenger deaths per 100 mil passenger mi. (3) Preliminary.

Cost of Unintentional Injuries, 1994

Source: National Safety Council, estimates

The cost of...	is equivalent to...
...all injuries ($440.9 bil)	80 cents of every dollar paid in 1994 federal personal income taxes, *or* 65 cents of every dollar spent on food in the U.S. in 1994.
...motor vehicle accidents ($176.5 bil)	purchasing 800 gallons of gasoline per registered vehicle in the U.S., *or* a $19,100 rebate on each new car sold in 1994.
...work injuries ($120.7 bil)	59 cents of every dollar of 1994 corporate dividends to stockholders, *or* 23 cents of every dollar of 1994 pre-tax corporate profits.
...home injuries ($94.3 bil)	a $78,700 rebate on each new single-family home built in 1994, *or* 49 cents of every dollar of property taxes paid in 1994.
...public injuries[1] ($63.2 bil)	a $7.0 million grant to each public library in the U.S., *or* an $86,900 bonus for each police officer and firefighter.

(1) Any accident, other than a motor vehicle or a work-related accident, that occurs in public use of any premises, such as accidents during recreation (swimming, hunting, etc.), due to natural disasters, or in a public building.

U.S. Fires, 1994
Source: National Fire Protection Assn.

Fires
- Public fire departments responded to 2,054,500 fires in 1994, a decrease of 5.2% from 1993.
- There were 614,000 structure fires in 1994, a very slight decrease of 1.2% from the 1993 figure.
- 74% of all structure fires, or 451,000 fires, occurred in residential properties.
- There were 422,000 vehicle fires in 1994. This is virtually the same number as the previous year.
- There were 1,018,500 fires in outside properties, an increase of 11.9% from 1993.
- The South, with 9.3 fires per 1,000 population, had the highest fire incidence rates in the nation.

Civilian deaths
- There were 4,275 civilian fire deaths in 1994, a decrease of 7.8% from 1993.
- The number of fire deaths in the home decreased by 7.9% to 3,425.
- About 80% of all fire deaths occurred in the home.
- The South had the highest regional death rate, with 22.4 civilian deaths per million population.
- Nationwide, someone died in a fire every 123 minutes.

Civilian injuries
- There were 27,250 civilian fire injuries in 1994, a decrease of 10.6% from the year before. About one-third of the decrease reflects the fact that no incident in 1994 was comparable to the 1993 fire and explosion at the World Trade Center in New York City, which injured more than 1,000 people. Overall, the actual numbers of injuries in 1993 and 1994 may have been higher due to underreporting of civilian injuries to the fire service.

- 20,025 civilian injuries, or 73.5%, occurred in residential properties; 11.4%, or 3,100 injuries, occurred in nonresidential structure fires.
- The North Central region had the highest civilian injury rate, with 130.6 civilian injuries per million population.
- Nationwide, a civilian was injured in fire every 19 minutes.

Property damage
- Property damage resulting from fires in 1994 decreased by 4.6%, to an estimated $8.151 billion.
- Structure fires accounted for 84% of all property damage, or $6.867 billion.
- 63% of all structure property loss occurred in residential properties. The cost totaled $4.317 billion.
- The Northeast had the highest property loss rate in the nation: $36.20 per person.

Incendiary and suspicious fires
- 14.0% of all structure fires, or an estimated 86,000 fires, were deliberately set or were suspected of being deliberately set. This represented a slight increase of 1.8% from 1993.
- Incendiary or suspicious structure fires resulted in the deaths of 550 people in 1994, a slight decrease of 1.8% from the year before. These fires cost $1.447 billion in property damage, representing 21.1% of all property loss from structure fires. However, the cost of such fires decreased by 38.5% from 1993, reflecting the fact that no fires in 1994 were comparable to the wildfires in Southern California and the fire and explosion at the World Trade Center, which resulted in combined estimated losses of $1.039 billion in 1993.
- Vehicle fires of incendiary or suspicious origin in 1994 decreased by 4.8% from 1993 to 43,500. They caused $156 million in property damage, up 13.9% from the previous year.

Physicians by Age, Sex, and Specialty, 1994
Source: American Medical Assn., as of Jan. 1, 1994

	Total Physicians[1]		Under 35 yr		35-44 yr		45-54 yr		55-64 yr	
	Male	Female	Male	Female	Male	Female	Male	Female	Male	Female
All Specialties	551,151	133,263	90,528	43,204	154,658	50,834	121,644	21,990	83,348	8,244
Aerospace Medicine	593	43	109	11	165	25	140	5	120	1
Allergy & Immunology	3,048	681	282	140	855	295	903	159	601	46
Anesthesiology	25,779	6,037	6,255	1,715	9,433	2,281	5,269	1,287	3,279	551
Cardiovascular Disease	17,280	1,157	2,528	289	6,605	578	4,514	196	2,421	63
Child Psychiatry	3,282	1,930	374	353	999	769	1,014	473	589	222
Colon/Rectal Surgery	920	45	73	9	322	31	271	4	139	1
Dermatology	6,112	2,241	746	802	1,723	953	1,873	343	1,139	107
Diagnostic Radiology	15,675	3,500	3,948	1,382	5,648	1,523	4,148	468	1,454	98
Emergency Medicine	14,834	2,910	3,019	986	6,425	1,345	3,812	451	1,040	101
Family Practice	43,030	11,679	7,740	4,427	17,186	5,260	8,865	1,405	5,124	392
Forensic Pathology	352	120	15	12	116	51	92	35	81	18
Gastroenterology	8,443	644	1,422	190	3,292	346	2,418	87	955	15
General Practice	16,164	2,290	257	95	1,516	546	2,959	765	4,527	480
General Preventive Med.	885	381	104	92	280	175	224	62	160	28
General Surgery	34,871	3,031	8,565	1,627	8,280	1,042	7,828	262	6,174	64
Internal Medicine	65,162	19,789	18,338	8,945	21,221	7,562	12,198	2,329	7,547	630
Neurological Surgery	4,537	173	841	65	1,255	83	1,116	19	916	6
Neurology	8,927	1,994	1,445	598	3,324	895	2,475	359	1,227	111
Nuclear Medicine	1,216	253	97	52	351	104	367	60	285	28
Obstetrics/Gynecology	23,394	9,237	3,577	3,944	6,514	3,553	6,477	1,234	4,699	358
Occupational Medicine	2,550	449	110	71	641	202	537	99	576	47
Ophthalmology	15,118	2,026	2,362	721	4,379	870	4,145	286	2,887	98
Orthopedic Surgery	20,932	601	4,089	246	6,319	280	5,504	49	3,611	14
Otolaryngology	8,191	594	1,499	259	2,286	253	2,206	58	1,622	17
Pathology-Anat./Clin.	13,160	4,621	1,762	1,103	3,626	1,864	3,261	1,068	2,973	385
Pediatrics	23,523	18,383	4,531	6,994	7,016	6,647	5,874	3,183	3,813	1,055
Pediatric Cardiology	962	282	176	102	345	88	220	51	156	26
Physical Med./Rehab.	3,607	1,617	1,018	516	1,221	550	673	337	385	154
Plastic Surgery	4,806	400	507	74	1,605	221	1,539	76	869	19
Psychiatry	27,781	9,921	2,982	2,227	6,914	3,678	7,379	2,212	5,982	1,076
Public Health	1,411	499	37	29	274	157	358	101	335	91
Pulmonary Diseases	6,442	747	969	238	2,715	346	1,868	106	596	32
Radiation Oncology	2,779	714	603	222	883	270	730	168	393	43
Radiology	7,055	877	395	118	1,031	309	2,019	283	2,414	122
Thoracic Surgery	2,268	40	263	11	616	21	548	5	530	3
Urological Surgery	9,524	203	1,477	83	2,461	100	2,796	14	1,993	6
Other	6,522	1,121	417	123	1,614	423	1,472	258	1,508	157
Unspecified	4,460	1,748	2,641	1,130	1,022	414	391	138	189	42

(1) Includes physicians 65 and older, those living in U.S. possessions, those "Inactive," "Not Classified," and "Address Unknown."

Ownership of Life Insurance in the U.S. and Assets of U.S. Life Insurance Companies, 1940-94

Source: American Council of Life Insurance

(millions of dollars)

Year	Purchases of life insurance				Insurance in force					Assets
	Ordinary	Group	Industrial	Total	Ordinary	Group	Industrial	Credit	Total	
1940	6,689	691	3,350	10,730	79,346	14,938	20,866	380	115,530	30,802
1950	17,326	6,068	5,402	28,796	149,116	47,793	33,415	3,844	234,168	64,020
1960	52,883	14,645	6,880	74,408	341,881	175,903	39,563	29,101	586,448	119,576
1965	83,485	51,385*	7,296	142,166*	499,638	308,078	39,818	53,020	900,554	158,884
1970	122,820	63,690*	6,612	193,122*	734,730	551,357	38,644	77,392	1,402,123	207,254
1975	188,003	95,190*	6,729	289,922*	1,083,421	904,695	39,423	112,032	2,139,571	289,304
1980	385,575	183,418	3,609	572,602	1,760,474	1,579,355	35,994	165,215	3,541,038	479,210
1985	910,944	319,503	722	1,231,169	3,247,289	2,561,595	28,250	215,973	6,053,107	825,901
1987	986,660	365,529	324	1,352,513	4,139,071	3,043,782	26,668	242,977	7,452,498	1,044,459
1989	1,020,719	420,707	252	1,441,678	4,939,964	3,469,498	24,446	260,107	8,694,015	1,299,756
1990	1,069,660	459,271	220	1,529,151	5,366,982	3,753,506	24,071	248,038	9,392,597	1,408,208
1991	1,041,508	573,953*	198	1,615,659*	5,677,777	4,057,606	22,475	228,478	9,986,336	1,551,201
1992	1,048,135	440,143	222	1,488,500	5,941,810	4,240,919	20,973	202,090	10,405,792	1,664,531
1993	1,101,327	576,823	149	1,678,299	6,428,434	4,456,338	20,451	199,518	11,104,741	1,839,127
1994	1,107,216	549,984	232	1,657,432	6,835,239	4,608,746	20,145	209,491	11,673,621	1,942,273

*Includes Servicemen's Group Life Insurance $27.8 billion in 1965, $17.1 billion in 1970, $1.7 billion in 1975, and $166.7 billion in 1991.

U.S. Health Expenditures, 1960-93

Source: Health Care Financing Administration, Office of the Actuary; data from Office of National Health Statistics

(in billions of dollars)

Type of expenditure	1960	1970	1980	1985	1987	1989	1990	1991	1992	1993
National health expenditures	$27.1	$74.3	$251.1	$434.5	$506.2	$623.9	$696.6	$755.8	$820.3	$884.2
Health services & supplies	25.4	69.0	239.4	418.1	487.9	601.8	672.2	730.8	792.9	855.2
Personal health care	23.9	64.8	220.1	380.5	453.8	550.5	612.4	670.8	729.7	182.5
Hospital care	9.3	28.0	102.7	168.2	194.1	231.8	256.5	282.3	306.0	326.6
Physician services	5.3	13.6	45.2	83.6	104.1	127.3	140.5	150.3	161.8	171.2
Dental services	2.0	4.7	13.3	21.7	25.3	28.6	30.4	31.7	34.7	37.4
Other professional services	0.6	1.4	6.4	16.8	22.6	32.2	36.0	40.4	46.4	51.2
Home health care	0.0	0.2	1.9	4.9	5.9	6.1	11.1	13.2	16.8	20.8
Drugs & other medical nondurables	4.2	8.8	21.6	37.4	45.4	54.4	61.2	67.1	70.8	75.0
Vision products & other medical durables	0.8	2.0	4.5	7.1	8.1	9.6	10.5	11.3	12.0	12.6
Nursing home care	1.0	4.9	20.5	34.9	40.6	48.9	54.8	60.6	65.5	69.6
Other personal health care	0.7	1.3	4.0	6.1	7.7	9.5	11.4	13.8	15.8	18.2
Program administration & net cost of private health insurance	1.2	2.8	12.1	25.3	19.4	32.3	38.3	37.0	39.5	48.0
Government public health activities	0.4	1.4	7.2	12.3	14.6	19.0	21.6	22.9	23.7	24.7
Research & construction	1.7	5.3	11.6	16.4	18.3	22.1	24.3	24.8	27.4	29.0
Research[1]	0.7	2.0	5.6	7.8	9.1	11.3	12.2	12.9	14.2	14.4
Construction	1.0	3.4	6.2	8.6	9.2	10.8	12.1	11.9	13.2	14.6
Average annual % change from previous year shown										
National health expenditures	—	10.6	12.9	11.6	7.9	11.0	11.6	8.5	8.6	7.8
Health services & supplies	—	10.5	13.2	11.8	8.0	11.1	11.7	8.7	8.5	7.9
Personal health care	—	10.5	13.0	11.6	9.2	10.1	11.2	9.5	8.8	7.2
Hospital care	—	11.7	13.9	10.4	7.4	9.3	10.7	10.0	8.4	6.7
Physician services	—	9.9	12.8	13.1	11.6	10.6	10.3	7.0	7.6	5.8
Dental services	—	9.1	11.1	10.2	8.2	6.3	6.1	4.2	9.6	7.7
Other professional services	—	8.8	16.3	21.2	16.6	19.4	11.8	12.3	14.8	10.4
Home health care	—	14.5	26.3	21.3	9.5	16.8	38.9	19.2	27.4	23.8
Drugs & other medical nondurables	—	7.6	9.4	11.8	10.2	9.5	12.5	9.5	5.5	5.9
Vision products & other medical durables	—	9.6	8.3	9.5	7.2	8.5	10.0	7.2	6.4	5.3
Nursing home care	—	17.4	15.5	11.3	7.6	9.8	12.0	10.9	7.8	6.3
Other personal health care	—	6.5	12.0	8.8	12.1	11.4	19.1	21.4	14.4	15.0
Program administration & net cost of private health insurance	—	9.1	15.9	15.9	−12.3	28.9	18.7	−3.3	8.6	21.5
Government public health activities	—	13.9	18.0	11.3	9.0	14.0	13.3	6.4	3.4	4.2
Research & construction	—	12.2	8.1	7.1	5.7	9.9	10.0	1.8	10.8	5.8
Research[1]	—	10.9	10.8	7.5	7.9	11.1	8.5	5.6	10.3	1.1
Construction	—	12.9	6.2	6.7	3.6	8.7	11.5	−1.9	11.4	10.8

Note: Numbers may not add to totals because of rounding. (1) Research and development expenditures of drug companies and other manufacturers and providers of medical equipment and supplies are excluded from "research expenditures," but included in the expenditure class in which the product falls.

Health Insurance Coverage, by State, 1994

Source: Bureau of the Census, U.S. Dept. of Commerce

(in thousands)

State	Total population	Covered by health insurance	Not covered by health insurance	Per- centage not covered	State	Total population	Covered by health insurance	Not covered by health insurance	Per- centage not covered
AL	4,305	3,479	826	19.2	MT	845	730	115	13.6
AK	592	513	79	13.3	NE	1,649	1,472	177	10.7
AZ	4,235	3,379	856	20.2	NV	1,524	1,284	240	15.7
AR	2,415	1,995	420	17.4	NH	1,132	997	135	11.9
CA	31,730	25,020	6,710	21.1	NJ	7,929	6,895	1,034	13.0
CO	3,746	3,280	466	12.4	NM	1,687	1,298	389	23.1
CT	3,194	2,861	333	10.4	NY	18,245	15,329	2,916	16.0
DE	681	589	92	13.5	NC	6,906	5,988	918	13.3
DC	611	511	100	16.4	ND	629	576	53	8.4
FL	14,273	11,816	2,457	17.2	OH	11,162	9,932	1,230	11.0
GA	7,241	6,066	1,175	16.2	OK	323	2,657	575	17.8
HI	1,107	1,005	102	9.2	OR	3,165	2,750	415	13.1
ID	1,139	980	159	14.0	PA	11,995	10,727	1,268	10.6
IL	11,845	10,490	1,355	11.4	RI	968	857	111	11.5
IN	5,986	5,355	631	10.5	SC	3,658	3,137	521	14.2
IA	2,817	2,545	272	9.7	SD	740	666	74	10.0
KS	2,527	2,201	326	12.9	TN	5,349	4,805	544	10.2
KY	3,852	3,268	584	15.2	TX	18,932	14,352	4,580	24.2
LA	4,364	3,525	839	19.2	UT	1,928	1,707	221	11.5
ME	1,203	1,045	158	13.1	VT	593	542	51	8.6
MD	5,052	4,414	638	12.6	VA	6,630	5,832	798	12.0
MA	6,011	5,259	752	12.5	WA	5,261	4,594	667	12.7
MI	9,523	8,495	1,028	10.8	WV	1,805	1,512	293	16.2
MN	4,495	4,067	428	9.5	WI	5,008	4,561	447	8.9
MS	2,590	2,130	460	17.8	WY	486	411	75	15.4
MO . . .	5,114	4,488	626	12.2	**U.S. . . . .**	**262,106**	**222,388**	**39,718**	**15.2**

Months Without Health Insurance Coverage, by Selected Characteristics

Source: Bureau of the Census, U.S. Dept. of Commerce

(in months)

Characteristic	1991-93	1990-92	Characteristic	1991-93	1990-92
Total	7.1	6.0	**Residence**		
Race and Hispanic origin[1]			Metropolitan	7.0	5.8
White	7.0	5.4	Central city	7.4	6.2
Not of Hispanic origin	6.0	4.9	suburbs	5.8	5.4
Black	7.1	7.3	Nonmetropolitan	7.2	6.7
Hispanic	7.7	7.2	**Region**		
Not of Hispanic origin	6.1	5.7	Northeast	7.1	5.1
Age			Midwest	4.7	4.7
Under 18 years	5.1	4.8	South	7.5	7.2
18 to 24 years	7.3	6.4	West	6.8	5.3
25 to 34 years	7.1	5.4	**Employment status**		
35 to 44 years	7.2	7.4	(persons 18 years and older)		
45 to 64 years	7.7	6.4	Employed full time	5.7	4.6
65 years and older	(2)	(2)	Employed part time	7.5	6.8
Sex			Unemployed	7.7	7.8
Male	7.2	6.6	Not in labor force	8.8	7.2
Female	6.6	5.5	**Receipt of public assistance**		
Educational attainment			Received public assistance	6.5	7.4
(persons 18 years and older)			Did not receive public assistance	7.1	5.7
Less than 4 years of high school	10.0	7.6	**Poverty status**		
High school graduate, no college	7.2	7.1	Below poverty	7.5	7.2
1 or more years of college	5.1	4.0	Above poverty	6.3	4.9

Note: Findings reported in this table are part of the Bureau of the Census's Survey of Income and Program Participation (SIPP). The SIPP is a longitudinal survey that interviews a representative sample of the U.S. noninstitutional population periodically to track trends among the U.S. population. Estimates in this table represent those persons observed to begin a period of time without any form of health insurance coverage, public or private, during the 32-month period prior to the survey. (1) Persons of Hispanic origin may be of any race. (2) Size of the survey is too small to be truly representative of this sector of the population for this question.

Hospice and Home Health Care, 1993

Source: National Center for Health Statistics, U.S. Dept. of Health and Human Services; preliminary data

- Hospice services are provided to patients who are in the terminal stage of illness. In 1993, about 50,000 patients a day received services from 1,000 hospice agencies throughout the U.S.

- The majority of hospice patients are elderly. In 1993, more than 70% of hospice patients were 65 years of age or older. Nearly 20% of hospice patients were 45-64 years of age. Women accounted for 59% of hospice patients.

- In 1993 the most common first-listed admission diagnosis for hospice patients was malignant neoplasms (71% of all patients). Human immunodeficiency virus (HIV) accounted for 3% of hospice patients.

- Home health care was provided to about 1.4 million patients a day by 7,400 home health agencies in 1993.

- Three-quarters of home health patients were 65 years of age and older, and almost 20% of home health patients were 85 years of age and older. Two-thirds of home health patients were women.

- Among home health patients in 1993, about one-half of the admission diagnoses were accounted for by the following 6 conditions: diseases of heart and hypertension (17%); injury and poisoning (9%); diabetes (7%); and cerebrovascular diseases, maglignant neoplasms, and respiratory diseases (6% each).

Top 20 Reasons Given by Patients for Emergency Room Visits, 1992

Source: National Center for Health Statistics, U.S. Dept. of Health and Human Services

Principal reason for visit	No. of visits (1,000)	Percent-age of total	Principal reason for visit	No. of visits (1,000)	Percent-age of total
All visits to emergency rooms	90,266	100.0	Earache or ear infection	1,804	2.0
Stomach and abdominal pain,			Vomiting	1,757	1.9
cramps, and spasms	5,106	5.7	Laceration and cuts—facial area	1,631	1.8
Chest pain and related symptoms	4,503	5.0	Injury, other and unspecific type—		
Fever	4,426	4.9	head, neck, and face	1,385	1.5
Headache, pain in the head	2,544	2.8	Hand and finger symptoms	1,383	1.5
Injury—upper extremity	2,312	2.6	Labored or difficult breathing		
Cough	2,144	2.4	(dyspnea)	1,314	1.5
Back symptoms	2,044	2.3	Neck symptoms	1,305	1.4
Symptoms referable to throat	2,013	2.2	Skin rash	1,122	1.2
Pain, site not referable to a			Head and finger injury	1,035	1.1
specific body system	1,955	2.2	Vertigo (dizziness)	1,029	1.1
Shortness of breath	1,877	2.1	All other reasons	47,577	52.7

Top 20 Reasons Given by Patients for Physicians' Office Visits, 1993

Source: National Center for Health Statistics, U.S. Dept. of Health and Human Services

Principal reason for visit	Number of visits (1,000)	Total	Female	Male
		Percentage distribution		
All visits	717,191	100.0	100.0	100.0
General medical examination	38,185	5.3	5.7	4.7
Routine prenatal examination	25,893	3.6	6.0	NA
Cough	24,642	3.4	2.9	4.3
Progress visit, not otherwise specified	20,836	2.9	2.5	3.6
Postoperative visit	18,129	2.5	2.4	2.7
Symptoms referable to throat	17,263	2.4	2.5	2.3
Earache or ear infection	16,130	2.2	2.0	2.6
Well-baby examination	14,023	2.0	1.7	2.3
Stomach pain, cramps, and spasms	13,027	1.8	2.0	1.6
Back symptoms	12,768	1.8	1.5	2.2
Vision dysfunctions	12,416	1.7	1.9	1.4
Skin rash	12,138	1.7	1.5	1.9
Headache, pain in the head	10,736	1.5	1.8	1.0
Head cold, upper respiratory infection (coryza)	10,160	1.4	1.3	1.5
Fever	10,006	1.4	1.2	1.7
Nasal congestion	9,872	1.4	1.3	1.5
Chest pain and related symptoms	9,535	1.3	1.2	1.5
Hypertension	9,503	1.3	1.2	1.5
Knee symptoms	8,824	1.2	1.1	1.5
Depression	8,758	1.2	1.3	1.0
All other reasons	414,347	57.8	57.0	59.2

NA = not applicable.

The 20 Drugs Most Frequently Prescribed in Physicians' Offices, 1993

Source: National Center for Health Statistics, U.S. Dept. of Health and Human Services; in thousands

Rank	Name of drug and principal generic substance[1]	Number of times prescribed	Therapeutic use
1.	Amoxicillin	19,212	Antibiotic
2.	Tylenol (acetaminophen)	11,225	Analgesic
3.	Premarin (estrogens)	10,675	Estrogen replacement therapy
4.	Lasix (furosemide)	10,578	Diuretic, antihypertensive
5.	Amoxil (amoxicillin)	10,569	Antibiotic
6.	Prednisone	10,562	Steroid replacement therapy, anti-inflammatory agent
7.	Zantac (ranitidine)	9,303	Duodenal or gastric ulcer
8.	Cardizem (ditiazem)	8,977	Angina/calcium channel blocking agent
9.	Allergy relief or shots	8,029	Diagnostics
10.	Influenza virus vaccine	7,685	Immunization
11.	Procardia (nifedipine)	7,575	Angina (calcium channel blocking agent)
12.	Lanoxin (digoxin)	7,177	Congestive heart failure, irregular heartbeat
13.	Synthroid (levothyroxine)	7,169	Thyroid hormone therapy
14.	Vasotec (enalapril)	7,032	Antihypertensive
15.	Diphtheria tetanus toxoids pertussis	6,994	Immunization
16.	Ventolin (albuterol)	6,940	Bronchodilator, antiasthmatic
17.	Prenatal formula	6,902	Vitamins, minerals
18.	Naprosyn (naproxen)	6,769	Nonsteroidal anti-inflammatory agent
19.	Proventil (albuterol)	6,626	Bronchodilator
20.	Prozac (fluoxetine hydrochloride)	6,462	Antidepressant
	All other	737,042	

(1) The trade or generic name used by the physician on the prescription or other medical records. The use of trade names is for identification only and does not imply endorsement by the Public Health Service or the U.S. Department of Health and Human Services.

Estimated New Cancer Cases and Deaths, by Sex, for Leading Sites, 1995

Source: American Cancer Society

The estimates of new cancer cases are offered as a rough guide and should not be regarded as definitive. About 800,000 basal and squamous cell skin cancers and 120,000 carcinoma in situ cases are not included in the totals. About 2,100 nonmelanoma skin cancer deaths occurred in 1995.

Estimated New Cases

Total		Women		Men	
All Sites	1,252,000	All Sites	575,000	All Sites	677,000
Prostate	244,000	Breast	182,000	Prostate	244,000
Breast	182,000	Lung	73,900	Lung	96,000
Lung	169,900	Colorectal	67,500	Colorectal	70,700
Colorectal	138,200	Uterus	48,600	Bladder	37,300
Lymphoma	58,700	Ovary	26,600	Lymphoma	34,000

Estimated Deaths

Total		Women		Men	
All Sites	547,000	All Sites	258,000	All Sites	289,000
Lung	157,400	Lung	62,000	Lung	95,400
Colorectal	55,300	Breast	46,000	Prostate	40,400
Breast	46,000	Colorectal	28,100	Colorectal	27,200
Prostate	40,400	Ovary	14,500	Pancreas	13,200
Pancreas	13,200	Pancreas	13,800	Lymphoma	12,800

Trends in Cancer Death Rates, 1959-61 and 1989-91

Source: American Cancer Society

Sites	Sex	Death rate[1] 1959-61	1989-91	Percentage change	Number of deaths 1961	Number of deaths 1991
All Sites	Male	183.0	220.7	21	147,157	272,380
	Female	136.0	141.9	†	126,345	242,277
Colon and rectum	Male	25.1	23.3	−23	19,607	28,178
	Female	22.5	15.8	†	20,755	29,017
Colon	Male	17.2	19.9	16	13,518	23,927
	Female	17.4	13.8	−21	16,147	25,208
Rectum	Male	8.0	3.4	−57	6,089	4,251
	Female	5.2	2.0	−62	4,608	3,809
Lung	Male	38.2	75.0	96	33,211	91,690
	Female	5.7	31.6	451	5,718	52,068
Melanoma of skin	Male	1.4	3.1	127	1,194	4,017
	Female	1.1	1.5	44	989	2,434
Breast	Male	0.3	0.2	−33	231	1,559
	Female	25.8	27.4	6	24,311	648
Cervix uteri	Female	9.1	3.4	−63	8,504	4,514
Other uterus	Female	6.6	1.0	−85	5,878	5,950
Ovary	Female	8.8	7.9	−10	8,116	13,247
Prostate	Male	20.5	26.3	28	14,941	33,564
Bladder	Male	7.2	5.7	−21	5,405	7,027
	Female	2.7	1.7	−36	2,420	3,379
Non-Hodgkin's lymphoma	Male	4.9	8.0	62	4,015	6,441
	Female	3.2	5.1	58	2,839	4,333
Hodgkin's lymphoma	Male	2.3	0.7	−68	1,953	928
	Female	1.3	0.4	−67	1,185	697

†Not statistically significant. **Note:** Even though some death rates declined, the number of deaths increased because the population has become larger and older. The U.S. population increased 38% from 1961 to 1991. (1) Death rates are per 100,000 persons and were adjusted to the age distribution of the 1970 U.S. census population.

Cardiovascular Diseases Statistical Summary, 1993

Source: American Heart Association, Dallas, TX

Prevalence — 63,340,000 Americans had one or more forms of heart and blood vessel disease.
* high blood pressure — more than 55,000,000
* coronary heart disease — more than 13,000,000
* stroke — 3,820,000
* rheumatic heart disease — 1,360,000

Hypertension (high blood pressure) — afflicted 55,000,000 Americans age 6 and above, including about 1 in 4 adults, in 1993.

Mortality[1] — 954,138 in 1993 (42.1% of all deaths).
* Someone died from cardiovascular disease every 33 seconds in the U.S. in 1993.

(1) Mortality estimates for 1993 are based on provisional data released by National Center for Health Statistics, U.S. Dept. of Health and Human Services.

Congenital or inborn heart defects —
* Mortality from such heart defects was 5,500 in 1993.

Coronary heart disease (heart attack) — caused 489,970 deaths in 1993.
* 13,000,000 people alive today have a history of heart attack and/or angina pectoris.
* As many as 1,500,000 Americans had a heart attack in 1993, about one-third of them fatal.

Stroke — killed about 149,740 in 1993; afflicted 3,820,000.

Rheumatic heart disease — afflicted 1,360,000 in 1993.
* killed 5,590 in 1993.

AIDS Deaths and New AIDS Cases in the U.S., 1985-94

Source: *Health United States 1994*, National Center for Health Statistics, U.S. Dept. of Health and Human Services

	All years[1]	1985	1988	1989	1990	1991	1992	1993	1994[2]
TOTAL DEATHS	284,249	6,961	21,019	27,653	31,339	36,246	40,072	42,572	44,052[3]
NEW AIDS CASES									
All races	410,532	8,160	30,716	33,643	41,761	43,771	45,961	103,463	61,301
Male									
All males, 13 years and older . . .	352,092	7,539	27,106	29,666	36,475	37,722	39,223	86,469	49,887
White, not Hispanic	192,158	4,781	16,041	17,543	21,000	20,675	20,899	43,892	18,089
Black, not Hispanic	106,167	1,713	7,188	8,055	10,300	11,149	12,209	28,714	23,211
Hispanic	49,786	986	3,637	3,737	4,773	5,467	5,625	12,782	18,089
American Indian[2]	841	6	38	61	78	84	102	289	7,954
Asian or Pacific Islander[4]	2,528	49	162	216	262	259	285	670	135
13-19 years	1,184	31	84	92	106	98	94	362	397
20-29 years	61,926	1,471	5,393	5,694	6,813	6,457	6,387	14,456	186
30-39 years	162,922	3,619	12,699	13,940	16,885	17,481	18,014	39,513	7,622
40-49 years	89,238	1,656	6,127	6,846	8,977	9,657	10,392	23,382	22,932
50-59 years	27,047	602	1,993	2,247	2,664	2,909	3,097	6,590	13,750
60 years and over	9,775	160	840	847	1,030	1,120	1,239	2,166	4,031
Female									
All females, 13 years and over. . .	52,778	520	3,040	3,380	4,560	5,373	5,980	16,113	10,693
White, not Hispanic	13,448	141	860	944	1,225	1,352	1,479	4,077	2,437
Black, not Hispanic	30,092	280	1,655	1,903	2,561	3,110	3,409	9,193	6,318
Hispanic.	8,728	96	492	499	736	863	1,023	2,670	1,854
American Indian[3]	152	2	6	9	9	11	17	57	35
Asian or Pacific Islander[4]	279	1	22	16	19	25	39	96	40
13-19 years	586	4	22	29	63	55	55	194	134
20-29 years	12,462	174	768	889	1,105	1,219	1,381	3,692	2,308
30-39 years	24,657	233	1,512	1,625	2,109	2,542	2,747	7,654	4,838
40-49 years	10,194	45	412	506	787	998	1,244	3,269	2,524
50-59 years	2,941	27	151	171	276	338	338	871	610
60 years and over	1,938	37	175	160	220	221	215	433	279
Children									
All children, under 13 years	5,662	131	570	597	726	676	758	881	721
White, not Hispanic	1,122	26	148	114	160	147	129	146	102
Black, not Hispanic	3,348	86	307	339	389	408	483	538	478
Hispanic	1,130	19	111	137	169	114	139	184	131
American Indian[4]	17	–	–	2	4	2	3	3	–
Asian or Pacific Islander[5]	32	–	4	3	4	4	1	5	8
Under 1 year	2,183	56	192	241	288	255	318	324	233
1-12 years	3,479	75	378	356	438	421	440	557	488

Note: The AIDS case definition was changed in 1985, 1987, and 1993, as more was learned about AIDS-associated diseases and conditions and to expand the spectrum of human immunodeficiency virus-associated diseases reportable as AIDS. Excludes residents of U.S. territories. Data are updated periodically because of reporting delays. Data for all years have been updated through Sept. 30, 1994. (1) Includes cases and deaths prior to 1985 and years not shown. (2) Jan. to Sept. 1994 unless otherwise noted. (3) Jan. to Dec. 1994. (4) Includes Aleut and Eskimo. (5) Includes Chinese, Japanese, Filipino, Hawaiian and part-Hawaiian, and other Asian or Pacific Islander.

New AIDS Cases in the U.S., 1985-94, by Transmission Category

Source: *Health United States 1994*, National Center for Health Statistics, U.S. Dept. of Health and Human Services

Sex and transmission category	All years[1]	1985	1988	1989	1990	1991	1992	1993	1994[2]
Male	352,092	7,539	27,106	29,666	36,475	37,722	39,223	86,469	49,887
Men who have sex with men	218,587	5,393	17,794	19,668	23,966	24,020	24,509	49,756	26,711
Injecting drug use	72,203	1,102	5,236	5,427	7,001	7,684	8,073	20,227	11,959
Men who have sex with men and inject-ing drug use	26,290	643	2,209	2,382	2,681	2,884	2,904	6,311	2,843
Hemophilia/coagulation disorder. . . .	3,431	68	294	278	330	304	319	1,063	401
Heterosexual contact[3]	9,004	32	328	492	712	878	1,270	3,103	1,959
Sex with injecting drug user	4,262	25	226	359	460	503	652	1,217	655
Transfusion[4]	3,888	105	485	425	462	404	366	639	357
Undetermined[5]	18,689	196	760	994	1,323	1,548	1,782	5,320	5,657
Female	52,778	520	3,040	3,380	4,560	5,373	5,980	16,113	10,693
Injecting drug use	25,464	282	1,641	1,799	2,321	2,752	2,879	7,752	4,431
Hemophilia/coagulation disorder. . . .	95	1	4	7	11	10	5	26	17
Heterosexual contact[3]	18,417	116	874	1,001	1,536	1,883	2,304	6,007	3,861
Sex with injecting drug user	9,760	82	637	704	1,040	1,188	1,328	2,718	1,489
Transfusion[4]	2,670	63	329	291	338	241	265	517	256
Undetermined[5]	6,132	58	192	282	354	487	527	1,811	2,128

Note: The AIDS case definition was changed in 1985, 1987, and 1993, as more was learned about AIDS-associated diseases and conditions and to expand the spectrum of human immunodeficiency virus-associated diseases reportable as AIDS. Excludes residents of U.S. territories. Data are updated periodically because of reporting delays. Data for all years have been updated through Sept. 30, 1994. (1) Includes cases prior to 1985 and years not shown. (2) Jan. to Sept. 1994. (3) Includes persons who have had heterosexual contact with a person with human immunodeficiency virus (HIV) infection or at risk of HIV infection. (4) Receipt of blood transfusion, blood components, or tissue. (5) Includes persons for whom risk information is incomplete, persons still under investigation, men reported only to have had heterosexual contact with prostitutes, and interviewed persons for whom no specific risk is identified.

Years of Life Expected at Birth

Source: National Center for Health Statistics

Year[1]	All Races Total	Male	Female	White Total	Male	Female	Black and Other Total	Male	Female
1920............	54.1	53.6	54.6	54.9	54.4	55.6	45.3	45.5	45.2
1930............	59.7	58.1	61.6	61.4	59.7	63.5	48.1	47.3	49.2
1940............	62.9	60.8	65.2	64.2	62.1	66.6	53.1	51.5	54.9
1950............	68.2	65.6	71.1	69.1	66.5	72.2	60.8	59.1	62.9
1960............	69.7	66.6	73.1	70.6	67.4	74.1	63.6	61.1	66.3
1965............	70.2	66.8	73.7	71.0	67.6	74.7	64.1	61.1	67.4
1970............	70.8	67.1	74.7	71.7	68.0	75.6	65.3	61.3	69.4
1975............	72.6	68.8	76.6	73.4	69.5	77.3	68.0	63.7	72.4
1976............	72.9	69.1	76.8	73.6	69.9	77.5	68.4	64.2	72.7
1977............	73.3	69.5	77.2	74.0	70.2	77.9	68.9	64.7	73.2
1978............	73.5	69.6	77.3	74.1	70.4	78.0	68.1	63.7	72.4
1979............	73.9	70.0	77.8	74.6	70.8	78.4	69.8	65.4	74.1
1980............	73.7	70.0	77.5	74.4	70.7	78.1	69.5	65.3	73.6
1981............	74.2	70.4	77.8	74.8	71.1	78.4	70.3	66.2	74.4
1982............	74.5	70.9	78.1	75.1	71.5	78.7	70.9	66.8	74.9
1983............	74.6	71.0	78.1	75.2	71.7	78.7	70.9	67.0	74.7
1984............	74.7	71.2	78.2	75.3	71.8	78.7	71.1	67.2	74.9
1985............	74.7	71.2	78.2	75.3	71.9	78.7	67.0	64.8	69.3
1986............	74.8	71.3	78.3	75.4	72.0	78.8	70.9	66.8	74.9
1987............	75.0	71.5	78.4	75.6	72.2	78.9	66.9	65.0	69.1
1988............	74.9	71.5	78.3	75.6	72.3	78.9	70.8	66.7	74.8
1989............	75.1	71.7	78.5	75.9	72.5	79.2	70.9	66.7	74.9
1990............	75.4	71.8	78.8	76.1	72.9	79.4	71.2	67.0	75.2
1991............	75.5	72.0	78.9	76.3	72.9	79.2	71.5	67.4	75.5
1992............	75.5	72.1	78.9	76.4	73.0	79.5	71.7	67.5	75.8
1993[p]........	75.5	72.1	78.9	76.3	73.0	79.5	71.5	67.4	75.5
1994[p]........	75.7	72.3	79.0	76.4	73.2	79.6	71.8	67.7	75.7

p= preliminary. (1) Data prior to 1940 for death-registration states only.

Average Height and Weight for Children

Source: Physicians Handbook, 1990

Age Years	Boys Height ft	in	cm	Weight lb	kg	Age Years	Girls Height ft	in	cm	Weight lb	kg
(Birth)	1	8	50.8	7 ½	3.4	(Birth)	1	8	50.8	7 ½	3.4
½	2	2	66.0	17	7.7	½	2	2	66.0	16	7.2
1	2	5	73.6	21	9.5	1	2	5	73.6	20	9.1
2	2	9	83.8	26	11.8	2	2	9	83.8	25	11.3
3	3	0	91.4	31	14.0	3	3	0	91.4	30	13.6
4	3	3	99.0	34	15.4	4	3	3	99.0	33	15.0
5	3	6	106.6	39	17.7	5	3	5	104.1	38	17.2
6	3	9	114.2	46	20.9	6	3	8	111.7	45	20.4
7	3	11	119.3	51	23.1	7	3	11	119.3	49	22.2
8	4	2	127.0	57	25.9	8	4	2	127.0	56	25.4
9	4	4	132.0	63	28.6	9	4	4	132.0	62	28.1
10	4	6	137.1	69	31.3	10	4	6	137.1	69	31.3
11	4	8	142.2	77	34.9	11	4	8	142.2	77	34.9
12	4	10	147.3	83	37.7	12	4	10	147.3	86	39.0
13	5	0	152.4	92	41.7	13	5	0	152.4	98	45.5
14	5	2	157.5	107	48.5	14	5	2	157.5	107	48.5

This table gives a general picture of American children at specific ages. Heights and weights given represent the mean of those children in the study. When used as a standard, the individual variation in children's growth should not be overlooked. In most cases the height-weight relationship is probably a more valid index of weight status than a weight-for-age assessment.

Overweight Adults, by Age, 1960-91

Source: *Health United States 1994*, National Center for Health Statistics, U.S. Dept. of Health and Human Services

Overweight is defined for men as body mass index greater than or equal to 27.8 kilograms/meter^2, and for women as body mass index greater than or equal to 27.3 kilograms/meter^2. These cut points were used because they represent the sex-specific 85th percentiles of all persons 20-29 years of age in the 1976-80 National Health and Nutrition Examination Survey. Height was measured without shoes; two pounds were deducted from the 1960-62 data to allow for weight of clothing. Pregnant women were excluded from the survey.

Overweight persons, 20 years of age and older	Percentage of U.S. population 1960-62	1971-74	1976-80	1988-91
Male				
20-34 years of age......................	19.6	19.2	17.3	22.2
35-44 years of age......................	22.8	29.4	28.9	35.3
45-54 years of age......................	28.1	27.6	31.0	35.6
55-64 years of age......................	26.9	24.8	28.1	40.1
65-74 years of age......................	21.8	23.0	25.2	42.9
75 years and older......................	NA	NA	NA	26.4
Female				
20-34 years of age......................	13.2	14.8	16.8	25.1
35-44 years of age......................	24.1	27.3	27.0	36.9
45-54 years of age......................	30.7	32.3	32.5	41.6
55-64 years of age......................	43.2	38.5	37.0	48.5
65-74 years of age......................	42.9	38.0	38.4	39.8
75 years and older......................	NA	NA	NA	30.9

NA = not available.

Offbeat News Stories

But Is It Art?—A New York City hotel was hosting an art fair in which individual artists set up their wares in hotel rooms as patrons roamed the hallways. While one artist's employees left their card game to attend to some customers, other customers commented on the card layout as if it were a work on display. Another art display was ruined when a cleaning lady made the artist's bed by mistake.

Agave americana—When the air conditioning failed at the Oxford University Botanic Gardens and temperatures in the greenhouse climbed, this rare cactus bloomed for the first time since 1896.

I Don't Think So—In Feb. 1995, Rolando Sanchez, a Tampa doctor, amputated the left foot of a patient who was supposed to have his right one removed. Then, in the summer he repeated the error with regard to a patient's toes. Although he has been suspended from practice indefinitely, he has denied making a mistake in the second operation. His version of the story, which he told to a nursing supervisor, was that "the toe fell off."

Woman Carried Dead Baby 60 Years—At the age of 32, she became pregnant, developed abdominal pain, and recovered. Her menstrual periods resumed. When she died in 1995 at the age of 92, doctors at the University of Vienna Medical School discovered a large abdominal mass extending from the pelvis to the right upper abdomen. Radiography revealed a stone child. Stone babies occur about once in every 250,000 pregnancies, but this was the first case of a woman carrying a calcified fetus for such a long time.

Happy 120th Birthday—On Feb. 21, 1995, Jeanne Calment, the oldest person alive whose age had been verified with official documents, celebrated her 120th birthday in Arles, in southern France. Although confined to a wheelchair since a fall five years earlier, she rode her bicycle through the streets of Arles until she turned 100. Mrs. Calment was known in Arles for vigorous walks and her consumption of more than 2 lb of chocolate a week. She quit smoking at the age of 117. When she was born, the automobile, the airplane, and electric lighting in homes were unknown. When asked what kind of future she expected, she said, "A very short one."

The Quack Heard 'Round the World—In Jan. 1992 a storm near the international date line washed 29,000 plastic ducks and other bathtub toys into the North Pacific. About 10 months later, the first yellow ducks, blue turtles, red beavers, and green frogs showed up on beaches in Sitka, Alaska. During the next 10 months, 400 toys were found along a stretch of coast along the Gulf of Alaska. As a result of the toys being found, and they were found about 6 months earlier than had been predicted, a computer model of the North Pacific tides had to be adjusted to include the effect of the wind. Ultimately, some of the plastic toys are likely to pass through the Bering Strait, make their way in ice packs across the Arctic Ocean, and end up in the North Atlantic.

A Thoroughly Modern Wedding—The Jewish bridegroom and the non-Jewish bride wrote their wedding ceremony, which was performed by their friend, a young lesbian. The bridegroom promised to obey the bride; the bride promised to boss the bridegroom. After their vows, the bride crushed a glass with her foot, and the couple embraced. At the reception the bride removed her flowing skirt to reveal a matching miniskirt. The couple traveled separately to their honeymoon destination. Each had frequent flier miles on different airlines.

Your Mother Warned You—When Francis Reichert of Stuart, FL, was 8 years old, he stuck cherry pits in each nostril to impress his friends. And for 50 years, one of them remained lodged in his proboscis until, during a visit to an eye, ear, and throat specialist, it dropped into his mouth. The doctor thinks it may be the oldest object discovered in anyone's nose.

Where the Misfits Fit—This is the motto of Eureka Springs, a quaint hillside hamlet in Arkansas. The town's 1900 inhabitants are divided over whether to embrace its tourism industry or to attempt to abolish it. A winner in this debate was Louise Berry who, in Nov. 1994, was elected to the city council even though she was dead. In Arkansas, it is perfectly legal for an otherwise qualified dead person to run for office. Although a local judge ordered a new election, the Arkansas Supreme Court reversed his decision in July 1995, saying that the dead woman was the lawful winner.

Miscellaneous Facts

—The Generation Gap in 1996: Generation Xers will be ages 20 to 32; Baby Boomers will be ages 33 to 50; the Silent Generation will be ages 51 to 64; and the Depression Generation will be ages 65 and older.

—The 5 most common U.S. surnames are (1) Smith, (2) Johnson, (3) Williams, (4) Jones, and (5) Brown.

—For an entry fee of about $46 and extra costs of renting beach paraphernalia, in Japan you can spend the day at an indoor beach park, which features 90-degree weather, 86-degree artificial waves, 86-degree artificial sand on a rubberized floor, and time-controlled sunlight.

—California's Jan. 1994 earthquake officially killed 61 people. Within 6 months, however, the state had received 400 requests for the $6,000 burial grants, by people claiming their dead relatives perished because of the quake.

—At 2 AM on Nov. 25, 1994, in Minneapolis, MN, Dan Hirschman became the youngest bridge player to be ranked life master by the American Contract Bridge League. He was 10 years, 2 months, and 20 days old.

—What time is it when the big hand is on the 10 and the little hand is on the 2? It's 10:10 on an analog watch, and it's time for the watch to be photographed for an ad. Nobody knows exactly why watches in print advertisements, digital as well as analog, almost always give the time as 10:10. One possibility proffered by an ad agency is that the open hands connote a warm and enveloping feeling similar to a person's outstretched and welcoming arms. One commercial photographer believes that 10:10 was the time Abraham Lincoln was shot. Another industry insider says 10:10 is more a happy face than a sad one. Or, maybe it's just easier to read this way. So, then, why are watches with a date feature set for Wednesday, Oct. 14?

—According to the Mar. 6, 1995, issue of *Fortune* magazine, Rubbermaid is the most-admired corporation in the U.S. Along with Rubbermaid, the top 5 included, in order, Microsoft, Coca-Cola, Motorola, and Home Depot.

—Some 1994 winter holiday facts: Hot toy, Mighty Morphin Power Ranger. Hot gift car, Ford Mustang, $20,000. (Hot gift car 1964, Ford Mustang, $2,500.) People employed as Santa, 10,000. Turkeys sold, 97 million. Gallons of gravy consumed, 21 million. Best-selling gift at "Skeletons in the Closet," a store run by the Los Angeles County Coroner's office, beach towel with chalk outline of a body, $20.

—In any given year, the number of people who visit New York City art museums exceeds the number of people who attend all New York professional sports games combined. In the fiscal year ending June 30, 1995, 4.9 million people visited the Metropolitan Museum of Art. A U.S. Census Bureau 1992 survey revealed that 49.6 million people had visited an art museum or gallery within the past year.

—In the past decade, collecting Zippo lighters has become an international hobby. Most prized are lighters made in 1932-33, the company's first year of production. Back then the lighters sold for $1; today collectors regularly pay $2,500 for one in mint condition.

QUICK REFERENCE INDEX

ABBREVIATIONS, U.S. POSTAL. 633
ACADEMY AWARDS 336-338
ACTORS, ACTRESSES 366-381
AEROSPACE. 315-322
AGRICULTURE 137-145
AIR MAIL, INTERNATIONAL 634-635
ANIMALS 189-190, 192, 638-639
AREA CODES, U.S. 396-426
    INTERNATIONAL 848
ARTISTS, PHOTOGRAPHERS, SCULPTORS 342-344
ARTS AND MEDIA 249-263
ASSOCIATIONS AND SOCIETIES 619-630
ASTRONOMICAL DATA, 1996. 274-308
AWARDS, MEDALS, PRIZES 323-339
BIRTHSTONES 726
BRIDGES. 702-705
BUDGET, U.S. 110-111
BUILDINGS, TALL 696-702
BUSINESS DIRECTORY. 714-719
CABINET, U.S. 104-109
CALENDARS 297-314, 647-648
CHEMICAL ELEMENTS 177-178
CHRONOLOGY, 1994-95 42-71
CITIES OF THE U.S. 390-391, 686-695
CLINTON ADMINISTRATION 78-81
COLLEGES AND UNIVERSITIES 224-248
COMPOSERS 360-362
COMPUTERS. 167-173
CONGRESS. 37-39, 82-91
CONSTITUTION 515-522
CONSUMER INFORMATION. 713-729
COPYRIGHT LAW 724-725
COST OF LIVING 112-114
COUNTIES, U.S. 388, 427-445
CRIME. 956-960
DECLARATION OF INDEPENDENCE 512-514
DISASTERS 264-273
DIVORCE LAWS. 729
ECONOMICS 110-136
EDUCATION 217-248
ELECTIONS. 82-90, 446-478
EMMY AWARDS (1994-95) 335-336
EMPLOYMENT. 146-157
ENDANGERED SPECIES 188-189
ENERGY 201-205
ENVIRONMENT 187-192
EXPLORATION AND GEOGRAPHY 586-599
FIRST AID 608
FLAGS OF THE WORLD (COLOR) 481-484
FOODS, NUTRITIVE VALUE 610-611
FORMS OF ADDRESS 641
GEOGRAPHICAL DATA 588-599
GOVERNORS 99-103
GRAMMY AWARDS 339
HEADS OF STATE 577-585, 737-776, 785-837
HEALTH. 608-618
    WHERE TO GET HELP. 616-618
HEIGHT AND WEIGHT TABLES 612
HISTORICAL ANNIVERSARIES 73-75
HISTORICAL FIGURES. 577-585
HOLIDAYS 312, 314, 647-648
HOUSE OF REPRESENTATIVES, U.S. 84-91
IMMIGRATION LAW 840-841
IMMUNIZATION 613
INDEX, GENERAL 4-32
INTEREST LAWS, RATES 721-722
INTERNET 167-170
INVENTIONS AND DISCOVERIES 174-178
JUDICIARY, U.S. 92-95
LABOR UNION DIRECTORY. 156-157
LANGUAGE 636-643
LATITUDE, LONGITUDE, & ALTITUDE OF CITIES . . 593-595

LIBRARIES 223, 539
MANUAL ALPHABET 643
MAPS (COLOR) 485-496
MARRIAGE LAWS 728
MAYORS 96-99
METEOROLOGICAL DATA. 179-186
METRIC SYSTEM 600-604
MILEAGE, AIR 216
    ROAD 215
MINERALS. 132-134
MISCELLANEOUS FACTS 975
MONEY 120-121
MORTGAGE RATES 726
MOUNTAINS 590-591
MOVIES. 249-250, 336-338
MUSICIANS 363-365
NATIONAL DEFENSE. 158-166
NATIONAL MONUMENTS. 548-549, 684-685
NATIONAL PARKS. 546-549
NATIONS OF THE WORLD 737-776, 785-848
NEWS PHOTOS, 1995 (COLOR). 193-200, 777-784
NEWS STORIES, 1994-95 . . . . 33, 42-71
NOBEL PRIZES 40, 323-325
OBITUARIES 76-77
OFF-BEAT NEWS STORIES 975
PASSPORTS 723
PEN NAMES 642
PERSONALITIES, NOTED 340-381
PLANETS 277-286, 290, 292-294
POPES 650
POPULATION, U.S. 382-445
    METROPOLITAN AREAS 389
    WORLD. 737-776, 785-839
POSTAL INFORMATION. 631-635
PRESIDENTIAL ELECTIONS 446-478
PRESIDENTS, U.S. 477-480, 530-539
PULITZER PRIZES 325-333
QUOTES OF THE YEAR. 72
RELIGION 644-654
RIVERS 596-597
SCIENCE AND TECHNOLOGY 174-178
SCIENTISTS 353-355
SENATE, U.S. 82-83, 90-91
SOCIAL SECURITY 708-712
SPACE FLIGHTS, NOTABLE 315-317
STATE NAMES, ORIGIN. 544
STATES OF THE UNION 655-685
STOCK MARKETS 130-131
SUPREME COURT, JUSTICES 92
    DECISIONS. 40, 523-524
TAXES. 730-736
TERRORISM 35-37, 960
TIME DIFFERENCES 313-314
TONY AWARDS (1994-95) 336
TOP TEN NEWS STORIES, 1995 33
TRADE AND TRANSPORTATION 206-216
TUNNELS 705-706
UNITED NATIONS 843-845
U.S. CAPITAL 680-681, 684-685
U.S. FACTS 540-550
U.S. FLAG 525-527
U.S. GOVERNMENT. 78-109
U.S. HISTORY 497-539
VICE PRESIDENTS 477, 479-480
VITAL STATISTICS 961-974
WEATHER 179-186
WEDDING ANNIVERSARIES 726
WEIGHTS AND MEASURES 600-607
WORLD HISTORY 551-576
WRITERS 356-360
ZIP CODES 396-426
ZOOLOGICAL PARKS 191

QUICK REFERENCE SPORTS INDEX

AUTO RACING. 929-931
BASEBALL. 936-955
BASKETBALL
    COLLEGE 912-917
    PROFESSIONAL 904-911
BOWLING 898-899
BOXING. 932-934
FISHING 919-920
FOOTBALL
    COLLEGE 879-886
    PROFESSIONAL 867-878

GOLF 921-923
HOCKEY. 887-894
HORSE RACING 895-898
OLYMPICS 849-865
PERSONALITIES. 924-926
SKIING 918
SWIMMING 903
TEAM DIRECTORY, PROFESSIONAL 901-902
TENNIS. 927-929
TOP TEN SPORTS EVENTS 849
TRACK AND FIELD 865-866

For complete Index, see pp. 4-32.